W9-AMS-857

THOMAS MIDDLETON

THE COLLECTED WORKS

General Editors

GARY TAYLOR AND JOHN LAVAGNINO

Associate General Editors

MACDONALD P. JACKSON, JOHN JOWETT,

VALERIE WAYNE, AND ADRIAN WEISS

CLARENDON PRESS • OXFORD

THE OXFORD MIDDLETON

Thomas Middleton (1580–1627)—'our other Shakespeare'—is the only other Renaissance playwright who created acknowledged masterpieces of comedy, tragedy, and history; his revolutionary English history play, *A Game at Chess*, was also the greatest box-office hit of early modern London. His achievements extend beyond these traditional genres to tragicomedies, masques, pageants, pamphlets, epigrams, and Biblical and political commentaries, written alone or in collaboration with Thomas Dekker, John Ford, Thomas Heywood, William Rowley, William Shakespeare, John Webster, and others. Compared by critics to Aristophanes and Ibsen, Racine and Joe Orton, he has influenced writers as diverse as Aphra Behn, Anthony Trollope, and T. S. Eliot. Though repeatedly censored in his own time, Middleton has since come to be particularly admired for his representations of the intertwined pursuits of sex, money, power, and God.

The Oxford Middleton, prepared by seventy-five scholars from a dozen countries, follows the precedent of The Oxford Shakespeare in being published in two volumes, an innovative but accessible *Collected Works* and a comprehensive scholarly *Companion*. Though closely connected, each volume can be used independently of the other.

The Collected Works brings together for the first time in a single volume all the works currently attributed to Middleton. The texts are printed in modern spelling and punctuation, with critical introductions and foot-of-the-page commentaries; they are arranged in chronological order, with a special section of Juvenilia. The volume is introduced by essays on Middleton's life and reputation, on early modern London, and on the varied theatres of the English Renaissance. Extensively illustrated, it incorporates much new information on Middleton's life, canon, texts, and contexts; twenty per cent of the works included have never before been annotated. A self-consciously 'federal edition', *The Collected Works* applies contemporary theories about the nature of literature and the history of the book to editorial practice; its unusual features are described and explained in 'How to Use This Book' (p. 18).

Thomas Middleton and Early Modern Textual Culture: A Companion to The Collected Works. Because Middleton is more representative than any of his contemporaries of the full range of textual practices in early modern England, his works provide an ideal focus for understanding the history of the book, and its relation to the larger history of culture, in this pivotal period. The *Companion* begins, accordingly, with eleven original essays placing Middleton's career in the context of larger cultural patterns governing the creation, reproduction, regulation, circulation, and reception of texts. These essays are followed by a textual introduction and full editorial apparatus for each work, including an account of evidence for its authorship and date of composition. This combination of detail and context provides a foundation for future studies both of Middleton and of early modern culture.

http://thomasmiddleton.org

Facetious Middleton, thy witty muse
Hath pleasèd all that books or men peruse.
Wit's Recreations (1640)

OXFORD
UNIVERSITY PRESS

Great Clarendon Street, Oxford OX2 6DP

Oxford University Press is a department of the University of Oxford.
It furthers the University's objective of excellence in research, scholarship,
and education by publishing worldwide in

Oxford New York

Auckland Cape Town Dar es Salaam Hong Kong Karachi
Kuala Lumpur Madrid Melbourne Mexico City Nairobi
New Delhi Shanghai Taipei Toronto

With offices in

Argentina Austria Brazil Chile Czech Republic France Greece
Guatemala Hungary Italy Japan Poland Portugal Singapore
South Korea Switzerland Thailand Turkey Ukraine Vietnam

Oxford is a registered trade mark of Oxford University Press
in the UK and in certain other countries

Published in the United States
by Oxford University Press Inc., New York

First published 2007

British Library Cataloguing in Publication Data
Data available

Library of Congress Cataloging in Publication Data
Data available

Printed in Italy
on acid-free paper by
Rotolito Lombarda SpA

ISBN 978–0–19–922588–0 (Set)
ISBN 978–0–19–818569–7 (Complete Works)
ISBN 978–0–19–818570–3 (Textual Companion)

1 3 5 7 9 10 8 6 4 2

CONTRIBUTORS

Gary Taylor (General Editor), Florida State University
John Lavagnino (General Editor), King's College London

MacDonald P. Jackson (University of Auckland)
John Jowett (Shakespeare Institute, University of Birmingham)
Valerie Wayne (University of Hawai'i at Mānoa)
Adrian Weiss (independent scholar)

Susan Dwyer Amussen (Union Institute & University)
David M. Bergeron (University of Kansas)
Michael Berlin (Birkbeck, University of London)
†Julia Briggs (De Montfort University)
Douglas Bruster (University of Texas at Austin)
Paul Bushkovitch (Yale University)
Swapan Chakravorty (Jadavpur University)
Thomas Cogswell (University of California, Riverside)
Ralph Alan Cohen (Mary Baldwin College)
Celia R. Daileader (Florida State University)
Lawrence Danson (Princeton University)
Michael Dobson (Birkbeck, University of London)
†Inga-Stina Ewbank (University of Leeds)
Doris Feldmann (Friedrich-Alexander-Universität Erlangen–Nürnberg)
Lori Anne Ferrell (Claremont Graduate University)
Julia Gasper (Open University)
Suzanne Gossett (Loyola University Chicago)
Donna B. Hamilton (University of Maryland, College Park)
Ton Hoenselaars (Universiteit Utrecht)
R. V. Holdsworth (University of Manchester)
Grace Ioppolo (University of Reading)
Maija Jansson (Yale University)
†M. T. Jones-Davies (Université de Paris—Sorbonne)
Coppélia Kahn (Brown University)
Ivo Kamps (University of Mississippi)
James Knowles (Keele University)
Theodore B. Leinwand (University of Maryland, College Park)
Kate D. Levin (City College of New York)
Jerzy Limon (Uniwersytet Gdański)
Ania Loomba (University of Pennsylvania)
Lawrence Manley (Yale University)
Robert Maslen (University of Glasgow)
Jeffrey Masten (Northwestern University)
C. E. McGee (St Jerome's University)
†Scott McMillin (Cornell University)
Paul Mulholland (University of Guelph)
Marion O'Connor (University of Kent at Canterbury)
Sharon O'Dair (University of Alabama)
Anthony Parr (University of the Western Cape)
Annabel Patterson (Yale University)
Bryan Reynolds (University of California, Irvine)
Neil Rhodes (University of St Andrews)
Nikolai Rogozhin (Russian State Archive of Ancient Documents)
Peter Saccio (Dartmouth College)
Paul S. Seaver (Stanford University)
G. B. Shand (Glendon College, York University)
Debora Shuger (University of California, Los Angeles)
R. Malcolm Smuts (University of Massachusetts, Boston)
Kurt Tetzeli von Rosador (Westfälische Wilhelms-Universität Münster)
Leslie Thomson (University of Toronto)
Daniel J. Vitkus (Florida State University)
Wendy Wall (Northwestern University)
Michael Warren (University of California, Santa Cruz)
Stanley Wells (Shakespeare Birthplace Trust)
Susan Wiseman (Birkbeck, University of London)
Linda Woodbridge (Pennsylvania State University)
Paul Yachnin (McGill University)

TABLE OF CONTENTS

ALPHABETICAL CONTENTS

Full titles, common abbreviations, and alternative titles are all given.
Asterisks mark the abbreviations used in this edition.

INDEX OF TITLES BY GENRE

Civic Pageantry

Comedies

English History Plays

Masques

Pamphlets and Poems

Tragedies

LIST OF ILLUSTRATIONS

HOW TO USE THIS BOOK

Gary Taylor

This edition of *The Collected Works of Thomas Middleton* is designed to make the full range of his work accessible to modern readers, in a way which will encourage both a wider appreciation of his achievement and a new understanding of the English Renaissance. As a result, it differs from other editions in a number of respects. Shakespeare's plays have been available in reasonably reliable and reasonably complete editions since 1623; by contrast, this book is the first one-volume collection of Middleton's works ever published. More generally, editorial paradigms based upon the unusual conditions of the Shakespeare canon are of limited relevance to Middleton (and many other writers). Rather than simply applying to Middleton modes of editorial practice developed to represent another author, we have sought to present Middleton's works in the manner most appropriate to their nature.

In finding their way around a relatively unfamiliar author in a relatively unfamiliar editorial format, readers may be helped by the following description of this book's special features.

Act Divisions. (See also SCENE DIVISIONS.) Unlike the plays of Marlowe and Shakespeare, the plays of their younger contemporary Middleton were not normally written for uninterrupted performance. Most of Middleton's plays were performed by companies which provided four musical intervals between the five acts of a play. Act divisions in such plays therefore reflect both authorial intention and early performance conditions. We mark act divisions in such plays by a special symbol (❁), and by recurring Latin phrases ('*Explicit Actus Primus*' and '*Incipit Actus Secundus*'), which Middleton regularly employed in his own manuscripts. By contrast, for early plays like *The Patient Man and the Honest Whore* and *Timon of Athens*, apparently written for continuous performance, we do not interpolate editorial act divisions or act numbers.

Acting Companies. Middleton, like most dramatists, wrote his plays for a variety of acting companies and theatres; these different venues had different physical arrangements, audiences, performance conventions, and talents. Moreover, the performance of any play depends upon active collaboration between the author(s) of the script and the other theatrical professionals who embody the text and transform it into visual and aural action. Therefore, on the first page of each play, we identify not only the title and author(s), but the acting company: 'Thomas Middleton, *The Puritan Widow*, for Paul's Boys' or 'Thomas Middleton, *The Revenger's Tragedy*, for the King's Men'.

Annotations. Many of Middleton's works have never before been annotated, or never adequately annotated, and the commentaries in this edition therefore contain much original scholarship. For most of the works, a glossarial commentary is provided at the foot of the page; these annotations are comparable to those in many one-volume textbook editions of Shakespeare. However, textbooks often homogenize commentaries to the level of a 'lowest common denominator' of readers. In order to avoid such flattening, and to remain sensitive to the different demands that certain texts make on the modern reader, this edition aims to make a virtue out of multivocality, illustrating a range of possible approaches to annotation by providing special commentaries for certain works. The notes to *Your Five Gallants* pay particular attention to theatrical problems, options, and opportunities. The commentary to *The Widow* provides extended notes on 'key words'—idioms with a complex historical significance, not easily indicated by a simple gloss. A detailed economic commentary is attached to *The Triumphs of Honour and Industry*. In *The Two Gates of Salvation* and *The Peacemaker*, annotation focuses upon the relationship between Middleton's text and its sources. The commentary to *A Game at Chesse: An Early Form* is dedicated to the play's historical and political referents; by contrast, the commentary to *A Later Form* of the same play is systematically literary and theatrical. Varieties of feminist commentary are provided for *A Mad World, My Masters*, *A Trick to Catch the Old One*, *The Roaring Girl*, and *A Chaste Maid in Cheapside*. The commentary to *Old Law*, adopting the protocols of recent historicist and materialist criticism, mixes textual apparatus with annotation and photography with type. Middleton's adaptation of *Macbeth*, already widely available, is printed here without any glossarial commentary, giving readers the (contrasting) experience of a 'plain text'. Not all readers will find all these approaches equally valuable, but juxtaposing them within the covers of one volume will, we hope, call attention to the ways in which annotation itself shapes our experience of a text.

Authorship. This edition contains texts of all Middleton's known surviving works, and brief descriptions of what we know about his various lost ones. It includes works written by Middleton alone, works written by Middleton in COLLABORATION with other writers, and works by other writers which Middleton later adapted. The exact division of labour between authors is often difficult to determine, but the Introduction to each text summarizes what is generally believed about the attribution of particular scenes or passages. In some early works—particularly *The Whole Royal and Magnificent Entertainment* and *News from Gravesend*—Middleton's share of the text seems to have been relatively small, but we have included the entire work, in the belief that Middleton's contribution can only be understood in its full context. This edition omits three plays—*Blurt, Master Constable* and *The Honest Whore, Part Two* (by Thomas Dekker) and *The Family of Love* (by Lording Barry)—which were attributed to Middleton in nineteenth-century editions. Decisions about which works to include have been based on a variety of documentary and stylistic evidence, laid out in full in the *Companion* (p. 331).

Character Names. In the original texts, many characters are not given personal names, but identified by generic social labels (Tyrant, Queen, Lady, Clown, White Queen's Pawn). At other times, a proper name is given somewhere in the text, but speech prefixes and stage directions use the generic label. In the eighteenth century, editors of Shakespeare and other English dramatists began systematically supplying personal names for dramatic characters, whenever they could be found. We have normally retained the original generic labels in STAGE DIRECTIONS and SPEECH PREFIXES, believing they reflect an emphasis upon social and theatrical roles rather than unique individuals. However, in exceptional circumstances—for one character in *A Trick to Catch the Old One* and several in *A Game at Chess: A Later Form*—it has seemed more important to provide proper names. (See CONSISTENCY.)

Chronology. The works are arranged in *The Collected Works* in what we believe to be their order of composition, from 1602 to 1627 (with the juvenilia of 1597–1601 placed in a separate sequence at the end). The order of 'authorial making' closely resembles the order of 'making public', since the plays and pageants were written for immediate performance, and all the pamphlets were apparently published soon after their composition. The evidence for the dating of individual works is given in full in the 'Canon and Chronology' section of the *Companion* (p. 331). Although the exact sequence of texts in a given year may be debatable, the broad outlines of the chronology are not disputed. This temporal arrangement makes it possible, for those readers interested in individual agency and artistry, to follow the author's own development; but it also enables others to situate each work in its historical and social moment. Moreover, because Middleton's pamphlets and pageants are less familiar than his plays, an arrangement by GENRES might ghettoize those works; a chronological arrangement, by contrast, juxtaposes familiar with unfamiliar texts, and shows the range of genres Middleton could juggle at one time.

Collaboration. The exact division of AUTHORSHIP in collaborative works is sometimes easy, sometimes difficult, to determine. Nevertheless, in the table of contents and on the title-pages of individual collaborative works we have listed the authors' names in an order which reflects our assessment of the relative size of their contribution to the work. Thus, Dekker's name is listed before Middleton's in *The Patient Man and the Honest Whore*, because Dekker seems to have written more of that play; but Middleton's name is listed before Dekker's in *The Roaring Girl*, because Middleton seems to have written more of that play.

Consistency. This edition does not attempt to provide or impose a unified view of Middleton or his works. The contributors come from different disciplines (literature, history, theatre, and theology); the ANNOTATIONS focus upon different aspects of the texts; different EDITORIAL PRACTICES are adopted for different works; and the critical introductions adopt different critical perspectives (from the performance orientation of *A Mad World, My Masters* to the postcolonial focus of *The Triumphs of Honour and Virtue*). This diversity is deliberate. It derives from a belief that authors and their readers are better served by a 'federal' than a 'unified' edition. By calling attention to the variety of ways in which the works of an author may be interpreted and edited, a 'federal' edition celebrates the play of difference and acknowledges the foreclosure of possibilities entailed in every act of choice.

Cross-reference. Each text in *The Collected Works* is provided with a textual introduction and apparatus in the *Companion*. The relevant page numbers are given at the end of each critical introduction in *The Collected Works*.

Doubling. Early modern plays were designed for performance by relatively small companies of actors, who were accustomed to doubling roles. Doubling offered opportunities for virtuoso acting; moreover, the need to double often influenced authorial decisions about the presence or absence of certain characters in certain scenes (since the same actor could not simultaneously play two different characters). Charts of doubling possibilities are printed after *Anything for a Quiet Life, The Changeling, A Chaste Maid in Cheapside, A Fair Quarrel, The Lady's Tragedy, Macbeth, A Mad World, My Masters, Measure for Measure, Michaelmas Term, More Dissemblers Besides Women, No Wit/Help like a Woman's, The Phoenix, The Roaring Girl, The Spanish Gypsy, Timon of Athens, The Widow, Wit at Several Weapons, The Witch, Women, Beware Women, The World Tossed at Tennis*; the very few doubling possibilities in *A Game at Chess: A Later Form* are noted in the commentary to its list of Persons.

Dramatis Personae. The history of dramatis personae lists in English drama, up to 1680, is traced in the *Companion* in the essay called 'The Order of Persons' (p. 31). Within the Middleton canon, a few dramatic texts—*The Roaring Girl, Masque of Heroes, A Chaste Maid in Cheapside, The Bloody Banquet*—were originally published with preliminary lists (which appear to be authorial) of their fictional characters. But most were published without such lists, or with lists apparently added by scribes or editors. In constructing editorial lists for plays that lack them, or modifying unauthoritative seventeenth-century lists, we have adopted the principles of organization used in the authorial lists. Accordingly, in most of the lists in this edition CHARACTER NAMES are grouped in households, not divided by gender, or even by rank. For the convenience of modern readers, the label given the character in SPEECH PREFIXES is printed in small capitals in the list of Persons.

Editorial Practices and Principles. The *Companion* includes full bibliographical descriptions of the early documents, critical analysis of their transmission and relationships, and a detailed textual apparatus for each work. *A Game at Chess* survives in more early independent documents than any play of the English Renaissance. By contrast, most of Middleton's works have come down to us in only a single authoritative early manuscript or printed edition, from which all later texts derive. For such single-text works, the editor's primary task is to reproduce, accurately, the substance of that earliest document, and at the same time to make it accessible to modern readers. (See PUNCTUATION, SPELLING, and STAGE DIRECTIONS.) However, all forms of early modern textual transmission introduced errors; accordingly, texts have been emended where the editors believe that such an error has occurred. How many emendations have been made in any given work depends in large part upon the quality of the early document, but also in part upon the attitude of the individual editor: some editors are more interested in detecting error, and more adventurous in correcting it, than others. All such emendations, and all variants in authoritative early texts, are recorded in the *Companion*; emendations and variants are not marked in the text of this volume. However, so that readers of the *Collected Works* may sample the kinds of editorial decision-making that affect all the texts in this book (and all modern texts of other Renaissance writers), we have foregrounded the editorial process in a few cases. In *Old Law*, textual notes are incorporated in the on-page commentary. For the Occasional Poems, each edited text is accompanied by a photograph of at least one relevant early document. We also reproduce two pages of a manuscript in Middleton's own handwriting (see *A Game at Chesse: An Early Form*).

Genres. Early seventeenth-century collections of the works of Ben Jonson and William Shakespeare divided their texts into distinct literary genres. Although Middleton's canon is even more diverse, there is no comparable early collection of his works, and so no such early division into traditional formal categories. Those interested in such groupings may prefer to organize their reading by consulting the editorial Index of Titles by Genre (p. 11).

Illustrations. Middleton's plays were illustrated more often than those of any other Renaissance playwright; this volume reproduces all the relevant title-pages, and in the spirit of Middleton's own practice also incorporates other visual material from the period. We do not, however, preserve the exact size of the original images, and some images are cropped; we have seldom retained unprinted margins in their full extent. Modern reproductions of early book pages often remove show-through and offset and enhance the contrast between dark ink and white paper, so that they resemble the pages of present-day books more closely; in some cases we have left the signs of earlier printing processes in place. For example, the background in the plates from *The Arches of Triumph* (p. 225) is not processed to make it uniform.

Indexes. Because both the canon and CHRONOLOGY of Middleton's work will be unfamiliar to most readers, for finding a particular text the main Table of Contents may be less useful than the Alphabetical Contents (p. 9), or the Index of Titles by Genre (p. 11). The 'key words' indexed in *The Widow* (p. 1123) occur in many other texts.

Metrical Markers. We indicate obsolete pronunciations when they seem necessary to the metre of verse lines. A diaeresis indicates that the 'ï' in words like 'conversatïon' should be pronounced as a separate unstressed syllable, so that 'conversatïon' has five syllables instead of the modern four. Every such diaeresis is editorial. An accent over the 'e' in words like 'injurèd' indicates that the past participle should be pronounced as a separate syllable, so that 'injurèd' has three syllables instead of the modern two. Middleton's early texts usually distinguish orthographically the obsolete from the modern pronunciation.

Modernization. See PUNCTUATION and SPELLING.

Music and Dance. Whenever an early score or choreography has survived, cross-references at the end of the Critical Introduction will alert readers to the relevant pages of the *Companion* where they are reproduced and discussed.

Punctuation. For most works, the text has been modernized to make it more intelligible for contemporary readers. Readers interested in how Middleton himself punctuated his texts may consult *A Game at Chesse: An Early Form*, most of which is based on autograph manuscripts. For parts of *Game*, and all his other works, we do not have Middleton's own handwritten copy, and the earliest surviving document mixes the punctuation practices of the author(s) with those of scribe(s) and/or printing-house compositor(s). Moreover, every act of punctuation, whether made by an early copyist or a modern editor, necessarily involves arbitrary choices, which will encourage one pronunciation or interpretation over another; every system of punctuation to some degree disambiguates a text which may be deliberately ambiguous. Readers interested in how a familiar but deeply ambiguous text would look without the arbitrary choices imposed by punctuation may consult Middleton's adaptation of Shakespeare's *Macbeth*, here printed without punctuation. This unpointed text is initially hard to read, but anyone desiring a more user-friendly *Macbeth* can easily find one.

Revised Versions. Middleton, like other writers, sometimes revised his own work, and sometimes had it altered by other people, with or without his consent. To illustrate such transformations, we have adopted distinct editorial strategies for different works. *The Nightingale and the Ant* (a.k.a. *Father Hubburd's Tales*) illustrates how a literary work may have been reshaped in the collaborative interactions between an author and publisher. The two texts of *The Lady's Tragedy*, printed in parallel, illustrate how a play developed in the normal transition between an author's original manuscript and an acting company's final (censored) promptbook. The two versions of *A Game at Chess*, printed separately in sequence, illustrate an authorial and theatrical transformation so radical and extensive that the two texts in some ways constitute two distinct works. In *Measure for Measure* and *Macbeth*, though we present only a single text, the typography of our 'genetic text' emphasizes the process of adaptation rather than the original or final state of the text. In *Penniless Parliament*, the commentary tracks Middleton's abridgements and expansions of the original pamphlet.

Scene Divisions. (See also ACT DIVISIONS.) In early modern theatrical practice, a 'scene' is not a unit of fictional space (defined by a location) but a unit of action (defined by the movement of actors). Middleton's theatres did not use scenic backdrops, and the fictional location of the onstage action was indicated by dialogue or props, and sometimes not at all; moreover, a scene which begins in one fictional place may sometimes shift to another, or abandon scenic fictions altogether, foregrounding instead the situation of an actor on a platform facing an audience. Consequently, the text of this edition does not provide a novelistic or Cartesian locale for each scene ('Another Part of the Polis'). However, for ease of reference we do identify and number, in the margins, separate scene-units. One scene ends whenever all the characters/actors present leave the playing space; a new scene begins with the subsequent entry of one or more characters/actors. In most cases, these scene divisions and numbers were not supplied in the earliest texts. In *A Game at Chesse: An Early Form*, we follow Middleton's own practice in marking act divisions, but not scene divisions.

Speech Prefixes. In seventeenth-century texts, speech prefixes are usually abbreviated, and written immediately to the left of the first words of the speech; this practice is retained in *A Game at Chesse: An Early Form*. In all other plays—and in *A Game at Chess: A Later Form*—for convenience and intelligibility we give the CHARACTER NAMES in full. When the first words of the speech are a full verse line, the use of an unabbreviated speech prefix would almost inevitably have the effect of making speech prefix and verse line together too long to fit the column, thus producing turn-overs at the beginning of thousands of speeches; to avoid this, the speech prefix is placed above the first line, rather than beside it. For prose speeches, or speeches which complete a verse line begun by another speaker, the prefix is placed on the same line as the character's first words. (See also SPLIT VERSE LINES.)

Spelling. Those who wish to read Middleton in the spelling of his time may do so by turning to the photographs of Occasional Poems, or to *A Game at Chesse: An Early Form*. But because this edition aims to make Middleton accessible to anyone interested in literature and drama, we have in all other cases modernized spelling (even when we know Middleton usually spelled a word differently), in accordance with the principles adopted for the Oxford Shakespeare. The running TITLES, at the top of each page, offer a different spelling, based on one or more original documents; we hope these will remind users of this edition that they are reading a text which has been modernized. Those interested in the editorial process of modernization may consult the commentary to *Old Law* in this volume, or the textual notes to other works in the *Companion*, which discuss problematic cases of modernization.

Split Verse Lines. Middleton, like other verse dramatists, often divided a verse line between two or more speakers. Early modern texts seldom represent this formal feature visually, and we retain the typical early modern typographical arrangement in *A Game at Chesse: An Early Form*. But elsewhere for the convenience of modern readers we have editorially indented the concluding part(s) of such a divided verse line in order to show the metrical integrity of the line. For instance, in the manuscript of *The Lady's Tragedy* the end of one character's speech and the beginning of the next speech (1.1.208) were written as follows:

see it effected.
———————
Mem. wth best care, my lord

This is clearly intended as a single iambic pentameter line, which we print as follows:

See it effected.
MEMPHONIUS With best care, my lord.

However, in some cases three part-lines are written in such a way that the middle part-line could form a complete verse line with either the preceding or the following part-line. For instance, an exchange in *The Widow* (4.2.197–99) was printed this way in the 1652 first edition:

Bra. I'm all well there.
La. You feel no grief i'th' kidney.
Bra. Sound, sound, sound sir.

The middle speech is an 'amphibious' part-line, which would make an acceptable Middleton verse line in either direction: either

I'm all well there.
You feel no grief i'th' kidney?

or

You feel no grief i'th' kidney?
Sound, sound, sound, sir.

Since both arrangements are equally acceptable, and since the fluidity of the verse in fact depends upon the metrical ambiguity of the amphibious part-line, it would be arbitrary and misleading to adopt either of the two alternative indentations. Accordingly, in such cases all three part-lines are printed immediately to the right of the speech prefix, without indentation.

BRANDINO I'm all well there.
LATROCINIO You feel no grief i'th' kidney?
BRANDINO Sound, sound, sound, sir.

Visually, such arrangements are indistinguishable from three short prose speeches, but the surrounding context should alert readers to whether they are dealing with prose or verse. (Middleton sometimes moves in and out of verse even within a single speech, so if the context does not clarify whether short lines are verse or prose, then the visual ambiguity reflects a formal ambiguity.)

Stage Directions. With Middleton as with other playwrights of his time, early texts are often deficient in describing stage action, even at so basic a level as the entrance and exit of actors. This edition's stage directions are designed to provide the minimum assistance necessary to make the text theatrically intelligible. All editorial additions of debatable directions (including, for instance, most asides, indications of the person addressed by a particular speech, and gestures) are printed in the text within square brackets, but are not recorded in the *Companion*. The *Companion* does include, for every play, a list of every original stage direction, in its original SPELLING and PUNCTUATION, keyed to its position in this edition and (where different) to its exact original location.

Texts/Events. Middleton's works occupy a continuum which runs from objects (printed pamphlets) to unique events (pageants only performed once). To the extent that a work is an object, the specific material forms which concretely embody its language may themselves constitute part of its meaning. (See TYPOGRAPHY.) To the extent that a work is a unique event, where it takes place is part of its meaning: those locations are described in the introductory essays on London (by Paul Seaver) and on the London theatres (by Scott McMillin). Moreover, the same event may be described differently by different witnesses: hence we include alternative descriptions of two pageants, *The Triumphs of Truth* and *The Triumphs of Honour and Industry*, by foreign ambassadors. More generally, an event may be described in more than one object; hence, we include in our 'text' of *The Whole Royal and Magnificent Entertainment* commemorative scripts of the event originally printed in three different publications by three of its collaborative creators, and we include accounts of the Lord Mayor's pageant of 1623 published separately by Thomas Middleton and his collaborator Anthony Munday. Finally, because play texts fall somewhere between these two categories—they are objects purchased by solitary readers, and at the same time they are attempts to represent and regulate recurring events—they can be edited and understood as objects and/or events: see ACT DIVISIONS, PUNCTUATION, SPELLING, and STAGE DIRECTIONS.

Titles. Because Middleton's works are not burdened by overfamiliarity, modern editors may restore their original titles without offending traditional taste. In one case, the only early text has no title at all, and we have supplied a conjectural title of our own (*The Lady's Tragedy*), to replace an earlier, grossly inaccurate conjecture (*The Second Maiden's Tragedy*). Generally the editorial problem is not dearth, but surplus. A number of Middleton's works are given—in separate early documents, or even within the same document—more than one title. In such cases, the running titles in our edition vary from page to page, thereby preserving the titular instability of the work throughout the experience of reading it. Thus, on any given opening, the reader may see '*The Nice Valour*' above the left-hand page, and the alternative title '*The Paſſionate Mad-man*' above the right-hand page, of the same play. We believe readers are capable of thinking stereoscopically, and that no real confusion should result from this practice, which preserves and foregrounds evidence which traditional editions routinely suppress.

Typography. All written and printed texts are embodied forms of language: the size, layout, calligraphy or typography of a text all signal its relationships to other texts, and encode the relationships of its parts to one another. No single book can incorporate the great and deliberate variety of embodiments of Middleton's early texts, and in any case those early embodiments would be unfamiliar and unintelligible to most modern readers. However, this edition does call attention to the range and significance of those early embodiments, in part by photographic illustrations, in part by preserving in a modern form the typographical distinctions of the original texts. Thus, the distinctive 1604 title-page of *The Black Book* is reproduced at the beginning of our introduction to it; the original's use of 'black letter' type for certain sections of the work is indicated here by use of a sans serif font (which suggests the emblematic visual 'blackening' of the text, but does so in a form more intelligible to modern readers); the original gothic font is reproduced in the running TITLES, where readers can be reminded of its function without being disturbed by its (to them) illegibility. Likewise, we preserve the extraordinary six-column openings of *The Two Gates of Salvation*, but do so in modern typefaces and modern SPELLING.

Website. At http://thomasmiddleton.org we publish further information relevant to Middleton and his texts, including additional indexes, illustrations, and links to other sites. It is hoped that this expanding site will eventually contain a concordance to *The Collected Works*.

Works Cited. In the various introductions and commentaries in this volume, references to other works are given in an abbreviated form within parentheses. Full citations for these authors and works can be found at the end of the textual introductions in the *Companion*. This arrangement enables us to document our scholarly sources and obligations, while minimizing the distraction caused to ordinary readers by the courtesy rituals of academic culture.

MIDDLETON AND HIS WORLD

THOMAS MIDDLETON: LIVES AND AFTERLIVES

Gary Taylor

Thomas Middleton and William Shakespeare were the only writers of the English Renaissance who created plays still considered masterpieces in four major dramatic genres: comedy, history, tragedy, and tragicomedy. Middleton was the only playwright trusted by Shakespeare's company to adapt Shakespeare's plays after his death. Middleton wrote the biggest hit performed by Shakespeare's company (or any other company in their lifetimes): the most talked-about dramatic work of its era, with the longest consecutive run, the most manuscript copies, the most surreptitious editions, the first engraved title-pages. But Middleton's triumphs were not confined to one company of actors: he wrote successful scripts for more theatrical venues than any of his contemporaries. The only seventeenth-century printed anthology of memorable passages from English plays quoted the Middleton canon more often than the works of any other playwright. He wrote the period's most popular theatrical song. The first English play translated into Dutch was by Middleton; his work was performed in Amsterdam and Dublin, and accounts of it were dispatched to Brussels, The Hague, Madrid, Florence, Rome, Venice, and Moscow. On and off the commercial stage, Middleton mastered more genres than any English writer of his time. Middleton was the greatest stylist of the Jacobean pamphlet, as Thomas Nashe had been of the Elizabethan pamphlet; as Ben Jonson dominated the court masque, Middleton dominated civic revels. Satirist, polemicist, ghost-writer for a king, co-author of the first masque transferred to the commercial stage, author of the most expensive and elaborate Lord Mayor's pageant that had ever been produced, Middleton was also the first officially appointed Chronologer of London.

'The Hogarth of the pen', he would be called, in a review of the first collected edition of his work (1840); Swinburne praised his 'perfect Hogarthian comedy' (1886), and the first *Dictionary of National Biography* crowned him the 'most veracious painter' of London life (1894). Middleton anticipates Hogarth's sharp ironic eye, his precise capacious vision of the exploding crowded mixedness of urban life. But the anonymous Victorian who compared Middleton to Hogarth was ambivalent about them both: both could be too 'gross' for his own admittedly 'fastidious' taste. Middleton has always made some people uncomfortable. In his own lifetime, his work was publicly burned, condemned from the pulpit in the yard of St Paul's Cathedral, banned by the Privy Council, compared to toilet paper. Cities, Hogarth and Middleton rudely remind us, require sewers—and brothels.

Hogarth's first popular success was *A Harlot's Progress*. The word 'pornographer' literally means 'prostitute-depicter', and in that sense both Hogarth and Middleton qualify. Their worlds wriggle with mistresses, courtesans, whores and whoremongers and whore managers. Middleton sexed language, and languaged sex, more comprehensively and creatively than any other writer in English. He dramatized literal incest in *The Revenger's Tragedy* and *Women, Beware Women*, an adult son's obsession with his mother's sexuality in *A Fair Quarrel*, a husband happily pimping his wife in *A Chaste Maid in Cheapside*, another literally selling his in *The Phoenix*. Middleton depicted the allure of a male transvestite in *Microcynicon* and a female transvestite in *The Roaring Girl*, stalking and sexual blackmail in *The Changeling*, castration and a sexually abusive priest in *A Game at Chess*, marital rape in *Hengist, King of Kent*, male impotence in *The Witch*, masochism in *The Nice Valour*, necrophilia in *The Lady's Tragedy*, pedophilia in *Anything for a Quiet Life*, an adulteress compelled to eat the corpse of her lover in *The Bloody Banquet*. He invoked 'back door' sex, male and female, more often than any of his contemporaries. He inventively—in *A Mad World, My Masters*, *The Roaring Girl*, and *No Wit/Help like a Woman's*—circumvented the prohibition on live onstage sex (fornication, masturbation, lesbianation). Hogarth saves pornography for morality by burying his syphilitic harlot at age 23. Middleton is more generous to his Molls, giving them ethics and eloquence, and dismissing them to whatever happiness can be afforded by marriage to their customers.

But by comparing Middleton to Hogarth, we extract him from the world he represents. The artists of his own time provide better parallels for his life and work. The anonymous *Young Man with a Skull*, depicted by Frans Hals, could have been inspired by the first scene of *The Revenger's Tragedy*. Middleton's tragedies can be as lurid, brutal, and demystifying as Caravaggio's *David and Goliath* or *Judith and Holofernes*. Caravaggio's torn, furrowed-browed *Doubting Thomas*, caught red-handed in that electric moment when scepticism thrusts its finger into faith, could be doubting Thomas Middleton's Captain Ager ('That man should hazard all upon things doubtful') or Vindice ('O, I'm in doubt, whether I'm myself or no') or Timon ('I must ever doubt, though ne'er so sure'). In Middleton's *The Widow*, as in Caravaggio's great painting *The Tooth-Drawer in a Tavern*, a con-artist extracts a painful rotten tooth; both *Your Five Gallants* and Caravaggio's *The Cardsharps* show us a naïve young

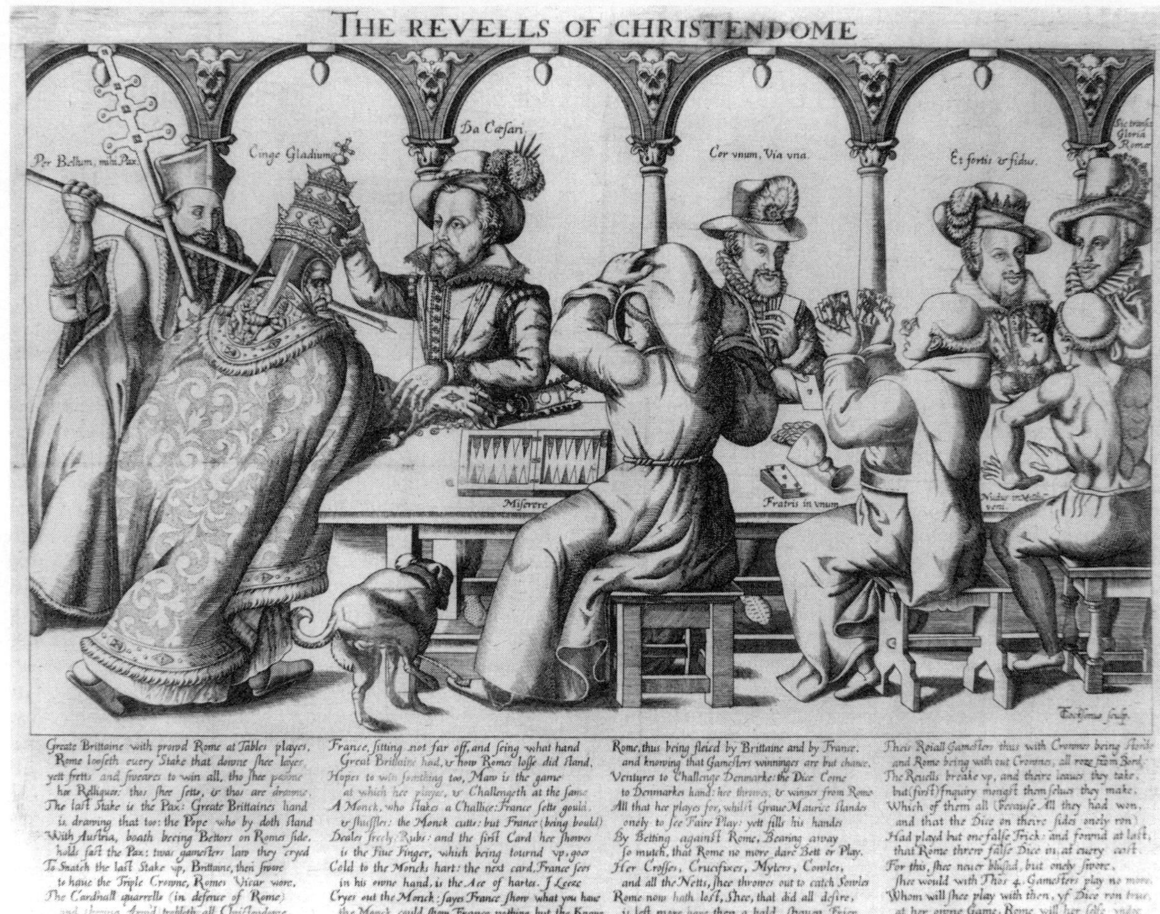

1. *The Revells of Christendome* (1609)—engraved by Thomas Cockson, with verses by an unidentified English poet, 'sold by Mary Oliver in Westminster Hall'—includes caricatures of King James (third from left), Henri IV of France, Prince Maurice, Christian IV of Denmark, the Pope, a Jesuit Cardinal, etc.

man being cheated in a card game; Caravaggio's *Fortune Teller* could be illustrating a scene from *The Spanish Gypsy*. But Middleton could also, like Peter Paul Rubens, portray King James as Solomon, animate allegorical figures like Envy and Peace, dedicate his art to the production of an ephemeral royal parade. As Middleton did in his outdoor pageants and indoor entertainments, Frans Hals painted official group portraits of serious urban dignitaries; but Hals could also crowd canvasses like *Merrymakers at Shrovetide* with the same seemingly spontaneous carnival abundance that Middleton packed into *A Chaste Maid in Cheapside*. The genre paintings of Caravaggio and Hals and the comedies of Middleton do not represent ancient gods and legendary heroes at moments of world-historical significance; instead, we see people like ourselves and our neighbours, doing things we and our neighbours do every day (and night).

Like these painters, Middleton belonged to an expansive European culture. But he also, like them, belonged to a partisan locality. In the 1609 engraving *The Revels of Christendom* (Illus. 1), as in the 1625 engraved title-page of Middleton's *A Game at Chess* (Illus. 2), the official group portrait is satirically superimposed upon an indecorous genre scene. The most powerful men in Europe are imagined as mere gamesters around a table, playing with the fate of nations and the kingdom of heaven. Recognizable individuals inhabit an allegorical action; genres clash; words breed with images. A visual artist collaborates with a poet; both collaborate with the technicians of print; they all collaborate with an entrepreneur who markets their work to a mass public.

However unique Middleton's achievement, it depended upon such middlemen: actors, producers, publishers, printers, carpenters, composers, choreographers, collabor-

2. The title-page of *A Game at Chess* (1625) does not identify the author (Middleton), printer (Nicholas Okes), or engraver, but features caricatures of Prince Charles (bottom right), the Spanish ambassador Gondomar (middle), and the Archbishop of Spalato (left); others seated at the table include Felipe IV of Spain (top left) and King James (top right).

ators of all kinds. Like everyone else's, Middleton's life took place in the middle of other lives. Consider, for example, the inaugural record of his existence (Illus. 3). In it, he is linked directly to his father (no mother being mentioned), and less directly to the names of other children born into the same parish that year: age-mates like Mary Dunscombe, whose mother was buried six days after her baby's baptism, or Anthony Brisley, who would die in a plague epidemic when they were thirteen. In emerging from a womb, Middleton entered a community. Therefore, his entry on this list does not commemorate his birth. It records his baptism: not a private biological event but a public linguistic ceremony, by which a child officially entered into language, was christened and received 'into the congregation of Christ's flock'. Indeed, this list of names existed as a consequence of the Reformation of Christ's flock: in 1538, Henry VIII had ordered every English community to keep a record of its conformity to the new state religion. As a result, every parish had its own bureaucratic 'church book', like the one which becomes a major comic prop in *Old Law*, like the one which records Middleton's emergence from his mother's

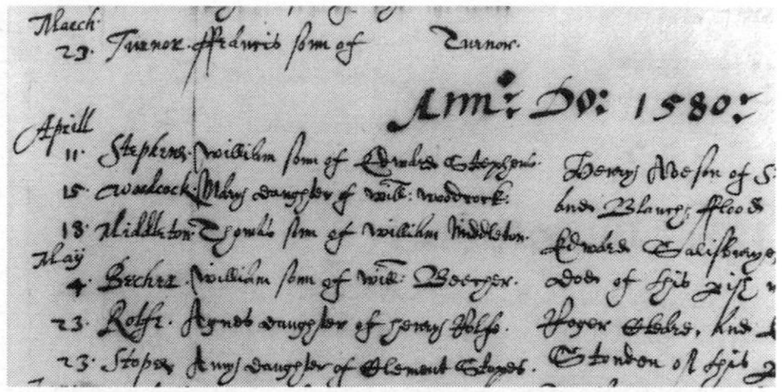

3. Parish register with record of Middleton's baptism.

womb into a parish. On 18 April in the year of our Lord 1580—the year that Jesuits first entered England, in an attempt to roll back the Reformation—Thomas Middleton's godparents, as prescribed by the Book of Common Prayer, vowed to teach him 'the Creed, the Lord's Prayer, and the Ten Commandments in the English tongue, and all other things which a Christian man ought to know and believe to his soul's health', so that he might inherit 'everlasting salvation'. As in Isaak Walton's celebrated biographies of John Donne and George Herbert, as in the private diaries of a London tradesman like Nehemiah Wallington, Thomas Middleton's life was, from its first moments, understood in relation to an after-life.

Any story about Middleton's life and after-life is thus, inevitably, a story of more than one life, of connected lives, of the lives in particular of men who could write their names in the emergent market-place of textual capitalism. But it is also the story of one man's singularity, and of his relationship to what was excluded from that record of his baptism: women.

Generation

In 1580, Anne Middleton was forty-one or forty-two. She presumably gave birth at home, attended by a midwife, who would have tightly wrapped the new-born in swaddling clothes, to keep him warm and immobile. Infant mortality being high, babies were given the benefits of Christianity almost immediately, and Thomas was baptized—probably within days of his birth—in the adjacent church of St Lawrence Jewry. This is the parish church where his parents had been married, where three other Middleton children were baptized and where two of them were soon buried, where his father would be buried, where his mother would remarry.

St Lawrence Jewry (so called 'because of old time many Jews inhabited thereabout') was a 'fair and large' church where, in 1501, Thomas More had given a famous series of lectures on St Augustine's *De Civitate Dei*. It is also a church where, until at least the 1590s, a child could have looked up and seen, 'fastened to a post of timber', the ancient shin-bone 'of a man (as it is taken)', which measured '25 inches in length by the rule' and was of a remarkable 'thickness, hardness and strength'. But if the past of the church was Catholic

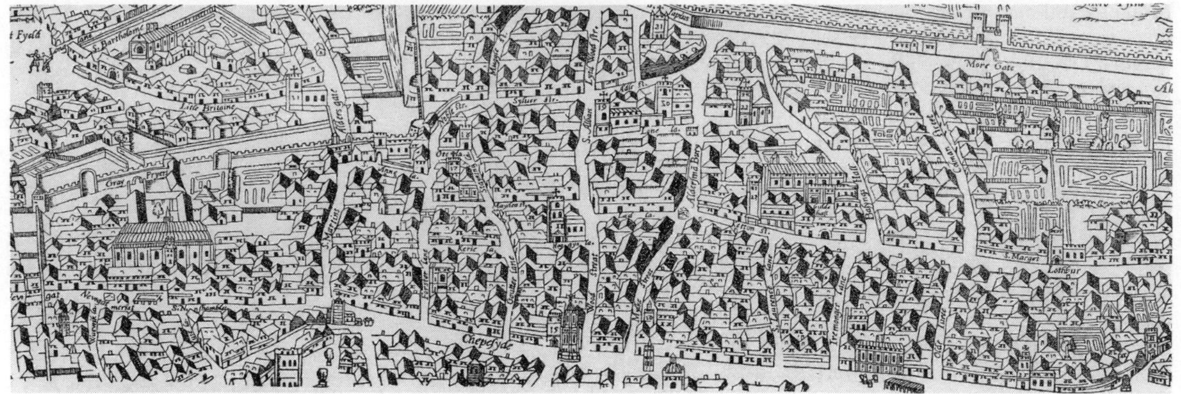

4. William Middleton lived on 'Catteton Strete' (in 1582) and on 'Ironmonger Lane' (in 1586); probably both documents refer to the same house, on the south-west corner of the intersection of the two streets. As a boy Thomas could have walked to Cheapside (bottom) in a minute and a half, and to St Paul's churchyard (far left) in less than five.

and magical, its present was determinedly Protestant. The minister who baptized Middleton was old Robert Crowley, a famous preacher and non-conformist, chosen by the parishioners themselves. For most of Middleton's childhood (1581–94), the vicar was George Dickins, an MA from Christ Church, Oxford, who held prebendaries at St Paul's Cathedral. Dickins was succeeded by another Oxford graduate, Thomas Sanderson of Balliol, whose education had been funded by scholarships from the Haberdashers' Company; Sanderson would become one of the translators of the 1611 'King James' Bible and the author of an anti-Catholic polemic. Unlike many parts of the country, prosperous London parishes were served by the best-educated ministers the Church of England could produce. Their parishioners wanted, and were willing to pay for, extra sermons every week.

Neither Dickins nor Sanderson seems to have been what contemporaries would have called, disparagingly, a 'Puritan' (or a 'presbyterian'); neither advocated further reforms in the rituals or ecclesiastical government of the English Church. But both ministers, like the Church hierarchy until the early seventeenth century, would have internalized and propagated some version of the theology of Jean Calvin (1509–64), a French refugee in Geneva, and the most popular writer in England during Middleton's lifetime. Calvin himself was an eclectic thinker, a tortured humanist who never achieved personal peace or intellectual closure; the best theological minds of early modern Europe wrestled with the problems Calvin posed. Middleton's introduction to such ideas would have taken the simplified form of a memorized catechism, like the one printed in thirty-nine English editions of the Geneva Bible between 1579 and 1616:

> *Question*: Are not all ordained unto eternal life?
> *Answer*: Some are vessels of wrath ordained unto destruction, as others are vessels of mercy prepared to glory.
> *Question*: How standeth it with God's justice that some are appointed unto damnation?
> *Answer*: Very well because all men have in themselves sin which deserveth no less, and therefore the mercy of God is wonderful in that he vouchsafeth to save some of that sinful race and to bring them to the knowledge of the truth.

Human nature was universally depraved. Its depravity began in the womb: 'we may be damned', John Donne insisted, 'though we be never born', and Calvin observed that 'in children many things are corrupt'. Such attitudes obviously affected how parents treated their children, and how children imagined themselves. No one could merit salvation. No amount of good work, no mere exercise of will, could close the gap between human possibility and divine law. God nevertheless, by an undeserved gift of his grace, had predestined some for election to heaven. Most were foreordained to damnation. These may seem abstruse philosophical issues, but an Italian visitor to England in the 1580s reported that 'the very women and shopkeepers were able to judge of predestination'.

To get to the church where such doctrines were taught, the Middletons had only to cross the street, and walk a block. They lived at the intersection of Ironmonger Lane and Catteton Street, in the prosperous Old Jewry area of the city, just north of the really wealthy houses and shops along the wide main thoroughfare of Cheapside (Illus. 4). Middleton grew up in the ward of Cheapside, the setting of one of his most famous plays. The centre of London government, the Guildhall, was—and still is—just behind the church of St Lawrence Jewry, and the processions celebrating the annual installation of a new Lord Mayor would have passed within a block of the Middleton home. In 1592, the mayor so celebrated was Sir William Roe, an ironmonger, neighbour, and fellow parishioner. In 1582 William Middleton (assessed at £20 in the tax roll) was the wealthiest of the nineteen named householders on Catteton Street, and among the wealthiest 10 per cent of Londoners overall; however, more than twenty members of the parish were assessed at £50, and one at £200. But although Ben Jonson's play *Every Man in his Humour* (1598) could thus plausibly allude to 'the rich merchant in the Old Jewry', the neighbourhood, like most neighbourhoods at the time, had a diverse population. The impressive timbered Tudor houses along the main streets were backed by tenements in the warren of narrow unpaved alleys and lanes which contemporary maps do not show, and even in the better homes masters and mistresses lived with their apprentices and servants. A single household could contain its own miniature social order.

In church all classes sang the same psalms. The gospel promised salvation to 'men of every sort'. But although the parish population may have been mixed by the distributions of geography and grace, it was conspicuously stratified by rank and status. Parishioners were arranged in their pews 'in order, in their degrees and callings'. Common people would often rise and bow when their betters entered the church and made their progress to the front pews. These rituals of obeisance were practised not only between families in public, but within families in private. Little Tom would have learned, early, to bow to his parents.

His parents had belonged to this neighbourhood since before 1574, when the parish clerk recorded the marriage of 'William Middleton & Anne Snowe of this parish'. It was apparently William's second marriage. His first wife, Margaret Barwicke, died in 1570 or 1572. She had married William on 21 November 1563; earlier that autumn, during twenty-five days in September and October, all five members of her family had died in the great plague epidemic of 1563, which carried off one-quarter of London's population. William Middleton married a woman who had just lost her entire family, and who almost certainly inherited whatever they owned.

A decade later, when William married Anne Snowe, he was a certified gentleman. On 23 April 1568, Sir Gilbert Dethicke, Garter King of Arms, 'ratified, confirmed, assigned, and allowed' to William Middleton 'and to his posterity forever' a coat of arms (Illus. 5). As a young man, William had—like many London residents—immigrated to the metropolis to take up an apprenticeship; in the unknown elsewhere of his birth, he had 'been of long time one of the bearers of these arms'. Whether this pedigree was the truth or an enabling fiction, it ensured that Thomas Middleton, William's first and only son, was born a gentleman. The gentry constituted perhaps only 2 per cent of England's population. Middleton began life as a member of the governing élite. The abbreviation 'Mr', after all, stood for 'Master'.

By the 1580s, William Middleton, gentleman, was also a prosperous businessman and landholder. He owned copyhold on property in Bishop's Hatfield, Hertfordshire; he also owned a lease for nearly five hundred years on a house and wharf in the eastern suburb of Limehouse.

5. Middleton coat of arms.

In the northern suburb of Shoreditch, he had acquired a fifty-year lease on property adjoining the Curtain Theatre ('where now commonly the plays be played'), then converted a dairy house there into several tenements, from which he received 'a great yearly rent'. In January 1586, his net worth was calculated at just over £335. Such assets would hardly have supported the lifestyle of a substantial country gentleman, but (at a time when an average family could subsist on £11–14 a year) it did put the Middletons squarely in the ranks of the urban 'middle sort', described in 1581 as those who 'neither welter in too much wealth, nor wrestle with too much want'.

William Middleton had achieved this prosperity as a member of the Worshipful Company of Tilers and Bricklayers, one of the less important London guilds. Almost certainly, he had served an apprenticeship of seven and a half years before becoming a freeman of the company, and thereby a citizen of London. A bricklayer's apprentice earned, by law, only seven pence a day, and the profession was neither prestigious nor gentlemanly. But William Middleton profited from the residential construction boom which accompanied the Elizabethan explosion of London's population. He became what we would call a building contractor, training apprentices and employing journeymen. On 5 February 1577 he had been promoted to the company's livery, and at the next company election became one of their Wardens (who were allowed more apprentices than other members). His double elevation was obviously disputed, because it was achieved only as the result of a court order. The Middleton family thus belonged, not only to a parish and a neighbourhood, but to a guild, a group of less than a hundred London households with its own rules, its own hierarchy, its own squabbles, and its own social rituals (like the company dinners at the Mermaid tavern in Cornhill).

On 24 January 1586, members of that guild put on their company livery and attended the funeral of William Middleton. Death may have taken him by surprise, for he had no time to prepare or sign a written will; he spoke his bequests as he lay dying. The cause of death is, as usual, not given, but we do not need incidents like that in St Dunstan's in the West on 1 March 1617—'John Price bricklayer, slain with the fall of a chimney'—to remind us that the construction industry has always had casualties, which a primitive medical technology could seldom help. In any event, to a five-year-old boy the death of his father is almost always unexpected and unexplainable. Who is to know what he made of the words George Dickins, in his gown and surplice, read aloud at the graveside that Monday, as the corpse was made ready to be laid in the cold earth? 'In the midst of life we be in death; of whom may we seek for succour but of thee, O Lord, which for our sins justly art displeased.'

Later that year, on 5 November, the more important corpse of Sir Philip Sidney arrived in London from the Netherlands, where he had died as part of a larger Protestant effort to help the Dutch rebellion against Catholic Spain. But while much of England mourned the death of chivalry, poetry, and 'the very hope of our age', the house on Ironmonger Lane was celebrating a wedding. Most London widows re-married within a year, and an affluent propertied widow like Anne Middleton would have been regarded as a real catch. The man who caught her was Thomas Harvey, a young gentleman who had completed his apprenticeship in 1582 and become a freeman of the Grocers' Company, one of the most powerful London guilds. On 27 July, 'Master Thomas Harvey' had returned to England with Sir Francis Drake, after spending 'the space of one whole year and more in very miserable case' as chief merchant to Sir Walter Ralegh's abortive colony at Roanoke; for his pains his name would be immortalized in the first edition of Richard Hakluyt's *The Principal Navigations, Voyages and Discoveries of the English Nation* (1589). Thomas Middleton thus became the first important English writer to be personally exposed, in childhood, to the backwash of European global expansion. Returning colonists told stirring stories of famous men, of weeks voyaging on the vast Atlantic, of the unmapped hot lush fragrant coast

6. Roanoke woman and child, from an original watercolour painted in 1585 by one of Thomas Harvey's fellow voyagers. The scanty clothing, boyish haircut, and tattoos of the mother, the dark skin and nudity of the child, would all have been scandalously exotic.

of what is now North Carolina, of the strange dress and habits of the Roanoke natives (Illus. 6); maybe Harvey was among those who were later said to 'have spoken of more than ever they saw'. Certainly, like his fellow traveller, the scientist and reputed atheist Thomas Harriot, Harvey had good reason to try to impress folks back home, and to make the most of this disappointing start to England's imperial future. Harvey himself had 'spent or lost whatsoever he embarked and shipped in', and was now 'poor and unable to pay his creditors'. He needed Anne's money. He visited her 'often'; she made enquiries about him through friends on 'whom she relied'; in the end, she 'settled her liking towards him, as a fit man for her to make choice of'. On 7 November, the forty-eight-year-old Anne Middleton vowed to 'obey him and serve him, love, honour, and keep him', and Thomas Harvey, a 'young man' perhaps twenty years her junior, took her 'for better, for worse, for richer, for poorer'.

The 'worse' and 'poorer' began almost immediately. In English common law, wives had no separate property; once married, a woman forfeited all her goods to her husband. But Anne, apparently following William Middleton's dying advice, had taken care to protect the interests of her two young children, Thomas and Avis. Between them, they were entitled to one-third of the estate; Anne 'of her free grant' increased that sum to 66 pounds, 13 shillings, and 4 pence (two-thirds of £100) apiece. In June, she had, with the help of three Inns of Court lawyers, created a complex trust to protect those bequests. Several months later, before her remarriage, the three trustees met with Harvey at Anne's house in Ironmonger Lane, and 'before supper, we all sitting there together', they explained the legal instruments 'given over in trust unto us'; 'Harvey gave his consent, and seemed also at that time not to dislike of anything'. But as soon as the marriage was blessed and consummated, Harvey asserted his prerogative. In an attempt to gain control of the children's portions, he demanded the papers, was refused, 'grew into great choler', and appealed to the Lord Mayor. Anne fought back, turning a wife's lack of independent legal status to her own advantage. Within a month of her marriage, she had herself arrested for defaulting on her financial commitment to the children; Harvey, as husband, was responsible for *her* debts, and so was forced to pay the Lord Mayor's Court, in cash, a sum equal to both bequests. To raise the money, he was compelled 'to suffer his goods to be sold at an outcry at his door'. Within a month of his marriage, the angry greedy Harvey had been ('by the cunning means of his wife') legally and financially humiliated in the very public venues of the Guildhall and the street where they lived.

So began a classic dysfunctional marriage in a country without divorce. There were times of 'peaceable and quiet continuance together' when 'they kept the deceased Middleton's children at their own charge'; Harvey set up shop as a grocer and trained apprentices, probably working, as most small retailers did, from the family home. But for most of the next fifteen years that home was in turmoil. Husband and wife fought, in and out of different courts. Harvey was imprisoned for debt. When he got out, he abandoned the family that did not want him, committing his body to the continuing English war against the Spanish empire. After the defeat of the Armada in 1588, a profitable victory abroad may have seemed likelier than any victory in Ironmonger Lane. Harvey joined the 1589 expedition against Portugal, then served in the Low Countries. Anne refused to send him 'one penny'. When he returned to London, he went back into business as a grocer, taking an apprentice in July 1592, but he was soon arrested for debt again, and spent at least four months in prison (December 1592 to April 1593). In September 1595, he was imprisoned again, this time for plotting to poison Anne. A month later Anne, through an intermediary, paid Harvey £56 to take to sea, in exchange for a deed ceding all the property which had belonged to William Middleton. Harvey left England for most of three years. He was reported dead. But by 1598 he was back in London, alive, and in 1600 he was back in court, suing his wife again—and five other people, including his stepson Thomas. From the beginning, the struggle for conjugal mastery had rippled outward, as neighbours and friends and relatives of both parties joined the tug of war, as tenants and creditors and debtors on the sidelines became involuntary participants, victims of the uncertainty over who controlled the contested properties.

But the most constant victims were Thomas and Avis—inevitably witnesses, and often parties, to an emotional and legal turmoil which lasted from their early childhood all the way through adolescence. Avis, baptized on 3 August 1582, was only three when her father died, four when her mother remarried. Just before she turned sixteen, she contracted a marriage as aggravating as her mother's. Her new husband, Allen Waterer of the parish of St Leonard Shoreditch, was twenty-five, and claimed to belong to the Clothworkers' guild; as soon as he could accumulate enough capital, he could set himself up in business. Avis's inheritance, which Anne had so fiercely protected from her own husband, could not be protected from her daughter's husband. In fact, Anne had some trouble protecting her own assets from her new son-in-law. Newlyweds were expected to set up house on their own, but Allen and Avis moved in with Anne, who gave them 'friendly entertainment'. But 'Allen Waterer and his mother-in-law could not agree together', and a new round of lawsuits commenced. Anne alleged that Allen sought 'to thrust her out of her house, and forbade her tenants to pay her any rent'; Allen alleged that Anne, by 'devilish and subtle practices', sought to deceive 'her own children'. Both Thomas Middleton and Thomas Harvey were soon embroiled in this struggle between Anne and her son-in-law. Allen moved to Holywell Lane (where the famous actor Richard Burbage would have been one of his neighbours); when Harvey went to Holywell Lane to serve a writ, Allen 'did rail, revile, and threaten the plaintiff with whipping... and thrust him out of his ground by the head and shoulder'. In June 1601, Allen assaulted Harvey again, wounding him so badly that his life was despaired of; in December, Allen was again arrested, this time for abusing a constable (who was a friend of Harvey's). From Avis herself, in all these documents, we hear nothing; she was busy elsewhere, bearing three children in three years.

Education

Her elder brother Thomas was luckier. While Avis was trapped at home with her embattled mother, Thomas could escape to grammar school, to the disciplined predictability of hourglass, clock, bell, ten or more hours a day, six days a week, for six or more years. By his seventh birthday, the familiar world of his early childhood had disintegrated: his father was dead, his father's apprentices were dispersed, his mother had married a nightmare, in prison or abroad most of the time, who when he did come home was more likely than not to find 'the doors were shut against' him. I don't know when Thomas entered grammar school; seven was normal, as late as nine was possible, but in any case it must have been in the first three years of his mother's second marriage. I don't know which London grammar school he attended, but all would have been within walking distance. In the years when infancy crossed into manhood, he crossed back and forth between a female vernacular household and a male classical schoolroom.

Even before entering grammar school, he would have learned, like his father, to read and write his mother tongue. His own mother (like 84 per cent of London women in the 1580s) signed her name with a mark; she probably could not write. But she did ensure that young Thomas, at home or at a local petty school, grasped and mastered the material technology and bodily routines of writing, routines which would occupy much of every working day for the rest of his life. 'A hand gets me my living', a professional writer says in *The Widow* (5.1.190): writing was a manual skill, enabling a fully socialized hand to manipulate expensive handmade tools (paper, ink, pens). Francis Clement, in *The Petty School* (1587), explained how to prepare a quill, taken from the feather of a bird, for use as a pen: 'Enter a rift with the edge of your knife even in the mid-back of your quill, then rive the same scissure half an inch into the quill—but, I say, just in the back, lest haply it show ragged and grinning teeth, for then will it never prove good.' There was a 'good' way to sharpen a pen, and a 'bad' way—just as there were good and bad ways of holding it. Proper sharpening and manual posture, careful adjustments to the viscosity of the ink, would enable the student's pen to 'glide or swim upon the paper'. Writing, in the era of inkwell and quill, was a liquid art.

The difference between good and bad in these physical routines was physically enforced. The sovereign schoolmaster rapped and whipped, and set his students to compete against each other for his favour. For the subjects of Tudor pedagogy, there was not only a distinction between good and bad, but a clear hierarchy within the good, and at the top of that hierarchy stood Latin, which was taught in grammar schools. The dominant (and literary) class was bilingual, and its political and economic power would be legitimized, increasingly, by its possession of the cultural capital conferred by literacy and Latinity. We know much of what Middleton learned in school, despite our ignorance of which petty or grammar school he attended, because all schools operated within a narrow range of authorized uniformity. In the 1530s and 1540s, Henry VIII had combined the newly concentrated powers of the Tudor state with the dispersive powers of the new technology of print to commission and impose a set of standardized national textbooks: a primer, a catechism, a grammar, a Book of Common Prayer. By early in the reign of Elizabeth I these had all, after much revision and evolution, hardened into enduring forms. The style and curriculum of English grammar schools was not wholly legislated, but, despite incidental local variations, all followed an educational model articulated by the Dutch humanist Desiderius Erasmus (*c.*1467–1536). This model can be seen, in all its naturalized simplicity, in the summary of an English schoolmaster like William Kempe, writing in 1588 of *The Education of Children*:

> first the scholar shall learn the precepts; secondly, he shall learn to note the examples of the precepts in unfolding other men's works; thirdly, to imitate the examples in some work of his own; fourthly and lastly, to make somewhat alone without an example.

The 'precepts' here are both moral and stylistic; the 'other men's works' come from the literature of classical antiquity; the goal is the production of some written 'work' of one's own, first by imitation, then by invention. This educational regime slighted women, mathematics, science, technology, any vocational skill; it was designed to produce male eloquence.

It produced Middleton. It did so, in part, by demanding that literature be perceived and experienced as a complex interlocking system of widely distributed printed texts. Rather than diet upon a single admired model, like Cicero, Erasmus demanded that one feed as widely as possible upon the writers and genres of antiquity: oratory, philosophy, epic, satire, comedy, tragedy, fable. By memorizing, 'unfolding', and imitating, the student internalized this cornucopia of texts as a storehouse of human possibilities and verbal strategies, which could be immediately accessed and applied, as occasion demanded. All thought was textual, and textuality was modular, broken down into parts which could themselves be broken down into subparts (genres, authors, works, speeches, phrases), broken down to be recycled, every component susceptible to recombination, fragments becoming ornaments, collaged into handbooks and anthologies, reconnected in a net of polytextual cross-referencing, inexhaustible, interminable.

What the ideal student achieves by this process is *copia*, myriad-kinded copiousness. What Middleton achieved was an ability to write prose, verse, comedy, tragedy, tragicomedy, history, allegory, masque, pageant, satire, poetry commendatory or commemorative, biblical commentary, annals. Moreover, this abundance of works is matched by an abundance within works, a pleasure in the piling up of plots, voices, classes, things, an everywhere multipliciousness—in the unexampled conspicuous consumption of *The Triumphs of Truth*, the carnivalian fertility of *A Chaste Maid in Cheapside*, the panoply of parody in *The*

Owl's Almanac, the comprehensive mortality of *Women, Beware Women*. Here, indeed, is Erasmus's plenty.

The link between the past *copia* of the grammar school canon and the future *copia* of the grammar school graduate was copying. 'Nature has implanted', Erasmus observed, 'in the youngest child an ape-like instinct of imitation'. Selves would best be fashioned by mimicking a fashion they could see: students enacted dialogues which taught them the proper fashion for everything from wiping their nose to polishing their prose. More advanced school exercises regularly included instructions like 'make some *parodiae*, or imitations of Latin verses'. Middleton—whose family crest was a chained ape (Illus. 5)—was compelled to mimic. We do not possess any of the innumerable school compositions he must have written in the 1590s, but his apprenticeship by *imitatio* was continued in the works he wrote between the ages of sixteen and twenty-two: *The Wisdom of Solomon* (an exercise in paraphrase and amplification), *Microcynicon* (Roman satire), *The Ghost of Lucrece* (Ovidian epistle), *The Penniless Parliament of Threadbare Poets* (compilation on a set theme), *Two Shapes* (Roman history). However effective these works are, their shared artistic agenda was the prescribed imitation of prescribed models.

But the end of imitation is an ability 'to make somewhat alone without an example'. Erasmus advised his students, '*teipsum ... exprimis*' ('express yourself'). Elizabethan grammar schools studied authors as unalike as Virgil and Lucian, and produced students as unalike as Sidney and Nashe, Shakespeare and Herbert, Heywood and Jonson. Uniqueness is common, and no one, then or since, writes quite like Middleton. Through all the diversity of his genres and characters there persists a particularity—a register of words, a registering of the world—as distinctive as his signature.

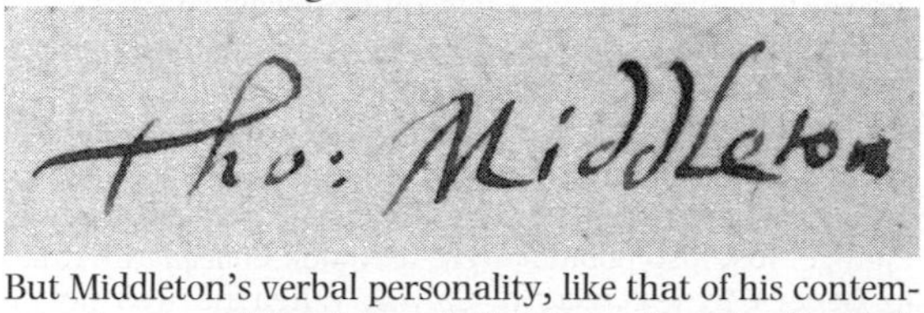

But Middleton's verbal personality, like that of his contemporaries, was defined by relation to a shared, reiterated, enforced, memorized, dead ideal. Sidney's quantities, Jonson's armature of abstruse art, the polysyllability of Shakespeare, of Milton the grammar alien and grace alluding—these are all approaches to the common goal of making English classical.

Tom Middleton read the same authors and learned to use the same figures. But whereas other writers of his time were described as 'our Virgil' (Spenser), 'the English Petrarch' (Sidney), 'a second Ovid' (Greene), 'England's Horace' (Jonson), or a compound of Theocritus, Virgil, Ovid, Lucan, Orpheus, and Homer (Drayton), Middleton did not make or attract such comparisons. He instead celebrates 'modern use' (*The Triumphs of Integrity* 85). Writing 'in these latter days', he has only a fallen language for a fallen world. That language is more immediately intelligible to twenty-first century readers, less encumbered with classical allusions or obsolete linguistic forms, than the writing of any of his contemporaries.

As often as I look upon that treasure,
And know it to be mine—there lies the blessing—
It joys me that I ever was ordained
To have a being, and to live 'mongst men:
Which is a fearful living, and a poor one,
Let a man truly think on't.
To have the toil and griefs of fourscore years
Put up in a white sheet, tied with two knots:
Methinks it should strike earthquakes in adulterers,
When e'en the very sheets they commit sin in
May prove, for aught they know, all their last garments.
O what a mark were there for women then!
But beauty able to content a conqueror
(Whom earth could scarce content) keeps me in compass.
I find no wish in me bent sinfully
To this man's sister or to that man's wife:
In love's name let 'em keep their honesties
And cleave to their own husbands, 'tis their duties.
Now when I go to church, I can pray handsomely,
Not come like gallants only to see faces,
As if lust went to market still on Sundays.

(*Women, Beware Women* 1.1.14–34)

William Hazlitt, who in 1808 began the resurrection of Middleton's reputation, praised his scenes as 'an immediate transcript from life'. But to call him a transcriber or—as T. S. Eliot would later do—'merely a great recorder', is to misrecognize art as artlessness. No English writer before Middleton had ever achieved such sustained transparency, or constructed such seemingly unconstructed representations of the shifting currents of ordinary speech. What the cultural arbiters of Middleton's lifetime admired in *The Countess of Pembroke's Arcadia* or Josuah Sylvester's translations of Sieur du Bartas was aristocratic artifice, consciously modelled on the monumentality of written texts more than a thousand years old. Middleton learned to listen instead to the transcience of the vernacular, to the human preoccupation not only with eternity but with ephemera: news, almanacs, fads and affectations, the slippery emotional wave-front of daily, hourly, life. Recommending *The Roaring Girl* to potential readers, his introductory epistle does not invoke the comedies of Aristophanes, Plautus, or Terence, but instead compares 'the fashion of play-making' to 'the alteration of apparel'; the most he will say of his own work is that it is 'a kind of light-colour summer stuff', 'fit for the times'. Even when he wants to commend someone else's play—like *The Duchess of Malfi*—he uses the language not of permanent stone but of perishable fabric. 'Thy note | Be ever plainness', he advises his friend John Webster, ''tis the richest coat.'

Immediately below these English verses 'upon this masterpiece of tragedy', Middleton writes a couplet in Latin '*In Tragœdiam*'. This movement between two languages is typical of grammar school routines; however grand the design, much of the daily grind involved translation from Latin into English, English into Latin—or (later) either into Greek, Greek into either. Middleton's first published work, *The Wisdom of Solomon*, is a translation, as is *Sir Robert Sherley*; he can quote Ovid in *Microcynicon*, Seneca in *The Revenger's Tragedy*, Horace and Virgil in *A Game at Chess*; his plays adapt material from Plautus and Terence which he probably read in Latin in school. But *No Wit/Help like a Woman's* demonstrates his fondness for Petronius, a Roman writer too raunchy for the curriculum—and also establishes his familiarity with a play, published only a few years before, by the Italian writer Giambattista della Porta. A command of Latin made romance languages easy to acquire, and Middleton was especially interested in modern European writers: he read the anti-Petrarchan Pietro Aretino, the satirical Miguel de Cervantes, the realist Niccolò Machiavelli, and many others now less familiar.

But the ability to read and write other languages may have been less formative than the linguistic habits associated with translation itself. People who are fully bilingual do not translate one of their languages into the other; they simply switch, as occasion demands, from the first self-contained vocabulary and syntax to the second (like an ambidextrous ballplayer, catching with her left hand, then her right). But Tudor grammar school had less to do with learning to use languages than with learning to translate them. Middleton spent six or seven years wrestling with the insolubles of translation. Of course, the sometimes extended family of meanings housed in one word in one language will seldom coalesce in any single word in another language; young Middleton and his fellow translators will, inevitably, often have been defeated by desired meanings left out, or undesired meanings thrust in. One effect of such repeated frustrations is a heightened sensitivity to puns, double meanings, complex words; another is an awareness of the uncontrollability of reference.

The Latin word *translatio* can be translated by the Greek word μεταφορά ('metaphor'), and a third effect of years of *translatio* is an interest in the effect of conflating dissimilar contexts. Middleton read the satires of Horace alongside those of Joseph Hall; he mixed Lucian with Nashe. In the summer of 1593, he and his schoolmates translated dead texts, while the bubonic plague translated their neighbours into graves. (In six months the ground around St Lawrence Jewry accommodated seventy-seven fresh corpses, sometimes in clusters: Alice Tilstone, for instance, lost both her children and her husband; Henry Ainsworth, haberdasher, lost two children and two servants.) Middleton might have been reading Virgil's *Georgics* at any time between 1594 and 1597, when two poor harvests were succeeded by two years of dearth; prices in London rose 10 per cent a year—the most concentrated burst of inflation in the entire sixteenth century, and particularly devastating for families (like his own) on fixed incomes. In 1597 he paraphrased *The Wisdom of Solomon*—and joined his mother in selling the reversion of a lease on the Curtain properties; he received twenty shillings for his share, and was allegedly a party to her expulsion of several tenants. Did the judgement of Solomon comfort or condemn him?

The next year he escaped to Oxford, where it should have been easier to ignore such disparities between the word and the world. He arrived there in April of 1598, a few days short of eighteen, a common age for matriculation. At least a full day's journey from his family and the other 200,000 residents of London, Oxford was a townlet of only about 6,000 inhabitants—most of them associated, one way or another, with the University. Middleton's fellow residents at Queen's College were, of course, all men; they included Thomas Overbury (later an influential figure in the court of James I) and a number of future divines: preachers like Robert Johnson and John Moore, the noted Puritan Robert Mandevill, the argumentative Richard Pilkington, and Barnabas Potter, who would become a chaplain to Prince Charles. George Abbot, then at University College, would in 1611 become Archbishop of Canterbury; he is probably represented as the White Bishop in *A Game at Chess*. But the man who more than any other had shaped the personality of Queen's College since 1586 was John Rainolds, leader of the Puritan party in Oxford and, arguably, in all of England. Rainolds moved to Corpus Christi College at about the time Middleton arrived, but his influence on Queen's, and the students and fellows he had attracted, long remained. In March 1599 Henry Airay, like Rainolds a champion of evangelical Calvinism, and unlike Rainolds an admired neo-Latin poet, was elected Provost of the college.

Elizabethan England was a nation dominated by an enforced state religion, and Protestantism was a part of every aspect of Middleton's education, beginning with the memorized catechisms of petty school. In grammar schools the day often began, at six o'clock, with 'prayers on bended knees'; Virgil and Horace were sometimes supplemented by such 'Christian poets' as Juvencus, Prudentius, and Palingenius; also popular were textbook *Colloquies* written in Geneva by followers of Calvin. When he was not in school, Middleton, if he resembled other Londoners, paid at least as much attention to sermons as plays. In the decade of the 1580s, 113 sermons were printed (as compared to only 16 plays); by 1600, religious lecturers in London were preaching 100 sermons a week, in addition to the regular weekly sermons offered in parish churches.

Many of those sermons were preoccupied with the question posed by the famous preacher William Perkins: 'How a man may know whether he be a child of God, or no?' Calvin's division of the human world into those predestined to damnation and those elected to salvation made this the most urgent of personal questions—far more important, for most believers, than doctrinal disputes or ecclesiastical politics. It was a question which often provoked a crisis of identity, particularly among young adults. Mere outward piety was no proof of election; as another preacher observed, often enough a beautiful apple 'at the core is rotten'. You must examine the core, your inner self, for signs of its spiritual state, which would forecast your eternal destination. Failure to do so—persistence in what Calvin castigated as 'self-ignorance'—was itself a sign of the reprobate. Believers therefore tied themselves to 'daily self-examination', scanning for latent content, anxiously anatomizing 'those evil desires that do gently tickle the mind'. The word 'psychology' was first used, in 1575, by the Protestant theologian Melanchthon; in the next seventy-five years, English collected a store of new compounds beginning with the word 'self', including several apparently coined by Middleton (self-affecting, self-changing, self-conceiving, self-disparagement, self-scandal, and self-treason).

This reading and rereading of the self attended an equally endless and intense reading of the Bible, for Protestants not only the key to salvation but also the greatest of the ancient classics. 'Upon this book I will found my church', Luther might as well have said, and upon its *copia* could be modelled many literary genres. Solomon and David were celebrated as the two chief authors of what tradition and Sir Philip Sidney called 'the poetical part of the Scripture'. Sidney himself, with his sister the Countess of Pembroke, translated all the Psalms; Donne declared their putative author, David, 'a better poet than Virgil'. Such readings of Scripture inspired a Protestant poetics which informed the spiritual lyrics of Donne and Herbert, the epics of Spenser and Milton, the satires of Marston and Hall. All these writers struggled to combine a classical with a biblical tradition; so did Middleton.

If it seems sacrilegious for any author to see himself in a mirror supplied by Solomon or David, the country pastor Herbert or the blind titan Milton may at least appear likelier candidates than lewd metropolitan Middleton—so fascinated by the fiscal and the physical, so familiar with debased genres of writing and living. But neither biblical poet was an innocent; both were great sinners, both transgressed publicly and privately. Their example authorized an implicated, political, metrosexual poetry, a poetry aware of its own sinful place in an imperfect human order. It was, after all, the author Solomon who 'looked on all the works that [his] hands had wrought' and realized 'all was vanity and vexation of spirit' (Eccl. 2:11), realized that 'of making many books there is no end' (12:12). Middleton's portrayal of authors—in *The Black Book, The Puritan Widow, The Nice Valour, A Game at Chess*—suggests that he was equally conscious of the devices and vices of the textual trade.

The texts and devices of the legal trade kept intruding on Middleton's efforts to study Aristotle's *Rhetoric* and other staples of the university curriculum. Sometime in 1598 he 'came from his place in Oxford to help his mother in those troubles' between her and his brother-in-law Allen Waterer. New students were supposed to remain resident in Oxford for a full uninterrupted year, and absconders could lose their scholarships; one witness thought Middleton, by answering his mother's call 'lost his fellowship at Oxford', which had allegedly been secured for him by his stepfather. Certainly, family troubles kept interfering with his intellectual life, and the pursuit of an intellectual life kept eroding his inheritance. In the summer of 1599 he was again in London, a party to further legal wrangling between his mother and his brother-in-law; on 3 December 1599 he sold Waterer his half-share in the Limehouse lease. On 10 June 1600, his stepfather Harvey began two lawsuits, designed to secure control of all the family properties; these would drag on for almost a year. Long before the verdict (in Harvey's favour), Middleton had, on 28 June 1600, sold Waterer his share of the other properties in return for money 'paid and disbursed for my advancement and preferment in the University of Oxford, where I am now a student, and for my maintenance with meat, drink, and apparel, and other necessaries'—including, presumably, books.

The books he was buying, though, were not necessarily the ones recommended by the University authorities. It's tempting to read autobiographically his account of a poor student: he 'daily rose before the sun, talked and conversed with midnight, killing many a poor farthing-candle', reading 'Aristotle's works', but he was then 'unfruitfully led to the lickerish study of poetry, that sweet honey-poison that swells a supple scholar with unprofitable sweetness and delicious false conceits,' and as a result eventually became 'one of the Poor Knights of Poetry' (*Father Hubburd's Tales* 1125–51). Certainly, by the summer of 1600, Middleton had sold, for an Oxford education, the entire landed inheritance his mother had fought so many years to preserve. Seven months later, he had lost Oxford, too. On 8 February 1601, the Earl of Essex, the man to whom Middleton had dedicated his first work, launched an abortive rebellion, in London, after commissioning a special performance of Shakespeare's old play about deposing a king, *Richard II*; on 8 February 1601, Middleton too was 'in London, daily accompanying the players'. The end of the Earl's life coincided, fortuitously, with the end of Middleton's academic career. Like most gentlemen—like his fellow playwrights Francis Beaumont, John Fletcher, and Philip Massinger—he left the university without taking a degree.

On 21 April 1601, before the Lord Mayor and Aldermen, Middleton acknowledged receipt of £25 which had been set aside for him at the time of his father's death, and held in trust until his twenty-first birthday. Middleton was the protected orphan of a citizen of London; but the City had now discharged its duty. He was a gentleman; but he had no land and no guaranteed income. He was the son, stepson, and brother-in-law of tradesmen; but he had no vocation. He had been to grammar school and university; but he had no career. He had £25 and talent.

Vocation

Sidney had described poetry as his 'unelected vocation', and Middleton had the same calling. But he did not have Sidney's income or leisure. He would be defined, by himself and others, in legal records and in print, as a 'poet'—a word then applied to any kind of writer, in verse or prose. Whether poets are born or made, Middleton had been one since 1597. But four years later, he became a poet in another sense, never pertinent to Sidney. To write, Middleton had to eat; to eat, now, he had to find someone who would pay him to write. Middleton in 1601 became a professional poet. Unlike Sidney or Donne or Ralegh, or himself at an earlier age, Middleton was now 'merely' (wholly and only) a poet. For such men, there were three possibilities: patronage, print, and plays.

Writers were sometimes subsidized by aristocratic connoisseurs. Thomas Nashe had been, briefly, the guest of Sir George Carey; Samuel Daniel was being supported by the Countess of Pembroke; Ben Jonson would be maintained for thirty years by notables minor and notables major. Middleton apparently lacked the ability or the effrontery to insert himself into personal favour with the aristocracy. By 1604 literary patrons were epitomized, for him, by Sir Christopher Clutchfist, 'the Muses' bad paymaster'; they 'never give the poor Muse-suckers a penny'.

In the absence of estates or patrons, a poet must set his 'wit to sale'. Wit was retailed in bookshops and theatres. Both these outlets were relatively new; both depended on new textual technologies, which could only flourish in cities. Concentrated urban populations provided a dense enough market to support a capital-intensive leisure industry. Gutenberg's development of movable type and viscous ink in the mid fifteenth century eventually transformed the book trade; but the high cost of an investment in presses, type fonts, and paper stocks bankrupted any printer who did not have ready access to a market large enough to buy up quickly or predictably hundreds of copies of a single book. Likewise, enclosed purpose-built theatres transformed the economics of playing, by enabling actors to charge in advance for admission and to hierarchize prices in relation to a fixed hierarchy of architectural space; but a profitable return on such investments in the purchase or lease of land and buildings could only be sustained in areas where thousands of people were able and willing to pay for admission many times each year. Once these industries were established, both actors and printers generated a demand for fresh wit, which in turn transformed the economics of authorship.

The first books printed in England had appeared a century before Middleton's birth. By multiplying copies and reducing costs, print increased the accessibility of texts; what technology made possible, ideology made desirable, as the Reformation urged individual Christians to learn to read, so they could encounter the Word of God at first hand. Supply and demand began to spiral around each other in an ascending double helix. From Middleton's birth to Elizabeth I's death (1580–1603), half again as many new titles were published as in the years from her accession to his birth (1558–1579). The market was still dominated by theological books (half of all extant titles between 1583 and 1623) and by stock secular work like primers, almanacs, and proclamations, but a small market for original vernacular literature had emerged, to be filled by writers such as Robert Greene, Thomas Nashe, and Samuel Rowlands.

But man could not live by print alone. Authors did not own copyright and received no royalties. Monsieur Lepet's pamphlet, *The Uprising of the Kick*, promises to become 'a stock book', like 'the almanacs ... and the *Book of Cookery*'; but ''tis the bookseller | That has the money for 'em', not the masochistic author (*The Nice Valour* 5.3.9–16). A commercial success like *The Owl's Almanac* (two editions within four months) earned Middleton no more money than *The Two Gates of Salvation* (copies of which still remained unsold eighteen years after its publication). For each pamphlet Middleton would have been paid up to £2, a flat fee which remained constant for more than sixty years, oblivious to inflation. In lieu of or addition to this fee, he might receive a certain number of copies to sell on his own: Nashe is described 'fiddling [his] pamphlets from door to door like a blind harper for bread and cheese, presenting [his] poems like old brooms to every farmer'. The author as door-to-door salesman was forcefully reminded that his texts were merchandise; however finely made, literary commodities were of less utility than the housewares which local manufacturers were producing in unprecedented quantities.

A more dignified form of salesmanship was the dedication. Middleton had dedicated *The Wisdom of Solomon* to the Earl of Essex (1597), and *The Ghost of Lucrece* to Baron Compton (1600). The dedicatee, honoured by this unsolicited homage, was supposed to reciprocate with a cash gift. A lucky dedication might net as much as £3; an unlucky one, nothing. The return on a dedication was thus higher, but less predictable, than a bookseller's fee. Taken together, fees, sales, and dedications over the course of twenty years earned the prolific Elizabethan pamphleteer Richard Robinson only about £3 annually—not even a subsistence income for a single adult.

By contrast, for what was apparently his first full-length play, *The Tragedy of Randolph, Earl of Chester*, Middleton was paid £7. In 1601, more experienced dramatists might receive £8 per play, and by 1613 a single script could be worth as much as £20. Between 1598 and mid-1603, professional dramatists like Henry Chettle, Thomas Dekker, and William Haughton were earning about £25 a year in fees from a single company—and they could also have been selling to other companies. In addition, they pocketed the surplus profits from the second or third performance. Each purpose-built Elizabethan theatre manufactured and sold vicarious emotion to hundreds or thousands of customers, six days a week: for the first time in European history, the commercial playhouses and their acting companies mass-produced and routinized the commodification of affect. The new technology needed new scripts, and a successful playwright could make two or three times as much as most university graduates.

Given the economics of patronage, print, and playing, it is not surprising that Middleton chose plays. As Francis Meres observed in 1598, 'for lack of patrons—O ingrateful and damned age!—our poets are solely or chiefly maintained, countenanced, and patronized by our witty comedians and stately tragedians'. But the theatre's appeal was not just financial. One of Middleton's collaborators on his first recorded play, Michael Drayton, confessed that his 'pride of wit' and 'heat of blood' could not help being moved by the 'shouts and claps at every little pause, | When the proud round on every side hath rung...' Moreover, the applause of the audience was enhanced by the exciting company of other playwrights. In 1601, Middleton could see new plays by Dekker, Heywood, Jonson, Marston, and Shakespeare, not to mention revivals of Marlowe, Kyd, and Nashe. In 1602, he was paid to write his own prologue and epilogue for a revival of Robert Greene's best play, *Friar Bacon and Friar Bungay*. Backstage, he was initiated into a fraternity of wit.

Unlike the guilds of Bricklayers or Grocers, that fraternity had no royal charter, no statutory privileges, no governing body, no incremental structure of professional advancement. Nevertheless, there was a pattern to playwrights' careers. They worked for companies of actors; they did not run their own businesses; they did not sell directly to the public. If the theatres had been organized as a guild, its masters would have been the actor-sharers who co-owned a joint-stock theatrical company like the Admiral's or the Chamberlain's Men. Playwrights were normally journeymen, 'hired men' like the freelance actors paid for their role in mounting a given play. Like other hired men, playwrights were not guaranteed regular employment; they received no share of the company's profits; they owned none of its real or chattel property. Like journeymen, they often did piecework, writing 'new additions' to a valuable old property—as Middleton did to Shakespeare's *Macbeth* and *Measure for Measure*, as others did to Middleton's *The Bloody Banquet*, *No Wit/Help like a Woman's*, and *The Nice Valour*.

Upon the standards of the dead (the classics studied in school, or play scripts written by earlier authors) were superimposed the standards of the living (the actors and audiences to be pleased now). Whether doing piecework or writing masterpieces, playwrights had to fit their product to the company's market profile: regular actors of a known number and type working in a particular theatre serving regular customers of a certain kind. Companies, if dissatisfied with the attempted fit, could demand that a script be altered or shortened. Ben Jonson, John Webster, and Richard Brome complained about such changes to their texts; Middleton did not—either because his scripts were less self-indulgent, or because he was more hospitable to criticism of them, or more persuasive in answering it. Successful companies had to be flexible enough to welcome initiatives and take risks, but a playwright had to persuade a company that his initiative was worth their risk. He had no power beyond his ability to persuade. And he became more persuasive with each successful play. Thus, although a playwright did not earn royalties, successful work paid future dividends by enhancing his credibility, his 'credit', with companies of actors. Most playwrights acquired a stock of credit by an apprenticeship, in which they collaborated with older, more experienced men. Middleton between 1602 and 1605 collaborated with Munday (twenty years his senior), Drayton (seventeen years), Shakespeare (sixteen), and Dekker (perhaps ten).

All playwrights worked within the same structure, but they had different relations to it, and to each other. In the first place, the fraternity was small—smaller than a guild—and all of its members must have known each other. More than half the known plays written between 1590 and 1640 were the work of just twenty-two men. Of these, several were amateurs, people who were not dependent on the theatre for a permanent livelihood and who did not stay in it long. Mr John Marston composed satires and satirical plays while attending the Inns of Court and awaiting his inheritance, but he would not have considered himself a professional writer; Mr Francis Beaumont after a short smart career as a playwright secured a marriageable heiress and retired to her country estate. When John Webster inherited his father's successful business as a saddler, he still worked on plays—including *Anything for a Quiet Life*, with Middleton—but he could do so at his leisure. If some men of means wrote plays on the side, so did some actors: Nathan Field, Thomas Heywood, Samuel Rowley, William Rowley, and William Shakespeare. These men enjoyed an unusually privileged position, being shareholders in the companies which bought and performed their plays. But they were not the only writers with sustained relationships to a single company. Beginning perhaps with Henry Chettle in 1602, some playwrights who were not actors signed contracts binding them to a company, giving it exclusive rights to their work, and promising to supply an agreed number of plays for a fixed annual sum. In later decades, John Fletcher, Philip Massinger, John Shirley, and Richard Brome were apparently monopolized in this way.

Middleton was not an actor, he could not afford to be an amateur, and as a newcomer he could not expect an exclusionary contract. He began writing plays as a freelance, learning through collaboration with veterans, staking a claim to professional status. But if that much was almost inevitable, other decisions were not. Though he often collaborated, Middleton never, to our knowledge, teamed up to write a play with Beaumont, Fletcher, Jonson, Chapman, Marston, or Massinger; he certainly must have known them all, but he did not run with that crowd. Though Middleton wrote brilliantly for companies of very young actors, he clearly preferred Paul's to what Thomas Heywood called the 'bitterness, and liberal invectives' of the rival children's company at the Blackfriars. Middleton began 'accompanying the players' during the War of the Theatres (a public jeering match between acting companies and their playwrights), and it was almost impossible not to be situated within the attendant rivalries and personal pairings. By collaborating with Dekker, he aligned himself against Jonson, and that alignment soured relations between Jonson and Middleton for the next quarter-century. But Middleton's early partnership with Dekker represents more than a personal rejection of—or by—Jonson. After all, young Middleton (whose father had been a bricklayer) might seem to have more in common with the satirical Jonson (whose stepfather was a bricklayer, and who was himself a dues-paying member of that company) than with the good-hearted Dekker; he might seem to have even more in common with the satirical educated gentleman Marston. But Dekker, like Shakespeare and Rowley and Heywood after him, by his very difference complements Middleton. Jonson rejected difference; Middleton collaborated with it.

So Middleton in 1601 or 1602 became a 'stagewright', a profession held in no more esteem than acting (which most people considered a vicious frivolity). But Middleton remained a gentleman, a distinction regularly advertised on his title-pages. He shared this mixed status—a compound of the élite and the contemptible—with Francis Beaumont, John Fletcher, John Marston, and William Rowley. Ben Jonson was not born, and never became, a gentleman, nor did he marry into a gentry family; so that when, in 1619, he gossiped that Middleton was 'a base fellow', his disdain had the edge (and the envy) of an *arriviste*, berating his social superiors for not living up to their rank.

Within two years of becoming a dramatist, Master Middleton's life had been transformed. By the end of 1603, his mother was dead, Queen Elizabeth was dead, his brother-in-law was dead; he was married, his wife was pregnant, and he was laid off.

He had married Mistress Marbeck, a woman baptized in 1575 as 'Magdalen' but later called 'Mary'; either name could be reduced to the nickname 'Moll', and both could be combined as Mary Magdalene, or 'Mary which was called Magdalen' (Luke 8:2), the female disciple of Jesus. Granddaughter of a famous musician, once persecuted for his Protestantism, who became royal organist at Windsor (John Marbeck, *c.*1505–1585?), and niece of the chief physician to Elizabeth I, who was also a tobacco-advocate and chronicler of the 1596 expedition against Cadiz (Roger Marbeck, 1536–1605), Mistress Marbeck was the daughter of one of the Six Clerks in the Court of Chancery, Edward Marbeck. She was born in the parish of St Dunstan in the West, where her father died in December 1581. Middleton and Marbeck probably met, not by way of any of her distinguished relatives, but through her less distinguished brother, an actor; Tom Marbeck and Tom Middleton were both working for the Admiral's Men in 1602. Like her husband, Mistress Marbeck had been born in London, belonged to a gentry family, had lost her father at an early age, and had much youthful experience of life in the company of lawyers. They lived together for a quarter of a century, and by entering his life she decisively changed its plot. From about the age of seven to about the age of twenty-two, Middleton had attended an all-male grammar school, an all-male university, and theatres run by all-male companies of actors performing plays written by an all-male club of playwrights. Regular female companionship, by day and night, was itself a new experience.

This female, moreover, must in some respects at least have differed from those he had known since childhood. His mother Anne, like his Queen Elizabeth, was—by the standards of the time, and the standards of a child—already old when he was born; although he may have admired, and could hardly have ignored, the capable independence of both, their wrinkled parsimonious stubbornness was probably less attractive. 'Such a troublesome woman'—that is what hostile witnesses called Anne in the last decade of her life, and what if they dared they might have called Elizabeth. If Anne was too old and inflexible, Avis was too young and malleable: a wife at sixteen, a mother at seventeen, a silent property in the struggles between her husband and her other relatives. When Allen Waterer died in July 1603, Avis married again within two months—yet managed in the interim to be swindled by Allen's brother. By marrying Mistress Marbeck, Middleton chose a companion of a very different type.

Women normally married earlier than men, and were younger than their husbands; Mary (Magdalen), though, was five years older than Thomas—which made her seven years older than Avis. In seeking or accepting a gentleman-playwright as a husband she did not make a timid or conservative choice, but her judgement was sound enough. Unlike Avis, Mary (Magdalen) chose a man who was educated, witty, a good collaborator, a good provider who did not much trouble the courts or his neighbours, a man remarkable for his representations—in plays like *The Patient Man and the Honest Whore* and *Anything for a Quiet Life*, in pamphlets like *The Peacemaker*—of a masculinity defined by non-violence. And unlike Avis, Mary (Magdalen) did not exhaust her youth bearing and raising offspring: she had, to our knowledge, only one child, their son Edward, born between November 1603 and November 1604. Either she was lucky, or the Middletons, like increasing numbers of English couples in the seventeenth century, managed their sexual life in a way which emphasized conjugal 'comfort', not procreation.

Mary (Magdalen) was also responsible for a change of residence. They were not married at St Lawrence Jewry; and although I don't know where they set up house initially, by 1609 they were living in the village of Newington in Surrey, where they stayed for the rest of their lives (Illus. 7). The medieval village had changed little in the preceding three centuries, and as late as 1853 the American visitor Harriet Beecher Stowe found it a 'charming retreat' with a view from the window of sheep and lambs grazing in a meadow. Long famous for its peaches and gardens, praised for plentiful 'cakes and ale',

7. In this 1681 map, Newington has a few more buildings than it did in Middleton's time, but still contrasts strikingly with his childhood neighborhood, crowded a century earlier (Illus. 4). The road on the lower right, in Middleton's time called 'Blackman Street', led to Southwark and London Bridge. The road on the upper right led to Lambeth Palace. The River Thames is beyond the right edge of the map (north).

Newington was a short trip 'over the fields' on the marshy south side of the Thames, where family friend John Gerard (author of the famous *Herbal* published in 1597) found water violets in the ditches. When Middleton, in the *Honourable Entertainments*, visualized the 'field-empëress' Flora, her 'close-enfolded rose', her 'ruffling robin and lark's heel', he was celebrating the countryside still intact all around Newington. For most of his adult life, he had to walk through that stubbornly rural world to get to the urban rush-and-clutter of actors, alewives, and aldermen.

'Blackman Street', where the Middletons lived, was artificially raised above the surrounding floodplain, and lined on both sides with hedges; it was part of the old Roman road that crossed London Bridge, passed through Southwark, then headed south-west to Portsmouth (by way of Clapham, Wimbledon, and Kingston-on-Thames). Alternatively, you could reach Middleton's home by taking the horse-ferry from Westminster to Lambeth, and walking from there along Lambeth Palace Road. Newington was one of 'the city out-leaps for a spirt' (in 1639), a place Londoners could reach easily on foot on day-trips, particularly on Sundays, when they wanted to get away from it all. It was not far from the open-air theatres on the south bank, and for more than a decade had a theatre of its own, which hosted *Titus Andronicus* and *The Jew of Malta*, among other plays, in the 1590s. The parishes of Southwark—where Avis lived, after her first marriage—had come under the jurisdiction of the Mayor of London in 1550. Newington, by contrast, was still a separate village, but close enough to the City for easy commuting.

It was also growing. By October 1599 there were new 'houses where the playhouse did stand at Newington'; maybe the Middletons eventually lived in one of them. In 1576, the parish of St Mary's Newington had a population of about 2,000; fifty years later, it had increased to about 3,000. This parish was wealthy enough, and close enough to London, to attract as its 'parson' a doctor of divinity from Cambridge University, 'Master Doctor' Thomas Puckering, who had in 1572 matriculated at Queen's College, where he acquired his BA (1576), MA (1579), BD (1586), and DD (1591). Puckering was rector from at least 1594 to 1617. St Mary's Newington was able and anxious to attract an educated ministry, and to hear 'lectures' in addition to the weekly sermon. But Middleton, although a gentleman, was apparently not wealthy or important enough to play an active part in parish affairs: in the October 1624 subsidy roll of taxable incomes in Newington Butts, he had the lowest possible assessment; taxability put him, financially, in the top quarter of the population, but at three pounds, eight shillings he was worth only about one-sixth the amount his father had been, more than forty years before. Though he probably lived in Newington for more than two decades he was never mentioned in the vestry minutes. The vestry was dominated by George Cure (head of Newington's leading gentry family) and Thomas Edge (who might have been Middleton's step-uncle).

In late 1603 Middleton's recent marriage, however happy, and his new home, however pleasant, gave him at least one and possibly two more bodies to feed, house, and

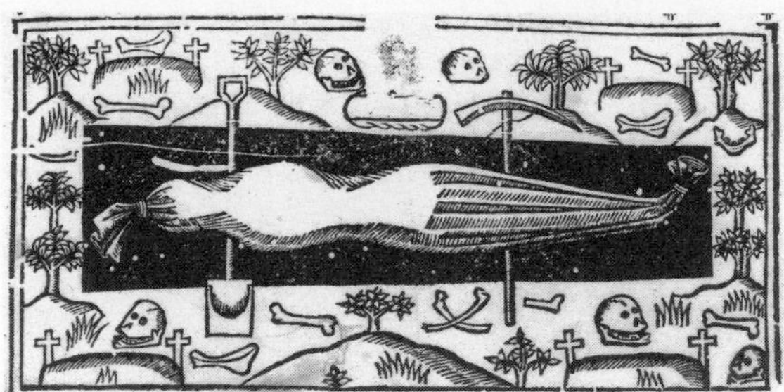

8. 'A sheet with two knots, and away' (*A Chaste Maid in Cheapside* 5.1.6). A corpse, wrapped in a knotted sheet, prepared for lowering into the grave.

worry about in a period of personal and social crisis. In May 1603, London suffered another outbreak of bubonic plague (described in *News from Gravesend* and *The Meeting of Gallants at an Ordinary*). Many people fled London, and if the Middletons had not already moved to Newington, the plague should have encouraged them to do so. In the first eight years of James I's reign the plague remained endemic in London. In 1625, another major outbreak occurred, but by then Newington was no longer a refuge: from 1 June to 8 August, it suffered 401 deaths (twenty times the average death rate), burying perhaps 13 per cent of the parish in 69 days (Illus. 8).

The plague did not kill Middleton or his family, but it did imperil his livelihood. In spring 1603, in response to the epidemic, municipal authorities closed the theatres, which apparently did not reopen until April 1604, and for the rest of the decade they were, by even the most optimistic estimates, closed more often than open. The London theatres had had nine years of uninterrupted and expanding prosperity, but the 1603 epidemic exposed the inherent insecurity of their market. Even during plague, acting companies could survive by touring provincial towns, but in such conditions they did not have the money or the need to buy new scripts. The plague was therefore particularly devastating for artisans like Middleton, whose income was entirely dependent on the economic climate in London. In the thirty-six months from January 1608 to December 1610, for instance, there may have been only eight months of public playing; his only known productions during those three years are two pamphlets and half a play.

Unlike bricklayers or grocers, playwrights had no guild to protect them from unfair competition, or to support them in hard times; because they were usually paid in advance, by installments, they were often working for money they had already spent. Dekker, Field, Jonson, and Massinger were all, at different times, imprisoned for unpaid debt; Middleton in 1609 defaulted on a debt of £6, and in 1606—depending on whom you believe—did or did not pay off a loan with the manuscript of a new play. If an uncontrolled market was one source of uncertainty, censorship was another: in 1605 Jonson and Chapman were imprisoned for writing a satirical play. In 1599, Middleton's own *Microcynicon* had been one of a number of satires burned by order of the Archbishop of Canterbury. For a nineteen-year-old, it can be both frightening and exhilarating to be considered dangerous, but the consequences were sometimes far more serious. In the same ecclesiastical crackdown, printers were forbidden to publish any more works by Nashe—thereby depriving him of his livelihood, and pitching him into the terminal poverty described by Middleton in *The Black Book*.

Middleton had some familiarity with poverty. In 1600 two witnesses described his stepfather Harvey as 'extreme poor'; in 1606, 1607, and 1608 his sister Avis and her husband were in court *in forma pauperis*, seeking to recover money they had lost in 1603. Avis's second husband, the cutler John Empson, was apparently no more successful as a businessman than Anne's second husband had been. As their examples demonstrate, people—including 'gentlemen' like Harvey—moved in and out of poverty, and many paupers were 'poor householders which be ashamed to beg and be no common beggars' or 'poor able labouring folk' who could not find work, or were 'not able to live off' the work they could find. The numbers of the poor in England, the depth of their poverty, the gap between wages and the cost of living, all rose steadily during the sixteenth century, reaching a brutal nadir in the years from 1580 to 1630. Middleton could have seen the human consequences on his own doorstep. In 1612, the overwhelmed 'inhabitants and parishioners of the town of Newington' petitioned the national Privy Council 'to have some contribution towards the maintenance of their poor'; in recognition of the severity of their need, they were granted £15 yearly, from county funds, for relief of the indigent. In 1618 several members of the Fishmongers' Company built twenty-two almshouses for the poor at the corner of Lambeth Road and Blackman Street, which must have been very near Middleton's home on Blackman Street; Middleton celebrated this act of charity in *The Peacemaker* (ll. 175–7), published that year.

Poverty was, of course, the cruelly literal opposite of the *copia* which humanist rhetoric treated as a metaphor. 'A good thrifty man will gather his goods together in time of plenty, and lay them out again in time of need', Sir Thomas Wilson noted in *The Art of Rhetoric*, 'and shall not an orator have in store good matter, in the chest of his memory, to use and bestow in time of necessity?' For Middleton, 1603 was a 'time of need', in which he drew upon the 'good matter' he had laid up during his education and apprenticeship. But the relation between plenty and paucity was not just temporal; if in one sense they alternated in time, in another they cohabited, structurally bound together, both socially and rhetorically.

Rhetorically, *brevitas* complements *copia*, as scarcity does abundance. They had often been opposed, but Erasmus insisted that good authors yoke concision to amplitude, and he demonstrated their interdependence in his influential *Adagia*, a huge textbook compendium of aphorisms. If *copia* best describes the scale and variety of

Middleton's matter, *brevitas* better describes his manner. His first successful publication, *The Penniless Parliament of Threadbare Poets* (1601), abridges and reshapes an earlier sprawling work three times its length; later, he probably trimmed as much as 25 per cent off Shakespeare's *Macbeth*, and abridged his own *A Game at Chess* to two-thirds its performed length. In 1611, he contrasted the 'huge bombasted plays' of Elizabeth's reign, 'quilted with mighty words to lean purpose', with the 'spruceness' of 'neater inventions' which had become fashionable under James I. This generational shift from the long-winded to the tight-lipped belonged to a larger European reaction against the Ciceronian accumulation of tropes and clauses, a reaction stimulated by the Flemish humanist Lipsius and the French dialectician Ramus, which found its first important English advocate in Francis Bacon. Sidney and Lyly heaped; Herbert and Middleton honed. But for professional writers this turning of the tide of literary fashion also reflected an economic shift. Spenser's epic amplitude had appealed to the self-aggrandizement of potential patrons. But why write long plays or pamphlets, when you got paid the same amount for short ones? Shakespeare could afford to elaborate, because he was a major shareholder in a profitable acting company; so could Jonson, because his main income came from court masques. Both had the leisure to embellish, and expected their work to embellish the leisure of others. Middleton did not. He was one of the first inhabitants of a commercial and mental world he summed up in three words: 'hurry hurry hurry' (*Revenger's Tragedy* 2.1.200).

Socially, Middleton's lifetime straddled the centre of a century-long deepening of the divide between rich and poor: the poor got poorer while the rich got richer, partly because the population grew more rapidly than the economy. A surplus of labour depressed wages, but created new opportunities for an expansive merchant capitalism. Theatres themselves illustrate this evolution. Joint-stock companies like the Chamberlain's Men were originally formed by actors who between them owned the assets and divided the profits from a new industry supported by a multiplying population. But as these founders retired or died their valuable shares, like stocks, could be inherited or bought by people who did not work in the theatre, but profited from the labour of those who did. Those who did work were, even so, the lucky ones, for there were soon more would-be players than there were parts to play. Edward Alleyn, one of London's first leading actors, made a fortune large enough to endow the founding of Dulwich College; none of his successors did so well.

The situation for working writers was even worse. Writers belonged to an intellectual class in part deliberately created by a state-sponsored educational boom. During the first two or three decades of Elizabeth's reign the expanding needs of the Protestant church, the state bureaucracy, and the legal profession created relatively buoyant opportunities for educated young men. But the supply of intellectuals soon exceeded demand for their services. When the first enclosed theatres were built in London, in the years just before Middleton's birth, the need to perform regularly in a fixed location created a sudden ravenous demand for new plays; this commodity hunger, which helped compensate for the shortfall in state employment, fuelled the careers of the first generation of dramatists—men like Greene, Peele, Kyd, Marlowe, and Shakespeare. But as the decades passed, acting companies acquired, in their chests and memories, stocks of old reliables, which could be revived without paying living playwrights for new scripts. By the reign of Charles I, almost three-fourths of known court performances were revivals of old plays. Middleton's generation of dramatists, attracted by the theatrical prosperity and achievement of the last decade of Elizabeth's reign, found themselves in an increasingly constricted and competitive marketplace. Success for one meant failure for another; worse, a playwright with a long career was eventually competing with his own past successes. Playwrights became less, as shareholders became more, secure.

Consummation

What security was achievable for a writer, Middleton had achieved by the end of 1604. His comedy *The Phoenix* was performed at court in February of that year. In March, he was named as part-author of *The Magnificent Entertainment*, commissioned by the City of London to honour their new king. He sold five pamphlets to London publishers; two were popular enough to be reprinted within the year. Even before he had sold the last pamphlet, he had begun collaborating with Dekker on *The Patient Man and the Honest Whore*, a play printed within months of its first performances, and which remained popular, on stage and in print, for more than thirty years. His apprenticeship was over, and he had fashioned a career which would engage virtually every aspect of early modern textual culture.

The shape of that career is most easily seen by stepping back from the annual succession of texts—which can, in any case, be read, for the first time, in the chronological parade of this edition—and looking instead at certain recurrent features of Middleton's working life. Most obvious is the diversity of his Renaissance self-marketing: the embodiment of 'Wit at Several Weapons', Middleton made plays for different companies, pageants for the city, pamphlets for the book trade. In all these venues, he worked in collaboration, often with other writers, always with groups which had their own corporate interests. Outside these professional networks, his career brought him into complicated relationships with different artistic constituencies: the legal community, the City authorities, the royal court, and—beyond all those, most important and least definable—the shifting community of readers and spectators, the great laity of literature, the daily physical world which preachers and proclamations could only imperfectly regulate. In relation to such issues, the work of 1604 epitomizes the next two decades of Middleton's professional life.

By 1604, if not before, Middleton had reduced his vulnerability and dependence on any one literary market by diversifying his portfolio. *The Phoenix* was performed by an all-boy company playing indoors at St Paul's; *The Patient Man and the Honest Whore*, by Prince Henry's Men, playing outdoors at the Fortune Theatre. Middleton worked in all for at least seven companies; his plays exploit the varied artistic opportunities offered by different casts, theatres, audiences. He may also have exploited—as Robert Daborne did—the rivalry between companies, getting a higher price for his product by offering to sell it to a competitor.

He supplemented his income as a playwright by writing pageants and pamphlets. The pageants were the outdoor sector of a larger market in subsidized theatre, which also included indoor shows written for the City (*Honourable Entertainments*), the royal court (*Masque of Cupids*), or the Inns of Court (*Masque of Heroes*). Competition for such lucrative work was direct and intense: in the case of Lord Mayor's shows, for instance, a guild committee considered scenarios for pageants submitted by several writers, and chose one. Not surprisingly, most of the successful bids came from playwrights who had proven their talent in the theatres; play-writing served as an apprenticeship for pageant-writing.

Moreover, as in the theatres, a would-be pageant-writer might get his start by working as a junior collaborator with a more experienced colleague. Middleton assisted Dekker in 1604, and for his first Lord Mayor's show, in 1613, he worked with Anthony Munday (who did not write the pageant but did produce it, and received a much larger share of the fee). Middleton wrote and produced six of the nine annual shows between 1617 and 1626. His first two, in 1613 and 1617, were both written for the Grocers, and his family connection with that guild may have helped him win the contract: Sir Thomas Myddelton, the Lord Mayor he celebrated in 1613, was about the same age as his stepfather Harvey, and like Harvey was involved in various overseas ventures in the 1580s and 1590s. As in the theatre, success increased a writer's credit with his employers, and made it likelier that he would be commissioned again. But, also as in the theatre, writers were paid for one job, with no guarantee that they would receive another. The City offered nothing comparable to the monopoly enjoyed by Ben Jonson at court, who between 1616 and 1625 was paid for fifteen masques. Nonetheless, Middleton was the City's chief writer from 1616 to 1626, responsible for Lord Mayor's parades, indoor revels, and civic celebrations of the monarchy. Those pageants, rather than his plays or poems, also brought him the only personal financial patronage he is known to have ever received: in November 1613 'Mr. Middleton the poet' received ten shillings (half a pound) from another Thomas Myddelton (1586–1666), the son of the Lord Mayor for whom our man Middleton had written *The Triumphs of Truth*, performed a few weeks before. The relationship indicated by this little gift may have been important to Middleton's future career: Mayor Myddelton remained prominent in London until the late 1620s, and was one of the city's four members of Parliament from 1624 to 1626, and his eldest son (who like the poet had matriculated at Queen's College, Oxford) would be elected to Parliament in 1624 and 1625—and in the 1640s would become an important officer in the Parliamentary army.

For men like Mayor Myddelton the poet Middleton not only wrote and produced civic revels; he also—unlike Jonson—published them. He prepared a narrative description of all his pageants, dedicating each to the Mayor it celebrated. He collected ten of his indoor shows into a volume of *Honourable Entertainments*. This practice no doubt reflected Middleton's sense of the 'perfection' to which civic pageantry could aspire, and his commitment to the political and social values of the City. But it also provided him with another source of income and another relationship to the book trade.

To book-buyers as to theatre-goers, Middleton's appeal was protean. In his lifetime, his publications ranged in format from the diminutive octavo of *Microcynicon* to the imposing large folio which included *The Life of Timon of Athens*, in typeface from the black letter of *The Black Book* to the roman of *Meeting of Gallants at an Ordinary* and the italic used for speeches in all the pageants, in visual design from the simplicity of *Plato's Cap* to the six-columned complexity of *The Two Gates of Salvation*, in price from a penny for *The Penniless Parliament of Threadbare Poets* to the sixpence that an early purchaser paid for a freshly-printed copy of *A Mad World, My Masters* to the shilling (twelve pence) apiece paid for bound second-hand copies of *The Phoenix* and *A Trick to Catch the Old One* in 1628. These material embodiments of his texts are not simply stamped by printers upon passive authorial flesh; Middleton actively exploited the potencies of print. Like the difference between theatrical spaces, the difference between textual spaces created opportunities for imaginative play. The size of *Microcynicon*, for instance, is characteristic of poetry books in the 1590s, but it also reflects its title, which itself reflects its author's youth; black letter is used in parodies of black letter genres; type, length, and price help to define the size and social status of a work's readership, which in turn helps to define the author's stance, from *Plato's Cap*, doffing his cap 'To all those that are laxative of laughter', to *Honourable Entertainments*, gravely addressing 'his worthy and honourable patrons'.

The Black Book, printed twice in 1604, sported a special black title-page, and this use of original visual designs would characterize every Middleton play published from 1611 until his death. *The Roaring Girl* was not the first commercial play printed with a title-page woodcut—there were a few scattered precedents between 1590 and 1609—but Middleton became the only dramatist of his time to make such illustrations a regular feature of printings of his plays. *The World Tossed at Tennis* (1620) was the first masque with an illustrated title-page; *The Triumphs of Health and Prosperity* (1626), the first Lord Mayor's show;

A Game at Chess (1625), the first individual English play printed with an original title-page engraving—actually, with two separate engravings in editions by different printers. Middleton may have been influenced by woodcuts on the title-pages of pamphlets, like the one which he read when writing *A Yorkshire Tragedy*: then as now, a striking cover can effectively promote the text it contains. But such visual accompaniments were particularly appropriate to dramatic texts, where they part-supplied, part-suggested, the spectacle of a full performance.

Middleton himself was clearly involved in the publication of *The Roaring Girl* in 1611—just as in 1604 Dekker had been involved in preparing *The Magnificent Entertainment* for the press, and as Middleton in that year prepared pamphlets to sell to printers. What changed between 1604 and 1611 was the application to a play of routines previously used for pageants and pamphlets. Nine of Middleton's plays were printed between 1604 and 1608, but there is no evidence that he participated in their publication; some are anonymous, others misattributed, and none contains a preface, epistle, or dedication. Most were probably sold to printers by two acting companies which broke up between 1606 and 1608. Middleton in that decade apparently accepted the view expressed by the actor-dramatist Thomas Heywood in 1608, who suspected the 'honesty' of men who made 'a double sale of their labours, first to the stage and after to the press'. Either Middleton avoided reselling his plays, or at least he wanted to conceal his doing so, and so avoided any sign of personal involvement in their publication. By 1611, such squeamishness had vanished, as part of a larger gradual shift in the literary status of plays. In that year, Middleton and Dekker published *The Roaring Girl* with an illustrated title-page, an authorial epistle, and a list of Dramatis Personae; Heywood himself published his play *The Golden Age*, to be followed two years later by *The Silver Age* and *The Brazen Age*; and Jonson for the first time dedicated the text of a play (*Catiline*) to an individual patron. Not everyone recognized this social-climbing genre, of course. Sir Thomas Bodley, founder of the great library at Oxford, still lumped playbooks with 'almanacs' and other 'riff-raffs', and thought that including such 'baggage books' in the University's library would cause a 'scandal'. But in some quarters at least English plays had begun to be taken seriously as literary works, as commodities with a small but growing clientele in the book trade, and as labour which authors could honestly offer to the reading public.

The Roaring Girl, the first of his plays which Middleton prepared for the press, was printed by Nicholas Okes for the bookseller Thomas Archer. Okes had a hand in more Middleton books than any other stationer, sometimes as printer, sometimes as publisher: he published all but one of Middleton's civic pageants, and printed two unlicensed editions of *A Game at Chess*, apparently from a manuscript supplied by the author. In the early seventeenth century a stationer's shop was a small business, dominated by the character and interests of its owner, and Middleton must have known Okes personally, perhaps as well as he knew the actor Richard Burbage (whose epitaph he wrote) or the impresario Philip Henslowe (whose account book he appears in): these were all men with whom he had sustained professional associations.

Okes was, like Middleton, a native Londoner, Middleton's age, married at about the same time, with an eldest son just a little younger than Middleton's. In December 1603 he ended his apprenticeship in the Stationers' Company, the guild which controlled the book trade, and got married; for the next three years he must have worked as a journeyman printer, until in January 1607, for £70 or more, he acquired a press of his own and became, at the unusually young age of twenty-seven, a 'Master Printer'. This is a sign of his status within the guild; it does not imply that he was a distinguished craftsman. English printers were much less accomplished in the art of fine bookmaking than their continental counterparts, and Okes was often sloppy even by English standards. But he did have a taste for plays. In his first year of independent operation he printed the first edition of *King Lear*, and later would print the first edition of *Othello*; he was also eventually responsible for work by Beaumont, Daborne, Daniel, Dekker, Donne, Fletcher, Ford, Heywood, Jonson, Munday, Taylor, Webster, and Wither. In working on these authors, and Middleton, Okes reflected and encouraged changes in the book-buying market.

Okes was not the only printer Middleton knew. Most Jacobean stationers were the owners of small shops, where Middleton the reader presumably browsed and bought books from the same men to whom Middleton the writer occasionally sold manuscripts: men like William Stansby (who printed Middleton's *Masque of Heroes* and Jonson's *Works*), Edward Allde (who printed a surreptitious edition of *A Game at Chess* in 1625, four years after he had been imprisoned for an equally scandalous book about the King of Bohemia), and Thomas Archer (who published not only *The Roaring Girl* but a series of texts on 'the woman question')—to name only three of the forty-three stationers who dealt in Middleton texts during his lifetime. Of course, these men all knew each other, too. The book trade was often collaborative: in 1608, Okes was one of two printers who shared the manufacturing of Middleton's *A Mad World, My Masters*, which was retailed by a third. Work on the first edition of *The Magnificent Entertainment*, in 1604, was divided among four separate printers, as was *The Patient Man and the Honest Whore*, also in 1604.

Such shared printing was part of a larger pattern of collaboration within the culture. Dekker, Middleton, and Jonson all composed parts of James I's royal entry into London, several other people wrote and delivered individual speeches, Stephen Harrison was 'the sole inventor of the Architecture', hundreds of craftsmen contributed. Later, when publishing accounts of his Lord Mayor's shows, Middleton went out of his way to acknowledge his collaboration with craftsmen such as Garret Christmas. Pageants were pervasively collaborative.

So were plays. Again, Middleton's collaboration with Dekker in 1604 is typical: a third of his known plays and masques were written with one or more partners. In context this statistic is not surprising, since from one-half to two-thirds of all plays written between 1590 and 1642 are of plural authorship, and in other periods and genres of literary production collaboration has been far more common than Romantic myths of solitary genius lead us to expect. These working partnerships could develop into, or out of, intensely personal relationships: Francis Beaumont and John Fletcher allegedly shared a bed and a woman, and when Beaumont retired to the country Philip Massinger became Fletcher's chief collaborator, eventually being buried in the same grave. After Ben Jonson and Inigo Jones had collaborated for decades, their break-up was as venomous as the worst divorce. In the Renaissance theatre, inspiration was often (perhaps always) social, a process of reciprocal stimulation. The division of imaginative labour in the sweatshops of wit could make the making of plays dramatic, an unpredictable performance of give-and-take, collaborate-and-compete, connect-and-contrast. What began as apprenticeship could develop into fellowship: by 1611, when they co-wrote *The Roaring Girl*, Middleton and Dekker were equal partners.

When Dekker was imprisoned for the debts he accumulated while producing the 1612 Lord Mayor's show, Middleton found another collaborator—or another collaborator found him. William Rowley was, unlike Dekker, a gentleman, and almost certainly younger than Middleton. He was also an actor, apparently described in a ballad of 1612 as 'the fat fool of the Curtain' [Theatre]. Certainly, his known roles are remarkable for their jolly obesity. He 'personated' Jaques, 'a simple clownish gentleman' in his own play *All's Lost by Lust*, and through almost every play which Rowley wrote or co-wrote bustles an endearing idiot, apparently created for Rowley to recreate—Bustopha in *The Maid in the Mill*, Young Cuddy Banks in *The Witch of Edmonton*; Pompey Doodle, Chough, Gnotho, Simplicity, Lollio, Sancho, in plays in this volume. Part of the appeal for an audience of this gallery of harmless happiness is the very familiarity of the actor in the new role. When the Fat Bishop says, 'I've all my lifetime played The fool till now' (*A Game at Chess* 2.2.92–3), or when Sancho is asked 'What parts dost use to play?' and replies that he could 'fit you' in the role of 'a coxcomb' (*The Spanish Gypsy* 4.2.73–5), we hear, through and in the character, the great clown Rowley.

But the clown was no fool, and he could play more than one part. Rowley's first known play was published in 1607; like most of his work, it was written in collaboration, and over the course of his career he teamed up with the best in the business—Day, Dekker, Fletcher, Ford, Heywood, Webster, and Wilkins. But he also wrote, occasionally, on his own, and his (lost) *Hymen's Holiday* was successful enough to be selected for court performance in February 1612. After Rowley's success and Dekker's arrest, in 1613, Rowley and Middleton began collaborating, and over the next decade they wrote at least six scripts together. Rowley by then belonged to the Prince's Men; since 1609, the patron of his company of actors had been Prince Charles, who with the death of his brother Henry in 1612 became heir to the throne. In 1616, Rowley became leader of the Prince's company, and in the same year Middleton wrote *Civitatis Amor* to celebrate Charles's investiture as Prince of Wales. This shared connection was strengthened in 1620, when Prince Charles commissioned Rowley and his company to create a masque, *The World Tossed at Tennis*, which Rowley wrote with Middleton. In 1624 Middleton wrote, and Rowley acted in, *A Game at Chess*, a play which—like the earlier masque—probably pleased Prince Charles as much as it annoyed his father. But the Prince was only a small part of the complex collaboration between Middleton and Rowley. Most critics consider them the best doubles team in the history of European drama.

One of the plays they wrote together was *Old Law*; one of the roles Middleton wrote for Rowley was performed at the law-school of the Inner Temple. The London legal community was one of the most important constituencies for drama and dance. In fact, the relationship between actors and lawyers goes back at least as far as the fifth century BCE, when Athenian tragedy and comedy were both influenced by the rhetoric, forms, and cases in Athenian law courts. This connection, made at the beginning of European drama, was also made at the beginning of Middleton's career: *The Phoenix* contains some of his funniest satire of lawyers, whose manœuvres he had been watching since he was six. Some such distrust of legalistic modes of thought was encouraged by Protestant theology, with its insistence upon the superiority of grace to law. On the other hand, many members of Middleton's audiences—especially at St Paul's—were lawyers, and he probably had personal relationships with some of them. In addition to the lawyers who helped his mother construct her trust fund, Middleton certainly knew attorney Michael Moseley, who represented him in court, and his wife Mary (Magdalen) Marbeck had been born into the legal community. As a 'Six Clerk' Edward Marbeck had been involved in almost every aspect of proceedings in the Court of Chancery. Although Mary's father had died twenty years before she met Middleton, her family must still have had law-world friends: each of the six Six Clerks had as many as eight under-clerks, and in 1594 it was estimated that the office was worth £3,000 per annum.

Such income derived from a structure of collaboration, masquerading as rivalry: though one client might lose, both lawyers would always win. Dramatists and actors, likewise, whatever their personal or professional rivalries, joined forces to relieve clients of their assets—as Middleton shows, openly and comically enough, in *A Mad World, My Masters* and *Hengist, King of Kent*. The common player and the common lawyer—increasingly well paid, increasingly professionalized, increasingly conspicuous in the daily life of early modern London—were both verbal performers for an audience which had to pay whatever the outcome. Playhouses and courthouses proved, from *The Phoenix* to the end of Middleton's career, difficult to disentangle. *Michaelmas Term* (1604–5) is named for, and begins with a personification of, the first term of the annual legal season; *A Yorkshire Tragedy* (1605) is based upon a scandalous court case; *Old Law* (1619?) defends common law against arbitrary prerogative; *Masque of Heroes* (1619) entertained the Inner Temple; Middleton gave copies of *A Game at Chess* (in 1625) and *The Witch* (in 1625?) to Inns of Court lawyers; some of his poems circulated in manuscript miscellanies apparently compiled in the same milieu. Some of the stationers who dealt in Middleton texts, like John Browne and George Eld, had shops near the Inns, and catered to lawyers and law students. As a critic facetiously concluded in 1885, if 'Shakespeare was [Sir Francis] Bacon, we can only say that it is quite certain that Middleton was [Sir Edward] Coke'. (Coke was the better lawyer, but James I preferred Bacon's more absolutist legal theories.)

Middleton recorded Bacon's impeachment by Parliament, and Coke's imprisonment by the King, in his *Annals* for the year 1621. Both entries testify to Middleton's continuing interest in lawyers, but the manuscript which contains those entries was written as part of his new job as official Chronologer of the City of London. If lawyers were one constituency to which Middleton appealed, the wholesale merchants who governed London were another: *The Marriage of the Old and New Testament* was dedicated, in 1620, to two such merchants, John Browne and Richard Fishbourne. John Stow had received a subsidy from the City for research on his *Survey of London* (1598, 1603), as had Anthony Munday for revising Stow's work in 1618; but Middleton in September 1620 became the first writer to be promised an annual City salary for recording contemporary London life for posterity. It was a job he had in fact been doing two decades before the post was created. Middleton spent a good part of his career representing Londoners to themselves—idealistically in his civic pageants, ironically in his equally numerous city comedies. The popular comedies of the 1590s had dramatized, typically, times and places in the misty distance of romance; but from *Michaelmas Term* to *Anything for a Quiet Life*, Middleton depicted contemporary London with its pants down, usually with a hand in someone else's pocket or placket. In 1623, he signed himself *Poëta et Chron. Londinensis*, 'Poet and Chronicler of London', a phrase as ambiguous in Latin as in English.

Though written for the City, *The Whole Royal and Magnificent Entertainment* celebrated the accession of James I, and *The Phoenix*, though written for a London theatre, was also performed before the new royal court—which presumably enjoyed its vision of a vigorous new ruler, replacing one who, after 'forty-five years' in office, had grown tired and out of touch. In play and pageant, Middleton represented the court of James I to itself and others. In subsequent years, *A Trick to Catch the Old One*, *No Wit/Help like a Woman's*, *Masque of Cupids*, *A Fair Quarrel*, *Old Law*, *The Widow*, *More Dissemblers Besides Women*, *The Changeling*, and *The Spanish Gypsy* would all follow *The Phoenix* and be performed before

9. *Mistress Turner's Farewell to All Women* (1615). Middle-class Anne Turner was hanged for helping Lady Frances Howard ('Vanity') murder Sir Thomas Overbury. Howard was the most scandalous woman of her time.

the Stuart royal family. Such command performances were the most prestigious critical recognition a play could receive. In 1618, James I authorized a special patent for publication of Middleton's *The Peacemaker*—a pamphlet condemning violence, which pretended to be the work of the King himself. James I was indeed a peacemaker; soon after his accession, he proclaimed an end to the ideologically-driven sometimes-hot sometimes-cold war with Spain which had dominated English minds for decades. A negotiated settlement was finalized in 1604, the year when Middleton came of artistic age; for the next twenty years, England was at peace.

Peace, though, encouraged renewed attention to domestic affairs, and attention spawned criticism. The political nation soon became disillusioned with the new king it had welcomed so enthusiastically. What had at first seemed munificence was reinterpreted as profligacy, once the bills came due, and kept coming due, and kept getting bigger. In *The Revenger's Tragedy*, *The Lady's Tragedy*, *Hengist, King of Kent*, and *Women, Beware Women*, Middleton depicted a series of sexually, politically, and financially corrupt courts. None of these plays impersonated or explicitly criticized the reigning monarch or his ministers, but comparisons were not hard to make. Not surprisingly, though they have been hailed by critics as masterpieces, none of these plays is known to have been performed before the King.

Court tragedies, like city comedies, represent a world beyond the boundaries of official morality, beyond the inaugural parade and the regal proclamation, a world of backdoors, bedrooms, and alleyways, where the immediate gossip of neighbours matters more than the eternal judgement of God. 'All the whole street will hate us', the cruel father worries in *A Chaste Maid in Cheapside* (5.2.97); 'O what will people think?' the would-be adulteress cries in *The Widow* (3.3.138). Middleton wrote, above all, of and for those nameless 'people' on that nameless 'street'. The constituency most important to his career was not the official singular but the irregular plural: not the few identifiable individuals to whom works were dedicated or for whom masques and pageants were written, but the unspecified thousands who attended his shows and bought his books. Not the polished élite attending a commemorative service in St Paul's Cathedral, but the customers milling in the dozens of bookshops in the cathedral yard, or applauding a play performed by boy actors in an indoor theatre in the cathedral precincts, or simply strolling through the aisles of the cathedral itself, as they do in *Your Five Gallants*, on the make. This is the company Middleton must have kept satisfying.

Volatile, ephemeral, unrespectable, reconstituted in different combinations every time, the audience Middleton addressed resembles in many ways the audience for street ballads. During his lifetime, innumerable ballads were printed on broadsides, which (like admission to the open-air theatres) cost a penny, and which (like Middleton's title-pages) were normally illustrated with woodcuts (Illus. 9). But although ballads could be purchased and read, they were (like plays) primarily an oral and performed art. London reverberated to the sound of balladmongers, music teachers, dancing schools, shopkeepers singing to passing customers ('What is't you lack, you lack, you lack?'). The performance of a play was almost always followed by a jig—a miniature comedy, written in ballad-measure, and sung and danced to ballad-tunes by two to four actors. The influence of these afterpieces can be seen in the songs inside Middleton's plays, which often, like jigs, combine rhyme and music to enact a story. In Act 3 of *The Widow*, for instance, Latrocinio distracts and then robs Ansaldo with a song; Ansaldo, turning the tables, forces Latrocinio to sing at gunpoint on his way to jail; Philippa and Violetta musically debate whether it is better to be 'a fool's mistress | Or an old man's wife?'

Not surprisingly, the authors of plays sometimes wrote ballads, and more often alluded to them. The alternative title of *The Puritan Widow*—'The Widow of Watling Street'—is taken from a ballad printed in 1597, and the history of *Hengist, King of Kent* had been balladed in 1589 ('Of the lewd life of Vortiger, King of Britain, and of the first coming of Hengist and the Saxons into the land'). This overlap between the two genres was sometimes simultaneous: the Calverley murders stimulated instant ballads as well as Middleton's instant *Yorkshire Tragedy*, and *Anything for a Quiet Life* was the title of a ballad of about the same date as Middleton and Webster's play. Like modern tabloids and television docudramas, ballads fed on sensational news, and what *The World Tossed at Tennis* says of the subject matter of street songs could also be said of early modern plays: 'one hangs himself today, another drowns himself tomorrow, a sergeant stabbed next day... fashions, fictions, felonies, fooleries—a hundred havens has the balladmonger to traffic at, and new ones still daily discovered' (29–35). Certainly, to cultural authorities the two forms were equally vulgar. In *Satyres and Satyricall Epigrams* (1617), Henry Fitzgeffrey condemned

> Books, made of ballads; 'Works', of plays;
> Sights, to be read, of my Lord Mayor's days

—thus lumping together Ben Jonson's proud 1616 collection of his 'Works', anthologies of ballads, and Lord Mayor's shows like Middleton's 1617 *Triumphs of Honour and Industry*. In 1600, Sir William Cornwallis read ballads in his privy and then used them to wipe himself; in 1640 a petition signed by 15,000 citizens complained of 'The swarming of lascivious, idle, and unprofitable books and pamphlets, playbooks, and ballads', which caused the 'withdrawing of people from reading, studying, and hearing the Word of God and other good books'.

The Word of God was at odds with more than plays and ballads. In 1584 London contained more than a hundred churches, but George Whetstone noted that this was less than the number of 'ordinary tables' for playing dice. Middleton stages dice games in *Michaelmas Term* and *Your Five Gallants*, trap-stick in *Women, Beware Women*, law-games in *The Phoenix*, dancing lessons in *More Dissemblers Besides Women*; he manipulates adult-size puppets in *The Revenger's Tragedy* and *Wit at Several Weapons*; he imagines *The World Tossed at Tennis* or at stake in *A Game at Chess*. In *A Chaste Maid in Cheapside*, social rituals of precedence or jealousy are transfigured into bizarre repetitive moves and countermoves: 'The game begins already' (1.2.79). His language dances and parries with images of a world at play. The very words 'game' and 'sport' flirt with sexual meanings, and the climax of *The Changeling* is an image of barley-brake (5.3.163).

Not only mentally but geographically, there was at least as much room in Middleton's world for playing as for praying. In 1628 an observer counted 'above thirty hundred alehouses, tippling houses, tobacco shops, etc.' in London. Houses of recreation were not only more numerous but more popular than houses of religion: 'come into a church on the Sabbath day, and ye shall see but few', a bishop recorded in 1560, 'but the alehouse is ever full'. These secular resorts are not featured so prominently on maps, but from Middleton's childhood home on Ironmonger Street it was as easy to walk to the Windmill Tavern or Blossom's Inn as to St Lawrence Jewry or the Guildhall. Actors usually gathered in a favourite ordinary to hear a playwright read his new script; the wine they drank there was a business expense, recorded in the company's account books. Middleton himself was a regular customer at 'a very great haunted inn' owned by Ewen Hebsen; he was in debt to Hebsen for a bond of £26, most of which he had paid by July 1609, when Hebsen died. In 1612 Hebsen's heir wrote off the remaining £7 as a 'desperate' (uncollectable) debt.

No one proposed the complete abolition of alehouses; without modern water treatment plants, it was healthier to drink beer than water. But if alehouses were a necessary evil, playhouses were superfluously satanic. In 1608, preaching at Paul's Cross, William Crashaw condemned 'ungodly plays and interludes'—and was particularly outraged that *The Puritan Widow* had dared satirize 'names of two churches of God'. In 1623, in a printed sermon that probably influenced *A Game at Chess*, Thomas Scott complained of the 'Neutralist, who is of all religions, or no religion; who goes ... to a play with greater delight and love, than to a sermon'. There was nothing original about such complaints: pulpits had been spitting at stages before Middleton was born. 'Will not a filthy play, with the blast of a trumpet, sooner call thither a thousand', another preacher at Paul's Cross had asked, in 1578, 'than an hour's tolling of a bell bring to the sermon a hundred?' Certainly, plays were popular: between 1567 and 1642, more than fifty million visits were made to thirteen London theatres. The plays performed in those theatres were 'filthy' in part because they brought together, on stage and in the audience, unsupervised idle women and men, who had congregated to spend their money in the pursuit of pleasure. In 1604 Dekker and Middleton made a prostitute the eponymous co-protagonist of their play, but long before then playhouses had been stigmatized as haunts of prostitution.

Such 'markets of bawdry' catered to a demand for unauthorized sex, real or imagined, that the social structure of early modern London had intensified. Half of its inhabitants were aged twenty-five or under. The active sexual energies of this young population could not be satisfied licitly for simple demographic reasons: there were 115 men for every 100 women. Moreover, 15 per cent of the total population were male apprentices, adolescents and young adults who could not marry. Although Middleton was probably only twenty-two when he married his twenty-seven-year-old bride, they were both atypical: London-born women were likely to be married by the age of twenty-one, and the average age of marriage for London men was twenty-eight. The demand for sex before or without marriage must have been explosively high. Poverty increased both demand and supply: poor young men were less likely to marry, poor young women were more likely to become prostitutes. Illegitimate births peaked in the decades from 1590 to 1620. But if poverty stimulated the economy of desire, so could wealth and power: the court of James I was notoriously unchaste (Illus. 9). James himself apparently had sexual partners of both genders, as do characters in *Michaelmas Term*. In the world of the theatre, particularly, where young boys dressed as women, homophobia was sure that men often 'played the sodomites, or worse'.

Middleton had an extraordinarily active sexual imagination. The range of his practice may or may not have matched that of his pen. (Which is more inspiring, consummation or frustration?) But his body, so irrelevant to us, was for him a constant stimulant or irritant, an inescapable presence familiarly collaborating with the books he read, the sermons he heard, the buildings he inhabited. Many of the books, sermons, and buildings have survived, still visible, touchable. The body is gone.

All that remains to us of the physical Middleton is a single half-length portrait (Illus. 10). It displays a man with a finely shaded face, shoulder-length curls, and a trim beard—a head distinctly unlike Shakespeare's dome, Jonson's rough round, Sidney's polished arrogance, Chapman's Homeric beard and muscled neck. This Middleton also differs, most revealingly, from the formal unhandsome Massinger etched by the same artist (Illus. 11). The day after Middleton's death, Massinger had begun writing exclusively for the King's Men; the timing suggests that he replaced Middleton as the company's house dramatist. But the two men apparently never collaborated, and the contrast between their portraits might suggest why. Massinger's portrait—with its straight lines, blocked letters, awkward contrasts, pasty face and disconnected nimbus—is perfectly stolid. Middleton looks altogether more stylish. Is he observing out of a window or interrogating a mirror? The engraving almost certainly derives from one of the portrait miniatures fashionable in Middleton's lifetime, an object of intimacy and vanity, often encased within a jewelled setting. The subject in this object, the object subjected to our gaze, wears his crown of laurel as naturally as one might don a low-slung, feathered hat. His left arm must be propped akimbo on his hip, a posture associated with authority or even vanity—but any arrogance is tucked away in the gown that conceals the arm; the gesture is not displayed but implied. Part of the function of any gown, of course, is to conceal. Middleton's body is hidden under layers of artifice: the flesh beneath the shirt beneath the gown, which is itself doubled over. As fluid as his pen, the dark gown, like his dark hair and his white collar, flows around him in waves and folds. It could be legal or academic, classical or modish, masculine or effeminate, warm or swank. If this dark-dressed dark-faced man were a character in *A Game at Chess*, he would obviously belong to the Black House; it's easy to picture him on the title-page, in place of the black-bearded black-gowned Black Knight (Illus. 2). Gowns are great sartorial playthings, inviting constant adjustment, gathering, folding, swishing—fashion in motion. His mother Anne owned 'a turkey grogram gown and a silk grogram kirtle' worth £7 at her death—as much as Middleton earned for his first play; his sister Avis, when newly widowed, bought 'a silk rash gown'. But this taste for expensive gowning was by no means confined to Middleton's family. The wardrobe of Sir Edmund Tilney, Master of the Revels until his death in

10. Engraved portrait of Middleton, used as a frontispiece for *Two New Playes... Written by Tho. Middleton, Gent.* (published by Humphrey Moseley in 1657).

11. Engraved portrait of Massinger, used as a frontispiece for *Three New Playes... Written by Philip Massenger, Gent.* (published by Humphrey Moseley in 1655).

1610, was so elaborate that he felt compelled to repent it in his will.

When this engraving was printed, the body hidden beneath the gown had been beneath the ground for thirty years. He made his final curtain call in the parish church of Newington, Surrey. St Mary's church 'is very small', the famous antiquarian John Aubrey recorded, later in the century, 'built of brick and boulder (which is irregular or unsquare stone put in a wall), a double roof covered with tile, and the walls with a rough cast; the windows are of a modern Gothic; the floor is paved with stone'. There were five bells in the church tower, and its turrets were sixty feet high, like the 'steep towers and turrets' that Middleton imagined his happy witches flying over, 'in moonlight nights'. On 30 June 1627 'a man out of the street' was buried, anonymously, in St Mary's churchyard; the bells tolled again, on 4 July, when the same minister committed the body of 'Mr Thomas Middleton' to the ground—'earth to earth, ashes to ashes, dust to dust'. There were presumably more mourners at Middleton's burial, but none of them could be sure whether the gentleman ascended into bliss, descended into torment, or simply rotted in place.

Reputation

The humanist educational system insisted on the persisting life of the works of authors who had been dead for millennia; it held out the promise that texts written now might likewise 'live' for ever. So Spenser describes his 'Epithalamium' as 'an endless monument'; Jonson is confident that 'this art shall live'; Daniel anticipates that 'th'unborn shall' read his 'authentic' verse 'in time to come'; Drayton proclaims that his 'world-outwearing rhymes' constitute an 'immortal song'. Middleton—or, as Thomas Heywood tells us he preferred to be called, 'plain

Tom'—did not praise himself in this way. The future of his soul may have mattered more to him than the future of his texts; or maybe neither mattered; perhaps (as his parody of almanacs suggests) he was amused and sceptical about any attempt to fix futures.

This attitude toward posterity—whether we attribute it to humility, other-worldliness, carelessness, or scepticism—shaped the history of Tom's posthumous reputation. He did not, as Spenser and Milton did, elect himself England's laureate; he did not, as Jonson did, build a monument to himself in his own lifetime, by publishing his works in folio; he did not, as Donne did, stage-manage his own death. Nor did he make it easy for others to improve the value of his literary estate after his death. Shakespeare was a corporation man, a shareholder in the same joint-stock company of actors for at least twenty years; his lifelong friends, the senior partners who survived him, collected and published his plays, which were company property, in 1623. In 1647, an ambitious royalist bookseller could acquire virtually all of the unpublished plays of Beaumont and Fletcher from the same single source, the King's Men. Middleton, by contrast, worked freelance; his plays were scattered among many companies. No one owned him.

Sidney's manuscripts were left in the possession of his sister, the Countess of Pembroke; Donne's works were posthumously edited by his son; Shakespeare's family paid for a monument in Holy Trinity Church. Middleton's family was not so well positioned to enhance his reputation. His stepfather, Thomas Harvey, had probably been dead for twenty years: he last paid his dues to the Grocers in 1605–6. Of his younger sister Avis no records have been found after 1609. In 1603 she had one surviving daughter; no children of her second marriage were baptized in the parish of St George the Martyr in Southwark. A John Empson (who may have been her husband) was buried there on 18 July 1625; another John Empson (who could have been her son or stepson) was married there on 24 June 1628. Even if she were alive, Avis, wife or widow of a feckless cutler, was not in a position to champion her elder brother's work. His friend and favourite collaborator William Rowley, who would have been better placed, had predeceased him in February 1626.

In February 1628, Magdalen Middleton, widow 'of Thomas Middleton deceased, late Chronologer of this City', upon her 'humble petition' to the Alderman's Court, was granted twenty nobles (two-thirds of £20), presumably to relieve her poverty. Middleton had never acquired landed property, and after his death (Mary) Magdalen would have had no income; such widows were particularly vulnerable to destitution. Fifty-two years old, and not wealthy, she would have had difficulty finding a second husband, and she would have been foolish not to sell books and manuscripts for whatever they would fetch. Her problems did not last long, however: she was buried a year after her husband, on 18 July 1628, at St Mary's in Newington.

Any remaining literary property would have descended to their only son, Edward. 'Edward Middleton of Newington, gent.' died in 1649; his will does not mention a wife or children of his own, instead beginning with another man's wife ('First I bequeath unto my loving friend Elizabeth Browne, wife of Edmond Browne, £5 to buy her mourning after my decease . . . '). Elizabeth's youngest son got £10, and her husband was named executor of his estate. He had, apparently, no wife or children of his own. Edward had been nineteen in November 1623; in September 1624 he was arrested and questioned by the Privy Council about the whereabouts of his father, then in hiding after the crackdown on *A Game at Chess*. This is not an experience likely to encourage most twenty-year-olds to interest themselves further in literary politics.

In the mid-1620s, Middleton needed champions. In August 1624, *A Game at Chess* became not only the greatest success of Middleton's career, but the most spectacularly and scandalously popular play of the English Renaissance. After its suppression, Middleton went into hiding, then into prison. He was released, but to our knowledge never wrote another play. John Marston, in 1608, had also been imprisoned for representing King James on stage; he too was released, but never wrote another play. Middleton died in 1627, but his dramatic career apparently ended in 1624. His career as a writer of pageants was simultaneously eclipsed. In prison or hiding, he could not write or produce the Lord Mayor's show of October 1624, and the 1625 show was cancelled. The pageant to celebrate Charles I's royal entry into London, written by Middleton and scheduled for summer 1625, was delayed and delayed and finally aborted by the King himself. Middleton did write the 1626 Lord Mayor's show, but this pageant, his first in three years, was bedevilled by the financial problems of the Company of Drapers; the cheapest show since 1609, it was not a success. Middleton did not get a chance to bounce back from that failure, because by the next October he was dead.

As a result of this enforced or fortuitous three-year silence, Middleton was for some time defined retrospectively as the author of a single work, *A Game at Chess*—a burst of light which by its magnitude and finality tended to obscure what preceded it. Moreover, Middleton's departure from the theatre coincided with Ben Jonson's return to it, after a ten-year absence. In 1626, Jonson coupled Middleton with another object of his contempt, the radical satirist George Wither, and imagined 'the poor English play' ('*The Game at Chess*') being used for toilet paper ('cleansing his posteriors'). Middleton's career as a playwright ended in 1624 with an unparaleled success; Jonson's ended, from 1626 to 1631, in a series of embarrassing failures. Nevertheless, Jonson's rejection by 'the loathed stage' actually enhanced his literary reputation, provoking odes of praise and defence by the poets Thomas Randolph and Thomas Carew, the Oxford don Richard James, and several others. Middleton's success became scatological; Jonson's failure, a badge of integrity. Jonson's former secretary, Richard

Brome, alluded to the same Middleton play in 1629, and in the first posthumous reference to Middleton by name, in 1632, William Heminges (another Jonson acolyte, writing a poem to Randolph) included in a list of modern poets 'squoblinge Middleton'. Heminges thus epitomized Middleton either as the author of spectacular plays and pageants full of firecrackers ('squibs') or the author of satirical 'squibs' (like *A Game at Chess*). Heminges went on to describe Middleton, 'with tears', telling the story of an amputated finger (like that in *The Changeling*?). This image of a weeping Middleton may have seemed as unmanly to the testosterone wits of the 1630s as it does now; modern male critics prefer an ever-ironic, intellectual, unsentimental Middleton. Certainly, Heminges in successive couplets contrasted Jonson (who made Puritans 'quake') with Middleton, whom they 'seemed much to adore' for his 'learnèd exercise' against Catholic Spain (*A Game at Chess*, again).

The hostility of Jonson and the approval of Puritans were, in the literary court of Caroline England, doubly damning. Middleton was as isolated, in this cavalier coterie, as Milton—but without Milton's massive defensive appropriation of classical authority. His plays continued to be revived in the theatre, and to influence the playwrights of the late 1620s and 1630s, from Massinger and Shirley to less familiar figures like Brome, Davenport, Glapthorne, and Richards. But the troubled state of his reputation is evident in an epigram printed in 1640 in the anthology *Wit's Recreations*:

> Facetious Middleton, thy witty muse
> Hath pleasèd all that books or men peruse.
> If any thee despise, he doth but show
> Antipathy to wit in daring so.
> Thy fame's above his malice, and 'twill be
> Dispraise enough for him to censure thee.

The opening couplet, with its assurance of unconditional and universal delight, is contradicted by the following four lines, which wittily defend Middleton against the antipathy, malice, and censure of those who despise him. This is embattled praise.

Middleton could be so readily and radically diminished by 'malice' in part because most of his work was unavailable or unidentified. This problem, which began in the first decades after his death, persisted into the twentieth century. Of the thirteen pamphlets in this edition, five were published anonymously; three were identified only by the initials 'T.M.' attached to a preface, one by the same initials on the title-page, three by the full name attached to a preface, and only one—the very first—by the full name on the title-page. Three-quarters of the pamphlets were thus attributed ambiguously if at all. Of the thirty plays in this edition, two were not published in the seventeenth century at all; four were published anonymously; four were misattributed to other playwrights; five named Middleton's collaborator as sole author; two attributed parts of the play to fictitious collaborators. Such confusions affected half of his surviving theatrical canon.

More grievously, much of that canon did not survive at all, in part because the middle decades of the seventeenth century were particularly disruptive of England's social and literary fabric. The Calvinist consensus of the English church, which had lasted half a century, was shattered in the last years of Middleton's life by the rise of a faction influenced by the Dutch theologian Jacobus Arminius (who argued that salvation was not predetermined, but could be influenced by individual action). Within a year of the accession of Charles I, Arminians effectively dominated the Church hierarchy. The reformist Protestant humanism of much of the laity collided with the new conservatism of the episcopate. The Thirty Years War, which began in central Europe in 1618, led to increasingly bitter divisions over foreign policy. The shortfall in government revenue, disguised by Elizabeth's unmarried parsimony, intensified into a perpetual crisis for the more lavish and fertile Stuarts; efforts to remedy the crisis were perceived, more and more widely, as corrupt or illegal. Fifteen years after Middleton's death, the annual Lord Mayor's shows had been suspended, ballads had been banned, the theatres were closed, and the Commons was at war with the Crown.

This dissolution affected Middleton's reputation, in part because it determined how and by whom he would be interpreted. Charles I was reading Shakespeare and Jonson in prison in the weeks before his execution; it is hard to imagine him reading Middleton. When his son Charles II returned to London in 1660, the Restoration's programmatic cultural nostalgia was more receptive to the gallant Beaumont and Fletcher, the neoclassical Jonson, the royal Shakespeare, than to vulgar critical Middleton. But the turmoil of these decades also had simpler, physical consequences for Middleton's reputation. On 2 September 1642, Parliament closed the theatres, condemning plays as 'spectacles of pleasure, too commonly expressing lascivious mirth and levity'. The acting companies held on for a while, but eventually disintegrated. On 15 April 1644, the Globe theatre was pulled down; on 6 August 1655, the Blackfriars; on 25 March 1656, the Hope—empty playhouses replaced by profitable tenements for a continually expanding urban population. In 1666, the Fire of London destroyed not only the church of St Lawrence Jewry, but most of the old City within the walls, including innumerable books and manuscripts.

Because Middleton's works had not been collected, they were particularly susceptible to chance destruction in these social cataclysms. If Shakespeare's *Comedies, Histories, and Tragedies* had not been published together in 1623, we could easily have lost half of his canon—including *Julius Caesar*, *As You Like It*, *Twelfth Night*, *Macbeth*, *Antony and Cleopatra*, *Coriolanus*, *The Winter's Tale*, and *The Tempest*. (Obviously, the fact that a play had not been printed is no reflection on its artistic virtue.) We can still read these works because, after 1623, perhaps 750 copies of thirty-six Shakespeare plays were widely dispersed in a single expensive volume, likely to be preserved in the library of a wealthy family or institution. Middleton's works

12. Restoration Middleton emphasized isolated single characters and fond memories of innocent vulgar clowning, as in this 1662 visual anthology, which includes *The Changeling* (upper left).

13. Elegant eighteenth-century Middleton: the masque in *Wit at Several Weapons*, 5.2, as illustrated in a frontispiece from Gerard Langbaine's 1711 edition of *The Works of Mr Francis Beaumont and Mr John Fletcher*, volume 6. Conflating 5.2.45–7 and 5.2.74–6, this illustration shows Cunningame (front left) stealing off leading the Niece (centre) under the approving eyes of Wittypate (right); behind them a reluctant Guardianess (left) is urged to dance by an energetic Lady Ruinous (right), while the Old Knight dances obliviously on at the rear. Priscian and Sir Ruinous are the two central figures in the musicians' gallery, above the spectators who crowd the stage boxes. The anonymous engraver may well have been influenced by the staging of this scene in Colley Cibber's adaptation, *The Rival Fools*, performed at Drury Lane in 1709.

were interred in no such monumental tome, and it is hard to be sure what quantity or quality of comedies, histories, and tragedies perished as a result.

The casualties must have been substantial. We can specify five lost plays, one lost masque, one lost royal pageant, two lost prose works, one lost prologue and epilogue. There were no doubt more. In 1611 alone, he wrote three surviving plays; for 1610 and 1612, not a single play survives. From spring 1602 to spring 1608, Middleton wrote all or part of fourteen known plays, averaging more than two plays per year; he also produced five known pamphlets. This period is probably representative of his usual productivity, which we can observe because of the survival of Henslowe's account books and the collapse of two acting companies, leading to the publication of an unusual number of plays. Even during this period, Middleton almost certainly wrote other material which has not survived; our knowledge of more than one-fifth of these plays is, after all, fortuitous. But even if we assume that the figures for these six years are complete, then from 1609 to 1624, at a comparable rate, he would have turned out, alone or in collaboration, in addition to civic pageants and a few pamphlets, another thirty-five dramatic texts. By this conservative estimate, we can read, now, only about half of Middleton's plays and masques. If 1611 is typical, then between 1601 and 1624 he would have written at least sixty-nine plays. Nor is this conclusion surprising. More than forty plays by Dekker are lost; of the plays written by Philip Massinger between 1625 and 1640, only about half survive. If Middleton's writing had been collected and published shortly after his death, that edition would probably have doubled the canon available to us—and maybe have tripled it.

We cannot judge work that has not survived. But we cannot ignore it, either, when estimating the relative scale of an author's achievement. In 1675 Edward Phillips, who compiled the first biographical encyclopedia of English poets, described Middleton as 'a copious writer'; he little realized how copious. Four years before, when the bookseller Francis Kirkman had ranked the top ten English playwrights in order of importance, that order had been determined largely by the number of their extant works; 'Middleton and Rowley' were sixth. The top three, not surprisingly, were Shakespeare, 'Beaumont and Fletcher', and Jonson—whose canons had been preserved, virtually complete, in folios. Genius cannot be statistically determined, but by any criteria Middleton belongs among the most productive dramatists of early modern England.

That status could hardly be appreciated in the years after 1660. When the monarchy returned and the theatres reopened, a reader could find virtually all of Jonson or Fletcher or Shakespeare in one book. By contrast, Middleton's work—like Marlowe's, Dekker's, Webster's, Ford's—was scattered in many separate cheap individual editions, each for sale in only a few remaining copies, or none, in a world without public libraries, without bibliographies, without journals for essays in criticism, without classes in English literature. In 1655, John Cotgrave's *English Treasury of Wit and Language* had quoted more excerpts from plays in the Middleton canon than from any other playwright—but he attributed none of his quotations, and until the twentieth century no reader of Cotgrave's anthology could have been aware of how much quotable Master Middleton contributed to it. In 1662 *The Changeling* was featured in a visual anthology of famous theatrical roles, but Middleton was not named (Illus. 12). In 1663, William Davenant could look back forty years, to a time when he was only eighteen, and remember the unparalleled 'crowd' that had rushed the doors to see Middleton's 'Play of *Gundamar*'—but the only published texts of *A Game at Chess* did not name its author, and neither did Davenant. After the Restoration, eight of Middleton's plays were successfully revived, but most were simply unknown. Those who knew them often took advantage of their unfamiliarity by borrowing from them, wholesale, without acknowledgement. As early as 1688, antiquarians like Gerard Langbaine complained about such robberies, but to no avail. To most readers or audiences, some of Middleton's virtues now appeared to be those of Shakespeare or Fletcher, whose folios included some of his plays (Illus. 13); other Middleton achievements were silently appropriated by Aphra Behn, Colley Cibber, and a dozen lesser writers. One of the most populist after-pieces of the eighteenth-century stage, 'The Slip', was lifted from *A Mad World, My Masters*, but its original creator was never credited. Middleton became virtually invisible for a century and a half. In that century and a half, the canon of English literature was established.

When Middleton resurfaced, in the nineteenth century, he entered a canonical system dominated by Shakespeare. This context has shaped the subsequent history of his reception. For eighteenth-century scholars from Lewis Theobald to George Steevens, Middleton's texts were simply raw linguistic data, collected for the better explication of Shakespeare; the revolutionary editor Edward Capell went out of his way to describe Middleton as 'no mean comic genius', but this remark was made in *The School of Shakespeare*, an anthology of extracts from 'diverse English books, that contribute to a due understanding of his writings' (1779). This pattern persisted into the twentieth century, Shakespeare serving as Middleton's chief patron. Those texts where Middleton's writing intertwines with Shakespeare's have been more widely edited, translated, produced, discussed, and illustrated than any of his other work (Illus. 14–16). Verdi made thrilling romantic opera out of Middleton's adaptation of the cauldron scene in *Macbeth*, Duke Ellington jazzed up Middleton's share of *Timon of Athens*. The most famous work of art inspired by Middleton is undoubtedly Dante Gabriel Rossetti's 'Mariana' (1870), based on a Middleton passage in *Measure for Measure*. In the nineteenth century, authorship problems in the Middleton canon were first seriously discussed in the meetings and transactions of the New Shakspere Society, and Shakespeare journals and conferences continue to be a main outlet for Middleton scholarship. Repertory companies founded primarily to produce Shakespeare have pioneered Middleton's restoration to the stage, from William Poel and his Elizabethan Stage Society, responsible for the only nineteenth-century performance of a Middleton play, to the Royal Shakespeare Company, which mounted the first professional revival since the early seventeenth century of *Women, Beware Women*. And though some contributors to this edition hail from departments of history, drama, or theology, most are teachers of English literature, and most were hired specifically to teach Shakespeare. Middleton has thus inevitably been understood and described—misleadingly—in terms of his similarities to or differences from Shakespeare. After all, every modern reader of Middleton is someone who has already read Shakespeare.

In order for there to be any such modern readers of Middleton, his work had to be reprinted and edited. In the eighteenth century, fragments of Middleton had been anthologized in collections of quotations like *The British Muse* and *Beauties of the English Drama*, and a handful of his plays had been printed entire in successive editions of *A Select Collection of Old Plays*. But most of his work was available only to wealthy collectors. In 1707 a copy

14. Spectacular Victorian Middleton: Bernard Partridge's painting of Middleton's chorus of witches in *Macbeth*, based on the 1898 production by Henry Irving.

of *The Roaring Girl* was purchased for three pounds nine shillings—78 times its original price, and two and a half times the price of a Shakespeare First Folio sold in the same decade. Edmond Malone, who bought books for the first Earl of Charlemont, 'picked up' *A Chaste Maid in Cheapside* in Dublin in 1797, but was unable to 'secure' a copy of *Old Law*, and complained that George III's buyers were pushing up auction prices for rare books. The first editions of Middleton's work, originally cheap and accessible, had become rare and expensive, while the expensive upmarket folios of Jonson, Shakespeare, and Fletcher had made their work readily obtainable.

Middleton's achievement did not begin to be visible, or imaginable, until 1840, when Edward Lumley of Chancery Lane, London, published a five-volume limited edition of *The Works of Thomas Middleton, Now first collected, with some account of the author, and notes, by the Reverend Alexander Dyce*. Dyce (1798–1869) was a resident of Gray's Inn (part of the London legal community Middleton had satirized and entertained); his lifetime of scholarship was supported by his parents' investments in the East India Company (which Middleton had celebrated in *The Triumphs of Honour and Industry* and other pageants). In 1840, Dyce was already an experienced editor of Renaissance plays, having worked on Peele, Webster, Greene, and Shirley; he would go on to edit Beaumont and Fletcher, Marlowe, Ford, and Shakespeare. All the contemporaries of Shakespeare whom Dyce edited, including Middleton, had been quoted and praised in Charles Lamb's influential anthology of *Specimens of English Dramatic Poets, Who Lived about the Time of Shakespeare* (1808). Dyce's Middleton was simply one part of a vast nineteenth-century archival project, carried out by many scholars, to recover systematically the culture of 'Elizabethan' England. His approach was archaeological, even anthropological: hence, 'As they faithfully reflect the manners and customs of the age, even the worst of Middleton's comedies are not without their value.'

By modern standards, Dyce's edition—like all nineteenth-century editions of Renaissance literature—leaves much to be desired. He guessed that Middleton had been born in 1570 (an error that still shows up in reference works) and conjectured that he was educated at the Inns of Court (an error that misled generations of critics into associating Middleton with coterie writers like Marston rather than popular writers like Shakespeare, Dekker and Heywood). More pervasively, Dyce froze the Middleton canon in the chaotic state created by the second half of the seventeenth century. He did not include some of Middleton's best work; he did include some mediocre work not by Middleton; he did little to disentangle Middleton from his collaborators. Nevertheless, Dyce's edition revolutionized perceptions of Middleton. His collection established, for the first time, a corpus, a body of work, an intertextual field susceptible to analysis of its structure, coherence, development, internal relations and articulations. His introductory life, citing manuscript sources never before consulted, made it possible to imagine a human body doing the work, a person, a personality; what Rowe's biography had done for Shakespeare in 1709, Dyce's biography did for Middleton. By reprinting as frontispiece the 1657 engraving (Illus. 10), Dyce put back into circulation an image of the poet, enabling readers like Swinburne to imagine his 'noble and thoughtful face, so full of gentle dignity and earnest composure'. Thanks to Dyce, the young American critic and poet James Russell Lowell in 1843 could draw 'an estimate' of Middleton's 'character', could casually quote ten of his plays, could situate their author among the poets whose words have 'a mysterious and oracular majesty' and whose 'tragic faculty' can 'bring up for us the snowy pearls which sleep in the deep abysses and caverns of the soul'. Thanks to Dyce, in 1854 the first African American novelist and playwright, William Wells Brown, could quote *Women, Beware Women* as well as Shakespeare. Thanks to Dyce, in 1878 the Aberdeen professor, journalist, and novelist William Minto could, in an article on Middleton in the famous ninth edition of the *Encyclopaedia Britannica*, affirm that 'in daring and happy concentration of imagery, and a certain imperial confidence in the use of words, [he] of all the dramatists of that time is the disciple that comes nearest to the master' [Shakespeare].

This praise came too late to save Middleton's physical remains. Two years before, the parish church of St Mary's Newington had been pulled down to make room for a wider road; all bodies were removed from the churchyard and interred together in a new vault. The surviving grave markers were meticulously transcribed, but the Middletons' must have disappeared long before, for they are not recorded. And if Victorian London did not much value what was left of Middleton's corpse, some Victorian critics were no tenderer toward his corpus. In the 1870s, Middleton's plays were being read not only by Minto and Swinburne, but also by the postmaster and novelist Anthony Trollope. Trollope read every play in Dyce's edition, and concluded that 'Perhaps of all the so-called Elizabethan dramatists Middleton was the worst.' In 1878, at about the time Minto's *Encyclopedia* article was coming off the press, Trollope was writing, at the end of *Your Five Gallants*, 'This piece is so tedious, so perplexed, so uninteresting and so bad, that one is at [a] loss to conceive

15. Pre-Raphaelite Middleton: Byam Shaw's illustration of the Middleton masque of ladies in *Timon of Athens*.

how such a man as Dyce could have given up his time to editing it. To have read it is a sin, in the wasting of time.'

Trollope was in the 1860s the most popular and 'the most English' of novelists; his revulsion from Middleton is representative of a class and a generation, but it also identifies certain real features of Middleton's work which any reader will soon observe. One of those features is Middleton's frank sexuality. Trollope was described by his contemporaries as 'the prose laureate of English girls of the better class' (1869); his heroines were praised for being 'like the honest English girls we know' (1867); Henry James remarked that 'the British maiden' of Trollope's novels has 'a kind of clinging tenderness, a passive sweetness' reminiscent of 'the fragrance of Imogen and Desdemona'. Middleton's women exude rather different fragrances (Illus. 15–19). In *The Nice Valour*, Middleton concludes that 'desire is of both genders' (5.3.180): both genders have powerful sexual appetites, and each may desire either—or both. Middleton would only begin to return to the theatrical repertory in the roaring twenties, a decade in which T. S. Eliot praised 'the indecencies of Elizabethan and Restoration drama' and Virginia Woolf confided to her diary that she 'adore[d] Shakespeare at his bawdiest'. She could have found even more bawdy in Middleton. By 1963, Kenneth Tynan could observe, in a family newspaper, that 'where sexual vagaries are concerned there is more authentic reportage in *The Changeling* and *Women Beware Women* than in the whole of' Shakespeare. In 1963—the year when sex was invented, in Philip Larkin's famously ironic chronology—Tynan's claim was praise; but Queen Victoria would not have been amused. Neither was Trollope.

But even Trollope could not avoid, at times, being impressed. The plot of his novel *The Fixed Period* (1882) is taken from *Old Law*, and in a moment of uncharacteristic weakness he conceded that Middleton, 'had he given himself fair chance by sustained labour, might have excelled all the Elizabethan dramatists except Shakespeare'. Others were more openly enthusiastic. In 1885–6 Dyce's edition was reprinted in eight volumes with a few changes (and more errors) by A. H. Bullen, who provided a new and more avid introduction; Bullen concludes that, if Middleton does not deserve to be called 'a great dramatist', then 'I know not which of Shakespeare's followers is worthy of that title'. Bullen's expensive limited edition, more widely reviewed than Dyce's, was followed in 1887–90 by Middleton's entry in the popular Mermaid series, a two-volume selection of ten plays edited by Havelock Ellis (soon to become famous for *Studies in the Psychology of Sex*). From then on, Middleton was treated, by editors and academic critics, as a major Renaissance dramatist. Individual plays have been translated into Dutch, German, French, Italian, Japanese, Polish, and Spanish.

His status has continued to rise. Each new decade has seen more revivals of his plays than the one before, including productions outside the English-speaking world (Gdańsk, Rome, Zurich). In 1922 *The Waste Land*'s most frequent, and in some ways most surprising, quotations were from Middleton and Webster; in 1927 Eliot wrote the most influential single essay on Middleton, describing him as 'one of the most voluminous, and one of the best, dramatic writers of his time', 'a great artist or artisan', dispassionately exposing the 'fundamental passions of any time and any place'. Not everyone accepted this assessment. The Cambridge don L. C. Knights, in 1936, judged Middleton far inferior to Jonson; Jonson has continued to attract much academic admiration, as he did in his own time. But whether Eliot inspired awe or dissent, he had put Middleton in the literary canon, on the critical agenda, in the university curriculum. After Eliot, English playwrights—Peter Barnes, Edward Bond, Barrie Keefe, Joe Orton—began to acknowledge Middleton as a precursor.

Eliot famously asserted that Middleton had 'no point of view', no 'peculiar personality'; 'He is merely the name which associates six or seven great plays.' Eliot's modernist misunderstanding of Middleton's work originated in ignorance of his biography. The central facts of Middleton's life were first established, by Mark Eccles, in 1931, four years after Eliot's essay was published. Middleton's seeming impersonality itself reflects a personality, a decision to reject the selfish rant of battling parents and battling poets. Aged twenty, he called himself 'Thomas Medius & Gravis Tonus', punning musically on his surname (*Ghost of Lucrece* 69–70); *medius* means 'in the middle' but also 'middling, ordinary' and 'neutral, ambiguous'—and 'central', and 'the common good'. *Gravis* teeters, ambiguously, between 'impressive' and 'base'. Middleton yokes opposites: his first surviving play, *The Phoenix*, is one of the first English tragicomedies, and later plays combined tragic plots (*Hengist, King of Kent*) and comic plots (*The Mayor of Queenborough*) so evenly that they boasted alternative titles. The emotional and intellectual complexity of Middleton's double plots, and multiple plots, first began to be appreciated in the twentieth century, in the work of critics like William Empson and Richard Levin. 'Was ever such a contrariety seen?' (*Old Law* 2.1.161).

The relationship between Middleton's life and his work requires more than a reliable biography; we also need to know which works Middleton wrote, and when he wrote them. We will respond to *The Wisdom of Solomon Paraphrased* differently, once we realize that most of it must have been written by a sixteen-year-old (not a twenty-six-year-old, as earlier scholars believed). The first sustained analysis of 'The Chronology of Middleton's Plays' (by R. C. Bald) was not published until 1937. The larger problem of the canon itself took much longer to solve. Most of the correct conclusions were reached by E. H. C. Oliphant between 1925 and 1929, but it took six decades for his intuitions to be confirmed by the more scientific methods of the American Cyrus Hoy, the Australian David Lake, the New Zealander MacDonald P. Jackson, and the Englishman R. V. Holdsworth. These decades of scholarship have made it possible for this edition to print his works in chronological order, beginning with his adult work and the reign of James I (with the Juvenilia gathered together in a separate section). It should make possible a new understanding of Middleton's artistic development. His early city comedies for the Children at Paul's were all written in his mid-twenties, with the brilliant surface virtuosity and drive of absolute youth, in exhilarated command of materials within the narrow circle of its own ego and experience. From that centre Middleton moved gradually outward, first beyond his own sex, eventually beyond his own neighbourhood to the larger European world. He never lost his lewd, ironic, grounded comic genius, but the later comedies and tragicomedies achieve a wider emotional range and a more complex orchestration of tones. Middleton wrote *The Revenger's Tragedy* when he was twenty-six (Shakespeare's age when he churned out *Henry the Sixth, Part Two*, John Osborne's when he spat out *Look Back in Anger*); *The Revenger's Tragedy* is a masterpiece unequalled in laser intensity,

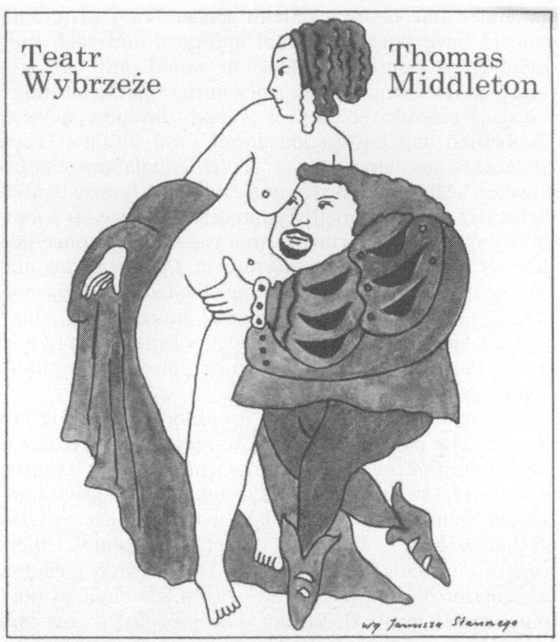

Twentieth-century Middleton. 16. Wyndham Lewis's 1912 modernist icon of Apemantus and the masque of ladies in *Timon of Athens* (upper left). 17. Janusza Stannego's post-modernist cover art for the programme of a 1988/89 production of *A Chaste Maid in Cheapside* at Teatr Wybrzeże, Poland (upper right). 18. Judi Dench (centre) as Bianca in the 1969 Royal Shakespeare Company production of *Women, Beware Women*, directed by Terry Hands, with a design reflecting the chess game (bottom).

but the forty-one-year-old who wrote *Women, Beware Women* commanded a broader spectrum of verbal and psychological light.

Eliot, typically, did not even mention Middleton's masques, pageants, or pamphlets. These works were, and still remain, less familiar than the plays. The first serious study of the genre of the masque was not published until 1927, and—like the later influential work of Stephen Orgel and Roy Strong—Enid Welsford concentrated upon *The Court Masque*. Even now, people are sometimes surprised to discover how many masques were not performed at court, not designed by Inigo Jones, and not written by Ben Jonson. This critical privileging of the court also helps to explain the neglect of pageants, which were written, by contrast, for the commonest possible public. Despite their wide and international audience—demonstrated by the Russian and Italian ambassadors whose reports are printed in this edition, and by the fact that the Anglophile Spanish ambassador Gondomar owned a copy of Middleton's *Triumphs of Truth*—the first serious study of Lord Mayor's shows, David Bergeron's *English Civic Pageantry 1558–1642*, was not published until 1971.

As for the genre of pamphlets, in the eighteenth and nineteenth centuries such works were reprinted, if at all, in historical anthologies like *The Harleian Miscellany* or *An English Garner*; in the twentieth century, early modern prose generally only interested critics seeking precursors of the novel. Middleton's pamphlets are not precursors of the novel. The one thing they have in common is that they do not fit our generic categories; we don't know which anthology should include them, or which course should teach them. Some of them—like *The Black Book* and *Father Hubburd's Tales*—are at least fabular or fictional, in ways which are almost familiar. Like short stories, these narratives depend on snapshot vignettes, resonant anecdotes, acute social observation, the creation of a distinct narrative voice. Like the short texts of Flannery O'Connor in particular, they are wickedly intelligent, observant, ironic. But Flannery O'Connor would not introduce Lucifer with a stage direction and a verse soliloquy. And other Middleton pamphlets abandon narrative altogether. It might be more useful to consider them experimental fiction, or postmodern non-novels. Like Michael Martone's *The Blue Guide to Indiana* (2001), Middleton's *The Owl's Almanac* (1618) takes a pedestrian non-fiction genre and transforms it into a literary fairground; but Martone does not switch-hit prose and verse, or rise to Middleton's playful complex typographic mimicry. Middleton's 'non-dramatic prose' is not consistently either. Like his plays, the pageants and the pamphlets mix rhyme, blank verse, and non-verse. Just as, in the plays, there is no tidy hierarchy of forms—prose for the lower orders, verse for the higher—so among the pamphlets there is no severe divide between 'literature' and 'unliterature'. The pamphlets embody the full unregulated variety of Renaissance discursive practices, mixing poetry and theology, politics and parody, journalism and *jouissance*.

19. Feminist Middleton: Helen Mirren's performance of Moll Cutpurse—in the Royal Shakespeare Company's 1983 production, directed by Barry Kyle—signalled a growing interest in Middleton's treatment of gender and sexuality.

The first attempt to render such a mixture available and intelligible was R. B. McKerrow's five-volume edition of *The Works of Thomas Nashe*, published between 1905 and 1910. Nashe was clearly an important influence on Middleton, and possibly a personal mentor, and McKerrow's work made critical appreciation of a career like Middleton's for the first time possible. But McKerrow also set standards for annotation and bibliographical description which were at the time virtually impossible for any editor of Middleton's much larger and more complicated canon to satisfy. McKerrow's friend, W. W. Greg, in 1906 reviewed Churton Collins's edition of the works of Robert Greene; the review was so damning and humiliating that it probably caused Collins to commit suicide, and certainly made it professional suicide for any serious scholar thereafter to edit an early modern writer without scrupulous attention to the new methods of analytical bibliography. Even McKerrow could not complete an edition of Shakespeare which satisfied such standards (though he died trying). From 1953 to 1961, Fredson Bowers produced a four-volume bibliographer's edition of Dekker, but the 'non-dramatic' canon was omitted and the commentary delegated to a junior collaborator, Cyrus Hoy, who would not publish his four volumes until 1980. Bowers's standards were even higher than Greg's had been, now including identification of compositors and sequence of typesetting. Such bibliographical perfectionism was self-defeating, and it defeated three postwar attempts to produce a new edition of Middleton.

That century of editorial constipation did not stop the march of Middleton's reputation, but scholarship and criticism have been hampered by the absence of a reliable text of the whole *œuvre*. The book you are now holding will, we hope, make it possible for many more people to experience what I felt in the summer of 1984, when for the first time I read all of Middleton. In one of the world's great research archives, founded in Middleton's lifetime at Middleton's university, I sat for days, surrounded by rare books, sometimes quietly moved to tears, sometimes unable to contain my laughter, so inappropriate in the venerable hush of the Duke Humphrey Library. And I thought, again and again, why was I never told to read this? Why was I never taught this? Why is this not on the shelves of ordinary libraries? Why have I never seen this performed? Why have I never heard this music? And why have I never been introduced to this Dickensian, Dostoevskian riot of life? Vindice, DeFlores, and Beatrice Joanna I'd encountered in college, but what about Allwit and all the rest? Lucifer, Candido, Quomodo, Sir Bounteous Progress, Dampit, Pieboard, Tailby, Weatherwise, Pompey Doodle, Captain Ager, Plumporridge, Simplicity, Simon, George, Lepet, the Yorkshire Husband, the Black Knight and Fat Bishop and White Queen's Pawn, the Tyrant, the Lady, the Young Queen, the Duchess of Milan, Mistress Low-water, Moll, Valeria, Hecate and Madge Owl, Livia and Bianca and Isabella—where have you people been all my life?

This edition does not claim to be definitive; we do not expect, or even hope, that it will last for ever. 'Nothing is perfect born' (*Roaring Girl* 9.227). Like Middleton himself, we are fallen authors, living in a fallen world, and the texts we produce are inevitably imperfect. Nevertheless, in at least one respect this edition should permanently transform our reading of Middleton. For the first time, you can find all that is left of him in one big book: this is 'the Middleton First Folio'. As that phrase suggests, this volume mimics many features of Shakespeare editions, and its visual design makes a larger cultural claim. As early as 1636, Shakespeare and Middleton were being coupled. Two gentlemen went to see Shakespeare's *Pericles*; one laughed and the other cried. Later, they went to see Middleton's *Mayor of Queenborough*; the first cried and the second laughed. Middleton is 'both a great comic writer and a great tragic writer': T. S. Eliot's phrase could be applied to only one other English playwright, and to very few in any language. Middleton is, David Frost concluded in 1968, 'Shakespeare's true heir', and *The Collected Works of Thomas Middleton* invites readers to think of our language as the home of two world champion playwrights, not just one. Our other Shakespeare has been, for centuries, scattered in a half-buried debris field; here, finally, the startling surviving pieces have all been unearthed, catalogued, authenticated, re-sequenced, and put back together in a single magic box that we can carry to our private desert islands and our collective urban wildernesses. We can now see the English Renaissance, stereoscopically, from the perspectives of two very different geniuses. We do not have to choose between them, any more than we need choose Mozart over Beethoven, or Michelangelo over Leonardo da Vinci. We are simply blessed, enriched, by their coexistence, their wrestling with each other and the world.

Middleton, of all writers, might have resisted the dignified uniformity asserted by the bulk and binding of such a book. His praise of *The Duchess of Malfi*, published in 1623, seems to contrast Webster's modest quarto with the 'cathedral palaces' of the monumental Shakespeare Folio, also published that year. Certainly, it would be misleading to impose upon Middleton's muchness the minimalism of a single critical voice-over, even if that voice were as hypnotizing as Samuel Johnson's. Editorially, this collection attempts to convey the formal individuality and variety of his early texts, and to offer a corresponding diversity of textual embodiment and annotation. Critically, the contributors have little in common but the republic of Middleton. It is a republic we invite you to join. For you are Middleton's, and our, most important collaborator. Only you, fallen reader, can open the magic box, and let the dead come out and dance.

SEE ALSO
Sources for Middleton's life and reputation: *Companion*, 449

MIDDLETON'S LONDON

Paul S. Seaver

'I AM thy mother', announces the figure of London at the outset of Thomas Middleton's *The Triumphs of Truth*, and London was never far from this dutiful son's thoughts. The city is mentioned in more than thirty of his works, and specific locales—Watling Street, Paul's Wharf, Finsbury Fields—appear with even greater frequency. When it is not named, London is almost always implied, providing the model of urban experience most familiar to writer and audience. 'The fashion of play-making', wrote Middleton, 'I can properly compare to nothing so naturally as the alteration of apparel', reminding his readers by this comparison of the rapid changes visible everywhere in London's streets during this first age of fashion, but it was not only fashions in play-making and clothes that were undergoing constant change in Middleton's lifetime. London itself was changing at an unprecedented rate, providing a setting and a stage evidently at once frightening and exciting, framed by much that was old and familiar, but constantly threatening to outgrow that frame, as the medieval city was transformed into England's and Europe's greatest metropolis.

Middleton's London, apostrophized in 1616 as 'this queen of cities, lady of this isle', was in one sense an ancient crone—'a reverend mother' in Middleton's kinder comparison—its walls dating back to Roman times. But if the walls had contained the medieval city, this was no longer true, for Middleton was born into a metropolis undergoing explosive growth, growth which would continue for perhaps a generation after his death, before the rate slowed in the later decades of the seventeenth century. London's population, which numbered little more than 50,000 in Sir Thomas More's time, was in the neighbourhood of 80,000 to 100,000 by the time Middleton was born in 1580, and the metropolis grew to perhaps 300,000 by the time of his death; then the walls contained no more than perhaps a third of the metropolitan population.

In 1600 when the young Moravian Baron Waldstein visited London at the conclusion of his studies at Strasbourg, he noted in his diary that on 5th July he 'went along the Thames to the small town of Westminster, [but] although it is over a mile from the City, we went past buildings the whole way'. The young baron remarked upon the built-up strip along the Strand precisely because north of that highway and west of Chancery Lane were still green fields, an area which was to become rapidly urban in Middleton's last years as builders began to develop the Covent Garden area as far as St Martin's Lane and north into St Giles-in-the-Fields. In fact by the time of Middleton's birth urban sprawl had begun to the north-west of Aldersgate in Clerkenwell and to the north-east of Aldersgate in the rapidly growing parish of St Giles Cripplegate. Another strip development extended north from Bishopsgate and another east from Aldgate toward the village of Mile End, while along the river urban development moved beyond St Katherine's to Wapping, Shadwell, and the Radcliffe docks.

Urban growth on such an unprecedented scale frightened the Crown, and as early as 1580 Queen Elizabeth I issued the first of what became a series of royal proclamations that sought to limit further growth. The 'excess of people', if not checked, posed three dangerous consequences: first, the Queen foresaw a city that could not be well governed without the creation of 'new jurisdictions and officers'; second, 'such multitudes' could not be supplied with food 'upon reasonable prices'; and third, the influx of the poor into crowded tenements created the conditions in which a 'plague or popular sickness' could not only 'invade the whole city', but could endanger 'her majesty's own person'. For remedy it was proposed to forbid any new building within three miles of the city's gates or the subletting of any rooms not already let or occupied. Less than a year before her death the old Queen complained that 'partly by the covetous and insatiable dispositions of some persons, that without any respect of the common good and public profit of the realm do only regard their own particular lucre and gain, and partly by the negligence and corruption of others who by reason of their offices and places ought to see the said proclamation... performed', enforcement had been neglected and 'the said mischiefs and inconveniences do daily increase', for remedy of which the new proclamation not only reiterated the former order against new building or new subdividing, but ordered that all illegal new building be torn down or let to the poor at such rates as were set by the churchwardens and minister of the parish. James I and the plague arrived together in the summer of 1603, and from the safe distance of Woodstock the new king issued a new proclamation, noting 'that the great confluence and access of excessive numbers of idle, indigent, dissolute and dangerous persons, and the pestering of many of them in small and strait rooms... have been one of the chiefest occasions of the great plague and mortality', and reiterating former regulations, particularly as they applied to the creation of subdivided housing. But despite attempts to enforce the proclamations and the multiplication of new regulations and restrictions, the population of the metropolis continued to expand. In 1615 King James, in a gesture reminiscent of King Canute commanding the tides, proclaimed that 'now that our City of London is become the greatest, or the next greatest, city of the Christian world: it is more than time that there be an utter cessation of further new buildings, lest the surcharge and overflow of people do bring upon our said City infinite inconveniences'. James concluded on a rather plaintive note, expressing the wish that 'as it was said of the first emperor of Rome, that he found the city of Rome of brick and left it of marble, so that we whom God hath honoured to be the first king of Great Britain, mought be able to say in some proportion, that we had found our City and suburb of London of sticks, and left them of brick, being a material far more durable, safe from fire, beautiful, and magnificent'. Such a rebuilding of the metropolis was not to be in James I's or Thomas Middleton's lifetime but was only begun in earnest after the great fire of 1666 devastated almost all of the old walled city.

In fact, for all London's explosive growth, Middleton's city in its physical aspect would not have changed out of all recognition from that known by Sir Thomas More at the beginning of the sixteenth century, and even in essentials from the city known by Geoffrey Chaucer a century earlier. The walled city was still the centre of metropolitan life, and the six medieval gates were still closed and guarded at night. Despite the traffic, one could pass through Aldgate (to the north of the Tower on the eastern border of the walled city) and walk along Cornhill and Cheapside and out of Newgate into Fleet Street in the west in about twenty minutes, and the distance from the river and out of Bishopsgate, Moorgate or Aldersgate to the north was even shorter. As in Chaucer's time, London Bridge remained the only passage for foot traffic or carts across the Thames. As a consequence, much of the traffic not only across the river but in fact from one end of London to the other and beyond was by the small wherries manned by watermen. When in Middleton's *A Chaste Maid in Cheapside* Touchwood Junior and Moll seek to flee the City to Barn Elms upriver near Putney, Moll is dispatched to take boat at Trigg Stairs, and Touchwood promises to follow from Paul's Wharf. Aided by the easy passage across the river, the population of Southwark on the south bank grew from more than 19,000 in 1603 to almost 26,000 three decades later, forming a dense urban development clustered around the south end of the bridge, and a strip of housing extending to the east along the river to Bermondsey and Rotherhithe, and west to the bear- and bull-baiting rings, the theatres, and the Winchester rents stretching to Paris Garden, after which there were only green fields and marshes around the bend of the Thames to Lambeth opposite Westminster.

Viewed from Southwark, the city not only kept its medieval aspect because the bulk of the housing remained the traditional three- and four-storey half-timbered structures, but even more importantly because the most prominent landmarks that would strike the eye were principally of medieval origin. At the east end of the city just outside the walls the massive fortification of the Tower of London was still the most prominent masonry pile, a constant reminder of the royal presence. Along the waterfront, Baynard's Castle, another Norman structure, still stood, and just to the west of the Fleet River (still an open if unsanitary ditch) was Bridewell Palace, an early Tudor structure now converted to civic use as one of the city's system of municipal hospitals. Further to the west past the Inns of Court until one's view was cut off by the bend in the Thames were the palaces of the great lay and ecclesiastical lords, Arundel House, Somerset House, Durham House and so on, all built between the Strand and the river. But what would have been most recognizable to any Londoner from the fourteenth to the late seventeenth century was the skyline, dominated by old St Paul's and by the towers of more than a hundred churches within and just beyond the walls. St Paul's, one of the largest Gothic cathedrals in Europe, stretched from east to west 585 feet, and its tower (even after its steeple burned down during a thunderstorm in 1561) was visible as far upriver as Richmond and as far downriver as Greenwich. It is no wonder that the popular Elizabethan rags-to-riches story of Dick Whittington, the fifteenth-century Lord Mayor, who as a boy was summoned to return to his apprenticeship 'by London bells sweetly rung', still resonated for Londoners, for the sound of church bells must have been ubiquitous.

Whittington's story resonated in another, more profound way, for, according to the Elizabethan tale, he came to London as a poor apprentice from the north country, and in fact immigration was crucial to the growth of London throughout the early modern era. By the late Elizabethan period between 4,000 and 5,000 apprentices were bound each year and more than 80 per cent of them came from beyond the Home Counties. Given the fact that as the seventeenth century wore on, premiums for apprenticeships increased, as did the start-up costs of setting up even a household business, it is surprising that thousands of young people trooped into the city every year, particularly when so many succumbed to disease (some 10 per cent of Elizabethan apprentices perished from disease in the course of their service), and when an increasing percentage could only look forward to a lifetime of wage labour: as skilled journeymen, if they were persistent and lucky, and as mere wage labourers, if they were not so fortunate. Part of the answer lies in the fact that the population of rural England grew in the Elizabethan period faster than new labour could be absorbed by either rural agriculture or industry; part in the failure of urban centres outside London to grow appreciably until well into the seventeenth century; and part, surely, in the fact that wages in London were appreciably higher than those even in south-east England generally. Wages for journeymen and even mere labourers in the building trades in London, such as those employed by Middleton's father, a bricklayer, as well as by carpenters, masons, and plasterers, were by 1590 some 50 per cent higher than elsewhere, and even in the 1590s when toward the end of the decade bad harvests sent grain prices

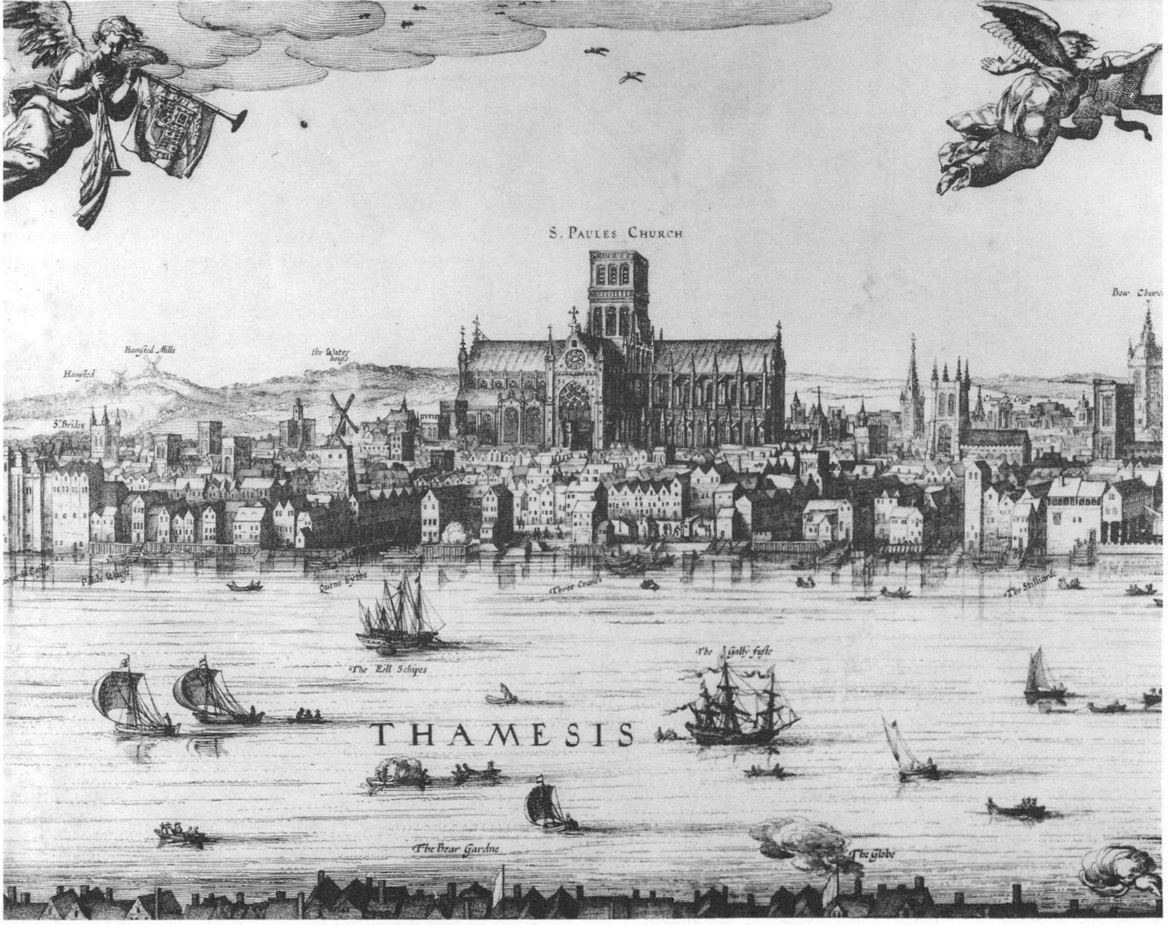

From a panorama of London by J. C. Visscher (1616).

skyrocketing, bread prices were lower in London than in the countryside.

It is reasonable to suppose that an equal number of young women came to the city seeking work as serving-maids in households, for maidservants were not the prerogative of the rich; most households, even of quite ordinary artisans, employed at least one maid. In the early seventeenth century even a mere London turner, who was never wealthy enough to enter the livery of that artisan company, employed a maidservant throughout his married life—two during the years when his wife was coping with small children as well as the household. In addition there were at least 5,000 alien immigrants in the city by the end of Elizabeth's reign. Middleton's London, like London today, was a polyglot capital, where one would encounter not only native English speaking unintelligible northern dialects, but also Welshmen, Irishmen, Scots, Flemings, Dutch, Germans from the Hanse, Norwegian sailors, French weavers, Spanish and Portuguese merchants, and a handful of more exotic American Indians and African blacks. In *A Chaste Maid in Cheapside* Sir Walter Whorehound enters Yellowhammer's goldsmith's shop accompanied by a Welsh gentlewoman, and in *A Fair Quarrel* the physician enters accompanied by a Dutch nurse, her nationality easily recognizable by her accent. But the full importance of immigration can only be appreciated when measured against the grim demographic history of the early modern city.

Thomas Middleton lived to be forty-seven, and both he and his sister lived to marry and have children. Survival itself was a minor miracle, but the fact that only two of William Middleton's children reached adulthood suggests that even the fortunate Middletons could not escape the appalling mortality rates that characterized early modern London. John Wallington, a London turner of William Middleton's generation, had twelve children by his first wife over the course of a marriage of twenty years, of whom only six survived to adulthood. The two sons each

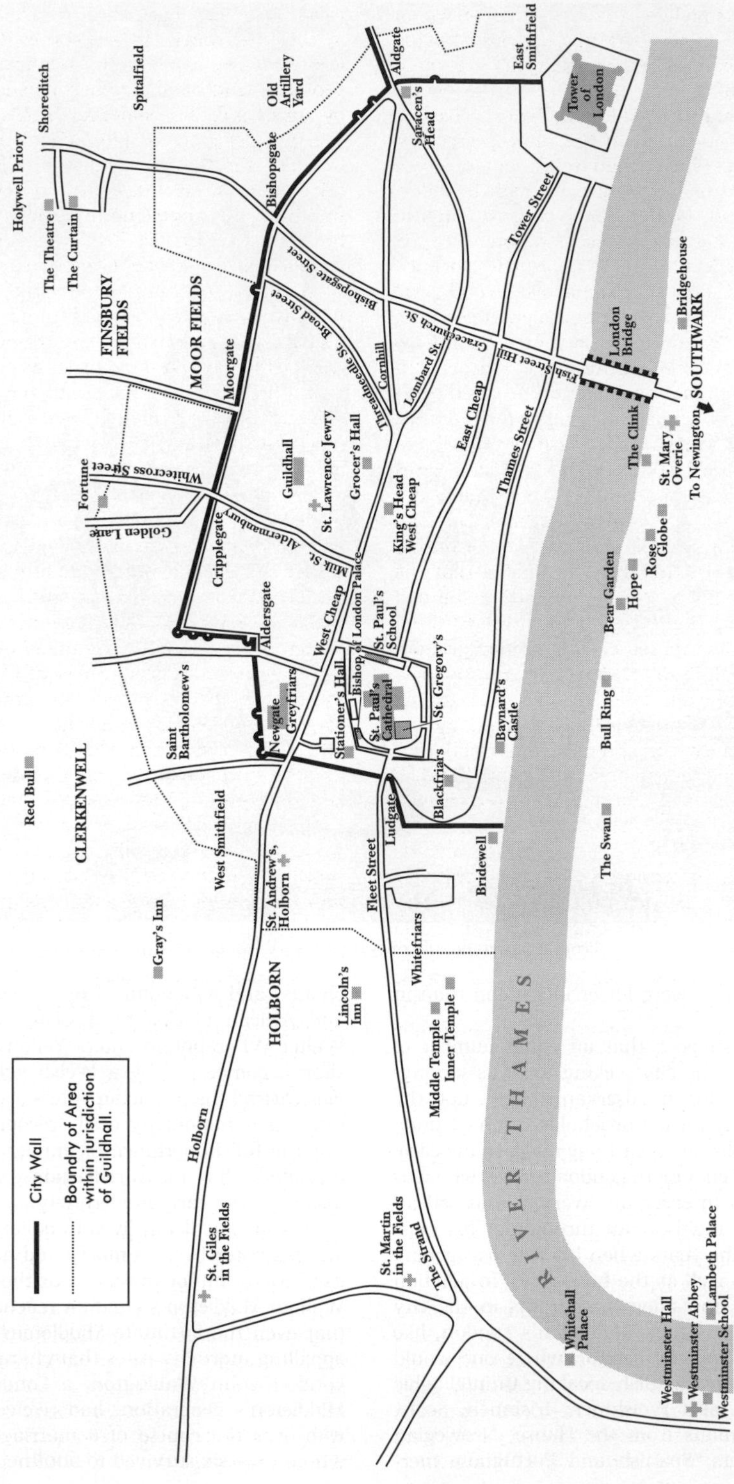
Holywell Priory
Shoreditch
Spitalfield
Old Artillery Yard
Aldgate
East Smithfield
Tower of London
Saracen's Head
Bishopsgate
The Theatre
The Curtain
Bishopsgate Street
Tower Street
Bridgehouse
FINSBURY FIELDS
MOOR FIELDS
Broad Street
Gracechurch St.
Fish Street Hill
London Bridge
SOUTHWARK
Moorgate
Threadneedle St.
Cornhill
Lombard St.
East Cheap
Thames Street
The Clink
St. Mary Overie
To Newington
Fortune
Whitecross Street
Golden Lane
Guildhall
St. Lawrence Jewry
Grocer's Hall
King's Head
West Cheap
Cripplegate
Aldermanbury
Milk St.
Hope
Rose
Globe
Bear Garden
Aldersgate
West Cheap
Bishop of London Palace
St. Paul's School
Saint Bartholomew's
Newgate
Greyfriars
Stationer's Hall
St. Paul's Cathedral
St. Gregory's
Baynard's Castle
Bull Ring
CLERKENWELL
Red Bull
West Smithfield
Ludgate
Blackfriars
Bridewell
The Swan
St. Andrew's, Holborn
Fleet Street
Gray's Inn
HOLBORN
Lincoln's Inn
Whitefriars
Middle Temple
Inner Temple
RIVER THAMES
City Wall
Boundry of Area within jurisdiction of Guildhall.
Holborn
St. Giles in the Fields
St. Martin in the Fields
The Strand
Whitehall Palace
Westminster Hall
Westminster Abbey
Westminster School
Lambeth Palace

married, the elder having five children, none of whom survived to the age of fifteen, the younger also having five children, only one, a daughter, living long enough to marry and have children in her turn. In the poorer parishes, fewer than half the male children survived to their fourteenth year, and even in the more prosperous and salubrious parishes fewer than seven out of every ten children born lived to celebrate a fifteenth birthday. London men, like most of the early modern English, married late, in part because citizenship, premised on freedom in a company, could not be achieved before the age of twenty-four, and so most men married several years later. In fact most young men were not apprenticed until their late teens, which would have prevented them from achieving their freedoms and setting up as independent householders until their late twenties. Hence, although the age at which London women first married was several years younger, in their early twenties rather than later, the average London family succeeded in baptizing fewer than three children. However, families were limited not so much by low fertility as by high mortality. In fact, more burials than baptisms took place in London during Middleton's lifetime, and it has been estimated that the deficit amounted to about 3,500 a year during the first half of the seventeenth century. London grew, then, not by natural, biological increase, but by immigration, and the best guess is that something over 10,000 new migrants entered the city annually, perhaps close to half the surplus of births over deaths for the whole of England.

Mortality was an ever-present spectacle and could never have been far from a Londoner's conscious thoughts. The London bells that summoned Whittington to return may well have been tolling a funeral. The plague which struck London thrice during Middleton's lifetime was only the most spectacular display of mortality. The comparatively minor incursion of 1593 carried off more than 10,000 Londoners, but those of 1603 and 1625 were responsible for the deaths of more than 25,000 on each occasion. Yet, dramatic and horrifying as these epidemics were, and in each of those three terrible years the plague accounted for the majority of all deaths in London, these spectacular visitations must be seen against the background of a constant high level of mortality that was to continue into the nineteenth century. In the parish of St Botolph without Aldgate, 24 per cent of those buried between 1558 and 1626 died of the plague, but another 22 per cent died of consumption, and various kinds of sickness identified as agues, fevers, fluxes, and colic carried off another 9 per cent. Smallpox carried off 2.4 per cent, and 1.5 per cent of the deaths were reported to be women in childbed. Elizabethans, of course, were presumed to perish from an excess of food and drink, and a Dutchman named Peter Yeop was reported in 1588 to have 'ended his life of a surfeit with drink'. Accidental deaths, although not as common as those attributable to disease, were common enough. Some twenty-one of the deaths recorded at St Botolph's were caused by drowning, one particularly pitiful case being a child of three whose chair in a privy 'whelmed backward', propelling her to her death in the town ditch. In 1590 one Richard Hawkesworth, a shoemaker, came along Aldersgate with a gun on his shoulder 'and having certain powder in his sleeve, which by mischance he, shooting of his said piece, fired the said powder', giving himself powder burns from which he died shortly after. Edward Frier, a bricklayer, like Middleton's father, died in 1618 'from a fall which he had from the top of the new church at Wapping, where he wrought'. In fact William Middleton himself almost perished in an accident three years before Thomas was born. While opening up a vault in the south aisle of St Lawrence Jewry for the tomb of Sir John Langley, Middleton and his men were digging too close to the supporting pillar and, but for a timely warning shout from the parish clerk, would have perished when the pillars, walls, and ceiling thundered down, carrying away the organ loft and destroying the pews in the adjacent chancel. It is not surprising that many at the time believed in an active Providence, intervening both to take life and to grant it, for death came suddenly and unexpectedly, and survival when so many died so young clearly seemed an act of special favour. Quite fittingly Thomas Beard, the Puritan divine, entitled his study of God's providence—which he found in the apparently arbitrary accidents of contemporary life—*The Theatre of God's Judgements*.

Yet despite the deadly play of God's judgements upon the city, particularly upon the young—and even in the plague year of 1593 more than 7,000 Londoners died of other causes, while in 1625, another plague year, more than 14,000 perished from other diseases and accidents—London continued to grow, so that in 1616 King James complained with perhaps pardonable exaggeration that 'with time England will only be London, and the whole country be left waste'. Indeed at the time it was recognized that this city of immigrants constituted a unique society, for Londoners 'are by birth for the most part a mixture of all countries of the same [realm], by blood gentlemen, yeomen and of the basest sort, without distinction, and by profession busy bees, and travellers for their living in the hive of this commonwealth', and this anonymous observer of Elizabethan London went on to describe the inhabitants of the city more prosaically as consisting 'of these three parts, merchants, handicraftsmen, and labourers'.

As might be expected in England's principal trading centre and port city, the merchants, the smallest of the three groups in number, were both the richest and the most politically powerful element in the city. Nevertheless, even in London the number of merchants active in overseas trade was very small. In 1606, for example, only 219 merchants were engaged in the trade in traditional woollen cloth to the northern European cloth markets, a trade monopolized by the Merchant Adventurers through all but the later years of Middleton's lifetime. This was in the seventeenth century a declining trade, and by 1640 only 103 merchants were still actively exporting cloth to Hamburg and the Netherlands. In those years the quantities of exported cloths dropped from 101,000

(1606) to 59,000 (1640). All merchants were not Merchant Adventurers, and the Levant Company merchants, trading in the eastern Mediterranean for silks and currants, were rapidly rising to prominence on the strength of the expanding trade in these luxuries. Raw silk imports, which had stood at a mere 12,000 pounds by weight in 1560 at the beginning of Elizabeth's reign, rose to 142,000 pounds in 1629, just after Middleton's death. Between 1611 and 1630 the Levant Company admissions book shows the entry of 203 into the ranks of the company. In 1559 sixteen (72 per cent) of the twenty-two richest Londoners, according to the subsidy of that year, were Merchant Adventurers. In 1640 the Crown raised a forced loan from 140 leading citizens; among them were 21 Merchant Adventurers, who contributed loans of an average of £155, and 31 Levant Company merchants, who paid an average of £275. Over several generations those engaged in the newer, long-distance trades—in the eastern Mediterranean, the East Indies, and the Americas—gradually replaced the Merchant Adventurers as the dominant economic force in the city, although trade with northern Europe continued to be an important component of London's business. It is no accident that Middleton's Lord Mayor's show for 1617, celebrating the mayoralty of George Bolles, a rich Grocer, begins with a scene in which 'a company of Indians, attired according to the true nature of their country, seeming for the most part naked, are set at work in an island of growing spices, some planting nutmeg trees, some other spice trees of all kinds, some gathering fruits, some making up bags of pepper'. The spices that once came to London markets by way of Mediterranean and Middle Eastern middlemen now reached the warehouses of the Grocers direct from the holds of the East India Company fleet, which had been sailing around the Cape to the Far East on a direct ocean route since the founding of the company at the end of Elizabeth I's reign.

Obviously all merchants did not belong to these two élite companies, and many were engaged in the expanding domestic trade. Feeding the growing population of London was itself a formidable business. Kentish ports alone shipped over 12,000 quarters of grain to the London market in 1587 and close to 28,000 in 1624, and whereas most of the cereals consumed by Londoners came from the south and east coast ports, much of the meat consumed came from the north and west, from Wales, Ireland, and Scotland, as well as the highland pastures of England. In 1662 more than 18,500 Scottish cattle passed through Carlisle on their way to southern markets, and by the end of the century it was estimated that Londoners were consuming one mutton per head each year. During Middleton's lifetime Londoners switched almost totally from using wood for fuel to coal, and although the trade in sea coal was infinitely less glamorous than the import of Levantine silk, the collier trade came to constitute a significant proportion of the shipping in the pool of London. Newcastle was shipping more than 120,000 tons of coal in the 1590s and close to 300,000 tons per year in the last decade of Middleton's life, by which time the coal trade engaged more than 28,000 tons of shipping, which must have been close to 20 per cent of the total tonnage of London shipping in that period.

As crucial as London's merchant community was to the growth and wealth of the city, an Elizabethan observer was surely correct in claiming that retail shopkeepers and artisans 'do far exceed' both the number of merchants and poor labourers together. Despite the dominant role of trade, London was also a major manufacturing centre, and the role of manufacturing in London's economy grew, leading to a shift in the balance of London imports away from luxury products to raw materials. In fact, one way to measure the increasing importance of manufacturing is to note the shift from the importing of manufactured goods to that of raw materials. In 1560 45 per cent of all imports were manufactured goods and only 26 per cent raw materials; by the 1630s the import of manufactured goods had slipped to 29 per cent of total imports, and the import of raw materials (exclusive of food in both cases) had risen to 35 per cent. What data we have suggests that a majority of Elizabethan Londoners were engaged in one or another form of production, and that in the early Stuart era manufacturing remained the dominant occupation of Londoners (rising from 58 per cent of London householders in the Elizabethan period to slightly more than 60 per cent in the early Stuart years), despite the great expansion of trade across the Atlantic and to the Far East. Further, as the proportion of those householders living within the walls and engaged in trade, distribution, and exchange of some kind increased from 28 per cent to 36 per cent of the intramural total, those engaged in manufacturing in the growing extramural parishes increased from 70 per cent of all occupations to more than 74 per cent. However, even within the walls more householders were engaged in production than in exchange, and the overwhelming number of those engaged in manufacturing worked in small shops presided over by a master and including the master's journeymen and apprentices. The fast-growing printing industry was one of these, numbering some dozen printing houses in 1550 and twenty-three in 1587, the twenty or so master printers employing about 150 journeymen and apprentices. The small number of print shops gives no sense of actual production, for in 1586 when a Star Chamber decree required the relicensing of all cheap broadside ballads, the Stationers' Company registered 237 titles in one year; it has been estimated that by the death of Elizabeth I some three million ballads had been printed, most of them, like most books, funnelled through the booksellers surrounding St Paul's Churchyard. A few industries had outgrown the streetfloor shop—shipbuilding, rope-making, glass- and brick-making, the larger tanneries and breweries, most of which were located outside the walls—but these large-scale operations were the exception, not the rule, even in the suburbs. The view of three small shops in a rank, where both manufacturing and retailing were carried on, with which the second act of *The Roaring Girl* opens, and the cry, 'What is't you lack, gentlemen, what is't you buy', was a scene familiar to even the most casual visitor to the metropolis and as much a part of the quotidian street scene as the church steeples were of the more distant prospect.

Elizabethans who attempted to map their society tended to see urban populations as an undifferentiated mass. William Harrison, despite having been born in London, spent pages (twenty in a modern edition) in his *Description of England* in a detailed anatomy of the major and minor nobility, that social pyramid that stretched from dukes and earls down to knights, esquires and mere gentlemen, but devoted scarcely two paragraphs to the 'citizens and burgesses ... who be those that are free within the cities and are of some likely substance to bear office in the same'. In fact London society was both stratified and complex. At its apex were the rich merchants and financiers, such as Middleton's contemporary and namesake, Sir Thomas Myddelton, a scion of a minor branch of that ramified Welsh family which had married into the Shropshire gentry and thus achieved an English patronymic. This Myddelton was apprenticed to Fernando Poyntz, a London grocer, and by the 1580s was deeply engaged in the sugar trade in Antwerp until its capture by Spanish forces put an end to English involvement in its economy. In the later 1580s Myddelton was frequently engaged in various partnerships with his father-in-law, Richard Saltonstall (father of the Massachusetts Bay adventurer), and by the 1590s Myddelton was investing in privateering enterprises that preyed on Spanish shipping and was increasingly engaged in money lending at 10 per cent—£20 to Job Throckmorton, the probable author of *Martin Marprelate* (the puritan satire on timeserving, careerist Elizabethan bishops), and more than a thousand pounds to the Earl of Shrewsbury. At the same time he was investing his profits in a Denbighshire estate, which by the end of Elizabeth's reign gave him a rent-roll of over £150. In the next reign he became alderman, lord mayor, and knight, his mayoralty ushered in by a lord mayor's show paid for by the Grocers' Company and scripted by Thomas Middleton, who shared his name if not his fortune.

Sir Thomas was not alone at the apex of this urban society. During the first quarter of the seventeenth century, 20 per cent of all merchants who were elected aldermen left fortunes of more than £20,000, and a handful of the spectacularly rich—Sir John Spencer, Sir William Craven, and Sir Baptist Hicks—were reputed to have fortunes of more than £100,000. In 1582 some seventy-five Londoners were assessed in the subsidy of that year at more than £200, the vast majority of whom were Merchant Adventurers. All but two of the twenty-six aldermen were numbered among this wealthy group. To be assessed in 1582 at £50 or more placed one among the richest 4.8 per cent of the metropolitan population. William Middleton, Thomas's father, already a wealthy property owner, was assessed at £20. To be assessed at all (the minimum was £3) placed one among the top 25 per cent of all London households.

There is another way to view the social pyramid. Altogether there were sixty companies ranked in an early precedence list dating from the twenty-third year of Henry VIII's reign, beginning with the Mercers and descending to the Blacksmiths, although only fifty-one of those companies had a livery. New companies were formed, such as the Apothecaries, who broke away from the Grocers and obtained a charter from James I. The peculiarity of the freedom of London was such that any citizen, free of a company, could carry on any trade or occupation. As a consequence, although overseas merchants came principally from the ranks of the twelve great livery companies—Mercers, Grocers, Drapers, Haberdashers, Merchant Taylors, Clothworkers, Goldsmiths, Skinners, Ironmongers, Salters, Fishmongers, and Vintners—members of the twelve did not have an exclusive monopoly even of the trades designated by their companies' names. Even the Merchant Taylors' Company, whose livery was dominated by wholesale traders overseas, nevertheless fiercely defended its handicraft members in the clothworking trades from the attempts by the Clothworkers' Company to force them under that company's jurisdiction, on the grounds that such an attempt at rationalization violated the traditional freedom of London citizens to engage in any legitimate occupation. Every livery company, whether one of the twelve, where the majority of the merchants were to be found, or among the vast number of craft and trade guilds, had an élite membership co-opted into 'the clothing' from whom the company officers were selected and who were expected to wear the company livery on company quarter days and court days and to vote in the Congregation. There were perhaps 2,500 liverymen in London at the end of Elizabeth's reign, and these members of the élite at least of their companies constituted the heads of about 10 per cent of the households in the city.

Not all Londoners were citizens, but it has been estimated that about three-quarters of the adult males were citizens in the 1550s and, despite the rapid growth of the city during the next generation, perhaps two-thirds were citizens in 1600 and about half in 1640. Citizenship mattered: one could live and work in the city without being a citizen, but one could not sell the product of one's labour without that privilege. Citizenship was obtained by becoming free of a company, and that freedom could be obtained by apprenticeship, patrimony (one could become free of one's father's company without having served a formal apprenticeship) or by purchase (also referred to as redemption). In the late decades of the sixteenth century 83 to 90 per cent of all those gaining their freedom did so by completing an apprenticeship.

As a consequence, social status was a complex issue. The son of a gentleman apprenticed to a Grocer and Merchant Adventurer was, despite his birth, a servant during his apprenticeship and did not achieve his freedom until his apprenticeship was completed. Nevertheless, the apprentice Grocer might find himself during the later years of his service acting as a factor living in a foreign port and buying and selling on his master's and sometimes his own behalf. Such a servant might end his career as a wealthy Grocer himself and an alderman, and if an alderman, almost inevitably, if he lived long enough, a Lord Mayor, a knight, and a justice of the peace, as all senior aldermen became automatically. The minutes of the election-day meeting of the Grocers' Court of Assistants on 11 July 1614 presented this ordered hierarchy at the head of that day's entry: at the top was listed Sir Thomas Myddelton, knight and Lord Mayor, followed by Sir Robert Napier, knight and baronet, Sir Stephen Soame, knight, and the three junior aldermen—Mr Nicholas Stiles, Mr George Bolles (soon to be Lord Mayor), and Mr Richard Pyott—followed by the three wardens of the company and the seventeen assistants in attendance, ranked according to seniority on the bench. Mobility, of course, was a two-way street, and a Vintner who failed in his trade might find himself suing for the privilege of being one of the company's licensed porters, unloading casks of wine at the crane and trundling those casks from the cart into the vaults of one of his more successful company brethren. As a porter, the Vintner would be performing the tasks of a mere labourer, but despite his bankruptcy, such a porter remained both a freeman of his company and a citizen of London.

The complexities of urban status did not end there. Journeymen were freemen of their companies who worked for masters for wages, usually on contracts that ran from year to year, the wages being paid at the conclusion of the contract; as wage labourers, journeymen differed little from other, unfree (non-citizen) wage labourers, except that they were citizens, free of a company, and therefore possessed the right, if they could accumulate the capital necessary to do so, to open a shop as an independent master and to take on apprentices and journeymen in their turn. Women present another anomaly, for in theory women had none of the rights of citizenship available to adult males, and this despite the obviously important economic role they played, either as maidservants or as housewives. And the housewife such as Anne Middleton, even the wife of an artisan, might find herself running a complex household, consisting of several maidservants, an apprentice and a journeyman, in addition to her husband and children. By Middleton's lifetime women had been excluded from all but a handful of apprenticeships (a few appear bound apprentice to cordwainers to learn the manufacture of perfumed gloves; a few appear bound in other trades jointly to the artisan's wife to learn such skills as lace-making or mantua-making—trades that paid too poorly for men to undertake). However, a small number of women appear in the records as partners of, for example, their citizen brothers, and as such opened shops and engaged in trade. More importantly, it was assumed that even without formal apprenticeship a woman might learn her husband's trade, and as the widow of a citizen, a woman had the right to keep open her husband's shop, to trade and to bind apprentices.

Middleton's London, viewed from the top, was properly oligarchical, a 'republic of wholesale merchants', as the Venetian ambassador described it. Neither Elizabeth I nor the early Stuart kings approved of 'popular' government, and the Crown had long been pleased to strengthen the powers of the governors of their principal city. An oligarchy based on merit, rather than heredity, and presided over by an annually elected mayor, who ruled at best as *primus inter pares*, was already sufficiently at odds with the principles of hereditary monarchy and aristocracy, even without being 'popular' or democratic, to pose a sharp contrast to prevailing concepts of politic rule. Essentially the city was ruled by its court of aldermen, twenty-six men representing the twenty-six wards of the city, who once selected were expected to serve for life. Although nominated by the ward in which a vacancy had occurred, the aldermanic court could reject nominees, which in effect gave the aldermen power to co-opt their membership. By custom aldermen were chosen from among the liveried members of the twelve great companies, and the few who rose from minor companies customarily transferred to one of the twelve certainly before election to the mayoralty. Thus Sir Edward Barkham, whose installation as Lord Mayor was celebrated in *The Sun in Aries*, began his rise as a Leatherseller and was then translated to the Drapers in 1621, the year of his election to the mayoralty. Although the lord mayor and the sheriffs were elected in the common hall or Congregation, to which all liveried members of the city companies had a right to attend, in fact one of the sheriffs was customarily selected from among the junior aldermen who had not yet held that office, and the Lord Mayor was invariably the oldest serving alderman who had not yet served as Lord Mayor. In fact it was the very predictability of such 'elections' that permitted the city company of the mayor elect to hire a Munday or Middleton, a Heywood or Dekker, to write the script for the pageant months in advance of its performance.

For all intents and purposes, the mayor and aldermen ran the city. They constituted the mayor's court, which governed as the executive council of the city, sat as the city's court of orphans and the sheriff's court, and those aldermen who had already served as mayor were named to the commission of the peace and served with the city recorder as justices of the peace in the city sessions court. Aldermen sat on all the boards of the five city hospitals—Christ's, Bridewell, St Bartholomew's, St Thomas's, and Bethlehem. All civic property was under the control of the City Lands Committee, which was composed of the city chamberlain and four to six aldermen. Although in a formal sense legislation and taxation required the consent of the Common Council, a body of 212, elected by the freemen of the wards, in fact the Common Council did not meet without the aldermen being present, and the aldermanic veto ensured that Common Council enacted nothing without their approval. In effect, Common Council gave the aldermanic bench a broader base of consent and legitimacy for important or controversial acts.

The mayor and aldermen represented an immense concentration of official power, but its exercise faced substantial limitations. From one direction they faced a steady stream of orders and reprimands from a concentration of political power even more formidable than their own. The presence of the Court and Privy Council on their doorstep was constantly felt, immensely helpful particularly in commercial matters, but a source of irritation and frustration in others. From the opening of the public theatres official London tried to close them and to confine playing to the Court, but perhaps nothing better illustrates the true limits of City power than the grovelling letter the Lord Mayor wrote on 25 February 1593 to Archbishop Whitgift in which he 'humbly and earnestly' beseeched that prelate to speak with the Queen's Master of Revels to see whether the archbishop might have better success than he, the Lord Mayor, had in persuading the Master to 'reform' the players by making them play in private in preparation for performances before the Queen, rather than in the public playhouses, and so free the city 'from these continued disorders which thereby do grow and increase daily among us'. The plague periodically closed the theatres, but the city never succeeded in doing so.

The mayor and aldermen found prostitution and bawdy-houses similarly objectionable, but equally difficult to control. While the governors of Bridewell even managed to inflict the humiliating punishment of whipping on members of the gentry caught fornicating, as they did on one occasion to Richard Denny of Bawdsey, Suffolk, for committing 'whoredom' with two maids at the sign of the Bell in Newgate market, despite his 'being very penitent for his said lewdness' (he had admitted that it had been his customary practice for the past ten or twelve years, when he had come to town), the city fathers were very much less successful in closing bawdy-houses and punishing prostitutes protected by the powerful. John Hollingbrig, who ran a brothel in Holborn, wore the livery of Lord Ambrose Dudley; a brothel was run out of Worcester House under the protection of that earl; and the punishment of Elizabeth Barlowe, sentenced for bawdry, was spared at the suit of 'Mr Browne which keepeth my Lord of Leicester's house'. Actors were not the only professional entertainers protected by the court aristocracy.

If the London magistrates were limited in one direction by the interests of a powerful Crown and Court, they were limited in the other direction by the multiplicity of subordinate communities upon whose cooperation their effective rule rested. London was a congeries of overlapping communities, the two most important of which were the guild and the parish. London citizens almost never appear in the records without mention of their company membership. Although apprenticeship was a private contract between master and apprentice, the company clerk kept a record of each apprentice binding, and the company court supervised the apprenticeship, transferring the apprentice to another master, if his first master failed in his business, failed to teach his apprentice his trade, or treated his apprentice with undue brutality. By the same token, masters who could not control their apprentices would have them brought before the company court for discipline, which might range from a reprimand to a public whipping. Every livery company presented its freemen with a ladder of honour and responsibility: from the yeomanry to the livery, and from the livery to the court assistants, the company wardens, and finally to the mastership of the company, officers elected yearly from among the liveried assistants who were themselves co-opted by the company court.

The livery companies presented the same set of anomalies and contradictions that the city government did, being at once both oligarchic and hierarchical and egalitarian and consensual: company minutes invariably list those in attendance according to the hierarchy of social estimation and political power. Sir Thomas Myddelton, nominated to the livery and chosen one of the assistants early in 1592, appears among the knighted aldermen at the top of the list of those attending the Grocers' court in 1612 and remained among that select company until he ceased to attend the court in the summer of 1631, shortly before his death. When the Merchant Taylors Company was assessed at £175 in 1565, 'for and towards the provision of wheat and other grain to be made for the use of the City', the company taxed its members according to the same hierarchy of social prestige and power: the three knighted aldermen were to pay £5. 18*s.* 4*d.* each; Mr Thomas Rowe, alderman, the four wardens of the company, and the other assistants were all assessed at £2. 3*s.* 4*d.*; and the thirty-seven liverymen not on the court of assistants were ordered to pay 33*s.* 4*d.* each. Privilege and power had its costs, and those in the yeomanry of the company were not assessed at all. At the same time companies saw all their members as brothers, and all grocers were expected to pay the annual 'brotherhood' fee in acknowledgement of their membership. Nothing better captures this guild ideal than the annual exhortation of the senior warden whom the company clerk records in July 1620 as giving, 'a very religious, brotherly and profitable speech for the good of this Company' in which he made 'a very earnest exhortation and persuasion to the whole assembly to live in brotherly love and unity amongst themselves and to be obedient to the lawful government and ordinances of this Company'.

Company courts of assistants met frequently, some as often as every other week, but all company members were expected to appear at their hall on quarter days to pay their quarterage in acknowledgement of their membership. Companies appointed searchers who inspected workshops to ensure that the quality of production was maintained and to confiscate shoddy goods, and company searches frequently extended beyond the Lord Mayor's jurisdiction to the two- to three-mile radius around the city specified in the company's royal charters. Companies served as quasi-governmental institutions; for example, Elizabethan and Caroline forced loans were apportioned by the mayor's court to the companies, which in turn were responsible for raising the assessed sums from among their wealthier members. Although companies ceased to be religious confraternities in King Edward's reign, the guilds remained administrators and repositories of charitable bequests, and in consequence performed a variety of social services, ranging from administering schools and almshouses, to providing scholarships to Oxford and Cambridge, loan funds to young and impecunious masters, small dowries to poor maids to enable them to marry, and alms to ancient members too old to work. Thomas Harvey, Middleton's stepfather, first appears in the records of the Grocers' Company as the second of nine 'young men' who were suitors for the company loan funds in a minute of 27 February 1587, less than three months after he married Middleton's mother (he was granted £50 for two years from the Sir Thomas Ramsey loan fund by the court of assistants on 4 December 1590). The companies were metropolitan institutions, and although divided between the livery and the yeomanry—and a liveried Haberdasher might well be a Merchant Adventurer trading to Hamburg, while a yeoman Haberdasher had a small shop retailing haberdashery—the combination of regulatory and supervisory powers and social services created a number of common interests that gave reality to the company identity no matter how casual most members might be about paying their quarterage regularly at the company hall. A master who failed to bring his apprentice before the company clerk to have his binding recorded could find himself in trouble both with his company and the City Chamberlain; a master who flouted a summons to appear before his company's court of assistants might find himself marched into their presence by a company of the Lord Mayor's servants. The companies eventually became businessmen's clubs, but in Middleton's lifetime they still played a key role in the life of Londoners and constituted one of every citizen's primary communities.

Although he was himself a university-educated gentleman, the world of tradesmen and guildsmen was one Middleton knew well and at first hand, as the son of a Tiler and Bricklayer, the stepson of a Grocer, and a brother-in-law both of a Cutler and of a Clothworker. Unlike Ben Jonson, he never became a member of his father's company, as he could easily have done by patrimony. He may have believed that the freedom of an artisan company ill consorted with his gentility; he may have concluded that such a company had little to offer in the way of patronage; but whatever his motives for not taking up citizenship and a company's freedom, he did not turn his back on the world of his birth, as the sympathetic presentation of the world of small artisans and shopkeepers in *A Chaste Maid in Cheapside* and other city plays suggests. As an established writer, he scripted three Lord Mayor's Shows for the Grocers, one of the wealthiest and most powerful of the great livery companies. It was a world with its share of villains (they people the disciplinary record of every company's court minutes) and Quomodo, the villainous Draper and moneylender of *Michaelmas Term*, was both a feared and familiar figure in a city in which banks had not yet come into existence but where small artisans and great merchants alike were in constant need of credit. The City also had its heroes—Dick Whittington, the fifteenth-century Lord Mayor, Sir Thomas Gresham, the early Elizabethan financier who built the New Exchange, and such contemporary figures as Sir Thomas Myddelton, who, although a moneylender like Quomodo, acquired his Welsh estates by purchase rather than by foreclosure on improvident gentry, and who among his other bequests left money to provide dowries to enable poor maidservants of Grocers to marry.

The other community to which every Londoner belonged, whether citizen or mere inhabitant, was the local parish. In origin parishes were medieval institutions, defining the geographical unit of parishioners who were expected to attend the obligatory religious services at their local parish church, to take communion at least once a year at Easter, and to support their incumbent minister—a rector, vicar, or stipendiary curate—with their tithe payments and other dues. London parishes within the walls were with a couple of exceptions extraordinarily small: St Stephen's Coleman Street, a parish of 26.7 acres, was by far the largest, while St Martin's Ironmonger Lane was a tiny 1.1 acre. St Lawrence Jewry, the parish in which Middleton was born, was at 5.6 acres larger than most of the 97 parishes within the walls but dwarfed by the large extramural parishes in the liberties, such as St Botolph Aldgate at 38.6 acres or St Botolph without Bishopgate at 44.5 acres. The average assessed rent in St Lawrence was £14.66 in 1638, which was above the average rent of £11.05 for the 113 parishes of the city and liberties, but that amount by no means placed it among the truly wealthy parishes in the city, such as Allhallows Lombard Street, which included the row of goldsmiths' shops along Lombard Street and which had an average rent of £38.92, or St Mary Magdalen Milk Street, where the average rent was £27.40. The wealthiest parishes tended to cluster in the centre of the city, along Cheapside and Lombard Street, whereas the poorest parishes were beyond the walls; St Botolph without Aldgate, for example, the large extramural parish east and north of Aldgate, had an average rental of only £3.67. Nevertheless, almost all parishes contained a mixed population of merchants, tradesmen, and artisans, the wealthy merchants and shopkeepers occupying residences along the principal streets and the artisans who sold their products to retailers resident in the back courts, alleys, and closes; the social segregation familiar to modern Londoners which sees a labouring population in the East End and a wealthy West End still lay in the future.

The church of St Lawrence Jewry fronted on Cateaton Street (now Gresham Street), a block north of Cheapside, and behind the church stood the Guildhall. St Lawrence was an impropriate rectory like many in the city: some were in the patronage of city companies—St Martin Outwich of the Grocers' Company, St Laurence Pountney of the Merchant Taylors—others in the gift of the Dean and Chapter of St Paul's and other ecclesiastical institutions. St Lawrence was in the gift of Balliol College, Oxford, which, as an absentee owner and patron, was content to lease the farm of the tithes to the parish itself, which paid Balliol as rector £20 and the vicar £20 as well. In 1575 the patron granted the next presentation to the parish, and in that year the parish elected as their vicar Robert Crowley, an Edwardian Protestant, a famous preacher, and a nonconformist who had been among those purged in 1566 at the height of the Vestiarian Controversy, when the Bishop of London was ordered to clamp down on those who had hitherto refused to wear the vestments prescribed by the ornaments rubric in the Book of Common Prayer. The parish supplemented Crowley's income with a lectureship, which paid £10 a year in addition to his vicarial stipend for a sermon beyond those required by his incumbency. In the 1570s Crowley was preaching lectures at St Margaret New Fish Street and at St Saviour, Southwark, as well. In 1581, during Middleton's first year of life, that old nonconformist resigned the living and lectureship, and although the parish tried to claim that it leased the advowson (the right to present or nominate the vicar) as well as the tithes, Balliol successfully reasserted its rights.

Although Londoners were notorious for denying their parish ministers the tithe income traditionally owed to the parish rector or vicar—by tradition Londoners paid tithes on a notional rent, rather than on their actual incomes, and kept rents low while increasing the fines paid on the renewal of leases to compensate for the inflation of property values—they also insisted on a preaching clergy and were willing to pay for lectureships in order to ensure the quantity and quality of preaching they desired. Much of the impetus behind this demand for preaching came from the Puritan members of the parish congregations, but the Puritans were not alone in wanting a preaching ministry. In the 1580s and 90s, in the years when Middleton was growing up in St Lawrence Jewry, between 30 and 40 London parishes (out of 113) hired lecturers, and perhaps 25 to 29 at any one time can clearly be identified as Puritans. St Lawrence had appointed Puritan preachers in the early Elizabethan years and would again in the 1620s, but there is no reason to suppose that all, or even a majority of the parishioners were Puritans, in that or most other London parishes, although clearly a majority of those active in the parish vestry wanted a preaching ministry and were willing to tax themselves to pay for it.

Parishes after the Reformation rapidly became civil as well as ecclesiastical institutions, and London parishes in particular soon had to cope with the growing numbers of the poor which accompanied the explosive growth of the metropolis. Even before the rood loft, the last vestige of the Catholic past, was dismantled in June 1566 and the first parish lecturer, propagating the new Protestantism, was hired in 1567, the vestry of St Lawrence Jewry, like other urban parishes, was appointing collectors for the poor. By the autumn of 1572 the system of parochial poor relief was backed by statute, supplementing such acts of private benevolence as that of Lady North, a native of Middleton's parish, who left a bequest in 1574 to provide fourpence weekly to six poor, 'honest' parishioners. Whatever hopes there had been for the great civic hospitals, erected largely out of the wreckage of the monastic dissolution—Bridewell was a former royal palace, but Christ's, which became the city orphanage, and St Bartholomew's, St Thomas's and Bethlehem were all erected on former religious foundations—the growth of urban poverty soon overwhelmed both the capacity of the hospitals and of private charity to cope, and long before the great codification of the Parliamentary poor law in 1598 and 1603, London had instituted a system of compulsory parochial poor rates and had ordered the livery companies to stockpile grain, which could be sold at below market rates to the poor in years of dearth and high prices.

Residence in a parish and membership in a company tell little about the actual level of involvement and the degree to which a resident's or guildsman's identity was wrapped up in those institutions. The Middletons presumably attended at least Sunday Morning Prayers at St Lawrence Jewry, paid their tithes and 'casualties', as the various church dues were called, and took communion in that church at least once a year, for failure to pay tithes would have invited a suit in a church court, and failure to take communion would have led to presentment as a recusant. On the other hand, there is no evidence that Middleton's father attended the vestry or served as one of the two churchwardens, the annually elected officers responsible for fiscal affairs of the parish and charged with tasks as varied as the payment of the clerk's wages, the repair of the chancel, and the provision of fire-fighting equipment and the parish pump. Company membership might mean equally minimal involvement. Middleton's father twice signed the Tilers and Bricklayers court minutes, which suggests that he was a member of that company's court of assistants, but Middleton's stepfather, Thomas Harvey, never rose above the yeomanry of the Grocers' Company and appears in their records merely as paying his annual brotherhood money. As for Middleton's brother-in-law, John Empson, Cutler, he too remained in the yeomanry of that minor company, paying his fees for opening his shop and binding apprentices, but otherwise appearing in the record only in the autumn of 1607 when he was fined 'for that he like a mad man very unorderly about 10 of the clock at night came to Mr Porte's house and there exclaimed and cried out against the master that he had undone him, and that he would bring his wife and children to our master, his doors', and again two years later, when he appeared in court to demand the return of his former apprentice, whom he had turned vagrant into the streets when Empson had gone out of town. Troublesome and vexatious as such associations might on occasion be, the parish and the guild provided most Londoners with a defined neighbourhood and a structured business community, a neighbourhood at once more intimate and face-to-face than one of the twenty-six wards of the city, and a set of associates joined at least by some common social and economic interests. Since most of London's inhabitants had left close family and kin behind when they migrated, these institutionalized communities probably played a larger role in most Londoners' lives than they might have in smaller and more stable places. In the absence of parishes and guilds it is hard otherwise to explain the capacity of the metropolis to absorb thousands of newcomers annually without creating the conditions for social revolution.

As Middleton's London grew, so both the Mayor's Court and the Crown's Privy Council became increasingly fearful of their capacity to maintain order, and yet the anticipated social anarchy never actually occurred. Vagrancy grew with poverty, and at times of high unemployment the alarmed magistrates instituted sweeps of the unemployed, who were whipped at Bridewell and sent out of town, presumably to return to their home parishes. Petty thievery was a constant problem; drinking and gambling at alehouses frequently led to brawling. Throughout Middleton's lifetime, apprentices regularly rioted at Shrovetide, despite mayoral precepts ordering masters to keep their apprentices at home, and despite the mobilizing of double watches and by James I's reign of one of the city regiments as well. (One suspects neither the watch nor the troops had much stomach for suppressing rioting sanctioned by custom, if not by the Lord Mayor, particularly when the riots were directed against theatres and bawdy-houses.) Weapons were readily available: many apprentices owned swords, although they could not wear them in their masters' shops, and all households were expected to own halberds and to be prepared to reinforce the watch. In 1626 a mayoral precept complained that 'much danger and hurt hath happened amongst the boys and youths of this City by their late meetings and marching together with pikes, shot and swords and the like'. The cry of 'clubs, apprentices' was well known, but Fishmongers' apprentices were reported to go at each other with their considerably more lethal fish-knives.

For all of that, the few riots that appeared to be dangerously out of control all seem directed at targets the City authorities were reluctant to defend. For example, on a late summer evening in 1618 a servant in the household of the Spanish ambassador, riding home up Chancery Lane, apparently knocked over a child playing in the road; a mob quickly collected and pursued the rider to the Barbican where he took refuge in the ambassadorial residence. The mob surrounded the house and smashed its windows and was preparing to force entrance when the Chief Justice, who had been at dinner nearby, and the sheriff arrived, took the rider into custody and dispersed the crowd. The ambassador protested, the Privy Council understandably wrote an angry missive to the Lord Mayor, complaining of this gross breach of ambassadorial immunity and of the length of time it had taken the City to mobilize its forces of law and order (they quite reasonably suspected the City authorities of taking their time in moving to defend so unpopular a target), and calling for the imprisonment and punishment of the ringleaders of the mob. Ten years later a mob of 'boys' set upon Dr John Lamb, the hated Duke of Buckingham's astrologer, whom they attacked as 'the duke's devil' as he was leaving a playhouse (possibly the Fortune, given the direction of his flight). They chased him through Moorgate to the Windmill Tavern where he took temporary refuge, and later, despite an escort of constables, stoned and beat him to death. The King was scandalized that a city mob would dare to murder the creature of his favourite in this brutal fashion on the very doorstep of the Court, and the Privy Council ordered the imprisonment of the constables and the Provost Marshal's men who were present or should have been present to prevent the outrage, but the culprits were never caught.

These were spectacular and widely noted riots, not because they posed any real threat to the social order, but because of their political implications. The drunken brawling, purse-cutting, 'picking' (as petty thievery was called), and riotous assaults, the beating of apprentices by brutal masters and the beating of masters by sturdy and unruly apprentices—all were charges that appear with some frequency in the records of Bridewell, of the City and Middlesex Sessions, and of guild courts. They posed no real threat to either the social or political order, and they rarely attracted the notice of Middleton's contemporaries, unless they were themselves the victims. Innocents from the country were warned to be wary of cheats and titillated with descriptions of a criminal underground by Dekker and others, but the record is instead of human failure and human viciousness: typical of many others, on 2 October 1574 the court at Bridewell heard the case of 'John Thomas, servant with Mr Austin, Skinner, sent in by Mr Starkie as a pilferer and one that will not at his master's commandment at no time serve God nor go to church, and for that he is otherwise riotous and disobedient'. He was ordered 'to have correction'.

This picture of an expanding metropolis of masters and servants, of citizens and their government, a bourgeois world of trade and manufacturing, has a significant piece missing: the non-citizen members of the learned professions of law, religion, and medicine and the resident armigerous gentry, such as Thomas Middleton himself. The physicians were the smallest component of the learned professions by far; university-trained, numbering just thirty in 1589, and organized in the Royal College of Physicians, they shared the actual practice of medicine with the much larger Barber Surgeons' Company, a city guild, and with the Apothecaries' Company, which broke away from the Grocers and received a royal charter in 1618. In theory these were complementary, not competitive practitioners, the medical doctors diagnosing illnesses and disease, the surgeons treating wounds and broken bones, and the apothecaries preparing medicines prescribed by physicians. Hence, in *A Fair Quarrel* the physician refers to the fact that doctors 'cast all waters', a Galenic diagnostic technique which was still standard practice, while the surgeon constantly refers to incisions, wounds, and sutures. In practice physicians had an élite practice and were rarely resorted to by ordinary people, who depended on folk medicine and practitioners—cunning men and women—supplemented by the advice of apothecaries and the skills of barber surgeons.

The clergy in London, also largely university-trained by this time (future clerics normally matriculated and proceeded to an MA, if not to one of the higher degrees in divinity), numbered perhaps two hundred or more. The parish clergy staffed the 122 parishes of the city and suburbs, to which number must be added the lecturing preachers who lacked a parish benefice, the schoolmasters of the more prestigious grammar schools, such as St Paul's and Merchant Taylors', and the Dean and Chapter of St Paul's Cathedral. The Bishop of London and the Archbishop of Canterbury were resident nearby in Fulham and Lambeth respectively, not actually in the City. Despite occasional purges of nonconformist Puritans, London never lacked for preaching at any time during Middleton's life. Sermons could be heard on any day of the week, and for those jaded by the local talent there was the weekly sermon at Paul's Cross, where Londoners could hear young talent straight from the universities, royal chaplains, present and future bishops, and other ecclesiastical luminaries. Competent preachers never lacked for an audience, and for the ambitious graduate London was a proving ground and an opportunity to attract and impress future patrons. Bishop John Earle in his *Microcosmography* described Paul's Walk in the Cathedral as a 'market of young lecturers, whom you may cheapen here at all rates and sizes'. John Poynter began his clerical career as curate and lecturer at St Mildred Bread Street in the City, but then went on to the living at Hanwell in Oxfordshire. After leaving Oxford with an MA Ezechial Culverwell, the son of a London Haberdasher of St Martin Vintry, spent the next three decades at various Essex livings until he was finally deprived in 1609 for nonconformity. He returned to London, preaching in the pulpits of various of his friends: St Anne Blackfriars, where his nephew, William Gouge, was preacher; Allhallows Bread Street, where Richard Stock was rector and preacher (Stock and Culverwell had edited Richard Rogers's *Seven Treatises*, a well-known guide to the godly life, for the press some years before, when Culverwell was Rector of Felsted, Essex, and Rogers was lecturer at nearby Wethersfield); and elsewhere. The clergy did not necessarily spend the whole of their professional lives in the City, but a small group did, forming close alliances with the godly merchants and craftsmen in their parishes and in the city companies, preaching their funeral sermons and remembered in their wills.

The lawyers were by far the largest, the fastest growing and the wealthiest of the professions, and although the centre of the profession was just to the west of the city in the Inns of Court, their influence in the city was pervasive. Between 1590 and 1639 more than 12,000 young men were admitted to one of the four Inns of Court—Lincoln's Inn, Gray's Inn, Inner and Middle Temple—where lawyers

From a diptych by John Gipkyn,
Preaching at St Paul's Cross, c.1616.

were trained in the common law, and during the same four decades more than 2,000 were called to the bar and were thus qualified to plead as barristers before the central courts—King's Bench, Common Pleas, and Exchequer—as well as the county Assizes. However, this gives a much too restrictive picture of their practices, for the same barristers also practised before the so-called English Bill courts—Chancery, Star Chamber, Requests, Wards and Duchy Chamber—and the ecclesiastical courts and admiralty alone remained the exclusive arena for the shrinking number of university-trained civil lawyers. In the city itself the Recorder of London was invariably a prominent lawyer, as was the City Serjeant; many of the company clerks of the more important guilds were lawyers as well, and since much of the business before the city courts involved issues of debt and contract, lawyers also practised before those courts. City companies retained learned counsel and consulted widely, when faced with difficult legal issues: for example, when the Grocers' Company was attempting to carry out the complex bequest of Lady Slany, the widow of a prominent Grocer and alderman, their Court of Assistants ordered that the company clerk, an attorney, and Mr Pheasant (doubtless Peter Pheasant, a prominent and pious barrister and eventual Serjeant-at-Law), the counsel retained by Lady Slany's executrixes, consult with Sir Thomas Coventry, the King's Solicitor General. The city companies tried to insist that their brethren settle disputes by arbitration before the company courts, before seeking remedies at common law, and regularly fined those who sued at law without permission, but London merchants and tradesmen were as litigious as the gentry in this very litigious age, and more than 70 per cent of the cases brought before King's Bench and Common Pleas were brought by litigants who were not landed gentry.

Heading the list of *Dramatis Personae* in the 1611 edition of Middleton and Dekker's *The Roaring Girl* is not Moll Cutpurse herself, or even the *cives & uxores*, but rather four knights. The gentry, like the nobility, had long been accustomed to come up to London to pursue business at Court and their law suits during term-time, but from the 1580s on increasing numbers of the landed élite apparently established residence in the City and suburbs for longer periods, much to the increasing alarm of the Crown. When Elizabeth I ordered those gentry home who were not pursuing legal business in a proclamation in 1596, the order came in the midst of a dearth that followed harvest failure, and the Crown was anxious that the landed classes return home and fulfil their traditional role of relieving their neighbourhoods. Elizabeth's Stuart successors continued to be concerned about the consequences of the 'decay of hospitality', but they also saw that the political as well as the social order was threatened 'by the absence of so many persons of quality and authority from their countries, whereby those parts are left destitute both of relief and government'. How many of the landed élite were actually resident in the metropolis it is impossible to tell, but two figures may be indicative of the situation in the last years of Middleton's life. In a newsletter the Reverend Joseph Mead wrote on 3 January 1623 he claimed that 'the two last proclamations have caused the remove from about this city, and Westminster, of 7,000 families, and with them 1,400 coaches . . . All tradesmen complain much, as do the poor, of their departure'. A decade later an official survey of those of the élite still in residence contrary to a recent royal proclamation discovered 37 of the nobility, 147 baronets and knights, and 130 squires and gentlemen. If more than 300 élite families were still in residence, despite the proclamation and the Christmas exodus—and it was customary for such families to keep open house at their principal country residence until after Twelfth Night—then a figure in the thousands resident at least briefly at other times does not seem unlikely.

If the need to pursue suits at law originally drew the landed élite to town, continued residence had other attractions. Since the obligations and expectations of hospitality were attached to the family seat and did not apply to life in London, the great crowd of servants and gentleman retainers associated with residence in a great house could be dispensed with for all but a handful of the court aristocracy. Many a gentleman found it easier to live on his rent-roll in London than on his estates, and with the improvement in the travelling coach in the early seventeenth century it became harder or at least less excusable to leave wife and children behind. But the attraction of London lay not only in such practical matters. For young gentlemen without professional ambitions the Inns of Court provided a respectable finishing school in which it was possible to meet and form social alliances with others of the same class, to visit the Court and take dancing and fencing lessons, to view the latest fashions, to visit the bookstalls at St Paul's and the public and private theatres, to gamble at cockfights and view the bear- and bull-baiting across the river, from which it was only a short distance to the houses of prostitution in the Winchester rents and at Holland's Leaguer, the notorious brothel located in the former manor house of Paris Garden. Above all London offered ready access to one's social equals: as the gallant Cockstone remarks in *Michaelmas Term* to the newly arrived Richard Easy, a gentleman from Essex, 'Here you may fit your foot, make choice of those whom your affection may rejoice in.'

For gentlemen the country offered the opportunity to exercise power over one's neighbours as a justice of the peace and to gossip with one's social equals at quarter sessions and the twice-yearly meetings of the Assize, and at least for the sturdy and athletic there were the pleasures of the chase; for wives and daughters only the opportunities of social intercourse on the occasion of long visits to distant kin broke the busy but isolated life of the country house. For the latter London spelled liberation. One gets a sense of the attractions of London in a chance observation by Margaret Cavendish, the Duchess of Newcastle, who recalled that in her youth (she was born about 1623) she and her sisters used 'in winter time to go sometimes to plays, or to ride in their coaches about the streets to see the concourse and recourse of people'. Similarly, after noting her pious upbringing (she was the daughter of the Provost of Eton), Anne, Lady Halkett observed that 'so scrupulous I was of giving any occasion to speak of me, as I know they did of others, that though I loved well to see plays and to walk in the Spring Garden sometimes . . . , yet I cannot remember 3 times that ever I went with any man besides my brothers, and if I did, my sisters or others better than myself was with me'. London fashions had become as important for women as for men. As Tawny Coat, the pedlar, remarks to Hobson, the London Haberdasher, in Heywood's play *If You Know Not Me, You Know Nobody, Part II*, 'Faith, Sir, our country girls are kin to your London courtiers, every month sick of a new fashion', and in 1621, when Thomas Knyvett, a Norfolk gentleman, was in London pursuing family legal business, he conscientiously wrote to his young wife at home, busy with her infant children, that her 'gown and things are a-making' and that 'all they wear at court is plain white aprons, among the great ladies', to which he added a postscript that waistcoats for women were now 'quite out of fashion'.

London's explosive growth during Middleton's lifetime made it a magnet attracting all sorts and degrees of people. For young men and women its guilds and households offered the opportunity for training and employment available in such numbers and variety nowhere else. For the ambitious cleric the city offered both readily available pulpits and the opportunity to demonstrate their preaching prowess before potential patrons. Proximity to the law schools and the central courts made London the inevitable focus for the legal profession which itself was growing at an unprecedented rate. The need to pursue legal business or to seek patronage at Court may have brought the gentry to town, but once there the opportunities of urban life and the amusements offered there kept increasing numbers in residence month after month. Proximity to the Court perhaps inevitably made London a centre of fashion and political news-gathering, but it was the growth of London that made possible the variety of commercialized entertainment, which anticipated the development of respectable amusements in the provinces by a century, and which, once in existence, could only be temporarily halted even by civil war and revolution.

Much of Middleton's London was old, however much it was transformed during his lifetime: the walled city with its medieval gates was still the centre of the metropolis, despite the erosion of its once independent liberties and the spread of its suburbs. Its economic life was still dominated by the livery companies, and its government structured by the mayor's Court of Aldermen and the wards, as it had been for centuries. But Thomas Middleton and his like represented something new in urban life; literate laymen writing for a largely literate lay mass audience was a way of life, whether seen as a trade or profession, little older than Middleton's engagement in it. The traditional religious culture survived but was transformed by Protestantism and the printing press, the masses and religious processions giving way to sermons preached and printed and the proliferating guides to a godly life. There was also a traditional culture of urban secular entertainment, of street entertainers—jugglers, acrobats, ballad singers—and of the alehouse, where dicing and card-playing accompanied drinking, which survived and flourished in Middleton's London and in fact long after. But alongside these traditional amusements were the new public theatres with their apparently insatiable appetite for new plays and the growing publishing industry prepared to satisfy an expanding literate laity both in London and throughout the rest of the country with an endless stream of new printed ballads, jest books, almanacs, plague pamphlets, crime stories, and plays. The new market opened the possibility of a new, if precarious, career alongside the traditional learned professions. Some straddled the traditional and the new, such as Ben Jonson, who wrote for the public stage but welcomed and gloried in his aristocratic and royal patronage, but others, such as Anthony Munday, Thomas Dekker, Thomas Heywood, and Thomas Middleton himself, found in the London theatre companies, publishing houses, and livery companies an urban market for their skills no longer dependent on the traditional power structure of Crown, Church, and nobility. For these writers—'poets', as they still called themselves—London was as much a new world to be explored and exploited as the New World beyond the ocean sea.

SEE ALSO

List of works cited: *Companion*, 457

MIDDLETON'S THEATRES

Scott McMillin

The London Theatre in 1601

SUPPOSE a young writer with a good ear and a knack for the stage—call him Thomas Middleton—had looked over the London theatre in 1601. What would he have seen?

He would have seen a theatre busy with controversy and competition, disreputable in the opinion of authority and magnetic to Londoners of all ranks. The two best-known acting companies were playing in splendid new theatres: the Chamberlain's Men at the Globe across the Thames from the city proper, a little beyond the reach of the authorities in one direction; and the Admiral's Men at the Fortune across the city to the north-west, beyond their reach in another. (The City fathers disliked crowds seeking entertainment, and the theatres were prudently built outside their jurisdiction.) These were the twin foundations of the London drama, the Chamberlain's Men and the Admiral's Men, the actors a generation of theatregoers had grown up with in the 1590s. The stage was known more by its acting companies and its star performers than by its playwrights. One went to see the great actor of the previous decade, Edward Alleyn, play a revival of *The Jew of Malta* at the Fortune (he had just returned to the stage after a hiatus of three years), or the Chamberlain's Men play *Henry V* at the Globe with Richard Burbage, Alleyn's rival, in the title role.

But the scene extended beyond the Globe and the Fortune. The Privy Council had tried for years to limit the number of adult companies to these two, but this pressure had not prevented a troupe under the patronage of the Earl of Derby from moving into a new inn-yard theatre at the Boar's Head in 1599 and becoming well enough known to be invited to Court for performances that winter. The great comic Will Kempe was soon to return after morris-dancing from London to Norwich on a wager and then acting on the continent. He had built his fame with the Chamberlain's Men, but now it was thought he would join a fourth company that was gaining a foothold in London, the Earl of Worcester's Men. With Worcester's Men vying for Kempe and negotiating to play at yet another playhouse, the Rose (not new but serviceable), the theatre was obviously outpacing the Privy Council's stated intentions. (Worcester was himself a Privy Counsellor.) To a young writer, the theatre must have looked like a growth industry.

These theatres—the Globe, the Fortune, the Rose, the Boar's Head—can become something more vivid than mere names if one thinks about where they stood and how they were reached. The map of London (see page 62) shows the locations. The Globe was on the Bankside, close to the Rose and another older theatre not yet mentioned, the Swan. They were reached on foot by walking down Gracechurch Street and across London Bridge, although some theatregoers treated themselves to the luxury of hiring a boatman to row them across the river—for a sixpenny fee that cost more than admission to the playhouse. The new Fortune stood north of the city, through Cripplegate to Golden Lane, to the west of the very first permanent playhouses that had been built in London just over a generation ago. (The Curtain was one of the earliest houses, and was still usable.) The Boar's Head was in Whitechapel, a few steps east of the city boundary, beyond the edge of the map. People living near St Paul's Cathedral could walk to the Fortune in minutes and the Boar's Head in half an hour. These were real places for theatre people, and Kempe, Alleyn, and Burbage were not only real, they were stars. To be able to choose among them would have been a theatregoer's delight. And then to walk to the theatre where Burbage (let us say) was acting, to see once again what a fine new theatre it was, to see that the rest of the company was largely the experienced professional troupe that one remembered from before (Kempe was gone, but Robert Armin had taken his place), then to see a play that was being talked about all over town—a theatregoer so blessed would think London the best place in the world for plays.

What theatre people may have talked about first in 1601, however, was the return of the children's companies. To the great advantage of Middleton's early career, two companies of boys were once again (after an absence of a decade) giving public performances in small exclusive playhouses recently refurbished in the centre of the city: one in the vicinity of St Paul's, the other a few streets toward the river, in the Blackfriars precinct. The adult troupes used boy actors to play the female roles in their plays, but the companies at St Paul's and Blackfriars were *entirely* made up of boys, who were choristers in training for the music at St Paul's or the Queen's Chapel, but had also been learning plays for performance at Court. Now their masters, on the pretence of holding open rehearsals, were charging high admissions for progressive and well-to-do patrons to see the plays, often even before the Queen could. These private theatres were roofed-over, heated in the winter, and intimate. Candlelight illuminated the stage. Some of the finest music in London could be heard during their act-intervals, an innovation that had not yet taken hold at the open-air theatres. Ordinary citizens could not usually afford this kind of entertainment, but the tone was being set for the London theatre of 1601 in these avant-garde houses, and people interested in theatre would have been talking about them. A shrewd observer would have sensed a change was in the making, although the form it would eventually take would have been hard to predict.

Five of the playhouses in use in 1601—the Fortune, the Globe, the Boar's Head, St Paul's, and the Blackfriars—were new or refurbished. Counting the children, up to six companies were putting on plays. The adult companies knew nothing of the long run or the classical revival. Everything they staged had been written within the last twenty years. The bill changed every day, and with the adult companies a play would usually not be repeated within the week. (The first long run would be of a Middleton play, *A Game at Chess*, which ran for nine consecutive performances in 1624.) Much of their repertory was new in the past two years, although the Admiral's Men were just now beginning a revival phase as they refurbished many of Alleyn's vehicles from the 1590s. Each adult company was putting on more than a dozen plays in daily rotation and introducing new plays with some regularity. The children's companies put on fewer plays, but they were known for doing the latest thing and wanted new scripts. An ambitious young writer could hardly ask for greater opportunities than Middleton found in London in 1601.

The sense of excitement the theatre always holds for young people must have seemed especially intense, for this industry was bold, imaginative, entertaining, risqué, profitable, and frowned upon by the authorities. The children's theatres were in respectable neighbourhoods, but the open-air theatres, especially the ones on the Bankside—the Globe, the Rose, and the Swan—stood in an area known for brothels, taverns, and bear-baiting pits. Writers in search of respectability would have thought twice about working in the theatre. Middleton was looking for an income, and although he seems to have wanted to change the world with even more determination than is usual among writers aged twenty-one, he would have seen the theatre as a market, the best literary market in town.

He would also have seen the other side of the theatre—it was filled with uncertainties and rife with opportunities for failure. The adult companies depended on box-office takings for their basic income, with extra money coming from command performances during the Christmas festivities at Court. They acted six days a week when conditions were in their favour—i.e., when the City authorities had no extraordinary reason, such as an outbreak of plague, to do what they wanted to do and close the theatres down. The children acted less frequently, probably three times a week. All these companies would have known how quickly disaster could strike. Many of the adult actors would remember the bad plague years of the early 1590s, when the London playhouses were closed for months at a time and long provincial tours were the means of survival. Such trouble may have seemed fairly distant in 1601, but it was still a worry; and from March 1603 the theatres would be shut down for more than a year, first by Queen Elizabeth's illness and death, then by a terrible new outbreak of plague.

The theatre building and refurbishing at the turn of the century was done in defiance of a Privy Council Order of 28 July 1597, which not only ordered all playhouses closed but insisted on their destruction. The order was not carried out, but it serves as a reminder of the political controversy surrounding the theatre industry. There was commercial uncertainty as well. Those splendid new theatres, the Globe and the Fortune, were not only signs of prosperity among the companies but also instruments of competition between them. When Shakespeare's company built the Globe across the river in the Bankside area, the Admiral's Men had been acting there for years, at the Rose. The most famous theatre ever built in England was not a polite undertaking. In danger of losing their lease, the Chamberlain's Men had torn down their old theatre (called the Theatre, north of the city) when their landlord was out of town for the Christmas holidays of 1598; they transported the heavy timbers across the river to the Bankside, and used them as the main structural units for the Globe, which they built less than two hundred yards from the Rose. Lovers of Shakespeare do not often dwell on this piece of commercial aggression and questionable legality. Perhaps the Admiral's Men were already planning to leave the Bankside, but in any case the Chamberlain's Men were solving the problem of losing their lease at the same time as they were putting pressure on the competition. Their new theatre was close enough to the Rose that crowd noise from one of these open-air theatres would have been heard in the other. Roslyn Knutson has shown that the Admiral's Men tried to meet the competition with an unusual outburst of new plays, but they must also have been looking to new locations. The Rose was now one of the older theatres, the Globe the newest: the Bankside theatre area had obviously changed. The Admiral's Men soon vacated the Rose. *Their* new theatre, the Fortune, was built across the city to the north-west. They were moving more or less in the direction from which their rivals had come.

The children's companies were another kind of rivalry. For ten years the adult companies had been free of competition from children's companies, but now a new generation of 'little eyases' (as they are called in *Hamlet*) or the 'nest of boys able to ravish a man' (as Middleton called them in *Father Hubburd's Tales*) were acting in two playhouses. These companies had an advantage: the boys were not paid for their acting. They were being trained for the Queen's musical and dramatic entertainments at the expense of the Church and the Crown. So these roofed-over and stylish theatres were operating on child labour under institutional subsidies, yet they could charge high admissions. The adult companies had to keep prices down because of their competition with each other, and because they had large theatres to fill. Drawing audiences was a daily contest. London was becoming the largest city in Europe, but its population was still under 200,000 at the turn of the century, even counting the suburbs and the City of Westminster. Up to six companies, each putting on three to six performances a week, were competing for a scarce resource, the full house. The best of them, it should be added, were making very good money despite all the competition.

For which of these companies would a young playwright have most wanted to write? We tend to think the answer should be the Chamberlain's Men, who in 1601 were creating some of our own world by staging *Hamlet*, followed over the next few years by the rest of Shakespeare's most famous tragedies. Hindsight always brings us around to ourselves, but to someone actually facing 1601 as a day-to-day business of opportunity and survival, Shakespeare and the Chamberlain's Men would have seemed very well established, prone to taking strange risks, and a little out of touch. Staging *Richard II* at the request of the Earl of Essex (as they did in February 1601) was a bizarre decision, whether or not they knew Essex would try to overthrow the government the next day. The *Henry V* in which Burbage was starring at the Globe was their *ninth* English history play by Shakespeare. The achievement was as stunning as it was old-fashioned. Fifteen years earlier, when Middleton was learning to *read*, history plays had been a new development, an innovation largely made by a company called the Queen's Men. Shakespeare and his company virtually took over that company's plots by rewriting plays on the reigns of Henry IV, Henry V, Richard III, and King John. This was how they worked, by beating others at their own game. That they were about to change the history of literature with Shakespeare's tragedies would not have been so apparent in 1601 as their commercial strength and the way they built it. *Hamlet* was a rewrite too, after all, although in this case the original property may have been their own.

That is not to say that Middleton steered around the Chamberlain's Men. A freelance takes his opportunities where he can, and at first Middleton found his opportunities elsewhere, with the Admiral's Men at the Fortune and the children's company at St Paul's. Within a few years, he would be writing for the Chamberlain's Men too, and collaborating with Shakespeare. He would also have learned a good deal about tragic characterization from *Hamlet*, with the long-term results to be most fully evident in *The Changeling*. But in 1601 the Admiral's Men and the revived children's companies presented great opportunities to a beginning writer, the adult company specializing in the older writer by whom Middleton was most deeply influenced—Marlowe, not Shakespeare—and the other specializing in the sort of satirical and avant-garde attitudes that a young writer would share and be quick to turn his own way.

Middleton obviously listened to Marlowe from an early age—one stanza of *The Wisdom of Solomon Paraphrased* (16.97–102) is a paraphrase of *Edward II* (5.1.11–15), for example—and his mature work deepened the relationship. His ironic tone in both comedy and tragedy draws upon *The Jew of Malta* and *The Massacre at Paris*; the sharp focus and relentlessness of his satire are secular versions of the religious intensity of *Doctor Faustus*. The refusal of Middleton's writing to admit the sentimental, its readiness for breaking and entering upon the established pieties, its tendency to be interrupted by outbursts of parody—these traits come from Marlowe more obviously than from Shakespeare. But what Middleton refused of Marlowe is important too, and the refusals would have been related to the Admiral's Men at the Fortune. Middleton did not follow Marlowe into the dominating central role, the Alleyn role—Tamburlaine, Faustus, Barabas—around which the rest of a play would be organized. The theatrical energy of a Middleton play circulates through many strong roles, as though it is the ensemble that matters most. And some of those strong roles are for female characters—another departure from Marlowe.

Middleton would have first heard Marlowe by hearing Alleyn, or hearing *about* Alleyn, whose performances in *The Jew of Malta*, *Doctor Faustus*, and *Tamburlaine* were extremely popular in the London of the 1590s. The teenaged Middleton must have seen these performances, heard about them, caught them from other conversations: teenagers know a hero when one appears, and Alleyn came into his prime when Middleton was the right age to be vastly impressed. By 1602–3, however, when he was *writing* for Alleyn and the Admiral's Men, his attitude might have been different. Alleyn had returned to acting when the company moved to the Fortune, and his famous roles from the 1590s were being revived one after another. The Admiral's Men were building an audience at their new theatre by resorting to past successes, and Marlowe's plays were prominent in the effort: *Doctor Faustus*, *The Jew of Malta*, and *The Massacre at Paris* were revived in 1601–2. Nostalgia was not among Middleton's stronger feelings. The career and the money lay in writing new plays, not in tinkering with revivals (as Middleton did in writing a new prologue and epilogue for Greene's *Friar Bacon*). The Alleyn revivals were cutting into the demand for new plays at the Fortune. Between 1600 and 1603, as Middleton was coming into their fold, the number of new plays produced by the Admiral's Men was well below their norm.

What a young writer would have prized at the Fortune was the opportunity to collaborate with experienced dramatists like Thomas Dekker, Henry Chettle, Anthony Munday, and Michael Drayton, men who could teach a novice the arts of commercial play-scripting as they worked together. These writers knew how to write for Alleyn, but they also knew how to write for the ensemble which Alleyn had built around him and which remained when Alleyn retired, again, in about 1603. One of Middleton's next ventures for the company became the earliest play by which he is known today, a collaboration with Dekker, *The Patient Man and the Honest Whore* of 1604. It is very much an ensemble piece, built on the interactions among important roles.

At the same time Middleton was writing for another troupe that specialized in ensemble performance, the children's company at St Paul's. Here he found the continuity to develop his own voice. He wrote at least five plays for the Paul's boys between 1603 and 1607 and one or two for the children's company at the Blackfriars—and all of the surviving plays he wrote for those two companies are comedies, resolutely new comedies, designed to make the romantic comedy of the previous decade look old. The new comedy, satiric in tone and urban in subject—'city comedy'—was not Middleton's alone (Jonson, Chapman, and Marston were also writing in this vein), and some of its early examples were staged at the public theatres. But Middleton's plays for the children's companies were the most sustained effort in the new mode, and no writer was more alert to the satirical and erotic characteristics of boy performers. Their charm and precocity allowed them to put on risqué satires about the London of their own day—unseemly or dangerous material if performed by adults. These boys were sharply trained, and talented. They could sing, they could play musical instruments, they could act. Their music was supposed to come first—it was for the appreciation of the Queen herself, occasionally. Their acting came a close second—it was for the profit of the Master who taught them their music. The Master knew he could charge high prices and still draw the wealthier, better educated theatregoers, the style-setters of the day, to see these charmers perform. While Middleton was not the only writer who supplied texts suited to these talents, he was the most consistent. And he was one of the two (Jonson was the other) best able to satirize the movers and shakers of a changing London even as some of them sat there and applauded the effort.

Public and Private Theatres

Middleton's early plays for the children's company at Paul's were the closest he ever came to being a 'house' writer. For the rest of his career he was freelancing, and his work was performed in most of the commercial theatres of his time (he is known to have written for the original Globe, the second Globe, the Rose, the Fortune, the Swan, the Phoenix, Blackfriars, and St Paul's, and we do not know the theatres for some of his plays). London also had a variety of non-commercial playing places for which Middleton wrote. One of these was the city itself—the streets of London, which were the setting for a processional kind of showmanship at which Middleton became a master. And his work was occasionally seen in the centres of power and influence at Court, in the law schools, or in the London residences of the élite: more than a half-dozen of his commercial plays were brought to Court for command performances; he wrote masques for the Inner Temple and for Denmark House, and he wrote a number of indoor entertainments and speeches for official functions of the City. No playwright of his time had his work performed on a greater variety of London stages.

A freelance dramatist has to know his theatres and the differences among them. In the dozen commercial playhouses operating in London during his time, Middleton would have encountered few contrasts greater than that between St Paul's and the Fortune, the two theatres where he began his career. These could well have been, respectively, the smallest and the largest commercial theatres in London. The Fortune stage is known to have run 43 feet across and 27 feet 6 inches deep, a very large platform of nearly 1,200 square feet. Richard Hosley has estimated the Fortune's audience capacity at about 3,000. No one can be sure how small St Paul's was, for the exact location of the playhouse is still disputed. Reavley Gair thinks the theatre was very small: a stage of about 170 square feet, and an audience of about 100 persons. An upward limit can be determined from the other private playhouse, the Blackfriars, said to have been larger than Paul's. Richard Hosley has estimated the stage at Blackfriars at 29 feet wide and 18 feet 6 inches deep, or 537 square feet. Between Gair's estimate of 170 square feet for Paul's and Hosley's of 537 square feet for Blackfriars, there is an enormous difference, of course, but even Blackfriars was not half the size of the Fortune, and Paul's was smaller than that.

All the commercial theatres Middleton wrote for would have ranged in size between the extremes of St Paul's and the Fortune. The open-air theatres were larger than the private houses, although the smallest of the public theatres, the Rose (in use only during Middleton's earliest years as a writer), had a stage about the same size as Hosley has estimated for the Blackfriars. (The Rose foundations were excavated in 1989 and offer abundant evidence that the public theatres could differ from one another.) Generally speaking, the public-theatre stages ran from 500 square feet upward to about 1,200 square feet and the private-theatre stages ran from 500 square feet downward to whatever size one can imagine for the yet-to-be-located St Paul's. Audience capacities were between 2,000 and 3,000 at the public theatres and under 1,000 at the private houses.

The Court stages were set up for the occasion in various halls and chambers. We cannot be certain where the Middleton command performances were staged; the range of possibilities is great. Tiny platforms were built at Hampton Court and Richmond during Queen Elizabeth's reign (twelve feet square and fourteen feet square respectively) and a forty-foot square masque stage was set up in the old Banqueting House at Whitehall in 1604–5. Those are perhaps the extremes of size, and they are even greater than the contrast between St Paul's and the Fortune. The new Banqueting House built in 1607 was the most prestigious building for entertainments (until it burned in 1619 and was replaced with the even more famous Banqueting House which still stands today). The masques of Jonson and Jones were the primary shows at the new Banqueting House, but plays were sometimes given there after 1610. When a document says that *The Changeling* was given 'at Whitehall' in 1624, the reference could be to the Banqueting House, the Great Chamber, the Hall, or the Cockpit, which were all used for plays. Hardly any information remains about the temporary stages erected in these spaces, although when the Cockpit was turned into a permanent theatre in 1629–30 (shortly after Middleton's death), it had a shallow apron stage 35 feet across backed by a concave façade reaching a maximum depth of about 16 feet. This size is in the private-theatre range.

A play staged at Court was attended by the rich and powerful, brilliantly attired, several hundred in number. Middleton would probably not have been invited. (His only recorded summons to Court was to be arrested for the scandalous *A Game at Chess* in 1624.) At the Fortune or the Globe, by contrast, the 2,000–3,000 spectators on a good day included some who paid a penny to stand in the yard ('groundlings'), others who paid an additional one or two pennies to obtain seats and some protection from bad weather in the roofed-over galleries, and a few of the wealthy or ostentatious who paid sixpence to sit in private boxes. Professional men like lawyers and courtiers, along with women from all ranks of London life, apprentices and journeymen taking time from work, and the occasional foreign traveller, would have been seen in the crowd. These public playhouses drew from all areas except royalty and perhaps the church, but they were basically cheap and accessible to the common playgoer. It was in a theatre like this—the Rose—that Middleton, coming of age, could have seen Alleyn play Marlowe.

The roofed-over private theatres liked to claim their audiences were 'select' and 'choice', and to a large extent this was true. Their admission prices are hard to pin down, but Michael Shapiro's examination of the evidence indicates that Blackfriars was the most expensive theatre in town, with an admission scale of six-, twelve-, or eighteen-pence—six times the prices of the public houses. Some gallants paid an extra sixpence to sit on stools along the edges of the stage. Paul's set itself between the extremes, sometimes charging sixpence throughout the house for an especially popular play, but normally charging two-, four-, or sixpence, twice the scale for the public theatres and distinctly less than Blackfriars. It may have held the smallest audience, but it was not the most select. The Paul's neighbourhood was expanding during the late sixteenth and early seventeenth centuries. Families headed by gentlemen, haberdashers, merchant tailors, weavers, barber-surgeons, booksellers, scriveners, and stationers were finding it a good place to live, and the middle aisle at St Paul's Cathedral was crowded with lawyers, booksellers, shopkeepers, and their clients and customers during the day (see *Your Five Gallants*, 4.4).

The most important characteristic Middleton found at Paul's was its ambience of familiarity with a small audience who knew they were in on a trend. One sign of that familiarity is the fluency with which the Paul's plays move from dialogue to soliloquy or aside, as though in such small space everything was tinged by a gesture to the audience. Another sign is the prologue to *Michaelmas Term*, a scathing attack on the legal profession—meant to be enjoyed by an audience well stocked with lawyers. The Children of Paul's specialized in satirizing the up-and-coming professionals of the day, many of whom lived within minutes of the theatre and who were reaching that stage of professional satisfaction where joining others of their own class in laughing at themselves was thought to be a pleasure.

That is where Middleton established himself—on what appeared to be the most progressive, modern side of the London theatre. In one sense, it was also the short-lived side. The satires performed by children's companies sometimes landed them in trouble with the Privy Council, one reason why their careers were brief. Another reason is that boy actors do not last long, and when their voices change there is no guarantee they will become good adult actors. (A notable exception was Nathan Field, who went from the children's company at Blackfriars to Lady Elizabeth's Men and then to the King's Men.) By 1607 voices must have been cracking at St Paul's and Blackfriars, and replacements were, one suspects, proving difficult to find. Five of Middleton's plays for the boy companies reached print in 1607–8, a sign of trouble in the producing organizations (who saw publication as a benefit only after a play ceased performance). But Middleton was not tied to Paul's. He still had links to the Fortune company, where the Admiral's Men had become the Prince's Men after the accession of King James; and by now some of his work was being staged at the Globe, where the Chamberlain's Men were now the King's Men. The new patronage did not mean the players and their writers were coming into a close relationship with royalty, but it was a connection royalty could tap on occasion: when Prince Charles requested *The World Tossed at Tennis*, it was the Prince's Men who received the commission.

Middleton's work with the King's Men was important to the next phase of his career. In 1608 and 1609, the King's Men were assisting the demise of the children's companies by calling in the Blackfriars lease, helping to bribe the manager at St Paul's to keep his boys from starting up again, and preparing to use the Blackfriars theatre as their second playhouse. No playwright was in a better position for this move than Middleton. When he later wrote *The Witch*, *The Widow*, and *Anything for a Quiet Life* for the King's Men at the Blackfriars, he was writing for the leading adult company in London, he was writing for the theatre where a children's company had staged *Your Five Gallants* and *A Trick to Catch the Old One*, and he was writing for the *kind* of theatre in which he had established himself as the most experienced and reliable playwright.

The move of the King's Men to the Blackfriars proved to be one of the decisive events not just in Middleton's time but in the course of English drama. The long-term future of the commercial drama lay in the private roofed-over playhouse. The reason is not hard to find, if we think about theatre-going in terms of real experience: the weather, for instance. Nothing can be more certain than that audiences and players at an outdoor house like the Globe often would rather have been indoors. The damp cold and gloom of a London winter can be suffered for an afternoon of playgoing, but suffered is the right word, and the English rain can bring misery in any season. That the early Elizabethan commercial drama survived these hazards of the air is perhaps the most amazing thing about it—some take it as a sign of British character. The adult troupes held to the open-air theatres not because they favoured bracing conditions, however, but because they were in business. Their finances were geared to audiences that numbered in the thousands, and indoor-theatre audiences numbered in the hundreds. The Globe and the Fortune had cheap admissions because of the company's need to draw sizeable audiences, they were large because those audiences had to have somewhere to stand or sit, and they were open to the skies because a theatre so large had to use the sun as its means of illumination. A shift in theatre economics was about to occur: establishing a daily repertory at Blackfriars prices would eventually prove to be more profitable than the public theatre system, and that is why we have roofs over our heads today when we can afford to go to the theatre. In 1608, however, this trend would not have been certain. Giving up the public-theatre venue would have been financially questionable, but adding a *second* playhouse, roofed and warm, would have been just the direction in which an expansive well-capitalized organization would want to travel.

The King's Men were the company to make the move. In a unique arrangement, the ownership of both the Globe and the Blackfriars was shared among the company's senior members. That gave the company a choice between their own public and private theatres, an advantage held by no other company of the time. Exactly how they divided their performances between the two playhouses is hard to say, although the proximity of Blackfriars to the Inns of Court and the royal courts at Whitehall, St James's, and Denmark House would have made it convenient for a large number of well-to-do patrons from the beginning of Michaelmas term in early October to the end of Easter term in early summer. From this, a leap of seasonal reasoning sometimes leads to the conclusion that the Globe was restricted to being a summer theatre after 1608, but the evidence for such a neat division is not solid, at least not during Middleton's lifetime. Drawing large crowds to the Globe would have been financially desirable in any season, and it is not likely the larger theatre stood empty for months at a time. Nevertheless, the company's prestige was now building around the Blackfriars operation, and other adult companies were looking toward private-theatre opportunities too. Between 1610 and the closing of the theatres by the outbreak of civil war in 1642, five private theatres were used by the adult companies. That is not to say that open-air theatres were being abandoned; indeed, new ones were being built. The Red Bull in Clerkenwell was a notable addition around 1605, and the Hope on the Bankside was opened in 1614. When the Globe burned to the ground in 1613, it was rebuilt, as was the Fortune after *it* burned down in 1621. But the trend was in the other direction. No *new* public theatre was opened after the Hope in 1614, but the new private theatres were the Phoenix in 1616, Salisbury Court in 1629, and the remodelled Cockpit-at-Court (not a commercial theatre) also in 1629. The private theatres were being established on the western side of an expanding London, in the direction of the Covent Garden and West End centres of today's commercial theatre. Influential men were building new residences, settling their families, and conducting their business in these areas. The theatre was moving up-market, and it was in the private playhouses that the move was being made. When a diarist named Thomas Crosfield jotted down the important London theatres in 1634, he named three private theatres (Blackfriars, the Phoenix, and Salisbury Court) and two public ones (the Red Bull and the Fortune). He did not mention the public theatre we think of as the most famous, the Globe, although it was still in use by the King's Men.

Staging Middleton: Preliminary Notes

The distinction between public and private theatres on which this discussion rests has always been the basis for Elizabethan–Jacobean theatre history. Like most paired terms standing in opposition, these can be misleading if one uses them heedlessly or thinks they tell the entire truth. It is not true, for example, that all the public theatres were like one another and different from all the private theatres. The private playhouse at St Paul's was small compared to the one at Blackfriars, the stage at the public Fortune had a different shape from the stage at the public Swan, the stage at the public Rose was not much larger than the stage at the private Blackfriars—we have noticed these variations and should assume there were others. It is also not true that the plays written for the private houses were all sophisticated, witty, and out-of-touch with the common people, while those for the open-air theatres were broad, democratic, and spotted with outbursts of vulgarity. Such generalizations do contain shades of accuracy, but they lose validity in the simplicity of binary thinking. By the time Crosfield made his note about the theatres referred to above, the Red Bull and the Fortune were known for rowdiness and sensationalism, the three private houses he named were known for sophistication and Court connections, and the Globe he did not name was somewhere between these extremes. Even then, however, and certainly earlier, during Middleton's career, both kinds of theatre belonged to the same commercial system, and plays were written to be suitable to that system and hence to both kinds of theatre. They were also adaptable to the various fit-up theatres at Court and in the law schools; sometimes they were taken on tour in the provinces. The acting companies

1. Arend van Buchell's copy of Johannes de Witt's sketch of the Swan playhouse, 1596.

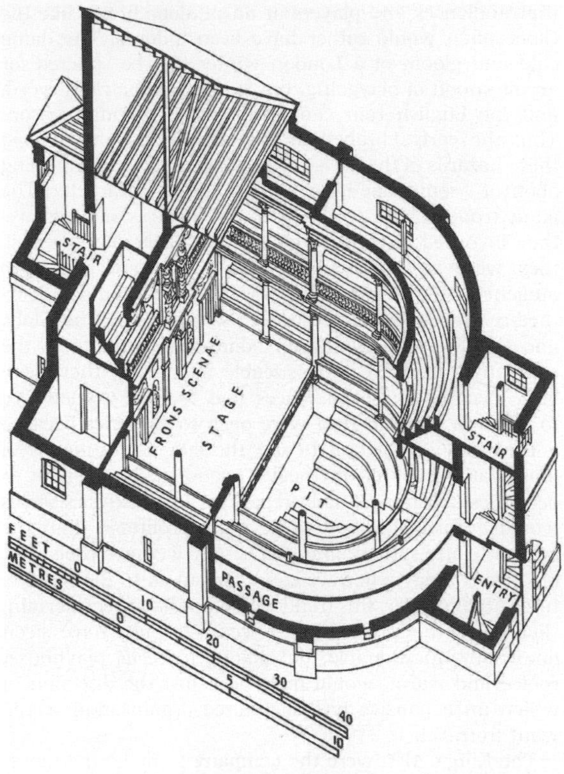

2. Scale reconstruction by Richard Leacroft of Inigo Jones's design for a private playhouse, possibly the Cockpit (also called the Phoenix) in Drury Lane.

had to be prepared for different venues, and their plays had to be flexible.

To gain a sense of how Middleton's plays were staged, the basic elements of Elizabethan-Jacobean theatre structure can be seen in the two most useful illustrations which have come down to us from the early playhouses, one from a public theatre and one from a private. The public-theatre illustration (Illus. 1) is a copy of a drawing of the open-air Swan theatre (where Middleton's *A Chaste Maid in Cheapside* was staged in 1613). The drawing was made by a visitor named Johannes De Witt in about 1596, when the Swan was the newest theatre in London, a tourist attraction. De Witt was so struck by the new playhouse that he sketched what he saw, put in some labels of features which reminded him of the classical theatre ('*mimorum aedes*' for the tiring-house, '*proscaenium*' for the stage, etc.), and wrote a description which mentions that the theatre could hold 3,000 spectators.

The other illustration comes from a set of plans drawn up by Inigo Jones for an unnamed indoor theatre of the seventeenth century (Illus. 3 and 4). John Orrell has made a case for identifying it as the Phoenix in Drury Lane, opened in 1617 (where *The Changeling* was staged in 1622), but the matter is not settled. It is best not to be specific about the playhouse and to take the drawings as Jones's design for some private theatre, whether it was realized or not (Illus. 2).

We recall that the private theatres were normally smaller than the public Swan, were roofed-over and more comfortable, lit by candle-power, attended to a noticeable extent by more fashionable audiences. One sees something else in the two illustrations: a basic similarity in the relationship between stage and audience. Both stages are set *into* the audience, so that actors would be seen from many angles. Both theatres bring their spectators around on three, or (counting the galleries to the rear) four sides of the actors. The Swan drawing gives a drastic version of this relationship: its stage is so assertive that it seems to interrupt the galleries that continue behind the tiring-house. (Some have thought the drawing was at fault for this effect, but there is no reason to doubt what De Witt was getting at, although his perspective is strained. If playing were brought to a permanent halt by order of the authorities, the theatrical unit shown in the

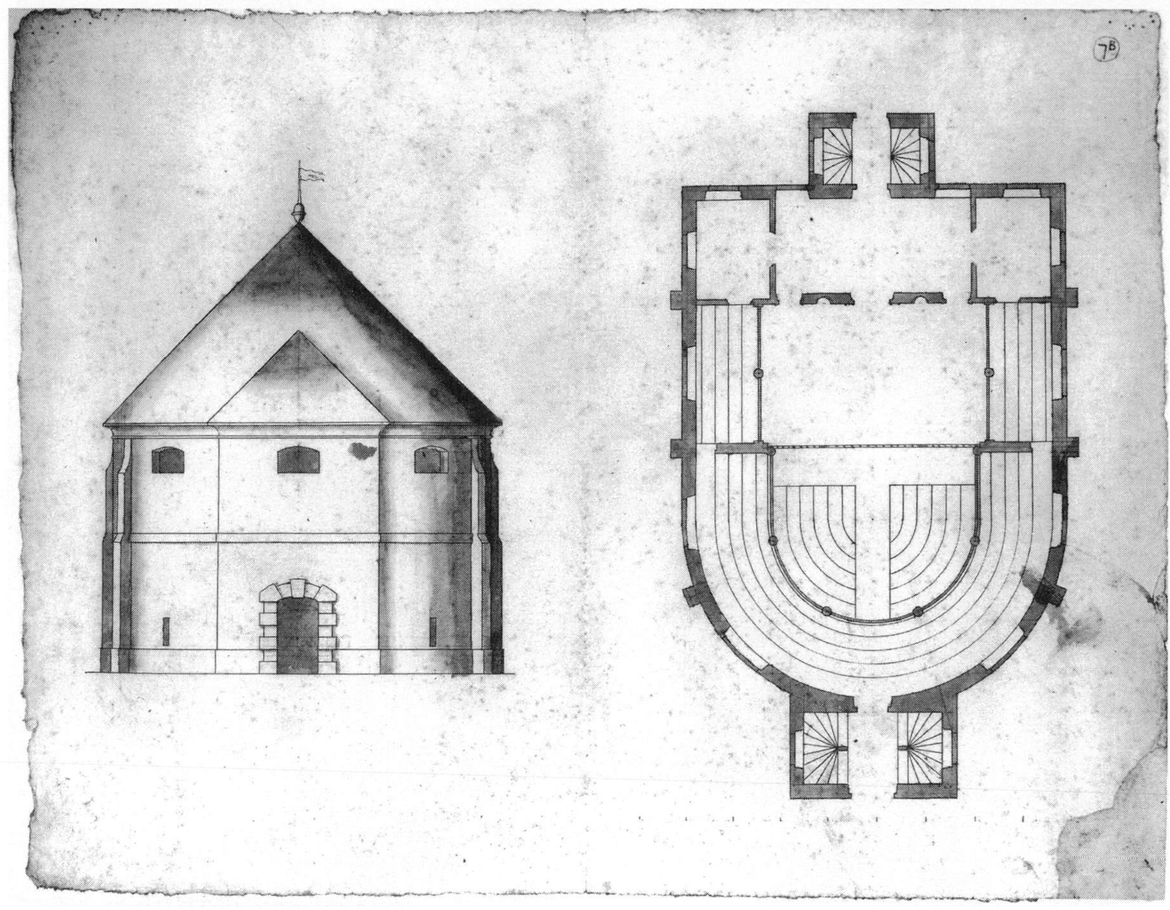

3. Elevation and plan from Inigo Jones's design for a private playhouse, *c.*1616.

drawing could be demounted, leaving a ring of galleries for bear-baitings and other spectator sports long associated with the Bankside.) Not all public theatres had such a severe downstage thrust. The recent excavation of the foundations of the Rose indicates a relatively shallow and wide stage, tapered at the front and closely integrated with the tiring-house façade to the rear. Yet both the Swan and the Rose had the basic characteristic of a stage that reached into a surrounding audience area. Both theatres were designed to place the actor in the centre of many points of view.

The Jones drawings of the private theatre show a similar stage-to-audience relationship: the spectator galleries extend along each side of the stage, so that the audience tends to surround the actor. Now, however, the auditorium and stage are a single architectural unit—this is a theatre built to stay that way. The Swan had two stage pillars supporting a roof-cover for part of the platform, but there is no need for that in the private theatre, which had its own roof. (The covering at the open-air theatres was called 'the heavens', the space under the stage was 'the hell', and these religious terms probably faded out from the private houses.) The pit where the groundlings would have stood for a penny at the Swan has been designed for seats in the private house, and these were among the more expensive seats. Keep in mind the different sizes of these arrangements. Where the Swan could accommodate up to 3,000 and used a stage which might have approached the nearly 1,200 square feet at the Fortune, the Inigo Jones drawing has been calculated to show a stage of 350 square feet and seating for between 500 and 700. The smaller theatre would have had a much more intimate feel to it. But the basic relationship of stage to audience obtains in all the commercial theatres for which we have any evidence.

In both the Swan and the private theatre a raised gallery is shown to the rear of the stage. This is the most obvious position for characters who are said to appear 'above' in the play texts, but it may have served other purposes too. The eight figures seated in the Swan drawing's gallery do

4. Sections from Inigo Jones's design for a private playhouse, *c.*1616.

not appear to be involved in the scene being acted on the platform. Who they are and what they are doing in the gallery are questions that have never been conclusively answered: they might be spectators, or musicians, or actors watching a rehearsal. De Witt's intentions have not reached us on this and on other matters. The clearest point about the Swan gallery is that it would have been useful whoever sat there. It is good space in a playhouse. Wealthy playgoers might pay more to sit behind the stage, wanting to be part of the show that the rest of the audience came to see. Musicians could accompany the action well enough from the gallery position, and if one section were set apart as a 'music room', there would be other sections for wealthy spectators too. Most important for our purposes is that an actor standing in one of the gallery compartments could claim to be at a window or on the walls of a city without generating disbelief, even if the other compartments were providing expensive seats for aristocrats or serving as a musicians' room. The same can be said of the gallery in the Jones drawing, although here the architecture seems to point up the centre of the gallery for acting, perhaps leaving the other sections for audiences or musicians.

The positioning of the highest-priced seats is always significant in a theatre. We know that special seats or boxes were reserved for wealthy patrons at both the public and private theatres. Exactly where those boxes were is a harder question. De Witt's drawing makes us think they were in the gallery, but this is by no means certain. Perhaps they were in the part of the galleries marked 'orchestra' on the Swan drawing, which should be imagined as being level with the stage and close to it. Herbert Berry has argued that the Blackfriars boxes were behind the stage but at stage level; Andrew Gurr and Richard Hosley think the evidence favours side boxes. No one can be quite certain, and the matter is complicated by the private-theatre custom of setting stools for high-paying spectators along the sides of the stage itself. The important point is that the highest-priced seats are *not* centrally positioned with sight lines to a visual stage picture. The centrally-positioned seat became important in the Court theatres: it was the King's seat, and it played its part in the long-term story of the theatre, as we will note. The King was seated according to sight-lines: his own sight-line, first of all, so that the effect of perspective scenes would be best observed by the eyes that mattered most; and the sight-lines of all the others, who were seated behind the chair of state, or along the sides of the room, able to see much of the stage and something of the King. (The Court convention held that no one should sit with his back to the King, so the area between the chair of state and the stage was kept clear of spectators. This was also the dancing area for masques.) But the exclusive seats in the commercial theatres of Middleton's time were in expensive boxes close to the actors, and they helped to create the 'surround' relationship between performer and spectator.

The Inigo Jones drawing adds one crucial feature that the Swan drawing lacks—a large central entrance to the platform, providing a third entrance and capable of being curtained for 'discovery' scenes that occur in the repertories of all the playhouses. Why the Swan drawing shows no central door has long puzzled stage historians, who know that Middleton's *A Chaste Maid in Cheapside*, the only extant play that can be confidently connected with the Swan, calls for a discovery scene at the very beginning, and that *The World Tossed at Tennis*, the only other play that can be connected with the Swan, calls for three doors. The Swan drawing is not helpful on this issue. Plays written for other playhouses, public and private, call for a central opening of the sort the Jones drawing shows, ample enough not only for discovery scenes but also for moving large standing properties like a bed or a throne onto the main stage. How discoveries were managed on the Swan arrangement has been the subject of much speculation, but it is clear that a third entrance was normal in the theatres. Middleton liked to bring characters on from different directions simultaneously (one of his favourite forms of stage direction is 'Enter X, meeting Y'), and his more crowded scenes are busy with comings and goings. His plays could all be played on the Swan stage if necessary, but they imply at least a third entrance and make modern directors glad to have more than that.

So the private and public theatres were alike in affording a central platform for most of the action and upstage spaces for rare effects of discovery and raised locations. Readers may wish to supplement these areas with their imaginations, on the understanding that actors feel free to use available space as they see fit. Perhaps surprise entrances were sometimes made through the audience, for example, or perhaps a canopied pavilion was built in front of one entrance door to stand for a repeatedly-used location. Theatre thrives on imagination in the first place, and actors do not feel bound to restrict themselves to the skimpy evidence that stage historians have to work with in reconstructing the past. Middleton specialized in the 'shop' scene, where some sort of representation of a tradesman's stall stood on the platform stage, and he could call upon a property tree or two for pastoral moments, or a throne to indicate the Court. But the printed and manuscript plays of the period do not reflect much in the way of variation beyond the basic use of the main platform and occasional raised or discovered scenes—and the raised or discovered characters nearly always address other characters on the platform stage, maintaining a flow of relationship from the upstage spaces out to the platform and thus into the space of the audience.

That was always the flow. Those entrance doors to the rear are an odd thing about the Elizabethan stage to modern ways of thinking. We like our actors to enter from different angles, at least from the sides as well as from upstage, and sometimes from the front or from the audience, but both the Swan drawing and the Jones plans show entrance doors only upstage. That means the actors entering the stage had only one direction to move, but that is the crucial direction for Elizabethan staging—toward the audience, down toward most of them, past those sitting along the sides, and away from anyone in the gallery. Such an actor is seen from many angles at once—thus, from many angles, he is at once expected to do something interesting. Alexander Leggatt has pointed out that one move the actor does not make in this kind of theatre is the little downstage curve required of entrances from the wings in a proscenium-arch theatre—the curve that allows a step in the direction of the audience as the actor moves into the garden, the parlour, or whatever the stage represents under the illusion it is not a stage. If you can picture actors entering from the upstage doors at the Swan or the Phoenix, then picture them moving downstage into a sort of criss-cross of views from the audience who see them from all angles, then you will be visualizing the basic system of Elizabethan–Jacobean staging in the public and private theatres.

If you also visualize the actors dressed in expensive costumes, you will catch one of the key features of Middleton's stage. The actor moving into the centre of a surrounding audience's gaze makes his costume crucial to the projection of his role. Middleton often writes significance into costumes themselves. The entry of the Duke and Bianca 'in great state' in *Women, Beware Women* 4.3 should reveal brilliance *and* decadence in their attire, with Bianca now displaying more than enough of the jewellery which was said to be 'locked up in [her] hidden virtues' when she entered in plain dress at the beginning of the play. When Frippery dresses up in the fine garb from his own pawn shop in the opening scene of *Your Five Gallants*, the stage business establishes his character as fully as anything in the dialogue. To visualize Middleton's plays, visualize costumed actors standing out as full-dimensioned figures. They *are* the scenic design, in their patterns of motion and colour.

We call the Elizabethan–Jacobean arrangement a 'thrust' stage today, to set it off from the normal proscenium-arch design, but for the Elizabethans a platform extending out into an audience was the norm, and names were needed for anything else: an actor on a raised gallery was 'above' and a set-scene revealed behind curtains was 'discovered'. These two kinds of upstage variation, action 'above' and action 'discovered', were used infrequently, but in the hands of a shrewdly visual dramatist (and because of their infrequency) they made an impact.

How Middleton used the basic arrangement of staging spaces is a subject waiting to be studied. The few suggestions that follow are only a sketch of the possibilities, intended to give some sense of the variations that could be played on the basic configuration of stage space described above. The place to begin is with the simplest Elizabethan staging, which is also the hardest for modern readers to grasp: a stage space that refuses to be anything but itself. We are trained by film and realistic theatre to read theatrical space in the image of some other kind of space, and we are not so familiar with theatrical space which signifies itself and is yet strictly subject to the names assigned it in the dialogue. In the realistic theatre, something said to take place in the forest will be accompanied by elaborate devices intended to make the stage look like a forest, while a film can be shot in the forest itself. The Jacobean stage did not disguise its basic contradiction but used it—the contradiction between a stage-obviously-itself and the language which called this space something else. The contradiction was amplified by such conventions as having boys play the women's roles and having adult actors double several roles within a play. Middleton's plays thrive on such doubleness of acting and staging: his stage does not 'stand' for something else so much as it allows different figures to be set forth in its own repeated space, rather as the boy actor playing a woman or the doubling actor playing several parts set forth different figures in their bodies. The identity of the woman who kills herself rather than yield to a tyrant's lust in *The Lady's Tragedy* is no settled matter when she is performed by a teenaged boy named Richard Robinson. *The Witch* is practically an experiment in double determinancies. It begins with a banquet laid out, signalling a location of the ruling class, but the dialogue is coy about which ruler it is (the King is referred to early in the scene, but a Duke comes along instead, and the Lord Governor finally turns out to be the host). When the stage clears at the end of the first scene, witches come into the same space 'with properties and habits fitting'. Their implements take the place of the banquet. This space that gained reluctant identification with authority only to be filled with witches known for a different kind of banquet is not about to stabilize itself for our comfort. Witches were probably played by adult actors, an exception to the practice of the boy actor, and in a large-cast play like this one, adult actors would have to double other roles. The players of the witches would turn up elsewhere as humans. We are meant to be kept guessing.

Consider now the two kinds of special upstage space: the entrance doors and the raised gallery. These are utilitarian spaces, of course, but actors and dramatists turn useful things to special effect. Middleton likes to place female characters 'above', for example. In a comedy like *The Widow*, the raised space is used repeatedly for Phillipa and Violetta to gain a vantage point over the affairs of the men and thus take some control of their situation. They are the only characters who appear 'above'—this becomes known as their space through repetition. Margot Heinemann has remarked that the new element in Middleton's women characters is their ability to reflect on their situations in general terms, an ability which takes on another social dimension when it is seen that the performers of the women are boys; and the use of the raised acting space as a vantage-point in their own houses is one way the women/boys become 'reflective' over the domestic space where they are ordinarily confined.

But in tragedy, the raised space gives a different meaning for women characters/boy performers. In *Women, Beware Women*, Bianca is first seen by the Duke when she is 'above', on the gallery. Twice in the later action she will appear on the same gallery, which is used to set forth different places, places in the control of others. It is on the gallery that she is surprised by the Duke in the rape scene, and it is on the gallery that she dies with him in the sensational, richly-costumed finale. The same 'above' that may give women a measure of control in the comedies can demonstrate their conspicuous vulnerability in the tragedies.

The central entrance door, which the Jones plans show as larger and more ornate than the other doors at the Phoenix, could have been curtained for the occasion and used for discovery scenes. Keeping in mind the downstage flow of Elizabethan staging, however, we can see another possibility. Standing properties like the throne could have been moved out from the sizeable central entrance onto the platform stage itself, where they would have been more visible and useful. A combination of the discovery and the moved-out standing property would have been a curtained pavilion or canopy jutting out onto the platform from the central entranceway. The important thing for readers to remember is that a standing property or curtained canopy might have been left in place during the entire performance, giving a symbolic visual focus to the stage. A throne standing in a central upstage position, waiting to be used in the appropriate scenes, would also provide a significant emblem of power and ambition throughout the play. Middleton's favourite standing property was the London shop, a structure for displaying a tradesman's wares which could be approached along the platform in a 'shop-and-street' arrangement. Something more than the central entrance/discovery space seems to have been used for the shop, for the business of setting out the goods or of shutting up the shop often attends the dialogue, as though the actors have a structure to work with. Middleton seems to have expected a standard 'stall' to have been available. Three stalls, a row of shops, are used in various scenes in *The Roaring Girl*, and it is likely that these were left in place during the entire play.

Michaelmas Term shows what could be done with the shop. Middleton establishes this shop-and-street combination in I.I: the action begins in a public concourse, pauses while an interlude takes place in Quomodo's shop, then continues in the public place. Quomodo's shop-business is to cozen a country gentleman named Easy, who comes along the street and gets taken in. Eventually Easy will obtain the shop and Quomodo will be left on the outside, but at first it seems that Easy hasn't a chance. He is fooled by all the disguises practised on him by Quomodo's henchmen, Shortyard and Falselight. His only hope comes from a raised area in Quomodo's place, a 'gallery' from which Quomodo's wife customarily observes the close dealings going on below. The raised space allows her to see the nature of her husband and to sympathize with poor Easy. The turning point comes when Quomodo goes a step too far and feigns his own death. From that point on, Quomodo (disguised as a Beadle, while his effigy is borne away as his corpse) must be outside the shop, where he discovers that his wife has married Easy upon hearing of her husband's death. Now the interior space is hers and Easy's. Quomodo must operate in the public concourse, where he is inadequate.

The final scene unites the shop structure and the concourse into one space, the judge's house. Perhaps this was accomplished by removing the shop structure. Perhaps the shop structure was turned into part of the judge's house. Readers can use their imaginations, but the basic visual idea is that the stage which was earlier divided into the street and the shop now is being unified, although perhaps not completely. A glance back to the Prologue will show what Middleton is getting at. In the Prologue, the entire stage was used for the cynical address of a character called Michaelmas Term, who shows how corrupt London's lawyers and law-schools are. At the end, the entire stage frames something better, a form of Justice that puts cynicism almost out of court.

An ironic twist is given to the 'shop-and-street' set-up in *The Patient Man and the Honest Whore*, where Candido's shop is replaced in the next scene with Bellafront's dressing room. Soon a third room is established—Hippolito's melancholy study. Each of these locations is introduced with the business of setting up the furniture and wares, and the point—that the tradesman, the whore, and the melancholic are engaging in similar trade—was probably reinforced by using one structure for all three locations. This would also be the curtained discovery space for the display of madmen at Bedlam hospital in the concluding scene, for the insane are put on display in much the same fashion as the wares of the various trades.

The idea running through all these examples of Middleton's staging is that theatrical spaces, costumes, properties, boys playing women, and adults playing more than one role must be read with a canny eye—the eye prepared for the pleasure and uncertainty of doubleness, reversal, and surprise, not the eye which looks for the security of settled identities. All theatre depends on a discrepancy between the sign that is made and the agent making the sign—between actor and character, between platform stage and fictional space—but Middleton's theatre carries the discrepancy further than we do, and plays with it harder. His theatre glories in the doubled and performed identity, turns it into the mode of production, and makes it one of the things the play is *about*.

The City As Theatre

The London of Middleton's time also had its non-commercial theatres, and these were sharply divided between the élite and the popular. Fabulously expensive masques were staged at Court, and word of these affairs, especially word of their cost, circulated through a public which never got to see one. What the public got to see were the great processional triumphs that marked events of political importance in London. The most elaborate of these was *The Whole Royal and Magnificent Entertainment* staged by the City in 1604 to celebrate the accession of James I. The more frequent kind of civic procession was the annual triumph for the newly-elected Lord Mayor, whose ceremonial journeys through the city were accompanied by pageant wagons and chariots displaying allegorical conflicts between the forces of good and evil. Gordon Kipling and Glynne Wickham have shown that these City processions were the secular descendants of the great medieval craft cycles and other early processions, where the dominant ideology of a city was dramatized in an outpouring of industry and cooperation.

Students of Shakespeare rarely hear of the city pageants or read a court masque, for the simple reason that Shakespeare did not write for these occasions. Most playwrights of the time did write for them, however: there were careers to be made in these non-commercial venues, money to be earned, and alliances to be built up during a time when tensions between City and Court were beginning to reflect antagonisms that would eventually contribute to the outbreak of civil war.

Middleton was a City writer. Beginning in 1613, he produced seven of the day-long Lord Mayor's pageants, along with entertainments for such civic events as the opening of a new waterworks or shooting-day at Bunhill and speeches for festive banquets honouring City officials. After 1620 he was City Chronologer, responsible for recording important events in the life of London and for devising the kinds of shows included in the ten *Honourable Entertainments* of 1620–1. At Court he was probably best recognized for the half-dozen of his commercial-theatre plays which were brought in for command performances at Christmastime. When he did write for Court interests, it was usually on commission from the City. He helped the City welcome King James in 1604 and celebrate its new Prince of Wales in 1616; he wrote the masque which the City was asked to produce for the Somerset–Howard marriage in 1614. These commissions brought Middleton into contact with some of the truly private theatres of Jacobean London, the by-invitation-only theatres that were set up for the occasion in the centres of influence themselves, such as the Great Hall of the Inner Temple (*Masque of Heroes*) or Merchant Taylors' Hall (*Masque of Cupids*). Yet these were not court masques of the kind Ben Jonson and Inigo Jones were devising for the Banqueting House at Whitehall. Jonson and Jones were preparing their masques at the political centre of the nation, and the most powerful people in the land attended them, even performed in them at times. Middleton's masques were designed for the fringes of court influence. *The World Tossed at Tennis* was intended for royal eyes, but the prologue announces without dismay that this performance did not take place, and its stage life seems to have occurred in commercial theatres instead. *Civitatis Amor*, the show for the installation of the Prince of Wales, was written on behalf of the City and called upon the same pageant-ship used for the Lord Mayor's show a few days before.

Court masques do occur *within* Middleton's plays, as part of the plot. They are marked by a fierce irony. The double masque at the end of *The Revenger's Tragedy*—a *repetition* of a masque, the second group of dancers not realizing their murderous entertainment has just been danced by another group—is a grotesque piece of humour at the expense of court conventions. *Women, Beware Women* is structured by the outdoor procession near the beginning and the indoor masque at the end: the action moves from the comparative innocence of the procession (where Bianca, on the gallery, is spotted by the Duke's roving eye) to the corruption and violence of the court masque at the climax: Bianca is again 'above', but now she is joined with the Duke as a spectator, both of them to die in the general slaughter that concludes this play. The wedding entertainment in *No Wit/Help like a Woman's*, as David Bergeron has noted, burlesques the staging which had been used for Middleton's speech for the King in the royal entry of 1604. When *No Wit/Help* was later performed at Court the King would have had a chance to see the parody, although that does not mean he caught the joke.

Middleton's pageantry for the City was extensive and profitable. His seven Lord Mayor's shows formed a substantial part of his career, and his first, *The Triumphs of Truth* in 1613, was the most expensive ever staged in the City. Its total cost came to £1,300, about the same amount as it cost the King's Men to rebuild the Globe Theatre after it burned to the ground in the same year. To understand what kind of play these civic 'ridings' amounted to, one must think about drama that comes to its audience. The 'theatre' is the city itself, its streets lined with spectators, and the episodes of the 'play' are carried on pageant wagons or chariots that move past this audience, heralded by trumpeters and attendants dressed as giants or devils bent on clearing the way. Churchbells ring throughout the city, and sometimes wine flows in the conduits. Processional drama is fundamentally different from commercial drama because no admission is charged (a large difference) and because it moves through the city in a demonstration of the theory that the public is involved in the play.

Picture the scene at the Little Conduit in Cheapside, one of the stations where Londoners lined the streets and looked out of house windows on 29 October 1613 to see the show come along—as though the very buildings were bowing to the Lord Mayor, as *The Owl's Almanac* puts it. In Middleton's extravaganza, the Mayor was accompanied by five 'islands' pulled by porters and decked with 'all manner of Indian fruit trees, drugs, spiceries'. There was a baptized king of the Moors and his queen, their conversion having been wrought 'by the religious conversation of English merchants, factors, travellers'. (This year's Mayor was a Grocer, and the Grocers were trading overseas—hence the Indian islands and the baptized Moorish king.) Truth, made to look naked and slender, was riding in a chariot joined by Zeal and an Angel on horseback, this virtuous team going before the Mayor; behind him, trying to get at him, ruin him if possible, came Error in a chariot, with Envy 'eating of a human heart, mounted on a rhinoceros, attired in red silk, suitable to the bloodiness of her manners, her left pap bare, where a snake fastens, her arms half naked, holding in her right hand a dart tincted in blood'.

Now, at the Little Conduit, the procession approaches a grand pageant wagon containing London's Triumphal Mount. The Mount is large enough to hold London (represented as a grey-haired mother), Religion, Liberality, Perfect Love, Modesty, Knowledge, Chastity, Fame, Simplicity, and Meekness, along with the charitable and religious works of the twelve Great Companies of London, 'especially the worthy Company of Grocers'. But no one can see these personages and items yet. They are covered by a mist which emanates from four monsters of Error—Ignorance, Impudence, Falsehood, and Barbarism—crouched at the corners of the pageant. The fog of Error covers London and all its accomplishments.

The Lord Mayor's procession is still held, but most Londoners do not turn out for it. Readers of Middleton do not have much experience with this kind of show today. In Mardi Gras processions, Thanksgiving Day parades, and various Midsummer and May Day celebrations, elaborate pageants move through our cities, but usually no conflict is acted out by which the forces of evil try to get at a political leader. At the Little Conduit in Middleton's 1613 show, Truth rides up to the mist-shrouded pageant, says something right-minded and confident to those four monsters and Error, then waves a fan of stars she holds in her right hand, and (thanks to the workmanship of the designer John Grinkin) the cloud of mist rises to become a 'bright-spreading canopy, stuck thick with stars, and beams of gold shooting forth', revealing London and all her cohorts. Do not think Error is finished yet. The cloud descends in time for the entire procession to move on to the cross in Cheapside, where the fog-clearing magic of Truth works its wonders for another crowd of spectators, then to the Standard, then to St Laurence-Lane end, and so on to the Guildhall. Still, that is not all. The entire parade accompanies the Lord Mayor back to Paul's later in the day, then escorts him to his home in the evening. There, outside the Mayor's door, the climax to the entire day occurs when Zeal reduces Error to embers with a great blast of flame from his head—a fireworks display which one hopes the children were allowed to stay up for.

A Glance Ahead

The technical sophistication of the Lord Mayor's shows was obviously important to Middleton's career, and it is worth asking—of a playwright who had Zeal reduce Error to ashes with a burst of fireworks in 1613—where he stood in relation to the long-term development of scenic extravagance which has marked the history of western drama down to our own time. Eye-widening technology and costs that run beyond the imagining of the average citizen are staples of the commercial drama in New York and London today. Did Middleton's Lord Mayor's shows participate in the early stages of this trend?

When one thinks about the advances that were being made in the Court masque, one realizes the answer has to be no. The influential experiments in lighting, movable scenery, and perspective views were in the hands of Inigo Jones and his literary collaborators, especially Ben Jonson. These experiments were being carried out in the area of the theatre where Middleton worked least, the Court. His Lord Mayor's shows did borrow techniques from the masque, to be sure. Glynne Wickham has pointed out that the Lord Mayor's shows 'gave to humble citizens something of the pleasure latent in a change of scene which Inigo Jones was offering in his decorations of masques to those courtiers privileged to attend them'. But the distinction in audiences makes all the difference. At Court, there was already in place an essential element of the modern scenic theatre, an exclusive audience of wealth and privilege. The audience for Middleton's Lord Mayor's shows consisted of the populace rather than the King and his courtiers, and the theatre was London itself rather than the Banqueting House at Whitehall.

The question of Middleton's modernism becomes more pointed when one recalls that artificial lighting was being practised in another venue of his career, the roofed-over private playhouse. It is a long journey from the candlelight of St Paul's and the Blackfriars to the computerized lighting-boards of the Royal Shakespeare Company, but artificial lighting is the technique in both cases, and higher admission prices a means of affording it. We have noted that Middleton was well positioned for the move of the King's Men to Blackfriars in 1608, and this was a consequential move in the direction of wealth and privilege. As Peter Thomson remarks about the King's Men at the Blackfriars, 'by assuming a private face, the country's leading group of players carried further the drift from the popular theatre of the Middle Ages toward the minority theatre with which we are familiar today'.

So the question is whether the private theatres for which Middleton wrote were experimenting with scenic innovation during his time. It is perhaps surprising to discover (the theatre usually being a trend-following industry) that they were not. Middleton's private theatre plays do not reflect the technological flamboyance of his Lord Mayor's shows. When he did write masques into his plays, the technical effects are tinged with travesty, disaster, or bleak comedy, and he calls only for the kinds of effects (a descending god, smoke, a burning star) which had long been available in the commercial theatres. More generally, there is no evidence that movable scenery, perspective views, and the other staging effects that become possible once the potential of artificial lighting is exploited were practised by anyone at Blackfriars and the other private playhouses until about 1635–40, after Middleton's death.

Why were the crucial experiments being conducted at Court? Money is the first reason, and sight-lines are the second. The most expensive Lord Mayor's show could cost as much as building a commercial playhouse, but a court masque under James I would routinely run into four figures, enough to build a little cluster of playhouses. This was the kind of wealth required for changing the direction of the English theatre. Perhaps the most revealing thing about the arrangements for the court masque is the position of the best seat in the house. We have noted the position of royalty in the banqueting and masquing houses. King James was seated just the right distance away from the stage, and at just the right elevation, to enjoy the perfect sight-lines for the illusion of perspective depth on a proscenium-arch stage with artificial lighting. At the commercial theatres, the most expensive seats were close to the stage, in the thick of things: in the private boxes behind or to the sides of the stage (gallants even paid extra for stools placed *on* the stage in the private theatres). Middleton wrote for the thick of things, and it is unlikely that perfect sight-lines were often on his mind.

The major technological change that occurred in the theatre of Middleton's time, then, rather passed by his plays and could be seen in his civic processions as a vivid reflection from Court. In its fullest perspective, that major change sends the theatre in the direction of concentrated wealth, technological progress, and a minority audience. Middleton is not our contemporary when it comes to these things. Suppose that having Zeal reduce Error to ashes was not only showmanship. Suppose it was what the writer sought to bring about. ''Tis the excellency of a writer to leave things better than he finds 'em', he wrote in his preface to *The Roaring Girl*, and although the comment in context is ironic enough to be read several ways, the straightforward way carries far into Middleton's overall career. At a time when some London playwrights and designers were finding the royal purse open to them—and at a time, too, when major advances in scenic technique were being made via that same purse—Middleton built his career mainly in the playhouses and pageants of the City. It is likely that this satirist of unprincipled men in the freewheeling get-what-you-can scene of early Stuart London saw that leaving the City 'better than he found it' was of greater use than helping to create new theatre technology by keeping the sight-lines clear for the King.

SEE ALSO

List of works cited: *Companion*, 459

COLLECTED WORKS 1602–1627

THE PHOENIX

Edited by Lawrence Danson and Ivo Kamps

'*The Phoenix*, As it hath been sundry times acted by the Children of Paul's, and presented before his Majesty': this is the potent advertising claim made on the title-page of the first printed edition (1607) of Thomas Middleton's first solo effort as a dramatist. That the play had been performed by the fashionable company of boy actors, and most of all that it had been performed before King James himself, were facts to recommend it to the book-buying public. As E. K. Chambers has noted, the most probable date of the performance before the King was 20 February 1604, so the play had to have been written before that. How long before? Topical allusions open only a small window of opportunity. Characters crack sardonic jokes about the cheapness of an aristocratic title—in Scene 6, for instance, Falso asks, 'Daughter, what gentleman might this be?' and she replies, 'No gentleman, sir, he's a knight'—jokes which take their point from King James's wholesale creation of knighthoods as he progressed from Edinburgh to London in the spring of 1603 to assume his English throne. And in the play's opening speech, the old Duke says, 'Forty-five years I've gently ruled this dukedom'. Elizabeth I had reigned for forty-five years when, following her death on 24 March 1603, James VI of Scotland became also James I of England. *The Phoenix* is, then, in various senses a Jacobean play: it was written in the first year of James's reign; it was performed at court in James's presence; and (going now beyond external circumstances) it is imbued with the anxiety and optimism of that time of political transition.

The play's engagement with this transition begins with its title and the name of its hero. To a Renaissance audience, the 'phoenix' bird suggested death but also renewal and rebirth. The bird, as legend had it, was periodically consumed by fire, but always miraculously rose anew from its ashes, a singular process suggesting that the whole kind (*genus*) of the phoenix was contained in the individual bird. The phoenix became a convenient image of royal succession in England, and Elizabeth I was especially so portrayed in art and literature. Contemplating the Queen's death, Fletcher and Shakespeare were to write in 1613 that when 'The bird of wonder dies—the maiden phoenix— | Her ashes new create another heir | As great in admiration as herself' (*All is True; or Henry VIII* 5.4.40–2). The new 'heir' was of course James I, and the point of the passage is that although England mourns the loss of its Virgin Queen, 'the Dignity' or 'singularity of the royal office' lives on in James—'*Dignitas nunquam perit, individua vero quotidie pereunt*, the Dignity never perishes, although individuals die every day' (Kantorowicz).

In Scene 1 of Middleton's play, the old ruler is not quite dead but certainly dying. His son and heir, Phoenix, to prepare himself for the succession, disguises his royalty, gives out the false news that he will be travelling in foreign countries, and, with his sidekick Fidelio, begins to explore his own territory, a place called 'Ferrara', where characters bearing Italian-sounding type-names participate in actions wholly native to the England of 1603. As a prince-in-disguise, Phoenix not only inserts himself into the life of his subjects, but into theatre history. He is one of several such disguised rulers on the Jacobean stage: the most notable others are Shakespeare's Duke Vincentio in *Measure for Measure* and Marston's Malevole in *The Malcontent*. Scholars have argued the question of historical priority, but there is in fact no way to be sure which playwright first used the device.

The Phoenix's membership in the class of disguised-ruler plays has, in this century, been one of its chief claims to fame—unfortunately, since the differences between Shakespeare's dramaturgy and Middleton's are more striking than the similarities; and because, given Shakespeare's prestige, the comparison inevitably introduces Shakespearean standards which are, at best, irrelevant to Middleton's practice and which, at worst, obscure or distort it. This much, however, *Measure for Measure* and *The Phoenix* have in common: their disguised rulers are an odd combination of the disarmingly ordinary (both Phoenix and Vincentio can be naïve or even bumbling, as when Phoenix finds himself in the dark with the Jeweller's Wife in Scene 13), and the politically powerful, their disguised omnipresence giving them an almost magical power to oversee and intervene in the affairs of their subjects. Phoenix, like Shakespeare's Duke, undergoes his own education; but as he does so he creates the image of an all-pervasive, all-surveilling power of the kind that might produce a politically effective anxiety in even the most obscure justice of the peace.

Recent scholarship has been critical of the figure of the ruler in disguise. *Measure for Measure*'s 'duke of dark corners', for instance, is viewed as a manipulative ruler who arouses anxiety in his subjects for the benefit of an oppressive culture. In *The Phoenix*, however, ducal surveillance and anxiety-arousing practices take on positive connotations; that is, Middleton appears to be capitalizing on the widespread, and perhaps excessive, expectations people had of the new King's abilities to transform English society for the better. Phoenix goes incognito to 'look into the heart and bowels of this dukedom' and 'mark all abuses ready for reformation or punishment' (1.102–4), but his efforts to clean up the legal system, stop sexual perversions, and avert a murder plot against his father are more obviously beneficial to the people than Vincentio's moralizing and callous manipulation of Isabella. If in *Measure for Measure* we, like Angelo and Isabella, learn to fear the hidden power of the spying Duke, in Middleton's play we are made to feel that an all-seeing, God-like authority is *necessary* to protect the people from a multitude of abuses. The reigning Duke of Ferrara says as much before transferring power to Prince Phoenix in the closing scene:

State is but blindness; thou hadst piercing art:
We only saw the knee, but thou the heart.
To thee then power and dukedom we resign;
He's fit to reign whose knowledge can refine.
(15.179–82)

The old Duke directly blames his own 'blindness' for the chaos in his dukedom; in sharp contrast to Vincentio who knew exactly what was going on in Vienna (he merely felt uncomfortable intervening directly), it is the Duke of Ferrara's inability to see, his ignorance, that has allowed corruption and treason to flourish. Phoenix's better sight is therefore crucial to Ferrara's health; but in Vienna the Duke's undercover escapades are primarily designed to stage and reassert his power. Hence, *The Phoenix* and *Measure for Measure* may draw on the same basic ruler-in-disguise motif, but they do so to different effects: Shakespeare may make us look anxiously over our shoulder; Middleton makes us feel that indeed we 'can sleep so soundly' knowing 'what watch the King keeps to maintain the peace' (*Henry V* 4.1.265, 280).

Comparisons to Shakespeare can only go so far. In the realm of character, for instance, nothing in *The Phoenix* reminds us of the tense psychosexual sparring of Angelo and Isabella. However, what Middleton extraordinarily accomplishes in this early play must be understood in its own terms and according to its own generic norms.

Those terms may be elusive for modern readers who see dramatic effects *either* as realistic *or* as allegorical, lifelike *or* symbolic, psychological *or* social. So Middleton has in this century been praised for the racy, cynical, richly individualized language of the Captain, and it has even been claimed—plausibly enough—that this remarkable character is drawn from life: Middleton's stepfather, Thomas Harvey, was a seafaring man, constantly in need of money which he tried to get by legal plunder of his wife, Anne Middleton. But the comically disturbing Scene 8, in which the Captain literally sells his wife, shows how, in Middleton's drama, an apparent imitation of the rough surface of daily life becomes ingeniously and richly symbolic of wider social issues. Middleton here shockingly literalizes the idea of woman as commodity and of marriage as a transaction of property. The Captain's very matter-of-factness as he carries out the grotesque action not only makes him a memorable character (in all senses of the word); it enacts Middleton's satiric idea, that in this nominal 'Ferrara', human beings have become equated with commodities and moral values with financial.

Middleton's language can be as cunningly double as his action. When the Lady protests, 'Have you no sense, neither of my good name | Or your own credit?' (8.5–6), her husband's response hinges on a quintessential Middletonian pun:

Credit? Pox of credit,
That makes me owe so much. It had been
Better for me by a thousand royals
I had lost my credit seven year ago.
'T'as undone me; that's it that makes me fly:
What need I to sea else, in the spring time,
When woods have leaves, to look upon bald oak?
Happier that man, say I, whom no man trusts;
It makes him valiant, dares outface the prisons,
Upon whose carcass no gowned raven jets:
O, he that has no credit owes no debts.
'Tis time I were rid on't. (8.6–17)

The Captain finds profit in being a man without either moral or financial 'credit': credit is trust, trust begets debt, so having good credit is a liability to this impecunious man who would prefer to exchange his chaste wife for ready cash.

Since his wife is concerned not only about his 'credit' but also about her 'good name' (Castiza or 'chastity'), we might expect her to separate the spiritual and material, or moral and financial, faces of the words 'credit' and 'chastity'. Instead they become, in her response, even more intricately implicated:

O, why do you
So wilfully cherish your own poison,
And breathe against the best of life, chaste credit?
Well may I call it chaste, for like a maid,
Once falsely broke, it ever lives decayed.
O, captain, husband, you name that dishonest
By whose good power all that are honest live;
What madness is it to speak ill of that,
Which makes all men speak well. Take away credit,
By which men amongst men are well reputed,
That man may live, but still lives executed. (8.17–27)

Now credit and chastity have become equated: both, once lost, can never be regained; both have been given value as commodities. All honest things, the Lady says, live by credit—and lest we think that she has succeeded in removing her 'credit' from the commercial realm where the Captain has placed his, she concludes with a pun on 'executed', meaning both 'killed' and 'signed, sealed, and delivered in law'.

But this scene's success does not depend only on verbal handy-dandy. The characters' disconcerting insistence on literalizing in action the rigidified logic implied in their punning language creates a bizarre, almost dream-like effect. If Shakespeare's Angelo astonishes us by his ability to look inward, the Captain astonishes us by his resistance to having any place inward to look.

The wife-selling scene in this early play already reveals many of Middleton's most characteristic dramatic skills. One is the deadpan presentation of a villainy all the more shocking for being made to seem only the way of the world. Here, Phoenix watches as Fidelio, disguised as a scrivener, is forced to read aloud the elaborate bill of his mother's sale. While Fidelio reads, the Captain counts his money and interjects the occasional huckster's line. The contract is addressed 'To all good and honest Christian people, to whom this present writing shall come', and delivers 'all the right, estate, title, interest, demand, possession, and term of years to come, which I the said captain have, or ought to have . . . [i]n and to Madonna Castiza, my most virtuous, modest, loving, and obedient wife—', and the Captain breaks in, 'By my troth, my lord, and so she is—three, four, five, six, seven—' (8.87–101). And it proceeds:

FIDELIO '*In primis*, the beauties of her mind, chastity, temperance, and, above all, patience—'
CAPTAIN You have bought a jewel, i'faith, my lord—nine-and-thirty, forty—
FIDELIO 'Excellent in the best of music, in voice delicious; in conference wise and pleasing; of age contentful, neither too young to be apish, nor too old to be sottish—'
CAPTAIN You have bought as lovely a penny-worth, my lord, as ere you bought in your life. (8.108–17)

The racy, specialized language of Middleton's rogues is more dramatically inventive than the highfalutin editorializing with which Prince Phoenix responds. But as a figure (however distantly suggested) for a newly installed reform-minded monarch, his speeches are worth listening to. Of the Captain's wife-selling, Phoenix says:

Of all deeds yet, this strikes the deepest wound
Into my apprehension.
Reverend and honourable matrimony,
Mother of lawful sweets, unshamed mornings,
Dangerless pleasures, thou that mak'st the bed
Both pleasant and legitimately fruitful: without thee,
All the whole world were soilèd bastardy.
Thou art the only and the greatest form,
That put'st a difference between our desires
And the disordered appetites of beasts,
Making their mates those that stand next their lusts.
(8.164–74)

Phoenix puts a different social value on matrimony than the Captain does—but still it is a social value, literally a 'form' which defines the 'lawful' and makes order out of actions which, in every outward way, are identical to the 'disordered appetites of beasts'. 'Matrimony' puts the exchange-value of sex under civic control; it creates the difference between 'soiled bastardy' and the 'legitimately fruitful' upon which other exchanges (including, for instance, Prince Phoenix's succession to his dying father's throne) depend. In Middleton, social value is not merely a surface covering a deeper reality, an externality that hides a more real internality; it creates form, meaning, difference, and thereby puts the 'human' in human life.

The plot of *The Phoenix* is episodic: it's one damned (literally) thing after another until the grand recognition scene when Phoenix reveals himself and metes out punishment. The various plots are linked, first of all by Phoenix's supervision of them, and second by interlocking character affiliations: for instance, the corrupt Justice Falso becomes the guardian (and would-be sexual partner) of his niece, who happens to be Fidelio's beloved; the Jeweller's Wife is Falso's daughter; the Captain tries to sell his wife to Proditor, who is also the aspiring assassin of the old Duke; and Tangle, who is Falso's competitor in legal shenanigans, draws up the bill of sale.

Of the villainies Phoenix encounters, Proditor's plot to assassinate the Duke (he hires Phoenix to be his hit man) is nominally the most heinous but dramatically less interesting than the actions involving what we might call society's middle class. Abuses of the legal system—abuses which Middleton himself might have encountered, and which he might look to a new monarch to reform—are especially prominent. The play is full of law-Latin and legalese. Scene 9, in which Justice Falso and the litigious Tangle engage in a legal as well as actual fencing match, is energetically ingenious and, for all its absurdity, frightening. In another instance of literalizing theatricality, the corrupt justice and the 'villainous law-worm' (4.44–5) try to outduel each other with rapiers, while simultaneously trying to outmanœuvre one another as if in a court of law. Legal words are weapons, the legal system a deadly game.

Abuses of the law and of sexual relations are closely related in the play, and both sorts of abuse are caught up in the satiric logic of commodification. In their adulterous affair, the Knight and the Jeweller's Wife use pet-names for one another: he is 'Pleasure' and she is 'Revenue'—where the 'pleasure' he supplies in exchange for her 'revenue' is social advancement as well as sexual gratification. In the final scene, when Phoenix brings each of the villains to book, the Jeweller's Wife is arraigned in terms that figure her sexual adventuring as a crime against the fabric of society (15.230–42). She is 'one of those | For whose close lusts the plague never leaves the city'; she deceives her 'husband, the world's eye, and the law's whip'; with her citizen gold she maintains aristocrats 'whom the court rejects'; she reverses the economic priorities of the gender system ('Now few but are by their wives' copies free'), and erases social distinctions ('now we see | City and suburbs wear one livery'). Like other anxious (male) Jacobean satirists, Middleton here seems to judge unconstrained female sexuality the opening wedge in the decline of civilization.

Adultery, incest, wife-selling, rampant theft, treason, bribery, social levelling, and attempted murder: these are some of the specific transgressions Phoenix encounters. In the register of fantastic satire they represent the actual social milieu in which the play was written. The last years of Elizabeth's reign were felt to be years of crisis. There were riots against enclosures, and the court had gained a reputation for corruption and political in-fighting. In 1601 the popular Earl of Essex revolted against the Queen, and was executed for his efforts. English spirits were dampened even further by poor harvests and high inflation, the latter brought on by the costly war with Spain. Yet in the spring of 1603, as the new King made his way down from Scotland, there was a strong feeling of anticipation and a sense that the nation had left behind a period of economic hardships and despair. Middleton's *The Phoenix* catches, in its mixed tone of angry denunciation and political optimism, the spirit of its time; and the ascent of the morally upright all-seeing Prince Phoenix from the ashes of an old rule gives the play a more upbeat conclusion than Middleton usually indulges.

SEE ALSO

Textual introduction and apparatus: *Companion*, 529
Authorship and date: *Companion*, 345
Measure for Measure, this volume, 1547

The Phoenix

[*for the Children of Paul's*]

THE PERSONS OF THE PLAY

DUKE of Ferrara
PHOENIX, his son
PRODITOR
LUSSURIOSO, a noble
INFESTO, a noble
LADY, also called Castiza
FIDELIO, her son
CAPTAIN, her husband
TANGLE
KNIGHT
FALSO, a justice of the peace
LATRONELLO, servant to Falso
FURTIVO, servant to Falso
FUCATO, servant to Falso
NIECE, to Falso
JEWELLER'S WIFE, daughter to Falso
QUIETO
Three SOLDIERS
GROOM
Two SUITORS (Scenes 4 and 6)
BOY
GENTLEMEN
CONSTABLE
Two OFFICERS
Two SUITORS (Sc. 12)
QUIETO'S BOY
MAID, to Jeweller's Wife

Nobles, attendants, servus, lackey, drawer, guards

Sc. 1 *Enter the old Duke of Ferrara, Nobles, Proditor, Lussurioso, and Infesto, with Attendants*

DUKE My lords,
Know that we, far from any natural pride
Or touch of temporal sway, have seen our face
In our grave council's foreheads, where doth stand
Our truest glass, made by time's wrinkled hand.
We know we're old, my days proclaim me so.
Forty-five years I've gently ruled this dukedom;
Pray heaven it be no fault,
For there's as much disease, though not to th'eye,
In too much pity as in tyranny.

INFESTO
Your grace hath spoke it right.

DUKE I know that life
Has not long course in me; 'twill not be long
Before I show that kings have mortal bodies
As well as subjects. Therefore, to my comfort,
And your successful hopes, I have a son
Whom I dare boast of—

LUSSURIOSO Whom we all do boast of,
A prince elder in virtues than in years.

1.0.1 *Proditor* traitor, villain
0.2 *Lussurioso* lecherous, wanton
3 **touch** taint
temporal sway political power
5 **glass** mirror
11 INFESTO odious, hateful

INFESTO
His judgement is a father to his youth.

PRODITOR [*aside*]
Ay, I would he were from court.

INFESTO
Our largest hopes grow in him.

PRODITOR
And 'tis the greatest pity, noble lord,
He is untravelled.

LUSSURIOSO 'Tis indeed, my lord.

PRODITOR
Had he but travel to his time and virtue—
[*Aside*] O, he should ne'er return again.

DUKE
It shall be so: what is in hope begun,
Experience quickens; travel confirms the man,
Who else lives doubtful, and his days oft sorry;
Who's rich in knowledge has the stock of glory.

PRODITOR
Most true, my royal lord.

DUKE
Someone attend our son.

Enter Prince Phoenix, attended by Fidelio

INFESTO
See, here he comes, my lord.

DUKE
O, you come well.

PHOENIX
'Tis always my desire, my worthy father.

DUKE
Your serious studies, and those fruitful hours
That grow up into judgement, well become
Your birth, and all our loves. I weep that you are my son,
But virtuously I weep, the more my gladness.
We have thought good and meet, by the consent
Of these our nobles, to move you toward travel,
The better to approve you to yourself,
And give your apter power foundation:
To see affections actually presented,
E'en by those men that owe them, yields more profit,
Ay, more content, than singly to read of them,
Since love or fear make writers partial.
The good and free example which you find
In other countries, match it with your own,
The ill to shame the ill, which will in time
Fully instruct you how to set in frame
A kingdom all in pieces.

PHOENIX Honoured father,
With care and duty I have listened to you.
What you desire, in me it is obedience;
I do obey in all, knowing for right,
Experience is a kingdom's better sight.

PRODITOR
O, 'tis the very lustre of a prince.
Travel! 'Tis sweet and generous.

DUKE
He that knows how to obey, knows how to reign;
And that true knowledge have we found in you.
Make choice of your attendants.

PHOENIX They're soon chosen;
[*Indicating Fidelio*] Only this man, my lord, a loving servant of mine.

DUKE
What, none but he?

PHOENIX I do entreat no more,
For that's the benefit a private gentleman
Enjoys beyond our state, when he notes all,
Himself unnoted.
For should I bear the fashion of a prince,
I should then win more flattery than profit;
And I should give 'em time and warning then
To hide their actions from me; if I appear a sun,
They'll run into the shade with their ill deeds,
And so prevent me.

PRODITOR [*aside*]
A little too wise, a little too wise to live long.

DUKE
You have answered us with wisdom: let it be.
Things private are best known through privacy.

Exeunt

Manent Phoenix and Fidelio

PHOENIX
Stay you, my elected servant.

FIDELIO My kind lord.

PHOENIX
The duke my father has a heavy burden
Of years upon him.

FIDELIO
My lord, it seems so, for they make him stoop.

PHOENIX
Without dissemblance he is deep in age,
He bows unto his grave. I wonder much
Which of his wild nobility it should be
(For none of his sad council has a voice in't)
Should so far travel into his consent
To set me over into other kingdoms
Upon the stroke and minute of his death?

FIDELIO
My lord, 'tis easier to suspect them all,
Than truly to name one.

PHOENIX Since it is thus,
By absence I'll obey the duke my father,
And yet not wrong myself.

19 **from** away from
23 **to** in addition to
26 **quickens** enlivens
28 **stock of glory** wealth of heaven
30.1 ***Phoenix*** (See Critical Introduction.) ***Fidelio*** faithful
40 **approve you to** make proof of
41 **apter** naturally well-suited
42 **affections** passions, appetites
43 **owe** own
44 **singly** only
46 **free** generous
49 **set in frame** restore order in
63 **state** high position
70 **prevent** forestall
74 **elected** chosen
81 **sad** serious, grave
83 **set me over** send me

FIDELIO Therein, my lord,
You might be happy twice.

PHOENIX So it shall be;
I'll stay at home, and travel.

FIDELIO Would your grace
Could make that good.

PHOENIX I can. And indeed a prince need not travel farther than his own kingdom, if he apply himself faithfully, worthy the glory of himself and expectation of others. And it would appear far nobler industry in him to reform those fashions that are already in his country than to bring new ones in, which have neither true form nor fashion; to make his court an owl, city an ape, and the country a wolf preying upon the ridiculous pride of either. And therefore I hold it a safer stern upon this lucky advantage, since my father is near his setting, and I upon the eastern hill to take my rise, to look into the heart and bowels of this dukedom, and in disguise mark all abuses ready for reformation or punishment.

FIDELIO
Give me but leave unfeignedly to admire you,
Your wisdom is so spacious and so honest.

PHOENIX So much have the complaints and suits of men seven, nay, seventeen years neglected, still interposed by coin and great enemies, prevailed with my pity, that I cannot otherwise think but there are infectious dealings in most offices, and foul mysteries throughout all professions. And therefore I nothing doubt but to find travel enough within myself, and experience, I fear, too much. Nor will I be curious to fit my body to the humblest form and bearing, so the labour may be fruitful: for how can abuses that keep low come to the right view of a prince? Unless his looks lie level with them, which else will be longest hid from him, he shall be the last man sees 'em.
For oft between king's eyes and subject's crimes
Stands there a bar of bribes; the under office
Flatters him next above it, he the next,
And so of most, or many.
Every abuse will choose a brother:
'Tis through the world, this hand will rub the other.

FIDELIO
You have set down the world briefly, my lord.

PHOENIX
But how am I assured of faith in thee?
Yet I durst trust thee.

FIDELIO Let my soul be lost
When it shall loose your secrets; nor will I
Only be a preserver of them, but,
If you so please, an assister.

PHOENIX It suffices.
That king stands sur'st who by his virtue rises
More than by birth or blood; that prince is rare,
Who strives in youth to save his age from care.
Let's be prepared—away.

FIDELIO I'll follow your grace;
Exit Phoenix
Thou wonder of all princes, precedent, and glory,
True phoenix, made of an unusual strain.
Who labours to reform is fit to reign.
How can that king be safe that studies not
The profit of his people? See where comes
The best part of my heart, my love.
Enter Niece

NIECE
Sir, I am bound to find you. I heard newly
Of sudden travel which his grace intends,
And only but yourself to accompany him.

FIDELIO
You heard in that little beside the truth.
Yet not so sudden as to want those manners
To leave you unregarded.

NIECE
I did not think so unfashionably of you.
How long is your return?

FIDELIO
'Tis not yet come to me, scarce to my lord,
Unless the duke refer it to his pleasure;
But long I think it is not. The duke's age,
If not his apt experience, will forbid it.

NIECE
His grace commands; I must not think amiss.
Farewell.

FIDELIO Nay, stay, and take this comfort:
You shall hear often from us. I'll direct
Where you shall surely know, and I desire you
Write me the truth, how my new father-in-law,
The captain, bears himself toward my mother;
For that marriage knew nothing of my mind,
It never flourished in any part of my affection.

NIECE
Methinks she's much disgraced herself.

FIDELIO Nothing so,
If he be good and will abide the touch.
A captain may marry a lady, if he can sail
Into her good will.

NIECE Indeed, that's all.

FIDELIO
'Tis all in all. Commend me to thy breast, farewell.
Exit Niece

98 **owl** (Because of its nocturnal habits, the owl was a symbol of solemn stupidity.)
99 **ape** foolish mimic
100 **safer stern** safer course ('stern' here standing for a ship's helm or rudder)
107 **suits** pleas
108 **still** always
interposed opposed, obstructed
111 **mysteries** secrets (with a pun: 'professions' were also called 'mysteries')
112 **nothing doubt but** expect
114 **Nor ... curious** I will not be too finicky
129 **loose** tell
136 **precedent** worthy example
137 **phoenix** (See Critical Introduction.)
146 **want** lack
148 **unfashionably** inappropriately
151 **refer ... pleasure** leaves it up to him
156–7 **direct ... know** write letters telling you where to find me
160 **knew ... mind** did not have my approval
163 **abide the touch** prove true (as real gold does when tested by a touchstone)

So by my lord's firm policy we may see,
To present view, what absent forms would be. *Exit*

Sc. 2 *Enter the Captain with soldiering fellows*

FIRST SOLDIER There's noble purchase, captain.

SECOND SOLDIER Nay, admirable purchase.

THIRD SOLDIER Enough to make us proud forever.

CAPTAIN Hah?

FIRST SOLDIER Never was opportunity so gallant.

CAPTAIN Why, you make me mad.

SECOND SOLDIER Three ships, not a poop less.

THIRD SOLDIER And every one so wealthily burdened, upon my manhood.

CAPTAIN Pox on't, and now am I tied e'en as the devil would ha't.

FIRST SOLDIER Captain, of all men living, I would ha' sworn thou wouldst ne'er have married.

CAPTAIN 'Sfoot, so would I myself, man. Give me my due; you know I ha' sworn all heaven over and over.

FIRST SOLDIER That you have, i'faith.

CAPTAIN Why, go to, then.

FIRST SOLDIER Of a man that has tasted salt water to commit such a fresh trick.

CAPTAIN Why 'tis abominable, I grant you, now I see't.

FIRST SOLDIER Had there been fewer women—

SECOND SOLDIER And among those women fewer drabs—

THIRD SOLDIER And among those drabs fewer pleasing—

CAPTAIN Then 't'ad been something.

FIRST SOLDIER But when there are more women, more common, pretty sweethearts, than ever any age could boast of—

CAPTAIN And I to play the artificer and marry: to have my wife dance at home, and my ship at sea, and both take in salt water together. O, lieutenant, thou'rt happy, thou keepest a wench.

FIRST SOLDIER I hope I am happier than so, captain, for o' my troth, she keeps me.

CAPTAIN How? Is there any such fortunate man breathing? And I so miserable to live honest? I envy thee lieutenant, I envy thee, that thou art such a happy knave. Here's my hand among you; share it equally; I'll to sea with you.

SECOND SOLDIER There spoke a noble captain.

CAPTAIN Let's hear from you. There will be news shortly.

FIRST SOLDIER Doubt it not, captain.

Exeunt [all but Captain]

CAPTAIN What lustful passion came aboard of me that I should marry—was I drunk? Yet that cannot altogether hold, for it was four o'clock i'th' morning. Had it been five, I would ha' sworn it. That a man is in danger every minute to be cast away, without he have an extraordinary pilot that can perform more than a man can do! And to say truth, too, when I'm abroad what can I do at home? No man living can reach so far. And what a horrible thing 'twould be to have horns brought me at sea, to look as if the devil were i'th' ship; and all the great tempests would be thought of my raising—to be the general curse of all merchants. And yet they likely are as deep in as myself, and that's a comfort. O, that a captain should live to be married! Nay, I that have been such a gallant salt-thief should yet live to be married. What a fortunate elder brother is he, whose father being a rammish plowman, himself a perfumed gentleman, spending the labouring reek from his father's nostrils in tobacco, the sweat of his father's body in monthly physic for his pretty queasy harlot; he sows apace i'th' country; the tailor o'ertakes him i'th' city; so that oftentimes before the corn comes to earing, 'tis up to the ears in high collars, and so at every harvest the reapers take pains for the mercers—ha! Why this is stirring happiness indeed. Would my father had held a plow so and fed upon squeezed curds and onions, that I might have bathed in sensuality. But he was too ruttish himself to let me thrive under him; consumed me before he got me, and that makes me so wretched now to be shackled with a wife, and not greatly rich, neither.

Enter his Lady

LADY Captain, my husband.

CAPTAIN 'Slife, call me husband again and I'll play the captain and beat you.

LADY
What has disturbed you, sir, that you now look
So like an enemy upon me?

CAPTAIN
Go, make a widower, hang thyself.

LADY
How comes it that you are so opposite

2.0.1 ***soldiering fellows*** soldiers on board a ship (distinguished from sailors)
1 **purchase** booty
10–11 **as the devil would ha't** (i.e., the converse of the commonplace that marriages are made in heaven)
14 **'Sfoot** by God's foot (a mild oath)
19 **fresh** unsophisticated
22 **drabs** prostitutes
28 **artificer** an artful or wily person, a trickster
30 **salt** lecherous, salacious
salt water (In the wife's case, salt water alludes to her lover's semen.)
32–3 **o' my troth** upon my truth, or honesty
35 **honest** virtuously
49 **do** (in the sexual sense)
50 **horns** (Cuckolds were said to wear horns on the brow.)
56 **salt-thief** pirate
58 **rammish** having a rank smell
60 **tobacco** (On the Renaissance stage, London fops were often represented as avid 'tobacco drinkers'.)
61 **monthly physic** (possibly a form of birth control, or a medicine for menstrual pains, or a medicine for venereal disease)
queasy sickly or nauseated
64 **earing** maturing to the point where the corn is ready to be picked
up . . . collars (A pun on the ears of corn and the ears of the brother, who is wearing expensive high-ruffed collars.)
65 **mercers** dealers in textile fabrics, especially in silks, velvets, and other expensive materials
69 **ruttish** lustful
70 **consumed me** spent my inheritance wastefully
72.1 **Lady** (Also called Castiza: her name means 'chaste'.)
74 **'Slife** God's life (a mild oath)
74–5 **play the captain** (Discipline on board was enforced by the captain.)

To love and kindness? I deserve more respect,
But that you please to be forgetful of it.
For love to you did I neglect my state,
Chide better fortunes from me,
Gave the world talk, laid all my friends at waste.

CAPTAIN
The more fool you. Could you like none but me?
Could none but I supply you?
I am sure you were sued to by far worthier men,
Deeper in wealth and gentry.
What could'st thou see in me to make thee dote
So on me, if I know I am a villain?
What a torment's this? Why didst thou marry me?
You think, as most of your insatiate widows,
That captains can do wonders, when, 'las,
The name does often prove the better man.

LADY
That which you urge should rather give me cause
To repent than yourself.

CAPTAIN Then to that end,
I do't.

LADY What a miserable state
Am I led into?

Enter Servus

CAPTAIN How now, sir?

SERVUS Count Proditor
Is now alighted. [*Exit Servus*]

CAPTAIN What! My lord? I must
Make much of him; he'll one day write me cuckold.
'Tis good to make much of such a man;
E'en to my face, he plies it hard—I thank him.

Enter Proditor

What, my worthy lord!

PRODITOR I'll come to you
In order, captain. [*Kisses Lady*]

CAPTAIN [*aside*] O, that's in order:
A kiss is the gamut to pricksong.

PRODITOR
Let me salute you, captain. [*Exit Lady*]

CAPTAIN My dear
Esteemèd count, I have a life for you.

PRODITOR
Hear you the news?

CAPTAIN What may it be, my lord?

PRODITOR
My lord, the duke's son, is upon his travel
To several kingdoms.

CAPTAIN May it be possible, my lord,
And yet so little rumoured?

PRODITOR Take't of my truth;
Nay, 'twas well managed, things are as they are handled:
But all my care is still, pray heaven, he return
Safe, without danger, captain.

CAPTAIN Why, is there
Any doubt to be had of that, my lord?

PRODITOR Ay, by my faith, captain.
Princes have private enemies, and great.
Put case a man should grudge him for his virtues,
Or envy him for his wisdom: why, you know
This makes him lie bare-breasted to his foe.

CAPTAIN
That's full of certainty, my lord. But who
Be his attendants?

PRODITOR Thence, captain, comes the fear.
But singly attended, neither—[*aside*] my best gladness—
Only by your son-in-law, Fidelio.

CAPTAIN Is it to be believed? I promise you, my lord, then I begin to fear him myself. That fellow will undo him. I durst undertake to corrupt him with twelve pence over and above, and that's a small matter. H'as a whorish conscience, he's an inseparable knave, and I could ne'er speak well of that fellow.

PRODITOR All we of the younger house, I can tell you, do doubt him much. The lady's removed; shall we have your sweet society, captain?

CAPTAIN Though it be in mine own house, I desire I may follow your lordship.

PRODITOR I love to avoid strife.
[*Aside*] Not many months Phoenix shall keep his life.
Exit

CAPTAIN
So, his way is in; he knows it:
We must not be uncourteous to a lord.
Warn him our house 'twere vile; his presence is an honour. If he lie with our wives, 'tis for our credit; we shall be the better trusted; 'tis a sign we shall live i'th' world. O, tempests and whirlwinds! Who but that man whom the forefinger cannot daunt, that makes his shame his living—who but that man, I say, could endure to be thoroughly married? Nothing but a divorce can relieve me. Any way to be rid of her would rid my torment. If all means fail, I'll kill or poison her, and

81 **But that** except that
82 **state** rank
84 **Gave...talk** gave the world cause for gossip
86 **supply** to furnish something needed or desired (here with sexual connotation)
88 **gentry** class of well-born people just below the nobility
94 **name** reputation
99.1 ***Servus*** servant
100 **alighted** dismounted, arrived
101 **write me cuckold** make a cuckold out of me
103 **plies it hard** works hard at it (i.e., cuckolding)
106 **gamut** the first or lowest note in the medieval scale of music
pricksong music sung from notes written or 'pricked'; sexual intercourse
108 **I...you** my life is at your disposal
118 **private** secret
119 **Put case** suppose that
127 **to fear him** to fear for him
130 **an inseparable knave** (Fidelio is inseparable from his whorish conscience.)
132 **the younger house** (the Ferraran House of Commons)
133 **doubt** fear
141 **Warn him** to bar him from
143–4 **live i'th' world** live well
145 **the forefinger** (i.e., pointing in scorn at a cuckold)

purge my fault at sea. But first I'll make gentle try of a divorce: but how shall I accuse her subtle honesty? I'll attach this lord's coming to her—take hold of that, ask counsel: and now I remember, I have acquaintance with an old crafty client, who by the puzzle of suits and shifting of courts has more tricks and starting holes than the dizzy pates of fifteen attorneys—one that has been muzzled in law like a bear and led by the ring of his spectacles from office to office.
Him I'll seek out with haste; all paths I'll tread,
All deaths I'll die ere I die marriéd. *Exit*

Sc. 3 *Enter Proditor with Lady (the Captain's wife)*

PRODITOR
Puh, you do resist me hardly.

LADY
I beseech your lordship, cease in this.
'Tis never to be granted. If you come as a friend unto my honour and my husband, you shall be ever welcome; if not, I must entreat it—

PRODITOR Why, assure yourself, madam, 'tis not the fashion.

LADY
'Tis more my grief, my lord; such as myself
Are judged the worse for such.

PRODITOR Faith, you're too nice:
You'll see me kindly forth.

LADY And honourably welcome.
Exeunt

Sc. 4 *Enter a Groom before Phoenix and Fidelio [in disguise], alighting into an inn*

GROOM Gentlemen, you're most neatly welcome.

PHOENIX You're very cleanly, sir; prithee, have a care to our geldings.

GROOM Your geldings shall be well considered.

FIDELIO Considered?

PHOENIX Sirrah, what guests does this inn hold now?

GROOM Some five-and-twenty gentlemen, besides their beasts.

PHOENIX Their beasts?

GROOM Their wenches, I mean, sir; for your worship knows those that are under men are beasts.

PHOENIX How does your mother, sir?

GROOM Very well in health; I thank you heartily, sir.

PHOENIX And so is my mare, i'faith.

GROOM I'll do her commendations indeed, sir.

FIDELIO Well kept up, shuttlecock.

PHOENIX But what old fellow was he that newly alighted before us?

GROOM Who, he? As arrant a crafty fellow as e'er made water on horseback: some say he's as good as a lawyer—marry, I'm sure he's as bad as a knave. If you have any suits in law, he's the fittest man for your company. He's been so towed and lugged himself, that he is able to afford you more knavish counsel for ten groats than another for ten shillings.

PHOENIX A fine fellow; but do you know him to be a knave, and will lodge him?

GROOM Your worship begins to talk idly. Your bed shall be made presently. If we should not lodge knaves, I wonder how we should be able to live honestly. Are there honest men enough, think you, in a term-time to fill all the inns in the town? And, as far as I can see, a knave's gelding eats no more hay than an honest man's—nay, a thief's gelding eats less, I'll stand to't. His master allows him a better ordinary—yet I have my eightpence, day and night. 'Twere more for our profit, Iwis, you were all thieves, if you were so contented. I shall be called for: give your worships good morrow. *[Exit]*

PHOENIX A royal knave, i'faith. We have happened into a godly inn.

FIDELIO Assure you, my lord, they belong all to one church.

PHOENIX *[Seeing Tangle in the doorway]* This should be some old, busy, turbulent fellow: villainous law-worm, that eats holes into poor men's causes.

Enter Tangle with two Suitors [and Groom]

FIRST SUITOR May it please your worship to give me leave?

TANGLE I give you leave, sir; you have your *veniam*. Now fill me a brown toast, sirrah.

GROOM Will you have no drink to't, sir?

TANGLE Is that a question in law?

GROOM Yes, in the lowest court, i'th' cellar, sir.

TANGLE Let me ha't removed presently, sir.

GROOM It shall be done, sir. *[Exit]*

TANGLE Now as you were saying, sir—I'll come to you immediately, too.

PHOENIX O, very well, sir.

TANGLE I'm a little busy, sir.

FIRST SUITOR But as how, sir?

TANGLE I pray, sir?

FIRST SUITOR He's brought me into the court; marry, my adversary has not declared yet.

TANGLE *Non declaravit adversarius*, sayst thou? What a villain's that. I have a trick to do thee good: I will

151 **subtle** cunning
honesty chastity
152 **attach** seize (with legal sense of taking into custody)
155 **starting holes** loopholes
3.1 **hardly** strongly
9 **nice** coy, reserved
4.0.2 ***alighting*** arriving
1 **neatly** (the first of the Groom's malapropisms)
14 **mare** (pun on the French word for mother, *mere*)
19–20 **made water** urinated
25 **groats** coins worth four pence each
shillings coins worth twelve pence each (one twentieth of a pound sterling)
31 **term-time** periods when courts of law are in session
35 **ordinary** a regular daily meal or allowance of food
36 **Iwis** certainly
47 ***veniam*** permission to do something
52 **removed** to transfer a cause or person for trial from one court of law to another
61 **declared** to make a declaration or statement of claim as plaintiff in an action
62 ***Non declaravit adversarius*** your adversary hasn't declared

get thee out a proxy, and make him declare with a pox to him.

FIRST SUITOR That will make him declare to his sore grief. I thank your good worship. But put case he do declare?

TANGLE *Si declarasset*, if he should declare there—

FIRST SUITOR I would be loath to stand out to the judgement of that court.

TANGLE *Non ad judicium*? Do you fear corruption? Then I'll relieve you again; you shall get a *supersedeas non molestandum*, and remove it higher.

FIRST SUITOR Very good.

TANGLE Now if it should ever come to a *testificandum*, what be his witnesses?

FIRST SUITOR I little fear his witnesses.

TANGLE *Non metuis testes*? More valiant man than Orestes!

FIRST SUITOR [*gives money*] Please you, sir, to dissolve this into wine, ale, or beer. I come a hundred mile to you, I protest, and leave all other counsel behind me.

TANGLE Nay, you shall always find me a sound card; I stood not o' th' pillory for nothing in eighty-eight; all the world knows that. Now let me dispatch you, sir; I come to you *presenter*.

SECOND SUITOR Faith, the party hath removed both body and cause with a *habeas corpus*.

TANGLE Has he that knavery? But has he put in bail above, canst tell?

SECOND SUITOR That, I can assure your worship, he has not.

TANGLE Why, then, thy best course shall be to lay out more money, take out a *procedendo*, and bring down the cause and him with a vengeance.

SECOND SUITOR Then he will come indeed.

TANGLE As for the other party, let the *audita querela* alone; take me out a special *supplicavit*, which will cost you enough, and then you pepper him. For the first party, after the *procedendo* you'll get costs; the cause being found, you'll have a judgement; *nunc pro tunc*, you'll get a *venire facies* to warn your jury, a *decem tales* to fill up the number, and a *capias ut lagatum* for your execution.

SECOND SUITOR I thank you, my learned counsel.

PHOENIX What a busy caterpillar's this? Let's accost him in that manner.

FIDELIO Content, my lord.

PHOENIX O, my old, admirable fellow, how have I all this while thirsted to salute thee? I knew thee in *octavo* of the duke—

TANGLE In *octavo* of the duke: I remember the year well.

PHOENIX By th' mass, a lusty, proper man.

TANGLE O, was I?

PHOENIX But still in law.

TANGLE Still in law? I had not breathed else now; 'tis very marrow, very manna to me to be in law: I'd been dead ere this else. I have found such sweet pleasure in the vexation of others, that I could wish my years over and over again, to see that fellow a beggar, that bawling knave a gentleman—a matter brought e'en to a judgement today, as far as e'er 'twas to begin again tomorrow: O, raptures! Here a writ of demur, there a *procedendo*, here a *sursurrara*, there a *capiendo*, tricks, delays, money-laws.

PHOENIX Is it possible, old lad?

TANGLE I have been a term-trotter myself any time this five-and-forty years; a goodly time and a gracious in which space I ha' been at least sixteen times beggared, and got up again, and in the mire again, that I have stunk again, and yet got up again.

PHOENIX And so clean and handsome now?

67 **put case** suppose
68 ***Si declarasset*** if he should declare
69 **stand out** to endure to the end, hold out against
71 ***Non ad judicium*** not to the judgement
72–3 ***supersedeas non molestandum*** writs staying proceedings at law because one of the parties is under the king's protection
75 ***testificandum*** testifying
78 ***Non metuis testes*** you don't fear witnesses
Orestes In Greek mythology, son of Agamemnon and Clytemnestra who avenged the death of his father by killing his mother.
82 **sound card** a person whose agency will ensure success
82–3 **I ... pillory** (Standing in the pillory was a punishment for men who made a living by giving false evidence.)
83 **eighty-eight** (1588, proverbial date for 'the old days', from the year when the Spanish Armada was defeated)
85 ***presenter*** immediately
87 ***habeas corpus*** a writ requiring the body of a person to be brought before the judge or into the court
88 **above** in a higher court
93 ***procedendo*** a writ issued by a superior court directing an inferior court to proceed to a final hearing
96 ***audita querela*** a writ initiating a process to introduce new evidence on behalf of the defendant after completion of the trial.
97 ***supplicavit*** a writ for taking surety of the peace against a person
100 **found** judged
nunc pro tunc now for then (i.e., not at the legally appointed time)
101 ***venire facies*** a writ directed to a sheriff requiring him to summon a jury to try a cause
decem tales a supply of men (in this case ten) to fill the jury
102 ***capias ut lagatum*** a writ commanding an officer to arrest an outlawed person
103 **execution** to put in force the sentence that the law has given
109–10 **in *octavo* ... duke** in the eighth year of the duke's reign
112 **lusty** cheerful, lively
proper handsome
114 **still** always
116 **marrow** rich and nutritious food
manna food miraculously provided for the Israelites in the wilderness (Exodus 16:14–36)
122 **demur** a motion to delay or suspend action because of a point of difficulty which the court must decide
123 ***sursurrara*** (Anglicized variant of *certiorari*) a writ, issuing from a superior court, upon the complaint of a party that he has not received justice in an inferior court, by which the records of the cause are called up for trial in the superior court
capiendo a writ of arrest
126 **term-trotter** one who frequented London in term-time

TANGLE You see it apparently; I cannot hide it from you. Nay, more, in *felici hora* be it spoken, you see I'm old, yet have I at this present nine-and-twenty suits in law.

PHOENIX Deliver us, man!

TANGLE And all not worth forty shillings.

PHOENIX May it be believed?

TANGLE The pleasure of a man is all.

PHOENIX An old fellow, and such a stinger?

TANGLE A stake pulled out of my hedge, there's one. I was well beaten, I remember; that's two. I took one abed with my wife against her will; that's three. I was called cuckold for my labour; that's four. I took another abed again; that's five. Then one called me wittol; that's six. He killed my dog for barking; seven. My maid-servant was knocked at that time; eight. My wife miscarried with a push; nine; and *sic de ceteris*. I have so vexed and beggared the whole parish with process, subpoenas, and suchlike molestations, they are not able to spare so much ready money from a term as would set up a new weathercock; the churchwardens are fain to go to law with the poor's money.

PHOENIX Fie, fie.

TANGLE And I so fetch up all the men every term-time, that 'tis impossible to be at civil cuckoldry within ourselves, unless the whole country rise upon our wives.

FIDELIO O' my faith, a pretty policy.

PHOENIX Nay, an excellent stratagem. But of all I most wonder at the continual substance of thy wit, that having had so many suits in law from time to time, thou hast still money to relieve 'em.

FIDELIO He's the best fortune for that; I never knew him without.

TANGLE Why do you so much wonder at that? Why, this is my course: my mare and I come up some five days before a term.

PHOENIX A good decorum.

TANGLE Here I lodge, as you see, amongst inns and places of most receipt—

PHOENIX Very wittily.

TANGLE By which advantage I dive into countrymen's causes, furnish 'em with knavish counsel, little to their profit, buzzing into their ears this course, that writ, this office, that *ultimum refugium*—as you know I have words enough for the purpose.

PHOENIX Enough i' conscience, i'faith.

TANGLE Enough i' law, no matter for conscience. For which busy and laborious sweating courtesy, they cannot choose but feed me with money, by which I maintain mine own suits. Ho, ho, ho.

PHOENIX Why, let me hug thee—caper in mine arms.

[*They caper around the stage*]

TANGLE Another special trick I have—nobody must know it—which is to prefer most of those men to one attorney whom I affect best, to answer which kindness of mine, he will sweat the better in my cause, and do them the less good. Take 't of my word, I helped my attorney to more clients the last term than he will dispatch all his life time: I did it.

PHOENIX What a noble, memorable deed was there!

Enter Groom

GROOM Sir.

TANGLE Now, sir.

GROOM There's a kind of captain very robustiously inquires for you.

TANGLE For me? A man of war? A man of law is fit for a man of war; we have no leisure to say prayers; we both kill o' Sunday mornings. [*To Phoenix*] I'll not be long from your sweet company.

PHOENIX O, no, I beseech you. *Exit Tangle* [*with Groom*]

FIDELIO What captain might this be?

PHOENIX

Thou angel sent amongst us, sober Law,
Maid with meek eyes, persuading action,
No loud immodest tongue, voiced like a virgin,
And as chaste from sale,
Save only to be heard, but not to rail:
How has abuse deformed thee to all eyes,
That where thy virtues sat, thy vices rise?
Yet why so rashly for one villain's fault
Do I arraign whole man? Admirèd law,
Thy upper parts must needs be sacred, pure,
And incorruptible; they're grave and wise.
'Tis but the dross beneath 'em, and the clouds
That get between thy glory and their praise,
That make the visible and foul eclipse.
For those that are near to thee are upright,
As noble in their conscience as their birth;
Know that damnation is in every bribe,
And rarely put it from 'em; rate the presenters,
And scourge 'em with five years imprisonment,
For offering but to tempt 'em.
Thus is true justice exercised and used:
Woe to the giver when the bribe's refused.
'Tis not their will to have law worse than war,
Where still the poor'st die first;
To send a man without a sheet to his grave,
Or bury him in his papers.
'Tis not their mind it should be, nor to have
A suit hang longer than a man in chains,
Let him be ne'er so fastened. They least know
That are above the tedious steps below.

133 ***felici hora*** in a happy hour
135 **Deliver us** tell us
144 **wittol** a man who knows of his wife's adultery and tolerates it
146 **knocked** beaten
147 ***sic de ceteris*** so with the rest
151 **churchwardens** laymen who execute a church's business
155 **within** among
169 **receipt** most frequented
174 ***ultimum refugium*** last refuge
183 **prefer** introduce or recommend
192 **robustiously** boisterously
203 **as...sale** (i.e., the law, like a virgin, is not for sale)
217 **presenters** bribers
224 **sheet** winding sheet
225 **papers** legal documents
227 **suit** law suit, with pun on clothes

I thank my time, I do.

FIDELIO
I long to know what captain this should be.

PHOENIX
See where the bane of every cause returns.

Enter Tangle with Captain

FIDELIO 'Sfoot, 'tis the captain, my father-in-law, my lord.

PHOENIX Take heed.

CAPTAIN The divorce shall rest then, and the five hundred crowns shall stand in full force and virtue.

TANGLE Then do you wisely, captain.

CAPTAIN Away sail I, fare thee well.

TANGLE A lusty crack of wind go with thee.

CAPTAIN But ah!

TANGLE Hah?

CAPTAIN Remember, a scrivener.

TANGLE I'll have him for thee. [*Exit Captain*]

Why, thus am I sought after by all professions. Here's a weatherbeaten captain, who not long since new married to a lady widow, would now fain have sued a divorce between her and him, but that her honesty is his only hinderance: to be rid of which, he does determine to turn her into white money; and there's a lord, his chapman, has bid five hundred crowns for her already.

FIDELIO How?

TANGLE Or for his part, or whole, in her.

PHOENIX Why, does he mean to sell his wife?

TANGLE His wife? Ay, by th' mass, he would sell his soul if he knew what merchant would lay out money upon 't—and some of 'em have need of one, they swear so fast.

PHOENIX Why, I never heard of the like.

TANGLE *Non audivisti,* didst ne'er hear of that trick? Why, Pistor, a baker, sold his wife t'other day to a cheesemonger, that made cake and cheese; another to a cofferer; a third to a common player. Why, you see 'tis common. Ne'er fear the captain; he has not so much wit to be a precedent himself. I promised to furnish him with an odd scrivener of mine own, to draw the bargain and sale of his lady. Your horses stand here, gentlemen.

PHOENIX Ay, ay, ay.

TANGLE I shall be busily plunged till towards bedtime above the chin in *profundis.* *Exit*

PHOENIX
What monstrous days are these?
Not only to be vicious most men study,
But in it to be ugly; strive to exceed
Each other in the most deformèd deed.

FIDELIO
Was this her private choice? Did she neglect
The presence and opinion of her friends, for this?

PHOENIX
I wonder who that one should be,
Should so disgrace that reverend name of lord,
So loathsomely to buy adultery?

FIDELIO
We may make means to know.

PHOENIX
Take courage, man; we'll beget some defence.

FIDELIO
I am bound by nature.

PHOENIX I by conscience.
To sell his lady! Indeed, she was a beast
To marry him, and so he makes of her.
Come, I'll thorough now I'm enterèd. *Exeunt*

Enter Jeweller's Wife with a Boy Sc. 5

JEWELLER'S WIFE Is my sweet knight coming? Are you certain he's coming?

BOY Certain, forsooth. I am sure I saw him out of the barber's shop, ere I would come away.

JEWELLER'S WIFE A barber's shop? O, he's a trim knight. Would he venture his body into a barber's shop when he knows 'tis as dangerous as a piece of Ireland? O, yonder, yonder, he comes. Get you back again and look you say as I advised you.

Enter Knight

BOY You know me, mistress.

JEWELLER'S WIFE My mask, my mask.

[*Exit Boy, after giving her a mask*]

KNIGHT My sweet Revenue!

JEWELLER'S WIFE My Pleasure, welcome. I have got single. None but you shall accompany me to the justice of peace, my father's.

KNIGHT Why, is thy father justice of peace, and I not know it?

235 **rest** remain to be dealt with
236 **crowns** coins worth five shillings each
239 **crack ... wind** fart
249 **white money** silver coins
250 **chapman** a man whose business is buying and selling
252 **part, or whole** (Tangle paraphrases a bill of sale, and puns on 'whole/hole', with sexual connotation.)
257 **fast** steadfastly
259 ***Non audivisti*** You didn't hear
260 **Pistor** baker
261 **cofferer** a builder of boxes or chests
269 ***profundis*** the depths (i.e. of legal matters)
275 **presence** company
282 **beast** a human being controlled by sexual appetite
284 **thorough** (go) through
5.1 **knight** (Originally a mounted soldier in service to the king, and in chivalry one who serves a lady, the title here indicates one of those newly raised to the knighthood by King James I. See Critical Introduction and 6.148, 9.2–4.)
3 **forsooth** truly
out of come out of
4 **barber's shop** (Barbers also pulled teeth and did minor medical operations.)
5 **trim** stylish (punning on 'freshly barbered')
7 **dangerous ... Ireland** (For the previous nine years, Ireland had been in an almost constant state of rebellion against the occupying English.)
11 **mask** (Small masks were worn by ladies of fashion as a sign of modesty, but also as an allure, and possibly to hide the scars of smallpox.)
12–13 **Revenue ... Pleasure** (The endearments spell out the terms of the relationship: the impecunious knight takes money from the middle-class woman, who takes sexual pleasure and social preferment in return.)

JEWELLER'S WIFE My father! I'faith, sir, ay; simply though I stand here a citizen's wife, I am a justice of peace's daughter.

KNIGHT I love thee the better for thy birth.

[*Enter the Knight's Lackey*]

JEWELLER'S WIFE Is that your lackey yonder, in the steaks of velvet?

KNIGHT He's at thy service, my sweet Revenue, for thy money paid for 'em.

JEWELLER'S WIFE Why, then, let him run a little before, I beseech thee, for, o' my troth, he will discover us else.

KNIGHT He shall obey thee; before sirrah, trudge.

[*Exit Lackey*]

But do you mean to lie at your father's all night?

JEWELLER'S WIFE Why should I desire your company else?

KNIGHT 'Sfoot, where shall I lie then?

JEWELLER'S WIFE What an idle question's that? Why, do you think I cannot make room for you in my father's house as well as in my husband's? They're both good for nothing else.

KNIGHT A man so resolute in valour as a woman in desire were an absolute leader. *Exeunt*

Sc. 6 *Enter two suitors with the Justice Falso*

FIRST SUITOR May it please your good worship, master justice—

FALSO Please me and please yourself; that's my word.

FIRST SUITOR The party your worship sent for will by no means be brought to appear.

FALSO He will not? Then what would you advise me to do therein?

FIRST SUITOR Only to grant your worship's warrant, which is of sufficient force to compel him.

FALSO No, by my faith! You shall not have me in that trap. Am I sworn justice of peace, and shall I give my warrant to fetch a man against his will? Why, there the peace is broken. We must do all quietly; if he come he's welcome, and, as far I can see yet, he's a fool to be absent—[*aside*] ay, by this gold is he, which he gave me this morning.

FIRST SUITOR Why, but may it please your good worship—

FALSO I say again, please me and please yourself; that's my word still.

FIRST SUITOR Sir, the world esteems it a common favour, upon the contempt of the party, the justice to grant his warrant.

FALSO Ay, 'tis so common, 'tis the worse again; 'twere the better for me 'twere otherwise.

FIRST SUITOR I protest, sir, and this gentleman can say as much, it lies upon my half undoing.

FALSO I cannot see yet that it should be so—I see not a cross yet.

FIRST SUITOR I beseech your worship show me your immediate favour, and accept this small trifle but as a remembrance to my succeeding thankfulness. [*Offers money*]

FALSO Angels? I'll not meddle with them. You give 'em to my wife, not to me.

FIRST SUITOR Ay, ay, sir.

FALSO But, I pray, tell me now, did the party *viva voce*, with his own mouth, deliver that contempt, that he would not appear, or did you but jest in't?

FIRST SUITOR Jest? No, o' my troth, sir, such was his insolent answer.

FALSO And do you think it stood with my credit to put up such an abuse? Will he not appear, says he? I'll make him appear with a vengeance. Latronello!

[*Enter Latronello*]

LATRONELLO Does your worship call?

FALSO Draw me a strong-limbed warrant for the gentleman speedily. He will be bountiful to thee. Go and thank him within.

FIRST SUITOR I shall know your worship hereafter.

Exeunt [*Suitors with Latronello*]

FALSO Ay, ay, prithee do. Two angels one party, four another; and I think it a great spark of wisdom and policy—if a man come to me for justice—first to know his griefs by his fees, which be light and which be heavy. He may counterfeit else, and make me do justice for nothing. I like not that, for when I mean to be just, let me be paid well for't: the deed so rare, purges the bribe.

[*Enter Furtivo*]

How now? What's the news thou art come so hastily? How fares my knightly brother?

FURTIVO Troth, he ne'er fared worse in his life, sir. He ne'er had less stomach to his meat since I knew him.

FALSO Why, sir?

FURTIVO Indeed, he's dead, sir.

FALSO How, sir?

FURTIVO Newly deceased, I can assure your worship. The tobacco-pipe new dropped out of his mouth before I took horse—a shrewd sign. I knew then there was no way but one with him. The poor pipe was the last man he took leave of in this world, who fell in three pieces before him, and seemed to mourn inwardly, for it looked as black i'th' mouth as my master.

FALSO Would he die so like a politician, and not once write his mind to me?

FURTIVO No, I'll say that for him, sir; he died in the perfect state of memory, made your worship his full and whole

22–3 **steaks of velvet** (velvet decorations, in thick strips like steaks, inset in his garment)
27 **discover** reveal
6.0.1 *Falso* false
21 **upon . . . party** when a person summoned before the court refuses to appear
26 **it lies upon** it is a matter of
28 **cross** coin bearing a cross stamped upon it; also, a coin generally
33 **Angels** gold coins worth ten shillings each
36 ***viva voce*** with the living voice
43 **Latronello** little thief
55.1 ***Furtivo*** furtive, sly
59 **stomach . . . meat** appetite for food
65–6 **no . . . one** (i.e., he must die)
69 **black . . . mouth** (because of (*a*) speaking slander or (*b*) the tobacco's tar)
70 **like a politician** cunningly

executor, bequeathing his daughter, and with her all his wealth only to your disposition.

FALSO Did he make such a godly end, sayest thou? Did he die so comfortably, and bequeath all to me?

FURTIVO Your niece is at hand, sir, the will, and the witnesses.

FALSO What a precious joy and comfort's this, that a justice's brother can die so well—nay, in such a good and happy memory—to make me full executor. Well, he was too honest to live, and that made him die so soon. Now, I beshrew my heart, I am glad he's in heaven, has left all his cares and troubles with me, and that great vexation of telling of money. Yet I hope he had so much grace before he died to turn his white money into gold, a great ease to his executor.

[*Enter Niece and two Gentlemen*]

FURTIVO See, here comes your niece, my young mistress, sir.

FALSO Ah, my sweet niece, let me kiss thee, and drop a tear between thy lips. One tear from an old man is a great matter; the cocks of age are dry. Thou hast lost a virtuous father, to gain a notable uncle.

NIECE
My hopes now rest in you next under heaven.

FALSO
Let 'em rest, let 'em rest.

FIRST GENTLEMAN
Sir—

FALSO
You're most welcome ere ye begin, sir.

FIRST GENTLEMAN
We are both led by oath and dreadful promise
Made to the dying man at his last sense,
First to deliver these into your hands,
The sureties and revealers of his state.
[*Gives papers to Falso*]

FALSO
Good.

FIRST GENTLEMAN
With this his only daughter and your niece,
Whose fortunes are at your disposing set;
Uncle and father are in you both met.

FALSO Good, i'faith, a well-spoken gentleman; you're not an esquire, sir?

FIRST GENTLEMAN Not, sir.

FALSO Not sir? More's the pity. By my faith, better men than you are, but a great many worse. You see I have been a scholar in my time, though I'm a justice now. Niece, you're most happily welcome, the charge of you is wholly and solely mine own; and since you are so fortunately come, niece, I'll rest a perpetual widower.

NIECE
I take the meaning chaster than the words;
Yet I hope well of both, since it is thus:
His phrase offends least that's known humorous.

FALSO [*reading the will*] 'I make my brother,' says he, 'full and whole executor'—honestly done of him i'faith. Seldom can a man get such a brother. And here again says he, very virtuously, 'I bequeath all to him and his disposing'—an excellent fellow. O' my troth, would you might all die no worse, gentlemen.

Enter Knight with Jeweller's Wife

FIRST GENTLEMAN But as much better as might be.

KNIGHT Bless your uprightness, master justice,

FALSO You're most soberly welcome, sir. [*Jeweller's Wife kneels*] Daughter, you've that ye kneel for; rise, salute your weeping cousin.

JEWELLER'S WIFE Weeping cousin?

NIECE Ay, cousin.

KNIGHT [*speaking apart with Jeweller's Wife*] Eye to weeping is very proper, and so is the party that spake it, believe me, a pretty, fine, slender, straight, delicate-knit body.
O, how it moves a pleasure through our senses!
How small are women's waists to their expenses!
I cannot see her face, that's under water yet.

JEWELLER'S WIFE News as cold to the heart as an old man's kindness: my uncle dead?

NIECE
I have lost the dearest father.

FALSO [*reading the will*] 'If she marry by your consent, choice and liking, make her dowry five thousand crowns.' [*Aside*] Hum, five thousand crowns? Therefore by my consent she shall ne'er marry. I will neither choose for her, like of it, nor consent to't.

KNIGHT [*aside*] Now, by the pleasure of my blood, a pretty cousin. I would not care if I were as near kin to her as I have been to her kinswoman.

FALSO Daughter, what gentleman might this be?

JEWELLER'S WIFE No gentleman, sir, he's a knight.

FALSO Is he but a knight? Troth, I would a' sworn he'd been a gentleman. To see, to see, to see!

JEWELLER'S WIFE He's my husband's own brother, I can tell you, sir.

FALSO Thy husband's brother? Speak certainly, prithee.

83 **honest** virtuous
93 **cocks** tearducts
98 **dreadful** reverential
99 **sense** moments of consciousness
101 **sureties** those who make themselves liable for another's debts
106 **esquire** a man belonging to the higher order of gentry, ranking immediately below a knight
116 **humorous** whimsical, odd, quaint
130–1 **Eye...proper** it is proper for an eye to weep
144 **blood** (the supposed seat of animal or sensual appetite)
145 **cousin** kinswoman (here niece)
148 **No...knight** Between his ascension and December 1604, James I almost tripled the number of knights in the realm, thereby cheapening the aura of the rank. The Jeweller's Wife refers to this cheapening when she states that the knight, who outranks a gentleman, is no gentleman.
151 **my...brother** (This is the only indication in the play that the Knight is related to the Jeweller; it makes possible the double entendre in the Jeweller's Wife's next line.)

JEWELLER'S WIFE I can assure you, father, my husband and he have lain both in one belly.

FALSO I'll swear then he is his brother indeed, and by the surer side. I crave hearty pardon, sweet kinsman, that thou hast stood so long unsaluted in the way of kindred.
Welcome to my board; I have a bed for thee.
My daughter's husband's brother shall command
Keys of my chests and chambers—I have stable
For thy horse, chamber for thyself,
And a loft above for thy lousy lackey.
All sit, away with handkerchiefs, dry up eyes;
At funeral we must cry; now let's be wise.

Exeunt [all but Knight and Jeweller's Wife]

JEWELLER'S WIFE
I told you his affection.

KNIGHT
It falls sweetly.

JEWELLER'S WIFE
But here I bar you from all plots tonight;
The time is yet too heavy to be light.

KNIGHT
Why, I'm content, I'll sleep as chaste as you,
And wager night by night who keeps most true.

JEWELLER'S WIFE
Well, we shall see your temper. *Exeunt*

Sc. 7 *Enter Phoenix and Fidelio [putting on new disguises]*

PHOENIX Fear not me, Fidelio; become you that invisible rope-maker, the scrivener, that binds a man as he walks, yet all his joints at liberty, as well as I'll fit that common folly of gentry, the easy-affecting venturer, and no doubt our purpose will arrive most happily.

FIDELIO Chaste duty, my lord, works powerfully in me, and rather than the poor lady my mother should fall upon the common side of rumour to beggar her name, I would not only undergo all habits, offices, disguised professions, though e'en opposite to the temper my blood holds, but in the stainless quarrel of her reputation, alter my shape forever.

PHOENIX I love thee wealthier, thou hast a noble touch. And by this means, which is the only safe means to preserve thy mother from such an ugly land- and sea-monster as a counterfeit captain is, he resigning and basely selling all his estate, title, right, and interest in his lady, as the form of the writing shall testify.
What otherwise can follow but to have
A lady safe delivered of a knave?

FIDELIO I am in debt my life to the free goodness of your inventions.

PHOENIX
O, they must ever strive to be so good;
Who sells his vow is stamped the slave of blood.

Exeunt

Enter Captain, his Lady following him Sc. 8

CAPTAIN
Away!

LADY
Captain, my husband—

CAPTAIN
Hence, we're at a price for thee, at a price,
Wants but the telling, and the sealing; then—

LADY
Have you no sense, neither of my good name
Or your own credit?

CAPTAIN Credit? Pox of credit,
That makes me owe so much. It had been
Better for me by a thousand royals
I had lost my credit seven year ago.
'T'as undone me; that's it that makes me fly:
What need I to sea else, in the spring time,
When woods have leaves, to look upon bald oak?
Happier that man, say I, whom no man trusts;
It makes him valiant, dares outface the prisons,
Upon whose carcass no gowned raven jets:
O, he that has no credit owes no debts.
'Tis time I were rid on't.

LADY O, why do you
So wilfully cherish your own poison,
And breathe against the best of life, chaste credit?
Well may I call it chaste, for like a maid,
Once falsely broke, it ever lives decayed.
O, captain, husband, you name that dishonest
By whose good power all that are honest live;
What madness is it to speak ill of that,
Which makes all men speak well. Take away credit,
By which men amongst men are well reputed,
That man may live, but still lives executed.
O, then show pity to that noble title
Which else you do usurp. You're no true captain,
To let your enemies lead you—foul disdain,
And everlasting scandal: O, believe it!
The money you receive for my good name

156–7 **the surer side** (proverbially, the mother's side)
166 **affection** disposition
169 **heavy** grave
light happy, wanton
7.1 **become you** pretend to be
2 **scrivener** notary (The disguise would probably include an inkhorn worn at his waist and a pen behind his ear.)
3 **fit** take the shape of
4 **gentry** class immediately below nobility; gentlemen
easy-affecting venturer careless investor
5 **arrive** turn out
6 **Chaste** virtuous
8 **common** vulgar
beggar impoverish
9 **habits** clothing
13 **noble touch** (like pure gold tested against a touchstone)
20 **of** from
21 **my life** throughout my life
22 **inventions** inventiveness; creative devices
24 **blood** passion
8.4 **Wants** lacks
telling counting
6 **Pox** (an exclamation of irritation or impatience)
8 **royals** gold coins worth fifteen shillings
14 **outface** to face boldly or defiantly
15 **gowned raven** (a judge or lawyer, who wears black robes)
jets to strut, swagger

Will not be half enough to pay your shame.

CAPTAIN
No, I'll sell thee then to the smock. See, here comes
My honourable chapman.

Enter Proditor [and Lackey]

LADY O, my poison!
Him, whom mine honour and mine eye abhors. *Exit*

PRODITOR
Lady—what so unjovially departed?

CAPTAIN [*aside*] Fine she-policy; she makes my back her bolster, but before my face she not endures him. Tricks!

PRODITOR
Captain, how haps it she removed so strangely?

CAPTAIN
O, for modesty's cause awhile, my lord,
She must restrain herself; she's not yours yet.
Beside, it were not wisdom to appear
Easy before my sight.
Faugh! Wherefore serves modesty but to pleasure a lady now and then, and help her from suspect? That's the best use 'tis put to.

PRODITOR Well observed of a captain.

CAPTAIN No doubt you'll be soon friends, my lord.

PRODITOR I think no less.

CAPTAIN And make what haste I can to my ship; I durst wager you'll be under sail before me.

PRODITOR A pleasant voyage, captain.

CAPTAIN Ay, a very pleasant voyage as can be. I see the hour is ripe. Here comes the prison's bawd, the bond-maker, one that binds heirs before they are begot.

PRODITOR And here are the crowns, captain. [*Giving money*] [*To Lackey*] Go, attend. Let our bay courser wait.

Enter Phoenix and Fidelio, both disguised

LACKEY It shall be obeyed. [*Exit*]

CAPTAIN [*aside to Fidelio*] A farmer's son, is't true?

FIDELIO [*aside to the Captain*] Has crowns to scatter.

CAPTAIN I give you your salute, sir.

PHOENIX I take it not unthankfully, sir.

CAPTAIN I hear a good report of you, sir—you've money.

PHOENIX I have so, true.

CAPTAIN An excellent virtue.

PHOENIX [*aside*] Ay, to keep from you—hear you me, captain? I have a certain generous itch, sir, to lose a few angels in the way of profit: 'tis but a game at tennis,
Where, if the ship keep above line, 'tis three to one;
If not, there's but three hundred angels gone.

CAPTAIN Is your venture three hundred? You're very preciously welcome; here's a voyage toward will make us all—

PHOENIX [*aside*] Beggarly fools and swarming knaves.

PRODITOR [*aside*] Captain, what's he?

CAPTAIN [*aside to Proditor*] Fear him not, my lord, he's a gull, he ventures with me; some filthy farmer's son. The father's a Jew, and the son a gentleman: faugh!—

PRODITOR [*aside to the Captain*] Yet he should be a Jew, too, for he is new come from giving over swine.

CAPTAIN [*aside to Proditor*] Why, that in our country makes him a gentleman.

PRODITOR Go to, tell your money, captain.

CAPTAIN Read aloft, scrivener. One, two—

FIDELIO [*reading the deed*] 'To all good and honest Christian people, to whom this present writing shall come: know you for a certain, that I, captain, for and in the consideration of the sum of five hundred crowns, have clearly bargained, sold, given, granted, assigned and set over, and by these presents do clearly bargain, sell, give, grant, assign and set over, all the right, estate, title, interest, demand, possession, and term of years to come, which I the said captain have, or ought to have—'

PHOENIX [*aside*] If I were as good as I should be—

FIDELIO 'In and to Madonna Castiza, my most virtuous, modest, loving, and obedient wife—'

CAPTAIN By my troth, my lord, and so she is—three, four, five, six, seven—

PHOENIX [*aside*] The more slave he that says it, and not sees it.

FIDELIO 'Together with all and singular those admirable qualities with which her noble breast is furnished.'

CAPTAIN Well said, scrivener, hast put 'em all in? You shall hear now, my lord.

FIDELIO '*In primis*, the beauties of her mind, chastity, temperance, and, above all, patience—'

CAPTAIN You have bought a jewel, i'faith, my lord—nine-and-thirty, forty—

FIDELIO 'Excellent in the best of music, in voice delicious; in conference wise and pleasing; of age contentful, neither too young to be apish, nor too old to be sottish—'

CAPTAIN You have bought as lovely a penny-worth, my lord, as ere you bought in your life.

34 **smock** a woman's undergarment
39 **bolster** pillow (The captain means that when his back is turned, his wife is much friendlier toward Proditor.)
40 **strangely** in an unfriendly manner
46 **from suspect** from being suspected
49 **friends** lovers
55–6 **prison's... begot** (i.e., the bail bondsman, like a pimp, caters to every debtor, whose children are born already owing him money)
58 **courser** a spirited or swift horse
69–71 **'tis... line** This is a complicated image which refers, first, to the line on an Elizabethan tennis court wall (the ball had to hit above the line to remain in play), and second, to shipping (where the 'line' refers to the proper line of flotation, the 'water line', when the ship is fully laden).
71 **three... one** (a profit of three to one on his investment)
73 **venture** investment
74 **toward** approaching
80 **Jew** (intended prejudicially: someone cunning and greedy)
82 **giving over** giving up
83–4 **Why... gentleman** (a gibe at the expense of upwardly mobile yeoman farmers and their sons)
86 **aloft** in a lofty tone
92 **these presents** these words or documents
102 **slave** a common term of abuse
108 ***In primis*** first
114–15 **neither... sottish** (i.e., neither so young as to be affected, nor so old as to be doltish)
116 **penny-worth** bargain

PRODITOR Why should I buy her else, captain?

FIDELIO 'And, which is the best of a wife, a most comfortable sweet companion—'

CAPTAIN I could not afford her so, i'faith, but that I am going to sea, and have need of money.

FIDELIO 'A most comfortable sweet companion—'

PRODITOR What, again? The scrivener reads in passion.

FIDELIO I read as the words move me. Yet if that be a fault it shall be seen no more—'which said Madonna Castiza lying, and yet being in the occupation of the said captain—'

CAPTAIN Nineteen—occupation? Pox on't, out with occupation, a captain is of no occupation, man.

PHOENIX [*aside*] Nor thou of no religion.

FIDELIO Now I come to the *habendum*: 'to have and to hold, use and—'

CAPTAIN
Use? Put out use, too, for shame,
Till we are all gone, I prithee.

FIDELIO 'And to be acquitted of and from all former bargains, former sales—'

CAPTAIN Former sales?—nine-and-twenty, thirty—by my troth my lord, this is the first time that ever I sold her.

PRODITOR Yet the writing must run so, captain.

CAPTAIN Let it run on then—nine-and-forty, fifty—

FIDELIO 'Former sales, gifts, grants, surrenders, re-entries—'

CAPTAIN For re-entries, I will not swear for her.

FIDELIO 'And furthermore, I the said, of and for the consideration of the sum of five hundred crowns to set me a board before these presents utterly disclaim for ever any title, estate, right, interest, demand, or possession, in or to the said Madonna Castiza, my late virtuous and unfortunate wife.'

PHOENIX [*aside*] Unfortunate indeed, that was well placed.

FIDELIO 'As also neither to touch, attempt, molest, or encumber any part, or parts whatsoever, either to be named or not to be named, either hidden or unhidden, either those that boldly look abroad, or those that dare not show their faces—'

CAPTAIN Faces? I know what you mean by faces; scrivener, there's a great figure in faces.

FIDELIO 'In witness whereof, I the said captain have interchangeably set to my hand and seal, in presence of all these, the day and date above written.'

CAPTAIN Very good, sir, I'll be ready for you presently—four hundred and twenty, one, two, three, four, five—

PHOENIX [*aside*]
Of all deeds yet, this strikes the deepest wound
Into my apprehension.
Reverend and honourable matrimony,
Mother of lawful sweets, unshamed mornings,
Dangerless pleasures, thou that mak'st the bed
Both pleasant and legitimately fruitful: without thee,
All the whole world were soilèd bastardy.
Thou art the only and the greatest form,
That put'st a difference between our desires
And the disordered appetites of beasts,
Making their mates those that stand next their lusts.
Then, with what base injury is thy goodness paid!
First, rare to have a bride commence a maid,
But does beguile joy of the purity,
And is made strict by power of drugs and art,
An artificial maid, a doctored virgin,
And so deceives the glory of his bed:
A foul contempt against the spotless power
Of sacred wedlock. But if chaste and honest,
There is another devil haunts marriage—
None fondly loves but knows it—jealousy,
That wedlock's yellow sickness,
That whispering separation every minute,
And thus the curse takes his effect or progress.
The most of men in their first sudden furies
Rail at the narrow bounds of marriage,
And call 't a prison; then it is most just,
That the disease o' th' prison, jealousy,
Should still affect 'em. But O! Here I am fixed
To make sale of a wife, monstrous and foul,
An act abhorred in nature, cold in soul.
Who that has man in him could so resign
To make his shame the posy to the coin?

CAPTAIN
Right, i'faith, my lord, fully five hundred.

PRODITOR I said how you should find it, captain; and with this competent sum you rest amply contented.

CAPTAIN Amply contented.

FIDELIO Here's the pen, captain: your name to the sale.

CAPTAIN 'Sfoot, dost take me to be a penman? I protest I could ne'er write more than A, B, C, those three letters, in my life.

FIDELIO Why, those will serve, captain.

CAPTAIN I could ne'er get further.

PHOENIX Would you have got further than A, B, C? [*Aside*] Ah, Base Captain, that's far enough, i'faith.

FIDELIO Take the seal off, captain.

CAPTAIN It goes on hardly, and comes off easily.

PHOENIX [*aside*] Ay, just like a coward.

FIDELIO Will you write witness, gentleman?

CAPTAIN He? He shall; prithee come and set thy hand for witness, rogue—thou shall venture with me?

124 **in passion** sorrowfully
127 **occupation** possession (with sexual connotation)
132 ***habendum*** to have and to hold
134 **Use** (use sexually)
142–3 **re-entries** the re-entering upon possession of lands, tenements, etc., previously granted or let to others
144 **re-entries** (the Captain's meaning is sexual)
158 **great figure** zero
171 **form** the essential determinant principle of a thing (in scholastic philosophy)
178 **strict** tight (referring to the bride's genitalia)
178–9 **power . . . virgin** artificial means by which women who had lost their virginity were made to appear as virgins
184 **fondly** foolishly
185 **yellow** (a colour often associated with jealousy)
196 **posy** a motto or short inscription

PHOENIX Nay, then I ha' reason, captain, that commands me. [*Writes*]

CAPTAIN [*aside*] What a fair fist the pretty whoreson writes, as if he had had manners and bringing up: a farmer's son? His father damns himself to sell musty corn, while he ventures the money. 'Twill prosper well at sea—no doubt he shall ne'er see't again.

FIDELIO So, captain, you deliver this as your deed?

CAPTAIN As my deed, what else, sir?

PHOENIX [*aside*] The ugliest deed that e'er mine eye did witness.

CAPTAIN So, my lord, you have her; clip her, enjoy her; she's your own. And let me be proud to tell you now, my lord, she's as good a soul, if a man had a mind to live honest, and keep a wench, the kindest, sweetest, comfortablest rogue—

PRODITOR [*aside to Captain*]
Hark in thine ear,
The baser slave art thou, and so I'll tell her.
I love the pearl thou sold'st, hate thee the seller.
Go, to sea, the end of thee—is lousy.

CAPTAIN
This is fine work, a very brave end, hum—

PRODITOR [*aside*]
Well thought upon, this scrivener may furnish me.
[*He takes Fidelio aside*]

PHOENIX [*aside*]
Why should this fellow be a lord by birth,
Being by blood a knave?—one that would sell
His lordship if he liked her ladyship.

FIDELIO Yes, my lord?

PHOENIX What's here now?

PRODITOR I have employment for a trusty fellow, bold, sure—

FIDELIO What if he be a knave, my lord?

PRODITOR There thou com'st to me—why he should be so, and men of your quill are not unacquainted.

FIDELIO Indeed all our chief living, my lord, is by fools and knaves. We could not keep open shop else: fools that enter into bonds, and knaves that bind 'em.

PRODITOR [*talking apart with Fidelio*] Why, now we meet.

FIDELIO And as my memory happily leads me, I know a fellow of a standing estate, never flowing:
I durst convey treason into his bosom,
And keep it safe nine years.

PRODITOR
A goodly time.

FIDELIO
And, if need were, would press to an attempt,
And cleave to desperate action.

PRODITOR
That last fits me;
Thou hast the measure right. Look I hear from thee.

FIDELIO
With duteous speed.

PRODITOR
Expect a large reward.
I will find time of her to find regard. *Exit*

CAPTAIN
The end of me is lousy?

FIDELIO [*aside to Phoenix*]
O, my lord!
I have strange words to tell you.

PHOENIX [*aside to Fidelio*] Stranger yet?
I'll choose some other hour to listen to thee;
I am yet sick of this. Discover quickly.

FIDELIO [*aside to Phoenix*]
Why, will you make yourself known, my lord?

PHOENIX [*aside to Fidelio*] Ay.
Who scourgeth sin, let him do't dreadfully.

CAPTAIN
Pox of his dissemblance: I will to sea.

PHOENIX [*aside*] Nay, you shall to sea, thou wouldst poison the whole land else—[*to the Captain*] why, how now, captain?

CAPTAIN In health.

FIDELIO What, drooping?

PHOENIX Or ashamed of the sale of thine own wife?

CAPTAIN You might count me an ass, then, i'faith.

PHOENIX If not ashamed of that, what can you be ashamed of, then?

CAPTAIN Prithee ha' done, I am ashamed of nothing.

PHOENIX [*aside*] I easily believe that.

CAPTAIN This lord sticks in my stomach.

PHOENIX How? Take one of thy feathers down, and fetch him up.

FIDELIO I'd make him come.

PHOENIX But what if the duke should hear of this?

FIDELIO Ay, or your son-in-law, Fidelio, know of the sale of his mother?

CAPTAIN What an they did, I sell none but mine own. As for the duke, he's abroad by this time, and for Fidelio, he's in labour.

PHOENIX He in labour?

CAPTAIN What call you travelling?

PHOENIX That's true. But let me tell you, captain, whether the duke hear on't, or Fidelio know on't, or both, or neither, 'twas a most filthy loathsome part.

FIDELIO A base, unnatural deed—

CAPTAIN Slave and fool—
[*Phoenix and Fidelio discover themselves, and grab him*]
Ha, who? O!—

PHOENIX Thou hateful villain; thou shouldst choose to sink
To keep thy baseness shrouded.
Enter his Lady

FIDELIO
Ugly wretch.

LADY
Who hath laid violence upon my husband?

226 **clip** embrace
234 **lousy** filthy, contemptible
236 **furnish** supply
245 **com'st to** understands
250 **meet** understand each other
252 **standing** stagnant
263 **Discover** let us take off our disguise
266 **dreadfully** so as to cause fear or awe
280 **down** i.e., down your throat
282 **I'd...come** I would make him vomit
286 **an** if
287 **duke** the future duke, Phoenix
298.1 ***his Lady*** Castiza

My dear, sweet captain—help!

PHOENIX
Lady, you wrong your value;
Call you him dear that has sold you so cheap?

LADY [*recognizing Phoenix and Fidelio*]
I do beseech your pardon, good my lord. [*Kneeling*]

PHOENIX
Rise.

FIDELIO
My abusèd mother.

LADY
My kind son, [*rising*]
Whose liking I neglected in this match.

FIDELIO
Not that alone, but your far happier fortunes.

CAPTAIN
Is this the scrivener and the farmer's son?
Fire on his lordship, he told me they travelled.

PHOENIX
And see the sum told out to buy that jewel
More precious in a woman than her eye, her honour.
Nay, take it to you, lady, and I judge it
Too slight a recompense for your great wrong,
But that his riddance helps it.

CAPTAIN
'Sfoot, he undoes me! I am a rogue and a beggar;
The Egyptian plague creeps over me already,
I begin to be lousy.

PHOENIX
Thus happily prevented, you're set free,
Or else made over to adultery.

LADY
To heaven and to you my modest thanks.

PHOENIX
Monster, to sea, spit thy abhorrèd foam,
Where it may do least harm—there's air and room.
Thou'rt dangerous in a chamber, virulent venom
Unto a lady's name and her chaste breath.
If past this evening's verge the dukedom hold thee,
Thou art reserved for abject punishment.

CAPTAIN I do beseech your good lordship, consider the state of a poor, downcast captain.

PHOENIX Captain? Off with that noble title; thou becomest it vilely. I ne'er saw the name fit worse; I'll sooner allow a pander a captain than thee.

CAPTAIN More's the pity.

PHOENIX Sue to thy lady for pardon.

LADY I give it without suit.

CAPTAIN I do beseech your ladyship not so much for pardon, as to bestow a few of those crowns upon a poor, unfeathered rover that will as truly pray for you—[*aside*] and wish you hanged—as any man breathing.

LADY
I give it freely all.

PHOENIX
Nay, by your favour,
I will contain you lady. [*Giving the Captain a few coins*]
Here, be gone.
Use slaves like slaves—wealth keeps their faults
unknown.

CAPTAIN
Well, I'm yet glad, I've liberty and these.
The land has plagued me, and I'll plague the seas.
Exit

PHOENIX
The scene is cleared, the bane of brightness fled;
Who sought the death of honour is struck dead.
Come, modest lady.

FIDELIO
My most honest mother.

PHOENIX
Thy virtue shall live safe from reach of shames.
That act ends nobly, preserves ladies' fames. *Exeunt*

Enter Justice Falso, Knight, and Jeweller's Wife Sc. 9

FALSO Why this is but the second time of your coming, kinsman. Visit me oftener. Daughter, I charge you bring this gentleman along with you. Gentleman? I cry ye mercy, sir! I call you gentleman still, I forget you're but a knight. You must pardon me, sir.

KNIGHT For your worship's kindness. Worship? I cry you mercy, sir. I call you worshipful still, I forget you're but a justice.

FALSO I am no more, i'faith.

KNIGHT You must pardon me, sir.

FALSO 'Tis quickly done, sir. You see I make bold with you, kinsman, thrust my daughter and you into one chamber.

KNIGHT Best of all, sir. Kindred, you know, may lie anywhere.

FALSO True, true, sir. Daughter, receive your blessing. Take heed the coach jopper not too much. Have a care to the fruits of your body—look to her, kinsman.

KNIGHT Fear it not, sir.

JEWELLER'S WIFE Nay, father, though I say it, that should not say it, he looks to me more like a husband than a kinsman.

FALSO I hear good commendations of you, sir.

KNIGHT You hear the worst of me, I hope, sir. I salute my leave, sir.

315 **Egyptian plague** (See Exodus 8:16–18)
339 **contain** restrain
9.3–5 **Gentleman? . . . knight** (another joke about the cheapening of the title; see 6.148)
6–8 **Worship? . . . justice** (The title belongs to a knight, but is questionable for a justice of the peace; Middleton satirizes the narrowing distance between the ranks.)
11 **make bold** take liberties
12 **kinsman** (Falso and the Knight are not really kinsmen, although they are morally akin. Falso's social-climbing adds a fiction of incest to the actual crimes of pandering and adultery.)
17 **coach** (Falso speaks as if his daughter and the Knight were about to leave on their wedding journey.)
jopper bump up and down
17–18 **Have . . . body** be careful not to get pregnant (but the same words might be used to tell a married woman to protect her lawful pregnancy)

FALSO You're welcome all over your body, sir.
[*Exeunt Knight and Jeweller's Wife*]
Nay, I can behave myself courtly, though I keep house i'th' country. What, does my niece hide herself? Not present, ha? Latronello!
[*Enter Latronello*]

LATRONELLO Sir.

FALSO Call my niece to me.

LATRONELLO Yes, sir. [*Exit*]

FALSO A foolish, coy, bashful thing it is. She's afraid to lie with her own uncle. I'd do her no harm i'faith. I keep myself a widower o' purpose, yet the foolish girl will not look into 't. She should have all, i'faith; she knows I have but a time, cannot hold long. See where she comes.
[*Enter Niece*]
Pray, whom am I, niece?

NIECE
I hope you're yourself,
Uncle to me and brother to my father.

FALSO O, am I so? It does not appear so, for surely you would love your father's brother for your father's sake, your uncle for your own sake.

NIECE I do so.

FALSO
Nay, you do nothing, niece.

NIECE
In that love which becomes you best, I love you.

FALSO
How should I know that love becomes me best?

NIECE
Because 'tis chaste and honourable.

FALSO
Honourable! It cannot become me then, niece,
For I'm scarce worshipful. Is this an age
To entertain bare love without the fruits?
When I received thee first, I looked
Thou shouldst have been a wife unto my house,
And saved me from the charge of marriage.
Do you think your father's five thousand pound would ha' made me take you else? No, you should ne'er ha' been a charge to me. As far as I can perceive yet by you, I've as much need to marry as e'er I had. Would not this be a great grief to your friends, think you, if they were alive again?

NIECE
'Twould be a grief indeed.

FALSO
You've confessed
All about house that young Fidelio,
Who in his travels does attend the prince,
Is your vowed love.

NIECE
Most true, he's my vowed husband.

FALSO And what's a husband? Is not a husband a stranger at first, and will you lie with a stranger before you lie with your own uncle? Take heed what ye do, niece, I counsel you for the best: strangers are drunken fellows, I can tell you. They will come home late o' nights, beat their wives, and get nothing but girls. Look to 't, if you marry, your stubbornness is your dowry. Five thousand crowns were bequeathed to you, true, if you marry with my consent, but if e'er you go to marrying by my consent, I'll go to hanging by yours. Go to, be wise and love your uncle.

NIECE
I should have cause then to repent indeed.
Do you so far forget the offices
Of blushing modesty? Uncles are half fathers.
Why, they come so near our bloods they're e'en part of it.

FALSO Why, now you come to me, niece. If your uncle be part of your own flesh and blood, is it not then fit your own flesh and blood should come nearest to you? Answer me to that, niece.

NIECE
You do allude all to incestuous will,
Nothing to modest purpose. Turn me forth,
Be like an uncle of these latter days,
Perjured enough, enough unnatural;
Play your executorship in tyranny,
Restrain my fortunes, keep me poor, I care not.
In this alone most women I'll excel,
I'll rather yield to beggary than to hell. *Exit*

FALSO Very good. O' my troth, my niece is valiant. She's made me richer by five thousand crowns, the price of her dowry. Are you so honest? I do not fear but I shall have the conscience to keep you poor enough, niece, or else I am quite altered o' late.
[*Enter Latronello*]
The news, may it please you, sir?

LATRONELLO Sir, there's an old fellow, a kind of law-driver, entreats conference with your worship.

26–7 **You're...courtly** (Falso makes an absurdly affected compliment, and then praises his own supposed sophistication.)
36 **should have all** would inherit my estate (if we marry and I then die)
50 **I'm scarce worshipful** ('Honourable' is an aristocratic title, while 'worshipful' pertains to the status of gentry, which he has barely attained. Falso makes the Niece's 'honourable' into a mere matter of social titles.)
54 **charge of marriage** (By marrying his own niece and ward, Falso would avoid the cost of paying her dowry to someone else.)
57 **by** from
59 **friends** relatives, her parents
71 **get** procreate
85 **will** sexual desire
87 **these...days** nowadays
94 **made me richer** (i.e., Falso gets to keep her dowry)
95 **honest** (*a*) law-abiding (*b*) chaste
99 **law-driver** (As Falso's repetition at 9.101 indicates, the phrase is Latronello's invention. Tangle drives the law as a coachman drives horses or an overseer drives slaves.)

FALSO A law-driver? Prithee, drive him hither. [*Exit Latronello*]

Enter Tangle [*with a Suitor*]

TANGLE [*to Suitor*] No, no I say, if it be for defect of appearance, take me out a special *significavit*.

SUITOR Very good, sir.

TANGLE Then if he purchase an *alias* or *capias*, which are writs of custom, only to delay time, your *procedendo* does you knight's service—that's nothing at all. Get your *distringas* out as soon as you can for a jury.

SUITOR I'll attend your good worship's coming out.

TANGLE Do, I prithee, attend me. I'll take it kindly, *a voluntate*. [*Exit Suitor*]

FALSO What, old signor Tangle!

TANGLE I am in debt to your worship's remembrance.

FALSO My old master of fence: come, come, come, I have not exercised this twelve moons; I have almost forgot all my law-weapons.

TANGLE They are under fine and recovery. Your worship shall easily recover them.

FALSO I hope so. [*To Latronello, within*] When there?

[*Enter Latronello*]

LATRONELLO Sir?

FALSO The rapier and dagger foils, instantly. [*Exit Latronello*]

And what's thy suit to me, old Tangle. I'll grant it presently.

TANGLE Nothing but this, sir, to set your worship's hand to the commendation of a knave whom nobody speaks well on.

FALSO The more shame for 'em. What was his offence, I pray?

TANGLE *Vestras deducite culpas*—nothing but robbing a vestry.

FALSO What, what! Alas, poor knave, give me the paper. He did but save the churchwardens a labour. Come, come, he has done a better deed in't than the parish is aware of, to prevent the knaves; he robs but seldom, they once a quarter. Methinks 'twere a part of good justice, to hang 'em at year's end, when they come out of their office, to the true terrifying of all collectors and sidemen.

TANGLE Your worship would make a fruitful commonwealth's man. The constable lets 'em alone, looks on, and says nothing.

FALSO Alas, good man, he lets 'em alone for quietness' sake, and takes half a share with 'em. They know well enough, too, he has an impediment in his tongue. He's always drunk when he should speak.

TANGLE Indeed, your worship speaks true in that, sir. They blind him with beer, and make him so narrow-eyed that he winks naturally at all their knaveries.

FALSO So, so, here's my hand to his commendations.

[*He signs the paper*]

TANGLE *A caritate*, you do a charitable deed in't, sir.

FALSO Nay, if it be but a vestry matter, visit me at any time, old signor law-thistle!

[*Enter Latronello with rapier and dagger foils*]

O, well done, here are the foils. [*Exit Latronello*]

Come, come, sir, I'll try a law-bout with you.

TANGLE I am afraid I shall overthrow you, sir, i'faith.

FALSO 'Tis but for want of use then, sir.

TANGLE Indeed, that same odd word, use, makes a man a good lawyer, and a woman an arrant. [*Takes some practice strokes*] Tuh, tuh, tuh, tuh, tuh, now am I for you, sir. But first to bring you into form, can your worship name all your weapons?

FALSO That I can, I hope. Let me see, longsword, what's longsword? I am so dulled with doing justice that I have forgot all i'faith.

TANGLE Your longsword, that's a writ of delay.

FALSO Mass, that sword's long enough, indeed. I ha' known it reach the length of fifteen terms.

TANGLE Fifteen terms, that's but a short sword.

FALSO Methinks 'tis long enough. Proceed, sir.

TANGLE A writ of delay, longsword. *Scandala magnatum*, backsword.

FALSO Scandals are backswords, indeed.

TANGLE *Capias comminus*, case of rapiers.

FALSO O, desperate!

102–3 **defect of appearance** failure to appear at a legal proceeding

103 ***significavit*** writ to stay a suit because of a prior excommunication alleged against the plaintiff

105 ***alias*** a second writ issued where one of the same kind has been issued before
capias a writ ordering the defendant's immediate arrest

106 **writs of custom** unwritten law
procedendo a writ issued by a superior court directing an inferior court to proceed to a final hearing

107 **knight's . . . nothing** (another jibe at the cheapening of aristocratic titles)

108 ***distringas*** a writ directing the sheriff to take a person's property and goods into custody to force compliance with an order

110–11 ***a voluntate*** at your pleasure

114 **fence** fencing (alluding to Tangle's ability to duel in law, which the rest of this scene makes literal)

117 **fine and recovery** (legal terms for the procedure of taking possession of property following a judicial verdict)

124 **hand** signature

129–30 ***Vestras*** . . . **vestry** reveal your own faults (with a pun on 'vestry', room where church vestments and sacred vessels are kept)

132 **churchwardens** laymen who execute a church's business

134 **prevent** anticipate

135 **quarter** quarter of a year, when rents and other quarterly charges are due

137–8 **collectors and sidemen** parish alms-collectors and the churchwardens' assistants

139–40 **commonwealth's man** good citizen (derived from derisive name given to radical reformers of the mid-sixteenth century)

150 ***A caritate*** for the sake of charity

152 **signor law-thistle** (Like the prickly plant, he hurts anyone who tries to handle him.)

157 **use** (*a*) practice (*b*) legal term for the right of one person to take the profits of land to which another has title (*c*) sexual intercourse

158 **arrant** notorious person (and implying 'errant', wandering)

167 **terms** periods when courts of law are in session

170 ***Scandala magnatum*** insulting words spoken about a peer or other great person of the realm

173 ***Capias comminus*** a writ ordering immediate arrest

TANGLE A *latitat*, sword and dagger. A writ of execution, rapier and dagger.

FALSO Thou art come to our present weapon, but what call you sword and buckler, then?

TANGLE O, that's out of use now! Sword and buckler was called a good conscience, but that weapon's left long ago. That was too manly a fight, too sound a weapon for these our days. 'Slid, we are scarce able to lift up a buckler now, our arms are so bound to the pox. One good bang upon a buckler would make most of our gentlemen fly i' pieces. 'Tis not for these linty times. Our lawyers are good rapier and dagger men; they'll quickly dispatch your—money.

FALSO Indeed, since sword and buckler time, I have observed, there has been nothing so much fighting. Where be all our gallant swaggerers? There are no good frays o' late.

TANGLE O, sir, the property's altered, you shall see less fighting every day than other, for everyone gets him a mistress, and she gives him wounds enough; and, you know, the surgeons cannot be here and there, too. If there were red wounds, too, what would become of the Rhenish wounds?

FALSO Thou sayst true, i'faith. They would be but ill-favouredly looked to then.

TANGLE Very well, sir.

FALSO I expect you, sir.

TANGLE I lie in this court for you, sir. My rapier is my attorney, and my dagger his clerk.

FALSO Your attorney wants a little oiling, methinks. He looks very rustily.

TANGLE 'Tis but his proper colour, sir. His father was an ironmonger. He will ne'er look brighter, the rust has so eat into him; he's never any leisure to be made clean.

FALSO Not in the vacation.

TANGLE *Non vacat exiguis rebus adesse Jovi.*

FALSO Then Jove will not be at leisure to scour him, because he ne'er came to him before.

TANGLE You're excellent at it, sir—and now you least think on't, I arrest you, sir.

[*Tangle thrusts at Falso, forcing him back*]

FALSO Very good, sir.

TANGLE Nay, very bad, sir, by my faith. I follow you still, as the officers will follow you as long as you have a penny.

FALSO You speak sentences, sir. By this time have I tried my friends, and now I thrust in bail—[*Lunges at Tangle*]

TANGLE [*parries*] This bail will not be taken, sir. They must be two citizens that are no cuckolds.

FALSO By'r Lady then I'm like to lie by it. I had rather 'twere a hundred that were.

TANGLE Take heed, I bring you not to a *Nisi prius*, sir.

FALSO I must ward myself as well as I may, sir.

TANGLE 'Tis court day now. *Declarat atturnatus*, my attorney gapes for money.

FALSO You shall have no advantage yet. I put in my answer.

TANGLE I follow the suit still, sir.

FALSO I like not this court, by'r Lady. I take me out a writ of remove, a writ of remove, do you see, sir?

TANGLE Very well, sir.

FALSO And place my cause higher.

TANGLE [*starts back*] There you started me, sir. Yet for all your demurs, *pluries*, and *sursurraras*, which are all longswords—that's delays—all the comfort is, in nine years a man may overthrow you.

FALSO You must thank your good friends then, sir.

TANGLE Let nine years pass, five hundred crowns cast away o' both sides, and the suit not twenty—my counsellor's wife must have another hood, you know, and my attorney's wife will have a new forepart—yet see at length law. I shall have law. Now beware, I bring you to a narrow exigent, and by no means can you avoid the proclamation—

[*Tangle knocks Falso's rapier from his hand*]

FALSO O!

TANGLE Now follows a writ of execution—a *capias utlagatum* gives you a wound mortal, trips up your heels, and lays you i'th' Counter. [*Overthrows him*]

FALSO O, villain!

175 ***latitat*** a writ summoning the defendant to appear before the so-called King's Bench
writ of execution order to the sheriff or other official to execute a legal judgement
178–9 **sword ... now** (Heavy swords and shields had been made old-fashioned by lighter rapiers and daggers.)
183 **pox** syphilis
185 **linty** soft (like lint or cotton fluff)
196 **red wounds** sexual wounds (i.e., symptoms of venereal disease)
197 **Rhenish wounds** (Rhenish wine is white; the 'wounds' are suppurating sores caused by venereal disease.)
202 **lie** wait
209 **vacation** time when law courts are not in session
210 ***Non ... Jovi*** 'Jove has no leisure to give heed to small things' (Ovid, *Tristia*, 2.216)
219 **sentences** wise sayings
223 **lie by it** stay in prison
225 ***Nisi prius*** a writ directing the sheriff to summon jurors
226 **ward** protect
227 ***Declarat atturnatus*** my attorney declares
232–3 **writ of remove** (i.e., to another court)
237 **demurs** motions to delay or suspend an action because of a point of difficulty which the court must decide
pluries a writ issued subsequently to a first and second of the same kind, which have proved ineffectual
sursurraras See 4.123
241–2 **five hundred ... twenty** five hundred crowns have been wasted in a cause worth less than twenty crowns
244 **forepart** ornamental covering for the breast
246 **exigent** a writ issued in the course of proceedings to declare a person an outlaw (immediately preceding the writ of *capias utlagatum*)
247 **proclamation** proclamation of outlawry (*utlagatum*)
249 **writ of execution** a writ to put in force the sentence that the law has given
249–50 ***capias utlagatum*** a writ commanding the officer to arrest an outlawed person
251 **Counter** name of two London prisons

TANGLE I cry your worship heartily mercy, sir. I thought we had been in law together, *adversarius contra adversarium*, by my troth.

FALSO O! Reach me thy hand, I ne'er had such an overthrow in my life.

TANGLE 'Twas long of your attorney there. He might 'a stayed the execution of *capias utlagatum*, and removed you with a *supersedeas non molestandum* into the court of equity.

FALSO Pox on him, he fell out of my hand when I had most need of him.

TANGLE I was bound to follow the suit, sir.

FALSO Thou couldst do no less than overthrow me. I must needs say so.

TANGLE You had recovered cost else, sir.

FALSO And now, by th' mass, I think I shall hardly recover without cost.

TANGLE Nay, that's *certo scio*—an execution is very chargeable.

FALSO Well, it shall teach me wit as long as I am a justice. I perceive by this trial if a man have a sound fall in law, he shall feel it in his bones all his life after.

TANGLE Nay, that's *recto* upon record, for I myself was overthrown in eighty-eight by a tailor, and I have had a stitch in my side ever since—O! *Exeunt*

c. 10

Toward the close of the music, the justice's three men prepare for a robbery, [*and exeunt*]
Enter Justice Falso, untrussed

FALSO Why, Latronello, Furtivo, Fucato—where be these lazy knaves that should truss me, not one stirring yet?

A CRY WITHIN Follow, follow, follow!

FALSO What news there?

A CRY WITHIN This way, this way, follow, follow!

FALSO Hark, you sluggish soporiferous villains. There's knaves abroad when you are a-bed. Are you not ashamed on't? A justice's men should be up first and give example to all knaves.

Enter two of his men, tumbling in, in false beards

LATRONELLO O, I beseech your good worship.

FUCATO Your worshipful worship.

FALSO Thieves, my two-hand sword! I'm robbed i'th' hall! Latronello, knaves, come down! My two-hand sword, I say!

LATRONELLO I am Latronello, I beseech your worship.

FALSO Thou Latronello? Thou liest. My men scorn to have beards.

LATRONELLO We forget our beards.
[*They take off their false beards*]
Now, I beseech your worship, quickly remember us.

FALSO How now?

FUCATO Nay, there's no time to talk of how now—'tis done.

A CRY WITHIN Follow, follow, follow.

LATRONELLO Four mark and a livery is not able to keep life and soul together. We must fly out once a quarter; 'tis for your worship's credit to have money in our purse. Our fellow Furtivo is taken in the action.

FALSO A pox on him for a lazy knave. Would he be taken?

FUCATO They bring him along to your worship; you're the next justice. Now or never show yourself a good master, an upright magistrate, and deliver him out of their hands.

FALSO Nay, he shall find me—apt enough to do him good, I warrant him.

LATRONELLO He comes in a false beard, sir.

FALSO 'Sfoot, what should he do here else? There's no coming to me in a true one, if he had one. The slave to be taken! Do I not keep geldings swift enough?

LATRONELLO The goodliest geldings of any gentleman in the shire.

FALSO Which did the whoreson knave ride upon?

LATRONELLO Upon one of your best, sir.

FUCATO Stand-and-Deliver.

FALSO Upon Stand-and-Deliver? The very gelding I choose for mine own riding, as nimble as Pegasus the flying horse yonder. Go shift yourselves into your coats, bring hither a great chair and a little table.

FUCATO With all present speed, sir.

FALSO And Latronello—

LATRONELLO Ay, sir.

FALSO Sit you down and very soberly take the examination.

LATRONELLO I'll draw a few horse heads in a paper, make a show. I hope I shall keep my countenance.
[*Exeunt Latronello and Fucato*]

FALSO Pox on him again. Would he be taken? He frets me. I have been a youth myself. I ha' seen the day I could have told money out of other men's purses—mass, so I can do now—nor will I keep that fellow about me that dares not bid a man stand, for as long as drunkenness is a vice, stand is a virtue. But I would not have 'em taken. I remember now betimes in a morning I would have peeped through the green boughs and have had the party presently, and then to ride away finely in fear;

254–5 ***adversarius contra adversarium*** adversary against adversary
258 **long of** because of
260 ***supersedeas non molestandum*** See 4.72–3
260–1 **court of equity** a system of English law existing, at this time, side by side with the court of common law and, on occasion, superseding it
270 ***certo scio*** I know it for certain
275 ***recto*** right
276 **eighty-eight** See 4.83
10.0.1 ***music*** the music being played during interval between the acts of a play in the indoor theatres. (No act divisions are indicated in the text.)
0.3 ***untrussed*** with the laces of his breeches undone
1 **Fucato** disguised
6 **soporiferous** sleepy
12 **two-hand sword** a large, heavy sword requiring two hands to wield
23 **mark** a coin worth 13*s.* 4*d.* or 2/3 of the pound sterling
livery the clothing and/or food dispensed to retainers or servants
29 **next** nearest
50–1 **examination** interrogation
56 **told** count
58–9 **drunkenness...virtue** (because one who is drunk cannot stand up; also, one who is drunk may become sexually impotent)

'twas e'en venery to me, i'faith, the pleasantest course of life. One would think every woodcock a constable and every owl an officer. But those days are past with me. And, o' my troth, I think I am a greater thief now and in no danger. I can take my ease, sit in my chair, look in your faces now, and rob you, make you bring your money by authority, put off your hat, and thank me for robbing of you. O, there is nothing to a thief under covert baron.

Enter Phoenix, Fidelio [disguised in robes], Constable, Officers, and the thief Furtivo

CONSTABLE Come, officers, bring him away.

FALSO [*aside*] Nay, I see thee through thy false beard, thou mid-wind-chined rascal! [*To Constable and Officers*] How now, my masters, what's he? Ha?

CONSTABLE Your worship knows, I never come but I bring a thief with me.

FALSO Thou hast left thy wont else, constable.

PHOENIX Sir, we understand you to be the only uprightness of this place.

FALSO But I scarce understand you, sir.

PHOENIX Why, then you understand not yourself, sir.

FALSO Such another word, and you shall change places with the thief.

PHOENIX A maintainer of equal causes, I mean.

FALSO Now I have you. Proceed, sir.

PHOENIX This gentleman and myself, being led hither by occasion of business, have been offered the discourtesy of the country, set upon by three thieves, and robbed.

FALSO What are become of the other two? Latronello and Fucato!

LATRONELLO [*within*] Here, sir!

PHOENIX They both made away from us, the cry pursues 'em, but as yet none but this taken.

[*Enter Latronello and Fucato, with chair and table*]

FALSO Latronello.

LATRONELLO Sir?

FALSO Take his examination.

LATRONELLO Yes, sir.

FALSO Let the knave stand single.

FURTIVO Thank your good worship.

FALSO He's been a suitor at court, sure. He thanks me for nothing.

PHOENIX He's a thief now, sure.

FALSO That we must know of him. What are you, sir?

FURTIVO A piece next to the tail, sir—a servingman.

FALSO By my troth, a pretty phrase and very cleanly handled. Put it down, Latronello. Thou mayst make use on't. Is he of honour or worship whom thou servest?

FURTIVO Of both, dear sir—honourable in mind, and worshipful in body.

FALSO Why would one wish a man to speak better?

PHOENIX O, sir, they most commonly speak best that do worst.

FALSO Say you so, sir? Then we'll try him further. Does your right worshipful master go before you as an example of vice, and so encourage you to this slinking iniquity? He is not a lawyer, is he?

FURTIVO He's the more wrong, sir. Both for his conscience and honesty, he deserves to be one.

FALSO Pity he's a thief, i'faith. I should entertain him else.

PHOENIX Ay, if he were not as he is, he would be better than himself.

FURTIVO No, 'tis well known, sir, I have a master the very picture of wisdom.

LATRONELLO [*aside*] For indeed he speaks not one wise word.

FURTIVO And no man but will admire to hear of his virtues.

LATRONELLO [*aside*] Because he ne'er had any in all his life.

FALSO You write all down, Latronello.

LATRONELLO I warrant you, sir.

FURTIVO So sober, so discreet, so judicious.

FALSO Hum.

FURTIVO And above all, of most reverend gravity.

FALSO I like him for one quality, he speaks well of his master; he will fare the better. Now, sir, let me touch you.

FURTIVO Ay, sir.

FALSO Why, serving a gentleman of such worship and wisdom, such sobriety and virtue, such discretion and judgement as your master is, do you take such a beastly course, to stop horses, hinder gentlewomen from their meetings, and make citizens never ride but o' Sundays, only to avoid morning prayer and you? Is it because your worshipful master feeds you with lean spits, pays you with Irish money, or clothes you in northern dozens?

FURTIVO Far be it from his mind, or my report. 'Tis well known he kept worshipful cheer the day of his wife's burial, pays our four marks a year as duly by twelve pence a quarter as can be.

PHOENIX [*aside*] His wisdom swallows it.

FURTIVO And for northern dozens—fie, fie, we were ne'er troubled with so many.

FALSO Receiving then such plenteous blessings from your virtuous and bountiful master, what cause have you to be thief now? Answer me to that gear.

FURTIVO 'Tis e'en as a man gives his mind to't, sir.

63 **venery** a source of great enjoyment; the indulgence of sexual desire

71 **covert baron** A legal term meaning that a wife is under the protection of her husband. (Falso means that it is easy to be a thief when you are protected by judicial authority.)

74 **mid-wind-chined** *Mid-wind* refers to one's breathing capacity, and *chined* is short for mourning of the chine, a horse desease.

79 **uprightness** a just person

85 **equal causes** impartial

97 **Take . . . examination** write down his interrogation

120 **entertain** hire

127 **admire** marvel

135 **touch** test (to test the purity of gold or silver by rubbing it upon a touchstone)

145 **Irish money** debased coins which the English imposed on Ireland from 1601 to 1603

145–6 **northern dozens** coarse woollen cloth

149 **marks** (one mark is worth 160 pence)

156 **gear** matter, business

FALSO How, sir?

FURTIVO For alas, if the whole world were but of one trade, traffic were nothing. If we were all true men, we should be of no trade. What a pitiful world would here be. Heaven forbid we should be all true men: then how should your worship's next suit be made? Not a tailor left in the land. Of what stuff would you have it made? Not a merchant left to deliver it—would your worship go in that suit still? You would ha' more thieves about you than those you have banished, and be glad to call the great ones home again to destroy the little.

PHOENIX A notable rogue.

FALSO O' my troth, a fine knave, and he's answered me gloriously. What wages wilt thou take after thou art hanged?

FURTIVO More than your worship's able to give. I would think foul scorn to be a justice then.

FALSO [*aside*] He says true, too, i'faith, for we are all full of corruption here—Hark you, my friends.

PHOENIX Sir?

FALSO By my troth, if you were no crueller than I, I could find in my heart to let him go.

PHOENIX Could you so, sir? The more pitiful justice you.

FALSO Nay, I did but to try you. If you have no pity, I'll ha' none. Away! He's a thief—to prison with him.

FURTIVO I am content, sir.

FALSO Are you content? Bring him back. Nay, then you shall not go. I'll be as cruel as you can wish. You're content? Belike you have a trick to break prison, or a bribe for the officers.

CONSTABLE For us, sir?

FALSO For you, sir? What colour's silver, I pray? You ne'er saw money in your life. I'll not trust you with him. Latronello and Fucato, lay hold upon him. To your charge I commit him.

FURTIVO O, I beseech you, sir.

FALSO Nay, if I must be cruel, I will be cruel.

FURTIVO Good sir, let me rather go to prison.

FALSO You desire that? I'll trust no prison with you. I'll make you lie in mine own house, or I'll know why I shall not.

FURTIVO Merciful sir.

FALSO Since you have no pity, I will be cruel.

PHOENIX Very good, sir. You please us well.

FALSO You shall appear tomorrow, sirs.

FURTIVO Upon my knees, sir.

FALSO You shall be hanged out o' th' way. Away with him, Latronello and Fucato. Officers, I discharge you my house; I like not your company.
Report me as you see me, fire and fuel;
If men be Jews, justices must be cruel.

Exeunt. [*Manent Phoenix and Fidelio*]

PHOENIX
So, sir, extremes set off all actions thus:
Either too tame, or else too tyrannous.
He being bent to fury, I doubt now
We shall not gain access unto your love,
Or she to us.

FIDELIO Most wishfully, here she comes.

Enter Niece

PHOENIX
Is that she?

FIDELIO This is she, my lord.

PHOENIX
A modest presence.

FIDELIO Virtue bless you, lady.

NIECE
You wish me well, sir.

FIDELIO
I'd first encharge this kiss, and next this paper;
You'll know the language, 'tis Fidelio's.

NIECE
My ever vowèd love! How is his health?

FIDELIO
As fair as is his favour with the prince.

NIECE
I'm sick with joy. Does the prince love him so?

FIDELIO
His life cannot requite it.
Not to wrong the remembrance of his love,
I had a token for you, kept it safe,
Till by misfortune of the way this morning
Thieves set upon this gentleman and myself,
And with the rest robbed that.

NIECE O me, I'm dearly
Sorry for your chance. Was it your loss?
They boldly look you in the face that robbed you;
No further villains than my uncle's men.

PHOENIX
What, lady?

NIECE 'Tis my grief I speak so true.

FIDELIO
Why, my lord!

PHOENIX
But give me pausing, lady. Was he one
That took the examination?

NIECE One and the chief.

PHOENIX
Henceforth hang him that is no way a thief:
Then I hope few will suffer.
Nay, all the jest was, he committed him
To the charge of his fellows, and the rogue
Made it lamentable, cried to leave 'em.
None live so wise but fools may once deceive 'em.

FIDELIO
An uncle so insatiate?

160 **traffic** commerce
162 **true** honest
208 **Jews** (Jews were stereotyped as strict interpreters of the law.)
211 **doubt** fear
213 **wishfully** according to wish or desire
217 **encharge** give in charge
228 **chance** unfortunate event

PHOENIX Ay, is't not strange, too,
That all should be by nature vicious,
And he bad against nature?

NIECE
Then you have heard the sum of all my wrongs.

PHOENIX
Lady, we have, and desire rather now
To heal 'em than to hear 'em.
For by a letter from Fidelio
Direct to us, we are entreated jointly
To hasten your remove from this foul den
Of theft and purposed incest.

NIECE I rejoice
In his chaste care of me; I'll soon be furnished.

FIDELIO
He writes that his return cannot be long.

NIECE
I'm chiefly glad. But whither is the place?

PHOENIX
To the safe seat of his late wrongèd mother.

NIECE
I desire it.
Her conference will fit mine; well you prevail.

PHOENIX
At next grove we'll expect you.

NIECE I'll not fail. *Exeunt*

Sc. 11 *Enter Knight and Jeweller's Wife*

KNIGHT It stands upon the frame of my reputation, I protest, lady.

JEWELLER'S WIFE Lady—that word is worth an hundred angels at all times, for it cost more. If I live till tomorrow night, my sweet Pleasure, thou shalt have them.

KNIGHT Could you not make 'em a hundred and fifty, think you?

JEWELLER'S WIFE I'll do my best endeavour to multiply, I assure you.

KNIGHT Could you not make 'em two hundred?

JEWELLER'S WIFE No, by my faith—

KNIGHT Peace, I'll rather be confined in the hundred and fifty.

JEWELLER'S WIFE Come e'en much about this time, when taverns give up their ghosts and gentlemen are in their first cast—

KNIGHT I'll observe the season.

JEWELLER'S WIFE And do but whirl the ring o'th' door once about. My maid-servant shall be taught to understand the language.

KNIGHT Enough, my sweet Revenue.

JEWELLER'S WIFE Good rest, my effectual Pleasure. *Exeunt*

Enter Proditor and Phoenix, [*the latter in disguise*] Sc. 1

PRODITOR Come hither, Phoenix.

PHOENIX What makes your honour break so early?

PRODITOR A toy, I have a toy.

PHOENIX A toy, my lord?

PRODITOR Before thou layest thy wrath upon the duke,
Be advised.

PHOENIX Ay, ay, I warrant you, my lord.

PRODITOR
Nay, give my words honour; hear me.
I'll strive to bring this act into such form
And credit amongst men, they shall suppose,
Nay, verily believe the prince his son
To be the plotter of his father's murder.

PHOENIX
O, that were infinitely admirable!

PRODITOR
Were't not? It pleaseth me beyond my bliss.
Then if his son meet death as he returns,
Or by my hired instruments turn up,
The general voice will cry. O happy vengeance!

PHOENIX
O blessed vengeance!

PRODITOR Ay, I'll turn my brain
Into a thousand uses, tire my inventions,
Make my blood sick with study, and mine eye
More hollow than my heart, but I will fashion,
Nay, I will fashion it. Canst counterfeit?

PHOENIX
The prince's hand? More truly, most direct;
You shall admire it.

PRODITOR Necessary mischief:
Next to a woman, but more close in secrets,
Thou'rt all the kindred that my breast vouchsafes.
Look into me anon. I must frame, and muse, and fashion.

Exit

PHOENIX
'Twas time to look into thee, in whose heart
Treason grows ripe, and therefore fit to fall.
That slave first sinks whose envy threatens all.
Now is his venom at full height.

Voices within

FIRST VOICE Lying or being in the said country in the tenure and occupation aforesaid—

243 **bad...nature** unnatural, immoral. (The incestuous Falso hopes to violate the customary relationship between uncle and niece.)
251 **furnished** provided for
254 **seat** residence
11.1 **stands upon the frame** is a matter of
4 **angels** gold coins worth ten shillings each
it (i.e., the title 'Lady')
8 **multiply** (*a*) get more money (*b*) have children
15 **give up their ghosts** closing time
16 **cast** vomit
22 **effectual** productive
12.1 **Phoenix** An error in the text: Proditor does not know the true identity of the disguised Phoenix.
2 **break** rise (like the sun at break of day)
3 **toy** an idle fancy or whim
15 **instruments** (men in Proditor's service)
turn up overthrow
19 **Make...study** (Too much study was thought to have an ill effect on the body.)
20 **fashion** contrive
31–2 **tenure...occupation** ownership, possession

SECOND VOICE No more, then. A writ of course upon the matter of—

THIRD VOICE Silence!

FOURTH VOICE Oho, O, O, yes! Carlo Turbulenzo, appear, or lose twenty mark in the suits.

PHOENIX Ha? Whither have my thoughts conveyed me? I am now within the dizzy murmur of the law.

FIRST VOICE So that then, the cause being found clear, upon the last citation—

FOURTH VOICE Carlo Turbulenzo, come into the court.

Enter Tangle with two [*Suitors*] *after him*

TANGLE Now, now, now, now, now, upon my knees I praise Mercury, the god of law, I have two suits at issue, two suits at issue.

FIRST SUITOR Do you hear, sir?

TANGLE I will not hear. I've other business.

FIRST SUITOR I beseech you, my learned counsel.

TANGLE Beseech not me, beseech not me. I am a mortal man, a client as you are. Beseech not me.

FIRST SUITOR I would do all by your worship's direction.

TANGLE Then hang thyself.

SECOND SUITOR Shall I take out a special *supplicavit?*

TANGLE Mad me not, torment me not, tear me not. You'll give me leave to hear mine own cause, mine own cause.

FIRST VOICE [*within*] Nay, moreover, and further—

TANGLE Well said, my lawyer, well said, well said.

FIRST VOICE [*within*] All the opprobrious speeches that man could invent, all malicious invectives, called wittol to his face.

TANGLE That's I, that's I. Thank you my learned counsel for your good remembrance. I hope I shall overthrow him horse and foot.

FIRST SUITOR Nay, but good sir.

TANGLE No more, sir. He that brings me happy news first, I'll relieve first.

BOTH SUITORS Sound executions rot thy cause and thee.

Exeunt

TANGLE Ay, ay, ay, pray so still, pray so still. They'll thrive the better.

PHOENIX I wonder how this fellow keeps out madness? What stuff his brains are made on?

TANGLE I suffer, I suffer, till I hear a judgement.

PHOENIX What, old signor?

TANGLE Prithee, I will not know thee now. 'Tis a busy time, a busy time with me.

PHOENIX What, not me, signor?

TANGLE O, cry thee mercy. Give me thy hand—fare thee well. He's no relief against me, then. His demurs will not help him, his *sursurraras* will but play the knaves with him.

Enter Justice Falso

PHOENIX The justice—'tis he.

FALSO Have I found thee, i'faith? I thought where I should smell thee out, old Tangle.

TANGLE What, old signor justicer—embrace me another time, an you can possibly. How does all thy wife's children?—well? That's well said, i'faith.

FALSO Hear me, old Tangle. [*Taking hold of him*]

TANGLE Prithee, do not ravish me. Let me go.

FALSO I must use some of thy counsel first.

TANGLE Sirrah, I ha' brought him to an exigent. Hark, that's my cause, that's my cause yonder. I twinged him, I twinged him.

FALSO My niece is stolen away.

TANGLE Ah, get me a *ne exeat regno* quickly. Nay, you must not stay upon 't. I'd fain have you gone.

FALSO A *ne exeat regno*. I'll about it presently—adieu.

[*Exit*]

PHOENIX You seek to catch her, justice? She'll catch you.

Enter First Suitor

FIRST SUITOR A judgement, a judgement!

TANGLE What, what, what?

FIRST SUITOR Overthrown, overthrown, overthrown.

TANGLE Ha, ah, ah.

Enter Second Suitor

SECOND SUITOR News, news, news.

TANGLE The devil, the devil, the devil!

SECOND SUITOR Twice Tangle's overthrown, twice Tangle's overthrown!

TANGLE Hold!

PHOENIX Now, old cheater of the law—

TANGLE Pray, give me leave to be mad.

PHOENIX Thou that hast found such sweet pleasure in the vexation of others.

TANGLE May I not be mad in quiet?

PHOENIX Very marrow, very manna to thee to be in law.

TANGLE Very syrup of toads and preserved adders.

PHOENIX Thou that hast vexed and beggared the whole parish, and made the honest churchwardens go to law with the poor's money.

TANGLE Hear me, do but hear me. I pronounce a terrible, horrible curse upon you all—and wish you to

33 **writ of course** an ordinary, customary writ
36 **Turbulenzo** troublemaker (Italian)
40 **cause** the case of one party in a suit
41 **citation** a reference to decided cases
44 **Mercury** (In Elizabethan comedy and rogue literature, he was usually the lightfooted protector of thieves.)
53 ***supplicavit*** a writ issuing out of the King's Bench or the Court of Chancery for taking surety of the peace against a person
59 **wittol** a man who knows of his wife's adultery and tolerates it
63 **horse and foot** completely
66 **relieve** free from an obligation
71 **on** of
79 ***sursurraras*** (see 4.123)
85 **an** if
91 **twinged** pinched, tweaked
94 ***ne exeat regno*** let him not leave the kingdom (a writ of restraint)
109–10 **Thou...others** (see 4.117–18)
112 **Very marrow, very manna** physical and spiritual nourishment; (see 4.116)
113 **preserved** kept in one's possession
114–16 **Thou...money** (see 4.150–1)
118–19 **wish...attorney** (a variation on 'wish you to the devil')

my attorney. See where a *praemunire* comes, a *dedimus potestatem*, and that most dreadful execution, *excommunicato capiendo*. There's no bail to be taken, I shall rot in fifteen jails. Make dice of my bones, and let my counsellor's son play away his father's money with 'em: may my bones revenge my quarrel! A *capias comminus*? Here, here, here, here: quickly dip your quills in my blood, off with my skin, and write fourteen lines of a side. There's an honest conscionable fellow; he takes but ten shillings of a bellows-mender. Here's another deals all with charity; you shall give him nothing, only his wife an embroidered petticoat, a gold fringe for her tail, or a border for her head. Ah, sirrah! You shall catch me no more in the springe of your knaveries. *Exit*

FIRST SUITOR Follow, follow him still. A little thing now sets him forward. *[Exeunt Suitors]*

PHOENIX
None can except against him. The man's mad
And privileged by the moon, if he say true:
Less madness 'tis to speak sin than to do.
This wretch that loved before his food his strife,
This punishment falls even with his life.
His pleasure was vexation, all his bliss
The torment of another.
Their heart, his health, their starvèd hopes his store:
Who so loves law dies either mad or poor.

Enter Fidelio

FIDELIO
A miracle, a miracle!
PHOENIX
How now, Fidelio?
FIDELIO
My lord, a miracle!
PHOENIX
What is't?
FIDELIO
I have found
One quiet, suffering, and unlawyered man,
An opposite, a very contrary
To the old turbulent fellow.
PHOENIX
Why, he's mad.

FIDELIO Mad? Why, he is in his right wits. Could he be madder than he was? If he be any way altered from what he was, 'tis for the better, my lord.

PHOENIX Well, but where's this wonder?

FIDELIO 'Tis coming, my lord, a man so truly a man, so indifferently a creature, using the world in his right nature but to tread upon; one that would not bruise the cowardliest enemy to man, the worm, that dares not show his malice till we are dead. Nay, my lord, you will admire his temper! See where he comes.
I promised your acquaintance, sir. Yon is
The gentleman I did commend for temper.

Enter Quieto

QUIETO
Let me embrace you simply,
That's perfectly, and more in heart than hand;
Let affectation keep at court.
PHOENIX
Ay, let it.
QUIETO
'Tis told me you love quiet.
PHOENIX
Above wealth.
QUIETO
Ay, above life. I have been wild and rash,
Committed many and unnatural crimes,
Which I have since repented.
PHOENIX
'Twas well spent.
QUIETO
I was mad, stark mad, nine years together.
PHOENIX
I pray! As how?
QUIETO
Going to law. I'faith, it made me mad.
PHOENIX
With the like frenzy, not an hour since
An aged man was struck.
QUIETO
Alas, I pity him.
PHOENIX
He's not worth pitying, for 'twas still his gladness
To be at variance.
QUIETO
Yet, a man's worth pity.
My quiet blood has blessed me with this gift:
I have cured some, and if his wits be not
Too deeply cut, I will assay to help 'em.
PHOENIX
Sufferance does teach you pity.

Enter his Boy

BOY O, master, master, your abominable next neighbour came into the house, being half in drink, and took away your best carpet.

QUIETO Has he it?

BOY Alas, sir.

QUIETO Let him go, trouble him not. Lock the door quietly after him, and have a safer care who comes in next.

PHOENIX But, sir, might I advise you, in such a cause as this a man might boldly, nay, with conscience, go to law.

QUIETO O, I'll give him the table too first. Better endure a fist than a sharp sword. I had rather they should pull

119 ***praemunire*** *praemunire facias*, a writ summoning a person accused
119–20 ***dedimus potestatem*** we have given the power; a writ empowering one who is not a judge to do some act in place of a judge
120–1 ***excommunicato capiendo*** a write of arrest for someone who stands excommunicated for forty days
124 **quarrel** cause
capias comminus a writ ordering the defendant's immediate arrest
127–8 **ten shillings** (For a bellows-mender, ten shillings would be at least two weeks' wages.)
130 **tail** the bottom of a gown that reaches nearly to the ground
131 **border** ornamental work around the edge of a cap
135 **except** take exception
136 **privileged...moon** exempt by reason of lunacy
142 **store** possessions
154 **his** its
160.1 ***Quieto*** quiet, calm
177 **assay** attempt
178 **Sufferance** suffering
181 **carpet** tablecloth

off my clothes than flay off my skin and hang that on mine enemy's hedge.

PHOENIX
Why, for such good causes was the law ordained.

QUIETO
True, and in itself 'tis glorious and divine—
Law is the very masterpiece of heaven.
But see yonder.
There's many clouds between the sun and us,
There's too much cloth before we see the law.

PHOENIX
I'm content with that answer. Be mild still,
'Tis honour to forgive those you could kill.

QUIETO
There do I keep.

PHOENIX
Reach me your hand. I love you,
And you shall know me better.

QUIETO
'Tis my suit.

PHOENIX
The night grows deep, and—

Enter two Officers

FIRST OFFICER Come away, this way, this way.

PHOENIX Who be those? Stand close a little.

[*As they retire,*] *Phoenix jars the ring of the door; the Maid enters, catches him*

MAID O, you're come as well as e'er you came in your life. My master's new gone to bed. Give me your knightly hand, I must lead you into the blind parlour. My mistress will be down to you presently.

She takes in Phoenix, amazed

FIRST OFFICER I tell you our safest course will be to arrest him when he comes out o'th' tavern, for then he will be half drunk, and will not stand upon his weapon.

SECOND OFFICER Our safest course, indeed, for he will draw.

FIRST OFFICER That he will, though he put it up again, which is more of his courtesy than of our deserving.

Exeunt [*Officers*]

QUIETO
The world is nothing but vexation,
Spite, and uncharitable action.

FIDELIO
Did you see the gentleman?

QUIETO
Not I.

FIDELIO
Where should he be? It may be he's passed by.
Good sir, let's overtake him. *Exeunt*

Sc. 13

Enter Phoenix with the Maid

MAID Here, sir, now you are there, sir. She'll come down to you instantly. I must not stay with you—my mistress would be jealous. You must do nothing to me, my mistress would find it quickly. *Exit*

PHOENIX 'Sfoot, whither am I led? brought in by th' hand? I hope it can be no harm to stay for a woman, though indeed they were never more dangerous. I have ventured hitherto and safe, and I must venture to stay now. This should be a fair room, but I see it not: the blind parlour calls she it?

Enter Jeweller's Wife

JEWELLER'S WIFE Where art thou? O, my knight!

PHOENIX Your knight? I am the duke's knight.

JEWELLER'S WIFE I say you're my knight, for I'm sure I paid for you.

PHOENIX Paid for you? Hum—'Sfoot, a light!

[*Phoenix lights a candle; Jeweller's Wife extinguishes it*]

JEWELLER'S WIFE Now out upon the marmoset. Hast thou served me so long, and offer to bring in a candle?

PHOENIX [*aside*] Fair room, villainous face, and worse woman. I ha' learned something by a glimpse o'th' candle.

JEWELLER'S WIFE How happened it you came so soon? I looked not for you these two hours. Yet, as the sweet chance is, you came as well as a thing could come, for my husband's newly brought abed.

PHOENIX And what has Jove sent him?

JEWELLER'S WIFE He ne'er sent him anything since I knew him. He's a man of a bad nature to his wife; none but his maids can thrive under him.

PHOENIX Out upon him.

JEWELLER'S WIFE Ay, judge whether I have a cause to be a courtesan or no? to do as I do? An elderly fellow as he is, if he were married to a young virgin, he were able to break her heart, though he could break nothing else. Here, here, there's just a hundred and fifty. [*Giving money*] But I stole 'em so hardly from him, 'twould e'en have grieved you to have seen it.

PHOENIX So 'twould, i'faith.

JEWELLER'S WIFE Therefore, prithee, my sweet Pleasure, do not keep company so much. How do you think I am able to maintain you? Though I be a jeweller's wife, jewels are like women: they rise and fall. We must be content to lose sometimes to gain often, but you're

198 **too much cloth** too many lawyers (here referred to by their professional garb)
205 **close** (i.e., close to the wall of the Jeweller's house)
208 **blind** windowless
212 **stand upon** rely on
13.16 **marmoset** monkey
25 **what . . . him** (Phoenix assumes that the Jeweller has been 'brought abed' with an illness; the Jeweller's Wife continues the exchange in a sexual vein, suggesting his sterility or impotence.)
26–7 **knew him** had sexual relations with him
27–8 **bad . . . him** (Her husband is sexually incompetent with her but not with the maid-servants.)
31 **courtesan** in this usage, a mistress or a woman who has extramarital sexual relations
33–4 **nothing else** (i.e., her hymen)
35 **hardly** with difficulty
41 **rise and fall** (i.e., in price [jewels] and sexually [women])

content always to lose and never to gain. What need you ride with a footman before you?

PHOENIX O, that's the grace.

JEWELLER'S WIFE The grace? 'Tis sufficient grace that you've a horse to ride upon. You should think thus with yourself every time you go to bed: if my head were laid, what would become of that horse? He would run a bad race then, as well as his master.

PHOENIX Nay, an you give me money to chide me—

JEWELLER'S WIFE No, if it were as much more, I would think it foul scorn to chide you. I advise you to be thrifty, to take the time now, while you have it. You shall seldom get such another fool as I am, I warrant you. Why, there's Metrezza Aureola keeps her love with half the cost that I am at. Her friend can go afoot like a good husband, walk in worsted stockings, and inquire for the sixpenny ordinary.

PHOENIX Pox on't, and would you have me so base?

JEWELLER'S WIFE No, I would not have you so base neither. But now and then, when you keep your chamber, you might let your footman out for eighteen pence a day—a great relief at year's end, I can tell you.

PHOENIX [*aside*] The age must needs be foul when vice reforms it.

JEWELLER'S WIFE Nay, I've a greater quarrel to you yet.

PHOENIX I'faith, what is't?

JEWELLER'S WIFE You made me believe at first the prince had you in great estimation, and would not offer to travel without you—nay, that he could not travel without your direction and intelligence.

PHOENIX I'm sorry I said so, i'faith, but sure I was overflown when I spoke it. I could ne'er have said it else.

JEWELLER'S WIFE Nay, more: you swore to me that you were the first that taught him to ride a great horse and tread the ring with agility.

PHOENIX By my troth, I must needs confess I swore a great lie in that, and I was a villain to do it, for I could ne'er ride great horse in my life.

JEWELLER'S WIFE Why lo, who would love you now but a citizen's wife?—so inconstant, so forsworn! You say women are false creatures, but take away men and they'd be honester than you. Nay, last of all, which offends me most of all, you told me you could countenance me at court, and you know we esteem a friend there more worth than a husband here.

PHOENIX What I spake of that, lady, I'll maintain.

JEWELLER'S WIFE You maintain? You seen at court?

PHOENIX Why, by this diamond—

JEWELLER'S WIFE O, take heed, you cannot have that; 'tis always in the eye of my husband.

PHOENIX I protest I will not keep it, but only use it for this virtue: as a token to fetch you and approve my power, where you shall not only be received, but made known to the best and chiefest.

JEWELLER'S WIFE O, are you true?

PHOENIX Let me lose my Revenue else.

JEWELLER'S WIFE That's your word indeed, and upon that condition take it, this kiss, and my love forever.

PHOENIX Enough!

JEWELLER'S WIFE Give me thy hand, I'll lead thee forth.

PHOENIX [*aside*]
I'm sick of all professions. My thoughts burn.
He travels best that knows when to return. *Exeunt*

Enter Knight, two Officers after him Sc. 14

KNIGHT Adieu, farewell, to bed you, I to my sweet city-bird, my precious Revenue. The very thought of a hundred and fifty angels increases oil and spirit, ho!

FIRST OFFICER [*catching him*] I arrest you, sir.

KNIGHT O!

FIRST OFFICER You have made us wait a goodly time for you. Have you not, think you? You are in your rouses and mullwines—a pox on you!—and have no care of poor officers staying for you.

KNIGHT I drunk but one health, I protest, but I could void it now. At whose suit, I pray?

FIRST OFFICER At the suit of him that makes suits, your tailor.

KNIGHT Why, he made me the last—this, this that I wear.

FIRST OFFICER Argo! Nay, we have been scholars, I can tell you. We could not have been knaves so soon else, for as in that notable city called London stand two most famous universities, Poultry and Wood Street, where some are of twenty years' standing, and have took all their degrees from the master's side down to the mistress' side, the Hole, so in like manner—

KNIGHT Come, come, come, I had quite forgot the hundred and fifty angels.

SECOND OFFICER 'Slid, where be they?

KNIGHT I'll bring you to the sight of 'em presently.

45 **grace** stylish touch
48–9 **if...laid** if I were dead
56 **Metrezza** Miss (in pseudo-Italian) **Aureola** halo (Italian)
58 **worsted** woollen
59 **sixpenny ordinary** inexpensive tavern
62 **keep your chamber** stay at home
74 **overflown** drunk
77 **great horse** war-horse
78 **ring** riding ring
81 **great horse** (with a pun on 'whores')
87 **countenance** introduce
90 **maintain** uphold (his word and his position at court)
95 **approve** prove
104 **professions** occupations
14.1 **Adieu, farewell** (The Knight is saying goodbye to his drinking companions in the tavern from which he is emerging.)
7 **rouses** carousals
8 **mullwines** drinking warmed ('mulled') wine
10 **void** evacuate (the stomach)
15 **Argo** Slang for the scholarly Latin *ergo* = therefore
18 **Poultry and Wood Street** London's two debtors' prisons. (A prisoner of means could live quite well in either institution.)
21 **the Hole** The worst ward of the debtors' prison, in which prisoners had to pay for their own food. If they had no money or could not secure outside aid, they might starve to death.
24 **'Slid** God's eyelid (a mild oath)

FIRST OFFICER A notable lad, and worthy to be arrested. We'll have but ten for waiting, and then thou shalt choose whether thou wilt run away from us, or we from thee.

KNIGHT A match at running? Come, come, follow me.

SECOND OFFICER Nay, fear not that.

KNIGHT Peace, you may happen to see toys, but do not see 'em.

FIRST OFFICER Pah!

KNIGHT That's the door.

FIRST OFFICER This?

He knocks on the door

KNIGHT 'Sfoot, officer, you have spoiled all already.

FIRST OFFICER Why?

KNIGHT Why? You shall see. You should have but whirled the ring once about, and there's a maid servant brought up to understand it.

MAID Who's at door?

KNIGHT All's well again. Phist, 'tis I, 'tis I.

MAID You? What are you?

KNIGHT Puh, where's thy mistress?

MAID What of her?

KNIGHT Tell her one—she knows who—her Pleasure's here, say.

MAID Her pleasure? My mistress scorns to be without her pleasure at this time of night. Is she so void of friends, think you? Take that for thinking so!

[*Maid gives him*] *a box* [*on the ear and shuts the door*]

FIRST OFFICER The hundred and fifty angels are locked up in a box. We shall not see 'em tonight.

KNIGHT How's this? Am I used like a hundred-pound gentleman? Does my Revenue forsake me? Damn me if ever I be her Pleasure again! Well, I must to prison.

FIRST OFFICER Go prepare his room; there's no remedy. I'll bring him along; he's tame enough now.

[*Exit Second Officer*]

KNIGHT Dare my tailor presume to use me in this sort? He steals and I must lie in prison for't.

FIRST OFFICER Come, come away, sir.

Enter a Gentleman with a Drawer

GENTLEMAN Art sure thou sawest him arrested, drawer?

DRAWER If mine eyes be sober.

GENTLEMAN And that's a question. Mass, here he goes! He shall not go to prison. I have a trick shall bail him—away! [*Exit Drawer*]

He blinds the Officer; [*and the Knight escapes*]

FIRST OFFICER O!

GENTLEMAN Guess, guess, who am I? Who am I?

FIRST OFFICER Who the devil are you? Let go—a pox on you! Who are you? I have lost my prisoner.

GENTLEMAN Prisoner? I've mistook. I cry you heartily mercy. I have done you infinite injury. O' my troth, I took you to be an honest man.

FIRST OFFICER Where were your eyes? Could you not see I was an officer? Stop, stop, stop, stop!

GENTLEMAN Ha, ha, ha, ha! *Exit* [*pursued by Officer*]

Enter Proditor and Phoenix [*the latter in disguise*] Sc. 15

PRODITOR
Now, Phoenix.
PHOENIX Now, my lord.
PRODITOR Let princely blood
Nourish our hopes; we bring confusion now.
PHOENIX
A terrible sudden blow.
PRODITOR Ay. What day
Is this hangs over us?
PHOENIX By th' mass, Monday.
PRODITOR
As I could wish. My purpose will thrive best.
'Twas first my birthday, now my fortune's day.
I see whom fate will raise needs never pray.
PHOENIX
Never.
PRODITOR
How is the air?
PHOENIX O, full of trouble.
PRODITOR
Does not the sky look piteously black?
PHOENIX
As if 'twere hung with rich men's consciences.
PRODITOR
Ah, stuck not a comet like a carbuncle
Upon the dreadful brow of twelve last night?
PHOENIX
Twelve? No, 'twas about one.
PRODITOR About one? Most proper,
For that's the duke.
PHOENIX [*aside*] Well shifted from thyself.
PRODITOR
I could have wished it between one and two,
His son and him.
PHOENIX
I'll give you comfort, then.
PRODITOR
Prithee.
PHOENIX
There was a villainous raven seen last night
Over the presence chamber in hard jostle
With a young eaglet.

32 **toys** sportive or frisky movements
54–5 **hundred-pound gentleman** the minimum property required for one who aspired to be called a gentleman
61.1 ***Drawer*** tapster or bartender
66.1 ***blinds the Officer*** (holds his hands over the officer's eyes)
15.1 **Phoenix** See note to 12.1.
2 **confusion** destruction
14 **that's the duke** (the comet portends the death of the dukedom's 'number one')
shifted from thyself (Phoenix suggests that Proditor has cleverly misread the comet's meaning, which is the fall of the number one conspirator.)
20 **jostle** combat

PRODITOR
A raven! That was I. What did the raven?
PHOENIX
Marry, my lord, the raven—to say truth,
I left the combat doubtful.
PRODITOR So 'tis still,
For all is doubt, till the deed crown the will.
Now bless thy loins with freedom, wealth and honour;
Think all thy seed young lords, and by this act
Make a foot-clothed posterity. Now imagine
Thou seest thy daughters with their trains born up,
Whom else despisèd want may curse to whoredom,
And public shames, which our state never threat:
She's never lewd that is accounted great.
PHOENIX [*aside*]
I'll alter that court axiom, thus renewed:
She's never great that is accounted lewd.
[*Enter several nobles*]
PRODITOR
Stand close, the presence fills. Here, here the place.
And at his rising let his fall be base,
Beneath thy foot.
PHOENIX How for his guard, my lord?
PRODITOR
My gold and fear keeps with the chief of them.
PHOENIX
That's rarely well.
[*Phoenix hides behind the Duke's presence-chair*]
PRODITOR [*aside*]
Bold, heedless slave, that dares attempt a deed
Which shall in pieces rend him—
Enter Lussurioso and Infesto
My lords both!
LUSSURIOSO
The happiness of the day.
PHOENIX [*aside*] Time my returning;
Treasons have still the worst, yet still are spurning.
[*Enter the Duke attended*]
PRODITOR
The duke!
PHOENIX [*aside*]
I ne'er was gladder to behold him.
ALL
Long live your grace!
DUKE I do not like that strain:
You know my age affords not to live long.
PRODITOR [*aside*]
Spoke truer than you think for.
DUKE
Bestow that wish upon the prince our son.
PHOENIX [*aside to Proditor*]
Nay, he's not to live long neither.
PRODITOR
Him as the wealthy treasure of our hopes,
You as possession of our present comfort,
Both in one heart we reverence in one.
PHOENIX [*aside*]
O, treason of a good complexion.
[*A*] *Horn* [*sounds within*]
Enter Fidelio
DUKE
How now, what fresher news fills the court's ear?
PRODITOR
Fidelio!
FIDELIO
Glad tidings to your grace.
The prince is safe returned and in your court.
DUKE
Our joy breaks at our eyes; the prince is come!
PRODITOR
Soul-quicking news—[*aside*] pale vengeance to my blood.
FIDELIO
By me presenting, to your serious view,
A brief of all his travels.
[*He delivers a paper*]
DUKE 'Tis most welcome.
It shall be dear and precious to our eye.
PRODITOR [*aside to Phoenix*]
He reads, I'm glad he reads.
Now take thy opportunity, leave that place.
PHOENIX [*aside to Proditor*]
At his first rising let his fall be base.
PRODITOR [*aside to Phoenix*]
That must be altered now.
PHOENIX [*aside to Proditor*]
Which? his rising or his fall?
PRODITOR [*aside to Phoenix*] Art thou dull now?
Thou hear'st the prince is come.
DUKE What's here?
PRODITOR My lord?
DUKE [*reads*] 'I have got such a large portion of knowledge, most worthy father, by the benefit of my travel—'
PRODITOR
And so he has, no doubt, my lord.
DUKE [*reads*] 'That I am bold now to warn you of Lord Proditor's insolent treason, who has irreligiously seduced a fellow and closely conveyed him e'en in the presence-chair to murder you.'
PHOENIX O, guilty, guilty!
[*Phoenix steps forward and drops his weapon*]
DUKE
What was that fell? What's he?
PHOENIX I am the man.

26 **loins** children
28 **foot-clothed posterity** heirs wealthy enough to have fancy trappings for their horses
35 **presence** presence-chamber
38 **gold . . . them** (They've been bribed and threatened.)
39 **rarely** very
42 **Time my returning** time for me to return
43 **spurning** spreading
47 **think for** expect
64 **At . . . base** (Phoenix repeats Proditor's instructions, see 15.36)

PRODITOR
O, slave!
PHOENIX
I have no power to strike.
PRODITOR
I'm gone, I'm gone.
DUKE
Let me admire heaven's wisdom in my son.
PHOENIX
I confess it, he hired me—
PRODITOR
This is a slave!
'Tis forged against mine honour and my life;
For in what part of reason can 't appear,
The prince, being travelled, should know treasons here?
Plain counterfeit—
DUKE
Dost thou make false our son?
PRODITOR
I know the prince will not affirm it.
FIDELIO
He can
And will, my lord.
PHOENIX
Most just, he may.
DUKE
A guard!
[*Guards secure Proditor*]
LUSSURIOSO
We cannot but in loyal zeal ourselves
Lay hands on such a villain.
DUKE
Stay you. I find you here, too.
LUSSURIOSO
Us, my lord?
DUKE [*reads*] 'Against Lussurioso and Infesto, who not only most riotously consume their houses in vicious gaming, mortgaging their livings to the merchant, whereby he with his heirs enter upon their lands—from whence this abuse comes, that in short time the son of the merchant has more lordships than the son of the nobleman, which else was never born to inheritance: but that which is more impious, they most adulterously train out young ladies to midnight banquets, to the utter defamation of their own honours and ridiculous abuse of their husbands.'
LUSSURIOSO
How could the prince hear that?
PHOENIX
Most true, my lord;
My conscience is a witness 'gainst itself,
For to that execution of chaste honour
I was both hired and led.
LUSSURIOSO
I hope the prince, out of his plenteous wisdom,
Will not give wrong to us! As for this fellow, [*points at Phoenix*]
He's poor and cares not to be desperate.

Enter Justice Falso

FALSO
Justice, my lord! I have my niece stol'n from me.
She's left her dowry with me, but she's gone;
I'd rather have had her love than her money, I.
This, this is one of them. [*Points at Phoenix*] Justice, my lord!
I know him by his face; this is the thief.
PRODITOR
Your grace may now in milder sense perceive
The wrong done to us by this impudent wretch,
Who has his hand fixed at the throat of law,
And therefore durst be desperate of his life.
DUKE
Peace! You're too foul; your crime is in excess;
One spot of him makes not your ulcers less.
PRODITOR O!
DUKE [*to Phoenix*]
Did your violence force away his niece?
PHOENIX
No, my good lord, I'll still confess what's truth.
I did remove her from her many wrongs,
Which she was pleased to leave, they were so vile.
DUKE [*to Falso*]
What are you named?
FALSO
Falso, my lord, Justice Falso.
I'm known by that name.
DUKE
Falso, you came fitly,
You are the very next that follows here.
FALSO
I hope so, my lord. My name is in all the records,
I can assure your good grace.
[*Enter Niece and Lady behind*]
DUKE [*reads*] 'Against Justice Falso—'
FALSO Ah!
DUKE [*reads*] 'Who, having had the honest charge of his niece committed to his trust by the last will and testament of her deceased father, and with her all the power of his wealth, not only against faith and conscience detains her dowry, but against nature and humanity assays to abuse her body.'
NIECE [*comes forward*]
I'm present to affirm it, my loved lord.
FALSO
How? What make I here?
NIECE
Either I must agree
To loathèd lust or despised beggary.
DUKE
Are you the plaintiff here?
FALSO
Ay, my good lord,
For fault of a better.
DUKE
Seldom comes a worse.

92 **livings** estates
97 **train** entice
113 **milder** more indulgent
118 **spot of** stain on
138 **What . . . here?** What am I doing here?
141 **fault** lack

[*Reads*] 'And, moreover, not contained in this vice only, which is odious too much, but against the sacred use of justice, maintains three thieves to his men—'

FALSO Cuds me!

DUKE [*reads*] 'Who only take purses in their master's liberty, where if any one chance to be taken, he appears before him in a false beard, and one of his own fellows takes his examination—'

FALSO [*aside*] By my troth, as true as can be, but he shall not know on't.

DUKE [*reads*] 'And in the end will execute justice so cruelly upon him, that he will not trust him in a prison, but commit him to his fellows' chamber.'

FALSO [*aside*] Can a man do nothing i' the country but 'tis told at court? There's some busy informing knave abroad, o' my life.

PHOENIX
That this is true, and these, and more, my lord,
Be it under pardon spoken for mine own.
He the disease of justice, these of honour,
And this of loyalty and reverence:
The unswept venom of the palace.

PRODITOR Slave!

PHOENIX
Behold the prince to approve it.

PRODITOR O, where?

PHOENIX
Your eyes keep with your actions, both look wrong.
[*Discovering himself*]

PRODITOR
An infernal to my spirit!

ALL My lord the prince!

PRODITOR
Tread me to dust, thou in whom wonder keeps.
Behold, the serpent on his belly creeps. [*Prostrating himself*]

PHOENIX
Rankle not my foot—away!
Treason, we laugh at thy vain-labouring stings,
Above the foot thou hast no power o'er kings.

DUKE
I cannot with sufficient joy receive thee,
And yet my joy's too much.

PHOENIX My royal father,
To whose unnatural murder I was hired,
I thought it a more natural course of travel,
And answering future expectation,
To leave far countries and inquire mine own.

DUKE
To thee let reverence all her powers engage,
That art in youth a miracle to age.
State is but blindness; thou hadst piercing art:
We only saw the knee, but thou the heart.
To thee then power and dukedom we resign;
He's fit to reign whose knowledge can refine.

PHOENIX
Forbid it, my obedience.

DUKE Our word's not vain;
I know thee wise, canst both obey and reign.
The rest of life we dedicate to heaven.

ALL
A happy and safe reign to our new duke!

PHOENIX
Without your prayers safer and happier.
Fidelio.

FIDELIO
My royal lord.

PHOENIX
Here, take this diamond.
You know the virtue on't. It can fetch vice.
Madam Castiza—

FIDELIO She attends, my lord.
[*Lady comes forward; exit Fidelio*]

PHOENIX
Place a guard near us.
[*To Lady*] Know you yon fellow, lady?

LADY My honour's evil.

PRODITOR
Torment again?

PHOENIX So ugly are thy crimes,
Thine eye cannot endure 'em.
And that thy face may stand perpetually
Turned so from ours, and thy abhorrèd self
Neither to threaten wrack of state or credit,
An everlasting banishment seize on thee.

PRODITOR
O, fiend!

PHOENIX
Thy life is such it is too bad to end.

PRODITOR
May thy rule, life, and all that's in thee glad,
Have as short time as thy begetting had.

PHOENIX Away, thy curse is idle. *Exit Proditor*
The rest are under reformation, and therefore
Under pardon.

LUSSURIOSO, INFESTO, FALSO, *and* SEVERAL NOBLES
Our duties shall turn edge upon our crimes.

FALSO [*aside*] 'Slid, I was afraid of nothing, but that for my thievery and bawdry I should have been turned to an innkeeper.

Enter Jeweller's Wife with Fidelio

My daughter! I am ashamed her worship should see me.

JEWELLER'S WIFE Who would not love a friend at court? What fine galleries and rooms am I brought through? I

145 **Cuds** God's (an oath)
147 **liberty** part of a county exempt from the jurisdiction of the sheriff
166 **wonder keeps** marvels dwell
179 **State** high rank
180 **knee** (i.e., the courtier's bended knee)
198 **wrack** destruction
207 **turn edge upon** make blunt

had thought my knight durst not have shown his face here, I.

PHOENIX
Now, mother of pride and daughter of lust,
Which is your friend now?

JEWELLER'S WIFE Ah, me!

PHOENIX I'm sure you are not so unprovided to be without a friend here; you'll pay enough for him first.

JEWELLER'S WIFE This is the worst room that ever I came in.

PHOENIX I am your servant, mistress; know you not me?

JEWELLER'S WIFE Your worship is too great for me to know. I am but a small-timbered woman when I'm out of my apparel, and dare not venture upon greatness.

PHOENIX
Do you deny me, then? Know you this purse?

JEWELLER'S WIFE That purse? O, death! Has the knight served me so? given away my favours?

PHOENIX
Stand forth—thou one of those
For whose close lusts the plague never leaves the city.
Thou worse than common—private, subtle harlot,
That dost deceive three with one feignèd lip:
Thy husband, the world's eye, and the law's whip.
Thy zeal is hot, for 'tis to lust and fraud,
And dost not dread to make thy book thy bawd.
Thou'rt curse enough to husband's ill-got gains,
For whom the court rejects, his gold maintains.
How dear and rare was freedom wont to be,
Now few but are by their wives' copies free,
And brought to such a head that now we see
City and suburbs wear one livery.

JEWELLER'S WIFE 'Tis 'long of those, an't like your grace, that come in upon us, and will never leave marrying of our widows till they make 'em all as free as their first husbands.

PHOENIX I perceive you can shift a point well.

JEWELLER'S WIFE Let me have pardon, I beseech your grace, and I'll peach 'em all, all the close women that are; and upon my knowledge there's above five thousand within the walls and the liberties.

PHOENIX
A band? They shall be sent against the Turk:
Infidels against infidels.

JEWELLER'S WIFE I will hereafter live so modestly I will not lie with mine own husband, nor come near a man in the way of honesty.

FALSO I'll be her warrant, my lord.

PHOENIX
You are deceived. You think you're still a justice.

FALSO 'Sfoot, worse than I was before I kneeled. I am no justice now. I know I shall be some innkeeper at last.

JEWELLER'S WIFE
My father! 'Tis mine own father.

PHOENIX
I should have wondered else, lust being so like.

NIECE
Her birth was kin to mine; she may prove modest.
For my sake, I beseech you pardon her.

PHOENIX
For thy sake I'll do more. Fidelio, hand her.
My favours on you both; next, all that wealth
Which was committed to that perjured's trust.

FALSO
I'm a beggar now, worse than an innkeeper.

Enter Tangle, mad

TANGLE Your *mittimus* shall not serve: I'll set myself free with a *deliberandum*, with a *deliberandum*, mark you.

DUKE
What's he? A guard!

PHOENIX Under your sufferance,
Worthy father, his harm is to himself;
One that has loved vexation so much,
He cannot now be rid on't.
He's been so long in suits that he's law-mad.

TANGLE A judgement, I crave a judgement, yea! *Nunc pro tunc, corruptione alicuius*. I peeped me a raven in the face, and I thought it had been my solicitor: O, the pens prick me.

Enter Quieto

PHOENIX
And here comes he, wonder for temperance,
Will take the cure upon him.

---

225 **small-timbered** small-framed (a house instead of a palace)
225–6 **out of my apparel** (not wearing a social-climber's elaborate costume, with a joke about literal nakedness)
226 **venture upon greatness** make pretence to social eminence (with pun on having sex)
227 **purse** (i.e., the one she gave Phoenix in sc. 13)
231 **close** secret
236 **book** (i.e, the Bible; a sardonic comment on affected piety)
238 **whom...rejects** (i.e., disgraced aristocrats like the Jeweller's Wife's knight)
240 **by...free** (The husbands are only 'free' by virtue of the wives' permission to be as promiscuous as they are. 'Copy' is a legal term, as in 'copyhold': an estate held at the will of the lord and subject to his decisions.)
241 **head** (with a pun on the cuckold's horns)
242 **City...livery** (Middle-class city dwellers dress indistinguishably from prostitutes who live in the suburbs.)
243 **'long of** because of
those (i.e., courtiers like the Knight)
245 **free** promiscuous
247 **shift a point** turn an argument
249 **peach** inform against, impeach
250–1 **within...liberties** within the City and the adjacent district subject to municipal control
265 **hand her** take her by the hand
269 ***mittimus*** a warrant of commitment to prison
270 ***deliberandum*** deliberating (also the writ known by that name)
276–7 ***Nunc...alicuius*** now for then (i.e., not at the legally appointed time) by the corruption of someone

QUIETO
A blessing to this fair assembly.
TANGLE Away, I'll have none on't; give me an *audita querela*, or a *testificandum*, or a dispatch in twelve terms: there's a blessing, there's a blessing.
PHOENIX
You see the unbounded rage of his disease.
QUIETO
'Tis the foul fiend, my lord, has got within him.
The rest are fair to this; this breeds in ink,
And to that colour turns the blood possessed.
For instance, now your grace shall see him dressed.
TANGLE
Ah ha, I rejoice; then he's puzzled, and muzzled, too.
Is't come to a *cepi corpus*?
QUIETO Ah, good sir,
This is for want of patience.
[*Quieto binds Tangle*]
TANGLE That's a fool:
She never saw the dogs and the bears fight—
A country thing.
QUIETO This is for lack of grace.
TANGLE
I've other business, not so much idle time.
QUIETO
You never say your prayers.
TANGLE
I'm advised by my learnèd counsel.
QUIETO
The power of my charm come o'er thee,
Place by degrees thy wits before thee;
With silken patience here I bind thee,
Not to move till I unwind thee.
TANGLE
Yea! Is my cause so muddy? Do I stick? Do I stick fast?
Advocate, here's my hand—pull, art made of flint?
Wilt not help out?—alas, there's nothing in't.
PHOENIX
O, do you sluice the vein now?
QUIETO Yes, my honoured lord.
PHOENIX
Pray, let me see the issue.
QUIETO
I therefore seek to keep it.
[*Opens Tangle's vein over a basin*]
Now burst out,
Thou filthy stream of trouble, spite, and doubt.
TANGLE O, an extent, a proclamation, a summons, a recognizance, a tachment, an injunction, a writ, a seizure, a writ of 'praisement, an absolution, a *quietus est.*
QUIETO
You're quieter, I hope, by so much dregs.
Behold, my lord.
[*Holds up basin to Phoenix*]
PHOENIX This, why it outfrowns ink.
QUIETO
'Tis the disease's nature, the fiend's drink.
TANGLE O, sick, sick, signor Ply-fee, sick. Lend me thy nightcap, O!
QUIETO [*gives medicine to Tangle*]
The balsam of a temperate brain
I pour into this thirsty vein,
And with this blessed oil of quiet,
Which is so cheap that few men buy it,
Thy stormy temples I allay.
Thou shalt give up the devil and pray.
Forsake his works, they're foul and black,
And keep thee bare in purse and back.
No more shalt thou in paper quarrel,
To dress up apes in good apparel.
He throws his stock and all his flock
Into a swallowing gulf
That sends his goose unto his fox,
His lamb unto his wolf.
Keep thy increase,
And live at peace,
For war's not equal to this battle:
That eats but men, this men and cattle.
Therefore no more this combat choose,
Where he that wins does always lose,
And those that gain all, with this curse receive it,
From fools they get it, to their sons they leave it.
TANGLE
Hail, sacred patience. I begin to feel
I have a conscience now, truth in my words,
Compassion in my heart, and, above all,
In my blood peace's music. Use me how you can,
You shall find me an honest, quiet man.
O, pardon, that I dare behold that face.
Now I've least law, I hope I have most grace.
PHOENIX
We both admire the workman and his piece.
Thus, when all hearts are tuned to honour's strings,
There is no music to the choir of kings.
[*Exeunt omnes*]

Finis

283–4 ***audita querela*** a writ initiating a process to introduce new evidence on behalf of the defendant after completion of the trial
284 ***testificandum*** testifying
dispatch legal settlement
288 **The...to this** All others are good compared to this one (meaning either the fiend or Tangle).
290 **dressed** given medical treatment
292 ***cepi corpus*** I have taken the body (the response of an officer who has arrested a person upon a writ of *capias*)
293 **That's** (i.e., 'patience' is)
310–13 **extent...*est*** (These are the legal terms being carried away with Tangle's blood; the last one means 'it is done'.)
319 **balsam** medicinal resin
328 **apes** pretenders to gentility
336 **cattle** property
348 **piece** masterpiece
350 **to** compared to

THE PARTS

Boys

PHOENIX (532 lines): drawer; Soldier *or* Servus; [Knight] *or* [Gentleman]

FALSO (387 lines): Groom; Boy; noble *or* attendant; Captain *or* Soldier; Gentleman *or* Drawer *or* Officer; Servus (*or* Captain); lackey (*or* Captain); Constable (*or* Officer); Quieto's boy (*or* Officer); Maid (*or* Officer)

TANGLE (312 lines): Boy; Soldier; Servus; noble *or* attendant, Proditor (*or* Servus) *or* lackey; Maid *or* Officer *or* Gentleman *or* Drawer; Quieto's boy (*or* Officer); Furtivo (*or* Gentleman *or* Officer) *or* Fucato (*or* Officer) *or* Constable (*or* Officer)

CAPTAIN (231 lines): any but Phoenix, Fidelio, Lady, Proditor, Tangle, Soldier, Suitor (scenes 4 and 6), Servus, lackey, [Niece]

FIDELIO (187 lines): drawer; Soldier *or* Servus; [Jeweller's Wife] *or* [Knight] *or* [Boy] *or* [Gentleman] (*or* drawer); Maid (*or* Knight)

PRODITOR (159 lines): any but Phoenix, Lussurioso, Infesto, Duke, Fidelio, Falso, Niece, Lady, Captain, guard, lackey, Servus, noble, attendant

JEWELLER'S WIFE (141 lines): any but Phoenix, Fidelio, Duke, Falso, Lussurioso, Infesto, Niece, Lady, Boy, Tangle, Quieto, Knight, Furtivo, Gentleman, guard

DUKE (112 lines): any but Proditor, Lussurioso, Infesto, Phoenix, Fidelio, Falso, Niece, Lady, Jeweller's Wife, Tangle, Quieto, noble, attendant, guard

QUIETO (72 lines): any but Phoenix, Fidelio, Duke, Lussurioso, Infesto, Falso, Niece, Lady, Jeweller's Wife, Tangle, Quieto's boy, Officer, guard

KNIGHT (69 lines): any but Jeweller's Wife, Niece, Falso, Furtivo, Maid, Boy, Drawer, Gentleman, Officer, [Phoenix *or* Fidelio], [Proditor *or* Phoenix], [Suitor], [Latronello], [Lady]

NIECE (55 lines): any but Duke, Proditor, Lussurioso, Infesto, Phoenix, Fidelio, Lady, Falso, Tangle, Jeweller's Wife, Quieto, Knight, Latronello, Furtivo, gentleman, guard, [Captain], [Soldier]

FURTIVO (54 lines): any but Falso, Niece, Gentleman, Knight, Jeweller's Wife, Phoenix, Fidelio, Latronello, Fucato, Constable, Officer

LADY (51 lines): any but Proditor, Phoenix, Lussurioso, Infesto, Duke, Fidelio, Niece, Jeweller's Wife, Tangle, Quieto, Captain, lackey, Servus, guard, [Knight], [Groom]

SUITORS (scenes 4 and 6; 39 lines): any but Phoenix, Fidelio, Tangle, Groom, Captain, Falso, Latronello, [Jeweller's Wife], [Boy], [Knight]

OFFICER (37 lines): any but Falso, Phoenix, Fidelio, Latronello, Furtivo, Fucato, Constable, Quieto, Quieto's boy, Maid, [Jeweller's Wife]

GROOM (Sc. 4; 32 lines): any but Phoenix, Fidelio, Tangle, Suitor (scenes 4 and 6), [Proditor], [Lady]

LATRONELLO (28 lines): any but Falso, Suitor (scenes 4 and 6), Tangle, Fucato, Phoenix, Fidelio, Furtivo, Constable, Officer, [Knight *or* Jeweller's Wife]

SOLDIERS (Sc. 2; 22 lines): any but Captain, [Niece]

MAID (14 lines): any but Phoenix, Knight, Officer, Fidelio, Quieto, Quieto's boy

SUITORS (Sc. 12; 13 lines): any but Phoenix, Tangle, Falso

LUSSURIOSO (11 lines): any but Proditor, Duke, Infesto, Phoenix, Fidelio, Falso, Niece, Lady, Jeweller's Wife, Tangle, Quieto, noble, attendant, guard

GENTLEMAN (10 lines): any but Falso, Furtivo, Niece, Knight, Jeweller's Wife, Officer, drawer, [Proditor]

FUCATO (Sc. 10; 8 lines): any but Falso, Latronello, Furtivo, Phoenix, Fidelio, Constable, Officer

Quieto's BOY (Sc. 12; 4 lines): any but Phoenix, Fidelio, Quieto, Officer, Maid

CONSTABLE (Sc. 10; 4 lines): any but Falso, Phoenix, Fidelio, Latronello, Furtivo, Fucato, Officer

INFESTO (4 lines): any but Proditor, Lussurioso, Duke, Phoenix, Fidelio, Falso, Niece, Lady, Jeweller's Wife, Tangle, Quieto, noble, attendant, guard

BOY (Sc. 5; 3 lines): any but Jeweller's Wife, Knight, [Phoenix], [Fidelio]

SERVUS (Sc. 2; 2 lines): any but Captain, Lady, Proditor

DRAWER (Sc. 14; 1 line): any but Gentleman, Knight, Officer

LACKEY (Sc. 8; 1 line): any but Captain, Lady, Proditor, Phoenix, Fidelio

ATTENDANT (Sc. 1; no lines): any but Duke, Proditor, Lussurioso, Infesto, Phoenix, Fidelio, noble

GUARD (Sc. 15; no lines): any but Proditor, Phoenix, Lussurioso, Infesto, Duke, Fidelio, Falso, Niece, Lady, Jeweller's Wife, Tangle, Quieto

NOBLE (Sc. 1; no lines): any but Duke, Proditor, Lussurioso, Infesto, Phoenix, Fidelio, attendant

Most crowded scene: 5.1: 12 characters (+3? mute guards)

NEWS FROM GRAVESEND: SENT TO NOBODY

Text edited by Gary Taylor, annotated and introduced by Robert Maslen

PLAGUE has always served as the most shocking of metaphors for political crisis. Pestilence reenacts the successive stages of the rise of Nazism in Albert Camus' *La Peste* (1947), while in Mary Shelley's *The Last Man* (1826) an apocalyptic plague puts an end to conventional forms of government before annihilating all but one of the earth's inhabitants. Plague is also the most urban of catastrophes. The need to contain it demarcates the boundaries of a city as remorselessly as a siege. In Daniel Defoe's *A Journal of the Plague Year* (1722) refugees from London are recognized wherever they go as residents of the infected city, despite all their efforts to disguise their provenance. Meanwhile those who choose to stay behind resort to listing the dead of each parish with obsessive accuracy, as if numbers had the power to preserve the city's identity in the face of depopulation and economic ruin. The modest pamphlet *News from Gravesend* (1604), written by Thomas Dekker and Thomas Middleton in response to the outbreak of 1603, shares with these later texts an acute awareness of the politics of plague and a horrified sensitivity to its redefinition of the urban community. Its authors make use of grotesque anecdotes and monstrous metaphors as vehicles for sometimes aggressive social satire. Their subject is the acute division between rich and poor which was aggravated by plague in the early years of the seventeenth century. The pamphlet anatomizes the social diseases of seventeenth-century London as minutely as it scrutinizes the physical symptoms of pestilence.

One of the peculiarities of texts associated with plague is their resistance to classification in terms of genre. Boccaccio's *Decameron*, which opens with its aristocratic narrators sequestering themselves from a plague-infested populace, ranges through every shade of comedy, tragedy and satire in its efforts to reconstruct the world abandoned by the storytellers. *The Journal of the Plague Year* masquerades as the memoirs of a London saddler, but incorporates demographic statistics, dramatic dialogue and investigative journalism into its account of the catastrophe. *La Peste* mixes the conventions of realist narrative with the experimental dislocations of modernism. It is as if plague had the power to disrupt the hierarchy of the imagination as easily as it disrupts the organization of a state. The Elizabethan precursors of *News from Gravesend* are as heterogeneous as its successors. William Bullein's *Dialogue against the Fever Pestilence* (1564) is a lively fusion of genres which combines factual reportage with medical tract and moral interlude with tall tales told by travellers, in the course of recounting the adventures of a citizen and his wife as they flee from the afflicted capital. The *Dialogue* ends with the moral interlude in the ascendant: the citizen repents and dies, humbly submitting to the will of Providence. In the process the text brings the epidemic under control. The plague becomes the instrument of divine authority, and death takes on the role of God's obedient junior minister. Bullein's text is modelled on the pastorals of Baptista Mantuanus (1498), but the pamphlets of Middleton and Dekker derive from a more recent and more unsettling model, the prose of Thomas Nashe.

Nashe's works are riddled with disease: from *Summer's Last Will and Testament* (1592), where Summer dies to the mournful accompaniment of the cry of the plague victims, 'Lord have mercy upon us', to the hallucinations that torment the bedridden fever-sufferer in *The Terrors of the Night* (1594). Nashe was familiar with Bullein's *Dialogue*, but his own uneasy medley of disparate genres has more disturbing implications. In *The Unfortunate Traveller* (1594) the narrative veers vertiginously from one geographical location to the next and from one genre to another. Chronicle history lapses into anecdote, epic is undercut by farce, romance by journalistic voyeurism, and in the process the workings of Providence, which lend a semblance of coherence to the muddle of European politics, rapidly recede into obscurity. The text is punctuated by plagues. Its presiding monarch is Henry VIII, the 'fever quartane of the French', and its protagonist Jack Wilton sets out on his travels to escape the sweating sickness in the English camp only to encounter the 'moist scorching steam' of bubonic plague in Rome. An incident that occurs during the Roman epidemic horrifically confirms the inaccessibility of Providence. Heraclide, having lost her husband and children in the plague, is raped and murdered by the robber Esdras despite an impassioned plea for divine protection. Jack Wilton can find no justification for her agony; when Esdras dies towards the end of the book Jack has nothing better to say than that 'Strange and wonderful are God's judgements'. *The Unfortunate Traveller* ultimately fails to provide arbitrary suffering with a convincing providential function.

Thomas Dekker's first plague pamphlet, *The Wonderful Year* (1603), shares the witty eclecticism of Nashe's satires. Like *The Unfortunate Traveller* it veers from comic to tragic, from elegaic lyricism to graveyard humour as it charts the 'chances, changes, and strange shapes that this protean climacterial year hath metamorphosed himself into'. The pamphlet passes few judgements on the behaviour of London's citizens during the epidemic. Instead Dekker anthropomorphizes the plague—or as he says 'anthropophagizes' it—into a flesh-eating lord of misrule, the hero of the pamphlet and its villain, who stands conventions on their heads and plays ghastly practical jokes on a powerless public.

But Dekker later became increasingly critical of the role of the authorities and the flight of the rich from the stricken capital. In 1625 he wrote a pamphlet designed as an active intervention in the city's affairs. The title of *A Rod for Runaways* proclaims its desire to scourge the retreating backsides of the wealthy fugitives. It is dedicated to a surgeon who is responsible for the only worthwhile works of art produced during an epidemic—the restoration of the sick to life; and it proposes that a guard be set at the city gates to prevent officials from abandoning their civic duties. *News from Gravesend* prepares the way for the radical interventionism of *A Rod for Runaways*. From the carnivalesque metamorphoses recounted in *The Wonderful Year* it turns its attention to the actions of the ruling classes during the plague and presents itself as a witness on behalf of the ordinary citizen. In doing so it records a subtle shift of power within London and within Jacobean society as a whole for which the plague provides a lurid backdrop.

The authors of *News from Gravesend* must have known they were playing a dangerous game. Any imitator of Nashe would have been aware that his works had been burned by the church authorities in 1599. And writers who chose to discuss the origins of plague had been recently warned of the state's intolerance of such discussions. In November 1603, the month before the composition of *News from Gravesend*, Henoch Clapham was jailed for preaching that the plague could not be cured by natural means and that government efforts to contain it were not only futile but blasphemous. *News from Gravesend*, then, with its echoes of Nashe and its speculations on the metaphysical origins of the plague, had good reasons for appearing anonymously.

At the same time it made clever use of its anonymity. The pamphlet is divided into two roughly equal parts: an Epistle Dedicatory in prose, and an account of the plague in octosyllabic couplets. This even-handed distribution of prose and verse lays unusual emphasis on the dedication, and hence on the social status of the text. The epistle is addressed to a non-existent knight, 'Sir Nicholas Nemo, alias Nobody' (8–9), the only responsible nobleman left in the city. At the centre of the pamphlet is a vacuum waiting to be filled: the vacuum left by the flight of the rich from the epidemic and the subsequent breakdown of the patronage system. The letter is signed by 'Somebody', one of a company of professional writers who have been left stranded, without a place, without an occupation, looking for a new readership to replace the aristocratic readers who have deserted them. In *The Wonderful Year* Dekker describes a dedication as a 'livery' like the ones worn by companies of players to protect them from the charge of vagrancy. But according to *News from Gravesend*, during the plague it is the rich who are the vagrants, and the ordinary countryfolk, the 'russet boor and leathern hind', who police their movements in the absence of any effective legislation against their flight (813). The pamphlet pours scorn on the aristocratic livery which traditionally lent a text its respectability: 'Out upon't! the fashion of such dedications is more stale than kissing' (11–15). Instead it offers itself to Nobody 'like a Whitefriars punk' (14–16), a whore whose illegitimate services contribute more to the city's economy than all the 'empty-fisted Maecen-asses' who ran away (2–3).

This literary whoredom is reinforced by the merciless scrutiny of the diseased body with which the text is filled. As his name implies, Somebody regards the bodies of the plague victims as material evidence of the government's irresponsibility, and the swelling plague-sores as physical manifestations of a deep-rooted moral corruption among the civic authorities. And the text's insistence on its joint authorship—the verses that make up the second half of the pamphlet repeatedly refer to the writers as 'we' and 'us'—implies that it articulates the indignation of the bulk of the London populace; that the Londoners themselves, in fact, comprise a single composite body. Internal evidence suggests that Dekker wrote most of the pamphlet and that Middleton's contribution is concentrated in about a hundred lines of poetry (972–1078), but Somebody's plural identity remains implicit throughout.

The transference of power by which the 'russet boor' polices the wealthy vagrant is only one of many effected by the plague in the epistle. The recurring implication is that the flight of the rich has proved that they are no longer necessary to the economy of London. 'Somebody' drives the point home when he describes his recent survey of maps of the world. In theory, printed maps gave the poorest of educated readers access to territories which had traditionally been colonized only by the wealthy, and Somebody's reading of 'universal maps' (37–9) gives the ordinary Londoner equal status with the aristocratic privateer. With the cartographers' help he crosses the world 'in a shorter time than a sculler can row from Queenhithe to Wapping' (40–3), and gets to know Constantinople 'as perfectly as Jobbin the malt-man's horse of Enfield knows the way to London' (46–8). The point of the survey is to demonstrate that the rich throughout the globe have ceased to patronize writers. In the process it suggests that the unique status accorded to the rich in official histories—'the white paper-gallery of a large chronicle' (60–2)—has no practical basis; and that the impressive coats of arms of noble houses are therefore effectively 'senseless' (60–1), devoid of meaning, like the empty motto '*Nec quidquam nec cuiquam*' ('nothing dedicated to Nobody') which decorates the pamphlet's title-page.

So far the argument resembles Nashe's deflation of the pretensions of chronicle history in *The Unfortunate Traveller*. But Somebody's engagement with the emptiness of aristocratic posturings has a more direct bearing on practical government than the misadventures of Jack Wilton. Nashe's protagonist returns at last to the service of the monarch; but Somebody dissociates himself forever from the patronage of the ruling classes. Instead he joins forces with writers who cater for other classes of reader, the 'rhymesters, play-patchers, jig-makers, ballad-mongers, and pamphlet-stitchers' who are the 'yeomanry' of the authors' company (153–7), and urges them to follow him in expunging the names of 'dukes, earls, lords and ladies' from their dedications (174–6). This is no empty threat. It is a statement of the urgent need for a reformation of the social structure, the replacement of an outmoded semi-feudal economic system with a system of mutual help which will enable the urban community to tackle emergencies like the plague both efficiently and humanely. In an energetic passage, Somebody compares the ruling classes to a ship's officers who have abandoned their crew in the middle of a sea battle: 'when the pilot, boatswains, master and master's mates, with all the chief mariners that had charge in this goodly argosy of government leapt from the stern ... [and] suffered all to sink or swim, crying out only "Put your trust in God, my bullies, and not in us!"' (185–96). At the same time, under the guise of praising the one responsible aristocrat, Nobody, he lists the policies which ought to have been put into effect: a proper food supply for quarantined households, a disciplined body of surgeons standing by to administer to the sick, and adequate land set aside for the burial of plague victims. These are policies similar to those recommended by the Privy Council in their book of national plague orders, *Orders thought meet by her Majesty and her Privy Council to be executed throughout the Counties of this Realm in such ... places as are ... infected with the plague*, first issued in 1583; but Somebody's ironic restatement of them supports the findings of the historian Paul Slack, who argues that very few of these policies were implemented in the capital during the 1603 epidemic.

The last part of the epistle demonstrates the ease with which the displacement of the ruling classes might be accomplished. It presents itself as the latest news from Winchester, the town to which the London law courts moved for the duration of the epidemic, and is largely taken up with tricks played by the locals on the unfortunate lawyers. By adapting their prices to the demand created by the sudden influx of Londoners, the people of Winchester contrive to snatch the legal and economic initiative away from the capital: 'having the law in their own hands, they ruled the roost how they listed; insomuch, that ... Winchester now durst (or at least hoped to) stand upon proud terms with London' (391–409). The transference of the law courts from the capital to the provinces results in the transference of power from gentlemanly lawyers to the landlords, tradesmen, and servants who supply their needs. The epistle ends with a mocking threat to make use of the new solidarity between different classes of writers to have the 'limping prose' of the dedication converted into the popular ballad form, the perfect medium for the dissemination of gossip (432–5). In this way the news of the discomfiture of the rich will quickly spread throughout the urban population, 'that it shall do any true-born citizen's heart good to hear such doings sung to some filthy tune' (435–8). *The Wonderful Year* represented the plague as a monstrous carnival during which the social order was temporarily reversed. The dedication of *News from Gravesend* suggests that the respect and even the economic ascendancy once enjoyed by the wealthy fugitives might be less easy to reinstate than they might think.

The poem that makes up the second half of the pamphlet exhibits shifts in tone that enact a still more dramatic series of reversals. The effect of these sudden shifts in tone and topic is to make all its conclusions open-ended, guarding it from possible accusations of either condemning or endorsing government policies. The verses begin by invoking the art of 'Physic' as their muse as if to affirm the efficacy of natural methods of combatting the epidemic. Hence a reader might initially assume that the pamphlet aligns itself with the national plague orders of 1583, whose stress on the incarceration of infected households implied that the plague was a natural disease like any other and that it spread by contagion. But after a few lines the poem abruptly changes tack and points out that medicine has proved powerless in the face of the epidemic: 'Sick is Physic's self to see | Her aphorisms proved a mockery' (486–7). At line 492 the poem effectively begins again, invoking tragedy instead of physic as its muse, and begging her to infuse its verse with the power to move the ruling classes, 'Till rich heirs meeting our strong verse | May not shrink back before it pierce | Their marble eyeballs' (508–10). Once again the official version of events has been replaced with an assault on the irresponsible rich.

Further abrupt transitions follow. The next section (523–730) begins with an account of one current theory of the plague's transmission, the theory of miasma, which held that the disease was communicated by a corruption of the air. But the passage concludes that miasma has nothing to do with the present epidemic, since if plague were transmitted by the atmosphere then its effects would be universal: 'Then rivers would drink poisoned air; | Trees shed their green and curlèd hair; | Fish swim to shore full of disease | (For pestilence would fin the seas)' (567–70). The poem espouses a more dangerous theory—dangerous because it seems to corroborate Henoch Clapham's opinion that the pestilence was a supernatural visitation. It argues that the causes of the plague are internal ones, that 'every man within him feeds | A worm, which this contagion breeds' (621–2) and that God has inflicted the plague on England as a punishment for 'some capital offence' (627). The ensuing catalogue of possible offences lays responsibility squarely at the door of England's governors:

> Whether they be princes' errors
> Or faults of peers, pull down these terrors, ...
> The courtier's pride, lust, and excess,
> The churchman's painted holiness,
> The lawyer's grinding of the poor ... (639–45)

Despite the poem's earlier assertion that every man bears some responsibility for the disaster, the catalogue implies that the ruling classes have a near monopoly on guilt, as they do on so much else.

As one might expect, the sting of the accusation is swiftly drawn; the list of abuses ends with a celebration of the crowning of James I, an event Dekker and Middleton commemorated in *The Magnificent Entertainment*. Briefly the miasma of James's fame supplants the miasma of infection, and restores, as it spreads across Europe, the damaged credibility of princes. But the following section, entitled simply 'The horror of the plague' (732–1067), reads like the script of a hideous alternative entertainment, made up of a series of miniature tragedies which have spilled out of the confined space of the theatre to infect the bodies of every class of citizen. At one point Somebody compares the pest-house, the hospital set aside for treating cases of the plague, to a private playhouse which has proved unequal to the task of containing the tragedy of the epidemic:

These are the tragedies, whose sight
With tears blot all the lines we write.
The stage, whereon the scenes are played,
Is a whole kingdom. What was made
By some (most provident and wise)
To hide from sad spectators' eyes
Acts full of ruth, a private room
To drown the horror of death's doom,
That building now no higher rear:
The pest-house standeth everywhere,
For those that on their biers are borne
Are numbered more than those that mourn. (934–45)

The tragic players described in 'The horror of the plague' range from the city itself to the bizarre parade of tormented citizens in Middleton's section of the poem (972–1078), whose plague-sores offer a commentary on their vices. For Middleton, pestilence provides the 'aptest' of deaths for the self-indulgent rich (988), who perish in horrified contemplation of the correspondence between the deformity of their lives and the physical repulsiveness of death by plague. Middleton's characters—a usurer, a drunkard, and a lecher—find themselves forced to inspect the corruption of their minds and bodies as they die, like the dying duke in *The Revenger's Tragedy*. The usurer 'must behold | His pestilent flesh' as it mimicks the coins which have been his consuming passion (980–1); the drunkard must 'view' the symptoms of plague as they mockingly reproduce the symptoms of alcoholism; and the lecher's dying vision is the most appallingly complex of all. With merciless clarity he notes the resemblance between the heat of his lust in the past, the fire of his present fever, and the flames of hell which await him after death—all of which make him 'freeze with horror' (1032)—while the pimps and whores who have catered to his sexual tastes celebrate their immunity from contagion by getting drunk, protected as they are from plague by the prior infection of syphilis. This morbid celebration combines with the carnival mounted by the lecher's conscience as he watches the 'horrid shapes' of his former misdeeds dancing round his deathbed in a hideous parody of the coronation entertainments (1058–67). Where Dekker chooses to examine the corporate reaction of the urban population to the plague, Middleton transfers our attention from the general to the particular, from the city to specific citizens, and in doing so anticipates the terrible isolation that afflicts the rich at the moment of death in the comedies and tragedies he wrote for the stage.

The penultimate section (1069–126) praises the efforts of the physicians to combat the disease by natural means, and urges the public to take moral and spiritual action to help them in their struggle: 'Only this antidote apply: | Cease vexing heaven, and cease to die' (1119–20). But the poem ends by proposing that plague is as much a product of economic collapse as of moral or physical delinquency. The last section, 'The necessity of a plague' (1128–63), argues that the epidemic constitutes a devastating final solution to the breakdown of the city's economic structure, which stems both from overpopulation and from the unproductive lives of its superfluous inhabitants. Before the plague can cease, individual citizens—from the wealthiest to the most indigent—must follow the example of the pamphlet's industrious authors and set to work to reconstruct the shattered fortunes of the capital. In this way the poem returns to the argument of the epistle, which contended that plague and economic ruin are two sides of the same coin, and that clear-sighted writers like Middleton and Dekker occupy the vanguard of a new, dynamic urban community, where the analysis and treatment of social ills take precedence over pandering to the appetites of the idle rich. *News from Gravesend* finishes with a pun that knits the writers' vision of a new society to the nation's inflated hopes for its new monarch. The poets pray 'That this last line may truly reign: | The plague's ceased; heaven is friends again' (1162–3), and so forges a material link between the last line of the poem and the incipient Stuart dynasty. The pamphlet ends as it began, with its plural author acting both as the mock-heroic spokesman for his devastated city and as the visionary advocate of a healthier, more democratic political regime.

SEE ALSO

Textual introduction and apparatus: *Companion*, 474
Authorship and date: *Companion*, 346
Other Middleton–Dekker works: *Caesar's Fall*, 328; *Meeting*, 183; *Magnificent*, 219; *Patient Man*, 280; *Banquet*, 637; *Roaring Girl*, 721; *Gypsy*, 1723

THOMAS DEKKER and THOMAS MIDDLETON

News from Gravesend: Sent to Nobody

Nec quidquam nec cuiquam.

The Epistle Dedicatory

To him that (in the despite and never-dying dishonour of all empty-fisted Maecen-asses) is the gracious, munificent, and golden rewarder of rhymes, singular paymaster of songs and sonnets, unsquint-eyed surveyor of heroical poems, chief rent-gatherer of poets and musicians, and the most valiant confounder of their desperate debts, and (to the comfort of all honest Christians) the now-only only-supper-maker to ingles and players' boys, Sir Nicholas Nemo, alias Nobody:

Shall I creep like a drowned rat into thy warm bosom, my benefic patron, with a piece of some old musty sentence in my mouth, stol'n out of Lycosthenes' *Apophthegms*, and so accost thee? Out upon't! The fashion of such dedications is more stale than kissing. No, no, suffer me, good Nobody, to dive, like a Whitefriars punk, into thy familiar and solid acquaintance at the first dash, and instead of 'Worshipful sir' come upon thee with 'Honest Jew, how dost?' Wonder not that out of the whole barrel of pickled patrons, I have only made choice of thee, for I love none really but thee and myself. For us two do I only care, and therefore I conjure thee, let the payment of thine affection be reciprocal.

They are rhymes that I have boiled in my leaden inkpot for thine own eating. And now, rarest Nobody, taste the reason why they are served up to thee (in the tail of the plague) like caviar or a dish of anchovies after supper. Know then, monsieur verse-gilder, that I have sailed (during this storm of the pestilence) round about the vast island of the whole world, which when I found to be made like a football—the best thing in it, being but a bladder of man's life, lost with a little prick—I took up my foot and spurned at it, because I have heard that none but fools make account of the world. But mistake me not, thou spur-royal of the muses, for it was neither in Sir Francis Drake's nor in Ca'ndish's voyage that I swam through so much salt water, but only with two honest cardmakers (Peter Plancius and Gerard Mercator) who in their universal maps (as in a barber's looking-glass, where a number of most villainous ungodly faces are seen in a year, and especially now at Christmas) did (like country fellows—that is to say, very plainly) and in a shorter time than a sculler can row from Queenhithe to Wapping, make a brave discovery unto me as well of all the old rain-beaten as of the spick-and-span new-found worlds, with every particular kingdom, dukedom, and popedom in their lively colours, so that I knew Constantinople as perfectly as Jobbin the malt-man's horse of Enfield knows the way to London, and could have gone to the great Turk's *seraglio* (where he keeps all his wenches) as tolerably, and far more welcome, than if I had been one of his eunuchs. Prester John and the Sophy were never out of mine eye (yet my sight was not a pin the worse). The Sultan of

Motto ***Nec quidquam nec cuiquam*** 'Nothing dedicated to nobody'

3 ***Maecen-asses*** Maecenas (*c.*70–8 BC) was a famous Roman patron of the arts; the plural form puns on 'asses'

7 **desperate debts** 'bad' debts, unlikely ever to be paid

8 **only-supper-maker** sole provider of square meals
ingles companions; homosexual lovers

9 **players' boys** boy-actors. The placing of players' boys alongside 'ingles' may refer to the idea (spread by vociferous critics of the stage and endorsed by some playwrights) that the acting of women's parts by boys in the Elizabethan theatre encouraged sodomy.
Nemo Nobody

11 **benefic** beneficent

11–12 **old musty sentence** worn-out aphorism or saying

12–13 **Lycosthenes' *Apophthegms*** An adaptation by Conrad Lycosthenes (1518–61) of Erasmus' *Apophthegmata*, which was widely used in schools.

15 **Whitefriars punk** prostitute operating from the sanctuary of the former Whitefriars nunnery

17–18 **Honest Jew** a term of affection

19 **pickled patrons** (substitutes 'patrons' for 'herrings', which were pickled in barrels)

21 **conjure** urge, beg

27 **verse-gilder** one who gives money for verses

30 **football** i.e. soccer ball

34 **spur-royal** gold coin worth fifteen shillings

35 **Sir . . . voyage** Sir Francis Drake (1540?–96) sailed round the world from 1577 to 1580; Sir Thomas Cavendish (1555?–92) did it from 1586 to 1588.

37 **cardmakers** mapmakers, cartographers
Peter Plancius and Gerard Mercator Peter Plancius (1552–1622) published his first *Orbis terrarum typus* in 1590; Mercator (1512–94) published one 'universal map' in 1538 and another in 1569.

42 **sculler** oarsman
from Queenhithe to Wapping a distance of about a mile and a half, rowing down the Thames. Queenhithe was one of the chief watergates of the city; Wapping was the place where pirates were hanged.

46 **lively colours** maps of the world were often coloured after printing. Peter Plancius' widely-distributed maps were bordered with lively engravings of the four continents.

47 **malt-man's** a maker of malt. The distance from Enfield to Shoreditch church in London was about 10 miles.

49 **seraglio** harem

51 **Prester John** a legendary Christian king of Asia
Sophy ruler of Persia.

Egypt I had with a wet finger; from whence, I travelled as boldly to the courts of all the kings in Christendom as if I had been an ambassador (his pomp only excepted).

Strange fashions did I pick (like worms) out of the fingers of every nation, a number of fantastic popinjays and apes (with faces like men) itching till they had got them. And (besides fashions) many wonders, worthy to be hung up (like shields with senseless bald impreses) in the white paper-gallery of a large chronicle. But this made me fret out worse than gummed taffeta: that neither in any one of those kingdoms (no, nor yet within the walls and waterworks of mine own country) could I either find or hear (for I gave a crier a King Harry groat to make an oyez), no nor read, of any man, woman or child left so well by their friends, or that carried such an honest mind to the commonwealth of the Castalians, as to keep open house for the seven poor liberal sciences, nor once (which even the rich cubs and fox-furred curmudgeons do) make them good cheer so much as at Christmas, when every cobbler has license (under the broad seal of hospitality) to sit cheek by jowl at the table of a very alderman's deputy.

What woodcocks then are these seven wise masters to answer to that worm-eaten name of 'liberal', seeing it has undone them? It's a name of the old fashion. It came up with the old religion, and went down with the new. Liberality has been a gentleman of a good house, and an ancient house, but now that old house (like the players' old hall at Dowgate) is fall'n to decay, and to repair it requires too much cost. My seven Latin-sellers have been liberal so long to others that now they have not a rag (or almost nothing but rags) left for themselves. Yea, and into such pitiful predicaments are they fallen that most of our gentry (besides the punies of the Inns of Court and Chancery) takes them for the seven deadly sins, and hate them worse than they hate whores. How much happier had it been for them to have changed their copies, and from sciences been bound to good occupations, considering that one London occupier (dealing uprightly with all men) puts up more in a week than seven Bachelors of Art (that every day go barely a-wooing to them) do in a year.

Hath not the plague, incomparable Nobody (and therefore 'incomparable', because with an Aeneas-like glory thou hast redeemed the golden tree of poesy, even out of the hellish scorn that this world, out of her Luciferan pride, hopes to damn it with)—hath it not, I say, done all men knight's service in working the downfall of our greatest and greediest beggars? *Dicite Io Pæan*, you young sophistical fry of the universities! Break Priscian's pate (if he cross you) for joy. For had not the plague stuck to you in this case, six of your seven academical sweethearts (if I said all seven, I should not lie upon them) had long ere this (but that some doctors withstood it) been begged (not for wards—yet some of them have lodged, I can tell you,

53 **with a wet finger** with ease; as easily as turning the pages of a book after wetting one's finger with the tongue
56 **Strange fashions** It was proverbial that Englishmen picked up different styles of clothing from all over the world in the course of their travels.
worms ticks or mites
57 **popinjays** parrots
60 **senseless bald impreses** meaningless devices or mottoes used on coats-of-arms
61 **white paper-gallery** a reference to pages of coats-of-arms printed in colour on one side of the paper in some books of heraldry and chronicles
62 **fret out worse than gummed taffeta** Taffeta was gummed to make it glossy, but the process damaged the fabric.
64 **waterworks** sea-walls, piers, defences against force of water
65 **King Harry groat** coin worth four pence from the reign of Henry VIII
66 **oyez** 'hear ye', the call of a London crier
68 **Castalians** those who have drunk from the fountain of Castalia on Mount Parnassus, sacred to the muses. In this case, university-educated writers.
69 **seven poor liberal sciences** The seven liberal arts or 'sciences' were the seven parts of the educational curriculum.
70 **cubs** troublesome youngsters
fox-furred curmudgeons wealthy usurers (often depicted wearing fur gowns)
70–1 **make them good cheer** entertain them
73 **alderman's** magistrate in charge of one of the London districts or 'wards'
74 **woodcocks** suckers, dupes
seven wise masters (punning on the title of a still-popular old jestbook, *The Seven Wise Masters of Rome*)
77 **the old religion** Catholicism (as opposed to the 'new', Protestantism)
79–80 **the players' old hall at Dowgate** Dowgate was one of the wards or administrative divisions of London. There may once have been a hall which served as a theatre on the street called Dowgate.
81 **seven Latin-sellers** the seven liberal arts, here characterized as vendors of intellectual goods. The phrase may incorporate a pun on 'latten', a mixed metal of yellow colour.
85 **punies** new students; freshmen
85–6 **the Inns of Court and Chancery** institutions where the law was studied
86–7 **seven deadly sins** sins punishable by damnation according to the Catholic church; here mockingly associated with the seven liberal arts
88–9 **changed their copies** altered their style or behaviour
89 **occupations** trades, businesses
90 **occupier** merchant, tradesman; also a term for a pimp
91 **puts up** pockets
92 **barely** bareheaded, hat in hat like a beggar
95 **Aeneas-like** The hero Aeneas carried a golden tree or bough as an offering to the goddess of the underworld, Proserpina, when he visited hell (*Aeneid* 6.136 ff.).
99 **knight's service** sterling service; a good turn
100 **greatest and greediest beggars** unemployed young men educated at university who follow the muses, that is, write for a living. Perhaps with particular reference to playwrights, since players were condemned as 'sturdy beggars' by the anti-theatrical lobby, and theatres were forced to close in times of plague
Dicite Io Pæan 'shout hurrah' (Ovid, *Ars amatoria*, 2.1)
100–1 **young sophistical fry** youngsters who play games with logic
101 **Priscian's** (AD 419–518) author of a Latin grammar much used in schools and universities
pate head
103 **six . . . sweethearts** It is not clear which of the liberal arts is here being exempted from the charge of folly.
104 **lie upon them** tell a lie about them; perhaps puns on 'lie with them'
105–7 **been begged . . . for** Since the mentally ill ('fools') were wards in Chancery, 'to beg for a fool' was to petition the Court of Wards for his custody, which involved not only the charge of the person but also the complete control of such a one's estate.
106 **wards** (*a*) someone under another person's protection; (*b*) 'fool'

in the Knight's Ward) but for mere Stones and Chesters. Fools, fools, and jesters! Because, whereas some of their chemical and alchemical raw disciples have learned (at their hands) to distil gold and silver out of very tavern bushes, old greasy knaves of diamonds, the dust of bowling alleys—yea, and, like Aesop's Gallus Gallinaceus, to scrape precious stones even out of dunghills—yet they themselves (poor harlotries) had never the grace nor the face to carry one penny in their own purses.

But to speak truth, my noble curer of the poctical madness for nothing, where should they have it? Let them be sent into the courts of princes, there they are so lordly that (unless they were bigger and taller of their hands than so many of the Guard) everyone looks over them, or if they give them anything, it's nothing but good looks. As for the city, that's so full of craftsmen there is no dealing with their mysteries. The nine muses stand in a brown study, when they come within their liberties, like so many mad wenches taken in a watch and brought before a bench of brown bills. *O cives, cives! quærenda pecunia primum! Virtus post Nummos*: 'first open your purses, and then be virtuous; part not with a penny.' The rich misers hold their own by this canon law. And for those (whom in English we call poor snakes), alas, they are barred (by the statute against beggars) from giving a dandiprat or a bawbee. In the camp there is nothing to be had but blows and provant, for soldiers had never worse doings. My sweet captain bestows his pipe of rich trinidado (taking the muses for Irish chimney-sweepers), and that's his talent.

Being in this melancholy contemplation, and having wept a whole inkhorn full of verses in bewailing the miseries of the time, on the sudden I started up, with my teeth bit my writings (because I would eat my words), condemned my pen-knife to the cutting of powder-beef and brewes, my paper to the drying and inflaming of tobacco, and my retirements to a more gentleman-like recreation, *viz.* Duke Humphrey's walk in Paul's—swearing five or six poetical furious oaths, that the goose-quill should never more gull me to make me shoot paper bullets into any stationer's shop or to serve under the weather-beaten colours of Apollo, seeing his pay was no better. Yet rememb'ring what a notable good fellow thou wert, the only Atlas that supports the Olympian honour of learning, and (out of thy horn of abundance) a continual benefactor to all scholars (thou matchless Nobody!), I set up my rest, and vowed to consecrate all my blotting papers only to thee. And not content to dignify thee with that love and honour of myself, I summoned all the rhymesters, play-patchers,

107 **the Knight's Ward** One of the better apartments in the Counter, a debtors' prison in London. It was occupied by prisoners with the means to pay for their upkeep.
Stones and Chesters Stone was a professional jester; Charles Chester a well-known braggart of the 1590s.

109 **chemical . . . disciples** amateur practitioners of the sciences of chemistry and alchemy. Alchemists hoped to 'distil gold and silver' (110–11) out of base metals. Here innkeepers (who make money from alcohol) and gamblers (who make money from cards and bowling alleys) are identified as the most successful alchemists in Jacobean England.

110–11 **tavern bushes** Many taverns advertised themselves with a bush instead of a sign.

111 **greasy knaves of diamonds** gambling with cards

112 **Aesop's Gallus Gallinaceus** Aesop (6th century BC) was a Greek writer famous for his animal fables. In his fable of *gallus gallinaceus* or 'the dunghill cock', a cock failed to recognize the value of a jewel it dug out of the dung on which it lived.

114 **harlotries** knaves or whores

119 **taller of their hands** more accomplished fighters

120 **looks over them** (pun on 'overlooks them')

123 **mysteries** skills, sometimes secret ones, involved in practising trade and manufacturing crafts

124 **brown study** daze
come within their liberties enter the district over which they (the craftsmen) have jurisdiction

125 **mad wenches** prostitutes
taken in a watch arrested in a night

126 **bench of brown bills** panel of night watchmen, who carried long-handled weapons called 'brown bills'

126–7 ***O cives . . . Nummos*** 'O citizens, citizens! Seek money first of all! Virtue after Wealth' (Horace, *Epistles*, 1.1.53–4)

130 **poor snakes** poor people
they i.e. the rich

131 **statute against beggars** Act 'for the suppressing of rogues, vagabonds and sturdy beggars' (1598)
dandiprat small coin worth three halfpence

132 **bawbee** Scottish coin worth about half a penny
In the camp among the military

133 **provant** soldiers' rations

134 **trinidado** the best tobacco, imported from Trinidad

135 **Irish chimney-sweepers** seem to have been common in London. Chimney-sweeps were often associated with smoking, perhaps because tobacco was thought to offer some protection against the lung diseases to which their work made them vulnerable.
talent wealth; i.e. that's all he can afford

140 **pen-knife** used continually to trim the tip of a pen made from a goose-quill as it became blunt in the course of writing

140–1 **powder-beef and brewes** salted beef, and bread soaked in the broth made from it

143 **Duke Humphrey's walk in Paul's** one of the aisles in St Paul's cathedral, where the tomb of Humphrey Duke of Gloucester was supposed to stand: a popular meeting-place for gallants, i.e. fashionable, idle men

144 **poetical furious oaths** swearing outrageous oaths was a necessary skill for gallants
goose-quill pen made from the quill of a goose

145 **gull** trick, con
bullets possible pun on 'billets', small documents or papers, which could also be written 'bullets'. Probably a reference to offering manuscripts to a publisher

146–7 **colours of Apollo** military flag of Apollo, god of poetry

148 **good fellow** good companion, usually a drinking partner
Atlas in Greek mythology, a Titan condemned to carry the heavens on his head and hands

149 **Olympian** Mount Olympus was the home of the Greek gods.

150 **horn of abundance** cornucopia, the horn of the goat Amalthea which suckled the infant Zeus. A metaphor for limitless fertility or generosity, the cornucopia was also used by early modern writers to signify writerly inventiveness.

151 **set up my rest** staked everything

154–5 **play-patchers . . . pamphlet-stitchers** perhaps those who cobble together plays and pamphlets from other people's work

jig-makers, ballad-mongers, and pamphlet-stitchers (being the yeomanry of the company) together with all those whom Theocritus calls the muses' birds (being the Masters and head Wardens) and before them all made an encomiastical oration in praise of Nobody (*scilicet* your proper self), pronouncing them asses, and threat'ning to have them pressed to serve at sea in the Ship of Fools, if ever hereafter they taught their lines (like water spaniels) to fetch any thing that were thrown out of them, or to dive into the unworthy commendations of Lucius Apuleius, or any *Golden Ass* of them all, being for their pains clapped only on the shoulder and sent away dropping, whenas thy leathern bags stand more open than seacoal sacks, more bounteously to reward them.

I had no sooner cut out thy virtues in these large cantles but all the synagogue of scribes gave a *plaudite*, crying out *viva voce*, with one loud throat, that all their verses should henceforth have more feet and take longer strides than if they went upon stilts, only to carry thy glorious praises over the earth, and that none but Nobody should lick the fat of their inventions; that dukes, earls, lords and ladies should have their ill-liberal names torn out of those books whose authors they sent away with a flea in their ear, and the style of Nobody in capital roman letters bravely printed in their places.

Hereupon crowding their heads together, and amongst themselves canvassing more and more thy inexplicable worth, all of them (as inspired) burst suddenly forth and sung extemporal odes in thine honour and palinodes in recantation of all former good opinions held of niggardly patrons—one of them magnifying thee, for that in this pestiferous shipwreck of Londoners, when the pilot, boatswains, master and master's mates, with all the chief mariners that had charge in this goodly argosy of government leapt from the stern, struck all the sails from the mainyard to the mizzen, never looked to the compass, never sounded in places of danger, nor so much as put out their close-fights when they saw a most cruel man-of-war pursue them, but suffered all to sink or swim, crying out only 'Put your trust in God, my bullies, and not in us!', whilst they either hid themselves under hatches or else scrambled to shore in cockboats, yet thou, undaunted Nobody, then, even then, didst stand stoutly to thy tackling, step courageously to the helm, and manfully run up and down, encouraging those (with comfortable words) whose hearts lay coldly in their bellies. Another lifted thee up above the third heaven for playing the constable's part so rarely—and not as your common constables (charging poor sick wretches that had neither meat nor money 'in the King's name' to keep their houses, that's to say, to famish and die), but discharging whole baskets full of victuals (like volleys of shot) in at their windows, thou, only thou, most charitable Nobody, madest them as fat as butter and preserved'st their lives. A third extolled thy martial discipline in appointing ambushes of surgeons and apothecaries to lie close in every ward, of purpose to cut off any convoy that brought the plague succour. A fourth swore at the next impression of *The Chronicles* to have thy name, with the year of our Lord (and certain hexameter verses underneath) all in great golden letters, wherein thy fame should be consecrated to eternal memory for carefully purchasing convenient plots of ground only for

155 **jig-makers, ballad-mongers** writers of popular verses often set to music.
156 **yeomanry** junior members of a guild, or company; in this case, writers of plays, jigs, ballads, and pamphlets
157 **Theocritus** Greek poet (*c*.270 BC)
the muses' birds i.e. bad but arrogant poets (Theocritus, idyll 7.47–8: 'I hate the birds of the muses, who struggle to rival Homer with their cackling')
157–8 **Masters and head Wardens** chief officials of a guild
158–9 **encomiastical oration** formal speech of praise
159–60 ***scilicet* your proper self** 'that is, your own self'
161 **the Ship of Fools** title of a popular book by Alexander Barclay (1475?–1552), published in 1509. It was a translation of Sebastian Brandt's *Narrenschiff* (1494).
162 **water spaniels** spaniels trained to put up birds from water for marksmen to shoot at, as opposed to 'land spaniels' which sought out game on land
164 **Lucius Apuleius** author (AD *c*.155) of *The Golden Ass*, the story of a writer who is changed by magic into a randy donkey
166 **dropping** drooping, disconsolate; with a pun on dripping, as a spaniel would after chasing something thrown into water
167 **seacoal sacks** sacks for carrying coal ('seacoal' was ordinary, mineral coal as opposed to charcoal)
169 **cantles** sections
170 ***plaudite*** shout of approval
171 ***viva voce*** loudly
175 **inventions** i.e. verses
177 **with a flea in their ear** proverbial: with biting words. An attack on aristocratic dedicatees who refuse to reward authors for dedicating books to them
178 **style** correct form of address
in capital roman letters in a modern typeface, as opposed to Gothic type or 'black letter'
181 **canvassing** discussing
183 **palinodes** poems or songs in which something that has been said is retracted; versified recantations
188 **argosy** large merchant-ship
191 **sounded** To 'sound' is to measure the depth of the water in shallow or rocky places, using a lead weight attached to a knotted rope or cord
192 **close-fights** canvas cloths or wooden gratings designed to screen a ship's crew from an enemy
man-of-war fighting ship
194 **bullies** friends, mates
196 **cockboats** small boats carried on shipboard
197–8 **tackling** block and tackle, and ropes used to control the sails
201 **the third heaven** the paradise to which St Paul was lifted (2 Corinthians 12:2)
202 **rarely** well
203–4 **'in the King's name'** the phrase by which Jacobean constables asserted their authority to arrest offenders
204 **keep their houses** stay indoors (the usual period of quarantine for plague was forty days)
205 **famish** starve
210 **lie close** lie hidden (in ambush)
ward administrative division of the city
212 ***The Chronicles*** *A Summary of English Chronicles*, by John Stow (1525–1605), was first published in 1565, and continued to be republished in an abridged form until 1618. Stow's *The Chronicles of England* (1580) was reprinted and expanded (as *The Annals of England*) in 1592 and 1601.
213–14 **hexameter verses** verses of six metrical feet
214 **great golden letters** extremely rare printing with gold ink and a 40-point titling font

burials (and those out of the City too, as they did in Jerusalem) to the intent that threescore (contrary to an Act of Common Council against inmates) might not be pestered together in one little hole where they lie and rot, but that a poor man might for his money have elbow-room, and not have his guts thrust out to be eaten up with paltry worms, lest when in hot and dry summers (that are yet not dreamed on), those musty bodies putrefying, the inavoidable stench of their strong breath be smelled out by the sun—and then there's new work for clerks and sextons.

Thus had everyone a flirt at thy praises. If thou hadst been begged to have played an anatomy in Barber Surgeons' Hall, thy good parts could not have been more curiously ripped up. They dived into the very bowels of thy hearty commendations. So that I—that (like a match) scarce gave fire before to the dankish powder of their apprehensions—was now burnt up myself in the flames of a more ardent affection towards thee, kindled by them. For presently the court broke up and (without a quarter dinner) all parted, their heads being great with child and aching very pitifully till they were delivered of hymns, hexasticons, paeans, and such other panegyrical stuff, which everyone thought seven year till he had brought forth, to testify the love that he bore to Nobody. In advancement of whose honour—and this was sworn upon a pen and inkhorn instead of a sword; yet they all write *Tam marti quàm mercurio*, but how lawfully let the heralds have an eye to't—they vowed and swore very terribly to sacrifice the very lives of their invention. And when they wanted ink (as many of them do, wanting money) or had no more (like a Chancery man) but one pen in all the world, parcel of their oath was to write with their blood and a broomstick before they would sit idle.

Accept therefore (for handsel-sake) these curtal rhymes of ours, thou capon-feaster of scholars. I call them *News from Gravesend*. Be it known unto thy non-residence that I come not near that Gravesend which takes his beginning in Kent, by twenty miles at least. But the end of those graves do I shoot at, which were cast up here in London to stand as landmarks for every parish, to teach them how far they were to go, laying down (so well as I can) the manner how death and his army of pestilent archers entered the field, and how every arrow that they drew did almost cleave a heart in sunder. Read over but one leaf, dear Nobody, and thou put'st upon me an armour of proof against the rankling teeth of those mad dogs (called book-biters) that run barking up and down Paul's churchyard and bite the muses by the shins. Commend thou my labours, and I will labour only to commend thee—for, thy humour being pleased, all the mewing critists in the world shall not fright me. I know the stationers will wish me and my papers burnt (like heretics) at the Cross, if thou dost (now) but enter into their shops by my means. It would fret their hearts to see thee at their stalls reading my *News*. Yet therein they deal doubly, and like notable dissemblers, for all the time of this plaguy alarum they marched only under thy colours, desired none but thy company, none but thyself wert welcome to them, none but Nobody (as they all cried out to thine immortal commendations) bought books off them. Nobody was their best and most bounteous customer. Fie on this hollow-hearted world! Do they shake thee off now? Be wise, and come not near them by twelve score at least; so shalt thou not need to

217–18 **as they did in Jerusalem** The tomb that belonged to Joseph of Arimathea, where Christ was buried, stood outside the walls of Jerusalem.

218–19 **Act of Common Council** The Court of Common Council passed several laws against filling houses with inmates—that is, with more than one family or household.

226–7 **new work for clerks and sextons** new graves to be dug (by sextons) and burial services read (by clerks), as a result of the contagion spread by sloppily buried corpses

228 **flirt** sharp blow; rap

229 **have played an anatomy** served as a subject for anatomical demonstrations

236 **court** assembly

236–7 **quarter dinner** dinner held once a quarter

239 **hexasticons** groups of six lines of verse
paeans songs of praise or thanksgiving
panegyrical stuff material for praising Nobody

244 ***Tam marti quàm mercurio*** 'Dedicated as much to Mars (the god of war) as to Mercury (the god of learning)'. A motto legitimately used by writers such as George Gascoigne (1539?–1577), who had served in the army.

246 **invention** creativity

247 **wanted** lacked

248 **Chancery man** attorney or clerk at the Inns of Chancery. Chancery lawyers acted for the poor, and were considered to be of a lower social status than those of the Inns of Court; hence the Chancery man's poverty.

249 **parcel** part

251 **for handsel-sake** as a handsel, i.e. a thing given in advance, as a promise of future gifts
curtal rhymes octosyllabic couplets. A 'curtal' was a horse with its tail docked.

252 **capon-feaster of scholars** one who feasts academics with chickens

253 ***Gravesend*** a town in Kent at the mouth of the Thames, visited by ships entering and leaving the port of London. In 1568 Sir Robert Martyn proposed that ships from infected harbours should be quarantined there for forty days, and this proposal was sporadically put into practice from then on. The German traveller Thomas Platter visited Gravesend in 1599, and reported that 'there is very little to be seen'.

255–6 **the end . . . shoot at** a metaphor from archery: 'I mean the graves'

257 **landmarks** objects set up to mark a boundary line

260–1 **every arrow . . . almost** almost every arrow

262 **armour of proof** armour whose resistance to bullets had been proved by having bullets fired at it

263–4 **book-biters** pun on 'backbiters', slanderers

264 **Paul's churchyard** the churchyard of St Paul's Cathedral, where most London printers and booksellers had their shops

267 **humour** inclination, taste
critists critics

269 **the Cross** Paul's Cross in Paul's churchyard, where books offensive to the church authorities were burned, as they were on one famous occasion in 1599: see *Microcynicon*

272 **deal doubly** engage in double-dealing

273 **alarum** a call to arms

274 **colours** banner, flag

280 **twelve score** Few archers could hit a target at twelve score (240) yards.

care what disgraces they shoot at thee. But leaving them to their old tune of 'What new books do you lack?', prick up thine ears like a March hare (at the sudden cry of a kennel of hounds) and listen what news the post that's come from Winchester Term winds out of his horn.

O that thou hadst taken a lease there, happy Nobody, but for one month! The place had, for thy sake, been well spoken of for ever. Many did heartily pray—especially watermen and players, besides the drawers, tapsters, butchers, and innholders, with all the rest of the hungry commonalty of Westminster—for thy going thither. Ten thousand in London swore to feast their neighbours with nothing but plum porridge and mince pies all Christmas (that now for anger will not bestow a crust on a beggar) upon condition that all the judges, serjeants, barristers and attorneys had not set a foot out of doors, but that thou only (in pomp), saving them that labour, hadst rode that journey, so greedily did they thirst after thy preferment. For hadst thou been there, those black buckram tragedies had never been seen that there have been acted. Alas! It's a beastly thing to report. But—truth must out!—poor dumb horses were made mere jades, being used so villainously that they durst neither whinny nor wag tail. And though the riders of them had grown never so choleric and chaffed till they foamed again, an ostler to walk them was not to be had for love or money. Neither could the geldings (even of gentlemen) get leave (for all they sweat till they dropped again) to stand as they had wont at rack and manger—no, no, 'twas enough for their masters to have that honour; but now, against all equity, were they called (when they little thought of any such matter) to a dear reckoning for all their old wild oats.

A conspiracy there was amongst all the innkeepers that Jack Straw (an ancient rebel) should choke all the horses—and the better to bring this to pass, a bottle of hay was sold dearer than a bottle of wine at London. A truss cost more than Master Mayor's truss of Forditch, with the sleeves and belly-piece all of bare satin to boot. Which knavery being smelled out, the horsemen grew politic, and never sat down to dinner, but their nags were still at their elbows. So that it grew to be as ordinary a question to ask 'What shall I pay for a chamber for myself and my gelding all night?' (because they would not be jaded any more) as in other country towns '—for my wife and myself'. For a beast and a man were entertained both alike, and that in such wonderful sort that they'll speak of it *in æternam rei memoriam*. For most of their rooms were fairly built (out of the ground, but not out of the dirt) like Irish hovels, hung round about with cobweb-lawn very richly, and furnished no alderman's parlour in London like them. For here's your bed, there a stable, and that a hog-sty, yet so artificially contrived that they stand all under one roof, to the amazement of all that behold them.

But what a childishness is it to get up thus upon their hobby-horses! Let them bite o' the bridle, whilst we have about with the men. As for the women, they may laugh and lie down; it's a merry world with them, but somebody pays for it. O Winchester! Much mutton hast thou to answer for, which thou hast made away (being sluttishly fried out in steaks, or in burnt carbonadoes). Thy maid-servants best know how, if they were called to an account. It was happy for some that four of the returns were cut off, for if they had held together many a one had never returned from thence his own man. O beware! Your

282 **'What . . . lack?'** 'What do you lack?' was a familiar seller's cry.

283 **March hare** March is the mating season for hares, when they are said to go mad.

284 **post** letter-bearer, who blows a horn to signal his arrival

285 **Winchester Term** During the plague of 1604 the Michaelmas term (beginning 10 October; one of the four terms during which the London law courts were in session) was held at Winchester.

289 **watermen** oarsmen who ferry passengers up and down the Thames
drawers, tapsters those who draw liquor for customers at a tavern

291 **commonalty** the common people; those below the rank of gentry

299 **black buckram tragedies** buckram was a coarse cloth; black buckram the traditional wear for tragedies

302 **made mere jades** To make a horse a jade is to exhaust it by working it too hard; 'to make a jade of' people is to fool them. The passage refers to the exorbitant prices charged for the upkeep of horses while the lawcourts met at Winchester.

303–4 **they durst . . . tail** proverbial: the horses didn't dare to draw attention to themselves

307–8 **for all . . . dropped again** despite the fact that they worked till the sweat dripped off them

308–9 **stand . . . at rack and manger** live in plenty, want for nothing

314 **Jack Straw** one of the leaders of the Rising of the Commons in 1381. Here his name refers to the triumph of the commons over the gentry at Winchester, where the cost of straw for gentlemen's horses was artificially raised by innkeepers.

315–16 **bottle of hay** bundle of hay

317 **truss . . . truss** puns on two meanings of truss: 'a bundle' and 'a closely fitting jacket or breeches'
Forditch may refer to Fordwich near Canterbury

318 **belly-piece** the part of the jacket that covers the belly

320 **politic** cunning

321 **ordinary** (*a*) frequent or regular; (*b*) a regular daily meal or allowance of food

324 **jaded** conned

327 ***in æternam rei memoriam*** 'in perpetual remembrance of the thing'

329 **cobweb-lawn** very fine linen: mockingly refers to the cobwebs bedecking the seedy chambers made available to gentlemen at Winchester

334–5 **get . . . hobby-horses** play the fool. A hobby-horse was a figure of fun in a morris dance.

335 **bite o' the bridle** restrain themselves

336 **have about with** have a go at

337 **laugh and lie down** a card game (with a sexual quibble), in which the women are collecting all the winnings

338 **mutton** (*a*) women's genitals; (*b*) whores

340 **sluttishly** sloppily; a 'slut' is a whore
carbonadoes meat scored across and grilled

342–3 **four . . . cut off** There were eight returns in Michaelmas term (10th October–28th November); that is, eight days on which the Sheriffs' reports were returned to the law courts. In 1603 the first four of these returns did not take place at Winchester.

Winchester goose is ten times more dangerous to surfeit upon than your St Nicholas Shambles capon.

You talk of a plague in London, and red crosses set upon doors, but ten plagues cannot melt so many crosses of silver out of lawyers' purses as the Winchesterians (with a hey-pas! repas!) juggled out of theirs to put into their own. Patient they were, I must needs confess, for they would pocket up anything, came it never so wrongfully, insomuch that very good substantial householders have oftentimes gone away with cracked crowns and never complained of them that gave them. If ever money were current (*a currendo*, of running away), now was the time. It ran from the poor clients to the attorneys and clerks of bands in small troops (here ten, and there twenty), but when the leaguers of Winchester cried 'Charge, charge!', the lawyers paid for't; they went to the pot full dearly, and the townsmen still carried away all the noble and royal victories. So that, being puffed up with an opinion that the Silver Age was crept into the world again, they denied (in a manner) the King's coin, for a penny was no money with them. Whensoever there shall come forth a prest for soldiers, thither let it be sent, for by all the opinion of the best captains that had a charge there, and have tried them, the men of Winchester are the only serviceable men this day in England. The reason is, they care no more to venture among small shots than to be at the discharging of so many cans of beer. Tush! 'tis their desire to see those that enter upon them to come off soundly, that when they are gone all the world may bear witness they came to their cost.

And being thus night and day employed, and continually ent'ring into action, it makes them have mighty stomachs, so that they are able to soak and devour all that come in their way. A rapier and a cloak have been eaten up at a supper as clean (and carried away well, too) as if they had been but two rabbit-suckers. A nag served but one servingman to a breakfast, whilst the saddle and bridle were brewed into a quart of strong beer.

This intolerable destroying of victuals being looked into, the inhabitants laid their heads together and agreed among themselves (for the general good of the whole town) to make it a town of garrison. And seeing the desperate termers, that strove in law together, in such a pitiful pickle, and every day so dirty that when they met their counsel they looked like the black guard fighting with the Inns of Court, that therefore all the householders should turn Turk and be victuallers to the camp. By this means, having the law in their own hands, they ruled the roost how they listed; insomuch, that a common jug of double beer scorned to kiss the lips of a knight under a groat. Six hours' sleep could not be bought under five shillings. Yea, in some places a night's lodging was dearer than the hire of a courtesan in Venice twice so long. And having learned the tricks of London sextons, there they laid four or five in a bed, as here those other knaves of spades thrust nine and ten into one grave—beds keeping such a jostling of one another in every room that in the day time the lodgings looked like so many upholsters' shops, and in the night time like the Savoy, or St Thomas' hospital. At which, if any guest did but once bite his lip or grumble, he was cashiered the company for a mutinous fellow; the place was not for him; let him trudge. A number stood with petitions ready to give money for the reversion of it, for Winchester now durst (or at least hoped to) stand upon proud terms with London. And this, thou beloved of all men, is the very pith and marrow of the

345 **Winchester goose** a swelling in the groin caused by syphilis. The brothels of Southwark came within the jurisdiction of the Bishop of Winchester.

346 **St Nicholas Shambles capon** The poulterers of London moved to St Nicholas Shambles in 1603. A capon is a castrated cockerel.

347 **red crosses** (used to mark the doors of houses infected by plague)

348–9 **crosses of silver** coins stamped with the figure of a cross

350 **hey-pas! repas!** terms used by jugglers

354 **cracked crowns** broken heads; also, worthless coins. Coins were stamped with a ring inside which the sovereign's head was placed. A coin containing a crack extending inside the ring was unfit for currency.

356 **current (*a currendo*, of running away)** The writer claims that the word 'current' is derived from the Latin verb *currere*, to run, because currency is always escaping from people's grasp.

357–8 **clerks of bands** 'bands' are collars such as lawyers wore. 'Clerks of bands' may mean unqualified attorneys who acted on behalf of those who could not afford to hire lawyers educated at the Inns of Court.

359 **leaguers** members of a league or gang
Charge, charge! a battle-cry; also puns on charging for room, board, and other services

360 **went . . . dearly** paid a lot for a drink

361 **noble and royal** (pun on two coins)

362–3 **the Silver Age** in classical mythology, the second of the seven ages of the world; i.e. the people of Winchester would not take anything less than silver for their services

363–4 **denied . . . King's coin** refused to accept legal currency, by regarding a penny as worthless

365 **prest** forced enlistment

367 **had a charge** commanded troops

368 **the only serviceable men** the only men fit for military service

370 **small shots** musket bullets, as opposed to cannon balls

372 **come off soundly** pay dearly for it

376–7 **mighty stomachs** (*a*) great courage; (*b*) inordinate greed

380 **rabbit-suckers** young rabbits

386 **town of garrison** town under military command

387 **termers** those who attend the law courts in term-time

389 **black guard** lowest-paid domestic servants; scullions, kitchen-boys etc., whose work involved getting dirty

391 **turn Turk** become apostates, i.e. change their profession
victuallers suppliers of food

395 **groat** coin worth four pennies. The usual price of a quart of best beer was a penny.

399–400 **knaves of spades** refers to the practices of London sextons or gravediggers who crammed nine or ten bodies into one grave to save money and labour, and who therefore cheated their customers as gamblers cheat their opponents at cards

403–4 **the Savoy, or St Thomas' hospital** two London hospitals

405 **cashiered** thrown out of (literally, dismissed from military or domestic service in disgrace)

408 **reversion of it** right of obtaining it at some future time

best and latest news (except the unmasking of certain treasons) that came with the post from Winchester, where if thou hadst hired a chamber—as would to heaven thou hadst!—thou wouldst never have gone to any barber's in London whilst thou hadst lived, but have been trimmed only there, for they are the true shavers; they have the right Neapolitan polling.

To whose commendations, let me glue this piece more: that it is the most excellent place for dispatching of old suits in the world—for a number of riding suits (that had lain long in lavender) were worn out there, only with serving amongst the hot shots that marched there up and down. Let Westminster therefore, Temple Bar, and Fleet Street, drink off this draught of *rosa solis* to fetch life into them again after their so often swooning that those few jurors that went thither (if any did go thither) have ta'en an oath never to sit at Winchester ordinary again, if they can choose, but rather to break their fasts in the old abbey behind Westminster with pudding pies and furmenty.

Deliver copies of these *News*, good Nobody, to none of thy acquaintance (as thou tender'st me), and thou shalt command any service at my hands. For I have an intent to hire three or four ballad-makers who, I know, will be glad for sixpence and a dinner to turn all this limping prose into more perfectly-halting verse, that it shall do any true-born citizen's heart good to hear such doings sung to some filthy tune. And so farewell. Turn over a new leaf, and try if I handle the plague in his right kind.

Devoted to none but thyself,
Somebody

News from Gravesend

To sickness and to queasy times
We drink a health in wholesome rhymes.
Physic, we invoke thy aid,
Thou that (born in heaven) art made
A lackey to the meanest creature;
Mother of health, thou nurse of nature,
Equal friend to rich and poor,
At whose hands kings can get no more
Than empty beggars; O thou wise
In nothing but in mysteries!
Thou that hast of earth the rule,
Where (like an academe, or school)
Thou read'st deep lectures to thy sons,
Men's demigods, physicïans,
Who thereby learn the abstruse powers
Of herbs, of roots, of plants, of flowers,
And suck from poisonous stinking weed
Preservatives, man's life to feed.
Thou nearest to a god—for none
Can work it, but a god alone—
O grave enchantress, deign to breathe
Thy spells into us, and bequeath
Thy sacred fires, that they may shine
In quick and virtual medicine.
Arm us to convince this foe,
This king of dead men, conquering so,
This hungry plague, cater to death,
Who eats up all, yet famisheth.
Teach us how we may repair
These ruins of the rotten air,
Or if the air's pollution can
So mortal strike through beast and man,
Or if in blood corrupt Death lie,
Or if one dead cause others die.
Howe'er, thy sovereign cures disperse,
And with that glory crown our verse,
That we may yet save many a soul
(Perchance, now merry at his bowl)
That ere our tragic song be done
Must drink this thick contagïon.
But—O grief!—why do we accite
The charms of Physic? Whose numbed sprite
Now quakes, and nothing dare or can,
Checked by a more dread magicïan.
Sick is Physic's self to see
Her aphorisms proved a mockery.

412 **treasons** In November 1603 Lord Grey of Wilton, Lord Cobham and Sir Walter Raleigh were tried for treason at Winchester.
415 **trimmed** cheated. Barbers were supposed to be inveterate cheats.
416–17 **the right Neapolitan polling** 'Polling' means both the cutting of hair and extortion. Naples was associated with syphilis, whose treatment caused loss of hair. Presumably, the inhabitants of Winchester sent Londoners home with the clap as well as with empty pockets.
419–20 **dispatching of old suits** bringing old lawsuits to a conclusion
422 **hot shots** cannon balls heated up so as to set fire to any combustible substance they struck; hence, hotheads, troublemakers
423–4 **Temple Bar, and Fleet Street** streets adjacent to the Inns of Court, where business would have been badly affected by the lawyers' absence
424 ***rosa solis*** a medicine originally made with the juice of the plant sundew, and later with brandy
429 **furmenty** a dish made of wheat boiled in milk, seasoned with sugar and spice
437–8 **Turn . . . leaf** (The verses began on a new page.)
442 **queasy** unhealthy
453 **academe** academy
465 **virtual** effective
466 **convince** defeat
468 **cater** caterer
471 **rotten air** plague was sometimes thought to have been caused, or at least aggravated, by corrupt atmospheric conditions
472 **Or if** whether
479 **at his bowl** drinking. It was widely believed that heavy drinking could protect the body against plague.
482 **accite** summon, call on
483 **sprite** spirit
487 **aphorisms** (alluding to various medical treatises with that title, including the *Aphorismes* of the ancient Greek medical writer Hippocrates)

For, whilst she's turning o'er her books
And on her drugs and simples looks,
She's run through her own armèd heart,
Th'infection flying above art.
Come, therefore, thou the best of nine
(Because the saddest), every line
That drops from sorrow's pen is due
Only to thee; to thee we sue.
Thou tragic maid, whose fury's spent
In dismal and most black ostent,
In uproars and in fall of kings,
Thou of empire's change that sings,
Of dearths, of wars, of plagues, and laughs
At funerals and epitaphs,
Carouse thou to our thirsty soul
A full draught from the Thespian bowl,
That we may pour it out again
And drink, in numbers, juice to men,
Striking such horrors through their ears
Their hair may upright stand with fears
Till rich heirs meeting our strong verse
May not shrink back before it pierce
Their marble eyeballs, and there shed
One drop (at least) for him that's dead.
To work which wonder, we will write
With pens pulled from that bird of night,
The shrieking owl; our ink we'll mix
With tears of widows, black as Styx;
The paper where our lines shall meet
Shall be a folded winding-sheet;
And that the scene may show more full,
The standish is a dead man's skull.
Inspire us therefore how to tell
The horror of a plague, the hell.

The cause of the plague

Nor drops this venom from that fair
And crystal bosom of the air,
Whose ceaseless motion clarifies
All vaporous stench that upward flies,
And with her universal wings
Thick poisonous fumes abroad she flings
Till (like to thunder), rudely tossed,
Their malice is (by spreading) lost.
Yet must we grant that—from the veins
Of rottenness and filth that reigns
O'er heaps of bodies slain in war,
From carrion (that endangers far),
From standing pools, or from the wombs
Of vaults, of muckhills, graves, and tombs,
From bogs, from rank and dampish fens,
From moorish breaths and nasty dens—
The sun draws up contagious fumes
Which, falling down, burst into rheums
And thousand maladies beside,
By which our blood grows putrefied.
Or, being by winds not swept from thence,
They hover there in clouds condense
Which, sucked in by our spirits, there flies
Swift poison through our arteries,
And (not resisted) straight it chokes
The heart with those pestiferous smokes.
Thus Physic and Philosophy
Do preach, and (with this) salves apply,
Which search, and use with speed. But now
This monster breeds not thus. For how
(If this be proved) can any doubt
But that the air does (round about)
In flakes of poison drop on all,
The sore being spread so general?
Nor dare we so conclude. For then
Fruits, fishes, foul, nor beasts nor men
Should 'scape untainted. Grazing flocks
Would feed upon their graves; the ox
Drop at the plough; the travelling horse
Would for a rider bear a corse;
Th'ambitious lark (the bird of state),
Whose wings do sweep heaven's pearlèd gate,
As she descended then would bring
Pestilent news under each wing;
Then rivers would drink poisoned air;
Trees shed their green and curlèd hair;
Fish swim to shore full of disease
(For pestilence would fin the seas),
And we should think their scaly barks,
Having small speckles, had the marks.
No soul could move. But sure there lies
Some vengeance more than in the skies.
Nor (as a taper, at whose beams
Ten thousand lights fetch golden streams,
And yet itself is burnt to death)
Can we believe that one man's breath

489 **simples** medicines
492 **best of nine** best of the nine muses
497 **ostent** appearance
503 **Thespian bowl** Thespis (6th century BC) was credited with being the founder of Greek tragedy. The Thespian bowl is therefore the cup of tragedy.
505 **numbers** metre, verse
juice bodily fluids, necessary to combat disease
514 **shrieking owl** considered a bad omen
515 **Styx** in Greek and Roman mythology, one of the rivers of the underworld
517 **winding-sheet** cloth in which corpses were wrapped
519 **standish** ink-stand
534 **far** from a distance
537 **dampish** vaporous
538 **moorish breaths** fumes from swamps
540 **rheums** colds
542 **grows putrefied** festers; becomes putrid or gangrenous
544 **condense** thick
545 **spirits** breath
549 **Philosophy** natural science
550 **salves** remedies
556 **sore . . . general** the disease being spread so universally
562 **corse** corpse
563 **lark** (considered ambitious because it soars heavenwards as it sings)
572 **marks** otherwise known as tokens: physical symptoms of plague
575–7 **taper . . . death** a taper which is used to light ten thousand candles but which burns up as it does so

Infected, and being blown from him,
His poison should to others swim—
For then who breathed upon the first?
Where did th'imbulkèd venom burst?
Or how 'scaped those that did divide
The self-same bits with those that died?
Drunk of the self-same cups, and lay
In ulcerous beds as close as they?
Or those who, every hour (like crows)
Prey on dead carcasses, their nose
Still smelling to a grave, their feet
Still wrapped within a dead man's sheet?—
Yet, the sad execution done,
Careless among their cans they run,
And there (in scorn of death or fate)
Of the deceased they wildly prate,
Yet snore untouched, and next day rise
To act in more new tragedies.
Or (like so many bullets flying)
A thousand here and there being dying,
Death's text-bill clapped on every door,
Crosses on sides, behind, before,
Yet he (i'th' midst) stands fast—from whence
Comes this? You'll say, 'From providence'.
'Tis so, and that's the common spell
That leads our ignorance (blind as hell),
And serves but as excuse to keep
The soul from search of things more deep.
No, no, this black and burning star
(Whose sulphured drops do scald so far)
Does neither hover o'er our heads,
Nor lies it in our bloods, nor beds;
Nor is it stitched to our attires,
Nor like wild balls of running fires
Or thunderbolts, which where they light
Do either bruise or kill outright,
Yet by the violence of that bound
Leap off, and give a second wound.
But this fierce dragon, huge and foul,
Sucks virid poison from our soul,
Which, being spit forth again, there reigns
Showers of blisters and of blains,
For every man within him feeds
A worm, which this contagion breeds.
Our heavenly parts are plaguy sick,
And there such leprous spots do stick
That God in anger fills his hand
With vengeance, throwing it on the land.
Sure, 'tis some capital offence,
Some high high treason doth incense
Th'eternal king, that thus we are
Arraigned at death's most dreadful bar,
Th'indictment writ on England's breast—
When other countries, better blest,
Feel not the judge's heavy doom,
Whose breath (like lightning) doth consume
And (with a whip of planets) scourges
The veins of mortals, in whom surges
Of sinful blood, billows of lust,
Stir up the pow'rs to acts unjust.
Whether they be princes' errors
Or faults of peers, pull down these terrors,
Or (because we may not err
Let's sift it in particular)
The courtier's pride, lust, and excess,
The churchman's painted holiness,
The lawyer's grinding of the poor,
The soldier's starving at the door
(Rag'd, lean, and pale through want of blood,
Sold cheap by him for country's good),
The scholar's envy, farmer's curse—
When heav'n's rich treasurer doth disburse
In bounteous heaps (to thankless men)
His universal blessings, then
This delving mole for madness eats
Even his own lungs, and strange oaths sweats
Because he cannot sell for pence
Dear years in spite of providence.
Add unto these the city-sin
(Brought by seven deadly monsters in)
Which doth all bounds and blushing scorn,
Because 'tis in the freedom born.
What trains of vice (which even hell hates)
But have bold passage through her gates?
Pride in diet, pride in clothing,
Pride in building, pure in nothing—

582 **th'imbulkèd** contained in the body
burst i.e. first break out
584 **bits** portions of food
589 **smelling to** seeking out graves by the smell of the corpses
592 **cans** jugs of beer
599 **text-bill** placard serving as an advertisement
603 **common spell** usual story
607 **black and burning star** refers to the plague, or its unknown cause, as a star or planet which has an evil influence on human affairs
608 **sulphured** sulphurous
618 **virid** green
620 **blains** swellings, sores
623 **heavenly parts** eternal soul; intellect and conscience
624 **spots** sins
633 **doom** sentence
635 **whip of planets** refers to the theological view that the Providential Will intervened in human affairs both directly (through miracles etc.) and indirectly, through astrological conjunctions
641 **because** so that
642 **sift** analyse
644 **painted** fake
647 **Rag'd** 'in rags' (not necessarily the same thing as 'ragged')
653 **delving** burrowing: applied to the rich farmer who works the soil
656 **Dear years** that is, the produce of 'dear years' or years when grain was in short supply. The farmer who wants to sell 'Dear years in spite of Providence' is one who wants to treat every year as a year of shortages by selling his produce at the highest possible price, thus usurping Providence's prerogative of controlling the seasons.
657 **city-sin** (punning on 'citizen')
658 **seven deadly monsters** i.e. the Seven Deadly Sins
660 **the freedom** a district of London which enjoyed special privileges: exemption from certain taxes, etc.

And that she may not want disease,
She sails for it beyond the seas.
With Antwerp will she drink up Rhine,
With Paris act the bloodiest scene,
Or in pied fashions pass her folly,
Mocking at heaven, yet look most holy.
Of usury she'll rob the Jews;
Of luxury, Venetian stews.
With Spaniards, she's an Indianist;
With barbarous Turks, a sodomist.
So low her antique walls do stand,
These sins leap o'er, even with one hand.
And he—that all in modest black,
Whose eyeball strings shall sooner crack
Than seem to note a tempting face,
Measuring streets with a dove-like pace—
Under that oily visor wears
The poor man's sweat and orphan's tears.
Now whether these particular fates,
Or general moles (disfiguring states),
Whether one sin alone, or whether
This main battalion joined together,
Do dare these plagues, we cannot tell,
But down they beat all human spell.
Or, it may be, Jehovah looks
But now upon those audit books
Of forty-five years' hushed account
For hours misspent (whose sums surmount
The price of ransomed kings), and there,
Finding out grievous debts, doth clear
And cross them under his own hand,
Being paid with lives through all the land.
For since his maiden-servant's gone
And his new viceroy fills the throne,
Heaven means to give him (as his bride)
A nation new and purified.
  Take breath awhile, our panting muse,
And to the world tell gladder news
Than these of burials; strive awhile
To make thy sullen numbers smile.
Forget the names of graves and ghosts,
The sound of bells, the unknown coasts
Of death's vast kingdom, and sail o'er
With fresher wind to happier shore.
For now the maiden isle hath got
A royal husband (heavenly lot).
Fair Scotland does fair England wed,
And gives her for her maidenhead
A crown of gold, wrought in a ring
With which she's married to a king.
Thou beldam (whisperer of false rumours),
Fame, cast aside those antic humours:
Lift up thy golden trump, and sound
Even from Tweed's utmost crystal bound
And from the banks of silver Thames
To the green ocean, that King James
Has made an island (that did stand
Half-sinking) now the firmest land.
Carry thou this to Neptune's ear
That his shrill Tritons it may bear
So far, until the Danish sound
With repercussive voice rebound,
That echoes (doubling more and more)
May reach the parchèd Indian shore,
For 'tis heav'n's care so great a wonder
Should fly upon the wings of thunder.

The horror of the plague

O thou my country, here mine eyes
Are almost sunk in waves that rise
From the rough wind of sighs, to see
A spring that lately courted thee
In pompous bravery, all thy bowers
Gilt by the sun, perfumed with flowers,
Now like a loathsome leper lying,
Her arbors with'ring, green trees dying,
Her revels and May merriments
Turned all to tragic dreariments.
And thou, the mother of my breath,
Whose soft breast thousands nourisheth,
Altar of Jove, thou throne of kings,
Thou fount, where milk and honey springs,

Apostrophe ad civitatem

667 **Rhine** wine from the Rhine region
668 **Paris . . . scene** refers to the St Bartholomew's Day massacre of 1572, when Protestants were massacred by Catholics. Christopher Marlowe (1564–1593) wrote a play about it in the early 1590s, *The Massacre at Paris*, so the 'scene' had been 'acted' on the English stage. 'Scene' puns on 'Seine'.
669 **pied fashions** motley fashions; the kind of parti-coloured clothes worn by professional jesters
her Paris's
672 **stews** brothels
673 **Indianist** possibly a smoker of tobacco, known as the Indian weed
674 **sodomist** sodomite
678 **eyeball strings** the muscles, nerves or tendons of the eye. These were supposed to crack at death.
681 **visor** mask
684 **moles** blemishes on the skin
686 **main battalion** the body of an army
687 **dare** provoke
688 **spell** (*a*) charm; (*b*) explanation
691 **forty-five . . . account** Elizabeth I died in the forty-fifth year of her reign. Despite war with Spain, fighting in Ireland and occasional rebellions, this was widely spoken of as a period of unbroken peace.
694–5 **clear And cross them** pay them and cross them out in the audit-book
697 **his maiden-servant's gone** the death of Elizabeth I, the virgin queen
698 **new viceroy** i.e. James I
706 **sound of bells** (tolled at funerals)
710 **lot** fortune, luck
711 **Scotland . . . wed** (James I united the kingdoms of Scotland and England)
715 **beldam** old woman
716 **antic humours** absurd activities
717 **trump** trumpet
718 **Tweed's** river in Scotland
723 **Neptune's** Roman god of the sea, whose servants are the Tritons
725 **sound** channel or strait (with pun on 'noise')
726 **repercussive** reverberating
740 **May merriments** traditional pastimes which took place in the month of May
741 **dreariments** mournful expressions
742.n ***Apostrophe ad civitatem*** words addressed to the City (of London)

Europe's jewel, England's gem,
Sister to great Jerusalem,
Neptune's minion ('bout whose waist
The Thames is like a girdle cast),
Thou that (but health) canst nothing want,
Empress of cities, Troynovant!
When I thy lofty towers behold
(Whose pinnacles were tipped with gold,
Both when the sun did set and rise,
So lovely wert thou in his eyes)
Now like old monuments forsaken
Or (like tall pines) by winter shaken;
Or, seeing thee gorgeous as a bride
Even in the height of all thy pride
Disrobed, disgraced, and when all nations
Made love to thee in amorous passions,
Now scorned of all the world; alone,
None seek thee, nor must thou seek none,
But like a prisoner must be kept
In thine own walls, till thou hast wept
Thine eyes out, to behold thy sweet
Dead children heaped about thy feet—
O dearest! say, how can we choose
But have a sad and drooping muse
When corpses do so choke thy way
That now thou look'st like Golgotha.
But thus, the alt'ring of a state
Alters our bodies and our fate,
For princes' deaths do even bespeak
Millions of lives; when kingdoms break,
People dissolve, and (as with thunder)
Cities' proud glories rend asunder.
Witness thy walls, whose stony arms
But yesterday received whole swarms
Of frighted English. Lord and loon,
Lawyer and client, courtier, clown,
All sorts did to thy buildings fly
As to the safest sanctuary,
And he that through thy gates might pass,
His fears were locked in towers of brass.
Happy that man; now happier they
That from thy reach get first away—
As from a shipwreck to some shore;
As from a lost field, drowned in gore;
As from high turrets, whose joints fail;
Or rather, from some loathsome jail.
But note heav'n's justice: they, by flying
That would cozen death and save a dying,
How like to chaff abroad they're blown,
And (but for scorn) might walk unknown.
Like to plumed ostriches they ride,
Or like sea-pageants, all in pride
Of tacklings, flags, and swelling sails,
Borne on the loftiest wave, that vails
His purple bonnet, and in dread
Bows down his snowy curlèd head,
So from th'infected city fly
These swallows in their gallantry,
Looking that wheresoe'er they light
Gay summer (like a parasite)
Should wait on them, and build 'em bowers,
And crown their nests with wreathèd flowers,
And swains to welcome them should sing
And dance, as for their Whitsun king.
Feather of pride, how art thou tossed!
How soon are all thy beauties lost!
How eas'ly golden hopes unwind!
The russet boor and leathern hind
That two days since did sink his knee
And (all uncovered) worshipped thee,
Or being but poor and meanly clothed
Was either laughed to scorn or loathed,
Now thee he loathes and laughs to scorn,
And though upon thy back be worn
More satin than a kingdom's worth
He bars his door and thrusts thee forth.
And they whose palate land nor seas,
Whom fashions of no shape, could please,
Whom princes have (in ages past)
For rich attires and sumptuous waste
Never come near, now sit they round
And feed (like beggars) on the ground,

748 **minion** lover
751 **Troynovant** New Troy, the name given to London by its legendary founder, Brutus
771 **Golgotha** 'the place of the skull', where Christ was crucified
774 **bespeak** order in advance
780 **loon** rogue, idler
781 **clown** peasant
785 **towers of brass** proverbially, the safest place of all. The friar and magician Roger Bacon (*c.*1214–*c.*1294) was said to have had a plan to wall England round with brass.
789 **lost field** military defeat
793 **cozen death ... dying** cheat death by keeping from him what they owe him: that is, a 'dying'
795 **(but for scorn)** if it were not for the contempt in which they are held (or possibly, in which they hold other people)
796 **plumed ostriches** (the ostrich was an emblem of pride)
797 **sea-pageants** ships displaying all their finery
799 **vails** removes, as a sign of respect
803 **gallantry** ostentatious clothing
805 **parasite** servant, sycophant
808 **swains** country folk
809 **Whitsun king** On Whit Sunday, the seventh Sunday after Easter, festivals called 'Whitsun ales' were held, presided over by a Whitsun king or lord.
813 **The russet boor and leathern hind** Countryfolk (here metaphorically associated with animals hunted by the rich for sport, the 'boar' and the 'hind') wore clothes made of leather and of russet, which was coarse homespun woollen cloth. 'Boor' and 'hind' were also terms for peasants, farm labourers.
815 **uncovered** hatless, a sign of respect
825 **sumptuous waste** wasteful extravagance; perhaps punningly refers to the sumptuary laws which had been more or less rigidly enforced in England since the reign of Edward III, regulating the expenditure on clothing permissible for different social classes. The implication is that the rich who have spent more on their clothes than princes have been committing offences against the Elizabethan sumptuary laws.

A field their bed, whose dankish sheets
Is the green grass. And he that meets
The flatt'ring'st fortune does but lie
In some rude barn or loathsome sty,
Forsook of all, flouted, forlorn.
Own brother does own brother scorn;
The trembling father is undone,
Being once but breathed on by his son.
Or if, in this sad pilgrimage,
The hand of vengeance fall in rage
So heavy upon any's head,
Striking the sinful body dead,
O shame to ages yet to come!
Dishonour to all Christendom!
In hallowed ground no heapèd gold
Can buy a grave, nor linen fold
To make—so far is pity fled—
The last apparel for the dead.
But as the fashion is for those
Whose desperate hands the knot unloose
Of their own lives, in some highway
Or barren field their bones they lay,
Even such his burial is. And there,
Without the balm of any tear
Or pomp of soldiers, but—O grief!—
Dragged like a traitor, or some thief,
At horses' tails, he's rudely thrown,
The corpse being stuck with flowers by none,
No bells (the dead man's consort) playing,
Nor any holy churchman saying
A funeral dirge, but swift they're gone,
As from some noisome carrion.
O desolate city! Now thy wings
(Whose shadow hath been loved by kings)
Should feel sick feathers on each side,
Seeing thus thy sons (got in the pride
And heat of plenty, in peace born)
To their own nation left a scorn.
Each cowherd fears a ghost him haunts,
Seeing one of thine inhabitants,
And does a Jew or Turk prefer
Before that name of Londoner.
Would this were all! But this black curse,
Doing ill abroad, at home does worse.
For in thy (now dispeopled) streets
The dead with dead so thickly meets
As if some prophet's voice should say
'None shall be citizens, but they'.
Whole households and whole streets are stricken;
The sick do die, the sound do sicken,
And, 'Lord have mercy upon us' crying,
Ere mercy can come forth, they're dying.
No music now is heard but bells,
And all their tunes are sick men's knells,
And every stroke the bell does toll
Up to heaven it winds a soul.
O, if for every corpse that's laid
In his cold bed of earth were made
A chime of bells, if peals should ring
For everyone whom death doth sting,
Men should be deaf, as those that dwell
By Nilus' fall. But now one knell
Gives with his iron voice this doom:
That twenty shall but have one room.
There friend and foe, the young and old,
The freezing coward and the bold,
Servant and master, foul and fair,
One livery wear, and fellows are,
Sailing along in this black fleet,
And at the new Gravesend do meet,
Where churchyards banquet with cold cheer,
Holding a feast once in ten year,
To which comes many a pilgrim worm,
Hungry and faint, beat with the storm
Of gasping famine, which before
Only picked bones, and had no more,
But now their messes come so fast
They know not where or which to taste,
For before 'Dust to dust' be spoken
And thrown on one, more graves be broken.
Thou jealous man, I pity thee:
Thou that liv'st in hell to see
A wanton's eye cheapening the sleek
Soft jewels of thy fair wife's cheek,

828 **dankish** wet
832 **flouted** mocked
842 **hallowed ground** ground consecrated for burials
843 **linen fold** fold linen to make a winding-sheet ('The last apparel for the dead')
847–8 **the knot...lives** i.e. commit suicide
856 **consort** music, small group of musicians
858 **dirge** song of mourning
859 **noisome** noxious
863 **got** conceived
870 **black curse** the plague
871 **abroad** away from home
878 **'Lord have mercy upon us'** the traditional cry of the plague victims
883 **Up...soul** The metaphor is derived from stage machinery: a winch was used to wind angels, gods and other characters up to 'heaven', the upper part of the theatre.
889 **Nilus' fall** Seneca (*c.*2 BC–AD *c.*65) speaks of a people who live where the river Nile transforms itself into a mighty waterfall, and who are rendered congenitally deaf by the noise (*Naturales quaestiones*, 4.2.5).
890 **doom** sentence
895 **livery** the uniform of a noble house
898–900 **banquet with cold cheer...pilgrim worm** i.e. the corpses furnish a fleshly feast for travelling worms
899 **ten year** The plague seems to have struck with particular virulence every ten years during this period. There were major outbreaks in 1563, 1592–3 and 1603, and minor ones in 1573–4 and 1582.
904 **messes** dishes of food
906 **'Dust to dust'** a text of particular importance in the funeral service, followed by the casting of a handful of earth on the corpse
910 **wanton's** lecher's
cheapening considering the value of; putting in a bid for

My verse must run through thy cold heart:
Thy wife has played the woman's part
And lain with death. But—spite on spite!—
Thou must endure this very night
Close by her side the poorest groom
In self-same bed and self-same room.
But ease thy vexed soul. Thus behold:
There's one who, in the morn, with gold
Could have built castles; now he's made
A pillow to a wretch that prayed
For ha'p'ny alms with broken limb.
The beggar now is above him.
So he that yesterday was clad
In purple robes, and hourly had
(Even at his finger's beck) the fees
Of barèd heads and bending knees,
Rich men's fawnings, poor men's prayers
(Though they were but hollow airs),
Troops of servants at his calling,
Children (like to subjects) falling
At his proud feet—lo, now he's taken
By death, he lies of all forsaken.
These are the tragedies, whose sight
With tears blot all the lines we write.
The stage, whereon the scenes are played,
Is a whole kingdom. What was made
By some (most provident and wise)
To hide from sad spectators' eyes
Acts full of ruth, a private room
To drown the horror of death's doom,
That building now no higher rear:
Pest-house
The pest-house standeth everywhere,
For those that on their biers are borne
Are numbered more than those that mourn.
But you grave patriots, whom fate
Makes rulers of this wallèd state,
We must not lose you in our verse,
Whose acts we one day may rehearse
In marble numbers that shall stand
Above time's all-destroying hand—
Only, methinks, you now do err
In flying from your charge so far.
So coward captains shrink away;
So shepherds do their flocks betray;
So soldiers, and so lambs, do perish;
So you kill those you're bound to cherish.
Be therefore valiant, as you're wise:
Come back again. The man that dies
Within your walls is even as near
To heav'n, as dying anywhere;
But if—O pardon our bold thought!—
You fear your breath is sooner caught
Here than aloof, and therefore keep
Out of death's reach, whilst thousands weep
And wring their hands for thousands dying,
No comfort near the sick man lying,
'Tis to be feared (you petty kings),
When back you spread your golden wings,
A deadlier siege (which heaven avert)
Will your replenished walls ingirt.
'Tis now the beggars' plague, for none
Are in this battle overthrown
But babes and poor. The lesser fly
Now in this spider's web doth lie.
But if that great and goodly swarm
(That has broke through, and felt no harm)
In his envenomed snares should fall,
O pity! 'twere most tragical.
For then the usurer must behold
His pestilent flesh, whilst all his gold
Turns into tokens, and the chest
They lie in, his infectious breast.
How well he'll play the miser's part
When all his coin sticks at his heart!
He's worth so many farthings then
That was a golden god 'mongst men.
And 'tis the aptest death—so please
Him that breathed heaven, earth, and seas—
For every covetous rooting mole
(That heaves his dross above his soul
And doth in coin all hopes repose)
To die with corpse stamped full of those.

913 **played the woman's part** According to misogynistic tradition, the role played by women in marriage was that of the unfaithful partner.
921–2 **wretch ... limb** a man who begged for charity by displaying his injuries
925 **purple** splendid, gaudy
926 **beck** gesture
929 **hollow airs** meaningless sounds
940 **ruth** sorrow
private room refers to the so-called 'private' theatres such as the Blackfriars, more expensive than 'public' theatres like the Globe and therefore playing to a more restricted audience
943 **pest-house** The London pest-house, a hospital in which plague victims were sequestered, was built in Bath Street in 1594–5.
947 **this wallèd state** the city of London
950 **marble numbers** commendatory verses carved on a marble monument
964 **aloof** at a distance
968 **petty** miniature
969 **golden wings** presumably, wealth
970 **deadlier siege** at present the plague assaults only the poor (''Tis now the beggars' plague'); but if it should attack (or lay siege to) the rich, the results would be more dreadful still. The next section of the poem describes what would happen.
971 **ingirt** enclose
972 **'Tis ... plague** From this line until line 1078 internal evidence for Middleton's authorship is most abundant.
982 **tokens** physical symptoms of plague
986 **farthings** coins of lower value than a penny; the sense is that the plague-stricken usurer is not worth much
989 **breathed** God 'breathed' heaven, earth, and seas in two senses: they were created by his command (he literally breathed them into existence), and he gave the breath of life to all the creatures in them.
990 **covetous rooting mole** one who is as blindly obsessed with gold as a mole is obsessed with other kinds of earth
991 **dross** worthless earth, rubbish; here material possessions valued more highly than the salvation of his immortal soul
993 **of those** i.e. of sores that resemble coins

Then the rich glutton, whose swoll'n eyne
Look fiery red (being boiled in wine),
And in his meals adores the cup
(For when he falls down, that stands up—
Therefore a goblet is his saint,
To whom he kneels with small constraint;
When his own goblet skull flows o'er,
He worships Bacchus on all four,
For none's his God but Bacchus then,
Who rules and guides all drunken men),
When he shall wake from wine and view
More than tavern-tokens new
Stamped upon his breast and arms
In horrid throngs and purple swarms,
Then will he loathe his former shapes,
When he shall see blue marks mock grapes
And hang in clusters on each vein
Like to wine bubbles, or the grain
Of staggering sin, which now appears
In the December of his years,
His last of hours, when he'll scarce have
Time to go sober to his grave.
And then to die—dreadful to think!—
When all his blood is turned to drink.
And who knows not this sentence given?
''Mongst all sins, none can reel to heaven.'
But woe to him that sinks in wine
And dies so (without heaved-up eyne)
And buried so! O loathsome trench!
His grave is like a tavern bench.
'Tis fearful, and most hard to say,
How he shall stand at latter day.
The adulterous and luxurious spirit
Pawned to hell and sin's hot merit,
That bathes in lust his leprous soul,
Acting a deed without control
Or thought of deity, through whose blood
Runs part of the infernal flood,
How will he freeze with horror!—lying
In dreadful trance before his dying,
The heat of all his damned desires
Cooled with the thought of gnashing fires,
His riots ravished, all his pleasures,
His marrow wasted with his treasures;
His painted harlots (whose embraces
Cost him many silver faces,
Whose only care and thought was then
To keep them sure from other men),
Now they dance in ruffians' hands,
Lazy lieutenants without bands,
With muffled half-faced panders laughing
Whilst he lies gasping, they sit quaffing,
Smile at this plague and black mischance,
Knowing their deaths come o'er from France.
'Tis not their season now to die:
Two gnawing poisons cannot lie
In one corrupted flesh together,
Nor can this poison then fly thither.
There's not a strumpet 'mongst them all
That lives and rises by her fall
Dreads this contagion or his threats,
Being guarded with French amulets.
Yet all this while thyself li'st panting,
Thy luxurious hours recanting,
Whilst before thy face appears
Th'adulterous fruit of all thy years
In their true form and horrid shapes:
So many incests, violent rapes,
Chambered adulteries, unclean passions,
Wanton habits, riotous fashions,
And all these antics dressed in hell
To dance about the passing bell

994 **eyne** eyes
997 **that** i.e. the cup
1000 **goblet skull** by analogy, when too much booze has been poured into his mouth, he vomits on all fours
1001 **Bacchus** Roman god of wine
all four all fours
1005 **tavern-tokens** small pieces of brass or copper issued by innkeepers and tradesmen for use as small change
1007–11 **horrid throngs . . . bubbles** outbreak of plague symptoms
1011–12 **the grain . . . sin** the harvest of his years of drunkenness; also refers to the grain used to make beer, as opposed to the grape used to make wine
1013 **the December of his years** usually, his old age; in this case, his last moments of life
1018 **sentence** aphorism, saying containing matter of substance
1019 **reel** stagger
1021 **heaved-up eyne** eyes lifted to heaven
1025 **How he shall stand** (*a*) in what position he shall find himself; (*b*) how he shall manage to get to his feet
latter day judgement day
1026 **luxurious** lecherous
1027 **merit** deserts; punishment
1029 **control** restraint
1031 **infernal flood** a river of fire, such as might be found in hell. May refer to the burning pains of venereal disease
1037 **His marrow wasted** by syphilis, which was thought to attack the bones (one of its alternative names was 'the Neapolitan bone-ache')
1038 **harlots** whores
1039 **silver faces** silver coins
1043 **lieutenants . . . bands** lieutenants without commissions; unemployed army officers
1044 **muffled . . . panders** pimps who half-cover their faces (perhaps with their cloaks) to avoid being recognized
1045 **quaffing** boozing
1047 **Knowing . . . France** Syphilis was associated with France as well as with Naples, and it was widely believed that those who had the clap were immune to other infections, since 'Two gnawing poisons cannot lie | In one corrupted flesh'. The belief was still current during the Great Plague of 1665. There is no truth to it.
1053 **fall** (*a*) lying prone for sexual intercourse; (*b*) moral decline
1054 **his** the contagion's (but perhaps also suggesting: the dying former lover's)
1055 **French amulets** syphilitic boils which serve as charms against the plague
1060–1 **In their true form . . . rapes** echoes a couplet in Christopher Marlowe's *Hero and Leander* (1598): 'There might you see the gods in sundry shapes, | Committing heady riots, incest, rapes' (First Sestiad, lines 143–4)
1062 **Chambered** private
1064 **antics** grotesquely comic actors
1065 **passing bell** bell tolled for the dead

And clip thee round about the bed
Whilst thousand horrors grasp thy head.

The cure of the plague

And therefore this infectious season
That now arrests the flesh for treason
Against heaven's everlasting king
(Anointed with th'eternal spring
Of life and power), this stroke of force
That turns the world into a corse,
Feeding the dust with what it craves,
Emptying whole houses to fill graves,
These speckled plagues (which our sins levy)
Are as needful as they're heavy.
Whose cures to cite, our muse forbears,
Though he the Daphnean wreath that wears
(Being both poesy's sovereign king
And God of medicine) bids us sing
As boldly of those policies,
Those onsets and those batteries
By physic cunningly applied
To beat down plagues so fortified,
And of those arms defensive
To keep th'assaulted heart alive,
And of those wards and of those sleights
Used in these mortal single fights,
As of the causes that commence
This civil war of pestilence,
For poets' souls should be confined
Within no bounds; their tow'ring minds
Must (like the sun) a progress make
Through art's immensive zodiac,
And suck (like bees) the virtuous power
That flows in learning's seven-fold flower,
Distilling forth the same again
In sweet and wholesome juice to men.
But for we see the army great
Of those whose charge it is to beat
This proud invader, and have skill
In all those weapons that do kill
Such pestilent foes, we yield to them
The glory of that stratagem—
To whose oraculous voice repair,
For they those Delphic prophets are
That teach dead bodies to respire
By sacred Aesculapian fire.
We mean not those pied lunatics,
Those bold fantastic empirics,
Quacksalvers, mushroom mountebanks
That in one night grow up in ranks
And live by pecking physic's crumbs.
O, hate those venomous broods; there comes
Worse sores from them, and more strange births,
Than from ten plagues or twenty dearths.
Only this antidote apply:
Cease vexing heaven, and cease to die.
Seek therefore (after you have found
Salve natural for the natural wound
Of this contagion) cure from thence
Where first the evil did commence,
And that's the soul. Each one purge one,
And England's free, the plague is gone.

The cure

The necessity of a plague

Yet to mix comfortable words,
Though this be horrid, it affords
Sober gladness and wise joys,
Since desperate mixtures it destroys.
For if our thoughts sit truly trying
The just necessity of dying,
How needful (though how dreadful) are
Purple plagues or crimson war.
We would conclude (still urging pity):
A plague's the purge to cleanse a city.
Who amongst millions can deny
(In rough prose, or smooth poesy)
Of evils 'tis the lighter brood—
A dearth of people, than of food!
And who knows not, our land ran o'er
With people, and was only poor

1066 **clip** surround
1074 **corse** corpse
1077 **speckled** spotty
1080 **the Daphnean wreath** laurel wreath worn by the god Apollo in honour of the nymph Daphne, who changed into a laurel bush when he tried to rape her. Apollo was the Roman god of poetry and of medicine.
1084 **onsets** assaults
batteries attacks
1087 **arms defensive** defensive weapons
1089 **wards** parries (with a sword)
sleights tricks
1093–6 **poets' souls…zodiac** refers to Sir Philip Sidney's definition of the poetic imagination in his *Defence of Poesy* (1595), where the poet is described as 'freely ranging only within the zodiac of his own wit'
1094 **tow'ring** soaring (a metaphor from falconry)
1096 **immensive** vast
1098 **learning's seven-fold flower** The flower of learning has seven parts because it consists of the seven liberal arts (see note to 68–70).
1107 **oraculous** prophesying
1108 **Delphic** The Delphic oracle was the supreme oracle of Greece, presided over by Apollo.
1109 **respire** breathe again
1110 **Aesculapian fire** Aesculapius was the classical god of healing, who was snatched by Apollo from the fire that consumed his mother.
1111 **pied lunatics** fools in their traditional parti-coloured or 'pied' suit
1112 **fantastic empirics** quacks who make outrageous claims for their medicines
1113 **Quacksalvers** bogus practitioners
mushroom mountebanks charlatans who spring up overnight, like mushrooms
1117 **strange births** deformed babies or monstrous new-born animals, read by many as signs of God's judgement
1118 **dearths** bad harvests leading to food shortages
1122 **Salve natural** cures based on natural principles, as opposed to magic or miracles
1125 **purge** cleanse
1131 **desperate mixtures** dangerous combinations of elements. The body was supposed to be composed of four humours; a 'desperate mixture' was a dangerous imbalance of the constituent elements of the body which caused disease or death.
1137 **purge** purifying agent, enema

In having too too many living,
And wanting living—rather giving
Themselves to waste, deface and spoil,
Than to increase (by virtuous toil)
The bankrupt bosom of our realm,
Which naked births did overwhelm.
This begets famine and bleak dearth,
When fruits of wombs pass fruits of earth;
Then famine's only physic, and
The med'cine for a riotous land
Is such a plague. So it may please
Mercy's distributor to appease
His speckled anger, and now hide
Th'old rod of plagues, no more to chide
And lash our shoulders and sick veins
With carbuncles and shooting blains.
Make us the happiest amongst men,
Immortal by our prophes'ing pen,
That this last line may truly reign:
The plague's ceased; heaven is friends again.

1145 **wanting living** unemployed
1147 **increase** make prosperous
1149 **naked births** children born destitute
1152 **physic** medicine
1155 **Mercy's distributor** God
1156 **speckled anger** anger as expressed in the marks of the plague
1157 **rod** stick used to punish children or criminals
1159 **carbuncles** spot or boil **shooting blains** agonizing sores
1161 **prophes'ing** prophesying
1162 **last line** (*a*) final line of verse; (*b*) dynasty which will never be superseded

THE NIGHTINGALE AND THE ANT *and* FATHER HUBBURD'S TALES

Edited by Adrian Weiss

THIS EDITION presents two versions of Middleton's work to illustrate its evolution from manuscript to the final printed form as seen in the second edition (CREEDE 2). The reconstructed manuscript version, *The Nightingale and the Ant*, is printed in a single typeface to replicate the 'look' of a manuscript so as to recreate (to a limited extent) the 'manuscript reading experience'. In contrast, the final completed version, *Father Hubburd's Tales*, exploits the typographical variations of a printed edition and includes textual materials specific to printed editions such as a title-page text and prefatory letters. The reader is encouraged to read the two versions in sequence in order to appreciate the significant differences that occurred both in the text and in Middleton's concept of his work.

While the movement from manuscript to printed edition always involved the introduction of typographical and layout variations and the addition of prefatory texts, the evolution of this work represents an exceptional case: the first edition (CREEDE 1) represents a transitional stage between the manuscript version and the final expanded version as seen in CREEDE 2. Middleton's text was entered in the Stationers' Register on 3 January 1604 with the variant title *The Nyghtingale and the Ante. A Jove surgit opus.* The Ovidian epigraph also appears in *Wisdom of Solomon*, and clearly must have come from Middleton's manuscript since it does not appear in either printed edition. As a general rule, the appearance of such a variant title in the Register entry is evidence that a manuscript whose title-page had not yet been modified for the printing project was presented at Stationers' Hall for licensing. The printed editions bear the variant titles *The Ant and the Nightingale, or Father Hubburd's Tales* (CREEDE 1) and *Father Hubburd's Tales, or the Ant and the Nightingale* (CREEDE 2). The re-ordering of the two sections of the title in CREEDE 2 reflects the final prominence of the title character Oliver Hubburd.

In preparing *The Nightingale and the Ant* for printing, Middleton expanded the text in two stages. For the first edition, Middleton added 'The Epistle Dedicatory', 'To the Reader', and the interpolated prose transition to the first tale (276–90; throughout this edition, line references are to *Father Hubburd's Tales*). The two prefatory texts reveal a significant change in Middleton's original concept of his work as found in the manuscript version. Both characters have suffered outrageous injustices in human society—Philomel, who was transformed into a nightingale after being raped by Tereus, and the ant, who possesses a magical ability to transform himself into a human, in his experiences as a ploughman and a soldier. But their sympathetic interaction is permeated by an elegaic, stoic tone which mutes the satire.

In contrast, 'The Epistle Dedicatory' introduces the character Oliver Hubburd as well as a new mode of satire in his angry and vicious railing against Christopher Clutch-Fist about the latter's treatment of poets and their books. Only in the caustic sarcasm of 'To the Reader' does Middleton reveal that Oliver Hubburd is actually the ant (75–7). However, the reader of CREEDE 1 is left puzzled about the cause of Oliver's anger and, more importantly, why he attacks Clutch-Fist's treatment of poets and their books—because CREEDE 1 contains no reference whatever to poets and expensively bound books. Something obviously is missing. (A reader of this edition is encouraged to experience the incongruity by skipping over the following three sections in a first reading of the final version. The Textual Introduction contains a more detailed analysis of the relationship of the versions.) Three sections were added to the body of the text in CREEDE 2: the transitional verses which introduce the new third tale (1073–92), The Scholar's Tale (1093–257), and its concluding stanza (1258–66). The final paragraph of the third tale solves the mystery by identifying Oliver Hubburd as a poet whose expensively bound book was torn apart by Clutch-Fist. In short, the sections added in CREEDE 1 and CREEDE 2 were undoubtedly conceived of as a single unit by Middleton and absolutely must appear together to make sense. That leaves an ultimately unanswerable question: why did Middleton agree to the printing of an incomplete version of his expanded work in the first edition? Regardless, the additions fundamentally change the concept of the work seen in the manuscript version both in terms of content as well as narrative structure.

Narrative Structure

The narrative structure of the manuscript version is simple and straightforward. Middleton is identified as the author, and presumably as the omniscient narrator, of the text by his 'posie' as recorded in the Stationers' Register—'A Jove Surgit Opus' (i.e., 'the work is inspired by Jove'). The text presents a self-contained work in which the ant's tales as ploughman and soldier are framed by a verse narrative where the interaction between the nightingale and the ant is portrayed.

Normally, prefatory letters added to a manuscript for print publication are extraneous to the work. However, in this case, 'The Epistle Dedicatory' and 'To the Reader' become part of the work and fundamentally modify its narrative structure as well as its basic fiction (as noted above). Verbal echoes, repetition of subject matter and specific details in the prefatory letters and The Scholar's Tale, and aspects of narrative structure show that Thomas Nashe's *Pierce Penniless his Supplication to the Devil* (1592) provided Middleton with the inspiration for his expansion of the manuscript version.

Pierce Penniless launches into his sweeping kaleidoscopic excoriation of society's vices abruptly without benefit of either a dedication or an epistle to the reader. The rambling narrative leads to the main text, Pierce's supplication to the devil. Sixty-eight pages later (in the second edition of *Pierce*, 1592, sig. I2^{v}; 128 pages later in G. B. Harrison's edition), having momentarily purged his revulsion at corruption in the world, Pierce finally turns to the reader, 'Gentle reader *tandem aliquando*, I am at leisure to talk to thee' and explains the situation which occasioned his supplication. The out-of-place epistle (Harrison, 128–137) wanders onto the subject of unappreciative patrons and concludes with a digression in which Pierce upbraids 'heavenly Spenser' for failing to include a dedication (among the dozen or so accidentally appended to the *Faerie Queen*) to 'Amyntas' (135–136), which Pierce then provides before breaking 'off this endless argument of speech abruptly' (137).

Obviously, the dedicatory verse to Amyntas and the epistle to the reader belong at the front of Pierce's book. This notion of clarifying the beginning at the end is duplicated in the expansions in *Father Hubburd's Tales*. But Middleton's adaptation of the structural concept is more sophisticated than in *Pierce*, where the concluding section simply provides the preliminary texts which conventionally begin a book: given the rambling, digressive structure of *Pierce*, this final section of *Pierce* is not at all essential and its absence would not be detected by even the most critical and perceptive reader. In contrast, the conclusion of The Scholar's Tale is utterly essential. In *Father Hubburd's Tales*, the reader is abruptly plunged, in the dedication to Sir Christopher Clutch-Fist, into a Pierce-like satirical quagmire of anger and threats of revenge with no introductory explanation whatever. Until the revelations of the final paragraph of The Scholar's Tale, the invective of the dedication floats untethered to any circumstance. Structurally, Middleton's narrative folds back on itself, providing the information which grounds the dedication in specific causative details.

The approach and function of the dedication are also clearly indebted to *Pierce*. In his belated epistle to the reader, Pierce considers the issue of finding 'a good patron', who 'will pay for all', to whom his work can be dedicated, and adds some advice: 'wherefore I would counsel my friends to be more considerate in their Dedications, and not cast away so many months labour on a clown that knows not how to use a scholar' (Harrison, 131). This is exactly the mistake made by the ant as Oliver Hubburd the poet in dedicating his 'elaborate poetical building' (1241) to Clutch-Fist, whose appreciation of poetry goes no farther than the scavengeable materials used to make an expensive book. Middleton took his cue for 'The Epistle Dedicatory' from Pierce's earlier attack on such patrons and how he would handle them: 'if I be evil intreated, or sent away with a flea in mine ear, let him look that I will rail on him soundly, not for an hour or a day while the injury is fresh in my memory, but in some elaborate polished poem, which I will leave to the world when I am dead to be a living image to all ages of his beggarly parsimony and ignoble illiberalty. . . .' (Harrison, 61). In *Father Hubburd's Tales*, the dedication does just that, especially in combination with Oliver's concluding sarcastic reference at the end of the book to 'Sir Christopher Clutch-Fist, whose bountiful virtue I blaze in my first epistle' (1248–9). However, Middleton overlooked—or perhaps intentionally created—a significant structural contradiction. Oliver's Epistle could only have been written after the concluding event of the final paragraph of The Scholar's Tale. After fainting at the sight of his 'book dismembered very tragically' (1252–4), Oliver awakens in his original form as an ant in which, he reports, 'ever since I have kept me' (1256–7). How, then, did the ant write a dedicatory epistle that appears in a printed book?

The Verse Frame

The combination of a verse frame and prose tales is Middleton innovation in a long tradition of framed tales stretching back to Boccaccio's *Decameron*, which had many imitators in Elizabethan prose fiction. The choice of Philomel as the spokes-bird of justice who presides over the ant's tales is traditional. From Ovid's depiction of her transformation into a nightingale in *The Metamorphoses* onward, Philomel (a royal victim of rape by her brother-in-law, King Tereus of Thrace) was a conventional symbol of the injustice suffered by the weak at the hands of the strong and mighty. Middleton embodies in Philomel the ideal of justice balanced by mercy and truth in a four-stanza section (138–61) after Philomel has caught the ant in her beak to kill him as a suspected spy. In contrast to 'many silken men' placed in positions of judgement by their wealth and rank who 'condemn at random' and 'often kill before the cause they know', Philomel's 'mercy was above her heat (i.e., emotions)'. Her patience permits the ant to explain himself and thus gain his escape from impending death. The two discover a common bond as oppressed individuals. Philomel's story of her rape occasions the ant's tales about his victimization in society in his human transformations.

Interestingly, Philomel engages in a twenty-line eulogy of Thomas Nashe, the muck-racking pamphleteer who epitomizes everything that the aristocracy found crude and characteristic of commoners (252–70). Nonetheless, she forbids him 'to rail like Nashe' (252; i.e., vent his anger and bitterness) in his tales, requiring him to assume a virtuous stance of stoic patience and resignation. As a result, the characteristic components of vicious satire—

anger, bitterness, envy, and the desire for revenge—are entirely absent from the manuscript version with its two tales. Philomel remains a sympathetic, commiserating auditor, and the ant narrates his tales as the naïve, almost cheerful victim of the world's vices.

However, the additions in CREEDE 1 and CREEDE 2 fundamentally change the tone of the manuscript version of the work by framing it with the very kind of vicious satiric invective that is characteristic of Nashe's satire. The expanded version begins and ends with the greed-driven Oliver's anger and desire for revenge upon Clutch-Fist. The impact upon the verse frame is momentary. The new transitional verses that appear at 1073–92 in CREEDE 2 (inserted after 1075 of the manuscript version) occasion a shift in Philomel's character. To this point, she has condemned the greed-driven lawyers, aldermen, wealthy bourgeois, and military officers responsible for the ant's victimization. But in response to the ant's decision to become a scholar, she castigates him for his choice: 'I thought, thou'dst leaped into a law-gown ... No academe makes a rich alderman' (1087–90). Philomel's implicit approval of the vice of greed as a motivation for the ant is inconsistent with her character. However, Philomel's consolation (''Tis better be a little ant | Than a great man and live in want', 1262–3) in the new transitional verses (1259–66) at the end of The Scholar's Tale is a return to her previous role.

The Ploughman's Tale

Middleton chooses a journalistic approach with the narrative told from the viewpoint of the fully-developed personality of the simple ploughman who struggles to comprehend the actions that he observes following the death of the old landlord. The ploughman's world obviously is turned topsy-turvy, but he cannot yet appreciate the long-term impact of the change until he and his fellows are summoned to London to witness the pawning of the estate by the young profligate heir for the velvet finery and dissolute lifestyle of the London gallant. In the remainder of the tale, which occurs between the end of September (Michaelmas Term) and early January (Hilary Term), Middleton zooms in on the forces and agents which contribute to the decay of the old land-based agrarian society that was structured according to the hierarchical network of reciprocal obligations of landlord and tenant (see G. R. Hibbard, 15–23). The ant as ploughman, however, is unaware of the broader implications of these specific events as he searches for words to explain what he observes in similes and metaphors that are drawn from his own experience and are mediated by continual contrasting glances at the old way of life exemplified in the deceased old landlord's regime and values. The end result is verbal exaggeration akin to the virulent description of the extremes of vice in formal satires such as *Microcynicon*. But the ploughman (and later, the soldier) lacks the heightened emotional revulsion from vice that is characteristic of formal satire.

At stage centre are the lawyers, merchants, and scriveners who negotiated the transition from old to new and thus were the frequent targets of satiric attack in the literature of the period. However, Middleton refrains from directly attacking them, couching his criticism in an eyewitness report from the simple perspective of the ploughman—whose spontaneous responses to the events that he witnesses are more effective than any direct satire. Middleton observes stylistic decorum in that the ploughman's verbal virtuosity, the peculiar strength of the narrative here as well as in The Soldier's Tale, is confined to the rhetorical low style appropriate to the uneducated classes of society. Without exception, the ploughman's wit consists of exploiting homophonic verbal associations (e.g., 'husbandman'/'husband', 293–7; etc.). His similes and metaphors reflect his pragmatic experience. In his effort to verbally convey the size of the profligate heir's breeches, he moves from 'as deep as the middle of winter' to 'the roadway between London and Winchester' to 'might very well put all his lands in them', and finally, 'you may imagine they were big enough when they would outreach a thousand acres' (386–91). Indeed, the land has been traded for the breeches. His pragmatic approach to life is the standard by which he measures the transactions: 'a dash of the pen stood for a thousand acres' (485–6), the largest denomination imaginable to the ploughman. Similarly, the mercer and merchant, the villainous agents destroying the ploughman's world, march away from the meeting 'heavier by a thousand acres' (541–2), the young heir 'a great man in both their books' (345) by virtue of the mortgage bonds. While this kind of wordplay and punning cannot compare with Nashe's verbal virtuosity, Middleton's characterization is quite successful within the rhetorical stylistic constraints of the ploughman's character.

Likewise, Middleton has the ploughman walk the high road by disassociating him from any negative reactions such as anger or even resentment at his exploitation by the heir. He unquestioningly accepts the principle that rank has privilege. His concluding description of the profligate heir's headlong plunge into 'all that might be in dissolute villainy' (722–3) remains on a detached level untainted by negative emotions. The ugliness of the vice being described is somehow magnified by the modesty of the ploughman's simple response: 'we did so much blush at his life and were so ashamed of his base courses that ever after we loathed to look after them' (724–6). The implicit moral judgement is far more damning than anything possible either in formal verse satire as seen in *Microcynicon* or in Nashe's kind of prose satire where the satirist's violent revulsion is almost as repulsive as the vice that he attacks.

Moreover, the ploughman and his mates reaffirm their natural dignity when their unfamiliarity with the quill is laughed at by the lawyer, scrivener, and mercer—middle-class bourgeois whose livelihood depends upon the written word. The ploughmen, however, live in another tradition, that of the old world where the visual image was far more important than the written sign in communicating truths, such as those fundamental to salvation which blazoned the stained-glass windows of churches and cathedrals. The new world's privileging of writing over visual image provides the ploughmen with an opportunity to 'bite their thumbs' at their oppressors as they legally witness the mortgage (488) by signing with emblems denoting the destruction of their world (i.e., the upside-down plough, 499–504) and the cause (i.e., the unbridled colt, 504–12). The ploughmen walk away from the ceremony with a sense of self-affirmation. The exploiters' perception that they are little more than beasts of burden obscures the fact that the ploughmen are men with souls and wit. From their view, they have mocked the others and maintained their dignity in a situation in which they were powerless. Nonetheless, the exploitive power contained in the word 'fines' is real. The lawyer's announcement of the actual amount of these fees renders their existence as ploughmen intolerable and they revert to the form of ants (731–7). As Philomel reminds them, they are better off as lowly ants who do not pay rent to support the profligate heir's dicing and whoring (755–76).

The Soldier's Tale

Although this tale deals with real military injustices (see Read, 429–463), Middleton chooses to temper the seriousness of the narrative by maintaining the focus upon the humorous aspect of the stereotypical soldier of the 'miles gloriosus' comic tradition which stretches back to Terence. As such, the ant's narrative style changes to bragging, boasting, and exaggeration in his accounts of his experience which exhibit the delightful flow of punning homophonic associations (e.g., 'for I thought, at first, that they had gathered something for me, but I found, at last, they did only but gather about me', 959–62) that characterize the verbal display sustained throughout the first two tales. The ant's decision to become a soldier is clearly tainted: 'not contented long (a vice cleaving to all worldlings) with this little estate of an ant, but stuffed with envy and ambition, as small as I was, desired to venture into the world again' (812–15). The choice to become a soldier held the promise of 'War's sweating fortunes' which included wages, shares in spoils, and glory.

The shift from the persona of the humble ant begins immediately with the soldier's crude reference ('the first that brought up prick-song') to Philomel's 'pitiful ravishment', a most insensitive comment, but in keeping with his character as a soldier (810–13). Once in the field, the ant's early near-escapes are appropriately exaggerated: 'the bullets came within a hair of my coxcomb even like a barber scratching my pate, and perhaps took away the left limb of a vermin, and so departed' (919–21). When his luck runs out, the maiming that results is beyond the usual level of exaggeration and renders him a ludicrous physical improbability. Lacking a right arm to counterpoise the remaining left leg with a crutch and produce forward movement, any kind of erect physical movement is impossible, except for hopping (987–8). The maiming becomes the vehicle for Middleton's exposure of the lack of charity in Christian society.

In regard to his military service, his commanders have spent his pay on gunpowder (941–4), and thus reward his sacrifice of limbs with nothing more than a begging passport, a legal instrument conferred by military representatives of the government. However, as the conclusion of the tale indicates, the ant assumes that the approaching watch would have no respect for his begging passport (1040–5). The society at large treats him with similar disrespect, mocking his crab-like locomotion as he scoots sideways on his stomach (960–7). Charity itself becomes a target in the persona of Mistress Charity, whom he encounters after strategically placing himself in Finsbury Fields with a southerly view down Windmill Hill for prospective alms-givers (985–1023). But after his comic 'premeditated speech', delivered in praise of her beauty in the fashion of a courtly lover (997–1005), the 'warm-lapped' Mistress Charity arrogantly casts her penny distastefully on the ground just as she would brush away a flea. The maimed soldier is merely an annoyance to her, not a suffering human being. The amazing aspect of the ant as a soldier is his boundless optimism in the face of these ever-worsening circumstances. Although he finally falls 'into passionate, but not railing speeches' about his rejection at the hands of society, he reminds himself that others have suffered greater misfortunes, and decides 'to be constant in calamity and valiant against the battering siege of misery' (1028–40). But his commitment to stoic virtue is unsustainable against the onslaught of injustice in the form of the approaching watch, so the soldier escapes by transforming himself back into an ant.

As part of his characterization of the ant as a soldier, Middleton interrupts the forward flow of the narrative with the 'starchwoman' digression (852–900). Such digressions, which usually expose underworld practices, occur commonly in the pamphlet literature (Nashe inserts several in *Pierce*). Behind the digression lies the symbiotic codependency between soldiers and prostitutes. The subsequent narrative is replete with sexual *doubles entendres* driven by the soldier's adolescent fascination with bawds posing as starchwomen engaged in the seduction of young wives. In this instance, the young wife is the adolescent's ideal fantasy, promising not only 'all C's else' (i.e., cunt, sex) but also providing the requested money as well. As a soldier, the ant does not sense the possibility that Philomel will find both his adolescent fascination with the subject, and the subject itself, a stark reminder of her own human experience as a rape victim at the hands of king Tereus. Nonetheless, she overlooks his attitude and rewards the ant with the promised canzonet. After all, he is just an ant.

In general, Middleton's characterization of the ploughman and the soldier transforms the literary tradition of the satiric prose pamphlet by creating a new kind of satiric voice. The ant's naïve, stoic narratives, untainted by anger or resentment, displace the invective of satire, leaving only the details of his victimization for Philomel's and the reader's judgement. In the final analysis, the ant is unequipped to survive in the corrupt world of human society.

The Scholar's Tale

The Scholar's Tale is fundamentally different from the previous two because the ant himself as Oliver Hubburd becomes the target of Middleton's satire rather than functioning as the golden mean, or standard against which the vices of the world are to be measured. His inflated self-esteem and greed-driven anger emerge as the vices which are most satirized in the tale.

At first, the ant as Oliver Hubburd the scholar exhibits (or seems to) the sober, pragmatic values that have dominated his narratives as ploughman and soldier. He seems cast in the mold of Nashe's Pierce Penniless, the poverty-stricken scholar who appeals to Lucifer for redress. But Oliver's greed creates a fundamental contrast. Pierce pursued learning as a good in itself rather than as a means to an end, and his anger is a reaction to a corrupt society in general. Unlike Pierce's railing, Oliver's harangue reveals a distortion of scholarly values: 'Yet for all my weighty and substantial arguments, being able to prove anything indeed by logic, I could prove myself never the richer, make the best syllogism I could' (1123–6). For Oliver, learning is thus a means to the end of acquiring wealth, a way 'out of penurious scarcity' which promises 'future advancement' (1141–3).

This flaw in Oliver's motivation causes the radical shift in the tone of the narrative when he addresses Philomel: 'But shall I tell you lady? O, here let me sigh out a full point and take leave of ... my wealthy hopes' and turns to the subject of his 'fall' into the study of poetry (1144–240). The tale thus abruptly switches from a historical account of his studies to the railing and ranting of a disgruntled satirist driven by the very vices (i.e., greed and envy) which he attacks. The subsequent events which lead up to the concluding paragraph are thus left untold.

As the anger aroused by the memory of his downfall into using poetry as a means to wealth surges into consciousness, his 'bursting into extremities' constitutes the material of his satiric harangue as he is swept into the nightmarish world of unresolved passions where the distinction between the real and the imaginary collapses, where the passion-driven Oliver eventually argues with, rails against, and finally pleads with the poetic personification of gold as if it were a real, present person and, in self-hatred, ends up exclaiming 'Why do I lose myself in seeking thee?' (1231–2). Middleton's tracing of the ant's rapid disintegration into this state of madness is masterful, a foreshadowing of his later dramatic power in depicting characters such as De Flores.

Despite Oliver's negative passions, the portrait remains sympathetic because he still is nothing more than a simple ant who has wandered into a trap. At the same time, his vice is real and worth excoriating. The problem has resulted from his naïve, bookish misunderstanding of patronage in the Golden Age of Augustan Rome when, he believes, kings 'Hung jewels at the ear of every rhyme' (1164). Translated into his own frame of reference, 'In those golden days ... a virtuous writer ... might have ... expended more by the revenue of his verse than any riotous elder brother upon the wealthy quarterages of three times three hundred acres', an echo of his experience as a ploughman (1154–9). He overlooks the reality of patronage both in ancient Rome and contemporary England in dedicating himself to poetry in the desperate hope of material advancement.

The situation is complicated by his unrealistic opinion of his talents as a poet. For example, he introduces his rhyming doggerel about the demise of the 'Golden Age' with his critical judgement: 'the excellent report of these lines' (1159). However, within these few lines occur outrageous instances of the mangling of the central conceit. Middleton's combination of defective rhetoric and Oliver's inflated opinion of his talents is similar to Marston's satiric technique in *The Metamorphosis of Pygmalion's Image and Certain Satires* (see Weiss, 1972). Overall, this section of the tale is a virtuoso performance in the 'vices', or misuses, of rhetorical tropes and figures as Oliver juggles various topoi (e.g., subjects–adjuncts, cause–effect) to produce the stream of ludicrous images.

Middleton took the idea for the major conceit of the ant's harangue and verses directly from a passage in *Pierce*: 'By which means, the mighty controller of fortune and imperious subverter of destiny, delicious gold, the poor man's God and idol of princes (that look pale and wan through long imprisonment), might at length be restored to his powerful monarchy and eftsoon be set at liberty to help his friends that have need of him' (Harrison, 18). Oliver's primary wish is that gold 'be let free to every virtuous and therefore poor scholar' (1195–6) and to 'keep company with a scholar that truly knows how to use thee' (1239–40). Nashe's 'long imprisonment' generates Oliver's observation that 'Gold lies now as prisoner in an usurer's great iron chest' (1171–2). Middleton plays with other elements of Nashe's conceit as well.

Given the quality of his verse, we can assume that Oliver's study of poetry followed the same method as his study of logic and was based upon the notion that simple hard work produces good poetry. He terms the process 'musical rhyming study' (1242–3). That is exactly what he has done, and because he has mastered the technique of 'running rhymes in rattling rows' (in Sir Philip Sidney's terms), he considers himself an accomplished poet worthy of patronage. This illusion looms over the project: he thinks that the product—that 'elaborate poetical building'—merits patronage because it is 'industriously heaped with weighty conceits, precious phrases and wealthy numbers' (1241–8). Despite his experience with Clutch-Fist, Oliver never realizes that a poet does not build a book like a husbandman builds a barn or a haystack. Ultimately, Oliver's understanding of good poetry is no better than the 'poor latinless authors' ridiculed by Nashe: 'They no sooner spy a new ballad and his name to it that compiled it, but they put him in for one of the learned men of our time' (Harrison, 60).

Although Clutch-Fist is a parsimonious patron worthy of condemnation, Oliver's desire for revenge in 'The Epistle Dedicatory' stems directly from his undiminished esteem for the worthiness of his own 'industriously heaped' poems. But Clutch-Fist's opinion of Oliver's verse is not the issue; rather, Oliver's thwarted greed frames the Epistle, beginning with the salutation 'Most guerdonless sir... the muses' bad paymaster that owest' (10–11) for all the works dedicated to him, and ends with the sarcastic advice 'make your men break their pates, and give them ten groats apiece' (43–6). It is true that Oliver chose the wrong patron, but the sad fact is that his poetry is unworthy of even ten groats. In the end, he departs the world of humans in this self-deluded state, believing that he is justified in blazoning to the world the truth about Clutch-Fist, 'a clown that knows not how to use a scholar' in Nashe's words. But Oliver should not have become a scholar to 'get rich' in the first place—that is the first cause of all ensuing effects. Nonetheless, Oliver retains Philomel's sympathy as well as the reader's. As Philomel observes (1259–64), he is better off as an ant.

The concluding verses common to both versions (1267–82) evoke a paranoia about the danger of satirically attacking those in positions of power and rank. Philomel feels 'betrayed' after noticing that 'all the birds', having awakened at dawn, perhaps have overheard part of 'their pretty chat'. Her fear is that 'they abroad will blab our words'. The ants understand the danger and 'held their tongues' after returning to work. Perhaps Middleton's own experience with the burning of *Microcynicon* and the ensuing ban on satires (1599) underlies this concluding scenario. It is a reminder that the fictional world of a satire intersects with reality. Middleton defends himself against criticism with a traditional 'apology' in 'To the Reader'. His 'mirth' is 'harmless', and the 'very bitterest' in him is nothing worse than a wholesome 'frost' (68–72). The satire in the work, in short, is meant to be funny although it will indeed touch tender spots in some readers—as satire always does. The only readers who will miss this point are 'some riotous vomiting Kit or some gentleman-swallowing Malkin' (73–4). Finally, the salutation—'Yours, if you read without spelling or hacking'—cautions the reader against trying to 'hack' (i.e., interpret) the descriptions of characters in an attempt to link them with real-world counterparts. That, indeed, is the real danger in publishing a satire.

SEE ALSO

Textual introduction and apparatus: *Companion*, 476
Authorship and date: *Companion*, 348

The Nightingale and the Ant

A Jove surgit opus

The west-sea's goddess in a crimson robe,
Her temples circled with a coral wreath,
Waited her love, the light'ner of earth's globe;
The wanton wind did on her bosom breathe,
  The nymphs of springs did hallowed water pour;
  Whate'er was cold helped to make cool her bower.

And now the fiery horses of the sun
Were from their golden-flaming car untraced,
And all the glory of the day was done,
Save here and there some light moon-clouds en-
    chased;
  A parti-coloured canopy did spread
  Over the sun and Thetis' amorous bed.

Now had the shepherds folded in their flocks,
The sweating teams uncoupled from their yokes.
The wolf sought prey, and the sly-murdering fox
Attempts to steal, fearless of rural strokes.
  All beasts took rest that lived by lab'ring toil;
  Only such ranged as had delight in spoil.

Now in the pathless region of the air
The wingèd passengers had left to soar,
Except the bat and owl, who bode sad care,
And Philomel, that nightly doth deplore,
  In soul-contenting tunes, her change of shape,
  Wrought first by perfidy and lustful rape.

This poor musician, sitting all alone
On a green hawthorn, from the thunder blest,
Carols in varied notes her antique moan,
Keeping a sharpened briar against her breast:
  Her innocence this watchful pain doth take,
  To shun the adder and the speckled snake.

These two, like her old foe the Lord of Thrace,
Regardless of her dulcet changing song,
To serve their own lust have her life in chase.
Virtue by vice is offered endless wrong.

Beasts are not all to blame, for now and then
We see the like attempted amongst men.

Under the tree whereon the poor bird sat,
There was a bed of busy, toiling ants,
That in their summer, winter's comfort got,
Teaching poor men how to shun after-wants;
Whose rules if sluggards could be learned to keep,
They should not starve awake, lie cold asleep.

One of these busy brethren, having done
His day's true labour, got upon the tree,
And with his little nimble legs did run.
Pleased with the hearing, he desired to see
What wondrous creature nature had composed,
In whom such gracious music was enclosed.

He got too near, for the mistrustful bird
Guessed him to be a spy from her known foe.
Suspicion argues not to hear a word;
What wiseman fears not that's inured to woe?
Then blame not her. She caught him in her beak,
About to kill him ere the worm could speak.

But yet her mercy was above her heat.
She did not—as a many silken men
Called by much wealth, small wit, to judgement's seat—
Condemn at random. But she pitied then
When she might spoil: would great ones would do so,
Who often kill before the cause they know.

O, if they would, as did this little fowl,
Look on their lesser captives with even ruth,
They should not hear so many sentenced howl,
Complaining Justice is not friend to Truth,
But they would think upon this ancient theme:
"Each right extreme, is injury extreme!"

Pass them to mend, for none can them amend
But heaven's lieutenant and earth's Justice-King.
"Stern will, hath will." "No great one wants a friend."
"Some are ordained to sorrow, some to sing."
And with this sentence let thy griefs all close:
"Whoe'er are wronged, are happier than their foes."

So much for such. Now to the little ant
In the bird's beak and at the point to die.
Alas for woe, friends in distress are scant!
None of his fellows to his help did hie.
They keep them safe; they hear, and are afraid:
'Tis vain to trust in the base number's aid.

Only himself unto himself is friend.
With a faint voice his foe he thus bespake:
'Why seeks your gentleness a poor worm's end?
O, ere you kill, hear the excuse I make!
I come to wonder, not to work offence:
There is no glory to spoil innocence!

'Perchance you take me for a soothing spy
By the sly snake or envious adder fee'd.
Alas, I know not how to feign and lie,
Or win a base intelligencer's meed,
That now are Christians, sometime Turks, then Jews,
Living by leaving heaven for earthly news.

'Trust me: I am a little emmet born to work,
Oft-times a man, as you were once a maid.
Under the name of man much ill doth lurk,
Yet of poor me, you need not be afraid.
Mean men are worms on whom the mighty tread;
Greatness and strength your virtue injurèd.'

With that she opened wide her horny bill,
The prison where this poor submissant lay;
And seeing the poor ant lie quivering still,
'Go wretch', quoth she, 'I give thee life and way.
The worthy will not prey on yielding things.
Pity's enfeoffed to the blood of kings!

'For I was once, though now a feathered veil
Cover my wrongèd body, queen-like clad;
This down about my neck was erst a rail
Of byss embroidered. Fie on that we had!
Unthrifts and fools and wrongèd ones complain
Rich things were theirs, must ne'er be theirs again.

'I was, thou know'st, the daughter to a king,
Had palaces and pleasures in my time.
Now mine own songs I am enforced to sing.
Poets forget me in their pleasing rhyme;
Like chaff they fly, tossed with each windy breath,
Omitting my forced rape by Tereus' death!

'But 'tis no matter: I myself can sing
Sufficient strains to witness mine own worth.
They that forget a queen, soothe with a king;
Flattery's still barren, yet still bringeth forth;
Their works are dews, shed when the day is done,
But sucked up dry by the next morning's sun.

'What more of them? They are like Iris' throne,
Commixed with many colours in moist time:
Such lines portend what's in that circle shown;
Clear weather follows showers in every clime,
Averring no prognosticator lies,
That says, "Some great ones fall, their rivals rise."

'Pass such for bubbles; let their bladder-praise
Shine and sink with them in a moment's change:
They think to rise when they the riser raise.
But regal wisdom knows it is not strange
For curs to fawn; base things are ever low;
The vulgar eye feeds only on the show.

'Else would not soothing glossers oil the son,
Who, while his father lived, his acts did hate.
They know all earthly day with man is done
When he is circled in the night of fate.
  So, the deceasèd they think on no more,
  But whom they injured late, they now adore.

'But there's a manly lion now can roar,
Thunder more dreaded than the lioness;
Of him let simple beasts his aid implore,
For he conceives more than they can express.
  The virtuous politic is truly man;
  Devil, the atheist politicïan.

'I guessed thee such a one: but tell thy tale.
If thou be simple, as thou hast expressed,
Do not with coinèd words set wit to sale,
Nor with the flatt'ring world use vain protest.
  Sith man thou sayst thou wert, I prithee tell,
  While thou wert man, what mischiefs thee befell.'

'Princess! You bid me buried cares revive',
Quoth the poor ant, 'Yet sith by you I live,
So let me in my daily lab'rings thrive
As I myself do to your service give.
  I have been oft a man, and so to be,
  Is often to be thrall to misery.

'But if you will have me my mind disclose,
I must entreat you that I may set down
The tales of my black fortunes in sad prose.
Rhyme is uneven, fashioned by a clown.
  I first was such a one: I tilled the ground,
  And amongst rurals verse is scarcely found.'

'Well, tell thy tales, but see thy prose be good.
For if thou Euphuize, which once was rare
And of all English phrase the life and blood,
In those times for the fashion past compare,
  I'll say thou borrow'st, and condemn thy style,
  As our new fools that count all following vile.

'Or if in bitterness thou rail like Nashe—
(Forgive me, honest soul, that term thy phrase
"Railing", for in thy works thou wert not rash,
Nor didst affect in youth thy private praise;
  Thou hadst a strife with that Trigemini:
  Thou hurt'st not them till they had injured thee.

'Thou wast indeed too slothful to thyself,
Hiding thy better talent in thy spleen.
True spirits are not covetous in pelf;
Youth's wit is ever ready, quick, and keen.
  Thou didst not live thy ripened autumn day,
  But wert cut off in thy best blooming May.

'Else hadst thou left, as thou indeed hast left,
Sufficient test, though now in others' chests,
T'improve the baseness of that humorous theft,
Which seems to flow from self-conceiving breasts.
  Thy name they bury, having buried thee;
  Drones eat thy honey: thou wert the true bee.

'Peace keep thy Soul.)—And now to you, Sir Ant:
On with your prose, be neither rude nor nice;
In your discourse let no decorum want;
See that you be sententious and concise,
  And, as I like the matter, I will sing
  A canzonet to close up everything.'

The Ant's Tale when he was a Ploughman.

I was sometimes, most chaste Lady Nightingale, or rather, Queen Philomel the ravished, a brow-melting husbandman. To be man and husband is to be a poor master of many rich cares, which, if he cannot subject and keep under, he must look forever to undergo as many miseries as the hours of his years contain minutes. Such a man I was and such a husband, for I was linked in marriage. My havings was small and my means less, yet charge came on me ere I knew how to keep it; yet did I all my endeavours, had a plough and land to employ it, fertile enough if it were manured, and for tillage I was never held a truant.

But my destruction and the ruin of all painful husbandmen about me began by the prodigal downfall of my young landlord, whose father, grandfather, and great-grandfather for many generations had been lords of the town wherein I dwelt and many other towns near adjoining; to all which belonged fair commons for the comfort of the poor, liberty of fishing, help of fuel by brush and underwood never denied, till the old devourer of virtue, honesty, and good neighbourhood—Death—had made our landlord dance after his pipe, which is so common that every one knows the way though they make small account of it. Well, die he did, and as soon as he was laid in his grave, the bell might well have tolled for hospitality and good housekeeping; for whether they fell sick with him and died and so were buried, I know not, but I am sure in our town they were never seen since, nor that I can hear of in any other part; especially about us they are impossible to be found.

Well, our landlord being dead, we had his heir, gentle enough and fair conditioned, rather promising at first his father's virtues than the world's villainies, but he was so accustomed to wild and unfruitful company about the court and London (whither he was sent by his sober father to practise civility and manners) that in the country he would scarce keep till his father's body was laid in the cold earth. But as soon as the hasty funeral was solemnized, from us he posted, discharging all his old father's servants (whose beards were even frost-bitten with age) and was attended only by a monkey and a marmoset, the one being an ill-faced fellow as variable as Newfangle for fashions, the other an imitator of anything, however villainous, but utterly destitute of all goodness. With this French page and Italianate servingman was our young landlord only waited on, and all to save charges in servingmen to pay it out in harlots. And we poor men had news of a far greater expense within less than a quarter, for we were sent for to London and found our great landlord in a little room about the Strand, who told us that, whereas we had lived tenants at will and might in his forefather's days been hourly turned out, he, putting on a better conscience to usward, intended to make us leases for years; and for advice 'twixt him and us, he had made choice of a lawyer, a mercer, and a merchant to whom he was much beholden, who that morning were appointed to meet in the Temple Church.

Temple and church, both one in name, made us hope of a holy meeting; but there is an old proverb, "The nearer the Church, the farther from God." To approve which saying, we met the mercer and the merchant that, loving our landlord or his land well, held him a great man in both their books. Some little conference they had; what the conclusion was we poor men were not acquainted with; but being called at their leisure and when they pleased to think upon us, told us they were to dine together at the Horn in Fleet Street, being a house where their lawyer resorted; and if we would there attend them, we should understand matter much for our good; and in the mean time they appointed us near the old Temple Garden to attend their counsellor, whose name was master Prospero—not the great rider of horse (for I have heard there was once such a one), but a more cunning rider who had rid many men till they were more miserable than beasts, and our ill hap it was to prove his hackneys. Well, though the issue were ill, on we went to await his worship, whose chamber we found that morning fuller of clients than I could ever see suppliants to heaven in our poor parish church (and yet we had in it three hundred households); and I may tell it with reverence, I never saw more submission done to God than to that great lawyer. Every suitor there offered gold to this gowned idol, standing bareheaded in a sharp-set morning (for it was in booted Michaelmas term), and not a word spoke to him but it was with the bowing of the body and the submissive flexure of the knee. Short tale to make, he was informed of us what we were and of our coming up, when, with an iron look and shrill voice, he began to speak to the richest of our number, ever and anon jerking out the word 'fines', which served instead of a full point to every sentence.

But that word 'fines' was no fine word, methought, to please poor labouring husbandmen that can scarce sweat out so much in a twelvemonth as he would demand in a twinkling. At last, to close up the lamentable tragedy of us ploughmen, enters our young landlord, so metamorphosed into the shape of a French puppet that, at the first, we started and thought one of the baboons had marched in in man's apparel. His head was dressed up in white feathers like a shuttlecock, which agreed so well with his brain (being nothing but cork), that two of the biggest of the guard might very easily have tossed him with battledores and made good sport with him in his majesty's great hall. His doublet was of a strange cut, and to show the fury of his humour, the collar of it rose up so high and sharp as if it would have cut his throat by daylight. His wings, according to the fashion now, was as little and diminutive as a puritan's ruff, which showed he ne'er meant to fly out of England nor do any exploit beyond sea, but live and die about London though he begged in Finsbury. His breeches, a wonder to see, were full as deep as the middle of winter or the roadway between London and Winchester, and so large and wide withal that I think within a twelvemonth he might very well put all his lands in them, and then you may imagine they were big enough when they would outreach a thousand acres. Moreover, they differed so far from our fashioned hose in the country and from his father's old gascoynes that his back part seemed to us like a monster, the roll of the breeches standing so low that we conjectured his house of office, sir-reverence, stood in his hams.

All this while his French monkey bore his cloak of three-pounds-a-yard, lined clean through with purple velvet, which did so dazzle our coarse eyes that we thought we should have been purblind ever after, what with the prodigal aspect of that and his glorious rapier and hangers, all bossed with pillars of gold, fairer in show than the pillars in Paul's or the tombs at Westminster; beside, it drunk up the price of all my ploughland in very pearl, which stuck as thick upon those hangers as the white measles upon hog's flesh. When I had well viewed that gay gaudy cloak and those unthrifty wasteful hangers, I muttered thus to myself: 'That is no cloak for the rain sure, nor those no hangers for Derrick.' When, of a sudden casting mine eyes lower, I beheld a curious pair of boots of King Philip's leather in such artificial wrinkles, sets, and pleats as if they had been starched lately and came new from the laundresses—such was my ignorance and simple acquaintance with the fashion, and I dare swear my fellows and neighbours here are all as ignorant as myself. But that which struck us most into admiration: upon those fantastical boots stood such huge and wide tops which so swallowed up his thighs that had he sworn, as other gallants did, this common oath: 'Would I might sink as I stand!', all his body might very well have sunk down and been damned in his boots. Lastly, he walked the chamber with such a pestilent jingle that his spurs over-squeaked the lawyer and made him reach his voice three notes above his fee. But after we had spied the rowels of his spurs, how we blessed ourselves!—they did so much and so far exceed the compass of our fashion that they looked more like the forerunners of wheelbarrows.

Thus was our young landlord accoutred in such a strange and prodigal shape that it amounted to above two year's rent in apparel. At last approach the mercer and the merchant, two notable arch-tradesmen who had fitted my young master in clothes whilst they had clothed themselves in his acres, and measured him out velvet by the thumb whilst they received his revenues by handfuls; for he had not so many yards in his suit as they had yards and houses bound for the payment, which now he was forced to pass over to them or else all his lands should be put to their book and to their forfeiting neck-verse. So my youngster was now at his pension, not like a gentleman pensioner, but like a gentleman scrivener.

Whereupon entered Master Bursebell the royal scrivener with deeds and writings hanged, drawn, and quartered for the purpose. He was a valiant scribe. I remember his pen lay mounted between his ear like a Tower gun, but not charged yet till our young master's patrimony shot off, which was some third part of an hour after. By this time the lawyer, the mercer, and the merchant were whispering and consulting together about the writings and passage of the land in very deep and sober conference.

But our 'wiseacres' all the while, as one regardless of either land or money, not hearkening or inquisitive after their subtle and politic devices, held himself very busy about the burning of his tobacco pipe (as there is no gallant but hath a pipe to burn about London) though we poor simple men ne'er heard of the name till that time; and he might very fitly take tobacco there, for the lawyer and the rest made him smoke already. But to have noted the apish humour of him and the fantastical faces he coined in the receiving of the smoke, it would have made your ladyship have sung nothing but merry jigs for a twelvemonth after—one time winding the pipe like a horn at the pie-corner of his mouth, which must needs make him look like a sow-gelder, and another time screwing his face like one of our country players, which must needs make him look like a fool; nay, he had at least his dozen of faces, but never a good one amongst them all—neither his father's face, nor the face of his grandfather, but yet more wicked and riotous faces than all the generation of him.

Now their privy whisperings and villainous plots began to be drawn to a conclusion when presently they called our smoky landlord in the midst of his draught, who in a valiant humour dashed his tobacco pipe into the chimney corner, whereat I started, and beckoning his marmoset to me, asked him if those long white things did cost no money; to which the slave replied very proudly: 'Money! Yes sirrah, but I tell thee my master scorns to have a thing come twice to his mouth.' 'Then', quoth I, 'I think thy master is more choice in his mouth than in any member else: it were good if he used that all his body over—he would never have need, as many gallants have, of any sweating physic.' 'Sweating physic?', replied the marmoset, 'What may thy meaning be? Why, do not you ploughmen sweat too?' 'Yes', quoth I, 'most of any men living. But yet there is difference between the sweat of a ploughman and the sweat of a gentleman, as much as between your master's apparel and mine. For when we sweat, the land prospers and the harvest comes in, but when a gentleman sweats, I wot how the gear goes then.' No sooner were these words spoken but the marmoset had drawn out his poinard halfway to make a show of revenge, but at the smart voice of the lawyer he suddenly whipped it in again.

Now was our young master with one penful of ink doing a far greater exploit than all his forefathers, for what they were a-purchasing all their lifetime, he was now passing away in the fourth part of a minute; and that which many thousand drops of his grandfather's brows did painfully strive for, one drop now of a scrivener's inkhorn did easily pass over. A dash of a pen stood for a thousand acres—how quickly they were dashed in the mouth by our young landlord's prodigal fist! It seemed he made no more account of acres than of acorns. Then were we called to set our hands for witnesses of his folly, which we poor men did witness too much already. And because we were found ignorant in writing and never practised in that black art (which I might very fitly term so because it conjured our young master out of all), we were commanded, as it were, to draw any mark with a pen, which should signify as much as the best hand that ever old Peter Bales hung out in the Old Bailey. To conclude, I took the pen first of the lawyer, and turning it arsy-versy like no instrument for a ploughman, our youngster and the rest of the faction burst into laughter at the simplicity of my fingering. But I, not so simple as they laughed me for, drew the picture of a knavish emblem, which was *A Plough with the Heels Upward*, signifying thereby that the world was turned upside down since the decease of my old landlord, all hospitality and good housekeeping kicked out of doors, all thriftiness and good husbandry tossed into the air, ploughs turned into trunks, and corn into apparel. Then came another of our husbandmen to set his mark by mine; he, holding the pen clean at the one side towards the merchant and the mercer showing that all went on their sides, drew the form of an unbridled colt so wild and unruly that he seemed with one foot to kick up the earth and spoil the labours of many toiling beasts, which was fitly alluded to our wild and unbridled landlord, which (like the colt) could stand upon no ground till he had no ground to stand upon.

These marks, set down under the shape of simplicity, were the less marked with the eyes of knavery, for they little dreamed that we ploughmen could have so much satire in us as to bite our young landlord by the elbow. Well, this ended, master Bursebell the calfskin scrivener was royally handled—that is, he had a royal put in his hand by the merchant. And now I talk of calfskin: 'tis great pity, Lady Nightingale, that the skins of harmless and innocent beasts should be as instruments to work villainy upon, entangling young novices and foolish elder brothers which are caught like woodcocks in the net of the law; for 'tis easier for one of the greatest fowls to slide through the least hole of a net than one of the least fools to get from the lappet of a bond.

By this time the squeaking lawyer began to reiterate that cold word 'fines' which struck so chill to our hearts that it made them as cold as our heels, which were almost frozen to the floor with standing. 'Yea', quoth the merchant and the mercer, 'you are now tenants of ours; all the right, title, and interest of this young gentleman, your late landlord, we are firmly possessed of, as you yourselves are witnesses. Wherefore, this is the conclusion of our meeting: such fines as master Prospero here, by the valuation of the land, shall out of his proper judgement allot to us, such are we to demand at your hands. Therefore we refer you to him to wait his answer at the gentleman's best time and leisure.' With that they stifled two or three angels in the lawyer's right hand—'right hand' said I? Which hand was that, trow ye? For it is impossible to know which is the right hand of a lawyer because there are but few lawyers that have right hands, and those few make much of them. So, taking their leaves of my young landlord that was and that never shall be again, away they marched, heavier by a thousand acres at their parting than they were before at their meeting.

The lawyer then, turning his Irish face to usward, willed us to attend his worship the next term, when we should further understand his pleasure. We poor souls thanked his worship and paid him his fee out in legs, when, in sight of us, he embraced our young gentleman (I think, for a fool) and gave him many riotous instructions how to carry himself, which he was prompter to take than the other to put into him: told him he must acquaint himself with many gallants of the Inns of Court and keep rank with those that spend most, always wearing bountiful disposition about him, lofty and liberal; his lodging must be about the Strand, in any case, being remote from the handicraft scent of the City; his eating must be in some famous tavern, as the Horn, the Mitre, or the Mermaid, and then after dinner, he must venture beyond sea, that is, in a choice pair of noblemen's oars to the Bankside where he must sit out the breaking up of a comedy or the first cut of a tragedy; or rather (if his humour so serve him), to call in at the Blackfriars where he should see a nest of boys able to ravish a man. This said, our young goosecap, who was ready to embrace such counsel, thanked him for his fatherly admonitions (as he termed them), and told him again that he should not find him with the breach of any of them, swearing and protesting he would keep all those better than the ten commandments. At which word he buckled on his rapier and hangers, his monkey-face casting on his cloak by the book; after an apish congee or two, passed downstairs without either word or nod to us, his old father's tenants.

Nevertheless, we followed him, like so many russet servingmen, to see the event of all and what the issue would come to, when, of a sudden, he was encountered by a most glorious-spangled gallant which we took at first to have been some upstart tailor because he measured all his body with a salutation from the flow of the doublet to the fall of the breeches. But at last we found him to be a very fantastical sponge that licked up all humours, the very ape of fashions, gesture, and compliment—one of those indeed (as we learned afterward) that fed upon young landlords, riotous sons, and heirs till either he or the Counter in Wood Street had swallowed them up; and would not stick to be a bawd or pander to such young gallants as our young gentleman, either to acquaint them with harlots or harlots with them, to bring them a whole dozen of taffeta punks at a supper; and they should be none of these common Molls neither, but discontented and unfortunate gentlewomen whose parents being lately deceased, the brother ran away with all the land, and they, poor squalls, with a little money which cannot hold out long without some comings in; but they will rather venture a maidenhead than want a headtire; such shuttlecocks as these which, though they are tossed and played withal, go still like maids all white on the top; or else decayed gentlemen's wives, whose husbands (poor souls) lying for debt in the King's Bench, they go about to make monsters in the King's Head tavern, for this is a general axiom: all your luxurious plots are always begun in taverns to be ended in vaulting houses; and after supper when fruit comes in, there is small fruit of honesty to be looked for—for you know that the eating of the apple always betokens the fall of Eve.

Our prodigal child, accompanied with this soaking swaggerer and admirable cheater (who had supped up most of our heirs about London like poached eggs), slips into Whitefriars nunnery whereas, the report went, he kept his most delicate drab of three hundred a year—some unthrifty gentleman's daughter who had mortgaged his land to scriveners sure enough from redeeming again. For so much she seemed by her bringing up, though less by her casting down. Endued she was (as we heard) with some good qualities, though all were converted then but to flattering villainies. She could run upon the lute very well, which in others would have appeared virtuous but in her lascivious, for her running was rather jested at because she was a light runner besides. She had likewise the gift of singing very deliciously, able to charm the hearer, which so bewitched away our young master's money that he might have kept seven noise of musicians for less charges, and yet they would have stood for servingmen too, having blue coats of their own. She had a humour to lisp often like a flatt'ring wanton and talk childish like a parson's daughter, which so pleased and rapt our old landlord's lickerish son that he would swear she spoke nothing but sweetmeats and her breath then sent forth such a delicious odour that it perfumed his white-satin doublet better than sixteen milliners.

Well, there we left him with his devouring cheater and his glorious cockatrice, and being almost upon dinner-time, we hied us and took our repast at thrifty Mother Walker's, where we found a whole nest of pinching bachelors crowded together upon forms and benches in that most worshipful three-halfpenny ordinary, where presently they were boarded with hot Monsieur Mutton-and-Porridge (a Frenchman by his blowing); and next to them, we were served in order, everyone taking their degree. And I tell you true, lady, I have known the time when our young landlord's father hath been a three-halfpenny eater there; nay more, was the first that acquainted us with that sparing and thrifty ordinary, when his riotous son hath since spent his five pound at a sitting. Well, having discharged our small shot (which was like hail-shot in respect of our young master's cannon-reckonings in taverns), we plodded home to our ploughs, carrying these heavy news to our wives, both of the prodigality of our old landlord's son as also of our oppressions to come by the burden of uncharitable fines. And, most musical Madam Nightingale, do but imagine now what a sad Christmas we all kept in the country without either carols, wassail-bowls, dancing of Sellinger's Round in moonshine nights about maypoles, shoeing the mare, hoodman-blind, hot-cockles, or any of our old Christmas gambols; no, not so much as choosing king and queen on Twelfth Night. Such was the dullness of our pleasures, for that one word 'fines' robbed us of all our fine pastimes.

This sour-faced Christmas thus unpleasantly past over, up again we trotted to London—in a great frost, I remember, for the ground was as hard as the lawyer's conscience. And arriving at the luxurious Strand some three days before the term, we inquired for our bountiful landlord, or the fool in the full, at his neat and curious lodging. But answer was made us by an old chambermaid that our gentleman slept not there all the Christmastime, but had been at court and at least in five masques. Marry now, as she thought, we might find him at master Poopes his ordinary with half-a-dozen of gallants more at dice. 'At dice? At the devil!', quoth I, 'for that is a dicer's last throw!' Here I began to rail like Thomas Nashe against Gabriel Harvey, if you call that railing; yet I think it was but the running a tilt of wits in booksellers' shops on both sides of John of Paul's churchyard, and I wonder how John escaped unhorsing. But when we were entered the door of the ordinary, we might hear our lusty gentleman shoot off a volley of oaths some three rooms over us, cursing the dice and wishing the pox were in their bones, crying out for a new pair of square ones, for the other belike had cogged with him and made a gull of him. When, the host of the ordinary coming downstairs, met us with this report after we had named him: 'Troth, good fellows, you have named now the most unfortunatest gentleman living—at passage, I mean; for I protest, I have stood by myself as a heavy eyewitness and seen the beheading of five hundred crowns, and what pitiful end they all made!' With that he showed us his embossed girdle and hangers new-pawned for more money, and told us beside (not without tears), his glorious cloak was cast away three hours before overboard, which was, off the table. At which lamentable hearing, we stood still in the lower room and durst not venture upstairs for fear he would have laid all us ploughmen to pawn too; and yet I think all we could scarce have made up one throw. But to draw to an end as his patrimony did, we had not lingered the better part of an hour, but down came the host fencing his glittering rapier and dagger as if he had been newly shoulder-clapped by a pewter-buttoned sergeant and his weapons seized upon. At last, after a great peal of oaths on all sides, the court broke up and the worshipful bench of dicers came thundering downstairs, some swearing, some laughing, some cursing, and some singing, with such a confusion of humours that, had we not known before what rank of gallants they were, we should have thought the devils had been at dice in an ordinary. The first that appeared to us was our most lamentable landlord dressed up in his monkey's livery cloak (that he seemed now rather to wait upon his monkey than his monkey upon him), which did set forth his satin suit so excellent scurvily that he looked for all the world like a French lord in dirty boots; when, casting his eye upon us, being desirous (as it seemed) to remember us now if we had any money, broke into these fantastical speeches: 'What, my whole warren of tenants?'—thinking indeed to make conies of us—'my honest nest of ploughmen, the only kings of Kent! More dice, ho! then, i'faith, let's have another career, and vomit three dice in a hand again.' With that I plucked his humour at one side and told him we were indeed his father's tenants, but his (we were sorry) we were not. And as for money to maintain his dice, we had not sufficient to stuff out the lawyer. Then replied our gallant in a rage, tossing out two or three new-minted oaths: 'These ploughmen are politicians, I think; they have wit, the whoresons; they will be tenants, I perceive, longer than we shall be landlords!' And fain he would have swaggered with us but that his weapons were at pawn. So, marching out like a turned gentleman, the rest of the gallants seemed to cashier him and throw him out of their company like a blank die—the one having no black pips, nor he no white pieces. Now was our gallant the true picture of the prodigal, and having no rents to gather now, he gathered his wits about him, making his brain pay him revenues in villainy. For it is a general observation that your sons and heirs prove seldom wisemen till they have no more land than the compass of their noddles. To conclude, within few days' practice, he was grown as absolute in cheating and as exquisite in pandarism that he outstripped all Greene's books *Of the Art of Cony-catching*; and where before he maintained his drab, he made his drab now maintain him; proved the only true captain of vaulting-houses and the valiant champion against constables and searchers, feeding upon the sin of Whitefriars, Pickt-hatch, and Turnbull Street. Nay, there was no landed novice now but he could melt him away into nothing, and in one twelvemonth make him hold all his land between his legs, and yet but straddle easily neither. No wealthy son of the city but, within less than a quarter, he could make all his stock not worth a Jersey stocking. He was all that might be in dissolute villainy and nothing that should be in his forefathers' honesty. To speak troth, we did so much blush at his life and were so ashamed of his base courses that ever after we loathed to look after them.

But returning to our stubble-haired lawyer, who reaped his beard every term-time (the lawyer's harvest), we found the mercer and the merchant crowded in his study amongst a company of law books, which they jostled so often with their coxcombs that they were almost together by the ears with them; when, at the sight of us, they took an *habeas corpus* and removed their bodies into a bigger room. But there we lingered not long for our torments, for the mercer and the merchant gave fire to the lawyer's tongue with a rope of angels, and the word 'fines' went off with such a powder that the force of it blew us all into the country, quite changed our ploughmen's shapes, and so we became little ants again.

This, Madam Nightingale, is the true discourse of our rural fortunes, which, how miserable, wretched, and full of oppression they were, all husbandmen's brows can witness that are fined with more sweat still year by year; and I hope a canzonet of your sweet singing will set them forth to the world in satirical harmony.

The remorseful nightingale, delighted with the ant's quaint discourse, began to tune the instrument of her voice, breathing forth these lines in sweet and delicious airs.

The Nightingale's Canzonet.

Poor little ant,
Thou shalt not want
The ravished music of my voice!
Thy shape is best,
Now thou art least;
For great ones fall with greater noise,
And this shall be the carriage of my song:
Small bodies can have but a little wrong.

Now thou art securer
And thy days far surer;
Thou pay'st no rent upon the rack
To daub a prodigal landlord's back,
Or to maintain the subtle running
Of dice and drabs, both one in cunning;
Both pass from hand to hand to many,
Flatt'ring all, yet false to any;
Both are well linked, for, throw dice how you can,
They will turn up their pips to every man.

Happy art thou and all thy brothers
That never feel'st the hell of others:
The torment to a luxur due,
Who never thinks his harlot true;
Although upon her heels he stick his eyes,
Yet still he fears that though she stands, she lies.

Now are thy labours easy,
Thy state not sick or queasy;
All drops thou sweat'st are now thine own;
Great subsidies be as unknown
To thee and to thy little fellow ants;
Now none of you under that burden pants.

Lo, for example, I myself, poor worms,
That have outworn the rage of Tereus' storms,
Am ever blessed now in this downy shape
From all men's treachery or soul-melting rape;
And when I sing *Tereu, Tereu*
Through every town and so renew
The name of *Tereus*, slaves, through fears,
With guilty fingers bolt their ears;
And all ravishers do rave and e'en fall mad,
And then such wronged souls as myself are glad.

So thou, small wretch, and all thy nest,
Are in those little bodies blest,
Not taxed beyond your poor degree
With landlord's fine and lawyer's fee.
But tell me, pretty toiling worm,
Did that same ploughman's weary form
Discourage thee so much from others,
That neither thou, nor those thy brothers,
In borrowed shapes durst once again
Venture amongst perfidious men?

Ant.

'Yes lady', the poor ant replied,
'I left not so, but then I tried
War's sweating fortunes, not alone
Condemning rash all states for one,
Until I found by proof and knew by course
That one was bad, but all the rest were worse.'

Nightingale.

Didst thou put on a rugged soldier then,
A happy state because thou fought'st 'gainst men?
Prithee discourse thy fortunes, state, and harms.
Thou wast, no doubt, a mighty man-at-arms.

The Ant's Tale when he was a Soldier.

Then thus: most musical and prickle-singing madam (for, if I err not, your ladyship was the first that brought up prick-song, being nothing else but the fatal notes of your pitiful ravishment), I, not contented long (a vice cleaving to all worldlings) with this little estate of an ant, but stuffed with envy and ambition, as small as I was, desired to venture into the world again, which I may rather term the upper hell, or *frigida gehenna*, the cold-charitable hell wherein are all kind of devils too, as your gentle devil, your ordinary devil, and your gallant devil; and all these can change their shapes too, as today in cowardly white, tomorrow in politic black, a third day in jealous yellow; for believe it, sweet lady, there are devils of all colours. Nevertheless I, covetous of more change, leaped out of this little skin of an ant and hung my skin on the hedge, taking upon me the grisly shape of a dusty soldier. Well made I was, and my limbs valiantly hewn out for the purpose: I had a mazard, I remember, so well-lined in the inside with my brain it stood me in better stead than a double headpiece, for the brain of a soldier, differing from all other sciences, converts itself to no other use but to line, fur, and even quilt the coxcomb, and so makes a pate of proof. My face was well-leavened which made my looks taste sour, the true relish of a man of war; my cheeks, dough-baked, pale, wan, and therefore argued valour and resolution; but my nose somewhat hard-baked and a little burnt in the oven, a property not amiss in a soldier's visage who should scorn to blush but in his nose. My chin was well thatched with a beard which was a necessary shelter in winter and a fly-flap in summer, so brushy and spreading that my lips could scarce be seen to walk abroad, but played at all-hid and durst not peep forth for starting a hair. To conclude, my arms, thighs, and legs were so sound, stout, and weighty (as if they had come all out of the timber yard) that my very presence only was able to still the bawlingest infant in Europe. And I think, madam, this was no unlikely shape for a soldier to prove well: here was mettle enough, for four shillings a week, to do valiant service till it was bored as full of holes as a skimmer.

Well, to the wars I betook me, ranked myself amongst desperate hot-shots—only, my carriage put on more civility, for I seemed more like a spy than a follower, an observer rather than a committer of villany. And little thought I, madam, that the camp had been supplied with harlots too as well as the Curtain, and the guarded tents as wicked as garden tenements, trulls passing to and fro in the washed shape of laundresses as your bawds about London in the manner of starchwomen, which is the most unsuspected habit that can be to train out a mistress. And if your ladyship will not think me much out of the way, though I take a running leap from the camp to the Strand again, I will discover a pretty knavery of the same breeding between such a starchwoman and a kind wanton mistress, as there are few of those ballassed vessels nowadays but will have a love and a husband.

The woman crying her ware by the door (a most pitiful cry and a lamentable hearing that such a stiff thing as starch should want customers), passing cunningly and slyly by the stall, not once taking notice of the party you wot on, but being by this some three or four shops off. 'Mass', quoth my young mistress to the weathercock her husband, 'such a thing I want, you know.' Then she named how many puffs and purls lay in a miserable case for want of stiffening. The honest, plain-dealing jewel her husband sent out a boy to call her (not 'bawd', by her right name, but 'starchwoman'); into the shop she came, making a low counterfeit curtsy, of whom the mistress demanded if the starch were pure gear and would be stiff in her ruff, saying, she had often been deceived before when the things about her have stood as limber as eelskins. The woman replied as subtly: 'Mistress', quoth she, 'take this paper of starch of my hand, and if it prove not to your mind, never bestow penny with me!'—which paper, indeed, was a letter sent to her from the gentleman, her exceeding favourite. 'Say you so?' quoth the young dame, 'and I'll try it i'faith.' With that she ran upstairs like a spinner upon small cobweb ropes, not to try or arraign the starch, but to construe and parse the letter (whilst her husband sat below by the counter like one of these brow-bitten catchpoles that wait for one man all day, when his wife can put five in the Counter before him), wherein she found many words that pleased her. Withal the gentleman writ unto her for a certain sum of money, which no sooner was read but was ready to be sent; wherefore, laying up the starch and that and taking another sheet of clean paper in her hand, wanting time and opportunity to write at large, with a penful of ink, in the very middle of the sheet writ these few quaint monosyllables: 'Coin, Cares, and Cures, and all C's else are yours.' Then rolling up the white money like the starch in that paper very subtly and artificially, came tripping downstairs with these colourable words: 'Here's goodly starch indeed! Fie, fie—trust me husband—as yellow as the jaundice! I would not have betrayed my puffs with it for a million! Here, here, here!' (giving her the paper of money). With that the subtle starchwoman, seeming sorry that it pleased her not, told her, within few days she would fit her turn with that which should like her (meaning, indeed, more such sweet news from her lover). These and suchlike, madam, are the cunning conveyances of secret, privy, and therefore unnoted harlots that so avoid the common finger of the world when less committers than they are publicly pointed at.

So, likewise in the camp, whither now I return borne on the swift wings of apprehension, the habit of a laundress shadows the abomination of a strumpet, and our soldiers are like glovers, for the one cannot work well nor the other fight well without their wenches. This was the first mark of villainy that I found sticking upon the brow of War. But after the hot and fiery copulation of a skirmish or two, the ordnance playing like so many Tamburlaines, the muskets and calivers answering like drawers, 'Anon, anon, sir, I cannot be here and there too'—that is, in the soldier's hand and in the enemy's belly—I grew more acquainted and, as it were, entered into the entrails of black-livered policy. Methought indeed, at first, those great pieces of ordnance should speak English, though now by transportation turned rebels; and what a miserable and pitiful plight it was, lady, to have so many thousands of our men slain by their own countrymen the cannons—I mean not the harmless canons of Paul's, but those cannons that have a great singing in their heads.

Well, in this onset I remember I was well smoke-dried but neither arm nor leg perished, not so much as the loss of a petty finger, for when I counted them all over, I missed not one of them, and yet sometimes the bullets came within a hair of my coxcomb even like a barber scratching my pate, and perhaps took away the left limb of a vermin, and so departed; another time shouldering me like a bailiff against Michaelmas term and then shaking me by the sleeve as familiarly as if we had been acquainted seven years together. To conclude, they used me very courteously and gentleman-like awhile, like an old cunning bowler to fetch in a young ketling gamester, who will suffer him to win one sixpenny-game at the first, and then lurch him in six pounds afterward; and so they played with me, still training me with their fair promises into far deeper and deadlier battles where, like villainous cheating bowlers, they lurched me of two of my best limbs, *viz.* my right arm and right leg, that so, of a man of war, I became in show a monster of war, yet comforted in this because I knew war begot many such monsters as myself in less than a twelvemonth.

Now I could discharge no more, having paid the shot dear enough, I think, but rather desired to be discharged, to have pay and be gone: whereupon I appeared to my captain and other commanders, kissing my left hand which then stood for both (like one actor that plays two parts), who seemed to pity my unjointed fortunes and plaster my wounds up with words, told me I had done valiant service in their knowledge; marry, as for pay, they must go on the score with me, for all their money was thumped out in powder. And this was no pleasing salve to a green sore, madam; 'twas too much for me, lady, to trust calivers with my limbs and then cavaliers with my money. Nevertheless, for all my lamentable action of one arm like old Titus Andronicus, I could purchase no more than one month's pay for a ten-month's pain and peril; nor that neither, but to convey away my miserable clamours that lay roaring against the arches of their ears, marry, their bountiful favours were extended thus far: I had a passport to beg in all countries.

Well, away I was packed, and after a few miseries by the way, at last I set one foot into England again (for I had no more then to set), being my native though unnatural country for whose dear good I pawned my limbs to bullets, those merciless brokers that will take the vantage of a minute, and so they were quite forfeited, lost, and unrecoverable. When I was on shore, the people gathered, which word 'gathering' put me in hope of good comfort that afterward I failed of. For I thought, at first, they had gathered something for me, but I found, at last, they did only but gather about me, some wondering at me as if I had been some sea monster cast ashore, some jesting at my deformity, whilst others laughed at the jests. One amongst them, I remember, likened me to a sea-crab because I went all of one side; another fellow vied it and said I looked like a rabbit cut up and half-eaten because my wing and leg (as they termed it) were departed. Some began to pity me, but those were few in number, or at least their pity was as penniless as Pierce, who writ to the devil for maintenance. Thus passing from place to place like the motion of Julius Caesar or the city Nineveh, though not altogether in so good clothes, I overtook the city from whence I borrowed my first breath and in whose defence I spent and laid out my limbs by whole sums to purchase her peace and happiness, nothing doubting but to be well entreated there, my grievous maims tenderly regarded, my poor broken estate carefully repaired, the ruins of my blood built up again with redress and comfort. But woe the while, madam! I was not only unpitied, succourless, and rejected, but threatened with the public stocks, loathsome jails, and common whipping-posts, there to receive my pay (a goodly reward for my bleeding service) if I were once found in the city again.

Wherefore I was forced to retire towards the Spital and Shoreditch, which, as it appeared, was the only Cole Harbour and sanctuary for wenches and soldiers; where I took up a poor lodging o' trust till the Sunday, hoping that then Master Alms and Mistress Charity would walk abroad and take the air in Finsbury.

At which time I came hopping out from my lodging like old lame Giles of Cripplegate; but when I came there, the wind blew so bleak and cold that I began to be quite out of hope of Charity, yet, like a torn map of misery, I waited my single halfpenny fortunes; when, of a sudden, turning myself about and looking down the Windmill Hill, I might espy afar off a fine-fashioned dame of the city with her man bound by indenture before her; whom no sooner I caught in mine eyelids, but I made to with all possible speed, and with a premeditated speech for the nonce, thus most soldier-like I accosted her:

'Sweet lady, I beseech your beauty to weigh the estate of a poor unjointed soldier that hath consumed the moiety, or the one half of his limbs, in the dismembering and devouring wars that hath cheated me of my flesh so notoriously. I protest I am not worth at this instant the small revenue of three farthings, besides my lodging unpleased and my diet unsatisfied. And had I ten thousand limbs, I would venture them all in your sweet quarrel rather than such a beauty as yourself should want the least limb of your desire.'

With that, as one being rather moved by my last words of promise than my first words of pity, she drew her white bountiful hand out of her marry-muff and quoited a single halfpenny, whereby I knew her then to be cold Mistress Charity both by her chill appearance and the hard frozen pension she gave me. She was warm lapped, I remember, from the sharp injury of the biting air: her visage was benighted with a taffeta mask to fray away the naughty wind from her face, and yet her very nose seemed so sharp with cold that it almost bored a hole quite through. This was frost-bitten Charity: her teeth chattered in her head and leaped up and down like virginal-jacks, which betrayed likewise who she was. And you would have broken into infinite laughter, madam (though misery made me leaden and pensive), had you been present to have seen how quickly the muff swallowed her hand again, for no sooner was it drawn forth to drop down her pitiful alms but, for fear the sun and air should have ravished it, it was extempore whipped up again. This is the true picture of Charity, madam, which is as cold as ice in the middle of July.

Well, still I waited for another fare. But then I bethought myself again that all the fares went by water o' Sundays to the bear-baiting, and o' Mondays to Westminster Hall, and therefore, little to be looked for in Moorfields all the week long.

Wherefore I sat down by the rails there and fell into these passionate, but not railing speeches: 'Is this the farthest reward for a soldier? Is valour and resolution, the two champions of the soul, so slightly esteemed and so basely undervalued? Doth reeling fortune not only rob us of our limbs, but of our living? Are soldiers then both food for cannon and for misery?' But then, in the midst of my passion, calling to memory the peevish turns of many famous popular gallants whose names were writ even upon the heart of the world (it could not so much as think without them, nor speak but in the discourse of them), I began to outdare the very worst of cruel and disaster chances and determined to be constant in calamity and valiant against the battering siege of misery. But note the cross star that always dogged my fortunes. I had not long rested there but I saw the tweering constable of Finsbury with his bench of brown billmen making towards me, meaning indeed to stop some prison hole with me, as your soldiers, when the wars have done with them, are good for nothing else but to stop holes withal; at which sight,

I scrambled up of all two, took my skin off the hedge, cozened the constable, and slipped into an ant again.

The Nightingale.

'O, 'twas a pretty quaint deceit'
(The Nightingale began to sing),
'To slip from those that lie in wait,
Whose touch is like a raven's wing,
Fatal and ominous, which, being spread
Over a mortal, aims him dead.

'Alas, poor emmet! thou wast tossed
In thousand miseries by this shape,
Thy colour wasted, thy blood lost,
Thy limbs broke with the violent rape
Of hot impatient cannons, which desire
To ravish lives, spending their lust in fire.

'O, what a ruthful sight it is to see,
Though in a soldier of the mean'st degree,
That right member perished,
Which thy body cherished;
That limb dissevered, burnt, and gone,
Which the best part was borne upon;
And then the greatest ruth of all,
Returning home in torn estate,
Where he should rise, there most to fall,
Trod down with envy, bruised with hate:
Yet wretch, let this thy comfort be,
That greater worms have fared like thee.'

By this the day began to spring
And seize upon her watchful eyes,
When more tree-choristers did sing,
And every bird did wake and rise;
Which was no sooner seen and heard,
But all their pretty chat was marred.
And then she said,
'We are betrayed,
The day is up, and all the birds,
And they abroad will blab our words.'
With that she bade the ants farewell,
And all they likewise Philomel.
Away she flew,
Crying *Tereu*!
And all the industrious ants in throngs
Fell to their work, and held their tongues.

FINIS.

Father Hubburd's Tales

Or, The Ant and the Nightingale

The Epistle Dedicatory.

To the true general patron of all muses, musicians, poets, and picture-drawers, Sir Christopher Clutch-Fist, knighted at a very hard pennyworth, neither for eating musk-melons, anchovies, or caviar, but for a costlier exploit and a hundred-pound feat of arms, Oliver Hubburd, brother to the nine waiting-gentlewomen, the muses, wisheth the decrease of his lands and the increase of his legs, that his calves may hang down like gamashoes.

Most guerdonless sir, pinching patron, and the muses' bad paymaster, thou that owest for all the pamphlets, histories, and translations that ever have been dedicated to thee since thou wert one-and-twenty and couldst make water upon thine own lands—but beware, sir! You cannot carry it away so, I can tell you, for all your copper-gilt

3 **Sir Christopher Clutch-Fist** perhaps with reference to William, second Baron Compton, of Compton Wynyates, Warwickshire (see Adams, pp. xxiii–xxxi). Middleton had dedicated *Ghost* to Compton, but apparently failed to merit his patronage in the form of the usual 'tip' of £3 for a dedication; Adams argues that the references to Clutch-Fist in the third tale may be autobiographical. Interestingly enough, Spenser's *Prosopoia, or Mother Hubburd's Tale* was dedicated to Lady Compton.

4–5 ***musk-melons . . . caviar*** delicacies which may refer to Compton's fondness for personal display and fine living

6 ***hundred-pound feat of arms*** allusion to the wholesale selling of knighthoods by James I during his progress to London for his coronation in 1603 and thereafter

7–8 ***decrease . . . calves*** satiric inversion of standard dedication terminology, in which an increase in lands is wished upon the dedicatee

9 ***gamashoes*** loose drawers or stockings worn outside the legs over the other clothing

10 **guerdonless** i.e., not giving a reward or payment

15 **copper-gilt** copper-plated, i.e., cheap imitation of gold-plated (see 39–41)

spurs and your brood of feathers. For there are certain line-sharkers that have coursed the countries to seek you out already, and they nothing doubt but to find you here this Candlemas term which, if it should fall out so (as I hope your worship is wiser than to venture up so soon to the chambers of London), they have plotted together with the best common play-plotter in England to arrest you at the muses' suit (though they shoot short of them) and to set one of the sergeants of poetry, or rather the Poultry, to claw you by the back, who with one clap on your shoulder will bruise all the taffeta to pieces. Now, what the matter is between you, you know best yourself, sir. Only, I hear that they rail against you in booksellers' shops very dreadfully that you have used them most unknightly in offering to take their books and would never return so much as would pay for the covers, beside the gilding too, which stands them in somewhat, you know, and a yard and a quarter of broad sixpenny ribbon—the price of that you are not ignorant of yourself because you wear broad shoestring. And they cannot be persuaded but that you pull the strings off from their books and so maintain your shoes all the year long; and think, verily, if the book be in folio, that you take off the parchment and give it to your tailor but save all the gilding together, which may amount in time to gild you a pair of spurs withal. Such are the miserable conceits they gather of you because you never give the poor muse-suckers a penny. Wherefore, if I might counsel you, sir, the next time they came with their gilded dedications, you should take the books, make your men break their pates, then give them ten groats apiece, and so drive them away.

Your worship's, if you embrace my counsel,
Oliver Hubburd.

FATHER
Hubburds Tales:
OR
THE ANT,
And the Nightingale.

LONDON
Printed by T. C. for William Cotton, and are to be ſolde at his Shop neare adioyning to Ludgate. 1604.

Title-page of CREEDE 2.

16 **brood of feathers** large, ostentatious feathers in a hat

17 **line-sharkers** *OED* cites this passage but cannot explain the meaning. The context suggests an inferior class of plagiarizing poets who have dedicated books of patchwork poems to Clutch-Fist.
countries i.e., counties

19 **Candlemas term** February 2, the time appointed for the sessions of certain law courts, and the payment of rents and wages. Clutch-Fist apparently travelled to London during court terms to attend to legal matters rather than using the local courts, partly to avoid local bias and partly for a visit to the city.

22 **best ... play-plotter** the reference may be to Anthony Munday. Francis Meres refers to him as '*Anthony Mundye* our best plotter' (*Palladis Tamia*, 1598). Henslowe's *Diary*, May 1602, records that Munday, Middleton, and others were working together on the play *Caesar's Fall*.

24 **sergeants ... Poultry** A sergeant was a sheriff's officer who made arrests; the Poultry was one of two city prisons. The line-sharkers have plotted to have Clutch-Fist arrested for debt, i.e., failure to remunerate them for their dedications and the materials scavenged from their books.

26 **taffeta** shoulder-padding in Clutch-Fist's outer garment

28 **rail** abuse verbally

32–3 **yard ... ribbon** very expensive ribbon at six pennies (the price of a play quarto) per yard, perhaps a half-inch in width. In a large book such as a folio (see note to l. 38), several such ribbons were stitched into the spine of the book at the top. A reader inserted the ribbons between pages as place markers.

38 **folio** the largest size of printed book in which the large printed sheet was folded once to form the leaves of the book. The gilding, ribbon, and parchment here indicate the most expensive kind of binding (see notes to ll. 1243–5).

39–40 **gilding ... spurs** the very thin gold leaf impressed on the cover of the book (see note to l. 1244). Clutch-Fist scrapes off the gold leaf and saves it until he has enough for gold-plating a pair of spurs.

41 **conceits** conception, image

42 **muse-suckers** i.e., poets ('line-sharkers'), who nurse at the breasts of the muses

44 **gilded dedications** The first letter of a dedicatory epistle frequently was printed with a large block capital, as was the 'M' in 'Most guerdonless sir ...' in both editions of Middleton's text. In very rare instances, the letter was printed in gold ink, thereby 'gilding' the dedication; figuratively, loading it with exaggerated praise.

45 **pates** heads
groats a paltry, insulting sum of money, usually the lowest going price; in context, probably less than a penny

To the Reader.

Shall I tell you what, reader?—But first I should call you gentle, courteous, and wise. But 'tis no matter, they're but foolish words, of course, and better left out than printed. For if you be so, you need not be called so; and if you be not so, there were law against me for calling you out of your names. By John of Paul's Churchyard I swear (and that oath will be taken at any haberdasher's), I never wished this book better fortune than to fall into the hands of a true-spelling printer and an honest-minded bookseller; and if honesty could be sold by the bushel like oysters, I had rather have one Bushel of honesty than three of money.

Why I call these *Father Hubburd's Tales* is not to have them called in again, as the *Tale of Mother Hubburd*: the world would show little judgement in that, i'faith, and I should say then *plena stultorum omnia*, for I entreat here neither of ragged bears or apes, no, nor the lamentable downfall of the old wife's platters. I deal with no such metal: what is mirth in me is as harmless as the quarter-jacks in Paul's that are up with their elbows four times an hour and yet misuse no creature living. The very bitterest in me is but like a physical frost that nips the wicked blood a little and so makes the whole body the wholesomer; and none can justly except at me but some riotous vomiting Kit or some gentleman-swallowing Malkin. Then, to condemn these tales following because Father Hubburd tells them in the small size of an ant is even as much as if these two words, *God* and *Devil*, were printed both in one line, to skip it over and say that line were naught because the devil were in it. *Sat sapienti*. And I hope there be many wisemen in all the twelve Companies.

Yours, if you read without spelling or hacking,
T.M.

The Ant and the Nightingale

The west-sea's goddess in a crimson robe,
Her temples circled with a coral wreath,
Waited her love, the light'ner of earth's globe;
The wanton wind did on her bosom breathe,
  The nymphs of springs did hallowed water pour;
  Whate'er was cold helped to make cool her bower.

And now the fiery horses of the sun
Were from their golden-flaming car untraced,
And all the glory of the day was done,
Save here and there some light moon-clouds enchased;
  A parti-coloured canopy did spread
  Over the sun and Thetis' amorous bed.

Now had the shepherds folded in their flocks,
The sweating teams uncoupled from their yokes.
The wolf sought prey, and the sly-murdering fox
Attempts to steal, fearless of rural strokes.
  All beasts took rest that lived by lab'ring toil;
  Only such ranged as had delight in spoil.

Now in the pathless region of the air
The wingèd passengers had left to soar,
Except the bat and owl, who bode sad care,
And Philomel, that nightly doth deplore,
  In soul-contenting tunes, her change of shape,
  Wrought first by perfidy and lustful rape.

This poor musician, sitting all alone
On a green hawthorn, from the thunder blest,
Carols in varied notes her antique moan,
Keeping a sharpened briar against her breast:
  Her innocence this watchful pain doth take,
  To shun the adder and the speckled snake.

55 **John of Paul's** a haberdasher situated in Paul's Churchyard

60 **Bushel of honesty** a complimentary pun on the name of the publisher of the first edition, Thomas Bushell

63 **called in again** the process whereby the High Commission, the Archbishop of Canterbury, the Bishop of London, or the Privy Council banned a book and ordered all copies to be brought to Stationers' Hall or the Bishop's residence
Tale of Mother Hubburd Although Edmund Spenser published a viciously satiric poem with this subtitle in 1591, no record is extant of it being called in. While an ape is a major figure in the poem, it contains no mention of 'ragged bears' or 'old wife's platters'.

65 ***plena stultorum omnia*** from Cicero's *Epistolae ad Familiares*: 'All things are full of fools', or 'fools are everywhere'

67–8 **platters . . . metal** i.e., the old wife's plates are metal (pewter?)

68–9 **quarter-jacks** the 'jacks' are the figures who strike a bell on the quarter-hour as part of a large, tower-mounted, public clock; typically a hammer is raised by the arm of the figure and brought down onto a bell

71–2 **physical frost . . . wholesomer** The notion that satire is like a physical purgative is also found in Thomas Dekker's epistle in *The Wonderful Year* (1603): 'If you read, you may happily laugh; 'tis my desire you should, because mirth is both physical and wholesome against the plague . . . .'

73 **Kit** loose woman

74 **Malkin** female personal name applied typically to a woman of the lower-class; a lewd woman

79 ***Sat sapienti*** shortened version of 'verbum sapienti sat est', or, 'a word to the wise is sufficient'

80 **Companies** the various trades were organized into twelve major and 32 minor self-regulating guilds, or 'companies'

81 **hacking** the mangling of words or sense, i.e., twisting or misinterpreting the author's words; currently 'computer-hacking', i.e., decoding the mechanisms which protect against illegal entry to computer systems

84 **goddess** the sea-nymph Thetis

91 **untraced** to free [horses] from the traces, or the leather straps or ropes by which the collar of a draught-animal is connected with the splinter-bar or swingletree

93 **enchased** inlaid with gold, gems, etc.

94 **parti-coloured** multi-coloured, i.e., a rainbow

99 **rural strokes** blows from the clubs or implements of farmers protecting their livestock

106 **change of shape** after being raped by Tereus, Philomel was transformed into a nightingale

111 **sharpened briar** Philomel sang all night with a thorn pressed against her breast in order to stay awake and remain vigilant against predators (snakes)

These two, like her old foe the Lord of Thrace,
Regardless of her dulcet changing song,
To serve their own lust have her life in chase.
Virtue by vice is offered endless wrong.
  Beasts are not all to blame, for now and then
  We see the like attempted amongst men.

Under the tree whereon the poor bird sat,
There was a bed of busy, toiling ants,
That in their summer, winter's comfort got,
Teaching poor men how to shun after-wants;
  Whose rules if sluggards could be learned to keep,
  They should not starve awake, lie cold asleep.

One of these busy brethren, having done
His day's true labour, got upon the tree,
And with his little nimble legs did run.
Pleased with the hearing, he desired to see
  What wondrous creature nature had composed,
  In whom such gracious music was enclosed.

He got too near, for the mistrustful bird
Guessed him to be a spy from her known foe.
Suspicion argues not to hear a word;
What wiseman fears not that's inured to woe?
  Then blame not her. She caught him in her beak,
  About to kill him ere the worm could speak.

But yet her mercy was above her heat.
She did not—as a many silken men
Called by much wealth, small wit, to judgement's seat—
Condemn at random. But she pitied then
  When she might spoil: would great ones would do so,
  Who often kill before the cause they know.

O, if they would, as did this little fowl,
Look on their lesser captives with even ruth,
They should not hear so many sentenced howl,
Complaining Justice is not friend to Truth,
  But they would think upon this ancient theme:
  "Each right extreme, is injury extreme!"

Pass them to mend, for none can them amend
But heaven's lieutenant and earth's Justice-King.
"Stern will, hath will." "No great one wants a friend."
"Some are ordained to sorrow, some to sing."
  And with this sentence let thy griefs all close:
  "Whoe'er are wronged, are happier than their foes."

So much for such. Now to the little ant
In the bird's beak and at the point to die.
Alas for woe, friends in distress are scant!
None of his fellows to his help did hie.
  They keep them safe; they hear, and are afraid:
  'Tis vain to trust in the base number's aid.

Only himself unto himself is friend.
With a faint voice his foe he thus bespake:
'Why seeks your gentleness a poor worm's end?
O, ere you kill, hear the excuse I make!
  I come to wonder, not to work offence:
  There is no glory to spoil innocence!

'Perchance you take me for a soothing spy
By the sly snake or envious adder fee'd.
Alas, I know not how to feign and lie,
Or win a base intelligencer's meed,
  That now are Christians, sometime Turks, then Jews,
  Living by leaving heaven for earthly news.

'Trust me: I am a little emmet born to work,
Oft-times a man, as you were once a maid.
Under the name of man much ill doth lurk,
Yet of poor me, you need not be afraid.
  Mean men are worms on whom the mighty tread;
  Greatness and strength your virtue injurèd.'

With that she opened wide her horny bill,
The prison where this poor submissant lay;
And seeing the poor ant lie quivering still,
'Go wretch', quoth she, 'I give thee life and way.
  The worthy will not prey on yielding things.
  Pity's enfeoffed to the blood of kings!

114 **Lord of Thrace** King Tereus, husband of Procne, Philomel's sister
115 **dulcet** sweet to the ear, pleasing, soothing, gentle
123 **after-wants** their industrious summer activity aims at supplying the winter's necessities. The ant colony was commonly used analogically as an ideal paradigm for the harmonious structuring of human society.
124 **learned** taught
137 **worm** frequently used in the sense of 'poor wretch'
138 **mercy** in this and the following stanza, Philomel embodies the ideal in Middleton's attack on injustice in human society
heat passion, anger
145 **ruth** pity, compassion
151 **heaven's lieutenant . . . earth's Justice-King** The reference is ambiguous. In the Christian mythos, Jesus Christ, the son of God, has the responsibility and the power of judging the living and the dead and is the only one who can ultimately 'amend' all earthly injustice. The possibility that the referent is James I is diminished by the later reference to him as the 'manly lion' (222).
154 **sentence** *sententia*, or a wise, witty saying
168 **soothing** flattering, smooth-talking
169 **fee'd** hired for a fee
171–3 **intelligencer's . . . earthly news** a spy or informer, presumably a Christian, who has no moral qualms about posing as an infidel, thereby sinning mortally and putting his soul in danger of damnation
174 **emmet** ant
181 **submissant** one who submits
185 **enfeoffed** put in possession of the fee-simple or fee-tail of lands, tenements etc. Pity and mercy are the obligation of kings.

'For I was once, though now a feathered veil
Cover my wrongèd body, queen-like clad;
This down about my neck was erst a rail
Of byss embroidered. Fie on that we had!
  Unthrifts and fools and wrongèd ones complain
  Rich things were theirs, must ne'er be theirs again.

'I was, thou know'st, the daughter to a king,
Had palaces and pleasures in my time.
Now mine own songs I am enforced to sing.
Poets forget me in their pleasing rhyme;
  Like chaff they fly, tossed with each windy breath,
  Omitting my forced rape by Tereus' death!

'But 'tis no matter: I myself can sing
Sufficient strains to witness mine own worth.
They that forget a queen, soothe with a king;
Flattery's still barren, yet still bringeth forth;
  Their works are dews, shed when the day is done,
  But sucked up dry by the next morning's sun.

'What more of them? They are like Iris' throne,
Commixed with many colours in moist time:
Such lines portend what's in that circle shown;
Clear weather follows showers in every clime,
  Averring no prognosticator lies,
  That says, "Some great ones fall, their rivals rise."

'Pass such for bubbles; let their bladder-praise
Shine and sink with them in a moment's change:
They think to rise when they the riser raise.
But regal wisdom knows it is not strange
  For curs to fawn; base things are ever low;
  The vulgar eye feeds only on the show.

'Else would not soothing glossers oil the son,
Who, while his father lived, his acts did hate.
They know all earthly day with man is done
When he is circled in the night of fate.
  So, the deceasèd they think on no more,
  But whom they injured late, they now adore.

'But there's a manly lion now can roar,
Thunder more dreaded than the lioness;
Of him let simple beasts his aid implore,
For he conceives more than they can express.
  The virtuous politic, is truly man;
  Devil, the atheist politicïan.

'I guessed thee such a one: but tell thy tale.
If thou be simple, as thou hast expressed,
Do not with coinèd words set wit to sale,
Nor with the flatt'ring world use vain protest.
  Sith man thou sayst thou wert, I prithee tell,
  While thou wert man, what mischiefs thee befell.'

'Princess! You bid me buried cares revive',
Quoth the poor ant, 'Yet sith by you I live,
So let me in my daily lab'rings thrive
As I myself do to your service give.
  I have been oft a man, and so to be,
  Is often to be thrall to misery.

'But if you will have me my mind disclose,
I must entreat you that I may set down
The tales of my black fortunes in sad prose.
Rhyme is uneven, fashioned by a clown.
  I first was such a one: I tilled the ground,
  And amongst rurals verse is scarcely found.'

'Well, tell thy tales, but see thy prose be good.
For if thou Euphuize, which once was rare
And of all English phrase the life and blood,
In those times for the fashion past compare,
  I'll say thou borrow'st, and condemn thy style,
  As our new fools that count all following vile.

'Or if in bitterness thou rail like Nashe—
(Forgive me, honest soul, that term thy phrase
"Railing", for in thy works thou wert not rash,

188–9 **rail | Of byss** a collar or neckerchief of finely embroidered linen
192 **king** King Pandion of Athens
195–7 **Poets ... death** The sense of the passage is that poets are fickle and only write about the latest 'newsworthy' events. Hence, they forget about Philomel's rape and now write about Tereus' death.
196 **chaff** husks of wheat and other grains separated from the edible part by threshing or winnowing; the wind blows away the lighter chaff
200 **queen ... king** presumably a reference to the displacement of grief about Elizabeth's death by the joy of James's recent accession to the throne
soothe i.e., flatter the king
204 **Iris' throne** the rainbow
208 **prognosticator** one who foretells the future (principally the weather for the coming year) in almanacs, which are the satiric target of Middleton *The Owl's Almanac*
210 **bladder-praise** praise that is inflated and insincere, like a bladder (or balloon) filled with hot air
216 **glossers** literally one who glosses a text by explaining words and meaning; here, a flatterer or brown-noser
222–3 **manly lion ... lioness** a reference contrasting James I to Elizabeth I
225 **he conceives** James I had published treatises on witchcraft and kingship which revealed his theological and political knowledge as well as his commitment to the pursuit of virtuous politics.
230 **coinèd words** a reference to the fad of 'coining', or inventing, new words; many authors, including Shakespeare, engaged in the practice; here, an exercise in showing off one's supposed genius
247 **Euphuize** to write in the outdated, highly affected, and ornate style introduced by John Lyly in *Euphues, The Anatomy of Wit* (1578) and *Euphues and His England* (1580)
rare considered choice or exquisite; fashionable
251 **new fools ... vile** the 'coiners' (l. 230) who scorn the imitation of literary models from the past
252 **Nashe** Thomas Nashe, a famous pamphleteer of the 1590s, noted for his particularly virulent and imaginative satiric writing.

Nor didst affect in youth thy private praise;
  Thou hadst a strife with that Trigemini:
  Thou hurt'st not them till they had injured thee.

'Thou wast indeed too slothful to thyself,
Hiding thy better talent in thy spleen.
True spirits are not covetous in pelf;
Youth's wit is ever ready, quick, and keen.
  Thou didst not live thy ripened autumn day,
  But wert cut off in thy best blooming May.

'Else hadst thou left, as thou indeed hast left,
Sufficient test, though now in others' chests,
T'improve the baseness of that humorous theft,
Which seems to flow from self-conceiving breasts.
  Thy name they bury, having buried thee;
  Drones eat thy honey: thou wert the true bee.

'Peace keep thy Soul.)—And now to you, Sir Ant:
On with your prose, be neither rude nor nice;
In your discourse let no decorum want;
See that you be sententious and concise,
  And, as I like the matter, I will sing
  A canzonet to close up everything.'

With this, the whole nest of ants, hearing their fellow was free from danger, like comforters when care is over, came with great thanks to harmless Philomel and made a ring about her and their restored friend, serving instead of a dull audience of stinkards sitting in the penny-galleries of a theatre and yawning upon the players, whilst the ant began to stalk like a three-quarter sharer and was not afraid to tell tales out of the villainous school of the world, where the devil is the schoolmaster, and the usurer, the under-usher; the scholars, young dicing landlords that pass away three hundred acres with three dice in a hand, and after the decease of so much land in money, become sons and heirs of bawdy-houses; for it is an easy labour to find heirs without land, but a hard thing indeed to find land without heirs. But for fear I interrupt this small actor in less than *decimo sexto*, I leave, and give the ant leave to tell his tale.

The Ant's Tale when he was a Ploughman.

I was sometimes, most chaste Lady Nightingale, or rather, Queen Philomel the ravished, a brow-melting husbandman. To be man and husband is to be a poor master of many rich cares, which, if he cannot subject and keep under, he must look forever to undergo as many miseries as the hours of his years contain minutes. Such a man I was and such a husband, for I was linked in marriage. My havings was small and my means less, yet charge came on me ere I knew how to keep it; yet did I all my endeavours, had a plough and land to employ it, fertile enough if it were manured, and for tillage I was never held a truant.

But my destruction and the ruin of all painful husbandmen about me began by the prodigal downfall of my young landlord, whose father, grandfather, and great-grandfather for many generations had been lords of the town wherein I dwelt and many other towns near adjoining; to all which belonged fair commons for the comfort of the poor, liberty of fishing, help of fuel by brush and underwood never denied, till the old devourer of virtue, honesty, and good neighbourhood—Death—had made our landlord dance after his pipe, which is so common that every one knows the way though they make small account of it. Well, die he did, and as soon as he was laid in his grave, the bell might well have tolled for hospitality and good housekeeping; for whether they fell sick with him and died and so were buried, I know not, but I am sure in our town they were never seen since, nor that I can hear of in any other part; especially about us they are impossible to be found.

Well, our landlord being dead, we had his heir, gentle enough and fair conditioned, rather promising at first his father's virtues than the world's villainies, but he was so accustomed to wild and

256 **Trigemini** literally 'triple birth', a reference to the brothers Gabriel, Richard, and John Harvey. Nashe waged an ongoing literary battle with Gabriel in a series of pamphlets culminating in Nashe's *Have with you to Saffron Walden* (1596), a masterpiece of personal invective that destroyed any pretension that Harvey had to respectability. The Bishop of London called in the pamphlets in the famous decree of 1599 which banned satire and forbade publication of their works in the future.

260 **pelf** wealth, possessions

263 **cut off... May** Nashe probably died in (or before) 1601 when he was thirty-four years old, roughly equivalent to 'summer' in terms of Elizabethan life expectancy. Middleton obviously had great respect for Nashe and believed that he would have gone on to produce noteworthy writings in his 'autumn' years.

266 **T'improve** to prove
humorous theft an obscure reference to a purported theft of Nashe's work, possibly from his papers after his death, by Samuel Rowlands

271 **nice** affected, too refined

272 **decorum** adherence to the literary requirements of genre

273 **sententious** laden with meaning, matter, wisdom

275 **canzonet** literally, a short song

280 **penny-galleries** unexplainable reference, either intentionally erroneous, or possibly due to compositorial omission of 'two' during setting. 'Groundlings' paid the fee of one penny for the privilege of standing on the open ground in front of the stage; a twopenny fee was required for admittance to the lowest level of seating rooms or 'galleries'.

281 **three-quarter sharer** an individual who owned three-quarters of a share of stock in an acting company

284 **under-usher** assistant to a schoolmaster or head teacher

289 ***decimo sexto*** literally 'sixteen'; a very small book format in which each sheet is folded to produce sixteen leaves containing thirty-two printed pages. The term was used to refer to the boy actors of Paul's and Blackfriars who competed with the adult acting companies; the ant is even smaller than a *decimo sexto*.

293 **husbandman** one who tills or cultivates the soil; in Middleton's time, a tenant or renter; in the socio-economic hierarchy, just below the gentleman farmer who owned the land that he tilled

306 **commons** rations, allowance of victuals, daily fare; the Christian duty of alms-giving in the form of feeding the poor, the period's equivalent of the modern 'soup kitchen'

307–8 **liberty... underwood** the deceased landlord permitted tenants to fish on his estate, presumably in stocked ponds, as well as to gather wood for cooking and heating

309–10 **Death... dance** reference to the *dance macabre*, a familiar emblematic image of the grim reaper playing upon a recorder while leading his newly-dead charges in a serpentine dance

unfruitful company about the court and London (whither he was sent by his sober father to practise civility and manners) that in the country he would scarce keep till his father's body was laid in the cold earth. But as soon as the hasty funeral was solemnized, from us he posted, discharging all his old father's servants (whose beards were even frost-bitten with age) and was attended only by a monkey and a marmoset, the one being an ill-faced fellow as variable as Newfangle for fashions, the other an imitator of anything, however villainous, but utterly destitute of all goodness. With this French page and Italianate servingman was our young landlord only waited on, and all to save charges in servingmen to pay it out in harlots. And we poor men had news of a far greater expense within less than a quarter, for we were sent for to London and found our great landlord in a little room about the Strand, who told us that, whereas we had lived tenants at will and might in his forefather's days been hourly turned out, he, putting on a better conscience to usward, intended to make us leases for years; and for advice 'twixt him and us, he had made choice of a lawyer, a mercer, and a merchant to whom he was much beholden, who that morning were appointed to meet in the Temple Church.

Temple and church, both one in name, made us hope of a holy meeting; but there is an old proverb, "The nearer the Church, the farther from God." To approve which saying, we met the mercer and the merchant that, loving our landlord or his land well, held him a great man in both their books. Some little conference they had; what the conclusion was we poor men were not acquainted with; but being called at their leisure and when they pleased to think upon us, told us they were to dine together at the Horn in Fleet Street, being a house where their lawyer resorted; and if we would there attend them, we should understand matter much for our good; and in the mean time they appointed us near the old Temple Garden to attend their counsellor, whose name was master Prospero—not the great rider of horse (for I have heard there was once such a one), but a more cunning rider who had rid many men till they were more miserable than beasts, and our ill hap it was to prove his hackneys. Well, though the issue were ill, on we went to await his worship, whose chamber we found that morning fuller of clients than I could ever see suppliants to heaven in our poor parish church (and yet we had in it three hundred households); and I may tell it with reverence, I never saw more submission done to God than to that great lawyer. Every suitor there offered gold to this gowned idol, standing bareheaded in a sharp-set morning (for it was in booted Michaelmas term), and not a word spoke to him but it was with the bowing of the body and the submissive flexure of the knee. Short tale to make, he was informed of us what we were and of our coming up, when, with an iron look and shrill voice, he began to speak to the richest of our number, ever and anon jerking out the word 'fines', which served instead of a full point to every sentence.

But that word 'fines' was no fine word, methought, to please poor labouring husbandmen that can scarce sweat out so much in a twelvemonth as he would demand in a twinkling. At last, to close up the lamentable tragedy of us ploughmen, enters our young landlord, so metamorphosed into the shape of a French puppet that, at the first, we started and thought one of the baboons had marched in in man's apparel. His head was dressed up in white feathers like a shuttlecock, which agreed so well with his brain (being nothing but cork), that two of the biggest of the guard might very easily have tossed him with battledores and made good sport with him in his majesty's great hall. His doublet was of a strange cut, and to show the fury of his humour, the collar of it rose up so high and sharp as if it would have cut his throat by daylight. His wings, according to the fashion now, was as little and diminutive as a puritan's ruff, which showed he ne'er meant

322 **practise civility** common custom of the provincial gentry aimed at learning 'city manners'

327 **marmoset** any small monkey. Middleton's coat of arms bore a marmoset.

328 **Newfangle** allusion to Nicholas Newfangle, the 'Vice' in the old interlude *Like will to Like* (1568)

330 **French page** French pages were held in high estimation
Italianate implies 'immoral' or 'depraved'

333 **quarter** a quarter of a year; in England and Ireland the quarter days on which rents were paid were Lady Day (25 March), Midsummer Day (24 June), Michaelmas (29 September), and Christmas

334 **the Strand** street running west from Middle Temple; fashionable area for lodgings

335 **tenants at will** tenants who hold property at the pleasure of the lessor

337 **usward** archaic form of the modern 'toward us'

339 **mercer** merchant who deals in textile fabrics—silks, velvets, and other costly materials

340 **Temple Church** lawyers and their clients used the Round in Temple Church as a meeting place (like the middle aisle of St Paul's)

345 **books** the young landlord's 'great' debts are noted in both the merchant's and the mercer's account books

348 **Horn** pub in Fleet Street near the Temple

352 **Temple Garden** small landscaped park between the Temple buildings and the Thames

353 **Prospero . . . horse** reference to a famous equestrian trainer

356 **hackneys** horses kept for hire

363 **booted Michaelmas term** the term or session of the High Court of Justice in England, and also of Oxford, Cambridge, and various other universities, beginning soon after the feast of St Michael (29 September); one of the four quarter-days of the English business year; hence, an allusion to the footwear of persons who rode to London on law business in winter

368 **jerking** speaking spasmodically
fines a fee (as distinguished from rent) paid by the tenant or vassal to the landlord on some alteration of the tenancy, as on the transfer or alienation of the tenant right

377 **shuttlecock** small spherical piece of cork fitted with a crown or circle of feathers, used in the game of battledore and shuttlecock; similar to that used in badminton

379 **battledores** small rackets used to hit the shuttlecock back and forth between players

380 **doublet** close-fitting vest-like garment, with or without sleeves, worn by men; the length varied according to fashion, as did the ornamental aspects of its design

383 **wings** wing-like projections on the shoulders of a doublet

384 **ruff** stiffly starched, pleated cloth worn around the neck. The Puritan's short ruffs were the target of ridicule.

to fly out of England nor do any exploit beyond sea, but live and die about London though he begged in Finsbury. His breeches, a wonder to see, were full as deep as the middle of winter or the roadway between London and Winchester, and so large and wide withal that I think within a twelvemonth he might very well put all his lands in them, and then you may imagine they were big enough when they would outreach a thousand acres. Moreover, they differed so far from our fashioned hose in the country and from his father's old gascoynes that his back part seemed to us like a monster, the roll of the breeches standing so low that we conjectured his house of office, sir-reverence, stood in his hams.

All this while his French monkey bore his cloak of three-pounds-a-yard, lined clean through with purple velvet, which did so dazzle our coarse eyes that we thought we should have been purblind ever after, what with the prodigal aspect of that and his glorious rapier and hangers, all bossed with pillars of gold, fairer in show than the pillars in Paul's or the tombs at Westminster; beside, it drunk up the price of all my ploughland in very pearl, which stuck as thick upon those hangers as the white measles upon hog's flesh. When I had well viewed that gay gaudy cloak and those unthrifty wasteful hangers, I muttered thus to myself: 'That is no cloak for the rain sure, nor those no hangers for Derrick.' When, of a sudden casting mine eyes lower, I beheld a curious pair of boots of King Philip's leather in such artificial wrinkles, sets, and pleats as if they had been starched lately and came new from the laundresses—such was my ignorance and simple acquaintance with the fashion, and I dare swear my fellows and neighbours here are all as ignorant as myself. But that which struck us most into admiration: upon those fantastical boots stood such huge and wide tops which so swallowed up his thighs that had he sworn, as other gallants did, this common oath: 'Would I might sink as I stand!', all his body might very well have sunk down and been damned in his boots. Lastly, he walked the chamber with such a pestilent jingle that his spurs over-squeaked the lawyer and made him reach his voice three notes above his fee. But after we had spied the rowels of his spurs, how we blessed ourselves!—they did so much and so far exceed the compass of our fashion that they looked more like the forerunners of wheelbarrows.

Thus was our young landlord accoutred in such a strange and prodigal shape that it amounted to above two year's rent in apparel. At last approach the mercer and the merchant, two notable arch-tradesmen who had fitted my young master in clothes whilst they had clothed themselves in his acres, and measured him out velvet by the thumb whilst they received his revenues by handfuls; for he had not so many yards in his suit as they had yards and houses bound for the payment, which now he was forced to pass over to them or else all his lands should be put to their book and to their forfeiting neck-verse. So my youngster was now at his pension, not like a gentleman pensioner, but like a gentleman scrivener. Whereupon entered Master Bursebell the royal scrivener with deeds and writings hanged, drawn, and quartered for the purpose. He was a valiant scribe. I remember his pen lay mounted between his ear like a Tower gun, but not charged yet till our young master's patrimony shot off, which was some third part of an hour after. By this time the lawyer, the mercer, and the merchant were whispering and consulting together about the writings and passage of the land in very deep and sober conference.

But our 'wiseacres' all the while, as one regardless of either land or money, not hearkening or inquisitive after their subtle and politic devices, held himself very busy about the burning of his tobacco pipe (as there is no gallant but hath a pipe to burn about London) though we poor simple men ne'er heard of the name till that time; and he might very fitly take tobacco there, for the lawyer and the rest made him smoke already. But to have noted the apish humour of him and the fantastical faces he coined in the receiving of the smoke, it would have made your ladyship

386 **Finsbury** open fields north of the city wall, accessible through Cripplegate and Moorgate; used for recreation by Londoners (walking, archery, etc.), and frequented by beggars
breeches padded pants-like garment covering the loins and thighs; later reaching to the knees or just below

393 **gascoynes** wide breeches reaching to the knee; in *Pierce Penniless*, Nashe mentions 'their Dad, goes sagging every day in his round Gascoynes of white cotton, and hath much ado (poor penny-father) to keep his unthrift elbows in reparations' (10); the sons 'do nothing but devise how to spend and ask counsel of the Wine and Capons, how they may quickliest consume their patrimonies'

395 **sir-reverence** colloquial mangling of 'Save Reverence', an apologetic phrase used here to ask pardon for referring to the 'house of office' (i.e., anus)
hams part of the leg at the back of the knee... by extension: the back of the thighs; the thigh and buttock collectively

396–7 **of three-pounds-a-yard** made of extremely expensive cloth

399 **purblind** dim-sighted

400 **hangers** loop or strap on a sword-belt from which the sword was hung, often richly ornamented
bossed studded, ornamented; roughly equivalent to modern 'embossed'

406 **Derrick** the common hangman at Tyburn

408 **King Philip's leather** soft Spanish leather, considered superior to English leather

420 **rowels** small serrated disk at the end of a spur

432 **neck-verse** a verse (usually the beginning of the fifty-first psalm) presented to a condemned criminal who claimed 'benefit of clergy' (i.e., literacy); by reading it, he might save his neck from the noose

434 **scrivener** professional writer or scribe; a notary; an important professional in an age when writing literacy lagged significantly behind reading literacy. The growing dependency upon credit records by landowners and merchants required the expertise of the scrivener in drawing up 'articles' and 'bonds', or the documents in which the particulars were legally stated and witnessed. In this instance, the lawyer, who presumably could perform the function, hires the scrivener to do it, much in the same manner as many law offices today retain full-time legal secretaries.

435 **hanged, drawn, and quartered** The executed criminal was first hanged by the neck but cut down before expiring, laid out and gutted like an animal, and then the body was cut into four pieces. (Public executions were a common form of entertainment at the time.)

445 **tobacco pipe** The smoking of tobacco in clay pipes had become extremely fashionable during the sixteenth century, and controversy raged about both the beneficial and ill effects of 'drinking tobacco'. James I is thought to be the author of the famous pamphlet *A Counter-blast to Tobbaco* (1604).

449 **coined** i.e., 'invented' various contortions of the face while smoking

have sung nothing but merry jigs for a twelvemonth after—one time winding the pipe like a horn at the pie-corner of his mouth, which must needs make him look like a sow-gelder, and another time screwing his face like one of our country players, which must needs make him look like a fool; nay, he had at least his dozen of faces, but never a good one amongst them all—neither his father's face, nor the face of his grandfather, but yet more wicked and riotous faces than all the generation of him.

Now their privy whisperings and villainous plots began to be drawn to a conclusion when presently they called our smoky landlord in the midst of his draught, who in a valiant humour dashed his tobacco pipe into the chimney corner, whereat I started, and beckoning his marmoset to me, asked him if those long white things did cost no money; to which the slave replied very proudly: 'Money! Yes sirrah, but I tell thee my master scorns to have a thing come twice to his mouth.' 'Then', quoth I, 'I think thy master is more choice in his mouth than in any member else: it were good if he used that all his body over—he would never have need, as many gallants have, of any sweating physic.' 'Sweating physic?', replied the marmoset, 'What may thy meaning be? Why, do not you ploughmen sweat too?' 'Yes', quoth I, 'most of any men living. But yet there is difference between the sweat of a ploughman and the sweat of a gentleman, as much as between your master's apparel and mine. For when we sweat, the land prospers and the harvest comes in, but when a gentleman sweats, I wot how the gear goes then.' No sooner were these words spoken but the marmoset had drawn out his poinard halfway to make a show of revenge, but at the smart voice of the lawyer he suddenly whipped it in again.

Now was our young master with one penful of ink doing a far greater exploit than all his forefathers, for what they were a-purchasing all their lifetime, he was now passing away in the fourth part of a minute; and that which many thousand drops of his grandfather's brows did painfully strive for, one drop now of a scrivener's inkhorn did easily pass over. A dash of a pen stood for a thousand acres—how quickly they were dashed in the mouth by our young landlord's prodigal fist! It seemed he made no more account of acres than of acorns. Then were we called to set our hands for witnesses of his folly, which we poor men did witness too much already. And because we were found ignorant in writing and never practised in that black art (which I might very fitly term so because it conjured our young master out of all), we were commanded, as it were, to draw any mark with a pen, which should signify as much as the best hand that ever old Peter Bales hung out in the Old Bailey. To conclude, I took the pen first of the lawyer, and turning it arsy-versy like no instrument for a ploughman, our youngster and the rest of the faction burst into laughter at the simplicity of my fingering. But I, not so simple as they laughed me for, drew the picture of a knavish emblem, which was *A Plough with the Heels Upward*, signifying thereby that the world was turned upside down since the decease of my old landlord, all hospitality and good housekeeping kicked out of doors, all thriftiness and good husbandry tossed into the air, ploughs turned into trunks, and corn into apparel. Then came another of our husbandmen to set his mark by mine; he, holding the pen clean at the one side towards the merchant and the mercer showing that all went on their sides, drew the form of an unbridled colt so wild and unruly that he seemed with one foot to kick up the earth and spoil the labours of many toiling beasts, which was fitly alluded to our wild and unbridled landlord, which (like the colt) could stand upon no ground till he had no ground to stand upon.

These marks, set down under the shape of simplicity, were the less marked with the eyes of knavery, for they little dreamed that we ploughmen could have so much satire in us as to bite our young landlord by the elbow. Well, this ended, master Bursebell the calfskin scrivener was royally handled—that is, he had a royal put in his hand by the merchant. And now I talk of calfskin: 'tis great pity, Lady Nightingale, that the skins of harmless and innocent beasts should be as instruments to work villainy upon, entangling young novices and foolish elder brothers which are caught like woodcocks in the net of the law; for 'tis easier for one of the greatest fowls to slide through the least hole of a net than one of the least fools to get from the lappet of a bond.

By this time the squeaking lawyer began to reiterate that cold word 'fines' which struck so chill to our hearts that it made them as cold as our heels, which were almost frozen to the floor with standing. 'Yea', quoth the merchant and the mercer, 'you are now tenants of ours; all the right, title, and interest of this young gentleman, your late landlord, we are firmly possessed of, as you

451 **jigs** songs or ballads of lively, jocular, or mocking (often scurrilous) character

452 **pie-corner** corner of Giltspur Street and Cock Lane in West Smithfield where cook shops were located. The simile apparently is based upon the fact that the intersection of the two streets formed an acute angle.

453 **sow-gelder** one who gelds or spays sows, i.e., removes the ovaries

464 **slave** derogatory term for servant

469 **sweating physic** medical prescription to induce sweating; probably a reference to a treatment for syphilis

476 **gear** indefinite noun, i.e., stuff, matter, things, business

477 **marmoset** see note to l. 327–8
poinard dagger

495 **Peter Bales** famous calligraphist and shorthand writer (1547?–1610?), widely known for his feat of engraving, in Latin, the Lord's Prayer, the Creed, and the Ten Commandments on a penny which he presented to Queen Elizabeth in 1575. He kept a writing school in the Old Bailey.

496 **arsy-versy** backwards

499 **emblem** A drawing or picture expressing a moral fable or allegory. Emblem books, originating in Italy, became popular in Middleton's age, the foremost of these being Geffrey Whitney's *A Choice of Emblems*. Typically, a detailed woodcut or engraving containing allegorical subject matter was accompanied by an explanation, often in verse, of the moral point of the image. The ant's explanation of the marks made by himself and his partner performs the latter function.

504 **trunks** short breeches; the heels or blades of the upside-down plough look like upside-down breeches

517 **calfskin scrivener** the most expensive vellum was made from calfskin; hence, Bursebell's fees are high
royally...royal a royal was a gold coin worth ten shillings (i.e., two royals to the pound); the ant's typical kind of punning

524 **lappet** a loose or overhanging part of a garment, forming a flap or fold; the edge of a folded paper to which a seal is affixed. The implication here is that once one has been caught in the folds of the paper containing the bond, it was impossible to escape.

yourselves are witnesses. Wherefore, this is the conclusion of our meeting: such fines as master Prospero here, by the valuation of the land, shall out of his proper judgement allot to us, such are we to demand at your hands. Therefore we refer you to him to wait his answer at the gentleman's best time and leisure.' With that they stifled two or three angels in the lawyer's right hand—'right hand' said I? Which hand was that, trow ye? For it is impossible to know which is the right hand of a lawyer because there are but few lawyers that have right hands, and those few make much of them. So, taking their leaves of my young landlord that was and that never shall be again, away they marched, heavier by a thousand acres at their parting than they were before at their meeting.

The lawyer then, turning his Irish face to usward, willed us to attend his worship the next term, when we should further understand his pleasure. We poor souls thanked his worship and paid him his fee out in legs, when, in sight of us, he embraced our young gentleman (I think, for a fool) and gave him many riotous instructions how to carry himself, which he was prompter to take than the other to put into him: told him he must acquaint himself with many gallants of the Inns of Court and keep rank with those that spend most, always wearing bountiful disposition about him, lofty and liberal; his lodging must be about the Strand, in any case, being remote from the handicraft scent of the City; his eating must be in some famous tavern, as the Horn, the Mitre, or the Mermaid, and then after dinner, he must venture beyond sea, that is, in a choice pair of noblemen's oars to the Bankside where he must sit out the breaking up of a comedy or the first cut of a tragedy; or rather (if his humour so serve him), to call in at the Blackfriars where he should see a nest of boys able to ravish a man. This said, our young goosecap, who was ready to embrace such counsel, thanked him for his fatherly admonitions (as he termed them), and told him again that he should not find him with the breach of any of them, swearing and protesting he would keep all those better than the ten commandments. At which word he buckled on his rapier and hangers, his monkey-face casting on his cloak by the book; after an apish congee or two, passed downstairs without either word or nod to us, his old father's tenants.

Nevertheless, we followed him, like so many russet servingmen, to see the event of all and what the issue would come to, when, of a sudden, he was encountered by a most glorious-spangled gallant which we took at first to have been some upstart tailor because he measured all his body with a salutation from the flow of the doublet to the fall of the breeches. But at last we found him to be a very fantastical sponge that licked up all humours, the very ape of fashions, gesture, and compliment—one of those indeed (as we learned afterward) that fed upon young landlords, riotous sons, and heirs till either he or the Counter in Wood Street had swallowed them up; and would not stick to be a bawd or pander to such young gallants as our young gentleman, either to acquaint them with harlots or harlots with them, to bring them a whole dozen of taffeta punks at a supper; and they should be none of these common Molls neither, but discontented and unfortunate gentlewomen whose parents being lately deceased, the brother ran away with all the land, and they, poor squalls, with a little money which cannot hold out long without some comings in; but they will rather venture a maidenhead than want a headtire; such shuttlecocks as these which, though they are tossed and played withal, go still like maids all white on the top; or else decayed gentlemen's wives, whose husbands (poor souls) lying for debt in the King's Bench, they go about to make monsters in the King's Head tavern, for this is a general axiom: all your luxurious plots are always begun in taverns to be ended in vaulting houses; and after supper when fruit comes in, there is small fruit of honesty to be looked for—for you know that the eating of the apple always betokens the fall of Eve.

Our prodigal child, accompanied with this soaking swaggerer and admirable cheater (who had supped up most of our heirs about London like poached eggs), slips into Whitefriars nunnery whereas, the report went, he kept his most delicate drab of three hundred a year—some unthrifty gentleman's daughter who had

536 **angels** another gold coin worth about ten shillings; so called because it bore the image of the Archangel Michael
right hand the ant puns on 'right vs. wrong', i.e., lawyers have no concern for morality
544 **Irish face** coarse
547 **paid . . . legs** a courteous bow involved bending the legs
551 **Inns of Court** the four law schools and lodgings of lawyers, located some distance along Fleet Street to the west of St Paul's Cathedral
555–6 **Horn, the Mitre . . . Mermaid** local pubs near the Temple in Fleet Street and Bread Street, frequented by gallants, lawyers, writers
557 **oars** i.e., rent an expensive launch to cross the Thames to Bankside, the location of theatres (the Globe, the Rose, the Hope, the Swan), the bull- and bear-baiting pits, and the Paris Garden; otherwise, it was a long walk east to London Bridge for the crossing
558 **breaking up** disruption, disintegration
559 **cut** excision or omission of a part
560 **Blackfriars . . . boys** a private theatre just east of the Inns of Court area, the venue of a company of boy actors (The Children of the Queen's Revels) famous for their ability to perform seductive female roles
561 **goosecap** fool, simpleton
567 **casting . . . book** putting on his cloak with exaggerated courtly formality
congee ceremonial bow upon taking leave of a person
570 **russet** coarse homespun woollen cloth of reddish-brown, grey, or neutral colour, used for the dress of peasants and country folk
571 **event** from Latin *eventus*, 'the outcome, or issue'. Middleton has the ant comically combine the term and its English meaning: 'event of all and what the issue would come to'.
579 **Counter** debtors' prison
583 **taffeta punks** overdressed prostitutes
584 **Molls** prostitutes
586 **squalls** small or insignificant persons; usually a term of derision
592 **King's Bench** debtors' prison
monsters i.e., cuckolds, emblematically imaged as a man with horns in his forehead that are visible to all but himself
593 **luxurious** lustful
594 **vaulting houses** slang for brothels
595 **honesty** chastity
598 **swaggerer** quarrelsome bully
600 **Whitefriars nunnery** previously a monastic precinct just east of the Inner Temple. Although the church had been pulled down, the privilege of sanctuary from officers of the law continued, so the area attracted prostitutes and criminals; hence the slang usage of 'nunnery' = 'brothel'.
601 **drab** prostitute
602–4 **gentleman's . . . again** i.e., the father had squandered his estate, leaving the daughter destitute and hence a candidate for prostitution

mortgaged his land to scriveners sure enough from redeeming again. For so much she seemed by her bringing up, though less by her casting down. Endued she was (as we heard) with some good qualities, though all were converted then but to flattering villainies. She could run upon the lute very well, which in others would have appeared virtuous but in her lascivious, for her running was rather jested at because she was a light runner besides. She had likewise the gift of singing very deliciously, able to charm the hearer, which so bewitched away our young master's money that he might have kept seven noise of musicians for less charges, and yet they would have stood for servingmen too, having blue coats of their own. She had a humour to lisp often like a flatt'ring wanton and talk childish like a parson's daughter, which so pleased and rapt our old landlord's lickerish son that he would swear she spoke nothing but sweetmeats and her breath then sent forth such a delicious odour that it perfumed his white-satin doublet better than sixteen milliners.

Well, there we left him with his devouring cheater and his glorious cockatrice, and being almost upon dinner-time, we hied us and took our repast at thrifty Mother Walker's, where we found a whole nest of pinching bachelors crowded together upon forms and benches in that most worshipful three-halfpenny ordinary, where presently they were boarded with hot Monsieur Mutton-and-Porridge (a Frenchman by his blowing); and next to them, we were served in order, everyone taking their degree. And I tell you true, lady, I have known the time when our young landlord's father hath been a three-halfpenny eater there; nay more, was the first that acquainted us with that sparing and thrifty ordinary, when his riotous son hath since spent his five pound at a sitting. Well, having discharged our small shot (which was like hail-shot in respect of our young master's cannon-reckonings in taverns), we plodded home to our ploughs, carrying these heavy news to our wives, both of the prodigality of our old landlord's son as also of our oppressions to come by the burden of uncharitable fines. And, most musical Madam Nightingale, do but imagine now what a sad Christmas we all kept in the country without either carols, wassail-bowls, dancing of Sellinger's Round in moonshine nights about maypoles, shoeing the mare, hoodman-blind, hot-cockles, or any of our old Christmas gambols; no, not so much as choosing king and queen on Twelfth Night. Such was the dullness of our pleasures, for that one word 'fines' robbed us of all our fine pastimes.

This sour-faced Christmas thus unpleasantly past over, up again we trotted to London—in a great frost, I remember, for the ground was as hard as the lawyer's conscience. And arriving at the luxurious Strand some three days before the term, we inquired for our bountiful landlord, or the fool in the full, at his neat and curious lodging. But answer was made us by an old chambermaid that our gentleman slept not there all the Christmastime, but had been at court and at least in five masques. Marry now, as she thought, we might find him at master Poopes his ordinary with half-a-dozen of gallants more at dice. 'At dice? At the devil!', quoth I, 'for that is a dicer's last throw!' Here I began to rail like Thomas Nashe against Gabriel Harvey, if you call that railing; yet I think it was but the running a tilt of wits in booksellers' shops on both sides of John of Paul's churchyard, and I wonder how John escaped unhorsing. But when we were entered the door of the ordinary, we might hear our lusty gentleman shoot off a volley of oaths some three rooms over us, cursing the dice and wishing the pox were in their bones, crying out for a new pair of square ones, for the other belike had cogged with him and made a gull of him. When, the host of the ordinary coming downstairs, met us with this report after we had named him: 'Troth, good fellows, you have named now the most unfortunatest gentleman living—at passage, I mean; for I protest, I have stood by myself as a heavy eyewitness and seen the beheading of five hundred crowns, and what pitiful end they all made!' With that he showed us his embossed girdle and hangers new-pawned for more money, and told us beside (not without tears), his glorious cloak was cast away three hours before overboard, which was, off the table. At which lamentable hearing, we stood still in the lower room and durst not venture upstairs for fear he would have laid all us ploughmen to pawn too; and yet I think all we could scarce have made up one throw. But to draw to an end as his patrimony did, we had not lingered the better part of an hour, but down came the host fencing his glittering rapier and dagger as if he had been newly shoulder-clapped by a pewter-buttoned sergeant and his weapons seized upon. At last, after a great peal of oaths on all sides, the court broke up and the worshipful bench of dicers came thundering downstairs, some swearing, some laughing, some cursing, and some singing, with such a confusion of humours that, had we not known before what

607 **run upon the lute** smoothly and gracefully play arpeggios, or notes of a chord plucked individually in very rapid succession
609 **light runner** loose woman; easily persuaded to sexual activity
612 **noise of musicians** a consort or ensemble, as in 'The King's Noise'
616 **lickerish** lecherous
621 **cockatrice** mythical beast able to kill with a glance; colloquially, a whore or mistress able to bewitch or 'kill' with her eyes
623 **forms** benches without back rests
624 **three-halfpenny ordinary** public eating house, or 'pub', where meals were provided at a fixed price, here one of the cheapest; other literary references cite twelve-penny and eighteen-penny ordinaries. Fashionable gallants frequented the more expensive class of ordinary where dinner was usually followed by gambling.
632 **hail-shot** buckshot or pellets, contrasted with cannon balls
639 **Sellinger's Round** old country dance
640–1 **shoeing the mare . . . hot-cockles** several social games
641 **gambols** a leap or spring in dancing; a caper, a frisk
648 **term** Hilary Term, which usually commenced on January 13
652 **masques** type of social dramatic entertainment in which the roles are played by members of a social gathering rather than by professional actors
655–8 **Nashe . . . unhorsing** suggests that the booksellers' shops which respectively sold Thomas Nashe's and Gabriel Harvey's pamphlets were on either side of the haberdasher John of Paul's shop in St Paul's churchyard
663 **cogged** 'fixing' dice by filing some corners round to raise the probability of certain numbers coming up
666 **passage** game at dice played by two opponents casting three dice
668 **crowns** gold coin worth five shillings bearing an image of a crown
669 **girdle** belt
670 **hangers** see note to l. 400
677–9 **down . . . seized** the host, likened to the sergeant who has arrested the landlord, carries the latter's weapons

rank of gallants they were, we should have thought the devils had been at dice in an ordinary. The first that appeared to us was our most lamentable landlord dressed up in his monkey's livery cloak (that he seemed now rather to wait upon his monkey than his monkey upon him), which did set forth his satin suit so excellent scurvily that he looked for all the world like a French lord in dirty boots; when, casting his eye upon us, being desirous (as it seemed) to remember us now if we had any money, broke into these fantastical speeches: 'What, my whole warren of tenants?'—thinking indeed to make conies of us—'my honest nest of ploughmen, the only kings of Kent! More dice, ho! then, i'faith, let's have another career, and vomit three dice in a hand again.' With that I plucked his humour at one side and told him we were indeed his father's tenants, but his (we were sorry) we were not. And as for money to maintain his dice, we had not sufficient to stuff out the lawyer. Then replied our gallant in a rage, tossing out two or three new-minted oaths: 'These ploughmen are politicians, I think; they have wit, the whoresons; they will be tenants, I perceive, longer than we shall be landlords!' And fain he would have swaggered with us but that his weapons were at pawn. So, marching out like a turned gentleman, the rest of the gallants seemed to cashier him and throw him out of their company like a blank die—the one having no black pips, nor he no white pieces. Now was our gallant the true picture of the prodigal, and having no rents to gather now, he gathered his wits about him, making his brain pay him revenues in villainy. For it is a general observation that your sons and heirs prove seldom wisemen till they have no more land than the compass of their noddles. To conclude, within few days' practice, he was grown as absolute in cheating and as exquisite in pandarism that he outstripped all Greene's books *Of the Art of Cony-catching*; and where before he maintained his drab, he made his drab now maintain him; proved the only true captain of vaulting-houses and the valiant champion against constables and searchers, feeding upon the sin of Whitefriars, Pickt-hatch, and Turnbull Street. Nay, there was no landed novice now but he could melt him away into nothing, and in one twelvemonth make him hold all his land between his legs, and yet but straddle easily neither. No wealthy son of the city but, within less than a quarter, he could make all his stock not worth a Jersey stocking. He was all that might be in dissolute villainy and nothing that should be in his forefathers' honesty. To speak troth, we did so much blush at his life and were so ashamed of his base courses that ever after we loathed to look after them.

But returning to our stubble-haired lawyer, who reaped his beard every term-time (the lawyer's harvest), we found the mercer and the merchant crowded in his study amongst a company of law books, which they jostled so often with their coxcombs that they were almost together by the ears with them; when, at the sight of us, they took an *habeas corpus* and removed their bodies into a bigger room. But there we lingered not long for our torments, for the mercer and the merchant gave fire to the lawyer's tongue with a rope of angels, and the word 'fines' went off with such a powder that the force of it blew us all into the country, quite changed our ploughmen's shapes, and so we became little ants again.

This, Madam Nightingale, is the true discourse of our rural fortunes, which, how miserable, wretched, and full of oppression they were, all husbandmen's brows can witness that are fined with more sweat still year by year; and I hope a canzonet of your sweet singing will set them forth to the world in satirical harmony.

The remorseful nightingale, delighted with the ant's quaint discourse, began to tune the instrument of her voice, breathing forth these lines in sweet and delicious airs.

The Nightingale's Canzonet.

Poor little ant,
Thou shalt not want
  The ravished music of my voice!
Thy shape is best,
Now thou art least;
  For great ones fall with greater noise,
And this shall be the carriage of my song:
Small bodies can have but a little wrong.

  Now thou art securer
  And thy days far surer;
Thou pay'st no rent upon the rack
To daub a prodigal landlord's back,
  Or to maintain the subtle running
  Of dice and drabs, both one in cunning;
Both pass from hand to hand to many,
Flatt'ring all, yet false to any;
Both are well linked, for, throw dice how you can,
They will turn up their pips to every man.

692 **warren** a group of game animals or fowls such as rabbits, partridges, etc.
693 **conies** rabbits, hares; figuratively, gullible dupes, easily swindled or conned
694 **only kings of Kent** the Kentish boasted that Kent had never been conquered; here, 'only' in the sense of 'the very'
695 **career** literally, a short gallop at full speed; charge at a tournament; figuratively, a quick game
704 **turned** changed circumstances, i.e., lost his money and possessions
cashier dismiss
706 **black pips** a blank die has no black spots or 'pips'
white pieces i.e., coins, money
711 **noddles** back of the head
713 **pandarism** functions of a pimp
Greene's books Robert Greene (d. 1592), a famous Elizabethan pamphleteer renowned for his series of pamphlets about London con-artists: *A Notable Discovery of Cozenage* (1591), *The Second Part of Cony-catching* (1591), *The Third and Last Part of Cony-catching* (1592), and *A Disputation between a He Cony-catcher and a She Cony-catcher* (1592).
717 **Pickt-hatch** area north of Aldersgate; favourite haunt of prostitutes and thieves
718 **Turnbull Street** street (i.e., Turnmill Street) running north from Smithfield; the most notorious, disreputable street in London
722 **Jersey stocking** Jersey was famous for the knitting of stockings
727–8 **stubble-haired... harvest** contorted analogy between the 'stubble', or stalks, left in the ground after reaping, and the short bristly growth of the lawyer's recently shaven beard. Literally, he shaved at the beginning of the term-time during which he 'reaped' his 'harvest' of fees.
730 **coxcombs** caps worn by a professional fool, like a cock's comb in shape and colour; ludicrous appellation for the head
732 ***habeas corpus*** legal term meaning 'you may take the body'; another instance of the ant's comic malapropistic verbal mimicry
743 **quaint** clever, ingenious
753 **carriage** meaning carried by words; in the musical sense, a refrain

Happy art thou and all thy brothers
That never feel'st the hell of others:
The torment to a luxur due,
Who never thinks his harlot true;
Although upon her heels he stick his eyes,
Yet still he fears that though she stands, she lies.

Now are thy labours easy,
Thy state not sick or queasy;
All drops thou sweat'st are now thine own;
Great subsidies be as unknown
To thee and to thy little fellow ants;
Now none of you under that burden pants.

Lo, for example, I myself, poor worms,
That have outworn the rage of Tereus' storms,
Am ever blessed now in this downy shape
From all men's treachery or soul-melting rape;
And when I sing *Tereu, Tereu*
Through every town and so renew
The name of *Tereus*, slaves, through fears,
With guilty fingers bolt their ears;
And all ravishers do rave and e'en fall mad,
And then such wronged souls as myself are glad.

So thou, small wretch, and all thy nest,
Are in those little bodies blest,
Not taxed beyond your poor degree
With landlord's fine and lawyer's fee.
But tell me, pretty toiling worm,
Did that same ploughman's weary form
Discourage thee so much from others,
That neither thou, nor those thy brothers,
In borrowed shapes durst once again
Venture amongst perfidious men?

Ant.

'Yes lady', the poor ant replied,
'I left not so, but then I tried
War's sweating fortunes, not alone
Condemning rash all states for one,
Until I found by proof and knew by course
That one was bad, but all the rest were worse.'

Nightingale.

Didst thou put on a rugged soldier then,
A happy state because thou fought'st 'gainst men?
Prithee discourse thy fortunes, state, and harms.
Thou wast, no doubt, a mighty man-at-arms.

The Ant's Tale when he was a Soldier.

Then thus: most musical and prickle-singing madam (for, if I err not, your ladyship was the first that brought up prick-song, being nothing else but the fatal notes of your pitiful ravishment), I, not contented long (a vice cleaving to all worldlings) with this little estate of an ant, but stuffed with envy and ambition, as small as I was, desired to venture into the world again, which I may rather term the upper hell, or *frigida gehenna*, the cold-charitable hell wherein are all kind of devils too, as your gentle devil, your ordinary devil, and your gallant devil; and all these can change their shapes too, as today in cowardly white, tomorrow in politic black, a third day in jealous yellow; for believe it, sweet lady, there are devils of all colours. Nevertheless I, covetous of more change, leaped out of this little skin of an ant and hung my skin on the hedge, taking upon me the grisly shape of a dusty soldier. Well made I was, and my limbs valiantly hewn out for the purpose: I had a mazard, I remember, so well-lined in the inside with my brain it stood me in better stead than a double headpiece, for the brain of a soldier, differing from all other sciences, converts itself to no other use but to line, fur, and even quilt the coxcomb, and so makes a pate of proof. My face was well-leavened which made my looks taste sour, the true relish of a man of war; my cheeks, dough-baked, pale, wan, and therefore argued valour and resolution; but my nose somewhat hard-baked and a little burnt in the oven, a property not amiss in a soldier's visage who should scorn to blush but in his nose. My chin was well thatched with a beard which was a necessary shelter in winter and a fly-flap in summer, so brushy and spreading that my lips could scarce be seen to walk abroad, but played at all-hid and durst not peep forth for starting a hair. To conclude, my arms, thighs, and legs were so sound, stout, and weighty (as if they had come all out of the timber yard) that my very presence only was able to still the bawlingest infant in Europe. And I think, madam, this was no unlikely shape for a soldier to prove well: here was mettle enough, for four shillings a week, to do valiant service till it was bored as full of holes as a skimmer.

Well, to the wars I betook me, ranked myself amongst desperate hot-shots—only, my carriage put on more civility, for I seemed more like a spy than a follower, an observer rather than a committer of villany. And little thought I, madam, that the camp had been supplied with harlots too as well as the Curtain, and the guarded tents as wicked as garden tenements, trulls passing to and fro in the washed shape of laundresses as your bawds about London in

767 **luxur** lecher

810 **prickle-singing** Philomel sang pricked by the thorn at her breast; the thorn's function was to keep her alert and awake.

811 **prick-song** literally, a song sung from notes written down, or 'pricked', in musical notation on paper rather than being sung from memory. In context, the ant exploits the homophonic association between 'pricked' and 'prick', i.e., penis, to attribute the notes of Philomel's song to her rape by Tereus.

816 ***frigida gehenna*** literally 'frozen hell'; reference to 2 Kings 23:10

816–17 **cold-charitable hell** ant's comic play with the translation of *frigida gehenna*

825 **mazard** head

837 **all-hid** possibly a reference to a game such as 'hide and seek'

842 **mettle** high-spirited temperament; implicit pun on 'metal'

844 **skimmer** a shallow metal utensil usually perforated with holes, used in skimming off the surface of a liquid; like a sieve

846 **hot-shots** reckless, hot-headed men

849 **Curtain** playhouse in Shoreditch just north-west of the Spitalfields, outside the city wall; a haunt of prostitutes (Middleton's father owned a tenement house near by)

850 **garden tenements** haunts of prostitutes and fallen women
trulls prostitutes

851–2 **laundresses . . . starchwomen** apparently prostitutes and bawds posed as such for easy access to male lodgings under the guise of collecting and delivering bed linens

the manner of starchwomen, which is the most unsuspected habit that can be to train out a mistress. And if your ladyship will not think me much out of the way, though I take a running leap from the camp to the Strand again, I will discover a pretty knavery of the same breeding between such a starchwoman and a kind wanton mistress, as there are few of those ballassed vessels nowadays but will have a love and a husband.

The woman crying her ware by the door (a most pitiful cry and a lamentable hearing that such a stiff thing as starch should want customers), passing cunningly and slyly by the stall, not once taking notice of the party you wot on, but being by this some three or four shops off. 'Mass', quoth my young mistress to the weathercock her husband, 'such a thing I want, you know.' Then she named how many puffs and purls lay in a miserable case for want of stiffening. The honest, plain-dealing jewel her husband sent out a boy to call her (not 'bawd', by her right name, but 'starchwoman'); into the shop she came, making a low counterfeit curtsy, of whom the mistress demanded if the starch were pure gear and would be stiff in her ruff, saying, she had often been deceived before when the things about her have stood as limber as eelskins. The woman replied as subtly: 'Mistress', quoth she, 'take this paper of starch of my hand, and if it prove not to your mind, never bestow penny with me!'—which paper, indeed, was a letter sent to her from the gentleman, her exceeding favourite. 'Say you so?' quoth the young dame, 'and I'll try it i'faith.' With that she ran upstairs like a spinner upon small cobweb ropes, not to try or arraign the starch, but to construe and parse the letter (whilst her husband sat below by the counter like one of these brow-bitten catchpoles that wait for one man all day, when his wife can put five in the Counter before him), wherein she found many words that pleased her. Withal the gentleman writ unto her for a certain sum of money, which no sooner was read but was ready to be sent; wherefore, laying up the starch and that and taking another sheet of clean paper in her hand, wanting time and opportunity to write at large, with a penful of ink, in the very middle of the sheet writ these few quaint monosyllables: 'Coin, Cares, and Cures, and all C's else are yours.' Then rolling up the white money like the starch in that paper very subtly and artificially, came tripping downstairs with these colourable words: 'Here's goodly starch indeed! Fie, fie—trust me husband—as yellow as the jaundice! I would not have betrayed my puffs with it for a million! Here, here, here!' (giving her the paper of money). With that the subtle starchwoman, seeming sorry that it pleased her not, told her, within few days she would fit her turn with that which should like her (meaning, indeed, more such sweet news from her lover). These and suchlike, madam, are the cunning conveyances of secret, privy, and therefore unnoted harlots that so avoid the common finger of the world when less committers than they are publicly pointed at.

So, likewise in the camp, whither now I return borne on the swift wings of apprehension, the habit of a laundress shadows the abomination of a strumpet, and our soldiers are like glovers, for the one cannot work well nor the other fight well without their wenches. This was the first mark of villainy that I found sticking upon the brow of War. But after the hot and fiery copulation of a skirmish or two, the ordnance playing like so many Tamburlaines, the muskets and calivers answering like drawers, 'Anon, anon, sir, I cannot be here and there too'—that is, in the soldier's hand and in the enemy's belly—I grew more acquainted and, as it were, entered into the entrails of black-livered policy. Methought indeed, at first, those great pieces of ordnance should speak English, though now by transportation turned rebels; and what a miserable and pitiful plight it was, lady, to have so many thousands of our men slain by their own countrymen the cannons—I mean not the harmless canons of Paul's, but those cannons that have a great singing in their heads.

Well, in this onset I remember I was well smoke-dried but neither arm nor leg perished, not so much as the loss of a petty finger, for when I counted them all over, I missed not one of them, and yet sometimes the bullets came within a hair of my coxcomb even like a barber scratching my pate, and perhaps took away the left limb of a vermin, and so departed; another time shouldering me like a bailiff against Michaelmas term and then shaking me by the sleeve as familiarly as if we had been acquainted seven years together. To conclude, they used me very courteously and gentleman-like awhile, like an old cunning bowler to fetch in a

853 **train out** teach young wives about having adulterous affairs
856 **kind** foolish
857 **ballassed** variant (obs.) of 'ballusted'; here, weighted down with a husband
860 **stiff thing** bawdy reference to erection
862 **wot on** know of
864 **weathercock** easily turned by the wind, i.e., her deceitful verbal expressions
865 **puffs** parts of a garments sewn in such a way as to appear inflated or puffed-up **purls** fringes or pleats
870 **gear** stuff, i.e., high quality starch
870–2 **ruff . . . eelskins** *double entendre* linking vagina (i.e., 'ruff') and limp penis
873 **paper of starch** starch rolled up in paper like flat, thin pastry dough
877 **spinner** spider
880 **catchpoles** sheriff's deputies or sergeants who arrest criminals
881 **Counter** debtors' prison; probably a pun on female genitalia
888 **all C's else** allusion to 'cunt'
890 **colourable** specious, feigned, plausible-sounding
896 **like** please
903 **glovers** glove makers or sellers
907 **ordnance** cannon, artillery **Tamburlaines** reference to the towering hero of Christopher Marlowe's two plays of that name
908 **calivers** lightweight muskets that could be aimed and fired without a rest **drawers** bartenders
911 **black-livered policy** In the physio-psychology of the time, the liver processed the digested fluid (chyle) from the stomach into the four humours, of which melancholia had the qualities of black, semi-excremental, sour, thick, and heavy. Its preponderance in the body produced a lean and pale appearance, a grim and frowning visage, and a mind given to envy, obstinacy, churlishness, and greed. The melancholic, or 'malcontent', was a politically dangerous type driven by a sense of injustice or unrequited merit and often plotted ('made policy') for revenge or the destruction of the good fortune enjoyed by others.
913 **transportation** the sale and export of ordnance to foreign countries
916 **canons** clergymen (including clerks in minor orders) living with others in a clergy-house, i.e., in one of the houses within the precincts, or 'close', of a cathedral; often choir members
922 **pate** head
923 **vermin** e.g., lice, fleas

young ketling gamester, who will suffer him to win one sixpenny-game at the first, and then lurch him in six pounds afterward; and so they played with me, still training me with their fair promises into far deeper and deadlier battles where, like villainous cheating bowlers, they lurched me of two of my best limbs, *viz.* my right arm and right leg, that so, of a man of war, I became in show a monster of war, yet comforted in this because I knew war begot many such monsters as myself in less than a twelvemonth.

Now I could discharge no more, having paid the shot dear enough, I think, but rather desired to be discharged, to have pay and be gone: whereupon I appeared to my captain and other commanders, kissing my left hand which then stood for both (like one actor that plays two parts), who seemed to pity my unjointed fortunes and plaster my wounds up with words, told me I had done valiant service in their knowledge; marry, as for pay, they must go on the score with me, for all their money was thumped out in powder. And this was no pleasing salve to a green sore, madam; 'twas too much for me, lady, to trust calivers with my limbs and then cavaliers with my money. Nevertheless, for all my lamentable action of one arm like old Titus Andronicus, I could purchase no more than one month's pay for a ten-month's pain and peril; nor that neither, but to convey away my miserable clamours that lay roaring against the arches of their ears, marry, their bountiful favours were extended thus far: I had a passport to beg in all countries.

Well, away I was packed, and after a few miseries by the way, at last I set one foot into England again (for I had no more then to set), being my native though unnatural country for whose dear good I pawned my limbs to bullets, those merciless brokers that will take the vantage of a minute, and so they were quite forfeited, lost, and unrecoverable. When I was on shore, the people gathered, which word 'gathering' put me in hope of good comfort that afterward I failed of. For I thought, at first, they had gathered something for me, but I found, at last, they did only but gather about me, some wondering at me as if I had been some sea monster cast ashore, some jesting at my deformity, whilst others laughed at the jests. One amongst them, I remember, likened me to a sea-crab because I went all of one side; another fellow vied it and said I looked like a rabbit cut up and half-eaten because my wing and leg (as they termed it) were departed. Some began to pity me, but those were few in number, or at least their pity was as penniless as Pierce, who writ to the devil for maintenance. Thus passing from place to place like the motion of Julius Caesar or the city Nineveh, though not altogether in so good clothes, I overtook the city from whence I borrowed my first breath and in whose defence I spent and laid out my limbs by whole sums to purchase her peace and happiness, nothing doubting but to be well entreated there, my grievous maims tenderly regarded, my poor broken estate carefully repaired, the ruins of my blood built up again with redress and comfort. But woe the while, madam! I was not only unpitied, succourless, and rejected, but threatened with the public stocks, loathsome jails, and common whipping-posts, there to receive my pay (a goodly reward for my bleeding service) if I were once found in the city again.

Wherefore I was forced to retire towards the Spital and Shoreditch, which, as it appeared, was the only Cole Harbour and sanctuary for wenches and soldiers; where I took up a poor lodging o' trust till the Sunday, hoping that then Master Alms and Mistress Charity would walk abroad and take the air in Finsbury.

At which time I came hopping out from my lodging like old lame Giles of Cripplegate; but when I came there, the wind blew so bleak and cold that I began to be quite out of hope of Charity, yet, like a torn map of misery, I waited my single halfpenny fortunes; when, of a sudden, turning myself about and looking down the Windmill Hill, I might espy afar off a fine-fashioned dame of the city with her man bound by indenture before her; whom no sooner I caught in mine eyelids, but I made to with all possible speed, and with a premeditated speech for the nonce, thus most soldier-like I accosted her:

'Sweet lady, I beseech your beauty to weigh the estate of a poor unjointed soldier that hath consumed the moiety, or the one half of his limbs, in the dismembering and devouring wars

928 **ketling** inexperienced
929 **lurch** overwhelmingly outscore an opponent. In bowling games played for wagers, the highly skilled player intentionally loses the first game and proceeds to win subsequent games until the inexperienced player has no more money.
943 **score** record of a debt; 'put it on the tab'
946 **cavaliers** gentlemen trained for military service on horseback; officers
947 **Titus Andronicus** The hero of Shakespeare's *Titus Andronicus* whose right hand is cut off in the third act; hence, subsequent manual activities are severely curtailed, but not nearly so much as his daughter's (i.e., both hands cut off).
951–2 **passport to beg** soldiers or sailors carrying such a passport were exempted from the act of 1598 which classified wandering beggars as rogues who were to be whipped and extradited to the parish of their birth
952 **countries** i.e., counties
957 **vantage** advantage
964–5 **likened . . . sea-crab** Certain species of crabs crawl sideways rather than forward; the image suggests that the soldier pulled himself sideways while prone on the ground, but the exaggerated image of his maiming defies any clear insight into his exact method of locomotion. He also mentions 'I came out hopping' (987), presumably with a stick for support.
965–6 **vied it** matching, raising, or calling the bet of an opponent in a card game such as stud poker in the confidence that one's hand will win; outdo another
969 **penniless as Pierce** In Nashe's *Pierce Penniless his Supplication to the Devil*, the poverty-stricken Pierce, who has devoted his life to learning, writes to Lucifer suggesting that the removal of the souls of a number of usurers and misers who have encroached on Lucifer's prerogatives would put more gold in circulation and thus help impoverished but deserving individuals like Pierce.
970–1 **motion of . . . Nineveh** two popular puppet shows; the maimed soldier's physical movements are jerky and unnatural like those of puppets
980 **pay** i.e. punishment
982–3 **Spital and Shoreditch** St Mary Spittle, a hospital north of the city wall on Bishopsgate Street, accessible through Bishopsgate; Shoreditch is immediately to the north. Nashe claimed that 'every second house' in the area was a brothel (*Pierce Penniless*).
983 **Cole Harbour** site in Upper Thames Street near Allhallows church which had acquired the right of sanctuary
988 **Cripplegate** city gate providing access to Finsbury Field; west of Bishopsgate and Moorgate; supposedly named after St Giles, the patron saint of cripples
992 **Windmill Hill** the north-south road leading past the windmills that had been erected in Finsbury Field during the reign of Elizabeth

that hath cheated me of my flesh so notoriously. I protest I am not worth at this instant the small revenue of three farthings, besides my lodging unpleased and my diet unsatisfied. And had I ten thousand limbs, I would venture them all in your sweet quarrel rather than such a beauty as yourself should want the least limb of your desire.'

With that, as one being rather moved by my last words of promise than my first words of pity, she drew her white bountiful hand out of her marry-muff and quoited a single halfpenny, whereby I knew her then to be cold Mistress Charity both by her chill appearance and the hard frozen pension she gave me. She was warm lapped, I remember, from the sharp injury of the biting air: her visage was benighted with a taffeta mask to fray away the naughty wind from her face, and yet her very nose seemed so sharp with cold that it almost bored a hole quite through. This was frost-bitten Charity: her teeth chattered in her head and leaped up and down like virginal-jacks, which betrayed likewise who she was. And you would have broken into infinite laughter, madam (though misery made me leaden and pensive), had you been present to have seen how quickly the muff swallowed her hand again, for no sooner was it drawn forth to drop down her pitiful alms but, for fear the sun and air should have ravished it, it was extempore whipped up again. This is the true picture of Charity, madam, which is as cold as ice in the middle of July.

Well, still I waited for another fare. But then I bethought myself again that all the fares went by water o' Sundays to the bear-baiting, and o' Mondays to Westminster Hall, and therefore, little to be looked for in Moorfields all the week long.

Wherefore I sat down by the rails there and fell into these passionate, but not railing speeches: 'Is this the farthest reward for a soldier? Is valour and resolution, the two champions of the soul, so slightly esteemed and so basely undervalued? Doth reeling fortune not only rob us of our limbs, but of our living? Are soldiers then both food for cannon and for misery?' But then, in the midst of my passion, calling to memory the peevish turns of many famous popular gallants whose names were writ even upon the heart of the world (it could not so much as think without them, nor speak but in the discourse of them), I began to outdare the very worst of cruel and disaster chances and determined to be constant in calamity and valiant against the battering siege of misery. But note the cross star that always dogged my fortunes. I had not long rested there but I saw the tweering constable of Finsbury with his bench of brown billmen making towards me, meaning indeed to stop some prison hole with me, as your soldiers, when the wars have done with them, are good for nothing else but to stop holes withal; at which sight, I scrambled up of all two, took my skin off the hedge, cozened the constable, and slipped into an ant again.

The Nightingale.

'O, 'twas a pretty quaint deceit'
(The Nightingale began to sing),
'To slip from those that lie in wait,
Whose touch is like a raven's wing,
Fatal and ominous, which, being spread
Over a mortal, aims him dead.

'Alas, poor emmet! thou wast tossed
In thousand miseries by this shape,
Thy colour wasted, thy blood lost,
Thy limbs broke with the violent rape
Of hot impatient cannons, which desire
To ravish lives, spending their lust in fire.

'O, what a ruthful sight it is to see,
Though in a soldier of the mean'st degree,
That right member perished,
Which thy body cherished;
That limb dissevered, burnt, and gone,
Which the best part was borne upon;
And then the greatest ruth of all,
Returning home in torn estate,
Where he should rise, there most to fall,
Trod down with envy, bruised with hate:
Yet wretch, let this thy comfort be,
That greater worms have fared like thee.'

1002 **unpleased** unpaid bill
1008 **marry-muff** cylindrical piece of clothing made from fur or silk into which the hands were inserted from either end, similar in function to gloves
quoited as in playing at quoits, a game played with 'a heavy flattish ring of iron, slightly convex on the upper side and concave on the under, so as to give it an edge capable of cutting into the ground when it falls, if skilfully thrown'. The sense is that Mistress Charity threw the coin on the ground rather than handing it to the ant.
1011 **lapped** wrapped in layers of clothing
1012 **benighted** covered, hidden from the light
fray frighten away
1016 **virginal-jacks** the keys of a virginal, a small keyboard instrument (a predecessor of the harpsichord) popular in aristocratic homes
1025–6 **bear-baiting** Bears were pitted against mastiffs at the Bear Garden in Southwark (across the Thames by the Globe) in a very popular form of entertainment which left the bears in what could be described as a 'ragged' condition (see 'To the Reader').
1027 **Moorfields** marshy area north of Moorgate between Finsbury Field on the west and Spitalfields on the east; haunt of beggars
1029 **railing** verbally abusive
1034–5 **peevish turns** the reference to 'reeling fortune' (1032) evokes the common image of the whimsical, unpredictable turning of Fortune's wheel which brings low those in high places. In the context of the *de casibus* literary tradition, only the 'peevish' or downward turns of Fortune 'were writ upon the heart of the world' as in the collection of histories in *The Mirror for Magistrates*.
1042 **tweering** spying
billmen members of the watch who carried spears or pikes with hooked points, or 'bills'. The ant uses the term 'bench' here and in the dicing episode to indicate a group, an obscure association.
1046 **cozened** cheated, defrauded through deceit
1061 **ruthful** pitiful

So here thou left'st, bloodless and wan,
Thy journeys thorough man and man;
These two crossed shapes, so much oppressed,
Did fray thy weakness from the rest.

Ant.

No, madam, once again my spleen did thirst
To try the third, which makes men blessed or curst;
That number, three, many stars wait upon,
Ushering clear hap or black confusïon.
Once more I ventured all my hopes to crown,
But, aye me, leaped into a scholar's gown.

Nightingale.

A needy scholar? Worse than worst,
Less fate in that than both the first:
I thought, thou'dst leaped into a law-gown, then
There had been hope to have swept up all again.
But a lank scholar? Study how you can,
No academe makes a rich alderman.
Well, with this comfort yet thou mayst discourse:
When fates are worst, then they can be no worse.

The Ant's Tale when he was a Scholar.

You speak oracle, madam. And now suppose, sweet lady, you see me set forth like a poor scholar to the university, not on horseback but in Hobson's wagon, and all my pack contained in less than a little hood-box; my books not above four in number, and those four were very needful ones too, or else they had never been bought; and yet I was the valiant captain of a grammar school before I went, endured the assault and battery of many unclean lashes, and all the battles I was in stood upon points much, which, once let down, the enemy (the schoolmaster) would come rearward and do such an exploit 'tis a shame to be talked of. By this time, madam, imagine me slightly entertained to be a poor scholar and servitor to some Londoner's son, a pure cockney that must hear twice a week from his mother, or else he will be sick ere the Sunday of a university-mullygrub. Such a one, I remember, was my first puling master by whose peevish service I crept into an old batteler's gown and so began to be a jolly fellow. There was the first point of wit I showed, in learning to keep myself warm; to the confirming of which, you shall never take your true philosophers without two nightcaps at once, and better, a gown of rug with the like appurtenances; and who be your wisemen, I pray, but they? Now as for study and books, I had the use of my young master's, for he was all day a courtier in the tennis-court tossing of balls instead of books, and only holding disputation with the court-keeper how many dozen he was in. And when any friend of his would remember him to his book with this old moth-eaten sentence, *nulla dies sine linea*, 'True', he would say, 'I observe it well, for I am no day from the line of the racket-court.'

Well, in the mean time, I kept his study warm and sucked the honey of wit from the flowers of Aristotle, steeped my brain in the smart juice of logic, that subtle virtue, and yet for all my weighty and substantial arguments, being able indeed to prove anything by logic, I could prove myself never the richer, make the best syllogism I could. No, although I daily rose before the sun, talked and conversed with midnight, killing many a poor farthing-candle that sometimes was ungently put to death when it might have lived longer, but most times living out the full course and hour and the snuff dying naturally in his bed. Nevertheless, I had entered as yet but the suburbs of a scholar and sat but upon the skirts of learning. Full often I have sighed when others have snorted, and when baser trades have securely rested in their linens, I have forced mine eyes open and even gagged them with capital letters, stretching them upon the tenters of a broad text-line when night and sleep have hung pound-weights of lead upon my eyelids.

How many such black and ghastly seasons have I passed over, accompanied only with a demure watching-candle that blinked upon Aristotle's works and gave even sufficient glimmering to read

1096 **Hobson's wagon** Thomas Hobson drove a freight wagon between London and Cambridge weekly from 1564 to 1630. John Milton immortalized him in two poems. Several extant invoices and letters from bookseller Thomas Chard of London (1580s) to his Cambridge buyer refer to delivery via Hobson's wagon.

1097 **hood-box** box for storing a hood (i.e., head-covering)

1099–103 **valiant captain ... talked of** Students progressed through the eight forms of the English grammar school before graduation; the curriculum focused upon the mastery of Latin grammar and rhetoric, followed by Greek. The ant was the chief misbehaver and hence the recipient of corporal punishment consisting of an undoing of the 'points', or laces, which attached the breeches to the doublet, thus exposing his buttocks for whipping with various instruments such as a stick or a bundle of birch twigs.

1101 **lashes** whipping

1105 **servitor** lowest rank of student: very poor students earned their keep as servants of well-off students

1107 **university-mullygrub** A mullygrub was a state of depression. Here, the ant's employer, a newly arrived student, experiences severe homesickness for his mother. Nashe satirizes the type as 'A young heir or cockney, that is his mother's darling'.

1108 **puling** whining or complaining like an infant

1109 **batteler's** rank of student below commoners; not entitled to commons, but had to purchase food from the cook and butler

1113 **rug** coarse woollen material

1117 **was in** apparently a fee for balls paid by the dozen

1119 **sentence** *sententia*, a wise saying ***nulla dies sine linea*** 'no day without a line'; a reference to drawing that originated with Pliny, recorded in an anecdote about the ancient Greek painter Apelles; alternately, since the context is 'his book', a reference to the practice in the Elizabethan grammar school of requiring students to memorize new lines of a classical text each day. The standard assignment beginning in the fourth form was the memorization of several lines of Ovid's *Metamorphoses*, the whole to be completed by the end of the eighth form.

1124 **substantial** containing substance or significant matter

1126 **syllogism** formal logical argument containing a major and a minor premise which share a common element (the 'middle term'), and together either affirm or deny the third part, the conclusion, which also contains the middle term

1128 **farthing-candle** candle costing a farthing, a coin (usually silver) worth one-quarter of a penny

1135 **tenters** wooden framework on which cloth was stretched after being milled, so that it would set or dry evenly without shrinking (a familiar sight to Londoners, given the large number of tenters situated just north of the city wall through Moorgate)

by, but none to spare. Hitherto my hopes grew comfortable upon the spreading branches of art and learning, rather promising future advancement than empty days and penurious scarcity. But shall I tell you, lady? O, here let me sigh out a full point and take my leave of all plenteous hours and wealthy hopes, for in the spring of all my perfections, in the very pride and glory of all my labours, I was unfruitfully led to the lickerish study of poetry, that sweet honey-poison that swells a supple scholar with unprofitable sweetness and delicious false conceits until he burst into extremities and become a poetical almsman, or at the most, one of the Poor Knights of Poetry, worse by odds than one of the Poor Knights of Windsor. Marry, there was an age once, but alas, long since dead and rotten, whose dust lies now in lawyers' sandboxes! In those golden days, a virtuous writer might have lived, maintained himself, better upon poems than many upon ploughs, and might have expended more by the year by the revenue of his verse than any riotous elder brother upon the wealthy quarterages of three times three hundred acres, according to the excellent report of these lines:

There was a Golden Age! who murdered it?
How died that Age, or what became of it?
Then poets, by divinest alchemy,
Did turn their ink to gold; kings in that time
Hung jewels at the ear of every rhyme.
But O, those days are wasted, and behold
The Golden Age that was, is coined to gold.
And why time now is called an iron man,
Or this an Iron Age, 'tis thus expressed:
The Golden Age lies in a iron chest.

Or,

Gold lies now as prisoner in an usurer's great iron-barred chest, where the prison-grates are the locks and the keyholes, but so closely mewed, or rather damned up, that it never looks to walk abroad again unless there chance to come a speedy rot among usurers, for, I fear me, the piddling gout will never make them away soon enough, for your rank money masters live their threescore and ten years as orderly as many honester men; and it is a great pity, Lady Philomel, that the gout should be such a long courtier in a usurer's great toe, revelling and domineering above thirty years together in his rammish blood and his fusty flesh. And I wonder much, madam, that gold, being the spirit of the Indies, can couch so basely under wood and iron, two dull slaves, and not muster up his legion of angels, burst through the wide bulk of a coffer, and so march into bountiful and liberal bosoms, shake hands with virtuous gentlemen, industrious spirits, and true deserving worthies, detesting the covetous clutches and loathsome fangs of a goat-bearded usurer, a sable-soul broker, and an infectious law-fogger.

O, but I chide in vain, for gold wants eyes,
And like a whore cares not with whom it lies.

Yet that which makes me most admire his baseness are these verses following wherein he proudly sets forth his own glory, which he vaunts so much of, that I shame to think any ignoble spirit or copper disposition should fetter his smooth golden limbs in boisterous and sullen iron, but rather be let free to every virtuous and therefore poor scholar (for poverty is niece to virtue); so should each elegant poem be truly valued, and divine Poesy sit crowned in gold as she ought, where now she only sits with a paper on her head as if she had committed some notorious trespass, either for railing against some brawling lawyer, or calling some justice of peace a wiseman; and how magnificently Gold sings of his own fame and glory, these his own verses shall stand for witnesses.

——————————Know I am Gold,
The richest spirit that breaths in earth or hell,
The soul of kingdoms and the stamp of souls;
Bright angels wear my livery, sovereign kings
Christen their names in gold and call themselves
Royal and sovereign after my gilt name.
All offices are mine, and in my gift
I have a hand in all: the statist's veins
Flow in the blood of gold, the courtier bathes
His supple and lascivious limbs in oil
Which my brow sweats. What lady brightly sphered
But takes delight to kiss a golden beard?
Those pleaders, forenoon players, act my parts
With liberal tongues and desperate fighting spirits
That wrestle with the arms of voice and air;
And lest they should be out, or faint, or cold,
Their innocent clients hist them on with gold.

1143 **penurious** indigent, destitute
1147 **lickerish** sweet, tempting, attractive
1149 **conceits** imaginative, fanciful, ingenious, witty expressions of some idea, concept, or poetic image
1152 **Poor Knights of Windsor** pensions and apartments in Windsor Castle were alloted to a certain number of impoverished military men
1154 **sandboxes** box with perforated top used for sprinkling sand to blot wet ink
1158 **quarterages** quarterly rents
1173 **mewed** shut up, concealed
1175 **piddling** trifling, petty
gout a disease (usually in males) characterized by painful inflammation of the smaller joints, especially that of the great toe
1180 **rammish** rank, strong, highly disagreeable (smell, taste); figuratively, lascivious or lustful
fusty mouldy or stale-smelling
1183 **angels** pun on the coin and heavenly angels
1192 **he** i.e., Gold, who is now personified as a poet writing praises of himself
1198–9 **paper on her head** obscure reference, probably to some form of punishment for naughty students such as being required to wear a 'dunce's cap' and sit in the corner
1207–9 **angels . . . Royal and sovereign** pun on the three coins
1209 **sovereign** gold coin worth about 10–11 shillings
1214 **lady brightly sphered** figurative reference to the nine heavenly spheres of the Elizabethan cosmos. Poets frequently 'ensphered' their ladies in the eighth sphere, that of the fixed stars, in their poems of courtship and praise. This represents the highest location in creation. Hence, even highly esteemed and beloved ladies, praised usually for their ethereal virtue among other qualities, bow to greed if enough gold is offered.
1216 **pleaders, forenoon players** lawyers
1220 **hist** sound made to urge on a dog or other animal

What holy churchman's not accounted even,
That prays three times to me, ere once to heaven?
Then, to let shine the radiance of my birth,
I am the enchantment both in hell and earth.

Here's golden majesty enough, I trow. And, Gold, art thou so powerful, so mighty, and yet snaffled with a poor padlock? O base drudge and too unworthy of such an angel-like form, much like a fair, sleek-faced courtier without either wit or virtue; thou that throwest the earthen bowl of the world, with the bias the wrong way, to peasantry, baseness, ingentility, and never givest desert his due or shakest thy yellow wings in a scholar's study! But why do I lose myself in seeking thee, when thou art found of few but illiterate hinds, rude boors, and hoary penny-fathers that keep thee in perpetual durance, in vaults, under false boards, subtle-contrived walls, and in horrible dark dungeons; bury thee most unchristian-like, without 'Amen' or the least noise of a priest or clerk, and make thee rise again at their pleasure many a thousand time before Doomsday; and yet, will not all this move thee once to forsake them and keep company with a scholar that truly knows how to use thee?

By this time I had framed an elaborate poetical building, a neat, choice, and curious poem, the first fruits of my musical rhyming study, which was dispersed into a quaint volume, fairly bound up in principal vellum, double-filleted with leaf-gold, strung most gentleman-like with carnation silk ribbon; which book, industriously heaped with weighty conceits, precious phrases, and wealthy numbers, I, Oliver Hubburd, in the best fashion I might, presented to Sir Christopher Clutch-Fist, whose bountiful virtue I blaze in my first Epistle. The book he entertained but, I think, for the cover's sake because it made such a goodly show on the backside. And some two days after, returning for my remuneration, I might espy (O lamentable sight! madam) my book dismembered very tragically, the cover ripped off (I know not for what purpose), and the carnation silk strings pulled out and placed in his Spanish-leather shoes; at which ruthful prospect I fell down and swooned, and when I came to myself again, I was an ant, and so ever since I have kept me.

The Nightingale.

'There keep thee still;
Since all are ill,
Venture no more;
'Tis better be a little ant
Than a great man and live in want,
And still deplore.
So rest thee now,
From sword, book, or plough.'
By this the day began to spring
And seize upon her watchful eyes,
When more tree-choristers did sing,
And every bird did wake and rise;
Which was no sooner seen and heard,
But all their pretty chat was marred.
And then she said,
'We are betrayed,
The day is up, and all the birds,
And they abroad will blab our words.'
With that she bade the ants farewell,
And all they likewise Philomel.
Away she flew,
Crying *Tereu*!
And all the industrious ants in throngs
Fell to their work, and held their tongues.

FINIS.

1226 **snaffled** simple form of bridle-bit, having less restraining power than one provided with a curb (the chain or strap passing under the horse's lower jaw)
1229 **bowl** ball used in the game played on a bowling green
bias to throw the bowl in such a way as to cause it to follow an oblique or curved trajectory; similar to 'putting english' on a cue ball or controlling the spin of a baseball to produce a curved trajectory, i.e., 'throwing a curve-ball'
1233 **penny-fathers** misers
1243 **quaint** ornate, expensive, finely crafted
1244 **principal vellum** the finest grade of leather parchment made from hides of calves, lambs, or kids; usually used for writing, painting, or binding books
double-filleted two lines forming rectangular frames around the perimeter of the book's cover; made by impressing strips of extremely thin ('leaf') gold upon the vellum
1245 **carnation silk ribbon** expensive pinkish or flesh-coloured ribbon (see note to l. 32–3)
1245–7 **industriously heaped . . . wealthy numbers** The ant measures the value of his 'elaborate poetic building' quantitatively in terms of detailed 'conceits', ornate images, and profusion of stanzas.
1249 **first Epistle** i.e., Epistle Dedicatory at the beginning of *Father Hubburd's Tales*
1250–1 **backside** unclear reference to some aspect of the book
1251 **remuneration** Oliver expected a reward for dedicating the book to Clutch-Fist.
1255 **prospect** sight
swooned fainted

THE MEETING OF GALLANTS AT AN ORDINARY; OR, THE WALKS IN PAUL'S

Edited by Paul Yachnin

Thy spring shall in all sweets abound,
Thy summer shall be clear and sound,
Thy autumn swell the barn and loft
With corn and fruits—ripe, sweet and soft;
And in thy winter, when all go,
Thou shalt depart as white as snow.

—*Masque of Heroes* (1619)

IN Harmony's perfectly flowing song of blessing for the new year of 1619 in Middleton's *Masque of Heroes*, there is one detail that causes a slight disruption for the modern reader. This disruption, not metrical but semantic, consists in the prediction that summer will be 'clear and sound'. 'Clear' seems like a straightforward reference to the weather, but the meaning of 'sound' is at first obscure for us. In contrast, what any hearer in the early seventeenth century would have grasped instantly was that Harmony's blessing represented a poetic attempt to ward off the plague. In this context, 'sound' means 'healthy' (as in 'sound of limb'), and 'clear' is not a reference to the weather at all, but rather expresses a wish that the atmosphere will be clear of the corruption which was often thought to precipitate the plague. 'This sickness of the plague', Thomas Lodge wrote in 1603, 'is commonly engendered of an infection of the air, altered with a venomous vapour, dispersed and sowed in the same.' In 1619, by the way, Middleton and his audience were fortunate because, although there was virulent plague in Rouen and two ships from there were quarantined at Tilbury for twenty-five days, there was no epidemic that year in England. The year of Lodge's *A Treatise of the Plague*, however, was not 'clear and sound'. The bubonic epidemic of 1603–4, toward the end of which time Middleton wrote *The Meeting of Gallants at an Ordinary*, killed more than one-sixth of the population of London. The most recent great epidemic had taken place ten years earlier, when Middleton was thirteen. The years from 1597 to 1600 were 'clear', although there were still a few plague-deaths annually during all those years. There was also sickness on the Continent: Lisbon in 1599, Spain in 1601, the Low Countries in 1602. In summer 1602, authorities prevented refugees from the contaminated city of Amsterdam from landing in England, and in September trade with the port town of Yarmouth and with Amsterdam was suspended by the Lord Mayor of London.

In spite of these and other precautions, however, the sickness eventually began to take hold in the city, first in the suburbs (deaths were reported in Southwark, south of the Thames, in early March) and then in London itself. By April, orders had been given both to restrict the movement of 'rogues and vagabonds' and to provide charity among the infected poor. The deaths for the week ending 26 May were thirty, but by July 1603 the weekly rate of mortality for London and the Liberties had reached the hundreds, and during the last week of that month, more than a thousand people died from the disease.

The new King celebrated his coronation on 25 July, but arrived at and departed from Westminster by water and, once crowned, left the city to return to Hampton Court about fifteen miles west of London. The toll in the city and out-parishes rose through the summer to a peak of over three thousand for the week ending 1 September. Michaelmas Term, the autumn session of the law courts (10 October to 28 November), was relocated to the town of Winchester. As *The Meeting of Gallants* tells us, St Paul's was deserted of the splendidly attired would-be courtiers who frequented it in healthier times ('What, Signor Jinglespur, the first gallant I met in Paul's, since the one-and-thirty day, or the decease of July' [124–5]). John Chamberlain, who lived his adult life in the neighbourhood of the Cathedral, wrote: 'Paul's grows very thin, for every man shrinks away and I am half ashamed to see myself left alone.' Eventually, the sickness began to abate, the weekly toll dropping below a thousand for the week ending 20 October. By Christmas, weekly deaths from the pestilence had fallen to fewer than a hundred. Hilary Term (23 January to 12 February) took place back in London. It was just around this time that Middleton, with help from Dekker, wrote *The Meeting of Gallants*.

Plague changed the face of life in the city. Although the English had had three hundred years' experience of recurrent bubonic plague, each new epidemic provided a grim surprise for whose physical and psychological effects no one could adequately prepare. Public life was disrupted. Those who could afford to, fled the city, the runaways often including doctors, ministers of the Church, and public officials; regular commerce diminished (businesses where the infection was detected were closed for a minimum of twenty-eight days). There was a feeling of panic. Thomas Lodge was besieged by crowds of citizens who mistook his house for that of a charlatan whose advertisements promised immunity from infection: 'everyone that read them came flocking to me, conjuring me by great proffers and persuasions to store them with my promised preservatives and relieve their sick with my cordial waters'. The terror aroused by the sickness could not be relieved, even with all the nostrums, prayer meetings, and public health measures carried out by the authorities. The terror was in part a result of the extreme speed and brutality of the sickness. Leeds Barroll explains its typical course:

> The bacillus of the bubonic plague, once it has penetrated the body of a human being, is vigorous and aggressive. It reproduces itself rapidly and spreads throughout the entire biological system.... the onset is sudden. Body temperature rises to at least 102°F, pulse increases, the victim breathes faster than usual and needs to lie down.... severe headache also strikes in the early stages. There are pains in the back and legs, and often in places where the lymph glands are located: the groin, the armpits, or the neck. A victim who tries to walk at this juncture is not well coordinated, often staggering as if drunk. Victims also begin to feel very thirsty.... accumulations of bacilli in the bloodstream begin to obstruct the tiny dilated capillaries, causing hemorrhage and bruises on the skin.... One's skin becomes hot and dry. Miniature blisters begin to appear on the hands, feet, and chest, becoming small, poxlike skin irruptions or coalescing into carbuncles sometimes as large as an inch in diameter. Sometimes, too, ulcers form on the skin near the lymph glands, and these ulcers may eat deeply enough into the skin to cause hemorrhage as the vein or artery is exposed.... Victims either become apathetic or go into wild deliriums marked by an impulse to wander or even run away.... frequently sufferers may experience air hunger that causes them to wish to leave an enclosed room in order to sit or lie down outside.... Death comes from heart failure.

In addition to the sheer impressiveness of the physical deterioration of one's neighbours and family members, the plague terrified on account of the mystery of its origin, the invisibility of its spread and the apparent randomness with which it selected its victims. 'How often', Dekker wrote in *The Wonderful Year* (1603), 'hath the amazed husband waking, found the comfort of his bed lying breathless by his side! His children at the same instant gasping for life!' Questions about the origin and capriciousness of the plague added a distinctly private, spiritual dimension to the worrying public concerns about the prevention of large assemblies of people, the disposal of corpses, the danger of the infected evading quarantine, and the problems of crushing poverty and food shortages brought on by the disruption in trade, especially the trade in woollen cloth which was England's primary export. (Cloth was thought to carry the infection; in fact, it often did carry infective fleas.) Writers such as Dekker and Middleton, having been cut off from their regular source of income as dramatists on account of the prohibition against theatrical performances, turned their energy toward writing for the popular press. While a physician-poet such as Lodge might publish his advice on how to treat the actual disease, Dekker and Middleton articulated the moral and spiritual questionings aroused by the epidemic. So in *News from Gravesend* (1604), mostly by Dekker with a section by Middleton, we have the following:

> Can we believe that one man's breath
> Infected, and being blown from him,
> His poison should to others swim,
> For then who breathed upon the first?
> Where did the imbulked venom burst?
> Or how 'scaped those that did divide
> The selfsame bits with those that died?
> Drunk of the selfsame cups, and lay
> In ulcerous beds, as close as they?

Dekker struggles with the fact that the plague exists rather than with the practical problems of its cure and control. How is it that some die and some survive? Where does the plague come from and how is the sickness passed from one person to another? In the end, the pamphlet concludes that the plague's origins are metaphysical rather than physical. In this view, and because the author loses sight of the problem of the randomness of mortality, the sickness is made to make moral sense because it is said to be a divine punishment visited upon a sinful nation ('God in anger fills his hand | With vengeance, throwing it on the land'), and the fundamental remedy therefore must lie in prayer rather than in any medical innovation:

> Only this antidote apply:
> Cease vexing Heaven, and cease to die.
> ...Each one purge one,
> And England's free, the plague is gone.

In *The Meeting of Gallants*, Middleton takes a tack different from that of *News from Gravesend*. The latter pamphlet develops a highly typical view. 'The plague', Lodge wrote in a similar vein, 'is a manifest sign of the wrath of God conceived against us'. It is important to remember, incidentally, that Dekker and Middleton were friends and collaborators and, in particular, that each man's part in *News from Gravesend* has not been definitively established. At any rate, *The Meeting of Gallants* differs from *News from Gravesend* because, first of all, it is not a theoretical inquiry into the causes and nature of the plague. Instead, since *The Meeting of Gallants* consists of a dramatized debate between personified causes of death (War, Famine, and Pestilence) and concludes with a series of 'tales', its view of the moral significance of the plague is implicit rather than explicit; its handling of the meaning of the sickness is woven into the dialogue and dramatically-framed narratives rather than proffered straightforwardly.

The Meeting of Gallants opens with a spirited verbal contest between personified versions of Death; this allegorical flyting leads to a scene in Paul's Cathedral set in the present time (January–February 1604) of Middleton's original readers and replete with local details of the very horror they had just endured; finally, the scene shifts to an 'ordinary', or tavern, where a series of tales about the plague is recounted. The overall effect of this arrangement of material is to put in question any conventional theodicy. Rather than suppressing the problem of the apparent arbitrariness with which the plague chooses its victims, *The Meeting of Gallants*'s jests highlight the capriciousness and consequent moral senselessness of the scourge. In this respect, Middleton's view is like the Earl of Gloucester's in *The History of King Lear* (1605–6) since the 'gods' of 'War, Famine and the Pestilence' do precisely 'kill us for their sport'. On the other hand, Middleton, though he gives full weight to the fear of random and invisible death, takes a much drier, tougher, and funnier view. We witness the 'gods' having their sport rather than seeing only the suffering of their victims. Furthermore, the debate is funny in itself, although chillingly or even infuriatingly funny. War, Famine, and Pestilence are represented as arrogant aristocrats who thoughtlessly place their interests over the interests of the people whom they destroy. Each wishes to be seen as the sovereign bringer of death, so each accuses the others of striking in peace-time, or of killing worthless victims ('a tailor is the farthest man thou kill'st', 13), or of destroying an insufficient number, or of taking life too quickly or too painlessly ('Not worthy to be named a torturing death', 103). Pestilence actually seems to enlist her victims as her allies or subjects, cataloguing their sufferings as testimonials to her dignity:

Beware, War, how thou speakest of me,
I have friends here in England, though some dead,
Some still can show where I was born and bred;
Therefore be wary in pronouncing me.
Many have took my part, whose carcases
Lie now ten fathom deep: many alive
Can show their scars in my contagious quarrel:
War, I surpass the fury of thy stroke.

How many swarms
Of bruised and cracked people did I leave,
Their groins sore pierced with pestilential shot,
Their armpits digged with blains, and ulcerous sores
Lurking like poisoned bullets in their flesh?
Othersome shot in the eye with carbuncles,
Their lids as monstrous as the Saracens'.

Middleton's gallows humour also distinguishes him from his colleague Dekker. Whereas Dekker voices a moving sympathy which sometimes shades into maudlin sentimentality, Middleton is characteristically tougher-minded in his treatment of loss and fear. It is not, of course, that Dekker is humourless; on the contrary, Middleton no doubt followed the example of *The Wonderful Year* in concluding with what his collaborator refers to as 'a merry epilogue to a dull play, certain tales . . . cut out in sundry fashions'; and indeed Dekker himself contributed some of the tales to *The Meeting of Gallants*. But while the 'merry tales' in *The Wonderful Year* culminate in a description of a poor servant boy who lay 'grovelling and groaning on his face . . . there continued all night, and died miserably for want of succour', Middleton's story-telling Host has an untender, funny and realistic point of view. In the following passage, at the conclusion of *The Meeting of Gallants*, Middleton is able to use the boisterous Host both to convey the horror and the normative Christian response to that horror (a response characteristic of Dekker and many others), and also to critique such responses as inadequate for the purposes of the living:

> Men on horseback riding thither [to the country], strangely stricken in the midst of their journeys, forced either to light off or fall off and die. And for certain and substantial report, many the last year were buried near unto highways in the same order, in their clothes as they were, booted and spurred even as they lighted off. Rolled into ditches, pits and hedges so lamentably, so rudely and unchristianlike, that it would have made a pitiful and remorseful eye bloodshot to see such a ruthful and disordered object, and a true heart bleed outright—but not such a one as mine, gallants, for my heart bleeds nothing but alegar. How commonly we saw here the husband and the wife buried together, a weeping spectacle containing much sorrow, how often were whole households emptied to fill up graves, and how sore the violence of that stroke was that struck ten persons out of one house, being a thing dreadful to apprehend and think upon, with many marvellous and strange accidents. But let not this make you sad, gallants. Sit you merry still. Here, my dainty bullies, I'll put you all in one goblet, and wash all these tales in a cup of sack.

It might be useful, finally, to imagine the state of mind of typical Londoners in February 1604. They had just witnessed appalling events, had heard perhaps too many theodicist rationalizations of the senseless suffering, had seen and been touched by that suffering (for few could have lived through the summer and autumn of 1603 without some momentous loss), and perhaps also felt some guilt for having survived at all when so many others had not. To readers in that state of mind, *The Meeting of Gallants* must have provided an acerbic tonic—a witnessing of the pestilence which neither sentimentalized nor suppressed nor rationalized what had happened; and which nonetheless did not slight the fact that the survivors had cause and need to be 'merry still'.

SEE ALSO

Textual introduction and apparatus: *Companion*, 491

Authorship and date: *Companion*, 349

Other Middleton–Dekker works: *Caesar's Fall*, 328; *Gravesend*, 128; *Magnificent*, 219; *Patient Man*, 280; *Banquet*, 637; *Roaring Girl*, 721; *Gypsy*, 1723

THOMAS MIDDLETON and THOMAS DEKKER

The Meeting of Gallants at an Ordinary; or, The Walks in Paul's

A Dialogue between War, Famine, and the Pestilence, blazing their several Evils

THE GENIUS OF WAR

Famine and Pestilence, cowards of hell,
That strike in peace, when the whole world's unarmed:
Tripping up souls of beggars, limbless wretches,
Hole-stopping prisoners, miserable catchpoles,
Whom one vocation stabs, dare you Furies
Confront the ghost of crimson passing War?
Thou bleak-cheeked wretch, one of my plenteous wounds
Would make thee a good colour.

FAMINE

I defy
Thy blood and thee, 'tis that which I destroy;
I'll starve thee, War, for this.

WAR

Alas, weak Famine;
Why, a tailor is the farthest man thou kill'st
That lives by bread; thou dar'st not touch a farmer,
No, nor his griping son-in-law that weds
His daughter with a dowry of stuffed barns,
Thou run'st away from these, such makes thee fly,
And there thou light'st upon the labourer's maw,
Break'st into poor men's stomachs, and there drivest
The sting of hunger like a dastard.

FAMINE

Bastard.
Peace, War, lest I betray thy monstrous birth:
Thou know'st I can derive thee.

PESTILENCE

And I both.

WAR

And I repugn you both, you hags of realms,
Thou witch of Famine, and drab of plagues:
Thou that mak'st men eat slovenly, and feed
On excrements of beasts, and at one meal
Swallow a hundred pound in very dove's dung.

FAMINE

Therein thou tell'st my glory and rich power.

WAR

And thou.

PESTILENCE

Beware, War, how thou speak'st of me,
I have friends here in England, though some dead,
Some still can show where I was born and bred;
Therefore be wary in pronouncing me.
Many have took my part, whose carcasses
Lie now ten fathom deep; many alive
Can show their scars in my contagious quarrel.
War, I surpass the fury of thy stroke.
Say that an army forty thousand strong
Enter thy crimson lists, and of that number,
Perchance the fourth part falls, marked with red death?
Why, I slay forty thousand in one battle,
Full of blue wounds, whose cold clay bodies look
Like speckled marble.
As for lame persons, and maim'd soldïers,
There I outstrip thee too. How many swarms
Of bruisèd and cracked people did I leave,
Their groins sore pierced with pestilential shot,
Their armpits digged with blains, and ulcerous sores
Lurking like poisoned bullets in their flesh?
Othersome shot in the eye with carbuncles,
Their lids as monstrous as the Saracens'.

WAR

Thou plaguy woman, cease thy infectious brags,
Thou pestilent strumpet, base and common murd'ress,
What men of mark or memory have fell
In thy poor purple battle? Say thou'st slain
Four hundred silkweavers, poor silkworms, vanished
As many tapsters, chamberlains, and ostlers,

Title *Ordinary* an eating-house or tavern where meals were provided at a fixed price
the Walks in Paul's Paul's Walk was the middle aisle, or nave, of the church; from 1550 to 1650 it was used as a meeting-place for all kinds of people.
1 **blazing** proclaiming
6 **catchpoles** a petty officer of justice; esp. a warrant officer who arrests for debt
7 **Whom one vocation stabs** ? who are all summoned by the call of Death
8 **passing** surpassing, excellent
13 **tailor** tailors were said to be effete and cowardly
farthest most powerful
15 **griping** avaricious
16 **stuffed barns** probably referring to the hoarding of foodstuffs in anticipation of a rise in prices—a common and reviled practice. In *Black Book*, 578, Middleton has the Devil 'shift' into 'the habit of a covetous barn-cracking farmer'.
18 **maw** stomach
20 **dastard** despicable coward
22 **derive** to show the derivation or pedigree
23 **repugn** to fight against, to resist or repel
24 **drab** prostitute
32 **pronouncing** proclaiming authoritatively
38 **lists** place of combat
42 **speckled** bearing the marks of moral or physical infection
47 **blains** inflammatory swellings
49 **carbuncles** inflammatory, malignant tumour, caused by inflammation of the skin
50 **Saracens'** belonging to Turks or Muslims; see Breton, *Wonders Worth the Hearing* (1602): 'a Sarazins face . . . his eyes like a Smithes forge'
55 **vanished** caused to disappear
56 **tapsters** those who draw the beer in public houses
chamberlains attendants at an inn
ostlers those who tend to horses at an inn

Darest thou contend with me, thou freckled harlot,
And match thy dirty glories with the splendour
Of kingly tragedies acted by me?
When I have dyed the green stage of the field
Red with the blood of monarchs and rich states,
How many dukes and earls have I drunk up
At one courageous rouse? O summer-devil,
Thou wast but made as ratsbane to kill bawds,
To poison drunkards, vomiting out their souls
Into the bulk of hell, to infect the corps
Of pewter-buttoned sergeants. Such as these
Venom whole realms; and as physicians say,
Poisons with poison must be forced away.

PESTILENCE
War, twit not me with double-damnèd bawds,
Or prostituted harlots, I leave them
For my French nephew, he reigns over these:
I'll show you both how I excel you both.
Who ever read that usurers died in war
Grasping a sword, or in an iron year,
Languished with famine? But by me surprised
Even in their countinghouses, as they sat
Amongst their golden hills: when I have changed
Their gold into dead tokens, with the touch
Of my pale-spotted and infectious rod,
When with a sudden start and ghastly look,
They have left counting coin, to count their flesh,
And sum up their last usury on their breasts,
All their whole wealth, locked in their bony chests.

WAR
Are usurers then the proudest acts thou played'st?
Pack-penny fathers, covetous rooting moles,
That have their gold thrice higher than their souls:
Is this the top of all thy glorious laughters,
To aim them at my princely massacres?
Poor dame of Pestilence, and hag of Famine,
I pity your weak furies.

FAMINE O I could eat you both,
I am so torn with hunger and with rage.
What, is not flinty Famine, gasping dearth,
Worthy to be in rank with dusty War
And little Pestilence? Are not my acts
More stony-pitiless than thine, or thine?
What is't to die stamped full of drunken wounds,
Which makes a man reel quickly to his grave,
Without the sting of torments, or the sense
Of chewing death by piecemeal? Undone and done,
In the fourth part of a poor short minute?
'Tis but a bloody slumber, a red dream,
Not worthy to be named a torturing death.
Nor thine, thou most infectious city dame,
That for thy pride art plagued, bear'st the shape
Of running Pestilence; those which thou strikest
Wear death within few days upon their hearts,
Or else presage amendment. When I reign,
Heaven puts on a brass, to be as hard in blessing
As the earth fruitless in increasing. O
I rack the veins and sinews, lank the lungs,
Freeze all the passages, plough up the maw:
My torment lingers like a suit in law.
What are you both to me? Insolent evils.
Join both your furies, they weigh light to mine.
And what art thou, War, that so want'st thy good?
But like a barber-surgeon that lets blood.

WAR Out, Lenten harlot.

PESTILENCE
Out on you both, and if all matter fails,
I'll show my glory in these following tales.

Finis

The Meeting of Gallants at an Ordinary
Where the Fat Host tells Tales at the upper end of the Table

SIGNOR SHUTTLECOCK What, Signor Jinglespur, the first gallant I met in Paul's, since the one-and-thirty day, or the decease of July, and I may fitly call it the decease, for there deceased above three hundred that day—a shrewd prologue, marry, to the tragedy that followed. And yet I speak somewhat improperly

61 **states** aristocrats
63 **rouse** bout of drinking
summer-devil both an ironic phrase (like 'fair weather friend') and a reference to the fact that plague was most active during summer
64 **bawds** panders
66 **bulk** hold of a ship or main body or nave of a church
corps punning on the corps, 'body', of sergeants and the bodies of the individual officers
68 **Venom** to injure by means of venom
72 **French nephew** the so-called 'French disease', i.e., syphilis
75 **iron** harsh, cruel
79 **tokens** spots on the body indicating disease, esp. the plague
86 **Pack-penny fathers** old misers
88 **laughters** subjects or matters for laughter
97 **stamped** crushed by stamping
100 **chewing** also corroding, wearing down
106 **running** suppurating
109 **brass** a type of hardness, insensibility; also a sepulchral tablet of brass... laid down on the floor or set up against the wall of a church
111 **lank** make shrunken or shrivelled
112 **plough up the maw** tear up the stomach
117 **barber-surgeon** barbers were also practitioners in surgery and dentistry
118 **Lenten** Famine is 'Lenten' because of Lent's association with fasting.
123 **Host** here an innkeeper
upper... Table the best company occupies the upper end, as distinct from the part of the table below the salt-cellar
124 **SHUTTLECOCK** small piece of cork, or similar light material, fitted with a crown or circle of feathers, used in the games of battledore, shuttlecock, and badminton. In *Hubburd*, 376–8, Middleton describes a gallant whose 'head was dressed up in white feathers like a shuttlecock, which agreed... well with his brain, being nothing but cork'.
Jinglespur referring to the fashionable wearing of spurs; in *Hubburd*, 417–18, one gallant 'walked the chamber with such a pestilent jingle, that his spurs over-squeaked the lawyer'
126–7 **deceased above three hundred** 1,396 died of plague during the last week of July 1603 (the Bills of Mortality provide only the weekly death-toll)
127 **shrewd** malignant, ominous

to call it a prologue, because those that died were all out of their parts. What, dare you venture, Signor, at the latter end of a fray now? I mean not at a fray with swords and bucklers, but with sores and carbuncles. I protest, you are a strong-mettled gentleman, because you do not fear the dangerous featherbeds of London, nor to be tossed in a perilous blanket, or to lie in the fellows of those sheets that two dead bodies were wrapped in some three months before. Nay, I can tell you, there is many an honest house in London well stocked before with large linen, where now remains not above two sheets and a half, and so the good man of the house driven to lie in the one sheet for shift, till the pair be washed and dried: for you know, ten wound out of one house must for shame carry five pair of sheets with them, being coffined and put to board-wages—the only knight's policy to save charges in victuals. But soft, Signor, what may he be that stalked by us now in a ruinous suit of apparel, with his page out at elbows? 'Tis a strange sight in Paul's, Signor, methinks, to see a broken page follow a seam-rent master.

SIGNOR JINGLESPUR What, do you wonder at that sight now? 'Tis a limb of the fashion, and as commendable to go ragged after a plague as to have an ensign full of holes and tatters after a battle. And I have seen five hundred of the same rank in apparel, for most of your choice and curious gallants came up in clothes, because they thought it very dangerous to deal with satin this plague-time, being devil enough without the plague. Besides, there hath been a great dearth of tailors, the property of whose deaths were wonderful, for they were took from hell to heaven. All these were motives sufficient to persuade gentlemen, as they loved their lives, to come up in their old suits, and be very respective and careful how they make themselves new ones. And to venture upon a Birchen Lane hose and doublet, were even to shun the villainous jaws of Charybdis and fall into the large swallow of Scylla, the devouring catchpole of the sea: for their bombast is wicked enough in the best and soundest season, and there is as much peril between the wings and the skirts of one of their doublets as in all the liberties of London, take St Tooles Parish, and all the most infected places of England.

Well, I have almost marred their market, for gentlemen especially, those that love to smell sweet, for they are the worst milliners in a kingdom, and their suits bear the mustiest perfume of anything breathing, unless it were an usurer's nightcap again. And indeed that scent's worse than the strong breath of Ajax, where his sevenfold shield is turned to a stool with a hole in it. But see yonder, Signor Stramazon and Signor Kickshaw now of a sudden alighted in Paul's with their dirty boots. Let's encounter them at the fifth pillar; in them you shall find my talk verified, and the fashion truly pictured. What, Signor, both well met upon the old worn brass, the moon hath had above six great bellies since we walked here last together, and lain in as often. Methinks, Signors, this middle of Paul's looks strange and bare, like a long-haired gentleman new polled, washed and shaved. And I may fitly say shaved, for there was never a lusty shaver seen walking here this half year; especially if he loved his life, he would revolt from Duke Humphrey, and rather be a wood-cleaver in the country than a chest-breaker in London. But what gallants march up a pace now, Signors, how are the high ways filled to London?

SIGNOR SHUTTLECOCK Every man's head here is full of the Proclamation, and the honest black gentleman the Term hath

129–30 **out of their parts** both out of their bodily parts (i.e., dead) and breaking the illusion of the stagey roles they assumed in life

131 **bucklers** small round shields

132 **carbuncles** boil-like sores

133 **dangerous featherbeds** On 19 January 1604, the Venetian Ambassador observed that the plague showed signs of increasing because of the carelessness with which the bedding and clothes of plague-victims were being used by the living. In fact, while the cloth itself was harmless, cotton and wool often harboured infective fleas.

134 **tossed in a perilous blanket** The proverbial punishment of being tossed in a blanket is exacerbated here by the peril of infection.

138 **two sheets and a half** i.e., one and a half pairs

142 **board-wages** wages which allowed servants only to keep themselves supplied with food

145 **out at elbows** proverbial

148 **limb of the fashion** a punning phrase, referring to the page's elbow, the page himself (limb=young rascal), and the page and master together as the apogee of fashion

149 **ensign** flag

151 **curious** careful as to the standard of excellence

152 **clothes** i.e., their own clothes

153 **satin** playing on Satan

156 **hell** the tailor's 'hell', into which cuttings were thrown

158 **respective** careful

159–60 **Birchen Lane** running north from Lombard Street to Cornhill, was occupied chiefly by drapers and second-hand clothes dealers

161 **Charybdis . . . Scylla** the monstrous whirlpool and the six-headed monster between which Odysseus must pass; the names and the perils are here reversed (Charydis is the whirlpool that 'swallows' ships)

162 **bombast** cotton wool used as padding for clothes

164 **wings . . . doublets** A doublet was a closely fitting garment for the upper body; 'wings' at the armholes hid the points which tied the sleeves to the garment, and 'skirts' were the flared bottom to which the hose were attached.

165 **liberties** areas in the City not under its authority
St Tooles Parish St Olave's Parish; James Bamford, the minister of the parish, wrote that 2,640 died between 7 May and 13 October

172 **Ajax** playing on 'a jakes', a privy

173 **Stramazon** a vertical downward cut in fencing
Kickshaw from French *quelque chose*; a trifle

177 **the old worn brass** The condition of the brass is explained in *Black Book*, 86–7: 'with their heavy trot and iron stalk | They have worn off the brass in the mid-walk'.

180 **polled** cropped or sheared

183 **Duke Humphrey** Duke Humphrey's Walk was a part of St Paul's Church on the south side of the nave, where there was a monument supposed to be that of Duke Humphrey of Gloucester. From the custom of persons in want of a dinner taking themselves to St Paul's to see if they could meet with someone who would invite them arose the phrase 'to dine with Duke Humphrey', which meant to do without dinner.

184 **wood-cleaver** wood-cutter
chest-breaker a breaker of money-chests, a spendthrift

187–8 **Proclamation** probably that issued 11 January 1604 announcing the king's intention to summon Parliament

188 **Term** the period appointed for the sitting of the courts of law. Hilary Term was held at Westminster from 23

kept a great hall at Westminster again. All the taverns in Kings Street will be emperors—inns and alehouses at least marquises apiece. Now cooks begin to make more coffins than carpenters, and bury more whole meat than sextons; few bells are heard anights besides old John Clapper's, the bellman's. And, gentlemen, 'twas time for you to come, for I know many an honest tradesman that would have come down to you else, and set up their shops in the country, had you not ventured up the sooner; and he that would have braved it, and been a vainglorious silken ass all the last summer, might have made a suit of satin cheaper in the plague-time, than a suit of marry-muff in the term-time. There was not so much velvet stirring as would have been a cover to a little book in octavo, or seamed a lieutenant's buff-doublet. A French-hood would have been more wondered at in London than the Polonians with their long-tailed gaberdines. And which was most lamentable, there was never a gilt spur to be seen all the Strand over, never a feather wagging in all Fleet Street, unless some country fore-horse came by, by mere chance, with a rain-beaten feather in his costrill, the street looking for all the world like a Sunday morning at six of the clock, three hours before service, and the bells ringing all about London as if the Coronation day had been half a year long.

SIGNOR STRAMAZON Trust me, gentlemen, a very sore discourse.

SIGNOR SHUTTLECOCK I could tell you now the miserable state and pitiful case of many tradesmen whose wares lay dead on their hands by the burying of their servants, and how those were held especially very dangerous and perilous trades that had any woollen about them, for the infection being for the most part a Londoner, loved to be lapped warm, and therefore was said to skip into woollen clothes, and lie smothering in a shag-haired rug, or an old-fashioned coverlid. To confirm which, I have heard of some this last summer that would not venture into an upholsterer's shop amongst dangerous rugs and feather-bed-ticks, no, although they had been sure to have been made aldermen when they came out again. Such was their infectious conceit of a harmless necessary coverlid, and would stop their foolish noses when they passed through Watling Street by a rank of woollen drapers. And this makes me call to memory the strange and wonderful dressing of a coach that scudded through London the ninth of August, for I put the day in my table-book because it was worthy the registering.

This fearful, pitiful coach was all hung with rue from the top to the toe of the boot, to keep the leather and the nails from infection. The very nostrils of the coach-horses were stopped with herb-grace, that I pitied the poor beasts being almost windless, and having then more grace in their noses than their master had in all his bosom, and thus they ran through Cornhill just in the middle of the street, with such a violent trample as if the Devil had been coachman.

SIGNOR KICKSHAW A very excellent folly, that the name of the plague should take the wall of a coach, and drive his worship down into the channel.

But see how we have lost ourselves. Paul's is changed into gallants, and those which I saw come up in old taffeta doublets yesterday are slipped into nine yards of satin today.

SIGNOR STRAMAZON And, Signors, we in especial care have sent our pages to inquire out a pair of honest clean tailors, which are hard to be found because there was such a number of botchers the last summer. And I think it one of Hercules's Labours to find two whole tailors about London that hath not been plagued for their stealing, or else for sowing of false seeds, which peep out before their seasons.

SIGNOR JINGLESPUR But what, dare you venture to an ordinary? Hark, the quarter-jacks are up for eleven. I know an honest host about London that hath barrelled up news for gallants, like

January to 12 February; Michaelmas Term, 10 October–28 November, had in part been adjourned to Winchester on account of plague in London.
189 **Westminster** the courts of law
189–90 **Kings Street** main thoroughfare from the Court of St James's to Westminster; narrow and ill-paved
191 **coffins** in cookery, a pie crust
192 **sextons** church-officers responsible for the upkeep of the building, also for bell-ringing and grave-digging
193 **John Clapper's** a generic name for a bellman
199 **marry-muff** a cheap fabric
201 **octavo** one of the smaller formats in printing, each page being one eighth of a sheet
202 **buff-doublet** a close-fitting leather garment with detachable sleeves
French-hood a head covering for women, pleated, of velvet, tissue, or other silk
203 **Polonians** the Polish ambassador and his retinue were in London in December 1603
203–4 **gaberdines** long coats, worn loose or girdled, with longsleeves
205 **Strand** running west from Temple Bar to Charing Cross; fashionable residential area
206 **Fleet Street** running west from the bottom of Ludgate Hill to Temple Bar; the Inns of Court and houses of many nobles along the Strand made Fleet Street a fashionable suburb
207 **costrill** head
209 **bells ringing** the bells rang for those dead from plague
210 **Coronation day** the coronation of King James took place 25 July 1603
214–15 **wares . . . servants** i.e., the wares were thought to be infectious and so were unsaleable
219 **shag-haired** shaggy, having a long, rough nap
222–3 **feather-bed-ticks** cases or covers containing feathers or the like, forming mattresses or pillows
225 **conceit** idea
226 **Watling Street** ran east from the south-east corner of St Paul's Churchyard; the principal inhabitants were drapers, retailers of woollen cloths.
230 **table-book** pocket notebook
231 **rue** In *The Herbal* (1597), John Gerard writes, 'The leaves of rue eaten with the kernels of walnuts or figs stamped together and made into a mass or paste, is good against all evil airs, the pestilence or plague'.
232 **boot** uncovered space on or by the steps on each side
234 **herb-grace** another name for rue
236 **Cornhill** running east from the end of the Poultry past the Royal Exchange to Leadenhall Street
240–1 **take . . . channel** City streets, usually unpaved, slanted down from the walls of the houses to a channel running down the centre; the wall-side was cleaner and so to be preferred, but here 'his worship' rides in the muddy channel because of his fear of the infection.
242–3 **Paul's . . . gallants** i.e., Paul's is full of gallants
247 **botchers** tailors who do repairs; unskilful workmen
250 **sowing of false seeds** playing on sow/sew and seed/seam
253 **quarter-jacks** mechanical figures of men which strike the quarter-hours on a bell outside a clock

pickled oysters; marry, your ordinary will cost you two shillings, but the tales that lie in brine will be worth sixpence of the money. For you know 'tis great charges to keep tales long, and therefore he must be somewhat considered for the laying out of his language. For blind Gue, you know, has sixpence at the least for groping in the dark.

SIGNOR STRAMAZON Yea, but Signor Jinglespur, you see we are altogether unfurnished for an ordinary till the tailor cut us out and new mould us. And to rank amongst gallants in old apparel, why their very apish pages would break jests upon our elbows, and domineer over our worn doublets most tyrannically.

SIGNOR JINGLESPUR Puh, Signor Stramazon, you turn the bias the wrong way, you doubt where there is no doubt. I will conduct you to an ordinary where you shall eat private amongst Essex gentlemen of your fashioned rank in apparel, who as yet wait for fresh clothes, as you for new tailors, and account it more commendable to come up in seam-rent suits and whole bodies, than to have infectious torn bodies and sound suits.

SIGNOR KICKSHAW If it be so, Signor (hark! a quarter strikes) we are for you. We will follow you, for I love to hear tales when a merry corpulent host bandies them out of his flop-mouth. But how far must we march now like tattered soldiers, after a fray, to their nuncheons?

SIGNOR SHUTTLECOCK Why, if you throw your eyes but a little before you, you may see the sign and token that beckons his guest to him. Do you hear the clapper of his tongue now?

SIGNOR STRAMAZON 'Sfoot, the mad bulchin squeaks shriller than the saunce bell at Westminster.

SIGNOR SHUTTLECOCK Nay, now you shall hear him ring lustily at our entrance. Stop your ears if you love them, for one of his words will run about your brains louder than the drum at the Bear Garden.

Entering into the Ordinary

HOST What, gallants, are you come, are you come? Welcome, gentlemen, I have news enough for you all, welcome again, and again: I am so fat and pursy, I cannot speak loud enough, but I am sure you hear me, or you shall hear me. Welcome, welcome, gentlemen, I have tales and quails for you. Seat yourselves, gallants. (*Enter boys and beards with dishes and platters.*) I will be with you again in a trice ere you look for me.

SIGNOR SHUTTLECOCK Now, Signors, how like you mine host? Did I not tell you he was a mad, round knave, and a merry one, too? And if you chance to talk of fat Sir John Oldcastle, he will tell you he was his great-grandfather, and not much unlike him in paunch, if you mark him well by all descriptions. And see where he appears again; he told you he would not be long from you. Let his humour have scope enough, I pray, and there is no doubt but his tales will make us laugh ere we be out of our porridge. How now, mine Host?

HOST O my gallant of gallants, my top and top gallant, how many horses hast thou killed in the country with the hunting of harlotries? Go to, was I with you, you mad wags? And I have been a merry knave this six-and-forty years, my bullies, my boys.

SIGNOR KICKSHAW Yea, but my honest-larded Host, where be these tales now?

HOST I have them at my tongue's end, my gallant bullies of five-and-twenty, my dainty liberal landlords, I have them for you. You shall never take me unprovided for, gentlemen, I keep them like anchovies to relish your drink well. Stop your mouths, gallants, and I will stuff your ears, I warrant you, and first I begin with a tipsy vintner in London.

Of a Vintner in London, dying in a humour

This discourse that follows, gentlemen-gallants, is of a light-headed vintner who, scorning to be only drunk in his own cellar, would get up betimes in the morning to be down of his nose thrice before evening. He was a man of all taverns, and excellent musician at the sackbut, and your only dancer of the canaries. This strange wine-sucker had a humour this time of infection to feign himself sick, and indeed he had swallowed down many tavern-tokens and was infected much with the plague of drunkenness. But howsoever, sick he would be, for the humour had possessed him, when to the comforting of his poor heart, he poured down eleven shillings in Rose of Solace, more than would have cheered all the sick persons in the pest-house. And yet for all that he felt himself ill at his stomach

259 **blind Gue** a contemporary clown
266–7 **bias the wrong way** referring to the game of bowls; bowls either contained an off-centre lead weight or were shaped so that they ran obliquely
272 **bodies** punning on 'bodice'
275 **flop-mouth** variant of flap-mouth: a mouth with broad, hanging lips
276 **tattered** punning on 'tottered', unsteady
277 **nuncheons** light refreshment taken between meals; a lunch
281 **'Sfoot** God's foot
bulchin bull-calf
282 **saunce bell** sanctus bell, rung at the Sanctus at Mass; in post-Reformation times often used to summon the people to church
285–6 **drum ... Garden** The Bear Garden, on the Bankside, Southwark (next to the Globe) was the primary arena for bear-baiting.
290 **pursy** short-winded, also fat
293 **beards** men
297 **Sir John Oldcastle** an allusion to Shakespeare's Falstaff, originally named Oldcastle. Oldcastle's descendants, the Cobham family, forced the change of name by 1598, but 'Oldcastle' evidently persisted in the public mind.
302–3 **ere ... porridge** before we have finished our soup
305–6 **hunting of harlotries** pursuing harlots or, more generally, jests and scurrility
312 **liberal** generous, high-born
317 **humour** eccentric or unusual temperament, a sense popularized by Ben Jonson's 'humour' comedies
320 **betimes** early
320–1 **down of his nose** the phrase is difficult, but context makes clear that it means 'drunk'
322 **sackbut** both a musical instrument like a trumpet and also a butt of sack (i.e., a cask of wine)
323 **canaries** both a lively dance and also a light sweet wine from the Canary Islands
324–5 **swallowed ... tavern-tokens** tavern-tokens were given in change by a tavern-keeper, and could be used to buy drinks; hence, the phrase means to get drunk
328 **Rose of Solace** *rosa solis* ('rose of the sun'), a cordial made from or flavoured with the plant sundew and also containing spirits such as brandy
329–30 **pest-house** The London pest-house was in the parish of St Giles-without-Cripplegate. Infected persons were also housed in private buildings appropriated for the purpose or, more usually, shut in their own dwellings along with the healthy.

afterwards, wherefore his request was, reporting himself very feeble, to have two men hired with sixpence apiece to transport him over the way to his friend's house. But when he saw he was deluded and had nobody to carry him, he flung his gown about him very desperately, took his own legs, and away he went with himself as courageously as the best stalker in Europe. Where being alighted not long after, he rounded one in the ear in private, and bade that the great bell should be tolled for him, the great bell of all, and with all possible speed that might be. That done, he gagged open the windows, and when the bell was tolling, cried, 'Louder yet; I hear thee not, Master Bell.' Then, strutting up and down the chamber, spake to the audience in this wise:

'Is't possible a man should walk in such perfect memory and have the bell toll for him? Sure I never heard of any that did the like before me.'

Thus, by tolling of the great bell, all the parish rang of him, diverse opinions went of him, and not without cause or matter to work upon. In conclusion, within few days after, he was found to be the man indeed whose part he did but play before. His pulses were angry with him, and began to beat him, all his pores fell out with him, the bell tolled for him in sadness, rung out in gladness, and there was the end of his drunken madness. Such a ridiculous humour of dying was never heard of before, and I hope never shall be again, now he is out of England.

SIGNOR STRAMAZON This was a strange fellow, mine Host, and worthy Stow's *Chronicle*.

HOST Nay, gallants, I'll fit you, and now I will serve in another as good as vinegar and pepper to your roast beef.

SIGNOR KICKSHAW Let's have it; let's taste on it, mine Host, my noble fat actor.

How a young fellow was even bespoke and jested to death by harlots

There was a company of intolerable light women assembled together, who all the time of infection lived upon citizens' servants—young novices that made their masters' bags die of the plague at home, whilst they took sanctuary in the country. Mistake me not, I mean not the best rank of servants, but underlings and boggish sots such as have not wit to distinguish companies, and avoid the temptation of harlots, which make men more miserable than Derrick. These light-heeled wagtails, who were armed (as they term it) against all weathers of plague and pestilence, carrying always a French supersedeas about them for the sickness, were determined, being half tipsy and as light now in their heads as anywhere else, to execute a jest upon a young, unfruitful fellow which should have had the banns of matrimony asked between him and a woman of their religion, which would have proved bane indeed, and worse than ratsbane—to have been coupled with a harlot. But note the event of a bespeaking jest: these women gave it out that he was dead, sent to the sexton of the church in all haste to have the bell rung out for him, which was suddenly heard, and many coming to enquire of the sexton, his name was spread over all the parish (he little dreaming of that dead report being as then in perfect health and memory). On the morrow, as the custom is, the searchers came to the house where he lay to discharge their office, asking for the dead body and in what room it lay. Who, hearing himself named, in such a cold shape almost struck dead indeed with their words, replied, with a hasty countenance (for he could play a ghost well), that he was the man. At which, the searchers started, and thought he had been new risen from under the table, when, vomiting out some two or three deep-fetched oaths, he asked what villain it was which made that jest of him. But whether the conceit struck cold to his heart or whether the strumpets were witches, I know not (the next degree to a harlot is a bawd or a witch), but this youngster danced the shaking of one sheet within few days after, and then the searchers lost not their labours, and therefore I conclude thus:

'That Fate lights sudden that's bespoke before;
A harlot's tongue is worse than a plague-sore.'

[SIGNOR JINGLESPUR] Well rhymed, my little round and thick Host, have you any more of these in your fat budget?

HOST I have them, my gallant bullies, and here comes one fitly for sauce to your capon.

Of one that fell drunk off from his horse, taken for a Londoner, dead

In a certain country town not far off, there was a boon companion lighted amongst good fellows, as they call good fellows nowadays, which are those that can drink best, for your excellent drunkard is your notable gallant, and he that can pass away clear without paying the host in the chimney corner, he

334 **nobody to carry him** No one was willing to touch him because he was thought to be sick with plague.
336 **stalker** robber; also an actor, the sense of Middleton's use in *Black Book*, 415–18: 'The spindle-shank spiders . . . went stalking over his head as if they had been conning of *Tamburlaine*'
337 **rounded** whispered
357 **Stow's *Chronicle*** John Stow's *Chronicles of England*, first published in 1580
358 **fit** provide what is fit
362 **bespoke** bespeak: to speak (a person) into some state
364 **light** unchaste
369 **boggish** inclined to bluster or brag
369–70 **distinguish companies** distinguish between good and bad company
371 **Derrick** the hangman at Tyburn, *c.*1600
wagtails harlots
373 **supersedeas** writ commanding the stay of legal proceedings; used figuratively for 'Something which stops, stays, or checks'. For the idea that syphilis protects one from plague, see *Black Book*, 366–9: 'Sergeant Carbuncle, one of the plague's chief officers, dares not venture within three yards of an harlot because Monsieur Dry-bone the Frenchman is a ledger before him.'
377–8 **woman of their religion** i.e., a prostitute
380 **event** outcome
386 **searchers** officers responsible for examining corpses in order to determine if the person had died of plague
390 **hasty** quick-tempered
397 **danced . . . sheet** playing on the popular ballad 'Can you dance the shaking of the sheets?'
403 **budget** wallet
412 **host . . . chimney corner** The joke is perhaps that the chimney corner was the place of the old and infirm—a depiction of an innkeeper quite unlike the high-spirited Host.

is the king of cans and the emperor of alehouses. This fellow, tying his horse by the bridle upon the red lattice of the window, could not bridle himself so well, but afterward proved more beast than his horse, being so overwhelmed with whole cans, hoops, and such drunken devices that his English crown weighed lighter by ten grains at his coming forth than at his entering in. And it was easier now for his horse to get up atop of Paul's than he to get up upon his horse. The stirrup played mock holiday with him and made a fool of his foot. At last, with much ado, he fell flounce into the saddle and away he scudded out at town's end, where he thought every tree he saw had been rising up to stop him. So strangely are the senses of drunkards tossed and transported that at the very instant they think the world's drowned again; so this staggering monster imagined he was riding upon a sea-mare. But before he was ten gallops from the town-side, his brain played him a jade's trick and kicked him over. Down he fell. When the horse, soberer than the master, stood still and wondered at him for a beast, but durst not say so much. By and by, passengers passing to and fro, beholding his lamentable downfall, called out to one another to view that pitiful spectacle. People flocked about him more and more, but none durst venture within two poles' length, nor some within the length of Paul's. Everyone gave up his verdict, and all concluding in one that he was some coward Londoner who thought to fly from the sickness, which, as it seemed, made after him amain and struck him beside his horse. Thus all agreed in one tale, some bemoaning the death of the man, othersome wishing that all curmudgeons, penny-fathers, and fox-furred usurers were served of the same sauce, who taking their flight out of London, left poor silkweavers, tapsters, and waterbearers to fight it out against sore enemies. In a word, all the town was in an uproar. The constable standing aloof off, stopping his nose like a gentleman-usher, durst not come within two stones' cast by no means—no, if he might presently have been made constable in the hundred. Every townsman at his wise nonplus, nothing but looking and wondering, yet some wiser than some, and those I think were the watchmen, told them flatly and plainly that the body must be removed in any case, and that extempore. It would infect all the air round about else. These whoresons seemed to have some wit yet, and their politic counsel was took and embraced amongst them, but all the cunning was how to remove him without taking the wind of him. Whereupon, two or three weather-wise stinkards plucked up handfuls of grass and tossed them into the air, and then whooping and hollowing, told them the wind blew sweetly for the purpose, for it stood full on his back-part. Then all agreed to remove him with certain long instruments, sending home for hooks and strong ropes, as if they had been pulling down a house of fire. But this was rather a tilt-boat cast away and all the people drowned within. To conclude, these long devices were brought to remove him without a writ; when by mere chance passed by one of the wisest of the town next the constable, for so it appeared afterwards by the hotness of his device, who being certified of the story and what they went about to do, brake into these words openly:

'Why, my good fellows, friends and honest neighbours, trow you what you venture upon, will you needs draw the plague to you, by hook or by crook? You will say perhaps your poles are long enough. Why, you never heard or read that long devices take soonest infection, and that there is no vilder thing in the world than the smell of a rope to bring a man to his end, that you all know.

'Wherefore, to avoid all further inconveniences, dangerous and infectious, hearken to my exploit. If you drag him along the fields, our hounds may take the scent of him, a very dangerous matter. If you bury him in the fields, a hundred to one but the ground will be rotten this winter. Wherefore, your only way must be to let him lie as he doth, without moving, and every good fellow to bring his armful of straw, heap it upon him and round about him, and so in conclusion burn out the infection as he lies.'

Every man threw up his old cap at this, straw was brought and thrown upon him by armfuls. All this while, the drowned fellow lay still without moving, dreaming of full cans, tapsters, and beer barrels, when presently they put fire to the straw, which kept such a bragging and a cracking that up started the drunkard like a thing made of fireworks, the flame playing with his nose, and his beard looking like flaming Apollo's, as our

413 **cans** drinking-vessels
414 **red lattice** a window of red lattice-work; a commonplace feature of alehouses
417 **hoops** the bands on a drinking-pot; hence the liquor between two bands
crown both 'coin' and 'head'; the wordplay continues in the following line in the allusion to the illegal clipping of precious metal coins
419–20 **horse... Paul's** Morocco, the famous stunt-horse, climbed the stairs to the top of the tower in 1601
427 **sea-mare** a nonce word (not in *OED*)
428 **jade's trick** jade: a horse of inferior breed
438 **amain** with full force
440 **curmudgeons** misers
penny-fathers misers
441 **fox-furred usurers** usurers are often depicted wearing fur
445 **gentleman-usher** gentleman acting as usher to a person of superior rank
447 **constable in the hundred** 'high constable', an officer of a large administrative district or *hundred*, a subdivision of a county or shire, having its own court
448 **at his wise nonplus** wise = manner, and nonplus = a state in which no more can be said or done; hence, the phrase means 'perplexed'
455 **taking the wind** a sailing and hunting term meaning to be to the windward of something
457 **hollowing** shouting
461 **pulling... fire** Appropriate to the context, the practice of pulling down houses to stop the spread of the fire was used in the suburbs or villages around London rather than in London itself, where it was impractical owing to both the stone construction and proximity of dwellings to each other.
462 **tilt-boat** a large rowing boat having a tilt or awning, formerly used on the Thames, especially as a passenger boat between London and Gravesend
477 **exploit** enterprise
491 **flaming** (a stock epithet for Apollo in Renaissance poetry)

poets please to term it, who burst into these reeling words when he spied the fire hizzing about his pate:

'What, is the top of Paul's on fire again? Or is there a fire in the Paul-Head? Why then, drawers, quench me with double beer.'

The folks in the town all in amaze, some running this way, some that way, knew him at last by his staggering tongue, for he was no far dweller, though they imagined he had dwelt at London. So, stopping his horse, which ran away from the fiery planet his master as though the Devil had backed him, everyone laughed at the jest, closed it up in an alehouse, where before evening the most part of them were all as drunk as himself.

And now I return to more pleasant arguments, gentlemen-gallants, to make you laugh ere you be quite out of your capon. This that I discourse of now is a pretty, merry accident that happened about Shoreditch, although the intent was sad and tragical, yet the event was mirthful and pleasant. The goodman (or rather as I may fitlier term him, the badman of a house), being sorely pestered with the death of servants, and to avoid all suspicion of the pestilence from his house above all others, did very craftily and subtly compound with the masters of the pest-cart to fetch away by night as they passed by all that should chance to die in his house, having three or four servants down at once, and told them that he knew one of them would be ready for them by that time the cart came by. And to clear his house of all suspicion, the dead body should be laid upon a stall, some five or six houses off, where there they should entertain him and take him in amongst his dead companions. To conclude, night drew onward and the servant concluded his life, and according to their appointment was installed to be made knight of the pest-cart. But here comes in the excellent jest, gentlemen-gallants of five-and-twenty. About the dark and pitiful season of the night, a shipwreck drunkard (or one drunk at the sign of The Ship), new cast from the shore of an alehouse and his brains sore beaten with the cruel tempests of ale and beer, fell flounce upon a low stall hard by the house. There being little difference in the carcass, for the other was dead, and he was dead-drunk (the worse death of the twain), there taking up his drunken lodging, and the pest-cart coming by, they made no more ado, but taking him for the dead body, placed him amongst his companions, and away they hurried with him to the pest-house. But there is an old proverb, and now confirmed true—a drunken man never takes harm. To the approbation of which, for all his lying with infectious bedfellows, the next morning a little before he should be buried, he stretched and yawned as wholesomely as the best tinker in all Banbury, and returned to his old vomit again, and was drunk in Shoreditch before evening.

SIGNOR JINGLESPUR This was a pretty comedy of errors, my round Host.

HOST O my bullies, there was many such a part played upon the stage both of the city and the suburbs.

Moreover, my gallants, some did noble exploits whose names I shame to publish, in hiring porters and base vassals to carry their servants out in sacks to Whitechapel and such out-places, to poor men's houses that work to them, and therefore durst do no otherwise but receive them, though to their utter ruins, and detestable noisomeness, fearing to displease them for their revenge afterwards, as in putting their work from them to others for their utter undoing. How many such pranks think you have been played in the same fashion only to entertain customers, to keep their shops open, and the foreheads of their doors from 'Lord have mercy upon us'? Many I could set down here and publish them to the world, together with all their strange shifts and uncharitable devices.

Whereof one especially notable and politic may even lead you to the rest and drive you into imagination of many the like. For one to bury four or five persons out of his house, and yet neither the sexton of the same parish nor any else of his neighbours in the street where he dwells in to have intelligence of it (but all things be they never so lurking, break forth at the last). This being the cunning and close practice: politicly to indent with the sexton of some other church (as dwelling in one parish) to see the sexton of another by a pretty piece of silver, to bury all that die in the same house in his churchyard, which void all suspicion of the plague from his shop, which may be at the least some six or seven parish churches off. Or at another to practise the like—nothing but compounding with a ravenous sexton that lives upon dead carcasses. For no trades were so much in use as coffin-makers and sextons; they were the lawyers the last vacation and had their bountiful fees of their grave clients. Wherefore, they prayed as the country folks at Hertford did (if report be no liar) very impiously and

493 **hizzing** hissing or whizzing
pate head
494 **Paul's on fire** Paul's steeple was destroyed by fire in 1561 and was never rebuilt; the church perished in the Great Fire of 1666.
495 **Paul-Head** tavern near Paul's Chain, a lane running south from Paul's Churchyard
double strong
498 **staggering** stammering
506 **ere... capon** before you have finished the main course
508 **Shoreditch** parish in north-east London, lying south of Old Street, between City Road and Bethnal Green; a haunt of whores and bad characters generally
522–3 **installed... pest-cart** a jocular version of formal phrases such as 'to be installed Knight of the Garter', with a glance at the *stall* upon which the servant has been laid
539 **tinker** craftsman who 'mend[ed] pots, kettles, and other household utensils'; held in low repute
Banbury market-town in Oxfordshire. Banbury tinkers had a proverbially bad reputation.
returned... vomit (proverbial)
541 **comedy of errors** probably an allusion to Shakespeare's play
547 **Whitechapel** parish in London, east of Aldgate
554–5 **foreheads of their doors** Authorities marked infected dwellings with a red cross and fastened a paper with the inscription 'Lord have mercy upon us' on the lintel; infected houses were quarantined for twenty-eight days.
557 **shifts** stratagems
563 **lurking** secretive
564 **close** covert
565 **indent** enter into an engagement
565–7 **sexton... churchyard** The practice is close indeed: probably the citizen contracts with one sexton (i.e., gravedigger), not of the citizen's own church, to arrange burial with still another sexton further away.
573 **vacation** period during which law courts are suspended

barbarously, that the sickness might last till the last Christmas. And this was their uncharitable meanings and the unchristian effect of their wishes: that they might have the Term kept at Hertford, and the sextons their term still here in London. But Winchester made a goose of Hertford and ended the strife. Thus, like monsters of nature, they wished in their barbarous hearts that their desires might take such effects, and for the greedy lucre of a few private and mean persons to suck up the life of thousands.

Many other marvellous events happened, both in the city and elsewhere. As, for example, in Dead Man's Place at St Mary Overies, a man-servant being buried at seven of the clock in the morning, and the grave standing open for more dead commodities, at four of the clock in the same evening, he was got up alive again by strange miracle—which to be true and certain, hundreds of people can testify that saw him act like a country ghost in his white 'peckled sheet. And it was not a thing unknown on the other side that the countries were stricken, and that very grievously, many dying there. Many going thither likewise fell down suddenly and died. Men on horseback riding thither, strangely stricken in the midst of their journeys, forced either to light off or fall off and die. And for certain and substantial report, many the last year were buried near unto highways in the same order, in their clothes as they were, booted and spurred even as they lighted off. Rolled into ditches, pits and hedges so lamentably, so rudely and unchristianlike, that it would have made a pitiful and remorseful eye bloodshot to see such a ruthful and disordered object, and a true heart bleed outright—but not such a one as mine, gallants, for my heart bleeds nothing but alicant. How commonly we saw here the husband and the wife buried together, a weeping spectacle containing much sorrow, how often were whole households emptied to fill up graves, and how sore the violence of that stroke was that struck ten persons out of one house, being a thing dreadful to apprehend and think upon, with many marvellous and strange accidents. But let not this make you sad, gallants. Sit you merry still. Here, my dainty bullies, I'll put you all in one goblet, and wash all these tales in a cup of sack.

Sit you merry still, gentlemen-gallants, your dish of tales is your best cheer, and to please you, my noble bullies, I would do that I did not this thirty years—caper, caper, my gallant boys, although I crack my shins and my guts sink a handful lower. I'll do't, my lusty lads, I'll do't.

With that, the Host gave a lazy caper and broke his shins for joy, the reckoning was appeased, the room discharged, and so I leave them in Paul's where I found them.

Finis

579 **Hertford** county town of Hertsfordshire, nineteen miles north of London. The inhabitants of Hertford are said to have prayed for the continuation of plague in London so that the law term, with its attendant business, would be moved to their town as it had been in 1592; however, part of Michaelmas Term 1603 was held in Winchester rather than Hertford.

580 **Winchester made a goose** a quibble: 'Winchester goose' is proverbial for 'a venereal disorder; a prostitute' (Tilley G366)

586–92 **As . . . sheet** The same story appears in Thomas Dekker, *The Wonderful Year* (1603).

586–7 **Dead . . . Overies** an alley led from Deadman's Place to the Globe Playhouse near by; St Mary Overies was an ancient church on the west side of the Borough High Street, Southwark, just over London Bridge. It is now known as Southwark Cathedral.

592 **'peckled** speckled, spotted

605 **alicant** wine made at Alicante in Spain

614–22 **Sit . . . them** In the 1604 edition, this passage, although clearly intended as the conclusion, precedes the Host's tale of the 'merry accident . . . about Shoreditch' (506–8). In its position in the present edition, the passage constitutes an ending similar to that of *Black Book* (822–31). See Textual Notes.

617 **crack** ? bruise (on the furniture?), or induce cramps

620 **reckoning was appeased** bill was settled

PLATO'S CAP

Edited by Paul Yachnin

Plato's Cap is one of the most interesting mock-almanacs, or mock-prognostications, of the early seventeenth century. The subgenre of the mock-almanac, together with dramatic satires of the readers and authors of almanacs, represents a significant critique of popular superstition in the early modern period. In addition to *Plato's Cap*, the play *No Wit/Help like a Woman's* and the pamphlet *The Owl's Almanac* are examples of the two satirical forms. While burlesque almanacs developed a sceptical response to questionable beliefs, however, they did not come into being because certain forward-looking writers felt impelled to speak out against the 'science' of prognostication. There was a literature critical of the popularity of astrology and almanacs, but it argued on behalf of an austere faith that refused to spy on God's providence. In contrast with these Christian polemical texts, the mock-almanac, as well as the almanac itself, was a creation of the book-trade. Almanacs were periodical publications which owed their existence to market-place demand. For this reason, the re-use of certain elements was normal practice. The same predictions, the same practical information, the same engravings, and the same words of wisdom appeared again and again from one year to the next. Mock-almanacs also recirculated certain standard material. An important difference between the two forms was that whereas almanacs were marketed on the strength of the reputations of their authors, burlesque almanacs were anonymous, and for this reason were a commodity of the book-trade even more than the almanacs themselves. As a creation of the market in popular literature, the subgenre of the almanac parody was an authorless adjunct to the huge industry in legitimate almanacs.

Almanacs and mock-almanacs were texts in which high and low culture met. By 1600, almanacs were the most popular and populist of English books, even though, with their use of Latin and their conjuring with exotic authorities, they held out to their readers the attractions of élite culture and exotic knowledge. Burlesque almanacs attacked these pretensions, satirizing what 'Adam Fouleweather' calls 'the authentical censures of Albumazar and Ptolomey', and affirming the value of popular, native culture, everyday forms of language and normal ways of understanding the world. That is the underlying point of satirical prognostications which 'predict' what is already the normal state of affairs. 'But when the sun enters into Virgo', Adam Eavesdropper says, 'take heed, maids, that you have no daughters. I fear me there will be but a few virgins in the Whitefriars for I find by strange art that in suchlike places this year maidenheads will be cheaper than mackerels.'

Anonymity, the recirculation of conventional material, and the hybridization of high and low culture are central to an historical understanding of any mock-almanac, but an account of *Plato's Cap* needs also to consider Middleton's particular handling of the conventions of the form. While he did not violate the rules of the subgenre, he did play innovatively within its formal boundaries in order to create something original and expressive of his literary ambitions. The question that faced Middleton was twofold: how to make his mark in a form that prescribed anonymity? how to write in an original fashion when mock-almanacs depended on the repetition of material? To a large degree, he overcame the limitations of the form and made an original contribution to the subgenre. Indeed the issues are not all that different from those that concern historians of the Elizabethan and Jacobean drama, that much more extensive body of work which also was largely authorless, commercialized, conventional, and culturally hybrid. How did writers of Middleton's time make a name for themselves in commodified literary forms which enforced the alienation of the makers from the texts that they made?

A gentleman and for several years a student at Oxford, Middleton dedicated two early publications to wealthy aristocratics in an attempt to win patronage and perhaps high-level notice. Both these texts bear his name. They represent a bid to enter a patronage system that was distinct, at least notionally, from the business of writing for the commercial theatre and the popular press. But with *Plato's Cap*, Middleton descended to a lower level in the literary factory. The primary fact about the pamphlet is anonymity. When, in 1604, readers bought *Plato's Cap* from Jeffrey Chorlton's stall at the North door of St. Paul's, they were not looking for the work of a particular author. The title-page that no doubt was pinned up near the stall advertised 'PLATOES Cap. | Cast at this Yeare 1604, | *being Leape-yeere*', and identified the publisher and the place and date of publication. It made no mention of the author. Currency, social and astrological satire, and low price, rather than the mystique of Middletonian authorship, were the attractions of the pamphlet. This is not to suggest that Middleton was actually disallowed from naming himself on the title-page. It was rather that his name was not important. Nor is it likely that he was distraught at not being named or by not having his name in demand. He might have suffered pangs concerning his general situation, since he was, while not wealthy, yet nevertheless a gentleman who was ambitious in letters and life. More important than analysing his psychology, however, is understanding how his talent and intelligence, and his ambition, altered and enriched the form of the burlesque almanac.

While original in many ways, *Plato's Cap* did recirculate conventional material. Phrases, sentences, and paragraphs were lifted from a 1591 mock-prognostication, *The Fearful and Lamentable Effects of Two Dangerous Comets*, by 'Simon Smell-knave'. The Oxford English Dictionary tells us that the word 'plagiarism' was not in use before 1621, but there is no question that people knew what the practice was. In *The Ant and the Nightingale*, Middleton castigates those who, he claims, have pirated Thomas Nashe's work: 'Thy name they bury, having buried thee; | Drones eat thy honey—thou wert the true bee'. This is a complicated matter, because the use of other writers' work was a legitimate literary practice in certain circumstances, such as Ben Jonson's translation of Tacitus in Cordus's speech on freedom of expression in *Sejanus* (1605). Legitimate imitation required clear evidence of creative engagement with the imitated work. That is not the case in *Plato's Cap*, and Middleton's workmanlike use of the earlier pamphlet suggests the degree to which he was re-using rather than inventing the honey of literary imagination.

To be fair to *Plato's Cap*, however, it needs to be said again that borrowing was standard practice, and it needs to be pointed out that Middleton recirculated less material than did his fellow almanac-satirists. His borrowings are clustered in the concluding section, where they extend the length and broaden the social ambit of the pamphlet. Also, he was not the only writer to imitate Simon Smell-knave's *Fearful and Lamentable Effects*. Anthony Nixon's *The Black Year* (1606), as F. P. Wilson has documented, is exhaustively copied from Simon and several other texts. Indeed, not even *Fearful and Lamentable Effects* is wholly original. Simon himself borrowed from Adam Fouleweather's *A Wonderful... Astrological Prognostication* (1591), although not so extensively as the others borrowed from him. Given the highly commercial conditions of production, what is most surprising is that so much of *Plato's Cap* is original.

One strength of Middleton's pamphlet is its wit. The usual humour of mock-almanacs depends on prophecies of the obvious: 'Mars being placed near unto the sun showeth that there shall be a great death among people', predicts *A Wonderful... Astrological Prognostication*, 'old women that can live no longer shall die of age'. *Plato's Cap* has its share of this: 'The bakers, woodmongers, butchers, and brewers shall fall to a mighty conspiracy this year, so that no man shall have bread, fire, flesh, or drink without credit or ready money.' While these jokes certainly embody a politics of plainness, much of the humour in *Plato's Cap* is more complex and funnier: 'Many men shall be so venturously disposed that they shall go into brothel-houses and yet come out again as honestly as when they went first in.' Much of it develops Nashe's exuberant and socially engaged style. According to Middleton's Adam Eavesdropper, the sun's entry into Taurus foretells 'the deposing of Lent and the overthrow of salt salmon... and... the restoring again of heroic-valiant beef, that ancient and surly courtier that never appears without a mess of mustard, his gentleman-usher bareheaded before him'. The passing of the Lenten season becomes a political contest between the ethos of old-fashioned court culture and the survivalist economy of the country: 'Red herring may go hang himself then for a twelvemonth upon the rusty beam of some farmer's chimney, until the hungry ploughboys cut him down and quarter him.'

The value of *Plato's Cap* depends upon more than its superior sense of humour. While, like other mock-almanacs, it is written in prose and organized according to the astrological calendar, it is also unified poetically by Middleton's interweaving of theme and imagery. The pamphlet thematizes the hybridization of high and low culture that was central to almanacs and mock-almanacs. It does so through a pattern of imagery focused on 'the cap', a pattern that leads from the obtrusively hybrid title through to the mockery of 'foisting John', the well-known hat-maker whose shop in Paul's Churchyard was not far from Chorlton's bookstall. The title, *Plato's Cap*, yoked together classical with common, élite culture with the culture of the market-place. Plato was the quintessential exotic authority and high-culture figure whereas Adam Eavesdropper's 'button-cap' was old-fashioned and native. In 1593, Henry Chettle remembered Richard Tarlton by 'his suit of russet, his buttoned cap', and mourned his passing as the end of true mirth. The pamphlet develops an opposition between caps and hats - Adam 'put[s] off Plato's Cap' to the reader but 'the true Frenchman seldom doffs his hat'; 'old-fashioned honest cap[s]' are pitted against 'new-fashioned prodigal hat[s]'. This fashion contest between traditional, English, and popular caps and new-fangled, foreign, and courtly hats connects with Englishwomen who wear the fashion of the French bodice and who are 'a scorn and by-jest to all riotous nations'. Presiding over these images of cultural contest is the figure of 'Plato's cap' itself with its yoking of élite and common, foreign and native; it announces the pamphlet's own hybridization and playfully reflects on the commercial nature of mock-almanacs in general. They embody a traditional view of the world, but they do so in the latest fashion.

Plato's Cap also foregrounds authorship and issues of interpretation in ways that are unlike the straightforward style of address typical of mock-almanacs.

The title is a figure of emulation and therefore expressive of Middleton's literary ambition. It derives from a pamphlet by Middleton's friend and collaborator Thomas Dekker. In *The Wonderful Year* (1603), Dekker wrote: 'Plato's *mirabilis annus* (whether it be past already, or to come within these four years) may throw Plato's cap at *mirabilis*, for the title wonderful is bestowed upon 1603.' 'Plato's wondrous year', as Marlowe's Tamburlaine calls it, was thought to be the millennial conjunction when the planets would return to their original positions in the heavens. 'To cast one's cap at something' is to despair of overtaking it; since Plato casts his cap at it, 1604 'caps' even the wondrous year of the celestial return. The title is a boast: it suggests that the pamphlet itself 'caps' the form by outdoing all previous mock-almanacs. Middleton plays with 'cap' as both an actual cap and the pamphlet itself: 'there is great difference between reading and reading well', Adam says in the dedication, 'for those who read well have a good tongue of their own, and spoil nothing in the spelling, and to such I cast up my cap'. 'To cast up one's cap' is to rejoice, so Adam celebrates those who read competently. 'To cast up' also means to publish; hence what is being 'cast' is the pamphlet itself as well as its author's cap. Finally, 'cast up' means to vomit, a sense picked up later in the description of 'wine-suckers' who 'cast it up again before the vintner's face'. Middleton's wordplay is not only a compliment to the reader but also a sly impertinence. His playing on the word 'cast' allows him to vent some hostility towards his readers and to register some ambivalence about the work itself.

Adding to these expressions of ambivalence is the way that comic polysemy helps reconfigure reading practices. The pamphlet attempts to reorient the experience of reading a mock-prognostication from a straightforward relationship between reader and text to a more complex relationship between reader and author mediated by the text. It is not merely that Middleton tries to make the conventional anonymity of the form into a game of guessing the name of the writer. 'Martin Merry-mate' had enticed readers to try to divine Simon Smell-knave's true identity thirteen years before 'Mihell Mercury' pretended not to know the name of the author of *Plato's Cap*. More pervasive than the attempt to mystify authorship is the pamphlet's emphasis on the process of reading and interpretation. In order to engage the reader with the author rather than directly with the text, Middleton develops a playful, interpretively unstable style. His irony is unlike the straightforward 'wit' of pamphlets such as *Fearful and Lamentable Effects*. In the following passage, we seem at first to be dealing with a stable set of good/bad oppositions—merchants vs. spend-alls, charity vs. self-display, old-fashioned honest caps vs. new-fashioned prodigal hats. But the word 'carped' (contended, prated) sends an interpretive tremor through the neat symmetrical structure, and that tremor (how admirable *were* the 'carping' merchants?) ramifies backwards through the passage, rippling ironically through a word such as 'profitable' (beneficial or money-making?), raising questions about just how generous was the 'sixpenny dole'. And this ironic reversal of the first interpretation connects the passage with the representation of sharp business practices—of cheating grocers who 'turn the scale with a false finger' and rich men who neglect to build up the 'low, old and rotten' houses of the poor. It is not that the passage undoes itself, revealing a satire 'behind' a merely apparent encomium; rather, Middletonian irony works by leaving intact and available mutually exclusive interpretative possibilities:

> And therefore you, the widows of rich, deceased merchants, mercers and grocers, whose husbands in their lifetimes have been large benefactors to hospitals and alms-houses and elevated many profitable buckets in their parish churches, with arms most quaintly painted upon them, beside sixpenny dole at their funerals, and the blue consort of Hospital Boys singing their dirges. You, I say, their weeping widows, this fearful conjunction threatens most, for many riotous spend-alls go about to inquire for you. And therefore all you that love yourselves better than a satin suit, and prefer your careful states before a white feather, let my prognosticating skill fray you from such brisk, perfumed wooers. Let not a new-fashioned prodigal hat waste and consume that which an old-fashioned honest cap carped and cared for all his lifetime before.

The particular nature of the irony of *Plato's Cap* had its origins, then, in the position of the author Middleton in the face of an anonymous subgenre. He undertook to reframe the form in terms of some of the emerging conventions of literary writing and reading. Not only does the pamphlet deploy irony in order to suggest a playful and knowing author, but it also develops a degree of reflexiveness on its own nature and conditions of production. It would no doubt be overstating the case to suggest that Middletonian irony transformed the reading experience for the Londoners who purchased the pamphlet in 1604, changing that experience from casual amusement at an authorless pamphlet into engagement with an authored work. No doubt *Plato's Cap* was read and interpreted in much the same way as were other mock-almanacs, not to mention the many other satirical pamphlets of the period. Nevertheless, it is important to acknowledge that *Plato's Cap* contributed, to however modest a degree, to the development of specifically literary reading practices, according to which interpretation must always work towards fullness of meaning in the shadow of the figure of the author. To understand how *Plato's Cap* participated in the growth of the domain of literature is to begin to grasp how Thomas Middleton, even though he was not named in the pamphlet he wrote, nevertheless made his presence felt in this commodified product of the early modern literary market-place.

SEE ALSO

Textual introduction and apparatus: *Companion*, 492
Authorship and date: *Companion*, 349

Plato's Cap

Cast at this year 1604, being leap year

To all those that are laxative of laughter

Gentlemen, I put off Plato's Cap to you, and keep on mine own after the French fashion, for your true Frenchman seldom doffs his hat (but upon large composition) for fear of dismembering his hair, and to speak truth, he that useth that and other things, shall lose much hair by the year, I assure you. I would fain have you merry, because your commons are thin this Lent, and scarce so thick as a good leg of mutton. Your oyster pie is your only reveller now, and domineers in all ordinaries, usurping the place of higher and more ambitious bake-meats. And if your complexions be not too rugged and boisterous, your brows too full of Saturn, that sullen planet that never laughs in a whole twelvemonth together, neither at Mercury's witty shifts, nor at Vulcan's Sellinger's-Round dancing with nimble Venus, till all the states smile at him, if your glances be not too full of iron-moulds, I presume you will fling one smile at our button-cap, and I wish no higher. For

A smile is constant and doth gild each style,
But laughter is the fool of every smile.

The wonders we entreat of here have little harm in them. You may take more hurt in a barber's shop, if you sit there fasting, than all my prognosticating comedy or comic prognostication aims at. And if these events chance to happen, they will be but merry ones, for they wish ill to none, but to those that wish ill to themselves, and none can justly except at this, but those that cannot well read it. For there is great difference between reading and reading well, for those that read well have a good tongue of their own, and spoil nothing in the spelling, and to such I cast up my cap, both in Paul's Churchyard, Popeshead Alley, and at Temple Bar.

Yours for a rainy day,
Adam Eavesdropper.

Mihell Mercury the 'pothecary in praise of the book.

If I have skill,
This book's not ill,
But chaste and pleasant.
If I knew the author,
I swear by my daughter,
I'd give him a pheasant.
Nor do you wonder,
You writers of thunder,
I know not the poet.
'Tis the book's praise I write.
But I would not for a mite
Have he himself know it,
For if he should spy it,
I'd flatly deny it.
He would fret, chafe, and nestle,
Stamp more in a minute
Than I in a sennight
At home with my pestle.
Therefore my best way
Is not long here to stay,
Because I'm no fighter.
This course then I took,
To commend the book,
But not meddle with the writer.
And because his art

Title see Introduction
1 **laxative of laughter** unable to contain one's laughter
3 **French fashion** The French were said to be impudent; what follows suggests that Frenchmen leave on their hats so as to conceal the loss of hair consequent upon syphilis—the so-called 'French disease'.
4 **upon large composition** by contractual arrangement
8 **commons** daily fare; 'commons' would naturally be 'thinner' than mutton during Lent since the eating of meat was not permitted
9 **oyster pie** seafood was standard fare during Lent
10 **ordinaries** eating-houses or taverns where public meals are provided at a fixed price
11 **bake-meats** pastries or pies, usually containing meat
12 **complexions** temperaments
13 **Saturn** the melancholy planet
15 **shifts** tricks
Sellinger's-Round St Leger's round; a rough country dance; mentioned as one of 'our old Christmas gambols' in *Hubburd*, 639
16 **states** high-ranking officials; here, the gods and goddesses
17 **iron-moulds** spots or discolourations on cloth
18 **button-cap** old-fashioned round headgear with a slight brim turned up and fastened by buttons; fashionable from the 1520s through 1550s, but replaced by hats in the seventies
28 **except** take exception
32 **Paul's Churchyard** the area surrounding St Paul's Cathedral, the centre of the book trade
Popeshead Alley lane running south from Cornhill to Lombard Street; occupied early in the seventeenth century by booksellers' shops
33 **Temple Bar** name of barrier or gateway closing the entrance into London from the Strand
35 **Adam** a name associated with mock prognostications, and also with populist writings because of the first Adam's association with hard, physical work
36 ***Mihell Mercury*** name combining old form of 'Michael', punning on 'my hell'; (as in 'Mihell Money-god' in *Black Book*, 808) with 'Mercury', which was used to treat syphilis
51 **nestle** to be uneasy or restless; to fidget
53 **sennight** a week (seven-night)

Is so pretty and tart
And his ink so well-favoured,
I swear by my simples,
A nose full of pimples
Is very ill-favoured.
For so he doth prognosticate and shows
A white flax beard wastes with a fiery nose.
See where he comes, I dare not stay, I fly,
So
All envy's poison go with Mercury.

The same hand again.

Plato's Cap

The revolution of this present year 1604 takes his beginning at what time the sun enters into the first minute of Aries, when many a scold shall be found in Ram Alley, whose tongues will never lin jangling until the sun enter into another sign, as the Miter or rather some boozing tap-house, where they must all drink themselves friends again till they are able to speak no more than a drowned rat, and then by that time I hope they will be quiet.

Next I find that the sun entering into Taurus, it will be exceeding good this year for the Butchers, both in Southwark, Eastcheap and Saint Nicholas Shambles, for he takes his entrance just upon Easter Tuesday, to the deposing of Lent and the overthrow of salt salmon and fresh cod, and to the restoring again of heroic-valiant beef, that ancient and surly courtier that never appears without a mess of mustard, his gentleman-usher bareheaded before him. Red herring may go hang himself then for a twelvemonth upon the rusty beam of some farmer's chimney, until the hungry ploughboys cut him down and quarter him. For Oliver Offal the butcher will be fat and flourish, and Gregory Gizzard the poulter will bring forth his progenies of partridges, plovers, and blackbirds. And what a pitiful sight it will be for poor waiters and trencher-bearers to see wise men and their masters feed upon woodcocks.

From thence the sun travels into Gemini, not into Germany (as some mechanic-readers will read Germany for Gemini) and then maids beware of two at once or two at a birth, if you love to preserve your own credits. But you especially this double sign threatens most, that live in merchants' houses amongst wanton springals your fellow servants, and are at midnight at the massacre and sacking of a posset, when your sober master and continent mistress are in their first sleep, and little dream of your cinnamon and sugar which are always the two sweet presenters of a sack-posset, the scene being laid in a bowl or a basin and the actors some half a dozen of silver spoons which seldom are out of their parts until all be eaten. There is much peril and danger in this sign, you damosels of seventeen and one-and-twenty. Therefore if I might counsel you, you should be your own 'pothecaries and preserve your honesties better than Barbaries. Go to bed presently after your master and mistress, save candles and caudles, sleep alone without company till you rise again, and if there be any hurt in this forty weeks after, never trust me again for an almanac-maker.

But when the sun rides a progress into Cancer, woe be to you that dwell in Crooked Lane, and sell shoeing-horns, for you shall take no money of those that have kibed heels, for the skin being off, they will rather go to the Skinners and buy them a fur, if they be wise, than hold by the horn while their brows run all of a water. In this crabbed sign Cancer, buttered crabs will be good meat, if you have money enough, and a very wholesome dish that can be, if you be sound when you eat them.

After this the sun takes a lion's stride and stalks into Leo, and then there will be more lions in the Tower than those that are seen for a penny. In this sign there will start up many false and

64 **simples** medicine composed of only one constituent
68 **fiery nose** inflamed due to drinking or syphilis
74 **revolution** the turning of the year
75 **minute** one-sixtieth of the arc of one of the twelve astrological signs
Aries (the sun enters Aries, the Ram, about 21 March; the new year began on 25 March)
76 **scold** woman who disturbs the peace by her constant scolding
Ram Alley narrow court on south side of Fleet Street; claimed the right of sanctuary and hence acquired a bad reputation
77 **lin jangling** stop talking
78 **tap-house** ale-house
81 **Taurus** (the sun enters Taurus, the Bull, about 21 April)
82 **Southwark** borough on the south side of the Thames between Lambeth and Deptford
Eastcheap 'a flesh [i.e., meat] market of butchers there dwelling, on both sides of the street' (Stow, 1.216)
83 **Saint Nicholas Shambles** a slaughter-house and meat-market on the north side of Newgate Street
87 **mess** portion
88 **Red herring** smoked herring
89 **rusty** having the colour of rust
beam . . . chimney presumably the horizontal piece of timber over the hearth on which meats and fish were smoked; chimney = fireplace
92 **plovers** pigeons
94 **trencher-bearers** servers
95 **woodcocks** known as a particularly stupid bird; unsuitable dish for wise men
96 **Gemini** the Twins, beginning about 21 May
97 **mechanic-readers** unschooled, laborious readers
101 **springals** young men
102 **posset** hot milk curdled with ale, wine, or other liquor, often with sugar, spices; 'sacking' refers both to drinking the posset and to adding sack, a sweet, white wine, to the posset
104 **presenters** actors who speak the prologue of a play
110 **Barbaries** inhabitants of Barbary, barbarians, pagans; with a glance at 'barberies' as 'barber shops', suggested by ''pothecaries'; both barber-surgeons and apothecaries were paramedical practitioners and both 'preserved' the health of their clients
111 **caudles** warm drinks
113 **forty weeks after** the time of gestation
115 **progress** a state journey made by a royal or noble personage
Cancer the Crab, beginning about 21 June
116 **Crooked Lane** street running from New Fish Street to St Michael's Lane
117 **kibed** chapped or ulcerated
118 **Skinners** The Company of Skinners prepared and traded in hides and pelts.
119 **hold by** rely on
horn . . . water horn: shoehorn, suggesting the 'brows' of the cuckold which were said to be horned; here the sufferer sweats in discomfort
123 **Leo** beginning about 21 July
124 **lions** Lions were kept in the Tower of London; from the practice of taking visitors to see these actual lions, the word came also to mean 'sights worth seeing'.

counterfeit coiners that will stamp so long till they stare at the gallows. Many prisoners and wretches will stop holes in the White Lion, to the setting up of the bailiffs and shoulder-clappers.

But when the sun enters into Virgo, take heed, maids, that you have no daughters. I fear me there will be but a few virgins in the Whitefriars for I find by strange art that in suchlike places this year maidenheads will be cheaper than mackerels, at their first coming in especially. This sign also is a shrewd threatener of you young wanton wenches in the Pawn, that ever and anon cry, 'What do you lack, gentlemen? What is't you buy, see a fine shirt!' Fie! Maidens should not name such a word methinks, without a crimson blush at least, because that linen word is always within an inch of immodesty.

From thence the sun takes a running leap into Libra, and then look well to the grocer lest he turn the scales with a false finger. Have an eye to the chandler's weights, you good housewives that buy your soap and salt butter by the pound and the half pound, for there is craft nowadays in weighing of candles and great policy in the uttering of puddings.

Next the sun takes his journey into the stinging sign Scorpio, and then beware of brokers, usurers, and pettifoggers—the scorpions of a kingdom. Come not in their villainous clutches all that month especially, for they will make you pay well for it, more in one month than you shall be able to recover again a whole twelvemonth after.

But entering into Sagittarius, it will be passing good for the fletchers in Grub Street and all the cavaliered bowyers. Twelve score pricks will be in season and those may shoot at Bunhill that are non-suited at Westminster Hall.

After this the sun mounts into Capricorn and then woe be unto you that are horn-mad and have three acres at Cuckold's Haven. You are well landed then, for one acre there is more than ever you will be able to make away as long as you live. This sign rains jealousy upon men and women, upon old frosty men that have young lusty wives, and upon old rivelled women that have young beardless husbands, for the true poison of jealousy swells the bosoms of unequal bedfellows. And a piece of a unicorn's horn can help any man but a cuckold. Whereby that old moth-eaten proverb is verified, which says, 'one man's meat is another man's poison'. For if he should take it down, he would think it would breed more horns within him. Such is the strange property of invincible jealousy, that is stronger than the great Spanish Armado in eighty-eight.

Next the sun enters into Aquarius, and then there will be good doings for water-men, many wanton meetings at Brentford, freshwater voyages to Blackwall and Greenwich, revelling and domineering among amiable lads and young wenches over the water. But that which I find most lamentable in this watery sign Aquarius, and most to be feared of all those that love valiant liquor, is the single-sole disposition of brewers, that will put too much Thames in their beer, and I fear me make it hop but of one leg, and that so lamely too, that a little thing will make it hop quite into the Thames again. And because ale-brewers and they are brothers, it is as much to be doubted on the other side, that each ale-brewer will play the Jew of Malta, and put but a little malt in the ale. So I hope there will be fewer red noses this year than was of a year a great while amongst the baser rank. And as for tavern-whiffers, I do not think but the honest,

126 **stamp . . . stare** 'to stamp and stare' was a phrase indicating rage; here 'stamp' refers primarily to the counterfeiting of coins (counterfeiting might be included under Leo because the 'lion' was a Scottish gold coin down to the reign of King James)

127–8 **White Lion** a tavern converted about 1560 into a prison for the county of Surrey

128 **shoulder-clappers** sheriff's officers

129 **Virgo** the Virgin, beginning about 21 August

131 **Whitefriars** a precinct in London that was outside the city's jurisdiction and so became known for lawlessness

134 **the Pawn** covered arcade in the Royal Exchange, 'furnished with all sorts of the finest wares in the City' (Stow, 1.193)

135–8 **shirt . . . immodesty** Shirts were undergarments; to wrap up in clean linen meant 'to deliver sordid or uncleanly matter in decent language' (Tilley, who gives the earliest instance as 1678).

139 **Libra** the Scales, beginning 23 September

141 **chandler's** chandlers were candle-makers and sellers; the word also referred, somewhat contemptuously, to retail dealers in groceries

144 **uttering** selling

145 **Scorpio** the Scorpion, beginning about 23 October

146 **brokers** any kind of intermediary, in commercial, legal or sexual dealings
pettifoggers legal practitioners of inferior status

152 **Grub Street** running from Fore Street to Chiswell Street, inhabited by bowyers, fletchers, and bowstring-makers; bowyers make bows, fletchers make arrows
cavaliered ? a nonce word, possibly suggesting the affected swaggering of the bowyers

152–3 **Twelve score pricks** targets placed 240 paces from the archers (the regular distance for archery practice)

153–4 **shoot . . . Hall** shoot with bow and arrow after having been shot down in a lawsuit; Bunhill Fields, north of the city, were used for archery practice, Westminster Hall housed the law courts; 'shoot' and 'suit' were homonyns

155 **Capricorn** the He-Goat, begins about 21 December

156 **horn-mad** enraged at having been made a cuckold
three . . . Haven According to legend, the Miller of Charlton, having discovered King John kissing his wife, demanded compensation, and was granted all the land he could see from his door. He claimed all as far as a point on the Thames below Greenwich, which was thereafter called Cuckold's Point; to have three acres at Cuckold's Haven is to be thoroughly a cuckold.

160 **rivelled** wrinkled

162 **unicorn's horn** thought to be an antidote against poison

165 **take it down** swallow powdered unicorn's horn; also referring to detumescence following ejaculation

167 **Armado** the 'Invincible Armada' sent by Philip II of Spain against England in 1588

169 **Aquarius** the Water-Carrier, begins 21 January

170 **Brentford** town in Middlesex at the junction of the Brent and the Thames, eight miles west of London

171 **Blackwall** suburb of London, four miles east of St Paul's
Greenwich town in Kent on the south bank of the Thames

176 **Thames in their beer** water their beer, so as to reduce the usual quantities of hops and malt in beer and ale respectively

177 **little thing** ? privy member, private parts

179 **doubted** feared

180 **Jew of Malta** eponymous character in Marlowe's play

183 **tavern-whiffers** to whiff = to drink liquor

virtuous vintners will take an order, and assuage the desperate and furious humours of their wines with a good, sober quantity of fair, temperate water. Nor can I much blame them, for after the reckoning hath been discharged and all, you should have some cast it up again before the vintner's face and think themselves misreckoned in the pottle, until they see two gallons apparently lie upon the floor before their eyes. And then they will believe it. And therefore good, sober vintners, I will not condemn, but rather applaud the watering of your wine. For by that honest-profitable policy, those that are your common wine-suckers will surfeit and be sick ten times ere they be drunk once. And so much for the sun's taking barge in Aquarius.

The twelve and last is when he turns golden angler and catches Pisces. And then woe be unto you that are dissolute full-mouthed swearers, for you will never catch haddocks as long as you breath. For you shall never hear a true fisher indeed swear beyond 'codsfish', and no oath at all that hath any flesh in it. In this last and finny sign Pisces, there will be odd doings in Old Fish Street. Lobsters will be no meat for lobcocks, as long as they pass for two shillings apiece. Maids will be no fish for harlots, nor soles for brokers—the one wanting continence and the other conscience. Marry, gudgeons will be your only dish for country gentlemen such as are come to their lands before they come to their wit, and are one-and-twenty year old in acres but scarce seven in discretion or manners. Such as these may fitly dwell at Fisher's Folly when they have made away all their fish ponds in the country. And this shall suffice for the sun's twelve strides into the twelve signs.

Now for general dispositions,
in all ranks of people whatsoever,
bred by variable, womanish and unconstant planets

The great conjunction of Saturn and Jupiter, changed from the watery triplicity to the fiery is to be noted specially (as our prognostigators would have it). Nevertheless, I hope there will be small hurt done by fire this year, because faggots, billets, and charcoal bear such a price that no poor snake is able to purchase them, and the most danger for fire lies in their cottages because for the most part they are low, old and rotten. And as for rich men, they could build up their houses again. But those which most prevent this great and fiery conjunction are usurers and niggards, both which are sure to have no sparkle flying or lying about their houses, for they will have never a coal in their chimneys.

This hot conjunction being but badly affected, shows that those which were widows the last year will be catched up this year, more for wealth and spending-money than for love and honesty. They shall have many gallant suitors that will carry all their lands upon their backs and yet swear they have grounds, backsides, and yards, when they have no more ground than the king's highway, no more backsides than one, and no more yard than what they have in their hose and doublets. And the tailor deceives them of one and a half too, to mend the matter, and by that shift makes the gallants forswear themselves.

Thus shall rich widows be beguiled, if they be not the craftier. And what their first husbands sweat for in honest, profitable labours, these their second, hot lovers will sweat out at dice in ordinaries, or in French balls at the tennis court—to the rotting of many fine cambric shirts and the bandying out of taffeta elbows. But politic-crafty Mercury ever and anon falling in among the bunch of planets shows that some London widows will be subtle enough for country gentlemen, and either be made lusty jointures or else never join battle with them. Their profitable wits I applaud well, and I hope witty Mercury will be good to their mourning gowns, and not suffer their brittle sex to repent within less than a month after their marriage day again.

And therefore you, the widows of rich, deceased merchants, mercers, and grocers, whose husbands in their lifetimes have been large benefactors to hospitals and alms-houses and elevated

184 **an order** a particular course of action
189 **pottle** a measure of capacity for liquids, equal to two quarts; a vessel containing a pottle
197 **Pisces** the Fishes, beginning about 20 February
197–200 **woe . . . it** The passage depends on associations between the eating of fish, Lent, and holy living on one side and the eating of flesh (i.e., meat) and carnal sinfulness on the other.
200 **'codsfish'** codfish; playing on 'cod's', a perversion of 'God's' in oaths and exclamations
201 **Old Fish Street** ran west from Bread Street to Old Change; the location of the fish market and of many taverns
202 **lobcocks** country bumpkins
203 **soles** punning on 'soul' and perhaps on 'sol' or 'sou', a French coin
205 **Marry** a form of Mary, the Virgin, used as an interjecton
gudgeons small fish used for bait
208 **Fisher's Folly** 'folly' preceded by possessive noun or proper noun was a popular name of any costly structure considered to have shown folly in the builder
213 ***womanish*** women were commonly thought to be capricious
215 **triplicity** In astrology, the signs are divided into four triplicities, each named after one of the elements, earth, air, water and fire; the watery triplicity comprises Cancer, Scorpio, and Pisces; the fiery triplicity is Aries, Leo, and Sagittarius.
217 **billets** pieces of wood used for fuel
218 **snake** needy or humble person
223 **sparkle** spark
225 **badly affected** ill-liked
228–9 **suitors . . . backs** young heirs who spend the worth of their lands on clothing
229 **backsides** back premises, back yard, outbuildings; also, posteriors
231 **yard** 'yard' of land; also playing on 'yard' of cloth and 'yard' = penis
232 **hose and doublets** stockings and close-fitting body-garments
232–4 **And . . . themselves** The tailor charges them for 'yards' of cloth, but uses less than two to sew their doublets. The gallants are forsworn because they claimed to have 'yards'.
238 **French** (by association, in the view of Jacobean popular culture, with dissolute pastimes)
239 **cambric** a fine linen
bandying hitting to and fro
out of taffeta elbows to be 'out at [or of] elbows' means to be poor and ragged; taffeta is a kind of silk
242 **jointures** the male equivalent of a woman's dowry
249–50 **elevated many profitable buckets** ? paid for the erection of beneficial or useful beams; i.e., contributed towards the refurbishing of their churches

many profitable buckets in their parish churches, with arms most quaintly painted upon them, beside sixpenny dole at their funerals, and the blue consort of Hospital Boys singing their dirges. You, I say, their weeping widows, this fearful conjunction threatens most, for many riotous spend-alls go about to enquire for you. And therefore all you that love yourselves better than a satin suit, and prefer your careful states before a white feather, let my prognosticating skill fray you from such brisk, perfumed wooers. Let not a new-fashioned prodigal hat waste and consume that which an old-fashioned honest cap carped and cared for all his lifetime before.

Moreover this dangerous and perilous conjunction portends many sudden and furious tempests this year, one thousand, six hundred and four. Tavern pots shall fly from one end of the room to the other and do much hurt if they light upon men's pates. Many cracked crowns shall pass current through Cheapside by goldsmith stalls, and yet never suspected. Many terrible frays in Smithfield between sergeants and gentlemen. Marry, sergeants will win the day and get the victory, especially if they be six to one. Then there is no remedy, but the Counter in Wood Street must part the fray. There shall be a dreadful war between the wife and the husband for superiority, in so much that the good man shall be fain to give over first, cry 'mum!' and let her do what she will all the year after.

Shrewd tempests shall arise about Cole Harbour, and many a maid shall be cast away about Westminster. There shall be a battle between the four knaves at cards for superiority, and between the false dice and true for antiquity.

Women that wear long gowns shall be glad to take up their clothes in the street when it rains, although a hundred men stand and look upon them. Yet they shall blush no more to hold them up if it be very dirty than men to make water in broad day at the Pissing Conduit if they have need.

The bakers, woodmongers, butchers, and brewers shall fall to a mighty conspiracy this year, so that no man shall have bread, fire, flesh, or drink without credit or ready money. Barbers shall be mightily out of work this year by reason of the French disease, for many shall lose their hair before they can come to their shops and so put them quite out of work. And beards shall be commodities hard to be gotten but more hard to be kept, for many hairs will start out this year that will never come in again, but perish and drop down by the way. And amongst all other trades and occupations, masons (poor souls) shall be troubled with the stone this year if there chance to be any great buildings, as by my skill I find no less. Marry, I doubt Paul's will scarce have a new steeple this year and in that, I think, I shall be the truest prognosticator that writ almanacs this twenty twelvemonths. The gout, I find, will keep a foul racket this year, and play at tennis in a usurer's puffed toe. But his gaping son and heir shall have little hope of his dying, I'll put him in that comfort, because he may linger yet above seven years longer, and his toe serve out above four 'prenticeships to the gout.

Tailors shall be mightily troubled with the stitch and sew many false seeds which shall peep out before a moon come about. And having a hell of their own, being but a bare board between, woe be to pieces of white fustian linings, for they fall in with their heels upward. Satin is the chiefest devil there and domineers over all inferior blacks. Velvet that old reveller and brave courtier lies there most tragically dismembered. Poor perpetuano is perpetually damned and, desperate-rash, falls in headlong.

Only in this all tailors are most true,
They damn false bodice and give them their due.

And what a lamentable thing it is on the other side that so many of our Englishwomen should wear French bodice and be a scorn and by-jest to all riotous nations.

251 **sixpenny** (commonly a term of depreciation)
dole the distribution of charity
252 **blue consort of Hospital Boys** the 'charity' scholars of Christ's Hospital, on the north side of Newgate, east of the Old Bailey, were often hired to sing at funerals. In *Michaelmas Term*, 4.4.13, their attendance at Quomodo's funeral suggests his high status and his wife's devotion since they are said to have charged the considerable sum of five pounds for their services.
256 **white feather** The landlord's son in *Hubburd*, 376–7, trades his father's estate for fashionable frivolities, one of which is a hat of 'white feathers'.
257 **fray** frighten
258–9 **hat . . . cap** Hats replaced caps as fashionable headgear in the later sixteenth century.
259 **carped** contended, prated
265 **cracked crowns** punning on damaged coins as well as broken heads
Cheapside on the south side was Goldsmith's Row
267 **Smithfield** an open space of five acres, lying in the triangle formed by Holborn, Aldersgate Street, and Charterhouse Street; a usual place of frays
269 **Counter** prison for debtors
274 **Cole Harbour** a place of sanctuary (and hence of wicked goings-on) in Upper Thames Street
275 **Westminster** refers specifically to the Abbey (two miles from St Paul's), but also the village which grew in its neighbourhood, extending in the sixteenth century from Temple Bar to Kensington, and from the Thames to Marylebone, becoming a city in 1540; notorious as a haunt of bad characters
275–7 **battle . . . antiquity** (suggesting the inherent knavery and falsity of games of chance)
276 **knaves** jacks
282 **Pissing Conduit** Conduits were erected so as to provide water to the public; the little Conduit, or Pissing Conduit, was near the Royal Exchange.
286 **French disease** syphilis, one of whose effects was hair loss
294 **new steeple** the steeple of St Paul's Cathedral was destroyed by fire in 1561
297 **puffed** swollen (due to gout)
300 **four 'prenticeships** twenty-eight years
302–3 **sew many false seeds** the sew/sow, seams/seeds punning implies that tailors will father bastard offspring
303–4 **before . . . about** within a month
304 **hell** the tailor's 'hell', into which cuttings were thrown
305 **fustian** a coarse cloth made of cotton and flax, used often because, until 1603, only gentry were legally permitted to wear silk linings
306 **fall . . . upward** In addition to the sense of an irredeemable fall, this phrase possibly continues the bawdy punning of 'sewing seeds', since 'heels upward' might suggest the proverbial 'light heels' of wanton women.
Satin punning on Satan
309 **perpetuano** a durable woollen fabric
312 **false bodice** poorly made garment(s); playing on 'bodies', the usual Jacobean spelling of 'bodice'. The spelling permitted a relaxed handling of the singular and plural.
314 **bodice** playing on 'bodies'; possibly suggesting that Englishwomen prefer French lovers

But shall I discover to the world wondrous events indeed, and tell you how muscadine in vintners' cellars shall indict their masters this year of commixtion, and arraign them at their own bar. And how bailiffs and marshals' men shall be content to arrest any man, if they can catch him.

Poor men shall be accounted knaves without occasion, and those that flatter least shall speed worst and never be worth three hundred a year, if they should live until Doomsday. Many shall eat upon other men's trenchers and surfeit upon other men's costs, but scarce feed upon Holland cheese in their own chambers.

The palsy shall be a very shrewd disease this year, for some will have it in their heads and shake so long till they have no more wit in their brains than Will the bell-ringer. Some shall have a palsy in their teeth, in so much that they shall eat more in a week than they will be able to pay for in a twelvemonth. Othersome shall be troubled with a palsy in their hands, and those are your riotous elder brothers that can keep nothing fast but will shake all the money out of their hands that comes into them, *videlicet*, in taverns, tennis-courts, and dicing-houses. And lastly some shall have a palsy in their feet, and will not be able to stand to anything but shake and reel from the stall into the channel—your excellent reel-pots. And so I leave them full in a puddle.

Some there shall be which shall have such a smell in their nostrils that no feast shall escape them without they have share in it.

But consumptions this year are dangerously threatened by the fiery copulation of those two surly and ambitious planets, for some shall be so consumed in their members, as they shall find never a good tongue in their heads, some so consumed in conscience that they will take above forty in the hundred and more too if they can get it, othersome so consumed by inchastity that if the constable should search them, he should find about them very little honesty.

Those that sing basses this year shall love to take liquor soundly and trumpeters that sound trebles shall stare by custom.

There shall be many fortune-tellers that shall shut a knave in a circle, and looking about for a devil, find him locked in their bosoms.

Many strange events shall happen and befall this year in those houses where Virgo is predominant with a master, but wants a mistress to look narrowly unto her. For the influence of the grocers' shops being elevated within a few sweet degrees presageth that some shameless drabs shall be still gadding about the streets for figs, almonds, and confects, and that without regard of either wit or honesty.

Great mists and fogs will arise and fall this year, so that some shall not see but to take their neighbour's bed for their own. And if watch-candles could tell tales, they would make you laugh, though your wives went to burying.

Many men shall be so venturously disposed that they shall go into brothel-houses and yet come out again as honestly as when they went first in.

Bakers shall thrive by two things this year—scores well paid and millers that are honest, which are as rare to be found nowadays as black swans and white ravens. Long-bearded men shall not be the wisest. Nor the most gravest in looks, the most holy in life.

The haberdashers, by the natural operation of this conjunction, are very fortunate. For old hats new trimmed shall not last long, and new hats for the most part shall have old trimming. And so by this means, foisting John shall thrive better by his knavery than any plain-dealing John about London by the talent of his honesty. And so I end, wishing all the felts in his shop no more wickeder block than his own pate. And then I am sure they will be so far from good fashion, that no honest man in England would be hired to wear them. And so farewell John, 'tis good luck sometimes, they say, to end with an etc.

FINIS

317 **muscadine** a form of 'muscatel': a strong sweet wine
318 **commixtion** mixing together
325 **Holland cheese** In *Pierce Penniless* (1592), Thomas Nashe asks, 'Is it not a pitiful thing that a fellow ... comes to the eighteen pence ordinary, because he would be seen amongst cavaliers and brave courtiers, living otherwise all the year long with salt butter and Holland cheese in his chamber' (1.170).
326 **palsy** a disease of the nervous system, characterized by impairment or suspension of muscular action or sensation, especially of voluntary motion, and, in some forms, by involuntary tremors of the limbs
328 **Will** ? a generic name for a bell-ringer
333 ***videlicet*** namely
336 **from the stall into the channel** from the market stall or shop into the gutter
337 **reel-pots** drunkards
341 **consumptions ... threatened** people are threatened with consumptions (i.e., wasting diseases)
342 **planets** here Saturn and Jupiter
345 **above ... hundred** a usurious rate of interest
349 **take liquor soundly** drink deeply, consonant with their deep voices
350 **trumpeters ... custom** possibly 'trumpeters who imbibe three drinks at one time will commonly rage drunkenly' (punning on sound = get to the bottom (of the glass), trebles = three of something)
351–2 **shut ... circle** Magicians protected themselves from the demons they conjured by staying within an enchanted circle; here the fortune-tellers are themselves the knaves.
355 **Virgo** the Virgin
predominant astrological term for the planet and constellation having greatest influence at any one time
356 **narrowly** with close attention
356–7 **influence ... presageth** more playing with astrological terminology
358 **drabs** slatterns or prostitutes
359 **confects** sweetmeats made of fruit and/or seed, preserved in sugar
363 **watch-candles** candles used for 'watching', that is, staying awake, rather than for reading or working
374 **new ... trimming** i.e., hats sold as new will be trimmed with second-hand materials
375 **foisting** cheating
John probably the haberdasher, John of Paul's churchyard; mentioned also in *Hubburd*, 55 and in Dekker's *Gull's Hornbook* (1609)
377 **felts** refers both to the felt material used to make hats and to hats themselves made of any material
378 **block** a mould for a hat
379 **would be hired** i.e., you could not pay anyone to wear them

THE BLACK BOOK

Edited by G. B. Shand

> I hear say there be obscure imitators, that go about to frame a second part of it, and offer to sell it in Paul's Churchyard, and elsewhere, as from me.... Indeed, if my leisure were such as I could wish, I might haps (half a year hence) write the return of the Knight of the Post from hell, with the Devil's answer to the *Supplication*: but as for a second part of *Pierce Penniless*, it is a most ridiculous roguery.

Thomas Nashe's epistle to the second edition of his *Pierce Penniless* (1592) evidently threw down a gauntlet so alluring that Middleton could not finally refuse to take it up, particularly at a moment when plague-silenced theatres and patronage-denying Clutchfists threatened his income. So *The Black Book* appeared in 1604, an exuberant sequel by a not-so-obscure imitator whose powers of supplementary invention had already, in *The Wisdom of Solomon Paraphrased* and *The Ghost of Lucrece*, been liberally honed on well-known pre-existing texts. As its two 1604 editions would suggest, *The Black Book*'s vigorous prose agreed better with the reading public than had those earlier poetic endeavours at adaptation.

Middleton's pamphlet is simply conceived. In *Pierce Penniless* a starving writer (Nashe's transparent stand-in) is driven to post a satirical plea to Hell for patronage; in *The Black Book* Lucifer rises in person at the Globe Theatre to answer Pierce's pitiful supplication. Like a night-walking John Stow, perambulating the civic wards in his *Survey of London* (1598), Lucifer bustles through the City's underworld, assembling his chief earthly followers and anatomizing their negative contributions to London life with a directness owing much to Nashe and the sharp-pointed satirical tradition of Pietro Aretino in which Nashe consciously wrote. Adding Pierce to his company, Lucifer plays a final scene in which he publishes the details of his last will and testament, including, 'for his redress, | A standing pension to Pierce Penniless' (108–9). This pension, be it noted, takes the ironic form of a rake-off from all the city's bawdy-houses, along with 'the playing in and out of all wenches at thy pleasure' (804). Minuscule though it be, Pierce's percentage of London's booming sex-trade ensures that he will 'never have need to write *Supplication* again' (806).

Even if no sequel to *Pierce Penniless* had ever appeared, a turn-of-the-century satirical work called *The Black Book* was probably inevitable. Robert Greene had promised one in his *Disputation Between a He Cony-catcher and a She Cony-catcher* (1592), and had titled another pamphlet of that year *The Black Book's Messenger*. In *Pierce Penniless* itself, the beleaguered Nashe had warned his detractors, 'Write who will against me, but let him look his life be without scandal; for if he touch me never so little, I'll be as good as The Black Book to him and his kindred.' Middleton's pamphlet is nothing like the gallery of roguish exploits seemingly promised by Greene, but he surely capitalizes on Greene's advance publicity for his title, and in *The Black Book*'s compassion for Pierce, and its implied scorn for the world that has so abused him, it is perhaps possible to catch a shadowy glimpse of the retribution threatened by Nashe. In form, however, Middleton's is more like an earlier pamphlet, *The Will of the Devil* (*c.*1548, reprinted three times by 1580). This is a rather nasty little assault on Roman Catholicism, but it does turn from attacking various luminaries of the Catholic hierarchy to speak of current vices, and it is framed as a diabolical will and testament spoken by Beelzebub who, 'sick in body and soul', lists his satirical bequests *Item* by *Item*, and ends (in the three reprints) with a guarantee that if his ten detestable commandments be followed 'straight to my kingdom thou shalt be led'. The superficial similarities with the conclusion of *The Black Book* are obvious.

Numerous other satirical pamphlets generally akin to *The Black Book* had appeared in the preceding decades, taking both safe and dangerous sides of political, social, and religious issues. It is conventional to speak of how the entertainment energy of these pamphlets regularly subverts the avowed moral intent, but such subversion does not occur here, despite *The Black Book*'s vivid comedy. Middleton sets out, as he says in the opening Epistle, to 'unmask the world's shadowed villainies', to anatomize the 'deceit and luxury' (i.e., lechery) of a world of 'panders, harlots and ruffians', and that is just what he does, assailing the monetary and carnal greed of London society by presenting its members uniformly, from fashionable gallants through mercantile citizens down to bawds, cheats, and thieves, as kinsmen and adherents of the Devil. Even the pamphlet's material design focuses self-reflexively on this end, as Gary Taylor has argued. *The Black Book* is literally a 'black book', from the solidly inked panel of its woodcut title-page, through the heavy black-letter typeface of its main body of text. Already somewhat archaic by 1604, and thus a potential signifier in itself (harking back to an older and better England), black letter links *The Black Book* visually to the physical style of earlier satirical pamphlets, and it also glances audaciously at those contemporary theological works which were still appearing in the traditional typeface. But its immediate function here is to help create an appropriate physical vehicle to house the pamphlet's relentlessly black world, a vehicle specifically acknowledged when the Black Book itself asks, in its Epilogue: 'Am I black enough, think you, dressed up in a lasting suit of ink? Do I deserve my dark and pitchy title?' (824–6).

This uniformity of aim and design supports a striking degree of internal cohesion which *The Black Book* gets mainly from narrative and character rather than from the formal structures of expository rhetoric. Though its satirical descriptions are often enthusiastically expansive, Middleton's pamphlet does not share the digressive anthologizing discursiveness which characterizes other works in this genre (one might cite *Pierce Penniless*'s own tedious anticlimactic discourse on spirits). Theatrically anchored in the consistent voice and experience of its vividly-realized protagonist, and in the economy of its inevitable narrative progress, this text has little time for readerly side-trips which might dilute the force of its satire. If there is anything self-subversive at work, it is the author's apparently deep and angry sympathy with innocent victims, and in particular with the miserable fate of Thomas Nashe himself, whose last days, sometime in 1601, seem to have been passed in exactly the penurious neglect experienced by Pierce, and feared by all professional writers, an obscurity as cold as the hearth of the miserable usurer whose tale Lucifer inserts at 242–86. There is a softness approaching (but never reaching) sentimentality in *The Black Book*'s attitude to Pierce, which paradoxically both anchors and undercuts the satirical anger of the work. It is surely of a piece with Middleton's intimately felt defence of Nashe in *The Ant and the Nightingale*, and it is tempting to think that we have here a protest not merely over a wronged fellow writer, but over a wronged friend.

As we might expect, *The Black Book* is highly theatrical in its imagining. Identifying itself as a *Moral*—the contemporary term for an interlude or play of *mores* (as Alan Dessen has demonstrated)—it stages Lucifer's arrival in a verse prologue spoken from the platform of the Globe, and proceeds to a first-person narrative of his travels through the London underworld. Lucifer has been given the vivaciously colloquial voice of a fully realized theatrical persona, sophisticated well beyond the similarly spoken styles of Dekker and Greene, and worthy of comparison with Nashe. Sprinkled with reported dialogue, with cant phrases, with contractions and colloquialisms, and with constant narrative connectives, his prose has a breathless forward momentum which is helped along by extensive adverbial compounding (especially using *when*). These devices, combined with an intensely tactile and visual savouring of descriptive detail, and with highly personalized adjectival choices, produce a story-telling voice so distinctively sustained that the pamphlet might almost be the script for a Jacobean one-man show:

> This said, the slave hugged himself and bussed the bawd for joy, when presently I left them in the midst of their wicked smack and descended to my bill-men that waited in the pernicious alley for me, their master constable. And marching forward to the third garden-house, there we knocked up the ghost of Mistress Silver-pin, who suddenly risse out of two white sheets and acted out of her tiring-house window. But having understood who we were, and the authority of our office, she presently, even in her ghost's apparel, unfolded the doors and gave me my free entrance, when in policy I charged the rest to stay and watch the house below whilst I stumbled up two pair of stairs in the dark, but at last caught in mine eyes the sullen blaze of a melancholy lamp that burnt very tragically upon the narrow desk of a half bedstead, which descried all the pitiful ruins throughout the whole chamber (396–410).

Even the extended general set-pieces on usurers, brokers, merchants, and various gallants which form the first third of *The Black Book* proper are not permitted to slow the pace. Instead, they are integrated into a single, sternly spoken scolding of Lieutenant Frig-beard which is only really interrupted once, where Lucifer turns aside to tell us the story of the 'frozen charity of a usurer's chimney' (242–86). Later, when the building momentum of the action is jeopardized by yet another set-piece, Lucifer actually cuts short his conventional catalogue of the twelve roguish companies in Master Bezzle's ordinary, naming only four of them before abruptly resuming his narrative line: 'and in all, your twelve tribes of villainy, who no sooner understood the quaint form of such an uncustomed legacy but they all pawned their vicious golls to meet there at the hour prefixed' (542–5).

Middleton further exploits his burgeoning playwriting skills here by giving Lucifer a bravura series of lightning-like costume and scene changes which might be the envy of Mephistophilis, and which depend for their satiric impact on the transgressive reputation of both the actor and the stage. Ascending to the Globe platform, Lucifer shifts his shape from flaming devil to constable, and goes first at night to the Pickt-hatch brothel of Mistress Wimble-chin, where he locates and summons Lieutenant Frig-beard, then to the adjacent brothel of Mistress Silver-pin, possibly in Rotten Row, where the lamentable Pierce is added to the company. In the morning, metamorphosing into a musty fur-bedecked usurer so miraculously that his watchmen 'staggered and all their bills fell down in a swoon' (473), he proceeds to the Royal Exchange where he summons the 'rammish penny-father' Mihell Money-god and Master Cog-bill the scrivener. Thence (having switched to a suit and weapons stolen from a Birchin Lane tailor and an unspecified cutler), he marches as a captain to Master Bezzle's ordinary (perhaps, given his later quibble on 'Bezzle-bub', the Devil Tavern in Fleet Street by Temple Bar). Here he finds many more of his followers at dice, and from them he summons a parcel of highway robbers, cutpurses, cheating bowlers and dicers, and even one Barnaby Burning-glass, 'Arch tobacco-taker of England' (777–8). After a briefly-mentioned tour to review his troops in 'many a second house in the city and suburbs' (554–5), and in Paul's Walk, Lucifer assembles these underworld luminaries back at his 'convocation house' (466), Mistress Silver-pin's establishment, which quickly begins to seem more like the stage of the Globe once again, with its tiring-house and its staged finale. Here he takes on one last role, this time costumed in the country nightgown and sick cap of a grain-hoarding Kentish farmer named Dick Devil-barn. He enters feebly between Pierce and Mistress Silver-pin, is helped into 'a wicked chair' (584–6), and proceeds to a climactic series of bequests forming a thin comic veneer over the author's outrage at the vicious practices and values they represent.

The London through which Lucifer bustles in his many shapes is (as usual) gendered female, but as will already be clear, this 'lusty dame and mistress of the land' (341) is no nurturing matron. Rather, Middleton depicts the urban environment Gail Kern Paster has characterized as predatory. The distant or absent City of God is antithetically mirrored by Lucifer's ironic fellowship of parasitic knaves and gulls. Monetary and sexual greed motivate one and all, with perhaps the partial exception of the legitimately needy Pierce. Though this cold and grasping underworld taints all the institutions of the actual city, the Devil's tour is something of a triumphal entry at the backdoor, a regal progress through the sewers, rather than a public visitation of conquest. Comically mediated, contained by the need for disguise and by the unrelieved company of bawds, cheats, and fools, Lucifer is most at home in the city's most marginal and transgressive locales, the stage of the Globe in Southwark, the suburban tenements of Pickt-hatch, 'the very skirts of all brothel-houses' (117). And yet, Middleton's satire is not muted, primarily because he inscribes a fictive City of Lucifer so like the actual London as to be virtually indistinguishable from it, and thus endows his satiric characters and events with the disturbing power of actuality.

Middleton's achievement, then, is anything but the 'ridiculous roguery' Nashe feared. Instead, it is a worthy continuation. 'It is the best of the imitations of Nashe's grotesque manner, ... [but] in a clearer narrative and dramatic framework than Nashe attempts to create' (Rhodes). It is secular, playful, vividly localized and inspired. Witness, finally, its laconic and remarkably layered handling of closure. As he entered into Lucifer's voice by way of a third-person stage direction at the beginning of the *Moral*, Middleton exits by abruptly dropping his diabolical persona for a brief impersonal narrative, of the sort occasionally preserved in post-production play texts: '*This said, he departed to his molten kingdom, the wind risse, the bottom of the chair flew out, the scrivener fell flat upon his nose, and here is the end of a harmless moral*' (818–20). The effect is deft. We see, briefly but vividly, a scene which would have made a wonderful stage finale, following which Middleton completes his departure by immediate transition to an Epilogue in a completely new voice: that of the smugly self-satisfied (and tantalizingly self-referential) *Black Book* itself.

SEE ALSO

Textual introduction and apparatus: *Companion*, 493
Authorship and date: *Companion*, 350

The Black Book

The Epistle to the Reader;
or, The True Character of this Book

To all those that are truly virtuous, and can touch pitch and yet never defile themselves, read the mischievous lives and pernicious practices of villains and yet be never the worse at the end of the book, but rather confirmed the more in their honest estates and the uprightness of their virtues, to such I dedicate myself, the wholesome intent of my labours, the modesty of my phrases, that even blush when they discover vices and unmask the world's shadowed villainies. And I account him as a traitor to virtue who, diving into the deep of this cunning age, and finding there such monsters of nature, such speckled lumps of poison as panders, harlots and ruffians do figure, if he rise up silent again, and neither discover or publish them to the civil rank of sober and continent livers who thereby may shun those two devouring gulfs, to wit, of deceit and luxury, which swallow up more mortals than Scylla and Charybdis, those two cormorants and Woolners of the sea, one tearing, the other devouring. Wherefore, I freely persuade myself, no virtuous spirit or judicial worthy but will approve my politic moral where, under the shadow of the Devil's legacies, or his bequeathing to villains, I strip their villainies naked, and bare the infectious bulks of craft, coz'nage and panderism, the three bloodhounds of a commonwealth. And thus far I presume, that none will or can except at this, which I call *The Black Book* (because it doubly damns the Devil), but some tainted harlot, noseless bawd, obscene ruffian and such of the same black nature and filthy condition that poison the towardly spring of gentility, and corrupt with the mud of mischiefs the pure and clear streams of a kingdom. And to spur-gall such, who reads me shall know I dare, for I fear neither the ratsbane of a harlot nor the poniard of a villain.

T. M.

A Moral

Lucifer, ascending as Prologue to his own play:

Now is hell landed here upon the earth,
When Lucifer, in limbs of burning gold,
Ascends this dusty theatre of the world
To join his powers. And, were it numbered well,
There are more devils on earth than are in hell.
Hence springs my damnèd joy. My tortured spleen
Melts into mirthful humour at this fate,
That heaven is hung so high, drawn up so far,
And made so fast, nailed up with many a star,
And hell the very shop-board of the earth,
Where, when I cut out souls, I throw the shreds
And the white linings of a new-soiled spirit,
Pawned to luxurious and adulterous merit.
Yea, that's the sin, and now it takes her turn,
For which the world shall like a strumpet burn.
And for an instance to fire false embraces
I make the world burn now in secret places.
I haunt invisible corners as a spy,
And in adulterous circles there rise I.
There am I conjured up through hot desire,
And where hell rises there must needs be fire.

Title See Introduction for probable origins; here, an exposé of roguish practices; originally, and also pertinent here, an official list of rogues and criminals; also, a book of black arts (cf. Webster, *The White Devil*, 4.1.33–36: 'And some there are which call it my black book: | Well may the title hold: for though it teach not | The art of conjuring, yet in it lurk | The names of many devils').
2 **Character** moral nature
3–4 **touch pitch...defile** proverbial
10 **discover** reveal
18 **luxury** lechery
19 **Scylla and Charybdis** fearsome rock and whirlpool off the coast of Sicily
cormorants (*fig.*) avaricious men, usurers; gluttons
Woolners Richard Woolner was a notorious Elizabethan glutton
29 **noseless** a common effect of advanced syphilis
33 **spur-gall** to scrape severely with spurs
34 **ratsbane** rat-poison
poniard dagger
37 **Moral** (*a*) interlude or play of manners (*mores*) (*b*) ironic appropriation of the term for an exposition of the moral teaching contained in a literary composition
38 ***Lucifer...play*** The entire *Moral* is conceived theatrically; see Introduction. Cf. the theatrical casting of Dekker's *Wonderful Year* (Hibbard, 168–171), but note that the voice of Dekker's pamphlet appears not to be a persona or character, but simply that of the author, where the voice of *The Black Book*, from the *Moral* until the penultimate sentence of the black-letter text proper, is vividly and consistently Lucifer's.
40 **limbs** armour
41 **theatre of the world** with a first glance at the Globe; cf. 60–2
44 **spleen** the traditional seat of laughter
46 **heaven** with a reference to the theatrical heavens or shadow, the roof protecting the stage, which continues in 47's carpentry figure: 'nailed up with many a star'
48 **hell...shop-board** the tailor's hell, beneath his shop-board or table, where his scraps were discarded; and playing on 'hell' as the place beneath the stage, leading to references to diabolical trap-entries between 57 and 61
49 **cut out** with the added sense of 'excise' or 'eliminate'
souls punning on 'soles', as (*a*) bottoms of shoes (*b*) bottoms of stockings or socks
51 **merit** due reward or punishment, with a glance at *meretrix* (L. harlot)
52 **that's the sin** i.e., lechery/adultery
57 **adulterous circles** (*a*) glancing, as with 'conjured up', 'where hell rises' and 'vaulted up' in the succeeding three lines, at the stage trap, from which devils consistently appeared; (*b*) playing on 'vaginas'

And now that I have vaulted up so high
Above the stage rails of this earthen Globe,
I must turn actor, and join companies
To share my comic sleek-eyed villainies,
For I must weave a thousand ills in one
To please my black and burnt affectïon.
Why, every term-time I come up to sow
Dissension betwixt ploughmen that should sow
The field's vast womb and make the harvest grow.
So comes it oft to pass, dear years befall
When ploughmen leave the field to till the Hall.
Thus famine and bleak dearth do greet the land
When the plough's held between a lawyer's hands.
I fat with joy to see how the poor swains
Do box their country thighs, carrying their packets
Of writings, yet can neither read nor write.
They're like to candles if they had no light,
For they're as dark within, in sense and judgement,
As is the Hole at Newgate, and their thoughts
Are like the men that lie there, without spirit.
This strikes my black soul into ravishing music,
To see swains plod, and shake their ignorant skulls
(For they are naught but skull, their brain but burr,
Wanting wit's marrow and the sap of judgement),
And how they grate with their hard naily soles
The stones in Fleet Street, and strike fire in Paul's.
Nay, with their heavy trot and iron stalk
They have worn off the brass in the mid-walk.
But let these pass for bubbles, and so die,
For I rise now to breathe my legacy
And make my last will, which I know shall stand
As long as bawd or villain strides the land.
For which I'll turn my shape quite out of verse,
Moved with the *Supplication* of poor Pierce,
That writ so rarely villainous from hence
For spending money to my excellence,
Gave me my titles freely, for which giving
I rise now to take order for his living.
The black Knight of the Post shortly returns
From hell, where many a tobacc'nist burns,
With news to smoky gallants, riotous heirs,
Strumpets that follow theatres and fairs,
Gilded-nosed usurers, base-metalled panders,
To copper-captains and Pickt-hatch commanders,
To all infectious catchpoles through the town,
The very speckled vermin of a crown,
To these and those, and every damnèd one,
I'll bequeath legacies to thrive upon.
Amongst the which, I'll give, for his redress,
A standing pension to Pierce Penniless.

The Black Book

No sooner was 'Pierce Penniless' breathed forth but I, the light-burning Sergeant Lucifer, quenched my fiery shape and whipped into a constable's nightgown, the cunning'st habit that could be, to search tipsy taverns, roosting inns and frothy alehouses, when, calling together my worshipful bench of bill-men, I proceeded toward Pickt-hatch, intending to begin there first, which, as I may fitly name it, is the very skirts of all brothel-houses. The watchmen, poor night crows, followed, and thought still they had had the constable by the hand when they had the Devil by the gown-sleeve. At last I, looking up to the casements of every suspected mansion, and spying a light twinkling between hope and desperation, guessed it to be some sleepy snuff, ever and anon winking and nodding in the socket of a candlestick as if the

61 **stage rails** There is no indisputable evidence of such a feature on the Globe stage, although stage rails did exist in such private and indoor theatres as Blackfriars.

62 **join companies** While 'to join company' is to get together for travel, the collocation here with 'actor' and 'share' implies, more specifically, joining a theatrical corps; the plural may simply be dictated by the rhyme.

63 **sleek-eyed** fawning, dissembling; cf. *Hubburd* (1228): 'sleek-faced courtier'

66 **term-time** period appointed for sitting of courts of law

70 **Hall** Westminster Hall, the courts of law

73 **swains** country or farm labourers

78 **Hole at Newgate** the cheapest and worst quarters in London's chief prison

82 **burr** a hollow passage

85 **Fleet Street** where, in Middleton's time, the legal profession was concentrated; the proximity of a multitude of taverns was no doubt mere coincidence
Paul's St Paul's Cathedral; its 'mid-walk' or centre aisle (87) was heavily frequented by the unemployed (and the shadily employed).

93 ***Supplication* of poor Pierce** Thomas Nashe's *Pierce Penilesse His Supplication to the Divell* (1592); note the play, here and elsewhere, on *purse*.

94–5 **writ...excellence** wrote from hence to me, asking for spending money

96 **my titles** Nashe's Pierce addresses himself to Lucifer with four lines of the devil's titles and honours.

98 **Knight of the Post** (*a*) dispatched to hell by Pierce to carry his supplication to Lucifer (see 428–30) (*b*) a professional giver of false evidence

99 **tobacc'nist** tobacco was already seen as a diabolical plague

102 **Gilded-nosed** from keeping one's nose constantly in one's gold; but Elizabethan usage associated a metallic sheen on the nose with a life of debauchery as well.
base-metalled continuing the obvious lexical set, in which metallic qualifiers indicate low estate; and with a clear derivation from and play on 'base-mettled'; the joke is in the spelling

103 **copper-captains** counterfeit officers
Pickt-hatch suburban brothel district, just south-east of the intersection of Goswell Road and Old Street

104 **catchpoles** the much-despised warrant officers or bum-bailiffs who made arrests for debt; proximity to 'infectious' suggests a play on 'catch' meaning 'to contract a disease'

105 **crown** both the kingdom and the head

111 **breathed forth** i.e., spoken aloud at the end of the *Moral*

111–12 **light-burning** etymologically false glance at 'Lucifer' (meaning 'light-bringing' or 'light-bearing')

114 **roosting** (*a*) harbouring, lodging (*b*) possibly playing on 'rousting', i.e., 'bellowing, roaring'

115 **bench** common misappropriation of the term for a court of justice, or for a collection of judges or magistrates
bill-men watchmen armed with bills (pikes or halberds)

119–20 **by the hand...gown-sleeve** proverbial (unrecorded variant of Tilley G260)

121–2 **between hope and desperation** i.e., between hope of burning and fear of going out

122 **snuff** (*a*) burnt wick (*b*) candle end

flame had been a-departing from the greasy body of Simon Snuff the stinkard. Whereupon I, the black constable, commanded my white guard not only to assist my office with their brown bills, but to raise up the house extempore. With that, the dreadful watchmen, having authority standing by them, thundered at the door whilst the candle lightened in the chamber, and so between thund'ring and light'ning the bawd risse, first putting the snuff to an untimely death, a cruel and a lamentable murder, and then, with her fat-sag chin hanging down like a cow's udder, lay reeking out at the window, demanding the reason why they did summon a parley. I told her in plain terms that I had a warrant to search from the sheriff of Limbo.

'How? From the sheriff of Lime Street?' replied Mistress Wimble-chin (for so she understood the word Limbo, as if Limbo had been Latin for Lime Street). 'Why then all the doors of my house shall fly open and receive you, master constable.'

With that, as being the watchword, two or three vaulted out of their beds at once, one swearing stocks and stones he could not find his stockings, others that they could not hit upon their false bodice when, to speak truth and shame myself, they were then as close to their flesh as they could, and never put them off since they were twelve year old. At last they shuffled up and were shut out at the back part as I came in at the north part. Up the stairs I went to examine the feather beds and carry the sheets before the justice, for there was none else then to carry, only the floor was strewed with busk-points, silk garters and shoe-strings, scattered here and there for haste to make away from me, and the farther such run, the nearer they come to me.

Then, another door opening rearward, there came puffing out of the next room a villainous lieutenant without a band, as if he had been new cut down like one at Wapping, with his cruel garters about his neck, which fitly resembled two of Derrick's necklaces. He had a head of hair like one of my devils in *Doctor Faustus* when the old Theatre cracked and frighted the audience. His brow was made of coarse bran, as if all the flour had been bolted out to make honester men, so ruggedly moulded with chops and crevices that I wonder how it held together, had it not been pasted with villainy. His eyebrows jetted out like the round casement of an alderman's dining-room, which made his eyes look as if they had been both damned in his head, for if so be two souls had been so far sunk into hell-pits, they would never have walked abroad again. His nostrils were cousin-germans to coral, though of a softer condition and of a more relenting humour. His crow-black mustachios were almost half an ell from one end to the other, as though they would whisper him in the ear about a cheat or a murder, and his whole face in general was more detestable ugly than the visage of my grim porter Cerberus, which showed that all his body besides was made of filthy dust and sea-coal ashes. A down countenance he had, as if he would have looked thirty mile into hell and seen Sisyphus rolling and Ixion spinning and reeling. Thus, in a pair of hoary slippers, his stockings dangling about his wrists, and his red buttons like foxes out of their holes, he began like the true champion of a vaulting-house, first to fray me with the bugbears of his rough-cast beard, and then to sound base in mine ears like the Bear Garden drum, and this was the humour he put on, and the very apparel of his phrases:

'Why, master constable, dare you balk us in our own mansion, ha? What, is not our house our Cold Harbour, our castle of come-down and lie-down? Must my honest wedded punk here, my glory-fat Audrey, be taken napping, and raised up by the thunder of bill-men? Are we disannulled of our first sleep, and cheated of our dreams and fantasies? Is there not law too for stealing away a man's slumbers, as well as for sheets off from hedges? Come you to search an honest bawdy-house, this seven-and-twenty years in fame and shame? Go to, then, you shall search. Nay, my very boots, too. Are you well now? The least hole in my house, too. Are you pleased now? Can we not take our ease in our inn, but we must

126 **white guard** pale with fear, looking ahead to 'dreadful' (127–8)
130 **risse** rose
136 **Lime Street** one of the residential quarters of the merchants of London
136–7 **Wimble-chin** wimble = nimble
140 **With that** with the uttering of 'constable'
141 **stocks and stones** imprecation meaning 'gods of wood and stone'
143 **bodice** with a play on 'bodies', which in fact was the contemporary spelling
to speak truth and shame myself ironic variant of the proverb 'Speak truth and shame the devil'
146 **north part** the devil's traditional entry point
149 **busk-points** tagged laces which secured the stays of corsets, etc.
153 **band** collar, playing on the sense 'group of followers, military regiment'
154 **Wapping** location of Execution Dock on north bank of the Thames, where pirates were chained up to be drowned by the rising tide
cruel garters common term for the hangman's rope, playing on 'crewel', a worsted yarn
155 **Derrick's** Derrick was the hangman at Tyburn, *c.*1600
156 ***Doctor Faustus*** Performances of the Christopher Marlowe play had a reputation for being accompanied by supernatural events.
157 **Theatre** James Burbage's playhouse in Shoreditch, which operated from 1576 to 1597
159 **chops** cracks, fissures
161 **casement** window, window-frame
163 **damned** deeply sunk, as in the next clause; with a play on 'dammed' (to which Dyce and Bullen politely emend)
165 **cousin-germans** near relations
166 **relenting** literally, melting, turning to liquid; i.e., running; 'humour' is also used here in its liquid sense
167 **ell** an obsolete unit of measure, 45 inches in England
170 **Cerberus** many-headed dog guarding the gate of hell
171 **sea-coal** mineral coal shipped to London by sea
172 **down** downcast, directed downwards
173 **Sisyphus** condemned forever to roll a heavy rock up a steep hill
Ixion chained to a revolving burning wheel in hell
175 **wrists** ankles; insteps
176 **vaulting-house** brothel
fray (*a*) frighten (*b*) chafe
177 **bugbears** hobgoblins
rough-cast roughly contrived, coarse (like the lime-and-gravel plaster of the same name)
178 **Bear Garden** Southwark enclosure where bear-baiting was carried on; its drum was notoriously loud. Compare *Meeting*, 285–6.
180 **balk** disappoint (expectations)
181 **Cold Harbour** sanctuary in Upper Thames Street
182 **punk** whore
183 **glory-fat** blubbery; from 'glore', loose or excessive fat
189 **hole** with obvious sexual sense
190 **take our ease in our inn** proverbial

come out so quickly? Nawd, go to bed, sweet Nawd. Thou wilt cool thy grease anon and make thy fat cake.'

This said, by the virtue and vice of my office I commanded my bill-men downstairs, when in a twinkling discovering myself a little, as much as might serve to relish me and show what stuff I was made of, I came and kissed the bawd, hugged her excellent villainies and cunning rare conveyances. Then, turning myself, I threw mine arms like a scarf or bandoleer cross the lieutenant's melancholy bosom, embraced his resolute phrases and his dissolute humours, highly commending the damnable trade and detestable course of their living, so excellent filthy and so admirable villainous. Whereupon, this lieutenant of Pickt-hatch fell into deeper league and farther acquaintance with the blackness of my bosom, sometimes calling me Master Lucifer the headborough, sometimes Master Devillin the little black constable, then telling me he heard from Limbo the eleventh of the last month, and that he had the letter to show, where they were all very merry. Marry, as he told me, there were some of his friends in Phlegethon troubled with the heart-burning ('Yea, and with the soul-burning, too,' thought I, 'though thou little dream'st of the torment.'), then complaining to me of their bad takings all the last plaguy summer, that there was no stirrings, and therefore undone for want of doings. Whereupon, after many such inductions to bring the scene of his poverty upon the stage, he desired in cool terms to borrow some forty pence of me. I stuffed with anger at that base and lazy petition, knowing that a right true villain and an absolute practised pander could not want silver damnation, but, living upon the revenues of his wits, might purchase the Devil and all. Half conquered with rage, thus I replied to his baseness:

'Why, for shame! A bawd and poor? Why then, let usurers go a-begging, or like an old Greek stand in Paul's with a porringer! Let brokers become whole honest then, and remove to heaven out of Houndsditch! Lawyers turn feeless, and take ten of a poor widow's tears for ten shillings! Merchants never forswear themselves, whose great perjured oaths o' land turn to great winds and cast away their ships at sea, which false perfidious tempest splits their ships abroad and their souls at home, making the one take salt water, and the other salt fire! Let mercers then have conscionable thumbs when they measure out that smooth glittering devil satin, and that old reveller velvet, in the days of Monsieur, both which have devoured many an honest field of wheat and barley that hath been metamorphosed and changed into white money! Pooh, these are but little wonders, and may be easily possible in the working. A usurer to cry bread and meat is not a thing impossible, for indeed your greatest usurer is your greatest beggar, wanting as well that which he hath as that which he hath not: then who can be a greater beggar? He will not have his house smell like a cook's shop, and therefore takes an order no meat shall be dressed in it, and because there was an house upon Fish Street Hill burned to the ground once, he can abide by no means to have a fire in his chimney ever since.'

(To the confirming of which, I will insert here a pretty conceit of a nimble-witted gentlewoman that was worthy to be ladified for the jest, who, ent'ring into a usurer's house in London to take up money upon unmerciful interest for the space of a twelvemonth, was conducted through two or three hungry rooms into a fair dining-room by a Lenten-faced fellow, the usurer's man, whose nose showed as if it had been made of hollow pasteboard, and his cheeks like two thin pancakes clapped together. A pitiful knave he was, and looked for all the world as if meal had been at twenty shillings a bushel. The gentlewoman, being placed in this fair room to await the usurer's leisure—who was casting up ditches of gold in his counting-house—and being almost frozen with standing, for it was before Candlemas frost-bitten term, ever and anon turning about to the chimney where she saw a pair of corpulent gigantical andirons that stood like two burgomasters at both corners, a hearth briskly dressed up, and a great cluster of charcoal piled up together like black puddings, which lay for a dead fire, and in the dining-room, too: the gentlewoman wond'ring it was so long a-kindling, at last she caught the miserable conceit of it, and calling her man to her, bade him seek out for a piece of chalk or some peeling of a white wall, whilst in the mean time she conceited the device, when, taking up the six former coals one after another, she chalked upon each of them a satirical letter, which six were these: 'T. D. C. R. U. S.', explained thus: 'These Dead Coals Resemble Usurers' Souls'; then placing them in the same order again, turning the chalked sides inward to try conclusions, which, as it happened, made up the jest the better. By that time

192 **cake** congeal
194 **discovering** revealing
197 **conveyances** tricks
198 **bandoleer** broad belt worn over the shoulder and across the breast
204 **headborough** parish officer identical to petty constable
205 **Devillin** variant of 'deviling', a young devil; an imp
206 **eleventh** the traditional number of transgression
208 **Phlegethon** one of the five rivers of fire in Hades; hell
211–12 **last plaguy summer** of 1603, a virulent plague year
212–13 **stirrings…doings** sexual activity
215 **stuffed** became out of breath
218–19 **purchase…all** proverbial
221 **Greek** a cheat, sharper
porringer (*a*) porridge or soup basin (*b*) a hat similarly shaped
222 **brokers** dealers in second-hand apparel, based mainly in Houndsditch (as in 223), which ran north-west along the line of the old city moat from Aldgate to Bishopsgate
whole wholly, completely
228 **salt fire** bitter, vexatious fire, i.e., hell fire
mercers dealers in costly fabrics
228–9 **conscionable** scrupulous; equitable
230 **satin** playing on Satan; the pun is common; but cf. *Plato's Cap*, 306; and note that *Plato's Cap* then proceeds to 'Velvet that old reveller'
Monsieur a seemingly gratuitous glance back at François de Valois, brother of Charles IX and Duke of Alençon and Anjou, the conclusion of whose controversial courtship of Elizabeth I (February 1582) continued to be remembered as an English escape from diabolical temptation. Compare Middleton's later animus against the Spanish marriage in *Game*.
232 **white money** silver
234 **cry** beg loudly
239–40 **Fish Street Hill** running south from East Cheap to Lower Thames Street
242 **conceit** ingenious stylistic decoration (acknowledging that this is a digression)
248 **pasteboard** wood substitute made by pasting sheets of paper together
250–1 **twenty shillings a bushel** about five times the going rate in 1603–4
254 **Candlemas** 2 February, in Hilary Term, which Middleton refers to as 'Candlemas term' in *Hubburd* (19)
258 **black puddings** blood sausages
263 **former** foremost, front
267 **to try conclusions** to experiment

the usurer had done amongst his golden heaps, and entertaining the gentlewoman with a cough a quarter of an hour long, at last, after a rotten hawk and a hem, he began to spit and speak to her. To conclude, she was furnished of the money for a twelvemonth, but upon large security and most tragical usury. When keeping her day the twelvemonth after, coming to repay both the money and the breed of it—for interest may well be called the usurer's bastard—she found the hearth dressed up in the same order with a dead fire of charcoal again, and yet the Thames was half frozen at that time with the bitterness of the season, when turning the foremost rank of coals, determining again, as it seemed, to draw some pretty knavery upon them too, she spied all those six letters which she chalked upon them the twelvemonth before, and never a one stirred or displaced, the strange sight of which made her break into these words: 'Is it possible,' quoth she, 'a usurer should burn so little here, and so much in hell? Or is it the cold property of these coals to be above a twelvemonth a-kindling?' So much to show the frozen charity of a usurer's chimney.)

'And then a broker to be an honest soul, that is, to take but sixpence a month, and threepence for the bill-making. A devil of a very good conscience. Possible too to have a lawyer bribeless and without fee, if his clientess, or female client, please his eye well. A merchant to wear a suit of perjury but once a quarter or so. Mistake me not, I mean not four times an hour. That shift were too short. He could not put it on so soon, I think. And lastly, not impossible for a mercer to have a thumb in folio, like one of the biggest of the guard, and so give good and very bountiful measure. But which is most impossible, to be a right bawd and poor! It strikes my spleen into dullness and turns all my blood into cool lead. Wherefore was vice ordained but to be rich, shining and wealthy, seeing virtue, her opponent, is poor, ragged and needy? Those that are poor are timorous honest and foolish harmless, as your carolling shepherds, whistling ploughmen and such of the same innocent rank, that never relish the black juice of villainy, never taste the red food of murder or the damnable suckets of luxury, whereas a pander is the very oil of villains and the syrup of rogues—of excellent rogues, I mean, such as have purchased five hundreds a year by the talent of their villainy. How many such gallants do I know, that live only upon the revenue of their wits! Some whose brains are above an hundred mile about, and those are your geometrical thieves, which may fitly be called so because they measure the highways with false gallops, and therefore are heirs of more acres than five-and-fifty elder brothers. Sometimes they are clerks of Newmarket Heath, sometimes the sheriffs of Salisbury Plain, and another time they commit brothelry when they make many a man stand at Hockley in the Hole. These are your great head landlords indeed, which call the word *robbing* the gathering in of their rents, and name all passengers their tenants at will.

'Another set of delicate knaves there are, that dive into deeds and writings of lands left to young gull-finches, poisoning the true sense and intent of them with the merciless antimony of the common law, and so by some crafty clause or two shove the true foolish owners quite beside the saddle of their patrimonies, and then they hang only by the stirrups, that is, by the cold alms and frozen charity of the gentlemen-defeaters, who, if they take after me, their great-grandfather, will rather stamp them down in the deep mire of poverty than bolster up their heads with a poor wisp of charity. Such as these corrupt the true meanings of last wills and testaments, and turn legacies the wrong way, wresting them quite awry like Grantham Steeple.

'The third rank, quainter than the former, presents us with the race of lusty vaulting gallants, that instead of a French horse practise upon their mistresses all the nimble tricks of vaulting, and are worthy to be made dukes for doing the Somerset so lively. This nest of gallants, for the natural parts that are in them, are maintained by their drawnwork dames and their embroidered mistresses, and can dispend their two thousand a year out of other men's coffers, keep at every heel a man, beside a French lackey (a great boy with a beard) and an English page which fills up the place of an ingle. They have their city-horse, which I may well term their stone-horse or their horse upon the stones, for indeed

270–1 **cough . . . spit** conventional phlegmatic attributes of the usurer in satire (phlegm, in humour theory, is cold, moist, dull, and slothful)
288 **bill-making** writing up the charges or the promissory note
292 **shift** change of clothes, with a play on the article of clothing
294 **have a thumb in folio** give generous measure
295 **biggest of the guard** King James's beefeaters, his household guard, were known for their great size.
302 **black juice** bile, linked with melancholy
303 **suckets** sweetmeats; presumably with an obscene glance at 'sockets'
309 **geometrical** literally, measuring earth
310 **false gallops** (*a*) canters (*b*) *fig.* illicit excursions
312–14 **Newmarket . . . Hole** all three were notorious for highway robbery
314 **stand** halt; with a play on male sexual arousal
316–17 **tenants at will** tenants who occupy a property at the pleasure of the landlord
318 **delicate** precise; given to pleasure
319 **gull-finches** simpletons
320 **antimony** ordinarily an emetic rather than a poison; exploiting the punning link with 'patrimonies' (322)
321 **clause** playing on 'claws'; see Textual Notes
329 **Grantham Steeple** There are numerous contemporary references to the apparent twisting of the steeple of the 13th-century parish church at Grantham.
330 **quainter** more cunning; but also glancing at 'quaint' as 'cunt'
331 **vaulting gallants** gigolos; note the subsequent play on 'vaulting' as both gymnastic and sexual feats
French horse Venereal diseases were frequently categorized as French, and a 'horse' is a vaulting block; hence a play on 'whores', leading to the ponderous quibbles with 'horse' and 'stones' (339–42).
333 **Somerset** common alteration of 'somersault', but a generic glance at the Seymours as well: Sir Edward, 1st Duke of Somerset, had his marital difficulties in the 1560s; son Edward married without permission in 1582; and grandson William, heir to the dukedom, had apparently begun a torrid affair with Arabella Stuart in 1602
334 **natural parts** (*a*) native ability (*b*) genital endowment
335 **drawnwork** ornamental work in fabrics, produced by drawing out some of the threads
338 **great boy with a beard** a very late learner; see *Pierce*: 'you shall see a great boy with a beard learn his A B C and sit weeping under the rod, when he is thirty years old' (1.179)
339 **ingle** homosexual boy-favourite
340 **stone-horse** stallion

the city, being the lusty dame and mistress of the land, lays all her foundation upon good stone-work, and somebody pays well for't, where'er it lights, and might with less cost keep London Bridge in reparations every fall than Mistress Bridget his wife; for women and bridges always lack mending, and what the advantage of one tide performs comes another tide presently and washes away.

'Those are your gentleman gallants, that seethe uppermost and never lin galloping till they run over into the fire, so gloriously accoutred that they ravish the eyes of all wantons and take them prisoners in their shops with a brisk suit of apparel. They strangle and choke more velvet in a deep-gathered hose than would serve to line through my lord what-call-ye-him's coach.

'What need I infer more of their prodigal glisterings and their spangled damnations, when these are arguments sufficient to show the wealth of sin, and how rich the sons and heirs of Tartary are? And are these so glorious, so flourishing, so brimful of golden lucifers or light angels, and thou a pander and poor? A bawd and empty, apparelled in villainous packthread, in a wicked suit of coarse hop-bags, the wings and skirts faced with the ruins of dish-clouts? Fie, I shame to see thee dressed up so abominable scurvy. Complain'st thou of bad doings, when there are harlots of all trades and knaves of all languages? Knowest thou not that sin may be committed either in French, Dutch, Italian or Spanish, and all after the English fashion? But thou excusest the negligence of thy practice by the last summer's pestilence. Alas, poor shark-gull, that put off is idle. For Sergeant Carbuncle, one of the plague's chief officers, dares not venture within three yards of an harlot because Monsieur Dry-bone the Frenchman is a ledger before him.'

At which speech the slave burst into a melancholy laugh which showed for all the world like a sad tragedy with a clown in't, and thus began to reply: 'I know not whether it be a cross or a curse, noble Philip of Phlegethon, or whether both, that I am forced to pink four ells of bag to make me a summer suit, but I protest, what with this long vacation and the fidging of gallants to Norfolk and up and down countries, Pierce was never so penniless as poor Lieutenant Frig-beard.'

With those words he put me in mind of him for whom I chiefly changed myself into an officious constable, poor Pierce Penniless, when presently I demanded of this lieutenant the place of his abode, and when he last heard of him, though I knew well enough both where to hear of him and find him. To which he made answer: 'Who? Pierce? Honest Penniless? He that writ the madcap's *Supplication*? Why, my very next neighbour, lying within three lean houses of me at old Mistress Silver-pin's, the only door-keeper in Europe. Why, we meet one another every term-time, and shake hands when the Exchequer opens, but when we open our hands the devil of penny we can see.'

With that I cheered up the drooping slave with the aqua vitae of villainy and put him in excellent comfort of my damnable legacy, saying I would stuff him with so many wealthy instructions that he should excel even Pandarus himself and go nine mile beyond him in panderism, and from thence forward he should never know a true rascal go under his red velvet slops and a gallant bawd indeed below her loose-bodied satin!

This said, the slave hugged himself and bussed the bawd for joy, when presently I left them in the midst of their wicked smack and descended to my bill-men that waited in the pernicious alley for me, their master constable. And marching forward to the third garden-house, there we knocked up the ghost of Mistress Silver-pin, who suddenly risse out of two white sheets and acted out of her tiring-house window. But having understood who we were, and the authority of our office, she presently, even in her ghost's apparel, unfolded the doors and gave me my free entrance, when in policy I charged the rest to stay and watch the house below whilst I stumbled up two pair of stairs in the dark, but at last caught in mine eyes the sullen blaze of a melancholy lamp that burnt very tragically upon the narrow desk of a half bedstead, which descried all the pitiful ruins throughout the whole chamber. The bare privities of the stone walls were hid with

342 **stone-work** sexual activity
344 **fall** (*a*) autumn (*b*) a sexual lapse
346 **presently** immediately
347–8 **seethe . . . fire** cf. Geffrey Whitney's emblem, *Qui se exaltat, humiliabitur*, figured as a cauldron which boils over and puts out its own fire (1586)
348 **lin** cease
353 **infer** report
354 **spangled** (*a*) decorated, glittering (*b*) speckled, spotted
355 **Tartary** Tartarus, hell
357 **light angels** underweight or clipped gold coins
359 **wings** lateral projections on the shoulder of a garment, designed to hide the points attaching the sleeves
360 **dish-clouts** dish-rags
365 **shark-gull** both knave and dupe
366 **Carbuncle** plague sore
367 **yards** with a glance, given the context, at 'yard' as 'penis'
368 **Dry-bone** syphilitic
ledger (*a*) resident (*b*) ambassador
372 **cross** vexation
374 **pink** decorate fabric by cutting eyelet-holes or figures
375 **long vacation** the summer vacation, which began early in 1603 when Trinity Term was adjourned on 23 June because of the plague
fidging . . . Norfolk presumably with reference to the restless flight ('fidging') out of London, by those who could afford it, to avoid the plague
376 **countries** counties
377 **Frig-beard** one who rubs or chafes his beard (hence its 'rough-cast' quality, 176–7); and with the bawdy senses of 'frig' in play as well
385 **lean houses** with a play on 'penthouses'?
Mistress Silver-pin's Joan Silver-pin, who also appears in Gilbert Walker's *A manifest detection of the most vyle and detestable use of Diceplay* (1552), seems to have been the type of the Tudor whore. Her name may glance at disease through the use of 'pin' to designate a small hard swelling.
385–6 **door-keeper** bawd
387 **Exchequer** Westminster department concerned with collection and administration of royal revenues
392 **Pandarus** the go-between in Shakespeare's *Troilus and Cressida* (1602–3)
394 **slops** wide baggy breeches
395 **loose-bodied** convenient for concealing pregnancy, and thus commonly associated with the dress of prostitutes
396 **bussed** kissed
398 **pernicious alley** with a glance at Rotten Row, immediately adjacent to Pickt-hatch?
400 **garden-house** (*a*) small house erected on the garden of a previously existing property (*b*) brothel
401 **white sheets** like a stage ghost?
402 **tiring-house** the actors' interior area (tiring = dressing) behind the upstage façade of the stage platform
406 **pair** flights
408–9 **half bedstead** a bedstead of half the usual size

two pieces of painted cloth, but so ragged and tattered that one might have seen all nevertheless, hanging for all the world like the two men in chains between Mile End and Hackney. The testern, or the shadow over the bed, was made of four ells of cobwebs, and a number of small spinners' ropes hung down for curtains. The spindle-shank spiders, which show like great lechers with little legs, went stalking over his head as if they had been conning of *Tamburlaine*. To conclude, there was many such sights to be seen, and all under a penny, beside the lamentable prospect of his hose and doublet which, being of old Kendal green, fitly resembled a pitched field upon which trampled many a lusty corporal. In this unfortunate tiring-house lay poor Pierce upon a pillow stuffed with horse-meat, the sheets smudged so dirtily as if they had been stolen by night out of St Pulcher's churchyard when the sexton had left a grave open and so laid the dead bodies woolward. The coverlet was made of pieces o' black cloth clapped together, such as was snatched off the rails in King's Street at the Queen's funeral. Upon this miserable bed's-head lay the old copy of his *Supplication* in foul written hand which my black Knight of the Post conveyed to hell, which no sooner I entertained in my hand, but with the rattling and blabbing of the papers poor Pierce began to stretch and grate his nose against the hard pillow, when after a rouse or two he muttered these reeling words between drunk and sober, that is, between sleeping and waking: 'I should laugh, i'faith, if for all this I should prove a usurer before I die and have never a penny now to set up withal. I would build a nunnery in Pickt-hatch here and turn the walk in Paul's into a bowling alley. I would have the Thames leaded over, that they might play at cony-holes with the arches under London Bridge. Well,' and with that he waked, 'the Devil is a mad knave still.'

'How now, Pierce?' quoth I. 'Dost thou call me knave to my face?' Whereat the poor slave started up with his hair a-tiptoe. To whom by easy degrees I gently discovered myself, who, trembling like the treble of a lute under the heavy finger of a farmer's daughter, craved pardon of my damnable excellence and gave me my titles as freely as if he had known where all my lordships lay and how many acres there were in Tartary. But at the length, having recovered to be bold again, he unfolded all his bosom to me, told me that the Knight of Perjury had lately brought him a singed letter sent from a damned friend of his, which was thus directed as followeth: 'From Styx to Wood's Close, or the Walk of Pickt-hatch'.

After I saw poor Penniless grow so well acquainted with me and so familiar with the villainy of my humour, I unlocked my determinations and laid open my intents in particulars, the cause of my up-rising being moved both with his penetrable petition and his insufferable poverty, and therefore changed my shape into a little wapper-eyed constable, to wink and blink at small faults and, through the policy of searching, to find him out the better in his cleanly tabernacle, and therefore gave him encouragement now to be frolic for the time was at hand, like a pickpurse, that Pierce should be called no more Penniless, like the Mayor's Bench at Oxford, but rather Pierce Penny-fist because his palm shall be pawed with pence. This said, I bade him be resolved and get up to breakfast, whilst I went to gather my noise of villains together and made his lodging my convocation house. With that, in a resulting humour, he called his hose and doublet to him (which could almost go alone, borne like a hearse upon the legs of vermin), whilst I thumped downstairs with my cow-heel, embraced Mistress Silver-pin and betook me to my bill-men, when, in a twinkling before them all, I leapt out of master constable's nightgown into an usurer's fusty furred jacket, whereat the watchmen staggered and all their bills fell down in a swoon, when I walked close by them, laughing and coughing like a rotten-

411 **painted cloth** a poor substitute for costly tapestry
412–13 **the two men in chains between Mile End and Hackney** presumably an event in the vicinity of Cambridge Heath; criminals were hung in chains at Mile End Green, but I find no other reference to the indecent exposure implied here. Mile End was east of Whitechapel, a mile from Aldgate. The village of Hackney was almost due north of Mile End.
414 **shadow** canopy, with playful use of the term for the roof over the stage in public playhouses
415 **spinners'** spiders'
416 **spindle-shank** having long skinny legs
417 **conning** memorizing
418 ***Tamburlaine*** Marlowe's play; the conqueror was played by the great Edward Alleyn, whose long-legged martial gait in the role was much remarked on, as for example by Joseph Hall who speaks of 'The stalking steps of his great personage' (*Virgidemiarum*, I.iii.16).
420 **Kendal green** green woollen cloth
423 **horse-meat** horse-feed (chaff was sometimes used as pillow-stuffing by poor country folk); but with a possible echo of *Pierce*'s 'side of bacon that you might lay under your head' (1.216)
424 **St Pulcher's churchyard** the quite nearby graveyard of St Sepulchre's, heavily used during plague years, and the usual burial place of criminals executed at Tyburn
425 **woolward** wearing wool next to the skin, esp. as a penance; but also, often, in the absence of a clean shirt
427 **King's Street** the way to Westminster Abbey, from Charing Cross
427–8 **Queen's funeral** 28 April 1603
428–9 **old copy . . . foul written hand** the rough copy or foul papers
433 **rouse** (*a*) shake (*b*) draught of liquor
436 **nunnery** brothel
439 **cony-holes** suggests a bowling game like nine-holes or pigeon-holes; literally, rabbit burrows; and a 'cony' in popular usage might be either a dupe or a loose woman.
440 **Devil . . . knave** proverbial
451 **Styx** like Phlegethon, one of the rivers of hell
Wood's Close a village about three and a half miles north of Islington
Walk perhaps playing with 'walk' meaning 'a tract of forest land'
455 **in particulars** in detail
456 **penetrable** capable of penetrating (i.e., affecting)
458 **wapper-eyed** sore-eyed, blinking
460 **tabernacle** referring ironically to the cobweb-canopy over Pierce's bed
461 **at hand . . . pickpurse** proverbial
462–3 **Mayor's Bench at Oxford** Penniless Bench, a seat at the east end of old Carfax Church, set aside for loungers and paupers; this phrase has been inked over by hand in the Folger copy, perhaps by some overly sensitive mayor!
464 **pawed** rudely covered, by the Devil's paw
465 **noise** company or band of musicians
467 **in a resulting humour** i.e., revived
469–70 **cow-heel** the cloven hoof of the Devil
472 **fusty** stale-smelling

lunged usurer to see what Italian faces they all made when they missed their constable and saw the black gown of his office lie full in a puddle.

Well, away I scudded in the musty moth-eaten habit, and being upon Exchange-time, I crowded myself amongst merchants, poisoned all the Burse in a minute and turned their faiths and troths into curds and whey, making them swear those things now which they forswore when the quarters struck again, for I was present at the clapping up of every bargain, which did ne'er hold no longer than they held hands together. There I heard news out of all countries in all languages: how many villains were in Spain, how many luxurs in Italy, how many perjureds in France and how many reel-pots in Germany.

At last I met, at half-turn, one whom I had spent mine eyes so long for, an hoary money-master that had been off and on some six-and-fifty years damned in his counting-house, for his only recreation was but to hop about the Burse before twelve to hear what news from the Bank and how many merchants were bankrupt the last change of the moon. This rammish penny-father I rounded in the left ear, winded in my intent, the place and hour, which no sooner he sucked in but smiled upon me in French and replied:

O Monsieur Diabla,
I'll be chief guest at your tabla.

With that we shook hands, and as we parted I bade him bring Master Cog-bill the scrivener along with him, and so I vanished out of that dressing. And passing through Birchin Lane amidst a camp royal of hose and doublets, Master Snip's backside being turned where his face stood, I took excellent occasion to slip into a captain's suit, a valiant buff doublet stuffed with points like a leg of mutton with parsley, and a pair of velvet slops scored thick with lace which ran round about the hose like ringworms, able to make a man scratch where it itched not. And thus accoutred, taking up my weapons o' trust in the same order at the next cutler's I came to, I marched to Master Bezzle's ordinary, where I found a whole dozen of my damned crew sweating as much at dice as many poor labourers do with the casting of ditches, when presently I set in a stake amongst them. Round it went, but the crafty dice having peeped upon me once, knew who I was well enough and would never have their little black eyes off o' me all the while after. At last came my turn about, the dice quaking in my fist before I threw them. But when I jerked them forth, away they ran like Irish lackeys as far as their bones would suffer them, I sweeping up all the stakes that lay upon the table. Whereat some stamped, others swore, the rest cursed and all in general fretted to the gall that a newcomer, as they termed me, should gather in so many fifteens at the first vomit.

Well, thus it passed on, the dice running as false as the drabs in Whitefriars, and when anyone thought himself surest, in came I with a lurching cast and made them all swear round again. But such gunpowder oaths they were that I wonder how the ceiling held together without spitting mortar upon them.

''Swounds, Captain,' swore one to me, 'I think the Devil be thy good lord and master.'

'True,' thought I, 'and thou his gentleman-usher.'

In conclusion, it fatted me better than twenty eighteenpence ordinaries to hear them rage, curse and swear like so many Emperors of Darkness. And all these twelve were of twelve several companies. There was your gallant extraordinary thief, that keeps his college of good-fellows and will not fear to rob a lord in his coach for all his ten trencher-bearers on horseback; your deep-conceited cutpurse, who by the dexterity of his knife will draw out the money and make a flame-coloured purse show like the bottomless pit, but with never a soul in't; your cheating bowler, that will bank false of purpose and lose a game of twelvepence to

475 **what . . . made** how they all ran away; an 'Italian face' is a backside
476 **full** completely, with a playful glance at its actual emptiness
478 **scudded** ran briskly
479 **Exchange-time** from 11:00 a.m. to 12:00 noon
480 **Burse** Royal Exchange
480–1 **turned . . . whey** made all their sworn oaths worthless
482 **quarters** quarter-hours
486 **luxurs** lechers
487 **reel-pots** drunkards
488 **half-turn** 11:30
492 **Bank** in the usual financial sense, but with a possible glance at the Bankside and its brothels
493 **rammish** rank
penny-father miser; more particularly a usurer, returning to the idea of interest as the usurer's bastard; presumably this is the 'Mihell Money-god, usurer' who is later named executor of the will (807–11).
494 **rounded** whispered
left ear the Devil's side, naturally
winded (*a*) blew (*b*) insinuated
495 **in French** continuing the characterization of the French as 'perjureds' (486)
500 **Cog-bill** To 'cog' is to cheat; thus 'Cog-bill' will write up false documents of obligation.
501 **dressing** costume (of a usurer)
Birchin Lane between Lombard Street and Cornhill, occupied mainly by drapers and second-hand clothes dealers
502 **camp royal** a great body of troops; a great number
502–3 **Master . . . stood** i.e., the tailor had his back to the devil, or to the front of his shop (or his head where the sun does not shine?)
504 **buff doublet** military jacket of oxhide
508 **o' trust** on the honour system
509 **Bezzle's** a 'bezzle' is a heavy drinker; also with a possible glance at Beelzebub (as at 593), and hence at the Devil Tavern in Fleet Street
ordinary eating-house or tavern
511 **casting** (*a*) digging (*b*) glancing at the casting of dice
516 **jerked** flung
516–17 **Irish lackeys** Irishmen were commonly employed as running-footmen.
517 **bones** legs (dice were made of bone)
519 **fretted to the gall** *fig.*, chafed to the point of soreness or irritation
520 **fifteens** playful reference to the common tax of one-fifteenth on personal property
521 **vomit** cast
523 **Whitefriars** notorious as the refuge of prostitutes ('drabs')
524 **lurching** winning
525 **gunpowder** explosive; easily inflamed
527 **'Swounds** 'God's wounds' (one of the most profane of oaths)
530–1 **eighteenpence ordinaries** costly meals
532–3 **twelve several companies** glancing at the twelve principal companies or guilds in the City of London
534 **college of good-fellows** collection of thieves
535 **trencher-bearers** servants; a trencher is a plate or platter
535–6 **deep-conceited** exceedingly clever
538 **bottomless pit** hell
soul with a play on *sol* or *sou*, French coins

purchase his partner twelve shillings in bets, and so share it after the play; your cheverel-gutted catchpole, who like a horse-leech sucks gentlemen; and in all, your twelve tribes of villainy, who no sooner understood the quaint form of such an uncustomed legacy but they all pawned their vicious golls to meet there at the hour prefixed. And to confirm their resolution the more, each slipped down his stocking, baring his right knee, and so began to drink a health half as deep as Mother Hubburd's cellar (she that was called in for selling her working bottle-ale to bookbinders and spurting the froth upon courtiers' noses). To conclude, I was their only captain, for so they pleased to title me, and so they all risse, *poculis manibusque* applauding my news. Then, the hour being more than once and once reiterated, we were all at our hands again, and so departed.

I could tell now that I was in many a second house in the city and suburbs afterward, where my entertainment was not barren nor my welcome cheap or ordinary, and then how I walked in Paul's to see fashions, to dive into villainous meetings, pernicious plots, black humours and a million of mischiefs which are bred in that cathedral womb and born within less than forty weeks after. But some may object, and say, 'What? Doth the Devil walk in Paul's then?'

Why not, sir, as well as a sergeant, or a ruffian, or a murderer? May not the Devil, I pray you, walk in Paul's as well as the horse go a-top of Paul's? For I am sure I was not far from his keeper. Pooh, I doubt where there is no doubt, for there is no true critic indeed that will carp at the Devil.

Now the hour posted onward to accomplish the effects of my desire, to gorge every vice full of poison that the soul might burst at the last and vomit out herself upon blue cakes of brimstone, when, returning home for the purpose in my captain's apparel of buff and velvet, I struck mine hostess into admiration at my proper appearance, for my polt-foot was helped out with bombast, a property which many worldlings use whose toes are dead and rotten, and therefore so stuff out their shoes like the corners of wool-packs.

Well, into my tiring-house I went, where I had scarce shifted myself into the apparel of my last will and testament, which was the habit of a covetous barn-cracking farmer, but all my striplings of perdition, my nephews of damnation, my kindred and alliance of villainy and sharking, were ready before the hour to receive my bottomless blessing. When entering into a country nightgown with a cap of sickness about my brows, I was led in between Pierce Penniless and his hostess, like a feeble farmer ready to depart England and sail to the kingdom of Tartary, who setting me down in a wicked chair, all my pernicious kinsfolks round about me, and the scrivener between my legs (for he loves always to sit in the Devil's cot-house), thus, with a whey countenance, short stops and earthen-dampish voice, the true counterfeits of a dying cullion, I proceeded to the black order of my legacies.

The Last Will and Testament of Lawrence Lucifer,
the old wealthy bachelor of Limbo,
alias Dick Devil-barn, the griping farmer of Kent.

In the name of Bezzle-bub, amen.

I, Lawrence Lucifer, alias Dick Devil-barn, sick in soul but not in body, being in perfect health to wicked memory, do constitute and ordain this my last will and testament irrevocable, as long as the world shall be trampled on by villainy.

Imprimis, I, Lawrence Lucifer, bequeath my soul to hell and my body to the earth. Amongst you all divide me and share me equally, but with as much wrangling as you can, I pray, and it will be the better if you go to law for me.

As touching my worldly-wicked goods, I give and bequeath them in most villainous order following:

First, I constitute and ordain Lieutenant Frig-beard, Archpander of England, my sole heir of all such lands, closes and gaps as lie within the bounds of my gift. Beside, I have certain houses, tenements and withdrawing-rooms in Shoreditch, Turnbull Street, Whitefriars and Westminster, which I freely give and bequeath to the aforesaid lieutenant and the base heirs truly begot of his villainous body, with this proviso, that he sell none of the land when he lacks money, nor make away any of the houses to impair and weaken the stock, no, not so much as to alter the property of any of them, which is to make them honest against their wills, but to train and muster his wits upon the Mile End of his mazard, rather to fortify the territories of Turnbull Street and enrich the county of Pickt-hatch with all his vicious endeavours, golden

541 **cheverel-gutted** Cheverel, kid-leather, is noted for its stretchiness; so the phrase may mean 'pot-bellied' or 'insatiable'.

544 **pawned . . . golls** pledged with their hands

547 **Mother Hubburd's cellar** The fact that Spenser's *Mother Hubberds Tale* (1591) was satiric, that it excited comment from Harvey and Nashe, and that it was likely called in, all render unnecessary Adams' theory of a second satirical work of the same name in early 1604 (*Ghost of Lucrece*, xxvi, n.1). If there is little clear connection between the substance of Spenser's poem and Middleton's references, the reason might be that Middleton knew the poem only by reputation. If *Hubburd*'s Clutchfist is Compton, as Adams suggests, there might be a link with the fact that *Mother Hubberds Tale* had been dedicated to Lady Compton.

548 **called in** recalled or confiscated by an official act of censorship

551 ***poculis manibusque*** with cups and hands

554 **second house** a playful glance at *Pierce* (1.216), where it is ventured that 'every second house in *Shoreditch* is maintained' by prostitution

563–4 **horse . . . Paul's** Morocco, the famed stunt horse, was reputed to have climbed to the top of St Paul's *c.*1600.

572 **polt-foot** club-foot
bombast cotton-wool stuffing; hence the rhetorical term

575 **wool-packs** large fleece bags

578 **barn-cracking** engrossing grain until the barn is filled to splitting

585 **wicked** with a play on 'wicker'?

587 **cot-house** shed, shelter
short stops of the breath; panting

588 **cullion** base fellow; *lit.* testicle

590 **Lawrence Lucifer** his name in *Pierce* as well; cf. Tilley D289.

592 **griping** grasping

599–600 **divide . . . equally** a black glance at the Last Supper

605 **closes** enclosed fields
gaps openings in hedges or walls

607 **tenements** flats, suites, single rooms let out as separate dwellings
withdrawing-rooms rooms to retire to (for illicit activities)

607–8 **Shoreditch . . . Westminster** here, all sites of prostitution

614 **Mile End** the green was a militia training ground
mazard head

enticements and damnable practices. And, lieutenant, thou must dive, as thou usest to do, into landed novices, who have only wit to be lickerish and no more, that so their tenants, trotting up to London with their quarterages, they may pay them the rent, but thou and thy college shall receive the money.

Let no young wriggle-eyed damosel, if her years have struck twelve once, be left unassaulted, but it must be thy office to lay hard siege to her honesty and to try if the walls of her maidenhead may be scaled with a ladder of angels, for one acre of such wenches will bring in more at year's end than an hundred acres of the best harrowed land between Deptford and Dover. And take this for a note by the way: you must never walk without your deuce or deuce-ace of drabs after your boot-heels, for when you are abroad you know not what use you may have for them. And lastly, if you be well-fee'd by some riotous gallant, you must practise, as indeed you do, to wind out a wanton velvet cap and bodkin from the tangles of her shop, teaching her (you know how) to cast a cuckold's mist before the eyes of her husband, which is telling him she must see her cousin new come to town, or that she goes to a woman's labour, when thou knowest well enough she goes to none but her own, and being set out of the shop with her man afore her to quench the jealousy of her husband, she by thy instructions shall turn the honest simple fellow off at the next turning and give him leave to see *The Merry Devil of Edmonton* or *A Woman Killed with Kindness*, when his mistress is going herself to the same murder. Thousand of such inventions, practices and devices I stuff thy trade withal, beside the luxurious meetings at taverns, ten-pound suppers and fifteen-pound reckonings, made up afterwards with riotous eggs and muscadine. All these female vomits and adulterous surfeits I give and bequeath to thee, which I hope thou wilt put in practice with all expedition after my decease, and to that end I ordain thee wholly and solely my only absolute, excellent, villainous heir.

Item, I give and bequeath to you, Gregory Gauntlet, high thief on horseback, all such sums of money that are nothing due to you, and to receive them in whether the parties be willing to pay you or no. You need not make many words with them, but only these two, 'Stand and deliver.' And therefore a true thief cannot choose but be wise, because he is a man of so very few words.

I need not instruct you, I think, Gregory, about the politic searching of crafty carriers' packs or ripping up the bowels of wide boots and cloak-bags. I do not doubt but you have already exercised them all. But one thing I especially charge you of, the neglect of which makes many of your religion tender their wine-pipes at Tyburn at least three months before their day: that if you chance to rob a virtuous townsman on horseback with his wife upon a pillion behind him, you presently speak them fair to walk a turn or two at one side where, binding them both together like man and wife, arm in arm very lovingly, be sure you tie them hard enough for fear they break the bonds of matrimony, which if it should fall out so, the matter would lie sore upon your necks the next sessions after, because your negligent tying was the cause of that breach between them.

Now, as for your Welsh hue and cry, the only net to catch thieves in, I know you avoid well enough because you can shift both your beards and your towns well, but for your better disguising henceforward I will fit you with a beard-maker of mine own, one that makes all the false hairs for my devils and all the periwigs that are worn by old courtiers who take it for a pride in their bald days to wear yellow curls on their foreheads when one may almost see the sun go to bed through the chinks of their faces.

Moreover, Gregory, because I know thee toward enough, and thy arms full of feats, I make thee Keeper of Coombe Park, Sergeant of Salisbury Plain, Warden of the standing-places and lastly, Constable of all heaths, holes, highways and cony-groves, hoping that thou wilt execute these places and offices as truly as Derrick will execute his place and office at Tyburn.

Item, I give and bequeath to thee, Dick Dog-man, Grand Catch-pole, over and above thy bare-bone fees that will scarce hang wicked flesh on thy back, all such lurches, gripes and squeezes as may be wrung out by the fist of extortion. And because I take pity on thee, waiting so long as thou usest to do ere thou canst land one fare at the Counter, watching sometimes ten hours together in an ale-house, ever and anon peeping forth and sampling thy nose with the red lattice, let him whosoever that falls into thy clutches at night pay well for thy standing all day. And, cousin Richard, when thou hast caught him in the mousetrap of thy liberty with the cheese of thy office, the wire of thy hard fist being clapped down upon his shoulders, and the back of his estate almost broken to pieces, then call thy cluster of fellow vermins together, and sit in triumph with thy prisoner at the upper end of a tavern table where, under the colour of showing him favour, as you term it, in waiting for bail, thou and thy counter-leech may swallow down six gallons of charnico and then begin to chafe that

618 **landed novices** naïve young heirs of lands
619 **lickerish** wanton
620 **quarterages** quarterly payments
622 **wriggle-eyed** fluttery-eyed, flirtacious; or 'rigol-eyed' (round-eyed), innocent
625 **angels** coins; with a glance at Jacob's ladder
627 **between Deptford and Dover** from one end of Kent to the other
629 **deuce-ace** a threesome
632 **wind out** lure
632–3 **velvet cap and bodkin** well-to-do female shopkeeper
635 **cousin** playing on 'cozen'; and cf. *Five Gallants*, where a secret lover is a 'cousin out o'th' country' (1.1.38)
640–1 ***The Merry . . . Kindness*** The first play, anonymous, was written 1599–1603; the second, by Heywood, is from 1603.
645–6 **eggs and muscadine** aphrodisiacs; 'muscadine' is muscatel
661 **Tyburn** place of execution for Middlesex criminals
663 **pillion** pad or cushion attached to rear of ordinary saddle
670 **Welsh hue and cry** A 'hue and cry' is an outcry calling for pursuit of a felon; 'Welsh' carries connotations of thievery, of lechery, of noisy incomprehensible babble, but may be suggested here by the pun on 'Hugh', a typical Welsh name.
671 **avoid** escape
679 **Coombe Park** in Surrey; yet another regular site for highway robberies, as in *Five Gallants*, 3.1
680 **Salisbury Plain** ditto; see 312–13
684 **Dog-man** from 'dog', to pursue or track, especially with hostile intent
686 **lurches** scams
689 **Counter** debtors' prison
690 **sampling** putting in comparison, matching
691 **red lattice** formerly a common mark of an ale-house
694 **liberty** district over which a person's privilege extends
700 **charnico** sweet Portuguese wine

he makes you stay so long before Peter Bail comes. And here it will not be amiss if you call in more wine-suckers and damn as many gallons again, for you know your prisoner's ransom will pay for all—this is if the party be flush now, and would not have his credit coppered with a scurvy counter.

Another kind of 'rest you have which is called shoe-penny—that is when you will be paid for every stride you take, and if the channel be dangerous and rough, you will not step over under a noble; a very excellent lurch to get up the price of your legs between Paul's Chain and Ludgate.

But that which likes me beyond measure is the villainous nature of that arrest which I may fitly term by the name of cog-shoulder, when you clap o' both sides like old Rowse in Cornhill, and receive double fee both from the creditor and the debtor, swearing by the post of your office to shoulder-clap the party the first time he lights upon the lime-twigs of your liberty when, for a little usurer's oil, you allow him day by day free passage to walk by the wicked precinct of your noses, and yet you will pimple your souls with oaths till you make them as well-favoured as your faces, and swear he never came within the verge of your eyelids. Nay more, if the creditor were present to see him arrested on the one side, and the party you wot on over the way at the other side, you have such quaint shifts, pretty hindrances and most lawyer-like delays ere you will set forward, that in the mean time he may make himself away in some by-alley, or rush into the bowels of some tavern or drinking-school, or if neither, you will find talk with some shark-shift by the way and give him the marks of the party, who will presently start before you, give the debtor intelligence, and so a rotten fig for the catchpole—a most witty, smooth and damnable conveyance. Many such running devices breed in the reins of your offices. Beside, I leave to speak of your unmerciful dragging a gentleman through Fleet Street to the utter confusion of his white feather and the lamentable spattering of his pearl-colour silk stockings, especially when some six of your black dogs of Newgate are upon him at once. Therefore, sweet cousin Richard, for you are the nearest kinsman I have, I give and bequeath to you no more than you have already, for you are so well gorged and stuffed with that, that one spoonful of villainy more would overlay your stomach quite and, I fear me, make you kick up all the rest.

Item, I give and bequeath to you, Benedick Bottomless, most deep cutpurse, all the benefit of pageant days, great market days, ballad places, but especially the sixpenny rooms in playhouses, to cut, dive or nim with as much speed, art and dexterity as may be handled by honest rogues of thy quality. Nay, you shall not stick, Benedick, to give a shave of your office at Paul's Cross in the sermon time. But thou holdst it a thing thou mayst do by law, to cut a purse in Westminster Hall. True, Benedick, if thou be sure the law be on that side thou cut'st it on.

Item, I give and bequeath to you, old Bias, alias Humphrey Hollow-bank, true cheating bowler and lurcher, the one half of all false bets, cunning hooks, subtle ties and cross-lays that are ventured upon the landing of your bowl, and the safe arriving at the haven of the mistress, if it chance to pass all the dangerous rocks and rubs of the alley and be not choked in the sand like a merchant's ship before it comes halfway home, which is none of your fault, you'll say and swear, although in your own turned conscience you know that you threw it above three yards short out of hand upon very set purpose.

Moreover, Humphrey, I give you the lurching of all young novices, citizens' sons and country gentlemen that are hooked in by the winning of one twelvepenny game at first, lost upon policy, to be cheated of twelve pounds worth o' bets afterward. And, old Bias, because thou art now and then smelt out for a coz'ner, I would have thee sometimes go disguised (in honest apparel) and so drawing in amongst bunglers and ketlers, under

701 **Peter Bail** apparently playing on Peter Bales, a well-known scrivener
702 **damn** in your respective bottomless pits
704 **flush** plentifully supplied with money
705 **credit** reputation, financial and general
coppered devalued
counter (*a*) counterfeit coin (*b*) the prison
706 **'rest** arrest
shoe-penny punning on *cioppini*, a current (and etymologically incorrect) pronunciation of *chopine*—absurdly tall cork-columned shoes favoured by stylish ladies of Venice and Spain, and whimsically appropriate for stepping over dangerous channels or drainage gutters
709 **noble** gold coin worth 6*s*. 8*d*.
710 **Paul's Chain** running south from the churchyard to Carter Lane
Ludgate with reference to the debtors' prison at the gate
712–13 **cog-shoulder** a cheating (cogging) arrest
713 **clap** (*a*) strike a bargain, contract (*b*) seize
Rowse suggested by the Bardolph-like description of Dog-man above (i.e. 'rouse'—a draught of drink, a bout of drinking)? The reference might be to an actual catchpole. Dyce speculated that a Cornish wrestler is intended (see Textual Note re 'Cornhill')
Cornhill street running east from the end of the Poultry to Leadenhall Street, passing by the Royal Exchange
715 **shoulder-clap** arrest
716 **lime-twigs** twigs smeared with birdline for catching birds
717 **usurer's oil** money
722 **wot on** know about
729 **fig** something valueless, contemptible
730–1 **running ... reins** with a reference to urinary discharge ('running of the reins', i.e., the kidneys, loins), usually associated with gonorrhea
735 **black dogs of Newgate** a popular name for diabolical catchpoles: Luke Hutton published a rogue pamphlet, *The Blacke Dogge of Newgate*, in 1596, and a two-part play of that title was written by Day, Hathaway, Went. Smith, and 'the other poet' for Worcester's Men between 24 November 1602 and 26 February 1603.
742–3 **pageant ... places** occasions and locations of large public gatherings
743 **sixpenny rooms** probably the lords' rooms
744 **cut ... nim** styles of theft
746 **shave** a shaving, by way of a sample
Paul's Cross the pulpit
750 **Bias** bowling term, referring to the oblique construction of the bowl
751 **Hollow-bank** with reference to his skill in relieving people of their money
752 **hooks** traps
ties obligations, restraints; matches
cross-lays cheating wagers
754 **mistress** the small target ball, or jack, in bowls
755 **rubs** impediments by which a bowl is hindered in its proper course; 'rocks' appears to be a fanciful embellishment of the same term
766 **bunglers and ketlers** oafs and tinkers, clumsy folk; especially, here as with 'ketling' in *Hubburd* (928), unskilled bowlers; and see *Five Gallants*, where the foolish country cousin of Mistress Newcut, who has 'the leisure to follow all new fashions—ply the brothels, practise salutes and cringes' (2.1.63–4), is named 'Bungler'.

the plain frieze of simplicity thou mayst finely couch the wrought velvet of knavery.

Item, I give and bequeath to your cousin-german here, Francis Finger-false, Deputy of Dicing-houses, all cunning lifts, shifts and couches that ever were, are and shall be invented, from this hour of eleven clock upon black Monday until it smite twelve o' clock at Doomsday. And this I know, Francis, if you do endeavour to excel as I know you do, and will truly practise falsely, you may live more gallanter far upon three dice than many of your foolish heirs about London upon thrice three hundred acres.

But turning my legacy to youward, Barnaby Burning-glass, Arch Tobacco-taker of England, in ordinaries, upon stages both common and private, and lastly in the lodging of your drab and mistress: I am not a little proud, I can tell you, Barnaby, that you dance after my pipe so long, and for all counterblasts and tobacco-Nashes, which some call railers, you are not blown away, nor your fiery thirst quenched with the small penny-ale of their contradictions, but still suck that dug of damnation with a long nipple, still burning that rare Phoenix of Phlegethon, tobacco, that from her ashes burnt and knocked out may arise another pipeful. Therefore I give and bequeath unto thee a breath of all religions save the true one, and tasting of all countries save His own, a brain well sooted, where the muses hang up in the smoke like red herrings. And look how the narrow alley of thy pipe shows in the inside, so shall all the pipes through thy body. Besides, I give and bequeath to thee lungs as smooth as jet and just of the same colour, that when thou art closed in thy grave the worms may be consumed with them and take them for black puddings.

Lastly, not least, I give and bequeath to thee, Pierce Penniless, exceeding poor scholar, that hath made clean shoes in both universities, and been a pitiful batteler all thy lifetime, full often heard with this lamentable cry at the butt'ry-hatch: 'Ho, Lancelot! A cue of bread and a cue of beer,' never passing beyond the confines of a farthing nor once munching commons, but only upon gaudy-days: to thee, most miserable Pierce, or pierced through and through with misery, I bequeath the tithe of all vaulting-houses, the tenth *denier* of each 'Hey-pass, come aloft!', beside the playing in and out of all wenches at thy pleasure, which I know as thou mayst use it will be such a fluent pension that thou shalt never have need to write *Supplication* again.

Now, for the especial trust and confidence I have in both you, Mihell Money-god, usurer, and Leonard Lavender, broker or pawn-lender, I make you two my full executors, to the true disposing of all these my hellish intents, wealthy villainies and most pernicious damnable legacies.

And now, kinsmen and friends, wind about me. My breath begins to cool, and all my powers to freeze. And I can say no more to you, nephews, than I have said, only this: I leave you all like ratsbane to poison the realm. And I pray, be all of you as arrant villains as you can be, and so farewell, be all hanged and come down to me as soon as you can.

This said, he departed to his molten kingdom, the wind risse, the bottom of the chair flew out, the scrivener fell flat upon his nose, and here is the end of a harmless moral.

FINIS

Epilogue spoken by the Black Book:

Now sir, what is your censure now? You have read me, I am sure. Am I black enough, think you, dressed up in a lasting suit of ink? Do I deserve my dark and pitchy title? Stick I close enough to a villain's ribs? Is not Lucifer liberal to his nephews in this his last will and testament? Methinks I hear you say nothing, and therefore I know you are pleased and agree to all, for *Qui tacet consentire videtur*. And I allow you wise and truly judicious, because you keep your censure to yourself.

767 **frieze** coarse woollen cloth
couch hide (as in ambush); cf. couches (secret tricks) below (771)
772 **eleven** at night; see note to 206
black Monday Easter Monday, traditionally an unlucky day; the unspoken implication is that the Antichrist Lucifer, who has evidently been in London for a single day, rose from hell on Easter Sunday!
777 **Barnaby** an apparent dig either at Barnaby Rich, enemy of tobacco-taking, or at Barnabe Barnes, who sided with Harvey against Nashe, and is attacked in Nashe's *Have With You to Saffron Walden* (1596)
Burning-glass a lens for igniting fires
781 **counterblasts** with apparent reference to King James's *A counter-blast to tobacco*, which however was itself only published in 1604
782 **tobacco-Nashes** playing on 'ashes', on the supposedly railing attacks of Nashe, and conceivably on 'gnashes'
783 **small penny-ale** weak ale, hence sold at a penny a gallon
788 **His** 'God's' or 'Christ's' seems likely, given the parallel with 'true' religion.
794 **consumed** destroyed
797 **batteler** a member of the lowest economic rank of undergraduates (specific to Oxford)
798 **butt'ry-hatch** the half-door over which provisions from the college buttery (bread, butter and ale) are served
799 **cue** half a farthing (denoted by *q* in college accounts)
800 **munching commons** eating at the common table
801 **gaudy-days** holidays, at Oxford
or that is to say (rephrasing 'most miserable Pierce')
803 ***denier*** worth about a tenth of an English penny
'Hey-pass, come aloft!' juggler's cry or trick, used here to designate tricks turned in the vaulting-houses; to come aloft is to have an erection, or to mount sexually.
805 **fluent** generous, flowing
808 **Mihell** obsolete form of 'Michael', playing on 'my hell'
Lavender 'to lay in lavender' is to pawn.
823 **censure** judgement
829–30 ***Qui . . . videtur*** legal maxim: he who remains silent will be seen to consent

THE WHOLE ROYAL AND MAGNIFICENT ENTERTAINMENT

Edited by R. Malcolm Smuts

The Whole Royal and Magnificent Entertainment, with the Arches of Triumph describes one of the two or three greatest spectacles of early seventeenth-century England: an event staged before tens of thousands of spectators, involving hundreds of participants and a massive display of ostentation. Expenditures by the Crown alone amounted to over £36,000—a sum comparable to the cost of twenty court masques, or roughly double that of constructing the Whitehall Banqueting House. London's guilds contributed £4,100 more, while the Borough of Westminster and the many peers and gentry who marched in the royal procession invested unknown but substantial sums. Modern scholarship has persistently associated the opulent culture of the Stuart court with indoor theatricals and collections of paintings. In reality, however, great outdoor pageants like James I's coronation procession consumed much more money and reached far more people than the masques of Ben Jonson and Inigo Jones or the portraits of Van Dyck. To understand what royal majesty meant in this period, and how poets contributed to the construction of a public image of kingship, we need to begin with such events.

Thomas Middleton's contribution—a speech for the figure Zeal (ll. 2122–81) at the sixth of eight pageants James encountered along his route—can only be understood within the whole context of which it formed a part. The text that follows this introduction provides the fullest possible account of James's entry that can be reconstructed from the original sources. It combines separate descriptions published shortly after the event by the poets, Thomas Dekker and Ben Jonson, and the London joiner Stephen Harrison, who had overseen construction of the pageant arches, along with additional material from printed and manuscript sources (see textual introduction).

Readers should not approach *The Whole Royal and Magnificent Entertainment*, however, as a completely accurate description of the entry on 15 March nor even a dramatic script for that event. It derives from three highly shaped texts, crafted by the individuals chiefly responsible for planning the day's arches and pageants. These emphasize poetic and iconographical elements that probably seemed less important to eyewitnesses, while minimizing or omitting other features of the entry, like the fireworks display on the Thames. Our text also presents a more cohesive and unified impression than any spectator could have achieved of events that took place along a route nearly two miles long, before a noisy crowd that sometimes almost drowned out the speeches. Even James must have had trouble absorbing all the speeches and iconographical details amidst the noise and other distractions; spectators who tried to follow the procession on foot must sometimes have failed to get close enough to understand what was going on. This was certainly the case with Gilbert Dugdale, who produced an independent narrative of the entry based on his own observations.

Our text thus provides an ideal reconstruction, rather than an account of what anyone saw or heard on 15 March 1604. That reconstruction is historically important in its own right, since the published accounts were read by many people who had not watched the entry, or who desired a comprehensive summary after the fact. Dekker's volume sold especially well, going through three editions—including one in Edinburgh—within a few months. Any interpretation must, however, begin by recognizing that the relationship between our composite account and the event it records is even more problematical than that of a printed play to an original performance. Instead of taking the textual description at face value, we ought to pose a number of questions concerning the historical traditions that lay behind James's coronation entry, the manner in which such an event was organized and constructed, and the role of theatrical and visual elements within the larger spectacle. Doing this will also serve to bring out differences between our three authors and to situate Middleton in relationship to them.

The Royal Entry Ritual

The royal entry developed during the late Middle Ages from procedures used when a ruler entered his capital or any other large city subject to his authority. By the fifteenth century a set formula had evolved, not only in England but—with important local variations—in several European states, notably France and the Holy Roman Empire. An entry always consisted of a procession by the royal household and nobles attending the monarch, before an audience consisting partly of civic dignitaries and partly of an undifferentiated public. It combined elements of chivalric cavalcade, civic pageant, liturgical ceremony and popular festival, in ways that simultaneously emphasized feudal and religious traditions of monarchy, the corporate structure of urban society and spontaneous popular devotion to the ruler.

The court and nobility processed in a strict order of precedence, with relatively insignificant officials like messengers and footmen placed at the front and the greater officers of state and highest noblemen and women at the rear, around the royal family. The procession therefore provided a mirror of the proper ordering of the social élite under royal authority, that defined both the sovereign's pre-eminence and the precise place of every participant in relation to him. This hierarchical image also embodied a deep sense of tradition. The commission appointed to determine the order of march searched the Crown's archives for precedents, and the great feudal offices of High Constable and Earl Marshal were filled with temporary appointees who marched in the places prescribed by medieval tradition, even though the former had been vacant for centuries. Such archaic features emphasized the deep historical roots of the monarchy, to a society that tended to equate authority with ancient lineages and immemorial custom.

The procession furnished the ruler with an extraordinarily large and splendid entourage, an essential expression of rank and power in late medieval and early modern society. Splendour was conveyed above all by sumptuous costumes, a prominent feature of court life since the twelfth century. Household servants wore standardized but extremely rich liveries. The King's yeomen and messengers sported scarlet coats with embroidered insignia and spangles made of real gold that glistened in the sunlight as they marched. The costumes of courtiers and noblemen were considerably more lavish, often requiring yards of embroidered cloth garnished with pearls and jewels. In April of 1603 one observer reported that some knights and noblemen had spent £4,000 or £5,000 each on suits for James's upcoming coronation—for which the entry was originally planned—so that a relatively poor lord might 'endanger his estate' by striving to keep up. Banners, painted chariots, embroidered velvet saddle cloths and the rich canopy carried over the King rounded out the effect, turning an entry into a massive display of wealth.

If the court and nobility dominated the procession, the civic community of London's guilds took pride of place among the watching crowd. One side of the processional route was reserved for them. Each guild assembled at its appointed place in ceremonial livery, beneath heraldic banners bearing its coat of arms and behind rails draped in blue cloth. In front of the rails stood specially appointed whifflers or marshals. The Mayor, Recorder, and aldermen of London also waited along the route, in crimson robes of office. As the monarch reached them the Recorder always delivered an oration expressing the city's devotion and presented a gift, consisting in 1604 of three gold cups. The King replied with a brief speech of thanks, whereupon the mayor and aldermen joined the procession. In effect the civic community, headed by its chief officers, became the King's host, as if London was a great country house and the mayor its lord. Dekker's text underlines the point by describing the City as the 'court royal' during the entry and equating the sites of the pageants with specific rooms in royal apartments at Whitehall and other palaces. The parallel between the city's hospitality and that of a nobleman's household may also explain the custom of placing tapestries on the outside of houses along the route, as if the city streets had become a gigantic gallery.

The guild representatives, however, formed only a small part of a crowd that John Stow described as consisting of 'the chiefest gentry of every country [county], and great number of strangers from beyond seas ... [and] such great multitudes of people from all places as the like in London was never seen until that day'. Then as now, great spectacles were international tourist attractions. Wealthier spectators rented space in windows overlooking the route, while their humbler counterparts took whatever vantage point they could find, normally along the side of the street opposite to that occupied by the guilds, which was also railed in but left free for spectators. English crowds customarily greeted public appearances of their rulers with raucous enthusiasm, which James found disconcerting after the more subdued public behaviour he had experienced in Scotland. During the coronation entry, however, he had little choice but to suffer his subjects' loud enthusiasm (no doubt increased by the free wine that flowed all day from the city's water conduits). The tolling of bells from the 123 parish churches in London and its suburbs added further to the noisy air of festive celebration that conveyed, more effectively than any set speeches, popular devotion toward the new king.

Pageants and Iconographic Programmes

Royal entries did not, therefore, require theatrical embellishment to express the majesty of kingship and loyalty of the people. From the Middle Ages, however, a tradition had grown up of accompanying particularly important entries with street pageants, sponsored by the host city or by individual guilds and other corporate groups. These commented allegorically on the meaning of the entry and sometimes alluded to specific political issues. During Elizabeth's coronation entry in 1559 London Protestants, almost certainly after prior consultation with leading figures at court, produced pageants hinting broadly at the Queen's Protestant inclinations and her intention to repudiate her Catholic sister's policies.

For James's coronation entry the City of London produced five pageants, and the Borough of Westminster and the foreign communities of Dutch and Italian merchants one each. We do not know how this apportionment of labour was decided or whether any significant consultation took place between the various civic groups and the court, although planning began very shortly after the new King's accession on 24 March 1603, as David Bergeron has shown. Dekker informs us that the London Corporation appointed a committee of four aldermen and twelve other prominent citizens to supervise its pageants. These luminaries, in turn, set up a bureaucratic structure presiding over a workforce of well over 200. Harrison was put in charge of the construction of the arches that would form the pageant settings; Dekker and Jonson were commissioned to devise the pageants themselves. Initially the entry was planned to coincide with James's coronation on 25 July 1603. An outbreak of plague led, however, to a decision to separate the entry from the coronation and postpone it until the epidemic had subsided. In late January of 1604 the court decided to proceed with the entry on 4 March, a date later pushed back to the fifteenth.

Harrison, Dekker, and Jonson each display a distinctive attitude toward the pageants, suggesting different interpretations of the role of visual and poetic imagery. Harrison's descriptions betray an obvious pride in the visual impression made by the arches and the technical architectural lore that went into their design, especially the science of measurement and a knowledge of the five classical orders. This emphasis seems almost superfluous today, when schoolchildren know how to read scaled drawings and recognize a Corinthian column. Architectural theory and methods of draftsmanship remained relatively esoteric subjects in the England of 1604, however, where buildings were still normally erected through artisanal methods in a vernacular tradition. In his stress on precise measurement and classical proportions, Harrison anticipates a more famous London joiner and self-styled architect, Inigo Jones, whose career as a designer of court masques began one year later. Harrison's prominent use of the squat Tuscan order in the first arch, which he associates with the 'shortness and thickness' of Atlas, provides another intriguing parallel. This order received little prominence in Italian architectural treatises but it fascinated Jones, who used it as the basis for his Covent Garden designs. It is difficult to know how much weight to place on this shared interest; but Harrison's text, with its beautiful engravings, its assertive pride and its determination to preserve a permanent record of ephemeral structures designed and erected by London tradesmen, provides a glimpse into the autodidact artisanal culture from which Jones also emerged. It shows that an interest in European visual culture and architectural classicism was not an exclusively aristocratic taste in Jacobean England.

Harrison oversaw the building of the arches; but as Dekker tells us, the poets devised the underlying 'inventions' or allegorical programmes. The Jacobean pageants deployed a more complex symbolism than Elizabeth's entry pageants, including extensive references to classical sources, that must have made them more difficult for the crowds to decipher. In this respect *The Magnificent Entertainment* marks a significant transition. It looks back to inherited medieval forms of public display and allegory; but it also anticipates the development of a cosmopolitan, classisizing and relatively exclusive court culture under the early Stuarts.

Revealingly, Dekker consistently plays down the more erudite and exclusive features of the iconographic programme, whereas Jonson emphasizes them in every possible way. Both agree on one point: classical allusions only bewilder the multitude. This observation leads Dekker to adopt a dismissive and almost apologetic tone concerning the learned dimensions of his verse. 'To make a false flourish here with the borrowed weapons of all the old masters of the noble Science of Poesy', he announces at the outset, '... only to show how nimbly we can carve up the whole mess of the poets, were to play the executioner, and to lay out the city's household god on the rack, to make him confess how many pair of Latin sheets we have shaken and cut into shreds to make him a garment' (ll. 278–86). Instead of stressing his own learning, Dekker emphasizes the enthusiastic participation of large numbers of mostly ordinary people in preparing to welcome the King. 'Not a finger but had an office' (l. 393), he writes of the city's preparations of the arches: 'even children, might they have been suffered, would gladly have spent their little strength about the engines that mounted up the frames, such a fire of love and joy was kindled in every breast' (ll. 406–9). He weaves descriptions of the watching 'world of people' into his narrative, evoking its bustle and impatience to catch sight of the King: 'The streets seemed to be paved with men; stalls instead of rich wares were set out with children; open casements filled up with women ...' (ll. 414–17). He also includes descriptions of speeches he did not himself write, by the spokesmen for the Dutch and Italian merchants, the Recorder of London, a boy speaking on behalf of St Paul's School, and Middleton. Dekker's text thus provides a relatively full narrative, written as a celebration of civic duty and popular devotion. His own contributions are modestly subsumed within this frame, as facets of a larger, communal event.

By contrast Jonson never provides a narrative of the crowd, although he does emphasize its devotion to the King in the symbolism and speeches he devised for the Fenchurch arch. Jonson thus subsumes the crowd within his visual and poetic 'invention', instead of acknowledging its independent existence. He also takes every opportunity to parade his scholarship. In a theoretical aside he distinguishes between his learned iconography and the crude symbolism of the popular tradition: 'Neither was it becoming, or could it stand with the dignity of these shows, after the most miserable and desperate shift of the puppets, to require a truchman or (with the ignorant painter) one to write, "This is a dog" or "This is a hare", but so to be presented as upon the view they might without cloud or obscurity declare themselves to the sharp and learned. And for the multitude, no doubt but their grounded judgements gazed, said it was fine and were satisfied' (ll. 756–64). In the printed text he does not rely even on 'the sharp and learned' to pick out the full range of his classical allusions but loads his verse with scholarly notes that crowd the margins and sometimes threaten to overwhelm the verse in erudite commentary. Typographically his text looks less like a typical book of Renaissance verse than a work of humanist philology, such as an annotated edition of a classical author. Sometimes Jonson takes an almost perverse delight in abstruseness, as in his use of a pagan goddess who happened to share the name of James's Queen. 'Who this Anna should be (with the Romans themselves) hath been no trifling controversy' (l. 2438.n) his explanatory note begins, before examining several ancient theories and finally arriving at Jonson's own conclusion. Elsewhere the notes take off on long and almost irrelevant tangents, commenting on topics like the primitive Roman custom of using ploughs to mark the bounds of newly founded cities, or the pointed caps worn by Roman priests. This strategy served to dissociate Jonson from the popular medium of street pageants, from city poets like Dekker and Middleton and from his own origins as a Westminster bricklayer's apprentice, linking him instead to the environment of academies and courtly humanism. Although the pageants took place in public, under the patronage of London and Westminster, Jonson does not treat them as a form of popular or civic culture. He presents them instead as products of a classicist high tradition, sheltered by its formidable erudition from the indignity of close contact with the multitude.

If we turn to the speeches and iconographic programmes, the contrast becomes more subtle and complex but nevertheless remains. Middleton emerges as a poet less interested than Jonson in intricate classical learning, but more adept than Dekker at integrating iconographic imagery into a lucid and decorous speech. Only 23, he already displays a remarkably mature and distinctive sense of how to craft panegyric verse for a great public ritual.

The pageants are generally consistent in their ideological and political orientation, stressing common themes that would soon become firmly associated with James's rule, such as the King's defence of the realm's peace and his union of the English and Scottish crowns into a new imperial British monarchy. The one striking exception is the third pageant, sponsored by the Dutch community. As Julia Gasper has shown, this employed a Protestant iconography very different from that used elsewhere in the entry, and implicitly argues against the Anglo-Spanish peace then being negotiated in nearby Westminster. Since there is no firm evidence that Dekker worked on this pageant, however, Gasper's attempt to see it as an expression of his Protestant internationalism is unconvincing. The Catholic Jonson and staunchly Protestant Dekker certainly disagreed over some fundamental issues, but only subtle and inconclusive hints of ideological differences emerge when we compare the pageants they undoubtedly devised. It is probably significant, for example, that Dekker uses more Tudor and medieval imagery than Jonson, whose historical allusions derive almost exclusively from the ancient world. Dekker no doubt felt more comfortable with neo-chivalric and high Elizabethan ideals than Jonson. The pageants themselves did not, however, attempt to link contrasting classical and medieval images of monarchy to divergent policies. They use somewhat different cultural languages but—the Dutch pageant aside—enunciate a fairly uniform message, centring upon the kingdom's joy at James's accession and the anticipation of an age of peace and prosperity under his rule.

We are on firmer ground in identifying contrasting approaches to the construction of iconographic schemes. All three poets combine classical imagery with conventional symbols that can have given plebeian spectators little trouble. By and large, however, Dekker's iconography is more traditional and less complex than Jonson's. In an initial pageant 'laid by' because James did not enter London in the expected place (ll. 362–5), Dekker represents England and Scotland through the familiar figures of St George and St Andrew, holding hands in token of friendship. The fourth arch near St Mildred's-in-the-Poultry employs another conventional image: a Fountain of Virtue that has dried up after the recent death of a 'Phoenix', a standard symbol for Elizabeth I. On the approach of James, a new Phoenix who has risen from the ashes of the old, it begins to flow again, overwhelming the efforts of Detractio and Oblivio to suck it dry. At the next arch a sylvan or wood god presented James with the devotion of Peace and her daughter Plenty, identified by a cornucopia and other relatively transparent emblems of fertility.

Jonson's first arch in Fenchurch Street, by contrast, deployed a more intricate symbology. The central figure of *Monarchia Britannica* could have been easily identified by her two crowns adorned with the arms of England and Scotland. But it would have been much harder to decipher some of the accompanying figures, and more difficult still to recognize the allusions to passages from Virgil, Ovid, and Claudian conveyed by Latin mottoes. In addition, the arch defines British Monarchy as a complex philosophical ideal, combining political, theological, and geographical elements. She rules with the support of the six daughters of the Genius of London, over a little world divided from the European continent. She also depends upon Divine Wisdom, who is represented holding a dove and a serpent as emblems of innocence and prudence. A speech by the Genius of London does little to clarify this programme but instead adds another, historical layer of imagery. The Genius welcomes James as heir to all who have ruled the island since before the Roman conquest, a king predestined to govern peacefully in a land that has often been subject to wars of conquest. In *Basilikon Doron* James referred to the bloodless unification of England and Scotland under his rule, after centuries of warfare and failed attempts at conquest, as an act of Providence. Jonson echoes and builds upon this royal claim.

While doing so, however, he also constructs a representation of the zealous devotion of the London populace. The city's devotion is personified by the river Thames—an image justified by a line from Ovid stating that even rivers have felt the power of love. Jonson further symbolizes London's loyalty through the figures of *Euphorsyne* (Gladness), *Sebasis* (Veneration), *Prothymia* (Promptitude), *Agrypina* (Vigilance), and *Agape* (Loving Affection). His verses refer to the spectators' 'sparkling eyes' and shouts that 'cleave the air'. Nothing in Dekker's pageants compares to this elaborate representation of public loyalty, in which, as Jonson boasted, 'the very site, fabric, strength, policy, dignity and affections of the city were all laid down to life: the nature and property of these devices being to present always some one entire body or figure consisting of distinct members, and each of those expressing itself in its own active sphere, yet all with that general harmony so connected and disposed, as no one little part can be missing to the illustration of the whole'. Despite his professed disdain for 'the multitude' and its 'grounded judgements', Jonson remained alive to the entry's significance as a civic and public event. He seems far more interested, however, in fashioning appropriate images of the crowd's feelings, supported by a dazzling array of classical citations, than in the actual crowd.

If we turn next to Middleton's speech for Zeal at the sixth arch (ll. 2122–81) we find a subtly different approach. Middleton also manages to integrate a fairly complex symbolic scheme into a speech that blends royal panegyric with references to the public's devotion. He seems far less concerned with precise iconographic detail than Jonson, however, and more intent on elucidating the relationship of symbolic images to the basic themes of his speech. The Fleet Street arch, for which Middleton wrote his speech, was topped by a globe 'filled with all the different degrees and states that are in the land', and by *Astraea*, the goddess of justice and of the mythical Golden Age, who had often been associated with Elizabeth. Figures representing the four elements turned the globe as James approached, so he could see the image inside it. Below *Astraea* stood *Arete* or Virtue and below her *Fortuna* standing on a turning globe and *Invidia* or Envy, looking on fearfully. Lower still sat personifications of the particular virtues of Justice, Fortitude, Temperance, and Prudence, and of James's four kingdoms, England, Scotland, France, and Ireland.

Middleton may not have devised this scheme but he crafted a speech that managed to allude to all the symbolic features on the arch, without straying from its central theme of royal virtue and public zeal. That speech revolves around a presentation of the King as the unifying spirit of the body politic and ultimate source of justice and harmony, whose virtues make civil life possible: a theme reflecting the ideal of monarchy James himself had expounded in *Basilikon Doron*. Zeal begins by alluding to public anxiety and disquiet following Elizabeth's death. Fears of a succession crisis complicated by class animosities had haunted England during the Queen's last years, but in 1603 the political nation quickly united around James, assuring a smooth succession. Zeal attributes this happy outcome entirely to the King himself, wrongly implying that his arrival halted an upsurge of social conflict, and attributing to his 'regal eye' a stability that really owed more to prompt action by the Privy Council and the political nation's horror of civil war. The speech proceeds to credit James with bringing peace not only to the kingdom but the cosmos, by quelling the natural enmity of the four elements of earth, air, fire, and water. Through his high fortune and still higher virtue, he dominates the world. Envy—a vice traditionally associated with popular resentment of the rich and powerful—cannot harm him and so consumes her own venom in frustration. James has united the four kingdoms of France, England, Scotland, and Ireland into an empire whose glories have caused *Astraea* to return to earth. Middleton probably felt it needless to explain what most schoolboys knew: that in Virgil's *Eclogues* the return of Astrea meant the renewal of the Golden Age, under the auspices of a wise and just emperor.

With its hyperbolic praise of the King's power to impose peace not only on his people but on nature itself, this speech anticipates many Jacobean masques and panegyrics. In doing so, however, it also manages to highlight public devotion to the King in a way that is not typical of Jacobean court entertainments. 'All estates, whose proper arts | Live by the breath of Majesty' burn with 'holy zeal' to greet James. The 'painted flames' of Zeal's robe are but outward signs of what the city and its people feel. Middleton is thus able to conclude with a decorous allusion to *the crowd's* zeal, that probably served as a cue for loud acclamations: 'with reverberate shouts our globe shall ring, | The music's close begins thus: God save our King!' Where Jonson represented public devotion through a self-contained structure of symbol and poetry, Middleton deliberately ends by turning outward, gesturing toward the unprogrammed enthusiasm of James's subjects.

The Whole Royal and Magnificent Entertainment is, therefore, not only a composite text but one that sometimes turns out, on close inspection, to be pulling in different directions. This becomes even more apparent if we notice passages in Dugdale's narrative that reveal James's impatience with the crowd. Jonson's discomfort with having to appeal to 'the multitude' corresponded to James's own lack of ease in public, just as his passion for classical learning fit in well with the King's scholarly interests.

In providing a record of the first great public ritual of Stuart monarchy, this text therefore also helps us understand why such lavish outdoor events were so rarely repeated. In James's reign only the creation of Henry as Prince of Wales (1610) and the wedding of Princess Elizabeth (1613) compared in scale and splendour with the 1604 entry. In 1627 Charles cancelled his own coronation entry, for which the city had already erected triumphal arches, so as 'to save the expense'. By then, of course, Jonson had developed a less unwieldy vehicle for the symbology of Stuart kingship in the court masque, with its spectacular stage sets and élite audience.

The true successor to the royal entry was not the masque, however, but the annual Lord Mayor's pageant, which involved a similar processional ceremony and comparable street pageants. If Jonson's erudite approach to the entry pageants anticipates his later development of the masque, Dekker's more tolerant and inclusive attitude found its true heir in the mayoral shows, foremost among them those of Thomas Middleton.

SEE ALSO

Textual introduction and apparatus: *Companion*, 498
Authorship and date: *Companion*, 351
Other Middleton–Dekker works: *Caesar's Fall*, 328; *Gravesend*, 128; *Meeting*, 183; *Patient Man*, 280; *Banquet*, 637; *Roaring Girl*, 721; *Gypsy*, 1723
Other Middleton–Webster works: *Caesar's Fall*, 328; *Quiet Life*, 1593; '*The Duchess of Malfi*', 1886

THOMAS DEKKER, STEPHEN HARRISON, BEN JONSON, and THOMAS MIDDLETON

The Whole Royal and Magnificent Entertainment of King James through the City of London, 15 March 1604, with the Arches of Triumph

To the Right Honourable Sir Thomas Bennet Knight, Lord Mayor of this city, the right worshipful the aldermen his brethren, and to those worshipful commoners elected committees for the managing of this business

The love which I bear to your honour and worships, and the duty wherewith I am bound to this honourable city, makes me appear in this boldness to you, to whom I humbly consecrate these fruits of my invention, which time hath now at length brought forth and ripened to this perfection. That magnificent royalty and glorious entertainment—which you yourselves for your part, out of a free, a clear and very bounteous disposition, and so many thousands of worthy citizens out of a sincere affection and loyalty of his Majesty, did with the sparing of no cost bestow but upon one day—is here new wrought up again and shall endure forever. For albeit those monuments of your loves were erected up to the clouds and were built never so strongly, yet now their lastingness should live but in the tongues and memories of men, but that the hand of art gives them here a second more perfect being, advanceth them higher than they were before and warrants them that they shall do honour to this city, so long as the city shall bear a name. Sorry I am that they come into the world no sooner, but let the hardness of the labour and the small number of hands that were busied about them make the fault, if it be a fault, excusable. I would not care if these unpainted pictures were more costly to me, so that they might appear curious enough to your lordship and worships; yet in regard that this present age can lay before you no precedent that ever any in this land performed the like, I presume these my endeavours shall receive the more worthy liking of you. And thus dedicating my labours and love to your honourable and kind acceptations, I most humbly take my leave this 16 of June 1604.

Most affectionately devoted to
your lordship and worships,
Stephen Harrison

Ode

Babel that strove to wear
A crown of clouds and up did rear
Her forehead high,
With an ambitious lust to kiss the sky,
Is now or dust or not at all;
Proud Nimrod's wall
And all his antique monuments,
Left to the world as precedents,
Cannot now show (to tell where they did stand)
So much in length as half the builder's hand.

The Mausolean tomb,
The sixteen curious gates in Rome,
Which times prefer,
Both past and present; Nero's Theatre
That in one day was all gilt o'er;
Add to these more
Those columns and those pyramids that won
Wonder by height, the Coloss' of the sun,
Th'Egyptian obelisks, are all forgotten.
Only their names grow great; themselves be rotten.

Dear friend! What honour then
Bestow'st thou on thy countrymen?
Crowning with praise
By these thy labours, as with wreaths of bays,
This royal city, where now stand
(Built by thy hand)
Her arches in new state, so made
That their fresh beauties ne'er shall fade.
Thou of our English triumphs rear'st the fame
'Bove those of old, but above all thy name.

Tho Dekker

Ode

Triumphs were wont with sweat and blood be
crowned.
To every brow
They did allow

This Commentary focuses upon classical sources and issues of rank and precedence.

8 **invention** the overall scheme of the pageants

25 **them** the engravings

44 **Nimrod's** Babylonian ruler, builder of the Tower of Babel

49 **Mausolean tomb** The tomb of Mausolus, Satrap of Caria in Persia (377–353 BC); one of the Seven Wonders of the World.

56 **Coloss' of the sun** celebrated 105-foot-high bronze statue at Rhodes, another of the Seven Wonders

71 **Triumphs** given in ancient Rome to honour great military exploits

Exercitationes Virtutum in omni ætate minificos afferunt fructus

THE ARCHS OF TRIVMPH
Erected in honor of the High and mighty prince. Iames. the first of that name. King, of England. and the sixt of Scotland. at his Maiesties Entrance and passage through his Honorable Citty & chamber of London. vpon the 15th day of march 1603

Invented and published by Stephen Harrison Ioyner and Architect: and graven by William Kip.

Monimentum Ære Perennius

Are to be sould at the white hort, in Popes head Alley, by Iohn Sudbury and George Humble.

Title-page from Harrison's *Arches of Triumph*.

The living laurel which begirted round
Their rusty helmets and had power to make
The soldier smile, while mortal wound did ache.

But our more civil passages of state,
Like happy feast
Of inured rest,
Which bells and woundless cannons did relate,
Stood high in joy, since warlike triumphs bring
Remembrance of our former sorrowing.

The memory of these should quickly fade
(For pleasure's stream
Is like a dream,
Passant and fleet as is a shade)
Unless thyself, which these fair models bred,
Had given them a new life when they were dead.

Take then, good countryman and friend, that merit
Which folly lends,
Not judgement sends,
To foreign shores for strangers to inherit.
Perfection must be bold with front upright,
Though Envy gnash her teeth whilst she would bite.

John Webster

The True Order of his Majesty's Proceeding through London on Thursday the 15 of March anno domini 1604, as it was marshalled by the Lords in Commission for the Office of Earl Marshal of England

Messengers of the Chamber in their Coats
Gentlemen Harbingers and Serjeant Porters
Pursuivants at Arms — Gentlemen and Esquires, the Prince's Servants — Pursuivants at Arms
Gentlemen and Esquires, the Queen's Servants
Gentlemen and Esquires, the King's Servants
Sewers, the King's Servants
Quarter Waiters
Gentlemen Ushers in Ordinary
Clerks Signet
Privy Seal
Council
Parliament
Crown
Chaplains having dignities
Aldermen of London
The Prince's Council at Law
The Prince's Serjeant to go with another Serjeant
Heralds at Arms — The King's Advocate and the Queen's Attorney — Heralds at Arms
The King's Attorney and Solicitor
Serjeants of the Law
The King's Serjeants
Masters of the Chancery

86 **Passant** passing, fleeting

87 **models** of the arches

96–199 ***The True Order*...follow** Public Record Office (London) State Papers Domestic 14, volume 6, item 97. This has been emended in a few places after comparison with the order of the procession printed in Nichols, pp. 325–28. Nichols stated that his Order derived from two manuscripts, one in private hands and the other among the Cotton Manuscripts of the British Museum. We have not attempted to locate these or additional lists that may still be extant. The PRO document was probably a working draft but it agrees with Nichols's Order except in a few relatively minor details. The correct date in the title also suggests that it was compiled not long before the event itself. It therefore seems unlikely that the actual processional order differed significantly from the one here recorded.

98–9 **Commission for the Office** The Earl Marshal was an officer of the Crown responsible for overseeing all matters pertaining to inherited honours, including the ordering of court processions. The office had been vacated by the execution of its holder, the Earl of Essex, for treason in 1601. Its duties were therefore exercised by a commission appointed in February 1604, consisting of the Duke of Lenox, the earls of Nottingham, Suffolk, and Worcester, and Lords Buckhurst and Henry Howard.

100 **Messengers of the Chamber** The order of the procession reflects a strict sense of rank, with lowest officers coming first and those of highest rank grouped around the King. The Messengers of the Chamber, of whom there were normally forty, delivered official messages and orders and occasionally made arrests in the King's name. They wore scarlet coats beautifully embroidered with the initials JR under an imperial crown.

101 **Gentlemen Harbingers** Officers of the Household below stairs under the Lord Steward, a department responsible for the various menial tasks necessary to sustain the court. The harbingers managed the removal of the court from one place to another, for example during summer progresses.

104 **Gentlemen and Esquires** functionaries of the Chamber, which oversaw court ceremony and the personal life of the King. Because they conferred access to the King and were also highly visible, posts in the Chamber, unlike most of those in the Lord Steward's department, tended to be filled by gentlemen and peers. The Gentlemen and Esquires of the Chamber had originated as personal attendants to the King, but by this period had been relegated to a ceremonial role. The Queen and Prince had their own households, with the same structure as the King's but smaller in size.

106 **Sewers** ceremonial officers of the Chamber who served the King when he dined in public

107 **Quarter Waiters** functionaries of the Chamber

108 **Gentlemen Ushers** doorkeepers in the Chamber and its more intimate offshoot, the Privy Chamber (see below, note to l. 145–6)

109 **Signet** a small seal of medieval origin, attached to an office that formed part of the royal bureaucracy for issuing official documents

110 **Privy Seal** another such seal

111–13 **Council | Parliament | Crown** i.e. clerks of the Council, Parliament, and Crown

114 **Chaplains having dignities** Royal chaplains holding other major ecclesiastical offices

117 **The Prince's Serjeant** a legal advisor, subordinate to the chief counsel

120 **The King's Attorney and Solicitor** Edward Coke and Francis Bacon, the senior legal counsellors of the Crown

121 **Serjeants of the Law** barristers with the right to plead in the Court of Common Pleas, the most active of the central common law courts

122 **King's Serjeants** assistant legal counsellors to the Crown

123 **Masters of the Chancery** Judges in Chancery, the kingdom's chief equity court under the jurisdiction of the Lord Chancellor.

Secretaries for the French and Latin Tongues
Knights Bachelors
Esquires for the body, sewers,
carvers and cupbearers in ordinary
Pursuivants | The Queen's Council at Law | Pursuivants
Masters of standing Offices being no Counsellors, *viz.* { Tents
Revels
Armoury
Wardrobe
Jewel House
Ordinance
Masters of Requests
The Chamberlains of the Exchequer
Barons of the Exchequer and Judges of the laws
Heralds at Arms | The Lord Chief Baron and Lord Chief Justice of the Common Pleas | Heralds at Arms
The Lord Chief Justice of England
The Serjeant Trumpeter with his Mace

Trumpets sounding
Knights and Gentlemen of the
Privy Chamber and Bedchamber
Knights of the Bath
Knights that have been Lord Ambassador
Lords Presidents and Lord Deputies
The Master of the Jewel House
and the Prince's Governor
The Dean of the King's Chapel
Barons' younger sons
Viscounts' younger sons
Knights of the Privy Council
Knights of the Garter
Heralds at Arms | Barons' eldest sons | Heralds at Arms
Earls' younger sons
Viscounts' eldest sons
Treasurer and Controller amongst
Barons according to their creations
Barons of the Parliament

124 **Secretaries for the French and Latin Tongues** responsible for official correspondence in those languages. The Latin secretary was Sir Thomas Smith.

125 **Knights Bachelors** knights who were not members of one of the chivalric orders

126–7 **Esquires . . . ordinary** functionaries of the Chamber, six in number

129 **Masters of standing Offices** heads of ancient administrative departments, attached to the Household or Chamber, or independent
being no Counsellors not belonging to the Privy Council, the chief administrative and policy-making organ of royal government

130 **Tents** a department of the Chamber

131 **Revels** department of the Chamber responsible for court entertainments and the licensing of plays

132 **Armoury** independent department responsible for armour and small arms

133 **Wardrobe** independent department affiliated with the Household, responsible for procuring and stockpiling cloths and related materials used by the court and issuing official robes to many Crown officials

134 **Jewel House** department of the Chamber that kept the royal jewels

135 **Ordinance** independent department responsible for procuring and storing munitions

136 **Masters of Requests** officers in charge of receiving and forwarding petitions to the King

137 **Chamberlains of the Exchequer** officers of the chief royal treasury

138 **Barons of the Exchequer** judges of the exchequer court, having jurisdiction over taxes: at this date Sir Thomas Fleming and Sir Lawrence Tanfield.
Judges of the laws presided in the common law courts of King's Bench and Common Pleas

139–40 **Lord Chief Baron and Lord Chief Justice** Sir William Periam and Sir Edward Anderson, who headed the courts of the Exchequer and Common Pleas

142 **Lord Chief Justice** Sir John Popham, Chief Justice of the King's Bench, the highest common law court

145–6 **Gentlemen of the Privy Chamber and Bedchamber** Gentlemen charged with attending upon the King within the more restricted sections of royal palaces, in which he actually lived. The Privy Chamber had emerged from the Chamber under Henry VII. Until 1603 its gentlemen (and ladies under Elizabeth I) were the monarch's chief personal attendants. Its Scottish counterpart was the Bedchamber. In 1603 James incorporated this institution and its Scottish staff within the English Privy Chamber, whose gentlemen thereby lost their intimate connection to the monarch, being displaced to a ceremonial role. James's court above stairs thus had a tripartite structure of Bedchamber, Privy Chamber, and Chamber proper, reflected both in the physical layout of his palaces and the institutional arrangements. The Scots monopoly over the Bedchamber, which lasted until 1618, caused considerable jealousy among English courtiers and office-holders, especially after the Bedchamber staff emerged as brokers of royal patronage, with privileged access to the King's sometimes extravagant bounty.

147 **Knights of the Bath** Sixty knights created and inducted into the Order of the Bath at royal coronations.

148 **Knights that have been Lord Ambassador** knights who had once served in that capacity. Their relatively high ceremonial prestige, reflected by their position in the procession, stemmed from their role as the personal representatives of English monarchs to foreign sovereigns.

149 **Lords Presidents and Lord Deputies** Heads, respectively, of the Councils of the North and of Wales and of royal government in Ireland

150 **Master of the Jewel House** Sir Edward Carey, official keeper of the King's jewels

151 **Prince's Governor** Sir Thomas Chaloner, appointed to take charge of the person and household of the Prince in August 1603

152 **Dean of the King's Chapel** James Montague, titular head of the staff of chaplains

155 **Knights of the Privy Council** members of the Privy Council holding the rank of knight

156 **Knights of the Garter** members of the great chivalric Order of the Garter, established by Edward III and based at Windsor Castle

160 **Treasurer and Controller** financial officers of the household below stairs, reporting to the Lord Steward

161 **according to their creations** The order of march was based on the date at which the baron's titles had been granted, with older titles taking precedence over more recent ones.

162 **Barons of the Parliament** lay members of the House of Lords without higher titles

The Principal Secretary being a baron
Bishops
Marquesses' younger sons
Earls' eldest sons
Viscounts
Dukes' younger sons
Marquesses' eldest sons
Earls
The Lord Admiral and Lord Chamberlain being not otherwise employed
Dukes' eldest sons
Marquesses
Dukes

Serjeants of Arms but not to pass the swords	Clarenceaux and Norroy kings of arms together	Serjeants of Arms but not to pass the swords

Lord Treasurer and Lord Chancellor together
Lord Mayor of London—Garter Chief King at Arms—Chief Gentleman Usher

The Prince's Footmen	The Prince of Wales	The Prince's Footmen
The Lord High Constable	The sword borne by the Earl Marshal	The Lord Great Chamberlain
Gentlemen Pensioners, Footmen and Equerries of the Stable	The King's Majesty	Gentlemen Pensioners, Footmen and Equerries of the Stable

The Master of the Horse leading a spare horse
Vice Chamberlain to the King
The Queen's Vice Chamberlain

163 **Principal Secretary** Robert Cecil, created Baron Essendon in May of 1603. The Principal Secretary was the more senior of two secretaries of state responsible for both diplomatic and domestic correspondence and a range of related duties. Cecil was at this time the single most powerful and important minister of the King.

171 **Lord Admiral** Charles Howard, Earl of Nottingham, commander of the royal navy, a post he had held during the famous victory over the Armada in 1588 **Lord Chamberlain** Thomas Howard, Earl of Suffolk, the administrative head of the Chamber and its offshoot, the Privy Chamber

176–8 **Clarenceaux and Norroy kings of arms** William Camden, the antiquarian, and Richard St George. Kings of Arms were heralds, responsible for overseeing grants of arms and adjudicating issues relating to rank, under the supervision of the Earl Marshal.

179 **Lord Treasurer** Thomas Sackville, Earl of Dorset, head of the Exchequer **Lord Chancellor** Sir Thomas Egerton. The Lord Chancellor was both the chief judge of the Court of Chancery and head of the administrative department that controlled the Great Seal, needed to authenticate legal writs and some other official documents. The Lord Chancellor and Lord Treasurer were the senior administrative officers of the Crown, since they headed the oldest administrative departments of royal government, dating from the twelfth century.

180 **Lord Mayor of London** Sir William Bennet. Dugdale describes him wearing 'a crimson velvet gown, bearing his enamelled golden mace upon his shoulder' and states that he 'ushered the King, Queen and Prince ... to Temple Bar, [where] he took his leave and received many thanks of the King and Queen, who was after met by the Aldermen and Sheriffs, who came to guard him home'.

180–1 **Garter Chief King at Arms** the highest ranking herald, William Noroy, who would have worn the robe of crimson satin he received when invested with his post in February 1604. Along with the Chief Gentlemen Usher he was placed here to attend upon the Lord Mayor, who was himself escorting the King through the City.

181 **Chief Gentleman Usher** in charge of the gentlemen ushers of the Privy Chamber

182–3 **Prince of Wales** James's eldest son Henry Frederick (1594–1612). Dugdale states: 'The young hopeful Henry Frederick or Frederick Henry, Prince of Wales, smiling as overjoyed, to the peoples' eternal comfort, salute[d] them with many a bend.'

184 **Lord High Constable** This medieval office had been vacant since 1521, but the Earl of Nottingham was appointed to fill it during the coronation and the entry into London.

185 **Earl Marshal** The Earl of Worcester, again appointed only for the Coronation and the entry.

186 **Lord Great Chamberlain** Edward de Vere, Earl of Oxford. This ancient office had long since become purely ceremonial in nature. The Lord High Constable, Earl Marshal and Lord Great Chamberlain were all relics of an earlier stage in the development of both the royal household and royal governance, when both retained many feudal characteristics. Their inclusion at this, the climactic point, of the royal procession reflects a deep sense of tradition rather than the organization of the court in the early seventeenth century. That sense of tradition was itself significant, however. Late in Elizabeth's reign, the Earl of Essex had attempted to revive the prestige of the Earl Marshal's Office as part of a broader reassertion of aristocratic privilege. A manuscript antiquarian treatise, apparently written under his auspices, had canvassed the ancient authority of both the Earl Marshal and the Constable, which arguably included, in the latter case, the right to arrest the King himself in the name of the nobility. The presence of archaic elements in the entry ceremony can legitimately be related to a wider preoccupation with medieval procedures and precedents that profoundly shaped the political culture of James's reign. **Gentlemen Pensioners** an élite guard equipped with black uniforms and gilt halberds, recruited from leading gentry families. Established in 1539, they staffed the Presence Chamber, a throne room immediately beyond the privy apartments, and also performed other ceremonial duties. **Equerries** functionaries of the royal stable, present as part of the King's escort

186–7 **The King's Majesty** James rode on a saddle of purple velvet embroidered with pearls and silver twist, beneath a canopy consisting of 38 yards of exceptionally fine yellow cloth worth £10 a yard, fastened to a wooden frame with gilt nails. The canopy was further adorned with gold fringe, ten large plumes and fifty yards of ribbon. In all the saddle, canopy and related paraphernalia cost just over £550 (PRO LC2/4(5)).

188 **Master of the Horse** Edward Somerset, Earl of Worcester. Head of the King's stables, the Master of the Horse had the right to ride with him during hunts and on other occasions.

189 **Vice Chamberlain** Sir John Stanhope. The second ranking officer of the Chamber, under the Chamberlain.

190 **Queen's Vice Chamberlain** Sir George Carew

The Queen's Lord Chamberlain

Gentlemen Ushers Footmen Pensioners	The Queen's Majesty	Gentlemen Ushers Footmen Pensioners

Master of the Horse leading a spare horse
Ladies according to their degrees, *viz.*
duchesses, marquesses, countesses,
viscountesses, baronesses, knights' wives
Maids of honour with the Mother of the Maids
The Captain of the Guard, with the Guard to follow

THE MAGNIFICENT ENTERTAINMENT Given to King James, Queen Anne his wife, and Henry Frederick the Prince, upon the day of his Majesty's triumphant passage (from the Tower) through his honourable city (and chamber) of London, being the 15 of March 1604. *As well by the English as by the strangers: with the speeches and songs delivered in the several pageants.*

Templa Deis, mores populis dedit, otia ferro,
Astra suis, Caelo sidera, serta Jovi

Martial

A DEVICE

(projected down, but till now not published) that should have served at his Majesty's first access to the city.

The sorrow and amazement that like an earthquake began to shake the distempered body of this island, by reason of our late sovereign's departure, being wisely and miraculously prevented, and the feared wounds of a civil sword (as Alexander's fury was with music) being stopped from bursting forth by the sound of trumpets that proclaimed King James, all men's eyes were presently turned to the north, standing even stone still in their circles, like the points of so many geometrical needles, through a fixed and adamantine desire to behold this forty-five years' wonder now brought forth by time; their tongues neglecting all language else, save that which spake zealous prayers and unceaseable wishes for his most speedy and longed-for arrival. Insomuch that the night was thought unworthy to be crowned with sleep, and the day not fit to be looked upon by the sun, which brought not some fresh tidings of his Majesty's more near and nearer approach.

At the length Expectation (who is ever waking and that so long was great) grew near the time of her delivery, Rumour coming all in a sweat to play the midwife, whose first comfortable words were that this treasure of a kingdom, a man ruler, hid so many years from us, was now brought to light and at hand.

Et populi vox erat una, Venit.

Martial

And that he was to be conducted through some utter part of this his city to his royal castle the Tower, that in the age of a man, till this very minute, had not been acquainted nor borne the name of a king's court. Which entrance of his in this manner being famed abroad, because his loving subjects the citizens would give a taste of their duty and affection, the device following was suddenly made up as the first service to a more royal and serious ensuing entertainment; and this, as it was then purposed, should have been performed about the bars beyond Bishopsgate.

The Device

Saint George, Saint Andrew, the patrons of both kingdoms, having a long time looked upon each other with

191 **Queen's Lord Chamberlain** Sir Henry Sydney. The Queen's household was staffed mainly by women but its chief officers were men.

192–3 **The Queen's Majesty** Anne of Denmark (1574–1619). Dugdale commented: 'Our gracious Queen Anne, mild and courteous, placed in a chariot of exceeding beauty, did all the way so humbly and with mildness salute her subjects, never ceasing to bend her body to them, this way and that, that women and men in my sight wept with joy.' The chariot—painted, gilt, covered with cloth of gold and topped by ostrich plumes—cost £351 (PRO LC2/4(5)).

194 **horse** The horse was equipped with an ornate saddle stuffed with down, covered with two yards of purple tissue cloth costing over £57, adorned with twist laces and fringes of gold, silver, and silk. The material for the saddle cloth cost £20 the yard and so must have been even finer than that used for the King's canopy. The bridle was covered in cloth of gold, fringed with gold and silver lace; there was also a large plume costing £10 (PRO LC2/4(5)).

195 **Ladies** rode in two chariots covered in crimson velvet fringed with gold and silk, topped by 18 plumes (PRO LC2/4(5)). Nichols lists them: The Lady Arabella, The Countess of Oxford, The Countess of Northumberland, The Countess of Shrewsbury, The Lady Rich by special commandment, The Countess of Derby, The Countess of Worcester, The Countess of Rutland, The Countess of Cumberland, The Countess of Sussex, The Countess of Bath, The Countess of Southamptom the elder, The Countess of Bedford, The Countess of Pembroke, The Countess of Hertford, The Countess of Essex, The Countess of Nottingham, The Countess of Suffolk, The Countess of Dorset, The Lady Lawarre, The Lady Lumlye, the Lady Dacres of the North, The Lady Mordant, The Lady North, The Lady Hunsdon, The Lady Wotton.

199 **Captain of the Guard** Sir Thomas Erskine. Like the Gentlemen Pensioners, the Guard belonged to the Chamber.

205 **strangers** Foreign residents

207–8 ***Templa...Jovi*** Temples he gave the Gods, morals to the people, rest to the sword, immortality to his own kin, to heaven stars, wreaths to Jove (Martial, *Epigrams*, 9.101.21)

210 ***DEVICE*** design

212 **access** entry into

215–16 **wisely and miraculously prevented** i.e. by the peaceful accession of James I. There had been widespread anxiety over a possible struggle for the succession.

217 **Alexander's...music** unidentified allusion

221 **geometrical needles** compasses

223 **forty-five years'** length of Elizabeth's reign (1558–1603)

237 ***Et...Venit*** And one voice of the people goes up, 'Does he come?' (Martial, *Epigrams*, 10.6.8)

239 **utter** outlying

246 **first service** as in a banquet

249 **bars** marking the city limits **Bishopsgate** on the northern face of the city wall, toward the east. See map, p. 62.

251 **Saint George, Saint Andrew** Patron saints of England and Scotland. Dugdale recorded an appearance by the two saints at Jonson's pageant in Fenchurch Street (below, note to l. 453). Was a truncated version of Dekker's pageant transferred there?

countenances rather of mere strangers than of such near neighbours, upon the present aspect of his Majesty's approach toward London were, in his sight, to issue from two several places on horseback and in complete armour, their breasts and caparisons suited with the arms of England and Scotland as they are now quartered, to testify their leagued combination and new sworn brotherhood. These two armed knights, encount'ring one another on the way, were to ride hand-in-hand till they met his Majesty. But the strangeness of this newly-begotten amity flying over the earth, it calls up the *Genius* of the city, who, not so much mazed as wond'ring at the novelty, intercepts their passage.

And most aptly, in our judgement, might this *domesticum numen*, the *Genius* of the place, lay just claim to this preeminence of first bestowing salutations and welcomes on his Majesty—*Genius* being held *inter fictos deos* to be god of hospitality and pleasure, and none but such a one was meet to receive so excellent and princely a guest.

Or if not worthy for those two former respects, yet being *deus generationis* and having a power as well over countries, herbs and trees as over men, and the city having now put on a regeneration or new birth, the induction of such a person might without a warrant from the court of critists pass very current.

To make a false flourish here with the borrowed weapons of all the old masters of the noble science of poesy, and to keep a tyrannical coil in anatomizing *Genius* from head to foot, only to show how nimbly we can carve up the whole mess of the poets, were to play the executioner, and to lay our city's houshould god on the rack, to make him confess how many pair of Latin sheets we have shaken and cut into shreds to make him a garment. Such feats of activity are stale and common among scholars, before whom it is protested we come not now, in a pageant, to play a master's prize, for *nunc ego ventosae plebis suffragia venor.*

The multitude is now to be our audience, whose heads would miserably run a-wool-gathering if we do but offer to break them with hard words. But suppose by the way, contrary to the opinion of all the doctors, that our *Genius* (in regard the place is feminine and the person itself, drawn *figura humana, sed ambiguo sexu*) should at this time be thrust into woman's apparel. It is no schism: be it so. Our *Genius* is then a female, antique and reverend both in years and habit: a chaplet of mingled flowers, interwoven with branches of the plane tree crowning her temples; her hair long and white; her vesture a loose robe, changeable and powdered with Stars. And being on horseback likewise, thus furnished, this was the tune of her voice.

GENIUS LOCI

Stay, we conjure you, by that potent name
Of which each letter's now a triple charm;
Stay and deliver us of whence you are,
And why you bear alone th'ostent of war,
When all hands else rear olive boughs and palm,
And halcyonean days assure all's calm;
When every tongue speaks music, when each pen
(Dulled and dyed black in gall) is white again
And dipped in nectar, which by Delphic fire
Being heated, melts into an Orphean choir.
When Troy's proud buildings show like fairy bowers
And streets, like gardens, are perfumed with flowers,
And windows glazed only with wond'ring eyes
(In a king's look such admiration lies!),
And when soft-handed Peace so sweetly thrives
That bees in soldiers' helmets build their hives;
When Joy a-tiptoe stands on Fortune's wheel
In silken robes, how dare you shine in steel?

258 **now quartered** on the arms of James I
263 **Genius** guardian spirit, incarnation of the city's essential character
266–7 ***domesticum numen*** household god
269 ***inter fictos deos*** among false or fictitious gods
273 ***deus generationis*** god of engendering
277 **critists** critics
280 **coil** disturbance, tumult
anatomizing describing minutely. Almost certainly a glance at Jonson's marginal note explaining the Genius at the Fenchurch arch (below, l. 567), which had appeared in print shortly before the publication of Dekker's text.
282 **mess** course or serving of food
288 **play ... prize** as in a university play
288–9 ***nunc ... venor*** 'I am now to hunt for the votes of a fickle public', paraphrasing Horace, *Epistles* 1.19.37. Dekker inverted the sense by substituting *Nunc* (now) for *Non* (not). Probably another barb aimed at Jonson, who liked to call himself the English Horace and who shared Horace's disdain for popularity.
295 ***figura ... sexu*** As a human figure but of ambiguous sex. Middleton followed this precedent in creating a female Genius for *Triumphs of Truth.*
296 **schism** heresy
297 **antique** ancient, referring both to classical antiquity and the Genius's appearance
298 **chaplet** wreath
299 **plane tree** an ornamental tree of Persian origin. Cesare Ripa, *Iconologia*, describes '*Genio Buono secondo i Gentilli*' as a youth crowned with a wreath of plane.
301 **powdered** sprinkled
307 ***th'ostent*** the appearance
308 ***olive boughs and palm*** conventional symbols of peace
309 ***halcyonean*** the halcyon, a mythical bird that builds its nest on the ocean and so has power to calm the waves; hence a symbol of a peace-giver
311 ***gall*** bile, venom
312 ***Delphic*** sacred to Apollo
313 ***Orphean*** of Orpheus, the mythological musician-poet whose lyre charmed even the gods of Hell
314 ***Troy's*** London's. The medieval chronicler Geoffrey of Monmouth traced the descent of the British people to a band of Trojans. Although repeatedly disputed, this theory sanctioned poetic allusions to the nation's Trojan origin. Dekker later refers to London as Troynovant (ll. 357, 1535).
buildings an allusion to the appearance of the triumphal route.
fairy bowers Thanks in large part to Spenser, fairies had become patriotic symbols.
319 ***bees in soldiers' helmets*** icon of peace, probably derived from emblem 45 in Andrea Alciati, *Emblemata Libellas*, 'Ex bello pax', showing several bees next to a helmet

SAINT GEORGE
Lady, what are you that so question us?
GENIUS
I am the place's Genius, whence now springs
A vine whose youngest branch shall produce kings:
This little world of men, this precious stone
That sets out Europe; this, the glass alone,
Where the neat sun each morn himself attires
And gilds it with his repercussive fires;
This jewel of the land, England's right eye,
Altar of Love and sphere of Majesty;
Green Neptune's minion, 'bout whose virgin waist
Isis is like a crystal girdle cast:
Of this are we the Genius. Here have I
Slept, by the favour of a deity,
Forty-four summers and as many springs,
Not frighted with the threats of foreign kings;
But held up in that gownèd state I have,
By twice twelve fathers politic and grave,
Who with a sheathèd sword and silken law
Do keep, within weak walls, millions in awe.
I charge you therefore say for what you come?
What are you?
BOTH *Knights at arms.*
SAINT GEORGE *Saint George.*
SAINT ANDREW *Saint Andrew.*
For Scotland's honour I.
SAINT GEORGE *For England's I,*
Both sworn into a league of unity.
GENIUS
I clap my hands for joy and seat you both
Next to my heart. In leaves of purest gold
This most auspicious love shall be enrolled.
Be joined to us and as to earth we bow,
So to those royal feet bend your steeled brow.
In name of all these Senators on whom
Virtue builds more than those of antique Rome,
Shouting a cheerful welcome—since no clime
Nor age that has gone o'er the head of time
Did e'er cast up such joys, nor the like sum
(But here) shall stand in the world, years to come—
Dread King, our hearts make good what words do want,
To bid thee boldly enter Troynovant.
Rerum certa salus, Terrarum gloria Caesar! Martial
Sospite quo, magnos credimus esse Deos:
Dilexere prius pueri, iuvenesque senesque, Idem
At nunc infantes te quoque Caesar amant.

This should have been the first off'ring of the city's love, but his Majesty not making his entrance according to expectation it was, not utterly thrown from the altar, but laid by.

Iam Crescunt media Paegmata celsa via.
Martial

By this time imagine that poets, who draw speaking pictures, and painters, who make dumb poesy, had their heads and hands full, the one for native and sweet invention, the other for lively illustration of what the former should devise; both of them emulously contending, but not striving, with the prop'rest and brightest colours of wit and art, to set out the beauty of the great triumphant day.

For more exact and formal managing of which business, a select number both of aldermen and commoners (like so many Roman *Aediles*) were *communi consilio* chosen forth, to whose discretion the charge, contrivings, projects and all other dependences owing to so troublesome a work was entirely and judicially committed.

Many days were thriftily consumed to mould the bodies of these triumphs comely and to the honour of the place, and at last the stuff whereof to frame them was beaten out: the soul that should give life and a tongue

324 ***vine*** symbolizing lineage
328 ***repercussive*** reflected
331 ***Neptune's*** God of the seas
332 ***Isis*** Egyptian goddess, protector of the dead and the sick, also associated with royal power
335 ***Forty-four summers*** since Elizabeth's accession
337 ***gownèd*** symbolizing peace
338 ***twice twelve*** alluding to the aldermen of London, of whom there were actually 26
politic versed in the mysteries of politics.
340 ***weak walls*** of London. Foreign visitors sometimes remarked on the absence of strong defences around English cities, attributable to the long domestic peace of the Tudor period.
350 ***Senators*** the Council of London.
357 ***Troynovant*** New Troy. See note at 314.
358–9 ***Rerum . . . Deos*** Sure saviour of our state, the world's glory, Caesar, from whose safety we win belief that the great gods exist (Martial, *Epigrams*, 2.91.1–2). An early example of the use of Roman imperial imagery to celebrate Jacobean kingship.
360–1 ***Dilexere . . . amant*** Boys loved thee before, and young men, and aged sires; but now infants, too, love thee, Caesar (Martial, *Epigrams*, 9.8.9–10).
366 ***Iam . . . via*** And the high stages grow in the middle of the street (Martial, *de Spectaculis* 2.2).
368–9 **poets . . . painters** a Renaissance commonplace, deriving ultimately from Horace's *Art of Poetry*
371 **invention** the selection and arrangement of materials for the entertainment
378 **Aediles** Roman municipal officers whose functions included overseeing shows and spectacles
communi consilio out of the common council
382 **Many days** glossing over the delay of eight months caused by the plague. Harrison states: 'These five [actually seven] triumphal arches were first taken in hand in the beginning of April 1603, presently after his Majesty was proclaimed, it being expected that his passage would have been through his honourable city and chamber to his coronation upon Saint James his day following [25 July]. But by reason of the sickness it pleased his Majesty to be solemnly crowned at Westminster, without sight of these triumphs. Notwithstanding, the business being set on foot went on with all expedition till Bartholomewtide [24 August], and then ceased because of the great mortality. Forty days more was given for the preparing of this triumphal arch.'
384 **stuff** material
385 **soul** inner spirit and meaning, contrasted with the outward form, supplied by the workmen

to this entertainment being to breathe out of writers' pens, the limbs of it to lie at the hard-handed mercy of mechanicians.

In a moment, therefore, of time are carpenters, joiners, carvers, and other artificers sweating at their chisels.

Accingunt Omnes operi.
Virgil

Not a finger but had an office: he was held unworthy ever after to 'suck the honeydew of peace' that 'against his coming, by whom our peace wears a triple wreath,' would offer to play the drone. The streets are surveyed: heights, breadths, and distances taken, as it were to make fortifications, for the solemnities. Seven pieces of ground like so many fields for a battle are plotted forth, upon which these arches of triumph must show themselves in their glory; aloft, in the end do they advance their proud foreheads.

Circum pueri, innuptaeque puellae,
Sacra canunt, funemque manu contingere gaudent.
Virgil

Even children, might they have been suffered, would gladly have spent their little strength about the engines that mounted up the frames, such a fire of love and joy was kindled in every breast.

The day for whose sake these wonders of wood climbed thus into the clouds is now come, being so early up (by reason of artificial lights which wakened it) that the sun overslept himself and rose not in many hours after, yet bringing with it into the very bosom of the city a world of people. The streets seemed to be paved with men; stalls instead of rich wares were set out with children; open casements filled up with women.

All glass windows taken down but in their places sparkled so many eyes that had it not been the day the light which reflected from them was sufficient to have made one. He that should have compared the empty and untrodden walks of London, which were to be seen in that late mortally-destroying deluge, with the thronged streets now, might have believed that upon this day began a new creation and that the city was the only workhouse wherein sundry nations were made.

A goodly and civil order was observed in marshalling all the companies according to their degrees, the first beginning at the upper end of Saint Mark's Lane and the last reaching above the Conduit in Fleet Street; their seats, being double-railed, upon the upper part whereon they leaned; the streamers, ensigns and bannerets of each particular company decently fixed. And directly against them, even quite through the body of the city, so high as to Temple Bar, a single rail, in fair distance from the other, was likewise erected to put off the multitude. Amongst whose tongues, which in such consorts never lie still, though there were no music, yet as the poet says:

Vox diversa sonat, populorum est vox tamen una.
Martial

Nothing that they speak could be made anything, yet all that was spoken sounded to this purpose, that still his Majesty was coming. They have their longings. And behold, afar off they spy him, richly mounted on a white jennet, under a rich canopy, sustained by eight Barons of the Cinque Ports, the Tower serving that morning but for his withdrawing chamber, wherein he made him ready, and from thence stepped presently into his City of London, which for the time might worthily borrow the name of his

388 **mechanicians** practitioners of mechanical crafts. The contrast here between writers and mechanicians seems at odds with the parallel of poets and painters in ll. 368–75. Poets had traditionally enjoyed a higher status than artists and architects because they dealt with ideas rather than manual skills. This distinction had been challenged by several European theorists, especially the Florentine painter and art historian Giorgio Vasari. Dekker's phrase implicitly affirms the traditional superiority of literature over the manual arts.
391 ***Accingunt*...*operi*** All equip themselves for the work (Virgil, *Aeneid* 2.235)
394–5 **suck**...**wreath** Unidentified quotations
394 **honeydew** a sticky substance found on leaves and stems of plants
against in anticipation of
403–4 ***Circum*...*gaudent*** Around it boys and unwedded girls chant holy songs and delight to touch the cable with their hands (Virgil, *Aeneid*, 2.238–239)
407 **engines** probably the arches themselves, rather than machines used to erect them
413 **overslept** The day was overcast.
415 **stalls** common along London streets
417 **casements** Street stalls and windows along the route were rented out to gentry and other affluent spectators.
423 **mortally-destroying deluge** the plague of 1603
427–8 **civil**...**degrees** the orderly arrangement of liveried members of the guilds along the route. See Introduction.
429 **Saint Mark's Lane** in the eastern part of the City near the Tower of London
431 **double-railed** closed in with a double rail
435 **Temple Bar** to the west, marking the boundary between London and Westminster along the Strand
439 ***Vox*...*una*** Many voices sounded, but the voice of the people was as one. Adapted from Martial, *De spectaculis libra* 3, l. 11.
445 **jennet** a small Spanish horse
445–6 **Barons of the Cinque Ports** Royal officers responsible for oversight of seven ports and adjacent land along the coast of Kent and Sussex, incorporated under the Crown in the early Middle Ages because of their strategic importance. The Barons of the Cinque Ports had successfully claimed the right to hold the canopy over James at the coronation in the previous year, on the basis of medieval precedent.
447 **withdrawing chamber** A room or rooms between the privy chamber and bedchamber in the King's apartments in various royal palaces, to which the topography of the city is here being compared.

court royal. His passage alongst that court offering itself for more state through seven gates.

g. 2

The Device called Londinium

The first *pegme* was erected in Fenchurch Street, the back of it so leaning on the east end of the church that it overspread the whole street. And thus we describe it.

It was a flat square, builded upright. The perpendicular line of the whole frame (that is to say, the distance from the bottom to the top) as the ground line, is (also in this, so in all the rest) to be found out and tried by the scale, divided by 1, 2, 3, 4 and 5, and set at the lower end of the piece. By which figures feet are represented, so that in all the descriptions, where mention is to be made of heights, breadths or any other commensurable proportions, you shall find them left thus — with a blank, because we wish you rather to apply them to the scale yourself, than by setting them down to call either your skill or judgement in question.

And note withal that the ground-plot hath not the same scale which the upright hath, for of the two scales which you see annexed the lesser is of the ground and standeth in the ground-plot, the greater for the edifice or building itself.

This gate of passage then, into which his Majesty made his first entrance, was derived from the *Tuscana*, being the principal pillar of those five upon which the noble frame of architecture doth stand, for the Tuscan column is the strongest and most worthy to support so famous a work as this fabric was, considering that upon his rustic pillars the goodliest houses, turrets, steeples, etc. within this city were to be borne. And those models stood as a coronet on the forehead or battlements of this great and magnificent edifice.

The cheeks or sides of the gate were, as it were, doubly guarded with the portraitures of Atlas, King of Mauritania, who, according to his own shortness and thickness, from the *symmetry* of his foot caused a pillar to be made, whose height with base and capital was six times the thickness in height. And so is this of ours, bearing the name of *Tuscana*, as we said before, and reaching to the very point of the arch, from whence we did derive *Dorica*, which bore up the architrave, frieze, and cornice, and was garnished with corbels or *croxtels* fitting such work, besides the beauty of pyramids, beasts, water, tables and many other enrichments which you may find expressed in the piece itself.

From a gallery directly over the gate the sound of loud music, being the waites and oboes of the city, was sent forth.

The Pegme at Fenchurch

Presented itself in a square and flat upright, like to the side of a city; the top thereof, above the vent and crest, adorned with houses, towers and steeples, set off in perspective. Upon the battlements, in a great capital letter, was inscribed,

LONDINIVM

451 **state** ceremonial magnificence
gates. Arches. Dekker goes on to describe the Fenchurch arch: see Additional Passage B.

453 **pegme** Arch. Dugdale comments: 'In Fenchurch Street was erected a stately trophy or pageant, at the city's charge, on which stood such a show of workmanship and glory as I never saw the like. Top and topgallant, whereon were shows so embroidered and set out as the cost was incomparable, who speaking speeches to the King of that excellent eloquence and as (while I live) I commend. The City of London very rarely and artificially made, where no church, house nor place of note but your eye might easily find out, as the Exchange, Cole harbour, Paul's, Bowe Church, etc. There also Saint George and Saint Andrew, in complete armour, met in one combat and fought for the victory, but an old hermit passing by, in an oration joined them hand-in-hand and so forever hath made them as one heart, to the joy of the King, the delight of the lords, and the unspeakable comfort of the commonalty.' The old hermit, mentioned in none of the other texts, was probably Dekker's Genius: her long robe must have given her a hermit-like appearance, since Dugdale appears to be describing a version of the pageant originally planned for Bishopsgate, which had perhaps been transferred to a site between the Tower and Fenchurch.

464 **a blank** Dekker often supplies the missing measurement. The use of the scale lent an aura of technical sophistication to the drawings, making them similar to architectural plots.

474 **Tuscana** The Tuscan order, discussed by Vitruvius and some Renaissance architectural manuals. Normally regarded as the oldest and sturdiest of the classical orders, suitable for barns and outbuildings, it was used by Inigo Jones in the 1630s as the basis for Covent Garden.

480 **coronet** small crown worn by a nobleman or noblewoman

490 **did derive *Dorica*** the Tuscan was replaced by the Doric order above the keystone of the arch

491 **architrave, frieze, and cornice** parts of the entablature, resting on the columns

492 **corbels** projecting beams. Large wooden corbels were a peculiar feature of the Tuscan order, prominently used by Jones in St Paul's Church, Covent Garden.

497 **waites and oboes** city musicians

501 **vent** crenellated top of the arch

503 **perspective** Perspective was not well understood by English painters at this date, although it would soon become an innovative feature of Inigo Jones's masque designs. Jonson, who ignores most of the architectural features reported by Harrison, notices this one technical feature which Harrison overlooked.

The device called Londinium, in Fenchurch Street, for pageant 2.

a *Annals* liber 14.

b Camden *Britannia*, p. 374.

c Liber 8 *Epigrammaton* 36.

According to Tacitus: *At Suetonius mira constantia, medios inter hosteis Londinium perrexit, cognomento quidem Coloniae non insigne, sed copia negotiatorum, et commeatu maxime celebre.*[a] Beneath that, in a less and different character, was written

CAMERA REGIA

Which title immediately after the Norman conquest it began to have, and by the indulgence of succeeding princes hath been hitherto continued.[b] In the frieze over the gate it seemeth to speak this verse:

PAR DOMVS HAEC COELO,
SED MINOR EST DOMINO.[c]

Taken out of Martial, and implying that though this city for the state and magnificence might, by hyperbole, be said to touch the stars and reach up to heaven, yet was it far inferior to the master thereof, who was his Majesty, and in that respect unworthy to receive him. The highest person advanced therein was

MONARCHIA BRITANNICA

and fitly, applying to the above mentioned title of the city, the King's chamber, and therefore here placed as in the proper seat of the empire: for so the glory and light of our kingdom, Master Camden, speaking of London, saith she is, *totius Britanniae Epitome, Britannicique imperii sedes, Regumque Angliae Camera, tantum inter omneis eminet, quantum (ut ait ille) inter viburna cupressus.* She was a woman richly attired in cloth-of-gold and tissue; a rich mantle; over her state two crowns hanging, with pensile shields through them, the one limned with the particular coat of England, the other of Scotland; on either side also a crown, with the like scutcheons and peculiar coats of France and Ireland. In her hand she holds a sceptre; on her head a fillet of gold interwoven with palm and laurel; her hair bound into four several points, descending from her crowns; and in her lap a little globe, inscribed upon

ORBIS BRITANNICVS

And beneath the word

506–9 ***At...celebre*** Suetonius, on the other hand, with remarkable firmness, marched straight through the midst of the enemy upon London; which, though not distinguished by the title of the colony, was none the less a busy centre, chiefly through its crowd of merchants and stores (Tacitus, *Annals* 14.33). The quotation, taken from Tacitus' account of London's destruction in Boadecia's rebellion, seems irrelevant, unless Jonson wanted to justify the use of the Latin form of the city's name.

511 **CAMERA REGIA** King's Chamber.

514.n **Camden *Britannia*** William Camden, *Britannia sive florentissimorum Rengnorum Anglia, Scotiae, Hiberniae et Insularum adjaentium ex intime antiquitate Chorographica Descriptio* (1586 and later editions). Camden was Jonson's tutor at Westminster and lifetime friend.

516–17 **PAR...DOMINO** whose summit touches the stars, rivals heaven, but is not so great as its lord (Martial, *Epigrams*, 8.36.12)

524 **MONARCHIA BRITANNICA** James's accession created the British monarchy by uniting the crown of Scotland to those of England and Ireland. Britain was still an unfamiliar Latinate name in 1603 and the notion that they should now think of themselves as British rather than English—and Scots as fellow countrymen rather than barbaric foreigners—horrified many of James's new subjects. The King, however, saw the dynastic union of England and Scotland as a providentially ordained event, meant to open the way to a more complete integration of laws, customs, and peoples. His strong feelings on the topic encouraged writers seeking court patronage to compose their own treatises and panegyrics on the union of England and Scotland. Numerous allusions to the unification throughout the pageant thus represent James's views, but not necessarily those of the audience.

528 **Master Camden** see above note to l. 514.n

529–31 ***totius...cupressus*** 'the epitome of all Britain, the seat of the British empire, the chamber of the English monarchy, so that, as the proverb has it, she rears her head as high among all other cities as the cypresses do among ossiers' (a paraphrase of Virgil's description of Rome, *Eclogues*, 1.25).

532 **tissue** fine cloth

533 **mantle** sleeveless garment. The gold robe and crown parallel those of the figure Divine Justice in Ripa's *Iconologia*

state throne

pensile pendant, hanging

534 **limned** painted

536 **peculiar** particular

541 **ORBIS BRITANNICVS** British world

DIVISVS AB ORBE

To show that this empire is a world divided from the world, and alluding to that of Claudian

Et nostro diducta Britannia mundo [a]

and Virgil

Et penitus toto divisos orbe Britannos. [b]

The wreath denotes victory and happiness, the sceptre and crowns sovereignty; the shields, the precedency of the countries and their distinctions. At her feet was set

THEOSOPHIA,

or Divine Wisdom, all in white, a blue mantle seeded with stars, a crown of stars on her head. Her garments figured truth, innocence and clearness. She was always looking up. In her one hand she sustained a dove, in the other a serpent: the last to show her subtlety, the first her simplicity, alluding to that text of scripture, *Estote ergo prudentes sicut serpentes, et simplices sicut columbae.* [c] Her word

PER ME REGES REGNANT. [d]

Intimating how by her all kings do govern and that she is the foundation and strength of kingdoms, to which end she was here placed upon a cube at the foot of the monarchy, as her base and stay. Directly beneath her stood

GENIVS VRBIS [e]

A person attired rich, reverend and antique, his hair long and white, crowned with a wreath of plane tree, which is said to be *arbor genialis*; his mantle of purple and buskins of that colour. He held in one hand a goblet, in the other a branch full of little twigs, to signify increase and indulgence. His word

HIS ARMIS

pointing to the two that supported him, whereof the one on the right hand was

BOULEVTES

figuring the Council of the city, and was suited in black and purple, a wreath of oak [f] upon his head; sustaining for his ensigns on his left arm a scarlet robe, and in his

a *De Manlio Theodoro Consulo Panegyricus.*

b *Eclogae* I.

c Matthew 10:16.

d Proverbs 8:15.

e *Antiqui Genium omnium gignendarum rerum existimarunt Deum: et tam urbibus quam hominibus vel caeteris rebus natum.* Lilius Gregorius Geraldus in *Syntagma deorum* 15. and Rosinus *Antiquitatis Romae* liber 2 caput 14.

f *Civica corona fit e fronde querna, quoniam cibus, victusque antiquissimus querceus capi solitus sit.* Rosinus, liber 10 caput 27.

543 **DIVISVS AB ORBE** divided from the world

546 ***Et . . . mundo*** And Britain, so far removed from our continent (Claudian, *Panegyricus dictus Manlio Theodero Consuli*, l. 51)

548 ***Et . . . Britannos*** And the Britons, wholly sundered from all the world (*Eclogues* 1.66)

553 **all in white** Ripa, *Iconologia* prescribes a white robe for Innocence and for one of four possible representations of Truth. The blue mantle and stars have no parallels in Ripa's descriptions of *Religione*, *Sapienza* or *Chiarezza*.
seeded sprinkled

556 **dove** Ripa depicts Divine Justice (*Justitia Divina*) with a dove.

557 **serpent** Perhaps suggested by Ripa's description of *religione finta* (feigned religion), who holds a gold cup from which a serpent rises.

558–9 ***Estote . . . columbae*** Be ye wise as serpents and innocent as doves

561 **PER . . . REGNANT** By me Kings reign

564 **cube** Ripa describes the figure *Religione* as standing on a squared stone, representing 'Christ our Lord, who is the true foundation stone taken from the builders of the old law and placed in the principal corner of His holy Church' (*Christo Signor nostro, il quale e la vera pitra anglare, che disse il profeta riprovata da gli Edificatori de la vecchia Legge, & e per esser posta poi nel principal contone della sua santa Chiesa*).

567 **GENIVS VRBIS** Genius (or spirit) of the city

567.n ***Antiqui . . . natum*** The ancients judged that God was the Genius of all created things, innate in men as in cities and other things.
Syntagma deorum *Historiae deorum gentilium syntagma.* Jonson owned Geraldus' *Opera Omnia*, (1580), which contained this work in volume 1.
Rosinus *Antiquitatis Romae* Johannes Rosinus, *Romae antiquitatis* (1583)

570 ***arbor genialis*** the nuptial tree, alluding to James's marriage to his kingdom

571 **buskins** boots worn by actors in Athenian tragedy

574 **HIS ARMIS** by these arms

578–9 **black and purple** Ripa represents Council as dressed in dark vestments of reddish colour.

579.n ***Civica . . . sit*** 'the civic crown should be from leaves of oak, inasmuch as nourishment and sustenance were customarily taken in the most ancient times from the oak.' The Romans believed that their remote ancestors subsisted largely on a diet of acorns.

right hand the *fasces*,[a] as tokens of magistracy, with this inscription:

SERVARE CIVES

The other on the left hand,

POLEMIVS

The warlike force of the city in an antique coat or armour, with a target and sword; his helm on and crowned with laurel, implying strength and conquest. In his hand he bore the standard of the city, with this word

EXTINGVERE ET HOSTEIS

Expressing by those several mots connected, that with those arms of counsel and strength the *Genius* was able to extinguish the King's enemies and preserve his citizens, alluding to those verses in Seneca,

Extinguere hostem, maxima est virtus ducis.
Servare cives, maior est patriae, patri. [b]

Underneath these in an aback thrust out before the rest lay

TAMESIS,

the river, as running along the side of the city in a skin-coat made like flesh, naked and blue. His mantle of sea green or water colour, thin and bolne out like a sail; bracelets about his wrists of willow and sedge; a crown of sedge and reed upon his head, mixed with water lilies, alluding to Virgil's description of Tiber:

Deus ipse loci, fluvio Tyberinus amoeno,
Populeas inter senior se attollere frondes
Visus, eum tenuis glauco velabat amictu
Carbasus, et crineis umbrosa tegebat Arundo. [c]

His beard and hair long and overgrown, he leans his arm upon an earthen pot, out of which water with live fishes are seen to run forth and play about him. His word

FLVMINA SENSERVNT IPSA [d]

a hemistich of Ovid's, the rest of the verse being

quid esset amor

affirming that rivers themselves and such inanimate creatures have heretofore been made sensible of passions and affections, and that he now no less partook the joy of his Majesty's grateful approach to this city than any of those persons to whom he pointed, which were the daughters of the *Genius* and six in number; who in a

a *Fasciculi virgarum, intra quas obligata securis erat, sic, ut ferrum in summo fasce extaret,* Rosinus l. 7 caput 3. *Ubi notandum est, non debere praecipitem, et solutam iram esse magistratus. Mora enim allata, et cunctatio, dum sensim virgae soluuntur, identidem consilium mutavit de plectendo. Quando autem vitia quaedam sunt corrigibilia, deplorata alia; castigant virgae, quod revocari valet, immendabile secures praecidunt,* Plutarch, *Problematae Romanae* 82.

b *Octavia*, Act 2.

c *Aeneid* liber 8.

d *Amores* liber 3 clausula 6.

581 **fasces** bundles of sticks enclosing an axe, the Roman symbol of magistracy

581.n ***Fasciculi . . . praecidunt*** Bundles of sticks in which axes are fastened, so that the heads project from the bundle, to show a magistrate's anger ought not to be rash and ungrounded. While the rods are loosened the magistrates deliberate and delay their anger, so that oftentimes they delay their punishment. Now, since some badness is curable, but other badness is past remedy, the rods correct that which may be amended and the axes cut off the incorrigible (Plutarch, *Roman Questions* 82, normally published as *Moralia* 283). We have supplied our own translation of Jonson's Latin for the first two sentences, rather than following the Loeb rendering of Plutarch's original Greek, which differs slightly in emphasis.

583 **SERVARE CIVES** to save citizens

587 **target** shield

590 **EXTINGVERE . . . HOSTEIS** and to extinguish enemies

595–6 ***Extinguere . . . patri*** '—To destroy foes is a ruler's greatest virtue. | —For the father of his country to save citizens is greater still.' An exchange between Nero and Seneca in the Senecan play *Octavia* (ll. 443–4), after the former ordered the execution of two erstwhile associates.

597 **aback** square tablet or compartment

599 **TAMESIS** Thames

602 **bolne** swelled

606–9 ***Deus . . . Arundo*** Before him the very god of the place, Tiberinus of the pleasant stream, seemed to raise his aged head amid the poplar leaves; thin lawn draped him in mantle of grey, and shady reeds crowned his hair (Virgil, *Aeneid* 8.31–4).

612 **word** motto

613–15 **FLVMINA . . . *amor*** what love is, rivers themselves have felt (*Amores* 3.6.24). Jonson incorrectly cited liber 3, cl. 5.

614 **hemistich** part of a line of verse, divided by a caesura

spreading ascent upon several greces help to beautify both the sides. The first

EVPHROSYNE

or Gladness was suited in green, a mantle of diverse colours, embroidered with all variety of flowers; on her head a garland of myrtle; in her right hand a crystal cruse filled with wine, in the left, a cup of gold; at her feet a timbrel, harp and other instruments, all ensigns of gladness,

Natis in usum laetitia scyphis, etc. [a]

And in another place,
Nunc est bibendum, nunc pede libero
Pulsanda Tellus, etc. [b]

Her word.

HÆC ÆVI MIHI PRIMA DIES [c]

as if this were the first hour of her life and the minute wherein she began to be, beholding so long coveted and looked for a presence. The second

SEBASIS

or Veneration was varied in an ash-coloured suit and dark mantle, a veil over her head of ash colour; her hands crossed before her and her eyes half closed. Her word

MIHI SEMPER DEUS [d]

implying both her office of reverence and the dignity of her object, who, being as God on earth, should never be less in her thought. The third

PROTHYMIA

or Promptitude was attired in a short tucked garment of flame colour, wings at her back; her hair bright and bound up with ribbons; her breast open, virago-like; her buskins so ribboned. She was crowned with a chaplet of trifolium, to express readiness and openness every way. In her right hand she held a squirrel, as being the creature most full of life and quickness; in the left a close round censer, with the perfume suddenly to be vented forth at the sides. Her word

QUA DATA PORTA [e]

taken from an other place in Virgil, where Eolus at the command of Juno lets forth the wind

a Horace *Carminum* liber 1, 27.

b Et Ode 37.

c Statius *Sylvae* 4, Eucharisticon Domitianum.

d Virgil, *Eclogae* I.

e *Aeneid* I.

622 **spreading ascent upon several greces** several steps that became wider as they ascended

626 **embroidered . . . flowers** Ripa describes the robes of *Contento Armoroso* (Amorous Contentment) and *Allegrezza* (Cheerfulness) as embroidered with flowers and explains in the latter case that this is 'because meadows laugh when covered with flowers'. Like Jonson's figure, *Allegrezza* holds a crystal goblet containing red wine and a gold cup, 'demonstrating that cheerfulness cannot hide herself but freely communicates' with others. Ripa does not mention the musical instruments or the verses by Horace.

628 **cruse** small jar or pot

631 **Natis . . . scyphis** 'Goblets meant for pleasure's service' (line 1)

633–4 ***Nunc . . . Tellus*** 'Now is the time to drain the flowing bowl, now with unfettered foot to beat the ground with dancing.' The first lines of an ode celebrating Octavius' final victory over Cleopatra, which effectively ended the civil wars following Caesar's assassination and opened the way for Octavian to become Emperor. The allusion thus suggests a celebration of newly founded imperial authority that overcomes civil discord and brings peace.

636 **HÆC . . . DIES** 'This is my natal day', Statius' cry of joy upon his first invitation to a great imperial banquet (*Silvae* 4.2, 'Eucharisticon ad Imperatorem Augustum Germanicum Domitianum', line 13).

644 **MIHI SEMPER DEUS** 'For a god he shall always be to me' (line 7); spoken of Augustus, 'the god who has wrought us this peace.'

646 **God on earth** Compare the opening couplet of the sonnet prefaced to James's *Basilikon Doron*: 'God gives not kings the style of Gods in vain | For on his throne his sceptre do they sway.' Jonson reinterprets the Roman habit of deifying emperors to conform with James's own theories of kingship.

649 **tucked** gathered up in folds

650 **flame colour** bright orange or yellow

651 **open** uncovered
virago-like virago: a heroine or female warrior

653 **trifolium** leguminous plant with trifoliate leaves

657 **word** motto

658 **QUA DATA PORTA** where passage is given

659 **Eolus** god charged with keeping the winds locked in a deep cave

ac venti velut agmine facto
Qua data porta ruunt, et terras turbine perflant [a]

and showed that she was no less prepared with promptitude and alacrity than the winds were, upon the least gate that shall be opened to his high command. The fourth

AGRYPNIA

or Vigilance in yellow, a sable mantle seeded with waking eyes, and silver fringe; her chaplet of heliotropium or turnsole; in her one hand a lamp or cresset, in her other a bell. The lamp signified search and sight, the bell warning, the heliotropium care and respecting her object. Her word

SPECULAMUR IN OMNEIS

alluding to that of Ovid, where he describes the office of Argus,

Ipse procul montis sublime cacumen
Occupat, unde sedens partes speculatur in omneis [b]

and implying the like duty of care and vigilance in herself. The fifth

AGAPE

or Loving Affection, in crimson fringed with gold, a mantle of flame colour, her chaplet of red and white roses; in her hand a flaming heart. The flame expressed zeal, the red and white roses a mixture of simplicity with love; her robes freshness and fervency. Her word

NON SIC EXCVBIÆ [c]

out of Claudian, in following

Nec circumstantia pila
Quam tutatur amor.

inferring that though her sister before had protested watchfulness and circumspection, yet no watch or guard could be so safe to the estate or person of a prince as the love and natural affection of his subjects, which she in the city's behalf promised. The sixth

OMOTHYMIA

or Unanimity in blue, her robe blue and buskins, a chaplet of blue lilies, showing one truth and entireness of mind. In her lap lies a sheaf of arrows bound together, and she herself sits weaving certain small silver twists. Her word

FIRMA CONSENSVS FACIT.
Auxilia humilia firma, etc. [d]

intimating that even the smallest and weakest aids by consent are made strong; herself personating the unan-

a *Aeneid* I.

b *Metamorphoses* I.

c *De Quarto Consulatu Honorii Augusti Panegyricus.*

d Publilius Syrus, *Sententiae Mimi.*

661–2 ***ac...perflant*** when lo! the winds, as if in armed array, rush forth where passage is given, and blow in storm blasts across the world (*Aeneid* 1.82, 3)

668 **seeded** sprinkled

669–70 **heliotropium or turnsole** plant whose flowers turn to follow the sun. (In *Sejanus* Jonson used the turnsole to symbolize a sycophant.)

670 **cresset** iron vessel containing oil or pitch, which can be lit to provide light

676–7 ***Ipse...omneis*** There he perched himself apart upon a high mountain top, where at his ease he could keep watch on every side (Ovid, *Metamorphoses* 1.666–7)

683–5 **flame...fervency** See Middleton's reference to 'Holy Zeal's immaculate fires' in l. 2170.

683–4 **red and white roses** symbols of the houses of York and Lancaster, whose union in the Tudor line ended the dynastic wars of the fifteenth century

686 **NON SIC EXCVBIÆ** Neither watch nor guard (line 281)

688–9 ***Nec...amor*** a continuation of the quotation from l. 686: 'nor yet a hedge of spears can secure thee safety; only the people's love can do that'. Claudian goes on to extol the power of love, by which 'the elements, not united by violence, are forever at harmony among themselves'. The equation of royal authority and love—which brings peace both to society and nature—foreshadows another theme of Jacobean symbology, employed by Jonson in several masques.

696 **buskins** boots

chaplet wreath

700 **FIRMA CONSENSVS FACIT** United feeling makes strength. The full line reads *Auxilia humilia firma consensus facit*, united feeling makes strength out of humble aids (line 4).

imity or consent of soul in all inhabitants of the city to his service.

These are all the personages or live figures, whereof only two were speakers (*Genius* and *Tamesis*); the rest were mutes. Other dumb complements there were, as the arms of the kingdom on the one side, with this inscription

HIS VIREAS

With these mayst thou flourish.

On the other side the arms of the city, with

HIS VINCAS

With these mayst thou conquer.

In the centre or midst of the pegme there was an aback or square, wherein this elogy was written:

Maximus hic rex est, et luce serenior ipsa
Principe quae talem cernit in urbe ducem;
Cuius Fortunam superat sic unica virtus,
Unus ut is reliquos vincit utraque viros.
Praeceptis alii populos, multaque fatigant
Lege; sed exemplo nos rapit ille suo.
Cuique frui tota fas est uxore marito,
Et sua fas simili pignora nosse patri.
Ecce ubi pignoribus circumstipata coruscis
It comes, et tanto vix minor ANNA viro.
Haud metus est, regem posthac ne proximus heres,
Neu successorem non amet ille suum.

This and the whole frame was covered with a curtain of silk painted like a thick cloud, and at the approach of the King was instantly to be drawn. The allegory being that those clouds were gathered upon the face of the city through their long want of his most wished sight but now, as at the rising of the sun, all mists were dispersed and fled. When suddenly upon silence made to the musics, a voice was heard to utter this verse

Totus adest oculis, aderat qui mentibus olim[a]

signifying that he now was really objected to their eyes, who before had been only, but still, present in their minds.

Thus far the complimental part of the first, wherein was not only laboured the expression of state and magnificence, as proper to a triumphal arch, but the very site, fabric, strength, policy, dignity and affections of the city were all laid down to life: the nature and property of these devices being to present always some one entire body or figure consisting of distinct members, and each of those expressing itself in their own active sphere, yet all with that general harmony so connected and disposed as no one little part can be missing to the illustration of the whole; where also is to be noted that the symbols used are not, neither ought to be, simply hieroglyphics, emblems

[a] Claudian *De Consulata Stilichonis*, liber 3.

715 **aback** square tablet or compartment
717–28 ***Maximus . . . suum*** This King is the greatest, and more serene than the sun itself which beholds him as such a leader in the city. And as unique virtue can overcome Fortune, just so this man by himself overcomes all the rest of mankind. Other rulers weary their people with commands and many laws, but he carries us along by his own example. It is right for the husband to enjoy his wife; and it is right for the same father to recognize his offspring. Behold his consort comes, surrounded by a brilliant retinue, Queen Anne, scarcely less magnificent than her great husband. There is no fear that the next heir does not love the King, nor that the King does not love the successor.
737 ***Totus . . . olim*** Full before thine eye is he who was long before thy mind (*De Consulata Stilichonis* 3.(24).5).
738 **objected** presented
749 **illustration** meaning
751 **hieroglyphics** symbols having a hidden meaning
emblems images expressing moral meanings

or impresa, but a mixed character, partaking somewhat of all and peculiarly apted to these more magnificent inventions, wherein the garments and ensigns deliver the nature of the person, and the word the present office. Neither was it becoming, or could it stand with the dignity of these shows, after the most miserable and desperate shift of the puppets, to require a truchman or (with the ignorant painter) one to write, 'This is a dog' or 'This is a hare', but so to be presented as upon the view they might without cloud or obscurity declare themselves to the sharp and learned. And for the multitude, no doubt but their grounded judgements gazed, said it was fine and were satisfied.

The speeches of gratulation

GENIVS

Time, Fate and Fortune have at length conspired
To give our age the day so much desired.
What all the minutes, hours, weeks, months and years
That hang in file upon these silver hairs
Could not produce beneath the Briton[a] *stroke,*
The Roman, Saxon, Dane, and Norman[b] *yoke,*
This point of time hath done. Now London rear
Thy forehead high and on it strive to wear
Thy choicest gems. Teach thy steep towers to rise
Higher with people. Set with sparkling eyes
Thy spacious windows, and in every street
Let thronging joy, love and amazement meet.
Cleave all the air with shouts, and let the cry
Strike through as long and universally
As thunder, for thou now art blissed to see
That sight for which thou didst begin to be.
When Brutus'[c] *plough first gave thee infant bounds,*
And I, thy GENIUS, walked auspicious rounds
In every furrow,[d] *then did I forlook*
And saw this day marked white[e] *in Clotho's*[f] *book.*

a As being the first, free and natural government of this island, after it came to civility.

b In respect they were all conquests and the obedience of the subject more enforced.

c Rather than the city should want a founder, we choose to follow the received story of Brute, whether fabulous or true, and not altogether unwarranted in poetry, since it is a favour of antiquity to few cities to let them know their first authors. Besides, a learned poet of our time, in a most elegant work of his, *Coniugium Tamesis et Isis*, celebrating London, hath this verse of her: *Aemula maternae tollens sua lumina Troia.* Here is also an ancient rite alluded to in the building of cities, which was to give them their bounds with a plough, according to Virgil *Aeneid* liber 10. *Interea Aeneas urbem designat Aratro.* And Isidore liber 15, caput 2 *Urbs vocata ab orbe, quod antiquae civitates in orbem fiebant; vel ab urbo parte aratri, quo muri designabantur, unde est illud. Optavitque locum regno et concludere sulco.*

d *Primigenius sulcus dicitur, qui in condenda nova urbe, tauro et vacca designationis causa imprimitur;* Hitherto respects that of Camden *Britannia*, p. 368, speaking of this city, *quicunque autem condiderit, vitali genio, constructam fuisse ipsius fortuna docuit.*

e For so all happy days were. Pliny caput 40 liber 7 *Naturalis Historia*, to which Horace alludes, liber 1, ode 36. *Cressa ne careat pulchra dies nota.* And the other Pliny *Epistola*: 2, liber 6, *O diem laetum, notandumque mihi candidissimo calculo.* With many other in many places. Martial *liber 8 epigramma 45; liber 9, epigramma 53; liber 10, epigramma 38; liber 11, epigramma 37.* Statius, *liber 4, Silvae, 6.* Persius, *Satura 2.* Catullus, *epigramma 69*, etc.

f The *Parcae* or Fates, Martianus calls them *scribas ac librarias superum* whereof Clotho is said to be the eldest, signifying in Latin *Evocatio.*

752 **impresa** images, usually accompanied by an appropriate motto
753–4 **inventions** devices
754 **ensigns** badges, standards
755 **office** function
758 **shift** expedient
truchman interpreter
759 **ignorant painter** Jonson alludes to a proverbial story of a painter so clumsy that in his picture a dog could not be distinguished from a hare. He therefore placed a label under each figure.
763 **grounded** low, base: perhaps alluding to the groundlings who stood in the open pit of a popular theatre.
765 **gratulation** congratulation, welcome
770 ***Briton . . . stroke*** violent rule of the ancient Britons
772 ***This point of time hath*** That which this time has
782.n ***Coniugium Tamesis et Isis*** 'The Marriage of the Thames and Isis'
Aemula . . . Troia lifting up her eyes, which are jealous of the Trojan motherland
Interea Meanwhile Aeneas had marked out the bounds of the city with a plough (*Aeneid* 5.725). Jonson incorrectly cited *Aeneid* 10.
Urbs . . . sulco 'City [*urbs*] is so-called from orb (*orbe*), because ancient civic foundations were circular; or from the beam [*urbs*] of the plough, by which walls were described, from whence comes this: And he chose a site and enclosed it by a furrow.' The phrase after the colon is from *Aeneid* 3.109.
784.n ***Primigenius . . . imprimitur*** the furrow is said to be *primigenius* [of the origins] which is impressed upon the ground by a bull and a heifer to describe the outline of a new city
quicunque . . . docuit whosoever it was who founded the city, her very fortune has taught us that she was built under the auspices of a life-giving spirit [*vitali genio*—an allusion to the Genius in the pageant]
785.n ***Cressa . . . nota*** Let this fair day not lack a mark of white (Horace, 1.36)
O diem . . . calculo It was a day of exquisite happiness, which I shall ever distinguish with the whitest mark (Pliny, *Epistola* 2.11).
scribas . . . superum the scibes and copyists of the gods.

The several circles[a] *both of change and sway*
Within this isle, there also figured lay,
Of which the greatest, perfectest and last
Was this, whose present happiness we taste.
Why keep you silence, daughters? What dull peace
Is this inhabits you? Shall office cease
Upon th'aspect of him, to whom you owe
More than you are or can be? Shall Time know
That article wherein your flame stood still,
And not aspired? Now heaven avert an ill
Of that black look. Ere pause possess your breasts
I wish you more of plagues: 'Zeal when it rests
Leaves to be Zeal.' Up thou tame river, wake,
And from thy liquid limbs this slumber shake.
Thou drown'st thyself in inofficious sleep
And these thy sluggish waters seem to creep,
Rather than flow. Up, rise and swell with pride
Above thy banks. 'Now is not every tide.'

TAMESIS

To what vain end should I contend to show
My weaker powers, when seas of pomp oe'rflow
The city's face and cover all the shore
With sands more rich than Tagus'[b] *wealthy ore?*
When in the flood of joy that comes with him
He drowns the world, yet makes it live and swim
And spring with gladness. Not my fishes here,
Though they be dumb, but do express the cheer
Of these bright streams. No less may these[c] *and I*
Boast our delights, albe't we silent lie.

GENIVS

Indeed, true gladness doth not always speak:
'Joy bred and born but in the tongue is weak.'
Yet lest the fervour of so pure a flame
As this my city bears might lose the name,
Without the apt eventing of her heat,
Know greatest James (and no less good than great)
In the behalf of all my virtuous sons
Whereof my eldest[d] *there thy pomp foreruns,*
(A man without my flatt'ring, or his pride,
As worthy as he's blest[e] *to be thy guide)*
In his grave name, and all his brethren's right,
Who thirst to drink the nectar of thy sight,
The council, commoners and multitude—
Glad that this day so long denied is viewed—
I tender thee the heartiest welcome yet,
That ever king had to his empire's seat.[f]
Never came man more longed for, more desired,
And being come, more reverenced, loved, admired.

a Those before mentioned of the Briton, Roman, Saxon, etc. and to this register of the Fates allude those verses of Ovid *Metamorphoses* 15: *Cornes illic molimine vasto. Ex are, et solido rerum tabularia ferro: Qua neque concussum coeli, neque fulminis iram, Nec metuunt ullas tuta atque; aeterna ruinas. Invenies illic incisa adamante perenni Fata etc.*

b A river dividing Spain and Portugal and by the consent of poets styled *aurifer*.

c Understanding Euphrosyne, Sebasis, Prothymia, etc.

d The Lord Mayor who for his year hath senior place of the rest, and for the day was chief serjeant to the King.

e Above the blessing of his present office, the word had some particular allusion to his name, which is Benet and hath, no doubt, in time been the contraction of Benedict.

f The city, which title is touched before.

786.n ***Cornes . . . Fata*** Thou shalt there behold the records of all that happens on tablets of brass and solid iron, a massive structure, tablets which fear neither the crashings of the sky, nor the lightnings' fearful power, nor any destructive shocks which may befall, being eternal and secure. There shalt thou find engraved on everlasting adamant thy descendants' fates (*Metamorphoses* 15.809–13)
787 ***figured*** represented
789 ***taste*** experience
791 ***office*** duty
792 ***th'aspect*** (seeing) the face
794 ***flame*** spirit
804 ***vain*** worthless
818 ***eventing*** venting
821 ***foreruns*** foretells
826 ***council, commoners and multitude*** The Common Council of London, the Common Hall of London (consisting of all guild members, enjoying the freedom of the city) and the unprivileged.
827 ***so long denied*** because of plague
828 ***tender*** offer

a To the Prince.

b An attribute given to great persons, fitly above other humanity, and in frequent use with all the Greek poets, especially Homer. *Iliad* α—δῖος Ἀχίλλευς. And in the same book—καὶ ἀντίθεον Πολυφῆμον.

c As Lactantatius calls Parnassus, *Umbilicum terrae.*

d To the Queen.

e An emphatical speech and well reinforcing her greatness, being by this match more than either her brother, father etc.

f Daughter to Frederick II King of Denmark and Norway; sister to Christian IV now there reigning; and wife to James our sovereign.

g The Prince Henry Frederick.

h Charles Duke of Rothberg and the Lady Elizabeth.

Hear and record it: 'In a prince it is
No little virtue to know who are his.'
With like devotions[a] *do I stoop t'embrace*
This springing glory of thy Godlike[b] *race;*
His country's wonder, hope, love, joy and pride.
How well doth he become the royal side
Of this erected and broad-spreading tree,
Under whose shade may Britain ever be.
And from this branch may thousand branches more
Shoot o'er the main and knit with every shore
In bonds of marriage, kindred and increase,
And style this land the navel[c] *of their peace.*
This is your servant's wish, your city's vow,
Which still shall propagate itself with you,
And free from spurs of hope that slow minds move:
He seeks no hire that owes his life to love.
And here she[d] *comes that is no less a part*
In this day's greatness than in my glad heart.
Glory of queens and glory of your name,[e]
Whose graces do as far outspeak your fame
As fame doth silence when her trumpet rings,
You daughter, sister, wife[f] *of several kings;*
Besides alliance and the style of mother,
In which one title you drown all your other.
Instance be that fair shoot,[g] *is gone before,*
Your eldest joy and top of all your store,
With those[h] *whose sight to us is yet denied*
But not our zeal to them, or aught beside
This city can to you. For whose estate
She hopes you will be still good advocate
To her best lord. So, whilst you mortal are,
No taste of sour mortality once dare
Approach your house; nor Fortune greet your Grace
But coming on, and with a forward face.

---

g. 3 Too short a time (in their opinions that were glued there together so many hours to behold him) did his Majesty dwell upon this first place. Yet too long it seemed to other happy spirits that higher up in these Elysian fields awaited for his presence. He sets on therefore, like the sun in his zodiac, bountifully dispersing his beams amongst particular nations, the brightness and warmth of which was now spent first upon the Italians and next upon the *Belgians*: the space of ground, on which their magnificent arches were builded, being not unworthy to bear the name of the great hall to this our court royal, wherein was to be heard and seen the sundry languages and habits of strangers, which under princes' roofs render excellent harmony.

In a pair of scales do I weigh these two nations and find them neither in hearty love to his Majesty, in advancement of the city's honour, nor in forwardness to glorify these triumphs, to differ one grain.

To dispute which have done best were to doubt that one had done well. Call their inventions therefore twins, or if they themselves do not like that name (for happily

832 ***In a prince*** Martial, *Epigrams*, 8.15.8: *Principus est virtus maxima nosse suos*
838 ***erected*** elevated, upright
843.n ***Umbilicum terrae*** navel of the world
847 ***He seeks*** Claudian, *Panegyricus de vi Consulatus Honorii* l. 610: *Non quaerit praetium vitam qui debet amori.*
848 ***is*** which is
858 ***whose . . . denied*** Princess Elizabeth and Prince Charles were not present
860 ***can*** can give
estate state or condition
862 ***her best lord*** James
865 ***coming . . . face*** i.e. may Fortune never turn her back on you
869 **Elysian fields** in classical mythology, the dwelling place of the blessed after death
873–4 **Italians** . . . ***Belgians*** communities of foreign merchants that erected the arches. Belgians here means Dutch.
876 **great hall** Traditionally the largest and most public room in a palace, under the Lord Steward's jurisdiction; thus an appropriate place for strangers to pay homage to the king.

they are emulous of one glory) yet thus may we speak of them.

Facies non omnibus una,
Ovid *Nec diversa tamen, qualem decet esse sororum.*

Because whosoever (*fixis oculis*) beholds their proportions,

Virgil *Expleri mentem nequit, ardesitque tuendo.*

Gracious Street The street upon whose breast this Italian jewel was worn was never worthy of that name which it carries till this hour, for here did the King's eye meet a second object that enticed him by tarrying to give honour to the place. And thus did the quaintness of the engine seem to discover itself before him.

The Italians' Pageant

The building took up the whole breadth of the street, of which the lower part was a square, garnished with four great columns, in the midst of which square was cut out a fair and spacious high gate, arched, being twenty-seven foot in the perpendicular line, and eighteen at the ground line. Over the gate in golden characters these verses (in a long square) were inscribed:

Tu Regere Imperio populos Iacobe memento,
Hae tibi erunt artes, pacique imponere morem,
Parcere subjectis, et debellare superbos.

And directly above this was advanced the arms of the Kingdom, the supporters fairly cut out to the life; over the lion, some pretty distance from it, was written,

IACOBO REGI MAGN.

And above the head of the unicorn, at the like distance, this:

HENRICI VII ABNEP

In a large square erected above all these, King Henry the seventh was royally seated in his imperial robes, to whom King James (mounted on horseback) approaches and receives a sceptre; over both their heads these words being written,

HIC VIR, HIC EST.

Between two of the columns on the right hand was fixed up a square table, wherein in lively and excellent colours was limned a woman, figuring Peace; her head securely leaning on her left hand, her body modestly bestowed (to the length) upon the earth. In her other hand was held an olive branch, the ensign of peace; her word was out of Virgil, being thus,

Deus nobis haec otia fecit.

Beneath that piece was another square table, reaching almost to the bases of the two columns, in which two seeming sea personages were drawn to the life, both of them lying, or rather leaning, on the bosom of the earth, naked; the one a woman, her back only seen; the other a man, his hand stretching and fast'ning itself upon her shoulder. The word that this dead body spake was this

I Decus I Nostrum.

Upon the left-hand side of the gate, between the other two columns, were also two square tables, in the one of which were two persons portrayed to the life, naked and wild in looks; the word,

Expectate solo Trinobanti.

And over that in another square, carrying the same proportion, stood a woman upright, holding in her hand a shield, beneath whom was inscribed in golden characters,

Spes o fidissima rerum.

And this was the shape and front of the first great square, whose top being flat was garnished with pilasters, and upon the roof was erected a great pedestal, on which stood a person carved out to the life, a woman, her left hand leaning on a sword with the point downward and her right hand reaching forth a diadem, which she seemed, by bowing of her knee and head, to bestow upon his Majesty.

On the four corners of this upper part stood four naked portraitures in great, with artificial trumpets in their hands.

In the arch of the gate was drawn, at one side, a company of palm trees, young and as it were but newly springing, over whose branches two naked winged angels, flying, held forth a scroll which seemed to speak thus,

Spes altera.

On the contrary side was a vine, spreading itself into many branches and winding about olive and palm trees; two naked winged angels hanging likewise in the air over

889–90 ***Facies . . . sororum*** They have not all the same appearance, and yet not altogther different; as it should be with sisters (Ovid, *Metamorphoses* 2.13–14)
891 **fixis oculis** with fixed eyes
892 ***Expleri . . . tuendo*** 'cannot satiate her soul, but takes fire as she gazes . . .' (Virgil's description of Dido falling in love, *Aeneid* 1.713)
893.n **Gracious Street** ran from Cornhill south toward London Bridge
897 **quaintness** cleverness, ingenuity
engine arch
907–9 ***Tu . . . superbos*** Paraphrasing *Aeneid* 6.851: 'O James, to rule the nations with thy sway—these be thine arts—to crown Peace with Law, to spare the humbled, and to tame in war the proud!' James had quoted the original Virgilian lines at the very end of *Basilikon Doron* as a summation of the 'craft' of kingship.
913 **IACOBO REGI MAGN.** Of Great James's Reign
916 **HENRICI VII ABNEP** Great-grandson of Henry VII (from whom James derived his claim to the English throne)
922 **HIC . . . EST** This is the man, this is he
925 **limned** painted
930 ***Deus . . . fecit*** It is a god who wrought for us this peace (*Eclogues* 1.6). Like Jonson in the Fenchurch pageant, Dekker here uses a Latin tag to evoke an image of royal authority as both sacred and peace-giving.
938 ***I Decus I Nostrum*** glory of our age . . . (paraphrasing Ovid, *Ex ponto* 2.8.25: *parce, precor, saecli decus indelible nostri*)
943 ***Expectate solo Trinobanti*** Sole expectation of the Trinobanti—a term for the citizens of London, probably based on a marginal note in Stow's *Survey of London*, 1.2.
947 ***Spes o fidissima rerum*** surest hope of the state
963 ***Spes altera*** Virgil, *Aeneid* 12.168: *magnae spes altera Romae* ('second hope of great Rome'). In Virgil the phrase is dynastically applied to Ascanius, the son and heir of Aeneas; in Renaissance emblem books it is often applied more generally to life springing from death (stalks of wheat shedding grains upon ground littered with bones, etc.)

The arch for the Italians' Pageant (pageant 3) in Gracechurch Street.

them, and holding a scroll between them filled with this inscription,

Uxor tua, sicut vitis abundans,
Et filii tui, sicut palmites olivarum.

If your imaginations, after the beholding of these objects, will suppose that his Majesty is now gone to the other side of this Italian trophy, do but cast your eyes back, and there you shall find just the same proportions which the forepart or breast of our arch carrieth, with equal number of columns, pedestals, pilasters, limned pieces and carved statues. Over the gate, this *distichon* presents itself.

Nonne tuo imperio satis est Iacobe potiri?
Imperium in Musas, aemule quaeris? Habes.

Under which verses a wreath of laurel seemed to be ready to be let fall on his Majesty's head as he went under it, being held between two naked antique women, their bodies stretching at the full length to compass over the arch of the gate. And above those verses, in a fair azure table, this inscription was advanced in golden capitals:

EXPECTATIONI ORBIS TERRARVM
REGIB. GENITO NVMEROSISS
REGVM GENITORI FAELICISS
REGI MARTIGENARVM AVGVSTISS
REGI MVSARVM GLORIOSISS

Itali statuerunt laetitiae et cultus Signum

On the right hand of this back part, between two of the columns, was a square table in which was drawn a Woman, crowned with beautiful and fresh flowers, a *caducaeus* in her hand, all the notes of a plenteous and lively Spring being carried about her. The soul that gave life to this speaking picture was,

Omnis feret omnia Tellus.

Above this piece in another square was portrayed a triton, his trumpet at his mouth, seeming to utter thus much:

Dum caelum stellas.

Upon the left hand of this back part in most excellent colours, antiquely attired, stood the four kingdoms—England, Scotland, France and Ireland—holding hands together, this being the language of them all:

Concordes stabili Fatorum numine.

The middle great square that was advanced over the *frieze* of the gate held Apollo with all his ensigns and properties belonging unto him, as a sphere, books, a *caducaeus*, an octahedron, with other geometrical bodies, and a harp in his left hand; his right hand with a golden wand in it, pointing to the battle of Lepanto fought by the Turks, of which his Majesty hath written a poem; and to do him honour Apollo himself doth here seem to take upon him to describe. His word,

Fortunate Puer.

These were the mutes and properties that helped to furnish out this great Italian theatre, upon whose stage the sound of no voice was appointed to be heard but of one, and that in the presence of the Italians themselves, who in two little opposite galleries under and within the arch of the gate, very richly and neatly hung, delivered thus much Latin to his Majesty:

The Italians' Speech in Latin

Salve, rex magne, salve. Salutem Maiestati tuae Itali, faelicissimum adventum laeti, faelices sub te futuri, precamur. Ecce hic omnes, exigui munere, pauculi numero: sed magni erga maiestatem tuam animi, multi obsequii. At nec Atlas, qui coelum sustinet, nec ipsa coeli convexa, altitudinem attingant meritorum regis optimi. Hoc est eius quem de teipso expressisti doctissimo (Deus!) et admirabili penicillo: Beatissimos populos, ubi et philosophus regnat et rex philosophatur. Salve, rex nobilissime, salve, vive, rex potentissime, faeliciter. Regna, rex sapientissime, faeliciter, Itali optamus omnes, Itali clamamus omnes, omnes, omnes.

The Italians' Speech in English

All hail mighty monarch! We the Italians, full of joy to behold your most happy presence, and full of hopes to enjoy a felicity under your royal wing, do wish and pray for the health of your Majesty. Behold here we are all: mean in merit, few in number, but towards your sovereign self in our loves great, in our duties more. For neither Atlas, who bears up heaven, no nor the arched roof itself of heaven, can by many, many degrees reach to the top and glorious height of a good and virtuous king's deservings. And such a one is he whom (good God!) most lively, most wisely and in wonderful colours, you did then pencil down in your own person, when you said that those

969–70 ***Uxor . . . olivarum*** Psalm 128:3: 'Your wife shall be as a fruitful vine | And thy children will be like olive shoots.' (Dekker, who was probably quoting from memory, substituted *palmites* for *nobellae*, with little effect on the meaning.)

973 **trophy** Arch

977 ***distichon*** couplet

978–9 ***Nonne . . . Habes*** Do you not see it is enough that James acquires your power? Do you seek jealously for a ruler of the Muses? You have him!

986–90 **EXPECTATIONI . . . GLORIOSISS** To the expectation of the world, To him who is by many kings engendered, To the most happy father of kings, To the most august of warrior kings, To the most glorious King of the Muses

991 ***Itali . . . Signum*** Italians erect a sign of their joy and devotion

995 ***caducaeus*** wand, carried by an ancient herald and by Mercury

998 ***Omnis . . . Tellus*** Every land shall bear all fruits (Virgil, *Eclogues* 4.39)

1000 ***triton*** sea deity, son of Poseidon and Amphritrite

1002 ***Dum caelum stellas*** 'While the sky breeds its stars.' From Tibullus, 1.4.66: 'Supported by the Muses a man shall live as long as earth breeds oaks, the sky its stars and rivers water.'

1007 ***Concordes . . . numine*** Voicing in unison the fixed will of Destiny (Virgil, *Ecolgues*, 4.47)

1013 **Lepanto** great naval victory of a combined Christian fleet over the Ottoman navy in the Mediterranean 1571

1014 **poem** Published as 'The Lepanto of James VI, King of Scotland' in *His Majesties Poetical Exercises at Vacant Hours* (Edinburgh, 1591).

1017 ***Fortunate Puer*** Happy lad (Virgil, *Eclogues* 5.49)

1038 **All hail** The translation appeared in the second edition of *Magnificent Entertainment*; it is not clear who was responsible for it.

people were blessed where a philosopher rules and where the ruler plays the philosopher. All hail, thou royalest of kings. Live, thou mightiest of princes, in all happiness. Reign, thou wisest of monarchs, in all prosperity. These are the wishes of us Italians, the hearty wishes of us all; thus we cry, all, all, even all.

g. 4 Having hoisted up our sails and taken leave of this Italian shore, let our next place of casting anchor be upon the land of the seventeen provinces, where the *Belgians*, attired in the costly habits of their own native country, without the fantastic mixtures of other nations, but more richly furnished with love, stand ready to receive his Majesty; who, according to their expectation, does most graciously make himself and his royal train their princely guests. The house which these strangers have builded to entertain him in is thus contrived.

The Pageant of the Dutchmen, by the Royal Exchange.

The foundation of this was, as it were by fate, laid near unto a royal place, for it was a royal and magnificent labour. It was bounded in with the houses on both sides the street, so proudly (as all the rest also did) did this extend her body in breadth. The passage of state was a gate, large, ascending eighteen foot high, aptly proportioned to the other limbs and twelve foot wide, arched; two lesser posterns were, for common feet, cut out and opened on the sides of the other.

Within a small frieze, (and kissing the very forehead of the gate) the *aedifice* spake thus:

Unicus a Fato surgo non degener haeres.

Whilst lifting up your eye to an upper larger frieze, you may there be enriched with these golden Capitals:

IACOBO, ANGL. SCOT. FRANC. HIBERN.
REGI OPT. PRINC. MAX. BELGAE ded.

But bestowing your sight upon a large azure table, lined quite through with characters of gold, likewise you may for your pains receive this inscription:

ORBIS RESTITVTOR. PACIS FVND. RELIG. PROPVG. D. IAC. P. F. REGI. P. P.
D. ANNAE REGIAE CONIVG. SOR. FIL. NEPTI. ET D. HENRI CO. I.FIL. PRINC. IVVENT.
IN PVBL. VRBIS ET ORBIS LAETITIA, SECVLIQVE FAELICITAT. XVII. BELGIAE PROV. MERCATORES BENIGNE REGIA HAC IN VRBE EXCEPTI, ET
S.M. VESTRAE OB ANTIQ. SOCIALE FOEDVS, ET D. ELIZ. BENEFICENT. DEVOTI.
FAVSTA OMNIA ET FOELICIA AD IMPERII AETERNITAT. PRECANTVR.

Above which (being the heart of the trophy) was a spacious square room left open, silk curtains drawn before it, which upon the approach of his Majesty being put by, seventeen young damsels, all of them sumptuously adorned after their country fashion, sat as it were in so many chairs of state, and figuring in their persons the seventeen provinces of *Belgia*, of which every one carried in a scutcheon (excellently pencilled) the arms and coat of one.

Above the upper edge of this large square room and over the first battlement, in another front advanced for the purpose, a square table was fastened upright, in which was drawn the lively picture of the King in his imperial robes, a crown on his head, the sword and sceptre in his hands. Upon his left side stood a woman, her face fixed upon his, a burning heart in her right hand, her left hanging by, a heron standing close unto her. Upon his other side stood upright, with her countenance directed likewise upon him, another woman, winged, and in a

1055 **even all.** Dugdale describes a further incident that occurred during this pageant: see Additional Passage C.
1058 **seventeen provinces** Of the Netherlands, north and south
1066 ***The Pageant of the Dutchmen*** Dugdale continues: 'Along Cornhill they [the royal procession] trooped with great majesty, but his Highness being right over the Exchange smiled looking toward it, belike remembering his last being there, the grace of the merchants and the rudeness of the multitude, and casting his eye up to the third trophy or pageant, admired it greatly. It was so goodly top and top many storeys, and so high as it seemed to fall forward. On the top you might behold the sea dolphins as dropping from the clouds on the earth, or looking to behold the King; pictures of great art, cost and glory, as a double ship that being two was so cunningly made as it seemed but one, which figured Scotland and England in one, with the arms of both in one scutcheon, sailing on two seas at once. Here was a speech of wonder delivered too: but the glory of this show was in my eye as a dream, pleasing to the affection, gorgeous and full of joy, and so full of show and variety that when I held down my head as wearied with looking so high, methought it was a grief to me to awaken so soon.'
Royal Exchange Main commercial market of London, in Cornhill.
1068 **royal place** the Exchange
1069 **bounded in with the houses** i.e. the arch took up the full street, abutting the houses on either side
1071 **passage of state** ceremonial passage, through which James would pass
1074 **common feet** the passage of ordinary pedestrians
1078 ***Unicus . . . haeres*** I rise by Fate your ownly heir, but one not unworthy
1081–2 **IACOBO . . . *ded.*** To James, the Great and Best King of England, Scotland, France and Ireland, the Belgians give
1086–98 **ORBIS RESTITVTOR . . . PRECANTVR** Restorer of the world, founder of peace, champion of religion, Prince James Defendor of the Faith; to the King, Father of the Country; To Lady Anne, wife, sister and granddaughter of kings and to Lord Henry, Prince, glory of the city and the world, who brought happiness to the age, we merchants of the Seventeen Provinces, who have been kindly received into this royal city, are devoted to your majesty, thanks to an ancient treaty of alliance and the benevolence of Lady Elizabeth. Dedicated as we are we pray that everything will be glorious and prosperous for the everlasting duration of your kingdom.
1099 **trophy** arch
1104 **chairs of state** throne-like chairs under canopies
1106 **scutcheon** heraldic shield
pencilled coloured, painted

The arch for the Dutch pageant (pageant 4), by the Royal Exchange.

frieze beneath them, which took up the full length of this square, this inscription set out itself in golden words:

Utroque Satellite Tutus.

Suffer your eyes to be wearied no longer with gazing up so high at those sunbeams, but turn them aside to look below through the little posterns whose state swelled quickly up to a greatness, by reason of two columns that supported them on either side. In a table over the right-hand portal was in perfect colours drawn a serpent pursued by a lion; between them, adders and snakes chasing one another, the lion scornfully casting his head back to behold the violence of a black storm that heaven poured down to overtake them. The sound that came from all this was thus:

Sequitur gravis ira feroces.

The opposite body to this (on the other side and directly over the other portal, whose pomp did in like manner lean upon and uphold itself by two main columns) was a square piece, in which were to be seen sheep browsing, lambs nibbling, birds flying in the air, with other arguments of a serene and untroubled season, whose happiness was proclaimed in this manner:

Venit alma cicuribus aura.

Directly above this, in a square table, were portrayed two kings, reverently and antiquely attired, who seemed to walk upon these golden lines:

Nascitur in nostro Regum par nobili Rege
Alter Iesiades, alter Amoniades.

From whom lead but your eye in a straight line to the other side, over the contrary postern, and there in a second upper picture you may meet with two other kings, not fully so antique but as rich in their ornaments; both of them, out of golden letters, composing these words:

Lucius ante alios, Edwardus, et inde IACOBUS
Sextus, et hic sanxit, sextus et ille fidem.

And these were the nerves by which this great triumphal body was knit together, in the inferior parts of it. Upon the shoulders whereof, which were garnished with rows of pilasters that supported lions rampant, bearing up banners, there stood another lesser square, the head of which wore a coronet of pilasters also; and above them, upon a pedestal, curiously closed in between the tails of two dolphins, was advanced a woman, holding in one hand a golden warder and pointing with the forefinger of the other hand up to heaven. She figured Divine Providence, for so at her feet was written

Provida Mens Coeli.

Somewhat beneath which was to be seen an imperial crown, two sceptres being fastened crosswise unto it, and delivering this speech

Sceptra hac concredidit uni.

At the elbows of this upper square stood, upon the four corners of a great pedestal, four pyramids, hollow and so neatly contrived that in the night time, for anger that the sun would no longer look upon these earthly beauties, they gave light to themselves and the whole place about them; the windows from whence these artificial beams were thrown being cut out in such a fashion that (as Ovid, describing the palace of the sun, says)

Clara micante auro, flammasque; imitante pyropo.

So did they shine afar off like crysolites, and sparkled like carbuncles. Between those two pyramids that were lifted up on the right hand stood Fortitude, her pillar resting itself upon this golden line:

Perfero curarum pondus, discrimina temno.

Between the two pyramids on the other side, Justice challenged her place, being known both by her habit and by her voice that spake thus:

Auspice me dextra solium regale perennat.

We have held his Majesty too long from ent'ring this third gate of his Court Royal. It is now high time that those eyes, which on the other side ache with rolling up and down for his gladsome presence, should enjoy that happiness. Behold, he is in an instance passed through; the objects that there offer themselves before him being these.

1120 ***Utroque . . . Tutus*** due to both followers secure

1132 ***Sequitur . . . feroces*** strong rage pursues the fierce

1140 ***Venit . . . aura*** A favourable breeze comes to the meek

1144–5 ***Nascitur . . . Amoniades*** 'There is born in our time one equal to the noble King of Kings, another son of Jesse, another son of Amon.' Jesse was the biblical father of David; Amon a North African god, sometimes equated with Jupiter. *Iesiades* can also mean 'descendant of Jesse' and, in association with the title King of Kings, strongly suggests the Messiah. This couplet is probably meant to be interpreted in conjunction with its counterpart on the opposite side of the arch (ll. 1151–2) to represent the roles played by various kings—including the Messiah Himself—in the origins of Christianity, its establishment in ancient Britain and subsequent purification during the Scottish and English Reformations.

1151–2 ***Lucius . . . fidem*** 'Lucius before all and then Edward and James, both the former and the latter the Sixth of that name; each preserved the faith inviolable.' In legend, Lucius was the first Christian King of Great Britain in about AD 180; Edward VI (r. 1547–1552) presided over the institution of a fully Protestant Church in England; James was the first Protestant King of Scotland, where he ruled as James VI.

1164 ***Provida . . . Coeli*** Foreseeing mind of heaven

1165–6 **imperial crown** A crown closed at the top, unlike the open crowns of medieval kings. Its use here implies the creation of a new British Empire from the old kingdoms of England and Scotland. Imperial crowns had been used in English royal iconography, however, since at least the fifteenth century, as a symbol of the Crown's independence from any foreign secular jurisdiction.

1168 ***Sceptra . . . uni*** either 'this crown causes both sceptres to give allegiance to one man' or, more probably, 'this man causes both sceptres to give allegiance to one crown'.

1177 ***Clara . . . pyropo*** Bright with glittering gold and bronze that show like fire (Ovid, *Metamorphoses* 2.2)

1178 **crysolites** green gems, emeralds

1179 **carbuncles** rubies

1182 ***Perfero . . . temno*** I bear with patience a weight of cares, I spurn divisions.

1186 ***Auspice . . . perennat*** The royal throne keeps me safe, thanks to an auspicious sign.

Our *Belgic* statue of triumph wears on her back as much riches as she carried upon her breast, being altogether as glorious in columns, standing on tiptoe, on as lofty and as proud pyramids; her walks encompassed with as strong and as neat pilasters; the colours of her garments are as bright, her adornments as many. For:

In the square field, next and lowest, over one of the portals were the Dutch country people toiling at their husbandry: women carding of their hemp, the men beating it, such excellent art being expressed in their faces, their stoopings, bendings, sweatings, etc., that nothing is wanting in them but life (which no colours can give) to make them be thought more than the works of painters.

Lift up your eyes a little above them and behold their Exchange, the countenances of the merchants there being so lively that bargains seem to come from their lips.

But instead of other speech this is only to be had:

PIO INVICTO,
R. IACOBO,
QVOD FEL. EIVS AVSPICIIS VNIVERSVM
BRIT. IMPERIVM PACAT, MARE TVTVM
PORTVS APERIT.

Over the other portal, in a square proportioned to the bigness of those other, men, women and children in Dutch habits are busy at other works: the men weaving, the women spinning, the children at their hand-looms, etc. Above whose heads you may with little labour walk into the mart, where as well the *frau* as the *burger* are buying and selling, the praise of whose industry (being worthy of it) stands published in gold, thus:

QVOD MVTVIS COMMERCIIS, ET
ARTIFICVM, NAVTARVMQVE SOLERTIA
CRESCAT, DESIDIA EXVLAT, MVTVAQVE
AMICITIA CONSERVETVR.

Just in the midst of these four squares and directly over the gate, in a large table whose feet are fastened to the frieze, is their fishing and shipping lively and sweetly set down; the skipper, even though he be hard tugging at his net, loudly singing this:

Quod celebre hoc emporium prudenti industria suos,
Quovis Terrarum Negotiatores emittat, exteros
Humaniter admittat, foris famam, domi divitias augeat.

Let us now climb up to the upper battlements, where at the right hand Time stands; at the left (in a direct line) his daughter Truth; under her foot is written, *Sincera*. And under his, *Durant*.

Sincera Durant.

In the midst of these two, three other persons are ranked together: Art, Sedulity, and Labour; beneath whom, in a frieze roving along the whole breadth of that square, you may find these words in gold:

Artes Perfecit Sedulitate Labor.

As on the foreside, so on this, and equal in height to that of Divine Providence, is the figure of a woman advanced, beneath whom is an imperial crown, with branches of olive fixed crosswise unto it, and gives you this word:

Sine caede et sanguine.

And thus have we bestowed upon you all the dead colours of this picture, wherein notwithstanding was left so much life as can come from art. The speaking instrument was a boy attired all in white silk, a wreath of laurel about his temples. From his voice came this sound:

Sermo ad Regem

Quae tot Sceptra tenes forti, Rex maxime, dextra,
Provida mens summi; numinis illa dedit.
Aspice ridentem per gaudia plebis Olympum,
Reddentem et plausus ad sua verba suos,
Tantus honos paucis, primi post secula mundi
Obtigit, et paucis tantum onus incubuit,
Nam regere imperiis populum faelicibus unum,
Ardua res, magnis res tamen apta viris.
At non unanimes nutu compescere gentes,
Non hominis pensum, sed labor ille Dei,
Ille ideo ingentes qui temperat orbis habenas,
Adiungit longas ad tua fraena manus.
Et menti de mente sua praelucet, et artem
Regnandi, regnum qui dedit ille, docet.
Crescentes variis cumulat virtutibus annos,
Quas inter pietas, culmina summa tenet.
Hac proavos reddis patriae, qui barbara gentis
Flexere inducto numine corda ferae.
Hac animos tractas rigidos, subigisque rebelles,
Et leve persuades quod trahis ipse iugum,
Illi fida comes terram indignata profanam,
At nunc te tanto rege reversa Themis.
Assidet et robusta soror, ingentibus ausis
Pro populo carum tradere prompta caput.
Quin et regis amor, musae et dilectus Apollo,
Regali gaudent subdere plectra manu.
Aurea et ubertas solerti nata labore,
Exhibet aggestas ruris et urbis opes.
Sunt haec dona poli, certa quae prodita fama
Miratum ut veniat, venit uterque polus.

1208 **Exchange** (of Amsterdam), a famous centre of international commerce, symbolizing Dutch prosperity and enterprise

1211–15 **PIO . . . APERIT** To the unconquered, pious and upright King James, because under his happy auspices peace has been brought to the entire British empire, the sea has been made safe, the ports have been opened.

1218 **habits** costumes

1221 ***frau . . . burger*** housewife . . . townsman

1224–7 **QVOD . . . CONSERVETVR** Because by mutual commerce industry, navigation and ingenuity grow, idleness is banished and mutual friendship preserved.

1233–5 ***Quod . . . augeat*** Let this crowded market-place with prudent industry send its merchants through the world and admit foreigners with kindness. Let it increase our fame abroad and our wealth at home.

1239–40 ***Durant . . . Durant*** Endure | The Pure Endure.

1245 ***Artes . . . Labor*** Labour perfects the arts by application

1250 ***Sine . . . sanguine*** Without slaughter and blood

1251 **dead** (because lacking the ability to speak or move). Speech gives life to art by actively communicating meaning.

Venimus et Belgae, partiis gens exul ab oris
Quos fovit tenero mater Eliza sinu.
Matri sacratum, patri duplicamus amorem,
Poscimus et simili posse favore frui.
Sic diu Panthaici tibi proferat alitis aevum,
Sceptra per innumeros qui tibi tradit avos.
Sic regina tui pars altera, et altera proles,
Spes populi longum det capiatque decus.

Which verses utter thus much in English prose:

Great King, those so many scepters which even fill thy right hand are all thine own only by the providence of heaven. Behold, heaven itself laughs to see how thy subjects smile and thunders out loud plaudits, to hear their *aves*. This honour of sovereignty, being at the beginning of the world bestowed but upon few, upon the heads of few were the cares of a crown set; for to sway only but one empire (happily) as it is a labour hard, so none can undergo the weight but such as are mighty. But (with a beck as it were) to control many nations (and those of different dispositions too) O! the arm of man can never do that, but the finger of God. God therefore, that guides the chariot of the world, holds the reigns of thy kingdom in his own hand. It is he whose beams lend a light to thine. It is he that teaches thee the art of ruling, because none but he made thee a king. And therefore, as thou grow'st in years thou waxest old in virtues, of all thy virtues Religion sitting highest. And most worthy, for by Religion the hearts of barbarous nations are made soft. By Religion Rebellion has a yoke cast about her neck and is brought to believe that those laws to which thou submittest even thy royal self are most easy. With Religion Justice keeps company, who once fled from this profane world, but hearing the name of King James she is again returned. By her side sits her sister Fortitude, whose life is ready (in heroic actions) to be lavishly spent for the safety of thy people. Besides, to make these virtues full Apollo and the Muses resign, the one his golden lyre, the other their laurel, to thy royal hands, whilst Plenty (daughter to Industry) lays the blessings both of country and city in heaps at thy feet. These are the gifts of heaven, the fame of them spreading itself so far that (to wonder at them) both the poles seem to come together. We, the *Belgians*, likewise come to that intent: a nation banished from our own cradles, yet nursed and brought up in the tender bosom of princely mother Eliza. The love which we once dedicated to her (as a mother) doubly do we vow it to you, our sovereign and father, entreating we may be sheltered under your wings now, as then under hers; our prayers being that he who through the loins of so many grandfathers hath brought thee to so many kingdoms, may likewise multiply thy years and lengthen them out to the age of a phoenix; and that thy Queen, who is one part of thyself, with thy progeny, who are the second hopes of thy people, may both give to and receive from thy kingdom immortal glory.

Pag. 5

Whilst the tongues of the strangers were employed in extolling the gracious aspect of the King and his princely behaviour towards them, his Majesty, by the quickness of Time and the earnestness of Expectation, whose eyes ran a thousand ways to find him, had won more ground and was gotten so far as to St Mildred's Church in the Poultry, close to the side of which a scaffold was erected, where, at the city's cost, to delight the Queen with her own country music, nine trumpets and a kettle drum did very sprightly and actively sound the Danish march, whose cunning and quick stops, by that time they had touched the last lady's ear in the train, behold, the King was advanced up so high as to Cheapside, into which place (if Love himself had entered and seen so many gallant gentlemen, so many ladies and beautiful creatures, in whose eyes glances, mixed with modest looks, seemed to dance courtly measures in their motion) he could not have chosen to have given the room any other name than the Presence Chamber.

Soper Lane

The stately entrance into which was a fair gate in height eighteen foot, in breadth twelve; the thickness of the passage under it being twenty-four. Two posterns stood wide open on the two sides, either of them being four foot wide and eight foot high. The two portals that jutted out before these posterns had their sides open four several ways and served as pedestals of rustic to support two pyramids, which stood upon four great balls and four great lions: the pedestals, balls and pyramids, devouring in their full upright height, from the ground line to the top, just sixty foot. But burying this mechanic body in silence,

1296 **Great King** The translation is again taken from the second edition of Dekker's tract, *Whole Magnificent Entertainment*.
1300 ***aves*** salutations
1329–30 **banished from our own cradles** (because of Spanish conquest and tyranny)
1333 **entreating** The Netherlands remained at war with Spain and feared desertion by its ally, England. The Protestant imagery of both speech and arch iconography—which contrasts with the more classical and religiously neutral tenor of the rest of the pageant—implicitly emphasized the ideological bonds between British and Dutch in the face of Catholic Spain, as did allusions to the Elizabethan alliance and Spanish oppression.
1346 **had won more ground** Dugdale again records a speech at this point of the procession missing from all other accounts: see Additional Passage D.
1347 **the Poultry** street connecting Cheapside and Cornhill
1349 **her own country** Denmark
1354 **Cheapside** the main commercial street of London
1359–60 **Presence Chamber** room in royal palaces, adjacent to the privy chamber, containing the King's throne
1361.n **Soper Lane** running south from Cheapside. Dugdale comments: 'There was cost both curious and comely, but the devices of that afar off I could not conjecture, but by report it was exceeding. It made no huge high show like the other, but as pompous both for glory and matter: a stage standing by, on which were enacted strange things, after which an oration delivered of great wisdom. Both the sides of this pageant were decked gallantly and furnished as all the broad street as the King passed showed like a paradise.'
1367 **rustic** unfinished stone
1371 **mechanic** erected by manual labour

The arch in Soper Lane, for pageant 5.

let us now take note in what fashion it stood attired. Thus then it went apparelled.

The Device at Soper Lane end

Within a large compartment mounted above the forehead of the gate, over the frieze, in capitals was inscribed this title:

NOVA FÆLIX ARABIA.

Under that shape of Arabia this island being figured, which two names of 'New' and 'Happy' the country could by no merit in itself challenge to be her due, but only by means of that secret influence accompanying his Majesty wheresoever he goes and working such effects.

The most worthy personage advanced in this place was *Arabia Britannica*, a woman attired all in white, a rich mantle of green cast about her, an imperial crown on her head, and a sceptre in one hand; a mound in the other, upon which she sadly leaned; a rich veil under the crown, shadowing her eyes, by reason that her countenance (which till his Majesty's approach could by no worldly object be drawn to look up) was pensively dejected; her ornaments were marks of chastity and youth; the crown, mound, and sceptre, badges of sovereignty.

Directly under her in a cant by herself, Fame stood upright, a woman in a watchet robe, thickly set with open eyes and tongues; a pair of large golden wings at her back; a trumpet in her hand; a mantle of sundry colours traversing her body: all these ensigns displaying but the property of her swiftness and aptness to disperse rumours.

In a descent beneath her, being a spacious concave room, were exalted five mounts, swelling up with different ascensions, upon which sat the five senses, drooping: *viz.*

1. *Auditus*, Hearing
2. *Visus*, Sight
3. *Tactus*, Feeling
4. *Olfactus*, Smelling
5. *Gustus*, Taste

apparelled in robes of distinct colours proper to their natures, and holding scutcheons in their hands, upon which were drawn hieroglyphical bodies to express their qualities.

Some pretty distance from them (and as it were in the midst before them) an artificial laver or fount was erected, called the *Fount of Arete* (Virtue), sundry pipes (like veins) branching from the body of it, the water receiving liberty but from one place, and that very slowly.

At the foot of this fount two personages, in greater shapes than the rest, lay sleeping; upon their breasts stuck their names, *Detractio*, *Oblivio*. The one holds an open cup, about whose brim a wreath of curled snakes were winding, intimating that whatsoever his lips touched was poisoned. The other held a black cup covered, in token of an envious desire to drown the worth and memory of noble persons.

Upon an ascent, on the right hand of these, stood the three Charities or Graces, hand in hand, attired like three sisters.

Aglaia		Brightness or Majesty
Thalia	Figuring	Youthfulness, or flourishing
Euphrosine		Cheerfulness or gladness.

They were all three virgins, their countenances labouring to smother an innated sweetness and cheerfulness that apparelled their cheeks, yet hardly to be hid. Their garments were long robes of sundry colours, hanging loose; the one had a chaplet of sundry flowers on her head, clustered here and there with the fruits of the earth; the second, a garland of ears of corn; the third, a wreath of vine branches, mixed with grapes and olives.

Their hair hung down over their shoulders, loose and of a bright colour, for that *epithite* is properly bestowed upon them by Homer in his hymn to Apollo:

PULCHRICOMEÆ CHARITES

'The bright-haired Graces'

They held in their hands pencilled shields. Upon the first was drawn a rose, on the second, three dice; on the third, a branch of myrtle.

	Pleasantness
Figuring	Accord
	Flourishing

In a direct line against them stood the three hours, to whom in this place we give the names of Love, Justice, and Peace. They were attired in loose robes of light colours painted with flowers, for so Ovid apparels them:

Conveniunt pictis incinctae vestibus Horae.

Wings at their feet expressing their swiftness, because they are lackeys to the Sun: *Iungere equos Tytan velocibus imperat Horis* (Ovid).

Each of them held two goblets: the one full of flowers, as ensign of the spring, the other full of ripened figs, the cognisance of summer.

Upon the approach of his Majesty (sad and solemn music having beaten the air all the time of his absence, and now ceasing), Fame speaks.

FAMA

Turn into ice mine eyeballs, whilst the sound
Flying through this brazen trump may back rebound

1378 **NOVA FÆLIX ARABIA** Happy New Arabia
1385 ***Arabia Britannica*** British Arabia
1386 **mantle** loose sleeveless cloak
1394 **cant** niche
1395 **watchet** light blue
1397 **sundry** several
1403 **ascensions** risings
1410 **scutcheons** heraldic shields
1411 **hieroglyphical** emblematic
1414 **laver** basin of a fountain
1426 **ascent** step or rise
1433 **innated** inward
1436 **chaplet** wreath
1441 ***epithite*** title
1445 **pencilled** coloured, painted
1451 **against** opposite to
1455 ***Conveniunt . . . Horae*** The hours assemble, clad in dappled weeds (Ovid, *Fasti* 5.217)
1457–8 ***Iungere . . . Horis*** Titan bade the swift hours to yoke his steeds (Ovid, *Metamorphoses* 2.118.)

To stop Fame's hundred tongues, leaving them mute
As in an untouched bell or stringless lute.
For Virtue's fount, which late ran deep and clear,
Dries and melts all her body to a tear.
You Graces! and you hours that each day run
On the quick errands of the golden sun,
O say! to Virtue's fount what has befell,
That thus her veins shrink up.

CHARITES HORAE *We cannot tell.*

EUPHROSINE

Behold the five-fold guard of sense, which keeps
The sacred stream, sit drooping. Near them sleep
Two horrid monsters. Fame! summon each sense,
To tell the cause of this strange accidence.

Hereupon Fame sounding her trumpet, *Arabia Britannica* looks cheerfully up, the senses are startled, Detraction and Oblivion throw off their iron slumber, busily bestowing all their powers to fill their cups at the fount with their old malicious intention to suck it dry; but a strange and heavenly music suddenly striking through their ears, which, causing a wildness and quick motion in their looks, drew them to light upon the glorious presence of the King; they were suddenly thereby daunted and sunk down. The fount in the same moment of time flowing fresh and abundantly through several pipes, with milk, wine and balm, whilst a person (figuring Circumspection) that had watched day and night, to give note to the world of this blessed time which he foresaw would happen, steps forth on a mounted stage extended thirty foot in length from the main building, to deliver to his Majesty the interpretation of this dumb mystery.

This presenter was a boy, one of the choristers belonging to Paul's.

His Speech

Great monarch of the West, whose glorious stem
Doth now support a triple diadem,
Weighing more than that of thy grand grandsire Brute;
Thou that mayst make a king thy substitute,
And dost, besides the red rose and the white,
With the rich flower of France thy garland dight,
Wearing above kings now or those of old
A double crown of laurel and of gold,
O let my voice pass through thy royal ear
And whisper thus much, that we figure here
A new Arabia, in whose spicèd nest
A phoenix lived and died in the sun's breast.
Her loss made Sight in tears to drown her eyes;
The ear grew deaf; Taste like a sick man lies,
Finding no relish; every other sense
Forgot his office, worth and excellence;
Whereby this Fount of Virtue 'gan to freeze,
Threatened to be drunk by two enemies,
Snaky Detraction and Oblivion;
But at thy glorious presence both are gone,
Thou being that sacred phoenix that dost rise
From th'ashes of the first: beams from thine eyes
So virtually shining that they bring
To England's new Arabia, a new spring.
For joy whereof, nymphs, senses, hours and fame,
Echo loud hymns to his imperial name.

At the shutting up of this speech his Majesty (being ready to go on) did most graciously feed the eyes of beholders with his presence, till a song was spent: which to a loud and excellent music, composed of violins and an other rare artificial instrument, wherein besides sundry several sounds effused (all at one time) were also sensibly distinguished the chirpings of birds, was by two boys (choristers of Paul's) delivered in sweet and ravishing voices.

Cantus

Troynovant is now no more a city.
O great pity! Is't not pity?
And yet her towers on tiptoe stand,
Like pageants built on Fairyland,
And her marble arms,
Like to magic charms,
Bind thousands fast unto her,
That for her wealth and beauty daily woo her,
Yet for all this, is't not pity?
Troynovant is now no more a city.

2

Troynovant is now a summer arbour,
Or the nest wherein doth harbour
The eagle, of all birds that fly
The Sovereign, for his piercing eye.
If you wisely mark,
'Tis besides a park
Where runs (being newly born)
With the fierce lion, the fair unicorn,
Or else it is a wedding hall
Where four great kingdoms hold a festival.

3

Troynovant is now a bridal chamber,
Whose roof is gold, floor is of amber,
By virtue of that holy light
That burns in Hymen's hand, more bright
Than the silver moon
Or the torch of noon.
Hark what the echoes say!
Britain til now ne'er kept a holiday:
For Jove dwells here: And 'tis no pity,
If Troynovant be now no more a city.

Nor let the screw of any wresting comment upon these words,

1478 **accidence** accident
1501 ***Brute*** mythical founder of Britain
1502 ***king*...substitute** privilege of an emperor, who alone outranks a king
1510 ***phoenix*** (often symbolizing Elizabeth)
1521 ***virtually*** with virtue or power
1530 **effused** spread
1535 ***Troynovant*** New Troy, i.e. London (an allusion to the claim of Geoffrey of Monmouth that the British descended from a band of Trojans).
1548 ***eagle*** (symbol of kingship)
1553 ***lion*...*unicorn*** heraldic supporters of the royal arms
1567 **wresting** perverting or distorting

Troynovant is now no more a city,

enforce the author's invention away from his own clear, straight and harmless meaning, all the scope of this fiction stretching only to this point: that London, to do honour to this day wherein springs up all her happiness, being ravished with unutterable joys, makes no account (for the present) of her ancient title, to be called a city, because that during these triumphs she puts off her formal habit of trade and commerce, treading even thrift itself underfoot, but now becomes a reveller and a courtier. So that, albeit in the end of the first stanza 'tis said,

Yet for all this, is't not pity
Troynovant is now no more a city.

by a figure called *castigatio* or the mender, here follows presently a reproof, wherein titles of summer arbour, the eagle's nest, a wedding hall, etc., are thrown upon her, the least of them being at this time by virtue of poetical heraldry, but especially in regard of the state that now upholds her, thought to be names of more honour than that of her own. And this short apology doth our verse make for itself, in regard that some (to whose settled judgement and authority the censure of these devices was referred) brought, though not bitterly, the life of those lines into question. But appealing with Machaetas to Philip, now these reasons have awakened him, let us follow King James, who having passed under this our third gate is by this time graciously receiving a gratulatory oration from the mouth of Sir Henry Montagu, Recorder of the city; a square low gallery, set round about with pilasters, being for that purpose erected some four foot from the ground and joined to the front of the Cross in Cheap; where likewise stood all the Aldermen, the Chamberlain, Town Clerk and Council of the city.

The Recorder's Speech

High Imperial Majesty, it is not yet a year in days since with acclamation of the people, citizens and nobles, auspiciously here at this Cross was proclaimed your true succession to the crown. If then it was joyous with hats, hands and hearts, lift up to heaven to cry 'King James!', what is it now to see King James? Come, therefore, O worthiest of kings, as a glorious bridegroom through your royal chamber. But to come nearer, *Adest quem querimus.* Twenty and more are the sovereigns we have served since our conquest but, conqueror of hearts, it is you and your posterity that we have vowed to love and wish to serve whilst London is a city. In pledge whereof my Lord Mayor, the aldermen and commons of this city, wishing a golden reign unto you, present your greatness with a little cup of gold.

At the end of the oration three cups of gold were given in the name of the Lord Mayor and the whole body of the city to his Majesty, the young Prince and the Queen.

All which, but above all (being gifts of greater value) the loyal hearts of the citizens being lovingly received, his Grace was (at least it was appointed he should have been) met on his way near to the Cross by Sylvanus dressed up in green ivy, a cornett in his hand, being attended on by four other sylvans in ivy likewise, their bows and quivers hanging on their shoulders, and wind instruments in their hands.

Upon sight of his Majesty they make a stand, Sylvanus breaking forth into this abrupt passion of joy.

SYLVANUS *Stay, sylvans, and let the loudest voice of music proclaim it, even as high as heaven, that he is come.*

Alter Apollo redit, novus en, iam regnat Apollo.

Which acclamation of his was borne up into the air and there mingled with the breath of their musical instruments, whose sound being vanished to nothing, thus goes our speaker on.

SYLVANUS *Most happy Prince pardon me, that being mean in habit and wild in appearance (for my richest livery is but leaves, and my stateliest dwelling but in the woods) thus rudely with piping Sylvans I presume to intercept your royal passage. These are my walks: yet stand I here not to cut off your way but to give it a full and a bounteous welcome, being a messenger sent from the Lady Eirene, my mistress, to deliver an errand to the best of all these worthies, your royal self. Many kingdoms hath the Lady sought out to abide in, but from them all hath she been most churlishly*

1592–3 **Machaetas to Philip** According to Plutarch, Philip of Macedon had almost fallen asleep while hearing a case in which he awarded damages against Machaetas. When Machaetas appealed Philip indignantly demanded to whom. Machaetas replied, 'from Philip badly informed to Philip better informed'. Philip refused to rehear the case but paid the damages out of his own funds after being convinced that he had made the wrong judgement.

1596 **Sir Henry Montagu** grandson of the Lord Chief Justice Montagu and a member of the Middle Temple; nominated by James for the post of Recorder 25 May 1603; knighted 23 July; later Chief Justice of the King's Bench (1616), Lord High Treasurer (1620), and Lord Privy Seal (1628).

Recorder Chief legal officer of London, responsible for representing the City to the court. 'But here his Grace might see the love of his subjects, who at that time are exceeding in the shows. Passing by the Cross, beautifully gilded and adorned, there the Recorder and aldermen on a scaffold delivered him a gallant oration: and withal a cup of beaten gold.' (Dugdale)

1603 **not yet a year** (since the coronation, 25 July 1603)

1606 **If then it was joyous** if the proclamation was joyously received then

1606–7 **hats, hands and hearts** throwing of hats in the air and lifting up of hands and hearts to heaven

1607 **lift** lifted

1609 **bridegroom** to marry the realm

1610 ***Adest...querimus*** He is here whom we seek

1624 **Sylvanus** god of the woods. Dugdale continues: 'So he [James] passed on to the pageant at the Little Conduit, very artificial indeed, of no exceeding height but pretty and pleasing in the manner of an arbor, wherein were placed all manner of wood inhabitants, diverse shows of admiration, as pompions, pomegranates and all kind of fruit, which the lords highly commended, where after strange musics hath given plenty of harmony he passed towards Fleet Street through Ludgate.'

1626 **sylvans** forest gods

1633 ***Alter...Apollo*** Another Apollo returns, for look a new Apollo reigns

1644 ***Eirene*** Peace

The arch at the Little Conduit, for pageant 5.

banished: not that her beauty did deserve such unkindness, but that, like the eye of heaven, hers were too bright and there were no eagles breeding in those nests that could truly behold them.

At last here she arrived, Destiny subscribing to this warrant, that none but this land should be her inheritance. In contempt of which happiness, Envy shoots his impoisoned stings at her heart but his adders, being charmed, turn their dangerous heads upon his own bosom. Those that dwell far off pine away with vexing to see her prosper, because all the acquaintance which they have of her is this, that they know there is such a goodly creature as Eirene in the world, yet her face they know not; whilst all those that here sleep under the warmth of her wings adore her by the sacred and celestial name of Peace, for number being (as her blessings are) infinite.

Her daughter Euporia, well known by the name of Plenty, is at this present with her, being indeed never from her side. Under yonder arbour they sit, which after the daughter's name is called Hortus Euporiae, Plenty's Bower. Chaste are they both and both maidens, in memory of a Virgin to whom they were nurse children, for whose sake, because they were bound to her for their life, me have they charged to lay at your imperial feet, being your hereditary due, the tribute of their love. And with it thus to say:

That they have languished many heavy months for your presence, which to them would have been (and proud they are that it shall be so now) of the same operation and influence that the sun is to the spring, and the spring to the earth. Hearing therefore what treble preferment you have bestowed upon this day, wherein besides the beams of a glorious sun, two other clear and gracious stars shine cheerfully on these her homely buildings, into which, because no duty should be wanting, she hath given leave even to strangers to be sharers in her happiness, by suffering them to bid you likewise welcome. By me (once hers, now your vassal) she entreats, and with a knee sinking lower than the ground on which you tread do I humbly execute her pleasure, that ere you pass further you would deign to walk into yonder garden. The Hesperides live not there but the Muses, and the Muses no longer than under your protection. Thus far am I sent to conduct you thither, prostrately begging this grace (since I dare not, as being unworthy, lackey by your royal side), in that yet these my green followers and myself may be joyful forerunners of your expected approach. Away, Sylvans.

And being, in this their return, come near to the arbour, they gave a sign with a short flourish from all their cornetts that his Majesty was at hand, whose princely eye, whilst it was delighting itself with the quaint object before it, a sweet pleasure likewise courted his ear in the shape of music sent from the voices of nine boys, all of them choristers of Paul's, who in that place presenting the nine Muses, sang the ditty following to their viols and other instruments.

But, lest leaping too bluntly into the midst of our garden at first we deface the beauty of it, let us send you round about it and survey the walls, alleys and quarters of it as they lie in order.

This being the fashion of it:

The passages through it were two gates, arched and grated arbour-wise, their height being eighteen foot, their breadth twelve from the roof, and so on the sides, down to the ground; cucumbers, pompions, grapes and all other fruits growing in the land hanging artificially in clusters. Between the two gates a pair of stairs were mounted with some twenty ascents. At the bottom of them on two pillars were fixed two satyrs carved out in wood; the sides of both the gates, being strengthened with four great French terms standing upon pedestals, taking up in their full height twenty foot.

The upper part also carried the proportion of an arbour, being closed with their round tops, the midst whereof was exalted above the other two, Fortune standing on the top of it. The garnishments for the whole bower being apples, pears, cherries, grapes, roses, lillies, and all other both fruits and flowers, most artificially moulded to the life. The whole frame of this summer banqueting house stood, at the ground line, upon forty-four foot; the perpendicular stretching itself to forty-five. We might that day have called it the music room, by reason of the change of tunes that danced round about it; for in one place were heard a noise of cornetts, in a second a consort; the third (which sat in sight) a set of viols, to which the Muses sang.

The principal persons advanced in this bower were *Eirene* (Peace) and *Euporia* (Plenty), who sat together.

Eirene

Peace was richly attired, her upper garment of carnation hanging loose, a robe of white under it powdered with stars and girt to her; her hair of a bright colour, long and hanging at her back but interwoven with white ribbons and jewels. Her brows were encompassed with a wreath compounded of the olive, the laurel and the date tree. In one hand she held a *caducaeus*, or Mercury's rod, the god of eloquence; in the other ripe ears of corn gilded; on her

1668 ***Virgin*** Elizabeth I
1679 ***two other... stars*** Queen Anne and Prince Henry
1681 ***wanting*** missing
1682 ***suffering*** allowing
1687 ***Hesperides*** daughters of Hesperus who, accompanied by a watchful dragon, guard the garden of the Isles of the Blest, in the far west
1691 ***lackey*** run in the manner of a footman or lackey
1696 **cornetts** trumpets
1697 **quaint** beautifully made
1701 **ditty** song
1711 **pompions** pumpkins
1714 **ascents** steps
1717 **terms** busts or statues like those of the god Terminus
1719 **proportion** part, used to stand for the whole
1733 **Peace** Ripa gives several formulas, none corresponding exactly to Dekker's figure. One, based on a medal of Vespasian, holds a caduceus in one hand and ears of corn in the other
1736 **powdered** sprinkled, spangled
1737 **girt** fastened about the waist

lap sat a dove, all these being ensigns and furnitures of Peace.

Euporie

Plenty, her daughter, sat on the left hand in changeable colours, a rich mantle of gold traversing her body, her hair large and loosely spreading over her shoulders; on her head a crown of poppy and mustard seed, the antique badges of fertility and abundance; in her right hand a *cornucopia*, filled with flowers, fruits etc.

Chrusos

Directly under these sat *Chrusos*, a person figuring Gold, his dressing a tinsel robe of the colour of gold.

Argurion

And close by him *Argurion*, Silver, all in white tinsel, both of them crowned and both their hands supporting a globe between them, in token that they commanded over the world.

Pomona

Pomona, the goddess of garden fruits, sat at the one side of Gold and Silver, attired in green, a wreath of fruitages circling her temples, her arms naked, her hair beautiful and long.

Ceres

On the other side sat Ceres, crowned with ripened ears of wheat, in a loose straw-coloured robe.

In two large descents a little below them were placed at one end,

The nine Muses	Clio Enterpe Thalia Melpomene Terpsicore Erato Polymnia Uranio Calliope	With musical instruments in their hands, to which they sung all the day.

At the other end

The seven liberal arts	Grammar Logic Rhetoric Music Arithmetic Geometry Astrology	Holding shields in their hands, expressing their several offices

Upon the very upper edge of a fair large frieze, running quite along the full breadth of the arbor and just at their feet, were planted ranks of artificial artichokes and roses.

To describe what apparel these arts and muses wore were a hard labour and when it were done all were but idle. Few tailors know how to cut out their garments. They have no wardrobe at all; not a mercer nor merchant, though they can all write and read very excellently well, will suffer them to be great in their books. But (as in other countries, so in this of ours) they go attired in such thin clothes that the wind every minute is ready to blow through them. Happy was it for them that they took up their lodging in a summer arbour and that they had so much music to comfort them. Their joys (of which they do not every day taste) being notwithstanding now infinitely multiplied in this, that where before they might have cried out till they grew hoarse and none would hear them, now they sing:

Aderitque vocatus Apollo.

Chorus in full voices answering it thus:

Ergo alacris sylvas, et caetera rura voluptas
Panaque pastoresque tenet, Driadasque puellas,
Nec lupus insidias pecori, nec retia cervis
Ulla dolum meditantur, amat bonus otia Daphnis;
Ipsi laetitia voces ad sidera iactant
Intonsi montes: ipsae iam carmina rupes,
Ipsa sonant arbusta, Deus, Deus, ille!

Sylvanus (as you may perceive by his office before) was but sent of an errand; there was another of a higher calling, a traveller and one that had gone over much ground, appointed to speak to his Majesty: his name Vertumnus, the master gardener, and husband to Pomona. To tell you what clothes he had on his back were to do him wrong, for he had, to say truth, but one suit. Homely it was, yet meet and fit for a gardener. Instead of a hat his brows were bound about with flowers, out of whose thick heaps here and there peeped a queen apple, a cherry, or a pear. This boon-grace he made of purpose to keep his face from heat because he desired to look lovely; yet the sun found him out and by casting a continual eye at him, whilst the old man was dressing his arbours, his cheeks grew tawny, which colour, for the better grace, he himself interpreted blushing. A white head he had and sunburned hands. In the one he held a weeding hook, in the other a grafting knife, and this was the tenor of his speech: that he was bound to give thanks to heaven, in that the arbour

1746 **Plenty** Perhaps loosely modelled after Ripa's Abondanza, who is dressed in green adorned with gold and holds a cornucopia.
changeable showing different colours under different aspects
1754 **tinsel** material interwoven with gold or silver thread, so as to sparkle
1756 **white** silver
1762 **fruitages** fruits
1765 ***Ceres*** Roman goddess of agriculture
1805 ***Aderitque . . . Apollo*** Apollo will be present at thy call (Virgil, *Aeneid* 3.395)
1807–13 ***Ergo . . . ille*** Therefore frolic glee seizes the woods and all the countryside and Pan and the shepherds, and the Dryad maids. The wolf plans no ambush for the flock and nets no snare for the stag; kindly Daphnis loves peace. The very mountains, with woods unshorn, joyously fling their voices starward; the very rocks, the very groves ring out the song. A god is he, a god (Virgil, *Eclogues* 5.58–64).
1817 **Vertumnus** Roman god of the changing season and developing vegetation
1824 **boon-grace** a shade worn on the front of a cap to protect the complexion from the sun

and trees which growing in that fruitful Cynthian garden began to droop and hang down their green heads and to uncurl their crisped forelocks, as fearing and in some sort feeling the sharpness of autumnian malice, are now on the sudden by the divine influence apparelled with a fresh and more lively verdure than ever they were before. The nine muses that could expect no better entertainment than sad banishment, having now lovely and amiable faces; arts that were threatened to be trod under foot by barbarism, now—even at sight of his Majesty, who is the Delian patron both of the muses and arts—being likewise advanced to most high preferment, whilst the very rural and sylvan troops danced for joy. The Lady, therefore, of the place, *Eirene* (his mistress), in name of the Praetor, Consuls and Senators of the city, who carefully prune this garden (weeding out all hurtful and idle branches that hinder the growth of the good) and who are indeed *Ergatai Pistoi*, faithful labourers in this piece of ground, she doth in all their names (and he in behalf of his lady) offer themselves, this arbour, the bowers and walks, yea her children Gold and Silver, with the loving and loyal hearts of all those the sons of peace, standing about him, to be disposed after his royal pleasure. And so wishing his happy arrival at a more glorious bower, to which he is now going, yet welcoming him to this and praying his Majesty not to forget this poor arbour of his lady, music is commanded to carry all their prayers for his happy reign, with the loud amen of all his subjects, as high as heaven.

Cantus

ONE

Shine, Titan, shine.
Let thy sharp rays be hurled
Not on this under world,
For now tis none of thine

These first four lines were sung by one alone, the single lines following, by a chorus in full voices.

CHORUS

No, no, 'tis none of thine.

2

ONE

But in that sphere,
Where what thine arms enfold
Turns all to burnished gold,
Spend thy gilt arrows there.

CHORUS

Do, do, shoot only there.

3

ONE

Earth needs thee not:
Her childbed days are done
And she another sun
Fair as thyself has got.

CHORUS

A new new sun is got.

4

ONE

O this is he!
Whose new beams make our spring,
Men glad, and birds to sing
Hymns of praise, joy and glee.

CHORUS

Sing, sing, O this is he!

5

ONE

That in the north
First rising, shone so far
Bright as the morning star
At his gay coming forth.

CHORUS

See, see, he now comes forth.

6

ONE

How soon joys vary!
Had still he stayed! O then
Happy both place and men,
But here he list not tarry.

CHORUS

O grief! he list not tarry.

7

ONE

No, no, his beams
Must equally divide
Their heat to orbs beside,
Like nourishing silver streams.

CHORUS

Joys slide away like streams.

8

ONE

Yet in this lies
Sweet hope: how far soever
He bides, no clouds can sever
His glory from our eyes.

CHORUS

Dry, dry your weeping eyes.

9

ONE

And make heaven ring
His welcomes shouted loudly,
For heaven itself looks proudly
That earth has such a king.

CHORUS

Earth has not such a king.

1833 **Cynthian** Pertaining to Cynthia, goddess of the moon and of chastity, often a symbol of Elizabeth. We have found no other references to Cynthian gardens.
1843 **Delian** from Delos (sacred to Apollo)
1844 **preferment** advancement, office
1846 **Praetor** Roman official
1850 ***Ergatai Pistoi*** faithful workmen (Greek)
1901 ***divide*** (between England and Scotland)

His Majesty dwelt here a reasonable long time, giving both good allowance to the song and music, and liberally bestowing his eye on the workmanship of the place. From whence at the length departing, his next entrance was, as it were, into the closet or rather the privy chamber to this our court royal, through the windows of which he might behold the cathedral temple of Saint Paul, upon whose lower battlements an anthem was sung by the choristers of the church, to the music of loud instruments. Which being finished, a Latin oration was *viva voce* delivered to his grace by one of Master Mulcaster's scholars at the door of the free school founded by the Mercers.

Oratio habita, et ad Regem, et coram Rege prae schola Paulina.

(...)

Brevis ero, ne ingratus sim, Rex serenissime, licet et plane, et plene putem Regem tam prudentem, in tam profusa suorum laetitia, ita se hodie patientia contra taedium armavisse, ne ullius toe dii ipsum posset toedere. Aedificium hoc magno sumptu suo extructum Dominus Johannes Collettus Eccelsiae Paulinae Decanus, sub Henrico septimo, maiestatis tuae prudentissimo abavo, erudiendae pueritiae consecravit, ut huius scholae infantia tuo in Regnum Anglicanum iure coetanea existat. Tanta magnificentia conditum parique magnificentia dotatum fidelissimae Mercerorum huius urbis primariae semper, hodie etiam Praetoriae societati tuendum testamento moriens commendavit. Quae societas, et demortui fundatoris spei, et nostrae educationis studio fidem suam sanctissime exoluit. Hic nos cum multis aliis erudimur, qui communi nomine totius pueritiae Anglicanae, a Domino Rege, licet sponte sua ad omnia optima satis incitato, humillime tamen contendimus, ut quemadmodum sua aetatis ratione, in omni re adultioribus prospicit, ita in summae spei Principis Henrici gratiam tenerioribus, parique cum ipso aetate pueris, in scholarum cura velit etiam consulere. Virgae enim obsequium, sceptri obedientiam et parit, et praeit inquit preceptor meus. Quique metu didicit iuvenis parere puerque, grandibus imperiis officiosus erit. Habent scholae Anglicanae multa, in quibus Regiam maiestatis correctionem efflagitant, ne inde in Academias implumes evolent unde in Rempublicam implumiores etiam e prima nuditate emittantur. Quod malum a preceptore nostro accepimus: qui annos iam quatuor supra quinquaginta publice, privatimque erudiendae pueritiae praefuit, et haec scholarum errata, cum aliquo etiam dolore suo, et passim, et sparsim deprehendit. Nostra haec schola fundatorem Collettum hominem tam pium; tutores Merceros homines tam fidos cousequuta, quam esset foelix, si placeret, Domino etiam Regi, quod Regibus Angliae, ad summam apud suos charitatem saepissime profuit, huic Mercerorum principi societati, fratrem se, et concivem adscribere. Quantum huic urbi ornamentum, quantum societati honestamentum, quantum scholae nostrae emolumentum? Quantus etiam Regi ipsi honos inde accederet, mavult, qui hoc vult alias inter alia per otium Regi suo apperire, quam hodie cum taedio et praeter aream eidem explicare. Omnipotens Deus Jesus Christus et cum eo, ac per eum noster et Pater et Deus, serenissimum Regem Jacobum, honoratissimam Reginam Annam, nobilissimum Principem Henricum, reliquamque Regiae stirpis ad omnia summa natam sobolem diu nobis ita incolumes tueatur, ut cum huius vitae secundissimum curriculum confeceritis, beatissimam vitae caelestis aeternitatem consequamini. Dixi.

THE ORATION DELIVERED at Paul's School by one of Master Mulcaster's Scholars

Most gracious sovereign, my speech shall not be long for fear it appear loathsome, yet do I fully and freely believe that a king so crowned with wisdom as yourself hath this day put on such strong armour of patience to bear off tediousness in this so main and universal meeting of joy in his subjects, that the extension and stretching out of any part of time can by no means seem irksome unto him. This building received her foundation from the liberal purse of John Colet (Dean of Paul's Church under Henry VII, great grandfather to your Majesty) and was by him consecrated to learning for the erudition of youth, to the intent that the infancy of this school may now, by your right to the kingdom of England, grow up to a full and ripe age. Which work of his, so magnificent for the building, so commendable for the endowments, he by last will and testament bequeathed to the faithful Society and Brotherhood of the Mercers, always the chiefest and now this year, by reason of a Lord Mayor who is a member amongst them, more than the chiefest of the companies of this city. Which Society have most religiously performed all rites both due to the hopes of our deceased founder and to the ornaments of our education. Within these walls we, with many other, suck the milk of learning, and in the general name of all the youth in England most humbly entreat of our lord the King (who of himself, we know, is forward enough to advance all goodness) that as by reason of his manly years his chiefest care is spent about looking to and governing men, so (notwithstanding) in favour of that his royal son Henry, prince of unspeakable hopes, he would a little suffer his eye to descend and behold our school, and therein to provide that those who are but green in years and of equal age with that his princely issue may likewise receive a virtuous education. For the obedience which is given to the rod brings along with it obedience to the sceptre, nay (as our master tells us) it goes even before it.

Quique metu didicit iuvenis parere puerque,

1918 **liberally** graciously
1921 **closet** small, intimate room
privy chamber room in the palace adjacent to the bedchamber (see l. 145–6).
1927 **Mulcaster's** Richard Mulcaster, master of St Paul's grammar school and former master of the Merchant Taylors' School
1928 **free school** (held in the chapel of the Mercers' Company on the north side of Cheapside)
1988 **John Colet** (1467?–1519) dean of St Paul's, scholar and educational reformer; one of those responsible for reforming English grammar school curricula along humanist lines
2016–17 ***Quique . . . erit*** Whosoever has learned as a youth and as a boy to obey out of fear will be dutiful in greater tasks

Grandibus imperiis officiosus erit.

Our schools of England are in many limbs deformed, whose crookedness require the hand of a king to set them straight, lest out of these young nests those that are there bred, flying without their feathers into universities, should afterward light upon the branches of the commonwealth more naked than at first, by reason they were not perfectly fledged. Which evil hath been discovered by the observation of our teacher, who now by the space of more than fifty-four years, both publicly and privately, hath instructed youth, and with no little grief of his own hath both here and abroad sifted out these gross vices that are mingled amongst schools. O how happy therefore should this our nursery of learning be if—after having first met with Colet, a founder so religious, and secondly the Mercers our patrons, men so faithful and virtuous—our lord the King would now at last also be pleased (considering many kings of England by doing so have won wonderful love from their subjects) to suffer his royal name to be rolled amongst the citizens of London, by vouchsafing to be free of that worthy and chiefest Society of Mercers. What glory should thereby rise up to the city? What dignity to that Society? To this our school what infinite benefit? What honour besides our sovereign himself might acquire, he that makes this wish now, wisheth rather (in fitter place and at fitter hours) to discover to his prince, than now, clean beyond his aim, to overshoot himself by tediousness. The Almighty etc.

g. 6 Our next arch of triumph was erected above the Conduit in Fleet Street, into which (as into the long and beauteous gallery of the city) his Majesty being entered, afar off (as if it had been some swelling promontory, or rather some enchanted castle guarded by ten thousand harmless spirits) did his eye encounter another tower of pleasure.

Presenting itself

Fourscore and ten foot in height and fifty in breadth; the gate twenty foot in the perpendicular line and fourteen in the ground line. The two posterns were answerable to these that are set down before. Over the posterns risse up in proportionable measures two turrets, with battlements on the tops. The midst of the building was laid open to the world, and great reason it should be so, for the globe of the world was there seen to move, being filled with all the degrees and states that are in the land: and these were the mechanical and dead limbs of this carved body.

As touching those that had the use of motion in it and for a need durst have spoken, but that there was no stuff fit for their mouths, the principal and worthiest was *Astraea* (Justice), sitting aloft, as being newly descended from heaven, gloriously attired; all her garments being thickly strewed with stars, a crown of stars on her head, a silver veil covering her eyes. Having told you that her name was Justice, I hope you will not put me to describe what properties she held in her hands, sithence every painted cloth can inform you.

Directly under her, in a cant by herself, was *Arete* (Virtue) enthroned, her garments white, her head crowned, and under her *Fortuna*, her foot treading on the globe that moved beneath her: intimating that his Majesty's fortune was above the world, but his virtues above his fortune.

Invidia

Envy, unhandsomely attired all in black, her hair of the same colour, filleted about with snakes, stood in a dark and obscure place by herself, near unto Virtue but making show of a fearfulness to approach her and the light; yet still and anon casting her eyes sometimes to the one side beneath—where on several greces sat the four cardinal virtues:

Viz. { *Justitia*, *Fortitudo*, *Temperantia*, *Prudentia* } In habiliments, fitting to their natures.

and sometimes throwing a distorted and repining countenance to the other opposite seat, on which his Majesty's four kingdoms were advanced:

Viz. { England, Scotland, France, Ireland }

all of them in rich robes and mantles, crowns on their heads and sceptres with pencilled scutcheons in their hands, lined with the coats of the particular kingdoms.

2025 **our teacher** Mulcaster (1530?–1611; then probably seventy-four years old); first headmaster of the Merchant Taylors' School and subsequently of St Paul's (1596–1608)

2044 **etc.** The text concludes: 'Almighty God Jesus Christ, and with him and through him our both Father and God, long safeguard amongst us our most serene King James, most honoured Queen Anne, most noble Prince Henry and the rest of the royal lineage, destined for the highest purposes; and when you [James and his family] shall have drawn to the end of the most fortunate course of this life, may you attain a blessed eternity of heavenly life.'

2045 **Our next arch** Despite its nearly undecipherable syntax, Dugdale's description conveys the court's admiration for this pageant: 'When he [James] came to the trophy in Fleet Street the lords considered that the same for royalty was so richly beautified and so plenteous of show that with the breadth of the street it seemed to them to have gone back again, and [were] but then at the Cross in Cheap, but otherwise saluted, as with variety of speeches and all sundry sorts of musics by the city appointed two [too?], as that at the Little Conduit and all else but the Exchange and Gracious Street; on top of this pageant was placed a globe of a goodly preparation.'

2060 **degrees and states** ranks and conditions

2065 **Astraea** goddess of justice, said to have left the earth at the end of the Golden Age from disgust at the vices of mankind. Her return will herald return of the Golden Age.

2070 **properties** props—scales of justice and a sword

2072 **cant** niche

2083 **greces** steps

2097 **pencilled scutcheons** painted shields

2098 **lined with the coats** covered with heraldic arms

The arch in Fleet Street, for pageant 6.

For very madness that she beheld these glorious objects, she stood feeding on the heads of adders.

The four elements in proper shapes, artificially and aptly expressing their qualities, upon the approach of his Majesty went round in a proportionable and even circle, touching that cantle of the Globe (which was open) to the full view of his Majesty, which being done, they bestowed themselves in such comely order, and stood so, as if the engine had been held up on the tops of their fingers.

Upon distinct ascensions, neatly raised within the hollow womb of the globe, were placed all the states of the land, from the nobleman to the ploughman, among whom there was not one word to be heard, for you must imagine as Virgil saith:

Astraea *Magnus ab integro seclorum nascitur ordo.*
Iam redit et virgo redeunt Saturnia regna.

Aeglogues 4

That it was now the golden world, in which there were few praters.

All the tongues that went in this place was the tongue of Zeal, whose personage was put on by W. Bourne, one of the servants to the young Prince.

And thus went his speech

The populous globe of this our English isle
Seemed to move backward at the funeral pile
Of her dead female majesty. All states,
From nobles down to spirits of meaner fates,
Moved opposite to nature and to peace,
As if the same had been th'Antipodes.
But see the virtue of a regal eye,
Th'attractive wonder of man's majesty.
Our globe is drawn in a right line again,
And now appear new faces and new men.
The elements (earth, water, air and fire),
Which ever clipped a natural desire
To combat each with other, being at first
Created enemies to fight their worst—
See at the peaceful presence of their king
How quietly they move, without their sting:
Earth not devouring, fire not defacing,
Water not drowning, and the air not chasing,
But propping the quaint fabric that here stands,
Without the violence of their wrathfull hands.
Mirror of times, lo where thy fortune sits
Above the world and all our human wits,
But thy high virtue above that. What pen,
Or art, or brain can reach thy virtue then?
At whose immortal brightness and true light
Envy's infectious eyes have lost their sight.
Her snakes not daring to shoot forth their stings
'Gainst such a glorious object, down she flings
Their forks of venom into her own maw,
Whilst her rank teeth the glittering poisons chew;
For 'tis the property of Envy's blood
To dry away at every kingdom's good,
Especially when she had eyes to view
These four main virtues figured all in you:
Justice in causes, Fortitude 'gainst foes,
Temp'rance in spleen, and Prudence in all those;
And then so rich an empire, whose fair breast
Contains four kingdoms by your entrance blessed,
By Brute divided but by you alone
All are again united and made one.
Whose fruitfull glories shine so far and even
They touch not only earth but they kiss heaven,
From whence Astraea is descended hither;
Who, with our last Queen's spirit, fled up thither,
Foreknowing on the earth she could not rest
Till you had locked her in your rightfull breast.
And therefore all estates, whose proper arts
Live by the breath of majesty, had hearts
Burning in holy Zeal's immaculate fires,
With quenchless ardours and unstained desires,
To see what they now see, your powerful grace
Reflecting joys on every subject's face.
These painted flames and yellow burning stripes
Upon this robe being but as shows and types
Of that great zeal. And therefore in the name

2103 **proportionable** well proportioned
2104 **cantle** section
2106 **comely** becoming
2108 **distinct ascensions** steps
2113–14 ***Magnus...regna*** 'The great line of the centuries begins anew. Now the virgin returns, the reign of Saturn returns' (Virgil, *Eclogues* 5.5–6). The virgin here is Astraea and the context a prophecy that a child is about to be born who will rule over a united world and restore the golden age. This prophecy was subsequently connected to the imperial mission of Rome, the peace of Augustus and—by Christian writers beginning with the Emperor Constantine—with the birth of Christ. The tradition was adapted by later European monarchs, esp. the Habsburg Emperor Charles V and his son Philip II of Spain, and by many Elizabethan apologists, who identified the return of the virgin goddess of justice with the Queen. The iconography of the arch is therefore grounded in a deep, multi-layered tradition of religious and imperial imagery. The theme remained prominent in the culture of the early Stuart court, e.g. in Jonson's masque, *The Golden Age Restored*.
2119 **Zeal** Described by Ripa as a man in a priest's garments, holding a lash in one hand and a lamp in the other. Middleton's figure evidently wore a gown decorated with an image of flames. The appearance of Zeal here complements the reference to the city's zeal at the Fenchurch arch (ll. 797–8).
W. Bourne also known as William Birde, an actor with the Admiral's Men
2120 **young Prince** Henry
2124 ***states*** ranks
2127 ***the same*** Nature and peace
th'Antipodes opposite side of the globe, hence exact opposites
2132 ***elements*** The theory that all things in nature derive from combinations of these elements was given its classic expression by Aristotle.
2133 ***clipped*** embraced
2140 ***quaint*** well-made
2150 ***maw*** stomach
2151 ***chew*** pronounced 'chaw'
2160 ***Brute*** Mythical ancient king of Britain, who divided his realm among his sons
2164 ***Astraea is descended*** heralding the return of the Golden Age
2167 ***her*** Astraea, who is also Justice
2168 ***arts*** skills

Of this glad city, whither no Prince ever came
More loved, more longed for, lowly I entreat
You'd be to her as gracious as you're great.
So with reverberate shouts our globe shall ring,
The music's close being thus: God save our King!

If there be any glory to be won by writing these lines, I do freely bestow it (as his due) on Thomas Middleton, in whose brain they were begotten, though they were delivered here: *Quae nos non fecimus ipsi, vix ea nostra voco.*

But having pieced up our wings now again with our own feathers, suffer us a while to be pruning them, and to lay them smooth whilst this song, which went forth at the sound of oboes and other loud instruments, flies along with the train.

Cantus

[FIRST SINGER]
Where are all these honours owing?
Why are seas of people flowing?
Tell me, tell me, Rumour,
Though it be thy humour
More often to be lying
Than from thy breath to have truth flying:
Yet alter now that fashion
And without the stream of passion
Let thy voice swim smooth and clear:
When words want gilding, then they are most dear.

[RUMOUR]
'Behold where Jove and all the States
Of heav'n, through heaven's seven silver gates,
All in glory riding,
Backs of clouds bestriding,
The Milky Way do cover;
Which starry path being measured over,
The deities convent
In Jove's high court of Parliament.'

[FIRST SINGER]
—Rumour—thou dost lose thine aims
This is not Jove, but one as great, King James.

And now take we our flight up to Temple Bar, the other end of this our gallery, where by this time his Majesty is upon the point of giving a gracious and princely farewell to the Lord Mayor and the city, but that his eye meeting a seventh beautiful object is invited by that to delay awhile his lamented departure.

The Device called Templum Jani, Temple of Janus. Pag.

The seventh and last *pegme* within the city was erected at Temple Bar, being adjoined close to the gate. The building was in all points like a temple, and dedicated to *Ianus Quadrifrons.*

Beneath that four-faced head of Janus was advanced the arms of the kingdom, with the supporters cut out to the life, from whence being removed they now are placed in the Guildhall.

The walls and gates of this temple were brass, the pillars silver, their capitals and bases gold. All the frontispiece, downward from those arms, was beautified and supported by twelve rich columns, of which the four lowermost, being great Corinthian pillars, stood upon two large pedestals, with a fair *vaux* over them instead of architrave, frieze and cornice. Above them eight columns more were likewise set, two and two, upon a large pedestal: for as our work began for his Majesty's entrance with rustic, so did we think it fit that this our temple should end with the most famous column, whose beauty and goodliness is derived both from the Tuscan, Doric, Ionic and Corinthian, and received his full perfection from Titus Vespasian, who advanced it to the highest place of dignity in his Arch Triumphal, and (by reason that the beauties of it were a mixture taken from the rest) he gave it the name of *composita* or *Italica.*

In the highest point of all was erected a Janus head, and over it written

IANO QUADRIFRONTI SACRVM.

Which title of *Quadrifrons* is said to be given him,[a] as he respecteth all climates and fills all parts of the world with his majesty; which Martial would seem to allude unto in that *hendecasyllable,*

Et lingua pariter locutus omni.[b]

a *Bassus apud Macro*: liber 1. *Saturae* caput 9.

b Liber 8, *Epigrammaton*, 2.

2185 ***Quae ... voco*** That which we do not ourselves make we will never call ours
2212 **Temple Bar** marking the boundary between London and Westminster along the Strand
2218 ***The Device*** Dugdale describes it as 'neither great nor small but finely furnished. Some compared it to an Exchange shop, it shined so in that dark place and was so pleasing to the eye, whereon a young man, an actor of the city, so delivered his mind and the manner of all in an oration that a thousand give him his due deserving commendations.' Dekker's description appears as Additional Passage E.
2221–2 ***Ianus Quadrifrons*** Janus of four faces.
2224 **supporters** the lion and unicorn (introduced in James's reign)
2232 ***vaux*** projecting band over the lower columns
2239 **Titus Vespasian** Roman emperor, AD 69–79
2246 ***IANO ... SACRVM*** sacred to Janus of the four faces
2250 **hendecasyllable** verse line of eleven syllables
2251 ***Et ... omni*** And, speaking alike with every tongue (*Epigrams*, 8.2.5).

The arch at Temple Bar, for pageant 7.

Others have thought it by reason of the four elements which broke out of him, being Chaos, for Ovid is not afraid to make Chaos and Janus the same, in those verses:

Me Chaos antiqui (nam sum res prisca) vocabant;
Adspice, etc. [a]

But we rather follow (and that more particularly) the opinion of the ancients, [b] who have entitled him *Quadrifrons* in regard of the year, which under his sway is divided into four seasons—spring, summer, autumn, winter—and adscribe unto him the beginnings and ends of things. See Marcus Cicero [c] *Cumque in omnibus rebus vim haberent maximam prima et extrema, principem in sacrificando Janum esse voluerunt, quod* [d] *ab eundo nomen est deductum: ex quo transitiones perviae Iani, foresque in liminibus profanarum aedium, Januae nominantur, etc.* As also the charge and custody of the whole world, by Ovid:

Quicquid ubique vides coelum, mare, nubila, terras,
Omnia sunt nostra clausa patentque manu:
Me penes est unum vasti custodia mundi,
Et ius vertendi cardinis omne meum est. [e]

About his four heads he had a wreath of gold, in which was graven this verse.

TOT VVLTVS MIHI NEC SATIS PVTAVI [f]

signifying that though he had four faces, yet he thought them not enough to behold the greatness and glory of that day. Beneath, under the head was written

ET MODO SACRIFICO CLVSIVS ORE VOCOR. [g]

For being open he was styled Patulcius, but then upon the coming of his Majesty, being to be shut, he was to be called Clusius. Upon the outmost front of the building was placed the entire arms of the kingdom with the Garter, crown and supporters, cut forth as fair and great as the life, with an *hexastich* written underneath, all expressing the dignity and power of him that should close that temple.

QVI DVDVM ANGVSTIS TANTVM REGNAVIT IN ORIS
PARVOQVE IMPERIO SE TOTI PRÆBVIT ORBI
ESSE REGENDO PAREM, TRIA REGNA (VT NVLLA DEESSET
VIRTVTI FORTVNA) SVO FELICITER VNI
IVNCTA SIMVL SENSIT: FAS VT SIT CREDERE VOTIS
NON IAM SANGVINEA FRVITVROS PACE BRITANNOS.

a *Fasti,* liber 1.

b *Lege Marlianum* liber 4, caput 8. Albricus, *in deorum imagine.*

c *De natura deorum, liber* 2.

d *quasi Eanus.*

e *Fasti, ibid.*

f Martial, *liber 8, Epigrammaton* 2.

g Ovid, *Fasti,* 1.

2255–6 ***Me...Adspice*** The ancients called me Chaos, for a being from of old am I; observe the long, long ages of which my song shall tell (Ovid, *Fasti,* 1.103, 4).

2262–6 ***Cumque...nominantur*** Also, as the beginning and the end are the most important parts of all affairs, they held that Janus is the leader in a sacrifice, the name being derived from *eundo* [going], hence the names *jani* for archways and *januae* for the front doors of secular buildings (Cicero, *De Natura Deorum,* 2.27).

2268–71 ***Quicquid...est*** Whate'er you see anywhere—sky, sea, clouds, earth—all things are closed and opened by my hand. The guardianship of this vast universe is in my hands alone, and none but me may rule the wheeling pole (*Fasti,* 1.117–20)

2274 TOT...PVTAVI he deemed his many faces were not enough for him (*Epigrams,* 8.2.3)

2278 ET...VOCOR for on his sacrificial lips I'm now Clusius called (*Fasti,* 1.130)

2284 ***hexastich*** group of six lines of verse

2287–92 **QVI...BRITANNOS** He who has reigned so long within narrow bounds and in a small kingdom now shows himself equal to ruling the world, and he now senses that three kingdoms (so that no good fortune should be lacking to his Virtue) are happily joined under his single care; and Britons, who are about to enjoy peace, not bloodshed, rightly believe in their prayers.

In a great frieze below, that ran quite along the breadth of the building, were written these two verses out of Horace

IVRANDASQVE SVVM PER NOMEN PONIMVS ARAS
NIL ORITVRVM ALIAS, NIL ORTVM TALE FATENTES[a]

The first and principal person in the Temple was

IRENE

or Peace. She was placed aloft in a *cant*, her attire white, semined with stars; her hair loose and large; a wreath of olive on her head; on her shoulder a silver dove. In her left hand she held forth an olive branch with a handful of ripe ears, in the other a crown of laurel, as notes of victory and plenty. By her stood

PLVTVS

or Wealth, a little boy, bare headed, his locks curled and spangled with gold, of a fresh aspect;[b] his body almost naked, saving some rich robe cast over him; in his arms a heap of gold ingots to express riches, whereof he is the god. Beneath her feet lay

ENYALIVS

or Mars, grovelling, his armour scattered upon him in several pieces, and sundry sorts of weapons broken about him. Her word to all was

UNA TRIVMPHIS IN NVMERIS POTIOR.

pax optima rerum
Quas homini novisse datum est, pax una Triumphis
Innumeris potior.[c]

signifying that peace alone was better, and more to be coveted than innumerable triumphs. Besides, upon the right hand of her, but with some little descent, in a *hemicycle* was seated

ESYCHIA

or Quiet, the first handmaid of peace, a woman of a grave and venerable aspect, attired in black; upon her head an artificial nest, out of which appeared storks' heads to manifest a sweet repose. Her feet were placed upon a cube, to show stability, and in her lap she held a perpendicular or level, as the ensign of evenness and rest. On the top of it sat a halcyon or kingfisher. She had lying at her feet

TARACHE

a Liber 2 *Epistularum* I *ad Augusto*.

b So Cephisodotus hath feigned him. See Pausanius *in Boeoti. et Phil. in Imag.* contrary to Aristophanes Theognetus Lucian and others, that make him blind and deformed.

c Silius Italicus.

2295–6 **IVRANDASQVE** … *FATENTES* betimes set up alters to swear by in your name, and confess that naught like you will hereafter arise or has arisen ere now (Horace, *Epistles*, 2.1.16–17)
2298 **IRENE** This figure does not correspond to any of those Ripa describes to represent Peace.
2299 **cant** niche
2300 **semined** sprinkled
loose and large loose and flowing
2305 **PLVTVS** Ripa represents Wealth by a female figure.
2307.n **Cephisodotus** Athenian sculptor of the fourth century BC
Pausanius Greek writer of the second century AD, best known for a travelogue, translated into Latin as *de situ Graeciae libri decem*. *In Boeti* is book 9. Jonson in this note is reviewing personifications of wealth by ancient poets to justify his own, unconventional choice of a boy.
Theognetus author of Hellenistic comedies of which only fragments survive.
2315 UNA … POTIOR One more powerful in numerous triumphs
2316–18 *pax … potior* Peace is the best thing that man may know; peace alone is better than a thousand triumphs (*Punica*, 11.592–94). A passage from an oration by the Carthaginian, Hanno, urging his countrymen to make peace with Rome instead of pressing the advantage given by Hannibal's victories in the Second Punic War. He was shouted down but the ultimate outcome proved him right.
2322 *hemicycle* semi-circular recess
2323 **ESYCHIA** a composite of Ripa's two figures for *Quiete*, one of which stands on a square and holds a perpendicular, while the other has a stork's nest on her head
2328 **perpendicular** plumb line or similar instrument
2331 **TARACHE** The multi-coloured garments and disordered hair correspond to Ripa's description of *Confusione* and are said to represent disordered actions and many varied thoughts which confuse the intellect.

or Tumult, in a garment of diverse but dark colours, her hair wild and disordered, a foul and troubled face. About her lay staves, swords, ropes, chains, hammers, stones and suchlike, to express turmoil. The word was

PERAGIT TRANQVILLA POTESTAS

Quod violenta nequit mandataque fortius urget
Imperiosa quies. [a]

Claudian

To show the benefits of a calm and facile power, being able to effect in a state that which no violence can. On the other side the second handmaid was

ELEVTHERIA

or Liberty, her dressing white and somewhat antique, but loose and free; her hair flowing down her back and shoulders. In her right hand she bore a club, on her left a hat, the characters of freedom and power. At her feet a cat was placed, the creature most affecting and expressing liberty. She trod on

DOVLOSIS

or Servitude, a woman in old and worn garments, lean and meagre, bearing fetters on her feet and hands; about her neck a yoke to insinuate bondage, and the word

NEC VNQVAM GRATIOR

alluding to that other of Claudian

Nunquam libertas gratior extat,
Quam sub Rege pio [b]

and intimated that liberty could never appear more graceful and lovely than now under so good a prince. The third handmaid was

SOTERIA

or Safety, a damsel in carnation, the colour signifying cheer and life. She sat high. Upon her head she wore an antique helm and in her right hand a spear for defence; in her left a cup for medicine; at her feet was set a pedestal, upon which a serpent, rolled up, did lie. Beneath was

PEIRA

or Danger, a woman despoiled and almost naked; the little garment she hath left her of several colours, to note her various disposition. Besides her lies a torch out and a sword broken, the instruments of her fury, with a net and wolf-skin, the ensigns of her malice, rent in pieces. The word

TERGA DEDERE METVS

borrowed from Martial [c] and implying that now all fears have turned their backs and our safety might become security, danger being so wholly depressed and unfurnished of all means to hurt. The fourth attendant is

EVDAIMONIA

a *De Manlio Theodoro Consulo Panegyricus.*

b *De Laudibus Stilichonis*, liber 3.

c Liber 12 *Epistulae* 6.

2334 **staves** shafts of lances
2336 PERAGIT TRANQVILLA POTESTAS Quiet authority accomplishes
2337–8 ***Quod...quies*** Quiet authority accomplishes what violence cannot, and that mandate compels more which comes from a commanding calm (ll. 240–1)
2343 **ELEVTHERIA** Very similar to Ripa's *Liberta*, who holds a sceptre instead of a club, however. Jonson perhaps felt the sceptre an inappropriate emblem for Liberty in a royal entry.
2350 **DOVLOSIS** similar to the first of three formulas for *Servitu* in Ripa
2354 NEC VNQVAM GRATIOR and not at any time more pleasing
2356–7 ***Nunquam...pio*** Never does liberty show more fair than beneath a pious king (*De Laudibus Stilichonis*, 3.114–15)
2361 **SOTERIA** Ripa gives five possible formulas for *Sicurezza* or *Sicurta*, none corresponding very exactly to Jonson's, though all but one hold a spear.
2368 **despoiled** stripped of possessions
2374 TERGA DEDERE METVS fear has turned its back
2379 **EVDAIMONIA** The caduceus and cornucpoia belong to Ripa's *Felicita* or *Felicitas Publica.*

or Felicity, varied on the second hand and apparelled richly in an embroidered robe and mantle; a fair golden tress. In her right hand a caduceus, the note of peaceful wisdom; in her left a cornucopia filled only with flowers, as a sign of flourishing blessedness, and crowned with a garland of the same. At her feet

DYSPRAGIA

or Unhappiness, a woman bareheaded; her neck, arms, breast and feet naked; her look hollow and pale; she holds a cornucopia turned downward with all the flowers fallen out and scattered; upon her sits a raven, as the augury of ill fortune; and the soul was

REDEVNT SATVRNIA REGNA.

out of Virgil,[a] to show that now those golden times were returned again, wherein peace was with us so advanced, rest received, liberty restored, safety assured and all blessedness appearing in every of these virtues her particular triumph over her opposite evil. This is the dumb argument of the frame, and illustrated with this verse of Virgil, written in the under frieze:

NVLLA SALVS BELLO
PACEM TE POSCIMVS OMNES.[b]

The speaking part was performed, as within the temple where there was erected an altar, to which at the approach of the King appears the *Flamen*

MARTIALIS[c]

and to him

GENIVS VRBIS

The *Genius* we attired before. To the *Flamen* we appoint this habit: a long crimson robe to witness his nobility; his tippet and sleeves white, as reflecting on purity in his religion; a rich mantle of gold with a train, to express the dignity of his function; upon his head a hat[d] of delicate wool, whose top ended in a cone and was thence called *apex*, according to that of Lucan, liber I

Atollensque apicem generoso vertice flamen.

This *Apex* was covered with a fine net[e] of yarn which they named *apiculum*, and was sustained with a bowed twig[f] of pomegranate tree. It was also in the hot time of summer to be bound with ribbons and thrown behind them as Scaliger[g] teacheth. In his hand he bore a golden

a *Eclogae* 4.

b *Aeneid* liber 11.

c One of the three *flamines* that as some think Numa Pompilius first instituted, but we rather with Varro take him of Romulus' institution, whereof there were only two, he and Dialis, to whom he was next in dignity. He was always created out of the nobility and did perform the rites to Mars, who was thought the Father of Romulus.

d Scaliger *in Coniectura in Varro* saith *Totus Pileus, vel potius velamenta, Flammeum dicebatur, unde Flamines dicti.*

e To this looks that other conjecture of Varro liber 4: *de lingua Latina Flamines, quod licio in Capite velati erant semper, ac caput cinctum habebant filo, Flamines dicti.*

f Which in their attire was called *stroppus*, in their wives' *inarculum.*

g Scaliger *ibid in Coniectura: Pone enim regerebant apicem, ne gravis esset summis aestatis caloribus. Amentis enim, quae offendices dicebantur sub mentum adductis, religabant; ut cum vellent, regererent, et pone pendere permitterent.*

2381 **mantle** sleeveless robe
2391 **soul** meaning—i.e. the inner life or spirit of the emblem
2392 REDEVNT SATVRNIA REGNA Saturn's reign returns (indicating the return of the Golden Age)
2400–1 NVLLA ... OMNES No safety is in war; for peace we pray thee one and all (l. 362)
2403 **altar** 'with burning incense upon it' (Harrison)
2404 **Flamen** Roman priest
2412.n ***Totus ... dicti*** This cap or rather small covering used to be called the *flameum*, from which the term *flamines* is derived (Joseph Scaliger [1540–1609], *Coniectura in T. Varronem de lingua latina* [Paris, 1565], a work of humanist scholarship by one of the greatest classicists of the period). This etymology is no longer considered correct.
2415 ***Atollensque ... flamen*** And the flamen, raising aloft on his high-borne head the pointed cap (*Pharasalia*, 1.604). The context—an augury of future anguish and bloodshed for the Roman state—seems singularly inappropriate. Jonson was presumably interested only in the technical description of the flamen's cap.
2416.n ***de lingua ... dicti*** From the Latin language *Flamines*, because they were allowed to always have a covering on their head, and having their head girded with a band of wool were called *Flamines*. (The meaning here is clarified by Jonson's note to l. 2412, explaining that the cap was called a *flameum*.)
2420.n ***Pone ... permitterent*** They used to put the pointed cap behind, so that it might deflect the heat of the oppresive summer. These hats they tied by means of ribbons (*amentis*) which were called *offendices* when drawn under the chin; and when they wanted they would push them back and allow them to hang behind.

censer with perfume, and censing about the altar, having first kindled his fire on the top, is interrupted by the *Genius*.

GENIUS
Stay, what art thou that in this strange attire
Dar'st kindle stranger and unhallowed fire
Upon this altar?
FLAMEN *Rather what art thou*
That darest so rudely interrupt my vow?
My habit speaks my name.
GENIUS *A flamen?*
FLAMEN *Yes,*
And Martialis[a] *called.*
GENIUS *I so did guess*
By my short view, but whence didst thou ascend
Hither? or how? or to what mystic end?
FLAMEN
The noise and present tumult of this day
Roused me from sleep and silence where I lay
Obscured from light; which, when I waked to see,
I wond'ring thought what this great pomp might be.
When (looking on my calendar) I found
The Ides of March[b] *were entered, and I bound*
With these to celebrate the genial feast
Of Anna[c] *styled Perenna, Mars*[d] *his guest;*
Who, in this month of his, is yearly called
To banquet at his altars and installed
A Goddess[e] *with him, since she fills the year,*
And knits the oblique scarf that girts the sphere.[f]
Whilst four-faced Janus turns his vernal look[g]
Upon their meeting hours, as if he took
High pride and pleasure.
GENIUS *Sure thou still dost dream,*
And both thy tongue and thought rides on the stream
Of fantasy: Behold here he nor she
Have any altar, fane or, deity.
Stoop, read but this inscription:[h] *and then view*
To whom the place is consecrate. 'Tis true
That this is Janus' Temple, and that now
He turns upon the year his freshest brow;
That this is Mars his month, and these the Ides
Wherein his Anne was honoured. Both the tides,
Titles, and place we know; but these dead rites
Are long since buried and new power excites
More high and hearty flames. Lo, there is he
Who brings with him a greater Anne[i] *than she,*
Whose strong and potent virtues have defaced[j]
Stern Mars his statues, and upon them placed
His and the world's blessed blessings:[k] *This hath brought*
Sweet Peace to sit in that bright state she ought,
Unbloody or untroubled; hath forced hence

a Of Mars, whose rites (as we have touched before) this flamen did specially celebrate.

b With us the 15 of March, which was the present day of this triumph, and on which the great feast of *Anna Perenna* (among the Romans) was yearly and with such solemnity remembered: Ovid *Fasti* 3 *Idibus est Annae festum geniale Perrenae, Haud procul a ripis, etc.*

c Who this Anna should be, with the Romans themselves hath been no trifling controversy. Some have thought her fabulously the sister of Dido; some, a nymph of Numicius; some Io; some Themis; others an old woman of Bouillae that fed the seditious multitude *in monte sacro* with wafers and fine cakes in time of their penury, to whom afterward (in memory of the benefit) their peace being made with the nobles, they ordained this feast. Yet they that have thought nearest have missed all these and directly imagined her the Moon. And that she was called Anna, *Quia mensibus impleat annum.* (Ovid *ibid*). To which, the vow that they used in her rites somewhat confirmingly alludes; which was, *ut Annare, et perennare commode liceret* (Macrobius *Saturnalia* liber 1 caput 12).

d So Ovid *ibid. Fasti* makes Mars speaking to her: *Mense meo coleris, iunxi mea tempora tecum.*

e *Nuper erat dea facta, etc. ibid* Ovid.

f Where is understood the meeting of the zodiac in March, the month wherein she is celebrated.

g That face wherewith he beholds the spring.

h Written upon the altar, for which we refer you to the page 272.

i The Queen, to answer which in our inscription we spake to the King *MARTE MAIORI.*

j The Temple of Janus we apprehend to be both the house of war and peace: of war when it is open, of peace when it is shut; and that there, each over the other is interchangeably placed, to the vicissitude of times.

k Which are peace, rest, liberty, safety, etc. and were his actively but the world's passively.

2430 ***mystic*** religious
2436.n ***Idibus...ripis*** On the Ides is held the jovial feast of Anna Perenna, not far from thy banks, O Tiber, who comes from afar (Ovid, *Fasti*, 3.523–4)
2438.n ***in monte sacro*** onto the sacred mount
Quia...annum because she fills the measure of the year by her months (*Fasti*, 3.653)
ut...liceret that throughout the year and for years to come it shall be permitted. (The point is that the name Anna derives from *annare*.)
Mense...tecum Thou art worshipped in my month, I have joined my season to thine (*Fasti*, 3.679)
2441.n ***Nuper...facta*** She was lately made a goddess (*Fasti*, 3.677)
2443 ***vernal*** springtime
2448 ***fane*** temple
2458.n ***MARTE MAIORI*** Greater than Mars

All tumults, fears, or other dark portents
That might invade weak minds; hath made men see
Once more the face of welcome liberty;
And doth (in all his present acts) restore
That first pure world, made of the better ore.
Now innocence shall cease to be the spoil
Of ravenous greatness, or to steep the soil
Of rais'd peasantry with tears and blood.
No more shall rich men, for their little good,
Suspect to be made guilty, or vile spies
Enjoy the lust of their so murd'ring eyes.
Men shall put off their iron minds and hearts,
The time forget his old malicious arts
With this new minute, and no print remain
Of what was thought the former age's stain.
Back, flamen, with thy superstitious fumes
And cense not here; thy ignorance presumes
Too much in acting any ethnic rite
In this translated temple. Here no wight
To sacrifice, save my devotion, comes
That brings instead of those thy masculine[a] *gums,*
My city's heart, which shall for ever burn
Upon this altar, and no time shall turn
The same to ashes. Here I fix it fast:
Flame bright, flame high, and may it ever last
Whilst I, before the figure of thy peace,
Still tend the fire and give it quick increase
With prayers, wishes, vows; whereof be these
The least and weakest: that no age may lose
The memory of this so rich a day,
But rather that it henceforth yearly may
Begin our spring, and with our spring the prime
And first account of years, of months,[b] *of Time:*[c]
And may these Ides as fortunate appear
To thee as they to Caesar[d] *fatal were.*
Be all thy thoughts born perfect and thy hopes
In their events still crowned beyond their scopes.
Let not wide heaven that secret blessing know
To give, which she on thee will not bestow.
Blind Fortune be thy slave, and may her store
(The less thou seek'st it) follow thee the more.

a Somewhat a strange epithet in our tongue, but proper to the thing, for they were only masculine odours which were offered to the altars. Virgil *Eclogae* 8: *Verbenasque adole pingueis, et mascula tura.* And Pliny, *Naturalis Historia*, liber 12, caput 32 speaking of these, hath *Quod ex eo rotunditate guttae pependit masculum vocamus, cum alias non fere mas vocetur ubi non sit foemina; religioni tributum ne sexus alter usurparetur. Masculum aliqui putant a specie testium dictum.* See him also, liber 34, caput 2: and Arnobius liber 7 *Adversus Gentes. Non si mille tu pondera masculi turis incendas, etc.*

b According to Romulus his institution, who made March the first month and consecrated it to his Father, of whom it was called Martius: Varro, *Festii in Fragmentae Martius mensis initium annis fuit, et in Latio, et post Romam conditam etc.* And Ovid, *Fasti* 3: *A te principium Romano dicimus anno: primus de patrio nomine mensis erit. Vox rata fit; etc.* See Macrobius, liber 1 *Saturnalia* caput 12 and Solin in Polybius *Historia* caput 3: *Quod hoc mense mercedes exoluerint magistris, quas completus annus deberi fecisset, etc.*

c Some to whom we have read this have taken it for a tautology, thinking time enough expressed before, in 'years' and 'months'. For whose ignorant sakes we must confess to have taken the better part of this travail in noting, a thing not usual, neither affected of us, but where there is necessity, as here, to avoid their dull censures: where in 'years' and 'months' we alluded to that is observed in our former note; but by 'time' we understand the present, and that from this instant we should begin to reckon and make this the first of our time. Which is also to be helped by emphasis.

d In which he was slain in the Senate.

2468 ***better ore*** gold
2473 ***Suspect to be made guilty*** be accused of guilt, in order to furnish an excuse for confiscating their property. Jonson may have been thinking of Tacitus's description of Rome during the unstable period following Nero's overthrow: 'Nobility, wealth, the refusal of the acceptance of office, were grounds for accusation' (*History*, 1.2).
2481 ***ethnic*** pagan
2482 ***translated*** transferred from one condition to another
wight being
2484.n ***Verbenasque ... tura*** burn rich herbs and masculine gums (frankincense) (*Eclogues*, 8.65).
Quod ... dictum Frankincense that hangs suspended in a globular drop we call male frankincense, although in other connections the term 'male' is not usually employed where there is no female; but it is said to have been due to religious scruple that the name of the other sex was not employed in this case. Some people think that male frankincense is so called from its resemblance to the testes. (Pliny, *Natural History*, 12.32.61. Jonson incorrectly cited 12.14). Jonson's note exemplifies his passion for accurate detail in borrowing from classical sources. He also referred to 'masculine odors' in describing a religious rite in *Sejanus* (5.91).
Non ... incendas Not if you burn a thousand weights of masculine gum.
2492 ***lose*** pronounced 'leese'
2496.n ***Martius ... conditam*** The month of Mars was the beginning of the year, both in Latium and after its foundation in Rome (Varro, *Sexti Pompeii Festii librorum Fragmenta*).
A te ... etc. We name the beginning of the Roman year after thee; the first month shall be called by my father's name. The promise was kept, etc. (l. 75)
Quod ... fecisset 'Because in this month they paid off all their commercial debts (*mercedes*) to the magistrates—those debts that is which the complete year had caused to become due.' An alternative etymology, the idea being that *Martius* (March) derived from *mercedes*.

Much more I would: but see, these brazen gates
Make haste to close, as urgèd by thy fates;
Here ends my city's office, here it breaks;
Yet with my tongue and this pure heart she speaks
A short farewell; and lower than thy feet,
With fervent thanks, thy royal pains doth greet.
Pardon if my abruptness breed dis-ease:
He merits not t'offend, that hastes to please.

Over the altar was written this Inscription:

D.I.O.M.
BRITANNIARVM. IMP.
PACIS. VINDICI. MARTE. MAIORI. P. P.
F. S. AVGVSTO. NOVO. GENTIVM. CON-
IVNCTARVM. NVMINI. TVTELARI.
D. A.
CONSERVATRICI. ANNÆ. IPSÆ. PERENNÆ.
DEABVSQVE. VNIVERSIS. OPTATIORI. SVI
FORTVNATISSIMI. THALAMI. SOCIÆ. ET
CONSORTI. PVLCHERRIMÆ. AVGVSTISSIMÆ.
ET
H. F. P.
FILIO. SVO. NOBILISSIMO. OB. AD-
VENTVM. AD VRBEM. HANC. SVAM. EX-
PECTATISSIMVM. GRATISSIMVM. CE-
LEBRATISSIMVM. CVIVS. NON. RADII. SED
SOLES. POTIVS. FVNESSIMAM. NVPER.
ÆRIS. INTEMPERIEM. SERENARVNT
S. P. Q. L.
VOTIS. X. VOTIS. XX. ARDENTISSIMIS.
L. M.
HANC. ARAM.
P.

And upon the Gate being shut,

2505 ***brazen gates*** (of the temple)

2515–37 **D.I.O.M. . . . P** To Lord James the Best and Greatest (*D[omino] I[acobo] O[ptimo] M[aximo]*), Emperor of the Britons, guarantor of peace, greater than Mars, father of his country, saviour of the faith (*P[atri] P[atriae] F[idei] S[ervatori]*), new Augustus, protecting guardian of all the people; To Lady Anne (*D[ominae] A[nnae]*) Anna Perenna herself, more desirable than all the pagan goddesses, associate of his most blessed wedding chamber and most beautiful and most distinguished consort and | To Prince Henry Frederick (*H[enrico] F[rederico] P[rincipi]*) his most noble son whose arrival in the city has been long awaited and is most welcome and most spectacularly celebrated, and who—not like the sun's rays but more like the sun itself—has lately cleared the funereal and most intemperate air. The Senate and People of London (*S[enatus] P[opulusque] L[ondenensis]*) by their ten—no twenty—most heartfelt pledges, gladly to the deserving (*L[ibens] M[erito]*, a traditional formula for a thank offering), have set up (*P[osuit]*) this altar.

IMP. IACOBVS MAX.
CÆSAR AVG. P. P.
PACE POPVLO BRITANNICO
TERRA MARIQVE PARTA
IANVM CLVSIT. S. C.

Thus hath both court, town and country reader our portion of device for the city. Neither are we ashamed to profess it, being assured well of the difference between it and pageantry. If the mechanic part yet standing give it any distaste in the wry mouths of the time, we pardon them, for their own ambitious ignorance doth punish them enough. From hence we will turn over a new leaf with you, and lead you to the *pegme* in the Strand, a work thought on, begun and perfected in twelve days. **Pag. 8**

The invention was a rainbow: the moon, sun and those seven stars, which antiquity hath styled the *Pleiades*, or *Vergilia*, advanced between two magnificent pyramids of seventy foot in height, on which were drawn his Majesty's several pedigrees, English and Scottish. To which body (being framed before) we were to apt our soul. And finding that one of these seven lights, *Electra*, is rarely or not at all to be seen—as Ovid liber 4, *Fasti* affirmeth:

Pleiades incipient humeros relevare paternos:
Quae septem dici, sex tamen esse solent.

And by and by after,

Sive quod Electra Troiae spectare ruinas
Non tulit: ante oculos opposuitque manum.

And Festus Avienus[a]

Fama vetus septem memorat genitore creatas
Longaevo: sex se rutila inter sidera tantum
Sustollunt, etc.

And beneath

...cerni sex solas carmine Mynthes
Asserit: Electram coelo abscessisse profundo, etc.

a Paraphraste in Arati Phaenomena.

2540–4 **IMP...S. C.** 'James the greatest emperor, Caesar Augustus Father of his Country. Because peace has been brought forth for the British people on land and sea, a decree of the Senate (*S[enatus] C[onsulto]*) closes the gate.' This appears to allude to a famous prophecy in the *Aeneid* (1.284–97) concerning the rise of the Julian dynasty and the establishment of world peace under its auspices: 'From this noble line shall be born the Trojan Caesar, who shall limit his empire with the ocean, his glory with the stars, a Julius, a name descended from the great Julus. Him in days to come shalt thou, anxious no more, welcome to heaven, laden with eastern spoils; he too shall be invoked in vows. Then shall wars cease and the rough ages soften; hoary Faith and Vesta, Quirinus with his brother Remus, shall give laws. The gates of war, grim with iron and close-fitting bars, shall be closed; within impious rage, sitting on savage arms, his hands fast bound behind with a hundred brazen knots, shall roar in the ghastliness of blood-stained lips.'

2549 **pageantry** showy display (here contrasted with Jonson's learning and poetry)
mechanic part physical remains of the pageant

2553 ***pegme*** stage. Dugdale implies that this was a failure: 'In the Strand was also another of small motion, a pyramid fitly beseeming time and place, but the day far spent and the King and states, I am sure, wearied with the shows—as the stomach may glutton the daintiest [courses]—stayed not long but passed forward to the place appointed.'

2555 **invention** design. Dekker's summary is printed as Additional Passage F.

2560 **apt** adapt
soul Literary and intellectual meaning.

2563–4 ***Pleiades...solent*** Pleiades will commence to lighten the burden that rests on their father's shoulders; seven are they usually called, but six they usually are (Ovid, *Fasti*, 4.169–70).

2566–7 ***Sive...manum*** or whether it be that Electra could not brook to behold the fall of Troy, and so covered her eyes with her hand (Ovid, *Fasti*, 4.177–8).

2568 **Festus Avienus** Rufus Festus Avienius, Roman poet of the fourth century

2569–71 ***Fama...Sustollunt*** Ancient rumour proclaims their father Longavus created them seven: but only six hold themselves among the reddish stars.

2573–4 ***cerni...profundo*** He brought it about that only six are able to be seen and he says that one of them, Electra, retired to the deepest sky.

We ventured to follow this authority and made her the speaker, presenting her hanging in the air in figure of a comet, according to Anonymous: *Electra non sustinens videre casum pronepotum fugerit; unde et illam dissolutis crinibus propter luctum ire asserunt, et propter comas quidam Cometen appellant.*

The Speech

ELECTRA

The long laments,[a] *I spent for ruin'd Troy*
Are dried, and now mine eyes run tears of joy.
No more shall men suppose Electra dead,
Though from the consort of her sisters fled
Unto the Arctic circle,[b] *here to grace*
And gild this day with her serenest[c] *face*
And see my daughter Iris[d] *hastes to throw*
Her roseate wings, in compass of a bow,
About our state as sign[e] *of my approach,*
Attracting to her seat from Mithra's[f] *coach*
A thousand different and particular hues,
Which she throughout her body doth diffuse.
The sun, as loth to part from this half sphere,
Stands still, and Phoebe labours to appear
In all as bright (if not as rich) as he;
And for a note of more serenity
My six fair sisters[g] *hither shift their lights,*
To do this hour the utmost of her rites,
Where lest the captious or profane might doubt
How these clear heavenly bodies come about,
All to be seen at once, yet neither's light
Eclipsed or shadowed by the other's sight.
Let ignorance know, great King, this day is thine,
And doth admit no night, but all do shine
As well nocturnal as diurnal fires
To add unto the flame of our desires.
Which are (now thou hast closed up Janus' gates,[h]
And giv'n so general peace to all estates)
That no offensive mist or cloudy stain
May mix with splendour of thy golden reign;
But, as thou'st freed thy chamber[i] *from the noise*
Of war and tumult, thou wilt pour those joys
Upon this place,[j] *which claims to be the seat*[k]
Of all thy kingly race, the cabinet
To all thy counsels and the judging chair

a Festus Avienus *Paraphrases: pars ait Idaeae deflentem incendia Troiae, Et numerosa suae lugentem funera gentis, Electram tetris moestum dare nubibus orbem.* Besides the reference to antiquity, this speech might be understood by allegory of the town here that had been so ruined with sickness, etc.

b Hyginus: *Sed postquam Troia fuit capta, et progenies eius quae a Dardano fuit eversa, dolore permotam ab his se removisse, et in circulo qui Arcticus dicitur constitisse, etc.*

c 'Electra' signifies 'Serenity itself' and is compounded of ἥλιος which is the sun and αἴθριος that signifies serene. She is mentioned to be *Anima sphaerae solis* by Proclus, *Commentarii in Hesiod.*

d She is also feigned to be the mother of the rainbow: *Nascitur enim Iris ex aqua et serenitate, e refractione radiorum scilicet:* Aristotle *In Meteorologia.*

e Valerius Flaccus *Argonauticon* 1, makes the rainbow *indicem serenitatis. Emicuit reserata dies, coelumque resolvit Arcus, et in summos redierunt nubila montes.*

f A name of the sun: Statius, *Thebais*, liber 1, *torquentem cornua Mithran*, And Martianus Capella liber 3 *De Nuptiis Mercurii et Philologiae, Te Serapim Nilus, Memphis veneratur Osirin; Dissona sacra Mithran, etc.*

g Alcyone, Celaeno, Taygete, Asterope, Merope, Maia, which are also said to be the souls of the other spheres, as Electra of the sun (Proclus *ibid. in commentarii): Alcyone Veneris. Celaeno Saturni. Taygete Lunae. Asterope Iovis. Merope Martis. Maia Mercurii.*

h Alluding back to that of our temple.

i London.

j His city of Westminster, in whose name, and at whose charge, together with the Duchy of Lancaster, this arch was erected.

k Since here they not only sat being crowned, but also first received their crowns.

2577–80 ***Electra . . . appellant*** Electra fled, not bearing to see her grandson's death, and this is why people say that she went, hair streaming behind her, because of her grief. And because of her hair (*comas*) some people call her the comet.
2582.n ***pars . . . orbem*** others say that while bitterly weeping over the burning of Idaean Troy and mourning the deaths of countless of her own people Electra offered herself as a grieving star.
2586.n ***Sed . . . constitisse*** But after Troy had been captured and her descendants through Dadanus overthrown, moved by grief she [Electra] left them and took her place in the circle called Arctic (*Myths of Hyginus*, 2, 21).
2587.n ***Anima sphaerae solis*** the soul of the sphere of the sun
2588.n ***Nascitur . . . scilicet*** Iris arises from water and fair weather [*serenitate*], evidently from the refraction of the sun's rays
2590.n ***indicem . . . montes*** the sign of peace. The unloosed day bursts out and clears the sky. The clouds return to the mountain heights.
2591.n ***torquentem cornua Mithran*** Mithra brandishing her horns
Te . . . Mithran The Nile venerates you Serapis and the city of Memphis venerates you Osiris and clamourous rituals venerate you Mithra
2595 ***Phoebe*** the moon
2598.n **Proclus . . . *Mercurii*** Proclus in the same in the commentary. Of the planet Venus, Alcyone. Caelano of Saturn. Taygete of the Moon. Asterope of Jupiter. Merope of Mars. Maia of Mercury.
2606 ***diurnal*** daytime
2615 ***cabinet*** small private room, often adjacent to a bedroom; hence a place where the king may receive secret or intimate advice.
2616 ***judging chair*** magistrate's seat

To this thy special kingdom. Whose so fair
And wholesome laws in every court shall strive
By equity and their first innocence to thrive.
The base and guilty bribes of guiltier men
Shall be thrown back, and Justice look as when
She loved the earth, and feared not to be sold
For that which worketh all things to it, gold. [a]
The dam of other evils, avarice,
Shall here lock down her jaws, and that rude vice
Of ignorant and pitied greatness, pride,
Decline with shame; ambition now shall hide
Her face in dust, as dedicate to sleep,
That in great portals wont her watch to keep.
All ills shall fly the light; thy court be free
No less from envy than from flattery.
All tumult, faction, and harsh discord cease,
That might perturb the music of thy peace.
The querulous nature shall no longer find
Room for his thoughts. One pure consent of mind
Shall flow in every breast, and not the air,
Sun, moon or stars shine more serenely fair.
This from that loud, blessed oracle I sing
Who here, and first, pronounced thee Britain's king.
Long mayst thou live and see me thus appear,
As ominous a comet, [b] *from my sphere*
Unto thy reign, as that did auspicate [c]
So lasting glory to Augustus' state.

a Horace *Carminae* liber 4, Ode 9: *Ducentis ad se cuncta pecuniae.*

b For our more authority to induce her thus, see Festus Avienus paraphrases in Arat. speaking of Electra: *Nonnumquam Oceani tamen istam surgere ab undis, In convexa poli, sed sede carere sororum; Atque os discretum procul edere, detestatam, Germanosque choros sobolis lachrimare ruinas, Diffusamque comas cerni, crinisque soluti Monstrari effigie, etc.*

c All comets were not fatal; some were fortunately ominous, as this to which we allude, and wherefore we have Pliny's testimony (*Naturalis Historia, liber 2, caput 23*): *Cometes in uno totius orbis loco colitur in templo Romae, admodum faustus Divo Augusto iudicatus ab ipso, qui incipiente eo, apparuit ludis quos faciebat Veneri Genetrici, non multo post obitum patris Caesaris, in collegio ab eo instituto. Namque his verbis id gaudium prodidit.* Iis ipsis ludorum meorum diebus, sidus crinitum per septem dies in regione coeli, quae sub septentrionibus est, conspectum. Id oriebatur circa undecimam horam diei, clarumque et omnibus terris conspicuum fuit. Eo sidere significari vulgus credidit, Caesaris animam inter deorum immortalium numina receptam: quo nomine id insigne simulacro capitis eius, quod mox in foro consecravimus adiectum est. *Haec ille in publicum, interiore gaudio sibi illum natum, seque in eo nasci interpretatus est. Et si verum fatemur, salutare id terris fuit.*

And thus have we (lowly and aloof) followed our sovereign through the seven triumphal gates of this his court royal, which name, as London received at the rising of the sun, so now at his going from her, even in a moment she lost that honour. And being, like an actor on a stage, stripped out of her borrowed majesty, she resigns her former shape and title of city; nor is it quite lost, considering it went along with him to whom it is due. For such virtue is begotten in princes that their very presence hath power to turn a village to a city and to make a city appear great as a kingdom. Behold how glorious a flower happiness is, but how fading. The minutes that lackey at the heels of Time run not faster away than do our joys. What tongue could have expressed the raptures on which the soul of the city was carried beyond itself, for the space of many hours? What wealth could have allured her to have closed her eyes at the coming of her king, and yet see her bridegroom is but stepped from her, and in a minute (nay in shorter time than a thought can be born) is she made a widow. All her consolation being now to repeat over by rote those honours, which lately she had perfectly by heart, and to tell of those joys which but even now she really beheld.

2621 ***Justice*** Astraea, alluding to the Golden Age when she lived on earth
2622 ***feared not to be sold*** Jonson suggests that the selling of justice for gold ended the Golden Age.
2623.n ***Ducentis . . . pecuniae*** Money that leads all things to herself
2628 ***dedicate*** devoted
2641 ***ominous*** portentous
2641.n ***Nonnumquam . . . etc.*** Sometimes that one [Electra] rises from the waters of the ocean into the convex sky, but avoids the seat of her sisters and shows her face apart from afar. Despising the twin chorus of the Pleiades, she weeps for the ruins of her Trojan race. She is distinguished by her spreading locks, by the image of her loosened hair, etc.
2642.n ***Cometes . . . fuit*** The only place in the whole world where a comet is the object of worship is a temple at Rome. His late majesty Augustus had deemed this comet very propitious to himself; as it had appeared at the beginning of his rule at some games which, not long after the decease of his father Caesar, as a member of the college founded by him he was celebrating in honour of Mother Venus. In fact he made public the joy it gave him in these very words: 'On the very days of my Games a comet was visible for seven days in the northern part of the sky. It was rising about an hour before sunset, and was a bright star, visible in all lands. The common people believed that this star signified the soul of Caesar received among the spirits of the immortal gods, and on this account the emblem of a star was added to the bust of Caesar that we shortly afterwards dedicated in the Forum.' This was his public utterance, but privately he rejoiced because he interpreted the comet as having been born for his own sake and containing his own birth within it; and to confess the truth it did have a health-giving influence over the world (*Natural History*, 2.93, 4).
2655 **lackey** run attending

Yet thus of her absent beloved do I hear her gladly and heartily speaking.

In freta dum Fluvii Current; dum montibus umbrae,
Lustrabunt Convexa, Polus dum sidera pascit,
Semper Honos, Nomenque tuum Laudesque manebunt.
Virgil

As touching those five [arches] which the city builded, the arbour in Cheapside and the temple of Janus at Temple Bar were both of them begun and finished in six weeks. Thc rest were taken in hand first in March last, after his Majesty was proclaimed, upon which, at that time, they wrought till a month after St James his day following, and then gave over by reason of the sickness. At this second setting upon them, six weeks more were spent.

The city elected sixteen committees, to whom the managing of the whole business was absolutely referred: of which number four were aldermen, the other grave commoners.

There were also committees appointed as overseers and surveyors of the works:

Artificium Operariumque in hoc tam
celebri apparatu, summa.
summa

The city employed in the framing, building and setting up of their five arches these officers and workmen:

A clerk that attended on the committees.
Two officers that gave summons for their meetings etc.
A clerk of the works.
Two master carpenters.
Painters.

Of which number, those that gave the main direction and undertook for the whole business were only these seven.

William Friselfield
George Mosse
John Knight
Paul Isacson
Samuel Goodrick
Richard Wood
George Heron
Carvers 24

Over whom Stephen Harrison, joiner, was appointed chief, who was the sole inventor of the architecture, and from whom all directions for so much as belonged to carving, joining, molding, and all other work in those five pageants of the city (painting excepted) were set down.

Joiners 80
Carpenters 60
Turners 6
Labourers to them 6
Sawyers 12
Labourers during all the time, and for the day of the Triumph 70

Besides these there were other artificers, as plumbers, smiths, molders.

To the Reader

Reader, you must understand that a regard being had that his Majesty should not be wearied with tedious speeches, a great part of those which are in this book set down were left unspoken. So that thou dost here receive them as they should have been delivered, not as they were.

FINIS.

Lectori Candido.

Reader, the limbs of these great triumphal bodies, lately disjointed and taken in sunder, I have thou seest (for thy sake) set in their apt and right places again, so that now they are to stand as perpetual monuments, not to be shaken in pieces or to be broken down by the malice of that envious destroyer of all things, time. Which labours of mine, if they yield thee either profit or pleasure, thou art, in requital thereof, to pay many thanks to this honourable city, whose bounty towards me, not only in making choice of me to give directions for the entire workmanship of the five triumphal arches builded by the same, but also in publishing these pieces, I do here gladly acknowledge to have been exceeding liberal.

Nor shall it be amiss in this place to give thee intelligence of some matters, by way of notes, which were not fully observed nor freely enough set down in the printed book of these triumphs, amongst which these that follow are chiefest.

His Majesty departed from the Tower between the hours of eleven and twelve, and before five had made his royal passage through the city, having a canopy borne over him by eight knights.

The first object that his Majesty's eye encountered after his entrance into London was part of the children of Christ's Church Hospital, to the number of three hundred,

2668–70 ***In*... *manebunt*** While rivers run into the sea, while on the mountains shadows move over the slopes, while heaven feeds the stars, ever shall thy honour, thy praises, thy name endure.
2675 **March last** March 1603, when Elizabeth died and James was first proclaimed
2677 **month after St James his day** *c.*25 August
2678–9 **second setting** presumably in February and March 1604, after the entry was rescheduled
2686–8 ***Artificium*... *summa*** The directors of the workmanship and workmen in that so famous and sumptuous undertaking.
2726 ***Lectori Candido*** To the candid reader
2727 **triumphal bodies** the arches
2742–3 **printed book** Dekker's *Magnificent Entertainment*
2745 **the Tower** The royal family entered the Tower on March 12, being greeted by a Latin oration (printed in Nichols, pp. 329–332). Dugdale supplies additional detail: see Additional Passage A.
2751 **Christ's Church Hospital** A hospital established in the mid-Tudor period for the care of orphans and poor children. It normally housed around 600 children at any time and was a crucial link in the city's well-organized system of poor relief.

who were placed on a scaffold erected for that purpose in Barking Churchyard by the Tower.

The way from the Tower to Temple Bar was not only sufficiently gravelled, but all the streets lying between those two places were on both sides, where the breadth would permit, railed in at the charges of the City, Paul's Churchyard excepted.

The liveries of the companies, having their streamers, ensigns and bannerets spread on the tops of their rails before them, reached from the middle of Mark Lane to the *pegme* at Temple Bar.

Two marshals were chosen for the day to clear the passage, both of them being well mounted and attended on by six men (suitably attired) to each marshal.

The conduits of Cornhill, of Cheap and of Fleet Street that day ran claret wine very plenteously, which by reason of so much excellent music, that sounded forth not only from each several *pegme* but also from diverse other places, ran the faster and more merrily down into some bodies' bellies.

As touching the oration uttered by Sir Henry Mountague, Recorder of the City, with the gifts bestowed on the King, the Queen and the Prince (being three cups of gold), as also all such songs as were that day sung in the several arches, I refer you to the book in print where they are set down at large.

And thus much you shall understand, that no manner of person whatsoever did disburse any part towards the charge of these five triumphs, but only the mere citizens, being all freemen; heretofore the charge being borne by fifteens and the Chamber of London (as may appear by ancient precedents) but now it was levied amongst the companies. The other two arches erected by merchant strangers (*viz.* the Italians and Dutchmen) were only their own particular charge.

The City elected sixteen committees to whom the managing of the whole business was absolutely referred, of which number four were aldermen, the other twelve commoners, *viz.* one out of each of the twelve companies. Other committees were also appointed as overseers and surveyors of the work. Farewell.

ADDITIONAL PASSAGES

A *Dugdale's account of the events at the Tower (see ll. 2745–8):*

The Tower was emptied of his prisoners, and I beheld the late Sir Walter Ralegh, the late Lord Cobham, the late Lord Gray [and] Markham, with others conveyed, some to the Marshelsea, others to the gatehouse, and others appointed prisoners. The Tower itself prepared with that pomp as eye never saw, such glory in the hangings, such majesty in the ornaments of the chambers, and such necessary provision as when I beheld it I could no less than say

God gives King James the place
And glory of the day,
As never king possessed like place,
That came the northern way:
And since the heavens will have it so,
What living soul dares answer no.

Upon the Thames the water works for his entertainment were miraculous, and the fireworks on the water passed pleasing, as a castle or fortress builded on two barges, seeming as a settled fort of an island, planted with much munition of defence: and two pinnaces, ready rigged, armed likewise to assault the castle, that had you beheld the managing of that fight with onset on the castle, repulse from the castle and then the taking of it in, it was a show worthy the sight of many princes: being there placed at the cost of the Cinque Ports, whereat the King all pleased made

2754 **Tower to Temple Bar** the route through the City of London, as far as the boundary with the Borough of Westminster on the Strand
2759 **liveries of the companies** ceremonial costume of the London guilds. Dugdale comments: 'the companies of London, in their liveries, placed in street double railed for them and the passengers, the whifflers they in their costly suits and chains of gold walking up and down'.
2762 ***pegme*** a stage or framework for a pageant. The Latinate word consistently used by Harrison, Dekker, and Jonson.
2766 **conduits** for water. Dugdale states, 'not a conduit betwixt the Tower and Westminster but ran wine, drink who will', and that near Ludgate 'the conduits dealt so plenteously both before and after he [James] was passed as many were shipped to the Isle of Sleep, that had no leisure for snorting to behold the day's triumph'.
Cornhill . . . Cheap . . . Fleet Street see map, p. 62
2772 **Sir Henry Montagu** nominated for the office of Recorder by James on 25 May 1603
2776 **book in print** Dekker's *Magnificent Entertainment*
2780 **five** the number of pageants had been increased from five to seven during the course of preparations. Harrison evidently forgot to emend his text.
2781 **freemen** of the guilds and City of London.
2782 **fifteens** a standard tax
Chamber of London the City's central treasury
2784 **companies** guilds. The guilds were assessed twice, for £2500 and £400. *Memorials of the Guild of Merchant Taylors of the Fraternity of St John the Baptist in the City of London* (London, 1875) reproduces the original assessment list, recording payments by 298 members, ranging from £5 6*s*. 8*d*. down to 6*s*., for a total contribution of £320 6*s*. 4*d*.
2789–90 **commoners** i.e. citizens of London who were not aldermen
2790 **twelve companies** the twelve great guilds or companies, from whose membership the Lord Mayor and aldermen were always chosen
A.8 **hangings** tapestries
14 **northern way** from Scotland
21 **pinnaces** small ships

A

answer that their love was like the wild fire unquenchable. And I pray God it may ever be so.

Well from the Tower he came. Here cost was quite careless, desire that was fearless and content flourished in abundance: but so royally attended as if the gods had summoned a Parliament and were all in their steps of triumph to Jove's high court.

B

Dekker's description of the Fenchurch arch and pageant follows on from l. 451:

His passage alongst that court offering itself for more state through seven gates, of which the first was erected at Fenchurch.

Thus presenting itself:

Fenchurch

It was an upright flat-square (for it contained fifty foot in the perpendicular, and fifty foot in the groundline) the upper roof thereof (on distinct greces) bore up the true models of all the notable houses, turrets and steeples within the city. The gate under which his Majesty did pass was twelve foot wide and eighteen foot high; a postern likewise (at one side of it) being four foot wide and eight foot in height. On either side of the gate stood a great French term of stone, advanced upon wooden pedestals; two half pilasters of rustic standing over their heads. I could shoot more arrows at this mark, and teach you without the carpenter's rule how to measure all the proportions belonging to this fabric, but an excellent hand being at this instant curiously describing all the seven, and bestowing on them their fair prospective limbs, your eye shall hereafter rather be delighted in beholding those pictures, than now be wearied in looking upon mine.

The personages (as well mutes as speakers) in this pageant were these: viz.

1 The highest person was The Britain Monarchy.
2 At her feet sat Divine Wisdom.
3 Beneath her stood The Genius of the City, a man.
4 At his right hand was placed a personage, figuring The Counsel of the City.
5 Under all these lay a person representing *Thamesis* the River.

Six other persons (being daughters to *Genius*) were advanced above him, on a spreading ascent, of which the first was

1 Gladness.
2 The second, Veneration.
3 The third, Promptitude.
4 The fourth, Vigilance.
5 The fifth, Loving affection.
6 The sixth, Unanimity.

Of all which personages, *Genius* and *Thamesis* were the only speakers, *Thamesis* being presented by one of the children of Her Majesty's Revels: *Genius* by Master Alleyn, servant to the young Prince. His gratulatory speech (which was delivered with excellent action, and a well-tuned audible voice) being to this effect:

That London may be proud to behold this day, and therefore in name of the Lord Mayor and aldermen, the council, commoners and multitude, the heartiest welcome is tendered to his Majesty, that ever was bestowed on any king, etc.

The waits and oboes of London

Which banquet being taken away with sound of music, there, ready for the purpose, his Majesty made his entrance into this his Court Royal. Under this first gate, upon the battlements of the work, in great capitals was inscribed thus:

LONDINIVM.

And under that, in a smaller (but not different) character was written,

CAMERA REGIA:

The King's Chamber.

C

Dugdale describes an incident during the Italians' Pageant (see ll. 866–1055):

Through [the arch] our King and his train passed, and at the corner of the street stood me one, an old man with a white beard, of the age of three score and nineteen, who had seen the change of four kings and Queens and now beheld the triumphs of the fifth, which by his report exceeded all the rest. Wherefore as hopeful never to behold the like, yet he would of his own accord do that which should show his duty and old love. That was to speak a few lines that his son had made him, which lines were to this purpose, he himself attired in green.

Peerless of honour, hear me speak a word.
Thy welcomed glory and enthroned renown
Being in peace, of earthly pomp and state
To furnish forth the beauties of thy crown.
Age thus salutes thee, with a downy pate.
Threescore and nineteen is thy servant's years,
That hath beheld thy predecessors four,
All flourishing green, whose deaths the subjects' tears,
Mingled with mine, did many times deplore:
But now again, since that our joys are five,
Five hundred welcomes I do give my King,
And may thy change, to us that be alive,
Never be known a fifth extreme to bring.
My honest heart be pattern of the rest.
Whoever prayed for them before, now thee,
Both them and thine, of all joy be possessed,
Whose lively presence we all bless to see,
And so pass on. God guide thee on thy way,
Old Hinde concludes, having no more to say.

But the narrow way and the pressing multitude so overshadowed him, and the noise of the show, that opportunity was not favourable to him, so that the King passed by. Yet noting his zeal I have publicly imprinted it, that all his fellow subjects may see this old

B.15 **term** a statue or bust atop a pillar or pedestal, from which it appears to spring

44–5 **Master Alleyn** Edward Alleyn (1566–1626), renowned Elizabethan actor, head of the Lord Admiral's Company, and co-owner, with his father-in-law, Philip Henslowe, of the Fortune Theatre. Alleyn retired from the stage about this time; his appearance in the pageant may have been his last as an actor. In James's reign he became a patron of poets, Dekker among them.

man's forwardness, who missed of his purpose by the concourse of people. Beside, the King appointed no such thing but at several stays and appointed places.

D *Dugdale's account of a speech at the Conduit (see l. 1346):* Still the street stood railed and the liveries of all the companies on both sides guarding the way, and the strong stream of people violently running in the midst toward Cheapside, there our triumphant rides garnished with troops of royalty and gallant personages, and passing by the great Conduit on the top thereof stood a prentice in a black coat, a flat cap servant-like, as walking before his master's shop. Now whether he spake this or no, I heard not it, but the manner of his speech was this, coming to me at the third or second hand.

What lack you gentlemen? What will you buy? Silks,
satins, taffetas, etc.?
But stay, bold tongue, stand at a giddy gaze;
Be dim, mine eyes. What gallant train are here
That strikes minds mute, and puts good wits in maze?
O 'tis our King, royal King James I say.
    Pass on in peace and happy be thy way!
    Live long on Earth, England's great Crown to sway!
    Thy city, gracious King, admires thy fame
    And on their knees prays for thy happy state;
    Our women for thy Queen Anne, whose rich name
    Is their created bliss, and sprung of late.
    If women's wishes may prevail thus being,
    They wish you both long lives, and good agreeing.

Children for children pray before they eat,
At their uprising and their lying down:
Thy sons and daughters, princely all, complete,
Royal in blood, children of high renown.
    But generally together they incline,
    Praying in one, great King, for thee and thine.

Whether he were appointed or of his own accord I know not, but howsoever forward love is acceptable, and I would the King had heard them, but the sight of the trophy at Soper Lane end made him the more forward.

E *Dekker's account of the arch and pageant at Temple Bar (see l. 2218):*
The building being set out thus:

The front or surface of it was proportioned in every respect like a temple, being dedicated to Janus, as by this inscription over the Janus head may appear:

Iano Quadrifronti
Sacrum

The height of the whole edifice, from the ground line to the top, was fifty-seven foot, the full breadth of it eighteen foot, the thickness of the passage twelve.

The personages that were in this temple are these:

1. The principal person, Peace.
2. By her stood Wealth.
3. Beneath the feet of Peace lay Mars (War) grovelling.
4. And upon her right hand (but with some little descent) was seated Quiet, the first handmaid of Peace.
5. She had lying at her feet Tumult.
6. On the other side was the second handmaid, Liberty, at whose feet lay a cat.
7. This person trod upon Servitude.
8. The third handmaid was Safety.
9. Beneath her was Danger.
10. The fourth attendant was, Felicity.
11. At her feet, Unhappiness.

Within the Temple was an Altar, to which, upon the approach of the King, a flamen appears, and to him, the former Genius of the city.

The effect of whose speech was, that whereas the flamen came to perform rites there in honour of one Anna, a goddess of the Romans, the Genius vows that none shall do sacrifice there but himself, the off'ring that he makes being the heart of the city, etc.

F *Dekker's account of the pageant in the Strand (see l. 2555):* The city of Westminster and Duchy of Lancaster, perceiving what preparation their neighbour city made to entertain her sovereign, though in greatness they could not match her, yet in greatness of love and duty they gave testimony that both were equal; and in token they were so, hands and hearts went together, and in the Strand, erected up a monument of their affection.

The invention was a rainbow, the moon, sun and the seven stars, called the Pleiades, being advanced between two pyramids: Electra (one of those seven hanging in the air, in figure of a comet) was the speaker, her words carrying this effect:

That as his Majesty had left the city of London happy, by delivering it from the noise of tumult, so he would crown this place with the like joys, which being done, she reckons up a number of blessings that will follow upon it.

The work of this was thought upon, begun and made perfect in twelve days.

C.36 **King . . . thing** The incident reveals James's discomfort with the sort of unplanned spontaneous expressions of popular loyalty that Elizabeth had often welcomed.

THE PATIENT MAN AND THE HONEST WHORE

Edited by Paul Mulholland

THE popularity of *The Patient Man and the Honest Whore* in its own time renders the play exceptional in the canons of either of the collaborating playwrights. Among their dramatic works, only Dekker's *Shoemakers' Holiday* and Middleton's *Game at Chess* can lay claim to surpass the attention generated by this comedy. Its multiple editions in the space of just over thirty years, a citation of a revival by 'Her Majesty's servants with great applause' on the title-page of the 1635 edition, and Dekker's studied duplication of successful elements in his sequel very likely written close on the original play's heels, all point to a remarkable stirring of interest. A contemporary theatregoer, Edward Pudsey, apparently in the habit of jotting down memorable phrases from plays he had attended, saw fit to record in his commonplace book seventeen brief passages drawn from *The Patient Man and the Honest Whore*'s final six scenes. Pudsey's citations range from the ribald, 'Made haste as though my looks had worked with him to give him a stool' (12.38–9), to the sententious, 'Wisely to fear is to be free from fear' (15.11), and share company with others from plays by Jonson, Marston, Chapman, Dekker, and Shakespeare.

The Patient Man and the Honest Whore was probably first performed at the Fortune Theatre some time between April (when the theatres reopened after an extended plague outbreak) and October 1604 (before the Stationers' Register entry in early November). If the allusion at 10.31–2 to relief of the siege of Ostend (11 September 1604) is not a revision, composition and early performances can be dated even more accurately. The later revival cited above presumably concerns a staging by Queen Henrietta's company at the Phoenix Theatre, although the possibility that Queen Anne's company mounted it prior to Charles I's accession, at the Phoenix or the Red Bull, cannot be ruled out. Despite the play's early theatrical success, few productions are on record since the seventeenth century. The first of these was staged with sly irony at the intimate Boulevard Theatre, part of the Raymond Revue Bar complex, in the heart of London's Soho by the Six O Six Theatre Company, 13 November to 5 December 1992. Director Gordon Anderson set the action in 1950s bohemian Soho accompanied by a jazz-blues musical score. The choice of venue, in which 'bump and grind' music occasionally intruded from next door, and its surrounding district provided a concrete context for matters raised chiefly in the Bellafront plot, a locale that could accommodate the play's diversity of characterization, and an environment that, in the director's words, helped to circumvent an overly reverential response to a Jacobean text. A second production played at Shakespeare's Globe Theatre on London's Bankside, 13 August to 18 September 1998. This adaptation by director, Jack Shepherd, and the Globe's artistic director, Mark Rylance, who also played Hippolito, compressed *The Patient Man and the Honest Whore* and Dekker's sequel, *The Honest Whore, Part 2*, into what *Time Out* termed a three-hour 'spare rib to Dekker's T-bone steak'. Reminiscent of its Six O Six predecessor, designer Hayden Griffin set the first part in 1950s Soho, and the second a decade later. Generally favourable reviews regularly singled out Rylance, Lilo Baur (likened by one critic to Anna Magnani) as a 'fragile, beautiful, poignant, but also tough and sexy' Bellafront, and Sonia Ritter as an embittered Infelice. Although advance publicity promised an adaptation that would eliminate the Candido plot, much of it survived. Appreciative commendations garnered by Marcello Magni (Candido) and Kathryn Pogson (Viola) vindicated retention of these scenes. In a complementary venture the Globe also presented 'staged readings' (with a different cast) of the two plays uncut on 6 and 13 September 1998. A seed sown by this editor in conversation with director/dramatist Peter Hinton some years ago seems to have germinated into a substantially adapted revival at the Ludger-Duvernay Theatre of Canada's National Theatre School, Montreal, 7–11 December 2004. This graduating-class production, styled by Hinton as '*Kill Bill* meets *Coronation Street*', among other changes, switched the gender of the central blocking character from Duke to Duchess in a 'gritty yet noble evocation of early seventeenth-century London'. Three productions within a relatively brief time-span augur well for theatrical exposure in the future.

The title of this Dekker–Middleton collaboration underwent several alterations in the course of its early history; and editorial convention since 1840 has assigned the play the title, *The Honest Whore, Part 1*. Although this serves to distinguish it from its sequel, there can be little doubt that the comedy was not known as *Part 1* at the time of its writing and first performance any more than other works that have generated sequels were known as *Part 1* at the point of their original release, publication, or performance. By adopting *The Patient Man and the Honest Whore*, this edition—the first to do so—aims to recover a title that on the testimony of contemporaries had currency at or near the time of the play's original stage performance. This title restores the balance of the play, giving a unified double paradox where the editorially conventional title provides a single paradox and a consequent sense of incompleteness. Henslowe's entry concerning an advance for 'the patient man and the honest whore' in addition to providing the earliest record of the play very likely situates its main interests in the circumstances of theatrical production.

The proverbial expression cited at 2.74, 'he who cannot be angry is no man', establishes the paradoxical basis of 'the patient man' and the terms by which he is intended to match 'the honest whore'. Patience is conventionally seen as a feminine attribute, as, for example, in Dekker's *Patient Grissil*, and is incompatible with common conceptions of virility. In Candido the play explores the unusual and unlikely combination of patience and manhood just as in Bellafront it explores the unusual and unlikely combination of honesty and whoredom. The other male characters are more conventionally susceptible to rage. Most appear in circumstances in which they succumb to the promptings of hot blood and surrender rational control. Seen against such eruptions Candido's imperturbable patience calls in question violent, aggressive behaviour construed as a sign of manliness as well as its ideological construction in proverbial form.

At the base of the various stratagems bent on provoking Candido to anger lies a problematic of gender construction and identity. The male characters who try to rouse a choleric outburst from him seek a confirmation of his male identity in terms consonant with those they recognize in themselves. Most of the characters who strive to strike sparks of anger from Candido reveal elsewhere a capacity for aggressive sparring among themselves that sets off their impulse to locate a corresponding capacity in him. Similar interests inform Viola's actions. Her longing for an expression of anger from her husband registers her adherence to the conventional codes that define manhood and patriarchal authority within and beyond marriage. Further, Viola, in accordance with patriarchal convention, defines her own position as wife in relation to the self-definition provided by her husband. His submissive and yielding nature gives rise to domineering and imperious qualities in her. Candido's design, however, entails a redefinition of the codes of virility and of spousal relations. Bellafront too engages in a struggle to redefine the terms by which honesty is conventionally understood.

The contrasting actions of the play's title—the often farcical story of a linen-draper who weathers an escalating series of assaults calculated to move his immovable patience and the moral study of a whore's conversion to honesty—are framed by a melodramatic-romantic plot involving a villainous duke and thwarted lovers. No source has been identified for any of these actions or characters; but some isolated elements appear to derive from *The Bachelor's Banquet* (1603), an anonymous translation of a French work, *Les Quinze joies de mariage*, that in setting out women's wiles to achieve dominance in marriage self-congratulatingly promotes bachelorhood. In its exuberant accounts of wives' extra-marital sexual adventures the work's distinctly lubricious quality pitched at voyeurism is shared by erotic elements of especially the play's initial brothel scene (Sc. 6). The title of Chapter 6, 'The humour of a woman that strives to master her husband', provides a telling perspective on Viola's unacknowledged intentions. Pioratto's account of Candido's entertainment of 'certain Neapolitan lords' (4.30–47) corresponds to strategies employed by a wife who deliberately impedes attempted preparations to feast the husband's friends. And the situation of Viola's refusal to surrender the key to a chest in which Candido's gown is locked, and subsequent exchanges between Candido and George (7.196–221), may also have been prompted by material in this chapter of *The Bachelor's Banquet*.

Structural, figurative, and thematic parallels and other devices link the various plots and confer coherence on the play's diverse elements. Imagery, styles of language, idioms, and terms associated with one action or setting emerge in another and invite a transfer of values and attitudes. Preparatory to the main brothel scene, for example, imagery drawn from prostitution invades the linen-draper's shop as the three gallants haggle over a virgin piece of lawn in terms borrowed from procuring (5.20–45). The reverse also occurs: the courtesan Bellafront contemptuously disparages a client through reference to apparel (6.129–31), and Fluello likens her skin to satin and lawn (6.210–11). After Bellafront has renounced whoredom, Hippolito's servant keeps the trade comically in view through a range of bawdy references and by playfully impersonating a brothel door-keeper prior to her entrance disguised as a page in Scene 10. Two related threads of imagery—involving the whore's body treated as vendible merchandise or as a beast of burden for hire—run through the play. The implied moral condemnation is extended by repeated associations of whoredom with disease and the brothel and whores with damnation and hell.

A further skein of imagery centres on the relationship between body and soul. The debate between Bellafront and Hippolito is founded on this question. In his encounter with the bravoes, Crambo and Poh, Candido wishes all souls were as 'innocent white' as his cloth. And in a similar vein Fustigo's plays on 'cousin' and 'cozen' at 2.133–46 and 7.168–85 are answered in the Bellafront plot with Roger's remark to Madonna Fingerlock at 8.52.

Bellafront's conversion from whoredom to citizen values and attitudes is the first and most dramatically charged of several metamorphoses. Candido's example of patience in the face of knockabout farcical incitements and more serious assaults on his equanimity brings about a corresponding change in Viola; and in a parallel transformation, the ruthless, revenge-play Duke undergoes in the final scene an alteration of character that renders him gentle and benevolent. (Both changes are significantly connected with Bethlehem/Bedlam.) Infelice and Hippolito at different points are supposed dead and 'return' to life. At the end of Scene 10 Bellafront speaks of being 'new born' and therein articulates the thematic correlative of rebirth that accompanies her own, Hippolito's, and, at least by implication, Infelice's transformations. Changes of smaller magnitude but of a similar order occur in other characters.

The play sets individual integrity, bonds of family and friendship, generosity of spirit, and trust fostered in such

Thomas Coryat with Margarita Emiliana, a Venetian courtesan, from Coryat's *Crudities* (1611).

relations, against forms of self-interest. Pursuit of personal advantage above concern for others—rampant in the dealings of characters in each plot—is ultimately represented as a species of madness. In addition, patience bolstered by reason, tolerance, and faith in the reforming and regenerative power of love wins the day against uncontrolled, generally self-serving, passion. As Alexander Leggatt has pointed out, the play concerns itself 'with social structures and institutions: marriage, the family, the shop, the hospital'. Candido stands as a figure central to each. His constancy serves as a reference point marking the tides of change witnessed elsewhere; and, although at times he is made to appear foolish, his selfless patience and reason finally overcome challenges that spring from interests and factions that cut across society. Patience underpins his devotion and duty to his wife, his apprentices, and his shop, and rides out successive provocations dreamed up by Viola and others. His 'conversion' to a prentice in Scene 12 in a modest way parallels Bellafront's conversion from whoredom; both characters are mistreated and suffer abuse of various kinds in the same section of the play.

Bellafront's progress through her action partakes of most of the essential features associated with the myth of the penitent harlot observed in stories of Mary Magdalen and other figures cast in a similar mould such as Thaïs, Pelagia, and Mary of Egypt. That Middleton's wife's name may have been Mary Magdalen points to a range of possible connections in this regard. The version of the saint's life current in the Middle Ages and Renaissance conflated several distinct women who figure in the Gospel accounts of Christ's ministry—the unnamed sinner of Luke 7:39–50; Mary of Bethany, Lazarus's sister; and the Mary Magdalen present at the Resurrection—augmented and elaborated from legend. Apart from her appearance in medieval Corpus Christi cycles, two dramatizations of events from the life of Mary Magdalen survive: the Digby saint's play, *Mary Magdalen* (*c.*1480–1520), and Lewis Wager's interlude, *The Life and Repentance of Mary Magdalen* (*c.*1550–66). In addition, two lost fifteenth-century plays bearing the saint's name are known and may be supplemented by a lost *Mary Magdalen Mask*. In the Digby play as in *The Patient Man and the Honest Whore* the central female character encounters the individual who will change her life as she awaits the arrival of more clients.

Like her hallowed predecessors, Bellafront is a beautiful and much sought-after prostitute. The dramatic suddenness of her transformation from a sinful life accords precisely with the mythic pattern and, as with Mary Magdalen, Thaïs, and Pelagia, is effected by a male of exemplary moral standing. Also like the saintly models, Bellafront after her conversion renounces the temptations and material rewards of whoredom (in a song at the beginning of Scene 9 and subsequently at the asylum in Scene 15). She too undergoes a period of suffering and deprivation which may be linked to penance for her earlier transgressions. Mortification of the flesh is typically associated with the penitent whore's life of denial and is connected with the inevitable withering of the flower of youth; although not physically represented in the play, it is featured in Hippolito's account of a prostitute's wretched prospects and accordingly reflects on Bellafront's perilous state. Similarly, tales of the archetypal figures give special attention to the women's deaths, dwelling on the ravages of time and care on their former beauty and their release from physical torment. Hippolito's citation of the deaths of harlots in Scene 6 and his later meditations on the supposed death of Infelice accompanied by a skull as a *memento mori* in Scene 10 coordinate with reports of the degeneration of the body in the hagiography of the penitent whore, though his remarks do not extend so far as to register deliverance from fleshly affliction common in lives of the saints.

The twelfth-century canonist Gratian disallowed marriage to a whore who persisted in her trade, but permitted such a marriage for the purpose of reformation. Marriage thus offered a means by which a prostitute could escape her plight, and an at least potentially more appealing and realizable alternative to the asceticism of the saints. The notion appears to underlie Tim's '*Uxor non est meretrix*' (a wife is not a whore) in *A Chaste Maid in Cheapside*. Although Erasmus in 'Of the young man and the evil-disposed woman' leaves his reformed prostitute in the care of 'a faithful honest matron', the colloquy was published in an English translation entitled *A Modest Mean to Marriage*. And Robert Greene in 'The Conversion of an English Courtesan', a partial reworking of the Erasmus dialogue and a possible influence on *The Patient Man and the Honest Whore*, marries his wayward and rebellious young woman to the young man who brings about her conversion.

Mary Magdalen's submission to carnality and subsequent repentance undoubtedly augmented her prominence and popularity. In contrast to the remote figure of purity and human perfection represented by the Virgin, the Magdalen through her fall and conversion was perceived as both more accessibly human and a reassuring comfort in offering the promise of grace to sinners. The qualities that made Mary Magdalen appealing very likely contributed potently to the popularity in its own time of the Dekker–Middleton play.

As a prostitute Bellafront pursues capitalist interests that challenge the roles normally available to women and threaten the patriarchal status quo. She has won a measure of economic and personal independence and is 'in bonds to no man' (6.310). But mercenary interests, especially on the part of panders and bawds at least as far back as Roman comedy, are generally treated as reprehensible. Roger and Bellafront's bilking of their clients of the price of a pottle of wine in Scene 6 and the haggling between Roger and Mistress Fingerlock over their respective fees in Scene 8, while entertaining, conform to the Plautine pattern. The reformed harlot makes no further reference to money in the context of competitive materialism. Misogyny, much of it directed at Bellafront, links up with a fear of women and traditional attitudes that associate women's beauty and supposed frailty with the perils and degradation of the flesh, attitudes evoked also by her saintly antecedents. From a condition of intense remorse Bellafront herself articulates the conventional position, 'Women at best are bad; make them not worse' (9.114), poignantly tempered moments later by her citation of male agency: 'You love to make us lewd, but never chaste' (9.123). Self-contempt at this point appears to resonate with the process of her adjustment to a patriarchal world which demands surrender of her independence and self-control and her submission to abuse in recompense for earlier transgressions. Although not acted upon, her intention to return to her father (10.202–4) signals her reintegration into such a world and looks forward to her embrace of the subservient role of Matteo's wife.

The opening of the first brothel scene, Scene 6, has been justly admired by Peter Ure and other critics for its wealth of suggestive realistic detail. Bellafront's skittish exchanges with Roger, her sharply observed racy denunciations, and her plangent wit constitute a freshly realized exercise in verisimilitude. This coarse, sharply etched realism shifts into a more formal, stylized mode in the process of the whore's conversion, however. Blank verse supersedes her sprightly vernacular prose and, except for her feigned 'mad' speech in Scene 15, persists to play's end. In later scenes with Roger and Mistress Fingerlock, and with the gallants, the continued high tone underscores her distance from the world she has forsaken. Bellafront's contrasting modes of speech substantially account for the problem of sustaining the illusion of continuity of character: the stereotypes of 'whore' and 'convert' upon which her two natures are founded produce discontinuous styles.

Hippolito's lecture in Scene 6, which makes of her life a case history, awakens Bellafront to the perils and the inevitable decline that await her, and succeeds in deflecting her attention from her body to her soul. His apparent invulnerability to her charms throws her off guard and thereby prepares the ground for his sermonizing in concert, ironically, with her own romantic attraction to him to have their effect. In answer, her sexual vanity leads her to interpret his cool detachment in kind as she wonders what 'blemish' he has discovered 'Eclipsing all [her] beauties' (6.494). Bellafront's transformation to honesty involves a radical change in character—a change the violence of which partakes of the kind of stylization that attends her alteration in speech. Her sudden romantic interest drives out whatever malignant forces had her in their grip, and renders her particularly susceptible to Hippolito's persuasive rhetoric; her reprise of his arguments in subsequent scenes bespeaks the depth of his influence. The precise point at which she subdues the whore that had taken possession of her effectively coincides with her application of Hippolito's sword in a gesture of suicide—in light of her romantic interest, her erstwhile profession, and her surroundings, a gesture loaded with ironically apt sexual suggestion.

Bellafront threatens a return to whoredom if Hippolito refuses to save her soul; but a hitherto unvoiced course of action springs from his spurning of her and demonstrates that her honesty was not after all in jeopardy—a revelation that in turn interrogates the intent of her threat. Further surprises are in store: in place of her declared intention to leave 'this undoing city' and return to her father, she next appears as a newly admitted inmate at Bethlehem Monastery.

Although it confers honesty on Bellafront, marriage to Matteo also heaps on her a legion of new tribulations, which Dekker explores in *The Honest Whore, Part 2*. While romance convention informs this match (which duplicates the conclusion of the Hippolito/Infelice action), it nevertheless carries deeper implications in its reflection of traditional attitudes: the stigma that tenaciously clings to the reclaimed whore permits a match only with a figure distinctly less appealing than her rescuer—an abiding reminder of the difficulty of successfully negotiating a move from the margins of society closer to its centre.

Once her conversion has taken hold, Bellafront's unshakable resolve and perseverance resonate with the long-suffering Candido's, especially in light of the misogyny and anti-matrimonial sentiment that rumble ominously in several characters' utterances and give some measure of her ordeal. Various critics have interpreted the suffering Bellafront endures as penance for her earlier transgressions and evidence of Dekker's conservative subscription to the prevailing morality. Placement of her transformation early in the action highlights the trials consequent upon it. In the play's closing moments Candido frames a defence of his position in terms reminiscent of Senecan stoicism (particularly as set out in *Of Anger*) in which he likens his patience to Christ's. Bellafront, in her Magdalen-like career, stands with the linen-draper as a model of Christian fortitude. The late association of Candido with Christ fulfils a series of hints among which is the application of the term, 'lamb', to both characters. Bellafront's transformation from 'mutton'—slang for 'whore'—to 'lamb' accordingly grafts spiritual rebirth onto the reductive view of the body.

The Bethlehem of the final scene combines the asylum of Bedlam—the first of many representations on the English stage—with the monastery from which it historically sprang; it accordingly aims to link the shelter and treatment of the insane with spiritual healing. Several of the play's central characters here experience disorientation or a violently altered frame of mind; the madhouse in part emblematizes their subjective experience. Viola's desperate final bid to satisfy her humour involves a substitution of one madness (insanity) for another (rage). Unable to stir Candido to anger, she has him committed to Bedlam presumably in the hope that an externally imposed designation will bring the wished-for madness into being and appease her longing. Bedlam is double-edged, however, and more clearly exhibits the unreason of this, as of other selfish acts. Viola's inordinate craving is matched by the Duke's irrational rejection of Hippolito. The Duke gives personal animosity rein over family and state interests (to the extent of arranging the murder of Hippolito). With Viola the question of the usurpation of male authority in the family and the shop is explored, and probes the interests of the wife as a figure normally bound within the marginal confines, set in contrast to whoredom, of woman's subordination. Substitution takes a variety of forms and operates on several levels in the play: Bellafront finally takes Matteo, her original seducer, as her husband in place of Hippolito; and in different ways dynamic character changes witnessed in Bellafront, the Duke, and Viola involve the substitution of one humour and/or set of attitudes or values for another.

The abundant references to and analogies with madness anticipate and find resolution in this final scene. Caught between his master and his mistress on a social and entrepreneurial level, George's position carries political dimensions that parallel the circumstances of those surrounding the Duke. Like George, who rebels against Viola, Doctor Benedict finally follows his own lights against the will of his would-be master and pursues instead a course sympathetic to Hippolito's interests. The Sweeper's remarks touching all manner of inmates from citizens' sons to

Sir Philip Sidney's hearse carried by fourteen yeomen, the corners of the pall held by four of his friends. From Thomas Lant, *The Funeral Roll of Sir Philip Sidney* (1587).

courtiers, Puritans, whores, and merchants' wives make clear the general reference of Bedlam: 'we have blocks for all heads' (15.146). As with other plays that explore this opposition, notably *The Changeling*, the world of the insane stands in parodic relation to the allegedly sane world, but despite the administration of whips and punishments is more humane and tolerant. The asylum accordingly provides an appropriate setting for the settlement of transgressions of various descriptions initiated in the world at large. Candido's figure, 'the world's upside down' (12.69), carries implications for circumstances beyond his own. But however laudable and successful may be his forbearance in effecting his wife's transformation and in redefining the terms of manhood, the play shrinks in the end from whole-heartedly endorsing it as the Duke remarks in closing, ''Twere sin all women should such husbands have, | For every man must then be his wife's slave.' Although the Duke proposes to use him as an example to 'teach our court to shine', Candido's accommodation into the play world is conditional on a recognition that he is unique.

SEE ALSO

Music: *Companion*, 137
Textual introduction and apparatus: *Companion*, 507
Authorship and date: *Companion*, 351
Other Middleton–Dekker works: *Caesar's Fall*, 328; *Gravesend*, 128; *Meeting*, 183; *Magnificent*, 219; *Banquet*, 637; *Roaring Girl*, 721; *Gypsy*, 1723

THOMAS DEKKER and THOMAS MIDDLETON

The Patient Man and the Honest Whore

[*for Prince Henry's Men at The Fortune*]

THE PERSONS OF THE PLAY

Gasparo Trebazzi, DUKE of Milan
INFELICE, daughter to the Duke
HIPPOLITO, in love with Infelice
MATTEO, Hippolito's friend
BELLAFRONT, the honest whore
CASTRUCCIO, PIORATTO, FLUELLO, SINEZI } gallants
DOCTOR Benedict
CANDIDO, a linen-draper
Viola, Candido's WIFE
GEORGE, journeyman to Candido
FUSTIGO, brother to Candido's Wife
Two PRENTICES to Candido
ROGER, servant to Bellafront
Mistress Fingerlock, a BAWD
CRAMBO, POH } bravoes
SERVANT to Hippolito
SERVANT to Doctor Benedict
PORTER
Father ANSELMO
SWEEPER
Three MADMEN
OFFICERS, Gentlemen

c. 1

Enter at one door a funeral, a coronet lying on the hearse, scutcheons and garlands hanging on the sides, attended by Gasparo Trebazzi, Duke of Milan, Castruccio, Sinezi, Pioratto, Fluello, and others. At another door enter Hippolito in discontented appearance, Matteo, a gentleman, his friend, labouring to hold him back

DUKE [*seeing Hippolito*]
Behold yon comet shows his head again!
Twice hath he thus at cross-turns thrown on us

1.0.2 *scutcheons* shields with armorial bearings
1 **comet** i.e. Hippolito; comets were regarded as ominous
2 **cross-turns** presumably points in the procession's progress where its path is intersected by another and there is a change of direction; Hippolito speaks of meeting it at *next turn* at 1.70.

Prodigious looks; twice hath he troubled
The waters of our eyes. See, he's turned wild.
Go on in God's name.

ALL THE MOURNERS On afore there, ho.

DUKE
Kinsmen and friends, take from your manly sides
Your weapons to keep back the desp'rate boy
From doing violence to the innocent dead.

HIPPOLITO
I prithee, dear Matteo.—

MATTEO Come, you're mad.

HIPPOLITO [*to Duke*]
I do arrest thee, murderer! Set down,
Villains, set down that sorrow, 'tis all mine.

DUKE
I do beseech you all, for my blood's sake,
Send hence your milder spirits, and let wrath
Join in confederacy with your weapons' points.
If he proceed to vex us, let your swords
Seek out his bowels: funeral grief loathes words.

ALL THE MOURNERS
Set on.

HIPPOLITO
Set down the body!

MATTEO O my lord,
You're wrong! I'th'open street? You see she's dead.

HIPPOLITO
I know she is not dead.

DUKE Frantic young man,
Wilt thou believe these gentlemen?—Pray speak.—
Thou dost abuse my child, and mock'st the tears
That here are shed for her. If to behold
Those roses withered that set out her cheeks,
That pair of stars that gave her body light
Darkened and dim for ever, all those rivers
That fed her veins with warm and crimson streams
Frozen and dried up: if these be signs of death,
Then is she dead. Thou unreligious youth,
Art not ashamed to empty all these eyes
Of funeral tears—a debt due to the dead
As mirth is to the living? Sham'st thou not
To have them stare on thee? Hark, thou art cursed
Even to thy face, by those that scarce can speak.

HIPPOLITO
My lord—

DUKE What wouldst thou have? Is she not dead?

HIPPOLITO
O, you ha' killed her by your cruelty.

DUKE
Admit I had, thou kill'st her now again,
And art more savage than a barbarous Moor.

HIPPOLITO
Let me but kiss her pale and bloodless lip.

DUKE O, fie, fie, fie!

HIPPOLITO
Or if not touch her, let me look on her.

MATTEO
As you regard your honour—

HIPPOLITO Honour? Smoke!

MATTEO
Or if you loved her living, spare her now.

DUKE
Ay, well done, sir; you play the gentleman.
[*To other Mourners*] Steal hence. [*To Matteo*] 'Tis nobly done. [*To Mourners*] Away. [*To Matteo*] I'll join
My force to yours to stop this violent torment.—
Pass on.

Exeunt with funeral [*all but Duke, Hippolito, and Matteo*]

HIPPOLITO
Matteo, thou dost wound me more.

MATTEO
I give you physic, noble friend, not wounds.

DUKE
O, well said, well done, a true gentleman!
Alack, I know the sea of lovers' rage
Comes rushing with so strong a tide it beats
And bears down all respects of life, of honour,
Of friends, of foes. Forget her, gallant youth.

HIPPOLITO
Forget her?

DUKE Nay, nay, be but patient,
Forwhy death's hand hath sued a strict divorce
'Twixt her and thee. What's beauty but a corpse?
What but fair sand-dust are earth's purest forms?
Queens' bodies are but trunks to put in worms.

MATTEO [*to Duke*] Speak no more sentences, my good lord, but slip hence. You see they are but fits; I'll rule him, I warrant ye. Ay, so, tread gingerly, your grace is here somewhat too long already. [*Exit Duke*] [*Aside*] 'Sblood, the jest were now, if having ta'en some knocks o'th' pate already, he should get loose again, and like a mad ox toss my new black cloaks into the kennel. I must humour his lordship.—[*To him*] My Lord Hippolito, is it in your stomach to go to dinner?

HIPPOLITO Where is the body?

MATTEO The body, as the Duke spake very wisely, is gone to be wormed.

HIPPOLITO
I cannot rest; I'll meet it at next turn.

3 **Prodigious** ominous, portentous
23 **set out** adorned, set off
24 **stars** i.e. eyes
41 **Honour? Smoke!** in reference to the expression, 'smoke of honour' = vain delusions of honour
47 **physic** medicine
51 **respects** considerations
54 **Forwhy** because
56 **sand-dust** ashes, the mouldered remains of a dead body
58 **sentences** sententious sayings, maxims
62–3 **having ta'en ... already** Matteo refers to his effort of restraining Hippolito.
64 **black cloaks** mourning garments (metonymy for 'mourners')
65 **kennel** gutter
66 **stomach** inclination
69 **wormed** eaten by worms

I'll see how my love looks.

Matteo holds him in's arms

MATTEO How your love looks?—Worse than a scarecrow. Wrestle not with me: the great fellow gives the fall for a ducat.

HIPPOLITO I shall forget myself.

MATTEO Pray, do so; leave yourself behind yourself, and go whither you will. 'Sfoot, do you long to have base rogues, that maintain a Saint Anthony's fire in their noses by nothing but twopenny ale, make ballads of you? If the Duke had but so much mettle in him as is in a cobbler's awl, he would ha' been a vexed thing: he and his train had blown you up but that their powder has taken the wet of cowards. You'll bleed three pottles of alicant, by this light, if you follow 'em; and then we shall have a hole made in a wrong place, to have surgeons roll thee up like a baby in swaddling clouts.

HIPPOLITO What day is today, Matteo?

MATTEO Yea, marry, this is an easy question; why today is—let me see—Thursday.

HIPPOLITO O, Thursday.

MATTEO Here's a coil for a dead commodity.—'Sfoot, women when they are alive are but dead commodities, for you shall have one woman lie upon many men's hands.

HIPPOLITO She died on Monday then.

MATTEO And that's the most villainous day of all the week to die in. An she was well, and ate a mess of water-gruel on Monday morning—

HIPPOLITO Aye, it cannot be
Such a bright taper should burn out so soon.

MATTEO O yes, my lord. So soon? Why I ha' known them that at dinner have been as well, and had so much health that they were glad to pledge it, yet before three o'clock have been found dead—drunk.

HIPPOLITO
On Thursday buried! And on Monday died!
Quick haste, by'r Lady. Sure her winding sheet
Was laid out fore her body; and the worms
That now must feast with her were even bespoke,
And solemnly invited like strange guests.

MATTEO Strange feeders they are indeed, my lord, and like your jester or young courtier, will enter upon any man's trencher without bidding.

HIPPOLITO
Cursed be that day for ever that robbed her
Of breath, and me of bliss! Henceforth let it stand
Within the wizard's book—the calendar—
Marked with a marginal finger, to be chosen
By thieves, by villains, and black murderers,
As the best day for them to labour in.
If henceforth this adulterous bawdy world
Be got with child with treason, sacrilege,
Atheism, rapes, treacherous friendship, perjury,
Slander (the beggar's sin), lies (sin of fools),
Or any other damned impieties,
On Monday let 'em be deliverèd.
I swear to thee, Matteo, by my soul,
Hereafter weekly on that day I'll glue
Mine eyelids down, because they shall not gaze
On any female cheek. And being locked up
In my close chamber, there I'll meditate
On nothing but my Infelice's end,
Or on a dead man's skull draw out mine own.

MATTEO You'll do all these good works now every Monday because it is so bad; but I hope upon Tuesday morning I shall take you with a wench.

HIPPOLITO
If ever, whilst frail blood through my veins run,
On woman's beams I throw affectïon,
Save her that's dead, or that I loosely fly
To th' shore of any other wafting eye,
Let me not prosper, heaven! I will be true
Even to her dust and ashes. Could her tomb
Stand whilst I lived so long that it might rot,
That should fall down, but she be ne'er forgot.

73–4 **great fellow . . . ducat** Matteo either alludes mockingly to himself, warning Hippolito of his prowess at wrestling, or sardonically advises him to wrestle with the Duke (instead of himself), who will overthrow him for a modest fee.

74 **ducat** an Italian silver coin worth about 4*s*. 8*d*. in 1608 (with a possible pun on 'Duke')

78 **Saint Anthony's fire** erysipelas, a local inflammation producing a deep red colour on skin

80 **mettle** spirit (punning on the 'metal' of the *cobbler's awl*)

82 **train** (*a*) retinue; (*b*) line of gunpowder laid as a fuse

but except

82–3 **their . . . cowards** i.e. the duke's dangerous power (*powder* = 'gunpowder') has been dampened by the urine of cowards among his retinue

83 **pottles** liquid measure (= two quarts)

84 **alicant** Spanish wine from Alicante

91 **coil** fuss, commotion

92 **dead commodities** unsaleable merchandise, with a pun on *dead commodity* = dead thing, 1.91

96 **most villainous** perhaps because Monday is the first day of the week; or because Monday is proverbially unlucky, as in 'Monday's child is full of woe'

97 **mess** dish, portion

water-gruel thin gruel made with water instead of milk

99 **Aye** alas

103 **health** with a pun on 'a toast drunk in a person's honour'

105–6 **Thursday . . . haste** A lapse of several weeks between the death of a prominent aristocrat and burial of the embalmed body was not unusual at this time.

106 **by'r Lady** by our Lady (an oath)

111 **enter upon** (*a*) dispossess; (*b*) begin an attack on

112 **trencher** plate and the food it bears (metonymy for 'subsistence')

116 **marginal finger** the pointing hand printed in the margins of books to draw attention to particular passages

120 **with treason** by treason

129 **close** private

130 **Infelice's** Infelice: Italian for 'unhappy' or 'unlucky'

131 **draw out** (*a*) delineate, trace out; (*b*) prolong, extend

134 **take** catch, come upon

135 **frail** liable to sin

136 **beams** glances

137 **that** if

138 **wafting** guiding; signalling

MATTEO If you have this strange monster, honesty, in your belly, why so jig-makers and chroniclers shall pick something out of you; but an I smell not you and a bawdy house out within these ten days, let my nose be as big as an English bag-pudding. I'll follow your lordship, though it be to the place aforenamed. *Exeunt*

Sc. 2

Enter Fustigo in some fantastic sea-suit at one door; a Porter meets him at another

FUSTIGO How now, porter, will she come?

PORTER If I may trust a woman, sir, she will come.

FUSTIGO [*giving money*] There's for thy pains. God-a-mercy, if ever I stand in need of a wench that will come with a wet finger, porter, thou shalt earn my money before any *clarissimo* in Milan. Yet, so God sa' me, she's mine own sister, body and soul, as I am a Christian gentleman. Farewell, I'll ponder till she come. Thou hast been no bawd in fetching this woman, I assure thee.

PORTER No matter if I had, sir; better men than porters are bawds.

FUSTIGO O God, sir, many that have borne offices. But porter, art sure thou went'st into a true house?

PORTER I think so, for I met with no thieves.

FUSTIGO Nay, but art sure it was my sister Viola?

PORTER I am sure by all superscriptions it was the party you ciphered.

FUSTIGO Not very tall?

PORTER Nor very low—a middling woman.

FUSTIGO 'Twas she, faith, 'twas she; a pretty plump cheek like mine?

PORTER At a blush, a little very much like you.

FUSTIGO Gods-so, I would not for a ducat she had kicked up her heels, for I ha' spent an abomination this voyage—marry, I did it amongst sailors and gentlemen.—[*Giving money*] There's a little modicum more, porter, for making thee stay; farewell, honest porter.

PORTER I am in your debt, sir; God preserve you.

FUSTIGO Not so, neither, good porter. *Exit* [*Porter*]

Enter Viola, Candido's Wife

God's lid, yonder she comes.—[*To her*] Sister Viola, I am glad to see you stirring. It's news to have me here, is't not, sister?

WIFE Yes, trust me. I wondered who should be so bold to send for me. You are welcome to Milan, brother.

FUSTIGO Troth, sister, I heard you were married to a very rich chuff, and I was very sorry for it that I had no better clothes, and that made me send; for you know we Milaners love to strut upon Spanish leather. And how does all our friends?

WIFE Very well. You ha' travelled enough now, I trow, to sow your wild oats.

FUSTIGO A pox on 'em!—Wild oats? I ha' not an oat to throw at a horse. Troth, sister, I ha' sowed my oats, and reaped two hundred ducats if I had 'em here. Marry, I must entreat you to lend me some thirty or forty till the ship come. By this hand, I'll discharge at my day, by this hand.

WIFE These are your old oaths.

FUSTIGO Why, sister, do you think I'll forswear my hand?

WIFE Well, well, you shall have them. Put yourself into better fashion, because I must employ you in a serious matter.

FUSTIGO I'll sweat like a horse if I like the matter.

WIFE You ha' cast off all your old swaggering humours?

FUSTIGO I had not sailed a league in that great fish-pond, the sea, but I cast up my very gall.

WIFE I am the more sorry, for I must employ a true swaggerer.

FUSTIGO Nay, by this iron, sister, they shall find I am powder and touch-box if they put fire once into me.

WIFE Then lend me your ears.

FUSTIGO Mine ears are yours, dear sister.

WIFE I am married to a man that has wealth enough, and wit enough.

FUSTIGO A linen-draper, I was told, sister.

143 **honesty** chastity
144 **jig-makers** ballad-writers
147 **bag-pudding** a haggis-like pudding made from an animal's stomach stuffed and boiled
2.0.1 *Fustigo* from the Italian *fustigóne*, a fumbler, a groper; a close-prying fellow; a clumsy fellow
2 **come** with a pun on the bawdy sense, 'reach orgasm'
3 **God-a-mercy** God have mercy (i.e. God reward you), an expression of thanks
4–5 **with a wet finger** easily, with little effort; without hesitation, readily. Underlying sexual innuendo suggests digital stimulation; or perhaps *finger* is a euphemism for 'penis'. The phrase may derive from a licked finger used to facilitate page-turning; here it may denote a finger moistened as a 'come-on'.
6 ***clarissimo*** Italian grandee
sa' save
13 **a true house** He seems to mean, 'the right house'; but the Porter understands *true* in the sense 'honest'.
22 **blush** glance (punning on a *blush* of the *cheek*)
23 **Gods-so** a corruption either of the oath, 'by God's soul', or of *cazzo*, Italian slang for 'penis'
23–4 **kicked up her heels** died (proverbial: Tilley H392)
24 **abomination** disgusting amount
30 **God's lid** 'by God's (eye-)lid' (a common oath)
36 **chuff** (*a*) miser; (*b*) with a possible reference to 'chough', a small, chattering member of the crow family
38 **Spanish leather** highly valued and commonly associated with effeminate opulence
46 **discharge** repay (punning on the sense, 'unload', in reference to *ship*)
53 **matter** with a sexual pun
59 **iron** sword
60 **touch-box** box for carrying touch (priming powder) used in fire-arms
61 **lend... ears** proverbial (Tilley E18)

WIFE Very true, a grave citizen; I want nothing that a wife can wish from a husband. But here's the spite: he has not all things belonging to a man.

FUSTIGO God's my life, he's a very mandrake, or else, God bless us, one o' these whiblins—and that's worse—and then all the children that he gets lawfully of your body, sister, are bastards by a statute.

WIFE O, you run over me too fast, brother. I have heard it often said that he who cannot be angry is no man. I am sure my husband is a man in print for all things else save only in this: no tempest can move him.

FUSTIGO 'Slid, would he had been at sea with us, he should ha' been moved and moved again, for I'll be sworn, la, our drunken ship reeled like a Dutchman.

WIFE No loss of goods can increase in him a wrinkle, no crabbed language make his countenance sour, the stubbornness of no servant shake him; he has no more gall in him than a dove, no more sting than an ant. Musician will he never be—yet I find much music in him—but he loves no frets; and is so free from anger that many times I am ready to bite off my tongue because it wants that virtue which all women's tongues have—to anger their husbands. Brother, mine can by no thunder turn him into a sharpness.

FUSTIGO Belike his blood, sister, is well brewed then.

WIFE I protest to thee, Fustigo, I love him most affectionately, but—I know not; I ha' such a tickling within me, such a strange longing; nay, verily I do long.

FUSTIGO Then you're with child, sister, by all signs and tokens; nay, I am partly a physician, and partly something else. I ha' read Albertus Magnus, and Aristotle's *Emblems*.

WIFE You're wide o'th' bow-hand still, brother; my longings are not wanton, but wayward. I long to have my patient husband eat up a whole porcupine, to the intent the bristling quills may stick about his lips like a Flemish mustachio, and be shot at me; I shall be leaner than the new moon, unless I can make him horn-mad.

FUSTIGO 'Sfoot, half a quarter of an hour does that: make him a cuckold.

WIFE Puh, he would count such a cut no unkindness.

FUSTIGO The honester citizen he. Then make him drunk and cut off his beard.

WIFE Fie, fie; idle, idle! He's no Frenchman to fret at the loss of a little scald hair. No, brother, thus it shall be—you must be secret.

FUSTIGO As your midwife, I protest, sister, or a barber-surgeon.

WIFE Repair to the Tortoise here in St Christopher's Street; I will send you money; turn yourself into a brave man: instead of the arms of your mistress, let your sword and your military scarf hang about your neck.

FUSTIGO I must have a great horseman's French feather too, sister.

WIFE O, by any means, to show your light head, else your hat will sit like a coxcomb. To be brief, you must be in all points a most terrible, wide-mouthed swaggerer.

FUSTIGO Nay, for swaggering points let me alone.

WIFE Resort then to our shop, and in my husband's presence kiss me, snatch rings, jewels, or anything—so you give it back again, brother, in secret.

66 **want** lack
68 **things** with an inevitable but presumably unintended sexual pun
69 **God's my life** God save my life
mandrake Although famed as an aphrodisiac and associated with sexual potency, the dominant sense here is apparently a 'bugger' or 'sodomite', i.e. a homosexual (Daalder and Moore).
70 **whiblins** cheaters or double-dealers: i.e. bigamists (Daalder and Moore)
71 **gets** begets
72 **bastards by a statute** in reference to the Bigamy Act of 1603, which protected the interests of children by a previous marriage. If Candido were discovered to have had children by an earlier, unknown marriage, Viola's children, hitherto thought to have been begotten lawfully, would be disinherited. This consequence explains why Fustigo considers a *whiblin* worse than a *mandrake* (Daalder and Moore).
73 **run over** read, interpret
74 **he ... no man** proverbial (Tilley M172)
75 **man in print** exemplary man (as might be depicted in a book; proverbial: Tilley M239)
76 **save** except
78 **la** exclamation, used here to introduce or call attention to an emphatic statement
79 **Dutchman** commonly associated with drunkenness
82–3 **no more gall ... than a dove** proverbial (Tilley D574)
85 **frets** a common pun on (*a*) the metal bars on the necks of guitars and similar instruments; and (*b*) vexations
90 **brewed** diluted
92 **tickling** craving
95–6 **something else** Fustigo evades the anticipated 'fool' familiar from the proverbial 'Every man is either a fool or a physician to himself' (Tilley M125).
96–7 **Albertus Magnus ... Aristotle's *Emblems*** authorities commonly cited by pretenders to knowledge. Fustigo presumably refers to the work on the secrets of women, *Secreta Mulierum*, by Albertus Magnus; *Emblems* is his ignorant error for *Problems*, a work ascribed to Aristotle and published in an English translation in 1595.
98 **wide o'th' bow-hand** far from the mark (literally, on the left or bow-hand side; proverbial: Tilley B567)
102–3 **leaner than the new moon** presumably because her longing so obsesses her that she has no appetite
103 **horn-mad** mad with rage (with a play on the horns of the new moon); the term's occasional association with cuckoldry prompts Fustigo's response
106 **cut** with a sexual pun on 'cunt'
110 **scald** 'scabby' or 'scurvy', contemptuous and suggesting a symptom of venereal disease (associated with the French)
112–13 **midwife ... barber-surgeon** in allusion to the popular perception of midwives and barbers as purveyors of news and gossip
114 **Repair** go
St Christopher's Street Although Milan is the nominal setting, this name may derive from Christopher Street, London, running between Finsbury Square and Clifton Street.
115 **brave** finely arrayed
118–20 **feather ... head** Fustigo wants a feather as a token of bravado; but Viola regards a feather as a mark of a fool.
121 **coxcomb** fool's cap
122 **swaggerer** quarreller
123 **let me alone** leave it to me

FUSTIGO By this hand, sister.

WIFE Swear as if you came but new from knighting.

FUSTIGO Nay, I'll swear after four hundred a year.

WIFE Swagger worse than a lieutenant among freshwater soldiers, call me your love, your ingle, your cousin, or so, but 'sister' at no hand.

FUSTIGO No, no, it shall be 'cousin', or rather 'coz'—that's the gulling word between the citizens' wives and their madcaps that man 'em to the Garden; to call you one o'my naunts, sister, were as good as call you arrant whore. No, no, let me alone to cousin you rarely.

WIFE He's heard I have a brother, but never saw him; therefore put on a good face.

FUSTIGO The best in Milan, I warrant.

WIFE Take up wares, but pay nothing; rifle my bosom, my pocket, my purse, the boxes, for money to dice withal; but, brother, you must give all back again in secret.

FUSTIGO By this welkin that here roars I will, or else let me never know what a secret is. Why, sister, do you think I'll cony-catch you, when you are my cousin? God's my life, then I were a stark ass. If I fret not his guts, beg me for a fool.

WIFE Be circumspect, and do so then. Farewell.

FUSTIGO The Tortoise, sister, I'll stay there. Forty ducats!

WIFE
Thither I'll send. *Exit [Fustigo]*
—This law can none deny,
Women must have their longings, or they die. *Exit*

Sc. 3

Enter Gasparo the Duke, Doctor Benedict, two Servants

DUKE [*to Servants*]
Give charge that none do enter; lock the doors;
And fellows, what your eyes and ears receive,
Upon your lives trust not the gadding air
To carry the least part of it. [*To Doctor*] The glass,
The hour-glass.

DOCTOR
Here my lord.

DUKE
Ah, 'tis near spent.
But Doctor Benedict, does your art speak truth?
Art sure the soporiferous stream will ebb,
And leave the crystal banks of her white body
Pure as they were at first, just at the hour?

DOCTOR
Just at the hour, my lord.

DUKE
Uncurtain her.

[*The Servants draw back curtains, revealing Infelice, as dead*]

Softly! See, doctor, what a coldish heat
Spreads over all her body.

DOCTOR
Now it works.
The vital spirits that by a sleepy charm
Were bound up fast and threw an icy crust
On her exterior parts now 'gin to break.
Trouble her not, my lord.

DUKE [*to Servants*] Some stools!—[*To Doctor*] You called
For music, did you not? [*Music sounds*] O ho, it speaks,
It speaks! Watch, sirs, her waking; note those sands.—
Doctor, sit down. A dukedom that should weigh
Mine own down twice, being put into one scale,
And that fond desperate boy, Hippolito,
Making the weight up, should not at my hands
Buy her i'th' t'other, were her state more light
Than hers who makes a dowry up with alms.
Doctor, I'll starve her on the Apennine
Ere he shall marry her. I must confess
Hippolito is nobly born; a man—
Did not mine enemy's blood boil in his veins—
Whom I would court to be my son-in-law.
But princes whose high spleens for empery swell
Are not with easy art made parallel.

SECOND SERVANT
She wakes, my lord.

DUKE
Look, Doctor Benedict.—
I charge you on your lives, maintain for truth
Whate'er the doctor or myself aver;

128 **new from knighting** alluding to James I's profuse creation of knights
129 **after four hundred a year** i.e. in the manner of one of such an income
130 **freshwater** untrained; unskilled
131 **ingle** minion, bosom friend
132 **at no hand** on no account
133–6 **cousin ... naunts** terms commonly used for convenience in illicit romantic or sexual dealings; *my naunts* = mine aunts ('aunt' regularly carried the sense 'bawd' or 'whore')
135 **man** escort
the Garden the Bear Garden or Paris Garden, on the Bankside in Southwark
137 **cousin** a pun on 'cozen' = cheat
141 **rifle** plunder, rob
144 **welkin** sky, in allusion to the vault of the heavens above the stage
welkin ... roars Although the reference suggests the possibility of an accompanying sound effect of thunder, the oath is more likely an instance of Fustigo's swaggering, and the roaring its echo or that of his laughter from the heavens over the stage.
146 **cony-catch** cheat
147 **fret not his guts** do not vex him deeply (recalls 2.85, adding *guts* as in musical strings)
147–8 **beg me for a fool** take me for a fool (proverbial: Tilley F496); originally in reference to the practice of petitioning the Court of Wards for custody of wealthy idiots whose inheritance fell to the disposition of their guardians
152 **Women ... longings** proverbial (Tilley W723)
3.7 **soporiferous** sleep-inducing
8 **crystal** conventionally associated with purity
10 **Uncurtain her** The Duke calls for the drawing of a curtain which has concealed the still-sleeping Infelice from view in a discovery space.
19–24 **A dukedom ... alms** The Duke proclaims his high valuation of his daughter and low appraisal of Hippolito: even if Hippolito's worth were added to twice the value of his dukedom in one scale, the total would in his estimate be insufficient to purchase Infelice endowed with an estate poorer than a pauper's in the other.
21 **fond** foolish, mad
24 **hers ... alms** i.e. a beggar's
25 **Apennine** the chain of mountains running down the centre of Italy
30 **high spleens** resolute spirits or minds
empery absolute dominion
31 **made parallel** equalled, made to conform

For you shall bear her hence to Bergamo.
INFELICE [*awakening*]
O God, what fearful dreams?
DOCTOR Lady.
INFELICE Ha!
DUKE Girl.
Why, Infelice, how is't now, ha? Speak.
INFELICE
I'm well—What makes this doctor here?—I'm well.
DUKE
Thou wert not so even now; sickness' pale hand
Laid hold on thee even in the midst of feasting;
And when a cup crowned with thy lover's health
Had touched thy lips, a sensible cold dew
Stood on thy cheeks, as if that death had wept
To see such beauty alter.
INFELICE I remember
I sat at banquet, but felt no such change.
DUKE
Thou hast forgot, then, how a messenger
Came wildly in with this unsavoury news:
That he was dead?
INFELICE What messenger? Who's dead?
DUKE
Hippolito. Alack, wring not thy hands.
INFELICE
I saw no messenger, heard no such news.
DOCTOR
Trust me, you did, sweet lady.
DUKE La, you now!
BOTH SERVANTS
Yes, indeed, madam.
DUKE La, you now!
[*Aside to Servants*] 'Tis well, good knaves!
INFELICE
You ha' slain him, and now you'll murder me.
DUKE
Good Infelice, vex not thus thyself;
Of this the bad report before did strike
So coldly to thy heart that the swift currents
Of life were all frozen up—
INFELICE It is untrue;
'Tis most untrue, O most unnatural father!
DUKE
And we had much to do by art's best cunning
To fetch life back again.
DOCTOR Most certain, lady.
DUKE [*to Infelice*]
Why, la, you now, you'll not believe me?—Friends,
Sweat we not all? Had we not much to do?
SECOND SERVANT Yes, indeed, my lord, much.
DUKE
Death drew such fearful pictures in thy face
That were Hippolito alive again,
I'd kneel and woo the noble gentleman
To be thy husband. Now I sore repent
My sharpness to him and his family.
Nay, do not weep for him; we all must die.—
Doctor, this place where she so oft hath seen
His lively presence hurts her, does it not?
DOCTOR
Doubtless, my lord, it does.
DUKE It does, it does.
Therefore, sweet girl, thou shalt to Bergamo.
INFELICE
Even where you will; in any place there's woe.
DUKE
A coach is ready. Bergamo doth stand
In a most wholesome air; sweet walks, there's deer—
Ay, thou shalt hunt and send us venison,
Which, like some goddess in the Cyprian groves,
Thine own fair hand shall strike.—Sirs, you shall teach her
To stand, and how to shoot; ay, she shall hunt.—
Cast off this sorrow. In, girl, and prepare
This night to ride away to Bergamo.
INFELICE
O most unhappy maid. *Exit*
DUKE [*to Servants*] Follow her close.
No words that she was buried, on your lives,
Or that her ghost walks now after she's dead.
I'll hang you if you name a funeral.
FIRST SERVANT
I'll speak Greek, my lord, ere I speak that deadly word.
SECOND SERVANT
And I'll speak Welsh, which is harder than Greek.
DUKE
Away, look to her. *Exeunt [Servants]*
Doctor Benedict,
Did you observe how her complexion altered
Upon his name and death? O, would 'twere true.
DOCTOR
It may, my lord.
DUKE May? How? I wish his death.
DOCTOR
And you may have your wish; say but the word,
And 'tis a strong spell to rip up his grave.
I have good knowledge with Hippolito;
He calls me friend. I'll creep into his bosom
And sting him there to death; poison can do't.

35 **Bergamo** the capital of the province of this name in northern Italy, 30 miles north-east of Milan
38 **makes** does
42 **sensible** perceptible
62 **Sweat we not all** did we not all suffer severely
69 **we all must die** proverbial (Tilley M505)
77–8 **hunt . . . groves** a curious collocation of Venus, who is associated with Cyprus, and Diana, goddess of the hunt
87 **Greek** i.e. unintelligibly (proverbial: Tilley G439)
94 **rip up** dig
95 **good knowledge** considerable intimacy
96 **creep into his bosom** work my way into his confidence (proverbial: Tilley B546)

DUKE
Perform it; I'll create thee half mine heir.

DOCTOR
It shall be done, although the fact be foul.

DUKE
Greatness hides sin. The guilt upon my soul! *Exeunt*

Sc. 4

Enter Castruccio, Pioratto, and Fluello

CASTRUCCIO Signor Pioratto, Signor Fluello, shall's be merry? Shall's play the wags now?

FLUELLO Ay, anything that may beget the child of laughter.

CASTRUCCIO Truth, I have a pretty sportive conceit new crept into my brain will move excellent mirth.

PIORATTO Let's ha't, let's ha't; and where shall the scene of mirth lie?

CASTRUCCIO At Signor Candido's house, the patient man, nay, the monstrous patient man. They say his blood is immovable, that he has taken all patience from a man, and all constancy from a woman.

FLUELLO That makes so many whores nowadays.

CASTRUCCIO Ay, and so many knaves too.

PIORATTO Well, sir?

CASTRUCCIO To conclude, the report goes he's so mild, so affable, so suffering, that nothing indeed can move him. Now do but think what sport it will be to make this fellow, the mirror of patience, as angry, as vexed, and as mad as an English cuckold.

FLUELLO O, 'twere admirable mirth, that; but how will't be done, signor?

CASTRUCCIO Let me alone, I have a trick, a conceit, a thing, a device, will sting him, i'faith, if he have but a thimbleful of blood in's belly, or a spleen not so big as a tavern token.

PIORATTO Thou stir him? Thou move him? Thou anger him? Alas, I know his approved temper. Thou vex him? Why, he has a patience above man's injuries; thou mayst sooner raise a spleen in an angel than rough humour in him. Why, I'll give you instance for it. This wonderfully tempered Signor Candido upon a time invited home to his house certain Neapolitan lords of curious taste and no mean palates, conjuring his wife, of all loves, to prepare cheer fitting for such honourable trencher-men. She—just of a woman's nature, covetous to try the uttermost of vexation, and thinking at last to get the start of his humour—willingly neglected the preparation, and became unfurnished, not only of dainty, but of ordinary dishes. He, according to the mildness of his breast, entertained the lords, and with courtly discourse beguiled the time, as much as a citizen might do. To conclude, they were hungry lords, for there came no meat in; their stomachs were plainly gulled, and their teeth deluded, and, if anger could have seized a man, there was matter enough i'faith to vex any citizen in the world! If he were not too much made a fool by his wife!

FLUELLO Ay, I'll swear for't. 'Sfoot, had it been my case, I should ha' played mad tricks with my wife and family. First I would ha' spitted the men, stewed the maids, and baked the mistress, and so served them in.

PIORATTO
Why 'twould ha' tempted any blood but his.—
And thou to vex him? Thou to anger him
With some poor shallow jest?

CASTRUCCIO 'Sblood, Signor Pioratto—you that disparage my conceit—I'll wage a hundred ducats upon the head on't, that it moves him, frets him, and galls him.

PIORATTO Done, 'tis a lay: join golls on't [*shaking hands with Castruccio*] .—Witness, Signor Fluello.

[*Fluello shakes hands with them*]

CASTRUCCIO Witness; 'tis done:
Come, follow me; the house is not far off.
I'll thrust him from his humour, vex his breast,
And win a hundred ducats by one jest. *Exeunt*

Sc. 5

Enter [Viola,] Candido's Wife; [she discovers] George, and two Prentices in the shop

WIFE Come, you put up your wares in good order here, do you not, think you? One piece cast this way, another that way! You had need have a patient master indeed.

GEORGE [*aside*] Ay, I'll be sworn, for we have a curst mistress.

WIFE You mumble? Do you mumble? I would your master or I could be a note more angry: for two patient folks

99 **fact** deed, crime

4.0.1 ***Castruccio*** The term in Tuscan dialect means 'pig-sty'; but the name may be associated with the Italian, *struccio*, ostrich—possibly intended to emblematize the character's ostentatious dress (an additional play on 'castrated' is possible).

1 **shall's** i.e. shall us = shall we

9 **blood** disposition, temper

12 **That** i.e. the loss of constancy

18 **mirror** paragon

22 **conceit** idea

24 **spleen** regarded as the seat of anger

25 **tavern token** small copper or brass piece circulated within a tavern or eating house as small change

27 **approved** tried, tested

33 **curious** delicate, fastidious

34 **of all loves** for love's sake

35 **trencher-men** feeders, eaters; *trencher* may mean 'knife' or 'plate'

37 **get the start of** gain superiority over
humour disposition, temperament
willingly wilfully

43 **meat** food

50 **spitted** thrust through with a spit; stabbed
stewed with a sexual pun derived from stews = brothel

51 **baked** possibly carrying the innuendo, 'made pregnant'
served them in dished them up (possibly with the sexual innuendo, 'sexually penetrated them')

56 **upon the head** rashly, precipitately

58 **lay** bet
golls hands (a cant term)

59 **Witness** bear witness

5.0.1–2 ***Enter... shop*** Candido's Wife presumably enters from a stage door and proceeds to initiate the 'opening up' of the shop in the discovery space; merchandise associated with the draper's trade would likely be set in view.

4 **curst** perversely disagreeable or cross, shrewish

7 **note** sign, token

in a house spoil all the servants that ever shall come under them.

FIRST PRENTICE [*aside*] You patient! Ay, so is the devil when he is horn-mad.

Enter Castruccio, Fluello, and Pioratto

ALL THREE IN THE SHOP Gentlemen, what do you lack? What is't you buy? See fine hollands, fine cambrics, fine lawns.

GEORGE What is't you lack?

SECOND PRENTICE What is't you buy?

CASTRUCCIO Where's Signor Candido, thy master?

GEORGE Faith, signor, he's a little negotiated; he'll appear presently.

CASTRUCCIO Fellow, let's see a lawn, a choice one, sirrah.

GEORGE The best in all Milan, gentlemen, and this is the piece. I can fit you gentlemen with fine calicoes, too, for doublets, the only sweet fashion now, most delicate and courtly, a meek, gentle calico, cut upon two double affable taffetas—ah, most neat, feat, and unmatchable.

FLUELLO A notable voluble-tongued villain.

PIORATTO I warrant this fellow was never begot without much prating. [*George presents the cloth*]

CASTRUCCIO What, and is this she, sayst thou?

GEORGE Ay, and the purest she that ever you fingered since you were a gentleman. Look how even she is, look how clean she is, ha!—as even as the brow of Cynthia, and as clean as your sons and heirs when they ha' spent all.

CASTRUCCIO Puh, thou talk'st—pox on't, 'tis rough.

GEORGE How? Is she rough? But if you bid pox on't, sir, 'twill take away the roughness presently.

FLUELLO Ha, signor, has he fitted your French curse?

GEORGE Look you, gentleman, here's another. Compare them, I pray, *compara Virgilium cum Homero*: compare virgins with harlots.

CASTRUCCIO Puh, I ha' seen better, and as you term them, evener and cleaner.

GEORGE You may see further for your mind, but trust me, you shall not find better for your body.

Enter Candido

CASTRUCCIO [*aside to Gallants*]
O, here he comes; let's make as though we pass.—
[*Aloud*] Come, come, we'll try in some other shop.

CANDIDO How now? What's the matter?

GEORGE The gentlemen find fault with this lawn, fall out with it, and without a cause, too.

CANDIDO Without a cause!
And that makes you to let 'em pass away!—
Ah, may I crave a word with you, gentlemen?

FLUELLO
He calls us.

CASTRUCCIO
Makes the better for the jest.

CANDIDO
I pray come near; you're very welcome, gallants.
Pray pardon my man's rudeness, for I fear me
He's talked above a prentice with you.—Lawns!
Look you, kind gentlemen; this—no—ay, this—
Take this upon my honest-dealing faith
To be a true weave, not too hard nor slack,
But e'en as far from falsehood as from black.

CASTRUCCIO Well, how do you rate it?

CANDIDO Very conscionably, eighteen shillings a yard.

CASTRUCCIO That's too dear. How many yards does the whole piece contain, think you?

CANDIDO Why, some seventeen yards, I think, or thereabouts. How much would serve your turn, I pray?

CASTRUCCIO Why, let me see—would it were better, too—

CANDIDO Truth, 'tis the best in Milan, at few words.

CASTRUCCIO Well, let me have then—a whole pennyworth.

CANDIDO Ha, ha! You're a merry gentleman.

CASTRUCCIO A penn'orth, I say.

CANDIDO Of lawn?

CASTRUCCIO Of lawn, ay, of lawn, a penn'orth. 'Sblood, dost not hear? A whole penn'orth. Are you deaf?

CANDIDO
Deaf? No, sir; but I must tell you,
Our wares do seldom meet such customers.

CASTRUCCIO Nay, an you and your lawns be so squeamish, fare you well. [*Offering to leave*]

CANDIDO Pray stay; a word, pray, signor. For what purpose is it, I beseech you?

CASTRUCCIO 'Sblood, what's that to you? I'll have a pennyworth.

CANDIDO A pennyworth! Why you shall: I'll serve you presently.

SECOND PRENTICE 'Sfoot, a pennyworth, mistress!

11 **horn-mad** mad with rage (with a quibble on the devil's horns)
13–16 **What... buy?** traditional street cries
18 **negotiated** engaged
21 **best... Milan** Milan was famous for ribbons, hats, lace and other items of haberdashery. The nominal setting in Milan which bears unmistakable features of London may be designed to play off 'the best on sale in town' against 'the finest imports'.
22 **piece** playing on the sense 'woman' or 'girl' (picked up by Castruccio at 5.29)
calicoes cotton cloths imported from the East
23 **doublets** close-fitting body-garments, with or without sleeves, worn by men
25 **affable** presumably, 'supple'
feat neat, trim
32, 33 **clean** pure, clear of obstructions; with a pun on the sense 'stripped of money' in 5.33
32 **Cynthia** Diana, maiden goddess of chastity
36–7 **bid pox... roughness** in reference to an effect of venereal disease (causing hair to fall out)
38 **fitted** applied, inserted (an image from venereal disease)
French Syphilis, or the pox, was known as the French disease.
40 ***compara... Homero*** compare Virgil with Homer (Latin); adapted from William Lily's Latin Grammar, Part 2, sig. E8
44 **for your mind** according to your taste or liking
61 **black** The traditional whiteness of the best lawns (5.57) is contrasted with its opposite.
85 **presently** immediately

WIFE
A pennyworth! Call you these gentlemen?
CASTRUCCIO [*directing Candido*]
No, no, not there.
CANDIDO What then, kind gentleman?
What, at this corner here?
CASTRUCCIO No, nor there neither;
I'll have it just in the middle, or else not.
CANDIDO
Just in the middle!—Ha!—You shall too. What,
Have you a single penny?
CASTRUCCIO Yes, here's one.
CANDIDO
Lend it me, I pray.
FLUELLO An exc'llent-followed jest.
WIFE
What, will he spoil the lawn now?
CANDIDO Patience, good wife.
[*Candido starts to cut the cloth*]
WIFE
Ay, that patience makes a fool of you.—Gentlemen,
You might ha' found some other citizen
To have made a kind gull on besides my husband.
CANDIDO
Pray, gentlemen, take her to be a woman;
Do not regard her language.—[*To Wife*] O kind soul,
Such words will drive away my customers.
WIFE Customers with a murrain! Call you these customers?
CANDIDO Patience, good wife.
WIFE Pox o'your patience.
GEORGE 'Sfoot, mistress, I warrant these are some cheating companions.
CANDIDO
Look you, gentleman, there's your ware. I thank you;
I have your money here. Pray know my shop;
Pray, let me have your custom.
WIFE Custom, quoth 'a!
CANDIDO Let me take more of your money.
WIFE You had need so.
PIORATTO [*aside to Castruccio*]
Hark in thine ear: thou'st lost an hundred ducats.
CASTRUCCIO [*aside to Pioratto*]
Well, well, I know't. Is't possible that *homo*
Should be nor man nor woman? Not once moved?
No, not at such an injury, not at all!
Sure he's a pigeon, for he has no gall.
FLUELLO [*to Candido*]
Come, come, you're angry, though you smother it:
You're vexed, i'faith—confess.
CANDIDO Why, gentlemen,
Should you conceit me to be vexed or moved?
He has my ware, I have his money for't,
And that's no argument I am angry; no,
The best logician cannot prove me so.
FLUELLO
O, but the hateful name of a pennyworth of lawn,
And then cut out i'th'middle of the piece!
Pah, I guess it by myself: 'twould move a lamb—
Were he a linen-draper, 'twould, i'faith.
CANDIDO
Well, give me leave to answer you for that.
We are set here to please all customers,
Their humours and their fancies, offend none;
We get by many, if we leese by one.
Maybe his mind stood to no more than that;
A penn'orth serves him; and 'mongst trades 'tis found,
Deny a penn'orth, it may cross a pound.
O, he that means to thrive with patient eye
Must please the devil if he come to buy.
FLUELLO
O wondrous man, patient 'bove wrong or woe!
How blest were men, if women could be so.
CANDIDO
And to express how well my breast is pleased,
And satisfied in all—George, fill a beaker—
Exit George
I'll drink unto that gentleman who lately
Bestowed his money with me.
WIFE God's my life,
We shall have all our gains drunk out in beakers,
To make amends for pennyworths of lawn.
Enter George [*with a beaker of wine*]
CANDIDO
Here, wife, begin you to the gentleman.
WIFE
I begin to him?
[*She spills the wine*]
CANDIDO George, fill't up again.—
'Twas my fault, my hand shook.
Exit George [*with the beaker*]

93 **Lend it me, I pray** i.e. to cut a piece of cloth the size of a coin
97 **gull** fool, simpleton
101 **murrain** plague
106 **companions** fellows
114–15 ***homo* . . . woman** Although normally masculine, the Latin '*homo*' ('man' or 'human being'), depending on its reference, could also be feminine in gender.
117 **pigeon . . . gall** proverbial (Tilley D574)
120 **conceit** imagine
126 **Pah** exclamation of disgust
126–7 **I guess . . . linen-draper** Fluello registers his admiration of Candido's patience: he reckons that his provocation would have angered a linen-draper as mildly disposed as a lamb.
126 **by myself** i.e. by my example
131 **leese** lose
132 **stood to** was resolutely fixed on (i.e. Candido's loss in this transaction)
134 **cross** thwart, prevent
140 **beaker** large open cup or goblet
145 **begin** i.e. drinking

PIORATTO How strangely this doth show!
A patient man linked with a waspish shrew.
FLUELLO [*aside*]
A silver and gilt beaker; I have a trick
To work upon that beaker; sure 'twill fret him;
It cannot choose but vex him. [*Aside to Castruccio*]
Signor Castruccio,
In pity to thee I have a conceit
Will save thy hundred ducats yet; 'twill do't,
And work him to impatience.
CASTRUCCIO [*aside to Fluello*] Sweet Fluello,
I should be bountiful to that conceit.
FLUELLO [*aside to Castruccio*]
Well, 'tis enough.
Enter George [*with a beaker of wine*]
CANDIDO Here, gentleman, to you,
I wish your custom; you're exceeding welcome.
CASTRUCCIO
I pledge you, Signor Candido;
[*He drinks*]
Here to you, that must receive a hundred ducats.
PIORATTO
I'll pledge them deep, i'faith, Castruccio.
[*He drinks*]
Signor Fluello.
FLUELLO Come, play't off; to me—
I am your last man.
CANDIDO George, supply the cup.
[*George refills the beaker*]
FLUELLO So, so, good honest George.—
[*He drinks*]
Here, Signor Candido, all this to you.
[*He offers the beaker*]
CANDIDO
O, you must pardon me, I use it not.
FLUELLO
Will you not pledge me then?
CANDIDO Yes, but not that:
Great love is shown in little.
FLUELLO Blurt on your sentences!—
'Sfoot, you shall pledge me all.
CANDIDO Indeed, I shall not.
FLUELLO
Not pledge me? 'Sblood, I'll carry away the beaker
then.
CANDIDO
The beaker? O, that at your pleasure, sir!
FLUELLO
Now by this drink, I will.
CASTRUCCIO [*to Candido*] Pledge him, he'll do't else.
FLUELLO [*finishing his wine*]
So, I ha' done you right, on my thumb-nail.
What, will you pledge me now?
CANDIDO You know me, sir;
I am not of that sin.
FLUELLO Why then, farewell;
I'll bear away the beaker, by this light.
CANDIDO That's as you please, 'tis very good.
FLUELLO Nay, it doth please me, and as you say, 'tis a very good one. Farewell, Signor Candido.
PIORATTO Farewell, Candido.
CANDIDO
You're welcome, gentlemen.
CASTRUCCIO Heart! Not moved yet?
I think his patience is above our wit.
Exeunt [*Gallants*]
GEORGE I told you before, mistress, they were all cheaters.
WIFE [*to Candido*] Why, fool, why, husband, why, madman, I hope you will not let 'em sneak away so with a silver and gilt beaker, the best in the house too.—[*To Prentices*] Go, fellows, make hue and cry after them.
CANDIDO Pray let your tongue lie still; all will be well.—
Come hither, George, hie to the constable,
And in calm order wish him to attach them.
Make no great stir, because they're gentlemen,
And a thing partly done in merriment.
'Tis but a size above a jest thou know'st,
Therefore pursue it mildly. Go, begone.
The constable's hard by; bring him along.
Make haste again. *Exit George*
WIFE O, you're a goodly patient woodcock, are you not now? See what your patience comes to: everyone saddles you and rides you—you'll be shortly the common stone-horse of Milan. A woman's well holped up with such a meacock! I had rather have a husband that would swaddle me thrice a day than such a one that will be gulled twice in half an hour. O, I could burn all the wares in my shop for anger.
CANDIDO
Pray wear a peaceful temper, be my wife,
That is, be patient; for a wife and husband

155 **I should . . . conceit** i.e. if your idea proves successful, I'll reward you
161 **play't off** toss it off, finish it
to me Fluello asks for the beaker to be passed to him after Pioratto has finished his drink (in order to follow through with his plan of taking the beaker to vex Candido).
163 **supply** fill
166 **I use it not** i.e. I am unaccustomed to such drinking. Candido has already pledged them (5.156) and refuses to drink more.
168 **Blurt on** 'snort on' or 'a fig for' (an exclamation of contempt)
sentences wise sayings
169 **all** i.e. (by drinking) all the wine
173 **on my thumb-nail** i.e. to the last drop; alluding to the practice of drinking supernaculum, in which the emptied glass was turned up over the left thumb-nail to show that no liquor remained
193 **a size** one measure
196 **again** back
197 **woodcock** fool, 'birdbrain'
200 **stone-horse** stallion (and therefore in general demand)
holped helped
201 **meacock** effeminate person; coward, weakling
202 **swaddle** beat
206–7 **a wife . . . between them** probably derived from Genesis 2:24 or Matthew 19:5–6

Share but one soul between them; this being known,
Why should not one soul then agree in one?

WIFE
Hang your agreements! But if my beaker be gone—
Exit

Enter Castruccio, Fluello, Pioratto, and George

CANDIDO O, here they come.

GEORGE The constable, sir, let 'em come along with me, because there should be no wond'ring; he stays at door.

CASTRUCCIO Constable?—Goodman Abram!

FLUELLO Now Signor Candido, 'sblood, why do you attach us?

CASTRUCCIO 'Sheart! Attach us!

CANDIDO Nay, swear not, gallants,
Your oaths may move your souls, but not move me.
You have a silver beaker of my wife's.

FLUELLO
You say not true: 'tis gilt.

CANDIDO Then you say true.
And being gilt, the guilt lies more on you.

CASTRUCCIO
I hope you're not angry, sir.

CANDIDO Then you hope right,
For I am not angry.

PIORATTO No, but a little moved.

CANDIDO
I moved! 'Twas you were moved, you were brought hither.

CASTRUCCIO
But you, out of your anger and impatience,
Caused us to be attached.

CANDIDO Nay, you misplace it;
Out of my quiet sufferance I did that,
And not of any wrath. Had I shown anger,
I should have then pursued you with the law
And hunted you to shame; as many worldlings
Do build their anger upon feebler grounds—
The more's the pity—many lose their lives
For scarce so much coin as will hide their palm,
Which is most cruel. Those have vexèd spirits
That pursue lives. In this opinion rest:
The loss of millions could not move my breast.

FLUELLO
Thou art a blest man, and with peace dost deal;
Such a meek spirit can bless a commonweal.

CANDIDO
Gentlemen, now 'tis upon eating time,
Pray part not hence, but dine with me today.

CASTRUCCIO
I never heard a courtier yet say nay
To such a motion. I'll not be the first.

PIORATTO Nor I.

FLUELLO Nor I.

CANDIDO
The constable shall bear you company.
George, call him in. Let the world say what it can,
Nothing can drive me from a patient man.
Exeunt [George at one door, the others at another door]

Sc. 6

Enter Roger with a stool, cushion, looking-glass, and chafing-dish; those being set down, he pulls out of his pocket a vial with white colour in it, and two boxes, one with white, another red, painting. He places all things in order and a candle by them, singing with the ends of old ballads as he does it. At last Bellafront, as he rubs his cheek with the colours, whistles within

ROGER Anon, forsooth.

BELLAFRONT [*within*] What are you playing the rogue about?

ROGER About you, forsooth; I'm drawing up a hole in your white silk stocking.

BELLAFRONT [*within*] Is my glass there? And my boxes of complexion?

ROGER Yes, forsooth, your boxes of complexion are here, I think—yes, 'tis here: here's your two complexions—and if I had all the four complexions, I should ne'er set a good face upon't. Some men, I see, are born under hard-favoured planets as well as women. Zounds, I look worse now than I did before, and it makes *her* face glister most damnably. There's knavery in daubing, I hold my life, or else this is only female pomatum.

212 **because** so that
213 **Abram** lunatic, madman; an Abraham-man feigned madness for the purpose of begging.
214 **attach** arrest
234 **spirits** Very likely pronounced 'sprites', as also at 5.238.
239 **now 'tis** i.e. 'now that it is'
247 **from** from being
6.0.2 ***chafing-dish*** used for heating the curling-iron and the poking-stick (*poker*, 6.16)
0.4 ***painting*** cosmetic pigment
10 **four complexions** four temperaments or humours (sanguine, phlegmatic, choleric, melancholy), quibbling also on *complexion* meaning 'face', 'natural skin colour', and 'cosmetic pigment'
10–11 **set a good face upon't** (in reference to his own face, which he has been daubing with red and white cosmetics) improve its appearance (proverbial: Tilley F17); with a play on *face* = complexion
11–12 **born ... planets** proverbial (Tilley P386)
12 **hard-favoured** playing on (*a*) ugly, of disagreeable appearance, and (*b*) ill disposed, unlucky
Zounds corruption of 'by God's wounds' (a strong oath)
14 **glister** sparkle, glitter
15 **pomatum** scented ointment

Enter Bellafront not full ready, without a gown. She sits down; with her bodkin curls her hair; colours her lips

BELLAFRONT Where's my ruff and poker, you block-head?

ROGER Your ruff and your poker are engendering together upon the cupboard of the court, or the court-cupboard.

BELLAFRONT Fetch 'em.—Is the pox in your hams, you can go no faster?

[*She throws an object at him*]

ROGER Would the pox were in your fingers, unless you could leave flinging. Catch!

[*He throws an object at her*]

Exit

BELLAFRONT I'll catch you, you dog, by and by. Do you grumble?

She sings

Cupid is a god,
As naked as my nail;
I'll whip him with a rod,
If he my true love fail.

[*Enter Roger with ruff and poker*]

ROGER There's your ruff. Shall I poke it?

BELLAFRONT Yes, honest Roger—no, stay; prithee, good boy, hold here.

[*Roger holds looking-glass and candle*]
[*She sings*]

Down, down, down, down, I fall
Down, and arise I never shall.

ROGER Troth, mistress, then leave the trade if you shall never rise.

BELLAFRONT What trade, Goodman Abram?

ROGER Why, that of down and arise, or the falling trade.

BELLAFRONT I'll fall with you by and by.

ROGER If you do, I know who shall smart for't: troth, mistress, what do I look like now?

[*He holds up the looking-glass to Bellafront*]

BELLAFRONT Like as you are: a panderly sixpenny rascal.

ROGER I may thank you for that; no, faith, I look like an old proverb, 'Hold the candle before the devil.'

BELLAFRONT Ud's life, I'll stick my knife in your guts an you prate to me so!—Wha-at?

She [*paints her face and*] *sings*

Well met, pug, the pearl of beauty, umh, umh.
How now, sir knave, you forget your duty, umh, umh.
Marry-muff, sir, are you grown so dainty? Fa, la, la, (*etc.*)
Is it you, sir? The worst of twenty; fa la, la, leera la.

Pox on you, how dost thou hold my glass?

ROGER Why, as I hold your door: with my fingers.

BELLAFRONT Nay, pray thee, sweet honey Roger, hold up handsomely.

[*She sings*]

Sing, pretty wantons, warble, (*etc.*)

We shall ha' guests today, I lay my little maidenhead, my nose itches so.

ROGER I said so too last night, when our fleas twinged me.

BELLAFRONT So poke my ruff now.—My gown, my gown; have I my fall? Where's my fall, Roger?

ROGER Your fall, forsooth, is behind.

One knocks

BELLAFRONT God's my pittikins, some fool or other knocks.

ROGER Shall I open to the fool, mistress?

BELLAFRONT And all these baubles lying thus? Away with it quickly. [*They gather up the paints etc.*] Ay, ay, knock and be damned, whosoever you be.—So, give the fresh salmon line now, let him come ashore; he shall serve for my breakfast, though he go against my stomach.

Roger fetches in Fluello, Castruccio, and Pioratto

FLUELLO [*to Bellafront*] Morrow, coz.

CASTRUCCIO [*to Bellafront*] How does my sweet acquaintance?

PIORATTO [*to Bellafront*] Save thee, little marmoset; how dost thou, good pretty rogue?

BELLAFRONT Well, God-a-mercy, good pretty rascal.

15.1 ***gown*** overgarment, often made of costly fabrics; but possibly in reference to a 'night-gown', a less elaborate, warmer outer garment not restricted to night-time wear. Bellafront would presumably be dressed in a kirtle, consisting either of a floor-length dress or of a bodice and skirt, over which a gown was commonly worn.

15.2 ***bodkin*** curling iron

16 **poker** poking-stick (a small steel rod which was heated and used for setting the pleats of a ruff)

18 **court-cupboard** a movable sideboard or cabinet used for the display of plate and storage of fruit, wine, spoons, and linen

24 **grumble** growl faintly

26 **naked as my nail** proverbial (Tilley N4)

29 **ruff...poke it** with a bawdy innuendo

32–3 **Down...shall** The concluding refrain of 'Sorrow, sorrow stay' from John Dowland's *Second Book of Songs or Ayres* (1600); see *Companion*, p. 137.

33 **arise** prosper

36 **Abram** lunatic; see 5.213 and note.

37 **down...falling trade** with sexual innuendoes; *falling trade* can also mean 'failing business' and 'declining path'

38 **fall with** assail with blows; settle with. Bellafront makes a forced pun on Roger's *falling* as she does with *catch*, 6.23.

41 **sixpenny** so named for the sixpences he receives for procuring clients; explained at 8.88–9

43 **Hold...devil** i.e. 'help the devil by holding a candle while he works' (proverbial: Tilley C42): Roger refers to himself holding a candle and mirror (emblematic of vanity) for Bellafront.

45 **Wha-at** expressing Bellafront's prolonged disdain

46 **pug** (*a*) a term of endearment; (*b*) courtesan, harlot

48 **Marry-muff** a derisive exclamation (originally a kind of cheap fabric)

51 **hold your door** conventional function of a pander (i.e. control access to your body)

56–62 **nose itches...fool** 'If your nose itches you will kiss a fool' (proverbial: Tilley N224).

59 **fall** falling band or collar

60 **fall** punning on 'sexual fall'
behind punning on 'in the past'

61 **pittikins** a diminutive of 'pity'

64–5 **knock and be damned** in reference to the brothel as hell (proverbial?)

65–6 **fresh salmon** fool, prey (often with a sexual suggestion)

67 **stomach** (*a*) appetite, taste; (*b*) abdomen (punning on *go* = copulate)

71 **marmoset** monkey (a term of endearment or playful reproach)

FLUELLO Roger, some light, I prithee.

ROGER You shall, signor, for we that live here in this vale of misery are as dark as hell. *Exit for a candle*

CASTRUCCIO Good tobacco, Fluello?

FLUELLO Smell.

Enter Roger [with a candle]

PIORATTO It may be tickling gear, for it plays with my nose already.

ROGER Here's another light angel, signor.

BELLAFRONT What, you pied curtal, what's that you are neighing?

ROGER I say, God send us the light of heaven, or some more angels.

BELLAFRONT Go fetch some wine, and drink half of it.

ROGER I must fetch some wine, gentlemen, and drink half of it?

FLUELLO [*offering money*] Here, Roger.

CASTRUCCIO [*offering money*] No, let me send, prithee.

FLUELLO Hold, you cankerworm.

ROGER You shall send both, if you please, signors.

PIORATTO Stay, what's best to drink o' mornings?

ROGER Hippocras, sir, for my mistress, if I fetch it, is most dear to her.

FLUELLO Hippocras! [*Giving money*] There, then, here's a teston for you, you snake.

ROGER Right, sir; here's three shillings and sixpence for a pottle and a manchet. *Exit*

CASTRUCCIO Here's most Herculean tobacco; ha' some, acquaintance?

BELLAFRONT Faugh, not I.—Makes your breath stink like the piss of a fox. Acquaintance, where supped you last night?

CASTRUCCIO At a place, sweet acquaintance, where your health danced the canaries, i'faith: you should ha' been there.

BELLAFRONT I there among your punks! Marry, faugh, hang 'em; scorn't. Will you never leave sucking of eggs in other folks' hens' nests?

CASTRUCCIO Why, in good troth, if you'll trust me, acquaintance, there was not one hen at the board; ask Fluello.

FLUELLO No, faith, coz, none but cocks. Signor Malavolta drunk to thee.

BELLAFRONT O, a pure beagle; that horse-leech there?

FLUELLO And the knight, Sir Oliver Lollio, swore he would bestow a taffeta petticoat on thee, but to break his fast with thee.

BELLAFRONT With me! I'll choke him then. Hang him, mole-catcher! It's the dreaming'st snotty-nose.

PIORATTO Well, many took that Lollio for a fool; but he's a subtle fool.

BELLAFRONT Ay, and he has fellows; of all filthy, dry-fisted knights, I cannot abide that he should touch me.

CASTRUCCIO Why, wench, is he scabbed?

BELLAFRONT Hang him, he'll not live to be so honest, nor to the credit to have scabs about him; his betters have 'em. But I hate to wear out any of his coarse knighthood, because he's made like an alderman's night-gown, faced all with cony before, and within nothing but fox. This sweet Oliver will eat mutton till he be ready to burst, but the lean-jawed slave will not pay for the scraping of his trencher.

PIORATTO Plague him! Set him beneath the salt, and let him not touch a bit till every one has had his full cut.

FLUELLO Sordello, the gentleman usher, came in to us too—marry, 'twas in our cheese, for he had been to borrow money for his lord, of a citizen.

CASTRUCCIO What an ass is that lord, to borrow money of a citizen.

79 **tickling** i.e. an effect of tobacco
gear stuff

81 **angel** (*a*) in reference to the candle as an angel bringing light to the *vale of misery*; (*b*) beautiful creature, who is wanton (*light*)

82 **curtal** (*a*) horse with a docked tail; (*b*) rogue who wears a short cloak

85 **angels** with a pun on the gold coin so named

86 **fetch some wine** one of the duties of a whore's attendant

87–8 **I must ... of it** Roger is presumably waiting for money.

94 **Hippocras** a spiced and sweetened wine so named for the cloth bag known as Hippocrates' sleeve through which it was strained

97 **teston** sixpence

99 **pottle** liquid measure (= two quarts)
manchet small loaf or roll of the finest wheaten bread

100 **Herculean** strong, powerful

106 **danced the canaries** punning on the Spanish dance and sweet Canary wine

108 **punks** prostitutes
Marry, faugh common expression of contempt (cf. the character, Mary Faugh, in Marston's *Dutch Courtesan*)

109–10 **sucking ... nests** i.e. characterizing Castruccio as a weasel or cuckoo.

112 **board** table

114 **Malavolta** playing on the *lavolta*, a lively dance

116 **beagle** a term of abuse (possibly with sexual innuendo)
horse-leech a term of abuse: (*a*) aquatic sucking worm, commonly used medically; (*b*) rapacious, insatiable person

117 **Lollio** Possibly derived from the Italian, *lóglio*, a darnel or cockle in corn. Middleton may have recalled it in writing *Changeling*.

121 **mole-catcher** term of abuse (probably with sexual innuendo associated with phallic suggestion of *mole*)

124 **dry-fisted** miserly

126 **scabbed** syphilitic

128 **credit** honour, trustworthiness

130 **night-gown** dressing gown (with a pun on *knighthood*)
faced covered, trimmed

131 **cony ... fox** playing on the proverbial innocence and foolishness of a rabbit (*cony*) and the cleverness and ruthlessness of a fox; cf. a wolf in sheep's clothing.
cony rabbit fur

131–2 **This sweet Oliver** alluding to a popular ballad, now lost, 'O sweet Oliver, leave me not behind thee' (proverbial: Tilley O40)

132 **eat mutton** enjoy, use prostitutes

135 **the salt** A register of social rank: persons of higher station were seated above the central large salt-cellar at table while those of inferior status were positioned below it.

136 **cut** slice or portion (with a bawdy pun on *cut* = cunt)

138 **in our cheese** at the end of our meal

BELLAFRONT Nay, God's my pity, what an ass is that citizen to lend money to a lord!

Enter Matteo and [after him] Hippolito, who, saluting the company, as a stranger walks off. Roger comes in sadly behind them with a pottle-pot, and stands aloof off

MATTEO Save you, gallants. Signor Fluello, exceedingly well met, as I may say.

FLUELLO Signor Matteo, exceedingly well met too, as I may say.

MATTEO And how fares my little pretty mistress?

BELLAFRONT E'en as my little pretty servant; sees three court dishes before her, and not one good bit in them. [*To Roger*] How now? Why the devil stand'st thou so? Art in a trance?

ROGER [*coming forward*] Yes, forsooth.

BELLAFRONT Why dost not fill out their wine?

ROGER Forsooth, 'tis filled out already: all the wine that the signor has bestowed upon you is cast away. A porter ran a-tilt at me, and so faced me down that I had not a drop.

BELLAFRONT I'm accursed to let such a withered artichoke-faced rascal grow under my nose. Now you look like an old he-cat going to the gallows.—I'll be hanged if he ha' not put up the money to cony-catch us all.

ROGER No, truly, forsooth, 'tis not put up yet.

BELLAFRONT How many gentlemen hast thou served thus?

ROGER None but five hundred, besides prentices and servingmen.

BELLAFRONT Dost think I'll pocket it up at thy hands?

ROGER Yes, forsooth, I fear you will pocket it up.

BELLAFRONT [*to Matteo*] Fie, fie, cut my lace, good servant, I shall ha' the mother presently, I'm so vexed at this horse-plum.

FLUELLO Plague, not for a scald pottle of wine.

MATTEO Nay, sweet Bellafront, for a little pig's wash!

CASTRUCCIO [*giving money*] Here, Roger, fetch more.—A mischance, i'faith, acquaintance.

BELLAFRONT [*to Roger*] Out of my sight, thou ungodly puritanical creature.

ROGER For the t'other pottle?—Yes, forsooth.

BELLAFRONT [*aside to Roger*] Spill that too. *Exit [Roger]*
What gentleman is that, servant—your friend?

MATTEO Gods-so, a stool, a stool.

[Hippolito comes forward]

If you love me, mistress, entertain this gentleman respectively, and bid him welcome.

BELLAFRONT He's very welcome.—Pray sir, sit.

HIPPOLITO Thanks, lady.

FLUELLO Count Hippolito, is't not?—Cry you mercy, signor, you walk here all this while, and we not heed you? Let me bestow a stool upon you, beseech you. You are a stranger here; we know the fashions o'th' house.

CASTRUCCIO Please you be here, my lord.

[He offers] tobacco

HIPPOLITO No, good Castruccio.

FLUELLO You have abandoned the court, I see, my lord, since the death of your mistress. Well, she was a delicate piece.—[*To Bellafront*] Beseech you, sweet.—[*To Hippolito*] Come, let us serve under the colours of your acquaintance still, for all that. Please you to meet here at the lodging of my coz, I shall bestow a banquet upon you.

HIPPOLITO
I never can deserve this kindness, sir.
What may this lady be whom you call coz?

FLUELLO Faith, sir, a poor gentlewoman, of passing good carriage; one that has some suits in law, and lies here in an attorney's house.

HIPPOLITO Is she married?

FLUELLO Ha, as all your punks are: a captain's wife, or so.—Never saw her before, my lord?

HIPPOLITO Never; trust me, a goodly creature.

FLUELLO By gad, when you know her as we do, you'll swear she is the prettiest, kindest, sweetest, most bewitching honest ape under the pole. A skin—your satin is not more soft, nor lawn whiter.

HIPPOLITO Belike, then, she's some sale courtesan.

FLUELLO Troth, as all your best faces are, a good wench.

HIPPOLITO Great pity that she's a good wench.

143.2 ***walks off*** withdraws or retires to the rear or another part of the stage
143.4 ***aloof off*** at a distance
149 **servant** lover
157 **faced me down** browbeat me
161 **gallows** i.e. where stray animals were hanged
162 **put up** pocketed
cony-catch cheat
163 **put up** stowed away (Roger quibbles on the meaning of Bellafront's term as below at 6.168).
167 **pocket it up** put up with it
168 **pocket it up** i.e. in reference to the swindle, in accordance with which Roger will hand the money over to Bellafront
169 **cut my lace** i.e. cut my stays (so I can breathe more freely and forestall swooning)
170 **the mother** hysteria
171 **horse-plum** small red variety of plum (term of contempt)
172 **scald** paltry, contemptible
173 **pig's wash** swill of a brewery given to pigs (contemptuously used in reference to weak, inferior liquor)
183 **respectively** (*a*) attentively; (*b*) respectfully
186 **Cry you mercy** I beg your pardon, forgiveness
190 **Please . . . my lord** Castruccio presumably merely offers tobacco, though he might also offer Hippolito his stool.
191–214 **No, good Castruccio . . . good wench** Bellafront and Matteo are presumably dallying or talking apart, as signalled by Matteo's non-sequitur statement at 6.215.
201 **passing** exceedingly
202 **carriage** demeanour
suits in law i.e. the pretence of law business in term-time would provide a conventional cover for prostitution
205 **captain's wife** i.e. a husband away at sea used as a cover for prostitution
212 **sale courtesan** (with a quibble on 'sale cloth'—meaning either 'cloth for sale' or 'inferior cloth'—making light of Fluello's likening of Bellafront's skin to fabrics)
214 **good wench** prostitute (Hippolito plays on the literal sense, 'virtuous woman')

MATTEO [*to Bellafront*] Thou shalt have it, i'faith, mistress.—How now signors? What? Whispering? [*To Hippolito*] Did not I lay a wager I should take you within seven days in a house of vanity?

HIPPOLITO You did, and I beshrew your heart, you have won.

MATTEO How do you like my mistress?

HIPPOLITO Well, for such a mistress; better, if your mistress be not your master. I must break manners, gentlemen, fare you well.

MATTEO 'Sfoot, you shall not leave us.

BELLAFRONT The gentleman likes not the taste of our company.

ALL THE GALLANTS Beseech you stay.

HIPPOLITO Trust me, my affairs beckon for me; pardon me.

MATTEO Will you call for me half an hour hence here?

HIPPOLITO Perhaps I shall.

MATTEO Perhaps? Faugh! I know you can; swear to me you will.

HIPPOLITO Since you will press me, on my word, I will. *Exit*

BELLAFRONT What sullen picture is this, servant?

MATTEO It's Count Hippolito, the brave count.

PIORATTO As gallant a spirit as any in Milan, you sweet Jew.

FLUELLO O, he's a most essential gentleman, coz.

CASTRUCCIO Did you never hear of Count Hippolito, acquaintance?

BELLAFRONT Marry-muff o'your counts, an be no more life in 'em!

MATTEO He's so malcontent, sirrah Bellafront. An you be honest gallants, let's sup together, and have the count with us.—Thou shalt sit at the upper end, punk.

BELLAFRONT Punk? You soused gurnet!

MATTEO King's truce! Come, I'll bestow the supper to have him but laugh.

CASTRUCCIO He betrays his youth too grossly to that tyrant melancholy.

MATTEO All this is for a woman.

BELLAFRONT A woman?—Some whore! What sweet jewel is't?

PIORATTO Would she heard you.

FLUELLO Troth, so would I.

CASTRUCCIO And I, by heaven.

BELLAFRONT Nay, good servant, what woman?

MATTEO Pah!

BELLAFRONT Prithee tell me, a buss and tell me. I warrant he's an honest fellow, if he take on thus for a wench. Good rogue, who?

MATTEO By th'Lord, I will not, must not, faith, mistress.—Is't a match, sirs? This night at th' Antelope; for there's best wine and good boys.

ALL THE GALLANTS It's done; at th' Antelope.

BELLAFRONT I cannot be there tonight.

MATTEO Cannot? By th'Lord, you shall.

BELLAFRONT By the Lady, I will not. Sha-all!

FLUELLO Why then, put it off till Friday: woo't come then, coz?

BELLAFRONT Well.

Enter Roger

MATTEO You're the waspishest ape.—Roger, put your mistress in mind—your scurvy mistress here—to sup with us on Friday next. You're best come like a madwoman, without a band, in your waistcoat, and the linings of your kirtle outward, like every common hackney that steals out at the back gate of her sweet knight's lodging.

BELLAFRONT Go, go, hang yourself!

CASTRUCCIO It's dinner-time, Matteo, shall's hence?

ALL THE GALLANTS Yes, yes.—Farewell, wench.

BELLAFRONT Farewell, boys. *Exeunt* [*Gallants*]
Roger, what wine sent they for?

ROGER Bastard wine, for if it had been truly begotten, it would not ha' been ashamed to come in. Here's six shillings to pay for nursing the bastard.

BELLAFRONT A company of rooks! O, good sweet Roger, run to the poulter's and buy me some fine larks.

ROGER No woodcocks?

BELLAFRONT
Yes, faith, a couple, if they be not dear.

Enter Hippolito

ROGER
I'll buy but one; there's one already here. *Exit*

HIPPOLITO
Is the gentleman, my friend, departed, mistress?

BELLAFRONT
His back is but new turned, sir.

HIPPOLITO
Fare you well.

BELLAFRONT
I can direct you to him.

HIPPOLITO
Can you, pray?

BELLAFRONT
If you please stay, he'll not be absent long.

238 **Jew** playful use of a conventional term of opprobrium
239 **essential** thorough, entire
244 **sirrah** often used in reference to women
247 **soused gurnet** pickled gurnet (gurnard), (term of abuse)
248 **King's truce** a cry for the discontinuance of a game
260 **buss** kiss
264 **Antelope** possibly in allusion to, or suggestive of, the Antelope Inn on the west side of West Smithfield, London
269 **Sha-all** signifying Bellafront's protracted indignation; cf. *Wha-at* (6.45)
270 **woo't** wilt
276 **band** collar
waistcoat A waist-length undergarment; worn without a covering garment, it was considered a sign of dishabille and frequently associated with prostitutes.
277 **kirtle** A floor-length garment worn as a dress over petticoats and occasionally with an outer gown. The *linings outward* presumably signify that the garment was put on in the dark or that the wearer was inebriated.
hackney prostitute
284 **Bastard wine** a sweet Spanish wine, with a play on the sense, 'illegitimate offspring', at 6.284–6.
285 **come in** i.e. to a brothel
287 **rooks** fools, gulls
291 **there's one** quibbling on a second sense of *woodcock* = fool, simpleton

HIPPOLITO
I care not much.
BELLAFRONT Pray sit, forsooth.
HIPPOLITO I'm hot.
If I may use your room, I'll rather walk.
BELLAFRONT
At your best pleasure.—Whew!—[*Calling offstage*]
Some rubbers there!
HIPPOLITO
Indeed, I'll none—indeed, I will not, thanks.
Pretty fine lodging. I perceive my friend
Is old in your acquaintance.
BELLAFRONT Troth, sir, he comes
As other gentlemen, to spend spare hours.
If yourself like our roof, such as it is,
Your own acquaintance may be as old as his.
HIPPOLITO
Say I did like; what welcome should I find?
BELLAFRONT
Such as my present fortunes can afford.
HIPPOLITO
But would you let me play Matteo's part?
BELLAFRONT
What part?
HIPPOLITO Why, embrace you, dally with you, kiss.
Faith, tell me, will you leave him, and love me?
BELLAFRONT
I am in bonds to no man, sir.
HIPPOLITO Why then,
You're free for any man; if any, me.
But I must tell you, lady, were you mine,
You should be all mine: I could brook no sharers;
I should be covetous, and sweep up all.
I should be pleasure's usurer; faith, I should.
BELLAFRONT
O fate!
HIPPOLITO
Why sigh you, lady? May I know?
BELLAFRONT
'T has never been my fortune yet to single
Out that one man whose love could fellow mine,
As I have ever wished it. O my stars!
Had I but met with one kind gentleman
That would have purchased sin alone to himself
For his own private use, although scarce proper,
Indifferent handsome, meetly legged and thighed,
And my allowance reasonable, i'faith,
According to my body, by my troth,
I would have been as true unto his pleasures,
Yea, and as loyal to his afternoons,
As ever a poor gentlewoman could be.
HIPPOLITO
This were well now, to one but newly fledged,
And scarce a day old in this subtle world:
'Twere pretty art, good birdlime, cunning net;
But come, come, faith, confess: how many men
Have drunk this selfsame protestatïon
From that red 'ticing lip?
BELLAFRONT Indeed, not any.
HIPPOLITO
'Indeed', and blush not?
BELLAFRONT No, in truth, not any.
HIPPOLITO
'Indeed', 'in truth'—How warily you swear!
'Tis well, if ill it be not; yet, had I
The ruffian in me, and were drawn before you
But in light colours, I do know indeed
You would not swear 'indeed', but thunder oaths
That should shake heaven, drown the harmonious
spheres,
And pierce a soul that loved her maker's honour
With horror and amazement.
BELLAFRONT Shall I swear?
Will you believe me then?
HIPPOLITO Worst then of all;
Our sins by custom seem at last but small.
Were I but o'er your threshold, a next man,
And after him a next, and then a fourth,
Should have this golden hook and lascivious bait
Thrown out to the full length. Why, let me tell you,
I ha' seen letters sent from that white hand
Tuning such music to Matteo's ear.
BELLAFRONT
Matteo! That's true, but if you'll believe
My honest tongue, my eyes no sooner met you
But they conveyed and led you to my heart.
HIPPOLITO
O, you cannot feign with me! Why, I know, lady,
This is the common fashion of you all,
To hook in a kind gentleman, and then
Abuse his coin, conveying it to your lover;
And in the end you show him a French trick,
And so you leave him, that a coach may run
Between his legs for breadth.
BELLAFRONT O, by my soul,
Not I! Therein I'll prove an honest whore,
In being true to one, and to no more.
HIPPOLITO
If any be disposed to trust your oath,
Let him; I'll not be he. I know you feign

298 **rubbers** towels
322 **scarce proper** hardly good-looking
323 **meetly** fairly well, tolerably
331 **birdlime** sticky substance applied to tree twigs for catching birds
334 **'ticing** enticing
335 **Indeed** an interjection associated with Puritans (and hence hypocrisy)
345 **Our sins . . . small** derived from St Augustine's '*Consuetudo peccati tollit sensum peccandi*': the custom of sinning takes away the feeling of sin; proverbial (Tilley C934)
359 **show . . . trick** infect him with venereal disease
360–1 **a coach . . . breadth** in allusion to an effect of venereal disease (*French trick*, 6.359)
362 **honest** chaste

All that you speak; ay, for a mingled harlot
Is true in nothing but in being false.
What, shall I teach you how to loathe yourself?
And mildly too, not without sense or reason?

BELLAFRONT
I am content; I would fain loathe myself,
If you not love me.

HIPPOLITO Then if your gracious blood
Be not all wasted, I shall assay to do't.
Lend me your silence, and attentïon.—
You have no soul:
That makes you weigh so light; heaven's treasure bought it,
And half a crown hath sold it. For your body,
It's like the common shore, that still receives
All the town's filth. The sin of many men
Is within you; and thus much, I suppose,
That if all your committers stood in rank,
They'd make a lane, in which your shame might dwell,
And with their spaces reach from hence to hell.
Nay, shall I urge it more? There has been known
As many by one harlot maimed and dismembered
As would ha' stuffed an hospital; this I might
Apply to you, and perhaps do you right.
O, you're as base as any beast that bears;
Your body is e'en hired, and so are theirs.
For gold and sparkling jewels, if he can,
You'll let a Jew get you with Christian.
Be he a Moor, a Tartar, though his face
Look uglier than a dead man's skull,
Could the devil put on a human shape,
If his purse shake out crowns, up then he gets:
Whores will be rid to hell with golden bits.
So that you're crueller than Turks, for they
Sell Christians only; you sell yourselves away.
Why, those that love you, hate you, and will term you
Lickerish damnation; wish themselves half sunk
After the sin is laid out, and e'en curse
Their fruitless riot—for what one begets
Another poisons; lust and murder hit.
A tree being often shook, what fruit can knit?

BELLAFRONT
O me unhappy!

HIPPOLITO I can vex you more:
A harlot is like Dunkirk, true to none,
Swallows both English, Spanish, fulsome Dutch,
Back-doored Italian, last of all the French;
And he sticks to you, faith, gives you your diet,
Brings you acquainted first with monsieur doctor,
And then you know what follows.

BELLAFRONT Misery.
Rank, stinking, and most loathsome misery.

HIPPOLITO
Methinks a toad is happier than a whore.
That with one poison swells, with thousands more
The other stocks her veins.—Harlot? Fie, Fie!
You are the miserablest creatures breathing,
The very slaves of nature. Mark me else:
You put on rich attires, others' eyes wear them;
You eat but to supply your blood with sin,
And this strange curse e'en haunts you to your graves:
From fools you get, and spend it upon slaves.
Like bears and apes you're baited and show tricks
For money, but your bawd the sweetness licks.
Indeed, you are their journeywomen, and do
All base and damned works they list set you to;
So that you ne'er are rich—for do but show me,
In present memory or in ages past,
The fairest and most famous courtesan,
Whose flesh was dear'st, that raised the price of sin
And held it up, to whose intemperate bosom
Princes, earls, lords—the worst has been a knight,
The mean'st a gentleman—have offered up
Whole hecatombs of sighs, and rained in showers
Handfuls of gold; yet for all this, at last
Diseases sucked her marrow, then grew so poor
That she has begged, e'en at a beggar's door.
And—wherein heaven has a finger—when this idol
From coast to coast has leaped on foreign shores,
And had more worship than th' outlandish whores,
When several nations have gone over her,
When for each several city she has seen
Her maidenhead has been new and been sold dear,

366 **mingled** promiscuous
375 **heaven's . . . it** Christ redeemed your soul
376 **For** as for
377 **shore** sewer
still constantly
380 **your committers** in a sexual sense: those who have had sexual relations with you
382 **spaces** accumulated distances from body to body
390 **get you . . . Christian** make you pregnant with a child who, because born to an at least nominal Christian or in a Christian land, will be brought up as one (the father having absconded)
395 **Whores** punning on 'horse'
rid ridden
bits (*a*) mouthpieces of horses' bridles; (*b*) coins
399 **Lickerish** lecherous
402 **hit** agree together
405 **Dunkirk** Notorious as a haven of freebooters who preyed indiscriminately on sailing vessels of all nations.
407 **Back-doored Italian** alluding to the alleged sexual proclivities of Italians for sodomy
French as bearers of venereal disease
413 **poison** Toads were thought to be venomous.
417 **others' . . . them** The sense seems to be that Bellafront's wearing of expensive clothes is appreciated chiefly by others.
423 **journeywomen** women working at a trade for daily wages
424 **list** please, choose
432 **hecatombs** vast numbers
436 **idol** i.e. the *courtesan* of l. 427
437 **leaped** (*a*) danced, skipped; (*b*) fornicated
438 **outlandish** foreign
440 **several** separate, different

Did live well there, and might have died unknown
And undefamed, back comes she to her own;
And there both miserably lives and dies,
Scorned even of those that once adored her eyes;
As if her fatal-circled life thus ran:
Her pride should end there where it first began.
What, do you weep to hear your story read?
Nay, if you spoil your cheeks, I'll read no more.

BELLAFRONT O yes, I pray proceed:
Indeed, 'twill do me good to weep indeed.

HIPPOLITO
To give those tears a relish, this I add:
You're like the Jews, scattered, in no place certain;
Your days are tedious, your hours burdensome,
And were't not for full suppers, midnight revels,
Dancing, wine, riotous meetings, which do drown
And bury quite in you all virtuous thoughts,
And on your eyelids hang so heavily
They have no power to look so high as heaven,
You'd sit and muse on nothing but despair,
Curse that devil Lust, that so burns up your blood,
And in ten thousand shivers break your glass
For his temptation. Say you taste delight
To have a golden gull from rise to set,
To mete you in his hot luxurious arms;
Yet your nights pay for all: I know you dream
Of warrants, whips, and beadles, and then start
At a door's windy creak, think every weasel
To be a constable, and every rat
A long-tailed officer. Are you now not slaves?
O, you have damnation without pleasure for it!
Such is the state of harlots. To conclude,
When you are old, and can well paint no more,
You turn bawd and are then worse than before.
Make use of this; farewell.

BELLAFRONT O, I pray stay.

HIPPOLITO
I see Matteo comes not; time hath barred me.
Would all the harlots in the town had heard me.
Exit [leaving his sword]

BELLAFRONT
Stay yet a little longer. No—quite gone!
Cursed be that minute—for it was no more,
So soon a maid is changed into a whore—
Wherein I first fell; be it for ever black.
Yet why should sweet Hippolito shun mine eyes,
For whose true love I would become pure-honest,
Hate the world's mixtures, and the smiles of gold?
Am I not fair? Why should he fly me then?
Fair creatures are desired, not scorned of men.
How many gallants have drunk healths to me
Out of their daggered arms, and thought them blest
Enjoying but mine eyes at prodigal feasts!
And does Hippolito detest my love?
O, sure their heedless lusts but flattered me;
I am not pleasing, beautiful, nor young.
Hippolito hath spied some ugly blemish
Eclipsing all my beauties; I am foul.
'Harlot'! Ay, that's the spot that taints my soul.—
His weapon left here? O fit instrument
To let forth all the poison of my flesh!
Thy master hates me, 'cause my blood hath ranged;
But when 'tis forth, then he'll believe I'm changed.
[She prepares to stab herself]
Enter Hippolito

HIPPOLITO
Madwoman, what art doing?

BELLAFRONT Either love me,
Or cleave my bosom on thy rapier's point;
Yet do not, neither, for thou then destroy'st
That which I love thee for—thy virtues. Here, here,
[She gives the sword to Hippolito]
Thou'rt crueller, and kill'st me with disdain;
To die so sheds no blood, yet 'tis worse pain.
Exit Hippolito
Not speak to me! Not look! Not bid farewell!
Hated! This must not be; some means I'll try.
Would all whores were as honest now as I. *Exit*

Enter Candido, [Viola,] his Wife, George, and two Prentices in the shop; Fustigo enters, walking by Sc. 7

GEORGE See, gentleman, what you lack. A fine holland, a fine cambric, see what you buy.

FIRST PRENTICE Holland for shirts, cambric for bands, what is't you lack?

FUSTIGO *[aside]* 'Sfoot, I lack 'em all, nay more, I lack money to buy 'em: let me see, let me look again; mass, this is the shop.—*[To Wife]* What, coz! Sweet coz! How dost, i'faith, since last night after candlelight? We had

443 **own** i.e. country
449 **read** lecture, sermonize
462 **shivers** splinters
glass mirror
464 **To have . . . set** to have a rich fool from sunrise to sunset
465 **mete** measure (i.e. embrace)
luxurious lustful
467 **whips** Whores were whipped for their offences by beadles.
start recoil suddenly in alarm
470 **long-tailed** possibly in reference to a whip or rope (*officer* could mean 'jailer' or 'executioner' as well as 'petty officer of justice' or 'constable')
476 **time . . . me** the passage of time has prevented me (from staying)
484 **mixtures** promiscuous sexual relations
487–8 **drunk healths . . . arms** One of the extravagant gestures of a gallant to his mistress consisted of piercing with his dagger a vein in his arm to procure a cupful of blood (sometimes mixed with wine), which was then drunk to her health.
498 **blood** sexual passion
ranged been inconstant
7.0.1–2 ***Enter . . . walking by*** As at the start of Sc. 5, those associated with the shop presumably reveal it and set it out in the discovery space—probably the central door providing access to the stage (if, as seems likely, the Fortune Theatre was equipped with three doors).
1 **holland** linen fabric, originally from the province of Holland in the Netherlands
2 **cambric** fine white linen, originally made at Cambray in Flanders

good sport, i'faith, had we not? And when shall's laugh again?

WIFE When you will, cousin.

FUSTIGO Spoke like a kind Lacedemonian. I see yonder's thy husband.

WIFE Ay, there's the sweet youth, God bless him.

FUSTIGO And how is't cousin? And how? How is't, thou squall?

WIFE Well, cousin; how fare you?

FUSTIGO How fare I? Troth, for sixpence a meal, wench, as well as heart can wish, with calves' chawdrons and chitterlings; besides I have a punk after supper, as good as a roasted apple.

CANDIDO Are you my wife's cousin?

FUSTIGO I am, sir; what hast thou to do with that?

CANDIDO O, nothing, but you're welcome.

FUSTIGO The devil's dung in thy teeth! I'll be welcome whether thou wilt or no, I.—What ring's this, coz? Very pretty and fantastical, i'faith; let's see it.

WIFE Puh! Nay, you wrench my finger.

FUSTIGO [*taking the ring*] I ha' sworn I'll ha't, and I hope you will not let my oaths be cracked in the ring, will you?—I hope, sir, you are not melancholy at this, for all your great looks. Are you angry?

CANDIDO
Angry? Not I, sir; nay, if she can part
So easily with her ring, 'tis with my heart.

GEORGE Suffer this, sir, and suffer all. A whoreson gull, to—

CANDIDO
Peace, George; when she has reaped what I have sown,
She'll say one grain tastes better of her own
Than whole sheaves gathered from another's land:
Wit's never good till bought at a dear hand.
[*Fustigo and Wife kiss*]

GEORGE But in the mean time she makes an ass of somebody.

SECOND PRENTICE See, see, see, sir, as you turn your back they do nothing but kiss.

CANDIDO
No matter, let 'em; when I touch her lip
I shall not feel his kisses, no, nor miss
Any of her lip; no harm in kissing is.
Look to your business, pray make up your wares.

FUSTIGO Troth, coz, and well remembered, I would thou wouldst give me five yards of lawn to make my punk some falling bands o' the fashion—three falling one upon another, for that's the new edition now. She's out of linen horribly, too; troth, sh'has never a good smock to her back neither, but one that has a great many patches in't, and that I'm fain to wear myself for want of shift, too. Prithee, put me into wholesome napery, and bestow some clean commodities upon us.

WIFE Reach me those cambrics and the lawns hither.

CANDIDO What to do, wife? To lavish out my goods upon a fool?

FUSTIGO Fool! 'Snails, eat the 'fool', or I'll so batter your crown that it shall scarce go for five shillings.

SECOND PRENTICE Do you hear, sir? You're best be quiet, and say a fool tells you so.

FUSTIGO [*to Candido*] Nails, I think so, for thou tell'st me.

CANDIDO
Are you angry, sir, because I named thee fool?
Trust me, you are not wise in mine own house
And to my face to play the antic thus.
If you'll needs play the madman, choose a stage
Of lesser compass, where few eyes may note
Your actions' error; but if still you miss,
As here you do, for one clap, ten will hiss.

FUSTIGO Zounds, cousin, he talks to me as if I were a scurvy tragedian.

SECOND PRENTICE [*aside to George*] Sirrah George, I ha' thought upon a device how to break his pate, beat him soundly, and ship him away.

GEORGE [*aside to Second Prentice*] Do't.

SECOND PRENTICE [*aside to George*] I'll go in, pass thorough the house, give some of our fellow prentices the watchword when they shall enter, then come and fetch my master in by a wile, and place one in the hall to hold him in conference, whilst we cudgel the gull out of his coxcomb.

GEORGE [*aside to Second Prentice*] Do't; away, do't.

WIFE Must I call twice for these cambrics and lawns?

CANDIDO Nay, see, you anger her, George, prithee dispatch.

SECOND PRENTICE Two of the choicest pieces are in the warehouse, sir.

CANDIDO Go fetch them presently.

FUSTIGO Ay, do, make haste, sirrah. *Exit Second Prentice*

12 **Lacedemonian** wanton (i.e. like Helen of Troy, who abandoned her husband in Lacedemon)
16 **squall** wench (a term of both endearment and opprobrium)
19 **chawdrons** entrails used for food
20 **chitterlings** smaller intestines stuffed with forcemeat and fried or boiled
30 **cracked in the ring** If a coin had a crack which extended from its edge beyond the ring which encircled the sovereign's head, it was no longer acceptable as currency.
32 **great looks** serious countenance
40 **Wit's . . . hand** proverbial (Tilley W567)
51 **falling bands** collars worn falling flat around the neck
52 **new edition** latest style
57 **napery** personal linen
61 **'Snails** by God's nails
eat (*a*) retract; (*b*) literally 'eat' (punning on *fool* as sweet dessert)
62 **crown** punning on 'head' and 'an English coin worth five shillings'
go (*a*) be accepted, pass; (*b*) sell
65 **for** because
68 **antic** fool
69–72 **choose a stage . . . hiss** a metatheatrical allusion to the indoor theatres used by the children's companies, which held fewer spectators than the public amphitheatres
79 **thorough** through

CANDIDO
Why were you such a stranger all this while,
Being my wife's cousin?

FUSTIGO Stranger? No sir, I'm a natural Milaner born.

CANDIDO I perceive still it is your natural guise to mistake me, but you are welcome, sir; I much wish your acquaintance.

FUSTIGO My acquaintance? I scorn that, i'faith; I hope my acquaintance goes in chains of gold three-and-fifty times double—you know who I mean, coz: the posts of his gate are a-painting, too.

Enter the Second Prentice

SECOND PRENTICE [*to Candido*] Signor Pandulfo the merchant desires conference with you.

CANDIDO
Signor Pandulfo? I'll be with him straight.
Attend your mistress and the gentleman. *Exit*

WIFE [*to Prentices*] When do you show those pieces?

FUSTIGO [*to Prentices*] Ay, when do you show those pieces?

ALL THE PRENTICES Presently, sir, presently; we are but charging them.

FUSTIGO Come, sirrah, you flat-cap, where be these whites?

GEORGE Flat-cap! Hark in your ear, sir—[*aside to Fustigo*] you're a flat fool, an ass, a gull, and I'll thrum you.—[*Aloud*] Do you see this cambric, sir?

FUSTIGO [*to Wife*] 'Sfoot, coz, a good jest! Did you hear him? He told me in my ear I was 'a flat fool, an ass, a gull, and I'll thrum you.—Do you see this cambric, sir?'

WIFE What, not my men, I hope?

FUSTIGO No, not your men, but one of your men, i'faith.

FIRST PRENTICE [*showing a piece of cloth*] I pray, sir, come hither; what say you to this? Here's an excellent good one.

FUSTIGO Ay, marry, this likes me well; cut me off some half-score yards.

SECOND PRENTICE [*aside to Fustigo*] Let your whores cut. You're an impudent coxcomb, you get none, and yet I'll thrum you.—[*Aloud*] A very good cambric, sir.

FUSTIGO Again, again, as God judge me! [*To Wife*] 'Sfoot, coz, they stand thrumming here with me all day, and yet I get nothing.

FIRST PRENTICE A word, I pray, sir; you must not be angry: prentices have hot bloods—young fellows. What say you to this piece? Look you, 'tis so delicate, so soft, so even, so fine a thread, that a lady may wear it.

FUSTIGO 'Sfoot, I think so: if a knight marry my punk, a lady shall wear it. Cut me off twenty yards; thou'rt an honest lad.

FIRST PRENTICE Not without money, gull, and I'll thrum you too.

ALL THE PRENTICES Gull, we'll thrum you.

FUSTIGO
O Lord, sister, did you not hear something cry thump?
Zounds, your men here make a plain ass of me.

WIFE What, to my face so impudent?

GEORGE
Ay, in a cause so honest we'll not suffer
Our master's goods to vanish moneyless.

WIFE
You will not suffer them?

SECOND PRENTICE No, and you may blush
In going about to vex so mild a breast
As is our master's.

WIFE [*to Fustigo*] Take away those pieces.
Cousin, I give them freely.

FUSTIGO Mass, and I'll take 'em as freely.

ALL THE PRENTICES We'll make you lay 'em down again more freely.

[*Prentices beat Fustigo with clubs*]

WIFE
Help, help, my brother will be murderèd!

Enter Candido

CANDIDO
How now, what coil is here? Forbear, I say.

GEORGE
He calls us flat-caps, and abuses us.

CANDIDO
Why, sirs? Do such examples flow from me?

92 **stranger** Candido asks why Fustigo did not reveal his identity; but in his reply Fustigo interprets *stranger* to mean 'foreigner'.

94 **natural** native (but in Candido's response 'inborn')

95 **mistake** misunderstand

97 **acquaintance** knowledge beyond recognition but less than intimacy (but Fustigo in his response professes his *acquaintance* to be with a specific wealthy and influential city official)

99 **chains of gold** either as worn by a well-dressed gentleman or associated with a city office

100–1 **the posts . . . a-painting** Posts were erected outside mayors', sheriffs', or aldermen's houses for exhibiting proclamations and were newly painted at the start of the official's term of office.

109 **charging** loading (the goods), with a pun on 'charging with gunpowder' playing on *pieces* = fire-arms

110 **flat-cap** A slighting term for a citizen and tradesmen, from the woollen caps apprentices were required to wear. **whites** white cloths or fabrics

112 **flat** punning also on the senses (*a*) dull, stupid; (*b*) downright **thrum** beat

123 **likes** pleases

124 **yards** Second Prentice interprets as 'penises'

125 **cut** castrate

129 **thrumming** (*a*) i.e. threatening to 'thrum' or 'beat'; (*b*) provoking (literally, 'striking something with the fingers as if playing on a musical instrument')

141 **cry thump** make a thumping sound; thump

152.1 ***Prentices . . . clubs*** Although Second Prentice at ll. 79–84 had set out the strategy for prentices other than George and First and Second Prentices to enter, additional assistance seems uncalled for to overpower Fustigo, especially since the same three apparently get the better of Crambo and Poh at 12.99.1.

154 **coil** fuss, commotion

WIFE
They are of your keeping, sir.—Alas, poor brother.

FUSTIGO I'faith, they ha' peppered me, sister: look, does 't not spin? Call you these prentices? I'll ne'er play at cards more when clubs is trump: I have a goodly coxcomb, sister, have I not?

CANDIDO
Sister and brother? Brother to my wife?

FUSTIGO If you have any skill in heraldry, you may soon know that; break but her pate, and you shall see her blood and mine is all one.

CANDIDO A surgeon, run, a surgeon! [*Exit First Prentice*]
Why then wore you that forgèd name of cousin?

FUSTIGO Because it's a common thing to call 'coz' and 'ningle' nowadays all the world over.

CANDIDO
Cousin! A name of much deceit, folly, and sin,
For under that common-abusèd word,
Many an honest-tempered citizen
Is made a monster, and his wife trained out
To foul adulterous action, full of fraud.
I may well call that word a city's bawd.

FUSTIGO Troth, brother, my sister would needs ha' me take upon me to gull your patience a little; but it has made double gules on my coxcomb.

WIFE
What, playing the woman? Blabbing now, you fool?

CANDIDO
O, my wife did but exercise a jest upon your wit.

FUSTIGO
'Sfoot, my wit bleeds for't, methinks.

CANDIDO
Then let this warning more of sense afford.
The name of cousin is a bloody word.

FUSTIGO I'll ne'er call coz again whilst I live, to have such a coil about it. This should be a coronation day, for my head runs claret lustily. *Exit*

Enter an Officer

CANDIDO
Go wish the surgeon to have great respect.—
[*Exit Second Prentice*]
How now, my friend? What, do they sit today?

OFFICER
Yes, sir, they expect you at the senate-house.

CANDIDO
I thank your pains, I'll not be last man there.—
Exit Officer
My gown, George; go, my gown.—A happy land,
Where grave men meet, each cause to understand;
Whose consciences are not cut out in bribes
To gull the poor man's right, but in even scales
Peise rich and poor, without corruption's vails.—
Come, where's the gown?

GEORGE I cannot find the key, sir.

CANDIDO Request it of your mistress.

WIFE Come not to me for any key.
I'll not be troubled to deliver it.

CANDIDO
Good wife, kind wife, it is a needful trouble,
But for my gown.

WIFE Moths swallow down your gown!
You set my teeth on edge with talking on't.

CANDIDO
Nay, prithee, sweet, I cannot meet without it;
I should have a great fine set on my head.

WIFE
Set on your coxcomb! Tush, fine me no fines.

CANDIDO
Believe me, sweet, none greets the senate-house
Without his robe of reverence, that's his gown.

WIFE
Well, then, you're like to cross that custom once.
You get nor key nor gown; and so depart.
[*Aside*] This trick will vex him sure, and fret his heart.
Exit

CANDIDO
Stay, let me see, I must have some device.—
My cloak's too short: fie, fie, no cloak will do't;
It must be something fashioned like a gown,
With my arms out.—O, George, come hither, George,
I prithee lend me thine advice.

GEORGE Troth, sir, were it any but you, they would break open chest.

CANDIDO
O, no. Break open chest? That's a thief's office.
Therein you counsel me against my blood:
'Twould show impatience, that. Any meek means
I would be glad to embrace. Mass, I have got it:
Go, step up, fetch me down one of the carpets—
The saddest coloured carpet, honest George—
Cut thou a hole i'th'middle for my neck,
Two for mine arms. Nay, prithee, look not strange.

GEORGE
I hope you do not think, sir, as you mean.

CANDIDO
Prithee, about it quickly, the hour chides me;
Warily, George, softly, take heed of eyes. *Exit George*
Out of two evils he's accounted wise

158 **peppered** severely beaten
't i.e. his head
160 **clubs is trump** proverbial (Tilley C453)
169 **ningle** boy-favourite, catamite; intimate
170 **Cousin** with a pun on 'cozen'
173 **monster** cuckold (horned)
trained lured
178 **gules** red (heraldic term)—possibly punning on 'gull'
185–6 **coronation day . . . claret** Fustigo likens his blood to wine flowing in the city's conduits to celebrate a coronation day; and he has a bloody 'crown'.
187 **wish** desire, request
respect deferential regard, care
192 **cause** (*a*) matter in dispute; (*b*) charge, accusation
195 **Peise** balance, weigh
vails casual profits, gratuities; perquisites
204 **set on my head** imposed on me (but Candido's Wife takes *head* literally)
208 **cross** contravene
222 **carpets** table-covers
223 **saddest** soberest

That can pick out the least; the fine imposed
For an ungownèd senator is about
Forty crusadoes, the carpet not 'bove four.
Thus have I chosen the lesser evil yet,
Preserved my patience, foiled her desperate wit.

Enter George [with the carpet]

GEORGE Here, sir, here's the carpet.

CANDIDO
O, well done, George, we'll cut it just i'th'midst.
[They cut a hole in the carpet]
'Tis very well, I thank thee; help it on.

GEORGE It must come over your head, sir, like a wench's petticoat.

[Candido puts the carpet on]

CANDIDO
Thou'rt in the right, good George, it must indeed.
Fetch me a night-cap, for I'll gird it close,
As if my health were queasy. 'Twill show well
For a rude careless night-gown, will't not, think'st?

GEORGE Indifferent well, sir, for a night-gown, being girt and pleated.

CANDIDO Ay, and a night-cap on my head.

GEORGE
That's true, sir.—I'll run and fetch one, and a staff.
Exit

CANDIDO
For thus they cannot choose but conster it:
One that is out of health takes no delight,
Wears his apparel without appetite,
And puts on heedless raiment without form.—
Enter George [with a night-cap and staff]
So, so, kind George, *[putting on the night-cap and taking the staff]* be secret now, and prithee
Do not laugh at me till I'm out of sight.

GEORGE I laugh? Not I, sir.

CANDIDO Now to the senate-house:
Methinks I'd rather wear, without a frown,
A patient carpet than an angry gown. *Exit*

GEORGE Now looks my master just like one of our carpet-knights, only he's somewhat the honester of the two.

Enter [Viola,] Candido's Wife [with a key]

WIFE What, is your master gone?

GEORGE Yes, forsooth, his back is but new turned.

WIFE
And in his cloak? Did he not vex and swear?

GEORGE *[aside]* No, but he'll make you swear anon.—*[To her]* No, indeed, he went away like a lamb.

WIFE
Key, sink to hell! Still patient, patient still!
I am with child to vex him. Prithee, George,
If e'er thou look'st for favour at my hands,
Uphold one jest for me.

GEORGE Against my master?

WIFE 'Tis a mere jest, in faith. Say, wilt thou do't?

GEORGE Well, what is't?

WIFE
Here, take this key. Thou know'st where all things lie.
Put on thy master's best apparel, gown,
Chain, cap, ruff, everything, be like himself,
And 'gainst his coming home, walk in the shop;
Fain the same carriage, and his patient look.
'Twill breed but a jest thou know'st; speak, wilt thou?

GEORGE
'Twill wrong my master's patience.

WIFE Prithee, George.

GEORGE Well, if you'll save me harmless, and put me under covert-baron, I am content to please you, provided it may breed no wrong against him.

WIFE
No wrong at all. Here, take the key; begone.
If any vex him, this; if not this, none.
Exeunt [Candido's Wife at one door, George at another]

Sc. 8

Enter a Bawd and Roger

BAWD O Roger, Roger, where's your mistress, where's your mistress? There's the finest, neatest gentleman at my house but newly come over. O, where is she, where is she, where is she?

ROGER My mistress is abroad, but not amongst 'em. My mistress is not the whore now that you take her for.

BAWD How? Is she not a whore? Do you go about to take away her good name, Roger? You are a fine pander, indeed.

ROGER I tell you, Madonna Fingerlock, I am not sad for nothing; I ha' not eaten one good meal this three-and-thirty days: I had wont to get sixteen pence by fetching a pottle of Hippocras, but now those days are past. We had as good doings, Madonna Fingerlock—she within doors and I without—as any poor young couple in Milan.

BAWD God's my life, and is she changed now?

ROGER I ha' lost by her squeamishness more than would have builded twelve bawdy houses.

232 **crusadoes** Portuguese coins stamped with a cross, worth about 2*s*. 4*d*.
233 **lesser evil** proverbial (Tilley E207)
241 **gird ... close** fasten tightly, or tie firmly
243 **night-gown** an overgarment worn indoors and out both during the day and at night
244 **Indifferent** moderately
248 **conster** explain, interpret
256–7 **Methinks ... gown** Candido prefers to express his patience in wearing the improvised table-cloth than to submit to anger in demanding his gown.
258–9 **carpet-knights** one knighted on a carpet before the throne in peacetime rather than on the battle-field; often implying a voluptuary; the term had particular topicality in 1604 since James I created more than 1000 knights in his first year as king.
266 **am with child** long inordinately
275 **'gainst** in readiness for
280 **covert-baron** protection (originally a legal term relating to the condition of a wife under the cover, authority, or protection of her husband)
8.3 **come over** arrived from abroad
10 **Fingerlock** Possibly in reference to tight curls (a *lock* twisted on the finger), but the name also carries clear bawdy innuendoes.
14 **doings** business (sexual pun)

BAWD And had she no time to turn honest but now? What a vile woman is this! Twenty pound a night, I'll be sworn, Roger, in good gold and no silver. Why, here was a time; if she should ha' picked out a time, it could not be better! Gold enough stirring; choice of men, choice of hair, choice of beards, choice of legs, and choice of every, every, everything. It cannot sink into my head that she should be such an ass. Roger, I never believe it.

ROGER Here she comes now.

Enter Bellafront

BAWD O sweet madonna, on with your loose gown, your felt and your feather! There's the sweetest, prop'rest, gallantest gentleman at my house; he smells all of musk and ambergris, his pocket full of crowns, flame-coloured doublet, red satin hose, carnation silk stockings, and a leg and a body, O!

BELLAFRONT
Hence, thou, our sex's monster, poisonous bawd,
Lust's factor, and damnation's orator,
Gossip of hell! Were all the harlots' sins
Which the whole world contains numbered together,
Thine far exceeds them all; of all the creatures
That ever were created, thou art basest.
What serpent would beguile thee of thy office?
It is detestable; for thou liv'st
Upon the dregs of harlots, guard'st the door,
Whilst couples go to dancing: O coarse devil!
Thou art the bastard's curse—thou brand'st his birth;
The lecher's French disease, for thou dry-suck'st him;
The harlot's poison, and thine own confusion.

BAWD Marry, come up, with a pox! Have you nobody to rail against but your bawd now?

BELLAFRONT
And you, knave pander, kinsman to a bawd—

ROGER [*to Bawd*] You and I, madonna, are cousins.

BELLAFRONT
Of the same blood and making, near allied,
Thou, that slave to sixpence, base-mettled villain.

ROGER Sixpence? Nay, that's not so; I never took under two shillings fourpence—I hope I know my fee.

BELLAFRONT
I know not against which most to inveigh,
For both of you are damned so equally.
Thou never spar'st for oaths, swear'st anything,
As if thy soul were made of shoe-leather:
'God damn me, gentleman, if she be within!'
When in the next room she's found dallying.

ROGER If it be my vocation to swear, every man in his vocation; I hope my betters swear and damn themselves, and why should not I?

BELLAFRONT Roger, you cheat kind gentlemen.

ROGER The more gulls they.

BELLAFRONT Slave, I cashier thee.

BAWD An you do cashier him, he shall be entertained.

ROGER Shall I?—[*To Bellafront*] Then blurt o' your service.

BELLAFRONT [*to Bawd*]
As hell would have it, entertained by you!
I dare the devil himself to match those two. *Exit*

BAWD Marry gup, are you grown so holy, so pure, so honest, with a pox?

ROGER Scurvy honest punk! But stay, madonna, how must our agreement be now, for you know I am to have all the comings-in at the hall-door, and you at the chamber-door.

BAWD True, Roger, except my vails.

ROGER Vails, what vails?

BAWD Why, as thus: if a couple come in a coach, and light to lie down a little, then, Roger, that's my fee; and you may walk abroad, for the coachman himself is their pander.

ROGER Is 'a so? In truth, I have almost forgot, for want of exercise. But how if I fetch this citizen's wife to that gull, and that madonna to that gallant, how then?

BAWD Why then, Roger, you are to have sixpence a lane: so many lanes, so many sixpences.

ROGER Is't so? Then I see we two shall agree and live together.

BAWD Ay, Roger, so long as there be any taverns and bawdy houses in Milan. *Exeunt*

24 **stirring** available, in circulation
30 **loose gown** (the conventional dress of prostitutes)
31 **felt** hat
prop'rest handsomest
33 **ambergris** perfume (a substance secreted in the intestines of the sperm-whale)
flame-coloured traditionally associated with sexual encounters
34 **hose** breeches
carnation a shade of red resembling the colour of raw flesh
silk stockings Preferred by fashionable gallants because they showed off their shapely legs better than woollen hose.
37 **factor** agent, representative
38 **Gossip** companion, crony
54 **base-mettled** mean spirited (with a pun on the metal of the *sixpence* coin)
60 **soul** with a pun on 'sole'
63–4 **If... vocation** Cf. 'Let euery man abide in the same vocation wherein he was called', 1 Cor. 7:20 (Geneva Bible).
69 **entertained** employed, taken into service
70 **blurt o'** 'snort on' or 'a fig for'
72 **devil... two** Cf. 'There cannot lightly come a worse except the devil come himself' (proverb: Tilley W910).
73 **Marry gup** a corruption of 'Marry' (i.e. by Mary) 'go up' (get along)
77 **comings-in** takings (the prospective client made payments at each stage of access to a prostitute)
79 **vails** casual profits, gratuities; perquisites
82 **light** descend (from the coach)
85 **'a** he
89 **lanes... sixpences** i.e. sixpence for each lane passed through in conducting them hither

Sc. 9

Enter Bellafront with a lute, pen, ink, and paper being placed before her [on a table].

Song

BELLAFRONT [*singing*]
The courtier's flatt'ring jewels,
Temptations only fuels;
The lawyer's ill-got moneys,
That suck up poor bees' honeys;
The citizen's son's riot,
The gallant's costly diet:
Silks and velvets, pearls and ambers,
Shall not draw me to their chambers.
Silks and velvets, (*etc.*)

She writes

O, 'tis in vain to write: it will not please;
Ink on this paper would ha' but presented
The foul black spots that stick upon my soul,
And rather make me loathsomer, than wrought
My love's impression in Hippolito's thought.
No, I must turn the chaste leaves of my breast,
And pick out some sweet means to breed my rest.
Hippolito, believe me, I will be
As true unto thy heart, as thy heart to thee,
And hate all men, their gifts, and company.

Enter Matteo, Castruccio, Fluello, and Pioratto

MATTEO You, goody punk, *subaudi* cockatrice, O you're a sweet whore of your promise, are you not, think you? How well you came to supper to us last night! Mew, a whore and break her word! Nay, you may blush, and hold down your head at it well enough. 'Sfoot, ask these gallants if we stayed not till we were as hungry as sergeants.

FLUELLO Ay, and their yeomen too.

CASTRUCCIO Nay, faith, acquaintance, let me tell you, you forgot yourself too much. We had excellent cheer, rare vintage, and were drunk after supper.

PIORATTO And when we were in our woodcocks, sweet rogue, a brace of gulls, dwelling here in the city, came in and paid all the shot.

MATTEO Pox on her, let her alone.

BELLAFRONT
O, I pray do, if you be gentlemen;
I pray depart the house. Beshrew the door
For being so easily entreated. Faith,
I lent but little ear unto your talk—
My mind was busied otherwise, in troth—
And so your words did unregarded pass.
Let this suffice: I am not as I was.

FLUELLO 'I am not what I was!'—No, I'll be sworn thou art not, for thou wert honest at five, and now thou'rt a punk at fifteen. Thou wert yesterday a simple whore, and now thou'rt a cunning, cony-catching baggage today.

BELLAFRONT
I'll say I'm worse; I pray forsake me then.
I do desire you leave me, gentlemen,
And leave yourselves. O, be not what you are—
Spendthrifts of soul and body.
Let me persuade you to forsake all harlots:
Worse than the deadliest poisons, they are worse,
For o'er their souls hangs an eternal curse.
In being slaves to slaves, their labours perish.
They're seldom blessed with fruit, for ere it blossoms,
Many a worm confounds it.
They have no issue but foul ugly ones
That run along with them, e'en to their graves;
For 'stead of children, they breed rank diseases,
And all you gallants can bestow on them
Is that French infant, which ne'er acts but speaks.
What shallow son and heir, then, foolish gallants,
Would waste all his inheritance to purchase
A filthy, loathed disease, and pawn his body
To a dry evil? That usury's worst of all
When th'interest will eat out the principal.

MATTEO [*aside*] 'Sfoot, she gulls 'em the best! This is always her fashion, when she would be rid of any company that she cares not for, to enjoy mine alone.

FLUELLO What's here? Instructions, admonitions, and caveats? Come out, you scabbard of vengeance.

[*He draws his sword*]

MATTEO Fluello, spurn your hounds when they fist; you shall not spurn my punk; I can tell you my blood is vexed.

FLUELLO Pox o' your blood; make it a quarrel.

MATTEO [*drawing his sword*] You're a slave! Will that serve turn?

ALL THE REST 'Sblood, hold, hold!

CASTRUCCIO Matteo, Fluello, for shame, put up.

MATTEO Spurn my sweet varlet!

BELLAFRONT O how many thus
Moved with a little folly have let out
Their souls in brothel-houses, fell down, and died
Just at their harlot's foot, as 'twere in pride!

FLUELLO Matteo, we shall meet.

9.0.1–2 **Enter...table** Presumably the items cited are placed in front of (*before*) Bellafront on a table rather than in advance of her entry, although the latter is possible.
11 **presented** represented
20 **goody** term of civility for a woman of humble station (here used ironically) ***subaudi*** understand, supply (Latin) **cockatrice** prostitute
22 **Mew** a mocking exclamation (imitative of a cat's cry)
31 **in our woodcocks** (*a*) 'eating our woodcocks', i.e. as a course of dinner; (*b*) a 'woodcock's head' was a kind of tobacco pipe, so named from its shape, so the sense may be 'smoking our pipes'; (*c*) 'being foolish' (from *woodcock* as a type of stupidity)
32 **brace** pair, couple
33 **shot** reckoning
36 **Beshrew** confound
45 **baggage** strumpet
61 **that French infant** i.e. venereal disease **ne'er...speaks** i.e. speaks (breaks out) whenever he acts
65 **dry** (*a*) withered; (*b*) sterile, unfruitful **evil** (*a*) malady, disease; (*b*) calamity, misfortune
71 **scabbard of vengeance** in reference to Bellafront
72 **fist** fart
79 **put up** sheathe your swords

MATTEO [*sheathing his sword*] Ay, ay, anywhere, saving at church; pray take heed we meet not there.

FLUELLO [*to Bellafront, sheathing his sword*]
Adieu, damnation.

CASTRUCCIO [*to Bellafront*]
Cockatrice, farewell.

PIORATTO
There's more deceit in women than in hell.

Exeunt [*Castruccio, Fluello, Pioratto*]

MATTEO Ha, ha, thou dost gull 'em so rarely, so naturally. If I did not think thou hadst been in earnest! Thou art a sweet rogue for't, i'faith.

BELLAFRONT
Why are not you gone too, Signor Matteo?
I pray depart my house. You may believe me,
In troth, I have no part of harlot in me.

MATTEO How's this?

BELLAFRONT
Indeed, I love you not, but hate you worse
Than any man, because you were the first
Gave money for my soul. You brake the ice,
Which after turned a puddle; I was led
By your temptation to be miserable.
I pray seek out some other that will fall,
Or rather, I pray, seek out none at all.

MATTEO Is't possible, to be impossible: an honest whore? I have heard many honest wenches turn strumpets with a wet finger, but for a harlot to turn honest is one of Hercules' labours. It was more easy for him in one night to make fifty queans than to make one of them honest again in fifty years. Come, I hope thou dost but jest.

BELLAFRONT
'Tis time to leave off jesting; I had almost
Jested away salvation. I shall love you
If you will soon forsake me.

MATTEO God buy thee.

BELLAFRONT
O, tempt no more women! Shun their weighty curse.
Women at best are bad; make them not worse.
You gladly seek our sex's overthrow,
But not to raise our states. For all your wrongs,
Will you vouchsafe me but due recompense,
To marry with me?

MATTEO How, marry with a punk, a cockatrice, a harlot?
Marry, faugh, I'll be burnt thorough the nose first.

BELLAFRONT
Why, la, these are your oaths! You love to undo us,
To put heaven from us, whilst our best hours waste;
You love to make us lewd, but never chaste.

MATTEO
I'll hear no more of this. This ground upon
Thou'rt damned: for alt'ring thy religïon. *Exit*

BELLAFRONT
Thy lust and sin speak so much. Go thou, my ruin,
The first fall my soul took. By my example
I hope few maidens now will put their heads
Under men's girdles. Who least trusts is most wise:
Men's oaths do cast a mist before our eyes.
My best of wit be ready; now I go,
By some device to greet Hippolito. [*Exit*]

Sc. 10

Enter a Servant setting out a table, on which he places a skull, a picture, a book, and a taper

SERVANT So, this is Monday morning, and now must I to my housewifery. Would I had been created a shoemaker, for all the gentle craft are gentlemen every Monday by their copy, and scorn then to work one true stitch. My master means sure to turn me into a student, for here's my book, here my desk, here my light, this my close chamber, and [*pointing to the picture*] here my punk; so that this dull, drowsy first day of the week makes me half a priest, half a chandler, half a painter, half a sexton, ay, and half a bawd, for all this day my office is to do nothing but keep the door. To prove it, look you, this good face and yonder gentleman, so soon as ever my back's turned, will be naught together.

Enter Hippolito

HIPPOLITO Are all the windows shut?

SERVANT Close, sir, as the fist of a courtier that hath stood in three reigns.

HIPPOLITO
Thou art a faithful servant, and observ'st
The calendar both of my solemn vows
And ceremonious sorrow. Get thee gone.
I charge thee on thy life, let not the sound
Of any woman's voice pierce through that door.

SERVANT
If they do, my lord, I'll pierce some of them.
What will your lordship have to breakfast?

HIPPOLITO Sighs.

90 **rarely** splendidly, finely

105–6 **with a wet finger** easily, with little effort; without hesitation, readily. See note to 2.4–5.

107–8 **Hercules' labours . . . queans** Hercules ravished King Thespius's fifty daughters in a single night.

108 **queans** harlots

112 **God buy thee** good-bye. Matteo presumably intends to leave Bellafront at this point; but her response postpones his exit.

120 **burnt . . . nose** i.e. in the advanced stages of the ravages of syphilis

128–9 **heads . . . girdles** i.e. in subjection (originally in reference to the practice of wearing keys at a girdle); proverbial (Tilley H248)

10.0.1 ***setting out a table*** Since a table is required in the previous scene, *setting out* may mean 'furnishing' or 'putting things on' rather than 'bringing on stage'.

2 **housewifery** housekeeping, management of household affairs

3 **the gentle craft** the trade of shoemaking

3–4 **gentlemen every Monday** Shoemakers kept Monday a holiday; the Servant associates their idleness on this day with gentlemanly behaviour.

4 **copy** indentures

7 **close** private, secluded

12 **good face** person with a smooth or fair face

yonder gentleman i.e. Hippolito

13 **naught** naughty (with bawdy innuendo)

15 **stood** endured; flourished

18 **calendar** register, record

SERVANT What to dinner?

HIPPOLITO Tears.

SERVANT The one of them, my lord, will fill you too full of wind, the other wet you too much. What to supper?

HIPPOLITO That which now thou canst not get me, the constancy of a woman.

SERVANT Indeed, that's harder to come by than ever was Ostend.

HIPPOLITO Prithee away.

SERVANT I'll make away myself presently, which few servants will do for their lords, but rather help to make them away. Now to my door-keeping; I hope to pick something out of it. *Exit*

HIPPOLITO [*studying the picture*]
My Infelice's face: her brow, her eye,
The dimple on her cheek; and such sweet skill
Hath from the cunning workman's pencil flown,
These lips look fresh and lively as her own,
Seeming to move and speak. 'Las! Now I see
The reason why fond women love to buy
Adulterate complexion: here 'tis read,
False colours last after the true be dead.
Of all the roses grafted on her cheeks,
Of all the graces dancing in her eyes,
Of all the music set upon her tongue,
Of all that was past woman's excellence
In her white bosom—look! A painted board
Circumscribes all. Earth can no bliss afford.
Nothing of her but this? This cannot speak.
It has no lap for me to rest upon,
No lip worth tasting; here the worms will feed,
As in her coffin. Hence, then, idle art,
True love's best pictured in a true-love's heart.
Here art thou drawn, sweet maid, till this be dead,
So that thou liv'st twice, twice art burièd.
Thou figure of my friend, lie there. [*Taking skull*]
What's here?
Perhaps this shrewd pate was mine enemy's.
'Las! Say it were, I need not fear him now.
For all his braves, his contumelious breath,
His frowns, though dagger-pointed, all his plots,
Though ne'er so mischievous, his Italian pills,
His quarrels, and that common fence, his law:
See, see, they're all eaten out; here's not left one!
How clean they're picked away! To the bare bone!
How mad are mortals then to rear great names
On tops of swelling houses! Or to wear out
Their fingers' ends in dirt, to scrape up gold!—
Not caring, so that sumpter-horse, the back,
Be hung with gaudy trappings, with what coarse,
Yea, rags most beggarly, they clothe the soul.
Yet, after all, their gayness looks thus foul.
What fools are men to build a garish tomb
Only to save the carcass whilst it rots,
To maintain't long in stinking, make good carrion,
But leave no good deeds to preserve them sound;
For good deeds keep men sweet, long above ground.
And must all come to this? Fools, wise, all hither?
Must all heads thus at last be laid together?
Draw me my picture then, thou grave, neat workman,
[*To skull*] After this fashion, [*to picture*] not like this;
these colours
In time, kissing but air, will be kissed off.
[*To skull*] But here's a fellow—that which he lays on
Till doomsday alters not complexïon.
Death's the best painter then; they that draw shapes,
And live by wicked faces, are but God's apes.
They come but near the life, and there they stay.
This fellow draws life too; his art is fuller:
The pictures which he makes are without colour.

Enter his Servant

SERVANT Here's a person would speak with you, sir.

HIPPOLITO Ha!

SERVANT A person, sir, would speak with you.

HIPPOLITO Vicar?

SERVANT Vicar? No sir, h'as too good a face to be a vicar yet—a youth, a very youth.

HIPPOLITO
What youth? Of man or woman? Lock the doors.

SERVANT If it be a woman, marrowbones and potato pies keep me for meddling with her, for the thing has got the breeches; 'tis a male varlet sure, my lord, for a woman's tailor ne'er measured him.

HIPPOLITO
Let him give thee his message and be gone.

29–30 **That which ... woman** Cf. the proverbs, 'Women are as wavering (changeable, inconstant) as the wind' (Tilley 698), and 'A woman's mind (a woman) is always mutable' (Tilley W674).

32 **Ostend** besieged by Spanish forces from 5 July 1601 to 11 Sept. 1604

34, 35–6 **make ... away** (*a*) put out of the way; (*b*) put to death

43 **fond** foolish

44 **Adulterate** (*a*) counterfeit; (*b*) adulterous

59 **figure** representation
friend beloved

64 **Italian pills** poisons

65 **common ... law** recorded by Edward Pudsey in his Commonplace Book: 'law the common fence'
fence defence; protection

66–7 **one ... bone** a rhyming couplet; as elsewhere in the speech rhymes confer an element of formality

68–9 **How mad ... houses** Hippolito mocks the vanity of human aspirations to greatness built on foundations of pride and arrogance.

69 **swelling** proud, haughty

71 **so** so long as
sumpter-horse pack-horse

72 **coarse** coarse cloth, garments

83 **this fashion ... this** i.e. the skull ... Infelice's portrait

85 **lays on** applies (i.e. paint)

88 **wicked** possibly with a pun on 'wicks' = lips

91 **colour** punning on the sense 'false appearance'

94 **person** pronounced in the same way as 'parson'

99 **marrowbones and potato pies** believed to be aphrodisiacs

101 **male varlet** 'masculine whore' in Thersites' phrase (*Troilus and Cressida*, 5.1.15–17)

SERVANT He says he's Signor Matteo's man, but I know he lies.

HIPPOLITO How dost thou know it?

SERVANT 'Cause h'as ne'er a beard. 'Tis his boy, I think, sir, whosoe'er paid for his nursing.

HIPPOLITO Send him, and keep the door. *[Exit Servant]*

[He] reads

Fata si liceat mihi
fingere arbitrio meo,
temperem zephyro levi
vela.

I'd sail, were I to choose, not in the ocean.
Cedars are shaken, when shrubs do feel no bruise.

Enter Bellafront, like a page, [with a letter]

How? From Matteo?

BELLAFRONT *[giving a letter]*
Yes, my lord.

HIPPOLITO Art sick?

BELLAFRONT
Not all in health, my lord.

HIPPOLITO Keep off.

BELLAFRONT I do.
[Aside] Hard fate when women are compelled to woo.

HIPPOLITO
This paper does speak nothing.

BELLAFRONT Yes, my lord,
Matter of life it speaks, and therefore writ
In hidden character; to me instruction
My master gives, and, 'less you please to stay
Till you both meet, I can the text display.

HIPPOLITO
Do so: read out.

BELLAFRONT I am already out.
Look on my face, and read the strangest story!

HIPPOLITO What, villain, ho!

Enter his Servant

SERVANT Call you, my lord?

HIPPOLITO Thou slave, thou hast let in the devil.

SERVANT Lord bless us, where? He's not cloven, my lord, that I can see; besides, the devil goes more like a gentleman than a page. Good my lord, *buon coraggio.*

HIPPOLITO
Thou hast let in a woman in man's shape,
And thou art damned for't.

SERVANT Not damned, I hope, for putting in a woman to a lord.

HIPPOLITO
Fetch me my rapier.—Do not: I shall kill thee.
Purge this infected chamber of that plague
That runs upon me thus; slave, thrust her hence.

SERVANT Alas, my lord, I shall never be able to thrust her hence without help.—Come, mermaid, you must to sea again.

BELLAFRONT
Hear me but speak; my words shall be all music.
Hear me but speak.

[Knocking within]

HIPPOLITO Another beats the door;
T'other she-devil, look.

SERVANT Why then, hell's broke loose.

HIPPOLITO
Hence, guard the chamber; let no more come on:
One woman serves for man's damnatïon.— *Exit [Servant]*
Beshrew thee, thou dost make me violate
The chastest and most sanctimonious vow
That e'er was entered in the court of heaven.
I was on meditation's spotless wings
Upon my journey thither; like a storm
Thou beat'st my ripened cogitatïons
Flat to the ground, and like a thief dost stand
To steal devotion from the holy land.

BELLAFRONT *[kneeling]*
If woman were thy mother, if thy heart
Be not all marble—or if't marble be,
Let my tears soften it, to pity me—
I do beseech thee, do not thus with scorn
Destroy a woman.

HIPPOLITO Woman, I beseech thee,
Get thee some other suit; this fits thee not.
I would not grant it to a kneeling queen;
I cannot love thee, nor I must not. See
The copy of that obligatïon
Where my soul's bound in heavy penalties.

BELLAFRONT *[rising]*
She's dead, you told me; she'll let fall her suit.

HIPPOLITO
My vows to her fled after her to heaven.
Were thine eyes clear as mine, thou might'st behold her
Watching upon yon battlements of stars
How I observe them. Should I break my bond,
This board would rive in twain, these wooden lips
Call me most perjured villain. Let it suffice
I ha' set thee in the path; is't not a sign
I love thee, when with one so most, most dear,
I'll have thee fellows? All are fellows there.

BELLAFRONT
Be greater than a king: save not a body,
But from eternal shipwreck keep a soul.

110–13 ***Fata...vela*** Seneca, *Oedipus*, 882–5: 'If it were possible to fashion fate according to my will, I would raise my sails to gentle winds.'

115 **Cedars...bruise** proverbial (Tilley C208)

bruise hurt, injury

124 **out** on display (i.e. *she* is the text)

129–30 **He's...see** recorded by Edward Pudsey in his Commonplace Book: 'he's not cloven that I can see'

131 ***buon coraggio*** good courage (Italian); *coraggio* very likely picks up a common sense of 'courage': sexual vigour, lust.

140 **mermaid** prostitute

149 **sanctimonious** sacred

156–7 **heart...marble** proverbial (Tilley H311)

169 **yon battlements of stars** in reference to the theatre 'heavens'

171 **This board** i.e. the picture

If not, and that again sin's path I tread,
The grief be mine, the guilt fall on thy head.

HIPPOLITO
Stay, and take physic for it: read this book,
Ask counsel of this head what's to be done;
He'll strike it dead, that 'tis damnatïon
If you turn Turk again. O, do it not!
Though heaven cannot allure you to do well,
From doing ill let hell fright you, and learn this:
The soul whose bosom lust did never touch
Is God's fair bride, and maidens' souls are such;
The soul that, leaving chastity's white shore,
Swims in hot sensual streams, is the devil's whore.

Enter his Servant [*with a letter*]

How now, who comes?

SERVANT No more knaves, my lord, that wear smocks. Here's a letter from Doctor Benedict. I would not enter his man, though he had hairs at his mouth, for fear he should be a woman, for some women have beards; marry, they are half witches.—'Slid, you are a sweet youth to wear a codpiece, and have no pins to stick upon't.

HIPPOLITO
I'll meet the doctor, tell him; yet tonight
I cannot; but at morrow rising sun
I will not fail. Go.—Woman, fare thee well.

Exeunt [*Hippolito and Servant*]

BELLAFRONT
The lowest fall can be but into hell.
It does not move him; I must therefore fly
From this undoing city, and with tears
Wash off all anger from my father's brow.
He cannot, sure, but joy seeing me new born.
A woman honest first, and then turn whore,
Is, as with me, common to thousands more;
But from a strumpet to turn chaste: that sound
Has oft been heard, that woman hardly found. *Exit*

Enter Fustigo [*with his head bound in a cloth*], *Crambo, and Poh*

FUSTIGO Hold up your hands, gentlemen: [*giving money*] here's one, two, three—nay, I warrant they are sound pistoles, and without flaws; I had them of my sister, and I know she uses to put up nothing that's cracked—three, four, five, six, seven, eight, and nine. By this hand, bring me but a piece of his blood and you shall have nine more. I'll lurk in a tavern not far off and provide supper to close up the end of the tragedy. The linen-draper's, remember. Stand to't, I beseech you, and play your parts perfectly.

CRAMBO Look you, signor, 'tis not your gold that we weigh.

FUSTIGO Nay, nay, weigh it and spare not; if it lack one grain of corn, I'll give you a bushel of wheat to make it up.

CRAMBO But by your favour, signor, which of the servants is it, because we'll punish justly.

FUSTIGO Marry, 'tis the head man—you shall taste him by his tongue—a pretty, tall prating fellow, with a Tuscalonian beard.

POH Tuscalonian? Very good.

FUSTIGO Cod's life, I was ne'er so thrummed since I was a gentleman; my coxcomb was dry-beaten as if my hair had been hemp.

CRAMBO We'll dry-beat some of them.

FUSTIGO Nay, it grew so high that my sister cried 'murder' out very manfully. I have her consent, in a manner, to have him peppered, else I'll not do't to win more than ten cheaters do at a rifling. Break but his pate or so, only his mazer, because I'll have his head in a cloth as well as mine—he's a linen-draper, and may take enough. I could enter mine action of battery against him, but we mayhaps be both dead and rotten before the lawyers would end it.

CRAMBO No more to do, but ensconce yourself i'th' tavern; provide no great cheer—couple of capons, some pheas-

178 **that** if
180 **physic for it** medicine to cure you of sinning
this book i.e. the skull
182–3 **He'll ... again** i.e. the skull will strike your sin dead by showing you that if you turn infidel again (return to whoredom), you cannot escape damnation.
191 **knaves ... smocks** i.e. women disguised as men
192 **enter** show in
196–7 **codpiece ... upon't** Alluding to a contemporary fashion; but also punning on *pins*/penis.
202–4 **I must ... brow** An intention not acted upon; Bellafront next appears in Bedlam.
203 **undoing** ruinous
208–9 **sound ... found** i.e. news of such transformations is frequently circulated, but is very rarely true
11.3 **pistoles** Spanish gold coins worth 16*s*. 6*d*. to 18*s*. each (with a possible pun on 'pizzles')
4 **she ... cracked** in allusion to a crack in the ring of a coin (with a bawdy reference to vagina), which would render it unacceptable as currency
put up stow away (with bawdy innuendo)
12–14 **if it lack ... make it up** i.e. if the amount Fustigo has given is short in the smallest degree, he will make amends by overcompensation
19 **Tuscalonian** Tuscan, i.e. golden yellow or straw-coloured—an instance of Fustigo's swaggering bombast
21 **Cod's** God's
22–3 **my coxcomb ... hemp** recorded by Edward Pudsey in his Commonplace Book: 'His coxcomb was dry-beaten as if his hair had been hemp'.
22 **dry-beaten** beaten as to dry clothes (*hemp* would require a lot of such beating)
23 **hemp** coarse, strong fibre used for rope and stout fabrics
24 **dry-beat** possibly with a pun on the sense 'beat severely without drawing blood'
27–8 **not do't ... rifling** recorded by Edward Pudsey in his Commonplace Book: 'not to win more than ten cheaters do at a rifling'
28 **cheaters** (*a*) false dice; (*b*) those who win money with false dice
rifling A gambling game in which the highest roll of the dice takes all money wagered.
29 **mazer** head, face
32 **mayhaps** may perhaps
34–6 **No more ... pie or so** Crambo asks Fustigo to order a meal with which to celebrate their success in the venture for which he and Poh have been hired.

ants, plovers, an orangeado pie or so. But how bloody soe'er the day be, sally you not forth.

FUSTIGO No, no; nay, if I stir, somebody shall stink. I'll not budge, I'll lie like a dog in a manger.

CRAMBO Well, well, to the tavern; let not our supper be raw, for you shall have blood enough—your bellyful.

FUSTIGO That's all, so God sa' me, I thirst after: blood for blood, bump for bump, nose for nose, head for head, plaster for plaster; and so farewell. What shall I call your names, because I'll leave word if any such come to the bar.

CRAMBO My name is Corporal Crambo.

POH And mine, Lieutenant Poh. *Exit*

CRAMBO Poh is as tall a man as ever opened oyster; I would not be the devil to meet Poh. Farewell.

FUSTIGO Nor I, by this light, if Poh be such a Poh.

Exeunt [Crambo following Poh, Fustigo at another door]

Sc. 12 *Enter [Viola,] Candido's Wife in her shop, and the two Prentices*

WIFE
What's o'clock now?

SECOND PRENTICE 'Tis almost twelve.

WIFE That's well.
The senate will leave wording presently,
But is George ready?

SECOND PRENTICE Yes, forsooth, he's furbished.

WIFE
Now as you ever hope to win my favour,
Throw both your duties and respects on him
With the like awe as if he were your master;
Let not your looks betray it with a smile
Or jeering glance to any customer;
Keep a true-settled countenance, and beware
You laugh not, whatsoever you hear or see.

SECOND PRENTICE I warrant you, mistress; let us alone for keeping our countenance; for if I list, there's never a fool in all Milan shall make me laugh, let him play the fool never so like an ass, whether it be the fat court fool, or the lean city fool.

WIFE
Enough, then, call down George.

SECOND PRENTICE I hear him coming.

WIFE
Be ready with your legs, then. Let me see
How court'sy would become him.—

Enter George [in Candido's apparel]

Gallantly!
Beshrew my blood, a proper seemly man,
Of a choice carriage, walks with a good port.

GEORGE I thank you, mistress; my back's broad enough, now my master's gown's on.

WIFE
Sure, I should think it were the least of sin
To mistake the master, and to let him in.

GEORGE 'Twere a good comedy of errors that, i'faith.

SECOND PRENTICE Whist, whist, my master.

WIFE You all know your tasks.

Enter Candido [dressed in the carpet], and exit presently

—God's my life, what's that he has got upon's back?
Who can tell?

GEORGE [*aside*] That can I, but I will not.

WIFE Girt about him like a madman. What, has he lost his cloak, too? This is the maddest fashion that e'er I saw. What said he, George, when he passed by thee?

GEORGE Troth, mistress, nothing; not so much as a bee, he did not hum; not so much as a bawd, he did not 'hem'; not so much as a cuckold, he did not 'ha'; neither hum, hem, nor ha; only stared me in the face, passed along, and made haste in, as if my looks had worked with him to give him a stool.

WIFE
Sure he's vexed now; this trick has moved his spleen.
He's angered now, because he uttered nothing;
And wordless wrath breaks out more violent.
Maybe he'll strive for place when he comes down;
But if thou lov'st me, George, afford him none.

GEORGE Nay, let me alone to play my master's prize, as long as my mistress warrants me. I'm sure I have his best clothes on, and I scorn to give place to any

36 **orangeado** candied orange-peel
38 **somebody shall stink** i.e. presumably as a result of a wound; but perhaps Fustigo threatens to damage Crambo's and Poh's reputations in the event of failure
39 **dog in a manger** churlish person who will neither use something himself nor allow others to do so (proverbial from Aesop's fable: Tilley D513)
47 **Crambo** a game in which one player gives a word to which each of the others must provide a rhyme
48 **Poh** an ejaculation of contemptuous rejection
49 **tall** brave, valiant
12.2 **wording** speaking, talking
5 **Throw . . . him** recorded by Edward Pudsey in his Commonplace Book: 'Throw your duties and respects on him'.
17 **legs** bows
18 **court'sy** in reference either to the bows of the two Prentices or to George's 'courteous comportment' in imitation of Candido, which Viola comments on in the remainder of the speech
24 **mistake . . . in** i.e. falsely suppose George to be the master and to admit him in that capacity
25 **comedy of errors** Possibly in allusion to Shakespeare's play, 2.2–3.1, in which Antipholus of Syracuse, mistaken for his twin, is allowed to enter, and the local Antipholus is kept at bay.
26 **Whist** a command for silence
35 **hem** clear one's throat (i.e. give a signal or warning such as bawds used)
38–9 **made haste . . . stool** recorded by Edward Pudsey in his Commonplace Book: 'made haste as though my looks had worked with him to give him a stool'
39 **give . . . stool** cause him to evacuate his bowels/send him to the privy
45 **play my master's prize** A quibble drawn from fencing, which had three degrees—in descending order, Master's, Provost's, Scholar's—each attained in a public prize or competition.

that is inferior in apparel to me; that's an axiom, a principle, and is observed as much as the fashion. Let that persuade you, then, that I'll shoulder with him for the upper hand in the shop, as long as this chain will maintain it.

WIFE Spoke with the spirit of a master, though with the tongue of a prentice.

Enter Candido like a prentice

Why, how now, madman? What, in your tricksy-coats?

CANDIDO O peace, good mistress.

Enter Crambo and Poh

See what you lack! What is't you buy? Pure callicoes, fine hollands, choice cambrics, neat lawns! See what you buy? Pray come near, my master will use you well, he can afford you a pennyworth.

WIFE Ay, that he can, out of a whole piece of lawn, i'faith.

CANDIDO Pray see your choice here, gentlemen.

WIFE O fine fool! What, a madman? A patient madman! Who ever heard of the like? Well, sir, I'll fit you and your humour presently. What? Cross-points?—I'll untie 'em all in a trice, I'll vex you, faith. Boy, take your cloak, quick, come. *Exit [with First Prentice]*

[George takes off his hat to Candido]

CANDIDO
Be covered, George; this chain and welted gown,
Bare to this coat? Then the world's upside down.

GEORGE Um, um, hum.

CRAMBO That's the shop, and there's the fellow.

POH Ay, but the master is walking in there.

CRAMBO No matter, we'll in.

POH 'Sblood, dost long to lie in limbo?

CRAMBO An limbo be in hell, I care not.

CANDIDO Look you, gentlemen, your choice: cambrics?

CRAMBO No, sir, some shirting.

CANDIDO You shall.

CRAMBO Have you none of this striped canvas for doublets?

CANDIDO None striped, sir, but plain.

SECOND PRENTICE I think there be one piece striped within.

GEORGE Step, sirrah, and fetch it, hum, hum, hum.

[Exit Candido and returns with cloth]

CANDIDO Look you, gentlemen, I'll make but one spreading; here's a piece of cloth—fine, yet shall wear like iron. 'Tis without fault, take this upon my word, 'tis without fault.

CRAMBO Then 'tis better than you, sirrah.

CANDIDO
Ay, and a number more. O, that each soul
Were but as spotless as this innocent white,
And had as few breaks in it.

CRAMBO 'Twould have some, then; there was a fray here last day in this shop.

CANDIDO
There was indeed a little flea-biting.

POH A gentleman had his pate broke: call you that but a flea-biting?

CANDIDO He had so.

CRAMBO Zounds, do you stand in't. *(He strikes him)*

GEORGE 'Sfoot, clubs, clubs! Prentices, down with 'em! Ah you rogues, strike a citizen in's shop?

[Prentices beat and disarm Crambo and Poh]

CANDIDO
None of you stir, I pray; forbear, good George.

CRAMBO I beseech you, sir, we mistook our marks; deliver us our weapons.

GEORGE Your head bleeds, sir; cry clubs.

CANDIDO
I say you shall not; pray be patïent.
Give them their weapons. Sirs, you're best be gone;
I tell you here are boys more tough than bears.
Hence, lest more fists do walk about your ears.

CRAMBO *and* POH
We thank you, sir. *Exeunt [Crambo and Poh]*

CANDIDO You shall not follow them;
Let them alone, pray; this did me no harm.
Troth, I was cold, and the blow made me warm,
I thank 'em for't. Besides, I had decreed
To have a vein pricked—I did mean to bleed—
So that there's money saved. They are honest men,
Pray use 'em well when they appear again.

GEORGE Yes, sir, we'll use 'em like honest men.

CANDIDO Ay, well said, George, like honest men, though they be arrant knaves, for that's the phrase of the city. Help to lay up these wares.

Enter [Viola,] Candido's Wife, with Officers

WIFE Yonder he stands.

48–9 **that's ... fashion** recorded by Edward Pudsey in his Commonplace Book: 'It is observed as a principle and as much as the fashion, not to give place to any that is inferior in apparel'.

55 **tricksy-coats** (*a*) prankish behaviour; (*b*) smart coats (ironic). *Coats* refers specifically to the garments (and station) of an apprentice.

65 **Cross-points** (*a*) a dance step in the galliard; (*b*) contrary intentions; (*c*) tagged laces used for fastening articles of clothing; (*d*) tricks

68 **Be covered** put your hat on

welted trimmed, fringed; or possibly, faced

70 **Um, um, hum** George is apparently at a loss for words and thereby registers his discomfort.

74 **limbo** i.e. jail (with a play on the literal sense, region bordering on hell)

75 **An** if

80 **but** only

84–5 **wear like iron** proverbial

91 **fray** fight, brawl (with a pun on a *fray* in the cloth)

93 **flea-biting** small hurt, damage (proverbial for wounds not worth speaking of; Tilley F355)

97 **stand in't** persist in your account

98 **clubs** the rallying cry of the London apprentices

101 **marks** targets

111 **decreed** decided

112 **bleed** i.e. deplete excess blood believed to be the source of an imbalance in the body's humours. Bleeding was often performed to reduce choler.

115 **honest men** Punning on its use as a vague term of praise, in patronizing reference to inferiors.

OFFICER What, in a prentice coat?

WIFE Ay, ay, mad, mad, pray take heed.

CANDIDO How now? What news with them? What make they with my wife? Officers? Is she attached?—Look to your wares.

WIFE He talks to himself; O, he's much gone indeed.

OFFICER Pray pluck up a good heart, be not so fearful.—
Sirs, hark, we'll gather to him by degrees.

WIFE Ay, ay, by degrees, I pray. O me! What makes he with the lawn in his hand, he'll tear all the ware in my shop.

OFFICER Fear not, we'll catch him on a sudden.

WIFE O, you had need do so; pray take heed of your warrant.

OFFICER I warrant, mistress.—Now, Signor Candido?

CANDIDO Now, sir, what news with you, sir?

WIFE
'What news with you?' he says; O, he's far gone.

OFFICER
I pray, fear nothing; let's alone with him.—
Signor, you look not like yourself, methinks;
[*Aside to Second Officer*] Steal you o' t'other side. [*To Candido*] You're changed, you're altered.

CANDIDO Changed, sir? Why true, sir; is change strange? 'Tis not the fashion unless it alter. Monarchs turn to beggars, beggars creep into the nests of princes, masters serve their prentices, ladies their servingmen, men turn to women.

OFFICER And women turn to men.

CANDIDO Ay, and women turn to men, you say true. Ha, ha, a mad world, a mad world.

[*Officers seize Candido*]

OFFICER Have we caught you, sir?

CANDIDO Caught me? Well, well, you have caught me.

WIFE He laughs in your faces.

GEORGE A rescue, prentices, my master's catchpoled!

OFFICER I charge you, keep the peace, or have your legs gartered with irons. We have from the Duke a warrant strong enough for what we do.

CANDIDO
I pray, rest quiet; I desire no rescue.

WIFE
La, he desires no rescue; 'las, poor heart,
He talks against himself.

CANDIDO Well, what's the matter?

OFFICER Look to that arm;
Pray make sure work, double the cord.

[*Officers bind Candido*]

CANDIDO Why, why?

WIFE
Look how his head goes! Should he get but loose,
O, 'twere as much as all our lives were worth.

OFFICER
Fear not, we'll make all sure for our own safety.

CANDIDO
Are you at leisure now? Well, what's the matter?
Why do I enter into bonds thus? Ha?

OFFICER
Because you're mad, put fear upon your wife.

WIFE
O, ay, I went in danger of my life every minute.

CANDIDO
What? Am I mad, say you, and I not know it?

OFFICER
That proves you mad, because you know it not.

WIFE
Pray talk as little to him as you can;
You see he's too far spent.

CANDIDO Bound with strong cord!
A sewster's thread, i'faith, had been enough
To lead me anywhere.—Wife, do you long?
You are mad too, or else you do me wrong.

GEORGE
But are you mad indeed, master?

CANDIDO My wife says so,
And what she says, George, is all truth, you know.—
And whither now? To Bethlem Monastery?
Ha, whither?

OFFICER Faith, e'en to the madmen's pound.

CANDIDO
O' God's name, still I feel my patience sound.

Exeunt [*Officers with Candido*]

GEORGE Come, we'll see whither he goes. If the master be mad, we are his servants, and must follow his steps; we'll be madcaps too. Farewell, mistress, you shall have us all in Bedlam. *Exeunt* [*George and Prentices*]

WIFE
I think I ha' fitted now, you and your clothes.
If this move not his patience, nothing can;
I'll swear then I have a saint, and not a man. *Exit*

122–3 **make they** are they doing
123 **attached** arrested
126 **pluck up ... heart** proverbial (Tilley H323)
127 **gather** make way (nautical term)
141–2 **Monarchs ... princes** Possibly alluding to the legendary African King Cophetua who disdained all women; finally he married a beggar who proved to be a fair and virtuous queen.
143–4 **turn to** (*a*) incline towards; (*b*) turn into, become
147 **a mad ... world** cf. the proverbial, 'a mad world, my masters' (Tilley W880); recorded by Edward Pudsey in his Commonplace Book: ''Tis a mad world'
151 **catchpoled** arrested (after 'catchpoles', the sheriffs' officers who made arrests, mainly for debt)
153 **gartered with irons** fettered
172 **sewster's** seamstress's
177 **Bethlem Monastery** the Hospital of the Priory of St Mary of Bethlehem, outside Bishopsgate, founded in 1246 and used as an asylum for lunatics from 1402
183 **Bedlam** corruption of Bethlem/Bethlehem

13 *Enter Duke, Doctor, Fluello, Castruccio, Pioratto*

DUKE
Give us a little leave.
[*Exeunt Fluello, Castruccio, Pioratto*]
Doctor, your news.

DOCTOR
I sent for him, my lord; at last he came
And did receive all speech that went from me
As gilded pills made to prolong his health.
My credit with him wrought it; for some men
Swallow even empty hooks, like fools that fear
No drowning where 'tis deepest 'cause 'tis clear.
In th' end we sat and ate; a health I drank
To Infelice's sweet departed soul.
This train I knew would take.

DUKE 'Twas excellent.

DOCTOR
He fell with such devotion on his knees,
To pledge the same—

DUKE Fond superstitious fool!

DOCTOR
That had he been inflamed with zeal of prayer,
He could not pour't out with more reverence.
About my neck he hung, wept on my cheek,
Kissed it, and swore he would adore my lips
Because they brought forth Infelice's name.

DUKE Ha, ha, alack, alack.

DOCTOR
The cup he lifts up high, and thus he said,
'Here, noble maid', drinks, and was poisonèd.

DUKE
And died?

DOCTOR And died, my lord.

DUKE Thou in that word
Hast pieced mine agèd hours out with more years
Than thou hast taken from Hippolito.
A noble youth he was, but lesser branches
Hind'ring the greater's growth must be lopped off
And feed the fire. Doctor, we're now all thine,
And use us so; be bold.

DOCTOR Thanks, gracious lord;
My honoured lord—

DUKE Hm.

DOCTOR
I do beseech your grace to bury deep
This bloody act of mine.

DUKE Nay, nay, for that,
Doctor, look you to't; me it shall not move.
They're cursed that ill do, not that ill do love.

DOCTOR
You throw an angry forehead on my face,
But be you pleased backward thus far to look:
That for your good this evil I undertook—

DUKE Ay, ay, we conster so.

DOCTOR And only for your love.

DUKE Confessed: 'tis true.

DOCTOR
Nor let it stand against me as a bar
To thrust me from your presence; nor believe,
As princes have quick thoughts, that now my finger
Being dipped in blood, I will not spare the hand,
But that for gold—as what can gold not do?—
I may be hired to work the like on you.

DUKE
Which to prevent—

DOCTOR 'Tis from my heart as far—

DUKE
No matter, doctor, 'cause I'll fearless sleep;
And that you shall stand clear of that suspicion,
I banish thee for ever from my court.
This principle is old, but true as fate:
Kings may love treason, but the traitor hate. *Exit*

DOCTOR
Is't so? Nay then, Duke, your stale principle
With one as stale the doctor thus shall quit:
He falls himself that digs another's pit;
Enter the Doctor's Man
How now! Where is he? Will he meet me?

DOCTOR'S MAN Meet you, sir? He might have met with three fencers in this time and have received less hurt than by meeting one doctor of physic. Why, sir, he's walked under the old abbey wall yonder this hour till he's more cold than a citizen's country house in January. You may smell him behind, sir; la, you, yonder he comes.

Enter Hippolito

DOCTOR Leave me.

DOCTOR'S MAN I'th' lurch, if you will. *Exit*

DOCTOR
O, my most noble friend!

HIPPOLITO Few but yourself
Could have enticed me thus, to trust the air
With my close sighs. You send for me—what news?

DOCTOR
Come, you must doff this black, dye that pale cheek
Into his own colour; go, attire yourself
Fresh as a bridegroom when he meets his bride.
The Duke has done much treason to thy love;
'Tis now revealed, 'tis now to be revenged.

13.10 **train** stratagem
22 **pieced...out** eked out, extended
24–6 **lesser...fire** recorded by Edward Pudsey in his Commonplace Book: 'Little branches hindering growth of the greater must be lopped off and thrown into the fire'
31 **for** as for
33 **They're cursed...love** Cf. the proverbial 'If you do no ill do no ill like' (Tilley I29).
37 **conster** interpret, construe
42 **As** as well you may believe, since; for indeed
51 **Kings...hate** proverbial (Tilley K64)
54 **He falls...pit** proverbial (Tilley P356)
59–60 **more cold...January** recorded by Edward Pudsey in his Commonplace Book: 'as cold as citizen's country house in January'
60 **citizen's...January** i.e. when it is uninhabited
61 **behind** in due time
68 **his** its

Be merry, honoured friend, thy lady lives.
HIPPOLITO
What lady?
DOCTOR Infelice. She's revived;
Revived? Alack! Death never had the heart
To take breath from her.
HIPPOLITO Um, I thank you, sir;
Physic prolongs life when it cannot save.
This helps not my hopes, mine are in their grave;
You do some wrong to mock me.
DOCTOR By that love
Which I have ever borne you, what I speak
Is truth: the maiden lives; that funeral,
Duke's tears, the mourning, was all counterfeit.—
A sleepy draught cozened the world and you;
I was his minister, and then chambered up
To stop discovery.
HIPPOLITO O, treacherous Duke!
DOCTOR
He cannot hope so certainly for bliss,
As he believes that I have poisoned you.
He wooed me to't; I yielded, and confirmed him
In his most bloody thoughts.
HIPPOLITO A very devil!
DOCTOR
Her did he closely coach to Bergamo,
And thither—
HIPPOLITO Will I ride. Stood Bergamo
In the low countries of black hell, I'll to her.
DOCTOR
You shall to her, but not to Bergamo.
How passion makes you fly beyond yourself.
Much of that weary journey I ha' cut off,
For she by letters hath intelligence
Of your supposèd death, her own interment,
And all those plots which that false Duke, her father,
Has wrought against you; and she'll meet you—
HIPPOLITO O when?
DOCTOR
Nay, see how covetous are your desires.—
Early tomorrow morn.
HIPPOLITO O where, good father?
DOCTOR
At Bethlem Monastery; are you pleased now?
HIPPOLITO
At Bethlem Monastery. The place well fits—
It is the school where those that lose their wits
Practise again to get them. I am sick
Of that disease; all love is lunatic.
DOCTOR
We'll steal away this night in some disguise.
Father Anselmo, a most reverend friar,
Expects our coming, before whom we'll lay
Reasons so strong that he shall yield in bands
Of holy wedlock to tie both your hands.
HIPPOLITO This is such happiness,
That to believe it, 'tis impossible.
DOCTOR
Let all your joys then die in misbelief;
I will reveal no more.
HIPPOLITO O yes, good father,
I am so well acquainted with despair
I know not how to hope; I believe all.
DOCTOR
We'll hence this night. Much must be done, much said,
But if the doctor fail not in his charms,
Your lady shall ere morning fill these arms.
HIPPOLITO
Heavenly physician! Far thy fame shall spread,
That mak'st two lovers speak when they be dead.
Exeunt

[Enter Viola,] Candido's Wife [with a paper], and George; Pioratto, [entering from another door,] meets them Sc.

WIFE O, watch, good George, watch which way the Duke comes.
GEORGE Here comes one of the butterflies; ask him.
WIFE Pray sir, comes the Duke this way?
PIORATTO He's upon coming, mistress.
WIFE I thank you, sir. *Exit [Pioratto]*
George, are there many madfolks where thy master lies?
GEORGE O yes, of all countries some, but especially mad Greeks—they swarm. Troth, mistress, the world is altered with you; you had not wont to stand thus with a paper humbly complaining. But you're well enough served; provender pricked you, as it does many of our city wives besides.
WIFE Dost think, George, we shall get him forth?
GEORGE Truly, mistress, I cannot tell; I think you'll hardly get him forth. Why, 'tis strange! 'Sfoot, I have known many women that have had mad rascals to their husbands, whom they would belabour by all means possible to keep 'em in their right wits; but of a woman to long to turn a tame man into a madman, why the devil himself was never used so by his dam.
WIFE How does he talk, George, ha? Good George, tell me.
GEORGE Why, you're best go see.

76 **Physic** medicine, the healing art
89 **closely** secretly
91 **low countries of black hell** prompted by Hippolito's characterization of the Duke as *A very devil* (13.88)
96 **interment** i.e. the burial following the funeral procession of Sc. 1, knowledge of which was kept from Infelice (3.83–6)
99 **covetous** eager
109 **yield** consent
bands bonds
14.3 **butterflies** courtiers
5 **upon** on the point of
8–9 **mad Greeks** prankish and frolicsome people
11 **complaining** lamenting, moaning
12 **provender pricked you** 'good food incited you'; i.e. your whim sprang from high feeding (proverbial: Tilley P615)
15 **hardly** (*a*) with trouble or hardship; (*b*) barely

WIFE Alas, I am afraid.

GEORGE Afraid! You had more need be ashamed; he may rather be afraid of you.

WIFE But, George, he's not stark mad, is he? He does not rave, he's not horn-mad, George, is he?

GEORGE Nay, I know not that, but he talks like a justice of peace, of a thousand matters and to no purpose.

WIFE I'll to the monastery. I shall be mad till I enjoy him, I shall be sick till I see him; yet when I do see him, I shall weep out mine eyes.

GEORGE Ay, I'd fain see a woman weep out her eyes; that's as true as to say a man's cloak burns when it hangs in the water. I know you'll weep, mistress; but what says the painted cloth?—

Trust not a woman when she cries,
For she'll pump water from her eyes
With a wet finger, and in faster showers
Than April when he rains down flowers.

WIFE Ay, but George, that painted cloth is worthy to be hanged up for lying. All women have not tears at will, unless they have good cause.

GEORGE Ay, but mistress, how easily will they find a cause; and as one of our cheese-trenchers says very learnedly:

As out of wormwood bees suck honey,
As from poor clients lawyers firk money,
As parsley from a roasted cony,
So, though the day be ne'er so sunny,
If wives will have it rain, down then it drives;
The calmest husbands make the stormiest wives.

WIFE True, George, but I ha' done storming now.

GEORGE Why, that's well done. Good mistress, throw aside this fashion of your humour, be not so fantastical in wearing it, storm no more, long no more. This longing has made you come short of many a good thing that you might have had from my master. Here comes the Duke.

Enter Duke, Fluello, Pioratto, Sinezi

WIFE [*to Duke*]
O, I beseech you, pardon my offence
In that I durst abuse your grace's warrant;
Deliver forth my husband, good my lord.

DUKE
Who is her husband?

FLUELLO Candido, my lord.

DUKE
Where is he?

WIFE He's among the lunatics.
He was a man made up without a gall;
Nothing could move him, nothing could convert
His meek blood into fury, yet like a monster
I often beat at the most constant rock
Of his unshaken patience, and did long
To vex him.

DUKE Did you so?

WIFE And for that purpose
Had warrant from your grace to carry him
To Bethlem Monastery, whence they will not free him
Without your grace's hand that sent him in.

DUKE
You have longed fair; 'tis you are mad, I fear.
It's fit to fetch him thence, and keep you there.
If he be mad, why would you have him forth?

GEORGE An please your grace, he's not stark mad, but only talks like a young gentleman, somewhat fantastically, that's all. There's a thousand about your court, city, and country, madder than he.

DUKE
Provide a warrant; you shall have our hand.

GEORGE Here's a warrant ready drawn, my lord.

DUKE Get pen and ink, get pen and ink. [*Exit George*]

Enter Castruccio

CASTRUCCIO
Where is my lord, the Duke?

DUKE How now? More madmen?

CASTRUCCIO
I have strange news, my lord.

DUKE Of what? Of whom?

CASTRUCCIO Of Infelice, and a marrïage.

DUKE
Ha! Where? With whom?

CASTRUCCIO Hippolito.

[*Enter George with pen and ink*]

GEORGE [*offering the pen*] Here, my lord.

DUKE Hence with that woman, void the room.

FLUELLO [*to Candido's Wife*] Away, the Duke's vexed.

28 **horn-mad** mad with rage (with a play on the horns of a cuckold)

29–30 **talks . . . purpose** recorded by Edward Pudsey in his Commonplace Book

31 **enjoy him** have his company

37 **painted cloth** imitation tapestry, painted with scriptural or allegorical scenes, and often embellished with verses by way of motto or epigraph

38 **Trust . . . cries** proverbial (Tilley W638)

40 **With a wet finger** easily, with little effort; without hesitation, readily. Here the *wet finger* suggests contribution to the impression of tears. See note to 2.4–5.

41 **rains down flowers** Probably in reference to the suddenness with which an abundance of flowers appear, 'sends down flowers like rain'; but 'beats down flowers with rain' may be possible.

42–3 **that . . . lying** recorded by Edward Pudsey in his Commonplace Book: 'Ay, but the painted cloth is worthy to be hanged for lying'

43 **hanged up** with a play on the capital punishment sense

46 **cheese-trenchers** commonly inscribed with sententious maxims

47 **wormwood** plant proverbial for its bitter taste

48 **firk** rob, cheat

49 **cony** rabbit

55 **fantastical** fanciful, capricious

56–7 **longing . . . thing** In addition to the primary common sense, 'earnest yearning', *longing* carries sexual innuendo picked up also in *come, short*, and *thing* (also wordplay on *long, longing*, and *short*).

57–8 **made you . . . had** recorded by Edward Pudsey in his Commonplace Book: 'make you come short of many a good thing you might have had'

73 **Without . . . hand** i.e. your written authorization

74 **fair** completely, fully

GEORGE Whoop, come mistress, the Duke's mad too.

Exeunt [*Candido's Wife and George*]

DUKE
Who told me that Hippolito was dead?

CASTRUCCIO He that can make any man dead, the doctor. But, my lord, he's as full of life as wildfire, and as quick. Hippolito, the doctor, and one more rid hence this evening; the inn at which they light is Bethlem Monastery. Infelice comes from Bergamo and meets them there. Hippolito is mad, for he means this day to be married; the afternoon is the hour, and Friar Anselmo is the knitter.

DUKE
From Bergamo? Is't possible? It cannot be,
It cannot be.

CASTRUCCIO I will not swear, my lord,
But this intelligence I took from one
Whose brains works in the plot.

DUKE What's he?

CASTRUCCIO Matteo.

FLUELLO
Matteo knows all.

PIORATTO He's Hippolito's bosom.

DUKE How far stands Bethlem hence?

ALL THE REST Six or seven miles.

DUKE Is't even so?
Not married till the afternoon, you say?
Stay, stay, let's work out some prevention. How?
This is most strange; can none but madmen serve
To dress their wedding dinner? All of you
Get presently to horse; disguise yourselves
Like country gentlemen,
Or riding citizens or so, and take
Each man a several path, but let us meet
At Bethlem Monastery, some space of time
Being spent between the arrival each of other,
As if we came to see the lunatics.
To horse, away; be secret on your lives.
Love must be punished that unjustly thrives.

Exeunt [*all but Fluello*]

FLUELLO
'Be secret on your lives!' Castruccio,
You're but a scurvy spaniel. Honest lord,
Good lady; zounds, their love is just, 'tis good,
And I'll prevent you, though I swim in blood. *Exit*

Enter Friar Anselmo, Hippolito, Matteo, Infelice

HIPPOLITO
Nay, nay, resolve, good father, or deny.

ANSELMO
You press me to an act both full of danger
And full of happiness; for I behold
Your father's frowns, his threats, nay, perhaps death
To him that dare do this. Yet, noble lord,
Such comfortable beams break through these clouds
By this blessed marriage that, your honoured word
Being pawned in my defence, I will tie fast
The holy wedding knot.

HIPPOLITO Tush, fear not the Duke.

ANSELMO
O son,
Wisely to fear is to be free from fear.

HIPPOLITO
You have our words, and you shall have our lives
To guard you safe from all ensuing danger.

MATTEO Ay, ay, chop 'em up, and away.

ANSELMO
Stay, when is't fit for me, safest for you,
To entertain this business?

HIPPOLITO Not till the evening.

ANSELMO
Be't so; there is a chapel stands hard by
Upon the west end of the abbey wall:
Thither convey yourselves, and when the sun
Hath turned his back upon this upper world
I'll marry you; that done, no thund'ring voice
Can break the sacred bond. Yet, lady, here
You are most safe.

INFELICE Father, your love's most dear.

MATTEO Ay, well said; lock us into some little room by ourselves, that we may be mad for an hour or two.

HIPPOLITO
O good Matteo, no, let's make no noise.

MATTEO How! No noise! Do you know where you are? 'Sfoot, amongst all the madcaps in Milan; so that to throw the house out at window will be the better, and no man will suspect that we lurk here to steal mutton. The more sober we are, the more scurvy 'tis. And though the friar tell us that here we are safest, I'm not of his mind, for if those lay here that had lost their money, none would ever look after them; but here are none but those that have lost their wits, so that if hue and cry be made, hither they'll come, and my reason is, because none goes to be married till he be stark mad.

95 **quick** speedy (punning on 'alive')
96 **light** arrive
105 **bosom** confidant
116 **several** separate, different
119 **As if . . . lunatics** a favourite contemporary pastime
123 **spaniel** alluding to the breed's fawning, ingratiating behaviour

15.0.1 *Anselmo* In opposing his sovereign, he shares a trait with St Anselm who repeatedly stood against Henry I.
1 **resolve** make up your mind (to it)
4 **Your** i.e. Infelice's
11 **Wisely . . . fear** proverbial (Tilley F135); recorded by Edward Pudsey in his Commonplace Book
14 **chop 'em up** i.e. clasp hands to seal the bargain
29 **throw . . . window** make a great disturbance in a house (proverbial: Tilley H785)
31 **mutton** wench (i.e. female flesh)
scurvy i.e. suspicious

Enter Fluello

HIPPOLITO Muffle yourselves, yonder's Fluello.

MATTEO Zounds!

FLUELLO O my lord, these cloaks are not for this rain; the tempest is too great. I come sweating to tell you of it, that you may get out of it.

MATTEO Why, what's the matter?

FLUELLO What's the matter! You have mattered it fair; the Duke's at hand.

ALL THE REST
The Duke?

FLUELLO The very Duke.

HIPPOLITO Then all our plots
Are turned upon our heads, and we are blown up
With our own underminings. 'Sfoot, how comes he?
What villain durst betray our being here?

FLUELLO Castruccio—Castruccio told the Duke, and Matteo here told Castruccio.

HIPPOLITO
Would you betray me to Castruccio?

MATTEO 'Sfoot, he damned himself to the pit of hell if he spake on't again.

HIPPOLITO
So did you swear to me, so were you damned.

MATTEO Pox on 'em, and there be no faith in men, if a man shall not believe oaths. He took bread and salt, by this light, that he would never open his lips.

HIPPOLITO
O God, O God!

ANSELMO Son, be not desperate,
Have patience; you shall trip your enemy down
By his own sleights.—How far is the Duke hence?

FLUELLO He's but new set out; Castruccio, Pioratto, and Sinezi come along with him. You have time enough yet to prevent them, if you have but courage.

ANSELMO
You shall steal secretly into the chapel,
And presently be married. If the Duke
Abide here still, spite of ten thousand eyes,
You shall 'scape hence like friars.

HIPPOLITO O blest disguise,
O happy man!

ANSELMO
Talk not of happiness till your closed hand
Have her by th' forehead, like the lock of time.
Be not too slow nor hasty now you climb
Up to the tower of bliss, only be wary
And patient, that's all. If you like my plot
Build and dispatch; if not, farewell, then not.

HIPPOLITO
O yes, we do applaud it. We'll dispute
No longer, but will hence and execute.
Fluello, you'll stay here; let us be gone.
The ground that frighted lovers tread upon
Is stuck with thorns.

ANSELMO Come then, away; 'tis meet
To escape those thorns, to put on wingèd feet.

Exeunt [Anselmo, Hippolito, and Infelice]

MATTEO
No words, I pray, Fluello, for it stands us upon.

FLUELLO O, sir, let that be your lesson. *[Exit Matteo]*
Alas, poor lovers! On what hopes and fears
Men toss themselves for women! When she's got,
The best has in her that which pleaseth not.

Enter to Fluello, the Duke, Castruccio, Pioratto, and Sinezi from several doors, muffled

DUKE
Who's there?

CASTRUCCIO My lord.

DUKE Peace, send that 'lord' away,
A lordship will spoil all; let's be all fellows.
What's he?

CASTRUCCIO Fluello, or else Sinezi, by his little legs.

ALL THE REST All friends, all friends.

DUKE
What, met upon the very point of time?
Is this the place?

PIORATTO This is the place, my lord.

DUKE
Dream you on lordships? Come, no more 'lords', pray.
You have not seen these lovers yet?

ALL THE REST Not yet.

DUKE
Castruccio, art thou sure this wedding feat
Is not till afternoon?

CASTRUCCIO So 'tis given out, my lord.

DUKE
Nay, nay, 'tis like: thieves must observe their hours;
Lovers watch minutes like astronomers.
How shall the interim hours by us be spent?

FLUELLO
Let's all go see the madmen.

40 **these cloaks . . . rain** 'To have a cloak for the rain' is proverbial for 'to have an alibi for one's actions' (Tilley C417).

40–1 **these cloaks . . . great** recorded by Edward Pudsey in his Commonplace Book

44 **mattered it fair** made a fine matter of it

57 **took bread and salt** swore (i.e. ate it, to confirm his oath)

61 **sleights** subtle schemes

64 **prevent** anticipate

66 **presently** immediately

70–1 **closed hand . . . time** Alluding to the emblematic and proverbial representation of Time (originally 'opportunity') with a full shock of hair in the front but bald behind, signifying the necessity of taking advantage of an occasion when it arises and not delaying until it has passed (Tilley T311).

76 **dispute** discuss

82 **it stands us upon** it (the scheme) depends on us

83 **O, sir . . . lesson** Fluello, mindful of the earlier lapse, replies that silence should be Matteo's concern.

99 **like** probable

100 **Lovers . . . astronomers** recorded by Edward Pudsey in his Commonplace Book: 'Lovers observe very minutes (for meeting) like astronomers'.

ALL THE REST Mass, content.

Enter [the player,] Thomas Towne, like a Sweeper

DUKE
O, here comes one; question him, question him.

FLUELLO How now, honest fellow, dost thou belong to the house?

SWEEPER Yes, forsooth, I am one of the implements; I sweep the madmen's rooms, and fetch straw for 'em, and buy chains to tie 'em, and rods to whip 'em. I was a mad wag myself here once, but I thank Father Anselm, he lashed me into my right mind again.

DUKE
Anselmo is the friar must marry them.
[*To Castruccio*] Question him where he is.

CASTRUCCIO And where is Father Anselmo now?

SWEEPER Marry, he's gone but e'en now.

DUKE
Ay, well done. Tell me, whither is he gone?

SWEEPER Why, to God A'mighty.

FLUELLO Ha, ha, this fellow is a fool, talks idly.

PIORATTO [*to the Sweeper*] Sirrah, are all the mad folks in Milan brought hither?

SWEEPER How, all? There's a wise question indeed; why, if all the mad folks in Milan should come hither, there would not be left ten men in the city.

DUKE Few gentlemen or courtiers here, ha?

SWEEPER O, yes, abundance, abundance. Lands no sooner fall into their hands but straight they run out o' their wits. Citizens' sons and heirs are free of the house by their fathers' copy; farmers' sons come hither like geese in flocks, and when they ha' sold all their cornfields, here they sit and pick the straws.

SINEZI Methinks you should have women here as well as men.

SWEEPER O, ay, a plague on 'em; there's no ho with them, they are madder than march hares.

FLUELLO Are there no lawyers here amongst you?

SWEEPER O, no, not one; never any lawyer. We dare not let a lawyer come in, for he'll make 'em mad faster than we can recover 'em.

DUKE And how long is't ere you recover any of these?

SWEEPER Why, according to the quantity of the moon that's got into 'em, an alderman's son will be mad a great while, a very great while, especially if his friends left him well; a whore will hardly come to her wits again; a puritan—there's no hope of him unless he may pull down the steeple and hang himself i'th'bell-ropes.

FLUELLO I perceive all sorts of fish come to your net.

SWEEPER Yes, in truth, we have blocks for all heads; we have good store of wild oats here, for the courtier is mad at the citizen, the citizen is mad at the countryman, the shoemaker is mad at the cobbler, the cobbler at the carman, the punk is mad that the merchant's wife is no whore, the merchant's wife is mad that the punk is so common a whore.

Enter Anselmo [and Servants]

Gods-so, here's Father Anselm; pray say nothing that I tell tales out of the school. *Exit*

ALL THE VISITORS
God bless you, father.

ANSELMO Thank you, gentlemen.

CASTRUCCIO
Pray, may we see some of those wretched souls
That here are in your keeping?

ANSELMO Yes, you shall;
But gentlemen, I must disarm you then.
There are of madmen, as there are of tame,
All humoured not alike; we have here some
So apish and fantastic play with a feather,
And, though 'twould grieve a soul to see God's image
So blemished and defaced, yet do they act
Such antic and such pretty lunacies
That spite of sorrow they will make you smile.
Others again we have like hungry lions,
Fierce as wild bulls, untameable as flies,
And these have oftentimes from strangers' sides
Snatched rapiers suddenly and done much harm,
Whom, if you'll see, you must be weaponless.

ALL THE VISITORS
With all our hearts.
[*They disarm*]

ANSELMO [*to a Servant*]
Here, take these weapons in.—
[*Exit Servant with the weapons*]
Stand off a little, pray—so, so, 'tis well.
I'll show you here a man that was sometimes
A very grave and wealthy citizen;
He's served a prenticeship to this misfortune,
Been here seven years, and dwelt in Bergamo.

DUKE
How fell he from himself?

ANSELMO By loss at sea.
I'll stand aside; question him you alone,
For if he spy me, he'll not speak a word

102 **Mass** 'by the mass', a mild oath

102.1 ***Towne . . . Sweeper*** Thomas Towne, an actor with the Admiral's (later Prince Henry's) Men, 1594–1610

108 **rods . . . 'em** i.e. as part of the cure

117 **idly** incoherently, deliriously

126 **free of the house** possessed of certain rights and privileges within the house

127 **copy** with a pun on (*a*) abundance; and (*b*) in reference to rights granted by the fathers' possession of copyhold or a transcript of documents establishing their status as landowners or householders

132 **ho** end, stopping

133 **madder than march hares** proverbial (Tilley H148)

139 **moon** alluding to the *moon*'s supposed influence over mad persons (preserved in *luna*tics)

142 **left him well** i.e. left him well provided for by legacy or inheritance

146 **blocks** moulds for making hats (quibbling on 'blockhead')

147 **mad** 'angry', with a play on 'insane'

150 **carman** carrier, carter

154 **tell tales . . . school** proverbial (Tilley T54)

164 **antic** fantastic

173 **sometimes** formerly

176 **seven years** the term of apprenticeship

Unless he's throughly vexed.

[He] discovers [a Madman]: an old man, wrapped in a net

FLUELLO Alas, poor soul.

CASTRUCCIO A very old man.

DUKE [*to First Madman*] God speed, father.

FIRST MADMAN God speed the plough, thou shalt not speed me.

PIORATTO We see you, old man, for all you dance in a net.

FIRST MADMAN True, but thou wilt dance in a halter, and I shall not see thee.

ANSELMO O, do not vex him, pray.

CASTRUCCIO Are you a fisherman, father?

FIRST MADMAN No, I'm neither fish nor flesh.

FLUELLO What do you with that net then?

FIRST MADMAN Dost not see, fool? There's a fresh salmon in't; if you step one foot further, you'll be over shoes, for you see I'm over head and ear in the salt water; and if you fall into this whirlpool where I am, you're drowned, you're a drowned rat.—I am fishing here for five ships, but I cannot have a good draught, for my net breaks still, and breaks; but I'll break some of your necks an I catch you in my clutches. Stay, stay, stay, stay, stay; where's the wind, where's the wind, where's the wind, where's the wind? Out, you gulls, you goosecaps, you gudgeon-eaters! Do you look for the wind in the heavens? Ha, ha, ha, ha! No, no! Look there, look there, look there, the wind is always at that door; hark how it blows, pooff, pooff, pooff.

ALL THE VISITORS Ha, ha, ha!

FIRST MADMAN Do you laugh at God's creatures? Do you mock old age, you rogues? Is this grey beard and head counterfeit, that you cry 'ha, ha, ha'?—Sirrah, art not thou my eldest son?

PIORATTO Yes indeed, father.

FIRST MADMAN Then thou'rt a fool, for my eldest son had a polt-foot, crooked legs, a verjuice face, and a pear-coloured beard. I made him a scholar, and he made himself a fool.—[*To Duke*] Sirrah! Thou there! Hold out thy hand.

DUKE My hand? Well, here 'tis.

FIRST MADMAN Look, look, look, look: has he not long nails, and short hair?

FLUELLO Yes, monstrous short hair, and abominable long nails.

FIRST MADMAN Tenpenny nails are they not?

FLUELLO Yes, tenpenny nails.

FIRST MADMAN Such nails had my second boy. Kneel down, thou varlet, and ask thy father blessing.

[Duke kneels]

Such nails had my middlemost son, and I made him a promoter; and he scraped, and scraped, and scraped, till he got the devil and all; but he scraped thus, and thus, and thus, and it went under his legs, till at length a company of kites, taking him for carrion, swept up all, all, all, all, all, all, all.

[Duke rises]

If you love your lives, look to yourselves. See, see, see, see, the Turk's galleys are fighting with my ships! 'Bounce!' goes the guns; 'O, O, O!' cry the men; 'Rumble, rumble!' go the waters.—Alas! There! 'Tis sunk—'tis sunk! I am undone, I am undone; you are the damned pirates have undone me—you are, by th' Lord, you are, you are!—Stop 'em!—You are!

ANSELMO Why, how now, sirrah, must I fall to tame you?

FIRST MADMAN Tame me? No, I'll be madder than a roasted cat. See, see, I am burnt with gunpowder.—These are our close fights.

ANSELMO I'll whip you if you grow unruly thus.

FIRST MADMAN Whip me? Out, you toad!—Whip me? What justice is this to whip me because I'm a beggar?—Alas, I am a poor man, a very poor man. I am starved and have had no meat, by this light, ever since the great flood. I am a poor man.

ANSELMO Well, well, be quiet, and you shall have meat.

FIRST MADMAN Ay, ay, pray do; for look you, [*holding out the net*] here be my guts: these are my ribs—you may look through my ribs—see how my guts come out—these are my red guts, my very guts, O, O!

180.1 ***discovers*** i.e. by opening the curtains of the discovery space

184 **God speed the plough** i.e. God prosper the plough (proverbial: Tilley G223)

186 **dance in a net** The proverb, 'You dance in a net and think nobody sees you', meant 'to act with practically no disguise while expecting to escape notice' (Tilley N130).

187 **halter** rope for hanging malefactors

190 **fisherman** understood by First Madman as 'fish or man'

191 **neither ... flesh** proverbial (Tilley F319)

193 **fresh salmon** playing on the sense 'dupe, prey' (often with sexual suggestion)

194 **over shoes** deeply immersed

195 **salt water** playing on the sense 'tears'

198 **draught** catch, quantity taken with one drawing of the net

203 **goosecaps** boobies, fools

gudgeon-eaters gullible persons (a *gudgeon* is a small fish used for bait)

214 **polt-foot** club-foot

verjuice sour, crabbed

214–15 **pear-coloured** i.e. russet-red

215–16 **I made ... fool** recorded by Edward Pudsey in his Commonplace Book: 'His friends made him a scholar, and he made himself a fool'.

223 **Tenpenny nails** large nails sold at tenpence a hundred

228 **promoter** informer

231 **kites** rapacious persons, sharpers (playing also on the literal sense: birds of prey)

234 **galleys** low flat-built sea-going vessels with one deck

235 **Bounce!** bang!

240 **fall to** set to work, begin

243 **close fights** defensive structures erected as citadels on the decks of ships in anticipation of boarding engagements; First Madman presumably makes reference to the discovery space and imagines a skirmish with Anselmo as such an encounter.

248–9 **the great flood** i.e. the flood Noah survived (Genesis 7:17–24), an originating moment in human history; confused by the old man with his loss at sea

ANSELMO [*to a Servant*] Take him in there.
[*Exit Servant with First Madman*]

ALL THE VISITORS A very piteous sight.

CASTRUCCIO
Father, I see you have a busy charge.

ANSELMO
They must be used like children: pleased with toys,
And anon whipped for their unruliness.
I'll show you now a pair quite different
From him that's gone; he was all words, and these,
Unless you urge 'em, seldom spend their speech,
But save their tongues.
[*Enter Second Madman, and Third Madman with food and drink*]
La, you.—This hithermost
Fell from the happy quietness of mind
About a maiden that he loved, and died.
He followed her to church, being full of tears,
And as her body went into the ground
He fell stark mad. That is a married man
Was jealous of a fair but, as some say,
A very virtuous wife; and that spoiled him.

SECOND MADMAN All these are whoremongers, and lay with my wife: whore, whore, whore, whore, whore.

FLUELLO Observe him.

SECOND MADMAN Gaffer shoemaker, you pulled on my wife's pumps, and then crept into her pantofles; lie there, lie there.—This was her tailor—you cut out her loose-bodied gown, and put in a yard more than I allowed her; lie there by the shoemaker.—O, master doctor! Are you here? You gave me a purgation, and then crept into my wife's chamber to feel her pulses, and you said, and she said, and her maid said that they went pit-a-pat, pit-a-pat, pit-a-pat.—Doctor, I'll put you anon into my wife's urinal.—Hey, come aloft, Jack! This was her schoolmaster, and taught her to play upon the virginals, and still his jacks leapt up, up. You pricked her out nothing but bawdy lessons, but I'll prick you all—fiddler—doctor—tailor—shoemaker—shoemaker—fiddler—doctor—tailor—so! Lie with my wife again, now.

CASTRUCCIO See how he notes the other, now he feeds.

SECOND MADMAN Give me some porridge.

THIRD MADMAN I'll give thee none.

SECOND MADMAN Give me some porridge.

THIRD MADMAN I'll not give thee a bit.

SECOND MADMAN Give me that flap-dragon.

THIRD MADMAN I'll not give thee a spoonful. Thou liest, it's no dragon, 'tis a parrot that I bought for my sweetheart, and I'll keep it.

SECOND MADMAN Here's an almond for parrot.

THIRD MADMAN Hang thyself.

SECOND MADMAN Here's a rope for parrot.

THIRD MADMAN Eat it, for I'll eat this.

SECOND MADMAN I'll shoot at thee an thou't give me none.

THIRD MADMAN Woo't thou?

SECOND MADMAN I'll run a-tilt at thee an thou't give me none.

THIRD MADMAN Woo't thou? Do, an thou dar'st.

SECOND MADMAN Bounce!

THIRD MADMAN O! O! I am slain!—Murder, murder, murder! I am slain, my brains are beaten out.

ANSELMO How now, you villains?—[*To a Servant*] Bring me whips.—[*To Madmen*] I'll whip you.

THIRD MADMAN I am dead, I am slain! Ring out the bell, for I am dead.

DUKE [*to Second Madman*] How will you do now, sirrah? You ha' killed him.

SECOND MADMAN I'll answer't at sessions; he was eating of almond-butter, and I longed for't. The child had never been delivered out of my belly if I had not killed him. I'll answer't at sessions, so my wife may be burnt i'th'hand too.

ANSELMO [*to a Servant*] Take 'em in both; bury him, for he's dead.

THIRD MADMAN Ay, indeed, I am dead; put me, I pray, into a good pit hole.

SECOND MADMAN I'll answer't at sessions.
Exeunt [*Servant with Second and Third Madmen*]
Enter Bellafront, mad

ANSELMO How now, housewife, whither gad you?

BELLAFRONT A-nutting, forsooth. How do you, gaffer? How do you, gaffer? There's a French curtsy for you, too.

FLUELLO 'Tis Bellafront.

257 **charge** (*a*) order; (*b*) care, custody
274 **Gaffer** title of address, often with no intimation of respect
275 **pumps** single-soled, low-cut shoes generally unsuitable for streetwear (but here suggesting sexual conquest)
pantofles high, cork-soled shoes, with open backs, slipped on over *pumps* (here suggesting stealthy sexual transgression)
276 **tailor** Tailors had a reputation for lechery.
277 **yard** punning on the sense 'penis'
280 **chamber** punning on the sense 'vagina'
283–4 **come aloft, Jack** the master's cry to a trained ape (with bawdy innuendo)
285 **virginals** keyed instrument of the harpsichord class (with sexual innuendo)
jacks upright pieces of wood (in the virginals) connected to the key-lever; when the keys were depressed the *jacks* rose causing quills fitted to them to pluck the strings (with bawdy innuendo)
286 **pricked** wrote down in musical notation (with bawdy innuendo)
287 **prick** grieve, torment (with a play on *pricked*)
295 **flap-dragon** a raisin floating in a cup of flaming liquor
299–301 **an almond . . . rope for parrot** phrases commonly taught to parrots
303 **thou't** contraction of 'thou woo't' = 'thou wilt'
304 **Woo't** wilt
317 **sessions** quarter-sessions (i.e. in a law court)
318 **almond-butter** a preparation of cream and whites of eggs boiled, to which are added blanched almonds
320 **burnt i'th'hand** branded as a felon
327 **housewife** hussy, wench
328 **A-nutting** nut-gathering; but possibly with a glance at a romantic sense from *nutting* in contemporary use as a term of affection; in either sense presumably intended as a token of insanity
gaffer my good fellow, old fellow
329 **French curtsy** venereal disease, the French pox (coupled with an actual curtsy)

PIORATTO 'Tis the punk, by th'Lord.

DUKE
Father, what's she, I pray?

ANSELMO As yet I know not;
She came but in this day, talks little idly,
And therefore has the freedom of the house.

BELLAFRONT Do not you know me? Nor you? Nor you, nor you?

ALL THE VISITORS No, indeed.

BELLAFRONT Then you are an ass, and you are an ass, and you are an ass, for I know you.

ANSELMO Why, what are they? Come, tell me, what are they?

BELLAFRONT Three fishwives; will you buy any gudgeons?

Enter Hippolito, Matteo, and Infelice, disguised in the habits of friars

God's santy, yonder come friars; I know them too.—
How do you, friar?

ANSELMO
Nay, nay, away, you must not trouble friars.
[*Aside to Hippolito, Matteo, Infelice*] The Duke is here; speak nothing.

BELLAFRONT Nay, indeed, you shall not go: we'll run at barley-break first, and you shall be in hell.

MATTEO [*aside*] My punk turned mad whore, as all her fellows are?

HIPPOLITO [*aside to Infelice and Matteo*]
Speak nothing, but steal hence when you spy time.

ANSELMO [*to Bellafront*]
I'll lock you up if you're unruly, fie.

BELLAFRONT Fie! Marry, faugh! They shall not go, indeed, till I ha' told 'em their fortunes.

DUKE Good father, give her leave.

BELLAFRONT Ay, pray, good father, and I'll give you my blessing.

ANSELMO Well then, be brief, but if you are thus unruly, I'll have you locked up fast.

PIORATTO Come, to their fortunes.

BELLAFRONT Let me see: one, two, three, and four.—I'll begin with the little friar first. [*To Infelice*] Here's a fine hand indeed, I never saw friar have such a dainty hand: here's a hand for a lady, you ha' good fortune now.
O see, see, what a thread here's spun;
You love a friar better than a nun,
Yet long you'll love no friar, nor no friar's son.

[*Infelice*] *bows a little*

The line of life is out, yet I'm afraid,
For all you're holy, you'll not die a maid.
God give you joy.—Now to you, Friar Tuck.

MATTEO God send me good luck.

BELLAFRONT
You love one, and one loves you.
You are a false knave, and she's a Jew;
Here is a dial that false ever goes.

MATTEO
O, your wit drops.

BELLAFRONT Troth, so does your nose.
[*To Hippolito*] Nay, let's shake hands with you, too: pray open,
Here's a fine hand. Ho, friar, ho, God be here,
So He had need. You'll keep good cheer;
Here's a free table, but a frozen breast,
For you'll starve those that love you best.
Yet you have good fortune, for if I am no liar,

[*She*] *discovers them*

Then you are no friar, nor you, nor you, no friar.
Ha ha, ha ha.

DUKE
Are holy habits cloaks for villainy?
Draw all your weapons.

HIPPOLITO Do, draw all your weapons.

DUKE Where are your weapons? Draw.

ALL THE GALLANTS
The friar has gulled us of 'em.

MATTEO O, rare trick!
You ha' learned one mad point of arithmetic.

HIPPOLITO
Why swells your spleen so high? Against what bosom
Would you your weapons draw? Hers? 'Tis your daughter's.
Mine? 'Tis your son's.

DUKE Son?

MATTEO Son, by yonder sun.

HIPPOLITO [*to Duke*]
You cannot shed blood here but 'tis your own;
To spill your own blood were damnatïon.
Lay smooth that wrinkled brow, and I will throw
Myself beneath your feet;
Let it be rugged still and flinted o'er,
What can come forth but sparkles that will burn

342 **gudgeons** small fish used for bait (one who takes a *gudgeon* is a fool)
343 **santy** perhaps a corruption of 'sanctity'
348 **barley-break ... hell** A country game played originally by three couples, one at either end of a field and the third in the centre, termed 'hell'. The couples at the field's ends try to cross from one side to the other and are permitted to separate or 'break' when challenged by the central pair, and to switch partners in the process, but if caught by the occupants of 'hell' must exchange places with them. The game continues until all the couples have taken a turn in 'hell'.
349–50 **My punk ... are** possibly in allusion to the effects of syphilis
362 **little friar** i.e. Infelice
370 **Friar Tuck** Robin Hood's friar (who, like Matteo in his disguise, was not all his gown indicated)
373 **Jew** a term of opprobrium: a wicked person
374 **dial** (indicating Matteo's face)
375 **your wit drops** Cf. the proverbial 'His wit is in the wane' (Tilley W555). **so ... nose** i.e. probably either inclining his head in shame or to conceal his face more fully in the cowl of the friar's habit
377 **Ho** exclamation of surprise
379 **table** punning on the sense 'palm'
380 **For ... best** in allusion to Hippolito's rejection of her love
389 **spleen** anger
396 **it** i.e. your brow
397 **sparkles** sparks

Yourself and us? She's mine; my claim's most good;
She's mine by marriage, though she's yours by blood.

ANSELMO [*kneeling to Duke*]
I have a hand, dear lord, deep in this act,
For I foresaw this storm, yet willingly
Put forth to meet it. Oft have I seen a father
Washing the wounds of his dear son in tears,
A son to curse the sword that struck his father,
Both slain i'th'quarrel of your families.
Those scars are now ta'en off; and I beseech you,
To seal our pardon. All was to this end:
To turn the ancient hates of your two houses
To fresh green friendship, that your loves might look
Like the spring's forehead, comfortably sweet,
And your vexed souls in peaceful union meet.
Their blood will now be yours, yours will be theirs,
And happiness shall crown your silver hairs.

FLUELLO [*to Duke*]
You see, my lord, there's now no remedy.

ALL THE GALLANTS [*to Duke*] Beseech your lordship.

DUKE
You beseech fair; you have me in place fit
To bridle me.—Rise friar, you may be glad
You can make madmen tame, and tame men mad.
Since fate hath conquered, I must rest content;
To strive now would but add new punishment.
I yield unto your happiness. Be blest.
Our families shall henceforth breathe in rest.

ALL THE GALLANTS
O happy change!

DUKE Yours now is my content;
I throw upon your joys my full consent.

BELLAFRONT Am not I a fine fortune-teller? God's me, you are a brave man; will not you buy me some sugar plums for telling how the friar was i'th'well, will you not?

DUKE
Would thou hadst wit, thou pretty soul, to ask,
As I have will to give.

BELLAFRONT Pretty soul! A pretty soul is better than a pretty body. Do not you know my pretty soul?

MATTEO No.

BELLAFRONT Look, fine man—nay? I know you all by your noses; he was mad for me once, and I was mad for him once, and he was mad for her once, and were you never mad? Yes, I warrant. Is not your name Matteo?

MATTEO Yes, lamb.

BELLAFRONT Lamb! Baa! Am I lamb? There you lie: I am mutton. I had a fine jewel once, a very fine jewel, and that naughty man stole it away from me, fine jewel, a very fine jewel.

DUKE What jewel, pretty maid?

BELLAFRONT Maid, nay, that's a lie.—O, 'twas a golden jewel, hark, 'twas called a maidenhead, and that naughty man had it, had you not, leerer?

MATTEO
Out, you mad ass, away!

DUKE Had he thy maidenhead?
He shall make thee amends and marry thee.

BELLAFRONT Shall he? [*Singing*] 'O, brave Arthur of Bradley then, shall he!'

DUKE
And if he bear the mind of a gentleman,
I know he will.

MATTEO I think I rifled her of some such paltry jewel.

DUKE
Did you? Then marry her; you see the wrong
Has led her spirits into a lunacy.

MATTEO How, marry her, my lord? 'Sfoot, marry a madwoman? Let a man get the tamest wife he can come by, she'll be mad enough afterward, do what he can.

DUKE
Father Anselmo here shall do his best
To bring her to her wits, and will you then?

MATTEO I cannot tell, I may choose.

DUKE
Nay, then, law shall compel. I tell you, sir,
So much her hard fate moves me, you should not breathe
Under this air unless you married her.

MATTEO
Well, then, when her wits stand in their right place
I'll marry her.

BELLAFRONT
I thank your grace.—Matteo, thou art mine!
I am not mad, but put on this disguise
[*To Hippolito*] Only for you, my lord; for you can tell
Much wonder of me; but you are gone: farewell.
Matteo, thou first mad'st me black, now make me
White as before; [*kneeling*] I vow to thee I'm now
As chaste as infancy, pure as Cynthia's brow.

HIPPOLITO
I durst be sworn, Matteo, she's indeed.

MATTEO
Cony-catched, gulled! Must I sail in your fly-boat
Because I helped to rear your main-mast first?
Plague 'found you for't.—'Tis well.

427 **the friar was i'th'well** Alluding to a popular ballad of a friar's attempted seduction of a maid. Taking his money while keeping him at bay, the girl resolves to trick him. He duly falls down a well thinking to escape her father. At length she rescues him, but refuses to return the money.

434 **noses** i.e. inclining heads (in shame); possibly punning on the 'noes' received in answer to her questioning if any knows her. Also the noses are the only features clearly visible on account of the friar's habits (with phallic innuendo).

439 **mutton** prostitute

448–9 **'O, brave Arthur . . . shall he'** refrain of a popular ballad about this character's wedding; see *Companion*, p. 139

466 **I thank your grace** Whether Bellafront removes any part of her disguise as a madwoman is not clear, but probable.

472 **Cynthia's** i.e. Diana's, alluding to the maiden goddess of chastity

474 **fly-boat** a light, fast sailing vessel (with the innuendo of female genitals)

475 **main-mast** (with innuendo of penis)

476 **'found** confound

The cuckold's stamp goes current in all nations;
Some men have horns given them at their creations:
If I be one of those, why so; it's better
To take a common wench, and make her good,
Than one that simpers and at first will scarce
Be tempted forth over the threshold door,
Yet in one sennight, zounds, turns arrant whore.
Come wench, thou shalt be mine, give me thy golls,
[*Raising her*] We'll talk of legs hereafter.—See, my lord,
God give us joy.

ALL THE REST God give you joy.

Enter [Viola,] Candido's Wife and George

GEORGE Come, mistress, we are in Bedlam now, mass, and see, we come in pudding-time, for here's the Duke.

WIFE My husband, good my lord.

DUKE Have I thy husband?

CASTRUCCIO It's Candido, my lord, he's here among the lunatics; Father Anselmo, pray fetch him forth.

[*Exit Anselmo*]

This madwoman is his wife, and though she were not with child, yet did she long most spitefully to have her husband, that was as patient as Job, to be more mad than ever was Orlando; and because she would be sure he should turn Jew, she placed him here in Bethlem. Yonder he comes.

Enter Candido with Anselmo

DUKE Come hither, signor.—Are you mad?

CANDIDO You are not mad.

DUKE Why, I know that.

CANDIDO
Then may you know I am not mad, that know
You are not mad, and that you are the Duke.
None is mad here but one.—How do you, wife?
What do you long for now?—Pardon, my lord.

DUKE
Why, signor, came you hither?

CANDIDO O my good lord!
She had lost her child's nose else. I did cut out
Pennyworths of lawn—the lawn was yet mine own;
A carpet was my gown, yet 'twas mine own;
I wore my man's coat, yet the cloth mine own;
Had a cracked crown, the crown was yet mine own.
She says for this I'm mad; were her words true,
I should be mad indeed.—O foolish skill!
Is patience madness? I'll be a madman still.

WIFE [*kneeling*]
Forgive me, and I'll vex your spirit no more.

DUKE
Come, come, we'll have you friends; join hearts, join hands.

CANDIDO See, my lord, we are even.
[*To Wife*] Nay, rise, for ill deeds kneel unto none but heaven.

DUKE
Signor, methinks patience has laid on you
Such heavy weight that you should loathe it.

CANDIDO Loathe it?

DUKE
For he whose breast is tender, blood so cool
That no wrongs heat it, is a patient fool.
What comfort do you find in being so calm?

CANDIDO
That which green wounds receive from sovereign balm.
Patience, my lord, why, 'tis the soul of peace.
Of all the virtues, 'tis near'st kin to heaven.
It makes men look like gods; the best of men
That e'er wore earth about him was a sufferer:
A soft, meek, patient, humble, tranquil spirit,
The first true gentleman that ever breathed.
The stock of patience, then, cannot be poor.
All it desires, it has; what monarch more?
It is the greatest enemy to law
That can be, for it doth embrace all wrongs,
And so chains up lawyers' and women's tongues.
'Tis the perpetual prisoner's liberty,
His walks, and orchards. 'Tis the bondslave's freedom,
And makes him seem proud of each iron chain,
As though he wore it more for state than pain.
It is the beggar's music, and thus sings,
Although their bodies beg, their souls are kings.
O my dread liege! It is the sap of bliss
Rears us aloft, makes men and angels kiss;
And last of all, to end a household strife,
It is the honey 'gainst a waspish wife.

DUKE
Thou giv'st it lively colours; who dare say
He's mad whose words march in so good array?
'Twere sin all women should such husbands have,
For every man must then be his wife's slave.
Come, therefore, you shall teach our court to shine;
So calm a spirit is worth a golden mine.
Wives with meek husbands that to vex them long,
In Bedlam must they dwell, else dwell they wrong.

Exeunt

Finis

483 **sennight** week (i.e. seven [days and] nights)
484 **golls** hands (a cant term)
485 **legs** bows (Bellafront has been kneeling in gratitude)
489 **in pudding-time** in good time (originally, the time when puddings were to be had); proverbial (Tilley P634)
496–7 **mad...Orlando** i.e. in allusion to the title character of Ariosto's *Orlando Furioso*
498 **Jew** a term of opprobrium, but presumably intended here to signify irascibility
508 **had lost...nose** i.e. would have graduated from childish tactics to others with graver consequences
514 **skill** reason; cleverness
525 **green** fresh, raw
528 **best of men** i.e. Christ
540 **state** dignified appearance

LOST PLAYS: A BRIEF ACCOUNT

Doris Feldmann and Kurt Tetzeli von Rosador

THOMAS MIDDLETON is not the Seventeenth-Century Master of the Lost Play: five plays known to be lost with about thirty extant is not a bad ratio for a professional Jacobean playwright. Nor is he, at least with respect to his lost plays, the Master of the Tantalizing Title. (That he could invent these with satiric ease, the list of fictitious titles in *Hengist, King of Kent*, 5.1.106–14, sufficiently documents.) With the possible exception of one, the alternative title of *Caesar's Fall*, all the titles are of a kind pleasing to scholars. They instigate an orderly play of signification—not the fearful free play of the signifier, but one loosely structured and delimited by social conditions, literary traditions, and cultural prescriptions: (1) *Caesar's Fall/Two Shapes*, (2) *Randall, Earl of Chester*, (3) *The Viper and Her Brood*, (4) *The Conqueror's Custom, or The Fair Prisoner*, and (5) *The Puritan Maid, the Modest Wife, and the Wanton Widow*.

Still, there can be—as it were, by definition—no absolute certainty about the number of plays lost. There are, however, degrees of uncertainty, which can be lessened with the help of soft facts. Thus an entry into the Stationers' Register for 9 September 1653 by Humphrey Moseley attributes four plays to Middleton. Or is it five? The wording of one of the entries, 'A right woman, or women beware of women', would normally mean that the first and second parts are alternatives, but one cannot be quite sure with Moseley. He, well-known for such sharp practice, may have entered two titles as one in order to save paying two fees. If so, is *A Right Woman* by Middleton, as all the other four titles are? Or is it the identically titled play which Moseley entered on 29 June 1660 as by Francis Beaumont and John Fletcher and for which—in a fit of honesty?—he then paid the ordinary fee? There can be no certainty. Nor does the title itself, with its widely applicable, vaguely proverbial phrasing—'You are a right woman, sister: you have pity' (*The Two Noble Kinsmen*, 3.6.215)—help to clarify the matter. To attribute *A Right Woman* to Middleton remains a soft option.

Yet, if soft facts all cohere, some certainty can be arrived at. Such seems to be the case for an untitled play, for which, on 3 October 1602, Philip Henslowe advanced on behalf of Worcester's Men the sum of 20s. to Middleton. Even though no title is given, there is nothing unusual about this entry, neither the space left for the title, to be filled in later by Henslowe himself or by an associate like Thomas Downton, nor the amount of the advance, which could vary considerably as a reflection of both the status of the playwright and the state of the manuscript. Yet Henslowe's entry about this payment 'in earnest of a play' is not followed by the usual ones of part and full payment a few weeks later, at least not for a play by Middleton for Worcester's Men. There are, however, records of a payment of £4 to Middleton on 21 October 1602, in 'part of payment for his play called Chester tragedy' and of 40s. on 9 November 1602, in 'full payment of his play called Randall, Earl of Chester'. The progressive concretization of the title, the proximity of dates, the complementary nature of the statements about the payments, mirroring faithfully Henslowe's regular procedure, and the total of £7 itself, a good one, but well within Henslowe's limits for a new play, suggest quite forcefully that, within five weeks' time, the untitled play had been completed and entitled *Randall, Earl of Chester*, changing hands in the process from Worcester's to the Admiral's Men, Henslowe's other company (a not uncommon procedure, as the reverse movement of Thomas Dekker's *A Medicine for a Curst Wife* three months earlier testifies).

Randall, Earl of Chester, however, had not been Middleton's first work for Henslowe. On 22 May 1602, Henslowe paid £5 to the Admiral's Men 'to give unto Anthony Munday and Michael Drayton, Webster and the rest /Middleton/ in earnest of a book called Caesar's Fall'. That Middleton's name is interlined above 'rest' may mean very little, since 'the rest' also designated Thomas Dekker, in 1602 a dramatist of some standing. He surfaces in the complementary entry of 29 May 1602, when the sum of £3 was handed to 'Thomas Dekker, Drayton, Middleton and Webster and Munday in full payment for their play called Two Shapes'. There is nothing unusual about an Elizabethan or a Jacobean play advertising itself by alternative titles, nor, indeed, about there being instability between the two. The identity of authors, the closeness of dates, and the complementary nature of the payments, adding up to as much as Henslowe was willing to disburse for a new play, leave hardly any room for doubt that the titles are alternative. With five dramatists collaborating, a mechanical division of labour, one act each, may have suggested itself as the least troublesome. About the distribution of the money, whether each of the dramatists received an equal share or not, nothing whatsoever is known.

That the matter of Caesar possessed both cultural relevance and popular appeal during the 1590s is testified by the number of dramatizations, be they for the closet, such as Samuel Daniel's *Cleopatra* of 1593, the academic stage, such as Trinity College's *Caesar's Revenge* of *c.*1595, or the public theatres. The Admiral's Men contributed their fair share to the Caesarean theme. In November

1594, they staged an anonymous play of *Caesar and Pompey*, followed seven months later by a second part. Three years later, in 1598, Henry Chettle and Robert Wilson collaborated on *Catiline's Conspiracy* for them. If this plan ever materialized, the Admiral's Men would, with *Caesar's Fall*, have built up a dramatic tradition of good commercial value (having laid in stock, according to Henslowe's inventory of 1598, '1 senator's gown, 1 hood, and 5 senator's capes'). And they would have completed a Caesarean project of some magnitude, showing Caesar in the round: the martial hero outmanœuvring and defeating Pompey the Great and, in the sequel, Sextus, his son; the powerful rhetorician and wily statesman of Catiline's conspiracy; and the destined fate of the mighty, inescapably subject to the *de casibus* pattern, to the inevitable rise and fall brought about either by a turn of blind Fortune's wheel or the retribution of the gods. In accordance with a tradition of mighty lines and mighty acting the Admiral's Men would have highlighted the central figure—in contrast and rivalry to the marginalized centrality of that other Julius Caesar, put on in 1599 by their competitors, the Lord Chamberlain's Men.

How the Caesar of the Admiral's Men would have been presented is not clear. Neither can the writings of any of the five dramatists be read as containing a single, fixed image of Caesar, nor can even the smallest common denominator be discerned between the works. The condemnation of Caesar's assassins implied in *1 Sir John Oldcastle* (1599), in which Drayton had a hand, is simply not compatible with the condemnation of Caesar's 'ambitious ends' in his *Poly-Olbion* of 1612 (X, 299); and Dekker's praise of James I as a 'second *Caesar*' (*The Wonderful Year*, 1603) was followed by Middleton's presentation of Caesar's life as subject of a 'motion' in *Father Hubburd's Tales* (1604), to be totally subverted by Webster's Menippean satire of a 'Julius Caesar making hair buttons' (*The White Devil*, 5.6.109–10).

This multivalence of the moral and ideological perspective—which is no final indeterminacy, since the *de casibus* pattern articulated in the title of *Caesar's Fall* prescribes unambiguously the sense of an ending—can be somewhat delimited by analysing what is either a sub- or an alternative title: *Two Shapes*. For it, as for almost any other evaluation of Caesar, Plutarch could have provided the stimulus with his description of Caesar's political 'craft and malice, which he cunningly cloaked under the habit of outward courtesy and familiarity'. Such a duplicity is not only expressed by the title's numerical adjective, but also by the noun. In Middleton, whoever and whatever is characterized by it comes in a questionable shape, the result of deceit ('There is a cheater by professïon | That takes more shapes than the chameleon', *Microcynicon*, 4.3–4), or of (theatrical) disguise ('I have bethought the shape— | Some credulous scholar', *Your Five Gallants*, 1.2.91–2).

Whatever Middleton may have learned about the technical side of his craft while collaborating on *Caesar's Fall*, he must have realized some of the possibilities of traditional historical subjects, especially the opportunity to represent problems of contemporary cultural relevance in a protective guise—joining, as he himself will put it in the Prologue to *Hengist, King of Kent*, 'new times' love to old times' story'. Ancient Roman history with its numerous *exempla* of the conflicts of authority vs. freedom, the monarchy vs. the republic, the individual vs. the state and its institutions, with its power struggles and the problematics of the transfer of power, had long served such purposes—in Heywood's succinct summary from *An Apology for Actors* (1612): 'If we present a foreign history, the subject is so intended, that in the lives of Romans, Grecians, or others, either the virtues of our countrymen are extolled, or their vices reproved.' England's own history had frequently been used for identical purposes, and Middleton turned to it in October 1602, dramatizing the tragedy of Randall, Earl of Chester. The subject might well have been suggested to him by his colleague Anthony Munday. In *John a Kent and John a Cumber* (*c.*1590), Munday had put—in one of a number of variant spellings—a *Ranulphe*, Earle of Chester on the stage, partly as a parental blocking figure, partly to give a local habitation and a name to one of the play's major conflicts (English Art vs. Scottish black magic). Munday had, moreover, employed an Earl of Chester in both *The Downfall* and *The Death of Robert, Earl of Huntingdon* (1598). And, in *Look About You* (printed in 1600), the Earl makes another stage appearance in another play of the Admiral's Men in a similar, though even less prominent, function. Middleton may also have been aware, as Langland was, of popular traditions, of 'rymes of Robyn hood and Randolf Erl of Chestre' (*Piers Plowman*, V.395). In addition, there are the 32 performances between 1594–7 of *The Wise Man of West Chester* and the play's revival in 1601, which kept Chester and its earls alive in the minds of Elizabethan theatregoers.

Such insistent presentation of powerful English aristocrats may well have been part of the Admiral's Men's deliberate policy. In marked contrast to the monarchical plays of the Lord Chamberlain's Men, the nineties see a long procession of English noblemen, always heroically fighting, sometimes heroically dying, under the auspices of the Admiral's Men, such as *Captain Thomas Stukeley* (1596), *The Downfall* and *The Death of Robert, Earl of Huntingdon* (1598), the two parts of *Sir John Oldcastle* (1599), and *The Conquest of Spain by John of Gaunt* (1601). That these aristocratic patterns of patriotism and heroism had a clear political message about the true strength and roots of England's glory to convey during the last years of Elizabeth's reign and the mounting tension inherent in the question of succession, exploding in the Essex rising of 1601, can be taken for granted.

Hence, Middleton's choice of subject matter can hardly be called fortuitous. If he, once again, followed the plough through a well-cultivated literary terrain, he found his own furrow by turning for the general outline of plot and conflict and for a good number of details of characterization and rhetoric to that work out of which the English history play came into its own, Raphael Holinshed's *Chronicles of England, Scotland, and Ireland*. There, in the revised version, published in 1587, he found three Ranulfs, Earls of Chester, of whom one, Ranulf de Meschines, is just mentioned in passing (vol. 2, p. 33). But both Ranulf de Gernons (died 1153) and Ranulf de Blundevill (died 1232) are colourful figures, extensively and dramatically treated. Munday had used Holinshed's account of Blundevill's early career for his *Huntingdon* plays, in which the Earl figures as nothing but a robe-bearing, doggedly loyalist member of the royal retinue. The latter part of Blundevill's life had greater appeal. He was packed off on a crusade by the king, opposed after his return the king's tyrannical measures and the introduction into England of a tithe for Rome—'The Earl of Chester only stood manfully against the payment of those tenths' (p. 364)—and was set free from a besieged castle by a quickly collected rabble of 'foreigners, players, musicians' (p. 373). Still, his life, lacking the one, terminating ingredient, is hardly the stuff of tragedy. Ranulf de Blundevill died peacefully as one of England's most powerful barons.

The life of his grandfather, Ranulf de Gernons, has more tragic potential. He is the quintessential English Baron, 'a man of ... stoutness of stomach' (p. 103), ever, as in the battle of Lincoln, leading the 'fore ward' (p. 88), ever being driven by an amoral vitalism to pursue personal autonomy and political power. King's rule or barons' rule—this is a central conflict circumscribing many others. It climaxes at the battle of Lincoln with Ranulf first delivering a rousing battle speech, given in full by Holinshed, then personally charging King Stephen, finally taking him prisoner. And it is dramatically reversed when later he himself is 'craftily taken ... and could not be delivered till he had surrendered the city and castle of Lincoln, with other fortresses' (p. 96). Foreshortening the historical Ranulf's further alliances, intrigues, and battles, Middleton might have had him summarily killed—poisoned by William Peverell, whom, it is said, he had robbed of his land. This drama of madly ambitious men, of alliances treacherously broken and treacherously renewed, of order and anarchy, foreshadows *Hengist, King of Kent*. And the element of sexual violence or violent sexuality, never far from the centre of any of Middleton's tragedies, could have been forcefully provided by the rival claimant for the English throne, the Amazonian figure of the Empress Matilda.

The fact that there are two tragedies among Middleton's earliest dramatic writings may help to correct the cliché of an early *œuvre* written for the children's companies, possessing a realistic, no-point-of-view satirical unity. Middleton wrote within the genres most popular around 1600—and drama based on (pseudo)history certainly ruled the public stage then. He contributed to the revival of another pseudohistory, when, on 14 December 1602, he received 5*s*. from Henslowe 'for a prologue and a epilogue for the play of Bacon for the court'. The writing of the two pieces for this revival of Robert Greene's old play of *Friar Bacon and Friar Bungay* (*c.*1589) was, no doubt, if one can judge by those highly conventional pieces which Middleton affixed to his own later plays, such as *The Roaring Girl, Anything for a Quiet Life*, and *A Game at Chess*, competently executed along the approved lines of apostrophe, *captatio benevolentiae*, promises of profit and delight, introducing the play's matter and mode, asking for an impartial judgement, begging for applause. It may, however, have profited Middleton in a more indirect, yet more important way, by making him realize magic's persistent popular appeal, cultural relevance—especially after James's accession—and dramatic possibilities. These are possibilities which Middleton richly exploited throughout his playwriting career—from the appearance of a succuba in *A Mad World, My Masters* (4.1) to the introduction of Hecate into *Macbeth*, and from the presentation of a witches' coven in *The Witch* to the transformation of Bacon's 'glass prospective' (*Friar Bacon and Friar Bungay*, v.105) into the fake 'magical glass' of *A Game at Chess* (3.1.330, 4.1.94).

With time on his hands and the need to earn money by writing, Middleton certainly wrote other plays between the beginning of his career as a professional playwright in 1601–2 and the death of Elizabeth, more or less coinciding with the closing of the theatres because of the plague, in March 1603. Where better to look for those other plays than among the lost ones—filling in, as in all reading, the empty spaces with plausible approximations. And, indeed, the titles of Middleton's two undated lost plays, *The Puritan Maid, the Modest Wife, and the Wanton Widow* and *The Conqueror's Custom, or The Fair Prisoner*, are open to such an ordered play of signification, which lodges them quite plausibly within the literary traditions and the cultural problematics of the early years of the seventeenth century.

That *The Puritan Maid, the Modest Wife, and the Wanton Widow* did exist and was written by Middleton there can be no reasonable doubt. It was ascribed to him both in the long list of plays entered in the Stationers' Register on 9 September 1653, for Humphrey Moseley, and in John Warburton's list of manuscript plays that were burnt by his legendary cook. The three other plays entered in the Stationers' Register by Moseley and bracketed with *The Puritan Maid* as by Middleton, exist and are correctly ascribed. The doubts about Warburton's veracity and the authenticity of his list have been persuasively dispersed by John Freehafer. Hence, what is left is a minimal text, the title. Its length and its additive listing of three adjectivally stereotyped figures make it a highly unusual, possibly a singular one for Jacobean plays enacted on a public stage—only academic entertainments in Cambridge being occasionally entitled according to the same principle. Certainly no other title in the Middleton canon is formulated on the same principle—with one exception. The title of *The Patient Man and the Honest Whore* as entered in the Stationers' Register on 9 November 1604, or, in slight variation, as printed on the first quarto the same year, runs to even more words: 'The Humours of the Patient Man. The Longing Wife and the Honest Whore'. This marked parallelism of two exceptionally phrased titles suggests some kind of relationship to have existed between the two texts, beyond that of common authorship. Proximity of date may have been one, thematic correspondence another: if *The Honest Whore* puts Puritan ideas and ideals to a somewhat acid test, *The Puritan Maid* might have reflected them. Be that as it may, there can hardly be any doubt that both plays foreground those problems which long had troubled Elizabethan minds: the moral value and cultural prestige of virginity and/or (married and widowed) chastity; the sexual and economic threat of widowhood; the hierarchical ordering of women's 'natural' roles and the possibilities of containing their bodily functions; the 'dichotomy' of woman/wife and whore.

That those themes pervade and organize the majority of Middleton's plays is common knowledge. Hence, a case can be made for almost any date for *The Puritan Maid* within his writing career. An early one might be favoured, if topicality and cultural relevance are privileged as criteria for dating. For the time-honoured discussion about the hierarchy of woman's three estates, of who was the earthlier happy or the more divinely blessed, maid, wife, or widow, was bound to become ever more topical and complex under the reign of an ageing Virgin Queen whose cult was not compatible with the advance of either Puritan morality or the new satirical realism. The cult is represented in 1602 by Sir John Davies's 'A Contention between a Wife, a Widow, and a Maid for Precedence'. Staged at Sir Robert Cecil's house in the Strand on 6 December 1602 to honour a visit by the Queen, it moves through 240 stately verses to its foregone conclusion. Nothing else is, under such circumstances, to be expected than that wife and widow will in the end 'yield the honour and the place...to the maid' (233–4). But the place of performance subverts the official doctrine: public representation has receded into the exclusive space of an aristocrat's private house.

Yet though receding, the power of official doctrine inscribes itself even in a text like Samuel Rowlands's *'Tis Merry When Gossips Meet* (entered in the Stationers' Register on 15 September 1602; printed the same year), presenting the three female prototypes from a plebeian, satirical, carnivalesque point of view. Despite the low setting, a room in a tavern, despite the chatty tone and the everyday topics of conversation—certainly including the traditional one of the hierarchy of woman's estates, but extending to a gossipy variety of others like husbands, tobacco, food, dreams, and the goings-on about town—despite the improbability, that is, of the text reflecting however obliquely on the royal *virgo absoluta*, a commendatory poem sees the necessity of insisting that the book deals but with '*Maids* of mean'st degree', protesting that it is 'not seated in a sumptuous chair, | Nor do thy lines import of Majesty'. The disclaimer implicates Rowlands's text quite thoroughly in the ongoing debate. It presents the three women, maid, wife, and, especially, widow, as weak and leaky vessels, but with a vitality and dignity of their own; not altogether mere objects of misogynist or patriarchal satire, not altogether autonomous subjects of their sayings and doings.

It is within such contexts that Middleton's ten-word text must be placed in order to understand its topicality and subversive relevance. Still, the debate, even if it shifted focus after the death of the royal embodiment of maidenhood, continued unabatedly. Hence, as Middleton's repeated and emphatic treatment of the problematic relationship in his other plays demonstrates, no one date can be insisted on. To understand Middleton's ideological stand in the play, however, there is no need to trace the numerous representations of the three estates, their versions and subversions, throughout his *œuvre*—the title itself explicates his position pretty clearly. The list sets off the middle term by framing it with two negatively loaded adjectives, *puritan* (or: *puritanical*) being invariably used by Middleton in accordance with contemporary usage, not to describe the reformist religious party, but to imply sectarianism or prudery or hypocrisy or all three. Thus privileging the wife, Middleton places himself squarely within mainstream Puritanism, alongside such leading Puritan divines as William Perkins, who in his *Christian Economy*, published in 1609, unequivocally sets up the ideal: 'Marriage...is a state in itself, far more excellent than the condition of single life' (p. 11). Indeed, as Isabella decides in her song dealing with a woman's progression through the three estates: 'of these three | The middle's best' (*The Witch*, 2.1.137–8).

Similar contextual arguments can be brought forward to locate Middleton's other undated lost play, *The Conqueror's Custom, or The Fair Prisoner*, either around the time of James's accession or any time later. The play's title heads a list of fifty-one manuscript plays, compiled between 1677 and 1703 by Abraham Hill, a seventeenth-century antiquarian of wide interests and easy familiarity with numerous leading figures from the intellectual and the aristocratic world. The list, magisterially described by Joseph Quincy Adams, is quite possibly based on the holdings of an antiquarian bookseller or a collector of manuscripts. The attribution of the play to Middleton must be accepted, even if there is only Hill's authority for it, since all other verifiable ascriptions of plays in Hill's manuscript are correct or, as in the case of *The Witch of Edmonton*, reflect (informed) seventeenth-century opinion. That *The Conqueror's Custom* heads the list may mean that Hill or whoever had arranged the manuscripts thought of it as an early play, as a rather vague chronological order can be discerned among the datable items, and at least one play from the top of the list, number 6, Henry Chettle's *All Is Not Gold That Glisters* (1601), is definitely an early one.

A stronger case for an early date can, however, be made if the portrait of the young Middleton as determinedly learning the profession of dramatist, as a revisionist and a snatcher-up of well-considered subjects of popular appeal, possessing also a high degree of topicality and cultural relevance, bears some resemblance to reality. For the wording of the title encapsulates a motif frequently dramatized in different generic modes during the 80s and the 90s, in plays such as Farrant's (?) *The Wars of Cyrus*, Lyly's *Campaspe*, Marlowe's *1* and *2 Tamburlaine*, Kyd's *Soliman and Perseda*, the anonymous *Edward III*, and Shakespeare's *Henry V*, to name but a few. The Herculean motif of heroic man, warrior or monarch, captivated by beauteous woman, slave or queen, lends itself above all to two dramatic representations: as a mirror for princes, based on the conflict of love and lust, or as the battle of two value systems, those of love and honour. Even though these issues can hardly ever be separated clearly, Elizabethan plays emphatically foreground the conflict within the male, the prince. It is his (self-)conquest which is staged, his fall, as in Lyly's play, 'from the armour of Mars to the arms of Venus' (2.2.68–9) and his final triumph: 'I go to conquer kings, and shall I not then | Subdue myself' (*Edward III*, 893–4). The women are the seductresses or the objects of desire, their bodies to be besieged and taken like castles (with which in the Petrarchan tradition they had indeed become identified). But with the accession of James a 'change in . . . culture', as Linda Woodbridge has argued in *Women and the English Renaissance* (1984), took place, a change 'from "masculine" military values to peacetime values traditionally female' (p. 161). The doubleness of Middleton's title, placing conqueror and prisoner on an equal, alternative footing, may be an expression of this shift, of a new double perspective, formulated in that new mode of alternative perspectives, tragicomedy.

Tempting as it is to see Middleton as seismographically reacting to such cultural changes, James's accession and the transformations it signalled and furthered are but stages in an ongoing process—a process which the stage continuously reflected and into which it intervened with plays such as Shakespeare's *Antony and Cleopatra* or Fletcher's and Massinger's *The False One*. The play's cultural relevance, inherent in the motif's dramatic potential to represent affirmatively or subversively courtly life as one of manly courtesy or of effeminate, sensual ease, would not have been much less, say, in 1618–9, when James's peacemaking efforts—the praises of which Middleton had ghost-written in 1618—came increasingly under critical fire. Moreover, Middleton himself, never averse to reusing and revising motifs and themes, figures and scenes, once successfully employed, wrote another play for which the title *The Conqueror's Custom, or The Fair Prisoner* would be a perfect fit (as no other title of any of the lost plays would be for any other of the known ones). In *More Dissemblers Besides Women* (1614) there are two conquerors, Andrugio, the general, returning victoriously from battle, and Love, prettily personified in a Cupid: 'I am a little conqueror too' (1.3.77). There is also the widowed Duchess who first, during a seven years' spell of mourning, shuts herself off from the world in voluntary imprisonment but then, falling in love with Andrugio, takes the new 'Captivity cheerfully' (3.2.26). Middleton rings richly ironic variations on the theme of conquest/imprisonment; the play's imagery is suffused with it, the figures body it forth, the plot is structured to test it. Still, there is no necessity to think of *The Conqueror's Custom* as an alternative title of *More Dissemblers Besides Women*. After all, the motif was common and culturally important in Elizabethan and Jacobean times—a fact which makes it impossible to date the lost play with any certainty.

There is no doubt about the early date of *The Viper and Her Brood*. The lawsuit—as discovered, published, and analysed by H. N. Hillebrand—which Robert Keysar, manager of the Children of the Queen's Revels at the Blackfriars, brought against Middleton in 1609 for a debt of £16 proves that Middleton had written a play called *The Viper and Her Brood* by 1606; that this play was a tragedy (Keysar received a 'librum lusorium tragicum'); that Middleton thought it worth £8 10*s*., in part payment of the debt, and acceptable for a children's company. Also, of course, that by 1606, he had close dealings with the manager of the Revels Children (at approximately the same time as the Children of Paul's fade from sight). And that he was in debt.

The conjunctive/disjunctive nature of the title suggests strongly what matter Middleton selected for his tragedy, out of the richly varied traditions adhering to vipers (as somewhat distinct from those about serpents). From Herodotus and Pliny onwards the most striking fact about the female viper was her murderous lust. Natural history and emblematic tradition lovingly report, depict, and moralize the phenomenon. The relationship between the female viper and her brood, however, is—again based on Herodotus and Pliny—even more frequently dealt with in Renaissance literature (e.g. in Sidney's *Apology for Poetry* or in an anti-papist attack, such as *The Tragicocomedy of Serpents*, 1607). Allusions to it are virtually ubiquitous in the drama of the time, from Munday's *The Death of Robert, Earl of Huntingdon* (ll. 1541–3) to Shakespeare's and Wilkins's *Pericles* (1.1.107–8), to Jonson's *Magnetic Lady* (4.4.5–8). It is based on the belief that the viper's brood is hatched inside her belly and impatiently gnaws its way out, thus killing the mother. It is moralized as an emblem of ingratitude or of revenge.

Taken in conjunction, ancient and Renaissance natural history emblematized tells a pretty story. Edward Topsell, following Herodotus, summarizes it succinctly and graphically in 1608, saying 'that when the vipers begin to rage in lust, and desire to couple one with another, the male commeth and putteth his head into the mouth of the female, who is so insatiable in the desire of that copulation, that when the male hath filled her with all his seed-genital, and so would draw forth his head again, she biteth it off, and destroyeth her husband, whereby he dieth and never liveth more: but the female departeth and conceiveth her young in her belly, who every day according to nature's inclination, grow to perfection and ripeness, and at last in revenge of their father's death, do likewise destroy their mother, for they eat out her belly, and by an unnatural issue come forth into the light of this world' (p. 293). Henry Peacham's *Minerva Britanna* (1612) depicts the story in one emblem:

This is the detailed scenario of a drama replete with murderous passion and passionate murder, or in Freudian terms, of the Oedipal tragedy complete with primal scene, castration, and horde of brothers, with parri- and matricide. It is a tragedy based upon emblematic tradition and lending itself to emblematic staging, much in the manner of *The Changeling* (in which Beatrice uses the material: 'Murder, I see, is followed by more sins. | Was my creation in the womb so cursed, | It must engender with a viper first?', 3.4.167–9). And it is the third tragedy within the first four years of Middleton's career as a highly versatile professional dramatist.

Whether there is any thematic unity within this early career or not, there seem to be, as it were, latent, subterranean connections between the works. Anthony Munday seems to have been a key-figure for the early Middleton—as collaborator, but also as mentor providing ideas (magic) or matter (Chester) for dramatic representation. And is it mere chance that the material of viper and brood frequently surfaces in Elizabethan and Jacobean writings about Caesar and the matter of Rome? '*Caesar* at *Rome*' is the cautionary *exemplum* in the anonymous *Vindiciae contra Tyrannos* (1579), well-known in England, even though only translated into English in 1648, for those 'which are so horribly wicked, that they seek to enthral their own native country like the viperous brood which gnaw through the entrails of their mother' (p. 105). Shakespeare's Brutus shares this view ('therefore think him as a serpent's egg, | Which, hatched, would as his kind grow mischievous', 2.1.32–3), and Jonson, both in *The Poetaster* (1601) and *Sejanus* (1603), uses the metaphor in a Roman, Caesarean setting (not, however, applying it to Caesar). Could *The Viper and Her Brood* have been another classical history? Presenting the monstrous life and regiment of an Agrippina? Of course it could, but it need not have been. For here we move definitely into a realm of speculation in which signifying practice plays fast and loose with scholarly rules of plausible approximation.

SEE ALSO

Lost Pageant for Charles I: A Brief Account: this volume, 1898
Lost Political Prose, 1620–7: A Brief Account: this volume, 1907
Other Middleton–Dekker works: *Gravesend*, 128; *Meeting*, 183; *Magnificent*, 219; *Patient Man*, 280; *Banquet*, 637; *Roaring Girl*, 721; *Gypsy*, 1723
Other Middleton–Munday works: *Integrity*, 1766; *Golden Fleece*, 1772
Other Middleton–Webster works: *Magnificent*, 219; *Quiet*, 1593; '*The Duchess of Malfi*', 1886
List of works cited: *Companion*, 1122

MICHAELMAS TERM

Edited by Theodore B. Leinwand

Michaelmas Term takes its name from the court session that began in London on the ninth of October. The first term, or 'father' (1.1.35) of the court calendar, it was succeeded by Hilary, Easter, and Trinity terms. Yet, as the eponymous Michaelmas Term of the Induction tells us, 'he that expects any great quarrels in law to be handled here, will be fondly deceived' (1.1.70–2). And this caveat is largely borne out. Legal documents are signed and seconded and a judge is brought on stage at the last moment, but the plot is driven by commercial, not legal intrigue, and lawyers do not participate in it. The lawyers in the house at the first performance of *Michaelmas Term*, some time between late 1604 and early 1606, would instead have been sitting opposite the stage. For a significant portion of the audience probably consisted of law students drawn from the inns of court.

We know that as early as 1580, young men from the inns of court were playgoers. In that year, three of the Earl of Oxford's players committed 'disorders and frays upon the gentlemen of the Inns of the Court'. The inns men returned the favour in 1581: Parr Stafferton, a 'gentleman of Grays Inn', is noted in a City of London order 'for that he...brought a disordered company of gentlemen of the Inns of Court & others, to assault...players of Interludes within the City'. Some ten years later, Thomas Nashe, in his *Pierce Penniless* (1592), included inns of court men among those prone to 'bestow themselves upon pleasure...[by] seeing a Play'. Thus young John Donne, of Lincoln's Inn, was a frequent playgoer in the 1590s. In 1609, in *The Gull's Hornbook*, Dekker denigrates a law student sitting on a stool at the theatre next to a farmer's son. In the Induction to *Bartholomew Fair* (1614), Jonson's stage-keeper imagines 'witty young masters of the *Inns of Court*' sousing a prostitute 'with her stern upward' under a stage property pump. And in 1629, Francis Lenton caricatures the progress of an inns student who not only has sat upon the Blackfriars stage and visited both the Cockpit and the Globe, but has a copy of Jonson's 'book of Plays' too. No wonder that a father in Jonson's *Poetaster* (1601), fearing that his son lodged at one of the inns will become an actor, asks, 'What? shall I have my son a stager now? an ingle [catamite, or kept boy] for players?'

Middleton several times refers explicitly to the inns in *Michaelmas Term*. Twice in 2.3, Quomodo boasts that his son Sim, 'lately commenced at Cambridge', is now a 'Templar' (the Knights Templar formerly occupied the law societies' buildings). The woollen draper takes pleasure in his son's gentrification and in his own sponsorship of Sim's putative advance in status: 'I have placed [him] at Inns of Court.' But Quomodo's final mention of London's law schools entails a vaunt of another sort. Left alone on stage once the commodity scam he has masterminded is well launched, Quomodo ends the second act by commanding the audience's approbation: 'Admire me, all you students at Inns of Cozenage.' While the inns were virtually England's third university, Quomodo's bravado indicates an unacknowledged fourth school—London itself—where a 'fair free-breasted gentleman' like Richard Easy could get 'the city powd'ring'. As an early modern English anticipation of a corporate lawyer/executive, a graduate of Cambridge, a law school, *and* the city would be a truly new man. Surpassing the draper, surpassing even his hopes for Sim (4.4.24), the merchant-lawyer that inns of court satirist Everard Guilpin lampooned in his *Skialetheia* (1598) could be found both 'Toyling' at the 'Inns' and 'Moyling' at 'th'Exchange'. 'Will not he thrive (think ye) who can devise, | Thus to unite the law and merchandise? | Doubtless he will, or cozen out of doubt; | What matter's that? his law will bear him out.'

Particularly because it takes the form of direct audience address, Quomodo's exuberant gloating raises questions about the relationship between the characters as well as the actors and their audiences. For *Michaelmas Term* was not only performed *for* at least a fair number of young men, it was performed *by* young men. The play's 1607 title-page informs us that it was 'sundry times acted by the Children *of Pauls*'. In a theatre that held but a few hundred spectators, a company of adolescent boys faced a cadre of late adolescent or young adult men. Surely there were mature citizens and city wives and gallants, maybe an ambassador and a lord in the audience, and a comprehensive analysis would consider citizen spectators' responses to Quomodo, their wives' possible reactions to Thomasine, the gallants' reactions to the play's gentry, and so on. But it is the law students in the audience whom Middleton singles out. From which characters might they have distanced themselves in cool amusement, and with whom might they have identified as they heard the choristers' song school performance of *Michaelmas Term*?

Despite the fact that he is the play's only lawyer in the rough, smug and gullible Sim Quomodo's negligible part is hardly one with which the inns men would have wanted to affiliate themselves. His father, his father's 'spirit' Shortyard, and Richard Easy are, however, all plausible candidates. Quomodo's craftiness works in his favour even as his social status, his craft as citizen-draper, works against him. To the extent that he motivates, indeed scripts the play's unfolding scam, and because he represents just the sort of capital that was financing the very city playhouses inns men frequented, Quomodo successfully models urban and financial cunning. To the extent that he is but one among a horde of grasping 'tradesmen' (5.1.69) out to 'undo gentlemen daily' (2.3.60–1), a status climber who can barely control his lust to be 'divulged a landed man' (3.4.5), Quomodo is an inns man's nightmare metonymy for the 'man-devouring city' (2.2.21). While the Middle and Inner Templars in the choristers' audience may have admired Quomodo for his cozenage or delighted in his artless fantasies of landownership as we still do, they also would have had a stake in his comeuppance, his final reinsertion into the shop world that bred him.

Templars in the audience could also have derived pleasure from Shortyard, Quomodo's endlessly shape-shifting 'spirit'. Shortyard opens up for young men on the make a vision of unchecked mobility and, better still, an apprentice besting—if only momentarily—his master. And there is reason to believe that inns students were engaged in a sort of apprenticeship. They served seven years before they were introduced by 'Masters of the Bench' into the mysteries of their craft. During their 'indenture', they were not only subject to discipline at the hands of barristers both older and more powerful than they were, but, as Arthur Marotti has argued, they were 'socially, economically, and politically vulnerable' in London at large. We might try to imagine what an inns student would have had to bring into focus as he followed Shortyard from one act to the next: first and always, a chorister and so an immature boy, then Shortyard the young man or boy/servant/apprentice, Blastfield the London gallant, and finally an alderman's deputy. Active and passive, gulling and gulled, short yarded (impotent) and yet a seminal, 'pregnant spirit' (1.2.95), Shortyard might as easily delight as dismay, incite as well as assuage would-be pleaders' anxieties.

Of course, it is primarily Richard Easy to whom we may assume the non-citizenry at a performance of *Michaelmas Term* would have responded. Gallants, inns men, or country gentlemen in town for business or court matters would all have recognized Easy as both literary and historical type, as a dupe ripe for duping and a recent inheritor of his father's estate newly arrived in the city. A 'fair, free-breasted gentleman' (1.2.57), a 'fresh gallant' (1.2.116), Easy comes up to London not so much to marry as to be 'free' and live at 'liberty' (1.2.51–2). That he is almost immediately hooked like one of the 'fish ... tradesmen catch' (1.2.135) speaks to his vulnerability. That he finally, perhaps undeservedly, recoups his losses and inadvertently outwits Quomodo speaks to the song school playwrights' ideological investment in the fantasies of the youthful gentlemen in their audiences. And yet in *Michaelmas Term*, at least, Middleton strives for balance. Quomodo announces early on that 'They're [gentry] busy 'bout our wives, we [citizens] 'bout their lands' (1.2.112); however, Quomodo is in the end still landless, and Easy is neither very preoccupied with nor very energetic about winning Thomasine Quomodo. Neither wived nor wealthier, the Easy whom the inns of court spectators attend to through *Michaelmas Term* has been powdered. He has been cured in the sweating tub that was London. Easy is initiated into the urban mysteries that challenged all of the young men in the audience, and in the end, he has that to which they aspired: a fair chance of succeeding within the mostly male social and financial circuits of the city.

He also enters on their behalf into urban erotic currents—circuits in which status and gender and finance and sexual practices are variously configured (Leinwand, 1994). Powdering tubs were, after all, designed for sweating out venereal disease. And the nasty Lethe–Courtesan–Hellgill scenes introduce into *Michaelmas Term* a hardly comic world of grotesque men trading in women's flesh. Where heteroerotic relations arise in this plot, or in the related doings in regard to Susan Quomodo's marriage, crude and degrading sodomitical intentions prevail. We may recall Jonson's 'masters of the *Inns*' humiliating a prostitute 'with her stern upward' when Middleton's Courtesan, a 'backslider', is advised to wear her hair 'like a mock-face behind; 'tis such an Italian [sodomitical] world, many men know not before from behind' (3.1.19–21). For her part, Susan—who will eventually find herself married to a man named Rearage—is not sure what to 'do with a gentleman? I know not which way to lie with him' (2.3.58–9). Even Thomasine has not been 'use[d] ... so well as a man mought' by Quomodo (4.3.54–5).

But it is Easy, who rests too much upon his 'R's', his arse (2.3.385), whose name conjures up a privy (a stool of ease), who describes himself as having been 'easily possessed' by Cockstone (1.2.51) and is in turn said by that gallant to be 'somewhat too open' (1.2.57), who finds in Shortyard a 'sweet bedfellow' for whom he is 'sick' with 'a great desire' (2.3.151 and 3.5.47–9), and about whom Shortyard says, 'in a word, we're man and wife; they can but lie together, and so do we' (2.3.171–4)—it is Easy who enters into a sometimes comic, sometimes corrosive set of homosocial, often homoerotic relations. Heterosexuality may underwrite the intrigue in various other Middletonian comedies, but in *Michaelmas Term* Easy's desire for male camaraderie, male affection, and the 'entertainment' (3.2.14) Shortyard can provide predominates. Considering the audience, and Bruce Smith's plausible contention that the inns of court 'fostered the homosexual potentiality in male bonding', we should not be surprised. Varieties of male relations in early modern England were often merely ordinary. Philip Stubbes's conviction that playgoing led men to 'play sodomite' had no effect on profits at the playhouses, and King James I's evocation of 'marriage', 'sweet child and wife', as well as 'dear dad and husband' in a letter to George Villiers did not undermine his sovereignty.

There may, then, be nothing particularly troubling when homosociality crosses over into homoeroticism in *Michaelmas Term*, but there is a cause for concern when hierarchies based on social status or on subject (active) and object (passive) are unsettled. Whom do we imagine does what to whom when a gentleman from Essex, looking to live free but caught up in a sting, sleeps with a citizen's spirit/servant disguised as a gallant? And in what position might the inns students have imagined themselves? Or Middleton, who signed himself 'T. M. gent.' and whose father was a bricklayer, a citizen, and an 'allowed' gentleman? The play does, after all, make something in 2.3 of who 'enters' first (signs his name, but also penetrates); of whether Quomodo had a 'stomach to' (inclination, but also sexual appetite for) a 'somewhat hot' gentleman like Easy, when he 'might ha' had a good substantial citizen' (3.4.59–69); and of Shortyard, when disguised as a wealthy citizen, venturing his body for a 'gentleman's pleasure' (3.5.68).

Since the choristers were venturing their bodies in the playhouse for gentlemen's pleasure, it is possible that the inns students would in the end have sought to distance themselves from Easy. Not just a gull, a figure who might be taken—in both the financial and the erotic sense—but probably a handsome boy actor and so an object of attraction, neither Easy nor the actor who personated him could easily escape subjection. What remained within the chorister's purview would have had less to do with his acting skills or his sexual sophistication than with the two together, with what Middleton in *Father Hubburd's Tales* imagined was the Blackfriars boy actors' ability to 'ravish a man' (561). In their own defence, the inns men could imagine that they, unlike the boy actors, were not circumscribed by a stigmatized institution such as the children's companies. But the inns, which nurtured the vogue for satire, were often one of its targets. The theatrical transaction at the song school may therefore betray some tension: the sexual connotation of 'undo' (as in 'ravish') and the uncertainty as to who hosts or employs whom complicate the concern on William Prynne's part (1633) that 'inns of court men were undone but for players; that they are their chiefest guests and employment'. Were a law student to confirm Stubbes's worst fear and bring home a boy actor after a performance, social status, sexual practice, age difference, even gender roles (the boys did play the woman's part) all would have been in play, just as they were during the two hours within which Michaelmas Term aimed to 'dispatch' (send off, but also sexually satisfy) the audience.

In 1927, T. S. Eliot described Middleton as a playwright 'solicitous to please his audience with what they expect; but there is underneath the same steady impersonal passionless observation of human nature'. While there is much in this formulation with which we might quibble, it nonetheless answers well to the interplay of desire and calculation, of pleasure and discomfort, stimulated in and by *Michaelmas Term*. Stimulated, not observed or recorded (Eliot argues that 'Middleton's comedy was "photographic"'), because *Michaelmas Term* formulates, analyses, enchants and disenchants. In fusing the city with comedy into what we now call city comedy, a dramatist like Middleton was not merely reworking New Comedy or dramatizing cony-catching stories. Like Swinburne's Hogarth (Swinburne called *Michaelmas Term* 'an excellent Hogarthian comedy'), Middleton seems to have been more interested in animating the ideologies that inform tropes and types than in human depth or flesh and blood (Leinwand, 1986). To imagine audience members responding to (a chorister's) Easy or Quomodo may well be different from what we usually have in mind when we talk about identifying with, say, (Burbage's) Hamlet. In a city comedy like *Michaelmas Term*, the city precedes and then engenders character. For Gail Kern Paster, who renders 'man-devouring city' (2.2.21) as 'the predatory city', as Middleton's version of a 'Renaissance overreacher', London is 'the one commodity that transcends the fact of limit'. A somewhat more benign account would suggest that London thoroughly socializes character, pre-empting any possibility of individuality, and that *Michaelmas Term* is a sort of profound comic urban sociology. Again, not photorealism but sociology, with the stress on its 'logy', its constitutive theorizing and its implicated theorist.

But comic too. For while it is reasonable to conceive of a darkly shaded production of *Michaelmas Term*, one in which 'there can be no change in the closed circle of the [city's] predatory system, merely recycling' (Paster), we may also imagine a production which is at least moderately restorative. Such a suggestion may seem naïve or even callous in the face of Thomasine's forced reallotment (5.3.60) to Quomodo, but then even she seems to expect to regain what she briefly possessed (5.3.140–2). Given that the play's Induction leaves off with Michaelmas Term hoping 'there's no fools i'th'house!' (1.1.75), a production might well align itself with comedy's educative function. As Stephen Booth has suggested, '*Comedy*... demonstrates the proposition that there is a way things are and fools forget what it is'. Of course, history—in which this comedy is surely embedded—has proved to many that there is no reason to construe the 'way things are' to mean unchanging; if it does not denote tractable, it might still signify only resistant to change. Therefore although the fools in *Michaelmas Term* and its audiences forget its comic proposition, we may still note that the literal judgements of the final scene stand for a more flexible, sound judgement: less moral than analytical, at once sociological and aesthetic, available then and again in the reader's or playgoer's now.

SEE ALSO

Textual introduction and apparatus: *Companion*, 535
Authorship and date: *Companion*, 353

Michaelmas Term

[*for the Children of Paul's*]

THE PERSONS OF THE PLAY

Richard EASY, a gentleman from Essex
REARAGE, SALEWOOD, COCKSTONE — London gallants

Ephestian QUOMODO, a woollen draper
THOMASINE, Quomodo's wife
SIM, their son
SUSAN, their daughter
SHORTYARD, alias John Blastfield, etc., FALSELIGHT, alias Idem, etc. — Quomodo's spirits
BOY, Quomodo's servant
WINIFRED, Thomasine's maid

Andrew LETHE, born Andrew Gruel, a Scottish upstart
MOTHER GRUEL, Lethe's mother
Dick HELLGILL (Pander)
COUNTRY WENCH, also Courtesan and Harlot, Lethe's mistress

Country Wench's FATHER
MOTHER, an old woman
MISTRESS COMINGS, a tirewoman
TAILOR

JUDGE
DUSTBOX, a scrivener
DRAWER
Mourners
SERVANTS
OFFICERS
LIVERY
Hospital boys

MICHAELMAS TERM, BOY, his servant, HILARY, EASTER, and TRINITY TERMS, POOR FELLOW, PAGE, and PANDER, in dumb show — the Induction

---

1.1 *Incipit Actus Primus*
Induction
Enter Michaelmas Term in a whitish cloak, new come up out of the country, a Boy bringing his gown after him

MICHAELMAS TERM
Boy?

BOY Here sir!

MICHAELMAS TERM
Lay by my conscience,
Give me my gown, that weed is for the country,
We must be civil now, and match our evil;
Who first made civil black, he pleased the devil.
So, now know I where I am, me thinks already
I grasp best part of the autumnian blessing
In my contentious fathom; my hand's free,
From wronger and from wrongèd I have fee.
And what by sweat from the rough earth they draw,
Is to enrich this silver harvest, Law.
And so through wealthy variance, and fat brawl,
The barn is made but steward to the hall.
Come they up thick enough?

BOY
O, like hops and harlots sir!

MICHAELMAS TERM
Why dost thou couple them?

BOY O, very aptly, for as the hop well boiled will make a man not stand upon his legs, so the harlot in time will leave a man no legs to stand upon!

MICHAELMAS TERM
Such another and be my heir. I have no child,
Yet have I wealth would redeem beggary.

This commentary pays special attention to sexual innuendo.

1.1.0.3 ***Michaelmas Term*** court session that began on 9 October

2 **weed** his 'whitish' (signifying innocence) cloak; white is still the liturgical colour for Michaelmas (29 September) in Roman Catholic and Anglican churches

3 **civil** urbane; citified as opposed to countrified

4 **civil black** wealthy citizens often wore black, which was associated with the devil

7 **fathom** grasp, power (*fig.*)

11 **wealthy variance** costly discrepancy between two legal documents
fat said of a dispute at law capable of yielding abundant returns

12 **hall** law courts (Westminster Hall)

13 **Come they up** litigants travelling to London

16 **hop well boiled** dried flowers of hops give a bitter flavour to malt liquor

18 **no legs** a consequence of venereal disease

19 **Such another** another witticism like that

20 **beggary** possible play on 'buggery' (see 1.1.25–6)

I think it be a curse both here and foreign,
Where bags are fruitful'st, there the womb's most barren;
The poor has all our children, we their wealth.
Shall I be prodigal when my life cools,
Make those my heirs whom I have beggared, fools?
It would be wondrous; rather beggar more;
Thou shalt have heirs enough, thou keep'st a whore.
And here comes kindred too with no mean purses,
Yet strive to be still blest with clients' curses.

Music playing. Enter the other three Terms, the first bringing in a fellow poor, which the other two advance, giving him rich apparel, a page, and a pander

Exit [fellow]

MICHAELMAS TERM
What subtlety have we here? A fellow
Shrugging for life's kind benefits, shift and heat,
Crept up in three Terms, wrapped in silk and silver,
So well appointed too with page and pander;
It was a happy gale that blew him hither.

FIRST TERM
Thou father of the Terms, hail to thee.

SECOND TERM
May much contention still keep with thee.

THIRD TERM
Many new fools come up and see thee.

SECOND TERM
Let 'em pay dear enough that see thee.

FIRST TERM
And like asses use such men,
When their load's off, turn 'em to graze again.

SECOND TERM
And may our wish have full effect,
Many a suit, and much neglect.

THIRD TERM
And as it hath been often found,
Let the clients' cups come round.

SECOND TERM
Help your poor kinsmen when you ha' got 'em;
You may drink deep, leave us the bottom.

THIRD TERM
Or when there is a lamb fall'n in,
Take you the lamb, leave us the skin.

MICHAELMAS TERM
Your duty and regard hath moved us,
Never till now we thought you loved us;
Take comfort from our words, and make no doubt,
You shall have suits come sixteen times about.

ALL THREE TERMS
We humbly thank the patron of our hopes. *Exeunt*

MICHAELMAS TERM
With what a vassal-appetite they gnaw
On our reversions, and are proud
Coldly to taste our meats, which eight returns
Serve in to us as courses.
One day our writs, like wild-fowl, fly abroad,
And then return o'er cities, towns, and hills,
With clients like dried straws between their bills;
And 'tis no few, birds pick to build their nests,
Nor no small money that keeps drabs and feasts!
But, gentlemen, to spread myself open unto you, in cheaper Terms I salute you, for ours have but sixpenny fees all the year long, yet we dispatch you in two hours, without demur; your suits hang not long here after candles be lighted. Why do we call this play by such a dear and chargeable title, *Michaelmas Term*? Know it consents happily to our purpose, though perhaps faintly to the interpretation of many, for he that expects any great quarrels in law to be handled here, will be fondly deceived; this only presents those familiar accidents which happened in town in the circumference of those six weeks whereof Michaelmas Term is lord. *Sat sapienti*; I hope there's no fools i'th' house! *Exit [with Boy]*

1.2

Enter at one door Master Rearage, meeting Master Salewood

SALEWOOD What, Master Rearage?

REARAGE Master Salewood? Exceedingly well met in town; comes your father up this Term?

SALEWOOD Why he was here three days before the Exchequer gaped.

22 **bags** moneybags; also scrotums (see 1.1.28)
24 **cools** wanes
28 **no mean purses** considerable wealth, but also large scrotums
29.1 **three Terms** Hilary (winter), Easter (early spring), and Trinity (late spring); because it commences the legal calendar, Michaelmas is the 'father' (1.1.35)
31 **Shrugging** shuddering
shift clothes
45 **'em** 'clients' cups' or goblets (payment, perhaps in the form of bribes)
46 **bottom** possible play on 'buttocks'
47 **lamb** client; also 'lamb's-wool', hot ale mixed with the pulp of roasted apples
48 **skin** parchment or legal document
52 **come sixteen times about** that take four years to litigate
55 **reversions** leftovers
56 **meats** also 'prostitutes' or flesh of a prostitute (see 1.1.62)
returns There were eight 'days of return' in Michaelmas Term on which sheriffs returned writs (1.1.58) to the courts from which they were issued
62 **drabs** prostitutes
63 **spread...you** make myself known; also, make myself available for copulation
64 **ours** the boy actors, the Children of St Paul's
64–5 **sixpenny fees** minimum admission price at a hall playhouse
65 **dispatch** send off; also, sexually satisfy (see 1.2.134)
two hours In *Romeo and Juliet*, Prologue.12, Shakespeare refers to the 'two-hours' traffic of our stage', but Dekker, in *The Raven's Almanac*, writes of players 'glad to play three hours for two pence'.
66 **hang** idle
67 **candles be lighted** indoor playhouses were candle-lit
68 **dear and chargeable** costly, weighty
69 **happily** fortunately
71 **fondly** foolishly
74 ***Sat sapienti*** proverbial: *dictum sapienti sat est* ('a word to the wise is sufficient')
1.2.0.1 ***Rearage*** one who is in debt ('arrears')
0.2 ***Salewood*** one who has sold his family's estate
4–5 **Exchequer gaped** The court which dealt with revenue matters opened eight days before Michaelmas Term.

REARAGE Fie, such an early Termer?

SALEWOOD He's not to be spoke withal. I dare not ask him blessing till the last of November.

REARAGE And how looks thy little venturing cousin?

SALEWOOD Faith like a lute that has all the strings broke; no body will meddle with her.

REARAGE Fie, there are doctors enough in town will string her again, and make her sound as sweet as e'er she did. Is she not married yet?

SALEWOOD Sh'as no luck, some may better steal a horse than others look on. I have known a virgin of five bastards wedded. Faith, when all's done we must be fain to marry her into the North, I'm afraid.

REARAGE But will she pass so, think you?

SALEWOOD Puh, any thing that is warm enough is good enough for them; so it come in the likeness, though the devil be in't, they'll venture the firing.

REARAGE They're worthy spirits, i'faith. Heard you the news?

SALEWOOD Not yet.

REARAGE Mistress Difficult is newly fallen a widow.

SALEWOOD Say true, is Master Difficult, the lawyer, dead?

REARAGE Easily dead, sir.

SALEWOOD Pray, when died he?

REARAGE What a question's that! When should a lawyer die but in the vacation? He has no leisure to die in the Term-time; beside, the noise there would fetch him again.

SALEWOOD Knew you the nature of his disease?

REARAGE Faith, some say he died of an old grief he had, that the vacation was fourteen weeks long.

SALEWOOD And very likely. I knew 'twould kill him at last; 't'as troubled him a long time. He was one of those that would fain have brought in the heresy of a fifth Term, often crying with a loud voice, 'O, why should we lose Bartholomew week?'

REARAGE He savours, stop your nose; no more of him.

Enter Master Cockstone, a gentleman, meeting Master Easy of Essex

COCKSTONE Young Master Easy, let me salute you, sir. When came you?

EASY I have but inn'd my horse since, Master Cockstone.

COCKSTONE
You seldom visit London, Master Easy,
But now your father's dead, 'tis your only course;
Here's gallants of all sizes, of all lasts;
Here you may fit your foot, make choice of those
Whom your affection may rejoice in.

EASY
You have easily possessed me, I am free;
Let those live hinds that know not liberty.

COCKSTONE
Master Rearage?

EASY
Good Master Salewood, I am proud of your society.

REARAGE
What gentleman might that be?

COCKSTONE
One Master Easy, h'as good land in Essex,
A fair free-breasted gentleman, somewhat too open
(Bad in man, worse in woman,
The gentry-fault at first); he is yet fresh
And wants the city powd'ring. But what news?
Is't yet a match 'twixt Master Quomodo's
The rich draper's daughter and yourself?

REARAGE
Faith, sir, I am vilely rivaled!

COCKSTONE
Vilely? By whom?

REARAGE
One Andrew Lethe, crept to a little warmth,
And now so proud that he forgets all storms;
One that ne'er wore apparel but, like ditches,
'Twas cast before he had it, now shines bright
In rich embroideries. Him Master Quomodo affects,
The daughter him, the mother only me;
I rest most doubtful, my side being weakest.

COCKSTONE
Yet the mother's side
Being surer than the father's, it may prove,
'Men plead for money best, women for love.'

REARAGE
'Slid, Master Quomodo!

8 **last of November** the end of Michaelmas Term

9 **venturing** adventuring, copulating; now that she has been 'broke' (1.2.10, deflowered), no one will 'meddle' (1.2.11, copulate) with her

18 **North** Scotland

22 **venture the firing** take a shot (*fig.*); possibly, risk being aroused or risk being infected with venereal disease (fire)

31 **die** also, to have an orgasm

32 **fetch him** draw forth or bring him back from the dead; cause to ejaculate or achieve an erection (to resurrect)

35 **grief** also, disease or sickness (compare 'gripes' or *griffes*, colic pains)

41 **Bartholomew week** week in August given over to Bartholomew Fair

42.1 ***Cockstone*** a lecher (cock/penis + stone/testicle)

51 **possessed** convinced; also, to have sexually (this would make it part of a cluster of bawdy having to do with sodomy: see 'gallants of all sizes', 'foot', 'affection', 'free' and 'liberty')

52 **hinds** farm servants or cottagers

56 **Essex** The people of Essex were said to be naïve farmers.

57 **open** sincere or undisguised, but also sexually available (compare 1.2.48–52)

60 **wants** lacks

powd'ring animal flesh was 'powdered'—salted and pickled—in a powdering tub; in *Henry V*, 2.1.73, Shakespeare refers to a 'powd'ring tub', a sweating tub used to cure venereal disease

65 **warmth** comfort, security, prosperity

67 **ditches** for drainage; graves; also, from L. *scrobis*, a ditch or vulva (associated with prostitutes)

68 **cast** to dig or clear; to throw away ('apparel')

75 **'Slid** an oath, contracted from 'God's (eye)lid'

COCKSTONE
How then, afraid of a woollen draper?
REARAGE He warned me his house, and I hate he should see me abroad. [*They retire*]
[*Enter*] *Quomodo with his two spirits, Shortyard and Falselight*
QUOMODO O my two spirits, Shortyard and Falselight, you that have so enriched me, I have industry for you both!
SHORTYARD Then do you please us best, sir.
QUOMODO Wealthy employment.
SHORTYARD You make me itch, sir.
QUOMODO You, Falselight, as I have directed you—
FALSELIGHT I am nimble.
QUOMODO
Go, make my coarse commodities look sleek,
With subtle art beguile the honest eye;
Be near to my trap-window, cunning Falselight.
FALSELIGHT
I never failed it yet.
QUOMODO I know thou didst not.
Exit Falselight
But now to thee, my true and secret Shortyard,
Whom I dare trust e'en with my wife;
Thou ne'er didst mistress harm, but master good.
There are too few of thy name gentlemen,
And that we feel, but citizens in abundance.
I have a task for thee, my pregnant spirit,
To exercise thy pointed wits upon.
SHORTYARD
Give it me, for I thirst.
QUOMODO Thine ear shall drink it.
Know, then, I have not spent this long vacation
Only for pleasure's sake. Give me the man
Who out of recreation culls advantage,
Dives into seasons, never walks, but thinks,
Ne'er rides, but plots. My journey was toward Essex—
SHORTYARD
Most true.
QUOMODO Where I have seen what I desire.
SHORTYARD
A woman?
QUOMODO Puh, a woman! Yet beneath her,
That which she often treads on, yet commands her:
Land, fair neat land.
SHORTYARD What is the mark you shoot at?
QUOMODO
Why, the fairest to cleave the heir in twain;
I mean his title: to murder his estate,
Stifle his right in some detested prison.
There are means and ways enough to hook in gentry,
Besides our deadly enmity, which thus stands:
They're busy 'bout our wives, we 'bout their lands.
SHORTYARD
Your revenge is more glorious:
To be a cuckold is but for one life,
When land remains to you, your heir, or wife.
QUOMODO
Ah, sirrah, do we sting 'em? This fresh gallant
Rode newly up before me.
SHORTYARD I beseech his name.
QUOMODO
Young Master Easy.
SHORTYARD Easy? It may fall right.
QUOMODO
I have inquired his haunt.—Stay, ha!
Ay, that 'tis, that's he, that's he!
SHORTYARD Happily!
QUOMODO Observe, take surely note of him, he's fresh and free. Shift thyself speedily into the shape of gallantry. I'll swell thy purse with angels. Keep foot by foot with him, out-dare his expenses, flatter, dice, and brothel to him. Give him a sweet taste of sensuality. Train him to every wasteful sin, that he may quickly need health, but especially money. Ravish him with a dame or two, be his bawd for once; I'll be thine forever. Drink drunk with him, creep into bed to him, kiss him and undo him, my sweet spirit.
SHORTYARD
Let your care dwell in me, soon shall it shine;
What subtlety is in man, that is not mine? *Exit*
QUOMODO
O, my most cheerful spirit, go, dispatch.
Gentry is the chief fish we tradesmen catch. *Exit*
EASY What's here?

76 **woollen draper** cloth merchant
77 **warned me** forbid me from entering
78.1 ***Quomodo*** *L.* for how; may pun on the name of William Howe, a broker, convicted in Star Chamber, in 1596, of 'cozening diverse young gentlemen'
spirits chameleon-like assistants (*fig.*); also a suggestion of Quomodo's seminal fluid or vital forces
Shortyard a 'short yard', a clipped measuring stick or a small penis
82 **employment** service or work, but also intercourse (thus Shortyard's 'itch'—1.2.83—his sexual desire and his anticipated skin-irritation due to venereal disease)
88 **trap-window** hinged skylight or pent-house
94 **citizens** those who were admitted to the freedom of the city (see 1.3.48); tradesmen and merchants as opposed to gentlemen
citizens in abundance too many citizens with short yards
95 **pregnant** clever
101 **Dives into seasons** seizes opportunities
105 **treads** walks, but also copulates
106 **neat** trim, tidy
107 **heir** puns on 'hair'
108 **title** hereditary right to his property
109 **prison** debtors' prison (see 2.3.382)
116 **sting** defraud, enrage
124 **angels** gold coins; possible play on 'ingles' or catamites (see 1.2.147–8)
Keep foot by foot keep pace; also, keep up with him, 'fuck for fuck' (from Fr. *foutre*)
126 **Train** entice
130 **creep into bed to him** While it was not uncommon for men to share beds at taverns and inns, this line and the next ('Kiss him and undo him') may suggest a sexual relation; see 1.2.48–52, 2.3.151, 2.3.172–4, and 3.4.105.

SALEWOOD O, they are bills for chambers.

EASY [*reads*] 'Against Saint Andrew's, at a painter's house, there's a fair chamber ready furnished to be let, the house not only endued with a new fashion forepart, but, which is more convenient for a gentleman, with a very provident back door.'

SALEWOOD Why, here's virtue still. I like that thing that's necessary, as well as pleasant.

[*Enter Lethe, reading the bills*]

COCKSTONE What news in yonder paper?

REARAGE Ha! Seek you for news, there's for you!

SALEWOOD Who? 'Tis! In the name of the black angels, Andrew Gruel!

REARAGE No, Andrew Lethe.

SALEWOOD Lethe?

REARAGE He's forgot his father's name, poor Walter Gruel, that begot him, fed him, and brought him up.

SALEWOOD Not hither?

REARAGE No. 'Twas from his thoughts; he brought him up below.

SALEWOOD
But does he pass for Lethe?

REARAGE
'Mongst strange eyes
That no more know him than he knows himself;
That's nothing now, for Master Andrew Lethe,
A gentleman of most received parts,
Forgetfulness, lust, impudence, and falsehood,
And one especial courtly quality,
To wit, no wit at all. I am his rival
For Quomodo's daughter, but he knows it not.

SALEWOOD
He's spied us o'er his paper.

REARAGE
O, that's a warning
To make our duties ready.

COCKSTONE
Salute him? Hang him!

REARAGE
Puh, wish his health a while, he'll be laid shortly;
Let him gorge venison for a time, our doctors
Will bring him to dry mutton. Seem respective,
To make his pride swell like a toad with dew.

SALEWOOD Master Lethe!

REARAGE Sweet Master Lethe!

LETHE Gentlemen, your pardon; I remember you not.

SALEWOOD Why, we supped with you last night, sir!

LETHE
O, cry you mercy, 'tis so long ago,
I had quite forgot you; I must be forgiven.
Acquaintance, dear society, suits, and things
Do so flow to me,
That had I not the better memory,
'Twould be a wonder I should know myself.
'Esteem is made of such a dizzy metal.'
I have received of many, gifts o'er night
Whom I have forgot ere morning. Meeting the men,
I wished 'em to remember me again;
They do so, then if I forget again,
I know what helped before, that will help then.
This is my course; for memory I have been told
Twenty preserves, the best I find is gold.
Ay truly! Are you not knights yet, gentlemen?

SALEWOOD Not yet.

LETHE No, that must be looked into, 'tis your own fault. I have some store of venison, where shall we devour it, gentlemen?

SALEWOOD The Horn were a fit place.

LETHE
For venison fit,
The horn having chased it,
At the Horn we'll—
Rhyme to that?

COCKSTONE
Taste it.

SALEWOOD
Waste it.

REARAGE
Cast it.

LETHE That's the true rhyme, indeed. We hunt our venison twice, I tell you: first out o'th' park, next out o'th' belly.

COCKSTONE
First dogs take pains to make it fit for men,
Then men take pain to make it fit for dogs.

LETHE
Right.

137 **bills** advertisements; the scene is probably the middle aisle of St Paul's Cathedral, where men of fashion and unemployed servants gathered for business and display

138 **Against** near or opposite
painter's possibly a play on 'pander's' or 'prostitute's'

139 **chamber** bed chamber, but also vagina (compare, 3.1.191)

140 **forepart** perhaps a stone or brick front, but also a stomacher, the front part of a bodice

142 **back door** to escape creditors and constables or to facilitate liaisons; also associated with anal intercourse

147 **black angels** devils or fallen angels; plays on 'ingles'

148 **Andrew Gruel** stereotypical Scotsman (a satirical rendering of the courtiers who accompanied King James to London); St Andrew is the patron saint of Scotland, 'gruel' is a watery porridge favoured there

149 **Lethe** puns on the river of forgetfulness in Hades and on Leith, near Edinburgh

151 **Walter** pronounced 'water' (thus watered down 'gruel')

155 **below** in Scotland; as a commoner (see 1.2.261–2 and 298–9)

156 **strange** strangers', foreigners'

159 **received parts** recognized talents

165 **duties** homage

166 **laid** humbled; on his back

168 **dry mutton** consumed in the treatment of venereal disease
respective respectful

176 **suits** petitions

180 **dizzy** dizzying

183 **remember me** refresh my memory (with another gift)

187 **preserves** preservatives

188 **knights yet** Upon his arrival in England, James I immediately began creating an unprecedented number of knights.

193 **The Horn** Fleet Street tavern

195 **horn** the hunters' horn

200 **Cast** disgorge

202 **park** deer park

COCKSTONE
Why, this is kindness; a kind gallant, you,
And love to give the dogs more than their due.
We shall attend you, sir.

LETHE I pray do so.

SALEWOOD
The Horn.

LETHE Easily remembered that, you know!

Exeunt [*except Lethe*]

But now unto my present business. The daughter yields, and Quomodo consents; only my Mistress Quomodo, her mother, without regard runs full against me, and sticks hard. Is there no law for a woman that will run upon a man at her own apperil? Why should not she consent, knowing my state, my sudden fortunes? I can command a custard, and other bake-meats, death of sturgeon; I could keep house with nothing. What friends have I! How well am I beloved, e'en quite throughout the scullery. Not consent? 'Tis e'en as I have writ; I'll be hanged an she love me not herself, and would rather preserve me as a private friend to her own pleasures, than any way advance her daughter upon me to beguile herself. Then how have I relieved her in that point? Let me peruse this letter. [*Reads*] 'Good Mistress Quomodo, or rather, as I hope ere the Term end, Mother Quomodo, since only your consent keeps aloof off and hinders the copulation of your daughter, what may I think, but that it is a mere affection in you, doting upon some small inferior virtue of mine, to draw me in upon yourself? If the case stand so, I have comfort for you; for this you may well assure yourself, that by the marriage of your daughter I have the better means and opportunity to yourself, and without the least suspicion.' This is moving stuff, and that works best with a citizen's wife. But who shall I get to convey this now? My page I ha' lent forth; my pander I have employed about the country, to look out some third sister, or entice some discontented gentlewoman from her husband, whom the laying out of my appetite shall maintain. Nay, I'll deal like an honourable gentleman. I'll be kind to women; that which I gather i'th' day, I'll put into their purses at night. You shall have no cause to rail at me; no, faith, I'll keep you in good fashion, ladies; no meaner men than knights shall ransom home your gowns and recover your smocks. I'll not dally with you. Some poor widow woman would come as a necessary bawd now; and see where fitly comes—

[*Enter Mother Gruel*]

My mother! Curse of poverty! Does she come up to shame me, to betray my birth, and cast soil upon my new suit? Let her pass me; I'll take no notice of her. Scurvy murrey kersey!

MOTHER GRUEL By your leave, an like your worship—

LETHE [*aside*] Then I must proudly venture it.—To me, good woman?

MOTHER GRUEL I beseech one word with your worship.

LETHE Prithee, be brief then.

MOTHER GRUEL Pray, can your worship tell me any tidings of one Andrew Gruel, a poor son of mine own?

LETHE I know a gallant gentleman of the name, one Master Andrew Gruel, and well received amongst ladies.

MOTHER GRUEL That's not he, then. He is no gentleman that I mean.

LETHE Good woman, if he be a Gruel, he's a gentleman i'th' mornings, that's a gentleman o'th' first; you cannot tell me.

MOTHER GRUEL No, truly, his father was an honest upright tooth-drawer.

LETHE O, my teeth!

MOTHER GRUEL An't please your worship, I have made a sore journey on't, all this vacant time, to come up and see my son Andrew. Poor Walter Gruel, his father, has laid his life, and left me a lone woman; I have not one husband in all the world. Therefore my coming up is for relief an't like your worship, hoping that my son Andrew is in some place about the kitchen—

LETHE Kitchen! Puh, fah!

MOTHER GRUEL Or a servingman to some knight of worship.

LETHE [*aside*] O, let me not endure her!—Know you not me, good woman?

MOTHER GRUEL Alas, an't please your worship, I never saw such a glorious suit since the hour I was christened.

LETHE [*aside*]
Good, she knows me not, my glory does disguise me;

209 **Easily remembered** Horns were a familiar sign of cuckoldry.
213 **sticks** persists, resists
214 **apperil** peril, risk
216 **custard** form of 'crustade'; meat (or fruit) pie covered with mixture of milk, eggs, and spices
216–17 **death of sturgeon** possibly an oath, or a keg of sturgeon
219 **scullery** kitchen or dishwashing room (at Court) where he got his venison
220 **an** if
226–7 **keeps aloof off** must yet be won
227 **copulation** union with
230 **case stand so** with 'small ... virtue of mine', *doubles entendres* for vagina and penis
237 **look out** find
237–8 **third sister** who may have to wait some time to marry
239 **laying out** expenditure
241 **kind** act naturally with, have sexual intercourse with; put 'kind' (semen or a sexual organ) in women's 'purses' (1.2.241–2, vaginas)
242–6 **You ... you** women in the audience
244–5 **ransom home ... and recover** retrieve from pawn
245 **dally** flirt
251 **murrey kersey** purplish-red cloth dyed with mulberries; a term of contempt for a woman
252 **an** if it
263–4 **if ... mornings** gentlemen ate gruel for breakfast
264 **o'th' first** first rate
267 **tooth-drawer** dentist; butt of numerous jokes and, proverbially, a meagre figure (Tilley, T 434)
269 **An't** If it
270 **vacant time** vacation
272 **laid his life** died
282 **glory** expensive clothing

Beside, my poorer name being drenched in Lethe,
She'll hardly understand me. What a fresh air can do!
I may employ her as a private drudge
To pass my letters and secure my lust,
And ne'er be noted mine, to shame my blood,
And drop my staining birth upon my raiment.—
Faith, good woman, you will hardly get to the speech of Master Andrew, I tell you.

MOTHER GRUEL No? Marry, hang him, an't like your worship, I have known the day when nobody cared to speak to him.

LETHE You must take heed how you speak ill of him now, I can tell you; he's so employed.

MOTHER GRUEL Employed for what?

LETHE For his behaviour, wisdom, and other virtues.

MOTHER GRUEL His virtues? No, 'tis well known his father was too poor a man to bring him up to any virtues; he can scarce write and read.

LETHE He's the better regarded for that amongst courtiers, for that's but a needy quality.

MOTHER GRUEL If it be so, then he'll be great shortly, for he has no good parts about him.

LETHE Well, good woman, or mother, or what you will.

MOTHER GRUEL Alack the day, I know your worship scorns to call me mother; 'tis not a thing fit for your worship indeed, such a simple old woman as I am.

LETHE In pity of thy long journey, there's sixpence British. Tend upon me, I have business for you.

MOTHER GRUEL I'll wait upon your worship.

LETHE Two pole off at least.

MOTHER GRUEL I am a clean old woman, an't like your worship.

LETHE It goes not by cleanness here, good woman; if you were fouler, so you were braver, you might come nearer. *Exit*

MOTHER GRUEL Nay, and that be the fashion, I hope I shall get it shortly; there's no woman so old but she may learn, and as an old lady delights in a young page or monkey, so there are young courtiers will be hungry upon an old woman, I warrant you. *Exit*

1.3 *Enter Lethe's pander* [*Hellgill*], *with a Country Wench*

HELLGILL Come, leave your puling and sighing.

COUNTRY WENCH Beshrew you now, why did you entice me from my father?

HELLGILL Why? To thy better advancement. Wouldst thou, a pretty, beautiful, juicy squall, live in a poor thrummed house i'th' country in such servile habiliments, and may well pass for a gentlewoman i'th' city? Does not five hundred do so, think'st thou, and with worse faces? O, now, in these latter days, the devil reigning, 'tis an age for cloven creatures. But why sad now? Yet indeed 'tis the fashion of any courtesan to be seasick i'th' first voyage, but at next she proclaims open wars, like a beaten soldier. Why, Northamptonshire lass, dost dream of virginity now? Remember a loose-bodied gown, wench, and let it go; wires and tires, bents and bums, felts and falls, thou shalt deceive the world, that gentlewomen indeed shall not be known from others. I have a master to whom I must prefer thee after the aforesaid decking, Lethe by name, a man of one most admired property: he can both love thee, and for thy better advancement be thy pander himself, an exc'llent spark of humility.

COUNTRY WENCH Well heaven forgive you, you train me up to't.

HELLGILL Why, I do acknowledge it, and I think I do you a pleasure in't.

COUNTRY WENCH And if I should prove a harlot now, I should be bound to curse you.

HELLGILL Bound? Nay, and you prove a harlot, you'll be loose enough.

COUNTRY WENCH If I had not a desire to go like a gentlewoman, you should be hanged ere you should get me to't, I warrant you.

HELLGILL Nay, that's certain; nor a thousand more of you. I know you are all chaste enough, till one thing or other tempt you! Deny a satin gown and you dare now?

COUNTRY WENCH You know I have no power to do't, and that makes you so wilful; for what woman is there such a beast that will deny any thing that is good?

HELLGILL True, they will not, most dissemble.

COUNTRY WENCH No, an she bear a brave mind, she will not, I warrant you.

HELLGILL
Why, therefore take heart, faint not at all,
Women ne'er rise, but when they fall;

283 **poorer name** Gruel
drenched in Lethe submerged in the river of forgetfulness
284 **understand** recognize
air appearance
285 **drudge** lowly servant, slave
302 **needy quality** requirement for those who labour
304 **parts** attributes but also genitalia
309 **sixpence British** possibly a coin newly minted following the accession of James I, who styled himself King of Britain; a Scots sixpence was worth much less
312 **Two pole** 11 yards
316 **so** so long as
braver more fashionably dressed
1.3.1 **puling** whining
5 **squall** derogatory term for a young girl
thrummed thatched (see 2.2.3)
10 **cloven** devilish
13 **beaten soldier** veteran
14 **loose-bodied** a floor-length dress, said by spectator at one of Jonson's masques to be able to hide 'any deformity'; appropriate to a 'harlot' who will prove 'loose enough' (1.3.30, wanton)
15–16 **wires...falls** 'wires' are frames to support hair or a ruff; 'tires' are headdresses; 'bents' are bows or frames to extend dresses; 'bums' are padding about the posterior; 'felts' are hats; 'falls' are collars
18 **prefer** present, advance (see 1.3.4–5)
19 **decking** costuming
20 **property** quality
28 **bound** obliged; Hellgill pretends she means 'tied' or 'tight'
35 **thing** penis (also 1.3.39)
36 **Deny** refuse
44 **fall** have sexual intercourse

Let a man break, he's gone, blown up,
A woman's breaking sets her up;
Virginity is no city trade,
You're out o'th' freedom, when you're a maid;
Down with the lattice, 'tis but thin;
Let coarser beauties work within,
Whom the light mocks; thou art fair and fresh,
The gilded flies will light upon thy flesh.

COUNTRY WENCH
Beshrew your sweet enchantments, you have won.

HELLGILL [*aside*]
How easily soft women are undone.
So farewell wholesome weeds where treasure pants,
And welcome silks, where lies disease and wants.—
Come, wench, now flow thy fortunes in to bless thee,
I'll bring thee where thou shalt be taught to dress thee.

COUNTRY WENCH O, as soon as may be. I am in a swoon till I be a gentlewoman; and you know what flesh is man's meat till it be dressed.

HELLGILL Most certain, no more: a woman. *Exeunt*

Finis Actus Primus

2.1

Incipit Actus Secundus

Enter Rearage, Salewood, Lethe, Easy, with Shortyard, alias Blastfield, [and his Boy,] at dice

REARAGE Gentlemen, I ha' sworn I'll change the room. Dice? Devils!

LETHE You see I'm patient, gentlemen.

SALEWOOD Ay, the fiend's in't. You're patient, you put up all.

REARAGE Come, set me, gentlemen.

SHORTYARD An Essex gentleman, sir?

EASY An unfortunate one, sir.

SHORTYARD I'm bold to salute you, sir. You know not Master Alsup there?

EASY O, entirely well.

SHORTYARD Indeed, sir?

EASY He's second to my bosom.

SHORTYARD I'll give you that comfort then, sir, you must not want money as long as you are in town, sir.

EASY No, sir?

SHORTYARD I am bound in my love to him to see you furnished, and in that comfort I recover my salute again, sir.

EASY Then I desire to be more dear unto you.

SHORTYARD [*aside*] I rather study to be dear unto you.—Boy, fill some wine.—I knew not what fair impressure I received at first, but I began to affect your society very speedily.

EASY I count myself the happier.

SHORTYARD To Master Alsup, sir, to whose remembrance I could love to drink till I were past remembrance. [*Drinks*]

EASY I shall keep Christmas with him, sir, where your health shall likewise undoubtedly be remembered, and thereupon I pledge you. [*Drinks*] I would sue for your name, sir.

SHORTYARD Your suit shall end in one Term, sir; my name is Blastfield.

EASY Kind Master Blastfield, your dearer acquaintance. [*Drinks*]

REARAGE Nay, come, will ye draw in, gentlemen? Set me.

EASY Faith, I'm scattered.

SHORTYARD Sir, you shall not give out so meanly of yourself in my company for a million. Make such privy to your disgrace? You're a gentleman of fair fortunes; keep me your reputation. Set 'em all; there's crowns for you.

EASY Sir, you bind me infinitely in these courtesies.

SHORTYARD You must always have a care of your reputation here in town, Master Easy; although you ride down with nothing, it skills not.

EASY I'm glad you tell me that yet, then I'm indifferent. Well, come, who throws? I set all these.

SHORTYARD Why, well said.

SALEWOOD This same Master Lethe here begins to undo us again.

LETHE Ah, sir, I came not hither but to win.

SHORTYARD And then you'll leave us, that's your fashion.

LETHE He's base that visits not his friends.

SHORTYARD
But he's more base that carries out his winnings;
None will do so but those have base beginnings.

LETHE
It is a thing in use and ever was,
I pass this time.

SHORTYARD I wonder you should pass,
And that you're suffered.

45 **break** default
46 **breaking** defloration
48 **freedom** city limits (see 1.2.94, note)
49 **lattice** screen, shutter; hymen (*fig.*)
50 **within** indoors
52 **gilded flies** gallants, would-be gentlemen
55 **treasure pants** virtue breathes
61 **dressed** plays on 'clothed' and 'prepared for cooking'
2.1.1 **change the room** find a room that will be luckier for me
4–5 **put up all** win our money; 'put up with' our insults (see 3.1.123–4)
6 **set** put down a stake
9 **salute** removes his hat (see 2.1.18, where he puts his hat back on)
10 **Alsup** host to all (*fig.*)
13 **second** next
17 **him** Master Alsup
21 **dear** costly
22 **impressure** impression
34 **Blastfield** one who destroys estates, and women or wombs ('fields')
38 **scattered** broke; possibly, spread too thin
40 **such** such gallants, dicers
42 **crowns** gold coins
46 **down** back to your country estate
skills matters
57 **in use** customary
58 **pass** give up one's turn
59 **suffered** tolerated, allowed

LETHE Tut, the dice are ours
Then wonder not at those that have most powers.

REARAGE
The devil and his angels!

LETHE Are these they?
Welcome, dear angels, where you're cursed ne'er stay.
[*Retires*]

SALEWOOD Here's luck!

EASY Let's search him, gentlemen, I think he wears a smock.

SHORTYARD I knew the time he wore not half a shirt, just like a pea.

EASY No! How did he for the rest?

SHORTYARD Faith, he compounded with a couple of napkins at Barnet, and so trussed up the lower parts.

EASY 'Twas a pretty shift, i'faith.

SHORTYARD But Master Lethe has forgot that too.

EASY A mischief on't, to lose all. I could—

SHORTYARD Nay, but good Master Easy, do not do yourself that tyranny, I beseech you. I must not ha' you alter your body now for the purge of a little money; you undo me, an you do.

EASY 'Twas all I brought up with me, I protest, Master Blastfield; all my rent till next quarter.

SHORTYARD Pox of money, talk not on't, I beseech you. What said I to you? Mass, I am out of cash myself too.—Boy!

BOY Anon, sir.

SHORTYARD Run presently to Master Gum, the mercer, and will him to tell out two or three hundred pound for me, or more according as he is furnished. I'll visit him i'th' morning, say.

BOY It shall be said, sir. [*Going*]

SHORTYARD Do you hear, boy?

BOY Yes, sir.

SHORTYARD If Master Gum be not sufficiently ready, call upon Master Profit, the goldsmith.

BOY It shall be done, sir. [*Going*]

SHORTYARD Boy!

BOY [*aside*] I knew I was not sent yet; now is the time.

SHORTYARD Let them both rest till another occasion. You shall not need to run so far at this time. Take one nigher hand; go to Master Quomodo, the draper, and will him to furnish me instantly.

BOY Now I go, sir. [*Exit*]

EASY It seems you're well known, Master Blastfield, and your credit very spacious here i'th' city.

SHORTYARD Master Easy, let a man bear himself portly, the whoresons will creep to him o' their bellies, and their wives o' their backs. There's a kind of bold grace expected throughout all the parts of a gentleman. Then, for your observances, a man must not so much as spit but within line and fashion. I tell you what I ha' done: sometimes I carry my water all London over, only to deliver it proudly at the Standard; and do I pass altogether unnoted, think you? No, a man can no sooner peep out his head, but there's a bow bent at him out of some watchtower or other.

EASY So readily, sir?

SHORTYARD Push, you know a bow's quickly ready, though a gun be long a-charging, and will shoot five times to his once. Come, you shall bear yourself jovially: take heed of setting your looks to your losses, but rather smile upon your ill luck, and invite 'em tomorrow to another breakfast of bones.

EASY Nay, I'll forswear dicing.

SHORTYARD What? Peace. I am ashamed to hear you; will you cease in the first loss? Show me one gentleman that e'er did it. Fie upon't, I must use you to company, I perceive; you'd be spoiled else. Forswear dice? I would your friends heard you, i'faith.

EASY Nay, I was but in jest, sir.

SHORTYARD I hope so. What would gentlemen say of you? 'There goes a gull that keeps his money.' I would not have such a report go on you for the world, as long as you are in my company. Why, man, fortune alters in a minute. I ha' known those have recovered so much in an hour, their purses were never sick after.

REARAGE O, worse than consumption of the liver! Consumption of the patrimony!

SHORTYARD How now? Mark their humours, Master Easy.

61 **angels** Rearage puns on the name of the coin as he loses once again (see 1.2.147)
64–5 **wears a smock** wears women's undergarments; is effeminate ('to smock' was to render effeminate). 'He was lapped in his mother's smock' (Tilley, M 1203) is proverbial for 'he is very lucky'
67 **pea** nothing separates a pea from its pod and no shirt comes between Lethe and his outerwear
69 **compounded with** put together; came to terms with (*fig.*)
napkins table napkins or handkerchiefs
70 **Barnet** resort town north-west of London
lower parts genitalia
71 **shift** puns on shirt and clever trick
73 **I could** Having lost again, Easy is about to strike himself or to remove some garment that he can set as a stake.
76 **purge** loss
77 **undo** foil my plans
78 **up** to London
80 **Pox of** a common curse; 'pox' ('pocks') indicated syphilis
84 **mercer** a dealer in textiles, especially silk (which was either stiffened or glossed by coating it with 'gum')
85 **tell** count
103 **portly** grandly, majestically
104 **whoresons** i.e. merchants
109 **water** urine
110 **the Standard** the great water conduit in Cheapside
111 **pass** walk across London; urinate
111–17 **a man ... once** Shortyard claims that no sooner does a man expose his 'head' (l. 112, his penis, or prepuce) than 'a bow' (l. 112, vulva or vagina) is directed toward him. The 'bow' is 'quickly ready' (l. 115) and will 'shoot' (l. 115–16, achieve an orgasm) 'five times' (l. 115–17) in the time it takes a 'gun' (l. 115–16, a penis) to 'charge' (ejaculate) 'once' (l. 116–17).
115 **Push** pish (expression of disdain)
117–18 **take ... losses** disguise your true feelings
120 **bones** dice (see 2.1.143)
124 **use** accustom
125 **spoiled** despoiled, but also violated; see 'first loss' (2.1.123, loss of virginity)
136 **humours** temperaments

REARAGE Forgive me, my posterity yet ungotten!

SHORTYARD That's a penitent maudlin dicer.

REARAGE
Few know the sweets that the plain life allows;
Vile son that surfeits of his father's brows.

SHORTYARD Laugh at him, Master Easy.

EASY Ha, ha, ha!

SALEWOOD I'll be damned an these be not the bones of some quean that cozened me in her life, and now consumes me after her death.

SHORTYARD That's the true wicked, blasphemous, and soul-shuddering dicer, that will curse you all service time, and attribute his ill luck always to one drab or other.

[Enter Hellgill, talks apart with Lethe]

LETHE Dick Hellgill! The happy news?

HELLGILL I have her for you, sir.

LETHE Peace, what is she?

HELLGILL Young, beautiful, and plump; a delicate piece of sin.

LETHE Of what parentage?

HELLGILL O, a gentlewoman of a great house.

LETHE Fie, fie!

HELLGILL [*aside*] She newly came out of a barn; yet too good for a tooth-drawer's son.

LETHE Is she wife or maid?

HELLGILL That which is daintiest, maid.

LETHE I'd rather she'd been a wife.

HELLGILL A wife, sir? Why?

LETHE O, adultery is a great deal sweeter in my mind.

HELLGILL [*aside*] Diseases gnaw thy bones!—I think she has deserved to be a wife, sir.

LETHE
That will move well.

HELLGILL [*aside*] Her firstlings shall be mine.
Swine look but for the husks; the meat be thine.

[Enter Boy, talks apart with Shortyard and Easy]

SHORTYARD How now, boy?

BOY Master Quomodo takes your worship's greeting exceeding kindly, and in his commendations returns this answer, that your worship shall not be so apt to receive it, as he willing to lend it.

SHORTYARD Why, we thank him, i'faith.

EASY Troth, and you ha' reason to thank him sir; 'twas a very friendly answer.

SHORTYARD Push, a gentleman that keeps his days even here i'th' city, as I myself watch to do, shall have many of those answers in a twelvemonth, Master Easy.

EASY I promise you, sir, I admire your carriage, and begin to hold a more reverend respect of you.

SHORTYARD Not so, I beseech you. I give my friends leave to be inward with me.—Will you walk, gentlemen?

LETHE We're for you. [*To Hellgill*] Present her with this jewel, my first token.

Enter a Drawer

DRAWER There are certain countrymen without inquiring for Master Rearage and Master Salewood.

REARAGE Tenants!

SALEWOOD Thou reviv'st us, rascal.

REARAGE
When's our next meeting, gentlemen?

SHORTYARD Tomorrow night;
This gentleman, by me, invites you all.
Do you not, Master Easy?

EASY Freely, sir.

SALEWOOD
We do embrace your love.—[*Aside*] A pure, fresh gull.

SHORTYARD
Thus make you men at parting dutiful,
And rest beholding to you, 'tis the sleight
To be remembered when you're out of sight.

EASY
A pretty virtue. *Exeunt*

2.2

Enter the Country Wench's Father, that was enticed for Lethe

FATHER
Where shall I seek her now? O, if she knew
The dangers that attend on women's lives,
She would rather lodge under a poor thatched roof
Than under carved ceilings. She was my joy,
And all content that I received from life,
My dear and only daughter.
What says the note she left? Let me again
With staider grief peruse it.
[*Reads*] 'Father, wonder not at my so sudden departure, without your leave or knowledge. Thus, under pardon I excuse it: had you had knowledge of it, I know you would have sought to restrain it, and hinder me from what I have long desired. Being now happily preferred to a gentleman's service in London, about Holborn, if you please to send, you may hear well of me.'
As false as she is disobedient.

137 **ungotten** not yet born

140 **surfeits...brows** indulges himself at his father's expense

144 **quean** prostitute
cozened cheated

147 **service time** while church services are going on; while 'serving' (having sexual intercourse with) a 'drab'

164 **Diseases** venereal diseases

166 **move** attract, arouse sexually

166–7 **Her...thine** Hellgill will consume the Country Wench's first fruits, he will have her 'firstlings' (and so deflower the 'maid'); Lethe can have what is left over: the 'husks' fit for 'swine' and the 'meat' (the flesh of a prostitute).

176 **keeps his days even** repays his debts on time

179 **carriage** bearing or deportment; but also bearing weight during sexual intercourse (see 2.1.182, note)

182 **inward** intimate (since Easy has admired Shortyard's 'carriage', this may refer to sexual intimacy, with a play on 'innards' or bowels)

184.1 ***Drawer*** tapster

187–8 **Tenants...reviv'st us** The tenants have come to pay their rent.

194 **sleight** artifice, trick

2.2.14 **Holborn** known for licentious behaviour in its gardens and as a lawyers' quarter; prisoners were taken along Holborn to execution at Tyburn

I've made larger inquiry, left no place
Where gentry keeps, unsought, yet cannot hear,
Which drives me most into a shameful fear.
Woe worth th'infected cause that makes me visit
This man-devouring city, where I spent
My unshapen youth, to be my age's curse,
And surfeited away my name and state
In swinish riots, that now, being sober,
I do awake a beggar. I may hate her.
Whose youth voids wine, his age is cursed with water.
O heavens, I know the price of ill too well,
What the confusions are, in whom they dwell,
And how soon maids are to their ruins won;
One minute, and eternally undone.
So in mine may it, may it not be thus!
Though she be poor, her honour's precious.
May be my present form and her fond fear,
May chase her from me, if her eye should get me;
And therefore as my love and wants advise,
I'll serve, until I find her, in disguise.
Such is my care to fright her from base evils,
I leave calm state to live amongst you, devils. *Exit*

2.3 *Lethe's Mother enters with Quomodo's wife Thomasine, with the letter [from Lethe]*

THOMASINE Were these fit words, think you, to be sent to any citizen's wife: to enjoy the daughter, and love the mother too for a need? I would foully scorn that man, that should love me only for a need, I tell you. And here the knave writes again, that by the marriage of my daughter, a has the better means and opportunity to myself. He lies in his throat like a villain. He has no opportunity of me, for all that; 'tis for his betters to have opportunity of me, and that he shall well know. A base, proud knave! A has forgot how he came up, and brought two of his countrymen to give their words to my husband for a suit of green kersey. A has forgot all this. And how does he appear to me when his white satin suit's on, but like a maggot crept out of a nutshell, a fair body and a foul neck: those parts that are covered of him looks indifferent well, because we cannot see 'em. Else, for all his cleansing, pruning and paring, he's not worthy a broker's daughter, and so tell him.

MOTHER GRUEL I will indeed, forsooth.

THOMASINE And as for my child, I hope she'll be ruled in time, though she be foolish yet, and not be carried away with a cast of manchets, a bottle of wine, or a custard, and so, I pray, certify him.

MOTHER GRUEL I'll do your errand effectually.

THOMASINE Art thou his aunt, or his—

MOTHER GRUEL Alas, I am a poor drudge of his.

THOMASINE Faith, an thou wert his mother, he would make thee his drudge, I warrant him.

MOTHER GRUEL Marry, out upon him, sir-reverence of your mistress-ship.

THOMASINE Here's somewhat for thy pains, fare thee well. [*Gives money*]

MOTHER GRUEL 'Tis more than he gave me since I came to him. [*Exit*]

Enter Quomodo and his daughter Susan

QUOMODO How now, what prating have we here? Whispers? Dumb shows? Why, Thomasine, go to; my shop is not altogether so dark as some of my neighbours', where a man may be made cuckold at one end, while he's measuring with his yard at t'other.

THOMASINE Only commendations sent from Master Lethe, your worshipful son-in-law that should be.

QUOMODO O, and that you like not, he that can make us rich in custom, strong in friends, happy in suits, bring us into all the rooms o' Sundays, from the leads to the cellar, pop us in with venison till we crack again, and send home the rest in an honourable napkin—this man you like not, forsooth!

SUSAN But I like him, father.

QUOMODO My blessing go with thy liking.

SUSAN A number of our citizens hold our credit by't, to come home drunk, and say we ha' been at Court; then how much more credit is't to be drunk there indeed?

QUOMODO Tut, thy mother's a fool.—Pray, what's Master Rearage, whom you plead for so?

THOMASINE Why, first, he is a gentleman.

QUOMODO Ay, he's often first a gentleman that's last a beggar.

SUSAN My father tells you true. What should I do with a gentleman? I know not which way to lie with him.

QUOMODO 'Tis true, too. Thou know'st, beside, we undo gentlemen daily.

THOMASINE That makes so few of 'em marry with our daughters, unless it be one green fool or other. Next,

18 **unsought** unsearched
cannot hear have had no news of her
20 **Woe worth** woe unto
23 **name and state** reputation and inheritance
26 **voids** vomits
33 **fond** foolish
36 **serve** play the part of a servant
2.3.2 **enjoy** have a sexual relation with (see 5.2.9, note)
6 **a** he
10 **came up** to London; his low status
11 **countrymen** If Lethe is indeed from Scotland, this would be another derogatory reference to the recent influx of Scotsmen to London.
give their words act as guarantors
12 **kersey** coarse, wool cloth (see 1.2.251)
18 **broker's daughter** daughter of a lesser tradesman, perhaps a pawnbroker (see 2.3.423)
22 **cast of manchets** a batch of fine white bread
25 **aunt** bawd
29 **sir-reverence** 'saving your reverence'; she excuses herself for having said 'Marry'—by the Virgin Mary
36 **Dumb shows** mime
39 **measuring with his yard** working with his measuring rod; having sexual intercourse
43 **custom** business
happy in suits successful when petitioning at Court
44 **all the rooms** at Court
leads lead roof
45 **crack** fart
59 **lie with** have sexual intercourse with
63 **green** gullible

Master Rearage has land and living, t'other but his walk i'th' street, and his snatching diet. He's able to entertain you in a fair house of his own, t'other in some nook or corner, or place us behind the cloth like a company of puppets. At his house you shall be served curiously, sit down and eat your meat with leisure; there we must be glad to take it standing, and without either salt, cloth, or trencher, and say we are befriended too.

QUOMODO O, that gives a citizen a better appetite than his garden.

SUSAN So say I, father; methinks it does me most good when I take it standing. I know not how all women's minds are.

Enter Falselight

QUOMODO Faith, I think they are all of thy mind for that thing.—How now, Falselight?

FALSELIGHT I have descried my fellow, Shortyard, alias Blastfield, at hand with the gentleman.

QUOMODO O, my sweet Shortyard!—Daughter, get you up to your virginals. [*Exit Susan*]
By your leave, Mistress Quomodo.

THOMASINE Why, I hope I may sit i'th' shop, may I not?

QUOMODO That you may, and welcome sweet honey-thigh, but not at this season, there's a buck to be struck.

THOMASINE [*aside*] Well, since I'm so expressly forbidden, I'll watch above i'th' gallery, but I'll see your knavery. *Exit*

QUOMODO Be you prepared as I tell you.

FALSELIGHT You ne'er feared me. *Exit*

QUOMODO O, that sweet, neat, comely, proper, delicate parcel of land, like a fine gentlewoman i'th' waist, not so great as pretty, pretty; the trees in summer whistling, the silver waters by the banks harmoniously gliding. I should have been a scholar; an excellent place for a student, fit for my son that lately commenced at Cambridge, whom now I have placed at Inns of Court. Thus we that seldom get lands honestly, must leave our heirs to inherit our knavery. But whist, one turn about my shop and meet with 'em.

Enter Master Easy with Shortyard, alias Blastfield [and Boy]

EASY Is this it, sir?

SHORTYARD Ay, let me see, this is it—sign of Three Knaves—'tis it.

QUOMODO [*into the shop*] Do you hear, sir?—What lack you, gentlemen? See good kerseys or broadcloths here, I pray come near.—Master Blastfield!

SHORTYARD I thought you would know me anon.

[*Enter Thomasine above*]

QUOMODO You're exceeding welcome to town, sir. Your worship must pardon me, 'tis always misty weather in our shops here; we are a nation the sun ne'er shines upon. Came this gentleman with you?

SHORTYARD O, salute him fairly. He's a kind gentleman, a very inward of mine.

QUOMODO Then I cry you mercy, sir. You're especially welcome.

EASY I return you thanks, sir.

QUOMODO But how shall I do for you now, Master Blastfield?

SHORTYARD Why, what's the matter?

QUOMODO It is my greatest affliction at this instant, I am not able to furnish you.

SHORTYARD How, Master Quomodo? Pray, say not so; 'slud, you undo me then.

QUOMODO Upon my religion, Master Blastfield, bonds lie forfeit in my hands. I expect the receipt of a thousand every hour, and cannot yet set eye of a penny.

SHORTYARD That's strange, methinks.

QUOMODO 'Tis mine own pity that plots against me, Master Blastfield. They know I have no conscience to take the forfeiture, and that makes 'em so bold with my mercy.

EASY I am sorry for this.

QUOMODO Nevertheless, if I might entreat your delay but the age of three days, to express my sorrow now, I would double the sum, and supply you with four or five hundred.

SHORTYARD Let me see, three days?

QUOMODO Ay, good sir, and it may be possible.

EASY [*aside to Shortyard*] Do you hear, Master Blastfield?

SHORTYARD Ha?

EASY You know I've already invited all the gallants to sup with me tonight.

SHORTYARD That's true, i'faith.

EASY 'Twill be my everlasting shame, if I have no money to maintain my bounty.

SHORTYARD I ne'er thought upon that.—[*Aside*] I looked still when that should come from him.—We have

64 **living** rent, income
65 **snatching diet** leftovers (like Lethe's venison) grabbed at Court; also, a 'diet' of snatches, or quick sexual encounters
67 **cloth** arras or hanging at Court
67–8 **a company of puppets** at a puppet show
68–70 **served...standing** descriptions of hospitality but also of intercourse ('served' sitting or 'take it standing') in a gentleman's house or at Court; see 2.1.146–8, 2.3.58–9 and 75
68 **curiously** fastidiously
69 **there** at Court
71 **trencher** wooden platter or knife
72–3 **his garden** his vegetable garden, but also his wife's genitals
78 **thing** copulation; also, penis (see 5.1.53)
82 **virginals** spinet in a box, without legs, or keyed musical instrument
83 **By your leave** please leave us
86 **season** time
buck to be struck deer (gull) to be caught or killed
90 **feared** mistrusted
96 **commenced** took his degree
97 **Inns of Court** London's legal colleges
99 **whist** silence
102–3 **Three Knaves** Quomodo, Shortyard, and Falselight
104 **What lack you** tradesman's customary greeting
109 **misty weather** 'not altogether so dark' (2.3.37)
114 **cry you mercy** beg your pardon
121 **furnish** 'supply' (2.3.134); also, procure for
123 **'slud** common oath, 'God's blood'
undo ruin
126 **of** on
129–30 **take the forfeiture** foreclose
145–6 **I looked...him** I have been waiting for him to say that

strictly examined our expenses; it must not be three days, Master Quomodo.

QUOMODO No? Then I'm afraid 'twill be my grief, sir.

EASY Master Blastfield, I'll tell you what you may do now.

SHORTYARD What, good sweet bedfellow?

EASY Send to Master Gum or Master Profit, the mercer and goldsmith.

SHORTYARD Mass, that was well remembered of thee.—[*Aside*] I perceive the trout will be a little troublesome ere he be catched.—Boy!

BOY Here, sir.

SHORTYARD Run to Master Gum, or Master Profit, and carry my present occasion of money to 'em.

BOY I run, sir. [*Exit*]

QUOMODO Methinks, Master Blastfield, you might easily attain to the satisfaction of three days; here's a gentleman, your friend, I dare say will see you sufficiently possessed till then.

EASY Not I, sir, by no means. Master Blastfield knows I'm further in want than himself; my hope rests all upon him. It stands upon the loss of my credit tonight, if I walk without money.

SHORTYARD Why, Master Quomodo, what a fruitless motion have you put forth. You might well assure yourself this gentleman had it not, if I wanted it. Why, our purses are brothers; we desire but equal fortunes; in a word, we're man and wife; they can but lie together, and so do we.

EASY As near as can be, i'faith.

SHORTYARD And to say truth, 'tis more for the continuing of this gentleman's credit in town, than any incitement from mine own want only, that I covet to be so immediately furnished. You shall hear him confess as much himself.

EASY 'Tis most certain, Master Quomodo.

Enter Boy

SHORTYARD O, here comes the boy now.—How now, boy, what says Master Gum, or Master Profit?

BOY Sir, they're both walked forth this frosty morning to Brentford, to see a nurse-child.

SHORTYARD A bastard be it. Spite and shame!

EASY Nay, never vex yourself, sweet Master Blastfield.

SHORTYARD Bewitched, I think!

QUOMODO Do you hear, sir? [*Aside to Easy*] You can persuade with him?

EASY A little, sir.

QUOMODO Rather than he should be altogether destitute, or be too much a vexation to himself, he shall take up a commodity of cloth of me, tell him.

EASY Why, la! By my troth, 'twas kindly spoken.

QUOMODO Two hundred pounds worth, upon my religion, say.

SHORTYARD So disastrously!

EASY Nay, Master Blastfield, you do not hear what Master Quomodo said since, like an honest, true citizen, i'faith. Rather than you should grow diseased upon't, you shall take up a commodity of two hundred pounds worth of cloth.

SHORTYARD The mealy moth consume it, would he ha' me turn pedlar now? What should I do with cloth?

QUOMODO He's a very wilful gentleman at this time, i'faith. He knows as well what to do with it as I myself, iwis. There's no merchant in town but will be greedy upon't, and pay down money upo'th' nail. They'll dispatch it over to Middleburgh presently, and raise double commodity by exchange. If not, you know 'tis Term-time, and Michaelmas Term too, the drapers' harvest for footcloths, riding suits, walking suits, chamber gowns, and hall gowns.

EASY Nay, I'll say that, it comes in as fit a time as can be.

QUOMODO Nay, take me with you again ere you go, sir. I offer him no trash, tell him, but present money, say, where I know some gentlemen in town ha' been glad, and are glad at this time, to take up commodities in hawks' hoods and brown paper.

EASY O, horrible! Are there such fools in town?

QUOMODO I offer him no trash, tell him, upon my religion, you may say.—[*Aside*] Now, my sweet Shortyard, now the hungry fish begins to nibble; one end of the worm is in his mouth, i'faith.

THOMASINE [*aside*]
Why stand I here (as late our graceless dames
That found no eyes) to see that gentleman
Alive, in state and credit executed,
Help to rip up himself, does all he can?
Why am I wife to him that is no man?

159 **carry ... occasion** tell them of my pressing need

167 **stands upon** entails

168 **walk** depart from here

169–70 **fruitless motion** worthless proposal; also, in the context of 'satisfaction' (l. 163), 'possessed' (l. 164), 'stands upon' (l. 167), 'purses' (l. 172), and 'we're man and wife' (l. 173), a barren sexual encounter

185 **Brentford** a short ride west of London; notorious for assignations (hence the illegitimate 'nurse-child' hidden with its wet-nurse)

193–4 **take ... cloth** take a loan in the form of cloth instead of cash

201 **diseased** dis-eased

207 **iwis** certainly

209 **upo'th' nail** on the spot

210 **Middleburgh** Dutch port and wool mart for English merchants

210–11 **raise ... exchange** double their money

212 **harvest** opportunity to 'reap' big profits

213 **footcloths** saddlecloths

213–14 **chamber gowns, and hall gowns** clothes for private rooms and for ceremonies (in great halls)

216 **take ... go** make no doubt about it

218 **where** whereas

220 **hawks' hoods** Hunting hawks were hooded to keep them calm.

226–9 **Why ... can** Thomasine compares herself to women watching an execution (see 2.3.378–80)

227 **found no eyes** would not weep

229 **Help ... can** Easy helps the executioner who has hanged him, to quarter him ('rip up')

230 **no man** inhumane; impotent (see 4.3.56–8 and 5.1.52–3)

I suffer in that gentleman's confusion.

EASY Nay, be persuaded in that, Master Blastfield. 'Tis ready money at the merchants'; beside, the winter season and all falls in as pat as can be to help it.

SHORTYARD Well, Master Easy, none but you could have persuaded me to that.—Come, would you would dispatch then, Master Quomodo; where's this cloth?

QUOMODO Full and whole within, all of this piece, of my religion, Master Blastfield. Feel't, nay, feel't and spare not, gentlemen; your fingers and your judgement.

SHORTYARD Cloth's good.

EASY By my troth, exceeding good cloth; a good wale 't'as.

QUOMODO Falselight!

[*Enter Falselight*]

FALSELIGHT I'm ne'er out o' the shop, sir.

QUOMODO Go, call in a porter presently to carry away the cloth with the star mark.—Whither will you please to have it carried, Master Blastfield?

SHORTYARD Faith, to Master Beggarland, he's the only merchant now; or his brother, Master Stillyard-down, there's little difference.

QUOMODO You've happened upon the money men, sir; they and some of their brethren, I can tell you, will not stick to offer thirty thousand pound to be cursed still; great monied men, their stocks lie in the poor's throats. But you'll see me sufficiently discharged, Master Blastfield, ere you depart?

SHORTYARD You have always found me righteous in that.

QUOMODO Falselight!

FALSELIGHT Sir?

QUOMODO You may bring a scrivener along with you.

FALSELIGHT I'll remember that, sir. [*Exit*]

QUOMODO Have you sent for a citizen, Master Blastfield?

SHORTYARD No, faith, not yet.—Boy!

EASY What must you do with a citizen, sir?

SHORTYARD A custom they're bound to o' late by the default of evil debtors; no citizen must lend money without two be bound in the bond; the second man enters but for custom sake.

EASY No? And must he needs be a citizen?

SHORTYARD By th' mass, stay, I'll learn that.—Master Quomodo!

QUOMODO Sir?

SHORTYARD Must the second party, that enters into bond only for fashion's sake, needs be a citizen? What say you to this gentleman for one?

QUOMODO Alas, sir, you know he's a mere stranger to me; I neither am sure of his going or abiding; he may inn here tonight, and ride away tomorrow. Although I grant the chief burden lies upon you, yet we are bound to make choice of those we know, sir.

SHORTYARD Why, he's a gentleman of a pretty living, sir.

QUOMODO It may be so, yet, under both your pardons, I'd rather have a citizen.

EASY I hope you will not disparage me so. 'Tis well known I have three hundred pound a year in Essex.

SHORTYARD Well said! To him thyself. Take him up roundly.

EASY And how doubtfully soe'er you account of me, I do not think but I might make my bond pass for a hundred pound i'th' city.

QUOMODO What, alone sir?

EASY Alone, sir? Who says so? Perhaps I'd send down for a tenant or two.

QUOMODO Ay, that's another case, sir.

EASY Another case let it be then!

QUOMODO Nay, grow not into anger, sir.

EASY Not take me into a bond? As good as you shall, goodman goosecap.

QUOMODO Well, Master Blastfield, because I will not disgrace the gentleman, I'm content for once, but we must not make a practice on't.

EASY No, sir, now you would, you shall not.

QUOMODO [*aside*] Cuds me, I'm undone; he's gone again.

SHORTYARD [*aside*] The net's broke.

THOMASINE [*aside*] Hold there, dear gentleman.

EASY Deny me that small courtesy? 'Sfoot, a very Jew will not deny it me.

SHORTYARD [*aside*] Now must I catch him warily.

EASY A jest indeed; not take me into a bond, quo' they.

SHORTYARD [*aside to Easy*] Master Easy. Mark my words: if it stood not upon the eternal loss of thy credit against supper—

EASY Mass, that's true.

SHORTYARD The pawning of thy horse for his own victuals—

EASY Right, i'faith.

SHORTYARD And thy utter dissolution amongst gentlemen forever—

EASY Pox on't!

SHORTYARD Quomodo should hang, rot, stink—

QUOMODO [*aside*] Sweet boy, i'faith.

231 **confusion** destruction
242 **wale** texture
244 **I'm . . . shop** plays on his name
246 **star mark** merchant or weaver's insignia
249 **Stillyard-down** one whose scale ('steelyard') doesn't weigh accurately; another citizen who is always impotent
252 **stick** hesitate
253 **still** always, continually
254 **their . . . throats** they have profited at the expense of the poor
255 **discharged** released; a bond must be signed
260 **scrivener** notary, copyist
267 **without** unless
268 **enters** signs; in the context of 'going' and 'inn' (l. 277), 'ride' (l. 278), 'burden lies upon you' (l. 279), 'case' (ll. 294 and 295), and 'undone' (l. 303; see 2.1.77, note), this suggests intercourse
276 **mere** complete
279 **chief burden** see 2.3.360–73, where Easy signs first and Shortyard second, merely as a guarantor
281 **pretty living** considerable estate; his rent comes to 'three hundred pound a year' (2.3.285)
287 **roundly** without equivocation; bluntly
292 **I'd send down** if I were to send to Essex
298 **goodman goosecap** master simpleton
303 **Cuds me** oath, corrupted from 'God save me'
305 **Hold there** proceed no further
306 **'Sfoot** oath, contracted from 'God's foot'
309 **quo' they** said they

SHORTYARD Drop, damn.

QUOMODO [*aside*] Excellent Shortyard!

EASY I forgot all this. What meant I to swagger before I had money in my purse?—How does Master Quomodo? Is the bond ready?

QUOMODO O, sir!

Enter Dustbox, the scrivener

EASY Come, we must be friends. Here's my hand.

QUOMODO Give it the scrivener. Here he comes.

DUSTBOX Good day, Master Quomodo. Good morrow, gentlemen.

QUOMODO We must require a little aid from your pen, good Master Dustbox.

DUSTBOX What be the gentlemen's names that are bound, sir?

QUOMODO Master John Blastfield, esquire, i'th' wild of Kent; and what do they call your bedfellow's name?

SHORTYARD Master Richard Easy; you may easily hit on't.

QUOMODO Master Richard Easy, of Essex, gentleman; both bound to Ephestian Quomodo, citizen and draper of London; the sum, two hundred pound. What time do you take, Master Blastfield, for the payment?

SHORTYARD I never pass my month, you know.

QUOMODO I know it, sir. October sixteenth today; sixteenth of November, say.

EASY Is it your custom to return so soon, sir?

SHORTYARD I never miss you.

Enter Falselight, like a porter, sweating

FALSELIGHT I am come for the rest of the same piece, Master Quomodo.

QUOMODO Star mark, this is it. Are all the rest gone?

FALSELIGHT They're all at Master Stillyard-down's by this time.

EASY How the poor rascal's all in a froth!

SHORTYARD
Push, they're ordained to sweat for gentlemen;
Porters' backs and women's bellies bear up the world.
[*Exit Falselight with remaining cloth*]

EASY 'Tis true, i'faith; they bear men and money, and that's the world.

SHORTYARD You've found it, sir.

DUSTBOX I'm ready to your hands, gentlemen.

SHORTYARD Come, Master Easy. [*Gestures to Easy to sign*]

EASY I beseech you, sir.

SHORTYARD It shall be yours, I say.

EASY Nay, pray, Master Blastfield.

SHORTYARD I will not, i'faith.

EASY What do you mean, sir?

SHORTYARD I should show little bringing up, to take the way of a stranger.

EASY By my troth, you do yourself wrong though, Master Blastfield.

SHORTYARD Not a whit, sir.

EASY But to avoid strife, you shall have your will of me for once.

SHORTYARD Let it be so, I pray. [*Easy signs*]

QUOMODO [*aside*] Now I begin to set one foot upon the land. Methinks I am felling of trees already; we shall have some Essex logs yet to keep Christmas with, and that's a comfort.

THOMASINE
Now is he quart'ring out; the executioner
Strides over him; with his own blood he writes.
I am no dame that can endure such sights.
Exit [*above*]

SHORTYARD [*aside*]
So his right wing is cut, he will not fly far
Past the two city hazards, Poultry and Wood Street.

EASY How like you my Roman hand, i'faith?

DUSTBOX Exceeding well, sir, but that you rest too much upon your R's and make your E's too little.

EASY I'll mend that presently.

DUSTBOX Nay, 'tis done now, past mending. [*Shortyard signs*] You both deliver this to Master Quomodo as your deed?

SHORTYARD We do, sir.

QUOMODO I thank you, gentlemen. [*Exit Dustbox*]

SHORTYARD Would the coin would come away now. We have deserved for't.

Enter Falselight [*disguised as a porter*] *with the cloth*

FALSELIGHT By your leave a little, gentlemen.

SHORTYARD How now? What's the matter? Speak!

FALSELIGHT As fast as I can, sir. All the cloth's come back again.

QUOMODO How?

SHORTYARD What's the news?

FALSELIGHT The passage to Middleburgh is stopped, and therefore neither Master Stillyard-down nor Master Beggarland, nor any other merchant, will deliver present money upon't. [*Exit Falselight*]

QUOMODO Why, what hard luck have you, gentlemen!

322 **damn** be damned

327.1 ***Dustbox*** the 'dustbox' contains sand with which to blot ink

328 **hand** Easy offers to shake hands, but Quomodo tells him to give his signature ('hand') to the scrivener

336 **wild of Kent** forest ('weald') south-east of London

340 **Ephestian** compare Hephaestion, Alexander the Great's lover (all of Asia was ordered to mourn at his death); also Hephaestus, who, as the Roman god Vulcan, was made a cuckold by Venus and Mars

346 **return** repay

358 **it** my meaning

362 **It** the 'courtesy' of signing first

366–7 **to take the way of** precede

375 **felling of trees** deforestation; controversial 'improvement' meant to maximize profits

378 **quart'ring out** see 2.3.229; those guilty of treason were hanged, drawn, and quartered; Easy has betrayed his inheritance, his 'blood' (2.3.379)

382 **Poultry and Wood Street** debtors' prisons

383 **Roman** the fashionable 'Italian' style of handwriting, as opposed to Secretary or Court hand

385 **R's . . . E's** puns on 'arse' and 'ease'

392 **coin** payment for the cloth

400 **passage . . . stopped** the route is closed (perhaps due to a Spanish blockade or attack, or to an English export prohibition)

EASY Why, Master Blastfield!

SHORTYARD Pish!

EASY You're so discontented too presently, a man cannot tell how to speak to you.

SHORTYARD Why, what would you say?

EASY We must make somewhat on't now, sir.

SHORTYARD Ay, where? How? The best is, it lies all upon my neck.—Master Quomodo, can you help me to any money for't? Speak.

QUOMODO Troth, Master Blastfield, since myself is so unfurnished, I know not the means how. There's one i'th' street, a new setter up; if any lay out money upon't, 'twill be he.

SHORTYARD His name?

QUOMODO Master Idem. But you know we cannot give but greatly to your loss, because we gain and live by't.

SHORTYARD 'Sfoot, will he give anything?

EASY Ay, stand upon that.

SHORTYARD Will he give anything? The brokers will give nothing, to no purpose.

QUOMODO Falselight!

[*Enter Falselight above*]

FALSELIGHT Over your head, sir.

QUOMODO Desire Master Idem to come presently and look upo'th' cloth.

FALSELIGHT I will, sir. [*Exit above*]

SHORTYARD What if he should offer but a hundred pound?

EASY If he want twenty on't, let's take it.

SHORTYARD Say you so?

EASY Master Quomodo will have four or five hundred pound for you of his own within three or four days.

[*Enter Thomasine*]

SHORTYARD 'Tis true, he said so indeed.

EASY Is that your wife, Master Quomodo?

QUOMODO That's she, little Thomasine!

EASY Under your leave, sir, I'll show myself a gentleman.

QUOMODO Do, and welcome, Master Easy.

EASY I have commission for what I do, lady, from your husband. [*Kisses her*]

THOMASINE You may have a stronger commission for the next, an't please you, that's from myself.

Enter Sim

EASY You teach me the best law, lady.

THOMASINE [*aside*] Beshrew my blood, a proper springall and a sweet gentleman.

QUOMODO My son, Sim Quomodo! Here's more work for you, Master Easy; you must salute him too—[*Aside*] for he's like to be heir of thy land, I can tell thee.

SIM *Vim, vitam, spemque salutem.*

QUOMODO He shows you there he was a Cambridge man, sir, but now he's a Templar. Has he not good grace to make a lawyer?

EASY A very good grace to make a lawyer.

SHORTYARD [*aside*] For, indeed, he has no grace at all.

QUOMODO Some gave me counsel to make him a divine.

EASY Fie, fie!

QUOMODO But some of our livery think it an unfit thing, that our own sons should tell us of our vices; others, to make him a physician, but then, being my heir, I'm afraid he would make me away. Now, a lawyer, they're all willing to, because 'tis good for our trade and increaseth the number of cloth gowns, and indeed 'tis the fittest for a citizen's son, for our word is, 'What do ye lack?' and their word is, 'What do you give?'

EASY Exceeding proper.

Enter Falselight for Master Idem

QUOMODO Master Idem, welcome!

FALSELIGHT I have seen the cloth, sir.

QUOMODO Very well.

FALSELIGHT I am but a young setter up; the uttermost I dare venture upon't is threescore pound.

SHORTYARD What?

FALSELIGHT If it be for me so, I am for it; if not, you have your cloth and I have my money.

EASY Nay, pray, Master Blastfield, refuse not his kind offer.

SHORTYARD A bargain then, Master Idem, clap hands.—[*Aside*] He's finely cheated.—Come, let's all to the next tavern and see the money paid.

EASY A match!

QUOMODO I follow you, gentlemen; take my son along with you. *Exeunt* [*all but Quomodo*]

Now to my keys; I'm Master Idem, he must fetch the money. First have I caught him in a bond for two hundred pound, and [ ] my two hundred pounds' worth o' cloth again for threescore pound. Admire me, all you students at Inns of Cozenage. *Exit*

Finis Actus Secundus

416 **a new setter up** one newly established
419 **Idem** 'the same' (Quomodo himself, see 2.3.482)
419–20 **we ... loss** what we pay you must be less than what we have charged you for the same goods
422 **stand** insist
426 **Over your head** plays on his name
431 **want twenty on't** twenty less; i.e. eighty pounds
445 **springall** young man (variant of 'springald')
450 ***Vim ... salutem*** 'Let me salute strength, life, and hope'
452 **Templar** at one of the Inns of Court (see 2.3.96–7)
458 **livery** the woollen drapers' company
461 **make me away** kill me
463 **gowns** worn by lawyers (see 1.1.2)
466.1 ***for*** disguised as
476 **clap hands** shake hands and so make a deal
482 **keys** to where he keeps his money
484 **and ... my** the text is corrupt here; perhaps 'now have I' or 'have got' has dropped out
486 **Cozenage** cheating

3.1 *Incipit Actus Tertius*

Enter Lethe's pander, Hellgill, the Country Wench coming in [as a Courtesan] with a new fashion gown, dressed gentlewoman-like, the Tailor points it, and Mistress Comings, a tirewoman, busy about her head

HELLGILL You talk of an alteration; here's the thing itself. What base birth does not raiment make glorious? And what glorious births do not rags make infamous? Why should not a woman confess what she is now, since the finest are but deluding shadows, begot between tirewomen and tailors? For instance, behold their parents.

MISTRESS COMINGS Say what you will, this wire becomes you best.—How say you, tailor?

TAILOR I promise you 'tis a wire would draw me from my work seven days a week.

COURTESAN Why, do you work o' Sundays, tailor?

TAILOR Hardest of all, o' Sundays, because we are most forbidden.

COURTESAN Troth, and so do most of us women; the better day the better deed, we think.

MISTRESS COMINGS Excellent, exceeding, i'faith. A narrow-eared wire sets out a cheek so fat and so full, and if you be ruled by me, you shall wear your hair still like a mock-face behind; 'tis such an Italian world, many men know not before from behind.

TAILOR How like you the sitting of this gown now, Mistress Comings?

MISTRESS COMINGS It sits at marvellous good ease and comely discretion.

HELLGILL Who would think now this fine sophisticated squall came out of the bosom of a barn, and the loins of a hay-tosser?

COURTESAN Out, you saucy, pestiferous pander! I scorn that, i'faith.

HELLGILL Excellent, already the true phrase and style of a strumpet. Stay, a little more of the red, and then I take my leave of your cheek for four-and-twenty hours.—Do you not think it impossible that her own father should know her now, if he saw her?

COURTESAN Why, I think no less. How can he know me, when I scarce know myself?

HELLGILL 'Tis right.

COURTESAN But so well you lay wait for a man for me.

HELLGILL I protest I have bestowed much labour about it; and in fit time, good news, I hope.

Enter a Servant bringing in her Father in disguise to serve her

SERVANT I've found one yet at last, in whose preferment I hope to reap credit.

COURTESAN Is that the fellow?

SERVANT Lady, it is.

COURTESAN Art thou willing to serve me, fellow?

FATHER So please you, he that has not the heart to serve such a mistress as your beautiful self, deserves to be honoured for a fool or knighted for a coward.

COURTESAN There's too many of them already.

FATHER 'Twere sin then to raise the number.

COURTESAN Well we'll try both our likings for a month, and then either proceed, or let fall the suit.

FATHER Be it as you have spoke, but 'tis my hope a longer Term.

COURTESAN No, truly, our Term ends once a month. We should get more than the lawyers, for they have but four Terms a year, and we have twelve, and that makes 'em run so fast to us in the vacation.

FATHER [*aside*] A mistress of a choice beauty! Amongst such imperfect creatures I ha' not seen a perfecter. I should have reckoned the fortunes of my daughter amongst the happiest, had she lighted into such a service, whereas now I rest doubtful whom or where she serves.

COURTESAN [*gives money*] There's for your bodily advice, tailor; and there's for your head-counsel; and I discharge you both till tomorrow morning again.

TAILOR At which time our neatest attendance.

MISTRESS COMINGS I pray, have an especial care, howsoever you stand or lie, that nothing fall upon your hair to batter your wire. *Exeunt [Tailor and Mistress Comings]*

COURTESAN I warrant you for that.—Which gown becomes me best now, the purple satin or this?

HELLGILL If my opinion might rule over you—

Enter Lethe with Rearage and Salewood

LETHE Come, gallants, I'll bring you to a beauty shall strike your eyes into your hearts. What you see you shall desire, yet never enjoy.

REARAGE And that's a villainous torment.

SALEWOOD And is she but your underput, Master Lethe?

LETHE No more, of my credit; and a gentlewoman of a great house, noble parentage, unmatchable education, my plain punk. I may grace her with the name of a

3.1.0.4–5 ***points it*** ties the laces
0.5 ***Comings*** puns on 'combings' but coming and going also suggests that she is a bawd; Mistress Comings is a hairdresser, although a 'tirewoman' was commonly a lady's maid or a dressmaker
8 **wire** either the entire headdress or just its supporting wire frame (see 1.3.14–16)
20 **mock-face** provocative hair arrangement resembling a face; if 'face' is slang for 'arse' (see 3.1.201 note), then this phrase sets up the next
20–1 **Italian . . . behind** Italian men were said to engage in sodomy
27 **squall** see 1.3.4–6, note
29 **pestiferous** plaguy, pernicious
32 **red** rouge
39 **But so well** How well (ironical)
lay . . . man look out for a servant
41.1 ***Servant*** Hellgill's man
47 **serve** see 2.3.68–70, note
49 **knighted** see 1.2.188, note
52 **try . . . likings** see if we are suited to each other
58 **four Terms** see 1.1.29.1, note; this concludes the legal metaphor that begins with 'proceed' (3.1.53)
61 **such imperfect creatures** womankind
71 **stand or lie** see 2.3.58–9 and 2.3.68–70, note
80 **underput** mistress, courtesan
83 **punk** prostitute

courtesan, a backslider, a prostitution, or such a toy; but when all comes to all, 'tis but a plain punk. Look you gentlemen, that's she; behold her.

COURTESAN O, my beloved strayer! I consume in thy absence.

LETHE La, you now. You shall not say I'll be proud to you, gentlemen; I give you leave to salute her.—[*Aside*] I'm afraid of nothing now, but that she'll utterly disgrace 'em, turn tail to 'em, and place their kisses behind her. No, by my faith, she deceives me; by my troth, she's kissed 'em both with her lips. I thank you for that music, masters. 'Slid, they both court her at once, and see, if she ha' not the wit to stand still and let 'em! I think if two men were brewed into one, there is that woman would drink 'em up both.

REARAGE [*to Courtesan*] A coxcomb! He a courtier?

COURTESAN He says he has a place there.

SALEWOOD So has the fool, a better place than he, and can come where he dare not show his head.

LETHE Nay, hear you me, gentlemen—

SALEWOOD I protest, you were the last man we spoke on. We're a little busy yet; pray stay there awhile. We'll come to you presently.

LETHE [*aside*] This is good, i'faith; endure this and be a slave forever! Since you neither savour of good breeding nor bringing up, I'll slice your hamstrings, but I'll make you show mannerly!—Pox on you, leave courting. I ha' not the heart to hurt an Englishman, i'faith, or else—

SALEWOOD What else?

LETHE Prithee, let's be merry; nothing else.—[*To Servant*] Here, fetch some wine.

COURTESAN Let my servant go for't.

LETHE Yours? Which is he?

FATHER This, sir.—
(*Aside*) But I scarce like my mistress now; the loins
Can ne'er be safe where the flies be so busy.
Wit, by experience bought, foils wit at school;
Who proves a deeper knave than a spent fool?—
I am gone for your worship's wine, sir. [*Exit*]

HELLGILL [*aside to Lethe*] Sir, you put up too much indignity; bring company to cut your own throat. The fire is not yet so hot, that you need two screens before it; 'tis but new kindled yet. If 'twere risse to a flame, I could not blame you then to put others before you; but, alas, all the heat yet is comfortable, a cherisher, not a defacer.

LETHE Prithee, let 'em alone. They'll be ashamed on't anon, I trow, if they have any grace in 'em.

HELLGILL [*aside*] I'd fain have him quarrel, fight, and be assuredly killed, that I might beg his place, for there's ne'er a one void yet. [*Exit with Servant*]

Enter Shortyard with Easy

COURTESAN You'll make him mad anon.

SALEWOOD 'Tis to that end.

SHORTYARD Yet at last Master Quomodo is as firm as his promise.

EASY Did I not tell you still he would?

SHORTYARD Let me see, I am seven hundred pound in bond now to the rascal.

EASY Nay, you're no less, Master Blastfield, look to't. By my troth, I must needs confess, sir, you ha' been uncommonly kind to me since I ha' been in town; but Master Alsup shall know on't.

SHORTYARD That's my ambition, sir.

EASY I beseech you, sir.—Stay, this is Lethe's haunt, see, we have catched him.

LETHE Master Blastfield and Master Easy, you're kind gentlemen both.

SHORTYARD Is that the beauty you famed so?

LETHE The same.

SHORTYARD Who be those so industrious about her?

LETHE Rearage and Salewood. I'll tell you the unmannerliest trick of 'em, that ever you heard in your life.

SHORTYARD Prithee, what's that?

LETHE I invited 'em hither to look upon her, brought 'em along with me, gave 'em leave to salute her in kindness; what do they but most saucily fall in love with her, very impudently court her for themselves, and, like two crafty attorneys, finding a hole in my lease, go about to defeat me of my right?

SHORTYARD Ha' they so little conscience?

LETHE The most uncivil'st part that you have seen. I know they'll be sorry for't when they have done, for there's

84 **toy** trifle, whim
87 **consume** waste away
90 **salute** kiss
92 **tail** her anus or vagina
95 **music** loud kisses
99 **coxcomb** conceited fool, a fop
100 **place there** position at Court
101 **fool** jester; King James brought Archy Armstrong, his fool, with him from Scotland to England
105 **busy** plays on 'business', or sexual intercourse
110 **leave** enough, stop
111 **an Englishman** further evidence that Lethe is a Scotsman
119 **flies** see 1.3.52, note
120–1 **Wit...fool** Although they are bankrupt fools, these sophisticated knaves will easily outwit a novice like the courtesan.
123 **put up** put up with (see 2.1.4, note)
124 **fire** the courtesan's desire
125 **two screens** Rearage and Salewood
131 **trow** believe, know
133 **place** at Court (see 3.1.100)
135 **him** Lethe; Salewood and Rearage are still 'courting'
136 **'Tis to that end** that's what we are trying to do
138 **promise** that he would shortly have money to lend
140 **I...in** Shortyard, and Easy (see 3.4.62–3 and 183–5), have further indebted themselves to Quomodo
151 **famed** boasted of
158 **in kindness** cordially, but also in a sexual manner
161 **hole** loophole, vagina
162 **right** title to her
163 **conscience** plays on 'cunt science' or 'cunt knowledge'
164 **part** share, but also plays on male and female genitals (private parts)
165 **done** finished copulating

no man but gives a sigh after his sin of women; I know it by myself.

SHORTYARD [*to Rearage and Salewood*] You parcel of a rude, saucy and unmannerly nation—

LETHE [*aside*] One good thing in him, he'll tell 'em on't roundly.

SHORTYARD Cannot a gentleman purchase a little fire to thaw his appetite by, but must you, that have been daily singed in the flame, be as greedy to beguile him on't? How can it appear in you but maliciously, an that you go about to engross hell to your selves? Heaven forbid, that you should not suffer a stranger to come in; the devil himself is not so unmannerly. I do not think but some of them rather will be wise enough to beg offices there before you, and keep you out. Marry, all the spite will be, they cannot sell 'em again.

EASY
Come, are you not to blame? Not to give place—
To us, I mean.

LETHE A worse and a worse disgrace!

COURTESAN Nay, gentlemen, you wrong us both then. Stand from me, I protest I'll draw my silver bodkin upon you.

SHORTYARD Clubs! Clubs! Gentlemen, stand upon your guard.

COURTESAN A gentlewoman must swagger a little now and then, I perceive; there would be no civility in her chamber else. Though it be my hard fortune to have my keeper there a coward, the thing that's kept is a gentlewoman born.

SHORTYARD And to conclude, a coward, infallible of your side. Why, do you think, i'faith, I took you to be a coward? Do I think you'll turn your back to any man living? You'll be whipped first.

EASY And then indeed she turns her back to some man living.

SHORTYARD But that man shows himself a knave, for he dares not show his own face when he does it; for some of the Common Council in Henry the Eight's days thought it modesty at that time, that one visor should look upon another.

EASY 'Twas honestly considered of 'em, i'faith.

Enter Mother Gruel

SHORTYARD How now? What piece of stuff comes here?

LETHE [*aside*] Now, some good news yet to recover my repute, and grace me in this company.—Gentlemen, are we friends among ourselves?

SHORTYARD United.

[*Enter Father with wine*]

LETHE Then here comes Rhenish to confirm our amity.—Wagtail, salute them all, they are friends.

COURTESAN Then, saving my quarrel, to you all.

SHORTYARD To's all.

COURTESAN Now beshrew your hearts, an you do not.

SHORTYARD To sweet Master Lethe.

LETHE Let it flow this way, dear Master Blastfield.—Gentlemen, to you all.

SHORTYARD This Rhenish wine is like the scouring-stick to a gun, it makes the barrel clear. It has an excellent virtue, it keeps all the sinks in man and woman's body sweet in June and July; and, to say truth, if ditches were not cast once a year, and drabs once a month, there would be no abiding i'th' city.

LETHE Gentlemen, I'll make you privy to a letter I sent.

SHORTYARD A letter comes well after privy; it makes amends.

LETHE There's one Quomodo a draper's daughter in town whom for her happy portion I wealthily affect.

REARAGE And not for love?—[*To Salewood*] This makes for me, his rival; bear witness.

LETHE
The father does elect me for the man,
The daughter says the same.

SHORTYARD Are you not well?

LETHE
Yes, all but for the mother; she's my sickness.

166 **of** with
168 **parcel** 'lot', 'set,' or 'pack' (*fig.*; usually contemptuous)
169 **nation** English
172 **fire** passion, mistress (see. 3.1.124), but also suggestive of venereal disease (that which has 'singed' Rearage and Salewood in the past)
176 **engross** monopolize
hell the gates of hell (a vagina) or hell-fire (syphilitic pain)
177 **stranger** foreigner, a Scotsman like Lethe (see 1.2.156)
179 **them** the Scots; Englishmen complained that James I was packing the Court (filling 'offices') with his countrymen
181 **'em** the 'offices' they purchased
184 **us** Lethe and her
185 **bodkin** hair-pin, ornament
187 **Clubs!** call to London apprentices to assert their rights
191 **chamber** bed chamber, but also vagina
192 **keeper** door keeper or bawd
coward impotent; effeminate (the opposite of 'hard')
194–5 **infallible . . . side** meaning uncertain; perhaps because Lethe is a 'coward', the Courtesan needn't fall on her back or 'side' (buttocks) for him
196 **turn your back** show yourself a coward; allow yourself to be taken from behind like a coward (a male whore)
197 **whipped** prostitutes were sentenced to whipping
201 **show his own face** the official who whipped prisoners in public wore a mask; 'face' was used for buttocks and pubic area
202 **Common Council** representatives from London's twenty-six wards, answerable to the Court of Aldermen and the Lord Mayor
Henry the Eight's days 1509–47
203 **visor** mask; prostitute
206 **piece of stuff** person of little worth, prostitute
211 **Rhenish** Rhine wine
212 **Wagtail** prostitute, courtesan (meant as term of affection here)
213 **saving** except for
to you all they toast ('salute') one another
215 **an . . . not** if you do not (toast us)
220 **barrel** of a gun, but also belly and loins (*fig.*)
221 **sinks** organs of digestion and excretion
223 **cast** see 1.2.68, note
drabs . . . month see 3.1.56–8; perhaps a monthly medical purging
225 **make . . . to** let you in on a secret about
226 **A letter . . . privy** toilet tissue is helpful in an outhouse
229 **portion** dowry
230 **makes for** favours
233 **well** well set

SHORTYARD By'rlady, and the mother is a pestilent, wilful, troublesome sickness, I can tell you, if she light upon you handsomely.

LETHE
I find it so; she for a stranger pleads,
Whose name I ha' not learned.

REARAGE [*to Salewood*]
And e'en now he called me by it.

LETHE Now, as my letter told her, since only her consent kept aloof off, what might I think on't, but that she merely doted upon me herself!

SHORTYARD Very assuredly.

SALEWOOD [*to Rearage*] This makes still for you.

SHORTYARD Did you let it go so, i'faith?

LETHE You may believe it, sir.—Now, what says her answer?

SHORTYARD Ay, her answer.

MOTHER GRUEL She says you're a base, proud knave, an like your worship.

LETHE How?

SHORTYARD Nay, hear out her answer, or there's no goodness in you.

MOTHER GRUEL You ha' forgot, she says, in what pickle your worship came up, and brought two of your friends to give their words for a suit of green kersey.

LETHE Drudge, peace, or—[*Gestures threateningly*]

SHORTYARD Show yourself a gentleman; she had the patience to read your letter, which was as bad as this can be. What will she think on't? Not hear her answer?—Speak, good his drudge.

MOTHER GRUEL And as for her daughter, she hopes she'll be ruled by her in time, and not be carried away with a cast of manchets, a bottle of wine, and a custard, which once made her daughter sick, because you came by it with a bad conscience.

LETHE Gentlemen, I'm all in a sweat.

SHORTYARD That's very wholesome for your body; nay, you must keep in your arms.

MOTHER GRUEL Then she demanded of me whether I was your worship's aunt or no?

LETHE Out, out, out!

MOTHER GRUEL Alas, said I, I am a poor drudge of his.—Faith, an thou wert his mother, quoth she, he'd make thee his drudge, I warrant him.—Marry, out upon him, quoth I, an't like your worship.

LETHE Horror, horror! I'm smothered. Let me go, torment me not. *Exit*

SHORTYARD An you love me, let's follow him, gentlemen.

REARAGE *and* SALEWOOD Agreed. *Exeunt*

SHORTYARD I count a hundred pound well spent to pursue a good jest, Master Easy.

EASY By my troth, I begin to bear that mind too.

SHORTYARD Well said, i'faith. Hang money! Good jests are worth silver at all times.

EASY They're worth gold, Master Blastfield.

Exeunt [Easy, Shortyard, and Mother Gruel]

COURTESAN Do you deceive me so? Are you toward marriage, i'faith, Master Lethe? It shall go hard but I'll forbid the banns. I'll send a messenger into your bones, another into your purse, but I'll do it. *Exit*

FATHER
Thou fair and wicked creature, steeped in art,
Beauteous and fresh, the soul the foulest part.
A common filth is like a house possessed,
Where, if not spoiled, you'll come out 'fraid at least.
This service likes not me; though I rest poor,
I hate the basest use, to screen a whore.
The human stroke ne'er made him; he that can
Be bawd to woman never leapt from man;
Some monster won his mother.
I wished my poor child hither, doubled wrong.
A month and such a mistress were too long;
Yet here awhile in others' lives I'll see
How former follies did appear in me. *Exit*

Enter Easy with Shortyard's Boy 3.2

EASY Boy!

BOY Anon, sir.

EASY Where left you Master Blastfield, your master, say you?

BOY An hour since I left him in Paul's, sir.—[*Aside*] But you'll not find him the same man again, next time you meet him.

EASY Methinks I have no being without his company. 'Tis so full of kindness and delight, I hold him to be the only companion in earth.

BOY [*aside*] Ay, as companions go nowadays, that help to spend a man's money.

EASY So full of nimble wit, various discourse, pregnant apprehension, and uncommon entertainment; he might keep company with any lord for his grace.

235 **By'rlady** By our lady
the mother hysteria
246 **let it go so** write that to her
255 **pickle** predicament
270 **keep . . . arms** not hit Mother Gruel; conduct yourself as a gentleman, a man who bears arms
284 **bear that mind** share your opinion
288 **toward** leaning toward, planning
290 **banns** announcement in church of intended marriage
290–1 **send . . . purse** give you venereal disease and bankrupt you (see 1.1.28, note)
292 **art** artifice, cunning
294 **common filth** prostitute
possessed controlled by devils
295 **spoiled** undone
'fraid afraid because the house is haunted; puns on 'frayed' ('spoiled' by a prostitute); see 3.3.62 and 4.1.110
296 **likes** pleases
297 **use** occupation, 'service' as a 'bawd' (3.1.299)
298 **stroke** discharge, shot, or caress in intercourse
299 **leapt** sprang, was born
3.2.5 **Paul's** St Paul's Cathedral (see 1.2.137, note)

BOY [*aside*] Ay, with any lord that were past it.

EASY And such a good, freehearted, honest, affable kind of gentleman. Come, boy, a heaviness will possess me till I see him. *Exit*

BOY But you'll find yourself heavier then, by a seven hundred pound weight. Alas, poor birds that cannot keep the sweet country, where they fly at pleasure, but must needs come to London to have their wings clipped, and are fain to go hopping home again. *Exit*

3.3 *Enter Shortyard and Falselight, like a Sergeant and a Yeoman, to arrest Easy*

SHORTYARD So, no man is so impudent to deny that. Spirits can change their shapes, and soonest of all into sergeants, because they are cousin-germans to spirits; for there's but two kind of arrests till doomsday: the devil for the soul, the sergeant for the body; but afterward the devil arrests body and soul, sergeant and all, if they be knaves still and deserve it. Now, my Yeoman Falselight—

FALSELIGHT I attend you, good Sergeant Shortyard.

SHORTYARD No more Master Blastfield now. Poor Easy, hardly beset.

FALSELIGHT But how if he should go to prison? We're in a mad state, then, being not sergeants.

SHORTYARD Never let it come near thy belief that he'll take prison, or stand out in law, knowing the debt to be due, but still expect the presence of Master Blastfield, kind Master Blastfield, worshipful Master Blastfield, and at the last—

BOY [*within*] Master Shortyard. Master Falselight!

SHORTYARD The boy; a warning-piece! See where he comes.

Enter Easy with the Boy

EASY Is not in Paul's.

BOY He is not far off, sure, sir.

EASY When was his hour, sayst thou?

BOY Two, sir.

EASY Why, two has struck.

BOY No, sir, they are now a-striking.

SHORTYARD Master Richard Easy of Essex, we arrest you. [*Strikes Easy on shoulder*]

EASY Ha?

BOY Alas, a surgeon! He's hurt i'th' shoulder. [*Exit*]

SHORTYARD Deliver your weapons quietly, sir.

EASY Why, what's the matter?

SHORTYARD You're arrested at the suit of Master Quomodo.

EASY Master Quomodo?

SHORTYARD How strange you make it. You're a landed gentleman, sir. I know 'tis but a trifle, a bond of seven hundred pound.

EASY
La, I knew you had mistook; you should arrest
One Master Blastfield, 'tis his bond, his debt.

SHORTYARD Is not your name there?

EASY True, for fashion's sake.

SHORTYARD Why and 'tis for fashion's sake that we arrest you.

EASY Nay, an it be no more, I yield to that. I know Master Blastfield will see me take no injury as long as I'm in town, for Master Alsup's sake.

SHORTYARD Who's that, sir?

EASY An honest gentleman in Essex.

SHORTYARD O, in Essex! I thought you had been in London, where now your business lies; honesty from Essex will be a great while a-coming, sir; you should look out an honest pair of citizens.

EASY Alas, sir, I know not where to find 'em.

SHORTYARD No? There's enough in town.

EASY I know not one, by my troth. I am a mere stranger for these parts; Master Quomodo is all, and the honestest that I know.

SHORTYARD To him, then, let's set forward.—Yeoman Spiderman, cast an eye about for Master Blastfield.

EASY Boy!—Alas, the poor boy was frighted away at first.

SHORTYARD Can you blame him sir? We that daily fray away knights, may fright away boys, I hope. *Exeunt*

3.4 *Enter Quomodo with the Boy,* [*Thomasine above*]

QUOMODO
Ha! Have they him, sayst thou?

BOY
As sure as—

QUOMODO
The land's mine; that's sure enough, boy.
Let me advance thee, knave, and give thee a kiss;
My plot's so firm, I dare it now to miss.
Now shall I be divulged a landed man
Throughout the livery: one points, another whispers,
A third frets inwardly, let him fret and hang!
Especially his envy I shall have
That would be fain, yet cannot be, a knave,
Like an old lecher, girt in a furred gown,
Whose mind stands stiff, but his performance down.
Now come my golden days in.

16 **past it** past grace, irredeemable
18 **heaviness** sadness; but the Boy, punning on 'pound' (3.2.21), takes Easy literally
23 **clipped** cut short to disable flight; see 2.3.381
24 **fain** obliged
3.3.0.1 *Sergeant* London's two Sheriffs oversaw Sergeants, who in turn were assisted by Yeomen
2 **Spirits** see 1.2.78.1, note
3 **cousin-germans** first cousins
11 **beset** under attack
14–15 **take prison** agree to imprisonment
15 **stand out in law** fight it out in court
20 **warning-piece** signal gun (Easy imagines the boy is looking for Blastfield)
24 **his hour** Blastfield's time of arrival at St Paul's
27 **a-striking** plays on the 'stroke' of two and the arrest, during which Easy is 'hurt i'th' shoulder' (3.3.31)
32 **weapons** sword and dagger
53 **citizens** for bail
56 **mere** complete
62 **fray** frighten
3.4.3 **advance** promote
6 **livery** see 2.3.458, note
9 **fain** gladly
10 **girt** wrapped
11 **Whose . . . down** firm of mind but impotent

—Whither is the worshipful Master Quomodo and his fair bedfellow rid forth?—To his land in Essex!—Whence comes those goodly load of logs?—From his land in Essex!—Where grows this pleasant fruit, says one citizen's wife in the Row.—At Master Quomodo's orchard in Essex.—O, O does it so? I thank you for that good news, i'faith.

BOY Here they come with him, sir. [*Exit*]

QUOMODO Grant me patience in my joys, that being so great, I run not mad with 'em.

[*Enter Shortyard and Falselight, disguised as a Sergeant and a Yeoman, bringing in Easy*]

SHORTYARD Bless Master Quomodo!

QUOMODO How now, sergeants? Who ha' you brought me here—Master Easy!

EASY Why, la you now, sergeants, did I not tell you you mistook?

QUOMODO Did you not hear me say, I had rather ha' had Master Blastfield, the more sufficient man a great deal?

SHORTYARD Very true, sir. But this gentleman lighting into our hands first—

QUOMODO Why, did you so, sir?

SHORTYARD We thought good to make use of that opportunity, and hold him fast.

QUOMODO You did well in that, I must needs say, for your own securities. But 'twas not my mind, Master Easy, to have you first. You must needs think so.

EASY I dare swear that, Master Quomodo.

QUOMODO But since you are come to me, I have no reason to refuse you; I should show little manners in that, sir.

EASY But I hope you spake not in that sense, sir, to impose the bond upon me?

QUOMODO By my troth, that's my meaning, sir. You shall find me an honest man; you see I mean what I say. Is not the day past, the money untendered? You'd ha' me live uprightly, Master Easy?

EASY Why, sir, you know Master Blastfield is the man.

QUOMODO Why, sir, I know Master Blastfield is the man; but is he any more than one man? Two entered into bond to me, or I'm foully cozened.

EASY You know my entrance was but for fashion sake.

QUOMODO Why I'll agree to you; you'll grant 'tis the fashion likewise when the bond's due, to have the money paid again.

SHORTYARD So we told him, sir, and that it lay in your worship's courtesy to arrest which you please.

QUOMODO Marry, does it, sir. These fellows know the law. Beside, you offered yourself into bond to me, you know, when I had no stomach to you. Now beshrew your heart for your labour! I might ha' had a good substantial citizen that would ha' paid the sum roundly, although I think you sufficient enough for seven hundred pound, beside the forfeiture. I would be loath to disgrace you so much before sergeants.

EASY If you would ha' the patience, sir, I do not think but Master Blastfield is at carrier's to receive the money.

QUOMODO He will prove the honester man, then, and you the better discharged. I wonder he should break with me; 'twas never his practice. You must not be angry with me now, though you were somewhat hot when you entered into bond; you may easily go in angrily, but you cannot come out so.

EASY No, the devil's in't, for that!

SHORTYARD [*aside to Easy*] Do you hear, sir? O'my troth, we pity you. Ha' you any store of crowns about you?

EASY Faith, a poor store, yet they shall be at their service that will strive to do me good. We were both drunk last night, and ne'er thought upon the bond.

SHORTYARD I must tell you this, you have fell into the hands of a most merciless devourer, the very gull o' the city; should you offer him money, goods or lands now, he'd rather have your body in prison, he's o' such a nature.

EASY Prison? We're undone then!

SHORTYARD He's o' such a nature, look! Let him owe any man a spite, what's his course? He will lend him money today, o' purpose to 'rest him tomorrow.

EASY Defend me!

SHORTYARD H'as at least sixteen at this instant proceeded in both the Counters: some bach'lors, some masters, some doctors of captivity of twenty years' standing; and he desires nothing more than imprisonment.

EASY Would Master Blastfield would come away.

SHORTYARD Ay, then things would not be as they are. What will you say to us if we procure you two substantial subsidy citizens to bail you, spite on's heart, and set you at liberty to find out Master Blastfield?

EASY Sergeant, here, take all! I'll be dear to you, do but perform it.

SHORTYARD [*aside*] Much!

FALSELIGHT [*aside*] Enough, sweet sergeant, I hope I understand thee.

17 **Row** affluent Goldsmith's Row in Cheapside
29 **sufficient** solvent, able to meet liabilities
45 **untendered** unpaid
56 **courtesy** prerogative, purview
59 **stomach** inclination; in the context of 'entered' and 'entrance' (see 2.3.268, note), as well as 'hot', 'go in' and 'come out' (3.4.70–2), this may also mean 'sexual appetite'
61 **good substantial** wealthy, sufficient (see 3.4.29)
62 **roundly** directly
66 **carrier's** a designated inn where he could receive from provincial messengers ('carriers') money due him
80 **gull** throat (gullet); greedy man; possibly trickster or cheat
87 **'rest** arrest
89–90 **proceeded . . . Counters** advancing to a higher degree in the city's debtors' prisons (universities)
96 **subsidy citizens** men who paid a Parliamentary tax beyond the regular assessment; wealthy men (see 3.4.190)
98 **all** whatever crowns he has upon him
100 **Much** expressing contempt, as in 'little' or 'of course'; Shortyard either won't 'perform' anything for Easy or he dismisses Easy's 'crowns' as negligible

SHORTYARD I love to prevent the malice of such a rascal. Perhaps you might find Master Blastfield tonight.

EASY Why, we lie together, man, there's the jest on't.

SHORTYARD Fie! And you'll seek to secure your bail? Because they will be two citizens of good account, you must do that for your credit sake.

EASY I'll be bound to save them harmless.

SHORTYARD A pox on him, you cut his throat then. No words!

EASY What's it you require me, Master Quomodo?

QUOMODO You know that before this time, I hope, sir: present money, or present imprisonment.

SHORTYARD [*aside to Easy*] I told you so.

EASY We ne'er had money of you.

QUOMODO You had commodities, an't please you.

EASY Well, may I not crave so much liberty upon my word, to seek out Master Blastfield?

QUOMODO Yes, an you would not laugh at me. We are sometimes gulls to gentlemen, I thank 'em; but gentlemen are never gulls to us, I commend 'em.

SHORTYARD Under your leave, Master Quomodo, the gentleman craves the furtherance of an hour; and it sorts well with our occasion at this time, having a little urgent business at Guildhall; at which minute we'll return, and see what agreement is made.

QUOMODO Nay, take him along with you, sergeant.

EASY I'm undone then!

SHORTYARD He's your prisoner, and being safe in your house at your own disposing, you cannot deny him such a request. Beside, he hath a little faith in Master Blastfield's coming, sir.

QUOMODO Let me not be too long delayed, I charge you.

EASY Not an hour, i'faith, sir.

Exeunt [*Shortyard and Falselight*]

QUOMODO O, Master Easy, of all men living, I never dreamt you would ha' done me this injury: make me wound my credit, fail in my commodities, bring my state into suspicion. For the breaking of your day to me has broken my day to others.

EASY You tell me of that still, which is no fault of mine, Master Quomodo.

QUOMODO O, what's a man but his honesty, Master Easy? And that's a fault amongst most of us all. Mark but this note; I'll give you good counsel now: as often as you give your name to a bond, you must think you christen a child, and take the charge on't too; for as the one, the bigger it grows, the more cost it requires, so the other, the longer it lies, the more charges it puts you to. Only here's the difference: a child must be broke, and a bond must not; the more you break children, the more you keep 'em under, but the more you break bonds, the more they'll leap in your face. And therefore, to conclude, I would never undertake to be gossip to that bond which I would not see well brought up.

EASY Say you so, sir? I'll think upon your counsel hereafter for't.

QUOMODO [*aside*] Ah, fool, thou shouldst ne'er ha' tasted such wit, but that I know 'tis too late.

THOMASINE [*aside*] The more I grieve.

QUOMODO To put all this into the compass of a little hoop ring:

Make this account, come better days or worse,
So many bonds abroad, so many boys at nurse.

EASY A good medicine for a short memory. But since you have entered so far, whose children are desperate debts, I pray?

QUOMODO Faith, they are like the offsprings of stolen lust, put to the hospital; their fathers are not to be found; they are either too far abroad, or too close within. And thus for your memory's sake:

The desperate debtor hence derives his name,
One that has neither money, land, nor fame;
All that he makes prove bastards, and not bands,
But such as yours at first are born to lands.

EASY But all that I beget hereafter I'll soon disinherit, Master Quomodo.

QUOMODO [*aside*] In the mean time, here's a shrewd knave will disinherit you.

EASY Well, to put you out of all doubt, Master Quomodo, I'll not trust to your courtesy; I ha' sent for bail.

QUOMODO How? You've cozened me there, i'faith.

EASY Since the worst comes to the worst, I have those friends i'th' city, I hope, that will not suffer me to lie for seven hundred pound.

QUOMODO And you told me you had no friends here at all; how should a man trust you now?

107 **account** repute
109 **save them harmless** fully indemnify them
110–11 **No words** silence
119 **word** honour; promise not to escape
124 **sorts** fits
126 **Guildhall** central meeting place for municipal business; City Hall
128–9 **take...then** Easy thinks Quomodo would have them imprison him and so make it impossible for him to secure bail.
138 **state** reputation in the business community
139 **day** when his debt was due
144 **that's** probably refers to breaking one's word
145 **note** noteworthy advice
146 **christen** become godparent ('gossip') to, take on as one's own responsibility ('charge')
149 **lies** remains unpaid
150 **broke** forced to obey
161–2 **To...ring** to compose a brief rhyme of the sort engraved on a ring
164 **bonds abroad** debts outstanding
166 **entered** gone into this subject (but one also 'entered' into debt)
desperate defaulted
169 **hospital** home for foundlings
170 **either...within** either run off or in the Counter
171 **thus...sake** Quomodo turns to verse, as he did with the hoop ring posy, to make it easier for Easy to memorize his advice.
173 **fame** good reputation
174 **All** 'debts' (3.4.166)
bands variant of 'bonds' (rhymes with 'lands')
175 **born to lands** land 'fathers' Easy's debts
176 **disinherit** discharge (*fig.*)
184 **to lie** to be imprisoned

EASY That was but to try your courtesy, Master Quomodo.

QUOMODO [*aside*] How unconscionably he gulls himself.— They must be wealthy subsidy-men, sir, at least forty pound i'th' King's Books, I can tell you, that do such a feat for you.

Enter Shortyard and Falselight, like wealthy citizens in satin suits

EASY Here they come, whatsoe'er they are.

QUOMODO By'rlady, alderman's deputies! I am very sorry for you, sir; I cannot refuse such men.

SHORTYARD Are you the gentleman in distress?

EASY None more than myself, sir. [*Takes Shortyard and Falselight aside*]

QUOMODO [*aside*] He speaks truer than he thinks, for if he knew the hearts that owe those faces! A dark shop's good for somewhat.

EASY That was all, sir.

SHORTYARD And that's enough, for by that means you have made yourself liable to the bond, as well as that Basefield.

EASY Blastfield, sir.

SHORTYARD O, cry you mercy, 'tis Blastfield indeed.

EASY But, under both your worships' favours, I know where to find him presently.

SHORTYARD That's all your refuge.

[*Enter Boy*]

BOY News, good news, Master Easy!

EASY What, boy?

BOY Master Blastfield, my master, has received a thousand pound, and will be at his lodging at supper.

EASY Happy news! Hear you that, Master Quomodo?

QUOMODO 'Tis enough for you to hear that, you're the fortunate man, sir.

EASY Not now, I beseech your good worships.

SHORTYARD Gentleman, what's your t'other name?

EASY Easy.

SHORTYARD O, Master Easy. I would we could rather pleasure you otherwise, Master Easy; you should soon perceive it. I'll speak a proud word: we have pitied more gentlemen in distress than any two citizens within the freedom. But to be bail to seven hundred pound action is a matter of shrewd weight.

EASY I'll be bound to secure you.

SHORTYARD Tut, what's your bond, sir?

EASY Body, goods, and lands, immediately before Master Quomodo.

SHORTYARD Shall we venture once again, that have been so often undone by gentlemen?

FALSELIGHT I have no great stomach to't; it will appear in us more pity than wisdom.

EASY Why should you say so, sir?

SHORTYARD I like the gentleman's face well; he does not look as if he would deceive us.

EASY O, not I, sir!

SHORTYARD Come, we'll make a desperate voyage once again; we'll try his honesty, and take his single bond, of body, goods, and lands.

EASY I dearly thank you, sir.

SHORTYARD Master Quomodo!

QUOMODO Your worships.

SHORTYARD We have took a course to set your prisoner free.

QUOMODO Your worships are good bail; you content me.

SHORTYARD Come then, and be a witness to a recullisance.

QUOMODO With all my heart, sir.

SHORTYARD Master Easy, you must have an especial care now to find out that Blastfield.

EASY I shall have him at my lodging, sir.

SHORTYARD The suit will be followed against you else. Master Quomodo will come upon us, and forsake you.

EASY I know that, sir.

SHORTYARD Well, since I see you have such a good mind to be honest, I'll leave some greater affairs, and sweat with you to find him myself.

EASY
Here, then, my misery ends.
A stranger's kindness oft exceeds a friend's. *Exeunt*

THOMASINE
Thou art deceived, thy misery but begins;
"To beguile goodness, is the core of sins."
My love is such unto thee, that I die
As often as thou drink'st up injury,
Yet have no means to warn thee from't; for "he
That sows in craft does rape in jealousy."
[*Exit above*]

189 **unconscionably** egregiously
190 **subsidy-men** see 3.4.96, note
191 **King's Books** tax rolls
194 **alderman's deputies** London was governed by twenty-six powerful aldermen and a Lord Mayor.
200 **owe** own
210 **all your refuge** your only hope
218 **Not now** perhaps, 'Don't abandon me now'
225 **freedom** see 1.3.48, note
226 **shrewd** worrisome
229–30 **Body . . . Quomodo** a 'statute merchant'; Easy would guarantee ('secure') the loan with both his 'body' (they could imprison him, see 3.4.81–2) and his property; this new obligation would take precedence over his bond with Quomodo
231 **venture** In the context of 'undone', 'stomach' (see 3.4.59, note), and 'face' (see 3.1.201, note), this suggests sodomy (see 1.2.22, note).
240 **single** simple, sincere
248 **recullisance** recognizance, a document acknowledging a debt and the terms of the bond
254 **Master . . . you** Quomodo will have the £700 of us and we will then consider you in default (take your land).
265–6 **he . . . jealousy** the crafty man is a suspicious man (see 4.1.120–1); punning on 'reap', to 'rape' is to take by force

3.5 *[Enter Rearage and Salewood]*

REARAGE Now the letter's made up and all; it wants but the print of a seal, and away it goes to Master Quomodo. Andrew Lethe is well whipped in't; his name stands in a white sheet here, and does penance for him.

SALEWOOD You have shame enough against him, if that be good.

REARAGE First, as a contempt of that reverend ceremony he has in hand, to wit, marriage.

SALEWOOD Why do you say, 'to wit, marriage', when you know there's none will marry that's wise?

REARAGE Had it not more need, then, to have wit to put to't, if it be grown to a folly?

SALEWOOD You've won, I'll give't you.

REARAGE 'Tis no thanks now. But, as I was saying, as a foul contempt to that sacred ceremony, he most audaciously keeps a drab in town; and to be free from the interruption of blue beadles and other bawdy officers, he most politicly lodges her in a constable's house.

SALEWOOD That's a pretty point i'faith.

REARAGE And so the watch that should fetch her out are her chiefest guard to keep her in.

SALEWOOD It must needs be, for look how the constable plays his conscience, the watchmen will follow the suit.

REARAGE Why, well then.

Enter Easy with Shortyard, like a citizen

EASY All night from me? He's hurt, he's made away!

SHORTYARD Where shall we seek him now? You lead me fair jaunts, sir.

EASY Pray, keep a little patience, sir. I shall find him at last, you shall see.

SHORTYARD A citizen of my ease and substance to walk so long afoot!

EASY You should ha' had my horse, but that he has eaten out his head, sir.

SHORTYARD How? Would you had me hold him by the tail, sir, then?

EASY Manners forbid! 'Tis no part of my meaning, sir. O, here's Master Rearage and Master Salewood; now we shall hear of him presently.—Gentlemen both.

SALEWOOD Master Easy, how fare you, sir?

EASY Very well in health. Did you see Master Blastfield this morning?

SALEWOOD I was about to move it to you.

REARAGE We were all three in a mind, then.

SALEWOOD I ha' not set eye on him these two days.

REARAGE I wonder he keeps so long from us, i'faith.

EASY I begin to be sick.

SALEWOOD Why, what's the matter?

EASY Nothing, in troth, but a great desire I had to have seen him.

REARAGE I wonder you should miss on't lately; you're his bedfellow.

EASY I lay alone tonight, i'faith. I do not know how—

[Enter Lethe]

O here comes Master Lethe; he can dispatch me. Master Lethe!

LETHE What's your name, sir? O, cry you mercy, Master Easy.

EASY When parted you from Master Blastfield, sir?

LETHE Blastfield's an ass; I have sought him these two days to beat him.

EASY Yourself all alone, sir?

LETHE I, and three more. *Exit*

SHORTYARD *[aside]* I am glad I am where I am, then. I perceive 'twas time of all hands.

REARAGE *[to Salewood]* Content, i'faith, let's trace him.

Exeunt after Lethe

SHORTYARD What, have you found him yet? Neither? What's to be done now? I'll venture my body no further for any gentleman's pleasure; I know not how soon I may be called upon, and now to overheat myself—

EASY I'm undone!

SHORTYARD This is you that slept with him. You can make fools of us; but I'll turn you over to Quomodo for't.

EASY Good sir—

SHORTYARD I'll prevent mine own danger.

EASY I beseech you, sir—

SHORTYARD Though I love gentlemen well, I do not mean to be undone for 'em.

EASY Pray, sir, let me request you, sir. Sweet sir, I beseech you, sir— *Exeunt*

Music. Finis Actus Tertius

3.5.1 **letter's made up** We never again hear of this letter; instead, Rearage plots with the Father (4.3.45–7).
3–4 **stands...sheet** shames him in public
5 **shame** scandalous information
8 **in hand** in preparation
14 **'Tis...now** Thanks for nothing.
17 **blue beadles** parish officers who wore blue coats
17–18 **bawdy officers** overseers of sexual offences
18 **politicly** cunningly
constable's constable: a peace officer who serves writs, makes arrests, and supervises the 'watch' (3.5.21), the night patrol
21 **fetch her out** arrest her
23 **look how** however
24 **follow the suit** overlook the offence (the imagery is drawn from card playing)
26 **made away** murdered
28 **jaunts** fatiguing or troublesome journeys
33–4 **he...head** he was forfeited in payment for his board; see 2.3.314–15
43 **move...you** ask you that
54 **dispatch** relieve; plays on 'make away with' or kill
63 **where I am** in disguise
64 **of all hands** on all sides
65 **Content** agreed; they pursue ('trace') Lethe
67 **venture** hazard (see 3.4.231, note)
69 **called upon** summoned for official duty or by death
74 **prevent** avoid, anticipate
danger see 3.4.253–4

4.1 *Incipit Actus Quartus*

Enter Quomodo, his disguised spirits [Shortyard and Falselight as citizens], after whom Easy follows hard

SHORTYARD Made fools of us! Not to be found!

QUOMODO What, what?

EASY Do not undo me quite, though, Master Quomodo.

QUOMODO You're very welcome, Master Easy. I ha' nothing to say to you; I'll not touch you, you may go when you please. I have good bail here, I thank their worships.

EASY What shall I say, or whom shall I beseech?

SHORTYARD Gentlemen! 'Slid, they were born to undo us, I think; but, for my part, I'll make an oath before Master Quomodo here, ne'er to do gentlemen good while I live.

FALSELIGHT I'll not be long behind you.

SHORTYARD [*to Easy*] Away! If you had any grace in you, you would be ashamed to look us i'th' face, iwis! I wonder with what brow you can come amongst us. I should seek my fortunes far enough, if I were you, and neither return to Essex, to be a shame to my predecessors, nor remain about London, to be a mock to my successors.

QUOMODO [*aside*] Subtle Shortyard!

SHORTYARD Here are his lands forfeited to us, Master Quomodo; and to avoid the inconscionable trouble of law, all the assurance he made to us, we willingly resign to you.

QUOMODO What shall I do with rubbish? Give me money! 'Tis for your worships to have land, that keep great houses; I should be hoisted.

SHORTYARD But, Master Quomodo, if you would but conceive it aright, the land would fall fitter to you than to us.

EASY [*aside*] Curts'ing about my land!

SHORTYARD You have a towardly son and heir, as we hear.

QUOMODO I must needs say, he is a Templar indeed.

SHORTYARD We have neither posterity in town, nor hope for any abroad; we have wives, but the marks have been out of their mouths these twenty years, and, as it appears, they did little good when they were in. We could not stand about it, sir; to get riches and children too, 'tis more than one man can do. And I am of those citizens' minds that say, let our wives make shift for children an they will, they get none of us; and I cannot think but he that has both much wealth and many children, has had more helps coming in than himself.

QUOMODO I am not a bow wide of your mind, sir. And for the thrifty and covetous hopes I have in my son and heir, Sim Quomodo, that he will never trust his land in wax and parchment, as many gentlemen have done before him—

EASY [*aside*] A by-blow for me.

QUOMODO I will honestly discharge you, and receive it in due form and order of law, to strengthen it forever to my son and heir, that he may undoubtedly enter upon't without the let or molestation of any man, at his or our pleasure whensoever.

SHORTYARD 'Tis so assured unto you.

QUOMODO Why, then, Master Easy, you're a free man, sir. You may deal in what you please and go whither you will.

[*Enter Thomasine*]

Why, Thomasine, Master Easy is come from Essex; bid him welcome in a cup of small beer.

THOMASINE [*aside*] Not only vile, but in it tyrannous.

QUOMODO If it please you, sir, you know the house; you may visit us often, and dine with us once a quarter.

EASY

Confusion light on you, your wealth and heir;
Worms gnaw your conscience, as the moth your ware.
I am not the first heir that robbed or begged.

Exit [*with Thomasine following*]

QUOMODO

Excellent, excellent, sweet spirits!

SHORTYARD

Landed Master Quomodo!

QUOMODO

Delicate Shortyard, commodious Falselight,
Hug and away, shift, shift;
'Tis sleight, not strength, that gives the greatest lift.

[*Exeunt Shortyard and Falselight*]

4.1.3 **quite** completely
8 **undo** begins a cluster of *doubles entendres* that includes 'part', 'do', 'long behind' and 'come'
13 **iwis** certainly
14 **brow** effrontery, impudence
15 **far** far away
21 **inconscionable** unfair and unreasonable
22 **assurance** title to Easy's property (see 5.1.3)
26 **hoisted** overtaxed; assessed a surcharge
30 **Curts'ing** effusively polite
31 **towardly** promising
32 **Templar** see 2.3.452, note
34 **abroad** illegitimate children
marks depressions in the enamel of a horse's incisors which, as they gradually disappear, indicate the horse's advancing age
37 **stand about it** support it; have an erection
39 **make shift** manage
40 **get** beget
42 **has . . . himself** has been cuckolded
43 **bow wide** length of a bow, but Shortyard's bawdy may elicit this particular expression (see 2.1.111–17, note)
46 **wax and parchment** sealed documents
48 **by-blow** side-stroke; calamity; perhaps also playing on sense of 'illegitimate child'
52 **let** hindrance
59 **small** weak
61 **house** Easy's own estate
64 **ware** merchandise; but see 4.2.11, note
68 **commodious** profitable, handy
69 **Hug . . . shift** hug me, then shift shapes (change your disguises); also wrestling terms
70 **lift** means to trip up someone; elation; perhaps also playing on 'to lift', to rob

Now my desires are full—for this time.
Men may have cormorant wishes, but, alas,
A little thing, three hundred pound a year,
Suffices nature, keeps life and soul together.
I'll have 'em lopped immediately; I long
To warm myself by th' wood.

A fine journey in the Whitsun holidays, i'faith, to ride down with a number of citizens, and their wives, some upon pillions, some upon sidesaddles. I and little Thomasine i'th' middle, our son and heir, Sim Quomodo, in a peach-colour taffeta jacket, some horse-length or a long yard before us. There will be a fine show on's, I can tell you, where we citizens will laugh and lie down, get all our wives with child against a bank, and get up again.—Stay, ha! Hast thou that wit, i'faith? 'Twill be admirable. To see how the very thought of green fields puts a man into sweet inventions. I will presently possess Sim Quomodo of all the land. I have a toy and I'll do't. And because I see before mine eyes that most of our heirs prove notorious rioters after our deaths, and that cozenage in the father wheels about to folly in the son, our posterity commonly foiled at the same weapon at which we played rarely; and being the world's beaten word, what's got over the devil's back (that's by knavery) must be spent under his belly (that's by lechery); being awake in these knowings, why should not I oppose 'em now, and break destiny of her custom, preventing that by policy, which without it must needs be destiny? And I have took the course! I will forthwith sicken, call for my keys, make my will, and dispose of all. Give my son this blessing, that he trust no man, keep his hand from a quean and a scrivener, live in his father's faith, and do good to nobody. Then will I begin to rave like a fellow of a wide conscience, and, for all the world, counterfeit to the life that which I know I shall do when I die: take on for my gold, my lands, and my writings, grow worse and worse, call upon the devil, and so make an end. By this time I have indented with a couple of searchers, who, to uphold my device, shall fray them out o'th' chamber with report of sickness, and so, la, I start up, and recover again. For in this business I will trust, no, not my spirits, Falselight and Shortyard, but in disguise note the condition of all: how pitiful my wife takes my death, which will appear by November in her eye, and the fall of the leaf in her body, but especially by the cost she bestows upon my funeral, there shall I try her love and regard; my daughter's marrying to my will and liking; and my son's affection after my disposing. For, to conclude, I am as jealous of this land as of my wife, to know what would become of it after my decease. *Exit*

Enter Courtesan with her disguised Father 4.2

FATHER
Though I be poor, 'tis my glory to live honest.

COURTESAN
I prithee, do not leave me.

FATHER
To be bawd.
Hell has not such an office.
I thought at first your mind had been preserved
In virtue and in modesty of blood,
That such a face had not been made to please
The unsettled appetites of several men,
Those eyes turned up through prayer, not through lust;
But you are wicked, and my thoughts unjust.

COURTESAN Why thou art an unreasonable fellow, i'faith. Do not all trades live by their ware, and yet called honest livers? Do they not thrive best when they utter most, and make it away by the great? Is not wholesale the chiefest merchandise? Do you think some merchants could keep their wives so brave but for their wholesale? You're foully deceived an you think so.

FATHER
You are so glued to punishment and shame,
Your words e'en deserve whipping.

72 **cormorant** greedy
75 **'em** the trees (or their branches) on his property in Essex (see 2.3.375 and 3.4.15)
lopped cut or trimmed (for fuel)
77 **Whitsun** Whit Sunday (Pentecost), seventh Sunday after Easter
79 **pillions** light saddles, or cushions attached to ordinary saddles (usually for women)
81 **peach-colour taffeta** expensive, fine silk fabric in a colour associated with pretentiousness
82 **long yard** a cloth measure
83–4 **laugh...down** 'laugh and lay down' was the name of a card game
85 **bank** river bank; also pile of money or money dealer's table (continues gaming imagery); this nearly completes a cluster of *doubles entendres* that begins with 'ride' (l. 78, to mount in sexual intercourse) and includes 'pillions' (which were mounted to the rear), 'sidesaddles' (l. 79, mounted on the side), 'middle' (l. 80, genital area), 'horse-length or a long yard' (ll. 81–2, length of a long penis), 'lie' (l. 84, have sexual intercourse with), and 'get up again' (l. 85)
88 **possess** put in possession
89 **toy** trifle, whim
93 **rarely** with uncommon excellence
94 **beaten** hackneyed; compare 1.3.12–13
94–6 **what's...lechery** proverbial, see Tilley, D 316
98 **policy** craft, cunning
99–100 **took the course** found the way
100 **keys** see 2.3.482, note
104–5 **wide conscience** irrational, perhaps hypocritical nature
106 **take on** carry on
108 **By** prior to
109 **indented** compounded; made an agreement
searchers persons who examined dead bodies and reported on the cause of death
110 **device** scheme
fray frighten
111 **sickness** bubonic plague
115 **November...eye** tears, or gloom
116 **fall of the leaf** autumn; sadness
120 **jealous** compare 3.4.265–6
4.2.7 **several** various, sundry
9 **unjust** mistaken
11 **ware** merchandise, but also genitalia (of either sex; see 4.1.64)
12 **utter** sell
13 **wholesale** plays on 'hole sale' and 'make it away by the great'—in large quantities
15 **brave** dressed fashionably
18 **whipping** see 3.1.197, note

To bear the habit of a gentlewoman,
And be in mind so distant.

COURTESAN Why, you fool you, are not gentlewomen sinners? And there's no courageous sinner amongst us, but was a gentlewoman by the mother's side, I warrant you. Besides, we are not always bound to think those our fathers that marry our mothers, but those that lie with our mothers, and they may be gentlemen born, and born again, for ought we know, you know.

FATHER
True, corruption may well be generation's first;
'We're bad by nature, but by custom worst.' *Exeunt*

4.3 *A bell tolls, a confused cry within*

THOMASINE [*within*] O, my husband!

SIM [*within*] My father, O, my father!

FALSELIGHT [*within*] My sweet master, dead!

Enter Shortyard and the Boy

SHORTYARD Run boy, bid 'em ring out. He dead, he's gone.

BOY Then is as arrant a knave gone, as 'ere was called upon. [*Exit*]

SHORTYARD
The happiest good that ever Shortyard felt,
I want to be expressed, my mirth is such;
To be struck now, e'en when his joys were high.
Men only kiss their knaveries, and so die,
I've often marked it.
He was a famous coz'ner while he lived,
And now his son shall reap it; I'll ha' the lands,
Let him study law after; 'tis no labour
To undo him forever. But for Easy,
Only good confidence did make him foolish,
And not the lack of sense, that was not it;
'Tis worldly craft beats down a scholar's wit.
For this our son and heir now, he
From his conception was entailed an ass,
And he has kept it well, twenty-five years now.
Then the slightest art will do't; the lands lie fair:
'No sin to beggar a deceiver's heir.' *Exit*

Enter Thomasine with Winifred, her maid, in haste

THOMASINE Here, Winifred, here, here, here. I have always found thee secret.

WINIFRED You shall always find me so, Mistress.

THOMASINE Take this letter and this ring.

WINIFRED Yes, forsooth.

THOMASINE O, how all the parts about me shake! Inquire for one Master Easy at his old lodging i'th' Blackfriars.

WINIFRED I will indeed, forsooth.

THOMASINE Tell him the party that sent him a hundred pound t'other day to comfort his heart has likewise sent him this letter and this ring, which has that virtue to recover him again forever, say. Name nobody, Winifred.

WINIFRED Not so much as you, forsooth.

THOMASINE Good girl. Thou shalt have a mourning gown at the burial, of mine honesty.

WINIFRED And I'll effect your will, o' my fidelity. *Exit*

THOMASINE I do account myself the happiest widow that ever counterfeited weeping, in that I have the leisure now, both to do that gentleman good, and do myself a pleasure; but I must seem like a hanging moon, a little waterish awhile.

Enter Rearage, Courtesan's Father following

REARAGE
I entertain both thee and thy device;
'Twill put 'em both to shame.

FATHER That is my hope, sir.
Especially that strumpet. [*Exit*]

REARAGE Save you, sweet widow!
I suffer for your heaviness.

THOMASINE O, Master Rearage, I have lost the dearest husband that ever woman did enjoy.

REARAGE You must have patience yet.

THOMASINE O, talk not to me of patience an you love me, good Master Rearage.

REARAGE Yet, if all tongues go right, he did not use you so well as a man mought.

THOMASINE Nay, that's true indeed, Master Rearage. He ne'er used me so well as a woman might have been used, that's certain; in troth, 't'as been our greatest falling out, sir. And though it be the part of a widow to show herself a woman for her husband's death, yet when I remember all his unkindness, I cannot weep a stroke, i'faith, Master Rearage. And therefore wisely did a great widow in this land comfort up another: 'Go to, lady', quoth she, 'leave blubbering; thou thinkest upon thy husband's good parts when thou sheddest tears, do but remember how often he has lain from thee, and how many naughty slippery turns he has done thee,

19 **habit** clothing
28 **be...first** begin with original sin ('nature') or in the act of generation
29 **custom** habit
4.3.0.1 ***bell*** the 'passing bell' tolls as Quomodo approaches death; once Falselight announces his master's death, Shortyard tells the Boy to order the death knell, to 'bid 'em ring out' (4.3.4)
5 **arrant** thoroughgoing, unmitigated
5–6 **called upon** summoned by death
8 **want...expressed** haven't the words to express my joy
9 **struck** see 2.3.86, note
10 **kiss** approach but do not taste the fruits
12 **famous coz'ner** see 5.3.21
16 **good confidence** too much trust (compare 1.2.57)
19 **For** as for
20 **entailed** given to being as a result of his inheritance
21 **it** his asininity
22 **art** artifice, cunning
30 **Blackfriars** London precinct (or liberty) between St Paul's Cathedral and the Thames
38 **of mine honesty** oath; compare Winifred's 'o' my fidelity'
43 **hanging moon** indicates a change of weather; shaped like a horn, the crescent moon was associated with cuckoldry
45 **entertain** accept
46 **'em** Lethe and the Courtesan
54 **use** treat; have sexual relations with (compare 2.3.230 and 5.1.52–3)
55 **mought** might
60 **show...woman** weep
61 **unkindness** meanness, but also unnatural behaviour
65 **parts** see 3.1.164, note
67 **turns** devices, tricks

and thou wilt ne'er weep for him, I warrant thee.' You would not think how that counsel has wrought with me, Master Rearage; I could not dispend another tear now, an you would give me ne'er so much.

REARAGE Why, I count you the wiser widow. It shows you have wisdom, when you can check your passion. For mine own part, I have no sense to sorrow for his death, whose life was the only rub to my affection.

THOMASINE Troth, and so it was to mine. But take courage now; you're a landed gentleman, and my daughter is seven hundred pound strong to join with you.

REARAGE
But Lethe lies i'th' way.

THOMASINE Let him lie still;
You shall tread o'er him or I'll fail in will.

REARAGE Sweet widow! *Exeunt*

4.4 *Enter Quomodo like a Beadle*

QUOMODO What a beloved man did I live? My servants gall their fingers with wringing, my wife's cheeks smart with weeping, tears stand in every corner; you may take water in my house. But am not I a wise fool now? What if my wife should take my death so to heart, that she should sicken upon't, nay, swoon, nay, die? When did I hear of a woman do so? Let me see; now I remember me, I think 'twas before my time. Yes, I have heard of those wives that have wept, and sobbed, and swooned; marry, I never heard but they recovered again; that's a comfort, la, that's a comfort, and I hope so will mine. Peace, 'tis near upon the time. I see; here comes the worshipful livery. I have the Hospital Boys; I perceive little Thomasine will bestow cost of me.
I'll listen to the common censure now,
How the world tongues me when my ear lies low.

Enter the Livery [*and Hospital Boys*]

FIRST LIVERYMAN
Who, Quomodo? Merely enriched by shifts
And cozenages, believe it.

QUOMODO [*aside*]
I see the world is very loath to praise me,
'Tis rawly friends with me; I cannot blame it,
For what I have done has been to vex and shame it.
Here comes my son, the hope, the landed heir,
One whose rare thrift will say, "Men's tongues, you lie;
I'll keep by law what was got craftily."

[*Enter Sim*]

Methinks I hear him say so.
He does salute the livery with good grace
And solemn gesture.—
[*To Sim*] O, my young worshipful master, you have parted from a dear father, a wise and provident father.

SIM Art thou grown an ass now?

QUOMODO Such an honest father—

SIM Prithee, beadle, leave thy lying. I am scarce able to endure thee, i'faith. What honesty didst thou e'er know by my father? Speak. Rule your tongue, beadle, lest I make you prove it, and then I know what will become of you. 'Tis the scurviest thing i'th' earth to belie the dead so, and he's a beastly son and heir that will stand by and hear his father belied to his face; he will ne'er prosper, I warrant him. Troth, if I be not ashamed to go to church with him, I would I might be hanged; I hear such filthy tales go on him. O, if I had known he had been such a lewd fellow in his life, he should ne'er have kept me company.

QUOMODO [*aside*] O, O, O!

SIM But I am glad he's gone, though 'twere long first; Shortyard and I will revel it i'faith; I have made him my rent-gatherer already.

QUOMODO [*aside*] He shall be speedily disinherited; he gets not a foot, not the crown of a molehill. I'll sooner make a courtier my heir, for teaching my wife tricks, than thee. My most neglectful son! O, now the corse; I shall observe yet farther.

A counterfeit corse brought in, [*followed by*] *Thomasine,* [*Mother,*] *and all the mourners equally counterfeit*

O, my most modest, virtuous, and rememb'ring wife;
She shall have all when I die, she shall have all.

Enter Easy

THOMASINE [*aside*] Master Easy? 'Tis. O, what shift shall I make now? O! (*She falls down in a feigned swoon*)

QUOMODO [*aside*] Sweet wife, she swoons. I'll let her alone. I'll have no mercy at this time. I'll not see her; I'll follow the corse. *Exit*

EASY The devil grind thy bones, thou cozening rascal!

MOTHER Give her a little more air, tilt up her head.— Comfort thyself good widow; do not fall like a beast for a husband. There's more than we can well tell where to put 'em, good soul.

THOMASINE O, I shall be well anon.

MOTHER Fie, you have no patience, i'faith. I have buried four husbands, and never offered 'em such abuse.

THOMASINE Cousin, how do you?

EASY Sorry to see you ill, coz.

69 **wrought with** affected
70 **dispend** expend, shed
74 **sense** desire
75 **rub** obstacle (in bowls, an obstacle that turns aside the ball)
78 **seven hundred pound** her dowry (see 5.3.113)
4.4.0.1 *Beadle* see 3.5.17, note; beadles also oversaw funeral processions
1 **gall** chafe
4 **take water** travel by boat
12 **time** for the funeral procession to pass by
13 **livery** see 2.3.458, note
Hospital Boys the Boys of Christ's Hospital accompany the procession, singing psalms
15 **censure** estimate, judgement
16 **tongues me** speaks of me
17 **shifts** tricks, stratagems
20 **rawly** scarcely
42 **lewd** base, worthless
45 **'twere long first** it was long in coming
49 **foot** of land
50 **teaching . . . tricks** making me a cuckold
51 **corse** corpse
61 MOTHER an old woman, possibly a hired mourner
68 **Cousin** familiar form of address

THOMASINE
The worst is past, I hope.
Pointing after the coffin
EASY I hope so too.
THOMASINE
Lend me your hand, sweet coz, I have troubled you.
MOTHER No trouble indeed, forsooth.—[*To Easy*] Good cousin, have a care of her, comfort her up as much as you can, and all little enough, I warrant ye.
Exeunt [*Mother and Mourners*]
THOMASINE
My most sweet love!
EASY My life is not so dear.
THOMASINE
I have always pitied you.
EASY You've shown it here,
And given the desperate hope!
THOMASINE Delay not now,
You've understood my love; I have a priest ready;
This is the fittest season, no eye offends us.
Let this kiss
Restore thee to more wealth, me to more bliss.
EASY
The angels have provided for me. [*Exeunt*]
Finis Actus Quartus

5.1 *Incipit Actus Quintus et Ultimus*
Enter Shortyard with writings, having cozened Sim Quomodo
SHORTYARD
I have not scope enough within my breast
To keep my joys contained; I'm Quomodo's heir,
The lands, assurances, and all are mine.
I have tripped his son's heels up above the ground
His father left him. Had I not encouragement?
Do not I know, what proves the father's prey,
The son ne'er looks on't, but it melts away?
Do not I know, the wealth that's got by fraud,
Slaves share it like the riches of a bawd?
Why, 'tis a curse unquenchable, ne'er cools;
Knaves still commit their consciences to fools,
And they betray who owed 'em. Here's all the bonds,
All Easy's writings. Let me see.
Enter Quomodo's wife [*Thomasine*] *married to Easy*
THOMASINE
Now my desires wear crowns.
EASY My joys exceed;
Man is ne'er healthful, till his follies bleed.
THOMASINE
O, behold the villain, who in all those shapes
Confounded your estate.
EASY That slave! That villain!
SHORTYARD [*reading*]
So many acres of good meadow—
EASY
Rascal!
SHORTYARD
I hear you, sir.
EASY
Rogue, Shortyard, Blastfield, sergeant, deputy, cozener!
SHORTYARD
Hold, hold!
EASY
I thirst the execution of his ears.
THOMASINE
Hate you that office.
EASY
I'll strip him bare for punishment and shame.
SHORTYARD
Why do but hear me, sir; you will not think
What I have done for you.
EASY Given his son my lands!
SHORTYARD
Why look you, 'tis not so, you're not told true;
I have cozened him again merely for you,
Merely for you, sir; 'twas my meaning then
That you should wed her, and have all again.
O'my troth, it's true, sir; look you then here, sir.
Gives Easy the writings
You shall not miss a little scroll, sir. Pray, sir,
Let not the city know me for a knave;
There be richer men would envy my preferment,
If I should be known before 'em.
EASY
Villain, my hate to more revenge is drawn.
When slaves are found, 'tis their base art to fawn.—
[*Calls*] Within there!

72 **No trouble** Thomasine has asked Easy to help her up and then apologized to him, but the Mother assumes that Thomasine is apologizing to her; the mother thinks she is witnessing a taking of hands, a betrothal ceremony (4.4.72–4).
79 **offends** vexes
5.1.0.2 ***writings*** the deeds, conveyances of Easy's property, and original bonds; the 'assurances, and all' (5.1.3)
7 **son** puns on 'sun'
11 **consciences** the 'wide conscience[s]' (4.1.104–5) or hypocrisy they employ to benefit foolish heirs whom they hope will prove thrifty and lawful
12 **they . . . 'em** the fools betray the knaves who fathered, or 'owned', them
14 **exceed** are in excess of Thomasine's crowned desires
15 **bleed** drawing blood was a common medical treatment
16 **shapes** disguises
21 **deputy** see 3.4.194
23 **ears** criminals' ears were sometimes cut off (see 5.1.47)
24 **office** of the executioner
33 **little scroll** a single document
35 **preferment** promotion
36 **before 'em** to be more clever than they are
38 **found** discovered (also 5.1.41)

[*Enter Officers with Falselight bound*]

SHORTYARD
How now? Fresh warders!

EASY
This is the other. Bind him fast.—Have I found you,
Master Blastfield?

SHORTYARD This is the fruit of craft.
Like him that shoots up high, looks for the shaft,
And finds it in his forehead, so does hit
The arrow of our fate. Wit destroys wit;
The head the body's bane and his own bears.—
You have corn enough, you need not reap mine ears,
Sweet Master Easy.

EASY I loathe his voice. Away!

Exit [*Shortyard with Falselight and Officers*]

THOMASINE What happiness was here! But are you sure you have all?

EASY I hope so, my sweet wife.

THOMASINE What difference there is in husbands, not only in one thing, but all.

EASY Here's good deeds and bad deeds, the writings that keep my lands to me, and the bonds that gave it away from me.
These, my good deeds, shall to more safety turn,
And these, my bad, have their deserts and burn.
I'll see thee again presently; read there. [*Exit*]

THOMASINE
Did he want all, who would not love his care? [*Reads*]

Enter Quomodo [*disguised as Beadle*]

QUOMODO [*aside*] What a wife hast thou, Ephestian Quomodo. So loving, so mindful of her duty, not only seen to weep, but known to swoon. I knew a widow about Saint Antlings so forgetful of her first husband, that she married again within the twelvemonth; nay, some, by'rlady, within the month. There were sights to be seen! Had they my wife's true sorrows, seven months nor seven years would draw 'em to the stake. I would most tradesmen had such a wife as I; they hope they have, we must all hope the best. Thus in her honour:
A modest wife is such a jewel,
Every goldsmith cannot show it;
He that's honest and not cruel
Is the likeliest man to owe it.
And that's I. I made it by myself; and coming to her as a beadle for my reward this morning, I'll see how she takes my death next her heart.

THOMASINE Now, beadle.

QUOMODO
Bless your mistress-ship's eyes from too many tears
Although you have lost a wise and worshipful gentleman.

THOMASINE You come for your due, beadle, here i'th' house?

QUOMODO Most certain. The Hospital money and mine own poor forty pence.

THOMASINE I must crave a discharge from you, beadle.

QUOMODO Call your man. I'll heartily set my hand to a memorandum.

THOMASINE You deal the trulier.

QUOMODO [*aside*] Good wench still.

THOMASINE George!

[*Enter Servant*]

Here is the beadle come for his money. Draw a memorandum that he has received all his due he can claim here i'th' house after this funeral.

QUOMODO [*aside, while Servant writes*] What politic directions she gives him, all to secure herself. 'Tis time, i'faith, now to pity her. I'll discover myself to her ere I go; but came it off with some lively jest now, that were admirable. I have it! After the memorandum is written and all, I'll set my own name to't, Ephestian Quomodo. She'll start; she'll wonder how Ephestian Quomodo came thither, that was buried yesterday. You're beset, little Quomodo.

THOMASINE [*counting out money*] Nineteen, twenty; five pound; one two, three; and fourpence.

QUOMODO [*aside, while signing*] So, we shall have good sport when 'tis read. [*Exit Servant*]

[*Enter Easy*]

EASY How now, lady, paying away money so fast?

THOMASINE The beadle's due here, sir.

QUOMODO [*aside*]
Who? 'Tis Easy! What makes Easy in my house?
He is not my wife's overseer, I hope.

EASY What's here?

QUOMODO [*aside*] He makes me sweat.

40 **Fresh warders** more guards
41 **other** Shortyard, Falselight's accomplice
43 **shaft** arrow
46 **bane** destruction, woe
47 **corn** grain; wealth (*fig.*)
50 **all** the legal papers
53 **one thing** penis; compare 2.3.78 and 230, and 4.3.54–8
60 **Did . . . all** even if he had nothing; possible play on 'awl', for penis (see 5.1.50 and compare Master 'Alsup'—awl's up—2.1.10)
64 **Saint Antlings** St Antholin's Church, known for morning lectures attended by Puritans
74 **owe** own
76 **reward** payment
83 **Hospital money** Quomodo, as Beadle, has been deputed to collect the boy singers' fees.
84 **forty pence** fee for participating in the funeral procession
85 **discharge** receipt
94 **politic** see 3.5.18, note
96 **discover** reveal
101 **thither** on the discharge
beset under attack, assailed on all sides
102 **little Quomodo** Thomasine; because Quomodo frequently refers to 'little Thomasine' (see 2.3.437 and 4.4.14), this could be a compositor's error
103–4 **Nineteen . . . fourpence** The Hospital Boys get five pounds ('nineteen, twenty' are the last two shillings in the fifth pound; 20*s*. = one pound); the Beadle gets 3 shillings, 4 pence, or 40 pence ('one, two, three' are also shillings; 12 pence = 1*s*.).
110 **overseer** person appointed to supervise the executor of a will; for bawdy connotations, see 5.1.128, note

EASY [*reads*] 'Memorandum: that I have received of Richard Easy all my due I can claim here i'th' house, or any hereafter for me. In witness whereof, I have set to mine own hand: *Ephestian Quomodo*.'

QUOMODO [*aside*] What have I done? Was I mad?

EASY Ephestian Quomodo?

QUOMODO
Ay, well, what then, sir? Get you out of my house;
First, you Master Prodigal Had-land, away!

THOMASINE
What, is the beadle drunk or mad?
Where are my men to thrust him out o' doors?

QUOMODO
Not so, good Thomasine, not so.

THOMASINE
This fellow must be whipped.

QUOMODO Thank you, good wife.

EASY
I can no longer bear him.

THOMASINE Nay, sweet husband.

QUOMODO [*aside*] Husband! I'm undone, beggared, cozened, confounded forever! Married already?—Will it please you know me now, Mistress Harlot and Master Horner? Who am I now?

[*Discovers himself*]

THOMASINE O, he's as like my t'other husband as can be.

QUOMODO I'll have judgement; I'll bring you before a judge; you shall feel, wife, whether my flesh be dead or no. I'll tickle you, i'faith, i'faith. *Exit*

THOMASINE
The judge that he'll solicit knows me well.

EASY
Let's on then, and our grievances first tell. *Exeunt*

5.2 *Enter Lethe with Officers, taken with his Harlot;* [*Rearage and Susan looking on*]

REARAGE
Here they come.

SUSAN O, where?

LETHE Heart of shame!
Upon my wedding morning, so disgraced!
Have you so little conscience, officers,
You will not take a bribe?

COURTESAN Master Lethe, we may lie together lawfully hereafter, for we are coupled together before people enough, i'faith.

[*Exeunt Officers with Lethe and his Harlot*]

REARAGE
There goes the strumpet.

SUSAN
Pardon my wilful blindness, and enjoy me;
For now the difference appears too plain
Betwixt a base slave and a true gentleman.

REARAGE
I do embrace thee in the best of love.
[*Aside*] How soon affections fail, how soon they prove.
[*Exeunt*]

5.3 *Enter Judge, Easy and Thomasine in talk with him;* [*Shortyard and Falselight guarded by Officers*]

JUDGE
His coz'nages are odious; he the plaintiff!
Not only framed deceitful in his life,
But so to mock his funeral!

EASY Most just.
The livery all assembled, mourning weeds
Throughout his house e'en down to his last servant,
The herald richly hired to lend him arms
Feigned from his ancestors, which I dare swear knew
No other arms but those they laboured with.
All preparations furnished, nothing wanted
Save that which was the cause of all—his death.
If he be living!

JUDGE 'Twas an impious part.

EASY
We are not certain yet it is himself,
But some false spirit that assumes his shape
And seeks still to deceive me.

[*Enter Quomodo*]

QUOMODO [*to Easy and Thomasine*]
O, are you come?—
My lord!—[*Looks to Shortyard and Falselight*] They're here. Good morrow, Thomasine.

JUDGE
Now, what are you?

QUOMODO
I am Quomodo, my lord, and this my wife;
Those my two men, that are bound wrongfully.

JUDGE
How are we sure you're he?

QUOMODO
O, you cannot miss, my lord.

JUDGE I'll try you.
Are you the man that lived the famous coz'ner?

115 **any** anyone
120 **First . . . away** before I do anything else, get out
Had-land irresponsible heir
128 **Master Horner** one who gives a man horns, makes him a cuckold
133 **tickle** beat, chastise; also, excite sexually (his 'flesh', or penis, is not yet 'dead')
134 **knows** Has Thomasine had an affair with this judge?
5.2.0.1 ***Officers*** They have arrested Lethe and the Courtesan at Rearage's instigation (see 4.3.45–6).
9 **enjoy me** as your wife
13 **How . . . prove** 'how fickle is love' or 'the quick demise of one's trivial affections proves one's worthiness'
5.3.4 **weeds** clothes
6 **richly** at great cost; bribed
arms a coat of arms; puns on body part at 5.3.8
7 **Feigned from** as if derived from
11 **part** business, affair

QUOMODO
O no, my lord.
JUDGE
Did you deceive this gentleman of his right,
And laid nets o'er his land?
QUOMODO Not I, my lord.
JUDGE
Then you're not Quomodo, but a counterfeit.
Lay hands on him, and bear him to the whip.
QUOMODO
Stay, stay a little,
I pray; now I remember me, my lord,
I cozened him indeed, 'tis wondrous true.
JUDGE
Then I dare swear this is no counterfeit;
Let all doubts cease, this man is Quomodo.
QUOMODO
Why, la, you now, you would not believe this.
I am found what I am.
JUDGE
But setting these thy odious shifts apart,
Why did that thought profane enter thy breast,
To mock the world with thy supposèd death?
QUOMODO
Conceive you not that, my lord? A policy.
JUDGE
So.
QUOMODO
For, having gotten the lands, I thirsted still
To know what fate would follow 'em.
JUDGE
Being ill got.
QUOMODO Your lordship apprehends me.
JUDGE
I think I shall anon.
QUOMODO And thereupon,
I, out of policy, possessed my son,
Which since I have found lewd, and now intend
To disinherit him forever.
Not only this was in my death set down,
But thereby a firm trial of my wife,
Her constant sorrows, her rememb'ring virtues;
All which are dews; the shine of a next morning
Dries 'em up all, I see't.
JUDGE
Did you profess wise cozenage, and would dare
To put a woman to her two days' choice,
When oft a minute does it?
QUOMODO Less! A moment,
The twinkling of an eye, a glimpse, scarce something
does it.
Your lordship yet will grant she is my wife?
THOMASINE
O heaven!
JUDGE
After some penance, and the dues of law
I must acknowledge that.
QUOMODO I scarce like
Those dues of law.
EASY My lord,
Although the law too gently 'lot his wife,
The wealth he left behind he cannot challenge.
QUOMODO
How?
EASY
Behold his hand against it. [*Shows memorandum*]
QUOMODO
He does devise all means to make me mad,
That I may no more lie with my wife
In perfect memory. I know't, but yet
The lands will maintain me in my wits;
The land will do so much for me.
JUDGE [*reading*] 'In witness whereof I have set to mine own
hand: *Ephestian Quomodo*.'
'Tis firm enough your own, sir.
QUOMODO
A jest, my lord, I did I knew not what.
JUDGE
It should seem so. Deceit is her own foe,
Craftily gets, and childishly lets go.
But yet the lands are his.
QUOMODO I warrant ye.
EASY
No, my good lord, the lands know the right heir;
I am their master once more.
QUOMODO Have you the lands?
EASY
Yes, truly, I praise heaven.
QUOMODO Is this good dealing?
Are there such consciences abroad? How?
Which way could he come by 'em?
SHORTYARD My lord,
I'll quickly resolve you that, it comes to me.
This coz'ner, whom too long I called my patron,
To my thought dying, and the fool, his son,
Possessed of all, which my brain partly sweat for,
I held it my best virtue, by a plot
To get from him what for him was ill got—

33 **found . . . am** found to be myself, what I really am (a cozener)
41 **apprehends** understands, but also 'arrests'
44 **lewd** base, worthless
46 **set down** intended
49 **shine** sunshine
51 **profess** practice
58 **acknowledge** assent to the legal force of
60 **'lot** allot, dispose of
61 **challenge** lay claim to
66 **In perfect memory** because she has slept with Easy
75 **yet . . . his** the Essex estate is still Quomodo's
81 **resolve** explain, settle
that how Easy regained his estate
it . . . me the job of explaining is rightly mine
83 **To my thought** as far as I knew

QUOMODO
O, beastly Shortyard!

SHORTYARD When, no sooner mine,
But I was glad more quickly to resign.

JUDGE
Craft once discovered shows her abject line.

QUOMODO [*aside*]
He hits me everywhere, for craft, once known,
Does teach fools wit, leaves the deceiver none.
My deeds have cleft me, cleft me!

Enter Officers with Lethe and the Harlot, [*Rearage, Salewood, the pander Hellgill, Mother Gruel, and Susan follow*]

FIRST OFFICER
Room there!

QUOMODO [*aside*]
A little yet to raise my spirit.
Here's Master Lethe comes to wed my daughter.
That's all the joy is left me.—Ha! Who's this?

JUDGE
What crimes have those brought forth?

SALEWOOD The shame of lust;
Most viciously on this his wedding morning,
This man was seized in shame with that bold strumpet.

JUDGE
Why, 'tis she he means to marry.

LETHE No, in truth.

JUDGE
In truth, you do.
Who, for his wife, his harlot doth prefer,
Good reason 'tis that he should marry her.

COURTESAN
I crave it on my knees, such was his vow at first.

HELLGILL [*aside*]
I'll say so too, and work out mine own safety.—
Such was his vow at first, indeed, my lord,
Howe'er his mood has changed him!

LETHE O, vile slave!

COURTESAN
He says it true, my lord.

JUDGE Rest content,
He shall both marry and taste punishment.

LETHE O, intolerable! I beseech your good lordship; if I must have an outward punishment, let me not marry an inward, whose lashes will ne'er out, but grow worse and worse. I have a wife stays for me this morning with seven hundred pound in her purse. Let me be speedily whipped and be gone, I beseech your lordship.

SALEWOOD
He speaks no truth, my lord; behold the virgin,
Wife to a well-esteemed gentleman,
Loathing the sin he follows.

LETHE
I was betrayed, yes, faith.

REARAGE [*to the Judge, completing an aside*]
...His own mother, my lord,
Which he confessed, through ignorance and disdain,
His name so changed to abuse the world and her.

LETHE [*aside*] Marry a harlot, why not? 'Tis an honest man's fortune. I pray, did not one of my countrymen marry my sister? Why, well then, if none should be married but those that are honest, where should a man seek a wife after Christmas? I pity that gentleman that has nine daughters to bestow, and seven of 'em seeded already; they will be good stuff by that time.—
I do beseech your lordship to remove
The punishment. I am content to marry her.

JUDGE
There's no removing of your punishment.

LETHE
O, good my lord!

JUDGE Unless one here assembled,
Whom you have most unnaturally abused,
Beget your pardon.

LETHE Who should that be?
Or who would do't, that has been so abused?
A troublesome penance.—[*To Quomodo*] Sir—

QUOMODO
Knave in your face! Leave your mocking, Andrew;
Marry your quean and be quiet!

LETHE Master Easy—

EASY
I'm sorry you take such a bad course, sir.

LETHE Mistress Quomodo—

THOMASINE Inquire my right name against next time; now go your ways like an ass as you came.

LETHE [*aside*]
Mass! I forget my mother all this while.
I'll make her do't at first.—Pray, mother,
Your blessing for once.

MOTHER GRUEL Call'st me mother? Out,
I defy thee, slave.

LETHE Call me slave
As much as you will, but do not shame me now;
Let the world know you are my mother.

MOTHER GRUEL
Let me not have this villain put upon me,

89 **abject line** wretched ways
101 **for** instead of
103 **at first** when we first met
111 **ne'er out** never disappear
116 **Wife** Susan and Rearage have married between this and the previous scene.
119–21 **His...her** possibly a corrupt passage; Rearage is explaining Lethe's deceptions to the Judge
123 **countrymen** see 2.3.11, note
125 **honest** virgins
126 **after Christmas** after a period of festive license
127 **bestow** marry off
seeded impregnated
128 **stuff** see 3.1.206, note
137 **Knave...face** I call you knave to your face
141 **Inquire...time** Thomasine still aims to leave Quomodo for Easy.
146 **defy** repudiate, despise
149 **put upon** imposed on

I beseech your lordship.

JUDGE
He's justly cursed; she loathes to know him now,
Whom he before did as much loathe to know.
Wilt thou believe me, woman?

MOTHER GRUEL
That's soon done.

JUDGE
Then know him for a villain; 'tis thy son.

MOTHER GRUEL
Art thou Andrew, my wicked son Andrew?

LETHE
You would not believe me, mother.

MOTHER GRUEL
How art thou changed!
Is this suit fit for thee, a tooth-drawer's son?
This country has e'en spoiled thee since though cam'st hither. Thy manners then were better than thy clothes; but now whole clothes and ragged manners. It may well be said that truth goes naked, for when thou hadst scarce a shirt, thou hadst more truth about thee.

JUDGE
Thou art thine own affliction, Quomodo.
Shortyard we banish; 'tis our pleasure.

SHORTYARD
Henceforth no woman shall complain for measure.

JUDGE
And that all error from our works may stand,
We banish Falselight evermore the land. *Exeunt*

Finis

THE PARTS

EASY (323 lines): Induction parts; Winifred; Tailor or Comings; [servant (5.1)]

QUOMODO (563 lines): Induction parts; Drawer; Winifred; Father or servant (3.1) or Tailor or Comings

SHORTYARD (512 lines): Induction parts; Winifred; servant (5.1); mourner or mother or liveryman or hospital boy; Tailor or Comings or servant (3.1)

LETHE (236 lines): Induction parts; Winifred; servant (5.1); mourner or mother or liveryman or hospital boy; [Tailor or Comings or servant (3.1)]

FALSELIGHT (35 lines): Induction parts; Winifred; servant (5.1); Father or servant (3.1) or Tailor or Comings; mourner or mother or liveryman or hospital boy

FATHER (86 lines): Induction parts; Winifred; servant (5.1); officer or Judge or Falselight; Falselight or Cockstone or Boy or drawer or Susan or Sim; Sim or mourner or mother or liveryman or hospital boy

COUNTRY WENCH (79 lines): Induction parts; Cockstone; Drawer; Winifred; servant (5.1); Boy or Dustbox; Sim or mourner or mother or liveryman or hospital boy

THOMASINE (150 lines): Induction parts; Cockstone; Drawer; servant (3.1) or Tailor or Comings

REARAGE (112 lines): Dustbox; servant (5.1); Tailor or Comings; Sim or mourner or mother or liveryman or or hospital boy; Michaelmas Term or Induction Boy [or other Induction parts]; [Winifred]

SALEWOOD (75 lines): Dustbox; Winifred; servant (5.1); Tailor or Comings; Sim or mourner or mother or liveryman or hospital boy; Michaelmas Term or Induction Boy [or other Induction parts]

HELLGILL (88 lines): Induction parts; Cockstone; Dustbox; Winifred; servant (5.1); Tailor or Comings; Sim or mourner or mother or liveryman or hospital boy

BOY (38 lines): Induction parts; Cockstone; Winifred; servant (5.1); servant (3.1) or Tailor or Comings or Father; mourner or mother or liveryman or hospital boy; officer or Judge or Susan

SIM (18 lines): Induction parts; Winifred; servant (5.1); Susan or Rearage or Salewood or Cockstone; officer or Judge (or Susan); Father or servant (3.1) or Tailor or Comings [(or Rearage or Salewood)]

JUDGE (5.3; 51 lines): Induction parts; Cockstone; Winifred; servant (5.1); Boy or Dustbox; Drawer (or Boy); Father (or Boy); servant (3.1) or Tailor or Comings (or Father); Sim or mourner or mother or liveryman or hospital boy

MOTHER GRUEL (74 lines): Induction parts; Cockstone; Dustbox or Boy; Winifred; servant (5.1); Tailor or Comings or servant (3.1); Sim or mourner or mother or liveryman or hospital boy

SUSAN (13 lines): Induction parts; Cockstone; Winifred; servant (5.1); Boy or Dustbox; Drawer (or Boy); Father (or Boy); servant (3.1) or Tailor or Comings (or Father); Sim or mourner or mother or liveryman or hospital boy

OFFICER (1 line): (same as Judge)

COCKSTONE (1.1; 28 lines): any but Rearage; Salewood, Easy, Quomodo, Shortyard, Falselight, Lethe

DRAWER (2.1; 2 lines): any but Rearage, Salewood, Lethe, Easy, Shortyard, Hellgill; Boy, [Father]

DUSTBOX (2.3; 10 lines): any boy, Quomodo, Easy, Shortyard, Boy, Thomasine, Falselight

TAILOR (3.1; 7 lines): any but Comings, servant (3.1), Country Wench, Hellgill, Father, [Lethe, Shortyard, Rearage]

MISTRESS COMINGS (3.1; 12 lines): any but Tailor, servant (3.1), Country Wench, Hellgill, Father, [Lethe, Shortyard, Rearage]

158 **This country** England

162 **scarce a shirt** see 2.1.66

165 **measure** see 1.2.90–3

SERVANT (3.1; 3 lines): any but Tailor, Comings, Country Wench, Hellgill, Father, [Lethe, Shortyard, Rearage]

WINIFRED (4.3; 5 lines): any but Thomasine [Shortyard, Rearage, Father]

MOTHER (4.4; 9 lines): any but Quomodo, liveryman, hospital boy, Sim, Thomasine, mourner, Easy

FIRST LIVERYMAN (4.4; 2 lines): any but Quomodo, mother, hospital boy, Sim, Thomasine, mourner, Easy

MOURNER (4.4; no lines): any but Quomodo, liveryman, hospital boy, Sim, Thomasine, mother, Easy

HOSPITAL BOY (4.4; no lines): any but Quomodo, liveryman, mother, Sim, Thomasine, mourner, Easy

SERVANT (5.1; no lines): any but Quomodo, Thomasine, [Easy]

Induction roles (75 lines): any but another Induction part, [Rearage, Salewood]

A TRICK TO CATCH THE OLD ONE

Edited by Valerie Wayne

THIS play is one of Middleton's finest achievements in comedy. In 1886 Swinburne pronounced it 'by far the best play Middleton had yet written, and one of the best he ever wrote'; in 1927 T. S. Eliot included it among the five plays marking Middleton as a 'great' dramatist, only one other of which, *The Roaring Girl*, was a comedy. Gerard Langbaine thought it 'an Excellent Old Play' in 1691 (Sara Jayne Steen), and in 1960 R. H. Parker termed its plot 'a triumph of ironic construction'. Although Victorian critics questioned its morality—a reviewer of Bullen's *Works of Thomas Middleton* complained that the play's 'considerable humour... is of the kind that one cannot retell in polite society'—contemporary audiences, often less accustomed to *politesse* and more attuned to politics, have appreciated its treatments of early modern greed and the triumphs it offers to figures of youth and wit as they outmanœuvre age and avarice. The play represents mercenary marriage as a socially sanctioned form of theft, one that the courtesan successfully reappropriates in her own best interest through her disguise as a rich widow. When Hoard inadvertently marries a 'whore', the thieving usurer is then caught in his own trap.

Trick was successfully adapted during the seventeenth century for Lording Barry's *Ram Alley* (1607–8) and Philip Massinger's *A New Way to Pay Old Debts* (1625). A Restoration production of the play between 1662 and 1665 (John Downes) may have been prompted by parallels between its plot and events surrounding the notorious Mary Carleton, who was tried for bigamy in 1663 at the Old Bailey for disguising herself as a German princess in order to entrap John Carleton in marriage, who also tried to entrap her. The case gained such wide public attention that it occasioned fourteen pamphlets and a play in 1663 and more publications ten years later, when Mary was tried again and hanged for theft (Janet Todd and Elizabeth Spearing). Aphra Behn, the first professional woman dramatist, then reworked *A Trick to Catch the Old One* and *A Mad World, My Masters* for her 1682 comedy, *The City Heiress* (Marston Stevens Balch). Her play opens with the same conflict between an uncle and his profligate nephew and concludes with the uncle's discovery that he has married his heir's 'cast-off mistress'. Behn extends Middleton's critique of the economy of marriage by making its connections with rape and theft even more explicit and adding two more female leads. Yet Wilding, Witgood's counterpart, also grows into the Restoration rake, and the celebration of his rampant virility mutes the play's social critique and appropriates it for royalist politics (Wayne, 'Assuming Gentility').

The intimate collusion between an elegant young woman and a fine gentleman, who pays her for her sexual services while a maid arranges a bed in a well-appointed interior. The inscription warns the viewer of the harm that comes from touch. *Tactus* (Touch), from a series of five prints representing the senses by Cornelis van Kittensteyn, after Dirck Hals, engraved between 1630 and 1663.

Revivals of *Trick* in the second half of the twentieth century occurred on average every five or six years. A 1964 staging in Dorset used modern dress and an all-male cast; another at Toronto in 1976 used an all-female cast. Commercial productions were mounted at the Mermaid Theatre in London in 1952, at the Theatr Clwyd in Wales in 1978, and the Bear Gardens Museum in 1985 (Lisa Cronin and Marilyn Roberts). The playwright Peter Barnes prepared an adaptation for a BBC Radio production of 1985 by bringing the allusions and jokes alive for a modern audience (Bernard Dukore). A company called Instant Classics mounted a modern dress production at London's White Bear Pub in 1994 that cut the Dampit scenes, changed one of the creditors to a woman, and based the set design on the children's game of Snakes and Ladders (Michael Neuman).

The early performance and publication history of Middleton's play also indicates a good reception from its very first audiences. *Trick* was probably written in 1605; it was performed by the Children of Paul's before that company ceased playing in July of 1606, after which it was trans-

'He that doth his youth expose | To brothel, drink, and danger, | Let him that is his nearest kin | Cheat him before a stranger' (*Trick* 1.1.15–18). Engraving from *The Parable of the Prodigal Son*, a series of six prints. Number 3, 'The son wasting his heritage with riotous living'. By Crispijn de Passe the elder. Late 16th or early 17th century.

ferred to the other boys' company at the Blackfriars. Two of its title-pages refer to a New Year's night performance at court before James I, most likely in 1607 or 1608. The play was licensed for publication in October 1607 at the same time as *The Revenger's Tragedy* and presumably printed after that play late in 1607 or early in 1608. George Eld printed three title-pages for the edition dated 1608: the first, which was cancelled, identifies it as performed by the Children of Paul's; the revised title-pages exist in two different states, both of which add performances at Blackfriars and before the King, identify 'T.M.' as the author, and name Henry Rocket as the bookseller. The play was going through Eld's press just months after three other comedies that he printed had also been released for publication from Paul's, but only *Trick* had additional performances by the Blackfriars boys. A second edition appeared eight years later in 1616, suggesting that the first edition sold relatively well.

Trick is one of the citizen comedies that Middleton was especially known for developing at Paul's. Plays of that genre locate their action in London and in citizen culture, from which they offer urbane critiques of their society's manners and morals; they lack the 'satirical bite' of those designed for the Blackfriars, where 'railing' plays were being produced instead (Andrew Gurr). Yet this play's transfer to the Blackfriars shows its versatility and broad appeal. Both theatres provided small and select indoor settings, where seats were expensive and the audience consisted in large measure of students from the Inns of Court, more established aristocrats and gentry, some citizens and probably their wives. Michael Shapiro remarks that plays from the boys' companies 'ridiculed not only the usual collection of pedants, parasites, and parvenus, but figures of authority resembling more closely than ever what spectators were, might become, or thought themselves to be'. When Middleton represents a young man's drive to secure his fortune through inheritance and marriage, and an old man's relish for becoming a landed, country gentleman, he is staging the 'forces of appetite and materialist opportunism' that were released by the lure of social mobility and an inflationary economy increasingly fuelled by credit (Brian Gibbons).

Both Roman and English traditions are evident in the play. An affinity with urban life marks one connection with the comedies of Plautus and Terence (Gail Kern Paster), and although no single source for *Trick* has been found, many features of Roman comedy can be identified. Dryden's description of the New Comedy *adulescens* as a 'Debauch'd Son, kind in his Nature to his Mistress, but miserably in want of Money', suits Witgood quite well. He and Jane, his mistress, for whom there are countless counterparts among the courtesans of Roman comedy, succeed in overthrowing the plans of not one but two *senex* figures, Hoard and Lucre. Added to this Roman tradition is the English dramatic heritage of the morality play, used here in the form of the prodigal son parable, which was often staged in the sixteenth and early seventeenth centuries (A. B. Stonex, George Rowe). The play also draws on English social satire. Middleton knew the coney-catching pamphlets of Robert Greene, narratives of low-life characters who tricked or 'cozened' their unsuspecting prey, and he had used them in other early comedies. The usurer was also a frequent figure in verse satires of the 1590s. Even the jest books could have provided him with material.

The drive of *Trick* as it advances without pause from one intrigue to the next comes not only from Middleton's ability to imitate older literary conventions but from the rooting of its incidents in the material contrivances of his own day. The character of Dampit forms the centre of a graphic tableau of Jacobean London alive with lawyers claiming fees they have not earned and creditors bent on inducing debt. What has sometimes been called Middleton's 'realism' is a controlled representation of a society fractured by the sale of women in marriage and the theft of earnings and inheritance by the agents of usury. The play offers the pleasure of seeing those who engage in both kinds of theft—Hoard and Lucre in particular—duped by their own greed into acts of uncharacteristic generosity. The happy ending in which they learn they have been gulled implies a strong judgement against them and their vices, while the audience shares in the glee of those who gulled them.

So it is difficult to sympathize with Victorian laments of the absence of morality in this play. It is true that Witgood has led a dissolute life before the play begins. He and Jane are motivated more from desires for survival than selflessness, but not to like them is to resist the cleverest and even kindest characters in this dissolute community. Jane's indefinite past is another source of disapproval, because she has often been dismissed as a 'whore' without an understanding of the diverse ways that word was used in early modern culture. Laura Gowing explains that in the 'language of insult' then current, 'the word "whore" rarely meant a real prostitute'. As some of the play's critics have noted, and as Aphra Behn's adaption implies, Jane is not a professional prostitute but Witgood's mistress: she has been financially supported by him in return for sex and companionship without the prospect of marriage. In the very first scene she makes it clear that she lost her virginity to Witgood (1.1.37–40), and in the very last Witgood says she has slept only with him (5.2.159–60). Yet since virginity was a requirement for respectable first marriages and Jane has had sexual experience outside of marriage, in early modern culture she is considered a 'whore'.

Witgood says 'she's a whore' at 5.2.111, but when Hoard charges her with being a 'common strumpet' fifteen lines later, Witgood objects:

Nay, now
You wrong her, sir. If I were she, I'd have
The law on you for that. I durst depose for her
She ne'er had common use, nor common thought.
(5.2.125–8)

From her position as a wife at the play's conclusion, Jane would be capable of bringing a suit of slander against Hoard in an ecclesiastical court because she was not promiscuous nor had a reputation for being so. A common strumpet or prostitute was usually poorly compensated for her sexual services and worked with little protection or maintenance; as an insult the term 'strumpet' implied 'a (very) wanton woman' (Eric Partridge). The speech headings and stage directions in the early texts of *Trick* identify Jane as a 'courtesan', and courtesans were originally attached to the court, so the term had upper-class associations. In Edward Sharpham's 1606 satire *The Fleer*, the lead character remarks, 'Your whore is for every rascal, but your courtesan is for your courtier' (2.1.184–5). Yet the word 'courtesan' was more often used in England to name one who functioned as a mistress or had relatively few sexual partners. Even the female character named Frank Gullman, the courtesan in *A Mad World, My Masters* whose maidenhead has been sold fifteen times, has been 'kept' by various men rather than commonly available, which is why the sale of her virginity can continue and Follywit can be duped into marrying her. In G. R. Quaife's classification of English prostitutes, Middleton's courtesan is closest to a 'private whore' (others being 'vagrant', 'public', and 'village' whores); yet she is also very different from the famous Venetian courtesans described in *Coryat's Crudities* (1611). Whether Italian or English, professional or private, 'courtesans' were not usually seen as 'common' and were very different from 'strumpets', unless one was reducing women to their sexually lowest, most common denominator. Hoard's slander in the presence of witnesses was an actionable offence in early modern England.

Jane assumes three different subject positions in the play: she is Witgood's mistress, a feigned rich widow named Jane Meddler, and a wife named Jane Hoard. We never learn her 'real' name. But the speech heading 'courtesan' fixes her in ways that make it difficult for readers to observe these shifts in identity and grounds a misconception of the character's sexual inconstancy, constructing for the contemporary reader a woman who makes her living by sexual commerce and is generally available to men. This situation has led most readers to think like Hoard about the character, which makes the correction and exposure of Hoard largely incomprehensible. An editorial fidelity to the original text thereby produces, for a modern audience, a de facto collusion with Hoard's view of Jane. Yet in performance this character is constructed not by an abstract social label, but by the recurrence of a physical body. Members of a theatre audience can alter their perceptions of the character as she changes more readily than a silent reader can, since the textual label is a constant reminder of her first identity. A familiar proper name is, however, about as individualized as a physical body without specifying a social role. For all of these reasons (discussed more fully in Wayne, 'Sexual Politics'), I have altered the speech headings in this edition to 'Jane' so that the subject positions of the character are associated with a name rather than a misleading occupational or sexual category.

Without such a change, it has been impossible for almost everyone to understand Jane's own charge against Hoard at the end of the play:

> If in disgrace you share, I sought not you.
> You pursued me, nay, forced me.
> Had I friends would follow it,
> Less than your action has been proved a rape.
> (5.2.131–4)

Understanding this passage depends on recognizing the actions in scene 3.1 as a spousal or marriage contract between Hoard and Jane complete with a handfast, verbal agreements before witnesses, a kiss, and the naming of Jane by Hoard as 'wife'. The contract is later confirmed by a formal ceremony with a priest and is followed by a sexual consummation. We learn from a conversation between Hoard, Lamprey, and Spitchcock in 3.3 that Hoard's friends are proud of the way they pushed Jane into conceding to the spousal.

The forced marriage and rape of women of substance was sufficiently frequent in the fifteenth and sixteenth centuries to prompt a sequence of statutes against such practices. Given the ease and speed with which spousals in England could be contracted, women of substance who were unmarried or *femes soles* were at particular risk of being forced into marriage by men who wanted to gain control of their wealth. The function of scene 3.3 in the play is to provide support for Jane's charge that she was so compelled. We know that she prefers to be married to Hoard because he is her best option since she has lost her virginity to Witgood, and he actively encourages her to accept Hoard's offer because he will not marry her. Hoard does not know as much, however, so her accusation represents a serious threat. Jane's charge of rape has also been ignored because she was thought to have made her living by sexual commerce, yet early modern English legal texts show that even prostitutes were entitled to claim that they had been raped. According to Michael Dalton writing in the early seventeenth century and citing a thirteenth-century legal historian, a 'whore' who said 'no' to a man was not, at that time, considered to be a 'whore', so the legal definition of 'whore' was malleable and reflected the disposition of a woman's sexuality in a given instance more than her reputation or occupation. A judgement issued in the trial of the Earl of Castlehaven in 1631 showed less flexibility in defining 'whore' but granted legal rights to a woman so considered: 'it is the enforcing against the will which makes the Rape; and the common whore may be ravished against her will' (*Complete Collection of State Trials*; Wayne, 'Sexual Politics').

The word 'rape' at this time was also used to describe two different events: what we now call rape—forced sexual relations, and the act of abduction (T. E., *Law's Resolutions*). Jane's accusation of rape concerns Hoard's plan to take her to Cole Harbour for a quick marriage, which he explicitly plans to conduct like an abduction (3.1.220–5). Her assent to his plan is ambiguous (3.1.226), as is her agreement to the spousal, 'I promise you, I ha' nothing' (3.1.205). This response prevents Hoard from claiming that she has deceived him about her wealth, but he reads her 'nothing' as a sexual lure, a modest understatement, or both. Hoard's feigned attempt at abduction is therefore at risk of being transformed into a legal reality by a very clever woman whose knowledge of the law is so precise that she can use every opportunity that comes to hand against him. His readiness to manipulate her shows he has given no thought to whether she desires the spousal or participates willingly in the abduction and the sexual consummation, and in the end he is yoked to a wife who has her own desires and has in turn manipulated him. Jane effectively conceals her agency until her position as wife is secure; then she activates her new status in her own defence.

After her charge of rape, Jane weighs her own mistakes against Hoard's and finds her sexual sins no more reprehensible than his coercion. Hoard then admits that her public dishonour and his own are so inextricably linked that their names can only be cleared by his treating her as a respectable wife. The 'whoring' of Hoard calls into question the opposition between good women and whores, as Anthony Dawson has observed, for if a whore can play the role of rich widow so well that she actually becomes a wife, then the difference between the two collapses and the very men who insisted on it, having taken the one for the other, become the means by which the difference is undone. This imitation of a legitimate woman in the marriage market by a marginal figure termed a 'whore' manages to highlight the ways in which marriageable women are treated as whores, because they also are bought and sold like property and for property (Margot Heinemann). The malleability of women's identities in the play therefore threatens some important social institutions—marriage, property, and inheritance. Hence it is not only usury that is staged in *Trick*; the play also exhibits the early modern commodities market in women. Jane and Witgood promise reform in the playful rhymes of the play's last lines, but it is Hoard whose 'craft' has exposed him as the play's biggest 'fool' (5.2.204). Though some might call him a villain, Jane and Witgood both have reason to be more generous, so the play draws quickly to a comic and parodic close. And what could be more important than consuming the wedding meal before it cools?

SEE ALSO

Music: *Companion*, 140
Textual introduction and apparatus: *Companion*, 562
Authorship and date: *Companion*, 354

A Trick To Catch The Old One

[for the Children of Paul's]

THE PERSONS OF THE PLAY

Theodorus WITGOOD, a gentleman in debt
JANE, Witgood's mistress
HOST, friend to Witgood
Three CREDITORS of Witgood

Pecunius LUCRE, Witgood's uncle, a usurer
Jenny, WIFE to Lucre
SAM Freedom, son of Lucre's wife and suitor to Joyce
FIRST and SECOND GENTLEMEN, friends to Lucre
GEORGE, Lucre's servant

Walkadine HOARD, usurer and rival to Lucre
Joyce, NIECE to Walkadine and Onesiphorus Hoard
MONEYLOVE, suitor to Joyce
ONESIPHORUS Hoard, brother to Walkadine Hoard

LIMBER, friend to Onesiphorus Hoard
KIX, friend to Onesiphorus Hoard
SERVANT to Walkadine Hoard
ARTHUR, another servant to Walkadine Hoard
Lady FOXSTONE, friend to Walkadine Hoard

LAMPREY, a gentleman
SPITCHCOCK, a gentleman

Harry DAMPIT, a usurer
AUDREY, Dampit's servant
GULF, a usurer and acquaintance of Dampit
Sir LANCELOT, acquaintance of Dampit

Drawer, Vintner, Boy, Scrivener, Sergeants, Tailor, Barber, Perfumer, Falconer, Huntsman

---

1.1 *Incipit Actus Primus*

Enter Witgood, a gentleman, solus

WITGOOD All's gone! Still thou'rt a gentleman, that's all; but a poor one, that's nothing. What milk brings thy meadows forth now? Where are thy goodly uplands and thy downlands? All sunk into that little pit, lechery. Why should a gallant pay but two shillings for his ordinary that nourishes him, and twenty times two for his brothel that consumes him? But where's Long-acre? In my uncle's conscience, which is three years' voyage about. He that sets out upon his conscience ne'er finds the way home again—he is either swallowed in the quicksands of law quillets, or splits upon the piles of a *praemunire*. Yet these old fox-brained and ox-browed uncles have still defences for their avarice and apologies for their practices, and will thus greet our follies:

He that doth his youth expose
To brothel, drink, and danger,

This commentary foregrounds issues relating to women, marriage, social class, and sexual commerce.

Title A *trick* was an artifice or ruse used to deceive or cheat and could also refer to a course of lovemaking or a sexual act. Jane's appearance immediately after Witgood calls for 'any trick out of the compass of law' at 1.1.27–8 confirms her part in the scheme that she and Witgood devise for their elders, which certainly has a sexual component. However, the meaning of *trick* as a prostitute's client seems not to have been current until the twentieth century. *The old one* refers not only to Lucre and Hoard but to the devil. Usurers, including Dampit, are consistently associated with the devil in the play.

1.1.1 **gentleman** a man of good but not noble birth entitled to bear arms, whose wealth often derived from land

2–4 **milk ... pit** Witgood's imagery describes a feminized landscape where *milk* rather than rain promotes the growth of his meadows and *uplands*, *downlands*, and *little pit* evoke locations on the female body. The wealth of his lands has subsided into the genital site of woman's sexuality.

4 **lechery** promiscuous sexual indulgence

5 **two shillings** A shilling was worth twelve pence; twenty shillings made up a pound. Two shillings could buy a meal at a quite expensive eating house or service at an inexpensive brothel.

6 **ordinary** an eating house that served a fixed-price meal, or the meal itself

6–7 **nourishes ... consumes** The juxtaposition between food that nourishes for a small amount of money and sex that consumes at a much higher rate obscures Witgood's voluntary engagement in both activities. He is demonizing his expensive brothel and characterizing himself as its victim. *Brothel* could apply either to a place of prostitution or to the prostitute who worked there.

7 **Long-acre** a general term for an estate or patrimony

8–12 **conscience ... *praemunire*** Lucre's *conscience* is like the ocean that swallows one in legal quibbles or shipwrecks one on legal obstacles.

11 **quillets** legal quibbles or technicalities
piles pilings or rocks

12 ***praemunire*** a sheriff's writ
ox-browed (*a*) cuckolded, because of the ox's horns, (*b*) stupid, by association with the ox's bovine nature

13 **still** always

15–18 **He ... stranger** The passage inverts Deuteronomy 23: 19–20, which prohibits usurers from lending money to family members but not to strangers.

Let him that is his nearest kin
Cheat him before a stranger.

And that's his uncle, 'tis a principle in usury. I dare not visit the city. There I should be too soon visited by that horrible plague, my debts, and by that means I lose a virgin's love, her portion and her virtues. Well, how should a man live now, that has no living, hum? Why, are there not a million of men in the world that only sojourn upon their brain and make their wits their mercers? And am I but one amongst that million and cannot thrive upon't? Any trick out of the compass of law now would come happily to me.

Enter Jane

JANE My love.

WITGOOD My loathing! Hast thou been the secret consumption of my purse, and now com'st to undo my last means, my wits? Wilt leave no virtue in me and yet thou ne'er the better?
Hence courtesan, round-webbed tarantula,
That driest the roses in the cheeks of youth.

JANE I have been true unto your pleasure, and all your lands, thrice racked, was never worth the jewel which I prodigally gave you: my virginity.
Lands mortgaged may return and more esteemed,
But honesty, once pawned, is ne'er redeemed.

WITGOOD Forgive. I do thee wrong
To make thee sin, and then to chide thee for't.

JANE
I know I am your loathing now. Farewell.

WITGOOD
Stay, best invention, stay.

JANE I that have been the secret consumption of your purse, shall I stay now to undo your last means, your wits? Hence courtesan, away!

WITGOOD I prithee, make me not mad at my own weapon. Stay. (A thing few women can do, I know that, and therefore they had need wear stays.) Be not contrary. Dost love me? Fate has so cast it that all my means I must derive from thee.

JANE From me? Be happy then.
What lies within the power of my performance
Shall be commanded of thee.

WITGOOD Spoke like
An honest drab, i'faith; it may prove something.
What trick is not an embryo at first,
Until a perfect shape come over it?

JANE
Come, I must help you. Whereabouts left you?
I'll proceed.
Though you beget, 'tis I must help to breed.
Speak, what is't? I'd fain conceive it.

WITGOOD So, so, so. Thou shall presently take the name and form upon thee of a rich country widow, four hundred a year valiant, in woods, in bullocks, in barns,

20 **the city** London

22 **lose . . . virtues** Witgood assumes that he would not be able to marry Joyce if his indebtedness were known or if he were imprisoned for debt.
portion dowry. Witgood's interest in Joyce seems largely monetary. Her status as a virgin was also important to make her an acceptable marital partner.

25 **sojourn** reside temporarily

25–6 **make their wits . . . mercers** owe debts only to their wits for providing them with clothes. Mercers were vendors of textiles, and *The Mercer's Book* was proverbial for the debts of a gallant. Witgood is intent throughout the play on turning his intelligence into money, and his name calls attention to his mental agility.

27–8 **out . . . law** (*a*) not punishable by law (*b*) out of the reach of law, and possibly illegal

28.1 ***Jane*** All previous printings of the text identify the character here and in subsequent stage directions and speech prefixes as *Courtesan*. However, Middleton uses that term in this and other plays to refer to a woman who was a kept mistress rather than a professional prostitute, and subsequent events confirm this description of her role. Because the term *courtesan* has been frequently misunderstood and contributed to confusion about the character's self-defence at the end of the play, and because the character is disguised as Jane Meddler in Act 2 and then becomes Jane Hoard in Act 3, this edition uses the Christian name to mark her speeches and actions. See Introduction.

30–2 **Hast . . . wits** Witgood continues to displace his own role in consorting with a mistress by describing Jane as the agent of his undoing.

32 **virtue** (*a*) moral sense (*b*) intellectual capacities (*c*) sexual energies

34 **courtesan** a woman involved in an extra-marital relationship between persons of some social standing, as distinct from a common whore; often in English Renaissance drama, as here, referring to a woman who was kept by a man rather than generally available
round-webbed tarantula The wide-hooped farthingale is likened to a spider's web in its ability to entrap a man and destroy him.

35 **driest . . . youth** continues the consumption imagery of 1.1.7 and 1.1.30–1

37 **thrice racked** rented out at excessive rates

37–8 **jewel . . . virginity** Jane commodifies her virginity in the image of a jewel and then rates it as much higher in value than Witgood's lands.

40 **honesty** chastity, especially virginity for an unmarried woman

44 **invention** (*a*) device or contrivance for Witgood's scheme (*b*) Jane in particular, seen as a product of Witgood's devising and an agent for his plan

45–7 **I . . . away** The speech parodies Witgood's at 1.1.30–4, suggesting Jane's facility with mimicry.

48 **weapon** words

49–50 **A thing . . . stays** a misogynist allusion to women's inconstancy. Witgood jokingly asserts that women could be made more constant if their apparel were buttressed with 'stays' in a bodice stiffened with whale bone.

56 **drab** prostitute

57 **embryo** (*a*) something in a rudimentary stage or first beginning (*b*) a 'brainchild' of Witgood's devising

58 **perfect** fully formed

61 **Though . . . breed** Jane claims a share in this *embryo* by extending the procreative language.

62 **conceive** (*a*) understand (*b*) become pregnant with. The imagery of wits having a generative function continues at 3.1.108–10.

65 **valiant** worth
bullocks young bulls

and in rye-stacks. We'll to London and to my covetous uncle.

JANE I begin to applaud thee; our states being both desperate, they're soon resolute. But how for horses?

WITGOOD Mass, that's true. The jest will be of some continuance. Let me see. Horses now, a bots on 'em! Stay, I have acquaintance with a mad host, never yet bawd to thee. I have rinsed the whoreson's gums in mull-sack many a time and often. Put but a good tale into his ear now, so it come off cleanly, and there's horse and man for us, I dare warrant thee.

JANE Arm your wits then speedily. There shall want nothing in me, either in behaviour, discourse, or fashion, that shall discredit your intended purpose.
I will so artfully disguise my wants,
And set so good a courage on my state,
That I will be believed.

WITGOOD Why, then, all's furnished. I shall go nigh to catch that old fox, mine uncle. Though he make but some amends for my undoing, yet there's some comfort in't. He cannot otherwise choose (though it be but in hope to cozen me again) but supply any hasty want that I bring to town with me. The device well and cunningly carried, the name of a rich widow and four hundred a year in good earth, will so conjure up a kind of usurer's love in him to me that he will not only desire my presence, which at first shall scarce be granted him—I'll keep off o' purpose—but I shall find him so officious to deserve, so ready to supply. I know the state of an old man's affection so well. If his nephew be poor indeed, why, he lets God alone with him; but if he be once rich, then he'll be the first man that helps him.

JANE 'Tis right the world, for in these days an old man's love to his kindred is like his kindness to his wife: 'tis always done before he comes at it.

WITGOOD I owe thee for that jest. Be gone! [*Giving money*] Here's all my wealth; prepare thyself. Away! I'll to mine host with all possible haste, and with the best art and most profitable form, pour the sweet circumstance into his ear, which shall have the gift to turn all the wax to honey. [*Exit Jane*]
How now? O, the right worshipful seniors of our country!

[*Enter Onesiphorus Hoard, Limber, and Kix*]

ONESIPHORUS Who's that?

LIMBER
O, the common rioter. Take no note of him.

WITGOOD [*aside*]
You will not see me now. The comfort is,
Ere it be long, you will scarce see yourselves. [*Exit*]

ONESIPHORUS
I wonder how he breathes. He's consumed all
Upon that courtesan.

LIMBER We have heard so much.

ONESIPHORUS
You have heard all truth. His uncle and my brother
Have been these three years mortal adversaries.
Two old tough spirits, they seldom meet
But fight or quarrel when 'tis calmest.
I think their anger be the very fire
That keeps their age alive.

LIMBER What was the quarrel, sir?

ONESIPHORUS Faith, about a purchase fetching over a young heir. Master Hoard, my brother, having wasted much time in beating the bargain, what did me old Lucre but as his conscience moved him: knowing the poor gentleman, stepped in between 'em and cozened him himself.

LIMBER And was this all, sir?

ONESIPHORUS This was e'en it, sir. Yet for all this, I know no reason but the match might go forward betwixt his wife's son and my niece. What though there be a dissension between the two old men, I see no reason it should put a difference between the two younger. 'Tis as natural for old folks to fall out as for young to fall in.

69 **resolute** full of resolve
70 **Mass** abbreviation of 'by the Mass', a common oath
71 **continuance** duration
a bots on 'em expletive meaning 'a disease take them'. *Bots* was a common disease of worms that affected horses' gums.
72 **mad** merry
73 **bawd** Innkeepers sometimes acted as procurers. The Host does not know Jane.
74 **mull-sack** white wine heated, sweetened and spiced
75 **cleanly** cleverly, adroitly
80 **wants** (*a*) shortcomings (*b*) sexual desires, which Jane must disguise in order to take up a position in a new social group
81 **set . . . state** i.e. make so bold a showing of my estate
83 **I shall go nigh** i.e. I am going to make every effort
85 **for my undoing** for ruining me
87 **cozen** cheat
94 **officious to deserve** eager to be entitled to reward
96 **he lets . . . him** leaves him to God's mercy
99 **right the world** precisely the way of the world
100 **kindness to** sexual relations with
100–1 **'tis . . . it** (*a*) the wife has already had sexual relations with someone else (*b*) the husband either ejaculates too soon or fails to have an erection. I.e. an old man's gift of 'love' (or money) to members of his family is like the sex he has with his wife: by the time he is ready to give it, she no longer wants it.
106 **gift** power
wax the host's earwax, which would figuratively make him deaf to Witgood's persuasion, if it did not melt into honey
109.1 ***Onesiphorus . . . Kix*** *Onesiphorus* was a Puritan name that meant 'profit-making'; *Kix* is a dried-up stalk; *Limber* refers ironically to the character's age.
111 **common rioter** notorious profligate
114–15 **He's . . . courtesan** Onesiphorus sees Witgood as a consumer rather than one who has been consumed, as Witgood sees himself.
116 **His uncle . . . brother** Pecunious Lucre and Walkadine Hoard
122 **purchase** profit acquired by dubious means
fetching over getting the better of
124 **beating the bargain** haggling
131 **his . . . niece** Sam Freedom and Joyce, the niece of Walkadine and Onesiphorus Hoard
134 **fall in** (*a*) make up a quarrel (*b*) have sex

A scholar comes a-wooing to my niece: well, he's wise, but he's poor. Her son comes a-wooing to my niece: well, he's a fool, but he's rich.

LIMBER Ay, marry, sir?

ONESIPHORUS Pray now, is not a rich fool better than a poor philosopher?

LIMBER One would think so, i'faith.

ONESIPHORUS She now remains at London with my brother, her second uncle, to learn fashions, practise music. The voice between her lips and the viol between her legs, she'll be fit for a consort very speedily. A thousand good pound is her portion. If she marry, we'll ride up and be merry.

KIX A match, if it be a match! *Exeunt*

1.2 *Enter at one door, Witgood, at the other, Host*

WITGOOD Mine Host!

HOST Young master Witgood.

WITGOOD I have been laying all the town for thee.

HOST Why, what's the news, bully Hadland?

WITGOOD What geldings are in the house of thine own? Answer me to that, first.

HOST Why man, why?

WITGOOD Mark me, what I say. I'll tell thee such a tale in thine ear, that thou shalt trust me spite of thy teeth, furnish me with some money willy nilly, and ride up with me thyself *contra voluntatem et professionem.*

HOST How? Let me see this trick, and I'll say thou hast more art than a conjuror.

WITGOOD Dost thou joy in my advancement?

HOST Do I love sack and ginger?

WITGOOD Comes my prosperity desiredly to thee?

HOST Come forfeitures to a usurer, fees to an officer, punks to an host, and pigs to a parson desiredly? Why then, la.

WITGOOD Will the report of a widow of four hundred a year, boy, make thee leap and sing and dance and come to thy place again?

HOST Wilt thou command me now? I am thy spirit. Conjure me into any shape.

WITGOOD I ha' brought her from her friends, turned back the horses by a sleight. Not so much as one amongst her six men, goodly large yeomanly fellows, will she trust with this her purpose. By this light, all unmanned, regardless of her state, neglectful of vainglorious ceremony, all for my love. O, 'tis a fine little voluble tongue, mine Host, that wins a widow.

HOST No, 'tis a tongue with a great T, my boy, that wins a widow.

WITGOOD Now sir, the case stands thus. Good mine Host, if thou lov'st my happiness, assist me.

HOST Command all my beasts i'th' house.

WITGOOD Nay, that's not all neither. Prithee, take truce with thy joy and listen to me. Thou know'st I have a wealthy uncle i'th' city, somewhat the wealthier by my follies. The report of this fortune, well and cunningly carried, might be a means to draw some goodness from the usuring rascal, for I have put her in hope already of some estate that I have either in land or money. Now if I be found true in neither, what may I expect but a sudden breach of our love, utter dissolution of the match, and confusion of my fortunes forever.

HOST Wilt thou but trust the managing of thy business with me?

WITGOOD With thee? Why, will I desire to thrive in my purpose? Will I hug four hundred a year? I that know the misery of nothing? Will that man wish a rich widow that has ne'er a hole to put his head in? With thee, mine Host? Why, believe it, sooner with thee than with a covey of counsellors!

HOST Thank you for your good report, i'faith, sir. And if I stand you not in stead, why then let an host come off *hic et haec hostis*, a deadly enemy to dice, drink, and venery. Come, where's this widow?

WITGOOD Hard at Park End.

HOST I'll be her servingman for once.

135 **scholar** Moneylove
144 **viol . . . legs** The viola da gamba, like the modern cello, was played with legs spread apart. The instrument here, as in *Roaring Girl* 4.1, suggests the expression of female erotic desire.
145 **consort** (*a*) concert, group of musicians (*b*) sexual partner or spouse
148 **A match . . . match** agreed, if a marriage takes place
1.2.1 **Host** an innkeeper
3 **laying** searching
4 **bully Hadland** good fellow who once had land
5 **geldings** castrated horses
9 **spite of thy teeth** proverbial for 'despite yourself' (Tilley S764)
10 **willy nilly** whether you want to or not
11 ***contra . . . professionem*** Latin for 'against your will and profession'
13 **conjuror** sorcerer
15 **ginger** considered an aphrodisiac
17 **punks** prostitutes
18 **pigs to a parson** proverbial, referring to the payment of tithes to a parson in livestock
19 **la** exclamation accompanying an emphatic remark
26 **sleight** trick
29 **unmanned** without male attendants
32 **tongue . . . great T** *great* meant 'capital', and the phrase alludes to cunnilingus as well as being a phallic joke associating male genitals with the shape of 'T' and relating a man's ability to persuade or seduce a widow with the size of his penis
37–8 **take truce with** take a break from
52 **ne'er . . . in** proverbial for 'having neither house nor home' (Tilley H520). The image reinforces the suggestions of cunnilingus and intercourse at 1.2.32.
54 **covey** flock, group
56 **in stead** (*a*) as your deputy (*b*) with horses, steeds
57 ***hic . . . hostis*** punning on English 'host' and Latin *hostis*, enemy. I.e. if I don't stand you in good stead, then let me turn out to be an enemy to dice, drink, and venery. Barber says that *hic et haec* parodies declensions in contemporary grammar books that preceded nouns with the demonstrative as if it were the definite article. If the noun could be either masculine or feminine, as with *hostis*, it was preceded in the nominative by *hic et haec*.
58 **venery** lechery
59 **Hard at** close to

WITGOOD Why, there we let off together, keep full time. My thoughts were striking then just the same number.

HOST I knew't. Shall we then see our merry days again?

WITGOOD Our merry nights—which ne'er shall be more seen. *Exeunt*

1.3 *Enter at several doors old Lucre and old Hoard. [Lamprey, Spitchcock, Sam Freedom and Moneylove] coming between them to pacify 'em*

LAMPREY Nay, good Master Lucre, and you, Master Hoard, anger is the wind which you're both too much troubled withal.

HOARD Shall my adversary thus daily affront me, ripping up the old wound of our malice which three summers could not close up, into which wound the very sight of him drops scalding lead instead of balsamum?

LUCRE Why Hoard, Hoard, Hoard, Hoard, Hoard! May I not pass in the state of quietness to mine own house? Answer me to that, before witness, and why. I'll refer the cause to honest, even-minded gentlemen, or require the mere indifferency of the law to decide this matter. I got the purchase, true. Was't not any man's case? Yes. Will a wiseman stand as a bawd, whilst another wipes his nose of the bargain? No, I answer, no in that case.

LAMPREY Nay, sweet Master Lucre.

HOARD Was it the part of a friend? No, rather of a Jew. Mark what I say. When I had beaten the bush to the last bird, or as I may term it, the price to a pound, then, like a cunning usurer, to come in the evening of the bargain and glean all my hopes in a minute! To enter as it were at the back door of the purchase, for thou ne'er cam'st the right way by it.

LUCRE Hast thou the conscience to tell me so, without any impeachment to thyself?

HOARD Thou that canst defeat thy own nephew, Lucre, lap his lands into bonds and take the extremity of thy kindred's forfeitures because he's a rioter, a waste-thrift, a brothel-master, and so forth—what may a stranger expect from thee but *vulnera dilacerata*, as the poet says, dilacerate dealing?

LUCRE Upbraidst thou me with 'nephew'? Is all imputation laid upon me? What acquaintance have I with his follies? If he riot, 'tis he must want it; if he surfeit, 'tis he must feel it; if he drab it, 'tis he must lie by't. What's this to me?

HOARD What's all to thee? Nothing, nothing. Such is the gulf of thy desire and the wolf of thy conscience. But be assured, old Pecunious Lucre, if ever fortune so bless me that I may be at leisure to vex thee, or any means so favour me that I may have opportunity to mad thee, I will pursue it with that flame of hate, that spirit of malice, unrepressed wrath, that I will blast thy comforts.

LUCRE Ha, ha, ha!

LAMPREY Nay, Master Hoard, you're a wise gentleman.

HOARD I will so cross thee—

LUCRE And I thee.

HOARD So without mercy fret thee—

LUCRE So monstrously oppose thee.

HOARD Dost scoff at my just anger? O, that I had as much power as usury has over thee!

LUCRE Then thou wouldst have as much power as the devil has over thee.

HOARD Toad!

LUCRE Aspic!

61 **let...time** Witgood and the Host are like two clocks that strike at the same time, with a bawdy quibble.

1.3.0.1 ***several*** separate

0.2 ***Lamprey, Spitchcock*** The *lamprey* is a predatory eel-like fish, and *spitchcock* is a dish made of eel split open or cut in pieces and broiled or fried. Both names suggest slippery and menacing characters.

4 **affront** (*a*) encounter, face (*b*) give offence to

7 **balsamum** (*a*) balsam, an aromatic medicinal preparation (*b*) in a more general sense, balm

12 **mere indifferency** absolute impartiality. *Indifferency* is an obsolete term for *indifference*.

13 **purchase** profit acquired by dubious means

any man's case an opportunity open to anyone

14 **bawd** pander, go-between

14–15 **wipes his nose** cheats him

17 **Jew** Drawing on the early modern characterization of Jews as non-Christian aliens who take unfair advantage of others. The more specific association between Jews and usury is not a reason for Hoard to reject Lucre as a *friend*, since he is a usurer himself.

18–19 **beaten...bird** done all the hard work. 'One beats the bush and another catches the bird' was proverbial (Tilley B740).

19 **price to a pound** agreed upon an amount

20 **in the evening** at the end

22 **back door** with a suggestion of anal intercourse

25 **impeachment** accusation

26 **defeat** dispossess, defraud

27 **lap** enfold

bonds (*a*) legal deeds by which one person is bound to pay another (*b*) physical means by which one is shackled or confined

28 **waste-thrift** spendthrift

30 ***vulnera dilacerata*** Latin for 'lacerated wounds'. There is probably no source for the phrase, which instead reflects Hoard's pomposity.

31 **dilacerate** rent asunder, torn (Hoard's coinage)

34 **want it** lack it

35 **drab it** resort to prostitutes

lie by't (*a*) sleep with them (*b*) suffer the consequences

38 **gulf** voracious appetite, as in the name for the character in this play

wolf Usurers were likened to wolves by Sir Thomas Wilson in *A Discourse upon Usury* (1572).

39 **Pecunious** from Latin *pecuniarius*, of money, and English 'pecunious', meaning wealthy

42 **mad** infuriate

47 **cross** thwart

51–2 **as...thee** Hoard implies that while Lucre is an agent of usury, he is also a victim of its power. The suggestion applies to all the usurers in the play, including Hoard himself.

53 **devil** from an association between usurers and devils

55 **Toad** Usurers were compared to toads by Gerard de Malynes in *St George for England* (1601).

56 **Aspic** asp, a poisonous snake

HOARD Serpent!

LUCRE Viper!

SPITCHCOCK Nay, gentlemen, then we must divide you, perforce.

LAMPREY When the fire grows too unreasonable hot, there's no better way than to take off the wood.

Exeunt. Manent Sam and Moneylove

SAM A word, good signior.

MONEYLOVE How now, what's the news?

SAM 'Tis given me to understand that you are a rival of mine in the love of Mistress Joyce, Master Hoard's niece. Say me ay, say me no.

MONEYLOVE Yes, 'tis so.

SAM Then look to yourself, you cannot live long. I'm practising every morning. A month hence I'll challenge you.

MONEYLOVE Give me your hand upon't. There's my pledge I'll meet you!

Moneylove strikes Sam

Exit

SAM O, O. What reason had you for that, sir, to strike before the month? You knew I was not ready for you, and that made you so crank. I am not such a coward to strike again, I warrant you. My ear has the law of her side, for it burns horribly. I will teach him to strike a naked face, the longest day of his life. 'Slid, it shall cost me some money, but I'll bring this box into the Chancery. *Exit*

1.4

Enter Witgood and the Host [disguised as a servingman]

HOST Fear you nothing, sir. I have lodged her in a house of credit, I warrant you.

WITGOOD Hast thou the writings?

HOST Firm, sir.

Enter Dampit and Gulf, who talk apart

WITGOOD Prithee, stay and behold two the most prodigious rascals that ever slipped into the shape of men: Dampit, sirrah, and young Gulf, his fellow caterpillar.

HOST Dampit? Sure I have heard of that Dampit.

WITGOOD Heard of him? Why, man, he that has lost both his ears may hear of him. A famous infamous trampler of time—his own phrase. Note him well, that Dampit. Sirrah, he in the uneven beard and the serge cloak is the most notorious, usuring, blasphemous, atheistical, brothel-vomiting rascal that we have in these latter times now extant, whose first beginning was the stealing of a mastiff dog from a farmer's house.

HOST He looked as if he would obey the commandments well when he began first with stealing.

WITGOOD True. The next town he came at, he set the dogs together by th'ears.

HOST A sign he should follow the law, by my faith.

WITGOOD So it followed, indeed. And being destitute of all fortunes, staked his mastiff against a noble, and by great fortune his dog had the day. How he made it up ten shillings, I know not. But his own boast is that he came to town but with ten shillings in his purse, and now is credibly worth ten thousand pound!

HOST How the devil came he by it?

WITGOOD How the devil came he not by it? If you put in the devil once, riches come with a vengeance. He's been a trampler of the law, sir, and the devil has a care of his footmen. The rogue has spied me now. He nibbled me finely once, too; a pox search you.—O, Master Dampit, the very loins of thee! Cry you mercy, Master Gulf. You walk so low, I promise you I saw you not, sir!

GULF He that walks low, walks safe, the poets tell us.

WITGOOD [*aside*] And nigher hell by a foot and a half than the rest of his fellows.—But my old Harry!

75 **before the month** before the time agreed upon for their duel a month hence

76 **crank** cocky

77 **again** back

77–8 **My ear . . . side** my ear is so badly injured that I have grounds for legal action

79 **naked** defenceless, unprotected

'Slid contraction of 'God's (eye)lid', a mild oath

80 **box** (*a*) blow (*b*) case

81 **Chancery** court of the Lord Chancellor, the highest court of justice after the House of Lords, on the same level with the King's Bench and the Common Pleas. This was the court in which equity cases were most often heard.

1.4.1–2 **house of credit** reputable house

3 **writings** the spurious documents presented to Lucre at 2.1.37.

4.1 ***Dampit . . . Gulf*** *Dampit* is compounded of 'the damned' and the 'pit' mentioned in Audrey's song at 4.5.2, the places where and means by which he effects that damnation: brothels, women's mouths and genitals, taverns, debt, and ultimately hell. *Gulf* suggests the voracious appetite of the usurer that Hoard imputes to Lucre at 1.3.38.

7 **caterpillar** extortioner

9–10 **lost . . . ears** (*a*) the deaf (*b*) the criminal, who was frequently punished by having his ears cropped

11 **trampler of time** A go-between, attorney, or petty solicitor who practised during 'term-time', the four periods of the year when courts were in session—Hilary, Easter, Trinity and Michaelmas.

12–13 **serge cloak** woollen or worsted cloth. Dampit's unkempt beard and serge clothing may suggest that he pretends to be poor.

14 **brothel-vomiting** one who (*a*) is thrown out of brothels (*b*) vomits drunkenly in brothels (*c*) speaks the language of the brothel

19–20 **set . . . th'ears** proverbial for 'set everyone at variance' (Tilley E23)

23 **staked . . . noble** A noble was a gold coin valued at 11 shillings and 3 pence when it was issued for the third time in 1527, but it had probably dropped in value from inflation by the early seventeenth century. Dampit apparently arranged a dog fight and staked his own dog for his part of the wager, thereby winning a noble when his dog won. Watson observes that 'this account of Dampit's rise to fortune is like a parody of the success story of the typical Jacobean businessman'.

31 **trampler of the law** suggesting that Dampit abuses the law or treads on the rights of others using legal means

31–2 **the devil . . . footmen** proverbial, as in 'the devil is ever kind to his own' (Tilley D245). The reference to *footmen* continues the trampling imagery associated with Dampit.

32 **nibbled** caught, nabbed, pilfered

35 **low** Gulf is short and was perhaps played by a younger boy actor.

36 **He . . . safe** a recurrent maxim in Seneca. Gulf uses *low* to mean 'humbly'.

38 **old Harry** used sometimes of the devil

DAMPIT My sweet Theodorus!

WITGOOD 'Twas a merry world when thou cam'st to town with ten shillings in thy purse.

DAMPIT And now worth ten thousand pound, my boy. Report it: Harry Dampit, a trampler of time. Say he would be up in a morning and be here with his serge gown, dashed up to the hams in a cause, have his feet stink about Westminster Hall and come home again, see the galleons, the galleasses, the great armadas of the law. Then there be hoys and petty vessels, oars and scullers of the time. There be picklocks of the time, too. Then would I be here. I would trample up and down like a mule: now to the judges, 'May it please your reverend honourable fatherhoods'; then to my counsellor, 'May it please your worshipful patience'; then to the examiner's office, 'May it please your mastership's gentleness'; then to one of the clerks, 'May it please your worshipful lousiness', for I find him scrubbing in his codpiece. Then to the hall again, then to the chamber again—

WITGOOD And when to the cellar again?

DAMPIT E'en when thou wilt again. Tramplers of time, motions of Fleet Street, and visions of Holborn! Here I have fees of one, there I have fees of another. My clients come about me, the fooliaminy and coxcombry of the country. I still trashed and trotted for other men's causes. Thus was poor Harry Dampit made rich by others' laziness, who, though they would not follow their own suits, I made 'em follow me with their purses.

WITGOOD Didst thou so, old Harry?

DAMPIT Ay, and I soused 'em with bills of charges, i'faith. Twenty pound a year have I brought in for boathire, and I ne'er stepped into boat in my life.

WITGOOD Tramplers of time.

DAMPIT Ay, tramplers of time, rascals of time, bull-beggars!

WITGOOD Ah, thou'rt a mad old Harry! Kind Master Gulf, I am bold to renew my acquaintance.

GULF I embrace it, sir. *Music. Exeunt*

Finis Actus Primus

Incipit Actus Secundus 2.1

Enter Lucre

LUCRE My adversary evermore twits me with my nephew. Forsooth, my nephew! Why, may not a virtuous uncle have a dissolute nephew? What though he be a brotheller, a waste-thrift, a common surfeiter, and to conclude, a beggar, must sin in him call up shame in me? Since we have no part in their follies, why should we have part in their infamies? For my strict hand toward his mortgage, that I deny not. I confess I had an uncle's penn'orth. Let me see, half in half; true, I saw neither hope of his reclaiming nor comfort in his being, and was it not then better bestowed upon his uncle than upon one of his aunts? I need not say bawd, for everyone knows what aunt stands for in the last translation.

[*Enter Servant*]

Now, sir.

SERVANT There's a country servingman, sir, attends to speak with your worship.

LUCRE I'm at best leisure now. Send him in to me. [*Exit Servant*]

Enter Host like a servingman

HOST Bless your venerable worship.

LUCRE Welcome, good fellow.

HOST [*aside*] He calls me thief at first sight, yet he little thinks I am an host!

LUCRE What's thy business with me?

39 **Theodorus** meaning 'gift of God'. Taken together, Witgood's names mean that 'cleverness is God's gift'.
45 **dashed** spattered with mud
hams the back of the thighs
45–6 **have...stink** compare 3.4.76
46 **Westminster Hall** where the law courts were held until 1882
47 **galleons** ships that were used by the Spanish to transport treasures from the New World. All of the vessels that follow serve as metaphors for people of different degrees of importance that Dampit encountered in his work.
galleasses heavy vessels, larger than galleons, used chiefly as warships
armadas large warships
48 **hoys** small coastal vessels
48–9 **oars and scullers** small vessels propelled by rowing and sculling
49 **picklocks** thieves
52 **counsellor** the legal advocate
53–4 **examiner's office** the officer who took depositions of witnesses
56 **scrubbing** scratching, because of lice
codpiece a bagged appendage at the front of breeches
60 **motions** puppets or puppet shows
motions...Holborn Fleet Street and Holborn were favourite haunts of sharpers, mentioned in Audrey's song at 4.5.3. The two phrases compare the 'tramplers of time' moving frenetically on their errands along the thoroughfares in London's business districts to figures seen in a puppet show or a trance.
62 **fooliaminy and coxcombry** Dampit's coinages, the first from 'fool' and the second from 'coxcomb', a fool or simpleton; both apply to his clients.
63 **trashed** ran or walked through mud and mire
68 **soused** soaked or swindled
69–70 **Twenty...life** Dampit has made as much as £20 a year by charging his clients for his travelling expenses by boat when he never incurred those costs. Transportation by water from one location in London to another was common.
72 **tramplers of time** By now the phrase implies that Dampit abused his clients by charging them for time and services that he never rendered, although he presented a great show of activity on their behalves.
72–3 **bull-beggars** hobgoblins or objects of dread; imps or sprites that incite superstitious fear
2.1.1 **twits** censures, upbraids
2 **Forsooth** in truth
5 **conclude** (*a*) end the list (*b*) end his life
9 **an uncle's penn'orth** a swindler's pennyworth. 'To uncle' was to cheat.
half in half half the total amount. He calculates how much he has swindled from Witgood.
10 **reclaiming** (*a*) reforming (*b*) repaying his debts to take back his property
14 **last translation** most recent slang. Lucre is spelling out his use of *aunts* to mean *bawds*, which will become an important motif later in the play.
21 **thief** *good fellow* was a cant name for a thief

HOST Faith, sir, I am sent from my mistress to any sufficient gentleman indeed, to ask advice upon a doubtful point. 'Tis indifferent, sir, to whom I come, for I know none, nor did my mistress direct me to any particular man, for she's as mere a stranger here as myself. Only I found your worship within, and 'tis a thing I ever loved, sir, to be dispatched as soon as I can.

LUCRE [*aside*] A good blunt honesty. I like him well.—What is thy mistress?

HOST Faith, a country gentlewoman and a widow, sir. Yesterday was the first flight of us, but now she intends to stay till a little term business be ended.

LUCRE Her name, I prithee?

HOST It runs there in the writings, sir, among her lands. Widow Meddler.

LUCRE Meddler? Mass, have I ne'er heard of that widow?

HOST Yes, I warrant you, have you, sir. Not the rich widow in Staffordshire?

LUCRE Cods me, there 'tis indeed. Thou has put me into memory. There's a widow indeed. Ah, that I were a bachelor again.

HOST No doubt your worship might do much then. But she's fairly promised to a bachelor already.

LUCRE Ah, what is he, I prithee?

HOST A country gentleman too, one whom your worship knows not, I'm sure. He's spent some few follies in his youth, but marriage, by my faith, begins to call him home. My mistress loves him, sir, and love covers faults, you know. One Master Witgood, if ever you have heard of the gentleman.

LUCRE Ha? Witgood, sayst thou?

HOST That's his name indeed, sir. My mistress is like to bring him to a goodly seat yonder—four hundred a year, by my faith.

LUCRE But I pray, take me with you.

HOST Ay, sir?

LUCRE What countryman might this young Witgood be?

HOST A Leicestershire gentleman, sir.

LUCRE [*aside*] My nephew, by the mass, my nephew! I'll fetch out more of this, i'faith. A simple country fellow, I'll work't out of him.—And is that gentleman, sayst thou, presently to marry her?

HOST Faith, he brought her up to town, sir. H'as the best card in all the bunch for't, her heart. And I know my mistress will be married ere she go down, nay I'll swear that. For she's none of those widows that will go down first and be married after. She hates that, I can tell you, sir.

LUCRE By my faith, sir, she is like to have a proper gentleman and a comely. I'll give her that gift!

HOST Why, does your worship know him, sir?

LUCRE I know him! Does not all the world know him? Can a man of such exquisite qualities be hid under a bushel?

HOST Then your worship may save me a labour, for I had charge given me to enquire after him.

LUCRE Enquire of him? If I might counsel thee, thou shouldst ne'er trouble thyself further. Enquire of him of no more but of me. I'll fit thee! I grant he has been youthful, but is he not now reclaimed? Mark you that, sir. Has not your mistress, think you, been wanton in her youth? If men be wags, are there not women wagtails?

HOST No doubt, sir.

LUCRE Does not he return wisest that comes home whipped with his own follies?

HOST Why, very true, sir.

LUCRE The worst report you can hear of him, I can tell you, is that he has been a kind gentleman, a liberal and a worthy. Who but lusty Witgood, thrice noble Witgood!

HOST Since our worship has so much knowledge in him, can you resolve me, sir, what his living might be? My duty binds me, sir, to have a care of my mistress' estate.

24 **sufficient** well-to-do
28 **mere** (*a*) absolute (*b*) ordinary, inept
30 **dispatched** rid of a piece of business promptly, even hastily
34 **first flight** commonly used of fledglings leaving the nest, i.e. this is the first time the widow has left her estate
35 **term business** legal business transacted while the law courts were in session, with bawdy implications because prostitutes also congregated during term-time
38 **Meddler** The name implies one who (*a*) mingles or interferes in another person's business and (*b*) engages in sexual intercourse. A third meaning more directly suggests a 'whore' and stems from the word's association with the medlar tree, the fruit of which was eaten when it was partly rotten. The seventeenth-century texts spell the name as 'Medler' and 'Meddler'. See textual note.
41 **Staffordshire** a county in the English Midlands
42 **Cods me** corruption of 'God save me'
51 **home** (*a*) back to his former, more restrained identity (*b*) back to domestic life
covers conceals; i.e. love is blind
56 **seat** estate
58 **take me with you** tell me your meaning
67 **bunch** pack
68 **go down** (*a*) leave London for the country (*b*) have sex
70 **She hates that** The host defends the honour of his mistress by affirming that she will not have sex before marriage. There is obvious dramatic irony in the remark given what the audience knows about Jane.
72 **proper** handsome
73 **comely** pleasing, agreeable
give her that gift grant her that
76 **hid...bushel** An image from Matthew 5:15: 'Neither do men light a lamp and put it under a bushel, but on a candlestick, and it giveth light unto all that are in the house'.
78 **after** about
81 **fit** answer
84–5 **If...wagtails** *Wags* suggests rogues; *wagtails* licentious women or prostitutes. There is a considerable gap between the small guilt attributed to men in the sentence and that attributed to women, which reflects the sexual double standard and makes suspect Lucre's attempts to use a woman's transgressions to justify a man's.
87–8 **Does...follies** The argument is similar to Jane's observation at 5.2.151, 'She that knows sin, knows best how to hate sin'.
91 **kind** affectionate, loving, with bawdy implications
liberal (*a*) generous (*b*) licentious
92 **lusty** (*a*) agreeable, pleasing (*b*) full of sexual desire
94 **living** livelihood and estate

She has been ever a good mistress to me, though I say it. Many wealthy suitors has she nonsuited for his sake. Yet though her love be so fixed, a man cannot tell whether his nonperformance may help to remove it, sir. He makes us believe he has lands and living.

LUCRE Who, young Master Witgood? Why, believe it, he has as goodly a fine living out yonder—what do you call the place?

HOST Nay, I know not, i'faith.

LUCRE Hum, see like a beast if I have not forgot the name—puh! And out yonder again, goodly grown woods and fair meadows. Pox on't, I can ne'er hit of that place, neither. He? Why, he's Witgood of Witgood Hall; he an unknown thing!

HOST Is he so, sir? To see how rumour will alter. Trust me, sir, we heard once he had no lands, but all lay mortgaged to an uncle he has in town here.

LUCRE Push! 'Tis a tale, 'tis a tale.

HOST I can assure you, sir, 'twas credibly reported to my mistress.

LUCRE Why, do you think, i'faith, he was ever so simple to mortgage his lands to his uncle? Or his uncle so unnatural to take the extremity of such a mortgage?

HOST
That was my saying still, sir.

LUCRE
Puh, ne'er think it.

HOST
Yet that report goes current.

LUCRE
Nay, then you urge me,
Cannot I tell that best that am his uncle?

HOST How, sir! What have I done?

LUCRE Why, how now, in a swoon, man?

HOST Is your worship his uncle, sir?

LUCRE Can that be any harm to you, sir?

HOST I do beseech you, sir, do me the favour to conceal it. What a beast was I to utter so much! Pray, sir, do me the kindness to keep it in. I shall have my coat pulled o'er my ears, an't should be known, for the truth is, an't please your worship, to prevent much rumour and many suitors, they intend to be married very suddenly and privately.

LUCRE And dost thou think it stands with my judgement to do them injury? Must I needs say the knowledge of this marriage comes from thee? Am I a fool at fifty-four? Do I lack subtlety now, that have got all my wealth by it? There's a leash of angels for thee. Come, let me woo thee. Speak, where lie they?

HOST So I might have no anger, sir—

LUCRE Passion of me, not a jot. Prithee, come.

HOST I would not have it known it came by my means.

LUCRE Why, am I a man of wisdom?

HOST I dare trust your worship, sir. But I'm a stranger to your house, and to avoid all intelligencers, I desire your worship's ear.

LUCRE [*aside*] This fellow's worth a matter of trust.—Come, sir. [*Host whispers to Lucre*] Why, now, thou'rt an honest lad. Ah, sirrah nephew!

HOST Please you, sir, now I have begun with your worship, when shall I attend for your advice upon that doubtful point? I must come warily now.

LUCRE Tut, fear thou nothing. Tomorrow's evening shall resolve the doubt.

HOST The time shall cause my attendance. *Exit*

LUCRE Fare thee well. There's more true honesty in such a country servingman than in a hundred of our cloak companions. I may well call 'em companions, for since blue coats have been turned into cloaks, we can scarce know the man from the master. George!

[*Enter George*]

GEORGE Anon, sir.

LUCRE List hither. Keep the place secret. Commend me to my nephew. I know no cause, tell him, but he might see his uncle.

GEORGE I will, sir.

LUCRE And do you hear, sir, take heed you use him with respect and duty.

GEORGE [*aside*] Here's a strange alteration. One day he must be turned out like a beggar, and now he must be called in like a knight! *Exit*

LUCRE Ah, sirrah, that rich widow! Four hundred a year! Beside, I hear she lays claim to a title of a hundred more. This falls unhappily, that he should bear a grudge to me

97 **nonsuited** rejected. There is a pun on the legal meaning of the word, which described the cessation of a suit resulting from the voluntary withdrawal of the plaintiff, and on 'suitors' as wooers.

99 **nonperformance** failure to fulfil one's promises or live up to the terms of a contract

106 **puh** an expression of impatience or disgust

107 **hit of** remember

113 **Push** pish, an expression of contempt analogous to the current use of *fuck*

118 **take the extremity of** exact the full amount of

119 **That...still** that was the story I was told

120 **goes current** is in general circulation

urge provoke

128 **in** secret

128–9 **coat...ears** be stripped of my livery, the clothing of servants; i.e. lose my job

129 **an't** if it

137 **leash of angels** three gold coins, each worth from 10 to 11 shillings, having the figure of the archangel St Michael on one side

138 **lie** lodge

144 **intelligencers** spies

148 **sirrah** an expression of contempt for Witgood and a sign of Lucre's authority over him

150–1 **that doubtful point** i.e. Witgood's living

153 **resolve** dissolve, remove

156–7 **cloak companions** i.e. gentlemen or freed citizens whose cloaks distinguished them from servingmen until the fashion changed (see 2.1.158–9)

157 **'em** i.e. servingmen

158 **blue coats** the traditional livery or clothing of the servingman, which was discarded in the early seventeenth century for cloaks of various colours

158–9 **we...master** Clothing served to identify people by their class standing, so the disappearance of blue coats blurred the distinctions between masters and servants. Lucre deplores this development and then orders his own servant about immediately afterwards.

159 **the man** the servingman or servant

161 **List hither** i.e. listen over here

171 **title** deed of property

now, being likely to prove so rich. What is't, trow, that he makes me a stranger for? Hum. I hope he has not so much wit to apprehend that I cozened him. He deceives me, then? Good heaven, who would have thought it would ever have come to this pass! Yet he's a proper gentleman, i'faith, give him his due. Marry, that's his mortgage, but that I ne'er mean to give him. I'll make him rich enough in words, if that be good; and if it come to a piece of money, I will not greatly stick for't. There may be hope some of the widow's lands, too, may one day fall upon me, if things be carried wisely.

[*Enter George*]

Now, sir, where is he?

GEORGE He desires your worship to hold him excused. He has such weighty business, it commands him wholly from all men.

LUCRE Were those my nephew's words?

GEORGE Yes indeed, sir.

LUCRE When men grow rich, they grow proud, too: I perceive that. He would not have sent me such an answer once within this twelvemonth. See what 'tis when a man's come to his lands. Return to him again, sir. Tell him his uncle desires his company for an hour. I'll trouble him but an hour, say. 'Tis for his own good, tell him. And do you hear, sir, put 'worship' upon him. Go to, do as I bid you. He's like to be a gentleman of worship very shortly.

GEORGE [*aside*] This is good sport, i'faith. *Exit*

LUCRE Troth, he uses his uncle discourteously now. Can he tell what I may do for him? Goodness may come from me in a minute that comes not in seven year again. He knows my humour; I am not so usually good. 'Tis no small thing that draws kindness from me, he may know that, an he will. The chief cause that invites me to do him most good is the sudden astonishing of old Hoard, my adversary. How pale his malice will look at my nephew's advancement! With what a dejected spirit he will behold his fortunes, whom but last day he proclaimed rioter, penurious makeshift, despised brothel-master! Ha, ha! 'Twill do me more secret joy than my last purchase, more precious comfort than all these widow's revenues!

[*Enter George*]

Now, sir—

Enter Witgood

GEORGE With much entreaty he's at length come, sir. [*Exit*]

LUCRE O nephew, let me salute you, sir! You're welcome, nephew.

WITGOOD Uncle, I thank you.

LUCRE You've a fault, nephew: you're a stranger here.
Well, heaven give you joy.

WITGOOD
Of what, sir?

LUCRE Ha, we can hear.
You might have known your uncle's house, i'faith.
You and your widow, go to, you were to blame,
If I may tell you so without offence.

WITGOOD
How could you hear of that, sir?

LUCRE O, pardon me.
It was your will to have it kept from me,
I perceive now.

WITGOOD
Not for any defect of love, I protest, Uncle.

LUCRE
O, 'twas unkindness, nephew—fie, fie, fie!

WITGOOD
I am sorry you take it in that sense, sir.

LUCRE
Puh, you cannot colour it, i'faith, nephew.

WITGOOD Will you but hear what I can say in my just excuse, sir?

LUCRE Yes, faith, will I, and welcome.

WITGOOD You that know my danger i'th' city, sir, so well, how great my debts are, and how extreme my creditors, could not out of your pure judgement, sir, have wished us hither.

LUCRE Mass, a firm reason indeed.

WITGOOD Else my uncle's house, why, 't'ad been the only make-match.

LUCRE Nay, and thy credit.

WITGOOD My credit? Nay, my countenance. Push! Nay, I know, uncle, you would have wrought it so by your

173 **trow** do you suppose
175 **cozened** cheated
175–6 **He . . . then** I am deceived in him, then?
181 **stick for't** be reluctant to do it
190–1 **When . . . that** Lucre is the first in the play to observe a connection between a man's proud sense of himself and his acquisition of riches or land. The play offers other instances with Hoard's reaction to his newfound wealth at 4.4.1–91 and 5.2.1–13.
196 **put 'worship' upon him** call him 'your worship' as a sign of respect
203 **humour** disposition
205 **an** if
210 **penurious** destitute, poor
212 **my last purchase** Lucre's victory over Hoard that was the subject of their dispute at 1.3.4–23
222 **known** been acquainted with, i.e. used, visited
229 **unkindness** ingratitude; forgetful of the relationship due to a relative
231 **colour** disguise, misrepresent
240 **uncle's house** perhaps a slang term for the residence of an 'aunt' or bawd, and hence an appropriate place for sexual assignations
241 **make-match** place to make a match
243 **countenance** dignity, appearance of wealth. Witgood counters Lucre's assertion that his uncle's home is the only place for him to gain credit with the claim that it is the only place that will support his general pretensions to wealth and reputation.

wit. You would have made her believe in time the whole house had been mine.

LUCRE Ay, and most of the goods, too.

WITGOOD La, you there! Well, let 'em all prate what they will, there's nothing like the bringing of a widow to one's uncle's house.

LUCRE Nay, let nephews be ruled as they list, they shall find their uncle's house the most natural place when all's done.

WITGOOD There they may be bold.

LUCRE Life, they may do anything there, man, and fear neither beadle nor summoner. An uncle's house! A very Cole Harbour! Sirrah, I'll touch thee near now. Hast thou so much interest in thy widow, that by a token thou couldst presently send for her?

WITGOOD Troth, I think I can, uncle.

LUCRE Go to, let me see that.

WITGOOD Pray, command one of your men hither, uncle.

LUCRE George!

[*Enter George*]

GEORGE Here, sir.

LUCRE Attend my nephew! [*Aside, as Witgood talks to George*] I love a' life to prattle with a rich widow. 'Tis pretty, methinks, when our tongues go together, and then to promise much and perform little. I love that sport o' life, i'faith. Yet I am in the mood now to do my nephew some good, if he take me handsomely.

[*Exit George*]

What, have you dispatched?

WITGOOD I ha' sent, sir.

LUCRE Yet I must condemn you of unkindness, nephew.

WITGOOD Heaven forbid, uncle!

LUCRE Yes, faith, must I. Say your debts be many, your creditors importunate, yet the kindness of a thing is all, nephew. You might have sent me close word on't, without the least danger or prejudice to your fortunes.

WITGOOD Troth, I confess it, uncle. I was to blame there. But indeed, my intent was to have clapped it up suddenly, and so have broke forth like a joy to my friends and a wonder to the world. Beside there's a trifle of a forty pound matter toward the setting of me forth, my friends should ne'er have known on't. I meant to make shift for that myself.

LUCRE How, nephew? Let me not hear such a word again, I beseech you. Shall I be beholden to you?

WITGOOD To me? Alas, what do you mean, uncle?

LUCRE I charge you upon my love, you trouble nobody but myself.

WITGOOD You've no reason for that, uncle.

LUCRE Troth, I'll ne'er be friends with you while you live, an you do.

WITGOOD Nay, an you say so, uncle, here's my hand. I will not do't.

LUCRE Why, well said. There's some hope in thee when thou wilt be ruled. I'll make it up fifty, faith, because I see thee so reclaimed. Peace, here comes my wife with Sam, her t'other husband's son.

[*Enter Wife and Sam*]

WITGOOD Good Aunt—

SAM Cousin Witgood! I rejoice in my salute. You're most welcome to this noble city, governed with the sword in the scabbard.

WITGOOD [*aside*] And the wit in the pommel.—Good Master Sam Freedom, I return the salute.

LUCRE By the mass, she's coming, wife. Let me see now how thou wilt entertain her.

WIFE I hope I am not to learn, sir, to entertain a widow. 'Tis not so long ago since I was one myself.

[*Enter Jane disguised as a rich widow*]

WITGOOD Uncle—

LUCRE She's come, indeed!

WITGOOD My uncle was desirous to see you, widow, and I presumed to invite you.

JANE The presumption was nothing, Master Witgood. Is this your uncle, sir?

LUCRE Marry, am I, sweet widow, and his good uncle he shall find me. Ay, by this smack that I give thee, thou'rt welcome. [*Kissing her*] Wife, bid the widow welcome the same way again.

248 **prate** talk, boast
251 **list** please
256 **beadle** a parish constable, whose duties might include whipping prostitutes **summoner** a minor official who summoned people to court; also an officer who brought offenders before the ecclesiastical courts, where sexual offences were often tried. Taken together, *beadle nor summoner* suggests that an uncle's house is free of the agents of civil and ecclesiastical authority.
257 **Cole Harbour** A group of tenements on the north bank of the Thames and west of London Bridge that became known as a sanctuary for debtors and criminals and a place for hasty marriages. **touch** upset, annoy
258 **interest** claim on
266 **a' life** as life, i.e. as dearly as my life **prattle** chatter or talk at length
270 **take me handsomely** interprets me courteously
277 **close** secret
280 **clapped it up** made the match
282 **friends** relatives **Beside there's** if it were not for
283 **matter** i.e. debt **setting...forth** equipping me, fitting me out
285 **make shift for** manage, deal with
293, 294 **an** if
297 **make it up** raise a sum to a larger sum
299 **t'other** other. Lucre has already married a widow.
302–3 **sword...scabbard** Since the *scabbard* was a sheath for the sword, the phrase implies that punishment is restrained.
304 **wit...pommel** the amount of wit in the knob on the hilt of a sword, i.e. no wit at all
307 **entertain** receive
317 **smack** kiss

SAM [*aside*] I am a gentleman now too, by my father's occupation, and I see no reason but I may kiss a widow by my father's copy. Truly, I think the charter is not against it. Surely these are the words: 'The son, once a gentleman, may revel it, though his father were a dauber.' 'Tis about the fifteenth page. I'll to her.

[*He tries to kiss Jane, who rebuffs him*]

LUCRE [*to Sam*] You're not very busy now.—A word with thee, sweet widow.

[*They talk apart*]

SAM [*aside*] Cod's nigs! I was never so disgraced, since the hour my mother whipped me.

LUCRE [*to Jane*] Beside, I have no child of mine own to care for. She's my second wife—old, past bearing. Clap sure to him, widow. He's like to be my heir, I can tell you!

JANE Is he so, sir?

LUCRE He knows it already, and the knave's proud on't. Jolly rich widows have been offered him here i'th' city, great merchants' wives, and do you think he would once look upon 'em? Forsooth, he'll none. You are beholden to him i'th' country, then, ere we could be. Nay, I'll hold a wager, widow, if he were once known to be in town, he would be presently sought after. Nay, and happy were they that could catch him first.

JANE I think so!

LUCRE O, there would be such running to and fro, widow, he should not pass the streets for 'em. He'd be took up in one great house or other presently. Fah! They know he has it and must have it. You see this house here, widow; this house and all comes to him. Goodly rooms ready furnished, ceiled with plaster of Paris, and all hung above with cloth of arras. Nephew!

WITGOOD Sir.

LUCRE Show the widow your house. Carry her into all the rooms, and bid her welcome. You shall see, widow. [*Aside to Witgood*] Nephew? Strike all sure above, an thou be'st a good boy. Ah!

WITGOOD Alas, sir, I know not how she would take it.

LUCRE The right way, I warrant ye. A pox, art an ass? Would I were in thy stead! Get you up. I am ashamed of you. [*Exeunt Witgood and Jane*]

[*Aside*] So, let 'em agree as they will now. Many a match has been struck up in my house o' this fashion. Let 'em try all manner of ways, still there's nothing like an uncle's house to strike the stroke in. I'll hold my wife in talk a little.—Now, Jenny, your son there goes a-wooing to a poor gentlewoman but of a thousand portion. See my nephew, a lad of less hope, strikes at four hundred a year in good rubbish.

WIFE Well, we must do as we may, sir.

LUCRE I'll have his money ready told for him, against he come down. Let me see, too. By th' mass, I must present the widow with some jewel, a good piece o' plate, or such a device; 'twill hearten her on well. I have a very fair standing cup, and a good high standing cup will please a widow above all other pieces. *Exit*

WIFE [*aside*] Do you mock us with your nephew?—I have a plot in my head, son—i'faith, husband, to cross you.

SAM Is it a tragedy plot, or a comedy plot, good mother?

WIFE 'Tis a plot shall vex him. I charge you of my blessing, son Sam, that you presently withdraw the action of your love from Master Hoard's niece.

SAM How, mother?

WIFE Nay, I have a plot in my head, i'faith. Here, take this chain of gold and this fair diamond. Dog me the widow home to her lodging, and at thy best opportunity fasten 'em both upon her. Nay, I have a reach. I can tell you, thou art known what thou art, son, among the right worshipful—all the twelve companies.

SAM Truly, I thank 'em for it.

WIFE He, he's a scab to thee. And so certify her thou hast two hundred a year of thyself, beside thy good parts—a proper person and a lovely. If I were a widow, I could find in my heart to have thee myself, son. Ay, from 'em all.

SAM Thank you for your good will, mother, but indeed I had rather have a stranger. And if I woo her not in that violent fashion that I will make her be glad to take

320 **father's** Lucre's, Sam's stepfather

321 **occupation** referring to Lucre's status as a gentleman. Since status was traditionally conferred by birth rather than employment or merit, Sam's choice of words reflects the upward mobility that wealth and occupation increasingly conferred in Jacobean society. He argues that the right to sexual intimacy is inflected by class, and the higher one's rank, the more claim one has on women of a comparable position.

322 **copy** (*a*) example (*b*) right, as in the rights of a son to lands that his father held by custom of the manor, which were recorded on a copy of the court rolls

charter i.e. of a guild of craftsmen, referring to Sam's work

325 **dauber** (*a*) plasterer (*b*) impostor, from *daub*, meaning to conceal or cover with a plausible exterior

328 **Cod's nigs** an expression of surprise, probably meaning 'God's little pieces'

345 **presently** immediately

346 **it** i.e. Lucre's wealth

348 **ceiled** ceilinged

349 **above** i.e. upstairs

cloth of arras rich tapestries, in which figures and scenes were woven in colour

353 **Strike all sure** (*a*) seal the match (*b*) have sex with her

362 **strike the stroke** (*a*) make a bargain (*b*) thrust one's penis

364 **thousand portion** i.e. a dowry of £1,000

366 **rubbish** land

368 **told** counted

against by the time that

370 **plate** silver or gold object

372 **standing cup** a cup on a stem or base, with a pun on its phallic shape

377 **of** by

378–9 **action ... love** offer of marriage

382 **Dog me** follow

384 **reach** scheme, goal

386 **twelve companies** the twelve most important trade guilds in the City of London

388 **scab to** scoundrel compared with

394 **stranger** Sam picks up his mother's hint of incestuous desire at 2.1.390–2 and deflects it.

395 **violent** vehement

these gifts ere I leave her, let me never be called the heir of your body.

WIFE Nay, I know there's enough in you, son, if you once come to put it forth.

SAM I'll quickly make a bolt or a shaft on't. *Exeunt*

2.2 *Enter Hoard and Moneylove*

MONEYLOVE Faith, Master Hoard, I have bestowed many months in the suit of your niece. Such was the dear love I ever bore to her virtues. But since she hath so extremely denied me, I am to lay out for my fortunes elsewhere.

HOARD Heaven forbid but you should, sir. I ever told you my niece stood otherwise affected.

MONEYLOVE I must confess you did, sir, yet in regard of my great loss of time, and the zeal with which I sought your niece, shall I desire one favour of your worship?

HOARD In regard of those two, 'tis hard but you shall, sir.

MONEYLOVE I shall rest grateful. 'Tis not full three hours, sir, since the happy rumour of a rich country widow came to my hearing.

HOARD How? A rich country widow?

MONEYLOVE Four hundred a year landed.

HOARD Yea?

MONEYLOVE Most firm, sir. And I have learnt her lodging. Here my suit begins, sir. If I might but entreat your worship to be a countenance for me, and speak a good word—for your words will pass—I nothing doubt but I might set fair for the widow. Nor shall your labour, sir, end altogether in thanks. Two hundred angels—

HOARD So, so, what suitors has she?

MONEYLOVE There lies the comfort, sir. The report of her is yet but a whisper, and only solicited by young, riotous Witgood, nephew to your mortal adversary.

HOARD Ha! Art certain he's her suitor?

MONEYLOVE Most certain, sir. And his uncle very industrious to beguile the widow and make up the match!

HOARD So? Very good!

MONEYLOVE Now, sir, you know this young Witgood is a spendthrift, dissolute fellow.

HOARD A very rascal.

MONEYLOVE A midnight surfeiter.

HOARD The spume of a brothel-house.

MONEYLOVE True, sir! Which being well told in your worship's phrase, may both heave him out of her mind and drive a fair way for me to the widow's affections.

HOARD Attend me about five.

MONEYLOVE With my best care, sir. *Exit*

HOARD

Fool, thou hast left thy treasure with a thief,
To trust a widower with a suit in love!
Happy revenge, I hug thee. I have not only the means laid before me extremely to cross my adversary and confound the last hopes of his nephew, but thereby to enrich my state, augment my revenues, and build mine own fortunes greater. Ha, ha!
I'll mar your phrase, o'erturn your flatteries,
Undo your windings, policies and plots,
Fall like a secret and dispatchful plague
On your securèd comforts. Why, I am able
To buy three of Lucre, thrice outbid him,
Let my out-monies be reckoned and all.

Enter three Creditors

FIRST CREDITOR I am glad of this news.

SECOND CREDITOR So are we, by my faith.

THIRD CREDITOR Young Witgood will be a gallant again now.

HOARD [*aside, overhearing their conversation*] Peace!

FIRST CREDITOR I promise you, Master Cockpit, she's a mighty rich widow.

SECOND CREDITOR Why, have you ever heard of her?

FIRST CREDITOR Who, Widow Meddler? She lies open to much rumour.

THIRD CREDITOR Four hundred a year, they say, in very good land.

FIRST CREDITOR Nay, take 't of my word, if you believe that, you believe the least.

SECOND CREDITOR And to see how close he keeps it.

FIRST CREDITOR O, sir, there's policy in that to prevent better suitors.

THIRD CREDITOR He owes me a hundred pound, and I protest I ne'er looked for a penny.

FIRST CREDITOR He little dreams of our coming. He'll wonder to see his creditors upon him. *Exeunt*

HOARD

Good, his creditors; I'll follow. This makes for me.
All know the widow's wealth, and 'tis well known
I can estate her fairly, ay, and will.
In this one chance shines a twice happy fate:
I both deject my foe, and raise my state. *Music. Exit*

Finis Actus Secundus

398–400 **there's . . . on't** the lines have phallic connotations
400 **bolt . . . on't** do it one way or the other; literally, use a thick arrow or a slender one. The phrase is proverbial (Tilley S264).
2.2.7 **affected** inclined, disposed
11 **but** unless
20 **countenance** support
21 **pass** succeed
22 **set fair for** stand a good chance of winning
23 **Two hundred angels** over £100, a considerable sum
35 **surfeiter** one who indulges in excesses
36 **spume** foam, froth
38 **phrase** manner of expression
49 **phrase** praise
50 **windings** meanderings, twists and turns, referring to Moneylove's shift from Hoard's niece to the widow
51 **dispatchful** deadly
54 **out-monies** assets lent out or invested and not immediately liquid
57 **gallant** fine gentleman, man of fashion
63–4 **lies . . . rumour** is much talked about (punning on *lies open* as 'sexually available'). Another name for the medlar fruit was 'openarse'.
69 **he** i.e. Witgood
73 **looked for** expected
76 **makes for me** works in my favour
80 **deject** overthrow
state estate

3.1 *Incipit Actus Tertius*

[Enter] Witgood with his Creditors

WITGOOD Why, alas, my creditors, could you find no other time to undo me but now? Rather your malice appears in this than the justness of the debt.

FIRST CREDITOR Master Witgood, I have forborne my money long.

WITGOOD I pray, speak low, sir. What do you mean?

SECOND CREDITOR We hear you are to be married suddenly to a rich country widow.

WITGOOD What can be kept so close but you creditors hear on't? Well, 'tis a lamentable state that our chiefest afflicters should first hear of our fortunes. Why, this is no good course, i'faith, sirs. If ever you have hope to be satisfied, why do you seek to confound the means that should work it? There's neither piety, no, nor policy in that. Shine favourably now. Why, I may rise and spread again, to your great comforts.

FIRST CREDITOR He says truth, i'faith.

WITGOOD Remove me now, and I consume forever.

SECOND CREDITOR Sweet gentleman!

WITGOOD How can it thrive which from the sun you sever?

THIRD CREDITOR It cannot, indeed.

WITGOOD
O, then show patience. I shall have enough
To satisfy you all.

FIRST CREDITOR Ay, if we could
Be content, a shame take us.

WITGOOD For, look you,
I am but newly sure yet to the widow,
And what a rend might this discredit make.
Within these three days will I bind you lands
For your securities.

FIRST CREDITOR No, good Master Witgood,
Would 'twere as much as we dare trust you with!

WITGOOD I am to raise a little money in the city toward the setting forth of myself, for mine own credit and your comfort. Now, if my former debts should be divulged, all hope of my proceedings were quite extinguished!

FIRST CREDITOR *[aside to Witgood]* Do you hear, sir? I may deserve your custom hereafter. Pray, let my money be accepted before a stranger's. Here's forty pound I received as I came to you. If that may stand you in any stead, make use on't. Nay, pray sir, 'tis at your service.

WITGOOD *[aside to First Creditor]*
You do so ravish me with kindness that
I'm constrained to play the maid and take it!

FIRST CREDITOR *[aside to Witgood]* Let none of them see it, I beseech you.

WITGOOD *[aside to First Creditor]* Fah!

FIRST CREDITOR *[aside to Witgood]*
I hope I shall be first in your remembrance
After the marriage rites.

WITGOOD *[aside to First Creditor]*
Believe it firmly.

FIRST CREDITOR So.—What, do you walk, sirs?

SECOND CREDITOR I go. *[Aside to Witgood]* Take no care, sir, for money to furnish you. Within this hour, I'll send you sufficient.—Come, Master Cockpit, we both stay for you.

THIRD CREDITOR I ha' lost a ring, i'faith. I'll follow you presently. *[Exeunt First and Second Creditors]* But you shall find it, sir. I know your youth and expenses have disfurnished you of all jewels. There's a ruby of twenty pound price, sir: bestow it upon your widow.—What, man, 'twill call up her blood to you. Beside, if I might so much work with you, I would not have you beholden to those bloodsuckers for any money.

WITGOOD Not I, believe it.

THIRD CREDITOR They're a brace of cutthroats!

WITGOOD I know 'em.

THIRD CREDITOR Send a note of all your wants to my shop, and I'll supply you instantly.

WITGOOD Say you so? Why, here's my hand, then. No man living shall do't but thyself.

THIRD CREDITOR Shall I carry it away from 'em both, then?

WITGOOD I'faith, shalt thou!

THIRD CREDITOR Troth, then I thank you, sir.

3.1.4 **forborne** gone without

15 **Shine ... spread** The metaphor associates the creditors with the sun and Witgood with a plant. It continues at 3.1.20.

18 **Remove me** (*a*) take me out of circulation by sending me to prison (*b*) take my money away
consume waste away (*a*) physically (*b*) financially

25 **sure** betrothed

26 **rend** rent, split, division
discredit (*a*) disrepute (*b*) having his debts called in

29 **Would ... with** even if the lands you offer us as security were worth as much as we feel we can loan you. (The creditors are so gullible that at this point they decline Witgood's offer to secure his prior loans.)

30 **I am to raise** Eighteen lines have been omitted prior to this line and printed as an additional passage at the end of the text, on the grounds that they are an undramatic repetition of the preceding twenty-nine lines in the scene and may have been an earlier version of it.

35 **custom** business patronage

39 **ravish** (*a*) transport with ecstasy or delight (*b*) rape

40 **play ... it** proverbial misogyny for yielding after an initial display of resistance. The complete proverb was, 'Maids say nay and take it' (Tilley M34). In this context, it suggests that Witgood appears to resist what he really wants: the money; but the proverb also attributes a coyness to women that incites and excuses rape by implying that *taking it* is part of being female.

49 **stay** wait

54 **disfurnished** deprived

56 **call ... you** The widow's *blood* or sexual desire will be prompted by the colour and value of the ring.

67 **carry ... from** triumph over

WITGOOD Welcome, good Master Cockpit!

Exit [*Third Creditor*]

Ha, ha, ha! Why, is not this better, now, than lying a-bed? I perceive there's nothing conjures up wit sooner than poverty, and nothing lays it down sooner than wealth and lechery! This has some savour yet. O, that I had the mortgage from mine uncle as sure in possession as these trifles, I would forswear brothel at noon day, and muscadine and eggs at midnight.

Enter Jane [*as a rich widow*]

JANE Master Witgood? Where are you?

WITGOOD Holla!

JANE Rich news!

WITGOOD Would 'twere all in plate.

JANE There's some in chains and jewels. I am so haunted with suitors, Master Witgood, I know not which to dispatch first.

WITGOOD You have the better term, by my faith.

JANE
Among the number,
One Master Hoard, an ancient gentleman.

WITGOOD
Upon my life, my uncle's adversary!

JANE
It may well hold so, for he rails on you,
Speaks shamefully of him.

WITGOOD
As I could wish it.

JANE
I first denied him, but so cunningly,
It rather promised him assurèd hopes
Than any loss of labour.

WITGOOD
Excellent!

JANE
I expect him every hour, with gentlemen
With whom he labours to make good his words,
To approve you riotous, your state consumed,
Your uncle—

WITGOOD Wench, make up thy own fortunes now; do thyself a good turn once in thy days. He's rich in money, movables, and lands—marry him. He's an old doting fool, and that's worth all—marry him. 'Twould be a great comfort to me to see thee do well, i'faith—marry him. 'Twould ease my conscience well to see thee well bestowed. I have a care of thee, i'faith.

JANE Thanks, sweet Master Witgood.

WITGOOD I reach at farther happiness. First, I am sure it can be no harm to thee, and there may happen goodness to me by it. Prosecute it well. Let's send up for our wits. Now we require their best and most pregnant assistance!

JANE Step in. I think I hear 'em. *Exit* [*with Witgood*]

Enter Hoard, Lamprey and Spitchcock with the Host as servingman

HOARD [*to Host*] Art thou the widow's man, by my faith? Sh'as a company of proper men, then.

HOST I am the worst of six, sir. Good enough for blue coats.

HOARD Hark hither. I hear say thou art in most credit with her.

HOST Not so, sir.

HOARD Come, come, thou'rt modest. There's a brace of royals. Prithee, help me to th' speech of her.

HOST I'll do what I may, sir, always saving myself harmless.

HOARD Go to. Do't, I say. Thou shalt hear better from me.

HOST [*aside*] Is not this a better place than five mark a year standing wages? Say a man had but three such clients in a day, methinks he might make a poor living on't. Beside, I was never brought up with so little honesty to refuse any man's money, never. What gulls there are o' this side the world. Now know I the widow's mind. None but my young master comes in her clutches. Ha, ha, ha! *Exit*

HOARD
Now my dear gentlemen, stand firmly to me.
You know his follies and my worth.

LAMPREY
We do, sir.

SPITCHCOCK
But Master Hoard, are you sure he is not i'th' house now?

HOARD
Upon my honesty, I chose this time
O' purpose fit. The spendthrift is abroad.
Assist me. Here she comes.

[*Enter Jane. Witgood watches while concealed*]

Now, my sweet widow.

76 **forswear** renounce
77 **muscadine** a strong, sweet wine, considered an aphrodisiac when taken with eggs
84 **dispatch** get rid of
85 **You . . . term** Jane is like a lawyer in having a profitable legal term. The pun on the legal and amorous meanings of *suitor* reflects the profits that both lawyers and prostitutes made during the court sessions.
89 **hold so** be true
90 **him** i.e. Lucre
96 **approve** prove
100 **movables** personal property
106–8 **First . . . it** Witgood risks his plan to secure the mortgage from Lucre in order to assure Jane a future with some wealth and respectability, but he senses that this arrangement may work to his advantage as well.
108 **Prosecute** perform
109 **pregnant** (*a*) inventive, resourceful (*b*) generative, continuing the image of their *trick* as an *embryo* begun at 1.1.57–62
112 **man** servant
114 **blue coats** the livery of servingmen
118–19 **brace of royals** pair of coins, each worth 15 shillings
120–1 **saving myself harmless** i.e. provided I avoid trouble
122 **Thou . . . me** i.e. I will reward you with more money
123 **mark** a sum equal to two-thirds of a pound
124 **standing** fixed
125 **poor** used ironically, since receiving three braces of royals each day would be an enormous sum for a servant
127 **gulls** dupes
132 **his** Witgood's
135 **abroad** out of his lodgings, where this scene occurs

JANE
You're welcome, Master Hoard.
HOARD
Dispatch, sweet gentlemen, dispatch.
I am come, widow, to prove those my words
Neither of envy sprung, nor of false tongues,
But such as their deserts and actïons
Do merit and bring forth, all which these gentlemen
Well known and better reputed will confess.
JANE [*to Lamprey and Spitchcock*] I cannot tell
How my affections may dispose of me,
But surely if they find him so desertless,
They'll have that reason to withdraw themselves.
And therefore, gentlemen, I do entreat you,
As you are fair in reputation,
And in appearing form so shine in truth:
I am a widow and, alas, you know,
Soon overthrown; 'tis a very small thing
That we withstand, our weakness is so great;
Be partial unto neither, but deliver,
Without affection, your opinion.
HOARD And that will drive it home.
JANE
Nay, I beseech your silence, Master Hoard.
You are a party.
HOARD Widow, not a word!
LAMPREY
The better first to work you to belief,
Know neither of us owe him flattery,
Nor t'other malice, but unbribèd censure,
So help us our best fortunes.
JANE It suffices.
LAMPREY
That Witgood is a riotous, undone man,
Imperfect both in fame and in estate,
His debts wealthier than he, and executions
In wait for his due body, we'll maintain
With our best credit and our dearest blood.
JANE
Nor land nor living, say you? Pray take heed
You do not wrong the gentleman!
LAMPREY What we speak
Our lives and means are ready to make good.
JANE
Alas, how soon are we poor souls beguiled!
SPITCHCOCK
And for his uncle—
HOARD Let that come to me.
His uncle, a severe extortioner,
A tyrant at a forfeiture, greedy of others'
Miseries, one that would undo his brother,
Nay, swallow up his father, if he can
Within the fathoms of his conscience.
LAMPREY Nay, believe it, widow.
You had not only matched yourself to wants,
But in an evil and unnatural stock.
HOARD [*aside*]
Follow hard, gentlemen, follow hard!
JANE
Is my love so deceived, before you all?
I do renounce him. [*Kneeling*] On my knees I vow
He ne'er shall marry me.
WITGOOD [*aside*]
Heaven knows he never meant it!
HOARD [*aside to gentlemen*]
There, take her at the bound.
[*Jane rises*]
LAMPREY
Then with a new and pure affectïon
Behold yon gentleman, grave, kind, and rich,
A match worthy yourself. Esteeming him,
You do regard your state.
HOARD [*aside to gentlemen*] I'll make her a jointure, say.
LAMPREY
He can join land to land, and will possess you
Of what you can desire.
SPITCHCOCK [*moving Jane toward Hoard*]
Come, widow, come.
JANE
The world is so deceitful!
LAMPREY There 'tis deceitful
Where flattery, want, and imperfection lies.

138 **Dispatch** make haste
140 **envy** malice, enmity
141 **their** Witgood's and Lucre's
145 **dispose of** decide, determine
150 **appearing form** outward appearance
151–3 **I...great** Jane parodies the stereotype of widows as generally weak and vulnerable because of their sexual needs, thereby manipulating Hoard by appearing to confirm his assumptions about her.
152 **very small thing** (*a*) very little adversity (*b*) penis
153 **withstand** resist, oppose
155 **Without affection** impartially
158 **a party** a participant in the dispute, so possibly biased
160 **him** Hoard
161 **t'other** Witgood
censure judgement
162 **So...fortunes** The gentlemen stake their money as proof of their testimony rather than their integrity, as occurs in the more common formula, 'So help me God'.
163 **undone** ruined
165 **executions** warrants for seizure of the goods or person of a debtor in default of payment
166 **his due body** i.e. his imprisonment for debt
168–9 **Pray...gentleman** Jane implies that a misrepresentation of Witgood's estate could constitute slander, which was a legal offence.
174 **forfeiture** a legal procedure in which goods are seized when a debtor cannot pay his debts
176–7 **swallow...conscience** recalling the metaphor of Lucre's conscience as like an ocean at 1.1.8–12
179 **wants** deficiencies, debts
181 **Follow hard** i.e. keep pressing your arguments
186 **at the bound** at the first opportunity
190 **regard** take notice and care of
jointure an agreement that property be held in the name of both husband and wife, with a provision that the wife becomes sole owner in the event of her husband's death
193 **There** i.e. with Witgood

But none of these in him! Push!

JANE Pray, sir.

LAMPREY [*moving Jane closer to Hoard*] Come, you widows are ever most backward when you should do yourselves most good, but were it to marry a chin not worth a hair now, then you would be forward enough! Come, clap hands, a match.

[*He joins the hands of Jane and Hoard*]

HOARD
With all my heart, widow! Thanks, gentlemen.
I will deserve your labour, and thy love.

JANE
Alas, you love not widows but for wealth.
I promise you, I ha' nothing, sir.

HOARD Well said,
Widow, well said. Thy love is all I seek,
Before these gentlemen.

JANE Now I must hope the best.

HOARD
My joys are such they want to be expressed.

JANE But Master Hoard, one thing I must remember you of before these gentlemen, your friends. How shall I suddenly avoid the loathed soliciting of that perjured Witgood and his tedious, dissembling uncle, who this very day hath appointed a meeting for the same purpose too, where, had not truth come forth, I had been undone, utterly undone?

HOARD What think you of that, gentlemen?

LAMPREY 'Twas well devised.

HOARD Hark thee, widow. Train out young Witgood single. Hasten him thither with thee somewhat before the hour, where, at the place appointed, these gentlemen and myself will wait the opportunity, when, by some sleight removing him from thee, we'll suddenly enter and surprise thee, carry thee away by boat to Cole Harbour, have a priest ready, and there clap it up instantly. How lik'st it, widow?

JANE
In that it pleaseth you, it likes me well.

HOARD
I'll kiss thee for those words. Come, gentlemen,
Still must I live a suitor to your favours,
Still to your aid beholden.

LAMPREY We're engaged, sir.
'Tis for our credits now to see't well ended.

HOARD
'Tis for your honours, gentlemen. Nay, look to't.
Not only in joy, but I in wealth excel.
No more sweet widow, but sweet wife, farewell.

JANE Farewell, sir. *Exeunt Hoard, Lamprey and Spitchcock*

Enter Witgood

WITGOOD O, for more scope! I could laugh eternally! Give you joy, Mistress Hoard. I promise your fortune was good, forsooth. You've fell upon wealth enough, and there's young gentlemen enough can help you to the rest. Now it requires our wits. Carry thyself but heedfully now, and we are both—

[*Enter Host as a servingman*]

HOST Master Witgood, your uncle.

Enter Lucre

WITGOOD [*aside to Jane*] Cods me! Remove thyself awhile. I'll serve for him. [*Exeunt Jane and Host*]

LUCRE Nephew, good morrow, nephew!

WITGOOD The same to you, kind uncle.

LUCRE How fares the widow? Does the meeting hold?

WITGOOD O, no question of that, sir.

LUCRE I'll strike the stroke then for thee; no more days.

WITGOOD The sooner the better, uncle. O, she's mightily followed.

LUCRE And yet so little rumoured.

195 **him** Hoard
Push pish, an expression of impatience
196 **Pray, sir** an expression of resistance, indicated also by Lamprey's suggestion that the widow is *backward* at 3.1.198
199 **chin . . . hair** a young man, without a beard or wealth
200 **forward** eager, willing
200–3.1.201.1 **Come . . . [*He joins . . . Hoard*]** Lamprey is the means by which Jane and Hoard engage in a handfast, a joining of hands as a sign of the spousal or marriage contract. He later boasts that he performs this act at 3.3.33. The handfast, the promise before witnesses (3.1.202–5 and 3.1.226), and the kiss (3.1.227) were all parts of the formal spousal.
203 **deserve** (*a*) requite (*b*) be worthy of
204 **not . . . but** only
205 **nothing** (*a*) no lands or living (*b*) a vagina (Gordon Williams). Hoard may take the remark in the second sense and also assume that Jane is modestly understating her wealth; but her disclaimer is important to prevent the charge that she misrepresents her fortune to Hoard, which could invalidate the marriage.
207 **Before these gentlemen** referring to the gentlemen as witnesses to his remark
208 **want to be expressed** are inexpressible, lack expression
211 **suddenly** shortly
avoid get rid of
218 **Train out** entice, lure
single alone
223–4 **Cole Harbour** see note to 2.1.257
224 **clap it up** settle the arrangement. The benediction of a priest and his pronouncement that Jane and Hoard were man and wife would complete all elements of the formal marriage ceremony, although the priest's involvement was not necessary for legal purposes. What Hoard proposes in the foregoing passage is a feigned abduction.
226 **In . . . well** The response registers Jane's assent to the planned abduction and the marriage by appearing to surrender her option of dissent in deference to her husband. Jane is 'acting' the wife.
233 **wife** Hoard's use of this word confirms that a marital contract has taken place in the preceding lines, as does Witgood's reference to Jane as *Mistress Hoard* at 3.1.236.
236 **promise** assure
237–9 **You've . . . rest** Witgood envisions Jane's needs in terms of money and sex. Marriage will provide her with the former, and he presumes she will entertain extra-marital affairs for the latter. Her remarks at 4.4.151–2 reflect different assumptions about her intent.
242 **Cods me** corruption of 'God save me'
243 **serve for** i.e. deal with
248 **strike the stroke** proverbial for 'do the deed', meaning here that he will sign over the mortgage
more days postponements, days of grace. This is usurers' language for the time a debt was due.

WITGOOD Mightily! Here comes one old gentleman, and he'll make her a jointure of three hundred a year, forsooth. Another wealthy suitor will estate his son in his lifetime and make him weigh down the widow. Here a merchant's son will possess her with no less than three goodly lordships at once, which were all pawns to his father.

LUCRE Peace, nephew. Let me hear no more of 'em. It mads me. Thou shalt prevent 'em all. No words to the widow of my coming hither. Let me see, 'tis now upon nine. Before twelve, nephew, we will have the bargain struck. We will, i'faith, boy.

WITGOOD O my precious uncle! *Exit [with Lucre]*

3.2 *Enter Hoard and his Niece*

HOARD Niece, sweet niece, prithee have a care to my house. I leave all to thy discretion. Be content to dream awhile. I'll have a husband for thee shortly. Put that care upon me, wench, for in choosing wives and husbands, I am only fortunate. I have that gift given me. *Exit*

NIECE
But 'tis not likely you should choose for me,
Since nephew to your chiefest enemy
Is he whom I affect. But O, forgetful,
Why dost thou flatter thy affections so,
With name of him that for a widow's bed
Neglects thy purer love. Can it be so?
Or does report dissemble?
[Enter George]
How now, sir?

GEORGE
A letter with which came a private charge.

NIECE
Therein I thank your care. *[Exit George]*
I know this hand.
(*Reading*) *Dearer than sight, what the world reports of me, yet believe not. Rumour will alter shortly. Be thou constant. I am still the same that I was in love, and I hope to be the same in fortunes.*
Theodorus Witgood
I am resolved. No more shall fear or doubt
Raise their pale powers to keep affection out. *Exit*

Enter with a Drawer, Hoard, Lamprey and Spitchcock 3.3

DRAWER You're very welcome, gentlemen. Dick, show those gentlemen the Pomegranate there.

HOARD Hist!

DRAWER Up those stairs, gentlemen.

HOARD Pist, drawer!

DRAWER Anon, sir.

HOARD Prithee, ask at the bar if a gentlewoman came not in lately.

DRAWER William at the bar, did you see any gentlewoman come in lately? Speak you ay, speak you no.

WILLIAM (*within*) No, none came in yet but Mistress Florence.

DRAWER He says none came in yet, sir, but one Mistress Florence.

HOARD What is that Florence? A widow?

DRAWER Yes, a Dutch widow.

HOARD How?

DRAWER That's an English drab, sir. Give your worship good morrow. *[Exit]*

HOARD A merry knave, i'faith. I shall remember a Dutch widow the longest day of my life.

LAMPREY Did not I use most art to win the widow?

SPITCHCOCK You shall pardon me for that, sir. Master Hoard knows I took her at best vantage.

HOARD What's that, sweet gentlemen; what's that?

SPITCHCOCK He will needs bear me down that his art only wrought with the widow most.

HOARD O, you did both well, gentlemen; you did both well. I thank you.

LAMPREY
I was the first that moved her.

HOARD
You were, i'faith.

SPITCHCOCK
But it was I that took her at the bound.

HOARD
Ay, that was you. Faith, gentlemen, 'tis right.

LAMPREY
I boasted least, but 'twas I joined their hands.

HOARD
By th' mass, I think he did. You did all well,
Gentlemen, you did all well. Contend no more.

255 **weigh down** (*a*) outweigh in wealth (*b*) position his body on top of hers during sex
256 **possess** (*a*) endow (*b*) take possession of
257 **lordships** lords' estates
pawns pledges as security for debt
260 **prevent** anticipate, forestall
3.2.5 **only** uniquely, pre-eminently
9 **affect** love
12 **purer** because Joyce is a virgin
14 **private charge** an order to deliver the letter privately
15 **hand** handwriting, script
21 **resolved** decided
3.3.0.1 ***Drawer*** one who draws liquor at a tavern, a tapster
2 **Pomegranate** Rooms of inns were given names rather than numbers.
16 **Dutch widow** The term returns with added force at 5.2.107.
18 **drab** prostitute
24 **vantage** opportunity, position
30 **moved** (*a*) put forward the issue, appealed to her (*b*) aroused her response (*c*) physically pushed her toward Hoard
31 **at the bound** (*a*) with a leap forward (*b*) on the recoil, rebound. Both meanings imply some physical movement of Jane in the earlier scene and hence some pressure on her assent that verges on coercion. Spitchcock's role in the spousal seems to have been more physical than verbal, which could be made evident in the staging.
33 **joined their hands** The remark and Hoard's response to it show that the handfast was initiated by Lamprey rather than Hoard or Jane.

LAMPREY
Come, yon room's fittest.
HOARD True, 'tis next the door.
Exit [with Lamprey and Spitchcock]
Enter Witgood, Jane [as a rich widow], and Host [as a servingman, with Drawer]
DRAWER You're very welcome. Please you to walk upstairs. Cloth's laid, sir.
JANE Upstairs! Troth, I am weary, Master Witgood.
WITGOOD Rest yourself here awhile, widow. We'll have a cup of muscadine in this little room.
DRAWER A cup of muscadine? You shall have the best, sir.
[He starts to leave]
WITGOOD But do you hear, sirrah?
DRAWER Do you call? Anon, sir.
WITGOOD What is there provided for dinner?
DRAWER I cannot readily tell you, sir. If you please, you may go into the kitchen and see yourself, sir. Many gentlemen of worship do use to do it, I assure you, sir.
[Exit]
HOST A pretty, familiar, prigging rascal. He has his part without book!
WITGOOD Against you are ready to drink to me, widow, I'll be present to pledge you.
JANE Nay, I commend your care. 'Tis done well of you.
[Exit Witgood]
Alas, what have I forgot!
HOST What, mistress?
JANE I slipped my wedding ring off when I washed, and left it at my lodging. Prithee, run. I shall be sad without it.
[Exit Host]
So, he's gone! Boy!
[Enter Boy]
BOY Anon, forsooth.
JANE Come hither, sirrah. Learn secretly if one Master Hoard, an ancient gentleman, be about house.
BOY I heard such a one named.
JANE Commend me to him.
Enter Hoard with Lamprey and Spitchcock
HOARD I'll do thy commendations!
JANE
O, you come well. Away, to boat, be gone!
HOARD
Thus wise men are revenged: give two for one.
Exeunt
Enter Witgood and Vintner
WITGOOD I must request
You, sir, to show extraordinary care.
My uncle comes with gentlemen, his friends,
And 'tis upon a making.
VINTNER Is it so?
I'll give a special charge, good Master Witgood.
May I be bold to see her?
WITGOOD Who, the widow?
With all my heart, i'faith. I'll bring you to her!
VINTNER If she be a Staffordshire gentlewoman, 'tis much if I know her not.
WITGOOD How now? Boy! Drawer!
[Enter Boy]
VINTNER Hie!
BOY Do you call, sir?
WITGOOD Went the gentlewoman up that was here?
BOY Up, sir? She went out, sir.
WITGOOD Out, sir?
BOY Out, sir. One Master Hoard, with a guard of gentlemen, carried her out at backdoor a pretty while since, sir.
WITGOOD Hoard? Death and darkness! Hoard!
Enter Host [as a servingman]
HOST The devil of ring I can find!
WITGOOD How now, what news? Where's the widow?
HOST My mistress? Is she not here, sir?
WITGOOD More madness yet.
HOST She sent me for a ring.
WITGOOD A plot, a plot! To boat! She's stole away!
HOST What?
Enter Lucre with Gentlemen
WITGOOD Follow! Enquire old Hoard, my uncle's adversary—
[Exit Host]
LUCRE Nephew, what's that?
WITGOOD Thrice miserable wretch!
LUCRE Why, what's the matter?
VINTNER The widow's borne away, sir.
LUCRE Ha? Passion of me! A heavy welcome, gentlemen.
FIRST GENTLEMAN The widow gone?
LUCRE Who durst attempt it?

42 **muscadine** a strong, sweet wine
50 **pretty** fine, smart
familiar saucy
prigging crooked, thieving
51 **without book** by heart
52 **Against** by the time that
53 **pledge** toast
57 **wedding ring** The ambiguous source of this ring indicates Jane's transitional state at this point in the play. The ring may be from her feigned former husband, in which case she pretends to desire it for sentimental reasons and to mark her status as a widow. It may be from Hoard after the spousal, since she is already married to him, although she would have had to conceal its source from the Host. And it may be from Witgood in anticipation of the matchmaking that is supposed to take place immediately thereafter, perhaps even the ring given him by the Third Creditor at 3.1.54–6, which would give the Host another reason to fetch it. This confusion about whose ring she has worn reinforces the impression that Jane is a married woman even though the identity of her husband at this moment, among her many prospects, is obscure.
63 **ancient** (*a*) venerable, senior (*b*) old
68 **give two for one** give better than they get
68.2 ***Vintner*** a wine-merchant, or an innkeeper who sells wine
72 **making** matchmaking
76–7 **'tis much if** i.e. I'd be surprised if
85 **carried** (*a*) escorted (*b*) drove or forcibly impelled, in keeping with the planned, feigned abduction

WITGOOD Who but old Hoard, my uncle's adversary?
LUCRE How?
WITGOOD With his confederates.
LUCRE
Hoard, my deadly enemy! Gentlemen, stand to me.
I will not bear it. 'Tis in hate of me.
That villain seeks my shame, nay thirsts my blood.
He owes me mortal malice.
I'll spend my wealth on this despiteful plot
Ere he shall cross me and my nephew thus.
WITGOOD So maliciously!

Enter Host [*as a servingman*]

LUCRE How now, you treacherous rascal?
HOST That's none of my name, sir.
WITGOOD Poor soul, he knew not on't.
LUCRE I'm sorry. I see then 'twas a mere plot.
HOST
I traced 'em nearly—
LUCRE Well?
HOST And hear for certain,
They have took Cole Harbour.
LUCRE The devil's sanctuary.
They shall not rest. I'll pluck her from his arms.
Kind and dear gentlemen,
If ever I had seat within your breasts—
FIRST GENTLEMAN
No more, good sir. It is a wrong to us
To see you injured. In a cause so just
We'll spend our lives, but we will right our friends.
LUCRE
Honest and kind. Come, we have delayed too long.
Nephew, take comfort: a just cause is strong.
WITGOOD
That's all my comfort, uncle.

Exeunt [*Lucre, Gentlemen, Vintner and Boy*]

Ha, ha, ha!
Now may events fall luckily, and well.
He that ne'er strives, says wit, shall ne'er excel. *Exit*

3.4

Enter Dampit, the usurer, drunk

DAMPIT When did I say my prayers? In anno '88, when the great armada was coming; and in anno '99, when the great thundering and lightning was, I prayed heartily then, i'faith, to overthrow Powis' new buildings. I kneeled by my great iron chest, I remember.

[*Enter Audrey*]

AUDREY Master Dampit, one may hear you before they see you. You keep sweet hours, Master Dampit. We were all abed three hours ago.
DAMPIT Audrey.
AUDREY O, you're a fine gentleman.
DAMPIT So I am, i'faith, and a fine scholar. Do you use to go to bed so early, Audrey?
AUDREY Call you this early, Master Dampit?
DAMPIT Why, is't not one of clock i'th' morning? Is not that early enough? Fetch me a glass of fresh beer.
AUDREY Here, I have warmed your nightcap for you, Master Dampit.
DAMPIT Draw it on, then. I am very weak, truly. I have not eaten so much as the bulk of an egg these three days.
AUDREY You have drunk the more, Master Dampit.
DAMPIT What's that?
AUDREY You mote an you would, Master Dampit.
DAMPIT I answer you, I cannot. Hold your prating. You prate too much and understand too little. Are you answered? Give me a glass of beer.
AUDREY May I ask you how you do, Master Dampit?
DAMPIT How do I? I'faith, naught.
AUDREY I ne'er knew you do otherwise.
DAMPIT I eat not one penn'orth of bread these two years. Give me a glass of fresh beer. I am not sick; nor I am not well.
AUDREY Take this warm napkin about your neck, sir, whilst I help to make you unready.
DAMPIT How now, Audrey-prater, with your scurvy devices. What say you now?

107 **stand to me** i.e. stand by me
110 **owes** bears
111 **despiteful** contemptuous, scornful
117 **mere** i.e. performed without the help of others
118 **nearly** carefully, closely
119 **took** proceeded to
devil's sanctuary because criminals resided there. See note to 2.1.257.
3.4.0.1 *usurer* Dampit is spoken of as a lawyer and a usurer throughout the play. All the money he made as a lawyer provides the capital for his second occupation.
2 **great armada** the Spanish Armada of 1588, when England defeated Spain
2–3 **'99 ... was** No great thunderstorms are recorded for this year, although they are for '89 and '98. Some editors emend the date, but the passage emphasizes the long lapse of time between Dampit's prayers, as Spencer suggests; and there is no reason to rely on Dampit's memory in any event.
4 **Powis' new buildings** This has been interpreted as an allusion to the house of a leatherseller named Poovey in St Paul's Churchyard, which was built of wood after a proclamation of 1 March 1605 forbade the use of timber in building construction. However, it would make no sense for Dampit to have prayed in 1599 for the overthrow of a building built in 1605. Since the point of the remark is that Dampit has not prayed in a long time and has had long gaps between his prayers, the allusion to an event in 1605 is unlikely. Sugden's proposal of a reference to Powis House at Lincoln's Inn Fields is the best suggestion to date. Whatever is alluded to, the larger point of the phrase is that when Dampit prayed on this last occasion, his purpose was to invoke harm on someone else.
5 **kneeled ... chest** Dampit uses his chest, which might contain his money and valuables, as an altar.
16 **nightcap** a cap worn to bed
23 **mote** archaic form of 'might', 'could'
an if
24 **prating** chattering, blabbing
28 **naught** in a bad way, ruined, or in bad health. Audrey takes the word in its meaning of 'wickedly'.
30 **penn'orth** pennyworth
33 **napkin** a neckerchief, which was a cloth or scarf used to cover the neck or shoulders
34 **make you unready** undress you

AUDREY What say I, Master Dampit? I say nothing but that you are very weak.

DAMPIT Faith, thou hast more cony-catching devices than all London!

AUDREY Why, Master Dampit, I never deceived you in all my life!

DAMPIT Why was that? Because I never did trust thee.

AUDREY I care not what you say, Master Dampit.

DAMPIT Hold thy prating. I answer thee, thou art a beggar, a quean, and a bawd. Are you answered?

AUDREY Fie, Master Dampit! A gentleman and have such words!

DAMPIT Why, thou base drudge of infortunity! Thou kitchen-stuff drab of beggary, roguery and coxcombry, thou cavernesed quean of foolery, knavery and bawdreaminy! I'll tell thee what, I will not give a louse for thy fortunes!

AUDREY No, Master Dampit? And there's a gentleman comes a-wooing to me, and he doubts nothing but that you will get me from him.

DAMPIT Ay? If I would either have thee or lie with thee for two thousand pound, would I might be damned! Why, thou base impudent quean of foolery, flattery, and coxcombry, are you answered?

AUDREY Come, will you rise and go to bed, sir?

DAMPIT Rise, and go to bed too, Audrey? How does Mistress Proserpine?

AUDREY Fooh!

DAMPIT She's as fine a philosopher of a stinkard's wife as any within the liberties!—Fah, fah, Audrey!

AUDREY How now, Master Dampit?

DAMPIT Fie upon't! What a choice of stinks here is. What hast thou done, Audrey? Fie upon't. Here's a choice of stinks indeed. Give me a glass of fresh beer, and then I will to bed.

AUDREY It waits for you above, sir.

DAMPIT Foh! I think they burn horns in Barnard's Inn. If ever I smelt such an abominable stink, usury forsake me! *[Exit]*

AUDREY They be the stinking nails of his trampling feet, and he talks of burning of horns! *Exit*

Finis Actus Tertius

Incipit Actus Quartus 4.1

Enter at Cole Harbour Hoard and Jane [disguised as a rich widow], married now; Lamprey and Spitchcock

LAMPREY
Join hearts, join hands in wedlock's bands,
Never to part till death cleave your heart.
[To Hoard] You shall forsake all other women,
[To Jane] You lords, knights, gentlemen, and yeomen.
What my tongue slips, make up with your lips.

HOARD *[kissing her]*
Give you joy, Mistress Hoard! Let the kiss come about!
[Knocking within] Who knocks? Convey my little pig-eater out.

LUCRE *[within]* Hoard?

HOARD
Upon my life, my adversary, gentlemen!

LUCRE *[within]*
Hoard, open the door, or we will force it ope.
Give us the widow.

HOARD Gentlemen, keep 'em out.

LAMPREY
He comes upon his death that enters here.

LUCRE *[within]*
My friends assist me.

HOARD He has assistants, gentlemen.

LAMPREY
Tut. Nor him, nor them, we in this action fear.

LUCRE *[within]*
Shall I in peace speak one word with the widow?

JANE
Husband and gentlemen, hear me but a word.

HOARD
Freely, sweet wife.

39 **cony-catching** cheating
46 **quean** prostitute
bawd procuress
49 **infortunity** misfortune
50 **kitchen-stuff** refuse from the kitchen
drab prostitute
coxcombry foolery
51 **cavernesed** one of Dampit's coinages, probably meaning 'cavernous' or even 'cavern-arsed'
51–2 **bawdreaminy** a portmanteau coinage from 'bawdry' and 'dream', which conveys in one word Dampit's fantastical projection of bawdry onto Audrey
55 **doubts nothing but** fears nothing except
63 **Mistress Proserpine** an unclear reference in Dampit's drunken haze, perhaps to a bawd or prostitute, to Dampit's wife or landlady, or even to Audrey herself, any of whom might be associated with the Greek goddess who spent half the year in the underworld
65 **stinkard's** stinkard: a smelly or despicable person, such as Dampit
66 **the liberties** areas, especially in the suburbs of London, over which the city had jurisdiction but no effective control, and therefore places where prostitution, theatre, and other marginal activities flourished
73 **burn horns** Spoons, cups, lanterns, and other domestic utensils were often made of horn, and burning them may have produced an unpleasant smell; but this reference has never been adequately explained.
Barnard's Inn one of the Inns of Court, in Holborn

4.1.0.2 ***Cole Harbour*** see note to 2.1.257
1 **Join ... hands** The joining of hearts symbolically represented through the joining of hands refers back to the handfast at 3.1.200–3.1.201.1. A marriage ceremony in which Jane and Hoard made their vows in the presence of a priest has just concluded.
2 **cleave** (*a*) split (*b*) pierce, penetrate (*c*) separate, sever. The entire line echoes passages in the marriage ceremony.
5 **slips** neglects, omits
6 **come about** come around. Hoard is inviting Lamprey and Spitchcock to kiss the bride.
7 **pig-eater** a term of endearment, probably meaning *breeder*. Pregnant women were thought to crave pork.

JANE Let him in peaceably.
You know we're sure from any act of his.
HOARD Most true.
JANE
You may stand by and smile at his old weakness.
Let me alone to answer him.
HOARD Content.
'Twill be good mirth, i'faith. How think you, gentlemen?
LAMPREY
Good gullery!
HOARD Upon calm conditions let him in.
LUCRE [*within*]
All spite and malice—
LAMPREY Hear me, Master Lucre.
So you will vow a peaceful entrance
With those your friends, and only exercise
Calm conference with the widow, without fury,
The passage shall receive you.
LUCRE [*within*] I do vow it.
LAMPREY
Then enter and talk freely. Here she stands.
Enter Lucre [with Gentleman and Host]
LUCRE
O Master Hoard, your spite has watched the hour!
You're excellent at vengeance, Master Hoard.
HOARD
Ha, ha, ha!
LUCRE I am the fool you laugh at.
You are wise, sir, and know the seasons well.
Come hither, widow. [*They talk apart*] Why is it thus?
O, you have done me infinite disgrace,
And your own credit no small injury.
Suffer mine enemy so despitefully
To bear you from my nephew! O, I had
Rather half my substance had been forfeit,
And begged by some starved rascal.
JANE
Why, what would you wish me do, sir?
I must not overthrow my state for love.
We have too many precedents for that.
From thousands of our wealthy, undone widows
One may derive some wit. I do confess
I loved your nephew. Nay, I did affect him,
Against the mind and liking of my friends,
Believed his promises, lay here in hope
Of flattered living and the boast of lands.
Coming to touch his wealth and state, indeed
It appears dross. I find him not the man:
Imperfect, mean, scarce furnished of his needs.
In words, fair lordships; in performance, hovels.
Can any woman love the thing that is not?
LUCRE
Broke you for this?
JANE Was it not cause too much?
Send to enquire his state: most part of it
Lay two years mortgaged in his uncle's hands.
LUCRE
Why, say it did, you might have known my mind.
I could have soon restored it.
JANE Ay, had I
But seen any such thing performed, why
'Twould have tied my affection and contained me
In my first desires. Do you think, i'faith,
That I could twine such a dry oak as this,
Had promise in your nephew took effect?
LUCRE
Why, and there's no time passed. And rather than
My adversary should thus thwart my hopes, I
would—
JANE
Tut, you've been ever full of golden speech.
If words were lands, your nephew would be rich.
LUCRE
Widow, believe it. I vow by my best bliss,
Before these gentlemen I will give in
The mortgage to my nephew instantly
Before I sleep or eat.
FIRST GENTLEMAN We'll pawn our credits,
Widow. What he speaks shall be performed
In fullness.
LUCRE Nay more, I will estate him
In farther blessings. He shall be my heir.
I have no son.
I'll bind myself to that condition.

18 **You...his** Jane refers to the binding nature of the spousal and the ceremony that has just ended. The marriage would not be secure if it occurred after a precontract with another party (which becomes a possibility at 4.4.99) or if the bride were taken under duress (which relates to Jane's charge at 5.2.132–4). Even at this point in the play, Jane exhibits her precise knowledge of marital law.
23 **gullery** trickery
25 **So** so long as
30 **watched the hour** awaited its opportunity
33 **seasons** i.e. favourable occasions
36 **credit** reputation
38–40 **I...rascal** This alternative remains a more likely possibility than Lucre recognizes if one considers Witgood a 'starved rascal'.
46 **affect** love
49 **flattered** exaggerated in its worth
50 **touch** i.e. test
50, 56 **state** estate
51 **dross** the impurities separated from metal by melting. The sentence adapts the metaphor of the touchstone, which was used for testing the quality of gold or silver alloys by rubbing them against a dark stone such as jasper. Here Jane herself serves as the touchstone.
52 **mean** (*a*) poor, of little value (*b*) low in social rank, not noble or gentle
53 **performance** fulfilment of promises
hovels squalid dwellings
63 **twine...dry oak** The elm with the vine twined around it was a Renaissance emblem of the husband and wife in marriage. Jane changes the elm to a *dry oak* to emphasize Hoard's age.
65 **no time passed** i.e. there is still time
69 **best bliss** referring to the hope of heavenly bliss
72 **pawn our credits** pledge our reputations

JANE
When I shall hear this done, I shall soon yield
To reasonable terms.

LUCRE In the mean season,
Will you protest before these gentlemen,
To keep yourself as you are now at this present?

JANE
I do protest before these gentlemen,
I will be as clear then, as I am now.

LUCRE
I do believe you. Here's your own honest servant.
I'll take him along with me.

JANE Ay, with all my heart.

LUCRE
He shall see all performed and bring you word.

JANE That's all I wait for.

HOARD
What, have you finished, Master Lucre? Ha, ha, ha,
ha!

LUCRE
So, laugh, Hoard, laugh at your poor enemy; do.
The wind may turn. You may be laughed at, too.
Yes, marry, may you, sir.—Ha, ha, ha!
Exeunt [Lucre, Gentleman, and Host]

HOARD
Ha, ha, ha! If every man that swells in malice
Could be revenged as happily as I,
He would choose hate and forswear amity.
What did he say, wife, prithee?

JANE
Faith, spoke to ease his mind.

HOARD O, O, O!

JANE
You know now, little to any purpose.

HOARD
True, true, true.

JANE He would do mountains now.

HOARD
Ay, ay, ay, ay.

LAMPREY You've struck him dead, Master Hoard.

SPITCHCOCK
Ay, and his nephew desperate.

HOARD I know't, sirs; ay.
Never did man so crush his enemy! *Exeunt*

4.2

Enter Lucre with Gentlemen [and Host as a servingman], meeting Sam Freedom

LUCRE
My son-in-law, Sam Freedom! Where's my nephew?

SAM
O man in lamentation, father!

LUCRE How?

SAM He thumps his breast like a gallant dicer that has lost his doublet and stands in's shirt to do penance.

LUCRE Alas, poor gentleman.

SAM I warrant you may hear him sigh in a still evening to your house at Highgate.

LUCRE I prithee, send him in.

SAM Were it to do a greater matter, I will not stick with you, sir, in regard you married my mother. *[Exit]*

LUCRE Sweet gentlemen, cheer him up. I will but fetch the mortgage and return to you instantly.

FIRST GENTLEMAN
We'll do our best, sir. *Exit Lucre*
See where he comes,
E'en joyless and regardless of all form.
[Enter Witgood]

SECOND GENTLEMAN Why, how now Master Witgood, fie! You a firm scholar and an understanding gentleman, and give your best parts to passion?

FIRST GENTLEMAN
Come, fie!

WITGOOD O, Gentlemen!

FIRST GENTLEMAN
Sorrow of me, what a sigh was there, sir.
Nine such widows are not worth it.

WITGOOD
To be borne from me by that lecher, Hoard!

FIRST GENTLEMAN
That vengeance is your uncle's, being done
More in despite to him than wrong to you.
But we bring comfort now.

WITGOOD I beseech you, gentlemen.

SECOND GENTLEMAN
Cheer thyself, man. There's hope of her, i'faith.

WITGOOD
Too gladsome to be true.
Enter Lucre

LUCRE Nephew, what cheer?
Alas, poor gentleman, how art thou changed!

79 **mean season** meantime
81 **as you are now** Lucre assumes that Jane is still unmarried.
83 **clear** (*a*) disengaged, which Hoard takes to mean unmarried (*b*) virtuous
98 **do mountains** i.e. do anything to win Jane back for Witgood
4.2.1 **son-in-law** son by marriage, i.e. stepson
2 **O...lamentation** An allusion to an old song, 'O man in desperation', mentioned in Peele's *Old Wives' Tale* and Nashe's *Summer's Last Will and Testament.*
3–4 **gallant...shirt** one who has gambled away so much that he has bet and lost some of the clothes he has on
4 **doublet** a close-fitting body garment with or without sleeves
7 **Highgate** a village outside London, where wealthy citizens might have country houses
9 **stick** haggle, argue with
14 **regardless...form** i.e. careless of all appearances
17 **passion** i.e. sorrow, grief

Call thy fresh blood into thy cheeks again.
She comes—

WITGOOD Nothing afflicts me so much
But that it is your adversary, uncle,
And merely plotted in despite of you.

LUCRE Ay, that's it mads me, spites me! I'll spend my wealth ere he shall carry her so, because I know 'tis only to spite me. Ay, this is it. Here, nephew. [*Offering him a paper*] Before these kind gentlemen I deliver in your mortgage, my promise to the widow. See, 'tis done. Be wise. You're once more master of your own. The widow shall perceive now you are not altogether such a beggar as the world reputes you. You can make shift to bring her to three hundred a year, sir.

FIRST GENTLEMAN
By'r Lady, and that's no toy, sir.

LUCRE
A word, nephew.

FIRST GENTLEMAN [*to Host*]
Now you may certify the widow.

LUCRE
You must conceive it aright, nephew, now.
To do you good I am content to do this.

WITGOOD I know it, sir.

LUCRE
But your own conscience can tell I had it
Dearly enough of you.

WITGOOD Ay, that's most certain.

LUCRE
Much money laid out, beside many a journey
To fetch the rent. I hope you'll think on't, nephew.

WITGOOD
I were worse than a beast else, i'faith.

LUCRE
Although to blind the widow and the world
I out of policy do't, yet there's a conscience, nephew.

WITGOOD
Heaven forbid else!

LUCRE When you are full possessed,
'Tis nothing to return it.

WITGOOD
Alas, a thing quickly done, uncle.

LUCRE
Well said. You know I give it you but in trust.

WITGOOD
Pray, let me understand you rightly, uncle.
You give it me but in trust.

LUCRE No.

WITGOOD
That is, you trust me with it.

LUCRE True, true.

WITGOOD [*aside*] But if ever I trust you with it again, would I might be trussed up for my labour.

LUCRE You can all witness, gentlemen—and you, sir yeoman!

HOST My life for yours, sir. Now I know my mistress' mind too well toward your nephew. Let things be in preparation, and I'll train her hither in most excellent fashion. *Exit*

LUCRE A good old boy. Wife Jenny!

Enter Wife

WIFE What's the news, sir?

LUCRE The wedding day's at hand. Prithee, sweet wife, express thy housewifery. Thou'rt a fine cook, I know't. Thy first husband married thee out of an alderman's kitchen. Go to! He raised thee for raising of paste, what? Here's none but friends. Most of our beginnings must be winked at. Gentlemen, I invite you all to my nephew's wedding against Thursday morning.

FIRST GENTLEMAN
With all our hearts. And we shall joy to see
Your enemy so mocked.

LUCRE He laughed at me,
Gentlemen. Ha, ha, ha! *Exeunt [all but Witgood]*

WITGOOD He has no conscience, faith,
Would laugh at them; they laugh at one another!
Who then can be so cruel? Troth, not I.
I rather pity now than aught envỳ.
I do conceive such joy in mine own happiness,
I have no leisure yet to laugh at their follies.

31 **merely...you** planned solely to spite you
33 **carry** win
35 **deliver in** reconvey, i.e. return with the debt cancelled
39 **make shift** manage
41 **By'r Lady** an oath referring to the Virgin Mary
toy trifle
42 **certify** assure
47 **Dearly** expensively, with reference to the high cost
56 **in trust** (*a*) as a property still in Lucre's name that Witgood would eventually inherit from him, but without present ownership having been transferred (*b*) as a property now placed in Witgood's name that Lucre trusts him to return once he has married Jane. Witgood's response at 4.2.58, which Lucre denies, can be taken to mean either alternative but especially the first; his rephrasing at 4.2.59, to which Lucre assents, proposes only the second.
61 **trussed up** hanged, punning on *trust*
66 **train** conduct, entice
71 **express** show
72–3 **out...kitchen** Lucre reveals that his wife worked as a cook until she married her first husband. Given what else we know about Lucre, the information suggests that he may have married her because she was another rich widow.
73 **Go to!** Come, come. Jenny has objected to Lucre's reference to her lower class origins.
raised...paste elevated her to her husband's social rank by marriage because (*a*) she was a good baker, referring to dough that rises through the effect of yeast, and because (*b*) she moved him sexually
74 **beginnings** (*a*) social origins (*b*) moments of conception
75 **winked at** turned a blind eye toward
79 **He** Lucre
80 **Would** i.e. who would
them Hoard and his friends
they Lucre and Hoard
82 **aught envỳ** bear malice towards anyone

[He addresses the mortgage]
Thou soul of my estate, I kiss thee.
I miss life's comfort when I miss thee.
O, never will we part again
Until I leave the sight of men.
We'll ne'er trust conscience of our kin
Since cozenage brings that title in. *[Exit]*

4.3 *Enter three Creditors*

FIRST CREDITOR I'll wait these seven hours, but I'll see him caught.

SECOND CREDITOR Faith, so will I.

THIRD CREDITOR Hang him, prodigal. He's stripped of the widow.

FIRST CREDITOR O' my troth, she's the wiser. She has made the happier choice. And I wonder of what stuff those widows' hearts are made of, that will marry unfledged boys before comely thrum-chinned gentlemen.

Enter a Boy

BOY News, news, news!

FIRST CREDITOR What, boy?

BOY The rioter is caught!

FIRST CREDITOR So, so, so, so! *[Exit Boy]* It warms me at the heart. I love a' life to see dogs upon men. O, here he comes.

Enter Witgood with sergeants

WITGOOD My last joy was so great, it took away the sense of all future afflictions. What a day is here o'ercast! How soon a black tempest rises!

FIRST CREDITOR O, we may speak with you now, sir. What's become of your rich widow? I think you may cast your cap at the widow, may you not, sir?

SECOND CREDITOR He, a rich widow? Who? A prodigal, a daily rioter and a nightly vomiter. He, a widow of account? He a hole i'th' counter!

WITGOOD You do well, my masters, to tyrannize over misery, to afflict the afflicted. 'Tis a custom you have here amongst you. I would wish you never leave it, and I hope you'll do as I bid you.

FIRST CREDITOR Come, come, sir. What say you extempore now to your bill of a hundred pound? *[Handing him a paper]* A sweet debt, for frotting your doublets.

SECOND CREDITOR *[handing another paper]* Here's mine of forty.

THIRD CREDITOR *[handing another paper]* Here's mine of fifty.

WITGOOD Pray, sirs, you'll give me breath.

FIRST CREDITOR No, sir, we'll keep you out of breath still. Then we shall be sure you will not run away from us.

WITGOOD Will you but hear me speak?

SECOND CREDITOR You shall pardon us for that, sir. We know you have too fair a tongue of your own. You overcame us too lately. A shame take you! We are like to lose all that for want of witnesses. We dealt in policy then. Always, when we strive to be most politic, we prove most coxcombs. *Non plus ultra.* I perceive by us we're not ordained to thrive by wisdom, and therefore we must be content to be tradesmen.

WITGOOD Give me but reasonable time, and I protest I'll make you ample satisfaction.

FIRST CREDITOR Do you talk of reasonable time to us?

WITGOOD 'Tis true, beasts know no reasonable time.

SECOND CREDITOR We must have either money or carcass.

WITGOOD Alas, what good will my carcass do you?

THIRD CREDITOR O, 'tis a secret delight we have amongst us. We that are used to keep birds in cages have the heart to keep men in prison, I warrant you.

WITGOOD *[aside]* I perceive I must crave a little more aid from my wits. Do but make shift for me this once, and I'll forswear ever to trouble you in the like fashion hereafter. I'll have better employment for you, an I live. *[To creditors]* You'll give me leave, my masters, to make trial of my friends and raise all means I can?

FIRST CREDITOR That's our desires, sir.

Enter Host [as a servingman]

HOST Master Witgood!

WITGOOD O, art thou come?

HOST May I speak one word with you in private, sir?

[Sergeants hold Witgood back]

WITGOOD No, by my faith, canst thou. I am in hell here and the devils will not let me come to thee.

CREDITORS *[all talking at once]* Do you call us devils? You shall find us puritans! *[To sergeants]* Bear him away! Let

85 **Thou ... thee** Compare Volpone's opening address to his gold, 'O thou son of Sol, ... let me kiss, | With adoration, thee' in *Volpone* at 1.1.10–12.

90 **cozenage** (*a*) trickery (*b*) kinship, cousinship

that title (*a*) i.e. of *kin* (*b*) the mark of ownership or title to the mortgage

4.3.9 **thrum-chinned** bearded. The *thrum* was the row of threads left hanging on a piece of cloth and the loom on which it was woven after the cloth was cut off; it would resemble fringe.

14 **a' life** i.e. as much as my life

14–15 **dogs upon men** i.e. sergeants with men in their grasp

20–1 **cast ... at** give up

24 **account** punning on 'cunt'

hole ... counter one of the worst cells in the city prisons for debtors. *Counter* also puns on 'cunt'; and *hole* has similar associations.

29–30 **extempore now** immediately

31 **frotting** rubbing with perfume

42 **all that** i.e. the money and jewellery that the creditors gave to Witgood at 3.1.36–64

policy cunning

43–6 **Always ... tradesmen** Compare the play's final line at 5.2.204.

44 ***Non plus ultra*** no farther

50 **beasts ... time** i.e. animals are never rational, because humans alone are defined as *animal rationale*

51 **carcass** referring to Witgood's threatened imprisonment for debt

57 **make shift** work a scheme

58, 59 **you** i.e. his wits

68 **Creditors** The speech headings of the 1608 and 1616 editions read *Cit*, for citizens, which suggests that the creditors had the status of those associated with certain London trade guilds.

69 **puritans** i.e. strict in enforcing laws rather than, like *devils*, transgressing them

'em talk as they go. We'll not stand to hear 'em. [*To Witgood*] Ah, sir, am I a devil? I shall think the better of myself as long as I live! A devil, i'faith! *Exeunt*

4.4 *Enter Hoard*

HOARD What a sweet blessing hast thou, Master Hoard! Above a multitude! Wilt thou never be thankful? How dost thou think to be blessed another time? Or dost thou count this the full measure of thy happiness? By my troth, I think thou dost. Not only a wife large in possessions, but spacious in content. She's rich, she's young, she's fair, she's wise. When I wake, I think of her lands—that revives me. When I go to bed, I dream of her beauty, and that's enough for me. She's worth four hundred a year in her very smock, if a man knew how to use it. But the journey will be all, in troth, into the country—to ride to her lands in state and order following my brother and other worshipful gentlemen, whose companies I ha' sent down for already, to ride along with us in their goodly decorum beards, their broad velvet cassocks and chains of gold twice or thrice double. Against which time, I'll entertain some ten men of mine own into liveries, all of occupations or qualities. I will not keep an idle man about me. The sight of which will so vex my adversary, Lucre—for we'll pass by his door of purpose, make a little stand for nonce, and have our horses curvet before the window—certainly he will never endure it, but run up and hang himself presently!

[*Enter Servant*]

How now, sirrah, what news? Any that offer their service to me yet?

SERVANT Yes, sir. There are some i'th' hall that wait for your worship's liking and desire to be entertained.

HOARD Are they of occupation?

SERVANT They are men fit for your worship, sir.

HOARD Say'st so? Send 'em all in! [*Exit Servant*]

To see ten men ride after me in watchet liveries with orange-tawny caps, 'twill cut his comb, i'faith.

Enter [*Tailor, Barber, Perfumer, Falconer, and Huntsman*]

How now? Of what occupation are you, sir?

TAILOR A tailor, an't please your worship.

HOARD A tailor? O, very good. You shall serve to make all the liveries. What are you, sir?

BARBER A barber, sir.

HOARD A barber! Very needful. You shall shave all the house, and if need require, stand for a reaper i'th'summertime. You, sir?

PERFUMER A perfumer.

HOARD I smelt you before. Perfumers of all men had need carry themselves uprightly, for if they were once knaves, they would be smelt out quickly. To you, sir?

FALCONER A falconer, an't please your worship.

HOARD Sa ho, sa ho, sa ho! And you, sir?

HUNTSMAN A huntsman, sir.

HOARD There boy, there boy, there boy! I am not so old but I have pleasant days to come. I promise you, my masters, I take such a good liking to you that I entertain you all. I put you already into my countenance, and you shall be shortly in my livery. But especially you two—my jolly falconer and my bonny huntsman. We shall have most need of you at my wife's manor houses i'th' country. There's goodly parks and champaign grounds for you. We shall have all our sports within ourselves. All the gentlemen o'th' country shall be beholden to us and our pastimes.

FALCONER And we'll make your worship admire, sir.

HOARD Say'st thou so? Do but make me admire, and thou shalt want for nothing. My tailor?

TAILOR Anon, sir.

HOARD Go presently in hand with the liveries.

TAILOR I will, sir.

HOARD My barber?

BARBER Here, sir.

HOARD Make 'em all trim fellows. Louse 'em well, especially my huntsman, and cut all their beards of the Polonian fashion. My perfumer?

4.4.1–23 **What . . . presently** Hoard's speech voices the fantasy of owning a country estate and achieving the social status of the landed gentry.

6 **spacious in content** ample in her ability to content me

10 **in . . . smock** i.e. without her outer clothing or additional possessions. The assessment places a monetary value on Jane's body.

11 **use it** employ Jane's body for profit

12 **country** punning on 'cunt'. Hoard's journey to the widow's country lands is analogous to a journey into her body.

14 **companies** presence

15 **decorum** decorous, an adjectival use of the noun

16 **cassocks** long, loose coats

17–18 **entertain . . . liveries** employ as uniformed servants

18 **occupations or qualities** particular trades or abilities

21 **for nonce** expressly, for that purpose

22 **curvet** leap in such a way that the horses' fore-legs are raised together and equally advanced, and the hind-legs are raised with a spring before the fore-legs touch the ground

23 **up** perhaps upstairs

27 **entertained** i.e. taken into service

31 **watchet liveries** pale blue uniforms

32 **orange-tawny** Francis Bacon remarks in his essay 'Of Usury' that 'usurers should have orange-tawny bonnets, because they do Judaize', i.e. imitate Jews. The colour was also associated with courtiers and may symbolize pride.

cut his comb take him down, humiliate

36 **liveries** clothing for servants, one of Hoard's preoccupations given his new status

39 **reaper** one who harvests grain

46 **Sa ho** a cry used at the sighting of game in hunting hawks

48 **There boy** a hunting call

51 **countenance** favour

53 **falconer . . . huntsman** Hoard's preference for the falconer and huntsman reflects his desire for forms of recreation specific to the country and the status such sports bring, as he suggests at 4.4.56–8.

55 **champaign** level, open country

59 **admire** marvel, wonder

67 **Louse 'em** i.e. remove their lice

69 **Polonian** Polish, possibly referring to a style that was current at the time. The Poles were said by Fynes Moryson in 1617 to prefer closely-trimmed hair on the head except for a long forelock.

PERFUMER Under your nose, sir.

HOARD Cast a better savour upon the knaves, to take away the scent of my tailor's feet and my barber's lotium-water.

PERFUMER It shall be carefully performed, sir.

HOARD But you, my falconer and huntsman, the welcom'st men alive, i'faith!

HUNTSMAN And we'll show you that, sir, shall deserve your worship's favour!

HOARD I prithee, show me that. Go, you knaves all, and wash your lungs i'th' buttery. Go.

[Exeunt Tailor, Barber, Perfumer, Falconer, and Huntsman]

[*Calling something to mind*] By th' mass, and well remembered! I'll ask my wife that question. Wife, Mistress Jane Hoard!

Enter [Jane as Hoard's wife] altered in apparel

JANE Sir, would you with me?

HOARD I would but know, sweet wife, which might stand best to thy liking, to have the wedding dinner kept here or i'th' country?

JANE Hum. Faith, sir, 'twould like me better here. Here you were married; here let all rites be ended.

HOARD Could a marquise give a better answer? Hoard, bear thy head aloft: thou'st a wife will advance it.

[Enter Host as a servingman with a letter]

What haste comes here now? Yea, a letter. Some dreg of my adversary's malice. Come hither. What's the news?

HOST [*giving letter to Jane*] A thing that concerns my mistress, sir.

HOARD Why then it concerns me, knave!

HOST [*aside*] Ay, and you, knave, too.—Cry your worship mercy! You are both like to come into trouble, I promise you, sir. A precontract.

HOARD How? A precontract, say'st thou?

HOST I fear they have too much proof on't, sir. Old Lucre, he runs mad up and down and will to law as fast as he can. Young Witgood, laid hold on by his creditors, he exclaims upon you o' t'other side, says you have wrought his undoing by the injurious detaining of his contract.

HOARD Body o' me!

HOST
He will have utmost satisfaction.
The law shall give him recompense, he says.

JANE [*aside*] Alas, his creditors so merciless, my state being yet uncertain, I deem it not unconscionable to further him.

HOST True, sir.

HOARD
Wife, what says that letter? Let me construe it.

JANE [*tearing letter and stamping on it*]
Cursed be my rash and unadvisèd words!
I'll set my foot upon my tongue
And tread my inconsiderate grant to dust.

HOARD Wife—

HOST [*aside*] A pretty shift, i'faith. I commend a woman when she can make away a letter from her husband handsomely, and this was cleanly done, by my troth.

JANE [*to Hoard*] I did, sir.
Some foolish words I must confess did pass
Which now, litigiously, he fastens on me.

HOARD
Of what force? Let me examine 'em.

JANE
Too strong, I fear. Would I were well freed of him.

HOARD Shall I compound?

JANE
No, sir. I'd have it done some nobler way
Of your side. I'd have you come off with honour.
Let baseness keep with them. Why, have you not
The means, sir? The occasion's offered you.

HOARD Where? How, dear wife?

JANE He is now caught by his creditors. The slave's needy, his debts petty. He'll rather bind himself to all inconveniences than rot in prison. By this only means you may get a release from him. 'Tis not yet come to his uncle's hearing. Send speedily for the creditors. By this time he's desperate, he'll set his hand to anything. Take order for his debts, or discharge 'em quite. A pox on him! Let's be rid of a rascal!

HOARD Excellent!
Thou dost astonish me. Go! Run! Make haste!
Bring both the creditors and Witgood hither.

71 **savour** scent

73 **lotium-water** stale urine, used by barbers as a hair rinse

80 **wash...buttery** i.e. have a drink in the storeroom or pantry

90 **marquise** a noblewoman of the second rank of the peerage, below a duchess and above a countess, and therefore considerably more elevated in class than Hoard assumes Jane to be. The term *marquess* or *marquis* was used in the sixteenth and seventeenth centuries to refer to persons of both sexes, and a woman could hold the rank in her own right. The wife or widow of a marquess could be referred to in these ways or as a 'marchioness'.

99 **precontract** an agreement to marry, which would form an impediment to subsequent marriage to another person

105 **detaining** withholding

111 **uncertain** (*a*) unknown (*b*) undetermined, because Hoard has not yet learned she has no wealth

111–12 **I...him** The aside shows that Jane is no longer blindly loyal to Witgood but weighs the ethics of continuing to support their joint deception. See note to 4.4.180–2.

117 **inconsiderate grant** unconsidered or rash promise

121 **handsomely** cleverly
cleanly adroitly

127 **compound** (*a*) bargain (in a general sense) (*b*) settle by means of payment

136 **release** a document freeing someone from contractual obligations

139 **quite** entirely

HOST [*aside*]
This will be some revenge yet. [*Exit*]

HOARD
In the mean space, I'll have a release drawn. Within there!
[*Enter Servant*]

SERVANT Sir?

HOARD
Sirrah, come take directions. Go to my scrivener.

JANE [*aside as Hoard talks to Servant*]
I'm yet like those whose riches lie in dreams.
If I be waked, they're false. Such is my fate,
Who ventures deeper than the desperate state.
Though I have sinned, yet could I become new,
For where I once vow, I am ever true.

HOARD
Away! Dispatch! On my displeasure, quickly!
[*Exit Servant*]
Happy occasion. Pray heaven he be in the right vein now to set his hand to't, that nothing alter him. Grant that all his follies may meet in him at once to besot him enough.
I pray for him, i'faith. And here he comes!
[*Enter Witgood and three Creditors*]

WITGOOD
What would you with me now, my uncle's spiteful adversary?

HOARD
Nay, I am friends.

WITGOOD Ay, when your mischief's spent.

HOARD
I heard you were arrested.

WITGOOD Well, what then?
You will pay none of my debts, I am sure.

HOARD A wiseman cannot tell.
There may be those conditions 'greed upon,
May move me to do much.

WITGOOD Ay, when?
[*He sees Jane*]
'Tis thou, perjured woman—O, no name
Is vile enough to match thy treachery—
That art the cause of my confusion!

JANE Out, you penurious slave!

HOARD
Nay, wife, you are too froward.
Let him alone. Give losers leave to talk.

WITGOOD
Shall I remember thee of another promise
Far stronger than the first?

JANE I'd fain know that.

WITGOOD
'Twould call shame to thy cheeks.

JANE Shame!

WITGOOD [*aside*] Hark, in your ear.
[*They talk apart*]
Will he come off, think'st thou, and pay my debts roundly?

JANE Doubt nothing. There's a release a-drawing and all, to which you must set your hand.

WITGOOD Excellent.

JANE But methinks, i'faith, you might have made some shift to discharge this yourself, having in the mortgage, and never have burdened my conscience with it.

WITGOOD O' my troth, I could not, for my creditors' cruelties extend to the present.

JANE No more.
[*Speaking aloud*] Why, do your worst for that. I defy you.

WITGOOD
You're impudent. I'll call up witnesses.

JANE
Call up thy wits, for thou hast been devoted
To follies a long time.

HOARD Wife, you're too bitter.
Master Witgood, and you my masters, you shall
Hear a mild speech come from me now, and this it is.
'T'as been my fortune, gentlemen, to have
An extraordinary blessing poured
Upon me o' late, and here she stands. I have wedded her

144 **This ... yet** Since the Host is still concerned about Witgood's loss of Jane, he sees the payment of his master's debts as a way in which Witgood can be requited for what he has lost.

147 **scrivener** a notary who, like the lawyer and the usurer, was sometimes despised for making a living off the misfortunes of others

150 **Who ... state** Barber sees in this remark an indication that Jane has 'reached the state of despair and then gone beyond it'. She has just described Witgood as *desperate* at 4.4.138 and now says her actions take her beyond that state to a point of no return.
ventures (*a*) voyages (*b*) gambles

151–2 **Though ... true** an indication that Jane chooses to remain faithful to Hoard. Her reference to a *vow* in the second line suggests the decision is not a departure from her past practice; instead, this is her first commitment of marriage, her relation with Witgood having been of a different sort. The biblical connotations of *become new* reinforce the sense that Jane is ready to assume a new identity as wife.

154 **he** i.e. Witgood

156 **besot** overcome

170 **froward** perverse, refractory. The charge was commonly made by husbands of their wives, and the word was frequently applied to shrews. So Hoard is already perceiving Jane's actions in terms of early modern assumptions about marriage and a husband's supposed right to control his wife's behaviour.

171 **Give ... talk** proverbial (Tilley L458)

173 **the first** presumably the promise of Witgood's marriage to Jane referred to in the letter. The mention of a *stronger* promise is only a pretext to speak alone with Jane, but the reference may evoke the earlier liaison of Witgood and Jane.
fain gladly

176 **roundly** completely

180–2 **But ... it** Jane's remark shows her resistance to further complicity in Witgood's schemes and her *conscience* about her relation to him now that she is married. Her comments at 4.4.110–12 and 4.4.150–2 are consistent with this direct criticism of him.

194–5 **wedded ... her** These words signal that the marriage contract and ceremony have concluded in a sexual consummation.

And bedded her, and yet she is little the worse.
Some foolish words she hath passed to you in the country,
And some peevish debts you owe here in the city.
Set the hare's head to the goose giblet.
Release you her of her words, and I will
Release you of your debts, sir.

WITGOOD Would you so?
I thank you for that, sir. I cannot blame you, i'faith.

HOARD Why, are not debts better than words, sir?

WITGOOD Are not words promises, and are not promises debts, sir?

HOARD He plays at back-racket with me.

FIRST CREDITOR Come hither, Master Witgood, come hither. Be ruled by fools once.

[*Creditors talk apart with Witgood*]

SECOND CREDITOR We are citizens and know what belong to't.

FIRST CREDITOR Take hold of his offer. Pox on her! Let her go! If your debts were once discharged, I would help you to a widow myself worth ten of her.

THIRD CREDITOR Mass, partner, and now you remember me on't, there's Master Mulligrub's sister, newly fallen a widow.

FIRST CREDITOR Cods me, as pat as can be! There's a widow left for you. Ten thousand in money, beside plate, jewels, et cetera. I warrant it a match. We can do all in all with her. Prithee, dispatch. We'll carry thee to her presently.

WITGOOD My uncle will ne'er endure me when he shall hear I set my hand to a release.

SECOND CREDITOR Hark! I'll tell thee a trick for that. I have spent five hundred pound in suits in my time. I should be wise. Thou'rt now a prisoner. Make a release. Take't of my word: whatsoever a man makes, as long as he is in durance, 'tis nothing in law.

[*He snaps his fingers*]

Not thus much.

WITGOOD Say you so, sir?

THIRD CREDITOR I have paid for't. I know't.

WITGOOD Proceed then, I consent.

THIRD CREDITOR Why, well said.

HOARD How now, my masters? What have you done with him?

FIRST CREDITOR With much ado, sir, we have got him to consent.

HOARD Ah, ah, ah! And what came his debts to now?

FIRST CREDITOR Some eightscore odd pounds, sir.

HOARD Naw, naw, naw, naw, naw! Tell me the second time; give me a lighter sum. They are but desperate debts, you know, ne'er called in but upon such an accident. A poor needy knave, he would starve and rot in prison. Come, come. You shall have ten shillings in the pound and the sum down roundly.

FIRST CREDITOR You must make it a mark, sir.

HOARD Go to, then. [*Giving money*] Tell your money. In the mean time, you shall find little less there. Come, Master Witgood, you are so unwilling to do yourself good now.

[*Enter Scrivener*]

Welcome, honest scrivener. Now you shall hear the release read.

SCRIVENER [*reading*] 'Be it known to all men by these presents that I, Theodorus Witgood, gentleman, sole nephew to Pecunious Lucre, having unjustly made title and claim to one Jane Meddler, late widow of Anthony Meddler, and now wife to Walkadine Hoard, in consideration of a competent sum of money to discharge my debts, do forever hereafter disclaim any title, right, estate, or interest in or to the said widow, late in the occupation of the said Anthony Meddler, and now in the occupation of Walkadine Hoard, as also neither to lay claim, by virtue of any former contract, grant, promise or demise, to any of her manor, manor houses, parks, groves, meadowgrounds, arable lands, barns, stacks, stables, dove-holes, and coney-burrows; together with all her cattle, money, plate,

197 **peevish** silly, trifling
198 **Set...giblet** proverbial for 'give tit for tat' (Tilley H161)
202 **better** i.e. more binding
205 **back-racket** return of the ball at tennis
214 **Mulligrub's** an allusion to Master Mulligrub from Marston's *The Dutch Courtesan*, which was performed between 1603 and 1605 and printed in the latter year. The mulligrubs was a fit of melancholy or spleen.
223 **trick** In the play's first two editions, this word is capitalized and italicized here and at 4.4.297 (*Trick*), also at 4.5.95 (*Tricks*) in the first edition, to call attention to the connection between these tricks and the play's title.
226–7 **whatsoever...law** i.e. a contract made under duress can later be rendered invalid. Although this principle does not fully apply to Witgood, since the precontract between him and Jane is a fiction, it does apply to Jane's marriage to Hoard. Its articulation here prepares us to understand the implications of her charge at 5.2.132–4.
238 **eightscore odd pounds** about £160, which is less than the bills presented to Witgood at 4.3.29–34 for £190
239 **Tell me** count
240 **desperate** i.e. irretrievable
241–2 **ne'er...accident** i.e. would never be paid except in special circumstances such as these, because the debtor would instead be placed in prison
243–4 **ten...pound** i.e. half of the amount, since there were twenty shillings in a pound
244 **down roundly** reduced promptly
245 **mark** i.e. two-thirds of the amount, since a mark was worth 13*s*. 4*d*. or two-thirds of a pound. The amount comes to slightly over £106.
246 **Tell** count
251–2 **these presents** i.e. the present document
256 **competent** sufficient
259 **occupation** occupancy, possession. Since the word generally refers to property, its application to the widow in this exaggerated account of her fictional possessions suggests how thoroughly she is treated like an estate or territory that has been 'occupied' sexually and economically by her supposed first husband and then by Hoard (at 4.4.260).
262 **demise** conveyance
264 **dove-holes** dovecotes, structures housing doves or pigeons
264–5 **coney-burrows** rabbit warrens
265 **cattle** chattel, movable personal possessions

jewels, borders, chains, bracelets, furnitures, hangings, movables, or immovables, in witness whereof I, the said Theodorus Witgood, have interchangeably set to my hand and seal before these presents, the day and date above written.'

WITGOOD What a precious fortune hast thou slipped here, like a beast as thou art!

HOARD Come, unwilling heart, come.

WITGOOD
Well, Master Hoard, give me the pen. I see
'Tis vain to quarrel with our destiny.

HOARD O, as vain a thing as can be. You cannot commit a greater absurdity, sir.

[*Witgood writes*]

So, so, give me that hand now. Before all these presents, I am friends forever with thee.

WITGOOD Troth, and it were a pity of my heart now if I should bear you any grudge, i'faith.

HOARD Content. I'll send for thy uncle against the wedding dinner. We will be friends once again.

WITGOOD I hope to bring it to pass myself, sir.

HOARD [*to Creditors*] How now? Is't right, my masters?

FIRST CREDITOR 'Tis something wanting, sir; yet it shall be sufficient.

HOARD Why, well said. A good conscience makes a fine show nowadays. Come, my masters. You shall all taste of my wine ere you depart.

ALL We follow you, sir.

[*Exeunt Hoard, Jane, and Scrivener*]

WITGOOD [*aside*] I'll try these fellows now.—A word, sir. What, will you carry me to that widow now?

FIRST CREDITOR Why, do you think we were in earnest, i'faith? Carry you to a rich widow? We should get much credit by that! A noted rioter, a contemptible prodigal! 'Twas a trick we have amongst us to get in our money. Fare you well, sir. *Exeunt Creditors*

WITGOOD Farewell and be hanged, you short pig-haired, ram-headed rascals! He that believes in you shall ne'er be saved, I warrant him! By this new league, I shall have some access unto my love.

[*Niece*] *is above*

NIECE Master Witgood!

WITGOOD My life!

NIECE Meet me presently. That note directs you. I would not be suspected. Our happiness attends us. Farewell!

WITGOOD A word's enough. *Exeunt*

4.5

A curtained bed is thrust forth. Enter Audrey, who spins by the curtains and sings

[AUDREY]
Let the usurer cram him, in interest that excel,
There's pits enough to damn him, before he comes
to hell.
In Holborn some, in Fleet Street some,
Where'er he come, there's some, there's some.

DAMPIT [*within the bed*] *Trahe, traheto*, draw the curtain.

Enter Boy. He opens the curtains, discovering Dampit the usurer in his bed

Give me a sip of sack more.

[*Exit Boy, and reenters shortly with sack*]

Enter Lamprey and Spitchcock

LAMPREY Look you, did not I tell you he lay like the devil in chains, when he was bound for a thousand year?

SPITCHCOCK But I think the devil had no steel bedstaffs. He goes beyond him for that.

LAMPREY Nay, do but mark the conceit of his drinking. One must wipe his mouth for him with a muckender. Do you see, sir?

266 **borders** ornamental work on the edge of garments, which might be made of costly materials
267 **movables** personal property capable of being moved, unlike land or houses
268 **interchangeably** reciprocally
269 **presents** i.e. witnesses
271 **slipped** i.e. let slip
285 **Is't right** i.e. is the sum of money correct?
292 **try** test
299 **pig-haired** close-cropped, a hairstyle of citizens
300 **ram-headed** cuckolded
301 **new league** friendship, truce, referring to the agreement with Hoard
4.5.1–4 **Let... some** The song is by Thomas Ravenscroft, a chorister at St Paul's Church, and was printed in his *Melismata* of 1611, where it is called 'The Scrivener's servant's song of Holborn'. The play's version lacks the first two lines: 'The master is so wise, so wise, that he's proceeded wittol, | My Mistress is a fool, a fool, and yet 'tis the most get-all.' These lines were probably dropped because Dampit is not clearly married, much less a wittol (an acquiescent cuckold). Reavley Gair says that Ravenscroft may have performed the role of Audrey. For Ravenscroft's music, see *Companion*, 140.
1 **excel** surpasses that of others
2 **pits** (*a*) brothels (*b*) women's mouths and genitals (Proverbs 22.14) (*c*) taverns (*d*) debt, the pit he has dug for others (Proverbs 28.10) (*e*) hell
3 **Holborn... Fleet Street** These are the streets where Dampit tramps about on his business, stopping along the way at the *pits* mentioned in (*a*) and (*c*) in the previous note.
5 ***Trahe, traheto*** Latin commands to 'draw', applying to both the curtains of Dampit's bed and to drink. In early productions Dampit was lying in bed on the inner stage, and its curtains served as his bed curtains.
6 **sack** white wine from Spain or the Canary Islands
7–8 **devil... year** The allusion is to Revelations 22:1–2, where an angel binds the devil with a great chain for a thousand years. The chain seems to refer to Dampit's being held up or bound in bed, given the references to *steel bedstaffs* at 4.5.9 and 4.5.164–5, to his being set up *a peg higher* at 4.5.112, and to his being *hung alive in chains* at 4.5.164. Sampson proposes that Dampit may be lying on the *great iron chest* mentioned at 3.4.5, and it is at least likely that he is surrounded by chains and devices that suggest his avarice as well as the need for additional support in his drunken state.
9 **steel bedstaffs** metal slats laid horizontally across the bed frame to support the bedding
11 **conceit** personal vanity, here referring to the need for assistance from another person
12 **muckender** handkerchief

SPITCHCOCK Is this the sick trampler? Why, he is only bedrid with drinking!

LAMPREY True, sir. He spies us.

DAMPIT What, Sir Tristram? You come and see a weak man here, a very weak man—

LAMPREY If you be weak in body, you should be strong in prayer, sir.

DAMPIT O, I have preyed too much, poor man.

LAMPREY There's a taste of his soul for you.

SPITCHCOCK Fah, loathsome!

LAMPREY I come to borrow a hundred pound of you, sir.

DAMPIT Alas, you come at an ill time. I cannot spare it, i'faith. I ha' but two thousand i'th house.

AUDREY Ha, ha, ha!

DAMPIT Out, you girnative quean! The mullipode of villainy, the spinner of concupiscency!

Enter Sir Lancelot and another gentleman

LANCELOT [*to Lamprey and Spitchcock*] Yea, gentlemen, are you here before us? How is he now?

LAMPREY Faith, the same man still. The tavern bitch has bit him i'th' head.

LANCELOT We shall have the better sport with him. Peace!—And how cheers Master Dampit now?

DAMPIT O, my bosom Sir Lancelot! How cheer I? Thy presence is restorative.

LANCELOT But I hear a great complaint of you, Master Dampit, among gallants.

DAMPIT I am glad of that, i'faith. Prithee, what?

LANCELOT They say you are waxed proud o' late, and if a friend visit you in the afternoon, you'll scarce know him.

DAMPIT Fie, fie! Proud? I cannot remember any such thing. Sure I was drunk then.

LANCELOT Think you so, sir?

DAMPIT There 'twas, i'faith. Nothing but the pride of the sack, and so certify 'em.—Fetch sack, sirrah.

BOY [*aside*] A vengeance sack you once!

[*Exit, and returns shortly with sack*]

AUDREY Why, Master Dampit, if you hold on as you begin and lie a little longer, you need not take care how to dispose your wealth. You'll make the vintner your heir.

DAMPIT Out, you babliaminy! You unfeathered, cremitoried quean! You cullisance of scabiosity!

AUDREY Good words, Master Dampit, to speak before a maid and a virgin.

DAMPIT Hang thy virginity upon the pole of carnality!

AUDREY Sweet terms! My mistress shall know 'em.

LAMPREY [*to Spitchcock*] Note but the misery of this usuring slave. Here he lies like a noisome dunghill, full of the poison of his drunken blasphemies, and they to whom he bequeaths all grudge him the very meat that feeds him, the very pillow that eases him. Here may a usurer behold his end. What profits it to be a slave in this world, and a devil i'th' next?

DAMPIT Sir Lancelot? Let me buss thee, Sir Lancelot. Thou art the only friend that I honour and respect.

LANCELOT I thank you for that, Master Dampit.

DAMPIT Farewell, my bosom Sir Lancelot.

LANCELOT [*aside to Lamprey and Spitchcock*] Gentlemen, an you love me, let me step behind you, and one of you fall a-talking of me to him.

LAMPREY Content.—Master Dampit?

DAMPIT So, sir.

LAMPREY Here came Sir Lancelot to see you, e'en now.

DAMPIT Hang him, rascal!

LAMPREY Who, Sir Lancelot?

DAMPIT Pythagorical rascal!

LAMPREY Pythagorical?

DAMPIT Ay, he changes his cloak when he meets a sergeant.

LANCELOT What a rogue's this!

17 **Sir Tristram** After fifteenth-century revivals of the Tristan story, the famous lover's name was associated with any libertine. Dampit addresses him by the name because lampreys were supposed to be strong aphrodisiacs.

21 **preyed** made a prey of, plundered

28 **girnative** given to 'girning' or snarling, grinning

mullipode another coinage of Dampit's, perhaps meaning 'miserable toad' from 'mulligrubs', a fit of depression or low spirits, and 'pode', for toad

29 **spinner** probably referring to a spider. Audrey is spinning as the scene opens, and toads and spiders were thought to be venomous.

concupiscency lust, erotic desire

32–3 **tavern . . . head** The phrase, meaning 'he is drunk', suggests that the women who provide pleasure in taverns also exact their revenge, just as drinking does.

36 **bosom** dear friend

49 **sack** destroy

52 **vintner** wine merchant

53 **babliaminy** Dampit's word for a babbler

53–4 **unfeathered, cremitoried quean** i.e. balding, burnt out whore. *Cremitoried* might refer either to the exhaustion of a prostitute or to her syphilitic or burning condition, which would also account for the loss of hair. Dampit's curses on Audrey continue to project onto her a sexual deviance that has no support elsewhere in the play.

54 **cullisance** badge, meaning 'epitome', from a corruption of *cognizance*

scabiosity suffering from scabies, various skin diseases, here associated with syphilis

57 **pole of carnality** i.e. erect penis

58 **My mistress** a reference, perhaps, to Dampit's wife, who is not clearly mentioned elsewhere, or to his landlady; or an inconsistency in the text. Compare 3.4.63–6.

60 **noisome** harmful, foul-smelling

64 **slave** The usurer was frequently called a slave to his money.

66 **buss** kiss

79 **Pythagorical** An allusion to the Pythagorean doctrine of the transmigration of souls, which in this reductive formulation likens a soul taking on a different body to a person changing his clothes in order to avoid detection by the law.

LAMPREY [*to Dampit*] I wonder you can rail at him, sir. He comes in love to see you.

DAMPIT A louse for his love. His father was a comb maker. I have no need of his crawling love! He comes to have longer day, the superlative rascal!

LANCELOT 'Sfoot, I can no longer endure the rogue.— Master Dampit, I come to take my leave once again, sir.

DAMPIT Who? My dear and kind Sir Lancelot? The only gentleman of England! Let me hug thee. Farewell and a thousand!

LAMPREY Composed of wrongs and slavish flatteries!

LANCELOT Nay, gentlemen, he shall show you more tricks yet. I'll give you another taste of him.

LAMPREY Is't possible?

LANCELOT His memory is upon departing.

DAMPIT Another cup of sack!

LANCELOT Mass, then 'twill be quite gone. Before he drink that, tell him there's a country client come up and here attends for his learned advice.

LAMPREY Enough.

DAMPIT One cup more, and then let the bell toll. I hope I shall be weak enough by that time.

LAMPREY Master Dampit.

DAMPIT Is the sack spouting?

LAMPREY 'Tis coming forward, sir. Here's a countryman, a client of yours, waits for your deep and profound advice, sir.

DAMPIT A coxcombry! Where is he? Let him approach. Set me up a peg higher.

LAMPREY [*to Lancelot*] You must draw near, sir.

DAMPIT [*to Lancelot*] Now, good man fooliaminy, what say you to me now?

LANCELOT [*disguising his voice*] Please your good worship, I am a poor man, sir.

DAMPIT What make you in my chamber then?

LANCELOT I would entreat your worship's device in a just and honest cause, sir.

DAMPIT I meddle with no such matters. I refer 'em to Master No-man's office.

LANCELOT I had but one house left me in all the world, sir, which was my father's, my grandfather's, my great grandfather's, and now a villain has unjustly wrung me out and took possession on't.

DAMPIT Has he such feats? Thy best course is to bring thy *ejectione firmae*, and in seven year thou mayst shove him out by the law.

LANCELOT Alas, an't please your worship, I have small friends and less money.

DAMPIT Heyday! This gear will fadge well. Hast no money? Why then, my advice is thou must set fire o'th' house and so get him out.

LAMPREY That will break strife, indeed.

LANCELOT I thank your worship for your hot counsel, sir. [*Aside to Lamprey and Spitchcock*] Altering but my voice a little, you see he knew me not. You may observe by this that a drunkard's memory holds longer in the voice than in the person. But gentlemen, shall I show you a sight? Behold the little dive-dapper of damnation, Gulf the usurer, for his time worse than t'other.

Enter Hoard with Gulf

LAMPREY What's he comes with him?

LANCELOT Why, Hoard, that married lately the Widow Meddler.

LAMPREY O, I cry you mercy, sir.

HOARD Now gentlemen visitants, how does Master Dampit?

LANCELOT Faith, here he lies e'en drawing in, sir, good canary as fast as he can, sir. A very weak creature, truly. He is almost past memory.

HOARD Fie, Master Dampit. You lie lazing a-bed here, and I come to invite you to my wedding dinner. Up, up, up!

DAMPIT Who's this, Master Hoard? Who hast thou married, in the name of foolery?

HOARD A rich widow.

DAMPIT A Dutch widow?

HOARD A rich widow, one Widow Meddler.

DAMPIT Meddler? She keeps open house.

HOARD She did, I can tell you, in her t'other husband's days—open house for all comers. Horse and man was welcome, and room enough for 'em all.

DAMPIT There's too much for thee, then. Thou mayst let out some to thy neighbours.

GULF What, hung alive in chains? O, spectacle! Bedstaffs of steel! *O monstrum horrendum, informe, ingens cui lumen*

85 **comb maker** a member of one of the newer guilds, which had less prestige than the older guilds. Combs were used to remove lice.
86 **crawling** referring to head lice on combs
87 **longer day** more time to repay his debts
88 **'Sfoot** an oath, from God's foot
92–3 **Farewell . . . thousand** i.e. a thousand farewells
98 **upon** at the point of
100 **quite** utterly
104 **let the bell toll** i.e. for his funeral
111 **coxcombry** i.e. fool
114 **fooliaminy** i.e. foolishness
118 **make** do
119 **device** a feigned malapropism for 'advice'
127 **feats** crimes
128 ***ejectione firmae*** a writ permitting a person who had been ousted from lands or property to recover possession of it
132 **Heyday** an exclamation denoting surprise or wonder, here used ironically
gear will fadge business will succeed
135 **break** (*a*) cause (*b*) destroy, end
141 **dive-dapper** dabchick, a small diving waterfowl, referring to Gulf's diminutive height as well as his moral constitution
146 **O . . . sir** Lamprey's apology for not recognizing Hoard, who may be looking especially fine
149 **canary** a sweet wine from the Canary Islands
150 **past memory** (*a*) a former event, i.e. dead (*b*) beyond being remembered or commemorated (*c*) lacking the capacity to remember or exercise judgement
158 **She . . . house** i.e. is a whore. Dampit puns on the medlar fruit, another name for which was 'openarse'. Hoard takes the remark to mean she is a generous hostess.
162–3 **let out** lend, presumably for money
165–6 ***O . . . ademptum*** Latin for 'O horrible monster, deformed, huge, deprived of sight', from Virgil's *Aeneid* III.658.

ademptum! O Dampit, Dampit! Here's a just judgement shown upon usury, extortion, and trampling villainy!

LANCELOT This' exc'lent. Thief rails upon the thief.

GULF Is this the end of cutthroat usury, brothel, and blasphemy? Now mayst thou see what race a usurer runs.

DAMPIT Why, thou rogue of universality, do not I know thee? Thy sound is like the cuckoo, the Welsh ambassador. Thou cowardly slave that offers to fight with a sick man when his weapon's down! Rail upon me in my naked bed? Why, thou great Lucifer's little vicar, I am not so weak but I know a knave at first sight. Thou inconscionable rascal! Thou that goest upon Middlesex juries and will make haste to give up thy verdict because thou wilt not lose thy dinner, are you answered?

GULF An't were not for shame—

Draws his dagger

DAMPIT Thou wouldst be hanged then.

LAMPREY Nay, you must exercise patience, Master Gulf, always, in a sick man's chamber.

LANCELOT He'll quarrel with none, I warrant you, but those that are bedrid.

DAMPIT Let him come, gentlemen, I am armed. Reach my close-stool hither.

LANCELOT Here will be a sweet fray anon. I'll leave you gentlemen.

LAMPREY Nay, we'll along with you.—Master Gulf.

GULF Hang him, usuring rascal!

LANCELOT Push! Set your strength to his, your wit to his.

AUDREY Pray, gentlemen, depart. His hour's come upon him. [*To Dampit*] Sleep in my bosom; sleep.

LANCELOT Nay, we have enough of him, i'faith. Keep him for the house.
Now make your best.
For thrice his wealth, I would not have his breast.

GULF
A little thing would make me beat him, now he's asleep.

LANCELOT
Mass, then 'twill be a pitiful day when he wakes.
I would be loath to see that day. Come.

GULF
You overrule me, gentlemen, i'faith. *Exeunt*

Finis Actus Quartus

Incipit Actus Quintus 5.1

Enter Lucre and Witgood

WITGOOD
Nay, uncle, let me prevail with you so much.
I'faith, go, now he has invited you.

LUCRE I shall have great joy there, when he has borne away the widow!

WITGOOD Why, la! I thought where I should find you presently. Uncle, o' my troth, 'tis nothing so.

LUCRE What's nothing so, sir? Is not he married to the widow?

WITGOOD No, by my troth is he not, uncle.

LUCRE How?

WITGOOD Will you have the truth on't? He is married to a whore, i'faith!

LUCRE I should laugh at that.

WITGOOD Uncle, let me perish in your favour if you find it not so, and that 'tis I that have married the honest woman.

LUCRE Ha! I'd walk ten mile afoot to see that, i'faith!

WITGOOD And see't you shall, or I'll ne'er see you again.

LUCRE A quean, i'faith? Ha, ha, ha! *Exeunt*

Enter Hoard tasting wine, the Host following in a livery cloak 5.2

HOARD Pup, pup, pup, pup! I like not this wine. Is there never a better tierce in the house?

HOST Yes, sir, there are as good tierce in the house as any are in England.

HOARD Desire your mistress, you knave, to taste 'em all over. She has better skill.

HOST [*aside*] Has she so? The better for her, and the worse for you. *Exit*

HOARD Arthur!

[*Enter Arthur*]

Is the cupboard of plate set out?

ARTHUR All's in order, sir. [*Exit*]

HOARD I am in love with my liveries every time I think on 'em. They make a gallant show, by my troth. Niece!

[*Enter Niece*]

NIECE Do you call, sir?

HOARD Prithee, show a little diligence and overlook the knaves a little. They'll filch and steal today and send whole pasties home to their wives. An thou beest a good niece, do not see me purloined.

NIECE Fear it not, sir.

173–4 **cuckoo . . . ambassador** The cuckoo's harsh call signalled a cuckold. Gwyn Williams suggests that the relation between it and *the Welsh ambassador* may stem from the representation of the bird as a messenger of love in Welsh poetry; but the conjunction here is associated with an unpleasant sound.

176 **my naked bed** i.e. when I am naked in bed

178–9 **Middlesex juries** juries from this county near London were often mentioned as unreliable

188 **close-stool** a covered chamber pot set in a stool

199 **breast** i.e. conscience

5.1.5–6 **I thought . . . presently** i.e. I thought that is what you were thinking

5.2.2 **tierce** cask

3 **tierce** (*a*) a thrust in fencing (*b*) a band or company of soldiers

6 **skill** discrimination in judging wine. Hoard is more readily duped by Jane because he lacks the knowledge of someone of her supposed class.

10 **cupboard of plate** a sideboard or cabinet for displaying plate or dishes, or the service of plate itself

17 **pasties** pies

[*Aside*] I have cause. Though the feast be prepared for you,
Yet it serves fit for my wedding dinner, too. [*Exit*]

Enter Lamprey and Spitchcock

HOARD Master Lamprey and Master Spitchcock, two the most welcome gentlemen alive! Your fathers and mine were all free o'th' fishmongers.

LAMPREY They were indeed, sir. You see bold guests, sir, soon entreated.

HOARD And that's best, sir.

[*Enter Servant*]

How now, sirrah?

SERVANT There's a coach come to th' door, sir. [*Exit*]

HOARD My Lady Foxstone, o' my life. Mistress Jane Hoard, wife! Mass, 'tis her ladyship indeed!

[*Enter Lady Foxstone*]

Madam, you are welcome to an unfurnished house, dearth of cheer, scarcity of attendance.

LADY FOXSTONE You are pleased to make the worst, sir.

HOARD Wife!

[*Enter Jane*]

LADY FOXSTONE Is this your bride?

HOARD Yes, madam.—Salute my Lady Foxstone.

JANE Please you, madam, awhile to taste the air in the garden?

LADY FOXSTONE 'Twill please us well.

Exeunt [Jane and Lady Foxstone]

HOARD
Who would not wed? The most delicious life!
No joys are like the comforts of a wife!

LAMPREY So we bachelors think, that are not troubled with them!

[*Enter Servant*]

SERVANT Your worship's brother with another ancient gentleman are newly alighted, sir. [*Exit*]

HOARD Master Onesiphorus Hoard! Why, now our company begins to come in.

[*Enter Onesiphorus Hoard, Limber and Kix*]

My dear and kind brother, welcome, i'faith.

ONESIPHORUS You see we are men at an hour, brother.

HOARD Ay, I'll say that for you, brother. You keep as good an hour to come to a feast as any gentleman in the shire. What, old Master Limber and Master Kix! Do we meet, i'faith, jolly gentlemen?

LIMBER We hope you lack guests, sir?

HOARD O, welcome, welcome! We lack still such guests as your worships.

ONESIPHORUS Ah, sirrah brother, have you catched up Widow Meddler?

HOARD From 'em all, brother. And I may tell you, I had mighty enemies, those that stuck sore. Old Lucre is a sore fox, I can tell you, brother.

ONESIPHORUS Where is she? I'll go seek her out. I long to have a smack at her lips!

HOARD And most wishfully, brother. See where she comes.

[*Re-enter Jane and Lady Foxstone*]

Give her a smack now, we may hear it all the house over.

Both [Jane and Onesiphorus] turn back

JANE O heaven, I am betrayed! I know that face!

HOARD Ha, ha, ha! Why, how now? Are you both ashamed? Come, gentlemen, we'll look another way.

ONESIPHORUS Nay, brother, hark you. Come, you're disposed to be merry?

HOARD Why do we meet else, man?

ONESIPHORUS That's another matter. I was ne'er so feared in my life but that you had been in earnest.

HOARD How mean you, brother?

ONESIPHORUS You said she was your wife?

HOARD Did I so? By my troth, and so she is.

ONESIPHORUS By your troth, brother?

HOARD What reason have I to dissemble with my friends, brother? If marriage can make her mine, she is mine! Why?

ONESIPHORUS Troth, I am not well of a sudden. I must crave pardon, brother. I came to see you, but I cannot stay dinner, i'faith.

HOARD I hope you will not serve me so, brother.

LIMBER By your leave, Master Hoard.

HOARD What now? What now? Pray gentlemen, you were wont to show yourselves wise men.

LIMBER
But you have shown your folly too much here.

HOARD How?

KIX
Fie, fie! A man of your repute and name!
You'll feast your friends, but cloy 'em first with shame.

HOARD
This grows too deep. Pray let us reach the sense.

LIMBER In your old age, dote on a courtesan—

HOARD Ha?

KIX Marry a strumpet!

HOARD Gentlemen!

ONESIPHORUS And Witgood's quean!

24 **free o'th' fishmongers** members of the Fishmongers' Guild, as the names Lamprey and Spitchcock suggest

30 **Foxstone** 'Stones' were testicles, so the name refers to the testicles of a fox. When powdered, these were supposed to be an aphrodisiac.

32 **unfurnished** unprepared

45–6 **another ancient gentleman** The subsequent dialogue indicates that two gentlemen accompany Onesiporus Hoard.

50 **men at an hour** punctual

55 **lack** are without, have too few

61 **stuck sore** thrust forcefully. *Stuck* is a fencing term, from *stoccado*.

62 **sore** stern, hard

68 **I am...face** It is clear as early as 1.1.114–15 that Onesiphorus Hoard knew of the relationship between Jane and Witgood when they were all in Leicestershire.

74 **feared** afraid

86 **serve** treat

HOARD O! Nor lands, nor living?
ONESIPHORUS Living!
HOARD [*to Jane*] Speak!
JANE
Alas, you know at first, sir,
I told you I had nothing.
HOARD
Out, out! I am cheated! Infinitely cozened!
LIMBER Nay, Master Hoard—
Enter Witgood and Lucre [with the Niece]
HOARD
A Dutch widow, a Dutch widow, a Dutch widow!
LUCRE
Why, nephew, shall I trace thee still a liar?
Wilt make me mad? Is not yon thing the widow?
WITGOOD
Why, la! You are so hard o' belief, uncle.
By my troth, she's a whore.
LUCRE Then thou'rt a knave.
WITGOOD *Negatur argumentum*, uncle.

LUCRE *Probo tibi*, nephew. He that knows a woman to be a quean must needs be a knave. Thou sayst thou knowst her to be one. *Ergo*, if she be a quean, thou'rt a knave.

WITGOOD *Negatur sequela majoris*, uncle. He that knows a woman to be a quean must needs be a knave: I deny that.

HOARD Lucre and Witgood, you're both villains. Get you out of my house.

LUCRE
Why, didst not invite me to thy wedding dinner?
WITGOOD And are not you and I sworn perpetual friends
before witness, sir, and were both drunk upon't?
HOARD
Daintily abused! You've put a junt upon me!
LUCRE
Ha, ha, ha!
HOARD A common strumpet!
WITGOOD Nay, now
You wrong her, sir. If I were she, I'd have
The law on you for that. I durst depose for her
She ne'er had common use, nor common thought.
JANE [*to Hoard*]
Despise me, publish me: I am your wife.
What shame can I have now but you'll have part?
If in disgrace you share, I sought not you.
You pursued me, nay, forced me.
Had I friends would follow it,
Less than your action has been proved a rape.
ONESIPHORUS Brother!
JANE
Nor did I ever boast of lands unto you,
Money or goods. I took a plainer course,
And told you true I'd nothing.
If error were committed, 'twas by you.
Thank your own folly. Nor has my sin been
So odious but worse has been forgiven.

100 **Nor lands, nor living** These words echo Jane's question at 3.1.168 about Witgood.
104 **I...nothing** See 3.1.205 and note.
107 **Dutch widow** Hoard learned that the phrase referred to a prostitute at 3.3.18.
108 **trace** find
112 ***Negatur argumentum*** Latin for '[your] argument is denied', a phrase appropriate to disputations at the universities.
113 ***Probo tibi*** 'I will prove it to you.'
knows (*a*) perceives, recognizes (*b*) has carnal knowledge of through intercourse
115 ***Ergo*** therefore. The syllogistic and Latinate manner in which Witgood and Lucre dispute the disposition of Jane's sexuality parodies her objectification by Onesiphorus Hoard, Limber, and Kix in the previous lines. But Lucre's conclusion is that Witgood is equally to blame.
116 ***Negatur sequela majoris*** 'The implication of your major premise is denied.' Through denying the premise, Witgood avoids acknowledging his complicity in Jane's construction as a 'whore'.
124 **junt** trick, cheat
125 **common strumpet** The phrase suggested promiscuity in a way that *courtesan* did not, since courtesans in English Renaissance drama were often kept by a man rather than generally available. *Common* also implies a lower class of woman than one who would be described as a courtesan. See Introduction.
126–8 **I'd...thought** Witgood uses the language of legal defence to deny that Jane was ever commonly available as a sexual companion and to observe that Hoard's statement leaves him open to Jane's charge of slander in an ecclesiastical court. See Introduction.
127 **depose** offer testimony to a court, under oath
128 **common** (*a*) promiscuous (*b*) lower class
use i.e. for sexual purposes
thought reputation, i.e. was never considered to be generally available
129 **publish** publically denounce
132 **You pursued...forced me** Jane is referring to the coercion applied to her consent to the spousal at 3.1.192–225. She is charging that she was married under duress.
133 **friends** kinsmen, near relations, or advisors. As a married woman or *feme covert*, Jane would not be allowed to bring a suit on her own behalf in civil court. But were someone willing to bring the suit for her (and Witgood is a good candidate, since he witnessed the forced marriage at 3.1.192–225), the laws on record imply that she may have had some chance of success. Even though English law defined women who were unmarried but sexually experienced as 'whores', it also held that she who refused consent to a sexual act was not, at that time, a 'whore'. See the note on rape at 5.2.134 below and the Introduction for further discussion.
follow it prosecute the case
134 **Less...rape** The word 'rape' during the early modern period referred not only to forced sexual relations but to the act of abduction. Rich widows were especially vulnerable to abduction by men seeking to gain control of their wealth by forcing their consent to marriage. *Proved* in this passage implies that some suits by women against their abductors may have been successful. Hoard planned a feigned abduction of Jane at 3.1.218–25 and brought it off at 3.3.67–8. Although the latter scene is dramatized, there were no witnesses among characters in the play besides Hoard and his friends. Jane's resistance or compliance would therefore be difficult to establish in court. She does prefer to be married to Hoard, because he is her best option in a world that characterizes a woman in her situation as a 'whore'. Hence her charges of forced marriage and abduction are designed to pressure him into honouring his marriage as well as recognizing his own errors. See Introduction.

Nor am I so deformed but I may challenge
The utmost power of any old man's love.
She that tastes not sin before twenty,
Twenty to one but she'll taste it after.
Most of you old men are content to marry
Young virgins and take that which follows,
Where marrying one of us, you both save
A sinner, and are quit from a cuckold forever.
"And more, in brief, let this your best thoughts win:
She that knows sin, knows best how to hate sin."

HOARD
Cursed be all malice! Black are the fruits of spite,
And poison first their owners. O my friends,
I must embrace shame, to be rid of shame.
Concealed disgrace prevents a public name.
Ah Witgood! Ah Theorodus!

WITGOOD Alas, sir, I was pricked in conscience to see her well bestowed, and where could I bestow her better than upon your pitiful worship? Excepting but myself, I dare swear she's a virgin. And now by marrying your niece, I have banished myself forever from her. She's mine aunt now, by my faith, and there's no meddling with mine aunt, you know—a sin against my nuncle.

JANE
Lo, gentlemen, before you all,
In true reclaimèd form I fall.
[*She kneels*]
Henceforth forever I defy
The glances of a sinful eye,
Waving of fans, which some suppose
Tricks of fancy; treading of toes,
Wringing of fingers, biting the lip,
The wanton gait, th'alluring trip;
All secret friends and private meetings,
Close-borne letters and bawds' greetings;
Feigning excuse to women's labours
When we are sent for to th' next neighbours;
Taking false physic, and ne'er start
To be let blood, though sign be at heart;
Removing chambers, shifting beds
To welcome friends in husbands' steads;
Them to enjoy and you to marry,
They first served, while you must tarry,
They to spend and you to gather,
They to get and you to father.
These and thousand thousand more,
New reclaimed, I now abhor.
[*She rises*]

LUCRE
Ah, here's a lesson, rioter, for you.

WITGOOD
I must confess my follies. I'll down, too.
[*He kneels*]
And here forever I disclaim
The cause of youth's undoing: game.
Chiefly dice, those true outlanders
That shake out beggars, thieves and panders;
Soul-wasting surfeits, sinful riots,

142 **challenge** lay claim to. Jane is not modest about her power to win Hoard's affection.

148 **one of us** someone who is sexually experienced but unmarried, which was sufficient by the standards of the time to designate her a 'whore'

149 **quit ... forever** A man who marries a woman reputed to be a 'whore' is saved from the danger of becoming a cuckold because his wife's sexuality was not contained before the marriage began. **cuckold** a husband whose wife commits adultery. Horns were often set on a man's head as a sign of public ridicule for his being unable to control his wife's sexuality. The word derives from *cuculus*, which was Latin for the cuckoo bird.

150–1 **"And ... sin."** These lines appear in quotation marks in the play's first two editions.

159 **pitiful** compassionate

159–60 **Excepting ... virgin** The play provides no reason to doubt this assertion.

163 **aunt** (*a*) the wife of Witgood's uncle (*b*) mistress, prostitute, a meaning associated with the sexual meanings of 'meddling'
nuncle uncle

166–85 **Henceforth ... abhor** This speech does not reflect on Jane's past so much as her future, for the 'tricks' she abjures are those of married women. One might read it as suggesting how fully Jane has accepted her role as a wife since she was married in 3.1.

166 **defy** renounce

169 **fancy** love

169–70 **treading ... lip** Compare Dekker and Webster's *Northward Ho!* at 2.2.11–14: 'what treads of the toe, salutations by winckes, discourse by bitings of the lip, amorous glances, sweete stolne kisses when your husbands backs turn'd, would passe between them'.

170 **Wringing** clasping

171 **trip** quick, light movements of the feet

173 **Close-borne** secretly conveyed

174 **women's labours** childbirth

176 **physic** medical treatment

176–7 **ne'er ... heart** Jane promises to avoid the *physic* of blood-letting when the astrological sign is in Leo (i.e. *at heart*), since that sign and some others were considered 'most dangerous for blood-letting, the Moon being in them', according to almanacs and medical books such as *A prognostication everlasting of right good effect* (1576) by Leonard Digges. Given the context, the phrase *though sign be at heart* probably also refers to a wife's sexual desires, which could prompt her to use the treatment as an excuse for infidelity or for being sexually unavailable to her husband, thereby making the excuse a form of *false physic*.

178 **Removing ... beds** moving to different bedrooms

179 **friends** lovers

180–3 **Them ... father** The references to *them* and *they* in contrast to *you* relate to lovers as compared to husbands. Jane is directing much of this speech to her own husband, Hoard.

183 **get** beget
father i.e. to parent or raise as one's biological child

185 **abhor** (*a*) loathe, hate (*b*) literally, move away from being a whore. This speech is Jane's final, spirited performance as a faithful wife.

188–200 **And ... all** Witgood offers gambling, gallantry, and riotous indulgence as the counterpart to the deceits of wives, but unlike Jane's version of what she might eventually have the chance to do, Witgood gives an account of the life he already led. She renounces the future, he the past. Both speeches serve as parodic substitutes for the parallel marriage vows from a hero and heroine that conclude more conventional comedies.

189 **game** gambling

190 **outlanders** foreigners

191 **shake out** i.e. make

Queans' evils, doctors' diets,
'Pothecaries' drugs, surgeons' glisters,
Stabbing of arms for a common mistress,
Ribboned favours, ribald speeches,
Dear perfumed jackets, penniless breeches,
Dutch flapdragons, healths in urine,
Drabs that keep a man too sure in:
I do defy you all.
Lend me each honest hand, for here I rise
A reclaimed man, loathing the general vice.
[*He rises*]

HOARD
So, so, all friends. The wedding dinner cools.
Who seem most crafty prove oft times most fools.
[*Exeunt*]

Finis

ADDITIONAL PASSAGE

A [*Additional Passage between 3.1.29 and 3.1.30*]

WITGOOD
I know you have been kind; however now,
Either by wrong report, or false incitement,
Your gentleness is injured. In such a state
As this a man cannot want foes.
If on the sudden he begin to rise,
No man that lives can count his enemies.
You had some intelligence, I warrant ye,
From an ill-willer.

SECOND CREDITOR Faith, we heard you brought up a rich widow, sir, and were suddenly to marry her.

WITGOOD Ay, why there it was. I knew 'twas so. But since you are so well resolved of my faith toward you, let me be so much favoured of you, I beseech you all—

ALL O, it shall not need, i'faith, sir—

WITGOOD As to lie still awhile, and bury my debts in silence, till I be fully possessed of the widow. For the truth is, I may tell you as my friends—

ALL O, O, O—

193 **Queans' evils** venereal diseases, in contrast to the 'king's evil', scrofula
194 **glisters** enemas
195 **Stabbing of arms** drawing one's own blood and then mixing it with wine to drink a toast to one's mistress.
195–8 **Stabbing ... urine** Compare Marston's *Dutch Courtesan* 4.2.59–63: 'if I have not as religiously vowed my heart to you, been drunk to your health, swallowed flapdragons, eat glasses, drunk urine, stabbed arms, and done all the offices of protested gallantry for your sake ...'.
196 **Ribboned** knots of ribbon given as favours to lovers
198 **Dutch flapdragons** raisins or similar objects set on fire and drunk in brandy as they flamed
healths in urine wine mixed with urine used to toast one's mistress
199 **Drabs** prostitutes
too sure in i.e. too tightly controlled
200 **defy** renounce
202 **the general vice** i.e. all vices
204 **Who ... fools** The line approaches the sense of two proverbs, 'To a crafty man a crafty and a half' (Tilley M393) and 'He that deceives another is oft deceived himself' (Tilley D170).
A.4 **want** lack
9 **brought up** escorted to town
12 **resolved** convinced

A MAD WORLD, MY MASTERS

Text edited and introduced by Peter Saccio, annotated by Celia R. Daileader

DICK FOLLYWIT, a prodigal trickster, replenishes his purse by thrice robbing his grandfather Sir Bounteous Progress. Frank Gullman, a Courtesan, furnishes Penitent Brothel with the opportunity for sex with Mistress Harebrain; Penitent in turn helps her to fleece both Sir Bounteous and two young heirs, Inesse and Possibility. These plots are standard fare deriving from the competition for women and money in ancient Roman comedy, the prodigal stories of the Elizabethan stage, and the cony-catching pamphlets that describe the swindles and scams of sixteenth-century London. Middleton himself had included in *The Ant and the Nightingale* a brief variant of the Penitent/Harebrain plot: a starchwoman-bawd arranges adultery between a citizen's wife and a gentleman. In *A Mad World, My Masters* Middleton effectively joins his two major stories in the marriage of Follywit to the Courtesan, each deceived about the character of the other. Using the popular device of an internal play that reflects and resolves the main plots, Middleton brings his play to conclusion with a richly inventive and funny play-within-a-play that highlights *Mad World*'s concern with performance.

With its intrigues for money and sex, the play strongly resembles the other London comedies Middleton wrote for performance by the Children of Paul's. In this case, however, the action is not limited to London: nine of its nineteen scenes are set at the country house of Sir Bounteous, to which other characters travel. (The allusion to Newbury Assizes in 4.4 suggests a location in Berkshire.) The ten London scenes are less insistent on the topography and practices of the town than are other Middleton comedies: fewer landmarks are mentioned, and the plot does not dwell heavily on the occupations, social tensions, and financial chicanery of the city. The Courtesan plies her trade in both town and country, as has her Mother before her. The story of Penitent Brothel and the Harebrains follows the familiar pattern of a gentleman cuckolding a citizen, but although the cast list given in the second edition (1640) identifies Penitent as a gentleman and Harebrain as a citizen no explicit use is made in the script of their class difference. They meet as equals in Act 4 and are entertained without distinction by Sir Bounteous in Act 5. The emphasis of the cuckolding plot therefore falls upon the cleverness of the scheme rather than the social fissures it could reveal. Furthermore, no innocent person in *Mad World* is wholly despoiled of his property like Easy in *Michaelmas Term*—the chief victim of plunder, Sir Bounteous, is surprisingly cheerful about his losses—and no one suffers the complete degradation of Dampit in *A Trick to Catch the Old One*. *Mad World* is quite an amiable play.

Its characteristic dramatic actions lie in disguise and theatrical performance. The chief trickster, Follywit, appears as Lord Owemuch, as a masked burglar, as the Courtesan, and as a player in a travelling troupe who functions successively as manager, prologue, and actor improvising a play. Even in his final appearance 'in his own shape', kneeling before Sir Bounteous, he likens himself to an actor concluding a performance with a prayer for the company's patron. The opening dialogue, when Follywit wears no disguise, forms a kind of green-room scene in which he recalls earlier transformations of character and costume and prepares a new role. His comrades join his performances in appropriate supporting parts, planned or improvised. The other major intriguer, the Courtesan, adopts roles without disguise or name-change. To Inesse, Possibility, and eventually Follywit, she is a pious virgin. To Harebrain she is a spiritual director for his wife. In the central scene of the play she is (for Harebrain) a sick woman uttering her dying words and (for Sir Bounteous) his mistress undergoing the pangs of pregnancy, both roles being supported by Penitent's performance as doctor. She too has a green-room passage in the first scene, receiving stage directions from her Mother. Mistress Harebrain carries out in detail the Courtesan's advice for acting the role of chaste wife, and a devil impersonates Mistress Harebrain to tempt Penitent into further sin.

The complexities of performance ramify. When Follywit appears the morning after the robbery as Lord Owemuch bound in his bed; when the Courtesan delivers moral advice to a Mistress Harebrain who is actually in the next room committing adultery; when a devil appears as a blatantly lascivious Mistress Harebrain (clearly played by the same actor who plays the lustful but decorously behaved 'real' Mistress Harebrain); and when Penitent and Mistress Harebrain convert their repentance for adultery into a pretence for Harebrain's benefit that no adultery could occur, the dizzying vortex of performances spins into ever more imaginative scripts. It is appropriate that *Mad World* should end with a play-within-the-play, that the inner play, *The Slip*, should exist only as a last-ditch improvisation by Follywit and his Lieutenant, and that a genuine 'Constable i'th' commonwealth' should be taken as 'the Constable i'th' comedy' (5.2.172–5). The overall effect is one of scrambling ingenuity exerting itself in resourceful role-playing.

It is indeed a mad world—the schemes of the two chief intriguers become fantastic. The Courtesan's virginity has been sold some fifteen times, she has convinced the impotent Sir Bounteous of his sexual prowess, and in the sickroom scene she bilks three men and helps cuckold a fourth. Follywit goes to great lengths to rob Sir Bounteous of a mere watch, chain, and jewel when he has already twice stolen heaps of his grandsire's money and treasure. Follywit and the Courtesan so often play roles that we gain little idea of their real personalities. Follywit justifies his thefts by citing the stingy jealousy of old men and asking pointedly how they got their money, while the Courtesan adeptly exploits men's contradictory stereotypes of women (they are shy and modest, they easily fall ill, they are cunning contrivers), but one cannot find in their speeches the serious concern about economics or gender that some of Middleton's other characters express. These plucky opportunists make the best of their circumstances, plume themselves on their successes, and take setbacks with resilience.

More deeply rooted comic eccentricity appears in Sir Bounteous, Harebrain, and Penitent. Explicitly identified as a character whose 'humour' (2.1.3–4) is extravagant hospitality, Sir Bounteous is as prodigal as his grandson. His appearance—'a little short old spiny gentleman in a great doublet' (3.2.7)—suggests his self-inflation. Eager as a host (witness his repetitive phrasing), enormously pleased with his possessions and courtly manners, harmlessly testy with servants, Sir Bounteous is a comic rendition of the great country householder idealized in such poems as Jonson's 'To Penshurst'. His knighthood derives from wealth, not military distinction. His social ambition is clear in his obsequious address to Lord Owemuch and his effort to establish intimacy with him. His proud display of his 'organs' hints at a ludicrous wish for bodily familiarity; he recommends Follywit to Owemuch as if he were offering an attractive catamite; and his grief over the tying up of Owemuch ('Ah, the binding of my lord cuts my heart in two pieces' [2.6.17–19]) sounds like a misplaced meditation on the Passion of Christ. His welcome to the non-noble Harebrains and Penitent is also warm, however, and with all visitors, even footmen, he loves the role of tour-guide. Despite his keeping Follywit short of money and his self-deceived relation with the Courtesan, there is something innocent in his jovial bounty. In the final deception of *The Slip* he is large enough to move from momentary vexation to enjoyment of the jest, and to ask only that his guests not laugh at him 'seven year hence' (5.2.184).

Harebrain is involved in deeper ironies. While many husbands in Jacobean drama fear cuckoldom, with or without warrant, Harebrain's suspicion is strikingly 'fantastic but deserved' (1.1.108). It is deserved because his wife desires Penitent from the start—she requires no persuasion, only opportunity. It is fantastic because her conduct gives no overt cause for jealousy, and his precautions and tests both prove her fidelity to his satisfaction (yet he must test again) and afford her the chance to cuckold him. He 'innocently ... plot[s] his own abuse' (1.1.113–17). Vain (he would teach other husbands how to guard their wives), emotionally labile (witness his tears and kisses), insistent on his own absurd views (his verbal repetitions, unlike Sir Bounteous's, sound peevish), he is obsessed by sex. He remarks on the 'luscious' quality of Elizabethan erotic poetry (1.2.47–8), dismisses all non-sexual sins as trivial, bursts into lubricious *carpe diem* verse when describing the Courtesan's illness, and even remarks on the 'pretty' appearance of Follywit-as-Prologue (5.2.29). His eavesdropping in the sickroom scene makes him the aural equivalent of a voyeur upon the event he most fears, an event filtered through to his misunderstanding by the ambiguities of the Courtesan's monologue. In his concern with the tortures hell provides (for adulterers only) and his delight in the strict tests he sets his wife, pleasure is linked with pain. That both arise for him from his own inadequacies is suggested by an odd textual crux. In Act 5, his name is twenty times given as 'Shortrod' rather than 'Harebrain'. (One line, probably to be spoken by him, is assigned to a mysterious 'Nub'.) 'Shortrod' is too good a name for a sexually anxious cuckold to be a compositor's accident, and misreading 'Harebrain' as 'Shortrod' (or 'Nub'—a small bodily protruberance!) is a very unlikely printing-house mistake. In the Textual Introduction of this edition I have argued in more detail that both names are authorial, that the character's full name is Shortrod Harebrain. Evidently Middleton intended to label this character with genital deficiencies as well as folly. In *Michaelmas Term* there are puns to this effect on Shortyard's name, and both Shortyard and Shortrod Harebrain display unusual warmth when bonding with other males. Whatever his quirks, however, Harebrain retains sufficient self-esteem to enter into the final festivities as a genial guest.

The characterization of Penitent Brothel is more complex and problematic. Although he hesitates to take the role of physician, his masterful use of medical jargon and his ironical asides make him a trickster nearly as skilful as his ally the Courtesan. His ardour for Mistress Harebrain emerges occasionally in verse that rises out of the comic plotting as the lyrical descants of the young lovers in Verdi's *Falstaff* soar above the merriment of the Windsor wives. But he is the only person in *Mad World* with a vivid sense of sin, and the tonal dissonance between his fear of damnation and the play's amoral intrigue has puzzled modern critics. His first soliloquy runs the gamut from appreciation of Follywit's pranks through harsh self-condemnation to shrewd assessment of Harebrain. His spiritual anxiety climaxes in his spontaneous repentance, his horrified loathing of the devil who tempts him, and his persuasive sermon to Mistress Harebrain. The repentance cannot be insincere, and is particularly striking when he abandons his conventionally sexist condemnation of 'slime, corruption, woman' as the source of sin (4.1.18) to shoulder responsibility for both his sin and hers (4.5.48–52). Some readers have felt that his spiritual intensity, with its use of godly precepts ridiculed in earlier scenes, splits the play apart. Penitent himself is perplexed: the sudden intrusion of a devil is so surprising that he requires repeated assurances that Mistress Harebrain herself has not visited him. The audience must share his perplexity. We too see and hear some one whose face, dress, and voice are precisely those of Mistress Harebrain. She behaves very differently from the woman we have seen before, but sexual consummation can cause a release of inhibitions, and this is the first time the lovers have had the stage to themselves. Middleton's irony here enters the realm of the grotesque, for the spiritual anguish of the repentance scenes is studded with farcical effects. For anyone to shift abruptly from demure propriety to eager sexuality is in itself funny. This woman then rhymes (as several critics have noted) like Ogden Nash; Penitent's quotations from *Hamlet* clash bizarrely with her jocular familiarity; and his notion of a woman being 'part a virgin' (4.5.69) sounds as absurd as being 'slightly pregnant'. Middleton skilfully solders this grotesquerie back into the amoral irony of *Mad World*. Mistress Harebrain's already demonstrated ability to deal dryly with her husband's emotional outbursts and Penitent's skill at playing doctor prepare us for their smooth response to the unexpected entrance of the cuckold. Nothing is given away, Harebrain once again discards his jealousy, and the sequence comes blandly to rest in the play's characteristic effect of resourceful role-playing.

Having plunged into moral passion, *Mad World* glides out of it. The dominating pattern of the play is *quid pro quo*: the jealous husband is cuckolded, the ambitious host and the steward who would seduce his master's mistress are cheated of their own bribes, thief and whore ignorantly marry each other. *Quid pro quo* may inspire moral reflection in an audience, and is indeed invoked by some Jacobean characters in weighty contexts, as when Shakespeare's Edgar moralizes the blinding of Gloucester and Webster's Ferdinand concludes, 'Like diamonds we are cut with our own dust'. Here the principle rings out in the alarm of a stolen watch and is articulated in Follywit's shoulder-shrugging line, 'Tricks are repaid, I see' (5.2.305). It is an aesthetic more than a moral pattern: a comic recoil closer to Somerset Maugham's ironic *Circle* than to Jonson's judgemental *Volpone*. It invites, not censure and reform, but mildly rueful pleasure at the neatness of the thing and whimsical acceptance of the mad world. A constable earnestly doing his duty is bound and gagged by the comedy, and everyone else applauds. Providing applause for Follywit is half the function of his comrades; Penitent fills the sickroom scene with praise of the Courtesan's wit; Sir Bounteous and his guests intersperse *The Slip* with their half-misguided delight. Middleton cues the reaction he wants from his own audience, and the publisher's preface in the 1640 edition urges readers to applaud the action and to disregard as relics of old-fashioned convention the moralizing couplets that end some scenes.

The play suggests that we enjoy not only witty contrivance by minds but also resourceful activity of bodies. In the best recent edition of *Mad World*, Standish Henning rightly declares that 'the play revels in obscenity', body jokes that he finds too obvious to explicate. In the present edition Celia R. Daileader does annotate them (and continues discussion of the sexual issues in her recent book *Eroticism on the Renaissance Stage*). Bodily actions and allusions, both decent and obscene, form a large and vital element of the play. Comic physical action appears in many of the entrances and exits (the servants especially tend to be hasty or delayed or clumsy or abrupt); in the Courtesan's fake wrestling with Follywit and with her Mother; in the dancing of Sir Bounteous and of the devil; in Follywit's cross-dressing and the hints of polymorphous sexuality; in the very breath of Follywit, whose taint of alcohol and tobacco nearly gives away his female disguise. The robbery scenes of Act 2 hinge on 'binding', where the literal tying up of characters also evokes legal obligation and intestinal constipation. The body's abilities concentrate particularly in the sickroom scene, where the Courtesan's moans disguise the sounds of offstage sex, and she feigns some action that drives Inesse and Possibility hastily away. Puking and purging are the obvious alternatives, and although the former is more easily acted, the latter coheres with the dialogue about stools and the physician's function of 'loosing' his patients. If, at the centre of this play, a beautiful and much-courted woman fakes a sonorous bowel movement to the applause of one man and the disgust of two others, the world is indeed ingeniously mad.

So theatrical a play merits a richer stage history than *Mad World* has had. The title-pages of the two early editions note performances at Paul's around 1606 and at Salisbury Court by 1640. Restoration memoirists note performances at Oxford in 1661 and in London around 1662. Thereafter *Mad World* was subjected to adaptation and pillage. Aphra Behn borrowed parts of the Owemuch robbery for *The City Heiress* (1682). Christopher Bullock made a six-scene farcical afterpiece called *The Slip* (1715) out of the Owemuch robbery and the play-within-the-play. In the same year Charles Johnson combined the robbery scenes with parts of Fletcher's *Custom of the Country* to create the full-length *Country Lasses*, which in turn was pillaged by William Kenrick in 1778. Going back directly to *Mad World* in 1786, Leonard Macnally created a two-act farce called *The April Fool* out of parts of Middleton's Acts 1, 2, and 5. Two American revivals have occurred: one at Harvard University in 1940 (again the Follywit scenes only) and another off-Broadway at the Bouwerie Lane Theatre in 1978. In 1977 Barrie Keeffe used the title and the general notion of city confidence tricks to create a contemporary satire for the Joint Stock Company at the Young Vic. In 1998 Middleton's own text returned to the London stage, for the first time since the seventeenth century, in a lively production at Shakespeare's Globe. Sue Lefton, a director of remarkable inventiveness in stage movement, zestfully animated Middleton's farcical complications. Amid a generally able cast David Rintoul in particular made Penitent Brothel coherent by stressing the fanaticism with which he responded to the least impulse, whether he was playing doctor, sexually rampant, or bitterly repentant.

SEE ALSO

Music and dance: *Companion*, 142
Textual introduction and apparatus: *Companion*, 586
Authorship and date: *Companion*, 355

A Mad World, My Masters

[for the Children of Paul's]

THE PERSONS

SIR BOUNTEOUS Progress, an old rich country knight
GUNWATER, steward to Sir Bounteous

Dick FOLLYWIT, grandson to Sir Bounteous
LIEUTENANT Mawworm, ENSIGN Oboe } comrades to Follywit
Another comrade disguised as a FOOTMAN
Other COMRADES to Follywit

Master Shortrod HAREBRAIN, a jealous husband
WIFE to Master Harebrain
RAFE, servant to Master Harebrain
Master PENITENT Brothel, in love with Harebrain's Wife
JASPER, servant to Master Penitent

COURTESAN, Frank Gullman, mistress to Sir Bounteous, bawd to Master Penitent
MOTHER to the Courtesan, an old gentlewoman, bawd to her daughter
MAN, servant to the Courtesan

Master INESSE, Master POSSIBILITY } two eldest brothers and heirs, suitors to the Courtesan
Two KNIGHTS, visitors to Sir Bounteous

CONSTABLE
Two or three WATCHMEN, hired by Master Harebrain
SERVANTS to Sir Bounteous
NEIGHBOURS to Sir Bounteous

SUCCUBUS, a devil in the likeness of Harebrain's Wife

1.1 *Incipit Actus Primus*

Enter Dick Follywit and his consorts, Lieutenant Mawworm, Ensign Oboe, and others his comrades

LIEUTENANT O captain, regent, principal!

ENSIGN What shall I call thee? The noble spark of bounty, the lifeblood of society!

FOLLYWIT Call me your forecast, you whoresons. When you come drunk out of a tavern, 'tis I must cast your plots into form still, 'tis I must manage the prank, or I'll not give a louse for the proceeding. I must let fly my civil fortunes, turn wild-brain, lay my wits upo'th' tenters, you rascals, to maintain a company of villains whom I love in my very soul and conscience.

LIEUTENANT Aha, our little forecast!

FOLLYWIT Hang you, you have bewitched me among you. I was as well given till I fell to be wicked, my grandsire

Title *A Mad World, My Masters* (proverbial)
1.1.0.2 *consorts* companions
0.3 *Mawworm* an intestinal worm, a parasite, likely to provoke a peevish temper in its victim
Oboe indicating the high-pitched voice of the child actor
1 **captain** perhaps figurative, but Follywit and his consorts may be now-indigent military men returning to civilian life after the signing of the peace treaty with Spain in 1604—hence the reference to 'civil fortunes', below.
4 **forecast** forethought, prudence; one who forecasts, or predicts the future
6 **still** always
8 **civil fortunes** the chance of a civilian career, with a pun on 'civil' as decent or seemly in behaviour
9 **tenters** a frame for stretching cloth
10 **conscience** inmost thought; mind
12–24 **Hang ... measure** a parody of Sir John Oldcastle's speech in *1 Henry IV*: 'I was as virtuously given as a gentleman need to be: virtuous enough; swore little; diced not—above seven times a week; went to a bawdy-house not—above once in a quarter—of an hour; paid money that I borrowed—three or four times; lived well, and in good compass. And now I live out of all order, out of all compass' (3.3.13–19). Middleton's version adds a burlesque of piety by way of the religious references glossed below.

had hope of me. I went all in black, swore but o' Sundays, never came home drunk but upon fasting nights to cleanse my stomach. 'Slid, now I'm quite altered, blown into light colours, let out oaths by th' minute, sit up late till it be early, drink drunk till I am sober, sink down dead in a tavern, and rise in a tobacco shop. Here's a transformation: I was wont yet to pity the simple and leave 'em some money. 'Slid, now I gull 'em without conscience. I go without order, swear without number, gull without mercy, and drink without measure.

LIEUTENANT I deny the last, for if you drink ne'er so much, you drink within measure.

FOLLYWIT How prove you that, sir?

LIEUTENANT Because the drawers never fill their pots.

FOLLYWIT Mass, that was well found out: all drunkards may lawfully say they drink within measure by that trick. And now I'm put i'th' mind of a trick. Can you keep your countenance, villains? Yet I am a fool to ask that, for how can they keep their countenance that have lost their credits?

ENSIGN I warrant you for blushing, captain.

FOLLYWIT I easily believe that, Ensign, for thou lost thy colours once. Nay, faith, as for blushing, I think there's grace little enough amongst you all, 'tis Lent in your cheeks, the flag's down. Well, your blushing face I suspect not, nor indeed greatly your laughing face, unless you had more money in your purses. Then thus compendiously now, you all know the possibilities of my hereafter fortunes, and the humour of my frolic grandsire, Sir Bounteous Progress, whose death makes all possible to me. I shall have all when he has nothing; but now he has all, I shall have nothing. I think one mind runs through a million of 'em: they love to keep us sober all the while they're alive, that when they're dead we may drink to their healths. They cannot abide to see us merry all the while they're above ground, and that makes so many laugh at their fathers' funerals. I know my grandsire has his will in a box, and has bequeathed all to me when he can carry nothing away; but stood I in need of poor ten pounds now, by his will I should hang myself ere I should get it. There's no such word in his will, I warrant you, nor no such thought in his mind.

LIEUTENANT You may build upon that, captain.

FOLLYWIT Then since he has no will to do me good as long as he lives, by mine own will I'll do myself good before he dies, and now I arrive at the purpose. You are not ignorant, I'm sure, you true and necessary implements of mischief, first, that my grandsire Sir Bounteous Progress is a knight of thousands, and therefore no knight since one thousand six hundred; next, that he keeps a house like his name, bounteous, open for all comers; thirdly and lastly, that he stands much upon the glory of his complement, variety of entertainment, together with the largeness of his kitchen, longitude of his buttery, and fecundity of his larder, and thinks himself never happier than when some stiff lord or great countess alights to make light his dishes. These being well mixed together may give my project better encouragement and make my purpose spring forth more fortunate. To be short and cut off a great deal of dirty way, I'll down to my grandsire like a lord.

LIEUTENANT How, captain?

FOLLYWIT A French ruff, a thin beard, and a strong perfume will do't. I can hire blue coats for you all by Westminster clock, and that colour will be soonest believed.

14 **all in black** an allusion to the Puritan abhorrence of gaudy or colourful attire; ironically, however, black also represents evil.

14–15 **swore but o' Sundays** The only time Christians may speak God's name without blaspheming is in prayer; thus, even if Follywit illogically construes his public worship as swearing, this is a supremely ironic statement.

15–16 **fasting ... stomach** another pious justification for improper behaviour; drinking to induce vomiting was neither encouraged nor proscribed as a fasting-day ritual.

16 **'Slid** an oath derived from 'God's eyelid'

17 **blown ... colours** blossomed into garish colours; 'blown' may also suggest the flamboyantly padded costumes then in fashion.

19–20 **sink ... shop** a parody of the Resurrection; also an allusion to the legend that Queen Elinor, wife of Edward I, was swallowed by the earth at Charing Cross to rise up again at Queenhive

21 **leave ... money** Previously, Follywit would not steal *all* their money.

24 **measure** moderation

28 **drawers** bartenders

32 **keep ... countenance** control your facial expression; also, maintain your reputation/financial credit

35 **warrant ... blushing** guarantee I won't blush

36–7 **lost ... colours** Follywit alludes to the ensign's duty as flag bearer; to lose the flag (or 'colours') to the enemy was considered shameful.

38–9 **Lent ... down** Flags flown from playhouses during performances were taken down when acting was prohibited, as during Lent.

42 **compendiously** briefly, concisely

43 **humour** whim, temperament
frolic frolicsome

54 **will** (*a*) desire (*b*) legal document

63–4 **Sir Bounteous Progress** The name indicates Sir Bounteous's liberality as a host to noble guests. A 'progress' was a state journey made by a royal or noble personage.

64–5 **no ... hundred** In 1603 James I required that all landholders worth forty pounds a year be knighted or else pay a fine. The implication is that Bounteous has cash but not status.

66–72 **open ... dishes** The description is loaded with sexual innuendo. 'Open for all comers' suggests male ingress and ejaculation; 'stands' and 'stiff' allude to penile erection; 'great' can mean either pregnant or vaginally 'loose' (i.e. well-used); 'countess' was pronounced 'cunt-ess,' and 'light' was often used in the sense of promiscuous. Overall, Follywit depicts the nobility as a lascivious lot.

68 **complement** retinue, household personnel

75–6 **cut ... way** to be short (proverbial)

78 **French ruff** a deep ruff or ornamental linen collar fastened at the chin; considered more fashionable than the English ruff

79–80 **blue ... clock** Blue coats were the traditional dress of servants. Westminster, the site of the Court and Law Courts, would be a good place to look for poor servants willing to sell or loan their clothes.

LIEUTENANT But prithee, captain—

FOLLYWIT Push! I reach past your fathoms; you desire crowns.

LIEUTENANT From the crown of our head to the sole of our foot, bully.

FOLLYWIT Why, carry yourselves but probably, and carry away enough with yourselves.

Enter Master Penitent Brothel

ENSIGN Why, there spoke a Roman captain. Master Penitent Brothel—

PENITENT Sweet Master Follywit— *Exeunt all but Penitent*

Here's a mad-brain o'th' first, whose pranks scorn to have precedents, to be second to any, or walk beneath any madcap's inventions. He's played more tricks than the cards can allow a man, and of the last stamp too, hating imitation—a fellow whose only glory is to be prime of the company, to be sure of which he maintains all the rest. He's the carrion, and they the kites that gorge upon him.

But why in others do I check wild passions
And retain deadly follies in myself?
I tax his youth of common received riot,
Time's comic flashes and the fruits of blood,
And in myself soothe up adulterous motions
And such an appetite that I know damns me
(Yet willingly embrace it), love to Harebrain's wife,
Over whose hours and pleasures her sick husband,
With a fantastic but deserved suspect,
Bestows his serious time in watch and ward.
And therefore I'm constrained to use the means
Of one that knows no mean, a courtesan
(One poison for another) whom her husband
Without suspicion innocently admits
Into her company, who with tried art
Corrupts and loosens her most constant powers,
Making his jealousy more than half a wittol,
Before his face plotting his own abuse,
To which himself gives aim,
Whilst the broad arrow with the forkèd head
Misses his brow but narrowly.

Enter Courtesan

See, here she comes,
The close courtesan, whose mother is her bawd.

COURTESAN Master Penitent Brothel.

PENITENT My little pretty Lady Gullman, the news, the comfort?

COURTESAN You're the fortunate man, Sir Knight o' th' Holland Shirt. There wants but opportunity and she's wax of your own fashioning. She had wrought herself into the form of your love before my art set finger to her.

PENITENT
Did our affections meet? our thoughts keep time?

COURTESAN So it should seem by the music. The only jar is in the grumbling bass viol, her husband.

PENITENT O his waking suspicion!

COURTESAN Sigh not, Master Penitent. Trust the managing of the business with me; 'tis for my credit now to see't well finished. If I do you no good, sir, you shall give me no money, sir.

PENITENT I am arrived at the court of conscience. A courtesan! O admirable times! Honesty is removed to the common place. Farewell, lady. *Exit*

Enter Mother

MOTHER How now, daughter?

COURTESAN What news, mother?

MOTHER A token from thy keeper.

COURTESAN O, from Sir Bounteous Progress. He's my keeper indeed, but there's many a piece of venison stolen that my keeper wots not on. There's no park kept so warily but loses flesh one time or other; and no woman kept so privately but may watch advantage to make the best of her pleasure. And in common reason one keeper cannot be enough for so proud a park as a woman.

MOTHER Hold thee there, girl.

COURTESAN Fear not me, mother.

MOTHER Every part of the world shoots up daily into more subtlety: the very spider weaves her cauls with more art and cunning to entrap the fly.
The shallow ploughman can distinguish now

83 **Push** an exclamation of contempt with vaguely obscene connotations; i.e. 'shove it'
fathoms hints
84 **crowns** coins
86 **bully** a term implying friendly admiration between men; fine fellow, gallant
87 **carry . . . probably** put on a plausible act
89 **Roman captain** Follywit follows the custom of a Roman leader in allowing his troops to pillage whatever booty they can carry.
92 **o'th' first** in heraldry, the colour first mentioned in blazoning a coat of arms; here, a superlative
95 **last stamp** most recent mintage
102 **tax . . . riot** reproach him for the expected boisterousness of youth
103 **Time's comic flashes** i.e. the passing follies of youth
fruits of blood products of excessive passion. According to Renaissance medical theory, an excess of blood (one of the 'four humours' believed to make up human physiology) resulted in a passionate or lascivious temperament.
108 **suspect** suspicion
109 **watch and ward** traditional phrase for the duties of the sentinel or watchman
111 **mean** moderation
115 **powers** faculties of body and mind
116 **wittol** contented cuckold
118 **To . . . aim** which he directs. In archery, to give aim is to report the accuracy of the shot.
119 **broad . . . head** i.e. the cuckold's horns
121 **close** secret
123 **Gullman** The courtesan's surname highlights her talent for fooling men.
125–6 **Sir Knight o' th' Holland Shirt** a mock-romantic title referring to Penitent's expensive shirt. (Holland is fine quality linen.)
138 **court of conscience** Court of Requests, established in 1517 to deal with small claims
140 **common place** a pun on the Court of Common Pleas, one of the three major courts of law; the common place is land publicly owned and can be used as a metaphor for a whore
146 **wots not on** does not know about
150 **proud** (*a*) fine (*b*) arrogant (*c*) sexually aroused
154 **cauls** webs

'Twixt simple truth and a dissembling brow.
Your base mechanic fellow can spy out
A weakness in a lord and learns to flout.
How does't behoove us then that live by sleight
To have our wits wound up to their stretched height?
Fifteen times thou know'st I have sold thy maidenhead to make up a dowry for thy marriage, and yet there's maidenhead enough for old Sir Bounteous still. He'll be all his lifetime about it yet, and be as far to seek when he has done.
The sums that I have told upon thy pillow!
I shall once see those golden days again.
Though fifteen, all thy maidenheads are not gone:
The Italian is not served yet, nor the French;
The Britishmen come for a dozen at once,
They engross all the market. Tut, my girl,
'Tis nothing but a politic conveyance,
A sincere carriage, a religious eyebrow
That throws their charms over the worldlings' senses;
And when thou spi'st a fool that truly pities
The false springs of thine eyes
And honourably dotes upon thy love,
If he be rich, set him by for a husband.
Be wisely tempered and learn this, my wench:
Who gets th'opinion for a virtuous name
May sin at pleasure, and ne'er think of shame.

COURTESAN
Mother, I am too deep a scholar grown
To learn my first rules now.

MOTHER 'Twill be thy own.
I say no more. Peace, hark, remove thyself. O, the two elder brothers! [*Exit Courtesan*]

Enter Inesse and Possibility

POSSIBILITY A fair hour, sweet lady.

MOTHER Good morrow, gentlemen, Master Inesse and Master Possibility.

INESSE Where's the little sweet lady, your daughter?

MOTHER Even at her book, sir.

POSSIBILITY So religious?

MOTHER 'Tis no new motion, sir, she's took it from an infant.

POSSIBILITY May we deserve a sight of her, lady?

MOTHER Upon that condition you will promise me, gentlemen, to avoid all profane talk, wanton compliments, indecent phrases, and lascivious courtings (which I know my daughter would sooner die than endure), I am contented your suits shall be granted.

POSSIBILITY Not a bawdy syllable, I protest!

INESSE [*aside to Possibility*] Syllable was well placed there, for indeed your one syllables are your bawdiest words. Prick that down! *Exeunt*

Enter Master Shortrod Harebrain 1.2

HAREBRAIN
She may make nightwork on't: 'twas well recovered.
He-cats and courtesans stroll most i'th' night,
Her friend may be received and conveyed forth
nightly.
I'll be at charge for watch and ward,
For watch and ward i'faith. And here they come.

Enter two or three [*Watchmen*]

FIRST WATCHMAN Give your worship good even.

HAREBRAIN Welcome, my friends. I must deserve your diligence in an employment serious. The troth is, there is a cunning plot laid, but happily discovered,
To rob my house: the night uncertain when,
But fixed within the circle of this month,
Nor does this villainy consist in numbers
Or many partners, only some one
Shall in the form of my familiar friend
Be received privately into my house
By some perfidious servant of mine own,
Addressed fit for the practice.

FIRST WATCHMAN O abominable!

HAREBRAIN
If you be faithful watchmen, show your goodness,
And with these angels shore up your eyelids.
[*Giving money*]
Let me not be purloined, purloined indeed!
[*Aside*] The merry Greeks conceive me. There is a gem
I would not loose, kept by the Italian
Under lock and key: we Englishmen are careless
creatures.
[*To Watchmen*] Well, I have said enough.

158 **mechanic fellow** labourer
159 **flout** act or speak with disdain
160 **sleight** cunning
167 **told** counted up
172 **engross** buy up, monopolize
173 **politic conveyance** (*a*) tactful behaviour (*b*) cunning trickery
175 **worldlings** those devoted to worldly pursuits or pleasures; citizens of the world
181 **th'opinion** reputation
186 **elder brothers** elder brothers from separate families; therefore each expects an inheritance by primogeniture.
186.1 ***Inesse and Possibility*** The two names derive from inheritance law: an estate *in esse* (in being) gave actual possession of land, as distinct from an estate in possibility which would give actual possession later.
193 **motion** inclination
204 **Prick that down** note that down (with a pun on 'prick', one of the offending monosyllables)
1.2.0.1 ***Harebrain*** Hares were held to suffer a spring madness arising from sexual jealousy.
1 **recovered** called to mind
11 **within ... month** sometime this month. The expression alludes to a sorcerer's practice of raising and restricting evil spirits within the circumference of a circle. The conjuring circle was often used as a vaginal symbol.
17 **Addressed ... practice** prepared for the trick
19 **angels** gold coins
20 **purloined** a pun on 'pur', the knave in a card-game, plus 'loin', to copulate; thus, 'loined' by a knave
21 **merry Greeks** tricky fellows
22–3 **kept ... key** Italian husbands were reputed to keep their women locked up.

SECOND WATCHMAN And we will do enough, sir.
Exeunt [Watchmen]

HAREBRAIN
Why, well said, watch me a good turn now, so, so, so.
Rise villainy with the lark, why 'tis prevented,
Or steal't by with the leather-wingèd bat,
The evening cannot save it. Peace!
[Enter Courtesan]
O Lady Gullman, my wife's only company! Welcome, and how does the virtuous matron, that good old gentlewoman thy mother? I persuade myself, if modesty be in the world she has part on't: a woman of an excellent carriage all her lifetime, in court, city, and country.

COURTESAN She's always carried it well in those places, sir—*[aside]* witness three bastards apiece.—How does your sweet bedfellow, sir? You see I'm her boldest visitant.

HAREBRAIN And welcome, sweet virgin, the only companion my soul wishes for her. I left her within at her lute. Prithee give her good counsel.

COURTESAN Alas, she needs none, sir.

HAREBRAIN Yet, yet, yet a little of thy instruction will not come amiss to her.

COURTESAN I'll bestow my labour, sir.

HAREBRAIN Do labour her, prithee. I have conveyed away all her wanton pamphlets, as *Hero and Leander*, *Venus and Adonis*, O two luscious mary-bone pies for a young married wife! Here, here, prithee take the *Resolution* and read to her a little. *[Giving book]*

COURTESAN She's set up her resolution already, sir.

HAREBRAIN True, true, and this will confirm it the more. There's a chapter of Hell 'tis good to read this cold weather. Terrify her, terrify her, go, read to her the horrible punishments for itching wantonness, the pains allotted for adultery. Tell her her thoughts, her very dreams are answerable, say so. Rip up the life of a courtesan and show how loathsome 'tis.

COURTESAN *[aside]* The gentleman would persuade me in time to disgrace myself and speak ill of mine own function. *Exit*

HAREBRAIN
This is the course I take. I'll teach the married man
A new selected strain. I admit none
But this pure virgin to her company.
Puh, that's enough: I'll keep her to her stint,
I'll put her to her pension,
She gets but her allowance, that's a bare one.
Few women but have that beside their own.
Ha, ha, ha! Nay, I'll put her hard to't.
Enter [Harebrain's] Wife and Courtesan. [They talk apart]

WIFE Fain would I meet the gentleman.

COURTESAN Push! Fain would you meet him! Why, you do not take the course.

HAREBRAIN *[aside]* How earnestly she labours her, like a good wholesome sister of the Family. She will prevail, I hope.

COURTESAN Is that the means?

WIFE What is the means? I would as gladly to enjoy his sight, embrace it as the—

COURTESAN Shall I have hearing? listen!

HAREBRAIN *[aside]* She's round with her, i'faith.

COURTESAN
When husbands in their rank'st suspicions dwell,
Then 'tis our best art to dissemble well.
Put but these notes in use, that I'll direct you,
He'll curse himself that e'er he did suspect you.
Perhaps he will solicit you as in trial
To visit such and such: still give denial.
Let no persuasions sway you: they are but fetches
Set to betray you, jealousy's slights and reaches.
Seem in his sight to endure the sight of no man;
Put by all kisses till you kiss in common.
Neglect all entertain; if he bring in
Strangers, keep you your chamber, be not seen.
If he chance steal upon you, let him find
Some book lie open 'gainst an unchaste mind
And coted Scriptures, though for your own pleasure
You read some stirring pamphlet, and convey it
Under your skirt, the fittest place to lay it.
This is the course, my wench, to enjoy thy wishes.
Here you perform best, when you most neglect:
The way to daunt is to outvie suspect.

26 **prevented** forestalled
33 **carriage** conduct, deportment, with an unintended innuendo: 'carriage' can refer to a woman's sexual bearing of a man's weight, and/or to her bearing of children. The courtesan picks up on the latter sense in l. 35 below.
47–8 ***Hero . . . Adonis*** erotic Ovidian poems by Marlowe and Shakespeare
48 **mary-bone** marrow bone, an alleged aphrodisiac
49 ***Resolution*** *The First Book of the Christian Exercise Pertaining to Resolution* (1582), a popular book of devotion written by the Jesuit Robert Parsons.
63 **new selected strain** alluding to the breeding of livestock and plants; Harebrain will produce a new quality in his wife and offspring by preventing her contact with any impure social elements and by having her propagate with himself alone.
65 **stint** an allotted amount or measure; an allowance, here sexual
68 **Few . . . own** Most women have their marital sexual 'rations' supplemented by adulterous contacts.
74 **Family** The Family of Love, a religious sect which held that religion consisted chiefly in the exercise of love: they were suspected (with some cause) of disregarding conventional morality, and were frequently used by dramatists as a vehicle for attacking sexual hypocrisy.
80 **round** straightforward, blunt
87 **fetches** decoys, traps
88 **reaches** contrivances
90 **in common** generally; by many men
91 **entertain** entertainment
94 **Some . . . mind** some book attacking sexual vice that should lie conspicuously open nearby
95 **coted** annotated. Such Bibles were popular amongst Puritans.
96 **stirring** titillating
100 **daunt** overcome
suspect suspicion

Manage these principles but with art and life:
Welcome all nations, thou'rt an honest wife.

HAREBRAIN [*aside*]
She puts it home, i'faith, e'en to the quick;
From her elaborate action I reach that.
I must requite this maid—faith, I'm forgetful.

WIFE
Here, lady, convey my heart unto him in this jewel.
[*Giving jewel*]
Against you see me next, you shall perceive
I have profited. In the mean season tell him
I am a prisoner yet, o'th' master's side.
My husband's jealousy,
That masters him as he doth master me,
And as a keeper that locks prisoners up
Is himself prisoned under his own key.
Even so my husband in restraining me
With the same ward bars his own liberty.

COURTESAN
I'll tell him how you wish it, and I'll wear
My wits to the third pile, but all shall clear.

WIFE
I owe you more than thanks, but that I hope
My husband will requite you.

COURTESAN Think you so, lady?
He has small reason for't.

HAREBRAIN [*to Courtesan*] What, done so soon?
Away, to't again, to't again, good wench, to't again.
Leave her not so, where left you. Come.

COURTESAN Faith, I am weary, sir.
I cannot draw her from her strict opinion
With all the arguments that sense can frame.

HAREBRAIN No, let me come. Fie, wife, you must consent.
What opinion is't, let's hear?

COURTESAN
Fondly and wilfully she retains that thought,
That every sin is damned.

HAREBRAIN O fie, fie, wife! Pea, pea, pea, pea, how have you lost your time? For shame, be converted: there's a diabolical opinion indeed. Then you may think that usury were damned—you're a fine merchant, i'faith. Or bribery?—you know the law well. Or sloth?—would some of the clergy heard you, i'faith. Or pride?—you come at court. Or gluttony?—you're not worthy to dine at an alderman's table.
Your only deadly sin's adultery,
That villainous ring-worm, woman's worse requital;
'Tis only lechery that's damned to th' pit-hole.
Ah, that's an arch-offence, believe it, squall,
All sins are venial but venereal.

COURTESAN I've said enough to her.

HAREBRAIN And she will be ruled by you.

COURTESAN Fah!

HAREBRAIN
I'll pawn my credit on't. Come hither, lady,
I will not altogether rest ungrateful. [*Offering ruby*]
Here, wear this ruby for thy pains and counsel.

COURTESAN It is not so much worth, sir. I am a very ill counsellor, truly.

HAREBRAIN Go to, I say.

COURTESAN [*taking ruby*] You're to blame, i'faith, sir. I shall ne'er deserve it.

HAREBRAIN Thou hast done't already. Farewell, sweet virgin. Prithee, let's see thee oftener.

COURTESAN [*aside*] Such gifts will soon entreat me. *Exit*

HAREBRAIN
Wife, as thou lov'st the quiet of my breast,
Embrace her counsel, yield to her advices.
Thou wilt find comfort in 'em in the end;
Thou'lt feel an alteration, prithee think on't.
[*Weeping*] Mine eyes can scarce refrain.

WIFE Keep in your dew, sir,
Lest when you would, you want it.

HAREBRAIN
I've pawned my credit on't. Ah, didst thou know
The sweet fruit once, thou'dst never let it go.

WIFE
'Tis that I strive to get.

HAREBRAIN And still do so. *Exeunt*

Finit Actus Primus

102 **Welcome . . . wife** You can take lovers from all nations and still appear to be chaste.
104 **reach** conclude
107 **Against** when
109 **o'th' master's side** There were four wards in debtors' prison: the master's, the knight's, the twopenny, and the hole, in descending order of cost. Mistress Harebrain likens her marriage to a relatively comfortable prison cell.
117 **to . . . pile** to the bone; 'three-pile' is a costly, three-layer velvet
121 **to't again** Many of Harebrain's remarks carry an unconscious sexual innuendo. Here he seems to provoke sexual activity rather than spiritual instruction.
125 **sense** reason, with a pun on sensuality
128 **Fondly** foolishly
129 **every . . . damned** Middleton satirizes the Familist devaluation of moral law in favour of an emphasis upon the experience of Divine love.
130 **pea** an exclamation of contempt, like 'pooh'
137 **alderman's** a town magistrate, next in dignity to a mayor
139 **ring-worm** The circular patches on the skin caused by this disease resembled the 'French crown' caused by syphilis, woman's 'requital' or revenge for adultery.
140 **pit-hole** (*a*) Hell (*b*) vagina
141 **squall** a term of endearment similar to 'pet'
142 **All . . . venereal** Harebrain contradicts Christian doctrine, which lists Seven Deadly Sins of which Lechery is only one. Unrepented deadly sins, unlike venial sins, result in damnation.
148 **ruby** considered the most precious of gemstones
152 **to blame** In the 16–17th c. 'to' was often understood as 'too'; 'blame' here may be read as 'blameworthy'.
157 **as . . . breast** if you value my peace of mind
161 **refrain** refrain from weeping
161–2 **Keep . . . want it** Keep in your tears or else you may have none when you need them. Mistress Harebrain may be alluding either to her husband's salvation or to his impending cuckoldom.
164 **sweet fruit** fruit of repentance, or of sexual pleasure (alluding to Eve's apple)

❁

2.1 *Incipit Actus Secundus*

Enter Sir Bounteous Progress with two knights

FIRST KNIGHT You have been too much like your name, Sir Bounteous.

SIR BOUNTEOUS O not so, good knights, not so, you know my humour. Most welcome, good Sir Andrew Polecat, Sir Aquitaine Colewort, most welcome.

BOTH KNIGHTS Thanks, good Sir Bounteous.

Exeunt at one door

At the other [*door*], *enter in haste* [*one of Follywit's comrades dressed as*] *a footman*

FOOTMAN O cry your worship heartily mercy, sir.

SIR BOUNTEOUS How now, linen stockings and threescore mile a day, whose footman art thou?

FOOTMAN Pray, can your worship tell me, [*panting*] hoh, hoh, hoh, if my lord be come in yet.

SIR BOUNTEOUS Thy lord! What lord?

FOOTMAN My Lord Owemuch, sir.

SIR BOUNTEOUS My Lord Owemuch! I have heard much speech of that lord. H'as great acquaintance i'th' City. That lord has been much followed.

FOOTMAN And is still, sir. He wants no company when he's in London. He's free of the Mercers, and there's none of 'em all dare cross him.

SIR BOUNTEOUS An they did, he'd turn over a new leaf with 'em, he would make 'em all weary on't i'th' end. Much fine rumour have I heard of that lord, yet had I never the fortune to set eye upon him. Art sure he will alight here, footman? I am afraid thou'rt mistook.

FOOTMAN Thinks your worship so, sir? By your leave, sir. [*Leaving*]

SIR BOUNTEOUS Puh, passion of me, footman! Why, pumps, I say, come back!

FOOTMAN Does your worship call?

SIR BOUNTEOUS Come hither, I say. I am but afraid on't. Would it might happen so well. How dost know? Did he name the house with the great turret o'th' top?

FOOTMAN No, faith, did he not, sir. [*Leaving*]

SIR BOUNTEOUS Come hither, I say. Did he speak of a cloth o' gold chamber?

FOOTMAN Not one word, by my troth, sir. [*Leaving*]

SIR BOUNTEOUS Come again, you lousy seven mile an hour!

FOOTMAN I beseech your worship detain me not.

SIR BOUNTEOUS Was there no talk of a fair pair of organs, a great gilt candlestick, and a pair of silver snuffers?

FOOTMAN 'Twere sin to belie my lord. I heard no such words, sir. [*Leaving*]

SIR BOUNTEOUS A pox confine thee! Come again, puh.

FOOTMAN Your worship will undo me, sir.

SIR BOUNTEOUS Was there no speech of a long dining room, a huge kitchen, large meat, and a broad dresser board?

FOOTMAN I have a greater maw to that indeed, an't please your worship.

SIR BOUNTEOUS Whom did he name?

FOOTMAN Why, one Sir Bounteous Progress.

SIR BOUNTEOUS Ah, ah, ah, I am that Sir Bounteous, you progressive roundabout rascal!

FOOTMAN (*laughs*) Puh!

SIR BOUNTEOUS I knew I should have him i'th' end; there's not a lord will miss me, I thank their good honours. 'Tis a fortune laid upon me, they can scent out their best entertainment. I have a kind of complimental gift given me above ordinary country knights, and how soon 'tis smelt out, I warrant ye! There's not one knight i'th' shire able to entertain a lord i'th' cue or a lady i'th' nick like me, like me. There's a kind of grace belongs to't, a kind of art which naturally slips from me, I know not on't, I promise you, 'tis gone before I'm aware on't. Cuds me, I forget myself. Where!

[*Enter two Servants*]

FIRST SERVANT Does your worship call?

2.1.4 **humour** temperament
Polecat a term of abuse, especially for the lecherous; the animal was known for its fetid smell

5 **Colewort** a kind of cabbage, also with an offensive smell

8 **linen stockings** a sign of low social status

8–9 **threescore . . . day** A running footman ran before his master's coach, covering considerable distance.

15 **H'as great acquaintance** He is well known.
i'th' City in London (the old walled town, distinguished from the larger metropolis which had grown up around it)

17 **wants** lacks

18 **free of the Mercers** literally, a freeman of the clothsellers' guild, but 'being in the mercer's book' was used proverbially in the period for the debts of a gallant. Owemuch, as his name indicates, is heavily in debt.

19 **cross him** (*a*) thwart him (*b*) cross out his debts

20 **An** If
turn . . . leaf (*a*) start fresh (*b*) open a new account

26 **pumps** alluding to the footman's running shoes

31 **great turret** Most of the objects of which Bounteous brags are large and phallic. This plays into the stereotype, frequent in literature of the period, of the rich old man whose possessions compensate for his failing sexual potency.

33–4 **cloth o' gold** cloth containing gold thread; presumably, the chamber is lined with tapestries of this fabric.

38 **pair of organs** a single musical instrument, with further phallic connotations

39 **pair . . . snuffers** an instrument for snuffing candles; the concave (female) partner to the phallic candlesticks

45 **large meat** Eating meat was a frequent metaphor for sexual consumption, and was believed to increase sexual appetite.
dresser board a table for the preparation of food

46 **maw** appetite, inclination

51 **progressive** longwinded, punning on the progresses or journeys during which he accompanies his lord

56 **complimental** (*a*) that which supplies all needs (*b*) complimentary

59 **shire** region, county

59–60 **lord . . . nick** at short notice, punning on 'cue' (from the French 'queue') as the male member and 'nick', a variant of 'nock', as the female genitals.

63 **Cuds me** a mild oath

SIR BOUNTEOUS Run, sirrah, call in my chief gentleman i'th' chain of gold, expedite! [*Exit First Servant*] And how does my good lord? I never saw him before in my life. [*To Second Servant*] A cup of bastard for this footman.

FOOTMAN My lord has travelled this five year, sir.

SIR BOUNTEOUS Travailed this five year? How many children has he? [*To Servant*] Some bastard, I say!

FOOTMAN No bastard, an't please your worship.

SIR BOUNTEOUS A cup of sack to strengthen his wit. The footman's a fool. [*Exit Second Servant*]

[*Enter Gunwater*]

O come hither, Master Gunwater, come hither. Send presently to Master Pheasant for one of his hens. There's partridge i'th' house.

GUNWATER And wild duck, an't please your worship.

SIR BOUNTEOUS And woodcock, an't please thy worship.

GUNWATER And woodcock, an't please your worship. I had thought to have spoke before you.

SIR BOUNTEOUS Remember the pheasant, down with some plover, clap down six woodcocks: my lord's coming. Now, sir?

GUNWATER An't please your worship, there's a lord and his followers newly alighted.

SIR BOUNTEOUS Dispatch, I say, dispatch! [*Exit Gunwater*] Why, where's my music? He's come indeed.

Enter Follywit like a lord, with [*Lieutenant, Ensign, and*] *his comrades in blue coats*

FOLLYWIT Footman!

FOOTMAN My lord.

FOLLYWIT Run swiftly with my commendations to Sir Jasper Topas. We'll ride and visit him i'th' morning, say.

FOOTMAN Your lordship's charge shall be effected. *Exit*

FOLLYWIT That courtly comely form should present to me Sir Bounteous Progress.

SIR BOUNTEOUS You've found me out, my lord, I cannot hide myself. Your honour is mostly spaciously welcome.

FOLLYWIT In this forgive me, sir,
That being a stranger to your house and you,
I make my way so bold, and presume
Rather upon your kindness than your knowledge.
Only your bounteous dispositïon
Fame hath divulged, and is to me well known.

SIR BOUNTEOUS Nay, an your lordship know my disposition, you know me better than they that know my person. Your honour is so much the welcomer for that.

FOLLYWIT Thanks, good Sir Bounteous.

SIR BOUNTEOUS Pray pardon me, it has been often my ambition, my lord, both in respect of your honourable presence and the prodigal fame that keeps even stroke with your unbounded worthiness,
To have wished your lordship where your lordship is,
A noble guest in this unworthy seat.
Your lordship ne'er heard my organs?

FOLLYWIT Heard of 'em, Sir Bounteous, but never heard 'em.

SIR BOUNTEOUS They're but double-gilt, my lord. Some hundred and fifty pound will fit your lordship with such another pair.

FOLLYWIT Indeed, Sir Bounteous?

SIR BOUNTEOUS O my lord, I have a present suit to you.

FOLLYWIT To me, Sir Bounteous? And you could ne'er speak at fitter time, for I'm here present to grant you.

SIR BOUNTEOUS Your lordship has been a traveller.

FOLLYWIT Some five year, sir.

SIR BOUNTEOUS I have a grandchild, my lord. I love him, and when I die I'll do somewhat for him. I'll tell your honour the worst of him: a wild lad he has been.

FOLLYWIT So we have been all, sir.

SIR BOUNTEOUS So we have been all indeed, my lord, I thank your lordship's assistance. Some comic pranks he has been guilty of, but I'll pawn my credit for him, an honest trusty bosom.

FOLLYWIT And that's worth all, sir.

SIR BOUNTEOUS And that's worth all indeed, my lord, for he's like to have all when I die. *Imberbis iuvenis*, his chin has no more prickles yet than a midwife's: there's great hope of his wit, his hair's so long a-coming. Shall I be bold with your honour, to prefer this aforesaid Ganymede to hold a plate under your lordship's cup?

FOLLYWIT You wrong both his worth and your bounty, an you call that boldness. Sir, I have heard much good of that young gentleman.

SIR BOUNTEOUS Nay, h'as a good wit, i'faith, my lord.

FOLLYWIT He's carried himself always generously.

SIR BOUNTEOUS Are you advised of that, my lord? He's carried many things cleanly. I'll show your lordship my will. I keep it above in an outlandish box. The whoreson

65 **sirrah** a term used to address a social inferior
66 **chain of gold** insignia worn by stewards
68 **bastard** sweet Spanish wine
70–1 **travelled...Travailed** a common pun on 'travel' and 'to labour in childbirth'
74 **sack** sweet white wine
75.1 ***Gunwater*** alluding to semen or urine
80 **woodcock** a bird proverbial for its foolishness, and an epithet for a simpleton.
92–3 **Sir Jasper Topas** a fictional knightly personage; hero of Chaucer's mock-romance, 'The Tale of Sir Thopas'
103 **knowledge** acquaintance
112 **keeps even stroke** measures up to, with a bawdy pun
115 **seat** (*a*) domicile (*b*) seat of trousers
123 **present suit** immediate request
138 ***Imberbis iuvenis*** beardless youth
139 **midwife's** sometimes signifying an effeminate man
139–40 **there's...a-coming** alluding to the proverb 'more hair than wit'
142 **Ganymede** the beautiful boy abducted by Zeus to serve as his cupbearer; hence, an effeminate male
148–9 **He's...cleanly** managed things artfully, dextrously, with a pun on carrying as stealing
150 **outlandish** of foreign fashion

boy must have all: I love him, yet he shall ne'er find it as long as I live.

FOLLYWIT Well sir, for your sake and his own deserving, I'll reserve a place for him nearest to my secrets.

SIR BOUNTEOUS I understand your good lordship: you'll make him your secretary. My music, give my lord a taste of his welcome!

A strain played by the consort. Sir Bounteous makes a courtly honour to that lord and seems to foot the tune

So, how like you our airs, my lord? Are they choice?

FOLLYWIT They're seldom matched, believe it.

SIR BOUNTEOUS The consort of mine own household.

FOLLYWIT Yea, sir.

SIR BOUNTEOUS The musicians are in ordinary, yet no ordinary musicians. Your lordship shall hear my organs now.

FOLLYWIT O, I beseech you, Sir Bounteous!

SIR BOUNTEOUS My organist.

The organs play, and [*servants with*] *covered dishes march over the stage*

Come, my lord, how does your honour relish my organ?

FOLLYWIT A very proud air, i'faith, sir.

SIR BOUNTEOUS O, how can't choose? A Walloon plays upon 'em, and a Welshman blows wind in their breech.

Exeunt

A song to the organs

2.2 *Enter Sir Bounteous with Follywit* [*as Lord Owemuch, with Lieutenant, Ensign*] *and his consorts toward his lodging*

SIR BOUNTEOUS You must pardon us, my lord, hasty cates; your honour has had ev'n a hunting meal on't. And now I am like to bring your lordship to as mean a lodging, a hard down bed i'faith, my lord, poor cambric sheets, and a cloth o' tissue canopy. The curtains indeed were wrought in Venice, with the story of the prodigal child in silk and gold. Only the swine are left out, my lord, for spoiling the curtains.

FOLLYWIT 'Twas well prevented, sir.

SIR BOUNTEOUS Silken rest, harmonious slumbers, and venereal dreams to your lordship.

FOLLYWIT The like to kind Sir Bounteous.

SIR BOUNTEOUS Fie, not to me, my lord. I'm old, past dreaming of such vanities.

FOLLYWIT Old men should dream best.

SIR BOUNTEOUS Their dreams indeed, my lord, you've gi'n t'us. Tomorrow your lordship shall see my cocks, my fishponds, my park, my champaign grounds. I keep chambers in my house can show your lordship some pleasure.

FOLLYWIT Sir Bounteous, you ev'n whelm me with delights.

SIR BOUNTEOUS Once again a musical night to your honour. I'll trouble your lordship no more. *Exit*

FOLLYWIT Good rest, Sir Bounteous. [*To his comrades*] So, come, the visors, where be the masking suits?

LIEUTENANT In your lordship's portmanteau.

FOLLYWIT Peace, lieutenant.

LIEUTENANT I had rather have war, captain.

FOLLYWIT
Puh, the plot's ripe. Come, to our business, lad.
Though guilt condemns, 'tis gilt must make us glad.

LIEUTENANT Nay, an you be at your distinctions, captain, I'll follow behind no longer.

FOLLYWIT Get you before then, and whelm your nose with your visor, go. [*Exeunt all but Follywit*]

Now grandsire, you that hold me at hard meat
And keep me out at the dag's end, I'll fit you.
Under his lordship's leave, all must be mine
He and his will confesses: what I take then
Is but a borrowing of so much beforehand.
I'll pay him again when he dies, in so many blacks;
I'll have the church hung round with a noble a yard,
Or requite him in scutcheons. Let him trap me
In gold and I'll lap him in lead, *quid pro quo.*
I must look none of his angels i'th' face, forsooth,
Until his face be not worth looking on.
Tut, lads,

154 **secrets** (*a*) private affairs (*b*) private parts

156 **secretary** notary, scribe, but also suggesting the etymological sense of someone entrusted with secrets

157.1 **consort** group of musicians

157.2 **honour** bow

158 **airs** tunes

162 **in ordinary** belonging to the regular household staff

167 **relish** (*a*) enjoy (*b*) enjoy sexually

168 **proud** (*a*) fine (*b*) sexually aroused

169–70 **Walloon...breech** The Flemish were stereotyped as good musicians, the Welsh as braggarts—or possibly farters

2.2.1 **cates** provisions, food

2 **hunting meal** In theory, a rough repast, but in fact such meals were often lavish.

4 **cambric** fine white linen

5 **cloth o' tissue** a rich cloth, often interwoven with gold or silver threads

6–7 **prodigal child** ironically appropriate, since the prodigal son in Luke 15:11–32 'wasted his substance with riotous living'

18 **champaign grounds** open fields

26 **visors** masks

27 **portmanteau** travelling bag

31 **gilt** gold, money

32 **distinctions** a farting joke: 'de-stink-shuns', with the 'stink' perhaps pointed by a gesture

37 **at the dag's end** at a distance; a dag was a heavy pistol

41 **blacks** funeral draperies

42 **noble a yard** expensive cloth. A noble was a gold coin.

43 **scutcheons** hatchments, square or lozenge-shaped tablets for exhibiting the coat of arms of the deceased, hung over his door.
trap outfit, clothe

44 **lap...lead** wrap him in lead for burial
quid pro quo tit for tat

45 **angels** coins, with a pun on celestial ministers

Let sires and grandsires keep us low, we must
Live when they're flesh as well as when they're dust.
Exit

2.3 *Enter Courtesan with her man*

COURTESAN Go, sirrah, run presently to Master Penitent Brothel. You know his lodging, knock him up. I know he cannot sleep for sighing. Tell him I've happily bethought a mean
To make his purpose prosper in each limb,
Which only rests to be approved by him.
Make haste, I know he thirsts for it. *Exeunt*

2.4 A VOICE WITHIN O!

Enter, in a masking suit with a visor in his hand, Follywit

FOLLYWIT Hark, they're at their business.

FIRST SERVANT [*within*] Thieves, thieves!

FOLLYWIT Gag that gaping rascal! Though he be my grandsire's chief gentleman i'th' chain of gold, I'll have no pity of him.

Enter the rest [Lieutenant, Ensign, Footman, and others], visored

How now, lads?

LIEUTENANT All's sure and safe. On with your visor, sir. The servants are all bound.

FOLLYWIT [*donning his visor*] There's one care past then. Come follow me lads, I'll lead you now t'th' point and top of all your fortunes. Yon lodging is my grandsire's.

LIEUTENANT So, so, lead on, on.

[*Exeunt all but Ensign*]

ENSIGN Here's a captain worth the following and a wit worth a man's love and admiring!

Enter [Follywit, Lieutenant and others] with Sir Bounteous in his nightgown

SIR BOUNTEOUS O gentlemen, an you be kind gentlemen, what countrymen are you?

FOLLYWIT Lincolnshire men, sir.

SIR BOUNTEOUS I am glad of that, i'faith.

FOLLYWIT And why should you be glad of that?

SIR BOUNTEOUS O, the honestest thieves of all come out of Lincolnshire, the kindest-natured gentlemen. They'll rob a man with conscience. They have a feeling of what they go about, and will steal with tears in their eyes. Ah, pitiful gentlemen!

FOLLYWIT Push! Money, money, we come for money.

SIR BOUNTEOUS Is that all you come for? Ah, what a beast was I to put out my money t'other day! Alas, good gentlemen, what shift shall I make for you? Pray come again another time.

FOLLYWIT Tut, tut, sir, money!

SIR BOUNTEOUS O not so loud, sir, you're too shrill a gentleman. I have a lord lies in my house. I would not for the world his honour should be disquieted.

FOLLYWIT Who, my Lord Owemuch? We have took order with him beforehand. He lies bound in his bed and all his followers.

SIR BOUNTEOUS Who, my lord? Bound my lord? Alas, what did you mean to bind my lord? He could keep his bed well enough without binding. You've undone me in't already, you need rob me no farther.

FOLLYWIT Which is the key, come?

SIR BOUNTEOUS Ah, I perceive now you're no true Lincolnshire spirits. You come rather out of Bedfordshire, we cannot lie quiet in our beds for you. So take enough, my masters, spur a free horse. My name's Sir Bounteous—a merry world, i'faith—what knight but I keep open house at midnight? Well, there should be a conscience, if one could hit upon't.

FOLLYWIT Away now, seize upon him, bind him.

SIR BOUNTEOUS Is this your court of equity? Why should I be bound for mine own money? But come, come, bind me, I have need on't. I have been too liberal tonight. Keep in my hands, nay, as hard as you list. I am not too good to bear my lord company. You have watched your time, my masters. I was knighted at Westminster, but many of these nights will make me a knight of Windsor. You've deserved so well, my masters, I bid you all to dinner tomorrow. I would I might have your companies, i'faith, I desire no more.

FOLLYWIT [*finding money*] O ho, sir!

SIR BOUNTEOUS Pray meddle not with my organs, to put 'em out of tune.

FOLLYWIT [*jingling the coins*] O no, here's better music, sir.

SIR BOUNTEOUS Ah, pox feast you!

FOLLYWIT Dispatch with him, away!

[*Exeunt Ensign and others carrying Sir Bounteous*]

So, thank you, good grandsire. This was bounteously done of him, i'faith. It came somewhat hard from him at first, for indeed nothing comes stiff from an old man but money, and he may well stand upon that, when he has nothing else to stand upon. Where's our portmanteau?

LIEUTENANT Here, bully captain.

2.3.5 **in each limb** (*a*) in every way (*b*) in each body part
6 **rests** remains
2.4.1.1 ***masking suit*** costume worn to a masque or ball
6 **of him** for him
11 **point** pinnacle
21–2 **honestest . . . Lincolnshire** alluding to Robin Hood and his men, who though chiefly associated with Nottinghamshire, dressed in Lincoln green.
25 **pitiful** piteous
28 **put out** invest
29 **shift** expedient, provision
35–6 **took order with** taken care of
46 **spur . . . horse** an allusion to the proverb, 'Do not spur a free (i.e. willing) horse.'
52 **bound** (*a*) tied up (*b*) held under legal obligation
55–6 **watched your time** chosen the appropriate time
56 **at Westminster** i.e. at Court, rather than on the battlefield
57–8 **knight of Windsor** gentleman pensioners, who because of age and poverty are not fit for military service
68–71 **It came . . . upon** Follywit pokes fun at Sir Bounteous's presumed impotence; achieving an erection was often euphemized in terms of standing.

FOLLYWIT In with the purchase, 'twill lie safe enough there under's nose, I warrant you.

[*They put the money in the portmanteau*]

Enter Ensign [*and others*]

What, is all sure?

ENSIGN All's sure, captain.

FOLLYWIT You know what follows now: one villain binds his fellows. Go, we must be all bound for our own securities, rascals, there's no dallying upo'th' point. You conceit me: there is a lord to be found bound in the morning, and all his followers. Can you pick out that lord now?

LIEUTENANT O admirable spirit!

FOLLYWIT You ne'er plot for your safeties, so your wants be satisfied.

ENSIGN But if we bind one another, how shall the last man be bound?

FOLLYWIT Pox on't, I'll have the footman 'scape.

FOOTMAN That's I, I thank you, sir.

FOLLYWIT The footman of all other will be supposed to 'scape, for he comes in no bed all night, but lies in's clothes to be first ready i'th' morning. The horse and he lies in litter together. That's the right fashion of your bonny footman, and his freedom will make the better for our purpose, for we must have one i'th' morning to unbind the knight, that we may have our sport within ourselves. We now arrive at the most ticklish point, to rob and take our ease, to be thieves and lie by't. Look to't lads, it concerns every man's gullet. I'll not have the jest spoiled, that's certain, though it hazard a windpipe. I'll either go like a lord as I came, or be hanged like a thief as I am, and that's my resolution.

LIEUTENANT Troth, a match, captain, of all hands.

[*They shake hands and*] *exeunt*

2.5 *Enter Courtesan with Master Penitent Brothel*

COURTESAN O Master Penitent Brothel!

PENITENT What is't, sweet Lady Gullman, that so seizes on thee with rapture and admiration?

COURTESAN A thought, a trick, to make you, sir, especially happy, and yet I myself a saver by it.

PENITENT
I would embrace that, lady, with such courage
I would not leave you on the losing hand.

COURTESAN I will give trust to you, sir, the cause then why I raised you from your bed so soon, wherein I know sighs would not let you sleep. Thus understand it:
You love that woman, Master Harebrain's wife,
Which no invented means can crown with freedom
For your desires and her own wish, but this
Which in my slumbers did present itself.

PENITENT I'm covetous, lady.

COURTESAN
You know her husband, lingering in suspect,
Locks her from all society but mine.

PENITENT Most true.

COURTESAN I only am admitted, yet hitherto that has done you no real happiness. By my admittance I cannot perform that deed that should please you, you know. Wherefore thus I've conveyed it, I'll counterfeit a fit of violent sickness.

PENITENT Good.

COURTESAN Nay, 'tis not so good, by my faith, but to do you good.

PENITENT And in that sense I called it. But take me with you, lady, would it be probable enough to have a sickness so suddenly violent?

COURTESAN Puh, all the world knows women are soon down. We can be sick when we have a mind to't, catch an ague with the wind of our fans, surfeit upon the rump of a lark and bestow ten pound in physic upon't. We're likest ourselves when we're down. 'Tis the easiest art and cunning for our sect to counterfeit sick, that are always full of fits when we are well, for since we were made for a weak imperfect creature, we can fit that best that we are made for. I thus translated, and yourself slipped into the form of a physician—

PENITENT I a physician, lady? Talk not on't, I beseech you. I shall shame the whole college.

COURTESAN Tut, man, any quacksalving terms will serve for this purpose, for I am pitifully haunted with a brace of elder brothers, new perfumed in the first of their fortunes, and I shall see how forward their purses will be to the pleasing of my palate and restoring of my health. Lay on load enough upon 'em and spare 'em not, for they're good plump fleshly asses and may well enough bear it. Let gold, amber, and dissolved pearl be

73 **purchase** booty
78–9 **bound...securities** continuing the legal puns: placed under legal obligation on our own recognizance
80 **conceit** understand
81 **pick out** identify
84–5 **You...satisfied** you never have to plot for financial security, as long as your needs are satisfied
93 **litter** bed of straw or rushes, as for animals
96 **within** amongst
97 **ticklish** tricky, touchy
98 **lie by't** (*a*) lie beside the booty (*b*) brazen it out
100 **hazard a windpipe** risk hanging for theft
103 **match...hands** joining of hands
2.5.5 **saver** the winning card in certain games
7 **on the losing hand** (*a*) with the losing hand of cards (*b*) empty-handed
16 **covetous** (*a*) desirous to hear (*b*) desirous of Mistress Harebrain
23 **conveyed** planned
28–9 **take...you** let me understand you
32 **down** horizontal, for reasons more related to lust than to health
36 **sect** sex
37 **fits** seizures, probably hysterical
38 **were made for** (*a*) were made as (*b*) are held to be
39 **translated** transformed
42 **college** College of Physicians, founded in 1518, an examining and qualifying body designed to check superstition and quackery.
43 **quacksalving** counterfeit medicine; quackery
49 **fleshly asses** (*a*) fat beasts of burden (*b*) fat asses

common ingredients, and that you cannot compose a cullis without 'em. Put but this cunningly in practice, it shall be both a sufficient recompense for all my pains in your love, and the ready means to make Mistress Harebrain's way (by the visiting of me) to your mutual desired company.

PENITENT I applaud thee, kiss thee, and will constantly embrace it. *Exeunt*

2.6 *Voices within*

SIR BOUNTEOUS [*within*] Ho, Gunwater!

FOLLYWIT [*within*] Singlestone!

ANOTHER (*within*) Jenkin, wa, ha, ho!

ANOTHER (*within*) Ewen!

ANOTHER (*within*) Simcod!

FOLLYWIT [*within*] Footman! whew!

Enter Sir Bounteous [*in his nightgown*] *with a cord half unbound, Footman with him* [*unbinding him*]

FOOTMAN O good your worship, let me help your good old worship.

SIR BOUNTEOUS Ah poor honest footman, how didst thou 'scape this massacre?

FOOTMAN E'en by miracle, and lying in my clothes, sir.

SIR BOUNTEOUS I think so. I would I had lain in my clothes too, footman, so I had 'scaped 'em. I could have but risse like a beggar then, and so I do now, till more money come in. But nothing afflicts me so much, my poor geometrical footman, as that the barbarous villains should lay violence upon my lord. Ah, the binding of my lord cuts my heart in two pieces. [*Footman frees him*] So, so, 'tis well, I thank thee, run to thy fellows, undo 'em, undo 'em, undo 'em.

FOOTMAN Alas, if my lord should miscarry, they're unbound already, sir. They have no occupation but sleep, feed and fart. *Exit*

SIR BOUNTEOUS If I be not ashamed to look my lord i'th' face, I'm a Saracen. My lord—

FOLLYWIT [*within curtain*] Who's that?

SIR BOUNTEOUS One may see he has been scared. A pox on 'em for their labours!

FOLLYWIT [*within*] Singlestone!

SIR BOUNTEOUS Singlestone? I'll ne'er answer to that, i'faith.

FOLLYWIT [*within*] Suchman!

SIR BOUNTEOUS Suchman? Nor that neither, i'faith, I am not brought so low, though I be old.

FOLLYWIT [*within*] Who's that i'th' chamber?

[*Sir Bounteous pulls curtain to reveal Follywit, disguised as Lord Owemuch in his nightgown, bound in his bed*]

SIR BOUNTEOUS Good morrow, my lord, 'tis I.

FOLLYWIT Sir Bounteous, good morrow. I would give you my hand, sir, but I cannot come at it. Is this the courtesy o'th' country, Sir Bounteous?

SIR BOUNTEOUS
Your lordship grieves me more than all my loss.
'Tis the unnatural'st sight that can be found
To see a noble gentleman hard bound.

FOLLYWIT Trust me, I thought you had been better beloved, Sir Bounteous, but I see you have enemies, sir, and your friends fare the worse for 'em. I like your talk better than your lodging. I ne'er laid harder in a bed of down. I have had a mad night's rest on't. Can you not guess what they should be, Sir Bounteous?

SIR BOUNTEOUS Faith, Lincolnshire men, my lord.

FOLLYWIT How? Fie, fie, believe it not, sir, these lie not far off, I warrant you.

SIR BOUNTEOUS Think you so, my lord?

FOLLYWIT I'll be burnt an they do: some that use to your house, sir, and are familiar with all the conveyances.

SIR BOUNTEOUS This is the commodity of keeping open house, my lord, that makes so many shut their doors about dinner-time.

FOLLYWIT They were resolute villains. I made myself known to 'em, told 'em what I was, gave 'em my honourable word not to disclose 'em.

SIR BOUNTEOUS O saucy unmannerly villains!

FOLLYWIT And think you the slaves would trust me upon my word?

SIR BOUNTEOUS They would not?

FOLLYWIT Forsooth, no, I must pardon them. They told me lords' promises were mortal, and commonly die within half an hour after they are spoken. They were but gristles, and not one amongst a hundred come to any full growth or perfection, and therefore though I were a lord I must enter into bond.

SIR BOUNTEOUS Insupportable rascals!

FOLLYWIT Troth, I'm of that mind, Sir Bounteous, you fared the worse for my coming hither.

[*Sir Bounteous begins to unbind Follywit*]

SIR BOUNTEOUS Ah, good my lord, but I'm sure your lordship fared the worse.

FOLLYWIT Pray, pity not me, sir.

SIR BOUNTEOUS Is not your honour sore about the brawn of the arm? A murrain meet 'em, I feel it.

FOLLYWIT About this place, Sir Bounteous.

52 **cullis** nourishing broth
2.6.2 **Singlestone** pun on 'stones' as testicles; hence, 'One Ball'.
11 **lying ... clothes** i.e. ready to run
14 **risse** risen
16 **geometrical** ground measuring
21 **miscarry** suffer misfortune
21–2 **unbound** discharged from their employment, with a pun on the relief of constipation
25 **Saracen** i.e. a heathen
41 **hard bound** (*a*) tied fast (*b*) constipated
45 **laid harder** slept worse
53 **conveyances** passages
54 **commodity** profit
61 **slaves** term of opprobrium
67 **gristles** infants (whose bones are gristly)
69 **enter into bond** (*a*) be tied up (*b*) submit to legal bond. As a peer, and therefore a member of the upper house of Parliament, a lord could not be summonsed to appear in court and could not be sued for debt or committed to prison for it.
77 **murrain** a cattle disease, often used as an oath

SIR BOUNTEOUS You feel as it were a twinge, my lord?
FOLLYWIT Ay, e'en a twinge, you say right.
SIR BOUNTEOUS A pox discover 'em, that twinge I feel too.
FOLLYWIT But that which disturbs me most, Sir Bounteous, lies here.
SIR BOUNTEOUS True, about the wrist, a kind of tumid numbness.
FOLLYWIT You say true, sir.
SIR BOUNTEOUS The reason of that, my lord, is the pulses had no play.
FOLLYWIT Mass, so I get it.
SIR BOUNTEOUS A mischief swell 'em, for I feel that too.
FOLLYWIT 'Slid, here's a house haunted indeed.

[Enter Lieutenant]

LIEUTENANT A word with you, sir.
FOLLYWIT How now, Singlestone?
LIEUTENANT I'm sorry, my lord, your lordship has lost—
SIR BOUNTEOUS Pup, pup, pup, pup, pup—
FOLLYWIT What have I lost? Speak!
SIR BOUNTEOUS [*aside to Lieutenant*] A good night's sleep, say.
FOLLYWIT Speak, what have I lost, say?
LIEUTENANT A good night's sleep, my lord, nothing else.
FOLLYWIT That's true. [*Rises, unbound*] My clothes! Come! *[Exit.] Curtains drawn*
LIEUTENANT [*calling off*] My lord's clothes! His honour's rising.
SIR BOUNTEOUS Hist, well said. Come hither. What has my lord lost? Tell me, speak softly.
LIEUTENANT His lordship must know that, sir.
SIR BOUNTEOUS Hush, prithee tell me.
LIEUTENANT 'Twill do you no pleasure to know't, sir.
SIR BOUNTEOUS Yet again? I desire it, I say.
LIEUTENANT Since your worship will needs know't, they have stolen away a jewel in a blue silk ribbon of a hundred pound price, besides some hundred pounds in fair spur-royals.
SIR BOUNTEOUS That's some two hundred i'th' total.
LIEUTENANT Your worship's much about it, sir.
SIR BOUNTEOUS Come, follow me, I'll make that whole again in so much money. Let not my lord know on't.
LIEUTENANT O pardon me, Sir Bounteous, that were a dishonour to my lord. Should it come to his ear, I should hazard my undoing by't.
SIR BOUNTEOUS How should it come to his ear? If you be my lord's chief man about him, I hope you do not use to speak unless you be paid for't, and I had rather give you a counsellor's double fee to hold your peace. Come, go to, follow me, I say.
LIEUTENANT There will be scarce time to tell it, sir. My lord will away instantly.
SIR BOUNTEOUS His honour shall stay dinner, by his leave, I'll prevail with him so far. And now I remember a jest. I bade the whoreson thieves to dinner last night. I would I might have their companies, a pox poison 'em. *Exit*
LIEUTENANT Faith, and you are like to have no other guests, Sir Bounteous, if you have none but us. I'll give you that gift, i'faith. *Exit*

Finit Actus Secundus

Incipit Actus Tertius 3.1
Enter Master Shortrod Harebrain with [the] two elder brothers, Master Inesse and Master Possibility

POSSIBILITY You see bold guests, Master Harebrain.
HAREBRAIN You're kindly welcome to my house, good Master Inesse and Master Possibility.
INESSE That's our presumption, sir.
HAREBRAIN Rafe!

[Enter Rafe]

RAFE Here, sir.
HAREBRAIN Call down your mistress to welcome these two gentlemen my friends.
RAFE I shall, sir. *Exit*
HAREBRAIN [*aside*]
I will observe her carrïage and watch
The slippery revolutions of her eye.
I'll lie in wait for every glance she gives
And poise her words i'th' balance of suspect.
If she but swag she's gone, either on this hand
Overfamiliar, or on this too neglectful.
It does behoove her carry herself even.
POSSIBILITY
But Master Harebrain—
HAREBRAIN True, I hear you, sir.
Was't you said?
POSSIBILITY I have not spoke it yet, sir.
HAREBRAIN Right, so I say.
POSSIBILITY
Is it not strange that in so short a time
My little Lady Gullman should be so violently
handled?
HAREBRAIN
O sickness has no mercy, sir.
It neither pities lady's lip nor eye.
It crops the rose out of the virgin's cheek,
And so deflowers her that was ne'er deflowered.
Fools then are maids to lock from men that treasure
Which death will pluck and never yield them pleasure.
Ah gentlemen, though I shadow it, that sweet virgin's

95 **pup** Bounteous makes inarticulate sounds in order to silence the Lieutenant.
113 **spur-royals** gold coins imprinted with a blazing sun resembling a spur
116 **make that whole** compensate for the loss
124 **counsellor's double fee** The chief counsel in legal actions took double fee; here, a bribe.
126 **tell** count
3.1.4 **That's our presumption** (*a*) So we presume (*b*) That's our arrogance
11 **slippery** cunning
13 **poise . . . suspect** weigh her words in the scale of suspicion
14 **swag** sink down
16 **even** evenly, with moderation
21 **handled** treated (by illness)
28 **shadow** hide

sickness grieves me not lightly. She was my wife's only delight and company. Did you not hear her, gentlemen, i'th' midst of her extremest fit, still how she called upon my wife, remembered still my wife, 'Sweet Mistress Harebrain!' When she sent for me, o' one side of her bed stood the physician, the scrivener on the other: two horrible objects, but mere opposites in the course of their lives, for the scrivener binds folks and the physician makes them loose.

POSSIBILITY But not loose of their bonds, sir?

HAREBRAIN No by my faith, sir, I say not so. If the physician could make 'em loose of their bonds, there's many a one would take physic that dares not now for poisoning. But as I was telling of you, her will was fashioning,
Wherein I found her best and richest jewel
Given as a legacy unto my wife.
When I read that, I could not refrain weeping.
Well, of all other, my wife has most reason to visit her.
If she have any good nature in her, she'll show it there.
[*Enter Rafe*]
Now sir, where's your mistress?

RAFE She desires you and the gentlemen your friends to hold her excused. Sh'as a fit of an ague now upon her, which begins to shake her.

HAREBRAIN Where does it shake her most?

RAFE All over her body, sir.

HAREBRAIN
Shake all her body, sir? 'Tis a saucy fit,
I'm jealous of that ague. Pray walk in, gentlemen,
I'll see you instantly. [*Exeunt Inesse and Possibility*]

RAFE
Now they are absent, sir, 'tis no such thing.

HAREBRAIN What?

RAFE My mistress has her health, sir,
But 'tis her suit she may confine herself
From sight of all men but your own dear self, sir,
For since the sickness of that modest virgin,
Her only company, she delights in none.

HAREBRAIN
No? Visit her again, commend me to her,
Tell her they're gone, and only I myself
Walk here to exchange a word or two with her.

RAFE I'll tell her so, sir. *Exit*

HAREBRAIN
Fool that I am, and madman, beast! What worse?
Suspicious o'er a creature that deserves
The best opinion and the purest thought,
Watchful o'er her that is her watch herself,
To doubt her ways that looks too narrowly
Into her own defects. I, foolish-fearful,
Have often rudely, out of giddy flames,
Barred her those objects which she shuns herself.
Thrice I've had proof of her most constant temper.
Come I at unawares by stealth upon her,
I find her circled in with divine writs
Of heavenly meditations, here and there
Chapters with leaves tucked up, which when I see,
They either tax pride or adultery.
Ah, let me curse myself, that could be jealous
Of her whose mind no sin can make rebellious.
And here the unmatched comes.
[*Enter Wife*]
Now wife, i'faith, they're gone. Push! See how fearful 'tis. Will you not credit me? They're gone, i'faith. Why, think you I'll betray you? Come, come, thy delight and mine, thy only virtuous friend, thy sweet instructress is violently taken, grievous sick, and which is worse, she mends not.

WIFE Her friends are sorry for that, sir.

HAREBRAIN She calls still upon thee, poor soul, remembers thee still, thy name whirls in her breath. 'Where's Mistress Harebrain?' says she.

WIFE Alas, good soul.

HAREBRAIN She made me weep thrice. She's put thee in a jewel in her will.

WIFE E'en to th' last gasp a kind soul.

HAREBRAIN Take my man, go, visit her.

WIFE Pray pardon me, sir; alas, my visitation cannot help her.

HAREBRAIN O yet the kindness of a thing, wife. Still she holds the same rare temper. Take my man, I say.

WIFE I would not take your man, sir, though I did purpose going.

HAREBRAIN No? Thy reason?

WIFE
The world's condition is itself so vile, sir,
'Tis apt to judge the worst of those deserve not.
'Tis an ill-thinking age, and does apply
All to the form of it own luxury.
This censure flies from one, that from another;
'That man's her squire', says he; 'Her pimp', the t'other;
'She's of the stamp', a third; fourth, 'I ha' known her.'
I've heard this, not without a burning cheek.
Then our attires are taxed, our very gait
Is called in question, where a husband's presence

34 **scrivener** notary, who will record her will
35 **mere** absolute
36 **binds** legally binds
37 **loose** relieved of constipation
51 **ague** fever
61 **suit** request
73 **narrowly** strictly
75 **giddy flames** insane passions
78 **at unawares** unnoticed
79 **writs** writings
81 **tucked up** folded at the corners
82 **tax** condemn
87 **'tis** 'It' refers to the Wife; a colloquial diminutive
credit believe
110–11 **apply . . . luxury** judge all by its own lecherous standards
114 **of the stamp** generally recognized as 'current' or sexually available
known her known her carnally
116 **taxed** found objectionable
117 **where** whereas

Scatters such thoughts, or makes 'em sink for fear
Into the hearts that breed 'em. Nay, surely, if I went, sir,
I would entreat your company.

HAREBRAIN Mine? Prithee, wife, I have been there already.

WIFE That's all one. Although you bring me but to th' door, sir, I would entreat no farther.

HAREBRAIN Thou'rt such a wife! Why, I will bring thee thither then, but not go up, I swear.

WIFE I'faith, you shall not. I do not desire it, sir.

HAREBRAIN Why then, content.

WIFE Give me your hand—you will do so, sir?

HAREBRAIN Why, there's my lip, I will. [*Kissing her*]

WIFE Why then, I go, sir.

HAREBRAIN With me or no man! Incomparable such a woman! *Exeunt*

3.2 *Vials, gallipots, plate, and an hourglass by her, the Courtesan* [*is discovered*] *on a bed for her counterfeit fit.* [*Enter*] *to her, Master Penitent Brothel* [*dressed*] *like a Doctor of Physic*

PENITENT Lady?

COURTESAN Ha, what news?

PENITENT There's one Sir Bounteous Progress newly alighted from his footcloth, and his mare waits at door, as the fashion is.

COURTESAN 'Slid, 'tis the knight that privately maintains me, a little short old spiny gentleman in a great doublet.

PENITENT The same, I know 'im.

COURTESAN He's my sole revenue, meat, drink and raiment.
My good physician, work upon him, I'm weak.

PENITENT Enough.

[*Enter Sir Bounteous Progress*]

SIR BOUNTEOUS Why, where be these ladies, these plump soft delicate creatures, ha?

PENITENT Who would you visit, sir?

SIR BOUNTEOUS Visit? Who? What are you with the plague in your mouth?

PENITENT A physician, sir.

SIR BOUNTEOUS Then you are a loose liver, sir. I have put you to your purgation.

PENITENT [*aside*] But you need none. You're purged in a worse fashion.

COURTESAN Ah, Sir Bounteous.

SIR BOUNTEOUS How now? What art thou?

COURTESAN Sweet Sir Bounteous.

SIR BOUNTEOUS Passion of me, what an alteration's here! Rosamund sick, old Harry? Here's a sight able to make an old man shrink. I was lusty when I came in, but I am down now, i'faith. Mortality, yea? This puts me in mind of a hole seven foot deep, my grave, my grave, my grave. Hist, Master Doctor, a word, sir, hark, 'tis not the plague, is't?

PENITENT The plague, sir? No.

SIR BOUNTEOUS Good.

PENITENT [*aside*] He ne'er asks whether it be the pox or no, and of the twain that had been more likely.

SIR BOUNTEOUS How now, my wench, how dost?

COURTESAN [*coughing*] Huh, weak, knight, huh.

PENITENT [*aside*] She says true, he's a weak knight indeed.

SIR BOUNTEOUS Where does it hold thee most, wench?

COURTESAN All parts alike, sir.

PENITENT [*aside*] She says true still, for it holds her in none.

SIR BOUNTEOUS Hark in thine ear. Thou'rt breeding of young bones; I am afraid I have got thee with child, i'faith.

COURTESAN I fear that much, sir.

SIR BOUNTEOUS O, O, if it should! A young Progress, when all's done.

COURTESAN You have done your good will, sir.

SIR BOUNTEOUS [*aside*] I see by her 'tis nothing but a surfeit of Venus, i'faith, and though I be old, I have gi'n't her. [*To Courtesan*] But since I had the power to make thee sick, I'll have the purse to make thee whole, that's certain. [*To Penitent*] Master Doctor.

PENITENT Sir.

SIR BOUNTEOUS Let's hear, I pray, what is't you minister to her?

PENITENT Marry, sir, some precious cordial, some costly refocillation, a composure comfortable and restorative.

SIR BOUNTEOUS Ay, ay, that, that, that.

3.2 This scene was clearly inspired by Pietro Aretino's *Ragionamenti*: for details see Daileader 2007.

0.1 ***gallipots*** small medicine jars
plate metal utensils

0.2 ***discovered*** revealed

4 **footcloth** large ornamented cloth laid over the horse's back and hanging to the ground on each side; considered a sign of rank.

7 **spiny** spindly, thin
doublet upper-body garment worn by men

15–16 **with...mouth** speaking of the plague

18 **loose liver** an immoral person, or one with a disordered liver, which was regarded as the seat of passion. Physicians were often suspected of irreligion.

19 **purgation** proof, trial, but also punning on intestinal purgation

20–1 **in...fashion** i.e. by his whore (sexually and financially)

26 **Rosamund...Harry?** apparently a quotation from a lost ballad or play about Rosamond Clifford, the mistress of Henry II, supposedly poisoned by Henry's queen

27 **shrink** fearful, but suggesting the loss of an erection in the face of a 'hole seven foot deep'

38 **weak** (*a*) prone to temptation (*b*) impotent

49–50 **surfeit of Venus** too much sex

58 **refocillation** restorative cordial
composure mixture

PENITENT No poorer ingredients than the liquor of coral, clear amber or *succinum*, unicorn's horn six grains, *magisterium perlarum* one scruple—

SIR BOUNTEOUS Ah.

PENITENT *Ossis de corde cervi* half a scruple, *aurum potabile* or his tincture—

SIR BOUNTEOUS Very precious, sir.

PENITENT All which being finely contunded and mixed in a stone or glass mortar with the spirit of diamber—

SIR BOUNTEOUS Nay, pray be patient, sir.

PENITENT That's impossible. I cannot be patient and a physician too, sir.

SIR BOUNTEOUS O cry you mercy, that's true, sir.

PENITENT All which aforesaid—

SIR BOUNTEOUS Ay, there you left, sir.

PENITENT When it is almost exsiccate or dry, I add thereto *olei succini, olei masi*, and *cinnamoni*.

SIR BOUNTEOUS So sir, *olei masi*, that same oil of mace is a great comfort to both the Counters.

PENITENT And has been of a long time, sir.

SIR BOUNTEOUS Well, be of good cheer, wench. There's gold for thee. [*Giving money*] Huh, let her want for nothing, Master Doctor. A poor kinswoman of mine: nature binds me to have a care of her. [*Aside*] There I gulled you, Master Doctor. [*To Courtesan*] Gather up a good spirit, wench. The fit will away, 'tis but a surfeit of gristles. [*Aside*] Ha, ha, I have fitted her! An old knight and a cock o' th' game still! I have not spurs for nothing, I see.

PENITENT [*aside*] No, by my faith, they're hatched. They cost you an angel, sir.

SIR BOUNTEOUS Look to her, good Master Doctor, let her want nothing. I've given her enough already. Ha, ha, ha! *Exit*

COURTESAN So, is he gone?

PENITENT He's like himself, gone.

COURTESAN [*indicating the gold*] Here's somewhat to set up with. How soon he took occasion to slip into his own flattery, soothing his own defects. He only fears he has done that deed which I ne'er feared to come from him in my life. This purchase came unlooked for.

PENITENT Hist, the pair of sons and heirs.

COURTESAN O, they're welcome, they bring money.

Enter Master Inesse [*with blood on his collar*] *and Master Possibility*

POSSIBILITY Master Doctor.

PENITENT I come to you, gentlemen.

POSSIBILITY How does she now?

PENITENT Faith, much after one fashion, sir.

INESSE There's hope of life, sir?

PENITENT I see no signs of death of her.

POSSIBILITY That's some comfort. Will she take anything yet?

PENITENT Yes, yes, yes, she'll take still. Sh'as a kind of facility in taking. How comes your band bloody, sir?

INESSE You may see I met with a scab, sir.

PENITENT *Diversa genera scabierum*, as Pliny reports: there are divers kinds of scabs.

INESSE Pray, let's hear 'em, sir.

PENITENT An itching scab, that is your harlot. A sore scab, your usurer. A running, your promoter. A broad scab, your intelligencer. But a white scab, that's a scald knave and a pander. But to speak truth, the only scabs we are nowadays troubled withal are new officers.

60 **liquor of coral** a solution of coral in water

61 **clear ... succinum** white or yellow amber, cited by Pliny as beneficial for stomach ailments, ear and eye diseases
unicorn's horn the horn of a rhinoceros, narwhal, or other animal, reputedly derived from the unicorn, and regarded as an antidote to poison

62 ***magisterium perlarum*** precipitate of pearls from an acid solution
scruple one-third of a dram

64 ***Ossis de corde cervi*** small bones in the heart and womb of a deer, regarded as beneficial to pregnant women and those in labour.
aurum potabile nitromuriate of gold deoxidized in a volatile oil and drunk as a cordial

65 **tincture** essence

67 **contunded** pounded

68 **spirit of diamber** a stomachic and cordial containing ambergris, musk, and other aromatics

76 ***olei ... cinnamoni*** oils of yellow amber, mace, and cinnamon

77 **oil of mace** a pun alluding to the maces carried by the serjeants when they arrested debtors, who might replenish either of the Counters (City prisons); a parallel coinage is 'oil of whip', proverbially beneficial against idleness

85 **gristles** baby's bones, a reference to her supposed pregnancy

86 **fitted her** (*a*) served her appropriately (*b*) caused this fit

87 **cock ... nothing** alluding to cockfighting and the metal spurs attached to the legs of the birds, with a pun on 'cock of the game' as a sexual adept. 'Spurs' may also be a pun on the testicles.

89 **hatched** (*a*) as a chick (alluding to the child) (*b*) engraved, like the large, ornate spurs of a knight. There is also a numismatic pun: the spur, or spur-royal, a coin worth fifteen shillings, produces angels, coins worth ten shillings.

92 **enough** i.e. the supposed child

95 **gone** (*a*) departed (*b*) out of his wits

100 **purchase** profit

106 **after one fashion** the same

109 **take** eat

112 **taking** Penitent puns on a woman's taking a man during sexual intercourse; also a 'taker up' is one who in a gang of swindlers attracts and softens up the victim.
band a wide collar often worn with the ruff

113 **scab** punning on 'scab' as a low person

114 ***Diversa genera scabierum*** 'Ulcers as they be of many sorts, so are they cured after diverse manners' (Pliny, *Natural History*, XXXVI, xiv).

117 **itching** i.e. suffering the 'itch' of lust

118 **promoter** informer, a 'running' scab because he carries tales

119 **intelligencer** spy, one who gathers and distributes information, making secrets 'broad' or apparent
white scab Treating skin affected by syphilis, or the 'pox', left a white scab.
scald afflicted with a scabby skin disease (here, the pox); contemptible

121 **officers** constables

INESSE Why, now you come to mine, sir, for I'll be sworn one of them was very busy about my head this morning, and he should be a scab by that, for they are ambitious and covet the head.

PENITENT Why, you saw I derived him, sir.

INESSE You physicians are mad gentlemen.

PENITENT We physicians see the most sights of any men living. Your astronomers look upward into th' air—we look downward into th' body, and indeed we have power upward and downward.

INESSE That you have, i'faith, sir.

POSSIBILITY Lady, how cheer you now?

COURTESAN The same woman still—[*coughing*] huh.

POSSIBILITY That's not good.

COURTESAN Little alteration.

[*Possibility gives her money*]

Fie, fie, you have been too lavish, gentlemen.

INESSE Puh, talk not of that, lady, thy health's worth a million. Here, Master Doctor, spare for no cost.

[*Giving him money*]

POSSIBILITY Look what you find there, sir.

COURTESAN What do you mean, gentlemen? Put up, put up, you see I'm down and cannot strive with you. I would rule you else. You have me at advantage, but if ever I live, I will requite it deeply.

INESSE Tut, an't come to that once, we'll requite ourselves well enough.

POSSIBILITY Mistress Harebrain, lady, is setting forth to visit you too.

COURTESAN Ha!—huh!

PENITENT [*aside*] There struck the minute that brings forth the birth of all my joys and wishes. But see the jar now: how shall I rid these from her?

COURTESAN Pray, gentlemen, stay not above an hour from my sight.

INESSE 'Sfoot, we are not going, lady.

PENITENT [*aside*] Subtly brought about, yet 'twill not do, they'll stick by't. [*To them*] A word with you, gentlemen.

INESSE *and* POSSIBILITY What says Master Doctor?

PENITENT She wants but settling of her sense with rest. One hour's sleep, gentlemen, would set all parts in tune.

POSSIBILITY He says truth, i'faith.

INESSE Get her to sleep, Master Doctor. We'll both sit here and watch by her.

PENITENT [*aside*] Hell's angels watch you! No art can prevail with 'em. What with the thought of joys and sight of crosses, my wits are at Hercules' Pillars, *non plus ultra.*

COURTESAN Master Doctor, Master Doctor!

PENITENT Here, lady.

COURTESAN Your physic works! Lend me your hand!

[*Penitent supplies a chamber-pot. She feigns farting and excreting*]

POSSIBILITY Farewell, sweet lady.

INESSE Adieu, Master Doctor.

[*Exeunt Inesse and Possibility*]

COURTESAN So.

PENITENT Let me admire thee.
The wit of man wanes and decreases soon,
But women's wit is ever at full moon.

Enter Wife

There shot a star from heaven.
I dare not yet behold my happiness,
The splendour is so glorious and so piercing.

COURTESAN Mistress Harebrain, give my wit thanks hereafter. Your wishes are in sight, your opportunity spacious.

WIFE Will you but hear a word from me?

COURTESAN Whooh!

WIFE My husband himself brought me to th' door, walks below for my return. Jealousy is prick-eared, and will hear the wagging of a hair.

COURTESAN Pish, you're a faint liver. Trust yourself with your pleasure and me with your security. Go.

PENITENT
The fullness of my wish!

WIFE Of my desire!

123 **busy . . . head** busy hitting me on the head

125 **covet the head** The officers aspire to the post of headborough, a minor parish official. There is also an allusion to the tendency of skin ailments to afflict the scalp.

126 **derived** traced his lineage, also alluding to the medical term 'derive', which means to withdraw inflammation from a diseased body part by blistering or cupping.

131 **power . . . downward** power to purge upward from the stomach or downward through the bowels

141 **Put up** put your money away, but also punning on 'put up' as (*a*) sheathe a sword or (*b*) insert the penis in the vagina

143 **have . . . advantage** take advantage of me

145 **requite** i.e. sexually

151 **jar** obstacle

152 **these** these two, Inesse and Possibility

155 **'Sfoot** an oath, from 'God's foot'

160 **parts in tune** punning on the 'parts' of a musical piece and the parts of the courtesan's body; also alluding to Penitent's impending consummation with Mistress Harebrain

165–6 **thought . . . crosses** expectation of pleasure and awareness of obstacles

166 **Hercules' Pillars** Gibraltar and Mt Abyla, believed by the ancients to support the western boundary of the world; hence *non plus ultra*, 'no farther'.

185 **walks** paces, waiting

186–7 **prick-eared . . . hair** alertly listening, with obscene innuendos on 'prick' as penis, 'wagging' as copulation, and 'hair' as the female pudendum.

188 **faint liver** coward, with a pun on the liver as seat of sexual desire

PENITENT
Beyond this sphere I never will aspire!
Exeunt [Penitent and Wife]

Enter Master Harebrain [apart,] listening

HAREBRAIN
I'll listen. Now the flesh draws nigh her end,
At such a time women exchange their secrets
And ransack the close corners of their hearts.
What many years hath whelmed, this hour imparts.

COURTESAN [*feigning to address Wife*] Pray sit down, there's a low stool. Good Mistress Harebrain, this was kindly done—huh!—give me your hand—huh! Alas, how cold you are. E'en so is your husband, that worthy wise gentleman, as comfortable a man to woman in my case as ever trod—huh!—shoe leather. Love him, honour him, stick by him. He lets you want nothing that's fit for a woman, and to be sure on't, he will see himself that you want it not.

HAREBRAIN And so I do, i'faith, 'tis right my humour.

COURTESAN You live a lady's life with him, go where you will, ride when you will, and do what you will.

HAREBRAIN Not so, not so, neither, she's better looked to.

COURTESAN I know you do, you need not tell me that. 'Twere e'en pity of your life, i'faith, if ever you should wrong such an innocent gentleman. Fie, Mistress Harebrain, what do you mean? Come you to discomfort me? Nothing but weeping with you?

HAREBRAIN She's weeping, 't'as made her weep. My wife shows her good nature already.

COURTESAN Still, still weeping? Huff, huff, huff, why how now, woman? Hey, hy, hy, for shame, leave! Suh, suh, she cannot answer me for snobbing.

HAREBRAIN All this does her good, beshrew my heart, and I pity her. Let her shed tears till morning, I'll stay for her. She shall have enough on't by my good will, I'll not be her hindrance.

COURTESAN O no, lay your hand here, Mistress Harebrain. Ay there, o there, there lies my pain, good gentlewoman. Sore? O ay, I can scarce endure your hand upon't.

HAREBRAIN Poor soul, how she's tormented.

COURTESAN Yes, yes, I eat a cullis an hour since.

HAREBRAIN There's some comfort in that yet; she may 'scape it.

COURTESAN O, it lies about my heart much.

HAREBRAIN I'm sorry for that, i'faith; she'll hardly 'scape it.

COURTESAN Bound? No, no, I'd a very comfortable stool this morning.

HAREBRAIN I'm glad of that i'faith, that's a good sign. I smell she'll 'scape it now.

COURTESAN Will you be going then?

HAREBRAIN Fall back, she's coming.

COURTESAN Thanks, good Mistress Harebrain. Welcome, sweet Mistress Harebrain. Pray commend me to the good gentleman your husband.

HAREBRAIN I could do that myself now.

COURTESAN And to my Uncle Winchcomb, and to my Aunt Lipsalve, and to my Cousin Falsetop, and to my Cousin Lickit, and to my Cousin Horseman, and to all my good cousins in Clerkenwell and Saint John's.

Enter Wife with Master Penitent

WIFE
At three days' end my husband takes a journey.

PENITENT
O, thence I derive a second meeting.

WIFE
May it prosper still.
Till then I rest a captive to his will.
Once again, health, rest and strength to thee, sweet lady. Farewell, you witty squall. Good Master Doctor, have a care to her body if you stand her friend. I know you can do her good.

COURTESAN Take pity of your waiter, go. Farewell, sweet Mistress Harebrain. *[Exit]*

HAREBRAIN [*coming forward*] Welcome, sweet wife, alight upon my lip. [*Kissing her*] Never was hour spent better.

192 **nigh** near
end (*a*) death (*b*) purpose (*c*) bottom, with 'the flesh' alluding to Penitent's penis
193 **secrets** (*a*) confidences (*b*) private parts
194 **close** hidden
195 **whelmed** kept covered
197 **stool** (perhaps accompanied by a gesture toward the chamber-pot)
198 **cold** in relation to the courtesan's supposed fever; also, ironically, cold as in chaste, devoid of passions
199 **E'en ... husband** poking fun at Harebrain's coldness in bed
201 **trod** 'Treading' is a term for copulation, based on the mating action of the male bird.
202–3 **want ... woman** punning on the two senses of 'want', the obscene sense of 'thing' and the literal sense of 'to fit'. The statement can mean either (*a*) he makes sure you need nothing suitable for a woman, or (*b*) he will not permit you to desire any 'thing' that fits (into) a woman.
203 **see** (*a*) see to it (*b*) be deceived into seeing
207 **ride** (*a*) ride coaches (*b*) ride men (hence Harebrain's comment)
210 **pity ... life** the great regret of your life
216 **Huff, huff, huff** coughing sounds, intended to cover the sounds of the off-stage sex
218 **snobbing** sobbing—a re-interpretation of the Wife's vocalizations of pleasure
228 **eat** ate
cullis nutritive broth
230 **'scape it** escape death
234 **Bound** constipated
237 **smell** (*a*) sense (*b*) smell
239 **coming** (*a*) approaching (*b*) achieving orgasm
244–6 **Uncle ... Horseman** all names suggesting bawds and whores: 'Winchcomb', presumably combs for wenches; 'Lipsalve', a balm for chafed lips or genitals; 'Falsetop', a wig or padded brassiere; 'Lickit', suggesting fellatio and 'Horseman', sexual 'riding'
247 **Clerkenwell ... John's** The Priory of St Johns was the main landmark in Clerkenwell, an area notorious for thieves and prostitutes.
253 **stand her friend** (*a*) remain her friend (*b*) remain her lover, with a pun on a 'standing' or erect penis
255 **waiter** referring to Harebrain, waiting below. 'Waiter' could mean servant or admirer, but 'waiters' also kept watch at principal ports to search incoming vessels for Catholic recusants.

WIFE Why, were you within the hearing, sir?

HAREBRAIN Ay, that I was i'faith, to my great comfort. I deceived you there, wife, ha, ha!
I do entreat thee, nay, conjure thee, wife,
Upon my love, or what can more be said,
Oftener to visit this sick virtuous maid.

WIFE
Be not so fierce. Your will shall be obeyed.

HAREBRAIN
Why then I see thou lov'st me.
Exeunt [the Harebrains]

PENITENT Art of ladies!
When plots are e'en past hope and hang their head,
Set with a woman's hand, they thrive and spread.
Exit

3.3

Enter Follywit with Lieutenant Mawworm, Ensign Oboe, and the rest of his consorts

FOLLYWIT Was't not well managed, you necessary mischiefs? Did the plot want either life or art?

LIEUTENANT 'Twas so well, captain, I would you could make such another muss at all adventures.

FOLLYWIT Dost call't a muss? I am sure my grandsire ne'er got his money worse in his life than I got it from him. If ever he did cozen the simple, why, I was born to revenge their quarrel. If ever oppress the widow, I a fatherless child have done as much for him. And so 'tis through the world either in jest or earnest. Let the usurer look for't, for craft recoils in the end like an overcharged musket, and maims the very hand that puts fire to't. There needs no more but a usurer's own blow to strike him from hence to hell—'twill set him forward with a vengeance. But here lay the jest, whoresons: my grandsire, thinking in his conscience that we had not robbed him enough o'ernight, must needs pity me i'th' morning and give me the rest.

LIEUTENANT Two hundred pounds in fair rose-nobles, I protest.

FOLLYWIT Push! I knew he could not sleep quietly till he had paid me for robbing of him too. 'Tis his humour and the humour of most of your rich men in the course of their lives, for you know,
They always feast those mouths that are least needy,
And give them more that have too much already.
And what call you that but robbing of themselves a courtlier way? O!

LIEUTENANT Cuds me, how now, captain?

FOLLYWIT A cold fit that comes over my memory and has a shrewd pull at my fortunes.

LIEUTENANT What's that, sir?

FOLLYWIT Is it for certain, lieutenant, that my grandsire keeps an uncertain creature, a quean?

LIEUTENANT Ay, that's too true, sir.

FOLLYWIT So much the more preposterous for me. I shall hop shorter by that trick. She carries away the thirds at least. 'Twill prove entailed land, I am afraid, when all's done, i'faith. Nay, I have known a vicious old thought-acting father,
Damned only in his dreams, thirsting for game,
When his best parts hung down their heads for shame,
For his blanched harlot dispossess his son,
And make the pox his heir—'twas gravely done.
How hadst thou first knowledge on't, lieutenant?

LIEUTENANT
Faith, from discourse, yet all the policy
That I could use, I could not get her name.

FOLLYWIT Dull slave that ne'er couldst spy it.

LIEUTENANT But the manner of her coming was described to me.

FOLLYWIT How is the manner, prithee?

LIEUTENANT Marry, sir, she comes, most commonly, coached.

FOLLYWIT Most commonly coached indeed, for coaches are as common nowadays as some that ride in 'em. She comes most commonly coached—

265 **fierce** eager, ardent
266 **Art** skill, artfulness
267–8 **When . . . spread** The metaphor is from horticulture, but there are puns suggesting the effect of a woman's hand on a flaccid penis.
3.3.1–2 **necessary mischiefs** useful mischief-makers
4 **muss** scramble (a children's game)
at all adventures at any risk
11 **recoils** mischarges
12 **puts fire to't** triggered it
13 **usurer's own blow** i.e. his blow against another, which recoils against him. This also suggests the phallic 'blow' which may result in rebellious progeny like Follywit.
14 **set him forward** advance him
19 **rose-nobles** gold coins stamped with a rose
30 **cold fit** chill
31 **shrewd pull** a sharp pull, a fierce assault. The original spelling is 'shrode,' which allows for a funereal pun: 'shrode' is a variant of 'shrewd' and 'shroud.' Follywit suffers a premonition of ill fortune.
34 **uncertain** morally questionable, shady
quean whore
36 **preposterous** in its etymological sense of placing last what should be first
37 **hop shorter** as if on a shorter leash
37–8 **thirds . . . entailed** She may get a widow's third of the estate while she lives, making it entailed land, limited in its transference. The pun on 'in-tailed', or vested in a woman's 'tail', is a favourite of Middleton's.
39 **vicious** laden with vice
40 **thought-acting** capable of acting, sexually, only in fantasy
41 **game** sexual play
42 **best parts** (*a*) best qualities (*b*) private parts
43 **blanched** whitened by cosmetics, but also alluding to the treatment of skin affected by venereal disease
dispossess deprive of an inheritance
44 **gravely** soberly, punning on the grave which awaits the victim of syphilis
46 **discourse** rumour
policy machiavellian wiles
49 **her . . . coming** (*a*) her means of transportation (*b*) the way she achieves orgasm
52 **Marry** an oath, from the name of the Virgin Mary
52–3 **she . . . coached** she generally travels by coach
54–5 **coaches . . . common** punning on the pejorative sense of 'common'. By 1605 riding in a coach was no longer a mark of status; coaches were frequently used for prostitution.

LIEUTENANT True, there I left, sir: guarded with some leash of pimps.

FOLLYWIT Beside the coachman?

LIEUTENANT Right, sir. Then alighting, she's privately received by Master Gunwater.

FOLLYWIT That's my grandsire's chief gentleman i'th' chain of gold. That he should live to be a pander and yet look upon his chain and his velvet jacket!

LIEUTENANT Then is your grandsire rounded i'th' ear, the key given after the Italian fashion, backward, she closely conveyed into his closet, there remaining till either opportunity smile upon his credit, or he send down some hot caudle to take order in his performance.

FOLLYWIT
Peace, 'tis mine own, i'faith—I ha't!

LIEUTENANT How now, sir?

FOLLYWIT Thanks, thanks to any spirit
That mingled it 'mongst my inventïons.

ENSIGN Why, Master Follywit!

ALL Captain!

FOLLYWIT Give me scope and hear me.
I have begot that means which will both furnish me
And make that quean walk under his conceit.

LIEUTENANT That were double happiness, to put thyself into money and her out of favour.

FOLLYWIT And all at one dealing!

ENSIGN 'Sfoot, I long to see that hand played.

FOLLYWIT And thou shalt see 't quickly, i'faith. Nay, 'tis in grain, I warrant it hold colour. Lieutenant, step behind yon hanging. If I mistook not at my entrance, there hangs the lower part of a gentlewoman's gown, with a mask and a chin-clout. Bring all this way. Nay, but do't cunningly now: 'tis a friend's house, and I'd use it so. There's a taste for you. *[Exit Lieutenant]*

ENSIGN But prithee, what wilt thou do with a gentlewoman's lower part?

FOLLYWIT Why, use it.

ENSIGN You've answered me indeed in that. I can demand no farther.

[Re-enter Lieutenant with women's garments]

FOLLYWIT Well said. Lieutenant—

LIEUTENANT What will you do now, sir?

FOLLYWIT Come, come, thou shalt see a woman quickly made up here.

LIEUTENANT But that's against kind, captain, for they are always long a-making ready.

FOLLYWIT And is not most they do against kind, I prithee? To lie with their horsekeeper, is not that against kind? To wear half-moons made of another's hair, is not that against kind? To drink down a man—she that should set him up—pray, is not that monstrously against kind now? *[Lieutenant holds out skirt for Follywit]* Nay, over with it, lieutenant, over with it. Ever while you live, put a woman's clothes over her head. Cupid plays best at blindman buff.

LIEUTENANT *[putting skirt over Follywit's head]* You shall have your will, maintenance. I love mad tricks as well as you, for your heart, sir. But what shift will you make for upper bodice, captain?

FOLLYWIT *[settling skirt at his waist]* I see now thou'rt an ass. Why, I'm ready.

LIEUTENANT Ready?

FOLLYWIT Why, the doublet serves as well as the best and is most in fashion. We're all male to th' middle, mankind from the beaver to th' bum. 'Tis an Amazonian time—you shall have women shortly tread their husbands. I should have a couple of locks behind. Prithee, lieutenant, find 'em out for me and wind 'em about

57 **leash** three, as of hunting dogs
64 **chain . . . jacket** marks of high status amongst the servants
65 **rounded** whispered
66 **key . . . backward** The key is handed behind the back. Italians were reputed to favour anal intercourse, perhaps due to the pornographic poems of Pietro Aretino, which emphasize this practice.
67 **closet** bedroom
68–9 **either . . . performance** If opportunity alone does not boost his sexual potency, he sends for some caudle (a restorative drink) to give him vigour.
72 **inventïons** schemes
75 **Give me scope** give me your attention
76 **begot** conceived of
furnish me satisfy my needs
77 **walk . . . conceit** decline in his estimation
82–3 **'tis . . . colour** It is dyed in a fast colour; it is a sound plan.
85 **lower . . . gown** skirt or kirtle
86 **mask** veil
chin-clout scarf, muffler. Masks had become fashionable for all women in public, but chin-clouts were chiefly worn by the lower classes.
87 **friend's house** alluding to both the clothing and the locale
88 **There's . . . you** (perhaps directed at the audience)
90 **lower part** (*a*) skirt (*b*) genitals
97 **made up** (*a*) created (*b*) screwed, and possibly made pregnant
98 **kind** nature
99 **long a-making ready** (*a*) take long to get dressed (*b*) take long to make ready for intercourse
101 **lie . . . horsekeeper** against nature because it departs from hierarchical social order
102 **half-moons** wigs in the shape of a half-moon, perhaps used to make the natural hair look fuller
103 **drink . . . man** consume a man sexually
104 **set him up** (*a*) honour him (*b*) give him an erection
107–8 **put . . . buff** (*a*) undress her (*b*) pull her skirt up over her head (playing with the idea of love as blind)
110 **maintenance** one who maintains servants; a 'meal-ticket'
111 **shift** invention
112 **upper bodice** From the 1580s, the bodice was made very much like the masculine doublet.
118 **beaver to th' bum** hat to waist. A beaver was a hat made of beaver fur; a bum was a French farthingale, a roll placed around the hips to add fullness to a woman's skirts.
118–19 **Amazonian time** an age of masculine women; the Amazons were a legendary race of female warriors
119 **tread** to mount sexually, as of birds
120 **locks behind** locks of false hair wound around the hatband, apparently indicating sexual availability

my hatband. Nay, you shall see, we'll be in fashion to a hair, and become all with probability. The most musty-visage critic shall not except against me.

LIEUTENANT [*arranging Follywit's hair*] Nay, I'll give thee thy due behind thy back. Thou art as mad a piece of clay—

FOLLYWIT Clay! Dost call thy captain clay? Indeed, clay was made to stop holes, he says true. Did not I tell you rascals you should see a woman quickly made up?

ENSIGN I'll swear for't, captain.

FOLLYWIT Come, come, my mask and my chin-clout—come into th' court.

LIEUTENANT Nay, they were both i'th' court long ago, sir.

FOLLYWIT Let me see, where shall I choose two or three for pimps now? But I cannot choose amiss amongst you all, that's the best. Well, as I am a quean, you were best have a care of me and guard me sure. I give you warning beforehand, 'tis a monkey-tailed age. 'Life, you shall go nigh to have half a dozen blithe fellows surprise me cowardly, carry me away with a pair of oars, and put in at Putney!

LIEUTENANT We should laugh at that, i'faith.

FOLLYWIT Or shoot in upo'th' coast of Kew!

LIEUTENANT Two notable fit landing places for lechers, P and Q, Putney and Kew.

FOLLYWIT Well, say you have fair warning on't. The hair about the hat is as good as a flag upo'th' pole at a common playhouse to waste company, and a chin-clout is of that powerful attraction, I can tell you, 'twill draw more linen to't.

LIEUTENANT Fear not us, captain, there's none here but can fight for a whore as well as some Inns o' Court man.

FOLLYWIT Why, then, set forward, and as you scorn
two-shilling brothel,
Twelve-penny panderism, and such base bribes,
Guard me from bonny scribs and bony scribes.

LIEUTENANT Hang 'em, pensions and allowances, fourpence halfpenny a meal, hang 'em. *Exeunt*

Finit Actus Tertius

Incipit Actus Quartus 4.1

Enter in his chamber out of his study, Master Penitent Brothel, a book in his hand, reading

PENITENT

Ha! Read that place again: 'Adultery
Draws the divorce 'twixt heaven and the soul.'
Accursed man that standst divorced from heaven,
Thou wretched unthrift that hast played away
Thy eternal portion at a minute's game,
To please the flesh hast blotted out thy name.
Where were thy nobler meditations busied
That they durst trust this body with itself,
This natural drunkard that undoes us all
And makes our shame apparent in our fall?
Then let my blood pay for't, and vex and boil;
My soul, I know, would never grieve to th' death
The eternal spirit that feeds her with his breath.
Nay, I that knew the price of life and sin,
What crown is kept for continence, what for lust,
The end of man and glory of that end,
As endless as the giver,
To dote on weakness, slime, corruption, woman?
What is she, took asunder from her clothes?
Being ready, she consists of hundred pieces,
Much like your German clock, and near allied:
Both are so nice they cannot go for pride.
Beside a greater fault, but too well known,
They'll strike to ten when they should stop at one.
Within these three days the next meeting's fixed;
If I meet then, hell and my soul be mixed.
My lodging, I know constantly, she not knows.

123 **become all** (*a*) become whatever we choose (*b*) look good in any circumstance
124 **musty-visage** dour, prudish
except against object to
126 **behind thy back** punning on either anal intercourse or the front-to-back position
127 **clay** (*a*) human flesh (*b*) weak and cowardly person (*c*) material for plastering (*d*) the penis
129 **stop holes** i.e. the vagina
133 **court** (*a*) courtyard (*b*) royal court
139 **monkey-tailed** lascivious
142 **put in** alluding to penile penetration
142–4 **Putney...Kew** small towns outside of London, noted as pleasure haunts; both could be reached by boat on the Thames River.
144 **shoot in** penetrate sexually
145–6 **P and Q** initials for 'prick' and the French 'queue' meaning 'tail'
149 **waste company** bad company, with a pun on 'waist'
chin-clout a signal of sexual availability
150–1 **draw...to't** The reference is unclear. Perhaps the 'fine linen' refers to gallants in fine clothing who will be attracted.
153–4 **Inns...man** law student, residing at one of the London Inns of Court
156 **two-shilling** the standard price for an ordinary whore
158 **bonny scribs** pretty misers
bony scribes starving professional penmen
4.1.1 **place** passage
4 **unthrift** spendthrift
4–5 **played...portion** hazarded, as at dice, your divine inheritance
5 **minute's game** i.e. sexual intercourse
13 **her** the soul's
15 **crown** reward; glory
17 **giver** i.e. God
19 **took asunder from** removed from
20 **ready** dressed
21 **German clock** a reference to the first clocks, which were imported from Germany and notoriously irregular
22 **nice** delicate, over-refined
go (*a*) go out (*b*) walk. Women's fashions both made for elaborate preparation rituals and prevented them from walking properly, once dressed.
23 **fault** flaw; but the sense of 'fissure, crack' made for obscene punning on the female anatomy—hence, a 'fault... too well known', suggests the well-used vagina of a (literally) loose woman
24 **strike to** as a clock; the word was also used in a similar sense as 'screw', copulate with—hence, the difference between ten (men) and one
27 **I...constantly** I am sure

Sin's hate is the best gift that sin bestows.
I'll ne'er embrace her more—never—bear witness, never.
Enter the Devil in [Wife's] shape, claps him on the shoulder

SUCCUBUS
What? At a stand? The fitter for my company!

PENITENT
Celestial soldiers guard me!

SUCCUBUS
How now, man?
'Las, did the quickness of my presence fright thee?

PENITENT
Shield me, you ministers of faith and grace!

SUCCUBUS
Leave, leave, are you not ashamed to use
Such words to a woman?

PENITENT
Thou'rt a devil.

SUCCUBUS
A devil?
Feel, feel, man: has a devil flesh and bone?

PENITENT
I do conjure thee by that dreadful power—

SUCCUBUS
The man has a delight to make me tremble.
Are these the fruits of thy adventurous love?
Was I enticed for this? to be soon rejected?
Come, what has changed thee so, delight?

PENITENT
Away!

SUCCUBUS
Remember!

PENITENT
Leave my sight!

SUCCUBUS
Have I this meeting wrought with cunning
Which when I come I find thee shunning?
Rouse thy amorous thoughts and twine me,
All my interest I resign thee.
Shall we let slip this mutual hour
Comes so seldom in our power?
Where's thy lip, thy clip, thy fadom?
Had women such loves, would't not mad 'em?
Art a man, or dost abuse one?
A love, and knowst not how to use one?
Come, I'll teach thee—

PENITENT
Do not follow!

SUCCUBUS
Once so firm and now so hollow?
When was place and season sweeter?
Thy bliss in sight and dar'st not meet her?
Where's thy courage, youth and vigour?
Love's best pleased when't's seized with rigour.
Seize me then with veins most cheerful;
Women love no flesh that's fearful.
'Tis but a fit—come, drink't away,
And dance and sing, and kiss and play.
[*Dancing and singing*] Fa le la le la fa le la le la la fa le la fa la le la le la.

PENITENT Torment me not.

SUCCUBUS Fa le la fa le la fa la la lo.

PENITENT Fury!

SUCCUBUS Fa le la fa le la fa la la lo.

PENITENT
Devil! I do conjure thee once again
By that soul-quaking thunder to depart,
And leave this chamber freed from thy damned art!
Succubus stamps and exit
It has prevailed! O my sin-shaking sinews!
What should I think? Jasper, why, Jasper!
[*Enter Jasper*]

JASPER
Sir, how now? What has disturbed you, sir?

PENITENT
A fit, a qualm—is Mistress Harebrain gone?

JASPER
Who, sir? Mistress Harebrain?

PENITENT
Is she gone, I say?

JASPER Gone? Why, she was never here yet.

PENITENT No?

JASPER Why, no, sir.

PENITENT Art sure on't?

JASPER Sure on't? If I be sure I breathe and am myself.

PENITENT I like it not. Where kept'st thou?

JASPER I'th' next room, sir.

PENITENT Why, she struck by thee, man.

JASPER You'd make one mad, sir. That a gentlewoman should steal by me and I not hear her? 'Sfoot, one may hear the rustling of their bums almost an hour before we see 'em.

PENITENT
I will be satisfied, although to hazard.

30 SUCCUBUS a demon in female form supposed to have intercourse with men in their sleep
At a stand (*a*) in a state of perplexity (*b*) with an erect penis; also alluding to the proverb, 'Idleness is the mother of all evil.'
fitter better-suited, with a suggestion of the potential 'fit' of their genitals
36 **has...bone** Much debate surrounded the question of whether good or evil spirits were palpable.
45 **twine** embrace
46 **All...thee** Everything I possess I surrender.
47 **mutual hour** hour together
49 **clip** kiss
fadom embrace, with a suggestion of the navigational sense of 'fathom' as 'plumbing the depths'—meaning penetration and/or damnation
50 **mad 'em** madden them
51 **abuse** i.e. abuse the form of man, as the Devil himself does by taking a human form in this scene
54 **firm** (*a*) resolute (*b*) sexually aroused
hollow (*a*) craven (*b*) devoid of passion
55 **season** moment; opportunity
59 **veins** containing blood, the element associated with lust
60 **flesh** (*a*) man (*b*) penis
72 **sin-shaking** (*a*) shaking from fear of sin (*b*) shaking away sin (*c*) shaking from temptation to sin
82 **kept'st** were
84 **struck by** passed by
87 **bums** (*a*) farthingales (*b*) buttocks
89 **although to hazard** even if at risk

What though her husband meet me? I am honest.
When men's intents are wicked, their guilt haunts 'em;
But when they're just, they're armed, and nothing daunts 'em.
[*Exit*]

JASPER What strange humour call you this? He dreams of women and both his eyes broad open! *Exit*

4.2 *Enter at one door Sir Bounteous Progress, at another Gunwater*

SIR BOUNTEOUS Why, how now, Master Gunwater? What's the news with your haste?

GUNWATER I have a thing to tell your worship—

SIR BOUNTEOUS Why, prithee tell me, speak, man.

GUNWATER Your worship shall pardon me, I have better bringing up than so.

SIR BOUNTEOUS How, sir?

GUNWATER 'Tis a thing made fit for your ear, sir.

SIR BOUNTEOUS O, O, O, cry you mercy, now I begin to taste you. Is she come?

GUNWATER She's come, sir.

SIR BOUNTEOUS Recovered, well and sound again?

GUNWATER That's to be feared, sir.

SIR BOUNTEOUS Why, sir?

GUNWATER She wears a linen cloth about her jaw.

SIR BOUNTEOUS Ha, ha, haw! Why, that's the fashion, you whoreson Gunwater.

GUNWATER The fashion, sir? Live I so long time to see that a fashion,
Which rather was an emblem of dispraise.
It was suspected much in Monsieur's days.

SIR BOUNTEOUS Ay, ay, in those days, that was a queasy time. Our age is better hardened now, and put oftener in the fire. We are tried what we are. Tut, the pox is as natural now as an ague in the springtime. We seldom take physic without it. Here, take this key. You know what duties belong to 't. Go, give order for a cullis, let there be a good fire made i'th' matted chamber, do you hear, sir?

GUNWATER I know my office, sir. *Exit*

SIR BOUNTEOUS An old man's venery is very chargeable, my masters: there's much cookery belongs to't. *Exit*

4.3 *Enter Gunwater [wearing his gold chain] with Follywit in Courtesan's disguise and masked*

GUNWATER Come, lady, you know where you are now?

FOLLYWIT Yes, good Master Gunwater.

GUNWATER This is the old closet, you know.

FOLLYWIT I remember it well, sir.

GUNWATER There stands a casket. I would my yearly revenue were but worth the wealth that's locked in't, lady, yet I have fifty pound a year, wench.

FOLLYWIT Beside your apparel, sir?

GUNWATER Yes, faith, have I.

FOLLYWIT But then you reckon your chain, sir.

GUNWATER No, by my troth do I not, neither. Faith, an you consider me rightly, sweet lady, you might admit a choice gentleman into your service.

FOLLYWIT O pray, away, sir!

GUNWATER Pusha! Come, come, you do but hinder your fortunes, i'faith. I have the command of all the house, I can tell you. [*Groping Follywit*] Nothing comes into th' kitchen but comes through my hands.

FOLLYWIT Pray do not handle me, sir.

GUNWATER Faith, you're too nice, lady, and as for my secrecy, you know I have vowed it often to you.

FOLLYWIT Vowed it? No, no, you men are fickle.

GUNWATER Fickle? 'Sfoot bind me, lady—

FOLLYWIT [*grasping his gold chain*] Why, I bind you by virtue of this chain to meet me tomorrow at the Flower-de-luce yonder, between nine and ten.

GUNWATER And if I do not, lady, let me lose it, thy love and my best fortunes!

FOLLYWIT [*taking chain*] Why, now I'll try you, go to.

GUNWATER Farewell, sweet lady. *Kisses her. Exit*

FOLLYWIT Welcome, sweet coxcomb! By my faith, a good induction. I perceive by his overworn phrase and his action toward the middle region still, there has been some saucy nibbling motion, and no doubt the cunning quean waited but for her prey, and I think 'tis better bestowed upon me for his soul's health—and his body's too. I'll teach the slave to be so bold yet, as once to offer

4.2.10 **taste you** (*a*) understand you (*b*) relish your tidings
13 **feared** doubted
15 **cloth . . . jaw** a means of hiding the disfigurement caused by syphilis; Follywit's chin-clout also hides his identity.
21 **Monsieur's** The Duke of Anjou, brother of the French king Charles IX, who visited England several times in the 1570s, hoping to marry Elizabeth.
22 **queasy** i.e. prudish, morally uptight
23–4 **put . . . fire** Heat treatment was a frequent remedy for the pox. Also, an ironic allusion to Biblical metaphors of testing such as in Zechariah 13:9.
25 **ague** fever
26 **physic** a euphemism for coitus
31 **venery** lechery, but also hunting
chargeable expensive
32 **my masters** (a wink at the men in the audience)
4.3.12–13 **admit . . . service** i.e. accept as a lover
18 **comes** (*a*) is transported (*b*) achieves orgasm
20 **nice** coy
24–5 **by virtue of** i.e. if you hazard the cost of
25–6 **Flower-de-luce** There were several inns in London known by this emblem; Middleton most likely referred to the one on Turnmill Street, an area notorious for brothels.
29 **try** (*a*) test (*b*) try out
31 **coxcomb** philanderer; rogue
32 **induction** introduction, as of a dramatic work. The term derives from the Latin for 'lead in'.
overworn phrase over-rehearsed lines; i.e. the usual cliched come-ons
33 **action . . . region** pelvic activity. 'Action' is another dramatic term.
34 **saucy nibbling motion** i.e. heavy foreplay. 'Motion' can mean 'puppet-show'.
35 **waited . . . prey** simply waited for her prey
36–7 **for . . . too** Follywit's disguise will benefit Gunwater by saving him from damnation and venereal disease.

to vault into his master's saddle, i'faith. Now, casket, by your leave, I have seen your outside oft, but that's no proof. Some have fair outsides that are nothing worth. [*Breaking casket open*] Ha! Now by my faith, a gentlewoman of very good parts: diamond, ruby, sapphire, *onyx cum prole silexque*. If I do not wonder how the quean 'scaped tempting, I'm an hermaphrodite. Sure she could lack nothing but the devil to point to't, and I wonder that he should be missing. Well, 'tis better as it is: this is the fruit of old grunting venery. Grandsire, you may thank your drab for this. O fie, in your crinkling days, grandsire, keep a courtesan to hinder your grandchild! 'Tis against nature, i'faith, and I hope you'll be weary on't.
Now to my villains that lurk close below.
Who keeps a harlot, tell him this from me:
He needs nor thief, disease, nor enemy.
Exit [*with jewels*]

4.4 *Enter Sir Bounteous*

SIR BOUNTEOUS Ah sirrah, methink I feel myself well toasted, bumbasted, rubbed and refreshed. But i'faith, I cannot forget to think how soon sickness has altered her to my taste. I gave her a kiss at bottom o'th' stairs, and by th' mass, methought her breath had much ado to be sweet, like a thing compounded methought of wine, beer and tobacco. I smelt much pudding in't.
It may be but my fancy or her physic;
For this I know, her health gave such content,
The fault rests in her sickness or my scent.
[*Looking for Courtesan*] How dost thou now, sweet girl, what, well recovered?
Sickness quite gone, ha? Speak, ha? Wench! Frank Gullman!
[*Finding open casket*] Why, body of me, what's here? My casket wide open, broke open, my jewels stolen! Why, Gunwater!

GUNWATER [*within*] Anon, anon, sir.

SIR BOUNTEOUS Come hither, Gunwater.

GUNWATER [*within*] That were small manners, sir, i'faith. I'll find a time anon. Your worship's busy yet.

SIR BOUNTEOUS Why, Gunwater!

GUNWATER [*within*] Foh, nay then, you'll make me blush, i'faith, sir.

[*Enter Gunwater*]

SIR BOUNTEOUS Where's this creature?

GUNWATER What creature is't you'd have, sir?

SIR BOUNTEOUS The worst that ever breathes.

GUNWATER That's a wild boar, sir.

SIR BOUNTEOUS That's a vild whore, sir. Where didst thou leave her, rascal?

GUNWATER Who? Your recreation, sir?

SIR BOUNTEOUS My execration, sir.

GUNWATER Where I was wont, in your worship's closet.

SIR BOUNTEOUS
A pox engross her, it appears too true.
See you this casket, sir?

GUNWATER
My chain, my chain, my chain, my one and only chain!

Exit

SIR BOUNTEOUS
Thou runst to much purpose now, Gunwater, yea?
Is not a quean enough to answer for
But she must join a thief to't? A thieving quean!
Nay, I have done with her, i'faith. 'Tis a sign she's been sick o' late, for she's a great deal worse than she was. By my troth, I would have pawned my life upon't, did she want anything? Was she not supplied?
Nay, and liberally, for that's an old man's sin:
We'll feast our lechery though we starve our kin.
Is not my name Sir Bounteous, am I not expressed there?
Ah, fie, fie, fie, fie, fie, but I perceive
Though she have never so complete a friend,
A strumpet's love will have a waft i'th' end
And distaste the vessel. I can hardly bear this.
But say I should complain, perhaps she has pawned 'em—
'Sfoot, the judges will but laugh at it, and bid her borrow more money of 'em, make the old fellow pay for's lechery: that's all the 'mends I get. I have seen the same case tried at Newbury the last 'sizes.
Well, things must slip and sleep. I will dissemble it

38 **vault . . . saddle** a variation on the 'riding' metaphor
42 **of . . . parts** (*a*) good qualities (*b*) attractive body-parts. The passage as a whole equates the broaching of the casket with the sexual penetration of a woman.
43 ***onyx . . . silexque*** onyx with its compounds, and silica; both are forms of quartz, often used for cameos. The phrase is out of a Latin grammar book; this particular passage refers to nouns of ambiguous gender.
44 **hermaphrodite** a person with attributes of both sexes
47 **this** i.e. Follywit's act, the theft
48 **drab** slut
49 **crinkling** wrinkled
50 **hinder** i.e. from his inheritance
4.4.1 **sirrah** Bounteous presumably thinks Gunwater is in the room.
2 **bumbasted** bum-basted, roasted on the backside, but also punning on bombast or hot air
7 **pudding** a variety of tobacco, compacted into a sausage-shaped wad
8 **physic** medicine
9 **content** contentment
10 **scent** sense of smell
12 **Frank Gullman** Frank is a diminutive of Francis. Her first and last names together create the oxymoron 'honest trickster'.
13 **body of me** an oath derived from the body of Christ
18 **small manners** bad manners. Gunwater does not want to interrupt Bounteous and his mistress making love.
26 **wild boar** a reference to the wild boar who roots up the vineyard of Israel in Psalm 80:13: an image of Satan
27 **vild** vile; the original spelling has been kept here for the sake of the rhyme.
32 **engross** take
35 **to much purpose** for good reason
46 **friend** a euphemism for lover
47 **waft** bad odour; fart
48 **distaste** render offensive
52 **'mends** amends
53 **'sizes** assizes, court sessions
54 **things . . . sleep** i.e. let sleeping dogs lie
dissemble it cover it up, put on a bold face

Because my credit shall not lose her lustre.
But whilst I live, I'll neither love nor trust her.
I ha' done, I ha' done, I ha' done with her i'faith!
Exit

4.5 *Master Penitent Brothel knocking within; enter a Servus [Rafe]*

RAFE Who's that knocks?
PENITENT [*within*] A friend.
[*Enter Penitent*]
RAFE What's your will, sir?
PENITENT Is Master Harebrain at home?
RAFE No, newly gone from it, sir.
PENITENT Where's the gentlewoman his wife?
RAFE My mistress is within, sir.
PENITENT When came she in, I pray?
RAFE Who, my mistress? She was not out these two days, to my knowledge.
PENITENT No? Trust me, I'd thought I'd seen her. I would request a word with her.
RAFE I'll tell her, sir. [*Exit*]
PENITENT I thank you.—It likes me worse and worse.
Enter [Wife]

WIFE
Why, how now, sir? 'Twas desperately adventured.
I little looked for you until the morrow.
PENITENT
No? Why, what made you at my chamber then even now?
WIFE
I at your chamber?
PENITENT Puh, dissemble not,
Come, come, you were there.
WIFE By my life you wrong me, sir.
PENITENT What?
WIFE
First, you're not ignorant what watch keeps o'er me,
And for your chamber, as I live I know 't not.
PENITENT [*strikes himself*]
Burst into sorrow then and grief's extremes
Whilst I beat on this flesh!
WIFE What is't disturbs you, sir?
PENITENT
Then was the devil in your likeness there.
WIFE Ha?
PENITENT
The very devil assumed thee formally:
That face, that voice, that gesture, that attire
E'en as it sits on thee, not a pleat altered,
That beaver band, the colour of that periwig,
The farthingale above the navel, all
As if the fashion were his own invention.
WIFE
Mercy defend me.
PENITENT To beguile me more,
The cunning succubus told me that meeting
Was wrought o' purpose by much wit and art,
Wept to me, laid my vows before me, urged me,
Gave me the private marks of all our love,
Wooed me in wanton and effeminate rhymes,
And sung and danced about me like a fairy.
And had not worthier cogitations blest me,
Thy form and his enchantments had possessed me.
WIFE
What shall become of me? My own thoughts doom me.
PENITENT
Be honest: then the devil will ne'er assume thee.
He has no pleasure in that shape to abide
Where these two sisters reign not, lust or pride.
He as much trembles at a constant mind
As looser flesh at him. Be not dismayed:
Spring souls for joy, his policies are betrayed.
Forgive me, Mistress Harebrain, on whose soul
The guilt hangs double,
My lust and thy enticement: both I challenge
And therefore of due vengeance it appeared
To none but me to whom both sins inhered.
What knows the lecher when he clips his whore
Whether it be the devil his parts adore?
They're both so like that, in our natural sense,
I could discern no change nor difference.
No marvel then times should so stretch and turn:
None for religion, all for pleasure burn.
Hot zeal into hot lust is now transformed,
Grace into painting, charity into clothes,
Faith into false hair, and put off as often.
There's nothing but our virtue knows a mean.
He that kept open house now keeps a quean.
He will keep open still that he commends,
And there he keeps a table for his friends;

4.5.0.2 *Servus* servant
14 **It likes me** I like it
15 **adventured** risked
17 **what made you** what were you doing
26 **assumed thee formally** assumed your shape
29 **beaver band** hat band of beaver fur **periwig** wig
30 **farthingale... navel** the drum farthingale, which depended upon a hoop at waist level, popular in the last year of Elizabeth's reign.
36 **marks** signs; reminders
40 **his** the devil's
46 **looser** weaker, more lascivious
47 **Spring souls** if souls spring
48 **whose** (referring to himself)
50 **thy enticement** i.e. my enticement of you **challenge** claim
54 **parts** (*a*) flesh (*b*) private parts
55 **like** alike (the devil and a whore) **sense** perception
57 **stretch and turn** corrupt and distort
60 **painting** cosmetics
62 **mean** limit
64 **that** that which (i.e. his whore, whom he 'keeps open' for other men's use)
65 **keeps... friends** The 'table' shared with friends may be a metaphor for the shared whore, or the 'friends' may be read in the bawdy sense as mistresses who eat at his table.

And she consumes more than his sire could hoard,
Being more common than his house or board.

Enter Harebrain [apart]

Live honest and live happy, keep thy vows:
She's part a virgin whom but one man knows.
Embrace thy husband, and beside him none:
Having but one heart, give it but to one.

WIFE [*kneeling and weeping*]
I vow it on my knees with tears true bred:
No man shall ever wrong my husband's bed.

PENITENT
Rise, I'm thy friend forever.

[She rises]

HAREBRAIN [*coming to them*] And I thine
Forever and ever. Let me embrace thee, sir,
Whom I will love even next unto my soul,
And that's my wife.
Two dear rare gems this hour presents me with,
A wife that's modest and a friend that's right.
Idle suspect and fear, now take your flight.

PENITENT
A happy inward peace crown both your joys.

HAREBRAIN
Thanks above utterance to you.

[Enter Rafe]

Now, the news?

RAFE Sir Bounteous Progress, sir,
Invites you and my mistress to a feast
On Tuesday next. His man attends without.

HAREBRAIN
Return both with our willingness and thanks.

[Exit Rafe]

I will entreat you, sir, to be my guest.

PENITENT
Who, I, sir?

HAREBRAIN Faith, you shall.

PENITENT Well, I'll break strife.

HAREBRAIN
A friend's so rare, I'll sooner part from life. *[Exeunt]*

4.6 *Enter Follywit, the Courtesan striving from him*

FOLLYWIT What, so coy, so strict? Come, come.

COURTESAN Pray change your opinion, sir, I am not for that use.

FOLLYWIT Will you but hear me?

COURTESAN I shall hear that I would not. *Exit*

FOLLYWIT 'Sfoot, this is strange. I've seldom seen a wench stand upon stricter points. 'Life, she will not endure to be courted. Does she e'er think to prosper? I'll ne'er believe that tree can bring forth fruit that never bears a blossom. Courtship's a blossom and often brings forth fruit in forty weeks. 'Twere a mad part in me now to turn over. If ever there were any hope on't, 'tis at this instant. Shall I be madder now than ever I have been? I'm in the way, i'faith.
Man's never at high height of madness full
Until he love and prove a woman's gull.
I do protest in earnest, I ne'er knew
At which end to begin to affect a woman
Till this bewitching minute. I ne'er saw
Face worth my object till mine eye met hers.
I should laugh an I were caught, i'faith.
I'll see her again, that's certain, whate'er comes on't.

Enter the Mother

By your favour, lady.

MOTHER You're welcome, sir.

FOLLYWIT Know you the young gentlewoman that went in lately?

MOTHER I have best cause to know her. I'm her mother, sir.

FOLLYWIT O, in good time. I like the gentlewoman well, a pretty, contrived beauty.

MOTHER Ay, nature has done her part, sir.

FOLLYWIT But she has one uncomely quality.

MOTHER What's that, sir?

FOLLYWIT 'Sfoot, she's afraid of a man.

MOTHER Alas, impute that to her bashful spirit. She's fearful of her honour.

FOLLYWIT Of her honour? 'Slid, I'm sure I cannot get her maidenhead with breathing upon her, nor can she lose her honour in her tongue.

MOTHER True, and I have often told her so, but what would you have of a foolish virgin, sir, a wilful virgin? I tell you, sir, I need not have been in that solitary estate that I am, had she had grace and boldness to have put herself forward. Always timorsome, always backward, ah, that same peevish honour of hers has undone her and me both, good gentleman. The suitors, the jewels, the jointures that has been offered her—we had been made women forever! But what was her fashion? She could not endure the sight of a man, forsooth, but run and hole herself presently, so choice of her honour. I am persuaded, whene'er she has husband,

66 **consumes** either sexually or gastronomically; most likely both
67 **common** open to all
69 **knows** i.e. knows carnally
74 **friend** The double meaning casts a shadow on the moralistic resolution of the scene.
77 **And...wife** i.e. my wife is my soul
79 **right** true; loyal
88 **break strife** take a meal
4.6.5 **that...not** that which I would rather not hear
7 **points** principles
11 **forty weeks** the duration of a pregnancy
12 **turn over** reform
14 **in** on
16 **gull** fool
18 **At...woman** i.e. whether to love a woman for her face or her lower end
20 **worth my object** worthy of my attentions
29 **in good time** just in time
30 **contrived** delicately made
36 **fearful of** i.e. fearful of losing
43–4 **put herself forward** i.e. into the society of marriageable men
44 **timorsome** timorous, fearful
backward contrary
45 **peevish** silly, perverse
47 **jointures** marriage settlements
48 **made** wealthy, successful, with a pun on sexual 'making'
50 **hole** hide, with an allusion to the vagina
choice of particular about

She will e'en be a precedent for all married wives,
How to direct their actions and their lives.

FOLLYWIT Have you not so much power with her to command her presence?

MOTHER You shall see straight what I can do, sir. *Exit*

FOLLYWIT Would I might be hanged if my love do not stretch to her deeper and deeper. Those bashful maiden humours take me prisoner. When there comes a restraint upon flesh, we are always most greedy upon't, and that makes your merchants' wives oftentimes pay so dear for a mouthful. Give me a woman as she was made at first, simple of herself, without sophistication, like this wench. I cannot abide them when they have tricks, set speeches and artful entertainments. You shall have some so impudently aspected, they will outcry the forehead of a man, make him blush first and talk him into silence, and this is counted manly in a woman. It may hold so—sure womanly it is not, no.
If e'er I love or anything move me,
'Twill be a woman's simple modesty.

Enter Mother bringing in strivingly the Courtesan

COURTESAN Pray let me go. Why, mother, what do you mean? I beseech you, mother! Is this your conquest now? Great glory 'tis to overcome a poor and silly virgin.

FOLLYWIT
The wonder of our time sits in that brow.
I ne'er beheld a perfect maid till now.

MOTHER
Thou childish thing, more bashful than thou'rt wise,
Why dost thou turn aside and drown thine eyes?
Look, fearful fool, there's no temptation near thee.
Art not ashamed that any flesh should fear thee?
Why, I durst pawn my life the gentleman means
No other but honest and pure love to thee.
How say you, sir?

FOLLYWIT By my faith, not I, lady.

MOTHER
Hark you there, what think you now, forsooth?
What grieves your honour now?
Or what lascivious breath intends to rear
Against that maiden organ, your chaste ear?
Are you resolved now better of men's hearts,
Their faiths and their affections? With you none,
Or at most few, whose tongues and minds are one.
Repent you now of your opinion past.
Men love as purely as you can be chaste.
To her yourself, sir: the way's broke before you,
You have the easier passage.

FOLLYWIT Fear not, come,
Erect thy happy graces in thy look.
I am no curious wooer, but in faith
I love thee honourably.

COURTESAN How mean you that, sir?

FOLLYWIT
'Sfoot, as one loves a woman for a wife.

MOTHER
Has the gentleman answered you, trow?

FOLLYWIT
I do confess it truly to you both,
My estate is yet but sickly, but I've a grandsire
Will make me lord of thousands at his death.

MOTHER
I know your grandsire well. [*Aside*] She knows him better.

FOLLYWIT
Why then, you know no fiction. My state then
Will be a long day's journey 'bove the waste, wench.

MOTHER Nay, daughter, he says true.

FOLLYWIT
And thou shalt often measure it in thy coach,
And with the wheels' track make a girdle for't.

MOTHER Ah, 'twill be a merry journey.

FOLLYWIT
What, is't a match? If't be, clap hands and lips.
[*He kisses Courtesan*]

MOTHER 'Tis done, there's witness on't.

FOLLYWIT
Why then, mother, I salute you.
[*He kisses Mother*]

MOTHER Thanks, sweet son.
[*Taking Follywit aside*] Son Follywit, come hither. If I might counsel thee, we'll e'en take her while the good mood's upon her. Send for a priest, and clap't up within this hour.

FOLLYWIT By my troth, agreed, mother.

59–62 **When...mouthful** an allusion to Lenten prohibitions against meat-eating, which drove many to paying black market prices. The meat-eating metaphor for sex appears in numerous works by Middleton.
63 **simple of herself** guileless, innocent
65 **set** calculated, contrived
66 **impudently aspected** brash, brazen-faced
66–7 **outcry...man** outrage (with a threat of cuckolding, the forehead being the site of the horns)
68 **manly** admirable; masculine
74 **silly** defenceless
76 **time** era, age
79 **drown** lower
81 **fear** frighten
88 **maiden organ** another pun on the genitals, suggesting that the ear is perhaps her only chaste organ
89 **Are...now** Do you now think
90 **With you none** You believe there are none
94 **broke** open, cleared—with an ironic allusion to her broken hymen
95 **easier passage** (to her heart, or between her legs)
96 **Erect** Follywit's 'happy graces' may be 'erect' in more than his 'look'.
97 **curious** particular, sophisticated, but also with the sense of prying or probing
100 **trow** do you think?
104 **knows** punning, again, on carnal knowledge
106 **waste** wasteland, barren region; also punning on 'waist'
108 **measure it** travel the distance
111 **clap** join
112 **there's witness on't** i.e., I am the witness of it. The joining of hands before a witness was a legally binding marriage promise, hence Follywit addresses the bawd as 'mother'.
116 **clap't up** (*a*) make it binding (*b*) consummate it sexually

MOTHER
Nor does her wealth consist all in her flesh,
Though beauty be enough wealth for a woman.
She brings a dowry of three hundred pound with her.

FOLLYWIT
'Sfoot, that will serve till my grandsire dies.
I warrant you, he'll drop away at fall o'th' leaf. If ever he reach to All Hollantide, I'll be hanged.

MOTHER O yes, son, he's a lusty old gentleman.

FOLLYWIT Ah pox, he's given to women; he keeps a quean at this present.

MOTHER Fie!

FOLLYWIT Do not tell my wife on't.

MOTHER That were needless, i'faith.

FOLLYWIT He makes a great feast upon the 'leventh of this month, Tuesday next, and you shall see players there.—[*Aside*] I have one trick more to put upon him.—My wife and yourself shall go thither before as my guests and prove his entertainment. I'll meet you there at night. The jest will be here: that feast which he makes will, unknown to him, serve fitly for our wedding dinner. We shall be royally furnished, and geld some charges by't.

MOTHER An excellent course, i'faith, and a thrifty. Why, son, methinks you begin to thrive before you're married.

FOLLYWIT [*to Courtesan*]
We shall thrive one day, wench, and clip enough:
Between our hopes there's but a grandsire's puff.
Exit

MOTHER
So, girl, here was a bird well caught.

COURTESAN
If ever, here.
But what for's grandsire? 'Twill scarce please him well.

MOTHER
Who covets fruit ne'er cares from whence it fell.
Thou'st wedded youth and strength, and wealth will fall.
Last, thou'rt made honest.

COURTESAN
And that's worth 'em all.
Exeunt

Finit Actus Quartus

5.1

Incipit Actus Quintus et Ultimus
Enter busily Sir Bounteous Progress [with Gunwater, Servants] for the feast

SIR BOUNTEOUS Have a care, bluecoats. Bestir yourself, Master Gunwater, cast an eye into th' kitchen, o'erlook the knaves a little. [*Exit Gunwater*]
Every Jack has his friend today—this cousin and that cousin puts in for a dish of meat—a man knows not till he make a feast how many varlets he feeds. Acquaintances swarm in every corner, like flies at Bartholomewtide that come up with drovers. 'Sfoot, I think they smell my kitchen seven mile about.

[*Enter Master Shortrod Harebrain, Wife, and Master Penitent Brothel*]

Master Shortrod and his sweet bedfellow, you're very copiously welcome.

HAREBRAIN [*presenting Penitent*] Sir, here's an especial dear friend of ours. We were bold to make his way to your table.

SIR BOUNTEOUS Thanks for that boldness ever, good Master Shortrod. Is this your friend, sir?

HAREBRAIN Both my wife's friend and mine, sir.

SIR BOUNTEOUS Why then compendiously, sir, you're welcome.

PENITENT In octavo I thank you, sir.

SIR BOUNTEOUS Excellently retorted, i'faith, he's welcome for's wit. I have my sorts of salutes and know how to place 'em courtly. Walk in, sweet gentlemen, walk in. There's a good fire i'th' hall. You shall have my sweet company instantly.

HAREBRAIN Ay, good Sir Bounteous.
[*Exeunt the Harebrains and Penitent*]

SIR BOUNTEOUS You shall indeed, gentlemen.

Enter Servus [clumsily]

How now, what news brings thee in stumbling now?

SERVUS There are certain players come to town, sir, and desire to interlude before your worship.

SIR BOUNTEOUS Players? By the mass, they are welcome, they'll grace my entertainment well. But for 'certain' players, there thou liest, boy. They were never more uncertain in their lives, now up and now down. They know not when to play, where to play, nor what to play: not when to play for fearful fools, where to play for Puritan fools, nor what to play for critical fools. Go call 'em in. [*Exit Servant*]

123 **at...leaf** by Fall, or as quickly as a leaf falls
124 **All Hollantide** All Saints' Day, 1 November
130 **needless** (because she knows)
135 **prove** test, check out
138 **royally furnished** superbly treated
geld some charges i.e. cut expenses, save money on the meal
142 **clip enough** (*a*) embrace enough (*b*) seize enough profit (with an allusion to the 'clipping' of gold off the edges of coins)
143 **puff** (dying) breath
147 **fall** as fruit from the tree
148 **Last** finally
5.1.1 **bluecoats** servants
4 **Jack** fellow; glancing at the proverbial happy ending, 'All is well, Jack shall have Jill.'
6 **varlets** servants
8 **Bartholomewtide** 24 August, the time of the annual fair held in the suburb of Smithfield
drovers cattle-drivers; herdsmen
9.1 ***Shortrod*** i.e. 'Littledick'
18 **compendiously** briefly
20 **In octavo** briefly; octavo is a small size in which books were printed with each sheet folded in eight
30 **interlude** perform a play, as in the interval of a feast
35 **where to play** Puritans constantly attempted to inhibit acting
36 **fearful fools** When deaths from plague reached a certain number per week, dramatic performances were prohibited for fear of spreading infection.
37 **critical fools** literary critics

How fitly the whoresons come upo'th' feast. Troth, I was e'en wishing for 'em.

[Re-enter Servant with Follywit, Lieutenant, and their comrades disguised as players]

O welcome, welcome, my friends.

FOLLYWIT
The month of May delights not in her flowers
More than we joy in that sweet sight of yours.

SIR BOUNTEOUS Well acted, o' my credit. I perceive he's your best actor.

LIEUTENANT He has greatest share, sir, and may live of himself, sir.

SIR BOUNTEOUS [*to Follywit, who is removing his hat*] What, what? Put on your hat, sir, pray put on. Go to, wealth must be respected; let those that have least feathers stand bare. And whose men are you, I pray? Nay, keep on your hat still.

FOLLYWIT We serve my Lord Owemuch, sir.

SIR BOUNTEOUS My Lord Owemuch, by my troth, the welcomest men alive! Give me all your hands at once. That honourable gentleman? He lay at my house in a robbery once and took all quietly, went away cheerfully. I made a very good feast for him. I never saw a man of honour bear things bravelier away. Serve my Lord Owemuch? Welcome, i'faith. [*To servant*] Some bastard for my lord's players! [*Exit Servant*] Where be your boys?

FOLLYWIT They come along with the wagon, sir.

SIR BOUNTEOUS Good, good. And which is your politician amongst you? Now, i'faith, he that works out restraints, makes best legs at court, and has a suit made of purpose for the company's business, which is he? Come, be not afraid of him.

FOLLYWIT I am he, sir.

SIR BOUNTEOUS Art thou he? Give me thy hand. Hark in thine ear, thou rollest too fast to gather so much moss as thy fellow there—champ upon that, ah! And what play shall we have, my masters?

FOLLYWIT A pleasant witty comedy, sir.

SIR BOUNTEOUS Ay, ay, ay, a comedy in any case, that I and my guests may laugh a little. What's the name on't?

FOLLYWIT 'Tis called *The Slip.*

SIR BOUNTEOUS *The Slip?* By my troth, a pretty name and a glib one. Go all and slip into't, as fast as you can. [*To Servant*] Cover a table for the players. [*Exit Servant*] First take heed of a lurcher: he cuts deep, he will eat up all from you. [*Calling off*] Some sherry for my lord's players there! Sirrah, why this will be a true feast, a right Mitre supper, a play and all.

[Exeunt Follywit and his comrades]

More lights!

Enter Mother and Courtesan

I called for light—here come in two are light enough for a whole house, i'faith. Dare the thief look me i'th' face? O impudent times! Go to, dissemble it.

MOTHER Bless you, Sir Bounteous.

SIR BOUNTEOUS O welcome, welcome, thief, quean, and bawd, welcome all three.

MOTHER Nay, here's but two on's, sir.

SIR BOUNTEOUS [*indicating Courtesan*] O' my troth, I took her for a couple. I'd have sworn there had been two faces there.

MOTHER Not all under one hood, sir.

SIR BOUNTEOUS
Yes, faith, would I, to see mine eyes bear double.

MOTHER
I'll make it hold, sir, my daughter is a couple.
She was married yesterday.

SIR BOUNTEOUS Buz.

MOTHER
Nay, to no buzzard neither; a right hawk
Whene'er you know him.

SIR BOUNTEOUS
Away, he cannot be but a rascal.
Walk in, walk in, bold guests that come unsent for.

[Exit Mother]

39 **fitly** promptly
40 **e'en** just this moment
46 **has greatest share** (*a*) owns the most shares in the players' stock company (*b*) has taken the greatest share of the booty
46–7 **live of himself** support himself
50–1 **let ... bare** let those with fewer feathers in their hats (representing wealth) stand hatless.
57 **took all quietly** (*a*) bore the misfortune without complaining (*b*) stole everything silently
59 **bear ... away** another pun on bearing as stealing
64–5 **politician ... restraints** business agent for the company, whose job is to negotiate around 'restraints', or prohibitions from playing, as in Lent or during plague
66 **legs** bows
66–7 **suit ... for** request in the interest of
68 **of** for
71–2 **rollest ... there** an allusion to the proverb, 'A rolling stone gathers no moss', but the point is obscure. Perhaps the Lieutenant is disguised with a beard ('moss').
72 **champ upon that** chew on that; think that over
77 ***The Slip*** several meanings come into play: an act of evasion; an act of falling; an error in conduct; a skirt; a counterfeit coin
79 **glib** smooth, slippery
80 **Cover** prepare; cover with food
81 **lurcher** a glutton, one who takes more than his share of food; also, a swindler
84 **Mitre** a high-class tavern at the corner of Bread Street and Cheapside
86 **light** (*a*) wanton, loose (*b*) light-fingered, artful
92 **on's** of us
96 **under one hood** a denial of duplicity, alluding to the proverb 'He carries two faces under one hood.'
97 **bear double** see double
98 **make it hold** affirm it
100 **Buz** interjection of impatience, contempt
101 **buzzard** a hawk useless for hunting—hence, a worthless person

[*Aside*] Soft, I perceive how my jewels went now
To grace her marriage. [*Stopping Courtesan*]

COURTESAN Would you with me, sir?

SIR BOUNTEOUS
Ay, how happed it, wench, you put the slip upon me
Not three nights since? I name it gently to you:
I term it neither pilfer, cheat, nor shark.

COURTESAN
You're past my reach.

SIR BOUNTEOUS I'm old and past your reach,
Very good, but you will not deny this, I trust.

COURTESAN
With a safe conscience, sir.

SIR BOUNTEOUS Yea? Give me thy hand,
Fare thee well. I have done with her.

COURTESAN
Give me your hand, sir. You ne'er yet begun with me.
Exit

SIR BOUNTEOUS
Whew, whew! O audacious age!
She denies me and all, when on her fingers
I spied the ruby sit that does betray her
And blushes for her fact. Well, there's a time for't,
For all's too little now for entertainment,
Feast, mirth, ay, harmony, and the play to boot,
A jovial season.

Enter Follywit [as a player]

How now, are you ready?

FOLLYWIT Even upon readiness, sir. (*Taking* [*hat*] *off*)

SIR BOUNTEOUS Keep you your hat on.

FOLLYWIT I have a suit to your worship.

SIR BOUNTEOUS O cry you mercy, then you must stand bare.

FOLLYWIT We could do all to the life of action, sir, both for the credit of your worship's house and the grace of our comedy.

SIR BOUNTEOUS Cuds me, what else sir?

FOLLYWIT And for some defects (as the custom is) we would be bold to require your worship's assistance.

SIR BOUNTEOUS Why, with all my heart. What is't you want? Speak.

FOLLYWIT One's a chain for a Justice's hat, sir.

SIR BOUNTEOUS [*removing chain and giving it to Follywit*] Why, here, here, here, here, whoreson, will this serve your turn?

FOLLYWIT Excellent well, sir.

SIR BOUNTEOUS What else lack you?

FOLLYWIT We should use a ring with a stone in't.

SIR BOUNTEOUS Nay, whoop, I have given too many rings already. Talk no more of rings, I pray you. [*Removing a brooch and giving it*] Here, here, here, make this jewel serve for once.

FOLLYWIT O, this will serve, sir.

SIR BOUNTEOUS What, have you all now?

FOLLYWIT All now, sir—only Time is brought i'th' middle of the play, and I would desire your worship's watch for Time.

SIR BOUNTEOUS My watch? With all my heart, only give Time a charge that he be not fiddling with it. [*Giving watch*]

FOLLYWIT You shall ne'er see that, sir.

SIR BOUNTEOUS Well, now you are furnished, sir, make haste away. [*Exit*]

FOLLYWIT E'en as fast as I can, sir.—I'll set my fellows going first. They must have time and leisure or they're dull else. I'll stay and speak a prologue, yet o'ertake them. I cannot have conscience, i'faith, to go away and speak ne'er a word to 'em. My grandsire has given me three shares here. Sure I'll do somewhat for 'em. *Exit*

Enter Sir Bounteous and all the guests [Harebrain, Wife, Penitent, Courtesan, Mother, and Servants] 5.2

SIR BOUNTEOUS
More lights, more stools, sit, sit, the play begins.
[*Servants provide candles and stools. The guests sit*]

HAREBRAIN Have you players here, Sir Bounteous?

SIR BOUNTEOUS We have 'em for you, sir, fine nimble comedians, proper actors most of them.

PENITENT Whose men, I pray you, sir?

SIR BOUNTEOUS O, there's their credit, sir. They serve an honourable popular gentleman, yclept my Lord Owemuch.

HAREBRAIN My Lord Owemuch? He was in Ireland lately.

SIR BOUNTEOUS O, you ne'er knew any of the name but were great travellers.

HAREBRAIN How is the comedy called, Sir Bounteous?

SIR BOUNTEOUS Marry, sir, *The Slip.*

HAREBRAIN *The Slip?*

SIR BOUNTEOUS Ay, and here the Prologue begins to slip in upon's.

HAREBRAIN 'Tis so, indeed, Sir Bounteous.

Enter for a Prologue, Follywit

Prologue

FOLLYWIT
We sing of wandering knights, what them betide
Who nor in one place nor one shape abide.
They're here now, and anon no scouts can reach 'em,
Being every man well horsed like a bold Beacham.

106 **Would...me** Do you want something from me?
109 **shark** swindle
110 **past my reach** i.e. I don't get it
114 **You...me** (a sneer at his impotence)
118 **fact** deed
119 **all's too little** nothing is too much; we can't get enough
123 **Even upon readiness** Just about ready
127 **do...action** act the whole play convincingly
131 **And...defects** Due to some deficiencies
137–8 **serve your turn** serve your needs
158 **dull** inept
161 **somewhat** something or other
5.2.4 **proper** handsome
7 **yclept** named (an affected archaism)
9 **Ireland** a notorious refuge for English debtors
10 **of the name** i.e. named Owemuch
21 **bold Beacham** alluding to the proverb 'as bold as Beauchamp', deriving from the exploits of Thomas Beauchamp, first Earl of Warwick

The play which we present no fault shall meet
But one: you'll say 'tis short, we'll say 'tis sweet.
'Tis given much to dumbshows, which some praise,
And like the Term delights much in delays.
So to conclude and give the name her due,
The play being called The Slip, I vanish too. *Exit*

SIR BOUNTEOUS Excellently well acted and a nimble conceit.

HAREBRAIN The Prologue's pretty, i'faith.

PENITENT And went off well.

SIR BOUNTEOUS Ay, that's the grace of all, when they go away well, ah.

COURTESAN [*aside*] O' my troth, an I were not married, I could find in my heart to fall in love with that player now, and send for him to a supper. I know some i'th' town that have done as much, and there took such a good conceit of their parts into th' twopenny room, that the actors have been found i'th' morning in a less compass than their stage, though 'twere ne'er so full of gentlemen.

SIR BOUNTEOUS But, passion of me, where be these knaves? Will they not come away? Methinks they stay very long.

PENITENT O, you must bear a little, sir, they have many shifts to run into.

SIR BOUNTEOUS 'Shifts' call you 'em? They're horrible long things.

Follywit returns in a fury [*with the chain*]

FOLLYWIT [*aside*] A pox of such fortune, the plot's betrayed! All will come out. Yonder they come taken upon suspicion and brought back by a constable. I was accurst to hold society with such coxcombs. What's to be done? I shall be shamed forever, my wife here and all. Ah, pox—by light, happily thought upon, the chain! Invention, stick to me this once, and fail me ever hereafter. So, so—

SIR BOUNTEOUS 'Life, I say, where be these players? O, are you come? Troth, it's time, I was e'en sending for you.

HAREBRAIN
How moodily he walks. What plays he, trow?

SIR BOUNTEOUS
A Justice, upon my credit. I know by the chain there.

FOLLYWIT [*improvising as a Justice*]
Unfortunate Justice!

SIR BOUNTEOUS Ah, ah, ah—

FOLLYWIT *In thy kin unfortunate.*
Here comes thy nephew now upon suspicion,
Brought by a constable before thee, his vile associates with him,
But so disguised none knows him but myself.
Twice have I set him free from officers' fangs,
And for his sake his fellows. Let him look to't.
My conscience will permit but one wink more.
[*He sits*]

SIR BOUNTEOUS Yea, shall we take justice winking?

FOLLYWIT
For this time,
I have bethought a means to work thy freedom,
Though hazarding myself. Should the law seize him,
Being kin to me, 'twould blemish much my name.
No, I'd rather lean to danger than to shame.

Enter Constable with [*neighbours, bringing in Lieutenant, Ensign and others of Follywit's comrades*]

SIR BOUNTEOUS A very explete Justice.

CONSTABLE [*to neighbours*] Thank you good neighbours, let me alone with 'em now. [*Exeunt neighbours*]

LIEUTENANT [*noticing Follywit*] 'Sfoot, who's yonder?

ENSIGN Dare he sit there?

THIRD COMRADE Follywit!

FOURTH COMRADE Captain! Puh!

FOLLYWIT [*as Justice*] *How now, Constable, what news with thee?*

CONSTABLE [*to Sir Bounteous*] May it please your worship, sir, here are a company of auspicious fellows.

SIR BOUNTEOUS To me? Puh—turn to the Justice, you whoreson hobby-horse. [*To guests*] This is some new player now. They put all their fools to the constable's part still.

FOLLYWIT *What's the matter, Constable, what's the matter?*

CONSTABLE [*to Follywit*] I have nothing to say to your worship. [*To Sir Bounteous*] They were all riding a-horseback, an't please your worship.

SIR BOUNTEOUS Yet again? A pox of all asses still, they could not ride afoot unless 'twere in a bawdy-house.

CONSTABLE The ostler told me they were all unstable fellows, sir.

FOLLYWIT *Why, sure, the fellow's drunk.*

LIEUTENANT [*as the Justice's Nephew*] *We spied that weakness in him long ago, sir. Your worship must bear with him,*

24 **dumbshows** pantomimes forming part of the action of the play (becoming unfashionable by 1605)
25 **Term** law term
28 **nimble conceit** witty invention
35 **send... supper** It was apparently common for prostitutes to invite favourite players to dinner.
37 **good... parts** thorough understanding of their roles, with a pun on 'private parts' **twopenny room** a covered upper room in the theatre, used for entertainment after a performance; this was a disreputable part of the house, frequented by prostitutes
38–9 **less... stage** a smaller circumference than the stage, even when it is most crowded by spectators. Gallants habitually sat on the stage during a performance; the players, here, wake up in beds even more crowded.
41 **passion of me** an oath, alluding to Christ's passion
42 **stay** delay
44 **shifts** (*a*) costume changes (*b*) stratagems (*c*) linen smocks
48–9 **taken upon suspicion** arrested
50 **hold society** keep company
53 **Invention** Ingenuity
60 **nephew** the word can mean 'grandson': hence, Follywit's narration is ironically pertinent
72 **explete** complete; also, serving to compensate for a loss
82 **auspicious** malapropism for 'suspicious'
84 **hobby-horse** the person in morris dances who acted the part of the horse; hence, a buffoon
85–6 **put... part** have the fools of the company play the role of constable
92 **ride afoot** i.e., mount a whore
93 **ostler** stable attendant; groom (hence, 'unstable fellows' is a pun)

the man's much o'erseen. Only in respect of his office we obeyed him, both to appear conformable to law and clear of all offence, for I protest, sir, he found us but a-horseback.

FOLLYWIT *What, he did?*

LIEUTENANT *As I have a soul, that's all, and all he can lay to us.*

CONSTABLE I'faith, you were not all riding away then?

LIEUTENANT *'Sfoot, being a-horseback, sir, that must needs follow.*

FOLLYWIT *Why, true, sir.*

SIR BOUNTEOUS Well said, Justice. [*To guests*] He helps his kinsman well.

FOLLYWIT *Why, sirrah, do you use to bring gentlemen before us for riding away? What, will you have 'em stand still when they're up, like Smug upo'th' white horse yonder? Are your wits steeped? I'll make you an example for all dizzy constables, how they abuse justice.* [*Rising*] *Here, bind him to this chair.*

CONSTABLE Ha, bind him? Ho!

FOLLYWIT *If you want cords, use garters.*

CONSTABLE Help, help, gentlemen!

LIEUTENANT [*binding Constable to chair*] *As fast as we can, sir.*

CONSTABLE Thieves, thieves!

FOLLYWIT *A gag will help all this. Keep less noise, you knave.*

CONSTABLE O help, rescue the Constable! O, O!

[*They gag him*]

SIR BOUNTEOUS Ho, ho, ho ho!

FOLLYWIT *Why la, you, who lets you now?*
You may ride quietly. I'll see you to
Take horse myself. I have nothing else to do.

Exit [*with Lieutenant, Ensign, and comrades*]

CONSTABLE [*tries to talk through gag*] O, O, O!

SIR BOUNTEOUS Ha, ha, ha! By my troth, the maddest piece of justice that ever was committed.

HAREBRAIN I'll be sworn for the madness on't, sir.

SIR BOUNTEOUS I am deceived if this prove not a merry comedy and a witty.

PENITENT Alas, poor Constable, his mouth's open and ne'er a wise word.

SIR BOUNTEOUS Faith, he speaks now e'en as many as he has done: he seems wisest when he gapes and says nothing. Ha, ha, he turns and tells his tale to me like an ass. What have I to do with their riding away? They may ride for me, thou whoreson coxcomb, thou. Nay, thou art well enough served, i'faith.

PENITENT But what follows all this while, sir? Methinks some should pass by before this time and pity the Constable.

SIR BOUNTEOUS By th' mass, and you say true, sir. [*To Servant*] Go, sirrah, step in. I think they have forgot themselves. Call the knaves away. They're in a wood, I believe. [*Exit Servant*]

CONSTABLE Ay, ay, ay.

SIR BOUNTEOUS Hark, the Constable says, 'Ay, they're in a wood',—ha, ha!

HAREBRAIN He thinks long of the time, Sir Bounteous.

[*Enter Servant*]

SIR BOUNTEOUS How now? When come they?

SERVANT Alas, an't please your worship, there's not one of them to be found, sir.

SIR BOUNTEOUS How?

HAREBRAIN What says the fellow?

SERVANT Neither horse nor man, sir.

SIR BOUNTEOUS Body of me, thou liest.

SERVANT Not a hair of either, sir.

HAREBRAIN How now, Sir Bounteous?

SIR BOUNTEOUS Cheated and defeated! Ungag that rascal! I'll hang him for's fellows. I'll make him bring 'em out.

[*Servant ungags Constable*]

CONSTABLE Did not I tell your worship this before, brought 'em before you for suspected persons, stayed 'em at town's end upon warning given, made signs that my very jawbone aches? Your worship would not hear me, called me ass (saving your worship's presence), laughed at me.

SIR BOUNTEOUS Ha?

HAREBRAIN I begin to taste it.

SIR BOUNTEOUS Give me leave, give me leave. Why, art not thou the Constable i'th' comedy?

CONSTABLE I'th' comedy? Why, I am the Constable i'th' commonwealth, sir.

SIR BOUNTEOUS I am gulled, i'faith, I am gulled. When wast thou chose?

CONSTABLE On Thursday last, sir.

SIR BOUNTEOUS A pox go with't, there't goes.

PENITENT I seldom heard jest match it.

HAREBRAIN Nor I, i'faith.

SIR BOUNTEOUS Gentlemen, shall I entreat a courtesy?

HAREBRAIN What is't, sir?

SIR BOUNTEOUS Do not laugh at me seven year hence.

PENITENT We should betray and laugh at our own folly then, for of my troth none here but was deceived in't.

SIR BOUNTEOUS Faith, that's some comfort yet. Ha, ha, it was featly carried! Troth, I commend their wits! Before our faces, make us asses while we sit still and only laugh at ourselves.

PENITENT Faith, they were some counterfeit rogues, sir.

98 **o'erseen** (*a*) deluded (*b*) intoxicated
102–3 **lay to us** charge us with
110 **do you use** are you accustomed
112 **Smug ... horse** referring to a scene (missing from the extant version) of *The Merry Devil of Edmonton* in which Smug plays St George riding upon a white horse
113 **steeped** soaked, or drunk
dizzy foolish, giddy
117 **want** lack
122 **Keep** make
125 **lets** hinders
126 **quietly** unimpeded
147 **in a wood** in a muddle
163 **for's fellows** (*a*) instead of his companions (*b*) because of the company he keeps
166–7 **that ... aches** until my jawbone ached
171 **taste** understand
177 **chose** elected
188 **featly** deftly
191 **counterfeit** deceiving

SIR BOUNTEOUS Why, they confess so much themselves. They said they'd play *The Slip*. They should be men of their words. I hope the Justice will have more conscience, i'faith, than to carry away a chain of a hundred mark of that fashion.

HAREBRAIN What, sir?

SIR BOUNTEOUS Ay, by my troth, sir, besides a jewel, and a jewel's fellow, a good fair watch that hung about my neck, sir.

HAREBRAIN 'Sfoot, what did you mean, sir?

SIR BOUNTEOUS Methinks my Lord Owemuch's players should not scorn me so, i'faith. They will come and bring all again, I know. Push! They will, i'faith, but a jest, certainly.

Enter Follywit in his own shape, and all the rest [*Lieutenant, Ensign, and comrades*]

FOLLYWIT [*kneels*] Pray, grandsire, give me your blessing.

SIR BOUNTEOUS Who? Son Follywit?

FOLLYWIT [*aside*] This shows like kneeling after the play, I praying for my Lord Owemuch and his good countess, our honourable lady and mistress.

SIR BOUNTEOUS
Rise richer by a blessing—thou art welcome.

FOLLYWIT Thanks, good grandsire.

[*He rises and presents comrades*]

I was bold to bring those gentlemen, my friends.

SIR BOUNTEOUS They're all welcome. Salute you that side, and I'll welcome this side.

[*He greets Follywit's comrades while Follywit greets Sir Bounteous's guests*]

Sir, to begin with you. [*Greeting Lieutenant*]

HAREBRAIN Master Follywit. [*Greeting him*]

FOLLYWIT I am glad 'tis our fortune so happily to meet, sir.

SIR BOUNTEOUS Nay, then, you know me not, sir. [*Greeting Ensign*]

FOLLYWIT Sweet Mistress Harebrain. [*Greeting her*]

SIR BOUNTEOUS You cannot be too bold, sir. [*Greeting another comrade*]

FOLLYWIT [*aside to Courtesan*] Our marriage known?

COURTESAN [*aside to him*] Not a word yet.

FOLLYWIT [*aside to her*] The better.

SIR BOUNTEOUS Faith, son, would you had come sooner with these gentlemen.

FOLLYWIT Why, grandsire?

SIR BOUNTEOUS We had a play here.

FOLLYWIT A play, sir? No.

SIR BOUNTEOUS Yes, faith. A pox o'th' author!

FOLLYWIT Bless us all! Why, were they such vile ones, sir?

SIR BOUNTEOUS I am sure, villainous ones, sir.

FOLLYWIT Some raw simple fools.

SIR BOUNTEOUS Nay, by th' mass, these were enough for thievish knaves.

FOLLYWIT What, sir?

SIR BOUNTEOUS Which way came you, gentlemen? You could not choose but meet 'em.

FOLLYWIT We met a company with hampers after 'em.

SIR BOUNTEOUS O, those were they, those were they! A pox hamper 'em!

FOLLYWIT Bless us all again!

SIR BOUNTEOUS They have hampered me finely, sirrah.

FOLLYWIT How, sir?

SIR BOUNTEOUS How, sir? I lent the rascals properties to furnish out their play, a chain, a jewel, and a watch, and they watched out their time and rid quite away with them.

FOLLYWIT Are they such creatures?

[*The watch rings in Follywit's pocket*]

SIR BOUNTEOUS Hark, hark, gentlemen, by this light, the watch rings alarum in his pocket! There's my watch come again, or the very cousin-german to't.

[*He confronts Follywit and the comrades*]

Whose is't, whose is't? By th' mass, 'tis he. Hast thou one, son? Prithee bestow it upon thy grandsire. [*Searching Follywit*] I now look for mine again, i'faith. Nay, come with a good will or not at all! I'll give thee a better thing. [*Groping in his pocket*] A piece, a piece, gentlemen!

HAREBRAIN Great or small?

SIR BOUNTEOUS [*Pulling out the stolen articles*] At once I have drawn chain, jewel, watch, and all!

PENITENT By my faith, you have a fortunate hand, sir.

HAREBRAIN Nay, all to come at once.

LIEUTENANT A vengeance of this foolery!

FOLLYWIT Have I 'scaped the Constable to be brought in by the watch?

COURTESAN O destiny! Have I married a thief, mother?

MOTHER Comfort thyself. Thou art beforehand with him, daughter.

SIR BOUNTEOUS Why son, why gentlemen, how long have you been my Lord Owemuch his servants, i'faith?

FOLLYWIT Faith, grandsire, shall I be true to you?

195–6 **of . . . mark** worth a hundred marks (a mark was worth two-thirds of a pound)

196 **of that fashion** in that manner

199 **fellow** companion piece

208 **kneeling . . . play** Traditionally, players—who escaped vagabond status only through their 'service' to the aristocracy—would offer a prayer for their patron at the close of a performance. This practice may not have survived in the public theatres.

234 **raw** rough, unmannerly

240 **hampers after 'em** i.e. carrying baskets

242 **hamper** obstruct

248 **watched . . . time** bided their time; waited for the perfect moment
rid rode

253 **cousin-german** first cousin (but punning on the fact that the watches come from Germany: see 4.1.21)

257 **come . . . all** the last line of the nursery rhyme, 'Girls and Boys Come Out to Play'. Here, however, there are bawdy overtones, as Bounteous gropes in his grandson's pockets: 'come', a pun on orgasm, and 'thing' or 'piece', indicating his penis.

260 **Great or small?** referring to either his watch or his penis

267 **watch** punning on the body of citizens who policed the streets at night

269 **Thou . . . him** You have paid him in advance for it.

SIR BOUNTEOUS I think 'tis time. Thou'st been a thief already.

FOLLYWIT I, knowing the day of your feast and the natural inclination you have to pleasure and pastime, presumed upon your patience for a jest, as well to prolong your days as—

SIR BOUNTEOUS Whoop, why then, you took my chain along with you to prolong my days, did you?

FOLLYWIT Not so neither, sir, and that you may be seriously assured of my hereafter stableness of life, I have took another course.

SIR BOUNTEOUS What?

FOLLYWIT Took a wife.

SIR BOUNTEOUS A wife? 'Sfoot, what is she for a fool would marry thee, a madman? When was the wedding kept in Bedlam?

FOLLYWIT She's both a gentlewoman and a virgin.

SIR BOUNTEOUS Stop there, stop there! Would I might see her!

FOLLYWIT [*indicating Courtesan*] You have your wish. She's here.

SIR BOUNTEOUS Ah, ha, ha, ha! This makes amends for all.

FOLLYWIT How now?

LIEUTENANT Captain, do you hear? Is she your wife in earnest?

FOLLYWIT How then?

LIEUTENANT
Nothing but pity you, sir.

SIR BOUNTEOUS Speak, son, is't true?
Can you gull us and let a quean gull you?

FOLLYWIT Ha!

COURTESAN
What I have been is past. Be that forgiven,
And have a soul true both to thee and heaven.

FOLLYWIT
Is't come about? Tricks are repaid, I see.

SIR BOUNTEOUS
The best is, sirrah, you pledge none but me.
And since I drink the top, take her and hark,
I spice the bottom with a thousand mark.

FOLLYWIT By my troth, she is as good a cup of nectar as any bachelor needs to sip at.
Tut, give me gold, it makes amends for vice.
Maids without coin are caudles without spice.

SIR BOUNTEOUS
Come, gentlemen, to th' feast, let not time waste.
We have pleased our ear, now let us please our taste.
Who lives by cunning, mark it, his fate's cast:
When he has gulled all, then is himself the last.

Exeunt

Finis

THE PARTS

SIR BOUNTEOUS (591 lines): Watchman; Courtesan's Man; Inesse or Possibility [or Rafe]; [Jasper]

FOLLYWIT (568 lines): Watchman; Knight; Jasper; Inesse or Possibility [or Rafe]; [Courtesan's Man]

PENITENT (259 lines): Watchman; Knight; Gunwater; Courtesan's Man

HAREBRAIN (252 lines): Gunwater; Courtesan's Man; Jasper; [Knight]

COURTESAN (227 lines): Knight; Gunwater; Rafe; Jasper; [Watchman]

MOTHER (117 lines): Watchman; Knight; Gunwater; Courtesan's Man; Rafe; Jasper

WIFE/SUCCUBUS (105 lines): Watchman; Knight; Gunwater; Courtesan's Man; [Jasper]; [Inesse or Possibility]

LIEUTENANT (103 lines): Watchman; Knight; Jasper; Inesse or Possibility or Rafe; [Gunwater]; [Courtesan's Man]

GUNWATER (46 lines): any but Follywit, Sir Bounteous, Footman/Third Comrade; [Lieutenant or Ensign or Fourth Comrade]

FOOTMAN/THIRD COMRADE (31 lines): Watchman; Jasper; Rafe (or [Inesse] or [Possibility]); [Knight]; [Courtesan's Man]

CONSTABLE (5.2; 25 lines): Watchman; Knight; Gunwater; Courtesan's Man; Jasper; Inesse or Possibility or Rafe

RAFE (23 lines): any but Penitent, Inesse, Possibility, Harebrain, Servant, Wife/Succubus; [Follywit or Courtesan or Sir Bounteous]

INESSE (22 lines): any but Penitent, Courtesan, Mother, Possibility, Servant, Harebrain, Rafe; [Wife/Succubus]

POSSIBILITY (21 lines): any but Penitent, Courtesan, Mother, Inesse, Harebrain, Servant, Rafe; [Wife/Succubus]

ENSIGN (18 lines): same as Lieutenant

284 **took another course** started upon a new path in life
287 **what...fool** what kind of fool
289 **Bedlam** the hospital of St Mary of Bethlehem, a lunatic asylum
306–7 **you...top** The metaphor is that of drinking from the same cup (a vaginal symbol); Follywit gets the dregs.
308 **bottom** punning on her bottom
312 **caudles** a warm, spiced drink
316.1 ***Exeunt*** See *Companion*, p. 142, for music that may have accompanied a concluding dance.

JASPER (4.1; 12 lines): any but Penitent, Servant, Neighbour; [Sir Bounteous or Wife/Succubus], [Gunwater or Sir Bounteous]

SERVANTS (8 lines): Inesse, Possibility, Watchmen, Knights, Courtesan's Man, Rafe, Jasper, [Gunwater?]

WATCHMEN (1.2; 3 lines): any but Harebrain; [Courtesan]

FIRST KNIGHT (2.1; 2 lines): any but Sir Bounteous; [Footman/Third Comrade]

FOURTH COMRADE (1 line): same as Lieutenant

COURTESAN'S MAN (2.3; no lines): any but Courtesan; [Follywit or Lieutenant or Ensign or Footman/Third Comrade or Fourth Comrade]

NEIGHBOURS (5.2; no lines): same as servants

Most crowded scene 5.2: 12 characters + 2 (?) Servants + (?)Neighbours

A YORKSHIRE TRAGEDY

Edited by Stanley Wells

On 23 April 1605 Walter Calverley, a young man of good family, heir to the manor of Calverley and Pudsey in Yorkshire, murdered two of his three young sons, one aged around eighteen months, the other no more than five years, and wounded their mother, his wife. On the following day, examined before two justices of the peace, he admitted to the crimes, claiming that his wife had 'many times theretofore uttered speeches and given signs and tokens unto him whereby he might easily perceive and conjecture that the said children were not by him begotten, and that he hath found himself to be in danger of his life sundry times by his wife'. At his subsequent trial he refused to plead—probably in order to ensure that the whole of his estate would pass to his heirs; he was pressed to death at York on 5 August of the same year.

These unhappy events caused a national stir, provoking a number of publications of varying degrees of artistry and sophistication. First came an anonymous pamphlet, entered on the Stationers' Register on 12 June 1605, called *Two Most Unnatural and Bloody Murders*, providing an account of the Calverley murders along with one of a different, unrelated case. Although this is partly journalistic in intent, it is far from a simple report of what happened; indeed Sandra Clark describes the narrative as 'intensely contrived and metaphorical; this is no mere domestic drama to be allotted, as fitting, the low or middle style, but a high tragedy of passion'; Calverley is given 'the motivation of a dramatic villain'. Transmutation of history into drama was already under way.

On 3 June a ballad based on the case had been entered, and on 24 August, after Calverley's execution, an account of *The Arraignment, Condemnation, and Execution of Master Calverley at York in August 1605*; neither survives. The story was also briefly told in the 1607 edition of John Stow's *Summary of English Chronicles*.

In addition, two plays were based on the case. The first to appear in print was *The Miseries of Enforced Marriage*, by George Wilkins, entered on 31 July 1607 and published in the same year 'as it is now played by his majesty's servants'. *A Yorkshire Tragedy*, entered as having been written by 'William Shakespeare' on 2 May 1608, appeared later that year. The title-page describes it as 'not so new as lamentable and true', claims that it was 'acted by his majesty's players at the Globe', and ascribes it to 'W. Shakespeare'; the headtitle to the text itself reads 'All's One, or one of the four plays in one, called *A Yorkshire Tragedy*, as it was played by the King's majesty's players'. The expression 'All's One', meaning 'it's of no account', seems entirely inappropriate to so serious a play; it might conceivably be used in an attempt to indicate some kind of overall unity for four plays performed together, but the headtitle unequivocally presents it as an alternative title for this particular play. Some commentators have taken the heading to indicate that *A Yorkshire Tragedy* was the overall title for a four-part work, but this seems unlikely. The phrase 'not so new' may accurately reflect a date of composition between the publication of the pamphlet and Calverley's execution, since the Wife, in her last speech, declares her intention of suing for his pardon; Holdsworth, however, arguing that *A Yorkshire Tragedy* echoes *King Lear* and influenced *Timon of Athens*, dates the *Tragedy* to the first two months of 1606.

In part, no doubt, because of the ascription to Shakespeare, *A Yorkshire Tragedy* has a far more extensive publication history than any of the other accounts of the Calverley case. The publisher of the first edition, Thomas Pavier, also included it in his 1619 collection of Shakespearean and pseudo-Shakespearean quartos, and although Heminges and Condell omitted it from the Shakespeare First Folio of 1623 it was one of the seven apocryphal plays added in the third Folio of 1664, reprinted in 1685. Thereafter it has frequently appeared in collections of the Shakespeare apocrypha, in other anthologies, and independently.

In spite of the evidence of the Stationers' Register both on first publication and in subsequent transfers, and of the title-page of the quarto, ascription of the play to Shakespeare is undermined by its omission from the First Folio and by the bad reputation of Pavier, whose 1619 collection, undertaken in association with William Jaggard, included falsely dated quartos of five Shakespeare plays and fraudulently ascribed *1 Sir John Oldcastle* to Shakespeare. Throughout the nineteenth and twentieth centuries most commentators have been unable to believe that Shakespeare wrote *A Yorkshire Tragedy*: as Tucker Brooke wrote in 1908, 'Neither in characterization, nor in plot, nor in metrical peculiarities have the most ardent defenders of the *Yorkshire Tragedy*'s authenticity pretended that there is any approach to Shakespeare's manner subsequent to 1605.' Many other candidates have been put forward, especially Thomas Heywood, but detailed studies by David J. Lake, MacDonald P. Jackson, and Roger Holdsworth of the play's linguistic and other features have strengthened the case that Thomas Middleton wrote most or, more probably, all of it.

The opening scene presents a number of anomalous features which have been much discussed; they may be illuminated by a brief consideration of *The Miseries of Enforced Marriage*, a full-length play of genuine accomplishment, especially considering that Wilkins seems not to have written any other non-collaborative dramas. Though it lacks the emotional intensity and narrative drive of *A Yorkshire Tragedy*, it offers the most freely inventive treatment of the facts of the case. Wilkins takes the basic situation depicted in the pamphlet—a man, Scarborough (also a Yorkshire place-name) contracted to a girl he loves but then forced into a loveless marriage for financial reasons—as the starting point for a social drama portraying many invented characters, all with fictional names, and often adopting a comic perspective on the action. Initially the husband is sympathetically portrayed, and although his beloved kills herself, events end happily for him as his guardian, dying, acknowledges responsibility for the forced marriage and leaves his wealth to Scarborough and his family. There are no murders.

The author of *A Yorkshire Tragedy*, by contrast, sticks remarkably closely for all but his opening scene to the pamphlet. From Scene 2 onwards all the characters come from that source, and none of any consequence are added. The pamphlet's sequence of action is followed with only one significant change: the account of the Wife's visit to her uncle and guardian in London, narrated in the pamphlet at a point corresponding to her exit at 2.103, is advanced to form the opening episode of Scene 3, in which we see her immediately on her return, thus achieving greater concentration of action and place; her speeches here pick up words uttered by her uncle in the pamphlet. Through most of the play—the closing scene is the main exception—speeches are closely indebted to the pamphlet's wording. An example is the Wife's self-defence at 3.58–67. In the pamphlet this reads:

> My friends are fully possessed your land is mortgaged. If you think I have published anything to him with desire to keep the sale of my dowry from you, either for mine own good or my children's, though it fits I have a motherly care of them, you being my husband, pass it away how you please, spend it how you will, so I may enjoy but welcome looks and kind words from you.

Middleton draws closely on this, but transforms it into a passage of regular blank verse which nevertheless presents the issues with greater clarity, with more measured pace, and with a dignified pathos with which a performer can do much:

> Only my friends
> Knew of your mortgaged lands, and were possessed
> Of every accident before I came.
> If thou suspect it but a plot in me
> To keep my dowry, or for mine own good
> Or my poor children's—though it suits a mother
> To show a natural care in their reliefs—
> Yet I'll forget myself to calm your blood.
> Consume it as your pleasure counsels you,
> And all I wish e'en clemency affords.

Even stage directions take over the pamphlet's wording—'Catches up the youngest' (5.17.1)—'she caught up the youngest'—is one of many possible examples; and a revealing tiny detail is the Wife's interrupted speech 'And—' at 2.76, stimulated by the pamphlet's 'But as she would have gone forward he cut her off...'.

In spite of these and other close correspondences, it would be wrong to give the impression that Middleton's dependence on the pamphlet is slavish. So, for example, the episodes in Scene 3 in which gentlemen reprove the Husband are considerably expanded and developed from a few hints in the source, and the Wife's speech at 3.80, indebted to the formal conventions of the dramatic lament, finds words for the 'long-fetched sigh or two' with which Calverley's wife 'eased her heart'. Although the dramatist was working primarily from a clearly defined source, his play may be located too within the conventions of domestic tragedy (such as the anonymous *Arden of Faversham*) and of 'patient wife' plays.

Thematically the dramatist's main development of his source material lies in the notion that the Husband's actions result from demoniac possession. This theme was probably suggested by the talons on the hands and feet of the dark figure of an old man depicted beside the murderer on the title-page of the pamphlet (reproduced in the *Companion*, 130). It emerges slowly, perhaps because it grew in Middleton's mind as he wrote, but perhaps also because in the earlier scenes he does not wish to detract from the Husband's personal responsibility for his tragedy. In the opening speech of Scene 2 the Wife speaks of her husband as 'half mad | His fortunes cannot answer his expense' and later declares that his transformation from his former self is 'As if some vexèd spirit had got his form upon him'. The Husband himself begins to see his condition as that of one who has sold his soul to the devil shortly before first attacking one of his sons:

> Divines and dying men may talk of hell,
> But in my heart her several torments dwell,
> Slavery and misery. Who in this case
> Would not take up money upon his soul,
> Pawn his salvation, live at interest?

(The fact that the first couplet of this passage comes from Thomas Nashe's *Pierce Penniless* may act as a caution against underestimating the literary features of what is too easily regarded as a largely documentary drama.) But the most explicit, and powerful, expression of the idea comes in the Husband's speech of repentance to which he is moved in the final scene by his Wife's forgiveness, when he feels the devil losing possession of his body:

...thou hast devised
A fine way now to kill me, thou hast given mine eyes
Seven wounds apiece, now glides the devil from me,
Departs at every joint, heaves up my nails.
O, catch him new torments that were ne'er invented,
Bind him one thousand more, you blessèd angels,
In that pit bottomless, let him not rise
To make men act unnatural tragedies,
To spread into a father and, in fury,
Make him his children's executioners,
Murder his wife, his servants, and who not?
For that man's dark where heaven is quite forgot.

This eloquent speech, with its heightened language, its use of rhyme and half-rhyme, its vivid physical imagery, its self-conscious rhetoric comparable to Faustus's great final speech in Marlowe's play, shows the dramatist writing at the height of his power, and a similar degree of expressiveness informs the Husband's reaction to the sight of his two dead children 'laid forth upon the threshold':

Here's weight enough to make a heartstring crack.
O were it lawful that your pretty souls
Might look from heaven into your father's eyes
Then should you see the penitent glasses melt
And both your murders shoot upon my cheeks.
But you are playing in the angels' laps
And will not look on me
Who, void of grace, killed you in beggary.

And he refers again to the influence of the devil:

O, 'twas the enemy my eyes so bleared.

The Husband's final words retreat from the immediacy of what has gone before to draw a generalized moral:

Let every father look into my deeds,
And then their heirs may prosper while mine bleeds.

But while the bulk of the play, from Scene 2 onwards, reads as if it were written at white heat, the dramatist himself possessed by the challenge of transforming the pamphlet into a play, the opening scene, as has long been recognized, has an entirely different quality. Only here are the characters given names—and although Middleton more than most dramatists was often content to let even major characters be known only by type names, only the special case of *A Game at Chess* affords a parallel in his output for the complete namelessness of all the characters in this play from the beginning of the second scene. And here too the raw material of the scene, which is only slightly indebted to the pamphlet, is treated with a relaxed expansiveness, a freedom of invention, more akin to the manner of Wilkins's full-length play than to anything in the rest of *A Yorkshire Tragedy*.

Many attempts have been made to explain the anomalies of this scene, which are such that, as Sturgess reasonably comments, 'It seems doubtful whether one should include scene i in a modern revival' (p. 35); they are summarized in the Introduction to the Revels edition (pp. 13–15), to whose editors 'it seems safe to infer that Scene i was added later by a different playwright'. But their inference that because the scene lacks the close relationship with the pamphlet of the rest of the play its author did not know the pamphlet, and therefore had not written the rest of the play, is unnecessary: the scene makes clear allusions to the grief of the servants' 'young mistress' 'for the long absence of her love' which is eloquently described in the pamphlet. The Revels editors propose that the scene was added as a result of the decision to print the play independently; it seems no less plausible that it served as an induction, linking the body of the play, in a way that we cannot recover, to the four-part sequence as a whole.

A Yorkshire Tragedy is roughly 700 lines long. If performed with three other plays of equal length it would have made an entertainment substantial but not exceptional in duration by Jacobean standards. Its brevity renders it unsuitable for conventional performance, but is not a complete handicap; indeed the play has a fuller history of production than many Jacobean dramas, including *The Miseries of Enforced Marriage*. In 1720 Joseph Mitchell (apparently with assistance from Aaron Hill) adapted it into a sentimental one-act tragedy, *The Fatal Extravagance*, and this play in turn was transformed into a sentimental comedy, *The Prodigal*, by F. G. Waldron in 1794. *A Yorkshire Tragedy* was given in Boston, Massachusetts, as part of a triple bill in 1847 as a benefit for the actress (Harriet Bland, sister of Helen Faucit) playing the Wife—rather surprisingly since, although the role gives good acting opportunities, it is so clearly overshadowed by that of the Husband. A Russian translation was performed in 1895 and (apparently) 1904, but no performances in England are recorded until the 1950s. Since then it has received a number of amateur and professional productions, some by out-of-the-way groups in obscure circumstances, but others of a more prestigious nature: in 1987 it even reached the National Theatre, though only for a single performance in its studio auditorium, the Cottesloe; the play probably achieved its largest audiences in two BBC radio productions, in 1955 and 1957.

Though the ascription to Shakespeare no doubt formed part of the motivation for many of these performances, those involved must also have had enough faith in the script's inherent stage-worthiness to put it to theatrical test; at least one group saw modern parallels to the action, adapting it into 'a play on the subject of domestic violence against women in modern Yorkshire' (Revels). The concentration of the play's action gives it great pace, and the unsentimentality of the presentation even of those episodes that afford most opportunity for pathos, such as the sufferings of the Wife and the terror of the little boy on being attacked by his father, is genuinely affecting; but it is above all the role of the Husband, with its fluctuations in style from staccato prose, anguished in its repetitions, to elevated verse, that gives the play its fascination, facing the actor with the challenge of synthesizing the character's conflicting impulses of family pride, love for brother, wife, and children, obsessive extravagance, and self-loathing issuing in horrendous violence. In a letter dated 12 March 1919 T. S. Eliot wrote: 'Damn Swinburne, J. A. Symonds, Dekker, Heywood and domestic tragedy *except* "Yorkshire Tr".' This is no doubt his tribute to the play's stark unsentimentality compared with other plays in the genre to which it belongs. Its brevity is part of its greatness; nothing dilutes its emotional impact.

SEE ALSO

Textual introduction and apparatus: *Companion*, 592
Authorship and date: *Companion*, 355

A Yorkshire Tragedy

(*one of the four-plays-in-one, called All's One*)

[*for the King's Men at The Globe*]

THE PERSONS OF THE PLAY

HUSBAND
MASTER of the College
KNIGHT
OLIVER, RALPH, SAM } servingmen

WIFE
SON of the Husband and Wife
MAID, with their second child
Gentlemen, servants, and officers

c. 1 *Enter Oliver and Ralph, two servingmen*

OLIVER Sirrah Ralph, my young mistress is in such a pitiful passionate humour for the long absence of her love!

RALPH Why, can you blame her? Why, apples hanging longer on the tree than when they are ripe makes so many fallings: viz., mad wenches because they are not gathered in time are fain to drop of themselves, and then 'tis common, you know, for every man to take 'em up.

OLIVER Mass, thou sayst true, 'tis common indeed. But sirrah, is neither our young master returned nor our fellow Sam come from London?

RALPH Neither of either, as the Puritan bawd says.—'Slid, I hear Sam, Sam's come, here's—tarry—come, i'faith now my nose itches for news.

Persons Oliver, Ralph, and Sam of Sc. 1 might double with any of the adult parts, but would most logically become the anonymous Servants/Servingmen of the rest of the play. The younger servant Sam may be the 'lusty' Servant of Sc. 5, who is the First Servant in the list of parts. In the edited text of the play, the roles of the Gentlemen and Servants are left unnumbered except when the quarto numbers them ('First Gentleman', etc.). The only other doubling possibilities for the adult males also involve the three servants (doubling as the gentlemen). None of the three parts for boy actors (Wife, Son, Maid) can be doubled.

1.1 **Sirrah** sir (used from a superior to an inferior)
my young mistress This seems to refer not to the Wife of the play but to the young Yorkshire woman to whom Calverley was previously contracted, and whom he wronged. She is not mentioned after Sc. 1.

2 **passionate humour for** suffering condition because of

4 **makes** causes (the singular form because 'apples ... ripe' is thought of as the subject)

5 **fallings** windfalls (first recorded use in this sense)
viz. namely; a colloquial abbreviation of 'videlicet'

5–6 **mad ... drop** perhaps 'wenches who go mad because they have not been made love to when they were ready for it are apt to fall (in virtue)'

9 **Mass** by the mass (a mild oath)
common (as in 'common woman', a prostitute)

12 **Neither of either** neither the one nor the other
the Puritan bawd obscure; 'Puritan' could imply 'hypocritical'. There may be a lost allusion.
'Slid by God's eyelid; a common oath

13 **here's** here (he) is
tarry (perhaps implying that Oliver was beginning to walk away)

14–15 **my nose itches ... elbow** forerunners of news in common superstition

OLIVER And so does mine elbow.

SAM (*calls within*) Where are you there?

Enter Sam furnished with things from London

SAM [*calling*] Boy, look you walk my horse with discretion, I have rid him simply. I warrant his skin sticks to his back with very heat, if a should catch cold and get the cough of the lungs I were well served, were I not?—What, Ralph and Oliver!

RALPH *and* OLIVER Honest fellow Sam, welcome, i'faith! What tricks hast thou brought from London?

SAM You see I am hanged after the truest fashion, three hats and two glasses bobbing upon 'em, two rebato wires upon my breast, a cap-case by my side, a brush at my back, an almanac in my pocket, and three ballads in my codpiece—nay, I am the true picture of a common servingman.

OLIVER I'll swear thou art, thou mayst set up when thou wilt. There's many a one begins with less, I can tell thee, that proves a rich man ere he dies. But what's the news from London, Sam?

RALPH Ay, that's well said, what's the news from London, sirrah? My young mistress keeps such a puling for her love.

SAM Why, the more fool she, ay, the more ninny-hammer she.

OLIVER Why, Sam, why?

SAM Why, he's married to another long ago.

RALPH *and* OLIVER I'faith, ye jest.

SAM Why, did you not know that till now? Why, he's married, beats his wife, and has two or three children by her; for you must note that any woman bears the more when she is beaten.

RALPH Ay, that's true, for she bears the blows.

OLIVER Sirrah Sam, I would not for two years' wages my young mistress knew so much, she'd run upon the left hand of her wit and ne'er be her own woman again.

SAM And I think she was blest in her cradle that he never came in her bed. Why, he has consumed all, pawned his lands, and made his university brother stand in wax for him—there's a fine phrase for a scrivener! Puh, he owes more than his skin's worth.

OLIVER Is't possible?

SAM Nay, I'll tell you moreover he calls his wife whore as familiarly as one would call Mall and Doll, and his children bastards as naturally as can be. But what have we here? I thought 'twas somewhat pulled down my breeches, I quite forgot my two poting-sticks. These came from London, now anything is good here that comes from London.

OLIVER Ay, 'Far fetched . . . ', you know—

SAM But speak in your conscience i'faith, have not we as good poting-sticks i'th' country as need to be put i'th' fire? The mind of a thing is all, the mind of a thing's all, and as thou saidst e'en now, 'Far fetched is the best things for ladies.'

OLIVER Ay, and for waiting gentlewomen, too.

SAM But Ralph, what, is our beer sour this thunder?

OLIVER No, no, it holds countenance yet.

SAM Why then, follow me, I'll teach you the finest humour to be drunk in, I learned it at London last week.

RALPH *and* OLIVER I'faith, let's hear it, let's hear it.

SAM The bravest humour, 'twould do a man good to be drunk in't. They call it 'knighting' in London when they drink upon their knees.

RALPH *and* OLIVER Faith, that's excellent.

SAM Come, follow me, I'll give you all the degrees on't in order. *Exeunt*

Sc.

Enter Wife

WIFE

What will become of us? All will away,
My husband never ceases in expense
Both to consume his credit and his house,
And 'tis set down by heaven's just decree
That Riot's child must needs be Beggary.
Are these the virtues that his youth did promise—
Dice, and voluptuous meetings, midnight revels,
Taking his bed with surfeits ill beseeming
The ancient honour of his house and name?—

18 **simply** recklessly
19 **a** he (the unaccented form)
20 **cough of the lungs** i.e. cough from the lungs, a 'bad chest'; in Middleton often a sign of old age
I were well served it would serve me right
23 **tricks** trinkets, knick-knacks
24 **hanged** bedecked, adorned
25 **glasses** mirrors (carried in hats)
25–6 **rebato wires** wire frames supporting ruffs
26 **cap-case** travelling-case or bag
28 **codpiece** the baggy appendage to male hose or breeches worn over the genitals
30 **set up** set yourself up in business (and 'be proud')
35 **puling** whining
37 **ninny-hammer** simpleton (first recorded Nashe 1592)
44–5 **any woman . . . beaten** proverbial (cf. Tilley W 644)
48–9 **upon . . . wit** i.e. go mad
49 **be . . . woman** recover her sanity
52 **stand in wax** enter into a bond
53 **scrivener** notary (presumably Sam is mocking his own coinage of a phrase)
57 **call Mall and Doll** i.e. call them whore; these were familiar names for prostitutes
59 **somewhat** something (that)
60 **poting-sticks** rods of metal, wood, or bone used when heated to crimp linen (as in ruffs); in his next speech Sam uses the term with bawdy innuendo
63 **'Far fetched . . . '** The proverb is cited in full at ll. 67–8.
66 **mind . . . is all** view, opinion
69 **waiting gentlewomen** possibly punning, as the 'young mistress' is waiting for her lover to return from London
70 **this thunder** at this time of thunder; there was a belief that thunder turned beer sour
71 **holds countenance** keeps a calm, or sweet, appearance (punning on 'sour' as 'ill-countenanced')
75 **bravest** finest
76–7 **knighting . . . knees** referring to the practice of drinking toasts while on one's knees
79 **degrees** names of different degrees of drunkenness
2.1 **will away** will be lost
3 **Both to consume** enough to waste both
credit honour, reputation
8 **Taking** taking to
surfeits illnesses resulting from excess

And this not all, but that which kills me most,
When he recounts his losses and false fortunes,
The weakness of his state so much dejected,
Not as a man repentant but half mad
His fortunes cannot answer his expense.
He sits and sullenly locks up his arms,
Forgetting heaven, looks downward, which makes him
Appear so dreadful that he frights my heart,
Walks heavily, as if his soul were earth,
Not penitent for those his sins are past
But vexed his money cannot make them last—
A fearful melancholy, ungodly sorrow.
O, yonder he comes: now in despite of ills
I'll speak to him, and I will hear him speak,
And do my best to drive it from his heart.

Enter Husband

HUSBAND
Pox o'th' last throw, it made
Five hundred angels vanish from my sight.
I'm damned, I'm damned. The angels have forsook me,
Nay, 'tis certainly true, for he that has no coin
Is damned in this world, he's gone, he's gone.

WIFE Dear husband—

HUSBAND
O, most punishment of all, I have a wife.

WIFE
I do entreat you as you love your soul,
Tell me the cause of this your discontent.

HUSBAND
A vengeance strip thee naked, thou art cause,
Effect, quality, property, thou, thou, thou. *Exit*

WIFE Bad turned to worse!
Both beggary of the soul as of the body,
And so much unlike himself at first
As if some vexèd spirit had got his form upon him.

Enter Husband again

He comes again.
He says I am the cause—I never yet
Spoke less than words of duty and of love.

HUSBAND If marriage be honourable then cuckolds are honourable, for they cannot be made without marriage. Fool, what meant I to marry, to get beggars? Now must my eldest son be a knave or nothing; he cannot live upo' th' soil for he will have no land to maintain him. That mortgage sits like a snaffle upon mine inheritance and makes me chaw upon iron. My second son must be a promoter, and my third a thief, or an underputter, a slave pander.
O beggary, beggary,
To what base uses dost thou put a man!
I think the devil scorns to be a bawd.
He bears himself more proudly, has more care
On's credit.
Base, slavish, abject, filthy poverty!

WIFE
Good sir, by all our vows I do beseech you,
Show me the true cause of your discontent.

HUSBAND Money, money, money, and thou must supply me.

WIFE
Alas, I am the least cause of your discontent,
Yet what is mine, either in rings or jewels,
Use to your own desire; but I beseech you,
As you're a gentleman by many bloods,
Though I myself be out of your respect,
Think on the state of these three lovely boys
You have been father to.

HUSBAND Puh, bastards, bastards, bastards, begot in tricks, begot in tricks.

WIFE
Heaven knows how those words wrong me! But I may
Endure these griefs among a thousand more.
O, call to mind your lands already mortgaged,
Yourself wound into debts, your hopeful brother
At the university in bonds for you
Like to be seized upon. And—

HUSBAND Ha' done, thou harlot
Whom though for fashion sake I marrièd
I never could abide! Think'st thou thy words
Shall kill my pleasures? Fall off to thy friends,
Thou and thy bastards beg, I will not bate
A whit in humour. Midnight, still I love you
And revel in your company. Curbed in?
Shall it be said in all societies
That I broke custom, that I flagged in money?
No, those thy jewels I will play as freely
As when my state was fullest.

WIFE Be it so.

10 **this** elliptical for 'this is'
12 **dejected** lowered, cast down
14 **answer** match
19 **are** (that) are
25 **Pox o'th'** a pox on the (a common curse) **throw** (of the dice)
26 **angels** gold coins worth ten shillings (half of a pound) each. Stakes are high.
34 **A vengeance** an act of vengeance (a standard curse)
39 **vexèd . . . upon him** tormented spirit (devil) had inhabited his shape
45 **get** beget
46–7 **live upo' th' soil** make a living from the products of the earth. This is an emendation of the first printed edition's 'live upo' th' fool', which has been defended as meaning 'live a life of riot.'
48 **snaffle** bridle-bit
49 **chaw** champ, chew roughly
50 **promoter** informer (for money) **underputter** procurer, pander
51 **slave** slavish, contemptible
56 **On's credit** of his reputation
65 **bloods** noble ancestors
69 **tricks** intrigues, adultery
74 **hopeful** full of promise (and of hope)
75 **in bonds** legally bound (to pay debts)
76 **Like . . . upon** likely to be arrested
77 **for fashion sake** only because of social pressure
79 **Fall off to** go off to
80–1 **bate . . . humour** soften my attitude one jot
82 **revel** make merry
83 **societies** companies
84 **flagged in money** was slow to pay out, reduced my expenditure
85 **play** gamble with
86 **fullest** at its most prosperous

HUSBAND
Nay I protest (*spurns her*)—and take that for an earnest—
I will for ever hold thee in contempt
And never touch the sheets that cover thee,
But be divorced in bed till thou consent
Thy dowry shall be sold to give new life
Unto those pleasures which I most affect.

WIFE
Sir, do but turn a gentle eye on me,
And what the law shall give me leave to do
You shall command.

HUSBAND Look it be done. Shall I want dust
And like a slave wear nothing in my pockets
But my hands, to fill them up with nails?
(*Holding his hands in his pockets*) O, much against my blood! Let it be done.
I was never made to be a looker-on.
A bawd to dice? I'll shake the drabs myself
And make 'em yield. I say, look it be done.

WIFE
I take my leave; it shall. *Exit*

HUSBAND Speedily, speedily.
I hate the very hour I chose a wife,
A true trouble.
Three children like three evils hang upon me.
Fie, fie, fie, strumpet and bastards, strumpet and bastards!

Enter three Gentlemen hearing him

FIRST GENTLEMAN
Still do those loathsome thoughts jar on your tongue,
Yourself to stain the honour of your wife,
Nobly descended? Those whom men call mad
Endanger others, but he's more than mad
That wounds himself, whose own words do proclaim
Scandals unjust to soil his better name.
It is not fit; I pray forsake it.

SECOND GENTLEMAN
Good sir, let modesty reprove you.

THIRD GENTLEMAN
Let honest kindness sway so much with you.

HUSBAND Good e'en, I thank you, sir—how do you?—
Adieu—I'm glad to see you. *Exeunt Gentlemen*
Farewell instructions, admonitions!

Enter a Servant

HUSBAND How now, sirrah, what would you?

SERVANT Only to certify you, sir, that my mistress was met by the way by them who were sent for her up to London by her honourable uncle, your worship's late guardian.

HUSBAND
So sir, then she is gone, and so may you be.
But let her look that the thing be done she wots of,
Or hell will stand more pleasant than her house at home.

[*Exit Servant*]

Enter a Gentleman

GENTLEMAN Well or ill met, I care not.

HUSBAND No, nor I.

GENTLEMAN
I am come with confidence to chide you.

HUSBAND Who, me? Chide me? Do't finely, then. Let it not move me, for if thou chid'st me angry I shall strike.

GENTLEMAN
Strike thine own follies, for it is they
Deserve to be well beaten. We are now in private;
There's none but thou and I. Thou'rt fond and peevish,
An unclean rioter, thy lands and credit
Lie now both sick of a consumption.
I am sorry for thee. That man spends with shame
That with his riches does consume his name:
And such art thou.

HUSBAND Peace.

GENTLEMAN No, thou shalt hear me further.
Thy father's and forefathers' worthy honours,
Which were our country monuments, our grace,
Follies in thee begin now to deface.
The springtime of thy youth did fairly promise
Such a most fruitful summer to thy friends
It scarce can enter into men's beliefs
Such dearth should hang on thee. We that see it
Are sorry to believe it. In thy change
This voice into all places will be hurled:
Thou and the devil has deceived the world.

HUSBAND
I'll not endure thee.

GENTLEMAN But of all the worst,
Thy virtuous wife right honourably allied

87 *spurns* kicks
earnest foretaste
90 **be divorced in bed** refrain from sex
92 **affect** enjoy
96 **Look it be done** i.e. make sure your dowry is realized and handed over
want dust lack money
98 **nails** finger nails (perhaps implying things of no realizable value)
101 **bawd to dice** one who brings others to gamble
drabs harlots (the dice); perhaps with a suggestion that he will metaphorically copulate with the drabs and make them bring forth children (= money): ironically anticipating his own 'Strumpet and bastards'
118 **Good e'en** good evening (used any time after noon)
118–19 **Good...see you** ironically empty politenesses
122 **certify** assure
123–4 **by the way...uncle** on the way by those whom her honourable uncle sent from London to take her there
127 **wots of** knows about (the sale of her dowry)
129 **Well...care not** i.e. I don't care whether you're pleased to see me; presumably this is one of the gentlemen whom the husband has just dismissed
132 **finely** discreetly
133 **move** anger
chid'st me angry provoke me to anger by rebuking me
136 **fond and peevish** foolish and perverse
138 **consumption** (*a*) wasting disease (*b*) excessive expenditure
143 **country** local
150 **voice** opinion

Thou hast proclaimed a strumpet.
HUSBAND Nay, then, I know thee.
Thou art her champion, thou, her private friend,
The party you wot on.
GENTLEMAN O ignoble thought!
I am past my patient blood. Shall I stand idle
And see my reputation touched to death?
HUSBAND
'T'as galled you, this, has it?
GENTLEMAN No, monster, I will prove
My thoughts did only tend to virtuous love.
HUSBAND
Love of her virtues? There it goes.
GENTLEMAN Base spirit,
To lay thy hate upon the fruitful honour
Of thine own bed.
They fight, and the Husband's hurt
HUSBAND O!
GENTLEMAN Wilt thou yield it yet?
HUSBAND
Sir, sir, I have not done with you.
GENTLEMAN
I hope nor ne'er shall do.
Fight again
HUSBAND Have you got tricks?
Are you in cunning with me?
GENTLEMAN No, plain and right,
He needs no cunning that for truth doth fight.
Husband falls down
HUSBAND
Hard fortune! Am I levelled with the ground?
GENTLEMAN
Now, sir, you lie at mercy.
HUSBAND Ay, you slave.
GENTLEMAN
Alas, that hate should bring us to our grave!
You see my sword's not thirsty for your life.
I am sorrier for your wound than you yourself.
You're of a virtuous house, show virtuous deeds!
'Tis not your honour, 'tis your folly bleeds.
Much good has been expected in your life;
Cancel not all men's hopes. You have a wife
Kind and obedient; heap not wrongful shame
On her and your posterity. Let only sin be sore,
And by this fall, rise never to fall more.
And so I leave you. *Exit*
HUSBAND [*rising*] Has the dog left me then,
After his tooth hath left me? O, my heart
Would fain leap after him. Revenge, I say,
I'm mad to be revenged. My strumpet wife,
It is thy quarrel that rips thus my flesh
And makes my breast spit blood; but thou shalt bleed.
Vanquished? Got down? Unable e'en to speak?
Surely 'tis want of money makes men weak.
Ay, 'twas that o'erthrew me, I'd ne'er been down else.
Exit

Enter Wife in a riding-suit, with a Servingman Sc. 3

SERVINGMAN
Faith, mistress, if it might not be presumption
In me to tell you so, for his excuse
You had small reason, knowing his abuse.
WIFE I grant I had, but, alas,
Why should our faults at home be spread abroad?
'Tis grief enough within doors. At first sight
Mine uncle could run o'er his prodigal life
As perfectly as if his serious eye
Had numbered all his follies;
Knew of his mortgaged lands, his friends in bonds,
Himself withered with debts, and in that minute
Had I added his usage and unkindness
'Twould have confounded every thought of good;
Where now, fathering his riots on his youth,
Which time and tame experience will shake off,
Guessing his kindness to me—as I smoothed him
With all the skill I had—though his deserts
Are in form uglier than an unshaped bear,
He's ready to prefer him to some office
And place at court, a good and sure relief
To all his stooping fortunes. 'Twill be a means I hope
To make new league between us, and redeem
His virtues with his lands.
SERVINGMAN I should think so, mistress. If he should not now be kind to you and love you, and cherish you up, I should think the devil himself kept open house in him.
WIFE
I doubt not but he will. Now prithee leave me,
I think I hear him coming.
SERVINGMAN I am gone. *Exit*
WIFE
By this good means I shall preserve my lands
And free my husband out of usurers' hands.

155 **private friend** secret lover
157 **past . . . blood** beyond all patience
158 **touched** injured
159 **galled** annoyed
161 **There it goes** here we go! (sarcastic)
163 **yield it** admit defeat (and that you are in the wrong)
164 **done with** completed my business. (The Gentleman probably plays on the sense 'done for', 'killed'.)
166 **in cunning with** using occult art against?
174 **'Tis . . . bleeds** i.e. your wound harms your folly, not your honour
181 **tooth** i.e. sword
184 **quarrel** complaint, hostility
3.0.1 ***in a riding-suit*** a conventional means of indicating that a character has just undertaken a journey
2 **his excuse** excusing him (to her uncle)
3 **abuse** ill usage
6 **within doors** i.e. at home, within the family circle
8 **serious eye** i.e. thoughtful consideration
10 **friends** (could include relatives, such as the Husband's Brother)
in bonds See 2.75.
13 **confounded** destroyed
15 **tame** i.e. taming
16 **smoothed him** glossed over his faults
17 **deserts** demerits
18 **uglier . . . bear** alluding to the legend that a bear 'brings forth her young informous and unshapen, which she fashioneth after by licking them over' (Sir Thomas Browne, *Pseudodoxia Epidemica*, 1646, sig. P2[v])
19 **prefer** advance

Now there is no need of sale, my uncle's kind;
I hope, if aught, this will content his mind.
Here comes my husband.

Enter Husband

HUSBAND Now, are you come? Where's the money, let's see the money, is the rubbish sold, those wise-acres your lands? Why, when, the money, where is't? Pour't down, down with it, down with it, I say pour't o'th' ground, let's see't, let's see't.

WIFE
Good sir, keep but in patience and I hope
My words shall like you well. I bring you better
Comfort than the sale of my dowry.

HUSBAND Ha, what's that?

WIFE Pray do not fright me, sir, but vouchsafe me hearing. My uncle, glad of your kindness to me and mild usage—for so I made it to him—has in pity of your declining fortunes provided a place for you at court of worth and credit, which so much overjoyed me—

HUSBAND (*spurns her*) Out on thee, filth—over and overjoyed when I'm in torments! Thou politic whore, subtler than nine devils, was this thy journey to nunc, to set down the history of me, of my state and fortunes? Shall I, that dedicated myself to pleasure, be now confined in service to crouch and stand like an old man i'th' hams, my hat off, I that never could abide to uncover my head i'th' church? Base slut, this fruit bears thy complaints.

WIFE O heaven knows
That my complaints were praises and best words
Of you and your estate. Only my friends
Knew of your mortgaged lands, and were possessed
Of every accident before I came.
If thou suspect it but a plot in me
To keep my dowry, or for mine own good
Or my poor children's—though it suits a mother
To show a natural care in their reliefs—
Yet I'll forget myself to calm your blood.
Consume it as your pleasure counsels you,
And all I wish e'en clemency affords;
Give me but comely looks and modest words.

HUSBAND [*drawing his dagger*] Money, whore, money, or I'll—

Enters a Servant very hastily

(*To his manservant in a fear*) What the devil? How now? Thy hasty news!

SERVANT May it please you sir—

HUSBAND What! May I not look upon my dagger? Speak, villain, or I will execute the point on thee. Quick, short.

SERVANT Why, sir, a gentleman from the university stays below to speak with you.

HUSBAND From the university? So, university—that long word runs through me. *Exeunt [Husband and Servants]*

WIFE (*alone*)
Was ever wife so wretchedly beset?
Had not this news stepped in between, the point
Had offered violence to my breast.
That which some women call great misery
Would show but little here, would scarce be seen
Amongst my miseries. I may compare
For wretched fortunes with all wives that are.
Nothing will please him until all be nothing.
He calls it slavery to be preferred,
A place of credit a base servitude.
What shall become of me and my poor children,
Two here and one at nurse, my pretty beggars?
I see how ruin with a palsy hand
Begins to shake the ancient seat to dust.
The heavy weight of sorrow draws my lids
Over my dankish eyes. I can scarce see.
Thus grief will last, it wakes and sleeps with me.
[*Exit*]

Sc. 4

Enter the Husband with the Master of the College

HUSBAND Please you draw near, sir. You're exceeding welcome.

MASTER That's my doubt, I fear I come not to be welcome.

HUSBAND Yes, howsoever.

MASTER 'Tis not my fashion, sir, to dwell in long circumstance, but to be plain and effectual. Therefore to the purpose. The cause of my setting forth was piteous and lamentable. That hopeful young gentleman your brother, whose virtues we all love dearly, through your default and unnatural negligence lies in bond executed for your debt, a prisoner, all his studies amazed, his hope struck dead, and the pride of his youth muffled in these dark clouds of oppression.

HUSBAND Hmh, um, um.

35 **wise-acres** self-opinionated fools; used contemptuously with reference to lands
40 **like** please
45 **made** represented
47 **credit** honour
49 **politic** devious, scheming
50 **nine** (more normally used of angels)
nunc uncle (contemptuous)
52–3 **confined in service** kept as a servant
53 **i'th' hams** i.e. with bent knees
55 **fruit...complaints** i.e. your complaints bear this fruit, have this result
58 **estate** condition
59 **possessed** informed
60 **accident** happening
65 **blood** anger
66 **it** (her dowry)
67 **e'en clemency affords** (is what) mercy itself allows
71 ***in*** i.e. who is in
75 **execute** use
79 **runs** (like a (long) sword)
80 **beset** surrounded by danger
81 **this** commonly used with 'news', it could be a variant spelling of 'these'
82 **Had** would have
91 **beggars** (could be a term of endearment)
92 **palsy** palsied; an allusion to the 'gentleman's palsy' 4.67, a term, unknown elsewhere, referring to the shaking of the dice-box seen as a sickness
93 **seat** ancestral estate
95 **dankish** moist
4.5–6 **dwell...circumstance** waste time in evading the point
6 **effectual** to the point
10 **default** failure in duty
10–11 **in bond...debt** seized in execution of the bond for non-payment of the debt (*OED*'s only instance of 'execute' in this sense); perhaps also 'seized because of a bond put into effect as a result of your debt'
11 **amazed** thrown into confusion

MASTER O, you have killed the towardest hope of all our university, wherefore, without repentance and amends, expect ponderous and sudden judgements to fall grievously upon you. Your brother, a man who profited in his divine employments, might have made ten thousand souls fit for heaven, now by your careless courses cast in prison, which you must answer for, and assure your spirit it will come home at length.

HUSBAND O God! O!

MASTER Wise men think ill of you, others speak ill of you, no man loves you, nay, even those whom honesty condemns, condemn you; and—take this from the virtuous affection I bear your brother—never look for prosperous hour, good thought, quiet sleeps, contented walks, nor anything that makes man perfect till you redeem him. What is your answer? How will you bestow him—upon desperate misery, or better hopes? I suffer till I hear your answer.

HUSBAND Sir, you have much wrought with me. I feel you in my soul. You are your art's master. I never had sense till now. Your syllables have cleft me. Both for your words and pains I thank you. I cannot but acknowledge grievous wrongs done to my brother, mighty, mighty, mighty wrongs. [*Calling*] Within there!

Enter a Servingman

SERVINGMAN Sir?

HUSBAND

Fill me a bowl of wine. *Exit Servingman for wine*
Alas, poor brother,
Bruised with an execution for my sake!

MASTER

A bruise indeed makes many a mortal sore
Till the grave cure 'em.

Enter Servingman with wine

HUSBAND

Sir, I begin to you. You've chid your welcome.

MASTER

I could have wished it better for your sake.
I pledge you, sir: to the kind man in prison.

HUSBAND

Let it be so.

Drink both

Now, sir, if you so please
To spend but a few minutes in a walk
About my grounds below, my man here shall attend
you. I doubt not but by that time to be furnished of a sufficient answer, and therein my brother fully satisfied.

MASTER

Good sir, in that the angels would be pleased
And the world's murmurs calmed, and I should say
I set forth then upon a lucky day.

Exit [with Servingman]

HUSBAND O thou confused man, thy pleasant sins have undone thee, thy damnation has beggared thee! That heaven should say we must not sin, and yet made women!—gives our senses way to find pleasure which, being found, confounds us. Why should we know those things so much misuse us? O, would virtue had been forbidden! We should then have proved all virtuous, for 'tis our blood to love what we're forbidden. Had not drunkenness been forbidden, what man would have been fool to a beast and zany to a swine, to show tricks in the mire? What is there in three dice to make a man draw thrice three thousand acres into the compass of a round little table, and with the gentleman's palsy in the hand shake out his posterity, thieves or beggars? 'Tis done, I ha' done't i'faith, terrible, horrible misery.—How well was I left, very well, very well. My lands showed like a full moon about me, but now the moon's i'th'last quarter, waning, waning, and I am mad to think that moon was mine, mine and my father's and my forefathers' generations, generations. Down goes the house of us, down, down, it sinks. Now is the name a beggar; begs in me that name which hundreds of years has made this shire famous—in me, and my posterity runs out. In my seed five are made miserable besides myself. My riot is now my brother's jailor, my wife's sighing, my three boys' penury, and mine own confusion.

Tears his hair

Why sit my hairs upon my cursèd head?
Will not this poison scatter them? O, my brother's
In execution among devils that

15 **towardest** most promising
19 **divine employments** religious duties
might (who) might
20 **careless** thoughtless, inconsiderate
22 **come home** affect you deeply
29 **perfect** satisfied, contented
30 **redeem** rescue
31 **desperate** despairing
33 **wrought with** prevailed upon
34 **art's master** quibbling on the university term 'master of arts'
41 **execution** writ authorizing arrest for non-payment
42 **makes** (that) makes
44 **begin to** toast
chid found fault with
46 **pledge you** give you a toast
49 **below** The action is imagined as taking place in an upper room.
50 **furnished of** supplied with
51 **satisfied** given satisfaction, compensated
56–8 **That ... women** a common sentiment
60 **so ... us** (which) so greatly abuse us
62 **blood** inclination (the sentiment is proverbial)
64 **fool** jester
zany to clownish imitator of
tricks stupid deeds
66 **draw** (as if by magic)
67 **table** gaming table
gentleman's palsy See 3.92.
70 **left** provided for by inheritance
71 **about** around
72–3 **mad to think** crazed by the thought that
74 **generations** descendants
75 **house of us** our lineage
76 **in me** i.e. in my person
hundreds i.e. for hundreds
81 **confusion** destruction
83 **poison** figurative; some kinds of poison cause hair to drop out
84 **In execution** i.e. imprisoned
devils i.e. jailors

Stretch him and make him give, and I in want,
Not able for to live nor to redeem him.
Divines and dying men may talk of hell,
But in my heart her several torments dwell,
Slavery and misery. Who in this case
Would not take up money upon his soul,
Pawn his salvation, live at interest?
I, that did ever in abundance dwell,
For me to want exceeds the throes of hell.

Enters his little son with a top and a scourge

SON What ail you, father, are you not well? I cannot scourge my top as long as you stand so. You take up all the room with your wide legs. Puh, you cannot make me afeard with this. I fear no visors nor bugbears.

Husband takes up the child by the skirts of his long coat in one hand and draws his dagger with th'other

HUSBAND Up, sir, for here thou hast no inheritance left.

SON O, what will you do, father?—I am your white boy.

HUSBAND (*strikes him*) Thou shalt be my red boy. Take that!

SON O, you hurt me, father.

HUSBAND My eldest beggar. Thou shalt not live to ask an usurer bread, to cry at a great man's gate, or follow 'good your honour' by a crouch, no, nor your brother. 'Tis charity to brain you.

SON How shall I learn now my head's broke?

HUSBAND (*stabs him*)
Bleed, bleed, rather than beg, beg. Be not thy name's disgrace.
Spurn thou thy fortunes first if they be base.
Come view thy second brother. Fates, my children's blood
Shall spin into your faces; you shall see
How confidently we scorn beggary. *Exit with his son*

Sc. 5 *Enter a Maid with a child in her arms, the Wife by her asleep*

MAID
Sleep, sweet babe. Sorrow makes thy mother sleep.
It bodes small good when heaviness falls so deep.
Hush, pretty boy. Thy hopes might have been better;
'Tis lost at dice what ancient honour won:
Hard when the father plays away the son.
Nothing but misery serves in this house,
Ruin and desolation—

Enter Husband with the boy bleeding

O!

HUSBAND Whore, give me that boy.

Strives with her for the child

MAID O help, help, out, alas, murder, murder!

HUSBAND
Are you gossiping, prating sturdy quean?
I'll break your clamour with your neck. Downstairs,
Tumble, tumble, headlong!

Throws her down

So, the surest way to charm a woman's tongue
Is break her neck; a politician did it.

SON Mother, mother, I am killed, mother!

Wife wakes

WIFE Ha, who's that cried? O me, my children! Both, both, both bloody, bloody!

Catches up the youngest

HUSBAND
Strumpet, let go the boy, let go the beggar.

WIFE O my sweet husband!

HUSBAND Filth, harlot!

WIFE
O, what will you do, dear husband?

HUSBAND Give me the bastard.

WIFE
Your own sweet boy.

HUSBAND There are too many beggars.

WIFE
Good my husband—

HUSBAND Dost thou prevent me still?

WIFE
O God!

HUSBAND (*stabs at the child in her arms*)
Have at his heart!

WIFE O my dear boy!

HUSBAND (*gets it from her*) Brat, thou shalt not live to shame thy house.

WIFE
O heaven!

She's hurt and sinks down

HUSBAND And perish, now be gone.

85 **give** yield, playing on the sense 'give money'
86 **for to live** to find the means to keep myself? to live as I should like?
87–8 **Divines ... dwell** This couplet, first found on the first page of Thomas Nashe's *Pierce Penniless* (1592), seems to have acquired semi-proverbial status, being varied by Samuel Nicholson in *Acolastus his After-wit* (1600) and in *The Insatiate Countess* (by Marston and Barkstead, 1613).
88 **several** various
89 **case** plight
90 **take ... soul** borrow money with his soul as security
91 **live ... interest** live on the money lent as interest on his soul
93.1 ***scourge*** whip
96 **room** space
97 **visors** hard looks? spectres?
bugbears hobgoblins
99 **white boy** darling
104 **usurer** moneylender
cry beg
105 **'good your honour'** an obsequious plea for charity
crouch stooping, obeisance
109 **first** i.e. before begging
111 **spin** gush
5.0.1 The direction seems to imply a 'discovery.' 11–12 show that, as in the previous scene, the action is imagined as occurring in an upper room.
2 **heaviness falls** sadness sinks
6 **serves** suits
10 **sturdy quean** headstrong whore
12.1 ***Throws her down*** i.e. downstairs, implying an involuntary exit for the Maid
13 **charm** put a spell on, silence
14 **politician** schemer, machiavel (sometimes thought to allude to the Earl of Leicester's alleged murder of his wife, Amy Robsart)
24 **Have at** let me strike at

There's whores enough, and want would make thee one.
Enter a lusty Servant

SERVANT
O sir, what deeds are these?

HUSBAND
Base slave, my vassal,
Com'st thou between my fury to question me?

SERVANT [*holding him back*]
Were you the devil I would hold you, sir.

HUSBAND
Hold me? Presumption! I'll undo thee for't.

SERVANT 'Sblood, you have undone us all, sir.

HUSBAND
Tug at thy master?

SERVANT
Tug at a monster.

HUSBAND
Have I no power, shall my slave fetter me?

SERVANT
Nay, then the devil wrestles, I am thrown.

HUSBAND
O villain, now I'll tug thee, (*overcomes him*) now I'll tear thee,
Set quick spurs to my vassal, bruise him, trample him.
So, I think thou wilt not follow me in haste.
My horse stands ready saddled, away, away.
Now to my brat at nurse, my sucking beggar.
Fates, I'll not leave you one to trample on.
The Master meets him

MASTER How is't with you, sir? Methinks you look of a distracted colour.

HUSBAND Who, I, sir? 'Tis but your fancy.
Please you walk in, sir, and I'll soon resolve you.
I want one small part to make up the sum,
And then my brother shall rest satisfied.

MASTER
I shall be glad to see it. Sir, I'll attend you.
Exeunt [*Husband and Master*]

SERVANT [*rising*]
O, I am scarce able to heave up myself.
He's so bruised me with his devilish weight
And torn my flesh with his blood-hasty spur,
A man before of easy constitution
Till now hell's power supplied, to his soul's wrong.
O, how damnation can make weak men strong!
Enter Master and two Servants

MASTER'S SERVANT
O, the most piteous deed, sir, since you came!

MASTER
A deadly greeting! Has he summed up these
To satisfy his brother? Here's another,
And by the bleeding infants the dead mother.

WIFE O, O!

MASTER
Surgeons, surgeons! She recovers life.
One of his men all faint and bloodièd.

SERVANT
Follow, our murderous master has took horse
To kill his child at nurse. O, follow quickly!

MASTER
I am the readiest, it shall be my charge
To raise the town upon him.

SERVANT Good sir, do, follow him.
Exeunt Master and his two Servants

WIFE O, my children!

SERVANT
How is it with my most afflicted mistress?

WIFE
Why do I now recover, why half live
To see my children bleed before mine eyes?—
A sight able to kill a mother's breast
Without an executioner. [*To the Servant*] What, art thou mangled too?

SERVANT
I, thinking to prevent what his quick mischiefs
Had so soon acted, came and rushed upon him.
We struggled, but a fouler strength than his
O'erthrew me with his arms. Then did he bruise me,
And rent my flesh, and robbed me of my hair,
Like a man mad in execution
Made me unfit to rise and follow him.

WIFE
What is it has beguiled him of all grace
And stole away humanity from his breast,
To slay his children, purposed to kill his wife,
And spoil his servants?
Enters two Servants

BOTH SERVANTS
Please you leave this most accursèd place.
A surgeon waits within.

WIFE
Willing to leave it!
'Tis guilty of sweet blood, innocent blood.
Murder has took this chamber with full hands,
And will ne'er out as long as the house stands.
Exeunt

28.1 *lusty* strong, vigorous
29 **vassal** low servant
30 **between** i.e. between me and
32 **undo** do for
35 **fetter** restrain
41 **sucking** unweaned
46 **walk in** The action is now imagined as taking place outside the house.
resolve reassure
47 **sum** (of what is owing)
49 **attend** accompany
52 **blood-hasty** eager for blood
53 **easy constitution** gentle disposition
54 **hell's** hell has
wrong harm, undoing
56 This line would make most sense if the servant entered slightly before the Master.
57 **greeting** i.e. the spectacle before him
summed up (alluding to l. 47)
74 **mischiefs** injuries
79 **execution** giving effect to his passion
80 **Made** (he) made
81 **beguiled** cheated
84 **spoil** seriously injure
88 **took** occupied
full (of blood, alluding to the superstition that blood shed by murder cannot be eradicated)

Sc. 6 *Enter Husband as being thrown off his horse, and falls*

HUSBAND
O stumbling jade, the spavin overtake thee,
The fifty diseases stop thee!
O, I am sorely bruised. Plague founder thee,
Thou runn'st at ease and pleasure. Heart, of chance
To throw me now within a flight o'th' town
In such plain even ground! 'Sfoot, a man
May dice upon't and throw away the meadows.
Filthy beast!

Cry within, 'Follow, follow, follow'

Ha! I hear sounds of men like hue and cry.
Up, up, and struggle to thy horse, make on,
Dispatch that little beggar and all's done.

Cry within, 'Here, this way, this way!'

At my back? O,
What fate have I, my limbs deny me go,
My will is bated, beggary claims a part.
O, could I here reach to the infant's heart!

Enter Master of the College, three Gentlemen, and others with halberds. Find him

ALL BUT HUSBAND
Here, here,—yonder, yonder.

MASTER
Unnatural, flinty, more than barbarous.
The Scythians in their marble-hearted feats
Could not have acted more remorseless deeds
In their relentless natures than these of thine.
Was this the answer I long waited on,
The satisfaction for thy prisoned brother?

HUSBAND
Why, he can have no more on's than our skins,
And some of 'em want but flaying.

FIRST GENTLEMAN
Great sins have made him impudent.

MASTER
He's shed so much blood that he cannot blush.

SECOND GENTLEMAN
Away with him, bear him along to the Justices.
A gentleman of worship dwells at hand,
There shall his deeds be blazed.

HUSBAND
Why, all the better.
My glory 'tis to have my action known,
I grieve for nothing but I missed of one.

MASTER
There's little of a father in that grief.
Bear him away. *Exeunt*

Enters a Knight with two or three Gentlemen Sc. 7

KNIGHT
Endangered so his wife? Murdered his children?

KNIGHT'S GENTLEMAN
So the cry comes.

KNIGHT
I am sorry I e'er knew him,
That ever he took life and natural being
From such an honoured stock and fair descent,
Till this black minute without stain or blemish.

KNIGHT'S GENTLEMAN
Here come the men.

Enter the Master of the College and the rest, with the Husband as prisoner

KNIGHT
The serpent of his house!
I'm sorry for this time that I am in place of justice.

MASTER
Please you, sir—

KNIGHT
Do not repeat it twice. I know too much.
Would it had ne'er been thought on. [*To Husband*] Sir,
I bleed for you.

KNIGHT'S GENTLEMAN [*to Husband*]
Your father's sorrows are alive in me.
What made you show such monstrous cruelty?

HUSBAND
In a word, sir,
I have consumed all, played away long-acre,
And I thought it the charitablest deed I could do
To cozen beggary and knock my house o'th' head.

KNIGHT
O, in a cooler blood you will repent it.

HUSBAND
I repent now—that one's left unkilled,
My brat at nurse. O, I would full fain have weaned
him.

KNIGHT
Well, I do not think but in tomorrow's judgement
The terror will sit closer to your soul
When the dread thought of death remembers you;

6.1 **jade** horse (contemptuous)
spavin a horse tumour
3 **founder** make lame
4 **Heart** God's heart!
of by
5 **flight** arrow's flight
6 **plain...ground** To stumble on even ground was considered a bad omen.
'Sfoot by God's foot
7 **throw** gamble
10 **make** hasten
13 **deny me go** will not let me walk
14 **bated** blunted, lessened
claims a part is partly responsible
18 **Scythians** proverbially barbarous
feats deeds
23 **he can...skins** (proverbial)
on's of, from us
24 **want...flaying** only need to be flayed (he has nothing else left to give), perhaps with the implication that the skins are hanging off a famished body
25 **impudent** shameless
28 **worship** high position
29 **blazed** made known
31 **missed of** failed to get
7.2 **cry comes** story goes
7 **for...justice** i.e. that at this time I am in the office of justice
10 **thought on** even imagined
11 **father's sorrows** i.e. the sorrows your father would have felt if he had been alive
14 **played** gambled
long-acre properly, a long, narrow field containing an acre; allusively, landed estate, patrimony; first recorded in Middleton, *Trick*
16 **cozen** cheat
and knock...o'th' head by making my line extinct ('knock on the head', kill, put an end to)
19 **weaned** (by killing)
22 **remembers** recurs to

To further which, take this sad voice from me:
Never was act played more unnaturally.

HUSBAND
I thank you, sir.

KNIGHT Go lead him to the jail.
Where justice claims all, there must pity fail.

HUSBAND Come, come, away with me.

Exit Husband as prisoner, [guarded]

MASTER
Sir, you deserve the worship of your place;
Would all did so. In you the law is grace.

KNIGHT
It is my wish it should be so. Ruinous man,
The desolation of his house, the blot
Upon his predecessors' honoured name.
That man is nearest shame that is past shame.

Exeunt

Sc. 8 *Enter Husband with the officers, the Master, and Gentlemen, as going by his house*

HUSBAND
I am right against my house, seat of my ancestors.
I hear my wife's alive, but much endangered.
Let me entreat to speak with her
Before the prison gripe me.

Enter his Wife brought in a chair

GENTLEMAN See here she comes of herself.

WIFE
O my sweet husband, my dear distressèd husband,
Now in the hands of unrelenting laws,
My greatest sorrow, my extremest bleeding,
Now my soul bleeds.

HUSBAND How now, kind to me?
Did I not wound thee, left thee for dead?

WIFE
Tut, far greater wounds did my breast feel,
Unkindness strikes a deeper wound than steel.
You have been still unkind to me.

HUSBAND Faith, and so I think I have.
I did my murders roughly, out of hand,
Desperate and sudden, but thou hast devised
A fine way now to kill me, thou hast given mine eyes
Seven wounds apiece. Now glides the devil from me,
Departs at every joint, heaves up my nails.
O, catch him new torments that were ne'er invented,
Bind him one thousand more, you blessèd angels,
In that pit bottomless, let him not rise
To make men act unnatural tragedies,
To spread into a father and, in fury,
Make him his children's executioners,
Murder his wife, his servants, and who not?
For that man's dark where heaven is quite forgot.

WIFE O my repentant husband!

HUSBAND
My dear soul, whom I too much have wronged,
For death I die, and for this have I longed.

WIFE
Thou shouldst not, be assured, for these faults die
If the law could forgive as soon as I.

Children laid out

HUSBAND What sight is yonder?

WIFE
O, our two bleeding boys laid forth upon the threshold.

HUSBAND
Here's weight enough to make a heartstring crack.
O were it lawful that your pretty souls
Might look from heaven into your father's eyes
Then should you see the penitent glasses melt
And both your murders shoot upon my cheeks.
But you are playing in the angels' laps
And will not look on me
Who, void of grace, killed you in beggary.
O that I might my wishes now attain,
I should then wish you living were again
Though I did beg with you, which thing I feared.
O, 'twas the enemy my eyes so bleared.
O, would you could pray heaven me to forgive,
That will unto my end repentant live.

WIFE
It makes me e'en forget all other sorrows
And have part with this.

OFFICER Come, will you go?

HUSBAND
I'll kiss the blood I spilt, and then I go.
My soul is bloodied, well may my lips be so.
Farewell, dear wife, now thou and I must part.

23 **sad voice** serious opinion
28 **worship... place** respect due to your office
33 **nearest... past shame** most shameful who is past feeling shame
8.0.2 ***as... house*** Presumably this implies that he moves across the back of the stage, perhaps from one stage door in the direction of another.
4.1 ***in a chair*** A similar direction occurs in the quarto text of *Othello*, 5.2.288: '...Cassio [wounded] in a chair.' Some kind of invalid's carrying-chair is implied.
13 **still** constantly
18-19 **Seven wounds... nails** Samuel Harsnett's *Declaration of Egregious Popish Impostures* (1603) describes how exorcists gave a woman 'five blows, in remembrance of the five wounds of Christ, and seven in honour of the seven sacraments' (sig. Ff2^{v}) in order to expel evil spirits. He also describes how a priest commanded a devil to go 'into the dead' of a woman's nail.
20 **ne'er** never previously
21-2 **Bind... bottomless** Alluding to Revelations 20:2-3: 'And he [the Angel] took the dragon that old serpent which is the devil and Satan, and he bound him a thousand years: | And cast him into the bottomless pit.' John Jowett plausibly suggests (privately) that 'more' may be an error for 'year'.
30 **For** for causing
32.1 ***Children laid out*** Presumably the bodies should be brought on to the stage at this point; or they might be revealed from behind a door or hanging.
34 **bleeding** perhaps alluding to the superstition that bodies bleed in the presence of their murderer
38 **glasses** i.e. eyes
39 **both... shoot** This elliptical expression seems to mean that tears for the murders of both boys would spring forth on his cheeks.
45 **Though** even if
46 **enemy** i.e. the devil
50 **have part with** participate wholly in

I of thy wrongs repent me with my heart.

WIFE O stay, thou shalt not go!

HUSBAND

That's but in vain, you see it must be so.
Farewell, ye bloody ashes of my boys,
My punishments are their eternal joys.
Let every father look into my deeds,
And then their heirs may prosper while mine bleeds.

WIFE

More wretched am I now in this distress
Than former sorrows made me.

Exeunt Husband and Officers with halberds

MASTER O kind wife,

Be comforted. One joy is yet unmurdered.
You have a boy at nurse; your joy's in him.

WIFE

Dearer than all is my poor husband's life.
Heaven give my body strength, which yet is faint
With much expense of blood, and I will kneel,
Sue for his life, number up all my friends,
To plead for pardon my dear husband's life.

MASTER

Was it in man to wound so kind a creature?
I'll ever praise a woman for thy sake.
I must return with grief, my answer's set;
I shall bring news weighs heavier than the debt.
Two brothers: one in bond lies overthrown,
This, on a deadlier execution. [*Exeunt*]

Finis

54 **thy wrongs** the wrongs I have done you
57 **ashes** remains
58 **My ... joys** This seems to mean that his suffering in hell is the condition of his sons' eternal bliss.
71 **a woman** has been taken as an allusion to the Virgin, but might mean simply 'womanhood'
72 **set** determined
73 **debt** (for which the brother is 'in bond')
75 **execution** (*a*) arrest and imprisonment for debt; (*b*) capital punishment

THE LIFE OF TIMON OF ATHENS

Text edited and annotated by John Jowett, introduced by Sharon O'Dair

WITH the inclusion of *Timon of Athens* in this edition of Thomas Middleton's *Collected Works*, readers may experience a familiar play differently. No longer need we assume that *Timon* is unfinished, as Hermann Ulrici suggested in 1815; or that it is inferior Shakespeare, perhaps even a sign of a midlife crisis, as E. K. Chambers suggested in 1930. Instead, we can now experience *Timon* as we experience *The Two Noble Kinsmen* or *The Changeling*—as an artistic and commercial collaboration between two professional playwrights. Of course, to think of *Timon* as a play partly by Middleton will not solve at once the oft-noted problems about the play's structure or interpretation. But as we become more comfortable in thinking of *Timon* as adjacent not only to *King Lear* but also to *Michaelmas Term* (with its almost womanless, homosocial world) and to *A Trick to Catch the Old One* (with its ruthless creditors), and as a play whose sources include not only North's translation of Plutarch but also an anonymous pamphlet that Middleton used in writing *A Yorkshire Tragedy*, it is likely we will at least reconceptualize many of those problems.

The suggestion that the play was written collaboratively is not new. In 1838, the editor Charles Knight concluded that *Timon* might not be entirely Shakespeare's own work. Following Knight's lead, editors and critics suggested over the course of the nineteenth century a number of candidates for the role of Shakespeare's collaborator, including Chapman, Day, Middleton, Tourneur, and Wilkins. But only Middleton has survived sustained investigation. Studies of *Timon* by Lake (1975), Jackson (1979), Holdsworth (1982), Taylor (1987), and Hope (1994) examine the play in the context of Jacobean drama and offer 'extensive, independent, and compelling evidence' that Middleton composed about one-third of *Timon*, including all of scene 2, all of scenes 5 through 10, and probably parts of scenes 4, 13, and 14 as well (Taylor 1987).

Historically, most attempts to settle on another hand in *Timon* have tried to explain perceived deficiencies in a play assumed to be by Shakespeare—hence the repeated references in the critical and editorial literatures to an 'inferior author' or to parts of the play that do not measure up to 'the Shakespearean yardstick'. In a postmodern critical and theatrical climate, however, in which Shakespeare is not held to be without fault or peer, the search for a collaborator is no longer a search for a scapegoat. With the identification of Middleton as Shakespeare's collaborator, the questions are these: will Middleton's considerable and growing reputation lead to a more positive or favourable assessment of *Timon*? And if so, can such assessments influence positively what we see on stage, make for a *Timon* with more stage-worthiness?

Obviously neither question, and especially the latter, can be answered here and now. What we do know is that a focus on the play as exclusively Shakespearean has left critics, directors, and audiences frustrated and unsatisfied. Critics and audiences have long complained about the second half of the play, which *is* undramatic, a series of static encounters in which the misanthropic Timon rails at a variety of Athenians, thus taking revenge on those he knew when he was the generous and magnificent Timon. As a number of critics have noted, these are encounters that interest audiences intellectually more than emotionally, which is not generally a recipe for success on the stage. And they are encounters, it should be noted in this context, that undoubtedly were written by Shakespeare.

Critics and audiences have complained, too, about the confusing and ambiguous characterization of Alcibiades. Some have wondered why he appears in the play at all, apparently not impressed by H. J. Oliver's now-creaky modernist explanation: like other Shakespearean men of action (including Fortinbras, Octavius, or Aufidius), Alcibiades functions as a foil to the more contemplative Timon, and survives the hero 'partly because he has a clearer view of things and is more efficient, but partly because (it is the thought that recurs most often in Shakespeare) efficiency has been bought at the price of a certain loss of sensitivity'. And in the last quarter century, a chorus of critics and viewers have complained about the play's 'exclusion' of women. For these, Alcibiades' two whores and the Amazons who appear in the Masque of scene 2 are hardly significant, and indicate that what is going on in Athens is fundamentally unsound or distasteful, the extremes of which, as Karen Newman puts it, 'might be alliteratively described as capitalism and castration'.

Even contemporary audiences who have had opportunities to judge the play in performance find the play unsatisfying. *Timon* has been performed more often in the last 50 years than it was performed in the previous two and a half centuries. What this frequency reveals, however, is not increased popularity or greater receptivity to the play's themes and movements, but the influence of increasingly numerous Shakespeare festivals, with their tendencies not to shirk even one bit of the canon. At least two studies suggest that despite the higher absolute numbers of productions, despite the likelihood of finding *Timon* in Newfoundland or Utah or Prague, *Timon* remains one of the three or four plays in the Shakespearean canon that is least likely to be put on the stage (Sanders; Williams). And even when a production is 'of great originality and distinction,... and perfectly successful in its own terms' (Berry), such as that directed in 1983 by Robin Phillips in Ontario, *Timon* troubles the box office. Despite its critical success, audiences stayed away from Phillips's production: the house was 'so shrunken ultimately that seats in the balcony and side aisles were, by the cunning of the computer, made out of bounds, so that the poor devils on the stage might have some sense of a crowd to play to' (Mellamphy). *Timon*, it seems, always makes the 'box-office "black list" of... losers' (Thomson).

This is not to say that over the centuries *Timon* has not attracted spirited defenders and admirers, both theatrical and literary, such as William Hazlitt and Friedrich Schiller, and even philosophical and political, such as Karl Marx and (if Michael Simmonds is to be believed) John Ruskin. Contemporary directors and critics find much to admire in the play and seem to want the play to succeed theatrically. Even a bit of lobbying goes on: given life in the late twentieth century, the play *should* succeed theatrically. We *should* appreciate, if not enjoy, the play because we, too, live in 'times of lessened expectations and bleak horizons' (Ruszkiewicz), and can see 'in Timon a recognizable man, one without spiritual resources in a mean-spirited world, who makes his fiercest commitment of all to despair' (Williams). We should appreciate *Timon* because ours, too, is 'an opulent civilization in catastrophe' in which misanthropy seems the justified response to 'greed and materialism and self-interest' (Zinman).

Convinced, like the critics, that they know why *Timon* is 'so much the play for our times' (Zinman), contemporary directors have focused on constructing *Timon* as social satire. Beginning with Willard Stoker's modern dress production in 1947, in which the second half of the play was set beside a bomb crater, and Tyrone Guthrie's production at the Old Vic in 1952, in which Timon was 'the spoiled Darling of Fortune whom Fortune suddenly spurns' (Guthrie, cited by Williams), directors have sought to make *Timon* relevant to audiences by emphasizing the play's relationship to putative failures of Western society—its militarism, its materialism, its self-interest and greed. In 1974, Peter Brook staged the play in French at the Théâtre des Bouffes-du-Nord in Paris, an abandoned Victorian theatre, gutted and scarred long ago by fire. In the remains of the red and gilt theatre, Brook's *Timon*—abstract, austere, and informal, seemingly unconcerned with period consistencies or contemporary relevancies—nevertheless precisely conveyed an image of the doom of consumer society, of the decline of the West.

Brook's vision of the play is perhaps not surprising in a society that had been rocked by the first 'oil crisis'. But the decline of the West is not a theme tied by contemporary directors or critics to a certain date, and certainly not to 1974, with its emerging inflationary spiral. The decline of the West plays well, for seemingly the West is always already in decline, and if not 1974, then a director can find a suitable setting for *Timon* in the Edwardian era, as Phillips did in 1983, and which Ralph Berry judged 'the ideal frame for the drama of opulence and disintegration'. If not satisfied with the age of property, a director can turn to the roaring 1920s, as Michael Langham did in 1991 at Stratford, Ontario; and, with the help of a splendid score by Duke Ellington originally commissioned for Stratford's 1963 production, he can reveal Timon to be 'the Great Gatsby *de leurs jours*' (Zinman).

Or, if near-relevance is not enough, a director can set *Timon* in the present, as Trevor Nunn did for his production at the Young Vic in London, also in 1991. Nunn put onto the stage not only what reviewer Peter Holland calls 'the violent underbelly of... Thatcherite consumer capitalism'—including an armed robbery, plain-clothes policemen, tramps, a vacant lot, and six wrecked cars—but also Thatcherite capitalism's more satisfying upper middle-class surface, its accessible amenities, such as computers, cell phones, squash courts, and bottles of Evian water. Nunn materialized this *Timon* through an impressive accumulation of social detail and a strategic rewriting of the play, rewriting intended 'to clarify what is impossibly obscure, to expand what is impenetrably telescoped and to make dramatic what is inert in the story' (Nunn, cited by Holland).

It is a cliché to say that every age invents its own Shakespeare; but clichés develop because they are to some degree accurate about what they describe. In the eighteenth century, Timon became an object lesson about the consequences of ostentation and liberality, and in the nineteenth, Timon was idealized, conceived most often as a noble victim of a corrupt society (Butler). The late twentieth century has cast the play as social satire, with Timon himself conceived variously: by Phillips and Langham, as a disillusioned millionaire; by Brook, as a disillusioned liberal; by Guthrie, as a disillusioned spoiled fool; by all, as one for whom it is impossible to feel pity or fear.

In the search for contemporary relevance, a relevance that seems so obvious—what could be more socially responsible or satisfying than to denounce contemporary society's greed or brutality?—what tends to be overlooked, as I have argued elsewhere, is the play's historical specificity, its location in a moment of social and economic development. What tends to be overlooked, ironically, are the important lessons Karl Marx drew from Shakespeare and Middleton's presentation of Timon's fall. Consider Timon's paean to gold (14.28–42), that 'immense malediction of malediction', which Marx loved and absorbed 'with a kind of delight whose signs are unmistakable' (Derrida). For Marx, the speech crystallizes the structurally transformative power of gold or money; Marx is less concerned with the ways money affects a person's personality than with the ways money allows a person to affect society. In the *Economic and Philosophical Manuscripts* (1844), Marx explains this point: 'that which I am unable to do as a *man*, and of which therefore all my individual essential powers are incapable, I am able to do by means of *money*'. Money provides anyone who obtains it the power to 'overturn ... and confound ... all human and natural qualities,' to bring about 'the fraternization of incompatibles'. This power—what Timon describes as the power to make 'Black white, foul fair, wrong right, | Base noble, old young, coward valiant'—would alter profoundly the largely static and traditional societies of medieval Europe.

Such is the social revolutionary force of capital about which Marx and Timon complain: under its influence society can be transformed structurally, everything can be turned 'into its *contrary*' (Marx, *Manuscripts*). Money accomplishes a 'transfiguring alchemy', as Jacques Derrida notes, and it does so because it is 'a radical leveller', which 'extinguishes all distinctions' (Marx, *Capital*). Money will 'Pluck stout men's pillows from below their heads' and give a thief 'title, knee, and approbation', the kind of honour traditionally reserved for 'senators on the bench'. Money can bring blessing to the 'accursed and | Make the hoar leprosy adored'. With enough money, even 'the wappered widow' can find a new husband: 'She whom the spittle house and ulcerous sores | Would cast the gorge at, this embalms and spices | To th' April day again'. Money allows 'social power [to become] the private power of private persons', as Marx argued in *Capital*, and as such, money disrupts and eventually undermines static and hierarchical social orders. Timon turns misanthropic for good reasons: his friends' failure to rescue him from ruin forces him to confront the deeply transformative, and in his eyes, the deeply evil effects of rationalized economic behaviour.

Marx identifies in *Timon* an expression of the structural power of capital, but Shakespeare and Middleton achieve this result by focusing attention on a contemporary social problem, what Lawrence Stone calls 'the crisis of the aristocracy'—the nobility's need to adapt behaviourally to the emergence of capitalism, which itself depended on freeing economic decision-making from determination by ethics and morality or the control of religious institutions. One of the many divisive and lengthy battles in this liberation occurred over the legitimation of interest-taking on loans; in 1571, Parliament repealed the Act of 1552, which had reinforced medieval prohibitions on moneylending by outlawing 'the taking of any interest whatever, under pain of imprisonment and fine, in addition to the forfeiture of principal and interest' (Tawney). The compromise Act of 1571 clearly 'was a turning point', according to R. H. Tawney, because it distinguished between usury and interest and legalized the latter. Another of the battles in this liberation focused on sumptuary laws, which regulated according to ascribed social status the kinds of clothes a person could purchase and wear. Like the prohibitions on interest-taking, the legal regulation of dress was repeatedly reinforced by the state during the Elizabethan period, but unsuccessfully; in 1604, the sumptuary laws were eliminated. In both cases, Pandora had already opened the box. As Lisa Jardine points out with respect to the sumptuary laws, 'the affluent burghers with ready money to dress like the gentry were also the purveyors of the commodity being legislated about: expensive fabrics'.

The noble Timon ruins his estate and himself by holding to a set of economic and ethical norms that are not just under pressure but clearly no longer in force. Commensurate with the norm that usury is sinful, for example, Timon believes that a nobleman should give, and give freely, without expectation of immediate, or even of any, return:

> Why, I have often wished myself poorer, that I might come nearer to you. We are born to do benefits; and what better or properer can we call our own than the riches of our friends? O, what a precious comfort 'tis to have so many like brothers commanding one another's fortunes! (2.97–102)

As this passage and others make clear, Timon thinks about money differently from us. Money is not a personal matter for him: both giving money and getting it occur through a generalized exchange among a group of men that over time is equitable. In Timon's world, furthermore, money is a means to an end, which itself is vastly more important than money: that of displaying through conspicuous consumption one's status, one's position relative to others. In contrast, as Middleton's scenes in this play show, Timon's 'brothers' or peers have learned, perhaps from hard experience, to behave less like Antonio and Bassanio and more like Shylock, or us: they will not allow others to command their fortunes, but will judge for themselves when to lend money and when not to, 'especially upon bare friendship, | without security' (5.41–2).

Timon's honour and prestige is deeply staked to his gift-giving. Indeed, Timon's 'power depends on his bounty', as David Bevington and David L. Smith observe. His gift-giving is rivalrous, as is the potlatch for the chieftains of the tribes of the American north-west, described by Marcel Mauss in *The Gift*, or to a lesser degree, the seasonal balls given by the élites of late nineteenth-century America, described by Thorstein Veblen in *The Theory of the Leisure Class*. What I wish to emphasize here are not the particular similarities or dissimilarities between Timon and the chiefs or the corporate chiefs, but rather Mauss's point that gift exchange is economic as well as social activity. Furthermore, as Veblen implies, market exchange itself is imbued with the behavioural norms of non-market exchange, which is why Veblen addresses the history of the leisure class in order to assess its role in contemporary economic life and why he—and we—can compare the potlatch to the society ball or to Timon's banquets: 'conspicuous consumption of valuable goods is a means of reputability to the gentleman of leisure'.

It has been argued, using Langham's 1991, jazz-era *Timon* as evidence, that performance of 'a classical play must lead the audience to see itself in the action, or it will cease to be a work of art which impels society towards the creation of new standards, and becomes one which inhibits creation' (Hayes). Perhaps. But Shakespeare and Middleton knew that audiences are not uniform in their tastes or interests: relevance, or leading an audience to 'see itself in the action', must be an expansive and resonant effort. In the past half-century, our efforts with *Timon* have been narrowly focused on contemporary social satire, which has led not to 'the creation of new standards' but to frustration and disappointment. In productions of *Timon*, we might see ourselves—and the negative effects of capitalism—more clearly if we understand that Timon is not our contemporary. His failure in the face of capital is not an object lesson for us because, like other literary misanthropes, his experience has 'a determinate otherness, which is to say: not all misanthropes are alike. They have a history, which is a reflex of the history of social forms themselves' (Konstan). Timon's rage, therefore, is not the same as the rage of Menander's Knemon, or even of Moliére's Alceste. Still, this kind of historical difference may be crucial and may offer a different way to make *Timon* 'relevant' to us: as Brook Thomas observes, it is through 'an exchange with texts from the past' that we gain 'a sense of the otherness of our own point of view', an insight that can then lead us to imagine 'alternative ways of world-making'.

Timon 'is a straightforward tract for the times', as E. C. Pettet suggested over fifty years ago: a tract for the early seventeenth century, when capital begins to transform society structurally, moving society's élite from gift-exchange and conspicuous consumption to market-exchange and increasing rates of saving. In *Timon*, Shakespeare and Middleton urge consideration of a specific historical moment, when the emergence of a capitalist economy begins to transform a society structurally—unsettling the status quo and confusing 'in equivalency the proper and the improper, credit and discredit, faith and lie, the "true and the false", oath, perjury, and abjuration...' (Derrida).

Marx would like us to agree that Timon's transformation symbolizes society's transformation under the influence of money and capital. But to do so requires an idealization of Timon's liberality and, more importantly, of the old order of feudalism that guarantees his privilege. In this, Marx's reading is perfectly attuned with other nineteenth-century readings of the play. In contrast, Shakespeare and Middleton do not make this association: however much they lament Timon's fall and however harshly they judge those who decline to help him, the authors do not idealize Timon or the social order that supports his privilege.

Shakespeare and Middleton were well-positioned to describe the structural transformations they dramatize, not just here in *Timon* but elsewhere as well, as in Shakespeare's *The Merchant of Venice* or Middleton's *A Chaste Maid in Cheapside*, which display the effects on the social order generally, and on the nobility in particular, of an economy newly sprung open, of social mobility by people of 'the middling sort' like the playwrights themselves. Furthermore, Shakespeare and Middleton doubtless were quite aware of the social and economic possibilities of the professional theatre in which they worked and quite interested in promoting them, as Louis Montrose has emphasized. But Shakespeare and Middleton understood, too, that their success in promoting a professional theatre or themselves as, in Taylor's words, 'textual capitalists' ('Lives'), depended on dramatizing not just their own but a variety of points of view: Timon's as well as Shylock's; Orlando's as well as Yellowhammer's; and Petruccio's as well as the Roaring Girl's. Such variety inhibits—or should inhibit—the kinds of moralizing that has surrounded *Timon of Athens*, especially in the twentieth century. Newman is correct, I believe, to conclude that *Timon* offers a sexual narrative 'in which the absence of women is simply that, the absence of women'. We would do well to conclude, too, that in *Timon* the failure of the gift economy is simply that, the failure of the gift economy. It is not the end of a golden age of bounty and magnificence, an economic fall from which we can never recover.

SEE ALSO

Textual introduction and apparatus: *Companion*, 704
Authorship and date: *Companion*, 356
Other Middleton–Shakespeare works: *Macbeth*, 1165; *Measure*, 1542

WILLIAM SHAKESPEARE and THOMAS MIDDLETON

The Life of Timon of Athens

[*for the King's Men at The Globe*]

THE PERSONS OF THE PLAY

TIMON of Athens

ALCIBIADES, an Athenian captain
APEMANTUS, a churlish philosopher

Flavius, Timon's STEWARD
LUCILIUS, a gentleman of Timon's household
FLAMINIUS, one of Timon's servants
SERVILIUS, another
Timon's THIRD SERVANT
A FOOL
A PAGE

LUCIUS, LUCULLUS } two flattering lords
SEMPRONIUS, another flattering lord
Other LORDS
A POET
A PAINTER
A JEWELLER
A MERCHANT
A Mercer
An OLD ATHENIAN MAN

VENTIDIUS, one of Timon's false friends
One dressed as CUPID in the masque
LADIES: certain masquers dressed as Amazons
Certain SENATORS
Three STRANGERS, the second called Hostilius

LUCIUS' SERVANT
LUCULLUS' SERVANT
CAPHIS, ISIDORE'S SERVANT, Two of VARRO'S SERVANTS, TITUS' SERVANT, HORTENSIUS' SERVANT, PHILOTUS' SERVANT } several servants to usurers

PHRYNIA, TIMANDRA } whores with Alcibiades
The Banditti, certain THIEVES
A SOLDIER of Alcibiades' army
Other soldiers
MESSENGERS
With divers other servants and attendants

Sc. 1

Enter Poet [*at one door*], *Painter* [*carrying a picture, at another door; followed by*] *Jeweller, Merchant, and Mercer, at several doors*

POET
Good day, sir.

PAINTER
I am glad you're well.

POET
I have not seen you long. How goes the world?

PAINTER
It wears, sir, as it grows.

POET
Ay, that's well known.
But what particular rarity, what strange,
Which manifold record not matches?—See,
Magic of bounty, all these spirits thy power
Hath conjured to attend.
[*Merchant and Jeweller meet. Mercer passes over the stage, and exits*]
I know the merchant.

PAINTER
I know them both. Th' other's a jeweller.

1.0.2–3 *followed ... doors* The play opens with a convergence of clients attending on Timon. They establish two separate conversations (Poet and Painter, Merchant and Jeweller). The Mercer may be an accidental duplication of the Merchant, but can be understood to add to the substance and bustle of the gathering clients ('all these spirits', 1.6, and compare the passage over the stage of the Senators at 1.38.1–1.41.1). The Painter is identifiable because carrying a picture; the Poet might wear a crown of laurel.

3 **wears** wears away
4 **what strange** what that is strange
5 **record** memory, recorded history
6 **spirits** (*a*) supernatural beings (*b*) people
7 **conjured to attend** Applies to both magical conjuration of spirits and the influence of patronage.

MERCHANT [*to Jeweller*]
O, 'tis a worthy lord!
JEWELLER Nay, that's most fixed.
MERCHANT
A most incomparable man, breathed, as it were,
To an untirable and continuate goodness.
He passes.
JEWELLER [*showing a jewel*]
I have a jewel here.
MERCHANT
O, pray, let's see't. For the Lord Timon, sir?
JEWELLER
If he will touch the estimate. But for that—
POET [*to himself*]
'When we for recompense have praised the vile,
It stains the glory in that happy verse
Which aptly sings the good.'
MERCHANT [*to Jeweller*] 'Tis a good form.
JEWELLER
And rich. Here is a water, look ye.
PAINTER [*to Poet*]
You are rapt, sir, in some work, some dedication
To the great lord.
POET A thing slipped idly from me.
Our poesy is as a gum which oozes
From whence 'tis nourished. The fire i'th' flint
Shows not till it be struck; our gentle flame
Provokes itself, and like the current flies
Each bound it chafes. What have you there?
PAINTER
A picture, sir. When comes your book forth?
POET
Upon the heels of my presentment, sir.
Let's see your piece.
PAINTER [*showing the picture*]
'Tis a good piece.
POET
So 'tis. This comes off well and excellent.
PAINTER
Indifferent.
POET Admirable. How this grace
Speaks his own standing! What a mental power
This eye shoots forth! How big imagination
Moves in this lip! To th' dumbness of the gesture
One might interpret.
PAINTER
It is a pretty mocking of the life.
Here is a touch; is't good?
POET I will say of it,
It tutors nature. Artificial strife
Lives in these touches livelier than life.
Enter certain Senators
PAINTER How this lord is followed!
POET
The senators of Athens, happy men!
PAINTER Look, more.
[*The Senators pass over the stage, and exeunt*]
POET
You see this confluence, this great flood of visitors.
I have in this rough work shaped out a man
Whom this beneath world doth embrace and hug
With amplest entertainment. My free drift
Halts not particularly, but moves itself
In a wide sea of wax. No levelled malice
Infects one comma in the course I hold,
But flies an eagle flight, bold and forth on,
Leaving no tract behind.
PAINTER How shall I understand you?

9 **fixed** certain
10 **breathed** accustomed through training
11 **continuate** continual
12 **passes** excels
14 **touch the estimate** reach the expected price
15 **we** i.e. poets
16 **happy** fortunate in its subject
17 **form** (*a*) shape (*b*) kind, quality
18 **water** transparency, lustre
21–5 **Our ... chafes** Poets, the Poet claims, are not subject to external and spasmodic stimulations such as a patron's favour; their verse flows slowly, spontaneously, at any time.
22–3 **The ... struck** Varies the proverb 'In the coldest flint there is hot fire'.
24 **Provokes itself** i.e. stimulates itself without needing friction
24–5 **like ... chafes** The image is now of a river whose current bends away from a bank to avoid friction and turbulence.
24 **flies** rushes away from
25 **bound** bank
27 **Upon the heels of** immediately after
presentment i.e. presentation of the book to Timon
30 **this grace** the grace of this figure
31 **his** i.e. that of the person represented (presumably Timon)
32 **big** greatly
33 **Moves in** i.e. is expressed by the apparent movement (or expression) of
35 **pretty** neatly contrived
mocking imitation, counterfeit
36 **touch** brushstroke; fine, natural, or lifelike detail
37 **Artificial strife** i.e. art's attempt to outdo nature
39 **this lord** i.e. Timon
41.1 ***Senators*** The term as applied to members of the Athenian Council is unusual and does not derive from recognized sources. It might anticipate costumes of classical robes, perhaps in contrast with contemporary Jacobean costume for the tradesmen and artisans. In the English context, *senators* could imply Members of Parliament, but Middleton's civic works often describe the City of London Council as senators. In the play the Senate seems to be an exclusive governing council and its members typically have mercantile or financial connections. The status of Athens as a city state strengthens the analogy with the Lord Mayor and Aldermen of London rather than, or as well as, MPs. The roles are distinct from lords except after 11.104.1, '*Enter the Senators with other Lords*'.
44 **beneath world** mortal, changeable world (as distinct from the heavens)
45 **entertainment** welcome
46 **particularly** in individual cases
47 **of wax** growing, becoming more potent (probably also referring to the practice of writing on tablets of wax)
levelled aimed at particular people
48 **comma** (*a*) the punctuation mark (*b*) phrase
49–50 **But ... behind** Compare Wisdom of Solomon 5:10–11: 'as a bird that flieth through in the air ... whereas afterward no token of her way can be found'.
49 **flies** i.e. My free drift flies
50 **tract** trace; track

POET I will unbolt to you.
You see how all conditions, how all minds,
As well of glib and slipp'ry creatures as
Of grave and austere quality, tender down
Their service to Lord Timon. His large fortune,
Upon his good and gracious nature hanging,
Subdues and properties to his love and tendance
All sorts of hearts; yea, from the glass-faced flatterer
To Apemantus, that few things loves better
Than to abhor himself—even he drops down
The knee before him, and returns in peace,
Most rich in Timon's nod.

PAINTER I saw them speak together.

POET
Sir, I have upon a high and pleasant hill
Feigned Fortune to be throned. The base o' th' mount
Is ranked with all deserts, all kind of natures
That labour on the bosom of this sphere
To propagate their states. Amongst them all
Whose eyes are on this sovereign lady fixed
One do I personate of Lord Timon's frame,
Whom Fortune with her ivory hand wafts to her,
Whose present grace to present slaves and servants
Translates his rivals.

PAINTER 'Tis conceived to scope.
This throne, this Fortune, and this hill, methinks,
With one man beckoned from the rest below,
Bowing his head against the steepy mount
To climb his happiness, would be well expressed
In our condition.

POET Nay, sir, but hear me on.
All those which were his fellows but of late,
Some better than his value, on the moment
Follow his strides, his lobbies fill with tendance,
Rain sacrificial whisperings in his ear,
Make sacred even his stirrup, and through him
Drink the free air.

PAINTER Ay, marry, what of these?

POET
When Fortune in her shift and change of mood
Spurns down her late belovèd, all his dependants,
Which laboured after him to the mountain's top
Even on their knees and hands, let him fall down,
Not one accompanying his declining foot.

PAINTER 'Tis common.
A thousand moral paintings I can show
That shall demonstrate these quick blows of Fortune's
More pregnantly than words. Yet you do well
To show Lord Timon that mean eyes have seen
The foot above the head.

Trumpets sound. Enter Lord Timon [wearing a rich jewel], addressing himself courteously to every suitor, [a Messenger from Ventidius with him; Lucilius and other Servants]

TIMON [*to Messenger*] Imprisoned is he, say you?

MESSENGER
Ay, my good lord. Five talents is his debt,
His means most short, his creditors most strait.
Your honourable letter he desires
To those have shut him up, which failing,
Periods his comfort.

TIMON Noble Ventidius! Well,
I am not of that feather to shake off
My friend when he must need me. I do know him
A gentleman that well deserves a help,
Which he shall have. I'll pay the debt and free him.

MESSENGER Your lordship ever binds him.

TIMON
Commend me to him. I will send his ransom;
And, being enfranchised, bid him come to me.
'Tis not enough to help the feeble up,
But to support him after. Fare you well.

MESSENGER All happiness to your honour. *Exit*

Enter an Old Athenian

OLD MAN
Lord Timon, hear me speak.

53 **conditions** (*a*) social ranks (*b*) temperaments
55 **quality** (*a*) rank, nobility (*b*) character
56 **large fortune** great good fortune, illustriousness (hinting also at 'ample wealth')
58 **Subdues** makes subservient
properties appropriates
59 **glass-faced** mirror-faced (reflecting his patron's moods and opinions)
62 **returns** goes away
63 **Most . . . nod** (*a*) most gratified in Timon's approval (*b*) most enriched by Timon's assent
65 **Feigned** represented
66 **ranked** lined
all deserts people of every kind of merit
67 **this sphere** (the earth)
68 **propagate** increase
states possessions, fortunes
69 **this sovereign lady** i.e. Fortune. The Poet's depiction of Fortune's mount was traditional.
72 **Whose** i.e. Fortune's
present grace graciousness of the moment
to into
present slaves immediate slaves
73 **Translates** transforms
to scope to the purpose, aptly
77 **expressed** exemplified
78 **our condition** the circumstances we find around us
80 **his value** him in value (or status)
83 **stirrup** (held by followers when the rider mounts his horse)
83–4 **through . . . air** depend on him even for the air they breathe. Air was proverbially free.
89 **declining** falling, sinking
foot (as the part of the body others follow)
91 **moral** allegorical
92 **demonstrate** (accented on the second syllable)
quick vigorous, sharp. *Pregnantly* in 1.93 gives wordplay on 'with child'.
93 **pregnantly** cogently (and see previous note)
94 **mean eyes** the eyes of the lowly
95 **The foot . . . head** i.e. the foot of the fortunate of Fortune's hill advanced above the vulnerable aspirant's head
97 **Five talents** A considerable sum: a talent could be over 56 lbs of silver.
98 **strait** exacting
100–1 **which . . . comfort** if which fails, his hopes end
102 **feather** i.e. disposition
106 **ever binds him** makes him obliged for ever
110 **But** i.e. but also necessary
111.1 ***Athenian*** Another suggestion of specifically ancient Greek costume.

TIMON Freely, good father.
OLD MAN
Thou hast a servant named Lucilius.
TIMON I have so. What of him?
OLD MAN
Most noble Timon, call the man before thee.
TIMON
Attends he here or no? Lucilius!
LUCILIUS [*coming forward*] Here at your lordship's service.
OLD MAN
This fellow here, Lord Timon, this thy creature,
By night frequents my house. I am a man
That from my first have been inclined to thrift,
And my estate deserves an heir more raised
Than one which holds a trencher.
TIMON Well, what further?
OLD MAN
One only daughter have I, no kin else
On whom I may confer what I have got.
The maid is fair, o' th' youngest for a bride,
And I have bred her at my dearest cost
In qualities of the best. This man of thine
Attempts her love. I prithee, noble lord,
Join with me to forbid him her resort.
Myself have spoke in vain.
TIMON The man is honest.
OLD MAN Therefore he will be, Timon.
His honesty rewards him in itself;
It must not bear my daughter.
TIMON Does she love him?
OLD MAN She is young and apt.
Our own precedent passions do instruct us
What levity's in youth.
TIMON [*to Lucilius*] Love you the maid?
LUCILIUS
Ay, my good lord, and she accepts of it.
OLD MAN
If in her marriage my consent be missing,
I call the gods to witness, I will choose
Mine heir from forth the beggars of the world,
And dispossess her all.
TIMON How shall she be endowed
If she be mated with an equal husband?
OLD MAN
Three talents on the present; in future, all.
TIMON
This gentleman of mine hath served me long.
To build his fortune I will strain a little,
For 'tis a bond in men. Give him thy daughter.
What you bestow in him I'll counterpoise,
And make him weigh with her.
OLD MAN Most noble lord,
Pawn me to this your honour, she is his.
TIMON
My hand to thee; mine honour on my promise.
LUCILIUS
Humbly I thank your lordship. Never may
That state or fortune fall into my keeping
Which is not owed to you. *Exit* [*with Old Man*]
POET [*presenting a poem to Timon*]
Vouchsafe my labour, and long live your lordship!
TIMON
I thank you. You shall hear from me anon.
Go not away. [*To Painter*] What have you there, my friend?
PAINTER
A piece of painting, which I do beseech
Your lordship to accept.
TIMON Painting is welcome.
The painting is almost the natural man;
For since dishonour traffics with man's nature,
He is but outside; these pencilled figures are
Even such as they give out. I like your work,
And you shall find I like it. Wait attendance
Till you hear further from me.
PAINTER The gods preserve ye!
TIMON
Well fare you, gentleman. Give me your hand.
We must needs dine together. [*To Jeweller*] Sir, your jewel
Hath suffered under praise.
JEWELLER What, my lord, dispraise?
TIMON
A mere satiety of commendations.
If I should pay you for't as 'tis extolled
It would unclew me quite.
JEWELLER My lord, 'tis rated
As those which sell would give; but you well know
Things of like value differing in the owners
Are prizèd by their masters. Believe't, dear lord,

112 **father** (respectful form of address to an older man)
118 **creature** dependant (disparaging)
121 **more raised** of higher breeding
122 **one...trencher** i.e. a domestic servant. A *trencher* was a wooden dish or plate.
125 **for a bride** of marriageable age
127 **qualities** accomplishments
129 **her resort** recourse to her
131 **honest** honourable
132 **will be** i.e. will be honest. Based on the proverb 'Virtue is its own reward'.
133 **His...itself** proverbial
134 **bear** carry away with it
136 **apt** easily impressed
148 **bond** obligation
150 **with** equally with
151 **Pawn...honour** if you will pawn your honour to this
155 **owed to you** acknowledged as owing to your generosity (or 'due to you as a debt')
156 **Vouchsafe** deign to accept
162 **traffics** has dealings
163 **but outside** merely outer appearances
pencilled painted with brush-strokes
164 **Even...out** just what they appear to be
165 **find I like it** oblique for 'be well paid for it'
169 **Hath...praise** i.e. cannot hope to match the high praise it has been given. The Jeweller understands *under-praise*, 'depreciation'.
170 **mere** utter, absolute
172 **unclew** undo
172–3 **rated | As** put at a price that
175 **by** according to

You mend the jewel by the wearing it.

TIMON Well mocked.

MERCHANT
No, my good lord, he speaks the common tongue
Which all men speak with him.

Enter Apemantus

TIMON Look who comes here.
Will you be chid?

JEWELLER We'll bear, with your lordship.

MERCHANT He'll spare none.

TIMON
Good morrow to thee, gentle Apemantus.

APEMANTUS
Till I be gentle, stay thou for thy good morrow—
When thou art Timon's dog, and these knaves honest.

TIMON
Why dost thou call them knaves? Thou know'st them not.

APEMANTUS Are they not Athenians?

TIMON Yes.

APEMANTUS Then I repent not.

JEWELLER You know me, Apemantus?

APEMANTUS
Thou know'st I do. I called thee by thy name.

TIMON Thou art proud, Apemantus!

APEMANTUS Of nothing so much as that I am not like Timon.

TIMON Whither art going?

APEMANTUS To knock out an honest Athenian's brains.

TIMON That's a deed thou'lt die for.

APEMANTUS Right, if doing nothing be death by th' law.

TIMON How lik'st thou this picture, Apemantus?

APEMANTUS The best for the innocence.

TIMON
Wrought he not well that painted it?

APEMANTUS He wrought better that made the painter, and yet he's but a filthy piece of work.

PAINTER You're a dog.

APEMANTUS Thy mother's of my generation. What's she, if I be a dog?

TIMON Wilt dine with me, Apemantus?

APEMANTUS No, I eat not lords.

TIMON An thou shouldst, thou'dst anger ladies.

APEMANTUS O, they eat lords. So they come by great bellies.

TIMON
That's a lascivious apprehension.

APEMANTUS
So thou apprehend'st it, take it for thy labour.

TIMON
How dost thou like this jewel, Apemantus?

APEMANTUS Not so well as plain dealing, which will not cost a man a doit.

TIMON
What dost thou think 'tis worth?

APEMANTUS Not worth my thinking.
How now, poet?

POET How now, philosopher?

APEMANTUS Thou liest.

POET Art not one?

APEMANTUS Yes.

POET Then I lie not.

APEMANTUS Art not a poet?

POET Yes.

APEMANTUS Then thou liest. Look in thy last work, where thou hast feigned him a worthy fellow.

POET That's not feigned, he is so.

APEMANTUS Yes, he is worthy of thee, and to pay thee for thy labour. He that loves to be flattered is worthy o' th' flatterer. Heavens, that I were a lord!

TIMON What wouldst do then, Apemantus?

APEMANTUS E'en as Apemantus does now: hate a lord with my heart.

TIMON What, thyself?

APEMANTUS Ay.

TIMON Wherefore?

APEMANTUS That I had no angry wit but to be a lord.— Art not thou a merchant?

MERCHANT Ay, Apemantus.

APEMANTUS
Traffic confound thee, if the gods will not!

MERCHANT If traffic do it, the gods do it.

APEMANTUS
Traffic's thy god, and thy god confound thee!

Trumpet sounds. Enter a Messenger

TIMON What trumpet's that?

MESSENGER
'Tis Alcibiades, and some twenty horse
All of companionship.

176 **mend** increase the value of
177 **mocked** counterfeited (as a sales pitch)
181 **bear, with** suffer, along with
184 **stay...morrow** i.e. you will have to wait for a greeting
191 **thy name** i.e. *knave*
200 **for the** on account of its
innocence (*a*) artlessness, guilelessness (perhaps because Apemantus sees obvious faults in the person painted that the Painter has failed to conceal), or (*b*) harmlessness (of the painted figure, in contrast with the represented person)
202 **He** i.e. God
204 **dog** A general insult; also an allusion to Apemantus' cynic philosophy, as *cynic* is derived from the Greek for 'dog'.
205 **generation** breed, species (punning on 'age-group')
208 **eat not lords** i.e. do not consume the wealth that makes lords
210 **eat** Quibbles on sexual 'devouring', hence the *great bellies* of pregnancy.
211 **apprehension** idea
212 **So...labour** as you took possession of it, keep it as reward for your effort (punning on *apprehend* as 'understand')
214–15 **Not...doit** From the proverbs 'Plain dealing is a jewel, but they that use it die beggars' and 'Not worth a doit'.
215 **doit** (a coin of small value)
223–5 **Art...liest** From the proverb, 'Painters and poets have leave to lie'.
226 **him** i.e. Timon
237 **angry wit** wit in my anger
240 **Traffic** business, trade
confound ruin
244 **horse** horsemen
245 **of companionship** in one party

TIMON [*to Servants*]
Pray entertain them. Give them guide to us.
[*Exit one or more Servants*]
[*To Jeweller*] You must needs dine with me. [*To Poet*] Go not you hence
Till I have thanked you. [*To Painter*] When dinner's done
Show me this piece. [*To all*] I am joyful of your sights.
Enter Alcibiades with his horsemen. [*They greet Timon*]
Most welcome, sir!
APEMANTUS [*aside*] So, so, there.
Achës contract and starve your supple joints!
That there should be small love 'mongst these sweet knaves,
And all this courtesy! The strain of man's bred out
Into baboon and monkey.
ALCIBIADES [*to Timon*]
Sir, you have saved my longing, and I feed
Most hungrily on your sight.
TIMON Right welcome, sir!
Ere we depart, we'll share a bounteous time
In different pleasures. Pray you, let us in.
Exeunt [*all but Apemantus*]
Enter two Lords
FIRST LORD
What time o' day is't, Apemantus?
APEMANTUS
Time to be honest.
FIRST LORD That time serves still.
APEMANTUS
The most accursèd thou, that still omitt'st it.
SECOND LORD
Thou art going to Lord Timon's feast?
APEMANTUS
Ay, to see meat fill knaves, and wine heat fools.
SECOND LORD Fare thee well, fare thee well.
APEMANTUS
Thou art a fool to bid me farewell twice.
SECOND LORD Why, Apemantus?
APEMANTUS Shouldst have kept one to thyself, for I mean to give thee none.
FIRST LORD Hang thyself!
APEMANTUS No, I will do nothing at thy bidding. Make thy requests to thy friend.
SECOND LORD Away, unpeaceable dog, or I'll spurn thee hence.
APEMANTUS I will fly, like a dog, the heels o' th' ass. [*Exit*]
FIRST LORD
He's opposite to humanity. Come, shall we in,
And taste Lord Timon's bounty? He outgoes
The very heart of kindness.
SECOND LORD
He pours it out. Plutus the god of gold
Is but his steward; no meed but he repays
Sevenfold above itself; no gift to him
But breeds the giver a return exceeding
All use of quittance.
FIRST LORD The noblest mind he carries
That ever governed man.
SECOND LORD
Long may he live in fortunes! Shall we in?
FIRST LORD I'll keep you company. *Exeunt*

Sc. 2

Oboes playing loud music. A great banquet served in, [*Steward and Servants attending*]; *and then enter Lord Timon,* [*Alcibiades*], *the States, the Athenian Lords, Ventidius which Timon redeemed from prison. Then comes, dropping after all, Apemantus, discontentedly, like himself*

VENTIDIUS
Most honoured Timon,
It hath pleased the gods to rèmember
My father's age, and call him to long peace.
He is gone happy, and has left me rich.
Then, as in grateful virtue I am bound
To your free heart, I do return those talents,
Doubled with thanks and service, from whose help
I derived liberty.
TIMON O, by no means,
Honest Ventidius. You mistake my love.

246 **entertain** receive, welcome
248 **thanked** i.e. rewarded
249.1–2 ***Enter . . . Timon*** The staging of Alcibiades' arrival and greeting may be informed by Plutarch, who described him as 'a bold and insolent youth whom he [Timon] would greatly feast and make much of, and kissed him very glady'.
252 **Achës** disyllabic form of *aches*, referring to rheumatism, arthritis, etc.
starve paralyse, disable
254 **bred out** dissipated through over-breeding
256 **saved my longing** gratified my desire to be with you. Proverbial.
258 **depart** part company
259 **different** various
259.2 ***two Lords*** They might be Lucius and Lucullus.
261 **That time serves still** it is always an opportune time for that
264 **meat** food
273 **spurn** kick
275 **heels** hooves
276 **opposite to** (*a*) set in opposition to (*b*) the opposite of
279 **pours it out** i.e. is unrestrainedly generous
280 **meed** (*a*) gift, or (*b*) merit
283 **All use of quittance** repayment with full interest
2.0.1 ***A great banquet*** i.e. a full banquet, as distinct from a light dessert (as was more usual on stage, and the 'idle banquet' of 2.153). A loaded table and chairs need to be brought on stage. The dialogue after 2.235 provides a possible occasion for clearing them.
0.3 ***States*** persons of rank, senators
0.6 ***like himself*** in his usual manner
3 **long peace** death
6 **free** generous (with wordplay with 'bound', 2.5, and 'at liberty', 2.8)
6–7 **I . . . service** Has overtones of the parable of the talents, Matthew 25:20, etc: 'Master, thou delivered'st unto me five talents; behold, I have gained with them other five talents . . .'.
7 **service** respect, homage

I gave it freely ever, and there's none
Can truly say he gives if he receives.
If our betters play at that game, we must not dare
To imitate them. Faults that are rich are fair.

VENTIDIUS
A noble spirit!
[*The Lords stand with ceremony*]

TIMON
Nay, my lords, ceremony was but devised at first
To set a gloss on faint deeds, hollow welcomes,
Recanting goodness, sorry ere 'tis shown;
But where there is true friendship, there needs none.
Pray sit. More welcome are ye to my fortunes
Than my fortunes to me.
[*They sit*]

FIRST LORD
My lord, we always have confessed it.

APEMANTUS
Ho, ho, confessed it? Hanged it, have you not?

TIMON
O, Apemantus! You are welcome.

APEMANTUS No,
You shall not make me welcome.
I come to have thee thrust me out of doors.

TIMON
Fie, thou'rt a churl. Ye've got a humour there
Does not become a man; 'tis much to blame.
They say, my lords, *Ira furor brevis est*,
But yon man is ever angry.
Go, let him have a table by himself,
For he does neither affect company
Nor is he fit for't, indeed.

APEMANTUS
Let me stay at thine apperil, Timon.
I come to observe, I give thee warning on't.

TIMON I take no heed of thee; thou'rt an Athenian, therefore welcome. I myself would have no power: prithee, let my meat make thee silent.

APEMANTUS I scorn thy meat. 'Twould choke me, for I should ne'er flatter thee. O you gods, what a number of men eats Timon, and he sees 'em not! It grieves me to see so many dip their meat in one man's blood; and all the madness is, he cheers them up, too.
I wonder men dare trust themselves with men.
Methinks they should invite them without knives:
Good for their meat, and safer for their lives.
There's much example for't. The fellow that sits next him, now parts bread with him, pledges the breath of him in a divided draught, is the readiest man to kill him. 'T'as been proved. If I were a huge man, I should fear to drink at meals,
Lest they should spy my windpipe's dangerous notes.
Great men should drink with harness on their throats.

TIMON [*drinking to a Lord*]
My lord, in heart; and let the health go round.

SECOND LORD
Let it flow this way, my good lord.

APEMANTUS 'Flow this way'? A brave fellow; he keeps his tides well. Those healths will make thee and thy state look ill, Timon.
Here's that which is too weak to be a sinner:
Honest water, which ne'er left man i'th' mire.
This and my food are equals; there's no odds.
Feasts are too proud to give thanks to the gods.

Apemantus' grace

Immortal gods, I crave no pelf.
I pray for no man but myself.
Grant I may never prove so fond
To trust man on his oath or bond,
Or a harlot for her weeping,
Or a dog that seems a-sleeping,
Or a keeper with my freedom,
Or my friends if I should need 'em.
Amen. So fall to't.
Rich men sin, and I eat root.
[*He eats*]
Much good dich thy good heart, Apemantus.

TIMON Captain Alcibiades, your heart's in the field now.

ALCIBIADES My heart is ever at your service, my lord.

10–11 **and . . . receives** Echoes Luke 6:34, 'if ye lend to them of whom ye hope to receive, what thank shall ye have?', and Acts 20:35, 'It is a blessed thing to give, rather than to receive'.
13 **Faults . . . fair** From the proverb 'Rich men have no faults'.
15 **ceremony** conventional forms of deference
16 **faint** spiritless, reluctant, indistinct
21 **confessed** acknowledged. But Apemantus alludes to the proverb 'Confess and be hanged', in which the sense is 'admit guilt'.
26 **churl** unmannered peasant
humour disposition
28 ***Ira . . . est*** Latin for 'anger is a short madness'; from Horace, *Epistles*, 1.2.62; proverbial in English.
33 **apperil** peril
34 **observe** watch and make critical comments
41 **dip . . . blood** Reminiscent of the Last Supper of Christ: 'He that dippeth his hand with me in the dish, he shall betray me' (Matthew 26:23).
42 **cheers them up** encourages them
44 **without knives** Guests usually brought their own knives to eat with.
46–52 **The . . . throats** Merges Judas Iscariot's betrayal of Christ after the Last Supper (see note to 2.41) with the proverb 'To laugh in one's face and cut one's throat'.
47 **pledges the breath** drinks to the life
48 **divided** shared, passed from guest to guest
49 **huge** eminent
51 **dangerous** vulnerable
notes (*a*) musical sounds (as of a *pipe*) (*b*) distinguishing marks
52 **harness** armour
53 **in heart** (a toast of fellowship)
55–6 **keeps his tides** doesn't miss his opportunity. *Tides* is both 'times, occasions' and the sea's *flow*.
59 **left man i'th' mire** proverbial
60 **no odds** nothing to choose between them
61 **proud** (*a*) arrogant (*b*) lavish
62 **pelf** plunder
66 **Or . . . weeping** From the proverb, 'Trust not a woman when she weeps'.
72 **dich** do it (?); or perhaps *dight*, 'dress, array'

TIMON You had rather be at a breakfast of enemies than a dinner of friends.

ALCIBIADES So they were bleeding new, my lord, there's no meat like 'em. I could wish my best friend at such a feast.

APEMANTUS Would all those flatterers were thine enemies then, that then thou mightst kill 'em and bid me to 'em.

FIRST LORD [*to Timon*] Might we but have that happiness, my lord, that you would once use our hearts whereby we might express some part of our zeals, we should think ourselves for ever perfect.

TIMON O, no doubt, my good friends, but the gods themselves have provided that I shall have much help from you. How had you been my friends else? Why have you that charitable title from thousands, did not you chiefly belong to my heart? I have told more of you to myself than you can with modesty speak in your own behalf; and thus far I confirm you. 'O you gods,' think I, 'what need we have any friends if we should ne'er have need of 'em? They were the most needless creatures living, should we ne'er have use for 'em, and would most resemble sweet instruments hung up in cases, that keeps their sounds to themselves.' Why, I have often wished myself poorer, that I might come nearer to you. We are born to do benefits; and what better or properer can we call our own than the riches of our friends? O, what a precious comfort 'tis to have so many like brothers commanding one another's fortunes! O, joy's e'en made away ere't can be born: mine eyes cannot hold out water, methinks. To forget their faults, I drink to you.

APEMANTUS Thou weep'st to make them drink, Timon.

SECOND LORD [*to Timon*]
Joy had the like conception in our eyes,
And at that instant like a babe sprung up.

APEMANTUS
Ho, ho, I laugh to think that babe a bastard.

THIRD LORD [*to Timon*]
I promise you, my lord, you moved me much.

APEMANTUS Much!

Sound tucket [*within*]

TIMON What means that trump?

Enter a Servant

How now?

SERVANT Please you, my lord, there are certain ladies most desirous of admittance.

TIMON Ladies? What are their wills?

SERVANT There comes with them a forerunner, my lord, which bears that office to signify their pleasures.

TIMON I pray let them be admitted.

Enter one as Cupid

CUPID
Hail to thee, worthy Timon, and to all
That of his bounties taste! The five best senses
Acknowledge thee their patron, and come freely
To gratulate thy plenteous bosom. Th' ear,
Taste, touch, smell, all, pleased from thy table rise.
They only now come but to feast thine eyes.

TIMON
They're welcome all. Let 'em have kind admittance.
Music make their welcome! [*Exit Cupid*]

FIRST LORD
You see, my lord, how ample you're beloved.

[*Music.*] *Enter the masque of Ladies as Amazons* [*representing the five senses*], *with lutes in their hands, dancing and playing*

APEMANTUS Hoy-day!
What a sweep of vanity comes this way!
They dance? They are madwomen.
Like madness is the glory of this life

75–6 **of enemies . . . of friends** i.e. upon enemies . . . with friends

77 **bleeding new** freshly killed (proverbial)

81 **to** set to, eat

83 **use our hearts** make use of our affections

85 **perfect** contented

89 **charitable** loving

98 **nearer** (*a*) more closely tied (*b*) closer in rank

98–9 **We . . . benefits** From the proverb 'We are not born for ourselves'.

99 **benefits** favours, good deeds

101–2 **O . . . fortunes** Probably influenced by Psalms 133:1: 'Behold how good and joyful a thing it is, brethren, to dwell together in unity'.

103 **made away** killed. Joy instantly turns to tears.

106 **Thou . . . Timon** Apemantus compresses Timon's words to produce an epigram on sacrifice.

111.1 ***tucket*** flourish of trumpets. This marks the beginning of a masque presented to entertain the guests and compliment the host (but Timon appears to have arranged it himself: see note to 2.148).

118 **that office to signify** the office of announcing

121–5 **The . . . eyes** This 'banquet of the senses' is an antitype of the 'celestial banquet' of Plato's *Symposium* as expounded by Ficino.

123 **gratulate** (*a*) gratify (*b*) greet (*c*) congratulate

plenteous bounteous

128.1 ***Amazons*** Women in *Timon* are confined to the roles of Amazons and whores. Though there were no women actors on the professional stage, female courtiers appeared in court masques, so the representation of the lady masquers as Amazons seems to reflect a complex and partly misogynistic public-theatre reaction to women on stage at court. No indication is given in the dialogue that the ladies are dressed as Amazons; they would probably be indicated as such on stage by wearing swords and plumed helmets.

128.2 ***representing the five senses*** This is suggested by 2.121–5. The senses might be indicated by motifs of the ear, tongue, finger, nose and eye on the costumes (the effect might be anything from decorous to grotesque). However, in the elaborate Caroline court masque *Coelum Britannicum* the senses were represented emblematically as follows: Sight, a man holding a mirror and a shield showing an eagle staring at the sun; Hearing, a woman playing a lute with a hind near by; Taste, a woman holding a bowl of fruit; Touch, a woman holding a falcon; Smell, a youth standing in a stream of water. Mirror, lute, bowl of fruit, falcon, and bowl of liquid are possible properties on the public stage, though the stage-direction call for '*lutes in their hands*' would make it difficult for the ladies to hold other objects.

129 **Hoy-day** (an exclamation of astonishment)

132 **Like madness** just such a madness

As this pomp shows to a little oil and root.
We make ourselves fools to disport ourselves,
And spend our flatteries to drink those men
Upon whose age we void it up again
With poisonous spite and envy.
Who lives that's not depravèd or depraves?
Who dies that bears not one spurn to their graves
Of their friends' gift?
I should fear those that dance before me now
Would one day stamp upon me. 'T'as been done.
Men shut their doors against a setting sun.

The Lords rise from table, with much adoring of Timon; and to show their loves, each single out an Amazon, and all dance, men with women, a lofty strain or two to the oboes; and cease

TIMON
You have done our pleasures much grace, fair ladies,
Set a fair fashion on our entertainment,
Which was not half so beautiful and kind.
You have added worth unto't and lustre,
And entertained me with mine own device.
I am to thank you for't.

FIRST LADY
My lord, you take us even at the best.

APEMANTUS Faith; for the worst is filthy, and would not hold taking, I doubt me.

TIMON
Ladies, there is an idle banquet attends you,
Please you to dispose yourselves.

ALL LADIES Most thankfully, my lord. *Exeunt Ladies*

TIMON Flavius.

STEWARD My lord.

TIMON The little casket bring me hither.

STEWARD Yes, my lord. [*Aside*] More jewels yet?
There is no crossing him in's humour,
Else I should tell him well, i'faith I should.
When all's spent, he'd be crossed then, an he could.
'Tis pity bounty had not eyes behind,
That man might ne'er be wretched for his mind.
Exit

FIRST LORD Where be our men?

SERVANT Here, my lord, in readiness.

SECOND LORD Our horses. [*Exit Servant*]

[*Enter Steward with the casket. He gives it to Timon, and exits*]

TIMON O my friends,
I have one word to say to you. Look you, my good lord,
I must entreat you honour me so much
As to advance this jewel. Accept it and wear it,
Kind my lord.

FIRST LORD
I am so far already in your gifts.

ALL LORDS So are we all.

[*Timon gives them jewels.*]

Enter a Servant

FIRST SERVANT My lord, there are certain nobles of the senate newly alighted and come to visit you.

TIMON They are fairly welcome. [*Exit Servant*]

Enter Flavius the Steward

STEWARD I beseech your honour, vouchsafe me a word; it does concern you near.

TIMON
Near? Why then, another time I'll hear thee.
I prithee, let's be provided to show them entertainment.

STEWARD I scarce know how.

Enter another Servant

SECOND SERVANT
May it please your honour, Lord Lucius
Out of his free love hath presented to you
Four milk-white horses trapped in silver.

TIMON
I shall accept them fairly. Let the presents
Be worthily entertained. [*Exit Servant*]

Enter a third Servant

How now, what news?

THIRD SERVANT Please you, my lord, that honourable gentleman Lord Lucullus entreats your company tomorrow to hunt with him, and has sent your honour two brace of greyhounds.

TIMON
I'll hunt with him, and let them be received
Not without fair reward. [*Exit Servant*]

STEWARD [*aside*] What will this come to?
He commands us to provide and give great gifts,
And all out of an empty coffer;
Nor will he know his purse, or yield me this:

133 **As . . . to** as can be seen by comparing this pomp with
a little oil and root i.e. a subsistence vegetarian diet
135 **spend** (*a*) utter (*b*) part freely with (*c*) consume, exhaust
drink (*a*) drink the health of (*b*) consume
136 **age** old age
138 **depravèd** both 'vilified' and 'perverted'
139 **spurn** painful insult, rejection
143 **Men . . . sun** From the proverb, 'Men more worship the rising than the setting sun'.
143.1 ***adoring of*** reverential gesture towards
143.2 ***show their loves*** i.e. express their devotion to Timon
148 **And . . . device** Suggests that Timon commissioned the entertainment and proposed at least its theme.
device theatrical contrivance
150 **take . . . best** rate us at the highest possible
151–2 **would . . . taking** wouldn't withstand sexual intercourse (because rotten with venereal disease)
153 **idle** trifling
banquet dessert (usually of sweetmeats, fruit, and wine)
156 **Flavius** The Steward's pesonal name is subsequently abandoned.
160 **crossing** thwarting, challenging
humour perverse disposition
162 **crossed** crossed off the list of debtors (quibbling on the sense in 2.160)
164 **mind** wilfulness
171 **advance** (*a*) wear prominently; and so (*b*) increase the value of
184 **free** bountiful
185 **trapped in silver** with silver trappings
187 **worthily entertained** received with the honour they deserve
196 **yield** grant

To show him what a beggar his heart is,
Being of no power to make his wishes good.
His promises fly so beyond his state
That what he speaks is all in debt, he owes
For every word. He is so kind that he now
Pays interest for't. His land's put to their books.
Well, would I were gently put out of office
Before I were forced out.
Happier is he that has no friend to feed
Than such that do e'en enemies exceed.
I bleed inwardly for my lord. *Exit*

TIMON [*to the Lords*] You do yourselves
Much wrong, you bate too much of your own merits.
[*To Second Lord*] Here, my lord, a trifle of our love.

SECOND LORD
With more than common thanks I will receive it.

THIRD LORD
O, he's the very soul of bounty!

TIMON [*to First Lord*] And now I remember, my lord, you gave good words the other day of a bay courser I rode on. 'Tis yours, because you liked it.

FIRST LORD
O I beseech you pardon me, my lord, in that.

TIMON
You may take my word, my lord, I know no man
Can justly praise but what he does affect.
I weigh my friends' affection with mine own,
I'll tell you true. I'll call to you.

ALL LORDS O, none so welcome.

TIMON
I take all and your several visitations
So kind to heart, 'tis not enough to give.
Methinks I could deal kingdoms to my friends,
And ne'er be weary. Alcibiades,
Thou art a soldier, therefore seldom rich.
[*Giving a present*] It comes in charity to thee, for all thy living
Is 'mongst the dead, and all the lands thou hast
Lie in a pitched field.

ALCIBIADES Ay, defiled land, my lord.

FIRST LORD We are so virtuously bound—

TIMON And so am I to you.

SECOND LORD So infinitely endeared—

TIMON All to you. Lights, more lights!

FIRST LORD
The best of happiness, honour, and fortunes
Keep with you, Lord Timon.

TIMON Ready for his friends.

Exeunt Lords [*and all but Timon and Apemantus*]

APEMANTUS What a coil's here,
Serving of becks and jutting-out of bums!
I doubt whether their legs be worth the sums
That are given for 'em. Friendship's full of dregs.
Methinks false hearts should never have sound legs.
Thus honest fools lay out their wealth on curtseys.

TIMON
Now, Apemantus, if thou wert not sullen
I would be good to thee.

APEMANTUS No, I'll nothing; for if I should be bribed too, there would be none left to rail upon thee, and then thou wouldst sin the faster. Thou giv'st so long, Timon, I fear me thou wilt give away thyself in paper shortly. What needs these feasts, pomps, and vainglories?

TIMON Nay, an you begin to rail on society once, I am sworn not to give regard to you. Farewell, and come with better music. *Exit*

APEMANTUS So. Thou wilt not hear me now, thou shalt not then. I'll lock thy heaven from thee.
O, that men's ears should be
To counsel deaf, but not to flattery! *Exit*

Sc. 3

Enter a Senator [*with bonds*]

SENATOR
And late five thousand. To Varro and to Isidore
He owes nine thousand, besides my former sum,
Which makes it five-and-twenty. Still in motion
Of raging waste! It cannot hold, it will not.
If I want gold, steal but a beggar's dog
And give it Timon, why, the dog coins gold.
If I would sell my horse and buy twenty more
Better than he, why, give my horse to Timon—
Ask nothing, give it him—it foals me straight
And able horses. No porter at his gate,
But rather one that smiles and still invites
All that pass by. It cannot hold. No reason
Can sound his state in safety. Caphis ho!
Caphis, I say!

202 **put to their books** mortgaged to them
208 **bate . . . of** diminish
213 **courser** stallion
218 **affection** desires, liking
219 **call to** call on, visit
220 **all . . . visitations** the totality and the separate instances of your visits
227 **pitched field** battlefield with armies drawn up in formation to fight. In his reply Alcibiades quibbles by taking *pitched* as 'covered with pitch', alluding to Ecclesiasticus 13:1, 'He that toucheth pitch shall be defiled with it'.
228 **virtuously bound** bound by your virtue
231 **Lights, more lights** Needed to illuminate the Lords' way out of Timon's house.
235 **coil's** commotion's
236 **Serving** delivering
becks nods, bows
237 **legs** bows. Similarly at 2.239, but there with a pun on the limbs.
248 **society** social occasions
252 **heaven** salvation, happiness (as might be obtained through heeding advice)
3.1 **late** recently
3–4 **Still . . . waste** A metaphor of violent natural destruction—'in a ceaseless rush of furious devastation'—or of a stormy sea (compare 3.12–13). More literally, *raging* is 'riotous, extravagant'; *waste* is 'wasteful expenditure'.
9 **straight** (*a*) at once (qualifying *foals me*) (*b*) upright (qualifying *horses*)
13 **sound . . . safety** measure his financial condition reliably and without risk. *Sound* is literally 'test the depth of water with a plummet'. Timon's *state* is both shallow and in flux, creating danger of shipwreck.

Enter Caphis

CAPHIS Here, sir. What is your pleasure?

SENATOR
Get on your cloak and haste you to Lord Timon.
Importune him for my moneys. Be not ceased
With slight denial, nor then silenced when
'Commend me to your master', and the cap
Plays in the right hand, thus; but tell him
My uses cry to me, I must serve my turn
Out of mine own, his days and times are past,
And my reliances on his fracted dates
Have smit my credit. I love and honour him,
But must not break my back to heal his finger.
Immediate are my needs, and my relief
Must not be tossed and turned to me in words,
But find supply immediate. Get you gone.
Put on a most importunate aspect,
A visage of demand, for I do fear
When every feather sticks in his own wing
Lord Timon will be left a naked gull,
Which flashes now a phoenix. Get you gone.

CAPHIS I go, sir.

SENATOR
'I go, sir'? [*giving him bonds*] Take the bonds along with you,
And have the dates in. Come.

CAPHIS I will, sir.

SENATOR Go.

Exeunt [severally]

Sc. 4 *Enter Steward, with many bills in his hand*

STEWARD
No care, no stop; so senseless of expense
That he will neither know how to maintain it
Nor cease his flow of riot, takes no account
How things go from him, nor resumes no care
Of what is to continue. Never mind
Was to be so unwise to be so kind.
What shall be done? He will not hear till feel.
[*A sound of horns within*]
I must be round with him, now he comes from hunting.
Fie, fie, fie, fie!

Enter Caphis [at one door, and Servants of] Isidore and Varro [at another door]

CAPHIS
Good even, Varro. What, you come for money?

VARRO'S SERVANT Is't not your business too?

CAPHIS
It is; and yours too, Isidore?

ISIDORE'S SERVANT It is so.

CAPHIS
Would we were all discharged.

VARRO'S SERVANT I fear it.

CAPHIS Here comes the lord.

Enter Timon and his train [amongst them Alcibiades, as from hunting]

TIMON
So soon as dinner's done we'll forth again,
My Alcibiades.
[*Caphis meets Timon*]
With me? What is your will?

CAPHIS
My lord, here is a note of certain dues.

TIMON Dues? Whence are you?

CAPHIS Of Athens here, my lord.

TIMON Go to my steward.

CAPHIS
Please it your lordship, he hath put me off,
To the succession of new days, this month.
My master is awaked by great occasion
To call upon his own, and humbly prays you
That with your other noble parts you'll suit
In giving him his right.

TIMON Mine honest friend,
I prithee but repair to me next morning.

CAPHIS
Nay, good my lord.

TIMON Contain thyself, good friend.

VARRO'S SERVANT
One Varro's servant, my good lord.

ISIDORE'S SERVANT [*to Timon*]
From Isidore. He humbly prays your speedy payment.

CAPHIS [*to Timon*]
If you did know, my lord, my master's wants—

VARRO'S SERVANT [*to Timon*]
'Twas due on forfeiture, my lord, six weeks and past.

ISIDORE'S SERVANT [*to Timon*]
Your steward puts me off, my lord, and I
Am sent expressly to your lordship.

TIMON Give me breath.—
I do beseech you, good my lords, keep on.
I'll wait upon you instantly.

[*Exeunt Alcibiades and Timon's train*]

19 **thus** i.e. probably with shows of courtesy, but perhaps with gestures of impatience for the visitor to leave so that the cap can be put back on
20 **uses** needs
21 **mine own** my own money
22 **fracted** broken
30–1 **When ... gull** Proverbial, and quibbles on *gull* as 'credulous fool'.
30 **his** its
35 **have the dates in** The bonds perhaps specified a span of time without naming the dates.
4.3 **riot** wild revelling
4 **resumes** assumes
5–6 **Never ... unwise** there was never a mind that was so unwise
13 **we were all discharged** the debts were all settled with us (perhaps also 'we were all relieved of this duty')
fear it i.e. suspect otherwise
14 **forth again** (to hunting)
21 **To ... days** day after day
24 **with ... suit** you'll act in accordance with your other noble qualities

[*To Steward*] Come hither. Pray you,
How goes the world, that I am thus encountered
With clamorous demands of broken bonds
And the detention of long-since-due debts,
Against my honour?

STEWARD [*to Servants*] Please you, gentlemen,
The time is unagreeable to this business;
Your importunacy cease till after dinner,
That I may make his lordship understand
Wherefore you are not paid.

TIMON [*to Servants*] Do so, my friends.
[*To Steward*] See them well entertained. [*Exit*]

STEWARD Pray draw near.
Exit

Enter Apemantus and Fool

CAPHIS Stay, stay, here comes the Fool with Apemantus. Let's ha' some sport with 'em.

VARRO'S SERVANT Hang him, he'll abuse us.

ISIDORE'S SERVANT A plague upon him, dog!

VARRO'S SERVANT How dost, Fool?

APEMANTUS Dost dialogue with thy shadow?

VARRO'S SERVANT I speak not to thee.

APEMANTUS No, 'tis to thyself. [*To Fool*] Come away.

ISIDORE'S SERVANT [*to Varro's Servant*] There's the fool hangs on your back already.

APEMANTUS No, thou stand'st single: thou'rt not on him yet.

CAPHIS [*to Isidore's Servant*] Where's the fool now?

APEMANTUS He last asked the question. Poor rogues' and usurers' men, bawds between gold and want.

ALL SERVANTS What are we, Apemantus?

APEMANTUS Asses.

ALL SERVANTS Why?

APEMANTUS That you ask me what you are, and do not know yourselves. Speak to 'em, Fool.

FOOL How do you, gentlemen?

ALL SERVANTS Gramercies, good Fool. How does your mistress?

FOOL She's e'en setting on water to scald such chickens as you are. Would we could see you at Corinth.

APEMANTUS Good; gramercy.

Enter Page [*with two letters*]

FOOL Look you, here comes my master's page.

PAGE Why, how now, captain? What do you in this wise company? How dost thou, Apemantus?

APEMANTUS Would I had a rod in my mouth, that I might answer thee profitably.

PAGE Prithee, Apemantus, read me the superscription of these letters. I know not which is which.

APEMANTUS Canst not read?

PAGE No.

APEMANTUS There will little learning die then that day thou art hanged. This is to Lord Timon, this to Alcibiades. Go, thou wast born a bastard, and thou'lt die a bawd.

PAGE Thou wast whelped a dog, and thou shalt famish a dog's death. Answer not; I am gone. *Exit*

APEMANTUS E'en so thou outrunn'st grace. Fool, I will go with you to Lord Timon's.

FOOL Will you leave me there?

APEMANTUS If Timon stay at home. [*To Servants*] You three serve three usurers?

ALL SERVANTS Ay. Would they served us.

APEMANTUS So would I: as good a trick as ever hangman served thief.

FOOL Are you three usurers' men?

ALL SERVANTS Ay, Fool.

FOOL I think no usurer but has a fool to his servant. My mistress is one, and I am her fool. When men come to borrow of your masters they approach sadly and go away merry, but they enter my master's house merrily and go away sadly. The reason of this?

VARRO'S SERVANT I could render one.

APEMANTUS Do it then, that we may account thee a whoremaster and a knave, which notwithstanding thou shalt be no less esteemed.

VARRO'S SERVANT What is a whoremaster, Fool?

FOOL A fool in good clothes, and something like thee. 'Tis a spirit; sometime't appears like a lord, sometime like a lawyer, sometime like a philosopher with two stones more than 's artificial one. He is very often like a knight; and generally in all shapes that man goes up and down in from fourscore to thirteen, this spirit walks in.

VARRO'S SERVANT Thou art not altogether a fool.

36 **How goes the world** proverbial
38 **detention** withholding
53 **the fool** the name 'fool'
54 **hangs on your back** attaches to you (with a possible quibble on a posture for anal intercourse picked up in the following exchange)
55 **stand'st** (quibbling on 'have an erection')
58 **He** he that
68 **scald** Refers to (*a*) scalding chicken to remove the feathers (*b*) treatment given for venereal disease of sweating in a heated tub.
69 **Would...Corinth** 'Lais, an harlot of Corinth...was for none but lords and gentlemen that might well pay for it. Whereof came up a proverb that it was not for every man to go unto Corinth' (Udall, 1542).
74–5 **Would...profitably** From Proverbs 26:3–4, '...a rod [belongeth] to the fool's back. Answer not a fool according to his foolishness, lest thou also be like him' and Isaiah 11:4, 'the rod of his mouth'.
83–4 **famish a dog's death** proverbial ('Die a dog's death')
88 **If...home** Implies that there will be a fool at Timon's house as long as he is there.
95–6 **My mistress is one** A procuress could be seen as an usurer in the sexual economy; compare 4.59.
99 **go away sadly** After a visit to a brothel a man would have spent his money and might have picked up a disease, but according to a well-known post-classical Latin dictum, '*Post coitum omne animal triste*' (after coition every animal is sad).
107 **philosopher** alchemist (see following note)
stones testicles. But the *artificial one* is the 'philosopher's stone' of the alchemists, supposedly capable of turning base metals to gold.
109–10 **goes up and down in** (*a*) walks about in (*b*) gets and loses erections
111 **not altogether a fool** proverbial

FOOL Nor thou altogether a wise man. As much foolery as I have, so much wit thou lack'st.

APEMANTUS That answer might have become Apemantus.

ALL SERVANTS Aside, aside, here comes Lord Timon.

Enter Timon and Steward

APEMANTUS Come with me, Fool, come.

FOOL I do not always follow lover, elder brother, and woman: sometime the philosopher.

[*Exeunt Apemantus and Fool*]

STEWARD [*to Servants*]
Pray you, walk near. I'll speak with you anon.

Exeunt [*Servants*]

TIMON
You make me marvel wherefore ere this time
Had you not fully laid my state before me,
That I might so have rated my expense
As I had leave of means.

STEWARD
You would not hear me.
At many leisures I proposed—

TIMON
Go to.
Perchance some single vantages you took
When my indisposition put you back,
And that unaptness made your minister
Thus to excuse yourself.

STEWARD
O my good lord,
At many times I brought in my accounts,
Laid them before you; you would throw them off
And say you summed them in mine honesty.
When for some trifling present you have bid me
Return so much, I have shook my head and wept,
Yea, 'gainst th' authority of manners prayed you
To hold your hand more close. I did endure
Not seldom nor no slight checks when I have
Prompted you in the ebb of your estate
And your great flow of debts. My lovèd lord—
Though you hear now too late, yet now's a time—
The greatest of your having lacks a half
To pay your present debts.

TIMON
Let all my land be sold.

STEWARD
'Tis all engaged, some forfeited and gone,
And what remains will hardly stop the mouth
Of present dues. The future comes apace.
What shall defend the interim, and at length
How goes our reck'ning?

TIMON
To Lacedaemon did my land extend.

STEWARD
O my good lord, the world is but a word.
Were it all yours to give it in a breath,
How quickly were it gone.

TIMON
You tell me true.

STEWARD
If you suspect my husbandry of falsehood,
Call me before th' exactest auditors
And set me on the proof. So the gods bless me,
When all our offices have been oppressed
With riotous feeders, when our vaults have wept
With drunken spilth of wine, when every room
Hath blazed with lights and brayed with minstrelsy,
I have retired me to a wasteful cock,
And set mine eyes at flow.

TIMON
Prithee, no more.

STEWARD
'Heavens,' have I said, 'the bounty of this lord!
How many prodigal bits have slaves and peasants
This night englutted! Who is not Timon's?
What heart, head, sword, force, means, but is Lord Timon's?
Great Timon, noble, worthy, royal Timon!
Ah, when the means are gone that buy this praise,
The breath is gone whereof this praise is made.
Feast won, fast lost; one cloud of winter show'rs,
These flies are couched.'

TIMON
Come, sermon me no further.
No villainous bounty yet hath passed my heart.
Unwisely, not ignobly, have I given.
Why dost thou weep? Canst thou the conscience lack
To think I shall lack friends? Secure thy heart.
If I would broach the vessels of my love
And try the argument of hearts by borrowing,
Men and men's fortunes could I frankly use
As I can bid thee speak.

STEWARD
Assurance bless your thoughts!

TIMON
And in some sort these wants of mine are crowned
That I account them blessings, for by these
Shall I try friends. You shall perceive how you

117–18 **lover . . . woman** (seen as easy sources of employment)
125 **vantages** opportunities
127–8 **made . . . yourself** provided you with an agent who would excuse you thus
136 **checks** rebukes
137 **Prompted you in** reminded, urged you of
139 **now's a time** i.e. better late than never
142 **engaged** mortgaged
143 **stop the mouth** Suggests both feeding and silencing.
147 **Lacedaemon** Sparta
153 **So** as
154 **our offices** the servants' work-areas, the kitchens, etc.
oppressed crowded, overwhelmed
156 **spilth** spillage
157 **minstrelsy** music played by minstrels
158 **cock** spout, tap
159 **And . . . flow** The weeping is both caused by the waste of the spilt wine and analogous to it.
161 **prodigal bits** excessive bits of food. *Prodigal* is transferred from the eaters to the food.
162 **Timon's** Timon's friend, object at the disposal of Timon as patron
167 **fast lost** (*a*) lost when there is a fast instead of a feast (*b*) quickly lost
168 **are couched** lie hidden
169 **villainous** (*a*) vicious (*b*) slavish (anticipating *ignobly*, 4.170)
172 **Secure** (*a*) give confidence to (*b*) close up (referring to the tears as a leak, and anticipating *broach the vessels*, 4.173)
174 **try** test
argument summary (as might be printed at the beginning of a book)
175 **frankly** as freely
176 **Assurance . . . thoughts** may your thought be blessed by being right

Mistake my fortunes. I am wealthy in my friends.—
Within there, Flaminius, Servilius!

Enter three servants: [*Flaminius, Servilius, and a Third Servant*]

ALL SERVANTS
My lord, my lord.

TIMON I will dispatch you severally,
[*To Servilius*] You to Lord Lucius, [*To Flaminius*] to Lord Lucullus you—I hunted with his honour today—[*To Third Servant*] You to Sempronius. Commend me to their loves, and I am proud, say, that my occasions have found time to use 'em toward a supply of money. Let the request be fifty talents.

FLAMINIUS As you have said, my lord. [*Exeunt Servants*]

STEWARD
Lord Lucius and Lucullus? Hmh!

TIMON Go you, sir, to the senators,
Of whom, even to the state's best health, I have
Deserved this hearing. Bid 'em send o' th' instant
A thousand talents to me.

STEWARD I have been bold,
For that I knew it the most general way
To them, to use your signet and your name;
But they do shake their heads, and I am here
No richer in return.

TIMON Is't true? Can 't be?

STEWARD
They answer in a joint and corporate voice
That now they are at fall, want treasure, cannot
Do what they would, are sorry, you are honourable,
But yet they could have wished—they know not—
Something hath been amiss—a noble nature
May catch a wrench—would all were well—'tis pity;
And so, intending other serious matters,
After distasteful looks and these hard fractions,
With certain half-caps and cold-moving nods
They froze me into silence.

TIMON You gods reward them!
Prithee, man, look cheerly. These old fellows
Have their ingratitude in them hereditary.
Their blood is caked, 'tis cold, it seldom flows.
'Tis lack of kindly warmth they are not kind;
And nature as it grows again toward earth
Is fashioned for the journey dull and heavy.
Go to Ventidius. Prithee, be not sad.
Thou art true and honest—ingenuously I speak—
No blame belongs to thee. Ventidius lately
Buried his father, by whose death he's stepped
Into a great estate. When he was poor,
Imprisoned, and in scarcity of friends,
I cleared him with five talents. Greet him from me.
Bid him suppose some good necessity
Touches his friend, which craves to be remembered
With those five talents. That had, give't these fellows
To whom 'tis instant due. Ne'er speak or think
That Timon's fortunes 'mong his friends can sink.

STEWARD
I would I could not think it. That thought is bounty's foe:
Being free itself, it thinks all others so.

Exeunt [*severally*]

Sc. 5

[*Enter*] *Flaminius* [*with a box under his cloak*], *waiting to speak with a lord* [*Lucullus*]. *From his master, enters a Servant to him*

LUCULLUS' SERVANT I have told my lord of you. He is coming down to you.

FLAMINIUS I thank you, sir.

Enter Lucullus

LUCULLUS' SERVANT Here's my lord.

LUCULLUS [*aside*] One of Lord Timon's men? A gift, I warrant. Why, this hits right; I dreamt of a silver basin and ewer tonight.—Flaminius, honest Flaminius, you are very respectively welcome, sir. [*To his Servant*] Fill me some wine. [*Exit Servant*] And how does that honourable, complete, free-hearted gentleman of Athens, thy very bountiful good lord and master?

FLAMINIUS His health is well, sir.

LUCULLUS I am right glad that his health is well, sir. And what hast thou there under thy cloak, pretty Flaminius?

FLAMINIUS Faith, nothing but an empty box, sir, which in my lord's behalf I come to entreat your honour to supply, who, having great and instant occasion to use fifty talents, hath sent to your lordship to furnish him, nothing doubting your present assistance therein.

LUCULLUS La, la, la, la, 'nothing doubting' says he? Alas, good lord! A noble gentleman 'tis, if he would not keep so good a house. Many a time and often I ha' dined with him and told him on't, and come again to supper to him of purpose to have him spend less; and yet he would embrace no counsel, take no warning by my coming. Every man has his fault, and honesty is his. I ha' told him on't, but I could ne'er get him from't.

Enter Servant, with wine

SERVANT Please your lordship, here is the wine.

188 **fifty talents** A vast sum: see note to 1.97.
192 **to** to the limits of
195 **general** usual
200 **at fall** at a low ebb
204 **catch** accidentally suffer
205 **intending** (*a*) pretending, or (*b*) turning to
206 **hard** (*a*) harsh (*b*) difficult to understand
fractions fragments (of utterances)
207 **half-caps** reluctantly-doffed caps
210 **hereditary** as something 'inherited' with age
212 **kindly** natural (punning on *kind*, 'caring, generous')
213 **earth** i.e. the grave
228 **free** generous
it i.e. bounty
5.7 **ewer** pitcher
tonight last night
10 **complete** perfect, fully accomplished
18 **supply** fill
20 **nothing** not at all
23 **good** i.e. lavish
27 **Every . . . fault** proverbial
honesty generosity

LUCULLUS Flaminius, I have noted thee always wise. [*Drinking*] Here's to thee!

FLAMINIUS Your lordship speaks your pleasure.

LUCULLUS I have observed thee always for a towardly prompt spirit, give thee thy due, and one that knows what belongs to reason; and canst use the time well if the time use thee well. [*Drinking*] Good parts in thee! [*To his Servant*] Get you gone, sirrah. [*Exit Servant*] Draw nearer, honest Flaminius. Thy lord's a bountiful gentleman; but thou art wise, and thou know'st well enough, although thou com'st to me, that this is no time to lend money, especially upon bare friendship without security. [*Giving coins*] Here's three solidares for thee. Good boy, wink at me, and say thou saw'st me not. Fare thee well.

FLAMINIUS
Is't possible the world should so much differ,
And we alive that lived?
[*He throws the coins at Lucullus*]
Fly, damnèd baseness,
To him that worships thee.

LUCULLUS Ha! Now I see thou art a fool, and fit for thy master. *Exit*

FLAMINIUS
May these add to the number that may scald thee.
Let molten coin be thy damnation,
Thou disease of a friend, and not himself.
Has friendship such a faint and milky heart
It turns in less than two nights? O you gods,
I feel my master's passion! This slave
Unto this hour has my lord's meat in him.
Why should it thrive and turn to nutriment,
When he is turned to poison?
O, may diseases only work upon't;
And when he's sick to death, let not that part of
nature
Which my lord paid for be of any power
To expel sickness, but prolong his hour. *Exit*

Sc. 6 *Enter Lucius, with three Strangers*

LUCIUS Who, the Lord Timon? He is my very good friend, and an honourable gentleman.

FIRST STRANGER We know him for no less, though we are but strangers to him. But I can tell you one thing, my lord, and which I hear from common rumours: now Lord Timon's happy hours are done and past, and his estate shrinks from him.

LUCIUS Fie, no, do not believe it. He cannot want for money.

SECOND STRANGER But believe you this, my lord, that not long ago one of his men was with the Lord Lucullus to borrow so many talents—nay, urged extremely for't, and showed what necessity belonged to't, and yet was denied.

LUCIUS How?

SECOND STRANGER I tell you, denied, my lord.

LUCIUS What a strange case was that! Now before the gods, I am ashamed on't. Denied that honourable man? There was very little honour showed in't. For my own part, I must needs confess I have received some small kindnesses from him, as money, plate, jewels, and suchlike trifles—nothing comparing to his; yet had he not mistook him and sent to me, I should ne'er have denied his occasion so many talents.

Enter Servilius

SERVILIUS [*aside*] See, by good hap yonder's my lord. I have sweat to see his honour. [*To Lucius*] My honoured lord!

LUCIUS Servilius! You are kindly met, sir. Fare thee well. Commend me to thy honourable, virtuous lord, my very exquisite friend.

SERVILIUS May it please your honour, my lord hath sent—

LUCIUS Ha! What has he sent? I am so much endeared to that lord, he's ever sending. How shall I thank him, think'st thou? And what has he sent now?

SERVILIUS He's only sent his present occasion now, my lord, requesting your lordship to supply his instant use with so many talents.

LUCIUS
I know his lordship is but merry with me.
He cannot want fifty-five hundred talents.

SERVILIUS
But in the mean time he wants less, my lord.
If his occasion were not virtuous
I should not urge it half so faithfully.

LUCIUS
Dost thou speak seriously, Servilius?

SERVILIUS Upon my soul, 'tis true, sir.

LUCIUS What a wicked beast was I to disfurnish myself against such a good time when I might ha' shown myself honourable! How unluckily it happened that I should purchase the day before a little part, and undo a great deal of honour! Servilius, now before the gods I am not able to do, the more beast I, I say. I was sending to use Lord Timon myself—these gentlemen

32 **speaks your pleasure** i.e. is kind to say so
33 **towardly** forward, promising
34 **prompt** ready and willing
give thee thy due proverbial
35 **what...reason** i.e. how to act wisely
time moment, opportunity
36 **time** times, moment
Good parts in thee! to your fine qualities! (a toast)
42 **solidares** (a Latinism for 'shillings')
43 **wink at** turn a blind eye towards
45 **differ** (from its past self)
46 **baseness** (*a*) worthlessness (*b*) base metal
54 **turns** (*a*) curdles (*b*) changes
55 **passion** grief
60 **nature** i.e. his physical body
6.13 **belonged** pertained
36 **so many** as many (as *his present occasion*). Servilius may give Lucius a note stipulating the sum.
38 **fifty-five...talents** The sum is absurdly excessive, perhaps both because Middleton misunderstood the value of a talent and because the inflation from *fifty* (5.19) to *fifty-five hundred* is grotesquely comic.
47 **part** consignment

can witness—but I would not for the wealth of Athens I had done't now. Commend me bountifully to his good lordship; and I hope his honour will conceive the fairest of me because I have no power to be kind. And tell him this from me: I count it one of my greatest afflictions, say, that I cannot pleasure such an honourable gentleman. Good Servilius, will you befriend me so far as to use mine own words to him?

SERVILIUS Yes, sir, I shall.

LUCIUS
I'll look you out a good turn, Servilius. *Exit Servilius*
True as you said: Timon is shrunk indeed;
And he that's once denied will hardly speed. *Exit*

FIRST STRANGER
Do you observe this, Hostilius?

SECOND STRANGER Ay, too well.

FIRST STRANGER
Why, this is the world's soul, and just of the same piece
Is every flatterer's spirit. Who can call him his friend
That dips in the same dish? For, in my knowing,
Timon has been this lord's father
And kept his credit with his purse,
Supported his estate; nay, Timon's money
Has paid his men their wages. He ne'er drinks,
But Timon's silver treads upon his lip;
And yet—O see the monstrousness of man
When he looks out in an ungrateful shape!—
He does deny him, in respect of his,
What charitable men afford to beggars.

THIRD STRANGER
Religion groans at it.

FIRST STRANGER For mine own part,
I never tasted Timon in my life,
Nor came any of his bounties over me
To mark me for his friend; yet I protest,
For his right noble mind, illustrious virtue,
And honourable carriage,
Had his necessity made use of me
I would have put my wealth into donation
And the best half should have returned to him,
So much I love his heart. But I perceive
Men must learn now with pity to dispense,
For policy sits above conscience. *Exeunt*

Sc. 7

Enter a Third Servant [from Timon], with Sempronius, another of Timon's friends

SEMPRONIUS
Must he needs trouble me in't? Hmh! 'Bove all others?
He might have tried Lord Lucius or Lucullus;
And now Ventidius is wealthy too,
Whom he redeemed from prison. All these
Owes their estates unto him.

SERVANT My lord,
They have all been touched and found base metal,
For they have all denied him.

SEMPRONIUS How, have they denied him?
Has Ventidius and Lucullus denied him,
And does he send to me? Three? Hmh!
It shows but little love or judgement in him.
Must I be his last refuge? His friends, like physicians,
Thrive, give him over; must I take th' cure upon me?
He's much disgraced me in't. I'm angry at him,
That might have known my place. I see no sense for't
But his occasions might have wooed me first,
For, in my conscience, I was the first man
That e'er receivèd gift from him.
And does he think so backwardly of me now
That I'll requite it last? No.
So it may prove an argument of laughter
To th' rest, and I 'mongst lords be thought a fool.
I'd rather than the worth of thrice the sum
He'd sent to me first, but for my mind's sake.
I'd such a courage to do him good. But now return,
And with their faint reply this answer join:
Who bates mine honour shall not know my coin.
Exit

SERVANT Excellent. Your lordship's a goodly villain. The devil knew not what he did when he made man politic—he crossed himself by't, and I cannot think but in the end the villainies of man will set him clear. How fairly this lord strives to appear foul! Takes virtuous

53–4 **conceive . . . me** think of me in the best light
60 **I'll . . . turn** Based on the proverb 'One good turn deserves another'.
62 **hardly speed** prosper only with difficulty
64 **piece** cloth
66 **That . . . dish** Recalls Matthew 26:23, 'He that dippeth his hand with me in the dish, the same shall betray me' (Christ referring to Judas).
68 **kept his credit** kept him in credit
72–3 **O . . . shape** Based on the proverb 'Ingratitude is monstrous'.
73 **looks out** shows himself
74 **in respect of his** relative to his own possessions
77 **tasted Timon** i.e. had experience of Timon's bounty. The substance of Timon is his wealth, but *tasted* connects with the imagery of human sacrifice.
78 **over** down on
81 **carriage** conduct
83 **donation** giveable form, i.e. cash
87 **policy** cynical calculation
7.6 **touched** tested for purity
11–12 **like . . . over** Proverbially, 'Physicians enriched give over their patients'.
12 **Thrive** (on his money)
give him over abandon him, give up on him
14 **That** who
20 **argument of** subject matter for
23 **but . . . sake** if only on account of my inclination (i.e. my good will to him)
24 **courage** desire
26 **bates** abates, undervalues
29 **crossed himself** (*a*) thwarted himself (*b*) crossed himself off the list of debtors (hence *set him clear*, 7.30) (*c*) subscribed to Christian symbolism
31–2 **Takes . . . wicked** he copies virtuous behaviour as a pretext to be wicked. *Takes . . . copies* is literally 'copies out examples of edifying writing'.

copies to be wicked, like those that under hot ardent zeal would set whole realms on fire; of such a nature is his politic love.
This was my lord's best hope. Now all are fled
Save only the gods. Now his friends are dead.
Doors that were ne'er acquainted with their wards
Many a bounteous year must be employed
Now to guard sure their master;
And this is all a liberal course allows:
Who cannot keep his wealth must keep his house.
Exit

Sc. 8

Enter Varro's two Servants, meeting others', all [Servants of] Timon's creditors, to wait for his coming out. Then enter [Servants of] Lucius, [Titus], and Hortensius

VARRO'S [FIRST] SERVANT
Well met; good morrow, Titus and Hortensius.
TITUS' SERVANT The like to you, kind Varro.
HORTENSIUS' SERVANT
Lucius, what, do we meet together?
LUCIUS' SERVANT
Ay, and I think one business does command us all,
For mine is money.
TITUS' SERVANT So is theirs and ours.
Enter [a Servant of] Philotus
LUCIUS' SERVANT And Sir Philotus too!
PHILOTUS' SERVANT Good day at once.
LUCIUS' SERVANT Welcome, good brother.
What do you think the hour?
PHILOTUS' SERVANT Labouring for nine.
LUCIUS' SERVANT
So much?
PHILOTUS' SERVANT
Is not my lord seen yet?
LUCIUS' SERVANT Not yet.
PHILOTUS' SERVANT
I wonder on't; he was wont to shine at seven.
LUCIUS' SERVANT
Ay, but the days are waxed shorter with him.
You must consider that a prodigal course
Is like the sun's,
But not, like his, recoverable. I fear
'Tis deepest winter in Lord Timon's purse; that is,
One may reach deep enough, and yet find little.
PHILOTUS' SERVANT I am of your fear for that.
TITUS' SERVANT
I'll show you how t'observe a strange event.
Your lord sends now for money?
HORTENSIUS' SERVANT Most true, he does.
TITUS' SERVANT
And he wears jewels now of Timon's gift,
For which I wait for money.
HORTENSIUS' SERVANT It is against my heart.
LUCIUS' SERVANT Mark how strange it shows.
Timon in this should pay more than he owes,
And e'en as if your lord should wear rich jewels
And send for money for 'em.
HORTENSIUS' SERVANT
I'm weary of this charge, the gods can witness.
I know my lord hath spent of Timon's wealth,
And now ingratitude makes it worse than stealth.
VARRO'S FIRST SERVANT
Yes; mine's three thousand crowns. What's yours?
LUCIUS' SERVANT Five thousand, mine.
VARRO'S FIRST SERVANT
'Tis much deep, and it should seem by th' sum
Your master's confidence was above mine,
Else surely his had equalled.
Enter Flaminius
TITUS' SERVANT One of Lord Timon's men.
LUCIUS' SERVANT
Flaminius! Sir, a word. Pray, is my lord
Ready to come forth?
FLAMINIUS No, indeed he is not.
TITUS' SERVANT
We attend his lordship. Pray signify so much.
FLAMINIUS
I need not tell him that; he knows you are
Too diligent. *[Exit]*
Enter Steward, in a cloak, muffled
LUCIUS' SERVANT
Ha, is not that his steward muffled so?
He goes away in a cloud. Call him, call him.
TITUS' SERVANT *[to Steward]* Do you hear, sir?
VARRO'S SECOND SERVANT *[to Steward]* By your leave, sir.
STEWARD What do ye ask of me, my friend?
TITUS' SERVANT
We wait for certain money here, sir.
STEWARD Ay,
If money were as certain as your waiting,
'Twere sure enough.
Why then preferred you not your sums and bills
When your false masters ate of my lord's meat?
Then they could smile and fawn upon his debts,
And take down th' int'rest into their glutt'nous maws.

32 **those** religious fanatics. Sometimes thought to allude specifically to the Catholic Gunpowder Plot to blow up the King in Parliament.
under hiding behind
33 **set whole realms on fire** An extension of the proverb 'To set one's heart on fire'.
37 **wards** locks (literally the notched part that accepts the right key)
41 **keep . . . keep his house** retain . . . stay indoors (to avoid arrest for debt)
8.7 **at once** to you all
9 **Labouring for** going up to
11 **shine** rise (like the sun)
13 **prodigal course** (as applied to the sun, its high course in summer)
15 **his** its
19 **t'observe** to see and interpret
30 **stealth** stealing
41 **in a cloud** (*a*) muffled from sight (*b*) in a state of trouble and anxiety. The phrase was proverbial in sense (*a*) for an act of secret intrigue.
48 **preferred** brought forward
50–1 **his debts . . . th' int'rest** i.e. the entertainment giving rise to them

You do yourselves but wrong to stir me up.
Let me pass quietly.
Believe't, my lord and I have made an end.
I have no more to reckon, he to spend.

LUCIUS' SERVANT
Ay, but this answer will not serve.

STEWARD
If 'twill not serve 'tis not so base as you,
For you serve knaves. [*Exit*]

VARRO'S FIRST SERVANT How? What does his cashiered worship mutter?

VARRO'S SECOND SERVANT No matter what; he's poor, and that's revenge enough. Who can speak broader than he that has no house to put his head in? Such may rail against great buildings.

Enter Servilius

TITUS' SERVANT O, here's Servilius. Now we shall know some answer.

SERVILIUS If I might beseech you, gentlemen, to repair some other hour, I should derive much from't; for, take't of my soul, my lord leans wondrously to discontent. His comfortable temper has forsook him. He's much out of health, and keeps his chamber.

LUCIUS' SERVANT
Many do keep their chambers are not sick,
And if it be so far beyond his health
Methinks he should the sooner pay his debts
And make a clear way to the gods.

SERVILIUS Good gods!

TITUS' SERVANT We cannot take this for answer, sir.

FLAMINIUS [*within*]
Servilius, help! My lord, my lord!

Enter Timon in a rage

TIMON
What, are my doors opposed against my passage?
Have I been ever free, and must my house
Be my retentive enemy, my jail?
The place which I have feasted, does it now,
Like all mankind, show me an iron heart?

LUCIUS' SERVANT
Put in now, Titus.

TITUS' SERVANT My lord, here is my bill.

LUCIUS' SERVANT
Here's mine.

[HORTENSIUS' SERVANT]
And mine, my lord.

VARRO'S FIRST *and* SECOND SERVANTS
And ours, my lord.

PHILOTUS' SERVANT All our bills.

TIMON Knock me down with 'em, cleave me to the girdle.

LUCIUS' SERVANT Alas, my lord.

TIMON Cut my heart in sums.

TITUS' SERVANT Mine fifty talents.

TIMON
Tell out my blood.

LUCIUS' SERVANT Five thousand crowns, my lord.

TIMON
Five thousand drops pays that. What yours? And yours?

VARRO'S FIRST SERVANT My lord—

VARRO'S SECOND SERVANT My lord—

TIMON
Tear me, take me, and the gods fall upon you. *Exit*

HORTENSIUS' SERVANT Faith, I perceive our masters may throw their caps at their money. These debts may well be called desperate ones, for a madman owes 'em.

Exeunt

Enter Timon [and Steward] Sc.

TIMON They have e'en put my breath from me, the slaves.
Creditors? Devils!

STEWARD My dear lord—

TIMON What if it should be so?

STEWARD My lord—

TIMON
I'll have it so. My steward!

STEWARD Here, my lord.

TIMON
So fitly? Go bid all my friends again:
Lucius, Lucullus, and Sempronius—all luxurs, all.
I'll once more feast the rascals.

STEWARD O my lord,
You only speak from your distracted soul.
There's not so much left to furnish out
A moderate table.

TIMON Be it not in thy care.
Go, I charge thee, invite them all. Let in the tide
Of knaves once more. My cook and I'll provide.

Exeunt [severally]

Enter three Senators at one door Sc.

FIRST SENATOR
My lord, you have my voice to't. The fault's bloody.
'Tis necessary he should die.
Nothing emboldens sin so much as mercy.

SECOND SENATOR Most true; the law shall bruise 'im.

54 **made an end** agreed to part
60 **worship** Used ironically: the Steward no longer commands deference.
70 **comfortable** cheerful
72 **Many ... sick** See note to 7.41.
79 **free** generous (playing on 'at liberty')
85 **bills** notes of debt (but Timon understands the weapon: and axe or blade with a long handle)
88 **sums** pieces of fixed value
90 **Tell** count
96 **throw their caps at** A proverbial gesture expressing the impossibility of catching up.
97 **desperate** (*a*) hopeless (*b*) violently reckless
9.1 **e'en ... me** taken even my breath off me (drawing on the proverb 'air is free')
6 **I'll have it so** (referring to the plan he has thought of)
8 **luxurs** debauchees
10.1 **voice to't** vote for it
fault's crime's
3 **Nothing ... mercy** Proverbially, 'Pardon makes offenders'.

Enter Alcibiades at another door, with attendants

ALCIBIADES
Honour, health, and compassion to the senate!

FIRST SENATOR Now, captain.

ALCIBIADES
I am an humble suitor to your virtues;
For pity is the virtue of the law,
And none but tyrants use it cruelly.
It pleases time and fortune to lie heavy
Upon a friend of mine, who in hot blood
Hath stepped into the law, which is past depth
To those that without heed do plunge into't.
He is a man, setting his feat aside,
Of comely virtues;
Nor did he soil the fact with cowardice—
An honour in him which buys out his fault—
But with a noble fury and fair spirit,
Seeing his reputation touched to death,
He did oppose his foe;
And with such sober and unnoted passion
He did behave his anger, ere 'twas spent,
As if he had but proved an argument.

FIRST SENATOR
You undergo too strict a paradox,
Striving to make an ugly deed look fair.
Your words have took such pains as if they laboured
To bring manslaughter into form, and set quarrelling
Upon the head of valour—which indeed
Is valour misbegot, and came into the world
When sects and factïons were newly born.
He's truly valiant that can wisely suffer
The worst that man can breathe, and make his
wrongs his outsides
To wear them like his raiment carelessly,
And ne'er prefer his injuries to his heart
To bring it into danger.
If wrongs be evils and enforce us kill,
What folly 'tis to hazard life for ill!

ALCIBIADES
My lord—

FIRST SENATOR
You cannot make gross sins look clear.
To rèvenge is no valour, but to bear.

ALCIBIADES
My lords, then, under favour, pardon me
If I speak like a captain.
Why do fond men expose themselves to battle,
And not endure all threats, sleep upon't,
And let the foes quietly cut their throats
Without repugnancy? If there be
Such valour in the bearing, what make we
Abroad? Why then, women are more valiant
That stay at home if bearing carry it,
And the ass more captain than the lion, the fellow
Loaden with irons wiser than the judge,
If wisdom be in suffering. O my lords,
As you are great, be pitifully good.
Who cannot condemn rashness in cold blood?
To kill, I grant, is sin's extremest gust,
But in defence, by mercy, 'tis most just.
To be in anger is impiety,
But who is man that is not angry?
Weigh but the crime with this.

SECOND SENATOR You breathe in vain.

ALCIBIADES In vain?
His service done at Lacedaemon and Byzantium
Were a sufficient briber for his life.

FIRST SENATOR
What's that?

ALCIBIADES
Why, I say, my lords, he's done fair service,
And slain in fight many of your enemies.
How full of valour did he bear himself
In the last conflict, and made plenteous wounds!

SECOND SENATOR
He has made too much plenty with 'em.
He's a sworn rioter; he has a sin
That often drowns him and takes his valour prisoner.
If there were no foes, that were enough
To overcome him. In that beastly fury
He has been known to commit outrages
And cherish factions. 'Tis inferred to us
His days are foul and his drink dangerous.

4.1 *Enter . . . attendants* Alcibiades may alternatively appear at the beginning of the scene but not approach the Senators until here. The attendants are Senate officials.
6 **Now** Either 'now then' or an expression of surprise at Alcibiades' presumptuous greeting.
12 **past** out of
14 **feat** action, crime (perhaps also suggesting *fate*)
16 **fact** deed, crime
19 **touched** (*a*) hit, damaged (*b*) infected through contagion, besmirched
21 **unnoted** inconspicuous, restrained, unremarkable
22 **behave** manage, control
27 **form** (*a*) a formality of argument, or (*b*) acceptable behaviour
28 **Upon the head** (*a*) in the category, or (*b*) as the crowning instance
indeed in fact
32 **outsides** outer garments
33 **carelessly** casually
34 **prefer** advance, promote
heart (seen as (*a*) seat of feelings (*b*) the vital organ)
38 **clear** innocent
39 **but to bear** i.e. rather, to endure wrongs is valour
42 **fond** foolish
45 **repugnancy** resistance
46 **bearing** enduring (of wrongs). Leads on to a quibble on child-bearing.
46–7 **what make we | Abroad?** what's the point of venturing out?
48 **carry it** wins the day (with wordplay between *bearing* and *carry*)
52 **pitifully good** good in showing pity
53 **condemn . . . blood** (*a*) condemn a rash deed committed in cold blood, or (*b*) condemn in cold blood a rash deed
54 **gust** (*a*) taste, experience (*b*) outburst
55 **by mercy** if seen mercifully
57 **angry** Probably three syllables: 'angery'.
66 **a sin** i.e. drunkenness
71 **cherish factions** encourage factional violence

FIRST SENATOR
He dies.

ALCIBIADES
Hard fate! He might have died in war.
My lords, if not for any parts in him—
Though his right arm might purchase his own time
And be in debt to none—yet more to move you,
Take my deserts to his and join 'em both.
And for I know
Your reverend ages love security,
I'll pawn my victories, all my honour to you
Upon his good returns.
If by this crime he owes the law his life,
Why, let the war receive't in valiant gore,
For law is strict, and war is nothing more.

FIRST SENATOR
We are for law; he dies. Urge it no more,
On height of our displeasure. Friend or brother,
He forfeits his own blood that spills another.

ALCIBIADES
Must it be so? It must not be.
My lords, I do beseech you know me.

SECOND SENATOR How?

ALCIBIADES
Call me to your remembrances.

THIRD SENATOR What?

ALCIBIADES
I cannot think but your age has forgot me.
It could not else be I should prove so base
To sue and be denied such common grace.
My wounds ache at you.

FIRST SENATOR Do you dare our anger?
'Tis in few words, but spacious in effect:
We banish thee for ever.

ALCIBIADES Banish me?
Banish your dotage, banish usury
That makes the senate ugly.

FIRST SENATOR
If after two days' shine Athens contain thee,
Attend our weightier judgement; and, not to swell
your spirit,
He shall be executed presently.
Exeunt [Senators and attendants]

ALCIBIADES
Now the gods keep you old enough that you may live
Only in bone, that none may look on you!
I'm worse than mad. I have kept back their foes
While they have told their money and let out
Their coin upon large interest, I myself
Rich only in large hurts. All those for this?
Is this the balsam that the usuring senate
Pours into captains' wounds? Banishment!
It comes not ill; I hate not to be banished.
It is a cause worthy my spleen and fury,
That I may strike at Athens. I'll cheer up
My discontented troops, and lay for hearts.
'Tis honour with most lands to be at odds.
Soldiers should brook as little wrongs as gods. *Exit*

Enter divers [of Timon's] friends, [amongst them Lucius, Lucullus, Sempronius, and other Lords and Senators,] at several doors Sc. 1

FIRST LORD The good time of day to you, sir.

SECOND LORD I also wish it to you. I think this honourable lord did but try us this other day.

FIRST LORD Upon that were my thoughts tiring when we encountered. I hope it is not so low with him as he made it seem in the trial of his several friends.

SECOND LORD It should not be, by the persuasion of his new feasting.

FIRST LORD I should think so. He hath sent me an earnest inviting, which many my near occasions did urge me to put off, but he hath conjured me beyond them, and I must needs appear.

SECOND LORD In like manner was I in debt to my importunate business, but he would not hear my excuse. I am sorry when he sent to borrow of me that my provision was out.

FIRST LORD I am sick of that grief too, as I understand how all things go.

SECOND LORD Every man hears so. What would he have borrowed of you?

FIRST LORD A thousand pieces.

SECOND LORD A thousand pieces?

FIRST LORD What of you?

SECOND LORD He sent to me, sir—
[*Loud music*]
Here he comes.

Enter Timon and attendants

TIMON With all my heart, gentlemen both; and how fare you?

FIRST LORD Ever at the best, hearing well of your lordship.

74 **parts** (*a*) qualities (*b*) limbs (the sense taken up in *right arm*, 10.75)
75 **time** natural lifespan
79 **security** (alludes to both financial and military security)
81 **Upon . . . returns** as pledge that he will repay your mercy. *Returns* might also suggest both reformation and returns from battle.
83 **receive't . . . gore** i.e. receive the equivalent to it in the blood of enemies that he will valiantly spill
84 **nothing more** not at all otherwise
86 **On height of our** at risk of our highest
101 **presently** immediately
102–3 **live . . . bone** i.e. be living skeletons (too ugly to be looked at)
105 **they** (the senators)
108 **balsam** balm, ointment
113 **lay** set an ambush
11.0.1 *divers* various
0.2 *Lucius, Lucullus, Sempronius* They probably correspond to speaking Lords, perhaps the First, Second, and Third Lords respectively.
4 **tiring** feeding. Said especially of a bird of prey tearing flesh.
6 **several** various
10 **occasions** affairs (perhaps also 'pretexts')
11–12 **conjured . . . appear** Compare 1.7 and note.
17 **grief** (*a*) illness (*b*) offence (*c*) sorrow

SECOND LORD The swallow follows not summer more willing than we your lordship.

TIMON [*aside*] Nor more willingly leaves winter, such summer birds are men.—Gentlemen, our dinner will not recompense this long stay. Feast your ears with the music a while, if they will fare so harshly o' th' trumpets' sound; we shall to't presently.

FIRST LORD I hope it remains not unkindly with your lordship that I returned you an empty messenger.

TIMON O sir, let it not trouble you.

SECOND LORD My noble lord—

TIMON Ah, my good friend, what cheer?

The banquet brought in

SECOND LORD My most honourable lord, I am e'en sick of shame that, when your lordship this other day sent to me, I was so unfortunate a beggar.

TIMON Think not on't, sir.

SECOND LORD If you had sent but two hours before—

TIMON Let it not cumber your better remembrance.—Come, bring in all together.

[*Enter Servants with covered dishes*]

SECOND LORD All covered dishes.

FIRST LORD Royal cheer, I warrant you.

THIRD LORD Doubt not that, if money and the season can yield it.

FIRST LORD How do you? What's the news?

THIRD LORD Alcibiades is banished. Hear you of it?

FIRST *and* SECOND LORDS Alcibiades banished?

THIRD LORD 'Tis so, be sure of it.

FIRST LORD How, how?

SECOND LORD I pray you, upon what?

TIMON My worthy friends, will you draw near?

THIRD LORD I'll tell you more anon. Here's a noble feast toward.

SECOND LORD This is the old man still.

THIRD LORD Will't hold, will't hold?

SECOND LORD It does; but time will—and so—

THIRD LORD I do conceive.

TIMON Each man to his stool with that spur as he would to the lip of his mistress. Your diet shall be in all places alike. Make not a City feast of it, to let the meat cool ere we can agree upon the first place. Sit, sit. The gods require our thanks.

[*They sit*]

You great benefactors, sprinkle our society with thankfulness. For your own gifts make yourselves praised; but reserve still to give, lest your deities be despised. Lend to each man enough that one need not lend to another; for were your godheads to borrow of men, men would forsake the gods. Make the meat be beloved more than the man that gives it. Let no assembly of twenty be without a score of villains. If there sit twelve women at the table, let a dozen of them be as they are. The rest of your foes, O gods—the senators of Athens, together with the common tag of people—what is amiss in them, you gods, make suitable for destruction. For these my present friends, as they are to me nothing, so in nothing bless them; and to nothing are they welcome.—Uncover, dogs, and lap.

[*The dishes are uncovered, and seen to be full of steaming water and stones*]

SOME LORDS What does his lordship mean?

OTHER LORDS I know not.

TIMON

May you a better feast never behold,
You knot of mouth-friends. Smoke and lukewarm water
Is your perfection. This is Timon's last,
Who, stuck and spangled with your flattery,
Washes it off, and sprinkles in your faces
Your reeking villainy.

[*He throws water in their faces*]

Live loathed and long,
Most smiling, smooth, detested parasites,
Courteous destroyers, affable wolves, meek bears,
You fools of fortune, trencher-friends, time's flies,
Cap-and-knee slaves, vapours, and minute-jacks!
Of man and beast the infinite malady
Crust you quite o'er.

[*A Lord is going*]

What, dost thou go?
Soft, take thy physic first. Thou too, and thou.

29–32 **The...men** Proverbially, 'Swallows, like false friends, fly away upon the approach of winter'.

40.1 ***The banquet*** i.e., a table with place-settings and stools, as for the banquet

46 **cumber...remembrance** trouble your memory of better things

61 **old man** man of old

62 **hold** continue, prove true

63 **time will—** Perhaps intimating the proverb 'time will tell truth'

65 **spur** urgent speed (as when a horse is spurred)

67 **City feast** i.e. feast as given by dignitaries of the City of London

67–8 **to...place** Implies both that social precedence is contested in the City and all matters are subject to debate.

70–83 **You...welcome** Timon's grace is printed in italics as a set piece in the 1623 Folio.

70 **society** social gathering

72 **reserve still** always hold back something

78 **they** women generally

80 **tag** rabble

88 **mouth-friends** (*a*) friends in lip-service only (*b*) friends when it comes to eating
Smoke steam (characteristically insubstantial and diffusing to nothing). *Smoke* is also 'mere talk'.

89 **perfection** (*a*) finishing touch (*b*) perfect representation

90 **stuck and spangled** Both verbs apply to fixing jewels or ornaments.

92 **reeking** (*a*) steaming (*b*) stinking

95 **fools** dupes, playthings. *Fools of fortune* was proverbial.
trencher-friends friends in feasting
flies (only about in fair weather)

96 **Cap-and-knee** cap-doffing and knee-bending
minute-jacks over-punctilious time-servers. The *jack* was the mechanical human figure that struck the bell on medieval clocks—though not every minute. *Jack* is also 'knave'.

98 **Crust** (as with a scab)

99 **physic** medicine

[*He beats them*]
Stay, I will lend thee money, borrow none.
[*Exeunt Lords, leaving caps and gowns*]
What, all in motion? Henceforth be no feast
Whereat a villain's not a welcome guest.
Burn house! Sink Athens! Henceforth hated be
Of Timon man and all humanity! *Exit*
Enter the Senators with other Lords
FIRST LORD How now, my lords?
SECOND LORD
Know you the quality of Lord Timon's fury?
THIRD LORD
Push! Did you see my cap?
FOURTH LORD I have lost my gown.
FIRST LORD He's but a mad lord, and naught but humours sways him. He gave me a jewel th' other day, and now he has beat it out of my hat.
Did you see my jewel?
THIRD LORD Did you see my cap?
SECOND LORD
Here 'tis.
FOURTH LORD
Here lies my gown.
FIRST LORD Let's make no stay.
SECOND LORD
Lord Timon's mad.
THIRD LORD I feel't upon my bones.
FOURTH LORD
One day he gives us diamonds, next day stones.
Exeunt

Sc. 12 *Enter Timon*

TIMON
Let me look back upon thee. O thou wall
That girdles in those wolves, dive in the earth,
And fence not Athens! Matrons, turn incontinent!
Obedience fail in children! Slaves and fools,
Pluck the grave wrinkled senate from the bench
And minister in their steads! To general filths
Convert o' th' instant, green virginity!
Do't in your parents' eyes. Bankrupts, hold fast!
Rather than render back, out with your knives,
And cut your trusters' throats. Bound servants, steal!
Large-handed robbers your grave masters are,
And pill by law. Maid, to thy master's bed!
Thy mistress is o' th' brothel. Son of sixteen,
Pluck the lined crutch from thy old limping sire;
With it beat out his brains! Piety and fear,
Religion to the gods, peace, justice, truth,
Domestic awe, night rest, and neighbourhood,
Instruction, manners, mysteries, and trades,
Degrees, observances, customs, and laws,
Decline to your confounding contraries,
And yet confusion live! Plagues incident to men,
Your potent and infectious fevers heap
On Athens, ripe for stroke! Thou cold sciatica,
Cripple our senators, that their limbs may halt
As lamely as their manners! Lust and liberty,
Creep in the minds and marrows of our youth,
That 'gainst the stream of virtue they may strive
And drown themselves in riot! Itches, blains,
Sow all th' Athenian bosoms, and their crop
Be general leprosy! Breath infect breath,
That their society, as their friendship, may
Be merely poison!
[*He tears off his clothes*]
Nothing I'll bear from thee
But nakedness, thou dètestable town;
Take thou that too, with multiplying bans.
Timon will to the woods, where he shall find
Th' unkindest beast more kinder than mankind.
The gods confound—hear me you good gods all—
Th' Athenians, both within and out that wall;
And grant, as Timon grows, his hate may grow
To the whole race of mankind, high and low.
Amen. *Exit*

106 **quality** nature
107 **Push!** pish!
108 **humours** extremes of temperament
113 **upon my bones** a literalizing alteration of *in my bones*, 'intuitively'
12.1 **wall** The city wall of Athens. City walls were conventionally represented by the tiring-house wall at the rear of the stage. Timon would have entered through a door in it.
3 **incontinent** sexually unrestrained
6 **minister** execute their duties
filths defiled whores
7 **green** i.e. fresh, young, innocent
8 **hold fast** i.e. refuse to repay
12 **pill** plunder
13 **Thy...brothel** (implying either that marriage is a form of prostitution or that the wife is unfaithful)
14 **lined** padded
17 **Domestic awe** reverential obedience in the home
neighbourhood neighbourliness
18 **Instruction** directions, orders (i.e. lines of social authority)
mysteries institutionalized professional skills
trades organized occupational groups
19 **Degrees** social ranks
observances following of customary rules and duties
20 **confounding** self-destroying
21 **yet** still (i.e. despite the general death and destruction)
incident to apt to fall on
23 **for stroke** to be struck
25 **liberty** licentiousness, wild behaviour
26 **marrows** (proverbially 'burnt' or 'melted' by lust)
27 **'gainst...strive** From Ecclesiasticus 4:28 (Bishops'), 'strive thou not against the stream, but for righteousness take pains...'. Proverbial.
28 **riot** debauchery (and, in the metaphor, tumult or turbulence caused by opposing the *stream of virtue*)
blains sores, blisters
29 **Sow** scatter through
31 **their society** i.e. the company of Athenians
32 **merely** unadulterated
32.1 ***He...clothes*** This would be theatrically straightforward and effective if Timon were wearing a gown in classical Greek style.
34 **bans** curses

Sc. 13

Enter Steward, with two or three Servants

FIRST SERVANT
Hear you, master steward, where's our master?
Are we undone, cast off, nothing remaining?

STEWARD
Alack, my fellows, what should I say to you?
Let me be recorded: by the righteous gods,
I am as poor as you.

FIRST SERVANT Such a house broke,
So noble a master fall'n? All gone, and not
One friend to take his fortune by the arm
And go along with him?

SECOND SERVANT As we do turn our backs
From our companion thrown into his grave,
So his familiars to his buried fortunes
Slink all away, leave their false vows with him
Like empty purses picked; and his poor self,
A dedicated beggar to the air,
With his disease of all-shunned poverty,
Walks like contempt alone. More of our fellows.

Enter other Servants

STEWARD
All broken implements of a ruined house.

THIRD SERVANT
Yet do our hearts wear Timon's livery.
That see I by our faces. We are fellows still,
Serving alike in sorrow. Leaked is our barque,
And we, poor mates, stand on the dying deck
Hearing the surges' threat. We must all part
Into this sea of air.

STEWARD Good fellows all,
The latest of my wealth I'll share amongst you.
Wherever we shall meet, for Timon's sake
Let's yet be fellows. Let's shake our heads and say,
As 'twere a knell unto our master's fortunes,
'We have seen better days.'
[He gives them money]
Let each take some.
Nay, put out all your hands. Not one word more.
Thus part we rich in sorrow, parting poor.

Embrace, and [the Servants] part several ways

O, the fierce wretchedness that glory brings us!
Who would not wish to be from wealth exempt,
Since riches point to misery and contempt?
Who would be so mocked with glory, or to live
But in a dream of friendship,
To have his pomp and all what state compounds
But only painted like his varnished friends?
Poor honest lord, brought low by his own heart,
Undone by goodness! Strange, unusual blood
When man's worst sin is he does too much good!
Who then dares to be half so kind again?
For bounty, that makes gods, does still mar men.
My dearest lord, blessed to be most accursed,
Rich only to be wretched, thy great fortunes
Are made thy chief afflictions. Alas, kind lord!
He's flung in rage from this ingrateful seat
Of monstrous friends;
Nor has he with him to supply his life,
Or that which can command it.
I'll follow and enquire him out.
I'll ever serve his mind with my best will.
Whilst I have gold I'll be his steward still. *Exit*

Sc. 14

Enter Timon [from his cave] in the woods, [half naked, and with a spade]

TIMON
O blessèd breeding sun, draw from the earth
Rotten humidity; below thy sister's orb
Infect the air. Twinned brothers of one womb,
Whose procreation, residence, and birth
Scarce is dividant, touch them with several fortunes,
The greater scorns the lesser. Not nature,
To whom all sores lay siege, can bear great fortune
But by contempt of nature.
It is the pasture lards the brother's sides,
The want that makes him lean.
Raise me this beggar and demit that lord,
The senator shall bear contempt hereditary,
The beggar native honour. Who dares, who dares

13.2 **undone...remaining** Echoes Timon's divestment in the previous scene.
5 **house broke** household broken up
10 **his familiars to** Shifts from 'his intimate friends' to 'those familiar with'.
buried fortunes The *fortunes* are personified as the actual recipients of friendship, now dead. Timon's *fortunes* as 'luck' are figuratively *buried*, but it was his material *fortunes* that his friends were familiar with; the idea of buried treasure is developed in the next scene.
12 **picked** from which the money has been stolen
20 **mates** (*a*) subordinate naval officers (the full expression was *master's mate*) (*b*) fellows
21 **part** (*a*) separate (*b*) die
23 **latest** last
32 **point** lead
35 **what state compounds** that of which conspicuous splendour is compounded
36 **varnished** glossily painted (implying 'specious, pretended')
42 **to be** in order to be
45–6 **ingrateful...monstrous** Compare 6.72–3 and note.
45 **seat** centre, stronghold
14.0.1 ***from his cave*** The cave might be represented naturalistically by a stage property or conventionally by a door.
1 **breeding** Refers to the sun's supposed capacity to breed flies etc.
2 **Rotten** putrid
below...orb i.e. throughout the corruptible part of creation. *Thy sister* is the moon, whose sphere (*orb*) was supposed to divide the mutable from the celestial.
4 **residence** gestation in the womb
5 **dividant** divisible, distinguishable
touch them if they are touched
several different
6–8 **Not...of nature** i.e. it is not in human nature to *bear great fortune* except by despising one's natural self and familial origins, because the natural state of things is to be under siege by sickness and misfortune
9 **It** i.e. fortune (?)
pasture Suggests both pastoral feeding and possession of land.
lards that fattens
9–10 **the brother's...him** i.e. the one brother's...the other
11 **demit** humble, abase
12 **hereditary** as if he were born to it. Similarly *native*, 14.13.

In purity of manhood stand upright
And say 'This man's a flatterer'? If one be,
So are they all, for every grece of fortune
Is smoothed by that below. The learnèd pate
Ducks to the golden fool. All's obliquy;
There's nothing level in our cursèd natures
But direct villainy. Therefore be abhorred
All feasts, societies, and throngs of men.
His semblable, yea, himself, Timon disdains.
Destruction fang mankind. Earth, yield me roots.
[He digs]
Who seeks for better of thee, sauce his palate
With thy most operant poison.
[He finds gold]
What is here?
Gold? Yellow, glittering, precious gold?
No, gods, I am no idle votarist:
Roots, you clear heavens. Thus much of this will make
Black white, foul fair, wrong right,
Base noble, old young, coward valiant.
Ha, you gods! Why this, what, this, you gods? Why, this
Will lug your priests and servants from your sides,
Pluck stout men's pillows from below their heads.
This yellow slave
Will knit and break religions, bless th' accursed,
Make the hoar leprosy adored, place thieves,
And give them title, knee, and approbation
With senators on the bench. This is it
That makes the wappered widow wed again.
She whom the spittle house and ulcerous sores
Would cast the gorge at, this embalms and spices
To th' April day again. Come, damned earth,
Thou common whore of mankind, that puts odds
Among the rout of nations; I will make thee
Do thy right nature.
March afar off
Ha, a drum! Thou'rt quick;
But yet I'll bury thee.
[He buries gold]
Thou'lt go, strong thief,
When gouty keepers of thee cannot stand.
[He keeps some gold]
Nay, stay thou out for earnest.
Enter Alcibiades, with [soldiers playing] drum and fife, in warlike manner; and Phrynia and Timandra

ALCIBIADES
What art thou there? Speak.

TIMON
A beast, as thou art. The canker gnaw thy heart
For showing me again the eyes of man.

ALCIBIADES
What is thy name? Is man so hateful to thee
That art thyself a man?

TIMON
I am Misanthropos, and hate mankind.
For thy part, I do wish thou wert a dog,
That I might love thee something.

ALCIBIADES
I know thee well,
But in thy fortunes am unlearned and strange.

TIMON
I know thee too, and more than that I know thee
I not desire to know. Follow thy drum.
With man's blood paint the ground gules, gules.
Religious canons, civil laws, are cruel;
Then what should war be? This fell whore of thine
Hath in her more destruction than thy sword,
For all her cherubin look.

PHRYNIA
Thy lips rot off!

TIMON
I will not kiss thee; then the rot returns
To thine own lips again.

16 **grece** a step in a flight of stairs; specifically those standing on the step

17 **smoothed** flattered
pate head (as both seat of intellect and part of the body that bows)

18 **obliquy** deviousness

22 **His semblable** that which resembles himself

23 **fang** seize with fangs

23.1 ***He digs*** The hole beneath the trapdoor in the middle of the stage would probably be used.

24–8 **Who . . . heavens** Timon's prayer is answered, though against his intention and ironically. His humility is rewarded with riches, and it is he, not those who seek for better, who gets the earth's most operant poison. The irony depends on biblical teachings, particularly 'the desire of money is the *root* of all evil, which while some lusted after they erred from the faith and pierced themsleves with many sorrows' (1 Timothy 6:10).

25 **operant** potent

27 **idle** ineffective; insincere. Perhaps plays on *idol*.
votarist one bound by vow to a religious way of life

28 **clear** innocent, blameless

28–9 **make | Black white** proverbial

33 **Pluck . . . heads** (in order to throttle them)

36 **hoar** Refers to the greyish colour of leprous skin.
place thieves appoint thieves to office

39 **wappered** sexually worn-out

40 **the . . . sores** i.e. those in hospital and with ulcerous sores

41 **cast the gorge** vomit
embalms and spices Suggests preparation to preserve a corpse, though spices were also used as cosmetic perfumes.

43 **common whore** Alters the traditional figure of the earth as a common (general) mother (as at 14.178), and so debases the connotations of *common*. *Whore* is appropriate because land can be bought and sold; it is unlikely to have been so described under the feudal system.
puts odds creates conflict

44 **rout** rabble

45 **quick** sudden (to bring about strife). Also, punningly, 'alive', anticipating *bury*.

46 **go** walk away

47 **keepers** (*a*) owners (*b*) jailers

48 **for earnest** as a token for the rest

49 **canker** canker-worm (with the heart seen as a flower-bud)

56 **strange** unaquainted

59 **gules** Heraldic term for red. The repetition might suggest a red motif on a red background.

61 **fell** dreadful, savage

62 **destruction** Both physical (disease) and moral (damnation).

63 **Thy lips rot off** Alludes to an effect of syphilis.

64–5 **I . . . again** i.e. the curse could only be fulfilled by kissing Phrynia; as Timon refuses, he claims that the curse of rotten lips recoils onto the lips of the speaker.

ALCIBIADES
How came the noble Timon to this change?

TIMON
As the moon does, by wanting light to give.
But then renew I could not like the moon;
There were no suns to borrow of.

ALCIBIADES
Noble Timon, what friendship may I do thee?

TIMON
None but to maintain my opinion.

ALCIBIADES What is it, Timon?

TIMON Promise me friendship, but perform none. If thou wilt promise, the gods plague thee, for thou art a man. If thou dost not perform, confound thee, for thou art a man.

ALCIBIADES
I have heard in some sort of thy miseries.

TIMON
Thou saw'st them when I had prosperity.

ALCIBIADES
I see them now; then was a blessèd time.

TIMON
As thine is now, held with a brace of harlots.

TIMANDRA
Is this th' Athenian minion, whom the world
Voiced so regardfully?

TIMON
Art thou Timandra?

TIMANDRA Yes.

TIMON
Be a whore still. They love thee not that use thee.
Give them diseases, leaving with thee their lust.
Make use of thy salt hours: season the slaves
For tubs and baths, bring down rose-cheeked youth
To the tub-fast and the diet.

TIMANDRA
Hang thee, monster!

ALCIBIADES
Pardon him, sweet Timandra, for his wits
Are drowned and lost in his calamities.
I have but little gold of late, brave Timon,
The want whereof doth daily make revolt
In my penurious band. I have heard and grieved
How cursèd Athens, mindless of thy worth,
Forgetting thy great deeds, when neighbour states
But for thy sword and fortune trod upon them—

TIMON
I prithee, beat thy drum and get thee gone.

ALCIBIADES
I am thy friend, and pity thee, dear Timon.

TIMON
How dost thou pity him whom thou dost trouble?
I had rather be alone.

ALCIBIADES
Why, fare thee well.
Here is some gold for thee.

TIMON
Keep it. I cannot eat it.

ALCIBIADES
When I have laid proud Athens on a heap—

TIMON
Warr'st thou 'gainst Athens?

ALCIBIADES
Ay, Timon, and have cause.

TIMON
The gods confound them all in thy conquest,
And thee after, when thou hast conquerèd.

ALCIBIADES
Why me, Timon?

TIMON
That by killing of villains
Thou wast born to conquer my country.
Put up thy gold.
[*He gives Alcibiades gold*]
Go on; here's gold; go on.
Be as a planetary plague when Jove
Will o'er some high-viced city hang his poison
In the sick air. Let not thy sword skip one.
Pity not honoured age for his white beard;
He is an usurer. Strike me the counterfeit matron;
It is her habit only that is honest,
Herself's a bawd. Let not the virgin's cheek
Make soft thy trenchant sword; for those milk paps
That through the window-bars bore at men's eyes
Are not within the leaf of pity writ;
But set them down horrible traitors. Spare not the babe
Whose dimpled smiles from fools exhaust their mercy.
Think it a bastard whom the oracle
Hath doubtfully pronounced the throat shall cut,

73 **Promise...perform** From the proverb 'to promise much and perform little'.
80 **held with a brace** (*a*) spent with a pair (*b*) held together with a clamp
81 **minion** favourite. But as also a derogatory term for a woman, it brings Timon into equivalence with the speaker. Her name Timandra, which Timon speaks in the next line, has the same effect. In Sc. 4 the Page was bearing letters from the brothel to Timon and Alcibiades; we might perhaps infer that Timandra was Timon's whore ('They love thee not that use thee', 14.84).
84 **Be a whore still** Proverbially, 'Once a whore, always a whore'.
85 **lust** Seen as expended and deposited in the whore's body, like semen.
86 **salt hours** hours of lechery (also anticipating *season*, as with salt)
season prepare (and see previous note)
87 **tubs and baths** sweating-tubs and hot baths; i.e. treatments for venereal disease
88 **tub-fast** sexual abstinence during treatment with the sweating-tub
diet (another part of the therapy)
90 **lost** (as at sea)
96 **trod upon them** would have trod upon them. A victor symbolically *trod upon* a vanquished foe. The *sword and fortune* are both the war-aims of the neighbour states and the Athenian means for defence.
104 **in thy conquest** by being conquered by you
109 **a planetary plague** a plague or disaster induced by malign planetary influence
114 **habit** dress
116 **trenchant** cutting, sharp
117 **window-bars** open-work squares of a bodice (?)
118 **leaf of pity** Metonymic for 'book of pity'; perhaps recalling the biblical Book of Life.
120 **exhaust** draw forth
122 **doubtfully** ambiguously (see next note)
the throat shall cut The prophecy does not specify whether the child will be victim or agent.

And mince it sans remorse. Swear against objects.
Put armour on thine ears and on thine eyes
Whose proof nor yells of mothers, maids, nor babes,
Nor sight of priests in holy vestments bleeding,
Shall pierce a jot. There's gold to pay thy soldiers.
Make large confusion, and, thy fury spent,
Confounded be thyself. Speak not. Be gone.

ALCIBIADES
Hast thou gold yet? I'll take the gold thou giv'st me,
Not all thy counsel.

TIMON
Dost thou or dost thou not, heaven's curse upon thee!

PHRYNIA *and* TIMANDRA
Give us some gold, good Timon. Hast thou more?

TIMON
Enough to make a whore forswear her trade,
And to make wholesomeness a bawd. Hold up, you
sluts,
Your aprons mountant.
[*He throws gold into their aprons*]
You are not oathable,
Although I know you'll swear, terribly swear,
Into strong shudders and to heavenly agues
Th' immortal gods that hear you. Spare your oaths;
I'll trust to your conditions. Be whores still,
And he whose pious breath seeks to convert you,
Be strong in whore, allure him, burn him up.
Let your close fire predominate his smoke;
And be no turncoats. Yet may your pain-sick months
Be quite contrary, and thatch your poor thin roofs
With burdens of the dead—some that were hanged,
No matter. Wear them, betray with them; whore still;
Paint till a horse may mire upon your face.
A pox of wrinkles!

PHRYNIA *and* TIMANDRA
Well, more gold; what then?
Believe't that we'll do anything for gold.

TIMON Consumptions sow
In hollow bones of man, strike their sharp shins,
And mar men's spurring. Crack the lawyer's voice,
That he may never more false title plead
Nor sound his quillets shrilly. Hoar the flamen
That scolds against the quality of flesh
And not believes himself. Down with the nose,
Down with it flat; take the bridge quite away
Of him that his particular to foresee
Smells from the general weal. Make curled-pate
ruffians bald,
And let the unscarred braggarts of the war
Derive some pain from you. Plague all,
That your activity may defeat and quell
The source of all erection. There's more gold.
Do you damn others, and let this damn you;
And ditches grave you all!

PHRYNIA *and* TIMANDRA
More counsel with more money, bounteous Timon.

TIMON
More whore, more mischief first; I have given you
earnest.

ALCIBIADES
Strike up the drum towards Athens. Farewell, Timon.
If I thrive well, I'll visit thee again.

TIMON
If I hope well, I'll never see thee more.

ALCIBIADES I never did thee harm.

TIMON Yes, thou spok'st well of me.

ALCIBIADES Call'st thou that harm?

TIMON
Men daily find it. Get thee away,

123 **sans** without
objects objections
125 **proof** tested power
136 **mountant** lifted up. A heraldic term, suggesting that the lifted skirts are emblems of prostitution. Perhaps puns on sexual 'mounting'.
oathable able to keep an oath
138 **strong...agues** i.e. dismay and pain. The words suggest also, quibblingly, both orgasm and effects of venereal disease.
140 **trust...conditions** (*a*) take your quality on trust (*b*) trust what your occupations indicate (that as whores they are not to be trusted)
142 **burn him up** (with venereal disease)
143 **close fire** (*a*) the enclosed and so fierce fire of your lust (*b*) secret venereal disease
predominate prevail over
smoke (*a*) vacuous pieties (*b*) steaming in the sweating-tub
144 **be no turncoats** i.e. stay true to being whores
145 **quite contrary** entirely opposed to your well-being (and perhaps 'just the opposite in character': i.e. making them sick instead of active, cold (*thin roofs*) instead of hot)
thin roofs i.e. hairless scalps (a supposed symptom of venereal disease)
146 **burdens of the dead** i.e. wigs made from the hair of the dead
148 **Paint** apply cosmetics
mire upon get stuck in (as if in mud)
149 **A pox of** a pox on, to hell with
151 **Consumptions** consuming diseases (especially sexual ones)
152 **hollow bones** The anticipated result of *Consumptions*. Syphilis makes bones brittle and fragile.
sharp shins Again the anticipated result: perhaps painful nodes on the shins.
153 **spurring** (*a*) horse-riding (*b*) copulation
Crack...voice An ulcered larynx is another effect of syphilis.
155 **quillets** verbal niceties, quibbles
Hoar make greyish-white (with syphilis)
flamen priest. The Latinism is perhaps a concession to the setting in classical Greece, but may have been chosen to avoid censorship.
156 **quality of flesh** i.e. susceptibility of the flesh to sexual temptation
157 **Down with the nose** Syphilis caused collapse of the nose-bridge.
159 **his particular** his own self-interest
160 **from** apart from
general weal i.e. well-being of society at large
curled-pate ruffians curly-headed swaggerers
161 **unscarred braggarts** i.e. boastful cowards
163 **quell** destroy
164 **The...erection** i.e. the male sexual impulse
168 **earnest** a down-payment
172–3 **I...me** Proverbially, 'Praise by evil men is dispraise'.

And take thy beagles with thee.
ALCIBIADES We but offend him. Strike!
Exeunt [to drum and fife all but Timon]
TIMON
That nature, being sick of man's unkindness,
Should yet be hungry!
[He digs the earth]
Common mother—thou
Whose womb unmeasurable and infinite breast
Teems and feeds all, whose selfsame mettle
Whereof thy proud child, arrogant man, is puffed
Engenders the black toad and adder blue,
The gilded newt and eyeless venomed worm,
With all th' abhorrèd births below crisp heaven
Whereon Hyperion's quick'ning fire doth shine—
Yield him who all the human sons doth hate
From forth thy plenteous bosom, one poor root.
Ensear thy fertile and conceptious womb;
Let it no more bring out ingrateful man.
Go great with tigers, dragons, wolves, and bears;
Teem with new monsters whom thy upward face
Hath to the marbled mansion all above
Never presented.
[He finds a root]
O, a root! Dear thanks.
Dry up thy marrows, vines, and plough-torn leas,
Whereof ingrateful man with liquorish draughts
And morsels unctuous greases his pure mind,
That from it all consideration slips!—
Enter Apemantus
More man? Plague, plague!
APEMANTUS
I was directed hither. Men report
Thou dost affect my manners, and dost use them.
TIMON
'Tis then because thou dost not keep a dog
Whom I would imitate. Consumption catch thee!
APEMANTUS
This is in thee a nature but infected,
A poor unmanly melancholy, sprung
From change of fortune. Why this spade, this place,
This slave-like habit, and these looks of care?
Thy flatterers yet wear silk, drink wine, lie soft,
Hug their diseased perfumes, and have forgot
That ever Timon was. Shame not these woods
By putting on the cunning of a carper.
Be thou a flatterer now, and seek to thrive
By that which has undone thee. Hinge thy knee,
And let his very breath whom thou'lt observe
Blow off thy cap. Praise his most vicious strain,
And call it excellent. Thou wast told thus.
Thou gav'st thine ears like tapsters that bade welcome
To knaves and all approachers. 'Tis most just
That thou turn rascal. Hadst thou wealth again,
Rascals should have't. Do not assume my likeness.
TIMON
Were I like thee, I'd throw away myself.
APEMANTUS
Thou hast cast away thyself being like thyself—
A madman so long, now a fool. What, think'st
That the bleak air, thy boisterous chamberlain,
Will put thy shirt on warm? Will these mossed trees
That have outlived the eagle page thy heels
And skip when thou point'st out? Will the cold brook,
Candied with ice, caudle thy morning taste
To cure thy o'ernight's surfeit? Call the creatures
Whose naked natures live in all the spite
Of wreakful heaven, whose bare unhousèd trunks
To the conflicting elements exposed
Answer mere nature; bid them flatter thee.
O, thou shalt find—
TIMON A fool of thee! Depart.
APEMANTUS
I love thee better now than e'er I did.
TIMON
I hate thee worse.
APEMANTUS Why?
TIMON Thou flatter'st misery.

176 **beagles** dogs good at hunting by scent. The implication is 'bitches who sniff out their male prey'.
178 **Common mother** proverbial for the earth
180 **Teems** breeds
181 **puffed** inflated (with pride)
182–3 **toad...newt** (both thought poisonous)
183 **eyeless venomed worm** The blind-worm proper is not poisonous (and not blind), but the poisonous (and well-sighted) adder was sometimes also called the 'blind-worm'.
184 **crisp** clear, shining
185 **Hyperion's** *Hyperion* is here the sun, though more accurately in Greek mythology the sun's father.
quick'ning life-giving
188 **Ensear** dry up, wither away
191 **upward** upturned
192 **marbled mansion** i.e. the heavens. *Marbled* suggests both opulence of a building and luminosity of the sky.
194 **marrows** vital pulp
leas fields
195 **liquorish** (*a*) pleasant (*b*) lust-inducing
draughts drinks: (*a*) potions (*b*) swallowings
196 **unctuous** rich in fat
greases (*a*) makes gross and lewd (*b*) makes slippery (see next line)
197 **consideration** capacity for thought
200 **affect** (*a*) like (*b*) assume, imitate
206 **habit** costume
208 **perfumes** (metonymic for 'perfumed mistresses')
210 **putting...carper** assuming the guise of a professional fault-finder
213 **observe** obsequiously follow
216 **tapsters** barmen in inns (who would greet all-comers)
218–19 **rascal...Rascals** lean and solitary deer...rogues
223 **chamberlain** personal servant
225 **outlived the eagle** From the proverbial expression 'an eagle's old age'.
page thy heels follow at your heels like a (young) page
226 **skip** jump to it
point'st out indicate something you want
227 **Candied** sugar-frosted
caudle refresh with a caudle (a warm, spiced medicinal drink)
229 **in** exposed to
230 **wreakful** vindictive
232 **Answer** act in accordance with
mere unmitigated

APEMANTUS
I flatter not, but say thou art a caitiff.
TIMON
Why dost thou seek me out?
APEMANTUS To vex thee.
TIMON
Always a villain's office, or a fool's.
Dost please thyself in't?
APEMANTUS Ay.
TIMON What, a knave too?
APEMANTUS
If thou didst put this sour cold habit on
To castigate thy pride, 'twere well; but thou
Dost it enforcèdly. Thou'dst courtier be again
Wert thou not beggar. Willing misery
Outlives incertain pomp, is crowned before.
The one is filling still, never complete;
The other at high wish. Best state, contentless,
Hath a distracted and most wretched being,
Worse than the worst, content.
Thou shouldst desire to die, being miserable.
TIMON
Not by his breath that is more miserable.
Thou art a slave whom fortune's tender arm
With favour never clasped, but bred a dog.
Hadst thou like us from our first swathe proceeded
The sweet degrees that this brief world affords
To such as may the passive drudges of it
Freely command, thou wouldst have plunged thyself
In general riot, melted down thy youth
In different beds of lust, and never learned
The icy precepts of respect, but followed
The sugared game before thee. But myself,
Who had the world as my confectionery,
The mouths, the tongues, the eyes and hearts of men
At duty, more than I could frame employment,
That numberless upon me stuck, as leaves
Do on the oak, have with one winter's brush
Fell from their boughs, and left me open, bare
For every storm that blows—I to bear this,
That never knew but better, is some burden.
Thy nature did commence in sufferance, time
Hath made thee hard in't. Why shouldst thou hate men?
They never flattered thee. What hast thou given?
If thou wilt curse, thy father, that poor rag,
Must be thy subject, who in spite put stuff
To some she-beggar and compounded thee
Poor rogue hereditary. Hence, be gone.
If thou hadst not been born the worst of men
Thou hadst been a knave and flatterer.
APEMANTUS Art thou proud yet?
TIMON Ay, that I am not thee.
APEMANTUS I that I was
No prodigal.
TIMON I that I am one now.
Were all the wealth I have shut up in thee
I'd give thee leave to hang it. Get thee gone.
That the whole life of Athens were in this!
Thus would I eat it.
[*He bites the root*]
APEMANTUS [*offering food*]
Here, I will mend thy feast.
TIMON
First mend my company: take away thyself.
APEMANTUS
So I shall mend mine own by th' lack of thine.
TIMON
'Tis not well mended so, it is but botched;
If not, I would it were.
APEMANTUS What wouldst thou have to Athens?
TIMON
Thee thither in a whirlwind. If thou wilt,
Tell them there I have gold. Look, so I have.
APEMANTUS
Here is no use for gold.
TIMON The best and truest,
For here it sleeps and does no hirèd harm.
APEMANTUS Where liest a-nights, Timon?
TIMON Under that's above me. Where feed'st thou a-days, Apemantus?
APEMANTUS Where my stomach finds meat; or rather, where I eat it.
TIMON Would poison were obedient, and knew my mind!
APEMANTUS Where wouldst thou send it?
TIMON To sauce thy dishes.
APEMANTUS The middle of humanity thou never knewest, but the extremity of both ends. When thou wast in thy gilt and thy perfume, they mocked thee for too much curiosity; in thy rags thou know'st none, but art

236 **caitiff** wretch
244 **incertain** insecure
is crowned i.e. finds fulfilment
246 **Best state, contentless** the greatest prosperity, if it is without contentment
248 **the worst, content** the least prosperity, if it is contented
252 **bred** i.e. whom fortune bred
253 **swathe** swaddling-clothes (of infancy)
proceeded passed through
254 **degrees** steps on fortune's ladder (*sweet* because leading upward)
255 **such** i.e. such a height
259 **precepts of respect** (*a*) commands issued by those in authority (*b*) rules for maintaining a position of respect (*c*) soundly-judged moral principles
259–60 **followed ... thee** (womanizing seen as a *sugared* form of hunting)
263 **At duty** at my service
frame employment devise employment for
265 **brush** violent burst
273 **in spite** out of spite
273–4 **put stuff | To** copulated with, 'stuffed'
274 **compounded** begot
285–8 **mend ... mended** improve ... repaired
288 **it ... botched** (because Apemantus would still have himself to endure)
289 **What** what message. Timon takes as 'what things'.
302 **The ... knewest** Proverbially, 'Virtue is found in the middle'.
305 **curiosity** (*a*) delicacy, fastidiousness (*b*) desire for novelty

despised for the contrary. There's a medlar for thee; eat it.

TIMON On what I hate I feed not.

APEMANTUS Dost hate a medlar?

TIMON Ay, though it look like thee.

APEMANTUS An thou'dst hated meddlers sooner, thou shouldst have loved thyself better now. What man didst thou ever know unthrift that was beloved after his means?

TIMON Who, without those means thou talk'st of, didst thou ever know beloved?

APEMANTUS Myself.

TIMON I understand thee: thou hadst some means to keep a dog.

APEMANTUS What things in the world canst thou nearest compare to thy flatterers?

TIMON Women nearest; but men, men are the things themselves. What wouldst thou do with the world, Apemantus, if it lay in thy power?

APEMANTUS Give it the beasts, to be rid of the men.

TIMON Wouldst thou have thyself fall in the confusion of men, and remain a beast with the beasts?

APEMANTUS Ay, Timon.

TIMON A beastly ambition, which the gods grant thee t'attain to. If thou wert the lion, the fox would beguile thee. If thou wert the lamb, the fox would eat thee. If thou wert the fox, the lion would suspect thee when peradventure thou wert accused by the ass. If thou wert the ass, thy dullness would torment thee, and still thou lived'st but as a breakfast to the wolf. If thou wert the wolf, thy greediness would afflict thee, and oft thou shouldst hazard thy life for thy dinner. Wert thou the unicorn, pride and wrath would confound thee, and make thine own self the conquest of thy fury. Wert thou a bear, thou wouldst be killed by the horse. Wert thou a horse, thou wouldst be seized by the leopard. Wert thou a leopard, thou wert german to the lion, and the spots of thy kindred were jurors on thy life; all thy safety were remotion, and thy defence absence. What beast couldst thou be that were not subject to a beast? And what a beast art thou already, that seest not thy loss in transformation!

APEMANTUS If thou couldst please me with speaking to me, thou mightst have hit upon it here. The commonwealth of Athens is become a forest of beasts.

TIMON How, has the ass broke the wall, that thou art out of the city?

APEMANTUS Yonder comes a poet and a painter. The plague of company light upon thee! I will fear to catch it, and give way. When I know not what else to do, I'll see thee again.

TIMON When there is nothing living but thee, thou shalt be welcome. I had rather be a beggar's dog than Apemantus.

APEMANTUS
Thou art the cap of all the fools alive.

TIMON
Would thou wert clean enough to spit upon.

APEMANTUS
A plague on thee! Thou art too bad to curse.

TIMON
All villains that do stand by thee are pure.

APEMANTUS
There is no leprosy but what thou speak'st.

TIMON If I name thee.
I'll beat thee, but I should infect my hands.

APEMANTUS
I would my tongue could rot them off.

TIMON
Away, thou issue of a mangy dog!
Choler does kill me that thou art alive.
I swoon to see thee.

APEMANTUS Would thou wouldst burst!

TIMON Away, thou tedious rogue!
[*He throws a stone at Apemantus*]
I am sorry I shall lose a stone by thee.

APEMANTUS Beast!

TIMON Slave!

APEMANTUS Toad!

TIMON Rogue, rogue, rogue!
I am sick of this false world, and will love naught
But even the mere necessities upon't.
Then, Timon, presently prepare thy grave.
Lie where the light foam of the sea may beat
Thy gravestone daily. Make thine epitaph,
That death in me at others' lives may laugh.
[*He looks on the gold*]
O, thou sweet king-killer, and dear divorce
'Twixt natural son and sire; thou bright defiler
Of Hymen's purest bed; thou valiant Mars;
Thou ever young, fresh, loved, and delicate wooer,

306 **medlar** A kind of apple eaten when rotten; with a pun in 14.311 on *meddlers*.
313 **unthrift** good-for-nothing
326 **fall in** (*a*) take part in (whereby the beasts overthrow mankind), or (*b*) degenerate (into a beast) in **confusion** overthrow, destruction
334 **dullness** stupidity **still** all the time
337–9 **Wert ... fury** The legendary way to catch a unicorn was to stand in front of a tree then step aside when it charged, so that its horn stuck in the tree-trunk.
340 **bear** (supposedly hated by horses)
342 **german** closely related
343 **spots** crimes (of the lion; quibbling on the leopard's physical spots)
344 **were remotion** would lie in keeping well away
347 **in transformation** i.e. if you were transformed
353 **Yonder ... painter** This disconnected remark anticipates the episode at the beginning of Sc. 15, which is not imminent. Apemantus might be warning that other asses have broken the walls of Athens and are on their way, but the comment may have been deleted by the time the play reached the stage.
360 **cap** foremost example (punning on the fool's coxcomb)
386 **Hymen's** (god of marriage)
387 **delicate** graceful

Whose blush doth thaw the consecrated snow
That lies on Dian's lap; thou visible god,
That sold'rest close impossibilities
And mak'st them kiss, that speak'st with every tongue
To every purpose; O thou touch of hearts:
Think thy slave man rebels, and by thy virtue
Set them into confounding odds, that beasts
May have the world in empire.

APEMANTUS Would 'twere so,
But not till I am dead. I'll say thou'st gold.
Thou wilt be thronged to shortly.

TIMON Thronged to?

APEMANTUS Ay.

TIMON
Thy back, I prithee.

APEMANTUS Live, and love thy misery.

TIMON
Long live so, and so die. I am quit.

Enter [at a distance] the Banditti, [Thieves]

APEMANTUS
More things like men. Eat, Timon, and abhor them.

Exit

FIRST THIEF Where should he have this gold? It is some poor fragment, some slender ort of his remainder. The mere want of gold and the falling-from of his friends drove him into this melancholy.

SECOND THIEF It is noised he hath a mass of treasure.

THIRD THIEF Let us make the assay upon him. If he care not for't, he will supply us easily. If he covetously reserve it, how shall 's get it?

SECOND THIEF True, for he bears it not about him; 'tis hid.

FIRST THIEF Is not this he?

OTHER THIEVES Where?

SECOND THIEF 'Tis his description.

THIRD THIEF He, I know him.

ALL THIEVES [*coming forward*] Save thee, Timon.

TIMON Now, thieves.

ALL THIEVES
Soldiers, not thieves.

TIMON Both, too, and women's sons.

ALL THIEVES
We are not thieves, but men that much do want.

TIMON
Your greatest want is, you want much of meat.
Why should you want? Behold, the earth hath roots.
Within this mile break forth a hundred springs.
The oaks bear mast, the briars scarlet hips.
The bounteous housewife nature on each bush
Lays her full mess before you. Want? Why want?

FIRST THIEF
We cannot live on grass, on berries, water,
As beasts and birds and fishes.

TIMON
Nor on the beasts themselves, the birds and fishes;
You must eat men. Yet thanks I must you con
That you are thieves professed, that you work not
In holier shapes; for there is boundless theft
In limited professions. [*Giving gold*] Rascal thieves,
Here's gold. Go suck the subtle blood o' th' grape
Till the high fever seethe your blood to froth,
And so scape hanging. Trust not the physician;
His antidotes are poison, and he slays
More than you rob. Take wealth and lives together—
Do, villains, do, since you protest to do't,
Like workmen. I'll example you with thievery.
The sun's a thief, and with his great attraction
Robs the vast sea. The moon's an arrant thief,
And her pale fire she snatches from the sun.
The sea's a thief, whose liquid surge resolves
The moon into salt tears. The earth's a thief,
That feeds and breeds by a composture stol'n
From gen'ral excrement. Each thing's a thief.
The laws, your curb and whip, in their rough power
Has unchecked theft. Love not yourselves. Away,
Rob one another. There's more gold. Cut throats;
All that you meet are thieves. To Athens go,
Break open shops; nothing can you steal
But thieves do lose it. Steal less for this I give you,
And gold confound you howsoe'er. Amen.

THIRD THIEF He's almost charmed me from my profession by persuading me to it.

389 **Dian's** Roman goddess of chastity. There is a suggestion too of Danaë, who was seduced by Jupiter in a shower of gold.
390 **close** closely (qualifying *sold'rest*)
392 **touch** touchstone
393 **virtue** power
394 **confounding odds** mutually-destructive strife
399.1 ***Enter...Thieves*** These might logically be deserters from Alcibiades' army, as mentioned at 14.91–3.
401 **Where should he have** (*a*) from where can he have obtained (*b*) where might he keep
402 **ort** leftover (usually of food)
405 **noised** rumoured
406 **assay** (*a*) test (as for the presence and quality of gold in an alloy) (*b*) assault
416 **women's sons** Proverbial, here suggesting 'members of sinning humanity'. Contrast 14.494–5.
417 **much do want** are very needy
421 **mast** acorns (fed to swine)
423 **mess** serving of food
427 **you con** express to you
430 **limited professions** (*a*) regulated trades (*b*) less forthright admissions
431 **subtle** (*a*) fine, delicate (*b*) treacherous **blood o' th' grape** wine. But the image of sucking blood suggests a leech (*a*) in the pejorative sense 'extortioner', (*b*) as used in medical blood-letting (the bloodsucker here doesn't cure the patient but contracts a *high fever*).
435 **Take wealth and lives** steal wealth and end lives
438 **attraction** power of drawing up moisture
441–2 **The...tears** Alludes to the belief that tides were caused by the sea drawing moisture from the moon.
441 **resolves** melts, dissolves
446 **Has unchecked theft** have unlimited power to steal
450 **for** on account of
451 **howsoe'er** whatever you do

FIRST THIEF 'Tis in the malice of mankind that he thus advises us, not to have us thrive in our mystery.

SECOND THIEF I'll believe him as an enemy, and give over my trade.

FIRST THIEF Let us first see peace in Athens. There is no time so miserable but a man may be true.

Exeunt Thieves

Enter the Steward to Timon

STEWARD O you gods!
Is yon despised and ruinous man my lord,
Full of decay and failing? O monument
And wonder of good deeds evilly bestowed!
What an alteration of honour has desp'rate want made!
What viler thing upon the earth than friends,
Who can bring noblest minds to basest ends!
How rarely does it meet with this time's guise,
When man was wished to love his enemies!
Grant I may ever love and rather woo
Those that would mischief me than those that do!
He's caught me in his eye. I will present
My honest grief unto him, and as my lord
Still serve him with my life.—My dearest master.

TIMON
Away! What art thou?

STEWARD
Have you forgot me, sir?

TIMON
Why dost ask that? I have forgot all men;
Then if thou grant'st thou'rt a man, I have forgot thee.

STEWARD
An honest poor servant of yours.

TIMON
Then I know thee not.
I never had honest man about me; ay, all
I kept were knaves to serve in meat to villains.

STEWARD The gods are witness,
Ne'er did poor steward wear a truer grief
For his undone lord than mine eyes for you.

TIMON
What, dost thou weep? Come nearer then; I love thee
Because thou art a woman, and disclaim'st
Flinty mankind whose eyes do never give
But thorough lust and laughter. Pity's sleeping.
Strange times, that weep with laughing, not with weeping!

STEWARD
I beg of you to know me, good my lord,
T'accept my grief,
[*He offers his money*]
and whilst this poor wealth lasts
To entertain me as your steward still.

TIMON Had I a steward
So true, so just, and now so comfortable?
It almost turns my dangerous nature mild.
Let me behold thy face. Surely this man
Was born of woman.
Forgive my general and exceptless rashness,
You perpetual sober gods! I do proclaim
One honest man—mistake me not, but one,
No more, I pray—and he's a steward.
How fain would I have hated all mankind,
And thou redeem'st thyself! But all save thee
I fell with curses.
Methinks thou art more honest now than wise,
For by oppressing and betraying me
Thou mightst have sooner got another service;
For many so arrive at second masters
Upon their first lord's neck. But tell me true—
For I must ever doubt, though ne'er so sure—
Is not thy kindness subtle, covetous,
If not a usuring kindness, and, as rich men deal gifts,
Expecting in return twenty for one?

STEWARD
No, my most worthy master, in whose breast
Doubt and suspect, alas, are placed too late.
You should have feared false times when you did feast.
Suspect still comes where an estate is least.
That which I show, heaven knows, is merely love,
Duty and zeal to your unmatchèd mind,
Care of your food and living; and, believe it,
My most honoured lord,
For any benefit that points to me,
Either in hope or present, I'd exchange
For this one wish: that you had power and wealth
To requite me by making rich yourself.

TIMON
Look thee, 'tis so. Thou singly honest man,
[*He gives Steward gold*]
Here, take. The gods, out of my misery,

454 **in the malice of** out of hatred for
455 **mystery** profession
456 **as an enemy** i.e. not at all
458–9 **Let ... true** Implies either (*a*) he too will become honest once peace returns, or (*b*) he will not quit his trade (peace being unlikely) but remain *true* to his calling.
463 **wonder** astonishing example
467 **it** (the time recalled in the next line)
468 **love his enemies** Christ's commandment (Matthew 5:54)
485 **Flinty** To wring water out of flint was proverbially difficult.
give yield tears
486 **thorough** through
492 **comfortable** comforting
494–5 **Surely ... woman** From Job 14:1, where 'man that is born of woman' describes the human condition. Timon is surprised that being born of woman has, in the Steward's case, left traces in his 'womanish' behaviour.
496 **exceptless** indiscriminate
498–9 **One ... steward** The Steward contrasts with the biblical Unjust Steward, who is wise but worldly and dishonest (Luke 16:1–9).
500 **fain** willingly
507 **Upon ... neck** (*a*) by mounting on his first master's shoulders (*b*) having subjugated him (*c*) having betrayed him to execution
509 **subtle** treacherous
513 **suspect** suspicion
515 **still** always

Has sent thee treasure. Go, live rich and happy,
But thus conditioned: thou shalt build from men,
Hate all, curse all, show charity to none,
But let the famished flesh slide from the bone
Ere thou relieve the beggar. Give to dogs
What thou deniest to men. Let prisons swallow 'em,
Debts wither 'em to nothing; be men like blasted woods,
And may diseases lick up their false bloods.
And so farewell, and thrive.

STEWARD
O, let me stay and comfort you, my master.

TIMON If thou hat'st curses,
Stay not. Fly whilst thou art blest and free.
Ne'er see thou man, and let me ne'er see thee.

Exeunt [*Timon into his cave, Steward another way*]

Sc. 15

Enter Poet and Painter

PAINTER As I took note of the place, it cannot be far where he abides.

POET What's to be thought of him? Does the rumour hold for true that he's so full of gold?

PAINTER Certain. Alcibiades reports it. Phrynia and Timandra had gold of him. He likewise enriched poor straggling soldiers with great quantity. 'Tis said he gave unto his steward a mighty sum.

POET Then this breaking of his has been but a try for his friends?

PAINTER Nothing else. You shall see him a palm in Athens again, and flourish with the highest. Therefore 'tis not amiss we tender our loves to him in this supposed distress of his. It will show honestly in us, and is very likely to load our purposes with what they travail for, if it be a just and true report that goes of his having.

POET What have you now to present unto him?

PAINTER Nothing at this time, but my visitation; only I will promise him an excellent piece.

POET I must serve him so too, tell him of an intent that's coming toward him.

PAINTER Good as the best.

Enter Timon from his cave, [*unobserved*]

Promising is the very air o' th' time; it opens the eyes of expectation. Performance is ever the duller for his act, and but in the plainer and simpler kind of people the deed of saying is quite out of use. To promise is most courtly and fashionable. Performance is a kind of will or testament which argues a great sickness in his judgement that makes it.

TIMON [*aside*] Excellent workman, thou canst not paint a man so bad as is thyself.

POET [*to Painter*] I am thinking what I shall say I have provided for him. It must be a personating of himself, a satire against the softness of prosperity, with a discovery of the infinite flatteries that follow youth and opulency.

TIMON [*aside*] Must thou needs stand for a villain in thine own work? Wilt thou whip thine own faults in other men? Do so; I have gold for thee.

POET [*to Painter*] Nay, let's seek him.
Then do we sin against our own estate
When we may profit meet and come too late.

PAINTER True.
When the day serves, before black-cornered night,
Find what thou want'st by free and offered light.
Come.

TIMON [*aside*]
I'll meet you at the turn. What a god's gold,
That he is worshipped in a baser temple
Than where swine feed!
'Tis thou that rigg'st the barque and plough'st the foam,
Settlest admirèd reverence in a slave.
To thee be worship, and thy saints for aye
Be crowned with plagues, that thee alone obey.
Fit I meet them.

[*He comes forward to them*]

POET
Hail, worthy Timon!

PAINTER Our late noble master!

TIMON
Have I once lived to see two honest men?

POET
Sir, having often of your open bounty tasted,
Hearing you were retired, your friends fall'n off,
Whose thankless natures, O abhorrèd spirits,
Not all the whips of heaven are large enough—
What, to you,
Whose star-like nobleness gave life and influence
To their whole being! I am rapt, and cannot cover

527 **from** away from
532 **be men** let men be
blasted blighted, withered
533 **lick up** consume (and hinting that the diseases are like a dog licking a sick man's sores or wounds)
538.1 ***Exeunt*...*way*** Whether there is a scene-break depends on whether there is an on-stage cave property. If Timon remains visible in his cave, there is continuity of action, and he need not come forward again until after 15.29, as in the 1623 text.
15.9 **breaking** bankruptcy
11–12 **a...highest** Alludes to Psalms 92:11: 'The righteous shall flourish like a palm-tree'.
15 **travail** both 'labour' and 'travel'
16 **having** possessions
22.1 ***Enter*...*unobserved*** See note to 14.538.1.
23–9 **Promising...it** See note to 14.73.
23 **air** metaphoric for 'style, manner'
26 **the deed of saying** performance of what has been promised
37–8 **whip...men** From proverbial 'To find fault with others and do worse oneself'.
40 **estate** (*a*) social group (*b*) prosperity
43 **black-cornered** full of dark corners
46 **meet...turn** confront you when you turn the corner. Other relevant senses of *turn* are 'subtle device', 'opportunity', 'sudden veer of a hunted hare'.
47 **a baser temple** i.e. the human body
50 **admirèd reverence** an expression of reverential wonder
55 **once** really
57 **were retired** had withdrawn from society
58 **Whose** for whose
61 **influence** the supposed astrological effect of celestial bodies on humans

The monstrous bulk of this ingratitude
With any size of words.

TIMON
Let it go naked; men may see't the better.
You that are honest, by being what you are
Make them best seen and known.

PAINTER He and myself
Have travelled in the great show'r of your gifts,
And sweetly felt it.

TIMON Ay, you are honest men.

PAINTER
We are hither come to offer you our service.

TIMON
Most honest men. Why, how shall I requite you?
Can you eat roots and drink cold water? No.

POET *and* PAINTER
What we can do we'll do to do you service.

TIMON
You're honest men. You've heard that I have gold,
I am sure you have. Speak truth; you're honest men.

PAINTER
So it is said, my noble lord, but therefor
Came not my friend nor I.

TIMON
Good honest men. [*To Painter*] Thou draw'st a coun-
terfeit
Best in all Athens; thou'rt indeed the best;
Thou counterfeit'st most lively.

PAINTER So so, my lord.

TIMON
E'en so, sir, as I say. [*To Poet*] And for thy fiction,
Why, thy verse swells with stuff so fine and smooth
That thou art even natural in thine art.
But for all this, my honest-natured friends,
I must needs say you have a little fault.
Marry, 'tis not monstrous in you, neither wish I
You take much pains to mend.

POET *and* PAINTER Beseech your honour
To make it known to us.

TIMON You'll take it ill.

POET *and* PAINTER Most thankfully, my lord.

TIMON Will you indeed?

POET *and* PAINTER Doubt it not, worthy lord.

TIMON
There's never a one of you but trusts a knave
That mightily deceives you.

POET *and* PAINTER Do we, my lord?

TIMON
Ay, and you hear him cog, see him dissemble,
Know his gross patchery, love him, feed him,
Keep in your bosom; yet remain assured
That he's a made-up villain.

PAINTER I know none such, my lord.

POET Nor I.

TIMON
Look you, I love you well. I'll give you gold,
Rid me these villains from your companies.
Hang them or stab them, drown them in a draught,
Confound them by some course, and come to me,
I'll give you gold enough.

POET *and* PAINTER
Name them, my lord, let's know them.

TIMON
You that way and you this, but two in company;
Each man apart, all single and alone,
Yet an arch-villain keeps him company.
[*To Painter*] If where thou art two villains shall not be,
Come not near him. [*To Poet*] If thou wouldst not
reside
But where one villain is, then him abandon.
Hence; pack! [*Striking him*] There's gold. You came for
gold, ye slaves.
[*Striking Painter*] You have work for me; there's
payment. Hence!
[*Striking Poet*] You are an alchemist; make gold of
that.
Out, rascal dogs!

Exeunt [Poet and Painter one way, Timon into his cave]

Sc. 16

Enter Steward and two Senators

STEWARD
It is in vain that you would speak with Timon,
For he is set so only to himself
That nothing but himself which looks like man
Is friendly with him.

FIRST SENATOR Bring us to his cave.
It is our part and promise to th' Athenians
To speak with Timon.

SECOND SENATOR At all times alike
Men are not still the same. 'Twas time and griefs
That framed him thus. Time with his fairer hand
Offering the fortunes of his former days,
The former man may make him. Bring us to him,
And chance it as it may.

STEWARD Here is his cave.
[*Calling*] Peace and content be here! Lord Timon,
Timon,

64 **size** (*a*) quantity (*b*) glutinous wash applied to prepare paper or canvas for painting
76 **therefor** on that account
78 **counterfeit** (*a*) life-like picture (*b*) forgery. The idea that the Painter dissimulates is brought out in *counterfeit'st*, 15.80.
82 **swells with stuff** (*a*) swells with ideas (like a swollen river) (*b*) is inflated with padding (like a garment)
94 **cog** cheat, flatter
95 **patchery** knavery
97 **made-up** complete
102 **draught** cesspool
105 **but ... company** yet there is still a company of two
113 **You are an alchemist** (because as a poet he transmutes his subject into something finer)
16.2 **set** fixed, directed
only exclusively
5 **our ... promise** the role we promised to play

Look out and speak to friends. Th' Athenians
By two of their most reverend senate greet thee.
Speak to them, noble Timon.

Enter Timon out of his cave

TIMON
Thou sun that comforts, burn! Speak and be hanged.
For each true word a blister, and each false
Be as a cantherizing to the root o' th' tongue,
Consuming it with speaking.

FIRST SENATOR Worthy Timon—

TIMON
Of none but such as you, and you of Timon.

FIRST SENATOR
The senators of Athens greet thee, Timon.

TIMON
I thank them, and would send them back the plague
Could I but catch it for them.

FIRST SENATOR O, forget
What we are sorry for ourselves in thee.
The senators with one consent of love
Entreat thee back to Athens, who have thought
On special dignities which vacant lie
For thy best use and wearing.

SECOND SENATOR They confess
Toward thee forgetfulness too general-gross;
Which now the public body, which doth seldom
Play the recanter, feeling in itself
A lack of Timon's aid, hath sense withal
Of it own fall, restraining aid to Timon;
And send forth us to make their sorrowed render,
Together with a recompense more fruitful
Than their offence can weigh down by the dram;
Ay, even such heaps and sums of love and wealth
As shall to thee blot out what wrongs were theirs,
And write in thee the figures of their love,
Ever to read them thine.

TIMON You witch me in it,
Surprise me to the very brink of tears.
Lend me a fool's heart and a woman's eyes,
And I'll beweep these comforts, worthy senators.

FIRST SENATOR
Therefore so please thee to return with us,
And of our Athens, thine and ours, to take
The captainship, thou shalt be met with thanks,
Allowed with absolute power, and thy good name
Live with authority. So soon we shall drive back
Of Alcibiades th' approaches wild,
Who, like a boar too savage, doth root up
His country's peace.

SECOND SENATOR And shakes his threat'ning sword
Against the walls of Athens.

FIRST SENATOR Therefore, Timon—

TIMON
Well, sir, I will; therefore I will, sir, thus.
If Alcibiades kill my countrymen,
Let Alcibiades know this of Timon:
That Timon cares not. But if he sack fair Athens,
And take our goodly agèd men by th' beards,
Giving our holy virgins to the stain
Of contumelious, beastly, mad-brained war,
Then let him know, and tell him Timon speaks it
In pity of our agèd and our youth,
I cannot choose but tell him that I care not;
And—let him take't at worst—for their knives care
not
While you have throats to answer. For myself,
There's not a whittle in th' unruly camp
But I do prize it at my love before
The reverend'st throat in Athens. So I leave you
To the protection of the prosperous gods,
As thieves to keepers.

STEWARD [*to Senators*] Stay not; all's in vain.

TIMON
Why, I was writing of my epitaph.
It will be seen tomorrow. My long sickness
Of health and living now begins to mend,
And nothing brings me all things. Go; live still.
Be Alcibiades your plague, you his,
And last so long enough.

FIRST SENATOR We speak in vain.

TIMON
But yet I love my country, and am not
One that rejoices in the common wrack
As common bruit doth put it.

FIRST SENATOR That's well spoke.

TIMON
Commend me to my loving countrymen—

FIRST SENATOR
These words become your lips as they pass through
them.

16 **Speak and be hanged** Varies the proverb 'Confess and be hanged'.

17–18 **For...tongue** Proverbially, 'Report has a blister on her tongue' (because she tells lies).

18 **cantherizing** Probably a portmanteau meaning both (*a*) *cantharidizing*, 'blistering (as with cantherides, blister-flies)', and (*b*) *cauterizing*.

24 **in thee** i.e. in our treatment of you

33 **it** its
restraining in withholding

36 **by the dram** i.e. when measured with most exacting accuracy

39 **figures** (*a*) images, expressions (*b*) numbers, arithmetic

47 **Allowed** invested

50 **Who...up** From Psalms 80:13 (Bishops'): 'The wild boar out of the wood doth root it up'.

59 **contumelious** insolent

63 **take't at worst** From proverbial 'Take it as you list'.
care I care

64 **answer** provide what is required (quibbling on 'reply in speech')

65 **whittle** clasp-knife

66 **prize** value
at in terms of

73 **nothing...things** Echoes the ideal of Christian life in 2 Corinthians 6:10: 'as having nothing, and yet possessing all things'.

75 **so** in that state

77 **wrack** destruction

78 **common bruit** popular rumour

SECOND SENATOR
And enter in our ears like great triumphers
In their applauding gates.
TIMON Commend me to them,
And tell them that to ease them of their griefs,
Their fears of hostile strokes, their achës, losses,
Their pangs of love, with other incident throes
That nature's fragile vessel doth sustain
In life's uncertain voyage, I will some kindness do them.
I'll teach them to prevent wild Alcibiades' wrath.
FIRST SENATOR [*aside*]
I like this well; he will return again.
TIMON
I have a tree which grows here in my close
That mine own use invites me to cut down,
And shortly must I fell it. Tell my friends,
Tell Athens, in the sequence of degree
From high to low throughout, that whoso please
To stop affliction, let him take his haste,
Come hither ere my tree hath felt the axe,
And hang himself. I pray you do my greeting.
STEWARD [*to Senators*]
Trouble him no further. Thus you still shall find him.
TIMON
Come not to me again, but say to Athens,
Timon hath made his everlasting mansion
Upon the beachèd verge of the salt flood,
Who once a day with his embossèd froth
The turbulent surge shall cover. Thither come,
And let my gravestone be your oracle.
Lips, let four words go by, and language end.
What is amiss, plague and infection mend.
Graves only be men's works, and death their gain.
Sun, hide thy beams. Timon hath done his reign.
Exit [*into his cave*]
FIRST SENATOR
His discontents are unremovably
Coupled to nature.
SECOND SENATOR
Our hope in him is dead. Let us return,
And strain what other means is left unto us
In our dear peril.
FIRST SENATOR It requires swift foot. *Exeunt*

Enter two other Senators, with a Messenger Sc. 17
THIRD SENATOR
Thou hast painfully discovered. Are his files
As full as thy report?
MESSENGER I have spoke the least.
Besides, his expedition promises
Present approach.
FOURTH SENATOR
We stand much hazard if they bring not Timon.
MESSENGER
I met a courier, one mine ancient friend,
Whom, though in general part we were opposed,
Yet our old love made a particular force
And made us speak like friends. This man was riding
From Alcibiades to Timon's cave
With letters of entreaty which imported
His fellowship i'th' cause against your city,
In part for his sake moved.
Enter the other Senators
THIRD SENATOR Here come our brothers.
FIRST SENATOR
No talk of Timon; nothing of him expect.
The enemy's drum is heard, and fearful scouring
Doth choke the air with dust. In, and prepare.
Ours is the fall, I fear, our foe's the snare. *Exeunt*

Enter a Soldier, in the woods, seeking Timon Sc. 18
SOLDIER
By all description, this should be the place.
Who's here? Speak, ho! No answer? What is this?
[*He discovers a grave, with two inscriptions*]
'Timon is dead, who hath outstretched his span.
Some beast read this; there does not live a man.'
Dead, sure, and this his grave. What's on this tomb
I cannot read. The character I'll take with wax.
Our captain hath in every figure skill,
An aged interpreter, though young in days.
Before proud Athens he's set down by this,
Whose fall the mark of his ambition is. *Exit*

81 **great triumphers** those entering at a great triumphal welcome. The Roman practice of according a triumph to victorious generals was imitated in Renaissance civic welcomes for dignitaries.
90 **close** enclosure
102 **embossèd** foaming (often used of an exhausted hunted animal foaming at the mouth)
105 **four** (used as an indefinite small number)
110 **nature** his nature
17.1 **painfully discovered** (*a*) painstakingly reconnoitred, (*b*) told painful news
files (of troops)
3 **his expedition** the speed of his advance
6 **ancient** long-standing
7 **in general part** on matters of public concern
13 **moved** taken up, advanced
15 **scouring** military scourging
18.3 **outstretched his span** i.e. lived too long
5–6 **What's ... read** This is puzzling just after he has apparently read an epitaph. Perhaps the lines he takes in wax, as read in Sc. 19, are written in another language such as Latin, or another script.
6 **character** lettering
take take an impression of
7 **figure** kind of writing
8 **interpreter** (perhaps specifically 'translater')
9 **he's set down by this** his captain (presumably Alcibiades) has encamped by now. *Set down* and *mark* (18.10) perhaps glance illogically at writing.
10 **Whose** Refers to Athens.
mark target

Sc. 19 *Trumpets sound. Enter Alcibiades with his powers, before Athens*

ALCIBIADES
Sound to this coward and lascivious town
Our terrible approach.

Sounds a parley. The Senators appear upon the walls

Till now you have gone on and filled the time
With all licentious measure, making your wills
The scope of justice. Till now myself and such
As stepped within the shadow of your power
Have wandered with our traversed arms, and breathed
Our sufferance vainly. Now the time is flush
When crouching marrow, in the bearer strong,
Cries of itself 'No more'; now breathless wrong
Shall sit and pant in your great chairs of ease,
And pursy insolence shall break his wind
With fear and horrid flight.

FIRST SENATOR Noble and young,
When thy first griefs were but a mere conceit,
Ere thou hadst power or we had cause of fear,
We sent to thee to give thy rages balm,
To wipe out our ingratitude with loves
Above their quantity.

SECOND SENATOR So did we woo
Transformèd Timon to our city's love
By humble message and by promised means.
We were not all unkind, nor all deserve
The common stroke of war.

FIRST SENATOR These walls of ours
Were not erected by their hands from whom
You have received your grief; nor are they such
That these great tow'rs, trophies, and schools should fall
For private faults in them.

SECOND SENATOR Nor are they living
Who were the motives that you first went out.
Shame that they wanted cunning, in excess,
Hath broke their hearts. March, noble lord,
Into our city with thy banners spread.
By decimation and a tithèd death,
If thy revenges hunger for that food
Which nature loathes, take thou the destined tenth,
And by the hazard of the spotted die
Let die the spotted.

FIRST SENATOR All have not offended.
For those that were, it is not square to take,
On those that are, revenge. Crimes like lands
Are not inherited. Then, dear countryman,
Bring in thy ranks, but leave without thy rage.
Spare thy Athenian cradle and those kin
Which, in the bluster of thy wrath, must fall
With those that have offended. Like a shepherd
Approach the fold and cull th' infected forth,
But kill not all together.

SECOND SENATOR What thou wilt,
Thou rather shalt enforce it with thy smile
Than hew to't with thy sword.

FIRST SENATOR Set but thy foot
Against our rampired gates and they shall ope,
So thou wilt send thy gentle heart before
To say thou'lt enter friendly.

SECOND SENATOR Throw thy glove,
Or any token of thine honour else,
That thou wilt use the wars as thy redress,
And not as our confusion. All thy powers
Shall make their harbour in our town till we
Have sealed thy full desire.

ALCIBIADES [*throwing up a glove*]
Then there's my glove.
Descend, and open your unchargèd ports.
Those enemies of Timon's and mine own
Whom you yourselves shall set out for reproof
Fall, and no more; and to atone your fears
With my more noble meaning, not a man
Shall pass his quarter or offend the stream
Of regular justice in your city's bounds
But shall be remedied to your public laws
At heaviest answer.

19.0.2–19.2.2 ***before Athens*** ... ***upon the walls*** As in Sc. 12, the tiring-house wall would represent the city wall.
1 **Sound** i.e. proclaim by trumpet-call
2 **terrible** terrifying
4 **all licentious measure** every degree and kind of licentiousness
5 **scope** determining limit
7 **traversed arms** (*a*) folded arms (a sign of melancholy); or (*b*) weapons held crossed (as in military drill)
breathed spoken about
8 **sufferance** sufferings, grievances
flush in full flood
9 **crouching** cringing, subservient
marrow (source of vitality and strength)
10 **of itself** of its own accord
breathless short-winded (because old and fearful)
wrong i.e. wrong-doers, the senators
12 **pursy** fat and short-winded
insolence overbearing pride (i.e. those so characterized)
break his wind gasp for breath; fart
13 **horrid** horrifying
14 **griefs** grievances
20 **means** terms; compromises; wealth
25 **trophies** monuments
schools public buildings
27 **motives that** i.e. instigators of the grievances for which
28 **wanted** lacked
cunning i.e. sufficient cleverness to forestall Alcibiades' revolt
in excess An excess of a passion was believed capable of making the heart burst.
31 **decimation ... death** Both expressions mean 'execution of one person in ten'.
34 **die** (singular of *dice*)
35 **spotted** tainted, guilty
36 **were** lived before
square right, just
39 **without** outside (the walls)
41 **bluster** wild storm
44 **What** whatever
47 **rampired** (*a*) strengthened (as with ramparts) (*b*) blocked with earth piled behind them
48 **So** if only
54 **sealed** i.e. formally satisfied
55 **unchargèd ports** unassailed gates
58 **atone** reconcile
59 **meaning** intentions
man soldier
60 **pass his quarter** leave his allotted place
offend violate

BOTH SENATORS 'Tis most nobly spoken.

ALCIBIADES Descend, and keep your words.

[*Trumpets sound. Exeunt Senators from the walls*]

Enter a Soldier, [*with a tablet of wax*]

SOLDIER

My noble general, Timon is dead,
Entombed upon the very hem o' th' sea;
And on his gravestone this insculpture, which
With wax I brought away, whose soft impression
Interprets for my poor ignorance.

Alcibiades reads the epitaph

[ALCIBIADES]

'Here lies a wretched corpse, of wretched soul bereft.
Seek not my name. A plague consume you wicked caitiffs left!
Here lie I, Timon, who alive all living men did hate.
Pass by and curse thy fill, but pass and stay not here thy gait.'
These well express in thee thy latter spirits.
Though thou abhorred'st in us our human griefs,
Scorned'st our brains' flow and those our droplets which
From niggard nature fall, yet rich conceit
Taught thee to make vast Neptune weep for aye
On thy low grave, on faults forgiven.

[*Enter Senators through the gates*]

Dead
Is noble Timon, of whose memory
Hereafter more. Bring me into your city,
And I will use the olive with my sword,
Make war breed peace, make peace stint war, make each
Prescribe to other as each other's leech.
Let our drums strike.

[*Drums.*] *Exeunt* [*through the gates*]

Finis

THE PARTS

Men

TIMON (844 lines): 4 Senator; a Stranger; Soldier

APEMANTUS (247 lines): Lucilius; Old Man; a Stranger; Lucius' Servant; Lucullus' Servant; Varro's Second Servant *or* a Servant of Titus, Hortensius, *or* Philotus; Soldier

STEWARD (203 lines): a Senator *or* Soldier; a Stranger; Lucullus' Servant; Varro's Second Servant *or* a Servant of Lucius, Titus, Hortensius, *or* Philotus

ALCIBIADES (159 lines): Lucilius; Old Man; a Stranger; Lucius' Servant; Lucullus' Servant; Varro's Second Servant *or* a Servant of Titus, Hortensius, *or* Philotus; a Thief

POET (102 lines): any but Timon, Apemantus, Alcibiades, Steward, Timon's Servants, Lords, Painter, Jeweller, Merchant, Lucilius, Old Man, Messenger(s) (Sc. 1)

FIRST SENATOR (87 lines): any but Timon, Alcibiades, Apemantus, Steward, Flaminius, [Timon's other Servants], Lords, Poet, Painter, other Senators, Caphis, Soldier, Messenger

LUCIUS/FIRST LORD (85 lines): Fool *or* Page; a Stranger; Caphis *or* a Servant of Lucius, Isidore, Varro, Titus, Hortensius, *or* Philotus; a Thief; Soldier

LUCULLUS/SECOND LORD (78 lines): Fool *or* Page; Lucullus' Servant; Caphis *or* a Servant of Lucius, Isidore, Varro, Titus, Hortensius, *or* Philotus; a Thief; Soldier

PAINTER (66 lines): any but Timon, Apemantus, Alcibiades, Steward, Lucilius, Timon's Servants, Lords, Poet, Jeweller, Merchant, 1 and 2 Senators, Old Man, Messengers (Sc. 1)

SECOND SENATOR (61 lines): any but Timon, Alcibiades, Apemantus, Steward, Flaminius, [Timon's other Servants], Lords, Poet, Painter, other Senators, Soldier, Messenger

SEMPRONIUS/THIRD LORD (38 lines): Fool *or* Page; Lucullus' Servant; Caphis *or* a Servant of Lucius, Isidore, Varro, Titus, Hortensius, *or* Philotus; a Thief; Soldier

FLAMINIUS (Timon's First Servant; 37 lines): Fourth Senator *or* Soldier; a Stranger; a Thief

65.1 ***Exeunt . . . walls*** The descent from the upper acting area was by offstage ladders in the Jacobean theatre. So unless the Senators ignore Alcibiades they must exit, and unless there is an awkward break in the action they must be offstage when the epitaph is read. A flourish of trumpets would drown the noise of the Senators descending, and might even allow time for them to enter ceremonially before the Soldier arrives.

67 **hem** edge

68 **insculpture** inscription

71–4 **Here . . . gait** These are two separate epitaphs in Plutarch, one of them not written by Timon. They conflict in that 'Seek not my name' is contradicted in 'Here lie I, Timon'. Counting the one in Sc. 18, there are three epitaphs in all. The compulsion to repeat or rework may be attributed to either Timon or Shakespeare.

72 **caitiffs** wretches, villains

77 **brains' flow** i.e. tears (likewise *droplets*)

78 **niggard nature** parsimonious human nature (compared unfavourably with *vast Neptune*, 19.79)

conceit ingenuity, imagination

83 **the olive** (as emblem of peace)

84 **stint** put an end to

85 **leech** physician. Also the worm used in medical blood-letting; hence 'cure'. War purges corruption by spilling blood, peace draws out the blood of violence.

LUCIUS' SERVANT (Sc. 8; 31 lines): any but Timon, Steward, Timon's Servants, Servants of Varro, Titus, Hortensius and Philotus
FIRST STRANGER (Sc. 6; 30 lines): any but Timon's Servants, Sempronius, another Stranger
OLD MAN (Sc. 1; 29 lines): any but Timon, Apemantus, Alcibiades, Timon's Servants, Lords, Poet, Painter, Merchant, Jeweller, Lucilius, Messenger(s)
SERVILIUS (Timon's Second Servant; 28 lines): a Senator *or* Soldier; a Stranger; Lucullus' Servant; a Thief
FOOL (Sc. 4; 21 lines): any but Timon, Apemantus, Steward, Lords, 1 and 2 Senators, Caphis, Varro's and Isidore's Servants
CAPHIS (20 lines): any but Timon, Alcibiades, Apemantus, Steward, Fool, Page, 1 Senator, Isidore's Servant, Varro's First Servant
MESSENGER(S) (two separately in Sc. 1, one in Sc. 17; 20 lines): any but Timon, Apemantus, Alcibiades, Lords, Senators, Timon's Servants, Poet, Painter, Jeweller, Merchant, Lucilius, Soldier
SOLDIER (15 lines): any but Alcibiades, Senators, Messenger (Sc. 17)
TITUS' SERVANT (15 lines): any but Timon, Steward, Timon's Servants, Servants of Varro, Hortensius and Philotus
JEWELLER (Sc. 1; 12 lines): any but Timon, Apemantus, Alcibiades, Lucilius, Timon's Servants, Lords, Poet, Painter, Merchant, Old Man, Messenger(s)
FIRST THIEF (11 lines): any but Timon, Apemantus, Steward, another Thief
MERCHANT (Sc. 1; 11 lines): any but Timon, Apemantus, Alcibiades, Lucilius, Timon's Servants, Lords, Poet, Painter, Jeweller, Old Man, Messenger(s)
HORTENSIUS' SERVANT (10 lines): any but Timon, Steward, Timon's Servants, Servants of Varro, Titus and Philotus
TIMON'S THIRD SERVANT (10 lines): Lucullus' Servant, a Thief, Soldier
VENTIDIUS (Sc. 1; 9 lines): any but Timon, Alcibiades, Apemantus, Steward, Timon's Servants, Lords
VARRO'S FIRST SERVANT (8 lines): any but Timon, Alcibiades, Apemantus, Steward, Fool, Page, Caphis, Varro's Second Servant, Servants of Isidore, Lucius, Titus, Hortensius, and Philotus, Flaminius, Timon's Third Servant
ISIDORE'S SERVANT (7 lines): any but Caphis, Varro's First Servant
SECOND STRANGER (Sc. 6; 7 lines): any but Timon's Servants, Sempronius, another Stranger
PHILOTUS' SERVANT (6 lines): any but Timon, Steward, Timon's Servants, Servants of Varro, Titus, and Hortensius
THIRD THIEF (6 lines): any but Timon, Apemantus, Steward, another Thief
VARRO'S SECOND SERVANT (6 lines): any but Timon, Steward, Timon's Servants, Varro's First Servant, Servants of Titus, Hortensius, and Philotus
LUCILIUS (Sc. 1; 5 lines): any but Timon, Apemantus, Alcibiades, Timon's Servants, Lords, Poet, Painter, Merchant, Jeweller, Old Man, Messenger(s)
SECOND THIEF (5 lines): any but Timon, Apemantus, Steward, another Thief
THIRD SENATOR (4 lines): any but Timon, Alcibiades, Apemantus, Steward, Flaminius, [Timon's other Servants], Lords, other Senators, Soldier, Messenger
FOURTH LORD (Sc. 11; 3 lines): any but Timon, Alcibiades, [Timon's Servants], other Lords, [1–3] Senators
LUCULLUS' SERVANT (Sc. 5; 3 lines): any but Timon, Steward, Flaminius, Lucullus
FOURTH SENATOR (1 line): any but Timon, [Alcibiades], Apemantus, Steward, [Timon's Servants], [Lords], other Senators, Soldier, Messenger (Sc. 17)
THIRD STRANGER (Sc. 6; 1 line): any but Timon's Servants, Sempronius, another Stranger

Boys

PAGE (Sc. 4; 7 lines): Cupid *or* a Lady; Phrynia *or* Timandra
CUPID (Sc. 2; 6 lines): Page; Phrynia *or* Timandra
TIMANDRA (Sc. 14; 4 lines): Page; Cupid *or* a Lady
PHRYNIA (Sc. 14; 1 line): Page; Cupid *or* a Lady
LADIES (in the masque, Sc. 2; 1 line): Page; Phrynia *or* Timandra

Most crowded scene: Sc. 1: about 13 speaking roles (+ mute Mercer, Senators, and horsemen)

THE PURITAN WIDOW *or* THE PURITAN *or* THE WIDOW OF WATLING STREET

Edited by Donna B. Hamilton

IN *The Puritan Widow* nearly every character is an object of Middleton's satire. The Widow and her daughters want money, influence, and autonomy, and men too if men will facilitate these other projects; the citizen scholar George Pieboard, finding the world inhospitable to learning, turns his wit to the manipulation and deceit of others; and the nobleman 'from the court' who denounces the women for choosing unworthy husbands orders them to marry three knights whose base motives and shallow worth Middleton has also already exposed. But however unrelenting and comprehensive the play's satire, the main targets are Puritans and Catholics.

Catholics, or 'Romanists', were people who adhered to the beliefs and practices in place prior to the Protestant Reformation. They revered images, followed the rituals of seven sacraments, believed that good deeds were efficacious for salvation, and believed that the Pope in Rome (not a secular ruler) was the head of the church. Puritans were those Protestants who, discontent with the degree to which England had broken from Rome, continued to agitate to one degree or another for further reform to liturgical practices and even church government.

These issues are full of implication, not just for assessing the satire of *The Puritan Widow*, but also for identifying Middleton ideologically, and even for developing a secure sense of the Middleton canon. A case in point is the position that Margot Heinemann took in regard to Middleton's authorship of *The Puritan Widow*. The play, usually dated late 1606, was identified, in 1607, on the title-page of the first printed edition as having been written by 'W. S.'; the play was included in the Shakespeare folios of 1664 and 1685. No modern scholar thinks that Shakespeare was the author. Although a majority of scholars have, for more than a century, assigned the play to Middleton, Heinemann challenged that attribution on the grounds that it satirizes moderate Puritans, a stance she found to be inconceivable for Middleton. More recently, N. W. Bawcutt has argued that Middleton's persistent satire of Puritans might well provide our best evidence that the label 'Puritan' is not a satisfactory one for Middleton himself.

An alternative to that line of inquiry resides in locating the historical circumstances of 1606–7 that made all Puritanism, and especially its more extreme forms, subject to attack. Early in James I's reign, two sets of events conspired to become the shaping circumstances for Protestant politics and rhetoric: the Gunpowder Plot and the institution of an oath of allegiance directed at Catholics. Prior to the Gunpowder Plot, it had only been clear that the focus of James I's ecclesiastical policy would be to ensure a continuation of Elizabeth I's hard line on conformity. Following the Hampton Court Conference, 12–18 January 1604, a deadline of 30 November 1604 was established for ministers to subscribe to the new Canons. Deprivations of some eighty non-subscribing Protestant ministers followed in 1605. Then, on 5 November 1605, the Jesuit attempt to blow up King and Parliament was discovered, an event that refocused the attention of the nation on Catholics as the common enemy. In reaction, the 1605 session of Parliament passed four statutes: an act to declare 5 November an annual day of thanksgiving, an act to punish those involved in the Plot, and two acts setting forth measures for 'discovering and repressing' and 'avoiding the dangers that may grow by' popish recusants.

Included in these statutes was a provision requiring Catholics to take an oath of allegiance in which they swore loyalty to the king as their temporal ruler and swore that the pope did not possess a power to depose temporal rulers. Published on 25 June 1606, this oath prompted a reply in the form of a breve or letter from Pope Paul V, in which he ordered English Catholics not to take the oath. When George Blackwell, head of the English Catholics, countered by taking the oath and advising others to do the same, the Pope repeated, in a breve dated 23 August 1607, his first order. This sequence of events touched off an international paper war which ran for more than a decade, and which prompted James I to write at such length defending the oath that ultimately those writings would comprise nearly three-quarters of his corpus of political writing.

Whatever the long-range effect of the Plot and the oath, the immediate effect was to produce an increased sense of the need for solidarity among Protestants. Religious dissenters tended to fall silent, and even those who opposed James I on other issues defended his position on the Plot and the oath. One aspect of that defence was the publication, in 1606, of the account of the trial of Father Henry Garnet, the chief suspect in the Plot. Another aspect involved the reprinting of old books, as well as the production of new books, which defined England's anti-Catholicism. A Latin edition of John Jewel's *Apology, or Answer in Defence of the Church of England* (not printed since 1599), was reissued in 1606. James I's first work on the oath, *Triplici nodo, triplex cuneus, or an Apologie for the oath of allegiance*, was published in 1607. In 1609,

James I reissued his *Apology for the oath of allegiance*, along with a lengthy preface entitled, *A premonition to all most mighty monarchs*; other works included Lancelot Andrewes's *Tortura torti* (1609), William Barlow's *Answer to a Catholic Englishman* (1609), and John Donne's *Pseudo-martyr* (1610). There also appeared new editions of John Foxe's *Acts and monuments* (1610) and of Spenser's *Faerie Queene* (1609). Because literary scholars have tended to pay more attention to the Gunpowder Plot than the oath of allegiance, their lists of literary works associated with the Plot often exclude by default any acknowledgement that those texts may have a broader frame of reference. Works in that category include John Fletcher's *Philaster* (1609), Shakespeare's *Cymbeline* (1610), and Ben Jonson's *Catiline* (1611), all written in the wake of James I's second round of writing on the oath.

Also belonging to this group are Thomas Dekker's *Whore of Babylon* and Middleton's *The Puritan Widow*, both of which were printed in 1607. As sometime collaborators and as writers whose livelihood depended on their ability to capture the contemporary moment, Middleton and Dekker have much in common. In their responses to the Plot and the oath controversy, however, they took advantage of different rhetorical options. Dekker replicated the traditional anti-Catholic narrative encapsulated in Protestant readings of Revelation, depicting—as had Foxe in *Acts and Monuments* and Spenser in Book 1 of *The Faerie Queene*—the Roman church as the Whore of Babylon, who usurps the power and place of true religion. In her discussion of *The Whore of Babylon* as a Gunpowder Plot play, Julia Gasper has emphasized its representation of James I as a militant king protecting the church against Antichrist.

Middleton chose a different approach. He invented for *The Puritan Widow* a plot that associated Catholic practices with Puritan practices. This technique for demonizing both groups had been popular with the conformist church establishment and had been adopted by James I, who disliked the challenges that Puritan reform interests posed to hierarchy. After the Gunpowder Plot, a time when solidarity among Protestants was popular, this technique could be used to present the implications of the Catholic threat with unusual economy.

Examples from the writings of James I can illustrate how this rhetoric of association worked. Aiming to construct the conformist position as the broad and inclusive centre, James I had, beginning in *Basilikon Doron* (1599), represented nonconformity as a monolithic group of Puritan extremists and, at the same time, associated them with papists. Puritan and papist together thus became the extremes that should be avoided. In *Basilikon Doron*, reprinted at the time of his accession, he had described Puritans as the 'very pests in the church and commonweal, whom ... neither oaths or promises bind', and warned his son to beware of 'both the extremities' that currently existed within the English church, 'as well as ye repress the vain Puritan, so not to suffer proud Papal Bishops'. In 1604, at the Hampton Court Conference, he linked Puritan and papist in his statement on the need to operate the ecclesiastical court of High Commission in those dioceses that had 'the most troublesome and refractory persons, either Papists or Puritans'. In his first speech to Parliament, March 1604, he distinguished the true and lawful religion from two other sorts, those 'called Catholics, but truly Papists' and those he would 'call a sect rather than Religion ... the Puritans and Novelists'. These attitudes continued in his writings on the oath of allegiance, where, in the *Premonition*, he declared that the 'Jesuits are nothing but Puritan-papists'.

Such constructions could at times be offensive and threatening to Puritans who sought further church reform. Indeed during the 1580s and 1590s, when Archbishop John Whitgift and Richard Bancroft were putting together the machinery to repress dissent in the church, some felt that reforming Protestants were in greater danger from the state than Catholic recusants. The renewed Catholic threat represented by the Gunpowder Plot, however, created a rhetorical situation in which a broader range of Protestants placed a higher value on representing themselves as united.

In *The Puritan Widow*, Middleton plays to this developing consensus by taking the rhetoric one step beyond merely associating puritan and papist. Satire in *The Puritan Widow* consists of conflating the two, of literalizing the identification of one with the other, a system whereby Middleton manages, in the same actions, to satirize Puritans while also representing those Catholic practices which Protestants most abhorred. Especially important to this method is his defining all Puritans by the characteristics of those who were most extreme.

The details in the play that most quickly confirm this aspect of his strategy are the names Middleton gives to the servingmen, Nicholas St Antlings and Simon St Mary Overies, as Baldwin Maxwell pointed out some time ago. In these characters' surnames, Middleton names two parishes which, as Paul Seaver has shown, had acquired reputations for radicalism in religion. St Antholin's, on Watling Street within sight of St Paul's Cathedral, was described by William Dugdale as 'the grand nursery whence most of the seditious preachers were after sent abroad throughout England to poison the people with their antimonarchical principles'. Nicholas St Antlings also shares a name with Nicholas Felton, the minister at St Antholin's, 1592–1617, whose services were known as having been conducted in Genevan (that is, presbyterian) fashion. Additionally, the church had a long-established and well-endowed lectureship, by means of which the church could hire lecturers independently of whatever candidate it might receive by virtue of the system of advowson, whereby a patron controlled the parochial living.

The second parish represented in the name of one of the play's characters is St Mary Overie, also known as St Saviour's (and since 1905, as Southwark Cathedral), a parish located not far from the Globe. In 1604, one of its lecturers was Edmund Snape, a presbyterian nonconformist, who was forced out of St Saviour's when the Bishop of Winchester refused to give him a preaching licence. William Symonds, whose last name reappears in Middleton's Simon St Mary Overies, was appointed at St Saviour's in 1605, and cited for nonconformity in 1606; apparently, he then conformed. John Trundle, who also preached at St Saviour's, remained obstinate and refused to conform; in 1608, he would be found preaching to Brownists.

In Middleton's satiric portrait, Puritans are fools and hypocrites; self-righteous about their holiness, they are driven by lust, deceit, materialism, and self-interest. The Widow's former husband may have attended church dutifully, but he also made a career of cheating heirs of their inheritances. Similarly, servant Nicholas insists that he could never stoop to 'steal' Sir Godfrey's gold chain, but, he equivocates, he is quite willing to 'nim', or filch, it. Organizing these characters' overriding materialism around this nimming event, Middleton plays ironically on the equivocating style for which the Jesuit 'plotters' had become so well known. He also plays on the spiritual symbolism of a gold chain. In works belonging to the *catena* tradition—such as the frequently reprinted *The Golden Chain* (1591) by the well-known Calvinist theologian William Perkins—the chain was used metaphorically for the way to salvation. These Puritans, however, seek only for lost jewellery.

Through the intrigue surrounding the chain, Middleton develops two other aspects of his play, each of which allows him to sharpen the attack against Puritans while at the same time taking a broad swipe at Catholics. The first of these involves the presence and activities of Corporal Oath; the second involves the conjuring scene in the Widow's private house.

Admittedly, there is more than one way in which oaths are at issue in *The Puritan Widow*; in the exaggerated self-consciousness with which characters swear without using the name of God, the play refers to the passage in May 1606 of the Act to Restrain Abuses, which forbade players that licence. But the presence of Corporal Oath also introduces the matter of a 'corporal oath', an oath which is sworn with the hand touching a sacred object or the Bible. The 1606 oath of allegiance, the oath *ex officio mero*, and the oath of supremacy were all corporal oaths. In use in England until 1641, the oath *ex officio* was the first step in trials held in the ecclesiastical court of High Commission. This oath required defendants to swear to answer all questions truthfully prior to being told of what they were accused. In so far as this oath provided for self-incrimination, it became a chief means for entrapping religious dissenters, whether Catholic or Protestant. During the 1580s and 1590s, Protestant opposition to the oath had taken various forms, including refusal to take it, a step that made it impossible for the ecclesiastical trial to proceed. Looked at from the point of view of Protestant dissenters, the oath *ex officio* was a powerful symbol of the oppressive tactics of a too-powerful Protestant church hierarchy and of church courts that had overstepped their jurisdiction. From another point of view, the oath *ex officio*, inasmuch as the nonconformists had organized so much of their cause in opposition to it, had come virtually to represent the lengths to which dissenters would go to avoid proper obedience and uniformity. James I signalled his impatience with such opposition in his reference to Puritans as 'pests ... whom ... neither oaths or promises bind' and in his insistence, at the Hampton Court Conference, that the oath *ex officio mero* be retained for use on both Puritans and Catholics.

In *The Puritan Widow*, Corporal Oath is 'a vainglorious fellow'; Simon St Mary Overies and Nicholas St Antlings are dismayed at having to deal with him. As Nicholas explains, 'You are the man that we are forbidden to keep company withal' (1.3.1–2). Contemptuous of Nicholas for his obviously Puritan ways, Corporal Oath declares that it is within his skill to get the guilty Captain Idle out of prison. All he needs to succeed is a little help from Nicholas, Idle's cousin. In this combination of actions, wherein Middleton mocks the Puritan's fastidiousness about oaths, as well as his willingness to collude with Corporal Oath to get someone out of prison, Middleton represents Puritans as contemptuous both of the oath *ex officio* and of the court system that put dissenters in prison. But the situation of Catholics is represented as well, for by the date of the play, the oath of allegiance was being asked of Catholics, who, if they refused, were also subject to the oath *ex officio*. In fact, to represent a corporal oath on stage at this point in time, just after the oath of allegiance had been instituted, would seem to make this recent oath the first referent, and thus itself a means of making the very strong satiric link between Puritan and Catholic.

The conjuring scene in the Puritan Widow's house offers a similarly conflated satire against both Puritans and Catholics. The conjuring itself gives the scene—at least from the perspective of a seventeenth-century Protestant—a Catholic cast, for one of the central principles of Protestant attacks on the Roman church had been the accusation that Roman beliefs in exorcism and in eucharistic transubstantiation were nothing but hocus-pocus, practices that counterfeited magic and that the English church had rightfully eliminated. By having Captain Idle and George Piebord take up conjuring in the home of a Puritan, Middleton mocks Catholic practices, associates Puritans with Catholic practices, and constructs Puritan households as places inhabited by extremists like the well-known Puritan exorcist John Darrell, whom Richard Bancroft, Bishop of London, and his chaplain Samuel Harsnett had tried by the High Commission in 1598. Moreover, by having Sir Godfrey decide that the best place to conjure will be in the 'private house' of the Widow, Middleton also represents another distinguishing feature of English religious dissident movements. As Christopher Haigh has emphasized, Catholic priests often lived with

Catholic gentry, who worshipped in the private chapels of their country houses. Dissident Protestants also used private houses for worship and meetings.

Beginning especially in the 1570s, Protestants interested in further reform had fostered various means of providing the kinds of practices for worship—including preaching and opportunities for discussion and debate—that the reform movements favoured. These practices, as described by Patrick Collinson, proceeded under the labels of 'prophesyings', 'classes', 'fasts', and 'conventicles', none of which is a self-explanatory term. 'Prophesyings' (which had nothing to do with 'prophet' or 'prophecy') were public meetings for the education of clergy, intended to assist clergy in their ability to expound scripture and involved discussion of a series of sermons preached on a single text. In 1576, Queen Elizabeth had expressed her dislike of preaching by ordering Archbishop Grindal to suppress prophesying; his protest of this policy led to his being suspended from his archepiscopal powers. The *classis* movement was another name for the presbyterian movement, which focused its reform effort on replacing the episcopacy with a system that would foster parity among ministers. The 'classes' were clandestine meetings of local clergy sympathetic to such reform; a highly organized and widespread practice, classes were often held in someone's private house. (Edmund Snape, also of St Saviour's, had been a leader of the Northampton *classis*.) 'Fasts' were opportunities for fasting, but were sometimes held so as to disguise the continuation during these fasts of both prophesyings and classes. 'Conventicles' were any illegal private religious meeting. The church hierarchy viewed such meetings as subversive. In 1584, twenty-four articles, developed by Whitgift to assist the High Commissioners who were empowered to seek out nonconforming ministers (and reprinted by Strype), included interrogatories concerning whether 'you have used private conferences, and assembled or been present at conventicles' and 'taken upon you to preach, read or expound the Scriptures as well in public places as in private houses'. In 1593, Parliament passed a bill forbidding conventicles, and the Canons of 1604 (reprinted by Bullard) included the orders that 'No minister shall preach, or administer the holy communion, in any private house, except it be in times of necessity.'

In *The Puritan Widow*, Middleton represents Puritans as people who listen to the counterfeit fortune-teller Pieboard 'prophesy' (3.5.221) and who gather in a private house where they are taken in by counterfeit conjuring. This representation not only characterizes Puritans as those who take part in forbidden activities, but characterizes the activities as embarrassingly foolish, as the practices of people from whom most people would want to dissociate. This dramatization of utter foolishness is perhaps the distinguishing mark of Middleton's satire in this play, extending to many scenes not discussed here. One related detail that we might pause over, however, is Pieboard's convincing the Widow that her Puritan husband is in purgatory, a preposterous notion for her to accept, given that Protestants regarded purgatory as the chief fiction of Roman Catholicism, invented by the pope to increase his power and extort money from the people. But in *The Puritan Widow*, the identification of Puritan with papist knows no limit.

Because the Children of Paul's are not known to have played anything after their performance of *The Puritan Widow*, W. Reavley Gair has speculated that this satiric representation of Puritans contributed to the company's final demise, sometime after 6 July 1606. Contrary to E. K. Chambers who puts the end of Paul's Boys in July 1606, Gair considers that a particular objection to the play, a Puritan attack on the stage that cited *The Puritan Widow*, contributed to the end of Paul's Boys. Preaching at Paul's Cross on 14 February 1608, the moderate Puritan minister William Crashaw denounced 'ungodly plays and interludes' for bringing 'religion and holy things upon the stage' and for having represented 'hypocrites' by way of the names Nicholas St Antlings and Simon St Mary Overies, 'names of two churches of God'.

Leaving the precise date of the end of the company aside, the entire situation may have been more complex and somewhat different than these hypotheses suggest. First, Crashaw's sermon itself was written partly in response to the Gunpowder Plot (he speaks of the plotter Henry Garnet, who had been executed by hanging in Paul's churchyard) and in support of James I's reaction to it; listing the 'twenty wounds found to be in the body of the present Romish religion', Crashaw calls on 'all the kings and princes of the Christian world' to follow the 'example of the King and Prince of Great Britain, to hate the whore and make her desolate'. Important for our purposes is Crashaw's eagerness to position himself on the side of right, but also to take pains to defend the more extreme Puritans who were now especially under attack. Thus, he goes to the defence of St Antholin's and St Mary Overie, a move we may understand as an attempt to reset the edge of the margins. *His* extremists are not papists and Puritans, but papists and Brownists.

Second, his complaint against the play includes the charge that it brought 'religion and holy things upon the stage', a complaint that surely was motivated in part by the fact that the play's representation of religion is so farcically funny. However, there is nothing exclusively Puritan in Crashaw's complaint. To the contrary, that complaint had often been the position of religious authority, of whatever stripe, in regard to the stage, and especially at moments of heightened religious tension or controversy. In 1589, it had been Whitgift and Bancroft, reacting to the playing of Martin Marprelate on the stage, who had decreed that players were not to stage 'matters of divinity'. Nervous even about representations that satirized their opposition, they tried to shut down all playing of church affairs. As Chambers emphasized, that situation probably caused the demise of Paul's Boys after 1590. In 1599, when Whitgift and Bancroft silenced the satirists, they ended the career of Thomas Nashe (who had earlier written against Marprelate on their behalf); they also ordered Middleton's *Microcynicon* to be burned. The circumstances of 1606 and 1607 were similarly anxious moments for a church hierarchy already bent on holding the line on religious diversity, and made nervous by the Jesuit plotters. In such a context, satire on matters of divinity might have seemed particularly threatening, especially if an attack against Catholics hit also the very Protestants whom the establishment was trying to bring to heel. A threat of reprisal or actual reprisal against the author or players of such a play is not inconceivable. But whether or not the potential for reprisal was activated, *The Puritan Widow* stands as another example of Middleton playing with the limits of the possible, politically and theatrically.

SEE ALSO

Textual introduction and apparatus: *Companion*, 540
Authorship and date: *Companion*, 358

The Puritan Widow

[*for the Children of Paul's*]

THE PERSONS OF THE PLAY

WIDOW Lady Plus, a citizen's widow
FRANK, MOLL } her two daughters
EDMUND, son to the Widow Plus
SIR GODFREY, brother-in-law to the Widow Plus
George PIEBOARD, a scholar and a citizen
Peter SKIRMISH, an old soldier
CAPTAIN Idle, a highwayman
CORPORAL Oath, a vainglorious fellow
NICHOLAS St Antlings, SIMON St Mary Overies, FRAILTY } servingmen to the Widow Plus
Sir Oliver MUCKHILL, a suitor to the Widow Plus
Sir John PENNYDUB, a suitor to Moll
Sir Andrew TIPSTAFF, a suitor to Frank
SHERIFF of London
PUTTOCK, RAVENSHAW } two of the sheriff's serjeants
DOGSON, a yeoman
GENTLEMAN
NOBLEMAN
Two knights
SERVANT
Prison KEEPER
Officers
Musicians

1.1 *Incipit Actus Primus*
Enter the Lady Widow Plus, her two daughters Frank and Moll, her husband's brother an old knight Sir Godfrey, with her son and heir Master Edmond, all in mourning apparel, Edmond in a cypress hat. The Widow wringing her hands, and bursting out into a passion, as newly come from the burial of her husband

WIDOW O that ever I was born, that ever I was born.

SIR GODFREY Nay, good sister, dear sister, sweet sister, be of good comfort. Show yourself a woman, now or never.

WIDOW O, I have lost the dearest man. I have buried the sweetest husband that ever lay by woman.

SIR GODFREY Nay, give him his due. He was indeed an honest, virtuous, discreet wise man. He was my brother, as right, as right.

WIDOW O, I shall never forget him, never forget him. He was a man so well given to a woman—O.

SIR GODFREY Nay, but kind sister, I could weep as much as any woman, but alas our tears cannot call him again. Methinks you are well read sister, and know that death is as common as *Homo* a common name to all men. A

1.1.0.6 **cypress** fabric imported from Cyprus and used as a hat band in sign of mourning

man shall be taken when he's making water. Nay, did not the learned parson Master Pigman tell us even now that all flesh is frail, we are born to die, man has but a time—with suchlike deep and profound persuasions, as he is a rare fellow you know and an excellent reader. And, for example (as there are examples abundance), did not Sir Humphrey Bubble die t'other day? There's a lusty widow. Why, she cried not above half an hour, for shame, for shame. Then followed him old Master Fulsome, the usurer. There's a wise widow. Why, she cried ne'er a whit at all.

WIDOW O rank not me with those wicked women. I had a husband out-shined 'em all.

SIR GODFREY Ay, that he did i'faith, he out-shined 'em all.

WIDOW [*to Edmond*] Dost thou stand there and see us all weep and not once shed a tear for thy father's death? O thou ungracious son and heir, thou.

EDMOND Troth, Mother, I should not weep, I'm sure. I am past a child, I hope, to make all my old school fellows laugh at me. I should be mocked, so I should. Pray, let one of my sisters weep for me. I'll laugh as much for her another time.

WIDOW O thou past-grace thou, out of my sight, thou graceless imp. Thou grievest me more than the death of thy father. O thou stubborn only son, hadst thou such an honest man to thy father that would deceive all the world to get riches for thee, and canst thou not afford a little salt water? He that so wisely did quite overthrow the right heir of those lands, which now you respect not, up every morning betwixt four and five so duly at Westminster Hall every term-time, with all his cards and writings, for thee thou wicked Absalom—O dear husband.

EDMOND Weep, quoth a? I protest I am glad he's churched, for now he's gone I shall spend in quiet.

FRANK
Dear mother, pray cease. Half your tears suffice.
'Tis time for you to take truce with your eyes.
Let me weep now.

WIDOW O such a dear knight, such a sweet husband have I lost, have I lost. If blessed be the corpse the rain rains upon, he had it pouring down.

SIR GODFREY Sister, be of good cheer. We are all mortal ourselves. I come upon you freshly, I ne'er speak without comfort, hear me what I shall say. My brother has left you wealthy. You're rich.

WIDOW O.

SIR GODFREY I say you're rich. You are also fair.

WIDOW O.

SIR GODFREY Go to, you're fair, you cannot smother it, beauty will come to light. Nor are your years so far entered with you but that you will be sought after and may very well answer another husband. The world is full of fine gallants, choice enough, sister. For what should we do with all our knights, I pray, but to marry rich widows, wealthy citizens' widows, lusty fair-browed ladies? Go to, be of good comfort, I say. Leave snobbing and weeping. Yet my brother was a kind-hearted man.—[*Aside*] I would not have the elf see me now.—Come, pluck up a woman's heart. Here stands your daughters, who be well-estated and at maturity will also be inquired after with good husbands. So all these tears shall be soon dried up and a better world than ever. What, woman, you must not weep still. He's dead, he's buried.—[*Aside*] Yet I cannot choose but weep for him.

WIDOW
Marry again? No, let me be buried quick then.
And that same part of choir whereon I tread
To such intent, O may it be my grave,
And that the priest may turn his wedding prayers,
E'en with a breath, to funeral dust and ashes.
O out of a million of millions, I should ne'er find such a husband. He was unmatchable, unmatchable. Nothing was too hot nor too dear for me. I could not speak of that one thing that I had not. Beside, I had keys of all, kept all, received all, had money in my purse, spent what I would, went abroad when I would, came home when I would, and did all what I would. O my sweet husband, I shall never have the like.

SIR GODFREY Sister, ne'er say so. He was an honest brother of mine, and so, and you may light upon one as honest again, or one as honest again may light upon you, that's the properer phrase indeed.

WIDOW
Never. O, if you love me, urge it not,
[*She kneels*]
O, may I be the by-word of the world,
The common talk at table in the mouth
Of every groom and waiter, if e'er more
I entertain the carnal suit of man.

MOLL [*she kneels*]
(*Aside*) I must kneel down for fashion, too.

45 **term-time** a term during which law courts are in session
cards small sheets of paper; maps; charts
46 **Absalom** rebelled against his father David in 2 Samuel
48 **churched** received some rite of the church, here burial, with pun also on 'churched' as the ceremony (set forth in the Book of Common Prayer and to which nonconformists objected) whereby a woman who had given birth was ceremonially 'cleansed' upon returning to church following childbirth
54–5 **blessed...upon** proverbial
68 **all our knights** the standard joke referring to King James's having created a large number of knights
71 **snobbing** sobbing
72 **elf** poor devil
74 **well-estated** possessed of 'means' or property
81 **choir** the upper or eastern part of the church, appropriated to the singers and to the use of those who officiate in the services and separated from other parts by a railing or screen
87 **too hot nor too dear** too difficult of attainment (proverbial)
94, 95 **light upon** chance upon; also bawdy, referring to male in superior position

FRANK [*she kneels*]
(*Aside*) And I, whom never man as yet hath scaled,
E'en in this depth of general sorrow, vow
Never to marry to sustain such loss
As a dear husband seems to be once dead.
[*Mother and daughters rise*]

MOLL (*aside*)
I loved my father well too, but to say,
Nay, vow I would not marry for his death,
Sure I should speak false Latin, should I not?
I'd as soon vow never to come in bed.
Tut, women must live by th' quick and not by th' dead.

WIDOW [*drawing out her husband's picture*]
Dear copy of my husband, O let me kiss thee.
How like him is this model. This brief picture
Quickens my tears. My sorrows are renewed
At this fresh sight.

SIR GODFREY Sister.

WIDOW Away,
All honesty with him is turned to clay,
O my sweet husband, O.

FRANK My dear father.

Exeunt [*Widow*] *and Frank*

MOLL [*aside*] Here's a puling indeed. I think my mother weeps for all the women that ever buried husbands, for if from time to time all the widows' tears in England had been bottled up, I do not think all would have filled a three-half-penny bottle. Alas, a small matter bucks a handkerchief, and sometimes the spittle stands to nigh St Thomas à Waterings. Well, I can mourn in good sober sort as well as another. But where I spend one tear for a dead father, I could give twenty kisses for a quick husband. *Exit*

SIR GODFREY [*aside*] Well, go thy ways old Sir Godfrey, and thou mayst be proud on't. Thou hast a kind loving sister-in-law. How constant, how passionate, how full of April the poor soul's eyes are. Well, I would my brother knew on't. He should then know what a kind wife he had left behind him. Truth an 'twere not for shame that the neighbours at the next garden should hear me, between joy and grief, I should e'en cry outright. *Exit*

EDMOND So, a fair riddance. My father's laid in dust. His coffin and he is like a whole meat pie, and the worms will cut him up shortly. Farewell, old Dad, farewell. I'll be curbed in no more, I. I perceive a son and heir may quickly be made a fool an he will be one, but I'll take another order. Now she would have me weep for him forsooth, and why? Because he cozened the right heir, being a fool, and bestowed those lands upon me his eldest son, and therefore I must weep for him. Ha, ha. Why, all the world knows, as long as 'twas his pleasure to get me, 'twas his duty to get for me. I know the law in that point, no attorney can gull me. Well, my uncle is an old ass and an admirable coxcomb. I'll rule the roost myself, I'll be kept under no more. I know what I may do well enough by my father's copy. The law's in mine own hands now. Nay, now I know my strength, I'll be strong enough for my mother, I warrant you. *Exit*

Enter George Pieboard, a scholar and a citizen, and unto him an old soldier, Peter Skirmish 1.2

PIEBOARD What's to be done now, old lad of war, thou that wert wont to be as hot as a turn-spit, as nimble as a fencer, and as lousy as a schoolmaster, now thou art put to silence like a sectary? War sits now like a justice of peace and does nothing. Where be your muskets, calivers and hotshots? In Long Lane, at pawn, at pawn.

103 **scaled** mounted
112 **copy** picture
118 **puling** feeble wailing; weak querulousness
122 **bucks** soaks
123 **spittle** saliva, with pun on spittle ('spital' or 'hospital') as place for the reception of the indigent or diseased. The saliva reaches almost to St Thomas à Waterings; or, the hospital for the poor is too close to St Thomas à Waterings.
124 **Thomas à Waterings** a spittle in Southwark
130–1 **full of April** full of showers of tears
140–1 **take another order** pursue another course
142 **cozened** cheated
148 **admirable coxcomb** conceited fool
rule the roost have full sway or authority
150 **by my father's copy** with my inheritance of my father's holdings by copy or copyhold (copy being a species of estate at will, or customary estate in England, the only visible title to which consists of the copies of the court rolls, which are made out by the steward of the manor)
1.2.0.1 ***Pieboard*** named after George Peele, the words 'peele' and 'pieboard' being two words for the spadelike implement used for removing bread, pies, and other baking from a baker's oven. Pieboard's two schemes (played out in 3.3 and 3.4, and in 3.4 and 4.2) have analogues in Jests 2 and 11, in Peele's *The Merry Conceited Jests of George Peele*, entered in the Stationers' Register on 14 December 1605, and printed 1607. Because analogues to the jests can be found in other sources, and because there is also the possibility that Middleton saw *Jests* in manuscript, *Jests* itself does not add definitively to an ability to date the play more precisely than 1606. For summaries of the jests as they occur in Peele, see notes to 3.3.92–5, and 3.5.22–8.
a scholar and a citizen like George Peele, who was both a scholar of Oxford and a citizen of London by patrimony from his father
2 **turn-spit** one who turns the roasting spit; also a term of contempt
3 **lousy** infested by lice
4 **put to silence like a sectary** 'Sectary' was a term commonly applied by the church hierarchy to protestant dissenters (nonconformists as well as separatists) that emphasized their setting themselves apart from (sectioning themselves off from) conformists. On 10 April 1593, Parliament passed a bill providing that 'seditious sectaries' who 'dispute the queen's authority in Ecclesiastical Cases...or attend unlawful Conventicles' be treated as harshly as Catholic recusants. The Canons of 1604 took a similarly harsh position.
5–6 **muskets, calivers and hotshots** portable firearms listed in descending order according to weight. The 'hotshot', or 'harquebus', had the most rapid fire.
6 **Long Lane** a street in London running east from the north-east corner of West Smithfield, a place of fights and executions, and occupied by pawnbrokers, old-clothes dealers, a cattle market, and Bartholomew Fair

Now keys are your only guns, key-guns, key-guns, and bawds the gunners, who are your sentinels in peace and stand ready charged to give warning with hems, hums, and pocky coughs. Only your chambers are licensed to play upon you, and drabs enough to give fire to 'em.

SKIRMISH Well, I cannot tell, but I am sure it goes wrong with me, for since the cessure of the wars, I have spent above a hundred crowns out o' purse. I have been a soldier anytime this forty years, and now I perceive an old soldier and an old courtier have both one destiny, and, in the end, turn both into hobnails.

PIEBOARD Pretty mystery for a beggar, for indeed a hobnail is the true emblem of a beggar's shoe sole.

SKIRMISH I will not say but that war is a blood-sucker, and so, but in my conscience (as there is no soldier but has a piece of one, though it be full of holes like a shot ensign, no matter, 'twill serve to swear by) in my conscience, I think some kind of peace has more hidden oppressions and violent heady sins (though looking of a gentle nature) than a professed war.

PIEBOARD Troth, and for mine own part, I am a poor gentleman and a scholar. I have been matriculated in the university, wore out six gowns there, seen some fools and some scholars, some of the city and some of the country, kept order, went bare-headed over the quadrangle, eat my commons with a good stomach, and battelled with discretion. At last, having done many sleights and tricks to maintain my wit in use (as my brain would never endure me to be idle), I was expelled the university only for stealing a cheese out of Jesus College.

SKIRMISH Is't possible?

PIEBOARD O there was one Welshman, God forgive him, pursued it hard and never left till I turned my staff toward London, where, when I came, all my friends were pit-holed, gone to graves, as indeed there was but a few left before. Then was I turned to my wits to shift in the world, to tower among sons and heirs, and fools and gulls, and ladies' eldest sons, to work upon nothing, to feed out of flint, and ever since has my belly been much beholding to my brain. But now, to return to you, old Skirmish, I say as you say, and for my part wish a turbulency in the world, for I have nothing to lose but my wits, and I think they are as mad as they will be. And to strengthen your argument the more, I say an honest war is better than a bawdy peace as touching my profession. The multiplicity of scholars hatched and nourished in the idle calms of peace makes 'em like fishes, one devour another. And the community of learning has so played upon affections, and thereby almost religion is come about to fantasy and discredited by being too much spoken of in so many and mean mouths. I myself, being a scholar and a graduate, have no other comfort by my learning but the affliction of my words, to know how scholar-like to name what I want, and can call myself a beggar both in Greek and Latin. And therefore, not to cog with peace, I'll not be afraid to say, 'tis a great breeder but a barren nourisher, a great getter of children, which must either be thieves or rich men, knaves or beggars.

SKIRMISH Well, would I had been born a knave then when I was born a beggar. For if the truth were known, I think I was begot when my father had never a penny in his purse.

PIEBOARD Puh, faint not, old Skirmish. Let this warrant thee, *facilis descensus Averni*, 'tis an easy journey to a knave. Thou may'st be a knave when thou wilt, and peace is a good madam to all other professions and an arrant drab to us. Let us handle her accordingly, and by our wits thrive in despite of her. For since the law lives by quarrels, the courtier by smooth Godmorrows, and every profession makes itself greater by imperfections, why not we then by shifts, wiles, and forgeries? And seeing our brains are our only patrimonies, let's spend with judgement, not like a desperate son and heir, but like a sober and discreet Templar, one that will never march beyond the bounds of his allowance. And for our thriving means, thus, I myself will put on the deceit of a fortune-teller, a fortune-teller.

SKIRMISH Very proper.

7 **key-guns** small pistols disguised in the form of a key; also, 'key' and 'gun' mean 'penis', puns that appear in some of the names of Southwark brothels—Cross Keys and the Gun—listed in John Stow's *Survey of London* (1598).
8 **sentinels** those who keep guard like military sentinels
10 **pocky coughs** coughs of people infected with the pox, or syphilis
chambers ordnance used to fire salutes; male or female servants; male or female genitalia.
11 **drabs** prostitutes
13 **cessure** end
17 **hobnails** nails with massive heads used for protecting the soles of heavy shoes; *fig.* persons of low means
23 **ensign** flag; flag bearer
32 **quadrangle** identifies the university as Oxford, the usual term at Cambridge being 'court'. Going 'bare-headed over the quadrangle' marks Pieboard as a student of humble status. Middleton matriculated from Queen's College, Oxford, the date of his subscription being 7 April 1598.
commons rations, allowance of victuals
33 **battelled** was supplied with provisions from the college kitchen and buttery, being one of three grades of students at Oxford (a poor child, a servitor, and a batteler) who did not pay for commons. A batteler was partly self-supporting.
36–9 **Jesus College . . . Welshman** Jesus College, Oxford, was founded by Queen Elizabeth as a result of a petition by Dr Hugh Price, of Brecon, in 1571, who wished to bestow his estate for the maintenance of scholars from Wales.
42 **pit-holed** laid in the grave, buried
44 **to tower** to achieve, compete, stand out
46 **feed out of flint** to get something out of nothing, as in 'to wring water from a flint'
61 **want** lack
63 **cog with** flatter; dissemble
72 ***facilis descensus Averni*** *Aeneid* 6.126, the descent to the lower world is easy
82 **Templar** an Inns of Court man
84 **thriving means** means of thriving

PIEBOARD And you of a figure-caster or a conjuror.

SKIRMISH A conjuror.

PIEBOARD Let me alone. I'll instruct you and teach you to deceive all eyes but the devil's.

SKIRMISH O ay, for I would not deceive him an I could choose of all others.

PIEBOARD Fear not, I warrant you, and so by those means we shall help one another to patients, as the condition of the age affords creatures enough for cunning to work upon.

SKIRMISH O wondrous new fools and fresh asses.

PIEBOARD O fit, fit, excellent.

SKIRMISH What, in the name of conjuring?

PIEBOARD My memory greets me happily with an admirable subject to graze upon, the Lady Widow, who of late I saw weeping in her garden for the death of her husband. Sure sh'as but a waterish soul, and half on't by this time is dropped out of her eyes. Device well-managed may do good upon her. It stands firm, my first practise shall be there.

SKIRMISH You have my voice, George.

PIEBOARD She's a grey gull to her brother, a fool to her only son, and an ape to her youngest daughter. I overheard 'em severally, and from their words I'll derive my device. And thou, old Peter Skirmish, shall be my second in all sleights.

SKIRMISH Ne'er doubt me, George Pieboard, only you must teach me to conjure.

PIEBOARD Puh, I'll perfect thee, Peter.

Enter Captain Idle, pinioned and with a guard of Officers, passeth over the stage

How now? What's he?

SKIRMISH O George, this sight kills me. 'Tis my sworn brother, Captain Idle.

PIEBOARD Captain Idle.

SKIRMISH Apprehended for some felonious act or other. He has started out, he's made a night on't, lacked silver. I cannot but commend his resolution. He would not pawn his buff jerkin. I would either some of us were employed or might pitch our tents at usurers' doors to kill the slaves as they peep out at the wicket.

PIEBOARD Indeed, those are our ancient enemies. They keep our money in their hands and make us to be hanged for robbing of 'em. But come, let's follow after to the prison and know the nature of his offence, and what we can stead him in he shall be sure of. And I'll uphold it still that a charitable knave is better than a soothing puritan. *Exeunt*

Enter at one door Corporal Oath, a vainglorious fellow, and at the other, three of the Widow Puritan's servingmen, Nicholas St Antlings, Simon St Mary Overies, and Frailty, in black scurvy mourning coats and books at their girdles, as coming from church. They meet. 1.3

NICHOLAS What, Corporal Oath? I am sorry we have met with you next our hearts. You are the man that we are forbidden to keep company withal. We must not swear, I can tell you, and you have the name for swearing.

SIMON Ay, Corporal Oath, I would you would do so much as forsake us, sir. We cannot abide you, we must not be seen in your company.

FRAILTY There is none of us, I can tell you, but shall be soundly whipped for swearing.

CORPORAL Why, how now, we three, puritanical scrape-shoes, flesh o' good Fridays, a hand.

SIMON, FRAILTY, *and* NICHOLAS O.

87 **figure-caster** a pretender to astrology ('figure' is a horoscope)
conjuror A statute passed by Parliament in 1604 forbade conjuration and witchcraft (see 3.5.134–5, and 3.4 and 4.2 *passim*).

103 **waterish soul** enfeebled judgement

108 **grey gull** old fool

110 **severally** one after another

115.1 ***pinioned*** disabled by having the arms bound; shackled

121 **started out... made a night on't** cant phrases for 'robbed on the highway'

123 **buff jerkin** leather jacket. To refuse to pawn it was to be ready to fight for a livelihood if there was no other way to gain one.

125 **wicket** small door or gate in or beside a larger one

130 **stead** assist

131 **soothing** pacifying, flattering, hypocritical

1.3.0.3 ***Nicholas St Antlings*** St Antholin's, a church on Watling Street not far from St Paul's Cathedral, known as a puritan stronghold and for religious radicalism. Nicholas Felton was the minister, 1592–1617.

0.3–4 ***Simon St Mary Overies*** St Mary Overie (meaning over the Rie, or over the river), later St Saviour's, located in Southwark east from the Bishop of Winchester's house and not far from the Globe and some prisons, had, like St Antholin's, a reputation for permitting religious radicalism. One of its lecturers was William Symonds, cited for nonconformity in 1606.

0.4 ***scurvy*** shabby

0.5 ***books at their girdles*** Bibles at their belts

1 **Corporal Oath** A 'corporal oath' is any oath—oath of supremacy, oath of allegiance, oath *ex officio*, etc.—sworn with the hand touching a sacred object or the Bible.

1–2 **I am sorry we have met with you next our hearts** That we have met up with you will weigh on our consciences.

3 **We must not swear** The 1606 Act of Abuses forbade players in a play, Maygame or pageant to use the name of God jestingly or prophanely. Also, nonconformists, when arrested and questioned, routinely refused at the outset of the proceeding to take the oath *ex officio*, which would have sworn them to answer all questions, including those which would be self-incriminating.

10 **we three** a catch phrase in drama of the period. Two of the 'three' are manifest fools, and the third, the victim of a jest or an onlooker, is included in that category by the 'we'

10–11 **scrape-shoes** scrape is an awkward bow or salutation in which the foot is drawn backward on the ground

11 **flesh o' good Fridays** some puritans regarded as popish the practice of not eating meat on Fridays

CORPORAL Why, Nicholas St Antlings, Simon St Mary Overies, has the de'il possessed you, that you swear no better? You half-christened catamites, you ungodmothered varlets, does the first lesson teach you to be proud, and the second to be coxcombs, proud coxcombs, not once to do duty to a man of mark?

FRAILTY A man of mark, quoth a. I do not think he can show a beggar's noble.

CORPORAL A corporal, a commander, one of spirit, that is able to blow you up all dry with your books at your girdles.

SIMON We are not taught to believe that, sir, for we know the breath of man is weak.

Corporal breathes upon Frailty

FRAILTY Foh, you lie, Nicholas, for here's one strong enough. Blow us up, quoth a, he may well blow me above twelve score off o' him. I warrant, if the wind stood right, a man might smell him from the top of Newgate to the leads of Ludgate.

CORPORAL Sirrah, thou hollow book of wax candle.

NICHOLAS Ay, you may say what you will, so you swear not.

CORPORAL I swear by the—

NICHOLAS Hold, hold, good Corporal Oath, for if you swear once, we shall all fall down in a swoon presently.

CORPORAL I must and will swear, you quivering coxcombs. My captain is imprisoned, and by Vulcan's leather codpiece point—

NICHOLAS O Simon, what an oath was there.

FRAILTY If he should chance to break it, the poor man's breeches would fall down about his heels, for Venus allows him but one point to his hose.

CORPORAL With these my bully feet, I will thump ope' the prison doors and brain the keeper with the begging box, but I'll set my honest sweet Captain Idle at liberty.

NICHOLAS How, Captain Idle, my old aunt's son, my dear kinsman, in cappadochio?

CORPORAL Ay, thou church-peeling, thou holy-paring, religious outside thou. If thou hadst any grace in thee, thou wouldst visit him, relieve him, swear to get him out.

NICHOLAS Assure you, corporal, indeed la, 'tis the first time I heard on't.

CORPORAL Why, do't now then, marmoset. Bring forth thy yearly wages, let not a commander perish.

SIMON But if he be one of the wicked, he shall perish.

NICHOLAS Well, corporal, I'll e'en along with you to visit my kinsman. If I can do him any good, I will, but I have nothing for him. Simon St Mary Overies and Frailty, pray make a lie for me to the knight, my master, old Sir Godfrey.

CORPORAL A lie? May you lie then?

FRAILTY O ay, we may lie, but we must not swear.

SIMON True, we may lie with our neighbour's wife, but we must not swear we did so.

CORPORAL O an excellent tag of religion.

NICHOLAS O Simon, I have thought upon a sound excuse. It will go current. Say that I am gone to a fast.

SIMON To a fast, very good.

NICHOLAS Ay, to a fast, say, with Master Fullbelly, the minister.

SIMON Master Fullbelly? An honest man. He feeds the flock well, for he's an excellent feeder.

[Exeunt] Corporal [and] Nicholas

FRAILTY O ay, I have seen him eat up a whole pig and afterward fall to the pettitoes. *[Exeunt] Simon and Frailty*

1.4

The prison Marshalsea. Enter Captain Idle at one door, George Pieboard and old soldier Skirmish speaking within at another door

PIEBOARD Pray, turn the key.

15 **catamites** young men kept for sexual purposes; derives from the Latin Catamitus, a corrupt form of Ganymedes, name of Jupiter's cupbearer whom Jupiter kept for sexual purposes

15–16 **ungodmothered** Nonconformist baptismal practice objected to some of the provisions for baptism specified in the Book of Common Prayer, such as the use of the sign of the cross in baptism, private baptism, and godparents being asked to represent themselves as the voice of the child in taking the baptismal vows. Thus, the 24 Articles had queried whether a minister had 'not used the interrogatories to the godfathers and godmothers, in the name of the infant' as dictated by the Book of Common Prayer.

18–20 **a man of mark... a beggar's noble** a pun on mark, meaning distinction, and mark, a sum of money. A noble was a coin; a 'beggar's noble', a farthing.

22 **blow you up all dry** destroy without bloodshed

30 **Newgate to the leads of Ludgate** two gates in the western wall of London. Ludgate had a flat leaded roof.

31 **book of wax candle** rolls of candle wax coiled up in the form of a book

38–9 **Vulcan's leather codpiece point** a codpiece is an appendage to the front of the hose (or breeches); a point is a tagged lace or cord of yarn, silk, or leather, for attaching the hose to the doublet.

42–3 **Venus allows... one point to his hose** The goddess of love has given him only one lace to hold up his breeches.

44 **bully** epithet expressing admiring familiarity

45 **begging box** almsbox on prison grounds for the benefit of prisoners

48 **cappadochio** cant name for prison. Cappadocia was an ancient kingdom of Asia Minor, known for its slaves.

55 **marmoset** a small monkey; also a term of abuse or contempt

67 **tag** an automatically repeated or overused phrase

69 **go current** be acceptable
fast Although fasting was commonly practised in the English church, its unauthorized use was regarded suspiciously because fasting could also be used as a cover for other practices, including prophesyings and conventicles. Canon 72 in the Canons of 1604 ordered 'Ministers not to appoint public or private Fasts or Prophecies, or to Exorcise, but by authority;' see also 1.2.84–7; 3.5.134–5, 139, and Introduction.

74 **feeder** eater, parasite

76 **pettitoes** pig's trotters

1.4.0.1 ***Marshalsea*** a prison in Southwark, on Borough High Street and not far from St Mary Overie, connected with the Court of the King's Marshal, and used as a prison for debtors and persons charged with contempt of the Courts of the Marshal, the King's Palace, and the Admiralty

SKIRMISH Turn the key, I pray.

CAPTAIN Who should those be? I almost know their voices.

[Pieboard and Skirmish] entering

O my friends, you're welcome to a smelling room here. You newly took leave of the air. Is't not a strange savour?

PIEBOARD
As all prisons have smells of sundry wretches
Who, though departed, leave their scents behind 'em.
By gold, captain, I am sincerely sorry for thee.

CAPTAIN By my troth, George, I thank thee, but pish, what must be must be.

SKIRMISH Captain, what do you lie in for? Is't great? What's your offence?

CAPTAIN Faith, my offence is ordinary, common, a highway. And I fear me my penalty will be ordinary and common too, a halter.

PIEBOARD
Nay, prophesy not so ill. It shall go hard,
But I'll shift for thy life.

CAPTAIN Whether I live or die, thou'rt an honest George. I'll tell you, silver flowed not with me as it had done, for now the tide runs to bawds and flatterers. I had a start out and by chance set upon a fat steward, thinking his purse had been as pursy as his body. And the slave had about him but the poor purchase of ten groats, notwithstanding being descried, pursued, and taken. I know the law is so grim in respect of many desperate unsettled soldiers that I fear me I shall dance after their pipe for't.

SKIRMISH I am twice sorry for you, captain, first, that your purchase was so small and, now, that your danger is so great.

CAPTAIN Push! The worst is but death. Ha' you a pipe of tobacco about you?

SKIRMISH I think I have thereabouts about me.

Captain blows a pipe

CAPTAIN Here's a clean gentleman too to receive.

PIEBOARD [*aside*]
Well, I must cast about, some happy sleight.
Work brain, that ever didst thy master right.

Corporal and Nicholas [speak from] within

CORPORAL Keeper, let the key be turned.

NICHOLAS Ay, I pray, master keeper, give's a cast of your office.

[Enter Corporal and Nicholas]

CAPTAIN How now, more visitants? What, Corporal Oath?

PIEBOARD *and* SKIRMISH Corporal.

CORPORAL In prison, honest captain? This must not be.

NICHOLAS How do you, captain kinsman?

CAPTAIN [*to Corporal*] Good coxcomb, what makes that pure, starched fool here?

NICHOLAS [*to Captain*] You see, kinsman, I am somewhat bold to call in and see how you do. I heard you were safe enough, and I was very glad on't that it was no worse.

CAPTAIN
This is a double torture now. This fool by th' book
Does vex me more than my imprisonment.
What meant you, corporal, to hook him hither?

CORPORAL
Who he? He shall relieve thee and supply thee.
I'll make him do't.

CAPTAIN Fie, what vain breath you spend.
He supply? I'll sooner expect mercy from a usurer when my bond's forfeited, sooner kindness from a lawyer when my money's spent, nay, sooner charity from the devil than good from a puritan. I'll look for relief from him when Lucifer is restored to his blood and in heaven again.

NICHOLAS [*aside*] I warrant my kinsman's talking of me, for my left ear burns most tyrannically.

PIEBOARD Captain Idle, what's he there? He looks like a monkey upward and a crane downward.

CAPTAIN Pshaw, a foolish cousin of mine. I must thank God for him.

PIEBOARD Why, the better subject to work a 'scape upon. Thou shalt e'en change clothes with him and leave him here, and so.

CAPTAIN Push, I published him e'en now to my corporal. He will be damned ere he do me so much good. Why, I know a more proper, a more handsome device than that if the slave would be sociable. [*To Nicholas*] Now, goodman fleer-face.

NICHOLAS [*aside*] O my cousin begins to speak to me now. I shall be acquainted with him again, I hope.

SKIRMISH [*to Captain*] Look, what ridiculous raptures take hold of his wrinkles.

PIEBOARD Then, what say you to this device, a happy one, captain?

CAPTAIN Speak low, George, prison rats have wider ears than those in malt-lofts.

NICHOLAS [*to Captain*] Cousin, if it lay in my power, as they say, to do.

4 **smelling** stinking
18 **shift for** contrive on behalf of
21–2 **had a start out** went to rob on the highway
23 **pursy** fat
24 **purchase** theft, plunder
groats coins worth four pence
25 **descried** perceived from a distance
27 **dance** slang for how a felon appears hanging from the gallows
27–8 **after their pipe** to their tune; i.e. incur the same punishment
32 **Push!** an exclamation of disdain, as in 'Pish!' or 'Tush!'
34.1 ***blows*** smokes
35 **clean gentleman** clean pipe
39–40 **cast of your office** example of your authority
46 **starched** formal and precise
51 **by th' book** formulaic, constrained behaviour
60 **restored to his blood** restored to his former place of dignity in heaven among obedient spirits
71 **published** described
75 **fleer-face** mocking, sneering face
78–9 **ridiculous raptures . . . wrinkles** Compare the description of the puritan Malvolio in Shakespeare, *Twelfth Night*, 3.2.74–75: 'He does smile his face into more lines than is in the new map with the augmentation of the Indies'.
83 **malt-lofts** where prepared malt is stored

CAPTAIN [*to Nicholas*] 'Twould do me an exceeding pleasure indeed that. Ne'er talk farther on't. [*To the Corporal*] The fool will be hanged ere he do't.

CORPORAL Pox, I'll thump 'im to't.

PIEBOARD [*to Captain*] Why, do but try the fopster and break it to him bluntly.

CAPTAIN [*to Pieboard*] And so my disgrace will dwell in his jaws, an the slave slaver out our purpose to his master, for would I were but as sure on't as I am sure he will deny to do't.

NICHOLAS [*to Captain*] I would be heartily glad, cousin, if any of my friendships, as they say, might stand, ah.

PIEBOARD [*to Captain*] Why, you see he offers his friendship foolishly to you already.

CAPTAIN Ay, that's the hell on't. I would he would offer it wisely.

NICHOLAS Verily, and indeed la, cousin.

CAPTAIN [*to Nicholas*] I have took note of thy fleers a good while. If thou art minded to do me good—as thou gapst upon me comfortably and givst me charitable faces, which indeed is but a fashion in you all that are puritans—wilt soon at night steal me thy master's chain?

NICHOLAS O, I shall swoon.

PIEBOARD Corporal, he starts already.

CAPTAIN [*to Nicholas*] I know it to be worth three hundred crowns, and with the half of that I can buy my life at a broker's at second hand, which now lies in pawn to the law. If this thou refuse to do, being easy and nothing dangerous, in that thou art held in good opinion of thy master, why 'tis a palpable argument thou holdst my life at no price, and these thy broken and unjointed offers are but only created in thy lip, now born, and now buried, foolish breath only. What, wilt do't? Shall I look for happiness in thy answer?

NICHOLAS Steal my master's chain, quoth a? No, it shall ne'er be said that Nicholas St Antling's committed birdlime.

CAPTAIN Nay, I told you as much, did I not? Though he be a puritan, yet he will be a true man.

NICHOLAS Why, cousin, you know 'tis written, thou shalt not steal.

CAPTAIN Why, and fool, thou shalt love thy neighbour and help him in extremities.

NICHOLAS Mass, I think it be indeed. In what chapter's that, cousin?

CAPTAIN Why, in the first of Charity, the second verse.

NICHOLAS The first of Charity, quoth a. That's a good jest, there's no such chapter in my book.

CAPTAIN No, I knew 'twas torn out of thy book, and that makes so little in thy heart.

PIEBOARD [*taking Nicholas aside*] Come, let me tell you, you're too unkind a kinsman, i'faith, the captain loving you so dearly, ay, like the pomewater of his eye, and you to be so uncomfortable, fie, fie.

NICHOLAS Pray, do not wish me to be hanged. Anything else that I can do, had it been to rob, I would ha' done't, but I must not steal. That's the word the literal, thou shalt not steal. And would you wish me to steal then?

PIEBOARD No, faith, that were too much, to speak truth. Why, wilt thou nim it from him?

NICHOLAS That I will.

PIEBOARD Why, enough, bully, he shall be content with that, or he shall ha' none. Let me alone with him now. [*To Captain*] Captain, I ha' dealt with your kinsman in a corner, a good, kind-natured fellow, methinks. Go to, you shall not have all your own asking, you shall bate somewhat on't. He is not contented absolutely, as you would say, to steal the chain from him, but to do you a pleasure, he will nim it from him.

NICHOLAS Ay, that I will, cousin.

CAPTAIN Well, seeing he will do no more, as far as I see, I must be contented with that.

CORPORAL [*aside*] Here's no notable gullery.

PIEBOARD [*to Nicholas*] Nay, I'll come nearer to you, gentleman, because we'll have only but a help and a mirth on't. The knight shall not lose his chain neither, but it shall be only laid out of the way some one or two days.

NICHOLAS Ay, that would be good indeed, kinsman.

PIEBOARD For I have a farther reach to profit us better by the missing on't only, than if we had it outright, as my discourse shall make it known to you. When thou hast the chain, do but convey it out at backdoor into the garden, and there hang it close in the rosemary bank

90 **fopster** fool
93 **slaver** utter in a fawning, flattering manner
105 **comfortably** comfortingly
108 **chain** ornament worn around the neck
123 **birdlime** a glutinous substance spread upon twigs, by which birds may be caught and held fast; slang for stealing
126–9 **shalt not steal . . . shalt love thy neighbour . . . extremities** Nicholas and Captain cite, respectively, the seventh and ninth of the Ten Commandments, the Captain embellishing his with 'help him in extremities'.
139 **pomewater** large juicy kind of apple
143 **That's the word the literal** That's exactly what the Bible says and means.
146 **nim** steal, filch
152 **bate** reduce, abate
160 **come nearer to you** meet halfway
166 **reach** project
167 **the missing on't** the missing of it (see textual note to 1.2.103–4)
170 **close** hidden

but for a small season. And by that harmless device, I know how to wind Captain Idle out of prison, the knight thy master shall get his pardon and release him, and he satisfy thy master with his own chain and wondrous thanks on both hands.

NICHOLAS That were rare indeed la. Pray, let me know how.

PIEBOARD Nay, 'tis very necessary thou shouldst know because thou must be employed as an actor.

NICHOLAS An actor? O no, that's a player, and our parson rails against players mightily, I can tell you, because they brought him drunk upo'th' stage once, as he will be horribly drunk.

CORPORAL Mass, I cannot blame him then, poor church spout.

PIEBOARD Why, as an intermeddler then.

NICHOLAS Ay, that, that.

PIEBOARD Give me audience then. When the old knight thy master has raged his fill for the loss of the chain, tell him thou hast a kinsman in prison of such exquisite art that the devil himself is French lackey to him and runs bare-headed by his horse belly (when he has one), whom he will cause with most Irish dexterity to fetch his chain, though 'twere hid under a mine of seacoal, and ne'er make spade or pickaxe his instruments. Tell him but this, with farther instructions thou shalt receive from me, and thou show'st thyself a kinsman indeed.

CORPORAL A dainty bully.

SKIRMISH An honest bookkeeper.

CAPTAIN And my three-times-thrice-honey cousin.

NICHOLAS Nay, grace of God, I'll rob him on't suddenly and hang it in the rosemary bank. But I bear that mind, cousin, I would not steal anything methinks for mine own father.

SKIRMISH He bears a good mind in that, captain.

PIEBOARD Why, well said. He begins to be an honest fellow, faith.

CORPORAL In troth he does.

NICHOLAS You see, cousin, I am willing to do you any kindness, always saving myself harmless.

CAPTAIN Why, I thank thee. Fare thee well. I shall requite it. *Exit Nicholas*

CORPORAL 'Twill be good for thee, captain, that thou hast such an egregious ass to thy cousin.

CAPTAIN
Ay, is he not a fine fool, corporal?
But, George, thou talkst of art and conjuring.
How shall that be?

PIEBOARD Puh, be't not in your care.
Leave that to me and my directions.
Well, captain, doubt not thy delivery now,
E'en with the vantage, man, to gain by prison,
As my thoughts prompt me. Hold on brain and plot.
I aim at many cunning far events,
All which I doubt not but to hit at length.
I'll to the Widow with a quaint assault.
Captain, be merry.

CAPTAIN Who, I? Kerry, merry, buff jerkin.

PIEBOARD O, I am happy in more sleights, and one will knit strong in another. Corporal Oath—

CORPORAL Ho, bully.

PIEBOARD And thou old Peter Skirmish—I have a necessary task for you both.

SKIRMISH Lay't upon, George Pieboard.

CORPORAL What e'er it be, we'll manage it.

PIEBOARD I would have you two maintain a quarrel before the Lady Widow's door and draw your swords i'th' edge of the evening. Clash a little, clash, clash.

CORPORAL Fuh.
Let us alone to make our blades ring noon
Though it be after supper.

PIEBOARD Know you can.
And out of that false fire, I doubt not but to raise strange belief. And, captain, to countenance my device the better and grace my words to the widow, I have a good plain satin suit that I had of a young reveller t'other night, for words pass not regarded nowadays unless they come from a good suit of clothes, which the fates and my wits have bestowed upon me. Well, Captain Idle, if I did not highly love thee, I would ne'er

171 **that harmless device** This jest of Pieboard's has an analogue in Jest 11 of George Peele's *The Merrie Conceited Jests of George Peele*, in which Peele, accompanying his friends to an Oxford commencement and running out of money, hides the rapier and dagger of a companion, and then, borrowing from the same companion, goes to Oxford and returns with a scholar, 'one of the rarest men in England,' who sets about divining the location of the lost possessions, which, as all search for them, George himself then locates. An analogue to this trick is also described in Reginald Scot's *The discovery of witchcraft* (1584), where the trick is described as being used for finding a stolen horse. Scot's book denounced witchcraft as a popish device aimed at deceiving the public and making the clergy rich.

180–2 **our parson ... stage** the stock characterization of the drunk cleric (here used against a puritan, but also used conventionally in criticisms of bishops, monks, popes, etc.) combined with a reference to clerics who declaimed against theatre practices. Puritan ministers usually objected to playing on Sundays and to the bear-baiting held in the theatres. In 1589, the conformist church establishment, in an effort to cope with the Marprelate controversy, sought to have all 'matters of divinity' excluded from stage plays.

185 **spout** one who speaks at length without much matter

186 **intermeddler** intermediary

191 **French lackey** a lackey is a hanger-on; 'French' is usually associated with venereal disease.

192 **bare-headed** a symptom of syphilis
horse belly horse's belly

193 **Irish dexterity** an allusion to the Irish running footmen employed by many nobles; as in 'Away they ran like Irish lackeys' (*Black Book* 516–7).

194 **seacoal** ordinary, mineral coal as opposed to charcoal

200 **cousin** kinsman

220 **vantage** advantage

224 **quaint** cunning, crafty; vagina

226 **Kerry, merry, buff jerkin** kerry-merry-buff is a kind of blow or buffet; running on, Idle adds 'jerkin'

be seen within twelve score of a prison, for, I protest, at this instant, I walk in great danger of small debts. I owe money to several hostesses, and you know such Jills will quickly be upon a man's Jack.

CAPTAIN True, George.

PIEBOARD Fare thee well, captain. Come, corporal and ensign, thou shalt hear more news next time we greet thee.

CORPORAL More news, ay, by yon Bear at Bridgefoot in heaven, shalt thou. *Exeunt [all but Captain]*

CAPTAIN
Enough, my friends, farewell.
This prison shows as if ghosts did part in hell. [*Exit*]

Finis Actus Primus

❁

2.1 *Incipit Actus Secundus*

Enter Moll, youngest daughter to the Widow, alone

MOLL Not marry? Forswear marriage? Why, all women know 'tis as honourable a thing as to lie with a man, and I, to spite my sister's vow the more, have entertained a suitor already, a fine gallant knight of the last feather. He says he will coach me too, and well appoint me, allow me money to dice withal, and many such pleasing protestations he sticks upon my lips. Indeed, his short-winded father i'th' country is wondrous wealthy, a most abominable farmer. And therefore he may do't in time. Troth, I'll venture upon him. Women are not without ways enough to help themselves. If he prove wise and good as his word, why I shall love him and use him kindly, and if he prove an ass, why in a quarter of an hour's warning I can transform him into an ox. There comes in my relief again.

Enter Frailty

FRAILTY O Mistress Moll, Mistress Moll.

MOLL How now, what's the news?

FRAILTY The knight, your suitor, Sir John Pennydub.

MOLL Sir John Pennydub? Where, where?

FRAILTY He's walking in the gallery.

MOLL Has my mother seen him yet?

FRAILTY O no, she's spitting in the kitchen.

MOLL
Direct him hither softly, good Frailty.
I'll meet him halfway.

FRAILTY That's just like running a tilt, but I hope he'll break nothing this time. [*Exit Frailty*]

MOLL 'Tis happiness my mother saw him not.

Enter Sir John Pennydub

O we'come, good Sir John.

PENNYDUB I thank you, faith. Nay, you must stand me till I kiss you. 'Tis the fashion everywhere i'faith, and I came from court e'en now.

MOLL Nay, the fates forfend that I should anger the fashion.

PENNYDUB Then, not forgetting the sweet of new ceremonies, I first fall back, then recovering myself, make my honour to your lip thus, and then accost it. (*Kissing [Moll]*)

MOLL Trust me, very pretty and moving. You're worthy on't sir.

[Enter] Widow and Sir Godfrey

O my mother, my mother, now she's here, we'll steal into the gallery. *Exeunt [Moll and Pennydub]*

SIR GODFREY Nay, sister, let reason rule you, do not play the fool, stand not in your own light. You have wealthy offers, large tenderings. Do not withstand your good fortune. Who comes a wooing to you, I pray? No small fool. A rich knight o'th' city, Sir Oliver Muckhill, no small fool I can tell you. And furthermore, as I heard late by your maidservants (as your maidservants will say to me anything, I thank 'em) both your daughters are not without suitors, ay, and worthy ones too. One a brisk courtier, Sir Andrew Tipstaff, suitor afar off to your eldest daughter, and the third a huge wealthy farmer's son, a fine young country knight. They call him Sir John Pennydub, a good name. Marry, he may have it coined when he lacks money. What blessings are these, sister?

WIDOW Tempt me not, Satan.

SIR GODFREY Satan? Do I look like Satan? I hope the devil's not so old as I, I trow.

WIDOW
You wound my senses, brother, when you name
A suitor to me. O, I cannot abide it.
I take in poison when I hear one named.

248 **twelve score** twelve score yards
251 **Jills** women
Jack coat of mail; buff jacket or jerkin; penis
256–7 **Bear at Bridgefoot in heaven** Bear in heaven is a constellation; Bear at Bridgefoot was a tavern at the end of London Bridge. Corporal has his private name for the constellation, calling it after the tavern.
2.1.4–5 **of the last feather** of the latest fashion
5 **coach me** buy me a coach
6 **appoint** equip, fit out
7 **protestations** assertions
7–8 **sticks upon my lips** pledges himself, with kisses, to perform
9 **abominable** offensive, preposterously large
10 **do't** keep his word
10–11 **venture upon him** bet on him
15 **ox** a castrated bull used for draught purposes; cuckold
19 **Sir John Pennydub** the first of three knights in this scene, each suing for marriage. Their names satirize knighthood at a point in time when much was being made of James's having knighted so many. 'Pennydub' suggests the knight purchased his title. 'Tipstaff' is suggestive of a court bailiff or his staff, which was tipped with iron; also phallic. 'Muckhill' suggests a pile of dirt or excrement.
21 **gallery** a corridor or long room for exhibiting paintings and walking
23 **spitting** crying
30 **stand me** stand still for me; give me an erection
33 **forfend** forbid
35 **sweet** the culmination
37 **accost** approach; solicit a woman for sex

Enter Simon

How now, Simon? Where's my son Edmond?

SIMON Verily, madam, he is at vain exercise, dripping in the tennis court. *[Exit Simon]*

WIDOW At tennis court? O now his father's gone, I shall have no rule with him. O wicked Edmond, I might well compare this with the prophecy in the Chronicle, though far inferior. As Harry of Monmouth won all, and Harry of Windsor lost all, so Edmond of Bristow that was the father got all, and Edmond of London that's his son now will spend all.

SIR GODFREY Peace, sister, we'll have him reformed. There's hope on him yet, though it be but a little.

Enter Frailty

FRAILTY Forsooth, madam, there are two or three archers at door would very gladly speak with your ladyship.

WIDOW Archers?

SIR GODFREY Your husband's fletcher, I warrant.

WIDOW O
Let them come near. They bring home things of his.
Troth, I should ha' forgot 'em. How now?
Villain, which be those archers?

Enter the suitors Sir Andrew Tipstaff, Sir Oliver Muckhill, and Pennydub

FRAILTY Why, do you not see 'em before you? Are not these archers? What do you call 'em? Shooters? Shooters and archers are all one, I hope.

WIDOW Out, ignorant slave.

MUCKHILL Nay, pray be patient, lady,
We come in way of honourable love.

TIPSTAFF *and* PENNYDUB
We do.

MUCKHILL
To you.

TIPSTAFF *and* PENNYDUB
And to your daughters.

WIDOW O why will you offer me this, gentlemen? Indeed, I will not look upon you. When the tears are scarce out of mine eyes, not yet washed off from my cheeks, and my dear husband's body scarce so cold as the coffin, what reason have you to offer it? I am not like some of your widows that will bury one in the evening, and be sure to another ere morning. Pray, away. Pray, take your answers, good knights, an you be sweet knights. I have vowed never to marry, and so have my daughters too.

PENNYDUB *(aside)* Ay, two of you have, but the third's a good wench.

MUCKHILL Lady, a shrewd answer, marry. The best is, 'tis but the first, and he's a blunt wooer that will leave for one sharp answer.

TIPSTAFF Where be your daughters, lady? I hope they'll give us better encouragements.

WIDOW Indeed, they'll answer you so. Tak't a' my word, they'll give you the very same answer *verbatim*, truly la.

PENNYDUB *(aside)* Mum, Moll's a good wench still. I know what she'll do.

MUCKHILL Well, lady, for this time we'll take our leaves, hoping for better comfort.

WIDOW O never, never, an I live these thousand years. An you be good knights, do not hope. 'Twill be all vain, vain. Look you, put off all your suits an you come to me again. *[Exeunt Pennydub and Tipstaff]*

FRAILTY Put off all their suits, quoth a? Ay, that's the best wooing of a widow indeed, when a man's nonsuited, that is, when he's a bed with her.

Going out, Muckhill and Sir Godfrey

MUCKHILL Sir Godfrey, here's twenty angels more. Work hard for me. There's life in't yet.

SIR GODFREY Fear not, Sir Oliver Muckhill, I'll stick close for you. Leave all with me. *Exit Muckhill*

Enter George Pieboard, the scholar

PIEBOARD By your leave, Lady Widow.

WIDOW What, another suitor now?

PIEBOARD A suitor? No, I protest, lady, if you'd give me yourself, I'd not be troubled with you.

WIDOW Say you so, sir, then you're the better welcome, sir.

PIEBOARD Nay, heaven bless me from a widow unless I were sure to bury her speedily.

WIDOW Good bluntness. Well, your business, sir.

PIEBOARD Very needful if you were in private once.

WIDOW Needful? Brother, pray leave us, and you, sir. *[Exit Sir Godfrey]*

FRAILTY *[aside]* I should laugh now if this blunt fellow should put 'em all beside the stirrup and vault into the saddle himself. I have seen as mad a trick. *Exit Frailty*

WIDOW Now, sir, here's none but we.

Enter daughters Frank and Moll

Daughters forebear.

PIEBOARD O no, pray let 'em stay, for what I have to speak importeth equally to them as to you.

WIDOW Then you may stay.

PIEBOARD
I pray, bestow on me a serious ear,
For what I speak is full of weight and fear.

65 **dripping** sweating
69 **prophecy in the Chronicle** The chronicles of Grafton, Hall, and Holinshed record the prophecy that Harry of Monmouth, Henry V, victor of Agincourt and conqueror of Normandy, would win all, and that his son Harry of Windsor, Henry VI, would lose all.
71 **Bristow** Bristol
79 **fletcher** one who makes or sells arrows; an archer
85 **Shooters** one who shoots with a bow or firearms. 'Shooters' puns on 'suitors', with sexual innuendo similar to 'guns' (1.2.7).
97 **sure** betrothed
117 **suits** wooing
122 **angels** gold coins valued at 10 shillings
132 **bless me from** protect me from

WIDOW
Fear?

PIEBOARD
Ay,
If't pass unregarded and uneffected.
Else, peace and joy. I pray, attention.
Widow, I have been a mere stranger for these parts that you live in, nor did I ever know the husband of you and father of them, but I truly know by certain spiritual intelligence that he is in purgatory.

WIDOW Purgatory? Tuh, that word deserves to be spit upon. I wonder that a man of sober tongue as you seem to be should have the folly to believe there's such a place.

PIEBOARD Well, lady, in cold blood I speak it. I assure you that there is a purgatory in which place I know your husband to reside and wherein he is like to remain till the dissolution of the world, till the last general bonfire, when all the earth shall melt into nothing and the seas scald their finny labourers. So long is his abidance, unless you alter the property of your purpose, together with each of your daughters theirs, that is, the purpose of single life in yourself and your eldest daughter, and the speedy determination of marriage in your youngest.

MOLL [*aside*] How knows he that? What, has some devil told him?

WIDOW [*aside*] Strange he should know our thoughts.— Why, but daughter, have you purposed speedy marriage?

PIEBOARD You see she tells you 'ay', for she says nothing. Nay, give me credit as you please. I am a stranger to you, and yet you see I know your determinations, which must come to me metaphysically and by a supernatural intelligence.

WIDOW This puts amazement on me.

FRANK [*aside*] Know our secrets?

MOLL [*aside*] I'd thought to steal a marriage. Would his tongue had dropped out when he blabbed it.

WIDOW But, sir, my husband was too honest a dealing man to be now in any purgatories.

PIEBOARD
O do not load your conscience with untruths.
'Tis but mere folly now to gild 'em o'er
That has passed but for copper. Praises here
Cannot unbind him there. Confess but truth.
I know he got his wealth with a hard gripe,
O hardly, hardly.

WIDOW [*aside*]
This is most strange of all. How knows he that?

PIEBOARD
He would eat fools and ignorant heirs clean up,
And had his drink from many a poor man's brow,
E'en as their labour brewed it.
He would scrape riches to him most unjustly.
The very dirt between his nails was ill-got,
And not his own. O, I groan to speak on't.
The thought makes me shudder, shudder.

WIDOW [*aside*] It quakes me too, now I think on't.—Sir, I am much grieved that you, a stranger, should so deeply wrong my dead husband.

PIEBOARD O.

WIDOW A man that would keep church so duly, rise early before his servants, and e'en for religious haste go ungartered, unbuttoned, nay, sir-reverence, untrussed, to morning prayer.

PIEBOARD O uff.

WIDOW Dine quickly upon high days, and when I had great guests, would e'en shame me and rise from the table to get a good seat at an afternoon sermon.

PIEBOARD There's the devil, there's the devil, true. He thought it sanctity enough if he had killed a man, so 't'ad been done in a pew, or undone his neighbour, so 't'ad been near enough to th' preacher. O a sermon's a fine short cloak of an hour long and will hide the upper part of a dissembler. Church, ay, he seemed all church, and his conscience was as hard as the pulpit.

WIDOW I can no more endure this.

PIEBOARD Nor I, widow, endure to flatter.

WIDOW Is this all your business with me?

PIEBOARD
No, Lady, 'tis but the induction to't.
You may believe my strains, I strike all true.
And if your conscience would leap up to your tongue, yourself would affirm it. And that you shall perceive I know of things to come, as well as I do of what is present, a brother of your husband's shall shortly have a loss.

WIDOW A loss? Marry, heaven forfend. Sir Godfrey, my brother.

PIEBOARD Nay, keep in your wonders till I have told you the fortunes of you all, which are more fearful if not happily prevented. For your part and your daughters, if

154 **purgatory** in Roman Catholic belief, a condition or place in which the soul of those dying penitent are purified from venial sins, or undergo the temporal punishment which, after the guilt of mortal sin has been remitted, still remains to be endured by the sinner. From the early sixteenth century, protestants, believing that the soul went directly to heaven after death, had characterized purgatory as an invention of the pope (who prayed for souls to be released from purgatory), used to increase his power and extort money from the people. In his *Premonition* (1609), King James would refer to purgatory 'and all the trash depending thereupon' as 'not worth the talking of'.
162 **last general bonfire** Day of Judgement
164 **finny** provided with or having fins
165 **property** identity, essence
168 **determination** accomplishment
176 **determinations** what has been decided
177 **metaphysically** by way of the occult
189 **gripe** act of seizing tenaciously, oppressing by miserly or penurious treatment
205 **sir-reverence** a corruption of 'save reverence' (*salva reverentia*); with all respect for you (used by way of apology before an unseemly expression)
untrussed untied points holding up breeches or hose
208 **high days** days of high celebration; solemn or festal days
221 **induction** introduction
228 **forfend** forbid

there be not once this day some bloodshed before your door whereof the human creature dies, the elder two of you shall run mad.

WIDOW *and* FRANK O.

FRANK (*aside*) That's not I yet.

PIEBOARD And with most impudent prostitution, show your naked bodies to the view of all beholders.

WIDOW Our naked bodies. Fie, for shame.

PIEBOARD Attend me—and your younger daughter be strucken dumb.

MOLL Dumb? Out, alas, 'tis the worst pain of all for a woman. I'd rather be mad, or run naked, or anything. Dumb?

PIEBOARD Give ear. Ere the evening fall upon hill, bog and meadow, this my speech shall have passed probation, and then shall I be believed accordingly.

WIDOW If this be true, we are all shamed, all undone.

MOLL Dumb? I'll speak as much as ever I can possible before evening.

PIEBOARD But if it so come to pass (as for your fair sakes I wish it may) that this presage of your strange fortunes be prevented by that accident of death and bloodshedding which I before told you of, take heed upon your lives that two of you which have vowed never to marry seek you out husbands with all present speed. And you, the third, that have such a desire to outstrip chastity, look you meddle not with a husband.

MOLL A double torment.

PIEBOARD The breach of this keeps your father in purgatory, and the punishments that shall follow you in this world would with horror kill the ear should hear 'em related.

WIDOW Marry? Why, I vowed never to marry.

FRANK And so did I.

MOLL And I vowed never to be such an ass but to marry. What a cross fortune's this?

PIEBOARD Ladies, though I be a fortune-teller, I cannot better fortunes. You have 'em from me as they are revealed to me. I would they were to your tempers and fellows with your bloods. That's all the bitterness I would you.

WIDOW O 'tis a just vengeance for my husband's hard purchases.

PIEBOARD I wish you to bethink yourselves and leave 'em.

WIDOW I'll to Sir Godfrey, my brother, and acquaint him with these fearful presages.

FRANK For, Mother, they portend losses to him.

WIDOW O ay, they do, they do.
If any happy issue crown thy words,
I will reward thy cunning.

PIEBOARD
'Tis enough, Lady, I wish no higher.
[*Exeunt Widow and Frank*]

MOLL
Dumb, and not marry, worse.
Neither to speak nor kiss, a double curse. *Exit*

PIEBOARD So all this comes well about yet. I play the fortune-teller as well as if I had had a witch to my grandam. For by good happiness, being in my hostess's garden, which neighbours the orchard of the widow, I laid the hole of mine ear to a hole in the wall and heard 'em make these vows and speak those words upon which I wrought these advantages. And to encourage my forgery the more, I may now perceive in 'em a natural simplicity which will easily swallow an abuse if any covering be over it. And to confirm my former presage to the widow, I have advised old Peter Skirmish, the soldier, to hurt Corporal Oath upon the leg, and in that hurry I'll rush amongst 'em, and instead of giving the corporal some cordial to comfort him, I'll pour into his mouth a potion of a sleepy nature to make him seem as dead. For the which, the old soldier being apprehended and ready to be borne to execution, I'll step in and take upon me the cure of the dead man upon pain of dying the condemnèd's death. The corporal will wake at his minute, when the sleepy force has wrought itself, and so shall I get myself into a most admired opinion, and under the pretext of that cunning, beguile as I see occasion. And if that foolish Nicholas St Antlings keep true time with the chain, my plot will be sound, the captain delivered, and my wits applauded among scholars and soldiers forever. *Exit Pieboard*

Enter Nicholas St Antlings with the chain **2.2**

NICHOLAS O, I have found an excellent advantage to take away the chain. My master put it off e'en now to 'say on a new doublet, and I sneaked it away by little and little most puritanically. We shall have good sport anon, when he's missed it, about my cousin the conjuror. The world shall see I'm an honest man of my word. For now, I'm going to hang it between heaven and earth among the rosemary branches. *Exit*

Finis Actus Secundus

247 **have passed probation** have been proved
253 **presage** prediction
271 **tempers** temperaments
272 **bloods** the supposed seat of emotion, passion
276 **bethink yourselves** reflect on the matter
'em refers to 'hard purchases' (inheritance) in 275
288 **grandam** grandmother
2.2.1 **advantage** opportunity
2–3 **'say on** assay, try on
7 **hang . . . earth** ironic play on the catena (chain) tradition, in which biblical verses, passages from commentators, or chapters on different topics were assembled to interpret a related set of theological concepts, such as in Thomas Rogers, *A golden chain, taken out of the psalms of King David* (1579), or William Perkins, *A golden chain, or the description of theology, containing the order of the causes of salvation and damnation* (1591)

❁

3.1 *Incipit Actus Tertius*

Enter Simon St Mary Overies and Frailty

FRAILTY Sirrah, Simon St Mary Overies, my mistress sends away all her suitors and puts fleas in their ears.

SIMON Frailty, she does like an honest, chaste, and virtuous woman, for widows ought not to wallow in the puddle of iniquity.

FRAILTY Yet, Simon, many widows will do't, what so comes on't.

SIMON True, Frailty, their filthy flesh desires a conjunction copulative. What strangers are within, Frailty?

FRAILTY There's none, Simon, but Master Pilfer, the tailor. He's above with Sir Godfrey praising of a doublet, and I must trudge anon to fetch Master Suds, the barber.

SIMON Master Suds, a good man, he washes the sins of the beard clean.

Enter old Skirmish the soldier

SKIRMISH How now, creatures, what's o'clock?

FRAILTY Why do you take us to be Jack o'th' clockhouse?

SKIRMISH I say again to you, what's o'clock?

SIMON Truly la, we go by the clock of our conscience. All worldly clocks we know go false and are set by drunken sextons.

SKIRMISH Then what's o'clock in your conscience?

Enter Corporal

O, I must break off. Here comes the corporal.—[*To the Corporal*] Hum, hum, what's o'clock?

CORPORAL O'clock? Why, past seventeen.

FRAILTY Past seventeen? [*Aside*] Nay, he's met with his match now. Corporal Oath will fit him.

SKIRMISH Thou dost not balk or baffle me, dost thou? I am a soldier. Past seventeen.

CORPORAL Ay, thou art not angry with the figures, art thou? I will prove it unto thee: twelve and 1 is thirteen, I hope, 2 fourteen, 3 fifteen, 4 sixteen, and 5 seventeen. Then past seventeen, I will take the dial's part in a just cause.

SKIRMISH I say, 'tis but past five then.

CORPORAL I'll swear 'tis past seventeen then. Dost thou not know numbers? Canst thou not cast?

SKIRMISH Cast? Dost thou speak of my casting i'th' street?

Corporal and Skirmish draw

CORPORAL Ay, and in the market-place.

SIMON Clubs, clubs, clubs! *Simon runs in*

FRAILTY Ay, I knew by their shuffling clubs would be trump.

Enter Pieboard

Mass, here's the knave, an he can do any good upon 'em. Clubs, clubs, clubs! [*Exit Frailty*]

CORPORAL O villain, thou hast opened a vein in my leg.

PIEBOARD How now, for shame, for shame, put up, put up.

CORPORAL By yon blue welkin, 'twas out of my part, George, to be hurt on the leg.

Enter Officers

PIEBOARD O peace now, I have a cordial here to comfort thee.

OFFICERS Down with 'em, down with 'em, lay hands upon the villain.

SKIRMISH Lay hands on me?

PIEBOARD [*aside*] I'll not be seen among 'em now.

[*Pieboard stands aloof*]

CORPORAL
I'm hurt and had more need have surgeons
Lay hands upon me than rough officers.

OFFICER
Go carry him to be dressed then.

[*Exeunt some Officers with Corporal Oath*]

This mutinous soldier shall along with me to prison.

SKIRMISH
To prison? Where's George?

OFFICERS Away with him.

Exeunt [other Officers] with Skirmish

PIEBOARD [*stepping forward*] So,
All lights as I would wish. The amazèd widow
Will plant me strongly now in her belief
And wonder at the virtue of my words,
For the event turns those presages from 'em
Of being mad and dumb and begets joy
Mingled with admiration. These empty creatures,
Soldier and corporal, were but ordained
As instruments for me to work upon.
Now to my patient. Here's his potion. *Exit*

Enter the Widow with her two daughters Frank and Moll [and Frailty] 3.2

WIDOW
O wondrous happiness, beyond our thoughts,
O lucky fair event. I think our fortunes
Were blessed e'en in our cradles. We are quitted
Of all those shameful violent presages
By this rash bleeding chance. Go, Frailty, run, and know
Whether he be yet living or yet dead
That here before my door received his hurt.

3.1.2 **puts fleas in their ears** a stinging reproof
11 **praising** appraising
16 **Jack o'th' clockhouse** figure in a great clock of a church, which by mechanism strikes the hours
18 **conscience** Religious dissidents (Protestant and Catholic) appealed to conscience to defend nonconformity to established English church practices and to defend the refusal to take the oath *ex officio* and thus avoid self-incrimination. Simon uses appeals to conscience to justify his doing whatever he pleases.
20 **sextons** church officers who ring the bells
26 **fit** match
27 **balk** thwart, frustrate, quibble
baffle confuse, frustrate
36 **cast** count or calculate numbers; vomit; void excrement
39 **clubs!** the cry raised when arms are drawn in a quarrel in order to draw help from bystanders
40–1 **clubs would be trump** force would rule the day, with pun on clubs as the winning card
46 **welkin** sky
59 **lights** happens

FRAILTY Madam, he was carried to the superior, but if he had no money when he came there, I warrant he's dead by this time. *Exit Frailty*

FRANK Sure, that man is a rare fortune-teller. Never looked upon our hands, nor upon any mark about us. A wondrous fellow surely.

MOLL I am glad I have the use of my tongue yet, though of nothing else. I shall find the way to marry too, I hope, shortly.

WIDOW O where's my brother Sir Godfrey? I would he were here that I might relate to him how prophetically the cunning gentleman spoke in all things.

Enter Sir Godfrey in a rage

SIR GODFREY O my chain, my chain, I have lost my chain. Where be these villains, varlets?

WIDOW O he's lost his chain.

SIR GODFREY My chain, my chain.

WIDOW Brother, be patient, hear me speak. You know I told you that a cunning man told me that you should have a loss, and he has prophesied so true.

SIR GODFREY Out! He's a villain to prophesy of the loss of my chain. 'Twas worth above three hundred crowns. Besides, 'twas my father's, my father's father's, my grandfather's huge grandfather's. I had as lief ha' lost my neck as the chain that hung about it. O my chain, my chain.

WIDOW O brother, who can be against a misfortune? 'Tis happy 'twas no more.

SIR GODFREY No more? O goodly godly sister, would you had me lost more? My best gown, too, with the cloth of gold lace? My holiday gaskins and my jerkin set with pearl? No more?

WIDOW O brother, you can read.

SIR GODFREY But I cannot read where my chain is. What strangers have been here? You let in strangers, thieves and catchpoles. How comes it gone? There was none above with me but my tailor, and my tailor will not steal, I hope.

MOLL [*aside*] No, he's afraid of a chain.

Enter Frailty

WIDOW How now, sirrah, the news.

FRAILTY O mistress, he may well be called a corporal now, for his corpse are as dead as a cold capon's.

WIDOW More happiness.

SIR GODFREY Sirrah, what's this to my chain? Where's my chain, knave?

FRAILTY Your chain, sir?

SIR GODFREY My chain is lost, villain.

FRAILTY I would he were hanged in chains that has it then for me. Alas, sir, I saw none of your chain since you were hung with it yourself.

SIR GODFREY
Out, varlet. It had full three thousand links.
I have oft told it over at my prayers,
Over and over, full three thousand links.

FRAILTY Had it so, sir, sure it cannot be lost then. I'll put you in that comfort.

SIR GODFREY Why, why?

FRAILTY Why, if your chain had so many links, it cannot choose but come to light.

Enter Nicholas

SIR GODFREY
Delusion. Now, long Nicholas, where's my chain?

NICHOLAS Why, about your neck, is't not, sir?

SIR GODFREY
About my neck, varlet. My chain is lost,
'Tis stole away, I'm robbed.

WIDOW Nay, brother, show yourself a man.

NICHOLAS Ay, if it be lost or stole, if he would be patient, mistress, I could bring him to a cunning kinsman of mine that would fetch't again with a sesarara.

SIR GODFREY Canst thou? I will be patient. Say, where dwells he?

NICHOLAS Marry, he dwells now, sir, where he would not dwell an he could choose, in the Marshalsea, sir. But he's an ex'lent fellow if he were out. He's travelled all the world o'er, he, and been in the seven-and-twenty provinces. Why, he would make it be fetched, sir, if 'twere rid a thousand mile out of town.

SIR GODFREY An admirable fellow. What lies he for?

NICHOLAS Why, he did but rob a steward of ten groats t'other night, as any man would ha' done, and there he lies for't.

SIR GODFREY
I'll make his peace, a trifle. I'll get his pardon,
Besides a bountiful reward. I'll about it,
But see the clerks, the justice will do much.
I will about it straight. Good sister, pardon me,

3.2.8 **superior** superintendent or surgeon. Hospitals like Thomas's in Southwark, which had been monastic institutions during the reign of Henry VIII, were refounded as charitable and municipal institutions, but were still variously connected to the Church. For example, the Church still granted licences to practise medicine and surgery.
28 **crowns** coins worth five shillings
30 **huge grandfather's** comic error for great grandfather's
had as lief might as well
37 **gaskins** loose breeches
39 **you can read** For consolation, you can read religious works.
42 **catchpoles** officers who arrest debtors
45 **chain** for a prisoner; see 3.2.54
48 **corpse** often construed as a plural, as in 'remains'.
58 **told . . . prayers** Either Godfrey has used his chain as a rosary, or, while in an attitude of prayer, his mind has drifted instead to the task of estimating the value of his chain.
63–4 **links . . . light** pun on link, which also means a torch
72 **sesarara** corruption of 'certiorari' meaning 'to be informed, to be made certain in regard to'; a writ of certiorari was a writ of review or inquiry
78–9 **seven-and-twenty provinces** probably the seventeen Provinces of the Netherlands, where wars were fought against the Spaniards

All will be well, I hope, and turn to good.
The name of conjuror has laid my blood. *Exeunt*

3.3 *Enter two sergeants Puttock and Ravenshaw [with Yeoman Dogson] to arrest the scholar George Pieboard*

PUTTOCK His hostess where he lies will trust him no longer. She has fee'd me to arrest him, and if you will accompany me, because I know not of what nature the scholar is, whether desperate or swift, you shall share with me, Sergeant Ravenshaw. I have the good angel to arrest him.

RAVENSHAW Troth, I'll take part with thee then, sergeant, not for the sake of the money so much, as for the hate I bear to a scholar. Why, sergeant, 'tis natural in us, you know, to hate scholars, natural. Besides, they will publish our imperfections, knaveries, and conveyances upon scaffolds and stages.

PUTTOCK Ay, and spitefully too. Troth, I have wondered how the slaves could see into our breasts so much when our doublets are buttoned with pewter.

RAVENSHAW Ay, and so close without yielding. O they're parlous fellows. They will search more with their wits than a constable with all his officers.

PUTTOCK Whist, whist, whist, Yeoman Dogson, Yeoman Dogson.

DOGSON Ha, what says sergeant?

PUTTOCK Is he in the 'pothecaries shop still?

DOGSON Ay, ay.

PUTTOCK Have an eye, ay.

RAVENSHAW The best is, sergeant, if he be a true scholar, he wears no weapon, I think.

PUTTOCK No, no, he wears no weapon.

RAVENSHAW Mass, I am right glad of that. 'T'as put me in better heart. Nay, if I clutch him once, let me alone to drag him if he be stiff-necked. I have been one of the six myself that has dragged as tall men of their hands, when their weapons have been gone, as ever bastinadoed a sergeant. I have done, I can tell you.

DOGSON Sergeant Puttock, Sergeant Puttock.

PUTTOCK Hoh.

DOGSON He's coming out single.

PUTTOCK Peace, peace, be not too greedy. Let him play a little, let him play a little. We'll jerk him up of a sudden. I ha' fished in my time.

RAVENSHAW Ay, and caught many a fool, sergeant.

Enter Pieboard

PIEBOARD [*aside*]
I parted now from Nicholas. The chain's couched,
And the old knight has spent his rage upon't.
The Widow holds me in great admiration
For cunning art. 'Mongst joys I am e'en lost,
For my device can no way now be crossed,
And now I must to prison to the captain, and there—

PUTTOCK I arrest you, sir.

PIEBOARD [*aside*] O, I spoke truer than I was aware. I must to prison indeed.

PUTTOCK They say you're a scholar, nay sir? Yeoman Dogson, have care to his arms. You'll rail again sergeants and stage 'em. You tickle their vices.

PIEBOARD Nay, use me like a gentleman. I'm little less.

PUTTOCK You, a gentleman? That's a good jest, i'faith. Can a scholar be a gentleman when a gentleman will not be a scholar? Look upon your wealthy citizens' sons, whether they be scholars or no, that are gentlemen by their fathers' trades. A scholar a gentleman?

PIEBOARD Nay, let fortune drive all her stings into me, she cannot hurt that in me. A gentleman is *accidens inseparabile* to my blood.

RAVENSHAW A rabblement, nay, you shall have a bloody rabblement upon you, I warrant you.

PUTTOCK Go, Yeoman Dogson, before, and enter the action i'th' Counter. *Exit Dogson*

PIEBOARD Pray, do not hand me cruelly. I'll go whither you please to have me.

PUTTOCK O he's tame. Let him loose, sergeant.

PIEBOARD Pray, at whose suit is this?

PUTTOCK Why, at your hostess's suit where you lie, Mistress Cunnyburrow, for bed and board, the sum four pound five shillings and five pence.

PIEBOARD [*aside*]
I know the sum too true, yet I presumed
Upon a farther day. Well, 'tis my stars,
And I must bear it now, though never harder.
I swear, now my device is crossed indeed.
Captain must lie by't. This is deceit's seed.

PUTTOCK Come, come away.

PIEBOARD Pray, give me so much time as to knit my garter, and I'll away with you.

He makes to tie his garter

PUTTOCK Well, we must be paid for this waiting upon you. This is no pains to attend thus.

90 **laid my blood** allayed my anger; also, conjuring involved raising and laying spirits
3.3.0.1 ***Puttock and Ravenshaw*** A 'puttock' is a buzzard; a 'ravenshaw' is a thicket where ravens assemble and build.
2 **fee'd** paid
5 **angel** coin having as its device the archangel Michael piercing the dragon
11 **conveyances** underhanded dealings
15 **doublets** close-fitting body garments
17 **parlous** dangerous, clever
31–2 **tall men of their hands** stout
33 **bastinadoed** beaten with a stick
41 **couched** hidden
52 **tickle** chastise
60–1 ***accidens inseparabile*** term in logic meaning an attribute inseparable from its subject
62 **rabblement** a play upon ... *rabile* in the preceeding speech; Ravenshaw does not understand the Latin
64 **enter** record
65 **Counter** or compter, was a debtors' prison attached to a court, at this time in London in the Poultry and in Wood Street, and in Southwark on the site of the old Church of St Margaret
77 **lie by't** lie in prison
79 **knit** tie

PIEBOARD [*aside*] I am now wretched and miserable. I shall ne'er recover of this disease. Hot iron gnaw their fists! They have struck a fever into my shoulder, which I shall ne'er shake out again, I fear me, till with a true *habeas corpus* the sexton remove me. O, if I take prison once, I shall be pressed to death with actions, but not so happy as speedily. Perhaps I may be forty year a-pressing till I be a thin old man that, looking through the grates, men may look through me. All my means is confounded. What shall I do? Has my wit served me so long and now give me the slip, like a trained servant, when I have most need of 'em, no device to keep my poor carcass from these puttocks? Yes, happiness, have I a paper about me now. Yes, too, I'll try it, it may hit. 'Extremity is touchstone unto wit', ay, ay.

PUTTOCK 'Sfoot, how many yards are in thy garters, that thou art so long atying on them? Come away, sir.

PIEBOARD Troth, sergeant, I protest, you could never ha' took me at a worse time, for now at this instant, I have no lawful picture about me.

PUTTOCK 'Slid, how shall we come by our fees then?

RAVENSHAW We must have fees, sirrah.

PIEBOARD I could ha' wished, i'faith, that you had took me half an hour hence for your own sake, for I protest, if you had not crossed me, I was going in great joy to receive five pound of a gentleman for the device of a masque here, drawn in this paper. But now, come, I must be contented. 'Tis but so much lost and answerable to the rest of my fortunes.

PUTTOCK Why, how far hence dwells that gentleman?

RAVENSHAW Ay, well said, sergeant. 'Tis good to cast about for money.

PUTTOCK Speak, if it be not far.

PIEBOARD We are but a little past it, the next street behind us.

PUTTOCK 'Slid, we have waited upon you grievously already. If you'll say you'll be liberal when you ha't, give us double fees and spend upon's, why, we'll show you that kindness and go along with you to the gentleman.

RAVENSHAW Ay, well said still, sergeant. Urge that.

PIEBOARD Troth, if it will suffice, it shall be all among you. For my part, I'll not pocket a penny. My hostess shall have her four pound five shillings and bate me the five pence, and the other fifteen shillings, I'll spend upon you.

RAVENSHAW Why, now thou art a good scholar.

PUTTOCK An excellent scholar, i'faith. He's proceeded very well o'late. Come, we'll along with you.

Puttock and Ravenshaw exeunt with Pieboard. Passing in, they knock at the door with a knocker withinside

[*Enter Servant*] 3.4

SERVANT Who knocks, who's at door? We had need of a porter.

PIEBOARD [*within*] A few friends here.

[*Servant opens the door to Pieboard, Ravenshaw, Puttock, and Dogson*]

Pray, is the gentleman your master within?

SERVANT Yes, is your business to him?

PIEBOARD Ay, he knows it when he sees me. I pray you, have you forgot me?

SERVANT Ay, by my troth, sir, pray come near. I'll in and tell him of you. Please you to walk here in the gallery till he comes.

PIEBOARD We will attend his worship.— [*Exit Servant*] [*Aside*] Worship I think, for so much the posts at his door should signify, and the fair coming in, and the wicket, else I neither knew him nor his worship. But 'tis happiness he is within doors, what so e'er he be. If he be not too much a formal citizen, he may do me good.—Sergeant and yeoman, how do you like this house? Is't not most wholesomely plotted?

RAVENSHAW Troth, prisoner, an exceeding fine house.

PIEBOARD [*aside*] Yet I wonder how he should forget me, for he ne'er knew me. No matter, what is forgot in you will be remembered in your master.—[*To Ravenshaw, Puttock, and Dogson*] A pretty comfortable room this, methinks. You have no such rooms in prison now.

PUTTOCK O dog holes to't.

PIEBOARD Dog holes indeed. I can tell you I have great hope to have my chamber here shortly, nay, and diet

86–7 ***habeas corpus*** writ ordering a prisoner to come to court on a certain day, but here, referring to death and everlasting judgement

88 **pressed to death with actions** literally, to be slowly pressed, spreadeagled on the ground, with as much iron placed upon the body as was necessary to exact a plea or to cause death; *fig.* to indicate he knows that prisoners were made to pay their creditors as well as fees to the prison for their keep and to the gaolers for attendance

92–6 **What...hit.** The jest that Pieboard is about to perpetrate has an analogue in Jest 2 in Peele's *Merrie Conceited Jests*, where George borrows and then absconds with a lute belonging to a barber. When the barber comes looking for it, George tells him that a gentleman has borrowed it; once in the gentleman's home to retrieve it, George convinces the gentleman, on the pretence that the person accompanying him is trying to get him arrested, to let him escape out a backdoor.

95 **puttocks** birds of prey

102 **picture** coin

126 **bate me** deduct for me

131.3 ***withinside*** The fluidity of Middleton's staging allows the characters to go off stage, knock on the door of the gentleman's house from the 'within' side of the stage, and re-enter, with no stop in the action.

3.4.12 **posts** doorposts were symbols of civic authority set up by doors of mayors, sheriffs, and other magistrates

16 **formal** observant of forms, precise, ceremonious

18 **plotted** laid out

27 **chamber** room in a house appropriated to the use of one person

diet meals

too, for he's the most free-heartedst gentleman where he takes. You would little think it. And what a fine gallery were here for me to walk and study and make verses.

PUTTOCK O it stands very pleasantly for a scholar.

PIEBOARD Look, what maps and pictures, and devices and things, neatly, delicately.

Enter Gentleman

[*Aside*] Mass, here he comes. He should be a gentleman. I like his beard well. [*To Gentleman*] All happiness to your worship.

GENTLEMAN You're kindly welcome, sir.

PUTTOCK [*to Ravenshaw*] A simple salutation.

RAVENSHAW [*to Puttock*] Mass, it seems the gentleman makes great account of him.

PIEBOARD [*to Gentleman*] I have the thing here for you, sir.

GENTLEMAN [ ]

PIEBOARD [*aside to Gentleman*] I beseech you, conceal me, sir. I'm undone else.—I have the masque here for you, sir. Look you, sir.—[*Aside to Gentleman*] I beseech your worship first to pardon my rudeness, for my extremes makes me bolder than I would be. I am a poor gentleman and a scholar, and now most unfortunately fall'n into the fangs of unmerciful officers, arrested for debt, which though small, I am not able to compass by reason I'm destitute of lands, money, and friends. So that if I fall into the hungry swallow of the prison, I am like utterly to perish, and with fees and extortions be pinched clean to the bone. Now, if ever pity had interest in the blood of a gentleman, I beseech you vouchsafe but to favour that means of my escape which I have already thought upon.

GENTLEMAN [*aside to Pieboard*] Go forward.

PUTTOCK [*to Ravenshaw*] I warrant he likes it rarely.

PIEBOARD [*aside to Gentleman*] In the plunge of my extremities, being giddy and doubtful what to do, at last it was put into my labouring thoughts to make happy use of this paper. And to blear their unlettered eyes, I told them there was a device for a masque drawn in't, and that, but for their interception, I was going to a gentleman to receive my reward for't. They, greedy at this word and hoping to make purchase of me, offered their attendance to go along with me. My hap was to make bold with your door, sir, which my thoughts showed me the most fairest and comfortablest entrance, and I hope I have happened right upon understanding and pity. May it please your good worship, then, but to uphold my device, which is to let one of your men put me out at backdoor, and I shall be bound to your worship forever.

GENTLEMAN By my troth, an excellent device.

PUTTOCK An excellent device, he says. He likes it wonderfully.

GENTLEMAN O' my faith, I never heard a better.

RAVENSHAW Hark, he swears he never heard a better, sergeant.

PUTTOCK O there's no talk on't. He is an excellent scholar, and especially for a masque.

GENTLEMAN [*to Pieboard*] Give me your paper, your device. I was never better pleased in all my life. Good wit, brave wit, finely wrought. Come in, sir, and receive your money, sir. [*Exit Gentleman*]

PIEBOARD I'll follow your good worship.—You heard how he liked it now?

PUTTOCK Puh, we know he could not choose but like it. Go thy ways. Thou art a witty fine fellow, i'faith. Thou shalt discourse it to us at tavern anon, wilt thou?

PIEBOARD Ay, ay, that I will. Look, sergeants, here are maps, and pretty toys. Be doing in the mean time. I shall quickly have told out the money, you know.

PUTTOCK Go, go, little villain, fetch thy chink. I begin to love thee. I'll be drunk tonight in thy company.

PIEBOARD [*aside*]
This gentleman I may well call a part
Of my salvation in these earthly evils,
For he has saved me from three hungry devils. *Exit*

PUTTOCK Sirrah, sergeant, these maps are pretty painted things, but I could ne'er fancy 'em yet. Methinks they're too busy and full of circles and conjurations. They say all the world's in one of them, but I could ne'er find the Counter in the Poultry.

RAVENSHAW I think so. How could you find it? For you know it stands behind the houses.

DOGSON Mass, that's true. Then we must look a'th' backside for't. 'Sfoot, here's nothing, all's bare.

RAVENSHAW I warrant thee that stands for the Counter, for you know there's a company of bare fellows there.

PUTTOCK Faith, like enough, sergeant, I never marked so much before. Sirrah, sergeant and yeoman, I should love these maps out o' cry now if we could see men peep out of door in 'em. O we might have 'em in a morning to our breakfast so finely, and ne'er knock our heels to the ground a whole day for 'em.

RAVENSHAW Ay, marry, sir, I'd buy one then myself. But this talk is by the way. Where shall's sup tonight? Five pound received. Let's talk of that. I have a trick worth all. You two shall bear him to th' tavern, whilst I go close with his hostess and work out of her. I know she would be glad of the sum to finger money because she knows 'tis but a desperate debt and full of hazard. What

28 **free-heartedst** generous
29 **takes** brings a person into his service, protection, favour
33 **devices** emblematic figures or designs, such as a heraldic bearings
43 GENTLEMAN The printer has omitted a speech by the Gentleman.
50 **fangs** grasp
97 **chink** ready cash
106 **Counter in the Poultry** the debtors' prison located on the Poultry, a London street connecting Cheapside and Cornhill, and named for the poulterers who had their stalls there
108 **stands behind the houses** houses stood in front of the Counter in the Poultry, partially concealing it
115 **out o' cry** beyond everything
122 **bear him to th' tavern** to eat and drink at his expense; see 3.3.120
124 **finger** handle

will you say if I bring it to pass that the hostess shall be contented with one half for all and we to share t'other; fifty shillings, bullies.

PUTTOCK Why, I would call thee King of Sergeants, and thou shouldst be chronicled in the Counter book forever.

RAVENSHAW Well, put it to me. We'll make a night on't, i'faith.

DOGSON 'Sfoot, I think he receives more money, he stays so long.

PUTTOCK He tarries long indeed. Maybe I can tell you, upon the good liking on't, the gentleman may prove more bountiful.

RAVENSHAW That would be rare. We'll search him.

PUTTOCK Nay, be sure of it, we'll search him and make him light enough.

Enter the Gentleman

RAVENSHAW O here comes the Gentleman. By your leave, sir.

GENTLEMAN God you good e'en, sirs. Would you speak with me?

PUTTOCK No, not with your worship, sir. Only we are bold to stay for a friend of ours that went in with your worship.

GENTLEMAN Who? Not the scholar?

PUTTOCK Yes, e'en he, an it please your worship.

GENTLEMAN Did he make you stay for him? He did you wrong then. Why, I can assure you he's gone above an hour ago.

RAVENSHAW How, sir?

GENTLEMAN I paid him his money, and my man told me he went out at backdoor.

PUTTOCK Backdoor?

GENTLEMAN Why, what's the matter?

PUTTOCK He was our prisoner, sir. We did arrest him.

GENTLEMAN What? He was not. You, the sheriff's officers, you were to blame then. Why did you not make known to me as much? I could have kept him for you. I protest, he received all of me in Britain gold of the last coining.

RAVENSHAW Vengeance dog him with't.

PUTTOCK 'Sfoot, has he gulled us so?

DOGSON Where shall we sup now, sergeants?

PUTTOCK Sup, Simon, now, eat porridge for a month.—[*To Gentleman*] Well, we cannot impute it to any lack of goodwill in your worship. You did but as another would have done. 'Twas our hard fortunes to miss the purchase. But if e'er we clutch him again, the Counter shall charm him.

RAVENSHAW The Hole shall rot him.

DOGSON Amen. *Exeunt [all but the Gentleman]*

GENTLEMAN So,
Vex out your lungs without doors. I am proud
It was my hap to help him. It fell fit.
He went not empty neither for his wit.
Alas poor wretch, I could not blame his brain
To labour his delivery to be free
From their unpitying fangs. I'm glad it stood
Within my power to do a scholar good. *Exit*

3.5

Enter in the prison, meeting, George Pieboard and Captain, Pieboard coming in muffled.

CAPTAIN How now, who's that? What are you?

PIEBOARD The same that I should be, captain.

CAPTAIN George Pieboard, honest George, why camst thou in half-faced, muffled so?

PIEBOARD O captain, I thought we should ne'er ha' laughed again, never spent frolic hour again.

CAPTAIN Why, why?

PIEBOARD
I, coming to prepare thee and with news
As happy as thy quick delivery,
Was traced out by the scent. Arrested, captain.

CAPTAIN Arrested, George?

PIEBOARD Arrested. Guess, guess, how many dogs do you think I'd upon me?

CAPTAIN Dogs? I say, I know not.

PIEBOARD
Almost as many as George Stone the bear.
Three at once, three at once.

CAPTAIN How didst thou shake 'em off then?

PIEBOARD
The time is busy and calls upon our wits.
Let it suffice,
Here I stand safe and 'scaped by miracle.
Some other hour shall tell thee, when we'll steep
Our eyes in laughter. Captain, my device
Leans to thy happiness, for ere the day
Be spent to th' girdle, thou shalt be set free.
The Corporal's in his first sleep, the chain is missed,
Thy kinsman has expressed thee, and the old knight
With palsy hams now labours thy release.
What rests is all in thee to conjure, captain.

130 **Counter book** book that kept the records for the Counter

143 **God you good e'en** God give you a good evening

162 **Britain...coining** James I assumed the title of King of Great Britain in 1604, and an indenture was executed 11 November 1604 for a coinage whereon the king's new title, Mag. Brit., was to be adopted.

166 **Sup, Simon** In Thomas Deloney's *Thomas of Reading, or The Six Worthy Yeomen of the West*, chap. 5, the character Simon, supping his pottage, is told 'Sup, Simon, there's good broth.'

172 **The Hole** the appalling quarters reserved for destitute prisoners

3.5.0.2 ***muffled*** covered up about the face

15 **as many...bear** Contests between dogs and bears in Bear Garden included the famous bear George Stone who, according to a petition to the king by Philip Henslowe, then Keeper of the King's Bears, died during late July or early August, 1606, at a baiting before the king of Denmark. The detail is referred to in discussions of the play's date.

23–4 **ere the day | Be spent to th' girdle** before noon, the girdle signifying the waist or midpoint

26 **expressed** described

27 **palsy hams** tremoring thighs

CAPTAIN Conjure? 'Sfoot, George, you know the devil o' conjuring, I can conjure.

PIEBOARD The devil of conjuring, nay by my fay, I'd not have thee do so much, captain, as the devil o' conjuring. Look here, I ha' brought thee a circle ready charactered and all.

CAPTAIN 'Sfoot, George, art in thy right wits? Dost know what thou sayst? Why dost talk to a captain o' conjuring? Didst thou ever hear of a captain conjure in thy life? Dost call't a circle? 'Tis too wide a thing, methinks. Had it been a lesser circle, then I knew what to have done.

PIEBOARD Why, every fool knows that, captain. Nay, then I'll not cog with you, captain. If you'll stay and hang the next sessions, you may.

CAPTAIN No, by my faith, George, come, come, let's to conjuring, let's to conjuring.

PIEBOARD But if you look to be released, as my wits have took pain to work it and all means wrought to farther it, besides to put crowns in your purse to make you a man of better hopes. And whereas before you were a captain or poor soldier, to make you now a commander of rich fools, which is truly the only best purchase peace can allow you, safer than highways, heath, or cony groves, and yet a far better booty. For your greatest thieves are never hanged, never hanged, for, why, they're wise and cheat within doors. And we geld fools of more money in one night than your false-tailed gelding will purchase in a twelvemonth's running. Which confirms the old beldam's saying, he's wisest that keeps himself warmest, that is, he that robs by a good fire.

CAPTAIN Well opened, i'faith. George, thou hast pulled that saying out of the husk.

PIEBOARD Captain Idle, 'tis no time now to delude or delay. The old knight will be here suddenly. I'll perfect you, direct you, tell you the trick on't. 'Tis nothing.

CAPTAIN 'Sfoot, George, I know not what to say to't. Conjure? I shall be hanged ere I conjure.

PIEBOARD Nay, tell not me of that, captain. You'll ne'er conjure after you're hanged, I warrant you. Look you, sir, a parlous matter, sure, first to spread your circle upon the ground, then with a little conjuring ceremony, as I'll have an hackney-man's wand silvered o'er o' purpose for you, then arriving in the circle, with a huge word and a great trample. As for instance, have you never seen a stalking stamping player that will raise a tempest with his tongue and thunder with his heels?

CAPTAIN O yes, yes, yes, often, often.

PIEBOARD Why, be like such a one, for anything will blear the old knight's eyes. For you must note that he'll ne'er dare to venture into the room, only perhaps peep fearfully through the keyhole to see how the play goes forward.

CAPTAIN Well, I may go about it when I will, but mark the end on't. I shall but shame myself, i'faith, George. Speak big words and stamp and stare, an he look in at keyhole. Why, the very thought of that would make me laugh outright and spoil all. Nay, I'll tell thee, George, when I apprehend a thing once, I am of such a laxative laughter that, if the devil himself stood by, I should laugh in his face.

PIEBOARD Puh, that's but the babe of a man and may easily be hushed, as to think upon some disaster, some sad misfortune, as the death of thy father i'the country.

CAPTAIN 'Sfoot, that would be the more to drive me into such an ecstasy that I should ne'er lin laughing.

PIEBOARD Why, then think upon going to hanging else.

CAPTAIN Mass, that's well remembered. Now I'll do well, I warrant thee. Ne'er fear me now. But how shall I do, George, for boisterous words and horrible names?

PIEBOARD Puh, any fustian invocations, captain, will serve as well as the best, so you rant them out well. Or you may go to a 'pothecary's shop and take all the words from the boxes.

CAPTAIN Troth and you say true, George, there's strange words enough to raise a hundred quacksalvers, though they be ne'er so poor when they begin. But here lies the fear on't, how if in this false conjuration a true devil should pop up indeed.

PIEBOARD A true devil, captain, why there was ne'er such a one. Nay, faith, he that has this place is as false a knave as our last church warden.

CAPTAIN Then he is false enough o' conscience i'faith, George.

The Cry at Marshalsea [*is heard*]

CRY PRISONERS

Good gentlemen over the way, send your relief,
Good gentlemen over the way—good Sir Godfrey—

[*Enter Sir Godfrey, Edmond, and Nicholas*]

PIEBOARD He's come, he's come.

31 **fay** faith
33 **a circle ready charactered** circle already inscribed with magical or astrological symbolism
39 **lesser circle** conjuror's circle; also vagina
42 **cog** quibble
If you'll stay and hang If you want to stay and so hang as a result
43 **sessions** court sessions
52 **cony groves** land used for breeding game
55 **geld** castrate; strip away the essence
56 **false-tailed gelding** a highwayman's horse, with a false tail to take on and off
57 **purchase** gain
58 **beldam's** aged woman's
58–9 **he's wisest ... warmest** proverbial
60 **Well opened** well-expounded
60–1 **pulled that saying out of the husk** explained it
69 **parlous** cunning, mischievous
71 **hackney-man's wand** switch for urging on a horse, hackney-man being one who keeps horses for hire
87 **laxative** unable to contain
90 **babe** childishness
94 **lin** cease
99 **fustian** bombastic
104 **quacksalvers** quacks
112.1 *Cry* prisoners appealing for mercy or justice, shouting together

NICHOLAS Master, that's my kinsman yonder in the buff jerkin. Kinsman, that's my master yonder i'th' taffety hat. Pray salute him entirely.

Captain and Sir Godfrey salute, and Pieboard salutes Master Edmond

SIR GODFREY [*to Captain*] Now, my friend—

PIEBOARD [*to Edmond*] May I partake your name, sir?

EDMOND My name is Master Edmond.

PIEBOARD Master Edmond, are you not a Welshman, sir?

EDMOND A Welshman? Why?

PIEBOARD Because Master is your Christian name, and Edmond your surname.

EDMOND O no, I have more names at home. Master Edmond Plus is my full name at length.

PIEBOARD O cry you mercy, sir.

Edmond and Pieboard whisper [aside]

CAPTAIN [*to Sir Godfrey*] I understand that you are my kinsman's good master, and, in regard of that, the best of my skill is at your service. But had you fortuned a mere stranger and made no means to me by acquaintance, I should have utterly denied to have been the man, both by reason of the Act passed in Parliament against conjurors and witches, as also because I would not have my art vulgar, trite, and common.

SIR GODFREY I much commend your care therein, good Captain Conjuror, and that I will be sure to have it private enough, you shall do't in my sister's house, mine own house I may call it, for both our charges therein are proportioned.

CAPTAIN Very good, sir. What may I call your loss, sir?

SIR GODFREY O you may call't a great loss, sir, a grievous loss, sir, as goodly a chain of gold, though I say it, that wore it.—How say'st thou, Nicholas?

NICHOLAS O 'twas as delicious a chain o'gold, kinsman, you know—

SIR GODFREY You know? Did you know't, captain?

CAPTAIN [*aside*] Trust a fool with secrets.—Sir, he may say I know. His meaning is, because my art is such, that by it I may gather a knowledge of all things.

SIR GODFREY Ay, very true.

CAPTAIN [*aside*] A pox of all fools. The excuse stuck upon my tongue like ship pitch upon a mariner's gown, not to come off in haste.—By'r Lady, knight, to lose such a fair chain o' gold were a foul loss. Well, I can put you in this good comfort on't. If it be between heaven and earth, knight, I'll ha't for you.

SIR GODFREY A wonderful conjuror. O ay, 'tis between heaven and earth, I warrant you. It cannot go out of the realm. I know 'tis somewhere above the earth.

CAPTAIN [*aside*] Ay, nigher the earth than thou wotst on.

SIR GODFREY For, first, my chain was rich, and no rich thing shall enter into heaven, you know.

NICHOLAS And as for the devil, master, he has no need on't, for you know he has a great chain of his own.

SIR GODFREY Thou sayest true, Nicholas, but he has put off that now that lies by him.

CAPTAIN Faith, knight, in few words, I presume so much upon the power of my art that I could warrant your chain again.

SIR GODFREY O dainty captain.

CAPTAIN Marry, it will cost me much sweat. I were better go to sixteen hothouses.

SIR GODFREY Ay, good man, I warrant thee.

CAPTAIN Beside great vexation of kidney and liver.

NICHOLAS O 'twill tickle you hereabouts, cousin, because you have not been used to't.

SIR GODFREY No, have you not been used to't, captain?

CAPTAIN [*aside*] Plague of all fools still.—Indeed, knight, I have not used it a good while, and therefore 'twill strain me so much the more you know.

SIR GODFREY O it will, it will.

CAPTAIN [*aside*] What plunges he puts me to. Were not this knight a fool, I had been twice spoiled now. That captain's worse than accursed that has an ass to his kinsman. 'Sfoot, I fear he will drivel 't out before I come to't.—Now, sir, to come to the point indeed. You see I stick here in the jaw of the Marshalsea and cannot do't.

SIR GODFREY Tut, tut, I know thy meaning. Thou wouldst say thou'rt a prisoner. I tell thee thou'rt none.

CAPTAIN How none? Why, is not this the Marshalsea?

117 **taffety** glossy silk

134–5 **Act . . . against conjurors and witches** The 1604 statute against conjuration and witchcraft specifically forbade using sorcery to seek for lost goods, or 'treasure of gold or silver'.

139 **private . . . in my sister's house** play on puritan conference or conventicle movement, the meetings for which were often held in a 'private house', and regarded suspiciously by the authorities as promoting any number of extremist activities. Canon 72 of the Canons of 1604 ('Ministers not to appoint public or private fasts or prophecies, or to exorcise, but by authority') was specifically designed to counter such episodes as had occurred in conjunction with the exorcisms performed in the late 1590s by the puritan exorcist John Darrell. The Canon included stipulations against 'private houses' and against any attempt 'by fasting and prayer, to cast out any Devil or Devils, under pain of the imputation of imposture or cozenage, and deposition from the ministry'.

140 **charges** costs

156–71 **fair chain . . . chain again** passages play on a variety of secular and religious meanings of 'chain'; see 2.2.6–7

160 **warrant** assure

162 **wotst on** know about

163–4 **no rich thing . . . into heaven** Mark 10:24: 'It is easier for a camel to go through the eye of a needle than for a rich man to enter into the kingdom of God'.

165–6 **the devil . . . own** See Rev. 20:1, 2, 7, 8: 'And I saw an angel come down from heaven, having the key of the bottomless pit, and a great chain in his hand. And he took the dragon . . . which is the devil and Satan, and he bound him a thousand years . . . .And when the thousand years are expired, Satan shall be loosed out of his prison, and shall go out to deceive the people'.

170 **warrant** guarantee

172 **dainty** term of endearment

174 **hothouses** bathing-houses with hot baths; brothels

176 **vexation of kidney and liver** as a result of drinking too much alcohol

177 **tickle** excite, puzzle, amuse

184 **plunges** dilemmas

SIR GODFREY
Wilt hear me speak? I heard of thy rare conjuring.
My chain was lost. I sweat for thy release
As thou shalt do the like at home for me.
Keeper—

Enter Keeper

KEEPER Sir?

SIR GODFREY Speak. Is not this man free?

KEEPER Yes, at his pleasure, sir, the fees discharged.

SIR GODFREY Go, go, I'll discharge them, ay.

KEEPER I thank your worship. *Exit*

CAPTAIN Now trust me, you're a dear knight, kindness unexpected. O there's nothing to a free gentleman. I will conjure for you, sir, till froth come through my buff jerkin.

SIR GODFREY Nay, then, thou shalt not pass with so little a bounty, for at the first sight of my chain again, forty fine angels shall appear unto thee.

CAPTAIN 'Twill be a glorious show, i'faith, knight, a very fine show. But are all these of your own house? Are you sure of that, sir?

SIR GODFREY Ay, ay, no, no. What's he yonder talking with my wild nephew? Pray heaven, he give him good counsel.

CAPTAIN Who, he? He's a rare friend of mine, an admirable fellow, knight, the finest fortune-teller.

SIR GODFREY O 'tis he indeed that came to my lady sister and foretold the loss of my chain. I am not angry with him now, for I see 'twas my fortune to lose it. [*To Pieboard*] By your leave, Master Fortune-teller, I had a glimpse on you at home at my sister's, the widow's. There you prophesied of the loss of a chain. Simply though I stand here, I was he that lost it.

PIEBOARD Was it you, sir?

EDMOND [*to Sir Godfrey*] O' my troth, nuncle, he's the rarest fellow. He's told me my fortune so right. I find it so right to my nature.

SIR GODFREY What is't? God send it a good one.

EDMOND O 'tis a passing good one, nuncle, for he says I shall prove such an excellent gamester in my time that I shall spend all faster than my father got it.

SIR GODFREY There's a fortune indeed.

EDMOND Nay, it hits my humour so pat.

SIR GODFREY Ay, that will be the end on't. Will the curse of the beggar prevail so much that the son shall consume that foolishly which the father got craftily? Ay, ay, ay, 'twill, 'twill, 'twill.

PIEBOARD Stay, stay, stay.

Pieboard [*opens*] *an almanac, and* [*takes aside*] *the Captain*

CAPTAIN Turn over, George.

PIEBOARD June, July, here July, that's this month. Sunday thirteen, yesterday fourteen, today fifteen.

CAPTAIN Look quickly for the fifteen day. If within the compass of these two days there would be some boisterous storm or other, it would be the best. I'd defer him off till then, some tempest, an it be thy will.

PIEBOARD Here's the fifteen day: [*Reading*] 'hot and fair.'

CAPTAIN Puh, would 't'ad been hot and foul.

PIEBOARD The sixteen day, that's tomorrow: 'the morning for the most part fair and pleasant.'

CAPTAIN No luck.

PIEBOARD 'But about high noon ligh'ning and thunder.'

CAPTAIN Ligh'ning and thunder, admirable, best of all, I'll conjure tomorrow just at high noon, George.

PIEBOARD Happen but true tomorrow, almanac, and I'll give thee leave to lie all the year after.

CAPTAIN [*to Sir Godfrey*] Sir, I must crave your patience to bestow this day upon me that I may furnish myself strongly. I sent a spirit into Lancashire t'other day to fetch back a knave drover, and I look for his return this evening. Tomorrow morning, my friend here and I will come and breakfast with you.

SIR GODFREY O you shall be both most welcome.

CAPTAIN And about noon, without fail, I purpose to conjure.

SIR GODFREY Midnoon will be a fine time for you.

EDMOND Conjuring? Do you mean to conjure at our house tomorrow, sir?

CAPTAIN Marry, do I sir. 'Tis my intent, young gentleman.

EDMOND By my troth, I'll love you while I live for't. O rare, Nicholas, we shall have conjuring tomorrow.

NICHOLAS Puh, ay, I could ha' told you of that.

CAPTAIN [*aside*] La, he could ha' told him of that, fool, coxcomb, could ye?

EDMOND [*to Captain*] Do you hear me, sir? I desire more acquaintance on you. You shall earn some money of me now I know you can conjure. But can you fetch any that is lost?

CAPTAIN O anything that's lost.

199 **the fees discharged** when the fees are discharged

208 **angels** coins, with pun

233 **humour** temperament

234–5 **curse of the beggar** proverbial notion that, even as a poor person's children may be wealthy, so the generation following them may be poor again, or 'Twice clogs, once boots.'

241 **today fifteen** In 1606, 15 July was on a Tuesday, a fact that has been used for dating *Puritan* no earlier than 1606.

242 **the fifteen day** No almanac from 1606 has been found to correspond to what is said here about July weather, but Captain's hope for stormy weather on this date coincides with the tradition that rain on St Swithin's Day (15 July) will persist for forty days.

258 **I...Lancashire** an allusion to Lancashire as a Catholic stronghold, and to the well-known case of the puritan exorcist John Darrell, whose exorcisms included those, in 1597, of Anne and John Starkey of Lancashire. Authorities accused Darrell of perpetrating a fraud, tried and imprisoned him. Richard Bancroft and Samuel Harsnett, Bancroft's chaplain, were deeply involved in the case. Darrell apparently died in prison in 1602, having published several books on secret presses, one of which had been answered by Harsnett. Canon 72 of the Canons of 1604 results in part from the Darrell case; see 3.5.139.

265 **Midnoon** midday, noon.

EDMOND Why, look you, sir, I tell't you as a friend and a conjuror, I should marry a 'pothecary's daughter, and 'twas told me she lost her maidenhead at Stony Stratford. Now if you'll do but so much as conjure for't and make all whole again—

CAPTAIN That I will, sir.

EDMOND By my troth, I thank you la.

CAPTAIN *[to Sir Godfrey]* A little merry with your sister's son, sir.

SIR GODFREY O a simple young man, very simple. Come, Captain, and you, sir. We'll e'en part with a gallon of wine till tomorrow breakfast.

PIEBOARD *and* CAPTAIN Troth, agreed sir.

NICHOLAS Kinsman, scholar.

PIEBOARD Why, now thou art a good knave, worth a hundred Brownists.

NICHOLAS Am I indeed la? I thank you truly la. *Exeunt*

Finis Actus Tertius

4.1 *Incipit Actus Quartus*

Enter Moll and Sir John Pennydub

PENNYDUB But I hope you will not serve a knight so, gentlewoman, will you? To cashier him and cast him off at your pleasure? What, do you think I was dubbed for nothing? No, by my faith, lady's daughter.

MOLL Pray, Sir John Pennydub, let it be deferred awhile. I have as big a heart to marry as you can have, but as the fortune-teller told me.

PENNYDUB Pox o'th' fortune-teller. Would Derrick had been his fortune seven year ago to cross my love thus. Did he know what case I was in? Why, this is able to make a man drown himself in's father's fish pond.

MOLL And then he told me moreover, Sir John, that the breach of it kept my father in purgatory.

PENNYDUB In purgatory? Why, let him purge out his heart there. What have we to do with that? There's physicians enough there to cast his water. Is that any matter to us? How can he hinder our love? Why, let him be hanged now he's dead. Well have I rid post day and night to bring you merry news of my father's death and now—

MOLL Thy father's death? Is the old farmer dead?

PENNYDUB As dead as his barn door, Moll.

MOLL And you'll keep your word with me now, Sir John, that I shall have my coach and my coachman.

PENNYDUB Ay, 'faith.

MOLL And two white horses with black feathers to draw it.

PENNYDUB Too.

MOLL A guarded lackey to run befor't and pied liveries to come trashing after't.

PENNYDUB Thou shalt, Moll.

MOLL And to let me have money in my purse to go whither I will.

PENNYDUB All this.

MOLL Then come, whatsoe'er comes on't, we'll be made sure together before the maids o'the kitchen. *Exeunt*

Enter Widow with her eldest daughter Frank and Frailty 4.2

WIDOW How now, where's my brother Sir Godfrey? Went he forth this morning?

FRAILTY O no, madam, he's above at breakfast with, sir-reverence, a conjuror.

WIDOW A conjuror? What manner o' fellow is he?

FRAILTY O, a wondrous rare fellow, mistress, very strongly made upward, for he goes in a buff jerkin. He says he will fetch Sir Godfrey's chain again, if it hang between heaven and earth.

WIDOW What, he will not? Then he's an ex'lent fellow, I warrant.—*[Aside]* How happy were that woman to be blessed with such a husband, a man o' cunning.—How does he look, Frailty? Very swartly, I warrant, with black beard, scorched cheeks, and smoky eyebrows.

FRAILTY Foh, he's neither smoke-dried, nor scorched, nor black, nor nothing. I tell you, madam, he looks as fair to see to as one of us. I do not think but if you saw him once you'd take him to be a Christian.

FRANK So fair and yet so cunning. That's to be wondered at, Mother.

Enter Sir Oliver Muckhill and Sir Andrew Tipstaff

MUCKHILL Bless you, sweet lady.

TIPSTAFF And you, fair mistress. *Exit Frailty*

WIDOW Coads! What do you mean, gentlemen? Fie, did I not give you your answers?

MUCKHILL Sweet lady—

281–2 **Stony Stratford** a town in Buckinghamshire, on the River Ouse, 52 miles north-west of London, along Watling Street, with pun on 'stone' meaning 'testicle'

294 **Brownists** separatists who were followers of Robert Brown. Roger Waterer (brother to Middleton's brother-in-law Allen Waterer), one of the earliest separatists in London, was examined in 1593 prior to the execution of Brownists Henry Barrow and John Greenwood. He testified that he had been a prisoner in Newgate for three years and had attended an assembly near Bedlam. In 1609, he was indicted for attending an assembly and again put in Newgate. Middleton was not on good terms with the Waterers. Brownists were sometimes referred to as 'sectaries' or 'recusants'.

4.1.2 **cashier** discard

8 **Derrick** the hangman at Tyburn in the early 17th century

16 **cast his water** diagnose disease by the inspection of the urine

18 **rid post** travelled express with letters or messages

29 **guarded** livery ornamented with braid
lackey running footman
pied of more than one colour
liveries distinctive dress worn by a one's servants

30 **trashing** walking or running with exertion

35–6 **we'll . . . kitchen** We'll promise ourselves to each other in marriage in a spousal before witnesses.

4.2.6 **strongly** with strong effect

7 **made** attired

13 **swartly** black or blackish, from the practice of alchemy

23 **Coads** exclamation of surprise, as in 'gads!'

WIDOW [*to Muckhill*]
Well, I will not stick with you now for a kiss.
[*To Frank*] Daughter, kiss the gentleman for once.

FRANK
Yes, forsooth. [*She kisses Tipstaff*]

TIPSTAFF I'm proud of such a favour.

WIDOW Truly la, Sir Oliver, you're much to blame to come again when you know my mind so well delivered as a widow could deliver a thing.

MUCKHILL But I expect a farther comfort, lady.

WIDOW Why, la you now. Did I not desire you to put off your suit quit and clean when you came to me again? How say you? Did I not?

MUCKHILL But the sincere love which my heart bears you—

WIDOW Go to, I'll cut you off and, Sir Oliver, to put you in comfort afar off, my fortune is read me. I must marry again.

MUCKHILL O blest fortune!

WIDOW But not as long as I can choose. Nay, I'll hold out well.

MUCKHILL Yet are my hopes now fairer.

Enter Frailty

FRAILTY O madam, madam—

WIDOW How now, what's the haste?

[*Frailty whispers*] *in the Widow's ear*

TIPSTAFF [*to Frank*] Faith, Mistress Frances, I'll maintain you gallantly. I'll bring you to court, wean you among the fair society of ladies, poor kinswomen of mine, in cloth of silver. Beside you shall have your monkey, your parrot, your musk-cat, and your piss, piss, piss.

FRANK It will do very well.

WIDOW [*aside to Frailty*] What does he mean to conjure here then? How shall I do to be rid of these knights?— [*To Tipstaff and Muckhill*] Please you, gentlemen, to walk a while i'th' garden. Go gather a pink or a gillyflower.

TIPSTAFF *and* MUCKHILL With all our hearts, lady, and count us favoured.

Exeunt Tipstaff and Muckhill; [*Widow, Frank and Frailty go into an adjoining room*]

SIR GODFREY (*within*) Step in, Nicholas.

[*Enter Nicholas*]

Look, is the coast clear?

NICHOLAS O as clear as a cat's eye, sir.

SIR GODFREY (*within*) Then enter, Captain Conjuror.

Enter Sir Godfrey, Captain, Pieboard, and Edmond

[*to Captain*] Now, how like you your room, sir?

CAPTAIN O wonderful convenient.

EDMOND I can tell you, captain, simply though it lies here, 'tis the fairest room in my mother's house, as dainty a room to conjure in, methinks. Why, you may bid I cannot tell how many devils welcome in't. My father has had twenty here at once.

PIEBOARD What devils?

EDMOND Devils? No, deputies, and the wealthiest men he could get.

SIR GODFREY Nay, put by your chats now, fall to your business roundly. The fescue of the dial is upon the criss-cross of noon. But, O hear me, captain, a qualm comes o'er my stomach.

CAPTAIN Why, what's the matter, sir?

SIR GODFREY O how if the devil should prove a knave and tear the hangings?

CAPTAIN Fuh, I warrant you, Sir Godfrey.

EDMOND Ay, nuncle, or spit fire upo'th' ceiling.

SIR GODFREY Very true, too, for 'tis but thin plastered and 'twill quickly take hold o' the laths. And if he chance to spit downward too, he will burn all the boards.

CAPTAIN My life for yours, Sir Godfrey.

SIR GODFREY My sister is very curious and dainty o'er this room, I can tell, and therefore if he must needs spit, I pray desire him to spit i'th' chimney.

PIEBOARD Why, assure you, Sir Godfrey, he shall not be brought up with so little manners to spit and spaule o'th' floor.

SIR GODFREY Why, I thank you, good captain. Pray, have a care, ay, fall to your circle. We'll not trouble you, I warrant you. Come, we'll into the next room, and because we'll be sure to keep him out there, we'll bar up the door with some of the godlies' zealous works.

EDMOND That will be a fine device, nuncle. And because the ground shall be as holy as the door, I'll tear two or three rosaries in pieces and strew the leaves about the chamber. [*It thunders*] O the devil already—

[*Sir Godfrey, Edmond, and Nicholas*] *run in*[*to adjoining room*]

26 **stick** stay
35 **quit** free, clear
49 **wean** train, accustom to good habits
52 **musk-cat** small hornless ruminant of Central Asia, the male of which yields the perfume 'musk'
piss lap dog; also contemptuous reference to Frank's collection of exotic possessions
57 **gillyflower** a variety of a pink, a wall-flower
72 **deputies** in the City of London, members of the Common Council, who act instead of an alderman in his absence
74 **chats** chatter
75 **fescue** the shadow on a sundial
76 **criss-cross** The meridional line in the old dial plate was distinguished by a cross; in ELD, 'chrisse-crosse'
91 **spaule** expectorate
96–7 **bar ... works** mocking allusion to lengthy religious treatises by those eager for more reform. 'Zealous' and 'godly' were commonly used to stigmatize puritans.
100 **rosaries** another example of the play's conflation of puritan and papist. While the word 'rosary' was occasionally adopted by protestants (as in Philip Stubbes's book of prayers, *The rosarie of Christian praiers and meditations*, 1583), rosaries were primarily understood to be the prayer beads of Catholics. In 1606, one of the statutes responding to the Gunpowder Plot forbade anyone to import, buy, sell, or print any 'popish' primers, psalters, manuals, rosaries, catechisms, missals, breviaries, or lives of saints (3 Jac.I.c.5).
leaves pages

PIEBOARD 'Sfoot, captain, speak somewhat, for shame. It lightens and thunders before thou wilt begin. Why, when?

CAPTAIN Pray, peace, George. Thou'lt make me laugh anon and spoil all.

PIEBOARD O now it begins again. Now, now, now, captain.

CAPTAIN *Rumbos—ragdayon, pur, pur, colucundrion, Hois—Plois*

SIR GODFREY (*speaking through the keyhole within*) O admirable conjuror, he's fetched thunder already.

PIEBOARD Hark, hark, again, captain.

CAPTAIN *Benjamino,—gaspois—kay—gosgothoteron—umbrois*

SIR GODFREY [*within*] O I would the devil would come away quickly. He has no conscience to put a man to such pain.

PIEBOARD Again.

CAPTAIN *Flowste—Kakopumpos—dragone—Leloomenos—hodge-podge*

PIEBOARD Well said, captain.

SIR GODFREY [*within*] So long a coming? O would I had ne'er begun't now, for I fear me these roaring tempests will destroy all the fruits of the earth and tread upon my corn, O, i'th' country.

CAPTAIN *Gog de gog, hobgoblin, huncks, Hounslow, Hockley te Combe Park*

WIDOW [*within*] O, brother, brother, what a tempest's i'th' garden. Sure there's some conjuration abroad.

SIR GODFREY [*within*] 'Tis at home, sister.

PIEBOARD By and by, I'll step in, captain.

CAPTAIN *Nunck-Nunck—Rip—Gascoynes, Ipis, Drip—Dropite*

SIR GODFREY [*within*] He drips and drops, poor man, alas, alas.

PIEBOARD Now I come.

CAPTAIN *O Sulphure Soot-face*

PIEBOARD Arch-conjuror, what wouldst thou with me?

SIR GODFREY [*within*] O the devil, sister, i'th' dining chamber, sing, sister. I warrant you, that will keep him out, quickly, quickly, quickly.

Sir Godfrey goes in

PIEBOARD So, so, so, I'll release thee. Enough, captain, enough. Allow us some time to laugh a little. They're shuddering and shaking by this time as if an earthquake were in their kidneys.

CAPTAIN Sirrah, George, how was't, how was't? Did I do't well enough?

PIEBOARD Wilt believe me, captain? Better than any conjuror, for here was no harm in this and yet their horrible expectation satisfied well. You were much beholding to thunder and lightning at this time. It graced you well, I can tell you.

CAPTAIN I must needs say so, George. Sirrah, if we could ha' conveyed hither cleanly a cracker or a firewheel, 't'ad been admirable.

PIEBOARD Blurt, blurt, there's nothing remains to put thee to pain now, captain.

CAPTAIN Pain? I protest, George, my heels are sorer than a Whitsun morris dancer.

PIEBOARD All's past now, only to reveal that the chain's i'th' garden, where thou know'st it has lain these two days.

CAPTAIN But I fear that fox Nicholas has revealed it already.

PIEBOARD Fear not, captain. You must put it to th' venture now. Nay, 'tis time. Call upon 'em, take pity on 'em, for I believe some of 'em are in a pitiful case by this time.

CAPTAIN Sir Godfrey, Nicholas kinsman—'Sfoot, they're fast at it still George. Sir Godfrey—

[*Enter Sir Godfrey, Widow, and Nicholas*]

SIR GODFREY O is that the devil's voice? How comes he to know my name?

CAPTAIN Fear not, Sir Godfrey, all's quieted.

SIR GODFREY What, is he laid?

CAPTAIN Laid, and has newly dropped your chain i'th' garden.

SIR GODFREY I'th' garden? In our garden?

CAPTAIN Your garden.

SIR GODFREY O sweet conjuror, whereabouts there?

CAPTAIN Look well about a bank of rosemary.

SIR GODFREY Sister, the rosemary bank. Come, come, there's my chain, he says.

103 **lightens** flashes lightening

108 **Rumbos—ragdayon, pur, pur** The Captain's language of conjuring is a hodgepodge of comically feigned Greek-sounding words, with this first line coming the closest of any to containing real and appropriate Greek. 'Rumbos', for rhumbos or rhombos, is the term for the special wheel used in magical rites. 'Ragdayon' is from the adjective rhagdaios, meaning 'violent' or 'furious', as applied to rain storms and lightning. 'Pur' is pyr, or 'fire'.

113 **gosgothoteron** -oteron is a suffix for a comparative adjective or adverb form, but the root of the work is not recognizable Greek.

119 **Kakopumpos... Leloomenos** two pseudo-Greek words

126–7 **Hounslow, Hockley te Combe Park** These three towns—Hounslow (on the Western coach road in Middlesex), Hockley in the Hole (on the N. W. Road, or Watling Street) and Combe Park (in Surrey)—were known as the scenes of many highway robberies.

154 **cracker** firework which explodes with a sharp report

firewheel rotating firework

156 **blurt** exclamation of contempt

159 **Whitsun** a parish festival held during the season of Whit Sunday or Whitsuntide, Whit Sunday being the seventh Sunday after Easter, to mark Pentecost

morris dancer dancers in fancy costumes whose dance usually represents characters in the Robin Hood legend; a mumming performance involving fantastic dancing

173 **he laid** his spirit prevented from walking

WIDOW O happiness, run, run.

[Exeunt Sir Godfrey, Widow, and Nicholas]

EDMOND *(at keyhole)* Captain Conjuror?

CAPTAIN Who? Master Edmond?

EDMOND *[at keyhole]* Ay, Master Edmond. May I come in safely without danger, think you?

CAPTAIN
Fuh, long ago. 'Tis all as 'twas at first.
Fear nothing.
[Enter Edmond]
Pray, come near. How now, man?

EDMOND O this room's mightily hot, i'faith. 'Slid, my shirt sticks to my belly already. What a steam the rogue has left behind him. Foh, this room must be aired, gentlemen. It smells horribly of brimstone. Let's open the windows.

PIEBOARD Faith, Master Edmond, 'tis but your conceit.

EDMOND I would you could make me believe that, i'faith. Why, do you think I cannot smell his savour from another? Yet I take it kindly from you because you would not put me in a fear, i'faith. O' my troth, I shall love you for this the longest day of my life.

CAPTAIN Puh, 'tis nothing, sir. Love me when you see more.

EDMOND Mass, now I remember. I'll look whether he has singed the hangings or no.

PIEBOARD *[aside to the Captain]* Captain, to entertain a little sport till they come, make him believe you'll charm him invisible. He's apt to admire anything, you see. Let me alone to give force to't.

CAPTAIN *[aside to Pieboard]* Go, retire to yonder end then.

EDMOND *[to Captain]* I protest you are a rare fellow, are you not?

CAPTAIN O Master Edmond, you know but the least part of me yet. Why, now at this instant I could but flourish my wand thrice o'er your head and charm you invisible.

EDMOND What? You could not. Make me walk invisible, man? I should laugh at that, i'faith. Troth, I'll requite your kindness, an you'll do't, good Captain Conjuror.

CAPTAIN Nay, I should hardly deny you such a small kindness, Master Edmond Plus. Why, look you, sir, 'tis no more but this, and thus, and again, and now you're invisible.

EDMOND Am I, i'faith? Who would think it?

CAPTAIN You see the fortune-teller yonder at farther end o'th' chamber? Go toward him. Do what you will with him, he shall ne'er find you.

EDMOND Say you so? I'll try that, i'faith.

He jostles Pieboard

PIEBOARD How now, captain, who's that jostled me?

CAPTAIN Jostled you? I saw nobody.

EDMOND Ha, ha, ha. Say 'twas a spirit.

CAPTAIN Shall I? Maybe some spirit that haunts the circle.

Edmond pulls Pieboard by the nose

PIEBOARD O my nose, again. Pray conjure then, captain.

EDMOND Troth, this is ex'lent. I may do any knavery now and never be seen. And now I remember me, Sir Godfrey, my uncle abused me t'other day and told tales of me to my mother. Troth, now I'm invisible, I'll hit him a sound wherret o'th' ear when he comes out o'th' garden. I may be revenged on him now finely.

Enter Sir Godfrey, Widow, Frank, and Nicholas with the chain

SIR GODFREY
I have my chain again, my chain's found again,
O sweet captain, O admirable conjuror.
Edmond strikes Sir Godfrey
O what mean you by that, nephew?

EDMOND
Nephew? I hope you do not know me, uncle?

WIDOW
Why did you strike your uncle, sir?

EDMOND
Why, captain, am I not invisible?

CAPTAIN *[aside to Pieboard]*
A good jest, George.—
[To Edmond] Not now you are not, sir.
Why, did you not see me when I did uncharm you?

EDMOND
Not I, by my troth, captain.—
[To Sir Godfrey] Then, pray you, pardon me, uncle.
I thought I'd been invisible when I struck you.

SIR GODFREY
So, you would do't. Go, you're a foolish boy,
And were I not o'ercome with greater joy,
I'd make you taste correction.

EDMOND *[aside]* Correction, push. No, neither you nor my mother shall think to whip me as you have done.

SIR GODFREY Captain, my joy is such I know not how to thank you. Let me embrace you, hug you. O my sweet chain. Gladness e'en makes me giddy, rare man. 'Twas as just i'th' rosemary bank as if one should ha' laid it there. O cunning, cunning.

WIDOW Well, seeing my fortune tells me I must marry, let me marry a man of wit, a man of parts. Here's a worthy captain, and 'tis a fine title truly la to be a captain's wife, a captain's wife. It goes very finely. Beside all the world knows that a worthy captain is a fit companion to any lord. Then why not a sweet bedfellow for any lady. I'll have it so.

Enter Frailty

FRAILTY O mistress, gentlemen, there's the bravest sight coming along this way.

WIDOW What brave sight?

FRAILTY O one going to burying and another going to hanging.

WIDOW A rueful sight.

PIEBOARD *[aside to Captain]* 'Sfoot, captain, I'll pawn my life the corporal's coffined, and old Skirmish the soldier going to execution. And 'tis now full about the time of

192 **brimstone** sulphur
194 **conceit** imagination
196 **savour** aroma
235 **wherret** slap, blow

his waking. Hold out a little longer, sleepy potion, and we shall have ex'lent admiration, for I'll take upon me the cure of him.

Enter the coffin of the Corporal, the soldier Skirmish bound and led by Officers, the Sheriff there

FRAILTY O here they come, here they come.

PIEBOARD [*aside*] Now must I close secretly with the soldier, prevent his impatience, or else all's discovered.

WIDOW O lamentable seeing! These were those brothers that fought and bled before our door.

SIR GODFREY What? They were not, sister.

SKIRMISH [*aside to Pieboard*] George, look to't. I'll peach at Tyburn else.

PIEBOARD [*aside to Skirmish*] Mum.—Gentles all, vouchsafe me audience, and you especially, Master Sheriff.
Yon man is bound to execution
Because he wounded this that now lies coffined.

SHERIFF True, true, he shall have the law, an I know the law.

PIEBOARD But under favour, Master Sheriff, if this man had been cured and safe again, he should have been released then.

SHERIFF Why make you question of that, sir?

PIEBOARD Then I release him freely and will take upon me the death that he should die, if within a little season I do not cure him to his proper health again.

SHERIFF How, sir, recover a dead man? That were most strange of all.

Frank comes to Pieboard

FRANK Sweet sir, I love you dearly and could wish my best part yours. O do not undertake such an impossible venture.

PIEBOARD
Love you me? Then for your sweet sake I'll do't.
Let me entreat the corpse to be set down.

SHERIFF Bearers, set down the coffin. This were wonderful and worthy Stow's *Chronicle*.

PIEBOARD I pray, bestow the freedom of the air upon our wholesome art.—[*Aside*] Mass, his cheeks begin to receive natural warmth. Nay, good corporal, wake betime or I shall have a longer sleep than you. 'Sfoot, if he should prove dead indeed now, he were fully revenged upon me for making a property on him. Yet I had rather run upon the ropes than have the rope like a tetter run upon me.—O he stirs, he stirs again, look, gentlemen, he recovers, he starts, he rises.

SHERIFF O, O defend us, out alas.

PIEBOARD Nay, pray be still. You'll make him more giddy else. He knows nobody yet.

CORPORAL 'Swounds, who am I, covered with snow, I marvel?

PIEBOARD [*aside*] Nay, I knew he would swear the first thing he did, as soon as ever he came to his life again.

CORPORAL 'Sfoot, hostess, some hot porridge. O, O, lay on a dozen of faggots in the moon parlour there.

PIEBOARD [*to Widow*] Lady, you must needs take a little pity of him, i'faith, and send him in to your kitchen fire.

WIDOW [*to Pieboard*] O with all my heart, sir. Nicholas and Frailty, help to bear him in.

NICHOLAS Bear him in, quoth a? Pray call out the maids. I shall ne'er have the heart to do't, indeed la.

FRAILTY Nor I neither. I cannot abide to handle a ghost, of all men.

CORPORAL 'Sblood, let me see. Where was I drunk last night, heh?

WIDOW O, shall I bid you once again take him away?

FRAILTY Why, we're as fearful as you, I warrant you, O.

WIDOW Away, villains. Bid the maids make him a caudle presently to settle his brain, or a posset of sack, quickly, quickly.

[*Frailty and Nicholas*] *exeunt, pushing in the corpse*

SKIRMISH [*to Pieboard*] Sir, what so e'er you are, I do more than admire you.

WIDOW O ay, if you knew all, Master Sheriff, as you shall do, you would say then that here were two of the rarest men within the walls of Christendom.

SHERIFF Two of 'em? O wonderful! Officers, I discharge you. Set him free. All's in tune.

SIR GODFREY Ay, and a banquet ready by this time, Master Sheriff, to which I most cheerfully invite you and your late prisoner there. See you this goodly chain, sir? Mum, no more words. 'Twas lost and is found again. [*To Pieboard and Captain*] Come, my inestimable bullies, we'll talk of your noble acts in sparkling charneco, and instead of a jester, we'll ha' the ghost i'th' white sheet sit at upper end o'th' table.

SHERIFF Ex'lent merry man, i'faith. [*Exeunt all but Frank*]

FRANK
Well, seeing I am enjoined to love and marry,

276 **admiration** wonder, astonishment
277.1 ***Enter the coffin*** With the entrance of the coffin, the location of the action changes from inside the Widow's house to outside on the street. No scene division is called for in this instance of discontinuity in place but continuity in action.
279 **close...with** unite with
284 **peach** turn informer
285 **Tyburn** the place of execution by hanging, near the junction of Oxford Street and Edgeware Road
292 **under favour** with all submission, subject to correction
307 **Stow's *Chronicle*** John Stow's *Chronicle of England* (1580, and frequently reprinted)
313 **making a property on him** making him a means to an end
314 **run upon the ropes** take desperate risks; a metaphor from tight-rope walking
rope hangman's cord
315 **tetter** ringworm
320 **covered with snow** Corporal refers to his winding sheet
324 **porridge** (used as a hangover remedy)
339 **caudle** warm, sweetened and spiced gruel, mixed with wine or ale
340 **posset** hot milk curdled with ale or wine
354 **charneco** a kind of wine

My foolish vow thus I cashier to air,
Which first begot it. Now, love, play thy part.
The scholar reads his lecture in my heart. [*Exit*]

Finis Actus Quartus

5.1 *Incipit Actus Quintus*

Enter in haste Master Edmond and Frailty

EDMOND This is the marriage morning for my mother and my sister.

FRAILTY O me, Master Edmond, we shall ha' rare doings.

EDMOND Nay, go, Frailty, run to the sexton. You know my mother will be married at St Antling's. Hie thee. 'Tis past five. Bid them open the church door. My sister is almost ready.

FRAILTY What? Already, Master Edmond?

EDMOND Nay, go hie thee. First run to the sexton, and run to the clerk, and then run to Master Pigman, the parson, and then run to the milliner, and then run home again.

FRAILTY Here's run, run, run.

EDMOND But hark, Frailty.

FRAILTY What more yet?

EDMOND Has the maids rememb'red to strew the way to the church?

FRAILTY Fough, an hour ago. I help' 'em myself.

EDMOND Away, away, away, away then.

FRAILTY Away, away, away then. *Exit*

EDMOND I shall have a simple father-in-law, a brave captain able to beat all our street, Captain Idle. Now my lady mother will be fitted for a delicate name, my Lady Idle, my Lady Idle, the finest name that can be for a woman. And then the scholar Master Pieboard for my sister Francis. That will be Mistress Francis Pieboard, Mistress Francis Pieboard. They'll keep a good table, I warrant you. Now all the knights' noses are put out of joint. They may go to a bone-setter's now.

Enter Captain and Pieboard

Hark, hark. O who come here with two torches before 'em? My sweet captain and my fine scholar. O how bravely they are shot up in one night. They look like fine Britons now, methinks. Here's a gallant change, i'faith. 'Slid, they have hired men and all, by the clock.

CAPTAIN Master Edmond, kind, honest, dainty Master Edmond.

EDMOND Fough, sweet captain father-in-law, a rare perfume, i'faith.

PIEBOARD What, are the brides stirring? May we steal upon 'em, thinkst thou, Master Edmond?

EDMOND Fough, they're e'en upon readiness, I can assure you, for they were at their torch e'en now. By the same token, I tumbled down the stairs.

PIEBOARD Alas, poor Master Edmond.

Enter musicians

CAPTAIN O the musicians. I prithee, Master Edmond, call 'em in and liquor 'em a little.

EDMOND That I will, sweet captain father-in-law, and make each of them as drunk as a common fiddler. *Exeunt*

5.2 *Enter Sir John Pennydub, and Moll above lacing of her clothes*

PENNYDUB Whew, Mistress Moll, Mistress Moll.

MOLL Who's there?

PENNYDUB 'Tis I.

MOLL Who? Sir John Pennydub? O you're an early cock, i'faith. Who would have thought you to be so rare a stirrer?

PENNYDUB Prithee, Moll, let me come up.

MOLL No, by my faith, Sir John. I'll keep you down, for you knights are very dangerous if once you get above.

PENNYDUB I'll not stay, i'faith.

MOLL I'faith, you shall stay, for, Sir John, you must note the nature of the climates. Your northern wench in her own country may well hold out till she be fifteen, but if she touch the south once and come up to London, here the chimes go presently after twelve.

PENNYDUB O th'art a mad wench, Moll, but I prithee make haste, for the priest is gone before.

MOLL Do you follow him, I'll not be long after. *Exeunt*

5.3 *Enter Sir Oliver Muckhill, Sir Andrew Tipstaff, and old Skirmish talking*

MUCKHILL O monstrous unheard of forgery.

TIPSTAFF Knight, I never heard of such villainy in our own country in my life.

MUCKHILL Why, 'tis impossible. Dare you maintain your words?

SKIRMISH Dare we? E'en to their weasand-pipes. We know all their plots. They cannot squander with us. They have knavishly abused us, made only properties on's to advance theirselves upon our shoulders, but they shall rue their abuses. This morning they are to be married.

MUCKHILL 'Tis too true. Yet if the Widow be not too much besotted on sleights and forgeries, the revelation of their villainies will make 'em loathsome. And to that end,

359 **cashier** make void
5.1.10 **clerk** the lay officer of a parish church, who has charge of the church and precincts, and assists the clergyman in various parts of his duties
11 **milliner** vendor of bonnets, ribbons, gloves, esp. of such as were originally of Milan manufacture
16 **strew** scatter flowers or rushes on the ground
21 **simple** free from duplicity; straightforward
23 **delicate** fine, self-indulgent, indolent
28–9 **noses . . . out of joint** plans . . . spoiled
32 **bravely** magnificently
shot up risen
33 **Britons** Scots; Andrew Lethe in *Michaelmas Term*, is a Scot whose fortunes shoot up once he gets to England.
34 **by the clock** by the hour
42 **at their torch** dressing by torch light
5.2.4–9 extended sexual quibble
12–15 **Your northern wench . . . after twelve** Moll refers to the sexual practices of the more worldly London woman.
5.3.1 **forgery** deceit
6 **weasand-pipes** throats, windpipes
12 **besotted** infatuated

be it in private to you, I sent late last night to an honourable personage, to whom I am much indebted in kindness as he is to me, and therefore presume upon the payment of his tongue, and that he will lay out good words for me. And to speak truth, for such needful occasions, I only preserve him in bond. And sometimes he may do me more good here in the city by a free word of his mouth than if he had paid one half in hand and took doomsday for t'other.

TIPSTAFF In troth, sir, without soothing be it spoken, you have published much judgement in these few words.

MUCKHILL For you know, what such a man utters will be thought effectual and to weighty purpose, and therefore into his mouth we'll put the approved theme of their forgeries.

SKIRMISH And I'll maintain it, knight, if ye'll be true.

Enter a Servant

MUCKHILL How now, fellow.

SERVANT May it please you, sir, my lord is newly lighted from his coach.

MUCKHILL

Is my lord come already? His honour's early.
You see, he loves me well up before seven.
Trust me, I have found him night-capped at eleven.
There's good hope yet. Come, I'll relate all to him.

Exeunt

5.4 *Enter the two bridegrooms, Captain and scholar Pieboard. After them, Sir Godfrey and Edmond, Widow changed in apparel, Mistress Frank led between two knights, Sir John Pennydub and Moll. There meets them a Nobleman, Sir Oliver Muckhill, Sir Andrew Tipstaff,* [*and Skirmish*]

NOBLEMAN By your leave, lady.

WIDOW My lord, your honour is most chastely welcome.

NOBLEMAN Madam, though I came now from court, I come not to flatter you. Upon whom can I justly cast this blot but upon your own forehead, that know not ink from milk. Such is the blind besotting in the state of an unheaded woman that's a widow. For it is the property of all you that are widows (a handful excepted) to hate those that honestly and carefully love you to the maintenance of credit, state and posterity, and strongly to doat on those that only love you to undo you. Who regard you least are best regarded, who hate you most are best beloved. And if there be but one man amongst ten thousand millions of men that is accursed disastrous and evilly planeted, whom fortune beats most, whom God hates most, and all societies esteem least, that man is sure to be a husband. Such is the peevish moon that rules your bloods. An impudent fellow best woos you, a flattering lip best wins you, or in a mirth, who talks roughliest is most sweetest. Nor can you distinguish truth from forgeries, mists from simplicity. Witness those two deceitful monsters that you have entertained for bridegrooms.

WIDOW Deceitful?

PIEBOARD [*aside to Captain*] All will out.

CAPTAIN [*aside to Pieboard*] 'Sfoot, who has blabbed, George? That foolish Nicholas?

NOBLEMAN For what they have besotted your easy blood withal were naught but forgeries, the fortunetelling for husbands, the conjuring for the chain Sir Godfrey heard the falsehood of. All nothing but mere knavery, deceit and cozenage.

WIDOW O wonderful! Indeed, I wondered that my husband with all his craft could not keep himself out of purgatory.

SIR GODFREY And I more wonder that my chain should be gone and my tailor had none of it.

MOLL And I wondered most of all that I should be tied from marriage, having such a mind to't. Come, Sir John Pennydub, fair weather on our side. The moon has changed since yesternight.

PIEBOARD [*aside*] The sting of every evil is within me.

NOBLEMAN And that you may perceive I feign not with you, [*Pointing to Skirmish*] behold their fellow actor in those forgeries who, full of spleen and envy at their so sudden advancements, revealed all their plot in anger.

PIEBOARD [*aside*] Base soldier to reveal us.

WIDOW Is't possible we should be blinded so and our eyes open?

NOBLEMAN Widow, will you now believe that false which too soon you believed true?

WIDOW O to my shame, I do.

SIR GODFREY But under favour, my lord, my chain was truly lost and strangely found again.

NOBLEMAN Resolve him of that, soldier.

SKIRMISH In few words, knight, then, thou wert the arch-gull of all.

SIR GODFREY How, sir?

SKIRMISH Nay, I'll prove it, for the chain was but hid in the rosemary bank all this while, and thou gotst him out of prison to conjure for it who did it admirably, fustianly. For indeed, what need any others when he knew where it was?

SIR GODFREY O villainy of villainies. But how came my chain there?

SKIRMISH Where's 'Truly la, Indeed la', he that will not swear but lie, he that will not steal but rob, pure Nicholas St Antlings.

SIR GODFREY

O villain, one of our society,
Deemed always holy, pure, religious,

19 **in bond** indebted
21 **in hand** immediately
23 **soothing** flattering
24 **published** displayed
5.4.7 **property** characteristic
15 **evilly planeted** under an evil astrological sign
21 **mists** deceits
28 **easy blood** thoughtless, careless disposition
66 **'Truly la, Indeed la'** Nicholas, who uses these expressions

A puritan a thief? When was't ever heard?
Sooner we'll kill a man than steal, thou know'st.
Out, slave, I'll rend my lion from thy back
With mine own hands.

NICHOLAS
Dear master, O—

NOBLEMAN Nay, knight, dwell in patience.
[*To Widow*] And now, widow, being so near the church, 'twere great pity, nay, uncharity to send you home again without a husband. [*To Muckhill and Tipstaff*] Draw nearer, you of true worship, state, and credit that should not stand so far off from a widow and suffer forged shapes to come between you. Not that in these I blemish the true title of a captain or blot the fair margent of a scholar, for I honour worthy and deserving parts in the one and cherish fruitful virtues in the other. [*To Widow and Frank*] Come, lady, and you, virgin, bestow your eyes and your purest affections upon men of estimation both in court and city, that hath long wooed you and both with their hearts and wealth sincerely love you.

SIR GODFREY Good sister, do. Sweet little Frank, these are men of reputation. You shall be welcome at court, a great credit for a citizen, sweet sister.

NOBLEMAN Come, her silence does consent to't.

WIDOW I know not with what face.

NOBLEMAN Pah, pah, why, with your own face. They desire no other.

WIDOW [*to Muckhill and Tipstaff*] Pardon me, worthy sirs.
I and my daughter have wronged your loves.

MUCKHILL
'Tis easily pardoned, lady,
If you vouchsafe it now.

WIDOW
With all my soul.

FRANK And I with all my heart.

MOLL
And I, Sir John, with soul, heart, lights and all.

PENNYDUB
They are all mine, Moll.

NOBLEMAN Now, lady,
What honest spirit but will applaud your choice
And gladly furnish you with hand and voice,
A happy change which makes e'en heaven rejoice.
Come enter into your joys. You shall not want
For fathers now, I doubt it not, believe me,
But that you shall have hands enough to give ye.

Exeunt

Finis

73 **rend my lion from thy back** remove my crest from your livery
81 **forged shapes** impostors
82–3 **blot the fair margent of** damage the reputation of, or destroy the previously favourable commentary on (pun on marginalia, which were a means of comment)
94 **face** expression

THE REVENGER'S TRAGEDY

Edited by MacDonald P. Jackson

IN *Rosencrantz and Guildenstern are Dead* Tom Stoppard re-imagined *Hamlet* from the point of view of those two interchangeable stooges. *The Revenger's Tragedy* is like a version by Yorick—as jester, and as skull. Middleton had obviously been fascinated by Shakespeare's great tragedy of revenge, but his own masterpiece in that genre adds ingredients from Jacobean satiric comedy of chicanery and disguise and from the medieval Morality drama, with its emphasis on death and eternal judgement. The spirit of the Gravedigger's 'whoreson mad fellow', master of quip and jape, presides over Middleton's plot, and the emblem of what Yorick has become dominates the play's thought, complicates its values, permeates its poetry, and darkens its mood.

The standard precipitant of a revenge tragedy, as introduced to the English theatre by Thomas Kyd's *The Spanish Tragedy* about 1588, is the horrendous and unpunished killing of somebody close to the hero. In Henry Chettle's *Hoffman* (1602), written when both Chettle and Middleton were working for the Admiral's Men, the eponymous villain-hero retaliates ferociously for the judicial execution of his pirate father, but normally the avenger seeks retribution for murder, the obstacle to legal redress being the power of the perpetrators. The adversaries of Kyd's Hieronimo, murderers of his son, are the Prince of Portugal and a machiavellian blackguard whose father is Duke of Castile and whose uncle is King of Spain. Hamlet's 'mighty opposite', Claudius, guilty of fratricide and regicide, is the new king. In *The Revenger's Tragedy*, Vindice's grievance is against the Duke, who poisoned his betrothed because she would not yield to his sexual advances. But Middleton's protagonist has a trace, too, of Hamlet's motive, his father having died, Vindice believes, of 'discontent' engendered by the Duke's ill treatment of him. Moreover Vindice's brother Hippolito, along with other disaffected courtiers, swears to avenge the rape of the Lord Antonio's wife—a crime that drove her to suicide—since the rapist, being the Duchess's son, seems likely to evade the full rigour of the law. And by the end of 1.3 Vindice 'durst make a promise of' Lussurioso to his sword, because the lustful heir to the dukedom has made him vow to serve as pander to Castiza, Vindice's own sister. *The Revenger's Tragedy* is deeply indebted to the conventions and devices of the genre towards which its title gestures: the *memento vindictae*, ritual oath upon a sword, undercover scheming, heavenly portents, use of poison, young woman threatened or victimized, wholesale slaughter, hero's reliance upon an 'occasion' afforded by the enemy, portrayal of an unbalanced mind, catastrophe in which a court entertainment encroaches upon the reality of the play—all these elements Middleton inherited from his predecessors, who had been influenced, directly or through Kyd, by the gory dramas of the first-century Roman Stoic, Seneca. *Hamlet*'s incest reappears in *The Revenger's Tragedy* in the liaison between the Duchess and her husband's bastard, and, less overtly, in Vindice's wooing of Castiza. The scene in which Vindice and Hippolito berate their mother for her willingness to prostitute her daughter, and at dagger's point persuade her to repentance, is strongly reminiscent of the closet scene between Hamlet and Gertrude.

Yet the diversity of Vindice's objectives as avenger points to an essential difference between Shakespeare's play and Middleton's. 'Something is rotten in the state of Denmark', but the source of that corruption is Claudius, and when Hamlet kills him, Hamlet himself is dying and the play is almost over. But in *The Revenger's Tragedy* the whole royal family—the Duke's wife, son, stepsons, and illegitimate son—are vile. Vindice's chief foe, the Duke, is dispatched at the midpoint of the play, and Vindice's own death awaits the elimination of the whole wrangling brood: he dies after 'a nest of dukes'. *Hamlet* proceeds by a series of moves and countermoves of protagonist and antagonist—a struggle to the death, which both lose. But *The Revenger's Tragedy* has no such central conflict: the Duke and his (or his Duchess's) offspring are unaware of Vindice's plans, which are in one sense superfluous, since the sibling rivalry is itself murderous in intent. Nor does Vindice have Hamlet's need to check a ghost's word, or Hieronimo's to confirm a dubious message, before committing himself to lethal action: he tells us, in his opening soliloquy, that the Duke is the criminal, and we accept the information as given. The play lacks *Hamlet*'s 'detective' interest. Vindice has none of Hamlet's questing, probing, self-scrutinizing impulse, either. He is unconcerned about the ethics of revenge. So the play explores no internal conflict in the mind of its hero in relation to his purpose.

Does Hamlet delay? Vindice does—for nine years, but before the play begins. The suggestion of a long prior build-up of furious resentment, newly aggravated by his 'worthy father's funeral' (1.1.119), perhaps helps explain the explosive force with which that hatred erupts on to the stage. Middleton's plot seems driven by Vindice's manic energy. Is Hamlet mad? Antony Sher, who played Vindice in Di Trevis's Royal Shakespeare Company production at the Swan in Stratford-upon-Avon in 1987, thought Middleton's hero 'so damaged by the tragedy of Gloriana that he is quite crazy, really', adding that for an actor the key to the role is realization of 'some kind of joy' in what for Vindice is 'a process of redemption'. An apter word might be therapy. Vindice moves from smouldering bitterness and a feeling that his 'life's unnatural' to him, as if he 'should be dead' (1.1.120–1), through the play's frenzied bursts of activity, to contented acquiescence in the sentence of death that Antonio passes upon him. But if Vindice experiences catharsis, the audience does not. We do not watch him die. He is bundled off to the headsman's block with a brisk 'Adieu'. No flights of angels sing this hero to his rest. We feel much as we do when at the conclusion of *A Mad World, My Masters* the arch trickster Follywit receives his comeuppance and good-humouredly shrugs off the news that he has unwittingly married his uncle's cast-off whore.

In fact for most of the play our engagement with Vindice is as with one of Middleton's comic pranksters or such bustling Vice figures as Marlowe's Barabas, Jonson's Volpone, or Shakespeare's Richard Gloucester. We are implicated in their wiliness or wickedness, vicariously enjoy it, admire their bravura inventiveness, but are detached enough to judge them. In fact, in *The Revenger's Tragedy*, 'the basic method of dramatic articulation seems to belong to comic art', as New Mermaid editor Brian Gibbons asserted. Events are shaped less by the inevitability of tragedy than by the capricious complications, ironies, and solutions of comedy or farce. Vindice dies because he cannot keep his mouth shut, a folly he had been quick to mock in others. His hubris is that of the contriver bursting with pride in his cleverness. In Middleton's play 'purposes mistook | Fall'n on th'inventors' heads' become the very principle of construction. So Ambitioso and Supervacuo, plotting to release their younger brother from prison 'by a wile' and to hasten the execution of their stepbrother Lussurioso while feigning to try to prevent it, accidentally ensure Junior's well-deserved beheading. Ambitioso's 'Whose head's that then?' (3.6.72) sounds like a line out of Joe Orton's *Loot*. Some critics have seen the just hand of Providence in these apt reversals, but the spirit in which they are presented suggests less the Divine Judge than some Cosmic Ironist or Omnipotent Jester. As audiences soon discover, much of *The Revenger's Tragedy* is quite outrageously funny.

Its most likely date of composition (for the King's Men) is 1606, after Middleton had written his series of 'city comedies' for the Children of Paul's. In those plays London scoundrels fleece country boobies and impoverished young gallants intrigue to outwit tightwad elders in a 'mad world' of prodigal dissipation, predatory greed, and saleable sex. Middleton presents a venal London society with deadpan detachment. *The Revenger's Tragedy* is in many ways closer in tone to Ben Jonson's *Volpone*, which Middleton may already have seen on stage, and to one of that play's evident ancestors, Marlowe's *The Jew of Malta*, in which the ironic handling of a melodramatic plot creates what T. S. Eliot recognized as a kind of 'savage farce'. Marlowe's Barabas and his untrusty Turkish servant Ithamore are cartoon figures of gleeful villainy, the central vengeful intriguers in a self-contained dramatic milieu of unscrupulous political scheming defined in a prologue spoken by the soul of Machiavelli himself. And in *Volpone*, with its beast-fable Italian character-names and Venetian setting of voluptuous trade, Jonson offers a topsy-turvy community of grotesque humours animated solely by avarice and lust, a community destroyed by its own appetites.

The creation of an abnormal looking-glass world with its own principles of operation is a familiar ploy of the satirist, and *The Revenger's Tragedy* adopts something of this method, to become the sanguinary counterpart of *Volpone*, matching its breadth, intensity, and richness, sharing its mix of revulsion and an almost celebratory gusto, while perhaps attaining a less steady ethical stance. It too draws on a conventional Elizabethan–Jacobean image of Italy, as, in the words of Thomas Nashe, 'the academy of manslaughter... the apothecary shop of poison', and employs type figures called by the Italian equivalents of Lechery, Ambition, Vanity, and so on. They are walking abstractions, vitalized by Vindice's, and beyond him the author's, fascinated detestation of what they stand for. The play encloses them in their own unnatural world of 'noon at midnight'. In many of his speeches Vindice—like Marston's ousted Duke Altofronto, awaiting the opportunity to unsettle his factious enemies and regain his kingdom, while disguised as malcontent railer Malevole—serves as court scourge, inveighing against its sensuality, extravagance, and inner rottenness, and excoriating all the foibles and abuses of the contemporary social order. Middleton's is a more effective, less bizarre and eccentric dramatic language than Marston's, but in this play he cultivates similar collisions of laughter and horror, using startling dislocations of mode and mood to convey a Mannerist sense of an unstable, chaotic age.

The blend of wit and violence, mutilation and fun often seems to foreshadow twentieth-century 'black comedy'. Audiences cannot believe that Spurio's 'Old Dad dead?' (5.1.116) belongs to the original text. It is not only the jocular treatment of grisly material and the amusing one-liners that recall Orton, who quoted Vindice's 'Surely we're all mad people, and they | Whom we think are, are not' (3.5.80–1) as epigraph to *What the Butler Saw*, another play in which an amoral lunacy reigns. Both playwrights exploit the disparity between the propriety of their characters' sentiments and the delinquency of their behaviour; both wring humour from the incongruous utterance of conventional pieties. The royal family in *The Revenger's Tragedy* pay lip-service to morality in trite couplets that bear no relation to their actual deeds. The Duke's 'Age hot is like a monster to be seen; | My hairs are white and yet my sins are green' (2.3.129–30) is simply the prelude to his asking Vindice to procure him a sexual partner. Functionally, the short soliloquy that ends with this rhyme is analogous to Claudius's prayer in

Hamlet, 3.3: it confirms his guilt beyond doubt, since he admits to having poisoned 'many a beauty' who rejected his advances. But whereas Claudius's desperate monologue serves to show the conscience-stricken human being inside the suave usurper, and so prepares the audience emotionally for the postponement of revenge, the glibness of the Duke's confession reveals an automaton, whose imminent gruesome destruction by Vindice and Hippolito we can approve, and even relish. Like Orton, Middleton has an ear for the hypocritical unction and laughable indignation of the wicked. When, after Lussurioso has found his father's corpse and blamed 'Piato' for the slaying, Vindice himself mimics this tone of mock-outrage—'O rascal! Was he not ashamed | To put the Duke into a greasy doublet?' (5.1.71–2)—we seem to hear in the ludicrously misplaced concern for externals the authentic voice of some subversive, decorum-guying modern. Best of all, because so integral to the action, are Vindice's sardonic last words of advice to the expiring Lussurioso, after he has informed him of his deeds: 'Tell nobody' (5.3.80). Vindice's gloating epitaph over his enemy may seem the culmination of the theme of secrecy, but there is the further irony of his own self-destructive blabbing to follow.

But 'Middleton our contemporary', the disconcerting humorist, was also inheritor of a stern medieval tradition of Morality drama, homily and complaint, allegorical and emblematic art—of *de contemptu mundi*, *exemplum horrendum*, Danse Macabre, and *memento mori*. *The Revenger's Tragedy* has been seen as affording the traditional 'horrible example' of a society hurtling towards damnation. (Luchino Visconti's film *The Damned* would be a modern secular equivalent.) The type figures of *The Revenger's Tragedy*, as of *Volpone*, recall the Moralities, in which personified virtues and vices contend for the soul of Everyman in a 'theatre of God's judgement'. The play opens with Vindice as presenter of a torchlit procession of Duke, Duchess, and progeny—a royal progress, transformed into a parade of the Seven Deadly Sins. Vindice's initial comment, 'Duke, royal lecher, go, grey-haired adultery' (1.1.1), enforces this impression. By branding the Duke not 'adulterer' but 'adultery' Vindice equates him with his sin. Lust in this play is closely associated with gluttony (or drunkenness), and pride, envy, covetousness, and wrath are prominent. A Christian symbolism popularized through sixteenth-century emblem books lies behind some of the play's most striking images—notably the 'eternal eye | That sees through flesh and all' at 1.3.67–8—and there is frequent exploitation (noted in the commentary) of classical and biblical iconography or thought. Vindice's 'conceit in picture' of 'A usuring father... boiling in hell, and his son and heir with a whore dancing over him' (4.2.86–7) is in the medieval cautionary vein, though Middleton gives the theme his own characteristic twist; his preceding ruminations—on 'how a great rich man lies a-dying and a poor cobbler tolls the bell for him' (4.2.68–77)—are in a moralistic tradition harking back to the gospel parable of Lazarus and Dives. The masques of dancing avengers and murderers with which the play ends evoke the theme, ubiquitous in the art of medieval Europe, of the Dance of Death, in which capering skeletons guide their live doubles to the grave, often during pageants or revels.

Focusing Vindice's obsession with mortality, like a *memento mori* in a monk's cell, is the skull of Gloriana. The opening, in which flame-lit court pomp and finery are displayed in contrast to the lone figure holding the sallow 'shell of death', initiates a dominant theme. And the great meditation on the vanity of human wishes at 3.5.44–107 is unmatched in subsequent drama in English until *Waiting for Godot* gives us Lucky's monologue, which comes to rest, after its crazed digressions, on 'the skull the skull the skull the skull'. The charnel-house remnant of Vindice's 'poisoned love' stands as both the ultimate resting point in the frenetic social process whereby inherited estates dissolve in hedonistic riot as an agrarian economy yields to urban capitalism, and the stark reality that all pleasure-loving flesh is heir to. The skull is a symbol at once social, political, and religious.

Godot never comes, but the thunderous Divine Avenger invoked by Vindice's rhetoric finally makes himself heard. But Vindice greets the portent with a certain flippancy, first as 'big-voiced crier' appearing on cue and then, with a pun on 'claps', as satisfied spectator at a 'tragedy' (5.3.43–8). While the comparison of the world to a play on which God passes judgement is commonplace, Providence here elicits less than due awe. Although even the 'gargoylish grin' worn by his play has roots in the Middle Ages (as Ekeblad noted), Middleton deploys the orthodox omens and emblems with a Jacobean ambivalence. Even in the 'silkworm' speech (3.5.44–107) Vindice wields his 'bony lady' with the tormented histrionics of Gethin Price with his dummies in Trevor Griffiths's *Comedians*. And in fact Vindice's frequent use of theatrical terminology, his implicit or direct appeals to the audience, his stage-managing of his own invented dramas and of his changing roles within them (as in the stabbing of his alias self), and his general self-consciousness about levels of illusion add to *The Revenger's Tragedy*'s air of twentieth-century sophistication. Even our uneasiness at the sadism of Vindice's physical and mental torturing of the Duke is largely allayed by sheer pleasure in his artistry—in the neat ironies whereby, betrayed by his own lasciviousness, the poisoner is poisoned, the victim of his victim, the forcer forced to witness his cuckolding by the child of his own adultery.

The ways in which various dramatic and literary traditions are unified in *The Revenger's Tragedy* have been illuminated by Inga-Stina Ekeblad (Ewbank). Certain key components act as nodes. Vindice combines the functions of a Hamlet, a Volpone, and a Malevole, besides acting as both Good and Evil Angel in a Morality temptation of Chastity and Grace. Gloriana's skull is an incitement to revenge, like the skeleton of Hoffman's father, a prompt to satirical attacks on face-painting and court ostentation, a focus for meditative sermonizing on the transience of worldly pleasures and on corporeal decay, and a stage-prop for what in a different context might have been a merry prank in which the biter is bit. The masque, a costly palace entertainment, is at once a traditional device for ending a revenge tragedy and a Danse des Morts. And this interweaving by means of character, plot, and theatrical image is tightened by the play's complex poetry. Vindice's opening monologue, brilliantly mixing exposition, denunciation, and contemplation, brings Jacobean targets within its satirical range through the associations of its imagery: the adjective 'spendthrift' is applied to the 'veins of a... parched and juiceless luxur' (linking sexual and financial profligacy); the old Duke riots it 'like a son and heir', recalling the wastrels of Middleton's comedies; Gloriana was once so beautiful that a 'usurer's son', in an age when landholders were increasingly in pawn to moneylenders, would have consumed 'all his patrimony' for the sake of a kiss (1.1.8–27). At the same time, a phrase such as 'apparelled in thy flesh' evokes an ancient orthodoxy (1.1.31). Ekeblad quotes some lines from Vindice's later speech over the skull (3.5.84–7):

Does every proud and self-affecting dame
Camphor her face for this? And grieve her maker
In sinful baths of milk, when many an infant starves
For her superfluous outside—all for this?

As she notes, this goes far beyond the Jacobean misogynist's reflex snarling at cosmetics, as the words 'proud', 'grieve her maker', and 'sinful' make plain: 'as in the medieval Morality the imagery of finery is pursued down to its moral significance, to its connection with pride, the deadliest of the sins, and with the homiletic theme of waste and extravagance versus the suffering inflicted upon innocents'. Yet those 'baths of milk' evoke a Cleopatra's charisma.

Dramatic, literary, and artistic traditions constitute the play's most vital source material, and as Holdsworth (1990) has shown, it is also in large measure an inspired reworking of elements already present in Middleton's early prose pamphlets, poems, and plays. But there are analogues to some of its situations and incidents in accounts of the Medici and Este families and other pseudo-historical works: notably (to name only the English versions) William Painter's *The Palace of Pleasure* (1567), Barnaby Rich's *Farewell to Military Profession* (1581), and Thomas Underdowne's *An Aethiopian History* (1587). Middleton also shows awareness of facts concerning the assassination of Duke Alessandro of Florence in 1537 that could not have been gleaned from Painter.

The Revenger's Tragedy was published anonymously in 1607/8, and criticism has been bedevilled by the wholly unreliable Edward Archer's mistaken ascription, fifty years later, of Middleton's play to Cyril Tourneur. Nineteenth- and early twentieth-century commentary culminated in T. S. Eliot's account of it as a projection of its author's 'inner world of nightmare', his immature 'cynicism... loathing and disgust of humanity... horror of life itself' (1934). Later critics such as L. G. Salingar, disentangling the playwright from his characters, saw not 'psychopathic perversion' but an alert and coherent response to the 'commercialisation of the nobility' under James I and 'the disintegration of a whole social order' (1937–8). The emotional adolescent plagued by his fantasies became the controlled artist selecting from his literary inheritance to fashion an image of the times. But those who still thought of that artist as Tourneur now began to assimilate the play to the orthodox piety of *The Atheist's Tragedy*, exaggerating its conservatism and didacticism and minimizing its aggression, prurience, humour, and élan. Jonathan Dollimore's more recent account of *The Revenger's Tragedy* as parodying the providential viewpoint, 'sceptical of ideological policing', celebrating 'the artificial and the delinquent', and dominated by an air of 'subversive black camp' is an understandable reaction (1984). Yet this view also seems partial. It ignores, for example, the play's admiration for the steadfastness of Castiza, the seriousness of the biblical language applied to Gratiana's fall and conversion, and the cumulative force of such oft-repeated words as 'sin', 'damnation', 'heaven', 'doom', 'shame', 'devil', 'hell', and the like, whose reverberations create a moral framework, however complacent the court characters' utterance of them.

Placed within the Middleton canon, the play will assume further guises. However, fraught with Middleton's Calvinist conviction of human depravity but willing to laugh about it, at once repudiating and attracted to the flesh and Mammon, weighing the evanescent pleasure of the 'bewitching minute' of sex or vengeance against temporal and eternal consequences, acutely aware of social flux in 'this luxurious day wherein we breathe' (1.3.112) and nostalgic for the stability of a lost order, the play retains its ambivalence. Fredson Bowers showed that Chettle first incorporated elements of the villainous adversary into the revenge hero himself, and that *The Revenger's Tragedy* follows suit (1940). Vindice's ultimate recognition that 'we are ourselves our foes' (5.3.109) resonates beyond its immediate context. The two masques, of revengers and murderers, are visually indistinguishable. Yet, however warped Vindice's psyche and compromised his deeds, we experience the play largely through him and his roles (with their many asides) and are beguiled by his authorial flair. This adds to the complexity of our response. It is difficult too to know how to take Antonio. Is he a self-serving hypocrite, or does in his case a reluctant assumption of power represent 'silver age' integrity? Holdsworth's balanced discussion gives him the benefit of the doubt; but the doubt remains. And does not the affecting tableau of ravished virtue, complete with prayer-book as 'pillow to her cheek' (1.4.13)—with which Antonio, whether deliberately or not, incites Hippolito and his fellows to vengeance—seem just a little too stage-managed? By whom? Where dissimulation is so rife, the sincerest show becomes suspect. Yet the image of medical blood-letting, with which the play concludes, suggests a genuine cleansing.

Apparently unknown to the theatre for three and a half centuries after its Jacobean performances, the play has frequently been produced by amateur groups in recent decades. The Royal Shakespeare Company performed it in 1966 (directed by Trevor Nunn), as well as 1987. The first fully professional revival was that of Brian Shelton for the Pitlochry Festival in Scotland in 1965. Shelton found it 'a flamboyant and sensational piece which changes constantly: pungent, moralistic, melodramatic, comic, allegorical, violent, poetic, bawdy, tragic, absurd, ironic—the moods tumble over each other, blend and alternate in exuberant profusion'. He guessed that it had been written 'in a ferment of excitement'. Through its poetry, characters, and action it vividly transmits its author's complex vision of life at a particular point in his own, the theatre's, and Europe's history. Conceived in 'excitement', it retains its power to excite, on the page and in the theatre.

SEE ALSO
Textual introduction and apparatus: *Companion*, 548
Authorship and date: *Companion*, 360

The Revenger's Tragedy

[*for the King's Men at The Globe*]

THE PERSONS OF THE PLAY

The DUKE
The DUCHESS, the Duke's second wife
LUSSURIOSO, the Duke's son
SPURIO, the Duke's bastard
AMBITIOSO, the Duchess's eldest son and Duke's stepson
SUPERVACUO, the Duchess's second son and Duke's stepson
JUNIOR, the Duchess's youngest son and Duke's stepson

ANTONIO, a lord
PIERO, a lord, friend of Antonio

VINDICE, in one of his disguises known as Piato
HIPPOLITO, Vindice's brother
MOTHER, Vindice's mother, once referred to as Gratiana
CASTIZA, Vindice's sister

NENCIO, follower of Lussurioso
SORDIDO, follower of Lussurioso
DONDOLO, servant of Mother (Gratiana)

FIRST JUDGE, SECOND JUDGE
FIRST SERVANT, SECOND SERVANT
FIRST NOBLE, SECOND NOBLE, THIRD NOBLE, FOURTH NOBLE
FIRST OFFICER, SECOND OFFICER, THIRD OFFICER
Prison KEEPER
FIRST GENTLEMAN
FIRST LORD, SECOND LORD, THIRD LORD

Dead Wife of Antonio, Fourth Officer (Guard), Servants (Attendants), Musicians

1.1 *Incipit Actus Primus*
Enter Vindice [*holding a skull*]. *The Duke, Duchess, Lussurioso his son, Spurio the Bastard, with a train, pass over the stage with torch-light*

VINDICE
Duke, royal lecher, go, grey-haired adultery,
And thou his son, as impious steeped as he,
And thou his bastard, true-begot in evil,
And thou his duchess that will do with devil,

This commentary focuses particularly upon verbal imagery and linguistic play.

1.1.0.2–4 ***Enter . . . torch-light*** The stage direction specifies, and Vindice comments on, only the four members of the royal family. Directors usually include the Duchess's three sons in the procession, bringing the number up to seven (like the Deadly Sins).

0.2–3 ***Vindice . . . Lussurioso . . . Spurio*** The descriptive names are derived from Italian words defined in John Florio's dictionary, *A World of Words* (1598). Vindice: a revenger; Lussurioso: lecherous; Spurio: bastard.

1 **adultery** The Duke is adultery personified, with a hint of a Morality figure.

2 **impious steeped** saturated in impiety

3 **true-begot** Vindice is sardonically playing on notions of what is true or false (or illegitimate): Spurio, though falsely begotten (out of wedlock), is the true offspring of a sinful act; his nature truly reflects his origins.

4 **do** have sex; the alliteration in this line, and the reductiveness of that two-letter word, point up the contempt.

Four exc'llent characters! O that marrowless age
Should stuff the hollow bones with damned desires
And, 'stead of heat, kindle infernal fires
Within the spendthrift veins of a dry duke,
A parched and juiceless luxur! O God, one
That has scarce blood enough to live upon,
And he to riot it like a son and heir?
O, the thought of that
Turns my abusèd heartstrings into fret.
[*To the skull*] Thou sallow picture of my poisoned love,
My study's ornament, thou shell of death,
Once the bright face of my betrothèd lady,
When life and beauty naturally filled out
These ragged imperfectïons,
When two heaven-pointed diamonds were set
In those unsightly rings—then 'twas a face
So far beyond the artificial shine
Of any woman's bought complexïon
That the uprightest man—if such there be
That sin but seven times a day—broke custom
And made up eight with looking after her.
O, she was able to ha' made a usurer's son
Melt all his patrimony in a kiss
And what his father fifty yeärs told
To have consumed, and yet his suit been cold.
But O accursèd palace!
Thee, when thou wert apparelled in thy flesh,
The old Duke poisoned,
Because thy purer part would not consent
Unto his palsy lust; for old men lustful
Do show like young men—angry, eager, violent,
Outbid their limited performances.
O, 'ware an old man hot and vicïous:
"Age, as in gold, in lust is covetous."
Vengeance, thou murder's quit-rent, and whereby
Thou show'st thyself tenant to tragedy,
O, keep thy day, hour, minute, I beseech,
For those thou hast determined. Hum, whoe'er knew
Murder unpaid? Faith, give Revenge her due,
Sh'as kept touch hitherto. Be merry, merry;
Advance thee, O thou terror to fat folks,
To have their costly three-piled flesh worn off

5 **characters** examples of types of humanity (as in Jacobean writers' satirical portraits)

5–9 **O that... luxur** The concentrated imagery here draws on Renaissance physiology, which associated the marrow and the blood (dispersed through the veins) with the natural, vital, and animal spirits causing vigour and sexual desire; since semen was held to be generated by the blood (much blood being needed for a little semen), lechery drained the system. The passage contrasts the 'sanguine' warmth of healthy youthful passion with the hellish, unquenchable lust of a dessicated profligate. His ultimate punishment is brought into account with the charnel-house image of 'hollow bones' and the judgements implied in 'damned' and 'infernal fires'. But the most brilliantly chosen term is 'spendthrift veins', which links the Duke's sexual dissipation (his 'expense of spirit in a waste of shame', as Shakespeare's Sonnet 129 puts it) to a Jacobean world of reckless financial prodigality glanced at in lines 11 and 26–9.

9 **luxur** lecher (a coinage used in *Black Book* and confined to Middleton)

11 **riot... heir** The wastrel son and heir is a favourite target in Middletonian comedy. Through such comparisons *Revenger* fuses diverse dramatic genres and relates its Italianate action to English society of the time.

13 **heartstrings** literally the tendons or nerves supposed to brace the heart, but with a musical allusion (common at the time) taken up in 'fret'

fret vexation or distress, with wordplay on the ring of gut or ridge of wood set on the fingerboard of a stringed instrument such as a lute or guitar at the proper places for the fingers

14 **poisoned love** Besides the obvious meaning that the Duke poisoned Vindice's betrothed, there is an ironic intimation that the hero's love for Gloriana has been poisoned by bitterness and hatred.

15 **study's ornament** object of meditation, in the figurative sense, but also a literal *memento mori* in his room (as in paintings of monks' or scholars' cells)

19 **heaven-pointed** turned towards heaven, but with a suggestion of the sparkling facets of a diamond; also 'appointed by heaven', 'God-given'

20 **unsightly** (*a*) ugly, (*b*) non-seeing

rings punning on (*a*) the sockets of bone, and (*b*) a ring for the finger

22 **bought complexïon** face made up with cosmetics, with a hint that the woman herself may be bought

23–4 **uprightest... day** an echo of the biblical Proverbs, 24:16, probably by way of the William Perkins's Puritan *A Treatise* (1595). 'For a just man falleth seven times, and riseth up again: but the wicked shall fall into mischief'.

26 **usurer's son** developing the image of the riotous son and heir, while sketching in an English social background of capitalist profiteering, where the usurer could amass a sizable fortune

27 **Melt** The verb gives concreteness to our sense of the process by which the young man's estate dissolves, as though molten gold were flowing away; there is wordplay on the idea of a tender or 'melting' kiss (the collocation was not yet a cliché, but compare 4.4.147 and *Pericles*, 22.64–5).

28 **told** added up, accumulated

29 **his suit been cold** his advances been rejected

34 **palsy lust** The aged Duke is afflicted with spasms of lust, as from the involuntary trembling that is the chief symptom of palsy.

36 **Outbid... performances** i.e. they overestimate their physical (especially sexual) prowess; at 1.2.75 the Duchess stigmatizes the Duke as 'slack... in performance'.

38 **"Age... covetous."** This 'sentence' or pithy saying is set off with double commas in Eld's quarto, in accord with common contemporary practice.

39 **quit-rent** money paid by a freeholder to a landlord in lieu of services; vengeance is, as it were, murder's due; as Ross notes, the idea of substitute payment is less pertinent than play on 'quit' in the sense 'repay for injury'

40 **tenant** continuing the metaphor from 'quit-rent'; tragedy is the lord that revenge serves

42 **determined** decided on, with suggestions of inexorable purpose and, ironically, predestination

44 **touch** faith, her promise

45 **thee** the skull

46 **three-piled** alluding to the richest kind of velvet (with a thick pile, like that of a modern luxury carpet), and harking back to the metaphor in 'apparelled in thy flesh' in line 31

As bare as this; for banquets, ease, and laughter
Can make great men, as greatness goes by clay,
But wise men little are more great than they.
Enter his brother Hippolito

HIPPOLITO
Still sighing o'er death's visor?

VINDICE Brother, welcome.
What comfort bring'st thou? How go things at court?

HIPPOLITO
In silk and silver, brother, never braver.

VINDICE Puh,
Thou play'st upon my meaning. Prithee say,
Has that bald madam, Opportunity,
Yet thought upon's? Speak, are we happy yet?
Thy wrongs and mine are for one scabbard fit.

HIPPOLITO
It may prove happiness.

VINDICE What is't may prove?
Give me to taste.

HIPPOLITO Give me your hearing then.
You know my place at court.

VINDICE Ay, the Duke's chamber.
But 'tis a marvel thou'rt not turned out yet.

HIPPOLITO
Faith, I have been shoved at, but 'twas still my hap
To hold by th' Duchess' skirt; you guess at that;
Whom such a coat keeps up can ne'er fall flat.
But to the purpose.
Last evening, predecessor unto this,
The Duke's son warily enquired for me;
Whose pleasure I attended. He began
By policy to open and unhusk me
About the time and common rumour;
But I had so much wit to keep my thoughts
Up in their built houses, yet afforded him
An idle satisfaction without danger.
But the whole aim and scope of his intent
Ended in this, conjuring me in private
To seek some strange-digested fellow forth
Of ill-contented nature, either disgraced
In former times or by new grooms displaced
Since his stepmother's nuptials; such a blood,
A man that were for evil only good;
To give you the true word, some base-coined pander.

VINDICE
I reach you, for I know his heat is such,
Were there as many concubines as ladies,
He would not be contained, he must fly out.
I wonder how ill-featured, vile-proportioned
That one should be, if she were made for woman,
Whom at the insurrection of his lust
He would refuse for once. Heart, I think none,
Next to a skull, though more unsound than one.
Each face he meets he strongly dotes upon.

HIPPOLITO Brother, you've truly spoke him.
He knows not you, but I'll swear you know him.

VINDICE
And therefore I'll put on that knave for once
And be a right man then, a man o'th' time;
For to be honest is not to be i'th' world.
Brother, I'll be that strange-composèd fellow.

HIPPOLITO
And I'll prefer you, brother.

VINDICE Go to, then,
The small'st advantage fattens wrongèd men.
It may point out Occasion. If I meet her
I'll hold her by the foretop fast enough,
Or like the French mole heave up hair and all.

48 **great** quibbling on (*a*) large, (*b*) admirable
as greatness goes by clay i.e. 'in the corporeal sense of greatness'; with 'clay' (prominent as the rhyme word) as a reminder of the flesh's destiny

49 **wise... they** compare the proverb 'Wisdom is better than riches'; 'little' means 'lowly'

50 **visor** mask, or face suggestive of a mask

52 **In... braver** Hippolito pretends to have understood Vindice's 'How go things at court?' as 'How do court-creatures walk, parade themselves?'; braver means 'more ostentatiously'.

53 **Puh** exclamation of dismissal

55 **that... Opportunity** In Renaissance iconography and proverb lore Opportunity or Occasion was a bald, winged, figure with a single forelock, which had to be seized before she passed. By attributing Occasion's baldness to the sexual disease of a brothel 'madam' (here a prostitute rather than brothel-keeper), Vindice gives his own twist to a fusion of the emblem with that of strumpet Fortune.

69 **unhusk** (so as to expose the 'kernel' of truth)

70 **time and common rumour** probably a hendiadys = the latest gossip

72 **in their built houses** dwelling inside his own head, where the mind is 'housed' and thoughts occupy their allotted sections of the brain

76 **strange-digested** oddly constituted, and hence alienated; compare 'strange-composèd' in line 96

79 **blood** man of hot spirit; unless 'blood' simply means 'nature'

81 **base-coined** illegitimately conceived; or perhaps merely of low birth with a suggestion of the debased (like base coinage)

82 **reach** understand

86 **for woman** to be a woman

88–9 **none... skull** his lust extends almost to necrophily; an ironical foreshadowing of the Duke's tryst with Gloriana's skull in 3.5. Vindice's words draw attention to the object that he holds.

93 **put on** personate

94 **right** fitting the accepted standards
a man o'th' time The idea is similar to that in *History of King Lear*, 24.30–1, 'men | Are as the time is', though there the context is of murderous tough-mindedness, rather than of knavish duplicity and panderism. The play repeatedly insists on the depravity of 'our age' (1.3.23), 'this present minute' (1.3.25), 'nowadays' (1.3.157), 'this luxurious day wherein we breathe' (1.3.112), and so on. The effect is to evoke a hectic 'modern' society devoted to momentary pleasures.

97 **prefer** recommend, promote

100 **foretop** forelock; compare note to 1.1.55

101 **French mole** a sore on the scalp due to syphilis, which causes hair to drop out; with wordplay on the mole that undermines lawn or pasture

I have a habit that will fit it quaintly.
[*Enter Mother and Castiza*]
Here comes our mother.

HIPPOLITO
And sister.

VINDICE
We must coin.
Women are apt, you know, to take false money.
But I dare stake my soul for these two creatures,
Only excuse excepted—that they'll swallow,
Because their sex is easy in belief.

MOTHER
What news from court, son Carlo?

HIPPOLITO
Faith, Mother,
'Tis whispered there the Duchess' youngest son
Has played a rape on Lord Antonio's wife.

MOTHER On that religious lady!

CASTIZA
Royal blood! Monster, he deserves to die,
If Italy had no more hopes but he.

VINDICE
Sister, you've sentenced most direct and true.
The law's a woman, and would she were you.
Mother, I must take leave of you.

MOTHER
Leave for what?

VINDICE
I intend speedy travel.

HIPPOLITO
That he does, madam.

MOTHER
Speedy indeed!

VINDICE
For since my worthy father's funeral
My life's unnatural to me, e'en compelled,
As if I lived now when I should be dead.

MOTHER
Indeed, he was a worthy gentleman,
Had his estate been fellow to his mind.

VINDICE
The Duke did much deject him.

MOTHER
Much.

VINDICE
Too much.
And through disgrace oft smothered in his spirit
When it would mount. Surely I think he died
Of discontent, the nobleman's consumption.

MOTHER
Most sure he did.

VINDICE
Did he? 'Lack, you know all;
You were his midnight secretary.

MOTHER
No.
He was too wise to trust me with his thoughts.

VINDICE [*aside*]
I'faith then, father, thou wast wise indeed.
"Wives are but made to go to bed and feed."—
Come, mother, sister. You'll bring me onward,
brother?

HIPPOLITO
I will.

VINDICE [*aside to Hippolito*]
I'll quickly turn into another. *Exeunt*

1.2

Enter the old Duke, Lussurioso his son, the Duchess, Spurio the Bastard, the Duchess's two sons Ambitioso and Supervacuo, the third her youngest, Junior, brought out with Officers for the rape, two Judges

DUKE
Duchess, it is your youngest son; we're sorry.
His violent act has e'en drawn blood of honour
And stained our honours,
Thrown ink upon the forehead of our state,
Which envious spirits will dip their pens into
After our death, and blot us in our tombs;
For that which would seem treason in our lives
Is laughter when we're dead. Who dares now whisper
That dares not then speak out, and e'en proclaim
With loud words and broad pens our closest shame?

FIRST JUDGE
Your grace hath spoke like to your silver years,
Full of confirmèd gravity; for what is it to have
A flattering false insculption on a tomb

102 **habit** costume
quaintly finely, ingeniously
102.1 ***Castiza*** Chastity (from Italian *casta*, chaste)
103 **coin** dissemble, counterfeit (taken up in 'false money' in the next line)
105–7 **But ... belief** 'Vindice is sure Gratiana and Castiza will see through and reject hypocrisy or deceit, with one exception—they will believe a good excuse, for women are credulous that way' (Foakes).
108 **Carlo** either a pet name or the sole relic of the author's original plan for naming the character
112 **Royal blood!** a sarcastic ejaculation; the blood royal is characterized by 'blood' in the sense of 'carnal appetite'
113 **hopes** i.e. heirs to the dukedom
115 **The law's a woman** alluding to the image of Justice as a female figure holding a sword or pair of scales
122 **worthy** honourable (but with a pun on 'worthy' = rich)
124 **deject** abase, depress
129 **secretary** confidant, sharer of secrets
130–2 **He ... feed** The notion that women cannot keep secrets was enshrined in many a misogynistic proverb.
1.2.0.3 ***Ambitioso and Supervacuo*** Italian for Ambitious and Useless, Vain, Foolish
2 **drawn ... honour** i.e. wounded honour so that its blood flows. Though figuratively applied, the violent image, followed by 'stained', vividly evokes the brutality of the rape; 'honour' (as the Duke repeats the word in the plural) carries its full range of meanings: chastity, reputation, royal dignity, decent conduct. 'Blood' leads, by way of 'stain' (and the associations of 'drawn'), to 'ink', which sets off the strand of imagery threading through the rest of the speech.
4 **Thrown ... forehead** References to the 'forehead' recur, as (*a*) site of the cuckold's horns, (*b*) countenance capable of expressing shame, anger, or brazen impudence. For sexual sinfulness inscribed on the forehead see Revelations, 17:5.
5 **envious** malicious
10 **broad pens** frank or scurrilous writings
closest most secret
13 **insculption** carved inscription

And in men's hearts reproach? The bowelled corpse
May be cered in, but with free tongue I speak:
"The faults of great men through their cerecloths
break."

DUKE
They do; we're sorry for't. It is our fate
To live in fear and die to live in hate.
I leave him to your sentence. Doom him, lords—
The fact is great—whilst I sit by and sigh.

DUCHESS [*kneeling*]
My gracious lord, I pray be merciful,
Although his trespass far exceed his years.
Think him to be your own, as I am yours;
Call him not son-in-law: the law, I fear,
Will fall too soon upon his name and him.
Temper his fault with pity.

LUSSURIOSO Good my lord,
Then 'twill not taste so bitter and unpleasant
Upon the judges' palate, for offences
Gilt o'er with mercy show like fairest women,
Good only for their beauties, which washed off,
No sin is uglier.

AMBITIOSO I beseech your grace,
Be soft and mild; let not relentless law
Look with an iron forehead on our brother.

SPURIO [*aside*]
He yields small comfort yet. Hope he shall die,
And if a bastard's wish might stand in force,
Would all the court were turned into a corse.

DUCHESS
No pity yet? Must I rise fruitless then?
A wonder in a woman! Are my knees
Of such low metal that without respect—
[*She rises*]

FIRST JUDGE Let the offender stand forth.
'Tis the Duke's pleasure that impartial doom
Shall take fast hold of his unclean attempt.
A rape! Why, 'tis the very core of lust,
Double adultery.

JUNIOR So, sir.

SECOND JUDGE And, which was worse,
Committed on the Lord Antonio's wife,
That general-honest lady. Confess, my lord,
What moved you to't?

JUNIOR Why, flesh and blood, my lord.
What should move men unto a woman else?

LUSSURIOSO
O, do not jest thy doom. Trust not an axe
Or sword too far. The law is a wise serpent
And quickly can beguile thee of thy life.
Though marriage only has made thee my brother,
I love thee so far—play not with thy death.

JUNIOR
I thank you, troth; good admonitions, faith,
If I'd the grace now to make use of them.

FIRST JUDGE
That lady's name has spread such a fair wing
Over all Italy that, if our tongues
Were sparing toward the fact, judgement itself
Would be condemned and suffer in men's thoughts.

JUNIOR
Well then, 'tis done, and it would please me well
Were it to do again. Sure, she's a goddess,
For I'd no power to see her and to live.
It falls out true in this, for I must die.
Her beauty was ordained to be my scaffold;
And yet methinks I might be easier 'sessed.
My fault being sport, let me but die in jest.

FIRST JUDGE This be the sentence—

DUCHESS
O, keep't upon your tongue; let it not slip.
Death too soon steals out of a lawyer's lip.
Be not so cruel-wise.

FIRST JUDGE Your grace must pardon us,
'Tis but the justice of the law.

DUCHESS The law
Is grown more subtle than a woman should be.

SPURIO [*aside*]
Now, now he dies. Rid 'em away.

DUCHESS [*aside*]
O, what it is to have an old cool duke
To be as slack in tongue as in performance.

FIRST JUDGE
Confirmed, this be the doom irrevocable.

DUCHESS O!

14 **bowelled** disembowelled (for embalming)
15 **cered in** wrapped in cerecloths (waxed sheets)
19 **Doom** sentence
20 **fact** crime (as also at line 58)
24 **son-in-law** stepson (here with wordplay on 'law')
26–31 **Good . . . uglier** Lussurioso's simile deconstructs the argument he intends, or at least pretends. Either (*a*) he unconsciously reveals his true feelings, or (*b*) he is being publicly sarcastic, or (*c*) lines 30–1 are an aside. The first explanation seems most probable.
36 **corse** corpse; the old spelling is retained for the rhyme
37 **rise fruitless** The pun in 'fruitless' that leads to the Duchess's exclamation in line 38 is based on 'rise' = swell in pregnancy.
39 **low metal** base metal (of little value), but with a suggestion of 'mettle' = the quality of a person's disposition; punning also on the literal sense of low, since she is kneeling
41 **doom** judgement
42 **attempt** assault
46 **general-honest** wholly chaste
56 **spread . . . wing** The image combines the idea of the extent of her fame with suggestions of the angelic and the protective.
61–3 **Sure . . . die** The idea that mortals cannot survive contact with the divine (probably with a specific allusion to Exodus, 33:20) is complicated by a pun on 'die' = to have sexual intercourse; the figurative death leads to the actual.
65 **'sessed** assessed, judged
66 **sport** playing on the senses 'amorous dalliance' and 'jesting, merrymaking'
71–2 **law . . . woman** compare I.1.115 and note
75 **performance** i.e. in bed

FIRST JUDGE
Tomorrow early—
DUCHESS Pray be abed, my lord.
FIRST JUDGE
Your grace much wrongs yourself.
AMBITIOSO No, 'tis that tongue.
Your too much right does do us too much wrong.
FIRST JUDGE
Let that offender—
DUCHESS Live and be in health.
FIRST JUDGE
Be on a scaffold—
DUKE Hold, hold, my lord.
SPURIO [*aside*] Pox on't,
What makes my dad speak now?
DUKE
We will defer the judgement till next sitting.
In the mean time let him be kept close prisoner.
Guard, bear him hence.
AMBITIOSO [*to Junior*] Brother, this makes for thee.
Fear not, we'll have a trick to set thee free.
JUNIOR
Brother, I will expect it from you both,
And in that hope I rest.
SUPERVACUO Farewell, be merry.
Exit Junior with a Guard
SPURIO [*aside*]
Delayed, deferred; nay then, if judgement have cold blood,
Flattery and bribes will kill it.
DUKE
About it then, my lords, with your best powers.
More serious business calls upon our hours.
Exeunt, manet Duchess
DUCHESS
Was't ever known step-duchess was so mild
And calm as I? Some now would plot his death
With easy doctors, those loose-living men,
And make his withered grace fall to his grave
And keep church better.
Some second wife would do this, and dispatch
Her double-loathèd lord at meat or sleep.
Indeed, 'tis true an old man's twice a child:
Mine cannot speak. One of his single words
Would quite have freed my youngest, dearest son
From death or durance, and have made him walk
With a bold foot upon the thorny law,
Whose prickles should bow under him; but 'tis not,
And therefore wedlock faith shall be forgot.
I'll kill him in his forehead; hate there feed.
That wound is deepest, though it never bleed.
[*Enter Spurio at a distance*]
And here comes he whom my heart points unto,
His bastard son, but my love's true-begot.
Many a wealthy letter have I sent him,
Swelled up with jewels, and the timorous man
Is yet but coldly kind.
That jewel's mine that quivers in his ear,
Mocking his master's chillness and vain fear.
He's spied me now.
SPURIO Madam, your grace so private?
My duty on your hand.
[*He kisses her hand*]
DUCHESS
Upon my hand, sir? Troth, I think you'd fear
To kiss my hand too, if my lip stood there.
SPURIO
Witness I would not, madam.
[*He kisses her*]
DUCHESS 'Tis a wonder,
For ceremony has made many fools.
It is as easy way unto a duchess
As to a hatted dame, if her love answer,
But that by timorous honours, pale respects,
Idle degrees of fear, men make their ways
Hard of themselves. What have you thought of me?
SPURIO
Madam, I ever think of you in duty,
Regard, and—
DUCHESS Puh, upon my love, I mean.
SPURIO
I would 'twere love, but 't'as a fouler name than lust.
You are my father's wife. Your grace may guess now
What I could call it.
DUCHESS Why, thou'rt his son but falsely.
'Tis a hard question whether he begot thee.
SPURIO
I'faith, 'tis true too; I'm an uncertain man,
Of more uncertain woman. Maybe his groom
O'th' stable begot me; you know I know not.
He could ride a horse well—a shrewd suspicion, marry.
He was wondrous tall; he had his length, i'faith,
For peeping over half-shut holiday windows.

79 **too much right** excessive privilege (as a judge)
85 **makes for thee** works in your favour
95 **easy** compliant
97 **keep church better** The Duke, entombed, would be not just a more regular attender at church but a permanent one!
100 **old...child** proverbial
103 **durance** imprisonment
107 **kill...forehead** i.e. by committing adultery (and so furnishing his forehead with a cuckold's horns)
114 **jewel's...ear** A producer should ensure that Spurio wears a jewelled ear-ring.
115 **Mocking** probably 'imitating', rather than 'deriding', though possibly both; 'quivers' = glitters, but leading to the imputation of quivering timidity
123 **hatted dame** hats were worn by women of the lower orders
129 **fouler...lust** i.e. incest
132 **hard** difficult, but with a *double entendre*
136–7 **He could...length** The further sexual innuendo in 'ride' and 'length' is picked up by the Duchess in lines 142–3.
138 **peeping...windows** i.e. he was so tall that, mounted on a horse, he could peep over the bottom, shuttered parts of windows into the private dwellings of people relaxing on holidays

Men would desire him 'light. When he was afoot,
He made a goodly show under a penthouse,
And when he rid, his hat would check the signs
And clatter barbers' basins.

DUCHESS Nay, set you a-horseback once,
You'll ne'er 'light off.

SPURIO Indeed, I am a beggar.

DUCHESS
That's more the sign thou'rt great. But to our love:
Let it stand firm both in thy thought and mine
That the Duke was thy father—as no doubt then
He bid fair for't—thy injury is the more,
For had he cut thee a right diamond,
Thou hadst been next set in the dukedom's ring,
When his worn self, like age's easy slave,
Had dropped out of the collet into th' grave.
What wrong can equal this? Canst thou be tame
And think upon't?

SPURIO No, mad and think upon't.

DUCHESS
Who would not be revenged of such a father,
E'en in the worst way? I would thank that sin
That could most injury him, and be in league with it.
O, what a grief 'tis that a man should live
But once i'th' world and then to live a bastard,
The curse o'the womb, the thief of nature,
Begot against the seventh commandëment,
Half-damned in the conception by the justice
Of that unbribèd everlasting law.

SPURIO
O, I'd a hot-backed devil to my father.

DUCHESS
Would not this mad e'en patience, make blood rough?
Who but an eunuch would not sin, his bed
By one false minute disinherited?

SPURIO [*aside*]
Ay, there's the vengeance that my birth was wrapped in.
I'll be revenged for all. Now hate begin.
I'll call foul incest but a venial sin.

DUCHESS
Cold still? In vain then must a duchess woo?

SPURIO
Madam, I blush to say what I will do.

DUCHESS
Thence flew sweet comfort. Earnest, and farewell.
[*She kisses him*]

SPURIO
O, one incestuous kiss picks open hell.

DUCHESS
Faith, now, old Duke, my vengeance shall reach high.
I'll arm thy brow with woman's heraldry. *Exit*

SPURIO
Duke, thou didst do me wrong, and by thy act
Adultery is my nature.
Faith, if the truth were known, I was begot
After some gluttonous dinner. Some stirring dish
Was my first father, when deep healths went round
And ladies' cheeks were painted red with wine,
Their tongues, as short and nimble as their heels,
Uttering words sweet and thick; and when they risse
Were merrily disposed to fall again.
In such a whisp'ring and withdrawing hour,
When base male-bawds kept sentinel at stair-head,
Was I stol'n softly. O, damnation met
The sin of feasts, drunken adultery.
I feel it swell me. My revenge is just.
I was begot in impudent wine and lust.
Stepmother, I consent to thy desires.
I love thy mischief well, but I hate thee
And those three cubs thy sons, wishing confusion,
Death, and disgrace may be their epitaphs.
As for my brother, the Duke's only son,
Whose birth is more beholden to report
Than mine, and yet perhaps as falsely sown—
Women must not be trusted with their own—
I'll loose my days upon him, hate all I.
Duke, on thy brow I'll draw my bastardy;
For indeed, a bastard by nature should make cuckolds,
Because he is the son of a cuckold-maker. *Exit*

Enter Vindice and Hippolito, Vindice in disguise as Piato to attend Lord Lussurioso, the Duke's son 1.3

VINDICE
What, brother, am I far enough from myself?

139 **'light** alight, dismount
140 **penthouse** projecting upper storey of an Elizabethan house, or awning over a shop or stall
141 **check the signs** strike the shop-signs hung out over the street
142 **barbers' basins** distinctively shaped shaving dishes, often used as barbers' shop-signs
143 **beggar** alluding to the proverb 'Set a beggar on horseback and he will ride a gallop'; here with sexual innuendo
147 **bid fair for't** made a fair attempt at it
148 **cut . . . diamond** fathered you legitimately (the image leading to 'set', 'ring', and 'collet')
151 **collet** the hollow (in a ring) in which the precious stone is set
160 **seventh commandëment** which forbade adultery (Exodus, 20:14)
172 **Earnest** The kiss is an 'earnest' or pledge of favours to come.
175 **woman's heraldry** cuckold's horns
179 **stirring** stimulating
182 **tongues . . . heels** 'short-tongued' = lisping; 'short-heeled' = wanton (see Tilley, S397)
183 **risse** rose (a Middleton form)
183–4 **risse . . . again** i.e. they were tipsy and ready for sex
187 **stol'n** illicitly and slealthily conceived
189 **swell** The word, as it recurs (1.2.112, 1.3.79, 1.3.122, 2.2.92, 4.1.64), tends to link the sins of gluttony, avarice, lechery, wrath, and pride; here the 'swelling' of drunkenness and feasting leads to arousal for (*a*) sex, (*b*) violence.
190 **impudent** shameless
195–7 **only . . . mine** i.e. Lussurioso, the Duke's legitimate son, is more acceptable to public opinion
199 **loose . . . him** devote my time to working his ruin
1.3.1 **far . . . myself** sufficiently disguised

HIPPOLITO
As if another man had been sent whole
Into the world and none wist how he came.

VINDICE
It will confirm me bold, the child o'th' court.
Let blushes dwell i'th' country. Impudence,
Thou goddess of the palace, mistress of mistresses,
To whom the costly-perfumed people pray,
Strike thou my forehead into dauntless marble,
Mine eyes to steady sapphires; turn my visage,
And if I must needs glow, let me blush inward,
That this immodest season may not spy
That scholar in my cheeks, fool bashfulness,
That maid in the old time, whose flush of grace
Would never suffer her to get good clothes.
Our maids are wiser and are less ashamed.
Save Grace the bawd, I seldom hear grace named.

HIPPOLITO
Nay, brother, you reach out o'th' verge now—
[Enter Lussurioso with Attendants]
'Sfoot,
The Duke's son! Settle your looks.

VINDICE Pray, let me not be doubted.
[Vindice withdraws to one side]

HIPPOLITO
My lord—

LUSSURIOSO
Hippolito? *[To his Attendants]* Be absent, leave us.
[Exeunt Attendants]

HIPPOLITO
My lord, after long search, wary enquiries,
And politic siftings, I made choice of yon fellow,
Whom I guess rare for many deep employments.
This our age swims within him, and if Time
Had so much hair, I should take him for Time,
He is so near kin to this present minute.

LUSSURIOSO 'Tis enough.
We thank thee; yet words are but great men's blanks;
Gold, though it be dumb, does utter the best thanks.
[He gives Hippolito money]

HIPPOLITO
Your plenteous honour! An exc'llent fellow, my lord.

LUSSURIOSO
So, give us leave. *[Exit Hippolito]*
[To Vindice] Welcome.
Be not far off; we must be better acquainted.
Push! Be bold with us—thy hand.

VINDICE
With all my heart, i'faith. How dost, sweet musk-cat?
When shall we lie together?

LUSSURIOSO *[aside]* Wondrous knave!
Gather him into boldness? 'Sfoot, the slave's
Already as familiar as an ague,
And shakes me at his pleasure.—Friend I can
Forget myself in private, but elsewhere
I pray do you remember me.

VINDICE
O, very well, sir. I cònstrue myself saucy.

LUSSURIOSO
What hast been, of what professïon?

VINDICE A bone-setter.

LUSSURIOSO A bone-setter?

VINDICE
A bawd, my lord, one that sets bones together.

LUSSURIOSO *[aside]* Notable bluntness!
Fit, fit for me, e'en trained up to my hand.—
Thou hast been scrivener to much knavery, then?

VINDICE
Fool to abundance, sir; I have been witness
To the surrenders of a thousand virgins,

3 **wist** knew
6 **mistresses** quibbling on the sense 'kept women'
13–14 **That ... clothes** i.e. modesty is an old-fashioned virgin that would not flaunt herself in court finery (perhaps with the implication that she would not prostitute herself for wealth). The lines draw on the iconographical association of nakedness with simplicity, truth, and innocence (and a prelapsarian state). The classical figures are *Nuda Simplicitas*, *Antiquitas*, or *Veritas*.
16 **Grace the bawd** an ironic prefiguring of the role of Vindice's Mother, Gratiana (= Grace)
17 **reach out o'th' verge** go beyond the limit, go too far. But 'verge' also means 'the precincts of the court': Vindice's mention of 'Grace the bawd' takes him into a new area of satirical observation. **'Sfoot** oath contracted from 'God's foot'
23 **This ... him** i.e. he is a kind of vessel or medium for the *Zeitgeist* (and its depravity); with 'swims within' compare 'impious steeped' of Lussurioso at 1.1.2
23–4 **Time ... hair** The implicit picture may be of the familiar Old Father Time, here balding; but the more pertinent emblem is of Time as *Kairos* (the decisive moment), which merges with that of Occasion or Opportunity (1.1.55).
27 **blanks** either (*a*) a form of unsigned cheque, or (*b*) coinage not yet value-stamped, or (*c*) a lottery ticket that does not win a prize. Lussurioso's point is that verbal expressions of gratitude have no cash value.
30 **give us leave** leave us
32 **Push!** a variant of the exclamation 'Pish!', common in Middleton's writing and rare outside it
33 **musk-cat** literally the musk-deer from which the perfume is obtained, but the term was applied to a fop or prostitute
35 **Gather ... boldness?** The rhetorical question, stressed on 'him', is a comment on Vindice's forwardness; Lussurioso implies that there was no need to encourage Vindice to take his hand (line 32). Vindice either shakes it vigorously or embraces him.
39 **remember me** remember who I am (and pay due respect to my rank)
40 **cònstrue** consider
42 **bone-setter** The term was standard for one who treated fractures. Vindice's jocular application of it to the trade of bawd is a macabre reminder of the skeleton beneath the copulating flesh.
46 **to my hand** i.e. for my use; an image from the training of a falcon may lie behind Lussurioso's words
47 **scrivener to** recorder of, agent for
48 **Fool to abundance** accessory to an abundance (of knavery). 'Fool' is here used in the sense of 'one who is imposed upon by others' or 'a (voluntary) dupe'; the term is invited by 'knavery' in the previous line, and distinguishes—in a world 'divided into knaves and fools' (2.2.4)—'between knaves who perform it and their agents' (Ross).

And not so little.
I have seen patrimonies washed a-pieces,
Fruit-fields turned into bastards,
And in a world of acres
Not so much dust due to the heir 'twas left to
As would well gravel a petitïon.

LUSSURIOSO [*aside*]
Fine villain! Troth, I like him wondrously.
He's e'en shaped for my purpose.—Then thou know'st
I'th' world strange lust?

VINDICE
O, Dutch lust, fulsome lust!
Drunken procreation, which begets so many drunkards.
Some father dreads not, gone to bed in wine,
To slide from the mother and cling the daughter-in-law.
Some uncles are adulterous with their nieces,
Brothers with brothers' wives. O, hour of incest!
Any kin now next to the rim o'th' sister
Is man's meat in these days, and in the morning,
When they are up and dressed and their mask on,
Who can perceive this, save that eternal eye
That sees through flesh and all? Well, if anything
Be damned, it will be twelve o'clock at night.
That twelve will never scape.
It is the Judas of the hours, wherein
Honest salvation is betrayed to sin.

LUSSURIOSO
In troth, it is too. But let this talk glide.
It is our blood to err, though hell gaped loud.
Ladies know Lucifer fell, yet still are proud.
Now, sir, wert thou as secret as thou'rt subtle
And deeply fathomed into all estates,
I would embrace thee for a near employment,
And thou shouldst swell in money and be able
To make lame beggars crouch to thee.

VINDICE
My lord,
Secret? I ne'er had that disease o'th' mother,
I praise my father. Why are men made close
But to keep thoughts in best? I grant you this,
Tell but some woman a secret over night,
Your doctor may find it in the urinal i'th' morning.
But my lord—

LUSSURIOSO
So, thou'rt confirmed in me,
And thus I enter thee.
[*He gives Vindice money*]

VINDICE
This Indian devil
Will quickly enter any man—but a usurer;
He prevents that, by ent'ring the devil first.

LUSSURIOSO
Attend me. I am past my depth in lust,
And I must swim or drown. All my desires
Are levelled at a virgin not far from court,
To whom I have conveyed by messenger
Many waxed lines, full of my neatest spirit,
And jewels that were able to ravish her
Without the help of man; all which and more
She foolish-chaste sent back, the messengers
Receiving frowns for answers.

VINDICE
Possible?
'Tis a rare phoenix, whoe'er she be.
If your desires be such, she so repugnant,
In troth, my lord, I'd be revenged and marry her.

LUSSURIOSO
Push!
The dowry of her blood and of her fortunes
Are both too mean—good enough to be bad withal.
I'm one of that number can defend
Marriage is good, yet rather keep a friend.

51 **washed a-pieces** wrecked, as by a rough sea; but with a hint of drunken profligacy in 'washed'

52 **Fruit-fields . . . bastards** i.e. the estate squandered on adultery and whoring (and perhaps on maintaining illegitimate children); the imagery also involves 'the ideas of true inheritance declining to false (usurers) and natural fruit debased by grafting with inferior stock' (Gibbons).

55 **gravel** sprinkle sand on (to dry the ink)

58 **Dutch** The Dutch were reputed to be heavy drinkers, and in *Trick* 'a Dutch widow' is 'an English drab'.

61 **To . . . daughter-in-law** 'In the sound and placing of two words, "slide" and "cling", the whole stealthy action comes alive' (Salgādo).

64 **rim** (*a*) edge, limit, (*b*) (rim of the) womb, (*c*) vagina. Here 'next to' means 'short of' (with the implication, 'though only just'); the taboo on sexual relations between brother and sister is parenthetically affirmed, but not without prurience. The tensions in Vindice's acting as procurer of Castiza for Lussurioso are foreshadowed here.

67 **eternal eye** The all-seeing eye of God, from which the sinning Adam and Eve try vainly to hide, was commonly pictured in emblem books.

70 **twelve** i.e. the twelfth of the twelve hours, as Judas was the one among the Twelve Disciples who betrayed Christ

74 **gaped loud** Hell is imagined as a yawning abyss from which the cries of the damned are heard.

75 **Lucifer** The angel Lucifer fell through the sin of pride.

77 **estates** classes of people

78 **near** private (and intimately concerning Lussurioso)

81 **disease o'th' mother** i.e. gossiping indiscreetly; compare 1.1.130–2; there is a quibble on 'the mother' = hysteria. Vindice praises his father for begetting him as male, and so immune from the feminine weakness for blabbing.

82 **close** playing on 'close' = secret and the difference between male and female anatomy

85 **Your . . . morning** The reference is to the inspection of urine in the diagnosis of illness. Elements combined in Vindice's image are present in modern senses of the word 'leak'.

86 **confirmed in me** established in my trust

87 **enter** admit, initiate; in the next line Vindice takes up the word to play on its normal sense; there are suggestions, particularly in association with the religious overtones of 'confirmed', of a kind of parody of the Eucharist, or black mass.
Indian The Indies were sources of gold and silver, and of tales of heathen practices.

89 **prevents** forestalls

94 **waxed lines** sealed letters

99 **rare phoenix** paragon, after the unique mythical bird

100 **repugnant** resistant, hostile

105 **defend** contend

106 **friend** mistress

Give me my bed by stealth, there's true delight;
What breeds a loathing in't but night by night?

VINDICE
A very fine religion.

LUSSURIOSO Therefore thus:
I'll trust thee in the business of my heart,
Because I see thee well experienced
In this luxurious day wherein we breathe.
Go thou and with a smooth enchanting tongue
Bewitch her ears and cozen her of all grace.
Enter upon the portion of her soul,
Her honour, which she calls her chastity,
And bring it into expense; for honesty
Is like a stock of money laid to sleep,
Which, ne'er so little broke, does never keep.

VINDICE
You have gi'n't the tang, i'faith, my lord.
Make known the lady to me, and my brain
Shall swell with strange invention. I will move it
Till I expire with speaking and drop down
Without a word to save me; but I'll work—

LUSSURIOSO We thank thee, and will raise thee.
Receive her name: it is the only daughter
To Madam Gratiana, the late widow.

VINDICE [*aside*]
O, my sister, my sister!

LUSSURIOSO Why dost walk aside?

VINDICE
My lord, I was thinking how I might begin,
As thus, 'O lady'—or twenty hundred devices.
Her very bodkin will put a man in.

LUSSURIOSO Ay, or the wagging of her hair.

VINDICE No, that shall put you in, my lord.

LUSSURIOSO
Shall't? Why, content. Dost know the daughter, then?

VINDICE
O, exc'llent well—by sight.

LUSSURIOSO That was her brother
That did prefer thee to us.

VINDICE My lord, I think so;
I knew I had seen him somewhere.

LUSSURIOSO
And therefore, prithee, let thy heart to him
Be as a virgin, close.

VINDICE O, my good lord.

LUSSURIOSO
We may laugh at that simple age within him—

VINDICE Ha, ha, ha.

LUSSURIOSO
Himself being made the subtle instrument
To wind up a good fellow—

VINDICE That's I, my lord.

LUSSURIOSO That's thou.—
To entice and work his sister.

VINDICE A pure novice.

LUSSURIOSO
'Twas finely managed.

VINDICE Gallantly carried.
A pretty perfumed villain.

LUSSURIOSO I've bethought me:
If she prove chaste still and immovable,
Venture upon the mother, and with gifts,
As I will furnish thee, begin with her.

VINDICE
O fie, fie, that's the wrong end, my lord.
'Tis mere impossible that a mother by any gifts should
become a bawd to her own daughter.

LUSSURIOSO Nay then, I see thou'rt but a puny in the subtle
mystery of a woman.
Why, 'tis held now no dainty dish; the name
Is so in league with th'age that nowadays
It does eclipse three quarters of a mother.

VINDICE Does't so, my lord?
Let me alone, then, to eclipse the fourth.

LUSSURIOSO
Why, well said. Come, I'll furnish thee. But first
Swear to be true in all.

VINDICE True.

LUSSURIOSO Nay, but swear.

VINDICE
Swear? I hope your honour little doubts my faith.

LUSSURIOSO
Yet for my humour's sake, 'cause I love swearing.

VINDICE
'Cause you love swearing, 'slud, I will.

LUSSURIOSO Why, enough.
Ere long look to be made of better stuff.

VINDICE
That will do well indeed, my lord.

LUSSURIOSO Attend me. [*Exit*]

112 **luxurious** lecherous

115 **Enter** The word links the ideas of devil possession (as at lines 87–8 above) and sexual assault (as at line 133 below). Lussurioso's whole speech describes a Temptation by Satan, but, taking up the implications of 'business' in line 110, puts the seduction of body and soul in commercial terms.
portion birthright, dowry

117 **expense** use

119 **broke** The simple enough word catches various concerns and overtones: broken sleep, a stock of money broken into, the hymen broken, and (through 'broker') traffic both financial and sexual.

120 **gi'n't the tang** given the true taste of it

122 **move it** urge it, plead your case

127 **Gratiana** Italian equivalent of Grace (from *gratia*, grace)

131 **bodkin** ornamental hairpin
put a man in provide an opening, serve as a conversation piece

133 **put you in** obscenely punning on pubic hair and sexual penetration

143 **wind up** prepare, excite
good fellow (*a*) agreeable companion, (*b*) thief

154 **puny** greenhorn

156 **the name** i.e. of bawd

156–8 **the . . . mother** 'The name (of bawd) is so closely connected with every woman in the age in which we live that even a mother is naturally three parts of one already' (Collins).

165 **'slud** a corruption of the oath 'God's blood'

167 **Attend me** wait on me as an attendant

VINDICE O!
Now let me burst. I've eaten noble poison.
We are made strange fellows, brother, innocent
villains.
Wilt not be angry when thou hear'st on't, think'st
thou?
I'faith, thou shalt. Swear me to foul my sister!
Sword, I durst make a promise of him to thee:
Thou shalt disheir him; it shall be thine honour.
And yet, now angry froth is down in me,
It would not prove the meanest policy
In this disguise to try the faith of both.
Another might have had the selfsame office,
Some slave that would have wrought effectually,
Ay, and perhaps o'erwrought 'em; therefore I,
Being thought travelled, will apply myself
Unto the selfsame form, forget my nature,
As if no part about me were kin to 'em,
So touch 'em—though I durst almost for good
Venture my lands in heaven upon their blood. *Exit*

1.4 *Enter the discontented Lord Antonio, whose wife the Duchess's youngest son ravished; he discovering the body of her dead to certain lords; [Piero] and Hippolito*

ANTONIO
Draw nearer, lords, and be sad witnesses
Of a fair comely building newly fall'n,
Being falsely underminèd. Violent rape
Has played a glorious act. Behold, my lords,
A sight that strikes man out of me.

PIERO
That virtuous lady!

ANTONIO Precedent for wives!

HIPPOLITO
The blush of many women, whose chaste presence
Would e'en call shame up to their cheeks and make
Pale wanton sinners have good colours.

ANTONIO Dead.
Her honour first drunk poison, and her life,
Being fellows in one house, did pledge her honour.

PIERO
O grief of many!

ANTONIO I marked not this before—
A prayer-book the pillow to her cheek;
This was her rich confection; and another
Placed in her right hand, with a leaf tucked up
Pointing to these words:
Melius virtute mori, quam per dedecus vivere.
True and effectual it is indeed.

HIPPOLITO
My lord, since you invite us to your sorrows,
Let's truly taste 'em, that with equal comfort
As to ourselves we may relieve your wrong.
We have grief too, that yet walks without tongue:
Curae leves loquuntur, majores stupent.

ANTONIO You deal with truth, my lord.
Lend me but your attentions and I'll cut
Long grief into short words. Last revelling night,
When torch-light made an artificial noon
About the court, some courtiers in the masque,
Putting on better faces than their own,
Being full of fraud and flattery, amongst whom
The Duchess' youngest son, that moth to honour,
Filled up a room; and with long lust to eat
Into my wearing, amongst all the ladies
Singled out that dear form who ever lived
As cold in lust as she is now in death;
Which that step-duchess' monster knew too well;
And therefore in the height of all the revels,
When music was heard loudest, courtiers busiest,
And ladies great with laughter—O vicious minute,
Unfit, but for relation, to be spoke of!—
Then with a face more impudent than his visor

170 **fellows** parners, accomplices
174 **disheir him** prevent him from inheriting the kingdom (by killing him)
175 **angry...down** The image is presumably of the subsidence of a tempestuous (frothy) sea.
184 **touch** test
184–5 **I durst...blood** I should dare, almost as a final act, to stake my hopes of eternal salvation on their strength of character
1.4.0.3 ***discovering*** revealing. A curtained 'discovery space' (whether alcove in the rear wall or temporary arrangement) would have been necessary for this revelation of the dead wife, posed as monumental figure of ravaged virtue. Presumably the curtains would have been closed on her at the end of the scene.
2 **Of...fall'n** Another expression of the traditional idea of the body as house or temple; by such hints in the imagery the play sketches a realm of religious thought against which its actions are implicitly judged; at the same time, such an image evokes a changing society in which actual buildings are demolished or crumble from neglect.
4 **played...act** suggesting a stage action, and sharpening our awareness of the play as play (Foakes); compare 1.1.40
7 **blush of** i.e. cause of blushes in
9 **good colours** both 'more attractive' and 'more virtuous' (because blushing indicated they were aware of past sins) (Loughrey and Taylor)
10 **drunk poison** figuratively, with reference to the rape
11 **pledge** toast (by drinking poison literally)
14 **confection** medicinal preservative (here in the spiritual sense)
17 ***Melius...vivere*** Better to die in virtue than to live with dishonour
20–1 **that...ourselves** that with as much comfort to you as to ourselves
23 ***Curae...stupent*** Light cares speak out, greater ones are dumbfounded; misquoted from Seneca's *Phaedra*, line 607; common in Jacobean drama and current as a proverb. See also 4.2.193–8.
29 **better faces** the masks worn in court entertainments
31 **moth to honour** i.e. one who eats honour away
33 **wearing** clothing (continuing the moth image)
34 **Singled...form** The associations of 'dear'/'deer' reinforce the hunting sense of 'singled out' (common in Renaissance writing), meaning to separate one deer from the herd.
39 **great** swollen (as though with child)
40 **but for relation** were it not for its essential part in the story
41 **a face** an effrontery (but with wordplay on the literal face)

He harried her amidst a throng of panders
That live upon damnation of both kinds,
And fed the ravenous vulture of his lust.
O, death to think on't! She, her honour forced,
Deemed it a nobler dowry for her name
To die with poison than to live with shame.

HIPPOLITO
A wondrous lady, of rare fire compact!
She's made her name an empress by that act.

PIERO
My lord, what judgement follows the offender?

ANTONIO
Faith, none, my lord; it cools and is deferred.

PIERO Delay the doom for rape?

ANTONIO
O, you must note who 'tis should die:
The Duchess' son. She'll look to be a saver.
"Judgement in this age is near kin to favour."

HIPPOLITO
Nay then, step forth, thou bribeless officer.
[He draws his sword]
I bind you all in steel to bind you surely.
Here let your oaths meet, to be kept and paid,
Which else will stick like rust, and shame the blade.
Strengthen my vow, that if at the next sitting
Judgement speak all in gold and spare the blood
Of such a serpent, e'en before their seats,
To let his soul out, which long since was found
Guilty in heaven.

ALL We swear it and will act it.
[They swear upon the sword]

ANTONIO
Kind gentlemen, I thank you in mine ire.

HIPPOLITO 'Twere pity
The ruins of so fair a monument
Should not be dipped in the defacer's blood.

PIERO
Her funeral shall be wealthy, for her name
Merits a tomb of pearl. My lord Antonio,
For this time wipe your lady from your eyes.
No doubt our grief and yours may one day court it,
When we are more familiar with revenge.

ANTONIO
That is my comfort, gentlemen, and I joy
In this one happiness above the rest,
Which will be called a miracle at last,
That, being an old man, I'd a wife so chaste.
[He closes the curtains to conceal the body]
Exeunt

Finis Actus Primi

Incipit Actus Secundus 2.1
Enter Castiza, the sister of Vindice and Hippolito

CASTIZA
How hardly shall that maiden be beset
Whose only fortunes are her constant thoughts,
That has no other child's-part but her honour
That keeps her low and empty in estate.
Maids and their honours are like poor beginners.
Were not sin rich, there would be fewer sinners.
Why had not virtue a revènue? Well,
I know the cause: 'twould have impoverished hell.
[Enter Dondolo]
How now, Dondolo?

DONDOLO Madonna, there is one, as they say, a thing of flesh and blood, a man I take him by his beard, that would very desirously mouth to mouth with you.

CASTIZA What's that?

DONDOLO Show his teeth in your company.

CASTIZA I understand thee not.

DONDOLO Why, speak with you, madonna.

CASTIZA Why, say so, madman, and cut off a great deal of dirty way. Had it not been better spoke in ordinary words, that one would speak with me?

DONDOLO Ha, ha, that's as ordinary as two shillings. I would strive a little to show myself in my place. A gentleman-usher scorns to use the phrase and fancy of a serving-man.

CASTIZA
Yours be your own, sir. Go, direct him hither.
[Exit Dondolo]
I hope some happy tidings from my brother
That lately travelled, whom my soul affects.
Here he comes.
Enter Vindice her brother, disguised [and bearing a treasure chest]

VINDICE
Lady, the best of wishes to your sex,

42 **harried** ravished
43 **kinds** sexes
44 **And . . . lust** This image of predatory lust derives from the myth of Tityus, one of the four great sinners tortured in Hades, in his case for having attacked Latona, mother of Apollo and Diana; his punishment, similar to Prometheus's, was to have a vulture feed eternally on his liver, seat of carnal passion. Renaissance commentators read the myth as an allegory of the tortures caused by immoderate love.
48 **compact** composed
62 **their** i.e. the judges'
70 **pearl** Emblematic of what is pure, invaluable, and even divine, the 'pearl' leads, through association with teardrops, to the bold trope in the next sentence.
72 **court it** be shown at court
2.1.1 **hardly** severely
3 **child's-part** inheritance
8.1 ***Dondolo*** Italian for a gull or foolish servant, as in *Dissemblers* and Marston's *Fawn*
17–18 **cut . . . way** i.e. speak directly (avoid covering a lot of muddy ground)
20 **ordinary as two shillings** punning on a 'two-shilling ordinary', a tavern offering meals at the fixed price of two shillings
21 **place** office
22 **gentleman-usher** gentleman (rather than a member of the servant class) acting as usher to a person of superior rank
26 **affects** loves
27.1–2 ***bearing . . . chest*** The need for this is accepted by most directors; see 1.3.149–50, 2.1.85, 155, 187. The scene either imitates or inspired *Volpone*, 3.5, in which Volpone brings on a chest of treasure for his attempted seduction of Celia.

Fair skins and new gowns.
[*He gives her a letter*]
CASTIZA O, they shall thank you, sir.
Whence this?
VINDICE O, from a dear and worthy friend,
Mighty.
CASTIZA
From whom?
VINDICE The Duke's son.
CASTIZA Receive that.
A box o'th' ear to her brother
I swòre I'd put anger in my hand
And pass the virgin limits of myself
To him that next appeared in that base office,
To be his sin's attorney. Bear to him
That figure of my hate upon thy cheek
Whilst 'tis yet hot, and I'll reward thee for't.
Tell him my honour shall have a rich name
When several harlots shall share his with shame.
Farewell, commend me to him in my hate. *Exit*
VINDICE
It is the sweetest box that e'er my nose came nigh,
The finest drawn-work cuff that e'er was worn.
I'll love this blow for ever, and this cheek
Shall still henceforward take the wall of this.
O, I'm above my tongue! Most constant sister,
In this thou hast right honourable shown.
Many are called by their honour that have none.
Thou art approved for ever in my thoughts.
It is not in the power of words to taint thee.
And yet for the salvation of my oath,
As my resolve in that point, I will lay
Hard siege unto my mother, though I know
A siren's tongue could not bewitch her so.
[*Enter Mother*]
Mass, fitly here she comes. Thanks, my disguise.—
Madam, good afternoon.
MOTHER You're welcome, sir.
VINDICE
The next of Italy commends him to you,
Our mighty expectation, the Duke's son.
MOTHER
I think myself much honoured that he pleases
To rank me in his thoughts.
VINDICE So may you, lady.
One that is like to be our sudden duke—
The crown gapes for him every tide—and then
Commander o'er us all. Do but think on him;
How blessed were they now that could pleasure him
E'en with anything almost.
MOTHER Ay, save their honour.
VINDICE
Tut, one would let a little of that go too
And ne'er be seen in't, ne'er be seen in't, mark you.
I'd wink, and let it go.
MOTHER Marry, but I would not.
VINDICE
Marry, but I would, I hope. I know you would too
If you'd that blood now which you gave your daughter.
To her indeed 'tis, this wheel comes about.
That man that must be all this, perhaps ere morning
(For his white father does but mould away),
Has long desired your daughter.
MOTHER Desired?
VINDICE Nay, but hear me:
He desires now that will command hereafter;
Therefore be wise.
I speak as more a friend to you than him.
Madam, I know you're poor, and, 'lack the day,
There are too many poor ladies already.
Why should you vex the number? 'Tis despised.
Live wealthy. Rightly understand the world,
And chide away that foolish country girl
Keeps company with your daughter, Chastity.
MOTHER
O fie, fie, the riches of the world cannot hire
A mother to such a most unnatural task.
VINDICE
No, but a thousand angels can;
Men have no power, angels must work you to't.
The world descends into such base-born evils
That forty angels can make fourscore devils.
There will be fools still, I perceive, still fools.
Would I be poor, dejected, scorned of greatness,
Swept from the palace, and see other daughters

29.1 ***He gives her a letter*** mentioned by Castiza at 2.1.138–40

35 **attorney** i.e. one who pleads on sin's behalf

36 **figure** image, representation

41 **box** punning on (*a*) blow, (*b*) container for spices or fragrant ointment (hence 'sweetest' and 'nose')

42 **drawn-work cuff** shirt-sleeve cuff decorated with thread, with a pun on the cuff = blow that is 'worn' on his cheek; also 'drawn' picks up 'figure' (line 36)

44 **take the wall of** take precedence over (from the privilege of walking next to the wall as the cleaner and safer side of a pavement)

46 **right honourable** playing on the style of address proper to certain peers and dignitaries

51 **As ... point** Vindice is recalling his idea of testing his sister and mother (1.3.176–7).

53 **siren's tongue** In classical myth the sirens were sea-songstresses (half women, half birds, though later pictured as mermaids) whose enchanting voices lured sailors to destruction.

56 **next of Italy** i.e. first in line of succession

60 **sudden duke** duke at any moment

61 **gapes ... tide** is open to him at any time now. Vindice's formulation blends sinister and comic overtones. Proverbially, what 'gapes' at the 'tide' is the oyster, as in Ben Jonson's *Bartholomew Fair*: 'I have gaped as the oyster for the tide' (5.5.23). But the grave and hell also gape (1.3.74), eager to devour.

70 **wheel** wheel of fortune (turning to provide Castiza with an opportunity)

79 **vex the number** aggravate the situation by adding to the number

85 **angels** punning on the name of the gold coin bearing the figure of the Archangel Michael and worth half one pound

90 **dejected** abased, lowly

Spring with the dew o'th' court, having mine own
So much desired and loved—by the Duke's son?
No, I would raise my state upon her breast
And call her eyes my tenants; I would count
My yearly maintenance upon her cheeks,
Take coach upon her lip, and all her parts
Should keep men after men, and I would ride
In pleasure upon pleasure.
You took great pains for her, once when it was.
Let her requite it now, though it be but some.
You brought her forth; she may well bring you home.

MOTHER
O heavens! This overcomes me.

VINDICE [*aside*] Not, I hope, already?

MOTHER [*aside*]
It is too strong for me; men know that know us,
We are so weak their words can overthrow us.
He touched me nearly, made my virtues bate,
When his tongue struck upon my poor estate.

VINDICE [*aside*]
I e'en quake to proceed; my spirit turns edge.
I fear me she's unmothered, yet I'll venture.
"That woman is all male whom none can enter."—
What think you now, lady? Speak, are you wiser?
What said advancement to you? Thus it said:
'The daughter's fall lifts up the mother's head.'
Did it not, madam? But I'll swear it does
In many places. Tut, this age fears no man.
"'Tis no shame to be bad, because 'tis common."

MOTHER
Ay, that's the comfort on't.

VINDICE [*aside*] The comfort on't!—
I keep the best for last. Can these persuade you
To forget heaven and—
[*He gives her money*]

MOTHER
Ay, these are they—

VINDICE O!

MOTHER —that enchant our sex;
These are the means that govern our affections.
That woman
Will not be troubled with the mother long
That sees the comfortable shine of you.
I blush to think what for your sakes I'll do.

VINDICE [*aside*]
O suffering heaven, with thy invisible finger
E'en at this instant turn the precious side
Of both mine eyeballs inward, not to see myself!

MOTHER
Look you, sir.

VINDICE Holla.

MOTHER Let this thank your pains.
[*She gives him money*]

VINDICE O, you're a kind madam.

MOTHER
I'll see how I can move.

VINDICE [*aside*] Your words will sting.

MOTHER
If she be still chaste, I'll ne'er call her mine.

VINDICE [*aside*] Spoke truer than you meant it.

MOTHER
Daughter Castiza.
[*Enter Castiza*]

CASTIZA Madam.

VINDICE O, she's yonder. Meet her.
[*Aside*] Troops of celestial soldiers guard her heart!
Yon dam has devils enough to take her part.

CASTIZA
Madam, what makes yon evil-officed man
In presence of you?

MOTHER Why?

CASTIZA He lately brought
Immodest writing sent from the Duke's son
To tempt me to dishonourable act.

MOTHER
Dishonourable act? Good honourable fool,
That wouldst be honest 'cause thou wouldst be so,
Producing no one reason but thy will;
And 't'as a good report, prettily commended,
But pray, by whom? Mean people, ignorant people.
The better sort I'm sure cannot abide it;
And by what rule should we square out our lives
But by our betters' actions? O, if thou knew'st
What 'twere to lose it, thou wouldst never keep it;

94 **state** (*a*) rank, (*b*) estate (connecting with 'raise' = build, and 'tenants')
98 **keep men after men** maintain many servants (but with a suggestion of promiscuity)
100 **once when it was** i.e. during childbirth
102 **bring you home** i.e. to the (financial) state to which you belong; this may be an antedating of *OED*'s *Home*, *adv.*, 7.a, 'bring oneself home' = 'recover oneself (financially)' (first citation 1760); but the phrase also recalls an 'eternal home', ironically equating material and spiritual salvation.
106 **bate** abate, dwindle
108 **turns edge** grows blunt
109 **she's unmothered** she has lost her maternal feelings; compare 1.3.156–60
venture pronounced 'venter' (a common spelling)
110 **all male** with wordplay on 'mail' = armour
enter persuade, with the obvious sexual pun
115 **fears** frightens
123 **the mother** (*a*) hysteria (as a women's disease), (*b*) maternal concern
124 **comfortable** comforting
126 **thy invisible finger** the scriptural Hand of God, prominent in Christian iconography as symbol of the omnipotent will, and often shown as issuing, with rays of light, from a cloud, and with three fingers extended (to represent the Trinity)
130 **kind** with the sarcastic sub-meaning 'natural, maternal'
131 **move** persuade (Castiza)
136 **dam** contemptuous term for 'mother', common in reference to 'the devil's dam'
142 **honest** chaste
147 **square out** mark out, direct; a 'square' was a footrule, so 'by what rule' plays on the abstract and concrete kinds of rule: (*a*) principle, criterion, (*b*) instrument for measuring

But there's a cold curse laid upon all maids:
Whilst others clip the sun, they clasp the shades.
Virginity is paradise locked up.
You cannot come by yourselves without fee,
And 'twas decreed that man should keep the key.
Deny advancement, treasure, the Duke's son?

CASTIZA
I cry you mercy, lady, I mistook you.
Pray, did you see my mother? Which way went she?
Pray god I have not lost her.

VINDICE [*aside*] Prettily put by.

MOTHER
Are you as proud to me as coy to him?
Do you not know me now?

CASTIZA Why, are you she?
The world's so changed, one shape into another,
It is a wise child now that knows her mother.

VINDICE [*aside*]
Most right, i'faith.

MOTHER I owe your cheek my hand
For that presumption now, but I'll forget it.
Come, you shall leave those childish haviours
And understand your time. Fortunes flow to you.
What, will you be a girl?
If all feared drowning that spy waves ashore,
Gold would grow rich and all the merchants poor.

CASTIZA
It is a pretty saying of a wicked one.
But methinks now
It does not show so well out of your mouth,
Better in his.

VINDICE [*aside*]
Faith, bad enough in both,
Were I in earnest, as I'll seem no less.
[*To Castiza*] I wonder, lady, your own mother's words
Cannot be taken, nor stand in full force.
'Tis honesty you urge. What's honesty?
'Tis but heaven's beggar;
And what woman is so foolish to keep honesty
And be not able to keep herself? No,
Times are grown wiser and will keep less charge.
A maid that has small portion now intends
To break up house and live upon her friends.
How blessed are you; you have happiness alone.
Others must fall to thousands, you to one,
Sufficient in himself to make your forehead
Dazzle the world with jewels, and petitionary people
Start at your presence.

MOTHER O, if I were young,
I should be ravished.

CASTIZA Ay, to lose your honour.

VINDICE
'Slid, how can you lose your honour to deal with my lord's grace?
He'll add more honour to it by his title.
Your mother will tell you how.

MOTHER That I will.

VINDICE
O, think upon the pleasure of the palace,
Securèd ease and state, the stirring meats
Ready to move out of the dishes, that e'en now
Quicken when they're eaten;
Banquets abroad by torch-light, musics, sports,
Bare-headed vassals that had ne'er the fortune
To keep on their own hats, but let horns wear 'em,
Nine coaches waiting—hurry, hurry, hurry!

CASTIZA Ay, to the devil.

VINDICE [*aside*]
Ay, to the devil.—To th' Duke, by my faith.

MOTHER
Ay, to the Duke. Daughter, you'd scorn to think
O'th' devil an you were there once.

VINDICE [*aside*] True, for most
There are as proud as he for his heart, i'faith.—
Who'd sit at home in a neglected room,
Dealing her short-lived beauty to the pictures
That are as useless as old men, when those
Poorer in face and fortune than herself
Walk with a hundred acres on their backs,
Fair meadows cut into green foreparts? O,

151 **clip** embrace; Vindice's rhetoric puts the alternatives not only as warmth or cold, light or darkness, but as life (and the Prince, associated in Renaissance hierarchical thought with the sun) or death ('the shades' = the phantom world of Hades)
153 **come by yourselves** (*a*) arrive at paradise unaided, (*b*) fulfil yourselves; possibly also with a sexual innuendo taken up in 'key' = penis
159 **coy** disdainful
162 **It...mother** a sardonic variation on the proverb 'It is a wise child that knows his own father'
165 **haviours** manners
168 **ashore** i.e. from the shore
169 **Gold...rich** money would accumulate (and goldsmiths, who acted as bankers, become wealthy) because it was not ventured in trade
181 **keep less charge** take less care (of virtue), but punning on 'charge' = expense
187 **petitionary people** suppliants at court (common folk)
189 **ravished** filled with delight, but Castiza takes up the literal meaning
190 **'Slid** oath contracted from 'God's lid' (eyelid)
honour...grace playing on the worldly and moral kinds of 'honour' and on 'grace' as theological term and as courtesy-title
194 **stirring** stimulating, but the word also leads into 'move' and 'Quicken' to give a paradoxical (and grotesque) vitality and motion to this verbal 'still life' painting
196 **Quicken** (*a*) arouse, (*b*) come to life; there is an added hint of pregnancy
197 **musics** musical items
198–9 **Bare-headed...'em** Hats were taken off in the presence of a social superior, though worn at home or even at church; 'let horns wear 'em' puns on stag-horn hatstands and cuckoldry.
204 **an** if
205 **for his heart** a colloquial phrase, adding emphasis ('for the life of him'); here suggesting the devil's commitment to pride. 'As proud as Lucifer' was proverbial.
210–11 **Walk...foreparts** satiric allusion to the sale of farms for court-wardrobes; 'foreparts' = ornamental coverings for the breast

It was the greatest blessing ever happenèd to women
When farmers' sons agreed and met again
To wash their hands and come up gentlemen.
The commonwealth has flourished ever since.
Lands that were mete by the rod, that labour's spared;
Tailors ride down and measure 'em by the yard.
Fair trees, those comely foretops of the field,
Are cut to maintain headtires—much untold.
All thrives but Chastity—she lies a-cold.
Nay, shall I come nearer to you? Mark but this:
Why are there so few honest women but because 'tis the poorer profession? That's accounted best that's best followed; least in trade, least in fashion; and that's not honesty, believe it. And do but note the low and dejected price of it:
"Lose but a pearl, we search and cannot brook it;
But that once gone, who is so mad to look it?"

MOTHER
Troth, he says true.

CASTIZA False, I defy you both.
I have endured you with an ear of fire;
Your tongues have struck hot irons on my face.
Mother, come from that poisonous woman there.

MOTHER Where?

CASTIZA
Do you not see her? She's too inward, then.
[*To Vindice*] Slave, perish in thy office. You heavens, please
Henceforth to make the mother a disease,
Which first begins with me, yet I've outgone you.
Exit

VINDICE [*aside*]
O angels, clap your wings upon the skies
And give this virgin crystal plaudities!

MOTHER
Peevish, coy, foolish!—But return this answer:
My lord shall be most welcome when his pleasure
Conducts him this way. I will sway mine own.
Women with women can work best alone.

VINDICE Indeed, I'll tell him so.— *Exit Mother*
O, more uncivil, more unnatural
Than those base-titled creatures that look downward!
Why does not heaven turn black, or with a frown
Undo the world? Why does not earth start up
And strike the sins that tread upon't? O,
Were't not for gold and women there would be no damnation;
Hell would look like a lord's great kitchen without fire in't.
But 'twas decreed before the world began
That they should be the hooks to catch at man. *Exit*

2.2

Enter Lussurioso with Hippolito, Vindice's brother

LUSSURIOSO
I much applaud thy judgement; thou art well-read in a fellow,
And 'tis the deepest art to study man.
I know this, which I never learned in schools,
The world's divided into knaves and fools.

HIPPOLITO [*aside*]
Knave in your face, my lord—behind your back.

LUSSURIOSO
And I much thank thee that thou hast preferred
A fellow of discourse, well-minglèd,
And whose brain time hath seasonèd.

HIPPOLITO True, my lord.
[*Aside*] We shall find season once, I hope. O villain,
To make such an unnatural slave of me, but—
[*Enter Vindice disguised*]

LUSSURIOSO Mass, here he comes.

HIPPOLITO [*aside*]
And now shall I have free leave to depart.

LUSSURIOSO
Your absence; leave us.

HIPPOLITO [*aside*] Are not my thoughts true?
I must remove, but brother, you may stay.
Heart, we are both made bawds a new-found way!
Exit

LUSSURIOSO
Now we're an even number. A third man's dangerous,
Especially her brother. Say, be free,
Have I a pleasure toward?

VINDICE O, my lord.

LUSSURIOSO
Ravish me in thine answer. Art thou rare?
Hast thou beguiled her of salvatïon
And rubbed hell o'er with honey? Is she a woman?

VINDICE
In all but in desire.

LUSSURIOSO Then she's in nothing.

214 **come up gentlemen** come up to the court as gentlemen; 'up' also implies the rise in rank

216 **mete** measured
rod a unit of length (16.5 feet) or area

217 **yard** tailor's cloth-yard (the standard 3 feet in length)

218 **foretops** forelocks (often arranged to adorn the forehead)

219 **headtires** headdresses
untold not reckoned; i.e. much more might be said (Foakes)

227 **brook it** endure the loss

228 **that** virginity (the 'honesty' of line 225)

236 **make . . . disease** see notes on 1.3.81, 2.1.123

237 **begins with** attacks
outgone outdistanced; i.e. resisted (the 'disease' that her mother has become)

239 **crystal plaudities** i.e. heavenly applause, referring to the crystalline heavenly sphere of Ptolemaic cosmology

246 **base-titled . . . downward** animals (walking upright being an attribute of humans, and, in classical and Christian-humanist ideology, a sign of kinship with the divine)

2.2.7 **discourse** fluent conversation
well-minglèd well constituted

8 **seasoned** matured

9 **season** i.e. a fit time for revenge

18 **toward** imminent; stressed on the first syllable

19 **rare** of exceptional merit (having succeeded)

I bate in courage now.

VINDICE The words I brought
Might well have made indifferent honest naught.
A right good woman in these days is changed
Into white money with less labour far.
Many a maid has turned to Mahomet
With easier working. I durst undertake,
Upon the pawn and forfeit of my life,
With half those words to flat a puritan's wife.
But she is close and good; yet 'tis a doubt
By this time. O, the mother, the mother!

LUSSURIOSO
I never thought their sex had been a wonder
Until this minute. What fruit from the mother?

VINDICE [*aside*]
Now must I blister my soul, be forsworn,
Or shame the woman that received me first.
I will be true; thou liv'st not to proclaim;
Spoke to a dying man, shame has no shame.—
My lord.

LUSSURIOSO
Who's that?

VINDICE Here's none but I, my lord.

LUSSURIOSO
What would thy haste utter?

VINDICE Comfort.

LUSSURIOSO Welcome.

VINDICE
The maid being dull, having no mind to travel
Into unknown lands, what did me I straight
But set spurs to the mother. Golden spurs
Will put her to a false gallop in a trice.

LUSSURIOSO Is't possible that in this
The mother should be damned before the daughter?

VINDICE O, that's good manners, my lord. The mother for her age must go foremost, you know.

LUSSURIOSO
Thou'st spoke that true; but where comes in this
comfort?

VINDICE
In a fine place, my lord. The unnatural mother
Did with her tongue so hard beset her honour
That the poor fool was struck to silent wonder;
Yet still the maid, like an unlighted taper,
Was cold and chaste, save that her mother's breath
Did blow fire on her cheeks. The girl departed,
But the good ancient madam, half mad, threw me
These promising words, which I took deeply note of:
'My lord shall be most welcome—'

LUSSURIOSO Faith, I thank her.

VINDICE
'When his pleasure conducts him this way—'

LUSSURIOSO
That shall be soon, i'faith.

VINDICE 'I will sway mine own—'

LUSSURIOSO
She does the wiser. I commend her for't.

VINDICE
'Women with women can work best alone.'

LUSSURIOSO By this light, and so they can, give 'em their due; men are not comparable to 'em.

VINDICE No, that's true, for you shall have one woman knit more in an hour than any man can ravel again in seven-and-twenty year.

LUSSURIOSO
Now my desires are happy; I'll make 'em freemen
now.
Thou art a precious fellow; faith, I love thee.
Be wise, and make it thy revènue: beg, leg.
What office couldst thou be ambitious for?

VINDICE Office, my lord? Marry, if I might have my wish, I would have one that was never begged yet.

LUSSURIOSO Nay then, thou canst have none.

VINDICE Yes, my lord, I could pick out another office yet; nay, and keep a horse and drab upon't.

LUSSURIOSO Prithee, good bluntness, tell me.

VINDICE Why, I would desire but this, my lord: to have all the fees behind the arras, and all the farthingales that fall plump about twelve o'clock at night upon the rushes.

LUSSURIOSO Thou'rt a mad apprehensive knave. Dost think to make any great purchase of that?

VINDICE O, 'tis an unknown thing, my lord. I wonder 't'as been missed so long.

LUSSURIOSO
Well, this night I'll visit her, and 'tis till then

23 **bate in courage** decline in ardour
24 **made . . . naught** corrupted a woman who was moderately virtuous; the adjectival 'indifferent honest' is made to stand for the (limited) virtue and for the person possessing it, so that 'naught' is both 'wicked' and the 'nothing' to which a measure of chastity is reduced
26 **white money** silver; i.e. she is converted into a prostitute
27 **turned to Mahomet** converted to paganism (with a nod towards the Muslim harem); pagan was a cant term for prostitute
29 **pawn . . . life** one of the several examples of hendiadys in this play; Vindice would pawn his life, knowing that it would be forfeit should he fail
30 **flat** (*a*) overcome, (*b*) put her on her back
31 **close** not open to persuasion
35 **be forsworn** see 1.3.172
37 **thou** i.e. Lussurioso
39 **Who's that?** Presumably Vindice, preoccupied with the dilemma expressed in his aside, forgot his 'Piato' voice as he addressed 'My lord'.
42 **did me I** the 'ethic dative', colloquial and emphatic
43–4 **But . . . trice** playing on the associations of 'spur': the golden spurs of a knight, the golden coin called a 'spur-royal'
49 **this comfort** i.e. that promised in line 40
66 **knit** figuratively, probably in the sense 'unite or combine intimately'
ravel unravel
68 **happy** fortunate
70 **leg** bow
71–81 **What . . . rushes** satirically alluding to abuse in the distribution of monopolies
76 **drab** whore
79 **fees behind the arras** i.e. fees for arranging sexual assignations behind a tapestry screen
farthingales hooped petticoats
81 **rushes** commonly strewn on floors
82 **apprehensive** witty
83 **purchase** profit

A year in my desires. Farewell, attend.
Trust me with thy preferment.

VINDICE My loved lord.—

Exit Lussurioso

[*He draws his sword*]

O, shall I kill him o'th' wrong side now? No!
Sword, thou wast never a backbiter yet.
I'll pierce him to his face. He shall die looking upon me.
Thy veins are swelled with lust. This shall unfill 'em.
Great men were gods, if beggars could not kill 'em.
Forgive me, heaven, to call my mother wicked.
O, lessen not my days upon the earth.
I cannot honour her. By this I fear me
Her tongue has turned my sister into use.
I was a villain not to be forsworn
To this our lecherous hope, the Duke's son;
For lawyers, merchants, some divines, and all
Count beneficial perjury a sin small.
It shall go hard yet, but I'll guard her honour
And keep the ports sure.

Enter Hippolito

HIPPOLITO Brother, how goes the world?
I would know news of you. But I have news to tell you.

VINDICE
What, in the name of knavery?

HIPPOLITO Knavery, faith.
This vicious old Duke's worthily abused;
The pen of his bastard writes him cuckold.

VINDICE
His bastard?

HIPPOLITO Pray, believe it. He and the Duchess
By night meet in their linen. They have been seen
By stair-foot panders.

VINDICE O, sin foul and deep!
Great faults are winked at when the Duke's asleep.

[*Enter Spurio with two Servants*]

See, see, here comes the Spurio.

HIPPOLITO Monstrous luxur!

VINDICE
Unbraced, two of his valiant bawds with him.

[*A Servant whispers to Spurio*]

O, there's a wicked whisper; hell is in his ear.
Stay, let's observe his passage.

[*Vindice and Hippolito withdraw*]

SPURIO O, but are you sure on't?

SERVANT
My lord, most sure on't, for 'twas spoke by one
That is most inward with the Duke's son's lust
That he intends within this hour to steal
Unto Hippolito's sister, whose chaste life
The mother has corrupted for his use.

SPURIO
Sweet word, sweeter occasion! Faith, then, brother,
I'll disinherit you in as short time
As I was when I was begot in haste.
I'll damn you at your pleasure—precious deed!
After your lust, O, 'twill be fine to bleed.
Come, let our passing out be soft and wary.

Exeunt Spurio and Servants

VINDICE
Mark, there, there, that step, now to the Duchess.
This their second meeting writes the Duke cuckold
With new additions, his horns newly revived.
Night, thou that lookst like funeral heralds' fees,
Torn down betimes i'th' morning, thou hang'st fitly
To grace those sins that have no grace at all.
Now 'tis full sea abed over the world,
There's juggling of all sides. Some that were maids
E'en at sunset are now perhaps i'th' toll-book.
This woman in immodest thin apparel
Lets in her friend by water. Here a dame,
Cunning, nails leather hinges to a door

89 **o'th' wrong side** in the back

95–6 **O, lessen...her** referring to Exodus, 20:12, 'Honour thy father and thy mother: that thy days may be long upon the land which the Lord thy God giveth thee.'

96 **By this** by now

97 **use** (*a*) prostitution, (*b*) profit; usury and whoredom are closely linked in the satirical thinking of the time

100 **and all** Presumably this is the colloquial filler, meaning *et cetera*.

101 **beneficial perjury** referring to the doctrine justifying equivocation or lying under oath for a good cause (Ross)

102 **It...but** idiomatic phrase introducing a statement of what will happen unless overwhelming difficulties prevent it

103 **ports** gates; thus drawing out the latent metaphor in 'guard'

107 **pen** punning on the slang for penis

112 **the Spurio** Use of the definite article brings out the meaning of the name: 'the illegitimate one'.
luxur lecher

113 **Unbraced** unbuttoned, with clothes loosened

127 **Mark...Duchess** Vindice and Hippolito, having watched but not overheard Spurio and his servants, draw a false conclusion.

128–9 **writes...revived** continuing the image of line 107 and alluding to the 'new additions' sometimes penned for the revival of old plays and advertised on quarto title-pages; with a pun on 'additions' = titles

130 **funeral heralds' fees** Perhaps the herald's exorbitant fees are equated with the displays they organized—of black-framed escutcheons, shields, pennons, crested helms, and other trappings. The fees charged by heralds on funeral occasions were high. See also Textual Notes.

133 **full sea** high tide (in sexual activity)

134 **juggling** deception

135 **toll-book** literally a book recording the sale of animals at market; here an imagined register of prostitutes, or even of the damned

137 **friend** lover
by water A lover could arrive silently by boat at a London house backing onto the Thames. Also the probable currency of 'water' = semen adds to the sexual innuendo, especially in association with 'let in'.

To avoid proclamation. Now cuckolds are
A-coining, apace, apace, apace, apace,
And careful sisters spin that thread i'th' night
That does maintain them and their bawds i'th' day.

HIPPOLITO
You flow well, brother.

VINDICE Puh, I'm shallow yet,
Too sparing and too modest. Shall I tell thee?
If every trick were told that's dealt by night,
There are few here that would not blush outright.

HIPPOLITO
I am of that belief too.

VINDICE Who's this comes?
[*Enter Lussurioso*]
The Duke's son up so late? Brother, fall back,
And you shall learn some mischief.—
[*Hippolito withdraws*]
My good lord.

LUSSURIOSO
Piato! Why, the man I wished for. Come,
I do embrace this season for the fittest
To taste of that young lady.

VINDICE [*aside*] Heart and hell!

HIPPOLITO [*aside*] Damned villain!

VINDICE [*aside*]
I ha' no way now to cross it but to kill him.

LUSSURIOSO
Come, only thou and I.

VINDICE My lord, my lord!

LUSSURIOSO
Why dost thou start us?

VINDICE I'd almost forgot—
The bastard!

LUSSURIOSO What of him?

VINDICE This night, this hour,
This minute, now—

LUSSURIOSO What, what?

VINDICE Shadows the Duchess—

LUSSURIOSO
Horrible word!

VINDICE And like strong poison eats
Into the Duke your father's forehead.

LUSSURIOSO O!

VINDICE
He makes horn royal.

LUSSURIOSO Most ignoble slave!

VINDICE
This is the fruit of two beds.

LUSSURIOSO I am mad.

VINDICE
That passage he trod warily.

LUSSURIOSO He did!

VINDICE
And hushed his villains every step he took.

LUSSURIOSO His villains? I'll confound them.

VINDICE Take 'em finely, finely now.

LUSSURIOSO
The Duchess' chamber door shall not control me.
Exeunt Lussurioso and Vindice

HIPPOLITO
Good, happy, swift! There's gunpowder i'th' court,
Wildfire at midnight. In this heedless fury
He may show violence to cross himself.
I'll follow the event. *Exit*

Enter again [*Lussurioso, with sword drawn, and Vindice, disguised*] 2.3

LUSSURIOSO Where is that villain?

139 **proclamation** exposure as adulteress (having been betrayed by squeaking hinges)

140 **A-coining** being coined or created. Vindice gives a paradoxical twist to the idea of sexual activity as a 'coining' or engendering of children.
apace . . . apace The play catches a sense of frantic hedonism in its rhythms, as well as in its imagery; the repetition here suggests a scarcely controlled excitement. Compare the urgent insistence of Vindice's 'sales-talk' at 2.1.200, 'hurry, hurry, hurry!', which Castiza rightly hears as an invitation to join the heedless rush to 'the devil'.

141 **sisters** 'sisters of the game' whose housework is in 'houses of resort'. The imagery combines suggestions of the Fates with the bawdiness of Sir Toby Belch's 'spin it off' in *Twelfth Night*, 1.3.98–100. 'Sisters' is also a loaded word in view of Vindice's situation in respect to Castiza.

145 **trick** (*a*) card hand (sustained in 'told' = counted, and in 'dealt'), (*b*) stratagem, (*c*) act of intercourse

146 **here** in the audience

150 **Piato** Vindice's assumed name, which means 'hidden'

156 **start** startle

158 **Shadows** either (*a*) closely attends upon, or (*b*) covers (though *OED* records no specifically sexual sense)

159–60 **And . . . forehead** The simile unites two image motifs, of poison and the forehead (as expressing either shame or impudence and as site for the cuckolds horns).

161 **horn royal** i.e. a royal cuckold, with a pun on 'royal' as a branch of a stag's antlers (possibly used as an aphrodisiac); 'horn royal' is formed on the analogy of such expressions as 'battle royal'

162 **fruit of two beds** i.e. a result of the Duke's begetting Spurio in a bed other than his own and the Duchess's

164 **villains** servants

169 **Wildfire** highly inflammable substance used in war

170 **cross** thwart

2.3.0.1–2 ***Enter . . . disguised*** Di Trevis, director of the Royal Shakespeare Company's production at the Swan (1987), found 2.3 a 'dreadful scene' to stage. Presumably in the Jacobean theatre the bed was set up within the 'discovery space' (curtained alcove in the stage wall or curtained booth projecting from it), and the Duke and Duchess would soon have leapt out. The imaginary setting appears unobtrusively to change from the Duchess's bed-chamber to 'the court'. Use of the discovery space would allow the bed to be concealed as the action spilled out onto the main platform and involved most of the cast. On the other hand, Jacobean beds were themselves commonly curtained, so that the scene could have been managed through the thrusting of a bed out onto the stage. And even if, as this edition's stage directions assume, the discovery space was used, its curtains may have been opened at the beginning of the scene, and the furnishings of the bed pulled back at line 7.

VINDICE
Softly, my lord, and you may take 'em twisted.
LUSSURIOSO
I care not how.
VINDICE O, 'twill be glorious
To kill 'em doubled, when they're heaped. Be soft, my lord.
LUSSURIOSO
Away, my spleen is not so lazy. Thus and thus
I'll shake their eyelids ope, and with my sword
Shut 'em again for ever.—Villain! Strumpet!
[He pulls back the curtains of the discovery space to reveal the Duke and Duchess in bed]
DUKE
You upper guard defend us!
DUCHESS Treason, treason!
DUKE
O, take me not in sleep. I have great sins.
I must have days,
Nay months, dear son, with penitential heaves,
To lift 'em out and not to die unclear.
O, thou wilt kill me both in heaven and here.
LUSSURIOSO
I am amazed to death.
DUKE Nay, villain, traitor,
Worse than the foulest epithet, now I'll gripe thee
E'en with the nerves of wrath, and throw thy head
Amongst the lawyers. Guard!
Enter [Guards, who seize Lussurioso; Hippolito,] Nobles, and sons of the Duchess, Ambitioso and Supervacuo
FIRST NOBLE
How comes the quiet of your grace disturbed?
DUKE
This boy, that should be myself after me,
Would be myself before me, and in heat
Of that ambition bloodily rushed in,
Intending to depose me in my bed.
SECOND NOBLE
Duty and natural loyalty forfend!
DUCHESS
He called his father villain, and me strumpet,
A word that I abhor to file my lips with.
AMBITIOSO
That was not so well done, brother.
LUSSURIOSO I am abused.
I know there's no excuse can do me good.
VINDICE *[aside to Hippolito]*
'Tis now good policy to be from sight.
His vicious purpose to our sister's honour
Is crossed beyond our thought.
HIPPOLITO *[aside to Vindice]* You little dreamt
His father slept here.
VINDICE *[aside to Hippolito]*
O, 'twas far beyond me.
But since it fell so, without frightful words,
Would he had killed him; 'twould have eased our swords.
[Vindice and Hippolito] dissemble a flight [and steal away]
DUKE
Be comforted, our Duchess; he shall die.
[Exit Duchess]
LUSSURIOSO *[aside]*
Where's this slave-pander now? Out of mine eye,
Guilty of this abuse.
Enter Spurio with two Servants, his villains. [They talk apart.]
SPURIO You're villains, fablers.
You have knaves' chins and harlots' tongues. You lie,
And I will damn you with one meal a day.
FIRST SERVANT
O, good my lord!
SPURIO 'Sblood, you shall never sup.
SECOND SERVANT
O, I beseech you, sir!
SPURIO To let my sword
Catch cold so long and miss him.
FIRST SERVANT Troth, my lord,
'Twas his intent to meet there.
SPURIO Heart, he's yonder.
Ha, what news here? Is the day out o'th' socket,
That it is noon at midnight, the court up?
How comes the guard so saucy with his elbows?
LUSSURIOSO *[aside]* The bastard here?
Nay then, the truth of my intent shall out.—

5 **spleen** The spleen was viewed as seat of passions, such as violent anger.
8 **upper guard** the guard nearest the bedchamber
11 **heaves** sighs
14 **I am...death** Lussurioso may let fall his sword here. It is for actors and director to decide at what point the Duke and Duchess leap out of bed.
16 **nerves** sinews
23 **forfend** forbid
25 **file** defile
26 **abused** imposed upon
32 **frightful** frightening; Vindice probably means that he wishes Lussurioso had killed the Duke before alarming and warning him
33.1 ***dissemble a flight*** The phrase suggests an exaggerated miming of stealing away.
35 **slave-pander** i.e. Piato
Out of mine eye out of sight; nowhere to be seen
36–45 This dialogue is ignored by others on stage. It is a feature of Middleton's dramaturgy that when single characters or groups of characters enter they often fail—at first or, as in this case, at any time during the scene—to interact with those already on stage, as though they were isolated by their own concerns. Hence the prevalence of asides. But Spurio's explosive entry leads into dialogue 'apart', rather than aside.
37 **harlots'** a general term of abuse, applicable to either sex
43 **out o'th' socket** perhaps like Hamlet's 'The time is out of joint', i.e. in an abnormal state; but the phrase carries suggestions of the traditional analogy of the sun ('the day') to God's eye, displaced and shining/open at the wrong time
45 **his elbows** i.e. Lussurioso's, held by guards

My lord and father, hear me.
DUKE Bear him hence.
LUSSURIOSO I can with loyalty excuse—
DUKE Excuse? To prison with the villain.
Death shall not long lag after him.
SPURIO [*aside*]
Good, i'faith; then 'tis not much amiss.
LUSSURIOSO
Brothers, my best release lies on your tongues.
I pray, persuade for me.
AMBITIOSO It is our duties.
Make yourself sure of us.
SUPERVACUO We'll sweat in pleading.
LUSSURIOSO
And I may live to thank you.
Exeunt [*Lussurioso, Nobles, and Guards*]
AMBITIOSO [*aside*] No, thy death
Shall thank me better.
SPURIO [*aside*] He's gone. I'll after him
And know his trespass, seem to bear a part
In all his ills, but with a puritan heart.
Exit [*Spurio with his Servants*]
AMBITIOSO [*to Supervacuo*]
Now, brother, let our hate and love be woven
So subtly together that in speaking
One word for his life we may make three for his death.
The craftiest pleader gets most gold for breath.
SUPERVACUO [*to Ambitioso*]
Set on, I'll not be far behind you, brother.
DUKE Is't possible
A son should be disobedient as far as the sword?
It is the highest, he can go no further.
AMBITIOSO
My gracious lord, take pity.
DUKE Pity, boys?
AMBITIOSO
Nay, we'd be loth to move your grace too much;
We know the trespass is unpardonable,
Black, wicked, and unnatural.
SUPERVACUO In a son, O, monstrous!
AMBITIOSO Yet, my lord,
A duke's soft hand strokes the rough head of law
And makes it lie smooth.
DUKE But my hand shall ne'er do't.
AMBITIOSO
That as you please, my lord.
SUPERVACUO We must needs confess
Some father would have entered into hate
So deadly pointed that before his eyes
He would ha' seen the execution sound,
Without corrupted favour.
AMBITIOSO But, my lord,
Your grace may live the wonder of all times
In pard'ning that offence which never yet
Had face to beg a pardon.
DUKE [*aside*] Honey? How's this?
AMBITIOSO
Forgive him, good my lord, he's your own son—
And I must needs say 'twas the vilelier done.
SUPERVACUO
He's the next heir—yet this true reason gathers:
None can possess that dispossess their fathers.
Be merciful—
DUKE [*aside*] Here's no stepmother's wit.
I'll try 'em both upon their love and hate.
AMBITIOSO
Be merciful, although—
DUKE You have prevailed.
My wrath, like flaming wax, hath spent itself.
I know 'twas but some peevish moon in him.
Go, let him be released.
SUPERVACUO [*aside*] 'Sfoot, how now, brother?
AMBITIOSO
Your grace doth please to speak beside your spleen.
I would it were so happy.
DUKE Why, go, release him.
SUPERVACUO
O, my good lord, I know the fault's too weighty
And full of general loathing, too inhuman,
Rather by all men's voices worthy death.
DUKE 'Tis true too.
Here then, receive this signet. Doom shall pass.
Direct it to the judges. He shall die
Ere many days. Make haste.
AMBITIOSO All speed that may be.
We could have wished his burden not so sore.
We knew your grace did but delay before.
Exeunt Ambitioso and Supervacuo
DUKE
Here's envy with a poor thin cover o'er't,
Like scarlet hid in lawn, easily spied through.
This their ambition by the mother's side
Is dangerous and for safety must be purged.
I will prevent their envies. Sure it was
But some mistaken fury in our son,
Which these aspiring boys would climb upon.

59 **puritan** hypocritical
61 **subtly** pronounced as trisyllabic
77 **sound** fully performed
81 **Honey** sweet words
86 **no stepmother's wit** The Duke, who sees through the blatant hypocrisy of Ambitioso and Supervacuo, means that they lack the Duchess's shrewdness or 'mother wit'.
90 **peevish moon** senseless fit of frenzy (the moon provoking 'lunes' or lunatic behaviour)
92 **beside your spleen** with your anger set aside
98 **signet** a small seal (usually on a ring) employed to give authority, in this case to a merely verbal command
103 **envy** malice
104 **scarlet** rich, bright red cloth
lawn linen so fine as to be partially transparent
107 **prevent** forestall

He shall be rèleased suddenly.
Enter Nobles

FIRST NOBLE
Good morning to your grace.

DUKE
Welcome, my lords.
[*The Nobles kneel before the Duke*]

SECOND NOBLE
Our knees shall take away the office of our feet for ever,
Unless your grace bestow a father's eye
Upon the clouded fortunes of your son,
And in compassionate virtue grant him that
Which makes e'en mean men happy, liberty.

DUKE [*aside*]
How seriously their loves and honours woo
For that which I am about to pray them do.—
Why, rise, my lords, your knees sign his release.
We freely pardon him.

FIRST NOBLE
We owe your grace much thanks, and he much duty.
Exeunt Nobles

DUKE
It well becomes that judge to nod at crimes
That does commit greater himself and lives.
I may forgive a disobedient error
That expect pardon for adultery
And in my old days am a youth in lust.
Many a beauty have I turned to poison
In the denial, covetous of all.
Age hot is like a monster to be seen;
My hairs are white and yet my sins are green. [*Exit*]
Finis Actus Secundi

3.1 *Incipit Actus Tertius*
Enter Ambitioso and Supervacuo

SUPERVACUO
Brother, let my opinion sway you once.
I speak it for the best, to have him die
Surest and soonest. If the signet come
Unto the judges' hands, why then his doom
Will be deferred till sittings and court-days,
Juries and further. Faiths are bought and sold.
Oaths in these days are but the skin of gold.

AMBITIOSO
In troth, 'tis true too.

SUPERVACUO
Then let's set by the judges
And fall to the officers. 'Tis but mistaking
The Duke our father's meaning, and where he named
'Ere many days', 'tis but forgetting that
And have him die i'th' morning.

AMBITIOSO
Excellent,
Then am I heir—duke in a minute!

SUPERVACUO [*aside*]
Nay,
An he were once puffed out, here is a pin
Should quickly prick your bladder.

AMBITIOSO
Blessed occasion!
He being packed, we'll have some trick and wile
To wind our younger brother out of prison
That lies in for the rape. The lady's dead,
And people's thoughts will soon be burièd.

SUPERVACUO
We may with safety do't, and live and feed.
The Duchess' sons are too proud to bleed.

AMBITIOSO
We are, i'faith, to say true. Come, let's not linger.
I'll to the officers. Go you before
And set an edge upon the executioner.

SUPERVACUO
Let me alone to grind him.

AMBITIOSO
Meet! Farewell.—
Exit Supervacuo
I am next now; I rise just in that place
Where thou'rt cut off—upon thy neck, kind brother;
The falling of one head lifts up another. *Exit*

Enter with the Nobles, Lussurioso from prison 3.2

LUSSURIOSO
My lords, I am so much indebted to your loves
For this, O, this delivery.

FIRST NOBLE
But our duties,
My lord, unto the hopes that grow in you.

LUSSURIOSO
If e'er I live to be myself, I'll thank you.

110 **suddenly** immediately
113–14 **eye . . . clouded** The collocation evokes the analogy of ruler (and his eye) to the sun.
115 **virtue** power
124 **disobedient error** lapse into disobedience (neglect of filial duty); a transferred epithet
127–8 **turned . . . denial** poisoned when she rejected my advances
128 **all** i.e. all beautiful women
130 **green** youthful
3.1.7 **skin of gold** i.e. a mere cover for the true regulator of the judicial process, which is money
8 **set by** bypass
9 **fall to** proceed to
14 **puffed out** extinguished (like a flame), in so far as 'he' = Lussurioso; but in the sense 'blown up' the phrase also relates to the sudden inflation and deflation of Ambitioso's status
pin i.e. his sword
16 **packed** packed off
24 **set an edge upon** make keen (the executioner in the figurative sense, and the axe in the literal); 'grind' continues the wordplay
25 **Meet!** Right! ('meet' = fitting)
26–7 **I rise . . . brother** The wording recalls the fabulous snake-like monster Hydra, whose heads grew again as fast as they were cut off; compare 3.5.222–3. The 'kind brother' is Lussurioso, with play on 'kind' as natural, kindred.
28 **head** punning on literal head and (prospective) head of family and state
3.2.2 **But** merely
4 **myself** i.e. Duke

O liberty, thou sweet and heavenly dame!
But hell for prison is too mild a name. *Exeunt*

3.3 *Enter Ambitioso and Supervacuo with Officers*

AMBITIOSO
Officers, here's the Duke's signet, your firm warrant,
Brings the command of present death along with it
Unto our brother, the Duke's son. We are sorry
That we are so unnaturally employed
In such an unkind office, fitter far
For enemies than brothers.

SUPERVACUO But you know
The Duke's command must be obeyed.

FIRST OFFICER
It must and shall, my lord. This morning then;
So suddenly?

AMBITIOSO Ay, alas, poor good soul,
He must break fast betimes. The executioner
Stands ready to put forth his cowardly valour.

SECOND OFFICER Already?

SUPERVACUO
Already, i'faith. O sir, destruction hies,
And he that is least impudent soonest dies.

FIRST OFFICER
Troth, you say true, my lord. We take our leaves.
Our office shall be sound. We'll not delay
The third part of a minute.

AMBITIOSO Therein you show
Yourselves good men and upright officers.
Pray let him die as private as he may,
Do him that favour, for the gaping people
Will but trouble him at his prayers
And make him curse and swear, and so die black.
Will you be so far kind?

FIRST OFFICER It shall be done, my lord.

AMBITIOSO
Why, we do thank you. If we live to be,
You shall have a better office.

SECOND OFFICER Your good lordship.

SUPERVACUO
Commend us to the scaffold in our tears.

FIRST OFFICER
We'll weep, and do your commendations.
Exeunt [*Officers*]

AMBITIOSO
Fine fools in office!

SUPERVACUO Things fall out so fit.

AMBITIOSO
So happily. Come, brother, ere next clock
His head will be made serve a bigger block. *Exeunt*

3.4 *Enter in prison Junior Brother* [*and his Keeper*]

JUNIOR
Keeper.

KEEPER My lord.

JUNIOR No news lately from our brothers?
Are they unmindful of us?

KEEPER
My lord, a messenger came newly in
And brought this from 'em.
He gives him a letter

JUNIOR Nothing but paper comforts?
I looked for my delivery before this,
Had they been worth their oaths. Prithee, be from us.
[*Exit Keeper*]
Now, what say you, forsooth? Speak out, I pray.
[*He reads the*] *letter*

'Brother, be of good cheer.'—'Slud, it begins like a whore, with good cheer. 'Thou shalt not be long a prisoner.'—Not five-and-thirty year like a bankrupt, I think so! 'We have thought upon a device to get thee out by a trick.'—By a trick? Pox o' your trick, an it be so long a-playing! 'And so rest comforted. Be merry and expect it suddenly.'—Be merry? Hang merry, draw and quarter merry! I'll be mad! Is't not strange that a man should lie in a whole month for a woman? Well, we shall see how sudden our brothers will be in their promise. I must expect still a trick. I shall not be long a prisoner.

[*Enter Keeper*]
How now, what news?

KEEPER
Bad news, my lord; I am discharged of you.

JUNIOR
Slave, call'st thou that bad news? [*Aside*] I thank you, brothers.

KEEPER
My lord, 'twill prove so. Here come the officers
Into whose hands I must commit you.
[*Enter four Officers*]

JUNIOR Ha,
Officers? What, why?

FIRST OFFICER You must pardon us, my lord.
Our office must be sound. Here is our warrant,

3.3.5 **unkind** with the older sense of 'unnatural', as well as 'cruel'
10 **betimes** early in the morning
13 **hies** hurries
14 **impudent** lacking in shame or decency; the whole line is ironic both in relation to (*a*) the true nature of Lussurioso and (*b*) the fate of Junior (who 'soonest dies').
16 **sound** properly performed
22 **black** damned
24 **If we live to be** i.e. if I ('we' is the royal we) live to be Duke
30 **block** the executioner's block; quibbling on 'block' = size of hat
3.4.9 **good cheer** quibbling on the meaning 'good entertainment'
10 **Not . . . bankrupt** The bankrupt, imprisoned for debt, could not resort to bribery!
14–15 **Hang . . . quarter merry** alluding to the traditional punishment for treason: 'draw' = disembowel, 'quarter' = cut into quarters, dismember
16 **lie in** i.e. lie in prison, be confined; with the idea that it is more in the natural order of things for a woman to 'lie in' = be confined in childbed 'for a man' (because he has made her pregnant)
26 **sound** either 'valid' or 'fully carried out' (as at 3.3.16)

The signet from the Duke. You must straight suffer.
JUNIOR
Suffer? I'll suffer you to be gone. I'll suffer you
To come no more. What would you have me suffer?
SECOND OFFICER
My lord, those words were better changed to prayers.
The time's but brief with you. Prepare to die.
JUNIOR
Sure, 'tis not so.
THIRD OFFICER It is too true, my lord.
JUNIOR
I tell you, 'tis not, for the Duke my father
Deferred me till next sitting, and I look
E'en every minute, threescore times an hour,
For a release, a trick wrought by my brothers.
FIRST OFFICER
A trick, my lord? If you expect such comfort,
Your hope's as fruitless as a barren woman.
Your brothers were the unhappy messengers
That brought this powerful token for your death.
JUNIOR
My brothers? No, no.
SECOND OFFICER 'Tis most true, my lord.
JUNIOR
My brothers to bring a warrant for my death?
How strange this shows.
THIRD OFFICER There's no delaying time.
JUNIOR
Desire 'em hither, call 'em up, my brothers.
They shall deny it to your faces.
FIRST OFFICER My lord,
They're far enough by this, at least at court,
And this most strict command they left behind 'em.
When grief swum in their eyes, they showed like brothers,
Brim-full of heavy sorrow; but the Duke
Must have his pleasure.
JUNIOR His pleasure?
FIRST OFFICER
These were their last words which my memory bears:
'Commend us to the scaffold in our tears.'
JUNIOR
Pox dry their tears! What should I do with tears?
I hate 'em worse than any citizen's son
Can hate salt water. Here came a letter now,
New-bleeding from their pens, scarce stinted yet.
Would I'd been torn in pieces when I tore it.
Look, you officious whoresons, words of comfort:
'Not long a prisoner'.
FIRST OFFICER It says true in that, sir, for you must suffer presently.
JUNIOR A villainous dunce upon the letter, knavish exposition. Look you then here, sir: 'We'll get thee out by a trick', says he.
SECOND OFFICER That may hold too, sir, for you know a trick is commonly four cards, which was meant by us four officers.
JUNIOR
Worse and worse dealing.
FIRST OFFICER The hour beckons us;
The headsman waits. Lift up your eyes to heaven.
JUNIOR
I thank you, faith; good, pretty, wholesome counsel.
I should look up to heaven, as you said,
Whilst he behind me cozens me of my head.
Ay, that's the trick.
THIRD OFFICER You delay too long, my lord.
JUNIOR
Stay, good authority's bastards. Since I must
Through brothers' perjury die, O let me venom
Their souls with curses.
FIRST OFFICER Come, 'tis no time to curse.
JUNIOR
Must I bleed, then, without respect of sign? Well—
My fault was sweet sport, which the world approves;
I die for that which every woman loves. *Exeunt*

Enter Vindice [disguised] with Hippolito his brother 3.5

VINDICE
O, sweet, delectable, rare, happy, ravishing!
HIPPOLITO
Why, what's the matter, brother?
VINDICE O, 'tis able
To make a man spring up and knock his forehead
Against yon silver ceiling.
HIPPOLITO Prithee, tell me,
Why may not I partake with you? You vowed once
To give me share to every tragic thought.
VINDICE By th' mass, I think I did too.
Then I'll divide it to thee: the old Duke,

34 **sitting** court session
55 **hate salt water** because of the proverbial dangers of sea-travel (Tilley, S177), and perhaps the practice of pressing men (here townsmen) to serve in the navy; with obvious wordplay on salt tears
56 **stinted** staunched (i.e. 'dried'), taking up the image of the flowing ink as blood
57 **tore it** i.e. tore it open
62 **dunce** sophistical gloss; alluding to the medieval scholastic theologian Duns Scotus, notorious among his opponents for hair-splitting arguments
upon the letter with punning reference to strictly 'literal' interpretation of a text in disregard of its spirit
66 **trick** (*a*) cards played and won, (*b*) hand of cards; Middleton may have in mind the popular game of primero; lines 12–13 ('trick ... a-playing') have foreshadowed the wordplay, which is continued in 'dealing' (68)
71–3 **I should ... trick** alluding to the distractions used by thieves and cheats
74 **good ... bastards** Junior's phrase, which makes the officers the illegitimate sons of a personified authority, reflects the play's concerns with bastardy and the proper and improper uses of power.
75 **perjury** the violation of their promise to have him released
77 **without ... sign** without consideration of whether the astrological signs are favourable for therapeutic bleeding
3.5.4 **silver ceiling** (*a*) the sky, (*b*) the 'heavens' or painted canopy over the stage
8 **divide it to** share it with

Thinking my outward shape and inward heart
Are cut out of one piece—for he that prates
His secrets, his heart stands o'th' outside—
Hires me by price to greet him with a lady
In some fit place veiled from the eyes o'th' court,
Some darkened, blushless angle that is guilty
Of his forefathers' lusts and great folks' riots;
To which I easily (to maintain my shape)
Consented, and did wish his impudent grace
To meet her here in this unsunnèd lodge
Wherein 'tis night at noon; and here the rather
Because, unto the torturing of his soul,
The bastard and the Duchess have appointed
Their meeting too in this luxurious circle;
Which most afflicting sight will kill his eyes
Before we kill the rest of him.

HIPPOLITO
'Twill, i'faith. Most dreadfully digested.
I see not how you could have missed me, brother.

VINDICE
True, but the violence of my joy forgot it.

HIPPOLITO
Ay, but where's that lady now?

VINDICE O, at that word
I'm lost again; you cannot find me yet;
I'm in a throng of happy apprehensions.
He's suited for a lady. I have took care
For a delicious lip, a sparkling eye.
You shall be witness, brother.
Be ready; stand with your hat off. *Exit*

HIPPOLITO
Troth, I wonder what lady it should be.
Yet 'tis no wonder, now I think again,
To have a lady
Stoop to a duke that stoops unto his men.
'Tis common to be common through the world,
And there's more private common shadowing vices
Than those who are known both by their names and
prices.
'Tis part of my allegiance to stand bare
To the Duke's concubine—and here she comes.

Enter Vindice with the [*masked*] *skull of his love dressed up in tires*

VINDICE [*to the skull*]
Madam, his grace will not be absent long.
Secret? Ne'er doubt us, madam. 'Twill be worth
Three velvet gowns to your ladyship. Known?
Few ladies respect that. Disgrace? A poor thin shell.
'Tis the best grace you have to do it well.
I'll save your hand that labour; I'll unmask you.
[*He reveals the skull*]

HIPPOLITO Why, brother, brother!

VINDICE
Art thou beguiled now? Tut, a lady can,
At such all-hid beguile a wiser man.
Have I not fitted the old surfeiter
With a quaint piece of beauty? Age and bare bone
Are e'er allied in action. Here's an eye
Able to tempt a great man—to serve God;
A pretty hanging lip, that has forgot now to dis-
semble.
Methinks this mouth should make a swearer tremble,
A drunkard clasp his teeth, and not undo 'em
To suffer wet damnation to run through 'em.
Here's a cheek keeps her colour, let the wind go
whistle.
Spout rain, we fear thee not; be hot or cold,
All's one with us. And is not he absurd
Whose fortunes are upon their faces set
That fear no other god but wind and wet?

HIPPOLITO Brother, you've spoke that right.
Is this the form that living shone so bright?

VINDICE The very same.
And now methinks I could e'en chide myself
For doting on her beauty, though her death

10 **prates** blabs
14 **blushless angle** nook or corner suited to shameless acts
16 **shape** disguise
22 **luxurious circle** lecherous spot, with a possible sly glance at the 'wooden O' of the Globe
25 **dreadfully digested** concocted so as to terrify
26 **missed me** left me out
30 **apprehensions** conceptions, anticipations
31 **suited for** provided with
34 **hat off** as a mark of respect
38 **Stoop to . . . stoops unto** submit (sexually) . . . degrades himself to the level of
39 **common** quibbling on (*a*) usual, and (*b*) publicly available; the wordplay continues in the paradox 'private common' in the next line
40 **shadowing** keeping themselves secret
41 **those** The 'vices' assume a degree of personification that allows 'those' to refer to whores as well as their sins.
42 **stand bare** stand with hat removed (but with a bawdy quibble)
43.2 **tires** headdress or wig
47 **shell** i.e. empty thing, of no matter
52 **all-hid** hide and seek
54 **quaint** (*a*) pretty, (*b*) ingeniously contrived; the word also carries a suggestion of 'cunt', linking to 'eye', 'lip', and 'mouth'
57 **hanging** (*a*) pouting (with reference to the former lip), (*b*) jutting downwards (with reference to the lower jawbone that remains)
64 **set** staked
65 **That . . . wet** alluding to the use of cosmetics (a favourite target of satirists)

Shall be revenged after no common action.
Does the silkworm expend her yellow labours
For thee? For thee does she undo herself?
Are lordships sold to maintain ladyships
For the poor benefit of a bewitching minute?
Why does yon fellow falsify highways
And put his life between the judge's lips
To refine such a thing, keeps horse and men
To beat their valours for her?
Surely we're all mad people, and they
Whom we think are, are not—we mistake those:
'Tis we are mad in sense, they but in clothes.

HIPPOLITO
Faith, and in clothes too, we; give us our due.

VINDICE
Does every proud and self-affecting dame
Camphor her face for this? And grieve her maker
In sinful baths of milk, when many an infant starves
For her superfluous outside—all for this?
Who now bids twenty pound a night, prepares
Music, perfumes, and sweetmeats? All are hushed.
Thou mayst lie chaste now. It were fine, methinks,
To have thee seen at revels, forgetful feasts,
And unclean brothels. Sure, 'twould fright the sinner
And make him a good coward, put a reveller
Out of his antic amble,
And cloy an epicure with empty dishes.
Here might a scornful and ambitious woman
Look through and through herself. See, ladies, with
false forms
You deceive men, but cannot deceive worms.—
Now to my tragic business. Look you, brother,
I have not fashioned this only for show
And useless property. No, it shall bear a part
E'en in it own revenge. This very skull
Whose mistress the Duke poisoned with this drug,
The mortal curse of the earth, shall be revenged
In the like strain, and kiss his lips to death.
As much as the dumb thing can, he shall feel.
What fails in poison, we'll supply in steel.

HIPPOLITO
Brother, I do applaud thy constant vengeance,
The quaintness of thy malice above thought.
[*Vindice puts poison on the skull's mouth*]

VINDICE
So, 'tis laid on. Now come, and welcome, Duke;
I have her for thee. I protest it, brother,
Methinks she makes almost as fair a sign

71 **after . . . action** (*a*) in no ordinary way, (*b*) through no legal process in the common court, (*c*) with unusual histrionics

72–98 **Does . . . worms** After T. S. Eliot drew attention to this passage, it was frequently analysed, most fully by L. G. Salingar and F. R. Leavis.

72 **expend . . . labours** The phrase, in which the epithet is made to modify the 'labours' rather than their product, condenses several images. The silkworm spins a yellow-white cocoon, which recalls gold in colour and value. 'Expend', phonetically incorporating the expected verb 'spin', works to enhance the suggestion of riches and currency, while implying a self-annihilating expenditure of effort for the benefit of others who will themselves end up as skulls; so that the associations of 'yellow' with age and disease also become pertinent.

73 **For** 'Vindice's irony turns, in this speech, on the ambiguities of the word "for", referring both to equivalence in exchange and to purpose or result' (Salingar).
undo herself (*a*) unwind the thread from herself, (*b*) exhaust herself, destroy herself

74 **lordships . . . ladyships** i.e. are inherited baronial estates sold so that their owners can keep mistresses in ladylike finery. The effect of the line derives from the speciousness of its alliterative symmetry, the substance of an actual lordship being set against the social and moral vacuity of the whore tricked out as 'your ladyship'.

75 **benefit** with wordplay on the sense 'property rights' (Onions), so harking back to 'lordships'
bewitching charming and seductive, but with a literal edge, implying a soul in thrall to a malignant spell

76 **falsify highways** The expression is obscure, but most editors have understood it as an allusion to highway robbery; hence 'act the highwayman' or 'make highways unsafe', perhaps with a reference to the offender's 'altering signposts and diverting rich travellers into his predatory hands' (Gibbons), with 'fellow' carrying suggestions of 'good fellow' = thief. Middleton discourses on highway robbery in *Black Book*, and in another rogue-pamphlet, *Martin Markall* (1610), 'S.R.' describes how young 'gentlemen . . . cavalieros' rob on the highways in order to pay for 'banqueting with whores'; 'S.R.' also mentions their donning of 'artificial beards and heads of hair' as disguises and their cloaks that can be worn either side out—which may help to explain 'falsify'; but all the brands of falsity and falsification called to mind by that verb are pertinent to the broader context. Loughrey and Taylor, reading 'high ways', interpret 'impersonate the aristocracy', but the risk of capital punishment (line 77) suggests the more spectacular crime. And the existence of the colloquial term 'highway lawyers' for highway robbers may have sparked the associative process that created 'the judge's lips'.

77 **put . . . lips** Some commentators have detected in this brilliant line a hint of the Last Judgement, mention of sins on the highway already having activated memories of the biblical 'broad . . . way that leads to destruction' (Matthew, 7:13).

78 **refine** improve by adding refinements (and finery), pamper; but 'the gold image, coming through by way of "sold" (and the more effectively for never having been explicit), seems also to be felt here, with the suggestion that nothing can refine this dross' (Leavis).

79 **beat their valours** wear out their strengths, with play on 'valours' = values, and a possible near-homonymic pun on 'bate' = diminish, degrade; 'valour' (as prowess and boldness) seems to link the phrase with the dangerous escapades of the highway robber

84 **self-affecting** self-loving, vain

85 **Camphor** wash with camphor, a white aromatic vegetable oil used as skin-cleanser

91 **forgetful** i.e. of (*a*) morals, (*b*) cares, (*c*) mortality

94 **antic amble** grotesque movement in walking or dancing; 'silly walks'

97 **forms** appearances

98 **worms** The silkworm at the beginning of Vindice's meditation and homily turns into the graveyard worm at its conclusion.

101 **property** in the theatrical sense, as though Vindice were mounting a revenge play

102 **it** its

105 **strain** manner (literally, 'tune')

109 **quaintness** ingenuity

112 **sign** show

As some old gentlewoman in a periwig.
[*To the skull*] Hide thy face now for shame; thou hadst need have a mask now.
[*He readjusts the mask*]
'Tis vain when beauty flows, but when it fleets
This would become graves better than the streets.

HIPPOLITO
You have my voice in that.
[*Voices within*]
Hark, the Duke's come.

VINDICE
Peace, let's observe what company he brings
And how he does absent 'em, for you know
He'll wish all private. Brother, fall you back a little
With the bony lady.

HIPPOLITO That I will.

VINDICE So, so—
Now nine years' vengeance crowd into a minute.
[*They withdraw. Enter the Duke and Gentlemen*]

DUKE [*to Gentlemen*]
You shall have leave to leave us, with this charge,
Upon your lives: if we be missed by th' Duchess
Or any of the nobles, to give out
We're privately rid forth.

VINDICE [*aside*] O happiness!

DUKE
With some few honourable gentlemen, you may say;
You may name those that are away from court.

FIRST GENTLEMAN
Your will and pleasure shall be done, my lord.
[*Exeunt Gentlemen*]

VINDICE [*aside*]
'Privately rid forth'!
He strives to make sure work on't. [*To the Duke*] Your good grace.

DUKE Piato, well done. Hast brought her? What lady is't?

VINDICE Faith, my lord, a country lady, a little bashful at first, as most of them are, but after the first kiss, my lord, the worst is past with them. Your grace knows now what you have to do. Sh'as somewhat a grave look with her, but—

DUKE
I love that best. Conduct her.

VINDICE [*aside*] Have at all!

DUKE
In gravest looks the greatest faults seem less.
Give me that sin that's robed in holiness.

VINDICE [*to Hippolito*]
Back with the torch, brother; raise the perfumes.

DUKE
How sweet can a duke breathe? Age has no fault.
Pleasure should meet in a perfumèd mist.—
Lady, sweetly encountered. I came from court.
I must be bold with you.
[*He kisses the skull*]
O, what's this? O!

VINDICE
Royal villain, white devil!

DUKE O!

VINDICE Brother,
Place the torch here, that his affrighted eyeballs
May start into those hollows. Duke, dost know
Yon dreadful visor? View it well; 'tis the skull
Of Gloriana, whom thou poisonedst last.

DUKE O, 't'as poisoned me.

VINDICE
Didst not know that till now?

DUKE What are you two?

VINDICE
Villains all three. The very ragged bone
Has been sufficiently revenged.

DUKE O, Hippolito, call treason.

HIPPOLITO
Yes, my good lord. Treason, treason, treason!
Stamping on him

DUKE Then I'm betrayed.

115 **'Tis . . . flows** i.e. a mask is pointless vanity when beauty exists to be displayed; with 'flows' suggesting both graceful motion and the flow of blood in the veins
fleets passes away

116 **This . . . streets** a skull befits a grave better than a public place (so a mask is appropriate)

117 **voice** agreement, support

119 **absent** dismiss

121 **bony** punning on 'bonny'

130 **Privately rid forth** Vindice is exultant not only at the opportunity afforded by the Duke's vulnerabilty without a guard but at the unintended aptness of the sexual connotations of his phrase (as at 1.2.136–7) and of the meaning 'rid forth' = disposed of, killed off.

136 **grave** The pun is obvious, but, as Foakes notes, not obvious enough for the Duke.

138 **Have at all!** a colloquial phrase, initiating a risky venture, such as a fight or a throw of dice

142 **fault** physical inadequacy

146 **Royal villain** an oxymoron, like the next two words; playing on the difference of status between royalty and a villein = vassal
white devil hypocrite, the fair-seeming devil proverbially being worse than the black (the standard colour); punning on the Duke's white hair

148 **start . . . hollows** stare wildly into the skull's eye-sockets; as though springing into them to supply the lost eyeballs

149 **visor** face, mask

150 **Gloriana** also a favourite name for the idealized Queen Elizabeth whose death in 1603 ended an Age that through the haze of nostalgia already appeared 'Golden'
whom . . . last i.e. she was the latest of his victims (compare 2.3.127). We are probably not expected to notice that, in association with 3.5.122, this means that there have been no others in the last nine years: Middleton wants to stress both that Vindice's desire for revenge has been festering in his mind for a very long time, and that the Duke is given to such crimes as he committed in respect of Gloriana.

153 **all three** including the skull ('ragged bone')

156.1 ***Stamping on him*** 'as if he were the serpent or a damned soul being thrust into hell, a common subject for paintings and emblems' (Gibbons). But we should not moralize away the pure primitive satisfaction afforded by the sadistic violence, to the sardonic cry of 'Treason, treason, treason!' (probably little more than a whisper).

VINDICE
Alas, poor lecher, in the hands of knaves.
A slavish duke is baser than his slaves.
DUKE
My teeth are eaten out.
VINDICE Hadst any left?
HIPPOLITO I think but few.
VINDICE
Then those that did eat are eaten.
DUKE O, my tongue!
VINDICE
Your tongue? 'Twill teach you to kiss closer,
Not like a slobbering Dutchman. You have eyes still:
Look, monster, what a lady hast thou made me
My once betrothed wife.
DUKE Is it thou, villain?
Nay then—
VINDICE 'Tis I, 'tis Vindice, 'tis I.
HIPPOLITO
And let this comfort thee: our lord and father
Fell sick upon the infection of thy frowns
And died in sadness. Be that thy hope of life.
DUKE O!
VINDICE
He had his tongue, yet grief made him die speechless.
Puh, 'tis but early yet. Now I'll begin
To stick thy soul with ulcers. I will make
Thy spirit grievous sore. It shall not rest,
But like some pestilent man toss in thy breast.
Mark me, Duke:
Thou'rt a renownèd, high, and mighty cuckold.
DUKE O!
VINDICE
Thy bastard, thy bastard rides a-hunting in thy brow.
DUKE
Millions of deaths!
VINDICE Nay, to afflict thee more,
Here in this lodge they meet for damnèd clips;
Those eyes shall see the incest of their lips.
DUKE
Is there a hell besides this, villains?
VINDICE Villain!
Nay, heaven is just, scorns are the hires of scorns.
I ne'er knew yet adulterer without horns.
HIPPOLITO
Once ere they die 'tis quitted.
[*Music sounds within*]
VINDICE Hark, the music.
Their banquet is prepared, they're coming.
DUKE O, kill me not with that sight.
VINDICE
Thou shalt not lose that sight for all thy dukedom.
DUKE Traitors, murderers!
VINDICE
What, is not thy tongue eaten out yet?
Then we'll invent a silence. Brother, stifle the torch.
DUKE Treason, murder!
VINDICE
Nay, faith, we'll have you hushed. [*To Hippolito*] Now with thy dagger
Nail down his tongue, and mine shall keep possession
About his heart. If he but gasp, he dies.
We dread not death to quittance injuries.
Brother, if he but wink, not brooking the foul object,
Let our two other hands tear up his lids
And make his eyes like comets shine through blood.
When the bad bleeds, then is the tragedy good.
HIPPOLITO
Whist, brother. Music's at our ear; they come.
Enter the Bastard Spurio meeting the Duchess.
[*They kiss, as Musicians and Attendants with lights enter and stand apart*]
SPURIO
Had not that kiss a taste of sin, 'twere sweet.
DUCHESS
Why, there's no pleasure sweet but it is sinful.
SPURIO
True, such a bitter sweetness fate hath given;
Best side to us is the worst side to heaven.
DUCHESS
Push! Come; 'tis the old Duke thy doubtful father,
The thought of him, rubs heaven in thy way;
But I protest by yonder waxen fire,
Forget him, or I'll poison him.
SPURIO
Madam, you urge a thought which ne'er had life.

159 **slavish** employing various shades of meaning: (*a*) vile, (*b*) enslaved by his passions, (*c*) forced into submission by his vassals
162 **those...eaten** a truly 'mordant' literalization of 'the biter bit'
164 **slobbering Dutchman** The Dutchman slobbers (dribbles) because proverbially a heavy drinker.
165 **made me** made for me (from my betrothed)
176 **pestilent** suffering from the plague
180 **rides...brow** makes you a cuckold; 'a-hunting' links both with 'rides' (which also puns on the sexual sense) and, through the hunting of antlered deer, with the cuckold's horns, while 'brow' plays on (*a*) forehead, and (*b*) the brow of a hill.
182 **clips** embraces
185 **hires** rewards
187 **Once...quitted** i.e. some time before adulterers die their sin is requited (by the adultery of their spouses)
198 **quittance** repay
199 **brooking** being able to endure
object sight (of Spurio and the Duchess embracing)
201 **comets** The analogy of eye to sun is here transformed to an analogy between eye and traditional omen of disaster and bloodshed.
202 **bad...good** The wordplay opposes a negative ethical judgement to a positive aesthetic one.
203 **Whist** like 'Hush!', a command for silence
205 **Why...sinful** This might almost be the court motto: sin adds piquancy to their sexual appetites.
209 **rubs** stirs up thoughts of; here coloured by the bowling term, as in Hamlet's 'Ay, there's the rub' (3.1.67), where 'rub' = an impediment
210 **waxen fire** burning taper

So deadly do I loathe him for my birth
That if he took me hasped within his bed,
I would add murder to adultery
And with my sword give up his years to death.

DUCHESS
Why, now thou'rt sociable. Let's in and feast.
Loud'st music sound. Pleasure is banquet's guest.
Exeunt [*Duchess, Spurio, Musicians, and Attendants*]

DUKE
I cannot brook—
[*Vindice kills him*]

VINDICE The brook is turned to blood.

HIPPOLITO
Thanks to loud music.

VINDICE 'Twas our friend indeed.
'Tis state in music for a duke to bleed.
The dukedom wants a head, though yet unknown.
As fast as they peep up, let's cut 'em down. *Exeunt*

3.6 *Enter the Duchess' two sons, Ambitioso and Supervacuo*

AMBITIOSO
Was not his execution rarely plotted?
We are the Duke's sons now.

SUPERVACUO Ay, you may thank
My policy for that.

AMBITIOSO Your policy,
For what?

SUPERVACUO
Why, was't not my invention, brother,
To slip the judges? And, in lesser compass,
Did not I draw the model of his death,
Advising you to sudden officers
And e'en extemporal executïon?

AMBITIOSO
Heart, 'twas a thing I thought on too.

SUPERVACUO
You thought on't too? 'Sfoot, slander not your thoughts
With glorious untruth. I know 'twas from you.

AMBITIOSO
Sir, I say 'twas in my head.

SUPERVACUO Ay, like your brains then,
Ne'er to come out as long as you lived.

AMBITIOSO
You'd have the honour on't, forsooth, that your wit
Led him to the scaffold?

SUPERVACUO Since it is my due,
I'll publish't; but I'll ha't in spite of you.

AMBITIOSO
Methinks you're much too bold. You should a little
Remember us, brother, next to be honest duke.

SUPERVACUO [*aside*]
Ay, it shall be as easy for you to be duke
As to be honest, and that's never, i'faith.

AMBITIOSO
Well, cold he is by this time, and because
We're both ambitious, be it our amity,
And let the glory be shared equally.

SUPERVACUO I am content to that.

AMBITIOSO
This night our younger brother shall out of prison;
I have a trick.

SUPERVACUO A trick? Prithee, what is't?

AMBITIOSO
We'll get him out by a wile.

SUPERVACUO Prithee, what wile?

AMBITIOSO
No, sir, you shall not know it till't be done,
For then you'd swear 'twere yours.
[*Enter an Officer carrying a head in a bag*]

SUPERVACUO
How now, what's he?

AMBITIOSO One of the officers.

SUPERVACUO
Desirèd news.

AMBITIOSO How now, my friend?

OFFICER My lords,
Under your pardon, I am allotted
To that desertless office to present you
With the yet bleeding head—

SUPERVACUO [*aside to Ambitioso*]
Ha, ha, excellent.

AMBITIOSO [*aside to Supervacuo*]
All's sure our own. Brother, canst weep, think'st thou?
'Twould grace our flattery much. Think of some dame;
'Twill teach thee to dissemble.

SUPERVACUO [*aside to Ambitioso*]
I have thought.
Now for yourself.

214 **hasped** in coital embrace
219 **cannot brook** cannot stand (leading to Vindice's pun on 'brook' = stream)
220 **Thanks . . . music** for drowning out the noise of the Duke's final struggles
221 **'Tis . . . bleed** Vindice employs the various senses of 'state' to say, roughly, 'It is fitting to a Duke's high rank that he should die in state to the accompaniment of music'.
222 **wants a head** lacks a head of state
223 *Exeunt* If the discovery space was used as the 'darkened, blushless angle' (3.5.14) for the Duke's rendezvous, the body was probably stowed there and curtained off. If not, Vindice and Hippolito must have dragged the corpse with them as they left.
3.6.3 **policy** clever plotting
5 **slip** bypass
in lesser compass to a lesser extent (i.e. less importantly); with play on 'compass' = crafty device, and on the instrument for drawing circles (leading to 'draw the model' in the next line)
6 **model** plan
7 **sudden** swift in action
8 **extemporal** on the spot
11 **glorious** boastful
from you far from your thoughts
16 **but I'll** I alone shall
18 **honest** honoured; Supervacuo's aside (19–20) plays on the modern sense
27 **wile** sly ruse
33 **desertless** thankless

AMBITIOSO Our sorrows are so fluent,
Our eyes o'erflow our tongues. Words spoke in tears
Are like the murmurs of the waters, the sound
Is loudly heard but cannot be distinguished.
SUPERVACUO
How died he, pray?
OFFICER O, full of rage and spleen.
SUPERVACUO
He died most valiantly, then. We're glad
To hear it.
OFFICER We could not woo him once to pray.
AMBITIOSO
He showed himself a gentleman in that,
Give him his due.
OFFICER But in the stead of prayer
He drew forth oaths.
SUPERVACUO Then did he pray, dear heart,
Although you understood him not.
OFFICER My lords,
E'en at his last, with pardon be it spoke,
He cursed you both.
SUPERVACUO He cursed us? 'Las, good soul.
AMBITIOSO
It was not in our powers, but the Duke's pleasure.
[*Aside*] Finely dissembled o' both sides. Sweet fate,
O happy opportunity!
Enter Lussurioso
LUSSURIOSO
Now, my lords—
AMBITIOSO *and* SUPERVACUO
O!
LUSSURIOSO Why do you shun me, brothers?
You may come nearer now;
The savour of the prison has forsook me.
I thank such kind lords as yourselves, I'm free.
AMBITIOSO
Alive!
SUPERVACUO
In health!
AMBITIOSO Released! We were both e'en amazed
With joy to see it.
LUSSURIOSO I am much to thank you.
SUPERVACUO
Faith, we spared no tongue unto my lord the Duke.
AMBITIOSO
I know your delivery, brother,
Had not been half so sudden but for us.
SUPERVACUO
O, how we pleaded!
LUSSURIOSO Most deserving brothers,
In my best studies I will think of it. *Exit Lussurioso*
AMBITIOSO
O death and vengeance!
SUPERVACUO Hell and torments!
AMBITIOSO [*to Officer*]
Slave, cam'st thou to delude us?
OFFICER Delude you, my lords?
SUPERVACUO
Ay, villain; where's this head now?
OFFICER Why, here, my lord.
Just after his delivery, you both came
With warrant from the Duke to behead your brother.
AMBITIOSO
Ay, our brother, the Duke's son.
OFFICER The Duke's son,
My lord, had his release before you came.
AMBITIOSO Whose head's that then?
OFFICER
His whom you left command for, your own brother's.
[*He takes the head from the bag and displays it*]
AMBITIOSO Our brother's!
O furies!
SUPERVACUO
Plagues!
AMBITIOSO Confusions!
SUPERVACUO Darkness!
AMBITIOSO Devils!
SUPERVACUO
Fell it out so accursedly?
AMBITIOSO So damnedly?
SUPERVACUO [*to Officer*]
Villain, I'll brain thee with it.
OFFICER O, my good lord.
[*Exit Officer*]
SUPERVACUO
The devil overtake thee!
AMBITIOSO O, fatal!
SUPERVACUO
O, prodigious to our bloods!
AMBITIOSO Did we dissemble?
SUPERVACUO
Did we make our tears women for thee?
AMBITIOSO Laugh and rejoice for thee?
SUPERVACUO
Bring warrant for thy death?
AMBITIOSO Mock off thy head?
SUPERVACUO
You had a trick, you had a wile, forsooth.
AMBITIOSO A murrain meet 'em! There's none of these wiles that ever come to good. I see now there is nothing sure in mortality but mortality.
Well, no more words. 'Shalt be revenged, i'faith.

56 **savour** smell
79 **prodigious** ominous
80 **make...women** fake grief; compressing the notions of women as prone to weep and to dissemble
84 **murrain** plague; the imprecation is not uncommon
86 **mortality** quibbling on (*a*) mortal existence, (*b*) death

Come, throw off clouds now, brother. Think of ven-
  geance
And deeper settled hate.—Sirrah, sit fast;
We'll pull down all, but thou shalt down at last.
Exeunt

Finis Actus Tertii

4.1 *Incipit Actus Quartus*
Enter Lussurioso

LUSSURIOSO
Hippolito.
Enter Hippolito
HIPPOLITO
My lord. Has your good lordship
Aught to command me in?
LUSSURIOSO I prithee leave us.
HIPPOLITO [*aside*]
How's this, come, and leave us?
LUSSURIOSO Hippolito.
HIPPOLITO Your honour,
I stand ready for any duteous employment.
LUSSURIOSO
Heart, what mak'st thou here?
HIPPOLITO [*aside*] A pretty lordly humour:
He bids me to be present to depart.
Something has stung his honour.
LUSSURIOSO Be nearer, draw nearer.
You're not so good, methinks. I'm angry with you.
HIPPOLITO
With me, my lord? I'm angry with myself for't.
LUSSURIOSO
You did prefer a goodly fellow to me.
'Twas wittily elected, 'twas. I thought
He'd been a villain and he proves a knave,
To me a knave.
HIPPOLITO I chose him for the best, my lord.
'Tis much my sorrow if neglect in him
Breed discontent in you.
LUSSURIOSO Neglect? 'Twas will.
Judge of it:
Firmly to tell of an incredible act,
Not to be thought, less to be spoken of,
'Twixt my stepmother and the bastard, O,
Incestuous sweets between 'em.
HIPPOLITO Fie, my lord.
LUSSURIOSO
I, in kind loyalty to my father's forehead,
Made this a desperate arm, and in that fury
Committed treason on the lawful bed
And with my sword e'en rased my father's bosom,
For which I was within a stroke of death.
HIPPOLITO
Alack, I'm sorry.
Enter Vindice [disguised]
[*Aside*] 'Sfoot, just upon the stroke
Jars in my brother. 'Twill be villainous music.
VINDICE
My honoured lord.
LUSSURIOSO Away, prithee forsake us;
Hereafter we'll not know thee.
VINDICE
Not know me, my lord? Your lordship cannot choose.
LUSSURIOSO
Begone, I say. Thou art a false knave.
VINDICE
Why, the easier to be known, my lord.
LUSSURIOSO
Push! I shall prove too bitter with a word,
Make thee a perpetual prisoner
And lay this iron-age upon thee.
VINDICE [*aside*] Mum,
For there's a doom would make a woman dumb.
Missing the bastard, next him; the wind's come
  about;
Now 'tis my brother's turn to stay, mine to go out.
Exit
LUSSURIOSO
He's greatly moved me.
HIPPOLITO Much to blame, i'faith.
LUSSURIOSO
But I'll recover, to his ruin. 'Twas told me lately,
I know not whether falsely, that you'd a brother.
HIPPOLITO
Who, I? Yes, my good lord, I have a brother.
LUSSURIOSO
How chance the court ne'er saw him? Of what
  nature?
How does he apply his hours?
HIPPOLITO Faith, to curse fates,
Who, as he thinks, ordained him to be poor,
Keeps at home, full of want and discontent.
LUSSURIOSO [*aside*]
There's hope in him, for discontent and want

89–90 **Sirrah . . . last** aimed at the absent Lussurioso

4.1.12 **wittily elected** wisely chosen

13 **villain . . . knave** The joke lies in the equivalence of the terms (even in their neutral meaning of 'servant'); but Lussurioso had expected villainy towards others rather than knavishness towards himself.

16 **will** deliberate behaviour

22 **kind** predominantly 'natural', i.e. showing due filial concern

forehead again as site of a cuckold's horns

25 **rased** scratched

28 **Jars in** makes an untimely entrance, enters on a discordant note; taken up in 'villainous music' and eliciting a musical image from 'stroke' = musical beat ('to keep stroke' = to keep time)

36 **iron-age** mass of iron fetters (see 4.2.129); with an allusion to the Iron Age, which in classical mythology succeeded the Golden, Silver, and Brazen as last and worst.

Mum Silence!

38 **Missing . . . him** Vindice's scheme to have Spurio killed by Lussurioso in the Duchess's bed has failed, and Lussurioso himself has been pardoned for his unintended attack on the Duke.

Is the best clay to mould a villain of.—
Hippolito, wish him repair to us.
If there be aught in him to please our blood,
For thy sake we'll advance him and build fair
His meanest fortunes, for it is in us
To rear up towers from cottages.

HIPPOLITO It is so, my lord.
He will attend your honour. But he's a man
In whom much melancholy dwells.

LUSSURIOSO Why, the better.
Bring him to court.

HIPPOLITO With willingness and speed.
[*Aside*] Whom he cast off e'en now must now succeed.
Brother, disguise must off:
In thine own shape now I'll prefer thee to him.
How strangely does himself work to undo him. *Exit*

LUSSURIOSO
This fellow will come fitly. He shall kill
That other slave that did abuse my spleen
And made it swell to treason. I have put
Much of my heart into him. He must die.
He that knows great men's secrets and proves slight,
That man ne'er lives to see his beard turn white.
Ay, he shall speed him; I'll employ thee, brother.
Slaves are but nails to drive out one another.
He being of black condition, suitable
To want and ill content, hope of preferment
Will grind him to an edge.

The Nobles enter

FIRST NOBLE Good days unto your honour.

LUSSURIOSO
My kind lords, I do return the like.

SECOND NOBLE Saw you my lord the Duke?

LUSSURIOSO
My lord and father? Is he from court?

FIRST NOBLE He's sure from court,
But where, which way his pleasure took, we know not,
Nor can we hear on't.

[*Enter the Duke's Gentlemen*]

LUSSURIOSO Here come those should tell.
Saw you my lord and father?

FIRST GENTLEMAN
Not since two hoürs before noon, my lord,
And then he privately rid forth.

LUSSURIOSO
O, he's rode forth?

FIRST NOBLE 'Twas wondrous privately.

SECOND NOBLE
There's none i'th' court had any knowledge on't.

LUSSURIOSO
His grace is old and sudden. 'Tis no treason
To say the Duke my father has a humour
Or such a toy about him. What in us
Would appear light, in him seems virtuous.

FIRST GENTLEMAN 'Tis oracle, my lord. *Exeunt*

Enter Vindice and Hippolito, Vindice out of his disguise 4.2

HIPPOLITO
So, so, all's as it should be; you're yourself.

VINDICE
How that great villain puts me to my shifts!

HIPPOLITO
He that did lately in disguise reject thee
Shall, now thou art thyself, as much respect thee.

VINDICE
'Twill be the quainter fallacy. But, brother,
'Sfoot, what use will he put me to now, think'st thou?

HIPPOLITO
Nay, you must pardon me in that, I know not.
H'as some employment for you, but what 'tis
He and his secretary the devil knows best.

VINDICE
Well, I must suit my tongue to his desires,
What colour soe'er they be, hoping at last
To pile up all my wishes on his breast.

HIPPOLITO
Faith, brother, he himself shows the way.

VINDICE
Now the Duke is dead the realm is clad in clay.
His death being not yet known, under his name
The people still are governed. Well, thou his son
Art not long lived; thou shalt not joy his death.
To kill thee, then, I should most honour thee,

53 **in us** i.e. within my power
58 **succeed** (*a*) take his place as successor, (*b*) successfully deal with Lussurioso
62 **fitly** opportunely
63 **spleen** fiery temper
65 **heart** innermost thoughts and feelings
66 **slight** unworthy of trust (but providing a kind of false antithesis to 'great')
68 **speed** kill
69 **Slaves . . . another** alluding to the proverb, 'One nail drives out another'
70 **of black condition** melancholic, the physiology of 'humours' attributing melancholy to an excess of black bile
72 **grind . . . edge** incite him (to action); a common phrase, but here with an apt suggestion of the sharpening of a weapon for Lussurioso's use
85 **sudden** impetuous
86 **humour** whim
87 **toy** idle fancy
88 **light** frivolous
89 **oracle** absolute truth
4.2.2 **great villain** an oxymoron, playing on 'great' = of high estate, and 'villain' = servant
shifts (*a*) stratagems, (*b*) changes of clothing
5 **quainter fallacy** wittier deception
9 **secretary** confidant
12 **To . . . breast** Perhaps an image drawn from pressing to death with weights.
13 **shows the way** i.e. provides a model of how to dissemble
14 **realm . . . clay** the old regime is buried; an image condensing three commonplaces: the flesh as clothing (as in 1.1.31), the state as body, and the identity of ruler with realm
17 **joy** enjoy (by succeeding to the dukedom)

For 'twould stand firm in every man's belief
Thou'st a kind child and only died'st with grief.

HIPPOLITO
You fetch about well, but let's talk in present.
How will you appear in fashion different,
As well as in apparel, to make all things possible?
If you be but once tripped, we fall for ever.
It is not the least policy to be doubtful.
You must change tongue. Familiar was your first.

VINDICE
Why, I'll bear me in some strain of melancholy
And string myself with heavy-sounding wire,
Like such an instrument that speaks
Merry things sadly.

HIPPOLITO Then 'tis as I meant:
I gave you out at first in discontent.

VINDICE
I'll turn myself, and then—
[Enter Lussurioso]

HIPPOLITO 'Sfoot, here he comes.
Hast thought upon't?

VINDICE Salute him. Fear not me.

LUSSURIOSO
Hippolito.

HIPPOLITO
Your lordship.

LUSSURIOSO What's he yonder?

HIPPOLITO
'Tis Vindice, my discontented brother,
Whom, 'cording to your will, I've brought to court.

LUSSURIOSO
Is that thy brother? Beshrew me, a good presence.
I wonder he's been from the court so long.
[*To Vindice*] Come nearer.

HIPPOLITO
Brother, Lord Lussurioso, the Duke's son.

LUSSURIOSO
Be more near to us. Welcome. Nearer yet.

Vindice snatches off his hat and makes legs to him,
[while Hippolito moves aside]

VINDICE
How don you? God you god den.

LUSSURIOSO We thank thee.
[*Aside*] How strangely such a coarse, homely salute
Shows in the palace, where we greet in fire,
Nimble and desperate tongues. Should we name God
In a salutation 'twould ne'er be stood on—heaven!
Tell me, what has made thee so melancholy?

VINDICE Why, going to law.

LUSSURIOSO Why, will that make a man melancholy?

VINDICE Yes, to look long upon ink and black buckram. I went me to law in *anno quadragesimo secundo* and I waded out of it in *anno sextagesimo tertio.*

LUSSURIOSO What, three and twenty years in law?

VINDICE I have known those that have been five-and-fifty, and all about pullen and pigs.

LUSSURIOSO
May it be possible such men should breathe,
To vex the terms so much?

VINDICE 'Tis food to some, my lord. There are old men at the present that are so poisoned with the affectation of law words (having had many suits canvassed) that their common talk is nothing but Barbary Latin. They cannot so much as pray but in law, that their sins may be removed with a writ of error and their souls fetched up to heaven with a sasarara.

LUSSURIOSO It seems most strange to me,
Yet all the world meets round in the same bent.
Where the heart's set, there goes the tongue's consent.
How dost apply thy studies, fellow?

VINDICE Study? Why, to think how a great rich man lies a-dying and a poor cobbler tolls the bell for him; how he cannot depart the world and see the great chest stand before him; when he lies speechless, how he will point you readily to all the boxes; and when he

20 **Thou'st** thou wast
21 **fetch about** wander around the subject (in an inventive way)
in present i.e. of the immediate problem
22 **fashion** manner
25 **not . . . policy** i.e. the best policy
doubtful careful
27–30 **Why . . . sadly** The musical conceit begins with 'strain' = tune. Vindice ought to have in mind a bass viol (Shakespeare uses the pun in *Comedy of Errors*, 4.3.23).
32 **turn** transform, with a hint of tuning an instrument (by turning the pegs), to round off the conceit
37 **Beshrew me** an idly used imprecation, meaning roughly 'the devil take me!'
41.1 ***snatches . . . him*** i.e. Vindice scrapes and bows in a caricature of the gawky yokel.
42 **don** do
God you god den God give you good even; like 'don', indicating rustic speech
45 **desperate tongues** reckless expressions
46 **stood on** taken seriously
heaven! Lussurioso's reflex use of this word to express surprise enforces the point of his sentence; see Textual Notes.
50 **black buckram** a lawyer's bag made of coarse linen, its blackness associating it with melancholy (or black bile)
51 ***anno . . . secundo*** the forty-second year (of an imagined reign)
52 ***anno . . . tertio*** the sixty-third year
53 **three** The blunder is presumably Lussurioso's (whether as arithmetician or Latinist), not Middleton's. Partly because he is so easily and repeatedly duped by Vindice, Lussurioso appears something of a dullard.
55 **pullen** poultry
57 **terms** periods when the law courts are in session
61 **Barbary Latin** barbarous, or bad, Latin
62 **writ of error** a writ brought to procure the reverse of a judgement on the ground of error
63 **sasarara** colloquial anglicization of Latin 'certiorari': a writ from a superior court arising from a complaint that a party has not received justice in an inferior court
65 **meets . . . bent** shares the same tendency; with 'world' acting on 'round' and 'bent' (= curve) to enhance the sense of a global characteristic
70 **and see** and (still) see
chest treasure chest
72 **boxes** presumably money-boxes

is past all memory, as the gossips guess, then thinks he of forfeitures and obligations; nay, when to all men's hearings he whurls and rattles in the throat, he's busy threatening his poor tenants; and this would last me now some seven years' thinking or thereabouts. But I have a conceit a-coming in picture upon this—I draw it myself—which, i'faith la, I'll present to your honour. You shall not choose but like it, for your lordship shall give me nothing for it.

LUSSURIOSO Nay, you mistake me then,
For I am published bountiful enough.
Let's taste of your conceit.

VINDICE In picture, my lord?

LUSSURIOSO
Ay, in picture.

VINDICE Marry, this it is:
A usuring father to be boiling in hell and his son and heir with a whore dancing over him.

HIPPOLITO [*aside*] He's pared him to the quick.

LUSSURIOSO The conceit's pretty, i'faith,
But tak't upon my life 'twill ne'er be liked.

VINDICE No? Why, I'm sure the whore will be liked well enough.

HIPPOLITO [*aside*] Ay, if she were out o'th' picture he'd like her then himself.

VINDICE And as for the son and heir, he shall be an eyesore to no young revellers, for he shall be drawn in cloth of gold breeches.

LUSSURIOSO
And thou hast put my meaning in the pockets
And canst not draw that out. My thought was this:
To see the picture of a usuring father
Boiling in hell, our rich men would ne'er like it.

VINDICE O true, I cry you heartily mercy. I know the reason, for some of 'em had rather be damned indeed than damned in colours.

LUSSURIOSO [*aside*]
A parlous melancholy! H'as wit enough
To murder any man, and I'll give him means.—
I think thou art ill-moneyed.

VINDICE Money? Ho, ho!
'T'as been my want so long 'tis now my scoff.
I've e'en forgot what colour silver's of.

LUSSURIOSO [*aside*]
It hits as I could wish.

VINDICE I get good clothes
Of those that dread my humour, and for table-room
I feed on those that cannot be rid of me.

LUSSURIOSO Somewhat to set thee up withal.
[*He gives Vindice money*]

VINDICE
O, mine eyes!

LUSSURIOSO How now, man?

VINDICE Almost struck blind.
This bright unusual shine to me seems proud.
I dare not look till the sun be in a cloud.

LUSSURIOSO [*aside*]
I think I shall affect his melancholy.—
How are they now?

VINDICE The better for your asking.

LUSSURIOSO
You shall be better yet if you but fasten
Truly on my intent.
[*He beckons Hippolito forward*]
Now you're both present
I will unbrace such a close, private villain
Unto your vengeful swords, the like ne'er heard of,
Who hath disgraced you much and injured us.

HIPPOLITO
Disgraced us, my lord?

LUSSURIOSO Ay, Hippolito.
I kept it here till now that both your angers
Might meet him at once.

VINDICE I'm covetous
To know the villain.

LUSSURIOSO [*to Hippolito*]
You know him, that slave-pander
Piato, whom we threatened last
With irons in perpetual prisonment.

VINDICE [*aside*]
All this is I.

HIPPOLITO Is't he, my lord?

LUSSURIOSO I'll tell you;
You first preferred him to me.

VINDICE Did you, brother?

HIPPOLITO
I did indeed.

LUSSURIOSO And the ingrateful villain,
To quit that kindness, strongly wrought with me—
Being, as you see, a likely man for pleasure—
With jewels to corrupt your virgin sister.

73 **gossips** relatives and friends at the bedside

74 **forfeitures and obligations** legal terms with an ironic relevance to eternal matters: confiscations of estate or goods; bonds for the payment of moneys

75 **whurls** gurgles

78 **conceit** (*a*) artistic conception, (*b*) witty figure
in picture i.e. as a pictorial emblem

80–1 **You . . . for it** Perhaps the point is simply that Lussurioso is not entitled to criticize something he has not paid for.

88 **pared . . . quick** The colloqialism (meaning literally to cut the cuticle so deep as to reach the sensitive parts) registers Hippolito's recognition that the conceit is an exposure of Lussurioso's own position.

104 **colours** a painting; but 'colours' also means 'appearances'

105 **parlous** shrewd, keen, dangerous

117 **affect** grow fond of

118 **they** i.e. Vindice's eyes

121 **unbrace** disclose; but the literal meaning of 'undress' serves as ironic reminder that Piato was a role created by means of diguise.

125 **here** perhaps laying a hand on his heart or head

133 **quit** repay
wrought with worked on

HIPPOLITO
O, villain!
VINDICE He shall surely die that did it.
LUSSURIOSO
I, far from thinking any virgin harm,
Especially knowing her to be as chaste
As that part which scarce suffers to be touched,
Th' eye, would not endure him—
VINDICE Would you not,
My lord? 'Twas wondrous honourably done.
LUSSURIOSO
But with some fine frowns kept him out.
VINDICE Out, slave!
LUSSURIOSO
What did me he but, in revenge of that,
Went of his own free will to make infirm
Your sister's honour, whom I honour with my soul
For chaste respect, and not prevailing there
(As 'twas but desperate folly to attempt it),
In mere spleen, by the way, waylays your mother,
Whose honour being a coward, as it seems,
Yielded by little force.
VINDICE Coward indeed.
LUSSURIOSO
He, proud of their advantage, as he thought,
Brought me these news for happy, but I,
Heaven forgive me for't—
VINDICE What did your honour?
LUSSURIOSO In rage pushed him from me,
Trampled beneath his throat, spurned him, and
bruised.
Indeed I was too cruel, to say troth.
HIPPOLITO
Most nobly managed.
VINDICE [*aside*] Has not heaven an ear?
Is all the lightning wasted?
LUSSURIOSO If I now
Were so impatient in a modest cause,
What should you be?
VINDICE Full mad. He shall not live
To see the moon change.
LUSSURIOSO He's about the palace.
Hippolito, entice him this way that thy brother
May take full mark of him.
HIPPOLITO Heart, that shall not need, my lord;
I can direct him so far.
LUSSURIOSO Yet for my hate's sake,
Go wind him this way. I'll see him bleed myself.
HIPPOLITO [*aside to Vindice*] What now, brother?
VINDICE [*aside to Hippolito*]
Nay, e'en what you will; you're put to't, brother.
HIPPOLITO [*aside to Vindice*]
An impossible task, I'll swear,
To bring him hither that's already here. *Exit*
LUSSURIOSO
Thy name? I have forgot it.
VINDICE Vindice, my lord.
LUSSURIOSO
'Tis a good name that.
VINDICE Ay, a revenger.
LUSSURIOSO
It does betoken courage. Thou shouldst be valiant
And kill thine enemies.
VINDICE That's my hope, my lord.
LUSSURIOSO
This slave is one.
VINDICE I'll doom him.
LUSSURIOSO Then I'll praise thee.
Do thou observe me best, and I'll best raise thee.
Enter Hippolito
VINDICE
Indeed, I thank you.
LUSSURIOSO Now, Hippolito,
Where's the slave-pander?
HIPPOLITO Your good lordship
Would have a loathsome sight of him, much offensive.
He's not in case now to be seen, my lord.
The worst of all the deadly sins is in him,
That beggarly damnation, drunkenness.
LUSSURIOSO
Then he's a double slave.
VINDICE [*aside*] 'Twas well conveyed,
Upon a sudden wit.
LUSSURIOSO What, are you both
Firmly resolved? I'll see him dead myself.
VINDICE
Or else let not us live.
LUSSURIOSO You may direct
Your brother to take note of him.
HIPPOLITO I shall.
LUSSURIOSO
Rise but in this and you shall never fall.
VINDICE
Your honour's vassals.
LUSSURIOSO [*aside*] This was wisely carried.
Deep policy in us makes fools of such.

136 **He...it** doubly ironic: Vindice covertly avows his intention to kill Lussurioso, while unwittingly forecasting his own fate

138–40 **chaste...Th' eye** with the slight pause before 'Th' eye' allowing innuendo; compare Webster's *Duchess of Malfi*, 'And women like that part which, like the lamphrey, | Hath ne'er a bone in't... | I mean the tongue' (1.1.336–8)

143 **did me he** colloquial and emphatic, as at 2.2.42

146 **For chaste respect** out of regard for her chastity

148 **mere spleen** pure spite

151 **their advantage** the advantage to be reported in 'these news'

156 **spurned** kicked

160 **in a modest cause** in the cause of chastity, with the additional sense that it is of only modest (moderate) relevance to himself

164 **mark** note

167 **wind** draw, entice

177 **observe** gratify, treat with respect

181 **in case** in a condition

184 **conveyed** managed

185 **sudden** punning on 'sodden'

Then must a slave die, when he knows too much.
Exit

VINDICE
O, thou almighty patience! 'Tis my wonder
That such a fellow, impudent and wicked,
Should not be cloven as he stood,
Or with a secret wind burst open.
Is there no thunder left, or is't kept up
In stock for heavier vengeance? There it goes.

HIPPOLITO
Brother, we lose ourselves.

VINDICE
But I have found it.
'Twill hold, 'tis sure. Thanks, thanks to any spirit
That mingled it 'mongst my inventions.

HIPPOLITO
What is't?

VINDICE
'Tis sound and good. Thou shalt partake it.
I'm hired to kill myself.

HIPPOLITO
True.

VINDICE
Prithee, mark it:
And the old Duke being dead but not conveyed,
For he's already missed too, and you know
Murder will peep out of the closest husk—

HIPPOLITO
Most true.

VINDICE
What say you then to this device?
If we dressed up the body of the Duke—

HIPPOLITO
In that disguise of yours.

VINDICE
You're quick, you've reached it.

HIPPOLITO I like it wondrously.

VINDICE
And being in drink, as you have published him,
To lean him on his elbow as if sleep had caught him,
Which claims most interest in such sluggy men.

HIPPOLITO Good yet, but here's a doubt:
We, thought by th' Duke's son to kill that pander,
Shall, when he is known, be thought to kill the Duke.

VINDICE
Neither, O thanks, it is substantïal,
For that disguise being on him which I wore,
It will be thought I, which he calls the pander,
Did kill the Duke and fled away in his apparel,
Leaving him so disguised to avoid swift pursuit.

HIPPOLITO
Firmer and firmer.

VINDICE
Nay, doubt not, 'tis in grain;
I warrant it hold colour.

HIPPOLITO
Let's about it.

VINDICE
But by the way too, now I think on't, brother,
Let's conjure that base devil out of our mother.
Exeunt

Enter the Duchess, arm in arm with the Bastard 4.3
Spurio; he seemeth lasciviously to her. After them,
enter Supervacuo, running with a rapier; his
brother Ambitioso stops him

SPURIO
Madam, unlock yourself. Should it be seen,
Your arm would be suspected.

DUCHESS
Who is't that dares suspect or this or these?
May not we deal our favours where we please?

SPURIO
I'm confident you may. *Exeunt Duchess and Spurio*

AMBITIOSO
'Sfoot, brother, hold.

SUPERVACUO
Woult let the bastard shame us?

AMBITIOSO
Hold, hold, brother.
There's fitter time than now.

SUPERVACUO
Now, when I see it?

AMBITIOSO
'Tis too much seen already.

SUPERVACUO
Seen and known;
The nobler she's, the baser is she grown.

AMBITIOSO
If she were bent lasciviously, the fault
Of mighty women that sleep soft—O death!
Must she needs choose such an unequal sinner
To make all worse?

SUPERVACUO
A bastard, the Duke's bastard!
Shame heaped on shame.

AMBITIOSO
O, our disgrace!
Most women have small waist the world throughout,
But their desires are thousand miles about.

193–8 **O, thou . . . vengeance?** adapted from Seneca's *Phaedra*, lines 671–4; see also 1.4.23

198 **There it goes** That's it!, Eureka! Vindice has hit upon a plan, as he explains in his next speech (198–200).

199 **Brother . . . it** Hippolito's phrase means 'we are destroying ourselves' and (by dramatic irony) 'we are damning ourselves'; Vindice, giving it the literal sense 'we have lost our way', claims to have 'found it' (the way to extricate themselves from their predicament).

200 **hold** stand the test, work

204 **conveyed** disposed of

206 **Murder . . . husk** the proverbial 'Murder will out'

213 **sluggy** sluggish

217 **substantïal** firmly based, soundly conceived

222 **in grain** fast dyed, indelible

223 **hold colour** continuing the image while playing on the figurative sense of 'colour' = pretence: the pretence will be believed

225 **conjure** exorcise

4.3.0.2 ***seemeth*** acts

1 **unlock yourself** i.e. release your arm from mine

3 **or this or these** either this arm or these kisses (or caresses)

6 **Woult** wilt thou

9 **baser** quibbling on the social and moral senses

10 **bent lasciviously** intent on wantonness

12 **unequal** i.e. in rank and blood

SUPERVACUO
Come, stay not here; let's after and prevent,
Or else they'll sin faster than we'll repent. *Exeunt*

4.4 *Enter Vindice and Hippolito, bringing out their Mother, one by one shoulder and the other by the other, with daggers in their hands*

VINDICE
O thou for whom no name is bad enough!
MOTHER
What means my sons? What, will you murder me?
VINDICE
Wicked, unnatural parent.
HIPPOLITO Fiend of women.
MOTHER
O, are sons turned monsters? Help!
VINDICE In vain.
MOTHER
Are you so barbarous to set iron nipples
Upon the breast that gave you suck?
VINDICE That breast
Is turned to quarlèd poison.
MOTHER
Cut not your days for't. Am not I your mother?
VINDICE
Thou dost usurp that title now by fraud,
For in that shell of mother breeds a bawd.
MOTHER
A bawd? O name far loathsomer than hell!
HIPPOLITO
It should be so, knew'st thou thy office well.
MOTHER I hate it.
VINDICE
Ah, is't possible, thou only God on high,
That women should dissemble when they die?
MOTHER
Dissemble?
VINDICE Did not the Duke's son direct
A fellow of the world's condition hither,
That did corrupt all that was good in thee,
Made thee uncivilly forget thyself
And work our sister to his lust?
MOTHER Who, I?
That had been monstrous. I defy that man
For any such intent. None lives so pure
But shall be soiled with slander.
Good son, believe it not.
VINDICE O, I'm in doubt
Whether I'm myself or no!—
Stay, let me look again upon this face.
Who shall be saved when mothers have no grace?
HIPPOLITO
'Twould make one half despair.
VINDICE I was the man.
Defy me now. Let's see; do't modestly.
MOTHER O hell unto my soul!
VINDICE
In that disguise I, sent from the Duke's son,
Tried you and found you base metal,
As any villain might have done.
MOTHER O no,
No tongue but yours could have bewitched me so.
VINDICE
O, nimble in damnation, quick in tune.
There is no devil could strike fire so soon.
I am confuted in a word.
MOTHER O sons,
Forgive me. To myself I'll prove more true.
You that should honour me, I kneel to you.
[*She kneels and weeps*]
VINDICE
A mother to give aim to her own daughter!
HIPPOLITO
True, brother, how far beyond nature 'tis,
Though many mothers do't.
VINDICE
Nay, an you draw tears once, go you to bed.
Wet will make iron blush and change to red.
Brother, it rains. 'Twill spoil your dagger. House it.
HIPPOLITO 'Tis done.
VINDICE
I'faith, 'tis a sweet shower. It does much good.
The fruitful grounds and meadows of her soul
Has been long dry. Pour down, thou blessèd dew.
Rise, mother. Troth, this shower has made you
higher.

4.4.5 **iron nipples** i.e. their daggers
7 **quarlèd** curdled
8 **Cut** cut short (by being executed for murder); again alluding to Exodus, 20:12, as at 2.2.95–6
12 **office** duty, role
17 **of ... condition** i.e. worldly, materialistic; but the phrase carries something of the Calvinist sense of general depravity.
19 **uncivilly** barbarously
24–5 **I'm ... no** The joke raises a deeper question about his true identity than Vindice intends. As Piato, he had played the role of pander to perfection.
26 **Stay ... face** 'This face' is presumably his mother's, but line 25 would give some justification for taking it as Vindice's own, in which case the props would have to include a mirror or glass. A moment of reflection on his own self and salvation might be effective here.
27 **grace** recalling the mother's name, Italian for 'Grace'
35 **quick in tune** quick to attune to the situation
40 **give aim** a term from archery meaning to guide the aim of the shooter; depending on whether the following 'to' means 'for' or 'towards', the point could be either that she directs Castiza towards Lussurioso or that she aids his attempt on the target
43 **you** i.e. his dagger
to bed into its scabbard
44 **blush** with red rust
48–9 **The ... dry** The traditional imagery of spiritual sterility and fruitfulness is here complicated by the play's 'virtual identification of stable moral and social values with the landed order of the old-fashioned manor' (Ross).
50 **this ... higher** continuing the image of plant growth; through her tears of remorse Mother has attained a higher moral station, and she is here literally raised to her feet

[*He helps her up*]

MOTHER
O you heavens,
Take this infectious spot out of my soul.
I'll rinse it in seven waters of mine eyes.
Make my tears salt enough to taste of grace.
To weep is to our sex naturally given,
But to weep truly, that's a gift from heaven.

VINDICE
Nay, I'll kiss you now. Kiss her, brother.
Let's marry her to our souls, wherein's no lust,
And honourably love her.

HIPPOLITO
Let it be.

VINDICE
For honest women are so seld and rare
'Tis good to cherish those poor few that are.
O you of easy wax, do but imagine,
Now the disease has left you, how leprously
That office would have clinged unto your forehead.
All mothers that had any graceful hue
Would have worn masks to hide their face at you.
It would have grown to this: at your foul name
Green-coloured maids would have turned red with shame.

HIPPOLITO
And then our sister, full of hire and baseness.

VINDICE
There had been boiling lead again.
The Duke's son's great concubine,
A drab of state, a cloth o' silver slut!
To have her train borne up and her soul trail i'th' dirt!

HIPPOLITO
Graced, to be miserably great; rich, to be eternally wretched.

VINDICE O common madness!
Ask but the thriving'st harlot in cold blood,
She'd give the world to make her honour good.
Perhaps you'll say, 'But only to th' Duke's son
In private'. Why, she first begins with one
Who afterward to thousand proves a whore:
"Break ice in one place, it will crack in more."

MOTHER Most certainly applied.

HIPPOLITO
O brother, you forget our business.

VINDICE
And well remembered. Joy's a subtle elf.
I think man's happiest when he forgets himself.—
Farewell, once dried, now holy-watered mead.
Our hearts wear feathers that before wore lead.

MOTHER
I'll give you this, that one I never knew
Plead better for and 'gainst the devil than you.

VINDICE You make me proud on't.

HIPPOLITO
Commend us in all virtue to our sister.

VINDICE
Ay, for the love of heaven, to that true maid.

MOTHER
With my best words.

VINDICE
Why, that was motherly said.

Exeunt Vindice and Hippolito

MOTHER
I wonder now what fury did transport me.
I feel good thoughts begin to settle in me.
O, with what forehead can I look on her
Whose honour I've so impiously beset?
[*Enter Castiza*]
And here she comes.

CASTIZA
Now mother, you have wrought with me so strongly
That, what for my advancement as to calm
The trouble of your tongue, I am content.

MOTHER
Content to what?

CASTIZA
To do as you have wished me,
To prostitute my breast to the Duke's son
And put myself to common usury.

MOTHER
I hope you will not so.

53 **I'll... eyes** I'll cleanse it by much penitent weeping (like Mary Magdalen, the Early Modern archetype of the repentant weeper). The phrase 'seven waters' suggests ritual purification, as when the prophet Elisha bade the leper Naaman 'wash in the Jordan seven times' (2 Kings, 5:10); Jesus had cast seven devils out of Mary (Mark, 16:9) and Mother's number probably glances also at the seven biblical psalms designated as the Penitential Psalms.

54 **salt** a possible allusion to the use of salt in baptism as symbol of delivery from sin. The whole passage emphasizes true repentance as a sign of saving grace through faith.

60 **seld** seldom found

62 **of easy wax** who are pliable

65 **graceful** quibbling on physical and spiritual grace
hue appearance

68 **Green-coloured** immature, inexperienced

69 **hire** payment for (sexual) use

72 **drab** whore

74 **rich... wretched** The consonance enforces the point.

84 **subtle elf** spirit that works imperceptibly or insidiously

85 **I think... himself** The line hints at the involutions of Vindice's tormented psyche. Like Hamlet ('Heaven and earth, | Must I remember?', 1.2.142–3), Vindice as revenger is a 'rememberer', aware of a past and of an eternal future that the court, in its frenetic preoccupation with pleasures of the present minute, obliterates from consciousness. This is a society of 'forgetful feasts' (3.5.91), and in his role as tempter Vindice tries to make his Mother 'forget heaven' (2.1.119). Vindice veers between contemplative contempt for the world and strenuous immersion in it.

86 **mead** meadow; the line's imagery provides the poetic resolution of the theme set forth in lines 48–50.

96 **forehead** countenance, dignity

100 **what for** In this elliptical construction, the phrase is equivalent to 'as much for'.

104 **usury** here = use for hire, prostitution; the figurative use of the term 'usury' associates sexual corruption with a money economy; see note on 2.2.97

CASTIZA Hope you I will not?
That's not the hope you look to be saved in.
MOTHER
Truth, but it is.
CASTIZA Do not deceive yourself.
I am as you e'en out of marble wrought.
What would you now? Are ye not pleased yet with me?
You shall not wish me to be more lascivious
Than I intend to be.
MOTHER Strike not me cold.
CASTIZA
How often have you charged me on your blessing
To be a cursèd woman? When you knew
Your blessing had no force to make me lewd,
You laid your curse upon me. That did more;
The mother's curse is heavy. Where that fights
Sons set in storm and daughters lose their lights.
MOTHER
Good child, dear maid, if there be any spark
Of heavenly intellectual fire within thee,
O let my breath revive it to a flame.
Put not all out with woman's wilful follies.
I am recovered of that foul disease
That haunts too many mothers. Kind, forgive me;
Make me not sick in health. If then
My words prevailed when they were wickedness,
How much more now when they are just and good?
CASTIZA
I wonder what you mean. Are not you she
For whose infect persuasions I could scarce
Kneel out my prayers, and had much ado
In three hours' reading to untwist so much
Of the black serpent as you wound about me?
MOTHER
'Tis unfruitful, held tedious, to repeat what's past.
I'm now your present mother.
CASTIZA Push! Now 'tis too late.
MOTHER
Bethink again; thou know'st not what thou say'st.
CASTIZA
No? 'Deny advancement, treasure, the Duke's son?'
MOTHER
O see, I spoke those words, and now they poison me.
What will the deed do then?
Advancement? True—as high as shame can pitch!
For treasure, whoe'er knew a harlot rich?
Or could build by the purchase of her sin
An hospital to keep their bastards in?
The Duke's son? O, when women are young courtiers,
They are sure to be old beggars.
To know the miseries most harlots taste,
Thou'dst wish thyself unborn when thou art unchaste.
CASTIZA
O mother, let me twine about your neck
And kiss you till my soul melt on your lips.
I did but this to try you.
MOTHER O, speak truth!
CASTIZA
Indeed, I did not, for no tongue has force
To alter me from honest.
If maidens would, men's words could have no power.
A virgin honour is a crystal tower,
Which, being weak, is guarded with good spirits;
Until she basely yields, no ill inherits.
MOTHER
O happy child! Faith and thy birth hath saved me.
'Mongst thousand daughters happiest of all others,
Be thou a glass for maids and I for mothers. *Exeunt*
Finis Actus Quarti

106 **That's ... in** The stress is on 'you': her mother's 'hope' had appeared to be of a material salvation from poverty, at the expense of Castiza's chastity, not of Divine Salvation.
108 **I am ... wrought** Castiza is probably saying 'I am now as hardened (to the prospect of sinning) as you'; compare the 'dauntless marble' inspired by 'Impudence' at 1.3.8 and 'marble impudence' at 5.3.69.
116–17 **The ... lights** Since curses 'light' (alight) on those cursed (as in 'Confusion light on you!' in *Michaelmas*, 4.1.63) and people either win or 'lose' fights, one might naturally have expected the rhyme-words to appear in the reverse order. This would have created a kind of punning false antithesis in line 116: 'heavy ... lights'. But the transposition is deliberate, enforcing the pun on 'Sons'/'Suns', which in turn gives the concreteness of an image of heavenly bodies to the phrase 'lose their lights' = lose their sense of moral direction.
119 **intellectual** here, spiritual
123 **Kind** (*a*) kind one, (*b*) child (one of my kin); hence = 'kind daughter'
128 **infect** infected
130–1 **untwist ... me** another image that gains power from a pictorial and emblematic tradition featuring Satan as serpent in the Garden of Eden and the struggles of figures from classical mythology, such as Laocoön, who was crushed by the coils of two sea-serpents.
133 **present** i.e. true
140 **purchase** profit
141 **hospital** orphanage
149 **did not** i.e. did not speak truth before
151 **would** had the will (to be chaste)
154 **inherits** takes possession, resides there
155 **happy** blessed
157 **glass** mirror (i.e. model)

5.1 [*Incipit Actus Quintus*]

Enter Vindice and Hippolito [*carrying the corpse of the Duke dressed in Vindice's disguise as Piato; they set it in place*]

VINDICE So, so, he leans well. Take heed you wake him not, brother.

HIPPOLITO I warrant you, my life for yours.

VINDICE
That's a good lay, for I must kill myself.
Brother, that's I; that sits for me. Do you mark it?
And I must stand ready here to make away myself yonder—I must sit to be killed and stand to kill myself. I could vary it not so little as thrice over again. 'T'as some eight returns like Michaelmas Term.

HIPPOLITO That's enough, o' conscience.

VINDICE But sirrah, does the Duke's son come single?

HIPPOLITO No, there's the hell on't; his faith's too feeble to go alone. He brings flesh-flies after him that will buzz against supper-time and hum for his coming out.

VINDICE Ah, the fly-flop of vengeance beat 'em to pieces! Here was the sweetest occasion, the fittest hour, to have made my revenge familiar with him, show him the body of the Duke his father and how quaintly he died—like a politician in hugger-mugger, made no man acquainted with it—and in catastrophe slain him over his father's breast, and—O, I'm mad to lose such a sweet opportunity!

HIPPOLITO Nay, push! Prithee be content. There's no remedy present. May not hereafter times open in as fair faces as this?

VINDICE They may if they can paint so well.

HIPPOLITO Come now, to avoid all suspicion let's forsake this room and be going to meet the Duke's son.

VINDICE Content, I'm for any weather. Heart, step close, here he comes.

Enter Lussurioso

HIPPOLITO My honoured lord.

LUSSURIOSO O me! You both present?

VINDICE E'en newly, my lord, just as your lordship entered now. About this place we had notice given he should be, but in some loathsome plight or other.

HIPPOLITO Came your honour private?

LUSSURIOSO
Private enough for this. Only a few
Attend my coming out.

HIPPOLITO [*aside*] Death rot those few!

LUSSURIOSO Stay, yonder's the slave.

VINDICE
Mass, there's the slave indeed, my lord.
[*Aside*] 'Tis a good child; he calls his father slave.

LUSSURIOSO
Ay, that's the villain, the damned villain. Softly,
Tread easy.

VINDICE Puh, I warrant you, my lord,
We'll stifle in our breaths.

LUSSURIOSO That will do well.—
Base rogue, thou sleepest thy last. [*Aside*] 'Tis policy
To have him killed in's sleep, for if he waked
He would betray all to them.

VINDICE But my lord—

LUSSURIOSO
Ha, what say'st?

VINDICE Shall we kill him now he's drunk?

LUSSURIOSO Ay, best of all.

VINDICE Why then, he will ne'er live to be sober.

LUSSURIOSO No matter, let him reel to hell.

VINDICE But being so full of liquor, I fear he will put out all the fire.

LUSSURIOSO Thou art a mad-breast.

VINDICE [*aside*] And leave none to warm your lordship's golls withal.—For he that dies drunk falls into hell-fire like a bucket o' water, qush, qush.

LUSSURIOSO
Come, be ready, nake your swords, think of your wrongs.
This slave has injured you.

VINDICE Troth, so he has.
[*Aside*] And he has paid well for't.

5.1.0.4 ***set it in place*** leaning on his elbow as though asleep, if they adhere to Vindice's original plan (4.2.212), as seems confirmed by Vindice's opening remarks, though his next speech twice refers to sitting (but perhaps 'sits' = is placed). Again, use of the 'discovery space' seems likely. If the Duke's body had been stowed in the alcove at the end of 3.5, the actor playing the Duke could be back in the same spot for the beginning of this scene, so that Vindice and Hippolito would need only to draw the curtains and arrange the Duke's posture. Holdsworth (1990) notes the references to 'this room' (28) and 'that sad room' (89), and also the echoes (which create an 'ironic counterpointing') of the discovery of Antonio's wife: with 5.1.88 and 100 compare 1.4.1 and 1.1.4–5.

4 **lay** bet

9 **returns** i.e. rhetorical variations for describing the situation; punning on 'returns' as the days for sheriff's reports (also 'returns') to the law court upon writs.

13 **flesh-flies** blow-flies, i.e. parasites, hangers-on

14 **against** in expectation of, until

15 **fly-flop** fly-swatter

18 **quaintly** ingeniously

19 **politician** schemer
in hugger-mugger in secret

20 **in catastrophe** in conclusion, as the final act of the tragedy. Vindice is dramatizing the situation to himself.

24 **open in** exhibit

26 **paint** as with cosmetics

41 **'Tis . . . slave** perhaps again recalling the proverb 'It is a wise child that know his own father'; compare 2.1.162 and note.

54 **mad-breast** a coinage on the analogy of 'mad-brain'; Lussurioso is complimenting Vindice on his bizarre wit; compare 2.2.82

56 **golls** hands

58 **nake** make naked, i.e. unsheath

LUSSURIOSO
Meet with him now.
VINDICE You'll bear us out, my lord?
LUSSURIOSO
Puh, am I a lord for nothing, think you? Quickly now.
VINDICE
Sa, sa, sa, thump!
[He stabs the corpse]
There he lies.
LUSSURIOSO
Nimbly done.
[He approaches the corpse]
Ha! O, villains, murderers,
'Tis the old Duke my father!
VINDICE That's a jest.
LUSSURIOSO What, stiff and cold already?
O, pardon me to call you from your names;
'Tis none of your deed. That villain Piato,
Whom you thought now to kill, has murdered him
And left him thus disguised.
HIPPOLITO And not unlikely.
VINDICE
O rascal! Was he not ashamed
To put the Duke into a greasy doublet?
LUSSURIOSO
He has been cold and stiff who knows how long?
VINDICE *[aside]* Marry, that do I.
LUSSURIOSO
No words, I pray, of anything intended.
VINDICE O, my lord.
HIPPOLITO I would fain have your lordship think that we have small reason to prate.
LUSSURIOSO
Faith, thou say'st true. I'll forthwith send to court,
For all the nobles, bastard, Duchess, all,
How here by miracle we found him dead,
And in his raiment that foul villain fled.
VINDICE That will be the best way, my lord, to clear us all.
Let's cast about to be clear.
LUSSURIOSO
Ho, Nencio, Sordido, and the rest!
Enter all [his attendants, including Sordido and Nencio and Guards]
SORDIDO My lord.
NENCIO My lord.
LUSSURIOSO
Be witnesses of a strange spectacle:
Choosing for private conference that sad room,
We found the Duke my father gealed in blood.
SORDIDO
My lord the Duke?—Run, hie thee, Nencio,
Startle the court by signifying so much.
[Exit Nencio]
VINDICE *[aside]*
Thus much by wit a deep revenger can,
When murder's known, to be the clearest man.
We're furthest off and with as bold an eye
Survey his body as the standers-by.
LUSSURIOSO
My royal father, too basely let blood
By a malevolent slave.
HIPPOLITO *[aside]* Hark,
He calls thee slave again.
VINDICE H'as lost; he may.
LUSSURIOSO
O sight! Look hither, see, his lips are gnawn
With poison.
VINDICE How, his lips? By th' mass, they be!
LUSSURIOSO
O villain, O rogue, O slave, O rascal!
HIPPOLITO *[aside]*
O good deceit, he quits him with like terms!
FIRST NOBLE *[within]* Where?
SECOND NOBLE *[within]* Which way?
[Enter Ambitioso and Supervacuo with Nobles and Gentlemen]
AMBITIOSO
Over what roof hangs this prodigious comet
In deadly fire?
LUSSURIOSO Behold, behold, my lords.
The Duke my father's murdered by a vassal
That owes this habit and here left disguised.
[Enter Duchess and Spurio]
DUCHESS
My lord and husband!
SECOND NOBLE Reverend majesty!
FIRST NOBLE
I have seen these clothes often attending on him.

61 **Meet with him** (*a*) encounter him as an enemy, (*b*) requite him
bear us out back us up (against any ensuing charge)
63 **Sa, sa, sa** exclamation used by fencers when delivering a thrust (French 'ça')
65 **That's a jest** i.e. you are surely not serious
67 **to . . . names** for using the wrong terms to describe you
72 **doublet** close-fitting body garment for men
78 **prate** gossip
79 **send** send a message
84 **cast . . . clear** contrive to be free from suspicion
85 **Nencio, Sordido** Italian for an idiot (with a possible pun on Latin *nuntius*, messenger) and for corrupt, absurd, unclean
90 **gealed** congealed
93 **deep** profoundly cunning
can can do
94 **clearest** (seemingly) most innocent
95 **furthest off** i.e. from suspicion
103 **quits** repays. Foakes suggests that Hippolito thinks of Lussurioso as addressing the Duke, who had called him 'villain, traitor' at 2.3.14.
106 **prodigious** ominous
comet This figurative reference to the portent of disaster and the death of a ruler foreshadows the actual appearance of the comet in 5.3. Ambitioso's burst of metaphor is essentially a high-flown and hypocritical exclamation of horror at the calamity.
109 **owes** owns
111 **these clothes** i.e. the man who wore these clothes, Piato

VINDICE [*aside*] That nobleman
Has been i'th' country, for he does not lie.
SUPERVACUO [*aside to Ambitioso*]
Learn of our mother. Let's dissemble too.
I am glad he's vanished; so I hope are you.
AMBITIOSO [*aside to Supervacuo*]
Ay, you may take my word for't.
SPURIO [*aside*] Old Dad dead?
I, one of his cast sins, will send the fates
Most hearty commendations by his own son.
I'll tug in the new stream till strength be done.
LUSSURIOSO
Where be those two that did affirm to us
My lord the Duke was privately rid forth?
FIRST GENTLEMAN
O, pardon us, my lords; he gave that charge
Upon our lives, if he were missed at court,
To answer so. He rode not anywhere.
We left him private with that fellow, here.
VINDICE [*aside*] Confirmed.
LUSSURIOSO
O heavens, that false charge was his death.
Impudent beggars! Durst you to our face
Maintain such a false answer? Bear him straight
To executïon.
FIRST GENTLEMAN
My lord!
LUSSURIOSO Urge me no more.
In this, the excuse may be called half the murder.
VINDICE
You've sentenced well.
LUSSURIOSO Away, see it be done.
[*Exit First Gentleman under guard*]
VINDICE [*aside*]
Could you not stick? See what confession doth.
Who would not lie, when men are hanged for truth?
HIPPOLITO [*aside to Vindice*]
Brother, how happy is our vengeance.
VINDICE [*aside to Hippolito*] Why, it hits
Past the apprehension of indifferent wits.
LUSSURIOSO My lord, let post horse be sent
Into all places to entrap the villain.
VINDICE [*aside*] Post horse, ha, ha!
[FIRST] NOBLE
My lord, we're something bold to know our duty.
Your father's accidentally departed.
The titles that were due to him meet you.
LUSSURIOSO
Meet me? I'm not at leisure, my good lord.
I've many griefs to dispatch out o'th' way.
[*Aside*] Welcome, sweet titles!—Talk to me, my lords
Of sepulchres and mighty emperors' bones;
That's thought for me.
VINDICE [*aside*] So, one may see by this
How sov'reign markets go:
Courtiers have feet o'th' nines and tongues o'th'
twelves.
They flatter dukes and dukes flatter themselves.
[SECOND] NOBLE
My lord, it is your shine must comfort us.
LUSSURIOSO
Alas, I shine in tears, like the sun in April.
[FIRST] NOBLE You're now my lord's grace.
LUSSURIOSO
My lord's grace? I perceive you'll have it so.
[SECOND] NOBLE 'Tis but your own.
LUSSURIOSO
Then heavens give me grace to be so.
VINDICE [*aside*]
He prays well for himself.
[FIRST] NOBLE [*to the Duchess*]
Madam, all sorrows
Must run their circles into joys. No doubt but time
Will make the murderer bring forth himself.
VINDICE [*aside*]
He were an ass then, i'faith.
[FIRST] NOBLE In the mean season,
Let us bethink the latest funeral honours
Due to the Duke's cold body, and withal—
Calling to memory our new happiness
Spread in his royal son—lords, gentlemen,
Prepare for revels.

112–13 **That...lie** alluding to the proverbial contrast between court deceit and country simplicity and truth
117 **cast** (*a*) discarded; (*b*) disseminated (the sins being linked to the Duke's indiscriminate sowing of his seed)
117–18 **will...son** i.e. he will kill Ambitioso, as he does in 5.3
119 **tug** as on an oar; i.e. he will strive for his own advantage in this new current of events
126 **Confirmed** probably meaning both 'True enough' and 'My innocence is confirmed'
131 **excuse** i.e. the excuse the Gentleman provided for the Duke's absence
133 **stick** stop talking; the whole line has ironic application to Vindice's own final inability to remain silent about the Duke's death.
136 **indifferent wits** ordinary intellects
137 **post horse** speedy riders
140 **we're...duty** we are rather eager (to the point of risking impertinence) to know where our allegiance now lies
147–8 **So...go** This is presumably Vindice's sardonic comment on Lussurioso's feigned unwillingness to accept the dukedom, but the exact meaning is obscure. Foakes, citing the proverb 'You may know by the market men how the markets go', suggests that Vindice means 'that as the new duke behaves, so his courtiers will follow suit'. But Vindice's point seems to concern market strategy: by pretending to be a reluctant 'buyer' Lussurioso encourages the 'sellers' to be more pressing. 'Sov'reign markets' are, punningly, the best markests and markets in monarchs and in gold coins.
149 **Courtiers...twelves** i.e. courtiers' flattering tongues are three sizes larger than their feet (perhaps with a submerged pun on the tongue of a boot or shoe)
153 **my lord's grace** a courtesy-title given to a duke
160 **mean season** meantime
164 **Spread** extended; the 'royal son' spreads happiness, as the sun its warming rays; the preposition 'in' is used (rather than 'by') because his subjects are happy in this son/sun

VINDICE [*aside*] Revels?
[FIRST] NOBLE Time hath several falls;
Griefs lift up joys, feasts put down funerals.
LUSSURIOSO
Come then, my lords; my favours to you all.
[*Aside*] The Duchess is suspected foully bent.
I'll begin dukedom with her banishment.
Exeunt Duke [*Lussurioso, Sordido*], *Nobles,* [*Gentlemen, Attendants bearing the old Duke's body*], *and Duchess*
HIPPOLITO [*to Vindice*]
Revels!
VINDICE [*to Hippolito*]
Ay, that's the word; we are firm yet.
Strike one strain more and then we crown our wit.
Exeunt brothers Vindice and Hippolito
SPURIO [*aside*] Well, have at the fairest mark!—So said the Duke when he begot me—
And if I miss his heart or near about,
Then have at any; a bastard scorns to be out. [*Exit*]
SUPERVACUO Not'st thou that Spurio, brother?
AMBITIOSO Yes, I note him to our shame.
SUPERVACUO He shall not live. His hair shall not grow much longer. In this time of revels, tricks may be set afoot. Seest thou yon new moon? It shall outlive the new Duke by much.
This hand shall dispossess him, then we're mighty.
A masque is treason's licence—that build upon.
'Tis murder's best face when a visor's on. *Exit*
AMBITIOSO
Is't so? 'Tis very good.
And do you think to be duke then, kind brother?
I'll see fair play: drop one and there lies t'other. *Exit*

5.2 *Enter Vindice and Hippolito with Piero and other Lords*

VINDICE
My lords, be all of music; strike old griefs
Into other countries
That flow in too much milk and have faint livers,
Not daring to stab home their discontents.
Let our hid flames break out as fire, as lightning,
To blast this villainous dukedom vexed with sin.
Wind up your souls to their full height again.
PIERO
How?
FIRST LORD
Which way?
SECOND LORD Any way. Our wrongs are such,
We cannot justly be revenged too much.
VINDICE
You shall have all enough. Revels are toward,
And those few nobles that have long suppressed you
Are busied to the furnishing of a masque
And do affect to make a pleasant tale on't.
The masquing suits are fashioning. Now comes in
That which must glad us all—we to take pattern
Of all those suits, the colour, trimming, fashion,
E'en to an undistinguished hair almost;
Then, ent'ring first, observing the true form,
Within a strain or two we shall find leisure
To steal our swords out handsomely
And, when they think their pleasure sweet and good,
In midst of all their joys they shall sigh blood.
PIERO Weightily, effectually.
THIRD LORD Before the t'other masquers come—
VINDICE We're gone, all done and past.
PIERO
But how for the Duke's guard?
VINDICE Let that alone;
By one and one their strengths shall be drunk down.
HIPPOLITO
There are five hundred gentlemen in the action
That will apply themselves and not stand idle.
PIERO
O, let us hug your bosoms!
VINDICE Come, my lords,
Prepare for deeds; let other times have words.
Exeunt

165 **falls** In view of 'lift up' and 'put down', the most obvious meaning must be operative here; one might paraphrase, 'time produces different kinds of overthrow'.
166 **Griefs . . . funerals** griefs enhance joy, and feasts overcome the sadness of funerals
168 **foully bent** lewdly inclined
170 **firm** secure
171 **Strike . . . more** play one more tune or theme; i.e. perform one more action
172 **have at** a colloquial declaration of intent, as at 3.5.138
mark target (i.e. Lussurioso, the new duke); vulva (when applied to what the Duke said)
175 **out** out of the game, without office or influence
183 **masque** an entertainment at festive occasions at court or in great halls; it consisted of dancing and acting, performers being masked or visored.
5.2.1–2 **My . . . countries** continuing the music imagery from 5.1 and quibbling on 'strike' as 'play (a tune)'
3 **flow . . . milk** i.e. are too mild and gentle
livers punning on 'liver' as 'inhabitant' and as the seat of violent passions and courage
7 **Wind up** This image of preparation for action might be of a windlass (suggested in 'height') or of the tightening of a crossbow or strings of a musical instrument.
10 **toward** in preparation
13 **affect** aspire
tale i.e. the allegorical narrative of the masque
18 **observing . . . form** keeping to the set order of the dance
19 **strain** measure
20 **handsomely** 'conveniently' as well as 'elegantly'
23 **Weightily, effectually** i.e. the victims will sigh heavily and to good effect (i.e. they will die)
27 **drunk down** overcome by drink

5.3

In a dumb show, the possessing of the young Duke Lussurioso with all his Nobles; then sounding music. A furnished table is brought forth; then enters the Duke and his Nobles to the banquet

FIRST NOBLE
Many harmonious hours and choicest pleasures
Fill up the royal numbers of your years.

LUSSURIOSO
My lords, we're pleased to thank you, though we know
'Tis but your duty now to wish it so.

SECOND NOBLE
That shine makes us all happy.

THIRD NOBLE [*aside to other Nobles*]
His grace frowns.

SECOND NOBLE [*aside to other Nobles*]
Yet we must say he smiles.

FIRST NOBLE [*aside to other Nobles*]
I think we must.

LUSSURIOSO [*aside*]
That foul, incontinent Duchess we have banished.
The bastard shall not live. After these revels
I'll begin strange ones. He and the stepsons
Shall pay their lives for the first subsidies.
We must not frown so soon, else 't'ad been now.

FIRST NOBLE
My gracious lord, please you prepare for pleasure;
The masque is not far off.

LUSSURIOSO
We are for pleasure.

A blazing star appeareth

Beshrew thee! What art thou mad'st me start?
Thou hast committed treason.—A blazing star!

FIRST NOBLE
A blazing star? O, where, my lord?

LUSSURIOSO
Spy out.

SECOND NOBLE
See, see, my lords, a wondrous dreadful one.

LUSSURIOSO
I am not pleased at that ill-knotted fire,
That bushing, flaring star. Am not I duke?
It should not quake me now. Had it appeared
Before it, I might then have justly feared.
But yet they say, whom art and learning weds,
When stars wear locks they threaten great men's heads.
Is it so? You are read, my lords.

FIRST NOBLE
May it please your grace,
It shows great anger.

LUSSURIOSO
That does not please our grace.

SECOND NOBLE
Yet here's the comfort my lord: many times,
When it seems most, it threatens farthest off.

LUSSURIOSO
Faith, and I think so too.

FIRST NOBLE
Beside, my lord,
You're gracefully established with the loves
Of all your subjects; and for natural death,
I hope it will be threescore years a-coming.

LUSSURIOSO True. No more but threescore years?

FIRST NOBLE
Fourscore, I hope, my lord.

SECOND NOBLE
And fivescore, I.

THIRD NOBLE
But 'tis my hope, my lord, you shall ne'er die.

LUSSURIOSO
Give me thy hand. These others I rebuke.
He that hopes so is fittest for a duke.
Thou shalt sit next me. Take your places, lords.
We're ready now for sports; let 'em set on.
[*To the blazing star*] You thing, we shall forget you quite anon.

THIRD NOBLE
I hear 'em coming, my lord.

5.3.0.1–4 ***In . . . banquet*** Lussurioso and his entourage enter twice, first for the dumb-show of his enthronement and then for the banquet. The initial mime might perhaps use all available actors, but Lussurioso sits at table with only the three nobles who speak and who are killed with him at 5.3.41.2. In performance, the First and Second Noble may have been Sordido and Nencio, though at 5.1.85 these two named characters seem to be thought of as attendants rather than nobles.

0.1 ***possessing*** putting in possession, formal investiture

0.2 ***sounding*** resounding, sonorous

5 **shine** smiling aspect, implying the conventional analogy between ruler and sun

10 **subsidies** payment; a subsidy was literally a levy exacted by a monarch, or a fiscal aid granted to him or her by parliament.

11 **else . . . now** or else it would have been now (that I should have ordered their execution)

13.1 ***A blazing star*** a common Jacobean stage effect, consisting 'either of a firework on a line or flaming material suspended in an iron cage or cresset, and burned for up to a minute' (Holdsworth)

14 **thee . . . thou** Lussurioso apostrophizes the planet.

15 **committed treason** i.e. by threatening him, since comets portended princes' deaths

17 **dreadful** a stronger word than now: 'full of dread'

18 **ill-knotted** looking forward to the image of hair in line 23

19 **bushing** growing thick (used of hair, or, figuratively, of a comet's tail)

21 **it** my becoming duke

22 **whom . . . weds** who combine skill and learning

23 **When . . . locks** i.e. when they are comets

24 **read** well read

27 **seems most** is most manifest, makes the greatest display

Enter the masque of revengers, the two brothers Vindice and Hippolito, and two Lords more

LUSSURIOSO [*aside*] Ah, 'tis well.
Brothers and bastard, you dance next in hell.

The revengers dance; at the end, steal out their swords, and these four kill the four at the table in their chairs. It thunders

VINDICE Mark, thunder!
Dost know thy cue, thou big-voiced crier?
Dukes' groans are thunder's watchwords.

HIPPOLITO So, my lords,
You have enough.

VINDICE
Come, let's away, no ling'ring.

HIPPOLITO Follow! [*To the two Lords*] Go!

Exeunt Hippolito and the two Lords

VINDICE
No power is angry when the lustful die.
When thunder claps heaven likes the tragedy. *Exit*

Enter the other masque of intended murderers, stepsons Ambitioso and Supervacuo, Bastard Spurio, and a Fourth Man, coming in dancing. The Duke Lussurioso recovers a little in voice and groans—calls, 'A guard! Treason!' At which they all start out of their measure and, turning towards the table, they find them all to be murdered

LUSSURIOSO
O, O!

SPURIO
Whose groan was that?

LUSSURIOSO Treason! A guard!

AMBITIOSO
How now, all murdered?

SUPERVACUO Murdered!

FOURTH NOBLE
And those his nobles!

AMBITIOSO [*aside*] Here's a labour saved;
I thought to have sped him.—'Sblood, how came this?

SUPERVACUO
Then I proclaim myself; now I am Duke.

AMBITIOSO
Thou Duke? Brother thou liest.

[*He stabs Supervacuo*]

SPURIO Slave, so dost thou.

[*He stabs Ambitioso*]

FOURTH NOBLE
Base villain, hast thou slain my lord and master?

[*He stabs Spurio*]

Enter the first men, [*Vindice, Hippolito, and the two Lords of the masque of revengers*]

VINDICE
Pistols, treason, murder, help, guard! My lord
The Duke!

[*Enter Antonio with Attendants and Guards*]

HIPPOLITO Lay hold upon this traitor.

[*Guards seize the Fourth Noble*]

LUSSURIOSO O!

VINDICE
Alas, the Duke is murdered.

HIPPOLITO And the nobles.

VINDICE
Surgeons, surgeons! [*Aside*] Heart, does he breath so long?

ANTONIO
A piteous tragedy, able to make
An old man's eyes bloodshot.

LUSSURIOSO O!

VINDICE
Look to my lord the Duke. [*Aside*] A vengeance throttle him!—
Confess, thou murd'rous and unhallowed man,
Didst thou kill all these?

FOURTH NOBLE None but the bastard, I.

VINDICE
How came the Duke slain, then?

FOURTH NOBLE We found him so.

LUSSURIOSO
O, villain—

VINDICE Hark.

LUSSURIOSO Those in the masque did murder us.

VINDICE La you now, sir.
O, marble impudence! Will you confess now?

FOURTH NOBLE
'Sblood, 'tis all false.

ANTONIO Away with that foul monster,
Dipped in a prince's blood.

FOURTH NOBLE Heart, 'tis a lie.

40.2 ***two Lords more*** Presumably Piero is one of these, and returns with Vindice and Hippolito at 5.3.55.2

41 **dance ... hell** already pointing to the symbolism of the dance of masquers as a Dance of Death

42–3 **Mark ... crier?** This aural omen, following on the visual, is addressed with a levity that complicates its status and effect: 'cue' gestures knowingly towards the sound-effects men in the tiring-house; then God/Jove is reduced to town or court crier; and by line 48 he has become a satisfied spectator at a play: the idea of God as judicial spectator of the world stage is orthodox and commonplace, but there is a certain flippancy in Vindice's tone.

44 **watchwords** signals to begin an attack

45 **enough** i.e. enough revenge

48 **claps** punning on applause and a clap of thunder

48.4–7 ***The Duke ... murdered*** This second half of Middleton's long stage direction simply foreshadows the dialogue and action that follow.

52 **sped** killed

57.1 ***Enter ... Guards*** Since the Guards are needed to take away the Fourth Noble at 5.3.72.1 and Vindice and Hippolito at 5.3.125.1, unless Antonio is accompanied by other attendants he will have nobody to whom to address the play's closing lines. Presumably all available members of the cast enter with him here.

59 **Heart** exclamation (from 'God's heart')

68 **La you now** a mild exclamation

69 **marble** hardened

ANTONIO
Let him have bitter executïon.
[*Exit Fourth Noble under guard*]

VINDICE [*aside*]
New marrow! No, I cannot be expressed.—
How fares my lord the Duke?

LUSSURIOSO Farewell to all.
He that climbs highest has the greatest fall.
My tongue is out of office.

VINDICE Air, gentlemen, air!
[*They step back*]
[*Whispering to Lussurioso*] Now thou'lt not prate on't,
'twas Vindice murdered thee—

LUSSURIOSO O!

VINDICE
Murdered thy father—

LUSSURIOSO O!

VINDICE And I am he.
[*Lussurioso dies*]
Tell nobody.—So, so, the Duke's departed.

ANTONIO
It was a deadly hand that wounded him.
The rest, ambitious who should rule and sway,
After his death were so made all away.

VINDICE
My lord was unlikely.

HIPPOLITO Now the hope
Of Italy lies in your reverend years.

VINDICE
Your hair will make the silver age again,
When there was fewer but more honest men.

ANTONIO
The burden's weighty and will press age down.
May I so rule that heaven may keep the crown.

VINDICE
The rape of your good lady has been 'quited
With death on death.

ANTONIO Just is the law above.
But of all things it puts me most to wonder
How the old Duke came murdered.

VINDICE O, my lord.

ANTONIO
It was the strangeliest carried; I ne'er heard of the
like.

HIPPOLITO
'Twas all done for the best, my lord.

VINDICE
All for your grace's good. We may be bold
To speak it now. 'Twas somewhat witty-carried,
Though we say it. 'Twas we two murdered him.

ANTONIO You two?

VINDICE
None else, i'faith, my lord. Nay, 'twas well managed.

ANTONIO
Lay hands upon those villains.
[*Guards seize Vindice and Hippolito*]

VINDICE How, on us?

ANTONIO
Bear 'em to speedy executïon.

VINDICE
Heart, was't not for your good, my lord?

ANTONIO My good?
Away with 'em. Such an old man as he!
You that would murder him would murder me.

VINDICE
Is't come about?

HIPPOLITO 'Sfoot, brother, you begun.

VINDICE
May not we set as well as the Duke's son?
Thou hast no conscience; are we not revenged?
Is there one enemy left alive amongst those?
'Tis time to die when we are ourselves our foes.
When murd'rers shut deeds close, this curse does seal
'em:
If none disclose 'em they themselves reveal 'em.
This murder might have slept in tongueless brass,
But for ourselves, and the world died an ass.
Now I remember too, here was Piato
Brought forth a knavish sentence once:
'No doubt', said he, 'but time
Will make the murderer bring forth himself'.
'Tis well he died; he was a witch.
And now, my lord, since we are in for ever,

73 **marrow** used figuratively to mean 'delicious food for my revenge' (bone marrow being considered a delicacy)
be expressed put my feelings into words
84 **unlikely** unsuitable
86 **silver age** in classical mythology a time of simplicity and happiness; with a pun on Antonio's grey-white hair
89 **keep** protect
90 **'quited** requited, avenged
97 **witty-carried** cleverly executed
105 **come about** turned out so, but the phrase catches the sense of sudden reversal
106 **set** die, punning on 'son'/'sun'
107 **conscience** (*a*) sense of what is right, (*b*) understanding, (*c*) conviction. The word may well be used in ironic awareness of the contradictions, in the context, among the available meanings.
109 **'Tis time to die** recalling 'a time to be born, and a time to die' in Ecclesiastes, 3:2
110–11 **When . . . 'em** a variation on the proverbial 'Murder will out'; 'seal 'em' = seal their fate
112 **brass** the memorial tablets for the victims
114–17 **Now . . . himself** The sententious remark ('sentence') was really the First Noble's; Vindice's recognition here is of the irony of his response to it: 'He were an ass then, i'faith' (5.1.160); though not disguised as Piato, he did speak in an aside.
118 **witch** because of his prophetic powers
119 **are in** are involved in the business

This work was ours, which else might have been slipped,
And, if we list, we could have nobles clipped
And go for less than beggars; but we hate
To bleed so cowardly. We have enough, i'faith:
We're well, our mother turned, our sister true;
We die after a nest of dukes. Adieu.
Exeunt [Vindice and Hippolito under guard]

ANTONIO
How subtly was that murder closed! Bear up
Those tragic bodies. 'Tis a heavy season.
Pray heaven their blood may wash away all treason.
Exeunt

Finis

120 **slipped** neglected
121 **list** chose
nobles clipped noblemen beheaded (for their part in the masque of revengers); punning on the 'clipping' or fraudulent paring of the edges of the gold coins known as nobles
124 **turned** converted
125 **nest of dukes** suggesting a nest of snakes
126 **closed** concealed
126–7 **Bear ... bodies** Since 5.3 has turned seven characters into corpses, any attempt to get them all off the stage would involve either ludicrous comings and goings or at least fourteen bearers, so presumably the play ends without Antonio's command having been put into effect. At the Globe the actors playing the slaughtered men would simply have risen to take their bows.

YOUR FIVE GALLANTS

Text edited by Ralph Alan Cohen with John Jowett, annotated and introduced by Ralph Alan Cohen

Your Five Gallants plays better than it reads. This is especially true of the 1608 quarto edition printed by George Eld, the only version of the text available until 232 years later when Alexander Dyce published *The Works of Middleton*. Eld's quarto breaks the promise of the title-page to give the reader the play 'As it hath beene often in Action at the Black-friers' by transposing two of the play's scenes and thereby badly knotting up a story with an already tangled narrative line. Even leaving aside the sins of Eld's print shop, *Your Five Gallants* is a play in which Thomas Middleton's strengths as a playwright are not readily apparent on the printed page. Indeed, *Your Five Gallants* is worth serious consideration partly because it illustrates not only that a playwright can write a good play without leaving on the printed page many traces of the genius we associate with his most famous works, but also that the theatrical dimension invisible to us on the page can even be stronger in plays that appear 'thin' textually.

Your Five Gallants resembles Middleton's other early city comedies: it works as much to exhibit (or expose) the manners of contemporary London as to tell a story. For the contemporary Londoner the imagined city setting was not just the backdrop for these plays; it was the unseen connection between characters and the understood motivation for their behaviour. In part, these plays amounted to staged versions of prose works like Thomas Dekker's *The Gull's Hornbook* or the numerous writings of Robert Greene (whose motto Middleton glances at 1.1.205–6). These popular books warned of the follies and vices of the City in the same way that native New Yorkers complain proudly of the perils of Manhattan. Londoners who went to *Your Five Gallants* no more expected to see Aristotle's rules observed than does the viewer who turns on the television to watch comedy sketches from *Saturday Night Live* or Monty Python. What they expected to see was a comic representation of their world. Accordingly, in *Your Five Gallants* Middleton not only gave them characters drawn from London life, he also put those characters into familiar and specific places such as a gaming room at the Mitre tavern (2.4) and the middle aisle of St Paul's Cathedral (4.4). For Middleton's audience at the Blackfriars—some gentry, some law students from the Inns of Court, some from London's growing middle class, but all 'gallants'—much of the fun in the play derives from the same kind of topographical humour in any fraternity or college skit: they laughed to see themselves and their haunts staged.

Nevertheless, *Your Five Gallants* can succeed with modern audience unfamiliar with the world of early seventeenth-century London. In October 1991, *Your Five Gallants* was produced in James Madison University's Theater II, a 'black box' theatre—as far as we know, the only revival so far of the play. The rules of this production were meant to duplicate what might have been the case at an intimate indoor theatre of the Renaissance: universal lighting, an audience on three sides, two entrances upstage, a bare stage, a space 'above', a company of twelve (during the masque, the play requires seventeen people, but three of those have no lines), and a duration of two hours not including a ten-minute 'interlude'. In the context of university theatre, public response is hard to measure, but the reception of the play was more than usually enthusiastic. Maximum seating capacity was 140. Four of the six shows were sold out; opening night and the Saturday matinee drew over 100; and the production almost doubled the gate for any of the other sixteen shows in that space during the 1991–2 academic year. *Your Five Gallants* attracted and held those audiences because Middleton is a master of those aspects of the theatrical medium that do not readily appear on the page. In particular, Middleton's reliance on blocking, props, and costume—none of which are visible to a reader—results in a play that works on the stage in a way it cannot work on the page.

As to blocking, we cannot know how the Blackfriars Children (who staged the play in 1606 or 1607) arranged the movement of the actors, but three long scenes in which most of the play's characters remain on-stage (2.1 at Primero's bawdy-house, 2.4 at the Mitre tavern, and the final scene with its mock masque) show that Middleton designed the play to give his audience a crowded stage with a multiplicity of actions. When such group scenes occur in Shakespeare's works, they focus on main characters or on some central situation. For example, however many characters may be on stage for the Boar's Head scene in *1 Henry IV*, Falstaff and Hal are the focus of attention. Other large scenes such as the trial in *Merchant of Venice* or the assassination of Caesar or the 'Pyramus and Thisbe' scene point to one business. Even Ben Jonson, whose plays, like Middleton's, crowd a large number of characters into an imagined setting such as Smithfield in *Bartholomew Fair*, filters the action through some central observer (Adam Overdo) whose comments can help a reader's orientation. By contrast, in Middleton's play, there is no single business. The scene at Primero's bawdy-house, for example, comprises no fewer than twenty-four distinct actions; and, as the title of the play with its promise of five major characters suggests, there is neither a central character nor a central point of view. Such a carousel of activity, though difficult to follow on the page, is wonderfully abundant entertainment in the theatre where the space itself holds all the characters together and where an audience knows immediately what the silent characters in a scene are doing.

In the play's three crowded scenes, moreover, Middleton shows a variety of designs for the action. In Primero's brothel the movement is largely centripetal; Primero acts as a sort of ringmaster while the gallants and their whores move in pairs by turns to centre stage. By contrast, in the scene at the Mitre tavern, the movement appears to be centrifugal. The central action is the dice game where the gallants and the two gulls are gaming, but throughout the scene various actions—Tailby and Bungler pawning things to Frip for gambling money, Goldstone setting up scams, the Boy supplying Pursenet with money stolen from the players—spin off to the apron of the stage. Finally, the rules of the masque choreograph the dance-like movement of the last scene. Together these three scenes demonstrate Middleton's advanced understanding of stage movement and of the need for visual variety; they are non-verbal proofs of his theatrical ingenuity.

Your Five Gallants thus achieves on the stage a satisfying multiplicity that is difficult to perceive in the more linear medium of print. Nor does this multiplicity come at the cost of unity, because Middleton uses costumes and props as a visual glue to hold the various parts of the play together. For example, Goldstone filches a cloak from Fitzgrave (disguised as 'Bowser') and then pawns the cloak to Frip, whose practice of wearing his clients' pawned clothes gets him into trouble when Pursenet, seeing the cloak, mistakes him for Fitzgrave ('Bowser') and attacks him, at which point Fitzgrave himself enters and accuses Frip of theft. The sight of the cloak connects these characters and does so in a way that reminds an audience of their roles in the story—Goldstone, the shameless and lucky con-man; Frip, the conscienceless pawnbroker; Pursenet, the hot-headed and unlucky highwayman; and Fitzgrave, the victimized representative of true gallantry.

The play's key property—in the sense both of a possession and of a stage prop—is the chain of pearls that Fitzgrave gives to Katherine in the second scene of the play. Pursenet's Boy steals the chain of pearls from Katherine, and an audience watches it go from Katherine to the Boy, who gives it to Pursenet, who gives it to his whore, who gives it to Tailby, who has it robbed by Pursenet, who drops it to be found by Goldstone, who (rather than be arrested for stealing it) returns it to Pursenet, who pawns it to Frip, who presents it to Katherine, who recognizes it as 'the very chain of pearl was filched from me!' In this way, the chain of pearls, largely invisible to the reader, strings together the disparate parts of the play for the audience and simultaneously helps to provide the play's thematic content. When Pursenet discovers that he has stolen from Tailby the same chain of pearls that he had given to his whore, he reacts with a speech that sums up the vanity of possession while it connects that theme firmly to that chain of pearls (which, as a circle made up of circles, is an emblem of the circle of possession):

> Does my boy pick and I steal to enrich myself, to keep her, to maintain him? Why this is the right sequence of the world: a lord maintains her, she maintains a knight, he maintains a whore, she maintains a captain. So, in like manner, the pocket keeps my boy, he keeps me, I keep her, she keeps him; it runs like quicksilver from one to another. (3.1.131–8)

The ambiguous pronouns—he, she, her, him, one, another—clearly extend beyond the world of the play, and, in an acting space where the spectators are lit equally with the actors, such a speech irresistibly suggests to an actor that he search the audience for his referents. In the James Madison University production, Pursenet started pointing to different audience members to illustrate each noun and pronoun from 'a lord maintains her' through to the end of the speech. This assertion of a connection between the fictive and the real worlds was one of the production's funniest and most successful moments. It is a moment designed by a playwright who uses his understanding of the acting space, the actors, and the audience to comment on the fluidity of his social world and its relationship to property.

Middleton sets up this revelation about property from the play's first scene in Frip's pawn shop, a scene which takes over fifteen minutes in performance but which, until its final minute, does not even mention the play's main plot, the wooing of Katherine. What the scene does instead is show Frip, the pawnbroker, at work, and through him and his profession it allows Middleton to introduce the theme of the instability of property. Frip recites how much he lent out for certain specific pieces of clothing. He rejects clothes from a parish where he fears the plague is too active. He gives a small pawn for a gentlewoman's clothes. He welcomes Primero, the bawd, who has come to find clothing for his latest recruit. Frip offers to trade him clothes for lessons in a card trick. When Primero's young prostitute arrives, Frip gets her favour by showing her the clothes. Finally, Frip chooses a suit of pawned clothing to wear for the 'wooing business' at Katherine's. Broken into these parts, the scene is about clothing and money, clothing and the plague, clothing and card tricks, clothing and declined gentry, clothing and sex, clothing and sex again, and clothing and ambition.

In short, Middleton seems to have chosen to postpone any storyline for an atmospheric scene that would associate the vices and ills of London—greed, the plague, gambling, prostitution—with clothes that go from hand to hand. Having established that association, Middleton makes the continual exchange of clothes a metaphor for all of the other contagious ills of society: what goes around, comes around.

Middleton embodies this wisdom in his characterization of Tailby, the ladies' man who is a sort of seventeenth-century precursor of the surfer and who expresses his 'easy come, easy go' approach in his nonchalance about fortune either good or bad. At Primero's bawdy-house (2.1), the women compete to give him valuables. He asks them for nothing; they simply provide. Later at the Mitre tavern, he literally loses his shirt at the gambling table, but in the next scene, before he even gets out of bed, an unnamed mistress sends him a suit of clothes. And while his servant Jack is dressing him, Tailby remembers that he 'pawned a good beaver hat to master Frip last night' and adds that he feels 'the want of it now'. Precisely at that moment a knock at the door announces Mistress Newblock's servant, and we discover that she has sent Tailby 'a beaver hat—with a band best in fashion' (Interim 2.51–2). Tailby, so beloved of whores, happily accepts the idea that fortune is a strumpet, and Middleton makes him an emblem for the theme of the fickleness of property and the meaninglessness of finery.

Unlike Jonson, however, who uses his city comedies to apply the 'iron rod' to vice, Middleton is rarely the moralist, and whatever moral instruction *Your Five Gallants* provides is muted by the play's general good-naturedness. Tailby and Pursenet in particular are endearing rogues. Tailby is so worldly that he has reached a Zen-like state of calm and generosity, and Pursenet is a highwayman who is as naïve about the world as he is inept at his profession. He seems genuinely shocked by the world's bad manners: he objects to the victim who fights back—''Sfoot, this gull lays on without fear or wit' (3.2.3–4); he complains of a mark who, by keeping one hand in a pocket at a greeting, makes stealing a purse difficult—'are we grown so beasts, do we salute by halves?' (4.4.29–32); and he fumes at his courtesan for her infidelity—'you are a strumpet!' (3.4.22–3). Her amused reply—'O, news abroad, sir... you knew that the first night you lay with me' (3.4.22–3)—puts into perspective Pursenet's self-righteousness and is one of several occasions in the play when the whores in the play, whom Middleton has simply designated as '1 Courtesan', '2 Courtesan', '3 Courtesan', and 'Novice', assert their individuality. Middleton's portrayal of them, as for example at the beginning of Act 5 when they voice their resentment of privileged amateurs like Mistress Newcut, is neither judgemental nor sentimental, and contributes to the overall geniality of the play.

Throughout *Your Five Gallants* Middleton enhances that quality of detached good humour by acknowledging with a sort of metatheatrical wink the conventions of the theatre. When Primero reminds Frip at the end of the first scene that they have forgotten the 'wooing business', the playwright seems almost to say with a wink, 'oops, nearly forgot the plot!' In doing so, he reminds the audience of the playwright's prerogatives in the construction of his play. Twice, Middleton plays games with the arbitrariness of stage time. At the end of 4.1, when Goldstone exits with a cloak he has stolen from Fitzgrave's lodging and Frip enters instantly wearing the same cloak, Middleton has treated his Blackfriars audience to a theatrical 'jump cut' that derives its humour as much from the elasticity of theatrical time as it does from the joke that Frip is a fence who automatically ends up wearing any stolen property. Similarly, Middleton gives his audience a metatheatrical 'nudge nudge' when he has Pursenet suddenly shift from Tailby's London lodging to the geographically distant locale of Coombe Park in 3.1; whether this is managed on stage by an exit and immediate re-entry or, as seems more likely, by movement over the stage, the representation of time and space become the subject of a joke in itself. Middleton actually stresses his creative geography by having Pursenet refer to the speed of his movement from one scene to another: 'Walk my horse', he says to the Boy, 'behind yon thicket—' (3.1.34), and then he boasts to the audience of his 'gelding's celerity over hedge and ditch' (3.1.38–40).

These moments in which Middleton shares the fun of the theatre game with his audience are more than incidental to an understanding of how *Your Five Gallants* works on the stage—as 'in-jokes' they link the playwright to audience and the audience to one another. To understand the effect of such moments imagine the original production in its Blackfriars setting. Surrounding a platform on at least three sides was an audience of London's 'night people'—people with the leisure, the daring, and the resources to brave the city after dark, they were the equivalent of the club world in a big city. On-stage they saw a company of children speaking as they speak, dressing as they dress, and pursuing the activities that they themselves pursue, perhaps that very night. Around the stage they saw themselves; on the stage they saw themselves in miniature. Even the title of the play—*Your Five Gallants*—implicated them, London's gallantry, in the world before them and made them responsible for it: they were watching *their* 'five gallants'.

In the context of this gallery of mirror images, Middleton's constant reminders of the artifice of playmaking—the admitted postponement of the main plot, the absurd coincidences, the toying with theatrical time—serve to remind his audience that they are indeed looking in a mirror. That effect culminates in the masque which both resolves and concludes the play. In the three years since the Stuart royal family had come into their new kingdom, their delight in masques had made the form an ever more fashionable entertainment, and the appeal of masques to his upwardly mobile audience gave Middleton a voguish metatheatical tool—an entertainment within an entertainment—to extend the mirroring effect in the play. As the indoor sport of royalty, the masque also lends a kind of authority to the true gallant, Fitzgrave, who uses it as a trap for the five false gallants. What Fitzgrave calls their 'large impudence' entices Frip, Primero, Goldstone, Pursenet, and Tailby to believe that they should participate in a princely entertainment, but they lack the wit and the Latin to recognize the roles that they are playing. Since they cannot see themselves in the mirror of their own theatrical entertainment, the masque exposes them as rogues and simultaneously separates them from the true gallants in the audience, or at least from those true gallants with the wisdom to see themselves in Middleton's play.

Middleton aimed to put on a good show, and he wrought from the materials of theatre—performance, space, time, audience, and the event itself—a play which gives ample proof of his skill as dramatist. That skill brought to the stage a coherent and memorable work of contemporary satire. Readers who approach *Your Five Gallants* with the theatre and Middleton's audience clearly in mind will find a play well worth the reading. When the Victorian Anthony Trollope condemned the work as 'tedious' and 'bad', he had read it without seeing it. He missed the show.

SEE ALSO
Music and dance: *Companion*, 143
Textual introduction and apparatus: *Companion*, 575
Authorship and date: *Companion*, 363

Your Five Gallants

[*for the Children of the Chapel at The Blackfriars*]

THE PERSONS OF THE PLAY

PRESENTER

PRIMERO, the bawd-gallant
FRIP, the broker-gallant
TAILBY, the whore-gallant
PURSENET, the pocket-gallant
GOLDSTONE, the cheating-gallant

KATHERINE, an heiress

FITZGRAVE, a gentleman, later disguised as Bowser
BUNGLER, a gentleman from the country
PIAMONT, a gentleman
FIRST GENTLEMAN-GALLANT
SECOND GENTLEMAN-GALLANT
FIRST ANCIENT GENTLEMAN
SECOND ANCIENT GENTLEMAN

NOVICE Courtesan
FIRST COURTESAN
SECOND COURTESAN
THIRD COURTESAN

Mistress NEWCUT, a merchant's wife

VINTNER
FIRST DRAWER
SECOND DRAWER
TAILOR
PAINTER
FIRST FELLOW } clients of Frip
SECOND FELLOW } clients of Frip
FIRST CONSTABLE
SECOND CONSTABLE

Pursenet's BOY
Primero's BOY
ARTHUR, Frip's servant
JACK, Tailby's servant
FULK, Goldstone's servant

Hieronimo Bedlam, KATHERINE'S SERVANT
MARMADUKE, Mistress Newcut's Servant
MISTRESS CLEVELAND'S SERVANT
MISTRESS NEWBLOCK'S SERVANT
MISTRESS TIFFANY'S SERVANT

Prologue *Presenter or prologue [enters. The action on stage happens as he announces it]*

PRESENTER Passing over the stage: the bawd-gallant, with three wenches gallantly attired; meets him the whore-gallant, the pocket-gallant, the cheating-gallant; kiss these three wenches and depart in a little whisper and wanton action. Now, for the other, the broker-gallant, he sits at home yet, I warrant you, at this time of day, summing up his pawns. *Hactenus quasi inductio*, a little glimpse giving.

Exit, [having discovered the broker-gallant, Frip, in a wretched cloak, summing up his pawns in a shop-book of accounts]

1.1 *Actus Primus*

[Frip continues to sum up his pawns.] Enter a Fellow, [with Arthur]

ARTHUR Is your pawn good and sound, sir?

FIRST FELLOW I'll pawn my life for that, sir.

ARTHUR Place yourself there, then, I will seek to prefer it presently. My master is very jealous of the pestilence; marry, the pox sits at meat and meal with him.

[The Fellow] starts back

FRIP *[reading]* 'Lent the fifth day of September to Mistress Onset, upon her gown, taffeta petticoat with three broad silver laces: three pound fifteen shillings.

'Lent to Justice Cropshin, upon both his velvet jackets: five pound ten shillings.

'Lent privately to my lady Newcut, upon her gilt casting-bottle and her silver lye-pot: fifty-five shillings—'

ARTHUR Sir—

FRIP 'Lent to Sir Oliver Needy upon his taffeta cloak, beaver hat, and perfumed leather jerkin: six pound five shillings—'

ARTHUR May it please your worship—

FRIP 'Lent to Master Andrew Lucifer, upon his flame coloured doublet and blue taffeta hose—' *[To Arthur]* Top the candle, sirrah; methinks the light burns blue. When came that suit in?

ARTHUR 'T'as lain above the year now.

FRIP Fire and brimstone! cut it out into matches; the white linings will serve for tinder.

ARTHUR And with little help, sir; they are almost black enough already. *[Presenting the Fellow]* Sir, here's another come with a pawn.

FRIP Keep him aside awhile and reach me hither the bill of the last week.

ARTHUR 'Tis here at hand, sir.

FRIP Now, sir, what's your pawn?

FIRST FELLOW The second part of a gentlewoman's gown, sir; the lower half, I mean.

FRIP I apprehend you easily: the breeches of the gown.

FIRST FELLOW Very proper, for she wears the doublet at home. A guest that lies in my house, sir. She looks every hour for her cousin out o'th' country.

FRIP O, her cousin lies here? A may mistake in that. My friend, of what parish is your pawn?

FIRST FELLOW Parish? Why, St Clement's, sir.—*[To Arthur]* I'll come to you presently. *[Exit Arthur]*

FRIP What parish is your pawn, my friend? *[Reading from the bill]* St Bride's: five; St Dunstan's: none; St Clement's: three. Three at Clement's! Away with your pawn, sir; your parish is infected. I will neither purchase the plague for six pence in the pound and a groat bill-money, nor venture my small stock into contagious parishes. You have your answer; fare-you-well, as fast as you can, sir.

FIRST FELLOW The pox arrest you, sir, at the suit of the suburbs—

FRIP Ay, welcome, welcome.

Prologue.1 bawd-gallant Primero runs a brothel.

2–3 **whore-gallant** Tailby lives off his sexual affairs.

3 **pocket-gallant** Pursenet is a thief. He has a young boy to help him pick pockets. A *pursenet* was a net-like bag that closed with a drawstring and was used for trapping small animals, especially rabbits or conies, and in that sense the name is doubly apt for someone who snatches purses and preys on yokels, a practice called 'cony-catching'.

cheating-gallant Goldstone is a con man.

4 **three wenches** i.e. the Courtesans

5 **broker-gallant** Frip is a pawnbroker. His name is short for *Frippery*, either old clothes or the place where they were sold.

7 ***Hactenus quasi inductio*** to this point, so to speak, an induction

8.2 ***in a wretched cloak*** Perhaps specifically a usurer's cloak. The dramatic function is the transformation at 1.1.278.1.

1.1.3 **prefer** promote

4 **jealous of** vigilant about

the pestilence the plague, which broke out in London in summer months

5 **pox** plague (here not venereal disease)

sits...him i.e. is his constant companion, concerns him even at meals

9 **Cropshin** The name means 'one of the refuse sort of herrings' (Nashe), suggesting that, in contrast with Mistress Onset, he is sexually feeble.

11 **Newcut** The name of a card game. It could have a sexual implication; in Thomas Heywood's *A Woman Killed with Kindness* the husband says his wife is 'best at newcut', and the intending seducer comments, 'If you play at newcut I'm soonest hitter of any here' (ed. R. W. Van Fossen (1961), 8.152–5).

12 **casting-bottle** bottle for sprinkling perfumed waters (also hinting at the obscene sense 'penis' or 'dildo')

lye-pot decorative vessel for lye used as a hairwash

20 **taffeta** glossy silk fabric

21 **Top** snuff

burns blue Blue flames were supposed to be a bad omen; Frip is superstitious.

24 **matches** cloth strips dipped in sulphur, used as tinder

29 **bill** weekly account of plague deaths in each parish

35–6 **breeches...doublet** implying that she is domineering, as in proverbial 'she wears the breeches' (Dent, B645)

39 **A may mistake** Frip is suggesting that a country person who comes to London is apt to be victimized, or to die of plague.

47–8 **a groat bill-money** Frip's charge for the bill of exchange. A groat was worth fourpence.

52 **suburbs** the location of brothels. Hence *pox* is here 'venereal disease'.

FIRST FELLOW For I think plague scorns your company. *Exit*

FRIP I rank with chief gallants; I love to smell safely. 'Lent in the vacation to master proctor upon his spiritual gown: five angels; and upon his corporal doublet: fifteen shillings. Sum: three pound five shillings.'

Enter his man [Arthur], bringing a trunk

ARTHUR Sir.

FRIP Now, sir.

ARTHUR Here's one come in with a trunk of apparel.

FRIP Whence comes it?

ARTHUR From St Martin's in the Field.

FRIP St Martin's in the Field?—St Mary Maudlin: two; St Martin's: none. Here's an honest fellow; let him appear, sir.

ARTHUR [*calling*] You may come near, sir.

[*Enter a Second Fellow*]

FRIP O, welcome, welcome. What's your pawn, sir?

SECOND FELLOW Faith, a gentlewoman's whole suit, sir.

FRIP Whole suit? 'Tis well.

SECOND FELLOW A poor kind soul, troubled with a bad husband, one that puts her to her shifts here.

FRIP He puts her from her shifts, methinks, when she is fain to pawn her clothes.

SECOND FELLOW Look you, sir, a fair satin gown; new taffeta petticoat.

FRIP Stay, this petticoat has been turned?

SECOND FELLOW Often turned up and down, an you will, but never turned, sir.

FRIP Cry you mercy, indeed.

SECOND FELLOW A fine white beaver, pearl band, three falls. I ha' known her have more in her days.

FRIP Alas, an she be but a gentlewoman of any count or charge, three falls are nothing in these days; know that. Tut, the world's changed: gentlewomen's falls stand upright now; no sin but has a bolster that it may lie at ease. Well, what do you borrow of these, sir?

SECOND FELLOW Twelve pound, an you will, sir.

FRIP How!

SECOND FELLOW They were not hers for twenty.

FRIP Why, so: our pawn is ever thrice the value of our money, unless in plate and jewels. How should the months be restored and the use, else? We must cast it for the twelve month—so many pounds, so many months, so many eighteen pences; then the use of these eighteen pences; then the want of the return of those pounds. All these must be laid together, which well considered, the valuation of the pawn had need to sound treble. Can six pound pleasure the gentlewoman?

SECOND FELLOW It may please her, but like a man of three score—in the limberest degree.

FRIP I have but one word more to say in't: twenty nobles is all and the utmost that I will hazard upon't.

SECOND FELLOW She must be content with't. The less borrowed, the better paid. Come.

FRIP Arthur.

ARTHUR At hand, sir.

FRIP Tell out twenty nobles and take her name in a bill.

SECOND FELLOW I'm satisfied, sir.

[*Exeunt Second Fellow and Arthur*]

FRIP Welcome, good St Martin's in the Field, welcome. Welcome—I know no other name.

Enter bawd-gallant, Primero

PRIMERO What, so hard at your prayers?

FRIP A little, sir, summing up my pawns here. What, Master Primero? Is it you, sir gallant? And how does all the pretty sweet ladies, those plump, kind, delicate blisses, ha, whom I kiss in my very thoughts? How do they, gallant?

PRIMERO Why, gallant, if they should not do well in my house, where should it be done, boy? Have I not a glorious situation?

FRIP O, a gallant receipt, violet air, curious garden, quaint walks, fantastical arbors, three back doors, and a coach

56 **proctor** an administrator in ecclesiastical and civil law-cases
spiritual ecclesiastical. But the sense 'of the spirit' leads to the antonym *corporal*, which might mean 'large of body', 'worn on the body', or 'material'.
57 **angels** gold coins bearing the image of the archangel Michael; worth ten shillings, and an appropriate coin as payment for a 'spiritual' pawn.
69 **suit** evidently 'entourage, wardrobe'
72 **puts her to her shifts** proverbial for 'makes her take desperate measures' (Dent, S337). Frip's reply takes *shifts* as petticoats.
77 **turned** renovated by reversing the fabric
78 **up and down** in the bawdy sense of having been raised and lowered in sexual encounters
80 **Cry you mercy** pardon me
81 **beaver** fur hat
falls veils that hung from the back of a hat; but leads on to a bawdy pun on 'falling' to sexual temptation
83 **count** account (probably punning on *cunt*)
84 **charge** (*a*) costly expenditure, (*b*) sexual onslaught
85 **the world's changed** Proverbially, 'The world changes every day' (Dent, W892.1).
85–6 **stand upright** are accounted righteous
92–3 **the months** the amount of time lost for investment
93 **use** interest
93–9 **We ... gentlewoman** The logic of the calculation is (deliberately?) hard to follow. Eighteen pence per pound per month plus interest would make up about one pound per pound after a year, perhaps Frip's justification for offering half the second-hand price, or about one-third of the price new.
93 **cast** calculate
98 **valuation** value
99 **sound treble** i.e. (*a*) be three times the amount handed over, (*b*) be as high as a treble note in music
101 **limberest** limpest
102 **nobles** coins worth six shillings and eight pence; thus Frip raises his offer by thirteen shillings and four pence.
108 **Tell** count
111.1 ***Primero*** named after a popular card game in which four cards were dealt to each player and counted at three times their value; cf. ll. 144–5
118 **do well** Frip asks about the ladies' well-being; Primero gives a sexual implication to *do*.
121 **receipt** reception room, with overtones of commerce appropriate to a brothel
violet i.e. perfumed
curious ... quaint Both words suggest 'ingeniously artificed'.
122 **walks** pathways

gate. Nay, thou'rt admirably seated: little furniture will serve thee; thou'rt never without movables.

PRIMERO I praise my stars. Ah, the goodly virginities that have been cut up in my house, and the goodly patrimonies that have lain like sops in the gravy. And when those sops were eaten, yet the meat was kept whole for another, and another, and another. For, as in one pie twenty may dip their sippets, so upon one woman forty may consume their patrimonies.

FRIP Excellent, Master Primero.

PRIMERO
Well, I'll pray for women while I live.
They're the profitablest fools, I'll say that for 'em,
A man can keep about his house—the prettiest kind
fowl,
So tame, so gentle e'en to strangers' hands,
So soon familiar, suffer to be touched
Of those they ne'er saw twice. The dove's not like 'em.

FRIP Most certain, for that's honest. But I have a suit to you.

PRIMERO And so have I to you.

FRIP That happens well; grant mine, and I'll grant yours.

PRIMERO A match.

FRIP Make me perfect in that trick that got you so much at primero.

PRIMERO O, for the thread tied at your partner's leg, the twitch?

FRIP Ay, that 'twitch', an you call't so.

PRIMERO
That secret twitch got me five hundred pound
Ere 'twas first known, and since I ha' sold it well.
Five hundred pound laid down shall not yet buy
The fee simple of my twitch. I would be here with't;
'Twas a blessed invention.
I had been a beggar many a lousy year
But for my twitch. It was the prettiest twitch.
Many over-cheated gulls have fatted me
With the bottom of their patrimonies
E'en to the last sop, gaped while I fed 'em,
Who now live by that art that first undid 'em.
But I must swear you to be secret, close.

FRIP As a maid at ten.

PRIMERO Had you sworn but two years higher, I would ne'er ha' believed you.

FRIP Nay, I let twelve alone;
For, after twelve has struck, maids look for one.

PRIMERO I look for one, too, and a maid, I think.

FRIP What, to come hither?

PRIMERO Sure she follows me. A pretty fat-eyed wench with a Venus in her cheek. Did but raiment smile upon her, she were nectar for great dons, boy. And that's my suit to thee.

FRIP And that's granted already. Of what volume is this book, that I may fit a cover to't?

PRIMERO Faith, neither in folio nor in decimo sexto, but in octavo between both, a pretty middle-sized trug.

FRIP Then I have fitted her already in my eye, i'faith. Here came a pawn in e'en now will make shift to serve her as fit. Look you, sir gallant: satin, taffeta, beaver; fall and all.

PRIMERO Is it new?

FRIP New? You see it bears her youth as freshly—

PRIMERO A pretty suit of clothes, i'faith, but put case the party should come to redeem 'em of a sudden?

FRIP Pooh, then your wit's sickly. Have not I the policy, think you, to seem extreme busy and defer 'em till the morrow, against which time that pawn shall be secretly fetched home and another carried out to supply the place?

PRIMERO I like thy craft well there.

FRIP A general course. O, frippery is an unknown benefit, sir gallant!

PRIMERO And what must I give you for the hire now, i'faith?

FRIP Of the whole suit for the month?

PRIMERO Ay, for the month.

FRIP Go to, you shall give me but twelve pence a day, Master Primero; you're a friend, and I'll use you so. 'Tis got up at your house in an afternoon, i'faith, the hire of the whole month. Ye must think I can distinguish spirits and put a difference between you and others. You pay no more, i'faith.

PRIMERO I could have offered you no less myself.

FRIP Tut, a man must use a friend as a friend may use him. Your house has been a sweet house to me, both for

124 **movables** (*a*) pieces of furniture, (*b*) things able to be set in motion, i.e. prostitutes
127 **sops** piece of bread for soaking up gravy or sauce
130 **sippets** pieces of toasted bread
133 **pray for** Equivocates between 'pray on behalf of' and 'pray to have'.
138 **like** equal to
152 **fee simple** an estate inherited unconditionally. Primero is comparing the value of his card trick to a family estate.
I...with't I wish I had it with me
165 **look for one** i.e. are on the lookout for a man; but, in the clock image, 'expect one o'clock'. In l. 166, 'expect to meet someone'.
169 **Venus** wanton or sexually attractive look
170 **dons** distinguished men (more specifically, Spanish aristocrats); cf. l. 255. The predicated word is *gods*, as nectar was the drink of the gods.
173 **that...to't** Books were usually sold unbound.
174–5 **folio...decimo sexto...octavo** book sizes. An octavo is twice the size of a decimo sexto, but a quarter of the size of a folio.
175 **trug** trull
182 **put case** what if
190 **frippery...benefit** Mock-proverbial, as though *frippery* were *thrift*. The proverb 'Thrift is a great revenue' is not recorded until 1659, but as it translates Cicero it may already have been familiar.
unknown inestimable

pleasure and profit; I'll give you your due. '*Omne tulit punctum*—', you have always kept fine punks in your house, that's for pleasure, '—*qui miscuit utile dulci*', and I have had sweet pawns from 'em, that's for profit, now.

[*Enter Novice*]

PRIMERO You flatter, you flatter, sir gallant. But, whist, here she enters. I prithee, question her.—[*To Novice*] O, you're welcome.

FRIP Is this your new scholar, Master Primero?

PRIMERO Marry, is she, sir.

FRIP I'll commend your judgement in a wench, while I live. That face will get money; i'faith, 'twill be a get-penny, I warrant you.—[*To Novice*] Go to, your fortune was choice, pretty bliss, to fall into the regard of so kind a gentleman.

NOVICE I hope so, sir.

FRIP See what his care has provided already for you; you'll be simply set out to the world. If you'll have that care now to deserve his pains, O, that will be acceptable. And these be the rudiments you must chiefly point at: to counterfeit cunningly, to wind in gentlemen with powerful attraction, to keep his house in name and custom, to dissemble with your own brother, never to betray your fellows' imperfections nor lay open the state of their bodies to strangers, to believe those that give you, to gull those that believe you, to laugh at all under taffeta. And these be your rudiments.

PRIMERO There's e'en all, i'faith. We'll trouble you with no more; nay, you shall live at ease enough. For nimming away jewels and favours from gentlemen (which are your chief vails), I hope that will come naturally enough to you. I need not instruct you; you'll have that wit, I trust, to make the most of your pleasure.

NOVICE I hope one's mother-wit will serve for that, sir.

PRIMERO O, properest of all, wench: it must be a she wit that does those things, and thy mother was quick enough at it in her days.

FRIP Give me leave, sister, to examine you upon two or three particulars, an you make you ready. Be not ashamed, here's none but friends. Are you a maid?

NOVICE Yes, in the last quarter, sir.

FRIP Very proper; that's e'en going out. A maid in the last quarter; that's a whore in the first. Let me see: new moon on Thursday; she'll be changed by that time, too. Are you willing to pleasure gentlemen?

NOVICE We are all born to pleasure our country, forsooth.

FRIP Excellent. Can you carry yourself cunningly and seem often holy?

NOVICE O, fear not that, sir; my friends were all Puritans.

FRIP I'll ne'er try her further.

PRIMERO She's done well, i'faith. I fear not now to turn her loose to any gentleman in Europe.

FRIP You need not, sir. Of her own accord, I think she'll be loose enough without turning.—Arthur.

[*Enter Arthur*]

ARTHUR Here, sir.

FRIP Go, make haste; shift her into that suit presently.

ARTHUR It shall be done.

PRIMERO Arthur. Do't neatly, Arthur!

ARTHUR Fear't not, sir.

PRIMERO Follow him, wench.

NOVICE With all my heart, sir. [*Exeunt Novice and Arthur*]

PRIMERO But, master,
In what are we forgetful all this while?

FRIP
In what?

PRIMERO The wooing business, man.

FRIP Heart, that's true.

PRIMERO
The gallants will prevent us.

FRIP Are you certain?

PRIMERO
I can avouch it; there's a general meeting
At the deceased knight's house this afternoon.
There's rivalship enough.

FRIP No doubt in that.
Would either thou or I might bear her from 'em.

PRIMERO
My hopes are not yet faint.

FRIP Nor mine.

PRIMERO Tut, man,
Nothing in women's hearts sooner win place
Than a brave outside and an impudent face.

FRIP And for both those, we'll fit it.

PRIMERO
Ay, if the devil be not in't. Make haste.

FRIP I follow straight. *Exit Primero*

[*Frip takes off his cloak, revealing bright clothes*]

Vanish, thou fog, and sink beneath our brightness,
Abashèd at the splendour of such beams.

205 **I'll . . . due** proverbial (Dent, D634)

205–7 **'*Omne tulit punctum . . . qui miscuit utile dulci*'** 'He gets every vote who mixes the sweet and the useful' (Horace, *Ars Poetica*). Adopted as a motto by the playwright and pamphleteer Robert Greene (1560?–1592). Frip twists and puns on the meaning.

206 **punks** whores (Frip's mistranslation of '*punctum*')

221 **simply** finely

223 **point at** aim towards

225–6 **in name and custom** in reputation and in profitable business

229–30 **under taffeta** i.e. (*a*) who wear fine clothes; or (*b*) who wear less than fine clothes. By the sumptuary law, in theory at least those below the rank of knight or knight's son, or without substantial landed income, were not permitted to wear taffeta or satin cloaks.

232 **nimming** stealing, filching

233 **favours** presents

234 **vails** perquisites, gratuities

243 **here's none but friends** proverbial (Dent, F743.1)

244 **in the last quarter** in the last quarter of the moon; i.e. at least until recently. (Or 'during the last quarter', suggesting abstinence from sex during menstruation.)

245 **proper** fitting

that's e'en going out i.e. the last quarter of the moon is just finishing

249 **We . . . country** Echoes the proverb, 'We are not born for ourselves'.

252 **friends** here probably 'relatives'

277 **if the devil be not in't** proverbial (Dent, D250.11)

We scorn thee, base eclipser of our glories,
That wouldst have hid our shine from mortals' eyes.
Now, gallants, I am for you; ay, and perhaps before
you!
You can appear but glorious from yourselves,
And have your beams but drawn from your own
light;
But mine from many, many make me bright.

Here's a diamond that sometimes graced the finger of a countess; here sits a ruby that ne'er lins blushing for the party that pawned it; here a sapphire. O providence and fortune! My beginning was so poor, I would fain forget it, and I take the only course, for I scorn to think on't: slave to a trencher, observer of a salt-cellar, privy to nothing but a close-stool or such unsavoury secret. But as I strive to forget the days of my serving, so I shall once remember the first step of my raising. For having hardly raked five mark together, I rejoiced so in that small stock, which most providently I ventured by water—to Blackwall, among fishwives; and in small time, what by weekly return and gainful restitution, it risse to a great body, beside a dish of fish for a present that stately preserved me a seven-night.

Nor ceased it there, but drew on greater profit,
For I was held religious by those
That do profess like abstinence,
And was full often secretly supplied
By charitable Catholics,
Who censured me sincerely abstinate,
When merely I for hunger, not for zeal,
Ate up the fish—and put their alms to use.
Ha, ha, ha!
But those times are run out, and, for my sake,
Zealous dissemblance has since fared the worse.

Let me see now, whose cloak shall I wear today to continue change? O, Arthur.

[Enter Arthur]

ARTHUR Here, sir.

FRIP Bring down Sir Oliver Needy's taffeta cloak and beaver hat—I am sure he is fast enough in the Knight's Ward—and Andrew Lucifer's rapier and dagger with the embossed girdle and hangers—for he's in his third sweat by this time, sipping of the doctor's bottle or picking the ninth part of a rack of mutton dry-roasted, with a leash of nightcaps on his head like the Pope's triple crown, and as many pillows crushed to his back, with 'O, the needles!'—for he got the pox of a seamster, and it pricked so much more, naturally.

Quick, Arthur, quick. *[Exit Arthur]*
Now to the deceased knight's daughter,
Whom many gallants sue to, I 'mongst many. For
Since impudence gains more respect than virtue,
And coin than blood—which few can now deny—
Who're your chief gallants, then, but such as I?
Exit

Enter Mistress Katherine, with Fitzgrave, a gentleman 1.2

FITZGRAVE
You do your beauties injury, sweet virgin,
To lose the time they must rejoice in youth.
There's no perfection in a woman placed
But wastes itself, though it be never wasted.
Then judge your wrongs yourself.

KATHERINE Good Master Fitzgrave,
Through sorrow for the knight my father's death—
Whose being was the perfection of my joys
And crown of my desires—I cannot yet
But forcedly on marriage fix my heart.
Yet heaven forbid I should deject your hopes;
Conceive not of me so uncharitably.
I should belie my soul if I should say
You are the man I never should affect.
I understand you thus far: you're a gentleman
Whom your estate and virtues may command
To a far worthier breast than this of mine.

FITZGRAVE
O cease, I dare not hear such blasphemy.
What is without you worthy, I neglect;
In you is placed the worth that I respect.
Vouchsafe, unequalled virgin, to accept
This worthless favour from your servant's arm:
The hallowed beads whereon I justly kept
The true and perfect number of my sighs.

287 **sometimes** at one time
288 **lins** ceases
292–3 **slave...secret** Frip's occupations as serving-man were so menial that he describes himself in relation to the mere objects he worked with. The phrases also suggest ambition to curry favour and advancement. A *trencher-man* could be a parasite, and *observer* means 'obsequious follower'.
292 **trencher** wooden platter
293 **close-stool** chamber pot enclosed in a stool or a box (with a play on 'privy')
296 **five mark** A mark was worth two-thirds of a pound.
297–8 **ventured by water** pointedly not a large-scale and risky investment in a voyage of discovery
298 **Blackwall** busy dock just east of London
304 **like abstinence** i.e. eating fish instead of meat
307 **censured** judged
309 **to use** to loan at interest
311 **for my sake** on account of me
317–18 **Knight's Ward** section of the Counter, the debtors' prison, reserved for those who could afford somewhat better lodging
319 **girdle and hangers** belt and strap—often ornamental—from which hung a gentleman's sword
320 **sweat** Venereal disease was treated by sweating and fumigation in a 'sweating-tub', and the other medical regimes mentioned.
322 **leash** set of three
324 **pox** venereal disease
325 **naturally** by its nature
329 **blood** good lineage
1.2.4 **wastes** consumes, destroys
22 **hallowed beads** Described and used as if they were rosary beads. Fitzgrave's devotion to the 'virgin' also imitates Catholic worship. Compare the quasi-religious ritual in 5.2.
justly accurately
23 **perfect** full; exact

[He gives her a chain of pearl]

KATHERINE
Mine cannot equal yours, yet in exchange
Accept and wear it for my sake.
[She gives him a jewel]

FITZGRAVE Even as my soul I'll rate it.

Enter five gallants [Goldstone, Pursenet, Tailby, Frip, Primero] at the farther door, [Pursenet's Boy with them]

GOLDSTONE Heart! Fitzgrave in such bosom-single loves?
PURSENET So close and private with her?
TAILBY Observe 'em: he grows proud and bold.
FRIP Why, was not this a general meeting?
PRIMERO By her own consent. Death, how I could taste his blood!
KATHERINE *[to Fitzgrave]* See, the gentlemen
At my request do all present themselves.
GOLDSTONE
Manifold blisses wait on her desire
Whose beauty and whose mind so many honour!
KATHERINE
I take your wishes thankfully.—Kind gentlemen
All here assembled, over whose long suits
I ne'er insulted,
Nor, like that common sickness of our sex,
Grew proud in the abundance of my suitors
Or number of the days they sued unto me—
Dutiful sorrow for my father's death,
Not wilful coyness hath my hours detained
So long in silence.
I'm left to mine own choice; so much the more
My care calls on me. If I err through love,
'Tis I must chide myself; I cannot shift
The fault unto my parents—they're at rest—
And I shall sooner err through love than wealth.
GOLDSTONE
Good.
PURSENET
Excellent.
TAILBY
That likes me well.
PRIMERO
Hope still.

[During the following speech, Pursenet's Boy steals the chain of pearl that Fitzgrave gave her]

KATHERINE
And my affections do pronounce you all
Worthy their pure and most entire deserts.
Yet they can choose but one;
Nor do I dissuade any of his hopes,
Because my heart is not yet throughly fixed
On marriage or the man,
But crave the quiet respite of one month—
The month unto this night—against which time
I do invite you all to that election,
Which, on my unstained faith and virgin promise,
Shall light amongst no strangers, but yourselves.
May this content you?
GALLANTS
Glad and content.
KATHERINE
'Tis a good time to leave.
Till then commend us to your gentlest thoughts.
Exit

GALLANTS Enough.

[Exeunt all the gallants but Pursenet. As they go,] they look scurvily upon Fitzgrave, and he upon them

FITZGRAVE Ugh!
BOY *[to Pursenet]* Hist, master, hist.

The Boy in a corner with his master, pocket-gallant [Pursenet]

PURSENET Boy, how now?
BOY Look you, sir.
PURSENET Her chain of pearl.
BOY I snecked it away finely.
PURSENET Active boy,
Thy master's best revenue, his life and soul—
Thou keep'st 'em both together. Whip away!
[Exit Boy]
Fall back, fall belly; I must be maintained.
Hope is no purchase, nor care I if I miss her.
Why I rank in this design with gallants
There's full cause: policy invites me to it.
'Tis not for love, or for her sake alone;
It keeps my state suspectless and unknown. *Exit*
FITZGRAVE
Their looks run through and through me, and the stings
Of their snake-hissing whispers pierced my hearing.
They're mad she graced me with one private minute
Above their fortunes. I have observed 'em often
Most spitefully aspected toward my happiness
Beyond all others'; but the cause I know not.
A quiet month the virgin has enclosed
Unto herself. Suitors stand without till then;

26.2 ***at the farther door*** i.e. the stage door further away from Katherine and Fitzgrave. In the lines immediately following there are two separate groupings of figures.
27 **bosom-single loves** one-to-one amorous exchanges
28–9 **close and private ... proud and bold** with innuendos of sexual intimacy and arousal
39 **insulted** exulted
72 **snecked** took, snatched
76 **Fall back, fall belly** he who hesitates (falls back) starves. A punning variant on the proverbial conflict of interest between back and belly: 'The belly robs the back', 'The belly is starved by the back', or, as W. Averell (1588) imagined the back addressing the belly, 'Your disorder in feeding hath made the members weak and my garments bare' (Tilley, B290). The phrasing echoes the proverb 'Fall back, fall edge' (Dent, B12).
77 **is no purchase** is no plunder; i.e. brings no material benefit
82 **run** like a sword-blade
86 **aspected** Refers to their facial expressions, but also, metaphorically, to the astrological influence of planets in certain positions.

In which space cunningly I'll wind myself
Into their bosoms. I have bethought the shape—
Some credulous scholar, easily infected
With fashion, time, and humour. Unto such
Their deepest thoughts will, like to wanton fishes,
Play above water and be all parts seen;
For since at me their envy pines, I'll see
Whether their lives from touch of blame sit free.
Exit

Finis Actus Primus

2.1 *Actus Secundus*

Enter Primero, the bawd-gallant, meeting Mistress Newcut, a merchant's wife

PRIMERO Mistress Newcut, welcome. Here will be choice of gallants for you anon.

NEWCUT Is all clear? May I venture? Am I not seen of the wicked?

PRIMERO Strange absurdity, that you should come into my house and ask if you be not seen of the wicked. Push, I take't unkindly, i'faith! What think you of my house? 'Tis no such common receptacle.

NEWCUT Forgive me, sweet Master Primero; I can be content to have my pleasure as much as another, but I must have a care of my credit. I would not be seen—anything else. My husband's at sea, and a woman shall have an ill report in this world let her carry herself never so secretly. You know't, Master Primero. And what choice of gallants be they? Will they be proper gentlemen, think you?

PRIMERO Nay, sure they are as proper as they will be already.

NEWCUT I must have choice, you know; I come for no gain, but for sheer pleasure and affection.

PRIMERO You see your old spy-hole yonder? Take your stand; please your own eye. I'll work it so the gallants shall present themselves before you, and in the most conspicuous fashion.

NEWCUT That's all I can desire. [*Giving him some money*] Till better come, look you.

PRIMERO What mean you, lady?

NEWCUT A trifle, sir, to buy you silver spurs. Good sir, accept it. [*She withdraws*]

PRIMERO 'Silver spurs'—a pretty emblem. Mark it, all her gifts are about riding still. The other day she sent me boot-hose wrought in silk and gold; now, silver spurs. Well, go thy ways; thou'rt as profitable a spirit as e'er lighted into my house. [*Calling*] Come, ladies, come; 'tis late. To music, when?

[*Enter two Courtesans and the Novice, with musical instruments*]

FIRST COURTESAN You're best command us, sir. [*To the other women*] Our pimp's grown proud.

PRIMERO [*to audience*]
To fools and strangers these are gentlewomen
Of sort and worship, knights' heirs, great in portions,
Boarded here for their music.
And oftentimes 'tas been so cunningly carried
That I have had two stol'n away at once
And married at Savoy, and proved honest shopkeepers.
And I may safely swear they practised music:
They're natural at prick-song. A small mist
Will dazzle a fool's eye, and that's the world.
So I can thump my hand upon the table
With an austere grace and cry 'one, two, and three',
Fret, stamp, and curse, 'foh!', 'twill pass well for me.
[*Enter Primero's Boy*]
How now, sirrah.

BOY They're coming in, sir; and strangers in their company.

PRIMERO Tune apace, ladies. Be ready for the song, sirrah.

Enter all: [*the gallants Goldstone, Pursenet and his Boy, Tailby, and Frip; with Bungler, and Fitzgrave in disguise as a scholar named Bowser*]

GOLDSTONE [*presenting 'Bowser'*] Nay, I beseech you, gallants, be more inward with this gentleman; his parts deserve it.

PURSENET Whence comes he, sir?

GOLDSTONE Piping hot from the university; he smells of buttered loaves yet; an excellent scholar, but the arrantest ass. For this our solicitor, he's a rare fellow

90–1 **In ... bosoms** While Katherine is 'enclosed | Unto herself', Fitzgrave will penetrate the gallants' secrets.
wind ... bosoms proverbial (Dent, B546)
93 **time, and humour** i.e. the fads of the moment
96 **their envy pines** they suffer in their malice
2.1.3–4 **of the wicked** Puritan diction
6 **Push** a dismissive exclamation, as in 'pooh!'
8 **'Tis ... receptacle** i.e. I don't receive just anyone here. *Common receptacle* suggests analogy with a prostitute. Questions of number of people, social class, and moral probity are comically confused in the suggestion that no one wicked would be found at a classy brothel.
21 **your ... yonder** It is perhaps in the upper acting area above the stage, as suggested by *watchtowers* at 5.1.3–4.
31 **riding** with a sexual innuendo. Middleton's references to spurs often imply sexual goading.
33–4 **as profitable ... house** He sees her as like a lucky household fairy.
36 **You're best** you had best (sarcastic)
39 **sort** quality
portions dowries
43 **Savoy** a precinct west of the city which had the historical privilege of sanctuary and so was frequently used for irregular marriages to runaways and women of bad reputations
45 **natural** innately gifted. But the context suggests 'expert by training'.
prick-song performing written or 'pricked' music. The bawdy joke is clear.
46 **dazzle ... world** as in the proverb 'the world is full of fools'
47 **So** as long as
48 **'one ... three'** in imitation of a music master counting
55 **this gentleman** i.e. 'Bowser'
parts qualities
59 **buttered loaves** University students had buttered bread for breakfast.
60 **this our solicitor** i.e. Bungler, who is 'soliciting'
he's i.e. he's considered

five-and-forty mile hence, believe that. His friends are of the old fashion—all in their graves; and now has he the leisure to follow all new fashions—ply the brothels, practise salutes and cringes.

PURSENET O.

GOLDSTONE [*to Fitzgrave*] Now, dear acquaintance,
I'll bring you to see fashions.

FITZGRAVE What house is this, sir?

GOLDSTONE
O, of great name. Here music is professed;
Here sometimes ladies practise—and the meanest,
Daughters to men of worship—
Whom gentlemen such as ourselves may visit,
Court, clip, and exercise our wits upon.
It is a professed courtesy.

FITZGRAVE A pretty recreation, i'faith.

GOLDSTONE I seldom saw so few here; you shall have 'em sometimes in every corner of the house, with their viols betwixt their legs and play the sweetest strokes—'twould e'en filch your soul almost out of your bosom.

FITZGRAVE Pox on't, we spoil ourselves for want of these things at university!

GOLDSTONE You have no such natural happiness. Let's draw near.

PRIMERO Gentlemen, you are all most respectively welcome.

GOLDSTONE We are bold and insatiate suitors, sir, to the breath of your music and the dear sight of those ladies.

PRIMERO
And what our poor skill can invite you to,
You are kindly welcome. You must pardon 'em,
gentlemen:
Virgins, and bashful; besides, new beginners.
'Tis not a whole month since they were first entered.

GOLDSTONE [*aside*] Seven year in my knowledge.

PRIMERO
They blush at their very lessons; they will not endure
To hear of a stop, a prick, or a semiquaver.

FIRST COURTESAN O, out upon you!

PRIMERO
La, I tell you—you'll bear me witness, gentlemen,
If their complaints come to their parents' ears—
They're words of art; I teach 'em naught but art.

GOLDSTONE Why, 'tis most certain.

BUNGLER For all scholars know that *musica est ars.*

ALL THE COURTESANS O, beastly word!

PRIMERO Look to the ladies, gentlemen.

GOLDSTONE [*to a Courtesan*] Kiss again.

PURSENET [*to a Courtesan*] Come, another.

TAILBY This' a good interim. [*Exit*]

PRIMERO [*to Bungler*] What have you done, sir?

BUNGLER Why, what have I done?

PRIMERO Saw you their stomachs queasy, and come with such gross meat?

BUNGLER Why, is't not Latin, sir?

PRIMERO Latin? Why then let the next to't be Latin too.

PURSENET [*to a Courtesan*] So, enough.

GOLDSTONE [*to Primero*] Nay, I can assure you thus far: I that never knew the language have heard so much, that *ars* is Latin for 'art'. And it may well be, too, for there's more art in't nowadays than ever was.

PRIMERO Is't possible? I am sorry, then, I have followed it so far.

FIRST COURTESAN A scholar call you him?

PRIMERO Music must not jar; the offence is satisfied. Come, to the song. [*To his Boy*] Begin, sir.

[*Primero's Boy sings*] *the song,* [*the Courtesans accompanying*]; *and he* [*Primero*] *keeps time, shows several humours and moods.* [*Pursenet's*] *Boy in his pocket nims away Fitzgrave's jewel here, and exit*

BUNGLER Not a whole month since you were entered, ladies?

FITZGRAVE None that shall see their cunning will believe it.

PRIMERO It is no affliction, gentlemen?

BUNGLER I care not much, i'faith, if I write down to my father presently to send up my sister in all haste, that I may place her here at this music school.

NEWCUT [*to the audience, appearing at her hiding place*] 'Slid, 'tis the fool my cousin! I would not for the value of three recreations he had seen me here!

PRIMERO [*to Frip*] How like you your new prize?

FRIP Pray, give me leave; I have not yet sufficiently admired her.

[*He courts the Novice, giving her jewels*]

PRIMERO 'Slife, he's in a sick trance!

GOLDSTONE [*to the audience*] My wits must not stand idle.
A cheat or two among these mistresses
Would not be ill-bestowed. I affect none

61 **friends** relatives

69 **sometimes ladies** i.e. women who were formerly of high rank
meanest lowest-born

70 **men of worship** respectable men, gentlemen

72 **clip** embrace

73 **professed** openly declared, regularly practised

77 **viols** stringed instruments like violas and cellos. The bass viol was held between the legs; hence Goldstone's sexual innuendoes.

80 **at university** Music was taught as an academic subject, but the universities were all-male.

81 **You . . . happiness** Hints that the only happiness at university is 'unnatural': homosexual.

83 **respectively** respectfully

90 **entered** (*a*) initiated as students (*b*) sexually penetrated

93 **stop** the hole in a wind instrument or one of a series of organ pipes; in either case, a bawdy joke
prick a musical notation (with the obvious play on 'penis')
semiquaver a musical sixteenth note, but also in the bawdy sense of a sexual quiver

95 **I tell you** I told you so

99 ***musica est ars*** music is art. With a play on *arse*.

110 **let . . . too** i.e. you might as well say that what is next to the arse is Latin too

115 **in't** The inoffensive referent is music.

116 **followed it** pursued the matter

123 **cunning** skill. *Cun-* probably puns on *cunt*.

134.1 ***He . . . jewels*** See 4.2.1–3.

But for my prey, such are their affections.
I know it; how could drabs and cheaters live else?
Then since the world rolls on dissimulation,
I'll be the first dissembler.
[*He moves to the Second Courtesan*]

FIRST COURTESAN [*to Pursenet*] Prithee, love, comfort, choice, my only wish; in thee I am confined. Deny me anything? A slight chain of pearl?

PURSENET Nay, an't be but slight—

FIRST COURTESAN Being denied,
I prize it slight; but given me by my love,
Light shall not be so dear unto my eye,
Mine eye unto the body, as the gift.

PURSENET
How have I power to deny this to you,
That command all? My fortunes are thy servants,
And thou the mistress both of them and me.
[*He gives her the chain of pearl*]

FIRST COURTESAN
The truest that e'er breathed.

GOLDSTONE [*to the Second Courtesan*]
To a gentleman
That thus so long and has so sincerely loved you
As I myself, ne'er was less pity shown.

SECOND COURTESAN
Why, I never was held cruel.

GOLDSTONE But to me.

SECOND COURTESAN
Nor to you.

GOLDSTONE Go to, 't'as scarred you much.

SECOND COURTESAN
I'm sorry your conceit is so unkind
To think me so.

GOLDSTONE When had I other argument?
I've often tendered you my love and service—
And that in no mean fashion—
Yet were you never that requiteful mistress
That graced me with one favour.
'Slight, not so much as such a pretty ring.
[*He takes her ring*]
Pox on't, 't'as almost broke my heart!

SECOND COURTESAN He's took it off. 'Sfoot! Master Bowser!

GOLDSTONE Nay, where a man loves most, there to be scanted.

SECOND COURTESAN My ring. Come, come.

GOLDSTONE
What reckon I a satin gown or two
If she were wise.

SECOND COURTESAN
Life, my ring, sir, come.

GOLDSTONE
Have you the face, i'faith?

SECOND COURTESAN Give me my ring.

GOLDSTONE Prithee, hence. By this light, you get none on't.

SECOND COURTESAN How!

GOLDSTONE
I hold your favours of more pure esteem
Than to part from 'em. Faith, I do, howe'er
You think of me.

SECOND COURTESAN Push! Pray, sir.

GOLDSTONE Hark you, go to. You have lost much by unkindness; go your ways.

SECOND COURTESAN 'Sfoot!

GOLDSTONE But yet there's no time past; you may redeem it.

SECOND COURTESAN Come, I cannot miss it, i'faith. Beside, the gentleman that bestowed it on me swore to me it cost him twenty nobles.

GOLDSTONE Twenty nobles? Pox of twenty nobles.
But you must cost me more, you pretty villain—
Ah, you little rogue.

SECOND COURTESAN
Come, come; I know you're but in jest.

GOLDSTONE
In jest? No, you shall see.

SECOND COURTESAN [*to audience*]
No way will get it.
As good give it him now and hope for somewhat.

GOLDSTONE True love made jest?

SECOND COURTESAN I did but try thy faith, how fast thou'dst hold it. Now I see a woman may venture worthy favours to thy trust and have 'em truly kept; and I protest, had I drawn't from thee, I should ne'er ha' loved thee; I know that.

GOLDSTONE 'Sfoot, I was ne'er so wronged in my life.
Think you I am in jest with you? What, with my love?
I could find lighter subjects, you shall see;
And time will show how much you injure me.

SECOND COURTESAN
The ring, were't thrice worth, I freely give,
For I know you will requite it.

GOLDSTONE Will I live?

SECOND COURTESAN
Enough.

GOLDSTONE [*to audience*]
Why, this was well come off now.
Where's my old servingman? Not yet returned.
[*Enter Fulk*]
O, here he peeps. Now, sirrah?

FULK May it please your worship. [*Aside to Goldstone, showing him two beakers*] They're done artificially, i'faith, boy.

GOLDSTONE Both the great beakers?

FULK Both, lad.

GOLDSTONE Just the same size?

159 **conceit** thought, understanding
160 **argument** theme (his protestations of love)
167 **'Sfoot** 'God's foot', a common oath
183–4 **But...redeem it** i.e. it's not too late
185 **miss** do without
204 **Will I live?** proverbial (Dent, L374.1)
205 **well come off** referring to both the ring and the outcome of the contest
209 **artificially** artfully

FULK Ay, and the marks as just.

GOLDSTONE So, fall off respectively now.

FULK [*aloud to Goldstone*]
My lord desires your worship of all love—

GOLDSTONE
His lordship must hold me excused till morning;
I'll not break company tonight. Where sup we,
gallants?

PURSENET At' Mermaid.

GOLDSTONE
Sup there who list; I have forsworn the house.

FULK [*to audience*] For the truth is this plot must take effect at' Mitre. [*Exit*]

GOLDSTONE Faith, I'm indifferent.

BUNGLER So are we, gentlemen.

PURSENET Name the place, Master Goldstone.

GOLDSTONE Why, the Mitre, in my mind, for neat attendance, diligent boys and—push!—excels it far.

ALL THE REST Agreed, the Mitre, then.

PURSENET Boy! [*To audience*] Some goodness toward: the Boy's whipped away.

FITZGRAVE [*stamping*] The jewel! Heart, the jewel!

GOLDSTONE How now, sir? What moved you?

FITZGRAVE Nothing, sir.
A spice of poetry, a kind o' fury,
A disease runs among scholars.

GOLDSTONE Mass, it made you stamp.

FITZGRAVE [*stamping again*] Whoo!
'Twill make some stamp and stare, make a strange
noise,
Curse, swear, beat tire-men, and kick players' boys.
The effects are very fearful.

PURSENET Bless me from't!

FITZGRAVE
O, you need not fear it, sir.—Hell of this luck!

GOLDSTONE Hark, he's at it again.

PURSENET
Some pageant plot or some device for the tilt-yard;
Disturb him not.

FITZGRAVE [*to audience*]
How can I gain her love
When I have lost her favour?

PURSENET [*to Bungler*] Look you, sir.

GOLDSTONE [*showing Frip the Second Courtesan's ring*] What money hast about thee? I must be fain to pawn a fair stone here for ordinary expenses. A pox of my tenants; I give 'em twenty days after the quarter, and they cut out forty.

FRIP Why, you might take the forfeiture of their leases then.

GOLDSTONE I know I might, but what's their course? The rogues comes me up all together, with geese and capons and petitions in pigs' snouts, which would move any man, i'faith, were his stomach ne'er so great; and to see how pitifully the pullen will look, it makes me after relent and turn my anger into a quick fire to roast 'em. Nay, touch't, and spare it not.

FRIP 'Tis right. Well, what does your worship borrow of this, sir?

GOLDSTONE The stone's twenty nobles.

FRIP Nay, hardly.

GOLDSTONE As I am a right gentleman.

FRIP It comes near it, indeed. Well, here's five pound in gold upon't.

GOLDSTONE 'Twill serve; and the ring safe and secret?

FRIP As a virgin's.

GOLDSTONE
I wish no higher.—What, gallants, are you constant?
Does the place hold?

ALL THE REST The Mitre.

GOLDSTONE [*to Primero*] Sir, in regard of our continued boldness and trouble—which love to your music hath made us guilty of—shall we entreat your worship's company, with these sweet ladies, your professed scholars, to take part of a poor supper with myself and these gentlemen at the Mitre?

FRIP Pray, Master Primero.

PURSENET [*to Primero*] I beseech you, sir, let it be so.

PRIMERO O, pardon me, sweet gentlemen, the world's apt to censure; I have the charge of them, they're left in trust, they're virgins, and I dare not hazard their fames. The least touch mars 'em, and what would their right worshipful parents think if the report should fly to them that they were seen with gentlemen in a tavern?

GOLDSTONE All this may be prevented. What serves your coach for? They may come coached and masked.

PRIMERO You put me to't, sir.
Yet I must say again: I fear the drawers
And vintner's boys will be familiar with them,
And think 'em mistresses.

PURSENET
There are those places where respect seems slighter;

215 **fall off respectively** assume a respectful distance (as a servant)

219 **Mermaid** a famous tavern; along with the Mitre, a favourite of the literary and fashionable men about town. 'Marmaide', the spelling in the early printed edition, suggests its reputation.

222 **Mitre** See previous note. Middleton links the Mitre to the theatre audience in *Mad World*: 'this will be a true feast, a right Mitre supper, a play and all' (5.1.83–4).

229 **toward** on the way

235 **Mass** 'by the mass', an oath

236 **Whoo** Fitzgrave, realizing that he lost his composure and nearly gave away his disguise, stages this second 'fit' of the 'disease' of scholars.

238 **tire-men** theatrical costume-managers. Fitzgrave imagines himself as an abusive playwright.

242 **tilt-yard** the tilting-ground at Westminster. Jacobean tilts were occasions for masque-like pageantry scripted by playwrights.

244 **favour** her love token (the jewel Fitzgrave had from Katherine)

247 **ordinary** tavern

248 **quarter** quarterly date on which rent is due

248–9 **cut out** make out of it

253 **comes me** come

256 **pullen** poultry

266 **ring** Frip's reply jokes on the sense 'vagina'.

More censure is belonging to the Mitre.
You know that, sir.

PRIMERO Gentlemen, you prevail.

GOLDSTONE
We'll all expect you there.

PRIMERO And we'll not fail.

FRIP
The devil will ne'er dissemble with them so,
As you for them.

GOLDSTONE Come, sir.

FRIP What else? Let's go.
Exeunt [all but Primero, the Courtesans, and the Novice]

Enter whore-gallant [Tailby]

PRIMERO
How cheer you, sir?

TAILBY Faith, like the moon, more bright;
Decreased in body, but remade in light.
Here, thou shalt share some of my brightness with me.
[He gives him money]

PRIMERO
By my faith, they are comfortable beams, sir. *[Exit]*

FIRST COURTESAN
Come, where have you spent the time now from my sight?
I'm jealous of thy action.

TAILBY Push!
I did but walk a turn or two in the garden.

FIRST COURTESAN
What made you there?

TAILBY Nothing but cropped a flower.

FIRST COURTESAN Some woman's honour, I believe.

TAILBY *[giving her a flower]*
Foh, is this a woman's honour?

FIRST COURTESAN Much about one:
When both are plucked their sweetness is soon gone.

TAILBY
Prithee, be true to me.

FIRST COURTESAN When did I fail?

TAILBY
Yet I am ever doubtful that you're firm.

FIRST COURTESAN
I do account the world but as my spoil to adorn thee.
My love is artificial to all others,
But purity to thee. Dost thou want gold?
Here, take this chain of pearl, supply thyself.
[She gives him the chain of pearl]
Be thou but constant, firm, and just to me,
Rich heirs shall want e'er want come near to thee.

TAILBY
Upon thy lip I seal sincerity.
[He kisses her.] Exit [First Courtesan]

SECOND COURTESAN Was this your vow to me?

TAILBY
Pox, what's a kiss to be quite rid of her;
She's sued so long I was ashamed of her.
'Twas but her cheek I kissed neither, to save her longing.

SECOND COURTESAN
'Tis not a kiss I weigh.

TAILBY Had you weighed this,
'T'ad lacked above five ounces of a true one;
No kiss that e'er weighed lighter.

SECOND COURTESAN 'Tis thy love that I suspect.

TAILBY
My love? Why, by this—What shall I swear by?

SECOND COURTESAN *[giving him Fitzgrave's jewel]*
Swear by this jewel. Keep thy oath; keep that.

TAILBY
By this jewel, then, no creature can be perfect
In my love but thy dear self.

SECOND COURTESAN I rest.
[Exit Second Courtesan]

TAILBY *[seeing the Novice]* Ha, ha, ha!
Let's laugh at 'em, sweet soul.

NOVICE Ay, they may laugh at me;
I was a novice and believed your oaths.

TAILBY
Why, what do you think of me? Make I no difference
'Tween seven years' prostitution and seven days?
Why, you're but in the wane of a maid yet.
You wrong my health in thinking I love them;
Do not I know their populous imperfections?
Why, they cannot live till Easter. Let 'em show
The fairest side to th' world, like hundreds more whose clothes
E'en stand upright in silver, when their bodies
Are ready to drop through 'em. Such there be;
They may deceive the world; they ne'er shall me.

NOVICE Forgive my doubts,
And for some satisfaction wear this ring,
From which I vowed ne'er, but to thee, to part.
[She gives him the ring that Goldstone pawned to Frip]

TAILBY
With which thou ever bind'st me to thy heart.
Exeunt

292 **More censure** better judgement
300 **comfortable** comforting, cheering
302 **jealous of thy action** suspicious of what you've been doing
304 **What made you** what did you do
306 **Much about** very similar to
320 **neither** and no more
to save her longing in contrast with proverbial 'to lose one's longing' (Dent, L422)
332 **difference** distinction

2.2 *Enter Fitzgrave, [disguised as Bowser]*

FITZGRAVE
My pocket picked! This was no brothel house?
A music school? Damnation has fine shapes.
I paid enough for th' song: I have lost a jewel
To me more precious than their souls to them
That gave consent to filch it. I'll hunt hard,
Waste time and money, trace and wheel about,
But I will find these secret mischiefs out.
[Enter Katherine's Servant]
How now, what's he?
O, a servant to my love. Being thus disguised,
I'll learn some news. *[Giving money]* Now, sir, you belong to me.

KATHERINE'S SERVANT I do, sir, but I cannot stay to say so. Nay, good sir, detain me not; I am going in all haste to enquire or lay wait for a chain of pearl nimmed out of her pocket the fifth of November—a dismal day.

FITZGRAVE Ha, a chain of pearl, say'st thou?

KATHERINE'S SERVANT A chain of pearl, sir, which one Master Fitzgrave, a gentleman and a suitor, fastened upon her as a pledge of his love.

FITZGRAVE Ha?

KATHERINE'S SERVANT
Urge me no more; I have no more to say—
Your friend, Hieronimo Bedlam. *Exit*

FITZGRAVE Thou'rt a mad fellow indeed.
Some comfort yet that hers is missing too;
I feel my soul at much more ease: both stol'n.
When griefs have partners, they are better borne. *Exit*

2.3 *Enter whore-gallant [Tailby]*

TAILBY
O, the parting of us twain,
Hath caused me mickle pain,
And I shall ne'er be married
Until I see my muggle again.

NEWCUT *[appearing at her hiding place]* Hist!
[Enter Primero]

PRIMERO Ha?

NEWCUT The nimble gentleman in the celestial stockings!

PRIMERO H'as the best smock-fortune to be beloved of women.—
Valle loo lo lille lo lilo,
Vallee loo lee lo lillo.

TAILBY
Vallee loo lo lillee lilo,
Vallee loo lee lo lillo.

NEWCUT Ah, sweet gentleman, he keeps it up stately.

PRIMERO *[to Tailby]* Well held, i'faith, sir.—Mass, and now I remember too, I think you ne'er saw my little banqueting box above since I altered it.

TAILBY Why, have you altered that?

PRIMERO O, divinely sir; the pictures are all new run over again.

TAILBY Fie!

PRIMERO For what had the painter done, think you? Drew me Venus naked (which is the grace of a man's room, you know) and, when he had done, drew a number of oaken leaves before her. Had not lawn been a hundred times softer, made a better show, and been more gentlewoman-like?

TAILBY More ladylike, a great deal.

PRIMERO Come, you shall see how 'tis altered now. I do not think but you'll like her. *Exeunt*

2.4 *[Music within. A dicing-table is set forth. Then] enter all at once: [Primero, First and Second Courtesans, Goldstone, Novice, Pursenet, Tailby, Frip, Bungler, Fulk, Arthur, and Pursenet's Boy]*

PRIMERO Where be your liveries?

FIRST COURTESAN They attend without.

PRIMERO Go, call the coach! Gentlemen, you have excelled in kindness as we in boldness.

TAILBY So, you think amiss, sir?

GOLDSTONE
Kind ladies, we commit you to sweet dreams,
Ourselves unto the fortune of the dice.—
Dice, ho!

FIRST COURTESAN *[aside to Tailby]*
You rest firm mine?

TAILBY E'en all my soul to thee.
[Exit First Courtesan]

SECOND COURTESAN *[aside to Tailby]*
You keep your vows?

TAILBY Why, do I breathe or see?
[Exit Second Courtesan]

NOVICE *[aside to Tailby]*
Is your love constant?

TAILBY Ay, to none but thee.
[Exeunt Novice and Primero]

2.2.14 **fifth of November** date of the 1605 Gunpowder Plot, in which a group of Catholics planned to blow up Parliament
21 **Hieronimo Bedlam** A name doubly associated with insanity: Hieronimo goes insane in Thomas Kyd's *Spanish Tragedy*; and 'Bedlam', the Hospital of St Mary of Bethlehem, was an insane asylum.
2.3.2 **mickle** much
4 **muggle** a term of affection. The exact sense is unknown; perhaps a variant of *migale*, 'fieldmouse'.
8 **smock-fortune** luck with women
10–11 **Valle loo . . . lillo** Perhaps an imitation hunting call, as with a horn. It is Primero's signal to Tailby, who replies in kind.
14 **he . . . stately** with a sexual equivocation
17 **banqueting box** probably an alcove partitioned off for private entertainment, with *banquet* in the obsolete sense of a course of sweetmeats, fruit, and wine
19 **run over** retouched (antedates *OED*'s one illustration, 1677)
25 **lawn** sheer linen
2.4.0.1 ***Music within*** The editorial stage direction allows a space between Tailby and Primero leaving the stage and re-entering; it also sets the scene at the Mitre, where supper is drawing to a close within.
1 **liveries** uniformed servingmen. Primero is maintaining the fiction that the courtesans are ladies of rank.

Now gone? Ay, now I love nor them nor thee;
'Slife, I should be cloyed should I love one in three.

[*Enter Fitzgrave, disguised as Bowser*]

PURSENET O, here's Master Bowser now.

FITZGRAVE Save you, sweet gentlemen.

TAILBY Sweet Master Bowser, welcome!

PURSENET [*calling*] When come these dice?

VINTNER (*within*) Anon, anon, sir.

PURSENET Yet 'anon, anon, sir.'

GOLDSTONE [*aside to Fulk*] Hast thou shown art in 'em?

FULK [*aside to Goldstone*]
You shall be judge, sir: here be the tavern beakers, [*showing beakers concealed on his person*] and here peep out the fine alchemy knaves, looking like—well, sir, most of our gallants, that seem what they are not.

GOLDSTONE [*aloud*] Peace, villain, am not I in presence?

FULK [*aside to Goldstone*] Why, that puts me in mind of the jest, sir.

GOLDSTONE [*aloud*] Again, you quarreler?

[*They continue speaking aside*]

FULK Nay, compare 'em, and spare 'em not.

GOLDSTONE
The bigness of the bore, just the same size;
the marks, no difference. Away, put money in thy pocket, and offer to draw in upon the least occasion.

FULK I am no babe, sir. [*He starts to exit*]

GOLDSTONE Hist!

FULK What's the matter now?

GOLDSTONE Give me a pair of false dice, e'er you go.

FULK Pox on't, you're so troublesome, too; you cannot remember a thing before. If I stay a little longer, I shall be stayed anon. [*Exit*]

[*Enter Vintner*]

VINTNER Here be dice for your worships.

PURSENET O, come, come.

GOLDSTONE The vintner himself! [*To audience*] I'll shift away these beakers by a sleight.

[*He switches the beakers for counterfeits*]

VINTNER [*seeing Goldstone handle the beakers*] Master Goldstone!

GOLDSTONE How now, you conjuring rascal!

VINTNER Bless your good worship, you're in humours, methinks.

GOLDSTONE Humours! Say that again.

VINTNER I said no such word, sir—[*To audience*] Would I had my beakers out on's fingers!

GOLDSTONE What's thy name, vintner?

VINTNER Jack, an please your worship.

GOLDSTONE Turn knight like thy companions, scoundrel. Live upon usury; wear thy gilt spurs at thy girdle for fear of slubbering.

VINTNER O no, I hope I shall have more grace than so, sir. Pray, let me help your worship.

GOLDSTONE Cannot I push 'em together without your help?

VINTNER O, I beseech your worship; they're the two standards of my house.

GOLDSTONE Standards! There lie your standards.

[*He gives the Vintner the counterfeit beakers*]

VINTNER Good, your worship. [*To audience*] I am glad they are out of his fingers. My wife shall lock 'em up presently; they shall see no sun this twelve-month's day for this trick.

GOLDSTONE Let me come to the sight of your 'standards' again.

VINTNER Your worship shall pardon me. Now you shall not see 'em in haste, I warrant ye.

[*Exit Vintner with fake beakers*]

GOLDSTONE I do not desire't. Ha, ha!

FITZGRAVE Why, Master Goldstone!

GOLDSTONE I am for you, gallants. Master Bowser, cry you mercy, sir; why supped you from us?

FITZGRAVE Faith, sir, I met with a couple of my fellow pupils at university, and so we renewed our acquaintance and supped together.

GOLDSTONE Fie, that's none of the newest fashion, I must tell you that, Master Bowser. You must never take acquaintance of any o' th' university when you are at London, nor any of London when you're at university. You must be more forgetful, i'faith; every place ministers his acquaintance abundantly.

BUNGLER He tells you true, sir.

GOLDSTONE I warrant you, here's a gentleman will ne'er commit such an absurdity.

BUNGLER Who, I? No, 'tis well known, if I be disposed I'll forget any man in a seven-night and yet look him in the face. Nay, let him ride but ten mile from me and come home again, it shall be at my choice whether I'll remember him or no. I have tried that.

GOLDSTONE This is strange, sir.

BUNGLER 'Tis as a man gives his mind to't, sir. And, now you bring me in, I remember 'twas once my fortune to be cozened of all my clothes and, with my clothes, my

13 **cloyed** clogged, burdened (not, presumably, 'satiated')

14 **Bowser** The name means 'college bursar'.

18 **Anon, anon, sir** Perhaps recalling *1 Henry IV* 2.5.36–56, in which Hal and Poins tease a drawer.

21 **beakers** drinking vessels

23 **alchemy knaves** the fake beakers which Goldstone intends to switch for the Vintner's: *alchemy* because they are base metal that will be 'transformed' to silver or gold (compare the name *Goldstone*)

32 **draw in** i.e. join the dicing

39 **stayed** either 'prevented' or 'arrested'

47 **humours** an odd mood

54 **Turn . . . companions** James I had cheapened knighthood by selling the title; Goldstone is suggesting that other mere vintners have become knights. Probably also an allusion to Shakespeare's Sir Jack Oldcastle/Falstaff, especially in view of the joke on 'anon, anon, sir' at ll. 18–19.

55 **gilt spurs** the gaudy excess of newly-made knights

56 **slubbering** muddying. The *nouveaux* knights won't wear their expensive new spurs on their boots for fear of getting them dirty.

61 **standards** vessels authorized as holding a full measure of drink

62 **There lie your standards** Plays on *standards* as objects that stand.

83 **ministers his acquaintance** looks after those it knows

money. A poor shepherd, pitying me, took me in and relieved me.

GOLDSTONE 'Twas kindly done of him, i'faith.

BUNGLER Nay, you shall see, now: 'twas his fortune likewise, not long after, to come to me in much distress, i'faith, and with weeping eyes, and do you think I remembered him?

GOLDSTONE You could not choose.

BUNGLER By my troth, not I. I forgot him quite, and never remembered him to this hour.

GOLDSTONE And yet knew who he was?

BUNGLER As well as I know you, i'faith. 'Tis a gift giv'n to some above others.

GOLDSTONE [*to audience*] To fools and knaves; they never miss on't.

BUNGLER Does any make such a wonder at this? Why, alas, 'tis nothing to forget others; what say you to those that forget themselves?

[*Enter Fulk*]

GOLDSTONE Nay, then, to dice. Come, set me, gallants, set.

[*The gallants go to the table, and Pursenet's Boy picks their pockets the while*]

FRIP [*standing aside from gamesters*] Ay, fall to't, gentlemen. I shall hear some news from some of you anon. I have th'art to know which lose and ne'er look on; I'll be ready with all the worst money I can find about me.—Arthur!

ARTHUR Here, sir.

FRIP Stand ready.

ARTHUR Fear not me, sir.

GOLDSTONE [*offering his dice to Tailby*] These are mine, sir.

FRIP [*examining his coins*] Here's a washed angel; it shall
away. Here's Mistress Rose-noble
Has lost her maidenhead—cracked in the ring.
She's good enough for gamesters and to pass
From man to man, for gold presents at dice
Your harlot: in one hour won and lost thrice;
Every man has a fling at her.

TAILBY [*losing at dice*] Again!
Pox of these dice!

BUNGLER 'Tis ill to curse the dead, sir.

PURSENET Mew!

TAILBY
Where should I wish the pox but among bones?

FITZGRAVE He tells you right, sir.

TAILBY
I ne'er have any luck at these odd hands.
None here to make us six? Why, Master Frip?

FRIP I am very well here, I thank you, sir. I had rather be telling my money myself than have others count it for me. 'Tis the scurviest music in the world, methinks, to hear my money jingle in other men's pockets; I never had any mind to't, i'faith.

TAILBY 'Slud, play six or play four; I'll play no more.

GOLDSTONE 'Sfoot, you see there's none here to draw in.

FULK Rather than you should be destitute, gentlemen, I'll play my ten pound—if my master's worship will give me leave.

PURSENET Come.

TAILBY He shall, he shall.

GOLDSTONE Pray excuse me, gentlemen. [*To Fulk*] 'Sfoot! How now, goodman rascal? What, because you served my grandfather when he went ambassador, and got some ten pound by th' hand, has that put such spirit in you to offer to draw in among gentlemen of worship, knave?

TAILBY Pray, sir, let's entreat so much for once.

PURSENET [*to Goldstone*] 'Tis a usual grace, i'faith, sir; you've many gentlemen will play with their men.

BUNGLER Ay, and with their maids too, i'faith.

PURSENET [*to Goldstone*] Good sir, give him leave.

GOLDSTONE [*to Fulk*] Yes, come, an you be wary on't. I pray, draw near, sir.

FULK Not so, sir.

TAILBY Come, fool, fear nothing. I warrant thee; he's given thee leave. Stand here by me. Come, now. Set round, gentlemen, set.

PURSENET How the poor fellow shakes!—Throw lustily, man.

FULK At all, gentlemen.

[*He throws dice and wins*]

TAILBY Well said, i'faith.

PURSENET They're all thine.

TAILBY By my troth, I am glad the fellow has such luck; 'twill encourage him well.

FULK [*betting against Goldstone*] At my master's worship alone.

[*Fulk throws and wins*]

GOLDSTONE Now, Sir Slave!

FULK At my master's worship alone.

124 **washed** bathed in acid to dissolve gold off it, so of reduced value
angel a gold coin

125 **Rose-noble** a gold coin (*noble*) with a rose on it. Punningly taken as a woman's name (probably with *Rose* also in the sense 'vulva'). Throughout the play money that goes from hand to hand is likened to women who do the same.

126 **cracked in the ring** (*a*) of the coin: with a crack in the rim extending to the decorative ring around the rose, at which point the coin lost its value; (*b*) of the woman: 'lost her maidenhead', with *ring* as 'vagina'. Proverbial (Dent, R130.1).

127 **gamesters** (*a*) wenchers, (*b*) gamblers

128 **presents** represents

131 **'Tis ... dead** proverbial ('Speak well of the dead', Dent, D124)
Mew derisive exclamation

132 **Where ... bones** A common curse was to wish the pox on someone's bones. Dice were made of bones.

134 **these odd hands** i.e. an odd number of card-hands, hence players. Tailby is superstitious about odd numbers.

141 **'Slud** 'God's blood', a severe oath

149 **goodman** form of address to someone below the rank of gentleman, often prefixed to his occupation, as in 'goodman tailor'

151 **by th' hand** right away

156 **play** Bungler's riposte brings out the sense 'have sexual play'.

167 **At all** Accompanies the throwing of dice to signal that the game is on and all are included.

168 **Well said** well done

[*Fulk throws and wins*]

GOLDSTONE So, saucy rascal!

FULK At my master's worship alone.

[*Fulk throws and wins*]

GOLDSTONE You're a rogue and will ever be one!

FULK By my troth, gentlemen, at all again, for once.

[*Fulk throws and wins*]

TAILBY Take 'em to thee, boy, take 'em to thee. Thou'rt worthy of 'em, i'faith.

GOLDSTONE Gentlemen, faith, I am angry with you. Go and suborn my knave against me here, to make him proud and peremptory?

TAILBY Troth, that's but your conceit, sir. The fellow's an honest fellow and knows his duty, I dare swear for him.

PURSENET Heart, I am sick already. [*He leaves the table*]

GOLDSTONE Whither goes Master—

PURSENET Play on, I'll take my turn, sir. [*Aside*] Boy!

BOY Master?

PURSENET Pist.

[*The Boy secretly shows Pursenet the money he's stolen*]

A supply. Carry't closely, my little fogger. How much?

BOY Three pound, sir.

PURSENET Good boy. Take out another lesson. [*Returning to the gallants*] How now, gentlemen?

TAILBY Devil's in't; did you e'er see such a hand?

PURSENET I set you these three angels.

BOY [*to audience*] My master may set high, for all his stakes are drawn out of other men's pockets.

FULK As I said, gentleman?

PURSENET Deuce, ace.

FULK At all your right worshipful worships.

[*Fulk wins*]

ALL THE REST Death and vengeance!

GOLDSTONE Hell, darkness!

[*Goldstone pretends to strike Fulk*]

TAILBY Hold, sir.

PURSENET Master Goldstone!

GOLDSTONE Hinder me not, sweet gentlemen.—You rascal! I banish thee the board.

TAILBY I'faith, but you shall not, sir!

GOLDSTONE Touch a die, an thou dar'st. Come you in with your lousy ten pound, you slave, among gentlemen of worship, and win thirty at a hand?

TAILBY Why, will you kick against luck, sir?

BUNGLER As long as the poor fellow ventures the loss of his own money, who can be offended at his fortunes?

FULK I have a master here! Many a gentleman would be glad to see his man come forward. [*He is seized by Goldstone*] Aha!

PURSENET [*to Goldstone*] Pray, be persuaded, sir.

GOLDSTONE 'Slife, here's none cuts my throat in play but he, I have observed it. An unluckly slave 'tis.

BUNGLER Methinks his luck's good enough, sir.

GOLDSTONE Upon condition, gentlemen, that I may ever bar him from the board hereafter, I am content to wink at him.

PURSENET Faith, use your own pleasure hereafter; he's won our money now! [*To Fulk*] Come to th' table, sir, your master's friends with you.

FULK Pray, gentlemen.

TAILBY [*to the audience, leaving the table*] The fiend's in't, I think; I left a fair chain of pearl at my lodging too, like an ass, and ne'er remembered it; that would ha' been a good pawn now. [*Offering his rapier, dagger, and hangers*] Speak, what do you lend upon these, Master Frip? I care not much if you take my beaver hat, too, for I perceive 'tis dark enough already, and it does but trouble me here.

FRIP Very well, sir. Why, now I can lend you three pound, sir—

TAILBY Prithee, do't quickly then.

FRIP There 'tis in six angels.

TAILBY Very compendiously.

[*He returns to the table*]

FRIP Here, Arthur; run away with these presently; I'll enter 'em into th' shop-book tomorrow.

[*Exit Arthur. Frip records the sale*]

Item, one gilt-hatched rapier and dagger, with a fair embroidered girdle, and hangers, with which came also a beaver hat, with a correspondent band.

TAILBY [*to Goldstone*] Push! I'faith, sir, you're to blame; you have snibbed the poor fellow too much; he can scarce speak; he cleaves his words with sobbing.

FULK Haf—Haf—Haf—Haf at all, gentlemen.

[*He throws and wins*]

GOLDSTONE Ah, rogue! I'll make you know yourself.

FULK At the fairest.

[*He throw and loses*]

PURSENET Out, i'faith—two aces.

GOLDSTONE I am glad of that. Come, pay me all these, goodman Cloak-bag.

PURSENET Why, are you the fairest, sir?

GOLDSTONE You need not doubt of that, sir. [*To Fulk*] Five angels, you scoundrel.

192 **fogger** person given to underhand practices for gain; engrosser
194 **Take out another lesson** go back to your studying (i.e. picking pockets)
196 **Devil's in't** proverbial (Dent, D250.11)
201 **Deuce, ace** Pursenet's bet on the dice: a two and a one
216 **a master** i.e. a fine master (sarcastic)
221 **unluckly** bringing ill luck, malicious. Bungler takes Goldstone to mean that Fulk has ill luck himself.
224–5 **wink at** turn a blind eye to
242 **compendiously** expeditiously
245 **gilt-hatched** gold-engraved
249 **snibbed** rebuked
252 **make... yourself** i.e. make you recognize your lowly status by making you lose you winnings. 'Know thyself' was proverbial (Dent, K175).
253 **At the fairest** Evidently declares a game against the player with most money on the table.
256 **Cloak-bag** i.e. porter (named by what he carries)

TAILBY Fie o' these dice! Not one hand tonight.—There they go, gentlemen. At all, i'faith.

[*He throws and loses*]

PURSENET Pay all with two treys and a quatre.

TAILBY All curses follow 'em! Pay yourselves withal; I'll pawn myself to't, but I'll see a hand tonight. Not once hold in? [*Taking off his doublet*] Here, Master Frip, lend me your hand—quick, quick, so.

FRIP What, do you borrow of this doublet now?

TAILBY Ne'er saw the world three days.

FRIP Go to; in regard you're a continual customer, I'll use you well and pleasure you with five angels upon't.

TAILBY
Let me not stand too long i'th' cold for them.

BUNGLER
Had ever country gentleman such fortune?
All swooped away! I'd need repair to th' brokers.

TAILBY If you be in that mind, sir, there sits a gentleman will furnish you upon any pawn as well as the public'st broker of 'em all.

BUNGLER Say you so, sir? There's comfort in that, i'faith.

[*He goes to Frip*]

FRIP [*recording*] Item, upon his orange tawny satin doublet, five angels.

BUNGLER But by your leave, sir, next comes the britches—

FRIP O, I have a tongue fit for anything—

BUNGLER Saving your tail, sir. 'Tis given me to understand that you are a gentleman i'th' hundred and deal in the premises aforesaid.

FRIP Master Bungler, Master Bungler, you're mightily mistook. I am content to do a gentleman a pleasure for once, so his pawn be neat and sufficient.

BUNGLER Why, what say you to my grandfather's seal ring here?

FRIP Ay, marry, sir; this is somewhat like.

BUNGLER Nay, view it well. An ancient arms, I can tell you.

FRIP What's this, sir?

BUNGLER The great codpiece with nothing in't.

FRIP How!

BUNGLER The word about it: '*Parturiunt montes*'.

FRIP What's that, I pray, sir?

BUNGLER 'You promise to mount us.'

FRIP And belike he was not so good as his word.

BUNGLER So it should seem by the story, for so our names came to be Bunglers.

FRIP A lamentable hearing, that so great a house should shrink and fall to ruin.

[*Bungler exchanges the ring for money and joins the table again*]

PURSENET Two quatres and yet lose it! Heart! [*Aside*] Boy, i'faith, what is't?

BOY Five pound, sir.

PURSENET [*to audience*] By my troth, this boy goes forward well. Ye shall see him come to his preferment i'th' end!

GOLDSTONE [*looking at Tailby*] Why, how now, who's that, gentlemen, a barge-man?

TAILBY I never have any luck, gallants, till my doublet's off; I'm not half nimble enough. At this old cinquanter drivel-beard.

[*He throws and loses*]

FULK Your worship must pay me all these, sir.

TAILBY There, and feast the devil with 'em.

PURSENET Hell gnaw these dice.

GOLDSTONE What, do you give over, gallants?

FULK [*aside to Goldstone*] Is't not time?

TAILBY I protest I have but one angel left to guide me home to my lodging.

GOLDSTONE [*aside to Fulk*] How much, think'st?

FULK Some fourscore angels, sir.

GOLDSTONE Peace, we'll join powers anon and see how strong we are in the whole number. [*To audience*] Mass, yon gilt goblet stands so full in mine eye, the whoreson tempts me. It comes like cheese after a great feast, to digest the rest. He will hardly 'scape me, i'faith; I see that by him already.

[*Enter Vintner*]

Back for a parting blow now.—Boy!

VINTNER Anon, anon, sir.

GOLDSTONE Fetch a pennyworth of soft wax to seal letters.

VINTNER I will, sir. [*Exit*]

TAILBY Nay, had not I strange casting? Thrice together, two quatres and a deuce.

PURSENET Why, was not I as often haunted with two treys and a quatre?

[*Enter Vintner*]

VINTNER There's wax for your worship.—Anon, anon, sir. [*Exit*]

262 **two treys and a quatre** two threes and a four

268 **Ne'er ... days** i.e. not three days old

281 **a ... anything** i.e. a taste for any sort of clothing. Bungler makes that claim into a dirty joke ('a tongue good for anything except the anus').

283 **gentleman i'th' hundred** Bungler's euphemism for usurer, converging (*a*) one who charges a percentage (part of a hundred) in interest, (*b*) a respectable country gentleman (since a 'hundred' was a subdivision of a shire)

290 **this is somewhat like** proverbial (Dent, S623.11)

296 **'*Parturiunt montes*'** 'The mountains are in labour'. The quotation, from Horace's *Ars Poetica*, was proverbial (Dent, M1215). It continues: '... and a silly mouse will be born'. Bungler sees the engraved emblem of the opening mountain as a codpiece, and misunderstands the Latin motto.

298 **mount us** Bungler might understand this to mean 'raise us in honour' and miss its bawdy sense. *Bungler* can mean 'unperforming husband'.

299 **so good as his word** Plays on the proverb (Dent, W773.1) by turning *word* from 'promise' to 'motto'.

308 **preferment** promotion to a higher status or position

310 **barge-man** as would row a barge without his doublet

312 **cinquanter** man of fifty or more (hence *drivel-beard*). Probably puns on *cinque-quatre*, the numbers four and five on the dice.

316 **Hell gnaw these dice** Based on proverbial 'Hell gnaw his bones' (Dent, B527.10, queried).

325 **full** prominent (playing on the sense 'full of drink')

GOLDSTONE [*to Fulk*] Screen me a little, you whoreson old crossbiter.

[*Goldstone uses wax to stick the goblet beneath the table*]

FULK Why, what's the business? Filchiton, Hobgoblit.

PURSENET And what has Master Bowser lost?

FITZGRAVE Faith, not very deeply, sir; enough for a scholar, some half a score royals.

PURSENET 'Sfoot, I have lost as many with spurs at their heels.

[*Enter Vintner and two drawers*]

GOLDSTONE Come, gallants, shall we stumble?

TAILBY What's o'clock?

DRAWER [*to the other*] Here's none on't, Dick; the goblet's carried down.

GOLDSTONE [*to Tailby*] Nay, 'tis upon the point of three.—Boy, drawer, what's to be done, sirs?

VINTNER All's paid, and your worships are welcome; only there's a goblet missing, gentlemen, and cannot be found about house.

GOLDSTONE How, a goblet?

PURSENET What manner o' one?

VINTNER A gilt goblet, sir, of an indifferent size.

GOLDSTONE 'Sfoot, I saw such a one lately.

VINTNER It cannot be found now, sir.

GOLDSTONE Came there no strangers here?

VINTNER No, sir.

GOLDSTONE This' a marvellous matter, that a goblet should be gone, and none but we in the room. The loss is near all here as we are. Keep the door, vintner.

VINTNER No, I beseech your worship.

GOLDSTONE By my troth, vintner, we'll have a privy search for this. What? We are not all one woman's children.

VINTNER I beseech ye, gentlemen, have not that conceit of me that I suspect your worships.

GOLDSTONE Tut, you are an ass. Do you know every man's nature? There's a broker i'th' company.

PURSENET [*aside to his Boy*] 'Slife, you have not stole the goblet, boy, have you?

BOY Not I, sir.

PURSENET I was afraid. [*To the others*] 'Tis a good cause, i'faith. Let each man search his fellow.—We'll begin with you.

[*He searches his Boy*]

TAILBY I shall save somebody a labour, gentlemen, for I'm half searched already.

PURSENET I thought the goblet had hung here, i'faith. None here, nor here.

GOLDSTONE Seek about' floor. What was the goblet worth, vintner?

VINTNER Three pound ten shillings, sir. No more.

GOLDSTONE Pox on't, gentlemen, 'tis but angels apiece; it shall be a brace of mine rather than I would have our reputations breathed upon by all comers; for you must think they'll talk on't in all companies: such a night, in such a company, such a goblet. 'Sfoot, it may grow to a gangrene in our credits and be incurable.

TAILBY Faith, I am content.

FRIP So am I.

PURSENET There's my angel, too.

GOLDSTONE So, and mine. [*To Vintner*] I'll tell thee what: the missing of this goblet has dismayed the gentlemen much.

VINTNER I am sorry for that, sir.

GOLDSTONE [*Giving the Vintner the money he's collected*] Yet they send thee this comfort by me. If they see thee but rest satisfied and depart away contented, which will appear in thy countenance, not three times thrice the worth of the goblet shall hang between them and thee, both in their continual custom and all their acquaintances.

VINTNER I thank their worships all. I am satisfied.

GOLDSTONE Say it again.—Do you hear, gentlemen?

VINTNER I thank your worships all. I am satisfied.

[*Exeunt Vintner and drawers*]

GOLDSTONE Why, la, was not this better than hazarding our reputations upon trifles, and in such public as a tavern, such a questionable place?

TAILBY True.

PURSENET Faith, it was well thought on.

GOLDSTONE Nay, keep your way, gentlemen.—I have sworn, Master Bowser, I will be last, i'faith.

[*Exeunt all but Goldstone and Fulk*]

Rascal, the goblet.

FULK Where, sir?

GOLDSTONE Peep yon, sir, under.

FULK [*finding the goblet under the table*] Here, sir.

[*Exeunt Goldstone and Fulk*]

Finis Actus Secundus

Interim 1

In the midst of the music, enter one [*Mistress Cleveland's Servant*] *bringing in a suit of satin; knocks at Tailby's door. Enter his man* [*Jack*]

JACK Who knocks?

MISTRESS CLEVELAND'S SERVANT A Christian. Pray, is not this Master Tailby's lodging? I was directed hither.

339 **crossbiter** swindler, accomplice in swindling

340 **Filchiton, Hobgoblit** Probably imitation thieving cant. *Filchiton* is based on *filch*, 'steal, pilfer'. *Hobgoblit* is an alteration of *hobgoblin* playing on *goblet*. Fulk jestingly invokes a mischievous spirit to cheer on Goldstone's thievery.

343 **royals** coins worth ten shillings or half of a pound sterling; Fitzgrave is casually estimating that he's lost five pounds

344–5 **spurs . . . heels** i.e. spur-royals, coins worth fifteen shillings

364 **Keep** secure, lock

367 **one woman's children** i.e. equally honest

386 **brace** pair

Interim 1.0.1 ***In . . . music*** In the Blackfriars theatre where the play was originally performed, a musical interlude was regularly performed between acts. Here, exceptionally, the music is interrupted by the episodes identified in this edition as entr'acte scenes (i.e. scenes performed during the interlude).

JACK Yes, this is my master's lodging.

MISTRESS CLEVELAND'S SERVANT Cry you mercy, sir. Is he yet stirring?

JACK He's awake, but not yet stirring, for he played away half his clothes last night.

MISTRESS CLEVELAND'S SERVANT My mistress commends her secrets unto him and presents him, by me, with a new satin suit here.

JACK Mass, that comes happily.

MISTRESS CLEVELAND'S SERVANT And she hopes the fashion will content him.

JACK There's no doubt to be had of that, sir. Your mistress's name, I pray?

[*Mistress Cleveland's Servant whispers*]

You're much preciously welcome.

MISTRESS CLEVELAND'S SERVANT I thank you uncommonly, sir.

JACK The suit shall be accepted, I warrant you, sir.

MISTRESS CLEVELAND'S SERVANT That's all my mistress desires, sir.

JACK Fare you well, sir.

MISTRESS CLEVELAND'S SERVANT Fare you well, sir. [*Exit*]

JACK This will make my master leap out of the bed for joy, and dance Wigmore's Galliard in his shirt about the chamber. [*Exit*]

Interim 2 *The music plays on a while, then enter Tailby, [and] his man [Jack] after, trussing him*

TAILBY Came this suit from Mistress Cleveland?

JACK She sent it secretly, sir.

TAILBY A pretty, requiteful squall. I like that woman that can remember a good turn three months after the date; it shows both a good memory and a very feeling spirit.

JACK This came fortunately, sir, after all your ill luck last night.

TAILBY I'd beastly casting, Jack.

JACK O, abominable, sir; you had the scurviest hand; the old servingman swooped up all.

TAILBY I am glad the fortune lighted upon the poor fellow. By my troth, 't made his master mad!

JACK Did you mark that, sir? I warrant he has the dogged'st master of any poor fellow under the dog-sign. I'd rather serve your worship—I'll say that behind your back, sir—for nothing: as indeed I have no standing wages at all, your worship knows.

TAILBY O, but your vails, Jack, your vails considered when you run to and fro between me and mistresses.

JACK I must confess my vails are able to keep an honest man, go I where I list.

TAILBY Go to, then, Jack.

JACK But those vails stand with the state of your body, sir; as long as you hold up your head. If that droop once, farewell you, farewell I, farewell all; and droop it will, though all the caudles in Europe should put to their helping hands to't. 'Tis e'en as uncertain as playing: now up, now down; for if the bill rise to above thirty, here's no place for players, so if your years rise to above forty, there's no room for old lechers.

TAILBY And that's the reason all rooms are taken up for young Templars?

JACK You're in the right, sir.

TAILBY Pize on't, I pawned a good beaver hat to Master Frip last night, Jack; I feel the want of it now.

[*Knocking within*]

Hark, who's that knocks?

[*Enter Mistress Newblock's Servant*]

MISTRESS NEWBLOCK'S SERVANT Is Master Tailby stirring?

JACK What's your pleasure with him? He walks here i'th' hall.

MISTRESS NEWBLOCK'S SERVANT [*to Tailby*] Give your worship good morrow.

TAILBY Welcome, honest lad.

MISTRESS NEWBLOCK'S SERVANT A letter from my mistress.

TAILBY Who's thy mistress?

MISTRESS NEWBLOCK'S SERVANT Mistress Newblock.

TAILBY Mistress Newblock, my sincere love. How does she?

MISTRESS NEWBLOCK'S SERVANT Faith, only ill in the want of your sight.

TAILBY Alas, dear sweet, I've had such business; I protest I ne'er stood still since I saw her.

13 **fashion** style

26 **Wigmore's Galliard** A galliard was a particularly energetic and spirited dance. The line may be a cue for Wigmore's Galliard to be played between the entr'acte episodes. It was a popular tune, and is extant; see *Companion*, p. 143.

Interim 2.0.1 *music* Another musical interlude suggesting the passage of time, in this case a sort of 'jump cut' in which the audience is to imagine that Tailby has awakened and Jack has begun to dress him in the newly delivered suit. See previous note.

0.2 *trussing him* fastening his clothes

1 **Cleveland** with the sexual innuendo 'place of cleaving, cleft'

3 **squall** little creature

4 **turn** in Tailby's bawdy sense, a sexual encounter

8 **casting** Refers to both throwing of dice and shedding clothes.

14 **dogged'st** most currish, most cruel **dog-sign** The constellation *Canis Major*, held to be astrologically unlucky.

18 **vails** tips

24 **hold up your head** in the bawdy sense 'maintain your erection'

26 **caudles** warm medicinal drinks (and recipes for them)

26–7 **put...to't** proverbial (Dent, H97)

28 **if...thirty** A 1604 ordinance of the Privy Council required the closing of theatres when more than thirty deaths from plague were reported in a week.

32 **Templars** law students who took rooms at the Inner and Middle Temples or Inns of Court just west of the Blackfriars theatre. Tailby's joke—that the young Templars have all the women—presumably would have pleased many in his audience.

34 **Pize** probably a variant of 'pox'

37 **stirring** up and about (with a possible innuendo: 'engaged in sexual activity')

50 **ne'er stood still** have had no free time (with a bawdy play on *stand* as 'have an erection')

MISTRESS NEWBLOCK'S SERVANT She has sent your worship a beaver hat here, with a band best in fashion.

TAILBY How shall I requite this dear soul?

MISTRESS NEWBLOCK'S SERVANT 'Tis not a thing fit for me to tell you, sir, for I have three years to serve yet. Your worship knows how, I warrant you.

TAILBY I know the drift of her letter, and, for the beaver, say I accept it highly.

[He puts the letter in his pocket]

MISTRESS NEWBLOCK'S SERVANT O, she will be a proud woman of that, sir.

TAILBY And hark thee, tell thy mistress, as I'm a gentleman, I'll dispatch her out of hand the first thing I do, o' my credit. Canst thou remember these words, now?

MISTRESS NEWBLOCK'S SERVANT Yes, sir: as you are a gentleman, you'll dispatch her out of hand the first thing you do.

TAILBY Ay, o' my credit.

MISTRESS NEWBLOCK'S SERVANT O, of your credit; I thought not of that, sir.

TAILBY Remember that, good boy.

MISTRESS NEWBLOCK'S SERVANT Fear it not now, sir. *[Exit]*

TAILBY I dreamt tonight, Jack, I should have a secret supply out o'th' city.

JACK Your dream crawls out partly well, sir.

[Knocking within]

What news there now?

Enter another, [Mistress Tiffany's Servant]

MISTRESS TIFFANY'S SERVANT I have an errand to Master Tailby—

JACK Yonder walks my master. *[Exit Jack]*

MISTRESS TIFFANY'S SERVANT Mistress Tiffany commends her to your worship, and has sent you your ten pound in gold back again, and says she cannot furnish you of the same lawn you desire till after All-Hallowtide—

TAILBY Thank her she would let me understand so much.

[Exit Servant]

Ha! Ha! This wench will live. Why, this was sent like a workwoman now; the rest are botchers to her.
Faith, I commend her cunning. She's a fool
That makes her servant fellow to her heart;
It robs her of respect, dams up all duty,
Keeps her in awe e'en of the slave she keeps.
This takes a wise course; I commend her more:
Sends back the gold I never saw before.
Well, women are my best friends, i'faith. Take lands; give me
Good legs, firm back, white hand, black eye, brown hair,
And add but to these five a comely stature.
Let others live by art, and I by nature.

Exit. [The music concludes]

❀

Actus Tertius 3.1

Enter Tailby reading [the] letter [he had put in his pocket]

TAILBY (*reads*) 'My husband is rode from home; make no delay. I know if your will be as free as your horse, you will see me yet ere dinner. From Kingston, this eleventh of November.'—Ha! These women are such creatures, such importunate sweet souls, they'll scarce give a man leave to be ready. That's their only fault i'faith; if they be once set upon a thing, why, there's no removing of 'em till their pretty wills be fulfilled. O, pity thy poor oppressed client here, sweet Cupid, that has scarce six hours' vacation in a month, his causes hang in so many courts; yet never suffer my French adversary nor his big-swollen confederates to overthrow me,
Who without mercy would my blood carouse
And lay me in prison—in a doctor's house.
Thy clemency, great Cupid.—Peace, who comes here?

[Enter Pursenet]

PURSENET Sir gallant, well encountered.

TAILBY
I both salute and take my leave together.

PURSENET Why, whither so fast, sir?

TAILBY
Excuse me, pray, I'm in a little haste;
My horse waits for me.

PURSENET What, some journey toward?

TAILBY A light one, i'faith, sir.

PURSENET
I am sorry that my business so commands me
I cannot ride with you; but I make no question
You have company enough.

TAILBY
Alas, not any—nor do I desire it.
Why, 'tis but to Kingston yonder.

58–9 **highly . . . proud** Both words suggest sexual arousal, and the fur hat may allude to the female genitals.

62 **dispatch her out of hand** A vague but loaded turn of phrase; she is to understand 'relieve her right away'.

73 **out o'th' city** from outside the city

79 **Tiffany** Meaning a kind of transparent silk. Compare the *lawn* (sheer linen) she can be expected to supply (l. Interim 82).

82 **All-Hallowtide** All Hallow's Day, the first of November

85 **workwoman** (*a*) woman who does needlework, (*b*) proficient working woman, expert at her trade

89 **awe** fear

3.1.0.2 ***Enter Tailby*** He will now be fully dressed and wearing his cloak, establishing that the location is now outdoors.

6–8 **if . . . fulfilled** Plays on *thing* as 'penis' and *wills* as 'vaginas'.

9–11 **client . . . courts** Tailby gives this legal terminology a bawdy turn.

11 **my French adversary** i.e. syphilis, the 'French disease'

12 **big-swollen confederates** i.e. prostitutes swollen with venereal disease. Perhaps also suggests another occupational hazard: a pregnant mistress.

21 **light** (*a*) slight, short; (*b*) bawdy, promiscuous

26 **Kingston** Because it had the first bridge west of London, Kingston-on-Thames was an important thoroughfare and a favourite hunting-ground for highwaymen.

PURSENET O, cry you mercy, sir.

TAILBY
'Scape but one reach, there's little danger thither.

PURSENET
True, a little, of Coombe Park.

TAILBY
You've named the place, sir; that's all I fear, i'faith.

PURSENET
Farewell, sweet Master Tailby. *[Exit Tailby]*
This fell out happily.
I'll call this purchase mine before I greet him;
E'en where his fear lies most, there will I meet him.
[He crosses the stage and disguises himself with a scarf]
Boy.
[Enter Boy]

BOY Sir?

PURSENET Walk my horse behind yon thicket. Give a word if you descry.

BOY I have all perfect, sir. *[Exit Boy]*

PURSENET So, he cannot now be long. What, with my boy's dexterity at ordinaries and my gelding's celerity over hedge and ditch, but we make pretty shift to rub out a gallant. For I have learned these principles:
Stoop thou to th' world, 'twill on thy bosom tread;
It stoops to thee if thou advance thy head.
The mind being far more excellent than fate,
'Tis fit our mind then be above our state.
Why should I write my extremities in my brow,
To make them loathe me that respect me now?
If every man were in his courses known,
Legs that now honour him might spurn him down.
To conclude, nothing seems as it is but honesty, and that makes it so little regarded amongst us.

BOY *[within]* Eela! Ha! Ho!

PURSENET The boy! He's hard at hand; I'll cross him suddenly. And here he comes.
[Enter Tailby]
Stand!

TAILBY Ha!

PURSENET Deliver your purse, sir.

TAILBY I feared none but this place, i'faith. Nay, when my mind gives me a thing once—

PURSENET Quick! Quick, sir, quick!
I must dispatch three robberies yet ere night.

TAILBY I'm glad you have such good doings, by my troth, sir.

PURSENET You'll fare never a whit the better for your flattery, I warrant you, sir.

TAILBY I speak sincerely. 'Tis pity such a proper-parted gentleman should want—nor shall you, as long as I have't about me.
[Pursenet begins to search Tailby, taking from him the chain of pearl, a purse, and a folded letter]
Nay, search and spare not: there's a purse in my left pocket, as I take it, with fifteen pound in gold in't, and there's a fair chain of pearl in the other. Nay, I'll deal truly with you. It grieves me, i'faith, when I see such goodly men in distress; I'll rather want it myself than they should go without it.

PURSENET And that shows a good nature, sir.

TAILBY Nay, though I say it, I have been always accounted a man of a good nature; I might have hanged myself ere this time else. Pray, use me like a gentleman: take all, but injury not my body.

PURSENET You must pardon me, sir, I must a little play the usurer and bind you, for mine own security.

TAILBY Alas, there's no conscience in that, sir; shall I enter into bond and pay money too?

PURSENET Tut, I must not be betrayed.

TAILBY Hear me but what I say, sir: I do protest I would not be he that should betray a man, to be prince of the world.

PURSENET Mass, that's the devil, I thank you heartily, for he's called prince o' th' world.

TAILBY You take me still at worst.

PURSENET Swear on this sword, then, to set spurs to your horse, not to look back, to give no marks to any passenger.

TAILBY Marks? Why, I think you have left me ne'er a penny, sir.

PURSENET I mean no marks of any.

TAILBY I understand you, sir.

PURSENET Swear, then.

TAILBY I'faith, I do, sir.

PURSENET Away.

TAILBY I'm gone, sir. *[To audience]* By my troth, of a fierce thief he seems to be a very honest gentleman. *Exit*

PURSENET
Why, this was well-adventured: trim a gallant!
Now with a courteous and long-thirsting eye,
Let me behold my purchase,
And try the soundness of my bones with laughter.
How! Is not this the chain of pearl I gave
To that perjured harlot? 'Tis, 'sfoot, 'tis,
The very chain! O, damnèd mistress! Ha!
And this the purse which not five days before
I sent her filled with fair spur-royals?—Heart,

27 **'Scape** except for; if I escape
reach stretch
28 **Coombe Park** scene of frequent highway robberies
32.1 ***He ... stage*** The location thus shifts to Coombe Park.
40 **shift** fraudulent trick, stratagem, make-shift
46 **write ... brow** i.e. let my problems show in my face
49 **honour him** bend to him in a bow
spurn kick
66 **proper-parted** finely accomplished
73 **want** do without
80–1 **play ... you** punning between physical and legal bonds
90 **take me still at worst** keep putting the worst construction on my character and my words
92 **marks** signs (with a pun on the coin in Tailby's reply)
103 **trim** rob
111 **spur-royals** coins which bore an emblem resembling a spur and were worth five shillings more than a royal

The very gold! 'Slife, is this no robbery!
How many oaths flew toward heaven,
Which ne'er came halfway thither, but, like fire-drakes,
Mounted a little, gave a crack, and fell?—
Feigned oaths bound up to sink more deep to hell.
What folded paper's this? Death, 'tis her hand!
'Master Tailby, you know with what affection I love you.'—You do?—'I count the world but as my prey to maintain you.'—The more dissembling quean, you, I must tell you.—'I have sent you an embroidered purse here with fifty fair spur-royals in't,'—a pox on you for you labour, wench!—'and I desire you, of all loves, to keep that chain of pearl from Master Pursenet's sight.'—He cannot, strumpet; I behold it now, unto thy secret torture.—'So fare thee well, but be constant and want nothing.'—As long as I ha't, i'faith; methinks it should have gone so. Well, what a horrible age do we live in, that a man cannot have a quean to himself; let him but turn his back, the best of her is chipped away like a court loaf, that when a man comes himself, h'as nothing but bombast; and these are two simple chippings here. Does my boy pick and I steal to enrich myself, to keep her, to maintain him? Why, this is right the sequence of the world: a lord maintains her, she maintains a knight, he maintains a whore, she maintains a captain. So, in like manner, the pocket keeps my boy, he keeps me, I keep her, she keeps him; it runs like quicksilver from one to another. 'Sfoot, I perceive I have been the chief upholder of this gallant all this while. It appears true: we that pay dearest for our pasture are ever likely worse used. 'Sfoot, he has a nag can run for nothing, has his choice, nay, and gets by the running of him. O, fine world, strange devils, and pretty, damnable affections.

BOY [*within*] Lela! Ha! Ho!

PURSENET The boy again.
[*Enter Boy*]
What news there?

BOY Master! Pist, master!

PURSENET How now, boy?

BOY I have descried a prize.

PURSENET Another, lad?

BOY The gull. The scholar.

PURSENET Master Bowser?

BOY Ay, comes along this way.

PURSENET Without company?

BOY As sure as he is your own.

PURSENET Back to thy place, boy. [*Exit Boy*]
I have the luck today to rob in safety
Two precious cowards.—Whist! I hear him.
[*Enter Fitzgrave, disguised as Bowser*]
Stand!

FITZGRAVE You lie. I came forth to go.

PURSENET
Deliver your purse.

FITZGRAVE 'Tis better in my pocket.

PURSENET
How now, at disputations, Signor Fool?

FITZGRAVE
I've so much logic to confute a knave, a thief, a rogue.
[*He overpowers Pursenet, whose scarf slips from his face*]

PURSENET
Hold! Hold, sir, an you be a gentleman; hold, let me rise.

FITZGRAVE [*to audience*]
Heart, 'tis the courtesy of his scarf unmasked him to me
Above the lip by chance. I'll counterfeit.
[*To Pursenet*] Light, because I am a scholar! You think belike that scholars have no mettle in 'em, but you shall find—
[*Pursenet tries to run*]
I have not done with you, cousin.

PURSENET
As you're a gentleman—

FITZGRAVE As you're a rogue!

PURSENET
Keep on upon your way, sir.

FITZGRAVE You bade me stand.

PURSENET
I have been once down for that.

FITZGRAVE And then deliver.

PURSENET
Deliver me from you, sir.—O, pox on't,
He's wounded me! Eela! Ha! Ho! My horse! My horse, boy!
[*Exit, running, leaving the letter behind*]

FITZGRAVE
Have you your boy so ready? O, thou world,
How art thou muffled in deceitful forms!
There's such a mist of these, and still hath been,
The brightness of true gentry is scarce seen.
This journey was most happily assigned;
I have found him dross both in his means and mind.
What paper's this he dropped? I'll look on't as I go.
[*Exit*]

114 **fire-drakes** fireworks
120 **quean** prostitute
131 **court loaf** i.e. a loaf with the crusts or *chippings* (l. 98) cut off (implying that at court the best part of the bread is removed with the crust)
132 **bombast** literally 'cotton wool, stuffing'; describing the middle of the loaf
141 **we that pay dearest** Ironic for a thief, unless he is caught.
143 **has his choice** i.e. has the nag to ride whenever he wants
144 **him** Emendation to 'her' would make Pursenet's analogy clearer.

3.2 [*Enter Pursenet and his Boy*]

PURSENET A gull call you him? Let me always set upon wise men; they'll be afraid of their lives; they have a feeling of their iniquities, and knows what 'tis to die with fighting. 'Sfoot, this gull lays on without fear or wit. How deep's it, say'st thou, boy?

BOY By my faith, three inches, sir.

PURSENET La, this was long of you, you rogue!

BOY Of me, sir?

PURSENET Forgive me, dear boy; my wound ached, and I grew angry. There's hope of life, boy, is there not?

BOY Pooh, my life for yours.

PURSENET A comfortable boy in man's extremes! I was ne'er so afraid in my life but the fool would have seen my face; he had me at such advantage he might have commanded my scarf. I 'scaped well there; 't'ad choked me;
My reputation had been past recovery;
Yet live I unsuspected and still fit
For gallants' choice societies. But here I vow,
If e'er I see this Bowser when he cannot see me—
Either in by-lane, privilege place, court-alley—
Or come behind him when he's standing high,
Or take him when he reels from a tavern late,
Pissing again a conduit, wall, or gate;
When he's in such a plight, and clear from men,
I'll do that I am ashamed to speak till then. [*Exeunt*]

3.3 *Enter* [*Fitzgrave and*] *two* [*Gentleman-Gallants*]

FITZGRAVE Nay, read forward. I have found three of your gallants, like your bewitching shame, merely sophistical: there's your bawd-gallant, your pocket-gallant, and your whore-gallant.

A GENTLEMAN-GALLANT [*reading*] 'Master Tailby—'

FITZGRAVE That's he.

A GENTLEMAN-GALLANT 'I count the world but as my prey to maintain you.'

FITZGRAVE That's just the phrase and style of 'em all to him; they meet all together in one effect, and it may well hold, too, for they all jump upon one cause: *subaudi* lechery.

A GENTLEMAN-GALLANT
What shapes can flattery take! Let me entreat you,
Both in the virgin's right and our good hopes,
Since your hours are so fortunate, to proceed.

FITZGRAVE
Why, he's base that faints until he crown his deed.
Exeunt

3.4 *Enter* [*at one door*] *Pursenet* [*his arm bandaged*] *and* [*at another door*] *his First Courtesan*

PURSENET [*to audience*]
See that dissembling devil, that perjured strumpet.

FIRST COURTESAN
Welcome, my soul's best wish!—O, out alas,
Thy arm bound in a scarf? I shall swoon instantly.
[*She appears to faint*]

PURSENET Heart, and I'll fetch you again in the same tune:
O, my unmatchèd love, if any spark of life
Remain, look up, my comfort, my delight, my—

FIRST COURTESAN
O, good, O good!

PURSENET [*to audience*]
The organ of her voice is tuned again;
There's hope in women when their speech returns.
See, like the moon after a black eclipse,
She by degrees recovers her pure light.—
How cheers my love?

FIRST COURTESAN
As one new waked out of a deadly trance,
The fit scarce quiet.

PURSENET 'Twas terrible for the time;
I'd much ado to fetch you.

FIRST COURTESAN 'Shrew your fingers!
How came my comfort wounded? Speak.

PURSENET Faith, in a fray last night.

FIRST COURTESAN
In a fray? Will you lose your blood so vainly?
Many a poor creature lacks it. Tell me, how?
What was the quarrel?

PURSENET Loath to tell you that.

FIRST COURTESAN
Loath to tell me?

PURSENET Yet 'twas my cause of coming.

FIRST COURTESAN
Why then must not I know it?

PURSENET Since you urge it, you shall:
You're a strumpet.

FIRST COURTESAN O, news abroad, sir!

PURSENET Say you so?

FIRST COURTESAN Why, you knew that the first night you lay with me.

3.2.7 **long of you** your fault
11 **my life for yours** proverbial (Dent, L260.1)
15–16 **choked me** Probably implying 'caused me to be hanged'.
21 **privilege place** place of sanctuary
22 **standing high** (*a*) held in high esteem, (*b*) standing in a vulnerable position, (*c*) with an erect penis, sexually preoccupied
24 **again** against
3.3.2 **your bewitching shame** the shameful practice of witchcraft
2–3 **merely sophistical** utterly duplicitous
11 ***subaudi*** a Latin term telling the listener to supply in his or her mind the true word
3.4.4, 15 **fetch you** bring you round
7 **O, good, O good** Evidently she expects that the rhyme-word will be 'wife'. This prompts a quick recovery, perhaps because she *doesn't* want marriage.
15 **'Shrew your fingers** Pursenet has revived her by caressing her, or she exclaims at his injured fingers.

PURSENET Nay, not to me only, but to the world.
FIRST COURTESAN Speak within compass, man.
PURSENET Faith, you know none; you sail without.
FIRST COURTESAN I have the better skill, then.
PURSENET At my first step into a tavern-room to spy that chain of pearl, wound on a stranger's arm, you begged of me.
FIRST COURTESAN How, you mistook it, sure.
PURSENET By heaven, the very self-same chain.
FIRST COURTESAN O, cry you mercy, 'tis true; I'd forgot it: 'tis St George's Day tomorrow; I lent it to my cousin only to grace his arm before his mistress.
PURSENET Notable cunning.
FIRST COURTESAN And is this all now, i'faith?
PURSENET Not; I durst go further.
FIRST COURTESAN Why, let me never possess your love if you see not that again o' Thursday morning. I take't unkindly, i'faith, you should fall out with me for such a trifle.
PURSENET Better and better.
FIRST COURTESAN Come, a kiss, and friends.
PURSENET Away.
FIRST COURTESAN By this hand, I'll spoil your arm an you will not.
PURSENET More for this than the devil.
[They kiss.]
[Enter Goldstone, Tailby, Fitzgrave (disguised as Bowser), Bungler, Second Courtesan, and Pursenet's Boy]
GOLDSTONE Yea, at your book so hard.
PURSENET
Against my will. *[Aside, looking at Fitzgrave]* Are you there, Signor Logic?
A pox of you, sir.
GOLDSTONE Why, how now? What has fate sent us here, in the name of Venus, goddess of Cyprus.
PURSENET A freebooter's pink, sir, three or four inches deep.
GOLDSTONE No more? That's conscionable, i'faith.
TAILBY Troth, I'm sorry for't: pray, how came it, sir?
PURSENET Faith, by a paltry fray in Coleman Street.
FITZGRAVE *[to audience]* Coombe Park, he would say.
PURSENET No less than three at once, sir, made a triangle with their swords and daggers, and all opposing me.
FITZGRAVE And amongst those three, only one hurt you, sir?
PURSENET Ex for ex.
TAILBY Troth, and I'll tell you what luck I had, too, since I parted from you last.
PURSENET What, I pray?
TAILBY The day you offered to ride with me—I wish now I'd had your company—'sfoot, I was set upon in Coombe Park by three, too.
PURSENET Bah!
TAILBY Robbed, by this light, of as much gold and jewels as I valued at forty pound.
PURSENET Sure Saturn is in the fifth house.
TAILBY I know not that; he may be in the sixth an he will, for me. I am sure they were in my pocket, wheresoever they were; but I'll ne'er refuse a gentleman's company again when 'tis offered me, I warrant you.
GOLDSTONE I must remember you 'tis Mitre night, ladies.
SECOND COURTESAN Mass, 'tis indeed Friday today; I'd quite forgot; when a woman's busy, how the time runs away.
FIRST COURTESAN *[aside to Tailby]*
O, you've betrayed us both.
TAILBY I understand you not.
FIRST COURTESAN
You've let him see the chain of pearl I gave you.
TAILBY
Who? Him? Will you believe me? By this hand
He never saw it.
FIRST COURTESAN
Upon a stranger's arm, he swore to me.
TAILBY
Mass, that may be, for the truth is, i'faith,
I was robbed on't at Coombe Park.
FIRST COURTESAN 'Twas that betrayed it.
TAILBY Would I had stayed him;
He was no stranger; he was a thief, i'faith,
For thieves will be no strangers.
FIRST COURTESAN How shall I excuse it?
BUNGLER *[catching the Boy, who was picking his pocket]* Nay, I have you fast enough, boy. You rogue.
BOY Good sir, I beseech you, sir, let me go.

27 **within compass** within limits, with restraint (proverbial: Dent, C577). In l. 28 'without [compass]' implies both 'without restraint' and, as the navigational compass needle always points north, 'without constancy'.
36 **St George's Day** 23 April. The excuse, alluding to the festivities held on that day, is all the more implausible as we are elsewhere told the month is November (see 2.2.14 and 3.1.2–5).
45–6 **Better and better . . . a kiss, and friends** both proverbial (Dent, B329.11, F753)
56 **freebooter's** plunderer's
pink (*a*) hole cut for fashion, (*b*) stab wound
59 **Coleman Street** known for its prosperous and law-abiding residents.
65 **Ex for ex** Perhaps 'tit for tat'. Bullen asks, 'Can this expression mean *ecce*, for example?'. If so, *ex* might be short for *ecce signum*, 'behold the sign', 'here is the proof of it', perhaps playing on 'X' as the cross of Christian symbolism and the supposed shape of the exchanged wounds.
75 **Saturn is in the fifth house** Astrology divides the heavens into twelve 'houses' and for each planet ascribes particular influence to two of these 'houses'; Saturn 'in the fifth house' is a gloomy astrological situation.
80 **remember** remind

He thumps

BUNGLER A pickpocket! Nay, you shall, to Newgate, look you. [*To Pursenet*] Is this your boy, sir?

PURSENET How now, boy? A monster! Thy arm limed fast in another's pocket? Where learned you that manners? What company have you kept alate that you are so transformed into a rogue? That shape I know not. [*To Bungler*] Believe me, sir, I much wonder at the alteration of this boy, where he should get this nature. As good a child to see, too, and as virtuous; he has his creed by heart, reads me his chapter duly every night; he will not miss you one title in the nine commandments.

BUNGLER There's ten of 'em.

PURSENET I fear he skips o'er one: 'thou shalt not steal'.

BUNGLER Mass, like enough.

PURSENET
Else grace and memory would quite abash the boy.—
Thou graceless imp! Ah, thou prodigious child
Begot at some eclipse, degenerate rogue,
Shame to thy friends, and to thy master eke;
How far digressing from the noble mind
Of thy brave ancestors that lie in marble
With their coat-armours o'er 'em!

BUNGLER Had he such friends?

PURSENET The boy is well descended, though he be a rogue and has no feeling on't. Yet for my sake and for my reputation's, seek not the blood of the boy; he's near allied to many men of worship now yet living; a fine old man to his father; it would kill his heart, i'faith; he'd away like a chrisom.

BUNGLER Alas, good gentleman.

PURSENET [*to the Boy*]
Ah, shameless villain, complain'st thou? Dost thou want?

BOY No, no, no, no.

PURSENET
Art not well clad? thy hunger well resisted?

BOY Yes, yes, yes, yes.

PURSENET
But thou shalt straight to Bridewell.

BOY Sweet master!

PURSENET
Live upon bread and water, and chap-choke.

BOY I beseech your worship!

BUNGLER Come, I'll be his surety for once.

PURSENET You shall excuse me indeed, sir.

BUNGLER He will mend; a may prove an honest man for all this. I know gallant gentlemen now that have done as much as this comes to in their youth.

PURSENET Say you so, sir?

BUNGLER And as for Bridewell, that will but make him worse; a will learn more knavery there in one week than will furnish him and his heirs for a hundred year.

PURSENET Deliver the boy?

BUNGLER Nay, I tell you true, sir, there's none goes in there a quean but she comes out an arrant whore, I warrant you.

PURSENET The boy comes not there for a million.

BUNGLER No, you had better forgive him by ten parts.

PURSENET True, but a must not know it comes from me. [*To Boy*] Down o' your knees, you rogue, and thank this gentleman has got your pardon.

BOY [*to Bungler*] O, I thank your worship.

PURSENET [*aside to Boy*] A pox on you for a rogue; you put me to my set speech once a quarter.

GOLDSTONE [*to the other gallants*] Nay, gentlemen, you quite forget your hour. Lead, Master Bowser.

Exeunt all but Goldstone and [Second] Courtesan

SECOND COURTESAN Let me go; you're a dissembler.

GOLDSTONE How?

SECOND COURTESAN Did not you promise me a new gown?

GOLDSTONE Did I not? Yes, faith, did I, and thou shalt have it. [*Calling offstage*] Go, sirrah, run for a tailor presently.—Let me see, for the colour now: orange tawny? peach colour? What say'st to a watchet satin?

[*Enter Tailor*]

SECOND COURTESAN O, 'tis the only colour I affect.

TAILOR A very orient colour, an't please your worships; I made a gown on't for a gentlewoman t'other day, and it does passing well upon her.

GOLDSTONE A watchet satin gown—

TAILOR There your worship left, sir.

GOLDSTONE Laid about, tailor—

TAILOR Very good, sir.

GOLDSTONE With four fair laces.

TAILOR That will be costly, sir.

97 **Newgate** the most famous of London's prisons, and the way-station to the gallows at Tyburn

99 **A monster** The conjunction of Bungler and the Boy is seen as a strange and unnatural beast. There is a suggestion that the hand in the pocket is an act of sexual deviance.
limed caught, as with birdlime smeared on twigs to catch birds with its stickiness. The catcher has become the caught, for more usually a thief would be said to take his plunder with limed fingers.

106 **chapter** of the Bible

107 **title** heading; i.e. one commandment

112 **prodigious** of unnatural and ominous birth, monstrous

114 **eke** archaic word for 'also'. Pursenet's feigned horror is reflected in his overly traditional diction.

115 **digressing** departing, transgressing

116 **in marble** represented in marble funeral statuary

117 **coat-armours** coats of arms

118 **friends** relatives

124 **a chrisom** an infant who dies. Presumably suggests a quiet and unexpected 'cot death'.

130 **Bridewell** a prison

131 **chap-choke** *chaps* were cheeks; hence 'choke on your own caved-in cheeks'

146 **the . . . million** proverbial ('not for a million', Dent, M963.11)

147 **by ten parts** i.e. it would be ten times better

150 **has** that has

161–2 **orange tawny** orange-brown

162 **watchet** light blue

164 **orient** lustrous

168 **There your worship left** that's where your worship left off

GOLDSTONE How, you rogue, costly? Out o'th' house, you slip-shod, sham'-legged, brown-thread, penny-skeined rascal.

[He chases the Tailor away]

SECOND COURTESAN Nay, my sweet love.

GOLDSTONE Hang him, rogue; he's but a botcher neither. Come, I'll send thee a fellow worth a hundred of this if the slave were clean enough. *Exeunt*

Finis Actus Tertius

4.1 *Actus Quartus*

[During the music, a cloak is set on the stage.]

Enter Goldstone, calling 'Master Bowser'

GOLDSTONE Master Bowser, Master Bowser! Ha, ha, ho! Master Bowser!

FITZGRAVE *[within]* Holla!

GOLDSTONE What, not out of thy kennel, Master Bowser?

FITZGRAVE *[within]* Master Goldstone, you're an early gallant, sir!

GOLDSTONE *[to audience]* A fair cloak yonder, i'faith.—By my troth, abed, Master Bowser? You remember your promise well o'ernight!

FITZGRAVE *[within]* Why, what's o'clock, sir?

GOLDSTONE Do you ask that now? Why, the chimes are spent at St Bride's.

FITZGRAVE *[within]* 'Tis a gentleman's hour. Faith, Master Goldstone, I'll be ready in a trice.

GOLDSTONE Away, there's no trust to you.

FITZGRAVE *[within]* Faith, I'll come instantly.

GOLDSTONE *[aside]* Nay, choose whether you will or no; by my troth, your cloak shall go before you.

FITZGRAVE *[within]* Nay, Master Goldstone, I ha' sworn—do you hear, sir?

GOLDSTONE Away, away! Faith, I'm angry with you: pox, abed now! I'm ashamed of it.

[Exit Goldstone with the cloak]

[Enter Fitzgrave, in his shirt]

FITZGRAVE Foot, my cloak! My cloak! Master Goldstone, 'slife, what mean you by this, sir? You'll bring it back again, I hope. *[Getting no response]* No, not yet? By my troth, I care very little for such kind of jesting; methinks this familiarity now extends a little too far—unless it be a new fashion come forth this morning secretly; yesterday 'twould have shown unmannerly and saucily. I scarce know yet what to think on't. Well, there's no great profit in standing in my shirt; I'll on with my clothes; he's bound me to follow the suit. My cloak's a stranger; he was made but yesterday, and I do not love to trust him alone in company. *Exit*

Enter Frip [wearing Fitzgrave's cloak] 4.2

FRIP What may I conjecture of this Goldstone? He has not only pawned to me this cloak, but the very diamond and sapphire which I bestowed upon my new love at Master Primero's house. The cloak's new, and comes fitly to do me great grace at a wedding this morning to which I was solemnly invited. I can continue change more than the proudest gallant of 'em all; yet never bestow penny of myself, my pawns do so kindly furnish me. But the sight of these jewels is able to cloy me, did I not preserve my stomach the better for the wedding dinner. A gift could never have come in a more patient hour, nor to be better digested. Is she proved false?—But I'll not fret today, nor chafe my blood.

Enter Pursenet

PURSENET *[to audience]* Ha, yonder goes Bowser; the place is fit. *[Calling offstage]* Boy, stand with my horse at corner.—I owe you for a pink three inches deep, sir.

[He wounds Frip, who falls]

FRIP O, O, O!

PURSENET Take that in part of payment for Coombe Park!

FRIP O, O, O! *Exit [Pursenet]*

Enter Fitzgrave, [disguised as Bowser]

FITZGRAVE How now, who's this? 'Sfoot, one of our gallants knocked down like a calf. Is there such a plague of 'em here at London they begin to knock 'em o'th' head already?

FRIP O, Master Bowser, pray, lend me your hand, sir; I am slain.

FITZGRAVE

Slain and alive? O, cruel execution!
What man so savage-spirited durst presume
To strike down satin on two taffetas cut,
Or lift his hand against a beaver hat?

FRIP *[rising, with help from Fitzgrave]*

Some rogue that owes me money, and had no other means
To a wedding dinner. I must be dressed myself, methinks.

FITZGRAVE How! Why, this is my cloak! Life, how came my cloak hither?

FRIP Is it yours, sir? Master Goldstone pawned it to me this morning fresh and fasting, and borrowed five pound upon't.

174 **slip-shod** (*a*) wearing slippers (*b*) slovenly
sham'-legged shamble-legged, limping
penny-skeined A *skein* was a reel of thread.
177 **botcher** tailor who does repairs, probably badly
4.1.11–12 **the chimes are spent** the bells have all been rung. Unlikely to mean it is after midday, as (*a*) the *gentleman's hour* for lunch, let alone rising, was 11 o'clock, (*b*) see 4.2.34–5; it is not midday until 4.5. *St Bride's* might refer not to the church but to Bridewell near it: once a royal house, in Jacobean times a prison.
14 **in a trice** proverbial (Dent, T517)
17 **whether ... no** proverbial (Dent, W400.1)
4.2.7 **the proudest ... of 'em all** proverbial (Dent, P614)
9 **But** merely (?)
9–10 **did ... stomach** i.e. if it weren't that I'm keeping my appetite
31 **be dressed** (*a*) be properly attired (*b*) have my wound tended to
35 **fresh and fasting** i.e. before breakfast

FITZGRAVE How, pawned it? Pray, let me hear out this story; come, and I'll lend you to the next barber-surgeon's.—Pawned my cloak? *[Exeunt]*

4.3 *Enter Goldstone and [Bungler, meeting Marmaduke]*

BUNGLER How now, Marmaduke, what's the wager?

MARMADUKE Nay, my care is at end, sir, now I am come to the sight of you. My mistress your cousin entreats you to take part of a dinner with her at home at her house, and bring what gentleman you please to accompany you.

BUNGLER Thank my sweet coz; I'll munch with her, say.

MARMADUKE I'll tell her so.

BUNGLER Marmaduke.

MARMADUKE Sir?

BUNGLER Will there be any stock-fish, think'st thou?

MARMADUKE How, sir?

BUNGLER Tell my coz I've a great appetite to stock-fish, i'faith. *[Exit Marmaduke]*
Master Goldstone, I'll entreat you to be the gentleman that shall accompany me.

GOLDSTONE Not me, sir.

BUNGLER You, sir.

GOLDSTONE By my troth, concluded. What state bears thy coz, sirrah?

BUNGLER O, a fine merchant's wife—

GOLDSTONE Or rather: a merchant's fine wife.

BUNGLER Trust me, and that's the properer phrase here at London, and 'tis as absurd, too, to call him fine merchant, for, being at sea, a man knows not what pickle he is in.

GOLDSTONE Why, true—

BUNGLER Yet my coz will be served in plate, I can tell you; she has her silver jugs and her gilt tankards.

GOLDSTONE Fie!

BUNGLER Nay, you shall see a house dressed up, i'faith; you must not think to tread o'th' ground when you come there.

GOLDSTONE No? How then?

BUNGLER Why, upon paths made of fig-frails and white blankets cut out in steaks.

GOLDSTONE Away. *[To audience]* I have thought of a device.—Where shall we meet an hour hence?

BUNGLER In Paul's.

GOLDSTONE Agreed. *Exit Bungler*

Enter Fitzgrave, [at a distance, disguised as Bowser]

FITZGRAVE
The broker-gallant and the cheating-gallant;
Now I have found 'em all. I so rejoice
That the redeeming of my cloak I weigh not.
I have spied him.

GOLDSTONE Pox, here's Bowser.

FITZGRAVE Master Goldstone, my cloak! Come, where's my cloak, sir?

GOLDSTONE O, you're a sure gentleman, especially if a man stand in need of you; he may be slain in a morning to breakfast ere you vouchsafe to peep out of your lodging.

FITZGRAVE How!

GOLDSTONE No less than four gallants, as I'm a gentleman, drew all upon me at once and opposed me so spitefully that I not only lost your cloak i'th' fray—

FITZGRAVE *[to audience]* Comes it in there?

GOLDSTONE But my rich hangers, sirrah; I think thou hast seen 'em.

FITZGRAVE Never, i'faith, sir.

GOLDSTONE Those with the two unicorns all wrought in pearl and gold? Pox on't; it frets me ten times more than the loss of the paltry cloak. Prithee, an thou lov'st me, speak no more on't; it brings the unicorns into my mind, and thou wouldst not think how the conceit grieves me. I will not do thee that disgrace, i'faith, to offer thee any satisfaction, for in my soul I think thou scorn'st it; thou bear'st that mind, in my conscience; I have always said so of thee. Fare thee well; when shall I see thee at my chamber, when?

FITZGRAVE Every day, shortly.

GOLDSTONE I have fine toys to show thee.

FITZGRAVE You win my heart then. *Exit Goldstone*
The devil scarce knew what a portion he gave his children when he allowed 'em large impudence to live upon and so turned 'em into th'world. Surely he gave away the third part of the riches of his kingdom; revenues are but fools to't:
The filèd tongue and the undaunted forehead
Are mighty patrimonies, wealthier than those
The city sire or the court father leaves.
In these behold it: riches oft like slaves
Revolt; they bear their foreheads to their graves.
What soonest grasps advancement, men's great suits,
Trips down rich widows, gains repute and name,
Makes way where'er it comes, bewitches all?

38 **lend you** a jocular way of saying 'hand you over', appropriate to Frip as pawnbroker (unless 'lend' is a misprint for 'lead')

4.3.1 **wager** competition prize. 'What's the wager' is apparently a mocking comment on Marmaduke's haste.

4 **take part of** partake in

11 **stock-fish** fish cured in the open air without salt. Bungler absurdly views this cheap and abundant fish as a delicacy.

25–6 **what...in** proverbial (Dent, P276), playing on brine as a pickling liquid

28 **in plate** with silver and gold utensils

35 **fig-frails** woven floor mats

36 **steaks** strips

39 **Paul's** St Paul's Cathedral, the daily meeting place of gallants and would-be gallants, who used its middle aisle as a promenade

42 **found** revealed

49 **to** before

70 **toys** amusements

72 **portion** inheritance; fate, destiny

76 **to't** compared with it

77 **filèd tongue...undaunted forehead** proverbial: Dent, T400.2; F590.1 ('to have an impudent forehead')
filèd smooth, polished
forehead countenance; impudence

Thou, impudence, the minion of our days,
On whose pale cheeks favour and fortune plays!
Call you these your five gallants? Trust me, they're rare fellows:
They live on nothing. Many cannot live on something;
Here they may take example. Suspectless virgin,
How easy had thy goodness been beguiled!
Now only rests that, as to me they're known,
So to the world their base arts may be shown. *Exit*

4.4 *Enter Pursenet and his Boy*

PURSENET Art sure thou saw'st him receive't, boy?

BOY Forty pound in gold, as I'm a gentleman born.

PURSENET Thy father gave thee ram's-head, boy.

BOY No, you're deceived, my mother gave that, sir.

PURSENET What's thy mother's is thy father's.

Enter Piamont

BOY I'm sorry it holds in the rams-head. See, here he walks; I was sure he came into Paul's. The gold had been yours, master, long ere this, but that he wears both his hands in his pockets.

PURSENET How unfortunately is my purpose seated! What the devil should come in his mind to keep in his hands so long? The biting but of a paltry louse would do me great kindness now; I knew not how to requite it. Will no rascal creature assist me? Stay! What if I did impudently salute 'em out? Good. Boy, be ready, boy.

BOY Upon the least advantage, sir.

PURSENET [*to Piamont*] You're most devoutly met in Paul's, sir.

PIAMONT So are you, but I scarce remember you, sir.

PURSENET O, I cry you mercy, sir; I pray pardon me. I fear I have tendered an offence, sir; troth, I took you at the first for one Master Dumpling, a Norfolk gentleman.

PIAMONT There's no harm done yet, sir.

PURSENET [*to audience*] I hope he is there by this time.— How now, boy, hast it?

BOY No, by troth, have I not; this labour's lost; 'tis in the right pocket, and he kept that hand in sure enough.

PURSENET [*to audience*] Unpractised gallant! Salute me but with one hand, like a counterfeit soldier?
O, times and manners! Are we grown beasts?
Do we salute by halves? Are not our limbs at leisure?
Where's comely nurture, the Italian kiss,
Or the French cringe with the Polonian waist? Are all forgot?
Then misery follows. Surely fate forbade it;
Had he employed but his right hand, I'd had it.

[*Enter Bungler*]

It must be an everlasting device, I think, that procures both his hands out at once.

[*He feigns a swoon, Piamont and Bungler go to assist him, and the Boy picks Piamont's pocket*]

[*Exeunt Pursenet and Boy*]

PIAMONT [*to Bungler*] Do you walk, sir?

BUNGLER No, I stay a little for a gentleman's coming too.

PIAMONT Farewell then, sir; I have forty pound in gold about me, which I must presently send down into the country.

BUNGLER Fare you well, sir. [*Exit Piamont*]
I wonder Master Goldstone spares my company so long; 'tis now about the navel of the day, upon the belly of noon.

Enter Goldstone and his man [*Fulk*], *disguised both*

GOLDSTONE [*aside to Fulk*] See where he walks; be sure you let off at a twinkling now.

FULK [*aside to Goldstone*] When did I miss you? [*Aloud to Goldstone*] Your worship has forgot; you promised Mistress Newcut, your cousin, to dine with her this day.

GOLDSTONE Mass, that was well remembered.

BUNGLER I am bold to salute you, sir.

GOLDSTONE Sir.

BUNGLER Is Mistress Newcut your cousin, sir?

GOLDSTONE Yes, she's a cousin of mine, sir.

BUNGLER Then I am a cousin of yours by the sister's side.

GOLDSTONE Let me salute you then; I shall be glad of your farther acquaintance.

BUNGLER I am a bidden guest there, too.

GOLDSTONE Indeed, sir.

BUNGLER Faith, invited this morning.

GOLDSTONE Your good company shall be kindly embraced, sir.

BUNGLER I walk a turn or two here for a gentleman, but I think he'll either overtake me or be before me.

GOLDSTONE 'Tis very likely, sir. [*Giving money to Fulk*] There, sirrah; go to dinner, and about two wait for me.

4.4.1 **Art...boy** See 4.6.3–5.

3 **gave thee ram's-head** i.e. made you thick-headed. The Boy then implies that his mother cuckolded his father, alluding to the cuckold's horns.

12–13 **The...now** Piamont would have to take his hand out of his pocket to scratch.

22 **Dumpling** (*a*) ball of dough or suet associated with Norfolk cooking, (*b*) short, dumpy person. Hence 'country yokel'.

23–6 **There's no harm done...this labour's lost** proverbial (Dent, H165.11; L9)

29 **counterfeit soldier** Pursenet suggests that Piamont is pretending injury to one of his arms.

30 **O, times and manners** Echoes Cicero's '*O tempora, O mores*'.
grown perhaps disyllabic: 'growen'

32–3 **the Italian...waist** The mock-Ciceronian lament on the decline of manners has a practical motive. An elaborate Italian kiss, or a French or Polish bow (from the *waist*), would require Piamont to remove his hands from his pockets.

45–6 **the navel...noon** i.e. the middle of the day

48 **let off** discharge; i.e. start your performance
at a twinkling proverbial (Dent, T635)

49 **miss** fail

BUNGLER Nay, let him come between two and three, cousin, for we love to sit long at dinner i'th' City. *[Exit Fulk]*

GOLDSTONE Come, sweet cousin.

BUNGLER Nay, cousin; keep your way, cousin. Good cousin, I will not, i'faith, cousin. *Exeunt*

4.5

Enter Mistress Newcut and Marmaduke, [who is setting the dinner table]

NEWCUT Why, how now, sirrah, upon twelve of the clock and not the cloth laid yet? Must we needs keep Exchange time still?

MARMADUKE I am about it, forsooth.

NEWCUT You're 'about it, forsooth'! You're still about many things, but you ne'er do one well. I am an ass to keep thee in th' house now my husband's at sea; thou hast no audacity with thee, a foolish dreaming lad, fitter to be in the garret than in any place else; no grace nor manly behaviour. When didst thou ever come to me but with thy head hanging down? O, decheerful prentice, uncomfortable servant! *[Exit Marmaduke]* Pray heaven the gull my cousin has so much wit left as to bring Master Tailby along with him—my comfort, my delight—for that was the chiefest cause I did invite him. I bade him bring what gentleman he pleased to accompany him; as far as I durst go. Why may he not then make choice of Master Tailby? Had he my wit or feeling he would do't.

Enter Bungler and Goldstone, disguised

BUNGLER Where's my sweet cousin here? Does she lack any guests?

NEWCUT Ever such guests as you; you're welcome, cousin.

GOLDSTONE I am rude, lady.

NEWCUT You're most welcome, sir.

BUNGLER There will be a gallant here anon, coz; he promised faithfully.

NEWCUT Who is't? Master Tailby?

BUNGLER Master Tailby? No, Master Goldstone.

NEWCUT Master Goldstone? I could think well of that Goldstone were't not for one vile trick he has.

GOLDSTONE What's that, lady?

NEWCUT In jest he will pawn his punks for suppers.

GOLDSTONE That's a vile part in him, i'faith, an he were my brother.

NEWCUT Pray, gentlemen, sit awhile; your dinner shall come presently. *[Exit]*

GOLDSTONE *[to audience]*
Yea, Mistress Newcut, at first give me a trip?
A close bite always asks a secret nip.

BUNGLER My cousin here is a very kind-natured soul, i'faith, in her humour.

GOLDSTONE Pooh, you know her not so well as I, coz; I have observed her in all her humours. You ne'er saw her a little waspish, I think.

BUNGLER I have not i'faith.

GOLDSTONE Pooh, then ye ne'er saw pretty humour in your life. I can bring her into't when I list.

BUNGLER Would you could, i'faith.

GOLDSTONE Would I could? By my troth, an I were sure thou couldst keep thy countenance, coz, what a pretty jest have I thought upon already to entertain time before dinner.

BUNGLER Prithee, coz, what is't? I love a jest o' life, i'faith.

GOLDSTONE Ah, but I am jealous you will not keep your countenance, i'faith.

BUNGLER Why, ye shall see a pretty story of a humour.

GOLDSTONE Faith, I'll try you for once. You know my cousin will wonder when she comes in to see the cloth laid and ne'er a salt upon the board.

BUNGLER That's true, i'faith.

GOLDSTONE *[taking the silver salt-cellar]* Now will I stand a while out of sight with it, and give her humour play a little.

BUNGLER Coz, dost thou love me? An thou wilt ever do anything for me, do't.

GOLDSTONE Marry, I build upon your countenance.

BUNGLER Why, dost thou think I'm an ass, coz?

GOLDSTONE I would be loathe to undertake it else, for if you should burst out presently, coz, the jest would be spoiled.

BUNGLER Why, do not I know that? Away, stand close. So, so. Mum, cousin! *[Exit Goldstone with salt-cellar]* A merry companion, i'faith; here will be good sport anon.

[Enter Mistress Newcut]

Whist, she comes!

NEWCUT I make you stay long for a bad dinner here, cousin; if Master Goldstone were come, the meat's e'en ready.

BUNGLER Some great business detains him, cousin, but he'll not be long now.

NEWCUT Why, how now? Cud's my life—

BUNGLER Why?

NEWCUT Was ever mistress so plagued with a shittle-headed servant? Why, Marmaduke!

MARMADUKE *[within]* I come, forsooth.

NEWCUT Able to shame me from generation to generation.

[Enter Marmaduke]

MARMADUKE Did you call, forsooth?

---

75 **I will not, i'faith** Bungler is being polite and refusing to go before Goldstone—but Goldstone doesn't know the way.

4.5.2–3 **keep Exchange time** The bell at the Royal Exchange, the stock market built in 1566 by Thomas Gresham, announced lunch-time for merchants at noon. The custom with gentry and aristocrats was to eat at 11 am.

33–4 **an ... brother** proverbial (Dent, B686.1)

38 **asks** invites
nip also meant a pickpocket

52 **o' life** of all things

55 **story** painting or sculpture containing human figures

58 **salt** salt-cellar; generally the main ornament of a table

65 **build upon your countenance** depend on your keeping a straight face

80 **Cud's** a corruption of 'God's'

82–3 **shittle-headed** flighty

NEWCUT Come hither, forsooth. Did you lay this cloth?

MARMADUKE Yes, forsooth.

NEWCUT Do you use to lay a cloth without a salt? A salt, a salt, a salt, a salt, a salt?

MARMADUKE How many salts would you have? I'm sure I set the best i'th' house upon the board.

BUNGLER How, cousin?—(*Sings*) Cousin, cousin, did call cozen.

NEWCUT Did you see a salt upon the board when you came in?

BUNGLER [*bursting out in a laugh*] Pooh!

NEWCUT Come, come; I thought as much. Beshrew your fingers, where is't now?

BUNGLER Your cousin yonder—

NEWCUT Why, the man's mad.

BUNGLER [*calling offstage*] Cousin! Hist, cousin!

NEWCUT What say you?

BUNGLER Pooh, I call not you; I call my cousin. Come forth with th' salt, cousin. [*Looking offstage*] Ha? How? Nobody? Why, was not he that came in e'en now your cousin?

NEWCUT My cousin? O, my bell-salt! O, my great bell-salt!

Enter Goldstone [as himself]

BUNGLER The tenor bell-salt. O, here comes Master Goldstone now, cousin; he may tell us some news on him. [*To Goldstone*] Did you not meet a fellow about door, with a great silver salt under his arm?

GOLDSTONE No, sure, I met none such.

NEWCUT Pardon me, sir; I forgot all this while to bid you welcome. I shall loathe this room for ever. [*To Marmaduke*] Take hence the cloth, you unlucky maple-faced rascal. [*Exit Marmaduke*]
Come, you shall dine in my chamber, sir.

GOLDSTONE No better place, lady.

Exeunt [Newcut and Goldstone by one door, Bungler by another]

4.6 *Enter Piamont*

PIAMONT No less than forty pound in fair gold at one lift! The next shall swoon and swoon again till the devil fetch him, ere I set hand to him. Heart, nothing vexes me so much but that I paid the goldsmith for the change, too, not an hour before. Had I left it alone in the chain of silver as it was at first, it might have given me some notice at his departure. 'Sfoot, I could fight with a windmill now. Sure 'twas some unlucky villain. Why should he come and salute me wrongfully too, mistake me at noonday? Now I think on't in cold blood, it could not be but an induction to some villainous purpose. Well, I shall meet him.

Enter Pursenet

PURSENET [*to audience*] This forty pound came fortunately to redeem my chain of pearl from mortgage. I would not care how often I swooned to have such a good caudle to comfort me; gold and pearl is very restorative.

PIAMONT [*to audience*] See, yonder's the rogue I suspect for foul play. I'll walk muffled by him, offer some offence or cause of a quarrel, only to try his temper. If he be a coward, he's the likelier to be a rogue—an infallible note.

[*He muffles himself, then bumps into Pursenet*]

PURSENET What? A pox ail you, sir! Would I had been aware of you.

PIAMONT Sir, speak you to me?

PURSENET Not I, sir; pray keep on your way; I have nothing to say to you.

PIAMONT You're a rascal.

PURSENET You may say your pleasure, sir; but I hope I go not like a rascal.

PIAMONT Are you fain to fly to your clothes because you're gallant? Why, there's no rascal like your gallant rascal, believe that.

PURSENET You have took me at such an hour, faith, you may call me e'en what you please; nothing will move me.

PIAMONT No? I'll make somewhat move you!

[*He unmuffles and draws his sword*]

Draw! I suspected you were a rogue, and you have pursed it up well with a coward!

PURSENET [*to audience*] Who?—My patron.

PIAMONT Keep out, you rascal.

PURSENET [*to audience*] The guest that did me the kindness in Paul's.—Hold, as you are a gentleman. You'll give me breath, sir?

[*He runs away, dropping the chain of pearl*]

PIAMONT Are you there with me? A vengeance stop you; you have found breath enough to run away from me. I will never meet this slave hereafter in a morning but I will breathe myself upon him. Since I can have no

93–4 **Cousin ... cozen** Plays on the expression *to call cousins*, 'to call each other cousin, to assume familiarity'. Bungler fails to keep his countenance and gives the game away in a sing-song refrain that puns between *cousin* and *cozen*, 'cheat'.
108 **bell-salt** salt-cellar shaped like a bell
109 **tenor** as of a large bell
116–17 **maple-faced** spotty-faced
4.6.5 **change** i.e. removal of the gold from the chain of silver
7 **his** its
7–8 **fight with a windmill** Alludes to Cervantes's Don Quixote. Proverbial, though not recorded as such before Middleton (*Don Quixote* had not as yet been published in English).
8 **unlucky** mischief-making, malicious
16 **gold ... restorative** Plays on the fact that gold and pearl were indeed sometimes dissolved into restoratives.
21 **note** noteworthy point
28–9 **go not like a rascal** don't appear by my dress to be of low birth
38 **pursed it up** combined it (as by putting in the same purse)
39 **My patron** Piamont's 'patronage' upholds Pursenet's business.
40 **Keep out** draw your sword
41 **guest** fellow, customer (or 'stranger')
47 **breathe** exercise

other satisfaction, he shall save me that forty pound in fence-school. *Exit*

4.7 [*Enter Goldstone*]

GOLDSTONE
When things are cleanly carried, sign of judgement:
I was the welcom'st gallant to her alive
After the salt was stolen; then a good dinner,
A fine provoking meal which drew on apace
The pleasure of a day-bed, and I had it;
This here one ring can witness. When I parted,
Who but 'sweet Master Goldstone'? I left her in that trance.
What cannot wit, so it be impudent,
Devise and compass? I would fain know that fellow now
That would suspect me but for what I am;
He lives not. 'Tis all in the conveyance.
[*He sees the chain of pearl*]
What?
Thou look'st not like a beggar; what mak'st thou
On the ground? I have a hand to help thee up.—
A fair chain of pearl.
Surely, a merchant's wife gives lucky handsel.
They that find pearl may wear't at a cheap rate.
Marry, my lady dropped it from her arm
For a device to toll me to her bed:
I've seen as great a matter.
[*Enter Primero and Frip*]
Who be these? I'll be too crafty for you.—
O, Monsieur Primero, Signor Frip; is it you, gallants?

FRIP Sweet Master Goldstone!
[*Frip and Goldstone*] *whisper* [*apart*]. *Enter Tailby*

TAILBY [*to audience*] Every bawd exceeds me in fortune: Master Primero was robbed of a carcanet upon Monday last, laid the goldsmiths, and found it. I ha' laid goldsmith, jeweller, burnisher, broker, and the devil and all, I think, yet could never so much as hear of that chain of pearl. He was a notable thief; he works close.—Peace! Who be these? Ha, let me see: by this light, there it is! Back, lest they see thee. A happy minute. Goldstone! What an age do we breathe in! Who that saw him now would think he were maintained by purses? So, who that meets me would think I were maintained by wenches? As far as I can see, 'tis all one case, and holds both in one court; we are both maintained by the common roadway. Keep thou thine own heart thou liv'st unsuspected; I leese you again now. [*Exit Tailby*]

GOLDSTONE But I pray you, tell me,
Met you no gentlewomen by the way you came?

FRIP
Not any. What should they be?

GOLDSTONE Nay, I do but ask
Because a gentlewoman's glove was found
Near to the place I met you.

PRIMERO Faith, we saw none, sir.
[*Enter Tailby and two Constables*]

TAILBY Good officers, upon suspicion of felony.

FIRST CONSTABLE Very good, sir.

SECOND CONSTABLE What call you the thief's name you do suspect?

TAILBY Master Justinian Goldstone.

SECOND CONSTABLE [*to the other Constable*] Remember: Master Justice Goldstone. [*To the other Constable and Tailby*] A terrible world the whilst, my masters.

TAILBY Look you, that's he; upon him, officers.

SECOND CONSTABLE I see him not yet; which is he, sir?

TAILBY Why, that.

SECOND CONSTABLE He a thief, sir? Who, that gentleman i'th' satin?

TAILBY E'en he.

SECOND CONSTABLE Farewell, sir; you're a merry gentleman.

TAILBY As you will answer it, officers, I'll bear you out; I'll be your warrant.

SECOND CONSTABLE Nay, an you say so. What's his name then?

TAILBY Justinian Goldstone.

SECOND CONSTABLE Master Justinian Goldstone, we apprehend you, sir, upon suspicion of felony.

GOLDSTONE Me?

TAILBY You, sir.

FIRST CONSTABLE I charge you, in the King's name, gentlemen, to assist us.

GOLDSTONE Master Tailby?

TAILBY The same man, sir.

GOLDSTONE Life, what's the news?

TAILBY Ha' you forgot Coombe Park?

GOLDSTONE Coombe Park? No, 'tis in Kingston way.

TAILBY I believe you'll find it so.

GOLDSTONE I not deny it.

SECOND CONSTABLE Bear witness: he's confessed.

GOLDSTONE What have I confessed, pair of coxcombs indubitable?

TAILBY
I was robbed finely of this chain of pearl there,
And forty fair spur-royals.

GOLDSTONE Did I rob you?

49 **fence-school** i.e. tuition fees in fencing. Piamont will practise for free on Pursenet.

4.7.1 **cleanly** adroitly
carried (*a*) managed, (*b*) stolen

15 **handsel** good-luck present, pledge of good things to follow

18 **toll** lure

24 **carcanet** ornate necklace

25 **laid** beset, searched

26–7 **the devil and all** proverbial (Dent, D224.11)

36 **by the common roadway** i.e. by the public highway (theft of purses), by sexual commerce (prostitution)

36–7 **Keep... unsuspected** Spoken as to Goldstone.

37 **heart** understanding, conviction
leese (*a*) lose, part company with; (*b*) destroy, ruin. *OED* less plausibly glosses 'set free, deliver, release', quoting this line—which would seem to require a change of referent to the chain of pearl.

81 **finely** subtly

TAILBY There where I find my goods I may suspect, sir.
FRIP I dreamt this would be his end.
GOLDSTONE See how I am wronged, gentlemen:
As I have a soul, I found this chain of pearl
Not three yards from this place, just when I met you.
TAILBY Ha, ha!
FRIP [*to Goldstone*] Yet the law's such, if he but swear 'tis you, you're gone.
GOLDSTONE Pox on't that e'er I saw't!
FRIP [*to Tailby*] Can you but swear 'tis he? Do but that, and you tickle him, i'faith.
TAILBY Nay, an it come once to swearing, let me alone.
FRIP Say and hold; he called my jewels counterfeit and so cheated the poor wench of 'em.
SECOND CONSTABLE Come, bring him away. Come!
GOLDSTONE 'Twill call my state in question!
[*Enter Pursenet*]
PURSENET
I think what's got by theft doth never prosper;
Now lost my chain of pearl.
[*He sees Goldstone with the chain of pearl, and seizes it*]
Come, Master Goldstone,
Let't go; this' mine, i'faith.
GOLDSTONE The chain of pearl?
PURSENET By my troth, it's mine.
GOLDSTONE By my troth, much good do't you, sir.
[*He hands Pursenet the chain of pearl*]
FRIP I'm glad in my soul, sir.—(*Gnaws*)
FIRST CONSTABLE [*to Pursenet*] Deliver your weapons.
PURSENET How?
FIRST CONSTABLE You're apprehended upon suspicion of felony.
PURSENET Felony? What's that?
TAILBY Was it you, i'faith, sir, all this while, that did me that kindness to ease both my pockets at Coombe Park?
PURSENET I, sir? Pray, gentlemen, draw near; let's talk among ourselves.—[*To a Constable*] Stand apart, scoundrel.—Must every gentleman be upbraided in public that flies out now and then upon necessity, to be themes for pedlars and weavers? This should not be; 'twas never seen among the Romans, nor read we of it in the time of Brute. Are we more brutish now? Did I list to blab, do not I know your course of life, Master Tailby, to be as base as the basest, maintained by me, by him, by all of us, and a' second hand from mistresses?—I've their letters here to show.
Why should you be so violent to strip naked
Another's reputation to the world,
Knowing your own so leprous?
Beside, this chain of pearl and those spur-royals
Came to you falsely, for she broke her faith
And made her soul a strumpet with her body
When she sent those; they were ever justly mine.
[*To Primero*] Pray what moves you, sir? Why should you shake your head? You're clear? Sure, I should know you, sir; pray, are not you sometimes a pandar and oftener a bawd, sir? Have I never sinned in your banqueting boxes, your bowers and towers, you slave that keeps fornication upon the tops of trees? The very birds cannot engender in quiet for you. Why, rogue that goes in good clothes made out of wenches' cast gowns—
PRIMERO Nothing goes so near my heart as that!
PURSENET Do you shake your slave's noddle?
TAILBY [*turning to Frip*] And here's a rascal looked a-swash too—saving the presence of Master Goldstone—a filthy-slimey-lousy-nittical broker, pricked up in pawns from the hatband to the shoe-string; a necessary hook to hang gentlemen's suits out i'th' air, lest they should grow musty with long lying (which his pawns seldom are guilty of); a fellow of several scents and steams—French, Dutch, Italian, English—and therefore his lice must needs be mongrels. Why, bill-money—
GOLDSTONE I am sorry to hear this among you. You've all deceived me; truly, I took you for other spirits. You must pardon me henceforward; I have a reputation to look to; I must be no more seen in your companies.
FRIP Nay, nay, nay, nay, Master Goldstone; you must not 'scape so, i'faith. One word before you go, sir.
GOLDSTONE Pray, dispatch then; I would not for half my revenues, i'faith now, that any gallants should pass by in the mean time and find me in your companies. Nay, as quick as you can, sir.
FRIP You did not take away Master Bowser's cloak t'other morning, pawned it to me, and borrowed five pound upon't?
GOLDSTONE Ha?
FRIP 'Twas not you neither that finely cheated my little novice at Master Primero's house of a diamond and sapphire, and swore they were counterfeit, both glass, mere glass, as you were a right gentleman?
GOLDSTONE 'Slife, why were we strangers all this while? 'Sfoot, I perceive we are all natural brothers. A pox on's all; are we found, i'faith?
FRIP A cheater!

99 **what's...prosper** Proverbially, 'Ill-gotten gains never prosper' (Dent, G301).
104 **(*Gnaws*)** grimaces, speaks between clenched teeth
115–16 **themes...weavers** i.e. subject matter for popular ballads (or gossip)
118 **Brute** Aeneas' great-grandson Brutus, supposed by the English to have founded Britain
121 **a'** at
134 **bowers and towers** Probably the names or descriptions of rooms in Primero's house, suggestively vaginal and phallic.
135 **keeps...trees** i.e. gives fanciful arboral names to the upstairs rooms for fornication. Perhaps also refers to the timbers of which the brothel (and the theatre) were constructed.
141 **a-swash** swaggering; suspicious
142–3 **filthy-slimey-lousy-nittical** *nittical*: filled with nits, the eggs of lice
143 **pricked up** decked out
147 **steams** noxious vapours
149 **bill-money** a note of charges. Tailby seems to be equating Frip with the money he charges.

GOLDSTONE A thief, a lecher, a bawd, and a broker!

FIRST CONSTABLE [*to the other*] What mean they to be so merry? I'm afraid they laugh at us and make fools on's.

GOLDSTONE [*to gallants*] Push! Leave it to me.—[*To Constables*] How now, who would you speak withal?

FIRST CONSTABLE Speak withal? Have we waited all this while for a suspected thief.

GOLDSTONE How! You're scarce awake yet, I think. Look well: does any appear like a thief in this company? Away, you slaves; you stand loitering, when you should look to the commonwealth! You catch knaves apace now, do you not? They may walk by your nose, you rascals. [*Exeunt Constables*]

ALL THE REST Sweet Master Goldstone!

GOLDSTONE You lacked spirit in your company till I came among you. Here be five on's; let's but glue together.
[*They take hands*]
Why, now the world shall not come between us.

PURSENET If we be true among ourselves.

GOLDSTONE Why, true; we cannot lack to be rich, for we cannot lack riches, nor can our wenches want, nor we want wenches.

PRIMERO Let me alone to furnish you with them.

TAILBY And me.

GOLDSTONE
There's one care past. And as for the knight's daughter,
Our chiefest business and least thought upon—

PURSENET That's true, i'faith.

TAILBY How shall we agree for her?

GOLDSTONE With as much ease
As for the rest. Tomorrow brings the night;
Let's all appear in the best shape we may—
Truth is, we have need on't—
And when amongst us five she makes election,
As one she shall choose—

PURSENET True, she cannot choose.

GOLDSTONE
That one so fortunate amongst us five
Shall bear himself more portly, live regarded,
Keep house, and be a countenance to the rest.

ALL THE REST Admiral!

GOLDSTONE For instance:
[*To Pursenet*] Put case yourself, after some robbery done,
Were pursued hardly; why, there were your shelter,
You know your sanctuary. Nay, say you were taken;
His letter to the justice will strike't dead.
'Tis policy to receive one for the head.

ALL THE REST
Let's hug thee, Goldstone.

GOLDSTONE What have I begot?

PURSENET What, sir?

GOLDSTONE I must plot for you all; it likes me rarely.

TAILBY Prithee, what is't, sir?

GOLDSTONE 'Twould strike Fitzgrave pale,
And make the other suitors appear blanks.

FRIP
For our united mysteries!

GOLDSTONE
What if we five presented our full shapes
In a strange, gallant, and conceited masque?

PURSENET
In a masque? Your thoughts and mine were twins.

TAILBY
So the device were subtle, nothing like it.

FRIP Some poet must assist us.

GOLDSTONE Poet?
You'll take the direct line to have us staged!
Are you too well, too safe? Why, what lacks Bowser,
An absolute scholar, easy to be wrought;
No danger in the operation.

PURSENET But have you so much interest?

GOLDSTONE What, in Bowser? Why my least word commands him.

TAILBY Then no man fitter.

PURSENET And there's Master Frip, too, can furnish us of masquing suits enough.

FRIP
Upon sufficient pawn I think I can, sir.

PURSENET
Pawn? Jew, here take my chain.
[*He gives Frip the chain of pearl*]
Pawns among brothers? We shall thrive,
But we must still expect one rogue in five,
And think us happy too.
[*Enter Fitzgrave, disguised as Bowser*]

GOLDSTONE Last man we spoke on, Master Bowser.

ALL THE GALLANTS Little Master Bowser, sweet Master Bowser, welcome, i'faith!

FITZGRAVE Are your fathers dead, gentlemen, you're so merry?

GOLDSTONE By my troth, a good jest. Did not I commend his wit to you, gentlemen? Hark, sirrah Rafe Bowser, cousin Bowser, i'faith: there's a kind of portion in town, a girl of fifteen hundred, whom we all powerfully affect, and determine to present our parts to her in a masque.

FITZGRAVE In a masque?

204 **cannot choose** has no alternative
206 **portly** dignified, imposing
207 **be a countenance to** provide a false appearance of good reputation for
208 **Admiral** admirable. An appropriate portmanteau between *admirable* and noun *admiral* as the gallants are agreeing to choose a leader.
213 **strike't dead** proverbial for 'do magnificently, work wonders' (Dent, S933.11)
214 **receive one for the head** accept one as leader
221 **mysteries** guilds. Frip refers to the 'trades' of the five gallants.
222 **shapes** fine forms; theatrical parts
225 **So** provided that
device emblematic form of the masque, contrivance
228 **staged** i.e. played on the *professional* stage
232 **interest** influence
250 **portion** dowry; here, a woman with a dowry worth fifteen hundred pounds

GOLDSTONE Right, sir; now a little of thy brain for a device to present us firm, which we shall never be able to do ourselves, thou know'st that, and with a kind of speech wherein thou mayst express what gallants are bravely.

FITZGRAVE Pooh, how can I express 'em otherwise but bravely? Now for a Mercury and all were fitted.

PURSENET Could not a boy supply it?

FITZGRAVE Why, none better.

PURSENET I have a boy shall put down all the Mercuries i'th' town; a will play a Mercury naturally at his finger's end, i'faith.

FITZGRAVE Why then we are suited. For torch-bearers and shield-boys, those are always the writer's properties; you're not troubled with them.

GOLDSTONE Come, my little Bowser; do't finely now, to the life.

FITZGRAVE I warrant you, gentlemen.

FRIP [*taking Fitzgrave aside*] Hist! Give me a little touch above the rest, an you can possibly; for I mean to present this chain of pearl to her.

FITZGRAVE Now I know that, let me alone to fit you.

Exeunt

Finis Actus Quartus

5.1

Actus Quintus

Enter [*three*] *Courtesans* [*(including the Novice as the Third Courtesan), and Mistress Newcut, with a mourning veil*]

FIRST COURTESAN [*to Newcut*] Come forth, you wary, private-whispering strumpet! Have we found your close haunts, your private watchtowers, and your subtle means?

NEWCUT How then?

SECOND COURTESAN You can steal secretly hither, you mystical quean, you, at twilight, twitterlights;
You have a privilege from your hat, forsooth,
To walk without a man, and no suspicion;
But we poor gentlewomen that go in tires
Have no such liberty; we cannot do thus.
Custom grants that to you that's shame in us.

NEWCUT Have you done yet?

SECOND COURTESAN You broke the back of one husband already, and now th'other's dead with grief at sea with your secret expenses, close stealths, cunning filches, and continued banquets in corners. Then, forsooth, you must have your milk-baths to white you, your rose-leaves to sweeten you, your bean-flour bags to sleek you and make you soft, smooth, and delicate for lascivious entertainment.

NEWCUT So, and you think all this while you dance like a thief in a mist you're safe, nobody can find you? Pray, were not you a fellmonger's daughter at first, that run away with a new courtier for the love of gentlewomen's clothes, and bought the fashion at a dear rate, with the loss of your name and credit? Why, what are all of you, but rustical insides and City flesh, the blood of yeomen and the bum of gentlewomen—

Enter Fitzgrave, [*disguised as Bowser*]

SECOND COURTESAN What, shall we suffer a changeable fore-part to out-tongue us? Take that.

[*They attack Newcut*]

NEWCUT Murder! Murder!

FITZGRAVE How now? Why, ladies, a retreat! Come, you have shown your spirits sufficiently; you're all land captains, and so they shall find that come in your quarters; but have you the law-free now to fight and scratch among yourselves and let your gallants run away with others?

FIRST COURTESAN How!

SECOND COURTESAN Good—

FIRST COURTESAN Sweet Master Bowser.

NEWCUT Another?

FITZGRAVE Why then, I perceive you know nothing. Why, they are in the way of marriage: a knight's daughter here in town makes her election among 'em this night.

FIRST COURTESAN This night?

FITZGRAVE This very night, and they all present themselves in a masque before her. Know you not this?

SECOND COURTESAN O, traitor Master Goldstone.

THIRD COURTESAN Perjured Master Tailby.

NEWCUT Without soul!

FIRST COURTESAN
She will chase him.

FITZGRAVE You have more cause to join

259 **Mercury** i.e. a boy to act as Mercury the herald. At l. 262 the sense becomes 'thieves', as Mercury was associated with theft.

263–4 **at his finger's end** i.e. expertly (from the proverb, 'to have it as one's finger's ends', Dent, F245). See also note to 3.4.99.

266 **properties** proprietorships; also theatrical *properties* or props

274 **fit** find something that suits; secretly, 'fittingly punish'

5.1.0.2 **[*three*] *Courtesans*** The Third Courtesan might be the Novice of the earlier scenes, except that in 5.2 the five 'whores' must include three Courtesans, the Novice, and Mistress Newcut.

0.3 ***Mistress Newcut*** She now seems to be wearing mourning dress: see notes to ll. 8 and 31, and l. 64.

7 **twitterlights** twilight (perhaps playing on the verb *twitter*, 'quiver with excitement')

8 **your hat** The widow's hat and veil (or perhaps the plain hat of a merchants' wife) allows her more public freedom than the fancy *tires* of the supposed gentlewomen. Widows were relatively independent of male control.

19 **bean-flour bags** an early version of both the powder puff and deodorant pad

29 **bum** buttocks

31 **fore-part** ornamental covering for the breast (referring, perhaps, to her new widow's attire); also, bawdily, 'front part', i.e. genitals (in contrast with *bum*)

34–5 **land captains** i.e. brave warriors, but quibbling on the sense 'highwaymen'

36 **quarters** soldiers' lodgings; also 'hindquarters' or 'skirts'

have . . . law-free i.e. are you exempt from the laws (though *OED* records *law-free* only as an adjective)

And play the grounds of friendship 'mongst yourselves
Than rashly run division. I could tell you
A means to pleasure you.

FIRST COURTESAN Good Master Bowser!

FITZGRAVE
But that you're women and are hardly secret—

SECOND COURTESAN
We vow it seriously!

FITZGRAVE You should be all there in presence,
See all, hear all, and yet not they perceive you.

THIRD COURTESAN
So that—

NEWCUT Sweet Master Bowser, I—

FITZGRAVE I can stand you in stead,
For I frame the device—

ALL THE COURTESANS If ever—

FITZGRAVE Will you do't?
Hark you—
[They whisper]

FIRST COURTESAN
Content.

SECOND COURTESAN And I'll make one.

THIRD COURTESAN
And I another. We'll mar the match.

NEWCUT
When that good news came of my husband's death,
Goldstone promised me marriage and swear to me—

SECOND COURTESAN
I'll bring his oaths in question.

THIRD COURTESAN So will I.

FITZGRAVE
Agree among yourselves, for shame!

FIRST COURTESAN Are we resolved?

SECOND COURTESAN
In this who would not feign?

THIRD COURTESAN Friends all, for my part.

NEWCUT
Here's my lip for mine.

THIRD COURTESAN Round let it go.
[They kiss]

SECOND COURTESAN
All wrath thus quenched.

FIRST COURTESAN And I conclude it so.
Exeunt [women]

FITZGRAVE
How all events strike even with my wishes!
Their own invention damns them.
[Enter Piamont, Bungler, and the two Gentleman-Gallants]
Now, gentlemen,
Stands your assistance firm?

FIRST GENTLEMAN-GALLANT Why, 'tis our own case;
I'm sorry you should doubt.

SECOND GENTLEMAN GALLANT
We'll furnish you.

BUNGLER
Are these our gallants?

FITZGRAVE Are our gallants these?
[Enter Painter, with five shields]

PAINTER Here be five shields, sir.

FITZGRAVE Finished already? That's well. I'll see thy master shortly.

PAINTER I'm satisfied. *Exit*

PIAMONT Prithee, let's see, Master Fitzgrave.

FITZGRAVE I have blazed them.

FIRST GENTLEMAN-GALLANT What's this?

BUNGLER Fooh, you should be a gallant too, for you're no university scholar.

FITZGRAVE Look, this is Pursenet: the device, a purse wide open and the mouth downward; the word, '*Alienis ecce crumenis.*'

FIRST GENTLEMAN-GALLANT What's that?

FITZGRAVE 'One that lives out of other men's pockets.'

PIAMONT That's right.

FITZGRAVE Here's Goldstone's: three silver dice.

FIRST GENTLEMAN-GALLANT They run high: two cinques and a quatre!

FITZGRAVE They're high-men, fit for his purpose; the word, '*Fratremque patremque.*'

SECOND GENTLEMAN-GALLANT Nay, he will cheat his own brother; nay, his own father, i'faith.

FITZGRAVE So much the word imports. Master Primero—

BUNGLER Pox, what says he now?

FITZGRAVE The device, an unvalued pearl hid in a cave; the word, '*Occultos vendit honores.*'

53–4 **play the grounds ... run division** Puns on musical terminology: *ground* as the repeated bass phrase, *division* as the elaborate improvisatory treble line played over it.

60 **stand you in stead** put you in place

65 **swear** swore

69–70 **Here's ... so** The women either exchange kisses and speak of drink metaphorically, or actually pass round a goblet of wine.

71 **strike** Perhaps a metaphor of music sounding, or of bells striking on time.

72 **Their** i.e. the gallants'
invention (*a*) ingenuity, (*b*) device (the masque)

72.1–2 ***Piamont ... Gentleman-Gallants*** These four gallants, together with Fitzgrave, make up a virtuous fivesome in contrast with the knavish gallants of the play's title.

75 **Are ... these?** This shared line stresses the irony of the play's title and its overriding satirical point as Fitzgrave turns Bungler's enquiry to a rhetorical question: 'are *our* five gallants anything like these two?' Alternatively, the painter enters early enough for the line to refer to the emblems on the shields.

81 **blazed** (*a*) described heraldically, blazoned; (*b*) divulged, defamed

83 **should** must

86 **word** motto

86–7 ***Alienis ecce crumenis*** 'here he is with the purse of another'

94 **high-men** dice loaded to turn up high numbers

95 ***Fratremque patremque*** '(against) both brother and father'

100 **unvalued** (*a*) priceless, (*b*) hidden from valuation

101 ***Occultos vendit honores*** 'he sells hidden honours'. *Honours*, the English equivalent of *honores*, could mean 'chastities, maidenheads', as is reflected in Fitzgrave's translation.

FIRST GENTLEMAN-GALLANT What's that?

FITZGRAVE 'One that sells maidenheads by wholesale.'

SECOND GENTLEMAN-GALLANT Excellently proper.

FITZGRAVE Master Frip—

SECOND GENTLEMAN-GALLANT That Pythagorical rascal: in a gentleman's suit today, in a knight's tomorrow.

FITZGRAVE The device for him, a cuckoo sitting on a tree; the word, '*En avis ex avibus*'—'one bird made of many', for you know, as the sparrow hatches the cuckoo, so the gentleman feathers the broker.

FIRST GENTLEMAN-GALLANT Let me admire thee, Master Fitzgrave.

FITZGRAVE They will scorn, gentlemen; and to assist them the better, Pursenet's boy, that little precious pick-pocket, has a compendious speech in Latin, and, like a Mercury, presents their dispositions more liberally.

FIRST GENTLEMAN-GALLANT Never were poor gallants so abused.

FITZGRAVE Hang 'em; they're counterfeits; no honest spirit will pity 'em.
This is my crown:
So good men smile, I dread no rascal's frown.
Away, bestow yourselves secretly o'erhead; this is the place appointed for the rehearsal to practise their behaviours.

FIRST GENTLEMAN-GALLANT We are vanished.

[Exeunt all but Fitzgrave, and appear above]

[Enter below Goldstone, Pursenet, Tailby, Frip, Primero, and Pursenet's Boy]

GOLDSTONE Master Bowser.

PURSENET Well said, i'faith. Off with your cloaks, gallants; let's fall roundly to our business.

TAILBY Is the boy perfect?

FITZGRAVE That's my credit, sir, I warrant you.

FRIP If our little Mercury should be out, we should scarce be known what we are.

FITZGRAVE I have took a course for that; fear it not, sir. Look you, first here be your shields.

GOLDSTONE Ay, where be our shields?

PURSENET Which is mine?

TAILBY Which is mine, Master Bowser? This?

FITZGRAVE I pray, be contained a little, gentlemen; they'll come all time enough to you, I warrant.

PURSENET This Frip is grown so violent.

FITZGRAVE Yours to begin withal, sir?

PURSENET Well said, Master Bowser.

FITZGRAVE First, the device, a fair purse wide open, the mouth downward; the word, '*Alienis ecce crumenis.*'

PURSENET What's that, prithee?

FITZGRAVE 'Your bounty pours itself forth to all men.'

PURSENET And so it does, i'faith; that's all my fault—bountiful.

FITZGRAVE Master Goldstone, here's yours, sir: three silver dice; the word, '*Fratremque patremque.*'

GOLDSTONE And what's that?

FITZGRAVE 'Fortune of my side.'

GOLDSTONE Well said, little Bowser, i'faith.

TAILBY *[to Fitzgrave]* What say you to me, sir?

FITZGRAVE For the device, a candle in a corner; the word, '*Consumptio victus.*'

TAILBY The meaning of that, sir?

FITZGRAVE 'My light is yet in darkness, till I enjoy her.'

TAILBY Right, sir!

PRIMERO Now mine, sir?

FITZGRAVE The device, an unvalued pearl hid in a cave.

PRIMERO Ah, ha, sirs!

FITZGRAVE The word, '*Occultos vendit honores.*'

PRIMERO Very good, I warrant.

FITZGRAVE 'A black man's a pearl in a fair lady's eye.'

PRIMERO I said 'twas some such thing.

FRIP My turn must needs come now; am I fitted, Master Bowser?

FITZGRAVE Trust to me; your device here is a cuckoo sitting on a tree.

FRIP The Welsh lieger; good.

FITZGRAVE The word, '*En avis ex avibus.*'

FRIP Ay, marry, sir.

FITZGRAVE Why, do you know what 'tis, sir?

FRIP No, by my troth, not yet, sir.

FITZGRAVE O, 'I keep one tune; I recant not.'

FRIP I'm like the cuckoo in that, indeed; where I love, I hold.

FITZGRAVE Did I not promise you I would fit you?

GOLDSTONE They're all very well done, i'faith, and very scholar-like, though I say't before thy face, little Bowser; but I would not have thee proud on't now. Come, if this be performed well—

FITZGRAVE Who, the boy? He has performed deeper matters than this.

PIAMONT *[above]* Ay, a pox on him; I think was in my pocket now, an truth were known.

BUNGLER *[above]* I caught him once in mine.

103 **wholesale** puns on *hole-sale*
106 **Pythagorical** changing in identity (after Pythagoras' theory of transmigration of souls)
109 ***En avis ex avibus*** 'here is a bird out of other birds'. The cuckoo has its eggs hatched by other birds.
114 **They will scorn** i.e. the shields will deride the gallants
122 **crown** probably figured as a victor's wreath with an emblematic motto
125–6 **behaviours** deportment, acting of roles
129 **Well said** well done
131 **Is the boy perfect** has the boy memorized his lines
158 ***Consumptio victus*** 'a consumption of sustenance'
167 **A...eye** proverbial (Dent, M79) **black** Perhaps Primero wears black. The sense he fails to recognize is 'wicked'.
173 **The Welsh lieger** a name for the cuckoo (proverbial—Dent, A233—but not before Middleton)
178 **I keep one tune** The cuckoo proverbially has but one song (Dent, C894). **recant** probably both 'retract' and 'sing another tune'

FITZGRAVE Suppose the shields are presented, then you begin, boy.

BOY 'I, representing Mercury, am a pickpocket and have his part at my fingers' ends; page I am to that great and secret thief, *Magno illo et secreto latroni*.'

FITZGRAVE [*to Pursenet*] There you make your honour, sir.

BOY At '*latroni*'.

[*Pursenet bows*]

You have it, sir.

PURSENET '*Latroni*'; that's mine.

FITZGRAVE [*apart*] He confesses the thief's his.

PURSENET Remember, boy, you point '*latroni*' to me.

BOY To you, master; proceed.

FITZGRAVE 'These four are his companions, the one a notable cheater that will cozen his own father.' Master Goldstone.

GOLDSTONE Let me alone, Master Bowser; I can take mine own turn.

FITZGRAVE Why—

GOLDSTONE Peace!

[*He bows*]

FITZGRAVE 'The second, a notorious lecher maintained by harlots, *Cuius virtus consumptio corporis*.'

TAILBY That's I, Master Bowser.

FITZGRAVE There you remember your honour, sir.

[*Tailby bows*]

BOY '*Ille leno pretiosissimus, virgineos ob lucrum vendens honores*.'

PURSENET It sounds very well, i'faith.

BOY '*Postremus ille, quamvis apparatu splendidus*, is no otherwise but a broker; these feathers are not his own, *sed avis ex avibus*—'

[*Frip bows*]

'all which to be nothing but truth will appear by the event.'

FITZGRAVE I'faith, here's all now, gentlemen.

GOLDSTONE Short and pithy.

TAILBY A good boy, i'faith, and a pregnant.

PURSENET I dare put trust in the boy, sir.—Forget not, sirrah, at any hand, to point that same '*latroni*' to me.

BOY I warrant you, master.

GOLDSTONE Come, gentlemen, the time beckons us away.

FITZGRAVE Ay, furnish, gentlemen; furnish.

PURSENET Hark, one word, Master Bowser, what's that same '*latroni*'? I have a good mind to that word, i'faith.

FITZGRAVE '*Latroni*'? Why, 'sheriff of the shire'.

PURSENET I'faith? And I have shriven some shires in my days. *Exeunt* [*the five Gallants and the Boy*]

FITZGRAVE [*to those above*] Now, gentlemen, are you satisfied and pleased?

FIRST GENTLEMAN-GALLANT Never more amply.

FITZGRAVE

Amongst us now falls that desirèd lot,
For we shall blast five rivals with one plot. [*Exeunt*]

Enter the virgin [*Katherine*] *between two Ancient Gentlemen* 5.2

KATHERINE

Grave gentlemen, in whose approvèd bosoms
My deceased father did repose much faith,
You're dearly welcome. Pray sit, command music,
See nothing want to beautify this night,
That holds my election in her peaceful arms—
Feasts, music, hymns, those sweet celestial charms.

[*She sits*]

FIRST ANCIENT GENTLEMAN [*sitting*]

May you be blessed in this election.

SECOND ANCIENT GENTLEMAN [*sitting*]

That content may meet perfection.

Hymn

[SINGERS] [*within*]

Sound lute, bandora, gittern,
Viol, virginals, and cithern!

193–221 I ... **event** Evidently, the Boy and Fitzgrave share in rehearsing the Boy's Latin speech, which for the convenience of the audience has been mostly translated into English. The insults, which are intrinsic to the speech, are probably not understood by the gallants because they are imagined to hear the speech in Latin.

195 *Magno ... latroni* 'for that great and secret thief'

196 **honour** bow (punning on 'moral reputation')

211 *Cuius ... corporis* 'whose virtue is an employment (and a wasting away) of the body'

214–15 *Ille ... honores* 'this is a very rich pimp because he sells virgin reputations for money'

217 *Postremus ... splendidus* 'this is the most inferior, although sumptuous in his pomp'

218 **these ... own** proverbial, as in *Timon*, 3.30 (Dent, B375)

219 *sed* but

224 **pregnant** resourceful

226 **at any hand** on any account

229 **furnish** get ready

233 **shriven** robbed (punning on *sheriff*)

5.2.0.1 *the virgin* Suggests a ceremonial costume denoting Katherine as such, perhaps a white robe.

8.1–5.2.18.15 *Hymn ... action* The masque abandons the device rehearsed in 5.1 involving Pursenet's Boy as Mercury. He is nevertheless present because he is apprehended on suspicion of stealing the pearls, and so probably plays a shield-boy. The direction after l. 18 summarizes the entire masque, and anticipates the bowing, delivery of the shields, and dancing that occupy ll. 5.2.19–5.2.25.6. In substance this edition preserves the original text. The action may be reconstructed as follows. The hymn, to the accompaniment of offstage musicians, is sung by the torch-bearers and shield-boys, who enter as they are singing. The groups separate by the middle of the hymn, and in ll. 16–18 *you* is addressed by the singers to the masquers, and *that* to an appropriate shield. Contrary to the sequence suggested by the printed text, the cornetts probably sound before the masquers bow to Katherine. Perhaps a flourish of cornetts announces the presentation of each shield. After the presentations, the action goes on as described in ll. 5.2.25.1–6.

9 **bandora** stringed instrument like the lute but with a deeper sound
gittern stringed instrument like a guitar

10 **virginals** keyboard instrument similar to the harpsichord
cithern another guitar-like instrument

Voices spring and lift aloud
Her name that makes the music proud!
This night perfection
Makes her election.
Follow, follow, follow, follow round;
Look you to that; nay, you to that; nay, you to that:
Anon you will be found, anon you will be found,
Anon you will be found.

Cornetts.

Enter the masque, thus ordered: a torch-bearer, a shield-boy, then a masquer, so throughout; then the shield-boys fall at one end, the torch-bearers at the other; the masquers i'th' middle. The torch-bearers are the five gentlemen [*Fitzgrave, Piamont, Bungler, and the two Gentleman-Gallants*]*; the shield-boys, the whores in boys' apparel* [*the two Courtesans, the Novice, and Mistress Newcut; also Pursenet's Boy as the fifth*]*; the masquers, the five gallants* [*Goldstone, Pursenet, Tailby, Frip, Primero*]*. They bow to her* [*Katherine*]*; she rises and shows the like; they dance, but first deliver the shields up. She reads.*

	The speech	*Their action*
KATHERINE	'*Alienis ecce crumenis.*'	*Pursenet bows to her*
	'*Fratremque, patremque.*'	*Goldstone bows to her*
	'*Consumptio victus.*'	*Tailby bows to her*
	'*Occultos vendit honores.*'	*Primero bows to her*
	A cuckoo: '*En avis ex avibus.*'	*Frip bows to her*

Are you all as the speech and shields display you?

GOLDSTONE We shall prove so.

They going to dance, each unhasps his weapon from his side and gives 'em to the torch-bearers. Katherine seems distrustful, but then Fitzgrave whispers to her and falls back. At the end of which, all making an honour, Frip presents her with that chain of pearl

KATHERINE
The very chain of pearl was filched from me!

FITZGRAVE Hold! Stop the boy there!

[*The Boy is stopped and*] *Pursenet stamps*

KATHERINE Will none lay hands on him?

All lay hands on him [*Frip*]

GOLDSTONE How now?

FRIP Alas, I'm but a broker; 'twas pawned to me in my shop.

[*Fitzgrave, Piamont, Bungler, and the two gentlemen unmask*]

TAILBY Ha? Fitzgrave?

PURSENET Piamont and the rest.

GOLDSTONE Where's Bowser?

FITZGRAVE Here.

GOLDSTONE We are all betrayed.

FITZGRAVE Betrayed? You're no sort to be betrayed; you have not so much worth. Nay, struggle not with the net; you are caught for this world.

FIRST COURTESAN Would we were out.

FITZGRAVE [*to gallants*]
'Twas I framed your device, do you see, 'twas I!
The whole assembly has took notice of it:
[*To Goldstone*] That you are a gallant cheater—
So much the pawning of my cloak contains—
[*To Pursenet*] You a base thief—think of Coombe Park, and tell me—
[*To Tailby*] That you're a hirèd smockster. [*To Primero*] Here's her letter
In which we are certified that you are a bawd.

FIRST ANCIENT GENTLEMAN
The broker has confessed it.

SECOND ANCIENT GENTLEMAN
So has the boy.

TAILBY That boy will be hanged; he stole the chain at first and has thus long maintained his master's gallantry.

FITZGRAVE [*to Katherine*]
All which we here present, like captive slaves
Waiting that doom which their presumption craves.

KATHERINE
How easily may our suspectless sex
With fair-appearing shadows be deluded!
Dear sir, you have the work so well begun
That, took from you, small glory would be won.

FITZGRAVE
Since 'tis your pleasure to refer to me
The doom of these, I have provided so:
They shall not altogether lose their cost;
See, I have brought wives for 'em.

[*The three Courtesans, the Novice, and Mistress Newcut unmask*]

GOLDSTONE Heart, the strumpets!—Out, out!

TAILBY
Having assumed out of their impudence
The shape of shield-boys.

FRIP
To heap full confusion.

FIRST COURTESAN
Rather confine us to strict chastity,
A mere impossible task, than to wed these
Whom we loathe worse than the foul'st disease.

GOLDSTONE [*to Fitzgrave*]
O, grant 'em their requests.

FITZGRAVE
The doom is passed;
So, since your aim was marriage,
Either embrace it in these courtesans
Or have your base acts and felonious lives
Proclaimed to the indignation of the law,
Which will provide a public punishment.
As for the boy and that infectious bawd,

17 **found** found out, identified
18.3 ***so throughout*** i.e. in this order for each masquer
46 **smockster** womanizer
69 **these courtesans** Mistress Newcut seems to fall under the heading. As Primero is sent off for whipping, only four gallants need to be matched, but at ll. 82–6 Newcut includes herself in the marrying.

We put forth those to whipping.

PRIMERO Whipping? You find not that in the statute, to whip satin.

FITZGRAVE Away with him.

[*Primero and the Boy are taken off*]

GOLDSTONE Since all our shifts are discovered, as far as I can see 'tis our best course to marry 'em: we'll make them get our livings.

PURSENET He says true.

NEWCUT You see how we are threatened; by my troth, wenches, be ruled by me: let's marry 'em an it be but to plague 'em; for when we have husbands, we are under covert-baron and may lie with whom we list. I have tried that in my t'other husbands' days.

ALL THE COURTESANS A match.

FITZGRAVE
I'll be no more deferred; come, when do you join?

GOLDSTONE These forced marriages do never come to good.

FITZGRAVE
How can they, when they come to such as you?

PURSENET
They often prove the ruin of great houses.

FITZGRAVE
Nor, virgin, do I in this seek to entice
All glory to myself; these gentlemen,
Whom I am bound to love for kind assistance,
Had great affinity in the plot with me.

KATHERINE
To them I give my thanks; myself to thee,
Thrice worthy Fitzgrave.

FITZGRAVE I have all my wishes.

KATHERINE [*to audience*]
And I presume there's none but those can frown
Whose envies, like the rushes, we tread down.

[*Exeunt*]

Finis

THE PARTS

GOLDSTONE (488 lines): Painter; Second Fellow; Jack *or* a Servant of Mistress Cleveland, Newblock, *or* Tiffany; Katherine's Servant

PURSENET (403 lines): Tailor; Painter; Second Fellow; Jack *or* a Servant of Mistress Cleveland, Newblock, *or* Tiffany; Katherine's Servant; Marmaduke

FRIP (322 lines): Tailor; Painter; Jack *or* a Servant of Mistress Cleveland, Newblock, *or* Tiffany; Katherine's Servant

FITZGRAVE (315 lines): Presenter *or* First Fellow; Tailor; Second Fellow; a Constable; Jack *or* a Servant of Mistress Cleveland, Newblock, *or* Tiffany

TAILBY (287 lines): Tailor; Painter; Second Fellow; Marmaduke; Mistress Cleveland's Servant

PRIMERO (182 lines): Tailor; Painter; Jack *or* a Servant of Mistress Cleveland, Newblock, *or* Tiffany; Katherine's Servant; Marmaduke

BUNGLER (150 lines): Presenter *or* First Fellow; Tailor; Second Fellow; a Constable; Jack *or* a Servant of Mistress Cleveland, Newblock, *or* Tiffany; Katherine's Servant

NEWCUT (92 lines): Presenter *or* First Fellow; Vintner *or* Drawer *or* Fulk; Tailor; Painter; Second Fellow; a Constable; Jack *or* a Servant of Mistress Cleveland, Newblock, *or* Tiffany; Katherine's Servant; Marmaduke *or* Fulk

FIRST COURTESAN (77 lines): Vintner *or* Drawer; Tailor; Painter; a Fellow; a Constable; Jack *or* a Servant of Mistress Cleveland, Newblock, *or* Tiffany; Katherine's Servant; Marmaduke

KATHERINE (66 lines): any but Gallants, Fitzgrave, Bungler, Piamont, Gentleman-Gallants, Ancient Gentlemen, Novice, Courtesans, Newcut, Pursenet's Boy

SECOND COURTESAN (61 lines): Vintner *or* Drawer; Painter; a Fellow; a Constable; Jack *or* a Servant of Mistress Cleveland, Newblock, *or* Tiffany; Katherine's Servant; Marmaduke

Pursenet's BOY (50 lines): Presenter *or* First Fellow; Tailor; Painter; Second Fellow; a Constable; Jack *or* a Servant of Mistress Cleveland, Newblock, *or* Tiffany; Katherine's Servant; Marmaduke

FULK (48 lines): any but Gallants, Fitzgrave, Bungler, Novice, First and Second Courtesans, Newcut; Vintner, Drawer, Pursenet's Boy, Primero's Boy, Arthur, Marmaduke

PIAMONT (42 lines): any but Gallants, Katherine, Fitzgrave, Bungler, Gentleman-Gallants, Ancient Gentlemen, Novice, Courtesans, Newcut, Painter, Pursenet's Boy, Marmaduke

JACK (39 lines): any but Tailby, Servants of Mistress Cleveland, Newblock, and Tiffany

---

75–6 **statute . . . satin** Gentlemen would not be whipped. Primero is evidently not by birth a gentleman, and so not legally entitled to wear satin.

85 **covert-baron** the legally protected position of a married woman

95 **affinity** alliance

98–9 **And . . . down.** The original printed text sets this speech off as an epilogue by introducing blank space above it and printing it in italic.

98 **none . . . frown** inverted from 'none can frown but those'

99 **envies** malice

rushes strewn on floors as a covering

VINTNER (2.4; 35 lines): any but Gallants, Fitzgrave; Bungler; Drawer, Pursenet's Boy, Arthur, Fulk

ARTHUR (22 lines): any but Presenter, Gallants, Fitzgrave, Bungler, Novice, First and Second Courtesans, Newcut; Vintner, Drawer, Fellows, Pursenet's Boy, Fulk

MISTRESS NEWBLOCK'S SERVANT (Interim 2; 20 lines): any but Tailby, Jack, Mistress Tiffany's Servant

NOVICE (later THIRD COURTESAN; 18 lines): Vintner *or* Drawer; Tailor; Second Fellow; Painter; a Constable; Jack *or* a Servant of Mistress Cleveland, Newblock, *or* Tiffany; Katherine's Servant; Marmaduke

SECOND FELLOW (1.1; 16 lines): any but Primero, Frip, Arthur

SECOND CONSTABLE (4.7; 15 lines): any but a Gallant, First Constable

MARMADUKE (14 lines): any but Frip, Goldstone, Fitzgrave, Bungler, Piamont, Newcut, Fulk

MISTRESS CLEVELAND'S SERVANT (Interim 1; 14 lines): any but Jack

FIRST GENTLEMAN-GALLANT (13 lines): any but Gallants, Katherine, Fitzgrave, Bungler, Piamont, Second Gentleman-Gallant, Ancient Gentlemen, Novice, Courtesans, Newcut, Painter, Pursenet's Boy

FIRST FELLOW (1.1; 11 lines): any but Presenter, Gallants, Arthur

FIRST CONSTABLE (4.7; 10 lines): any but a Gallant, Second Constable

KATHERINE'S SERVANT (9 lines): any but Tailby, Fitzgrave

PRESENTER (Prologue; 8 lines): any but Gallants, Courtesans ('wenches'), 1 Fellow, Arthur

MISTRESS TIFFANY'S SERVANT (Interim 2; 6 lines): any but Tailby, Jack, Mistress Newblock's Servant

SECOND GENTLEMAN-GALLANT (6 lines): any but Gallants, Katherine, Fitzgrave, Bungler, Piamont, First Gentleman-Gallant, Ancient Gentlemen, Novice, Courtesans, Newcut, Painter, Pursenet's Boy

TAILOR (3.4; 6 lines): any but Goldstone, Second Courtesan

Primero's BOY (2.1; 2 lines): any but a Gallant, Fitzgrave, Bungler, Novice, Courtesans, Newcut, Pursenet's Boy, Fulk

DRAWER (2.4; 2 lines): any but Gallants, Fitzgrave; Bungler; Vintner, Pursenet's Boy, Arthur, Fulk

FIRST ANCIENT GENTLEMAN (5.2; 2 lines): any but Gallants, Katherine, Fitzgrave, Bungler, Piamont, Gentleman-Gallants, Second Ancient Gentleman, Novice, Courtesans, Newcut, Pursenet's Boy

PAINTER (5.1; 2 lines): any but Fitzgrave, Bungler, Piamont, Gentleman-Gallants

SECOND ANCIENT GENTLEMAN (5.2; 2 lines): any but Gallants, Katherine, Fitzgrave, Bungler, Piamont, Gentleman-Gallants, First Ancient Gentleman, Novice, Courtesans, Newcut, Pursenet's Boy

Most crowded scene: 5.2 (18 actors)

THE BLOODY BANQUET: A TRAGEDY

Text introduced and annotated by Julia Gasper, edited by Julia Gasper and Gary Taylor

THE title *The Bloody Banquet* draws attention to the final scene of this play, in which the Tyrant compels his wife, the young Queen Thetis, publicly to eat the corpse of her lover, Tymethes. The same title could serve for Seneca's tragedy *Thyestes*, or indeed for Shakespeare and Peele's tragedy, *Titus Andronicus*. *The Bloody Banquet* is greatly influenced by the tradition of Senecan horror, but its success is not to be judged by how closely it conforms to a classical model. This is a play which sets its own goals and, to a great extent, attains them.

The Bloody Banquet uses as its immediate source an Elizabethan prose novel, William Warner's *Pan his Syrinx*, in which a version of the gruesome banquet appears in a somewhat less horrific form than Seneca's. While its source can be called a diluted myth, *The Bloody Banquet* is an ambitious play whose authors, Dekker and Middleton, display not only their classical learning but also considerable originality and dramatic power. In their hands the gruesome banquet becomes a metaphor for all the gender and power relationships in the play.

The story of Atreus and Thyestes is only one of several Greek myths in which the motif of the gruesome, cannibalistic banquet recurs. In Greek legend, the Titan Cronos ate his children because he feared being supplanted. In the play, Armitrites expresses the same sentiment over the dead bodies of his son and daughter: 'Yes, and we safe, our death we need less fear, | Usurpers' issue oft proves dangerous, | We depose others, and they poison us.' Cronos' fears are self-fulfilling because his son Zeus, concealed by his mother Rhea, grows up to take revenge by poisoning him and forcing him to disgorge all his devoured offspring. No such kind reversal is possible in Thyestes' case, but the story suggests a conflation of the processes of digestion and gestation (both words deriving ultimately from the same Latin root *gesto*, to bear or carry) which elucidates the original meaning of the gruesome banquet myth. 'Incorporation... turns into a surrogate pregnancy', as Marina Warner has said.

A closely related legend concerns Tantalus, the son of Zeus and King of Lydia, the country which provides the setting for *The Bloody Banquet*. Tantalus is said to have served up his son Pelops to the gods in order to test whether they could tell human from animal flesh. He was suitably punished with starvation in the afterlife. Tantalus was traditionally the grandfather of Thyestes, and in Seneca's play there is an allusion to him in Act IV at the point where Atreus is carrying out the murder of Thyestes' three young sons, one of whom is called Tantalus after his ancestor.

Other versions of the myth include the story of King Astiages of Media, told by Herodotus: he killed the children of Harpagus and served them to their father in a pie, then for the second course brought in their heads, hands, and feet. This story is retold by Seneca in the third book of his moral essays, 'On Anger', which was a widely-studied text in the Renaissance. The extent of Seneca's influence on Elizabethan drama, particularly the drama written for the public stage, has been questioned by G. K. Hunter, and in some respects there may have been exaggeration and inexactitude (certainly in the case of T. S. Eliot's opinions). But there can be little doubt that Seneca and Ovid were the Latin authors through whom the gruesome banquet myth was known to Dekker, Middleton, and Shakespeare.

A further example is the legend of Philomela, told by Ovid and used as a source for *Titus Andronicus*. Philomela's sister Procne, discovering that her husband Tereus had raped Philomela, killed Itys, her own son by Tereus, and served him to Tereus, who ate him unknowingly.

There are three components of this myth. First, a father eats his own children. Second, he is a king. Third, he is deceived or he deceives others. Without the third element, it would seem an ideal metaphor for tyranny. Aristotle took it for granted that government was the extension of the father's authority over the family and household. So the father eating his own children would be a logical image of tyranny, the perversion of government. A strong Renaissance tradition characterized Seneca as a critic of tyranny, a view confirmed by recent opinion, which suggests that a similar political agenda animates Elizabethan and Jacobean emulations of Senecan horror. In a society whose concepts of the state were usually organic, an image of physiological horror which perverts family relationship represents tyranny, not as a cold abstraction, but as an atrocity.

However, there is also the deception component. It never occurs to Thyestes, any more than to Oedipus, to exonerate himself because his trespass was committed unintentionally. Guilt is guilt and they damn themselves ruthlessly. Thyestes' pollution can be understood by comparing it to a rape such as Philomela's or Lucretia's, in another story taken up by Middleton: Thyestes' body has been contaminated because this forbidden flesh has entered it. Likewise Proserpine swallowed the seeds of the pomegranate in ignorance but paid the penalty. Christian theology insists that Adam, when he ate the apple, was not deceived. Roman logic damns him even if he was. There is no escape for Thyestes from the terrible knowledge of what he has done, which is a hell in itself.

The tragedy of Thyestes indicates a culture with a highly developed sense of pollution, transgression, and guilt, but no doctrine of redemption. Moral guilt is not the whole issue, however: Thyestes is tortured because in ingesting his own children, he has done the last thing he would have wished to do. If the purpose of any living organism is to perpetuate its own genes, he has frustrated the object of his whole existence.

The gruesome banquet myth grapples with the problem of defilement, for which in the classical culture there was no solution but death. It would be unwise to limit the scope or the significance of this myth: it is a symbol which assumes new meanings in a succession of cultural metamorphoses. In the Christian culture, the gruesome banquet becomes transformed into the Communion, and takes on a soteriological significance. The problem of sin, which is subtly different from the pagan notion of defilement but closely related to it, is resolved through paradox, as the communicants eat the flesh and drink the blood, not of their own children, but of the Host's offspring. By doing this, their own defilement is washed away and they are, like Thyestes and his sons, incorporated into one body.

The only moral of *Thyestes* is 'never hope for reconciliation with your enemy.' Thyestes is destroyed through his idealism, his nobility, which did not seek revenge. Revenge, Seneca's play asserts, is the law of nature, and in abjuring it Thyestes only brings a more frightful injury on himself. Yet revenge is also mysterious and problematic. The motives of Atreus are obscure, and the Latin language does not distinguish clearly between private revenge, divine vengeance, and public penalty: it uses the words *poena* or *ultio* to mean any of these things.

Its relationship to rape provides one insight into the gruesome banquet myth—and is what gives the Philomela myth its inner logic. Tereus' crime against Philomela is avenged in a fashion that makes him understand what she has suffered. Titus Andronicus seeks revenge through the gruesome banquet for the many crimes endured by his family—but in the Elizabethan play the Mediterranean myth subtly shifts. The cruel Tamora eats her own children, and thus receives them back into her own body. She re-assimilates them, and her horror is derived from a contemplation of the mysterious relation of parent to child, in which the exact boundaries of the individual are impossible to define.

At this point we encounter a gender transformation. In all the vernacular Elizabethan examples of this myth, the banqueter is female, and she is compelled to eat a male victim. In all the classical examples, the banqueter is male, and so also are the victims; women may serve up the gruesome banquet, but they never partake of it until the Renaissance. Another change in the myth is that in later versions it is no longer the child, but the lover of the woman who is now eaten. In *The Bloody Banquet* Tymethes, by being betrothed to Amphridote, the stepdaughter of the Queen, could be regarded as the Queen's son as well as her lover. Such in-law relationships were taken very seriously in the Renaissance and figured in the tables of matrimonial exclusion. In other words, the sexual relationship between Tymethes and the Queen would have been regarded as incestuous, as well as adulterous. *The Bloody Banquet* thus anticipates Freud's linking of cannibalism to incest.

Classical and Renaissance features of the myth are combined in a neo-Latin play of 1592, William Alabaster's *Roxana*. In this play, which was closely based on an Italian source (Groto's *La Dalida*), a cannibalistic banquet is served to Oromasdes, king of Bactria, by his wife Atossa. When he has eaten it, she reveals that it contained the flesh of his mistress, Roxana, and Roxana's two children by him. This combines both the child-eating and the lover-eating versions, as in a sense does *The Bloody Banquet*. Furthermore, Roxana earlier has been compelled to carry out the murder of her own children, somewhat like Tamora who eats her own sons in *Titus*, or again like the Queen who actually murders Tymethes. It is as if Renaissance versions could not resist centring on a female figure. It is not impossible that Dekker or Middleton knew *Roxana*, which was performed at Trinity College, Cambridge, in 1592; they may have encountered a manuscript, and in *The Bloody Banquet* we find the unusual name Roxano for a character who does not in any way derive from Warner. In the play's cast list his name is oddly misspelled in a feminine form, 'Roxona', which may only be a misprint, but in a later play of Middleton's (*Hengist, King of Kent*) the name Roxana is used for a woman. There are also plot resemblances: for instance, in *Roxana* the heroine takes refuge in the forest when Bactria is invaded and conquered by Oromasdes, while in *The Bloody Banquet* the Old Queen does the same at the invasion of Armatrites. Whether or not Dekker and Middleton knew Alabaster's play, their play and his share typical Renaissance features of the myth.

Those features are also present in Dekker and Middleton's undoubted source, the story of Thetis in Warner's *Pan his Syrinx*. Warner's narrative was in itself a conflation of elements of the classical gruesome banquet with another story, the legend of Fair Rosamund which (as Wallace Bacon points out) goes back at least as far as Caxton's *Golden Legend*; analogues are found in the Gesta Romanorum, the *Heptameron* of Marguerite of Navarre (story 32), Painter's *Palace of Pleasure* (I, 57), and Whetstone's *Aurelia*. Another example appears in Machiavelli's *Florentine History*, Middleton's source for *The Witch* (a play with some interesting links to *The Bloody Banquet*, noted in the commentary). In the story of Rosamund and its analogues, an unfaithful wife is compelled to drink from the skull of her lover (or, in some versions, her father). Warner increased the gruesome banquet element by having her also forced to consume his flesh. However, the young Queen is never in any doubt about what she is eating and drinking, and so the deception element of the myth disappears. This change may relate to the difference between classical concepts of defilement and Christian concepts of guilt, knowledge being crucial for the latter. Her knowledge of what she eats makes the young Queen, in the final scene, an almost iconographic figure of what Julia Kristeva calls abjection, and what Gary Taylor (2002) calls 'the edible complex.'

While *The Bloody Banquet* is not slavishly Senecan, the dramatists did attempt to make it, in some respects, more Senecan than Warner's version. In the last scene, Dekker added some details which restore the deception element in another form: while it is the young Queen who is compelled to consume the remains of Tymethes, his father the Old King of Lydia enters as a guest and, upon hearing the story related, he realizes that the remains are those of his own son. The pieces of the myth are all there, but they are fragmented (like Tymethes himself, it is tempting to say). The play's ending turns a little too quickly from the horror to attempt what is almost a happy ending. It is not a tragicomedy, for too many deaths and disasters have taken place, but such problems of genre are quite typical of Dekker (who seems to have written the ending). It is also possible that this abruptness results from a Caroline abridgement, since—as Schoenbaum suggested—the play was apparently adapted and shortened at some point between its first performances and its publication in 1639.

Dekker and Middleton moved away from the Senecan model in an explicitly Christian direction, emphasizing redemption in the Lapyrus plot and suggesting the hand of Providence at work in the downfall of Armatrites' dynasty. This typical humanist eclecticism, mixing classical and Christian motifs, is one of the things that makes Renaissance drama stimulating, and without it the dramatists could not have created such a powerful scene as 4.3 with its blend of transmuted myth, theological mystery, and sheer theatrical shock. It surely deserves to be acted.

Moreover, the play has its own hidden coherence in a pattern of ideas concerning food, sex, vice, virtue, and the role of the female. There was a strongly held belief, stated by both Aristotle and Hippocrates, that sexual intercourse vitiated the male and nourished the female, because semen passed from the male to the female, resulting in loss and weakness to the man. This belief survived into the Victorian word for ejaculation ('spend') and also into the French term for the same thing (*la perte*, which has the further meanings of loss, ruin, and destruction). Since semen was believed to be made out of blood, lovemaking that was too frequent or too passionate led to the female effectively devouring the man: it would become a bloody banquet. At the same time it was believed that a woman's blood was turned into breast milk, and so a woman nourished her children with her own life-force. Middleton surely drew on this belief in the stanza from *The Ghost of Lucrece* that concludes 'Here's blood for milk...' (136–42). In *The Bloody Banquet*, the Old Queen is presented with two young children at the breast, but starving so that she cannot feed them. The young Queen feasts on men, while her virtuous antithesis feeds and nurtures them.

When Lapyrus has turned traitor by being tempted through a woman, Eurynome, he can redeem himself by renouncing the woman (she is never heard of again) and serving the good Old Queen: his expiation involves starving himself while he searches for food for her and her offspring. That good Queen renounces her roles as both wife and mother during the period of expiation, reducing herself to a mere wet-nurse (that is, a nourisher), of her one remaining child. In this way, strength is restored to the good king and queen, so that they eventually regain their throne with a surviving heir. Abstinence helps to restore potency.

When the Tyrant greets his young Queen, he says 'This night we'll banquet in these blissful arms', but the ironic implication is that his voracious desire will result in her consuming him, not the other way around. Uxoriousness is the first step in his destruction, his loss of potency. Tymethes is a wastrel who ends up being literally consumed by a woman. The play abounds in lines connected with this theme, linking its plot and imagery into one compelling whole. Even when Amphridote turns from virtue to despair, the means she uses is poison: when the good woman becomes bad, she ceases to be a nourisher and becomes a poisoner. Poison is the perversion of her gender role. Mazeres attempts to poison Tymethes, but fails miserably. This network of ideas provides one more link back to Seneca, for while in the classical gruesome banquet the parent devours the child, in the Lapyrus plot (which seems to have been written by Dekker) the wholesome antithesis, a mother feeding her children from her own body, is given centrality.

Middleton specialized in the depiction of wicked women, and even in a play where most of the men—the Tyrant, Tymethes, Mazeres, Roxano—are base and unscrupulous, the wickedness of the young Queen stands out. It has more dramatic impact, perhaps because it is more culturally transgressive. It is not unprepared. Act 4 scene 3—in which the young Queen makes Tymethes kneel in prayer by the side of her bed, then shoots him dead with two pistols—is the dramatic climax of the play. She has warned him of death often before, but somehow we do not quite expect this. We assume, if anything, that the furious husband or the obliging pander would carry out the execution, not the Queen herself. In Warner, the husband simply finds the guilty pair ('the naughty packs') in bed together, and beheads the lover on the spot. Middleton knew that was too hackneyed to have the kind of impact he desired. Everything in this scene wanders far from the source, introducing mythological elements and theological mysteries far beyond the scope of Warner.

Tymethes' mad determination to unmask his mysterious lover in her rich palace recalls the Cupid and Psyche legend: but the genders are reversed. Here it is the man whose curiosity proves his downfall, and the woman who sorrowfully withdraws her love from him. Psyche of course was not killed, but given a chance to expiate her sin. The young Queen instructs Tymethes to kneel and repent of his sins, which he imagines to be his only penalty until she pulls the trigger. In her soliloquy over his body she points out that she has treated him generously by letting him pray for mercy first so that he will go to heaven. It reminds us of Hamlet's inability to kill

Claudius while he was at prayer, and raises the question, so fascinating to Calvinists such as Middleton and Dekker and most of their audience: how could you ever be sure who was saved and who was damned?

Middleton also introduced the succeeding incident, with its black humour, when the young Queen tries to explain Tymethes' dead body to her intruding husband by claiming that he was a total stranger who had been trying to rape her. He exclaims: 'O let me embrace thee for a brave, unmatchable, Precious, unvalued, admirable whore!' The business of the false rape-charge is an ancient and oppressive myth. It goes back in classical culture at least as far as the story of Phaedra and Hippolytus, and in the Jewish-Christian tradition to that of Joseph and Potiphar's wife in Genesis 39 (stories whose similarities were noted by scholars of the Renaissance). The myth also persists in twentieth-century works (e.g. Forster's *A Passage to India*). Middleton probably had both the biblical and the classical stories in mind, particularly the latter since Seneca wrote a tragedy on the subject of Phaedra. We know that Middleton was acquainted with it because he quotes from it in Latin in *The Revenger's Tragedy*: *Curae leves loquuntur, ingentes stupent*. In *The Bloody Banquet*, the young Queen appears to be the second wife of the Tyrant, as Phaedra was of King Theseus; Hippolytus was thus Phaedra's stepson, while Tymethes is betrothed to the young Queen's stepdaughter. Phaedra indirectly causes Hippolytus' death, for in desperately fleeing her slanders his chariot overturns and he is killed. Phaedra commits suicide over his fragmented remains: 'Hippolytus! Is this how I must find you? | Is this what I have made of you? What creature— | Some Sinis, some Procrustes?—Cretan bull | Bellowing in a Daedalian labyrinth, | Horned hybrid—can have torn you into pieces?'

But the differences are very revealing. Tymethes is far from an innocent young man: he has accepted the queen's advances readily, along with a large cash payment, then boasted of his adventure to Zenarchus and given his virgin love a jewel actually filched from the sleeping Queen. Moreover, the young Queen does not lie from simple motives of malice, as Phaedra and the nameless wife of Potiphar do. She does so out of self-preservation, fearing a husband who has locked her up like an animal and can now kill her on the spot for her adultery. The Middleton story does not, as its antecedents did, confine moral blame only to the woman, and it offers more insight into the pressures and constraints which can lead men or women to resort to duplicity.

It is no accident that the jealous husband is referred to throughout the play as 'the tyrant', even by his own servants. He is a domestic as well as a public tyrant in every sense. He usurps Lydia, incarcerates his wife (Roxano is bluntly described as her 'keeper') and predictably opposes his daughter's choice of husband. In *Thyestes* it is Atreus who is the usurper, but Armatrites is a Machiavellian tyrant, rather than a Senecan one, because he brings specious justifications and pragmatic evaluations of everything that he does. Armatrites has invited his betrayal by the young Queen through his own previous treachery to the King of Lydia, without which Tymethes would never have had opportunity to get into this particular entanglement. The web of treachery, of cause and effect, is carefully woven.

The final scene of *The Bloody Banquet* presents a spectacle of tyranny overthrown, but it is also much more than that. The guilty young Queen is now presented as an object for compassion as she endures her public humiliation. In her, disparate strands of the myth are woven together: she is eating her lover but again in another sense eating her own child, and she is also a penitent eating in humility the child of her host, the Old King. Perhaps we are meant to believe that through it she achieves redemption before her death. At any rate, none of the horror is merely sensational and this scene is a complex achievement. The soldiers' cry of 'Speranza!' alludes back to the opening of the play, while the discharge of pistols which kills the Tyrant echoes the earlier one in the climactic central scene when Tymethes was dispatched by the young Queen.

This ending is more politically forthright than later plays in the Dekker canon: in *The Noble Spanish Soldier* the wicked King of France takes poison by accident rather than being killed by the conspirators. Middleton, on the other hand, had few inhibitions about dramatizing tyrannicide. His canon supplies a large proportion of the Jacobean genre that Albert Tricomi calls 'anti-court drama'. Chronologically, the tyrannicide in *The Bloody Banquet* apparently belongs to the period between those in *The Revenger's Tragedy* (1606) and *The Lady's Tragedy* (1611). Taylor (2002), on the basis of topical allusions and stylistic tests, places it *c.*1609.

In *The Lady's Tragedy* once more we have a female protagonist who lacks a baptismal name married to an usurper who is known generically as 'Tyrant'. That Tyrant's death in the final scene—fondling her corpse, poisoned by kissing the pigment he has commanded to be painted on her lips and cheeks—is a stroke of necrophiliac horror closely comparable to that in the final scene of *The Bloody Banquet*. Both can be compared to Vindice's fondling of the skull of his beloved, at the beginning of *The Revenger's Tragedy*, and his later use of that skull, appropriately painted with poison, to kill the lecherous and tyrannical Duke. Such comparisons do not prove that one man wrote all three plays; the proof of Middleton's authorship of all three comes from many kinds of interlocking stylistic evidence. In the case of *The Bloody Banquet*, Middleton's authorship of the Young Queen plot was first suggested by E. H. C. Oliphant in 1925, and confirmed by Gary Taylor in 2000; we provide further evidence in this edition. But the narrative, thematic, and emotional links between *The Revenger's Tragedy*, the Young Queen plot in *The Bloody Banquet*, and *The Lady's Tragedy* create an intelligible pattern of tragedies with a family resemblance, written between 1606 and 1611.

Like *The Bloody Banquet*, *The Lady's Tragedy* opens with the entrance of the new usurper of the kingdom. In the later play, Sophonirus tells the Tyrant that cuckoldry is good for one's health. He speaks from experience, declaring 'I draw my life out by the bargain | Some twelve years longer than the times appointed, | When my young prodigal gallant kick up's heels | At one-and-thirty, and lies dead and rotten | Some five-and-forty years before I'm coffined' (1.1.44–8). Here are the fundamental assumptions that underlie *The Bloody Banquet*: sexual activity vitiates the system, whereas male chastity conserves the body's strength. The penalty for sexual abandonment is, literally, death.

Both *The Bloody Banquet* and *The Lady's Tragedy* are plays of horror, a genre not nowadays rated very highly on the scale of aesthetic achievement. But their transgression of certain boundaries of 'good taste'—an ironic phrase, in this context—is surely as deliberate as that of, say, Oscar Wilde's *Salome*. The composition of more than one work in a similar vein probably indicates that the first was a success on stage. Nobody repeats a failure. The first anthology of memorable passages from English Renaissance drama—John Cotgrave's *English Treasury* (1655)—quotes *The Bloody Banquet* fifteen times: more than any other Middleton play but *The Revenger's Tragedy*, more than any Shakespeare play but *Hamlet*. Nobody quotes a failure. In its own time, *The Bloody Banquet* seems to have been a theatrical and literary success. Only good modern productions of high standard might help us understand why.

SEE ALSO

Textual introduction and apparatus: *Companion*, 1020
Authorship and date: *Companion*, 364
Other Middleton–Dekker works: *Caesar's Fall*, 328; *Gravesend*, 128; *Meeting*, 183; *Magnificent*, 219; *Patient Man*, 280; *Roaring Girl*, 721; *Gypsy*, 1723

THOMAS MIDDLETON and THOMAS DEKKER

The Bloody Banquet: A Tragedy

[*adapted for Beeston's Boys at The Phoenix*]

Hector adest secumque Deos in proelia ducit

Nos haec novimus esse nihil

DRAMATIS PERSONAE

The KING of Lydia
TYMETHES, his son
LAPYRUS, his nephew

The King of Lycia
Zantippus, his son
Eurimone, his daughter

Armatrites, King of Cilicia [and TYRANT of Lydia]
ZENARCHUS, his son
AMPHRIDOTE, his daughter
His young QUEEN [Thetis]
Her maid, [a LADY in waiting]
MAZERES, his favourite
ROXANO, the Young Queen's keeper

FIDELIO, AMORPHO } two faithful servants to the Lydian King

SERTORIO, LODOVICO } two unfaithful servants of his

The OLD QUEEN of Lydia
Her two little children

CHORUS
The CLOWN
Two SHEPHERDS
Four SERVANTS
Soldiers

Motto ***Hector*...*ducit*** 'Then Hector appeared, bringing his gods to do battle with him' [i.e. on his behalf] (Ovid, *Metamorphoses* XIII, 82). Ajax is recalling the Trojan war during his contention with Ulysses for the armour of Achilles.

Nos*...*nihil 'We know these things to be nothing' (Martial, *Epigrams*, XIII, 2). An authorial expression of modesty.

The Bloody Banquet.

Induction

Inductio

Flourish. Enter [Chorus, then] at one door the old King of Lydia, Tymethes his son, Lapyrus his nephew, and soldiers; at the other, the old King of Lycia, Zantippus his son, Eurymone his daughter, and soldiers. The two kings parley, and change hostages for peace. Lapyrus is given to the Lycian, and Zantippus to the Lydian. The Lycian seems to offer his daughter Eurymone to Lapyrus to fall from his uncle, and join with him; he accepts her, drawing his sword against his country and uncle. The Lydian sends his son Tymethes for aid; he enters again with Armatrites King of Cilicia, Zenarchus his son, and Mazeres a young Prince, the Cilician King's follower. All they draw against the Lycian's party, whereat they all with Lapyrus fly, the two other kings pursuing them. Then enter the old Queen of Lydia flying from her nephew Lapyrus, with two babes in her arms, he pursuing her with his drawn sword; [they cross the stage and exeunt]

CHORUS
After the waste of many thousand wounds
Given and received alike, in seven set battles,
Lydia's old King (upon conditions signed
For peace and truce), entered constrainèd league
With his fierce enemy the Lycian King,
Gave him in hostage as his pledge of faith
His nephew, Lord Lapyrus, and received
Noble Zantippus from the Lycian,
To make the contract full and honourable.
This Lord Lapyrus entertained and welcomed
By [ ],
But chiefly by the fair Eurymone,
The King's sole daughter, who unto Lapyrus
Offers her as his bride, so he would turn
A traitor to his country and his king.
Lapyrus, to obtain the beauteous maid,
Turns traitor to his king, and joins his force
Unto his fair love's father's, Lycia's king's;
Th'old King of Lydia, being so beset
By his own nephew's unexpected treacheries,
Sent forth his son Tymethes to crave aid
From Armatrites, King of great Cilicia,
Which he obtained—in a disastrous hour,
As the event will witness. In this trouble
The frighted Queen with her two infants fled
Into a forest, fearing the sad ruin
Hourly expected, until Armatrites
With a fresh army forced Lapyrus fly
And saved the King, doomed for worse treachery.
What follows shows itself; 'tis our full due,
If we with labour give content to you. *Exit*

[A throne.] Enter the two Kings of Lydia and Cilicia, Zenarchus (son to the Cilician), Tymethes (son to the Lydian), Mazeres, Fidelio, Amorpho, Sertorio, Lodovico, when they come unto the throne, the Tyrant of Cilicia puts by the old King, and ascends alone: all snatch out their swords, Mazeres crowns him, the old King and Tymethes stand amazed. Flourish 1.1

TYRANT *Speranza.*
OMNES Long live Armatrites, King of Lydia!
KING How?
TYRANT
Art thou amazed, old King, and all thy people
Mutually labouring in a fit of wonder?
Start from those pale dreams: we will prove all true.
Who wins the day, the brightness is his due.
KING
King of Cilicia—
TYRANT Ay, and Lydia now.
Bate us not our titles: we and ours
Have sweat and dearly earned them in our flesh.
KING
It savours not of nobleness nor virtue,
Religion, loyalty, heaven or nature's laws
So most perfidiously to enter, tyrant,
Where was expected honesty and honour,
Assistance from a friend, not a dissembler,
A royal neighbour and no politic foe.
What worse than this could th'enemy perform?
And when shines friendship best but in a storm?
TYRANT
Why, doting Lydia, is it of no virtue
To bring our army hither, and put in venture
Our person and their lives upon your foes?
Wasting our courage, weak'ning our best forces,
Impoverishing the heart of our munition,
And having won the honour of the battle
To throw our glory on unworthy spirits,
And so unload victory's honey thighs
To let drones feed?

Induction Probably written by an adapter, to replace several short battle scenes.
1.1 Dekker.
1 *Speranza* hope (Italian)
2 OMNES all (Latin)—presumably 'all the supporters of the Tyrant'
9 **Bate us not** do not leave out anything we are entitled to
10 **sweat** sweated
16 **politic** crafty
23 **Impoverishing . . . munition** expending our best forces

KING Will nothing satisfy but all?
TYRANT Without all, nothing.
The kingdom, and not under, suits our blood.
Flies are not eagles' preys, nor thanks our food.
And for Cilicia, our other sphere—
Our son Zenarchus, let thy beams move there.

ZENARCHUS
Rather, my lord, let me move pity here
Unto that reverend fate-afflicted king—
For whom, with his disconsolate son (my friend
And plighted brother) I here kneel as suitor.
[*Zenarchus and Tymethes kneel*]
O my most noble father, still retain
The seal of honour and religïon.
A kingdom rightfully possessed by course
Contains more joy than is usurped by force.

TYRANT [*aside*] The boy hath almost changed us.

MAZERES [*aside*]
He cools.—My lord, remember: you are possessed.

TYRANT What, with the devil?

MAZERES
The devil! The dukedom, the kingdom, Lydia.
All pant under your sceptre; the sway's yours.
Be not bought out with words. A kingdom's dear.
Kiss fortune, keep your mind, and keep your state.
You're laughed at if you prove compassionate.

TYRANT
Thanks to Mazeres; he hath refreshed our spirits.—
Zenarchus, 'tis thy death if thou proceed.
Thy words we threat; rise silent, or else bleed.
[*Zenarchus and Tymethes rise*]

KING
Who can expect but blood where tyrants govern?

TYRANT
We are not yet so cruel to thy fortune
As was Lapyrus, thy own nephew, treacherous—
That stole upon thy life, beseiged thee basely,
And had betrayed thee to thine enemies' anger
Had we not beat his strength to his own throat
And made him shrink before us. All can tell
In him 'twas monstrous; 'tis in us but... well,
A trick of war, advantage, policy—
Nay, rather recompense.
There's more deceit in peace: 'tis common there
T'unfold young heirs; the old may well stand bare.
You have your life, be thankful—and 'tis more
Than your perfidious nephew would consent to,
Had he surprised you first. Your fate is cast.
The sooner you be gone, 'twill prove the safer.

KING
On thee, Lapyrus, and thy treacheries, fall
The heavy burden of an old man's curse.

FIDELIO
Your Queen with her two infants fled the city,
Affrighted at this treason and new wars.

KING
News of more sadness than the kingdom's loss!
She fled upon her hour, for had she stayed
She'd either died, been banished or betrayed.—
I have some servants here.

AMORPHO All these, my lord.

KING All these? Not all. You did forget:
I am not worth the flattering. I am done,
Old and at set; honour the rising sun.
If any for love serve me, which is he?
Now let him shame the world and follow me.

FIDELIO
That's I, my lord.

AMORPHO And I.

KING What, two of you?—
Let it be enrolled
Two follow a king when he is poor and old.
Exit cum suis

SERTORIO Farewell, king.
I'll play the flounder: keep me to my tide.

LODOVICO
And so will I: this is the flowing side.

MAZERES [*to Tyrant*]
Those men are yours, my lord.

TYRANT We'll grace them chiefly.—
Wait for employment, place and eminence;
The like to each that to our bounty flies,
For he that falls to us shall surely rise.—
[*Menarchus and the Tyrant speak apart*]
His son Tymethes little frights our thoughts:
He's young, and given to pleasure, not to plots.

MAZERES
Your grace defines him right. He may remain;
The Prince, your son, binds him in a love-chain.
There's little fear of him.

TYRANT Their loves are dear.
Base boy, he leaves his father to live here.

MAZERES
His presence sets a gloss on your attempts;
They have their lustre from him.

TYRANT He's their countenance.

30 **not under** nothing less
32 **sphere** orbit of one of the planets (in the Ptolemaic astronomical system)
36 **my friend** The friendship of Xenarchus and Tymetes in the source (Warner, 117) does not go as far as this. The play's version resembles the friendship of David and Jonathan in 1 Samuel 20.
40 **course** lineal succession
43 **possessed** (*a*) in possession (of Lydia); (*b*) inhabited (by an evil spirit)
53 **but** anything but
tyrants i.e. usurpers
64 **T'unfold** to disclose or lay open to the view; to unwrap, hence to strip of their assets, to fleece.
stand bare (*a*) remove their hats, as a sign of deference; (*b*) are completely bereft of possessions
84 **enrolled** recorded in a roll, like an official document
85 **Two... old** Compare *King Lear* (1605).
85.1 ***cum suis*** with his followers (Latin)
87 **play the flounder** swim with the tide, not against it; i.e., support the winner.
99 **sets... attempts** gives the takeover an air of legitimacy

'Twas well observed and followed; he shall stay.
Mazeres, thou armest us that won the day.
Exit all but Zenarchus and Tymethes

ZENARCHUS
None but Mazeres, that court fly, could on
The virtues of the King blow such corruption.
Man falls to vice in minutes, runs and leaps,
But unto goodness he takes wary steps.
How soon a tyrant—
[*Tymethes lies upon the ground*]
Why, Tymethes! friend, brother!

TYMETHES
Peace, prithee, peace. You undo me if you wake me;
I hope I'm in a dream.

ZENARCHUS
Would 'twere so happy!

TYMETHES
No? Why then, wake, beggar!
[*He sits up*]
But the comfort is
I have brave seeming-kinsmen. Why, Zenarchus,
'Tis not the loss of kingdom, father's banishment,
Uncertainty of mother, afflicts me
With half the violence that those crossed affections
Betwixt your princely sister and ourself,
Who, upon fortune or her father's frown
Erecting the whole fabric of her love,
Either now will not, or else dare not, love me.

ZENARCHUS
Chance alters not affection: see in me
That hold thee dear still spite of tyranny.
Fate does but dim the gloss of a right man;
He still retains his worth, do what fate can.
Change faith for dross? I will not call her sister,
That shall hate virtue for afflictïon.
Enter Amphridote
And here she comes to clear those doubts herself.

AMPHRIDOTE
Strange alteration! Will the King my father
Go to his grave a ruffian and a treacher?
In his grey hairs turn tyrant to his friends?
Wasting his penitential times in plots,
Acting more sins than he hath tears to weep them?

TYMETHES
Alas, lady, fortune hath changed my state.
Can you love a beggar?

AMPHRIDOTE
Why, fortune hath the least command o'er love.
She cannot drive Tymethes from himself,
And 'tis Tymethes, not his painted glories,
My soul in her accomplished wish desires.

ZENARCHUS
What say you now, sir?

TYMETHES
Nothing but admire
That heaven can frame a creature like a woman
And she be constant, seeing most are common.

ZENARCHUS
Put by your wonder, sir; she proves the same.
I spoke her virtues for her ere she came,
And when my father dies I here do vow,
This kingdom now detainèd wrongfully
Shall then return unforcèdly to you,
In part thy dowry, but in all thy due.

TYMETHES Unmatchèd honest young man!
Enter Mazeres observing

ZENARCHUS
Come, let your lips meet, though your fortunes wander.
[*Tymethes and Amphridote kiss*]

MAZERES [*aside*]
Ha! Taste lips so bounteously with a beggar?

ZENARCHUS
Thus in firm state let your affections rest.
Time, that makes wretched, makes the same men blest.
Exeunt [*all but Mazeres*]

MAZERES
What's here? Either the princes (out of charity's rareness)
Are pleased to lay aside their glories, and refresh
The gasping fortunes of a desperate wretch;
Or if for larger bounties [
] I was mad
T'advise the King for his remaining here
That had been banished, and with him my fear.
I love the princess, and the King allows it.
If he should prove a rival to my love,
I have argued fair for his abiding here.
My plots shall work his ruin; if one fail
I'll raise a second, for I must prevail.
I that used policy to cause him stay
Can show like art to rid my fears away. *Exit*

Enter the old Queen [*in beggarly clothes*] *with two babes, as being hard pursued* 1.2

OLD QUEEN
O whither shall I fly with these poor babes?
Twice set upon by thieves within this forest,
Who robbed me of my clothes, and left me these,

103 **fly** (found where corruption is). Compare Mosca (= fly) in Jonson's *Volpone* (1606).
105–6 **leaps...steps** (a rhyme)
107.1 ***Tymethes...ground*** A conventional expression of despair. Tymethes must do something to prompt Zenarchus's self-interruption.
111 **seeming-kinsmen** Zenarchus, who is not ashamed to call Tymethes his brother, even after what has happened.
113 **Uncertainty of mother** The Old Queen has fled and her whereabouts are unknown.
151 **the princes** i.e. Zenarchus and Amphridote
157 **That...fear** (Tymethes was at first exiled along with his father, and if he had gone Mazeres would have had no rival in love.)
163 **policy** cunning
164 **like** similar
1.2 Dekker.
0.1 ***old*** former

Which better suit with my calamity.
What fate pursues the good old King my husband,
I cannot learn, which is my worst affliction.
O treacherous Lapyrus! Impious nephew!
All horrors of a guilty breast keep with thee!—
Either, poor babes, you must pine here for food,
Or have the wars drink your immaculate blood.
Cry within, 'Follow! Follow!'
O fly, lest life and honour be betrayed. *Exit*

1.3 *Enter Lapyrus disguised [with a false beard, etc.]*

LAPYRUS
Villain and fugitive, where wilt thou hide
Th'abhorrèd burden of thy wretched flesh?
In what disguise canst thou be safe and free,
Having betrayed thy country? Base Lapyrus!
[He prepares to kill himself]
Earth, stretch thy throat: take down this bitter pill,
Loathing the hateful taste of his own ill.
Enter the [old] Queen and two soldiers [now thieves] pursuing her

OLD QUEEN
O help! Good heaven, save a poor wretch from slaughter!

FIRST THIEF *[to Second Thief]*
Stop her mouth first. Soldiers must have their sport.
'Tis dearly earned; they venture their blood for't.

LAPYRUS *[aside]*
A mother so enforced by pitiless slaves?
Let me redeem my honour in her rescue,
And in this deed my former baseness die.

SECOND THIEF *[to Old Queen]* Come, come.

OLD QUEEN
If ever woman bore you—

LAPYRUS *[coming forward]* Whoe'er bore them,
Monsters begot them. Merciless damned villains!

BOTH [THIEVES]
Hold, hold, sir; we are soldiers, but do not love to fight.
Exeunt [soldiers]

OLD QUEEN *[to Lapyrus]*
Let me dissuade you from all hope of recompense
Save thanks and prayers, which are the beggar's gifts.

LAPYRUS
You cannot give me that I have more need of
Than prayers, for my soul hath a poor stock.
There's a fair house within, but 'tis ill furnished:
There wants true tears for hangings, penitent falls—
For without prayers, soldiers are but bare walls.
Whence are you? that with such a careful charge
Dare pass this dangerous forest?

OLD QUEEN Generous sir,
I was of Lydia once, as happy then
As now unfortunate, till one Lapyrus,
That traiterous villain, nephew to the King,
Sought the confusion of his state and him,
And with a secret army girt his land
When peace was plighted by his enemy's hand,
Little expecting such unnatural treason
From forth a kinsman's bosom; all admired
But I his miserable queen.

LAPYRUS *(aside)*
O sink into perdition! Let me hear no further.

OLD QUEEN
I'll tell you all—for your so late attempt
Confirms you honest, and my thoughts so keep you.
I, frighted at new wars and his false breath,
Chose rather with these babes this lingering death.

LAPYRUS *[aside]*
O, in her words I endure a thousand deaths!

OLD QUEEN
The truth of this sad story hath been yours;
Now, courteous sir, may I request your name?
That in my prayers I may place the same.

LAPYRUS *[aside]*
I'll put my death into her woeful hands.

OLD QUEEN
I hear you not, sir. I desire your name.

LAPYRUS
To add some small content to your distress,
Know that Lapyrus, whom your miseries
May rightly curse and be revengèd justly,
Lurks in this forest equally distressed.

OLD QUEEN
Lurks in this forest that abhorrèd villain?

LAPYRUS
These eyes did see him—and faith, lady, say
If you should meet that worst of villains here,
That treacher, monster, what would you attempt?

OLD QUEEN
His speedy death. I should forget all mercy,
Had I but means fully to express my vengeance.

LAPYRUS
You would not, Queen.

OLD QUEEN No? By these infants' tears
That weep for hunger, I would throughly do't.

LAPYRUS
See, yonder he comes.

OLD QUEEN O where?

LAPYRUS Here, take my sword.
Are you yet constant? Shame your sex, and be so.
Will you do't?

OLD QUEEN I see him not.

5 **What** whatever
10 **Or . . . blood** (anticipating the cannibalism of the final scene, but also suggesting its transmutation in the Christian communion)
1.3 Dekker.
9 **blood** (playing on the sense 'semen', and recalling 1.1.10–30)
22 **penitent falls** (Falling tears are likened to curtains or tapestries because both drop.)
24 **careful charge** burden requiring care, i.e. her children
33 **admired** were astonished.

LAPYRUS
Strike him through his guilt and treachery
And let him see the horrors of his perjured soul.
Are you ready?

OLD QUEEN Pray let me see him first.

[Lapyrus] pulls off his false beard and kneels

LAPYRUS
You see him now—now do't!

OLD QUEEN Lapyrus!
O fortunate revenge! Now all thy villanies
Shall be at once requited: thy country's ruin,
The King thy uncle's sorrow, my own miseries,
Shall at this minute all one vengeance meet.—
Alas, he doth submit, prays, and relents.
Who could wish more? None made from woman can.
Small glory 'twere to kill a kneeling man.
When he in penitent sighs his soul commends
Thou send'st him to the gods, thyself to th' fiends.—
But hearken to thy piteous infants' cries,
And they're for vengeance. Peace then: now he dies.
—Ungrateful woman, he delivered thee
From ravishment; canst thou his murd'ress be?
What's riches to thy honour? That rare treasure
Which worlds redeem not, yet 'tis lost at pleasure.
Kill him that preserved that? and in thy rescue
His noble rage so manfully behaved?—
Rise, rise! He that repents is ever saved.

LAPYRUS *[rising]*
Will misery yet a longer life afford,
To see a queen so poor, not worth her word?

OLD QUEEN
I am better than my word; my word was death.

LAPYRUS
Man's ne'er past grief, till he be past his breath.

OLD QUEEN
I pardon all, Lapyrus.

LAPYRUS Do not do't.

OLD QUEEN
And only to one penance I enjoin thee
For all thy faults past: while we here remain
Within this forest, this thy task shall be—
To procure succour to my babes and me.

LAPYRUS
And if I fail, may the earth swallow me.

OLD QUEEN
Thou'rt now grown good. Here could I ever dwell,
Were the old King, my husband, safe and well.

Exeunt

1.4

Enter Tymethes and Zenarchus

ZENARCHUS
Come, come, drive away these fits. Faith, I'll have thee merry.

TYMETHES
As your son and heir at his father's funeral.

ZENARCHUS
Thou seest my sister constantly affects thee.

TYMETHES
There were no mirth nor music else for me.

ZENARCHUS
Sir, in this castle the old King my father,
O'erworn with jealousy, keeps his beauteous wife;
I think thou never saw'st her.

TYMETHES No, not I.

ZENARCHUS
Why then, thy judgement's fresh. I'll visit her
O' purpose for thy censure.

TYMETHES I speak my affection.

ZENARCHUS
Nay on my knowledge she's worth jealousy,

Enter Roxano

Though jealousy be far unworth a king.

ROXANO
My loved lord?

ZENARCHUS How cheers the Queen?

They whisper

TYMETHES *[aside]*
Have I not seen this fellow before now?
He has an excellent presence for a pander;
I know not his office.

ZENARCHUS *[to Roxano]*
Use those words to her.

ROXANO
They shall be used, my lord—and any thing
That comes to using, let it come to me. *Exit*

TYMETHES What's he, Zenarchus?

ZENARCHUS
Who, Roxano? A fellow in great trust,
Elected by my father's jealousy.
But he and all the rest attend upon her
I think would turn her panders for reward—
For 'tis not watch nor ward keeps woman chaste,
If honour's watch in her mind be not placed.

TYMETHES
Right oracle! What gain hath jealousy?
Fruitless suspicion, sighs, ridiculous groans.
Hunger and lust will break through flesh and stones,
And like a whirlwind blows ope castle doors,
Italian padlocks, [ ].

71 **Small...man** She holds him at sword-point but is unable to kill him. For a woman with a weapon confronting a vulnerable man, compare 4.3.96.1, *Richard III* 1.2, and *Roaring Girl* sc. 5.

72–3 **When...fiends** Compare *Hamlet* 3.3 (Hamlet sparing the kneeling Claudius).

78 **honour** sexual integrity

1.4 Middleton.

1 **fits** capricious impulses, moods

2 **your** one's (general, not specific)

3 **affects** loves

9 **affection** true feelings (i.e., I'll give you an honest opinion).

12 **cheers** fares

16–17 **any thing...using** (sexual innuendoes)

29 **Italian padlocks** chastity belts. (Italian men were allegedly more jealous than Englishmen.)

ZENARCHUS
What mad lords are your jealous people then,
That lock their wives from all men but their men?
Make 'em their keepers, to prevent some greater.
So oft it happens to the poor's relief:
Keepers eat venison, when their lords eat beef.
Enter young Queen with a book in her hand
See, see, she comes.
TYMETHES [*aside*]
Honour of beauty! There man's wishes rise.
Grace and perfection lighten from her eyes;
Amazement is shot through me.
ZENARCHUS 'Tis Tymethes, lady,
Son to the banished King.
QUEEN Is this he?
ZENARCHUS It is, sweet lady.
QUEEN [*aside*]
I never knew the force of a desire
Until this minute struck within my blood.
I fear one look was destined to undo me.
ZENARCHUS
Why, Tymethes! Friend?
TYMETHES Ha?
ZENARCHUS A courtier,
And forget your first weapon? Go and salute
Our lady mother.
QUEEN [*aside*] He makes towards us.—
You're Prince Tymethes? So I understand.
TYMETHES
The same unfortunate, most gracious lady,
Supremest of your sex in all perfections.
QUEEN
Sir, you're forgetful. This is no place for courtship,
Nor we a subject for't. Return to your friend.
TYMETHES [*aside*] All hopes killed in their blossom.
QUEEN [*aside*]
Too cruelly, in faith, I put him by.—
Wine for our son Zenarchus! 'Twas done kindly.
Enter Roxano with wine
You, son, and our best visitant—
ZENARCHUS Duty binds me.
QUEEN
Begin to me, Zenarchus; I'll have't so.
[*Zenarchus pledges her, then gives her the cup*]
TYMETHES [*aside*]
Why then there's hope she'll take occasïon
To drink to me; she hath no means t'avoid it.
QUEEN [*aside*]
I'll prevent all loose thoughts, drink to myself.
Drinks and gives Roxano the cup
My mind walks yonder, but suspèct walks here.
TYMETHES [*aside*]
The devil's on that side and engrosses all,
Smiles, favours, common courtesies—none can fall
But he has a snatch at 'em. Not drink to me?
QUEEN [*to Roxano*]
Make you yon stranger drink.
Roxano offers it him
TYMETHES [*refusing the cup*] Pox on't, not I.
QUEEN [*aside*]
I speak strange words against my fantasy.
ZENARCHUS
Prithee, Tymethes, drink!
TYMETHES I am not dry.
ZENARCHUS
I think so too; dry, and so young? 'Twere strange.
Come prithee, drink to the Queen, my mother.
TYMETHES
You shall rule me.—Unto that beauteous majesty!
[*He pledges the Queen, then gives her the cup*]
QUEEN Thanks, noble sir.
[*Aside*] I must be wary; my mind's dangerous.—
I'll pledge you anon, sir.
Gives Roxano the cup. [*Exit Roxano*]
TYMETHES [*aside*]
Heart! How contempt ill fortune does pursue!
Not drink, nor pledge: what was she born to do?
I'll stay no longer, lest I get that flame
Which nothing but cold death can quench or tame.—
Zenarchus, come. *Exit*
ZENARCHUS I go.—
Music of mind to the Queen.
QUEEN To you no less.
ZENARCHUS
And all that you can wish, or I express. *Exit*
QUEEN Thanks to our son!—
Th'other took leave in silence, but left me
To speak enough both for myself and he.
Tymethes? That's his name. Poor heart, take heed:
Look well into th'event ere thou proceed.
Love, yet be wise; impossible, none can.
If e'er the wise man claim one foolish hour,

31 **their men** their servants
34.1 ***book*** (probably a prayer book or Bible: see 3.2)
46 **first weapon** i.e. tongue (but suggesting 'penis')
55 **son** stepson
57 **Begin** (For the woman to pledge first would suggest excessive familiarity or forwardness.)
58–9 **Why...t'avoid it** Normally pledging goes in a round: A (Zenarchus) pledges B (Young Queen), who pledges C (Tymethes), who pledges A (Zenarchus).
60 **I'll...myself** She drinks the second toast without pledging to anyone, disappointing Tymethes' expectation. He was hoping for this as a sign of flirtation.
61 **My...here** (Her thoughts are on Tymethes, but she fears observation by Roxano and Zenarchus.)
62 **devil's** i.e. Roxano
65 ***refusing the cup*** (because she has not pledged him first in the correct sequence. His show of pique is flirtatious in itself.)
66 **strange** unfriendly
fantasy inclination, desire
67 **dry** (*a*) thirsty; (*b*) deficient in semen
78 ***Exit*** Now that Tymethes has done the courteous thing and pledged the Queen, she postpones replying to him. He misinterprets this as a snub (because of his fallen social status), and retaliates by leaving without a word.
86 **th'event** consequence

'Tis when he loves; he's then in folly's power.
I need not fear the servants that o'erwatch me;
Their faiths lie in my coffers, in effect,
More true to me than to my lord's suspèct.
The fears and dangers that most threaten me
Live in the party that I must enjoy,
And that's Tymethes. Men are apt to boast.
He may in full cups blaze and vaunt himself
Unto some meaner mistress, make my shame
The politic engine to beat down her name,
And from thence force a way to the King's ears.
Strange fate: where my love keeps, there keep my
fears.

Enter Tyrant [apart]

TYRANT [*aside*]
Alone? Why, where's her guard? Suffer her alone?
Her thoughts may work; their powers are not her
own.
Women have of themselves no entire sway;
Like dial needles they wave every way,
And must be throughly taught to be kept right
And point to none but to their lord's delight.
Time to convey and plot? Leave her alone!—
Why, villains!

[*Enter Roxano and guard*]

[*To Queen*] Kiss me, my perfectïon.

[*They kiss*]

This night we'll banquet in these blissful arms.

QUEEN
Your nights are music, and your words are charms.

TYRANT Kiss me again, fair Thetis.

[*They kiss. He*] *walks off with her, and the guard follows*

ROXANO
My lady is scarce perfect in her thoughts,
Howe'er she framed a smile upon the tyrant.
I have some skill in faces—and yet they never were more deceitful. A man can scarce know a bawd from a midwife by the face, an hypocritical puritan from a devout Christian, if you go by the face. Well, all's not straight in my lady. She hath certain crooked cogitations, if a man had the liberty to search 'em. If aught point at my advice or performance, she may fortunately disclose it: she knows my mettle, and what it yields to an ounce. She cannot be deceived in't: here's service, and secrecy, and no lady can wish more, beside a monkey. She is assured of our faculties; there's none of us all that stand her smock-sentinels but would venture a joint to do her any pleasurable service, and I think that's as much as any woman desires.—Mass, here she comes.

Enter [young] Queen sad

'Tis some strange physic; I know by the working.

QUEEN [*aside*]
It cannot be kept down with any argument.
'Tis of aspiring force; sparks fly not downward,
No more this rèceived fancy of Tymethes.
I threaten it with my lord's jealousy,
Yet still it rises against all objections.
I see my dangers, in what fears I dwell;
There's but a plank on which I run to hell,
Yet were't thrice narrower I should venture on.
None dares do more for sin than woman can.
Misery of love—Roxano? I am observed.—
What news, Roxano?

ROXANO None that's good, madam.

QUEEN No? Which is the bad?

ROXANO
The worst of all is, madam, you are sad.

QUEEN Indeed I am not merry.

ROXANO
Would I knew the means would make you so!
I would turn myself into any shape or office
To be the author on't, sweet lady.

QUEEN Troth,
I have that hope of thee, I think thou wouldst.

ROXANO
Think it? 'Sfoot, you might swear safely in that action
And never hurt your oath. I ne'er failed yet.

QUEEN
'Twere sin to injure thee; I know thou didst not.

ROXANO
Nay, I know I did not.

QUEEN But, my trusty servant,
This plot requires art, secrecy and wit,
Yet out of all can hardly work one safety.

ROXANO
Not one? That's strange. I would 'twere put to me.
I'll make it arrive safe whate'er it be.

QUEEN
Thou couldst not, my Roxano. Why, admit I love,
Now I come to thee.

ROXANO Admit you love?
Why, all's safe enough yet.

95 **Men . . . boast** (Her scruples are pragmatic, not ethical.)
97–8 **make . . . name** mention his success with me in order to impress some other woman and persuade her to yield to him
101 **Alone?** (He not only incarcerates her, but demands that she be kept under constant observation.)
104 **dial** compass
105 **throughly** thoroughly
109 **banquet** feast (sexually)
116 **puritan** non-conformist Protestant: see *Puritan Widow*
121 **mettle** spirit (punning on 'metal')
123 **service** (sexual pun)
124 **monkey** expensive and fashionable pet (notoriously lecherous)
125 **stand** (punning on 'sexually erect') **smock-sentinels** guardians of her chastity. (Smocks were worn as undergarments or nightwear.)
126 **venture a joint** risk a limb (probably bawdy)

QUEEN Ay, but a stranger?

ROXANO Nay, now we are all spoiled, lady. I may look for my brains in my boots—now you have put home to me indeed, madam. A stranger? There's a hundred deaths i'th' very name, besides vantage.

QUEEN I said I should affright thee.

ROXANO Faith, no fool can fright me, madam, commonly called a stranger.

QUEEN
Hast thou the will? Or dar'st thou do me good?

ROXANO Do thee good, sweet lady? As far as I am able, ne'er doubt it. Let me but cast about for safety, and I'll do anything, madam.

QUEEN
Ay, ay, our safeties, which are mere impossibles.
Love forgets all things but its proper objects.

ROXANO What is he? And his name?

QUEEN
Tymethes, in a most unlucky minute
Led hither by our son-in-law Zenarchus.

ROXANO Hmm...is that the most fortunate, spider-catching, smock-wrapped gentleman?

QUEEN
Yet if he know me—

ROXANO
What then?

QUEEN
I am undone.

ROXANO And is it possible a man should lie with a woman, and yet not know her? And yet 'tis possible too—Thank my invention, follow that game still.

QUEEN
He must not know me. Then I love no further,
Although for not enjoying him I die.
My lord's pale jealousy does so o'erlook me
That if Tymethes know what he enjoys
It may make way unto my lord's mistrust;
Then, since in my desire such horrors move,
I'll die no other than the death of love.
She swoons, and Roxano holds her in his arms

ROXANO Lady! Madam, do you hear? Have you leisure to swoon now, when I have taken such pains i'th' business to take order for your safety, set all things right? Why, Madam!

QUEEN What says the man?

ROXANO Why, he says like a gentleman, every inch of him, and will perform the office of a gentleman: bring you together, put you together, and leave you together. What gentleman can do more?

QUEEN And all this safely?

ROXANO And all this safely. Ay, by this hand will I, or else would I might never do anything to purpose. If he have but the first part of a young gentleman in him, 'tis granted, madam. I have crotchets in my brain that you shall see him and enjoy him, and he not know where he is, nor who it is.

QUEEN How? Shall he not know me?

ROXANO Why 'tis the least part of my meaning he should, lady. Do you think you could possibly be safe, an he know you? Why, some of your young gallants are of that vainglorious and preposterous humour that if they lay with their own sisters you should hear 'em prate on't! This is too usual. There's no wonder in't. What I have said, I will swear to perform: you shall enjoy him ere night, and he not know you next morning.

QUEEN
Thou art not only necessary but pleasing,
There, catch our bounty.
[*She gives him gold*]
Manage all but right,
As now with gold, with honours we'll requite.

ROXANO
I am your creature, lady. [*Exit Queen*]
Pretty gold,
And by this light methinks most easily earned.
There's no faculty, say I, like a pander, and that makes so many nowadays die i'th' trade. I have your gold, lady,
And eke your service. I am one step higher;
This office makes a gentleman a squire. *Exit*
[*Finis Actus Primus*]

❁

[*Incipit Actus Secundus*] **2.1**
[*In the act-time, a tree with fruit set out, and the trapdoor is opened.*] *Enter Clown and two Shepherds* [*carrying boughs*]

FIRST SHEPHERD Come, fellow Corydon, are the pits digged?

159 **stranger** i.e. not her husband, or Roxano; but also 'foreigner'
160 **now...spoiled** (She has dashed his hopes. His preceding speeches have suggested that he would like to sleep with her himself.)
163 **besides vantage** and a little more (perhaps suggesting 'not counting my commission')
175 **son-in-law** stepson
176–7 **spider-catching** (comparing women to spiders, because they 'ensnare' men: Tymethes ensnares women, who normally ensnare men)
177 **smock-wrapped** (*a*) successful with women; (*b*) wrapped in a lady's smock like a spider's victim in a web
180 **not know her** (punning on the cognitive and sexual senses)
182 **Then** therefore
184 **o'erlook** supervise
188 **die** (punning on 'have an orgasm')
194 **inch** (alluding to penis measurements)
195 **perform...gentleman** (probably bawdy)
201 **first part** (*a*) prime personal quality or attribute; (*b*) most important body part, i.e. penis
202 **crotchets** fanciful devices
205, 208 **know** (punning again)
207 **an** if
217 **your creature** (*a*) your servant; (*b*) only what you have made me
219 **faculty** branch of art or science
223 **squire** pimp
2.1 Middleton, probably with Dekker.
1 **Corydon** (conventional name for a shepherd in pastoral literature)

CLOWN Ay, and as deep as an usurer's conscience, I warrant thee.

SECOND SHEPHERD Mass, and that's deep enough; 'twill devour a widow and three orphans at a breakfast. Soft, is this it?

FIRST SHEPHERD Ay, ay, this is it.

CLOWN Nay, for the deepness I'll be sworn. But come, my masters, and lay these boughs crossover, so, so, artificially, and may all those whoreson muttonmongers the wolves hole here, which eat our sheep.

[*The lay boughs over the open pit*]

SECOND SHEPHERD I wonder what wolves those are which eat our sheep, whether they be he-wolves or she-wolves?

CLOWN

They should be he-wolves by their loving mutton,
But by their greediness they should be she-wolves,
For the belly of a she-wolf
Is never satisfied till it be dammed up.

FIRST SHEPHERD

Why are the she-wolves worse than the he's?

CLOWN

Why, is not the dam worse than the devil, pray?

FIRST SHEPHERD You have answered me there indeed.

CLOWN Why, man, if all the earth were parchment, the sea ink, every stick a pen, and every knave a scrivener, they were not all able to write down the knaveries of she-wolves.

SECOND SHEPHERD A murrain on them, he's or she's! They suck the blood of none but our lambs.

CLOWN O always the weakest goes to the wall—as for example, knock down a sheep and he tumbles forwards, knock down a woman and she tumbles backwards.

FIRST SHEPHERD Sirrah, I wonder how many sorts of wolves there be?

CLOWN Marry, just as many sorts as there be knaves in the cards.

SECOND SHEPHERD Why, that's four.

CLOWN First, there are your court-wolves, and those be foul eaters and clean drinkers.

SECOND SHEPHERD And why 'clean drinkers'?

CLOWN Why, because when they be drunk they commonly cast up all, and so make cleansing work on't.

SECOND SHEPHERD So sir, those are clean drinkers, indeed.

CLOWN The next are your country-wolves: nothing chokes them but plenty. They sing like sirens when corn goes out by shipfulls, and dance after no tune but after 'an angel a bushel'.

FIRST SHEPHERD The halter take such corn-cutters!

SECOND SHEPHERD [*to Clown*] Are there no city-wolves?

CLOWN A rope on them! Yes, huge routs, you shall have Long Lane full of them. They'll feed upon any whore, carrion, thief, or anything.

FIRST SHEPHERD Have they such maws?

CLOWN Maws? Why, man, fiddlers have no better guts. I have known some of them eat up a lord at three bites.

SECOND SHEPHERD Three bonds, you mean.

CLOWN A knight is nobody with them; a young gentleman is swallowed whole, like a gudgeon.

FIRST SHEPHERD I wonder that gudgeon does not choke him.

CLOWN A gudgeon choke him? If the throat of his conscience be sound, he'll gulp down anything. Five of your silken gallants are swallowed easier than a damask prune—for our city-wolves do so roll my young prodigal first in wax (which is soft), till he look like a gilded pill, and then so finely wrap him up in satin (which is sleek), that he goes down without chewing, and thereupon they are called slippery gallants.

FIRST SHEPHERD I'll be no gentleman for that trick.

CLOWN The last is your sea-wolf, a horrible ravener too: he has a belly as big as a ship, and devours as much silk at a gulp as would serve forty dozen tailors against a Christmas Day or a running at tilt.

FIRST SHEPHERD Well, well, now our trap is set what shall we do with the wolves we catch?

CLOWN Why, those that are great ones and more than our matches we'll let go, and the lesser wolves we will hang: shall it be so?

BOTH SHEPHERDS Ay, ay, each man to his stand.

Exeunt [*severally*]

10 **artificially** with careful design
11 **hole here** fall in this hole
15 **mutton** (*a*) female sheep; (*b*) prostitutes
17 **belly** (*a*) stomach; (*b*) womb
18 **dammed up** stuffed full
20 **dam** mother
28 **weakest ... wall** proverbial: the weakest go under.
30 **backwards** i.e. onto her back, ready to be sexually mounted
39–40 **drunk ... all** (probably alluding to notorious incidents of drunken vomiting in the Jacobean court)
42–6 **nothing ... corn-cutters** The farmers export grain, either to get higher prices for it abroad, or to keep prices up at home by creating a shortage. (Such exports were forbidden by proclamation in June 1608.)
45 **angel** gold coin worth ten shillings
46 **corn-cutters** farmers (but punning on chiropodist, 'persons who cuts corns from the feet')
49 **Long Lane** street in the City of London (north of St Paul's, running from Smithfield to the Barbican) occupied by usurers, pawnbrokers and rogues
52 **guts** (*a*) stomachs, appetites; (*b*) animal guts used to make strings for musical instruments
53 **bites** (*a*) mouthfuls; (*b*) bits
62–3 **roll ... wax** i.e. get him to sign legal documents or bonds, which are sealed with wax
64 **satin** (*a*) cloth used in expensive fashionable clothing; (*b*) satin ribbons with which deeds and other legal documents were tied up
68 **sea-wolf** pirate (subject of sensational news accounts in 1609, and an increasing problem for English shipping)
71 **Christmas ... tilt** (occasions for which courtiers would order new clothes)
74–6 **great ones ... hang** (proverbial)

2.2 *Enter Lapyrus solus*

LAPYRUS
Foul monster-monger, who must live by that
Which is thy own destruction: why should men
Be nature's bond-slaves? Every creature else
Comes freely to the table of the earth;
That which for man alone doth all things bear
Scarce gives him his true diet anywhere.
What spiteful winds breathe here, that not a tree
Spreads forth a friendly arm? Distressèd Queen,
And most accursèd babes! The earth that bears you
Like a proud mother scorns to give you food.
[He sees fruit on the tree]
Ha!
Thanks, fate! I now defy thee, starveling hunger.
Blessed tree, four lives grow in thy fruit. Run, taste it then:
Wise men serve first themselves, then other men.
He falls in the pit
O me accursèd and most miserable!
Help, help! Some angel lay a list'ning ear
To draw my cry up!—None to lend help? O,
Then pine and die.
Enter Clown

CLOWN A wolf caught, a wolf caught!

LAPYRUS O help! I am no wolf, good friend.

CLOWN No? What art thou then?

LAPYRUS A miserable wretch.

CLOWN An usurer?

LAPYRUS No, no.

CLOWN A broker then?

LAPYRUS
Mock not a man in woe: in a green wound
Pour balsam, and not physic.

CLOWN 'Snails, he talks like a surgeon.—If you be one, why do you not help yourself, sir?

LAPYRUS
I am no surgeon, friend; my name's Lapyrus.

CLOWN How? A wolf caught, ho!—Lap what Lap ho!

LAPYRUS
Lapyrus is my name; dost thou not know me?

CLOWN Yes, for a wolfish rascal that would have worried his own country.

LAPYRUS
Torture me not, I prithee. I am that wretch;
A villain I was once, but I am now—

CLOWN The devil in the vault! You, sirrah, that betrayed your country and the old King your uncle, there lie till one wolf devour another, thou treacherous rascal.
[Cover the pit, and] exit

LAPYRUS
O me most miserable and wretched creature!
I now do find there's a revenging fate
That dooms bad men to be unfortunate.

2.3 *Enter Zenarchus, Tymethes, Amphridote, and Mazeres [following behind them]*

TYMETHES
We are observed.

ZENARCHUS By whom?

TYMETHES Mazeres follows us.

AMPHRIDOTE
O, he's my protested servant, your sole rival.

TYMETHES The devil he is!

AMPHRIDOTE
You'll make a hot suitor of him anon.

TYMETHES
He may be hot in th'end; his good parts sue for't.

ZENARCHUS
He eyes us still.

TYMETHES He does. You shall depart, lady.
I'll take my leave o' purpose in his presence.
He's jealous, and a kiss runs through his heart:
I'll make a thrust at him upon your lip.

MAZERES *[aside]*
Death! Minute favours? Every step a kiss?
I think they count how the day goes by kissing;
'Tis past four since I met 'em.

TYMETHES
I've hit him in the gall; instead of blood,
He sheds distractions, which are worse than wounds.

ZENARCHUS But sirrah!

2.2 Dekker.
0.1 ***solus*** alone (Latin)
1–6 **Foul . . . anywhere** Lapyrus wonders why Nature has made it so difficult for human beings to find anything edible in the wilds where he is: humans can only find or grow food by hard labour, which is 'thy own destruction', i.e. he has almost exhausted himself in the search. Men are 'Nature's bond-slaves' because they are required to work, unlike other animals.
5 **That . . . bear** (According to Genesis, man had dominion over all living things.)
9 **bears** (*a*) carries; (*b*) gives birth to
10 **proud mother** (Upper-class mothers rarely breast-fed their babies, employing wet-nurses instead.)
12 **Blessed tree** (alluding to the trees at opposite ends of Christian historical symbolism: the tree in Eden whose fruit Eve and Adam ate, and the 'tree'/cross on which Christ was crucified)
four lives himself, the Old Queen and her two children
13.1 ***pit*** (an image of hell, represented in the medieval and Renaissance plays by the space under the stage)
21 **miserable** (suggesting 'miser' to the Clown, hence 'usurer')
25 **green** fresh or recent
26 **balsam, and not physic** soothing medicine, not an unpleasant purgative
27 **'Snails** 'by God's nails', i.e. the nails used in the crucifixion (strong oath)
28 **help yourself** (recalling Biblical, 'Physician, heal thyself')
2.3 Middleton.
0.1 ***Enter*** (If the tree is still visible onstage, the courtiers are probably imagined strolling outdoors—where they can be accosted by a poor beggar.)
2 **protested servant** declared suitor
4 **hot** eager
5 **hot in th'end** end up in Hell
parts qualities (sarcastic)
13 **hit . . . gall** galled him
14 **distractions** mental disturbances (mad jealousy)

MAZERES [*aside*]
Stays he to prove my rival? Cursed be th'hour
Wherein I advised the King for his stay here!
I have set slaves t'entrap him, yet none prosper.
I'll lay no more my faith upon their works.
They're weak and loose and like a rotten wall;
Leaning on them may hazard my own fall.
I'll use a swifter course, cut off long journeys
And tedious ways that run my hopes past breath:
I'll take the plain roadway and hunt his death. *Exit*

TYMETHES
So, so, he departs with a knit brow! No matter.
When his frown begets earthquakes, haply then
'Twill shake me too. I shall stand firm till then.

Enter Roxano, disguised

ROXANO [*aside*]
Mass, here a walks. I am far enough from myself.
I challenge all disguises except drinking
To hide me better; I give way to that—
for that indeed will thrust a white gentleman into a suit of mud. But whist, I begin to be noted.

ZENARCHUS Ay, he changed upon't.

TYMETHES I marked him.

ROXANO [*coming forward, hat in hand*] Good your honours, your most comfortable charitable relief and devotion to a poor star-crossed gentleman.

TYMETHES Pox on thee!

ROXANO I'm bare enough already, if it like your honour.

TYMETHES [*to Zenarchus and Amphridote*] He did?

ROXANO [*aside*] 'Pox on thee'? Your young gallants love to give no alms, but that that will stick by a man; that's one virtue in 'em. He's not content to have my hat off, but he would have my hair off too. [*To Tymethes*] Thank your good lordship!

TYMETHES [*to Amphridote*] No! Was that his action?

AMPHRIDOTE It called him lord.

ZENARCHUS Nay, he's a villain.

ROXANO [*to them*] Good your honours! I have been a man in my time—

TYMETHES Why, what art thou now?

ROXANO —kept goodly beasts, had three wives, two men uprising, three maids down lying. O good your kind honours!

TYMETHES 'Sfoot, I am a beggar myself.

ROXANO Perhaps your lordship gets by it. Good your sweet honour!

TYMETHES [*to Zenarchus and Amphridote*]
This fellow would be whipped.

ROXANO Your Lordship has forgot since you were a beggar.

TYMETHES
I'll give thee somewhat for that jest in truth.
[*He goes to Roxano. They talk apart*]

ROXANO But now you are in private, shut your purse, and open your ear, sir.

TYMETHES How?

ZENARCHUS [*to Amphridote*]
He's dealing his devotion; hinder him not.

ROXANO I am not literally a beggar, as puritanical as I appear. The naked truth is you are happily desired—

TYMETHES Ha?

ROXANO —of the most sweet, delicate, divine, pleasing, ravishing creature—

TYMETHES Peace, peace, prithee peace!

ROXANO —that ever made man's wishes perfect.

TYMETHES
Nay, say not so. I saw one creature lately
Exceeds all human form for true perfection:
This may be beauteous—

ROXANO This for white and red, sir!
Her honour and my oath sue for that pardon:
You must not know her name, nor see her face.

TYMETHES How?

ROXANO
She rather chooseth death in her neglect
Than so to hazard life or lose respect.

TYMETHES
How shall I come at her?

ROXANO Let your will
Subscribe to the sure means already wrought,
She shall be safely pleased, you safely brought.

TYMETHES
Ha! And is this sheer faith, without any trick in't?

ROXANO
Let me perish in this office else; and I need wish
No more damnation than to die a pander.

TYMETHES Thou speakest well. When meet we?

ROXANO
Five is the fixèd hour, upon tomorrow's evening.

TYMETHES
So, the place?

ROXANO Near to the further lodge.

26 **When . . . earthquakes** (an impossible condition: 'when pigs fly')
28 **a** he (Tymethes)
31–2 **thrust . . . mud** make a pale well-dressed person of birth and means fall over in the filthy streets. Alcohol will also 'muddy' (i.e. cloud) his mental faculties.
31 **white** (indicating race or class, in contrast to the darker dirtier skin of a beggar)
32 **mud** (often associated with labourers)
33 **he** i.e. Mazeres
39 **bare** bareheaded, hatless
41–2 **to . . . man** instead of giving money (which would be spent) they give him venereal disease ('pox'), which will not go away
44 **hair off** (Syphilis could cause baldness.)
49 **man** person of some consideration
51 **what . . . now** (taking 'man' in its most literal sense)
52 **men** male household servants
53 **uprising** (punning on 'sexually erect') **maids** (*a*) female household servants; (*b*) virgins
56 **gets** gains financially
64 **dealing his devotion** giving alms, an act of charity
65 **puritanical** i.e., despising ornament, plainly dressed

TYMETHES
Go to then! It holds honest all the way?
ROXANO
Else does there live no honesty but in lawyers.
TYMETHES
Enough. Five? And the furthest lodge? I'll meet thee.
ROXANO
Enjoy the sweetest treasure in a woman. *Exit*
TYMETHES [*aside*]
Always excepting but the tyrant's gem.
ZENARCHUS What, have you done with the beggar?
TYMETHES
None that lives can say he has done with the beggar.
ZENARCHUS
Hold conference so long with such a fellow?
TYMETHES
How? Are your wits perfect? If one should refuse
To talk with every beggar, he might refuse
Brave company sometimes—gallants, i'faith. *Exeunt*

2.4 *Enter the old King, Fidelio, and Amorpho*

KING
The loss of my dear Queen afflicts me more
Than all Lapyrus' cursèd treacheries:
Inhuman monster!
LAPYRUS (*in the pit*)
If you have human forms to fit those voices
And hearts that may be pierced with misery's groans
Sent from a fainting spirit, pity a wretch,
A miserable man, prisoner to darkness!
Your charitable strengths this way repair,
And lift my flesh to the reviving air.
KING
Alas, some travelling man, by night outstripped,
Missing his way, into this danger slipped.
Set all our hands to help him.—Come, good man,
They that sit high may make their ends below.
[*They reach down into the pit to pull him up*]
LAPYRUS [*in the pit*] Millions of thanks and praises!
KING
You're heavy, sir, whoe'er you be.
LAPYRUS [*in the pit*]
There's weight within keeps down my soul and me.
KING One full strength more
Makes our pains happy; poor strength helps the poor.
[*They raise Lapyrus from the pit*]
So sir, you're welcome to—Lapyrus? O!
Lapyrus falls down
We do forgive thy treachery: revive.
'Tis pity, and not hate, makes goodness thrive.
LAPYRUS
O that astonishment had left me dead!
Shame, sitting on my brow, weighs down my head.
Even thus the guilt of my abhorrèd sin
Flashed in my face when I beheld the Queen.
KING
Our Queen! O, where, Lapyrus? Tell the rest.
LAPYRUS
Within this forest with her babes distressed.
KING
Which way? Lead, dear Lapyrus.
LAPYRUS Follow me then.
KING
Not only shall we quit thy soul's offence
But give thy happy labour recompense. *Exeunt*

2.5 *Dumb show*

Enter [Chorus, then] the old Queen weeping, with both her infants, the one dead. She lays down the other on a bank, and goes to bury the dead, expressing much grief. Enter the former shepherds, walking by carelessly; at last they espy the child and strive for it. At last the Clown gets it, and dandles it, expressing all signs of joy to them. Enter again the Queen; she looks for her babe and, finding it gone, wrings her hands. The shepherds see her, then whisper together, then beckon to her. She joyfully runs to them; they return her child; she points to her breasts, as meaning she should nurse it; they all give her money; the Clown kisses the babe and her, and so exeunt several ways. Then enter Lapyrus, the old King, Amorpho and Fidelio; they miss the Queen and so, expressing great sorrow, exeunt

CHORUS
The miserable Queen expecting still
The infants' succour from Lapyrus' hand
(Who wants himself), it chanced through èxtreme want
The youngest died, and this so near his end
That had not shepherds happily passed by
And on the babe cast a compassionate eye
And snatched the child out of the arms of death
(Where the sad mother left it), the same hour
Had been his grave that gives his life new power.
Thus the distressèd Queen, to them unknown,
Was as a nurse received unto her own—
Whose sight Lapyrus missing, having led

90 **lawyers** (proverbially dishonest)
93 **Always . . . gem** i.e. the 'sweetest' woman apart from the Young Queen. (Amphridote is forgotten.)
but only
94 **done** finished your business
95 **None . . . beggar** Nobody can be sure they will not end up destitute.
99 **Brave** excellent, well-dressed
gallants men about town, courtiers (sometimes actually penniless)
2.4 Dekker.
13 **below** i.e. in hell
18 **poor strength** (weakened because old, or from wandering in exile)
2.5 Probably written by the adapter to replace several scenes of the Lapyrus plot: one at the end of Act Two with the Old Queen, the Clown and shepherds, and another after 3.1 in which the Old King and Lapyrus fail to find the Old Queen.
10–11 **Queen . . . own** (She passes herself off as a wet-nurse to her own child, recalling the story of Moses in Exodus 2:1–10.)

The King her husband to this hapless place,
They all depart in èxtreme height of grief
To get unto their own sad wants relief.
Exit. [*Finis Actus Secundus. In the act-time the trapdoor closed and the tree removed*]

3.1 [*Incipit Actus Tertius*]
Enter Roxano with his disguise in his hand

ROXANO
This is the farther lodge, the place of meeting;
The hour scarce come yet. Well, I was not born to this.
There's not a hair to choose betwixt me and a pander in this case, shift it off as well as I can. I do envy this fellow's happiness now, and could cut his throat at pleasure. I could e'en gnaw feathers now to think of his downy felicity. I that could never aspire above a dairy wench, the very cream of my fortunes—that he should bathe in nectar, and I most unfortunate in buttermilk, this is good dealing now, is't?
Enter Mazeres, musing

MAZERES [*aside*]
I'll have some other, for he must not live.

ROXANO [*aside*]
Who's this? My lord Mazeres, discontent?
He's been to seek me twice, and privately.
I wonder at the business. I'm no statesman: if I be, 'tis more than I know. I protest therefore, I dare not call it in question. What should he make with me? I'll discover myself to him. If th'other come i'th' mean time, so I may be caught bravely; yet 'tis scarce the hour. I'll put it to the trial.

MAZERES [*aside*]
Roxano in my judgement had been fittest,
And farthest from suspèct of such a deed,
Because he keeps i'th' castle.

ROXANO [*coming forward*] My loved lord.

MAZERES
Roxano!

ROXANO The same, my lord.

MAZERES I was to seek thee twice.
Tell me Roxano, have I any power in thee?
Do I move there, or any part of me
Flow in thy blood?

ROXANO As far as life, my lord.

MAZERES As far as love, man,
I ask no further.

ROXANO Touch me then, my lord,
And try my mettle.

MAZERES First, there's gold for thee,
[*He gives him gold*]
After which follow favour, eminence,
And all those gifts which fortune calls her own.

ROXANO Well, my lord.

MAZERES
There's one Tymethes, son to the banished King,
Lives about court; Zenarchus gives him grace.
That fellow's my disease. I thrive not with him.
He's like a prison chain shook in my ears.
I take no sleep for him; his favours mad me.
My honours and my dignities are dreams
When I behold him. That right arm can ease me.
I will not boast my bounties, but forever
Live rich and happy. Thou art wise; farewell. *Exit*

ROXANO Hmm, what news is here now? 'Thou art wise; farewell'? By my troth, I think it is a part of wisdom to take gold when it is offered. Many wise men will do't: that I learned of my learnèd counsel. This is worth thinking on now. To kill Tymethes, so strangely beloved by a lady, and so monstrously detested by a lord? Here's gold to bring Tymethes, and here's gold to kill Tymethes. Ay, let me see, which weighs heaviest? By my faith, I think the killing gold will carry't! I shall, like many a bad lawyer, run my conscience upon the greatest fee: who gives most is like to fare best. I like my safety so much the worse in this business in that Lord Mazeres is his professed enemy. He's the King's bosom: he blows his thoughts into him. And I had rather be torn with whirlwinds than fall into any of their furies. Troth, as far as I can see, the wisest course is to play the knave, lay open this venery, betray him.—But see, my lord again.
Enter Mazeres

MAZERES
Hast thou thought of me? May I do good upon thee?
I'll out of recreation make thee worthy,
Play honours to thy hand.

ROXANO My lord?

MAZERES
Art thou resolved an I will be thy lord?

ROXANO It will appear I am so.
Be proud of your revenge before I name it.
Never was man so fortunate in his hate.
I'll give you a whole age but to think how.

3.1 Middleton. What is now 3.2 may originally have belonged here, thus contrasting the Young Queen and the Old Queen.
6 **gnaw feathers** chew his pillow (in frustration)
7 **downy** (*a*) made of down, like expensive bedding; (*b*) exquisitely soft, like skin
7–8 **dairy wench** (commoner, and hence considered less desirable, sexually, than a Queen)
18 **bravely** i.e. without his disguise
23 **I...thee** I've been to look for you
25–6 **Do...blood** Do I have any influence with you
30 **mettle** spirit (punning on 'metal')
46 **learnèd counsel** (another dig at the avarice of lawyers)
55 **bosom** confidant
62 **out of recreation** (*a*) from the sheer pleasure of doing it; (*b*) in recompense for the sexual recreation you enable
63 **Play** deal out to you (like cards)
hand (*a*) possession; (*b*) hand of cards, filled with high cards, which represent 'honoured' persons like kings, queens, etc.

MAZERES
Thou mak'st me thirst.
ROXANO Tymethes meets me here.
MAZERES
Here? Excellent! On, Roxano: he meets thee here...
ROXANO
I meant at first to betray all to you, sir:
Understand that, my lord.
MAZERES I'faith, I do.
ROXANO Then thus, my lord—he comes.
Enter Tymethes
MAZERES [*aside to Roxano*]
Withdraw behind the lodge; relate it briefly.
[*They withdraw*]
TYMETHES [*aside*]
A delicate sweet creature? 'Slight, who should it be?
I must not know her name, nor see her face?
It may be some trick to have my bones bastinadoed well, and so sent back again. What say you to a blanketting? Faith, so 'twere done by a lady and her chambermaids I care not, for if they toss me i'th' blankets I'll toss them i'th' sheets, and that's one for th'other. A man may be led into a thousand villainies. But the fellow swore enough, and here's blood apt enough to believe him.
MAZERES [*aside to Roxano*]
I both admire the deed, and my revenge.
ROXANO [*aside to Mazeres*]
My lord, I'll make your way.
MAZERES Thou mak'st thy friend.
Exit
[*Roxano puts on his disguise, and meets Tymethes*]
TYMETHES
Art come? We meet e'en jump upon a minute.
ROXANO
Ay, but you'll play the better jumper of the two;
I shall not jump so near as you by a handful.
TYMETHES
How! At a running leap?
ROXANO That is more hard:
At a running leap you may give me a handful.
TYMETHES So, so, what's to be done?
ROXANO
Nothing but put this hood over your head.
TYMETHES How? I never went blindfold before.
ROXANO You never went otherwise, sir, for all folly is blind.
Besides, sir, when we see the sin we act,
We think each trivial crime a bloody fact.
TYMETHES Well followed of a servingman.
ROXANO Servingmen always follow their masters, sir.
TYMETHES No, not in their mistresses.
ROXANO There I leave you, sir.
TYMETHES I desire to be left when I come there, sir.
But faith, sincerely, is there no trick in this?
Prithee deal honestly with me.
ROXANO
Honestly? if protestation be not honest,
I know not what to call it.
TYMETHES Why, if she affect me
So truly, she might trust me with her knowledge.
I could be secret to her chief actions: why, I love women too well—
ROXANO She'll trust you the worse for that, sir.
TYMETHES
Why, because I love women?
ROXANO O sir, 'tis most common:
He that loves women, is ne'er true to woman.
Experience daily proves he loveth none
With a true heart, that affects more than one.
TYMETHES
Your wit runs nimbly, sir; pray use your pleasure.
ROXANO
Why then, good night, sir.
He puts on the hood
TYMETHES Mass, the candle's out.
ROXANO
O sir, the better sports taste best i'th' night,
And what we do i'th' dark, we hate i'th' light.
TYMETHES
A good doer mayst thou prove, for thy experience.
Come, give me thy hand. Thou mayst prove an honest lad;
But however, I'll trust thee.
ROXANO O sir, first try me.
But we protract good hours. Come, follow me, sir.—
[*Aside*] Why, this is right your sportive gallants' prize:
Before they'll lose their sport, they'll lose their eyes.
Exeunt, [*Roxano leading Tymethes*]

Enter the [*young*] *Queen and four servants, she with a book in her hand* 3.2
QUEEN
O my fear-fighting blood! Are you all here?

76 **'Slight** contraction of 'by God's light' (oath)
78 **bastinadoed** thrashed
87 **jump** (Roxano's reply takes 'jump' in a bawdy sense, as in 'jump her bones'.)
98 **followed** replied, argued
of considering you are only
99 **follow** (*a*) walk behind; (*b*) imitate, copy
100 **in** (*a*) in relation to; (*b*) penetrating
103 **trick** (*a*) deception; (*b*) act of prostitution
105 **protestation** (*a*) solemn affirmation; (*b*) lover's assurances, wooing; (*c*) legal dissent to a statement which the witness cannot confidently confirm or deny
123 **right** exactly what
124 **lose...eyes** (Syphilis could cause blindness.)
3.2 Perhaps written by the adapter, or moved here from its original position before 3.1, in order to replace a scene in which Lapyrus (now a faithful servant) enters leading the Old King (his master) toward an intended rendezvous with the Old Queen; this would be in ironic contrast with Roxano's exit with Tymethes. If the lost scene contained further comment on the exiles' lack of food, it would also have contrasted with the extravagant banquet of 3.3. The scene's authorship is uncertain.
0.2 ***a book*** the Bible, on which she asks the servants to swear

FIRST SERVANT All at your pleasure, madam.
QUEEN
That's my wish, and my opinïon
Hath ever been persuaded of your truths,
And I have found you willing t'all employments
We put into your charge.
SECOND SERVANT In our faiths, madam.
THIRD SERVANT
For we are bound in duty to your bounty.
QUEEN
Will you to what I shall prescribe swear secrecy?
FOURTH SERVANT
Try us, sweet lady, and you shall prove our faiths.
QUEEN
To all things that you hear or see,
I swear you all to secrecy.
I pour my life into your breasts;
There my doom or safety rests.
If you prove untrue to all,
Now I rather choose to fall
With loss of my desire, than light
Into the tyrant's wrathful spite.
But in vain I doubt your trust.
I never found your hearts but just.
On this book your vows arrive,
And, as in truth, in favour thrive.
[The servants swear upon the book]
OMNES
We wish no higher; so we swear.
QUEEN
Like jewels all your vows I'll wear.
Here, take this paper; there those secrets dwell.
Go read your charge, which I should blush to tell.
[The servants take the paper and exeunt]
All's sure; I nothing doubt of safety now,
To which each servant hath combined his vow.
Roxano, that begins it trustily—
I cannot choose but praise him. He's so needful.
There's nothing can be done about a lady
But he is for it. Honest Roxano!
Even from our head to feet he's so officious.
The time draws on. I feel the minute's here.
No clock so true as love that strikes in fear. *[Exit]*

3.3

Soft music. [Two seats and] a table with lights set out, arras spread [by the Queen's servants]. Enter Roxano leading Tymethes, [hooded]. Mazeres meets them.

TYMETHES How far lack I yet of my blind pilgrimage?
MAZERES Whist, Roxano!
ROXANO You are at your—*[to Mazeres]* In, my lord, away:
I'll help you to a disguise.
MAZERES Enough. *Exit*
TYMETHES
Methinks I walk in a vault all underground.
ROXANO
And now your long lost eyes again are found.
Pulls off the hood
Good morrow, sir.
TYMETHES By the mass, the day breaks.
ROXANO
Rest here, my lord, and you shall find content
Catch your desires; stay here, they shall be sent.
TYMETHES
Though it be night, 'tis morning to that night
Which brought me hither.
Ha! The ground spread with arras? What place is this?
Rich hangings? Fair room gloriously furnished?
Lights and their lustre? Riches and their splendour?
'Tis no mean creature's, these dumb tokens witness.
Troth, I begin t'affect my hostess better.
I love her in her absence, though unknown,
For courtly form that's here observed and shown.
Loud music. Enter two [visored servants] with a banquet, other two [visored servants] with lights: they set 'em down and depart, making obeisance. Roxano takes one of them aside
ROXANO
Valesta? Yes, the same. 'Tis my lady's pleasure
You give to me your coat and visor, and attend without
Till she employ you. *[Exit one servant]*
So, now this disguise
Serves for my lord Mazeres, for he watches
But fit occasion.—Lecher, now beware.
Securely sit and fearless quaff and eat:
You'll find sour sauce still, after your sweet meat.
Exit [with coat and visor]
TYMETHES
The servants all in visors? By this light,
I do admire the carriage of her love—
For I account that woman above wise
Can sin and hide the shame from a man's eyes.
They never do their easy sex more wrong
Than when they venture fame upon man's tongue.
Yet I could swear concealment in love's plot,
But happy woman that believes me not.
Whate'er is spoke, o'er to be spoke seems fit.
All still concludes her happiness and wit.

20 **vows arrive** i.e. place your hands and swear
30–2 **nothing ... officious** (unintentionally suggesting his sexual interest)
32 **officious** eager to please
3.3 Middleton.
17 **t'affect** to love
26 **sour sauce** i.e. betrayal
28 **carriage** manner, management
32 **venture ... tongue** risk telling a man their name, enabling him to repeat it, and thereby ruin their reputation **man's tongue** (probably alluding to cunnilingus)
35 **Whate'er ... fit** anything that is spoken once, is fit to be spoken again

Loud music. Enter Roxano, Mazeres [visored and disguised] and the [three other visored] servants with dishes of sweetmeats. Roxano places them [on the table]. Each, having delivered his dish, makes low obeisance to Tymethes

ROXANO
This banquet from her own hand rèceived grace,
Herself prepared it for you—as appears
By the choice sweets it yields, able to move
A man past sense to the delights of love.
I bid you welcome as her most prized guest,
First to this banquet, next to pleasure's feast.

TYMETHES
Whoe'er she be, we thank her and commend
Her care and love to entertain a friend.

ROXANO
That speaks her sex's rareness, for to woman
The darkest path love treads is clear and common.
She wishes your content may be as great
As if her presence filled that other seat.

TYMETHES
Convey my thanks to her, and fill some wine.

MAZERES [*stepping forward to pour wine*]
My lord?

ROXANO [*aside*]
My lord Mazeres caught the office.
I can't but laugh to see how well he plays
The devil in a visor,
Damns where he crouches. Little thinks the prince
Under that face lurks his life's enemy.
Yet he but keeps the fashion: great men kill
As flatterers stab, who laugh when they mean ill.

MAZERES [*aside*]
Now could I poison him fitly, aptly, rarely.
My vengeance speaks me happy: there it goes.
[He poisons the cup]

TYMETHES
Some wine!

MAZERES It comes, my lord.
Enter a Lady with [another cup of] wine

LADY
My lady begun to you, sir, and doth commend
This to your heart, and with it her affection.

TYMETHES
I'll pledge her thankfully.
[Tymethes] spills the wine [Mazeres gave him, and pledges with the cup the lady brought]
There!—[*To Mazeres*] Remove that.

MAZERES
And in this my revenge must be removed
Where first I left it. Now my abusèd wrath
Pursues thy ruin in this dangerous path.

ROXANO [*aside*]
That cup hath quite dashed my lord Mazeres.

TYMETHES [*to the Lady*]
Return my faith, my reverence, my respect,
And tell her this, which courteously I find:
She hides her face, but lets me see her mind.
[Exit Lady]

ROXANO [*aside*] I would not taste of such a banquet to feel that which follows it for the love of an empress. 'Tis more dangerous to be a lecher than to enter upon a breach. Yet how securely he munches!
His thoughts are sweeter than the very meats before him.
He little dreams of his destructiön,
His horrid fearful ruin, which cannot be withstood.
The end of venery is disease or blood.
Soft music. Enter the [young] Queen masked in her nightgown, her maid with a shirt and a nightcap. [The maid puts down the shirt and nightcap. Exeunt the Queen and maid severally]

TYMETHES
I have not known one happier for his pleasure
Than in that state we are. 'Tis a strange trick,
And sweetly carried. By this light, a delicate creature!
And should have a good face, if all hit right.
For they that have good bodies and bad faces
Were all mismatched, and made up in blind places.

ROXANO
The wind and tide serve, sir; you have lighted
Upon a sea of pleasure. Here's your sail, sir,
And your top streamer: a fair-wrought shirt and nightcap.

TYMETHES I shall make
A sweet voyage of this.

ROXANO Ay, if you knew all, sir.

TYMETHES
Is not all known yet? What's to be told?

ROXANO
Five hundred crowns in the shirt sleeve in gold.

TYMETHES
How?

ROXANO
'Tis my good lady's pleasure.
No clouds eclipse her bounty; she shines clear.
Some like that pleasure best that costs most dear.
Yet I think your lordship is not of that mind now.
You like that best that brings a banquet with it,
And five hundred crowns.

TYMETHES Ay, by this light do I.
And I think thou art of my mind.

ROXANO We jump somewhat near, sir.

TYMETHES But what does she mean to reward me aforehand? I may prove a eunuch now, for aught she knows.

60 **begun to you** (flirtatiously taking the initiative, as she had refused to do at 1.4.55–78)

77.2 ***maid*** (probably the lady-in-waiting who appeared earlier in the scene)

89 **told** (*a*) said; (*b*) tolled, counted

ROXANO O sir, I ne'er knew any of your hair but he was absolute at the game.

TYMETHES Faith, we are much of a colour. But here's a note; what says it?

He reads

Our love and bounty shall increase
So long as you regard our peace.
Unless your life you would forego,
Who we are, seek not to know.
Enjoy me freely: for your sake
This dangerous shift I undertake.
Be therefore wise; keep safe your breath.
You cannot see me under death.

I'd be loth to venture so far for the sight of any creature under heaven.

ROXANO Nay, sir, I think you may see a thousand faces better cheap.

TYMETHES
Well, I will shift me instantly, and be content
With my groping fortune. *Exit*

ROXANO O sir, you'll grope to purpose. *Exit*

MAZERES [*removing his visor*] I'll after thee,
And see the measure of my vengeance upheaped.
His ruin is my charge. I have seen that
This night would make one blush thorough this visor.
Like lightning in a tempest her lust shows,
Or drinking drunk in thunder, horrible—
For on this act a thousand dangers wait.
The King will seize him in his burning fury
And seal his vengeance on his reeking breast.
Though I make pander's use of ear and eye,
No office' vile to damn mine enemy.
This course is but the first. 'Twill not rest there;
The next shall change him into fire and air. *Exit*

[*Finis Actus Tertius*]

4.1 [*Incipit Actus Quartus*]

Enter Tymethes and Zenarchus

TYMETHES Nay, did e'er subtlety match it?

ZENARCHUS
'Slight, led to a lady hoodwinked,
Placèd in state and banqueted in visors!

TYMETHES
All, by this light: but all this nothing was
To the delicious pleasures of her bed.

ZENARCHUS
Who should this be?

TYMETHES Nay, enquire not, brother.
I'd give one eye to see her with the other.
Seest thou this jewel? In the midst of night
I slipped it from her veil, unfelt of her.
'T may be so kind unto me as to bring
Her beauty to my knowledge.

ZENARCHUS Canst not guess at her,
Nor at the place?

TYMETHES At neither, for my heart.
Why, I'll tell thee, man, 'twas handled with such art,
Such admired cunning, what with my blindness
And their general darkness, that when mine eyes
Received their liberty I was ne'er the nearer.
To them in full form I appeared unshrouded,
But all their sights to me were masked and clouded.

Enter Tyrant and Mazeres, observing

ZENARCHUS
'Fore heaven, I do admire the cunning on't.

TYMETHES
Nay, you cannot outvie my admiration.
I had a feeling on't, beyond your passion.

ZENARCHUS
Well, blow this over; see, our sister comes.

Enter Amphridote

[*Tyrant and Mazeres speak apart*]

TYRANT
Art sure, Mazeres, that he courts our daughter?

MAZERES
I'm sure of more, my lord: she favours him.

TYRANT
That beggar?

MAZERES Worse my lord, that villain traitor—
And yet worse my lord.

TYRANT How?

MAZERES
Pardon, my lord, a riper time
Shall bring him forth. Behold him there, my lord.

Tymethes kisses her

TYRANT
Dares she so far forget respect to us,
And dim her own lustre to give him grace?

MAZERES
Favours are grown to custom 'twixt 'em both:
Letters, close banquets, whisperings, private meetings.

TYRANT I'll make 'em dangerous meetings.

AMPHRIDOTE [*to Tymethes*]
In faith, my lord, I'll have this jewel.

TYMETHES
'Tis not my gift, lady.

101–2 **any ... game** anybody with hair like yours who was not a superb lover
103 **we ... colour** your hair is pretty much the same colour as mine
110 **shift** (*a*) tricky business; (*b*) transfer of affections
112 **under death** without the penalty of death
116 **better cheap** at less cost
117 **shift me** (*a*) get moving; (*b*) transform myself
122 **charge** office, duty
that that thing, something which
125 **drunk in thunder** (*a*) incapacitated in dangerous circumstances; (*b*) defiantly immoral, despite threats from heaven
130 **No ... enemy** I'll stoop to anything to destroy Tymethes.
4.1 Middleton.
2 **'Slight** contraction for 'by God's light' (oath)
21 **feeling** physical sensation
22 **blow this over** keep quiet about this
36 **my gift** mine to give

TYRANT What's that, Mazeres?

MAZERES
Marry, my lord, she courtly begs a jewel of him,
Which he keeps back as courtly with fair words.

AMPHRIDOTE
I've sworn, my lord.

TYMETHES Why, upon that condition
You'll keep it safe and close from all strange eyes,
Not wronging me, 'tis yours.

AMPHRIDOTE I swear.

TYMETHES It shall suffice.

[He gives her the jewel.] They kiss, and exeunt Zenarchus and Amphridote

MAZERES
'Tis hers, my lord, at which they part in kisses.

TYRANT
I'll make those meetings bitter. Both shall rue.
We have found Mazeres to this minute true.

Exit cum Mazeres

TYMETHES
No trick to see this lady? Heart of ill fortune!
The jewel that was begged from me too was
The hope I had to gain her wished-for knowledge.
Well, here's a heart within will not be quiet.
The eye is the sweet feeder of the soul;
When the taste wants, that keeps the memory whole.
'Tis bad to be in darkness, all know well;
Then not to see her, what doth it want of hell?
What says the note?

[He reads]

Unless your life you would forego,
Whom we are, seek not to know.

Pish, all idle!
As if she'd suffer death to threaten me
Whom she so bounteously and firmly loves!
No trick? Excellent, 'twill fit; make use of that.

Enter Mazeres and Roxano [and speak apart]

MAZERES
Enough, thou'rt honest. I affect thee much.
Go, train him to his ruin.

ROXANO
Let me alone, my lord: doubt not I'll train him.

[Exit Mazeres]

Perhaps sir, I have the art.

TYMETHES O, I know thy mind.

ROXANO
The further lodge?

TYMETHES Enough, I'll meet thee presently.

ROXANO
Why so: I like one that will make an end—
[*Aside*] of himself at few words.
A man that hath a quick perseverance in ill,
A leaping spirit, he'll run through horror's jaws
To catch a sin. But to o'ertake a virtue
He softly paces, like a man that's sent
Some tedious, dark, unprofitable journey.
Corrupt is nature; she loves nothing more
Than what she most should hate. There's nothing springs
Apace in man but grey hairs, cares, and sins. *Exit*

TYMETHES
I'll see her, come what can. But what can prove?
She cannot seek my death that seeks my love. *Exit*

Enter Amphridote and Mazeres 4.2

AMPHRIDOTE
My lord, what is the matter?

MAZERES I know not what;
The King sent.

AMPHRIDOTE Well, we obey.

MAZERES Here comes his highness.

Enter Tyrant

TYRANT
How now, what's she?

AMPHRIDOTE I, my lord? Your highness
Knew me once: your most obedient daughter.

TYRANT
They lie that tell me so; this is not she.

AMPHRIDOTE
No, my lord?

TYRANT No, for as thou art I know thee not,
And I shall strive still to forget thee more.
Thou neither bear'st in memory my respects
Nor thy own worths. How can we think of thee
But as of a dejected worthless creature?—
So far beneath our grace and thy own lustre,
That we disdain to know thee.
Was there no choice 'mong our selected nobles
To make thy favourite, besides Tymethes?
Son to our enemy, a wretch, a beggar,
Dead to all fortunes, honours or their hopes;
Besides his breath, worth nothing. Abject wretch,
To place so vigorously thy affection
On him can ne'er requite it! Deny't not.
We know the favours thou hast given him:
Pledges of love, close letters, private meetings,
And whisperings are customary 'twixt you.
Come, which be his gifts? Whereabout lie his pledges?

AMPHRIDOTE
Your grace hath been injuriously informed.
I ne'er receivèd pledge.

TYRANT Impudent creature,
When in our sight and hearing shamefully
Undervaluing thy best honours and setting by
All modesty of blood thou begged'st a jewel of him.

AMPHRIDOTE
O pardon me, my lord, I had forgot: here 'tis.

52 **want** lack
61 **train** lead
67 **quick . . . ill** eager determination to do wrong
75 **prove** happen
4.2 Middleton.

[*She gives him the jewel*]
That is the same, and all that e'er was his.

TYRANT
Ha! This! How came this hither?

AMPHRIDOTE
I gave it you, my lord.

TYRANT
Who gave it thee?

AMPHRIDOTE
Tymethes.

TYRANT
He! Who gave it him?

AMPHRIDOTE
I know not that, my lord.

TYRANT
Then here it sticks.—Mazeres!

MAZERES
My lord?

TYRANT 'Tis my Queen's, my Queen's, Mazeres.
How to him came this?

MAZERES I can resolve your highness.

TYRANT Can Mazeres?

MAZERES
He is some ape: the husk falls from him now,
And you shall know his inside. He's a villain,
A traitor to the pleasures of your bed.

TYRANT
O, I shall burst with torment.

MAZERES
He's received this night
Into her bosom.

TYRANT
I feel a whirlwind in me
Ready to tear the frame of my mortality.

MAZERES
I traced him to the deed.

TYRANT
And saw it done?

MAZERES
I abused my eyes in the true survey on't,
Tainted my hearing with lascivious sounds;
My loyalty did prompt me to be sure
Of what I found so wicked and impure.

TYRANT
'Tis springtide in my gall. All my blood's bitter—
Puh, lungs too.

MAZERES
This night.

TYRANT
Lodovico!

Enter Lodovico

LODOVICO
My lord.

TYRANT How cam'st thou up? Let's hear.

LODOVICO
My lord, my first beginning was a broker.

TYRANT
A knave from the beginning; there's no hope of him.
Sertorio!

Enter Sertorio

SERTORIO
Here, my lord.

TYRANT
We know thee just.
How cam'st thou up? Let's hear.

SERTORIO
From no desert
That I can challenge but your highness' favour.

TYRANT
Thou art honest in that answer. Go:
Report we are forty leagues off rid forth:
Spread it about the castle cunningly.

SERTORIO
I'll do it faithfully, my lord.

TYRANT
Do't cunningly.
Go! If thou shouldst do't faithfully, thou liest.
[*Exit Sertorio*]
I'm lost by violence through all my senses.
I'm blind with rage.—Mazeres, guide me forth.
I tread in air, and see no foot nor path;
I've lost myself, yet cannot lose my wrath.
Exeunt all but Amphridote

AMPHRIDOTE
What have I heard? It dares not be but true.
Tymethes taken in adulterate trains,
And with the Queen, my mother? Now I hate him,
As beauty abhors years, or usurers charity.
He does appear unto my eye a leper
Enter Mazeres
Full of sin's black infection, foul adultery.
Cursèd be the hour in which I first did grace him
And let Mazeres starve in my disdain,
That hath so long observed me with true love,
Whose loyalty in this approves the same.

MAZERES Madam.

AMPHRIDOTE My love?
'My lord' I should say, but would say 'my love'.

MAZERES [*kneeling*]
I do beseech your grace for what I've done
Lay no oppressing censure upon me.
I could not but in honesty reveal it,
Not envying in that he was my rival
Nor in the force of any ancient grudge,
But as the deed in its own nature craved,
So 'mong the rest it was revealed to me,
Appearing so detested that yourself,
Gracious and kind, had you but seen the manner,
Would have thrown by all pity and remorse
And took my office, or one more in force.

AMPHRIDOTE
Rise, dear Mazeres, in our favours rise.
So far am I from censure to reprove thee
That in my hate to him I choose and love thee.

33 **sticks** pierces (his heart)
38 **ape . . . now** (proverbially, 'an ape will be an ape, though that ye clad him all in purple array')
49 **springtide** high tide
51 **cam'st thou up** did you rise to your present high position
55–6 **From . . . challenge** for no merit that I can allege
67 **trains** entanglements
68 **mother** step-mother
89 **took . . . force** taken the steps I did, or done something more forceful

MAZERES [*rising*]
If constant service may be called desert,
I shall deserve.
AMPHRIDOTE Man hath no better part.
MAZERES (*aside*)
Why, this was happily observed and followed.—
The King will to the castle late tonight
And tread through all the vaults; I must attend.
AMPHRIDOTE
I wish that at first sight thou'dst forced his end. *Exit*
MAZERES
'Tis better thus. So my revenge imports.
Now thrive my plots! The end shall make me great:
She mine, the crown sits here. I am then complete.
Exit

4.3 *Enter [young] Queen and her maid with a light*

QUEEN
So, leave us here awhile; bear back the light.
I would not be discovered if he come.
[*The maid shuts the lantern*]
You know his entertainment. So, be gone.
[*Exit maid*]
I am not cheerful, troth, what point soe'er
My powers arrive at. I desire a league
With desolate darkness, and disconsolate fancies.
There is no music in my soul tonight.
What should I fear, when all my servants' faiths
Sleep in my bounty, and no bribes nor threats
Can wake 'em from my safety? For the King,
He's forty leagues rode forth; I heard it lately.
Yet heaviness, like a tyrant, proud in night,
Usurps my power, rules where it hath no right.
She sleeps. Enter Roxano as she sleeps, with
Tymethes hoodwinked
TYMETHES
Methinks this a longer voyage than the first?
ROXANO
Pleasures once tasted makes the next seem worse.
TYMETHES
Is that the trick?
ROXANO O sir, experience proves it.
You came at first to enjoy what you ne'er knew;
Now all is but the same whate'er you do.
TYMETHES
I'll prove that false: the sight of her is new.
ROXANO
I have forgot a business to my lord Mazeres;
My safety to the King relies upon't.
You are in the house, my lord: this is the withdrawing room.
TYMETHES I see nothing.
ROXANO No matter, sir, as long as you have feeling enough.
TYMETHES
Is the hood off?
ROXANO 'Tis here in my hand, sir.
I must crave pardon, leave you here awhile.
But as you love my safety and your own
Remove not from this room till my return.
TYMETHES
Well, here's my hand: I will not.
ROXANO 'Tis enough, sir.
Exit
TYMETHES
Hist, art gone? Then boldly I step forth,
Cunning discoverer of an unknown beauty
As subtle as her plot. Thou art masked too:
Opens a dark lantern
Show me a little comfort, in this condensive darkness.
Play the flatterer: laugh in my face.
Why, here's enough to pèrfect all my wishes.
With this I taste of that forbidden fruit
Which, as she says, death follows; death, 'twill sting.
Soft, what room's this? Let's see, 'tis not the former
I was entertained in; no, it somewhat differs:
Rich hangings still, court deckings, ay, and all—
He spies the Queen
O all that can be in man's wish comprised
Is in thy love immortal, in thy graces!
[*He touches her*]
I am not the same flesh; my touch is altered.
She awakes
QUEEN
Hast thou betrayed me? What hast thou attempted?
TYMETHES
Nothing that can be prejudicïal
To the sweet peace of those illustrious graces.
QUEEN O my most certain ruin!
TYMETHES
Admirèd lady, hear me, hear my vow.
QUEEN
O miserable youth, none saves thee now.
TYMETHES
By that which man holds dearest, dreadful Queen,
And all that can be in a vow contained,
I'll prove as true, secret, and vigilant
As ever man observed with serious virtue
The dreadful call of his departing soul.
Your own soul to your secrets shall not prove more true
Than mine to it, to them, to all, to you.
QUEEN
O misery of affection built on breath!

93–4 **desert . . . part** (a rhyme)
100–1 **great . . . complete** (a rhyme)
101 **here** i.e. on his own head. (He would have to eliminate Zenarchus.)
4.3 Middleton. This scene is greatly elaborated from its brief source in Warner (p. 49), where the lover is killed by the jealous husband.
30 **Remove not** do not leave
33 **discoverer** unveiler. Middleton is here drawing on the Cupid and Psyche myth, but with the genders reversed.
35 **condensive** dense
44 **immortal** (comparing her to a goddess, as in the myth of Cupid and Psyche)

Were I as far past my belief in heaven
As in man's oaths, I were the foulest devil.

TYMETHES
May I eat and ne'er be nourishèd,
Live and know nothing, love without enjoying,
If ever—

QUEEN Come, this is more than needs.

TYMETHES There's comfort then.

QUEEN
You that profess such truth, shall I enjoin you
To one poor penance then to try your faith?

TYMETHES Be't what it will, command it.

QUEEN
Spend but this hour, wherein you have offended,
In true repentance of your sin, and all
Your hasty youth stands guilty of—and being clear,
You shall enjoy that which you hold most dear.

TYMETHES
And if this penance I perform not truly,
May I henceforth ne'er be received to favour.
[Tymethes kneels, as praying]

QUEEN
Why then, I'll leave you to your task awhile.
[She speaks aside]
Most wretched, doubtful, strange-distracted woman,
E'en drawn in pieces betwixt love and fear,
I weep in thought of both. Bold venturous youth,
Twice I writ death, yet would he seek to know me.
He'll make no conscience where his oaths bestow me.
Exit

TYMETHES
I'm glad all's so well past, and she appeased.
I swear I did expect a harder penance
When she began to enjoin me. Why, this is wholesome
For soul and body, though I seldom use it.
Her wisdom is as pleasing as her beauty.
I never knew affection hastier born,
With more true art and less suspicïon.
It so amazed me to know her my mistress,
I had no power to close the light again,
Enter the [young] Queen with two pistols
Unhappy that I was.—Peace, here she comes.
Down to thy penance: think of thy whole youth.
From the first minute that the womb conceived me
To this full-heapèd hour, I do repent me,
With heart as penitent as a man dissolving,
Of all my sins, born with me, and born of me,
Dishonest thoughts and sleights, the paths of youth.
So thrive in mercy as I end in truth!
She shoots him dead

QUEEN
Fly to thy wish! I pray it may be given.
Man in a twinkling is in earth and heaven.
I dealt not like a coward with thy soul,
Nor took it unprepared.
I gave him time to put his armour on
And sent him forth like a celestial champion.
I loved thee with more care and truer moan,
Since thou must die, to taste more deaths than one.
Too much by this pity and love confesses.
Had any warning fast'ned on thy senses,
[ ].
Rash, unadvisèd youth, whom my soul weeps for,
How oft I told thee this attempt was death!
Yet would'st thou venture on, fond man, and knew?
But what destruction will not youth pursue?
Here long mightst thou have lived, been loved, enjoyed,
Had not thy will thy happiness destroyed!
Thought'st thou by oaths to have thy deeds well borne?
Thou shouldst have come when man was ne'er forsworn.
They are dangerous now; witness this breach of thine.
Who's false to his own faith, will ne'er keep mine.
We must be safe, young man, the deeds unknown.
There are more loves; honours, no more than one.
Yet spite of death, I'll kiss thee.
[She kisses the corpse]
O strange ill,
That for our fears we should our comforts kill!
Whom shall I trust with this poor bleeding body?
Yonder's a secret vault runs through the castle;
There for a while convey him. Hapless boy,
That never knew how dear 'twas to enjoy!
Enter Tyrant with a torch
O I'm confounded everlastingly,
Damned to a thousand tortures in that sight.

65 **enjoin** command
70 **being clear** having been cleared (of your sins, by prayer and penance)
79 **make . . . me** not have any compunctions about breaking his promise and talking about me everywhere
92 **full-heapèd hour** hour full of accumulated sins
93 **dissolving** dying (the soul being the only part of a human not able to dissolve, therefore immortal)
96 **thrive . . . truth** Compare 1.3.82 where the Old Queen says to Lapyrus 'Rise, rise, he that repents is ever saved.' Repentance at the eleventh hour was not excluded by Calvinist beliefs: in Dekker's *The Virgin Martyr* the persecutor unexpectedly proves to be one of the elect, repenting at the last. But it is unclear whether Tymethes' final words are sincere; his prayer, like that of Claudius in *Hamlet*, may be only an empty form.
114 **well borne** tolerated
116 **this breach of thine** your broken promise
120.1 ***She . . . corpse*** A powerful tragic moment, anticipating the necrophilia of *The Lady's Tragedy*. Her soliloquy recalls Phaedra's over the body of Hippolytus in Seneca's tragedy *Phaedra* (from which Middleton quotes in *Revenger* 1.4.23, 4.2.193–8).

What shall I frame?—My lord!
She runs to him

TYRANT
What's she?

QUEEN O my sweet dearest lord!

TYRANT Thy name?

QUEEN
Thy poor affrighted and endangered Queen.

TYRANT O, I know thee now.

QUEEN
Did not your majesty hear the piteous shrieks
Of an enforcèd lady?

TYRANT Yes, whose were they?

QUEEN
Mine, my most worthy lord. Behold this villain,
Sealed with his just desert. Light here, my king.
This violent youth, whom till this night I saw not,
Being, as it seems, acquainted with the footsteps
Of that dark passage, broke through the vault upon me
And with a secret lantern searched me out,
And seized me at my orisons, alone,
And bringing me by violence to this room,
Far from my guard or any hope of rescue,
Intending here the ruin of my honour;
But in the strife, as the good gods ordained it,
Reaching for succour, I lighted on a pistol,
Which I presumed was not without his charge.
Then I redeemed mine honour from his lust,
So he that sought my fall lies in the dust.

TYRANT
O, let me embrace thee for a brave, unmatchable,
Precious, unvalued, admirable—whore.

QUEEN Ha! What says my lord?

TYRANT
Come hither. Yet draw nearer. How came this man
To's end? I would hear that. I would learn cunning.
Tell me that I may wonder, and so lose thee.
There is no art like this. Let me partake
A subtlety no devil can imitate.
Speak: why is all so contrary to time?
He down and you up? Ha, why thus?

QUEEN
I am sorry for my lord; I understand him not.

TYRANT
The deed is not so monstrous in itself
As is the art which ponders home the deed.
The cunning doth amaze me past the sin,
That he should fall before my rage begin.

QUEEN My lord?

TYRANT
Come hither yet. One of those left hands give me;
Thou hast no right at all.

QUEEN What would my lord?

TYRANT
Nothing but put a ring upon a finger.

QUEEN
That's a wrong finger for a ring, my lord.

TYRANT
And what was he on whom you bounteously
Bestowed this jewel?
[*He puts the jewel on her finger*]

QUEEN (*aside*) I do not like that word.

TYRANT
Look well upon't: dost know it? Ay, and start.

QUEEN O heaven, how came this hither?
Your highness gave me this; this is mine own.

TYRANT
'Tis the same ring, but yet not the same stone.
Mystical strumpet, dost thou yet presume
Upon thy subtle strength? Shak'st thou not yet?
Or is it only art makes women constant,
Whom nature makes so loose?
I looked for gracious lightning from thy cheeks
(I see none yet), for a relenting eye
(I can see no such sight). Lust keeps in all.—
My witness! Where's my witness? Rise in the same form.
Enter from below, Mazeres habited like Roxano

QUEEN O I'm betrayed.

TYRANT [*to Mazeres*]
Is not yon woman an adulteress?

MAZERES Yes, my good lord.

TYRANT
Was not this fellow catched for her desire?
Brought in a mist? Banqueted and received
To all her amplest pleasures!

MAZERES True, my lord:

128 **frame** invent
129 **What's she?...Thy name?** The Tyrant addresses his wife as if she were a stranger, because the revelation of her guilt has made him feel he does not know her. See also note to 5.1.229.
134–48 For this false rape-charge (not in the source story), see the myth of Phaedra and Hippolytus, and the story of Potiphar's wife in Genesis 39 (which were compared to each other by Renaissance Senecan scholars).
135 **Light** look, alight
150 **unvalued** impossible to value, priceless (with ironic suggestion of 'worthless')
154 **wonder** (punning on 'wander', and ironically suggesting 'and get rid of you in the same way')
158 **He...up** (sexual innuendo)
161 **ponders home** thinks through
165 **left hands** In Roman tradition, used to touch the private parts, and hence considered impure (as in modern 'sinister'); the Latin slang for masturbation was 'the left-hand whore'. The right hand was used for public acts such as greeting or swearing an oath (hence modern 'rectitude'). Her actions are so sinister and impure that he imagines she should have two left hands and no right hand.
167 **ring** (slang for 'vagina')
168 **wrong finger** (The Tyrant deliberately places the ring on the wrong finger, because she has allowed her 'ring' to be penetrated by the wrong man's 'finger'.)
170 **jewel** (often used as a symbol for a woman's sexual purity)
174 **stone** (punning on 'testicle')
179 **gracious lightning** blushing as a sign of the repentance caused by God's grace

I brought him, saw him feasted and received—
TYRANT
Down, down, we have too much.
QUEEN O 'tis Roxano.
MAZERES [*aside*]
So, by this sleight I have deceived 'em both.
I'm took for him I strive to make her loathe.
Exit [*below*]
TYRANT
Needs hear more witnesses? I'll call up more.
QUEEN
O no, here lies a witness 'gainst myself
Sooner believed than all their hirèd faiths.
Doom me unto my death, only except
The lingering execution of your look;
Let me not live tormented in that brow.
I do confess.
TYRANT O, I felt no quick till now.
All witnesses to this were but dead flesh;
I was insensible of all but this.
Would I had given my kingdom, so conditioned
That thou hadst ne'er confessed it.
Now I stand by the deed, see all in action,
The close conveyance, cunning passages,
The artful fetch, the whispering, close disguising,
The hour, the banquet, and the bawdy tapers,
All stick in mine eye together. Yet thou shalt live.
QUEEN
Torment me not with life; it asks but death.
TYRANT
O hadst thou not confessed! Hadst thou no sleight?
Where was thy cunning there?
I see it now in thy confessïon.
Thou shalt not die as long as this is meat.
Thou killed'st a buck which thou thyself shalt eat.
QUEEN
Dear sir?
TYRANT Here's deer struck dead with thy own hand;
'Tis venison for thy own tooth. Thou know'st the relish:
A dearer place hath been thy taster. Ho!
Sertorio! Lodovico!
They enter
AMBO Here, sir.
TYRANT
Drag hence that body; see it quartered straight.
[*Exeunt Sertorio and Lodovico with the body of Tymethes*]
No living wrath can I extend upon't,
Else torments, horrors, gibbets, racks and wheels
Had with a thousand deaths presented him
Ere he had tasted one.—Yet thou shalt live.
Here, take this taper lighted, kneel, and weep.
[*Queen kneels*]
I'll try which is spent first, that or thine eye.
I'll provide food for thee; thou shalt not die.
If there be hell for sins that men commit,
Marry a strumpet and she keeps the pit. *Exit*
QUEEN
I feared this misery long before it came.
My ominous dreams and fearful dreadfulness
Promised this issue long before 'twas born.
Enter Mazeres [*in his own clothes*]
MAZERES [*aside*]
Yonder she kneels, little suspecting me
The neat discoverer of her venery.
I were full safe had I Roxano's life,
Which in this stream I fish for.—How now, lady?
So near the earth suits not a living queen.
QUEEN
Under the earth were safer and far happier.
MAZERES
What is't that can drive you to such discomforts,
To prize your glories at so mean a rate?
QUEEN
The treachery of my servants, good my lord.
MAZERES
Dare they prove treacherous (most ignoble vassals!)
To the sweet peace of so divine a mistress?
QUEEN
I'm sure one villain, whom I dearly loved,
Of whom my trust had made election chief,
Perfidiously betrayed me to the fury
Of my tempestuous unappeasèd lord.
MAZERES
Let me but know him, that I may bestow
My service to your grace upon his heart,
And thence deserve a mistress like yourself.
Enter Roxano from below
QUEEN
O me, too soon behold him!
MAZERES Madam, stand by,
Let him not see the light.
ROXANO [*aside*] Now I expect reward.
MAZERES
He dies, were he my kinsman, for that guilt,
Though 'twere as far to's heart as 'tis to th' hilt.
ROXANO
Ha? What was that?
[*Mazeres*] *runs at Roxano* [*with his sword, and pierces him*]
There's a reward with a vengeance.
MAZERES
Fall villain, for betraying of thy lady.
Such things must never creep about the earth
To poison the right use of service—a treacher!

202 **so conditioned** on condition that
216–17 **relish . . . taster** (sexual innuendo, perhaps alluding to oral sex; but vaginal sex was classically perceived as female consumption of the male.)
218 AMBO both (Latin)
225 **I'll . . . eye** I'll see whether your eyes dry up from weeping before the taper is consumed by burning.

QUEEN
This is some poor revenge. Thanks, good my lord.
Into that cave with him, from whence he rose
Not long since and betrayed me to the King.

MAZERES [*to Roxano*]
O villain, in, and overtake thy soul.
[*He drops Roxano's body back into the pit*]

QUEEN
Here's a perplexèd breast: let that warm steel
Perform but the like service upon me,
And live the rarest friend to a queen's wish.

MAZERES
O pardon me, that were too full of evil.
I threat not angels, though I smite the devil:
Doubt not your peace; the King will be appeased.
There I'll bestow my service.

QUEEN
We are pleased.

MAZERES [*aside*]
As much as comes to nothing; I'll not sue
To urge the King from that I urged him to. *Exit*

QUEEN
Betrayed where I reposed most trust? O heaven,
There is no misery fit match for mine.
Enter Tyrant, Sertorio, Lodovico, bringing in Tymethes' limbs

TYRANT
So, bring 'em forward yet, there; there bestow 'em.
Before her eyes lay the divided limbs
Of her desirèd paramour. So. You're welcome,
Lady, you see your cheer: fine flesh, coarse fare.
Sweet was your lust; what can be bitter there?
By heaven, no other food thy taste shall have,
Till in thy bowels those corpse find a grave.
Which to be sure of, come: I'll lock thee safe
From the world's pity.—Hang those quarters up!—
[*Sertorio and Lodovico hang up Tymethes' limbs*]
The bottom drink's the worst in pleasure's cup.
Exeunt omnes

[*Finis Actus Quartus*]

5.1 [*Incipit Actus Quintus*]
Enter Zenarchus solus

ZENARCHUS
O my Tymethes! Truest joy on earth!
Hath thy fate proved so flinty, so perverse,
To the sweet spring both of thy youth and hopes?
This was Mazeres' spite, that cursèd rival.
And if I fail not, his own plot shall shower
Upon his bosom like a falling tower.
Enter Tyrant
My worthy lord.

TYRANT O, you should have seen us sooner.

ZENARCHUS Why my lord?

TYRANT
The quarters of your friend passed by in triumph,
A sight that I presume had pleased you well.

ZENARCHUS
I call a villain to my father's pleasure
No friend of mine. The sight had pleased me better
Had I, not like Mazeres, run my hate
Into the sin before it grew to act,
And killed it ere't had knotted. 'Twas rare service
(If your vexed majesty conceive it right)
In politic Mazeres, serving more
In this discovery his own vicious malice
Than any true peace that should make you perfect—
Suffering the hateful treason to be done
He might have stopped in his confusïon.

TYRANT
Most certain.

ZENARCHUS Good your majesty, bethink you
In manly temper and considerate blood:
Went he the way of loyalty or your quiet,
After he saw the courtesies exceed,
T'abuse your peace, and trust 'em with the deed?

TYRANT
O no, none but a traitor would have done it.

ZENARCHUS
For my lord, weigh't indifferently.

TYRANT
I do, I do.

ZENARCHUS
What makes it heinous, burdensome and monstrous,
Fills you with such distractions, breeds such furies
In your incensèd breast, but the deed doing?

TYRANT O!

ZENARCHUS
Th'intent had been sufficient for his death,
And that full satisfaction; but the act—

TYRANT Insufferable.—
Sertorio! Where's Sertorio?
Enter Sertorio

SERTORIO
My lord?

TYRANT
Seek out Mazeres suddenly. [*Exit Sertorio*]
Peace, Zenarchus.
Let me alone to trap him.

ZENARCHUS
It may prove.

261 **overtake thy soul** i.e. in the plunge downwards towards Hell, of which the vault provides an image. The soul has already set off at the moment Roxano died.
276 **cheer** (*a*) entertainment, food and drink; (*b*) happiness
coarse (punning on 'corse', corpse)
279 **corpse** remains, 'corps' (plural)
282 **bottom . . . cup** dregs are bitter
5.1.0.1–5.1.110.1 Middleton.
2 **flinty** hard
10 **passed . . . triumph** were paraded in public, as memorials of a conquest (ironic)
16 **knotted** i.e. knitted together in sexual union
rare service good work (sarcastic)
22 **his confusïon** its confounding

[He speaks aside to Tymethes' limbs]
Behold, my friend, how I express my love.

TYRANT
O villain! Had he pierced him at first sight,
Where I have one grief, I had missed ten thousand by't.

Enter Mazeres and Sertorio

MAZERES *[aside]* I dreamt of some new honours
For my late service, and I wondered how
He could keep off so long from my desert.

TYRANT
Mazeres?

MAZERES
My loved lord.

TYRANT
I am forgetful.
I am in thy debt some dignities, Mazeres.
What shift shall we make for thee? Thy late service
Is warm still in our memory and dear favour.
Prithee, discover to's the manner how
Thou took'st 'em subtly.

MAZERES
I was received
Into a waiter's room, my lord.

TYRANT
Thou wast!

MAZERES
And in a visor helped to serve the banquet.

TYRANT Ha, ha!

MAZERES
Saw him conveyed into a chamber privately.

TYRANT
And still thou let'st him run?

MAZERES
I let him play, my lord.

TYRANT Ha, ha, ha!

MAZERES
I watched still near, till her arms clasped him.

TYRANT And there thou let'st him rest?

MAZERES There he was caught, my lord.

TYRANT So art thou here.—
[To Sertorio] Drag him to execution. He shall die
With tortures 'bove the thought of tyranny.

Exit [Tyrant, with Mazeres borne off by Sertorio]

ZENARCHUS
No words are able to express my gladness.
'Tis such a high born rapture that the soul
Partakes it only.

Enter Amphridote and Lodovico [and speak apart]

AMPHRIDOTE
My lord Mazeres led
Unto his death?

LODOVICO
It proves too true, dear princess.
[Exit]

AMPHRIDOTE *[aside]*
Cursed be the mouth that doomed him, and forever
Blasted the hand that parts him from his life.
Was there none fit to practise tyranny on
But whom our heart elected? Misery of love!
I must not live to think on't.

ZENARCHUS *[aside]* Here's my sister.
I could not bring that news will please her better.—
My news brings that command over your passions,
You must be merry.

AMPHRIDOTE
Have you warrant for't, brother?

ZENARCHUS
Yes, strong enough, i'faith. Hear me: Mazeres
By this time is at his everlasting home.
Where'er his body lies, I struck the stroke.
I wrought a bitter pill that quickly choked him.

AMPHRIDOTE *[aside]*
O me, my soul will out!—Some wine there, ho!

ZENARCHUS
Wine for our sister!—for the news is worth it.

Enter Lodovico with wine

AMPHRIDOTE
It will prove dear to both.—So, give it me.
[She takes the wine]
Now leave us.
[Exit Lodovico]

ZENARCHUS
Revenge ne'er brought forth a more happy issue
Than I think mine to be.

She poisons the wine

AMPHRIDOTE *[aside]*
I'm setting forth, Mazeres.—Here, Zenarchus!
[She drinks]

ZENARCHUS
Thou art not like this hour, jovial.

AMPHRIDOTE
I shall be after this.

ZENARCHUS
That does't, if any.
Wine doth both help defects, and causeth many.
Here's to the deed, faith, of our last revenge.
[He drinks]

AMPHRIDOTE
Dying men prophesy: faith, 'tis our last end.
Now I must tell you, brother, that I hate you,
In that you have betrayed my loved Mazeres.

ZENARCHUS What's this?

AMPHRIDOTE
His deed was loyal, his discovery just:
He brought to light a monster and his lust.

ZENARCHUS Nay, if you grow
So strumpet-like in your behaviour to me,
I'll quickly cool that insolence.
[He threatens her]

AMPHRIDOTE
Peace, peace.
There is a champion fights for me unseen;
I need not fear thy threats.

ZENARCHUS
Indeed no harlot
But has her champion, besides bawd and varlet.
O!

52 **room** place, role
56 **run** continue
82 **dear** (punning on 'costly')
100 **harlot** whore (because she has switched her love from one man to another)

AMPHRIDOTE
Why, law you now! Such gear will ne'er thrive with you.
ZENARCHUS
I'm sick of thy society, poison to mine eyes.
AMPHRIDOTE
'Tis lower in thy breast the poison lies.
ZENARCHUS
How?
AMPHRIDOTE
'Tis for Mazeres.
ZENARCHUS O you virtuous powers!
What, a right strumpet? Poison, under love?
AMPHRIDOTE
That man can ne'er be safe that divides love.
She dies
ZENARCHUS
Nor she be honest can so soon impart.
O 'ware that woman that can shift her heart!
[He] dies
Thunder and lightning. A blazing star appears. Enter Tyrant
TYRANT
Ha? Thunder? And thou marrow-melting blast,
Quick-wingèd lightning, and thou blazing star,
I like not thy prodigious bearded fire.
Thy beams are fatal.
[He sees the bodies]
Ha! Behold the influence
Of all their malice in my children's ruins!
Their states malignant powers have envìed,
And both in haste, struck with their envies, died.
'Tis ominous.—Within there!
Enter Sertorio and Lodovico
LODOVICO Here, my lord.
TYRANT
Convey those bodies awhile from my sight.
SERTORIO Both dead, my lord.
TYRANT
Yes, and we safe; our death we need less fear.
[Exit Sertorio and Ludovico with bodies]
Usurper's issue oft proves dangerous:
We depose others, and they poison us.
I have found it on recòrds; 'tis better thus.

Enter the Old King, Lapyrus, Fidelio, Amorpho, all disguised like pilgrims [and speak apart]
LAPYRUS *[to old King]*
My lord, this castle is but slightly guarded.
KING
'Tis as I hoped and wished. Now bless us heaven!
What horrid and inhuman spectacle
Is yonder that presents itself to sight?
FIDELIO
It seems three quarters of a man hung up.
KING
What tyranny hath been exercised of late?
I dare not venture on.
AMORPHO
Fear not, my lord: our habits give us safety.
LAPYRUS
Behold, the tyrant maketh toward us.
TYRANT
Holy and reverent pilgrims, welcome!
KING
Bold strangers, by the tempest beaten in.
TYRANT Most welcome still.
We are but stewards for such guests as you:
What we possess is yours, to your wants due.
We are only rich for your necessities.
KING
A generous, free, and charitable mind
Keeps in thy bosom, to poor pilgrims kind.
TYRANT
'Tis time of day to dine, my friends.—Sertorio!
Enter Sertorio
SERTORIO
My lord?
TYRANT Our food.
SERTORIO 'Tis ready for your highness.
[Exit Sertorio]
Loud music. A banquet brought in, and by it a small table for the [young] Queen
TYRANT
Sit, pray sit, religious men, right welcome
Unto our cates. Grave sir, I have observed
You waste the virtue of your serious eye
Too much on such a worthless object as that is.
A traitor when he lived called that his flesh;
Let't hang. Here's to you! We are the oldest here.

103 **law you** (oath of uncertain meaning)
gear doings, goings-on (deliberately vulgar)
107 **right** genuine
under under cover of, in the name of
108 **that divides love** who comes between two people who love each other (i.e. Amphridote and Mazeres)
109 **Nor...impart** A woman cannot be virtuous if she so hastily confers [love].
110.2–5.1.248.1 *Thunder...omnes* Dekker.
110.2 ***blazing star*** nova or comet, regarded as ominous
121–4 **Yes...thus** This brutal speech recalls the Cronos myth, another version of the bloody banquet. The Titan Cronos devoured his own children out of fear that they would grow up to supplant him; he was (like the Tyrant) supplanted anyway.
124.2 ***pilgrims*** A useful disguise if you wanted to claim hospitality. One or more scenes in which Lapyrus and the Old King were welcomed by the King of Lycia, and Lapyrus married his daughter Euronome, were probably removed by the adapter; placed somewhere between 3.3 and 5.1, they probably would have prepared for the reappearance of these characters.
132 **habits...safety** (because no one will do violence to a pilgrim)
135 **by...in** forced to come in because of the storm
145 **cates** delicate food

[He pledges the old King, and passes the cup]
Round let it go. Feed, if you like your cheer.
Enter Sertorio

SERTORIO
My lord.

TYRANT How now?

SERTORIO Ready, my lord.

TYRANT *[to pilgrims]* Sit merry.
Exit [Tyrant and servants]

KING
Where'er I look, these limbs are in mine eye.

LAPYRUS
Some wretch on whom he wrought his tyranny.

FIDELIO
Hard was his fate to 'light into his mercy.

AMORPHO Peace, he comes.
Soft music. Enter the Tyrant with the [young] Queen, her hair loose; she makes a curtsy to the table. Sertorio brings in the flesh, with a skull all bloody. [She sits at the table, and begins to eat the flesh, and drink blood from the skull.] They all wonder

TYRANT
I perceive strangers more desire to see
An object than the fare before them set.
But since your eyes are serious suitors grown,
I will discourse; what's seen shall now be known.

KING
Your bounty every way conquers poor strangers.

TYRANT
Yon creature whom your eyes so often visit
Held mighty sway over our powers and thoughts;
Indeed we were all hers.
Besides her graces, there were all perfections:
Unless she spoke, no music; till her wishes
Brought forth a monster, a detested issue,
Poisoning the thoughts I held of her.
The old King sends forth [Fidelio]
She did from her own ardour undergo
Adulterous baseness with my professed foe.
Her lust strangely betrayed, I ready to surprise them,
Set on fire by the abuse, I found his life
Cunningly shifted by her own dear hand
And far enough conveyed from my revenge.
Unnaturally she first abused my heart,
And then prevented my revenge by art.
Yet there I left not. Though his trunk were cold,
My wrath was flaming, and I exercised
New vengeance on his carcass, and gave charge
The body should be quartered and hung up. 'Twas done.
This as a penance I enjoined her to:
To taste no other sustenance, no nor airs,
Till her love's body be consumed in hers.

KING
The sin was great; so is the penance grievous.

TYRANT
Our vow is signed.

KING And was he Lydian born?

TYRANT
He was no less. Son to mine enemy,
A banished king; Tymethes was his name.

KING *[aside]* O me, my son Tymethes!

LAPYRUS *[aside]*
Passion may spoil us.—Sir, we oft have heard
Of that old king, his father, and that justly
This kingdom was by right due to his sway.

TYRANT
It was; I think it was, till we (called in)
By policy and force deceived his confidence,
Showed him a trick of war and turned him out.

KING *[aside]*
Sin's boast is worse than sin.
Enter Fidelio [and speaks apart to the pilgrims]

FIDELIO All's sure, the guards are seized on.

LAPYRUS Good.

FIDELIO
The passage strongly guarded.

TYRANT Holy sir, what's he?

LAPYRUS
Our brother, a poor pilgrim, that gives notice
Of a religious father that attends
To bear us company in our pilgrimage.

TYRANT
O ho, 'tis good, 'tis very good.

KING Alas, poor lady!
It makes me weep to see what food she eats.
I know your mercy will remit this penance.

TYRANT
Never, our vow's irrevocable, never.
The lecher must be swallowed rib by rib.
His flesh is sweet; it melts, and goes down merrily.
[The pilgrims] discover themselves
Ha? What are these?

LAPYRUS *Speranza.*

TYRANT Ha?

KING
Villain, this minute looses thee, thou tyrant.

154 **'light into his mercy** fall into the Tyrant's merciless hands
155.2 ***hair loose*** (a theatrical symbol of female madness)
155.3–4 ***skull all bloody*** See Introduction.
187 **O me, my son Tymethes** The closest the play comes to the cannibal banquet in Seneca's *Thyestes*: the Old King realizes the human remains being consumed are those of his own son. In Warner's *Pan his Syrinx* there is no relation between the devoured body and the witnesses.
191 **(called in)** i.e. to help
202 **mercy** Before condemning the Tyrant, the Old King tests his mercy: compare 2.4.19.1–2.4.21, when the Old King forgave the treachery of Lapyrus.
206 ***Speranza*** (the same word the Tyrant used when he usurped the throne)
207 **looses thee** releases you, frees the soul from the body.

TYRANT
Pilgrims wear arms? The old King? And Lapyrus?
Betrayed? Confounded? O, I must die forsworn.
Break, vow; bleed, whore.
He kills his Queen
There is my jealousy flown.
O happy man, 'tis more revenge to me
Than all your aims: I have killed my jealousy.
I have nothing now to care for. More than hell
'T had been if you had struck me ere she fell.
I had left her to your lust; the thought is bitterness.
But she first fall'n— ha, ha, ha!

KING
Die, cruel murderous tyrant.
They all discharge at him

TYRANT
So laugh away this breath.
My lust was ne'er more pleasing than my death.
Dies

LAPYRUS [*to old King*]
As full possessed as ever, and as rich
In subjects' hearts and voices, we present thee
The complete sway of this usurpèd kingdom.

KING
I am so borne betwixt the violent streams
Of joy and passion, I forget my state.
To all: our thanks and favours, and what more
We are in debt, to all your free consent
We will discharge in happy government.
Enter the old Queen disguised, a boy with her

OLD QUEEN [*kneeling*]
The peaceful'st reign that ever prince enjoyed—

KING
Already a petition? Suitors begin betimes.
We are scarce warm in our good fortune yet. What
are you?

OLD QUEEN
Unworthiest of all the joys this hour brings forth.
She discovers

KING
Our dearest Queen?

OLD QUEEN
Your poor distressèd Queen.

KING
O let me light upon that constant breast,
And kiss thee till my soul melt on thy lips.
[*They embrace*]
Our joys were perfect, stood Tymethes there.
We *are* old; this kingdom wants a hopeful heir.

OLD QUEEN
Your joys are perfect, though he stand not there,
And your wish blessed: behold a hopeful heir!
Stand not amazed: 'tis Manophes.

KING
How just the gods are, who in their due time
Return what they took from us.

OLD QUEEN
Happy hour!
Heaven hath not taken all our happiness;
For though your elder met ill fate, good heaven
Hath thus preserved your younger for your heir.

KING [*to Amorpho and Fidelio*]
Prepare those limbs for honourable burial.—
And, noble nephew, all your ill is lost
In your late new-born goodness, which we'll reward.—
No storm of fate so fierce but time destroys,
And beats back misery with a peal of joys.
Exeunt omnes

215 **lust** (*a*) sexual appetite; (*b*) free disposal (and possible mercy)
217.1 ***discharge*** fire pistols or muskets
221 **sway** rule, government
223 **state** (*a*) political obligations; (*b*) subjects
229 **scarce warm in** (metaphor taken from clothing or beds)
What are you? The Old King does not recognize his wife at first: compare 4.3.128–30.

SIR ROBERT SHERLEY HIS ENTERTAINMENT IN CRACOVIA

Text edited and annotated by Jerzy Limon and Daniel J. Vitkus, introduced by Daniel J. Vitkus

MOST of Middleton's 1609 pamphlet on Sir Robert Sherley is a prose translation of a Latin poem by Andrew Leech, a Scottish Jesuit living in Poland. Leech must have met Sir Robert Sherley during the winter of 1608–9 in Cracow. Sherley, appointed by the Shah of Persia as ambassador to the princes of Europe, was travelling from court to court, seeking support for a Perso-Christian alliance against the Turks.

The literary career of Andrew Leech had begun in London in 1603 with Latin verses celebrating the accession of King James. But between 1606 and 1609 he published in Cracow, under his Latin name (Andreas Loeaechius), at least five books of Latin verse. Some of those texts link him to Habsburg patrons and to the court of the Polish-Lithuanian Commonwealth in Cracow where a sophisticated internationalist culture existed around the monarch, Sigismund III. Sigismund was a militant counter-Reformation Catholic who sponsored a tremendous expansion of the Jesuit movement within Poland and Lithuania. His long reign (1587–1632) represents the apex of the Polish-Lithuanian Commonwealth's power, affluence, and culture. Sigismund's support for an alliance with Persia against Turkey is not surprising, since his borders were often harassed by the Ottomans and their vassals (including slave-raiding parties from the Tatar khanate).

The Scottish expatriate community under Sigismund may have been extensive. John Chamberlain, writing from the English court on 24 March 1621, recounts that Polish ambassadors 'tell what numbers of Scots are fostered in Poland, which after their account are more than 30,000 families'. Leech belongs to the same Latin Renaissance of expatriate Catholic Scots that would produce John Barclay's *Argenis* (published in Paris in 1621), the last masterpiece of Latin literature, and the last international bestseller in Latin.

No such masterpiece, the neoclassical *Encomia Nominis & Negocii D. Roberti Sherlaeii* is an unusually anxious panegyric because it betrays so much concern about Sherley's exotic status. Leech commends Sherley's 'fame and honour' (295) and praises his 'honoured enterprises' (293), but much of the text raises questions (for English Protestant readers, at least) about Sherley's ties to Persia and his loyalty to England. Middleton's translation states that 'England may very justly accuse Persia of wrong for detaining him from her' (205–6); a personified Mother England tells Persia 'that against all law of nations, thou robbest me of my subject' (249–50); and Sherley himself celebrates his 'liberty' from England (271) while proclaiming at the same time, 'I am a servant to that great master' (274), the Shah.

Middleton acknowledges through a musical analogy that the *Entertainment* is a song of praise for Sherley played 'upon an instrument tuned and directed by another' (64–5), but he may have known nothing of 'Loeaechius' and his background. Middleton's text is not simply a word-for-word translation. He adds an original introductory section, including a letter 'To the Reader'; he removes some passages that might be read as offensive, cutting a couple of sections that might have been interpreted in England as treasonous; he inserts a translated passage from the ancient Greek author Strabo. The additions from Strabo (taken from the fifteenth book of his *Geographia*) present the Persians as virtuous pagans, thereby concealing their Islamic identity and praising their martial discipline and virility. Somewhat surprisingly, Middleton's translation retains some provocative statements suggesting that England was isolated from a cosmopolitan Christianity. 'What is the cause that Sherley has not all this while lived in the same country, that first lent him breath?' (302–3). The answer is that 'a spirit so great was not to be contained within so small a circle, as his country' (303–5). The Latin original belittles England, and suggests that Robert Sherley (and by analogy, Leech himself) is a great spirit who left Protestant England to join the greater, common cause of Christendom and to promote a grand alliance against the Turks.

Repackaging the Latin poem for English consumption, Middleton tried to allay and redirect xenophobic anxieties by stressing that Sherley's service as a Persian ambassador would bring honour to England and succour to Christians besieged by 'that hell-hound brood of Mahomet . . . the barbarous Turks' (164–6). Middleton opens the *Entertainment* with a general defence of travel that is an implicit defence of Robert Sherley's transgressive hybridity. Declaring that 'Travel is the golden mine that enriches the poorest country and fills the barrenest with abundant plenty' (49–50), Middleton enters into a contemporary debate about the effects of travel. Returned travellers and travel writers had to contend with domestic distrust of their tales and 'true reports'. For instance, William Parry, who accompanied Anthony and Robert Sherley on their voyage to Persia, wrote *A new and large discourse of the travels of Sir Anthony Sherley Knight . . . to the Persian empire* (1601), a text that begins with this sentence: 'It hath been, and yet is, a proverbial speech amongst us, that travellers may lie by authority.' It was not only lies that English homebodies feared, but also the contaminating importation of foreign goods and foreign ideas. That fear is evident, for example, in Bishop Joseph Hall's *Quo Vadis? A Just Censure of Travel* (1617). Hall articulates English xenophobia through the discourse of religious sectarianism. He concedes that there are two ethically justifiable purposes for travel, 'matter of traffic, and matter of state', but he warns merchant travellers to 'take heed, lest they go too far, that they leave God behind them; that whiles they buy all other things good cheap, they make not an ill match for their souls'.

Middleton's pamphlet acknowledges its alien origins (in Catholic Poland and in Shiite Persia) but plays down Sherley's Catholic connections and presents the Shah as a quasi-Christian figure. Its description of 'the Persian himself confessing and worshipping Christ' (89–90) is intentionally ambiguous. (The Shah was tolerant of Christians and rumoured to wear a cross, but remained a Muslim all his life.) Middleton's Christ-worshipping 'Persian' serves as an example of the compatibility and convertibility of foreign powers in the imagined 'league' (131) that would include both the Shah and the 'Christian kings' (129) of Europe. This trans-sectarian, international alliance is embodied by Robert Sherley himself, who converted to Catholicism while in Persia. Sherley is described by Leech as wearing 'rich garments... woven by Grecian workmen' (230–1), riding a 'Thracian courser' (234–5), and bearing a 'victorious scimitar' (237) that has spilled 'so much blood of those, that are enemies to the Persians' (238–9). Sherley had served in the Shah's army against the Turks, and he was now touring the Continent wearing a silken caftan and a turban decorated with a jewel-encrusted crucifix (see illustration). The Loeaechius poem was probably given to Middleton by Sherley's 'agent Master Moore', who had 'lately arrived in England' (358–9), also 'Attired in... Persian habits' (358). In his epistle 'To the Reader', Middleton compares the pamphlet to an exotic import, 'this Persian robe, so richly woven with the praises only of Sir Robert Sherley' (10–11), but he seeks to reassure his readers that this imported text(ile) comes 'at a low price' (12). In early modern England, anxiety about contact and exchange with foreign culture generated objections to the importation of luxury goods and to the presence of aliens in London. Consequently, Middleton attempts to present the hybridized Sherley, 'this famous English Persian' (360), in a positive light, as 'our famous English traveller' (375–6), a brave soul who had demonstrated English honour and virtue to the wider world without going 'too far'.

The object of Middleton's defensive praise was the youngest of three brothers whose controversial activities had already demonstrated to the English court that travel often breeds trouble, not moral or monetary profit. The eldest brother, Sir Thomas Sherley, captured and imprisoned by the Turks for piracy in 1603, was ransomed and returned to England in 1606—then in September 1607 committed to the Tower, accused of conspiring to divert the Levant trade from England to Venice. He was released in 1608 (but by 1611 would be in prison again,

Portrait engraving of Sir Robert Sherley by Diego de Astor, 1609

this time for debt). Sir Anthony Sherley led an abortive military expedition to Italy in 1598, then went from Venice to Persia, where the unauthorized English embassy was hospitably received by the Shah. Sponsored by Abbas I, Anthony left Persia in 1599 for Europe on a mission to persuade the princes of Europe to ally themselves with Persia against the Ottomans. He never returned to Persia, ending his days in poverty in Madrid.

Robert Sherley had accompanied his older brother Anthony to Persia in 1598, and stayed there until 1608, when the Shah assigned him the diplomatic mission Anthony had botched. Among the letters he carried was one from the Shah addressed to King James, which suggested that 'the Turk ought to be assaulted by diverse ways' and that a joint military operation 'to ruin him and to blot out his name' should be mounted (Shirley, App. C). Sherley journeyed first to Moscow, next to the court of Sigismund III, and then to the imperial court at Prague, to Florence, and to Rome. According to the Venetian ambassador in Rome, Sherley delivered an oration there in which he claimed that 'When the Turk was defeated and Constantinople taken... his master intended to become a Christian and to render entire obedience to the Apostolic See' (*Calendar of State Papers Venetian* 11: 648). He arrived in Spain in December 1609, but his prolonged negotiations there proved fruitless. Sherley's 'coming into England' (5), announced in the *Entertainment*, did not occur until June 1611, more than two years after publication of the pamphlet.

Given Middleton's known sympathies for an English brand of Calvinism and his affiliation with the Protestant citizens of London, why would he write what G. B. Shand has characterized as 'a piece of advance public relations work' for Robert Sherley, an orientalized Catholic who had been 'entertained' by the militant counter-Reformation court of Sigismund III? One motive may have been a pressing need for cash. We know that Middleton adapted and prepared the *Entertainment* before May 30, 1609, because on that day its publisher, John Budge, was fined for having had the pamphlet printed without permission. Legal records dating from December 1608 to July 1609 show Middleton—deprived of theatrical income by the closure of the theatres due to plague—being sued for failing to repay loans to two different creditors. Middleton may have been paid by Sherley's harbingers, including 'Master Moore', to translate a Latin poem for London publication; certainly, he would have been paid something by the London publisher. He must have hoped for patronage from Robert Sherley's brother and father, to whom he dedicated his text. Author and publisher probably noted the Sherleys' fame and popularity, whose exploits had been romanticized by other pamphlets and by a stage play, *The Travels of the Three English Brothers* (first performed in 1607). Merchants and courtiers may have scorned the Sherleys, but among the common people they had taken on, through the media of cheap print and stage performance, the image of heroic adventurers.

Middleton may also have been personally sympathetic to the idea of a 'Universal peace' (165) that would establish Christian amity throughout Europe—and enable a crusade against an Islamic empire that was pushing back the borders of Christendom. Furthermore, he had reason to believe that King James would favour Sherley's mission. As early as 1589, James had begun to promote religious reconciliation among Christian nations and express hostility toward the Ottoman sultanate. In 1601 James wrote to the Shah of Persia, Abbas I, praising him for his military success against the Ottomans and implying that soon James himself would offer assistance to Persia. In the same letter, James expressed admiration for Sir Anthony Sherley, the Shah's ambassador. As W. B. Patterson has shown in *King James VI and I and the Reunion of Christendom*, throughout his reign James pursued an accommodation between all Christian princes and sects. In 1618, the King was to sponsor Middleton's *The Peacemaker*, in which England is praised as 'the factory of peace'. The persistence beyond the Reformation of a 'Common Corps of Christendom' led to frequent calls for a crusade against the Turks, and James himself had developed a conciliar theology which prepared the way for a possible *rapprochement* with the Church of Rome. Under the threat of Spanish power, Elizabeth I and her councillors had forged an alliance with Turkey and had fostered the Levant trade, but when in 1603 James succeeded to the English throne, he immediately expressed his dislike of this affiliation with the Turks. According to Thomas Wilson, James 'denied absolutely' at the commencement of his reign in England to sign commercial agreements with the Ottomans, 'saying, that for merchant's causes he would not do things unfitting a Christian prince' (Baumer, 36n).

James's peacemaking policies in support of Christian solidarity and his hostility toward the Ottomans help to explain the warm welcome that Robert Sherley obtained at the Jacobean court in 1611. In the end, though, Sherley's efforts to drum up support for an anti-Ottoman alliance and a new commercial arrangement with Persia were decisively thwarted by powerful commercial interests committed to trade with Turkey. One English courtier, John Chamberlain, doubted the success of Sherley's 'projects', because 'the way is long and dangerous, the trade uncertain, and must quite cut off our traffic with the Turk'. English commerce with the Ottoman empire, ongoing since 1570, was controlled by the Levant Company, a powerful organization firmly opposed to any Anglo-Persian alliance against the Turks. Middleton's translation exhorted Christian princes to put martial valour and the sacred cause of a crusade before venal motives, but pro-Turkish mercantile priorities prevailed over Sherley's proposal. Middleton's *Entertainment* may have helped to publicize and promote Sherley's mission, but ultimately the effort to enlist James in a coalition against the Turks failed. Sherley left England for Spain (and then Persia) in early 1613.

The *Entertainment* marks the beginning of Middleton's interest in foreign affairs, but the next time that he would write about an ambassador coming from Spain to negotiate an alliance with England, it would be Gondomar in *A Game of Chess*, and Middleton would write in opposition, not support, of a partnership with foreign and Catholic powers.

SEE ALSO

Textual introduction and apparatus: *Companion*, 598
Authorship and date: *Companion*, 368

ANDREAS LOEAECHIUS, translated and adapted by THOMAS MIDDLETON

Sir Robert Sherley his Entertainment in Cracovia

Sent ambassador in the name of the King of Persia to Sigismond the Third, King of Poland and Swecia, and to other princes of Europe.

His royal entertainment into Cracovia, the chief city of Poland, with his pretended coming into England.

Also, the honourable praises of the same Sir Robert Sherley, given unto him in that kingdom, are here likewise inserted.

To the Reader

Reader, this Persian robe, so richly woven with the praises only of Sir Robert Sherley (thy countryman) comes to thee at a low price, though it cost him dear that wears it, to purchase so much fame, as hath made it so excellent. It is now his, forever, thine so long as it is his; for every good man (as I hope thou art) doth participate in the renown of those that are good, and virtuous.

He hath been a traveller a long time: give him now a welcome home; the arms of his own country embracing him will be more joyful to him than all those of so many foreign kingdoms, with which he hath so often been honoured.

If a man that hath ventured through the world may deserve thy love, thou canst not choose but bestow as much of it upon him, as upon any. Look upon him truly, and thou shalt find a large general chronicle of time writ in a little volume.

He comes laden with the trophies of war, and the honours of peace. The Turk hath felt the sharpness of his sword, and against the Turk is he now whetting the swords of Christian princes. Much more could I speak of him, but that I should do wrong to the common laws of civility, by taking away that reverence from strangers, whom (from countries afar off) you shall presently hear giving ample testimonies of his nobleness.

Vale:

News from Persia and Poland, touching Sir Robert Sherley, being sent ambassador to divers princes of Europe, famed as well for his wisdom and experience, as for his knowledge and understanding of many tongues.

Albeit that man can receive his birth but from one place, yet is he born a freeman of all the cities of the world. The whole earth is his country, and he that dwelleth farthest off, is by the laws of nature, as near to him in love as his kindred and acquaintance. This general charter being given by the King of this universal crown, to all nations, hath caused men from time to time (by the virtue of that privilege) to forsake the places of their first being, and to travel into other countries. The benefits that kingdoms have gotten by this means cannot in so small a volume (as this in hand) be comprehended. Travel is the golden mine that enriches the poorest country and fills the barrenest with abundant plenty. It is the chain that at first tied kingdoms together and the musical string that still maintains them in concord, in leagues and in unity. The Portuguese have hereby crowned themselves and their posterity with garlands of never dying honour. The Spaniards have their names (for this) so deeply engraven in the chronicles of fame, that they can never be forgotten. The French likewise and the Dutch, have raised their glories to a nobler height, only by these adventures. In imitation of all whose labours, or rather in emulation of all their fames, our Englishmen have not only stept as far as any of them all, but gone beyond the most and the best of them. And not to reckon those men of worth (in this kind) of our own nation, whose voyages and travels (by sea and land) to set down, were able to fill whole volumes, I will only at this time (not with a loud and shrill trumpet, as they deserve, but as it were upon an instrument tuned and directed by another) give only a soft touch of the praises of this worthy gentleman Sir Robert Sherley, of whose adventures, dangers, and various fortunes, both good and bad, to draw a true picture in the right and lively colours would as easily feed men's eyes with gazing admiration, as the large pictured tables of others have filled them with wonder.

Being therefore contented (at this time) to swim but in a shallow stream of his fame, sithence greater sails are likely hereafter (and that very shortly) to swell with the true report of his actions, you shall understand that Sir Robert Sherley, after a long, a chargeable, and a dangerous progress through most (if not all) the kingdoms in Europe, receiving entertainment from the princes of those dominions fitting to such a guest, desire of glory still more and more burning within him. At the length, he left Europe and travelled into Asia, receiving noble entertainment at the hands of the king of Persia. In whose court he so well and so wisely bore himself in all his actions, that the Persian (with much of his love, of which he tasted most plenteously) heaped on his head many honourable favours.

1 **ambassador** envoy
1–2 **the King of Persia** Shah Abbas I
2 **Sigismond the Third** Polish king of the Vasa dynasty; ruled between 1587 and 1632.
3 **Swecia** Sweden. In point of fact Sigismund III lost his Swedish throne in 1598.
princes monarchs
5 **pretended** intended
17–18 **give … home** Although Sherley's arrival was expected in England in 1610, he did not arrive until 1611.
28 **The Turk** the Ottoman sultan, Ahmed I
35 ***Vale*** Latin: farewell, adieu
44 **King of this universal crown** God
72 **sithence** sith = from this time on
75 **chargeable** burdensome; expensive

That common enemy of Christ and Christians, (the Turk) lifting up his sword continually (for the most part) not only against the Polack, the Hungarian, Bohemian, and other princes of Christendom, but also thirsting after the rich empire of Persia and showing a mortal hatred to that kingdom by being ever by in arms against it, it was thought fit that (the Persian himself confessing and worshipping Christ) aid should be required at the hands of Christian princes in the Persian's behalf, against so barbarous, so ambitious and so general an enemy. Hereupon honour of such an embassy was conferred (by the King of Persia) upon Sir Robert Sherley, as a man worthy and apt to treat with Christian princes in so weighty a business, he himself being a Christian born, and a gentleman that had travelled and by experience knew the conditions, state, and policies of most of their kingdoms.

First therefore was he employed into Poland, where by Sigismund (the King of Poland and of Swecia) he was received with great magnificence and applause, both of the Polack himself and of his people.

And because it is not fit that every common and popular ear should stand listening to the private business of princes in a designment that concerns the universal state of Christendom, we will not therefore at this time be interpreters of the Persian's embassy but rather wait his expected coming who hath in charge to deliver it by word of mouth himself.

In the mean time notwithstanding (forbearing to reckon up the rich presents given by the Poland king to Sir Robert, the honours done to him by the Polish lords, and the favours thrown upon him by the common people) you shall be witnesses only to those (not unworthy) praises of him, by which his fame (amongst scholars by those of the better sort) was lifted up at the time of his staying in Poland.

A fourfold anagram upon Sir Robert Sherley's name.

ROBERTVS SHERLÆIVS.

1. *Heus Labor, Tueris Res.*
2. *Servus, ast Hero Liber.*
3. *Libertas, ero Servus.*
4. *Virtus, Labores sere.*

Encomiums or praises, as well upon the name as negotiation, of Sir Robert Sherley, an English knight, sent ambassador from the King of the Persians, to the princes of Europe.

Mercurius, seeing the ambassador ready to take his journey, resigneth unto him his office, as being messenger or herald to the gods, according to the fiction of poets, and with that office bestoweth the gift of eloquence upon him, because he may have power to persuade the princes to whom he is sent. And withal adds a wish that those Christian kings whom he is to solicit may not be cold in joining their forces together, but that they may enter into an honourable, a pious and inviolable league against that common enemy, the Turk.

Mercury's speech.

Thou (O Sherley), being born an Englishman, art sent from the Persian empire to the kingdoms that lie in Europe. Thy place is full of honour, thy message of weight: discharge thou therefore boldly those things which the great Lord of Persia commands thee to do. It is not chance that throws this high office upon thee, but a full synod (or parliament) of all the gods do appoint thee to be their messenger to the great kings of the earth. For this cause, I that am heaven's winged messenger, seeing thee ready to depart, present myself thus before thee and uttering only so much, as in the letters of thy name lies mystically hidden, and that is this:

Heus Labor,—tu Res hoc ore Tueris Persarum.——

O exceeding labour! Yet thou art the man that must defend the state of the Persians, even by the force of my eloquence. Go on therefore, be thou Mercurius in the courts of kings. I give thee my place; I give it to thee, that art more worthy of it then myself. O that the princes of Europe would knit an indissoluble league together with thy master (the Persian monarch) and tie all their sinews to one arm, that a noble war may be begotten. Let Bellona (the goddess of battles) breath courage into the breasts of soldiers; and let no country be dishonoured by bearing men that have no hearts to come into the field. O let not that covetous dragon, which once watched the golden firmament, sleep in the bosoms of kings and with his poison infect them with that covetous disease of hoarding up gold. Cast off (O you princes) your sensual pleasures, and let it be your ambition to wear garlands of oak, which are the crowns of conquerors. Prefer immortal fame before all those dangers, over which you must of necessity pass, be they never so invincible in the show of undertaking, and aspire only to that life which shall remain when your bodies lie dead. Heaven (in your doing so) shall smile upon your enterprises. Hell shall be conquered, and that hell-hound brood of Mahomet be utterly confounded. Universal peace shall crown the world and the barbarous Turks feel the sinews and puissant arms of Europe.

89–90 **Persian . . . worshipping Christ** This, of course, was not true, except in the sense that all Muslims acknowledge Jesus as a prophet.
100 **Polack** the King of Poland
106 **his expected coming** Sir Robert was expected in England shortly after his visit to Poland, Bohemia, Italy, and Spain.
115–307 **A fourfold . . . kings** This entire passage is a free translation of Middleton's source, Andrew Leech's *Encomium*.
115 **anagram** In what follows each line should contain all the letters of Sherley's (Latinized) name.
117 ***Heus . . . Res*** Here's labour, you must care about things.
118 ***Servus . . . Liber*** Servant, but free for his sovereign.
119 ***Libertas, ero Servus*** Free, but servant to his sovereign.
120 ***Virtus, Labores sere*** Virtue, sow labour.
121 **Encomiums** praises
122 **English knight** Robert Sherley was never knighted in England. He was, however, knighted by the Emperor in Prague in June 1609; in addition, he was created a count palatine of the Holy Roman Empire. Two months later Sir Robert was created count of the sacred palace of the Lateran by the Pope (Paul V).
124 **Mercurius** messenger of the gods
144 **Heus . . . Persarum** this is translated by Middleton in the next line
154–5 **covetous dragon . . . firmament** In Greek mythology Ladon was the dragon that guarded the golden apples of the Hesperides. Ladon had a hundred heads and voices, and was killed by Heracles when he came to fetch the golden apples (his twelfth labour).
166 **puissant** mighty, powerful

To the nations (unto whom the ambassador is sent on great and serious affairs, as rightly may be conjectured) a desire and wish is made that all kings in Christendom may entertain this holy war with the same courage, constancy and zeal, that the Persian doth.

Hearken O you Polanders, Italians, French, and you Germans; enrich your chronicles with an act of a wonder never heard of in the world before: for behold, a Briton is sent on a royal message from the King of the Persians. A Briton is sent, but who is it? Such a one he is, as by his name (being before anagrammatized) he may apparently be deciphered.

Ast Liber, Servus Hero.

Free born and a servant only unto his sovereign.

He, even he, is sent to you (O you nations of Europe) from the confines of the Persians, bringing along with him the name of his Lord and with that name the sound of an approaching war.

The destinies begin to promise some great matter: the God of battles (hereupon) speaks cheerfully. God himself prepares the armour; muster yourselves together therefore (O you kings) and with a religious defence draw your swords against the Turks.

A gratulatory compendious speech, to Sir Robert Sherley, commending both his virtue and present fortune.

O Sherley, thou that art an honour to the Persians as well as to the Britons, within whose head dwelleth experience and wisdom, and upon whose tongue eloquence writeth her charms: whatsoever he was that at first durst say that Fortune was blind and that she bestowed extraordinary benefits upon undeserving men, let him know that all this while he hath been in an error. For Fortune had more eyes than Argus when she crowned this Englishman with so many Persian honours and offices. That monarch (O thou renowned Briton) whose sword is dreadful to the Thracian tyrant, makes thee a partner in the cares and burdens of his empire: for he hath seen, yea, he hath ever seen and found thee constant in execution of all his just and royal commands.

The empire of the Persian is here commended: the kings and princes of Europe being called to give witness how much glory the dexterity of Sir Robert Sherley hath added to the Persian monarchy; upon which, he appears to the Persians a gentleman of such merit, as that England may very justly accuse Persia of wrong for detaining him from her.

The fame of the Persian empire doth not grow up only in a mean soldier, for their cities are full of renowned and worthy captains: from the ancient discipline and stratagems of war, are the glories of the Persians sprung up and continue famous, but (O thou honoured Englishman) she derived her first principles from thy practice and knowledge. Far be my words from the base servitude of flattery: for within a short time, kings shall rise up as witnesses of what I speak. Let thine own country envy the kingdom of Persia for enjoying this honour (which by thee is given her). Yea, let her challenge thee to be delivered back again as her own, yet let her claim be made in such manner that England and Persia may not grow into quarrel about thee, but rather thus let them both share thee. Let rich Persia enjoy thy presence and reckon thee in the number of her citizens, and be proud in the possession of a man so worthy. Let England glory that she alone is happy in thy birth, and that she bears the honour of giving thee thy name. But howsoever (O thou, the dignity and lustre of two renowned kingdoms) go thou on in thine intended embassage, and perform these behests which the great Persian thy lord hath imposed upon thy integrity.

A short Speech uttered as it were by the whole body of the Polish court, to Robert Sherley, ambassador from the invincible King of the Persians.

It is not thy rich garments, embroidered so thick with gold and woven by Grecian workmen, that draws our eyes into admiration by beholding thee; it is not thy sparkling jewels, nor those costly precious stones that adorn thy robe, which dazzle our sight; it is not thy comely riding, nor skilful managing of that Thracian courser upon whose back thou sittest, whilst the proud beast itself champs on the glistering bit in disdain to be so curbed, that makes us to look after thee. It is not that victorious scimitar of thine, wherewith thou hast made the earth drunk so often with so much blood of those that are enemies to the Persians, that causes us to stand gazing at thy presence. No, it is the beauty of thy mind wherewith our eyes are enchanted. It is the excellent music of thy tongue, that so ties our ears to thy charms: thou being able to speak and to answer so many several nations in their own proper languages.

England's complaint to Persia for her Sherley.

O Persia! thou glorious kingdom, thou chief of empires; the palace sometimes where wisdom only kept her court, the land that was governed by none but by wisemen; yet must I tell thee, and with grief dost thou enforce me to tell thee, that against all law of nations, thou robbest me of my subject. Why should the right of another be thine? It is justice for every one to keep their own. But thou makest up thy gain by my loss. Is this equity? Is this tolerable? Cease to do it and send home (O Persia) that son of mine to me that am his mother: for to me only is he due. But (aye me) the

169 **all kings in Christendom** In the original source Pope Paul V is also mentioned; in Middleton's pamphlet the Pope is omitted on purpose.

178 **Ast Liber, Servus Hero** translated in the next sentence

181 **confines** borders

182 **war** Again, in the source we have a direct address to Paul V, here omitted.

187 **compendious** comprehensive though brief

195 **Argus** Argus had one hundred eyes, only two of which closed at any one time. He was killed by Hermes, and Hera saw to it that his eyes were placed in the peacock's tail.

197 **Thracian** Thrace was a large European country located to the south-west of the Black Sea and to the north of the Aegean Sea. Today, part of Turkey or Bulgaria. In Middleton's text 'Thracian' means simply 'Turkish'.

200 **commands** For some reason, Middleton did not include a translation of the passage that follows in the original, which consists of Sherley's address to his liberty, being an explication of the third line of his anagram: 'Libertas, ero Servus'.

223 **lustre** glory

225 **behests** vows, duties

226 **integrity** uncorrupted virtue

234 **Thracian** Turkish

235 **courser** a swift horse

236 **champs** bites

237 **scimitar** a curved, single-edged sword used by the Turks and Persians (and the Poles, as a matter of fact)

241–4 **It is . . . proper languages** Sir Robert's reputation as a linguist was confirmed by other writers, including Thomas Herbert (*Relation of Some Yeares Travaile*).

honours of his own country, and the palaces of my kingdom, are by him (belike) neglected and seem not worth the looking on; and though to the eye of the world I may perhaps appear beautiful and great, yet in his eye I show no bigger than a small corner of the world. I do envy thee therefore (O Persia) only for him; yet sithence I cannot enjoy him, fare thou well, O thou my darling, and with that farewell bear along with thee the praises which I give thee. I rob Persia, Persia robs not me: my loss is to me more honour, for the Persian empire borrows her brightness from the beams of one of the sons of England.

Sherley to his native country.

O thou my country, if I should pay back into thy hands so much as by bonds due unto thee from me, I should then lay down my life at thy feet. But my thoughts aim at greater matters: it is not breath I would pay thee, but fame; take thou from me so much honour as may make me live for ever. Liberty is the goal to which I run, but such a liberty it is, as may free me from the common baseness of the multitude and make me worthy to be respected by the eye of a king.

Servus hero, I am a servant to that great master, to whose feet all the Persians bow and do reverence: I am his servant that I may be his messenger and bear the treaties of such a king to other kings in Christendom. I am destined out to deliver his mind in their own languages, to foreign princes and to the monarchs of the earth. Let them therefore come together, and quickly shall the Turkish fury be calmed, and being weakened in her own strengths, shall be glad to kneel to the power and mercy of others. And thou (O my native country), if thou wouldst be pleased to knit thy forces in this just and universal war, to what dignities may thou advance thyself? Whatsoever is dishonourable hath a base descention and sinks beneath hell, but whatsoever is good and honest lifts up the unblemished brow on high and makes it level with the front of heaven.

The author's wish and request to Virtue that she would give unto Sherley such a fruitful harvest of his labours that, having conquered the hardness of them, his name may aspire to the full height of his desert.

O Virtue! the noblest and boldest guide, thou that givest to men the due crown of praises, prosper thou the honoured enterprises of Sherley; but touching those paths which must lead him to titles of fame and honour, make them even and certain before him: he hath no desire to have his name eaten out by the rust of idleness, no; he will never unworthily sink beneath his own proposed fortune.

Another of the same author, touching Sir Robert Sherley being called as it were by Fate to manage the affairs of foreign princes.

What is the cause that Sherley hath not all this while lived in the same country that first lent him breath? This is the reason: a spirit so great was not to be contained within so small a circle as his country. Besides,

He is the child of Fate and highly sings
Of kingly embassies to none but kings.

Crowned with these praises as you hear in Poland and leaving the fame of his memorable actions behind him, bending his course to other princes of Christendom with the same royal embassage of honourable and Christian confederacy against Mahomet and his adherents, it shall not be amiss here to speak of the kingdom of Persia, where Sir Robert received such honourable entertainment, suitable to his noble actions and the virtues of his mind, as also of the manners, fashions, rites, and customs that are and have been observed by the Persians. And first, for their religion which they have observed of old, doing worship and reverence in their upright zeal to the Sun, Moon, Venus, Fire, Earth, Water, and Winds, erecting neither altars nor statues, but in open fields offering their sacrifices, which sacrifices were superstitious and full of idle ceremonies too tedious to be here rehearsed. For their kings, the golden line of them is drawn out of one family. That custom amongst the Persians never as yet suffered change or alteration, and so severe their laws are in effect to the punishing of all rebellious, treasonable and disobedient people, that whosoever he be that is found repugnant in the least demeanor to the will and affection of the King, he is presently seized upon by the tormentors, his head and arms chopped off, and with his detested body thrown into some common field, without either grave or covering. And for their palaces and royal mansions, this hath ever been the continued custom among them, that every king hath had his seat royal erected on some high hill or mountain, the bowels of which he makes his safe treasure house, where all his riches, jewels, and tribute moneys are with exceeding carefulness kept hid and secret. And so much they do detest sterility and barrenness, that from the highest to the lowest they take many wives in marriage, counting the fruitful propagation of the empire, the only happiness they can raise to it, and so much they thirst after human fruitfulness, that the kings themselves propound great gifts and rewards to those that in one year brings forth the greatest harvest of mankind. From five year old to four-and-twenty the male children practise to ride great horses, to throw the vulnerable and inevitable dart, to shoot in arbalests or long steel bows, and all such manly exercises which shames many other Christian countries and may justly upbraid them of effeminacy and laziness.

Their victuals, for the most part, by which the common sort of people are fed and do live by, are acorns and hedge-pears, their bread coarse and hard, their drink the running spring. For their apparel, the princes and those that live in greatest respect amongst them adorn their bodies with a triple robe, and another garment in the fashion of a cloak hanging down to their knees, the inward linings all of white silks and the outward facing like

274 **Servus hero** see note to l. 118.
284 **descention** falling in rank
289–91 ***Sherley . . . desert*** This passage elaborates on the fourth line of Sherley's anagram; cf. note to l. 120.
306–7 **He is . . . kings** This couplet is the only part of the translation that reproduces the poetic form used by Loeaechius in the Latin original.
311–12 **Mahomet and his adherents** Middleton does not admit that Persia was in fact a Muslim country.
316–20 **And first . . . sacrifices** This passage is based on Strabo, p. 136.
325–9 **whosoever . . . covering** This passage is based on Strabo, p. 137.
326 **repugnant** resistant
335–7 **And so much . . . the empire** This passage is based on Strabo, p. 137.
341–3 **From five . . . bows** This passage is based on Strabo, p. 137.
345 **upbraid them of** reproach them for
346–57 **Their victuals . . . as tissue, etc.** This passage is based on Strabo, pp. 138–9.

powdered ermines. In summer for the most part they walk in purple; the winter refuses no colour; about their temples they wear a great tiara, being a stately ornament high and round with a cone at the top, from which descends a rich fair pendant of some costly embroidered stuff, as tissue, etc.

Attired in some of which ordinary Persian habits his agent Master Moore is lately arrived in England, bringing happy tidings of this famous English Persian, as also of his coming to England to the exceeding great joy of his native country, laden with honours through every kingdom, as the deserving ornaments of his virtue and labour. And thus, ingenuous reader, have I set down by true and most credible information a brief epitome of Sir Robert Sherley's entertainment into Cracovia, the chief city of Poland, together with all those several speeches delivered to him by the scholars of that country, which although they may seem to the nice ear of our times, not altogether so pure and polished as the refined labour of many English wits, yet therein they strived to express both their fashion and affection to the worthy virtues of Sir Robert, and for a taste of their style and manner of writing, it shall not be amiss if you cast your eye upon these verses following, composed by a scholar worthily reputed in that country, one Andreas Loeaechius, and those are they which at this I borrow to shut up the honourable praises of our famous English traveller.

Ad illustrissimum & maximi tum ingenij tum animi virum, Dom. Robertum Sherlaeum, Equitem Anglum Regis Persarum nomine ad Europae PP. legatum.

Aemule Honos Animo Proavis, Lux alta, Britannae,
Qui gentis pessum non sinis ire Decus;
Non uni dat Cuncta Polus, sed Carmina Apollo,
Mars vires, Arcas Nuncius Ingenium.
Haec cuncta unus habes, est vis, sunt ora diserta.
Numina avara aliis, prodiga facta tibi;
Persia se iactat gemino in te munere, Martis
Pectore belligeri; Palladis ingenio,
Tantus honore licet, te Scoti haud subtrahe Vena,
At Venam excedit pondere vatis Amor.
Immo Censendum satis est Cecinisse Poetam
Quod tibi se fassus carmine & ore rudem;
Parva loquor, ne te venturis subtrahe saeclis:
At Fidei, ut Famae suesce parare modum.

FINIS.

ADDITIONAL PASSAGES

A *To the worthy and well experienced gentleman, Sir Thomas Sherley, son to that happy father, Sir Thomas Sherley, and brother to that noble gentleman, Sir Robert.*

Worthy Sir,

The selfsame office of love and due praises which the world put itself into, at your long desired arrival in England, falls happily upon me to perform the like duty toward your worthy brother, nor can I recite more encomiums of his actions, then those of your own hath rightly and properly challenged to themselves; I'll speak thus much of you both, and the world shall judge it free from flattery: you well may be own brothers in birth, that are so near kin to one another in actions of fame and honour: so commending you both to eternizing memory of your own virtues and fortunes, I remain an unworthy observer of them both.

Your Worship's, in his most selected studies,
Thomas Middleton.

359 **Master Moore ... England** It is very likely that Moore (of whom nothing else is known) brought Leech's poem to England.

374 **Andreas Loeaechius** i.e. Andrew Leech, a Scottish Jesuit and a poet who found refuge in Poland

377–93 ***Ad*... modum** This poem opens Leech's work. Translation by Daniel J. Vitkus:

To the most illustrious Master Robert Sherley, a man both of the greatest spirit and of the greatest character; an English knight, and in the name of the king of Persia, ambassador to the princes of Europe.

O honoured man, rivalling the ancestral spirit, bright light, of Britain,
You who do not allow the glory of your people to perish:
Heaven [lit. 'the pole star'] does not give all things to one person,
But Apollo gives songs, Mars strength, Mercury financial genius.
You alone have all these things: strength is here, eloquent speech is here.
Others possess a jealous majesty; you have wondrous deeds.
Persia casts itself upon you with a double gift: with the heart of warlike Mars and the mind of Pallas.
So much honour is allowed you that the talent of a Scot can scarcely detract from it,
But the poet's love is weightier than his talent.
On the contrary, it is enough for the poet to have sung the praises of a man so worthy of esteem,
For he has confessed to you that he is unrefined both in song and in speech.
I say little, lest I detract from you in the centuries to come;
But I sing for my faith, so as to provide your wonted measure of fame.

A This dedicatory epistle appears in one surviving copy of *Sherley*; all other copies contain the dedicatory epistle printed here as Additional Passage B.

A.1–2 ***Sir Thomas Sherley*** (1564–1630?), the eldest son of Sir Thomas Sherley; ironically, two years after the publication of Middleton's pamphlet, Robert's brother found himself in prison.

A.2, B.1–2 ***Sir Thomas Sherley*** (1542–1612), the father of the three famous sons

A.6 **long desired arrival** Sir Thomas spent thirteen years abroad, between 1593 and 1607.

B *To the worthy and noble affected gentleman, Sir Thomas Sherley, father to that illustrious spark of honour and virtue, Sir Robert Sherley.*

Sir, not long since it was my happiness to meet with a little poem in Latin, as full freighted with the praises of your worthy renowned son, as is his breast with virtues; which no sooner mine eye had visited, but the general fame of his nobleness invited me to make his praises as general. And because it had been a great injury to his worthiness that but one tongue should sound forth his encomiums, who in so many tongues hath purchased glory, I thought it a part of humanity, and the office of a native countryman, since his honours were so spacious and general, to make his praises speak more tongues than one, and amongst all, especially, I chose the voice of his own country as the fittest trumpet of his fame, for whose honour he hath chiefly adventured his life and fortunes. To you therefore the happy father of so worthy a son, I dedicate both my love and labour, knowing the universal taste of his nobleness cannot come to the dear thirst of his country more pleasing than to your soul joyful.

THE TWO GATES OF SALVATION
or THE MARRIAGE OF THE OLD AND NEW TESTAMENT
or GOD'S PARLIAMENT HOUSE

Text edited and annotated by Paul Mulholland, introduced by Lori Anne Ferrell

HISTORY is rarely a matter of names and dates, but in the case of Thomas Middleton's 1609 text *The Two Gates of Salvation*, both nomenclature and chronology are essential to an understanding of the author's political and religious world-view. *Two Gates* was reissued in 1620 as *The Marriage of the Old and New Testament*; it was reissued a second time in 1627 as *God's Parliament House*. Here change over time is reflected, significantly, in titles transformed to suit a volatile political climate; here, too, is a simple reason for the relative obscurity of this particular piece. If Middleton's unique exploration of the relationship between the first and second testaments has remained unprinted since the seventeenth century, it is not because of its subject, or the work's anomalous position in the Middleton *œuvre*, but because of the confusion caused by its various and nonattributive title-pages. It has only recently been established that the 'Thomas Middleton' whose name appears in the preface to *Two Gates* is the poet, playwright, and chronologer of seventeenth century London.

The Two Gates of Salvation is a treatise of biblical typology, often called a 'harmony', which in two sections presents an arrangement of parallel scriptural texts. Throughout, the harmony of the Old and New Testaments is quite literally invoked by Middleton: 'Hearken therefore to the mutual sounds,' he writes, 'which their heavenly music sends forth' (a.I.6–8). The themes presented in this work thus conform to the expectations of the genre; it is to the rhetoric of the second section, and the overall format of the piece, that we must turn to discover the unique nature of *The Two Gates of Salvation* and to speculate about Middleton's own religious affiliations.

After a short section devoted to the prophecies of Christ's birth, life, and passion, Middleton extends his paradigm to represent the Old Testament anticipation of New Testament doctrine. This is a more unusual and complicated undertaking, something noted by Middleton himself, who writes at the end of the first section, 'what follows of him [Christ] now, shall appear more largely, though more irregularly'. This section, which comprises 39 of the original's 55 pages, is expansive in more ways than one. What Middleton calls 'largeness' is in fact theological speculation, in which the Old Testament does not so much prefigure Christ's teachings as provide a commentary to them. In a methodology reflective of

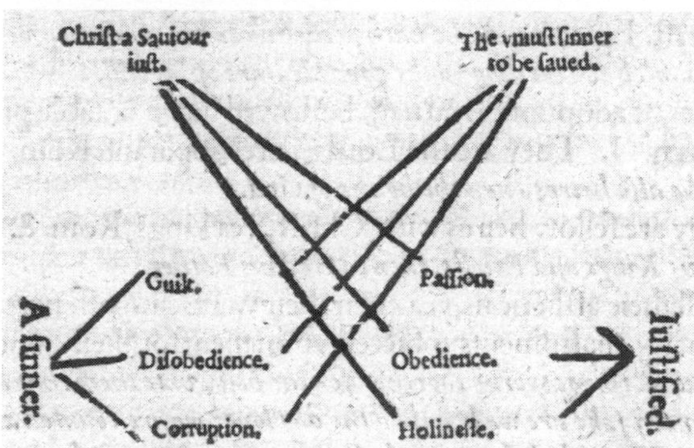

An example, from William Perkins's *A Golden Chain*, of the graphic depiction of salvation theology.

Calvin's in *Institutes of the Christian Religion*, the Law is pressed into the service of the Gospel in *The Two Gates of Salvation*.

While Middleton's rhetorical approach is typical of the theological concerns of protestantism, his parallel-text presentation of these concerns makes *Two Gates* remarkable in the context of early seventeenth-century religious prose. The 'harmony' of the testaments is presented to the reader in graphic form, by the literal juxtaposition of the scriptures on opposing pages. This polyphonic format is unusual, even in a world where various schemata were employed to explain doctrine, as in the church calendars affixed to the Bishops' Bible, or, more notably, in William Perkins's *A Golden Chain*, where the doctrinal path of election is travelled over connecting lines and geometric figures. Rather than use a diagrammatic outline of unfolding events or logical progression, Middleton instead depends on simultaneous presentation to make his 'harmony'.

This format of mutuality is especially necessary to the polemical intent of the second half of the work, which is political as well as religious. By displaying the testamental texts side by side, Middleton makes a stronger case for his theology, which is strongly Calvinist. Middleton's Calvinism, however, is less significant to a political reading of *The Two Gates of Salvation* than the kind of Calvinist Middleton appears to be. For Middleton's beliefs, as evinced in his only extant theological treatise, occupy a grey area, a characteristic danger zone where Calvinist religion could shade over into Puritan politics, goaded by the events of the volatile reign of James I.

The Civil War of the 1640s has been called by an earlier generation of historians 'England's Puritan Revolution' and by recent historians 'Britain's Wars of Religion'. During the time span represented by *Two Gate*'s three publication dates, the religious consensus that had loosely bound James I's loyal subjects began to unravel, as the King appeared increasingly conciliatory to continental Catholicism, and, upon his death, as relations broke down between Charles I and his Parliaments over religious issues. *The Two Gates of Salvation* displays a theology that would have appeared more confrontative in 1620 than it did in 1609, more so in 1627 than in 1620. Middleton's presentation of scriptural mutuality, therefore, graphically echoes and underscores the calls for alliance and cooperation that characterize the political treatises, published sermons, and parliamentary rhetoric of the period. This was, after all, a time when differences over religion were perceived and decried with increasing vigour: the age that created the idea of the 'Puritan' as a symbol of religious harmony gone discordant.

To examine the rhetorical—and nominal—strategies of this treatise is to realize the importance of understanding its politics as well as its theology. Middleton's desire for political harmony is essential to an understanding of the work as a reflection of the Jacobean milieu wherein it was conceived, written, published, and re-issued. The period used to be described in terms of doctrinal conflict between 'Puritans', who were Calvinists, and 'Anglicans', who were not. This is a dichotomy that is no longer credible in the face of extensive recent scholarship. Jacobean religion ran across a broader doctrinal spectrum than such arbitrary distinctions can negotiate. More importantly, perhaps, the Church of England was an entity as much secular as spiritual. In this context, theological nuance, political alliance, and simple timing could mean the difference between moderate Calvinism, stiff-necked Calvinism, and Puritanism.

This state of affairs could exist because Jacobean protestantism, in general, combined the rhetoric of Calvinism with the religious practices of an unreformed past. The Thirty-Nine Articles of Religion raised doctrinal ambiguity to a religious art form. While most of the Church of England's orthodox theologians were Calvinists, their adherence to Calvin's ideas as contained in his uncompromising *Institutes* was less clear-cut. Unfettered by a well-defined official orthodoxy, there existed in the Church varieties of Calvinism (as well as doctrinal opinions best described as anti-Calvinist), each distinguished in part by its treatment of the doctrine of predestination. Until the final years of his reign, the King tolerated a broad range of opinion on predestination, as long as the Royal Supremacy went unchallenged and order and uniformity governed the Church's ceremonies.

Generally speaking, Puritans and Calvinists in the Jacobean Church were united in terms of theology. But doctrine constitutes only part of a religious programme. What was called 'Puritanism' at this time was not primarily a matter of dogma—it was a cultural phenomenon with political connotations. What fashioned a Puritan out of a Calvinist in this period was the former's increasingly impatient attitude toward unreformed (and thus 'papist' or 'idolatrous') Church practices, conjoined with an inflexible style of Calvinism. At the time Middleton first published *The Two Gates of Salvation*, however, such opinions were usually absorbed into the Church of England's broad-based and ill-defined theological consensus.

Consensus, however, is not quiescence. In the absence of an official Calvinist gloss to the Articles of Religion, efforts to define the religion of England flourished in religious treatises and political tracts. *The Two Gates of Salvation* is representative of the politics of moderation that governed Jacobean polemic. But while Middleton's rhetoric is consensual, it is deceptively so. As with other printed works in this period, we must look beyond Calvinist doctrine to find Puritan tendencies. But instead of reading between the lines, we only have to glance across the page.

The first section of *The Two Gates of Salvation* is a straightforward biblical typology, in which the protestant tradition of the genre is somewhat refined in the preface. There Middleton's debt to the Reformed tradition can be seen in his claim that 'kings, priests, and prophets' (Preface.69) foreshadow the person of Christ; Calvin, following Martin Bucer, maintained in Book Two of the *Institutes* that these functions made up *triplex munus Christi*, the threefold ministry of Christ. There is, however, nothing peculiarly Calvinist in Middleton's treatment of prophecy in this section, or in its simple marginal glosses. Middleton's use of the Geneva Bible in *Two Gates* has been demonstrated, but there is nothing distinctively Calvinist in this—the Bishops' Bible and the Geneva Bible were used interchangeably in the early seventeenth century, even by such anti-Calvinists as Lancelot Andrewes.

The distinctive doctrinal content of *The Two Gates of Salvation* is found in its second section, where Middleton admits his approach is one that favours 'material fullness' rather than 'formal niceness'. Loosening his theological tie, Middleton moves comfortably across the broad range of religious belief available in Jacobean England. This section reveals not only the content of Middleton's Calvinism, therefore, but also just what kind of Calvinist Middleton was.

We can easily identify Middleton's theology in *Two Gates*'s exposition of predestination. Its preface introduces the doctrine:

> God, being throughly angered with *mankind* for disobedience, put a sharp bridle into his mouth. That bridle was the law; that law was a curst *judge* and ready to condemn. But the King of *heaven* being as full of mercy as of justice, abated the edge of the axe,

> and to a heavy *sentence* added a comfortable *pardon*. (Preface.33–9)

Here Middleton employs a common metaphor. The idea of the Law as a 'bridle' used to restrain creatures naturally unable to discipline themselves was most vividly described by Martin Luther in his *On the Bondage of the Will*, written 1525. Following Luther, protestant theologians viewed the Fall as destructive, not only of eternal life, but also of free-will. Since humankind could not presume to merit salvation, either by inclination or by effort, they were dependent on a gratuitous act of the divine free-will to obtain justification.

The doctrine of election in itself is not peculiarly Calvin's but it was Calvinist; in fact, allowing for differences of emphasis, it is a feature of all protestant doctrines of salvation, following Augustine's *On the Predestination of the Saints*. Protestant, even Calvinist theologians, however, tended to speak only of predestination to salvation. Not so Calvin himself, whose capacity to take arguments to their logical and extreme conclusions is displayed in Book Three of the *Institutes*: '[God] does not create all in like condition, but ordains eternal life for some and eternal damnation for others' (xxi.5). For Calvin, the omnipotence of God and the captivity of the human will meant that a special decision was also required in the case of the unregenerate. The divine will is thus doubly-binding: both Elect and Reprobate were predestined to their fate.

The doctrine of double predestination is a distinctive feature of Calvin's theology. It was also its most vulnerable tenet, constantly under attack by anti-Calvinists unscrupulous and combative enough to make it a straw man. Reformers more than willing to call themselves Calvinists at this time found it hard to explain why they thought God had summarily consigned the majority of the human race to damnation; most simply said that God's ways were inscrutable and not subject to inquiry. Willingness to explore and defend the double decree, therefore, identified bona fide, die-hard followers of Calvin. Their task became harder over time, as all styles of Calvinism drew increasing fire in the 1620s and 30s.

The Two Gates of Salvation follows the more rigorous line of Calvin. Citing Matthew 7:22–3, '... Then Christ will say unto them, I never knew you', Middleton explains in his marginal gloss that 'this is not of Ignorance, but because he will cast them away' (6.II.c). The text Middleton chooses to prefigure this passage, Psalm 6, 'the Lord hath heard the voice of my weeping', underscores the harshness of a deserved fate. But this choice of Old Testament text also softens the harsh edge of Calvin's theology, by emphasizing God's mercy towards the 'broken-hearted, ... that are lively touched with the feelings of their sins' (9.I.c). Here Middleton echoes the Calvinist William Perkins, who counselled his readers that these anguished 'prickings of the heart' could be the welcome sign of their election to salvation.

Middleton presents the decree of election as an action done on behalf of humanity, who have been absolved of the responsibility to fulfil the impossible demands of the Law. In this scheme, predestination is curative rather than punitive. He cites Ezekiel 34:12:

> As a shepherd searcheth out his flock when he hath been among his sheep that are scattered, so will I seek out my sheep, and will deliver them out of all places, where they have been scattered ... (39.I.1–4)

On the opposite page, Middleton cites as corresponding text Matthew 25:32, invoking the caretaking ideal of the Old Testament text, but then extending it to include the idea of judgement:

> [H]e shall separate them one from another, as a shepherd divideth his sheep from the goats, and he shall set the sheep on his right hand, and the goats on the left. (39.II.1–4)

Middleton's methodology reflects the Calvinist strategies of the Geneva Bible in providing marginal glosses to guide the reader through an interpretation of the texts. This does not mean, however, that he appropriates Geneva's marginalia; as Paul Mulholland has shown, Middleton's interpretation of the Matthew scripture, 'The Judgement-day, the Elect, and the Reprobate', is unique. By aligning this double-predestinarian reflection on Matthew with an Old Testament text glossed as 'a comfort to the Church in all dangers', Middleton echoes the language, if not the ambiguity, of the Thirty-Nine Articles, in which Article 17 describes predestination as a 'comfortable doctrine'.

Middleton's debt to Calvin and the Articles of Religion of the Church of England is an important reminder of the status of strict Calvinism in the reign of James I. Middleton reflects the protestant status quo when he defends the doctrine of election; when he defends the doctrine of double predestination, he reflects a rigorous but acceptable dogma. If pressed, most bishops, many court preachers, and other respectable religious polemicists in 1609 would have supported the same doctrine. At the time *Two Gates* was published, therefore, Middleton's intriguing combination of biblical typology, Calvin's rhetoric, and twin-text format would have been enlightening and quite possibly persuasive, but not very provocative.

The Two Gates of Salvation displays other, extra-doctrinal opinions, however, that identify Middleton as not only rigorously Calvinist but potentially puritan. He juxtaposes Isaiah 29:13–4, glossed here as 'a fearful judgement against hypocrites', to Matthew 15:7–8, 'This people ... honoureth me with their lips ... but in vain they worship me, teaching for doctrines, men's precepts' (20.I.c, 20.II.1–4). Middleton's comments on the New Testament text betray his disapproval of the sacramental and ceremonial practices of the Jacobean Church: 'They are condemned for hypocrisy, because they made the kingdom of God to stand in outward things.' This marginal condemnation of idolatry, aligned with the scriptural injunction against confusing 'men's precepts' with God's, blames the unreformed state of the Church of England on its government by bishops—or, by extension, on the Royal Supremacy itself.

These ideas, in conjunction with his belief in double predestination, can help to label Middleton as a Puritan, but they by no means make the label certain. It is more reliable to consider the effect this text would have had in its next two publications. By 1620, as opposition to the Spanish match grew, and ceremonialists and anti-Calvinists rose to hitherto unprecedented positions of power in the Church, the fragile religious peace established by James I was shattered. Puritan rhetoric, a censorious voice more or less absorbed into a still-reforming Church, began to be viewed by the King as the inharmonious noise of political opposition. *The Two Gates of Salvation* thus became increasingly discordant with each re-publication.

This brings us to the subsequent titles of *Two Gates* and its very late inclusion in the Middleton canon. Margot Heinemann has pointed to the publication of *The Marriage of the Old and New Testament* as evidence of Middleton's Puritanism in 1620; with the discovery of the 1609 version, it is tempting to roll back the date of Middleton's Puritanism as well. But Middleton's ideas need to be placed back into the historical contexts they occupied during a time of rapid social, cultural, and religious change. It might be best to see in *The Two Gates of Salvation* evidence of beliefs initially unremarkable, but that later would prove provocative. Like many other Jacobean Calvinists, Thomas Middleton became a Puritan over time—not because his ideas had radically changed, but because the times had.

SEE ALSO

Textual introduction and apparatus: *Companion*, 600
Authorship and date: *Companion*, 369

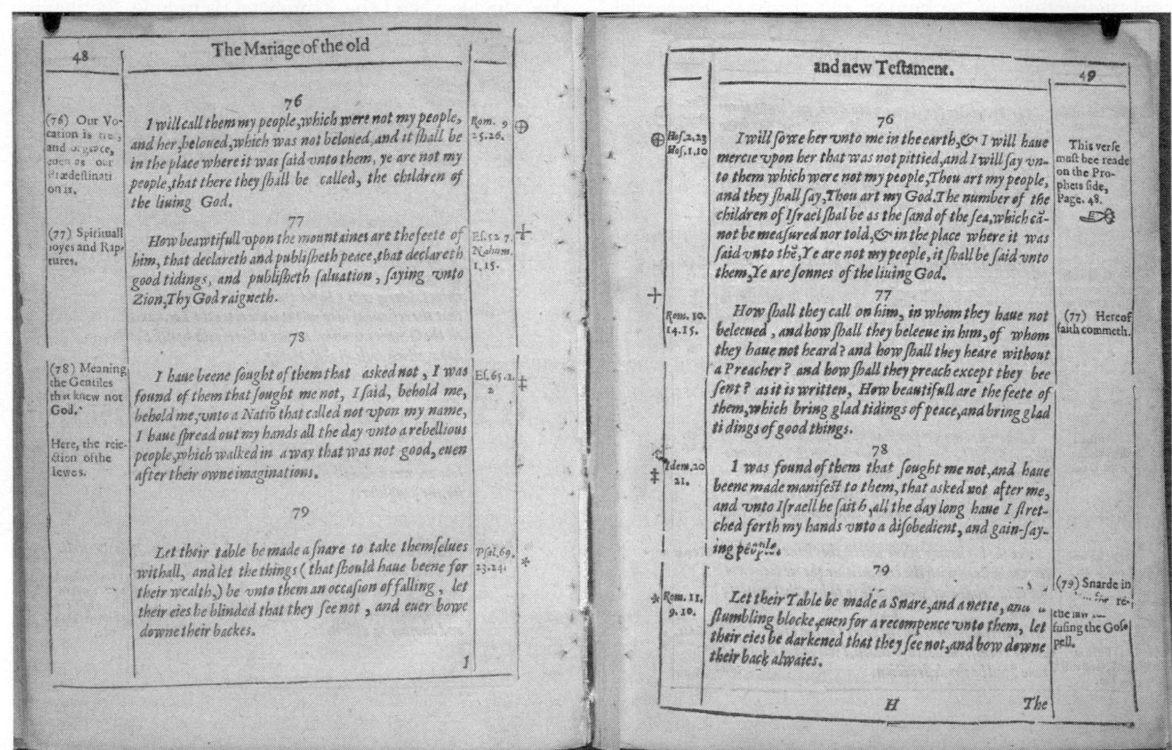

48 The Mariage of the old

76

(76) Our Vocation is [illegible] and [illegible] euen as our Prædestination is.

I will call them my people, which were not my people, and her, beloued, which was not beloued, and it ſhall be in the place where it was ſaid vnto them, ye are not my people, that there they ſhall be called, the children of the liuing God. Rom. 9. 25.26.

77

(77) Spirituall ioyes and Raptures.

How beawtifull vpon the mountaines are the feete of him, that declareth and publiſheth peace, that declareth good tidings, and publiſheth ſaluation, ſaying vnto Zion, Thy God raigneth. Eſ. 52. 7. Nahum. 1. 15.

78

(78) Meaning the Gentiles that knew not God.

Here, the reiection of the Iewes.

I haue beene ſought of them that asked not, I was found of them that ſought me not, I ſaid, behold me, behold me, vnto a Natiō that called not vpon my name, I haue ſpread out my hands all the day vnto a rebellious people, which walked in a way that was not good, euen after their owne imaginations. Eſ. 65. 1. 2.

79

Let their table be made a ſnare to take themſelues withall, and let the things (that ſhould haue beene for their wealth,) be vnto them an occaſion of falling, let their eies be blinded that they ſee not, and euer bowe downe their backes. Pſal. 69. 23. 24.

I

and new Teſtament. 49

76

Hoſ. 2. 23. Hoſ. 1. 10.

I will ſowe her vnto me in the earth, & I will haue mercie vpon her that was not pittied, and I will ſay vnto them which were not my people, Thou art my people, and they ſhall ſay, Thou art my God. The number of the children of Iſrael ſhal be as the ſand of the ſea, which cānot be meaſured nor told, & in the place where it was ſaid vnto thē, Ye are not my people, it ſhall be ſaid vnto them, Ye are ſonnes of the liuing God.

This verſe muſt bee reade on the Prophets ſide, Page. 48.

77

Rom. 10. 14. 15.

How ſhall they call on him, in whom they haue not beleeued, and how ſhall they beleeue in him, of whom they haue not heard? and how ſhall they heare without a Preacher? and how ſhall they preach except they bee ſent? as it is written, How beautifull are the feete of them, which bring glad tidings of peace, and bring glad tidings of good things.

(77) Hereof faith commeth.

78

Idem. 20. 21.

I was found of them that ſought me not, and haue beene made manifeſt to them, that asked not after me, and vnto Iſraell he ſaith, all the day long haue I ſtretched forth my hands vnto a diſobedient, and gain-ſaying people.

79

Rom. 11. 9. 10.

Let their Table be made a Snare, and a nette, and a ſtumbling blocke, euen for a recompence vnto them, let their eies be darkened that they ſee not, and bow downe their back alwaies.

(79) Snarde in [illegible] the law [illegible] fuſing the Goſpell.

H The

The G4^v/H1 opening as it appears in the 1620 issue—equipped with coordinating 'The Mariage of the old/and new Teſtament' running titles—showing the accidental reversal of Old and New Testament passages (76.I and 76.II) found in all copies. Since sheet G had almost certainly already been machined when the error was noticed, a marginal note was added to the corresponding passage on H1 to alert the reader to the correct positions.

The Two Gates of Salvation Set Wide Open

Or, The Marriage of the Old and New Testament

Animæ patria est Deus ipse. August.

Preface *The Marriage of the Old and New Testament*

God's *anger* is short, his *mercy* infinite; he seldom sendeth a *punishment* but presently after followeth a *pardon*. Read his everlasting chronicle, *The Bible*, and you shall find this true. First he chideth and then smileth, strikes and then cureth, drowns the world for sin and then gives the *rainbow* as a sign he will do so no more. But passing by the *least*, let our considerations stay upon the greatest. *Adam* was in *paradise*, and there fell; he no sooner fell there but he was driven from thence; he no sooner was *banished* but, to comfort him, *Christ* was promised. Though *Adam* fled from *God*, yet *God* fled not from him; but howsoever our first *father* stood condemned, we, his *posterity*, had a *reprieve* from Gen. 3:15 a *Messiah* that was to come. The blessing which we lost in *Adam* was to be recovered by the seed of Gen. 12:2 *Abraham*; *Moses* was the first witness to it, and after him all the *prophets*. In *Adam* were we both happy and miserable. Happy if we had continued in the first estate, and miserable if, like maimed soldiers, we had not been fetched off when we lay wounded by sin; but our surgeon was at hand. Man sinned and the son of man was to suffer. The treason of the first *Adam* put the second to death, and the death of the second quitted all the sins of the first. So that what we lost by the one we gained by the other;

This commentary pays particular attention to Middleton's sources. In composing *The Two Gates* Middleton appears to have had before him three versions of the Bible or, at the minimum, two versions of the complete Bible and yet another version of the New Testament: the Geneva Bible, the version of the New Testament 'Englished by L. Tomson' (possibly as part of a separate edition of the complete Geneva Bible), and the Bishops' Bible.

The Geneva Bible was a translation initiated by a group of Protestant refugees who had fled England and settled in Geneva during the reign of the Catholic Queen Mary (1553–8). The presence in Geneva of John Calvin and John Knox among others had helped to establish the city as a Protestant seat of learning and biblical scholarship. Originally printed and published in Geneva in 1560, the Bible was the first in English to divide scripture into verses. A prominent and distinguishing feature was its generous marginal commentary which betrayed a Calvinist or what would later be termed a Puritanical bias in matters of doctrine and scriptural interpretation and, especially in Revelation, anti-Roman Catholic sentiment. In its attempt to take account of Hebrew and Aramaic idiom in the Old Testament and Apocryphal texts and reference to the recent work of the age's foremost biblical scholar, Theodore Beza, on the New Testament the Geneva Bible marked a distinct advance in biblical scholarship over previous English versions. The Calvinist slant, despite the Bible's dedication to Elizabeth, however, prevented adoption for reading in English churches and the granting of royal approval. The Geneva Bible nevertheless became the standard version in English households; more than seventy complete editions as well as numerous separate editions of the New Testament were printed between 1560 and 1644, of which the first published in England is dated 1575.

A revised version of the Geneva New Testament by Laurence Tomson was first published in 1576. Tomson's translation proved popular and was subsequently frequently mated with the Geneva Old Testament and Apocrypha. It preserves much of its predecessor's phraseology and reproduces many, though not all, of the Geneva's annotations complete with that version's doctrinal posture and supplemented by the translator's own extensive contributions. Among the traits that set it apart from the Geneva New Testament is Tomson's idiosyncratic use of 'that' to translate the Greek article, τὶς, which is discernible in two of Middleton's citations.

Although the scholarship of the Geneva Bible was generally acknowledged to have superseded that of all earlier English translations, its failure to attract royal approval and authorization for use in churches left a conspicuous gap which the Bishops' Bible, first published in 1568, was intended to fill. The Bible's name derives from the distribution of the labours of translation and revision among sixteen or more bishops and other high-ranking churchmen overseen by Archbishop Matthew Parker. The Great Bible (1539), which had formerly been sanctioned for church use, was employed as the basis of the Bishops' Bible. In clear reference to the Geneva Bible, Parker remarked in a letter to Elizabeth's chief minister, Sir William Cecil, that the new Bible avoided provision of 'bitter notes upon any text'. Such notes as accompanied scriptural passages side-stepped controversy and confined themselves to matters calling for straightforward and unprovocative explanation. Within four years of initial publication the translation of the Psalms included in the Bible was replaced by that of the Book of Common Prayer, which in turn was essentially that of the Great Bible. This move was undoubtedly dictated by the form of the Psalms incorporated into the service of the Established Church since adoption of the Great Bible for church use. Psalm citations in *The Two Gates* uniformly match the wording of the Prayer Book Psalter and commonly printed in Bishops' Bible from 1572.

Motto ***Animæ ... ipse*** St Augustine, 'de Quantitate Animæ', 1.2 (Migne, *Patrologiæ Latinæ*, vol. 32, 1035–6): 'The soul's homeland is God himself.'

Preface.26 first *Adam* ... to death reference to the typological vision that sees Christ as the antitype of Adam

27 quitted repaid, requited

we were beaten out of *paradise* and entertained into *heaven*. The *tree* of *good* and *evil* brought forth an *apple* to cast us all away, and the *tree* of *shame* bore a fruit to save us all for ever.

God, being throughly angered with *mankind* for disobedience, put a sharp bridle into his mouth. That bridle was the law; that law was a curst *judge* and ready to condemn. But the King of *heaven* being as full of mercy as of justice, abated the edge of the axe, and to a heavy *sentence* added a comfortable *pardon*. The *balsamum* of grace healed the wounds of the law; law did both promise and threaten. The gospel should perform and reconcile. The bitterness of the law was tasted, but the sweetness of *grace* could not be relished but by hope. It was fit, therefore, that we lying so sick should be kept in hand that a *physician* was coming; and hereupon was *Christ* promised, even from the beginning. He was promised not once but often. Often, to show that God was mindful of our saving health; and by many mouths was the news brought to seal up the tidings with more assurance and credit.

Moses was the first that took upon him the office of a trumpeter and proclaimed the coming of a *Messiah* at least four thousand years before he set forth; and because he was to spring from the stock of *Judah*, he, like an industrious *herald*, took especial pains in drawing that *genealogy*. It rested not so, for old *Jacob* lying on his deathbed foretold that *Shiloh* should come; and who was that *Shiloh* but *Messiah*? Gen. 38 Gen. 49

Balaam, instead of cursing, altered his tunes through the charms of the most high, and sung sweetly of a saviour. Exod. 24:17

What is that ladder which *Jacob* saw in his dream, reaching from earth to heaven, but that scale of our ascending up thither (*Jesus Christ*)? Gen. 28:12

And what other *paschal lamb* stand we in need of than of him who is the true *Passover*? To preserve the memory of this expected *redeemer* more lively, sundry pictures of him, as it were, were drawn in the persons of others. Kings, priests, and prophets were appointed to be shadows of him that was the true and only substance. In *Isaac*, when he was ready to be sacrificed, was the figure of *Christ* going to be crucified. In *Joshua*, leading the children of *Israel* into the land of *Canaan*, was a *type* of our heavenly *Joshua*, *Christ Jesus*, conducting us to everlasting happiness. In the person of *David* he was the chief king and a conqueror. In *Solomon*, the builder up of the spiritual temple. In *Hezekiah*, the destroyer of all idolatry. Exod. 16:6 Gen. 22:8 Josh.

After these were faithful messengers sent out whose errands were prophecies, and their prophecies ending only in a *Messiah*.

Above the rest *Esay* sings loudest and clearest: he names *Christ's* forerunner and draws out *Christ's* kingdom in lively colours; his offices, his life, and his death are by him foretold. Isa. 40:3 Isa. 54

Jeremy celebrateth his birth, *Ezekiel* and *Daniel* boast of his coming. *Hosea* makes him a captain over *Judah* and *Israel*. *Joel*, a shepherd to gather the scattered sheep; *Amos*, a builder to raise up the tabernacle which was fallen; *Jonah* goes into the grave before him to show how many days he himself should lie there. *Obadiah*, *Micah*, *Nahum*, and all the rest of the heavenly *singers* bear a part in suchlike *hymns*: they have their voices in this high parliament, for the nearer the time approached in which Christ was to come, the louder did they proclaim him, and with more greedy eyes stood waiting for his presence, as people do for a strange king that is to take possession of a new kingdom. Jer. 31 & 33 Hos. 1:11 Joel 3 Amos 9:11 Jon. 17

They waited not in vain; neither was expectation deluded, for God, to prove that his prophets were no liars, was as good as his word: he kept his day, and sent a Saviour; in him the obligation of the *ritual* law was cancelled, in him all Jewish ceremony ended, in him all promises had performances, all foretellings their finishings. By him are *the gates of salvation set wide open*, in him alone all debts are

31 ***tree* of *shame*** i.e. the cross
37 **abated** blunted
39 ***balsamum*** balm; a conventional typological trope represents Christ as a physician and his grace as healing or curing balm
45 **hand** expectation
53 **four thousand years** difficult to reconcile with contemporary chronologies. Edmund Coote in *The English Schoolmaster* (1596), pp. 67–8, places Moses 1494 years before Christ; the Geneva Bible (1597) reckons this period to be 1514 years; and the Bishops' Bible (1602) calculates that 1510 years separate Moses's giving of the law and the nativity of Christ.
54–5 **stock of *Judah*** Geneva–Tomson glosses Matt. 1:1: 'Jesus Christ came of Abraham of the tribe of Judah, and of the stock of David, as God promised.'
56 **rested not so** did not continue or remain in that condition
57 ***Shiloh*** Gen. 49:10. The Geneva Bible interprets this reference as a prophecy of Christ.
60.n **Exod. 24:17** mistaken reference for Num. 24:17
65 ***paschal lamb*** lamb sacrificed at Passover; Christ
66 ***Passover*** paschal lamb
70–4 **shadows . . . figure . . . *type*** terms conventionally used in typological formulations
73–4 **leading . . . *Canaan*** Josh. 13 and 14
79 **destroyer . . . idolatry** chiefly set out in 2 Kgs. 18–20 and 2 Chr. 29–32
83 ***Esay*** a form of Isaiah that appears in Ecclesiasticus (Apocrypha) 48:20–2, and common in the Bishops' Bible
87 ***Jeremy*** Greek—and hence New Testament—form of Jeremiah
99–100 **people . . . new kingdom** possibly a reminiscence of the entry of James I into London on 15 March 1604 for which Middleton composed a speech: see *The Whole Royal and Magnificent Entertainment*.
104–6 ***ritual* law . . . ceremony ended** Joseph Hall, *The Passion Sermon*, sig. $\mathrm{C}2^{\mathrm{v}}$, p. 10: '*Christ is the end of the law.* What Law? Ceremonial, moral. Of the moral, it was kept perfectly by himself, satisfied fully for us. Of the ceremonial, it was referred to him, observed of him, fulfilled in him, abolished by him.'

paid, through his means the *prophets* and *evangelists* hold hands and embrace. It is he that hath *married the Old and New Testament* together; five thousand years and more hath a parliament been held about his birth-right, and both the *upper house* and the *lower house*, *heaven* and *earth*, are now agreed upon it. In conclusion, this chronicle he writes of himself, and this epitome do we set forth of his acts, *Consummatum est*, all is now finished.

What is finished? Whatsoever was foretold, all the prophets gave out that the prince of *heaven* should dwell upon earth, and lo, the omnipotent king, his father, hath sent him hither. Shall I set down the gests of his progress? These they are: he first set out from his celestial palace and lodged in the womb of a *virgin*, when he left that blessed habitation he lay next in a *manger*, from the *manger* he went to the *cross*, from the *cross* to the *sepulchre*, and from that *sepulchre* returned home again into *heaven*. Sweetly therefore hath it been sung by one of the most excellent singers in *David's* temple:

Hall, *in sermone Passionis Domini*

'*Nothing*', saith he, '*was ever foretold by the prophets of Christ which was not done; nothing was done by Christ which was not foretold. It would take up a life to compare the prophets and evangelists, the predictions and the history, and largely to discourse how the one foretells and the other answers.*'

Cast therefore your eyes upon this building, survey it from the foundation to the battlements; here shall you behold a wedding passing through

John 14:6. *Ego sum via.*

two gates, the one having sundry paths beaten out, and all leading to one way; the other directed by one path only whose steps do guide to all *happiness*.

The first is the *court-gate* at which prophets are the porters to open it, whilst angels are the footmen and forerunners, bringing news that the king is upon coming.

The second gate is an entrance to the very *palace* where the king shows himself in person after he is come. Four *evangelists* are the four *heralds* that sound forth his approaching and proclaim him king both of heaven and earth; here sits he crowned with the world at his feet, and his people round about him; he sits crowned with thorns, despised of the world, and betrayed by his people; but because you may take perfect knowledge of him, whom so they crowned, despised, and betrayed, a true relation shall be made of his honourable descent (being sprung from kings), of his marvellous birth (his mother being a pure *virgin*), of most base betraying him (the *traitor* feeding at his own table), of his ignominious death (the *tree* being accursed). And last of all, of his wondrous burial and most glorious resurrection, triumphing over *death* and *hell*. To prove all these things, behold witnesses stand ready on both sides who, *viva voce*, give in this evidence of him, *viz.*

Observations to be taken in reading this book

Upon every first page or leaf stand the prophets, and on the other page, right against it, are the evangelists: the one foretells the coming, the birth, the passion, etc., of Christ; the other shows wherein all the prophecies of him are fulfilled.

So that after you have read the words of the prophets at the upper end of the first leaf, marked thus ⊕, with a circled cross, you are, if you would truly follow the method of this book, next to read the words of the evangelists on the other side, marked likewise as the former ⊕, with a circled cross.

And so still if you read any verse quoted with any other marks, as + ‡ ¶, etc., behold the like mark on the other side just opposite to it; for the matter of the one is answerable to, and makes plain, the other.

In reading the prophets you shall find that they speak of things to come as if they were already past; but note that they do this of purpose to show the certainty of all their prophecies, which they know could not choose but happen because God himself was the revealer of those secrets to them.

T.M.

111–12 **five thousand years and more** The chronology corresponds roughly to some contemporary historical thinking. Edmund Coote in *The English Schoolmaster* (1596) gives the year 1596 as 5524 years from the creation, a figure more or less in keeping with the 1597 Geneva Bible's 5564 years; Thomas Buckminster's *Almanack and Prognostication for the Year 1598* sets the creation 5560 years earlier. The Bishops' Bible (1602) in its 'Genealogy of Adam' prefixed to the scriptures, however, places Christ's birth at 5199 years from the creation of the world.

117 ***Consummatum est*** i.e. 'it is finished', the Latin rendering of Christ's last words in the Vulgate Bible, John 19:30, and the text of Hall's *Passion Sermon*

122 **gests** stages of a journey

130.n **Hall, *in sermone Passionis Domini*** i.e. Joseph Hall, *The Passion Sermon*, delivered at Paul's Cross, 14 April 1609, and published in two issues of the first edition and a second edition in the same year. The passage cited, which is slightly inaccurate, appears on sig. B3, p. 5.

139.n ***Ego sum via*** from one of the Latin Bibles (e.g. Beza, Tremellius, Vulgate): 'I am the way'

142 ***court-gate*** the gate of a court or courtyard; the gate of the king's court

164 ***viva voce*** by word of mouth (Latin)

173–5 **marked thus . . . book** Although they essentially duplicate the numbers used to link parallel Old and New Testament passages, the early edition of the pamphlet also incorporates matching symbols set in the inner margins of facing pages. The present edition does not reproduce these symbols or the rules framing the text on each page: modern readers are more familiar with this kind of linked arrangement and do not need the extra help provided by these further typographical indications.

The first Gate.

On this side are placed the prophets, giving testimony of so much as is revealed to them of Christ; and because the stock of which, according to the flesh, he was to come is one of the first matters which they handle, you shall first see how the prophets derive his *pedigree*, and then, on the other side, how the evangelist confirms it. Hearken therefore to the mutual sounds which their heavenly music sends forth.

i

Christ is that blessing which was lost in *Adam*, and promised to be recovered in the seed of *Abram*.

The Lord said to Abram, *I will make of thee a great* nation, *and will bless thee and make thy name great, and thou shalt be a* blessing. Gen. 12:2

ii

The Lord visited Sarah, *as he had said, and did unto her according as he had promised: for* Sarah *conceived and bore* Abraham *a son in his old age at the same season that God told him; and* Abraham *called his son's name that was born unto him,* Isaac. Gen. 21:1, 2

iii

Out of Judah.

And thou, Bethlehem Ephratah, *art little to be amongst the thousands of* Judah, *yet out of thee shall he come forth unto me that shall be* ruler in Israel, *whose goings forth have been from the beginning and from everlasting.* Mic. 5:2

iv

Formam viri assumendo, et de fæmina nascendo, utrumque sexum hoc modo honorandum indicavit. Aug.

Therefore the Lord himself will give you a sign; behold the Virgin *shall conceive and bear a son, and he shall call his name* Immanuel. Isa. 7:14

v

For lo, thou shalt conceive and bear a son, and no razor shall come on his head, for the child shall be a Nazarite *unto God from his birth, and he shall begin to save* Israel *out of the hands of the* Philistines. Judg. 13:5, Sam. 1:11, Num. 6:3

vi

Christ his kingdom at the beginning is small and contemptible.

He shall grow up as a root out of a dry ground; he hath neither form nor beauty; when we shall see him, there shall be no form that we should desire him. He is despised and rejected of men. Isa. 53:2, 3

References to passages in the body of the work are by section number, testament (I for Old, II for New), and line number or marginal column (s for source, c for commentary). Thus 65.II.4 refers to section 65, New Testament passage, line 4. The early printed text contains two numbered sequences of sections, the first running from 1 to 17 and the second from 1 to 92; in this edition the first sequence is printed with roman numerals to distinguish it from the second. The introductory and concluding sections in these sequences are identified as a, xviia, o, and 92a in references.

i.I Geneva

c Geneva's commentary to 'a blessing' reads, 'The world shall recover by thy seed, which is Christ, the blessing which they lost in Adam.'

ii.I Geneva, with omission of 'which Sarah bore him' before '*Isaac*', 5

s The citation extends to Gen. 21:3.

iii.I Geneva, with 'among' altered to '*amongst*', 1, and 'the' omitted before 'ruler', 3

c untraced (a duplicate of iii.II.c)

iv.I Geneva, with a change of 'she' to '*he*' in the final clause

c The sense of this passage appears in St Augustine in various sermons (e.g. Sermon 51.3, Migne, *Patrologiæ Latinæ*, vol. 38, 334–5, Sermon 190.2, Migne, vol. 38, 1007–8), but the precise wording of the marginal notation has not been traced; 'He made known by taking the form of a man and by being born of a woman that each sex should in this way be honoured.'

v.I Geneva

vi.I Geneva

c Geneva glosses 'root': 'The beginning of Christ's kingdom shall be small, and contemptible in the sight of men, but it shall grow wonderfully, and flourish before God.'

On this side the evangelists are ready to subscribe to all that which the prophets set down. The one draws Christ in picture, the other shows him in person. His kindred are scattered amongst the prophets and reckoned together amongst the evangelists. *Moses* fetcheth his descent from *Abram* and *David*, not showing the direct line; but *Matthew*, the first work he doth, draws out his true *genealogy*.

i

Matt. 1:1 *This is the* book *of the* generation *of Jesus Christ, the son of* David, *the son of* Abram.

The Messiah sprung both from *Abraham* of the tribe of *Judah*, and from the stock of *David*.

ii

Idem, 1:2, 1:6, 1:16 Abraham *begat* Isaac, *and* Isaac *begat* Jacob, etc. Obed *begat* Jesse, *and* Jesse *begat* David, etc. Nathan *begat* Jacob, *and* Jacob *begat* Joseph, *the husband of* Mary, *of whom was born* Jesus, *that is called* Christ.

Read Luke 3:23, where the genealogy of Christ is likewise set down, proving his descent from *Adam*.

iii

Matt. 2:4 Herod *asked where* Christ *should be born, and they said unto him, At* Bethlehem *in* Judah, *for so it is written by the prophet; and thou,* Bethlehem, *in the land of* Judah, *art not the least amongst the princes of* Judah, *for out of thee shall come the governor that shall feed my people* Israel.

Out of Judah.

iv

Matt. 1:22 *And all this was done that it might be fulfilled which was spoken of the Lord by the prophet, saying, Behold, a virgin shall be with child and shall bear a son, and they shall call his name* Immanuel, *which is by interpretation,* God *with us.*

Nobilitas fuit Christi nascentis, in virginitate parientis; nobilitas parientis, in divinitate nascentis. Aug.

v

Matt. 2:23 *And* Joseph *went and dwelt in a city called* Nazareth, *that it might be fulfilled which was spoken by the prophets, which was that he should be called a* Nazarite.

vi

Luke 2:7 *And she brought forth her first begotten son, and wrapped him in swaddling clothes, and laid him in a* manger, *because there was no room for them in the inn.*

Ubi aula regia? Ubi thronus? Ubi curiæ regalis frequentia? Nunquid aula est stabulum? Thronus præsepium? Et totius curiæ frequentia Joseph et Maria?

i.II Bishops' (although it and other versions read 'Abraham')
c Geneva–Tomson comments on Matt. 1:1: 'Jesus Christ came of Abraham of the tribe of Judah, and of the stock of David, as God promised.'
ii.II Geneva or Geneva–Tomson; Middleton appears to have adopted Luke's 'Nathan' in place of Matthew's 'Matthan' in Christ's genealogy, Matt. 1:15.
s The cited fragments are from Matt. 1:2, 5–6, 15–16.
c untraced
iii.II The occurrence of 'Bethleem' in the unmodernized text of *The Two Gates* and in Geneva–Tomson (derived from Theodorus Beza) points to this version; with 'Herod' substituted for 'he', and 'of them' omitted after '*asked*', 1.
s The citation covers Matt. 2:4–6.
c untraced (a duplicate of iii.I.c)
iv.II Geneva or Geneva–Tomson
c St Augustine, sermon 200.2, 'In Epiphania Domini' (Migne, *Patrologiæ Latinæ*, vol. 38, 1029): 'Christ's nobility sprang from his virgin birth; his mother's nobility from her child's divinity.'
v.II Geneva or Geneva–Tomson, with 'Joseph' added before '*went*', 1
vi.II Geneva–Tomson, except for the substitution of 'manger' (Bishops') for 'cratch'
c source untraced, possibly St Augustine; 'Where is the royal palace? Where the throne? Where the royal assembly of the court? Is there no palace but a stable? No throne but a manger? And the assembly of the whole court but Joseph and Mary?'

vii

I shall see him, but not now; I shall behold him, but not near; there shall come a star of Jacob *and a scepter shall rise of Israel, and shall smite the coasts of* Moab, *and destroy all the sons of* Sheth. Num. 24:17

viii

The kings of Tarshish *and of the isles shall bring presents; the kings of* Arabia *and* Saba *shall bring gifts; all kings shall fall down before him; all nations shall do him service. He shall live, and unto him shall be given of the gold of* Sheba; *they shall also pray for him continually, and daily bless him.* Ps. 72:10

ix

When Israel *was a child, then I loved him, and called my son out of* Egypt. Hos. 11:1

x

Therefore the Lord thy God humbled thee, and made thee hungry, and fed thee with man *which thou knewest not, neither did thy fathers know it, that he might teach thee that man liveth not by bread only, but by every word that proceedeth out of the mouth of the Lord doth a man live.* Deut. 8:3

xi

There shall no evil happen unto thee, neither shall any plague come nigh thy dwelling: for he shall give his angels charge over thee, to keep thee in all thy ways; they shall bear thee in their hands, that thou hurt not thy foot against a stone. Ps. 91:11

vii.I Geneva, with an apparently accidental reversal of '*all the*' in the final clause in the early edition

viii.I The opening to '*gifts*', 2, is closer to Geneva (Bishops' has 'give' in place of '*bring*') except for provision of 'Arabia', which is the Bishops' reading; but Geneva provides a marginal gloss identifying 'Sheba' as a part of Arabia, which may have been responsible for the switch (cf. xvii.II). The phraseology of the next verse, Ps. 72:11, down to '*service*' is Bishops'; and the final verse, from Ps. 72:15, mixes Geneva ('*he shall live, and unto him*') and Bishops' ('*shall be given of the gold of*'), and then reverts to Geneva for 'Sheba' (Bishops' reads 'Arabia') to the end. Preservation of 'Sheba' is curiously at odds with the earlier change to 'Arabia'.

s The reference should read Ps. 72:10, 11, 15.

ix.I Geneva

x.I Geneva

2 **man** manna, the substance miraculously supplied as food to the Children of Israel during their progress through the wilderness

xi.I Bishops' (after '*dwelling*', 2, Bishops' and Geneva concur)

s The reference should be Ps. 91:10, 11, 12.

vii

Matt. 2:1 *When Jesus was born at* Bethlehem, *a city of* Jewry, *in the days of* Herod *the king, behold there came wise men from the east to* Jerusalem, *saying, Where is he that is born King of the Jews? For we have seen his star in the east, and are come to worship him.* Worshippers of Christ.

viii

Matt. 2:10, 11 *And when the wise men saw the star, they rejoiced with an exceeding great joy, and went into the house, and found the babe with* Mary, *his mother, and fell down and worshipped him, and opened their treasures, and presented unto him gifts, even gold and frankincense and myrrh.* *Aurum solvitur quasi regi magno, thus immolatur ut deo, myrrha præbetur tamquam pro salute omnium morituro.* Aug.

ix

Matt. 2:14 *So* Joseph *arose and took the babe and his mother by night, and departed into* Egypt, *and was there unto the death of* Herod, *that that might be fulfilled which is spoken of the Lord by the prophet, saying, Out of* Egypt *have I called my son.* Joseph's flight.

x

Matt. 4:2 *When Jesus had fasted forty days and forty nights, he was afterward hungry: then came unto him the tempter, and said, If thou be the son of God, command that these stones be made bread. But he answered, saying, Man shall not live by bread only, but by every word that proceedeth out of the mouth of God.* Christ is hungry.

xi

Matt. 4:6 *And the Devil said unto Christ, If thou be the son of God, cast thyself down: for it is written that he shall give his angels charge over thee, and with their hands they shall lift thee up, lest at any time thou shouldst dash thy foot against a stone.* Christ is tempted.

vii.II Bishops', except for the retention of 'Bethleem', a form favoured by Geneva (but modernized here to 'Bethlehem'), and the substitution of 'Jerusalem' for 'Hierusalem', which occurs in both Bishops' and Geneva
s The reference should read Matt. 2:1, 2.
c The Geneva-Tomson chapter-heading synopsis reads: 'The wise men, who are the first fruits of the Gentiles, worship Christ'.

viii.II '*frankincense*' points to Geneva-Tomson (Geneva reads 'incense'); although this term appears also in Bishops', this version's phraseology otherwise differs markedly.
c The sense of this passage appears in various locations in St Augustine (e.g. several Epiphany sermons: Sermon 202.2, Migne, *Patrologiæ Latinæ*, vol. 38, 1034; *Sermones Suppositii* 136.4, 6, Migne, vol. 39, 2014, 2015, and 139.2, Migne, vol. 39, 2018), but the source of this specific wording has not been traced; 'Gold is offered as to a great king, frankincense as to a god, myrrh is presented as to one who will die for the salvation of all.'

ix.II Geneva or Geneva-Tomson, with 'Joseph' in place of 'he'
s The reference should read Matt. 2:14, 15.
c The Geneva-Tomson chapter-heading synopsis for Matt. 2:14 reads: 'Joseph fleeth into Egypt with Jesus and his mother'

x.II Geneva or Geneva-Tomson, with minor alterations: ('*unto*' for 'to' at 2, and '*answered saying*' for 'he answering, said, It is written' at 4)
s The reference should read Matt. 4:2, 3, 4.
c presumably a paraphrase drawn from Matt. 4:2

xi.II Geneva or Geneva-Tomson, with the addition of '*the Devil*' and change of 'him' to '*Christ*' in the opening line, and a change of 'he will' to '*he shall*' at 2
c Both the Geneva-Tomson headline and the chapter-heading synopsis for Matt. 4:1 read 'Christ is tempted'

xii

The great light of the Gentiles.

Yet the darkness shall not be according to the affliction that it had, when at the first he touched lightly the land of Zabulon *and the land of* Nephthalim; *nor afterward when he was more grievous by the way of the sea beyond* Jordan *in* Galilee *of the Gentiles. The people that walked in darkness have seen a great light: they that dwelled in the land of the shadow of death, upon them hath the light shined.*

Isa. 9:1, 2

xiii

The spirit of the Lord is upon me, to preach the acceptable year of the Lord, and the day of vengeance of our God, to comfort all that mourn, to appoint unto them that mourn in Zion, *and to give unto them beauty for ashes, the oil of joy for mourning, the garment of gladness for the spirit of heaviness.*

Isa. 61:1

xiv

Christ's poverty and affliction.

Surely he hath borne our infirmities, and carried our sorrows; he was wounded for our transgressions, broken for our iniquities, the chastisement of our peace was upon him, and with his stripes we are healed.

Isa. 53:4

xv

His humility.

Rejoice greatly, O daughter Zion; *shout for joy, O daughter* Jerusalem: *behold, thy king cometh unto thee, even the righteous and saviour, poor and riding upon an* ass, *and upon a* colt, *the foal of an* ass.

Zech. 9:9, Isa. 62:11

xvi

Betraying.

Yea, even mine own familiar friend, whom I trusted, which did also eat of my bread, hath laid great wait for me.

Ps. 41:9

xvii

Sold for a price.

And I said unto them, If you think it good, give me my wages, and if no, leave off. And so they weighed for my wages thirty pieces of silver. And the Lord said unto me, Cast it unto the potter: a goodly price that I was valued at of them. And I took the thirty pieces of silver and cast them to the potter in the house of the Lord.

Zech. 11:12, 13

xii.I Geneva, with minor alterations (influenced by the New Testament passage)
4 ***grievous*** oppressive; severe
c presumably derived from the parallel passage from Matt.

xiii.I Geneva, with omission of the remainder of 61:1 following '*upon me*', 1
s The passage runs from the opening of 61:1 to 61:2 and part way through 61:3.

xiv.I Geneva, with omission of 'yet we did judge him as plagued, and smitten of God, and humbled. But' after '*sorrows*', 1, and 'he was' after '*transgressions*', 2
c possibly influenced by a headline above the parallel passage from Matt. 8 in Geneva and Geneva–Tomson: 'Christ's poverty'

xv.I Bishops'
c Geneva glosses Zech. 9:9: 'Which declareth that they should not look for such a king as should be glorious in the eyes of man, but should be poor, and yet in himself have all power to deliver his: and this is meant of Christ, as Matt. 21:5'; the marginal commentary to xv.II may be the direct source, however.

xvi.I Bishops'
c presumably influenced by the commentary for the parallel New Testament passage

xvii.I Geneva, except for the addition of '*And*' in the phrase '*And so they weighed*', 2
c Since it duplicates the commentary to xvii.II, that for xvii.I presumably either was deliberately designed to mirror the opposed passage (to emphasize the correspondence, for example), or signals an error in the manuscript or the setting.

xii

Matt. 4:13 *And Jesus leaving* Nazareth *went and dwelt in* Capernaum, *which is near the sea, in the borders of* Zabulon *and* Nephthalim, *that it might be fulfilled which was spoken by* Esaias *the prophet, saying, The land of* Zabulon *and the land of* Nephthalim *by the way of the sea, beyond* Jordan, Galilee *of the Gentiles; the people which sat in darkness saw great light, and to them which sat in the region and shadow of death, light is risen up.*

xiii

Matt. 5:1 *When Jesus saw the multitude, he went up into a mountain, and when he was set, his disciples came to him, and he opened his mouth and taught them, saying, Blessed are they that mourn, for they shall be comforted.*

xiv

Matt. 8:16, 17 *They brought unto Jesus many that were possessed with devils, and he cast out the spirits with his word, and healed all that were sick: that it might be fulfilled which was spoken by* Esaias *the prophet, saying, He took our infirmities and bore our sicknesses.*

This shows that in Christ only we should seek remedy in all our miseries.

xv

Matt. 21:4, 5 *All this was done that it might be fulfilled which was spoken by the prophets, saying, Tell ye the daughter of* Zion, *behold thy king cometh unto thee, meek, and sitting upon an ass, and a colt, the foal of the* ass *used to the yoke.*

Christ's humility.

xvi

Matt. 26:23 *Jesus said unto his disciples, He that dippeth his hand with me in the dish, he shall betray me.*

Betraying. Whom I vouchsafe to come to my table.

xvii

Matt. 27:9, 10 *Then was fulfilled that which was spoken by* Zecharias *the prophet, saying, And they took thirty silver pieces, the price of him that was valued, whom they of the children of* Israel *valued, and gave them for the potter's field, as the Lord appointed me.*

Sold for a price.

xii.II Geneva or Geneva–Tomson, with the addition of '*Jesus*' in the opening line
s The reference should read Matt. 4:13, 14, 15, 16.
xiii.II Geneva or Geneva–Tomson, with substitution of '*Jesus*' for 'he' and omission of Matt. 5:3
s The reference should read Matt. 5:1, 2, 4.
xiv.II Geneva or Geneva–Tomson
c Geneva–Tomson glosses Matt. 8:16: 'Christ, in healing divers diseases, showeth that he was sent of his Father, that in him only we should seek remedy in all our miseries'.
xv.II Geneva or Geneva–Tomson, with minor alterations ('*prophets*' for 'prophet', 'Zion' for 'Sion', and '*the* ass' for 'an ass')
c Geneva–Tomson glosses Matt. 21:1: 'Christ by his humility triumphing over the pride of this world, ascendeth to true glory by ignominy of the cross'; 'Christ's humility' appears as a headline to Geneva, Isa. 42.
xvi.II Geneva or Geneva–Tomson, with alteration of the opening of v. 23: 'And he answered and said'
c Geneva–Tomson glosses Matt. 26:23: 'That is to say, whom I vouchsafed to come to my table, alluding to the place, Ps. 41:10, which is not so to be understood, as though at the self-same instant that the Lord spoke these words Judas had his hand in the dish (for that had been an undoubted token) but it is meant of his tabling and eating with them'.
xvii.II Geneva or Geneva–Tomson, with the substitution of 'Zecharias' for 'Jeremias', possibly prompted by the accompanying gloss: 'Seeing this prophecy is read in Zech. 11:12 it cannot be denied but Jeremy's name crept into the text through the printer's fault, or by some other's ignorance: it may be also that it came out of the margin, by reason of the abbreviation of the letters, the one being "iou", the other "zou", which are not much unlike. But in the Syrian text the prophet's name is not set down at all', or by Hall's comment in *The Passion Sermon*, sig. B4, p. 7, quoting this passage, 'Zachary (miswritten Jeremy, by one letter mistaken in the abbreviation)'; 'they' also omitted from v. 10.
c Geneva–Tomson glosses Matt. 27:3: 'An example of the horrible judgement of God, as well against them which sell Christ, as against them which buy Christ'.

Lo, thus in order hath been presented to your best eye—your soul—from Christ's dear and miraculous birth to his base and *Jewish* undervaluing. What follows shall offer itself to your religious view more amply, though not so nicely.

Here now bestow your eyes, and that worthily, upon this heavenly *coherence* following, in those principal and saving effects of *the Old and New Testament*, that

Are now in marriage, knit in heavenly bands,
To which they join their everlasting hands.

I

God approveth not hereby that light divorcement, but permitteth it to avoid further inconvenience.

When a man taketh a wife and marrieth her, if so be she find no favour in his eyes because he hath espied some filthiness in her, then let him write her a bill of divorcement, and put it in her hand, and send her out of his house. Deut. 24:1

2

'Wilderness': that is, in *Babylon* and other places where they were kept in captivity and misery.

A voice crieth in the wilderness: Prepare ye the way of the Lord, make straight in the desert a path for our God. Isa. 40:3

3

Ye shall not swear by my name falsely, neither shalt thou defile the name of thy God: I am the Lord. Lev. 19:12, Exod. 20:7, Deut. 5:11

4

Thou shalt open thy hand unto thy poor brother, and shalt lend him sufficient for his need which he hath. Deut. 15:8

5

O cast thy burden upon the Lord, and he shall nourish thee, and shall not suffer the righteous to fall for ever. Ps. 55:23

6

Crying tears.

Away from me all you that work vanity, for the Lord hath heard the voice of my weeping. Ps. 6:8

xviia.I.5 **nicely** precisely, exactly
o.I.4 **marriage** disyllabic
heavenly disyllabic (confirmed by the corresponding term at o.II.4, 'sacred')
1.I Geneva
c Geneva glosses 'then . . . divorcement': 'Hereby God approveth not that light divorcement, but permitteth it to avoid further inconvenience, Matt. 19:7'.
2.I Geneva
c Geneva glosses 'wilderness': 'That is, in Babylon and other places where they were kept in captivity, and misery.'
3.I Geneva
4.I Geneva
5.I Although the wording and verse numbering (the cited passage is v. 22 in Geneva) of the Bishops' text and the Book of Common Prayer Psalter agree, the unmodernized spelling, '*burthen*', which appears in *The Two Gates*, occurs only in the Psalter. Reference to the Psalter is not assured, however, since Middleton appears to have independently employed the spelling, '*burthens*', for the second of two uses of this term in 57.II.
6.I opening clause ('*Away . . . vanity*'): Bishops'; the second clause ('*for . . . weeping*') could be either Bishops' or Geneva.

Thus have you received a heavenly taste of Christ, from his cradle to his cross. What follows of him now shall appear more largely, though more irregularly, wherein I rather observe material fulness than formal niceness.

Here now bestow your eyes, and that worthily, upon this heavenly *coherence* following, in those principal and saving effects of *the Old and New Testament*, that

Are now in marriage, knit in sacred bands,
To which they join their everlasting hands.

1

Matt. 1:19 *Then* Joseph, *her husband, being a just man, and not willing to make her a public example, was minded to put her away secretly.*

2

Matt. 3:3 *For this is he of whom it is spoken by the prophet* Esaias, *saying, The voice of him that crieth in the wilderness, prepare you the way of the Lord, make his paths straight.*

Make him a plain and smooth way.

3

Matt. 5:33 *Thou shalt not forswear thyself, but shalt perform thine oaths to the Lord.*

4

Matt. 5:42 *Give to him that asketh, and from him that would borrow of thee, turn not away.*

5

Matt. 6:25 *Therefore I say unto you, Be not careful for your life, what ye shall eat, or what you shall drink: nor yet for your body, what you shall put on; is not the life more worth than meat, and the body than raiment? Behold the fowls of the heavens,* etc.

The carefulness of this life is worthily checked by thinking on the providence of God.

6

Matt. 7:22, 23 *Many will say to me in that day, Lord, Lord, have we not by thy name prophesied, and by thy name cast out devils, and by thy name done many great works? Then Christ will say unto them, I never knew you: depart from me, ye that work iniquity.*

'I never knew you': this is not of ignorance, but because he will cast them away.

xviia.II.4 niceness precision, exactness
0.II.4 marriage disyllabic
1.II Geneva or Geneva–Tomson
2.II Omission of 'is' after '*wilderness*' points to Geneva–Tomson.
c cited directly from Geneva–Tomson
3.II Geneva or Geneva–Tomson
4.II Geneva or Geneva–Tomson
5.II Geneva or Geneva–Tomson
s The citation extends into Matt. 6:26.
c Geneva–Tomson glosses 'Therefore ... life': 'The froward carking carefulness for things of this life, is corrected in the children of God by an earnest thinking upon the providence of God'.
6.II Geneva (Geneva–Tomson has 'unto me', 1), with a change apparently introduced for clarity: '*Then Christ will say unto them*' for 'And then I will profess to them'
c Geneva–Tomson glosses 'I never knew you': 'This is not of ignorance, but because he will cast them away'.

7

By the word 'clean' is meant, of birds which were permitted to be eaten.

And the priest shall go out of the camp, and the priest shall consider him: and if the plague of leprosy be healed in the leper, then shall the priest command to take for him that is cleansed two sparrows alive and clean, and cedar wood, and a scarlet lace, and hyssop. Lev. 14:3, 4

8

The wickedness of times, and the danger.

Trust ye not in a friend, neither put ye confidence in a counsellor. Keep the doors of thy mouth from her that lieth in thy bosom; for the son revileth the father, the daughter riseth up against her mother, and the daughter-in-law against the mother-in-law, and a man's enemies are the men of his own house. Mic. 7:5, 6

9

'The broken-hearted' are those that are lively touched with the feeling of their sins.

'The captives': those which are in the bondage of sin.

The spirit of the Lord God is upon me, therefore hath the Lord anointed me, he hath sent me to preach the gospel unto the poor, to bind up the broken-hearted, to preach liberty to the captives, and to them that are bound, the opening of the prison. Isa. 61:1

10

'My messenger': that is meant of *John Baptist*, as Christ expoundeth it. Luke 7:27.

Behold, I will send my messenger, and he shall prepare the way before me; and the Lord whom you seek shall speedily come to his temple, even the messenger of the covenant whom you desire, behold, he shall come, saith the Lord of hosts. Mal. 3:1

11

Here *John Baptist*, both for his zeal and restoring of religion, is aptly compared to *Elias*.

Behold, I will send you Elias *the prophet before the coming of the great and fearful day of the Lord, and he shall turn the heart of the fathers to their children, and the heart of the children to their fathers, lest I come and smite the earth with cursing.* Mal. 4:5, 6

12

'The old way': wherein the patriarchs and prophets walked, directed by the word of God.

Thus saith the Lord, Stand in the ways, and behold, and ask for the old way, which is the good way, and walk therein, and you shall find rest for your souls. Jer. 6:16

13

Christ is called a 'servant' in respect of his manhood.

'He shall not cry nor lift up the voice,' *etc.*: that is, his coming shall not be with pomp and noise, as earthly princes'.

Behold, my servant: I will stay upon him: mine elect in whom my soul delighteth; I have put my spirit upon him; he shall bring forth judgement to the Gentiles; he shall not cry, nor lift up, nor cause his voice to be heard in the street, a bruised reed shall he not break, and the smoking flax shall he not quench; he shall bring forth judgement in truth. Isa. 42:1, 2, 3

7.I Geneva
c Geneva glosses 'clean': 'Of birds which were permitted to be eaten.'
8.I Geneva, with minor alterations (addition of '*and*' ('*and the daughter-in-law*') at 4, substitution of '*the mother-in-law*' for 'her mother-in-law' 4–5)
c Geneva gives 'The wickedness of those times' in the chapter-heading synopsis for Mic. 7:4.
9.I Geneva, with the substitution of '*the gospel*' for 'good tidings'
c Geneva glosses 'broken-hearted': 'To them that are lively touched with the feeling of their sins'; and 'captives': 'Which are in the bondage of sin'.
10.I Geneva
c Geneva glosses 'messenger': 'This is meant of John Baptist, as Christ expoundeth it, Luke 7:27'.
11.I Bishops' with some elements from Geneva; alteration of 'Elijah' to the New Testament Greek form, 'Elias', was presumably dictated by a wish to sharpen the agreement between the parallel passages.
c Geneva glosses 'Elijah': 'This Christ expoundeth of John Baptist, Matt. 11:13, 14, who both for his zeal, and restoring of religion is aptly compared to Elijah'.
12.I Geneva, with 'ye' altered to '*you*', 3
c Geneva glosses 'old way': 'Wherein the patriarchs and prophets walked, directed by the word of God: signifying that there is no true way, but that which God prescribeth'.
13.I Geneva
c Geneva glosses 'my servant': 'That is, Christ, who in respect of his manhood is called here, servant'; and 'cry . . . street': 'His coming shall not be with pomp and noise, as earthly princes'.'

7

Matt. 8:2, 3, 4 *And lo, there came a leper and worshipped him, saying, Master, if thou wilt, thou canst make me clean. And Jesus, putting forth his hand, touched him, saying, I will; be thou clean. And immediately his leprosy was cleansed. Then Jesus said unto him, See thou tell no man, but go and show thyself unto the priest, and offer the gift that* Moses *commanded for a witness to them.*

In this Christ shows that he abhorreth no sinner that comes unto him, be he never so unclean.

8

Matt. 10:34, 35, 36 *Think not that I am come to send peace into the earth, but the sword; for I am come to set a man at variance against his father, and the daughter against her mother, and the daughter-in-law against her mother-in-law, and a man's enemies shall be they of his own household.*

Civil dissensions follow the preaching of the gospel.

9

Matt. 11:4, 5 *And Jesus said, Go and show* John *what things you hear and see: the blind receive sight, the halt do walk, the lepers are cleansed, the deaf hear, the dead are raised up, and the poor receive the gospel.*

Christ shows by his works that he is the promised *Messiah*.

10

Idem 9, 10 *But what went you out to see? A prophet? Yea, I say unto you, and more than a prophet: for this is he of whom it is written, Behold, I send my messenger before thy face, which shall prepare thy way before thee.*

Christ's testimony of *John*.

11

Matt. 11:13, 14 *All the prophets and the law prophesied unto* John, *and if you will receive it, this is that* Elias, *which was to come. He that hath ears to hear, let him hear.*

12

Matt. 11:29 *Take my yoke on you, and learn of me, that I am meek and lowly in heart, and you shall find rest unto your souls.*

13

Matt. 12:18, 19, 20, 21 *Behold my servant whom I have chosen, my beloved in whom*
my soul delighteth: I will put my spirit on him, and he shall
19 *show judgement unto the Gentiles; he shall not strive nor cry,*
20 *neither shall any man hear his voice in the streets; a bruised*
reed shall he not break, and smoking flax shall he not quench
21 *until he bring forth judgement unto victory. And in his name*
shall the Gentiles trust.

By 'judgement' is meant a settled state, because Christ was to publish true religion among the Gentiles.

7.II Geneva or Geneva–Tomson
c Geneva–Tomson glosses Matt. 8:2: 'Christ in healing the leprous with the touching of his hand showeth that he abhorreth no sinners that come unto him, be they never so unclean.'
8.II Geneva or Geneva–Tomson, with the omission of 'I came not to send peace' after '*earth*', 1
c cited directly from the Geneva–Tomson gloss to Matt. 10:34
9.II Geneva–Tomson, with omission of 'answering' and 'unto them' respectively before and after '*said*', 1, 'ye hear' changed to '*you hear*', 1, omission of 'and' after '*sight*', 2, and '*cleansed*', 3. (Geneva uses preterites—'have heard and seen'—and some different wording.)
c Geneva–Tomson glosses Matt. 11:1: 'Christ showeth by his works, that he is the promised Messias.'
10.II Geneva or Geneva–Tomson, with a substitution of '*you*' for 'ye' in '*went you*', 1
c Both the headline and the chapter-heading synopsis in Geneva–Tomson read, 'Christ's testimony of John'.
11.II Geneva–Tomson, with alteration of 'ye' to '*you*', 1
s The reference should be Matt. 11:13, 14, 15.
12.II Geneva or Geneva–Tomson, with 'ye shall' altered to '*you shall*', 2
13.II Geneva or Geneva–Tomson, with alteration of 'to' to '*unto*' in '*unto the Gentiles*', 3
c Geneva–Tomson glosses 'judgement': 'By judgement is meant a settled state, because Christ was to publish true religion among the Gentiles . . .'
publish disseminate

14

Behold God's terrible judgement and incomprehensible mercy met together.

Now the Lord had prepared a great fish to swallow up Jonas: Jon. 1:17
and Jonas *was in the belly of the fish three days and three*
nights.

15

Through their own malice, the hearts of the wicked are hardened.

And the Lord said, Go, and say unto this people, you shall hear Isa. 6:9, 10
indeed, but you shall not understand; you shall plainly see, and
not perceive: make the heart of this people fat, make their ears 10
heavy, and shut their eyes, lest they see with their eyes, and
hear with their ears, and understand with their hearts, and
convert, and he heal them.

16

I will open my mouth in a parable, I will declare hard sentences Ps. 78:2, 3, 4
of old, which we have heard and known, and such as our 3
fathers have told us, that we should not hide them from the 4
children of the generations to come, but to show the honour of
the Lord, his mighty and wonderful works that he hath done.

17

Their wickedness full ripe.

Put in your scythes, for the harvest is ripe; come, get you Joel 3:13
down, for the winepress is full, yea, the winepresses run over,
for their wickedness is great.

18

Who have kept the true fear of God and his religion.

They that be wise shall shine as the brightness of the Dan. 12:3
firmament; and they that turn many to righteousness shall
shine as the stars for ever and ever.

19

Thou shalt not discover the shame of thy brother's wife, for it Lev. 18:16
is thy brother's shame.

20

A fearful judgement against hypocrites.

Therefore the Lord said, Because this people come near unto Isa. 29:13, 14
me with their mouth, and honour me with their lips, but have
removed their hearts far from me, and their fear toward me
was taught by the precept of men; therefore, behold, I will 14
again do a marvellous work in this people, even a marvellous
work and a wonder: for the wisdom of their wise men shall
perish, and the understanding of their prudent men shall be
hid.

14.I Geneva, with substitution of 'Jonas' for 'Jonah', presumably either influenced by or for consonance with the New Testament citation

c Geneva glosses 'belly . . . nights': 'Thus the Lord would chastise his prophet with a most terrible spectacle of death, and hereby also confirmed him of his favour and support in this his charge, which was enjoined him.'

15.I Geneva

c Geneva glosses Isa. 6:9: 'Whereby is declared that for the malice of man God will not immediately take away his word, but he will cause it to be preached to their condemnation, whenas they will not learn thereby to obey his will, and be saved: hereby he exhorteth the ministers to do their duty, and answereth to the wicked murmurers, that through their own malice their heart is hardened.'

16.I Bishops'

17.I Geneva

c Geneva glosses 'scythes': 'Thus he shall encourage the enemies when their wickedness is full ripe to destroy one another, which he calleth the valley of God's judgement.'

18.I Geneva

c cited directly from Geneva

19.I Geneva

1, 2 ***shame*** privy members, 'parts of shame'

20.I Geneva, with the alteration of 'heart' to '*hearts*', 3

c Geneva glosses 'people . . . lips': 'Because they are hypocrites and not sincere in heart.'

14

Idem 40 *As* Jonas *was three days and three nights in the* whale's *belly, so shall the son of man be three days and three nights in the heart of the earth.*

15

Matt. 13:14, 15 *So in them is fulfilled the prophecy of* Esay, *which saith, By*
hearing you shall hear, and shall not understand, and seeing,
15 *you shall see, and shall not perceive: for this people's heart is*
waxed fat, and their ears are dull of hearing, and with their eyes they have winked, lest they should see with their eyes, and hear with their ears, and understand with their hearts, and should return that I might heal them.

16

Matt. 13:34, 35 *All these things spoke Jesus unto the people in parables, and* By 'parables' is meant grave and sentententious proverbs.
without a parable spoke he not unto them, that it might be fulfilled which was spoken by the prophets, saying, I will open my mouth in parables, and will utter the things that have been kept secret from the foundation of the world.

17

Matt. 13:38, 39 *The field is the world, the good seed are the children of the kingdom; but the tares are the children of the wicked, and the enemy that soweth them is the devil, and the harvest is the end of the world, and the reapers be the angels.*

18

Matt. 13:43 *Then shall the righteous shine as the sun in the kingdom of their father. Who hath ears to hear, let him hear.*

19

Matt. 14:3, 4 Herod *had taken* John *and bound him and put him in prison for* Herodias' *sake, his brother* Philip's *wife. For* John *said unto him, It is not lawful for thee to have her.*

20

Matt. 15:7, 8 *O hypocrites!* Esaias *prophesied well of you, saying, This* They are condemned for hypocrisy
people draweth near unto me with their mouth, and honoureth because they made the kingdom of
me with their lips, but their heart is far off from me, but in God to stand in outward things.
vain they worship me, teaching for doctrines, men's precepts.

14.II Geneva or Geneva–Tomson

15.II Geneva or Geneva–Tomson, with 'Esaias' altered to 'Esay', 1, 'ye' to '*you*' ('*you shall hear*' ... '*you shall see*'), 2–3, and the omission of 'prophecy' after '*which*', 1, and 'should' before '*understand*', 6

4–5 ***with ... winked*** they have shut their eyes to impropriety, faults

16.II Bishops', at least to '*spoke he not unto them*' ('that it ... prophets' is common to both, except that 'prophet' is singular); the remainder, Geneva

c Geneva glosses 'parables': 'This word signifieth grave and sententious proverbs, to the end that the doctrine might have the more majesty, and the wicked might thereby be confounded.'

17.II chiefly Geneva and Geneva–Tomson, with some elements of Bishops' (omission of 'and' after '*world*', 1, and 'but' at the start of the clause '*but the tares ...*'); Geneva–Tomson alone omits 'they are' after '*good seed*', 1.

18.II Bishops'

19.II Geneva or Geneva–Tomson

20.II probably Geneva–Tomson on the basis of '*far off*' ('far' in Geneva), 3

s The cited passage extends to Matt. 15:9.

c Geneva–Tomson glosses 'hypocrites': 'The same men are condemned for hypocrisy and superstition, because they made the kingdom of God to stand in outward things.'

21

God doth never repent; but he speaketh after our capacity.

When the Lord saw that the wickedness of man was great in the earth, and all the imaginations of the thoughts of his heart were only evil continually: then it repented the Lord that he had made man in the earth, and he was sorry in his heart.

Gen. 6:5, 6

22

'In the wilderness': that is, in barren hearts and ignorant.

The eyes of the blind shall be lightened, and the ears of the deaf be opened. Then shall the lame man leap as an hart, and the dumb man's tongue shall sing: for in the wilderness shall waters break forth, and rivers in the desert.

Isa. 35:5, 6

23

One witness shall not rise against a man for any trespass, or for any sin, or for any fault that he offendeth in, but at the mouth of two witnesses, or at the mouth of three witnesses, shall the matter be stablished.

Deut. 19:15

24

'The man': *Adam.*

The man said, This now is bone of my bones, and flesh of my flesh, she shall be called woman, because she was taken out of man. Therefore shall man leave his father and his mother, and shall cleave to his wife, and they shall be one flesh.

Gen. 2:23, 24

25

Not that God alloweth divorcement, but of two faults he inferreth the less.

Keep yourselves in your spirit, and let none transgress against the wife of his youth. If thou hatest her, put her away, saith the Lord God of Israel; yet he covereth the injury under his garment: therefore keep yourselves in your spirit and transgress not.

Mal. 2:15, 16

26

Against unbelievers.

Thus saith the Lord of hosts, If the residue of this people think it to be unpossible in their eyes in these days, should it therefore be unpossible in my sight?

Zech. 8:6

27

He that hath said unto his father and to his mother, I have not seen him; and he that knew not his brethren, nor knew his own children: those are they that have observed thy word, and shall keep thy covenant.

Deut. 33:9

21.1 Geneva
c Geneva glosses 'repented the Lord': 'God doth never repent, but he speaketh after our capacity, because he did destroy him, and in that, as it were, did disavow him to be his creature.'
3 ***repented...Lord*** caused the Lord to feel regret
22.1 Geneva, with rephrasing of the opening clause, 'Then shall the eyes of the blind be lightened', and alteration of 'out' to '*forth*', 4
c Geneva glosses 'wilderness', 3: 'They that were barren and destitute of the graces of God, shall have them given by Christ.'
23.1 Geneva
4 ***stablished*** rendered indubitable
24.1 Geneva
c untraced
25.1 Geneva, with substitution of '*transgress*' in '*let none transgress*', 1, for 'trespass' (presumably influenced by 'transgress' at 5), and omission of 'saith the Lord of hosts' after '*garment*', 4
c Geneva glosses 'put her away': 'Not that he doth allow divorcement, but of the two faults he showeth which is the less.'
26.1 Bishops'
c Geneva glosses the initial 'unpossible': 'He showeth wherein our faith standeth, that is, to believe that God can perform that which he hath promised, though it seem never so unpossible to man'.
27.1 Bishops'

21

Matt. 15:19, 20 *Out of the heart come evil thoughts, murders, adulteries, fornications, thefts, false testimonies, slanders: these are the things which defile the man, but to eat with unwashen hands defileth not the man.*

22

Matt. 15:30 *And great multitudes came unto Jesus, having with them halt, blind, dumb, maimed, and many other, and cast them down at Jesus' feet, and he healed them.*

'Maimed': whose members were weakened with the palsy or by nature.

23

Matt. 18:15, 16 *Moreover if thy brother shall trespass against thee, go and tell him his fault between thee and him alone: if he hear thee, thou hast won thy brother; but if he hear thee not, take yet with thee one or two, that by the mouth of two or three witnesses every word may be confirmed.*

24

Matt. 19:4, 5 *Christ said, Have you not read that he which made them at the beginning made them male and female, and said, For this cause shall a man leave father and mother, and cleave unto his wife, and they which were two shall be one flesh.**

*This word *flesh* is by a figure taken for the whole man.

25

Idem 9 *Whosoever shall put away his wife, except it be for whoredom, and marrieth another, committeth adultery, and whosoever marrieth her that is divorced doth commit adultery.*

26

Idem 24, 26 *It is easier for a camel to go through the eye of a needle, than for a rich man to enter into the kingdom of God. The disciples said, Who then can be saved? But Jesus beheld them, and said unto them, With men this is unpossible, but with God all things are possible.*

Theophilact noteth that by this word *camel* is meant a cable, which though it be granted, it takes away nothing of the wonder.

27

Idem 29 *Whosoever shall forsake houses, or brethren, or sisters, or father, or mother, or wife, or children, or lands for my name's sake, he shall receive an hundred fold more, and shall inherit everlasting life.*

21.II Geneva or Geneva–Tomson
3 ***unwashen*** unwashed
22.II Geneva or Geneva–Tomson, with 'him' altered to '*Jesus*', 1
c Geneva–Tomson glosses 'maimed': 'Whose members were weakened with the palsy, or by nature, for afterward it is said, he healed them . . . '
23.II Geneva or Geneva–Tomson
24.II probably Geneva–Tomson, with 'And he answered and said unto them' altered to '*Christ said*'; Geneva–Tomson reads 'two' where Geneva reads 'twain', 4
c Geneva–Tomson glosses 'flesh': '. . . and this word flesh, is by a figure taken for the whole man, or the body after the manner of the Hebrews.'
25.II Geneva or Geneva–Tomson, with 'marry' altered to '*marrieth*' ('*marrieth another*'), 2, and 'which' to '*that*', 3
26.II Geneva or Geneva–Tomson, with a condensation of v. 25: 'And when his disciples heard it, they were exceedingly amazed, saying, Who then can be saved?'; '*but*', 3, is possibly from Bishops'.
c Geneva–Tomson glosses 'camel': 'Theophylact noteth that by this word is meant a cable rope, but Caninius allegeth out of the Talmudists, that it is a proverb, and the word, Camel, signifieth the beast itself.'
27.II Geneva or Geneva–Tomson, with 'hundreth' altered to '*hundred*'

28

Making religion their covering.

Is this house become a den of thieves whereupon my name is called before your eyes? Behold, even I see it, saith the Lord.

Jer. 7:11, Isa. 56:7

29

O Lord, our governor, how excellent is thy name in all the world, thou that hast set thy glory above the heavens! Out of the mouth of very babes and sucklings hast thou ordained strength, because of thine enemies, that thou mightst still the enemy and the avenger.

Ps. 8:1, 2

30

Meaning that he had planted his church in a place most plentiful and abundant.

Now will I sing to my beloved a song of my beloved to his vineyard. My beloved had a vineyard in a very fruitful hill; and he hedged it, and gathered out the stones of it, and he planted it with the best plants, and he built a tower in the midst thereof, and made a winepress therein; then he looked that it should bring forth grapes, but it brought forth wild grapes.

Isa. 5:1, 2

31

The same stone which the builders refused is become the headstone in the corner; this is the Lord's doing, and it is marvellous in our eyes.

Ps. 118:22, 23

32

Christ is a sanctuary to his elect, to the rest a stumbling stone.

And he shall be as a sanctuary; but as a stumbling stone and as a rock to fall upon to both the houses of Israel, and as a snare and as a net to the inhabitants of Jerusalem.

Isa. 8:14, Zech. 12:3, Dan. 2

33

Moreover, God appearing unto Moses *said, I am the God of thy fathers, the God of* Abraham, *the God of* Isaac, *and the God of* Jacob; *then* Moses *hid his face, for he was afraid to look upon God.*

Exod. 3:6

34

A son honoureth his father, and a servant his master: if then I be a father, where is mine honour? And if I be a master, where is my fear? saith the Lord of hosts.

Mal. 1:6

28.I Geneva
c Geneva glosses 'den of thieves': 'As thieves hid in holes and dens think themselves safe, so when you are in my temple, you think to be covered with the holiness thereof, and that I cannot see your wickedness.'
29.I Bishops'
30.I Geneva, with the addition of '*and*' in '*and he built*', 4
c Geneva's gloss on 'vineyard'
31.I Bishops'
32.I Geneva
s The reference in Dan. is 2:45.
c Geneva glosses 'sanctuary': 'He will defend you which are his elect, and reject all the rest, which is meant of Christ, against whom the lewd should stumble and fall.'
33.I Geneva, with a recasting of the opening from 'Moreover he said' and pluralization of '*father*'
34.I Geneva

28

Matt. 21:12, 13 *And Jesus went into the temple of God, and cast out all them*
that sold and bought in the temple, and overthrew the tables
of the money-changers, and the seats of them that sold doves,
13 *and said to them, It is written, my house shall be called the*
house of prayer; but you have made it a den of thieves.

29

Idem 16 *When the chief priests and scribes saw the marvels that Christ did, and the children crying in the temple and saying,* Hosanna *to the son of* David, *they disdained, and said unto him, Hearest thou what these say? Jesus said unto them, Yea, have you never read, By the mouth of babes and sucklings thou hast made perfect the praise?*

Established, grounded, made perfect: it is all one that the evangelist saith, for that is stable and sure which is most perfect.

30

Idem 33 *Jesus put forth a similitude: There was a certain householder which planted a vineyard, and hedged it round about, and made a winepress therein, and built a tower, and let it out to husbandmen, and went into a strange country, etc.*

31

Matt. 21:42 *Read you never in the scriptures, saith Jesus, the stone which the builders refused, the same is made the head of the corner; this was the Lord's doing, and it is marvellous in our eyes.*

'The head of the corner': which beareth up the joints of the whole building.

32

Idem 44 *Whosoever shall fall on this stone shall be broken; but on whomsoever it shall fall, it will dash him in pieces.*

33

Matt. 22:31, 32 *Concerning the resurrection of the dead, have you not read what is spoken to you of God, saying, I am the God of* Abraham, *and the God of* Isaac, *and the God of* Jacob; *God is not the God of the dead, but of the living.*

34

Matt. 23:9, 10 *Call no man your father upon the earth, for there is but one, your father which is in heaven; be not called doctor, for one is your doctor, even Christ.*

The scribes very greedily hunt after such titles.

28.II probably Geneva-Tomson (Geneva reads 'Mine house', 4), with 'ye' altered to '*you*', 5

29.II Geneva-Tomson and Bishops': with 'he' altered to '*Christ*', 1; otherwise the wording follows Geneva-Tomson except for '*have you never read*', 4–5, which is the Bishops' reading with '*you*' substituted for 'ye'.

s The reference should read Matt. 21:15, 16.

c Geneva-Tomson glosses 'made perfect the praise': 'We read in David, Thou hast established or grounded, and if the matter be considered well, it is all one that the evangelist saith, for that is stable and sure, which is most perfect.'

30.II Geneva-Tomson, except for the opening clause, which though apparently invented includes the term '*similitude*' found only in Bishops'.

31.II Geneva or Geneva-Tomson, with a modification of the opening: 'Jesus said unto them', and 'ye' altered to '*you*', 1

c Geneva-Tomson glosses 'the head of the corner': 'The chiefest stone in the corner, is called the head of the corner, which beareth up the couplings or joints of the whole building.'

32.II Geneva-Tomson, with 'he' omitted after '*stone*'

33.II Geneva or Geneva-Tomson, with minor changes of 'ye' to '*you*' in '*have you not*', 1, and 'unto' to '*to*', 2

34.II Geneva or Geneva-Tomson, with 'doctors' rendered singular, 2

c Geneva-Tomson glosses 'doctors': 'It seemeth that the Scribes did very greedily hunt after such titles, whom, verse 16, he calleth blind guides.'

35

Sacrifices ceasing, which Christ accomplished by his death and resurrection.

After threescore and two weeks shall Messiah *be slain, and shall have nothing, and the people of the prince that shall come shall destroy the city and the sanctuary; and the end thereof shall be with a flood, and unto the end of the battle it shall be destroyed by desolations. And he shall confirm the covenant with many for one week; and in the midst of the week he shall cause the sacrifice and the oblation to cease, and for the overspreading of the abominations he shall make it desolate, even until the consummation determined shall be poured upon the desolate.* Dan. 9:27

It desolate meaning *Jerusalem* and the sanctuary.

36

The deliverance of the church by Christ, called here by the name of the archangel *Michael.*

At that time shall Michael *stand up, the great prince, which standeth for the children of thy people, and there shall be a time of trouble, such as never was since there began to be a nation, unto that same time; and at that time thy people shall be delivered, every one that shall be found written in the book.* Dan. 12:1

37

All the powers of heaven and earth war against sinners.

Behold the day of the Lord cometh, cruel, with wrath, and fierce anger to lay the land waste, and he shall destroy the sinners out of it: for the stars of heaven, and the planets thereof shall not give their light; the sun shall be darkened in his going forth; and the moon shall not cause her light to shine. Isa. 13:9, 10, Ezek. 32:7, Joel 2:31

38

That 'ancient of days', is meant by God the Father, who gave to the blessed *Messiah* all dominion, as to the mediator.

As I beheld in visions by night, behold, one like the son of man came in the clouds of heaven, and approached unto the ancient of days, before whom they brought him, and he gave him dominion, and honour, and a kingdom, that all people, nations, and languages should serve him; his dominion is an everlasting dominion, which shall never be taken away; and his kingdom shall never be destroyed. Dan. 7:13, 14

39

A comfort to the church in all dangers.

As a shepherd searcheth out his flock when he hath been among his sheep that are scattered, so will I seek out my sheep, and will deliver them out of all places, where they have been scattered, in the cloudy and dark day. Ezek. 34:12

35.I Geneva
7 ***oblation*** offering of a sacrifice
s The reference should be Dan. 9:26, 27.
c Geneva glosses 'cease': 'Christ accomplished this by his death and resurrection'; and 'overspreading ... abominations': 'Meaning, that Jerusalem and the sanctuary should be utterly destroyed for their rebellion against God and their idolatry ...'
36.I Geneva
c Geneva glosses 'time ... stand up': 'The angel here noteth two things: first that the church shall be in great affliction and trouble at Christ's coming, and next that God will send his angel to deliver it, whom here he calleth Michael, meaning Christ, which is published by the preaching of the gospel.'
37.I Geneva
c Geneva glosses 'stars ... light': 'They that are overcome, shall think that all the powers of heaven and earth are against them.'
38.I Geneva, with a phrase imported from Bishops': '*before whom they brought him*', 3
c Geneva glosses 'dominion ... kingdom': 'This is meant of the beginning of Christ's kingdom, when God the Father gave unto him all dominion, as to the mediator, to the intent that he should govern here his church in earth continually, till the time that he brought them to eternal life.'
39.I Geneva
c Geneva glosses 'cloudy and dark day': 'In the day of their affliction and misery: and this promise is to comfort the church in all dangers.'

35

Matt. 24:14, 15, 16, 17 *This gospel of the kingdom shall be preached through the*
whole world for a witness unto all nations, and then shall
15 *the end come; when you therefore shall see the abomination*
of desolation spoken of by Daniel *the prophet set in the holy*
16 *place (let him that readeth consider it): then let them which*
17 *be in Judea fly into the mountains; let him which is on the*
house-top not come down to fetch anything out of his house,
etc.

'The gospel', which is the covenant before spoken of.

'Abomination of desolation': that is, idolatry and the fruits thereof. The great fear that shall ensue.

36

Idem 20, 21, 22 *Pray that your flight be not in the winter, neither on the sabbath day: for then shall be a great tribulation, such as was not from the beginning of the world, nor shall be; and except those days should be shortened, there should no flesh be saved: but for the elect's sake, those days shall be shortened.*

'Neither on the sabbath': it was not lawful to take a journey on the sabbath day. *Josephus, lib.* 13.

37

Matt. 24:29 *And immediately after the tribulations of those days shall the sun be darkened, and the moon shall not give her light, and the stars shall fall from heaven, and the powers of heaven shall be shaken.*

38

Idem 30, 31 *Then shall appear the sign of the son of man in heaven, and then shall all the kindreds of the earth mourn, and they shall see the son of man come in the clouds of heaven with power and great glory, and he shall send his angels with a great sound of a trumpet, and they shall gather together his elect from the four winds, and from the one end of the heavens unto the other.*

The exceeding glory and majesty of Christ.

'From the four winds': that is, from the four quarters of the world.

39

Matt. 25:32 *Before Christ shall be gathered all nations, and he shall separate them one from another, as a shepherd divideth his sheep from the goats, and he shall set the sheep on his right hand, and the goats on the left.*

The Judgement Day, the elect and the reprobate.

35.II probably Geneva–Tomson (Geneva reads 'standing' in place of '*set*', 4), with 'ye' altered to '*you*', 3, and 'flee' to '*fly*', 6

c Geneva–Tomson gives the following glosses on Matt. 24:15–17: 'The abomination of desolation, that is to say, which all men detest, and cannot abide, by reason of the foul and shameful filthiness of it; and he speaketh of the idols that were set up in the temple, or as other think, he meant the marring of the doctrine in the Church'; on 'clothes': 'This betokeneth the great fear that shall be.'

36.II Geneva or Geneva–Tomson, with omission of 'to this time' after '*world*', 3

c Geneva–Tomson glosses 'Sabbath day': 'It was not lawful to take a journey on the Sabbath day. Joseph, book 13.' The reference to Josephus is to *Jewish Antiquities*, 13.52 or 252.

37.II Geneva or Geneva–Tomson

38.II Geneva or Geneva–Tomson

c Geneva–Tomson glosses 'sign . . . heaven': 'The exceeding glory and majesty, which shall bear witness that Christ, the Lord of heaven and earth, draweth near to judge the world'; and 'four winds': 'From the four quarters of the world.'

39.II probably Bishops' on the basis of '*divideth*' (Geneva and Geneva–Tomson read 'separateth'); but '*and the goats*', 4, conforms to Geneva/Geneva–Tomson (Bishops' has 'but'); 'him' in the opening line has been altered to '*Christ*'.

s The reference should read Matt. 25:32, 33.

c possibly a conflation of glosses in Geneva (to 'foundations', Matt. 25:34): 'Hereby God declareth the certainty of our predestination, whereby we are saved because we were chosen in Christ before the foundations of the world', and Geneva–Tomson (to Matt. 25:31): 'A lively setting forth of the everlasting judgement which is to come'; Geneva also provides as both a headline and a chapter-head summary 'The last judgement'.

40

The true fast, which God requires.

Is not this the fasting that I have chosen? To deal thy bread to the hungry, and that thou bring the poor that wander unto thine house, when thou seest the naked that thou cover him, and hide not thyself from thine own flesh? Then shall thy light break forth as the morning, and thine health shall grow speedily, thy righteousness shall go before thee, and the glory of the Lord shall embrace thee.

'Thine own flesh': for in him thou seest thyself, if so afflicted.

Isa. 58:7, 8, Ezek. 18:7

41

The general resurrection.

Many of them that sleep in the dust of the earth shall awake, some to everlasting life, and some to shame and perpetual contempt.

Dan. 12:2

42

'My shepherd': meaning Christ, the head of all pastors.

Arise, O sword, upon my shepherd, and upon the man that is my fellow, saith the Lord of hosts, smite the shepherd and the sheep shall be scattered, and I will turn mine hand upon the little ones.

Zech. 13:7

43

Whoso sheddeth man's blood, by man shall his blood be shed; for in the image of God hath he made man.

Gen. 9:6, Ezek. 11:7, 8, 9, 10

44

By *Josiah*, called 'anointed' because he was a figure of Christ.

The breath of our nostrils, the anointed of the Lord was taken in their nets, of whom we said, Under his shadow we shall be preserved alive among the heathen.

Lam. 4:20

45

I gave my back unto the smiters, and my cheeks to the nippers, I hid not my face from shame and spitting.

Isa. 50:6

46

His willingness and patience in suffering.

He was oppressed, and he was afflicted; yet did he not open his mouth: he is brought as a sheep to the slaughter; and as a sheep before her shearer is dumb, so he openeth not his mouth.

Isa. 53:7

47

They part my garments among them, and cast lots upon my vesture; but be not thou far from me, O Lord: thou art my succour, haste thee to help me.

Ps. 22:18, 19

40.1 Geneva, with an omission of the rest of v. 6 and the start of v. 7 after '*chosen*', 1
c Geneva contains the headline 'Of the true fast', and glosses 'thine own flesh': 'For in him thou seest thyself as in a glass.'
s The opening line is actually from Isa. 58:6.
41.1 Geneva
c Geneva headline, and cited in the gloss to Dan. 12:2
42.1 Geneva
c Geneva glosses 'shepherd': 'The prophet warneth the Jews that before this great comfort should come under Christ, there should be an horrible dissipation among the people: for their governors and pastors should be destroyed, and the people should be as scattered sheep: and the evangelist applieth this to Christ, because he was the head of all pastors.'
43.1 Geneva
44.1 Geneva
c Geneva glosses Lam. 4:20: 'Our king, Josiah, in whom stood our hope of God's favour, and on whom depended our state and life, was slain, whom he calleth anointed, because he was a figure of Christ.'
45.1 Geneva
46.1 Geneva
c Geneva glosses Isa. 53:7: 'But willingly, and patiently obeyed his father's appointment.'
47.1 Bishops'

40

Matt. 25:34, 35, 36 *Come you blessed of my Father, take the inheritance of the* Of all the virtues, *charity* sits highest.
kingdom prepared for you from the foundation of the world:
35 *for I was a-hungered, and you gave me meat; I thirsted, and*
you gave me drink; I was a stranger, and you took me in unto
36 *you; I was naked, and you clothed me; I was sick, and you*
visited me; I was in prison, and you came unto me.

41

Idem 46 *These shall go into everlasting pain; and the righteous into life eternal.* The last day.

42

Matt. 26:31 *Jesus said unto his disciples, All you shall be offended because of me this night: for it is written, I will smite the shepherd, and the sheep of the flock shall be scattered.* Their flight forewarned.

43

Matt. 26:52 *One of them which was with Jesus stretched out his hand, and drew his sword; then said Jesus unto him, Put up thy sword into his place, for all that take the sword shall perish with the sword.* They take the sword, to whom the Lord hath not given it.

44

Idem 55, 56 *The same hour said Jesus to the multitude, You be come out as it were against a thief, with swords and staves to take me; I sat daily teaching in the temple among you, and you took me not: but all this was done that the scriptures of the prophets might be fulfilled.*

45

Idem 67, 68 *Then spat they on his face, and buffeted him, and other smote him with rods, saying, Prophesy to us, O Christ, who is he that smote thee?*

46

Matt. 27:13, 14 Pilate *said to Jesus, Hearest thou not how many things they lay against thee?—There is his affliction.—But Jesus answered him not to one word—there's his patience and long suffering—insomuch that the governor marvelled greatly.* Note his affliction, then his patience and long suffering.

47

Matt. 27:35 *And when they had crucified Jesus, they parted his garments, and did cast lots, that it might be fulfilled which was spoken by the prophet: they divided my garments among them, and upon my vesture did cast lots.*

40.II Geneva–Tomson, with 'ye' altered to '*you*' at various points
c derived presumably from 1 Cor. 13:13
41.II Geneva or Geneva–Tomson
c possibly drawn from the Geneva headline or chapter-head summary to Matt. 25: 'The last judgement'
42.II Bishops'
c Geneva–Tomson glosses Matt. 26:31: 'Christ being more careful of his disciples, than of himself, forewarneth them of their flight, and putteth them in better comfort.'
43.II Geneva or Geneva–Tomson, with alteration of 'were' to '*was*', 1, and omission of the remainder of v. 51 after '*sword*', 2
s The citation draws on Matt. 26:51 and 52.
c Geneva–Tomson glosses 'take the sword': 'They take the sword to whom the Lord hath not given it, that is to say, they which use the sword, and are not called to it.'
44.II Geneva or Geneva–Tomson, with alteration of 'ye be come' to '*You be come*', 1 and 'and ye' to '*and you*', 3
45.II probably Geneva–Tomson (Geneva reads 'their rods', 2)
46.II Geneva or Geneva–Tomson, with interpolated additions ('*There is his affliction*' and '*there's his patience and long suffering*') presumably by Middleton
c possibly derived from Isa. 53:7—i.e. to focus on the agreement of the parallel passages
47.II Geneva or Geneva–Tomson, with 'him' altered to '*Jesus*' in the opening line

48

'Experience': for the comfort of sinners.

He is despised, and abhorred of men; he is such a man as hath good experience of sorrows and infirmities; we have reckoned him so vile that we hid our faces from him. Isa. 53:3

49

My God, my God, look upon me, why hast thou forsaken me? And art so far from my health, and from the words of my complaint? Ps. 22:1

50

They gave me gall to eat; and when I was thirsty, they gave me vinegar to drink. Ps. 69:22

51

'Their worm': a continual gnawing of conscience, which shall never suffer them to rest.

From month to month, and from sabbath to sabbath, shall all flesh come to worship before me, saith the Lord. And they shall go forth and look upon the carcasses of the men that have transgressed against me, for their worm shall not die; neither shall their fire be quenched, and they shall be an abhorring unto all flesh. Isa. 66:24

52

The land shall never be without poor, and therefore I command thee, saying, Thou shalt open thy hand unto thy brother that is needy and poor in thy land. Deut. 15:11

53

For his humility, he shall receive glory.

Therefore will I give him a portion with the great, and he shall divide the spoil with the strong, because he hath poured out his soul unto death, and he was counted with the transgressors, and he bore the sin of many, and prayed for the trespassers. Isa. 53:12

54

Of Christ's birth and office.

Unto us a child is born, and unto us a son is given; upon his shoulder doth the rule lie, and he shall call his name Wonderful, the Giver of Counsel, the Mighty God, the Everlasting Father, the Prince of Peace; the increase of his government and peace shall have none end; he shall sit upon the throne of David, *and upon his kingdom, to order it, and to stablish it with equity and righteousness from henceforth for evermore.* Isa. 9:6, 7, Dan. 7:14, Mic. 4:7

55

The word of the Lord came unto Elias, *saying, Up and get thee to Sarepta, which is in Sidon, and remain there: behold I have commanded a widow there to sustain thee.* 1 Kgs. 17:8, 9

48.I Bishops'
c Geneva glosses 'infirmities': 'Which was by God's singular providence for the comfort of sinners.'
49.I Bishops'
50.I Bishops'
s The reference should read Ps. 69:21.
51.I Geneva
c The reference should read Isa. 66:23, 24. Geneva glosses 'worm . . . die': 'Meaning, a continual torment of conscience, which shall ever gnaw them and never suffer them to be at rest.'
52.I Bishops'
53.I Geneva
c Geneva glosses 'hath . . . death': 'Because he humbled himself, therefore he shall be exalted to glory.'
54.I either Bishops' or Geneva for the opening, '*Unto . . . given*'; '*upon . . . lie*': Bishops'; '*and he . . . Wonderful*': Geneva; '*the Giver of Counsel*': Bishops'; '*the Mighty . . . Peace*': either; '*the increase . . . stablish it with*': Geneva; '*equity . . . evermore*': Bishops'
7 ***stablish*** bring into settled order
c Geneva headline
55.I Geneva, with 'Elias' (in place of 'Elijah', used elsewhere in 1 Kgs.) substituted for 'him', 'Zarephath' altered to '*Sarepta*', and 'Zidon' to '*Sidon*', apparently to emphasize the correspondence between the verses from the two Testaments

48

Idem 39, 40 *They that passed by reviled him, wagging their heads and saying, Thou that destroyest the temple, and buildest it in three days, save thyself; if thou be the son of God, come down from the cross.*

49

Idem 46 *And about the ninth hour, Jesus cried with a loud voice, saying,* Eloi, Eloi, lama sabachtani, *that is to say, My God, my God, why hast thou forsaken me?*

'Forsaken': to wit, in this misery, never otherwise.

50

Idem 48 *And straightway one of them ran, and took a sponge and filled it with vinegar, and put it on a reed, and gave him to drink.*

51

Mark 9:43, 44 *If thy hand cause thee to offend, cut it off; it is better for thee*
to enter into life maimed, than having two hands to go into
44 *hell, into the fire that never shall be quenched: where their*
worm dieth not, and the fire never goeth out.

All hindrances to Christ cut off. The torments of the damned.

52

Mark 14:7 *You have poor with you always, and when you will you may do them good: but me shall you not have always.*

53

Mark 15:27, 28 *They crucified also with him two thieves, the one on the right hand, and the other on the left. Thus the scripture was fulfilled which saith, He was counted among the wicked, and they that went by, railed on him, etc.*

54

Luke 1:30, 31, 32, 33 *The angel said unto her, Fear not,* Mary*: for thou hast found*
favour with God; for lo, thou shalt conceive in thy womb, and
32 *bear a son, and shalt call his name Jesus. He shall be great,*
and shall be called the Son of the Most Highest, and the Lord
33 *God shall give unto him the throne of his father* David*; and*
he shall reign over the house of Jacob *for ever; and of his*
kingdom there shall be none end.

The angel sent to *Mary*.

55

Luke 4:25 *I tell you of a truth, many widows were in Israel in the days of* Elias, *when heaven was shut three years and six months, when great famine was throughout all the land, but unto none of them was* Elias *sent, save into Sarepta, a city of Sidon, unto a certain widow.*

48.II Geneva or Geneva–Tomson

49.II probably Bishops' (Geneva and Geneva–Tomson read 'that is' for '*that is to say*', 2), with alteration of the text of Christ's words to agree with Mark 15:34

c Geneva–Tomson glosses 'forsaken': 'To wit, in this misery: And this crying out is proper to his humanity, which notwithstanding was void of sin, but yet it felt the wrath of God, which is due to our sins.'

50.II Geneva or Geneva–Tomson

51.II Geneva or Geneva–Tomson, with 'thine' altered to '*thy*', 1.

c Geneva glosses 'hand': 'It is a manner of speech which signifieth, that we should cut off all things, which hinder us to serve Christ'; and 'worm': 'These similitudes declare the pains, and eternal torments of the damned.'

52.II Geneva or Geneva–Tomson, with 'ye' altered to '*you*' at several points, 'the' omitted before '*poor*', and 'ye shall' reversed ('*shall you*')

53.II Geneva or Geneva–Tomson, with some elements possibly drawn from Bishops': '*the left*' in place of Tomson's 'his left', and omission of Tomson's 'And' before '*he was counted*...', 3

s The cited passage extends into v. 29.

54.II Geneva, with elements drawn from Bishops': '*Most Highest*', 4, in place of Geneva's 'Most High', and the addition of '*there*' in the final line

c Geneva headline

55.II Geneva or Geneva–Tomson

s The reference should read Luke 4:25, 26.

56

Against the princes of *Israel*, living in voluptuousness.

Woe to them that are at ease in Zion, and trust in the mountain of Samaria, which were famous at the beginning of the nations, and the house of Israel came to them. Amos 6:1

57

Woe unto them that decree wicked decrees, and write grievous things, to keep back the poor from judgement, and to take away the judgement of the poor of my people, that widows may be their prey, and that they may spoil the fatherless. Isa. 10:1, 2

58

More Gentiles than Jews believers.

Rejoice, O barren that didst not bear; break forth into joy, and rejoice thou that didst not travail with child: for the desolate hath more children than the married wife, saith the Lord. Isa. 54:1

59

Moses *made a serpent of brass, and set it up for a sign; and when a serpent had bitten a man, then he looked to the serpent of brass and lived.* Num. 21:9

60

His heavenly care over the weak and tender.

He shall feed his flock like a shepherd: he shall gather the lambs with his arm, and carry them in his bosom, and shall guide them with young. Isa. 40:11

61

No stranger, except he be circumcised.

A stranger, or an hired servant shall not eat of the passover: in one house shall it be eaten; thou shalt carry none of the flesh out of the house, neither shall you break a bone thereof. Exod. 12:45, 46

62

Thou shalt not leave my soul in hell, neither shalt thou suffer thine holy one to see corruption. Ps. 16:11

63

I will make them one people in the land, upon the mountains of Israel; and one king shall be king to them all, and they shall be no more two peoples, neither be divided any more henceforth into two kingdoms. Ezek. 37:22

64

Let their habitation be void, and no man to dwell in their tents; when sentence is given upon him, let him be condemned: and let his prayer be turned into sin; let his days be few, and let another take his office. Ps. 69:26 and 109:6, 7

56.I Geneva
c Geneva gives as the chapter synopsis: 'Against the princes of Israel living in pleasures.'
57.I Geneva
58.I Geneva
c Geneva's chapter synopsis: 'More of the Gentiles shall believe the gospel than of the Jews.'
59.I Geneva
60.I Geneva
c Geneva glosses 'young': 'He shall show his care and favour over them that are weak and tender.'
61.I Geneva
c Geneva glosses 'no stranger' from v. 43: 'Except he be circumcised and only profess your religion.'
62.I Bishops'; apart from its different phraseology, the scriptural reference in Geneva is Ps. 16:10.
63.I Geneva
64.I Bishops'

56

Luke 6:24 *Woe be to you that are rich: for you have received your consolation.*

That put their confidence in riches.

57

Luke 11:46 *Woe unto you also, you lawyers, for you load men with burdens grievous to be borne, and you yourselves touch not the burdens with one of your fingers.*

58

Luke 23:29 *Behold, the days will come when men shall say, Blessed are the barren, and the wombs that never bore, and the paps that never gave suck.*

59

John 3:14, 15 *As* Moses *lift up the serpent in the wilderness, so must the son of man be lift up, that whosoever believeth in him should not perish, but have eternal life.*

'Lift up': that is, his power made manifest.

60

John 10:11 *I am that good shepherd: that good shepherd giveth his life for the sheep.*

61

John 19:34, 35, 36 *One of the soldiers with a spear pierced his side, and forthwith*
came there out blood and water; and he that saw it bore
record, and his record is true: and he knoweth that he saith
36 *true that you might believe it; for these things were done, that*
the scripture should be fulfilled, Not a bone of him shall be
broken.

62

John 20:9 *As yet the disciples knew not the scripture, that he must rise again from the dead.*

63

John 10:16 *Other sheep I have also, which are not of this fold: them also must I bring, and they shall hear my voice, and there shall be one sheepfold, and one shepherd.*

The Gentiles, which then were strangers to the church of God.

64

Acts 1:19, 20 *It is known unto all the inhabitants of Jerusalem, insomuch that that field is called in their own language* Aceldama, *that is, the field of blood: for it is written in the book of Psalms, Let his habitation be void, and let no man dwell therein; also, Let another take his charge.*

'His charge': that is, his office and his ministry.

56.II Geneva or Geneva–Tomson, with 'ye have' altered to '*you have*'
c Geneva glosses 'rich': 'That put your trust in your riches, and forget the life to come.'

57.II '*Woe . . . lawyers*': Bishops'; the remainder could be Bishops' or Geneva, with 'ye', which occurs in the latter three instances, altered to '*you*', and the second instance of 'burdens' changed to its unmodernized form, '*burthens*', 3.

58.II Geneva or Geneva–Tomson

59.II Geneva
1, 2 *lift* lifted
c Geneva glosses 'lift up': 'His power must be manifest which is not yet known.'

60.II Geneva–Tomson

61.II Geneva or Geneva–Tomson, with 'ye' changed to '*you*', 4

62.II Geneva or Geneva–Tomson

63.II Geneva or Geneva–Tomson
c Geneva glosses 'Other sheep': 'To wit, among the Gentiles, which then were strangers from the Church of God.'

64.II Geneva or Geneva–Tomson (the main distinction between them is 'Jerusalem' and 'Hierusalem' respectively)
c Geneva–Tomson glosses 'his charge': 'His office and ministry . . . '

65

'Pour out my spirit': that is, in greater abundance more generally than in times past, by Christ and the joyful tidings of the gospel.

By 'the remnant' are meant the Gentiles.

Afterward will I pour out my spirit upon all flesh, and your Joel 2:28, 29, 30, 31, 32
sons and your daughters shall prophesy, your old men shall
dream dreams, and your young men shall see visions; and also 29
upon the servants and upon the maids in those days will I pour
my spirit. And I will show wonders in the heaven and in the 30
earth, blood and fire, and pillars of smoke. The sun shall be 31
turned into darkness, and the moon into blood, before the great
and terrible day of the Lord come. But whosoever shall call on 32
the name of the Lord shall be saved, for in Mount Zion, and
in Jerusalem shall be deliverance, as the Lord hath said, and
in the remnant, whom the Lord shall call.

66

I have set God always before me, for he is on my right hand: therefore I shall not fall. Wherefore my heart was glad, and my glory rejoiced, my flesh also shall rest in hope. Ps. 16:9, 10

67

Meaning a continual succession of prophets, till Christ, the end of all prophets, come.

The Lord thy God will raise up unto thee a prophet like unto me, from among you, even of the brethren: unto him shall you hearken. Deut. 18:15

68

The world shall win by thy seed, Christ, the blessing which was lost in *Adam.*

I will make of thee a great nation, and will bless thee, and make thy name great; and thou shalt be a blessing: I will also bless them that bless thee, and curse them that curse thee; and in thee shall all families of the earth be blessed. Gen. 12:2, 3

69

Siccuth and *Chiun*: two idols, which as their king they carried about.

Have you offered unto me sacrifices and offerings in the Amos 5:25, 26, 27
wilderness forty years, O house of Israel? But you have borne 26
Siccuth *your king, and* Chiun *your images, and the star of*
your gods, which you made to yourselves. Therefore will I 27
cause you to go into captivity beyond Damascus, saith the
Lord, whose name is the God of hosts.

70

God's majesty is so great it filleth both heaven and earth.

Thus saith the Lord: The heaven is my throne, and the earth is my footstool; where is that house that you will build unto me? And where is that place of my rest? For all these things hath mine hand made, and all these things have been, saith the Lord. Isa. 66:1, 2

65.I Geneva
c Geneva glosses 'pour . . . spirit': 'That is, in greater abundance and more generally than in time past; and this was fulfilled under Christ whenas God's graces, and his spirit under the gospel was abundantly given to the church'; and 'the remnant': 'Meaning hereby the Gentiles.'
66.I Bishops'
67.I Geneva, with 'thy' altered to '*the*' and 'ye shall' to '*shall you*', 2–3
c Geneva's gloss on 'prophet'
68.I Geneva
c Geneva glosses 'a blessing': 'The world shall recover by thy seed, which is Christ, the blessing which they lost in Adam.'
69.I Geneva, with 'Have ye' altered to '*Have you*', 1, and 'which ye' to '*which you*', 4
s Geneva glosses 'Siccuth . . . images': 'That idol which you esteemed as your king, and carried about, as you did Chiun, in the which images you thought that there was a certain divinity.'
70.I Geneva
c Geneva glosses 'heaven . . . footstool': 'My majesty is so great that it filleth both heaven and earth, and therefore cannot be included in a temple like an idol: condemning hereby their vain confidence, which trusted in the temple and sacrifices.'

65

Acts 2:16, 17, 18, 19, 20, 21
This is that which was spoken by the prophet Joel*: And it shall*
be in the last days, saith God, I will pour out my spirit upon
all flesh, and your sons and your daughters shall prophesy;
and your young men shall see visions, and your old men shall
18 *dream dreams; and on my servants and on my handmaids I*
will pour out my spirit in those days, and they shall prophesy;
19 *and I will show wonders in heaven above, and tokens in the*
20 *earth beneath, blood and fire, and the vapour of smoke; the*
sun shall be turned into darkness, and the moon into blood,
21 *before that great and notable day of the Lord come; and it shall*
be, that whosoever shall call on the name of the Lord shall be
saved.

'All flesh': all without exception, both upon Jews and Gentiles.

'Call on' signifieth in holy scriptures, an earnest praying

66

Acts 2:25, 26

Thus David *saith concerning Jesus, I beheld the Lord always before me, for he is at my right hand, that I should not be shaken: therefore did mine heart rejoice, and my tongue was glad, and moreover also my flesh shall rest in hope.*

67

Acts 3:22

Moses *said unto the fathers, The Lord your God shall raise up unto you a prophet, even of your brethren, like unto me; you shall hear him in all things whatsoever he shall say unto you.*

This promise was of an excellent prophet, *Christ*.

68

Acts 3:25

Ye are the children of the prophets and of the covenant, which God hath made unto our fathers, saying to Abraham, *Even in thy seed shall all the kindreds of the earth be blessed.*

God to *Abraham*.

69

Acts 7:42, 43

Then God turned himself away, and gave them up to serve the host of heaven, as it is written in the book of the prophets, O house of Israel, have you offered to me slain beasts and sacrifices by the space of forty years in the wilderness? And ye took up the tabernacle of Moloch, *and the star of your god* Remphan, *figures which you made to worship them; therefore I will carry you away beyond Babylon.*

By 'the host of heaven' is meant the sun, moon, stars, etc.

70

Acts 7:48, 49, 50

The most high dwelleth not in temples made with hands, as saith the prophet, Heaven is my throne, and earth is my footstool; what house will you build for me? saith the Lord; or what place is it that I should rest in? Hath not mine hand made all these things?

65.II Although many correspondences in phraseology and wordings exist among Bishops', Geneva, and Geneva-Tomson for this passage, Geneva stands closest; 'of' was presumably omitted in the phrase 'pour out of my spirit' at 2 and 6 to register a closer correspondence with the parallel citation from Joel, where '*pour out my spirit*' is given additional support by a gloss on its meaning and significance.

c Geneva-Tomson glosses 'all': 'all without exception, both upon the Jews and Gentiles'; and 'call on': 'This word, Call on, signifieth in Holy Scripture, an earnest praying and craving for help at God's hand.'

66.II Geneva or Geneva-Tomson, with 'For' altered to '*Thus*' and 'him' to '*Jesus*', 1

67.II Geneva-Tomson, with 'ye shall hear' altered to '*you shall hear*', 2–3

c Geneva-Tomson glosses 'a prophet': 'This promise was of an excellent and singular prophet.'

68.II Geneva or Geneva-Tomson

c presumably derived from the citation

69.II Geneva or Geneva-Tomson, with 'have ye' altered to '*have you*', 3, and 'which ye' to '*which you*', 6

c Geneva-Tomson glosses 'host of heaven': 'By the host of heaven here, he meaneth not the angels, but the moon and sun, and other stars.'

70.II Geneva or Geneva-Tomson, with 'will ye' altered to '*will you*', 3

71

None shall be blinded with ignorance.

They shall teach no more every man his neighbour, and every man his brother, saying, Know the Lord: for they shall all know me from the least of them unto the greatest of them, saith the Lord; for I will forgive their iniquity, and will remember their sins no more.

Jer. 31:34, Mic. 7:18

72

They shall not believe their own ruins, because unbelievers of God's word.

Behold among the heathen, and regard, and wonder, and marvel: for I will work a work in your days, you will not believe it, though it be told you.

Hab. 1:5

73

I will send the *Messiah* promised, and restore by him the spiritual *Israel.*

In that day will I raise up the tabernacle of David *that is fallen down, and close up the breaches thereof; and I will raise up his ruins, and I will build it as in the days of old, that they may possess the remnant of* Edom, *and of all the heathen, because my name is called upon them, saith the Lord that doth this.*

Amos 9:11, 12

74

If we have forgotten the name of our God, and holden up our hands to any strange god, shall not God search it out? For he knoweth the very secrets of the heart; for thy sake also we are killed all the day long, and are counted as sheep appointed to be slain.

Ps. 44:21, 22

75

Against those that murmur against God in time of adversity.

Woe be unto him that striveth with his maker, the potsherd with the potsherds of the earth; shall the clay say to him that fashioneth it, What makest thou? Or thy work, It hath none hands? O house of Israel, cannot I do with you as this potter? saith the Lord. Behold, as the clay is in the potter's hand, so are you in mine hand, O house of Israel.

Isa. 45:9, Jer. 18:6

76

I will sow her unto me in the earth; and I will have mercy upon her that was not pitied; and I will say unto them which were not my people, Thou art my people; and they shall say, Thou art my God. The number of the children of Israel shall be as the sand of the sea, which cannot be measured nor told; and in the place where it was said unto them, Ye are not my people, it shall be said unto them, Ye are sons of the living God.

Hos. 2:23, 1:10

71.I Geneva
c Geneva glosses Jer. 31:34: 'Under the kingdom of Christ there shall be none blinded with ignorance, but I will give them faith, and knowledge of God for remission of their sins and daily increase the same ...'
72.I Geneva, with 'ye will' altered to '*you will*', 2
c Geneva glosses 'you will ... told you': 'As in times past you would not believe God's word, so shall ye not now believe the strange plagues which are at hand.'
73.I Geneva
c gloss to Geneva, Amos 9:11
74.I Bishops' except for a reversal of '*we are*' in v. 22
s The verse reference gives additional support for Bishops' since the passage is Ps. 44:20–2 in Geneva.
75.I Geneva
s The citations from Isaiah and Jeremiah are presented consecutively.
c Geneva glosses Isa. 45:9: 'Hereby he bridleth their impatiency, which in adversity and trouble murmur against God, and will not tarry his pleasure ...'
murmur grumble
76.I Geneva or Geneva-Tomson, with 'the' omitted before '*sons*', 7

71

Acts 10:42, 43 *Jesus commanded us to preach unto the people, and to testify that it is he that is ordained of God a judge of quick and dead; to him also give all the prophets witness, that through his name all that believe in him shall receive remission of sins.*

There is no other name under heaven to be saved by.

72

Acts 13:40, 41 *Beware, lest that come upon you, which is spoken of in the prophets: Behold, you despisers, and wonder, and vanish away, for I work a work in your days, you will not believe it, though it be told you.*

Against their incredulity.

73

Acts 15:16, 17 *After this I will return, and will build again the tabernacle of* David, *which is fallen down; and the ruins thereof will I build again, and I will set it up, that the residue of men might seek after the Lord, and all the Gentiles upon whom my name is called, saith the Lord, which doth all these things.*

The promise kept.

74

Rom. 8:35, 36 *Who shall separate us from the love of Christ? Shall tribulation or anguish? Or persecution, or famine, or nakedness, or peril, or sword? As it is written, For thy sake are we killed all day long; we are counted as sheep for the slaughter.*

'The love of Christ': that is, wherewith Christ loveth us.

75

Rom. 9:20, 21 *But, O man, who art thou which pleadest against God? Shall the thing formed say to him that formed it, Why hast thou made me thus? Hath not the potter power of the clay, to make of the same lump one vessel to honour, and another to dishonour?*

Predestination. This similitude aptly agreeth in the first creation of mankind.

76

Rom. 9:25, 26 *I will call them my people, which were not my people; and her, beloved, which was not beloved. And it shall be in the place where it was said unto them, Ye are not my people, that there they shall be called the children of the living God.*

Our vocation is free, and of grace, even as our predestination is.

71.II probably Geneva on the basis of the present tense of '*believe*', 4 (Geneva–Tomson reads 'believed')
c Geneva–Tomson glosses Acts 10:37: 'The sum of the gospel (which shall be made manifest at the latter day, when Christ himself shall sit as judge both of the quick and dead) is this, that Christ promised to the fathers, and exhibited in his time with the mighty power of God (which was by all means showed) and at length crucified to reconcile us to God, did rise again the third day, that whosoever believeth in him, should be saved through the remission of sins.'

72.II Geneva or Geneva–Tomson, with 'therefore' omitted after '*Beware*', 1, and 'ye despisers' altered to '*you despisers*', 2. The final line, '*you . . . told you*' conforms to none of the versions of the Bible and was presumably influenced by the parallel reading from Habakkuk.
c possibly designed as a response to the commentary to 72.I; not found in any of the Bibles used elsewhere

73.II Geneva or Geneva–Tomson
c apparently devised to respond to the commentary on Amos 9:11; not found in any of the Bibles used elsewhere

74.II Geneva or Geneva–Tomson
c Geneva–Tomson glosses 'love of Christ': 'Wherewith Christ loveth us.'

75.II Geneva or Geneva–Tomson, with 'another unto' altered to '*another to*', 4
c probably derived in part from the headline, 'Predestination', to Geneva, Rom. 9. Geneva–Tomson glosses Rom. 9:20–1: 'This similitude agreeth very fitly to the first creation of mankind.'

76.II Geneva or Geneva–Tomson
c Geneva–Tomson glosses Rom. 9:25: 'Our vocation or calling, is free and of grace, even as our predestination is . . .'

77

Spiritual joys and raptures.

How beautiful upon the mountains are the feet of him that declareth and publisheth peace, that declareth good tidings, and publisheth salvation, saying unto Zion, Thy God reigneth. Isa. 52:7, Nah. 1:15

78

Meaning the Gentiles that knew not God.

I have been sought of them that asked not; I was found of them that sought me not; I said, Behold me, behold me, unto a nation that called not upon my name. Isa. 65:1, 2

Here, the rejection of the Jews.

I have spread out my hands all the day unto a rebellious people, which walked in a way that was not good, even after their own imaginations.

79

Let their table be made a snare to take themselves withal, and let the things (that should have been for their wealth) be unto them an occasion of falling; let their eyes be blinded that they see not, and ever bow down their backs. Ps. 69:23, 24

80

The true deliverance from sin and Satan.

The Redeemer shall come unto Zion, and unto them that turn from iniquity in Jacob, saith the Lord. And I will make this my covenant with them, saith the Lord. My spirit that is upon thee, and my words, which I have put in thy mouth, shall not depart out of thy mouth, nor out of the mouth of thy seed, nor out of the mouth of the seed of thy seed, saith the Lord, from henceforth even for ever. Isa. 59:20, 21

81

God only wise.

His omnipotence.

Who hath measured the waters in his fist? And counted heaven Isa. 40:12, 13, 14
with the span, and comprehended the dust of the earth in a
measure? And weighed the mountains in a weight, and the
hills in a balance? Who hath instructed the Spirit of the 13
Lord? Or was his counsellor, or taught him? Of whom took he 14
counsel, and who instructed him, and taught him in the way
of judgement, or taught him knowledge, and showed unto him
the way of understanding?

82

All shall acknowledge me for God.

Look unto me, and you shall be saved: all the ends of the Isa. 45:22, 23
earth shall be saved, for I am God, and there is none other; I 23
have sworn by myself, the word is gone out of my mouth in
righteousness, and shall not return, That every knee shall bow
unto me, and every tongue shall swear by me.

77.1 Geneva
c Geneva glosses Isa. 52:7: 'Signifying, that the joy and good tidings of their deliverance should make their affliction in the mean time more easy: but this is chiefly meant of the spiritual joy.'

78.1 Geneva
c Geneva glosses 'asked not': 'Meaning the Gentiles which knew not God, should seek after him when he had moved their hearts with his holy spirit'; and Isa. 65:2: 'He showeth the cause of the rejection of the Jews . . .'

79.1 Bishops'
s Additional support for Bishops' is provided by the reference to Ps. 69:23, which is 69:22 in Geneva.

80.1 Geneva
c Geneva glosses Isa. 59:20: 'Whereby he declareth that the true deliverance from sin and Satan belongeth to none, but to the children of God, whom he justifieth.'

81.1 Geneva
2 ***span*** distance from the tip of the thumb to the tip of the little finger with the fingers and thumb of a hand spread apart
c The order of the Geneva glosses has apparently been inverted; Isa. 40:12: 'Declaring that as God only hath all power, so doth he use the same for the defence and maintenance of his church', and 40:13: 'He showeth God's infinite wisdom for the same end and purpose.'

82.1 Geneva, with 'ye shall' altered to '*you shall*', 1; see textual note.
c Geneva–Tomson glosses 'shall confess unto God', Rom. 14:11: 'Shall acknowledge me for God', which either by design or accident is set as commentary to the parallel citation from Isaiah.

77

Rom. 10:14, 15 *How shall they call on him, in whom they have not believed, and how shall they believe in him, of whom they have not heard? And how shall they hear without a preacher? And how shall they preach, except they be sent? As it is written, How beautiful are the feet of them which bring glad tidings of peace, and bring glad tidings of good things.*

Hereof faith cometh.

78

Idem 20, 21 *I was found of them that sought me not; and have been made manifest to them that asked not after me; and unto Israel he saith, All the day long have I stretched forth my hands unto a disobedient and gainsaying people.*

79

Rom. 11:9, 10 *Let their table be made a snare and a net and a stumbling-block, even for a recompense unto them: let their eyes be darkened, that they see not, and bow down their back always.*

Snared in the law for refusing the gospel.

80

Idem 26, 27 *All Israel shall be saved; as it is written, The Deliverer shall come out of Zion, and shall turn away the ungodliness from Jacob, and this is my covenant to them, when I shall take away their sins.*

Christ the Saviour.

81

Rom. 11:33, 34, 35, 36 *O the deepness of the riches, both of the wisdom and knowledge*
of God! How unsearchable are his judgements, and his ways
34 *past finding out! For who hath known the mind of the Lord?*
35 *Or who was his counsellor? Or who hath given unto him first,*
36 *and he shall be recompensed? For of him, and through him,*
and for him, are all things: to him be glory for ever. Amen.

Paul, ravished in spirit, crieth out as astonished with the wonderful wisdom of God.

82

Rom. 14:10, 11 *We shall all appear before the judgement seat of Christ. For*
11 *it is written, I live, saith the Lord, and every knee shall bow*
unto me, and all tongues shall confess unto God.

The knowledge of God, and the true worshipping, shall be through all the world.

77.II Geneva or Geneva–Tomson
 c Geneva–Tomson glosses Rom. 10:14: 'That is true faith, which seeketh God in his word, and that preached according as God hath appointed in the Church.'
78.II The reading, 'hands', 3, points to Bishops' since it is unique to this version.
79.II Geneva or Geneva–Tomson
 c Geneva–Tomson glosses Rom. 11:9: 'As unhappy birds are enticed to death by that which is their sustenance, so did that only thing turn to the Jews' destruction, out of which they sought life, to wit, the Law of God for the preposterous zeal whereof, they refused the Gospel.' A similar gloss, but with different wording, appears in Geneva.
80.II Geneva or Geneva–Tomson
 c untraced
81.II Geneva or Geneva–Tomson
 c Geneva–Tomson glosses Rom. 11:33: 'The apostle crieth out as astonished with this wonderful wisdom of God . . . '
82.II Geneva or Geneva–Tomson, with 'to me' altered to '*unto me*', 3
 c Geneva glosses the parallel passage from Isa. 45:23: 'The knowledge of God and the true worshipping shall be through all the world', which appears here as the commentary to Rom. 14:10, 11.

83

The wonderful love of God. *Since the beginning of the world they have not heard, nor understood with the ear, neither the eye seen another God beside thee, which doth so to him that waiteth for him.* Isa. 64:4

84

Even in death God will give life. *I will redeem them from the power of the grave; I will deliver them from death: O death, I will be thy death; O grave, I will be thy destruction.* Hos. 13:14

85

In an acceptable time have I heard thee, and in a day of salvation have I helped thee: and I will preserve thee, and will give thee for a covenant of the people, that thou mayst raise up the earth, and obtain the inheritance of the desolate heritages. Isa. 49:8

'A covenant', meaning Christ alone.

86

God in arms, to the delivering of his church. *He put on righteousness as an habergeon, and an helmet of salvation upon his head; and he put on the garments of vengeance for clothing, and was clad with zeal as a cloak.* Isa. 59:17

87

Meaning Christ; 'the rod of his mouth', which is his word. *With righteousness shall he judge the poor, and with equity shall he reprove for the meek of the earth; and he shall smite the earth with the rod of his mouth, and with the breath of his lips shall he slay the wicked.* *Idem* 11:4

88

Thou Lord in the beginning hast laid the foundation of the earth, and the heavens are the work of thy hands; they shall perish but thou shalt endure; they all shall wax old as doth a garment; and as a vesture shalt thou change them, and they shall be changed; but thou art the same, and thy years shall not fail. Ps. 102:25, 26, 27

89

Meant by Jerusalem. *Lo, I begin to plague the city, where my name is called upon, and should you go free? You shall not go quit: for I will call for a sword upon all the inhabitants of the earth, saith the Lord of hosts.* Jer. 25:29

83.I Geneva
c Geneva glosses Isa. 64:4: 'St Paul useth the same kind of admiration, 1 Cor. 2:9, marvelling at God's great benefit showed to his church by the preaching of the gospel.'
84.I Geneva
c Geneva glosses 'death': 'Meaning that no power shall resist God when he will deliver his, but even in death will he give them life.'
85.I Geneva
c adapted from a gloss to Geneva, Isa. 49:8: 'Meaning, Christ alone.'
86.I Geneva
1 ***habergeon*** sleeveless coat or jacket of mail or scale-armour
c Geneva glosses Isa. 59:17: 'Signifying, that God hath all means at hand to deliver his church, and to punish their enemies.'
87.I Geneva
c Geneva glosses Isa. 11:4: 'All these properties can agree to none but only unto Christ: for it is he that toucheth the hearts of the faithful, and mortifieth their concupiscences: and to the wicked he is the savour of death, and to them that shall perish: so that all the world shall be smitten with this rod, which is his word.'
88.I Bishops'
89.I Geneva, with 'ye shall' altered to '*You shall*', 2
c Geneva glosses 'the city': 'That is, Jerusalem'.
2 ***quit*** free

83

1 Cor. 2:9 *The things which eye hath not seen, neither ear hath heard, neither came into man's heart, are, which God hath prepared for them that love him.* Joys incomprehensible.

84

1 Cor. 15:54, 55 *Death is swallowed up into victory. O death, where is thy sting? O grave, where is thy victory?* The triumph over death.

85

2 Cor. 6:2 *I have heard thee in a time accepted, and in the day of salvation have I succoured thee: behold now the accepted time, behold now the day of salvation.* In a time of grace and free mercy.

86

Eph. 6:14, 15, 16, 17 *Stand therefore, and your loins gird about with verity, and having on the breastplate of righteousness, and your feet shod with the preparation of the gospel of peace, above all, take the shield of faith, wherewith you may quench all the fiery darts of the wicked; and take the helmet of salvation, and the sword of the spirit, which is the word of God.* Salvation, which was purchased by Jesus Christ.

87

2 Thess. 2:8 *The wicked man shall be revealed, whom the Lord shall consume with the spirit of his mouth, and shall abolish with the brightness of his coming.* By 'spirit', the word.

88

Heb. 1:10, 11, 12 *Thou Lord in the beginning hast established the earth; and the heavens are the works of thine hands: they shall perish; but thou dost remain; and they all shall wax old as doth a garment; and as a vesture shalt thou fold them up, and they shall be changed: but thou art the same, and thy years shall not fail.*

89

1 Pet. 4:17, 18 *The time is come that judgement must begin at the house of God: if it first begin at us, what shall the end be of them which obey not the gospel of God? And if the righteous scarcely be saved, where shall the ungodly and the sinner appear?* 'Saved': concerning temporal punishment.

83.II Geneva or Geneva–Tomson
c Geneva–Tomson glosses 1 Cor. 2:9: 'Man cannot so much as think of them, much less conceive them with his senses.'
84.II Geneva or Geneva–Tomson
c Various quarto editions of the Geneva–Tomson New Testament print 'Our victory' in the headline over the cited passage.
85.II Geneva or Geneva–Tomson
c Geneva–Tomson glosses 2 Cor. 6:2: 'In that that grace is offered, it is of the grace of God who hath appointed times and seasons to all things, that we may take occasion when it is offered'; and 'Which I of my free mercy and love towards thee liked of and appointed: at which time God poured out that his marvellous love upon us.'
86.II probably Geneva (Geneva–Tomson reads 'girded', 1), with 'ye' altered to '*you*', 4
c Geneva glosses 'salvation': 'The salvation purchased by Jesus Christ.'
87.II probably Geneva (Geneva–Tomson reads 'that wicked man'.)
c Geneva glosses 'with . . . mouth': 'That is, with his word.'
88.II Geneva or Geneva–Tomson
89.II Geneva or Geneva–Tomson
c Geneva glosses 'saved': 'As concerning this life where he is punished.'

90

Here by 'seraphins', angels.

Every one of the seraphin that stood upon the throne had six wings; with twain he covered his face, and with twain he covered his feet, and with twain he did fly; and one cried to another and said, Holy, holy, holy, is the Lord of hosts: the whole world is full of his glory. Isa. 6:2, 3, Ezek. 10:20

91

They shall not be hungry, neither shall they be thirsty; neither shall the heat smite them, nor the sun: for he that hath compassion on them shall lead them, even to the springs of waters shall he drive them. Isa. 49:10

92

By 'wine and milk', spiritual joy and nourishment.

Ho, everyone that thirsteth, come ye to the waters, and ye that have no silver, come, buy, and eat; come, I say, buy wine and milk without silver and without money. Isa. 55:1

Thus have you heard the heavenly music of the prophets and evangelists, at which every good man's soul springs and rejoices: never sweeter harmony, nor ever cheaper. Come, and hear, 'tis freely yours; come, and feast, yours all.

What heaven calls his, call yours: be glad, and feast;
There is no price set on a heavenly guest:
Milk, water, wine—life, grace, th'Eternal's love—
All three are free, and so I hope you'll prove.

FINIS.

Deo soli gloria sapienti.

90.I Geneva, with the opening part, '*Every . . . throne*', rephrased from 'The Seraphims stood upon it, every one', and incorporating the throne reference from Isa. 6:1
c Geneva glosses 'seraphim': 'They were angels, so called, because they were of a fiery colour, to signify that they burn in the love of God, or were light as fire to execute his will.'
91.I Geneva
92.I Geneva
c Geneva glosses Isa. 51:1: 'By waters, wine, milk and bread, he meaneth all things necessary to the spiritual life, as these are necessary to this corporal life.'
92a.I.11 ***Deo . . . sapienti*** glory to God, the only wise one (Latin)

90

Rev. 4:8 *The four beasts had each one of them six wings about him; and they were full of eyes within: and they ceased not day nor night, saying, Holy, holy, holy, Lord God Almighty, which was, and which is, and which is to come.*

91

Rev. 7:16, 17 *They shall hunger no more, neither thirst any more; neither shall the sun light on them, neither any heat; for the Lamb, which is in the midst of the throne, shall govern them, and shall lead them unto the lively fountains of waters: and GOD shall wipe away all tears from their eyes.*

All infirmity and misery shall be taken away.

92

Rev. *ult.*:16, 17 *I, Jesus, have sent mine angel to testify unto you these things in the churches. I am the root and the generation of* David, *and the bright morning star. And the spirit and the bride say, Come. And let him that heareth say, Come; and let him that is athirst come; and let whosoever will, take of the water of life freely.*

Come, you that desire heavenly graces and comfort.

Thus have you heard the heavenly music of the prophets and evangelists, at which every good man's soul springs and rejoices: never sweeter harmony, nor ever cheaper. Come, and hear, 'tis freely yours; come, and feast, yours all.

What heaven calls his, call yours: be glad, and feast;
There is no price set on a heavenly guest:
Milk, water, wine—life, grace, th'Eternal's love—
All three are free, and so I hope you'll prove.

FINIS.

Christo gloria.

90.II Geneva or Geneva-Tomson
91.II Geneva or Geneva-Tomson, with 'mids' expanded to '*middest*', 3
c Geneva glosses Rev. 7:16: 'For all infirmity and misery shall be then taken away.'
92.II Geneva or Geneva-Tomson
c Geneva glosses 'athirst': 'He that feeleth himself oppressed with afflictions, and desireth the heavenly graces and comfort.'
92a.II.11 ***Christo gloria*** glory to Christ (Latin)

ADDITIONAL PASSAGES

A

To the very worthy deserver of all true honours, and constant lover both of religion and learning,

[ ]

Worthy Sir,

Such fruits as, for the *diet* of the *soul*, I have prepared for myself do I most gladly bestow upon you. *Prophets* were the first grafters of them, *evangelists* the gatherers of them, and the *tree* on which they grow is Christ; it was a *heavenly pleasure* to me to climb up to these *branches*, and I hope it shall be a heavenly *banquet* to you to taste that which they bear. This book is as it were a *map* of a *large kingdom* wherein you may see so much drawn forth as was promised by the *King* of *heaven* and *earth* should be bestowed upon his only *begotten son*. The *city* of the soul is builded *above*, and through these two *gates* must she pass if she *travel* to *salvation*. The one *gate* was opened more than five thousand years ago (even presently after the world was made), for to *Adam* himself was a *Messiah* promised. At that *gate*, *prophets* stood waiting, and telling news of his coming. But to us the other *gate* is opened, and we are assured that our *shepherd* is come; Christ hath been a dweller with us upon earth. In whose *birth*, *life*, *words*, *deeds*, *passion*, *death*, *resurrection*, and *ascension* is fulfilled whatsoever of him was foretold. I am a mere stranger to your eye (though not to the good fame that lives of you familiarly conversant). But sithence the *voyage* of every professed Christian lies but one *way*, and that *way* is set down here by the principles of *spiritual navigation*, accept of my poor knowledge therein, I beseech you, which offers itself, not as a *guide* unto your journey (you no doubt having skill enough of your own), but as a perfect *circle* of my love, filled with many wishes that after you have gone through this first *gate* of a momentary life, you may enter in at that second, which leadeth to all eternity and happiness.

Devoted most affectionately to your

[ ]

B

To the two noble examples of friendship and brotherhood,

Mr *Richard Fishbourne* and Mr *John Browne*

This sacred work is consecrated, as a testimony of his love and service, to worth and virtue,

By *Tho. Middleton*, Chronologer for the honourable city of London

A This is the text of a dedication leaf that appears between the title-page and the Preface in the solitary extant copy of the 1609 issue of *Two Gates*.

2–3 **learning, [ ]** In the original dedication leaf a space follows 'learning,' for manuscript insertion of the dedicatee's name; the space is blank in the only surviving copy containing this leaf.

17 **more than . . . ago** See note to Preface.111–12 above.

26 **sithence** since

26–8 ***voyage . . . navigation*** i.e. in reference to the typological formulation that sees every Christian life as a correlative type or antitype

36–7 **Devoted . . . your [ ]** As in the case of the blank space for the dedicatee's name, a space is left at the conclusion of the dedicatory epistle for manuscript completion.

B This is the text of a dedication leaf that appears between the title-page and the Preface in the only extant copy of the 1620 issue of *Two Gates*.

3 ***Richard Fishbourne . . . John Browne*** prominent London merchants of Puritan sympathies (Mercer and Merchant Taylor respectively)

6–7 **Chronologer . . . London** a title acquired by Middleton 6 September 1620 and held until his death (1627)

THE ROARING GIRL *or* MOLL CUTPURSE

Edited by Coppélia Kahn

The Roaring Girle.
OR
Moll Cut-Purſe.
As it hath lately beene Acted on the Fortune-ſtage by *the Prince his Players.*
Written by *T. Middleton* and *T. Dekkar.*

My caſe is alter'd, I muſt worke for my liuing.

Printed at *London* for *Thomas Archer*, and are to be ſold at his ſhop in Popes head-pallace, neere the Royall Exchange. 1611.

MARY FRITH, the notorious London figure who inspired Middleton and Dekker to create the heroine of *The Roaring Girl*, may well have been the first English woman to perform in a public theatre. Sometime in the spring of 1611, according to church court records, she sat on the stage of the Fortune Theatre 'in the public view of all the people there present, in man's apparel, and played upon her lute and sang a song'. The Epilogue to *The Roaring Girl*, moreover, promises a repeat performance from her 'some few days hence... on this stage'. The 'original' of the play's roaring girl, a woman who dressed as a man, appears here in writing as a performer. And she could have made her stage debut in the very play that fictionalized her as a comic heroine, for (as allusions to contemporary events in the text indicate) *The Roaring Girl* was probably first performed at about the same time as Moll's stage appearance, in late April or early May of 1611, at the Fortune Theatre. Its printed version, entered in the Stationers' Register on 18 February, 1612, only nine days after Mary Frith appeared in the customary white robe at Paul's Cross to do penance for her behaviour at the theatre the preceding spring (and for other offences), was probably intended to capitalize on that public appearance. As reported by John Chamberlain, her penance was as much a performance as her singing and playing onstage at the Fortune:

> she wept bitterly and seemed very penitent, but it is since doubted [suspected] she was maudlin drunk, being discovered to have tippled of three quarts of sack before she came to her penance.

New evidence of Mary Frith's transgressiveness has recently come to light. On September 26, 1611 (between her performance at the Fortune and her penance at St Paul's), the London Court of Aldermen cites her for unspecified 'divers misdemeanours', probably other than cross-dressing, and sends her to Newgate.

A purportedly factual life of Mary Frith, much influenced by stereotypes of criminal biography, was published in 1662. Recent research by Gustav Ungerer reveals that unlike the play's heroine, Mary Frith married—and carried on a profitable business as broker of stolen goods while also serving as intermediary between pickpockets (of whom she had been one for many years), their victims, and the authorities. He suggests that her cross-dressing was indeed performance, through which she tried 'to carve a niche for herself... in the entertainment business of Southwark and the City of London'.

In effect, Dekker and Middleton's Moll Cutpurse is a nexus of interchanges between the living woman and the fictional character, the performed and the real. And within any one textual representation of her, we find ambiguities and inconsistencies that expose constructions of gender in this patriarchal society, despite their apparent rigidity, as shifting and multivalent. Moreover, 'like a fat eel through a Dutchman's fingers', Moll slips between classes as well as genders, as did Mary Frith. She is equally at home with nobles, middle-class artisans, or criminals, but interacts with all of them so as to expose and explore social tensions increased by extremes of wealth and poverty in an expanding, nascently capitalistic consumer economy. In collaborating on *The Roaring Girl* Dekker and Middleton, both deeply familiar with London's social topography, fused their talents; though one of the two probably wrote certain scenes, both writers shaped the whole play.

As Marjorie Garber suggests, cross-dressing like Moll's 'offers a challenge to easy notions of binarity, putting into question the categories of "female" and "male"'. Unlike the Shakespearean comic heroines who disguise themselves as boys so that they can covertly pursue the men they love, but abandon their assumed identities when obstacles to marriage are overcome, Moll never conceals her socially ascribed identity as a woman, doesn't stop dressing like a man, and refuses to marry. By wearing breeches and carrying a sword, she assumes the social position and prerogatives of a man—without either renouncing her social identity as a woman or conforming to its dictates. Thus she transgresses one of the most fiercely defended cultural boundaries of early modern Europe. In the final scene, when her fleeting disguise as a bride is plucked off, she puckishly declares to the bridegroom's appalled father, 'Methinks you should be proud of such a daughter— | As good a man as your son!' She has demonstrated that 'being a man' might be, as Judith Butler claims, 'a kind of persistent impersonation that passes as the real'. And the same proposition applies, of course, to 'being a woman'.

Indeed, in diverse kinds of cultural traditions women did impersonate men. Female cross-dressing flourished not only as a literary motif but also as a social practice, part of a struggle over women's place in early modern Europe that was just as characteristic of the period as the rhetoric of divinely ordered hierarchies frequently marshalled to quell it. In seventeenth and eighteenth century Holland, 119 cases of women living or trying to live as men over a period of years have been documented; in England, where female cross-dressing hasn't yet been fully researched, about fifty instances are known. Those in Holland who dressed and lived as men were usually poor, labouring class women under the age of twenty-five, orphaned or in conflict with their families, and away from home in pursuit of work. If they couldn't earn a living as servants, the usual alternatives were begging, vagrancy, and prostitution, so they joined an army or shipped off to sea as sailors, some accompanying husbands or lovers.

The English ballad figure of 'the warrior maid' closely parallels these instances of female cross-dressing in social life. 'Mary Ambree', the first of about one hundred such ballads written over the next three centuries, was published about a decade before *The Roaring Girl*'s first performance, in 1600. It tells the story of a woman who becomes a soldier to avenge her lover's death and fights valiantly as a man in the siege of Gaunt. In these ballads as in a fictional biography of 'Long Meg', a cross-dressing woman in Henry VIII's London, love is almost always the heroine's motive for 'manly' deeds, and fully compatible with them. Like *The Roaring Girl*, which pursues a conventional comic courtship plot while celebrating a manly heroine who rejects marriage, these ballads represent an unresolved combination of the erotic with the martial, the conventionally feminine with the (masculine) heroic.

In so far as cross-dressing women simply tried to be taken for men, they were conforming to gender norms—but in so far as they succeeded (and it is only those who were ultimately discovered that we know about), they tend to support Butler's claim that gender is a 'persistent impersonation'. Though Dekker and Middleton's characterization of Moll bears more than a trace of the warrior maid tradition, it also differs strikingly, for on only one occasion and for one specific purpose (exposing Laxton) does Moll try to pass as a man. Otherwise, she pursues her eccentric bi-modal career of speaking and acting on women's behalf while acting and speaking as she is dressed—'like a man'.

Moll wasn't the only woman in sixteenth or seventeenth century London, then, to wear a doublet. We can also find precedents for her dress among bourgeois or gentry women, for whom a 'broad-brimmed hat and wanton feather' topping 'ruffianly short locks' became the latest fashion in the 1570s and 1580s, and again around 1620. Unlike Moll—if we can believe hostile male witnesses—these women used men's clothes specifically to enhance their femininity, wearing 'the loose, lascivious civil embracement of a French doublet, being all unbuttoned to entice'. This description is taken from *Hic Mulier; or, The Man Woman* (1620), a pamphlet indicting the fashion and, even more, the behaviours it elicited from its wearers: 'vile and horrible profanations', 'ruffianly and uncivil actions' that make women

> man in body by attire, man in behaviour by rude complement, man in nature by aptness to anger, man in action by pursuing revenge, man in wearing weapons, man in using weapons . . . so much man in all things that they are neither men nor women, but just good for nothing.

Moll's male dress isn't designed for sexual enticement and she rejects all sexual advances. Nonetheless, in the play as in the pamphlet, clothes make the man, as it were. Men's clothes prompt or authorize the wearer to impersonate male behaviour, to perform a stylized kind of aggressive, self-assertive masculinity like that of the 'roaring boy', a recognized social type in early seventeenth century London on which Mary Frith patterned herself.

Hic Mulier (in Latin, an impossible phrase yoking a masculine pronoun to the feminine noun for woman) was promptly answered by *Haec Vir* (a similarly incorrect, oxymoronic Latin phrasing pertaining to a man). The woman in *Haec Vir* defends her right to dress as she pleases on the grounds that women 'are as freeborn as men, have as free election, and as free spirits'. She denies the dogma of female subjection, and dress as the sign of it. Instead, she calls clothing merely a matter of custom—absurd, foolish, and like the rest of the world, 'a warehouse of change', from which men and women alike are empowered by their creator to choose. This powerful argument, however, is followed by a conclusion that takes precisely the opposite tack, in which the woman argues that if men will only abandon their feminizing fashions and resume 'those manly things which you have forsaken', then women will 'like rich jewels hang at your eares to take our instructions'. Together this pair of pamphlets suggests the range of conflicting positions about gender difference as essence and as social construction that is dramatized in *The Roaring Girl*.

As Ann Rosalind Jones and Peter Stallybrass argue, among the various discourses that seek to distinguish male from female, 'gender is never grounded: there is no master discourse which is called upon to fix the essence of gender'. Certainly religion claimed that kind of authority by appealing to the Bible and reading Eve's creation as a paradigm for the hierarchy of male over female. According to Genesis, God made Eve to supply that 'help' that Adam wanted, and thus Adam and Eve were seen as the first husband and wife. In sermon after sermon, preachers insist that 'the husband is the head of the woman, as Christ is the head of the Church', making marriage the general model of women's subjection to patriarchal authority. Nonetheless, numerous handbooks of marriage specifying the roles of husband and wife arrive, as Catherine Belsey points out, at a confusing position for the woman, who is configured as 'an authoritative mistress' over servants and children but nonetheless 'a subjected wife' in relation to her husband, whose position within the family is always clearly that of governor. In *The Roaring Girl*, the troubled marriages of the Gallipots and the Openworks articulate a similar confusion of authority. For example, Mistress Gallipot claims higher social rank than her husband, and her role in attracting and serving customers is crucial to his business as apothecary, yet she rebukes him for being too 'cookish', too fond and subservient, as if goading him to enact his proper role as governor.

Given the actual instability in discourses that purport to be clear and authoritative about sexual difference, it is no surprise that clothing is called upon to serve as a 'sign distinctive to discern betwixt sex and sex', in the words of Philip Stubbes, writing against cross-dressing women in 1583. He continues: 'therefore one to wear the apparel of another sex is to... adulterate the verity of his own kind', implying that the woman who dons a doublet alters her gender, actually becoming partly male in nature—as if clothing had the magical power to alter flesh and spirit. (Dekker and Middleton play with this idea in the *double entendre* of scene 4, implying that the breeches for which the tailor measures Moll must accommodate a male organ.) Stubbes calls male-dressed women '*Hermaphroditi*, that is, monsters of both kinds, half women, half men', epithets applied to Moll by Sir Alexander and his friends, who say she is 'woman more than man, | Man more than woman.... A monster!' (2.132–3, 137). If women costumed as men may become virtual men and perform *as* men, they not only threaten male governance; they also call masculinity as a fixed essence into question.

Moreover, clothing was a 'sign distinctive' not only of gender but also of social rank. The male voice of *Hic Mulier* equates such appropriation of manliness in dress and behaviour with a collapse of all social difference, asking 'Must but a bare pair of shears pass between noble and ignoble, between the generous spirit and the base mechanic? Shall we all be coheirs of one honour, one estate, and one habit?' The sumptuary laws (in effect till 1604) and Elizabeth's royal proclamations frequently reiterating them were meant to maintain hierarchy in the face of unprecedented social mobility. When a prosperous merchant could afford to wear the velvet reserved for a lord, arguments against women's cross-dressing easily modulated into dire warnings against the levelling of ranks.

The Roaring Girl dramatizes the interdependency of fashion, money, gender, and rank that is a major preoccupation of city comedy. In the courtship plot that pits son against father and then reconciles them, Sir Alexander Wengrave, proud of his place and his wealth, opposes his son's match with Mary Fitzallard because he considers her dowry of 5000 marks (considerably larger than usual) insufficient. He equates the woman with her money. When she pursues Sebastian, disguising herself as a seamstress delivering an order of fashionable collars, the play superimposes the working woman who makes and sells commodities onto the bourgeois woman who is herself a commodity.

Just as strikingly, scene 3 opens with the three citizen wives framed in their shops, displaying themselves and their wares as objects of the gallants' acquisitive gaze. They are selling items necessary to the self-presentation of the stylish gentleman: tobacco, ruffs, feathers. 'Gentlemen, what is't you lack?' cries Mistress Openwork in the time-honoured language of street vendors (5.1), inadvertently suggesting that both status and gender can be signified through what men buy and wear. Laxton and Goshawk each hope to profit from these women, one financially, the other sexually. And the women seek from the gallants a sexual pleasure that the economic partnership of marriage doesn't afford them. Moll is the only female shopper, roving from stall to stall as freely as the men, but Laxton tries to buy her, too, giving her ten gold angels to join him in a rendezvous—the same ten angels he wheedled from Mistress Gallipot. Moll flings them back at him when they meet, with a stinging indictment of lechers who prey on 'distressed needlewomen and trade-fallen wives' (5.95).

Moll's masculine clothing enables her to intervene in the circulation of goods, money, and women that shores up masculine identities by keeping women in their place. Her costume and behaviour function like a 'persistent impersonation' that *isn't* meant to pass for the real. Rather, its point is precisely to show that a woman can act like a man, can perform masculinity and do what men do, but on her own behalf. 'I scorn to prostitute myself to a man', she cries as she challenges Laxton, 'I that can prostitute a man to me' (5.111–12). In a play world of male characters who intrigue, swindle, and fail to govern themselves or others well, ranging from gentlemen such as the greedy Sir Alexander and impotent Laxton to displaced rascals such as Trapdoor and Tearcat, 'honest Moll' stands up for herself. Scene 5, in which she turns her assignation with Laxton into a swordfight and a bruising denunciation of men like him, best demonstrates this strategy at work.

The scene recalls the figure of the warrior woman in Renaissance epics such as Spenser's *The Faerie Queene* and Ariosto's *Orlando Furioso* and in popular literature such as *Long Meg of Westminster*: the woman disguised as a warrior who challenges and defeats a braggart male in a swordfight, then reveals herself as a woman by removing her helmet and letting down her long hair. Thus she reaffirms her essential difference from the man, and shows him up as less than a man; she normalizes gender difference. Here the playwrights give the motif a new twist, in that the 'real' Moll revealed when she takes off her cloak isn't the 'normal' woman Laxton counts on, the woman who can be reduced to a sexual object, but rather one who fights like a man yet speaks as a woman identified with women, to defend them from men's slander.

'Thou'rt one of those', she charges, 'That thinks each woman thy fond flexible whore', a man who interprets any woman's behaviour as indicating her innate seducibility (5.72–3). Even worse, she says, he speaks of chaste, virtuous women as whorish, gives them 'a blasted name', and ruins them. In this speech, the longest in the play, Moll focuses not on dress but on language deployed by men as the power that subjects women, first by eroticizing them, and then by slandering them as unchaste. Here the play refracts a problem faced by women generally in early modern England, for whom chastity was the *sine qua non* of social acceptability. As Susan Amussen argues, citing defamation cases tried in church courts, 'Women's reputations were far more narrowly rooted in sexual behaviour ... [and] more easily threatened than men's'. Mistress Gallipot's false story of a precontracted marriage with Laxton is a desperate (and highly comic) expedient to protect her reputation. In a more serious vein, the play often makes a point of the disparity between Moll's reputation for whorishness and thievery, and her actual chastity and uprightness.

This brings us to a seeming contradiction, reminiscent of *Hic Mulier*, in the way male characters respond to Moll's male dress. Instead of simply making her more of a man and thus less appealing as a woman, it heightens her sexual attractiveness. Laxton sees her as a figure of extraordinary sexual potency who would challenge or even exhaust the virility of men who desire her. Though Sir Alexander considers Moll 'half woman, half man' and thus a monster, he also takes her apparel as a sign that she's a whore. (London court records show that women dressing as men were often accused of prostitution.) Thus he links it with the name Moll which, as he tells Sebastian, is typically a whore's name (4.160–2). That it is also a nickname for Mary suggests, as is the case in *A Chaste Maid in Cheapside*, that the virgin and the whore are both types of male desire, a bifurcated image of woman constructed by patriarchal discourse. This linkage is inscribed in the plot of *The Roaring Girl*, in which Sebastian pretends to court Moll for the sake of winning Mary, and the two women appear successively as his bride in the final scene.

In scene 8, however, when both Mary and Moll wear breeches, the playwrights explore a different configuration of desire. Sebastian says when he kisses Mary, 'Methinks a woman's lip tastes well in a doublet' (8.47)—possibly because the doublet recalls a male love object, a boy who could be the 'ingle' or sexual partner of a gallant, one of his many pleasures, like those in the list Sir Davy Dapper reels off: 'A noise of fiddlers, tobacco, wine, and a whore ... fencers and ningles' (7.64–8). The fact that both Mary and Moll would be played by boy actors makes it possible, as Lisa Jardine and others have argued, that boy actors playing female characters (especially those in male costume) might appeal to men homoerotically as well as heterosexually. The homoerotic implications of scene 8, however, are somewhat at odds with the heterosexual implications of the marriage plot, as are the 'two noble friends' Sir Beauteous Ganymede (ganymede being a synonym for ingle) and Sir Noland who escort the real bride in the final scene.

Though Moll promotes the marriage of Mary and Sebastian, she herself adamantly refuses to marry, which she explains and justifies in a sequence of contradictions that mirrors the controversy over women in texts like *Hic Mulier* and *Haec Vir*. On the one hand, she rejects marriage because 'a wife ought to be obedient', but she herself is 'too headstrong to obey'; she presents herself as an exception to a norm she doesn't question. On the other hand, she declares

> I have the head now of myself, and am man enough for a woman; marriage is but a chopping and changing, where a maiden loses one head, and has a worse i'th' place. (4.43–7)

Here she criticizes marriage, implying that it involves violence against women and submission to an unfit male authority. Yet in doing so, she draws on the hierarchical opposition of head to body that, in patriarchal discourse, subtends and reinforces that of male to female. She can find no other language than this in which to assert her headship, her autonomy. So long as Moll remains outside marriage and resists normalization as a woman, though, she modifies the threat she poses to men, for as a 'headstrong' woman who is nobody's wife, she challenges no husband's mastery. The price she pays for her freedom, however, is the abridgement of her own sexuality, which is dramatized in the play's most original scene—saturated with sexual *doubles entendres*—when she plays the viol and sings. Reversing the passive/active, female/male relationships usually imaged in literary representations of erotic activity, she plays rather than being played upon, but 'fingering' and stroking an instrument held between her legs can be interpreted both as heterosexual and as auto-erotic. The haunting, dream-like lyrics of her songs mysteriously suggest female autonomy in a community of women:

I dream there is a mistress,
And she lays out the money;
She goes unto her sisters,
And never comes at any. (8.103–6)

Like many of her speeches, they also protest the hypocrisy of those who impugn her chastity: 'Yet she began, like all my foes, | To call whore first' (8.122–3). 'Except in dreams', as Jean E. Howard suggests, 'Moll cannot be an autonomous sexual subject and escape being called a whore.'

Most readers have found her, nonetheless, irresistible as both focus and source of the play's energies. Oddly, both the Victorian editor Bullen and the modernist poet-critic T. S. Eliot share an uncritical delight in Moll Cutpurse. To Bullen she is an 'Amazon of the Bankside' with 'the thews of a giant and the gentleness of a child', while in his influential 1927 essay Eliot finds her 'a real and unique human being', yet also 'a type of the sort of woman who has renounced all happiness for herself and who lives only for a principle'. In a different vein, Eliot applied to Middleton Kathleen Lynch's thesis that Elizabethan–Jacobean comedy dramatized the rise of the merchant class to gentry status. Thus he helped to nudge interpretation away from its fascination with Moll toward the socio-economic approach to city comedy represented by L. C. Knights (1938). Knights, however, concentrates solely on the intrigues of citizens and gallants, ignoring Moll, while in the first book devoted to city comedy (1968), Brian Gibbons neglects to discuss the play at all. Five years later Alexander Leggatt's book on city comedy breaks this critical silence on Moll, arguing that the playwrights make her chastity not a docile submission to prevailing mores but 'the assertion of an individual will'. He locates this extraordinary assertiveness, however, entirely in her chastity, without even mentioning her male dress.

It is only with the advent of feminist criticism that *The Roaring Girl* is being understood as a probing critique of intersecting class and gender ideologies, rather than as a play about a historical curiosity. Recent essays by Rose (1984) and Howard (1988, 1992) set it in the context of a hierarchical social system trying to regulate both class and gender under the intense pressure of economic and cultural change. Shepherd (1981) and Helms (1989) view Moll as avatar of a classic literary type, the warrior woman, but like Rose and Howard, read that type in terms of a social contest over what gender means. Several critics focus on marriage as the key point in this contest: Comensoli (1987), Hendricks (1990), and Miller (1990) examine the commodifying effects of the exchange of women by men through marriage. Others, such as Dawson (1993), Nakayama (1993), and Orgel (1993), look at the performative dimensions of Moll's dual gender identity as part of an interplay among various cultural representations of gender. Garber (1991) interprets the play as a manifestation of cultural anxiety about masculinity as much as femininity, a play that, fascinated with fashion and clothing, theorizes in them the fashioning of gender. This rich, stimulating body of work places *The Roaring Girl* at the centre of cultural change in early modern England, opening it up to questions that are, at the same time, current in the 1990s: does cross-dressing subvert or recuperate an oppositional gender ideology? Can the performance of gender effectively challenge oppressive political and economic structures?

Until a 1951 production by the Brattle Street Theatre in Cambridge, Massachusetts, there is no record that *The Roaring Girl* was revived. The Brattle Street production pleased audiences as a fast-paced Restoration farce, with Nancy Walker playing Moll as 'a... combination of Groucho Marx and Mae West.' The intrigues between citizens and gallants were radically trimmed, but songs and a 'Keystone Cops' chase sequence were added. Of the six other performances since, two command special interest. Sue-Ellen Case's 1979 adaptation at the University of California, Berkeley, was the first that opened the play to feminist inquiry. Case emphasized the intersection of acting conventions with gendered power structures. Using a main stage for a 'straight' performance of the text and an adjacent stage for a concurrent dressing room drama, she cast the entire play with female actors. By intercutting dialogue from *The Roaring Girl* with the actors' mocking, probing backstage interrogations of it, she implied that the characters in the play, the all-male actors of Middleton's theatre, and the female actors were all playing gender roles scripted by male dominance and heterosexuality. The actress most critical of such structures is accused of scene-stealing, and bound and gagged by the others. Moll's part inspires provocative comment such as 'All plays are about male identification. But not about women doing it'. Her centrality as heroine is undermined, however, and attention re-focused on the patriarchal system that configures all characters: 'It's about money and how it buys sex... in the hands of the male'.

The 1983 Royal Shakespeare Company production of *The Roaring Girl*, directed by Barry Kyle and starring Helen Mirren as Moll, similarly emphasized the play's critique of the social order while trying to make it appealing as a comedy. A risky revival of a little-known play, it was paired with *The Taming of the Shrew* to increase box-office draw (thus also setting up the inevitable comparison with Shakespeare). Mirren won praise for her performance of Moll as a working class heroine with a Cockney accent who 'radiates mirth'. But some reviewers were put off by the implications of the set, which included 'a set of cog-wheels representing Tudor capitalism', in line with Kyle's interpretation of the play as 'a moral comedy about the class system breaking down in a Jacobean world of profiteering and self-interest'. Critical response, heavily influenced by the idealizing praise of Moll in Eliot's 1927 essay, betrays a certain disappointment with the play as a comedy and an edgy resistance to what is perceived as the obscurity of its wordplay and intrigues—which is surely no greater than that of Shakespeare. In the decade since 1983, however, feminist scholarship has made the play legible as a document of early modern culture contiguous with our own times. Moreover, the popular success of films such as *The Crying Game* (1992), and of plays such as *M. Butterfly* (1988) that challenge traditional thinking about gender as innate and fixed, may encourage performances of *The Roaring Girl* that release its intellectual and dramatic energies anew.

SEE ALSO

Textual introduction and apparatus: *Companion*, 610
Authorship and date: *Companion*, 369
Other Middleton–Dekker works: *Caesar's Fall*, 328; *Gravesend*, 128; *Meeting*, 183; *Magnificent*, 219; *Patient Man*, 280; *Banquet*, 637; *Gypsy*, 1723

THOMAS MIDDLETON and THOMAS DEKKER

The Roaring Girl

[*for Prince Henry's Men at The Fortune*]

THE PERSONS OF THE PLAY

Sir ALEXANDER Wengrave
NEATFOOT, his man
[SIR THOMAS Long]
SIR ADAM Appleton
SIR DAVY Dapper
SIR BEAUTEOUS Ganymede
LORD NOLAND
Young [SEBASTIAN] Wengrave
JACK DAPPER, and GULL his page
GOSHAWK
GREENWIT
LAXTON

TILTYARD and MISTRESS TILTYARD
OPENWORK and MISTRESS OPENWORK
GALLIPOT and MISTRESS GALLIPOT

MOLL, the Roaring Girl
TRAPDOOR
[TEARCAT]

SIR GUY Fitzallard
MARY Fitzallard, his daughter

CURTALAX, a Sergeant
HANGER, his Yeoman

Ministri [FELLOW with long rapier, PORTER, TAILOR, COACHMAN, 5 or 6 CUTPURSES]

Epistle *To the Comic Play-readers, Venery and Laughter*

The fashion of play-making I can properly compare to nothing so naturally as the alteration in apparel: for in the time of the great-crop doublet, your huge bombasted plays, quilted with mighty words to lean purpose, was only then in fashion; and as the doublet fell, neater inventions began to set up. Now in the time of spruceness, our plays follow the niceness of our garments: single plots, quaint conceits, lecherous jests dressed up in hanging sleeves; and those are fit for the times and the termers. Such a kind of light-colour summer stuff, mingled with diverse colours, you shall find this published comedy—good to keep you in an afternoon from dice, at home in your chambers; and for venery you shall find enough, for sixpence, but well couched an you mark it. For Venus, being a woman, passes through the play in doublet and

Persons.23 **Ministri** servants (Latin)
Epistle preface in form of a letter
0.1 **Venery** hunting game animals; pursuing sexual pleasure
3 **great-crop doublet** upper body garment worn by men, padded according to fashion
bombasted enlarged with cotton stuffing; padded with inflated language
6 **spruceness** neatness
7 **niceness** elegance
single separate
8 **quaint conceits** clever expressions
8–9 **hanging sleeves** long, open sleeves hanging to knee or foot
9 **termers** people who come to London for legal business, pleasure, or intrigue during terms, periods when courts are in session
14 **sixpence** price of a printed play
couched hidden; decorated
Venus goddess of love; here, Moll Cutpurse

breeches: a brave disguise and a safe one, if the statute untie not her codpiece point! The book I make no question but is fit for many of your companies, as well as the person itself, and may be allowed both gallery-room at the play-house and chamber-room at your lodging. Worse things, I must needs confess, the world has taxed her for than has been written of her; but 'tis the excellency of a writer to leave things better than he finds 'em; though some obscene fellow, that cares not what he writes against others, yet keeps a mystical bawdy-house himself, and entertains drunkards to make use of their pockets and vent his private bottle ale at midnight—though such a one would have ripped up the most nasty vice that ever hell belched forth, and presented it to a modest assembly, yet we rather wish in such discoveries where reputation lies bleeding, a slackness of truth, than fulness of slander.

Thomas Middleton.

Prologue

A play (expected long) makes the audience look
For wonders—that each scene should be a book,
Composed to all perfection; each one comes
And brings a play in's head with him: up he sums,
What he would of a roaring girl have writ—
If that he finds not here, he mews at it.
Only we entreat you think our scene
Cannot speak high, the subject being but mean.
A roaring girl, whose notes till now never were,
Shall fill with laughter our vast theatre:
That's all which I dare promise; tragic passion,
And such grave stuff, is this day out of fashion.
I see attention sets wide ope her gates
Of hearing, and with covetous listening waits
To know what girl this roaring girl should be—
For of that tribe are many. One is she
That roars at midnight in deep tavern bowls,
That beats the watch, and constables controls;
Another roars i'th' day-time, swears, stabs, gives
braves,
Yet sells her soul to the lust of fools and slaves:
Both these are suburb-roarers. Then there's besides
A civil, city-roaring girl, whose pride,
Feasting, and riding, shakes her husband's state,
And leaves him roaring through an iron grate.
None of these roaring girls is ours: she flies
With wings more lofty. Thus her character lies—
Yet what need characters, when to give a guess,
Is better than the person to express?
But would you know who 'tis? would you hear her
name?
She is called Mad Moll; her life, our acts proclaim.

Enter Mary Fitzallard disguised like a sempster with a case for bands, and Neatfoot a servingman with her, with a napkin on his shoulder, and a trencher in his hand as from table Sc. 1

NEATFOOT The young gentleman, our young master, Sir Alexander's son—is it into his ears, sweet damsel, emblem of fragility, you desire to have a message transported, or to be transcendent?

MARY A private word or two, sir, nothing else.

NEATFOOT You shall fructify in that which you come for: your pleasure shall be satisfied to your full contentation. I will, fairest tree of generation, watch when our young master is erected—that is to say up—and deliver him to this your most white hand.

16 **disguise** fashion; deceptive dress
statute could refer to misdemeanors, including male dress, for which Mary Frith was brought before a church court in January 1611/12 (see Introduction). Church laws, based on Deut. 22:5, prohibited women from dressing as men, but civil law did not.
17 **untie not her codpiece point** does not reveal that she is a woman (the codpiece, a cloth bag covering the male genitals, was tied to hose or breeches by laces called points)
19 **gallery-room** a place in the covered, tiered seating of the playhouse
24 **obscene** offensive
25 **keeps a mystical bawdy-house** secretly enjoys illicit sex
27 **vent** pour out
27–9 **though such a one ... modest assembly** Unlike the author, this writer is hypocritical; though personally immoral, he self-righteously exposes extreme vice to decent people.
Prologue.5 **a roaring girl** see Moll Cutpurse, 1.72, note
6 **mews** derides by imitating a cat's cry
7–8 **our scene ... but mean** Our play can't be tragic (high), because its subject (Moll) is of low social rank; see 11–12.
9 **whose notes ... never were** who has never been represented on stage before
10 **our vast theatre** the Fortune Theatre, in which the play was first performed; like other public theatres, it held approximately 2000–3000 persons
17 **bowls** drinking vessels
18 **constables** officers of the ward or parish responsible for keeping order
controls rebukes
19 **gives braves** defies, flouts
21 **suburb-roarers** Suburbs were areas outside the city walls, not subject to city authorities.
24 **through an iron grate** behind the iron-barred window of a cell in debtors' prison
26 **character** distinctive traits
30 **Mad Moll** wild, eccentric, not conforming to standards of female behaviour; cf. 1.102, note
1.0.1 **Mary Fitzallard** Mary connotes chastity, especially in conjunction with Moll (see 1.73, note).
sempster one who sews garments for a living, either man or woman
0.2 ***case for bands*** a box for neck-bands or collars
Neatfoot suggests skill and efficiency as a servant; pun on oxfoot prepared as food
0.4 ***trencher*** wooden plate or shallow dish, common in noble or fashionable households at this time
1–2 **The young gentleman ... son** Sebastian, Sir Alexander's son and heir, in love with Mary Fitzallard
Sir Alexander's Sir Alexander Wengrave; 'grave' suggests his dignity as Justice of the Peace. In the original quarto, spelled 'Went-grave' only in the dramatis personae, suggesting his response to Mary Fitzallard's dowry.
4 **transcendent** affected diction typical of Neatfoot
6 **fructify ... come for** suggests sexual consummation
8 **tree of generation** suggests Mary's desired union with Sebastian, which would make her part of his family tree
9 **erected** no longer seated, punning on erection as sexual arousal

MARY Thanks, sir.

NEATFOOT And withal certify him that I have culled out for him, now his belly is replenished, a daintier bit or modicum than any lay upon his trencher at dinner. Hath he notion of your name, I beseech your chastity?

MARY One, sir, of whom he bespake falling-bands.

NEATFOOT Falling bands, it shall so be given him. If you please to venture your modesty in the hall, amongst a curl-pated company of rude servingmen, and take such as they can set before you, you shall be most seriously, and ingeniously welcome.

MARY I have dined indeed already, sir.

NEATFOOT —Or will you vouchsafe to kiss the lip of a cup of rich Orleans in the buttery amongst our waiting-women?

MARY Not now in truth, sir.

NEATFOOT Our young master shall then have a feeling of your being here presently. It shall so be given him.

MARY
I humbly thank you, sir. *Exit Neatfoot*
But that my bosom
Is full of bitter sorrows, I could smile
To see this formal ape play antic tricks;
But in my breast a poisoned arrow sticks,
And smiles cannot become me. Love woven sleightly,
Such as thy false heart makes, wears out as lightly,
But love being truly bred i'th' soul, like mine,
Bleeds even to death at the least wound it takes.
The more we quench this, the less it slakes. O me!

Enter Sebastian Wengrave with Neatfoot

SEBASTIAN A sempster speak with me, sayst thou?

NEATFOOT Yes, sir, she's there, *viva voce*, to deliver her auricular confession.

SEBASTIAN With me, sweetheart? What is't?

MARY I have brought home your bands, sir.

SEBASTIAN Bands? Neatfoot!

NEATFOOT Sir.

SEBASTIAN Prithee look in, for all the gentlemen are upon rising.

NEATFOOT Yes, sir, a most methodical attendance shall be given.

SEBASTIAN And, dost hear, if my father call for me, say I am busy with a sempster.

NEATFOOT Yes, sir, he shall know it that you are busied with a needlewoman.

SEBASTIAN In's ear, good Neatfoot.

NEATFOOT It shall be so given him. *Exit*

SEBASTIAN Bands? You're mistaken, sweetheart, I bespake none. When, where, I prithee? What bands? Let me see them.

MARY
Yes, sir, a bond fast sealed with solemn oaths,
Subscribed unto, as I thought, with your soul,
Delivered as your deed in sight of heaven,
Is this bond cancelled? Have you forgot me?

SEBASTIAN
Ha! Life of my life! Sir Guy Fitzallard's daughter!
What has transformed my love to this strange shape?
Stay; make all sure; so. Now speak and be brief,
Because the wolf's at door that lies in wait
To prey upon us both. Albeit mine eyes
Are blessed by thine, yet this so strange disguise
Holds me with fear and wonder.

MARY
Mine's a loathed sight.
Why from it are you banished else so long?

SEBASTIAN
I must cut short my speech: in broken language,
Thus much, sweet Moll, I must thy company shun.
I court another Moll; my thoughts must run
As a horse runs that's blind: round in a mill,
Out every step, yet keeping one path still.

MARY
Um! Must you shun my company? In one knot

14 **modicum** small quantity of food
16 **falling-bands** collars worn flat (falling), with puns on bond (her precontract with Sebastian) and banns, part of the betrothal ritual (see 56–8, note)
19 **curl-pated** curly-headed
rude unmannerly
21 **ingeniously** graciously
24 **Orleans** French wine from region of Orleans
buttery storeroom for food
24–5 **waiting-women** female servants
28 **presently** immediately
29 **But** except
31 **formal ape** referring to Neatfoot's affectation or aping of formality
antic tricks grotesque gestures
33 **sleightly** craftily, skilfully
39 ***viva voce*** by word of mouth; in person
40 **auricular confession** normally used for confession of sins to a priest; here, insinuates confession of sexual misdemeanors
52 **needlewoman** needle could mean penis
56–8 **bands . . . bond** The two words were used interchangeably. Mary refers to her precontract with Sebastian, a ceremony in which the couple joined hands (with or without witnesses) to signify their union before God, after which they were regarded as husband and wife, but weren't considered fully married until a wedding ceremony took place in church. Before the ceremony, 'banns' had to be called in church on three successive Sundays, announcing the expected wedding ceremony so that those who knew of any impediment could voice their objection.
62 **Sir Guy Fitzallard's** recalls Guy of Warwick, hero of chivalric romance
65 **the wolf's at door** proverbial; refers to Sir Alexander
72 **Moll** nickname for Mary; see l. 73, note; 5.4, note
73 **Moll** the roaring girl. As a proper noun 'moll' means a whore, a thief's female companion, or a female thief. Moll's surname, Cutpurse, associates her with thieves who robbed people by cutting the cord that attached purses to clothing. Purse could also refer to the scrotum. Given Moll's appropriation of masculine prerogatives and the reactions it provokes, 'Cutpurse' hints at castration, the removal of the testicles. Roaring boys were swaggering, quarrelsome young men given to gaming, whoring, and thieving, in defiance of law and social mores.
74–5 **As a horse runs that's blind . . . keeping one path still** proverbial; blindfolded horses provided power for grist mills; suggests persistence

Have both our hands by th'hands of heaven been tied
Now to be broke? I thought me once your bride—
Our fathers did agree on the time when—
And must another bedfellow fill my room?

SEBASTIAN

Sweet maid, let's lose no time. 'Tis in heaven's book
Set down that I must have thee; an oath we took
To keep our vows; but when the knight, your father,
Was from mine parted, storms began to sit
Upon my covetous father's brows, which fell
From them on me. He reckoned up what gold
This marriage would draw from him, at which he
swore
To lose so much blood could not grieve him more.
He then dissuades me from thee, called thee not fair,
And asked, 'What is she but a beggar's heir?'
He scorned thy dowry of five thousand marks.
If such a sum of money could be found,
And I would match with that, he'd not undo it,
Provided his bags might add nothing to it;
But vowed, if I took thee—nay more, did swear it—
Save birth from him I nothing should inherit.

MARY

What follows then—my shipwreck?

SEBASTIAN Dearest, no.

Though wildly in a labyrinth I go,
My end is to meet thee: with a side wind
Must I now sail, else I no haven can find,
But both must sink forever. There's a wench
Called Moll, Mad Moll, or Merry Moll, a creature
So strange in quality, a whole city takes
Note of her name and person. All that affection
I owe to thee, on her, in counterfeit passion,
I spend to mad my father; he believes
I dote upon this roaring girl, and grieves
As it becomes a father for a son
That could be so bewitched; yet I'll go on
This crooked way, sigh still for her, feign dreams
In which I'll talk only of her: these streams
Shall, I hope, force my father to consent
That here I anchor, rather than be rent
Upon a rock so dangerous. Art thou pleased,
Because thou seest we are waylaid, that I take
A path that's safe, though it be far about?

MARY

My prayers with heaven guide thee!

SEBASTIAN Then I will on,

My father is at hand; kiss and be gone.
Hours shall be watched for meetings. I must now,
As men for fear, to a strange idol bow.

MARY

Farewell!

SEBASTIAN

I'll guide thee forth. When next we meet,
A story of Moll shall make our mirth more sweet.

Exeunt

Enter Sir Alexander Wengrave, Sir Davy Dapper, Sir Adam Appleton, Goshawk, Laxton, and Gentlemen Sc. 2

OMNES

Thanks, good Sir Alexander, for our bounteous cheer.

ALEXANDER

Fie, fie, in giving thanks you pay too dear!

SIR DAVY

When bounty spreads the table, faith, 'twere sin,
At going off, if thanks should not step in.

ALEXANDER

No more of thanks, no more. Ay marry, sir,
Th'inner room was too close; how do you like
This parlour, gentlemen?

OMNES O, passing well!

SIR ADAM

What a sweet breath the air casts here—so cool!

GOSHAWK

I like the prospect best.

LAXTON See how 'tis furnished.

SIR DAVY

A very fair sweet room.

ALEXANDER Sir Davy Dapper,

The furniture that doth adorn this room
Cost many a fair grey groat ere it came here;
But good things are most cheap when they're most
dear.
Nay, when you look into my galleries—

77 **our hands . . . tied** refers to precontract; see 56–8, note
80 **bedfellow** If they have had sexual intercourse (which could be implied here), then they would be considered married; could also refer to another match for Sebastian.
81 **heaven's book** refers to precontract as sacred, binding
91 **five thousand marks** worth £3,330, well above the average dowry offered by gentry in 1600–1624, and only slightly below the average offered by peers
94 **bags** money bags
102 **Mad Moll** mad in the sense of not conforming to conventions of behaviour for women; spirited, wild (cf. Prologue.30 and 1.73, note)
103 **quality** character; occupation
111 **streams** currents
113 **rent** torn apart
2.0.1 **Wengrave** see 1.1, note
0.1–2 **Sir Davy Dapper** Dapper suggests smart dress, brisk movements.
0.2 **Sir Adam Appleton** in alluding to the Adam of Genesis, suggests both venerable age and human fallibility
Goshawk female hawk used in falconry; refers to his predatory schemes
Laxton 'lacks stone' (testicle), implying his impotence and his landlessness (see 2.57, note)
5 **marry** exclamation denoting surprise or emphasis; from the Virgin Mary
7 **parlour** a spacious and handsomely furnished sitting room
9 **prospect** view of landscape
12 **fair grey groat** A groat was a silver coin worth fourpence; figuratively, any small sum. Sir Alexander, though, stresses its worth in 'fair'.
14 **galleries** long, narrow rooms in manor houses for the display of family portraits often hung very closely together

How bravely they are trimmed up—you all shall swear
You're highly pleased to see what's set down there:
Stories of men and women, mixed together
Fair ones with foul, like sunshine in wet weather.
Within one square a thousand heads are laid
So close that all of heads the room seems made;
As many faces there, filled with blithe looks,
Show like the promising titles of new books
Writ merrily, the readers being their own eyes,
Which seem to move and to give plaudities.
And here and there, whilst with obsequious ears
Thronged heaps do listen, a cutpurse thrusts and leers
With hawk's eyes for his prey—I need not show him:
By a hanging villainous look yourselves may know him,
The face is drawn so rarely. Then, sir, below,
The very floor, as 'twere, waves to and fro,
And like a floating island, seems to move
Upon a sea bound in with shore above.

Enter Sebastian and Greenwit

OMNES
These sights are excellent!

ALEXANDER I'll show you all;
Since we are met, make our parting comical.

SEBASTIAN
This gentleman—my friend—will take his leave, sir.

ALEXANDER
Ha? Take his leave, Sebastian? Who?

SEBASTIAN This gentleman.

ALEXANDER
Your love, sir, has already given me some time,
And if you please to trust my age with more,
It shall pay double interest—good sir, stay.

GREENWIT
I have been too bold.

ALEXANDER Not so, sir. A merry day
'Mongst friends being spent, is better than gold saved.
Some wine, some wine! Where be these knaves I keep?

Enter three or four Servingmen and Neatfoot

NEATFOOT
At your worshipful elbow, sir.

ALEXANDER You are
Kissing my maids, drinking, or fast asleep.

NEATFOOT
Your worship has given it us right.

ALEXANDER You varlets, stir!
Chairs, stools, and cushions.

Servants bring on wine, chairs, stools and cushions

Prithee, Sir Davy Dapper,
Make that chair thine.

SIR DAVY 'Tis but an easy gift,
And yet I thank you for it, sir; I'll take it.

ALEXANDER
A chair for old Sir Adam Appleton.

NEATFOOT
A backfriend to your worship.

SIR ADAM Marry, good Neatfoot,
I thank thee for it: backfriends sometimes are good.

ALEXANDER
Pray make that stool your perch, good Master Goshawk.

GOSHAWK
I stoop to your lure, sir.

ALEXANDER Son Sebastian,
Take Master Greenwit to you.

SEBASTIAN Sit, dear friend.

ALEXANDER
Nay, Master Laxton. (*To Servant*)—Furnish Master Laxton
With what he wants, a stone—a stool, I would say, a stool.

LAXTON
I had rather stand, sir.

Exeunt [Neatfoot and] Servants

ALEXANDER
I know you had, good Master Laxton. So, so—
Now here's a mess of friends; and gentlemen,
Because time's glass shall not be running long,
I'll quicken it with a pretty tale.

SIR DAVY Good tales do well
In these bad days, where vice does so excel.

SIR ADAM
Begin, Sir Alexander.

ALEXANDER Last day I met

19–24 **Within one square . . . give plaudities** Sir Alexander's description of his galleries modulates into a vision of the tiered galleries of the Fortune Theatre (the only public theatre built as a square) in which the faces of the audience crowded together resemble those in the galleries' portraits, and then, figuratively, the titles of books displayed on library shelves.

24 **plaudities** conflates *plaudite* (Latin), customary appeal for applause made by actors at end of play, with applause

26 **heaps** multitudes

26–7 **a cutpurse . . . for his prey** In court records and other writings, the Fortune was associated with cutpurses and pickpockets.

30–2 **The very floor . . . with shore above** likens the Fortune's floor, crowded with standing spectators, to a sea and the stage to an island

32.1 **Greenwit** suggests youth, naïvete

34 **comical** happy

45 **varlets** servants, or abusively, knaves

46 **Chairs, stools, and cushions** Even in wealthy houses chairs were not plentiful and were often reserved for those of highest rank.

50 **backfriend** chair supporting his back; pun on 'backfriend' as pretended or false friend, and on officer arresting debtor, laying hands on him from behind

52–3 **perch . . . lure** word play on Goshawk's name; in falconry, a hawk stoops to the lure when it comes down for its food

56 **a stone . . . a stool** a jab at Laxton's impotence, punning on 'wants' as lacks, and 'stone' as testicle

57 **stand** be capable of erection; refers to his impotence

59 **mess** proverbially, 'four make up a mess'; a group of four

60–1 **Because time's glass . . . a pretty tale** to make time seem short, I'll tell a story to please you

An aged man upon whose head was scored
A debt of just so many years as these
Which I owe to my grave: the man you all know.

OMNES
His name, I pray you, sir?

ALEXANDER Nay, you shall pardon me.
But when he saw me, with a sigh that brake,
Or seemed to break, his heart-strings, thus he spake:
'O my good knight', says he—and then his eyes
Were richer even by that which made them poor,
They had spent so many tears, they had no more—
'O sir', says he, 'you know it, for you ha' seen
Blessings to rain upon mine house and me.
Fortune, who slaves men, was my slave; her wheel
Hath spun me golden threads, for, I thank heaven,
I ne'er had but one cause to curse my stars.'
I asked him then what that one cause might be.

OMNES
So, sir.

ALEXANDER
He paused, and as we often see
A sea so much becalmed there can be found
No wrinkle on his brow, his waves being drowned
In their own rage; but when th'imperious winds
Use strange invisible tyranny to shake
Both heaven's and earth's foundation at their noise,
The seas swelling with wrath to part that fray
Rise up and are more wild, more mad, than they:
Even so this good old man was by my question
Stirred up to roughness; you might see his gall
Flow even in's eyes; then grew he fantastical.

SIR DAVY
Fantastical? Ha, ha!

ALEXANDER
Yes, and talked oddly.

SIR ADAM
Pray, sir, proceed. How did this old man end?

ALEXANDER
Marry, sir, thus:
He left his wild fit to read o'er his cards;
Yet then, though age cast snow on all his hairs,
He joyed, 'Because', says he, 'the god of gold
Has been to me no niggard. That disease
Of which all old men sicken, avarice,
Never infected me—'

LAXTON (*aside*) He means not himself, I'm sure.

ALEXANDER 'For like a lamp
Fed with continual oil, I spend and throw
My light to all that need it, yet have still
Enough to serve myself. O but', quoth he,
'Though heaven's dew fall thus on this aged tree,
I have a son that's like a wedge doth cleave,
My very heart-root.'

SIR DAVY Had he such a son?

SEBASTIAN (*aside*) Now I do smell a fox strongly.

ALEXANDER
Let's see; no, Master Greenwit is not yet
So mellow in years as he, but as like Sebastian,
Just like my son Sebastian—such another.

SEBASTIAN (*aside*) How finely, like a fencer, my father fetches his by-blows to hit me; but if I beat you not at your own weapon of subtlety—

ALEXANDER
'This son', saith he, 'that should be
The column and main arch unto my house,
The crutch unto my age, becomes a whirlwind
Shaking the firm foundation.'

SIR ADAM 'Tis some prodigal.

SEBASTIAN (*aside*) Well shot, old Adam Bell!

ALEXANDER
No city monster neither, no prodigal,
But sparing, wary, civil, and—though wifeless—
An excellent husband; and such a traveller,
He has more tongues in his head than some have teeth.

SIR DAVY
I have but two in mine.

GOSHAWK So sparing and so wary,
What then could vex his father so?

ALEXANDER O, a woman.

SEBASTIAN A flesh-fly: that can vex any man!

ALEXANDER
A scurvy woman,
On whom the passionate old man swore he doted.
'A creature', saith he, 'nature hath brought forth
To mock the sex of woman.' It is a thing

64 **scored** marked; word play on physical signs of age and 'score' as notch cut on stick in keeping accounts

75–6 **Fortune ... golden threads** combines the wheel of Fortune and the Fates' spinning wheel, both emblems of Fortune's control over human life; may also allude to Fortune Theatre (see 19–24, note)

88 **gall** bile, a bodily substance associated with bitterness; here, merged with tears

89 **fantastical** eccentric, strange

94 **read o'er his cards** take note of the hand fortune dealt him

101 **like a lamp** draws on a parable (Luke 8:16) which had become proverbial: 'a candle lights others and consumes itself'

106 **wedge** tool used for splitting wood or stone

108 **smell a fox** as in 'smell a rat', meaning suspect a trick; fox can also mean a kind of sword (see fencing imagery in 112–14)

113 **by-blows** side strokes with a sword

114 **subtlety** craftiness, cunning device

118 **prodigal** alludes to parable of the prodigal son (Luke 15:11–32), who squandered his paternal inheritance

119 **Adam Bell** refers to famous archer and outlaw; also plays on Sir Adam's name

122 **husband** plays on senses of 'spouse' and of 'household manager' who is thrifty, careful

122–3 **traveller ... teeth** Travellers' stories were thought to be exaggerated, fanciful.

126 **flesh-fly** fly that lives on and lays eggs in dead flesh; implies that Moll is a prostitute and by infecting her customers with venereal disease, makes her living from their 'dead flesh'

127 **scurvy** contemptible

130–2 **a thing ... | Ere she was all made** associates Moll's masculine dress with the monstrous, that which transgresses the laws of nature, by likening her to a deformed infant born prematurely

One knows not how to name: her birth began
Ere she was all made. 'Tis woman more than man,
Man more than woman, and which to none can hap,
The sun gives her two shadows to one shape;
Nay, more, let this strange thing walk, stand, or sit,
No blazing star draws more eyes after it.

SIR DAVY
A monster! 'Tis some monster!

ALEXANDER She's a varlet!

SEBASTIAN [*aside*] Now is my cue to bristle.

ALEXANDER
A naughty pack.

SEBASTIAN 'Tis false!

ALEXANDER Ha, boy?

SEBASTIAN 'Tis false!

ALEXANDER
What's false? I say she's naught.

SEBASTIAN I say that tongue
That dares speak so—but yours—sticks in the throat
Of a rank villain. Set yourself aside.

ALEXANDER
So, sir, what then?

SEBASTIAN Any here else had lied.
(*aside*)—I think I shall fit you.

ALEXANDER
Lie?

SEBASTIAN
Yes.

SIR DAVY
Doth this concern him?

ALEXANDER Ah, sirrah boy,
Is your blood heated? Boils it? Are you stung?
I'll pierce you deeper yet. O my dear friends,
I am that wretched father, this that son
That sees his ruin, yet headlong on doth run.

SIR ADAM
Will you love such a poison?

SIR DAVY Fie, fie!

SEBASTIAN You're all mad!

ALEXANDER
Thou'rt sick at heart, yet feel'st it not. Of all these,
What gentleman, but thou, knowing his disease
Mortal, would shun the cure? O Master Greenwit,
Would you to such an idol bow?

GREENWIT Not I sir.

ALEXANDER
Here's Master Laxton: has he mind to a woman
As thou hast?

LAXTON No, not I, sir.

ALEXANDER Sir, I know it.

LAXTON
Their good parts are so rare, their bad so common,
I will have naught to do with any woman.

SIR DAVY
'Tis well done, Master Laxton.

ALEXANDER O thou cruel boy,
Thou wouldst with lust an old man's life destroy.
Because thou seest I'm halfway in my grave,
Thou shovel'st dust upon me: would thou mightest have
Thy wish, most wicked, most unnatural!

SIR DAVY
Why sir, 'tis thought Sir Guy Fitzallard's daughter
Shall wed your son Sebastian.

ALEXANDER Sir Davy Dapper,
I have upon my knees wooed this fond boy
To take that virtuous maiden.

SEBASTIAN Hark you a word, sir.
You on your knees have cursed that virtuous maiden,
And me for loving her; yet do you now
Thus baffle me to my face? Wear not your knees
In such entreats! Give me Fitzallard's daughter!

ALEXANDER
I'll give thee ratsbane rather!

SEBASTIAN Well then, you know
What dish I mean to feed upon.

ALEXANDER Hark, gentlemen,
He swears to have this cutpurse drab to spite my gall.

OMNES
Master Sebastian!

SEBASTIAN I am deaf to you all!
I'm so bewitched, so bound to my desires,
Tears, prayers, threats, nothing can quench out those fires
That burn within me! *Exit*

ALEXANDER
Her blood shall quench it then.
Lose him not: O dissuade him, gentlemen!

SIR DAVY
He shall be weaned, I warrant you.

ALEXANDER Before his eyes
Lay down his shame, my grief, his miseries.

132–3 **woman...woman** Like a hermaphrodite, also considered a monstrosity, she belongs to both genders indeterminately.
134 **two shadows** possibly, a different shadow for each gender
136 **blazing star** comet
139 **naughty pack** person of bad character
140 **naught** immoral; wanton
141 **but** except
144 **I shall fit you** echoes the revenger-hero's famous line from Thomas Kyd's *The Spanish Tragedy* (*c*.1582–92): 'Why then, I'll fit you', 4.1.70 (ed. Mulryne)
158 **common** plays on senses of frequently found and promiscuous
159 **naught** See 140; 'to do naught' means to have sex with someone; Laxton equivocates, implying that he refuses to have sex, that he can't have sex (because of impotence), and that he will have it indiscriminately.
171 **baffle** subject to public disgrace; cheat
173 **ratsbane** rat poison
175 **drab** whore

OMNES
No more, no more; away!
Exeunt all but Sir Alexander

ALEXANDER
I wash a negro,
Losing both pains and cost. But take thy flight:
I'll be most near thee when I'm least in sight.
Wild buck, I'll hunt thee breathless: thou shalt run on,
But I will turn thee when I'm not thought upon.
Enter Ralph Trapdoor [with a letter]
Now, sirrah, what are you? Leave your ape's tricks and speak.

TRAPDOOR A letter from my captain to your worship.

ALEXANDER O, O, now I remember, 'tis to prefer thee into my service.

TRAPDOOR To be a shifter under your worship's nose of a clean trencher, when there's a good bit upon't.

ALEXANDER [*reads letter*]
Troth, honest fellow.—[*Aside*]—Hm—ha—let me see—
This knave shall be the axe to hew that down
At which I stumble: h'as a face that promiseth
Much of a villain; I will grind his wit,
And if the edge prove fine make use of it.
Come hither sirrah, canst thou be secret, ha?

TRAPDOOR As two crafty attorneys plotting the undoing of their clients.

ALEXANDER
Didst never, as thou hast walked about this town,
Hear of a wench called Moll—Mad, Merry Moll?

TRAPDOOR Moll Cutpurse, sir?

ALEXANDER The same; dost thou know her then?

TRAPDOOR As well as I know 'twill rain upon Simon and Judes day next. I will sift all the taverns i'th' city, and drink half-pots with all the watermen o'th' Bankside, but if you will, sir, I'll find her out.

ALEXANDER That task is easy; do't then. Hold thy hand up. What's this? Is't burnt?

TRAPDOOR No, sir, no: a little singed with making fireworks.

ALEXANDER There's money. Spend it; that being spent, fetch more.

TRAPDOOR O sir, that all the poor soldiers in England had such a leader! For fetching, no water-spaniel is like me.

ALEXANDER
This wench we speak of strays so from her kind
Nature repents she made her; 'tis a mermaid
Has tolled my son to shipwreck.

TRAPDOOR I'll cut her comb for you.

ALEXANDER
I'll tell out gold for thee then; hunt her forth,
Cast out a line hung full of silver hooks
To catch her to thy company: deep spendings
May draw her that's most chaste to a man's bosom.

TRAPDOOR The jingling of golden bells, and a good fool with a hobbyhorse, will draw all the whores i'th' town to dance in a morris.

ALEXANDER Or rather, for that's best, they say sometimes
She goes in breeches; follow her as her man.

TRAPDOOR And when her breeches are off, she shall follow me!

ALEXANDER Beat all thy brains to serve her.

TRAPDOOR Zounds, sir, as country wenches beat cream, till butter comes.

ALEXANDER Play thou the subtle spider: weave fine nets
To ensnare her very life.

TRAPDOOR
Her life?

ALEXANDER
Yes, suck
Her heart-blood if thou canst. Twist thou but cords
To catch her; I'll find law to hang her up.

TRAPDOOR
Spoke like a worshipful bencher!

ALEXANDER
Trace all her steps; at this she-fox's den
Watch what lambs enter; let me play the shepherd
To save their throats from bleeding, and cut hers.

TRAPDOOR
This is the goll shall do't.

185 **I wash a negro** proverbial: 'To wash an Ethiop (blackamoor, moor) white', meaning that an action is futile

189.1 **Ralph Trapdoor** Ralph puns on 'raff' (trash); Trapdoor refers to his efforts to trap Moll.

190 **ape's tricks** possibly refers to Trapdoor's attempt at courteous gestures

192 **letter...to your worship** Justices of the Peace such as Sir Alexander were responsible for administering laws concerning discharged soldiers who turned to begging and became vagrants.

195–6 **To be a shifter...clean trencher** to wait on table as your servant

209–10 **Simon and Judes day** 28 October, a feast day honouring the holy apostles, was closely associated with the annual Lord Mayor's Pageants held in London the following day; in 1605, the celebration was postponed because of rain and foul weather.

210 **sift** search closely

211 **watermen o'th' Bankside** boatmen who ferried passengers from the City across the Thames to the Bankside in Southwark, where many public theatres were located

214 **burnt** branded as a felon; common punishment for first offences

222 **mermaid** suggests Moll's allegedly dual nature as both woman and man (see 130–3, note); also associated with sirens who lured sailors to shipwreck by singing

224 **cut her comb** humiliate by destroying her 'masculine' potency

225 **tell out** count out

229–31 **The jingling of golden bells...dance in a morris** A hobbyhorse is both a figure in the morris dance who wears bells and figuratively a whore; Trapdoor suggests that the morris dancer's golden bells and lewd capers will attract whores, as like is drawn to like.

233 **her man** her servant

237 **Zounds** abbreviation of 'by God's (Christ's) wounds'; considered profane and banned from the stage in the Act of Abuses, 1606

237–8 **till butter comes** punning on come as orgasm

243 **bencher** magistrate

247 **goll** hand, in thieves' jargon or 'cant'; see 10.134–372

ALEXANDER Be firm and gain me
Ever thine own. This done, I entertain thee.
How is thy name?

TRAPDOOR
My name, sir, is Ralph Trapdoor—honest Ralph.

ALEXANDER
Trapdoor, be like thy name, a dangerous step
For her to venture on; but unto me—

TRAPDOOR
As fast as your sole to your boot or shoe, sir.

ALEXANDER
Hence then, be little seen here as thou canst;
I'll still be at thine elbow.

TRAPDOOR
The trapdoor's set.
Moll, if you budge you're gone. This me shall crown:
A roaring boy the Roaring Girl puts down.

ALEXANDER
God-a-mercy, lose no time. *Exeunt*

Sc. 3

The three shops open in a rank: the first a pothecary's shop, the next a feather shop, the third a sempster's shop. Mistress Gallipot in the first, Mistress Tiltyard in the next, Master Openwork and his wife in the third. To them enters Laxton, Goshawk, and Greenwit

MISTRESS OPENWORK Gentlemen, what is't you lack? What is't you buy? See fine bands and ruffs, fine lawns, fine cambrics. What is't you lack, gentlemen, what is't you buy?

LAXTON Yonder's the shop.

GOSHAWK Is that she?

LAXTON Peace!

GREENWIT She that minces tobacco?

LAXTON Ay: she's a gentlewoman born, I can tell you, though it be her hard fortune now to shred Indian pot-herbs.

GOSHAWK O sir, 'tis many a good woman's fortune, when her husband turns bankrupt, to begin with pipes and set up again.

LAXTON And indeed the raising of the woman is the lifting up of the man's head at all times: if one flourish, t'other will bud as fast, I warrant ye.

GOSHAWK Come, thou'rt familiarly acquainted there, I grope that.

LAXTON And you grope no better i'th' dark, you may chance lie i'th' ditch when you're drunk.

GOSHAWK Go, thou'rt a mystical lecher!

LAXTON I will not deny but my credit may take up an ounce of pure smoke.

GOSHAWK May take up an ell of pure smock! Away, go! [*Aside*] 'Tis the closest striker! Life, I think he commits venery forty foot deep: no man's aware on't. I, like a palpable smockster, go to work so openly with the tricks of art that I'm as apparently seen as a naked boy in a vial; and were it not for a gift of treachery that I have in me to betray my friend when he puts

248 **entertain** take as my servant
253 **fast** close-sticking; loyal
258 **roaring boy** see 1.73, note
259 **God-a-mercy** God have mercy in the sense of 'May God reward you'; exclamation of gratitude
3.0.1 ***three shops open in a rank*** Resembling stalls or booths, the shops might be represented by canvas-covered wooden frames, or by the three doors downstage against the tiring-house wall, as distinct from the usual two, that may have been a special feature of the Fortune stage. Tradesmen commonly set up stalls in front of their houses to display goods, which were made in workshops at home; their wives, pretty and well-dressed, attracted customers.
in a rank in a row
0.2 ***pothecary's shop*** An apothecary or pharmacist sold tobacco (widely popular since the 1590s, hailed as medicine and decried as a vanity) in addition to herbs and drugs.
feather shop Feathers, many imported from Africa and the Americas, were popular luxury items used extravagantly on hats.
0.3 ***sempster's shop*** sold made to order apparel, especially shirts, undergarments, etc.; see 1.0.1
Mistress Gallipot Mistress denotes a married woman; her first name, Prudence, ironically alludes to her imprudent intrigue with Laxton. Gallipot, a small pot for ointments and medicines, refers to her husband's livelihood as apothecary.
0.4 ***Mistress Tiltyard*** Her first name, Rosamond, is typical for heroines of romance, an ironic reference to her unromantic entanglement with Goshawk. Her surname denotes her husband's trade as feather-seller: a tiltyard is an enclosure for tilting (jousting with lances), a ceremonial, quasi-chivalric courtiers' pastime in which participants adorned their costumes with feathers.
Master Openwork His surname refers to the kind of needlework required in his and his wife's trade as sempsters, and to his honesty; see 1.0.1, note; also 246–8, note, on needlework as metaphor for sex.
1–4 **what is't you lack? . . . buy?** traditional street vendors' cries
11 **pot-herbs** herbs for cooking; here, tobacco
12–14 **good woman's fortune . . . set up again** suggests how women in trade helped restore their husbands' businesses; here, by selling tobacco (a highly popular commodity) to pipe-smoking male customers
15–17 **the raising of the woman . . . bud as fast** implies a connection between financial profit and sexual vigour, with wordplay on 'head' and 'bud' suggesting erection
19, 20 **grope** understand; feel, in sexual play
22 **mystical** secret; see Epistle.24–5
23 **credit** good reputation; sale on trust
24–5 **ounce of pure smoke . . . ell of pure smock** pun on smoke/smock, a shirt worn both as underwear and nightgown: Laxton implies that Mistress Gallipot sells him tobacco on credit, Goshawk that Laxton is having sex with her, i.e., lifts up her smock
25 **ell** measure of length: 45 inches
26 **closest** most secret; intimate
striker implies aggressive sexual conquest
27 **venery** sexual pleasure; in this context, with predatory implication; see Epistle.1
28 **smockster** lecher (see 24–5, note)
29–30 **a naked boy in a vial** Goshawk's attempts at secrecy in seduction turn out to be as open as the curiosities displayed in early collections or 'wonder cabinets', among them the 'embalmed child'—fetus displayed in glass as a curiosity—listed by Thomas Platter in 1599.

most trust in me—mass, yonder he is too—and by his injury to make good my access to her, I should appear as defective in courting as a farmer's son the first day of his feather, that doth nothing at Court but woo the hangings and glass windows for a month together, and some broken waiting-woman for ever after. I find those imperfections in my venery, that were it not for flattery and falsehood, I should want discourse and impudence; and he that wants impudence among women is worthy to be kicked out at bed's feet.—He shall not see me yet.

At the tobacco shop

GREENWIT Troth, this is finely shred.

LAXTON O, women are the best mincers!

MISTRESS GALLIPOT 'T had been a good phrase for a cook's wife, sir.

LAXTON But 'twill serve generally, like the front of a new almanac, as thus: calculated for the meridian of cooks' wives, but generally for all Englishwomen.

MISTRESS GALLIPOT Nay, you shall ha't sir: I have filled it for you.

She puts it to the fire

LAXTON The pipe's in a good hand, and I wish mine always so.

GREENWIT But not to be used o' that fashion!

LAXTON O pardon me, sir, I understand no French. [*Aside to Goshawk*] I pray be covered. Jack, a pipe of rich smoke.

GOSHAWK Rich smoke: that's sixpence a pipe, is't?

GREENWIT To me, sweet lady.

MISTRESS GALLIPOT [*aside to Laxton*] Be not forgetful; respect my credit; seem strange; art and wit makes a fool of suspicion; pray be wary.

LAXTON [*aside to Mistress Gallipot*] Push! I warrant you. [*To them*] Come, how is't, gallants?

GREENWIT Pure and excellent.

LAXTON I thought 'twas good, you were grown so silent. You are like those that love not to talk at victuals, though they make a worse noise i' the nose than a common fiddler's prentice, and discourse a whole supper with snuffling. [*Aside to Mistress Gallipot*] I must speak a word with you anon.

MISTRESS GALLIPOT [*aside to Laxton*] Make your way wisely then.

GOSHAWK O, what else, sir? He's perfection itself, full of manners, but not an acre of ground belonging to 'em.

GREENWIT Ay, and full of form; h'as ne'er a good stool in's chamber.

GOSHAWK But above all religious: he preyeth daily upon elder brothers.

GREENWIT And valiant above measure: he's run three streets from a sergeant.

LAXTON (*blowing smoke in their faces*) Puh, puh.

GREENWIT *and* GOSHAWK [*coughing*] O, puh, ho, ho. [*They move away*]

LAXTON So, so.

MISTRESS GALLIPOT What's the matter now, sir?

LAXTON I protest I'm in extreme want of money. If you can supply me now with any means, you do me the greatest pleasure, next to the bounty of your love, as ever poor gentleman tasted.

MISTRESS GALLIPOT What's the sum would pleasure ye, sir? Though you deserve nothing less at my hands.

LAXTON Why, 'tis but for want of opportunity thou knowest. [*Aside*] I put her off with opportunity still! By this light I hate her, but for means to keep me in fashion with gallants; for what I take from her, I spend upon other wenches, bear her in hand still. She has wit enough to rob her husband, and I ways enough to consume the money. [*To gallants*] Why, how now? What, the chincough?

GOSHAWK Thou hast the cowardliest trick to come before a man's face and strangle him ere he be aware. I could find in my heart to make a quarrel in earnest.

LAXTON Pox, an thou dost—thou knowest I never use to fight with my friends—thou'll but lose thy labour in't.

32 **mass** shortened form of 'by the mass', referring to Catholic church service
34–5 **the first day of his feather** on his first day attending the sovereign at court, where feathers were much worn
36 **hangings** tapestries or draperies hung against walls as decoration
37 **broken** sexually defiled
39 **discourse** ability to converse politely, pleasingly (for purpose of seduction)
39–40 **impudence . . . among women** presumptuous boldness; Goshawk implies that a man should abandon respect for women when seducing them
43 **mincers** best at chopping small; playing on sense of affectedly dainty
47 **almanac** a cheap, popular book containing astrological predictions, proverbs, medical advice, useful information of various kinds
meridian noon; referring to astrological calculations
47–8 **cooks' wives . . . all Englishwomen** parody of title-pages of almanacs, appealing to the widest market
51 **pipe's in a good hand** bawdy suggestion of pipe as penis
53 **o' that fashion** put to the fire, alluding to the symptoms of syphilis
54 **French** 'French pox' was a common term for venereal disease.
55 **be covered** replace your hat
56 **sixpence a pipe** six times the cost of the cheapest place in a playhouse
57 **To me** a pipe for me
59 **seem strange** don't be too familiar
61 **Push!** exclamation
65 **victuals** articles of food; here, meals
66–8 **noise i' the nose . . . snuffling** symptoms of venereal disease
67 **fiddler's prentice** Fiddles and fiddlers often suggest sexual play; prentice is a shortened form of apprentice.
73 **manners** punning on manors; Laxton possesses no land
74 **form** etiquette; pun on form meaning bench
76 **preyeth** pun implying that Laxton schemes to get lands from heirs (the eldest son usually inherited the father's estate; see 4.61–5, and 4.62–4, note)
78–9 **he's run three streets from a sergeant** implies that Laxton is both cowardly and deeply in debt (sergeants arrested debtors)
90 **nothing less** anything but money
91 **thou** Laxton switches from 'you' to the more intimate form
92–3 **By this light** daylight; an emphatic assertion
95 **bear her in hand** lead her on
98 **chincough** whooping cough; Laxton blows smoke in their faces

Enter Jack Dapper, and his man Gull

Jack Dapper!

GREENWIT Monsieur Dapper, I dive down to your ankles.

JACK DAPPER Save ye, gentlemen, all three, in a peculiar salute.

GOSHAWK He were ill to make a lawyer: he dispatches three at once!

LAXTON So well said! [*Receiving purse from Mistress Gallipot*] But is this of the same tobacco, Mistress Gallipot?

MISTRESS GALLIPOT The same you had at first, sir.

LAXTON I wish it no better: this will serve to drink at my chamber.

GOSHAWK Shall we taste a pipe on't?

LAXTON Not of this, by my troth, gentlemen; I have sworn before you.

GOSHAWK What, not Jack Dapper?

LAXTON Pardon me sweet Jack, I'm sorry I made such a rash oath, but foolish oaths must stand. Where art going, Jack?

JACK DAPPER Faith, to buy one feather.

LAXTON One feather? [*Aside*] The fool's peculiar still!

JACK DAPPER Gull.

GULL Master?

JACK DAPPER Here's three halfpence for your ordinary, boy; meet me an hour hence in Paul's.

GULL [*aside*] How? Three single halfpence? Life, this will scarce serve a man in sauce: a ha'p'orth of mustard, a ha'p'orth of oil, and a ha'p'orth of vinegar—what's left then for the pickle herring? This shows like small beer i'th' morning after a great surfeit of wine o'ernight. He could spend his three pound last night in a supper amongst girls and brave bawdy-house boys. I thought his pockets cackled not for nothing: these are the eggs of three pound. I'll go sup 'em up presently. *Exit Gull*

LAXTON [*aside*] Eight, nine, ten angels. Good wench, i'faith, and one that loves darkness well. She puts out a candle with the best tricks of any drugster's wife in England; but that which mads her, I rail upon opportunity still, and take no notice on't. The other night she would needs lead me into a room with a candle in her hand to show me a naked picture, where no sooner entered, but the candle was sent of an errand; now I, not intending to understand her, but like a puny at the inns of venery, called for another light innocently. Thus reward I all her cunning with simple mistaking. I know she cozens her husband to keep me, and I'll keep her honest, as long as I can, to make the poor man some part of amends. An honest mind of a whoremaster! [*To Gallants*] How think you amongst you? What, a fresh pipe? Draw in a third man.

GOSHAWK No, you're a hoarder: you engross by th'ounces!

At the feather shop now

JACK DAPPER

Puh, I like it not.

MISTRESS TILTYARD

What feather is't you'd have, sir?
These are most worn and most in fashion
Amongst the beaver gallants, the stone-riders,
The private stage's audience, the twelvepenny-stool gentlemen:
I can inform you 'tis the general feather.

JACK DAPPER

And therefore I mislike it—tell me of general!
Now a continual Simon and Jude's rain
Beat all your feathers as flat down as pancakes.

103.1 ***Jack Dapper*** Son of Sir Davy Dapper. Jack is a generic name for an ordinary fellow; the surname suggests smart dress and brisk movements similar to his father's (see 2.0.1–2, note).
his man Gull Man means manservant; a gull is a fool or simpleton.

105 **dive down** in an exaggerated bow, like a dive-dapper, bird that dives into water; playing on Dapper's name

106 **Save ye** short for 'God save ye'
peculiar single; special

108–9 **lawyer... three at once!** He would make a bad lawyer (ironically, because he is efficient, doesn't prolong business).

113 **drink** smoke

122 **one feather** Feathers were proverbially linked to fools, as in 'a feather for a fool'.

123 **peculiar** odd; playing on 106

126 **ordinary** eating house serving a fixed-price meal, or the meal itself, here a very cheap one; ordinaries were often considered meeting places for rogues and outlaws

127 **Paul's** probably Paul's Walk, the middle aisle of St Paul's Cathedral, a meeting place for high and low

128 **Life** short for 'God's life'

129 **in sauce** he can only buy sauce, not the meal itself
ha'p'orth halfpenny's worth

131–2 **small beer** weak beer, recommended for the morning after a night of heavy drinking

134 **brave** handsome

135–6 **his pockets cackled... eggs of three pound** The coins in Jack's pockets chinked like hens cackling before laying eggs; Gull's small change is like the eggs.

136 **presently** right now

137 **angels** the money he received from Mistress Gallipot; an angel, a coin worth ten shillings at this time, was named for its design of St Michael slaying the dragon

138 **loves darkness well... puts out a candle** implies that she is promiscuous

139 **drugster's** apothecary's

140 **rail... still** complain that circumstances keep us from having sex

144 **sent of an errand** put out

145 **understand** playing on stand as erection; have sex
puny freshman at university or Inns of Court, residential colleges of law

147 **cozens** tricks, deceives

148 **keep** support me; hold my affection

150 **whoremaster** lecher

153 **hoarder** Laxton hasn't shared the tobacco (actually, money) Mistress Gallipot gave him earlier (see 110–11)

156 **beaver gallants** gallants wearing fashionable, costly beaver hats; because the beaver was considered lustful, may suggest sexual desire, potency
stone-riders riders of stallions, playing on stone as testicle; implies masculine sexual potency

157 **private stage's** indoor theatres that charged more than public (outdoor) theatres; attended by wealthier people, of somewhat higher rank
twelvepenny-stool gentlemen Stools for sitting onstage were available in both public and private theatres, and were much favoured by gallants.

158 **the general feather** most fashionable feather

160 **Simon and Jude's rain** see 2.209–10

Show me—a—spangled feather.
MISTRESS TILTYARD O, to go a-feasting with!
You'd have it for a hench-boy; you shall.
At the sempster's shop now
OPENWORK
Mass, I had quite forgot!
His honour's footman was here last night, wife:
Ha'you done with my lord's shirt?
MISTRESS OPENWORK What's that to you, sir?
I was this morning at his honour's lodging
Ere such a snail as you crept out of your shell.
OPENWORK
O, 'twas well done, good wife.
MISTRESS OPENWORK I hold it better, sir,
Than if you had done't yourself.
OPENWORK Nay, so say I:
But is the countess's smock almost done, mouse?
MISTRESS OPENWORK
Here lies the cambric, sir, but wants, I fear me.
OPENWORK
I'll resolve you of that presently.
[*Makes sexual gesture*]
MISTRESS OPENWORK
Heyday! O audacious groom,
Dare you presume to noblewomen's linen?
Keep you your yard to measure shepherd's holland!
I must confine you, I see that.
At the Tobacco Shop now
GOSHAWK What say you to this gear?
LAXTON I dare the arrantest critic in tobacco to lay one fault upon't.
Enter Moll in a frieze jerkin and a black safeguard
GOSHAWK Life, yonder's Moll.
LAXTON Moll, which Moll?
GOSHAWK Honest Moll.
LAXTON Prithee let's call her. Moll!
ALL Moll, Moll, pist, Moll!
MOLL How now, what's the matter?
GOSHAWK A pipe of good tobacco, Moll?
MOLL I cannot stay.
GOSHAWK Nay Moll—puh—prithee hark, but one word, i'faith.
MOLL Well, what is't?
GREENWIT Prithee come hither, sirrah.
LAXTON [*aside*] Heart, I would give but too much money to be nibbling with that wench. Life, sh'as the spirit of four great parishes, and a voice that will drown all the city! Methinks a brave captain might get all his soldiers upon her, and ne'er be beholding to a company of Mile End milksops, if he could come on, and come off quick enough. Such a Moll were a marrowbone before an Italian: he would cry bona-roba till his ribs were nothing but bone. I'll lay hard siege to her—money is that *aquafortis* that eats into many a maidenhead: where the walls are flesh and blood, I'll ever pierce through with a golden auger.
GOSHAWK Now thy judgement, Moll—is't not good?
MOLL Yes, faith, 'tis very good tobacco. How do you sell an ounce? Farewell. God buy you, Mistress Gallipot.
GOSHAWK Why Moll, Moll!
MOLL I cannot stay now, i'faith; I am going to buy a shag ruff—the shop will be shut in presently.
GOSHAWK 'Tis the maddest, fantasticalest girl! I never knew so much flesh and so much nimbleness put together!
LAXTON She slips from one company to another like a fat eel between a Dutchman's fingers.—[*Aside*] I'll watch my time for her.
MISTRESS GALLIPOT Some will not stick to say she's a man, and some both man and woman.

162 **spangled** decorated with spangles; speckled
163 **hench-boy** page
you shall you shall have it
171 **mouse** term of endearment
172 **wants** isn't yet finished
176 **yard** measuring stick; penis
shepherd's holland coarse linen fabric first made in Holland
178 **gear** stuff; here, tobacco
180.1 ***frieze jerkin*** short coat with collar and (usually) sleeves, made of coarse woollen cloth; worn by men
safeguard outer skirt worn by women to protect clothing from dirt when riding horseback (Moll enters the play wearing both male and female dress)
192 **sirrah** often used to address women
193 **Heart** short form of 'God's heart', an exclamation
195 **four great parishes** possibly those of Southwark, composed of four parishes much larger than any of those within the city: St Savior's, St Olave's, St Thomas's, and St George's
196–7 **get all his soldiers upon her** Medical writers debated the contributions made by female and male in conceiving a child; some followed Aristotle in believing that the male gave it form or spirit, and the female, matter, while others followed Galen in thinking the female contributed both matter and form. Laxton reasons that a 'mannish' woman like Moll will produce only male children.
198 **Mile End** a field south of Mile End Road used as a drill ground for citizens' militia
come on, and come off military terms for advance and retire, with sense of sexual conquest
199–200 **marrowbone before an Italian** Bones containing marrow were considered a delicacy and an aphrodisiac; Italians were reputedly lustful.
200–1 **cry bona-roba . . . nothing but bone** Bona-roba is a term for prostitute; the (supposedly) lusty Italian would exhaust himself in having sex with her till his marrow, believed the seat of animal vitality, was consumed.
201 **lay hard siege** military language connoting aggressive sexual pursuit
202 ***aquafortis*** nitric acid, a powerful solvent and corrosive
204 **auger** long pointed tool for boring holes in wood; a phallic image
206 **How** at what price?
207 **God buy you** God redeem you; equivalent to 'good-bye'
209–10 **shag ruff** a fluted collar standing up around the neck, made of worsted or silk cloth with a velvet nap on one side
211 **fantasticalest** from fantastical, meaning eccentric or strange; see 2.89, note
214 **eel** a favourite food in Holland
216–17 **a man . . . both man and woman** Mistress Gallipot echoes Sir Alexander's remarks; see 2.129–30, 132–3.

LAXTON That were excellent: she might first cuckold the husband and then make him do as much for the wife!

The feather shop again

MOLL Save you—how does Mistress Tiltyard?

JACK DAPPER Moll!

MOLL Jack Dapper!

JACK DAPPER How dost, Moll?

MOLL I'll tell thee by and by—I go but to th'next shop.

JACK DAPPER Thou shalt find me here this hour about a feather.

MOLL Nay, an a feather hold you in play a whole hour, a goose will last you all the days of your life!

The sempster shop

Let me see a good shag ruff.

OPENWORK Mistress Mary, that shalt thou, i'faith, and the best in the shop.

MISTRESS OPENWORK How now?—Greetings! Love terms, with a pox between you! Have I found out one of your haunts? I send you for hollands, and you're i'the low countries with a mischief. I'm served with good ware by th'shift, that makes it lie dead so long upon my hands, I were as good shut up shop, for when I open it, I take nothing.

OPENWORK Nay, and you fall a-ringing once the devil cannot stop you; I'll out of the belfry as fast as I can. Moll.

MISTRESS OPENWORK Get you from my shop!

MOLL I come to buy.

MISTRESS OPENWORK I'll sell ye nothing; I warn ye my house and shop.

MOLL
You, goody Openwork, you that prick out a poor
 living
And sews many a bawdy skin-coat together,
Thou private pandress between shirt and smock,
I wish thee for a minute but a man:
Thou shouldst never use more shapes, but as th'art,
I pity my revenge. Now my spleen's up,
I would not mock it willingly.

Enter a fellow with a long rapier by his side

Ha, be thankful,
Now I forgive thee.

MISTRESS OPENWORK Marry, hang thee! I never asked forgiveness in my life.

MOLL You, goodman swine's face!

FELLOW What, will you murder me?

MOLL You remember, slave, how you abused me t'other night in a tavern?

FELLOW Not I, by this light.

MOLL No, but by candlelight you did: you have tricks to save your oaths, reservations have you, and I have reserved somewhat for you. [*Strikes him*] As you like that, call for more: you know the sign again.

FELLOW Pox on't! Had I brought any company along with me to have borne witness on't, 'twould ne'er have grieved me; but to be struck and nobody by, 'tis my ill fortune still. Why tread upon a worm, they say, 'twill turn tail; but indeed a gentleman should have more manners. *Exit*

LAXTON Gallantly performed, i'faith, Moll, and manfully! I love thee for ever for't. Base rogue, had he offered but the least counter-buff, by this hand, I was prepared for him.

MOLL You prepared for him? Why should you be prepared for him? Was he any more than a man?

218 **cuckold** A wife made her husband a cuckold by sleeping with another man; the term conveys scorn for the man who cannot keep his wife sexually satisfied. There is no fully equivalent term for the wife of an unfaithful husband.

227–8 **feather . . . goose** Moll evokes the traditional association between feathers, geese, and foolishness; see 123.

234–8 **I send you for hollands . . . I take nothing** an extended *double entendre* in which the sempster's language bears consistently sexual meaning. She claims that when she sends her husband to get cloth (hollands, linen from Holland) he pursues women with lecherous intent (low countries, for genitals). The ware (cloth, or sexual service) that he devises by this shift (subterfuge, or erotic play, shift meaning both an undergarment and a clever trick) leaves her dead (sexually unsatisfied) so that she takes in nothing (doesn't turn profits sexually or financially).

239 **fall a-ringing** proverbial language for the shrewish (articulate, assertive) wife

241 **Moll** Openwork fades from the dialogue to emerge at 313 talking to Goshawk; he then exits with Moll at 406

244 **warn ye** deny you entry to

246 **goody** goodwife
prick out Seamstresses didn't belong to guilds and were often quite poor, thus some eked out a living through prostitution (see 1.52, note, and 5.95).

247 **skin-coat** *double entendre* in which sewing also means bringing whore and customer together, and skin-coat stands for sexual intercourse

248 **Thou** Moll shows her contempt by shifting to the more intimate form; see 91–2, note.
private pandress secret bawd
shirt and smock man and woman

249 **but a man** transformed to a man (presumably so that Moll could challenge her with physical combat)

250 **shapes** she would no longer deceive people

251 **pity** forego
spleen's temper's

252.1 ***Enter a fellow . . . rapier*** See Persons.23–4; a quarrelsome gallant, the first of several bit parts comprised in the term *Ministri*, servants and others defined mainly by social role or vocation
long rapier long, pointed, two-edged sword

256 **goodman** title for yeomen and others beneath the rank of gentlemen

261–2 **tricks . . . reservations** ways of equivocating when you swear that a statement is true

266 **borne witness on't** witnessed my being struck (so that he would have grounds for retaliation)

268–9 **tread upon a worm . . . 'twill turn tail** proverbial; even the humblest person will resent an injury and retaliate (also plays on tail as male or female sexual parts)

273 **counter-buff** blow in return

LAXTON No, nor so much by a yard and a handful, London measure.

MOLL Why do you speak this, then? Do you think I cannot ride a stone-horse unless one lead him by th'snaffle?

LAXTON Yes, and sit him bravely, I know thou canst, Moll. 'Twas but an honest mistake through love, and I'll make amends for't any way; prithee, sweet plump Moll, when shall thou and I go out o' town together?

MOLL Whither? To Tyburn, prithee?

LAXTON Mass, that's out o' town indeed! Thou hangest so many jests upon thy friends still. I mean honestly to Brentford, Staines, or Ware.

MOLL What to do there?

LAXTON Nothing but be merry and lie together; I'll hire a coach with four horses.

MOLL I thought 'twould be a beastly journey. You may leave out one well; three horses will serve if I play the jade myself.

LAXTON Nay, push! Thou'rt such another kicking wench. Prithee be kind and let's meet.

MOLL 'Tis hard but we shall meet, sir.

LAXTON Nay, but appoint the place then. There's ten angels in fair gold, Moll: you see I do not trifle with you—do but say thou wilt meet me, and I'll have a coach ready for thee.

MOLL Why, here's my hand I'll meet you, sir.

LAXTON [*aside*] O good gold!—[*To her*] The place, sweet Moll?

MOLL It shall be your appointment.

LAXTON Somewhat near Holborn, Moll.

MOLL In Gray's Inn Fields then.

LAXTON A match.

MOLL I'll meet you there.

LAXTON The hour?

MOLL Three.

LAXTON That will be time enough to sup at Brentford.

Fall from them to the other

OPENWORK I am of such a nature, sir, I cannot endure the house when she scolds; sh'as a tongue will be heard further in a still morning than St Antholin's bell. She rails upon me for foreign wenching, that I, being a freeman, must needs keep a whore i'th' suburbs, and seek to impoverish the liberties. When we fall out, I trouble you still to make all whole with my wife.

GOSHAWK No trouble at all: 'tis a pleasure to me to join things together.

OPENWORK Go thy ways. [*Aside*] I do this but to try thy honesty, Goshawk.

The feather shop

JACK DAPPER How likest thou this, Moll?

MOLL O, singularly: you're fitted now for a bunch. [*Aside*] He looks for all the world with those spangled feathers like a nobleman's bedpost. The purity of your wench would I fain try: she seems like Kent unconquered, and I believe as many wiles are in her. O, the gallants of these times are shallow lechers: they put not their courtship home enough to a wench; 'tis impossible to know what woman is thoroughly honest, because she's ne'er thoroughly tried. I am of that certain belief there are more queans in this town of their own making than of any man's provoking: where lies the slackness then?

277 **a yard and a handful** punning on yard as penis; London mercers customarily gave a little more than the exact measure

280 **stone-horse** stallion (see 156); also figuratively a man, and an ironic reference to Laxton's impotence
th'snaffle a simple kind of bridle-bit, without a curb

285 **Tyburn** place of execution for criminals in London

288 **Brentford, Staines, or Ware** towns conveniently near London for a day's amusement or a sexual rendezvous. Ware, twenty miles north of London, housed the famous great bed of Ware (10 feet 9 inches square); Staines lay seventeen miles west and Brentford, the closest of the three, only ten miles west of the city.

294 **jade** a worn out, ill-tempered horse; 'to play the jade' means to act like a whore

297 **'Tis hard but** of course

306 **Holborn** a main thoroughfare of London, along which the inns of court (law schools) were located; gardens in its western part were locales for illicit sex

307 **Gray's Inn Fields** Gray's Inn was a distinguished law school; its open fields were frequented by criminal elements.

312.1 ***Fall from them to the other*** signals a shift of focus from one group to another

315 **St Antholin's bell** a church in Watling Street where Puritan preachers not under church jurisdiction held an early morning lecture for which the bell was rung at 5 a.m.; the noise was resented by some in the neighbourhood

317–18 **suburbs...liberties** The city had no control over the suburbs, so that prostitution supposedly could flourish more easily in them; the liberties (named because they were free from manorial rule or obligation to the crown) were territories both within and outside the city over which no single city or county authority had jurisdiction or control. Mistress Openwork ironically suggests that her husband, as a guild member and citizen of London, goes against his own interests by seeking his sexual pleasures in the suburbs.

318 **fall out** quarrel

319 **trouble you** ask you
make all whole make peace

320–1 **join things together** Goshawk ironically alludes to his own sexual interests

322 **Go thy ways** as you please

325 **singularly** very much; alluding to Jack's intention of buying a single feather (see 123, 225)

327 **nobleman's bedpost** The 'state beds' of the great manor houses built by the gentry and nobility had four posts supporting a canopy, or tester, which were often decorated with bunches of feathers.

328 **Kent unconquered** commonly said of this county, which unlike others, retained its original laws and customs pre-dating the Norman conquest

330–1 **put...home** They don't go far enough, get to the point (implying sexual penetration).

332 **honest** chaste; virtuous in a sexual sense

333 **tried** tested, put to the proof

334 **queans** loose (unchaste) women; whores

Many a poor soul would down, and there's nobody will push 'em!
Women are courted but ne'er soundly tried,
As many walk in spurs that never ride.

The sempster's shop

MISTRESS OPENWORK O abominable!

GOSHAWK Nay, more, I tell you in private, he keeps a whore i'th' suburbs.

MISTRESS OPENWORK O spittle dealing! I came to him a gentlewoman born: I'll show you mine arms when you please, sir.

GOSHAWK [*aside*] I had rather see your legs, and begin that way!

MISTRESS OPENWORK 'Tis well known he took me from a lady's service where I was well-beloved of the steward. I had my Latin tongue and a spice of the French before I came to him, and now doth he keep a suburban whore under my nostrils.

GOSHAWK There's ways enough to cry quit with him. Hark in thine ear. [*Whispers*]

MISTRESS OPENWORK There's a friend worth a million.

[*Before the feather shop*]

MOLL I'll try one spear against your chastity, Mistress Tiltyard, though it prove too short by the burr.

Enter Ralph Trapdoor

TRAPDOOR [*aside*] Mass, here she is! I'm bound already to serve her, though it be but a sluttish trick. [*To her*] Bless my hopeful young mistress with long life and great limbs, send her the upper hand of all bailiffs and their hungry adherents!

MOLL How now, what art thou?

TRAPDOOR A poor ebbing gentleman that would gladly wait for the young flood of your service.

MOLL My service! What should move you to offer your service to me, sir?

TRAPDOOR The love I bear to your heroic spirit and masculine womanhood.

MOLL So, sir, put case we should retain you to us: what parts are there in you for a gentlewoman's service?

TRAPDOOR Of two kinds right worshipful: movable and immovable—movable to run of errands, and immovable to stand when you have occasion to use me.

MOLL What strength have you?

TRAPDOOR Strength, Mistress Moll? I have gone up into a steeple and stayed the great bell as 't has been ringing; stopped a windmill going.

MOLL And never struck down yourself?

TRAPDOOR Stood as upright as I do at this present.

Moll trips up his heels; he falls

MOLL Come, I pardon you for this; it shall be no disgrace to you. I have struck up the heels of the high German's size ere now. What, not stand?

TRAPDOOR I am of that nature where I love, I'll be at my mistress' foot to do her service.

MOLL Why, well said! But say your mistress should receive injury: have you the spirit of fighting in you—durst you second her?

TRAPDOOR Life, I have kept a bridge myself, and drove seven at a time before me.

MOLL Ay?

TRAPDOOR (*aside*) But they were all Lincolnshire bullocks, by my troth.

MOLL Well, meet me in Gray's Inn Fields between three and four this afternoon, and upon better consideration we'll retain you.

TRAPDOOR I humbly thank your good mistress-ship. [*Aside*] I'll crack your neck for this kindness. *Exit*

Moll meets Laxton

LAXTON Remember three.

MOLL Nay, if I fail you, hang me.

LAXTON Good wench, i'faith.

Then Moll meets Openwork

MOLL Who's this?

OPENWORK 'Tis I, Moll.

MOLL Prithee tend thy shop and prevent bastards!

OPENWORK We'll have a pint of the same wine, i'faith, Moll. [*Exit Openwork with Moll*]

336 **would down** would 'fall' from chastity; have illicit sex

339 **walk in spurs that never ride** Horseriding often carries sexual meanings; here, many are ready to ride (have sex) who never have the chance.

343 **spittle** shortened form of hospital, probably referring to St Mary's Spittle which specialized in treating venereal disease, and its neighbourhood, frequented by thieves and prostitutes

344 **arms** the shield or emblem that signifies her family's status as gentry

349 **steward** person in charge of a gentle or noble household, responsible for expenditures, servants, etc.

350 **a spice of the French** a little French; associated with venereal disease, called the French pox and (especially in women) with loose sexual behaviour

353 **cry quit with** pay back, get back at

357 **burr** ring of iron behind handle of lance used in tilting (see 3.0.4, note); playing on 'Tiltyard'

364 **ebbing** unfortunate, impoverished

365 **young flood** flow of tide upriver
service the position of servant; here also implies sexual 'service'

370 **put case** suppose

371 **parts** abilities, talents; also, sexual organs (see 'stand', 374)

372–3 **movable and immovable** punning on 'parts', 371

380 **Stood as upright** punning on erection

382–3 **high German's size** a German fencer, tall and of great strength, in London at this time

385 **foot** playing on French *foutre*, to have sex with; continuing the implications of 'service' (see 364–5) that Moll will dominate him sexually

388 **second** support in attacking or defending

389–90 **kept a bridge . . . before me** military actions

392 **Lincolnshire bullocks** cattle from a county well known for them; undercuts his claim of valour in 389–90

402 **Who's this?** Seemingly, Openwork is eluding his wife.

405 **same wine** a common pun on bastard, a sweet Spanish wine

The bell rings

GOSHAWK Hark, the bell rings; come, gentlemen. Jack Dapper, where shall's all munch?

JACK DAPPER I am for Parker's Ordinary.

LAXTON
He's a good guest to'm, he deserves his board:
He draws all the gentlemen in a term-time thither.
We'll be your followers, Jack: lead the way.
Look you, by my faith, the fool has feathered his nest well.

Exeunt Gallants

Enter Master Gallipot, Master Tiltyard, and servants with water spaniels and a duck

TILTYARD Come, shut up your shops. Where's Master Openwork?

MISTRESS OPENWORK Nay, ask not me Master Tiltyard.

GALLIPOT Where's his water-dog? Puh—pist—hurr—hurr—pist.

TILTYARD Come wenches, come, we're going all to Hogsden.

MISTRESS GALLIPOT To Hogsden, husband?

GALLIPOT Ay, to Hogsden, pigsney.

MISTRESS TILTYARD I'm not ready, husband.

TILTYARD Faith, that's well. (*Spits in the dog's mouth*) Hum—pist—pist.

GALLIPOT Come Mistress Openwork, you are so long.

MISTRESS OPENWORK I have no joy of my life, Master Gallipot.

GALLIPOT Push! Let your boy lead his water spaniel along, and we'll show you the bravest sport at Parlous Pond. Hey Trug, hey Trug, hey Trug! Here's the best duck in England, except my wife.
Hey, hey, hey! Fetch, fetch, fetch!
Come, let's away:
Of all the year, this is the sportful'st day. [*Exeunt*]

Enter Sebastian solus Sc. 4

SEBASTIAN
If a man have a free will, where should the use
More perfect shine than in his will to love?
All creatures have their liberty in that;

Enter Sir Alexander and listens to him

Though else kept under servile yoke and fear,
The very bondslave has his freedom there.
Amongst a world of creatures voiced and silent,
Must my desires wear fetters?—[*Aside*] Yea, are you
So near? Then I must break with my heart's truth,
Meet grief at a back way. [*Aloud*] Well: why, suppose
The two-leaved tongues of slander or of truth
Pronounce Moll loathsome; if before my love
She appear fair, what injury have I?
I have the thing I like. In all things else
Mine own eye guides me, and I find 'em prosper;
Life, what should ail it now? I know that man
Ne'er truly loves—if he gainsay't, he lies—
That winks and marries with his father's eyes;
I'll keep mine own wide open.

Enter Moll and a Porter with a viol on his back

ALEXANDER [*aside*] Here's brave wilfulness.
A made match: here she comes; they met o' purpose.

PORTER Must I carry this great fiddle to your chamber, Mistress Mary?

MOLL Fiddle, goodman hog-rubber? Some of these porters bear so much for others, they have no time to carry wit for themselves.

PORTER To your own chamber, Mistress Mary?

408 **shall's** shall we
409 **Parker's Ordinary** see 126
410 **to'm** to him, i.e., to Parker
411 **term-time** when law courts were in session and London was full of visitors
413 **fool . . . feathered** referring to Jack Dapper's purchase of feathers; see 123
413.3 **water spaniels and a duck** type of dog used for retrieving water fowl; duck-hunting was a popular pastime
417–18 **Puh . . . pist** whistles or other sounds, for calling the dog
419–20 **Hogsden** Hoxton, an area north of London with open fields, popular for excursions
422 **pigsney** term of endearment, possibly playing on Hogsden
424 **Spits in the dog's mouth** expression of affection toward and means of befriending a dog
430 **Parlous Pond** pond in London popular for swimming, not far from the Fortune Theatre and on the way to Hogsden; so named because of drownings that occurred there (parlous is a corruption of 'perilous')
431 **Trug** name of dog; can also mean prostitute
435 **sportful'st day** an enthusiastic exclamation, or possibly a reference to May Day (1 May) or Shrove Tuesday (the pre-Lenten festivity) on which 'the pancake bell' rang at 11 a.m. and apprentices stopped work, sometimes rioting and destroying property
4.8 **break with** abandon, renounce (since his father is present, he must dissemble)
9 **Meet grief . . . way** express grief covertly
10 **two-leaved tongues** recalls both the forked tongue of the devil in the form of a serpent, who speaks a mixture of slander and truth, and Virgil's *Fama* or *Rumour* (*Aeneid* 4.173–97, Loeb ed.), who speaks both truth and untruth
17 **winks** closes his eyes
18.1 ***viol*** a stringed instrument played with a bow, very popular with both men and women at this time. Playing an instrument often carried the meaning of sexual play, with the player assumed to be either male or female and the 'instrument' of either sex; because the viol was held between the knees (hence Ital. *gamba*, leg) it was especially suggestive. Here a female player takes the active role of 'player' (cf. scene 8 and Introduction)
19 **made match** arranged meeting
20 **great fiddle** great could mean pregnant; to fiddle could mean to play sexually with a woman
22 **hog-rubber** abusive term for a swineherd

MOLL Who'll hear an ass speak? Whither else, goodman pageant bearer? They're people of the worst memories.

Exit Porter

SEBASTIAN Why, 'twere too great a burden, love, to have them carry things in their minds and o' their backs together.

MOLL Pardon me, sir, I thought not you so near.

ALEXANDER [*aside*] So, so, so.

SEBASTIAN
I would be nearer to thee, and in that fashion
That makes the best part of all creatures honest.
No otherwise I wish it.

MOLL Sir, I am so poor to requite you, you must look for nothing but thanks of me: I have no humour to marry. I love to lie o' both sides o'th'bed myself; and again o'th'other side, a wife, you know, ought to be obedient, but I fear me I am too headstrong to obey, therefore I'll ne'er go about it. I love you so well, sir, for your good will, I'd be loath you should repent your bargain after, and therefore we'll ne'er come together at first. I have the head now of myself, and am man enough for a woman; marriage is but a chopping and changing, where a maiden loses one head, and has a worse i'th' place.

ALEXANDER [*aside*]
The most comfortablest answer from a roaring girl,
That ever mine ears drunk in.

SEBASTIAN This were enough
Now to affright a fool forever from thee,
When 'tis the music that I love thee for.

ALEXANDER [*aside*]
There's a boy spoils all again!

MOLL Believe it, sir,
I am not of that disdainful temper,
But I could love you faithfully.

ALEXANDER [*aside*] A pox
On you for that word. I like you not now;
You're a cunning roarer, I see that already.

MOLL But sleep upon this once more, sir; you may chance shift a mind tomorrow: be not too hasty to wrong yourself. Never while you live, sir, take a wife running: many have run out at heels that have done't. You see, sir, I speak against myself, and if every woman would deal with their suitor so honestly, poor younger brothers would not be so often gulled with old cozening widows that turn o'er all their wealth in trust to some kinsman, and make the poor gentleman work hard for a pension. Fare you well, sir.

SEBASTIAN Nay, prithee one word more!

ALEXANDER [*aside*] How do I wrong this girl; she puts him off still.

MOLL Think upon this in cold blood, sir; you make as much haste as if you were a-going upon a sturgeon voyage. Take deliberation, sir, never choose a wife as if you were going to Virginia. [*Moves away from him*]

SEBASTIAN And so we parted, my too cursed fate! [*Retires*]

ALEXANDER [*aside*] She is but cunning; gives him longer time in't.

Enter a Tailor

TAILOR Mistress Moll, Mistress Moll! So ho ho, so ho!

MOLL There boy, there boy. What dost thou go a-hawking after me with a red clout on thy finger?

TAILOR I forgot to take measure on you for your new breeches. [*Takes measurements*]

ALEXANDER [*aside*] Heyday, breeches! What, will he marry a monster with two trinkets? What age is this? If the wife go in breeches, the man must wear long coats like a fool.

27 **pageant bearer** Pageants were spectacular displays or tableaux, either erected on fixed stages, placed on moving cars, or carried by porters in municipal celebrations.

33 **fashion** marriage

34 **the best part** most

37 **humour** inclination

38 **again** besides

39 **o'th'other side** ambiguously, the other side of the bed, or of the question of marriage

44 **have the head** a term from horsemanship that picks up the metaphor behind 'headstrong' (39): to give a horse his head means to let him go freely. Moll 'has the head of herself' in that she governs herself, without being subject to a husband (see 1 Cor. 11:3, 'the head of the woman is the man').

44–5 **man enough for a woman** echoes Sir Alexander's description of her as 'woman more than man, | Man more than woman' (2.132–3), but more positively implies that the 'masculine' trait of self-governance doesn't disturb her femaleness

45–7 **marriage . . . i'th' place** Chopping implies some violence in defloration or loss of maidenhead in marriage, and in the change to being governed by the husband as one's 'head'.

48 **roaring girl** see 1.72, note

59 **running** on the run

62–4 **younger brothers . . . cozening widows** Moll contrasts her frankness to the tactics of wealthy widows, who keep suitors (here, younger brothers with modest inheritance, or none) from their wealth by secretly transferring legal control over it to male relatives; otherwise, it would normally pass by law to their second husbands.

66 **pension** denied possession of his wife's estate, the husband must obey her wishes to get even an allowance

71–2 **sturgeon voyage** a long fishing voyage; i.e., you will actually have to live with the wife you choose

73 **Virginia** as if you were going on a long voyage to a faraway place with uncertain prospects. The Virginia Company established Jamestown, the first colony, in 1607; in its early years, more than half the settlers died within a few months of arrival.

74 **And so we parted . . . fate!** For his father's ears, Sebastian pretends to be downcast at being refused by Moll.

77 **So ho** cry in hare-hunting and falconry; hence 'a-hawking' in 78

79 **red clout** piece of cloth for measuring, or to stick pins and needles into

83 **a monster with two trinkets** see 2.132–3; having the features of both sexes, like a hermaphrodite

84 **breeches . . . long coats** proverbial; floor-length coats or skirts were worn by young children, women, and professional fools or jesters. Sir Alexander takes clothing to mark or even determine gender, and gender is dichotomized; male and female have mutually exclusive traits (cf. 2.129–36).

MOLL What fiddling's here? Would not the old pattern have served your turn?

TAILOR You change the fashion, you say you'll have the great Dutch slop, Mistress Mary.

MOLL Why sir, I say so still.

TAILOR Your breeches then will take up a yard more.

MOLL Well, pray look it be put in then.

TAILOR It shall stand round and full, I warrant you.

MOLL Pray make 'em easy enough.

TAILOR I know my fault now; t'other was somewhat stiff between the legs. I'll make these open enough, I warrant you.

ALEXANDER [*aside*] Here's good gear towards! I have brought up my son to marry a Dutch slop and a French doublet: a codpiece daughter.

TAILOR So, I have gone as far as I can go.

MOLL Why then, farewell.

TAILOR If you go presently to your chamber, Mistress Mary, pray send me the measure of your thigh by some honest body.

MOLL Well sir, I'll send it by a porter presently. *Exit*

TAILOR So you had need: it is a lusty one. Both of them would make any porter's back ache in England! *Exit*

SEBASTIAN [*comes forward*]
I have examined the best part of man—
Reason and judgement—and in love, they tell me,
They leave me uncontrolled. He that is swayed
By an unfeeling blood, past heat of love,
His springtime must needs err: his watch ne'er goes right
That sets his dial by a rusty clock.

ALEXANDER [*comes forward*]
So—and which is that rusty clock, sir, you?

SEBASTIAN
The clock at Ludgate, sir, it ne'er goes true.

ALEXANDER
But thou goest falser; not thy father's cares
Can keep thee right, when that insensible work
Obeys the workman's art, lets off the hour,
And stops again when time is satisfied;
But thou run'st on, and judgement, thy main wheel,
Beats by all stops as if the work would break,
Begun with long pains for a minute's ruin,
Much like a suffering man brought up with care,
At last bequeathed to shame and a short prayer.

SEBASTIAN
I taste you bitterer than I can deserve, sir.

ALEXANDER
Who has bewitched thee, son? What devil or drug
Hath wrought upon the weakness of thy blood
And betrayed all her hopes to ruinous folly?
O wake from drowsy and enchanted shame,
Wherein thy soul sits with a golden dream
Flattered and poisoned! I am old, my son—
O let me prevail quickly,
For I have weightier business of mine own
Than to chide thee. I must not to my grave
As a drunkard to his bed, whereon he lies
Only to sleep, and never cares to rise.
Let me dispatch in time; come no more near her.

SEBASTIAN
Not honestly? Not in the way of marriage?

ALEXANDER
What sayst thou? Marriage? In what place?—The sessions-house?
And who shall give the bride, prithee?—An indictment?

SEBASTIAN
Sir, now ye take part with the world to wrong her.

ALEXANDER
Why, wouldst thou fain marry to be pointed at?
Alas the number's great, do not o'erburden't.
Why, as good marry a beacon on a hill,
Which all the country fix their eyes upon,
As her thy folly dotes on. If thou long'st
To have the story of thy infamous fortunes
Serve for discourse in ordinaries and taverns,
Thou'rt in the way; or to confound thy name,
Keep on, thou canst not miss it; or to strike
Thy wretched father to untimely coldness,
Keep the left hand still, it will bring thee to't.
Yet if no tears wrung from thy father's eyes,

86 **fiddling's** fidgeting; sexual play (see 3.67, note). 'Tailor' could mean male or female sexual organ.
89 **great Dutch slop** wide-cut baggy breeches; see title-page woodcut of Moll
91 **yard** unit of measure; also penis
93 **stand round and full** as in erection; the tailor virtually attributes a penis to Moll
96 **stiff** again, refers to erection
98 **gear** doings; genitals
100 **codpiece daughter** again, implying that because she wears male dress, she must be a man anatomically—but at the same time, still a woman, combining what ought to be mutually exclusive; see 83–4, note; Epistle.16–18, note; and Introduction
107 **lusty** vigorous; lustful
112 **unfeeling blood** In Renaissance humours psychology, sexual passion derives from blood, a warm, moist humour which decreases with age; Sebastian objects to being 'swayed' by his father's cold, 'unfeeling blood' (referring also to their blood relationship).
113–14 **springtime ... rusty clock** plays on spring as a season and as part of a clock, both alluding to the human life cycle; youth can't develop properly if it moves to the rhythms of age
116 **clock at Ludgate** one of the ancient city gates, according to legend built by King Lud in 66 BC; made into a prison for debtors and bankrupts by Richard II
121–2 Sebastian's 'uncontrolled' (111) passion drives his judgement to run wildly till it breaks, like a clock running too fast and breaking down.
128 **blood** youthful passion
132 **Flattered** encourage with false hopes
134 **weightier business** presumably, setting his estate or his soul to rights before he dies
140 **sessions-house** court house
150 **in the way** on the way to it
name family name and reputation
152 **untimely coldness** premature death
153 **left hand** the opposite of the right; associated with error, evil, disaster

Nor sighs that fly in sparkles from his sorrows,
Had power to alter what is wilful in thee,
Methinks her very name should fright thee from her,
And never trouble me.

SEBASTIAN
Why is the name of Moll so fatal, sir?

ALEXANDER
Many one, sir, where suspect is entered,
Forseek all London from one end to t'other
More whores of that name than of any ten other.

SEBASTIAN
What's that to her? Let those blush for themselves;
Can any guilt in others condemn her?
I've vowed to love her: let all storms oppose me
That ever beat against the breast of man,
Nothing but death's black tempest shall divide us.

ALEXANDER
O folly that can dote on naught but shame!

SEBASTIAN
Put case a wanton itch runs through one name
More than another: is that name the worse
Where honesty sits possessed in't? It should rather
Appear more excellent and deserve more praise
When through foul mists a brightness it can raise.
Why, there are of the devil's, honest gentlemen,
And well descended, keep an open house;
And some o'th'good man's that are arrant knaves.
He hates unworthily that by rote contemns,
For the name neither saves nor yet condemns;
And for her honesty, I have made such proof on't
In several forms, so nearly watched her ways,
I will maintain that strict against an army,
Excepting you, my father. Here's her worst:
Sh'as a bold spirit that mingles with mankind,
But nothing else comes near it, and oftentimes
Through her apparel somewhat shames her birth;
But she is loose in nothing but in mirth:
Would all Molls were no worse!

ALEXANDER [*aside*]
This way I toil in vain and give but aim
To infamy and ruin: he will fall,
My blessing cannot stay him; all my joys
Stand at the brink of a devouring flood
And will be wilfully swallowed, wilfully!
But why so vain let all these tears be lost?
I'll pursue her to shame, and so all's crossed. *Exit*

SEBASTIAN
He is gone with some strange purpose whose effect
Will hurt me little if he shoot so wide
To think I love so blindly. I but feed
His heart to this match to draw on th'other,
Wherein my joy sits with a full wish crowned—
Only his mood excepted, which must change
By opposite policies, courses indirect:
Plain dealing in this world takes no effect.
This mad girl I'll acquaint with my intent,
Get her assistance, make my fortunes known:
'Twixt lovers' hearts she's a fit instrument,
And has the art to help them to their own.
By her advice, for in that craft she's wise,
My love and I may meet, spite of all spies. *Exit*

Sc. 5

Enter Laxton in Gray's Inn Fields with the Coachman

LAXTON Coachman!

COACHMAN Here, sir.

LAXTON [*gives money*] There's a tester more; prithee drive thy coach to the hither end of Marybone Park—a fit place for Moll to get in.

COACHMAN Marybone Park, sir?

LAXTON Ay, it's in our way, thou knowest.

COACHMAN It shall be done, sir.

LAXTON Coachman.

COACHMAN Anon, sir.

LAXTON Are we fitted with good frampold jades?

COACHMAN The best in Smithfield, I warrant you, sir.

LAXTON May we safely take the upper hand of any coached velvet cap or tuftaffety jacket? For they keep a wild swaggering in coaches nowadays—the highways are stopped with them.

155 **sparkles** implying that his heart is hardened by sorrow; Sebastian's conduct strikes it, producing sparks
160 **Many one . . . suspect** many an officer, when a person is suspected of an offence, or under surveillance
161 **Forseek** seek thoroughly, to the point of being weary
169 **Put case** imagine that
174 **of the devil's** those of the devil's party
176 **o'th'good man's** good men; also married men ('goodman' was title for married man)
179 **honesty** chastity
180 **nearly** closely
181 **strict** strictly, rigorously
183 **mankind** men; as adjective, denotes masculine quality in a woman, thus can also mean 'is somewhat mannish'
184 **But nothing . . . near it** in no other way does she approach men
188 **give . . . aim** in archery, to guide one's aim by charting the result of the previous shot
201 **By . . . courses indirect** i.e., by Sebastian pretending to court Moll, which will make his father more favourably inclined toward Mary
203 **mad** spirited, eccentric; see 1.102
208 **spite** in spite of
5.0.1 ***Gray's Inn Fields*** see 3.307, note
3 **tester** small coin worth sixpence
4 **Marybone Park** near Oxford Street; named for St Mary-le-Bourne (on the brook) or St Mary-le-Bonne (the good), also playing on 'marybone' for marrow-bone, marrow considered a seat of vitality and an aphrodisiac (see 3.199, note). The park was known as a centre of prostitution, thus its name evokes the same juxtaposition of whore and virgin as does Moll's name; see 1.73, note, and Introduction.
11 **frampold** spirited
12 **Smithfield** famous market for horses and cattle near London
13 **coached** travelling by coach, which was newly fashionable
14 **tuftaffety** taffeta with raised, velvety patterns in different colours from the ground colour; costly, worn by the wealthy

COACHMAN My life for yours, and baffle 'em too, sir! Why, they are the same jades—believe it sir—that have drawn all your famous whores to Ware.

LAXTON Nay, then they know their business; they need no more instructions.

COACHMAN They're so used to such journeys, sir, I never use whip to 'em; for if they catch but the scent of a wench once, they run like devils.

Exit Coachman with his whip

LAXTON Fine Cerberus! That rogue will have the start of a thousand ones, for whilst others trot afoot, he'll ride prancing to hell upon a coach-horse! Stay, 'tis now about the hour of her appointment, but yet I see her not. (*The clock strikes three*) Hark, what's this? One, two three: three by the clock at Savoy; this is the hour, and Gray's Inn Fields the place, she swore she'd meet me. Ha, yonder's two Inns-o'-Court men with one wench: but that's not she; they walk toward Islington out of my way. I see none yet dressed like her: I must look for a shag ruff, a frieze jerkin, a short sword, and a safeguard, or I get none. Why, Moll, prithee make haste or the coachman will curse us anon.

Enter Moll like a man

MOLL [*aside*] O here's my gentleman! If they would keep their days as well with their mercers as their hours with their harlots, no bankrupt would give sevenscore pound for a sergeant's place. For would you know a catchpole rightly derived: the corruption of a citizen is the generation of a sergeant. How his eye hawks for venery! [*To him*] Come, are you ready, sir?

LAXTON Ready? For what, sir?

MOLL Do you ask that now, sir? Why was this meeting 'pointed?

LAXTON
I thought you mistook me, sir.
You seem to be some young barrister;
I have no suit in law—all my land's sold,
I praise heaven for't, 't has rid me of much trouble.

MOLL Then I must wake you, sir; where stands the coach?

LAXTON Who's this?—Moll? Honest Moll?

MOLL So young, and purblind? You're an old wanton in your eyes, I see that.

LAXTON Thou'rt admirably suited for the Three Pigeons at Brentford. I'll swear I knew thee not.

MOLL I'll swear you did not: but you shall know me now!

LAXTON No, not here: we shall be spied i'faith! The coach is better; come.

MOLL Stay.

She puts off her cloak and draws

LAXTON
What, wilt thou untruss a point, Moll?

MOLL
Yes, here's the point
That I untruss: 't has but one tag, 'twill serve though
To tie up a rogue's tongue!

LAXTON
How?

MOLL [*putting down gold*]
There's the gold
With which you hired your hackney, here's her pace:
She racks hard and perhaps your bones will feel it.
Ten angels of mine own I've put to thine:
Win 'em and wear 'em!

LAXTON
Hold, Moll! Mistress Mary—

MOLL
Draw, or I'll serve an execution on thee
Shall lay thee up till doomsday.

LAXTON
Draw upon a woman? Why, what dost mean, Moll?

MOLL
To teach thy base thoughts manners! Thou'rt one of those
That thinks each woman thy fond flexible whore:
If she but cast a liberal eye upon thee,
Turn back her head, she's thine; or amongst company,
By chance drink first to thee, then she's quite gone,

17 **baffle** shame
18–19 **jades ... whores** a jade was a worn-out or mean-tempered horse; whores were often called jades
19 **Ware** town near London known as site for sexual rendezvous; see 3.288, note
25 **Cerberus** in classical mythology, three-headed dog guarding entrance to hell
30 **Savoy** hospital built on site of Savoy Palace, between the Thames and the Strand
33 **Islington** suburb north of London used for outings and sexual meetings
35–6 **shag ruff ... safeguard** Laxton remembers Moll much as she was dressed on her entrance (see 3.180.1), in both men's and women's garments
38–9 **keep their days** figuratively, pay their debts
39 **mercers** dealers in textiles, especially costly silks and velvets
42 **catchpole** sergeant who arrested people for debt
42–3 **rightly derived ... sergeant** Moll summarizes a cycle of downward social mobility; tradesmen who go bankrupt because gallants don't pay them become sergeants, who arrest gallants for debt.
43–4 **hawks for venery** see Epistle.1, note
47 **'pointed** appointed
49 **barrister** lawyer
50 **all my land's sold** perhaps suggests a parallel between his lack of stones (testicles), signifying impotence, and his lack of land, a kind of social impotence
54 **purblind** totally blind
56 **Three Pigeons** tavern in Brentford; see 3.288, note
58 **know me now** know what I really think of you; in lines 59–60, he thinks she means carnal knowledge, gained by having sex with someone
62 **untruss a point** undo a lace (laces fastened hose to doublet); Laxton may think, mistakenly, that by starting to remove her hat or cloak, Moll is trying to entice him
point sword point
63 **tag** hard end of lace, allowing it to be threaded through eyelet
65 **hackney** horse for ordinary riding; prostitute
pace speed; gait (playing on a prostitute's sexual movements)
66 **racks hard** runs fast, shaking the rider
68 **Win 'em and wear 'em** proverbial: take your chance
69–70 **serve ... lay thee up** deliver a writ that will put you in jail or incapacitate you (using legal language for a threat of physical force)
70 **doomsday** the day of judgement (playing on 'execution', 69)
73 **fond** foolishly infatuated
flexible malleable, impressionable
74 **liberal** generous; flirtatious

There's no means to help her. Nay, for a need,
Wilt swear unto thy credulous fellow lechers
That thou'rt more in favour with a lady
At first sight than her monkey all her lifetime.
How many of our sex by such as thou
Have their good thoughts paid with a blasted name
That never deserved loosely or did trip
In path of whoredom beyond cup and lip?
But for the stain of conscience and of soul,
Better had women fall into the hands
Of an act silent than a bragging nothing:
There's no mercy in't. What durst move you, sir,
To think me whorish? A name which I'd tear out
From the high German's throat if it lay ledger there
To dispatch privy slanders against me!
In thee I defy all men, their worst hates
And their best flatteries, all their golden witchcrafts
With which they entangle the poor spirits of fools—
Distressed needlewomen and trade-fallen wives,
Fish that must needs bite or themselves be bitten—
Such hungry things as these may soon be took
With a worm fastened on a golden hook.
Those are the lecher's food, his prey. He watches
For quarrelling wedlocks and poor shifting sisters:
'Tis the best fish he takes. But why, good fisherman,
Am I thought meat for you, that never yet
Had angling rod cast towards me? 'Cause you'll say
I'm given to sport, I'm often merry, jest;
Had mirth no kindred in the world but lust?
O shame take all her friends then! But howe'er
Thou and the baser world censure my life,
I'll send 'em word by thee, and write so much
Upon thy breast, 'cause thou shalt bear't in mind:
Tell them 'twere base to yield where I have conquered.
I scorn to prostitute myself to a man,
I that can prostitute a man to me!
And so I greet thee.

LAXTON Hear me!

MOLL Would the spirits
Of all my slanderers were clasped in thine,
That I might vex an army at one time!

They fight

LAXTON I do repent me; hold!

MOLL You'll die the better Christian then.

LAXTON I do confess I have wronged thee, Moll.

MOLL
Confession is but poor amends for wrong,
Unless a rope would follow.

LAXTON I ask thee pardon.

MOLL
I'm your hired whore, sir!

LAXTON I yield both purse and body.

MOLL
Both are mine and now at my disposing.

LAXTON
Spare my life!

MOLL I scorn to strike thee basely.

LAXTON
Spoke like a noble girl, i'faith.
—[*Aside*] Heart, I think I fight with a familiar, or the ghost of a fencer! She's wounded me gallantly. Call you this a lecherous voyage? Here's blood would have served me this seven year in broken heads and cut fingers, and it now runs all out together! Pox o' the Three Pigeons! I would the coach were here now to carry me to the surgeon's. *Exit*

MOLL
If I could meet my enemies one by one thus,
I might make pretty shift with 'em in time,
And make 'em know, she that has wit and spirit
May scorn to live beholding to her body for meat,
Or for apparel, like your common dame
That makes shame get her clothes to cover shame.
Base is that mind that kneels unto her body
As if a husband stood in awe on's wife;
My spirit shall be mistress of this house

77 **for a need** in a pinch
80 **monkey** monkeys were ladies' pets
84 **cup and lip** refers to pledging faith by drinking wine or beer in a betrothal ceremony, as a sign of marital union; figuratively, protests censure of women for having sex with their future husbands before the wedding ceremony (as in fact many women did)
85 **But for** except for
87 **act silent** man who has sex with a woman but doesn't talk about it
bragging nothing man who brags of having sex with a woman when he hasn't
89–90 **tear...throat** To lie in the throat means to lie deliberately, without justification.
90 **high German's** see 3.382
ledger ambassador
91 **privy** secret (as in secrets of state, playing on 90)
95 **trade-fallen** fallen in social rank, from gentry to merchant class; see 3.12–14, note
96 **Fish** proverbial: 'The great fish eat the small.' Moll reverses the usual emphasis, making predatory behaviour in women a response to circumstances rather than simply a vice in itself.
100 **wedlocks** wives
shifting deceiving
102 **meat** food, punning on 'meet', suitable, and suggesting 'whore'
113 **greet** as in 'salute'; also, attack
117 **Christian** If believers confess their sins before death, they are saved from damnation and may expect to enter heaven.
120 **rope** hanging; figuratively, any punishment
125 **familiar** a demon or evil spirit supposed to assist a witch
126 **gallantly** finely; like a gallant
127 **lecherous voyage** sexual adventure
133 **make...shift** dispose of them nicely
135 **to live...for meat** to feed herself by selling her body as a prostitute
136 **common dame** whore, or, ordinary housewife
137 **shame...shame** shamefully works as a prostitute to buy clothes to cover the 'shame' of her naked body; or, as shamefast (modest, chaste) wife 'earns' her clothes from her husband
139 **husband...wife** based on patriarchal comparison of the mind, which ideally should rule the body, to a husband, who ideally should rule over his wife; a prostitute allows her body to rule her mind (spirit, conscience)
140 **My spirit...mistress** cf. 138–40, in which 'mind' is figured as 'husband'; here, spirit is feminine and rules the house

As long as I have time in't.
Enter Trapdoor
O
Here comes my man that would be: 'tis his hour.
Faith, a good well-set fellow, if his spirit
Be answerable to his umbles. He walks stiff,
But whether he will stand to't stiffly, there's the point!
H'as a good calf for't, and ye shall have many a woman
Choose him she means to make her head by his calf;
I do not know their tricks in't. Faith, he seems
A man without; I'll try what he is within.

TRAPDOOR [*aside*]
She told me Gray's Inn Fields 'twixt three and four.
I'll fit her mistress-ship with a piece of service:
I'm hired to rid the town of one mad girl.
She jostles him
—[*To her*] What a pox ails you, sir?

MOLL He begins like a gentleman.

TRAPDOOR Heart, is the field so narrow, or your eyesight?—
She comes towards him
Life, he comes back again!

MOLL
Was this spoke to me, sir?

TRAPDOOR
I cannot tell, sir.

MOLL
Go, you're a coxcomb!

TRAPDOOR
Coxcomb?

MOLL
You're a slave!

TRAPDOOR
I hope there's law for you, sir!

MOLL
Yea, do you see sir?
Turns his hat

TRAPDOOR Heart, this is no good dealing. Pray let me know what house you're of.

MOLL
One of the Temple, sir.
Fillips him

TRAPDOOR
Mass, so methinks.

MOLL
And yet, sometime I lie about Chick Lane.

TRAPDOOR I like you the worse because you shift your lodging so often; I'll not meddle with you for that trick, sir.

MOLL
A good shift, but it shall not serve your turn.

TRAPDOOR
You'll give me leave to pass about my business, sir?

MOLL
Your business? I'll make you wait on me
Before I ha' done, and glad to serve me too!

TRAPDOOR How sir, serve you? Not if there were no more men in England!

MOLL But if there were no more women in England, I hope you'd wait upon your mistress then.

TRAPDOOR Mistress!

MOLL O you're a tried spirit at a push, sir.

TRAPDOOR What would your worship have me do?

MOLL You a fighter?

TRAPDOOR No, I praise heaven, I had better grace and more manners.

MOLL As how, I pray, sir?

TRAPDOOR Life, 't had been a beastly part of me to have drawn my weapons upon my mistress; all the world would 'a' cried shame of me for that.

MOLL Why, but you knew me not.

TRAPDOOR Do not say so, mistress; I knew you by your wide straddle as well as if I had been in your belly.

MOLL Well, we shall try you further; i'th' mean time, we give you entertainment.

TRAPDOOR Thank your good mistress-ship.

MOLL How many suits have you?

TRAPDOOR No more suits than backs, mistress.

MOLL
Well, if you deserve, I cast off this next week,
And you may creep into't.

TRAPDOOR
Thank your good worship.

MOLL
Come, follow me to St Thomas Apostles:
I'll put a livery cloak upon your back
The first thing I do.

TRAPDOOR
I follow my dear mistress. *Exeunt*

142 **man that would be** he who wants to be my manservant
144 **umbles** edible inward parts of an animal, usually a deer; figuratively, insides
stiff resolute, playing on erection
145 **stand to't** reference to erection
147 **to make her head by his calf** choose a husband by his calf, i.e., physical attractiveness
148 **tricks** stratagems for choosing
151 **fit** furnish
157 **coxcomb** fool
158 **law for you** law to deal with people like you
161 **what house** which one of the Inns of Court
162 **the Temple** a lawyer affiliated with the Middle Temple or the Inner Temple (named for the property of the Knights Templar which they leased)
162.1 ***Fillips him*** gives him a sharp blow
163 **Chick Lane** in the suburb of Smithfield, known as a haunt of thieves and ruffians
165 **I'll not meddle with you** because he fears one from Chick Lane
for that trick because you change lodging
167 **shift** punning on shift as change of residence and as trick, device
serve your turn suit your purpose
176 **tried** proven
at a push in an emergency; playing on 'push' as the sexual act
182 **part** piece of behaviour
187 **straddle** walking, standing, or sitting with legs wide apart
as well . . . in your belly as well as if you were my mother
189 **give you entertainment** engage you as a servant
195 **St Thomas Apostles** church located in neighbourhood of clothing shops

Sc. 6 *Enter Mistress Gallipot as from supper, her husband after her*

GALLIPOT What, Prue! Nay, sweet Prudence!

MISTRESS GALLIPOT What a pruing keep you! I think the baby would have a teat, it kyes so. Pray be not so fond of me, leave your city humours. I'm vexed at you to see how like a calf you come bleating after me.

GALLIPOT Nay, honey Prue, how does your rising up before all the table show? And flinging from my friends so uncivilly? Fie, Prue, fie! Come.

MISTRESS GALLIPOT Then up and ride, i'faith.

GALLIPOT Up and ride? Nay, my pretty Prue, that's far from my thought, duck. Why mouse, thy mind is nibbling at something. What is't? What lies upon thy stomach?

MISTRESS GALLIPOT Such an ass as you! Heyday, you're best turn midwife or physician; you're a pothecary already, but I'm none of your drugs.

GALLIPOT Thou art a sweet drug, sweetest Prue, and the more thou art pounded, the more precious.

MISTRESS GALLIPOT Must you be prying into a woman's secrets? Say ye?

GALLIPOT Woman's secrets?

MISTRESS GALLIPOT What? I cannot have a qualm come upon me but your teeth waters till your nose hang over it.

GALLIPOT It is my love, dear wife.

MISTRESS GALLIPOT Your love? Your love is all words; give me deeds! I cannot abide a man that's too fond over me, so cookish! Thou dost not know how to handle a woman in her kind.

GALLIPOT No, Prue? Why, I hope I have handled—

MISTRESS GALLIPOT Handle a fool's head of your own!—Fie, fie!

GALLIPOT Ha, ha, 'tis such a wasp, it does me good now to have her sting me, little rogue.

MISTRESS GALLIPOT Now fie how you vex me! I cannot abide these apron husbands: such cotqueans! You overdo your things; they become you scurvily.

GALLIPOT [*aside*] Upon my life, she breeds. Heaven knows how I have strained myself to please her night and day. I wonder why we citizens should get children so fretful and untoward in the breeding, their fathers being for the most part as gentle as milch kine. [*To her*] Shall I leave thee, my Prue?

MISTRESS GALLIPOT Fie, fie, fie.

GALLIPOT Though shalt not be vexed no more, pretty kind rogue; take no cold, sweet Prue. *Exit*

MISTRESS GALLIPOT As your wit has done! Now Master Laxton, show your head: what news from you? [*Produces a letter*] Would any husband suspect that a woman crying, 'Buy any scurvy-grass', should bring love letters amongst her herbs to his wife? Pretty trick! Fine conveyance! Had jealousy a thousand eyes, a silly woman with scurvy-grass blinds them all.
Laxton, with bays
Crown I thy wit for this: it deserves praise.
This makes me affect thee more, this proves thee wise;
'Lack, what poor shift is love forced to devise?
To the point.

She reads the letter

'O Sweet Creature'—a sweet beginning—'pardon my long absence, for thou shalt shortly be possessed with my presence. Though Demophon was false to Phyllis, I will be to thee as Pan-da-rus was to Cres-sida; though Aeneas made an ass of Dido, I will die to thee ere I do so. O sweetest creature, make much of me, for no man beneath the silver moon shall make more of a woman

6.0.1 ***as from supper*** presumably late afternoon or evening of the same day as scene 5

2 **pruing** pestering; nonce word derived from Prudence

3 **kyes** baby talk for 'cries'

4 **city humours** moods typical of husbands in city comedies, anxious about their wives' marital fidelity

9 **up and ride** exclamation of impatience, with sexual innuendo

12 **lies upon** has upset, with sexual innuendo

15 **drugs** playing on drudge, a menial servant

17 **pounded** as in preparation of medicines; also, refers to the sexual act

19 **secrets** playing on private parts, genitalia

21 **qualm** sudden faintness or feeling of illness

25–6 **words ... deeds** proverbial opposition

27 **cookish** like a woman fussing over her cooking

28 **in her kind** in the way she wants

29 **handled** in a sexual way

30 **a fool's head of your own** your own foolish head (in exasperation)

35 **cotqueans** men that act like housewives

36 **things** concerns; sexual organs
scurvily meanly

37 **breeds** is pregnant

39 **get** beget

40 **untoward** hard to manage
breeding bringing up

41 **milch kine** milk cows

45 **take no cold** don't catch cold; don't be cold toward me

46 **As your wit has done** i.e., caught cold, gotten sick

49 **scurvy-grass** spoonwort, an herb growing along the Thames; its juice was used as a remedy for scurvy

51 **a thousand eyes** alludes to Argus, a giant with eyes all over his body, whom Hera commanded to watch over Io when Zeus was enamored of her
silly simple, helpless

53 **bays** a garland of bay leaves, traditional reward for poetic achievement

55 **affect** love

56 **'Lack** alack, exclamation of despair
shift trick

60 **Demophon ... Phyllis** When Demophon sailed to Athens, promising to return to his wife Phyllis at a certain time, she gave him a box containing an object sacred to Rhea, the goddess of earth, which he was not to open unless he decided not to return. He settled in Cyprus, and Phyllis hanged herself; then he opened the box, was driven mad by its contents, and died by accidentally falling on his own sword.

61 **Pan-da-rus ... Cres-sida** (She hesitates over unfamiliar words.) Pandarus wasn't Cressida's lover but rather the go-between who assisted her love affair with Troilus; the reference ironically undercuts Laxton's profession of fidelity, and moreover implies that he will not be Mistress Gallipot's lover.

62 **Aeneas ... Dido** After Aeneas abandoned Dido to pursue his destiny of founding Rome, she killed herself.
die to thee become as though dead, with play on die meaning to have an orgasm

64–5 **make more ... of thee** be more loving, with ironic meaning of profiting from

than I do of thee. Furnish me therefore with thirty pounds—you must do it of necessity for me. I languish till I see some comfort come from thee. Protesting not to die in thy debt, but rather to live so, as hitherto I have and will,
Thy true Laxton ever.'
Alas, poor gentleman! Troth, I pity him.
How shall I raise this money? Thirty pound?
'Tis thirty sure: a three before an O—
I know his threes too well. My childbed linen?
Shall I pawn that for him? Then if my mark
Be known, I am undone! It may be thought
My husband's bankrupt. Which way shall I turn?
Laxton, what with my own fears, and thy wants,
I'm like a needle 'twixt two adamants.

Enter Master Gallipot hastily

GALLIPOT Nay, nay, wife, the women are all up—[*Aside*] Ha? How? Reading o' letters? I smell a goose, a couple of capons, and a gammon of bacon from her mother out of the country, I hold my life—
Steal—steal—

[*He sneaks behind her*]

MISTRESS GALLIPOT
O beshrew your heart!

GALLIPOT
What letter's that? I'll see't.

She tears the letter

MISTRESS GALLIPOT
O would thou hadst no eyes to see
The downfall of me and thyself! I'm for ever,
For ever I'm undone.

GALLIPOT
What ails my Prue?
What paper's that thou tear'st?

MISTRESS GALLIPOT
Would I could tear
My very heart in pieces, for my soul
Lies on the rack of shame that tortures me
Beyond a woman's suffering.

GALLIPOT
What means this?

MISTRESS GALLIPOT
Had you no other vengeance to throw down,
But even in height of all my joys—

GALLIPOT
Dear woman!

MISTRESS GALLIPOT
When the full sea of pleasure and content
Seemed to flow over me?

GALLIPOT
As thou desirest
To keep me out of Bedlam, tell what troubles thee!
Is not thy child at nurse fallen sick, or dead?

MISTRESS GALLIPOT
O no!

GALLIPOT
Heavens bless me! Are my barns and houses
Yonder at Hockley Hole consumed with fire?
I can build more, sweet Prue.

MISTRESS GALLIPOT
'Tis worse, 'tis worse!

GALLIPOT
My factor broke? Or is the *Jonas* sunk?

MISTRESS GALLIPOT
Would all we had were swallowed in the waves,
Rather than both should be the scorn of slaves!

GALLIPOT
I'm at my wit's end!

MISTRESS GALLIPOT
O my dear husband,
Where once I thought myself a fixed star
Placed only in the heaven of thine arms,
I fear now I shall prove a wanderer.—
O Laxton, Laxton, is it then my fate
To be by thee o'erthrown?

GALLIPOT
Defend me, wisdom,
From falling into frenzy! On my knees,
Sweet Prue, speak! What's that Laxton who so heavy
Lies on thy bosom?

MISTRESS GALLIPOT
I shall sure run mad!

GALLIPOT
I shall run mad for company then. Speak to me—
I'm Gallipot, thy husband. Prue! Why, Prue!
Art sick in conscience for some villainous deed
Thou wert about to act? Didst mean to rob me?
Tush, I forgive thee. Hast thou on my bed
Thrust my soft pillow under another's head?
I'll wink at all faults, Prue; 'las that's no more
Than what some neighbours near thee have done before.
Sweet honey Prue, what's that Laxton?

MISTRESS GALLIPOT
O!

GALLIPOT
Out with him!

73 **an O** zero; also, term for female genitals
74 **childbed linen** bed linen used for confinement and childbirth, sometimes finely embroidered and costly
75 **mark** sign of personal ownership
79 **adamants** hard stones confused with loadstones or magnets; she is pulled two ways, by her attraction to Laxton and her desire to stay married
80 **up** risen from the supper table
83 **hold** bet
84 **steal** his movement as he creeps behind her to read the letter over her shoulder
beshrew your heart common expression, often used lightly, meaning 'devil take your heart'
85–137 **O would thou hadst no eyes . . . never!** To deceive her husband, Mistress Gallipot adopts an extravagant style associated with tragedy; in this comic context, the style amounts to parody.
96 **Bedlam** corruption of Hospital of St Mary of Bethlehem in London, which treated the insane; bedlam came to mean any kind of madhouse
97 **child at nurse** The well-to-do customarily sent infants away from home to be suckled by wet nurses.
100 **Hockley Hole** Hockley-in-the-Hole, a village near London
102 **factor** financial representative
broke ruined financially
Jonas trading vessel in which Gallipot presumably has a financial interest; ironically named, since the cargo of the Biblical Jonah's ship was cast overboard in the storm (see Jonah 1:5)
106 **fixed star** one which appears to hold the same position, as distinguished from a wandering star or planet, which circles the sun
108 **wanderer** unfaithful, wanton
111 **On my knees** i.e., I beg you
120 **wink at** pretend not to see
'las Alas

MISTRESS GALLIPOT
O, he's born to be my undoer!
This hand which thou call'st thine, to him was given;
To him was I made sure i'th' sight of heaven.

GALLIPOT
I never heard this thunder!

MISTRESS GALLIPOT Yes, yes, before
I was to thee contracted, to him I swore.
Since last I saw him, twelve months three times told
The moon hath drawn through her light silver bow;
For o'er the seas he went, and it was said—
But rumour lies—that he in France was dead.
But he's alive! O he's alive! He sent
That letter to me, which in rage I rent,
Swearing with oaths most damnably to have me
Or tear me from this bosom. O heavens save me!

GALLIPOT
My heart will break—shamed and undone for ever!

MISTRESS GALLIPOT
So black a day, poor wretch, went o'er thee never!

GALLIPOT
If thou shouldst wrestle with him at the law,
Thou'rt sure to fall; no odd sleight, no prevention.
I'll tell him thou'rt with child.

MISTRESS GALLIPOT Um!

GALLIPOT Or give out
One of my men was ta'en abed with thee.

MISTRESS GALLIPOT
Um, um!

GALLIPOT
Before I lose thee, my dear Prue,
I'll drive it to that push.

MISTRESS GALLIPOT Worse, and worse still!
You embrace a mischief to prevent an ill.

GALLIPOT
I'll buy thee of him, stop his mouth with gold:
Think'st thou 'twill do?

MISTRESS GALLIPOT O me, heavens grant it would!
Yet now my senses are set more in tune,
He writ, as I remember in his letter,
That he in riding up and down had spent,
Ere he could find me, thirty pounds: send that,
Stand not on thirty with him.

GALLIPOT Forty, Prue.
Say thou the word, 'tis done. We venture lives
For wealth, but must do more to keep our wives.
Thirty or forty, Prue?

MISTRESS GALLIPOT Thirty, good sweet;
Of an ill bargain let's save what we can
I'll pay it him with my tears. He was a man,
When first I knew him, of a meek spirit:
All goodness is not yet dried up, I hope.

GALLIPOT
He shall have thirty pound; let that stop all.
Love's sweets taste best when we have drunk down gall.

Enter Master Tiltyard and his wife, Master Goshawk, and Mistress Openwork

Gods-so, our friends! Come, come, smooth your cheek;
After a storm, the face of heaven looks sleek.

TILTYARD Did I not tell you these turtles were together?

MISTRESS TILTYARD How dost thou, sirrah? Why, sister Gallipot!—

MISTRESS OPENWORK Lord, how she's changed!

GOSHAWK Is your wife ill, sir?

GALLIPOT Yes indeed, la, sir, very ill, very ill, never worse.

MISTRESS TILTYARD How her head burns; feel how her pulses work.

MISTRESS OPENWORK Sister, lie down a little: that always does me good.

MISTRESS TILTYARD In good sadness, I find best ease in that too. Has she laid some hot thing to her stomach?

MISTRESS GALLIPOT No, but I will lay something anon.

TILTYARD Come, come, fools, you trouble her. Shall's go, Master Goshawk?

GOSHAWK Yes, sweet Master Tiltyard.

[*Talks apart with Mistress Openwork*]

Sirrah, Rosamond, I hold my life Gallipot hath vexed his wife.

MISTRESS OPENWORK She has a horrible high colour indeed.

GOSHAWK We shall have your face painted with the same red soon at night, when your husband comes from his rubbers in a false alley; thou wilt not believe me that his bowls run with a wrong bias?

MISTRESS OPENWORK It cannot sink into me that he feeds upon stale mutton abroad, having better and fresher at home.

GOSHAWK What if I bring thee where thou shalt see him stand at rack and manger?

125 **made sure...heaven** betrothed, bound by a precontract (see 1.56–8, note)
129 **The moon...silver bow** The moon is identified with Diana as huntress; drawing her bow signifies the passage of one month.
139 **odd sleight** clever trick
143 **push** extremity
151 **Stand not on** don't refuse on principle to give him
154 **Thirty** see 209, note
160 **gall** bile, signifying bitterness
161 **Gods-so** corruption of 'by God's soul' or 'God save my soul'
163 **turtles** turtle-doves, associated with love
173 **good sadness** in all seriousness
174 **hot thing to her stomach** as medication; playing on hot as lustful, thing as penis, with sexual innuendo
184 **rubbers** a set of (usually three) games, playing on rub as sexual movement; in 183–5 Goshawk insinuates, as he has before, that Openwork is having an affair **false alley** bowling alley; figuratively, false woman or whore
185 **bowls...bias** he bowls with unnatural crookedness (bowling balls were normally made to move obliquely), meaning that he is unfaithful
187 **stale mutton** mutton is slang for whore
190 **stand at rack and manger** like a horse with plenty of food; plainly revealed as unfaithful

MISTRESS OPENWORK I'll saddle him in's kind and spur him till he kick again!

GOSHAWK Shall thou and I ride our journey then?

MISTRESS OPENWORK Here's my hand.

GOSHAWK No more.—[*To Tiltyard*] Come Master Tiltyard, shall we leap into the stirrups with our women and amble home?

TILTYARD Yes, yes; come wife.

MISTRESS TILTYARD In troth, sister, I hope you will do well for all this.

MISTRESS GALLIPOT I hope I shall. Farewell good sister, sweet Master Goshawk.

GALLIPOT Welcome, brother; most kindly welcome, sir.

OMNES Thanks, sir, for our good cheer.

Exeunt all but Gallipot and his Wife

GALLIPOT
It shall be so, because a crafty knave
Shall not outreach me, nor walk by my door
With my wife arm in arm, as 'twere his whore.
I'll give him a golden coxcomb: thirty pound.
Tush, Prue, what's thirty pound? Sweet duck, look cheerly.

MISTRESS GALLIPOT Thou art worthy of my heart, thou buy'st it dearly.

Enter Laxton muffled

LAXTON [*aside*] Uds light, the tide's against me! A pox of your pothecaryship! O for some glister to set him going! 'Tis one of Hercules' labours to tread one of these city hens, because their cocks are still crowing over them. There's no turning tail here; I must on.

MISTRESS GALLIPOT
O husband, see, he comes!

GALLIPOT
Let me deal with him.

LAXTON Bless you, sir.

GALLIPOT Be you blessed too, sir, if you come in peace.

LAXTON Have you any good pudding-tobacco, sir?

MISTRESS GALLIPOT
O pick no quarrels, gentle sir! My husband
Is not a man of weapon, as you are.
He knows all: I have opened all before him
Concerning you.

LAXTON [*aside*] Zounds, has she shown my letters?

MISTRESS GALLIPOT
Suppose my case were yours, what would you do?
At such a pinch, such batteries, such assaults,
Of father, mother, kindred, to dissolve
The knot you tied, and to be bound to him?
How could you shift this storm off?

LAXTON
If I know, hang me!

MISTRESS GALLIPOT
Besides a story of your death was read
Each minute to me.

LAXTON [*aside*] What a pox means this riddling?

GALLIPOT
Be wise, sir, let not you and I be tossed
On lawyers' pens: they have sharp nibs and draw
Men's very heart-blood from them; what need you, sir,
To beat the drum of my wife's infamy,
And call your friends together, sir, to prove
Your precontract, when she's confessed it?

LAXTON
Um, sir,—
Has she confessed it?

GALLIPOT
Sh'as, faith, to me, sir,
Upon your letter sending.

MISTRESS GALLIPOT
I have, I have.

LAXTON [*aside*]
If I let this iron cool, call me slave!
—[*To her*] Do you hear, you dame Prudence? Think'st thou, vile woman,
I'll take these blows and wink?

MISTRESS GALLIPOT
Upon my knees.—

LAXTON
Out, impudence!

GALLIPOT
Good sir—

LAXTON
You goatish slaves!—
No wild fowl to cut up but mine?

GALLIPOT
Alas, sir,
You make her flesh to tremble: fright her not;
She shall do reason, and what's fit.

191–2 **saddle him...kick again** continuing Goshawk's horse metaphors, meaning 'I'll get back at him for his misdeeds, using his own methods'

193–4 **Shall thou...my hand** they agree to have sex, parodying the betrothal ceremony

197 **amble** a leisurely horseriding pace

208 **coxcomb** derogatory term for head, implying foolishness; Gallipot threatens to beat Laxton along with paying him the money

209 **thirty pound** A fancy riding suit cost twenty pounds; a knighthood purchased from the king, thirty pounds; a small cottage, possibly forty pounds.

211.1 ***Enter Laxton muffled*** Here as in all his subsequent entrances, Laxton's concealment suggests that the drubbing he received from Moll in scene 5 has left him ashamed, injured, or vulnerable to creditors because of the ten angels he lost to her. (Debtors commonly concealed themselves so as to escape arrest.)

212 **Uds light** corruption of 'by God's light', a mild oath

213 **glister** suppository or enema

214 **Hercules' labours** the twelve extraordinary feats of strength and bravery performed by the legendary Greek hero **tread** copulate with; used of male bird with female

216 **turning tail** with sexual innuendo on tail as genitals

220 **pudding-tobacco** compressed tobacco in rolls resembling a pudding or sausage

224 **letters** the plural implies that their liaison has been going on for some time

232–3 **tossed | On lawyers' pens** financially drained by fees for prolonged legal manœuvres

235 **beat the drum of** make public

236–7 **call your friends...precontract** Gallipot imagines Laxton asserting the legal force of the alleged precontract by assembling the family members who witnessed it.

236 **friends** relatives

240 **iron cool** reference to the proverb, 'Strike while the iron is hot'; Laxton would play along with Mistress Gallipot's ruse, to blackmail her husband and extort more money

243 **goatish** lustful; goats were considered very sexually active

244 **wild fowl** a term for prostitutes

LAXTON I'll have thee,
Wert thou more common than an hospital
And more diseased—
GALLIPOT But one word, good sir!
LAXTON So, sir.
GALLIPOT
I married her, have lain with her, and got
Two children on her body: think but on that.
Have you so beggarly an appetite,
When I upon a dainty dish have fed,
To dine upon my scraps, my leavings? Ha, sir?
Do I come near you now, sir?
LAXTON Be lady, you touch me.
GALLIPOT
Would not you scorn to wear my clothes, sir?
LAXTON Right, sir.
GALLIPOT
Then pray, sir, wear not her, for she's a garment
So fitting for my body, I'm loath
Another should put it on: you will undo both.
Your letter, as she said, complained you had spent
In quest of her, some thirty pound: I'll pay it.
Shall that, sir, stop this gap up 'twixt you two?
LAXTON
Well, if I swallow this wrong, let her thank you.
The money being paid, sir, I am gone;
Farewell. O women, happy's he trusts none!
MISTRESS GALLIPOT
Dispatch him hence, sweet husband.
GALLIPOT Yes, dear wife.
Pray, sir, come in; [*To Wife*] ere Master Laxton part,
Thou shalt in wine drink to him.
MISTRESS GALLIPOT With all my heart.
Exit Gallipot

How dost thou like my wit?
LAXTON Rarely: that wile
By which the serpent did the first woman beguile
Did ever since all women's bosoms fill:
You're apple-eaters all, deceivers still! *Exeunt*

Enter Sir Alexander Wengrave, Sir Davy Dapper, Sir Adam Appleton at one door, and Trapdoor at another door Sc. 7

ALEXANDER
Out with your tale, Sir Davy, to Sir Adam—
A knave is in mine eye deep in my debt.
SIR DAVY Nay, if he be a knave, sir, hold him fast.
[*Sir Alexander talks apart with Trapdoor*]
ALEXANDER Speak softly; what egg is there hatching now?
TRAPDOOR A duck's egg, sir; a duck that has eaten a frog. I have cracked the shell and some villainy or other will peep out presently. The duck that sits is the bouncing ramp, that roaring girl, my mistress; the drake that must tread is your son, Sebastian.
ALEXANDER Be quick.
TRAPDOOR As the tongue of an oyster-wench.
ALEXANDER And see thy news be true.
TRAPDOOR As a barber's every Saturday night. Mad Moll—
ALEXANDER Ah!
TRAPDOOR Must be let in without knocking at your back gate.
ALEXANDER So.
TRAPDOOR Your chamber will be made bawdy.
ALEXANDER Good!
TRAPDOOR She comes in a shirt of mail.
ALEXANDER How, shirt of mail?
TRAPDOOR Yes, sir, or a male shirt, that's to say, in man's apparel.
ALEXANDER To my son?
TRAPDOOR Close to your son: your son and her moon will be in conjunction if all almanacs lie not. Her black safeguard is turned into a deep slop, the holes of her

247–8 **more common ... diseased** common, meaning sexually available, wanton; hospitals were sometimes associated with venereal disease
254 **come near you** do you see my point?
Be lady corruption of 'by our lady' (the Virgin Mary)
255 **wear my clothes** clothes marked social rank
256–8 **wear not her ... put it on** figuratively, suggests their intimacy as a couple, his affection for her, and a wife's function as social 'ornament' for her husband
259 **complained** lodged a complaint (in quasi-legal sense)
264 **O women ... trusts none** proverbial
265 **Dispatch him** settle the business and send him away
268–71 **that wile ... deceivers still** pictures Mistress Gallipot as Eve, attributing the serpent's guile in the garden of Eden to the woman he beguiled into eating the apple
7.2 **A knave ... in my debt** Sir Alexander conceals the real nature of his dealings with Trapdoor by inventing this reason for his presence.
in mine eye here before me
5 **A duck's egg ... frog** The duck (which may carry the sexual meaning of wild-fowl for prostitute; see 6.244) is Moll, who has swallowed the frog, i.e., Trapdoor's bait.
7 **bouncing** loud, blustering
8 **ramp** bold, vulgar, ill-behaved woman
9 **tread** used of male birds copulating with hens; see 6.213
11 **oyster-wench** woman who sells oysters, which were considered an aphrodisiac and a delicacy
13 **barber's every Saturday night** barbers, great sources of news, were busiest at this time
15–16 **back gate** sexual allusion to anal intercourse or *coitus a tergo*
18 **bawdy** made to look like a bawdy-house or brothel
20 **shirt of mail** garment made of mail, interlaced metal rings or overlapping plates; a type of armour
25–6 **Close to your son ... almanacs lie not** playing on astrological predictions in almanacs, with sexual innuendo in 'conjunction' (close proximity of heavenly bodies)
27–9 **safeguard ... codpiece** Moll has changed female clothing—safeguard (see 3.180.1, note), upper body or bodice fastened with laces in eyelets or holes, waistcoat, and placket—for male: deep slop or baggy breeches (see 4.89, and title-page woodcut), doublet fastened with buttons and button holes, and codpiece (see Epistle.14–17).

upper body to buttonholes, her waistcoat to a doublet, her placket to the ancient seat of a codpiece; and you shall take 'em both with standing collars.

ALEXANDER Art sure of this?

TRAPDOOR As every throng is sure of a pickpocket; as sure as a whore is of the clients all Michaelmas Term, and of the pox after the term.

ALEXANDER The time of their tilting?

TRAPDOOR Three.

ALEXANDER The day?

TRAPDOOR This.

ALEXANDER Away, ply it; watch her.

TRAPDOOR As the devil doth for the death of a bawd, I'll watch her; do you catch her.

ALEXANDER She's fast; here weave thou the nets. Hark—

TRAPDOOR They are made.

ALEXANDER I told them thou didst owe me money: hold it up, maintain't.

TRAPDOOR Stiffly, as a Puritan does contention. [*As in a quarrel*] Fox, I owe thee not the value of a halfpenny halter!

ALEXANDER Thou shalt be hanged in't ere thou 'scape so! Varlet, I'll make thee look through a grate!

TRAPDOOR I'll do't presently: through a tavern grate. Drawer! Pish! *Exit*

SIR ADAM
Has the knave vexed you, sir?

ALEXANDER
Asked him my money;
He swears my son received it! O that boy
Will ne'er leave heaping sorrows on my heart
Till he has broke it quite!

SIR ADAM
Is he still wild?

ALEXANDER
As is a Russian bear.

SIR ADAM
But he has left
His old haunt with that baggage.

ALEXANDER
Worse still and worse!
He lays on me his shame, I on him my curse.

SIR DAVY
My son, Jack Dapper, then shall run with him,
All in one pasture.

SIR ADAM
Proves your son bad too, sir?

SIR DAVY
As villainy can make him: your Sebastian
Dotes but on one drab, mine on a thousand!
A noise of fiddlers, tobacco, wine, and a whore,
A mercer that will let him take up more,
Dice, and a water-spaniel with a duck; O,
Bring him abed with these! When his purse jingles,
Roaring boys follow at's tail, fencers and ningles—
Beasts Adam ne'er gave name to—these horse-leeches suck
My son; he being drawn dry, they all live on smoke.

ALEXANDER
Tobacco?

SIR DAVY
Right; but I have in my brain
A windmill going that shall grind to dust
The follies of my son, and make him wise
Or a stark fool. Pray lend me your advice.

ALEXANDER *and* SIR ADAM
That shall you, good Sir Davy.

SIR DAVY
Here's the springe
I ha' set to catch this woodcock in: an action
In a false name—unknown to him—is entered
I'th' Counter to arrest Jack Dapper.

ALEXANDER *and* SIR ADAM
Ha, ha, he!

SIR DAVY
Think you the Counter cannot break him?

SIR ADAM
Break him?
Yes, and break's heart too, if he lie there long!

SIR DAVY
I'll make him sing a counter-tenor, sure.

SIR ADAM
No way to tame him like it; there he shall learn
What money is indeed, and how to spend it.

29 **placket** slit at top of skirt or petticoat to allow putting on; a feature typical of women's dress, it came to mean women *per se* and women's genitals. The word could also mean apron, petticoat, or pocket in a woman's skirt.
30 **standing collars** high straight collars worn by both sexes
33 **whore ... Michaelmas Term** When law courts were in session, visitors flooded London for legal business and for pleasure, and prostitution was said to increase; Michaelmas Term ran from 9 or 10 October to 28 or 29 November.
35 **tilting** see 3.0.4, note; with sexual innuendo
42 **fast** fastened; fixed to the spot
44–52 see 2, note: they resume their ruse
46 **Stiffly** sexual allusion to erection, playing on 'hold it up', 44
48 **halter** rope with a noose used for hanging
50 **grate** prison grating, barred window; see Prologue.24, note
51 **tavern grate** red lattice work of alehouse window
52 **Drawer** one who draws liquor from the tap in an alehouse or tavern
57 **Russian bear** imported to England for bear baiting, a popular spectator sport
58 **baggage** disreputable woman or strumpet
63 **drab** whore
64 **noise** group (of musicians)
65 **mercer** dealer in textiles; see 5.39, note **take up more** buy more on credit
66 **water-spaniel with a duck** see 3.413.3
67 **Bring him abed** let him be delivered of, be rid of; punning on childbirth
68 **Roaring boys** see 1.73, note **ningles** boy favourites or male lovers; satires of this period associate them with other pleasures and fashions enjoyed by gallants (see Sir Davy's list, 7.64–6)
69 **Beasts Adam ne'er gave name to** those indulging in sexual practices considered 'unnatural', not belonging to the animals in paradise to which Adam gave names **horse-leeches** extortioners; whores
72 **windmill** figuratively, visionary scheme
75 **That shall you** that shall you have
75–6 **springe ... woodcock** proverbial; snare for catching small birds, such as woodcocks, which are easily caught
76 **action** legal proceedings, which Sir Davy has instigated using a false name
78 **Counter** one of two debtors' prisons in London, both named after the streets where they were located, in Cheapside: the Poultry Counter and the Wood Street Counter
79 **break him** break his will, reform him
81 **counter-tenor** punning on Counter, a male voice higher than tenor; may also hint at castration, used to produce *castrati*, high-voiced male singers

SIR DAVY
He's bridled there.

ALEXANDER Ay, yet knows not how to mend it!
Bedlam cures not more madmen in a year
Than one of the counters does; men pay more dear
There for their wit than anywhere. A counter,
Why, 'tis an university! Who not sees?
As scholars there, so here men take degrees
And follow the same studies, all alike.
Scholars learn first logic and rhetoric;
So does a prisoner. With fine honeyed speech
At's first coming in he doth persuade, beseech
He may be lodged with one that is not itchy,
To lie in a clean chamber, in sheets not lousy.
But when he has no money, then does he try
By subtle logic and quaint sophistry
To make the keepers trust him.

SIR ADAM Say they do?

ALEXANDER
Then he's a graduate!

SIR DAVY Say they trust him not?

ALEXANDER
Then is he held a freshman and a sot,
And never shall commence; but, being still barred,
Be expulsed from the Master's Side to th'Twopenny Ward,
Or else i'th' Hole be placed.

SIR ADAM When then, I pray,
Proceeds a prisoner?

ALEXANDER When, money being the theme,
He can dispute with his hard creditors' hearts
And get out clear, he's then a Master of Arts!
Sir Davy, send your son to Wood Street College;
A gentleman can nowhere get more knowledge.

SIR DAVY
There gallants study hard.

ALEXANDER True: to get money.

SIR DAVY
'Lies by th'heels, i'faith. Thanks, thanks; I ha' sent
For a couple of bears shall paw him.

Enter Sergeant Curtalax and Yeoman Hanger

SIR ADAM Who comes yonder?

SIR DAVY
They look like puttocks; these should be they.

ALEXANDER I know 'em;
They are officers. Sir, we'll leave you.

SIR DAVY My good knights,
Leave me; you see I'm haunted now with sprites.

ALEXANDER *and* SIR ADAM Fare you well, sir.

Exeunt Sir Alexander and Sir Adam

CURTALAX This old muzzle chops should be he by the fellow's description. [*To Sir Davy*] Save you, sir.

SIR DAVY Come hither, you mad varlets; did not my man tell you I watched here for you?

CURTALAX One in a blue coat, sir, told us that in this place an old gentleman would watch for us, a thing contrary to our oath, for we are to watch for every wicked member in a city.

SIR DAVY You'll watch, then, for ten thousand! What's thy name, honesty?

CURTALAX Sergeant Curtalax, I sir.

SIR DAVY
An excellent name for a sergeant, Curtalax;
Sergeants indeed are weapons of the law:
When prodigal ruffians far in debt are grown,
Should not you cut them, citizens were o'erthrown.
Thou dwell'st hereby in Holborn, Curtalax?

CURTALAX That's my circuit, sir; I conjure most in that circle.

SIR DAVY And what young toward whelp is this?

HANGER Of the same litter; his yeoman, sir. My name's Hanger.

84 **how to mend it** how to cure his spendthrift habits

87–108 **counter ... university ... knowledge** a frequent comparison, between the prisoner's acquisition of survival skills in prison and the scholar's course of study from bachelor's to master's to doctor's degrees

91 **logic and rhetoric** logic, forms and rules of reasoning; rhetoric, rules derived from classical authors for using language eloquently, to persuade; along with grammar, these comprised the *trivium*, a triad of studies basic to the liberal arts curriculum of the medieval university that continued to shape the Renaissance curriculum

100 **freshman** beginning student
sot fool

101 **commence** take the full university degree of master or doctor
barred prevented from graduating, with a pun on prison bars

102–3 **Master's Side ... th'Twopenny Ward ... i'th' Hole** in descending order of comfort and expense, the different wards (sections) of debtors' prison; prisoners had to pay for their food and lodging, and as their money ran out, they moved from one ward to the next, 'the Hole' being notorious for filth, misery, and disease

104–5 **theme ... dispute** pedagogical terms; scholars were given 'themes', topics or propositions to be debated or 'disputed' in exercises

110 **'Lies by th'heels** in irons or the stocks; in jail

111 **bears shall paw him** figuratively, sergeants who arrested debtors by laying hands on their shoulders; they were sometimes called 'shoulder-clappers'

111.1 *Curtalax* short, broad sword; as a sergeant, he is an officer of the court who arrests debtors (see 111, note)
Yeoman Hanger a yeoman assisted an official; a hanger was a loop on the belt from which a sword hung (see title-page engraving of Moll) or a short sword hung from a belt; suggests his role as assistant

112 **puttocks** kites, birds of prey

114 **sprites** figuratively, sergeants who make bodily arrests, analogous to spirits who take possession of the soul

116 **muzzle chops** name for a man with prominent nose and jaw, like an animal's muzzle

118 **mad** foolish

120 **One in a blue coat** a servant

125 **honesty** an honest, honourable man

126–8 **Curtalax ... weapons of the law** playing on the sergeant's name; see III.1

130 **cut** strike sharply, playing on Curtalax

132 **circuit ... conjure** alluding to the magician's action of drawing a circle before conjuring

134 **toward** bold, or conversely, docile

SIR DAVY Yeoman Hanger.
One pair of shears, sure, cut out both your coats;
You have two names most dangerous to men's
throats.
You two are villainous loads on gentlemen's backs;
Dear ware, this Hanger and this Curtalax.

CURTALAX We are as other men are, sir; I cannot see but he who makes a show of honesty and religion, if his claws can fasten to his liking, he draws blood. All that live in the world are but great fish and little fish, and feed upon one another: some eat up whole men; a sergeant cares but for the shoulder of a man. They call us knaves and curs, but many times he that sets us on worries more lambs one year than we do in seven.

SIR DAVY Spoke like a noble Cerberus! Is the action entered?

HANGER His name is entered in the book of unbelievers.

SIR DAVY What book's that?

CURTALAX The book where all prisoners' names stand; and not one amongst forty when he comes in believes to come out in haste!

SIR DAVY Be as dogged to him as your office allows you to be.

CURTALAX *and* HANGER O sir!

SIR DAVY You know the unthrift Jack Dapper?

CURTALAX Ay, ay, sir, that gull? As well as I know my yeoman.

SIR DAVY And you know his father too, Sir Davy Dapper?

CURTALAX As damned a usurer as ever was among Jews! If he were sure his father's skin would yield him any money, he would, when he dies, flay it off and sell it to cover drums for children at Barthol'mew Fair!

SIR DAVY [*aside*] What toads are these to spit poison on a man to his face! [*To them*] Do you see, my honest rascals? Yonder Greyhound is the dog he hunts with: out of that tavern, Jack Dapper will sally. Sa, sa! Give the counter! On, set upon him!

CURTALAX *and* HANGER We'll charge him upo'th' back, sir.

SIR DAVY Take no bail; put mace enough into his caudle. Double your files! Traverse your ground!

CURTALAX *and* HANGER Brave, sir!

SIR DAVY Cry arm, arm, arm!

CURTALAX *and* HANGER Thus, sir.

SIR DAVY There boy, there boy, away: look to your prey, my true English wolves and—and so I vanish. *Exit*

CURTALAX Some warden of the sergeants begat this old fellow, upon my life! Stand close.

HANGER Shall the ambuscado lie in one place?

CURTALAX No, nook thou yonder.

Enter Moll and Trapdoor

MOLL Ralph.

TRAPDOOR What says my brave captain, male and female?

MOLL This Holborn is such a wrangling street.

TRAPDOOR That's because lawyers walks to and fro in't!

MOLL Here's such jostling as if everyone we met were drunk and reeled.

TRAPDOOR Stand, mistress, do you not smell carrion?

MOLL Carrion? No, yet I spy ravens.

TRAPDOOR Some poor wind-shaken gallant will anon fall into sore labour; and these men-midwives must bring him to bed i'the Counter: there all those that are great with child with debts lie in.

MOLL Stand up.

TRAPDOOR Like your new maypole!

HANGER [*to Curtalax*] Whist, whew!

138 **One pair of shears** proverbial for likeness, sameness

140 **villainous** regarded as vile, detestable **loads** referring to their mode of arrest, grabbing debtors from behind

141 **ware** metal goods, punning on their names

144–6 **All ... feed upon one another** proverbial; see 5.96, Moll's variation on the same idea

146–7 **a sergeant ... the shoulder of a man** again referring to his mode of arresting debtors; compare 111, 140

148 **worries** like wolves or dogs, seizes the throat of sheep with the teeth

150 **Cerberus** see 5.25, note; implicitly, compares debtors' prison to hell

152 **book of unbelievers** the register of prisoners (see 154); the opposite of the book of the faithful entering heaven

157 **dogged** strict, dutiful; playing on 'Cerberus'

164 **As damned a usurer ... among Jews** Jews were expelled from England in 1290 by Edward I. Though some Jews were living in London at this time, none could have practised usury legally because the office that regulated Jewish usurers was no longer in existence; Curtalax voices prejudice rather than known practice.

165–7 **his father's skin ... Barthol'mew Fair** Crimes commonly attributed to Jews may reflect a European fascination with the Jewish ritual of circumcision. At Bartholemew Fair, held in Smithfield on 24 August, St Bartholemew's Day, toys such as drums were sold (see Ben Jonson's comedy, *Bartholemew Fair* [1614]).

168 **toads ... poison** toads were proverbially poisonous

170 **Greyhound** probably the name of a tavern; the place where Jack Dapper can be found

171 **Sa, sa** exclamation used by fencers delivering a thrust

172 **counter** fencing term for circular motion of sword, or, hunting term for going in the opposite direction to the course taken by the game

174 **mace ... caudle** caudle, a warm drink of thin gruel, mixed with wine or ale, was often spiced with mace; pun on mace, the staff carried by sergeants as badge of office, with which they made their arrests

175 **Double ... ground** military terms: increase your file (row of soldiers) to double its length (absurd for only two soldiers), move from side to side

176 **Brave** excellent

177 **Cry arm** 'be ready for fight' or 'take up arms'

183 **ambuscado** force lying in ambush (sergeants waited in concealment at alehouses and other locales for debtors they arrested)

184 **nook** hide in a corner

187 **Holborn** see 3.306, note

192 **ravens** referring to lawyers as those who prey on people as ravens eat carrion

193 **wind-shaken** flawed in the centre, as timber cracked by high winds

194–6 **sore labour ... lie in** comparison of debtors to pregnant women (great with child) in the final stage (sore) of labour who are brought to bed (for delivery) in prison by men-midwives (sergeants), where they lie in (await the birth)

199 **Whist, whew** whistling sounds, to get his partner's attention

CURTALAX [*to Hanger*] Hump, no!

MOLL Peeping? It shall go hard, huntsmen, but I'll spoil your game. They look for all the world like two infected maltmen coming muffled up in their cloaks in a frosty morning to London.

TRAPDOOR A course, captain: a bear comes to the stake!

Enter Jack Dapper and Gull

MOLL It should be so, for the dogs struggle to be let loose.

HANGER [*to Curtalax*] Whew!

CURTALAX [*to Hanger*] Hemp!

MOLL Hark Trapdoor, follow your leader.

JACK DAPPER Gull.

GULL Master?

JACK DAPPER Didst ever see such an ass as I am, boy?

GULL No, by my troth, sir, to lose all your money, yet have false dice of your own! Why, 'tis as I saw a great fellow used t'other day: he had a fair sword and buckler, and yet a butcher dry-beat him with a cudgel!

MOLL *and* TRAPDOOR Honest sergeant! [*To Jack*] Fly! Fly, Master Dapper, you'll be arrested else!

JACK DAPPER Run, Gull, and draw!

GULL Run master! Gull follows you!

Exit Jack Dapper and Gull

CURTALAX [*Moll holding him*] I know you, well enough: you're but a whore to hang upon any man.

MOLL Whores then are like sergeants: so now hang you! [*To Trapdoor*] Draw, rogue, but strike not: for a broken pate they'll keep their beds and recover twenty marks damages.

CURTALAX You shall pay for this rescue! [*To Hanger*] Run down Shoe Lane and meet him!

TRAPDOOR Shoo! Is this a rescue, gentlemen, or no?

[*Exeunt Curtalax and Hanger*]

MOLL
Rescue? A pox on 'em Trapdoor, let's away;
I'm glad I have done perfect one good work today.
If any gentleman be in scrivener's bands,
Send but for Moll, she'll bail him by these hands!

Exeunt

Enter Sir Alexander Wengrave solus Sc. 8

ALEXANDER
Unhappy in the follies of a son,
Led against judgement, sense, obedience,
And all the powers of nobleness and wit—
O wretched father!

Enter Trapdoor

Now, Trapdoor, will she come?

TRAPDOOR
In man's apparel, sir; I am in her heart now,
And share in all her secrets.

ALEXANDER
Peace, peace, peace.
Here, take my German watch, hang't up in sight
That I may see her hang in English for't.

TRAPDOOR
I warrant you for that now, next sessions rids her, sir.
This watch will bring her in better than a hundred
constables.

ALEXANDER
Good Trapdoor, sayst thou so? Thou cheer'st my heart
After a storm of sorrow. My gold chain, too:
Here, take a hundred marks in yellow links.

TRAPDOOR
That will do well to bring the watch to light, sir,
And worth a thousand of your headborough's lan-
terns.

ALEXANDER
Place that o' the court-cupboard, let it lie
Full in the view of her thief-whorish eye.

TRAPDOOR
She cannot miss it, sir; I see't so plain
That I could steal't myself.

ALEXANDER
Perhaps thou shalt, too;

200 **Hump** return signal

202–3 **infected maltmen** During plague times, those who brought malt for sale to London returned to the countryside with contaminated rags for use as fertilizer, and became infected.

203 **muffled** as debtors often were, to avoid arrest

205 **course** in hunting, the animal being pursued (here, Jack Dapper)
stake post to which bear was tethered for bear baiting

206 **dogs** sergeants; compare 134–5

213–14 **to lose all . . . false dice** he came prepared to cheat others, but was cheated himself instead

214–16 **great fellow . . . dry-beat him with a cudgel** may allude to an actual occurrence at the Fortune Theatre on 26 February 1610/11, when two butchers 'abused' some gentlemen

217 **Honest sergeant** Moll tries to divert the sergeant's attention so that Jack Dapper can escape him.

222–3 **a whore to hang upon . . . like sergeants** Sergeants cling to debtors' shoulders as whores cling to customers; cf. 111, 140, 146–7.

224–6 **broken pate . . . damages** If debtors resist arrest, sergeants will claim injury, pretend to need recuperation (keep their beds), and sue debtors for damages.

224–5 **broken pate** cut head

225 **twenty marks** A mark was an amount (not a coin), two-thirds of a pound; twenty marks was a considerable sum.

228 **Shoe Lane** street running north from Fleet Street to Holborn

229 **Shoo** expression of mild contempt, punning on Shoe Lane

232 **in scrivener's bands** Scrivener could mean notary, or a broker who made loans for security; thus a debtor raising money to pay off debts might be further in debt to a scrivener.

233 **by these hands** an oath, or a reference to herself as agent of rescue

8.5 **in her heart** have her trust

7 **German watch** the earliest portable timekeepers were made in Germany around 1500

8 **in English** under English law

9 **sessions** court session

10 **watch** timepiece, punning on ward or parish officers who keep the watch at night

12 **gold chain** worn by well-dressed gentlemen; perhaps an emblem of his office as Justice of the Peace

13 **a hundred marks** £66 13*s.* 4*d.* (a mark was an amount worth two-thirds of a pound; see 1.91); an expensive item

15 **headborough's** parish police officer or constable; they carried lanterns on night watch

16 **court-cupboard** sideboard with three tiers of open shelves, used to display silver dishes, known as 'plate'

That or something as weighty. What she leaves,
Thou shalt come closely in and filch away,
And all the weight upon her back I'll lay.

TRAPDOOR
You cannot assure that, sir.

ALEXANDER
No? What lets it?

TRAPDOOR
Being a stout girl, perhaps she'll desire pressing;
Then all the weight must lie upon her belly.

ALEXANDER
Belly or back, I care not, so I've one.

TRAPDOOR
You're of my mind for that, sir.

ALEXANDER
Hang up my ruff band with the diamond at it;
It may be she'll like that best.

TRAPDOOR It's well for her that she must have her choice—[*Aside*] he thinks nothing too good for her!—[*To him*] If you hold on this mind a little longer, it shall be the first work I do to turn thief myself: would do a man good to be hanged when he is so well provided for!

ALEXANDER
So, well said! All hangs well; would she hung so too:
The sight would please me more than all their glisterings.
O that my mysteries to such straits should run,
That I must rob myself to bless my son! *Exeunt*

Enter Sebastian with Mary Fitzallard like a page, and Moll [*dressed as a man*]

SEBASTIAN
Thou hast done me a kind office, without touch
Either of sin or shame: our loves are honest.

MOLL
I'd scorn to make such shift to bring you together else.

SEBASTIAN
Now have I time and opportunity
Without all fear to bid thee welcome, love.
(*He kisses Mary*)

MARY
Never with more desire and harder venture.

MOLL
How strange this shows, one man to kiss another.

SEBASTIAN
I'd kiss such men to choose, Moll;
Methinks a woman's lip tastes well in a doublet.

MOLL
Many an old madam has the better fortune then,
Whose breaths grew stale before the fashion came:
If that will help 'em, as you think 'twill do,
They'll learn in time to pluck on the hose too!

SEBASTIAN
The older they wax, Moll. Troth, I speak seriously:
As some have a conceit their drink tastes better
In an outlandish cup than in our own,
So methinks every kiss she gives me now
In this strange form is worth a pair of two.
Here we are safe, and furthest from the eye
Of all suspicion: this is my father's chamber,
Upon which floor he never steps till night.
Here he mistrusts me not, nor I his coming;
At mine own chamber he still pries unto me.
My freedom is not there at mine own finding,
Still checked and curbed; here he shall miss his purpose.

MOLL
And what's your business, now you have your mind, sir?
At your great suit I promised you to come:
I pitied her for name's sake, that a Moll
Should be so crossed in love, when there's so many
That owes nine lays apiece, and not so little.
My tailor fitted her: how like you his work?

SEBASTIAN
So well, no art can mend it for this purpose;
But to thy wit and help we're chief in debt,
And must live still beholding.

MOLL
Any honest pity
I'm willing to bestow upon poor ring-doves.

SEBASTIAN
I'll offer no worse play.

MOLL
Nay, and you should, sir,

21 **closely** secretly
22 **all the weight ... lay** I'll accuse her of stealing what you steal
23 **lets** hinders
24 **stout** robust, large
pressing word play on pressing as *peine forte et dure*, a form of torture in which weights were loaded on the accused to force them to answer a charge, and with reference to the sexual act, the man 'pressing on' the woman
26 **so I've one** I don't care, so long as I incriminate her one way or the other
28 **ruff band** small ruff; see 3.209, note
37 **mysteries** pun on secret practices, and technical skills proper to his craft, as in 'secrets of the trade'
41 **shift** effort, with pun on shift as change of clothes (at Sebastian's request, she is disguised in order to pass as a male musician)
46 **to choose** by choice
48 **madam** derisive term for fashionable lady, implying affectation
49 **Whose breaths ... the fashion came** who aged before male dress for women became fashionable
50 **that** dressing as men
52 **The older they wax** they'll still get older
53 **conceit** fancy, notion
54 **outlandish** foreign, strange
56 **pair of two** set of two
65 **great suit** earnest pleading
66 **for name's sake** calling attention to the close conjunction of opposing images of women as whores and virgins (see 1.0.1, note; 1.73, note; and 5.4, note)
68 **owes nine lays** meaning uncertain: owes probably means owns, and lays can mean either wagers (they won prizes in a contest) or lodgings (they keep as many as nine lodgings for meeting customers)
72 **still** forever
beholding beholden
73 **ring-doves** wood-pigeons; figuratively, lovers
74 **play** sport; sexual play

I should draw first and prove the quicker man!
[*Draws*]

SEBASTIAN
Hold, there shall need no weapon at this meeting;
But 'cause thou shalt not loose thy fury idle,
[*Takes down and gives her a viol*]
Here, take this viol: run upon the guts
And end thy quarrel singing.

MOLL Like a swan above bridge:
For, look you, here's the bridge and here am I.

SEBASTIAN Hold on, sweet Moll.

MARY I've heard her much commended, sir, for one that was ne'er taught.

MOLL I'm much beholding to 'em. Well, since you'll needs put us together, sir, I'll play my part as well as I can: it shall ne'er be said I came into a gentleman's chamber and let his instrument hang by the walls!

SEBASTIAN Why well said, Moll, i'faith; it had been a shame for that gentleman then, that would have let it hang still, and ne'er offered thee it.

MOLL There it should have been still then for Moll, for though the world judge impudently of me, I ne'er came into that chamber yet where I took down the instrument myself.

SEBASTIAN Pish, let 'em prate abroad! Thou'rt here where thou art known and loved; there be a thousand close dames that will call the viol an unmannerly instrument for a woman, and therefore talk broadly of thee, when you shall have them sit wider to a worse quality.

MOLL Push, I ever fall asleep and think not of 'em, sir; and thus I dream.

SEBASTIAN Prithee let's hear thy dream, Moll.

The Song

MOLL
I dream there is a mistress,
And she lays out the money;
She goes unto her sisters,
She never comes at any.
Enter Sir Alexander behind them
She says she went to th'Burse for patterns;
You shall find her at St Kathern's,
And comes home with never a penny.

SEBASTIAN That's a free mistress, 'faith.

ALEXANDER [*aside*] Ay, ay, ay, like her that sings it; one of thine own choosing.

MOLL But shall I dream again?
Here comes a wench will brave ye,
Her courage was so great,
She lay with one o' the navy,
Her husband lying i' the Fleet.
Yet oft with him she cavilled;
I wonder what she ails;
Her husband's ship lay gravelled
When hers could hoise up sails.
Yet she began, like all my foes,
To call whore first; for so do those—
A pox of all false tails!

SEBASTIAN Marry, amen, say I!

75 **draw first...man** provoked by Sebastian's sexual innuendo, Moll draws her sword to defend her honour

76 **weapon** playing on sword and on weapon as penis

77 **loose thy fury idle** spend your energy (either aggressive, as in loosing an arrow, or sexual) to no purpose

78 **run upon the guts** pun on running through with a sword, and drawing bow across strings (made of animal guts)

79 **swan above bridge** alludes to the idea that swans sing just before they die; traditionally, swans drew Venus' chariot, and were also plentiful on the Thames around London
bridge pun on bridge of viol (piece of wood over which strings are stretched) and bridge over a river

85 **put us together...play my part** part in musical sense, but also implying a sexual encounter

87 **let his instrument hang by the walls** viols were fashionable instruments, especially for men, and often hung on chamber walls; also, word play on instrument as penis

88–90 **it had been a shame...ne'er offered thee it** intended as a compliment, implying that not to make sexual overtures to Moll would be the man's loss

92 **judge impudently** judge me (wrongly) to be forward, sexually aggressive, or, be impudent in judging me thus

93–4 **took down the instrument myself** approached a man sexually (Moll is again defending herself against a reputation for wanton behaviour)

96 **close** secret, close-mouthed

97 **call the viol an unmannerly instrument** punning on viol/vile/vial (penis), on unmannerly, and on instrument (see 87, 92–4): disapprove of women playing the viol/having sex with men

98 **talk broadly** disapprove

99 **sit wider to a worse quality** alluding to woman's position in playing the viol and in having sex: behave more unchastely

101 **dream** in addition to normal sense, means make melody

102 **dream** music, melody

103 **mistress** a woman who governs a family, household, state or territory, or establishment of any kind, having control over and care of children, servants, dependents, etc.

105 **sisters** ambiguously, female siblings; fellow members of a female religious order; fellow Christians who are female; fellow prostitutes; or, broadly, women who share her position in some sense

106 **never comes at** doesn't accost anyone, like a prostitute; doesn't profit from anyone

107 **th'Burse** from Fr. *bourse*, purse: the original name for the Royal Exchange, a financial centre built in 1566 and surrounded by arcades for small shops selling fashionable wares appealing to women; more likely, refers to the New Exchange built in 1609 on the Strand, also with arcades and similar kinds of shops
patterns models or specimens, perhaps of clothing or such fasionable items as were sold at the Burse, or decorative designs on china, carpets, wallpaper

108 **St Kathern's** dockside district along the Thames in east London, from the Tower of London to Ratcliff, known for alehouses and taverns

110 **free** generous, magnanimous; noble, gentle; may also imply sexual looseness

114 **brave** challenge, defy

116 **lay with** had sex with; playing on 'lying' (117), staying, lodging at

117 **the Fleet** Fleet Prison, near the junction of Ludgate Hill and Fleet Street

118 **cavilled** found fault with, quarrelled

119 **what she ails** what ails her

120 **gravelled** beached

121 **hoise up sails** i.e., when she could manage, make progress; sometimes used of prostitutes attracting customers

124 **false tails** derogatory for sexual partners who are false, fickle; punning on tales, to mean slander, false allegations

ALEXANDER [*aside*] So say I, too.

MOLL Hang up the viol now, sir; all this while I was in a dream: one shall lie rudely then, but being awake, I keep my legs together. A watch; what's a clock here?

ALEXANDER [*aside*] Now, now, she's trapped!

MOLL Between one and two; nay then, I care not. A watch and a musician are cousin-germans in one thing: they must both keep time well or there's no goodness in 'em. The one else deserves to be dashed against a wall, and t'other to have his brains knocked out with a fiddle-case.
What? A loose chain and a dangling diamond!
Here were a brave booty for an evening thief now;
There's many a younger brother would be glad
To look twice in at a window for't,
And wriggle in and out like an eel in a sandbag.
O, if men's secret youthful faults should judge 'em,
'Twould be the general'st execution
That e'er was seen in England!
There would be but few left to sing the ballads: there would be so much work, most of our brokers would be chosen for hangmen—a good day for them!—they might renew their wardrobes of free cost then!

SEBASTIAN [*to Mary*]
This is the roaring wench must do us good.

MARY [*to Sebastian*]
No poison, sir, but serves us for some use,
Which is confirmed in her.

SEBASTIAN Peace, peace—
Foot, I did hear him sure, where'er he be.

MOLL
Who did you hear?

SEBASTIAN My father:
'Twas like a sigh of his—I must be wary.

ALEXANDER [*aside*]
No? Will't not be? Am I alone so wretched
That nothing takes? I'll put him to his plunge for't.

SEBASTIAN [*aside to Moll and Mary*]
Life, here he comes!—[*Aloud to Moll*] Sir, I beseech you take it.
Your way of teaching does so much content me,
I'll make it four pound; here's forty shillings, sir.
I think I name it right. [*Aside to Moll*] Help me, good Moll.
—[*Aloud*] Forty in hand. [*Offering money*]

MOLL Sir, you shall pardon me,
I have more of the meanest scholar I can teach:
This pays me more than you have offered yet.

SEBASTIAN
At the next quarter,
When I receive the means my father 'lows me,
You shall have t'other forty.

ALEXANDER [*aside*] This were well now,
Were it to a man whose sorrows had blind eyes;
But mine behold his follies and untruths
With two clear glasses.
[*He comes forward*]
[*To Sebastian*] How now?

SEBASTIAN Sir?

ALEXANDER What's he there?

SEBASTIAN
You're come in good time, sir, I've a suit to you;
I'd crave your present kindness.

ALEXANDER What is he there?

SEBASTIAN A gentleman, a musician, sir: one of excellent fingering—

ALEXANDER Ay, I think so. [*Aside*] I wonder how they 'scaped her?

SEBASTIAN H'as the most delicate stroke, sir—

ALEXANDER A stroke indeed.—[*Aside*] I feel it at my heart!

SEBASTIAN Puts down all your famous musicians.

ALEXANDER Ay.—[*Aside*] A whore may put down a hundred of 'em!

SEBASTIAN Forty shillings is the agreement, sir, between us; now, sir, my present means mounts but to half on't.

ALEXANDER And he stands upon the whole.

SEBASTIAN Ay indeed does he, sir.

ALEXANDER And will do still; he'll ne'er be in other tale.

128 **rudely** crudely, immodestly, with reference to 'dream' as music and the position of the viol player's legs
132 **cousin-germans** first cousins, punning on the 'German watch' (7)
137 **brave** splendid, fine looking
138 **younger brother** without paternal inheritance
140 **eel...sandbag** sinuously, nimbly
142 **general'st execution** i.e., more people would be condemned as criminals, and executed
144 **ballads** those that commemorated prisoners condemned to be hanged; playing on execution, 142
145–7 **brokers...free cost then** hangmen traditionally received their victims' clothing; if hangmen were brokers (dealers in second hand clothing) they could profit greatly because they could replenish their stock without cost
149 **No poison...some use** proverbial; also an example of the Christian doctrine that everything in creation has a use
151 **Foot** abbreviation of mild oath, 'God's foot'
154 **Will't not be?** won't my scheme work?
155 **takes** takes effect
put him to his plunge I'll bring this crisis to a head
161 **have more of** get more money from
168 **What's he there?** who is that man there?
172–85 This series of *doubles entendres* referring to both musical and sexual playing could be read as a sequence: 'fingering' (172), 'delicate stroke' (175), 'puts down' (177), 'mounts to' (181), 'stands upon' (183), and 'tale' (185).
172 **fingering** in playing an instrument; in thieving; in sexual sense
173 **they** items displayed to tempt Moll: watch, chain, diamond
174 **'scaped** escaped
175 **delicate stroke** in bowing the viol; in sexual act
176 **stroke...at my heart** paralytic stroke
177 **Puts down** excels; Sir Alexander takes it in a sexual sense
180 **Forty shillings** two pounds; could buy an inexpensive horse
181 **mounts but to half** only amounts to half, i.e., twenty shillings instead of the forty he offered in lines 158 and 160; possibly playwrights' or scribe's error
183 **stands upon** insists on; playing on 'mounts' (181) in sexual sense
185 **ne'er be in other tale** will keep to the same story (as yours); with pun on tail as sexual parts

SEBASTIAN Therefore I'd stop his mouth, sir, an I could.
ALEXANDER Hum, true. There is no other way indeed.—
[*Aside*] His folly hardens; shame must needs succeed.—
[*To Moll*] Now sir, I understand you profess music.
MOLL I am a poor servant to that liberal science, sir.
ALEXANDER
Where is it you teach?
MOLL Right against Clifford's Inn.
ALEXANDER Hum, that's a fit place for it; you have many scholars?
MOLL And some of worth, whom I may call my masters.
ALEXANDER [*aside*] Ay, true, a company of whoremasters!—[*To Moll*] You teach to sing, too?
MOLL Marry, do I, sir.
ALEXANDER I think you'll find an apt scholar of my son, especially for prick-song.
MOLL I have much hope of him.
ALEXANDER [*aside*] I am sorry for't, I have the less for that.
[*To Moll*] You can play any lesson?
MOLL At first sight, sir.
ALEXANDER There's a thing called 'The Witch'—can you play that?
MOLL I would be sorry any one should mend me in't.
ALEXANDER
Ay, I believe thee. [*Aside*] Thou has so bewitched my son,
No care will mend the work that thou hast done.
I have bethought myself, since my art fails,
I'll make her policy the art to trap her.
Here are four angels marked with holes in them,
Fit for his cracked companions. Gold he will give her;
These will I make induction to her ruin,
And rid shame from my house, grief from my heart.
—[*To Sebastian*] Here, son, in what you take content and pleasure,
Want shall not curb you; [*Gives money*] pay the gentleman
His latter half in gold.
SEBASTIAN I thank you, sir.
ALEXANDER [*aside*]
O, may the operation on't end three:
In her, life; shame in him; and grief in me. *Exit*
SEBASTIAN
Faith, thou shalt have 'em; 'tis my father's gift:
Never was man beguiled with better shift.
MOLL
He that can take me for a male musician,
I cannot choose but make him my instrument
And play upon him! *Exeunt*

Enter Mistress Gallipot and Mistress Openwork Sc. 9

MISTRESS GALLIPOT Is then that bird of yours, Master Goshawk, so wild?
MISTRESS OPENWORK A goshawk, a puttock: all for prey! He angles for fish, but he loves flesh better.
MISTRESS GALLIPOT Is't possible his smooth face should have wrinkles in't, and we not see them?
MISTRESS OPENWORK Possible? Why, have not many handsome legs in silk stockings villainous splay feet for all their great roses?
MISTRESS GALLIPOT Troth, sirrah, thou sayst true.
MISTRESS OPENWORK Didst never see an archer, as thou'st walked by Bunhill, look asquint when he drew his bow?
MISTRESS GALLIPOT Yes, when his arrows have flown toward Islington, his eyes have shot clean contrary towards Pimlico.
MISTRESS OPENWORK For all the world, so does Master Goshawk double with me.
MISTRESS GALLIPOT O fie upon him! If he double once, he's not for me.

186 **stop his mouth** pay him off
190 **liberal science** In the seven liberal arts of the medieval curriculum, music was grouped with arithmetic, geometry, and astronomy in the four-part division called the *quadrivium*; see 7.91, note.
191 **Clifford's Inn** the oldest of the Inns of Chancery, law schools that trained lawyers for the court of Chancery; located on Fleet Street between Chancery Lane and Fetter Street
199 **prick-song** an accompanying melody written or 'pricked' down, as opposed to plainsong, which was improvised; with sexual sense
204 **'The Witch'** possibly a contemporary ballad; implying that Moll has bewitched Sebastian (see 207)
206 **mend me** excel me; correct me
210 **policy** stratagem of posing as a musician
211 **angels** gold coins worth ten shillings (see 3.137, note)
marked with holes making them no longer current; thus if Moll tried to pass them, she would break the law
212 **cracked** Metal was illicitly filed or 'clipped' from the edges of coins for profit; if clipping 'cracked' the circle around the sovereign's head embossed on the coin, it was no longer legal tender. 'Cracked' coinage became a metaphor for flawed moral conduct and especially for women's 'cracked' sexual virtue.
213 **induction** initial step, punning on sense of prologue to a play
222–4 **He that can take me...play upon him** Thus Middleton punningly alludes to several motifs in this scene: disguise, manipulation, and music.
9.3 **puttock** kite; see 7.112, note
8 **silk stockings** favoured by gallants because they showed off the leg better than woollen ones
splay feet flat feet that turn outwards
9 **great roses** ornamental knots of ribbon in the shape of a rose, tied to the shoe (see title-page woodcut of Moll)
12 **Bunhill** street near Moorfields, marshy area north of city walls that, when laid out in walks in 1606, became popular for summer excursions; also used as training ground for city militia, and for duels
asquint sideways
14–15 **Islington...Pimlico** He aims toward Islington in the north-west (see 5.33, note) but he looks toward Pimlico, the inn in Hogsden to the north-east. The inn's name derives from a Roanoke Island place-name, one of a number of links connecting Hogsden with tobacco and Virginia (Coates).
17 **double with** deceive, like the archer in 13–15

MISTRESS OPENWORK Because Goshawk goes in a shag-ruff band, with a face sticking up in't which shows like an agate set in a cramp-ring, he thinks I'm in love with him.

MISTRESS GALLIPOT 'Las, I think he takes his mark amiss in thee.

MISTRESS OPENWORK He has, by often beating into me, made me believe that my husband kept a whore.

MISTRESS GALLIPOT Very good.

MISTRESS OPENWORK Swore to me that my husband this very morning went in a boat with a tilt over it to the Three Pigeons at Brentford, and his punk with him under his tilt!

MISTRESS GALLIPOT That were wholesome!

MISTRESS OPENWORK I believed it; fell a-swearing at him, cursing of harlots, made me ready to hoise up sail and be there as soon as he.

MISTRESS GALLIPOT So, so.

MISTRESS OPENWORK And for that voyage, Goshawk comes hither incontinently; but sirrah, this water spaniel dives after no duck but me: his hope is having me at Brentford to make me cry quack!

MISTRESS GALLIPOT Art sure of it?

MISTRESS OPENWORK Sure of it? My poor innocent Openwork came in as I was poking my ruff; presently hit I him i'the teeth with the Three Pigeons. He forswore all, I up and opened all, and now stands he, in a shop hard by, like a musket on a rest, to hit Goshawk i'the eye when he comes to fetch me to the boat.

MISTRESS GALLIPOT Such another lame gelding offered to carry me through thick and thin—Laxton, sirrah—but I am rid of him now.

MISTRESS OPENWORK Happy is the woman can be rid of 'em all! 'Las, what are your whisking gallants to our husbands, weigh 'em rightly, man for man?

MISTRESS GALLIPOT Troth, mere shallow things.

MISTRESS OPENWORK Idle, simple things: running heads; and yet—let 'em run over us never so fast—we shopkeepers, when all's done, are sure to have 'em in our purse-nets at length, and when they are in, Lord, what simple animals they are!

MISTRESS OPENWORK Then they hang the head—

MISTRESS GALLIPOT Then they droop—

MISTRESS OPENWORK Then they write letters—

MISTRESS GALLIPOT Then they cog—

MISTRESS OPENWORK Then deal they underhand with us, and we must ingle with our husbands abed; and we must swear they are our cousins, and able to do us a pleasure at Court.

MISTRESS GALLIPOT And yet when we have done our best, all's but put into a riven dish: we are but frumped at and libelled upon.

MISTRESS OPENWORK O if it were the good Lord's will there were a law made, no citizen should trust any of 'em all!

Enter Goshawk

MISTRESS GALLIPOT Hush sirrah! Goshawk flutters.

GOSHAWK How now, are you ready?

MISTRESS OPENWORK Nay, are you ready? A little thing, you see, makes us ready.

GOSHAWK Us? [*To Mistress Openwork*] Why, must she make one i' the voyage?

MISTRESS OPENWORK O by any means: do I know how my husband will handle me?

GOSHAWK [*aside*] Foot, how shall I find water to keep these two mills going? Well, since you'll needs be clapped under hatches, if I sail not with you both till all split, hang me up at the mainyard and duck me. [*Aside*] It's but liquoring them both soundly, and then you shall see their cork heels fly up high, like two swans, when their tails are above water and their long necks under water,

20–1 **shag-ruff band** see 3.209–10, note
21–2 **with a face . . . cramp-ring** an image of a small head surrounded by a large ruff; small figures carved in agate decorated seals, used for sealing letters with wax. Cramp rings, charms against illness, were distributed by the monarch on Good Friday.
24 **mark** in archery, a target (continuing the archery image of 11–15); in falconry, a hawk's quarry or prey (playing on Goshawk's name)
26 **beating into me** repeatedly telling me (with suggestion of a bird's beating wings)
30 **tilt** awning over a boat
31 **Three Pigeons at Brentford** inn which Laxton suggested for a rendezvous with Moll (see 3.288, note; 5.56, note)
punk whore
35 **hoise up sail** get going; compare 8.121, note
39 **incontinently** immediately
39–41 **water spaniel . . . cry quack!** cf. 'wild fowl', 6.244, note
44 **poking my ruff** when soaked in starch, ruffs were pleated by being folded over poking sticks, on which they dried
44–5 **hit I him i'the teeth** aggressively accused him
46–7 **hard by** near by
47 **a musket on a rest** the barrels of heavy, unwieldy muskets were set into forked poles driven into the ground
53 **whisking** lively, smart
55, 56 **things** playing on thing as penis
56 **running heads** footmen, lackeys
59 **purse-nets** bag-shaped nets the mouths of which were drawn together; used especially for catching rabbits (conies), hence referring to cony-catching (illicitly duping naïve victims)
61–2 **hang the head . . . droop** become dejected; playing on detumescence (to get limp)
64 **cog** cheat; fawn, wheedle
66 **ingle** caress with; cajole (to deceive husbands)
67–8 **a pleasure at Court** a favour from some court official; such claims were stratagems used by wives having affairs with gallants, to deceive husbands
70 **all's . . . a riven dish** riven means broken; i.e., our efforts have gone for nothing
frumped at mocked
76 **little thing** i.e., we're almost ready (with reference to thing as penis)
81 **handle** treat (she claims to need Mistress Gallipot with her as protection)
82 **Foot** abbreviation of mild oath 'God's foot', with play on Fr. *foutre*, to have sex
82–3 **water . . . mills** *double entendre* for having sex; water is figuratively semen
83–4 **clapped under hatches** imprisoned on a ship; also refers to having sex
84 **split** go to pieces; shipwreck
85 **hang me up . . . duck me** traditional sailors' punishment
86 **liquoring . . . soundly** making them drunk
87 **cork heels** fashionable, and associated with women's lightness (wantonness)
87–9 **like two swans . . . diving to catch gudgeons** pictures the women in flagrant sexual postures, like swans diving for small fish

diving to catch gudgeons. [*To them*] Come, come! Oars stand ready; the tide's with us. On with those false faces. Blow winds, and thou shalt take thy husband casting out his net to catch fresh salmon at Brentford.

MISTRESS GALLIPOT I believe you'll eat of a cod's-head of your own dressing before you reach halfway thither.

[*They put on masks*]

GOSHAWK So, so, follow close. Pin as you go.

Enter Laxton muffled

LAXTON Do you hear? [*Talks apart with Mistress Gallipot*]

MISTRESS GALLIPOT Yes, I thank my ears.

LAXTON I must have a bout with your pothecary-ship.

MISTRESS GALLIPOT At what weapon?

LAXTON I must speak with you.

MISTRESS GALLIPOT No!

LAXTON No? You shall!

MISTRESS GALLIPOT Shall? Away soused sturgeon, half fish, half flesh!

LAXTON Faith, gib, are you spitting? I'll cut your tail, puss-cat, for this.

MISTRESS GALLIPOT 'Las poor Laxton, I think thy tail's cut already! Your worst!

LAXTON If I do not— *Exit*

GOSHAWK
Come, ha' you done?

Enter Master Openwork

[*To Mistress Openwork*] 'Sfoot, Rosamond, your husband!

OPENWORK
How now? Sweet Master Goshawk! None more welcome!
I have wanted your embracements. When friends meet,
The music of the spheres sounds not more sweet
Than does their conference. Who is this? Rosamond?
Wife?—[*To Mistress Gallipot*] How now, sister?

GOSHAWK
Silence, if you love me!

OPENWORK
Why masked?

MISTRESS OPENWORK
Does a mask grieve you, sir?

OPENWORK
It does.

MISTRESS OPENWORK
Then you're best get you a-mumming.

GOSHAWK [*aside to Mistress Openwork*]
'Sfoot, you'll spoil all!

MISTRESS GALLIPOT
May not we cover our bare faces with masks
As well as you cover your bald heads with hats?

OPENWORK
No masks; why, they're thieves to beauty, that rob eyes
Of admiration in which true love lies.
Why are masks worn? Why good? Or why desired?
Unless by their gay covers wits are fired
To read the vil'st looks. Many bad faces—
Because rich gems are treasured up in cases—
Pass by their privilege current; but as caves
Damn misers' gold, so masks are beauties' graves.
Men ne'er meet women with such muffled eyes,
But they curse her that first did masks devise,
And swear it was some beldame. Come, off with't.

MISTRESS OPENWORK
I will not!

OPENWORK
Good faces, masked, are jewels kept by sprites.
Hide none but bad ones, for they poison men's sights;
Show them as shopkeepers do their broidered stuff:
By owl-light; fine wares cannot be open enough.
Prithee, sweet Rose, come strike this sail.

MISTRESS OPENWORK
Sail?

OPENWORK
Ha?
Yes, wife, strike sail, for storms are in thine eyes.

MISTRESS OPENWORK
They're here, sir, in my brows, if any rise.

OPENWORK
Ha, brows? What says she, friend? Pray tell me why
Your two flags were advanced: the comedy?

90 **false faces** Masks made of velvet or other silk were worn by women of fashion to protect the complexion from the sun, to shield them from public gaze, or to conceal their identity.

92 **fresh salmon** figuratively, young whores

93 **cod's-head** fool's head, meaning that his plan will fail and expose him for a fool

95 **Pin** possibly, put on your masks

95.1 ***muffled*** see 6.211.1, note

98 **bout** round of fighting, with sexual implication

103 **soused** pickled, or soaked in liquor; an insult

103–4 **half fish, half flesh** proverbial for neither one thing nor another, referring to his impotence; if he lacks the sexual capacity of a man, he is assumed to be womanish

105 **gib** term for cat, especially male or castrated cat, used for woman as insult

107–8 **tail's cut already** alluding to his impotence

108 **Your worst!** do your worst (a challenge)

113 **wanted** missed

114 **The music of the spheres** In the Ptolemaic system, the planets, sun, moon, and fixed stars moved in concentric circles around the earth, creating friction which made music normally inaudible to human ears.

118 **a-mumming** Mummings, amateur performances for holiday festivities, were mimed; Mistress Openwork is telling her husband to be silent.

125–7 **Many bad faces . . . privilege current** Bad women (wicked, unchaste) pass for good because they wear expensive masks, making people think something valuable lies behind the mask.

127–8 **as caves . . . beauties' graves** Just as hoarding gold is morally wrong, so is hiding beauty behind a mask.

131 **beldame** hag

133 **sprites** spirits

135 **stuff** cloth of lesser quality

136 **owl-light** Dim light; drapers and sempsters were said to deceive customers by displaying wares in badly-lit shops.

137 **strike this sail** possibly, remove your mask, and prepare for trouble

139 **in my brows** Referring to a frown; Openwork pretends to think she means horns, conventional symbol of a cuckold.

141 **flags . . . advanced** Playhouses flew flags when open for performance.
comedy Openwork associates Goshawk's deception with play-acting.

Come, what's the comedy?

MISTRESS GALLIPOT *Westward Ho.*

OPENWORK How?

MISTRESS OPENWORK
'Tis *Westward Ho*, she says.

GOSHAWK Are you both mad?

MISTRESS OPENWORK
Is't market day at Brentford, and your ware
Not sent up yet?

OPENWORK What market day? What ware?

MISTRESS OPENWORK A pie with three pigeons in't—'tis drawn and stays your cutting up.

GOSHAWK As you regard my credit—

OPENWORK Art mad?

MISTRESS OPENWORK Yes, lecherous goat! Baboon!

OPENWORK Baboon? Then toss me in a blanket.

MISTRESS OPENWORK [*to Mistress Gallipot*] Do I it well?

MISTRESS GALLIPOT [*to Mistress Openwork*] Rarely!

GOSHAWK [*to Openwork*]
Belike, sir, she's not well; best leave her.

OPENWORK No,
I'll stand the storm now, how fierce soe'er it blow.

MISTRESS OPENWORK
Did I for this lose all my friends? Refuse
Rich hopes and golden fortunes to be made
A stale to a common whore?

OPENWORK This does amaze me.

MISTRESS OPENWORK
O God, O God! Feed at reversion now?
A strumpet's leaving?

OPENWORK Rosamond!

GOSHAWK [*aside*] I sweat; would I lay in Cold Harbour.

MISTRESS OPENWORK Thou hast struck ten thousand daggers through my heart!

OPENWORK Not I, by heaven, sweet wife.

MISTRESS OPENWORK Go, devil, go! That which thou swear'st by, damns thee!

GOSHAWK [*aside to Mistress Openwork*] 'S heart, will you undo me?

MISTRESS OPENWORK [*to Openwork*]
Why stay you here? The star by which you sail
Shines yonder above Chelsea; you lose your shore.
If this moon light you, seek out your light whore.

OPENWORK
Ha?

MISTRESS GALLIPOT
Push! Your western pug!

GOSHAWK Zounds, now hell roars!

MISTRESS OPENWORK
With whom you tilted in a pair of oars
This very morning.

OPENWORK Oars?

MISTRESS OPENWORK At Brentford, sir!

OPENWORK
Rack not my patience. Master Goshawk,
Some slave has buzzed this into her, has he not?—
I run a-tilt in Brentford with a woman?
'Tis a lie!
What old bawd tells thee this? 'Sdeath, 'tis a lie!

MISTRESS OPENWORK
'Tis one to thy face shall justify
All that I speak.

OPENWORK Ud' soul, do but name that rascal!

MISTRESS OPENWORK
No, sir, I will not.

GOSHAWK [*aside*] Keep thee there, girl. [*To them*] Then!

OPENWORK [*to Mistress Gallipot*]
Sister, know you this varlet?

MISTRESS GALLIPOT Yes.

OPENWORK Swear true;
Is there a rogue so low damned? A second Judas?
A common hangman? Cutting a man's throat?
Does it to his face? Bite me behind my back?
A cur-dog? Swear if you know this hell-hound!

142 ***Westward Ho*** cry of boatmen carrying passengers across the Thames; also title of a comedy by Dekker and Webster (1604)

144–5 **Is't market day ... up yet** likens the prostitutes supposedly waiting for her husband at Brentford, a market town located on the trade route from London in the south-west of England, to goods for sale (see 3.288, note)

146 **A pie with three pigeons in't** playing on the Three Pigeons Inn, the supposed site of his meeting; pigeons, like ducks (see 38–41) and swans (see 86–8), are terms for prostitutes

147 **stays** waits for
cutting up carving, as of roasted fowl, with sexual implication

150 **goat! Baboon!** both regarded as highly lustful

151 **toss me in a blanket** humiliating punishment

152 **Do I it well?** is my act convincing?

156 **friends** relatives (alluding to her social rank, supposedly higher than her husband's; see 3.12–14, 343–4, 348–50)

158 **stale** lover whose fidelity is mocked to amuse her rival ('common whore'); decoy

159–60 **Feed at reversion ... leaving** Why should I take a whore's leftovers (i.e., Openwork)?

161 **Cold Harbour** neighbourhood near London Bridge known as refuge for the poor and sanctuary for debtors hiding from arrest; also, pun on 'Cold', as remedy for sweating

167 **'S heart** abbreviation for 'God's heart', mild oath

170 **Chelsea** west from London, on the way to Brentford, where Openwork supposedly will meet a prostitute

171 **light ... light** pun on light as illumination and as fickle, wanton

172 **western pug** bargeman going westward from London; whore in Brentford, west of London

173 **tilted** pun on tilting as jousting with lances, as the sexual act, and as the boat covered with a tilt (see 30, note)
pair of oars boat rowed by two men

181 **Ud' soul** corruption of 'God bless my soul'

184 **Judas** from Judas Iscariot, the disciple who betrayed Christ; a betrayer who seems a friend

186 **Bite ... back** backbiter; one who vilifies another behind his back

187 **cur-dog** mongrel; term of contempt
hell-hound allusion to Cerberus, watchdog of hell (see 5.25, note)

MISTRESS GALLIPOT
In truth I do.
OPENWORK His name?
MISTRESS GALLIPOT Not for the world,
To have you to stab him.
GOSHAWK [*aside*] O brave girls: worth gold!
OPENWORK
A word, honest Master Goshawk.
Draws out his sword
GOSHAWK What do you mean, sir?
OPENWORK
Keep off, and if the devil can give a name
To this new fury, holla it through my ear,
Or wrap it up in some hid character.
I'll ride to Oxford and watch out mine eyes,
But I'll hear the Brazen Head speak; or else
Show me but one hair of his head or beard,
That I may sample it. If the fiend I meet
In mine own house, I'll kill him—the street,
Or at the church door—there, 'cause he seeks to untie
The knot God fastens, he deserves most to die!
MISTRESS OPENWORK
My husband titles him!
OPENWORK Master Goshawk, pray, sir,
Swear to me that you know him or know him not,
Who makes me at Brentford to take up a petticoat
Besides my wife's.
GOSHAWK By heaven, that man I know not.
MISTRESS OPENWORK
Come, come, you lie!
GOSHAWK Will you not have all out?
—[*To Openwork*] By heaven, I know no man beneath the moon
Should do you wrong, but if I had his name,
I'd print it in text letters.
MISTRESS OPENWORK Print thine own then;
Didst not thou swear to me he kept his whore?
MISTRESS GALLIPOT
And that in sinful Brentford they would commit
That which our lips did water at, sir? Ha?
MISTRESS OPENWORK
Thou spider, that hast woven thy cunning web
In mine own house t'ensnare me: hast not thou
Sucked nourishment even underneath this roof
And turned it all to poison, spitting it
On thy friend's face, my husband—he as 'twere, sleeping—
Only to leave him ugly to mine eyes,
That they might glance on thee?
MISTRESS GALLIPOT Speak, are these lies?
GOSHAWK
Mine own shame me confounds.
MISTRESS OPENWORK No more, he's stung.
Who'd think that in one body there could dwell
Deformity and beauty, heaven and hell?
Goodness, I see, is but outside. We all set
In rings of gold, stones that be counterfeit:
I thought you none.
GOSHAWK Pardon me.
OPENWORK Truth, I do.
This blemish grows in nature, not in you;
For man's creation stick even moles in scorn
On fairest cheeks. Wife, nothing is perfect born.
MISTRESS OPENWORK
I thought you had been born perfect.
OPENWORK
What's this whole world but a gilt rotten pill?
For at the heart lies the old core still.
I'll tell you, Master Goshawk, ay, in your eye
I have seen wanton fire; and then to try
The soundness of my judgement, I told you
I kept a whore, made you believe 'twas true,
Only to feel how your pulse beat, but find
The world can hardly yield a perfect friend.
Come, come, a trick of youth, and 'tis forgiven;
This rub put by, our love shall run more even.
MISTRESS OPENWORK
You'll deal upon men's wives no more?
GOSHAWK No. You teach me
A trick for that!
MISTRESS OPENWORK
Troth, do not; they'll o'erreach thee.
OPENWORK
Make my house yours, sir, still.
GOSHAWK No.

192 **this new fury** Openwork imagines his wife as one of the furies, Greco-Roman goddesses of vengeance who punished those who committed certain serious crimes.
holla shout
193 **hid character** secret code
194 **watch out mine eyes** stay awake watching, no matter how long
195 **Brazen Head** alluding to the legendary magical bronze head of Brasenose College, Oxford; by making it speak, Friar Bacon tried to wall England with brass, but missed hearing it and failed
197 **the fiend** the one who has supposedly lied about him
200 **The knot God fastens** the marital bond; compare 1.58–60
201 **titles** calls by the right name
203 **take up a petticoat** have sex
208 **text letters** capital letters
212–15 **Thou spider . . . poison** Spiders were associated with craftiness and treachery; cf. 2.239–40.
226 **moles** small pieces of velvet or silk cut in decorative shapes and attached to women's faces to cover blemishes or call attention to an attractive feature
229 **gilt rotten pill** some sweetmeats (candies) were decorated with an edible gold covering
237 **trick** habit; deception; prank
238 **rub** obstacle; term in the game of bowls for touch of a bowl against others or unevenness in its passage
put by set aside
239 **deal upon** work on, exploit
239–40 **teach me | A trick** i.e., your own trick has taught me not to
240 **o'erreach** overpower

OPENWORK I say you shall:
Seeing, thus besieged, it holds out, 'twill never fall!

Enter Master Gallipot, and Greenwit like a sumner; Laxton muffled, aloof off

OMNES How now?

GALLIPOT [*to Greenwit*] With me, sir?

GREENWIT You, sir. I have gone snuffling up and down by your door this hour to watch for you.

MISTRESS GALLIPOT What's the matter, husband?

GREENWIT I have caught a cold in my head, sir, by sitting up late in the Rose Tavern, but I hope you understand my speech.

GALLIPOT So, sir.

GREENWIT I cite you by the name of Hippocrates Gallipot, and you by the name of Prudence Gallipot, to appear upon *Crastino*—do you see—*Crastino Sancti Dunstani*, this Easter Term, in Bow Church.

GALLIPOT Where, sir? What says he?

GREENWIT Bow—Bow Church, to answer to a libel of precontract on the part and behalf of the said Prudence and another; you're best, sir, take a copy of the citation: 'tis but twelvepence.

OMNES A citation?

GALLIPOT You pocky-nosed rascal, what slave fees you to this?

LAXTON Slave? [*Comes forward; aside to Goshawk*] I ha' nothing to do with you, do you hear, sir?

GOSHAWK [*aside to Laxton*] Laxton, is't not? What vagary is this?

GALLIPOT
Trust me, I thought, sir, this storm long ago
Had been full laid, when—if you be remembered—
I paid you the last fifteen pound, besides
The thirty you had first—for then you swore—

LAXTON
Tush, tush, sir, oaths—
Truth, yet I'm loath to vex you.—Tell you what:
Make up the money I had an hundred pound,
And take your bellyful of her.

GALLIPOT An hundred pound?

MISTRESS GALLIPOT
What, a hundred pound? He gets none!
What a hundred pound?

GALLIPOT
Sweet Prue, be calm; the gentleman offers thus:
If I will make the moneys that are past
A hundred pound, he will discharge all courts
And give his bond never to vex us more.

MISTRESS GALLIPOT
A hundred pound? 'Las, take, sir, but threescore.
—[*Aside to Laxton*] Do you seek my undoing?

LAXTON I'll not bate one sixpence.
—[*Aside to Mistress Gallipot*] I'll maul you, puss, for spitting.

MISTRESS GALLIPOT Do thy worst!
—[*Aloud*] Will fourscore stop thy mouth?

LAXTON No.

MISTRESS GALLIPOT You're a slave!
Thou cheat; I'll now tear money from thy throat.
Husband, lay hold on yonder tawny-coat.

GREENWIT
Nay, gentlemen, seeing your women are so hot,
I must lose my hair in their company, I see.
[*Removes hair-piece*]

MISTRESS OPENWORK
His hair sheds off, and yet he speaks not so much
In the nose as he did before.

GOSHAWK He has had
The better surgeon. Master Greenwit,
Is your wit so raw as to play no better
A part than a sumner's?

GALLIPOT I pray, who plays
A Knack to Know an Honest Man in this company?

242.2 ***sumner*** summoner; officer of church court who summoned people to appear there
Laxton muffled see 6.211, note
aloof off at a distance
245 **snuffling** speaking through the nose; symptom of venereal disease associated with summoners
247 **What's... husband?** Mistress Gallipot addresses her husband, but Greenwit answers
252 **Hippocrates** a Greek physician born about 460 BC and considered the founder of medicine; ironically appropriate for an apothecary
254 ***Crastino... Dunstani*** the day after St Dunstan's Day, which was 19 May: 20 May
255 **Easter Term** session of church court beginning the fifteenth day after Easter and ending after Ascension Day
Bow Church church of St Mary le Bow, built in the reign of William the Conqueror (1066–1087), named for its bow-shaped stone arches, the first in London; the church court held here was called the Court of Arches
257–8 **libel of precontract** charge of marrying someone who was already betrothed to another by a precontract; see 1.56–8, note
259 **citation** summons (legal document summoning someone to appear in court)
262 **pocky-nosed** pocks or pustules were a symptom of venereal disease, and commonly attacked the nose; see 245, note
fees you to is paying you for
266 **vagary** prank
269 **laid** subsided
270 **last fifteen pound** Not dramatized; Laxton has evidently continued to bilk Gallipot since 6.259–60.
274 **Make up... an hundred pound** bring the total sum to a hundred pounds
280 **discharge all courts** Gallipot thinks Laxton threatens other legal actions besides the present one.
281 **give his bond** promise
283 **bate** abate; subtract
285 **stop thy mouth** satisfy you
286 **tear money from thy throat** implies Laxton is lying; compare 5.89–90, note
287 **tawny-coat** Greenwit, who wears a summoner's tawny-coloured livery
288 **hot** angry; implying sexual eagerness; alludes to burning sensations of syphilis
289 **lose my hair** playing on 'hot', 288, note
293 **wit so raw** playing on Greenwit's name
295 ***A Knack to Know an Honest Man*** Anonymous comedy of 1594 in which a character disguises himself to test the honesty of those he meets; as the action proceeds, the title becomes a catch phrase.

MISTRESS GALLIPOT
Dear husband, pardon me, I did dissemble,
Told thee I was his precontracted wife—
When letters came from him for thirty pound,
I had no shift but that.

GALLIPOT A very clean shift,
But able to make me lousy.—On.

MISTRESS GALLIPOT Husband, I plucked—
When he had tempted me to think well of him—
Gilt feathers from thy wings, to make him fly
More lofty.

GALLIPOT O' the top of you, wife. On.

MISTRESS GALLIPOT
He, having wasted them, comes now for more,
Using me as a ruffian doth his whore,
Whose sin keeps him in breath. By heaven, I vow,
Thy bed he never wronged more than he does now.

GALLIPOT
My bed? Ha, ha, like enough! A shop-board will serve
To have a cuckold's coat cut out upon;
Of that we'll talk hereafter.—[*to Laxton*] You're a
villain!

LAXTON
Hear me but speak, sir, you shall find me none.

OMNES
Pray, sir, be patient and hear him.

GALLIPOT I am
Muzzled for biting, sir; use me how you will.

LAXTON
The first hour that your wife was in my eye,
Myself with other gentlemen sitting by
In your shop tasting smoke, and speech being used
That men who have fairest wives are most abused
And hardly 'scaped the horn, your wife maintained
That only such spots in city dames were stained
Justly, but by men's slanders; for her own part,
She vowed that you had so much of her heart,
No man by all his wit, by any wile
Never so fine spun, should yourself beguile
Of what in her was yours.

GALLIPOT Yet Prue, 'tis well;
Play out your game at Irish, sir. Who wins?

MISTRESS OPENWORK
The trial is when she comes to bearing.

LAXTON
I scorned one woman, thus, should brave all men,
And—which more vext me—a she-citizen.
Therefore I laid siege to her: out she held,
Gave many a brave repulse, and me compelled
With shame to sound retreat to my hot lust.
Then seeing all base desires raked up in dust,
And that to tempt her modest ears I swore
Ne'er to presume again, she said her eye
Would ever give me welcome honestly;
And—since I was a gentleman—if it run low,
She would my state relieve, not to o'erthrow
Your own and hers; did so. Then seeing I wrought
Upon her meekness, me she set at naught;
And yet to try if I could turn that tide,
You see what stream I strove with. But sir, I swear
By heaven and by those hopes men lay up there,
I neither have nor had a base intent
To wrong your bed. What's done is merriment;
Your gold I pay back with this interest:
When I had most power to do't, I wronged you least.

GALLIPOT
If this no gullery be, sir—

OMNES No, no, on my life!

GALLIPOT
Then, sir, I am beholden—not to you, wife—
But Master Laxton, to your want of doing ill,
Which it seems you have not. Gentlemen,
Tarry and dine here all.

OPENWORK Brother, we have a jest
As good as yours to furnish out a feast.

GALLIPOT
We'll crown our table with it.—Wife, brag no more
Of holding out: who most brags is most whore.

Exeunt

299 **shift** Mistress Gallipot refers to her stratagem; her husband takes the word to mean both undergarment and change.
303 **O' the top of you** alluding to the sexual act
305 **ruffian** pimp
306 **keeps him in breath** supports him
308–9 **A shop-board ... cut out upon** A shopboard is a counter for displaying goods; a man can be made a cuckold in his own shop if his wife has sex with another man on the shopboard.
313 **Muzzled for biting** I will be quiet and listen to you.
318 **hardly 'scaped the horn** can't really avoid being cuckolded
319–20 **only such spots ... men's slanders** city wives should be censured (stained) for unchastity (spots) only if it isn't men's slanders that incriminate them
325 **Irish** board game similar to backgammon, played with dice and counters
326 **bearing** term in both Irish and backgammon for removing pieces at end of game; playing on childbearing
327 **scorned** objected that
brave defy
329–31 **laid siege ... lust** military metaphors for his aggressive sexual pursuit of her
332 **raked up in dust** like a fire covered with ashes to keep it from burning actively
334–5 **her eye ... honestly** She would befriend me but remain chaste.
336–8 **if it run low ... | Your own and hers** If my money (state) ran low, she would pay me not to ruin (o'erthrow) your marriage by talking about our relationship.
338 **did so** she paid me
338–9 **wrought | Upon her meekness** worked on her compassion
339 **set at naught** repulsed, rejected
340 **to try ... tide** to see if I could make her change
347 **gullery** trickey
351 **jest** in the sense of Fr. *geste*, tale of notable deeds, exploits
352 **furnish out** fill out; embellish

Sc. 10 *Enter Jack Dapper, Moll [dressed as a man], Sir Beauteous Ganymede, and Sir Thomas Long*

JACK DAPPER But prithee, Master Captain Jack, be plain and perspicuous with me: was it your Meg of Westminster's courage that rescued me from the Poultry puttocks indeed?

MOLL The valour of my wit, I ensure you, sir, fetched you off bravely when you were i' the forlorn hope among those desperates. Sir Beauteous Ganymede here and Sir Thomas Long heard that cuckoo—my man Trapdoor—sing the note of your ransom from captivity.

SIR BEAUTEOUS Uds-so, Moll, where's that Trapdoor?

MOLL Hanged, I think, by this time; a justice in this town, that speaks nothing but 'Make a mittimus, away with him to Newgate', used that rogue like a firework to run upon a line betwixt him and me.

OMNES How, how?

MOLL Marry, to lay trains of villainy to blow up my life: I smelt the powder, spied what linstock gave fire to shoot against the poor captain of the galley-foist, and away slid I my man like a shovel-board shilling. He struts up and down the suburbs, I think, and eats up whores, feeds upon a bawd's garbage.

SIR THOMAS Sirrah Jack Dapper—

JACK DAPPER What sayst, Tom Long?

SIR THOMAS Thou hadst a sweet-faced boy, hail-fellow with thee to your little Gull: how is he spent?

JACK DAPPER Troth, I whistled the poor little buzzard off o' my fist because when he waited upon me at the ordinaries, the gallants hit me i' the teeth still and said I looked like a painted alderman's tomb, and the boy at my elbow, like a death's head. Sirrah Jack, Moll.

MOLL What says my little Dapper?

SIR BEAUTEOUS Come, come, walk and talk, walk and talk.

JACK DAPPER Moll and I'll be i' the midst.

MOLL These knights shall have squire's places, belike then. Well, Dapper, what say you?

JACK DAPPER Sirrah Captain Mad Mary, the gull, my own father—Dapper, Sir Davy—laid these London boot-halers, the catchpoles, in ambush to set upon me.

OMNES Your father? Away, Jack!

JACK DAPPER By the tassels of this handkerchief, 'tis true; and what was his warlike stratagem, think you? He thought, because a wicker cage tames a nightingale, a lowly prison could make an ass of me.

OMNES A nasty plot!

JACK DAPPER Ay: as though a counter, which is a park in which all the wild beasts of the city run head by head, could tame me!

Enter the Lord Noland

MOLL Yonder comes my Lord Noland.

OMNES Save you, my lord.

LORD NOLAND Well met, gentlemen all: good Sir Beauteous Ganymede, Sir Thomas Long—and how does Master Dapper?

JACK DAPPER Thanks, my lord.

MOLL No tobacco, my lord?

LORD NOLAND No, faith, Jack.

10.0.2 ***Ganymede*** Jove's beloved cupbearer, renowned for his boyish beauty; in the Renaissance, a term for a lover of the same sex

Thomas Long conventional name for carrier of letters, goods, parcels

1 **Jack** generic name for a man; apparently used for Moll when she wears male clothing

2–3 **Meg of Westminster's courage** alludes to the legendary figure whose biography is a source for this play; see Introduction

3 **Poultry puttocks** officers of debtors' prison called the Poultry; for Poultry, see 7.78, note; for puttocks, see 7.112, note

5–6 **fetched you off** rescued you

6 **i' the forlorn hope** in military language, soldiers chosen to begin the attack; figuratively, persons in a desperate condition

8 **cuckoo** The cuckoo, a migratory bird, arrives in Britain in April and is considered a herald of spring; Trapdoor is first to suspect the sergeants who arrest Jack Dapper (see 7.191–5).

10 **Uds-so** corruption of 'God save my soul'

11 **a justice** Sir Alexander

12–13 **Make a mittimus ... Newgate** Proverbial expression for a severe magistrate. Named for its first word *mittimus* (Lat. we send), a mittimus is a legal warrant to commit someone to jail; Newgate, London's main prison, was used for felons and debtors.

13–14 **firework ... a line** a line of gunpowder used as a fuse to set off explosives

16 **trains ... to blow up my life** compares Trapdoor, who was planted by Sir Alexander to trap Moll into stealing, with a line of gunpowder used to blow her up (see 13)

16–19 **I smelt the powder ... shilling** not dramatized; Moll realized that Trapdoor was tricking her, and dismissed him

17 **linstock** staff with a forked head for holding the match used to light gunpowder in a musket

18 **captain of the galley-foist** derogatory terms; a galley-foist was a barge used by the Lord Mayor of London for state occasions

19 **shovel-board shilling** disk used in playing shuffle-board

20 **eats up** devastates; takes over (as a pimp); has sex with

21 **garbage** whores that pimps have abandoned; play on Ralph, Trapdoor's first name, and raff, trash (see 2.189.1, note)

24 **hail-fellow** on intimate terms

25 **spent** employed

26–7 **whistled ... o' my fist** released (falconry term); dismissed

28 **hit me i' the teeth** accused, insulted me

29–30 **painted alderman's tomb ... death's head** A coloured effigy of the deceased was placed on an alderman's tomb, along with a death's head as a *memento mori* (heads of guilds were magistrates in city government, next in dignity to the mayor).

34 **squire's places** Reversing the ceremonial position of a knight between two squires, Moll and Dapper walk in the middle with Sir Beauteous and Lord Noland flanking them.

37–8 **boot-halers** marauding soldiers; highwaymen

40 **tassels ... handkerchief** handkerchiefs about four inches square with buttons or tassels at each corner were worn, folded, in hats

45 **counter** debtors' prison; see 7.78, note

47.1 ***Noland*** derived from 'know' or 'noll' (head) and 'land', suggesting power and authority

54 **No tobacco** possibly alludes to James I's well-known opposition to tobacco, as expressed in *A Counterblaste to Tobacco* (1604)

JACK DAPPER My Lord Noland, will you go to Pimlico with us? We are making a boon voyage to that nappy land of spice cakes.

LORD NOLAND Here's such a merry ging, I could find in my heart to sail to the World's End with such company. Come gentlemen, let's on.

JACK DAPPER Here's most amorous weather, my lord.

OMNES Amorous weather? (*They walk*)

JACK DAPPER Is not amorous a good word?

Enter Trapdoor like a poor soldier with a patch o'er one eye, and Tearcat with him, all tatters

TRAPDOOR Shall we set upon the infantry, these troops of foot? Zounds, yonder comes Moll, my whorish master and mistress; would I had her kidneys between my teeth!

TEARCAT I had rather have a cow-heel.

TRAPDOOR Zounds, I am so patched up, she cannot discover me. We'll on.

TEARCAT *Coraggio*, then.

TRAPDOOR Good your honours and worships, enlarge the ears of commiseration, and let the sound of a hoarse military organ-pipe penetrate your pitiful bowels to extract out of them so many small drops of silver as may give a hard straw-bed lodging to a couple of maimed soldiers.

JACK DAPPER Where are you maimed?

TEARCAT In both our nether limbs.

MOLL Come, come, Dapper, let's give 'em something; 'las poor men, what money have you? By my troth, I love a soldier with my soul.

SIR BEAUTEOUS Stay, stay, where have you served?

SIR THOMAS In any part of the Low Countries?

TRAPDOOR Not in the Low Countries, if it please your manhood, but in Hungary against the Turk at the siege of Belgrade.

LORD NOLAND Who served there with you, sirrah?

TRAPDOOR Many Hungarians, Moldavians, Valachians, and Transylvanians, with some Sclavonians; and retiring home, sir, the Venetian galleys took us prisoners, yet freed us, and suffered us to beg up and down the country.

JACK DAPPER You have ambled all over Italy then?

TRAPDOOR O sir, from Venice to Roma, Vecchia, Bonogna, Romagna, Bologna, Modena, Piacenza, and Toscana with all her cities, as Pistoia, Volterra, Montepulciano, Arezzo, with the Siennese and diversc others.

MOLL Mere rogues, put spurs to 'em once more.

JACK DAPPER Thou lookest like a strange creature—a fat butter-box—yet speakest English. What art thou?

TEARCAT *Ick, mine here. Ick bin den ruffling Tearcat, den brave soldado. Ick bin dorick all Dutchlant gueresen. Der shellum das meere ine beasa, ine woert gaeb; Ick slaag um stroakes on tom cop, dastick den hundred touzun divel halle; frollick, mine here.*

SIR BEAUTEOUS Here, here—[*About to give money*] let's be rid of their jobbering.

MOLL Not a cross, Sir Beauteous. You base rogues, I have taken measure of you better then a tailor can, and I'll fit you as you—monster with one eye—have fitted me.

TRAPDOOR Your worship will not abuse a soldier!

MOLL Soldier?—Thou deservest to be hanged up by that tongue which dishonours so noble a profession.—Soldier, you skeldering varlet?—Hold, stand, there should be a trapdoor hereabouts.

56 **Pimlico** an inn and place of entertainment at Hogsden
57 **boon voyage** prosperous, happy trip; cf. Fr. *bon voyage*
nappy foaming, heady (used of ale); refers to strong ale for which Pimlico was famed
58 **spice cakes** eaten with ale
59 **ging** gang
60 **World's End** a long journey, as far as one could go; several London taverns were so named
62 **amorous** malapropism for amiable, as suggested by responses in 63–4
64.2 ***Tearcat* . . . *all tatters*** 'To tear a cat' means to rant like a swaggering hero; he is wearing ragged clothes.
66–7 **whorish master and mistress** Like Sir Alexander, he confounds the prostitute's supposed lust with the transgression of gender difference attributed to Moll's dress; see 2.132–3, 4.157–62.
69 **cow-heel** calf's foot jelly, a jellied broth used as a restorative
72 ***Coraggio*** Italian; have courage
75 **bowels** considered the source of pity, compassion
85 **Low Countries** England fought the forces of Spain, which occupied the present Holland and Belgium, from 1585 to 1587.
87–8 **in Hungary . . . Belgrade** Belgrade, capital of Serbia, was seized from Hungarian occupation by Solyman, Sultan of Turkey, in 1522; thus Trapdoor's claim is fallacious.
90–1 **Hungarians . . . Sclavonians** soldiers from the regions under Hungarian rule
93 **suffered** allowed
96–9 **Venice . . . others** As in 86–8, 90–4, Trapdoor provides many place names, mixing cities with regions indiscriminately, and English with Italian forms (as was common) so as to convince his listeners that he is a widely travelled soldier.
96 **Vecchia** Civitavecchia, the port of Rome
96–7 **Bonogna . . . Bologna** city in Romagna, in northern Italy
97 **Romagna** region in Italy north of Tuscany
Toscana region in Italy north of Rome; Tuscany in English
98 **Volterra** town in Tuscany
Montepulciano town in Tuscany
99 **Siennese** inhabitants of Siena, city in Tuscany
102 **butter-box** contemptuous term for a Dutchman
103–6 As Dekker advises in *The Gull's Hornbook* (1609), those who fear arrest should pretend to be from a country at peace with England, so that they cannot be examined by a magistrate; hence, Tearcat's pretence of being a native Dutch speaker. His speech isn't meant to be strictly understood. It means roughly: I, my lord? I am the ruffling Tearcat, the brave soldier. I have travelled through all Dutchland. [He is] the greater scoundrel who gives an angry word. I beat him directly on the head, that you take out a hundred thousand devils. [Be] merry, sir.
109 **jobbering** jabbering
110 **cross** coin with cross stamped on one side
111–12 **I'll fit you** Moll echoes the same well-known line from *The Spanish Tragedy* as Sebastian did (2.144); also plays on 'tailor' in 110–12.
112 **monster with one eye** may refer to stage convention of representing the devil as one-eyed
116 **skeldering** begging, sponging, swindling

Pulls off his patch

TRAPDOOR The balls of these glaziers of mine—mine eyes—shall be shot up and down in any hot piece of service for my invincible mistress.

JACK DAPPER I did not think there had been such knavery in black patches as now I see.

MOLL O sir, he hath been brought up in the Isle of Dogs, and can both fawn like a spaniel and bite like a mastiff, as he finds occasion.

LORD NOLAND [*to Tearcat*] What are you, sirrah? A bird of this feather too?

TEARCAT A man beaten from the wars, sir.

SIR THOMAS I think so, for you never stood to fight.

JACK DAPPER What's thy name, fellow soldier?

TEARCAT I am called by those that have seen my valour, Tearcat.

OMNES Tearcat?

MOLL A mere whip-jack, and that is, in the commonwealth of rogues, a slave that can talk of sea-fight, name all your chief pirates, discover more countries to you than either the Dutch, Spanish, French, or English ever found out; yet indeed all his service is by land, and that is to rob a fair, or some such venturous exploit. Tearcat—foot, sirrah, I have your name, now I remember me, in my book of horners: horns for the thumb, you know how.

TEARCAT No indeed, Captain Moll—for I know you by sight—I am no such nipping Christian, but a maunderer upon the pad, I confess; and meeting with honest Trapdoor here, whom you had cashiered from bearing arms, out at elbows under your colours, I instructed him in the rudiments of roguery, and by my map made him sail over any country you can name, so that now he can maunder better than myself.

JACK DAPPER So then, Trapdoor, thou art turned soldier now.

TRAPDOOR Alas, sir, now there's no wars, 'tis the safest course of life I could take.

MOLL I hope then you can cant, for by your cudgels, you, sirrah, are an upright man.

TRAPDOOR As any walks the highway, I assure you.

MOLL And Tearcat, what are you? A wild rogue, an angler, or a ruffler?

TEARCAT Brother to this upright man, flesh and blood, ruffling Tearcat is my name, and a ruffler is my style, my title, my profession.

MOLL Sirrah, where's your doxy?—Halt not with me.

OMNES Doxy, Moll? What's that?

MOLL His wench.

TRAPDOOR My doxy? I have, by the solomon, a doxy that carries a kinchin mort in her slate at her back, besides my dell and my dainty wild dell, with all whom I'll tumble this next darkmans in the strommel, and drink ben booze, and eat a fat gruntling-cheat, a cackling-cheat, and a quacking-cheat.

JACK DAPPER Here's old cheating!

TRAPDOOR My doxy stays for me in a boozing ken, brave captain.

MOLL He says his wench stays for him in an ale-house. [*To Trapdoor and Tearcat*] You are no pure rogues.

TEARCAT Pure rogues? No, we scorn to be pure rogues; but if you come to our libken, or our stalling-ken, you shall find neither him nor me a queer cuffin.

MOLL So, sir, no churl of you.

TEARCAT No, but a ben cove, a brave cove, a gentry cuffin.

LORD NOLAND Call you this canting?

JACK DAPPER Zounds, I'll give a schoolmaster half a crown a week and teach me this pedlar's French.

118 **glaziers** eyes, in cant (thieves' jargon)
122 **patches** referring to their clothes; playing on patches meaning fools, clowns
123 **Isle of Dogs** peninsula in the Thames; reportedly, the king's hounds were kept there
134 **whip-jack** rogue who masquerades as a former sailor, wandering, begging, and thieving
141 **book of horners** plays on the hornbook, consisting of a paper on which the alphabet and other rudiments of literacy were written, covered with a thin sheet of transparent horn and mounted on wood; used for teaching small children
horns for the thumb piece of horn shaped like a thimble to protect thumb from knife blade when thief cuts purse
144 **nipping** He who cuts the purse is called the nip.
144–5 **maunderer upon the pad** wanderer on the road
146–7 **cashiered from bearing arms** military terms for dismissing from service
147 **out at elbows** proverbial for being poor, destitute
under your colours in your service
155 **cant** speak in the jargon of vagabonds and rogues; dialogue is largely in cant to 238
156 **upright man** first or second in the hierarchy of rogues named in cant, who dominate lesser rogues and have their choice of women; tall, large, loud-voiced men who carry truncheons and travel together in all-male groups
158 **wild rogue** thief travelling in a large group that meets in barns at night to have sex and plan robberies
angler companion of upright man, who uses a long staff with a hook to angle (fish) through open windows for goods to steal
159 **ruffler** first or second in the hierarchy; much like upright man (see 156, note)
163 **doxy** general term for adult, sexually available woman who might also be a prostitute or pickpocket
166 **by the solomon** by the mass
167–8 **kinchin mort . . . wild dell** Ranks in the hierarchy of female rogues: kinchin mort, female infant carried on mother's back in a sheet; mort, mother who belongs sexually to one man; dell, teen-age girl or virgin; wild dell, either born on the road, or a servant or young woman of gentle birth forced into a wandering or criminal life by circumstances.
169 **darkmans** night
strommel straw
170 **ben booze** good drink
170–1 **gruntling-cheat . . . quacking-cheat** cheat means thing; gruntling-cheat, pig; cackling-cheat, chicken; quacking-cheat, duck
172 **old** great, abundant
173 **boozing ken** alehouse
178 **libken** sleeping place
stalling-ken house for receiving stolen goods
179–81 **queer cuffin . . . gentry cuffin** cuffin means man: queer cuffin, churl or Justice of the Peace; gentry cuffin, gentleman
181 **a ben cove, a brave cove** cove means man or fellow; ben cove, good fellow; brave cove, gentleman
184 **pedlar's French** underworld slang

TRAPDOOR Do but stroll, sir, half a harvest with us, sir, and you shall gabble your bellyful.

MOLL [*to Trapdoor*] Come you rogue, cant with me.

SIR THOMAS Well said, Moll.—[*To Trapdoor*] Cant with her, sirrah, and you shall have money—else not a penny.

TRAPDOOR I'll have a bout if she please.

MOLL Come on, sirrah.

TRAPDOOR Ben mort, shall you and I heave a booth, mill a ken, or nip a bung? And then we'll couch a hogshead under the ruffmans, and there you shall wap with me, and I'll niggle with you.

MOLL Out, you damned impudent rascal! [*Hits and kicks him*]

TRAPDOOR Cut benar whids, and hold your fambles and your stamps!

LORD NOLAND Nay, nay, Moll, why art thou angry? What was his gibberish?

MOLL Marry, this, my lord, says he: 'Ben mort'—good wench—'shall you and I heave a booth, mill a ken, or nip a bung?'—shall you and I rob a house, or cut a purse?

OMNES Very good!

MOLL 'And then we'll couch a hogshead under the ruffmans',—and then we'll lie under a hedge.

TRAPDOOR That was my desire, captain, as 'tis fit a soldier should lie.

MOLL 'And there you shall wap with me, and I'll niggle with you',—and that's all.

SIR BEAUTEOUS Nay, nay, Moll, what's that wap?

JACK DAPPER Nay, teach me what niggling is; I'd fain be niggling.

MOLL Wapping and niggling is all one: the rogue my man can tell you.

TRAPDOOR 'Tis fadoodling, if it please you.

SIR BEAUTEOUS This is excellent; one fit more, good Moll.

MOLL [*to Tearcat*] Come, you rogue, sing with me.

The Song

A gage of ben Rome-booze
In a boozing ken of Rome-ville

TEARCAT

Is benar than a caster,
Peck, pannam, lap, or popler
Which we mill in Deuce-a-ville.

MOLL *and* TEARCAT

O, I would lib all the lightmans,
O, I would lib all the darkmans,
By the solomon, under the ruffmans,
By the solomon, in the harmans,

TEARCAT

And scour the queer cramp-ring,
And couch till a palliard docked my dell,
So my boozy nab might skew Rome-booze well.

MOLL *and* TEARCAT

Avast to the pad, let us bing,
Avast to the pad, let us bing.

OMNES Fine knaves, i'faith.

JACK DAPPER The grating of ten new cart-wheels, and the gruntling of five hundred hogs coming from Romford market cannot make a worse noise than this canting language does in my ears. Pray, my Lord Noland, let's give these soldiers their pay.

SIR BEAUTEOUS Agreed, and let them march.

LORD NOLAND [*gives money*] Here, Moll.

MOLL [*to Trapdoor and Tearcat*] Now I see that you are stalled to the rogue and are not ashamed of your professions: look you, my Lord Noland here, and these gentlemen, bestows upon you two, two bords and a half: that's two shillings sixpence.

TRAPDOOR Thanks to your lordship.

TEARCAT Thanks, heroical captain.

MOLL Away.

TRAPDOOR We shall cut ben whids of your masters and mistress-ship wheresoever we come.

MOLL [*to Trapdoor*] You'll maintain, sirrah, the old justice's plot to his face?

TRAPDOOR Else trine me on the cheats: hang me!

MOLL Be sure you meet me there.

TRAPDOOR Without any more maundering, I'll do't.—Follow, brave Tearcat.

185 **harvest** season

192–5 **Ben mort . . . niggle with you** Modestly avoiding 'wap' and 'niggle', Moll translates this speech: see 202–5, 207–12. Wap and niggle both mean to have sex, the implications of which anger her at 196–7.

198–9 **Cut . . . stamps** speak better words, and hold your hands and legs

218 **fadoodling** nonce word, euphemism for having sex

219 **fit** part of poem or song; strain of music

221–34 Moll translates the song, excepting the last two lines, at 264–74. A literal translation follows: A quart pot of good wine in an ale-house of London is better than a cloak, meat, buttermilk (or whey) or porridge which we steal in the country. O I would lie all the day, I would lie all the night, by the mass, under the woods (or bushes), by the mass in the stocks, and wear bad bolts (or fetters), and lie till a rogue lay with my wench, so my drunken head might quaff wine well. Away to the highway, let us be off, etc.

231 **palliard** rogue, often Irish or Welsh, who wears patched clothing and travels with a wife and forged marriage document; may feign disease to draw pity

237 **Romford** town north-east of London that held a famous hog market every Tuesday (perhaps playing on 'Rome-ville')

244 **stalled to the rogue** initiated as rogues

246 **bords** shillings

251 **cut ben whids** speak good words

253–7 Moll and Trapdoor join forces against Sir Alexander, looking ahead to the denouement in scene 11

255 **trine me on the cheats** hang me on the gallows

TEARCAT *I prae, sequor*; let us go, mouse.

Exeunt they two, manet the rest

LORD NOLAND Moll, what was in that canting song?

MOLL Troth, my lord, only a praise of good drink, the only milk which these wild beasts love to suck, and thus it was:

A rich cup of wine,
O it is juice divine!
More wholesome for the head
Than meat, drink, or bread;
To fill my drunken pate,
With that, I'd sit up late;
By the heels would I lie,
Under a lousy hedge die,
Let a slave have a pull
At my whore, so I be full
Of that precious liquor—

and a parcel of such stuff, my lord, not worth the opening.

Enter a Cutpurse very gallant, with four or five men after him, one with a wand

LORD NOLAND What gallant comes yonder?

SIR THOMAS Mass, I think I know him: 'tis one of Cumberland.

FIRST CUTPURSE Shall we venture to shuffle in amongst yon heap of gallants, and strike?

SECOND CUTPURSE 'Tis a question whether there be any silver shells amongst them, for all their satin outsides.

OMNES Let's try!

MOLL Pox on him, a gallant? Shadow me, I know him: 'tis one that cumbers the land indeed. If he swim near to the shore of any of your pockets, look to your purses!

OMNES Is't possible?

MOLL This brave fellow is no better then a foist.

OMNES Foist? What's that?

MOLL A diver with two fingers: a pickpocket. All his train study the figging-law, that's to say, cutting of purses and foisting. One of them is a nip: I took him once i'the twopenny gallery at the Fortune; then there's a cloyer, or snap, that dogs any new brother in that trade, and snaps will have half in any booty. He with the wand is both a stale, whose office is to face a man i'the streets whilst shells are drawn by another, and then with his black conjuring rod in his hand, he, by the nimbleness of his eye and juggling stick, will in cheaping a piece of plate at a goldsmith's stall, make four or five rings mount from the top of his caduceus and, as if it were at leap-frog, they skip into his hand presently.

SECOND CUTPURSE Zounds, we are smoked!

OMNES Ha?

SECOND CUTPURSE We are boiled, pox on her; see Moll, the roaring drab!

FIRST CUTPURSE All the diseases of sixteen hospitals boil her! Away!

MOLL Bless you, sir.

FIRST CUTPURSE And you, good sir.

MOLL Dost not ken me, man?

FIRST CUTPURSE No, trust me, sir.

MOLL Heart, there's a knight, to whom I'm bound for many favours, lost his purse at the last new play i'the Swan—seven angels in't: make it good, you're best; do you see? No more.

FIRST CUTPURSE A synagogue shall be called, Mistress Mary: disgrace me not; *pocas palabras*, I will conjure for you. Farewell. [*Exeunt Cutpurses*]

MOLL Did not I tell you, my lord?

LORD NOLAND I wonder how thou camest to the knowledge of these nasty villains?

SIR THOMAS And why do the foul mouths of the world call thee Moll Cutpurse? A name, methinks, damned and odious.

MOLL

Dare any step forth to my face and say,
'I have ta'en thee doing so, Moll'? I must confess,
In younger days, when I was apt to stray,
I have sat amongst such adders, seen their stings—
As any here might—and in full playhouses
Watched their quick-diving hands, to bring to shame
Such rogues, and in that stream met an ill name.
When next, my lord, you spy any one of those—
So he be in his art a scholar—question him,
Tempt him with gold to open the large book

259 ***I prae, sequor*** Lat. go first, I will follow; a phrase from a play by Terence, Latin writer taught in grammar school
276.1 ***gallant*** smartly dressed
276.2 ***wand*** light walking stick or riding switch
278–9 **Cumberland** country in north-west England, probably chosen for the wordplay at 285–6
281 **strike** pick a pocket or cut a purse
283 **silver shells** money
289 **foist** pickpocket
292 **figging-law** cant for strategies used by cutpurses and pickpockets
293 **foisting** picking pockets
nip thief who actually cuts the purse
294 **twopenny gallery at the Fortune** gallery that cost two pennies for admission; for a description of the Fortune, see 2.19–24, note
294–6 **cloyer . . . any booty** thief who accompanies any novice, and divides booty with him
296–303 **He with the wand . . . hand presently** The stale has two jobs: he distracts a victim while another thief robs him, and he uses his wand to steal rings while bargaining for silver dishes at a goldsmith's shop.
302 **caduceus** the wand or staff with two serpents twined around it carried by Mercury, messenger of the gods and protector of thieves
304 **smoked** seen, identified as thieves
306 **boiled** same as smoked, 304, note
312 **ken** know
315–16 **i'the Swan** playhouse on the south bank of the Thames; the only extant contemporary drawing of a London theatre depicts the interior of the Swan
316 **angels** gold coins worth ten shillings; see 3.137, note
make it good get it back
318 **synagogue** meeting at which thieves choose officers, deal with business, etc.
319 ***pocas palabras*** common Spanish phrase meaning few words
conjure appeal on your behalf; beseech
330 **adders** poisonous snakes; figuratively, criminals, wicked people
335 **So** so long as

Of his close villainies; and you yourself shall cant
Better than poor Moll can, and know more laws
Of cheaters, lifters, nips, foists, puggards, curbers,
With all the devil's blackguard, than it is fit
Should be discovered to a noble wit.
I know they have their orders, offices,
Circuits, and circles, unto which they are bound,
To raise their own damnation in.

JACK DAPPER How dost thou know it?

MOLL
As you do: I show it you, they to me show it.
Suppose, my lord, you were in Venice.

LORD NOLAND Well.

MOLL
If some Italian pander there would tell
All the close tricks of courtesans, would not you
Hearken to such a fellow?

LORD NOLAND Yes.

MOLL And here,
Being come from Venice, to a friend most dear
That were to travel thither, you would proclaim
Your knowledge in those villainies, to save
Your friend from their quick danger: must you have
A black ill name because ill things you know?
Good troth, my lord, I am made Moll Cutpurse so.
How many are whores in small ruffs and still looks?
How many chaste whose names fill slander's books?
Were all men cuckolds, whom gallants in their scorns
Call so, we should not walk for goring horns.
Perhaps for my mad going, some reprove me;
I please myself, and care not else who loves me.

OMNES A brave mind, Moll, i'faith.

SIR THOMAS Come, my lord, shall's to the ordinary?

LORD NOLAND Ay, 'tis noon sure.

MOLL Good my lord, let not my name condemn me to you or to the world; a fencer, I hope, may be called a coward: is he so for that? If all that have ill names in London were to be whipped and to pay but twelvepence apiece to the beadle, I would rather have his office than a constable's.

JACK DAPPER So would I, Captain Moll: 'twere a sweet tickling office, i'faith. *Exeunt*

Sc. 11

Enter Sir Alexander Wengrave, Goshawk and Greenwit, and others

ALEXANDER
My son marry a thief! That impudent girl
Whom all the world stick their worst eyes upon!

GREENWIT
How will your care prevent it?

GOSHAWK 'Tis impossible!
They marry close; they're gone, but none knows
whither.

ALEXANDER
O gentlemen, when has a father's heart-strings
Held out so long from breaking?
Enter a Servant
—Now what news, sir?

SERVANT
They were met upo'th' water an hour since, sir,
Putting in towards the Sluice.

ALEXANDER The Sluice? Come gentlemen,
'Tis Lambeth works against us.

GREENWIT And that Lambeth
Joins more mad matches than your six wet towns
'Twixt that and Windsor Bridge, where fares lie
soaking.

ALEXANDER
Delay no time, sweet gentlemen: to Blackfriars!
We'll take a pair of oars and make after 'em.
Enter Trapdoor

TRAPDOOR
Your son and that bold masculine ramp, my mistress,
Are landed now at Tower.

ALEXANDER Heyday, at Tower?

TRAPDOOR
I heard it now reported. [*Exit*]

337 **close** secret
339 **cheaters** those who win money by using false dice
lifters those who steal valuable items such as plate (silver dishes), jewels, velvet, etc.
nips cutpurses
foists pickpockets
puggards thieves of an unspecified type
curbers thieves who use hooks to steal goods out of open windows
340 **the devil's blackguard** attendants black in character and dress who guard the devil (a parody of courtiers attending the sovereign)
343–4 **Circuits . . . raise their own damnation in** Magicians drew circles within which they raised spells.
346–54 **Suppose . . . you know?** Allusion to Thomas Coryate's questionable defence of himself for providing information on Venetian courtesans in *Coryate's Crudities* (1611)
348 **close tricks** secret stratagems
355 **I . . . so** I am given a bad reputation because I know about evil doings.
358–9 **cuckolds . . . horns** horns were the sign of a cuckold; see 3.218, note
360 **mad going** eccentric behaviour
365 **name** reputation
369–70 **beadle . . . constable's** The beadle, a minor officer of the parish church, punished petty offenders, usually by whipping them. Moll's point is that many people have bad reputations who, like her, don't deserve them; if they all were punished and fined, beadles would grow rich.
372 **tickling** pleasing
11.4 **close** secretly
8 **the Sluice** an embankment along the south side of the Thames protecting Lambeth Marsh, swampy open country west of Southwark, from flooding; a landing place for those going to Lambeth
9–10 **Lambeth . . . | Joins more mad matches** Couples could be married secretly outside of their home parishes in London by clergy in Lambeth.
10–11 **six wet towns . . . Windsor Bridge** possibly refers to several towns on the banks of the Thames that were popular for sexual rendezvous
12 **Blackfriars** Blackfriars Stairs was a landing stage on the north (city) side of the Thames, presumably the one closest to Sir Alexander's house.
14 **ramp** vulgar, ill-behaved woman; cf. 7.8, note
15 **Tower** at either the wharf or the landing stages at the Tower of London

ALEXANDER Which way, gentlemen,
Shall I bestow my care? I'm drawn in pieces
Betwixt deceit and shame.

Enter Sir Guy Fitzallard

SIR GUY Sir Alexander.
You're well met, and most rightly served;
My daughter was a scorn to you.

ALEXANDER Say not so, sir.

SIR GUY
A very abject she, poor gentlewoman!—
Your house has been dishonoured! Give you joy, sir,
Of your son's gaskin-bride; you'll be a grandfather shortly
To a fine crew of roaring sons and daughters:
'Twill help to stock the suburbs passing well, sir.

ALEXANDER
O, play not with the miseries of my heart!
Wounds should be dressed and healed, not vexed, or left
Wide open to the anguish of the patient,
And scornful air let in; rather let pity
And advice charitably help to refresh 'em.

SIR GUY
Who'd place his charity so unworthily,
Like one that gives alms to a cursing beggar?
Had I but found one spark of goodness in you
Toward my deserving child, which then grew fond
Of your son's virtues, I had eased you now;
But I perceive both fire of youth and goodness
Are raked up in the ashes of your age,
Else no such shame should have come near your house,
Nor such ignoble sorrow touch your heart.

ALEXANDER
If not for worth, for pity's sake assist me!

GREENWIT
You urge a thing past sense; how can he help you?
All his assistance is as frail as ours,
Full as uncertain where's the place that holds 'em.
One brings us water-news, then comes another
With a full-charged mouth like a culverin's voice,
And he reports the Tower: whose sounds are truest?

GOSHAWK
In vain you flatter him. Sir Alexander—

SIR GUY
I flatter him? Gentlemen, you wrong me grossly.

GREENWIT [*aside to Goshawk*]
He does it well, i'faith.

SIR GUY Both news are false,
Of Tower or water: they took no such way yet.

ALEXANDER
O strange: hear you this, gentlemen? Yet more plunges!

SIR GUY
They're nearer than you think for, yet more close,
Than if they were further off.

ALEXANDER How am I lost
In these distractions!

SIR GUY For your speeches, gentlemen,
In taxing me for rashness, for you all,
I will engage my state to half his wealth,
Nay, to his son's revenues, which are less,
And yet nothing at all till they come from him,
That I could, if my will stuck to my power,
Prevent this marriage yet, nay, banish her
For ever from his thoughts, much more his arms!

ALEXANDER
Slack not this goodness, though you heap upon me
Mountains of malice and revenge hereafter!
I'd willingly resign up half my state to him,
So he would marry the meanest drudge I hire.

GREENWIT [*to Sir Alexander*]
He talks impossibilities, and you believe 'em!

SIR GUY
I talk no more than I know how to finish;
My fortunes else are his that dares stake with me.
The poor young gentleman I love and pity;
And to keep shame from him—because the spring
Of his affection was my daughter's first,
Till his frown blasted all—do but estate him
In those possessions which your love and care
Once pointed out for him, that he may have room
To entertain fortunes of noble birth,
Where now his desperate wants casts him upon her;
And if I do not, for his own sake chiefly,
Rid him of this disease that now grows on him,
I'll forfeit my whole state, before these gentlemen.

GREENWIT [*to Sir Alexander*]
Troth, but you shall not undertake such matches;

21 **A very abject she** Sir Guy sarcastically mimics Sir Alexander's scorn for his daughter.
22 **dishonoured** by Sebastian's supposed marriage to Moll
23 **gaskin-bride** Gaskins were wide, knee-length breeches; as in 'codpiece daughter' (4.100), it is implied that male clothing makes Moll part man.
25 **suburbs** towns outside London where the city had no jurisdiction and crime could flourish
30 **refresh** restore, heal
34 **which** who (i.e., Mary)
45 **culverin's** large cannon's
46 **reports** punning on report, meaning to fire a gun
49 **He does it well** Sir Guy plays his part in the trick (making Sir Alexander believe that Sebastian has married Moll).
51 **plunges** dilemmas, playing on Sebastian's supposed travels by water; cf. 8.155, note
56 **engage...his wealth** pledge my estate to the value of half Sir Alexander's wealth
57 **Nay, to his son's...less** i.e., Sir Guy stands to lose more
58 **nothing...come from him** Sebastian won't have any money unless his father gives or bequeaths it to him.
68 **My fortunes else...dares stake with me** I'll wager my wealth to anyone who will stand by me in my pledge (to end the supposed marriage).
71 **his affection** Sebastian's, for Mary
72 **his frown** Sir Alexander's
estate him give or bequeath to him
76 **her** Moll
80 **matches** agreements

We'll persuade so much with you.
ALEXANDER [*to Sir Guy*] Here's my ring; [*Gives ring*]
He will believe this token. Fore these gentlemen
I will confirm it fully: all those lands
My first love 'lotted him, he shall straight possess
In that refusal.
SIR GUY If I change it not,
Change me into a beggar!
GREENWIT Are you mad, sir?
SIR GUY
'Tis done!
GOSHAWK Will you undo yourself by doing,
And show a prodigal trick in your old days?
ALEXANDER
'Tis a match, gentlemen.
SIR GUY Ay, ay, sir, ay!
I ask no favour, trust to you for none;
My hope rests in the goodness of your son. *Exit*
GREENWIT [*aside to Goshawk*]
He holds it up well yet.
GOSHAWK [*aside to Greenwit*]
Of an old knight, i'faith.
ALEXANDER
Cursed be the time I laid his first love barren,
Wilfully barren, that before this hour
Had sprung forth fruits of comfort and of honour;
He loved a virtuous gentlewoman.
Enter Moll [dressed as a man]
GOSHAWK
Life, here's Moll!
GREENWIT
Jack!
GOSHAWK
How dost thou, Jack?
MOLL How dost thou, gallant?
ALEXANDER
Impudence, where's my son?
MOLL Weakness, go look him!
ALEXANDER
Is this your wedding gown?
MOLL The man talks monthly:
Hot broth and a dark chamber for the knight;
I see he'll be stark mad at our next meeting. *Exit*
GOSHAWK
Why sir, take comfort now, there's no such matter;
No priest will marry her, sir, for a woman
Whiles that shape's on: an it was never known,
Two men were married and conjoined in one!
Your son hath made some shift to love another.
ALEXANDER
Whate'er she be, she has my blessing with her:
May they be rich and fruitful, and receive
Like comfort to their issue as I take
In them. H'as pleased me now, marrying not this,
Through a whole world he could not choose amiss.
GREENWIT
Glad you're so penitent for your former sin, sir.
GOSHAWK
Say he should take a wench with her smock-dowry:
No portion with her but her lips and arms?
ALEXANDER
Why, who thrive better, sir? They have most blessing,
Though other have more wealth, and least repent:
Many that want most know the most content.
GREENWIT
Say he should marry a kind youthful sinner?
ALEXANDER
Age will quench that; any offence but theft
And drunkenness, nothing but death can wipe away;
Their sins are green even when their heads are grey.
Nay, I despair not now, my heart's cheered, gentle-
men:
No face can come unfortunately to me.
Enter a Servant
Now sir, your news?
SERVANT Your son with his fair bride
Is near at hand.
ALEXANDER Fair may their fortunes be!
GREENWIT
Now you're resolved, sir, it was never she?
ALEXANDER
I find it in the music of my heart.
Enter Moll [in female dress] masked, in Sebastian's hand, and Sir Guy Fitzallard
See where they come.
GOSHAWK A proper lusty presence, sir.
ALEXANDER
Now has he pleased me right. I always counselled him
To choose a goodly personable creature:
Just of her pitch was my first wife, his mother.

82 **he** Sebastian (when Sir Guy tells him of his father's pledge)
84 **'lotted** allotted
straight immediately
85 **change it not** if I don't change Sebastian's marriage to Moll
87 **undo yourself by doing** reverse your position, or, ruin your finances, by making this agreement
88 **prodigal trick . . . old days** alludes to the parable of the prodigal son (cf. 2.118, note); like him, Sir Alexander might squander his wealth in this agreement
92 **holds it up well** keeps it going; see 49
98 **Jack!** generic name for man, addressed to Moll; see 10.1, note
99 **Impudence** implies her boldness in appearing before him, her immodesty in dressing as a man, and her supposed sexual misconduct
look look for
100 **monthly** plays on links between the moon, its monthly cycle, menstruation, and madness
101 **Hot broth and a dark chamber** common remedies for the agitations of mad people, intended to calm them
110 **issue** children
114 **smock-dowry** dowry consisting only of her smock (undergarment)
115 **portion** dowry
119 **sinner** unchaste woman
120–2 **Age will quench that . . . heads are grey** Sir Alexander first says that unchastity stops as one grows older, then reverses himself by claiming that, like all sins except thieving and drunkenness, it persists till death.
129 **lusty** gaily dressed; merry; lustful
132 **pitch** height

SEBASTIAN
Before I dare discover my offence, [*Kneels*]
I kneel for pardon.
ALEXANDER My heart gave it thee
Before thy tongue could ask it—
Rise; thou hast raised my joy to greater height
Than to that seat where grief dejected it.
[*Sebastian rises*]
Both welcome to my love and care for ever!
Hide not my happiness too long: all's pardoned;
Here are our friends. Salute her, gentlemen.
They unmask her
OMNES
Heart, who? This Moll!
ALEXANDER
O my reviving shame! Is't I must live
To be struck blind? Be it the work of sorrow
Before age take't in hand!
SIR GUY Darkness and death!
Have you deceived me thus? Did I engage
My whole estate for this?
ALEXANDER You asked no favour,
And you shall find as little: since my comforts
Play false with me, I'll be as cruel to thee
As grief to father's hearts.
MOLL Why, what's the matter with you,
'Less too much joy should make your age forgetful?
Are you too well, too happy?
ALEXANDER With a vengeance!
MOLL
Methinks you should be proud of such a daughter—
As good a man as your son!
ALEXANDER O monstrous impudence!
MOLL
You had no note before, an unmarked knight;
Now all the town will take regard on you,
And all your enemies fear you for my sake.
You may pass where you list, through crowds most thick,
And come off bravely with your purse unpicked!
You do not know the benefits I bring with me:
No cheat dares work upon you with thumb or knife,
While you've a roaring girl to your son's wife!
ALEXANDER
A devil rampant!
SIR GUY Have you so much charity
Yet to release me of my last rash bargain,
And I'll give in your pledge?
ALEXANDER No, sir, I stand to't:
I'll work upon advantage, as all mischiefs
Do upon me.
SIR GUY Content, bear witness all then,
His are the lands, and so contention ends.
Here comes your son's bride 'twixt two noble friends.
Enter the Lord Noland and Sir Beauteous Ganymede, with Mary Fitzallard between them, the Citizens and their Wives with them
MOLL [*to Sir Alexander*]
Now are you gulled as you would be: thank me for't,
I'd a forefinger in't.
SEBASTIAN Forgive me, father;
Though there before your eyes my sorrow feigned,
This still was she for whom true love complained.
ALEXANDER
Blessings eternal and the joys of angels
Begin your peace here to be signed in heaven!
How short my sleep of sorrow seems now to me,
To this eternity of boundless comforts
That finds no want but utterance and expression.
—[*To Lord Noland*] My lord, your office here appears so honourably,
So full of ancient goodness, grace, and worthiness,
I never took more joy in sight of man
Than in your comfortable presence now.
LORD NOLAND
Nor I more delight in doing grace to virtue
Than in this worthy gentlewoman, your son's bride,
Noble Fitzallard's daughter, to whose honour
And modest fame I am a servant vowed;
So is this knight.
ALEXANDER Your loves make my joys proud.
—[*To Servant*] Bring forth those deeds of land my care laid ready—
[*Servant fetches deeds*]
And which, old knight, thy nobleness may challenge,
Joined with thy daughter's virtues, whom I prize now,

133 **discover my offence** confess my fault, playing on unmasking Moll as his bride
141 **Heart** shortened form of 'God's heart', a mild oath
This Moll! Several meanings are possible: Moll's female identity is confirmed (this *is* Moll), or questioned (this is Moll?), or her appearance in female dress is simply distinguished from that in male dress (*this* Moll).
148 **I'll be as cruel to thee** I'll seize your estate because you haven't kept your part of our agreement.
150 **'Less** unless
153 **monstrous impudence** Monstrous recalls Sir Alexander's first account of Moll (see 2.130–2, note; 132–3, note); for impudence, see 99, note.
154 **note** distinction
unmarked unnoticed
158 **come off** escape
160 **No cheat... thumb or knife** No thief dares cut your purse; see 10.141, note.
162 **devil rampant** Playing on ramp, an abusive term used of Moll (see 7.8, note) and rampant, rearing on the hind legs to show fierceness, used of animals in heraldic emblems; indicates Sir Alexander's outrage at including Moll in his family lineage, signified by the heraldic emblems on a coat of arms.
164 **your pledge** your ring (given to him, 81); your promise to give your estate to Sebastian
169 **would be** wish to be
170 **forefinger** as in the proverbial 'finger in the pie', with sexual implications
174 **signed in heaven** refers to wedding ceremony; see 1.82, note.
179 **ancient** venerable, old-fashioned
181 **comfortable** cheering
188 **challenge** lay claim to (in the sense of take credit for, because he negotiated Sir Alexander's pledge of an estate to Sebastian)

As dearly as that flesh I call mine own.
—[*To Mary*] Forgive me, worthy gentlewoman, 'twas my blindness:
When I rejected thee, I saw thee not;
Sorrow and wilful rashness grew like films
Over the eyes of judgement, now so clear
I see the brightness of thy worth appear.

MARY
Duty and love may I deserve in those,
And all my wishes have a perfect close.

ALEXANDER
That tongue can never err, the sound's so sweet.
Here, honest son, receive into thy hands
The keys of wealth, possessions of those lands
Which my first care provided; they're thine own.
Heaven give thee a blessing with 'em! The best joys
That can in worldly shapes to man betide
Are fertile lands and a fair fruitful bride,
Of which I hope thou'rt sped.

SEBASTIAN
I hope so too, sir.

MOLL
Father and son, I ha' done you simple service here.

SEBASTIAN
For which thou shalt not part, Moll, unrequited.

ALEXANDER
Thou art a mad girl, and yet I cannot now
Condemn thee.

MOLL
Condemn me? Troth an you should, sir,
I'd make you seek out one to hang in my room:
I'd give you the slip at gallows and cozen the people.
[*To Lord Noland*] Heard you this jest, my lord?

LORD NOLAND
What is it, Jack?

MOLL
He was in fear his son would marry me,
But never dreamt that I would ne'er agree!

LORD NOLAND
Why? thou hadst a suitor once, Jack; when wilt marry?

MOLL
Who, I, my lord? I'll tell you when i'faith:
When you shall hear
Gallants void from sergeants' fear,
Honesty and truth unslandered,
Woman manned but never pandered,
Cheaters booted but not coached,
Vessels older ere they're broached;
If my mind be then not varied,
Next day following, I'll be married.

LORD NOLAND
This sounds like doomsday.

MOLL
Then were marriage best,
For if I should repent, I were soon at rest.

ALEXANDER
In troth, thou'rt a good wench; I'm sorry now
The opinion was so hard I conceived of thee:
Enter Trapdoor
Some wrongs I've done thee.

TRAPDOOR
Is the wind there now?
'Tis time for me to kneel and confess first,
For fear it come too late and my brains feel it.
—[*To Moll*] Upon my paws I ask you pardon, mistress.

MOLL
Pardon? For what, sir? What has your rogueship done now?

TRAPDOOR
I have been from time to time hired to confound you,
By this old gentleman.

MOLL
How?

TRAPDOOR
Pray forgive him;
But may I counsel you, you should never do't.
Many a snare to entrap your worship's life
Have I laid privily—chains, watches, jewels—
And when he saw nothing could mount you up,
Four hollow-hearted angels he then gave you,
By which he meant to trap you, I to save you.

ALEXANDER
To all which, shame and grief in me cry guilty.
—[*To Moll*] Forgive me; now I cast the world's eyes from me,
And look upon thee freely with mine own.
I see the most of many wrongs before thee
Cast from the jaws of Envy and her people,
And nothing foul but that. I'll never more
Condemn by common voice, for that's the whore

193 **films** morbid growths
201 **first** the estate he originally planned to give
205 **sped** provided
206 **simple service** a modest expression for 'I have served you well'
208–9 **Thou...thee** Sir Alexander shifts to the more familiar forms.
208 **mad** see 1.102, note
209 **an** if
210 **room** place (she would find a substitute)
217–24 **When you shall hear...married** parodies a form of religious prophecy that lists sins or social evils and makes their eradication the condition for the coming of God's final judgement, or reaching salvation, as line 225 indicates
218 **sergeants' fear** fear of being arrested for debt
219 **Honesty** chastity, with primary reference to women
220 **manned** escorted or ruled (by husbands)
221 **Cheaters...coached** thieves with enough money for boots to walk or ride horseback with, but not enough for the luxury of a coach
222 **Vessels...broached** In Christian thought, the body is the vessel (container) of the spirit (1 Thess. 4); when women aren't too soon penetrated—in marriage, or by rape—then Moll will marry.
223 **varied** changed
225 **doomsday** see 217–24, note
225–6 **marriage...at rest** alluding to proverb 'Marry in haste and repent at leisure' (Tilley M196)
229 **Is the wind there** has the situation changed?
232 **paws** dog-like, emphasizing his contrition
234 **confound** ruin, destroy
239 **mount you up** hang you on the gallows
240 **hollow-hearted angels** four coins 'marked with holes in them' (see 8.211–14 and note), thus 'hollow-hearted' in no longer being current, i.e., legally exchangeable as money
246 **Envy** malice, ill will
248 **voice** opinion; rumour

That deceives man's opinion, mocks his trust,
Cozens his love, and makes his heart unjust.

MOLL

Here be the angels, gentlemen: they were given me
As a musician; I pursue no pity—
Follow the law, and you can cuck me, spare not;
Hang up my viol by me, and I care not!

ALEXANDER

So far I'm sorry, I'll thrice double 'em
To make thy wrongs amends.
Come, worthy friends, my honourable lord,
Sir Beauteous Ganymede, and noble Fitzallard,
And you, kind gentlewomen, whose sparkling presence
Are glories set in marriage, beams of society,
For all your loves give lustre to my joys;
The happiness of this day shall be remembered
At the return of every smiling spring;
In my time now 'tis born, and may no sadness
Sit on the brows of men upon that day,
But as I am, so all go pleased away! *[Exeunt]*

Epilogue

A painter, having drawn with curious art
The picture of a woman—every part
Limned to the life—hung out the piece to sell.
People who passed along, viewing it well,
Gave several verdicts on it: some dispraised
The hair, some said the brows too high were raised,
Some hit her o'er the lips, misliked their colour,
Some wished her nose were shorter, some the eyes fuller;
Others said roses on her cheeks should grow,
Swearing they looked too pale, others cried no.
The workman, still as fault was found, did mend it,
In hope to please all; but, this work being ended,
And hung open at stall, it was so vile,
So monstrous and so ugly, all men did smile
At the poor painter's folly. Such we doubt
Is this our comedy: some perhaps do flout
The plot, saying, 'tis too thin, too weak, too mean;
Some for the person will revile the scene,
And wonder that a creature of her being
Should be the subject of a poet, seeing,
In the world's eye, none weighs so light; others look
For all those base tricks published in a book—
Foul as his brains they flowed from—of cutpurses,
Of nips and foists, nasty, obscene discourses,
As full of lies, as empty of worth or wit,
For any honest ear or eye unfit.
And thus,
If we to every brain that's humorous
Should fashion scenes, we, with the painter, shall,
In striving to please all, please none at all.
Yet for such faults, as either the writers' wit
Or negligence of the actors do commit,
Both crave your pardons: if what both have done
Cannot full pay your expectation,
The Roaring Girl herself, some few days hence,
Shall on this stage give larger recompense;
Which mirth that you may share in, herself does woo you,
And craves this sign: your hands to beckon her to you.
Finis

252 **pursue** seek
253 **cuck** Set me in a cucking stool, a chair into which women who vocally challenged male authority (designated 'scolds') were strapped, then publicly immersed several times in water; a legal punishment and social ritual.
Epilogue.1 **curious** skilful, elaborate
3 **Limned** painted; portrayed
to the life in a lifelike way
6 **brows** eyebrows
7 **hit her o'er the lips** criticized the lips
13 **open at stall** at an open stall, stand
15 **doubt** suspect, fear
17 **mean** involving people of low social rank; in a literary sense, unadorned, modest
18 **person** character, i.e., Moll
21 **weighs so light** is considered so trivial, playing on light as wanton
22–6 **book ... eye unfit** probably refers to a pamphlet by Samuel Rid taking issue with Dekker's pamphlet *The Belman* (1608), an exposé of the London underworld
24 **nips and foists** cutpurses and pickpockets; cf. 10.327–41
obscene repulsive
28 **humorous** afflicted with unsettled humours, fanciful, capricious
31–3 **writers' ... | Both** the two playwrights in collaboration, Dekker and Middleton
35–6 **The Roaring Girl ... larger recompense** Probably refers to the appearance of Mary Frith, the figure on whom Moll is based, singing and playing a lute on the stage of the Fortune in man's clothing, probably at a performance of this play several months before it was published (see Introduction).
37 **Which mirth ... share in** so that you may share in this mirth
38 **this sign** applause

The Roaring Girle.

THE PARTS

Adult Males

ALEXANDER (524 lines): Jack Dapper *or* Sir Thomas *or* Cutpurses (Sc. 10); Tearcat; Coachman (Sc. 5)

LAXTON (264 lines): Curtalax *or* Hanger; Tailor (Sc. 4); Porter (Sc. 4); Tearcat; Cutpurses (Sc. 10); Tiltyard *or* Sir Guy *or* Lord Noland *or* Sir Beauteous *or* Sir Thomas *or* Others (Sc. 11) *or* Servants (Sc. 11)

SEBASTIAN (246 lines): Curtalax *or* Hanger *or* Jack Dapper; Coachman (Sc. 5); Cutpurse (Sc. 10) *or* Jack Dapper; Tearcat; Sir Thomas

TRAPDOOR (217 lines): Neatfoot; Tailor (Sc. 4); Porter (Sc. 4); Coachman (Sc. 5); Cutpurses (Sc. 10)

GALLIPOT (155 lines): Neatfoot *or* Sir Davy *or* Curtalax *or* Hanger *or* Sir Adam *or* Jack Dapper *or* Gentlemen (Sc. 2) *or* Servingmen (Sc. 2); Porter (Sc. 4); Tailor (Sc. 4); Coachman (Sc. 5); Sir Thomas *or* Tearcat; Cutpurses (Sc. 10) *or* Sir Thomas; Tearcat *or* Sir Thomas

GOSHAWK (136 lines): Curtalax *or* Hanger; Gentlemen *or* Servingmen (Sc. 2); Servants (Sc. 3); Porter (Sc. 4); Tailor (Sc. 4); Coachman (Sc. 5); Sir Thomas; Tearcat; Cutpurses (Sc. 10); Servants *or* Others (Sc. 11)

OPENWORK (110 lines): Neatfoot *or* Sir Davy *or* Curtalax *or* Hanger *or* Sir Adam *or* Gentlemen (Sc. 2) *or* Servingmen (Sc. 2); Servants (Sc. 3); Porter (Sc. 4); Tailor (Sc. 4); Curtalax *or* Hanger *or* Sir Davy; Coachman (Sc. 5); Tearcat *or* Sir Thomas; Cutpurses (Sc. 10) *or* Sir Thomas

SIR DAVY (79 lines): any but Sebastian, Alexander, Sir Adam, Goshawk, Laxton, Gentlemen (Sc. 2), Greenwit, Neatfoot, Servingmen (Sc. 2), Trapdoor, Curtalax, Hanger

JACK DAPPER (69 lines): Alexander *or* Sebastian *or* Sir Guy *or* Gallipot *or* Neatfoot *or* Sir Davy *or* Tailor (Sc. 4) *or* Porter; Coachman (Sc. 5); Others *or* Servant (Sc. 11)

SIR GUY (58 lines): Neatfoot *or* Laxton *or* Sir Adam *or* Sir Davy *or* Curtalax *or* Hanger *or* Gentlemen (Sc. 2) *or* Servingmen (Sc. 2); Jack Dapper *or* Curtalax *or* Hanger *or* Cutpurses (Sc. 10) *or* Sir Thomas; Fellow (Sc. 3); Servants (Sc. 3); Porter (Sc. 4); Tailor (Sc. 4); Curtalax *or* Hanger *or* Sir Davy *or* Jack Dapper; Coachman (Sc. 5); Sir Thomas *or* Cutpurses (Sc. 10) *or* Jack Dapper; Cutpurses (Sc. 10) *or* Sir Thomas *or* Jack Dapper

GREENWIT (48 lines): Curtalax *or* Hanger; Porter (Sc. 4); Tailor (Sc. 4); Coachman (Sc. 5); Sir Thomas *or* Tearcat; Cutpurses (Sc. 10) *or* Sir Thomas; Tearcat *or* Sir Thomas

CURTALAX (35 lines): any but Hanger, Sir Adam, Sir Davy, Trapdoor, Jack Dapper

NEATFOOT (34 lines): any but Sebastian, Alexander, Sir Davy, Sir Adam, Goshawk, Laxton, Gentlemen (Sc. 2), Greenwit, Servingmen (Sc. 2)

LORD NOLAND (29 lines): Neatfoot; Sir Adam; Sir Davy; Gentlemen *or* Servingmen (Sc. 2); Laxton; Jack Dapper; Servants (Sc. 3); Fellow (Sc. 3); Tailor (Sc. 4); Porter (Sc. 4); Coachman (Sc. 5); Curtalax *or* Hanger

SIR ADAM (20 lines): any but Sebastian, Alexander, Sir Davy, Goshawk, Laxton, Gentlemen (Sc. 2), Greenwit, Neatfoot, Servingmen (Sc. 2), Trapdoor, Curtalax, Hanger

SIR THOMAS (13 lines): any but Jack Dapper, Sir Beauteous, Lord Noland, Trapdoor, Tearcat, Cutpurses (Sc. 10)

TILTYARD (10 lines): Neatfoot *or* Sir Adam *or* Sir Davy *or* Curtalax *or* Hanger *or* Laxton *or* Gentlemen (Sc. 2) *or* Servingmen (Sc. 2); Fellow (Sc. 3); Porter (Sc. 4); Tailor (Sc. 4); Coachman (Sc. 5); Jack Dapper *or* Curtalax *or* Hanger; Sir Thomas *or* Tearcat; Cutpurses (Sc. 10) *or* Sir Thomas *or* Jack Dapper; Tearcat *or* Sir Thomas

SIR BEAUTEOUS (8 lines): Laxton *or* Neatfoot *or* Sir Adam *or* Sir Davy *or* Gentlemen (Sc. 2) *or* Servingmen (Sc. 2); Servants (Sc. 3); Fellow (Sc. 3); Tailor (Sc. 4); Porter (Sc. 4); Coachman (Sc. 5); Curtalax *or* Hanger

HANGER (6 lines): any but Curtalax, Sir Adam, Sir Davy, Trapdoor, Jack Dapper

Adult males not listed in Dramatis Personae

TEARCAT (34 lines): any but Jack Dapper, Sir Beauteous, Sir Thomas, Lord Noland, Trapdoor

TAILOR (Sc. 4; 16 lines): any but Sebastian, Alexander

CUTPURSES (Sc. 10; 14 lines): any but Jack Dapper, Sir Beauteous, Sir Thomas, Lord Noland

COACHMAN (Sc. 5; 11 lines): any but Laxton

FELLOW (Sc. 3; 8 lines): any but Openwork, Laxton, Goshawk, Greenwit, Jack Dapper

Gentlemen (Sc. 2; 7 lines): any but Alexander, Sir Davy Dapper, Sir Adam, Goshawk, Laxton, Sebastian, Greenwit, Neatfoot, Servingmen (Sc. 2)

PORTER (Sc. 4; 3 lines): any but Sebastian, Alexander

Others (Sc. 11; 1 line): any but Alexander, Sebastian, Goshawk, Greenwit, Servant (Sc. 11), Sir Guy, Lord Noland, Sir Beauteous, Gallipot, Openwork, Tiltyard, Trapdoor

Servingmen (Sc. 2; no lines): the same, excluding themselves, including Gentlemen (Sc. 2)

SERVANTS (Sc. 3; no lines): any but Gallipot, Tiltyard

SERVANT (Sc. 11; no lines): any but Alexander, Sebastian, Goshawk, Greenwit, Sir Guy, Lord Noland, Sir Beauteous, Gallipot, Openwork, Tiltyard, Trapdoor

Boys

MOLL (547 lines): none

MISTRESS GALLIPOT (217 lines): none

MISTRESS OPENWORK (154 lines): none

MARY (36 lines): Gull

GULL (16 lines): Mary

MISTRESS TILTYARD (16 lines): none

Most crowded scene: Sc. 11, 17 characters

NO WIT/HELP LIKE A WOMAN'S; OR, THE ALMANAC

Edited by John Jowett

'*No Wit/Help like a Woman's*, a comedy by Thomas Middleton, Gent.' waited until 1657 before it appeared in print. But the play was clearly written decades earlier in 1611, for Weatherwise repeatedly quotes from actual almanacs for that year published by Thomas Bretnor and Jeffrey Neve (George, 1966). It is probably no coincidence that on 29 December of the same year, 1611 a play called *The Almanac* was acted by Prince Henry's Men at Whitehall before King James. In all probability this is the same play, or a court adaptation of it (Eccles, 1987).

If *No Wit* is indeed the Prince Henry's Men's play, the company would presumably have staged its original performances at the Fortune Theatre, within months of their production of *The Roaring Girl*. The title *No Wit/Help like a Woman's*, like *The Roaring Girl*, promises that the play will focus on one or more female characters, and in each play the principal female is a resourceful figure who dresses herself as a man and in that guise offends social probity. In *No Wit*'s world of scoundrels and fools, Mistress Low-water stands out as a character who, though disadvantaged by misfortune and by the social expectations of gender, is able to succeed remarkably well through her own resourceful wit. Thus the alternative titles place different emphasis on the play's balance. Women engineer the real plots of *No Wit*. Weatherwise, with his almanac, actually has no control over anything. He is butt of *The Almanac*'s anti-providential wit and mainspring of its theatricality.

The play is known to have been revived in 1638 by James Shirley for the short-lived St Weburgh Street Theatre in Dublin. Shirley gave the play a new prologue and inserted a reference to the year of his production at 7.293; act intervals were evidently introduced (unless they derive from the 1611 court performance or an unrecorded revival), and further changes cannot be entirely ruled out. In more respects than most plays of the period, *No Wit* anticipates Restoration comedy, and in 1677 a farcical adaptation called *The Counterfeit Bridegroom, or, The Defeated Widow* (attributed to Aphra Behn or Thomas Betterton) was acted at Dorset Garden. The Low-water plot was imitated from *The Counterfeit Bridegroom*, either directly or indirectly, in a number of eighteenth-century plays (Balch, 1980). Middleton's play thus fell by the wayside, and it evidently remained unperformed for over three hundred years. In a marginal note in his copy of Dyce's edition, Anthony Trollope gave an ill-tempered verdict on its theatrical potential; he observed 'a certain activity' about the play 'that may have made it attractive on the stage to an audience devoid of all taste'. The play was finally revived in 1985 in London by the Wayward Players at the Bear Gardens, where it formed an effective double bill with *Women, Beware Women* and revealed the women as 'astonishingly good natured' (Potter, 1985), and again in 1991 by a student group at the University of Toronto, a production that confirmed, according to its director Robert Irish, the stage prominence of Weatherwise.

Trollope's response was not typical of his century. A. W. Ward (1875) found a mix of lively, accomplished writing and dubious moral situation, a view the 1885 editor A. H. Bullen echoed. In 1887 Algernon Charles Swinburne wrote of 'the unfailing charm of a style worthy of Fletcher himself'. Such praise can turn to disparagement; a recent editor, Johnson (1976), laments what he sees as the blunting influence of Fletcherian romance on the incisive style found in Middleton's earlier city comedies. A more positive evaluation comes from Rowe (1979), who sees the play as repeatedly denying and interrogating comic resolutions. This is a useful approach, but it should not be allowed to obscure the charm noted by Swinburne. If the play absurdifies comic convention, it does so in a spirit that is itself comic. If it probes the limits of tolerance, it is perhaps itself finally tolerant.

No Wit might be described as a female-oriented continuation of male-oriented city comedy. The rapacious Goldenfleece has defrauded Low-water of his fortune; now Mistress Low-water pursues a new kind of confrontation with Goldenfleece's Widow. The key men are dead (Goldenfleece), ineffectual (Low-water) or contemptible (the Widow's suitors). Initially Mistress Low-water seeks revenge on a would-be seducer, Sir Gilbert Lambstone, who is also a favoured suitor to the Widow. Disguised as a plucky young gentleman, Mistress Low-water appears as an uninvited guest at Weatherwise's banquet in honour of the Widow, and reveals Sir Gilbert's duplicity to the assembled company. The Widow responds by falling in love with her saviour, and decides to marry for love rather than money. Mistress Low-water plays the game for her own advantage, and the couple are duly wed. Now the disguised woman's survival as the young gallant and her need for revenge converge, for the 'husband' must inflict emotional cruelty in order to avoid being taken to bed and discovered as a woman. The Widow has chosen love over money only to be emotionally and sexually defrauded. The frustrated and injured Widow turns her attention to Mistress Low-water's brother Beveril, enabling the sister to accuse the Widow of sexual dishonesty, just as she did Sir Gilbert before her. A restitution of the gains from her first husband's financial misdemeanours is required before the new love-match between her and Beveril can be solemnized.

This contest between Mistress Low-water and the Widow Lady Goldenfleece relates to a ballad in *The Exeter Garland* (1720) called 'No Wit Like to a Woman's; or, The Old Woman Fitted by her Daughter'. The extant ballad tells of a daughter whose dowry is withheld by her rich widowed mother; she tricks her mother of the wealth by disguising herself as a beau and causing her mother to fall in love with her. Either the Exeter ballad and the play have a common source in a lost ballad, or the play is itself the source for the ballad.

For the play's other plot, Middleton followed Giambattista Della Porta's 1584 Italian comedy *La Sorella* ('The Sister'), which he presumably read in the Italian. The location turns from Della Porta's Venice to London; accordingly the Turks are familiarized as England's co-religionists but trade rivals, the Dutch. The manservant Savourwit, a New Comedy witty rogue, is new to Middleton's play, and his cynicism helps to complicate *La Sorella*'s moral simplicity.

Before the stage-action begins, Philip's father sent Philip and Savourwit to the Low Countries to redeem Philip's long-lost Mother and sister from captivity with Dutch pirates. Having squandered the ransom, Philip returned home with a wife whom he now passes off as his redeemed sister Grace. This works well until his Mother is unexpectedly freed and returns home. Surprisingly, she agrees to connive with Philip against his father by pretending that Grace is his sister. But confusion multiplies when she meets Grace and discovers, to Philip's horror, that she is indeed that sister. It takes a second extraordinary twist of fate to set all to rights again.

Here are two causally independent plots. As the 1657 title itself suggests, the very idea of doubleness holds the play together. On the title-page the word 'wit' is bracketed above 'help', so as to give alternative readings. The 'wit' is above all the means by which Mistress Low-water helps herself, her husband, her brother Beveril, even, finally, the Widow. Philip's Mother is not particularly witty, but her lie on his behalf is of considerable help to him. Finally it takes the help of another woman, the Widow, to rescue Philip. The split title equates and contrasts the ideas of wit and help, and similarly correlates the two plots.

The apparent disjunction between the plots is in fact correlation in disguise. Both take financial loss in conjunction with the loss of a relative as a starting point. New marriages at first offer to compensate, but turn out to be disasters. Each plot hinges on a piece of female duplicity or role-playing—Mistress Low-water's disguise as a man, Philip's Mother's acceptance of Grace as her daughter—and push the pretence unnervingly towards becoming a reality. What is at issue is a false marriage—woman to woman, brother to sister. Each of these marriages becomes a meeting point for the laws of inheritance and wayward desire.

The outcomes are more secure marital resolutions in which confusion of identity is resolved by sleights of hand. It is important here that in both plots a character is available to double with one of the marriage partners. Philip's supposed and real sisters are dangerously interchangeable (Middleton gives the women's fathers the virtually synonymous names Sunset and Twilight), and the evasive device of the stand-in marital partner links this resolution with that for the Low-water plot. There it is the brother who is miraculously available to stand in for the sister and as it were reconstruct the homosexual marriage as heterosexual.

To put it another way, Grace, whose identity as Philip's sister is supposed to be the reality behind the false identity, who is repeatedly referred to as Philip's sister, and is specifically called '*Sister*' in the stage direction following 8.159, becomes Philip's legitimate wife; in contrast Mistress Low-water changes from the Widow's spouse to her 'sister' (9.570, 9.578), in the sense 'sister-in-law'. Della Porta's title provides a keyword for the denouement of both plots. The unacceptable marriages are resolved by taking the sisterhood out of the incestuous marriage and inserting it as a separator to prevent the other from constituting itself as a union of women.

Of course mistaken identity and romantic confusion as a result of cross-dressing are conventions of Renaissance comedy. But Middleton retrieves the issues of sexuality from the comic formalities in several ways. Any links between these two autonomous plots are bound to highlight their common core of significance. The extreme involutions of the action draw attention to its artificiality, and so draw attention to the desperate need to avoid certain outcomes. And incest and female homoeroticism are actually confronted. Philip despairingly fears damnation for incest, and these fears inhabit the same part of the play as the Widow's lust for the man who is really Mistress Low-water. Philip perhaps articulates an anxiety about illicit sex on behalf of both sets of characters. The masque scene raises the matter of Mistress Low-water's apparent and real gender. Sir Gilbert despises the young gentleman's effeminacy, and in scourging widows who marry such androgynes he states what is the actual situation in an outraged but supposedly hypothetical comparison:

> They marry now but the third part of husbands—
> Boys, smooth-faced catamites—to fulfil their bed,
> As if a woman should a woman wed. (9.90–2)

Much virtue in 'as if', especially as the actor playing Mistress Low-water would indeed have been a 'smooth-faced' boy. (And the actor playing the Widow would also have been a boy: the marriage perhaps threatens simultaneous collapse into both male and female homosexuality.) Rarely in Renaissance drama are such possibilities confronted so explicitly. It is all the more striking because, as Valerie Traub has pointed out, there was no Early Modern English word for lesbianism, a sexuality that was almost as Shirley imagines Dublin in his Prologue to *No Wit*, unchronicled, unmapped, invisible. And indeed even in the play it is incest rather than same-sex marriage that finds all too clear a place on the list of damnable sins.

The whole play can be seen as an action that forces incestuous and female-homoerotic marriage from actual event to similitude, 'as if'. Thanks to the doubling characters Beveril and Jane, incest and same-sex liaison are only temporary mistakes. The final outcomes may be taken as matters of fact, unless our sense of the factual has been so heavily undercut that they seem rather to be fantasies of normalization that bring about an acceptable ending. It is not beyond the bounds of Middleton's representation of human behaviour to suggest that earlier in the play Philip and the Widow get what they unconsciously desire. Marriages have taken place that, more or less to the audience's best knowledge, break the very laws on which marriage is founded. Incest doubles the family upon itself, and same-sex marriage denies the possibility of progeny. Like widowhood, lost or duplicitous mothers, and cross-dressing, they undermine male control of reproduction and inheritance. Every step towards recognizing these desires is a step away from a standard comedic ending, and they are not allowed finally to hold sway.

The stage-managed denouements may be read by the light of two earlier episodes that show the intractability of life to theatrical schemes. These are the major and sustained ensemble scenes of the banquet in Scene 4 and the subverted wedding masque in Scene 9. Weatherwise, central protagonist in the play as *The Almanac*, attempts to rule over both festivities, unintentionally or intentionally ensuring that the prescripted inner action of each is in the event twisted to a bizarre outcome.

For his 'conceited' banquet, Weatherwise arranges twelve places that correspond to the signs of the zodiac, each with a motto appropriate to the time of year represented by the sign. He devises sweet-dishes for his guests that are shaped like the twelve astrological signs. In allocating each guest to his or her seat he makes much play on the correspondence between person and sign, and on the part of the human body associated with each sign. The whole table becomes an emblem of the natural year, of human behaviour, and of the human body. The most immediate point of reference is the almanac lore to which Weatherwise is enslaved. Pocket-book almanacs usually included the figure of the 'anatomical man': a human body surrounded by a rectangular frame showing the twelve signs of the zodiac, each sign connected to the corresponding bodily limb or organ. This graphic table has become the banqueting table.

Almanacs were popular renditions of astrological learning. Weatherwise has produced a correspondingly debased rendition of aristocratic and royal feast-making. The zodiac signs are presumably confections of marzipan and sugar of the kind mentioned, and associated with lecherous feasting, in *Women, Beware Women* 3.1.270 and 3.2.74–5, where the bull, ram, and goat are again astrological signs. Sugar sculptures were standard items of conceited extravagance, and representative of the new levels of refinement and ingenuity being reached in food preparation. A court banquet would be a work of gastronomic contrivance designed to surprise and delight both eyesight and palate. An ingenious procession of dishes would manifest natural food substances in cunningly altered form. Thus the banquet could aspire to high artifice and even theatricality. At the Whitehall Banqueting Hall it might be prelude to a performance of a court masque—or indeed of a play such as *The Almanac*.

Weatherwise's banquet, here 'a course of sweetmeats, fruit, and wine, served...as a separate entertainment' (*OED*), is metonymic for such feasting. His pretentious vulgarity recalls Petronius Arbiter's Latin prose-and-verse fiction *Satyricon*. A lengthy section of this fragmented work describes Trimalchio's banquet. The Renaissance editions Middleton might have read preserve only small portions of this episode, but one of them is the opening passage which includes an account of a course of comestibles that are shaped like the signs of the zodiac or make punning reference to it. This text probably suggested to Middleton Weatherwise's edible zodiac signs. The parvenu Trimalchio, like Weatherwise, is superstitious, observing lucky and unlucky days. He has apparently mastered fortune (his wife is called Fortunata), and Weatherwise hopes to do likewise. Yet the astrologer falls well short of Trimalchio's lavish opulence. All and sundry crowd in to Trimalchio's feast, but Weatherwise needs to conscript his tenants to fill the empty seats. In the theatre the tenants would be mute hired men, and presumably filled the chairs whose backs faced the audience. But this theatrical pragmatism nicely coincides with a satire on Weatherwise's ill-disguised frugality. His tenants are pointedly marginalized, and plain foods such as beef and fish are only figuratively present on his table as Taurus and Pisces. Weatherwise fails in the mythical simple old-fashioned hospitality of the rural gentry, just as he fails to reproduce the style of princes.

The guests conspicuously lack the mannered courtliness that should crown the feast as a living art-form. Instead, conversation is marked by amusingly stilted incongruity. The Renaissance manners on display at the fictional repast in Book 4 of Stefano Guazzo's *Civil Conversation* (translated from the Italian by Bartholomew Young, 1586) offer a significant point of contrast. There are several correspondences between the conduct of the two banquets as social occasions. In *Civil Conversation*, a woman is appointed head of the feast, games are played with proverbial tags, and a drinking-vessel ingeniously shaped like a ship is passed round the guests. *No Wit* echoes these details, but where in Guazzo they were sources of compliment and delight, they are here occasions for awkwardness, embarrassment, and factional contempt for the inventor. Just as Middleton adds Savourwit to the personae of *La Sorella*, he augments Guazzo's feast with a sardonic Clown who ridicules the sun-cup Weatherwise produces to pass through his zodiac. Guazzo provides a fictional model of 'civil conversation' that Weatherwise imitates in accidental parody.

All of his conceits turn out to be unsuitable, and unhelpful in his attempts to woo the Widow. At first he simply plays into the hands of his rivals. By the end of the scene he and the other suitors have been displaced by Mistress Low-water, the supposed young gentleman humiliated at the foot of the table.

The wedding masque is the occasion for the suitors' revenge. When the Widow commissions the scholar Beveril to supply an entertainment, her former suitors offer their services as actors, in order to turn an extravagant public compliment into an equally extravagant insult. The masque is again based on a theme familiar to Weatherwise from his almanacs: the division of human temperament into four types or humours related to the four elements of Earth, Air, Fire, and Water. Middleton may have based Beveril's masque on a sequence in Thomas Dekker's portion of *The Magnificent Entertainment* (Bergeron, 1985; see 2047–2119). Weatherwise visually presides over the show, suspended from the heavens as Air. The suitors displace Beveril's text for the masque, which would inferably have shown the Widow's love for her supposed husband as a perfect figuration of all the elements combined in harmony. Their actual speeches are calculatedly nasty, though the sheer absurdity of the suitors' transformations ensures that they cannot be taken too seriously.

As with the banquet scene, the proposed idealized view of human nature designed to flatter the Widow becomes in the event the very opposite. Human nature is deeply imperfect in this play, especially where sexual passion is concerned. If the conventions of marriage masque are corrupted, so too are the conventions of romantic comedy. The disguised heroine cannot marry; she is the wrong gender for the match in question, and she already has a spouse. Mistress Low-water is neither Shakespeare's premarital Viola nor Middleton's anti-marital Moll. Though she claims the moral high ground, and even, as her fortunes improve, sees herself as a post-diluvian Noah favoured by God (6.253–7), her charm has more to do with wit than virtue. That wit is hard pushed to excuse some of her actions, especially as the Widow, her victim, is herself too verbally witty, too sexually vulnerable, and finally too dignified to capitulate, by association with her dead husband, to the role of villain.

A redistribution of wealth is the precondition for final happiness. As the Widow accepts a lowered position in the financial order of things, and is accepted as a member of the middling-gentry community, she becomes the key to resolving Philip and Grace's difficulties. That resolution defies belief, and in the celebration that follows it is the roguish Savourwit who says he 'could spring up and knock my head against yon silver ceiling for joy'. As in *Revenger's Tragedy* 3.5.2–4, where Vindice uses virtually the same words to express how he is ravished by his own success, or indeed Jonson's *Sejanus* 5.8–9, where the self-congratulatory would-be tyrant at each step feels his 'advanced head | Knock out a star in heaven', there are suggestions here of atheistic self-congratulation. Sejanus and Vindice meet their downfall, but the comic plot-machine of *No Wit* rewards those who wittily help themselves. The mysteries of concord between microcosm and macrocosm are reduced to an emblematic banqueting-table or debased in a show that consigns the Platonic ideal to the past; the science of astrology has retreated to banal almanac lore; the heavens are merely a painted ceiling. Weatherwise proves to be a lack-wit above all for his belief in schematic conceptualizations of the world; he is an urban-gentry Prospero who is chastened for his attempts at deploying providence for his own ends. As with Prospero, the Epilogue is left to him.

As the Epilogue centres on Weatherwise's almanac, it might hypothetically have been added for the court performance where the play was called *The Almanac*, or at any rate have been an optional afterthought to the original play. It distracts attention from the play's leading concerns to its leading comic character. Interestingly, though, in the final lines Weatherwise offers himself as a scapegoat for the play's faults:

> Some faults perhaps have slipped I am to answer;
> And if in anything your revenge appears,
> Send me in with all your fists about mine ears.

In other words, perhaps, don't blame the women. The final three lines of the main play have likewise been spoken by a male character, and have been analogously addressed to the 'gentlemen' assembled on stage. But it is a perfunctory summing-up. The last exchange specific to the play's action comes in two lines immediately before, where Mistress Low-water says of the Widow, 'I am her servant for't', the Widow replies, 'Ha, worthy sister!', and then adds, without any apparent change of addressee, 'The government of all I bless thee with.' This exchange between the women jokingly looks back on their courtship, in that 'servant' plays on the sense 'suitor, wooer', the role that has been replaced now that Mistress Low-water, as woman and as her brother's sister, has become the Widow's 'worthy sister'. Mistress Low-water doesn't get a wife, but she does get a dowry. Beveril has just offered to make the Widow's wealth readily available to his sister. In response, Mistress Low-water's 'I am her servant for't' sets aside Beveril's theoretical power as husband-to-be and insists on acknowledging deference to the Widow. The Widow not only gives Mistress Low-water access to her wealth but puts her fully in control of it. She thus establishes an alliance between the women that strips her future husband of his potential rights. If the Widow addresses whom she seems to address and means what she says, her endowment of her sister-in-law is an astonishing financial transaction, especially in context of a period when the restrictions on female ownership of property were very considerable. The play cannot propose woman-to-woman marriage as the basis for a socially inclusive comic ending, but it can and evidently does propose a woman-to-woman financial exchange as the basis for that comic ending. This switch from the sexual to the economic aspect of marriage is the play's last moment of doubleness and substitution. It might be a stunning twist to the conventions of comic closure, one that goes far beyond questions of form and artifice. Perhaps the distracting Epilogue was needed from the play's inception after all.

SEE ALSO

Textual introduction and apparatus: *Companion*, 1149

Authorship and date: *Companion*, 371

No {*Wit* / *Help*} *like a Woman's*

Or, The Almanac

[*for Prince Henry's Men at the Fortune*]

THE ACTORS' NAMES

PROLOGUE
SIR OLIVER Twilight, a rich old knight
PHILIP his son, servant to Mistress Grace
SANDFIELD, friend to Philip, servant to Mistress Jane
Master SUNSET, true father of Mistress Grace
MASTER LOW-WATER, a decayed gentleman
SIR GILBERT Lambstone, Master WEATHERWISE, Master PEPPERTON, Master OVERDONE } Suitors to the Lady Goldenfleece
Master BEVERIL, brother to Mistress Low-water
DUTCH MERCHANT
DUTCH BOY
SAVOURWIT, Sir Oliver's man
FOOTMAN
Peccadill, Lady Goldenfleece's CLOWN
SERVANTS
Six of Weatherwise's TENANTS

Lady Twilight, Philip's MOTHER
Lady Goldenfleece, a rich WIDOW
MISTRESS LOW-WATER
Mistress GRACE, Sunset's daughter, but supposed Twilight's
Mistress JANE, Twilight's daughter, but supposed Sunset's

In the masque, presenters of three of the Winds

Prologue [*Enter Prologue*]

PROLOGUE
How is't possible to suffice
So many ears, so many eyes?
Some in wit, some in shows
Take delight, and some in clothes;
Some for mirth they chiefly come,
Some for passion, for both some;
Some for lascivious meetings, that's their errand,
Some to detract, and ignorance their warrant.
How is't possible to please
Opinion tossed in such wild seas?
Yet I doubt not, if attention
Seize you above, and apprehension
You below, to take things quickly,
We shall both make you sad and tickle ye. [*Exit*]

Title ***No ... Woman's*** The main title has a proverbial flavour (compare 'A woman's wit helps at a pinch'). *Wit* is 'intelligence, craftiness', and may have a sexual pun: 'genitals'.

Persons Most of the names indicate the character type. See notes on their first appearances.

3, 4 **servant** lover

6 **decayed** impoverished

Prologue.1 suffice satisfy (rhymes with *eyes*)

6 **passion** grief, high emotion (the stuff of tragedy)

12–13 **you above ... You below** i.e. those in the audience sitting in the galleries and those standing in the yard. The disposition of the audience reflected the social hierarchy.

12 **apprehension** understanding

Sc. 1 *Enter Philip, Sir Oliver Twilight's son, with Savourwit, his father's man*

PHILIP I am at my wit's ends, Savourwit.

SAVOURWIT And I am e'en following after you as fast as I can, sir.

PHILIP My wife will be forced from me, my pleasure!

SAVOURWIT Talk no more on't, sir. How can there be any hope i'th' middle when we're both at our wits' end in the beginning? My invention was ne'er so gravelled since I first set out upon't.

PHILIP
Nor does my stop stick only in this wheel,
Though it be a main vexation; but I'm grated
In a dear absolute friend, young Master Sandfield—

SAVOURWIT
Ay, there's another rub too.

PHILIP Who supposes
That I make love to his affected mistress,
When 'tis my father works against the peace
Of both our spirits, and woos unknown to me.
He strikes out sparks of undeservèd anger
'Twixt old steel friendship and new stony hate,
As much forgetful of the merry hours
The circuits of our youth hath spent and worn
As if they had not been, or we not born.

Enter Sandfield

SAVOURWIT
See where he comes.

SANDFIELD Unmerciful in torment!
Will this disease never forsake mine eye?

PHILIP
It must be killed first if it grow so painful.
Work it out strongly at one time, that th'anguish
May never more come near thy precious sight.
If my eternal sleep will give thee rest,
Close up mine eyes with opening of my breast.

[*He offers his breast*]

SANDFIELD
I feel thy wrongs at midnight, and the weight
Of thy close treacheries. Thou hast a friendship
As dangerous as a strumpet's that will kiss
Men into poverty, distress, and ruin;
And to make clear the face of thy foul deeds,
Thou work'st by seconds.

[*He draws his sword*]

PHILIP
Then may the sharp point of an inward horror
Strike me to earth, and save thy weapon guiltless.

SANDFIELD
Not in thy father?

PHILIP O defend me, friendship!
How much is truth abused when 'tis kept silent!

SAVOURWIT [*to Sandfield*]
True, your anger's in an error all this while, sir.
But that a lover's weapon now hears reason,
'Tis out still like a mad man's. Hear but me, sir.
'Tis my young master's injury, not yours,
That you quarrel with him for; and this shows
As if you'd challenge a lame man the field,
And cut off's head because he has lost his legs.
His grief makes him dead flesh, as it appeared
By off'ring up his breast to you; for, believe it, sir,
Had he not greater crosses of his own,
Your hilts could not cross him—

SANDFIELD How?

SAVOURWIT Not your hilts, sir.
Come, I must have you friends. A pox of weapons!
There's a whore gapes for't; put it up i'th' scabbard.

SANDFIELD [*putting up his sword*]
Thou'rt a mad slave.

SAVOURWIT Come, give me both your hands.
You're in a quagmire both. Should I release you now,
Your wits would both come home in a stinking pickle;
Your father's old nose would smell you out presently.

PHILIP
Tell him the secret which no mortal knows
But thou and I, and then he will confess
How much he wronged the patience of his friend.

SAVOURWIT
Then thus the marigold opens at the splendour
Of a hot constant friendship 'twixt you both.
[*To Sandfield*] 'Tis not unknown to your ear, some ten years since,
My mistress his good mother, with a daughter
About the age of six, crossing to Jersey,
Was taken by the Dunkirks, sold both, and separated.
As the last news brings hot, the first and last
So much discovered; for in nine years' space
No certain tidings of their life or death

1.0.2 ***Savourwit*** The name is fitting for a flippant cynic.
6 **middle** i.e. (*a*) middle of an action or voyage (*b*) middle (sexual) region of the body
7 **invention** ingenuity
gravelled run aground (like a ship on sand), confounded
8 **set out** Draws specifically on the sense 'put to sea'.
9 **Nor . . . wheel** From the proverb 'to set a spoke in one's wheel'.
stop peg to stop a wheel turning
10 **grated** harassed, irritated
12 **rub** (*a*) irritation, reproof (*b*) obstacle
13 **make love to** woo
his affected mistress the woman he loves
17 **steel** (alluding to the proverb 'true as steel')
stony (alluding to the proverb 'as hard as a flint-stone')
24 **Work it out** get rid of it
at one time once and for all
33 **seconds** other people, agents
39 **lover's weapon** (with a phallic innuendo)
40 **still** always
48 **hilts** sword-hilt
50 **whore** i.e. the scabbard
52–3 **You're . . . pickle** From the proverbs 'to be in a sad pickle' and 'to lie in the mire'.
54 **smell you out** (proverbial)
presently straight away
58 **opens** opens its flower (with *hot constant friendship* as the sun); i.e. discloses secrets
63 **Dunkirks** Dunkirk pirates
64 **last . . . last** latest . . . final
brings is brought

Or what place held 'em, earth, the sea, or heaven,
Came to the old man's ears, the knight my master;
Till, about five months since, a letter came,
Sent from the mother, which related all
Their taking, selling, separation,
And never meeting; and withal required
Six hundred crowns for ransom, which my old master
No sooner heard the sound but tolled the sum,
Gave him the gold, and sent us both aboard.
We landing by the way, having a care
To lighten us of our carriage because gold
Is such a heavy metal, eased our pockets
In wenches' aprons. Women were made to bear,
But for us gentlemen 'tis most unkindly.

SANDFIELD
Well, sir?

PHILIP
A pure rogue still!

SAVOURWIT
Amongst the rest, sir,
'Twas my young master's chance there to dote finely
Upon a sweet young gentlewoman, but one
That would not sell her honour for the Indies
Till a priest struck the bargain, and then half
A crown dispatched it.
To be brief, wedded her and bedded her,
Brought her home hither to his father's house;
And with a fair tale of mine own bringing up,
She passes for his sister that was sold.

SANDFIELD
Let me not lose myself in wond'ring at thee.
But how made you your score even for the mother?

SAVOURWIT
Pish, easily. We told him how her fortunes
Mocked us as they mocked her. When we were o'th' sea
She was o'th' land; and, as report was given,
When we were landed she was gone to heaven.
So he believes two lies one error bred:
The daughter ransomed, and the mother dead.

SANDFIELD
Let me admire thee, and withal confess
My injuries to friendship.

PHILIP
They're all pardoned.
These are the arms I bore against my friend.
[*He embraces Sandfield*]

SAVOURWIT
But what's all this to th' present? This discourse
Leaves you i'th' bog still.

PHILIP
On, good Savourwit.

SAVOURWIT
For yet our policy has crossed ourselves;
For the old knave my master, little thinking her
Wife to his son, but his own daughter still,
Seeks out a match for her.

PHILIP
Here I feel the surgeon
At second dressing.

SAVOURWIT
And he's entertained,
E'en for pure need—for fear the glass should crack
That is already broken, but well soldered—
A mere sot for her suitor, a rank fox,
One Weatherwise, that woos by the almanac,
Observes the full and change, an arrant moon-calf.
And yet, because the fool demands no portion
But the bare dow'r of her smock, the old fellow,
Worn to the bone with a dry covetous itch
To save his purse and yet bestow his child,
Consents to masty lumps of almanac stuff
Kned with May-butter.—Now as I have thought on't,
I'll spoil him in the baking.

SANDFIELD
Prithee, as how, sirrah?

SAVOURWIT
I'll give him such a crack in one o'th' sides,
He shall quite run out of my master's favour.

PHILIP
I should but too much love thee for that.

SAVOURWIT
Thus then,
To help you both at once, and so good-night to you:
After my wit has shipped away the fool,
As he shall part I'll buzz into the ear
Of my old master that you, sir, Master Sandfield,
Dearly affect his daughter, and will take her
With little or no portion. Well stood out in't!
Methinks I see him caper at that news,
And, in the full, cry 'O!' This brought about
And wittily dissembled on both parts,
You to affect his love, he to love yours,
I'll so beguile the father at the marriage

74 **tolled** counted out
75 **him** i.e. Philip
77 **carriage** burden
78–9 **eased... aprons** Refers literally to the transfer of money, euphemistically to sexual acts the money paid for.
79 **Women... bear** Possible proverbial; the same joke occurs in *Taming of the Shrew*, 2.1.200.
bear Refers to (*a*) the position underneath in the sexual act (*b*) child-bearing (*c*) carrying money.
80 **unkindly** unnatural
87 **wedded her and bedded her** (proverbial)
93 **him** i.e. Philip's father
97 **one error bred** that were bred by one error
101 **arms** Puns on limbs and weapons.
102–3 **This... bog** See note to ll. 52–3.
111 **mere sot** utter fool
113 **arrant** (*a*) downright, rascally (*b*) *errant*: wandering, unfixed
moon-calf natural idiot (quibbling on the moon as the object whose changes Weatherwise *Observes*)
114 **portion** dowry
115 **dow'r** dowry
118 **masty** fed with mast, fatted, swinish
118–19 **lumps... May-butter** Describes the consistency of Weatherwise's mind.
119 **Kned** kneaded
May-butter unsalted butter left to stand in the sun during May and used medicinally. Mentioned here because rancid and cloudy. The proverb 'Mad as May-butter' may have been current.
121–2 **I'll... favour** The punning image is of a pie (see l. 120) whose contents *run out* through the crack.
129 **stood out** stood firm, upheld
131 **in the full** at full

That each shall have his own; and both being welcomed
And chambered in one house—as 'tis his pride
To have his children's children got successively
On his forefathers' feather beds—in the daytimes
To please the old man's eyesight you may dally
And set a kiss on the wrong lip. No sin in't;
Brothers and sisters do't, cousins do more;
But pray take heed you be not kin to them.
So in the night-time nothing can deceive you.
Let each know his own work; and there I leave you.

SANDFIELD
Let me applaud thee.

PHILIP [*to Savourwit*] Blest be all thy ends,
That mak'st armed enemies embracing friends.
About it speedily. *Exit* [*with Sandfield*]

SAVOURWIT I need no pricking.
I'm of that mettle so well paced and free,
There's no good riders that use spur to me.

Enter Grace Twilight

O, are you come?

GRACE Are any comforts coming?

SAVOURWIT I never go without 'em.

GRACE
Thou sport'st with joys that utterance cannot perfect.

[*A noise within*]

SAVOURWIT
Hark, are they risen?

GRACE Yes, long before I left 'em;
And all intend to bring the widow homeward.

SAVOURWIT
Depart then, mistress, to avoid suspect.
Our good shall arrive time enough at your heart.

[*Exit Grace*]

Poor fools that evermore take a green surfeit
Of the first-fruits of joys! Let a man but shake the tree,
How soon they'll hold up their laps to receive comfort!
The music that I struck made her soul dance.

Enter the Lady Widow Goldenfleece, with Sir Gilbert Lambstone, Master Pepperton, Master Overdone, suitors; after them the two old men Sir Oliver Twilight and Master Sunset, with their daughters Grace Twilight, Jane Sunset

Peace.
Here comes the lady widow, the late wife
To the deceased Sir Avarice Goldenfleece,
Second to none for usury and extortion,
As too well it appears on a poor gentleman,
One Master Low-water, from whose estate
He pulled that fleece that makes his widow weight.
Those are her suitors now, Sir Gilbert Lambstone,
Master Pepperton, Master Overdone.

WIDOW
Nay, good Sir Oliver Twilight, Master Sunset,
We'll trouble you no farther.

SUNSET *and* SIR OLIVER No trouble, sweet madam.

SIR GILBERT
We'll see the widow at home; it shall be our charge that.

WIDOW It shall be so indeed.
Thanks, good Sir Oliver, and to you both
I am indebted for those courtesies
That will ask me a long time to requite.

SIR OLIVER Ah, 'tis but your pleasant condition to give it out so, madam!

WIDOW
Mistress Grace and Mistress Jane, I wish you both
A fair contented fortune in your choices,
And that you happen right.

GRACE *and* JANE Thanks to you, good madam.

WIDOW
There's more in that word 'right' than you imagine.
I now repent, girls, a rash oath I took
When you were both infants, to conceal a secret.

GRACE What does't concern, good madam?

WIDOW
No, no; since you are both so well, 'tis well enough.
It must not be revealed. 'Tis now no more
Than like mistaking of one hand for t'other.
A happy time to you both.

GRACE *and* JANE The like to you, madam.

GRACE [*aside*]
I shall long much to have this riddle opened!

JANE [*aside*]
I would you were so kind to my poor kinswoman,
And the distressèd gentleman her husband,
Poor Master Low-water, who on ruin leans.
You keep this secret as you keep his means.

142 **kin to** like (quibbling on 'related to')
147 **pricking** spurring
151 **comforts** Grace means 'comforting news'; Sandfield understands 'sexual comforts'.
153 **sport'st with** are flippant about, joke about
utterance cannot perfect cannot be realized in speech
157 **Our good** (*a*) the good Philip and I intend (*b*) our merchandise
158 **green surfeit** i.e. (*a*) surfeit taken through eager inexperience (*b*) sickness caused by eating too much green fruit
161.1 ***Goldenfleece*** The name points to the wealth that the Widow's husband has filched (*fleeced*) from the Low-waters, and recalls the Greek myth of Jason's quest for the Golden Fleece, which he won with the help of the enchantress Medea.
161.2 ***Lambstone*** Suggests 'Lamb-stone', i.e. lamb's testicle, and so the character's virile lechery.
Pepperton He might be *peppered* in the sense 'infected with venereal disease'.
161.3 ***Overdone*** The name implies he is sexually exhausted.
161.4 ***Twilight . . . Sunset*** The names suggests their old age.
168 **He . . . fleece** See note to l. 161.1.
widow weight A variation of *widow right*, the part of a deceased husband's estate to which the widow has a right. The Widow has the financial load but not the right to it.
173 **see . . . home** i.e. escort the widow home
178 **condition** disposition
182 **you happen right** things turn out well for you

WIDOW Thanks, good Sir Oliver Twilight. Welcome, sweet Master Pepperton. Master Overdone, welcome.

Exeunt; manet Sir Oliver with Savourwit

SIR OLIVER
And goes the business well 'twixt those young lovers?

SAVOURWIT
Betwixt your son and Master Sunset's daughter
The line goes even, sir.

SIR OLIVER Good lad, I like thee.

SAVOURWIT
But, sir, there's no proportion, height, or evenness
Betwixt that equinoctial and your daughter.

SIR OLIVER
'Tis true, and I'm right glad on't.

SAVOURWIT Are you glad, sir,
There's no proportion in't?

SIR OLIVER Ay, marry am I, sir.
I can abide no word that ends in 'portion'.
I'll give her nothing.

SAVOURWIT Say you should not, sir—
As I'll ne'er urge your worship 'gainst your nature—
Is there no gentleman, think you, of worth and credit
Will open's bed to warm a naked maid?—
A hundred gallant fellows, and be glad
To be so set a-work. Virginity
Is no such cheap ware as you make account on
That it had need with portion be set off;
For that sets off a portion in these days.

SIR OLIVER Play on, sweet boy.
O, I could hear this music all day long
When there's no money to be parted from!
Strike on, good lad!

SAVOURWIT
Do not wise men and great often bestow
Ten thousand pound in jewels that lie by 'em?
If so, what jewel can lie by a man
More precious than a virgin? If none more precious,
Why should the pillow of a fool be graced
With that brave spirits which dearness have embraced?—
And then perhaps, ere the third spring come on,
Sends home your diamond cracked, the beauty gone,
And—more to know her, 'cause you shall not doubt her—
A number of poor sparks twinkling about her.

SIR OLIVER
Now thou play'st Dowland's 'Lachrimae' to thy master.

SAVOURWIT
But shall I dry your eyes with a merry jig now,
And make you look like sunshine in a shower?

SIR OLIVER
How, how, my honest boy, sweet Savourwit?

SAVOURWIT
Young Master Sandfield, gallant Master Sandfield—

SIR OLIVER
Ha, what of him?

SAVOURWIT Affects your daughter strangely.

SIR OLIVER
Brave Master Sandfield! Let me hug thy zeal
Unto thy master's house. Ha, Master Sandfield!
But he'll expect a portion.

SAVOURWIT Not a whit, sir,
As you may use the matter.

SIR OLIVER
Nay, an the matter fall into my using,
The devil a penny that he gets of me.

SAVOURWIT
He lies at the mercy of your lock and key, sir.
You may use him as you list.

SIR OLIVER
Sayst thou me so? Is he so far in doting?

SAVOURWIT Quite over head and ears, sir. Nay, more, he means to run mad and break his neck off some high steeple if he have her not.

SIR OLIVER Now bless the young gentleman's gristles! I hope to be a grandfather yet by 'em.

SAVOURWIT That may you, sir,
To, marry, a chopping girl with a plump buttock
Will hoist a farthingale at five years' old,
And call a man between eleven and twelve
To take part of a piece of mutton with her.

SIR OLIVER
Ha, precious wag! Hook him in finely, do.

SAVOURWIT
Make clear the way for him first; set the gull going.

SIR OLIVER
An ass, an ass; I'll quickly dash his wooing.

200 **line** verse, metre. Quibbles on the sense 'equatorial line,' anticipating *equinoctial*.
201 **proportion** (*a*) regular rhythm (*b*) due relation
height Implies (*a*) quality of poetic style (*b*) elevation of a heavenly body above the horizon.
202 **equinoctial** (*a*) celestial equator (a glance at Weatherwise's interest in astrology) (*b*) terrestrial equator (probably hinting that Weatherwise has a rotund figure)
217 **When...from** (referring to payment for musical entertainment in taverns)
218 **Strike** play
224 **which...embraced** i.e. that have been conjoined with high value (with quibbles on *dearness* as 'affection' and *embraced* in its sexual sense)
227 **more** the better
228 **sparks** gallants (playing on the sense 'jewels' or 'sparkles')
229 **Dowland's 'Lachrimae'** i.e. John Dowland's *Lachrimae, or Seven Tears* (1604), a music collection with seven pavans based on Dowland's melancholy song 'Flow my Tears'.
230–1 **But...shower** From the proverb 'to laugh and cry like rain and sunshine'.
238 **use the matter** take advantage of the situation
244 **over...ears** (proverbial)
247 **bless...gristles** (an alteration of *bless his bones* that picks up on *gristle* as 'youthful, delicate man' and as having a phallic overtone)
250 **chopping** healthy, strong
251 **farthingale** framework of hoops supporting a skirt, made of whalebone. A phallic innuendo is possible.
253 **take...mutton** i.e. partake in lovemaking
255 **gull** fool

SAVOURWIT
Why, now the clocks go right again. It must be a strange wit
That makes the wheels of youth and age so hit.
The one are dry, worn, rusty, furred, and soiled;
Love's wheels are glib, ever kept clean and oiled.
Exit

SIR OLIVER
I cannot choose but think of this good fortune.
That gallant Master Sandfield!

Enter Weatherwise [with his almanac]

WEATHERWISE [*aside*] Stay, stay, stay!
What comfort gives my almanac today?
Luck, I beseech thee!

[*He reads*]

'Good Days... Evil Days... June... July'. Speak a good word for me now, and I have her. Let me see. 'The fifth day, 'twixt hawk and buzzard. The sixth day, backward and forward.'—That was beastly to me, I remember.—'The seventh day, on a slippery pin. The eighth day, fire and tow. The ninth day, the market is marred.'—That's long of the hucksters, I warrant you. But now, the eleventh day. Luck, I beseech thee now, before I look into't! 'The eleventh day, against the hair'.—A pox on't, would that 'hair' had been left out! 'Against the hair'! That 'hair' will go nigh to choke me—had it been against anything but that, 'twould not have troubled me—because it lies cross i'th' way. Well, I'll try the fortune of a good face yet, though my almanac leave me i'th' sands.

SIR OLIVER [*aside*]
Such a match, too! I could not wish a better.

WEATHERWISE Mass, here he walks!—Save you, sweet Sir Oliver! Sir Oliver Twilight!

SIR OLIVER O, pray come to me a quarter of a year hence;
I have a little business now.

WEATHERWISE How, a quarter of a year hence? What, shall I come to you in September?

SIR OLIVER
Nor in November neither, good my friend.

WEATHERWISE You're not a mad knight; you will not let your daughter hang past August, will you? She'll drop down under tree then. She's no winter fruit, I assure you, if you think to put her in crust after Christmas!

SIR OLIVER
Sir, in a word, depart. My girl's not for you.
I gave you a drowsy promise in a dream,
But, broad awake now, I call't in again.
Have me commended to your wit. Farewell, sir.
[*Exit*]

WEATHERWISE Now the devil run away with you, and some lousy fiddler with your daughter! May Clerkenwell have the first cut of her, and Houndsditch pick the bones! I'll never leave the love of an open-hearted widow for a narrow-eyed maid again, go out of the roadway like an ass to leap over hedge and ditch. I'll fall into the beaten path again, and invite the widow home to a banquet. Let who list seek out new ways; I'll be at my journey's end before him.
My almanac told me true how I should fare:
Let no man think to speed against the hair. *Exit*

Enter Mistress Low-water Sc. 2

MISTRESS LOW-WATER
Is there no saving means, no help religious
For a distressèd gentlewoman to live by?
Has virtue no revènue? Who has all, then?
Is the world's lease from hell? The devil's head-landlord?
O, how was conscience, the right heir, put by?
Law would not do such an unrighteous deed,
Though with the fall of angels 't had been fee'd.
Where are our hopes in banks? Was honesty,

258 **hit** fall in with each other
259 **furred** encrusted
262.1 ***Weatherwise*** The name alludes to the character's interest in the predictions in almanacs (see Introduction).
266 **her** i.e. the Widow
266–77 **Let... way** Weatherwise's almanac has proverbial and sometimes cryptic mottoes for each day. Some derive from the 1611 almanac of Thomas Bretnor, which Middleton consulted.
267 **'twixt hawk and buzzard** From Bretnor: 'Beware the hawk and buzzard'.
267–8 **backward... remember** The motto suggests different coital techniques. *Backward* would be *beastly*.
269 **on... pin** From Bretnor.
pin peg
270 **tow** flax. 'Put not fire to tow' was proverbial.
the market is marred (proverbial)
271 **long of** because of
hucksters profiteers, middle-men, engrossers
272 **eleventh** Eleven was considered an unlucky number through its association with sin and death. Weatherwise evidently passes over the tenth day without reading it.
273 **against the hair** i.e. against the grain (proverbial). With a suggestion of 'adverse to the hair', taken up in *pox*: syphylis caused baldness.
hair Puns at ll. 275–8 on *hare*.
277 **cross i'th' way** To have a hare cross one's way was proverbially unlucky.
279 **i'th' sands** i.e. stuck in the quicksands. Proverbial; compare ll. 52–3 and note.
296–7 **the... daughter** Draws on the proverb 'The Devil rides on a fiddlestick'.
297 **Clerkenwell** A district of London known for thieves and prostitutes.
298 **cut** slice (as of a piece of meat). Also a euphemism for 'vulva'.
Houndsditch A London street with many second-hand clothes dealers. A *hound* would *pick the bones*.
299–300 **open-hearted... narrow-eyed** Suggests contrasting degrees of sexual generosity.
302 **banquet** repast of sweetmeats, fruit, and wine
306 **speed** be successful
against the hair against the grain
2.0.1 ***Low-water*** The name alludes to the low ebb in the couple's financial fortunes.
1 **saving** (*a*) redeeming, protecting (*b*) allowing accumulation of money
4 **Is... head-landlord** Inverts the common idea that life is loaned or tenanted from God.
7 **Though** even if
8 **banks** (*a*) sums of money (*b*) seats of justice

A younger sister without portion, left
No dowry in the Chamber beside wantonness?
O miserable orphan!
'Twixt two extremes runs there no blessèd mean,
No comfortable strain, that I may kiss it?
Must I to whoredom or to beggary lean,
My mind being sound? Is there no way to miss it?
Is't not injustice that a widow laughs,
And lays her mourning part upon a wife;
That she should have the garment, I the heart?
My wealth her husband left her, and me her grief.
Yet, stood all miseries in their loathèd'st forms
On this hand of me, thick like a foul mist,
And here the bright enticements of the world
In clearest colours, flattery, and advancement,
And all the bastard glories this frame jets in,
Horror nor splendour, shadows fair nor foul,
Should force me shame my husband, wound my soul.

Enter Mistress Jane, Sunset's daughter

Cousin, you're welcome. This is kindly done of you
To visit the despised.

JANE I hope not so, coz.
The want of means cannot make you despised.
Love, not by wealth, but by desert is prized.

MISTRESS LOW-WATER
You're pleased to help it well, coz.

JANE I am come to you,
Beside my visitation, to request you
To lay your wit to mine, which is but simple,
And help me to untie a few dark words
Made up in knots—they're of the widow's knitting,
That ties all sure—for my wit has not strength
Nor cunning to unloose 'em.

MISTRESS LOW-WATER Good, what are they?—
Though there be little comfort of my help.

JANE
She wished Sir Oliver's daughter and myself
Good fortune in our choices, and repented her
Of a rash oath she took when we were both infants
A secret to conceal; but since all's well,
She holds it best to keep it unrevealed.
Now what this is, heaven knows.

MISTRESS LOW-WATER Nor can I guess.
The course of her whole life, and her dead husband's,
Was ever full of such dishonest riddles
To keep right heirs from knowledge of their own.
And now I'm put i'th' mind on't, I believe
It was some prize of land or money given
By some departing friend upon their deathbed,
Perhaps to yourself; and Sir Oliver's daughter
May wrongfully enjoy it, and she hired—
For she was but an hireling in those days—
To keep the injury secret.

JANE The most likeliest
That ever you could think on!

MISTRESS LOW-WATER Is it not?

JANE
Sure, coz, I think you have untied the knot.
My thoughts lie at more ease. As in all other things,
In this I thank your help; and may you live
To conquer your own troubles and cross ends,
As you are ready to supply your friends.

MISTRESS LOW-WATER
I thank you for the kind truth of your heart,
In which I flourish when all means depart.

[*Jane begins to leave*]

Sure in that oath of hers there sleeps some wrong
Done to my kinswoman.

Enter Footman

JANE Who'd you speak withal?

FOOTMAN
The gentlewoman of this house, forsooth.

JANE
Whose footman are you?

FOOTMAN One Sir Gilbert Lambstone's.

JANE
Sir Gilbert Lambstone's!—There my cousin walks.

FOOTMAN
Thank your good worship. [*Exit Jane*]

MISTRESS LOW-WATER How now, whence are you?

FOOTMAN [*giving her a letter*]
This letter will make known.

MISTRESS LOW-WATER Whence comes it, sir?

FOOTMAN
From the knight my master, Sir Gilbert Lambstone.

MISTRESS LOW-WATER Return't; I'll receive none on't.

[*She throws down the letter and turns away*]

FOOTMAN [*aside*] There it must lie then. I were as good run to Tyburn afoot and hang myself at mine own charges as carry it back again. *Exit*

MISTRESS LOW-WATER
Life, had he not his answer? What strange impudence
Governs in man when lust is lord of him!
Thinks he me mad? 'cause I have no monies on earth
That I'll go forfeit my estate in heaven,
And live eternal beggar? He shall pardon me.
That's my soul's jointure; I'll starve ere I sell that.
O, is he gone, and left the letter here?

10 **Chamber** City of London Treasury (where orphans' inheritances were deposited until they came of age)
13 **strain** (*a*) kind, class, breed (*b*) melody (*comfortable* to the voice)
15 **My ... sound** i.e. despite my mind being sound
18 **heart** vital centre, feelings (of *grief*, l. 19)
20 **stood all miseries** even if all miseries stood
24 **bastard** i.e. false (but also a glance at the consequences of extramarital sex)
this frame i.e. the world
jets struts
25 **shadows ... foul** i.e. fair false appearances or foul dark shapes
26 **soul** Rhymes with *foul*.
32 **Beside my visitation** i.e. apart from my simple desire to visit you. *Visitation* has connotations of a charitable visit to the sick or needy.
59 **cross** thwarted
73 **Tyburn** (the place of execution by hanging)

Yet I will read it, more to hate the writer.
[*She picks it up and reads*]
'Mistress Low-water,
If you desire to understand your own comfort, hear me out ere you refuse me. I'm in the way now to double the yearly means that first I offered you; and, to stir you more to me, I'll empty your enemy's bags to maintain you; for the rich widow the Lady Goldenfleece, to whom I have been a longer suitor than you a long adversary, hath given me so much encouragement lately insomuch that I am perfectly assured the next meeting strikes the bargain. The happiness that follows this 'twere idle to inform you of. Only consent to my desires, and the widow's notch shall lie open to you. Thus much to your heart I know you're wise. Farewell.
Thy friend to his power,
And another's,
Gilbert Lambstone.'
In this poor brief what volumes has he thrust
Of treacherous perjury and adulterous lust!
So foul a monster does this wrong appear
That I give pity to mine enemy here.
What a most fearful love reigns in some hearts,
That dare oppose all judgement to get means,
And wed rich widows only to keep queans.
What a strange path he takes to my affection,
And thinks't the nearest way—'twill never be—
Goes through mine enemy's ground to come to me.
This letter is most welcome. I repent now
That my last anger threw thee at my feet.
My bosom shall receive thee.
[*She puts the letter in her bosom*]
Enter Sir Gilbert Lambstone

SIR GILBERT [*aside*] 'Tis good policy, too,
To keep one that so mortally hates the widow.
She'll have more care to keep it close herself;
And look what wind her revenge goes withal,
The self-same gale whisks up the sails of love.
I shall loose much good sport by that.—Now, my sweet mistress!

MISTRESS LOW-WATER
Sir Gilbert! You change suits oft; you were here
In black but lately.

SIR GILBERT My mind ne'er shifts though.

MISTRESS LOW-WATER [*aside*] A foul mind the whilst.—
But sure, sir, this is but a dissembling glass
You sent before you. 'Tis not possible
Your heart should follow your hand.

SIR GILBERT Then may both perish!

MISTRESS LOW-WATER
Do not wish that so soon, sir. Can you make
A three-months' love to a rich widow's bed,
And lay her pillow under a quean's head?
I know you can't, howe'er you may dissemble't.
You have a heart brought up better.

SIR GILBERT Faith, you wrong me in't.
You shall not find it so. I do protest to thee,
I will be lord of all my promises,
And ere't be long thou shalt but turn a key
And find 'em in thy coffer; for my love
In matching with the widow is but policy
To strengthen my estate and make me able
To set off all thy kisses with rewards,
That the worst weather our delights behold,
It may hail pearl and shower the widow's gold.

MISTRESS LOW-WATER
You talk of a brave world, sir.

SIR GILBERT 'Twill seem better
When golden happiness breaks forth itself
Out of the east port of the widow's chamber.

MISTRESS LOW-WATER
And here it sets.

SIR GILBERT Here shall the down-fall be.
Her wealth shall rise from her, and set in thee.

MISTRESS LOW-WATER
You men have th'art to overcome poor women.
Pray give my thoughts the freedom of one day,
And all the rest take you.

SIR GILBERT
I straight obey. [*Aside*] This bird's my own.
Exit

MISTRESS LOW-WATER
There is no happiness but has her season
Wherein the brightness of her virtue shines.
The husk falls off in time that long shuts up
The fruit in a dark prison; so sweeps by
The cloud of miseries from wretches' eyes,
That yet, though fall'n, at length they see to rise.
The secret powers work wondrously, and duly.
Enter Master Low-water

MASTER LOW-WATER
Why, how now, Kate?

85 **in the way** disposed
94 **notch** score, i.e. financial account (with a sexual quibble, playing on the common figuration of a woman's sex organs as a hidden treasure, and perhaps anticipating Mistress Low-water's disguise as a male suitor to the Widow)
95 **heart** desires (both financial and amorous)
96 **to** to the extent of
99 **brief** summary document
thrust crammed, insinuated
105 **queans** whores
114 **look what** whatever
116 **loose** set loose
118 **In black** (in fellow mourning with the Widow)
121 **this** i.e. the letter
125 **love** suit
126 **her pillow** i.e. what you have won from her bed; her money
quean's whore's
131–2 **turn ... coffer** There may be a suggestion of sexual penetration that clarifies the cost to Mistress Low-water.
138 **brave** splendid
139 **golden happiness** i.e. the Widow's money; also sexual bliss and even childbirth (both sustained in *breaks forth*, and see next notes)
140 **port** i.e. the figurative 'gateway' of both the sun's rising and the Widow's vagina
chamber (*a*) bedroom (*b*) vagina
146 **There ... season** From the proverb 'everything in its season'.
147 **virtue** good quality, efficacy

MISTRESS LOW-WATER O, are you come, sir? Husband,
Wake, wake, and let not patience keep thee poor.
Rouse up thy spirit from this falling slumber.
Make thy distress seem but a weeping dream,
And this the opening morning of thy comforts.
Wipe the salt dew off from thy careful eyes,
And drink a draught of gladness next thy heart
T'expel the infection of all poisonous sorrows.

MASTER LOW-WATER
You turn me past my senses.

MISTRESS LOW-WATER Will you but second
The purpose I intend, I'll be first forward.
I crave no more of thee but a following spirit.
Will you but grant me that?

MASTER LOW-WATER Why, what's the business
That should transport thee thus?

MISTRESS LOW-WATER Hope of much good,
No fear of the least ill. Take that to comfort thee.

MASTER LOW-WATER
Yea?

MISTRESS LOW-WATER
Sleep not on't; this is no slumbering business.
'Tis like the sweating sickness: I must keep
Your eyes still 'wake; you're gone if once you sleep.

MASTER LOW-WATER
I will not rest, then, till thou hast thy wishes.

MISTRESS LOW-WATER [*giving him the letter*]
Peruse this love-paper as you go.

MASTER LOW-WATER A letter? *Exeunt*

Sc. 3 *Enter Sir Oliver Twilight, with Master Sandfield, and Savourwit*

SIR OLIVER
Good Master Sandfield, for the great affection
You bear toward my girl, I am well pleased
You should enjoy her beauty. Heaven forbid, sir,
That I should cast away a proper gentleman,
So far in love, with a sour mood or so.
No, no, I'll not die guilty of a lover's neck-cracking.
Marry, as for portion, there I leave you, sir,
To the mercy of your destiny again;
I'll have no hand in that.

SANDFIELD Faith, something, sir,
Be't but t'express your love.

SIR OLIVER I have no desire, sir,
To express my love that way, and so rest satisfied.
I pray take heed in urging, that too much
You draw not my love from me.

SANDFIELD Fates foresee, sir.

SIR OLIVER
Faith, then you may go seek out a high steeple
Or a deep water; there's no saving of you.

SAVOURWIT [*aside*]
How naturally he plays upon himself!

SIR OLIVER
Marry, if a wedding dinner, as I told you,
And three years' board, well lodged in mine house,
And eating, drinking, and a sleeping portion
May give you satisfaction, I am your man, sir;
Seek out no other.

SANDFIELD I am content to embrace it, sir,
Rather than hazard languishment or ruin.

SIR OLIVER
I love thee for thy wisdom. Such a son-in-law
Will cheer a father's heart. Welcome, sweet Master Sandfield.
Enter Philip
Whither away, Philip?

PHILIP To visit my love, sir,
Old Master Sunset's daughter.

SIR OLIVER That's my Philip!
[*To Philip and Sandfield*] Ply't hard, my good boys both; put 'em to't finely.
One day, one dinner, and one house shall join you.

PHILIP *and* SANDFIELD
That's our desire, sir. *Exeunt Philip and Sandfield*

SIR OLIVER Pish! Come hither, Savourwit.
Observe my son, and bring me word, sweet boy,
Whether h'as a speeding wit or no in wooing.

SAVOURWIT
That will I, sir. [*Aside*] That your own eyes might tell ye.
I think it speedy your girl has a round belly. *Exit*

SIR OLIVER
How soon the comfortable shine of joy
Breaks through a cloud of grief!
The tears that I let fall for my dead wife
Are dried up with the beams of my girl's fortunes.
Her life, her death, and her ten years' distress
Are e'en forgot with me. The love and care
That I owed her, her daughter shows it all.
It can but be bestowed, and there 'tis well.
Enter Servant
How now, what news?

SERVANT
There's a Dutch merchant, sir, that's now come over,
Desires some conference with you.

SIR OLIVER How, a Dutch merchant?

165 **transport** (*a*) enrapture (*b*) move (as suggested by l. 162)
168 **the sweating sickness** (a fever causing profuse sweating and often quickly fatal)
3.6 **a... neck-cracking** See 1.244–6.
13 **Fates foresee** provide against disasters
16 **plays upon** (like a musical instrument)
19 **eating... portion** dowry of food, drink, and sleeping quarters
31 **speeding** successful
33 **speedy** (*a*) successful (*b*) soon
34 **comfortable** comforting
39 **e'en** entirely
40 **shows it all** i.e. manifests all the benefit of it. *Shows* might also suggest elided *she owes*, 'she possesses'.

Pray send him in to me. [*Exit Servant*]
What news with him, trow?
Enter Dutch Merchant, with a little Dutch Boy in great slops

DUTCH MERCHANT
Sir Oliver Twilight?

SIR OLIVER That's my name indeed, sir.
I pray be covered, sir. You're very welcome.

DUTCH MERCHANT
This is my business, sir: I took into my charge
A few words to deliver to yourself
From a dear friend of yours that wonders strangely
At your unkind neglect.

SIR OLIVER Indeed? What might he be, sir?

DUTCH MERCHANT Nay, you're i'th' wrong gender now.
'Tis that distressèd lady your good wife, sir.

SIR OLIVER
What say you, sir, my wife?

DUTCH MERCHANT Yes, sir, your wife.
This strangeness now of yours seems more to harden
Th'uncharitable neglect she taxed you for.

SIR OLIVER
Pray give me leave, sir: is my wife alive?

DUTCH MERCHANT
Came any news to you, sir, to th' contrary?

SIR OLIVER
Yes, by my faith, did there.

DUTCH MERCHANT Pray, how long since, sir?

SIR OLIVER
'Tis now some ten weeks.

DUTCH MERCHANT Faith, within this month, sir,
I saw her talk and eat; and those, in our calendar,
Are signs of life and health.

SIR OLIVER Mass, so they are in ours.

DUTCH MERCHANT
And these were the last words her passion threw me:
'No grief', quoth she, 'sits to my heart so close
As his unkindness and my daughter's loss.'

SIR OLIVER
You make me weep, and wonder, for I swear
I sent her ransom, and that daughter's here.

DUTCH MERCHANT
Here? That will come well to lighten her of one grief.
I long to see her for the piteous moan
Her mother made for her.

SIR OLIVER That shall you, sir.—
Within there!
[*Enter Servant*]

SERVANT Sir.

SIR OLIVER Call down my daughter.

SERVANT Yes, sir.
[*Exit*]

SIR OLIVER
Here's strange boggling! I tell you, sir,
Those that I put in trust were near me too.
A man would think they should not juggle with me.
My own son and my servant, no worse people, sir.

DUTCH MERCHANT
And yet oft-times, sir, what worse knave to a man
Than he that eats his meat?

SIR OLIVER Troth, you say true, sir.
I sent 'em simply, and that news they brought
My wife had left the world; and with that son
I sent to her, this brought his sister home.
Enter Grace
Look you, sir, this is she.

DUTCH MERCHANT If my eye sin not, sir,
Or misty error falsify the glass,
I saw that face at Antwerp in an inn
When I set forth first to fetch home this boy.

SIR OLIVER
How, in an inn?

GRACE [*aside*] O, I am betrayed, I fear.

DUTCH MERCHANT
How do you, young mistress?

GRACE Your eyes wrong your tongue, sir,
And makes you sin in both. I am not she.

DUTCH MERCHANT
No? Then I never saw face twice. Sir Oliver Twilight,
I tell you my free thoughts. I fear you're blinded.
I do not like this story. I doubt much
The sister is as false as the dead mother.

SIR OLIVER
Yea? Say you so, sir? I see nothing lets me
But to doubt so too, then.
[*To Grace*] So, to your chamber; we have done with you.

GRACE [*aside*]
I would be glad you had.—Here's a strange storm!
Sift it out well, sir. Till anon I leave you, sir. [*Exit*]

DUTCH MERCHANT
Business commands me hence, but as a pledge
Of my return I'll leave my little son with you,
Who yet takes little pleasure in this country,
'Cause he can speak no English; all Dutch he.

SIR OLIVER
A fine boy. He's welcome, sir, to me.

DUTCH MERCHANT [*to the Boy*]
Where's your leg and your thanks to the gentleman?

45 **trow** I wonder
45.2 ***slops*** baggy trousers
47 **be covered** put your hat on
57 **taxed** censured
62 **calendar** almanac
64 **passion** distress, anguish
65 **close** Rhymes with *loss*.
67 **swear** Rhymes with *here*.
73 **boggling** playing fast and loose
74 **near** closely related to
79 **simply** i.e. (*a*) trustingly, or (*b*) on their own
80 **with** as well as
81 **this** i.e. the sending of Philip
90 **free thoughts** Proverbially, 'thought is free'.
91 **doubt** suspect
93 **lets** hinders

Waar is je nijgen en je dank-je?
DUTCH BOY [*to Sir Oliver*]
Ik dank je voor Uw Edelman vriendelijkheid.
SIR OLIVER What says he, sir?
DUTCH MERCHANT He thanks you for your kindness.
SIR OLIVER Pretty knave!
DUTCH MERCHANT
Had not some business held me by the way,
This news had come to your ear ten days ago.
SIR OLIVER
It comes too soon now, methinks. I'm your debtor.
DUTCH MERCHANT
But I could wish it, sir, for better ware.
SIR OLIVER
We must not be our own choosers in our fortunes.
Exit Dutch Merchant
Here's a cold pie to breakfast: wife alive,
The daughter doubtful, and the money spent!
How am I juggled withal?
Enter Savourwit
SAVOURWIT It hits, i'faith, sir.
The work goes even.
SIR OLIVER O, come, come, come! Are you come, sir?
SAVOURWIT
Life, what's the matter now?
SIR OLIVER There's a new reckoning come in since.
SAVOURWIT [*aside*]
Pox on't, I thought all had been paid.
I can't abide these after-reckonings.
SIR OLIVER
I pray come near, sir; let's be acquainted with you.
You're bold enough abroad with my purse, sir.
SAVOURWIT
No more than beseems manners and good use, sir.
SIR OLIVER
Did not you bring me word some ten weeks since
My wife was dead?
SAVOURWIT Yes, true, sir, very true, sir.
SIR OLIVER
Pray stay, and take my horse along with you.
And, with the ransom that I sent for her,
That you redeemed my daughter?
SAVOURWIT Right as can be, sir.
I never found your worship in a false tale yet.
SIR OLIVER
I thank you for your good word, sir; but I'm like
To find your worship now in two at once.
SAVOURWIT
I should be sorry to hear that.
SIR OLIVER I believe you, sir.
Within this month my wife was sure alive—
There's six weeks bated of your ten-weeks' lie—
As has been credibly reported to me
By a Dutch merchant, father to that boy,
But now come over, and the words scarce cold.
SAVOURWIT [*aside*]
O strange! [*To Sir Oliver*] 'Tis a most rank untruth.
Where is he, sir?
SIR OLIVER
He will not be long absent.
SAVOURWIT [*aside*] All's confounded.
[*To Sir Oliver*] If he were here, I'll tell him to his face, sir,
He wears a double tongue that's Dutch and English.
Will the boy say't?
SIR OLIVER 'Las, he can speak no English.
SAVOURWIT [*aside*]
All the better. I'll gabble something to him.—
Hoyste kaloiste, kalooskin ee vou, dar sune, alla gaskin?
DUTCH BOY *Ik weet niet wat hij zegt.—Ik en verstaan U niet.*
SAVOURWIT
Why, la, I thought as much!
SIR OLIVER What says the boy?
SAVOURWIT He says his father is troubled with an imperfection at one time of the moon, and talks like a madman.
SIR OLIVER
What, does the boy say so?
SAVOURWIT I knew there was somewhat in't.
Your wife alive! Will you believe all tales, sir?
SIR OLIVER
Nay, more, sir: he told me he saw this wench
Which you brought home at Antwerp in an inn;
Tells me I'm plainly cozened of all hands:
'Tis not my daughter neither.
SAVOURWIT [*aside*] All's broke out.
[*To Sir Oliver*] How, not your daughter, sir? I must to't again.
[*To the Boy*] *Quisquinikin sadlamare, alla pisse kickin sows-clows,*
Hoff tofte le cumber shaw, bouns bus boxsceeno.
DUTCH BOY *Ik antwoord nooit geen klappende hik. Ik denk uit zijn zinnen.*

104 ***Waar . . . dank-je*** 'Where is your bow and your thank-you'
105 ***Ik . . . vriendelijkheid*** 'I thank you for your kindness'. *Edelman* is literally 'nobleman'; this deferential form of address was antiquated.
108 **knave** fellow, rogue (with no opprobium)
112 **for** exchanged for
114 **cold pie to breakfast** cold comfort (proverbial)
116 **hits** succeeds
126 **stay** wait
take . . . you i.e don't gallop off ahead of me. From proverbial 'take me with you'.
134 **bated** deducted
145 ***Ik weet . . . niet*** 'I don't know what he says.—I understand you not'
153 **Antwerp** (centre of the English wool trade in Flanders)
154 **of all hands** on all sides
159–60 ***Ik antwoord . . . zinnen*** 'I never answer beating hiccups [i.e. nonsense]. I think [he is] out of his mind'

SAVOURWIT O, *zein zennon*! Aha, I thought how 'twould prove i'th' end. The boy says they never came near Antwerp—a quite contrary way, round about by Parma.

SIR OLIVER What's the same '*zein zennon*'?

SAVOURWIT That is, he saw no such wench in an inn. 'Tis well I came in such happy time to get it out of the boy before his father returned again. Pray be wary, sir; the world's subtle. Come and pretend a charitable business in policy, and work out a piece of money on you!

SIR OLIVER Mass, art advised of that?

SAVOURWIT The age is cunning, sir; beside, a Dutchman will live upon any ground, and work butter out of a thistle.

SIR OLIVER
Troth, thou sayst true in that. They're the best thrivers
In turnips, artichokes, and cabbages;
Our English are not like them.

SAVOURWIT O, fie, no, sir!

SIR OLIVER
Ask him from whence they came, when they came hither.

SAVOURWIT That I will sir.—*Cullvaron lagooso, lageen, lagan, rufft, punkatee?*

DUTCH BOY *Neem U eige' te kakk'*.

SAVOURWIT What, what? I cannot blame him then.

SIR OLIVER What says he to thee?

SAVOURWIT The poor boy blushes for him. He tells me his father came from making merry with certain of his countrymen, and he's a little steeped in English beer; there's no heed to be taken of his tongue now.

SIR OLIVER Hoyda! How com'st thou by all this? I heard him speak but three words to thee.

SAVOURWIT O, sir, the Dutch is a very wide language; you shall have ten English words even for one. As for example, *gullder-goose*: there's a word for you, master.

SIR OLIVER
Why, what's that same *gullder-goose*?

SAVOURWIT
'How do you and all your generation?'

SIR OLIVER
Why, 'tis impossible! How prove you that, sir?

SAVOURWIT 'Tis thus distinguished, sir: gull, 'how do you'; der, 'and'; goose, 'your generation'.

SIR OLIVER
'Tis a most saucy language. How cam'st thou by't?

SAVOURWIT
I was brought up to London in an eel-ship;
There was the place I caught it first by th' tail.—
[*Aside*] I shall be tripped anon. Pox, would I were gone!—
I'll go seek out your son, sir; you shall hear
What thunder he'll bring with him.

SIR OLIVER Do, do, Savourwit.
I'll have you all face to face.

SAVOURWIT [*aside*] Cuds me!—What else, sir?—
An you take me so near the net again,
I'll give you leave to squat me. I have scaped fairly!
We are undone in Dutch; all our three-months' roguery
Is now come over in a butter firkin. *Exit*

SIR OLIVER
Never was man so tossed between two tales!
I know not which to take, not which to trust.
The boy here is the likeliest to tell truth,
Because the world's corruption is not yet
At full years in him. Sure he cannot know
What deceit means; 'tis English yet to him.
And when I think again, why should the father
Dissemble for no profit? He gets none,
Whate'er he hopes for, and I think he hopes not.
The man's in a good case, being old and weary,
He dares not lean his arm on his son's shoulder
For fear he lie i'th' dirt, but must be rather
Beholding to a stranger for his prop.

Enter Dutch Merchant

DUTCH MERCHANT
I make bold once again, sir, for a boy here.

SIR OLIVER
O, sir, you're welcome. Pray resolve me one thing, sir:
Did you within this month with your own eyes
See my wife living?

DUTCH MERCHANT I ne'er borrowed any.
Why should you move that question, sir? Dissembling
Is no part of my living.

SIR OLIVER I have reason
To urge it so far, sir—pray be not angry though—
Because my man was here since your departure,
Withstands all stiffly, and, to make it clearer,

163 **Parma** In north Italy: an implausible detour.
170 **Mass** (an oath: 'by the mass')
art advised of have you considered
172–3 **work ... thistle** productively farm land on which only thistles grow. Comically varies the proverb 'To wring milk from a stone' with a product associated with the Dutch (see l. 207).
180 ***Neem ... kakk'*** 'Make shit of yourself'; i.e. make a fool of yourself
187 **Hoyda** (an exclamation of surprise)
191 ***gullder-goose*** Suggests *gull the goose*, slang for 'cheat the idiot', or *guilder-goose*, from the Dutch coin guilder, 'fool with his money'.
193 **generation** offspring
197 **saucy** (*a*) cheeky (because of the imputations of *gullder-goose*) (*b*) savoury, sauce-like (suggested by *goose* as food)
198 **eel-ship** The Dutch were reputed to be fond of eels.
199 **by th' tail** (as eels might be caught; with a possible pun on *tale*, as in l. 207)
202 **thunder** i.e. angry words
203 **Cuds me** (an expletive; literally 'God's me')
204–5 **An ... squat me** Savourwit pictures himself as a tennis ball.
205 **squat** slam down, smash (as in the tennis stroke)
207 **come over** i.e. shipped to England
butter firkin small cask of butter (as a typical import from Holland, and perhaps suggestive of the Merchant's appearance)
213 **English** i.e. foreign
217 **in a good case** well off (ironic)
218 **He** i.e. who
220 **Beholding** beholden

Questioned your boy in Dutch, who, as he told me,
Returned this answer first to him: that you
Had imperfection at one time o'th' moon,
Which made you talk so strangely.

DUTCH MERCHANT How, how's this?—
Zeg, jongen, ik ben gekweld met een dolligheid, een ontijd van de maan, en koeterwalend?

DUTCH BOY *Wee ik! Hij liegt in zijn bakkes die't zegt.*

DUTCH MERCHANT
Why, la you, sir! Here's no such thing.
He says he lies in's throat that says it.

SIR OLIVER
Then the rogue lies in's throat, for he told me so,
And that the boy should answer at next question
That you ne'er saw this wench, nor came near
Antwerp.

DUTCH MERCHANT Ten thousand devils!—*Zei hij U ook niet, jongen, dat we niet kijf bij Antwerpen vandaan komen, noch zien de dochter daar?*

DUTCH BOY *Ik heb hem geen zulke dingen gezegd. Hij is een schelm, een rabauw!*

DUTCH MERCHANT He says he told him no such matter; he's a knave and a rascal.

SIR OLIVER Why, how am I abused! Pray tell me one thing:
What's *gullder-goose* in Dutch?

DUTCH MERCHANT How, *gullder-goose*? There's no such thing in Dutch; it may be 'an ass' in English.

SIR OLIVER Hoyda! Then am I that ass in plain English. I am grossly cozened, most inconsiderately.
Pray let my house receive you for one night,
That I may quit these rascals, I beseech you, sir.

DUTCH MERCHANT
If that may stead you, sir, I'll not refuse you.

SIR OLIVER A thousand thanks, and welcome!—
On whom can fortune more spit out her foam?
Worked on abroad, and played upon at home!

Exeunt

Sc. 4

Enter Weatherwise the gull, meeting the Clown and one or two servants bringing out a table [*with twelve trenchers*]

WEATHERWISE So, set the table ready. The widow's i'th' next room, looking upon my clock with the days and the months and the change of the moon. I'll fetch her in presently. [*Exit*]

CLOWN She's not so mad to be fetched in with the moon, I warrant you. A man must go roundlier to work with a widow than to woo her with the hand of a dial, or to stir up her blood with the striking part of a clock. I should ne'er stand to show her such things in chamber.

Exeunt

Enter Weatherwise, with the Widow, Sir Gilbert Lambstone, Master Pepperton, Master Overdone

WEATHERWISE Welcome, sweet widow, to a bachelor's house here. A single man I, but for two or three maids that I keep.

WIDOW Why, are you double with them then?

WEATHERWISE An exceeding good mourning wit! Women are wiser than ever they were, since they wore doublets. You must think, sweet widow, if a man keep maids they're under his subjection.

WIDOW That's most true, sir.

WEATHERWISE They have no reason to have a lock but the master must have a key to't.

WIDOW To him, Sir Gilbert; he fights with me at a wrong weapon now.

[*The Widow and Sir Gilbert talk apart*]

WEATHERWISE [*aside*]
Nay, an Sir Gilbert strike, my weapon falls.
I fear no thrust but his. Here are more shooters,
But they have shot two arrows without heads;
They cannot stick i'th' butt yet. Hold out, knight,
And I'll cleave the black pin in th' midst o'th' white.

Exit

WIDOW [*to Sir Gilbert*] Nay, and he led me into a closet, sir, where he showed me diet drinks for several months, as scurvygrass for April, clarified whey for June, and the like.

SIR GILBERT O madam, he is a most necessary property, an't be but to save our credit ten pound in a banquet.

WIDOW Go, you're a wag, Sir Gilbert!

234–5 ***Zeg . . . koeterwalend?*** 'Tell me, boy, I, am I tortured with a madness, a bad time of the moon, and raving?'

236 ***Wee . . . zegt*** 'Woe is me! He lies in his face that says it'

238 **lies in's throat** (proverbial)

242–4 ***Zei . . . daar?*** 'Didn't he tell you also, boy, that we certainly did not then come from Antwerp, nor saw the daughter there?' The sense required is 'Didn't you tell him . . .'.

245–6 ***Ik . . . rabauw*** 'I have said no such thing to him. He is a rogue and a rascal'

252 **an . . . English** See note to l. 191.

256 **quit** requite

257 **stead** help

4.5 **fetched in** (*a*) brought in (*b*) taken in, cheated

with the moon i.e. when the moon changes (with an allusion to menstruation)

6 **roundlier** more thoroughly

8 **the . . . clock** *Hand* and *striking part of a clock* have phallic innuendos, and *dial* suggests 'vulva'.

9 **stand** (*a*) put up with (*b*) have an erection

chamber (*a*) private room (*b*) vagina

13 **are you double with** (*a*) do you have two of (*b*) do you double up with

15 **wore doublets** A doublet was a man's body-garment. For women scandalously cross-dressing, see *Roaring Girl*. *Doublets* also plays on *double*, l. 13, and so suggests promiscuity.

19–20 **They . . . to't** (with a coital implication, developed in ll. 21–7)

24 **shooters** (pronounced the same as *suitors*)

25–6 **they . . . yet** Implies that Pepperton and Overdone are incapable of having an erection. *Butt* ('mark for archery practice') suggests 'vulva' or 'buttocks'.

27 **the . . . white** i.e. the peg in the middle of the inner white circle of the archer's target. 'Cleave the pin' was proverbial.

28 **he** i.e. Weatherwise

29 **diet** i.e. medicinal

30 **scurvygrass** (a plant believed effective against scurvy)

32 **property** means to an end, tool

34 **wag** mischievous joker

SIR GILBERT How many there be in the world of his fortunes that prick their own calves with briers to make an easy passage for others, or, like a toiling usurer, sets his son a-horseback in cloth-of-gold breeches, while he himself goes to th' devil a-foot in a pair of old strossers!
But shall I give a more familiar sign?
His are the sweetmeats, but the kisses mine.
[*He kisses her*]

OVERDONE [*aside*] Excellent! A pox o' your fortune!

PEPPERTON [*to Overdone*] Saucy courting has brought all modest wooing clean out of fashion. You shall have few maids nowadays got without rough handling, all the town's so used to't; and most commonly too they're joined before they're married, because they'll be sure to be fast enough.

OVERDONE
Sir, since he strives t'oppose himself against us,
Let's so combine our friendships in our straits,
By all means graceful to assist each other.
For I protest it shall as much glad me
To see your happiness and his disgrace
As if the wealth were mine, the love, the place.

PEPPERTON
And with the like faith I reward your friendship.
I'll break the bawdy ranks of his discourse
And scatter his libidinous whispers straight.—
Madam!

WIDOW How cheer you, gentlemen?

SIR GILBERT [*aside*] Pox on 'em!
They waked me out of a fine sleep; three minutes
Had fastened all the treasure in mine arms.

PEPPERTON
You took no note of this conceit, it seems, madam.

WIDOW
Twelve trenchers, upon every one a month:
January, February, March, April—

PEPPERTON
Ay, and their posies under 'em.

WIDOW
Pray what says May? She's the spring lady.
[*She reads*]
'Now gallant May in her array
Doth make the field pleasant and gay.'

OVERDONE [*reading*]
'This month of June use clarified whey
Boiled with cold herbs, and drink alway.'

WIDOW
'Drink't all away', he should say.

PEPPERTON
'Twere much better indeed, and wholesomer for his liver.

SIR GILBERT
September's a good one here, madam.

WIDOW
O, have you chose your month? Let's hear't, Sir Gilbert!

SIR GILBERT [*reading*]
'Now mayst thou physics safely take,
And bleed and bathe for thy health's sake.
Eat figs and grapes and spicery,
For to refresh thy members dry.'

WIDOW Thus it is still when a man's simple meaning lights among wantons. How many honest words have suffered corruption since Chaucer's days? A virgin would speak those words then that a very midwife would blush to hear now, if she have but so much blood left to make up an ounce of grace. And who is this long on but such wags as you, that use your words like your wenches? You cannot let 'em pass honestly by you but you must still have a flirt at 'em.

PEPPERTON You have paid some of us home, madam.

Enter Weatherwise

WEATHERWISE [*aside*] If conceit will strike this stroke, have at the widow's plumb-tree! I'll put 'em down all for a banquet.—Widow and gentlemen, my friends and servants, I make you wait long here for a bachelor's pittance.

WIDOW O, sir, you're pleased to be modest.

WEATHERWISE No, by my troth, widow; you shall find it otherwise.

Strike music. Enter [*the Clown and servants with the*] *banquet, and six of Weatherwise's tenants with the twelve signs, made like banqueting-stuff,* [*in order:*] *Aries, Taurus, Gemini, Cancer, Leo,*

38 **cloth-of-gold** cloth interwoven with gold thread
39 **strossers** trousers
48 **fast** (*a*) firmly *joined* (*b*) quick
56–7 **break...ranks...scatter** (military metaphor)
61 **conceit** ingenious contrivance
64 **posies** epigrams, mottoes
66–9 **Now...alway** Both posies are from the 1611 almanac of Jeffrey Neve.
68 **clarified whey** (drunk as a health remedy)
69 **alway** always. Needed for rhyme, but already archaic; hence the Widow's emendation. Neve supports Weatherwise's reading.
74–7 **Now...dry** Quoted word-for-word from Neve, except that Neve reads 'physic'.
74 **physics** medicines
75 **bleed** let blood
77 **members** (*a*) the parts of the body (the 'simple' meaning) (*b*) the penis.
78–9 **Thus...wantons** The suitors have responded to the sexual meaning.
79 **wantons** i.e. people with sex on the brain
80 **Chaucer's days** Seen as a time when language was pure; equivocal because Chaucer himself was a bawdy poet.
81 **midwife** Seen as sexually knowledgeable and so without the *grace* of innocence, and perhaps also as old and so with little blood in her veins.
83 **ounce of grace** The amount of blood needed to blush is seen as a minimal sign of *grace*.
long on because of
86 **flirt** (*a*) stroke of wit (*b*) flirtation
87 **home** Said of a sword-thrust that finds its mark and goes deep.
89 **plumb-tree** (slang for 'pudendum')
put...for defeat them all by means of
95.3 ***banqueting-stuff*** i.e. sweetmeats, fruit, etc.

Virgo, Libra, Scorpio, Sagittarius, Capricorn, Aquarius, and Pisces. [*The tenants set the signs on the table, with Aries at the head and Pisces at the foot*]

WIDOW What, the twelve signs!

WEATHERWISE These are the signs of my love, widow.

WIDOW
Worse meat would have served us, sir. By my faith,
I'm sorry you should be at such charges, sir,
To feast us a whole month together here.

WEATHERWISE
Widow, thou'rt welcome a whole month and ever.

WIDOW
And what be those, sir, that brought in the banquet?

WEATHERWISE
Those are my tenants. They stand for fasting days.

SIR GILBERT
Or the six weeks in Lent.

WEATHERWISE You're i'th' right, Sir Gilbert.—
Sweet widow, take your place at Aries here.
That's the head sign. A widow is the head
Till she be married.

WIDOW What is she then?

WEATHERWISE The middle.

WIDOW [*sitting*] 'Tis happy she's no worse.

WEATHERWISE
Taurus, Sir Gilbert Lambstone, that's for you.
They say you're a good town-bull.

SIR GILBERT [*sitting*] O, spare your friends, sir.

WEATHERWISE
And Gemini for Master Pepperton.
He had two boys at once by his last wife.

PEPPERTON [*sitting*]
I hear the widow find no fault with that, sir.

WEATHERWISE
Cancer the crab for Master Overdone,
For when a thing's past fifty it grows crookèd.

[*Overdone sits*]

WIDOW
Now for yourself, sir.

WEATHERWISE Take no care for me, widow;
I can be anywhere. Here's Leo, heart and back;
Virgo, guts and belly.
I can go lower yet, and yet fare better,
Since Sagittarius fits me the thighs.
I care not if I be about the thighs;
I shall find meat enough.

[*He sits*]

WIDOW But under pardon, sir,
Though you be lord o'th' feast and the conceit both,
Methinks it had been proper for the banquet
To have had the signs all filled, and no one idle.

WEATHERWISE I know it had; but whose fault's that, widow? You should have got you more suitors to have stopped the gaps.

WIDOW
Nay, sure, they should get us, and not we them.
There be your tenants, sir. We are not proud;
You may bid them sit down.

WEATHERWISE By th' mass, it's true, too. Then sit down, tenants, once, with your hats on; but spare the meat, I charge you, as you hope for new leases. I must make my signs draw out a month yet, with a bit every morning to breakfast, and at full-moon with a whole one that's restorative. Sit round, sit round; and do not speak, sweet tenants. You may be bold enough, so you eat but little.

[*The tenants sit*]

How like you this now, widow?

WIDOW It shows well, sir,
And like the good old hospitable fashion.

CLOWN How, like a good old hospital? My mistress makes an arrant gull on him.

WIDOW
But yet methinks there wants clothes for the feet.

95.6–8 *The ... foot* The formally correct positions for the remaining signs would be to have Gemini, Leo, Libra, Sagittarius, and Aquarius along the side of the table to the left of Aries, and Taurus, Cancer, Virgo, Scorpio, and Capricorn opposite them. The staging would be more straightforward if Gemini and Taurus were transposed, so that Lambstone and Weatherwise could both face the audience, and if Virgo and Libra were transposed, so that at ll. 117–22 Weatherwise could proceed down one side of the table.

98 **meat** food

103 **They ... days** (because they physically stand at various points in the zodiac 'year' to which no banqueting food is allotted)

105–6 **Aries ... sign** The astrological signs were each thought to govern parts of the body: Aries, the head and face. The sign for Aries at the head of the table might be thought an inappropriate place for a female guest, especially as the ram is a male animal; though in Guazzo's *Civil Conversation* (see Introduction) a woman is appointed head of the feast, and the Widow's name Goldenfleece suggests the sheep or ram.

106 **A ... head** (turning *head* to mean 'head of the family')

107 **The middle** (*a*) i.e. between husband and children in rank (*b*) pudendum

108 **no worse** i.e. (*a*) no lower in rank (*b*) not called a worse name

110 **town-bull** bull kept in turn by a village's farmers for servicing cows; 'stud'

116 **Take no care for** don't worry about

117–22 **Here's ... enough** Further examples of the association between signs and parts of the body, with a joking allusion to their edibility.

119 **lower** i.e. (*a*) at table (*b*) in the body

120–2 **Since ... enough** Weatherwise obliviously chooses a place where he is surrounded by tenants and at a distance from the Widow.

120 **fits me** accords with. *Me* is redundant except to emphasize the verb.

121 **about** (*a*) around, near (*b*) busy with

128 **stopped the gaps** (with a coital implication)

134 **draw out** last

143 **the feet** The part of the body associated with Pisces, whose place that *wants clothes* (i.e. is empty) is at the foot of the table. The Widow, four suitors, and six tenants fill the eleven occupied places.

WEATHERWISE That part's uncovered yet.—Push! No matter for the feet!

WIDOW Yes, if the feet catch cold the head will feel it.

WEATHERWISE Why then, you may draw up your legs, and lie rounder together.

SIR GILBERT He's answered you well, madam.

WEATHERWISE An you draw up your legs too, widow, my tenant will feel you there, for he's one of the calves.

WIDOW Better and better, sir; your wit fattens as he feeds.

CLOWN She's took the calf from his tenant and put it upon his ground now.

[Enter a Servant]

WEATHERWISE
How now, my lady's man, what's the news, sir?

SERVANT *[to the Widow]*
Madam, there's a young gentleman below
Has earnest business to your ladyship.

WEATHERWISE
Another suitor, I hold my life, widow.

WIDOW *[to the Servant]*
What is he, sir?

SERVANT He seems a gentleman.
That's the least of him, and yet more I know not.

WIDOW
Under the leave o'th' master of the house here,
I would he were admitted.

WEATHERWISE
With all my heart, widow. I fear him not,
Come cut and long tail. *[Exit Servant]*

SIR GILBERT I have the least fear,
And the most firmness; nothing can shake me.

WEATHERWISE If he be a gentleman, he's welcome. There's a sign does nothing, and that's fit for a gentleman. The feet will be kept warm enough now for you, widow, for if he be a right gentleman he has his stockings warmed, and he wears socks beside, partly for warmth, partly for cleanliness. And if he observe Fridays too, he comes excellent well; Pisces will be a fine fish dinner for him.

WIDOW Why then you mean, sir, he shall sit as he comes?

WEATHERWISE Ay; an he were a lord he shall not sit above my tenants. I'll not have two lords to them; so I may go look my rent in another man's breeches; I was not brought up to be so unmannerly!

Enter Mistress Low-water, as a gallant gentleman, her husband like a servingman after her

MISTRESS LOW-WATER *[aside]* I have picked out a bold time.—Much good do you, gentlemen.

WEATHERWISE You're welcome as I may say, sir.

MISTRESS LOW-WATER *[to the Widow]*
Pardon my rudeness, madam.

WIDOW No such fault, sir.
You're too severe to yourself; our judgement quits you.
Please you to do as we do?

MISTRESS LOW-WATER Thanks, good madam.

WIDOW Make room, gentlemen.

WEATHERWISE Sit still, tenants; I'll call in all your old leases and rack you else.

ALL TENANTS O, sweet landlord!

MISTRESS LOW-WATER *[to Master Low-water]*
Take my cloak, sirrah.—If any be disturbed,
I'll not sit, gentlemen. I see my place.

WEATHERWISE *[aside]* A proper woman turned gallant! If the widow refuse me I care not if I be a suitor to him. I have known those who have been as mad and given half their living for a male companion.

MISTRESS LOW-WATER
How, Pisces! Is that mine? 'Tis a conceited banquet.
[She sits]

WEATHERWISE If you love any fish, pray fall to, sir. If you had come sooner, you might have happened among some of the flesh signs, but now they're all taken up. Virgo had been a good dish for you, had not one of my tenants been somewhat busy with her.

MISTRESS LOW-WATER
Pray let him keep her, sir. Give me meat fresh;
I'd rather have whole fish than broken flesh.

SIR GILBERT
What say you to a bit of Taurus?

MISTRESS LOW-WATER No, I thank you, sir;
The bull's too rank for me.

SIR GILBERT How, sir?

MISTRESS LOW-WATER Too rank, sir.

SIR GILBERT
Fie, I shall strike you dumb, like all your fellows.

MISTRESS LOW-WATER
What, with your heels or horns?

144 **Push** pish (a strong expletive)
146 **if...it** (folk-wisdom that varies the proverb, 'The head and feet keep warm, the rest will take no harm')
151 **calves** (*a*) lower legs (*b*) dolts (by extension of the sense 'young cows')
152 **Better and better** (proverbial)
he it
153 **calf** (*a*) young cow (as an animal grazed on land) (*b*) the imputation of dolt
164 **Come...tail** Proverbial for 'come dogs of all kinds' (a *cut* is a dog with a docked tail), hence 'whatever happens, whoever comes'. Also suggests the genitals (*cut* meaning 'slit' or suggesting 'cunt', and *tail* able to apply to male or female organs), anticipating Mistress Low-water's disguised sexual identity.
167 **that's...gentleman** (because the gentry had no trade or occupation)
170 **socks** (part of a gentleman's costume)
171 **Fridays** Fish was customarily eaten instead of meat on Fridays.
173–5 **Why...tenants** Guests of higher social rank would usually sit nearer the head of the table.
175 **to** in exchange for
176 **look** seek
178–9 **bold time** time that calls for boldness
182 **quits** requites
186 **rack** charge excessive rent, extort
190 **A...gallant** A hyperbolic comment on the *gallant*'s effeminacy; Weatherwise does not actually see through the disguise.
198 **dish** The slang sense 'attractive woman' was not current, but the word is here used metaphorically to similar effect.
203 **rank** (*a*) foul, rancid (*b*) lustful
204 **your fellows** i.e. fish

SIR GILBERT Perhaps with both.
MISTRESS LOW-WATER
It must be at dead low water, when I'm dead, then.
MASTER LOW-WATER [*aside*]
'Tis a brave Kate, and nobly spoke of thee.

WEATHERWISE This quarrel must be drowned. Peccadill, my lady's fool!

CLOWN You're your own man, sir.

WEATHERWISE Prithee, step in to one o'th' maids—

CLOWN That I will, sir, and thank you too.

WEATHERWISE Nay, hark you, sir. Call for my sun-cup presently; I'd forgot it.

CLOWN How, your sun-cup?—Some cup, I warrant, that he stole out o'th' Sun Tavern! [*Exit*]

WIDOW [*aside, looking on Mistress Low-water*]
The more I look on him, the more I thirst for't.
Methinks his beauty does so far transcend,
Turns the signs back, makes that the upper end.
WEATHERWISE
How cheer you, widow? Gentlemen, how cheer you?
Fair weather in all quarters?
The sun will peep anon; I have sent one for him.
In the mean time, I'll tell you a tale of these.
This Libra here that keeps the scale so even
Was i'th' old time an honest chandler's widow,
And had one daughter which was callèd Virgo,
Which now my hungry tenant has deflowered.
This Virgo, passing for a maid, was sued to
By Sagittarius there, a gallant shooter,
And Aries, his head rival.
But her old crabbèd uncle Cancer here,
Dwelling in Crookèd Lane,
Still crossed the marriage, minding to bestow her
Upon one Scorpio, a rich usurer.
The girl, loathing that match, fell into folly
With one Taurus, a gentleman in Town-bull Street,
By whom she had two twins, those Gemini there;
Of which two brats she was brought a-bed in Leo:
At the Red Lion about Tower Hill.
Being in this distress, one Capricorn,
An honest citizen,
Pitied her case, and married her to Aquarius,
An old water-bearer.
And Pisces was her living ever after:
At Standard she sold fish, where he drew water.
ALL THE REST
It shall be yours, sir.
WIDOW Meat and mirth too; you're lavish!
Your purse and tongue has been at cost today, sir.

SIR GILBERT [*to Weatherwise*] You may challenge all comers at these twelve weapons, I warrant you.

Enter Clown, [*without his doublet, with a cypress over his face, and bearing the sun-cup*]

CLOWN Your sun-cup, call you it? 'Tis a simple voyage that I have made here: I have left my doublet within, for fear I should sweat through my jerkin, and thrown a cypress over my face, for fear of sun-burning.

WEATHERWISE How now, who's this?—Why, sirrah!

CLOWN Can you endure it, mistress?

WIDOW Endure what, fool?

WEATHERWISE [*taking the cup from the Clown*] Fill the cup, coxcomb.

CLOWN Nay, an't be no hotter I'll go put on my doublet again. *Exit*

WEATHERWISE What a whoreson sot is this! [*To Master Low-water*] Prithee, fill the cup, fellow, and give't the widow.

MISTRESS LOW-WATER [*to Master Low-water*] Sirrah, how stand you? Bestow your service there upon her ladyship.

[*Master Low-water fills the cup and offers it to the Widow*]

WIDOW
What's here, a sun?
WEATHERWISE It does betoken, madam,
A cheerful day to somebody.
WIDOW [*aside*] It rises
Full in the face of yon fair sign, and yet
By course he is the last must feel the heat.—
Here, gentlemen, to you all, for you know the sun must go through the twelve signs.

206 **It...then** Alludes to the stranding of fish on an exposed shore, quibbling on Mistress Low-water's name, and puns on *dead* as (*a*) absolute (*b*) not alive.

208 **drowned** (by drinking wine)
Peccadill An anglicization of *peccadillo*, alluding to the venial trespasses of a fool.

210 **You're...man** (implying Weatherwise is (*a*) not a servant (*b*) not married to *my lady*, so not in charge of the Clown (*c*) a decisive man)

211 **step in to** go inside to (but the Clown takes it as 'sexually enter')

213 **sun-cup** Evidently a goblet ornamented with a sun motif, to complement the zodiac signs.

216 **Sun Tavern** Located in London's New Fish Street.

219 **Turns** that it turns

223 **a tale of these** The signs are characterized in appropriate ways as London citizens.

229 **shooter** Refers to the bow and arrow of Sagittarius, and puns on *suitor*.

230 **head** chief (and referring to the head as the part of the body associated with Aries)

232 **Crookèd Lane** (adjoined New Fish Street)

234 **Scorpio** (appropriate as a usurer because of its sting)

236 **Town-bull Street** A comic alteration of the disreputable Turnbull Street. See note to l. 110.

239 **Red Lion** A tavern near the Tower of London.

240 **Capricorn** The word's association with goat's horns suggests someone who cuckolds.

242 **Pitied her case** Complicated by the quibble on *case* as 'vagina'.

245 **Standard** (a water conduit in Cheapside; with a phallic innuendo)
sold fish With the implication 'practised prostitution'.
water With the implication 'semen'. *Drew water* probably refers to pimping.

246 **It shall be yours** (a phrase used to acknowledge a victory)

249.1 ***cypress*** piece of light, transparent cloth. If black, it would usually denote mourning.

250 **simple** fine (ironic)

[*She drinks*]

WEATHERWISE
Most wittily, widow; you jump with my conceit right.
There's not a hair between us.

WIDOW [*to Master Low-water*] Give it Sir Gilbert.

SIR GILBERT
I am the next through whom the golden flame
Shines when 'tis spent in thy celestial ram.
The poor feet there must wait and cool a while.
[*He drinks*]

MISTRESS LOW-WATER
We have our time, sir; joy and we shall meet.
I have known the proud neck lie between the feet.
[*They drink in turn*]

WEATHERWISE So round it goes.

Enter Clown

CLOWN I like this drinking world well.

[*Pepperton drinks*]

WEATHERWISE [*to Master Low-water*] So fill t' him again.

PEPPERTON Fill t' me? Why, I drunk last, sir.

WEATHERWISE
I know you did, but Gemini must drink twice,
Unless you mean that one of them shall be choked.

WIDOW [*aside*]
Fly from my heart all variable thoughts!
She that's enticed by every pleasing object
Shall find small pleasure, and as little rest.
This knight hath loved me long; he's best and worthiest.
I cannot but in honour see him requited.—
Sir Gilbert Lambstone—

MISTRESS LOW-WATER How? Pardon me, sweet lady,
That with a bold tongue I strike by your words.—
Sir Gilbert Lambstone?

SIR GILBERT Yes, sir, that's my name.

MISTRESS LOW-WATER
There should be a rank villain of that name.
Came you out of that house?

SIR GILBERT How, Sir Slave!

MISTRESS LOW-WATER
Fall to your bull; leave roaring till anon.

WEATHERWISE Yet again! An you love me, gentlemen, let's have no roaring here. If I had thought that, I'd have sent my bull to the Bear Garden.

PEPPERTON Why, so you should have wanted one of your signs.

WEATHERWISE But I may chance want two now, an they fall together by the ears.

WIDOW
What's the strange fire that works in these two creatures?
Cold signs both, yet more hot than all their fellows.
[*The cup comes round to Mistress Low-water*]

WEATHERWISE Ho, Sol in Pisces! The Sun's in New Fish Street; here's an end of this course.

CLOWN [*to the Widow*] Madam, I am bold to remember your worship for a year's wages and an livery-cloak.

WIDOW
How, will you shame me? Had you not both last week, fool?

CLOWN Ay, but there's another year passed since that.

WIDOW
Would all your wit could make that good, sir.

CLOWN I am sure the sun has run through all the twelve signs since; and that's a year, these gentlemen can witness.

WEATHERWISE The fool will live, madam.

CLOWN Ay, as long as your eyes are open, I warrant him.

MISTRESS LOW-WATER [*to Master Low-water*] Sirrah!

MASTER LOW-WATER Does your worship call?

MISTRESS LOW-WATER
Commend my love and service to the widow;
Desire her ladyship to taste that morsel.
[*She gives him the letter*]

MASTER LOW-WATER [*aside*]
This is the bit I watched for all this while;
But it comes duly.
[*He takes the letter to the Widow*]

SIR GILBERT [*to Mistress Low-water*]
And wherein has this name of mine offended,
That you're so liberal of your infamous titles,
I but a stranger to thee? It must be known, sir,
Ere we two part.

MISTRESS LOW-WATER
Marry, and reason, good sir.

WIDOW [*reading the letter*]
O strike me cold! This should be your hand, Sir Gilbert?

SIR GILBERT Why, make you question of that, madam? 'Tis one of the letters I sent you.

WIDOW [*rising as if to leave*] Much good do you, gentlemen!

ALL THE SUITORS [*rising*] How now? What's the matter?

272 **jump** accord
conceit idea, whim
273 **not a hair between** (proverbial)
275 **when...ram** i.e. after it has passed through Aries
278 **neck** (associated with Taurus, hence Sir Gilbert)
feet (associated with Pisces, hence Mistress Low-water)
291 **strike by** i.e. sound the time as prompted by (taking *tongue* as 'bell-clapper')
295 **Fall to your bull** i.e. set to eating your banqueting-stuff. Sir Gilbert may have risen to his feet in the previous line.
roaring (*a*) bellowing (*b*) brawling
298 **Bear Garden** (a bull-baiting pit)
302 **fall...ears** (proverbial)
304 **Cold signs** The temperament associated with each sign was described in terms of heat and moisture. Taurus was considered cold and dry, Pisces cold and wet.
305 **Sol** the sun
305–6 **The...Street** See note to l. 216.
307 **remember** remind
315 **will live** i.e. must earn a living (but the Clown takes the words more literally)
316 **your eyes are open** i.e. you are alive
324 **infamous titles** insulting names
326 **reason** with good reason

WEATHERWISE Look to the widow; she paints white. Some aqua coelistis for my lady. [*To the Clown*] Run, villain!

CLOWN Aqua solister? Can nobody help her case but a lawyer, and so many suitors here?

WIDOW
O treachery unmatched, unheard of!

SIR GILBERT How do you, madam?

WIDOW
O impudence as foul! Does my disease
Ask how I do? Can it torment my heart,
And look with a fresh colour in my face?

SIR GILBERT
What's this, what's this?

WEATHERWISE I am sorry for this qualm, widow.

WIDOW
He that would know a villain when he meets him,
Let him ne'er go to a conjuror;
[*She shows him the letter*]
Here's a glass
Will show him without money, and far truer.
[*To Mistress Low-water*] Preserver of my state, pray tell me, sir,
That I may pay you all my thanks together,
What blest hap brought that letter to your hand
Frames me so fast locked in mine enemy's power?

MISTRESS LOW-WATER
I will resolve you, madam. I have a kinsman
Somewhat infected with that wanton pity
Which men bestow on the distress of women,
Especially if they be fair and poor.
With such hot charity, which indeed is lust,
He sought t'entice, as his repentance told me,
Her whom you call your enemy, the wife
To a poor gentleman, one Low-water—

WIDOW
Right, right, the same.

MASTER LOW-WATER [*aside*]
Had it been right, 't'ad now been.

MISTRESS LOW-WATER
And according to the common rate of sinners,
Offered large maintenance, which with her seemed nothing;
For if she would consent, she told him roundly,
There was a knight had bid more at one minute
Than all his wealth could compass; and withal
Plucked out that letter as it were in scorn;
Which by good fortune he put up in jest,
With promise that the writ should be returnable
The next hour of his meeting. But, sweet madam,
Out of my love and zeal I did so practise
The part upon him of an urgent wooer
That neither he nor that returned more to her.

SIR GILBERT [*aside*]
Plague o' that kinsman!

WEATHERWISE Here's a gallant rascal!

WIDOW [*to Mistress Low-water*]
Sir, you have appeared so noble in this action,
So full of worth and goodness, that my thanks
Will rather shame the bounty of my mind
Than do it honour. [*To Sir Gilbert*] O, thou treacherous villain!
Does thy faith bear such fruit?
Are these the blossoms of a hundred oaths
Shot from thy bosom? Was thy love so spiteful
It could not be content to mock my heart—
Which is, in love, a misery too much—
But must extend so far to the quick ruin
Of what was painfully got, carefully left me,
And 'mongst a world of yielding needy women
Choose no one to make merry with my sorrows,
And spend my wealth on in adulterous surfeits,
But my most mortal enemy? O, despiteful!
Is this thy practice? Follow it; 'twill advance thee.
Go, beguile on. Have I so happily found
What many a widow has with sorrow tasted,
Even when my lip touched the contracting cup,
E'en then to see the spider? 'Twas miraculous!
Crawl with thy poisons hence, and for thy sake
I'll never covet titles and more riches,
To fall into a gulf of hate and laughter.
I'll marry love hereafter; I've enough,
And wanting that, I have nothing. There's thy way.
[*She points to a door*]

OVERDONE
Do you hear, sir? You must walk.

PEPPERTON Heart, thrust him downstairs!

WEATHERWISE
Out of my house, you treacherous, lecherous rascal!

SIR GILBERT [*to them all*]
All curses scatter you! [*Exit*]

332 **paints white** turns pale (literally, 'whitens her face with make-up')
333 **aqua coelistis** A cordial. The *c* is pronounced 's'.
334 **solister** The Clown's mishearing allows a pun on *solicitor*.
case (*a*) situation (*b*) lawsuit (*c*) vagina
339 **look...face** (*a*) appear to give fresh colour to my face (referring to the metaphorical disease) (*b*) look, with its own fresh colour, at my [pale] face (referring to Sir Gilbert)
340 **qualm** fit of sickness
342 **glass** magic crystal
347 **Frames** that forms, articulates, shows
356 **Had...been** i.e. the story is no more true than Low-water's present appearance (?)
363 **put up** pocketed
364 **writ** letter
376 **Shot** (*a*) uttered (*b*) sprouted
386 **found** found out
388 **the contracting cup** i.e. betrothal, figured as drinking a pledge
389 **spider** Thought to produce poison. The image of the spider in the cup is associated with knowledge of a spouse's adultery in *Winter's Tale* 2.1.40–5.
392 **To** in order to
394 **that** i.e. love

WEATHERWISE Life, do you thunder here?
If you had stayed a little longer, I'd have ripped out some of my bull out of your belly again.

PEPPERTON [*to Mistress Low-water*] 'Twas a most noble discovery. We must love you for ever for't.

WIDOW [*to Weatherwise*]
Sir, for your banquet and your mirth we thank you;—
You, gentlemen, for your kind company;—
[*To Mistress Low-water*] But you, for all my merry days to come,
Or this had been the last else.

MISTRESS LOW-WATER Love and fortune
Had more care of your safety, peace, and state, madam.

WEATHERWISE [*aside*]
Now will I thrust in for't.

PEPPERTON [*aside*] I'm for myself now.

OVERDONE [*aside*]
What's fifty years? 'Tis man's best time and season.
Now the knight's gone, the widow will hear reason.

MASTER LOW-WATER [*aside to Mistress Low-water*]
Now, now the suitors flutter, hold on, Kate.
The hen may pick the meat while the cocks prate.
Exeunt

Sc. 5 *Enter Master Sandfield, Philip (Sir Oliver Twilight's son), with Savourwit*

PHILIP [*to Savourwit*]
If thou talk'st longer, I shall turn to marble,
And death will stop my hearing.

SANDFIELD Horrible fortune!

SAVOURWIT
Nay, sir, our building is so far defaced
There is no stuff left to raise up a hope.

PHILIP
O, with more patience could my flesh endure
A score of wounds, and all their several searchings,
Than this that thou hast told me.

SAVOURWIT Would that Flemish ram
Had ne'er come near our house! There's no going home
As long as he has a nest there, and his young one,
A little Flanders egg new-fledged. They gape
For pork, and I shall be made meat for 'em.

PHILIP
'Tis not the bare news of my mother's life—
May she live long and happy—that afflicts me
With half the violence that the latter draws.
Though in that news I have my share of grief,
As I had share of sin and a foul neglect,
It is my love's betraying that's the sting
That strikes through flesh and spirit; and since nor wit
From thee in whom I ne'er saw ebb till now
Nor comforts from a faithful friend can ease me,
I'll try the goodness of a third companion,
What he'll do for me.
[*He draws his sword and offers to kill himself*]

SANDFIELD Hold! Why, friend!

SAVOURWIT Why, master, is this all your kindness, sir: offer to steal into another country and ne'er take your leave on's? Troth, I take it unkindly at your hands, sir; but I'll put it up for once.
[*He puts up Philip's sword*]
Faith, there was no conscience in this, sir. Leave me here to endure all weathers, whilst you make your soul dance like a juggler's egg upon the point of a rapier? By my troth, sir, you're to blame in't. You might have given us an inkling of your journey; perhaps others would as fain have gone as you.

PHILIP
Burns this clay-lamp of miserable life,
When joy, the oil that feeds it, is dried up?
Enter his Mother, new landed, with Master Beveril (a gentleman scholar) and servants

MOTHER
He has removed his house.

BEVERIL So it seems, madam.

MOTHER
I'll ask that gentleman. [*To Philip*] Pray can you tell me, sir,
Which is Sir Oliver Twilight's?

PHILIP Few can better, gentlewoman.
It is the next fair house your eye can fix on.

MOTHER
I thank you, sir.—Go on. [*Exeunt servants*]
He had a son
About some ten years since.

PHILIP That son still lives.

MOTHER I pray, how does he, sir?

PHILIP
Faith, much about my health. [*Aside*] That's never worse.—
If you have any business to him, gentlewoman,
I can cut short your journey to the house.
I'm all that ever was of the same kind.

MOTHER
O my sweet son! Never fell fresher joy
Upon the heart of mother!—This is he, sir.

397 **thunder** Draws on thunder (*a*) as a sign of Jove's wrath and (*b*) in the sense 'roar'.
398–9 **I'd...again** Refers to the eaten sign of Taurus; and perhaps varies the proverb 'I wish it were in your belly', a way of retorting an insult.
5.3 **defaced** destroyed
6 **several** distinct, various
searchings probings (to cleanse and heal)
20 **friend** i.e. Sandfield
25 **put it up** (*a*) put up with it (*b*) put up the sword
32 **clay-lamp** The body was proverbially pictured as a house of clay.
33 **joy, the oil** The biblical 'oil of joy' was God's comfort for mourners (Isaiah 61:3).
33.1 ***new landed*** i.e. still dressed for the voyage. The servants may carry a trunk.

BEVERIL
My seven years' travel has e'en worn him out
Of my remembrance.
SAVOURWIT [*aside*] O, this gear's worse and worse!
PHILIP [*kneeling to his Mother*]
I am so wonder-struck at your blest presence
That through amazed joy I neglect my duty.
MOTHER [*raising him*]
Rise, and a thousand blessings spring up with thee!
SAVOURWIT [*aside*]
I would we had but one in the mean time;
Let the rest grow at leisure.
MOTHER
But know you not this gentleman yet, son?
PHILIP
I take it's Master Beveril.
BEVERIL My name's Beveril, sir.
PHILIP [*embracing him*]
Right welcome to my bosom!
MOTHER You'd not think, son,
How much I am beholding to this gentleman:
As far as freedom. He laid out the ransom,
Finding me so distressed.
PHILIP 'Twas worthily done, sir,
And I shall ever rest your servant for't.
BEVERIL
You quite forget your worth. 'Twas my good hap, sir,
To rèturn home that way after some travels,
Where finding your good mother so distressed,
I could not but in pity see her released.
PHILIP
It was a noble charity, sir. Heaven quit you!
SAVOURWIT [*aside*]
It comes at last.
BEVERIL I left a sister here
New married when I last took leave of England.
PHILIP
O, Mistress Low-water!
BEVERIL Pray, sir, how does she?
PHILIP
So little comfort I can give you, sir,
That I would fain excuse myself for silence.
BEVERIL
Why, what's the worst, sir?
PHILIP Wrongs has made her poor.
BEVERIL
You strike my heart. Alas, good gentlewoman!
PHILIP Here's a gentleman;
You know him: Master Sandfield.
BEVERIL [*to Sandfield*] I crave pardon, sir.
PHILIP
He can resolve you from her kinswoman.
SANDFIELD
Welcome to England, madam.
MOTHER Thanks, good sir.
[*The Mother, Beveril, and Sandfield speak apart*]
PHILIP [*aside to Savourwit*]
Now there's no way to scape; I'm compassed round.
My shame is like a prisoner set with halberds.
SAVOURWIT
Pish, master! Master, 'tis young flood again,
And you can take your time now. Away, quick!
PHILIP
Push! Thou'st a swimming head!
SAVOURWIT Will you but hear me?
When did you lose your tide when I set forth with
you?
PHILIP
That's true.
SAVOURWIT
Regard me then. Though you have no feeling,
I would not hang by th' thumbs with a good will.
PHILIP
I hang by th' heart, sir, and would fain have ease.
SAVOURWIT
Then this or none: fly to your mother's pity,
For that's the court must help you. You're quite gone
At common law; no counsellor can hear you
Confess your follies, and ask pardon for 'em.
Tell her the state of all things; stand not nicely.
The meat's too hard
To be minced now; she breeds young bones by this
time.
Deal plainly; heaven will bless thee. Turn out all,
And shake your pockets after it.
Beg, weep, kneel, anything; 'twill break no bones,
man.
Let her not rest, take breathing time, nor leave thee
Till thou hast got her help.
PHILIP Lad, I conceive thee.
SAVOURWIT
About it then; it requires haste. Do't well.
There's but a short street between us and hell.

49 **gear's** affair's
76 **resolve you from** dispell your uncertainty with information from
her kinswoman i.e. Jane
80 **young flood** rising tide (the best time to set sail)
82 **Push** pish
swimming (*a*) giddy (*b*) inclined to swim in the sea
84 **Though** even if
85 **hang by th' thumbs** (a form of torture)
88 **the court** (probably alluding to the ecclesiastical court, as distinct from *common law*)
gone lost
89 **counsellor** advocate
91 **stand not nicely** don't fastidiously hold off
93 **minced** The image is suggested by the expression 'to mince matters' (i.e. to extenuate them).
she breeds young bones i.e. she (Grace) is pregnant (proverbial).
bones (too hard to be *minced*)
96 **'twill...bones** (as is proverbially said of words)
98 **conceive** understand
100 **a short street** i.e. the distance to Twilight's house. Also glances at the proverb 'A short prayer penetrates heaven'.

BEVERIL [*to Sandfield*]
Ah, my poor sister!
MOTHER 'Las, good gentlewoman!
My heart e'en weeps for her.
Philip shogs his Mother
Ay, son, we'll go now.
PHILIP
May I crave one word, madam?
MOTHER With me, son?
The more, the better welcome.
SAVOURWIT [*aside*] Now, now, luck!
I pray not often; the last prayer I made
Was nine year old last Bartholomew-tide.
'Twould have been a jolly chopper an 't'ad lived
Till this time.
MOTHER [*to Philip*]
Why do your words start back? Are they afraid
Of her that ever loved them?
PHILIP I have a suit to you, madam.
MOTHER
You have told me that already; pray, what is't?
If't be so great my present state refuse it,
I shall be abler; then command and use it.
Whate'er't be, let me have warning to provide for't.
PHILIP [*kneeling*]
Provide forgiveness then, for that's the want
My conscience feels. O, my wild youth has led me
Into unnatural wrongs against your freedom once.
I spent the ransom which my father sent,
To set my pleasures free while you lay captive.
SAVOURWIT [*aside*]
He does it finely, faith.
MOTHER And is this all now?
You use me like a stranger; pray stand up.
PHILIP
Rather fall flat; I shall deserve yet worse.
MOTHER [*raising Philip*]
Whate'er your faults are, esteem me still a friend,
Or else you wrong me more in asking pardon
Than when you did the wrong you asked it for;
And since you have prepared me to forgive you,
Pray let me know for what; the first fault's nothing.
SAVOURWIT [*aside*]
'Tis a sweet lady, every inch of her.
PHILIP
Here comes the wrong then that drives home the rest.
I saw a face at Antwerp that quite drew me
From conscience and obedience. In that fray
I lost my heart; I must needs lose my way.
There went the ransom, to redeem my mind.
Stead of the money, I brought over her,
And, to cast mists before my father's eyes,
Told him it was my sister, lost so long,
And that yourself was dead. You see the wrong.
MOTHER
This is but youthful still.—O, that word 'sister'
Afflicts me when I think on't!—I forgive thee
As freely as thou didst it. For, alas,
This may be called good dealing to some parts
That love and youth plays daily among sons.
SAVOURWIT [*aside*]
She helps our knavery well; that's one good comfort.
PHILIP
But such is the hard plight my state lives in,
That 'twixt forgiveness I must sin again,
And seek my help where I bestowed my wrongs.
O mother, pity once, though against reason!—
'Cause I can merit none. Though my wrongs grieve ye,
Yet let it be your glory to relieve me.
MOTHER
Wherein have I given cause yet of mistrust,
That you should doubt my succour and my love?
Show me but in what kind I may bestow 'em.
PHILIP
There came a Dutchman with report this day
That you were living.
MOTHER Came he so lately?
PHILIP Yes, madam.
Which news so struck my father on the sudden
That he grows jealous of my faith in both.
These five hours have I kept me from his sight,
And wished myself eternally so hid;
And, surely, had not your blest presence quickened
The flame of life in me, all had gone out.
Now to confirm me to his trust again
And settle much aright in his opinion,
Say but she is my sister, and all's well.
MOTHER
You ask devotion like a bashful beggar
That pure need urges, and not lazy impudence;
And, to express how glad I am to pity you,
My bounty shall flow over your demand.
I will not only with a constant breath
Approve that, but excuse thee for my death.
SAVOURWIT [*aside*] Why, here's a woman made as a man would wish to have her!
PHILIP
O, I am placed higher in happiness
Than whence I fell before!

102.1 ***shogs*** jogs to attract attention
106 **Bartholomew-tide** St Bartholomew's day (24 August). The *prayer* was perhaps an entreaty for a sexual favour made at the notorious Bartholomew Fair.
107 **chopper** strong child
133 **redeem my mind** get what I wanted, release my mind from bondage
135 **cast...eyes** 'To cast mists before someone's eyes' was proverbial.
141 **to** compared to
145 **'twixt forgiveness** i.e. between the forgiveness obtained and that now sought for the new sin
156 **jealous** suspicious
both i.e. Philip's two assertions: that Grace was his sister and that his mother was dead
169 **Approve** confirm, corroborate

SAVOURWIT [*aside*] We're brave fellows once again, and we can keep our own.
Now hufty-tufty, our pipes play as loftily!

BEVERIL [*to Sandfield*] My sister fled?

SANDFIELD
Both fled; that's the news now. Want must obey;
Oppressions came so thick, they could not stay.

BEVERIL
Mean are my fortunes, yet had I been nigh
Distress nor wrong should have made virtue fly.

MOTHER
Spoke like a brother worthy such a sister.

BEVERIL
Grief's like a new wound: heat beguiles the sense;
For I shall feel this smart more three days hence.
Come, madam. Sorrow's rude, and forgets manners.

Exeunt; manet Savourwit

SAVOURWIT Our knavery is for all the world like a shifting bankrupt: it breaks in one place, and sets up in another. He tries all trades, from a goldsmith to a tobacco-seller; we try all shifts, from an outlaw to a flatterer. He cozens the husband and compounds with the widow; we cozen my master and compound with my mistress. Only here I turn o'th' right hand from him: he is known to live like a rascal, when I am thought to live like a gentleman.

Exit

Sc. 6

Enter Kate Low-water, with her man-husband, [both disguised as before]

MISTRESS LOW-WATER
I have sent in one to th' widow.

MASTER LOW-WATER Well said, Kate.
Thou ply'st thy business close. The coast is clear yet.

MISTRESS LOW-WATER Let me but have warning,
I shall make pretty shift with them.

MASTER LOW-WATER That thou shalt, wench.

Exit

[Enter Servant]

SERVANT
My lady, sir, commends her kindly to you,
And for the third part of an hour, sir,
Desires your patience.
Two or three of her tenants out of Kent
Will hold her so long busied.

MISTRESS LOW-WATER Thank you, sir.

[Exit Servant]

'Tis fit I should attend her time and leisure.
Those were my tenants once. But what relief
Is there in what hath been, or what I was?
'Tis now that makes the man. A last-year's feast
Yields little comfort for the present humour.
He starves that feeds his hopes with what is past.

[Enter Master Low-water, disguised as before]

How now?

MASTER LOW-WATER
They're come, newly alighted.

MISTRESS LOW-WATER Peace, peace.
I'll have a trick for 'em; look you second me well now.

MASTER LOW-WATER I warrant thee.

MISTRESS LOW-WATER
I must seem very imperious, I can tell you;
Therefore if I should chance to use you roughly,
Pray forgive me beforehand.

MASTER LOW-WATER With all my heart, Kate.

MISTRESS LOW-WATER
You must look for no obedience in these clothes;
That lies in the pocket of my gown.

MASTER LOW-WATER Well, well, I will not then.

MISTRESS LOW-WATER
I hear 'em coming; step back a little, sir.

[Master Low-water steps back.] Enter Master Weatherwise, Master Pepperton, and Master Overdone, suitors

Where be those fellows? Who looks out there? Is there ne'er a knave i'th' house to take those gentlemen's horses? Where wait you today? How, stand you like a dreaming goose in a corner? The gentlemen's horses, forsooth!

MASTER LOW-WATER Yes, an't like your worship. *[Exit]*

PEPPERTON [*to the other suitors*] What's here? A strange alteration!

WEATHERWISE A new lord! Would I were upon my mare's back again then!

MISTRESS LOW-WATER
Pray, gentlemen, pardon the rudeness of these grooms.
I hope they will be brought to better fashion.
In the mean time, you're welcome, gentlemen.

ALL THE SUITORS We thank you, sir.

WEATHERWISE Life, here's quick work! I'll hold my life he's struck the widow i'th' right planet.

176 **hufty-tufty** Expresses superiority and giddy behaviour; also imitative of the sound of pipes.
186 **shifting** (*a*) deceitful (*b*) changing abode
187 **breaks** (*a*) decamps (*b*) becomes bankrupt
189 **shifts** (*a*) expedients, tricks, frauds (*b*) livelihoods
190 **compounds** comes to an agreement
192 **o'th' right hand** (*a*) to the right-hand side (*b*) in the right direction

6.1 **said** done
2 **ply'st** (*a*) work away at (*b*) steer, tack (as with a sailing vessel)
close (*a*) rigorously (*b*) secretly (*c*) close to the wind
The coast is clear (proverbial)
4 **pretty** artful, clever
shift contrivance, stratagem
13 **'Tis . . . man** Varies the proverb 'manners make the man'.

14 **humour** mood, inclination
22 **these clothes** (her disguise)
23 **the . . . gown** i.e. (*a*) my female identity as constructed through clothing (*b*) my sexuality (evoked by a quibble on *pocket* and *gown* as 'vagina')
26 **looks out** is on duty
29 **goose** simpleton
41 **i'th' right planet** i.e. when the right planet is dominant

[*He looks in his almanac*]
Venus in Cauda! I thought 'twas a lecherous planet that goes to't with a caudle.

[*Enter Master Low-water, disguised as before*]

MISTRESS LOW-WATER How now, sir?

MASTER LOW-WATER The gentlemen's horses are set up, sir.

PEPPERTON No, no, no, we'll away.

WEATHERWISE We'll away.

MISTRESS LOW-WATER How? By my faith, but you shall not yet, by your leave! [*To Master Low-water*] Where's Bess? Call your mistress, sir, to welcome these kind gentlemen my friends. [*Exit Master Low-water*]

PEPPERTON *and* OVERDONE How, Bess? Peg?

WEATHERWISE Plain Bess! I know how the world goes then; he has been a-bed with Bess, i'faith. There's no trust to these widows; a young horsing gentleman carries 'em away clear.

[*Enter Master Low-water, disguised as before*]

MISTRESS LOW-WATER [*to Master Low-water*] Now where's your mistress, sir? How chance she comes not?

MASTER LOW-WATER Sir, she requests you to excuse her for a while; she's busy with a milliner about gloves.

MISTRESS LOW-WATER Gloves?

WEATHERWISE Hoyda, gloves too!

MISTRESS LOW-WATER [*to Master Low-water*] Could she find no other time to choose gloves but now when my friends are here?

PEPPERTON No, sir, 'tis no matter; we thank you for your good will, sir. To say truth, we have no business with her at all at this time, i'faith, sir.

MISTRESS LOW-WATER O, that's another matter. Yet stay, stay, gentlemen, and taste a cup of wine ere you go.

OVERDONE No thank you, sir.

MISTRESS LOW-WATER Master Pepperton? Master Weatherwise, will you, sir?

WEATHERWISE I'll see the wine in a drunkard's shoes first, and drink't after he has brewed it. But let her go; she's fitted, i'faith. A proud surly sir here; he domineers already; one that will shake her bones and go to dice with her money, or I have no skill in a calendar. Life, he that can be so saucy to call her 'Bess' already will call her 'prating quean' a month hence. *Exeunt suitors*

MASTER LOW-WATER
They have given thee all the slip.

MISTRESS LOW-WATER So, a fair riddance!
There's three rubs gone; I've a clear way to th'
mistress.

MASTER LOW-WATER
You'd need have a clear way, because you're a bad
pricker.

MISTRESS LOW-WATER
Yet if my bowl take bank, I shall go nigh
To make myself a saver.
Here's alley-room enough; I'll try my fortune.
I am to begin the world like a younger brother;
I know that a bold face and a good spirit
Is all the jointure he can make a widow;
And't shall go hard but I'll be as rich as he,
Or at least seem so, and that's wealth enough.
For nothing kills a widow's heart so much
As a faint bashful wooer. Though he have thousands,
And come with a poor water-gruel spirit
And a fish-market face, he shall ne'er speed.
I would not have himself left a poor widower.

MASTER LOW-WATER Faith, I'm glad I'm alive to commend thee, Kate. I shall be sure now to see my commendations delivered.

MISTRESS LOW-WATER
I'll put her to't, i'faith.

MASTER LOW-WATER But soft ye, Kate.
How an she should accept of your bold kindness?

MISTRESS LOW-WATER
A chief point to be thought on, by my faith.
Marry, therefore, sir, be you sure to step in, for fear I should shame myself, and spoil all.

MASTER LOW-WATER Well, I'll save your credit then for once, but look you come there no more.

MISTRESS LOW-WATER
Away; I hear her coming.

MASTER LOW-WATER I am vanished. *Exit*

42 **Cauda** Latin for 'tail'; here referring to the 'Dragon's Tail', almanac terminology for the passage of the Moon or a planet across the ecliptic from north of it to south (i.e. through the 'descending node'). The malevolent aspect of planets (for Venus, lust) was thought to be augmented at this time.

43 **caudle** warm, spiced drink, here seen as an aphrodisiac. Puns on *Cauda*.

45 **set up** put up in the stable

49 **Bess** Short forms of the first name were considered appropriate only from husband to wife, or to a whore.

52 **Peg** Another familiar name, emphasizing Overdone's astonishment at *Bess*.

60 **gloves** (customary gifts from the bride to the groom's men)

69 **that's another matter** that changes the situation

75 **brewed** (*a*) fermented (*b*) poured out (i.e. vomited)

76 **fitted** well matched, fittingly punished

77–8 **shake ... money** Dice were made of bone.

80 **prating quean** gossiping whore

82 **rubs** impediments. Specifically, unevennesses in the turf in a game of bowls. **mistress** (*a*) 'jack' or target bowl (*b*) wooed woman

83 **pricker** (*a*) horseman, rider (*b*) someone who aims at the prick or target (*c*) wielder of a penis

84 **bank** i.e. the raised bank of the bowling green, which could be used to curve the bowl round an obstacle (with a pun on the sense 'gaming stake')

85 **make ... saver** i.e. compensate for my loss

86 **alley-room** passage-way. An *alley* was an enclosure for bowls.

87 **younger brother** (who could expect little or no inheritance and would have to seek his fortune)

90 **but I'll** if I'll not

95 **fish-market** i.e. pale and watery (in contrast with *flesh-market*)

96 **a poor widower** (having married a wife both poor and sickly)

105 **credit** (*a*) credibility (as a man) (*b*) reputation (as a virtuous wife)

Enter Widow

MISTRESS LOW-WATER
How does my life, my soul, my dear sweet madam?

WIDOW
I have wronged your patience, made you stand too long here.

MISTRESS LOW-WATER
There's no such thing, i'faith, madam; you're pleased to say so.

WIDOW Yes, I confess I was too slow, sir.

MISTRESS LOW-WATER Why, you shall make me amends for that then with a quickness in your bed.

WIDOW That were a speedy 'mends, sir.

MISTRESS LOW-WATER Why then you are out of my debt. I'll cross the book, and turn over a new leaf with you.

WIDOW So with paying a small debt I may chance run into a greater.

MISTRESS LOW-WATER My faith, your credit will be the better then. There's many a brave gallant would be glad of such fortune, and pay use for't.

WIDOW Some of them have nothing else to do; they would be idle an 'twere not for interest.

MISTRESS LOW-WATER I promise you, widow, were I a setter-up, such is my opinion of your payment I durst trust you with all the ware in my shop.

WIDOW I thank you for your good will; I can have no more.

MISTRESS LOW-WATER [*aside*] Not of me, i'faith, nor that neither an you know all.—Come, make but short service, widow: a kiss and to bed. I'm very hungry, i'faith, wench.

WIDOW What are you, sir?

MISTRESS LOW-WATER O, a younger brother, has an excellent stomach, madam, worth a hundred of your sons and heirs that stay their wedding stomachs with a hot bit of a common mistress, and then come to a widow's bed like a flash of lightning. You're sure of the first of me, not of the five hundredth of them. I never took physic yet in my life; you shall have the doctor continually with them, or some bottle for his deputy: out flies your monies for restoratives and strength'nings. In me, 'tis saved in your purse, and found in your children. They'll get peevish pothecaries' stuff—you may weigh 'em by th' ounces—I, boys of war, brave commanders that shall bear a breadth in their shoulders and a weight in their hips, and run over a whole country with a pound o' beef and a biscuit in their belly. Ho, widow, my kisses are virgins, my embraces perfect, my strength solid, my love constant, my heat comfortable—but to come to the point, inutterable.

WIDOW
But soft ye, soft ye. Because you stand so strictly
Upon your purity, I'll put you to't, sir.
Will you swear here you never yet knew woman?

MISTRESS LOW-WATER [*kneeling*]
Never as man e'er knew her, by this light, widow.

WIDOW
What, what, sir? [*Aside*] 'Shrew my heart, he moves me much.

MISTRESS LOW-WATER
Nay, since you love to bring a man on's knees,
I take into the same oath thus much more:
That you're the first widow, or maid, or wife
That ever I in suit of love did court
Or honestly did woo. [*Rising*] How say you to that, widow?

WIDOW Marry, I say, sir, you had a good portion of chastity left you, though ill fortune run away with the rest.

MISTRESS LOW-WATER That I kept for thee, widow. She's of fortune, and all her strait-bodied daughters. Thou shalt have't, widow.
[*She embraces her*]

WIDOW Push! What do you mean?

MISTRESS LOW-WATER I cannot bestow't better.

WIDOW I'll call my servants.

MISTRESS LOW-WATER By my troth, you shall not, madam.

Enter Master Low-water [disguised as before]

MASTER LOW-WATER
Does your worship call, sir?

110 **pleased** kind, well-disposed
114 **'mends** amends
116 **cross the book** cancel the account
turn ... leaf (proverbial)
119 **credit** (*a*) positive reckoning of money (*b*) reputation
121 **fortune** (*a*) sum of money (*b*) good luck
use for't (*a*) interest on it (*b*) for the use of it
123 **interest** i.e. the money-lending system
124–5 **setter-up** beginner in business
129–30 **Not ... neither** i.e. not of my body ... nor of my good will
131 **service** (*a*) shop service (*b*) religious service, ceremony (*c*) sexual 'servicing'
134 **has** who has
136 **stay** (*a*) hold back, appease; or (*b*) sustain, strengthen
137 **bit** morsel
140 **physic** medicine
143 **'tis** The money is *saved* and the strength is *found*.
144 **get** beget
147–8 **a ... biscuit** (soldiers' rations)
149 **perfect** complete, undivided
150 **comfortable** cheering, pleasure-giving
155 **by this light** An asseveration; *this light* is the sun.
157 **on's** onto his
159 **widow ... wife** (the three proverbial classifications of women)
162 **portion** inheritance
163 **the rest** i.e. wealth
164–5 **of fortune** Chastity might be regarded as morally enriching, but at 1.211–14 Savourwit points out that it is also a commodity.
165 **strait-bodied** sexually restrained. Also 'narrow-bodied', i.e. young, virginal, boyish. As such the term is relevant to the opposite cross-dressing to Mistress Low-water's, and generally to the playing of women's roles by boy actors. Ironically, Mistress Low-water associates the chastity of her male disguised role with a slightly ambiguated female image. There may be a hint of sexual desirability, to some at least: Ben Jonson referred to 'strait-bodied [narrow-fitting] city attire' able to 'stir a courtier's blood'.
daughters female adherents. Glances at the impossibility of a chaste woman having literal daughters.
167 **Push** pish. Can also be equivalent to interjectory 'fuck', which may be relevant here.

MISTRESS LOW-WATER Ha, pox! Are you peeping?
Throws somewhat at him. [*Exit Master Low-water*]
[*Aside*] He came in a good time, I thank him for't.
WIDOW
What do you think of me? You're very forward, sir.
MISTRESS LOW-WATER
Extremity of love.
WIDOW You say you're ignorant;
It should not seem so, surely, by your play.
For aught I see, you may make one yourself;
You need not hold the cards to any gamester.
MISTRESS LOW-WATER
That love should teach men ways to wrong itself!
WIDOW
Are these the first-fruits of your boldness, sir?
If all take after these, you may boast on 'em.
There comes few such to market among women.
Time you were taken down, sir.—Within there!
MISTRESS LOW-WATER [*aside*] I've lost my way again.
There's but two paths that leads to widows' beds;
That's wealth or forwardness; and I've took the wrong one.
Enter a Servant, with the suitors
SERVANT [*to the suitors*]
He, marry my lady? Why, there's no such thought yet.
[*Exit*]
MISTRESS LOW-WATER [*aside*]
O, here they are all again too!
WIDOW Are you come, gentlemen?
I wish no better men.
WEATHERWISE O, the moon's changed now!
WIDOW
See you that gentleman yonder?
PEPPERTON Yes, sweet madam.
WIDOW
Then pray be witness all of you: with this kiss
I choose him for my husband—
[*She kisses Mistress Low-water*]
ALL THE SUITORS A pox on't!
WIDOW
And with this parted gold, that two hearts join.
[*She parts gold and gives one part to Mistress Low-water*]
MISTRESS LOW-WATER
Never with chaster love than this of mine.
WIDOW
And those that have the hearts to come to th' wedding,
They shall be welcome for their former loves. *Exit*
PEPPERTON
No, I thank you; you've choked me already.
WEATHERWISE I never suspected mine almanac till now. I believe he plays Cogging John with me. I bought it at his shop; it may learn the more knavery by that.
MISTRESS LOW-WATER
Now indeed, gentlemen, I can bid you welcome;
Before 'twas but a flourish.
WEATHERWISE Nay, so my almanac told me: [*Reading*] 'There should be an eclipse, but not visible in our horizon, but about the western inhabitants of Mexicana and California.'
MISTRESS LOW-WATER Well, we have no business there, sir.
WEATHERWISE Nor we have none here, sir; and so fare you well.
MISTRESS LOW-WATER You save the house a good labour, gentlemen. *Exeunt suitors*
The fool carries them away in a voider.—Where be these fellows?
Enter Servants: the Clown, and Master Low-water, [disguised as before,] and another Servant
SERVANT Sir.
CLOWN Here, sir.
SERVANT What your worship' pleasure?
MISTRESS LOW-WATER
O, this is something like. [*To Master Low-water*] Take you your ease, sir;
Here are those now more fit to be commanded.
MASTER LOW-WATER [*aside*] How few women are of thy mind! She thinks it too much to keep me in subjection for one day, whereas some wives would be glad to keep their husbands in awe all days of their lives, and think it the best bargain that e'er they made. [*Exit*]
MISTRESS LOW-WATER
I'll spare no cost for th' wedding; some device too,
To show our thankfulness to wit and fortune.
It shall be so. [*To the Clown*] Run straight for one o'th' wits.
CLOWN How, one o'th' wits? I care not if I run on that account. Are they in town, think you?
MISTRESS LOW-WATER Whither runn'st thou now?
CLOWN To an ordinary, for one of the wits.
MISTRESS LOW-WATER Why to an ordinary, above a tavern?

176 **make one** play the game
177 **hold the cards to** i.e. continue to play with a hidden hand of cards against
182 **taken down** (*a*) cut down, felled (like a fruit tree); put in your place; or (*b*) taken from the shelf (like the fruit). With a quibble on detumescence after sexual intercourse.
192 **parted gold** Parting gold in this way was a betrothal custom. The gold might be coins, a chain that unlinks, or the like.
198 **Cogging** cheating
201 **flourish** ostentatious gesture
202 **eclipse** (a portent of disaster)
204 **Mexicana** Mexico
208 **save . . . labour** i.e. deprive the household of entertaining you
210 **The . . . voider** i.e. they depart like leftovers from a feast carried out by the Clown
voider receptacle for clearing leftovers after a meal
215 **something like** more like it
216 **those . . . commanded** (quibbling on (*a*) more dutiful servants, and (*b*) those whose station it is to be servants)
222 **device** theatrical contrivance, show
228 **ordinary** eating-house. Wits would evidently in fact prefer a tavern, more expensive but more convivial.

CLOWN No, I hold your best wits to be at ordinary; nothing so good in a tavern.

MISTRESS LOW-WATER And why, I pray, sir?

CLOWN Because those that go to an ordinary dine better for twelve pence than he that goes to a tavern for his five shillings; and I think those have the best wits that can save four shillings, and fare better too.

MISTRESS LOW-WATER So, sir, all your wit then runs upon victuals.

CLOWN 'Tis a sign 'twill hold out the longer then.

MISTRESS LOW-WATER [*to Servant*]
What were you saying to me?

SERVANT Please your worship,
I heard there came a scholar over lately
With old Sir Oliver's lady.

MISTRESS LOW-WATER [*aside*]
Is she come?—
What is that lady?

SERVANT A good gentlewoman,
Has been long prisoner with the enemy.

MISTRESS LOW-WATER [*aside*]
I know't too well, and joy in her release.—
Go to that house then straight, and in one labour
You may bid them and entreat home that scholar.

SERVANT
It shall be done with speed, sir.

CLOWN I'll along with you,
And see what face that scholar has brought over:
a thin pair of parbreaking sea-water-green chops, I warrant you. [*Exeunt Servant and Clown*]

MISTRESS LOW-WATER
Since wit has pleasured me, I'll pleasure wit;
Scholars shall fare the better. O, my blessing!
I feel a hand of mercy lift me up
Out of a world of waters, and now sets me
Upon a mountain where the sun plays most,
To cheer my heart e'en as it dries my limbs.
What deeps I see beneath me, in whose falls
Many a nimble mortal toils
And scarce can feed himself. The streams of fortune,
'Gainst which he tugs in vain, still beat him down,
And will not suffer him, past hand-to-mouth,
To lift his arm to his posterity's blessing.
I see a careful sweat run in a ring
About his temples, but all will not do;
For till some happy means relieve his state,
There he must stick, and bide the wrath of fate.
I see this wrath upon an uphill land.
O, blest are they can see their falls, and stand!

Enter Beveril [and Servant]

How now?

SERVANT With much entreating, sir, he's come.

MISTRESS LOW-WATER
Sir, you're—[*aside*] My brother! Joys come thick together.—
Sir, when I see a scholar, pardon me,
I am so taken with affection for him
That I must run into his arms and clasp him.
[*She embraces him*]

BEVERIL
Art stands in need, sir, of such cherishers;
I meet too few. 'Twere a brave world for scholars
If half a kingdom were but of your mind, sir;
Let ignorance and hell confound the rest.

MISTRESS LOW-WATER
Let it suffice, sweet sir, you cannot think
How dearly you are welcome.

BEVERIL [*kneeling*] May I live
To show you service for't.

MISTRESS LOW-WATER [*raising him*]
Your love, your love, sir;
We go no higher, nor shall you go lower.
Sir, I'm bold to send for you to request
A kindness from your wit for some device
To grace our wedding. It shall be worth your pains;
And something more t'express my love to art,
You shall not receive all in bare embracements.

BEVERIL
Your love I thank; but pray, sir, pardon me;
I've a heart says I must not grant you that.

MISTRESS LOW-WATER
No? What's your reason, sir?

BEVERIL I'm not at peace
With the lady of this house. Now you'll excuse me.
She's wronged my sister, and I may not do't.

MISTRESS LOW-WATER The widow knows you not.

BEVERIL
I never saw her face, to my remembrance.
O, that my heart should feel her wrongs so much,
And yet live ignorant of the injurer!

MISTRESS LOW-WATER
Let me persuade thee, since she knows you not,
Make clear the weather, let not griefs betray you.
I'll tell her you're a worthy friend of mine—

244 **Has** who has
247 **bid** invite
250 **parbreaking** vomiting
chops cheeks
254–69 **I...stand** An emblematic description drawing at first on Noah's preservation from the Flood (Genesis 8:1–5), passing into an image of fortune's victim struggling to survive in raging seas. *Falls* and *streams* also suggest a river torrent; proverbially 'It is vain to strive against the stream'.
258 **deeps** deep waters (perhaps also 'abysses')
falls The falling waters are probably waves rather than waterfalls. The abstract sense is 'calamities, overthrows'.
262 **hand-to-mouth** subsistence living (proverbial)
263 **To...blessing** i.e. (*a*) to enable him to bless his descendants with prosperity (*b*) to earn the blessings of his descendants
lift his arm labour. Develops from both *he tugs in vain* (in the water) and *hand-to-mouth*.
264 **careful** afflicted with cares
266 **happy means** stroke of good fortune
268 **upon** i.e. being myself upon
283 **I'm bold** I presume
294 **to my remembrance** as far as I can remember
295 **her** i.e. Mistress Low-water's

[*Aside*] And so I tell her true; thou art indeed.
Enter Widow
Sir, here she comes.

WIDOW What, are you busy, sir?

MISTRESS LOW-WATER
Nothing less, lady. Here's a gentleman
Of noble parts, beside his friendship to me.
Pray give him liberal welcome.

WIDOW He's most welcome.

MISTRESS LOW-WATER
The virtues of his mind will dèserve largely.

WIDOW
Methinks his outward parts deserve as much then;
A proper gentleman it is.

MISTRESS LOW-WATER Come, worthy sir.

BEVERIL
I follow. [*Exeunt; manet Beveril*]
Check thy blood,
For fear it prove too bold to wrong thy goodness.
A wise man makes affections but his slaves.
Break 'em in time; let 'em not master thee.
O, 'tis my sister's enemy, think of that!
Some speedy grief fall down upon the fire,
Before it take my heart; let it not rise
'Gainst brotherly nature, judgement, and these wrongs.
Make clear the weather.
O, who could look upon her face in storms?
Yet pains may work it out. Griefs do but strive
To kill this spark; I'll keep it still alive. [*Exit*]

Sc. 7

Enter the three late suitors (*Weatherwise, Pepperton, and Overdone*) *joined with Sir Gilbert Lambstone*

WEATHERWISE
Faith, Sir Gilbert, forget and forgive.
There's all our hands to a new bargain of friendship.

PEPPERTON
Ay, and all our hearts to boot, Sir Gilbert.

WEATHERWISE Why, la you, there's but four suitors left on's in all th' world, and the fifth has the widow; if we should not be kind to one another, and so few on's, i'faith, I would we were all raked up in some hole or other.

SIR GILBERT
Pardon me, gentlemen; I cannot but remember
Your late disgraceful words before the widow
In time of my oppression.

WEATHERWISE Puh, Saturn reigned then, a melancholy, grumbling planet; he was in the third house of privy enemies, and would have bewrayed all our plots. Beside, there was a fiery conjunction in the Dragon's Tail that spoilt all that e'er we went about.

SIR GILBERT
Dragon or devil, somewhat 'twas, I am sure.

WEATHERWISE Why, I tell you, Sir Gilbert, we were all out of our wits in't. I was so mad at that time myself, I could have wished an hind-quarter of my bull out of your belly again, whereas now I care not if you had eat tail and all. I am no niggard in the way of friendship. I was ever yet at full moon in good fellowship, and so you shall find if you look into the almanac of my true nature.

SIR GILBERT
Well, all's forgiven for once. Hands apace, gentlemen.

WEATHERWISE Ye shall have two of mine to do you a kindness.
[*He clasps hands with Sir Gilbert*]
[*Aside*] Yet when they're both abroad, who shall look to th' house here?

PEPPERTON *and* OVERDONE Not only a new friendship, but a friend.
[*They clasp hands with Sir Gilbert*]

SIR GILBERT
But upon this condition, gentlemen:
You shall hear now a thing worth your revenge.

WEATHERWISE An you doubt that,
You shall have mine before-hand. I've one ready;
I never go without a black oath about me.

SIR GILBERT
I know the least touch of a spur in this
Will now put your desires to a false gallop,
By all means sland'rous, in every place
And in all companies, to disgrace the widow,
No matter in what rank so it be spiteful
And worthy your revenges. So now I.
It shall be all my study, care, and pains.
And we can lose no labour; all her foes

307 **proper** handsome, well-framed
310 **bold** eager
311 **affections** passions. Beveril has fallen in love with his sister's enemy.
312 **Break 'em** reduce them to obedience
319 **work it out** exhaust it, expell it
7.0.1 *late* former
1 **forget and forgive** (proverbial)
2–3 **There's ... boot** (from the proverb 'with heart and hand')
11 **oppression** trouble, distress
12 **reigned** had predominant influence
13 **third house** The heavens were notionally divided into segments known as houses, through which the heavenly bodies passed each day: six houses below the horizon and six in the visible sky. The house in which a planet was situated at a given time was thought to modify its influence. In fact the twelfth house was traditionally associated with enemies.
14 **bewrayed** revealed
15 **fiery conjunction** A *conjunction* is when two bodies appear in the same sign of the zodiac. It is *fiery* (or 'combust') when one of them is the sun. The other is presumably Venus, the planet in the Dragon's Tail at 6.40. With a sexual implication: 'hot-blooded copulation' (*OED*, *Conjunction*, 2b), which (*a*) refers to the supposed gentleman and the Widow, and (*b*) quibbles on *tail* as 'anus' (taken up in 'Dragon or devil'). **Dragon's Tail** See note to 6.42 and previous note.
30 **th' house** i.e. the almanac
37 **black** malignant, deadly
39 **false gallop** canter. Often used figuratively of unregulated speech; 'to run a false gallop' was proverbial.
42 **rank** (*a*) kind, manner (*b*) rankness
45 **lose no labour** (proverbial)

Will make such use on't that they'll snatch it from us
Faster than we can forge it, though we keep
Four tongues at work upon't and never cease.
Then, for the indifferent world, faith, they're apter
To bid a slander welcome than a truth.
We have the odds of our side. This in time
May grow so general, as disgrace will spread,
That wild dissension may divide the bed.

WEATHERWISE *and* PEPPERTON
Excellent!

OVERDONE
A pure revenge; I see no dregs in't.

SIR GILBERT
Let each man look to his part now, and not feed
Upon one dish all four on's, like plain maltmen;
For at this feast we must have several kickshaws
And delicate-made dishes, that the world
May see it is a banquet finely furnished.

WEATHERWISE
Why then, let me alone for one of your kickshaws.
I have thought on that already.

SIR GILBERT
Prithee, how, sir?

WEATHERWISE Marry, sir, I'll give it out abroad that I have lain with the widow myself. As 'tis the fashion of many a gallant to disgrace his new mistress when he cannot have his will of her, and lie with her name in every tavern though he ne'er came within a yard of her person; so I, being a gentleman, may say as much in that kind as a gallant: I am as free, by my father's copy.

SIR GILBERT This will do excellent, sir!

WEATHERWISE And moreover, I'll give the world thus much to understand beside: that if I had not lain with the widow in the wane of the moon at one of my Seven Stars houses when Venus was about business of her own and could give no attendance, she had been brought abed with two roaring boys by this time, and the Gemini being infants, I'd have made away with them like a step-mother, and put mine own boys in their places.

SIR GILBERT
Why, this is beyond talk; you outrun your master.

Enter Clown

CLOWN Whoop, draw home next time! Here are all the old shooters that have lost the game at pricks. What a fair mark had Sir Gilbert on't if he had shot home before the last arrow came in! Methinks these show to me now for all the world like so many lousy beggars turned out of my lady's barn, and have ne'er a hole to put their heads in.

WEATHERWISE
Mass, here's her ladyship's ass; he tells us anything.

SIR GILBERT
Ho, Peccadill!

CLOWN
What, Sir Gilbert Lambstone!
Gentlemen, outlaws all, how do you do?

SIR GILBERT
How! What dost call us? How goes the world at home, lad?
What strange news?

CLOWN This is the state of prodigals as right as can be: when they have spent all their means on brave feasts, they're glad to scrape to a servingman for a meal's meat.
So you that whilom like four prodigal rivals
Could goose or capon, crane or woodcock, choose,
Now're glad to make up a poor meal with news.
A lamentable hearing!

WEATHERWISE
He's in passion, up to the eyebrows for us.

CLOWN O, Master Weatherwise, I blame none but you. You are a gentleman deeply read in Pond's Almanac; methinks you should not be such a shallow fellow.
You knew this day the twelfth of June would come
When the sun enters into the Crab's room,
And all your hopes would go aside, aside.

48 **tongues** Puns on the instrument used in handling metal in the forge.
49 **for** as for
53 **That** so that
56 **maltmen** maltsters, beer-brewers
57 **kickshaws** dainty dishes
60 **let me alone** leave it to me
65 **lie** *(a)* go to bed *(b)* tell lies
66 **yard** Puns on the measurement of distance and the tavern courtyard.
68 **free** *(a)* of the class of gentleman and above *(b)* free-tongued, unconstrained
68–9 **by my father's copy** *(a)* as established in my father's legal document *(b)* by virtue of being a copy (i.e. son) of my father *(c)* by my father's rights as a copyholder (a recognized tenant on an estate, as distinct from a bondman). Sense *(c)* reflects the usual legal sense of *copy*, but undercuts Weatherwise's claim to gentry status.
73 **in . . . moon** Associated with age, and here with lack of vigour.
74 **houses** taverns (with a quibble on astrological houses)
Venus i.e. *(a)* the planet conducive to sexual love, and *(b)* the tavern maid
77 **Gemini** twins (in Weatherwise's astrological diction)
80 **your master** i.e. the almanac
81 **draw home** draw arrows that hit the target; i.e. better luck
82 **shooters** (pronounced the same as *suitors*)
at pricks *(a)* to hit the bull's-eye *(b)* with penises
83 **mark** *(a)* archery target *(b)* vulva
86–7 **have . . . in** Proverbial for homelessness; with a sexual innuendo.
90 **outlaws** i.e. banished men
96 **meat** food
97 **whilom** formerly
98 **goose . . . woodcock** The Clown probably indicates each suitor in turn. *Goose* and *woodcock* were by-words for stupidity; *capon* suggests impotence; the crane was notoriously clumsy in taking flight, and was considered greedy. All were highly esteemed as food.
100 **hearing** report, news. The strangest news is the suitors' eagerness for news.
103 **Pond's Almanac** Edward Pond began publishing almanacs in 1601. The information that follows is not from Pond, who is named, as *deeply* and *shallow* suggest, for a pun on a pond of water.
105 **the twelfth of June** (the summer solstice in the old-style calendar, when the sun entered Cancer)
107 **aside** Crabs move sideways.

WEATHERWISE The fool says true, i'faith, gentlemen. I knew 'twould come all to this pass. I'll show't you presently.

CLOWN
If you had spared but four of your twelve signs now,
You might have gone to a tavern and made merry
with 'em.

WEATHERWISE H'as the best moral meaning of an ass that e'er I heard speak with tongue. Look you here gentlemen.

[*He reads from his almanac*]

'Fifth day, neither fish nor flesh.'

CLOWN
No, nor good red herring an you look again.

WEATHERWISE 'Sixth day, privily prevented.'

CLOWN Marry, faugh!

WEATHERWISE 'Seventh day, shrunk in the wetting.'

CLOWN
Nay, so will the best ware bought for love or money.

WEATHERWISE 'The eighth day, over head and ears.'

CLOWN By my faith, he come home in a sweet pickle then!

WEATHERWISE 'The ninth day, scarce sound at heart.'

CLOWN What a pox ailed it?

WEATHERWISE 'The tenth day, a courtier's welcome.'

CLOWN That a cup of beer, an you can get it.

WEATHERWISE 'The eleventh day, stones against the wind.'

CLOWN Pox of an ass, he might have thrown 'em better!

WEATHERWISE Now the twelfth day, gentlemen—that was our day—'past all redemption'.

CLOWN Then the devil go with't.

WEATHERWISE
Now you see plainly, gentlemen, how we're used.
The calendar will not lie for no man's pleasure.

SIR GILBERT
Push! You're too confident in almanac posies.

PEPPERTON
Faith, so said we.

SIR GILBERT They're mere delusions.

WEATHERWISE How?
You see how knavishly they happen, sir.

SIR GILBERT
Ay, that's because they're foolishly believed, sir.

[*Sir Gilbert and the Clown talk apart*]

WEATHERWISE Well, take your courses, gentlemen, without 'em, and see what will come on't. You may wander like masterless men; there's ne'er a planet will care a halfpenny for you. If they look after you, I'll be hanged, when you scorn to bestow twopence to look after them.

SIR GILBERT [*to the Clown*] How, a device at the wedding, sayst thou?

CLOWN Why, have none of you heard of that yet?

SIR GILBERT 'Tis the first news, i'faith, lad.

CLOWN O, there's a brave travelling scholar entertained into the house o' purpose, one that has been all the world over, and some part of Jerusalem. H'as his chamber, his diet, and three candles allowed him after supper.

WEATHERWISE By my faith, he need not complain for victuals then, whate'er he be.

CLOWN He lies in one of the best chambers i'th' house, bravely matted; and to warm his wits as much, a cup of sack and an aqua vitae bottle stands just at his elbow.

WEATHERWISE He's shrewdly hurt, by my faith! If he catch an ague of that fashion, I'll be hanged.

CLOWN He'll come abroad anon.

SIR GILBERT Art sure on't?

CLOWN Why, he ne'er stays a quarter of an hour in the house together.

SIR GILBERT No? How can he study then?

CLOWN Fah, best of all: he talks as he goes, and writes as he runs. Besides, you know, 'tis death to a traveller to stand long in one place.

SIR GILBERT
It may hit right, boys!—Honest Peccadill,
Thou wast wont to love me.

CLOWN I'd good cause, sir, then.

SIR GILBERT [*giving money*]
Thou shalt have the same still; take that.

CLOWN Will you believe me now, I ne'er loved you better in my life than I do at this present.

SIR GILBERT
Tell me now truly, who are the presenters?
What persons are employed in the device?

109 **presently** at once
111 **tavern** Appropriate because taverns display inn-signs.
115–30 **Fifth . . . redemption** The mottoes are assembled from various 'evil days' between March and December in Bretnor's 1611 almanac, except the ambiguous 'a courtier's welcome', which is listed as a 'good day'.
115 **neither . . . flesh** Proverbial for 'neither one thing nor the other', but here suggesting 'nothing of any kind will come of it', alluding to fish as the food of fast-days; and with the bawdy suggestion of no sexual success.
116 **nor good red herring** A common amplification of the proverb, ruling out the flesh-like fish.
117 **privily prevented** The Clown picks up on the lavatory senses of *privy* and *vented*.
118 **faugh** An expression of disgust.
119 **shrunk in the wetting** (proverbial)
120 **for love or money** (proverbial)
121 **over head and ears** (proverbial for 'completely immersed')
122 **By . . . then** (implying that he is *over head and ears* in drink or mire)
in . . . pickle (proverbial)
125 **a courtier's welcome** Presumably polite but cold and meagre, as indicated by *a cup of beer*. The phrase is from Bretnor.
127 **stones against the wind** (proverbial for a futile act)
131 **Then . . . with't** (picking up on the religious sense of *redemption*)
133 **lie** tell lies (and quibbling on 'lie in bed for sex')
134 **Push** pish
140 **masterless men** unemployed itinerents
141 **look after** take care of (but in l. 133, 'seek after')
142 **twopence** (the price of an almanac)
156 **aqua vitae** i.e. spirits such as brandy
157 **shrewdly** cursedly, badly (used ironically)
158 **of that fashion** in that way
164 **goes** walks
171 **at this present** (*a*) right now (*b*) for this gift
173 **persons** (pronounced the same as *parsons*)

CLOWN Parsons? Not any, sir. My mistress will not be at the charge; she keeps none but an old Welsh vicar.

SIR GILBERT Prithee, I mean who be the speakers?

CLOWN Troth, I know none but those that open their mouths.

Enter Master Beveril, [*with a pasteboard*]

Here he comes now himself; you may ask him.

WEATHERWISE Is this he? By my faith, one may pick a gentleman out of his calves and a scholar out on's cheeks; one may see by his looks what's in him. I warrant you there has ne'er a new almanac come out these dozen years but he has studied it over and over.

SIR GILBERT [*to the Clown*] Do not reveal us now.

CLOWN Because you shall be sure on't, you have given me a ninepence here; and I'll give you the slip for't. *Exit*

SIR GILBERT
Well said. Now the fool's pleased, we may be bold.
[*The suitors talk apart*]

BEVERIL [*aside*]
Love is as great an enemy to wit
As ignorance to art. I find my powers
So much employed in business of my heart
That all the time's too little to dispatch
Affairs within me. Fortune too remiss,
I suffer for thy slowness. Had I come
Before a vow had chained their souls together,
There might have been some hope, though ne'er so little.
Now there's no spark at all, nor e'er can be,
But dreadful ones struck from adultery;
And if my lust were smothered with her will,
O, who could wrong a gentleman so kind,
A stranger made up with a brother's mind?

SIR GILBERT [*aside to the other former suitors*]
Peace, peace, enough. Let me alone to manage it.—
A quick invention, and a happy one,
Reward your study, sir.

BEVERIL Gentlemen, I thank you.

SIR GILBERT
We understand your wits are in employment, sir,
In honour of this wedding.

BEVERIL Sir, the gentleman
To whom that worthy lady is betrothed
Vouchsafes t'accept the power of my good will in't.

SIR GILBERT
I pray resolve us then, sir, for we're friends
That love and honour her—

ANOTHER SUITOR That humbly serve her—

SIR GILBERT
Whether your number be yet full or no
Of those which you make choice of for presenters.

BEVERIL
First, 'tis so brief, because the time is so,
We shall not trouble many; and, for those
We shall employ, the house will yield in servants.

SIR GILBERT
Nay then, under your leave and favour, sir,
Since all your pains will be so weakly graced,
And, wanting due performance, lose their lustre,
Here are four of us gentlemen her friends,
Both lovers of her honour and your art,
That would be glad so to express ourselves,
And think our service well and worthily placed.

BEVERIL
My thanks do me no grace for this large kindness;
You make my labours proud of such presenters.

SIR GILBERT
She shall not think, sir, she's so ill beloved
But friends can quickly make that number perfect.

BEVERIL
She's bound t'acknowledge it.

SIR GILBERT Only thus much, sir,
Which will amaze her most: I'd have't so carried,
As you can do't, that neither she nor none
Should know what friends we were till all were done.

WEATHERWISE
Ay, that would make the sport.

BEVERIL I like it well, sir.
My hand and faith amongst you, gentlemen,
It shall be so disposed of.

SIR GILBERT We are the men then.

BEVERIL
Then look you, gentlemen.
[*He shows them the pasteboard*]
The device is single,
Naked, and plain, because the time's so short,
And gives no freedom to a wealthier sport.
'Tis only, gentlemen, the four elements
In liveliest forms: Earth, Water, Air, and Fire.

WEATHERWISE
Mass, and here's four of us too.

BEVERIL It fits well, sir.
This is the effect: that, whereas all those four
Maintain a natural opposition

175 **charge** expense
vicar Originally a clergyman who stands in for a parson.
181 **calves** (i.e. the stockings on them, perhaps of silk or some such costly material)
182 **cheeks** (presumably pale)
185 **reveal us** (as the former suitors)
187 **a ninepence** i.e. an Irish shilling, worth only nine English pence. A veiled complaint.
give you the slip (*a*) slip away from you (*b*) give you a counterfeit coin (compare previous note)
196 **though** even if
199 **smothered** i.e. satiated
203 **quick** lively
invention creative faculty, inventiveness
happy fortunate (i.e. financially beneficial)
223 **large** generous
226 **perfect** full, complete
227 **thus much** i.e. with this qualification
234 **single** i.e. without preliminary episode, sub-plot, or the like
238 **In liveliest forms** i.e. most vividly represented in living form

And untruced war the one against the other,
To shame their ancient envies they should see
How well in two breasts all these do agree.

WEATHERWISE
That's in the bride and bridegroom; I am quick, sir.

SIR GILBERT
In faith, it's pretty, sir; I approve it well.

BEVERIL
But see how soon my happiness and your kindness
Is crossed together.

SIR GILBERT Crossed? I hope not so, sir.

BEVERIL
I can employ but two of you.

PEPPERTON How comes that, sir?

BEVERIL
Air and the Fire should be by men presented,
But the two other in the forms of women.

WEATHERWISE
Nay, then we're gone again. I think these women
Were made to vex and trouble us in all shapes.

SIR GILBERT [*to Beveril*]
Faith, sir, you stand too nicely.

WEATHERWISE [*to Beveril*] So think I, sir.

BEVERIL
Yet when we tax ourselves, it may the better
Set off our errors when the fine eyes judge 'em.—
But Water certainly should be a woman.

WEATHERWISE By my faith, then he is gelded since I saw him last. He was thought to be a man once, when he got his wife with child before he was married.

BEVERIL
Fie, you are fishing in another stream, sir.

WEATHERWISE But now I come to yours an you go to that, sir: I see no reason then but Fire and Water should change shapes and genders.

BEVERIL How prove you that, sir?

WEATHERWISE Why, there's no reason but Water should be a man, because Fire is commonly known to be a quean.

BEVERIL So, sir, you argue well.

WEATHERWISE Nay, more, sir. Water will break in at a little crevice; so will a man if he be not kept out. Water will undermine; so will an informer. Water will ebb and flow; so will a gentleman. Water will search any place; and so will a constable, as lately he did at my Seven Stars for a young wench that was stole. Water will quench fire, and so will Wat the barber. Ergo, let Water wear a codpiece point.

BEVERIL
Faith, gentlemen, I like your company well.

WEATHERWISE Let's see who'll dispute with me at the full o'th' moon.

BEVERIL No, sir; an you be vainglorious of your talent, I'll put you to't once more.

WEATHERWISE I'm for you, sir, as long as the moon keeps in this quarter.

BEVERIL Well, how answer you this then? Earth and Water are both bearers; therefore they should be women.

WEATHERWISE Why, so are porters and pedlars, and yet they are known to be men.

BEVERIL I'll give you over in time, sir; I shall repent the bestowing on't else.

WEATHERWISE If I that have proceeded in five-and-twenty such books of astronomy should not be able to put down a scholar now, the dominical letter being 'G', I stood for a goose.

SIR GILBERT
Then this will satisfy you: though't be a woman,
Ocèanus, the sea, that's chief of waters,
He wears the form of a man, and so may you.

BEVERIL
Now I hear reason, and I may consent.

SIR GILBERT
And so, though Earth challenge a feminine face,
The matter of which earth consists, that's dust,
The general soul of earth, is of both kinds.

BEVERIL
Fit yourselves, gentlemen; I've enough for me.
Earth, Water, Air, and Fire, part 'em amongst you.

243 **envies** malices
254 **stand too nicely** insist too much upon niceties
256 **Set off** put out of consideration
258–60 **By ... married** Puns on *water* and the name *Walter*, and quibbling on *water* as 'seminal fluid'.
262 **I ... that** i.e. we exchange 'streams'
267–8 **Fire ... quean** Alludes to fire as a figure for lust and as a euphemism for venereal disease.
268 **quean** prostitute
272–3 **ebb and flow** Applies to the *gentleman* as 'fluctuate in wealth'.
275 **Seven Stars** (the tavern name)
276 **Wat** (diminutive of *Walter*)
the barber Barber-surgeons would treat venereal disease (*fire*)
Ergo therefore (Latin)
286 **bearers** Playing on the senses 'child-bearers' and 'supporters'. The earth both supports those who stand upon it and is commonly figured as a 'mother' to all life; water supports floating vessels.
289 **give you over** give up on you
290 **bestowing on't** i.e. time spent on it
291 **proceeded in** advanced through, graduated in
293 **now** The original 1657 printed text reads 'now in One thousand six hundred thirty and eight', an interpolation referring to the year of James Shirley's revival of the play in Dublin.
dominical letter The letter used to denote Sundays in a given year; often printed in red or large type in almanacs. It was established by giving each day in the first week of the year a letter from A to G. The dominical letter for 1611, the almost certain year of first production, was in fact F, but that for 1638 (see previous note) happened to be G.
293–4 **stood for** would be reckoned as (quibbling on G as the initial letter of *goose*)
296 **Ocèanus** one of the Titans; father of the rivers of the world and of the ocean nymphs
299 **challenge** claim as its due
301 **of both kinds** i.e. composed of the dead of both sexes
302 **Fit yourselves** have it your way

WEATHERWISE
Let me play Air; I was my father's eldest son.
BEVERIL
Ay, but this air never possessed the lands.
WEATHERWISE I'm but disposed to jest with you, sir. 'Tis the same my almanac speaks on, is't not?
BEVERIL That 'tis, sir.
WEATHERWISE Then leave it to my discretion to fit both the part and the person.
BEVERIL
You shall have your desire, sir.
SIR GILBERT We'll agree
Without your trouble now, sir; we're not factious,
Or envy one another for best parts
Like quarrelling actors that have passionate fits;
We submit always to the writer's wits.
BEVERIL
He that commends you may do't liberally,
For you deserve as much as praise can show.
SIR GILBERT
We'll send to you privately.
BEVERIL I'll dispatch you.
SIR GILBERT [*aside*]
We'll poison your device. *Exit*
PEPPERTON [*aside*] She must have pleasures,
Shows, and conceits, and we disgraceful doom!
WEATHERWISE [*aside*]
We'll make your elements come limping home.
Exeunt suitors
BEVERIL
How happy am I in this unlooked-for grace,
This voluntary kindness from these gentlemen!
Enter Mistress Low-water and her man-husband,
[*both disguised as before, unobserved by Beveril*]
'Twill set off all my labours far more pleasing
Before the widow, whom my heart calls mistress,
But my tongue dares not second it.
MASTER LOW-WATER [*aside to Mistress Low-water*]
How say you now, Kate?
MISTRESS LOW-WATER [*aside to Master Low-water*]
I like this music well, sir.
BEVERIL O, unfortunate!
Yet though a tree be guarded from my touch,
There's none can hinder me to love the fruit.
MISTRESS LOW-WATER [*aside*]
Nay, now we know your mind, brother, we'll provide for you.
Exit [*with her man-husband*]
BEVERIL
O, were it but as free as late times knew it,
I would deserve if all life's wealth could do it! *Exit*

Sc. 8

Enter, at Sir Oliver's house, himself; old Sunset;
Sir Oliver's redeemed lady, Philip's Mother;
Master Sandfield; the Dutch Merchant; Philip, Sir
Oliver's son; and Savourwit aloof off; and Servants
SIR OLIVER [*to Philip's Mother*]
O, my reviving joy! Thy quick'ning presence
Makes the sad night of threescore and ten years
Sit like a youthful spring upon my blood.
I cannot make thy welcome rich enough
With all the wealth of words.
MOTHER It is expressed, sir,
With more than can be equalled. The ill store
Lies only on my side; my thanks are poor.
SIR OLIVER
Blest be the goodness of his mind for ever
That did redeem thy life! May it return
Upon his fortunes double! That worthy gentleman,
Kind Master Beveril! Shower upon him, heaven,
Some unexpected happiness to requite him
For these my joys unlooked for! O, more kind,
And juster far is a mere stranger's goodness
Than the sophistic faith of natural sons.
Here's one could juggle with me, take up the ransom,
He and his loose companion.
SAVOURWIT [*aside*] Say you me so, sir?
I'll eat hard eggs for that trick!
SIR OLIVER Spend the money,
And bring me home false news and empty pockets!
In that young gallant's tongue there, you were dead
Ten weeks before this day, had not this merchant
Brought first the truth in words, yourself in substance.
MOTHER
Pray let me stay you here ere you proceed, sir.
Did he report me dead, say you?
SIR OLIVER Else you live not.
MOTHER
See now, sir, you may lay your blame too rashly,
When nobody looked after it. Let me tell you, sir,
A father's anger should take great advice
Ere it condemn flesh of so dear a price.
He's no way guilty yet, for that report
The general tongue of all the country spread;
For, being removed far off, I was thought dead.
PHILIP
Can my faith now be taken into favour, sir?
Is't worthy to be trusted?
SAVOURWIT [*aside*] No, by my troth, is't not.
'Twould make shift to spend another ransom yet.
SIR OLIVER [*to Philip*]
Well, sir, I must confess you've here dealt well with me;
And what is good in you I love again.

304 **Air** Puns on *heir*.
305 **possessed the lands** i.e. (*a*) as inheritor (*b*) as an element distinct from earth
309–10 **fit . . . person** i.e. supply an appropriate costume and act the role fittingly
318 **dispatch you** i.e. answer you quickly
320 **conceits** fanciful devices
doom Rhymes with *home*.
327 **this music** i.e. Beveril's words
8.14 **juster** more honourable
mere complete
18 **I'll** i.e. I'll have to
26 **looked after** demanded, deserved
27 **advice** deliberation
34 **make shift** find a way

SAVOURWIT [*aside*]
Now am I halfways in, just to the girdle;
But the worst part's behind.

SIR OLIVER [*to Philip*] Marry, I fear me, sir,
This weather is too glorious to hold long.

MOTHER
I see no cloud to interpose it, sir,
If you place confidence in what I have told you.

SIR OLIVER
Nay, 'tis clear sky on that side; would 'twere so
All over his obedience! I see that,
And so does this good gentleman—

MOTHER [*to the Dutch Merchant*] Do you, sir?

SIR OLIVER
That makes his honesty doubtful.

MOTHER [*to the Dutch Merchant*] I pray, speak, sir.
The truth of your last kindness makes me bold with you.

DUTCH MERCHANT
The knight your husband, madam, can best speak.
He truliest can show griefs whose heart they break.

MOTHER [*to Sir Oliver*]
I'm sorry yet for more. Pray let me know't, sir,
That I may help to chide him, though 'twould grieve me.

SIR OLIVER
Why then, prepare for't. You came over now
In the best time to do't you could pick out.
Not only spent my money, but, to blind me,
He and his wicked instrument—

SAVOURWIT [*aside*] Now he fiddles me.

SIR OLIVER
Brings home a minion here—by great chance known—
Told me she was his sister; she proves none.

MOTHER [*to Philip*]
This was unkindly done, sir. Now I'm sorry
My good opinion lost itself upon you.
You are not the same son I left behind me;
More grace took him.—O, let me end in time,
For fear I should forget myself and chide him!
Where is she, sir? Though he beguiled your eyes,
He cannot deceive mine; we're now too hard for him.
For since our first unfortunate separation,
I've often seen the girl—[*aside*] would that were true!—
By many a happy accident, many a one,
But never durst acknowledge her for mine own;
And therein stood my joys distressed again.

SIR OLIVER
You rehearse miseries, wife!—Call the maid down.
[*Exit Servant*]

SAVOURWIT [*aside*]
She's been too often down to be now called so.
She'll lie down shortly and call somebody up.

MOTHER
He's now to deal with one, sir, that knows truth.
He must be shamed or quit; there's no mean saves him.

SIR OLIVER
I hear her come.

MOTHER [*aside to Philip*]
You see how hard 'tis now
To rèdeem good opinion, being once gone.
Be careful then, and keep it when 'tis won.
Now see me take a poison with great joy
Which, but for thy sake, I should swoon to touch.
Enter Grace

GRACE
What new affliction? Am I set to sale
For anyone that bids most shame for me?

SIR OLIVER [*to Philip's Mother*]
Look you, do you see what stuff they've brought me home here?

MOTHER
O bless her, eternal powers! My life, my comforts,
My nine years' grief, but everlasting joy now,
Thrice welcome to my heart! 'Tis she indeed.
[*She embraces Grace*]

SIR OLIVER
What, is it?

PHILIP I'm unfit to carry a ransom?

SAVOURWIT [*aside to Grace*]
Down on your knees, to save your belly harmless.
Ask blessing, though you never mean to use it
But give't away presently to a beggar wench.
[*Grace kneels*]

PHILIP [*to Sir Oliver*]
My faith is blemished, I'm no man of trust, sir?

MOTHER
Rise with a mother's blessing.
[*Grace rises*]

SAVOURWIT [*aside*] All this while
She's risse with a son's.

SIR OLIVER But soft ye, soft ye, wife!
I pray take heed you place your blessing right now.
This honest Dutchman here told me he saw her
At Antwerp in an inn.

MOTHER True, she was so, sir.

38 **the . . . behind** (proverbial)
45 **That** who
54 **instrument** agent, helper (but Savourwit takes it as 'musical instrument')
55 **minion** strumpet
known found out
60 **took** lit upon
71 **shortly** straight away
call somebody up (*a*) summon someone upstairs (*b*) provoke an erection in someone
86 **your belly** (alluding to Grace's pregnancy)
91 **risse** risen (another reference to pregnancy)

DUTCH MERCHANT
Sir, 'tis my quality what I speak once
I affirm ever. In that inn I saw her.
That lets her not to be your daughter now.
SIR OLIVER
O, sir, is't come to that?
SUNSET Here's joys ne'er dreamt on!
SIR OLIVER
O, Master Sunset, I am at the rising
Of my refulgent happiness!—Now, son Sandfield,
Once more and ever!
SANDFIELD I am proud on't, sir.
SIR OLIVER [*to Philip*]
Pardon me, boy; I have wronged thy faith too much.
SAVOURWIT [*aside*]
Now may I leave my shell and peep my head forth.
SIR OLIVER
Where is this Savourwit, that honest whoreson,
That I may take my curse from his knave's shoulders?
SAVOURWIT
O sir, I feel you at my very blade here.
Your curse is ten-stone weight, and a pound over.
SIR OLIVER
Come, thou'rt a witty varlet, and a trusty.
SAVOURWIT
You shall still find me a poor faithful fellow, sir,
If you have another ransom to send over,
Or daughter to find out.
SIR OLIVER I'll do thee right, boy.
I ne'er yet knew thee but speak honest English.
Marry, in Dutch I found thee a knave lately.
SAVOURWIT
That was to hold you but in play a little,
Till farther truths came over, and I strong.
You shall ne'er find me a knave in mine own tongue;
I have more grace in me. I go out of England
Still when I take such courses; that shows modesty,
sir.
SIR OLIVER
Anything full of wit, and void of harm,
I give thee pardon for; so was that now.
SAVOURWIT [*aside*]
Faith, now I'm quit I find myself the nimbler
To serve you so again, and my will's good,
Like one that lately shook off his old irons
And cuts a purse at bench to deserve new ones.
SIR OLIVER
Since it holds all the way so fortunate still,
And strikes so even with my first belief,
This is the gentleman, wife, young Master Sandfield
here,
A man of worthy parts beside his lands,
Whom I make choice of for my daughter's bed.
SAVOURWIT [*aside*]
But he'll make choice there of another bedfellow.
MOTHER
I wish 'em both the happiness of love, sir.
SIR OLIVER
'Twas spoke like a good lady. An your memory
Can reach it, wife—but 'tis so long ago too—
Old Master Sunset he had a young daughter
When you unluckily left England so,
And much about the age of our girl there,
For both were nursed together.
MOTHER 'Tis so fresh
In my remembrance, now you've wakened it,
As if twelve years were but a twelve hours' dream.
SIR OLIVER
That girl is now a proper gentlewoman,
As fine a body, wife, as e'er was measured
With an indenture cut in farthing steaks—
SUNSET
O, say not so, Sir Oliver. You shall pardon me, sir;
I'faith, sir, you are to blame.
SIR OLIVER Sings, dances, plays,
Touches an instrument with a motherly grace.
SUNSET
'Tis your own daughter that you mean that by.
SAVOURWIT [*aside*]
There's open Dutch indeed, an he could take it.
SIR OLIVER
This wench, under your leave—
SUNSET You have my love in't.
SIR OLIVER
Is my son's wife that shall be.
SAVOURWIT [*aside*] Thus I hold with't:
Is your son's wife that should be Master Sandfield's.
MOTHER
I come in happy time to a feast of marriages.
SIR OLIVER
And now you put's i'th' mind, the hour draws on
At the new-married widow's; there we're looked for.
There will be entertainments, sports, and banquets.

97 **lets** prevents
99–100 **O...happiness** (quibbling on Sunset's name)
100 **son** (said of Sandfield as potential son-in-law)
104 **whoreson** rogue, fellow (used playfully)
106 **blade** shoulder-blade
115 **I strong** i.e. until my position was strong
118 **Still** always
124 **bench** court of law
128 **parts** qualities
130 **he'll** i.e. Philip will
140 **proper** handsome
142 **With...steaks** i.e. by a young man just released from his indenture as apprentice, just graduated from youth
farthing steaks tiny strips
146 **'Tis...by** Picks up on *grace* as the daughter Grace.
147 **open Dutch** Dutch language intelligible to an English ear; i.e. words more transparently true than they might seem (because the supposed daughter Grace is *motherly* in that she will soon be a mother). Introduces possible sexual equivocations on *Touches an instrument*, *open* (sexually available), and *take*.
take understand (and see previous note)

There these young lovers shall clap hands together.
The seed of one feast shall bring forth another.

SUNSET
Well said, Sir Oliver.

SIR OLIVER [*to the Dutch Merchant*]
You're a stranger, sir.
Your welcome will be best.

DUTCH MERCHANT Good sir, excuse me.

SIR OLIVER
You shall along, i'faith; you must not refuse me.

Exeunt; manent Mother, Sister (Grace), Philip, and Savourwit

PHILIP
O, mother, these new joys that sets my soul up,
Which had no means, nor any hope of any,
Has brought me now so far in debt to you
I know not which way to begin to thank you.
I am so lost in all, I cannot guess
Which of the two my service most constrains,
Your last kind goodness or your first dear pains.

MOTHER
Love is a mother's duty to a son,
As a son's duty is both love and fear.

SAVOURWIT
I owe you a poor life, madam, that's all.
Pray call for't when you please; it shall be ready for
you.

MOTHER
Make much on't, sir, till then.

SAVOURWIT [*aside*] If buttered sack will.

MOTHER
Methinks the more I look upon her, son,
The more thy sister's face runs in my mind.

PHILIP
Belike she's somewhat like her; it makes the better,
madam.

MOTHER
Was Antwerp, say you, the first place you found her
in?

PHILIP
Yes, madam. Why do you ask?

MOTHER [*to Grace*] Whose daughter were you?

GRACE
I know not rightly whose, to speak truth, madam.

SAVOURWIT [*aside*]
The mother of her was a good twigger the whilst.
[*Philip and Savourwit talk apart*]

MOTHER [*to Grace*]
No? With whom were you brought up then?

GRACE With those, madam,
To whom, I've often heard, the enemy sold me.

MOTHER What's that?

GRACE
Too often have I heard this piteous story
Of a distressèd mother I had once,
Whose comfortable sight I lost at sea;
But then the years of childhood took from me
Both the remembrance of her and the sorrows.

MOTHER [*aside*]
O, I begin to feel her in my blood!
My heart leaps to be at her.—What was that mother?

GRACE
Some said an English lady—but I know not.

MOTHER
What's thy name?

GRACE Grace.

MOTHER May it be so in heaven,
For thou art mine on earth. Welcome, dear child,
Unto thy father's house, thy mother's arms,
After thy foreign sorrows.
[*She embraces Grace*]

SAVOURWIT [*showing Philip his Mother and Grace*]
'Twill prove gallant.

MOTHER
What, son, such earnest work: I bring thee joy now
Will make the rest show nothing, 'tis so glorious.

PHILIP
Why, 'tis not possible, madam, that man's happiness
Should take a greater height than mine aspires.

MOTHER
No, now you shall confess it; this shall quit thee
From all fears present or hereafter doubts
About this business.

PHILIP Give me that, sweet mother.

MOTHER
Here, take her then, and set thine arms a-work.
There needs no 'fection; 'tis indeed thy sister.

PHILIP
My sister!

SAVOURWIT [*aside*]
Cuds me, I feel the razor!

MOTHER
Why, how now, son, how comes a change so soon?

PHILIP
O, I beseech you, mother, wound me anywhere
But where you pointed last; that's present death.
Devise some other miserable torment,
Though ne'er so pitiless, and I'll run and meet it.
Some way more merciful let your goodness think on
May steal away my joys but save my soul.

155 **clap hands together** pledge themselves to each other before witnesses in a spousal
157–8 **You're . . . best** (from the proverbial advice, 'Give the stranger welcome')
166 **first dear pains** (of childbirth)
171 **buttered sack** i.e. mulled wine with melted butter
174 **makes** works out
178 **twigger** prolific breeder (hence 'woman with various sexual partners')
190–1 **May . . . earth** Echoing the Lord's Prayer: 'Thy will be done on earth as it is in heaven'. The point is probably that divine *grace* is necessary for this.
194 **earnest** weighty, important
197 **take** measure (as in gauging the altitude of a heavenly body)
aspires mounts up to
199 **hereafter** future
202 **'fection** affectation
210 **May** that may

I'll willingly restore back every one
Upon that mild condition; anything
But what you spake last will be comfortable.

MOTHER
You're troubled with strange fits in England here.
Your first suit to me did entreat me hardly
To say 'twas she, to have old wrath appeased;
And now 'tis known your sister, you're not pleased.
How should I show myself?

PHILIP
Say 'tis not she.

MOTHER
Shall I deny my daughter?

PHILIP
O, you kill me
Beyond all tortures!

MOTHER
Why do you deal thus with me?

PHILIP
She is my wife; I married her at Antwerp.
I have known the way unto her bed these three months.

SAVOURWIT [*aside*]
And that's too much by twelve weeks for a sister.

MOTHER
I understand you now, too soon, too plain.

PHILIP
O mother, if you love my peace for ever,
Examine her again, find me not guilty.

MOTHER
'Tis now too late; her words make that too true.

PHILIP
Her words! Shall bare words overthrow a soul?
A body is not cast away so lightly.
How can you know 'tis she? Let sense decide it:
She then so young, and both so long divided.

MOTHER
She tells me the sad story.

PHILIP
Does that throw me?
Many a distress may have the face of yours
That never was kin to you.

MOTHER
But however, sir,
I trust you are not married.

PHILIP
Here's the witness,
And all the wealth I had with her: this ring
That joined our hearts together.
[*He shows the ring*]

MOTHER
O, too clear now!
Thou'st brought in evidence to o'erthrow thyself.
Had no one word been spoke, only this shown,
'T had been enough to approve her for mine own.
See here two letters that begun my name
Before I knew thy father. This I gave her,
And as a jewel fastened to her ear.

GRACE
Pardon me, mother, that you find it stray.
I kept it till I gave my heart away.

PHILIP
O, to what mountain shall I take my flight,
To hide the monster of my sin from sight?

SAVOURWIT [*aside*]
I'll to Wales presently; there's the best hills
To hide a poor knave in.

MOTHER
O, heap not desperation upon guilt!
Repent yet, and all's saved. 'Twas but hard chance.
Amongst all sins, heaven pities ignorance;
She's still the first that has her pardon signed.
All sins else see their faults; she's only blind.
Go to thy chamber, pray, leave off, and win.
One hour's repentance cures a twelvemonth's sin.

GRACE
O my distressèd husband, my dear brother!
Exit Mother, cum filia (*Grace*)

PHILIP
O Savourwit, never came sorrow yet
To mankind like it! I'm so far distressed
I've no time left to give my heart attendance,
Too little all to wait upon my soul!
Before this tempest came, how well I stood,
Full in the beams of blessedness and joy!
The memory of man could never say
So black a storm fell in so bright a day.
I am that man that e'en life surfeits of;
Or, if to live, unworthy to be seen
By the savage eyesight. Give's thy hand.
Commend me to thy prayers.

SAVOURWIT
Next time I say 'em.

PHILIP
Farewell, my honest breast, that cravest no more
Than possible kindness. That I've found thee large in,
And I must ask no more. There wit must stay;
It cannot pass where fate stops up the way.
Joy thrive with thee; I'll never see thee more.
[*He starts to leave*]

SAVOURWIT
What's that, sir? Pray come back, and bring those words with you.
You shall not carry 'em so out of my company.
There's no last refuge when your father knows it;
There's no such need on't yet; stay but till then,
And take one with you that will imitate you
In all the desperate onsets man dare think on.

211 **restore back** Prompted by *steal away*, but now Philip is the thief.
215 **hardly** obdurately
216 **old** inveterate
229 **cast away** i.e. condemned to death. A single testimony was not considered sufficient proof in law.
236 **with her** along with her (by way of dowry)
240 **approve** prove
241 **here** (on the ring)
248 **Wales** (well known for its mountains)
254 **she's only** she alone is
255 **leave off** i.e. abstain from sex
257.1 *cum filia* with the daughter
260 **give . . . attendance** i.e. set my feelings in order
261 **all** at all
268 **savage eyesight** eyesight of savages
269 **Commend . . . prayers** Implies that Philip is contemplating suicide.

Were it to challenge all the wolves in France
To meet at one set battle, I'd be your half in't;
All beasts of venom, what you had a mind to,
Your part should be took still. For such a day
Let's keep ourselves in heart; then am I for you.
In the mean time, to beat off all suspicion,
Let's to the bride-house too; here's my petition.

PHILIP
Thou hast a learning art when all hopes fly.
Let one night waste; there's time enough left to die.

SAVOURWIT
A minute's as good as a thousand year, sir,
To pink a man's heart like a summer suit. *Exeunt*

Sc. 9

Enter two or three Servants, [setting forth a stage for the masque, and] placing things in order, with Peccadill the Clown like an overseer

CLOWN Bestir your bones nimbly, you ponderous beef-buttocked knaves! What a number of lazy hinds do I keep company withal! Where's the flesh-colour velvet cushion now, for my lady's peaseporridge-tawny satin bum? You, attendants upon revels?

FIRST SERVANT You can prate and domineer well, because you have a privilege place, but I'd fain see you set your hand to't.

CLOWN O base bone-pickers! I, set my hand to't? When did you e'er see a gentleman set his hand to anything, unless it were to a sheepskin and receive a hundred pound for his pains?

SECOND SERVANT And afterward lie in the Counter for his pleasure.

CLOWN Why, true, sir; 'tis for his pleasure indeed; for spite of all their teeths he may lie i'th' Hole when he list.

FIRST SERVANT Marry, and should, for me.

CLOWN Ay, thou wouldst make as good a bawd as the best jailer of them all; I know that.

FIRST SERVANT How, fool?

Loud music [*within*]

CLOWN Hark! I must call you knave within; 'tis but staying somewhat the longer for't. *Exeunt*

Enter the new-married Widow, and Kate Low-water [*as*] *her husband, both changed in apparel, arm in arm together; after them, Sir Oliver Twilight, Master Sunset, and the Dutch Merchant; after them, the Mother, Grace the daughter, sad, with Jane Sunset; after these, melancholy Philip, Savourwit, and Master Sandfield*

MISTRESS LOW-WATER
This fair assembly is most freely welcome.

ALL THE REST
Thanks to you, good sir.

WIDOW [*to the Mother*]
Come, my long-wished-for madam;
You and this worthy stranger take best welcome.
Your freedom is a second feast to me.

[*Enter Master Low-water, disguised as before*]

MISTRESS LOW-WATER [*aside to him*]
How is't with my brother?

MASTER LOW-WATER [*aside to her*]
The fit holds him still.
No love's more violent.

MISTRESS LOW-WATER [*aside to him*]
'Las, poor gentleman!
I would he had my office without money;
If he should offer any, I'd refuse it.

MASTER LOW-WATER [*aside to her*] I have the letter ready.
He's worthy of a place knows how to use it.

MISTRESS LOW-WATER
That's well said.—Come, ladies, gentlemen, Sir Oliver;
Good, seat yourselves. Shall we be found unreadiest?

[*They sit*]

What is yon gentleman with the funeral face there?
Methinks that look does ill become a bride-house.

SIR OLIVER
Who does your worship mean, sir, my son Philip?
I am sure he had ne'er less reason to be sad.—
Why are you sad, son Philip?

PHILIP
How, sir, sad?
You shall not find it so, sir.

SAVOURWIT [*aside to Philip*] Take heed he do not, then. You must beware how you carry your face in this company. As far as I can see, that young bridegroom has hawk's eyes. He'll go nigh to spell 'sister' in your face if your nose were but crooked enough to serve for an 'S'; he'd find an eye presently, and then he has more light for the rest.

PHILIP [*aside to Savourwit*] I'll learn then to dissemble.

282 **be your half** share the risk
283 **what** whatever
288 **learning art** skill in teaching
291 **pink** deck out, ornament (i.e., as applied to the heart, cheer up)
9.2 **hinds** servants
4 **peaseporridge-tawny** (mocking fanciful compounds for describing the colour of fabrics)
7 **privilege** (the Servant's mistake for *privileged*)
9 **bone-pickers** i.e. eaters of leftovers
11 **sheepskin** parchment, legal document (for a loan)
13 **Counter** (the name for either of the debtors' prisons; with a possible pun on *cunt*)
for (*a*) as amends for (*b*) to procure (the Clown's sense)
15–16 **spite ... teeths** in defiance of them all (proverbial). *Teeths* might also suggest the seizing powers of usury or the law.
16 **lie i'th' Hole** (*a*) be imprisoned in the Hole (the worst room in the debtors' prison) (*b*) have sexual intercourse
17 **for me** as far as I'm concerned
25 **this worthy stranger** i.e. the Dutch merchant
29 **without money** Public offices were often obtained with bribes.
31 **the letter** i.e. the letter Beveril receives at l. 296.1 (but quibbling on a letter of recommendation)
32 **worthy of a place** i.e. deserves the *office* purely on merit
34 **Shall we** i.e. who's going to
42 **As ... see** (proverbial)
43 **has hawk's eyes** (proverbial)
45 **an eye** i.e. (*a*) an eye in Philip's face (*b*) an eye to see *the rest* (*c*) a letter 'I'

SAVOURWIT [*aside to Philip*] Nay, an you be to learn that now you'll ne'er sit in a branched velvet gown as long as you live. You should have took that at nurse, before your mother weaned you; so do all those that prove great children and batten well.

Enter Master Beveril, with a pasteboard

Peace, here comes a scholar indeed; he has learnt it, I warrant you.

WIDOW [*to Beveril*]
Kind sir, you're welcome. You take all the pains, sir.

BEVERIL
I wish they were but worthy of the grace
Of your fair presence and this choice assembly.
Here is an abstract, madam, of what's shown,
Which I commend to your favour.
[*He gives her the pasteboard*]

WIDOW Thank you for't, sir.

BEVERIL [*aside*]
I would I durst present my love as boldly.

MISTRESS LOW-WATER [*aside, hearing him*]
My honest brother!

WIDOW [*showing Mistress Low-water the pasteboard*]
Look thee here, sweetheart.

MISTRESS LOW-WATER
What's there, sweet madam?

BEVERIL Music, and we're ready.

Loud music a while. A thing like a globe opens of one side o'th' stage and flashes out fire; then Sir Gilbert, that presents the part, issues forth with yellow hair and beard, intermingled with streaks like wild flames, a three-forked fire in's hand. And at the same time [*Weatherwise, presenting*] *Air, comes down, hanging by a cloud, with a coat made like an almanac, all the twelve moons set in it, and the four quarters, Winter, Spring, Summer, and Autumn, with change of weathers, rain, lightning, and tempest, etc.*

And from under the stage at both ends arises [*Overdone presenting*] *Water and* [*Pepperton presenting*] *Earth: Water with green flags upon his head standing up instead of hair, and a beard of the same, with a chain of pearl; Earth with a number of little things like trees, like a thick grove, upon his head, and a wedge of gold in his hand, his garment of a clay colour.*

The Fire speaking first, Beveril the scholar stands behind, gives him the first word, which he now follows

BEVERIL
'The flame of zeal—'

SIR GILBERT *as* FIRE The wicked fire of lust
Does now spread heat through water, air, and dust.

BEVERIL [*aside*]
How? He's out in the beginning.—'The wheel of time—'

WEATHERWISE [*aside*] The devil set fire o'th' distaff!

SIR GILBERT *as* FIRE
I that was wont in elder times to pass
For a bright angel—so they called me then—
Now so corrupted with the upstart fires
Of avarice, luxury, and inconstant heats
Struck from the bloods of cunning clap-fall'n daughters,
Night-walking wives, but, most, libidinous widows,
That I that purify e'en gold itself
Have the contemptible dross thrown in my face,
And my bright name walk common in disgrace:
How am I used o' late, that I am so handled,
Thrust into alleys, hospitals, and tubs!
I was once a name of comfort, warmed great houses
When Charity was landlord; I have given welcome
To forty russet yeomen at a time
In a fair Christmas hall. How am I changed!
The chimneys are swept up, the hearth as cold
As the forefathers' charity in the son.
All the good hospitable heat now turns
To my young landlord's lust, and there it burns.
Rich widows that were wont to choose by gravity
Their second husbands, not by tricks of blood,
Are now so taken with loose Aretine flames
Of nimble wantonness and high-fed pride,
They marry now but the third part of husbands—
Boys, smooth-faced catamites—to fulfil their bed,
As if a woman should a woman wed.
These are the fires o' late. My brightness darks,
And fills the world so full of beggarly sparks.

49 **branched . . . gown** (of a judge)
branched embroidered
50 **at nurse** at the nurse's breast
52 **great** (*a*) large (*b*) eminent, prosperous
batten put weight on, thrive
53 **has learnt it** knows his stuff
62.1 ***A thing . . . globe*** Probably a circular flat painted like a globe. Court masques sometimes made use of large globes from which masquers issued.
opens Probably here 'is disclosed (by drawing back curtains)'.
62.3 ***the part*** (of Fire)
62.7 ***comes down*** i.e. is lowered on a wire from a trapdoor in the stage roof or 'heavens'
62.8 ***moons*** months; i.e. signs of the zodiac
62.18 ***wedge*** ingot
65 **out** out of his lines
66 **distaff** staff on which the unspun flax was wound. 'To have tow on one's distaff' was proverbial for having work in hand.
67–8 **I . . . then** Suggested by Psalm 104:4: 'Who maketh his angels spirits, | His ministers a flaming fire'.
69 **upstart** (both socially upstart and physically rising up)
71 **clap-fall'n** stricken with gonorrhea
77 **tubs** sweating tubs (used for treatment of syphilis)
80 **russet** clad in coarse homespun reddish-brown woollen cloth
82–3 **the hearth . . . son** (developed from the proverb 'as cold as charity')
87 **tricks of blood** freakish turns of lust
88 **Aretine** in the manner of Pietro Aretino (1492–1556), famous for his licentious poetry; lustful
94 **sparks** (*a*) sparks of fire (*b*) gallants

BEVERIL [*aside*]
Heart, how am I disgraced! What rogue should this be?
WIDOW
By my faith, Monsieur Fire, you're a hot whoreson!
MISTRESS LOW-WATER [*aside*]
I fear my brother is beside his wits;
He would not be so senseless to rail thus else.
WEATHERWISE *as* AIR
After this heat, you madams fat and fair,
Open your casements wide, and take in Air.
But not that air false women make up oaths with;
No, nor that air gallants perfume their clothes with.
I am that air that keeps about the clouds.
None of my kindred was smelt out in crowds.
Not any of our house was ever tainted,
When many a thousand of our foes have fainted.
Yet some there are that be my chief polluters:
Widows that falsify their faith to suitors,
And will give fair words when the sun's in Cancer,
But at the next remove, a scurvy answer;
Come to the poor men's houses, eat their banquet,
And at night with a boy tossed in a blanket.
Nay, shall I come more near?—perhaps at noon;
For here I find a spot full in the moon.
I know youth's trick; what's she that can withstand it
When Mercury reigns, my lady's chamber planet?
He that believes a widow's words shall fail
When Venus' gown-skirts sweeps the Dragon's Tail.
Fair weather the first day she makes to any;
The second cloudy, and the third day rainy.
The fourth day a great storm, lightning and thunder;
A bolt strikes the suitor: a boy keeps her under.
BEVERIL [*aside*]
Life! These are some counterfeit slaves crept in their rooms,
O' purpose for disgrace; they shall all share with me.
Heart, who the devil should these be? *Exit*
WIDOW
My faith, gentlemen,
Air has perfumed the room well!
SIR OLIVER
So methinks, madam.
SAVOURWIT [*aside*]
A man may smell her meaning two rooms off,
Though his nose wanted reparations,
And the bridge left at Shoreditch as a pledge
For Rosa Solis in a bleaching-house.
MISTRESS LOW-WATER [*aside to Master Low-water*]
Life, what should be his meaning in't?
MASTER LOW-WATER
I wonder.
OVERDONE *as* WATER
Methinks this room should yet retain such heat
Struck out from the first ardour, and so glow yet,
You should desire my company, wish for water,
That offers here to serve your several pipes
Without constraint of mill or death of water-house.
What if I sprinkled on the widow's cheeks
A few cool drops to 'lay the guilty heat
That flashes from her conscience to her face?
Would't not refresh her shame? From such as she
I first took weakness and inconstancy.
I sometimes swell above my banks and spread;
They're commonly with child before they're wed.
In me the Sirens sing before they prey;
In her more witchcraft, for her smiles betray.
Where I'm least seen, there my most danger lies;
So in those parts hid most from a man's eyes—
Her heart, her love, or what may be more close.
I know no mercy; she thinks that no loss.
In her, poor gallants, pirates thrive in me.
I help to cast away, and so does she.
WIDOW
Nay, an you can hold nothing sweet, Sir Water,

100 **casements** window-frames (with a quibble on 'vulvas')
101 **air** i.e. breath
103 **keeps** dwells
104 **smelt out** (*a*) detected, caught (*b*) smelt
105 **house** (*a*) place of abode in the heavens (*b*) household
109 **Cancer** (associated with the emotional and protective)
110 **at the next remove** i.e. when shifted to the next sign. As planets move backwards through the zodiac, the next sign would be Gemini, associated with changeability.
112 **tossed** i.e. are tossed
114 **here** Weatherwise is commenting on the chart painted on his coat.
a...moon From the proverb, 'The moon is not without spots'.
116 **Mercury** Said to influence artfulness, trickery, and thieving; depicted as youthful. Here stands for the young gentleman.
118 **Dragon's Tail** See note to 6.42.
119–21 **Fair...thunder** Again refers to the depictions on Weatherwise's coat.
122 **keeps her under** (both physically and figuratively)
123 **rooms** places
126 **perfumed** (playing on the sense 'fumigated')
128 **wanted reparations** needed repairing. Refers to collapse of the nose through syphilis.
129 **Shoreditch** A London parish renowned for prostitution.
130 **Rosa Solis** An alcoholic cordial that would make the breath smell (punning on *Rosa Solace*, the supposed name of the woman whose *solace* has caused syphilis).
bleaching-house The bleachery, or brothel, where Rosa Solace was to be found; perhaps also a hospital for curing venereal disease.
132 **this room should** if this room should
135 **pipes** water-pipes (perhaps also 'tubular body-organs')
136 **water-house** building in which water was raised from a conduit to a reservoir
138 **'lay** allay
142 **I...spread** A river bursting its banks was a common image of unregulated behaviour. *Swell* and *spread* also quibble on the physical appearance of a woman *with child*.
144 **prey** With possible wordplay on *pray*, referring to (*a*) the alternation of singing and prayer in a church service, and (*b*) prayer as metonymic for the wedding ceremony, giving a closer parallel with the previous line (and with *sing* suggesting 'have sexual intercourse with').
146 **Where...lies** Refers to treacherous hidden currents.
148 **close** enclosed, secret
151 **cast away** (*a*) wreck ships (*b*) reject
152 **hold nothing** (*a*) bear nothing afloat (*b*) keep nothing secret
Water Puns on *Walter*.

I'll wash my hands o' you ever hereafter.

PEPPERTON *as* EARTH

Earth stands for a full point. Me you should hire
To stop the gaps of Water, Air, and Fire.
I love muck well, but your first husband better.
Above his soul he loved it, as his end
Did fearfully witness it. At his last gasp
His spirit flamed as it forsook his breast,
And left the sparkles quarrelling 'bout his lips.
Now of such metal the devil makes him whips.
He shall have gold enough to glut his soul;
And as for Earth, I'll stop his crane's-throat full.
The wealth he left behind him, most men know
He wrung inconscionably from the rights
Of poor men's livings. He drunk dry their brows.
That liquor has a curse, yet nothing sweeter.
When your posterity drinks, then 'twill taste bitter.

SIR GILBERT *as* FIRE

And now to vex, 'gainst nature, form, rule, place,
See once four warring elements all embrace.

[They embrace]

Enter four, [one of them Beveril,] at several corners, addressed like the four winds, with wings, etc., and dance all to the drum and fife. The four elements seem to give back, and stand in amaze. The South Wind has a great red face, the North Wind a pale bleak one, the Western Wind one cheek red and another white, and so the Eastern Wind. At the end of the dance, the winds shove off the disguises of the other four, which seem to yield and almost fall off of themselves at the coming of the winds; so all the four old suitors are discovered. Exeunt all the winds but one, which is Beveril the scholar in that disguise. So shows all

WIDOW

How, Sir Gilbert Lambstone, Master Overdone,
All our old suitors! You have took pains, my masters!

SIR GILBERT

We made a vow we'd speak our minds to you.

WEATHERWISE And I think we're as good as our words, though it cost some of our purses. I owe money for the clouds yet, I care not who knows it; the planets are sufficient enough to pay the painter an I were dead.

WIDOW *[to Beveril]* Who are you, sir?

BEVERIL *[taking off his disguise]*

Your most unworthy servant.

WIDOW Pardon me; is't you, sir?

BEVERIL

My disgrace urged my wit to take some form
Wherein I might both best and properliest
Discover my abusers and your own,
And show you some content before y'had none.

WIDOW

Sir, I owe much both to your care and love,
And you shall find your full requital worthy.
[To the old suitors] Was this the plot now your poor envy works out?
I do revenge myself with pitying on you.
[To Master Low-water] Take Fire into the buttery; he has most need on't.
Give Water some small beer, too good for him.
Air, you may walk abroad like a fortune-teller;
But take down Earth, and make him drink i'th' cellar.

[Exeunt the old suitors, with Master Low-water]

MISTRESS LOW-WATER

The best revenge that could be.

MOTHER *[to the Widow]* I commend you, madam.

SIR OLIVER I thought they were some such sneakers.

SAVOURWIT The four suitors! And here was a mess of mad elements!

MISTRESS LOW-WATER

Lights, more lights there! Where be these bluecoats?

[Enter Servants with lights]

WIDOW

You know your lodgings, gentlemen, tonight.

SIR OLIVER

'Tis bounty makes bold guests, madam.

WIDOW *[to Philip's Mother]* Good rest, lady.

SIR OLIVER

A most contentful night begin a health, madam,
To your long joys, and may the years go round with't.

WIDOW

As many thanks as you have wished 'em hours, sir,

153 **wash my hands o'** Proverbial for 'have nothing more to do with', and quibbling on 'wash my hands *with*'.
154 **full point** full stop, i.e. end (because (*a*) Earth is the last speaker, and (*b*) the dead return to earth)
156 **muck** (*a*) manure, mud (*b*) money **better** i.e. loved *muck* better
159–60 **His...lips** Alludes to the belief that after death the soul left the body through the mouth; but the husband's *spirit* has qualities of precious metal and jewels.
163 **crane's-throat** The crane's neck is long and swells when swallowing a fish.
167 **That liquor** i.e. the sweat of *poor men*
170.3 ***addressed*** dressed
170.4 ***dance...fife*** The fife is a pipe that could be played with one hand, leaving the other to accompany on the drum. The dance is probably an unruly jig.
170.11 ***fall...themselves*** fall away from each other of their own accord
170.14 ***shows all*** all is revealed
174 **as...words** (proverbial)
176–7 **the...dead** The planets of his costume are evidently made of coins.
187 **poor envy** petty malice **works out** devises
189 **Take...on't** Either fire is associated with alcoholic spirits or it induces thirst.
190 **small beer** watery beer
191 **Air...fortune-teller** Air is proverbially free
192 **cellar** (fittingly subterranean)
194 **sneakers** sneaks
195 **mess of** group of four
195–6 **mad elements** (with *elements* as in the 'four elements', but quibbling on 'constituents of madness')
197 **bluecoats** servants (so called from their livery)
199 **bold** i.e. confident of hospitality
200 **begin a health** (*a*) initiate prosperity (*b*) toast a health (taken up in *go round with't*, l. 201)
202 **'em** i.e. *joys*

Take to your lodging with you.
MISTRESS LOW-WATER A general rest to all.
Exeunt; [manent Philip, Savourwit, the Widow, and Mistress Low-water]
PHILIP [*aside to Savourwit*] I'm excepted.
SAVOURWIT [*aside to Philip*]
Take in another to you then; there's room enough
In that exception, faith, to serve us both.
The dial of my sleep goes by your eyes.
Exeunt; manent Widow and Mistress Low-water
WIDOW
Now like a greedy usurer, alone
I sum up all the wealth this day has brought me;
And thus I hug it.
[*She embraces her*]
MISTRESS LOW-WATER
Prithee!
WIDOW [*kissing her*] Thus I kiss it.
MISTRESS LOW-WATER
I can't abide these kissings.
WIDOW How, sir, not?
I'll try that, sure; I'll kiss you out of that humour.
MISTRESS LOW-WATER
Push! By my troth, I cannot.
WIDOW What cannot you, sir?
MISTRESS LOW-WATER
Not toy, nor bill and imitate house-pigeons.
A married man must think of other matters.
WIDOW
How, other matters, sir? What other matters?
MISTRESS LOW-WATER
Why, are there no other matters that belong to't?
Do you think you've married only a cock sparrow,
And fit but for one business, like a fool?
You shall not find it so.
WIDOW You can talk strangely, sir.
Come, will you to bed?
MISTRESS LOW-WATER No, faith, will not I.
WIDOW What, not to bed, sir?
MISTRESS LOW-WATER
An I do, hang me. Not to bed with you.
WIDOW
How, not to bed with me? Sir, with whom else?
MISTRESS LOW-WATER
Why, am not I enough to lie with myself?
WIDOW
Is that the end of marriage?
MISTRESS LOW-WATER No, by my faith;
'Tis but the beginning; yet death is the end on't,
Unless some trick come i'th' middle and dash all.
WIDOW
Were you so forward lately, and so youthful,
That scarce my modest strength could save me from you,
And are you now so cold?
MISTRESS LOW-WATER I've thought on't since.
It was but a rude part in me, i'faith,
To offer such bold tricks to any woman,
And by degrees I shall well break myself from't.
I feel myself well chastened since that time,
And not the third part now so loosely minded.
O, when one sees their follies, 'tis a comfort.
My very thoughts take more staid years upon 'em.
O, marriage is such a serious, divine thing!
It makes youth grave, and sweetly nips the spring.
WIDOW
If I had chose a gentleman for care
And worldly business, I had ne'er took you.
I had the offers of enough more fit
For such employment; I chose you for love,
Youth, and content of heart, and not for troubles;
You are not ripe for them. After you've spent
Some twenty years in dalliance, youth's affairs,
Then take a book in your hand and sum up cares.
As for wealth now, you know that's got to your hands.
MISTRESS LOW-WATER
But had I known't had been so wrongfully got,
As I heard since, you should have had free leave
To have made choice of another master for't.
WIDOW
Why, can that trouble you?
MISTRESS LOW-WATER It may too soon. But go.
My sleeps are sound; I love not to be started
With an ill conscience at the fall of midnight
And have mine eyes torn ope with poor men's curses.
I do not like the fate on't. 'Tis still apt
To breed unrest, dissension, wild debate;
And I'm the worst at quarrels upon earth.
Unless a mighty injury should provoke me,
Get you to bed, go.
WIDOW Not without you, in troth, sir.
MISTRESS LOW-WATER
If you could think how much you wrong yourself
In my opinion of you, you would leave me now
With all the speed you might. I like you worse
For this fond heat, and drink in more suspicion of you.
You high-fed widows are too cunning people
For a poor gentleman to come simply to.

207 **The . . . eyes** An image of a sundial, with Philip's eyes as the sun, or of two clocks, one set by the other.
213 **Push** See note to 6.167.
214 **toy** dally
218 **sparrow** (proverbially lustful)
226 **end** purpose (but 'conclusion' in l. 227)
227–8 **death is the end . . . all** Echoes the proverb, 'Death is the end of all'.
228 **Unless . . . middle** (with a sexual innuendo)
230 **my modest strength** the strength of my modesty
237 **their** Refers back to *bold tricks*, l. 233.
240 **spring** young shoot
248 **book** (*a*) account book (*b*) bible
267 **simply** (*a*) alone (*b*) artlessly, humbly

WIDOW
What's that, sir?
MISTRESS LOW-WATER
You may make a youth on him;
'Tis at your courtesy, and that's ill trusted.
You could not want a friend, beside a suitor,
To sit in your husband's gown and look over your writings.
WIDOW
What's this?
MISTRESS LOW-WATER
I say there is a time when women
Can do too much and understand too little.
Once more, to bed. I'd willingly be a father
To no more noses than I got myself.
And so good-night to you.
WIDOW Now I see the infection.
A yellow poison runs through the sweet spring
Of his fair youth already; 'tis distracted,
Jealous of that which thought yet never acted.—
[*Kneeling*] O dear sir, on my knees I swear to thee—
MISTRESS LOW-WATER
I prithee, use them in thy private chamber,
As a good lady should. Spare 'em not there;
'Twill do thee good. Faith, none 'twill do thee here.
WIDOW [*rising*]
Have I yet married poverty, and missed love?
What fortune has my heart? That's all I craved,
And that lies now a-dying. It has took
A speeding poison, and I'm ignorant how.
I never knew what beggary was till now.
My wealth yields me no comfort in this plight.
Had want but brought me love, I'd happened right.
Exit Widow
MISTRESS LOW-WATER
So, this will serve now for a preparative
To ope the pores of some dislike at first.
The physic will pay't home.
Enter Master Low-water, [disguised as before]
How dost thou, sir?
How goes the work?
MASTER LOW-WATER Your brother has the letter.
MISTRESS LOW-WATER
I find no stop in't then; it moves well hitherto.
Did you convey it closely?
MASTER LOW-WATER He ne'er set eye of me.
[*Enter Master Beveril,*] *above*, [*with a letter*]
BEVERIL
I cannot read too often.
MISTRESS LOW-WATER [*aside to Master Low-water*]
Peace; to your office.
[*Master Low-water steps back*]
BEVERIL
What blessèd fate took pity of my heart,
But with her presence to relieve me thus?
All the large volumes that my time hath mastered
Are not so precious to adorn my spirit
As these few lines are to enrich my mind.
I thirst again to drink of the same fountain.
[*He reads*]

'Kind sir, I found your care and love so much in the performance of a little wherein your wit and art had late employment that I dare now trust your bosom with business of more weight and eminence. Little thought the world that since the wedding dinner all my mirth was but dissembled, and seeming joys but counterfeit. The truth to you, sir, is, I find so little signs of content in the bargain I made i'th' morning that I began to repent before evening prayer; and to show some fruits of his wilful neglect and wild disposition more than the day could bring forth to me, he's now forsook my bed; I know no cause for't.'

MISTRESS LOW-WATER [*aside*] But I'll be sworn I do.

BEVERIL [*reading*] 'Being thus distressed, sir, I desire your comfortable presence and counsel, whom I know to be of worth and judgement, that a lady may safely impart her griefs to you and commit 'em to the virtues of commiseration and secrecy.

Your unfortunate friend,
The widow wife.

I have took order for your private admittance with a trusty servant of mine own, whom I have placed at my chamber door to attend your coming.' He shall not wait too long and curse my slowness.

MASTER LOW-WATER [*aside*] I would you'd come away then.

BEVERIL
How much am I beguiled in that young gentleman!
I would have sworn had been the perfect abstract
Of honesty and mildness; 'tis not so.
MISTRESS LOW-WATER [*aside*]
I pardon you, sweet brother; there's no hold
Of what you speak now; you're in Cupid's pound.
BEVERIL
Blest be the secret hand that brought thee hither;
But the dear hand that writ it, ten times blest. [*Exit*]
MASTER LOW-WATER
That's I still; he's blest me now ten times at twice.
Away; I hear him coming.
MISTRESS LOW-WATER Strike it sure now!
MASTER LOW-WATER
I warrant thee, sweet Kate; choose your best bow.
Exit Mistress Low-water

268 **make . . . him** contrive for him to be a youth
269 **at your courtesy** subject to your indulgence
270 **want** lack, do without
275 **got** begot
277 **yellow** i.e. jealous
279 **thought yet never acted** was never even thought
290 **Had . . . love** i.e. if I had been poor but found love
291 **preparative** potion taken to prepare the body for a medicine
293 **physic** medicine
296 **closely** secretly, unobtrusively
307 **eminence** distinction, honour
330 **abstract** epitome
337–8 **Strike . . . bow** *Strike* suggests a phallic arrow; *bow* correspondingly suggests 'vulva' (and rhymes with *now*).

Enter Master Beveril, [below]

BEVERIL
Who's there?

MASTER LOW-WATER
O, sir, is't you? You're welcome then.
My lady still expects you, sir.

BEVERIL
Who's with her?

MASTER LOW-WATER
Not any creature living, sir.

BEVERIL [*giving money*]
Drink that.
I've made thee wait too long.

MASTER LOW-WATER
It does not seem so now, sir. Sir, if a man
Tread warily, as any wise man will,
How often may he come to a lady's chamber
And be welcome to her!

BEVERIL
Thou giv'st me learnèd counsel for a closet.

MASTER LOW-WATER
Make use on't, sir, and you shall find no loss in't.
[*Exit Beveril to the Widow*]
So, you are surely in, and you must under.

Enter, [at another door,] Kate Low-water, [disguised as before, attended by Servants, and] with all the guests: Sir Oliver Twilight, Master Sunset, Twilight's wife (the Mother), daughter (Grace), [Jane]; [after them,] Philip, Sandfield, and Savourwit

MISTRESS LOW-WATER
Pardon my rude disturbance; my wrongs urge it.
I did but try the plainness of her mind,
Suspecting she dealt cunningly with my youth,
And told her the first night I would not know her;
But, minding to return, I found the door
Warded suspiciously, and I heard a noise
Such as fear makes, and guiltiness at th'approaching
Of an unlooked-for husband.

ALL THE GUESTS
This is strange, sir.

MISTRESS LOW-WATER [*trying the door*]
Behold, it's barred. I must not be kept out.

SIR OLIVER
There is no reason, sir.

MISTRESS LOW-WATER
I'll be resolved in't.
If you be sons of honour, follow me.

Break open door, rush in; [manet Savourwit]

SAVOURWIT Then must I stay behind, for I think I was begot i'th' woodyard, and that makes everything go so hard with me.

MISTRESS LOW-WATER (*within*)
That's he; be sure on him!

Enter confusedly [Mistress Low-water and Master Low-water, both disguised as before, and all the guests,] with the Widow and Mistress Low-water's brother Beveril the scholar

SIR OLIVER [*to Mistress Low-water*]
Be not so furious, sir.

MISTRESS LOW-WATER
She whispered to him to slip into her closet.
[*To the Widow*] What, have I taken you? Is not my dream true now?
Unmerciful adulteress: the first night!

SIR OLIVER
Nay, good sir, patience.

MISTRESS LOW-WATER
Give me the villain's heart,
That I may throw't into her bosom quick.
There let the lecher pant.

MOTHER
Nay, sweet sir!

MISTRESS LOW-WATER
Pardon me;
His life's too little for me.

WIDOW
How am I wrongfully shamed! [*To Beveril*] Speak your intent, sir,
Before this company; I pursue no pity.

MISTRESS LOW-WATER
This is a fine thievish juggling, gentlemen!
She asks her mate that shares in guilt with her.
Too gross, too gross!

BEVERIL
Rash mischief!

MISTRESS LOW-WATER
Treacherous sir,
Did I for this cast a friend's arm about thee,
Gave thee the welcome of a worthy spirit,
And lodged thee in my house, nay, entertained thee
More like a natural brother than a stranger;
And have I this reward? Perhaps the pride
Of thy good parts did lift thee to this impudence.
Let her make much on 'em; she gets none of me.
Because thou'rt deeply read in most books else,
Thou would'st be so in mine. [*Pointing to Widow*]
There it stands for thee;
Turn o'er the leaves, and where you left, go forward.
To me it shall be like the book of fate,
Ever clasped up.

SIR OLIVER
O dear sir, say not so!

MISTRESS LOW-WATER
Nay, I'll swear more. For ever I refuse her;
I'll never set a foot into her bed,
Never perform the duty of man to her,
So long as I have breath.

SIR OLIVER
What an oath was there, sir! Call't again.

345 **come...chamber** (quibbling on sexual penetration)
347 **closet** (*a*) lady's private room (*b*) study
349 **under** i.e. drown
355 **Warded** defended
359 **resolved** made certain
364 **be sure on him** i.e. keep him from escape
366 **taken** caught
369 **quick** alive
370 **the lecher** i.e. the plucked-out heart **pant** beat
375 **asks** examines judicially
382 **good parts** (*a*) scholarly talents (*b*) physical endowments
387 **book of fate** i.e. the biblical Book of Life, finally opened on the Day of Judgement (Revelation 20:12). Suggests that those who open and read the book find they are destined to be damned.
388 **clasped up** Larger books used to be held closed with a clasp.
393 **Call't again** revoke it

MISTRESS LOW-WATER
I knew by amorous sparks struck from their eyes
The fire would appear shortly in a blaze,
And now it flames indeed. [*To the Widow*] Out of my house,
And take your gentleman of good parts along with you.
That shall be all your substance. He can live
In any emperor's court in Christendom.
You know what you did, wench, when you chose him,
To thrust out me. You have no politic love;
You are to learn to make your market, you.
You can choose wit, a burden light and free,
And leave the grosser element with me:
Wealth, foolish trash, I thank you. Out of my doors!

SIR OLIVER Nay, good sir, hear her.

MOTHER *and* SUNSET Sweet sir!

MISTRESS LOW-WATER
Pray, to your chambers, gentlemen. I should be here
Master of what is mine.

SIR OLIVER Hear her but speak, sir!

MISTRESS LOW-WATER
What can she speak but woman's common language:
She's sorry and ashamed for't? That helps nothing.

WIDOW
Sir, since it is the hard hap of my life
To rèceive injury where I placed my love—

MISTRESS LOW-WATER
Why, la, I told you what escapes she'd have.

SIR OLIVER
Nay, pray, sir, hear her forward.

WIDOW Let our parting
Be full as charitable as our meeting was,
That the pale envious world, glad of the food
Of others' miseries, civil dissensions,
And nuptial strifes, may not feed fat with ours.
But since you are resolved so wilfully
To leave my bed and ever to refuse me,
As by your rage I find it your desire—
Though all my actions dèserve nothing less—
Here are our friends, men both of worth and wisdom;
Place so much power in them to make an evenness
Between my peace and yours. All my wealth within doors
In gold and jewels lie in those two caskets
I lately led you to, the value of which
Amounts to some five thousand pound apiece;
Exchange a charitable hand with me,
And take one casket freely. Fare thee well, sir.

SIR OLIVER [*to Mistress Low-water*]
How say you to that now?

MISTRESS LOW-WATER Troth, I thank her, sir!
Are not both mine already? [*To the Widow*] You shall wrong me,
And then make satisfaction with mine own?
I cannot blame you; a good course for you.

WIDOW
I know 'twas not my luck to be so happy.
My miseries are no starters, when they come
Stick longer by me.

SIR OLIVER [*to Mistress Low-water*]
Nay, but give me leave, sir:
The wealth comes all by her.

MISTRESS LOW-WATER So does the shame,
Yet that's most mine; why should not that be too?

SIR OLIVER
Sweet sir, let us rule so much with you:
Since you intend an obstinate separation
Both from her bed and board, give your consent
To some agreement reasonable and honest.

MISTRESS LOW-WATER
Must I deal honestly with her lust?

MOTHER Nay, good sir!

MISTRESS LOW-WATER
Why, I tell you, all the wealth her husband left her
Is not of power to purchase the dear peace
My heart has lost in these adulterous seas.
Yet, let her works be base, mine shall be noble.

SIR OLIVER
That's the best word of comfort I heard yet.

MISTRESS LOW-WATER
Friends may do much.—Go, bring those caskets forth.
[*Exeunt Servants*]
I hate her sight; I'll leave her though I lose by't.

SIR OLIVER
Spoke like a noble gentleman, i'faith.
I'll honour thee for this.

BEVERIL [*aside*] O, cursèd man!
Must thy rash heat force this division?

MISTRESS LOW-WATER [*to the Widow*]
You shall have free leave now, without all fear.
You shall not need oiled hinges, privy passages,
Watchings, and whisperings. Take him boldly to you.

WIDOW
O that I had that freedom, since my shame
Puts by all other fortunes, and owns him
A worthy gentleman! If this cloud were passed him
I'd marry him, were't but to spite thee only,
So much I hate thee now.

Enter Servants with two caskets, and the suitors: Sir Gilbert Lambstone, Weatherwise, Pepperton, and Overdone

SIR OLIVER
Here come the caskets, sir. Hold your good mind now,
And we shall make a virtuous end between you.

402 **make your market** From the proverb 'to make one's market', to determine one's own fortune.

403 **You ... free** Proverbially, words are but wind, and air is free.

404 **the grosser element** i.e. earth (from which wealth, as land or precious metals, is derived)

411 **nothing** not at all

437 **starters** deserters, wanderers

440 **that be** i.e. the wealth be

457 **passages** (*a*) goings on, passings to and fro (*b*) corridors

MISTRESS LOW-WATER
Though nothing less she merit but a curse
That might still hang upon her and consume her still—
As't has been many a better woman's fortune
That has deserved less vengeance, and felt more—
Yet my mind scorns to leave her shame so poor.

SIR OLIVER
Nobly spoke still!

SIR GILBERT This strikes me into music. Ha, ha!

PEPPERTON
Parting of goods before the bodies join?

WEATHERWISE This 'tis to marry beardless domineering boys. I knew 'twould come to this pass. Well fare a just almanac yet; for now is Mercury going into the second house near unto Ursa Major, that great Hunks the Bear at the Bridge-foot in heaven, which shows horrible bear-baitings in wedlock; and the sun near ent'ring into th' Dog sets 'em all together by th' ears.

SIR OLIVER [*to Mistress Low-water, opening a casket*]
You see what's in't.

MISTRESS LOW-WATER
I think 'tis as I left it.

WIDOW
Then do but gage your faith to this assembly
That you will ne'er return more to molest me,
But rest in all revenges full appeased
And amply satisfied with that half my wealth,
And take't as freely as life wishes health.

SIR OLIVER
La you, sir; come, come; faith, you shall swear that.

MISTRESS LOW-WATER
Nay, gentlemen, for your sakes now I'll deal fairly with her.

SIR OLIVER
I would we might see that, sir.

MISTRESS LOW-WATER I could set her free;
But now I think on't, she deserves it not.

SUNSET
Nay, do not check your goodness. Pray, sir, on with't.

MISTRESS LOW-WATER
I could release her ere I parted with her—
But 'twere a courtesy ill placed—and set her
At as free liberty to marry again
As you all know she was before I knew her.

SIR OLIVER
What, couldst thou, sir?

MISTRESS LOW-WATER
But 'tis too good a blessing for her.—
Up with the casket, sirrah.

WIDOW O, sir, stay!

MISTRESS LOW-WATER
I have nothing to say to you.

SIR OLIVER Do you hear, sir?
Pray let's have one word more with you for our money.

WIDOW [*to Mistress Low-water*]
Since you've exposed me to all shame and sorrow,
And made me fit but for one hope and fortune,
Bearing my former comforts away with you,
Show me a parting charity but in this:
For all my losses pay me with that freedom,
And I shall think this treasure as well given
As ever 'twas ill got.

MISTRESS LOW-WATER
I might afford it you,
Because I never mean to be more troubled with you.
But how shall I be sure of the honest use on't,
How you'll employ that liberty?—Perhaps sinfully,
In wantonness unlawful, and I answer for't.
So I may live a bawd to your loose works still,
In giving 'em first vent. Not I, 'shall pardon me;
I'll see you honestly joined ere I release you.
I will not trust you for the last trick you played me.
Here's your old suitors.

PEPPERTON Now we thank you, sir!

WEATHERWISE My almanac warns me from all cuckoldly conjunctions.

WIDOW [*to Mistress Low-water*]
Be but commander of your word now, sir,
And before all these gentlemen our friends
I'll make a worthy choice.

SUNSET [*to Mistress Low-water*]
Fly not ye back now.

MISTRESS LOW-WATER [*to the Widow*]
I'll try thee once. I am married to another.
There's thy release.

SIR OLIVER
Hoyda, there's a rèlease with a witness!
Thou'rt free, sweet wench.

WIDOW [*to Mistress Low-water*] Married to another?
Then in revenge to thee,
To vex thine eyes, 'cause thou hast mocked my heart
And with such treachery repaid my love,

475 **Mercury** (representing the young gentleman)
475–6 **the second house** (associated with money)
476 **Ursa Major** constellation of the Great Bear (named for the animal's association with surliness and bear-baiting)
Hunks Originally the name of a particular bear at Paris Garden bear-baiting amphitheatre, hence a by-word for bad temper and meanness.
477 **the Bridge-foot** Location of a tavern called the Bear, over the bridge from London in Southwark, and on the way to the bear-gardens.
shows indicates
479 **th' Dog** i.e. the constellation of Canis Major, and its brightest star Sirius, the 'Dog-star'. The sun does not pass through Canis Major. The 'dog-days' (the time of Sirius' heliacal rising; late July–early August) were associated with pernicious events and dogs running mad. The reference is also to bear-baiting dogs.
sets...ears (proverbial)
492 **But 'twere** if it were not
500 **one...fortune** i.e. dissolution of the marriage
516 **conjunctions** (quibbling on the astrological and marital senses)
522 **with a witness** (proverbial for 'for sure, with a vengeance')

This is the gentleman I embrace and choose.
[*She embraces Beveril*]

MISTRESS LOW-WATER
O, torment to my blood: mine enemy!
None else to make thy choice of but the man
From whence my shame took head!

WIDOW 'Tis done to quit thee.
Thou that wrong'st woman's love, her hate can fit thee.

SIR OLIVER
Brave wench, i'faith! Now thou hast an honest gentleman,
Rid of a swaggering knave, and there's an end on't.
A man of good parts. This t'other had nothing.
Life, married to another?

SIR GILBERT O, brave rascal with two wives!

WEATHERWISE Nay, an our women be such subtle animals, I'll lay wait at the carrier's for a country chambermaid, and live still a bachelor. When wives are like almanacs, we may have every year a new one. Then I'll bestow my money on 'em; in the mean time I'll give 'em over and ne'er trouble my almanac about 'em.

SIR GILBERT [*to Mistress Low-water*]
I come in a good time to see you hanged, sir,
And that's my comfort. Now I'll tickle you, sir.

MISTRESS LOW-WATER
You make me laugh indeed.

SIR GILBERT Sir, you remember
How cunningly you choked me at the banquet
With a fine bawdy letter?

MISTRESS LOW-WATER Your own fist, sir.

SIR GILBERT
I'll read the statute-book to you now for't.
Turn to the act in *anno Jacobi primo*;
There lies a halter for your windpipe.

MISTRESS LOW-WATER Fie, no!

SIR OLIVER
Faith, but you'll find it so, sir, an't be followed.

WEATHERWISE
So says my almanac, and he's a true man.
[*He shows Mistress Low-water the almanac*]
Look you: 'The thirteenth day, work for the hangman.'

MISTRESS LOW-WATER [*reading*]
'The fourteenth day, make haste.' 'Tis time you were there then.

WEATHERWISE
How, is the book so saucy to tell me so?

BEVERIL [*to Mistress Low-water*]
Sir, I must tell you now, but without gall,
The law would hang you if married to another.

MISTRESS LOW-WATER
You can but put me to my book, sweet brother,
And I've my neck-verse perfect here and here.
[*She takes off her disguise and appears as herself*]
Heaven give thee eternal joy, my dear sweet brother!

ALL THE OTHERS
Who's here?

SIR GILBERT O devil: herself! Did she betray me?
A pox of shame; nine coaches shall not stay me.
Exit

BEVERIL
I've two such deep healths in two joys to pledge,
Heaven keep me from a surfeit!

SIR OLIVER Mistress Low-water!
Is she the jealous cuckold all this coil's about?—
And my right worshipful servingman, is it you, sir?

MASTER LOW-WATER [*taking off his disguise*]
A poor wronged gentleman glad to serve for his own, sir.

SIR OLIVER
By my faith, you've served the widow a fine trick between you!

MISTRESS LOW-WATER
No more my enemy now: my brother's wife,
And my kind sister.

SIR OLIVER [*to the Widow*]
There's no starting now from't.
'Tis her own brother; did not you know that?

WIDOW
'Twas never told me yet.

SIR OLIVER I thought you'd known't.

MISTRESS LOW-WATER
What matter is't? 'Tis the same man was chose still,
No worse now than he was. [*To the Widow*] I'm bound to love you;
You've exercised in this a double charity
Which, to your praise, shall to all times be known:
Advanced my brother, and restored mine own—
Nay, somewhat for my wrongs, like a good sister;
For well you know the tedious suit did cost
Much pains and fees. I thank you 'tis not lost.

531 **quit** requite
532 **fit** fittingly punish
534 **there's an end on't** (proverbial)
538 **lay...chambermaid** i.e. seduce country girls as they arrive in town to work as chambermaids
544 **tickle** Euphemistic for 'chastize', but Mistress Low-water takes the usual sense.
547 **fist** handwriting
549 ***anno...primo*** Law-Latin for the first year of James's reign, i.e. 1603–4. The act was 'to restrain all persons from marriage until their former wives and former husbands be dead'.
553 **The...hangman** From Bretnor's 1611 almanac.
554 **there** i.e. at the hangman's scaffold
558 **put...book** test me. See following note.
559 **neck-verse** A condemned man seeking to escape execution by claiming 'benefit of clergy' was tested with a passage of Latin verse. Here the *neck-verse* that will exempt Mistress Low-water from bigamy is the revelation that she is a woman (specifically the baring of her neck).
562 **coaches** Often used for sexual liaisons.
565 **coil's** fuss's
570 **kind** i.e. bound to mutual affection by kinship
579 **suit** (*a*) lawsuit (as a metaphor) (*b*) wooing (i.e. Mistress Low-water's advancement of her brother's interest in the Widow)

You wished for love; and, faith, I have bestowed you
Upon a gentleman that does dearly love you.
That recompense I've made you; and you must think, madam,
I loved you well—though I could never ease you—
When I fetched in my brother thus to please you.

SIR OLIVER
Here's unity for ever strangely wrought.

WIDOW
I see too late there is a heavy judgement
Keeps company with extortion and foul deeds,
And, like a wind which vengeance has in chase,
Drives back the wrongs into the injurer's face.
My punishment is gentle, and to show
My thankful mind for't, thus I'll revenge this:
With an embracement here, and here a kiss.
[She embraces Mistress Low-water and kisses Beveril]

SIR OLIVER
Why, now the bells they go trim, they go trim!
[To Beveril] I wished thee, sir, some unexpected blessing
For my wife's ransom, and 'tis fall'n upon thee.

WEATHERWISE A pox of this; my almanac ne'er gulled me till this hour! 'The thirteenth day, work for the hangman', and there's nothing toward it. I'd been a fine ass if I'd given twelve pence for a horse to have rid to Tyburn tomorrow! But now I see the error: 'tis false-figured; it should be 'thirteen days and a half, work for the hangman', for he ne'er works under thirteen pence halfpenny. Beside, Venus being 'a spot in the sun's garment' shows there should be a woman found in hose and doublet.

SIR OLIVER Nay, faith, sweet wife, we'll make no more hours on't now; 'tis as fine a contracting time as ever came amongst gentlefolks.—Son Philip, Master Sandfield, come to the book here.

PHILIP *[aside to Savourwit]* Now I'm waked
Into a thousand miseries and their torments.

SAVOURWIT *[aside to Philip]* And I come after you, sir, drawn with wild horses. There will be a brave show on's anon if this weather continue.

SIR OLIVER *[to Grace and Jane]*
Come, wenches.—Where be these young gentlemen's hands now?

MOTHER *[aside]*
Poor gentleman my son!—Some other time, sir.

SIR OLIVER I'll have't now, i'faith, wife.

WIDOW What are you making here?

SIR OLIVER I have sworn, sweet madam,
My son shall marry Master Sunset's daughter,
And Master Sandfield mine.

WIDOW So, you go well, sir;
[Pointing to Jane] But what make you this way then?

SIR OLIVER This? For my son.

WIDOW
O, back, sir, back! This is no way for him.

SUNSET *and* SIR OLIVER How?

WIDOW
O, let me break an oath, to save two souls,
Lest I should wake another judgement greater.
You come not here for him, sir.

SIR OLIVER What's the matter?

WIDOW
Either give me free leave to make this match,
Or I'll forbid the banns.

SIR OLIVER Good madam, take it.

WIDOW
Here, Master Sandfield, then—
[She presents Jane to Sandfield]

SIR OLIVER Cud's bodkins!

WIDOW
Take you this maid.

SANDFIELD You could not please me better, madam.

SIR OLIVER
Hoyda! Is this your hot love to my daughter, sir?

WIDOW
Come hither, Philip; here's a wife for you.
[She presents Grace to him]

SIR OLIVER
Zounds, he shall ne'er do that: marry his sister?

WIDOW
Had he been ruled by you, he had married her,
But now he marries Master Sunset's daughter,
And Master Sandfield yours. I've saved your oath, sir.

PHILIP O, may this blessing hold!

SAVOURWIT Or else all the liquor runs out.

SIR OLIVER *[to the Widow]* What riddle's this, madam?

WIDOW
A riddle of some fourteen years of age now.
[To Philip's Mother] You can remember, madam, that your daughter
Was put to nurse to Master Sunset's wife?

MOTHER
True; that we talked on lately.

SIR OLIVER I grant that, madam.

584 **ease** sexually gratify
589 **has in chase** i.e. chases forward like a hunted animal. *Vengeance* is probably the subject, but might be the object.
594 **trim** finely, well
597 **gulled** made a fool of
603–4 **thirteen pence halfpenny** By custom, a thief could be hanged if he or she stole more than this.
604–5 **Venus . . . garment** Fanciful almanac language (from Bretnor's 1611 almanac) for the planet's transit in front of the sun. Here implies 'a woman blemishing (by wearing) a man's garment'.
606 **hose and doublet** (items of male attire)
607–8 **make . . . hours** delay no more
610 **come to the book** put your name to the document; i.e. join in with the marriage contracts (and perhaps also referring to the Book of Common Prayer with which marriages were solemnized)
614 **drawn** Refers specifically to dragging criminals at a horse's tail to execution. The idea of a public spectacle is developed in *brave show*.
631 **Cud's bodkins** An oath; a euphemized form of 'God's little body'.
635 **Zounds** A strong oath; literally 'God's wounds'.

WIDOW
Then you shall grant what follows. At that time
You likewise know old Master Sunset here
Grew backward in the world, till his last fortunes
Raised him to this estate.
SIR OLIVER Still this we know too.
WIDOW
His wife then nurse both to her own and yours,
And both so young, of equal years, and daughters,
Fearing the extremity of her fortunes then
Should fall upon her infant, to prevent it
She changed the children: kept your daughter with her,
And sent her own to you for better fortunes.
So long, enjoined by solemn oath unto't
Upon her deathbed, I have concealed this;
But now so urged, here's yours, and this is his.
SAVOURWIT Whoop! The joy is come of our side.
WEATHERWISE Hey, I'll cast mine almanac to the moon too, and strike out a new one for next year.
PHILIP
It wants expression, this miraculous blessing.
SAVOURWIT Methinks I could spring up and knock my head against yon silver ceiling now for joy.
WEATHERWISE By my faith, but I do not mean to follow you there; so I may dash out my brains against Charles's Wain, and come down as wise as a carman.
SIR OLIVER
I never wondered yet with greater pleasure.
MOTHER
What tears have I bestowed on a lost daughter,
And left her here behind me!
WIDOW This is Grace,
This Jane. Now each has her right name and place.
SUNSET
I never heard of this.
WIDOW I'll swear you did not, sir.
SIR OLIVER
How well I have kept mine oath against my will!
Clap hands, and joy go with you.
[*Philip and Sandfield clap hands with the former 'Grace' and 'Jane'*]
Well said, boys!
PHILIP [*to the former 'Grace'*]
How art thou blest from shame, and I from ruin!
SAVOURWIT [*aside*]
Ay, from the baker's ditch if I'd seen you in.
PHILIP
Not possible the whole world to match again
Such grief, such joy, in minutes lost and won.
BEVERIL
Who ever knew more happiness in less compass?
[*To Mistress Low-water*] Ne'er was poor gentleman so bound to a sister
As I am, for the neatness of thy mind!
Not only that thy due, but all our wealth,
Shall lie as open as the sun to man
For thy employments; so the charity
Of this dear bosom bids me tell thee now.
MISTRESS LOW-WATER
I am her servant for't.
WIDOW Ha, worthy sister!
The government of all I bless thee with.
BEVERIL
Come, gentlemen; on all, perpetual friendship.
Heaven still relieves what misery would destroy.
Never was night yet of more general joy.
[*Exeunt; manet Weatherwise*]

Epilogue

WEATHERWISE
Now, let me see what weather shall we have now.
Hold fair now, and I care not.
[*He reads his almanac*]
Mass, full moon too,
Just between five and six this afternoon.
This happens right: 'the sky for the best part clear,
Save here and there a cloud or two dispersed';
That's some dozen of panders and half a score
Pick-pockets—you may know them by their whistle;
And they do well to use that while they may,
For Tyburn cracks the pipe and spoils the music.
What says the destiny of the hour this evening?
Ha, 'fear no colours'. By my troth, agreed then.
The red and white looks cheerfully. For know ye all,
The planet's Jupiter: you should be jovial.
There's nothing lets it, but the sun i'th' Dog:
Some bark in corners that will fawn and cog,

648 **Grew . . . world** declined in prosperity
661 **strike out** i.e. cross off the note to buy
662 **wants expression** is inexpressible
664 **yon silver ceiling** i.e. the sky (and the stage canopy, conventionally painted with the zodiac)
666–7 **Charles's Wain** Another name for the constellation of the Plough or Great Bear. A *wain* is a wagon; hence *carman.*
667 **as wise as a carman** i.e. stupid
carman carrier, carter.
672 **of** the like of
674 **said** done
676 **baker's ditch** Dishonest bakers were punished by being dunked in ditches.
681 **neatness** ingenuity
686 **her servant** i.e. obliged to her (the Widow); with a suggestion of *servant* as 'professed lover, wooer', jokingly recalling Mistress Low-water's role in disguise
689 **still** always
Epilogue.1–23 **Now . . . ears** The astrological references suggest conflicting times of year between July and October.
3 **Just . . . afternoon** Presumably the present moment at the end of the play's afternoon performance.
9 **pipe** windpipe
11 **fear no colours** A proverbial military phrase for 'be fearless'; *colours* are (enemy) flags.
12 **red and white** i.e. (*a*) the English flags (*colours*) of St George (*b*) the audience's faces
13 **jovial** (the temperament associated with Jove or Jupiter)
14 **lets** hinders
i'th' Dog See note to 9.479. Here the *Dog* produces dog-like behaviour.
15 **cog** (synonymous with *fawn*)

Glad of my fragments for their ember-week.
The sign's in Gemini too: both hands should meet.
There should be noise i'th' air if all things hap,
Though I love thunder when you make the clap.
[ ] Cancer,
Some faults perhaps have slipped I am to answer;
And if in anything your revenge appears,
Send me in with all your fists about mine ears.
[*Exit*]

Finis

Shirley *James Shirley's Prologue for the 1631 revival in Dublin*

We are sorry, gentlemen, that with all our pains
To invite you hither, the wide house contains
No more. Call you this term? If the Courts were
So thin, I think 'twould make your lawyers swear,
And curse men's charity in whose want they thrive,
Whilst we by it woe to be kept alive.
I'll tell you what a poet says: two year
He has lived in Dublin, yet he knows not where
To find the city. He observed each gate,
It could not run through them, they are too strait.
When he did live in England, he heard say
That here were men loved wit and a good play,
That here were gentlemen and lords. A few
Were bold to say there were some ladies too.
This he believed, and though they are not found
Above, who knows what may be underground?
But they do not appear, and missing these,
He says he'll not believe your chronicles
Hereafter, nor the maps, since all this while
Dublin's invisible, and not Brazil;
And all that men can talk he'll think to be
A fiction now above all poetry.
But stay; you think he's angry? No, he prayed
Me tell you he recants what he has said.
He's pleased so you shall be, yes, and confess
We have a way 'bove wit of man to please;
For though we should despair to purchase it
By art of man, this is a woman's wit.

THE PARTS

Men

WEATHERWISE (423 lines): Prologue, Footman
SAVOURWIT (394 lines): Footman, [Prologue, a Tenant]
SIR OLIVER (340 lines): Prologue, Footman, a Tenant
SIR GILBERT (202 lines): Prologue, Footman
BEVERIL (195 lines): Prologue, Footman, a Tenant
PHILIP (195 lines): Footman, [Prologue, a Tenant]
CLOWN (118 lines): Prologue, Footman
DUTCH MERCHANT (65 lines): Prologue, Footman, a Tenant
MASTER LOW-WATER (63 lines): Prologue, Footman
PEPPERTON (52 lines): Prologue, Footman
OVERDONE (34 lines): Prologue, Footman
SANDFIELD (30 lines): Footman, a Tenant, [Prologue]
SERVANT(s) (30 lines): Prologue, Footman
PROLOGUE (14 lines): any [but Philip, Savourwit]
SUNSET (9 lines): Prologue, Footman, a Tenant
FOOTMAN (8 lines): any

Boys

MISTRESS LOW-WATER (573 lines): Dutch Boy
WIDOW (342 lines): Dutch Boy
MOTHER (153 lines): Dutch Boy
JANE (30 lines): Dutch Boy
GRACE (26 lines): Dutch Boy
DUTCH BOY (8 lines): Widow, Grace, Jane, Mistress Low-water, Mother

Most crowded scene: Sc. 9: 17 characters (+ 3 mutes)

16 **ember-week** period of fasting
17 **Gemini** (the sign associated with the hands)
19 **thunder** (associated with the god Jupiter)
20 **[ ] Cancer** The missing words probably referred to the crab's claws; conjecturally, 'Though claws pinch closest when the sign is Cancer'.
23 **with ... ears** proverbial for (*a*) applause (*b*) blows
Shirley.3 **term** one of the times of year when law courts were in session. The speaker goes on to compare the theatre with a court-room, but the immediate point is that the city should be busy during term.
5–6 **And ... alive** Charity is bad for lawyers' business, whereas the players have such low receipts that they depend on it.
7 **a poet** i.e. the writer, Shirley
9 **the city** i.e. the populace (but quibbling on the area within the gated walls)
10 **strait** narrow
20 **Dublin's ... Brazil** Brazil would more usually be accounted *invisible* because remote from most Englishmen's actual experience, apparently uncharted and unchronicled, so figuratively an empty space. Dublin is seen as more like this than like a civilized city such as London.
25 **so** if
26, 28 **man** Quibbles on 'human' and 'male'.
28 **this ... wit** Refers to the play.

THE LADY'S TRAGEDY: PARALLEL TEXTS

Edited by Julia Briggs

ON 31 October 1611, the Master of the Revels, Sir George Buc, read through, corrected and licensed a manuscript submitted to him by the King's Men, Shakespeare's company and the leading troupe of the day. On the last page, he wrote, 'This second Maydens tragedy (for it hath no name inscribed) may with the reformations bee acted publikely'. Buc gave the manuscript this provisional title because its theme of tyrannicide and its anti-court satire reminded him of Beaumont and Fletcher's *The Maid's Tragedy*, submitted by the same company in the previous year. *The Second Maiden's Tragedy*, as it has usually been called, was never printed, perhaps because of its anti-court sentiments, but it survived in the manuscript marked up first by Buc, and then by the King's Men, who used it as the prompt copy for their performances. In this edition, the play has been retitled *The Lady's Tragedy*, since its heroine, like the Duchess of Malfi, has no personal name, and is always referred to as the Lady, or else as Govianus's Lady. The heroine of the parallel plot also remains unnamed. Though she is usually identified as the Wife or Anselmus's Wife, she is four times referred to as 'Lady' or 'Anselmus's Lady' in the original stage directions (at A1.2.290/B1.2.289, 4.1.0.2, 5.1.37.2, and 5.1.120.2), while the word 'lady' itself occurs more than fifty times within the dialogue. Jacobean spelling (like modern pronunciation) did not distinguish between *The Lady's Tragedy* and *The Ladies' Tragedy*.

Surviving in a single manuscript without a title-page (though with the names of George Chapman, Thomas Goff, and William Shakespeare written in as later guesses as to authorship beneath Buc's licence), *The Lady's Tragedy* was first attributed to Thomas Middleton by the Victorian poet and dramatic critic Algernon Swinburne. His tentative suggestion has since been confirmed by a number of scholars, including E. H. C. Oliphant, R. H. Barker, and Samuel Schoenbaum and, in the 1970s, by David Lake and MacDonald P. Jackson, who used statistical linguistic tests and independently arrived at the same conclusion. Anne Lancashire's edition for Revels (1978), while shrinking from putting Middleton's name on the title-page, nevertheless found many verbal parallels with other plays of his, and in particular with *No Wit/Help like a Woman's*, written earlier in 1611; further parallels have been observed by Roger Holdsworth. In 1998, the play was finally published as the work of Thomas Middleton in a volume of *Four Jacobean Sex Tragedies* edited by Martin Wiggins, under the title *The Maiden's Tragedy* (although the word 'maiden' never actually appears in the play). In the present edition, the text is given in two versions—the first, in the left column, is as close as possible to Middleton's original composition, and the second, in the right column, is as it was performed, after various cuts and alterations had been incorporated. For the first time, the reader will be able to see how a Jacobean tragedy, written for the King's Men at the height of their success, underwent processes of censorship, addition, and revision before and during rehearsal.

Plot

The plot of *The Lady's Tragedy* resembles that of *The Changeling* in being constructed from two different narratives worked together to form a complex counterpoint: the Lady plot is assumed to have been Middleton's own invention. It draws on themes earlier dramatized in *The Revenger's Tragedy* (1606) such as court corruption and the fatal kiss of the dead, while the character of the Tyrant owes something to the sexually fixated Tyrant of *The Bloody Banquet* (1608–9). The Wife plot is adapted from Cervantes's story of 'The Curious Impertinent', included in the first part of *Don Quixote* (1605), and also published separately in a French translation alongside the Spanish text in 1608. This is a tale of the woes of marriage, characterized by ironies of misplaced confidence and sexual betrayal such as Middleton relished.

The play opens with the Tyrant ascending the throne and proposing to the Lady, who rejects him in favour of her betrothed—Govianus, the kingdom's rightful heir. The two are placed under house arrest, and the Tyrant sends her father Helvetius to woo the Lady on his behalf, but Helvetius repents when Govianus shoots him with a blank pistol, literally putting the fear of God in him. The next set of messengers lay siege to the house, and, in the midst of furious knocking, the Lady commits suicide to avoid abduction and rape, Govianus having failed to slay her at the crucial moment. The Tyrant, brooking no obstacle to his desires, breaks into the Cathedral and steals the Lady's corpse from its tomb. As Govianus mourns for her, her ghost appears to him, begging him to recover her body and re-inter it. Meanwhile in the Wife plot, Govianus's brother Anselmus is determined to test his Wife's fidelity, and so forces his best friend Votarius to tempt her. After some initial resistance, the Wife surrenders. The lovers set about deceiving Anselmus, but are betrayed to him by Leonella, the Wife's maid, who is eager to exonerate herself and create further mischief, especially as her own lover, Bellarius, is the sworn enemy of Votarius. The Wife attempts to convince her husband of her fidelity by staging a scene in which she fights off Votarius's unwanted advances, but she is again betrayed by Leonella, who poisons the sword with which the Wife defends herself. In the fighting that follows, everyone is killed. Govianus mourns for his brother Anselmus, and then sets off for the court where the Tyrant is paying homage to the Lady's corpse. Disguised as an artist, Govianus paints her dead lips with poison, so that the Tyrant dies from her kiss. A conspiracy of courtiers declares Govianus king, and the play ends with the Lady's funeral procession.

First Performance

Middleton wrote this play to be performed by the King's Men at their indoor theatre at Blackfriars, late in 1611: the boys' singing voices were one attraction there, and he included two songs—the mournful, 'If ever pity were well placed', sung by a page at 4.4.14–28, and the madrigal, 'O what is beauty that's so much adorèd?', sung offstage while the Tyrant worships the Lady's corpse at 5.2.14–19. The comparative darkness of the indoor theatre would have enhanced the effect in 4.3, where the ruffians break into the Cathedral with pickaxes and dark lanterns, and contributed to the *coup de théâtre* when 'a great light appears in the midst of the tomb' from behind or beneath the stage (4.4.42.2–3). Ceremonial music would have further emphasized the contrast between the Tyrant's worship of the Lady's corpse early in 5.2, and the dead march at its end. The Lady's tomb, 'richly set forth' (4.3.0.3–4), may even have included an effigy of the Lady herself, as Jacobean tombs often did (see illustration), perhaps also recalling the final scene of *The Winter's Tale*, which the King's Men had performed earlier that year. But unlike Hermione's statue, the Lady's corpse when taken from the tomb proves 'cold indeed' (4.3.94).

When Middleton had finished drafting his play, two copies would have been written out by a professional scrivener employed by the company. The copy which has survived was submitted to Sir George Buc, in accordance with government regulations. The second copy consisted of individual 'parts' for the actors. As the play went into rehearsal, Middleton was asked to supply some extra speeches. The same scrivener copied these onto a single folio page, twice. One of these was cut up and the slips were pinned onto the manuscript that Buc had sent back, marked up with his corrections; this now became the prompt copy. The other sheet was cut up to be distributed to the actors. The new speeches (at B1.1.198, B1.1.208–15, B2.1.3–10, B4.2.38–41, B4.2a.1–11, and B5.1.166–79) tidied up loose ends in the plot, making the shared house arrest of the Lady and Govianus more plausible, and covering the Tyrant's exit and immediate re-entry at the end of 4.2 and the beginning of 4.3 (disallowed by the stage practice of the day). The most striking of Middleton's additions gives Anselmus, the jealous husband, a moment of sudden reversal and discovery, an Aristotelian *peripateia*: instead of dying in the happy (if mistaken) belief that his Wife had proved her innocence by killing Votarius (5.1.136–42), he survives a few minutes longer to learn that his worst fears have been realized, and she had indeed cuckolded him (B5.1.166–79). The addition at B4.2a.1–11 prepared the audience for the reappearance of Helvetius in 5.2, but in production further substantial cuts were made, especially to the last scene, so that Helvetius's part in it disappeared entirely. The cutting of several long poetic speeches that hold up the action at crucial points (e.g. at A2.1.108–38, A5.2.127–38, A180–7) suggests that comparable long set speeches may have been cut from other plays of the period during rehearsal.

We do not know whether Middleton, having supplied the script and six additional passages, played any further part in the production of his play, but it seems unlikely. He was not an actor or a company shareholder, and so had no further reason to participate, once he had received payment for the script (probably around £6). The play text moved steadily away from his original conception as it passed through the hands, first of Buc, and later of the company, in the course of rehearsals. Sir George Buc had begun by correcting what he took to be a grammatical mistake (at 1.1.2), but then went on to delete a number of oaths (sixteen are deleted in all, five examples of 'Heart!', ten of 'Life!' and a 'By the mass!'), a reference to the recent death by torture of Henry IV's assassin, François Ravaillac (A5.2.141/B5.2.116), as well as a series of sarcastic comments on the court and its courtiers:

...heaven,
That glorious court of spirits, all honest courtiers!
(last three words deleted, 1.2.14–15)

I must put on
A courtier's face and do't. Mine own will shame me.
('courtier's' deleted, 'brazen' substituted, 1.2.164–5)

Push! Talk like a courtier, girl, not like a fool.
('courtier' deleted, 'woman' substituted, A2.1.69/B2.1.75)

There's many a good knight's daughter is in service
And cannot get such favour of her mistress
('knight's' deleted, 'men's' substituted [ungrammatically], 4.1.74–5)

I would not trust at court, an I could choose
('at court' deleted, 'but few' substituted, A5.2.80/B5.2.66)

In addition, a number of passages have been marked for omission that comment specifically on the sexual misbehaviour of court ladies (e.g. at A2.1.72–81, A3.1.219–21), and the play's final couplet has been spoiled by substituting the more general term 'virtuous' for 'honest' (which carried stronger connotations of sexual chastity). It had originally read

I would those ladies that fill honour's rooms
Might all be borne so honest to their tombs. (A5.2.212–13/B5.2.163–4).

Although the play's original cast list was not recorded, the bookkeeper entered the names of two of the King's Men on the play script in the course of adding further stage directions. One was that of Master (Robert) Gough, written in at B4.2a.0.1. Gough had been with the company since before 1605, and almost certainly played Memphonius, though the particular speech where his name appears lacks its speech heading. The Lady was played by Richard Robinson, named in the margin at the entry for her ghost (B4.4.42.7). Robinson was one of the company's boy apprentices, and may also have played Shakespeare's Hermione. His name was included in the cast-list for Jonson's *Catiline* (1611), where he probably played Fulvia. Five years later, in *The Devil is an Ass*, Engine recommends Dick Robinson's talents as a female impersonator to Merecraft (2.7.64–73), but he is actually replaced by Wittipol (no doubt also played by Robinson himself), who later appears in drag as 'the Spanish Lady'. By the 1620s, Robinson was taking adult roles such as the Cardinal in *The Duchess of Malfi*, and had his own apprentice. He remained an actor and shareholder with the company until the 1630s. The part of the Tyrant would have suited the company's leading actor, Richard Burbage, who had played the lip-gnawing Richard III, Macbeth and, probably, Leontes.

Later History

The manuscript in which all these changes have been recorded is one of sixteen surviving promptbooks used in the public theatres before 1642, and one of only four to have been marked up by the Master of the Revels in his capacity as censor. The detailed stage directions entered on the manuscript of *The Lady's Tragedy* by the bookkeeper provide evidence of its performance, in the absence of other records; so, too, does its impact on other dramatists, especially John Webster, who borrowed several of its effects for *The White Devil* (1612), including the poisonous kiss, and for his fifth-act climax, Govianus's trick with the blank pistol shots and also a violent reversal resulting from a revelation. The character of the Lady, with her love of 'goodness' rather than 'greatness', also influenced that of *The Duchess of Malfi* (*c.*1614).

After the theatres closed in 1642, the manuscript of *The Lady's Tragedy* passed, with other playbooks belonging to the King's Men, into the hands of the printer Humphrey Moseley who registered it for printing on 9 September 1653 with several other Middleton plays (though the order of his list suggests that he had not identified it as Middleton's); in any case he never actually got round to printing it. A century later it resurfaced in the collection of the antiquarian, John Warburton, who claimed that it was one of only three play manuscripts that escaped being burned, or baked under pies by his cook. From Warburton it passed to Lord Lansdowne, and thence to the British Museum Library in 1807. It was first published in 1824 and nine further editions have been produced since then, most notably W. W. Greg's old-spelling transcript for the Malone Society (1910) and Anne Lancashire's exemplary modern edition for Revels (1978).

After nearly four centuries of complete theatrical neglect, the twentieth century ended with a sudden flurry of performances of Middleton's play under a variety of titles. The first was in London, in 1984, as *The Tyrant's Tragedy*, in a production by the Troupe at the Upstream Theatre. Ten years later, this time billed as Middleton's *The Lady's Tragedy* and using the earlier (left-hand) text given here, it was performed by 'Show of Strength' at Bristol, under the direction of Alan Coveney, who also played the Tyrant, in a production memorable for its menacing atmosphere and intelligent verse-speaking. But earlier that year, the appearance of a new and highly eccentric edition of the play created renewed interest in it: in May 1994, Charles Hamilton published a version under the title *Cardenio, or The Second Maiden's Tragedy*, attributing it to William Shakespeare and John Fletcher and renaming the characters from the 'Cardenio' plot of Cervantes's *Don Quixote*. Hamilton claimed it was Shakespeare's lost late play, *Cardenio*, on the grounds that *Cardenio* and the Wife plot of *The Lady's Tragedy* both derived from (different) episodes in Cervantes. Hamilton also claimed that the manuscript of *The Lady's Tragedy* was in Shakespeare's hand. His edition was launched with a play-reading by the Allied Theatre Group at Fort Worth, Texas.

Once (re-)attributed to Shakespeare, the play rapidly acquired a new lease of life: it was translated into German and performed at the Globe Theater at Neuss, near Düsseldorf, in August 1994, and into Serbian in 1996, to be broadcast by Radio Belgrade, where its focus on political oppression had a special immediacy. Meanwhile, back in the USA in 1995, the Upstart Crow Theatre Company of Boulder, Colorado, performed a carefully authentic version under the play's traditional title, attributing it to Middleton. Two further performances took place that year, both as *Cardenio*, by the Unseam'd Shakespeare Company of Pittsburgh, Pennsylvania, and by the Palm Beach Shakespeare Festival, where Kevin Crawford produced and starred as the Tyrant; an off-Broadway run followed in 1996.

In 1998, Kate Buckley produced the play as *Cardenio* for the Next Theatre of Evanston, Illinois, and Melanie White directed the first English version as *Cardenio* at Essex University, and later at the Globe Theatre on Bankside. Her production used modern dress and a Gothic style, with off-stage screams and bright red blood and lipstick emphasized by a black and white set and costumes. In 2002, the Lone Star Ensemble played it as *Cardenio* in Los Angeles, again in modern dress, using newsreels and guns for swords in the manner of Baz Luhrmann's *Romeo + Juliet*. This version separated the two plots and performed them successively, with an interval between; soliloquies were videoed and Cardenio/Govianus's third-act swoon was drug-induced. The same year, the Ariel Society performed a *Cardenio* at Oxford with an almost all-female cast, Jessica Cullimore playing the Tyrant. In

October 2004, Blue Eyes played a modern-dress version at the White Bear Theatre. As Shakespeare's *Cardenio*, *The Lady's Tragedy* has found a new theatrical life, though it still awaits a strong mainstream professional production.

Structure

Despite increasing interest in it, the play has so far failed to attract the critical attention it deserves, though its strong and independent heroine, its percipient exploration of marital distrust and betrayal, its highly politicized treatment of the court will attract future critics, and no doubt theatrical directors as well. Until recently, the vivid psychological detail of the Wife plot has appealed more strongly than the Lady plot which Samuel Schoenbaum considered 'less interesting', finding it 'unconvincing', and lacking in realism. He disliked its use of archetypes, and its serious and uninhibited use of the supernatural, so unlike the naturalistic stage practice of his day. Schoenbaum also complained of 'the two stories being joined together in a clumsy and arbitrary fashion', though, as Richard Levin was to point out, this was no more true of *The Lady's Tragedy* than it was of *The Changeling*: in both plays, the two plots are cunningly interwoven, and scenes of temptation, sudden reversals, play-acting, disguise, treachery, even particular words or phrases echo one another closely throughout. In fact, like the rest of Middleton's *œuvre*, *The Lady's Tragedy* displays a deep theatrical self-awareness (as David Bergeron has demonstrated).

Both plots represent sexual desire as self-destructive and spiritually dangerous, recalling the imagery used of Narcissus's death in *The Wisdom of Solomon Paraphrased*: 'O sugared kiss, dyed with a poisoned lip' (13.86), a metaphor made literal when the Tyrant actually kisses the Lady's poisoned lips (as in *The Revenger's Tragedy*, where the Duke kisses Gloriana's poisoned skull [3.5.145]). Poison also figures in the Wife plot where the sword that Leonella has baited kills her as well as Votarius, Bellarius, and perhaps the Wife too; its poison rages like a fire through breast and blood, as a foretaste of punishments to come (5.1.108, 132–5). The gendered symbolism of poisoned lips and sword suggests the way in which the Tyrant's lust propels the Lady plot, and the Wife's desire drives the Wife plot, although her husband's jealousy and the several treacheries of Votarius and Leonella also contribute to her downfall.

Both plots present relationships under breaking strain: the love of Govianus and his Lady (they are apparently betrothed rather than married—a familiar state for many young couples in early modern England) is threatened by outside forces in the shape of the Tyrant and his henchmen, while Anselmus's marriage is threatened from within by his own obsessive fears, a point he himself makes at the outset: 'He's lost the kingdom, but his mind's restored; | Which is the larger empire?' (1.2.6–7). For Anselmus, the Lady's independent choice of Govianus gives his brother the 'peace and pleasure' (1.2.18) that he cannot find within his marriage. His words expose the hidden cost of patriarchy which, by reducing women's opportunities to make active choices, sets up troubling doubts and anxieties in their masters. When the Wife is play-acting for Anselmus's benefit, she compares herself with the Lady, threatening that unless her husband can save her from Votarius's (supposedly) unwanted attentions: '...here I vow | I'll imitate my noble sister's fate,... | And cast away my life as she did hers' (5.1.79–82). But by this point, the comparison merely emphasizes the difference between the Wife who has succumbed to temptation, and the Lady who has triumphed over it in death.

Staging Oppression

There is no obvious source for the dramatic confrontation between the Tyrant and the Lady in the opening scene—the meeting of an irresistible force with an immovable object—though it voices contemporary fears of absolute power, and of political or religious coercion, as Bushnell, and more recently, Allman, have shown. The Tyrant's transgressive desire reflects his refusal to submit to the law, a self-will so determined that it overrides fate and death. 'It is the mark of a tyrant,...', wrote Erasmus, in *The Education of a Christian Prince*, 'to follow the unbridled will of [his] mind.' Like his predecessor in *The Bloody Banquet*, the Tyrant descends from sexual obsession into full-blown mania.

At one level, the Lady's resistance is emblematic of the (religious) conscience. The encounter between a female victim and a male authority figure is a recurrent motif in Middleton, though more typically, masculine power prevails, as in the encounter between the Duke and Bianca in 2.2 of *Women, Beware Women*. The chaste wife who becomes the sexual victim of a man in power, sacrificing her life, was epitomized in the Roman legend of Lucrece (used by Middleton in *The Ghost of Lucrece*, written at the outset of his career). *The Revenger's Tragedy* (1606) reworks different elements of Lucrece's story: Gloriana's death provides the Revenger with his motive, Junior rapes Antonio's wife, triggering a political conspiracy against the Duke and his family, and Castiza defends her virtue. Tales of sexual intimidation were, in any case, popular on the Elizabethan stage, and the Roman heroines Lucrece and Virginia, as well as the Biblical Susannah were dramatized in Thomas Garter's *Most Virtuous and Godly Susanna* (1563–9), R. B.'s, and later Webster's *Appius and Virginia* (1564 and 1624, respectively) and Thomas Heywood's *The Rape of Lucrece* (1607). Comparable situations of sexual and political oppression also occur in Anthony Munday's *The Death of Robert, Earl of Huntingdon* (1598), whose heroine Matilda, like the Lady, is conspicuously dressed in black, as well as in Shakespeare's *Measure for Measure* (1604) and John Marston's *Sophonisba, the Wonder of Women* (1605).

Closest in atmosphere to *The Lady's Tragedy*, and a significant influence on it (see notes to A4.2.38 and B5.1.192) is John Fletcher's *Tragedy of Valentinian*, performed some time during 1610 or 1611: here, the chaste wife, Lucina, is raped by the Emperor, whose corrupt court is deeply complicit in her ruin. One of the age's most influential books, Foxe's 'Book of Martyrs' (*The Acts and Monuments*, 1570), had recorded the lives of a number of early Christian martyrs, including that of Sophronia who, like Middleton's Lady and her Roman prototype, Virginia, or Olympia in Marlowe's *Tamburlaine, Part Two*, avoided rape by committing suicide. Foxe represented the resistance of martyrs, among them women and the lower classes, as part of the long and ultimately victorious struggle of the Protestant church against Catholic persecution.

All or any of these narratives could have contributed to the story of the Tyrant and the Lady. The Tyrant's illegitimacy, lustfulness, and acts of desecration and idol atry link him with the Catholic Church as it appeared to committed Protestants like Middleton, while the sombrely dressed Lady represents the reformed Church, persecuted but unafraid. She is the daughter of Helvetius, perhaps named after the (Calvinist) United Swiss Provinces and referred to as 'the father of the state' (B4.2a.9), and she is betrothed to the rightful, virtuous and godly prince, Govianus. As John Stachniewski observed, the play also employs a number of characteristically Calvinist images, whereby spiritual states are described in terms of physical processes: at A2.1.149/B2.1.115 Govianus acts as a surgeon, restoring Helvetius to spiritual health by cutting away his worldly ambitions, an operation that the good governor may be obliged to perform upon a people corrupted by evil rule. In the Wife plot, the temptation to adultery is experienced by Votarius first as the threat of a 'dead sleep' (1.2.226), then of sickness (1.2.229). Later, thoughts of jealousy and revenge course like poison or alcohol through his blood (2.2.110, 149–50), until they are overtaken by the literal action of the poison itself (5.1.108).

The sexual passions of the Wife plot contrast with the transcendent love of Govianus and the Lady who take comfort in the thought of sharing eternal joy: 'we'll walk together | Like loving spirits' (4.4.82–3). The Lady does not consider suicide a sin (St Augustine had argued it was) but as an act necessary to preserve herself from the Tyrant whose 'lust may part thee from me, but death, never. | Thou canst not lose me there, for dying thine, | Thou dost enjoy me still. Kings cannot rob thee' (3.1.144–6). The intensely dramatic scene (3.1) in which she stabs herself to the accompaniment of frenzied offstage knocking wonderfully conveys the lovers' conflicting desires to be united both in life and in death. The violent break-in of Govianus's house, and subsequently of the Lady's tomb symbolically enact her threatened rape and make powerful theatre. For the Tyrant, the Lady's spirituality is merely an obstacle to his desires; their sinister nature is made fully apparent when he embraces her corpse, in a gruesome echo of the Dance of Death, at once anticipating and acting out his damnation.

Body and Spirit

Yet even in death her spirit still resists him. Her presence as a ghost creates a number of problems, some metaphysical, others practical and theatrical. There is the whole question of the legitimacy of ghosts within the Protestant tradition: as in *Hamlet*, the ghost threatens to be incompatible with a belief system that no longer allows a place of transit for its dead. Female ghosts were in any case unusual on the Jacobean stage, appearing more commonly in complaint poems in which legendary figures such as Fair Rosamund or Jane Shore lamented their lost virtue. Middleton's *The Ghost of Lucrece*, a poem belonging to this genre, effects an interesting negotiation between poetry and the theatre when its heroine writes out her wrongs as if on stage, and speaking a prologue; but otherwise she has little in common with the Lady's ghost who has anticipated and avoided Lucrece's fate. The ghost's plea for reburial was traditional, common to a wide range of cultures (see, for example, the ballad of 'The Unquiet Grave', or Virgil's Palinurus in the *Aeneid*, 6.337–383), though the Tyrant's necrophilia gives it a peculiarly gruesome twist. The notion that the spirit requires proper burial to be at peace is very ancient and not especially Christian, though Govianus offers a rationale for it in terms of the contemporary belief in the resurrection of the body: 'Thy body shall return to rise again' (A5.2.162/B5.2.137).

The Lady's ghost is given specifically Christian, and even angelic overtones, as if to allay any suspicions it might arouse. As Lancashire has pointed out, its appearance at the tomb dressed all in white, accompanied by a supernatural wind and a mysterious beam of light (4.4.42.1–6), recalls the appearance of the angel at Christ's empty tomb in the 'Resurrection' play of the suppressed Mystery cycles. Traditionally, the angel appeared to the four soldiers guarding the tomb, who shifted from coarse jesting to panic, much as the soldiers do in 4.3. Protestant objections to those plays had focused largely on their representation of the divine in gross material terms; yet even in the very different medium of the secular stage, the representation of the supernatural remained a problem. The Lady (or her spirit) responds to Govianus's prayer with the strange words, 'I am not here' (echoing the angel at Christ's empty tomb in the gospels: 'He is not here, for He is risen')—words that emphasize the shifting and ultimately elusive nature of the self as body or spirit, even as actor. The stage direction 'Enter Lady | Rich Robinson' marking the ghost's entry at B4.4.42.7 draws attention to the physical presence of the boy actor, his face whitened with flour as convention required, dressed 'all in white, stuck with jewels, and a great crucifix on her breast', to resemble the corpse 'as went out' in the previous scene (and, perhaps, the Lady's effigy upon her tomb). The relationship between the Lady's ghost and her physical remains becomes even more complicated in the play's last scene, where the two are required to appear on stage together.

Disappointingly, the stage directions give no indication as to whether the Lady's corpse in 5.2 was represented by another actor or, as seems more probable, by a dummy which could also have been used for her abduction from the tomb at 4.3.81.1. After death, the Lady's body is emptied of its spirit, and the actor who played her living

A Jacobean tomb effigy from the Church of St Margaret, Paston, England. Did the Lady's tomb, so 'richly set forth', include her effigy?

must now play her ghost, although body and spirit are dressed identically, first in the white of grave-clothes or eternal brightness in Act 4, and then in fashionable if deathly black velvet, with pearls in Act 5. The transience of flesh is the theme of the off-stage song at 5.2.17 ('The dainty preserv'd flesh, how soon it moulders'), underlined by the corpse's 'too constant paleness' (A5.2.28/B5.2.23) and its tendency to sag: 'Keep her up, | I'll have her swoon no more, there's treachery in it' (A5.2.115–16/ B5.2.101–2). The Tyrant's efforts to disguise from himself what he is worshipping reach a climax in the face-painting episode, which brings together various symbolic associations of deception (among them, the make-up used on the stage itself). In the opening scene, the Tyrant had attacked the Lady for wearing mourning garments, while she had responded by rejecting 'strange colours' (A1.1.113–25/B1.1.94–106). Now the Tyrant commands an artist to impose on her the colour she lacks. Face-painting in Jacobean drama is always linked with meretriciousness, the artifice of the prostitute. It was further associated with the Church of Rome through John Bale's identification of the Catholic Church with the Scarlet Woman of Babylon in the Apocalypse, in his *Image of Both Churches* (*c.*1545). The disguised Govianus paints the Lady's face with poison in order to kill the Tyrant and rescue her corpse, but to do so, he must first disguise her body as its own antithesis, the painted whore, so that in kissing the corpse, the Tyrant quite literally embraces death and sexual corruption. Such use of the Lady's body as the agent of destruction is deeply troubling, and not least for Govianus: 'A religious trembling shakes me by the hand | And bids me put by such unhallowed business' (A5.2.91–2/B5.2.77–8).

The Tyrant's sacrilegious desire to violate the Lady's body contrasts with Govianus's desire to honour it 'in memory | Of her admirèd mistress' (A5.2.197–8/ B5.2.153–4), and the gap between them may be intended to bring to mind contemporary debate as to the meaning of transubstantiation: while Catholics consumed the wafer as the literal body of Christ, the reformers took it 'in memory of' the Last Supper. If such meanings were present, it is likely that Middleton necessarily left them inexplicit, though they are hinted at by the contrasting ceremonies of the final scene. In the first, polyphonic music plays while the Tyrant and the soldiers make low bows to the Lady's corpse, and the Tyrant kisses her hand. In an aside, the first soldier denounces this as 'mere idolatry! I make curtsy | To my damnation', linking it with incomprehensible 'Latin prayers' (A5.2.20–3), as well as the polyphonic music, bowing and kneeling that had been part of the old mass. The second ceremonial was to have been performed at Govianus's command, 'Here place her in this throne, crown her our queen' (A5.2.201), but a line in the margin indicates a cut at this point—whether marked in by the Master of the Revels as politically unacceptable, or by the actors because the scene was already too long, is impossible to tell. However we interpret it, Stephen Greenblatt's description of *Hamlet* as 'the conjunction of gross physicality and pure abstracted spirituality, of Body and Word, of corruptible flesh and invulnerable ghost' may also be applied to *The Lady's Tragedy*, which weaves together Renaissance anxieties about the relationship of body and spirit, and their embodiment on the material stage—a medium in which the paradoxes within the process of representation itself were always palpable to the beholders.

SEE ALSO

Textual introduction and apparatus: *Companion*, 619
Authorship and date: *Companion*, 371

The Lady's Tragedy

[for the King's Men]

THE PERSONS OF THE PLAY

The TYRANT, a usurper
GOVIANUS, the rightful king
MEMPHONIUS and SOPHONIRUS, Nobles
HELVETIUS, an old courtier
The LADY, daughter of Helvetius

ANSELMUS, brother of Govianus
VOTARIUS, friend of Anselmus
The WIFE of Anselmus

LEONELLA, her waiting woman
BELLARIUS, lover of Leonella

Two NOBLES
SERVANT of the Lady
Three SOLDIERS (Guard of the Tyrant)
Two FELLOWS
PAGE of Govianus
Two SERVANTS of Anselmus
ATTENDANTS

1.1

Incipit Actus Primus
[The throne is set out]
Enter the new usurping Tyrant; the Nobles of his faction, Memphonius, Sophonirus, Helvetius, with others; the right heir, Govianus, deposed

TYRANT *[speaking from the throne]*
Thus high, my lords, your powers and constant loves
Hath fixed our glories like unmovèd stars
That know not what it is to fall or err.
We're now the kingdom's love, and he that was
Flattered awhile so stands before us now
Readier for doom than dignity.

GOVIANUS So much
Can the adulterate friendship of mankind,
False fortune's sister, bring to pass on kings,
And lay usurpers sunning in their glories
Like adders in warm beams.

TYRANT There was but one
In whom my heart took pleasure amongst women,
One in the whole creation, and in her

1.1

Incipit Actus Primus
[The throne is set out]
Enter the new usurping Tyrant; the Nobles of his faction, Memphonius, Sophonirus, Helvetius, with others; the right heir, Govianus, deposed
A sennet

TYRANT *[speaking from the throne]*
Thus high, my lords, your powers and constant loves
Have fixed our glories like unmovèd stars
That know not what it is to fall or err.
We're now the kingdom's love, and he that was
Flattered awhile so stands before us now
Readier for doom than dignity.

GOVIANUS So much
Can the adulterate friendship of mankind,
False fortune's sister, bring to pass on kings,
And lay usurpers sunning in their glories
Like adders in warm beams.

TYRANT There was but one
In whom my heart took pleasure amongst women,
One in the whole creation, and in her

Line references to both versions are given wherever possible; where the line number of a passage differs in the two versions, or where the passage exists in only one version, original-text (that is, left-hand column) line numbers are prefixed with A, and performance-text (right-hand column) line numbers are prefixed with B.

1.1.0.4 ***Helvetius*** 'man of Switzerland' (a country associated with the Protestant faith)

0.5 ***right*** true, as at 5.1.2
Govianus Pronounced 'Jovianus', and deriving from 'Jove' (i.e. the classical god), meaning king-like (and suggesting 'Giovanni', i.e. John).

B0.6 ***sennet*** trumpet fanfare, here accompanying the procession to the throne

A2 **Hath** the use of a singular verb with plural reference was not uncommon (as at A5.2.70/B5.2.56), but was here assumed to be a mistake and so corrected, apparently by Sir George Buc, the censor.

2 **unmovèd stars** According to the Ptolemaic system, the region of fixed stars was not subject to change. The Tyrant's elevation, both in terms of status and position on stage, and Govianus's degradation are emphasized throughout the scene.

6 **for . . . dignity** to be judged than honoured (as at l. 68)

6–8 **So . . . kings** Thus men's false friendship, like the related treachery of fortune, can bring about the fall of kings. The theme of false friendship links this scene with the next.

10 **adders . . . beams** Like poisonous snakes in the sunshine. Images of sunshine and storm recur in this scene, like those of height and depth.

You dared to be my rival! Was't not bold?
Now we are king, she'll leave the lower path
And find the way to us.—Helvetius,
It is thy daughter. Happier than a king
And far above him, for she kneels to thee
Whom we have kneeled to, richer in one smile
That came from her, than she in all thy blessings.
If thou be'st proud, thou art to be forgiven;
It is no deadly sin in thee. While she lives,
High lust is not more natural to youth
Than that to thee: be not afraid to die in't.
'Tis but the sin of joy. There is no gladness
But has a pride it lives by: that's the oil
That feeds it into flames.—Let her be sent for
And honourably attended, as beseems
Her that we make our queen. My lords Memphonius
And Sophonirus, take into your care
The royal business of my heart. Conduct her
With a respect equal with that to us.
If more, it shall be pardoned; so still err.
You honour us, but ourself honours her.

MEMPHONIUS [*aside*]
Strange fortune! Does he make his queen of her?
Exit

SOPHONIRUS [*aside*]
I have a wife. Would she were so preferred!
I could be but her subject—so I'm now.
I allow her her one friend, to stop her mouth
And keep her quiet, give him his table free,
And the huge feeding of his great stone-horse
With which he rides in pomp about the city,
Only to speak to gallants in bay-windows.
Marry, his lodging he pays dearly for:
He gets me all my children; there I save by't.
Beside I draw my life out by the bargain
Some twelve years longer than the times appointed,
When my young prodigal gallant kicks up's heels
At one-and-thirty, and lies dead and rotten
Some five-and-forty years before I'm coffined.
'Tis the right way to keep a woman honest:
One friend is barricado to a hundred
And keeps 'em out. Nay, more: a husband's sure
To have his children all of one man's getting,
And he that performs best can have no better.
I'm e'en as happy then that save a labour. *Exit*

TYRANT [*to Helvetius*]
Thy honours with thy daughter's love shall rise.

You dared to be my rival! Was't not bold?
Now we are king, she'll leave the lower path
And find the way to us.—Helvetius,
It is thy daughter. Happier than a king
And far above him, for she kneels to thee
Whom we have kneeled to, richer in one smile
That came from her, than she in all thy blessings.
If thou be'st proud, thou art to be forgiven;
'Tis no deadly sin in thee. While she lives,
High lust is not more natural to youth
Than that to thee: be not afraid to die in't.
'Tis but the sin of joy. There is no gladness
But has a pride it lives by: that's the oil
That feeds it into flames.—Let her be sent for
And honourably attended, as beseems
Her that we make our queen. My lords Memphonius
And Sophonirus, take into your care
The royal business of my heart. Conduct her
With a respect equal with that to us.
If more, it shall be pardoned; so still err.
You honour us, but ourself honours her.

MEMPHONIUS [*aside*]
Strange fortune! Does he make his queen of her?
Exit

SOPHONIRUS [*aside*]
I have a wife. Would she were so preferred!
I could be but her subject—so I'm now.
I allow her her own friend, to stop her mouth
And keep her quiet, gi' him his table free,
And the huge feeding of his great stone-horse
On which he rides in pomp about the city,
Only to speak to gallants in bay-windows.
Marry, his lodging he pays dearly for:
He gets me all my children; there I save by't.
Beside I draw my life out by the bargain
Some twelve years longer than the times appointed,
When my young prodigal gallant kicks up's heels
At one-and-thirty, and lies dead and rotten
Some five-and-forty years before I'm coffined.
'Tis the right way to keep a woman honest:
One friend is barricado to a hundred
And keeps 'em out. Nay, more: a husband's sure
To have his children all of one man's getting,
And he that performs best can have no better.
I'm e'en as happy then that save a labour. *Exit*

TYRANT [*to Helvetius*]
Thy honours with thy daughter's love shall rise.

20–6 **If . . . flames** Though pride can be a deadly sin, your pride in your daughter, while she lives, is as natural as the energy of the young, and as forgivable. Every happiness is fed by some kind of pride—it's the oil that feeds the flame.

28–9 **Memphonius . . . Sophonirus** Their names derive from Greek, Memphonius meaning 'a fault-finder' and Sophonirus meaning clever or wise of mind (with irony).

35–54 **I . . . labour** This soliloquy of the contented cuckold anticipates that of Allwit in *Chaste Maid* (1.2.12–56). It consists of a series of double meanings. Sophonirus wishes his wife might become queen, since he is already her obedient 'subject'. He persuades himself that this is to his advantage, since her present lover ('friend') performs all the sexual duties required of a husband. Mouth-stopping, feeding, riding, speaking (like 'intercourse') can all be used of the sexual act; a stone-horse is a stallion (like 'stud'); 'gallants in bay-windows' are ladies of fashion (or prostitutes). The lover pays for his 'lodging' (his possession of the wife's body) by begetting all her children, which he will pay for in another sense, since copulating was supposed to shorten one's life ('kicks up's heels', i.e. dies).

50 **barricado** barrier

I shall read thy deservings in her eyes.
HELVETIUS
O may they be eternal books of pleasure
To show you all delight.
[*The Tyrant consults his Nobles*]
GOVIANUS [*aside*]
The loss of her sits closer to my heart
Than that of kingdom, or the whorish pomp
Of this world's titles that with flattery swells us
And makes us die like beasts fat for destruction.
O she's a woman, and her eye will stand
Upon advancement, never weary yonder;
But when she turns her head, by chance, and sees
The fortunes that are my companïons,
She'll snatch her eyes off, and repent the looking.
TYRANT [*to Nobles*]
'Tis well advised. We doom thee, Govianus,
To banishment for ever from our kingdom.
GOVIANUS
What could be worse to one whose heart is locked
Up in another's bosom? Banishment?
And why not death? Is that too easy for me?
TYRANT But that the world would call
Our way to dignity a path of blood,
It should be the first act in all our reign.
GOVIANUS
She's lost for ever. [*To Nobles*] Farewell, virtuous men,
Too honest for your greatness. Now you're mightier
Than when we knew the kingdom, your styles heavier;
Then, ponderous nobility, farewell.
FIRST NOBLE How's that, sir?
GOVIANUS
Weighty and serious.—O, sir, is it you?
I knew you one-and-twenty and a lord,
When your discretion sucked; is't come from nurse yet?
You scorn to be a scholar, you were born better.
You have good lands, that's the best grounds of learning.
If you can cònstrue but your doctor's bill,
Pierce your wife's waiting women, and decline your tenants
Till they're all beggars, with new fines and rackings,
You're scholar good enough for a lady's son
That's born to living. If you list to read,
Ride but to th' city and bestow your looks
On the court library, the mercers' books;
They'll quickly furnish you. Do but entertain

I shall read thy deservings in her eyes.
HELVETIUS
O may they be eternal books of pleasure
To show you all delight.
[*The Tyrant consults his Nobles*]
GOVIANUS [*aside*]
The loss of her sits closer to my heart
Than that of kingdom, or the whorish pomp
Of this world's title that with flattery swells us
And makes us die like beasts fat for destruction.
O she's a woman, and her eye will stand
Upon advancement, never weary yonder;
But when she turns her head, by chance, and sees
The fortunes that are my companïons,
She'll snatch her eyes off, and repent the looking.
TYRANT [*to Nobles*]
'Tis well advised. We doom thee, Govianus,
To banishment for ever from our kingdom.
GOVIANUS
What could be worse to one whose heart is locked
Up in another's bosom? Banishment?
And why not death? Is that too easy for me?
TYRANT But that the world would call
Our way to dignity a path of blood,
It should be the first act in all our reign.
GOVIANUS
She's lost for ever. [*To Nobles*] Farewell, virtuous men,
Too honest for your greatness. Now you're mightier
Than when we knew the kingdom, your styles heavier;
Then, ponderous nobility, farewell. [*Going*]

62 **beasts ... destruction** animals fattened for slaughter
63–4 **stand | Upon** remain fixed on
78 **styles** titles
A83 **when ... yet** When your wisdom was being suckled—is it weaned now?
A84–96 **You ... called** In a sequence of complex puns, the young nobleman substitutes sexual and social exploitation for education, and in particular, learning Latin: he construes (i.e. inspects/translates) his doctor's bills, because he has caught a venereal infection; he pierces/parses (i.e. penetrates his wife's maids/identifies parts of speech) and declines (i.e. reduces the living standards of his tenants/inflects). Fines and rackings are fees and excessive rents charged. A living is an estate providing a source of income. Mercers' books are the account books of cloth-dealers. In an age of extravagant dress, tailors could expound (explain or comment on) the stuff (material, in both senses) and its title (i.e. the name, whether of a book or a type of cloth).

A tailor for your tutor, to expound
All the hard stuff to you, by what name and title
Soever they be called.

FIRST NOBLE I thank you, sir.

GOVIANUS
'Tis happy you have learned so much manners,
Since you have so little wit. Fare you well, sir. [*Going*]

TYRANT
Let him be stayed awhile.

SECOND NOBLE [*to Govianus*]
Stay!

FIRST NOBLE [*to Govianus*] You must stay, sir.

GOVIANUS [*aside*]
He's not so honest, sure, to change his mind,
Revoke his doom. Hell has more hope on him!

TYRANT
We have not ended yet: the worst part's coming.
Thy banishment were gentle, were that all,
But t'afflict thy soul, before thou goest
Thou shalt behold the heaven that thou must lose
In her that must be mine;
Then to be banished, then to be deprived,
Shows the full torment we provide for thee.

GOVIANUS [*aside*]
Here's a right tyrant now: he will not bate me
Th'affliction of my soul; he will have all parts
Suffer together.

Enter [*Memphonius*] *with the Lady, clad in black*

Now I see my loss.
I never shall recover't. My mind's beggared.

TYRANT
Black? Whence risse that cloud? Can such a thing be seen
In honour's glorious day? The sky so clear?
Why mourns the kingdom's mistress? Does she come
To meet advancement in a funeral garment?
Back! She forgot herself. 'Twas too much joy
That bred this error and we heartily pardon't.
[*To Attendants*] Go, bring me her hither like an illustrious bride
With her best beams about her. Let her jewels
Be worth ten cities—that beseems our mistress,
And not a widow's case, a suit to weep in.

LADY
I am not to be altered.

TYRANT How?

LADY I have a mind
That must be shifted ere I cast off these,
Or I shall wear strange colours. 'Tis not titles
Nor all the bastard honours of this frame
That I am taken with. I come not hither

TYRANT
Let him be stayed awhile.

SECOND NOBLE [*to Govianus*]
Stay!

FIRST NOBLE [*to Govianus*] You must stay, sir.

GOVIANUS [*aside*]
He's not so honest, sure, to change his mind,
Revoke his doom. Hell has more hope on him!

TYRANT
We have not ended yet: the worst part's coming.
Thy banishment were gentle, were that all,
But to afflict thy soul, before thou goest
Thou shalt behold the heaven that thou must lose
In her that must be mine;
Then to be banished, then to be deprived,
Shows the full torment we provide for thee.

GOVIANUS [*aside*]
Here's a right tyrant now: he will not bate me
Th'affliction of my soul; he'll have all parts
Suffer together.

Enter [*Memphonius*] *with the Lady, clad in black*

Now I see my loss.
I never shall recover't. My mind's beggared.

TYRANT
Whence risse that cloud? Can such a thing be seen
In honour's glorious day? The sky so clear?
Why mourns the kingdom's mistress? Does she come
To meet advancement in a funeral garment?
Back! She forgot herself. 'Twas too much joy
That bred this error and we heartily pardon't.
[*To Attendants*] Go, bring me her hither like an illustrious bride
With her best beams about her. Let her jewels
Be worth ten cities—that beseems our mistress,
And not a widow's case, a suit to weep in.

LADY
I am not to be altered.

TYRANT How?

LADY I have a mind
That must be shifted ere I cast off these,
Or I shall wear strange colours. 'Tis not titles
Nor all the bastard honours of this frame
That I am taken with. I come not hither

A101/B82 **Hell... him** Hell's hopes (of receiving him) are better than mine are (i.e. that he will change his mind).

A109/B90 **bate** spare, abate

A113/B94 **risse** rose (older form)

A125/B106 **strange colours** The Lady's black expresses her sobriety, as well as her mourning for the state. She would not be true to herself if she wore imposed colours (and see A5.2.72/B5.2.58, A124/B110).

A125–7/B106–8 **'Tis not... with** See ll. A171–2/B152–3, and *No Wit* 2.20–6, for comparison especially with l. A126/B107 here.

A126/B107 **frame** world

To please the eye of glory, but of goodness,
[*To the Tyrant*] And that concerns not you, sir. You're for greatness.
I dare not deal with you. [*Indicating Govianus*] I have found my match
And I will never lose him.

GOVIANUS
If there be man
Above a king in fortunes, read my story
And you shall find him there. Farewell, poor kingdom!
[*To the Tyrant*] Take it to help thee, thou hadst need on't now.
I see thee in distress, more miserable
Than some thou lay'st taxations on, poor subjects.
Thou art all beset with storms, more overcast
Than ever any man that brightness flattered.
'Tis only wretchedness to be there with thee,
And happiness to be here.

TYRANT [*aside*]
Sure some dream crowned me.
If it were possible to be less than nothing,
I wake, the man you seek for. There's the kingdom
Within yon valley fixed, while I stand here
Kissing false hopes upon a frozen mountain,
Without the confines. I am he that's banished.
The king walks yonder, chose by her affection,
Which is the surer side, for where she goes,
Her eye removes the court. What is he here
Can spare a look? They're all employed on her!—
[*To Helvetius*] Helvetius! Thou art not worth the waking, neither.
I lose but time in thee. Go, sleep again:
Like an old man, thou canst do nothing.
Thou tak'st no pain at all to earn thine honours.
Which way shall we be able to pay thee
To thy content, when we receive not ours?
The master of the work must needs decay
When he wants means, and sees his servant play.

HELVETIUS [*to the Lady*]
Have I bestowed so many blessings on thee,
And do they all return to me in a curse?
Is that the use I ha' for 'em? Be not to me
A burden ten times heavier than my years.
Thou'dst wont to be kind to me and observe
What I thought pleasing. Go, entreat the king.

LADY
I will do more for you, sir—you're my father.
I'll kiss him too. [*She kisses Govianus*]

HELVETIUS
How am I dealt withal!

LADY
[*Pointing to the Tyrant*] Why, that's the usurper, sir.
[*Pointing to Govianus*] This is the King.
I happened righter than you thought I had,
And were all kingdoms of the earth his own,

To please the eye of glory, but of goodness,
[*To the Tyrant*] And that concerns not you, sir. You're for greatness.
I dare not deal with you. [*Indicating Govianus*] I have found my match
And I will never lose him.

GOVIANUS
If there be man
Above a king in fortunes, read my story
And you shall find him there. Farewell, poor kingdom!
[*To the Tyrant*] Take it to help thee, thou hast need on't now.
I see thee in distress, more miserable
Than some thou lay'st taxations on, poor subjects.
Thou'rt all beset with storms, more overcast
Than ever any man that brightness flattered.
'Tis only wretchedness to be there with thee,
And happiness to be here.

TYRANT [*aside*]
Sure some dream crowned me.
If it were possible to be less than nothing,
I wake, the man you seek for. There's the kingdom
Within yon valley fixed, while I stand here
Kissing false hopes upon a frozen mountain,
Without the confines. I am he that's banished.
The king walks yonder, chose by her affection,
Which is the surer side, for where she goes,
Her eye removes the court. What is he here
Can spare a look? They're all employed on her!—
[*To Helvetius*] Helvetius! Thou art not worth the waking, neither.
I lose but time in thee. Go, sleep again:
Like an old man, thou canst do nothing.
Thou tak'st no pains at all to earn thine honours.
Which way shall we be able to pay thee
To thy content, when we receive not ours?
The master of the work must needs decay
When he wants means, and sees his servant play.

HELVETIUS [*to the Lady*]
Have I bestowed so many blessings on thee,
And do they all return to me in curses?
Is that the use I ha' for 'em? Be not to me
A burden ten times heavier than my years.
Thou'dst wont to be kind to me and observe
What I thought pleasing. Go, entreat the king.

LADY
I will do more for you, sir—you're my father.
I'll kiss him too. [*She kisses Govianus*]

HELVETIUS
How am I dealt withal!

LADY
[*Pointing to the Tyrant*] Why, that's the usurper, sir.
[*Pointing to Govianus*] This is the King.
I happened righter than you thought I had,
And were all kingdoms of the earth his own,

A130/B111 **match** partner
A145/B126 **Without** outside
A146/B127 **chose** chosen
A152/B133 **thou . . . nothing** You are useless ('Like an old man' may be read with the previous or the following clause).
A157/B138 **wants** lacks (its most usual meaning in the play, as at 1.2.98, 191, 195, etc.)
A160/B141 **use I ha'** the treatment I get; also, the capital interest I receive (i.e. on his blessings given)
A168/B149 **his own** i.e. the Tyrant's

As sure as this is not, and this dear gentleman
As poor as virtue and almost as friendless,
I would not change that misery for thy sceptre
Wherein I had part with him. Sir, be cheerful!
'Tis not the reeling fortune of great state
Or low condition that I cast mine eye at.
It is the man I seek; the rest I lose
As things unworthy to be kept or noted.
Fortunes are but the outsides of true worth.
It is the mind that sets his master forth.

TYRANT
Has there so many bodies been hewn down,
Like trees in progress, to cut out a way
That was ne'er known, for us and our affections,
And is our game so crossed? There stands the first
Of all her kind that ever refused greatness.
A woman to set light by sovereignty?
What age can bring her forth, and hide that book?
'Tis their desire most commonly to rule
More than their part comes to, sometimes their
husbands.

HELVETIUS
'Tis in your power, my lord, to force her to you
And pluck her from his arms.

TYRANT Thou talk'st unkindly.
That had been done before thy thought begot it,
If my affection could be so hard-hearted
To stand upon such payment. It must come
Gently and kindly, like a debt of love,
Or 'tis not worth receiving.

GOVIANUS Now, usurper,
I wish no happier freedom than the banishment
That thou hast laid upon me.

TYRANT [*aside*] O, he kills me
At mine own weapon. 'Tis I that live in exile,
Should she forsake the land. I'll feign some cause
Far from the grief itself, to call it back.—
[*To Govianus*] That doom of banishment was but lent
to thee
To make a trial of thy factious spirit
Which flames in thy desire. Thou would'st be gone.
There is some combination betwixt thee
And foreign plots; thou hast some powers to raise,
Which to prevent, thy banishment we revoke,
Confine thee to thy house nearest our court
And place a guard about thee. Lord Memphonius,
See it effected.

MEMPHONIUS With best care, my lord.

GOVIANUS
Confine me? Here's my liberty in mine arms.

As sure as this is not, and this dear gentleman
As poor as virtue and almost as friendless,
I would not change this misery for that sceptre
Wherein I had part with him. Sir, be cheerful!
'Tis not the reeling fortune of great state
Or low condition that I cast mine eye at.
It is the man I seek; the rest I lose
As things unworthy to be kept or noted.
Fortunes are but the outsides of true worth.
It is the mind that sets his master forth.

TYRANT
Has there so many bodies been hewn down,
Like trees in progress, to cut out a way
That was ne'er known, for us and our affections,
And is our game so crossed? There stands the first
Of all her kind that ever refused greatness.

HELVETIUS
'Tis in your power, my lord, to force her to you
And pluck her from his arms.

TYRANT Thou talk'st unkindly.
That had been done before thy thought begot it,
If my affection could be so hard-hearted
To stand upon such payment. It must come
Gently and kindly, like a debt of love,
Or 'tis not worth receiving.

GOVIANUS Now, usurper,
I wish no happier freedom than the banishment
That thou hast laid upon me.

TYRANT [*aside*] O, he kills me
At mine own weapon. 'Tis I that live in exile,
Should she forsake the land. I'll feign some cause
Far from the grief itself, to call it back.—
[*To Govianus*] That doom of banishment was but lent
to thee
To make a trial of thy factious spirit
Which flames in thy desire. Thou would'st be gone.
There is some combination betwixt thee
And foreign plots; thou hast some powers to raise,
Which to prevent, thy banishment we revoke,
Confine thee to thy house nearest our court
And place a guard about thee. Lord Memphonius,
See it effected.

MEMPHONIUS With best care, my lord.

GOVIANUS
Confine me? Here's my liberty in mine arms.

A171–2/B152–3 **I would...him** I would not exchange that misery which I might share with him (Govianus) for the sceptre (you offer). 'Thy' must be colloquial; a daughter would not normally use this intimate form of address to her father.

A180–1/B161–2 **Like...known** During a royal visit ('progress'), trees were cut down to create new routes.

A184–5 **A...book** A woman who does not take royal power seriously? What age can produce such a woman and then conceal the record ('that book') of her existence?

A189/B166 **unkindly** 'Kind' means both considerate and natural (kin being blood relatives), here and elsewhere.

A192/B169 **stand upon** to insist upon

A199/B176 **call it back** retract (i.e. the sentence of banishment)

I wish no better to bring me content.
Love's best freedom is close prisonment!
Exeunt Lady and Govianus [*with Memphonius*]

TYRANT [*aside*]
Methinks the day e'en darkens at her absence.
I stand as in a shade, when a great cloud
Muffles the sun whose beams shine afar off
On towers and mountains, but I keep the valleys,
The place that is last served.

HELVETIUS My lord!

TYRANT Your reason, sir?

HELVETIUS
Your grace is mild to all but your own bosom.
They should have both been sent to several prisons,
And not committed to each other's arms.
There's a hot durance! He'll ne'er wish more freedom.

TYRANT
Thou talk'st not like a statesman. Had my wrath
Took hold of such extremity at first,
They'd lived suspectful still, warned by their fears.
Where now that liberty makes 'em more secure,
I'll take 'em at my pleasure. It gives thee
Freer access to play the father for us
And ply her to our will.

HELVETIUS Mass, so it does.
Let a man think on't twice, your grace hath happened
Upon a strange way, yet it proves the nearest.

I do beseech your majesty, look cheerful.
You shall not want content, if it be locked
In any blood of mine: the key's your own,
You shall command the wards.

TYRANT Say'st thou so, sir?
I were ingrateful, then, should I see thee

I wish no better to bring me content.
Lovers' best freedom is close prisonment!
Exeunt Lady and Govianus [*with Memphonius*]

TYRANT [*aside*]
Methinks the day e'en darkens at her absence.
I stand as in a shade, when a great cloud
Muffles the sun whose beams shine afar off
On towers and mountains, but I keep the valleys,
The place that is last served.

HELVETIUS My lord!

TYRANT Your reason, sir?

HELVETIUS
Your grace is mild to all but your own bosom.
They should have both been sent to several prisons,
And not committed to each other's arms.
There's a hot durance! He'll ne'er wish more freedom.

TYRANT
'Tis true. Let 'em be both forced back.
[*To departing Attendants*] Stay, we command you!
[*To Helvetius*] Thou talk'st not like a statesman. Had my wrath
Took hold of such extremity at first,
They'd lived suspectful still, warned by their fears.
Where now that liberty makes 'em more secure,
I'll take 'em at my pleasure. It gives thee
Freer access to play the father for us
And ply her to our will.

HELVETIUS Mass, so it does.
Let a man think on't twice, your grace hath happened
Upon a strange way, yet it proves the nearest.

TYRANT
Nay, more to vex his soul, give command straight
They be divided into several rooms
Where he may only have a sight of her
To his mind's torment, but his arms and lips
Locked up like felons from her.

HELVETIUS Now you win me.
I like that cruelty passing well, my lord.

TYRANT
Give order with all speed.

HELVETIUS Though I be old,
I need no spur, my lord. Honour pricks me.
I do beseech your grace, look cheerfully.
You shall not want content, if it be locked
In any blood of mine: the key's your own,
You shall command the wards.

TYRANT Say'st thou so, sir?
I were ingrateful, then, should I see thee

A213–16/B190–3 **I ... served** Here the repeated images of sunshine and cloud and height versus lowliness are brought together.

A216/B193 **Your reason, sir?** i.e. for speaking,—What do you want?

A220/B197 **a hot durance** a harsh (also burning, passionate) imprisonment

B198 **'Tis true ... you;** B208–15 **Nay, ... pricks me.** The additional passages here respond to Helvetius's point, that the Tyrant's punishment will be ineffectual unless the lovers are kept apart. Despite his orders, they are shown freely together at 2.1, although a further addition at B2.1.3–10 explains why. Anne Lancashire points out that the order to keep them apart would have reminded the audience of the separate imprisonment of the royal lovers Arabella Stuart and William Seymour (both of whom had claims to the throne) in 1610–11.

A224/B202 **secure** confident

A229/B207 **nearest** most direct

A233/B219 **wards** the notches or guards on a lock so that only one key can open it (thus giving access to the Lady)

Want honour, that provides content for me. *Exeunt*

[*The throne is withdrawn*]

1.2

Enter Lord Anselmus, the deposed King's brother, with his friend Votarius

VOTARIUS

Pray, sir, confine your thoughts and excuse me.
Methinks the deposed king your brother's sorrow
Should find you business enough.

ANSELMUS How, Votarius?
Sorrow for him? Weak ignorance talks not like thee.
Why, he was never happier!

VOTARIUS Pray prove that, sir.

ANSELMUS

He's lost the kingdom, but his mind's restored;
Which is the larger empire? Prithee tell me.
Dominions have their limits: the whole earth
Is but a prisoner, nor the sea her jailer,
That with a silver hoop locks in her body.
They're fellow prisoners, though the sea look bigger
Because he is in office, and pride swells him.
But the unbounded kingdom of the mind
Is as unlimitable as heaven,
That glorious court of spirits, all honest courtiers!
Sir, if thou lov'st me, turn thine eye to me
And look not after him that needs thee not.
My brother's well attended. Peace and pleasure
Are never from his sight: he has his mistress.
She brought those servants and bestowed them on him,
But who brings mine?

VOTARIUS Had you not both long since
By a kind, worthy lady, your chaste wife?

ANSELMUS

That's it that I take pains with thee to be sure of.
What true report can I send to my soul
Of that I know not? We must only think
Our ladies are good people, and so live with 'em,
A fine security for them! Our own thoughts
Make the best fools of us; next to them, our wives.
But say she's all chaste, yet is that her goodness?
What labour is't for woman to keep constant
That's never tried or tempted? Where's her fight,
The wars within her breast, her honest anger
Against the impudence of flesh and hell?
So let me know the lady of my rest,
Or I shall never sleep well. Give not me

Want honour, that provides content for me. *Exeunt*
A flourish
[*The throne is withdrawn*]

Enter Lord Anselmus, the deposed King's brother, with his friend Votarius

1.2

VOTARIUS

Pray, sir, confine your thoughts and excuse me.
Methinks the deposed king your brother's sorrow
Should find you business enough.

ANSELMUS How, Votarius?
Sorrow for him? Weak ignorance talks not like thee.
Why, he was never happier!

VOTARIUS Pray prove that, sir.

ANSELMUS

He's lost the kingdom, but his mind's restored;
Which is the larger empire? Prithee tell me.
Dominions have their limits: the whole earth
Is but a prisoner, nor the sea her jailer,
That with a silver hoop locks in her body.
They're fellow prisoners, though the sea look bigger
Because he is in office, and pride swells him.
But the unbounded kingdom of the mind
Is as unlimitable as heaven,
That glorious court of spirits!
Sir, if thou lov'st me, turn thine eye to me
And look not after him that needs thee not.
My brother's well attended. Peace and pleasure
Are never from his sight: he has his mistress.
She brought those servants and bestowed them on him,
But who brings mine?

VOTARIUS Had you not both long since
By a kind, worthy lady, your chaste wife?

ANSELMUS

That's it that I take pains with thee to be sure of.
What true report can I send to my soul
Of that I know not? We must only think
Our ladies are good people, and so live with 'em,
A fine security for them! Our own thoughts
Make the best fools of us; next to them, our wives.
But say she's all chaste, yet is that her goodness?
What labour is't for woman to keep constant
That's never tried or tempted? Where's her fight,
The wars within her breast, her honest anger
Against the impudence of flesh and hell?
So let me know the lady of my rest,
Or I shall never sleep well. Give not me

B221.1 ***flourish*** i.e. of trumpets

1.2.0.2 ***Votarius*** His name means a worshipper or vow-maker, and has been altered from 'Lothario' in Cervantes's story, while that of 'Anselmo' has been retained.

1 **Pray . . . me** Votarius is replying to Anselmus's proposal, repeated at ll. 39–40.

6–7 **He's . . . empire** Unlike Govianus (though like the Tyrant), Anselmus cannot rule his own inner empire, his thoughts.

8–12 **the whole . . . him** The earth is imprisoned (because surrounded) by the sea, but the sea is also a prisoner (because governed by the moon), though the sea looks bigger because its power over the earth makes it swell with pride.

20 **those servants** i.e. peace and pleasure

27 **security** insurance; protection against unwelcome truths

28 **next . . . wives** after them, our wives (i.e. make fools of us)

34 **know** i.e. the truth about

The thing that is thought good, but what's approved
 so,
So wise men choose. O what a lazy virtue
Is chastity in a woman if no sin
Should lay temptation to't! Prithee set to her
And bring my peace along with thee.

VOTARIUS You put to me
A business that will do my words more shame
Than ever they got honour among women.
Lascivious courtings among sinful mistresses
Come ever seasonably, please best;
But let the boldest ruffian touch the ear
Of modest ladies with adulterous sounds,
Their very looks confound him and force grace
Into that cheek where impudence sets her seal.
That work is never undertook with courage
That makes his master blush. However, sir,
What profit can return to you by knowing
That which you do already, with more toil?
Must a man needs, in having a rich diamond,
Put it between a hammer and an anvil
And, not believing the true worth and value,
Break it in pieces to find out the goodness,
And, in the finding, lose it? Good sir, think on't.
Nor does it taste of wit to try their strengths
That are created sickly, nor of manhood.
We ought not to put blocks in women's ways
For some too often fall upon plain ground.
Let me dissuade you, sir.

ANSELMUS Have I a friend?
And has my love so little interest in him
That I must trust some stranger with my heart
And go to seek him out?

VOTARIUS Nay, hark you, sir,
I am so jealous of your weaknesses
That, rather than you should lie prostituted
Before a stranger's triumph, I would venture
A whole hour's shaming for you.

ANSELMUS Be worth thy word, then.

Enter Wife

Yonder she comes. [*Aside*] I'll have an ear to you
 both.
I love to have such things at the first hand!

[*He conceals himself*]

VOTARIUS [*aside*]
I'll put him off with somewhat. Guile in this
Falls in with honest dealing. O who could move
Adultery to yon face? So rude a sin
May not come near the meekness of her eye.
My client's cause looks so dishonestly

The thing that is thought good, but what's approved
 so,
So wise men choose. O what a lazy virtue
Is chastity in a woman if no sin
Should lay temptation to't! Prithee set to her
And bring my peace along with thee.

VOTARIUS You put to me
A business that will do my words more shame
Than ever they got honour among women.
Lascivious courtings among sinful mistresses
Come ever seasonably, please best;
But let the boldest ruffian touch the ear
Of modest ladies with adulterous sounds,
Their very looks confound him and force grace
Into that cheek where impudence sets her seal.
That work is never undertook with courage
That makes his master blush. However, sir,
What profit can return to you by knowing
That which you do already, with more toil?
Must a man needs, in having a rich diamond,
Put it between a hammer and an anvil
And, not believing the true worth and value,
Break it in pieces to find out the goodness,
And, in the finding, lose it? Good sir, think on't.
Nor does it taste of wit to try their strengths
That are created sickly, nor of manhood.
We ought not to put blocks in women's ways
For some too often fall upon plain ground.
Let me dissuade you, sir.

ANSELMUS Have I a friend?
And has my love so little interest in him
That I must trust some stranger with my heart
And go to seek him out?

VOTARIUS Nay, hark you, sir,
I am so jealous of your weaknesses
That, rather than you should lie prostituted
Before a stranger's triumph, I would venture
A whole hour's shaming for you.

ANSELMUS Be worth thy word, then.

Enter Wife

Yonder she comes. [*Aside*] I'll have an ear to you
 both.
I love to have such things at the first hand!

[*He conceals himself*]

VOTARIUS [*aside*]
I'll put him off with somewhat. Guile in this
Falls in with honest dealing. O who could move
Adultery to yon face? So rude a sin
May not come near the meekness of her eye.
My client's cause looks so dishonestly

36 **approved** proved
44 **seasonably** at a welcome moment
50 **However** in any case
58 **try** test
59 **created sickly** At this period, women were regarded as weaker in all respects (e.g. sexually, spiritually) than men.
60 **blocks** obstacles, as in a race; even so, some women can fall (i.e. succumb to sexual temptation) on a level course.
63 **interest in** claim upon
66–8 **jealous ... triumph** so anxious to conceal your weaknesses that, rather than you should sell (or submit) yourself to the power of a stranger
72 **somewhat** something, as at l. A274/B273
73 **Falls in** coincides
76–7 **My ... in't** Votarius speaks as a lawyer whose case looks so bad that he does not want to be seen arguing for it.

I'll ne'er be seen to plead in't.
WIFE
What, Votarius?
VOTARIUS
Good morrow, virtuous madam.
WIFE
Was my lord
Seen lately here?
VOTARIUS
He's newly walked forth, lady.
WIFE
How was he attended?
VOTARIUS
Faith, I think with none, madam.
WIFE
That sorrow for the king his brother's fortune
Prevails too much with him, and leads him strangely
From company and delight.
VOTARIUS [*aside*]
How she's beguiled in him!
There's no such natural touch, search all his bosom.
[*To Wife*] That grief's too bold with him indeed, sweet madam,
And draws him from the pleasure of his time,
But 'tis a business of affectïon
That must be done. We owe a pity, madam,
To all men's misery, but especially
To those afflictions that claim kindred of us.
We're forced to feel 'em. All compassion else
Is but a work of charity; this, of nature,
And ties our pity in a bond of blood.
WIFE
Yet, sir, there is a date set to all sorrows.
Nothing is everlasting in this world.
Your counsel will prevail. Persuade him, good sir,
To fall into life's happiness again
And leave the desolate path. I want his company.
He walks at midnight in thick shady woods
Where scarce the moon is starlight. I have watched him
In silver nights, when all the earth was dressed
Up like a virgin in white innocent beams,
Stood in my window, cold and thinly clad,
T'observe him through the bounty of the moon
That liberally bestowed her graces on me;
And when the morning dew began to fall,
Then was my time to weep. He's lost his kindness,
Forgot the way of wedlock, and become
A stranger to the joys and rites of love.
He's not so good as a lord ought to be.
Pray, tell him so from me, sir.
VOTARIUS
That will I, madam.
Exit Wife
Now must I dress a strange dish for his humour.
ANSELMUS [*aside*]
Call you this courting? Life, not one word near it!
There was no syllable but was twelve score off!

I'll ne'er be seen to plead in't.
WIFE
What, Votarius?
VOTARIUS
Good morrow, virtuous madam.
WIFE
Was my lord
Seen lately here?
VOTARIUS
He's newly walked forth, lady.
WIFE
How was he attended?
VOTARIUS
Faith, I think with none, madam.
WIFE
That sorrow for the king his brother's fortune
Prevails too much with him, and leads him strangely
From company and delight.
VOTARIUS [*aside*]
How she's beguiled in him!
There's no such natural touch, search all his bosom.
[*To Wife*] That grief's too bold with him indeed, sweet madam,
And draws him from the pleasure of his time,
But 'tis a business of affectïon
That must be done. We owe a pity, madam,
To all men's misery, but especially
To those afflictions that claim kindred of us.
We're forced to feel 'em. All compassion else
Is but a work of charity; this, of nature,
And ties our pity in a bond of blood.
WIFE
Yet, sir, there is a date set to all sorrows.
Nothing is everlasting in this world.
Your counsel will prevail. Persuade him, good sir,
To fall into life's happiness again
And leave the desolate path. I want his company.
He walks at midnight in thick shady woods
Where scarce the moon is starlight. I have watched him
In silver nights, when all the earth was dressed
Up like a virgin in white innocent beams,
Stood in my window, cold and thinly clad,
T'observe him through the bounty of the moon
That liberally bestowed her graces on me;
And when the morning dew began to fall,
Then was my time to weep. He's lost his kindness,
Forgot the way of wedlock, and become
A stranger to the joys and rites of love.
He's not so good as a lord ought to be.
Pray, tell him so from me, sir.
VOTARIUS
That will I, madam.
Exit Wife
Now must I dress a strange dish for his humour.
ANSELMUS [*aside*]
Call you this courting? Life, not one word near it!
There was no syllable but was twelve score off!

90 **kindred of us** relationship with us (because they belong to our relatives; also, because they are related to our own)

100 **scarce . . . starlight** where the moon gives scarcely as much light as the stars

107 **kindness** natural feeling, affection (see A1.1.189/B1.1.166)

112 **dress** prepare (food)

My faith, hot temptation! Woman's chastity
In such a conflict had great need of one
To keep the bridge—'twas dangerous for the time.
Why, what fantastic faiths are in these days
Made without substance! Whom should a man trust
In matters about love?
[*Anselmus comes forward*]

VOTARIUS [*aside*] Mass, here he comes, too!

ANSELMUS
How now, Votarius? What's the news for us?

VOTARIUS
You set me to a task, sir, that will find
Ten ages work enough, and then unfinished.
Bring sin before her? Why, it stands more quaking
Than if a judge should frown on't! Three such fits
Would shake it into goodness, and quite beggar
The under-kingdom! Not the art of man
Woman, or devil—

ANSELMUS [*interrupting*]
O, peace, man! Prithee, peace.

VOTARIUS
—Can make her fit for lust.

ANSELMUS Yet again, sir?
Where lives that mistress of thine, Votarius,
That taught thee to dissemble? I'd fain learn.
She makes good scholars.

VOTARIUS How, my lord?

ANSELMUS
Thou art the son of falsehood. Prithee, leave me.
How truly constant, charitable and helpful
Is woman unto woman in affairs
That touch affection and the peace of spirit,
But man to man, how crooked and unkind!
I thank my jealousy I heard thee all,
For I heard nothing.—Now thou'rt sure I did.

VOTARIUS
Now, by this light, then wipe but off this score,
Since you're so bent, and if I ever run
In debt again to falsehood and dissemblance
For want of better means, tear the remembrance of
me
From your best thoughts.

ANSELMUS For thy vow's sake, I pardon thee.
Thy oath is now sufficient watch itself
Over thy actions. I discharge my jealousy.
I ha' no more use for't now! To give thee way,
I'll have an absence made purposely for thee,
And presently take horse. I'll leave behind me
An opportunity that shall fear no starting.

My faith, hot temptation! Woman's chastity
In such a conflict had great need of one
To keep the bridge—'twas dangerous for the time.
Why, what fantastic faiths are in these days
Made without substance! Whom should a man trust
In matters about love?
[*Anselmus comes forward*]

VOTARIUS [*aside*] Mass, here he comes, too!

ANSELMUS
How now, Votarius? What's the news for us?

VOTARIUS
You set me to a task, sir, that will find
Ten ages work enough, and then unfinished.
Bring sin before her? Why, it stands more quaking
Than if a judge should frown on't! Three such fits
Would shake it into goodness, and quite beggar
The under-kingdom! Not the art of man
Woman, or devil—

ANSELMUS [*interrupting*]
O, peace, man! Prithee, peace.

VOTARIUS
—Can make her fit for lust.

ANSELMUS Yet again, sir?
Where lives that mistress of thine, Votarius,
That taught thee to dissemble? I'd fain learn.
She makes good scholars.

VOTARIUS How, my lord?

ANSELMUS
Thou art the son of falsehood. Prithee, leave me.
How truly constant, charitable and helpful
Is woman unto woman in affairs
That touch affection and the peace of spirit,
But man to man, how crooked and unkind!
I thank my jealousy I heard thee all,
For I heard nothing.—Now thou'rt sure I did.

VOTARIUS
Now, by this light, then wipe but off this score,
Since you're so bent, and if I ever run
In debt again to falsehood and dissemblance
For want of better means, tear the remembrance of
me
From your best thoughts.

ANSELMUS For thy vow's sake, I pardon thee.
Thy oath is now sufficient watch itself
Over thy actions. I discharge my jealousy.
I ha' no more use for't now! To give thee way,
I'll have an absence made purposely for thee,
And presently take horse. I'll leave behind me
An opportunity that shall fear no starting.

115–17 **Woman's... time** Her chastity was so fiercely besieged that, like Rome, she needed a hero like Horatius (famous for single-handedly defending the Roman bridge against the Etruscans): Anselmus is being sarcastic.
118 **fantastic faiths** unbelievable promises (as in *Revenger*, 3.1.6–7)
123 **Ten ages** i.e. for ten ages
124 **it** i.e. sin
125 **judge... frown** indicating that he will condemn the prisoner
126–7 **beggar | The under-kingdom** depopulate hell
130–1 **Where... learn** Where does the mistress live who taught you how to act a part? I'd like to learn myself.
138 **I... all** Thanks to my suspiciousness, I heard everything you said.
140 **wipe... score** Don't count what happened this time.
141 **bent** determined
147 **way** opportunity
149 **presently take horse** set out riding at once
150 **starting** sudden interruption

Let but thy pains deserve it.
VOTARIUS I am bound to't.
ANSELMUS
For a small time, farewell, then. Hark thee—
VOTARIUS [*interrupting*] O, good sir,
It will do wondrous well. *Exit Anselmus*
What a wild seed
Suspicion sows in him, and takes small ground for't.
How happy were this lord, if he would leave
To tempt his fate and be resolved he were so.
He would be but too rich.
Man has some enemy still that keeps him back
In all his fortunes, and his mind is his,
And that's a mighty adversary. I had rather
Have twenty kings my enemies than that part,
For let me be at war with earth and hell,
So that be friends with me.—I ha' sworn to make
A trial of her faith. I must put on
A courtier's face and do't. Mine own will shame me.
Enter Wife
WIFE
This is most strange of all! How one distraction
Seconds another!
VOTARIUS What's the news, sweet madam?
WIFE
He's took his horse, but left his leave untaken.
What should I think on't, sir? Did ever lord
Depart so rudely from his lady's presence?
VOTARIUS
Did he forget your lip?
WIFE He forgot all
That nobleness remembers.
VOTARIUS I'm ashamed on him.
Let me help, madam, to repair his manners,
And mend that unkind fault.
[*He tries to kiss her*]
WIFE Sir, pray forbear.
You forget worse than he.
VOTARIUS [*aside*] So virtue save me,
I have enough already.
WIFE 'Tis himself
Must make amends, good sir, for his own faults.
VOTARIUS [*aside*]
I would he'd do't, then, and ne'er trouble me in't.
[*To Wife*] But, madam, you perceive he takes the course
To be far off from that: he's rode from home,
But his unkindness stays, and keeps with you.
Let whos' will please his wife, he rides his horse;
That's all the care he takes. I pity you, madam:
You've an unpleasing lord. Would 'twere not so,
I should rejoice with you.

Let but thy pains deserve it.
VOTARIUS I am bound to't.
ANSELMUS
For a small time, farewell, then. Hark thee—
VOTARIUS [*interrupting*] O, good sir,
It will do wondrous well. *Exit Anselmus*
What a wild seed
Suspicion sows in him, and takes small ground for't.
How happy were this lord, if he would leave
To tempt his fate and be resolved he were so.
He would be but too rich.
Man has some enemy still that keeps him back
In all his fortunes, and his mind is his,
And that's a mighty adversary. I had rather
Have twenty kings my enemies than that part,
For let me be at war with earth and hell,
So that be friends with me.—I ha' sworn to make
A trial of her faith. I must put on
A brazen face and do't. Mine own will shame me.
Enter Wife
WIFE
This is most strange of all! How one distraction
Seconds another!
VOTARIUS What's the news, sweet madam?
WIFE
He's took his horse, but left his leave untaken.
What should I think on't, sir? Did ever lord
Depart so rudely from his lady's presence?
VOTARIUS
Did he forget your lip?
WIFE He forgot all
That nobleness remembers.
VOTARIUS I'm ashamed on him.
Let me help, madam, to repair his manners,
And mend that unkind fault.
[*He tries to kiss her*]
WIFE Sir, pray forbear.
You forget worse than he.
VOTARIUS [*aside*] So virtue save me,
I have enough already.
WIFE 'Tis himself
Must make amends, good sir, for his own faults.
VOTARIUS [*aside*]
I would he'd do't, then, and ne'er trouble me in't.
[*To Wife*] But, madam, you perceive he takes the course
To be far off from that: he's rode from home,
But his unkindness stays, and keeps with you.
Let whos' will please his wife, he rides his horse;
That's all the care he takes. I pity you, madam:
You've an unpleasing lord. Would 'twere not so,
I should rejoice with you.

151 **bound** committed
154 **ground** basis (and metaphorically, earth)
155–6 **leave | To tempt** leave off tempting
157 **but** only
159 **is his** i.e. is his enemy
162–3 **For...me** for I could be at war with earth and hell so long as my mind was friends with me.
167 **Seconds** follows
168 **his...untaken** without saying goodbye
182 **whos'** 'whoso(ever)', i.e. 'let whoever wants to, please...', and also 'let whoever's "will" (i.e. penis) please...'. For riding as having sex, see above, 1.1.40.

You're young, the very spring's upon you now,
The roses on your cheeks are but new blown—
Take you together, you're a pleasant garden
Where all the sweetness of man's comfort breathes.
But what is it to be a work of beauty
And want the heart that should delight in you?
You still retain your goodness in yourselves,
But then you lose your glory, which is all.
The grace of every benefit is the use,
And is't not pity you should want your grace?
Look you like one whose lord should walk in groves
About the peace of midnight? Alas, madam,
'Tis to me wondrous how you should spare the day
From amorous clips, much less the general season
When all the world's a gamester.
That face deserves a friend of heart and spirit,
Discourse and motion, indeed such a one
That should observe you, madam, without ceasing,
And not a weary lord.

WIFE Sure, I was married, sir,
In a dear year of love, when scarcity
And famine of affection vexed poor ladies,
Which makes my heart so needy. It ne'er knew
Plenty of comfort yet.

VOTARIUS Why, that's your folly,
To keep your mind so miserably, madam.
Change into better times. I'll lead you to 'em.
What bounty shall your friend expect for his?
O, you that can be hard to your own heart,
How would you use your friend's? If I thought kindly,
I'd be the man myself should serve your pleasure.

WIFE How, sir?

VOTARIUS
Nay, and ne'er miss you, too: I'd not come sneaking
Like a retainer, once a week or so,
To show myself before you for my livery.
I'd follow business like a household servant,
Carry my work before me and dispatch
Before my lord be up, and make no words on't,
The sign of a good servant.

WIFE 'Tis not friendly done, sir,
To take a lady at advantage thus,
Set all her wrongs before her, and then tempt her.

VOTARIUS [*aside*]
Heart, I grow fond myself! 'Twas well she waked me,

You're young, the very spring's upon you now,
The roses on your cheeks are but new blown—
Take you together, you're a pleasant garden
Where all the sweetness of man's comfort breathes.
But what is it to be a work of beauty
And want the heart that should delight in you?
You still retain your goodness in yourselves,
But then you lose your glory, which is all.
The grace of every benefit is the use,
And is't not pity you should want your grace?
Look you like one whose lord should walk in groves
About the peace of midnight? Alas, madam,
'Tis to me wondrous how you should spare the day
From amorous clips, much less the general season
When all the world's a gamester.
That face deserves a friend of heart and spirit,
Discourse and motion, indeed such a one
That should observe you, madam, without ceasing,
And not a weary lord.

WIFE Sure, I was married, sir,
In a dear year of love, when scarcity
And famine of affection vexed poor ladies,
Which makes my heart so needy. It ne'er knew
Plenty of comfort yet.

VOTARIUS Why, that's your folly,
To keep your mind so miserably, madam.
Change into better times. I'll lead you to 'em.
What bounty shall your friend expect for his?
O, you that can be hard to your own heart,
How would you use your friend's? If I thought kindly,
I'd be the man myself should serve your pleasure.

WIFE How, sir?

VOTARIUS
Nay, and ne'er miss you, too: I'd not come sneaking
Like a retainer, once a week or so,
To show myself before you for my livery.
I'd follow business like a household servant,
Carry my work before me and dispatch
Before my lord be up, and make no words on't,
The sign of a good servant.

WIFE 'Tis not friendly done, sir,
To take a lady at advantage thus,
Set all her wrongs before her, and then tempt her.

VOTARIUS [*aside*]
I grow fond myself! 'Twas well she waked me,

187 **new blown** just opened

193 **all** everything

194–5 **The . . . grace?** The value of every natural gift lies in its use, so isn't it a shame that you lack the proper appreciation?—There are further implications: if Anselmus is not making proper, i.e. sexual, use of his wife, he is not according proper value to her attractions (also, the Wife's frustration will contribute to her surrender and consequent loss of spiritual grace).

199 **clips** embraces

200 **a gamester** at (sexual) play

201–3 **a friend . . . you** these terms all carry sexual overtones: friend, i.e. lover (as at A2.1.65); spirit, i.e. semen (as in modern 'spunk'); discourse i.e. intercourse; motion i.e. during the sexual act; to observe is to attend on, pay court to.

205 **dear year** year of famine

209 **your . . . miserably** your own wishes so neglected

217–22 **Like . . . servant** This passage plays upon resemblances between the terms of domestic and sexual service: a retainer lived outside the household, only coming in for his 'livery', a payment of food or clothing (in this case, sex). Business and work can both refer to the sexual act; to dispatch is to finish, and 'up' means erect.

A225 **Heart** 'God's heart!' This and 'Life' (i.e. God's life!) are the two most frequently used oaths in the play. Both Buc, the official censor and others at the playhouse deleted a number of examples, in accordance with contemporary laws against blasphemy on the stage.

225 **fond** besotted

Before the dead sleep of adultery took me—
'Twas stealing on me. Up, you honest thoughts,
And keep watch for your master.—[*To Wife*] I must hence.
[*Aside*] I do not like my health; 't'as a strange relish.
Pray heaven I plucked mine eyes back time enough.
I'll never see her more. I praised the garden,
But little thought a bed of snakes lay hid in't.
[*He prepares to leave*]

WIFE [*aside*]
I know not how I am! I'll call my woman.—
[*To Votarius*] Stay! [*Aside*] For I fear thou'rt too far gone already.

VOTARIUS [*aside*]
I'll see her but once more. Do thy worst, love,
Thou art too young, fond boy, to master me.
[*To Wife*] I come to tell you, madam, and that plainly,
I'll see your face no more. Take't how you please!

WIFE
You will not offer violence to me, sir,
In my lord's absence? What does that touch you
If I want comfort?

VOTARIUS Will you take your answer?

WIFE
It is not honest in you to tempt woman
When her distresses takes away her strength:
How is she able to withstand her enemy?

VOTARIUS
I would fain leave your sight, an I could possible.

WIFE
What is't to you, good sir, if I be pleased
To weep myself away, and run thus violently
Into the arms of death, and kiss destruction.
[*She runs to him and kisses him*]
Does this concern you now?

VOTARIUS Aye, marry, does it. [*Returning her kiss*]
What serve these arms for but to pluck you back,
These lips but to prevent all other tasters,
And keep that cup of nectar for themselves?
[*Aside*] Heart, I'm beguiled again! Forgive me, heaven!
My lips have been naught with her! Sin's mere witchcraft!
Break all the engines of life's frame in pieces,
I will be master once, and whip the boy
Home to his mother's lap. [*To Wife*] Face, fare thee well!
Exit [*abruptly*]

Before the dead sleep of adultery took me—
'Twas stealing on me. Up, you honest thoughts,
And keep watch for your master.—[*To Wife*] I must hence.
[*Aside*] I do not like my health; 't'as a strange relish.
Pray heaven I plucked mine eyes back time enough.
I'll never see her more. I praised the garden,
But little thought a bed of snakes lay hid in't.
[*He prepares to leave*]

WIFE [*aside*]
I know not how I am! I'll call my woman.—
[*To Votarius*] Stay! [*Aside*] For I fear thou'rt too far gone already.

VOTARIUS [*aside*]
I'll see her but once more. Do thy worst, love,
Thou art too young, fond boy, to master me.
[*To Wife*] I come to tell you, madam, and that plainly,
I'll see your face no more. Take't how you please!

WIFE
You will not offer violence to me, sir,
In my lord's absence? What does that touch you
If I want comfort?

VOTARIUS Will you take your answer?

WIFE
It is not honest in you to tempt woman
When her distresses takes away her strength:
How is she able to withstand her enemy?

VOTARIUS
I would fain leave your sight, an I could possible.

WIFE
What is't to you, good sir, if I be pleased
To weep myself away, and run thus violently
Into the arms of death, and kiss destruction.
[*She runs to him and kisses him*]
Does this concern you now?

VOTARIUS Aye, marry, does it. [*Returning her kiss*]
What serve these arms for but to pluck you back,
These lips but to prevent all other tasters,
And keep that cup of nectar for themselves?
[*Aside*] I'm beguiled again! Forgive me, heaven!
My lips have been naught with her!

I will be master once, and whip the boy
Home to his mother's lap. [*To Wife*] Face, fare thee well!
Exit [*abruptly*]

226 **dead** heavy, also spiritually blind (used in the Psalms, 13:3 and 76:6)
229 **my ... relish** spiritual state; it has a strange taste. Calvinist discourse often described spiritual states in terms of physical health.
230 **time enough** in time
236 **fond boy** i.e. love, personified as Cupid
240 **touch** matter to
245 **I ... possible** I'd like to be out of your sight, if I possibly could.
254 **naught** sexually immoral (for having kissed her)
A254 **mere witchcraft** nothing but an evil spell
A255 **Break ... pieces** even if it may break all the parts of my body to pieces
A256–7/B255–6 **the boy ... lap** i.e. Cupid back to the lap of his mother Venus
A257/B256 **Face** Votarius associates the attractions of the Wife with her face (as also at 1.2.74, 201, 238).

WIFE
Votarius? Sir? My friend? Thanks, heaven, he's gone
And he shall never come so near again.
I'll have my frailty watched ever. Henceforward
I'll no more trust it single, it betrays me
Into the hands of folly. Where's my woman?
Enter Leonella
My trusty Leonella!
LEONELLA Call you, madam?
WIFE
Call I? I want attendance! Where are you?
LEONELLA
Never far from you, madam.
WIFE Pray be nearer,
Or there is some that will, and thank you, too;
Nay, perhaps bribe you to be absent from me.
LEONELLA
How, madam?
WIFE Is that strange to a lady's woman?
There are such things i'th' world, many such buyers
And sellers of a woman's name and honour,
Though you be young in bribes, and never came
To the flesh market yet.—Beshrew your heart,
For keeping so long from me!
LEONELLA What ail you, madam?
WIFE
Somewhat commands me, and takes all the power
Of myself from me!
LEONELLA What should that be, lady?
WIFE
When did you see Votarius?
LEONELLA [*aside*] Is that next?
Nay, then, I have your ladyship in the wind!
[*To Wife*] I saw him lately, madam.
WIFE Whom did'st see?
LEONELLA
Votarius.
WIFE What have I to do with him
More than another man? Say he be fair,
And his parts proper both of mind and body,
You praise him but in vain in telling me so.
LEONELLA [*aside*]
Yea, madam, are you prattling in your sleep?
'Tis well my lord and you lie in two beds!
WIFE [*aside*]
I was ne'er so ill. [*To Leonella*] I thank you, Leonella,
My negligent woman, here you showed your service.
LEONELLA [*aside*]
Life, have I power or means to stop a sluice
At a high water? What would sh'ave me do in't?

WIFE
Votarius? Sir? My friend? Thanks, heaven, he's gone
And he shall never come so near again.
I'll have my frailty watched ever. Henceforward
I'll no more trust it single, it betrays me
Into the hands of folly. Where's my woman?
Enter Leonella
My trusty Leonella!
LEONELLA Call you, madam?
WIFE
Call I? I want attendance! Where are you?
LEONELLA
Never far from you, madam.
WIFE Pray be nearer,
Or there is some that will, and thank you, too;
Nay, perhaps bribe you to be absent from me.
LEONELLA
How, madam?
WIFE Is that strange to a lady's woman?
There are such things i'th' world, many such buyers
And sellers of a woman's name and honour,
Though you be young in bribes, and never came
To the flesh market yet.—Beshrew your heart,
For keeping so long from me!
LEONELLA What ail you, madam?
WIFE
Somewhat commands me, and takes all the power
Of myself from me!
LEONELLA What should that be, lady?
WIFE
When did you see Votarius?
LEONELLA [*aside*] Is that next?
Nay, then, I have your ladyship in the wind!
[*To Wife*] I saw him lately, madam.
WIFE Whom did'st see?
LEONELLA
Votarius.
WIFE What have I to do with him
More than another man? Say he be fair,
And has parts proper both of mind and body,
You praise him but in vain in telling me so.
LEONELLA [*aside*]
Yea, madam, are you prattling in your sleep?
'Tis well my lord and you lie in two beds!
WIFE [*aside*]
I was ne'er so ill. [*To Leonella*] I thank you, Leonella,
My negligent woman, here you showed your service.
LEONELLA [*aside*]
Have I power or means to stop a sluice
At a high water? What would sh'ave me do in't?

A261/B260 **single** unaccompanied, alone
A262.1/B261.1 ***Leonella*** i.e. little lioness (named thus in Cervantes's story)
A266/B265 **there…too** There are others who want to be nearer me and would also thank you for the opportunity.
A271/B270 **young** inexperienced
A272/B271 **Beshrew your heart** curse you
A277/B276 **I…wind** I have picked up your scent (as in hunting).
A284/B283 **in two beds** presumably since Anselmus began to distrust his Wife
A285/B284 **ill** in such a bad state (physically or spiritually)
A287/B286 **sluice** a flood-gate (Leonella cannot stop the truth pouring out of the Wife)

WIFE
I charge thee, while thou liv'st with me, henceforward
Use not an hour's absence from my sight. *Exit*
LEONELLA
By my faith, madam, you shall pardon me,
I have a love of mine own to look to,
And he must have his breakfast. [*Calling offstage*] Psst!
Bellarius!
Enter Bellarius, muffled in his cloak
BELLARIUS Leonella?
LEONELLA
Come forth, and show yourself a gentleman,
Although most commonly they hide their heads,
As you do there, methinks!
And why a taffeta muffler? Show your face, man.
I'm not ashamed on you.
BELLARIUS I fear the servants.
LEONELLA
And they fear their mistress, and ne'er think on you.
Their thoughts are upon dinner, and great dishes.
If one thing hap, impossible to fail, too,
(I can see so far in't), you shall walk boldly, sir,
And openly in view through every room
About the house; and, let the proudest meet thee,
I charge you give no way to 'em.
BELLARIUS How thou talk'st!
LEONELLA
I can avoid the fool, and give you reason for't.
BELLARIUS
'Tis more than I should do, if I asked more on thee:
I prithee, tell me how?
LEONELLA With ease, i'faith, sir.
My lady's heart is wondrous busy, sir,
About the entertainment of a friend, too,
And she and I must bear with one another
Or we shall make but a mad house betwixt us.
BELLARIUS
I'm bold to throw my cloak off at this news,
[*He does so*]
Which I ne'er durst before, and kiss thee freelier!
[*He kisses Leonella*]
What is he, sirrah?
LEONELLA Faith, an indifferent fellow
With good long legs, a near friend of my lord's.
BELLARIUS
A near friend of my lady's, you would say!
His name, I prithee?
LEONELLA One Votarius, sir.

WIFE
I charge thee, while thou liv'st with me, henceforward
Use not an hour's absence from my sight. *Exit*
LEONELLA
By my faith, madam, you shall pardon me,
I have a love of mine own to look to,
And he must have his breakfast. [*Calling offstage*] Psst!
Bellarius!
Enter Bellarius, muffled in his cloak
BELLARIUS Leonella?
LEONELLA
Come forth, and show yourself a gentleman,
Although most commonly they hide their heads,
As you do there, methinks!
And why a taffeta muffler? Show your face, man.
I'm not ashamed on you.
BELLARIUS I fear the servants.
LEONELLA
And they fear their mistress, and ne'er think on you.
Their thoughts are upon dinner, and great dishes.
If one thing hap, impossible to fail, too,
(I can see so far in't), you shall walk boldly, sir,
And openly in view through every room
About the house; and, let the proudest meet thee,
I charge you give no way to 'em.
BELLARIUS How thou talk'st!
LEONELLA
I can avoid the fool, and give you reason for't.
BELLARIUS
'Tis more than I should do, if I asked more on thee:
I prithee, tell me how?
LEONELLA With ease, i'faith, sir.
My lady's heart is wondrous busy, sir,
About the entertainment of a friend, too,
And she and I must bear with one another
Or we shall make but a mad house betwixt us.
BELLARIUS
I'm bold to throw my cloak off at this news,
[*He does so*]
Which I ne'er durst before, and kiss thee freelier!
[*He kisses Leonella*]
What is he, sirrah?
LEONELLA Faith, an indifferent fellow
With good long legs, a near friend of my lord's.
BELLARIUS
A near friend of my lady's, you would say!
His name, I prithee?
LEONELLA One Votarius, sir.

A293/B292 **breakfast** any meal that ends a period of fast, but here ending his sexual fast
Bellarius His name means aggressive, warlike (he does not appear in Cervantes's story).
A296/B295 **hide their heads** i.e. keep their heads covered, or their hats on; gentlemen might hide their heads for any number of embarrassing reasons, including to avoid arrest for unpaid debts.
A302/B301 **If...fail** if a particular thing happens, which it can't fail to do
A305–6/B304–5 **let...'em** Even if the proudest confront you, I command you not to step aside for them.
A306/B305 **How...talk'st** What a lot of nonsense you talk.
A307/B306 **I can...for't** I'm not a fool, and I can explain what I've just said.
A308/B307 **'Tis more...thee** If I ask you to tell me more, I'll be the fool.
A312–13/B311–12 **And...us** She and I must put up with one another (also, take the weight of our lovers), or else between the two of us we'll turn the house upside down ('mad' has undertones of sexual obsession and lunacy, as in *Changeling*: e.g. 1.1.146).

BELLARIUS
What sayest thou?
LEONELLA He walks under the same title.
BELLARIUS
The only enemy that my life can show me!
LEONELLA
Your enemy? Let my spleen then alone with him.
Stay you your anger, I'll confound him for you.
BELLARIUS
As how, I prithee?
LEONELLA I'll prevent his venery.
He shall ne'er lie with my lady.
BELLARIUS Troth, I thank you!
Life, that's the way to save him! Art thou mad?
Whereas the other way, he confounds himself
And lies more naked to revenge and mischief.
LEONELLA
Then let him lie with her, and the devil go with him!
He shall have all my furtherance.
BELLARIUS
Why, now you pray heartily, and speak to purpose.
Exeunt
Finis Actus Primus

2.1 *Incipit Actus Secundus*
Enter the Lady of Govianus, with a servant
LADY
What's he would speak with me?
SERVANT My lord your father.
LADY
My father? Pray make haste; he waits too long.
Entreat him hither. [*Exit Servant*]

Enter Helvetius
Some mild news, I hope,
Comes with my father. No, his looks are sad.
There is some further tyranny.—Let it fall!
Our constant suff'rings shall amaze it.
[*She kneels before Helvetius*]
HELVETIUS Rise!

BELLARIUS
What sayest thou?
LEONELLA He walks under the same title.
BELLARIUS
The only enemy that my life can show me!
LEONELLA
Your enemy? Let my spleen then alone with him.
Stay you your anger, I'll confound him for you.
BELLARIUS
As how, I prithee?
LEONELLA I'll prevent his venery.
He shall ne'er lie with my lady.
BELLARIUS Troth, I thank you!
Life, that's the way to save him! Art thou mad?
Whereas the other way, he confounds himself
And lies more naked to revenge and mischief.
LEONELLA
Then let him lie with her, and the devil go with him!
He shall have all my furtherance.
BELLARIUS
Why, now you pray heartily, and speak to purpose.
Exeunt
Finis Actus Primus

2.1 *Incipit Actus Secundus*
Enter the Lady of Govianus, with a servant
LADY
Who is't would speak with us?
SERVANT My lord your father.
LADY
My father! Pray make haste; he waits too long.
Entreat him hither. [*Exit Servant*]
In despite of all
The Tyrant's cruelties, we have got that friendship
E'en of the guard that he has placed about us,
My lord and I have free access together,
As much as I would ask of liberty.
They'll trust us largely now, and keep sometimes
Three hours from us, a rare courtesy
In jailers' children.
Enter Helvetius
Some mild news, I hope,
Comes with my father. No, his looks are sad.
There is some further tyranny.—Let it fall!
Our constant suff'rings shall amaze it.
[*She kneels before Helvetius*]
HELVETIUS Rise!

A320/B319 **He . . . title** That's his name
A322/B321 **spleen** anger, spite
A323/B322 **confound** destroy, as at l. A327/B326, where Bellarius points out that easy access to sin will be more destructive than being hindered from it.
A324/B323 **venery** sexual pleasure
A331/B330 **to purpose** to the point
2.1.3 **Entreat him hither** The additional passage inserted at this point explains how the jailer's kindness has enabled the Lady and Govianus to be together.
B4 **got** gained
B8 **largely** greatly, freely
B9–10 **a rare . . . children** an unusually considerate gesture from a jailer's family
A6/B13 **Our . . . it** Our steadfastness in the face of suffering shall surprise (that tyranny).

I will not bless thee. Thy obedience
Is after custom, as most rich men pray
Whose saint is only fashion and vainglory:
So 'tis with thee in thy dissembled duty.
There is no religion in't, no reverent love,
Only for fashion and the praise of men.

LADY [*rising*]
Why should you think so, sir?

HELVETIUS
Think? You come too late
If you seek there for me. I know't and see't.
I'll sooner give my blessing to a drunkard
Whom the ridiculous power of wine makes humble,
As foolish use makes thee.—Base-spirited girl,
That canst not think above disgrace and beggary
When glory is set for thee and thy seed,
Advancement for thy father, beside joy
Able to make a latter spring in me
In this my fourscore summer, and renew me
With a reversion yet of heat and youth!
But the dejection of thy mind and spirit
Makes me, thy father, guilty of a fault
That draws thy birth in question, and e'en wrongs
Thy mother, in her ashes, being at peace
With heav'n and man. Had not her life and virtues
Been seals unto her faith, I should think thee now
The work of some hired servant, some house tailor,
And no one part of my endeavour in thee.
Had I neglected greatness, or not rather
Pursued, almost to my eternal hazard,
Thou'dst ne'er been a lord's daughter.

LADY
Had I been
A shepherd's, I'd been happier and more peaceful.

HELVETIUS
Thy very seed will curse thee in thy age
When they shall hear the story of thy weakness:
How in thy youth thy fortunes tendered thee
A kingdom for thy servant, which thou left'st
Basely, to serve thyself. What dost thou in this
But merely cozen thy posterity
Of royalty and succession, and thy self
Of dignity present?

LADY
Sir, your king did well
'Mongst all his Nobles to pick out yourself
And send you with these words. His politic grace
Knew what he did, for well he might imagine
None else should have been heard. They'd had their
answer
Before the question had been halfway through.
But, dearest sir, I owe to you a reverence,
A debt which both begins and ends with life,
Never till then discharged, 'tis so long lasting.

I will not bless thee. Thy obedience
Is after custom, as most rich men pray
Whose saint is only fashion and vainglory:
So 'tis with thee in thy dissembled duty.
There is no religion in't, no reverent love,
Only for fashion and the praise of men.

LADY [*rising*]
Why should you think so, sir?

HELVETIUS
Think? I know't and see't.
I'll sooner give my blessing to a drunkard
Whom the ridiculous power of wine makes humble,
As foolish use makes thee.—Base-spirited girl,
That canst not think above disgrace and beggary
When glory is set for thee and thy seed,
Advancement for thy father, beside joy
Able to make a latter spring in me
In this my fourscore summer, and renew me
With a reversion yet of heat and youth!
But the dejection of thy mind and spirit
Makes me, thy father, guilty of a fault
That draws thy birth in question, and e'en wrongs
Thy mother, in her ashes, being at peace
With heav'n and man. Had not her life and virtues
Been seals unto her faith, I should think thee now
The work of some hired servant, some house tailor,
And no one part of my endeavour in thee.
Had I neglected greatness, or not rather
Pursued, almost to my eternal hazard,
Thou'dst ne'er been a lord's daughter.

LADY
Had I been
A shepherd's, I'd been happier and more peaceful.

HELVETIUS
Thy very seed will curse thee in thy age
When they shall hear the story of thy weakness:
How in thy youth thy fortunes tendered thee
A kingdom for thy servant, which thou left'st
Basely, to serve thyself. What dost thou in this
But merely cozen thy posterity
Of royalty and succession, and thy self
Of dignity present?

LADY
Sir, your king did well
'Mongst all his Nobles to pick out yourself
And send you with these words. His politic grace
Knew what he did, for well he might imagine
None else should have been heard. They'd had their
answer
Before the question had been halfway through.
But, dearest sir, I owe to you a reverence,
A debt which both begins and ends with life,
Never till then discharged, 'tis so long lasting.

A7–9/B14–16 **Thy...vainglory** Your obedience is a matter of convention, just as most rich men pray in church but really worship only fashion and self-advancement.

A17/B23 **use** custom

A22/B28 **my fourscore summer** my eightieth year (a symbolic, rather than literal figure)

A23/B29 **reversion** return, recovery

A24/B30 **dejection** degradation, baseness

A29/B35 **seals** guarantees

A33/B39 **to...hazard** to the extent of risking my eternal salvation

A41–3/B47–9 **cozen...present** cheat your descendants of royalty and inheritance of the throne, and yourself of immediate honours

A45/B51 **politic** cunning, scheming

Yet could you be more precious than a father
Which, next a husband, is the richest treasure
Mortality can show us, you should pardon me
(And yet confess, too, that you found me kind)
To hear your words, though I withstood your mind.

HELVETIUS
Say you so, daughter? Troth, I thank you kindly.
I am in hope to rise well by your means,
Or you to raise yourself; we're both beholden to you.
Well, since I cannot win you, I commend you;
I praise your constancy and pardon you.
Take Govianus to you, make the most of him,
Pick out your husband there, so you'll but grant me
One light request that follows.

LADY
Heaven forbid else, sir.

HELVETIUS
Give me the choosing of your friend, that's all.

LADY
How, sir? My friend? A light request indeed!
Somewhat too light, sir, either for my wearing
Or your own gravity, an you look on't well.

HELVETIUS
Push! Talk like a courtier, girl, not like a fool.
Thou know'st the end of greatness, and hast wit
Above the flight of twenty feathered mistresses
That glister in the sun of princes' favours.
Thou hast discourse in thee fit for a king's fellowship,
A princely carriage and astonishing presence.
What should a husband do with all this goodness?
Alas, one end on't is too much for him,
Nor is it fit a subject should be master
Of such a jewel. 'Tis in the king's power
To take it for the forfeit!—But I come
To bear thee gently to his bed of honours,
All force forgotten. He commends him to thee
With more than the humility of a servant
That since thou wilt not yield to be his queen,
Be yet his mistress. He shall be content
With that, or nothing. He shall ask no more,
And with what easiness that is performed,
Most of your women know: having a husband,
That kindness costs thee nothing. You've that in,
All over and above to your first bargain,
And that's a brave advantage for a woman,

Yet could you be more precious than a father
Which, next a husband, is the richest treasure
Mortality can show us, you should pardon me
(And yet confess, too, that you found me kind)
To hear your words, though I withstood your mind.

HELVETIUS
Say you so, daughter? Troth, I thank you kindly.
I am in hope to rise well by your means,
Or you to raise yourself; we're both beholden to you.
Well, since I cannot win you, I commend you;
I praise your constancy and pardon you.
Take Govianus to you, make the most of him,
Pick out your husband there, so you'll but grant me
One light request that follows.

LADY
Heaven forbid else, sir.

HELVETIUS
Give me the choosing of your servant, that's all.

LADY
How, sir? My servant? A light request indeed!
Somewhat too light, sir, either for my wearing
Or your own gravity, an you look on't well.

HELVETIUS
Push! Talk like a woman, girl, not like a fool.
Thou know'st the end of greatness, and hast wit
Above the flight of twenty feathered mistresses.

The King commends him to thee
With more than the humility of a servant
That since thou wilt not yield to be his queen,
Be yet his mistress. He shall be content
With that, or nothing. He shall ask no more,
And with what easiness that is performed,
Most of your women know: having a husband,
That kindness costs thee nothing. You've that in,
All over and above to your first bargain,
And that's a brave advantage for a woman,

A53/B59 **next a husband** after a husband

A54–6/B60–2 **you...mind** You should forgive me for resisting your intentions, while acknowledging that you found me 'kind' (i.e. considerate and dutiful) in listening to you; also 'kind' (natural) in hearing you, but rejecting your advice (as unworthy of a father).

A64/B70 **light** small. 'Friend' (A65) signifies lover (as at 1.2.201), as does 'servant' (B71). When the Lady repeats her father's phrase, she picks up other meanings of 'light', in particular, 'wanton'; also 'thin' (as of material), and lacking in weight or seriousness.

A69/B75 **Push** Middleton's characteristic spelling of 'pish', an exclamation of impatience

A70–1/B76–7 **Thou...mistresses** You know where great ambitions lead, and your intelligence will carry you higher than the flock of court mistresses, for all their fine feathers

A73–4 **Thou...presence** 'Discourse' means conversation, but also sexual intercourse (as at 1.2.202); 'carriage' means bearing, but also taking a man's weight in the act of love (as at A1.2.312/B1.2.311) or being pregnant (carrying a child); 'presence' means (impressive) appearance.

A76 **one end on't** a part of it: i.e. she should bestow the other 'end' (her sexual parts, also suggested at A70/B76) elsewhere.

A79 **for the forfeit** as his by right, according to the custom of *droit de seigneur* (i.e. the lord's right to take the virginity of brides); or else due to him as a penalty, perhaps for her disobedience.

A88–9/B85–6 **You've...bargain** You have that advantage as well, in addition to what you receive from your first contract (with a sexual innuendo).

If she be wise, as I suspect not thee.
And having youth, and beauty, and a husband,
Thou'st all the wish of woman. Take thy time, then.
Make thy best market.

LADY Can you assure me, sir,
Whether my father spake this, or some spirit
Of evil-wishing that has, for a time,
Hired his voice of him to beguile me that way,
Presuming on his power and my obedience?
I'd gladly know, that I might frame my answer
According to the speaker.

HELVETIUS How now, baggage!
Am I in question with thee? Does thy scorn cast
So thick an ignorance before thine eyes
That I am forgotten too? Who is't speaks to thee
But I, thy father?

Enter Govianus, discharging a pistol. [*Helvetius falls*]

GOVIANUS The more monstrous he!
Art down but with the bare voice of my fury?
Up, ancient sinner, thou'rt but mocked with death.
I missed thee purposely, thank this dear creature.
O, hadst thou been anything beside her father,
I'd made a fearful separation on thee.
I would have sent thy soul to a darker prison
Than any made of clay, and thy dead body
As a token to the lustful king thy master.
Art thou struck down so soon with the short sound
Of this small earthen instrument, and dost thou
So little fear th'eternal noise of hell?
What's she? Does she not bear thy daughter's name?
How stirs thy blood, sir? Is there a dead feeling
Of all things fatherly and honest in thee?
Say thou couldst be content, for greatness' sake,
To end the last act of thy life in panderism
(As you perhaps will say your betters do),
Must it needs follow that unmanly sin
Can work upon the weakness of no woman
But hers, whose name and honour natural love
Bids thee preserve more charily than eyesight,
Health or thy senses? Can promotion's thirst
Make such a father? Turn a grave old lord
To a white-headed squire? Make him so base
To buy his honours with his daughter's soul
And the perpetual shaming of his blood?
Hast thou the leisure, thou forgetful man,
To think upon advancement at these years?
What wouldst thou do with greatness? Dost thou hope

If she be wise, as I suspect not thee.
And having youth, and beauty, and a husband,
Thou'st all the wish of woman. Take thy time, then.
Make thy best market.

LADY Can you assure me, sir,
Whether my father spake this, or some spirit
Of evil-wishing that has, for a time,
Hired his voice of him to beguile me that way,
Presuming on his power and my obedience?
I'd gladly know, that I might frame my answer
According to the speaker.

HELVETIUS How now, baggage!
Am I in question with thee? Does thy scorn cast
So thick an ignorance before thine eyes
That I am forgotten too? Who is't speaks to thee
But I, thy father?

Enter Govianus, discharging a pistol. [*Helvetius falls*]

GOVIANUS The more monstrous he!
Art down but with the bare voice of my fury?
Up, ancient sinner, thou'rt but mocked with death.
I missed thee purposely, thank this dear creature.

A91/B88 **as ... thee** as I don't doubt that you are

A94/B91 **Make ... market** Drive the best bargain you can.

A101/B98 **Am ... thee?** Are you questioning who I am?—When Gratiana tempts her daughter Castiza, in *Revenger*, 2.1.156–7, Castiza replies: 'I cry you mercy, lady, I mistook you. | Pray did you see my mother?'

A105/B102 **Art ... fury?** Have you been struck down merely by the sound of my anger?—The stage direction brings Govianus onto the stage at A104.1/B101.1, but he may enter earlier and overhear some of the preceding dialogue.

A109 **a fearful separation** i.e. of your body from your soul

A114 **this ... instrument** i.e. the pistol

A125 **more charily** more carefully, lovingly (the preciousness of a child is compared to eyesight in *Women Beware*, 1.1.1–3).

A128 **squire** a gentleman below a knight in status, but also slang for a pimp or procurer, as at A2.3.52

To fray death with't, or hast thou that conceit
That honour will restore thy youth again?
Thou art but mocked, old fellow, 'tis not so.
Thy hopes abuse thee. Follow thine own business,
And list not to the sirens of the world.
Alas, thou hadst more need kneel at an altar,
Than to a chair of state,
And search thy conscience for thy sins of youth:
That's work enough for age; it needs no greater.
Thou'rt called within; thy very eyes look inward
To teach thy thoughts the way, and thy affections.
But miserable notes that conscience sings,
That cannot truly pray, for flattering kings.

HELVETIUS
This was well searched indeed, and without favouring.
Blessing reward thee! Such a wound as mine
Did need a pitiless surgeon! Smart on, soul,
Thou'lt feel the less hereafter. Sir, I thank you.
I ever saw my life in a false glass
Until this friendly hour. With what fair faces
My sins would look on me, but now truth shows 'em
How loathsome and how monstrous are their forms.
[*He rises to his knees*]
Be you my king and master, still. Henceforward,
My knee shall know no other earthly lord.
Well may I spend this life to do you service
That sets my soul in her eternal way.

GOVIANUS
Rise, rise, Helvetius!

HELVETIUS
I'll see both your hands
Set to my pardon first.

GOVIANUS
Mine shall bring hers.

LADY
Now, sir, I honour you for your goodness chiefly.
You're my most worthy father. You speak like him.
The first voice was not his. My joy and reverence
Strive which should be most seen. Let our hands, sir,
[*They raise Helvetius to his feet*]
Raise you from earth thus high, and may it prove
The first ascent of your immortal rising,
Never to fall again.

HELVETIUS
A spring of blessings
Keep ever with thee, and the fruit thy lord's.

GOVIANUS
I ha' lost an enemy and have found a father. *Exeunt*

Alas, thou hadst more need kneel at an altar,
Than to a chair of state,
And search thy conscience for thy sins of youth:
That's work enough for age; it needs no greater.
Thou'rt called within; thy very eyes look inward
To teach thy thoughts the way, and thy affections.
But miserable notes that conscience sings,
That cannot truly pray, for flattering kings.

HELVETIUS
This was well searched indeed, and without favouring.
Blessing reward thee! Such a wound as mine
Did need a pitiless surgeon!
[*He rises to his knees*]
Be you my king and master, still. Henceforward,
My knee shall know no other earthly lord.
Well may I spend this life to do you service
That sets my soul in her eternal path.

GOVIANUS
Rise, rise, Helvetius!

HELVETIUS
I'll see both your hands
Set to my pardon first.

GOVIANUS
Mine shall bring hers.

LADY
Now, sir, I honour you for your goodness chiefly.
You're my most worthy father. You speak like him.
The first voice was not his. My joy and reverence
Strive which should be most seen. Let our hands, sir,
[*They raise Helvetius to his feet*]
Raise you from earth thus high, and may it prove
The first ascent of your immortal rising,
Never to fall again.

HELVETIUS
A spring of blessings
Keep ever with thee, and the fruit thy lord's.

GOVIANUS
I ha' lost an enemy and have found a father. *Exeunt*

A134 **fray** frighten, drive off
conceit fantasy, idea

A138 **the sirens** in classical mythology, mermaids whose singing distracted sailors, luring their ships onto the rocks

A140/B106 **chair of state** i.e. a throne

A143–4/B109–10 **thy ... way** The sunken eyes of old age seem to look inward, in order to lead the mind to contemplate the eternal life to come.

A145–6/B111–12 **But ... kings** Only poor music ('miserable notes') comes from that conscience which cannot truly pray because it is too busy flattering kings.

A147–9/B113–15 **well ... surgeon** well probed and without sparing (the patient). Helvetius acclaims Govianus as the surgeon who has examined his spiritual wound and restored him to health.

A164–7/B125–8 **Let ... again** Helvetius kneels to Govianus and the Lady, until they bless him and raise him to his feet (thus reversing the moment when the Lady knelt for a blessing at the opening of the scene). His rising prefigures his 'immortal rising' (eternal salvation), and the avoidance of a further fall (into sin).

A167/B128 **A spring** new growth

2.2

Enter Votarius sadly

VOTARIUS
All's gone! There's nothing but the prodigal left.
I have played away my soul at one short game
Where e'en the winner loses.
Pursuing sin, how often did I shun thee?
How swift art thou afoot, beyond man's goodness,
Which has a lazy pace: so was I catched.
A curse upon the cause! Man in these days
Is not content to have his lady honest,
And so rest pleased with her without more toil,
But he must have her tried, forsooth, and tempted,
And when she proves a quean, then he lies quiet:
Like one that has a watch of curious making,
Thinking to be more cunning than the workman,
Never gives over tamp'ring with the wheels
Till either spring be weakened, balance bowed,
Or some wrong pin put in, and so spoils all.
How I could curse myself! Most business else
Delights in the dispatch, that's the best grace to't;
Only this work of blind, repented lust
Hangs shame and sadness on his master's cheek;
Yet wise men take no warning—

Enter Wife

—Nor can I now.
Her very sight strikes my repentance backward.
It cannot stand against her. Chamber thoughts
And words that have sport in 'em, they're for ladies.

WIFE
My best and dearest servant!

VOTARIUS Worthiest mistress!

[*They embrace.*]

Enter Leonella

LEONELLA
Madam!

WIFE Who's that? My woman! She's myself.
Proceed, sir.

LEONELLA Not if you love your honour, madam.
I came to give you warning my lord's come.

VOTARIUS How?

WIFE My lord!

LEONELLA [*aside*]
Alas, poor vessels, how this tempest tosses 'em!

2.2

Enter Votarius sadly

VOTARIUS
All's gone! There's nothing but the prodigal left.
I have played away my soul at one short game
Where e'en the winner loses.
Pursuing sin, how often did I shun thee?
How swift art thou afoot, beyond man's goodness,
Which has a lazy pace: so was I catched.
A curse upon the cause! Man in these days
Is not content to have his lady honest,
And so rest pleased with her without more toil,
But he must have her tried, forsooth, and tempted,
And when she proves a quean, then he lies quiet:
Like one that has a watch of curious making,
Thinking to be more cunning than the workman,
Never gives over tamp'ring with the wheels
Till either spring be weakened, balance bowed,
Or some wrong pin put in, and so spoils all.
How I could curse myself! Most business else
Delights in the dispatch, that's the best grace to't;
Only this work of blind, repented lust
Hangs shame and sadness on his master's cheek;
Yet wise men take no warning—

Enter Wife

—Nor can I now.
Her very sight strikes my repentance backward.
It cannot stand against her. Chamber thoughts
And words that have sport in 'em, they're for ladies.

WIFE
My best and dearest servant!

VOTARIUS Worthiest mistress!

[*They embrace.*]

Enter Leonella

LEONELLA
Madam!

WIFE Who's that? My woman! She's myself.
Proceed, sir.

LEONELLA Not if you love your honour, madam.
I came to give you warning my lord's come.

VOTARIUS How?

WIFE My lord!

LEONELLA [*aside*]
Alas, poor vessels, how this tempest tosses 'em!

2.2.1–3 **All's...loses** Votarius compares himself to a spendthrift who has gambled away his soul at a game (of cards or dice), where even the winner (he has had sex with the Wife) loses. For similar imagery, see ll. 168–9 and Penitent Brothel's soliloquy in *Mad World*, 4.1.4–5, 'Thou wretched unthrift, that hast play'd away | Thy eternal portion at a minute's game'. This scene parallels and contrasts with 2.1: one of the tempters (Helvetius) is saved, the other (Votarius) is damned.

4 **Pursuing sin** sin that pursues (man)

7 **cause...days** 'the cause' was Anselmus's insistence that Votarius make trial of his Wife; Anselmus is typical of 'man in these days'.

11 **quean** promiscuous woman

15–16 **spring...all** The carefully made, easily broken watch signifies the Wife, spoiled by her husband's interference: the main spring drives the mechanism; the balance regulates the speed, but when a 'wrong pin' (peg, also penis) is 'put in' to her 'wheels', she is ruined. Watches were comparatively new at this time, like the 'German clock' which occurs with similar wordplay in Penitent Brothel's soliloquy, cited at ll. 1–3.

17–20 **Most...cheek** Most other activities are a source of pleasure after they are performed—that's the most attractive aspect of them; but illicit lovemaking leaves one feeling guilty and miserable (lust is blind because it does not rightly see its object or foresee its consequences, as at 1.2.226; see also *Solomon*, 6.114; *Game*, 5.2.75).

23 **Chamber thoughts** bedroom thoughts; see l. 76, and especially ll. 129, 138.

26 **She's myself** i.e. as secret as if she were me

31–6 **Alas...still** The lovers' excitement is brought down by Anselmus's return, like ships in a storm: the Wife's 'sails' fall as her arousal fades (and, perhaps, she

They're driven both asunder in a twinkling:
Down goes the sails here, and the main mast yonder.
Here rides a barque with better fortune yet;
I fear no tossing, come what weather will;
I have a trick to hold out water still.

VOTARIUS [*aside*]
His very name shoots like a fever through me,
Now hot, now cold. Which cheek shall I turn toward
him
For fear he should read guiltiness in my looks?
I would he would keep from home, like a wise man.
'Tis no place for him now. I would not see him
Of any friend alive! It is not fit
We two should come together. We have abused
Each other mightily: he used me ill
To employ me thus, and I ha' used him worse!
I'm too much even with him.

Enter Anselmus

Yonder's a sight on him.

WIFE
My loved and honoured lord! Most welcome, sir!
[*She kisses him*]

LEONELLA [*aside*]
O, there's a kiss! Methinks my lord might taste
Dissimulation rank in't, if he had wit:
He takes but of the breath of his friend's lip.
A second kiss is hers, but that she keeps
For her first friend. We women have no cunning.

WIFE
You parted strangely from me.

ANSELMUS
That's forgotten!
Votarius, I make speed to be in thine arms!
[*He embraces Votarius*]

VOTARIUS
You never come too soon, sir.

ANSELMUS [*taking Votarius aside*]
How goes the business?

VOTARIUS
Pray think upon some other subject, sir.
What news at court?

ANSELMUS
Pish! Answer me.

VOTARIUS
Alas, sir, would you have me work by wonders,
To strike fire out of ice? You're a strange lord, sir.
Put me to possible things and find 'em finished
At your return to me. I can say no more.

ANSELMUS
I see by this thou didst not try her throughly.

They're driven both asunder in a twinkling:
Down goes the sails here, and the main mast yonder.
Here rides a barque with better fortune yet;
I fear no tossing, come what weather will;
I have a trick to hold out water still.

VOTARIUS [*aside*]
His very name shoots like a fever through me,
Now hot, now cold. Which cheek shall I turn toward
him
For fear he should read guiltiness in my looks?
I would he would keep from home, like a wise man.
'Tis no place for him now. I would not see him
Of any friend alive! It is not fit
We two should come together. We have abused
Each other mightily: he used me ill
To employ me thus, and I ha' used him worse!
I'm too much even with him.

Enter Anselmus

Yonder's a sight on him.

WIFE
My loved and honoured lord! Most welcome, sir!
[*She kisses him*]

LEONELLA [*aside*]
O, there's a kiss! Methinks my lord might taste
Dissimulation rank in't, if he had wit:
He takes but of the breath of his friend's lip.
A second kiss is hers, but that she keeps
For her first friend. We women have no cunning.

WIFE
You parted strangely from me.

ANSELMUS
That's forgotten!
Votarius, I make speed to be in thine arms!
[*He embraces Votarius*]

VOTARIUS
You never come too soon, sir.

ANSELMUS [*taking Votarius aside*]
How goes the business?

VOTARIUS
Pray think upon some other subject, sir.
What news at court?

ANSELMUS
Pish! Answer me.

VOTARIUS
Alas, sir, would you have me work by wonders,
To strike fire out of ice? You're a strange lord, sir.
Put me to possible things and find 'em finished
At your return to me. I can say no more.

ANSELMUS
I see by this thou didst not try her throughly.

lowers her raised skirts), while Votarius's 'main mast' falls, in detumescence. Leonella, by contrast, is more 'seaworthy': she fears no 'tossing' (sexual activity). Her 'trick' to keep out water (also, semen) may be a stratagem to protect her love affair (such as she uses later in this scene), or possibly a device to avoid pregnancy ('vessel' and 'barque' can be used of women as sexual objects; 'trick' may also be a sexual act).

46 **I'm . . . him** I'm more than even with him.

48–52 **Methinks . . . cunning** If Anselmus were cleverer, he would notice that his Wife was pretending, giving him only the kiss that she received from his friend (Votarius), while she keeps a second, more intimate kiss for her first (best) friend. The final comment is ironic.

53 **strangely** in an unfriendly way

62–6 **I . . . so** Votarius claims he has tried the Wife out as thoroughly as he could (in all senses), and that she did not find him 'slack' (i.e. sexually limp, as in *Revenger*, 1.2.75).

62 **throughly** thoroughly, but also 'all the way through'

VOTARIUS
How, sir? Not throughly? By this light, he lives not
That could make trial of a woman better.
ANSELMUS
I fear thou wast too slack.
VOTARIUS Good faith, you wrong me, sir.
She never found it so.
ANSELMUS Then I've a jewel,
And nothing shall be thought too precious for her.
I may advance my forehead and boast purely.
Methinks I see her worth with clear eyes now.
O when a man's opinion is at peace,
'Tis a fine life to marry! No state's like it!
[*To Wife*] My worthy lady, freely I confess
To thy wronged heart, my passion had alate
Put rudeness on me, which I now put off.
I will no more seem so unfashionable
For pleasure and the chamber of a lady.
WIFE
I'm glad you're changed so well, sir.
VOTARIUS [*aside*] Thank himself for't.
Exeunt Wife and Anselmus
LEONELLA [*aside*]
This comes like physic when the party's dead!
Flows kindness now, when 'tis so ill deserved?
This is the fortune still. Well, for this trick,
I'll save my husband and his friend a labour:
I'll never marry as long as I'm honest,
For commonly queans have the kindest husbands.
Exit; manet Votarius
VOTARIUS
I do not like his company now; 'tis irksome.
His eye offends me. Methinks 'tis not kindly
We two should live together in one house,
And 'tis impossible to remove me hence.
I must not give way first: she is my mistress,
And that's a degree kinder than a wife.
Women are always better to their friends
Than to their husbands, and more true to them.
Then let the worst give place, whom she's least need
on,
He that can best be spared, and that's her husband.
I do not like his overboldness with her.
He's too familiar with the face I love.
I fear the sickness of affectïon.
I feel a grudging on't: I shall grow jealous
E'en of that pleasure which she has by law,
I shall go so near with her.

VOTARIUS
How, sir? Not throughly? By this light, he lives not
That could make trial of a woman better.
ANSELMUS
I fear thou wast too slack.
VOTARIUS Good faith, you wrong me, sir.
She never found it so.
ANSELMUS Then I've a jewel,
And nothing shall be thought too precious for her.
I may advance my forehead and boast purely.
Methinks I see her worth with clear eyes now.
O when a man's opinion is at peace,
'Tis a fine life to marry! No state's like it!
[*To Wife*] My worthy lady, freely I confess
To thy wronged heart, my passion had alate
Put rudeness on me, which I now put off.
I will no more seem so unfashionable
For pleasure and the chamber of a lady.
WIFE
I'm glad you're changed so well, sir.
VOTARIUS [*aside*] Thank himself for't.
Exeunt Wife and Anselmus
LEONELLA [*aside*]
This comes like physic when the party's dead!
Flows kindness now, when 'tis so ill deserved?
This is the fortune still. Well, for this trick,
I'll save my husband and his friend a labour:
I'll never marry as long as I'm honest,
For commonly queans have the kindest husbands.
Exit; manet Votarius
VOTARIUS
I do not like his company now; 'tis irksome.
His eye offends me. Methinks 'tis not kindly
We two should live together in one house,
And 'tis impossible to remove me hence.
I must not give way first: she is my mistress,
And that's a degree kinder than a wife.
Women are always better to their friends
Than to their husbands, and more true to them.
Then let the worst give place, whom she's least need
on,
He that can best be spared, and that's her husband.
I do not like his overboldness with her.
He's too familiar with the face I love.
I fear the sickness of affectïon.
I feel a grudging on't: I shall grow jealous
E'en of that pleasure which she has by law,
I shall go so near with her.

66 **Then I've a jewel** Anselmus celebrates his Wife's fidelity and the joys of marriage at exactly the moment he has lost them both (as do Hoard in *Trick*, 5.2.41–2, and Leantio in *Women Beware*, 3.1.82–94).

68 **advance my forehead** hold up my head (to show I have no cuckold's horns)

73 **my passion** my preoccupation, what was on my mind

alate of late

77 **Thank . . . for't** He has only himself to thank for it. (Anselmus is 'changed', i.e. betrayed, as a result of Votarius's deception, which he himself set up.)

81–3 **I'll . . . husbands** I'll save my husband and his friend a lot of trouble (or sexual activity) by not marrying as long as I'm faithful to one man, since it's usually promiscuous women who have the most indulgent husbands. Here, as at ll. 85, 89, several senses of 'kind' are played on, including generous, natural, intimate, akin, i.e. closely related.

90–1 **Women . . . them** Votarius unconsciously echoes Sophonirus's view at 1.1.49–53.

97 **grudging** first symptom

99 **go . . . her** become so intimate with her

Enter Bellarius, passing over the stage, [then exits]
Ha! What's he?
Life, 'tis Bellarius, my rank enemy,
Mine eye snatched so much sight of him. What's his business?
His face half-darkened, stealing through the house
With a whoremaster's pace—I like it not.
This lady will be served like a great woman
With more attendants, I perceive, than one.
She has her shift of friends. My enemy one?
Do we both shun each other's company
In all assemblies public, at all meetings,
And drink to one another in one mistress?
My very thought's my poison. 'Tis high time
To seek for help. Where is our head physician,
A doctor of my making, and that lecher's?
O woman, when thou once leav'st to be good,
Thou car'st not who stands next thee! Every sin
Is a companion for thee, for thy once-cracked honesty
Is like the breaking of whole money:
It never comes to good, but wastes away.
Enter Anselmus

ANSELMUS
Votarius?

VOTARIUS
Ha!

ANSELMUS We miss you, sir, within.

VOTARIUS
I missed you more without. Would you had come sooner, sir!

ANSELMUS
Why, what's the business?

VOTARIUS You should ha' seen a fellow,
A common bawdy-house ferret, one Bellarius,
Steal through this room, his whorish barren face
Three-quarters muffled. He is somewhere hid
About the house, sir.

ANSELMUS Which way took the villain,
That marriage felon, one that robs the mind
Twenty times worse than any highway striker?
Speak, which way took he?

VOTARIUS Marry, my lord, I think—
Let me see—which way was't, now? Up yon stairs.

ANSELMUS
The way to chamb'ring! Did not I say still
All thy temptations were too faint and lazy?

Enter Bellarius, passing over the stage, [then exits]
Ha! What's he?
'Tis Bellarius, my rank enemy,
Mine eye snatched so much sight of him. What's his business?
His face half-darkened, stealing through the house
With a whoremaster's pace—I like it not.
This lady will be served like a great woman
With more attendants, I perceive, than one.
She has her shift of friends. My enemy one?
Do we both shun each other's company
In all assemblies public, at all meetings,
And drink to one another in one mistress?
My very thought's my poison. 'Tis high time
To seek for help. Where is our head physician,
A doctor of my making, and that lecher's?
O woman, when thou once leav'st to be good,
Thou car'st not who stands next thee! Every sin
Is a companion for thee, for thy once-cracked honesty
Is like the breaking of whole money:
It never comes to good, but wastes away.
Enter Anselmus

ANSELMUS
Votarius?

VOTARIUS
Ha!

ANSELMUS We miss you, sir, within.

VOTARIUS
I missed you more without. Would you had come sooner, sir!

ANSELMUS
Why, what's the business?

VOTARIUS You should ha' seen a fellow,
A common bawdy-house ferret, one Bellarius,
Steal through this room, his whorish barren face
Three-quarters muffled. He is somewhere hid
About the house, sir.

ANSELMUS Which way took the villain,
That marriage felon, one that robs the mind
Twenty times worse than any highway striker?
Speak, which way took he?

VOTARIUS Marry, my lord, I think—
Let me see—which way was't, now? Up yon stairs.

ANSELMUS
The way to chamb'ring! Did not I say still
All thy temptations were too faint and lazy?

100 **rank** absolute (also, lustful)

105–6 **With...friends** Votarius suddenly suspects the Wife of having other lovers ('attendants'), and varying them like a change ('shift') of clothes.

109–10 **drink...poison** share the same vessel or cup, as a pledge of trust or friendship (since both may be having sex with the Wife). Votarius feels himself poisoned by this thought, and begins to experience Anselmus's irrational jealousy.

111 **head physician** Anselmus is the 'head physician', made thus (i.e. cuckolded) by Votarius and Bellarius, but now needed to cure (Votarius's) (fore)head of the pain of being horned, i.e. sexually betrayed.

114 **who...thee** is closest to you (to 'stand' is also to have an erection)

115–16 **for...money** Once women gave up sexual fidelity, they were supposed to have lost their value, like cracked coins which, when sufficiently damaged, were no longer legal tender.

122 **barren** ugly

125–6 **That...striker** That marriage thief takes away peace of mind, and so is far worse than the highwayman (who only takes money).

129 **chamb'ring** illicit lovemaking (as at l. 138)

Thou did'st not play 'em home.
VOTARIUS To tell you true, sir,
I found her yielding ere I left her last,
And wavering in her faith.
ANSELMUS Did not I think so?
VOTARIUS
That makes me suspect him.
ANSELMUS Why, partial man,
Could'st thou hide this from me, so dearly sought for,
And rather waste thy pity upon her?
Thou'rt not so kind as my heart praised thee to me.
[*Footsteps are heard offstage*]
Hark!
VOTARIUS
'Tis his footing, certain.
ANSELMUS Are you chambered?
I'll fetch you from aloft! *Exit*
VOTARIUS He takes my work
And toils to bring me ease. This use I'll make on him,
His care shall watch to keep all strange thieves out,
Whiles I familiarly go in and rob him
Like one that knows the house.
But how has rashness and my jealousy used me!
Out of my vengeance to mine enemy,
Confessed her yielding? I have locked myself
From mine own liberty with that key. Revenge
Does no man good, but to his greater harm.
Suspect and malice, like a mingled cup,
Made me soon drunk. I knew not what I spoke,
And that may get me pardon.
Enter Anselmus, a dagger in his hand, with Leonella
LEONELLA Why, my lord!
ANSELMUS
Confess, thou mystical panderess!
[*He threatens Leonella*]
—Run, Votarius,
To the back gate. The guilty slave leaped out
And 'scaped me so. This strumpet locked him up
In her own chamber. *Exit Votarius*
LEONELLA Hold, my lord! I might,
He is my husband, sir!
ANSELMUS O, soul of cunning!
Came that arch-subtlety from thy lady's counsel
Or thine own sudden craft? Confess to me
How oft thou hast been a bawd to their close actions,
Or all thy light goes out.
LEONELLA My lord, believe me,

Thou did'st not play 'em home.
VOTARIUS To tell you true, sir,
I found her yielding ere I left her last,
And wavering in her faith.
ANSELMUS Did not I think so?
VOTARIUS
That makes me suspect him.
ANSELMUS Why, partial man,
Could'st thou hide this from me, so dearly sought for,
And rather waste thy pity upon her?
Thou'rt not so kind as my heart praised thee to me.
[*Footsteps are heard offstage*]
Hark!
VOTARIUS
'Tis his footing, certain.
ANSELMUS Are you chambered?
I'll fetch you from aloft! *Exit*
VOTARIUS He takes my work
And toils to bring me ease. This use I'll make on him,
His care shall watch to keep all strange thieves out,
Whiles I familiarly go in and rob him
Like one that knows the house.
But how has rashness and my jealousy used me!
Out of my vengeance to mine enemy,
Confessed her yielding? I have locked myself
From mine own liberty with that key. Revenge
Does no man good, but to his greater harm.
Suspect and malice, like a mingled cup,
Made me soon drunk. I knew not what I spoke,
And that may get me pardon.
Enter Anselmus, a dagger in his hand, with Leonella
LEONELLA Why, my lord!
ANSELMUS
Confess, thou mystical panderess!
[*He threatens Leonella*]
—Run, Votarius,
To the back gate. The guilty slave leaped out
And 'scaped me so. This strumpet locked him up
In her own chamber. *Exit Votarius*
LEONELLA Hold, my lord! I might,
He is my husband, sir!
ANSELMUS O, soul of cunning!
Came that arch-subtlety from thy lady's counsel
Or thine own sudden craft? Confess to me
How oft thou hast been a bawd to their close actions,
Or all thy light goes out.
LEONELLA My lord, believe me,

131 **play 'em home** push them (in) far enough (Anselmus is unconscious of the innuendo)
135 **dearly** eagerly (also, expensively)—Anselmus fails to notice the ironic meaning of his words, but his keenness to hear of his wife's adultery is perverse.
138 **chambered** upstairs in the bed chamber, but also inside a woman's vagina; 'aloft' means sexually erect, as well as on high
147–8 **Revenge... harm** Any benefit revenge appears to offer is outweighed by the spiritual damage it does. (According to the Church, revenge was the prerogative of God alone, as in *Solomon* 18.227–8: 'Man did not overcome his foes with arms, | But with thy word, which conquers greater harms'.)
149 **Suspect** suspicion
mingled cup strong cocktail
152 **mystical** secret (as in 'mystical strumpet', *Banquet*, 4.3.175; 'mystical harlot', *Hengist*, 5.2.154)
155–6 **I... husband** I'm allowed to—he is my fiancé. Leonella pretends to be, or is perhaps, engaged, and thus entitled to refer to Bellarius as her 'husband'.
158 **sudden craft** quick invention
159 **close** secret, intimate
160 **thy light** i.e. of life

In troth I love a man too well myself
To bring him to my mistress.

ANSELMUS Leave thy sporting,
Or my next offer makes thy heart weep blood.
[He threatens to stab her]

LEONELLA *[on her knees]*
O, spare that strength my lord, and I'll reveal
A secret that concerns you, for this does not.

ANSELMUS Back, back, my fury, then.
It shall not touch thy breast.
[He sheathes his dagger]
Speak freely. What is't?

LEONELLA
Votarius and my lady are false gamesters.
They use foul play, my lord.

ANSELMUS Thou liest!

LEONELLA Reward me, then,
For all together, if it prove not so:
I'll never bestow time to ask your pity.

ANSELMUS
Votarius and thy lady! 'Twill ask days
Ere it be settled in belief.—So, rise.
[She rises]
Go, get thee to thy chamber. *Exit*

LEONELLA A pox on you!
You hindered me of better business, thank you.
He's frayed a secret from me. Would he were whipped!
Faith, from a woman a thing's quickly slipped! *Exit*

2.3

[The throne is set out]
Enter the Tyrant with Sophonirus, Memphonius and other Nobles
A flourish

TYRANT
My joys have all false hearts. There's nothing true to me
That's either kind or pleasant. I'm hardly dealt withal.
I must not miss her. I want her sight too long.
Where's this old fellow?

SOPHONIRUS
Here's one, my lord, of threescore and seventeen.

TYRANT
Push! That old limber ass puts in his head still!
Helvetius! Where is he?

MEMPHONIUS
Not yet returned, my lord.
Enter Helvetius

TYRANT Your lordship lies.
Here comes the kingdom's father. Who amongst you

In troth I love a man too well myself
To bring him to my mistress.

ANSELMUS Leave thy sporting,
Or my next offer makes thy heart weep blood.
[He threatens to stab her]

LEONELLA *[on her knees]*
O, spare that strength my lord, and I'll reveal
A secret that concerns you, for this does not.

ANSELMUS Back, back, my fury, then.
It shall not touch thy breast.
[He sheathes his dagger]
Speak freely. What is't?

LEONELLA
Votarius and my lady are false gamesters.
They use foul play, my lord.

ANSELMUS Thou liest!

LEONELLA Reward me, then,
For all together, if it prove not so:
I'll never bestow time to ask your pity.

ANSELMUS
Votarius and thy lady! 'Twill ask days
Ere it be settled in belief.—So, rise.
[She rises]
Go, get thee to thy chamber. *Exit*

LEONELLA A pox on you!
You hindered me of better business, thank you.
He's frayed a secret from me. Would he were whipped!
Faith, from a woman a thing's quickly slipped! *Exit*

2.3

[The throne is set out]
Enter the Tyrant with Sophonirus, Memphonius and other Nobles
A flourish

TYRANT
My joys have all false hearts. There's nothing true to me
That's either kind or pleasant. I'm hardly dealt withal.
I must not miss her. I want her sight too long.
Where's this old fellow?

SOPHONIRUS
Here's one, my lord, of threescore and seventeen.

TYRANT
Push! That old limber ass puts in his head still!
Helvetius! Where is he?

MEMPHONIUS
Not yet returned, my lord.
Enter Helvetius

TYRANT Your lordship lies.
Here comes the kingdom's father. Who amongst you

162 **sporting** joking, playing games

163 **offer** i.e. blow (with his dagger)

169–71 **Reward...pity** Punish me, then, for both claims (that Bellarius is my husband and Votarius is your Wife's lover), if they turn out not to be true. I won't waste time asking for your pity.

172 **'Twill ask days** it will take several days

175 **better business** i.e. from using her knowledge to blackmail the Wife

176 **frayed** frightened (as at A2.1.134)

177 **thing's** i.e. a secret, also penis

2.3.2–3 **I'm...long** I'm harshly treated. I must not be without her. I've lacked the sight of her for too long.

5 **threescore and seventeen** i.e. seventy-seven. Sophonirus seems to be referring to himself, and the Tyrant replies as if speaking of him.

6 **Push...still** Huh! That flabby old idiot is always butting in (suggesting his impotence).

Dares say this worthy man has not made speed?
I would fain hear that fellow.
SOPHONIRUS [*aside*] I'll not be he.
I like the standing of my head too well
To have it mended.
TYRANT [*to Helvetius*]
Thy sight quickens me.
I find a better health when thou art present
Than all times else can bring me. Is the answer
As pleasing as thyself?
HELVETIUS Of what, my lord?
TYRANT
Of what? Fie, no! He did not say so, did he?
SOPHONIRUS
O no, my lord, not he spoke no such word!
[*Aside*] I'll say as he would ha't, for I'd be loath
To have my body used like butcher's meat.
TYRANT
When comes she to our bed?
HELVETIUS Who, my lord?
TYRANT Hark!
You heard that plain amongst you?
SOPHONIRUS O, my lord,
As plain as my wife's tongue that drowns a saint's bell.
[*Aside*] Let me alone to lay about for honour.
I'll shift for one.
TYRANT When comes the lady, sir,
That Govianus keeps?
HELVETIUS Why, that's my daughter.
TYRANT
O, is it so? Have you unlocked your memory?
What says she to us?
HELVETIUS Nothing.
TYRANT How thou tempt'st us!
What did'st thou say to her, being sent from us?
HELVETIUS
More than was honest, yet it was but little.
TYRANT
How cruelly thou work'st upon our patience,
Having advantage 'cause thou art her father!
But be not bold too far. If duty leave thee,
Respect will fall from us.
HELVETIUS Have I kept life
So long, till it looks white upon my head,
Been threescore years a courtier, and a flatterer
Not above threescore hours, which time's repented
Amongst my greatest follies? And am I at these days
Fit for no place but bawd to mine own flesh?
You'll prefer all your old courtiers to good services,
If your lust keep but hot some twenty winters:
We are like to have a virtuous world of wives,

Dares say this worthy man has not made speed?
I would fain hear that fellow.
SOPHONIRUS [*aside*] I'll not be he.
I like the standing of my head too well
To have it mended.
TYRANT [*to Helvetius*]
Thy sight quickens me.
I find a better health when thou art present
Than all times else can bring me. Is the answer
As pleasing as thyself?
HELVETIUS Of what, my lord?
TYRANT
Of what? Fie, no! He did not say so, did he?
SOPHONIRUS
O no, my lord, not he spoke no such word!
[*Aside*] I'll say as he would ha't, for I'd be loath
To have my body used like butcher's meat.
TYRANT
When comes she to our bed?
HELVETIUS Who, my lord?
TYRANT Hark!
You heard that plain amongst you?
SOPHONIRUS O, my lord,
As plain as my wife's tongue that drowns a saint's bell.
[*Aside*] Let me alone to lay about for honour.
I'll shift for one.
TYRANT When comes the lady, sir,
That Govianus keeps?
HELVETIUS Why, that's my daughter.
TYRANT
O, is it so? Have you unlocked your memory?
What says she to us?
HELVETIUS Nothing.
TYRANT How thou tempt'st us!
What did'st thou say to her, being sent from us?
HELVETIUS
More than was honest, yet it was but little.
TYRANT
How cruelly thou work'st upon our patience,
Having advantage 'cause thou art her father!
But be not bold too far. If duty leave thee,
Respect will fall from us.
HELVETIUS Have I kept life
So long, till it looks white upon my head,
Been threescore years a courtier, and a flatterer
Not above threescore hours, which time's repented
Amongst my greatest follies? And am I at these days
Fit for no place but bawd to mine own flesh?

23 **saint's bell** rung to summon the congregation to church

24–5 **lay...one** Trust me to look around for advancement; I'll take care of number one.

26 **keeps** withholds; also, maintains

A40–5 **You'll...'em** You'll advance all your old courtiers to good positions, if you stay as lecherous as this for the next twenty years; we're likely to have all our virtuous women—wives, daughters, sisters, as well as relatives, cousins—carried off all over the place, wherever it pleases you to take them (i.e. sexually).

Daughters and sisters, besides kinswomen
And cousin-germans removed, up and down,
Where'er you please to have 'em! Are white hairs
A colour fit for panders and flesh-brokers,
Which are the honoured ornaments of age,
To which e'en kings owe reverence, as they're men,
And greater in their goodness than their greatness?
And must I take my pay all in base money?
I was a lord born, set by all court grace,
And am I thrust now to a squire's place?

TYRANT
How comes the moon to change so in this man,
That was at full but now in all performance
And swifter than my wishes? I beshrew that virtue
That busied herself with him: she might have found
Some other work. The man was fit for me
Before she spoiled him. She has wronged my heart in't
And marred me a good workman.—Now his art fails
him,
What makes the man at court? This is no place
For fellows of no parts. He lives not here
That puts himself from action when we need him.
[*To Helvetius*] I take off all thy honours and bestow
'em
On any of this rank that will deserve 'em.

SOPHONIRUS
My lord, that's I; trouble your grace no further.
I'll undertake to bring her to your bed
With some ten words. Marry, they're special charms.
No lady can withstand 'em. A witch taught me 'em.
If you doubt me, I'll leave my wife in pawn
For my true loyalty, and your majesty
May pass away the time till I return.
I have a care in all things.

TYRANT
That may thrive best
Which the least hope looks after. But, however,
Force shall help nature; I'll be too sure now.
Thy willingness may be fortunate. We employ thee.

SOPHONIRUS
Then I'll go fetch my wife and take my journey.

TYRANT
Stay, we require no pledge. We think thee honest.

SOPHONIRUS [*aside*]
Troth, the worse luck for me. We had both been made
by't.
It was the way to make my wife great too.

TYRANT [*to Helvetius*]
I'll teach thee to be wide and strange to me:

Are white hairs
A colour fit for panders and flesh-brokers,
Which are the honoured ornaments of age,
To which e'en kings owe reverence, as they're men,
And greater in their goodness than their greatness?

TYRANT
How comes the moon to change so in this man,
That was at full but now in all performance
And swifter than our wishes? I beshrew that virtue
That busied herself with him:

She has wronged my heart in't—Now his art fails
him,
What makes the man at court? This is no place
For fellows of no parts. He lives not here
That puts himself from action when we need him.
[*To Helvetius*] I take off all thy honours and bestow
'em
On any of this rank that will deserve 'em.

SOPHONIRUS
My lord, that's I; trouble your grace no further.
I'll undertake to bring her to your bed
With some ten words. Marry, they're special charms.
No lady can withstand 'em. A witch taught me 'em.
If you doubt me, I'll leave my wife in pawn
For my true loyalty, and your majesty
May pass away the time till I return.
I have a care in all things.

TYRANT
That may thrive best
Which the least hope looks after. But, however,
Force shall help nature; I'll be too sure now.
Thy willingness may be fortunate. We employ thee.

SOPHONIRUS
Then I'll go fetch my wife and take my journey.

TYRANT
Stay, we require no pledge. We think thee honest.

SOPHONIRUS [*aside*]
Troth, the worse luck for me. We had both been made
by't.
It was the way to make my wife great too.

TYRANT [*to Helvetius*]
I'll teach thee to be wide and strange to me:

A51–2 **I...place** I was born into the aristocracy, even if you ignore ('set by') my high status at court. (Alternatively, the phrase may mean 'set up with a high status at court', or else, 'how can you ignore my high status at court?') And am I now to be demoted to the position of a squire? (also meaning 'procurer', as at A2.1.128).

A59 **marred me** i.e. (Virtue) spoilt (a good workman) for me.

A59/B49 **his art** i.e. his skill as a courtier

A61/B51 **parts** abilities

A69–71/B59–61 **I'll...time** I'll leave my wife as a pledge of my good faith, so that your majesty may amuse yourself with her.

A73–4/B63–4 **however...nature** even so, force shall back up nature (in the form of Sophonirus's 'special charms')

A79/B69 **great** of high status; also, pregnant

A80/B70 **I'll...me** I'll teach you to be distant and stand-offish with me!

Thou'lt feel thyself light, shortly. I'll not leave thee
A title to put on, but the bare name
That men must call thee by, and know thee miserable.

HELVETIUS
'Tis miserable, king, to be of thy making
And leave a better workman. If thy honours
Only keep life in baseness, take 'em to thee
And give 'em to the hungry. [*Pointing to Sophonirus*]
There's one gapes.

SOPHONIRUS
One that will swallow you, sir, for that jest,
And all your titles after.

HELVETIUS
The devil follow 'em,
There's room enough for him, too.—Leave me, thou king,
As poor as truth (the gentlewoman I now serve,
And never will forsake her for her plainness),
That shall not alter me!

TYRANT
No? [*Calling*] Our guard, within there!

Enter Guard

GUARD My lord?

TYRANT
Bear that old fellow to our castle prisoner.
Give charge he be kept close.

HELVETIUS
Close prisoner?
Why, my heart thanks thee. I shall have more time
And liberty to virtue in one hour
Than all those threescore years I was a courtier.
So by imprisonment I sustain great loss;
Heav'n opens to that man the world keeps close.

Exit [*under guard*]

SOPHONIRUS [*aside*]
But I'll not go to prison to try that.
Give me the open world; there's a good air.

TYRANT
I would fain send death after him, but I dare not.
He knows I dare not: that would give just cause
Of her unkindness everlasting to me.
His life may thank his daughter.—Sophonirus!
Here, take this jewel. Bear it as a token
To our heart's saint. 'Twill do thy words no harm.
Speech may do much, but wealth's a greater charm
Than any made of words, and to be sure,
If one or both should fail, I provide further.
Call forth those resolute fellows whom our clemency

I'll not leave thee
A title to put on, but the bare name
That men must call thee by, and know thee miserable.

HELVETIUS
'Tis miserable, king, to be of thy making
And leave a better workman. If thy honours
Only keep life in baseness, take 'em to thee
And give 'em to the hungry. [*Pointing to Sophonirus*]
There's one gapes.

SOPHONIRUS
One that will swallow you, sir, for that jest,
And all your titles after.

HELVETIUS
The devil follow 'em,
There's room enough for him, too.—Leave me, thou king,
As poor as truth (the mistress I now serve,
And never will forsake her for her plainness),
That shall not alter me!

TYRANT
No? [*Calling*] Our guard, within there!

Enter Guard

GUARD My lord?

TYRANT
Bear that old fellow to our castle prisoner.
Give charge he be kept close.

HELVETIUS
Close prisoner?
Why, my heart thanks thee. I shall have more time
And liberty to virtue in one hour
Than all those threescore years I was a courtier.
So by imprisonment I sustain great loss;
Heav'n opens to that man the world keeps close.

Exit [*under guard*]

SOPHONIRUS [*aside*]
But I'll not go to prison to try that.
Give me the open world; there's a good air.

TYRANT
I would fain send death after him, but I dare not.
He knows I dare not: that would give just cause
Of her unkindness everlasting to me.
His life may thank his daughter.—Sophonirus!
Here, take this jewel. Bear it as a token
To our heart's saint. 'Twill do thy words no harm.
Speech may do much, but wealth's a greater charm
Than any made of words, and to be sure,
If one or both should fail, I provide further.
Call forth those resolute fellows whom our clemency

A81 **Thou'lt...shortly** You'll soon find yourself relieved, i.e. of the weight of your honours.

A85–6/B75–6 **And...thee** And abandon a better workman, i.e. God. If your honours only allow one to live basely, take them back.

A87/B77 **There's one gapes** There's someone with his mouth wide open (i.e. for honours).

A90–3/B80–3 **Leave...me** Even if you leave me, wretched king, as poor as Truth, that will not change me. (Helvetius personifies Truth as a woman of good family come down in the world, whose simple way of life will not deter him from his service to her. This image and his refusal to be altered recall the Lady's words at A1.1.123/B1.1.104 and A1.1.171/B1.1.152, and at A2.3.96–9/B2.3.86–9 he will echo Govianus at A1.1.210–11/B1.1.187–8 in welcoming his imprisonment.)

A93/B83 **Our guard** The guard called out here is apparently distinct from the 'resolute fellows' summoned at l. A113/B103 (see note on that line).

A96/B86 **close** closely confined

A107/B97 **His...daughter** He may thank his daughter for his life.

A113–15/B103–5 **fellows...offences** fellows whom my mercy saved from a shameful execution for war crimes committed on the battlefield. These men seem to be identical with the soldiers summoned at 4.2.37–8, 'The men I wished for, | For secrecy and employment', though by 5.2.11.1, they seem to have become the official guard.

Saved from a death of shame in time of war
For field offences. Give 'em charge from us
They arm themselves with speed, beset the house
Of Govianus round, that if thou fail'st,
Or stay'st beyond the time thou leav'st with them,
They may with violence break in themselves
And seize on her for our use.
Exeunt [Tyrant, Memphonius and Nobles]. Manet Sophonirus

SOPHONIRUS They're not so saucy
To seize on her for their own, I hope;
As there are many knaves will begin first
And bring their lords the bottom. I have been served so
A hundred times myself by a scurvy page
That I kept once; but my wife loved him, and
I could not help it. *Exit*

A flourish
[The throne is withdrawn]
Finit Actus Secundus

3.1 *Incipit Actus Tertius*
Enter Govianus with his Lady, and a Servant

GOVIANUS
What is he?

SERVANT An old lord come from the court.

GOVIANUS
He should be wise, by's years. He will not dare
To come about such business: 'tis not man's work.
Art sure he desired conference with thy lady?

SERVANT
Sure, sir.

GOVIANUS
Faith, thou'rt mistook. 'Tis with me, certain.
Let's do the man no wrong. Go, know it truly, sir.

SERVANT [*aside*]
This' a strange humour we must know things twice.
Exit

GOVIANUS
There's no man is so dull, but he will weigh
The work he undertakes, and set about it
E'en in the best sobriety of his judgement,
With all his senses watchful. Then his guilt
Does equal his for whom 'tis undertaken.
Enter Servant
What says he now?

SERVANT E'en as he said at first, sir.
He's business to my lady from the king.

Saved from a death of shame in time of war
For field offences. Give 'em charge from us
They arm themselves with speed, beset the house
Of Govianus round, that if thou fail'st,
Or stay'st beyond the time thou leav'st with them,
They may with violence break in themselves
And seize her for our use.
Exeunt [Tyrant, Memphonius and Nobles]. Manet Sophonirus

SOPHONIRUS They're not so saucy
To seize her for their own, I hope;
As there are many knaves will begin first
And bring their lords the bottom. I have been served so
A hundred times myself by a scurvy page
That I kept once; but my wife loved him, and
I could not help it. *Exit*

A flourish
[The throne is withdrawn]
Finit Actus Secundus

Incipit Actus Tertius 3.1
Enter Govianus with his Lady, and a Servant

GOVIANUS
What is he?

SERVANT An old lord come from the court.

GOVIANUS
He should be wise, by's years. He will not dare
To come about such business: 'tis not man's work.
Art sure he desired conference with thy lady?

SERVANT
Sure, sir.

GOVIANUS
Faith, thou'rt mistook. 'Tis with me, certain.
Let's do the man no wrong. Go, know it truly, sir.

SERVANT [*aside*]
This' a strange humour we must know things twice.
Exit

GOVIANUS
There's no man is so dull, but he will weigh
The work he undertakes, and set about it
E'en in the best sobriety of his judgement,
With all his senses watchful. Then his guilt
Does equal his for whom 'tis undertaken.
Enter Servant
What says he now?

SERVANT E'en as he said at first, sir.
He's business to my lady from the king.

A116/B106 **beset** besiege

A118/B108 **time...them** the time appointed, agreed with them

A122–3/B112–13 **As...bottom** Dishonest servants would drink their masters' wine and leave them the dregs. The analogy has a sexual twist, as in *Mad World*, 5.2.306–8, *Banquet*, 4.3.282, and *Changeling*, 5.3.170–1.

3.1.3 **such business** i.e. luring the Lady back to the court. Govianus is reluctant to recognize the danger that threatens her; he reacts slowly, and with disbelief.

7 **This'** i.e. This is, as at 4.1.87, 5.1.107

11–12 **Then...undertaken** In that case, he is as guilty as the man he acts for. Govianus's comment applies to the temptations of Helvetius and Votarius, as well as to that of Sophonirus.

GOVIANUS
Still from the king. He will not come near, will he?
SERVANT
Yes, when he knows he shall, sir.
GOVIANUS
I cannot think it!
Let him be tried.
SERVANT
Small trial will serve him, I warrant you, sir. [*Exit*]
GOVIANUS
Sure, honesty has left man. Has fear forsook him?
Yes, faith, there is no fear where there's no grace.
LADY
What way shall I devise to give him his answer?
Denial is not strong enough to serve, sir.
GOVIANUS
No, 't must have other helps.
Enter Sophonirus [*with a casket*]
I see he dares.
O patience, I shall lose a friend of thee!
SOPHONIRUS
I bring thee, precious lady, this dear stone
And commendations from the king my master.
GOVIANUS [*drawing his sword*]
I set before thee, panderous lord, this steel,
And much good do't thy heart. [*Offering to fight*] Fall
to, and spare not!
[*They fight. Govianus runs Sophonirus through. He falls*]
LADY
'Las, what have you done, my lord?
GOVIANUS
Why, sent a bawd
Home to his lodging, nothing else, sweet heart.
SOPHONIRUS
Well, you have killed me, sir, and there's an end.
But you'll get nothing by the hand, my lord,
When all your cards are counted. There be gamesters,
Not far off, will set upon the winner
And make a poor lord on you, ere they've left you.
I'm fetched in like a fool to pay the reck'ning,
Yet you'll save nothing by't.
GOVIANUS
What riddle's this?
SOPHONIRUS
There she stands by thee now, who yet ere midnight
Must lie by the king's side.
GOVIANUS
Who speaks that lie?
SOPHONIRUS
One hour will make it true. She cannot 'scape,
No more than I from death. You've a great gain on't,
An you look well about you, that's my comfort:

GOVIANUS
Still from the king. He will not come near, will he?
SERVANT
Yes, when he knows he shall, sir.
GOVIANUS
I cannot think it!
Let him be tried.
SERVANT
Small trial will serve him, I warrant you, sir. [*Exit*]
GOVIANUS
Sure, honesty has left man. Has fear forsook him?
Yes, faith, there is no fear where there's no grace.
LADY
What way shall I devise to gi'm his answer?
Denial is not strong enough to serve, sir.
GOVIANUS
No, 't must have other helps.
Enter Sophonirus [*with a casket*]
I see he dares.
O patience, I shall lose a friend of thee!
SOPHONIRUS
I bring thee, precious lady, this dear stone
And commendations from the king my master.
GOVIANUS [*drawing his sword*]
I set before thee, panderous lord, this steel,
And much good do't thy heart. [*Offering to fight*] Fall
to, and spare not!
[*They fight. Govianus runs Sophonirus through. He falls*]
LADY
'Las, what have you done, my lord?
GOVIANUS
Why, sent a bawd
Home to his lodging, nothing else, sweet heart.
SOPHONIRUS
Well, you have killed me, sir, and there's an end.
But you'll get nothing by the hand, my lord,
When all your cards are counted. There be gamesters,
Not far off, will set upon the winner
And make a poor lord on you, ere they've left you.
I'm fetched in like a fool to pay the reck'ning,
Yet you'll save nothing by't.
GOVIANUS
What riddle's this?
SOPHONIRUS
There she stands by thee now, who yet ere midnight
Must lie by the king's side.
GOVIANUS
Who speaks that lie?
SOPHONIRUS
One hour will make it true. She cannot 'scape,
No more than I from death. You've a great gain on't,
An you look well about you, that's my comfort:

15 **near** i.e. nearer
16 **shall** i.e may
20 **there...grace** Wicked men (i.e. who lack God's grace) are not afraid of sinning.
24 **patience...thee** I am about to lose my patience (literally, to lose patience as a friend).
28 **Fall to** Get on with it—an invitation to begin fighting. It is not clear whether Sophonirus defends himself (as my stage directions propose), or whether Govianus simply kills him without pity.
29 **bawd** pimp, procurer
30 **his lodging** where he belongs (i.e. hell)
32–7 **But...by't** You won't gain from your (winning) hand when all the cards are added up. There are players nearby who will attack you and rob you of your winnings, and ruin you before they've finished with you. Like a fool, I've been called in to foot the bill, yet that isn't going to help you.
41–2 **You've...you** You'll see how much you've gained from my death, if you take a good look around you (ironic).

The house is round beset with armèd men
That know their time, when to break in, and seize on
her.

LADY
My lord!

GOVIANUS [*to the Lady*]
'Tis boldly done, to trouble me
When I've such business to dispatch. [*Calling*]—
Within there!
Enter Servant

SERVANT
My lord?

GOVIANUS
Look out, and tell me what thou seest.
[*Exit Servant*]

SOPHONIRUS
How quickly now my death will be revenged,
Before the king's first sleep. I depart laughing
To think upon the deed.
[*He dies*]

GOVIANUS 'Tis thy banquet.
Down, villain, to thy everlasting weeping
That canst rejoice so in the rape of virtue
And sing light tunes in tempests, when we're ship-
wrecked,
And have no plank to save us.
Enter Servant
Now, sir, quickly!

SERVANT
Which way soe'er I cast mine eye, my lord,
Out of all parts o' th' house, I may see fellows
Gathered in companies and all whispering,
Like men for treachery busy—

LADY 'Tis confirmed.

SERVANT
Their eyes still fixed upon the doors and windows.

GOVIANUS
I think thou'st never done. Thou lov'st to talk on't.
'Tis fine discourse. Prithee find other business.

SERVANT
Nay, I am gone. I'm a man quickly sneaped. *Exit*

GOVIANUS
He's flattered me with safety for this hour.

LADY
Have you leisure to stand idle? Why, my lord,
It is for me they come.

GOVIANUS For thee, my glory,
The riches of my youth, it is for thee.

LADY
Then is your care so cold? Will you be robbed
And have such warning of the thieves? Come on, sir,
Fall to your business, lay your hands about you!

The house is round beset with armèd men
That know their time, when to break in, and seize on
her.

LADY
My lord!

GOVIANUS [*to the Lady*]
'Tis boldly done, to trouble me
When I've such business to dispatch. [*Calling*]—
Within there!
Enter Servant

SERVANT
My lord?

GOVIANUS
Look out, and tell me what thou seest.
[*Exit Servant*]

SOPHONIRUS
How quickly now my death will be revenged,
Before the king's first sleep. I depart laughing
To think upon the deed.
[*He dies*]

GOVIANUS 'Tis thy banquet.
Down, villain, to thy everlasting weeping
That canst rejoice so in the rape of virtue
And sing light tunes in tempests, when we're ship-
wrecked,
And have no plank to save us.
Enter Servant
Now, sir, quickly!

SERVANT
Which way soe'er I cast mine eye, my lord,
Out of all parts o' th' house, I may see fellows
Gathered in companies and all whispering,
Like men for treachery busy—

LADY 'Tis confirmed.

SERVANT
Their eyes still fixed upon the doors and windows.

GOVIANUS
I think thou'st never done. Thou lov'st to talk on't.
'Tis fine discourse. Prithee find other business.

SERVANT
Nay, I am gone. I'm a man quickly sneaped. *Exit*

GOVIANUS
He's flattered me with safety for this hour.

LADY
Have you leisure to stand idle? Why, my lord,
It is for me they come.

GOVIANUS For thee, my glory,
The riches of my youth, it is for thee.

LADY
Then is your care so cold? Will you be robbed
And have such warning of the thieves? Come on, sir,
Fall to your business, lay your hands about you!

46 **such...dispatch** so much to do
50 **'Tis thy banquet** Enjoy yourself (as in *Changeling*, 'My thoughts are at a banquet', 3.4.18).
59 **still** constantly
61 **'Tis...business** That's a fine topic of conversation (ironic). Please go and find something else to do.
62 **quickly sneaped** easily reproved, ticked off
69 **Fall...business** Get on with the job (i.e. of killing me).

Do not think scorn to work. A resolute captain
Will rather fling the treasure of his bark
Into whales' throats than pirates should be gorged with't.
Be not less man than he. Thou art master yet
And all's at thy disposing. Take thy time;
Prevent mine enemy. Away with me,
Let me no more be seen! I'm like that treasure,
Dangerous to him that keeps it; rid thy hands on't.

GOVIANUS
I cannot lose thee so.

LADY
Shall I be taken
And lost the cruell'st way? Then wouldst thou curse
That love that sent forth pity to my life,
Too late thou wouldst.

GOVIANUS
O, this extremity!
Hast thou no way to 'scape 'em but in soul?
Must I meet peace in thy destruction,
Or will it ne'er come at me?
'Tis a most miserable way to get it.
I had rather be content to live without it
Than pay so dear for't, and yet lose it too.

LADY
Sir, you do nothing. There's no valour in you.
You're the worst friend to a lady in affliction
That ever love made his companion!
For honour's sake, dispatch me! Thy own thoughts
Should stir thee to this act more than my weakness.
The sufferer should not do't. I speak thy part,
Dull and forgetful man, and all to help thee!
Is it thy mind to have me seized upon
And borne with violence to the tyrant's bed,
There forced unto the lust of all his days?

GOVIANUS
O no! Thou liv'st no longer, now I think on't.
[*He runs at her with his sword drawn*]
I take thee at all hazard!

LADY
O stay! Hold, sir!

GOVIANUS
Lady, what had you made me done now? You never cease
Till you prepare me cruel 'gainst my heart,
And then you turn't upon my hand and mock me.

LADY Cowardly flesh,
Thou show'st thy faintness still: I felt thee shake
E'en when the storm came near thee. Thou'rt the same;
But 'twas not for thy fear I put death by.
I had forgot a chief and worthy business,
Whose strange neglect would have made me forgotten

Do not think scorn to work. A resolute captain
Will rather fling the treasure of his bark
Into whales' throats than pirates should be gorged with't.
Be not less man than he. Thou art master yet
And all's at thy disposing. Take thy time;
Prevent mine enemy. Away with me,
Let me no more be seen! I'm like that treasure,
Dangerous to him that keeps it; rid thy hands on't.

GOVIANUS
I cannot lose thee so.

LADY
Shall I be taken
And lost the cruell'st way? Then wouldst thou curse
That love that sent forth pity to my life,
Too late thou wouldst.

GOVIANUS
O, this extremity!
Hast thou no way to 'scape 'em but in soul?
Must I meet peace in thy destruction,
Or will it ne'er come at me?
'Tis a most miserable way to get it.
I had rather be content to live without it
Than pay so dear for't, and yet lose it too.

LADY
Sir, you do nothing. There's no valour in you.
You're the worst friend to a lady in affliction
That ever love made his companion!
For honour's sake, dispatch me! Thy own thoughts
Should stir thee to this act more than my weakness.
The sufferer should not do't. I speak thy part,
Dull and forgetful man, and all to help thee!
Is it thy mind to have me seized upon
And borne with violence to the tyrant's bed,
There forced unto the lust of all his days?

GOVIANUS
O no! Thou liv'st no longer, now I think on't.
[*He runs at her with his sword drawn*]
I take thee at all hazard!

LADY
O stay! Hold, sir!

GOVIANUS
Lady, what had you made me done now? You never cease
Till you prepare me cruel 'gainst my heart,
And then you turn't upon my hand and mock me.

LADY Cowardly flesh,
Thou show'st thy faintness still: I felt thee shake
E'en when the storm came near thee. Thou'rt the same;
But 'twas not for thy fear I put death by.
I had forgot a chief and worthy business,
Whose strange neglect would have made me forgotten

70 **think scorn** think it shameful
74 **Take thy time** seize your opportunity
76 **Let . . . seen** Let me die (as in *Changeling*, 2.2.136).
79 **lost . . . way** i.e. by being raped by the Tyrant
82 **in soul** in spirit, i.e. through death
84 **Or . . . me** or else I will never find it (i.e. peace)
90 **That . . . companion** that ever became a lover
93 **The . . . do't** The one who must endure it should not perform it.
95 **thy mind** your intention
99 **at all hazard** at any risk
101–2 **Till . . . hand** until you've persuaded me to be cruel against my nature, and then you turn my heart against my hand
105–6 **Thou'rt . . . by** You (i.e. the Lady's flesh) are always fearful of death, yet it was not for that reason that I delayed it.

Where I desire to be remembered most.
I will be ready straight, sir.
[*She kneels to pray*]
GOVIANUS O poor lady,
Why might not she expire now in that prayer,
Since she must die, and never try worse ways?
'Tis not so happy, for we often see
Condemned men sick to death, yet 'tis their fortune
To recover to their execution,
And rise again in health, to set in shame!
What if I steal a death unseen of her now,
And close up all my miseries, with mine eyes?—O fie,
And leave her here alone? That were unmanly.
LADY [*rising*]
My lord, be now as sudden as you please, sir.
I am ready to your hand.
GOVIANUS But that's not ready!
'Tis the hard'st work that ever man was put to.
I know not which way to begin to come to't.
Believe me, I shall never kill thee well;
I shall but shame myself. It were but folly,
Dear soul, to boast of more than I can perform.
I shall not have the power to do thee right in't.
Thou deserv'st death with speed, a quick dispatch,
The pain but of a twinkling, and so sleep.
If I do't, I shall make thee live too long
And so spoil all that way. I prithee excuse me.
LADY
I should not be disturbed, an you did well, sir.
I have prepared myself for rest and silence
And took my leave of words. I am like one
Removing from her house, that locks up all
And rather than she would displace her goods,
Makes shift with anything for the time she stays.
Then look not for more speech: th'extremity speaks
Enough to serve us both, had we no tongues!

Hark!
VOICES WITHIN
Lord Sophonirus?
GOVIANUS Which hand shall I take?
LADY
Art thou yet ignorant? There is no way
But through my bosom.
GOVIANUS Must I lose thee, then?
LADY
They're but thine enemies that tell thee so:
His lust may part thee from me, but death, never.
Thou canst not lose me there, for dying thine,

Where I desire to be remembered most.
I will be ready straight, sir.
[*She kneels to pray*]
GOVIANUS O poor lady,
Why might not she expire now in that prayer,
Since she must die, and never try worse ways?
'Tis not so happy, for we often see
Condemned men sick to death, yet 'tis their fortune
To recover to their execution,
And rise again in health, to set in shame!
What if I steal a death unseen of her now,
And close up all my miseries, with mine eyes?—O fie,
And leave her here alone? That were unmanly.
LADY [*rising*]
My lord, be now as sudden as you please, sir.
I am ready to your hand.
GOVIANUS But that's not ready!
'Tis the hard'st work that ever man was put to.
I know not which way to begin to come to't.
Believe me, I shall never kill thee well;
I shall but shame myself. It were but folly,
Dear soul, to boast of more than I can perform.
I shall not have the power to do thee right in't.
Thou deserv'st death with speed, a quick dispatch,
The pain but of a twinkling, and so sleep.
If I do't, I shall make thee live too long
And so spoil all that way. I prithee excuse me.
LADY
I should not be disturbed, an you did well, sir.
I have prepared myself for rest and silence
And took my leave of words. I am like one
Removing from her house, that locks up all
And rather than she would displace her goods,
Makes shift with anything for the time she stays.
Then look not for more speech: th'extremity speaks
Enough to serve us both, had we no tongues!
[*A*] *knock*[*ing within*]
Hark!
VOICES WITHIN
Lord Sophonirus?
GOVIANUS Which hand shall I take?
LADY
Art thou yet ignorant? There is no way
But through my bosom.
GOVIANUS Must I lose thee, then?
LADY
They're but thine enemies that tell thee so:
His lust may part thee from me, but death, never.
Thou canst not lose me there, for dying thine,

109 **most** i.e. in heaven

113–16 **'Tis...shame** But it won't turn out as well as that, for we often see condemned men at death's door, yet it's just their luck to get better in time for their execution, so they get up from their sick-beds only to be brought down by a shameful death. The association of the setting sun with shame is characteristic of Middleton (see *Dissemblers*, 'an ill cause...sets in shame', 2.1.17–9), as is the metaphorical use of 'set', meaning 'to go down'.

117 **What...now** Supposing I were to kill myself now, while she isn't looking? Govianus's difficulty in 'dispatching' the Lady efficiently throughout this scene seems to him 'unmanly' (l. 119), and his fear of failure carries sexual undertones: to inflict death (also, to bring to orgasm) is 'more than I can perform' (126).

137 **Makes shift with** makes do with

140 **hand** course (i.e. what should I do?)

Thou dost enjoy me still. Kings cannot rob thee.

VOICES WITHIN
Do you hear, my lord?
LADY Is it yet time or no?
Honour remember thee.
GOVIANUS I must. Come, prepare thyself!
LADY
Never more dearly welcome!
[Govianus, with his sword drawn,] runs at her and falls by the way in a swoon
Alas, sir!
My lord, my love—O thou poor-spirited man!
He's gone before me. Did I trust to thee,
And hast thou served me so? Left all the work
Upon my hand, and stole away so smoothly?
There was not equal suffering shown in this,
And yet I cannot blame thee: every man
Would seek his rest. Eternal peace sleep with thee.
[She takes up Govianus's sword]
Thou art my servant now. Come, thou hast lost
A fearful master, but art now preferred
Unto the service of a resolute lady,
One that knows how to employ thee, and scorns death
As much as great men fear it. Where's hell's ministers,
The Tyrant's watch and guard?
'Tis of much worth
When with this key the prisoner can slip forth.
[She] kills herself [by falling on the sword]
A great knocking again
GOVIANUS *[awaking from his swoon]*
How now? What noise is this? I heard doors beaten.
Where are my servants? Let men knock so loud
Their master cannot sleep?
VOICES WITHIN The time's expired,
And we'll break in, my lord.
GOVIANUS Ha! Where's my sword?
I had forgot my business! *[Seeing the Lady]* O, 'tis done,
And never was beholden to my hand.
Was I so hard to thee, so respectless of thee
To put all this to thee? Why, it was more
Than I was able to perform myself
With all the courage that I could take to me.
It tired me. I was fain to fall and rest.
And hast thou, valiant woman, overcome
Thy honour's enemies with thine own white hand,
Where virgin-victory sits, all without help?
Eternal praise go with thee!—*[Calling]* Spare not now,

Thou dost enjoy me still. Kings cannot rob thee.
[A] knock[ing within]
VOICES WITHIN
Do you hear, my lord?
LADY Is it yet time or no?
Honour remember thee.
GOVIANUS I must. Come, prepare thyself!
LADY
Never more dearly welcome!
[Govianus, with his sword drawn,] runs at her and falls by the way in a swoon
Alas, sir!
My lord, my love—O thou poor-spirited man!
He's gone before me. Did I trust to thee,
And hast thou served me so? Left all the work
Upon my hand, and stole away so smoothly?
There was not equal suffering shown in this,
And yet I cannot blame thee: every man
Would seek his rest. Eternal peace sleep with thee.
[She takes up Govianus's sword]
Thou art my servant now. Come, thou hast lost
A fearful master, but art now preferred
Unto the service of a resolute lady,
One that knows how to employ thee, and scorns death
As much as some men fear it. Where's hell's ministers,
The Tyrant's watch and guard?
[A] knock[ing within]
'Tis of much worth
When with this key the prisoner can slip forth.
[She] kills herself [by falling on the sword]
A great knocking again
GOVIANUS *[awaking from his swoon]*
How now? What noise is this? I heard doors beaten.
Where are my servants? Let men knock so loud
Their master cannot sleep?
VOICES WITHIN The time's expired,
And we'll break in, my lord.
GOVIANUS Ha! Where's my sword?
I had forgot my business! *[Seeing the Lady]* O, 'tis done,
And never was beholden to my hand.
Was I so hard to thee, so respectless of thee
To put all this to thee? Why, it was more
Than I was able to perform myself
With all the courage that I could take to me.
It tired me. I was fain to fall and rest.
And hast thou, valiant woman, overcome
Thy honour's enemies with thine own white hand,
Where virgin-victory sits, all without help?
Eternal praise go with thee!—*[Calling]* Spare not now,

148 **Honour remember thee** May Honour remind you (or else reward you, or be remembered by you).
151 **He's . . . me** He's preceded me by dying first.
153 **Upon my hand** up to me
158 **fearful** apprehensive, full of fear
preferred promoted
163 **this key** i.e. the sword (which can release the prisoner from prison, just as it releases the soul from within the body)
165 **Let** allowing (i.e. how dare they allow)
169 **beholden** indebted
170 **respectless** careless
178 **Spare not** don't hesitate

Make all the haste you can.
[He drags the body of Sophonirus across the stage]
—I'll plant this bawd
Against the door, the fittest place for him,
That when with ungoverned weapons they rush in,
Blinded with fury, they may take his death
Into the purple number of their deeds,
And wipe it off from mine.
[He sets the body against the door, calling out]
How now? Forbear,
My lord's at hand.
VOICES WITHIN My lord, and ten lords more,
I hope the king's officers are above 'em all.
[The Fellows break down the door]
GOVIANUS
Life, what do you do? Take heed—
Enter the Fellows, well weaponed, [striking and stumbling over the body of Sophonirus]
Bless the old man—
My lord?
[He examines Sophonirus]
All-ass, my lord? He's gone!
FIRST FELLOW Heart, farewell he, then.
We have no eyes to pierce thorough inch boards.
'Twas his own folly. The king must be served
And shall. The best is, we shall ne'er be hanged for't,
There's such a number guilty.
GOVIANUS Poor my lord!
He went some twice ambassador, and behaved himself
So wittily in all his actions.
SECOND FELLOW *[seeing the Lady]*
My lord, what's she?
GOVIANUS Let me see,
What should she be? Now I remember her.
O she was a worthy creature
Before destruction grew so inward with her.
FIRST FELLOW
Well, for her worthiness, that's no work of ours.
You have a lady, sir. The king commands her
To court with speed, and we must force her thither.
GOVIANUS
Alas, she'll never strive with you. She was born
E'en with the spirit of meekness.—Is't for the king?
FIRST FELLOW
For his own royal and most gracious lust,
Or let me ne'er be trusted.
GOVIANUS Take her, then.
SECOND FELLOW
Spoke like an honest subject, by my troth.

Make all the haste you can.
[He drags the body of Sophonirus across the stage]
—I'll plant this bawd
Against the door, the fittest place for him,
That when with ungoverned weapons they rush in,
Blinded with fury, they may take his death
Into the purple number of their deeds,
And wipe it off from mine.
Knocking within. [He sets the body against the door, calling out]
How now? Forbear,
My lord's at hand.
VOICES WITHIN My lord, and ten lords more,
I hope the king's officers are above 'em all.
[The Fellows break down the door]
GOVIANUS
Life, what do you do? Take heed—
Enter the Fellows, well weaponed, [striking and stumbling over the body of Sophonirus]
Bless the old man—
My lord?
[He examines Sophonirus]
All-ass, my lord? He's gone!
SECOND FELLOW Farewell he, then.
We have no eyes to pierce thorough inch boards.
'Twas his own folly. The king must be served
And shall. The best is, we shall ne'er be hanged for't,
There's such a number guilty.
FIRST FELLOW Poor my lord!
He went some twice ambassador, and behaved himself
So wittily in all his actions.
SECOND FELLOW *[seeing the Lady]*
My lord, what's she?
GOVIANUS Let me see,
What should she be? Now I remember her.
O she was a worthy creature
Before destruction grew so inward with her.
FIRST FELLOW
Well, for her worthiness, that's no work of ours.
You have a lady, sir. The king commands her
To court with speed, and we must force her thither.
GOVIANUS
Alas, she'll never strive with you. She was born
E'en with the spirit of meekness.—Is't for the king?
FIRST FELLOW
For his own royal and most gracious lust,
Or let me ne'er be trusted.
GOVIANUS Take her, then.
SECOND FELLOW
Spoke like an honest subject, by my troth.

180 **fittest place** because holding the door was the pimp's job (prostitution was 'the hold-door trade')
183 **purple** bloody
184 **Forbear** wait a moment
185–6 **My . . . all** However many lords there are, I hope the King's officers will be recognized as taking precedence over them.
188 **All-ass** i.e. Sophonirus. All-fool, also punning on 'alas'.
191 **And . . . is** And he will be served. The best (of it) is . . .
193 **some . . . ambassador** a couple of times as an ambassador
194 **wittily** wisely, punning on 'wittolly', i.e. like a cuckold
198 **inward** intimate
199 **for . . . ours** as for her worthiness, that's none of our business

I'd do the like myself to serve my prince.
Where is she, sir?
GOVIANUS [*pointing to the Lady*]
Look but upon yon face,
Then do but tell me where you think she is.
SECOND FELLOW
Life, she's not here.
GOVIANUS She's yonder.
FIRST FELLOW Faith, she's gone
Where we shall ne'er come at her, I see that.
GOVIANUS
No, nor thy master, neither. [*Aside*] Now I praise
Her resolution. 'Tis a triumph to me
When I see those about her.
SECOND FELLOW How came this, sir?
The king must know.
GOVIANUS [*pointing to Sophonirus*]
From yon old fellow's prattling:
All your intents he revealed largely to her,
And she was troubled with a foolish pride
To stand upon her honour, and so died.
'Twas a strange trick of her. Few of your ladies
In ord'nary will believe it; they abhor it.
They'll sooner kill themselves with lust, than for it.
FIRST FELLOW
We have done the king good service to kill him,
More than we were aware on. But this news
Will make a mad court. 'Twill be a hard office
To be a flatterer now. His Grace will run
Into so many moods, there'll be no finding on him:
As good seek a wild hare without a hound now.
[*To Sophonirus*] A vengeance of your babbling! [*To the others*] These old fellows
Will hearken after secrets as their lives,
But keep 'em in, e'en as they keep their wives!
ALL
We have watched fairly.
Exeunt [*with the body of Sophonirus*]. *Manet Govianus*
GOVIANUS What a comfort 'tis
To see 'em gone without her. Faith, she told me
Her everlasting sleep would bring me joy,
Yet I was still unwilling to believe her,
Her life was so sweet to me. Like some man
In time of sickness that would rather wish,
To please his fearful flesh, his former health
Restored to him than death, when after trial,
If it were possible, ten thousand worlds
Could not entice him to return again

I'd do the like myself to serve my prince.
Where is she, sir?
GOVIANUS [*pointing to the Lady*]
Look but upon yon face,
Then do but tell me where you think she is.
SECOND FELLOW
She's not here.
GOVIANUS She's yonder.
FIRST FELLOW Faith, she's gone
Where we shall ne'er come at her, I see that.
GOVIANUS
No, nor thy master, neither. [*Aside*] Now I praise
Her resolution. 'Tis a triumph to me
When I see those about her.
SECOND FELLOW How came this, sir?
The king must know.
GOVIANUS [*pointing to Sophonirus*]
From yon old fellow's prattling:
All your intents he revealed largely to her,
And she was troubled with a foolish pride
To stand upon her honour, and so died.
FIRST FELLOW
We have done the king good service to kill him,
More than we were aware on. But this news
Will make a mad court. 'Twill be a hard office
To be a flatterer now. His Grace will run
Into so many moods, there'll be no finding on him:
As good seek a wild hare without a hound now.
[*To Sophonirus*] A vengeance of your babbling! [*To the others*] These old fellows
Will hearken after secrets as their lives,
But keep 'em in, e'en as they keep their wives!
ALL
We have watched fairly.
Exeunt [*with the body of Sophonirus*]. *Manet Govianus*
GOVIANUS What a comfort 'tis
To see 'em gone without her.

210 **she's not here** she's dead (anticipating 4.4.40: and see note)
yonder in heaven
214 **those...her** fellows like those standing around her
218 **stand upon** insist upon, worry about
A219–20 **ladies | In ord'nary** i.e. ladies-in-waiting at the court, punning on 'in the ordinary way'
A221 **for it** on account of it
A226/B223 **finding on him** keeping track of him (as in hare-coursing)
A228/B225 **A vengeance of** a curse on
A230/B227 **keep...wives** i.e. they can't keep secrets, any more than they can keep their wives to themselves
A231/B228 **We...fairly** We've done our best; or perhaps ironically, we've made a fine mess of this.
A235–41 **Like...flew** (I was) like a sick man who longs to get better rather than die, but who would not want to recover, if he were once able to experience the joys of the afterlife.

And walk upon the earth from whence he flew.
So stood my wish, joyed in her life and breath;
Now gone, there is no heav'n but after death!
[He takes the Lady's body in his arms]
Come, thou delicious treasure of mankind:
To him that knows what virtuous woman is
And can discreetly love her, the whole world
Yields not a jewel like her, ransack rocks
And caves beneath the deep.—O thou fair spring
Of honest and religious desires,
Fountain of weeping honour, I will kiss thee
After death's marble lip.
[He kisses her]
Thou'rt cold enough
To lie entombed now by my father's side;
Without offence in kindred there I'll place thee
With one I loved the dearest next to thee.
Help me to mourn, all that love chastity!
Exit [carrying the body of the Lady]
Finit Actus Tertius

❁

4.1 *Incipit Actus Quartus*
Enter Votarius with Anselmus's Wife

VOTARIUS
Prithee forgive me, madam. Come, thou shalt!
WIFE
I'faith, 'twas strangely done, sir.
VOTARIUS
I confess it.
WIFE
Is that enough to help it, sir? 'Tis easy
To draw a lady's honour in suspicion,
But not so soon recovered and confirmed
To the first faith again from whence you brought it.
Your wit was fetched out about other business
Or such forgetfulness had never seized you.
VOTARIUS
'Twas but an overflowing, a spring tide
In my affection, raised by too much love,
And that's the worst words you can give it, madam.
WIFE
Jealous of me?
VOTARIUS
Life, you'd 'a' sworn yourself, madam,
Had you been in my body, and changed cases:
To see a fellow with a guilty pace
Glide through the room, his face three-quarters
nighted,
As if a deed of darkness had hung on him.

[He takes the Lady's body in his arms]
Come, thou delicious treasure of mankind:
To him that knows what virtuous woman is
And can discreetly love her, the whole world
Yields not a jewel like her, ransack rocks
And caves beneath the deep.—O thou fair spring
Of honest and religious desires,
Fountain of weeping honour, I will kiss thee
After death's marble lip.
[He kisses her]
Thou'rt cold enough
To lie entombed now by my father's side;
Without offence in kindred there I'll place thee
With one I loved the dearest next to thee.
Help me to mourn, all that love chastity!
Exit [carrying the body of the Lady]
Finit Actus Tertius

❁

Incipit Actus Quartus 4.1
Enter Votarius with Anselmus's Wife

VOTARIUS
Prithee forgive me, madam. Come, thou shalt!
WIFE
I'faith, 'twas strangely done, sir.
VOTARIUS
I confess it.
WIFE
Is that enough to help it, sir? 'Tis easy
To draw a lady's honour in suspicion,
But not so soon recovered and confirmed
To the first faith again from whence you brought it.
Your wit was fetched out about other business
Or such forgetfulness had never seized you.
VOTARIUS
'Twas but an overflowing, a spring tide
In my affection, raised by too much love,
And that's the worst words you can give it, madam.
WIFE
Jealous of me?
VOTARIUS
You'd 'a' sworn yourself, madam,
Had you been in my body, and changed cases:
To see a fellow with a guilty pace
Glide through the room, his face three-quarters
nighted,
As if a deed of darkness had hung on him.

A246/B232 **discreetly** wisely
A247/B233 **ransack** i.e. even if one were to ransack
A253/B239 **Without offence in kindred** without breaking the rules as to who may be buried in the family tomb. The Lady was betrothed, but not yet married to Govianus, so would not normally have been buried with his family.

4.1.1 **shalt** must
2 **strangely done** an unfriendly thing to do
3 **to help it** set it right
3–6 **'Tis...it** It's easy to throw suspicion upon a lady's honour, but not so easy to restore it and re-establish the original trust which you destroyed.
7 **Your...business** your mind was distracted with some other matter
9–10 **a spring...affection** a high tide in my passion (love arouses feelings as the moon draws the sea)
13 **cases** places
14 **pace** step
15 **nighted** hidden
16 **deed of darkness** secret or illicit act

WIFE
I tell you twice, 'twas my bold woman's friend.
Hell take her impudence!
VOTARIUS Why, I have done, madam.
WIFE
You've done too late, sir. Who shall do the rest now?
Confessed me yielding? Was thy way too free?
Why didst thou long to be restrained? Pray speak, sir.
VOTARIUS
A man cannot cozen you of the sin of weakness,
Or borrow it of a woman for one hour,
But how he's wondered at; where, search your lives,
We shall ne'er find it from you. We can suffer you
To play away your days in idleness
And hide your imperfections with our loves
(Or the most part of you would appear strange
creatures),
And now 'tis but our chance to make an offer
And snatch at folly, running; yet to see
How earnest y'are against us, as if we had robbed you
Of the best gift your natural mother left you.
WIFE
'Tis worth a kiss, i'faith, and thou shalt ha't,
Were there not one more left for my lord's supper.
[*She kisses him*]
And now, sir, I've bethought myself—
VOTARIUS That's happy!
WIFE
You say we're weak, but the best wits on you all
Are glad of our advice, for aught I see,
And hardly thrive without us.
VOTARIUS I'll say so too,
To give you encouragement and advance your virtues.
[*Aside*] 'Tis not good always to keep down a woman.
WIFE
Well, sir, since you've begun to make my lord
A doubtful man of me, keep on that course
And ply his faith still with that poor belief
That I'm inclining unto wantonness.
Take heed you pass no further now.
VOTARIUS Why, dost think
I'll be twice mad together in one moon?
That were too much for any freeman's son
After his father's funeral.
WIFE Well, then thus, sir:

WIFE
I tell you twice, 'twas my bold woman's friend.
Hell take her impudence!
VOTARIUS Why, I have done, madam.
WIFE
You've done too late, sir. Who shall do the rest now?
Confessed me yielding? Was thy way too free?
Why didst thou long to be restrained? Pray speak, sir.
VOTARIUS
A man cannot cozen you of the sin of weakness,
Or borrow it of a woman for one hour,
But how he's wondered at; where, search your lives,
We shall ne'er find it from you. We can suffer you
To play away your days in idleness
And hide your imperfections with our loves
(Or the most part of you would appear strange
creatures),
And now 'tis but our chance to make an offer
And snatch at folly, running; yet to see
How earnest y'are against us, as if we had robbed you
Of the best gift your natural mother left you.
WIFE
'Tis worth a kiss, i'faith, and thou shalt ha't,
Were there not one more left for my lord's supper.
[*She kisses him*]
And now, sir, I've bethought myself—
VOTARIUS That's happy!
WIFE
You say we're weak, but the best wits on you all
Are glad of our advice, for aught I see,
And hardly thrive without us.
VOTARIUS I'll say so too,
To give you encouragement and advance your virtues.
[*Aside*] 'Tis not good always to keep down a woman.
WIFE
Well, sir, since you've begun to make my lord
A doubtful man of me, keep on that course
And ply his faith still with that poor belief
That I'm inclining unto wantonness.
Take heed you pass no further now.
VOTARIUS Why, dost think
I'll be twice mad together in one moon?
That were too much for any freeman's son
After his father's funeral.
WIFE Well, then thus, sir:

17 **twice** again
18 **I have done** I've no more to say
19 **You've...late** It's a bit late for that
20 **Confessed...free** So you confessed that I gave in to you? Was the passage (also, my sexual passage) too readily available to you?
22 **cozen you of** cheat, take from all you women
24–5 **where...you** whereas, if you examine your lives, we shall never find you free of it (i.e. the sin of weakness)
29–30 **'tis...running** if it happens to be our turn to have a go, and grab at something silly, in passing
32 **natural mother** your own mother, or perhaps Mother Nature
33–4 **'Tis...supper** Your argument deserves a kiss, and you shall have it, even if there were no more left to give my lord tonight.
35 **happy** lucky
36 **the best...you** the cleverest of you
38 **hardly** scarcely
40 **keep...woman** keep a women under (both sexually and socially)
42 **A doubtful...me** suspicious of me
45 **pass** go
45–8 **Why...funeral** Do you think that I'd behave like a madman twice in a single month? That would be too much, even for a freeman's son after his father's funeral. Freemen enjoyed a certain status—the freedom of the guild, city, etc.—, and were well off, so their sons could expect to inherit wealth. Madness was connected with the lunar cycle, and attacks were expected once a month.

Upholding still the same, as being emboldened
By some loose glance of mine, you shall attempt
(After you've placed my lord in some near closet)
To thrust yourself into my chamber rudely,
As if the game went forward to your thinking;
Then leave the rest to me. I'll so reward thee
With bitterness of words (but prithee pardon 'em),
My lord shall swear me into honesty
Enough to serve his mind all his life after.
Nay, for a need, I'll draw some rapier forth
That shall come near my hand, as 'twere by chance,
And set a lively face upon my rage—
But fear thou nothing. I too dearly love thee
To let harm touch thee.

VOTARIUS O, it likes me rarely.
I'll choose a precious time for't. *Exit*

WIFE Go thy ways.
I'm glad I had it for thee.

Enter Leonella

LEONELLA
Madam, my lord entreats your company.

WIFE Say ye?

LEONELLA 'Say ye?'
My lord entreats your company.

WIFE What now?
Are ye so short-heeled?

LEONELLA I am as my betters are, then.

WIFE
How came you by such impudence alate, minion?
You're not content to entertain your playfellow
In your own chamber closely, which I think
Is large allowance for a lady's woman.
There's many a good knight's daughter is in service
And cannot get such favour of her mistress
But what she has by stealth (she and the chamber-maid
Are glad of one between 'em), and must you
Give such bold freedom to your long-nosed fellow
That every room must take a taste of him?

LEONELLA
Does that offend your ladyship?

WIFE How think you, forsooth?

LEONELLA
Then he shall do't again.

WIFE What?

Upholding still the same, as being emboldened
By some loose glance of mine, you shall attempt
(After you've placed my lord in some near closet)
To thrust yourself into my chamber rudely,
As if the game went forward to your thinking;
Then leave the rest to me. I'll so reward thee
With bitterness of words (but prithee pardon 'em),
My lord shall swear me into honesty
Enough to serve his mind all his life after.
Nay, for a need, I'll draw some rapier forth
That shall come near my hand, as 'twere by chance,
And set a lively face upon my rage—
But fear thou nothing. I too dearly love thee
To let harm touch thee.

VOTARIUS O, it likes me rarely.
I'll choose a precious time for't. *Exit*

WIFE Go thy ways.
I'm glad I had it for thee.

Enter Leonella

LEONELLA
Madam, my lord entreats your company.

WIFE Say ye?

LEONELLA 'Say ye?'
My lord entreats your company.

WIFE What now?
Are ye so short-heeled?

LEONELLA I am as my betters are, then.

WIFE
How came you by such impudence alate, minion?
You're not content to entertain your playfellow
In your own chamber closely, which I think
Is large allowance for a lady's woman.
There's many a good man's daughter is in service
And cannot get such favour of her mistress
But what she has by stealth (she and the chamber-maid
Are glad of one between 'em), and must you
Give such bold freedom to your long-nosed fellow
That every room must take a taste of him?

LEONELLA
Does that offend your ladyship?

WIFE How think you, forsooth?

LEONELLA
Then he shall do't again.

WIFE What?

50 **loose** inviting
53 **to your thinking** according to your plans
56–7 **My...after** My lord shall swear that I am faithful with such confidence that it will satisfy his doubts for the rest of his life.
58 **for a need** if necessary (i.e. to convince him)
60 **lively face** life-like, realistic appearance
62–3 **O...for't** I'm delighted with it (i.e. the Wife's scheme). I'll find the perfect moment for it.
63–4 **Go...thee** Off you go. I'm glad I thought of it for you.
66 **Say ye?** What did you say? (Leonella repeats the question, making these the first of the Wife's words to be thrown back at her.)
69 **short-heeled** sexually promiscuous, perhaps also referring to Leonella's 'shortness', her offhand brevity
70 **alate** of late, recently
minion saucy woman (implying sexual misbehaviour and social inferiority)
71–3 **You're...woman** You're not satisfied with entertaining your lover secretly in your bedroom, which I think is a great privilege for a lady's maid.
A74 **knight's daughter** Daughters of knights and gentry were often sent into service as waiting ladies in grand households, though this may be a sidelong glance at the fact that James I was criticized for giving knighthoods away too cheaply. The censor altered 'knight's' to 'men's' (ungrammatically).
78 **long-nosed** The length of the nose was supposed to indicate the length of the penis.

LEONELLA And again, madam.
So often till it please your ladyship,
And when you like it, he shall do't no more.

WIFE
What's this?

LEONELLA I know no difference, virtuous madam,
But in love all have privilege alike.

WIFE
You're a bold quean!

LEONELLA And are not you my mistress?

WIFE This' well, i'faith!

LEONELLA
You spare not your own flesh no more than I:
Hell take me an I spare you!

WIFE [*aside*] O, the wrongs
That ladies do their honours when they make
Their slaves familiar with their weaknesses.
They're ever thus rewarded for that deed,
They stand in fear e'en of the grooms they feed.
I must be forced to speak my woman fair now
And be first friends with her; nay, all too little,
She may undo me at her pleasure else.
She knows the way so well, myself not better.
My wanton folly made a key for her
To all the private treasure of my heart.
She may do what she list. [*To Leonella*] Come, Leon-
ella,
I am not angry with thee.

LEONELLA Pish!

WIFE Faith, I am not.

LEONELLA
Why, what care I an you be?

WIFE Prithee forgive me.

LEONELLA I have nothing to say to you.

WIFE
Come, thou shalt wear this jewel for my sake.
A kiss and friends; we'll never quarrel more.
[*She gives Leonella the jewel, and offers to kiss her*]

LEONELLA [*accepting the jewel but refusing the kiss*]
Nay, choose you, faith. The best is, an you do,
You know who'll have the worst on't.

WIFE [*aside*] True, myself.

LEONELLA [*aside*]
Little thinks she, I have set her forth already!
I please my lord, and keep her in awe, too.

WIFE
One thing I had forgot: I prithee, wench,
Steal to Votarius closely, and remember him

LEONELLA And again, madam.
So often till it please your ladyship,
And when you like it, he shall do't no more.

WIFE
What's this?

LEONELLA I know no difference, virtuous madam,
But in love all have privilege alike.

WIFE
You're a bold quean!

LEONELLA And are not you my mistress?

WIFE This' well, i'faith!

LEONELLA
You spare not your own flesh no more than I:
Hell take me an I spare you!

WIFE [*aside*] O, the wrongs
That ladies do their honours when they make
Their slaves familiar with their weaknesses.
They're ever thus rewarded for that deed,
They stand in fear e'en of the grooms they feed.
I must be forced to speak my woman fair now
And be first friends with her; nay, all too little,
She may undo me at her pleasure else.
She knows the way so well, myself not better.
My wanton folly made a key for her
To all the private treasure of my heart.
She may do what she list. [*To Leonella*] Come, Leon-
ella,
I am not angry with thee.

LEONELLA Pish!

WIFE Faith, I am not.

LEONELLA
Why, what care I an you be?

WIFE Prithee forgive me.

LEONELLA I have nothing to say to you.

WIFE
Come, thou shalt wear this jewel for my sake.
A kiss and friends; we'll never quarrel more.
[*She gives Leonella the jewel, and offers to kiss her*]

LEONELLA [*accepting the jewel but refusing the kiss*]
Nay, choose you, faith. The best is, an you do,
You know who'll have the worst on't.

WIFE [*aside*] True, myself.

LEONELLA [*aside*]
Little thinks she, I have set her forth already!
I please my lord, and keep her in awe, too.

WIFE
One thing I had forgot: I prithee, wench,
Steal to Votarius closely, and remember him

86 **bold quean** impudent whore
87 **This' well** This is well, or, here's a fine thing (with irony).
88–9 **You . . . you!** You don't hold back where your pleasure's concerned any more than I do. Damn me if I hold back from telling you so!
91 **slaves** servants
93 **grooms** man-servants
94 **fair** politely, nicely
95 **be first friends** first make friends with her—or, make her my closest friend
100 **what she list** as she pleases
106 **choose . . . do** Just as you please. The best of it is, that if you do (i.e. quarrel), . . .
108 **Little . . . already** She's no idea that I've already given her away.
110 **wench** term of affection for a female inferior
111–13 **closely . . . fear** secretly, and remind him to put on some hidden armour at that time, so that I can pretend to be angry with him, without hurting him

To wear some privy armour then about him,
That I may fain a fury without fear.

LEONELLA
Armour? When, madam?

WIFE
See now, I chid thee,
When I least thought upon thee. Thou'rt my best hand;
I cannot be without thee.—Thus, then, sirrah:
To beat away suspicion from the thoughts
Of ruder list'ning servants about house
I have advised Votarius at fit time
Boldly to force his way into my chamber,
The admittance being denied him, and the passage
Kept strict by thee, my necessary woman
(La, there I should ha' missed thy help again!);
At which attempt I'll take occasion
To dissemble such an anger that the world
Shall ever after swear us to their thoughts
As clear and free from any fleshly knowledge
As nearest kindred are, or ought to be,
Or what can more express it, if that failed.

LEONELLA
You know I'm always at your service, madam.
But why some privy armour?

WIFE
Marry, sweet heart,
The best is yet forgotten: thou shalt hang
A weapon in some corner of the chamber,
Yonder, or there—[*pointing around the room*]

LEONELLA
Or anywhere. Why, i'faith, madam,
Do you think I'm to learn now to hang a weapon?
[*Aside*] As much as I'm uncapable of what follows,
I've all your mind without book. [*To the Wife*] Think it done, madam.

WIFE
Thanks, my good wench—I'll never call thee worse.
Exit Wife

LEONELLA
Faith, you're like to ha't again, an you do, madam.
Enter Bellarius

BELLARIUS
What, art alone?

LEONELLA
Cuds me, what make you here, sir?
You're a bold long-nosed fellow!

BELLARIUS
How?

LEONELLA
So my lady says.
Faith, she and I have had a bout for you, sir,
But she got nothing by't.

BELLARIUS
Did not I say still,

To wear some privy armour then about him,
That I may fain a fury without fear.

LEONELLA
Armour? When, madam?

WIFE
See now, I chid thee,
When I least thought upon thee. Thou'rt my best hand;
I cannot be without thee.—Thus, then, sirrah:
To beat away suspicion from the thoughts
Of ruder list'ning servants about house
I have advised Votarius at fit time
Boldly to force his way into my chamber,
The admittance being denied him, and the passage
Kept strict by thee, my necessary woman
(La, there I should ha' missed thy help again!);
At which attempt I'll take occasion
To dissemble such an anger that the world
Shall ever after swear us to their thoughts
As clear and free from any fleshly knowledge
As nearest kindred are, or ought to be,
Or what can more express it, if that failed.

LEONELLA
You know I'm always at your service, madam.
But why some privy armour?

WIFE
Marry, sweet heart,
The best is yet forgotten: thou shalt hang
A weapon in some corner of the chamber,
Yonder, or there—[*pointing around the room*]

LEONELLA
Or anywhere. Why, i'faith, madam,
Do you think I'm to learn now to hang a weapon?
[*Aside*] As much as I'm uncapable of what follows,
I've all your mind without book. [*To the Wife*] Think it done, madam.

WIFE
Thanks, my good wench—I'll never call thee worse.
Exit Wife

LEONELLA
Faith, you're like to ha't again, an you do, madam.
Enter Bellarius

BELLARIUS
What, art alone?

LEONELLA
Cuds me, what make you here, sir?
You're a bold long-nosed fellow!

BELLARIUS
How?

LEONELLA
So my lady says.
Faith, she and I have had a bout for you, sir,
But she got nothing by't.

BELLARIUS
Did not I say still,

114 **chid** scolded

115–18 **Thou'rt . . . house** You're my most valued helper; I can't manage without you. Now, this is how it is, girl: to drive out suspicion from the minds of the lower servants around the house, . . .

121–2 **the . . . woman** the entrance carefully guarded by you, my woman, so essential to my plans (De Flores is 'a wondrous necessary man' to Beatrice in *Changeling*, 5.1.92)

125 **dissemble** put on, pretend

127–9 **As . . . failed** as innocent of any sexual contact as the closest relatives are—or ought to be—or whatever comparison can put it more forcibly, if that one failed to

135–7 **Do . . . book** Do you think I need to learn how to handle a weapon (sword, penis), then? Just as I don't know what to do after that, and I don't understand what you're up to as well as if I'd learned it by heart ('without book')?

139 **to . . . do** to get it back again, if you do

140 **Cuds . . . sir?** Good God, what are you doing here, sir?

142 **had a bout** had a quarrel (a round in a fencing match)

Thou wouldst be too adventurous?
LEONELLA Ne'er a whit, sir!
I made her glad to seek my friendship first.
BELLARIUS
By my faith, that showed well: if you come off
So brave a conqueress, to't again and spare not.
I know not which way you should get more honour.
LEONELLA
She trusts me now to cast a mist, forsooth,
Before the servants' eyes. I must remember
Votarius to come once with privy armour
Into her chamber, when with a feigned fury
And rapier drawn (which I must lay o' purpose
Ready for her dissemblance), she will seem
T'act wonders for her juggling honesty.
BELLARIUS
I wish no riper vengeance! Canst conceive me?
Votarius is my enemy.
LEONELLA That's stale news, sir.
BELLARIUS
Mark what I say to thee: forget of purpose
That privy armour. Do not bless his soul
With so much warning, nor his hated body
With such sure safety. Here express thy love:
Lay some empoisoned weapon next her hand
That in that play he may be lost for ever.
I'd have him kept no longer. Away with him!
One touch will set him flying—let him go.
LEONELLA
Bribe me but with a kiss, it shall be so!
[*They kiss;*] *exeunt*

4.2 *Enter Tyrant, wondrous discontentedly;* [*Memphonius, and*] *Nobles afar off*

FIRST NOBLE
My lord.
TYRANT Begone, or never see life more.
I'll send thee far enough from court!
[*Exit First Noble*]
Memphonius!
Where's he, now?
MEMPHONIUS Ever at your highness' service.
TYRANT
How dar'st thou be so near, when we have threatened
Death to thy fellow? Have we lost our power?
Or thou thy fear? Leave us, in time of grace.
'Twill be too late anon.
MEMPHONIUS [*aside, going*]
I think 'tis so
With thee already.
TYRANT Dead! And I so healthful?

Thou wouldst be too adventurous?
LEONELLA Ne'er a whit, sir!
I made her glad to seek my friendship first.
BELLARIUS
By my faith, that showed well: if you come off
So brave a conqueress, to't again and spare not.
I know not which way you should get more honour.
LEONELLA
She trusts me now to cast a mist, forsooth,
Before the servants' eyes. I must remember
Votarius to come once with privy armour
Into her chamber, when with a feigned fury
And rapier drawn (which I must lay o' purpose
Ready for her dissemblance), she will seem
T'act wonders for her juggling honesty.
BELLARIUS
I wish no riper vengeance! Canst conceive me?
Votarius is my enemy.
LEONELLA That's stale news, sir.
BELLARIUS
Mark what I say to thee: forget of purpose
That privy armour. Do not bless his soul
With so much warning, nor his hated body
With such sure safety. Here express thy love:
Lay some empoisoned weapon next her hand
That in that play he may be lost for ever.
I'd have him kept no longer. Away with him!
One touch will set him flying—let him go.
LEONELLA
Bribe me but with a kiss, it shall be so!
[*They kiss;*] *exeunt*

Enter Tyrant, wondrous discontentedly; [*Memphonius, and*] *Nobles afar off* 4.2

FIRST NOBLE
My lord.
TYRANT Begone, or never see life more.
I'll send thee far enough from court!
[*Exit First Noble*]
Memphonius!
Where's he, now?
MEMPHONIUS Ever at your highness' service.
TYRANT
How dar'st thou be so near, when we have threatened
Death to thy fellow? Have we lost our power?
Or thou thy fear? Leave us, in time of grace.
'Twill be too late anon.
MEMPHONIUS [*aside, going*]
I think 'tis so
With thee already.
TYRANT Dead! And I so healthful?

146–8 **that...honour** that was impressive. If you come out of it so triumphantly, have another go, and don't hold back. I can't think of any way you could gain more respect.
154–5 **she...honesty** she will look as if she is working wonders for her dubious chastity
156 **Canst conceive me?** Do you follow me?
157 **stale** old
158 **of** on
161 **Here...love** Show your love for me in (doing) this.
162 **next** near, close to
163 **That...ever** so that in that game (swordplay, play-acting) he will die and be damned eternally
4.2.6–7 **in...anon** while you still can. Soon it will be too late.

There's no equality in this.—Stay!
MEMPHONIUS Sir?
TYRANT
Where is that fellow brought the first report to us?
MEMPHONIUS
He waits without.
TYRANT I charge thee, give command
That he be executed speedily,
As thou'd stand firm thyself.
MEMPHONIUS [*aside*] Now, by my faith,
His tongue has helped his neck to a sweet bargain.
Exit
TYRANT
Her own fair hand so cruel? Did she choose
Destruction before me? Was I no better?
How much am I exalted to my face,
And where I would be graced, how little worthy!
There's few kings know how rich they are in goodness
Or what estate they have in grace and virtue;
There is so much deceit in glozers' tongues,
The truth is taken from us. We know nothing
But what is for their purpose: that's our stint;
We are allowed no more. O wretched greatness!
I'll cause a sessions for my flatterers,
And have 'em all hanged up.—'Tis done too late.
O, she's destroyed, married to death and silence,
Which nothing can divorce—riches, nor laws
Nor all the violence that this frame can raise.
I've lost the comfort of her sight for ever.
I cannot call this life that flames within me,
But everlasting torment, lighted up
To show my soul her beggary!—A new joy
Is come to visit me, in spite of death.
It takes me, of that sudden. I'm ashamed
Of my provision, but a friend will bear.
[*Calling*] Within, there!
Enter [*three*] *soldier*[*s*]
FIRST SOLDIER Sir!
SECOND SOLDIER My lord!
TYRANT The men I wished for,
For secrecy and employment.—

There's no equality in this.—Stay!
MEMPHONIUS Sir?
TYRANT
Where is that fellow brought the first report to us?
MEMPHONIUS
He waits without.
TYRANT I charge thee, give command
That he be executed speedily,
As thou'd stand firm thyself.
MEMPHONIUS [*aside*] Now, by my faith,
His tongue has helped his neck to a sweet bargain.
Exit
TYRANT
Her own fair hand so cruel? Did she choose
Destruction before me? Was I no better?
How much am I exalted to my face,
And where I would be graced, how little worthy!
There's few kings know how rich they are in goodness
Or what estate they have in grace and virtue;
There is so much deceit in glozers' tongues,
The truth is taken from us. We know nothing
But what is for their purpose: that's our stint;
We are allowed no more. O wretched greatness!
I'll cause a sessions for my flatterers,
And have 'em all hanged up.—'Tis done too late.
O, she's destroyed, married to death and silence,
Which nothing can divorce—riches, nor laws
Nor all the violence that this frame can raise.
I've lost the comfort of her sight for ever.
I cannot call this life that flames within me,
But everlasting torment, lighted up
To show my soul her beggary!—A new joy
Is come to visit me, in spite of death.
It takes me, of that sudden. I'm ashamed
Of my provision, but a friend will bear.
[*Calling*] Within, there!
Enter [*four*] *soldiers*
FIRST SOLDIER Sir!
SECOND SOLDIER My lord!
TYRANT The men I wished for,
For secrecy and employment. [*To Fourth Soldier*] Go, give order
That Govianus be released.
FOURTH SOLDIER Released, sir?
TYRANT
Set free! And then I trust he will fly the kingdom
And never know my purpose. [*Exit Fourth Soldier*]

13 **As . . . thyself** if you wish to remain safe yourself
14 **sweet bargain** an attractive deal (ironic)
18 **would be graced** want to be thought well of
19–20 **how . . . virtue** how many good qualities they possess, or what their position is in terms of grace and virtue (the Tyrant regrets that no one dares speak truthfully to kings)
21 **glozers'** flatterers'
23 **But . . . stint** but whatever suits their purpose: that's all we're allowed
25 **sessions** trial, assize
29 **this frame** the world (as at A1.1.126/ B1.1.107)
35 **of that sudden** so suddenly
36 **Of . . . bear** of being so unprepared (for this new idea), but a friend will be understanding
38 **For . . . employment** In the passage added at this point, the Tyrant orders Govianus's release, in order to prevent his darker plans from being interrupted, though in fact it also enables Govianus to visit the Cathedral at 4.4.

[*To First Soldier*] Run, Afranius,
Bring me the keys of the Cathedral straight.

FIRST SOLDIER [*aside*]
Are you so holy now? Do you curse all day
And go to pray at midnight? *Exit*

TYRANT
Provide you, sirs, close lanterns and a pickaxe.
Away, be speedy!

SECOND SOLDIER [*aside*]
Lanterns and a pickaxe?
Life, does he mean to bury himself alive, trow?
[*Exeunt Second and Third Soldiers*]

TYRANT
Death nor the marble prison my love sleeps in
Shall keep her body locked up from mine arms.
I must not be so cozened. Though her life
Was like a widow's state made o'er in policy
To defeat me and my too confident heart,
'Twas a most cruel wisdom to herself,
As much to me that lov'd her.
Enter First Soldier, [*with keys*]
What, returned?

FIRST SOLDIER
Here be the keys, my lord.

TYRANT
I thank thy speed.
[*Enter Second and Third Soldiers, with lanterns and pickaxe*]
Here comes the rest, full furnished. Follow me
And wealth shall follow you. *Exit*

FIRST SOLDIER
Wealth! By this light,
We go to rob a church! I hold my life
The money will ne'er thrive. That's a sure saw,
'What's got from grace, is ever spent in law'.
Exeunt

[*To First Soldier*] Run, sir, you,
Bring me the keys of the Cathedral.

FIRST SOLDIER [*aside*]
Are you so holy now? Do you curse all day
And go to pray at midnight? *Exit*

TYRANT
Provide you, sirs, close lanterns and a pickaxe.
Away, be speedy!

SECOND SOLDIER [*aside*]
Lanterns and a pickaxe?
Does he mean to bury himself alive, trow?
[*Exeunt Second and Third Soldiers*]

TYRANT
Death nor the marble prison my love sleeps in
Shall keep her body locked up from mine arms.
I must not be so cozened. Though her life
Was like a widow's state made o'er in policy
To defeat me and my too confident heart,
'Twas a most cruel wisdom to herself,
As much to me that lov'd her.
Enter First Soldier, [*with keys*]
What, returned?

FIRST SOLDIER
Here be the keys, my lord.

TYRANT
I thank thy speed.
[*Enter Second and Third Soldiers, with lanterns and pickaxe*]
Here comes the rest, full furnished. Follow me
And wealth shall follow you. *Exit*

FIRST SOLDIER
Wealth! By this light,
We go to rob a church! I hold my life
The money will ne'er thrive. That's a sure saw,
'What's got from grace, is ever spent in law'.
Exeunt

Enter Mr Gough [*as Memphonius*] **4.2a**

[MEMPHONIUS]
What strange fits grow upon him! Here alate
His soul has got a very dreadful leader.
What should he make in the Cathedral now,

A38 **Run, Afranius** the name of the first soldier, only given in the original version, was taken from John Fletcher's recent *Tragedy of Valentinian*, where he is a captain loyal to the Emperor, and appears in 5.4 and 5.8.

A42/B45 **close lanterns** dark, i.e. shuttered lanterns

A44/B47 **trow** trow ye, i.e. do you think? or, I wonder?

A47/B50 **so cozened** so cheated (of her)

A47–9/B50–2 **Though...me** She gave up her life, like a widow who deliberately puts her (e)state in trust (i.e. in order to prevent it from falling into the hands of her second husband), to frustrate my plans.

A55–7/B58–60 **I hold...law** I'll wager my life that this money will come to no good. It's a sure saying, ill-gotten gains are always paid out in legal costs.

B4.2a This additional passage was partly inserted to avoid the Tyrant and his soldiers leaving the stage and immediately re-entering at a different location (at 4.3.0.1–2). The speaker's name appears in the margin as Mr Gough, an actor for the King's Men, and the speech was almost certainly spoken by Memphonius. It enlarges upon the Tyrant's mental breakdown and announces the conspiracy to release Helvetius, who was originally intended to reappear in the last scene, though at a later stage his part in it was cut altogether (see Introduction, 834).

B1 **alate** of late, recently

B2 **a very dreadful leader** i.e. the devil

B3 **make** do

B6–8 **He...long** He grows to be a weight upon his Nobles' minds; his moods are so difficult that they cannot put up with them, and are not prepared to do so much longer,

B9 **father of the state** the most senior and respected member of government

B11 **close policy** secret stratagem

4.3 *Enter the Tyrant again [followed by the soldiers] at a further door, which opened, brings him to the tomb where the Lady lies buried. The tomb here discovered, richly set forth*

TYRANT Softly, softly!
Let's give this place the peace that it requires.
The vaults e'en chide our steps with murmuring sounds
For making bold so late.—It must be done.

FIRST SOLDIER [*aside*] I fear nothing but the whorish ghost of a quean I kept once. She swore she would so haunt me I should never pray in quiet for her, and I have kept myself from church this fifteen year to prevent her.

TYRANT
The monument woos me; I must run and kiss it.
Now trust me if the tears do not e'en stand
Upon the marble. What slow springs have I?
'Twas weeping to itself before I came.
How pity strikes e'en through insensible things
And makes them shame our dullness.
Thou house of silence, and the calms of rest
After tempestuous life, I claim of thee
A mistress, one of the most beauteous sleepers
That ever lay so cold, not yet due to thee
By natural death, but cruelly forced hither
Many a year before the world could spare her.
We miss her 'mongst the glories of our court,
When they be numbered up. All thy still strength,
Thou grey-eyed monument, shall not keep her from us.
[*To Second Soldier*] Strike, villain, though the echo rail us all
Into ridiculous deafness. Pierce the jaws
Of this cold ponderous creature.

SECOND SOLDIER Sir!

TYRANT Why strik'st thou not?

SECOND SOLDIER
I shall not hold the axe fast; I'm afraid, sir.

The hour so deep in night? All his intents
Are contrary to man, in spirit or blood.
He waxes heavy in his Nobles' minds,
His moods are such, they cannot bear the weight,
Nor will not long, if there be truth in whispers!
The honourable father of the state,
Noble Helvetius, all the lords agree
By some close policy shortly to set free. [*Exit*]

4.3 *Enter the Tyrant again [followed by the soldiers] at a further door, which opened, brings him to the tomb where the Lady lies buried. The tomb here discovered, richly set forth*

TYRANT Softly, softly!
Let's give this place the peace that it requires.
The vaults e'en chide our steps with murmuring sounds
For making bold so late.—It must be done.

FIRST SOLDIER [*aside*] I fear nothing but the whorish ghost of a quean I kept once. She swore she would so haunt me I should never pray in quiet for her, and I have kept myself from church this fifteen year to prevent her.

TYRANT
The monument woos me; I must run and kiss it.
Now trust me if the tears do not e'en stand
Upon the marble. What slow springs have I?
'Twas weeping to itself before I came.
How pity strikes e'en through insensible things
And makes them shame our dullness.
Thou house of silence, and the calms of rest
After tempestuous life, I claim of thee
A mistress, one of the most beauteous sleepers
That ever lay so cold, not yet due to thee
By natural death, but cruelly forced hither
Many a year before the world could spare her.
We miss her 'mongst the glories of our court,
When they be numbered up. All thy still strength,
Thou grey-eyed monument, shall not keep her from us.
[*To Second Soldier*] Strike, villain, though the echo rail us all
Into ridiculous deafness. Pierce the jaws
Of this cold ponderous creature.

SECOND SOLDIER Sir!

TYRANT Why strik'st thou not?

SECOND SOLDIER
I shall not hold the axe fast; I'm afraid, sir.

4.3.0.3–4 ***here discovered*** i.e. revealed, probably by the drawing back of a curtain across the 'discovery space' at the back of the stage. The tomb remains on stage for this scene and the next, when the curtain would be redrawn.

3 **The vaults** the vaulting is probably that of the Cathedral itself. Jacobean tombs were often 'richly set forth', i.e. elaborately sculptured, with effigies of those buried within, and set along the aisle or in side chapels. The soldiers' sense of being in church suggests that this scene takes place in the Cathedral itself, rather than in the crypt beneath (which would also have been vaulted).

6 **quean** whore, as at 4.1.86

7 **for her** because of her

9–11 **The ... marble** The Tyrant's desire to run and kiss the monument suggests that it includes an effigy of the Lady which seems to be weeping. By contrast, the Tyrant's eyes are 'slow springs', i.e. slow to respond.

23 **grey-eyed** perhaps because stone-coloured (but grey eyes have been admired since the ancient Greeks)

24 **rail** scold, cry out against

TYRANT
O shame of men! A soldier and so limber?
SECOND SOLDIER
'Tis out of my element to be in a church, sir.
Give me the open field and turn me loose, sir.
TYRANT
True, there thou hast room enough to run away.
[*To First Soldier*] Take thou the axe from him.
FIRST SOLDIER I beseech your grace,
'Twill come to a worse hand. You'll find us all
Of one mind for the church, I can assure you, sir.
TYRANT [*to Third Soldier*]
Nor thou?
THIRD SOLDIER
I love not to disquiet ghosts
Of any people living, that's my humour, sir!
TYRANT
O slaves of one opinion!
[*He takes the axe from Second Soldier*]
Give me't from thee,
Thou man made out of [ ]
SECOND SOLDIER [*aside*] By my faith,
I'm glad I'm rid on't.—
I that was ne'er before in a Cathedral
And have the batt'ring of a lady's tomb
Lie hard upon my conscience at first coming,
I should get much by that! It shall be a warning to
me.
I'll ne'er come here again.
TYRANT [*striking at the tomb*]
No, wilt not yield?
Art thou so loath to part from her?
FIRST SOLDIER [*aside*] Life, what means he?
Has he no feeling with him? By this light, if I be not afraid to stay any longer, I'm a stone-cutter! Very fear will go nigh to turn me of some religion or other, and so make me forfeit my lieutenantship.
TYRANT [*loosening the stone*]
O, have we got the mastery? Help, you vassals!
Freeze you in idleness and can see us sweat?
SECOND SOLDIER
We sweat with fear as much as work can make us.
TYRANT
Remove the stone that I may see my mistress.
Set to your hands, you villains, and that nimbly,
Or the same axe shall make you all fly open!
ALL
O good my lord!
TYRANT I must not be delayed!

TYRANT
O shame of men! A soldier and so fearful?
SECOND SOLDIER
'Tis out of my element to be in a church, sir.
Give me the open field and turn me loose, sir.
TYRANT
True, there thou hast room enough to run away.
[*To First Soldier*] Take thou the axe from him.
FIRST SOLDIER I beseech your grace,
'Twill come to a worse hand. You'll find us all
Of one mind for the church, I can assure you, sir.
TYRANT [*to Third Soldier*]
Nor thou?
THIRD SOLDIER
I love not to disquiet ghosts
Of any people living.
TYRANT
O slaves of one opinion!
[*He takes the axe from Second Soldier*]
Give me't from thee,
Thou man made out of fear!
SECOND SOLDIER [*aside*] By my faith,
I'm glad I'm rid on't.—
I that was ne'er before in a Cathedral
And have the batt'ring of a lady's tomb
Lie hard upon my conscience at first coming,
I should get much by that! It shall be a warning to
me.
I'll ne'er come here again.
TYRANT [*striking at the tomb*]
No, wilt not yield?
Art thou so loath to part from her?
FIRST SOLDIER [*aside*] What means he?
Has he no feeling with him? By this light, if I be not afraid to stay any longer, I'm a villain! Very fear will go nigh to turn me of some religion or other, and so make me forfeit my lieutenantship.
TYRANT [*loosening the stone*]
O, have we got the mastery? Help, you vassals!
Freeze you in idleness and can see us sweat?
SECOND SOLDIER
We sweat with fear as much as work can make us.
TYRANT
Remove the stone that I may see my mistress.
Set to your hands, you villains, and that nimbly,
Or the same axe shall make you all fly open!
ALL
O good my lord!
TYRANT I must not be delayed!

A28 **limber** limp, feeble
B28 **fearful** 'Fie, my lord, fie—a soldier and afeared?' *Macbeth*, 5.1.34–5.
29 **out of my element** not natural to me
34 **for** with regard to
35–6 **I ... living** i.e. ghosts are the last people alive that I'd want to disturb.
A36 **that's my humour** that's the way I am (a popular catch-phrase of the day)
43 **I ... that** I should gain a great deal from that (ironic).
46 **with him** in him
A47 **stone-cutter** ironic, since the first soldier's reluctance to break into the tomb prevents him from becoming a stone-cutter, in the sense of a mason (it can also mean a surgeon who removes internal stones or cuts off 'stones', i.e. testicles)
47–9 **Very ... lieutenantship** Fear itself will almost convert me to some religion or other, and so force me to give up my lieutenancy (soldiers were often thought of as irreligious).
50 **vassals** slaves

FIRST SOLDIER This is ten thousand times worse than ent'ring upon a breach!
'Tis the first stone that ever I took off
From any lady. Marry, I have brought 'em many,
Fair diamonds, sapphires, rubies.
[*They remove the stone from the tomb*]
TYRANT [*gazing into the opened tomb*]
O, blest object!
I never shall be weary to behold thee.
I could eternally stand thus and see thee.
Why, 'tis not possible death should look so fair;
Life is not more illustrious when health smiles on't.
She's only pale, the colour of the court,
And most attractive. Mistresses most strive for't
And their lascivious servants best affect it.
[*To Soldiers*] Where be these lazy hands again?
ALL My lord!
TYRANT
Take up her body.
FIRST SOLDIER How, my lord?
TYRANT Her body!
FIRST SOLDIER
She's dead, my lord!
TYRANT True, if she were alive
Such slaves as you should not come near to touch her.
Do't, and with all best reverence place her here.
FIRST SOLDIER
Not only, sir, with reverence, but with fear.
You shall have more than your own asking once.
I am afraid of nothing but she'll rise
At the first jog, and save us all a labour.
SECOND SOLDIER
Then we were best take her up and never touch her?
FIRST SOLDIER
Life, how can that be? Does fear make thee mad?
I've took up many a woman in my days,
But never with less pleasure, I protest!
[*The soldiers lift the Lady's body out of the tomb*]
TYRANT
O, the moon rises! What reflection
Is thrown about this sanctifièd building,
E'en in a twinkling! How the monuments glister,
As if death's palaces were all massy silver
And scorned the name of marble!

FIRST SOLDIER This is ten thousand times worse than ent'ring upon a breach!
'Tis the first stone that ever I took off
From any lady. Marry, I have brought 'em many,
Fair diamonds, sapphires, rubies.
[*They remove the stone from the tomb*]
TYRANT [*gazing into the opened tomb*]
O, blest object!
I never shall be weary to behold thee.
I could eternally stand thus and see thee.
Why, 'tis not possible death should look so fair;
Life is not more illustrious when health smiles on't.
She's only pale, the colour of the court,
And most attractive. Mistresses most strive for't
And their lascivious servants best affect it.
[*To Soldiers*] Lay to your hands again!
ALL My lord!
TYRANT
Take up her body.
FIRST SOLDIER How, my lord?
TYRANT Her body!
FIRST SOLDIER
She's dead, my lord!
TYRANT True, if she were alive
Such slaves as you should not come near to touch her.
Do't, and with all best reverence place her here.
FIRST SOLDIER
Not only, sir, with reverence, but with fear.
You shall have more than your own asking once.
I am afraid of nothing but she'll rise
At the first jog, and save us all a labour.
SECOND SOLDIER
Then we were best take her up and never touch her?
FIRST SOLDIER
How can that be? Does fear make thee mad?
I've took up many a woman in my days,
But never with less pleasure, I protest!
[*The soldiers lift the Lady's body out of the tomb*]
TYRANT
O, the moon rises! What reflection
Is thrown about this sanctifièd building,
E'en in a twinkling! How the monuments glister,
As if death's palaces were all massy silver
And scorned the name of marble!

58 **ent'ring upon a breach** making an attack through a gap blown in fortifications during a siege (also sexual penetration)

59–61 **'Tis . . . rubies** The first soldier continues punning on 'stones', first as testicles (you couldn't take those off a woman), then as gemstones. It is not clear from the text whether the stone removed from the tomb is a side panel, or forms the lid (as ll. 131–2 suggest, though this might be awkward if the tomb had an effigy on top).

66 **pale** a fair (i.e. not sunburned) complexion was considered desirable at this period

68 **best affect it** imitate it, or aim for it most

70 **Take up** The Tyrant's order, that the soldiers 'take up' (i.e. lift up) the Lady's body, has a secondary sexual meaning, of the taking up of clothes before lovemaking, or simply the act itself, as does 'touch' at l. 72, which also means to make sexual contact. The soldiers play on these different senses in ll. 78, 80.

How, my lord What do you mean, my lord?

75 **You . . . once** You'll get more than you bargained for.

82 **the moon rises** i.e. her body is lifted from the tomb (a dummy may have been used for this—see note at 5.2.13.1)

86–7 **cold? . . . yet** Dead (or, sexually unresponsive)? I still can't believe it.

[*He receives the Lady's body from them*]
Art thou cold?
I have no faith in't yet; I believe none.
Madam! 'Tis I, sweet lady, prithee speak!
'Tis thy love calls on thee, the king thy servant.
No, not a word? All prisoners to pale silence?
I'll prove a kiss.
[*He kisses the body*]

FIRST SOLDIER [*aside*]
Here's fine chill venery!
'Twould make a pander's heels ache! I'll be sworn
All my teeth chatter in my head to see't.

TYRANT
By th' mass, thou'rt cold indeed; beshrew thee for't!
Unkind to thine own blood? Hard-hearted lady,
What injury hast thou offered to the youth
And pleasure of thy days! Refuse the court,
And steal to this hard lodging, was that wisdom?
O I could chide thee with mine eye brim-full,
And weep out my forgiveness when I ha' done.
Nothing hurt thee but want of woman's counsel:
Hadst thou but asked th'opinion of most ladies,
Thou'dst never come to this! They would have told thee
How dear a treasure life and youth had been:
'Tis that they fear to lose; the very name
Can make more gaudy tremblers in a minute
Than heaven, or sin, or hell—those are last thought on.
And where got'st thou such boldness from the rest
Of all thy timorous sex, to do a deed here
Upon thyself, would plunge the world's best soldier,
And make him twice bethink him, and again,
And yet give over? Since thy life has left me,
I'll clasp the body for the spirit that dwelt in't,
And love the house still for the mistress' sake.
Thou art mine now, 'spite of destruction
And Govianus; and I will possess thee.
I once read of a Herod whose affection
Pursued a virgin's love, as I did thine,
Who for the hate she owed him killed herself
(As thou too rashly didst) without all pity;
Yet he preserved her body dead in honey
And kept her long after her funeral.
But I'll unlock the treasure house of art
With keys of gold and bestow all on thee.
[*To the soldiers*] Here, slaves, receive her humbly from our arms;

[*He receives the Lady's body from them*]
Art thou cold?
I have no faith in't yet; I believe none.
Madam! 'Tis I, sweet lady, prithee speak!
'Tis thy love calls on thee, the king thy servant.
No, not a word? All prisoners to pale silence?
I'll prove a kiss.
[*He kisses the body*]

FIRST SOLDIER [*aside*]
Here's fine chill venery!
'Twould make a pander's heels ache! I'll be sworn
All my teeth chatter in my head to see't.

TYRANT
Thou'rt cold indeed; beshrew thee for't!
Unkind to thine own blood? Hard-hearted lady,
What injury hast thou offered to the youth
And pleasure of thy days! Refuse the court,
And steal to this hard lodging, was that wisdom?
O I could chide thee with mine eye brim-full,
And weep out my forgiveness when I ha' done.
Nothing hurt thee but want of woman's counsel:
Hadst thou but asked th'opinion of many ladies,
Thou'dst never come to this! They would have told thee
How dear a treasure life and youth had been:
'Tis that they fear to lose; the very name
Can make more gaudy tremblers in a minute
Than heaven, or sin, or hell—those are last thought on.
And where got'st thou such boldness from the rest
Of all thy timorous sex, to do a deed here
Upon thyself, would plunge the world's best soldier,
And make him twice bethink him, and again,
And yet give over? Since thy life has left me,
I'll clasp the body for the spirit that dwelt in't,
And love the house still for the mistress' sake.
Thou art mine now, 'spite of destruction
And Govianus; and I will possess thee.
I once read of a Herod whose affection
Pursued a virgin's love, as I did thine,
Who for the hate she owed him killed herself
(As thou too rashly didst) without all pity;
Yet he preserved her body dead in honey
And kept her long after her funeral.
But I'll unlock the treasure house of art
With keys of gold and bestow all on thee.
[*To the soldiers*] Here, slaves, receive her humbly from our arms;

90 **prisoners** i.e. her words are imprisoned within her by her death
91 **prove** try
91–2 **chill...ache** lovemaking so cold that it would make even a pimp's heels ache (pimps were supposed to 'cool their heels', while they waited for their clients)
94 **beshrew thee** curse you
105–7 **the...hell** the mere mention (of losing life and youth) can make more revellers tremble in a moment than can heaven or sin or hell
108 **from** unlike
110 **plunge** overwhelm
112 **yet give over** eventually give up
114 **house** i.e. body (as in *Roaring Girl*, 5.140–1): the body as the (now empty) house of the soul echoes the Tyrant's violation of the tomb, the (now empty) house of the body
117–22 **read...funeral** the full horror of the Tyrant's plan is finally revealed, through the legend of Herod's preservation of Mariamne's body—according to some versions, in order to have sex with it—as related in the *Works of Josephus* (trans. Thomas Lodge, 1602) and elsewhere

Upon your knees, you villains! All's too little,
If you should sweep the pavement with your lips.

FIRST SOLDIER [*aside*]
What strange brooms he invents!
[Soldiers kneel and take the body from the Tyrant]

TYRANT
So, reverently,
Bear her before us gently to our palace.
Place you the stone again where first we found it.
Exeunt [Second and Third Soldiers carrying the body]. Manet First Soldier

FIRST SOLDIER
Life, must this on now to deceive all comers
And cover emptiness?
[He replaces the tombstone]
'Tis for all the world
Like a great city-pie brought to a table
Where there be many hands that lay about.
The lid's shut close, when all the meat's picked out,
Yet stands to make a show and cozen people. *Exit*

4.4

Enter Govianus in black, a book in his hand, his page carrying a torch before him

GOVIANUS
Already mine eye melts. The monument
No sooner stood before it, but a tear
Ran swiftly from me, to express her duty.
Temple of honour, I salute thee early,
The time that my griefs rise. Chamber of peace,
Where wounded virtue sleeps, locked from the world,
I bring to be acquainted with thy silence
Sorrows that love no noise: they dwell all inward,
Where truth and love in every man should dwell.
[*To the page*] Be ready, boy; give me the strain again.
'Twill show well here, whilst in my grief's devotion
At every rest mine eye lets fall a bead
To keep the number perfect.
Govianus kneels at the tomb wondrous passionately. His page sings.
The song:
If ever pity were well placed
On true desert and virtuous honour,
It could ne'er be better graced;
Freely, then, bestow't upon her.

Never lady earned her fame
In virtue's war with greater strife.
To preserve her constant name
She gave up beauty, youth and life.
There she sleeps,

Upon your knees, you villains! All's too little,
If you should sweep the pavement with your lips.

FIRST SOLDIER [*aside*]
What strange brooms he invents!
[Soldiers kneel and take the body from the Tyrant]

TYRANT
So, reverently,
Bear her before us gently to our palace.
Place you the stone again where first we found it.
Exeunt [Second and Third Soldiers carrying the body]. Manet First Soldier

FIRST SOLDIER
Must this on now to deceive all comers
And cover emptiness?
[He replaces the tombstone]
'Tis for all the world
Like a great city-pie brought to a table
Where there be many hands that lay about.
The lid's shut close, when all the meat's picked out,
Yet stands to make a show and cozen people. *Exit*

4.4

Enter Govianus in black, a book in his hand, his page carrying a torch before him

GOVIANUS
Already mine eye melts. The monument
No sooner stood before it, but a tear
Ran swiftly from me, to express her duty.
Temple of honour, I salute thee early,
The time that my griefs rise. Chamber of peace,
Where wounded virtue sleeps, locked from the world,
I bring to be acquainted with thy silence
Sorrows that love no noise: they dwell all inward,
Where truth and love in every man should dwell.
[*To the page*] Be ready, boy; give me the strain again.
'Twill show well here, whilst in my grief's devotion
At every rest mine eye lets fall a bead
To keep the number perfect.
Govianus kneels at the tomb wondrous passionately. His page sings.
The song:
If ever pity were well placed
On true desert and virtuous honour,
It could ne'er be better graced;
Freely, then, bestow't upon her.

Never lady earned her fame
In virtue's war with greater strife.
To preserve her constant name
She gave up beauty, youth and life.
There she sleeps,

126–7 **All's . . . lips** Your reverence for her would be inadequate, even if you were to bow so low that you brushed the paving with your lips.

131 **this on** this (i.e. the stone) be put back on (the tomb)

133 **city-pie** pie made for the Lord Mayor's or Aldermen's feasts in the City of London. Sometimes elaborate pie-crusts were put back on the dishes after they had been emptied. The pie crust or lid was also known as the coffin.

134 **lay about** grab what they can

4.4.1–5 **Already . . . rise** Unlike the Tyrant, Govianus weeps at once. It is now early morning ('the time that my griefs rise'). The play's action takes place over twenty-four hours, although the movement of time is telescoped to create a sense of continuous action.

3 **her duty** i.e. my duty to her

10–13 **give . . . perfect** a strain is a musical passage (as in *Twelfth Night*, 1.1.4), which will 'show well' (fit appropriately) at this point. Rests are pauses in the music, and Govianus's falling tears (beads) keep the numbers (i.e. the measure) of the song in strict time.

And here he weeps,
The lord unto so rare a wife.

Weep, weep and mourn lament,
You virgins that pass by her,
For if praise come by death again,
I doubt few will lie nigh her.

GOVIANUS
Thou art an honest boy. 'Tis done like one
That has a feeling of his master's passions
And the unmatchèd worth of his dead mistress.
Thy better years shall find me good to thee
When understanding ripens in thy soul,
Which truly makes the man, and not long time.
Prithee withdraw a little and attend me
At cloister door.

PAGE It shall be done, my lord. [*Exit*]

GOVIANUS
Eternal maid of honour, whose chaste body
Lies here, like virtue's close and hidden seed,
To spring forth glorious to eternity
At the everlasting harvest—

VOICE WITHIN I am not here.

GOVIANUS
What's that? Who is not here? I'm forced to question
it.
Some idle sounds the beaten vaults send forth.

On a sudden in a kind of noise like a wind, the doors clattering, the tombstone flies open, and a great light appears in the midst of the tomb; his Lady, as went out, standing just before him all in white, stuck with jewels and a great crucifix on her breast

Mercy look to me! Faith, I fly to thee!
Keep a strong watch about me—now thy friendship!
O never came astonishment and fear
So pleasing to mankind! I take delight
To have my breast shake, and my hair stand stiff.
If this be horror, let it never die!
Came all the pains of hell in that shape to me,
I should endure 'em smiling. [*To the Lady*] Keep me
still
In terror, I beseech thee: I'd not change
This fever for felicity of man

And here he weeps,
The lord unto so rare a wife.

Weep, weep and mourn lament,
You virgins that pass by her,
For if praise come by death again,
I doubt few will lie nigh her.

GOVIANUS
Thou art an honest boy. 'Tis done like one
That has a feeling of his master's passions
And the unmatchèd worth of his dead mistress.
Thy better years shall find me good to thee
When understanding ripens in thy soul,
Which truly makes the man, and not long time.
Prithee withdraw a little and attend me
At cloister door.

PAGE It shall be done, my lord. [*Exit*]

GOVIANUS
Eternal maid of honour, whose chaste body
Lies here, like virtue's close and hidden seed,
To spring forth glorious to eternity
At the everlasting harvest—

VOICE WITHIN I am not here.

GOVIANUS
What's that? Who is not here? I'm forced to question
it.
Some idle sounds the beaten vaults send forth.

On a sudden in a kind of noise like a wind, the doors clattering, the tombstone flies open, and a great light appears in the midst of the tomb; his Lady, as went out, standing just before him all in white, stuck with jewels and a great crucifix on her breast.

Enter Lady: Rich. Robinson

Mercy look to me! Faith, I fly to thee!
Keep a strong watch about me—now thy friendship!
O never came astonishment and fear
So pleasing to mankind! I take delight
To have my breast shake, and my hair stand stiff.
If this be horror, let it never die!
Came all the pains of hell in that shape to me,
I should endure 'em smiling. [*To the Lady*] Keep me
still
In terror, I beseech thee: I'd not change
This fever for felicity of man

25 **mourn lament** sadly sing a lament. The words of the song show that the Lady was both 'wife', i.e. betrothed to Govianus, but also virgin (see also 37–8).

27–8 **if...her** if a virgin were to achieve praise again through death, I am sure that few would approach her in virtue

32 **better** later, older

35–6 **attend...door** wait for me at the door to the cloisters.

38–40 **like...harvest** like the seeds of virtue, secret and concealed, until they shall bear fruit at God's harvest of souls (i.e. be resurrected at the last judgement). Govianus's words refer to the doctrine of the resurrection of the body, a further powerful reason why the Lady's body must be saved from the Tyrant's lust.

40 **I am not here** According to the gospels, angels clothed in white told mourners at Christ's tomb, 'He is not here, for He is risen'. The mysterious offstage voice prepares us for the Lady's miraculous appearance two lines later, probably through a trapdoor, since she arrives 'standing just before him'.

42 **idle** meaningless
beaten echoing

42.4 ***as went out*** A baffling phrase, which looks as if it should mean 'as she left the stage', or 'as she was when she died', but since the Lady was then in black, and is now in white, 'stuck with jewels', this seems less likely.

B42.7 ***Enter Lady: Rich. Robinson*** Richard Robinson was a boy actor with the King's Men (see Introduction, 835).

44 **thy friendship** I need (faith's) friendship

Or all the pleasures of ten thousand ages.

LADY
Dear lord, I come to tell you all my wrongs.

GOVIANUS
Welcome! Who wrongs the spirit of my love?
Thou art above the injuries of blood,
They cannot reach thee now. What dares offend thee?
No life that has the weight of flesh upon't,
And treads as I do, can now wrong my mistress!

LADY
The peace that death allows me is not mine.
The monument is robbed. Behold, I'm gone,
My body taken up.

GOVIANUS [*looking into the tomb*]
'Tis gone indeed.
What villain dares so fearfully run in debt
To black eternity?

LADY He that dares do more—
The Tyrant!

GOVIANUS All the miseries below
Reward his boldness!

LADY I am now at court,
In his own private chamber. There he woos me
And plies his suit to me with as serious pains
As if the short flame of mortality
Were lighted up again in my cold breast;
Folds me within his arms and often sets
A sinful kiss upon my senseless lip;
Weeps when he sees the paleness of my cheek,
And will send privately for a hand of art
That may dissemble life upon my face
To please his lustful eye.

GOVIANUS O piteous wrongs,
Inhuman injuries, without grace or mercy!

LADY
I leave 'em to thy thought, dearest of men.
My rest is lost. Thou must restore't again.

GOVIANUS
O, fly me not so soon!

LADY Farewell, true lord. *Exit*

GOVIANUS
I cannot spare thee yet. I'll make myself
Over to death too, and we'll walk together
Like loving spirits—I prithee let's do so.
She's snatched away by fate and I talk sickly.
I must dispatch this business upon earth
Before I take that journey.
I'll to my brother for his aid or counsel.
So wronged! O heav'n, put armour on my spirit:
Her body I will place in her first rest
Or in th'attempt lock death into my breast. *Exit*

Finit Actus Quartus

Or all the pleasures of ten thousand ages.

LADY
Dear lord, I come to tell you all my wrongs.

GOVIANUS
Welcome! Who wrongs the spirit of my love?
Thou art above the injuries of blood,
They cannot reach thee now. What dares offend thee?
No life that has the weight of flesh upon't,
And treads as I do, can now wrong my mistress!

LADY
The peace that death allows me is not mine.
The monument is robbed. Behold, I'm gone,
My body taken up.

GOVIANUS [*looking into the tomb*]
'Tis gone indeed.
What villain dares so fearfully run in debt
To black eternity?

LADY He that dares do more—
The Tyrant!

GOVIANUS All the miseries below
Reward his boldness!

LADY I am now at court,
In his own private chamber. There he woos me
And plies his suit to me with as serious pains
As if the short flame of mortality
Were lighted up again in my cold breast;
Folds me within his arms and often sets
A sinful kiss upon my senseless lip;
Weeps when he sees the paleness of my cheek,
And will send privately for a hand of art
That may dissemble life upon my face
To please his lustful eye.

GOVIANUS O piteous wrongs,
Inhuman injuries, without grace or mercy!

LADY
I leave 'em to thy thought, dearest of men.
My rest is lost. Thou must restore't again.

GOVIANUS
O, fly me not so soon!

LADY Farewell, true lord. *Exit*

GOVIANUS
I cannot spare thee yet. I'll make myself
Over to death too, and we'll walk together
Like loving spirits—I prithee let's do so.
She's snatched away by fate and I talk sickly.
I must dispatch this business upon earth
Before I take that journey.
I'll to my brother for his aid or counsel.
So wronged! O heav'n, put armour on my spirit:
Her body I will place in her first rest
Or in th'attempt lock death into my breast. *Exit*

Finit Actus Quartus

59 **treads** walks on the earth

63–4 **What . . . eternity** Who is so wicked that he dares incur a debt that must be paid for eternally in hell?

65 **below** of hell

74 **a hand of art** the hand of an artist

75 **dissemble** give the appearance of

80 **fly me not** do not fly from me

88–90 **put . . . breast** give me spiritual protection. I will restore her body to its original resting-place, or die in the attempt.

5.1 *Incipit Actus Quintus*

Enter Votarius with Anselmus, the husband

VOTARIUS [*pointing out the closet*]
You shall stand here, my lord, unseen, and hear all.
Do I deal now like a right friend with you?

ANSELMUS
Like a most faithful.

VOTARIUS
You shall have her mind e'en as it comes to me,
Though I undo her by't. Your friendship, sir,
Is the sweet mistress that I only serve.
I prize the roughness of a man's embrace
Before the soft lips of a hundred ladies.

ANSELMUS
And that's an honest mind of thee.

VOTARIUS
Lock yourself, sir,
Into that closet and be sure none see you.
Trust not a creature. We'll have all run clear,
E'en as the heart affords it.

ANSELMUS
'Tis a match, sir.

[*He withdraws to the closet*]

VOTARIUS [*aside*]
Troth, he says true there: 'tis a match indeed.
He does not know the strength of his own words,
For if he did, there were no mast'ring on him.
He's cleft the pin in two with a blind man's eyes.
Though I shoot wide, I'll cozen him of the game.

Exit

[*Enter*] *Leonella above, in a gallery with her love Bellarius*

LEONELLA
Dost thou see thine enemy walk?

BELLARIUS
I would I did not.

LEONELLA
Prithee rest quiet, man. I have fee'd one for him,
A trusty catchpole, too, that will be sure on him.
Thou know'st this gallery well. 'Tis at thy use now;
'T'as been at mine full often. Thou mayst sit
Like a most private gallant in yon corner,
See all the play, and ne'er be seen thyself.

BELLARIUS
Therefore I chose it.

LEONELLA
Thou shalt see my lady
Play her part naturally, more to the life

5.1 *Incipit Actus Quintus*

Enter Votarius with Anselmus, the husband

VOTARIUS [*pointing out the closet*]
You shall stand here, my lord, unseen, and hear all.
Do I deal now like a right friend with you?

ANSELMUS
Like a most faithful.

VOTARIUS
You shall have her mind e'en as it comes to me,
Though I undo her by't. Your friendship, sir,
Is the sweet mistress that I only serve.
I prize the roughness of a man's embrace
Before the soft lips of a hundred ladies.

ANSELMUS
And that's an honest mind of thee.

VOTARIUS
Lock yourself, sir,
Into that closet and be sure none see you.
Trust not a creature. We'll have all run clear,
E'en as the heart affords it.

ANSELMUS
'Tis a match, sir.

[*He withdraws to the closet*]

VOTARIUS [*aside*]
Troth, he says true there: 'tis a match indeed.
He does not know the strength of his own words,
For if he did, there were no mast'ring on him.
He's cleft the pin in two with a blind man's eyes.
Though I shoot wide, I'll cozen him of the game.

Exit

[*Enter*] *Leonella above, in a gallery with her love Bellarius*

LEONELLA
Dost thou see thine enemy walk?

BELLARIUS
I would I did not.

LEONELLA
Prithee rest quiet, man. I have fee'd one for him,
A trusty catchpole, too, that will be sure on him.
Thou know'st this gallery well. 'Tis at thy use now;
'T'as been at mine full often. Thou mayst sit
Like a most private gallant in yon corner,
See all the play, and ne'er be seen thyself.

BELLARIUS
Therefore I chose it.

LEONELLA
Thou shalt see my lady
Play her part naturally, more to the life

5.1.2 **right** true. Votarius hides Anselmus in the closet so that he may overhear what ensues (as he had done earlier at 1.2.71.1, or as the deceived Harebrain does in *Mad World*, 3.2.191–5).

3 **have** know

8 **that's...thee** that shows an honourable attitude on your part.

10 **clear** smoothly, also openly or transparently

11–16 **'Tis...game** That's agreed. In an aside, Votarius plays on further meanings of this expression—that Anselmus and he are playing a match against one another for the Wife, but if Anselmus were to realize this, there would be no controlling his rage. Anselmus is like a blind man at an archery match who has accidentally managed to split the centre ('pin') of the target. Even if Votarius cannot beat him (shooting wide of the mark), he can still cheat him of the prize.

18–19 **I...him** I have paid an officer to arrest him (a catchpole was an officer who arrested debtors),—a reliable one who will make sure that he's got him.

22 **Like...corner** Gallants (men-about-town) sat on the stage and in the galleries of the theatre, partly in order to be seen. Bellarius, by contrast, will be 'private', i.e. invisible to the actors, but able to watch the performance about to take place on the stage below. The fifth act sets up a piece of play-acting which suddenly becomes reality, but unlike comparable scenes in *Mad World*, *Hengist* and *Women Beware*, this one is not presented as a formal entertainment.

25–6 **more...on** more realistically than she realizes

Than she's aware on.
BELLARIUS There must I be pleased.
Thou'rt one of the actors, thou'lt be missed anon.
LEONELLA
Alas, a woman's action's always ready.
Yet I'll down, now I think on't. *Descendet Leonella*
BELLARIUS Do, 'tis time, i'faith.
ANSELMUS [*apart, at the closet*]
I know not yet where I should plant belief,
I am so strangely tossed between two tales.
I'm told by my wife's woman the deed's done,
And in Votarius' tongue, 'tis yet to come:
The castle is but upon yielding yet,
'Tis not delivered up. Well, we shall find
The mystery shortly. I will entertain
The patience of a prisoner i'th' mean time.
[*He*] *locks himself in* [*the closet*]
Enter Anselmus' Wife with Leonella [*who hangs up the sword*]
WIFE [*aside to Leonella*]
Is all set ready, wench?
LEONELLA Push! Madam, all.
WIFE [*louder, as if replying to Leonella*]
Tell me not so. She lives not for a lady
That has less peace than I.
LEONELLA Nay, good sweet madam,
You would not think how much this passion alters
you:
It drinks up all the beauty of your cheek.
I promise you, madam, you have lost much blood.
WIFE
Let it draw death upon me, for till then
I shall be mistress of no true content.
Who could endure hourly temptation
And bear it, as I do?
LEONELLA Nay, that's most certain,
Unless it were myself again. I can do't,
I suffer the like daily. You should complain, madam.
WIFE
Which way, were that wisdom? Prithee, wench, to
whom?
LEONELLA
To him who makes all whole again, my lord.
To one that, if he be a kind, good husband,
Will let you bear no more than you are able.
WIFE
Thou know'st not what thou speak'st. Why, my lord's
he

Than she's aware on.
BELLARIUS There must I be pleased.
Thou'rt one of the actors, thou'lt be missed anon.
LEONELLA
Alas, a woman's action's always ready.
Yet I'll down, now I think on't. *Descendet Leonella*
BELLARIUS Do, 'tis time, i'faith.
ANSELMUS [*apart, at the closet*]
I know not yet where I should plant belief,
I am so strangely tossed between two tales.
I'm told by my wife's woman the deed's done,
And in Votarius' tongue, 'tis yet to come:
The castle is but upon yielding yet,
'Tis not delivered up. Well, we shall find
The mystery shortly. I will entertain
The patience of a prisoner i'th' mean time.
[*He*] *locks himself in* [*the closet*]
Enter Anselmus' Wife with Leonella [*who hangs up the sword*]
WIFE [*aside to Leonella*]
Is all set ready, wench?
LEONELLA Push! Madam, all.
WIFE [*louder, as if replying to Leonella*]
Tell me not so. She lives not for a lady
That has less peace than I.
LEONELLA Nay, good sweet madam,
You would not think how much this passion alters
you:
It drinks up all the beauty of your cheek.
I promise you, madam, you have lost much blood.
WIFE
Let it draw death upon me, for till then
I shall be mistress of no true content.
Who could endure hourly temptation
And bear it, as I do?
LEONELLA Nay, that's most certain,
Unless it were myself again. I can do't,
I suffer the like daily. You should complain, madam.
WIFE
Which way, were that wisdom? Prithee, wench, to
whom?
LEONELLA
To him who makes all whole again, my lord.
To one that, if he be a kind, good husband,
Will let you bear no more than you are able.
WIFE
Thou know'st not what thou speak'st. Why, my lord's
he

26 **There . . . pleased** I'm bound to be pleased about that.
28 **a woman's . . . ready** women are always ready to play their part; also, women's (sexual) parts are always ready.
31 **tossed . . . tales** 'Never was man so tossed between two tales! | I know not which to take, nor which to trust' (*No Wit*, 3.208–9).
34–5 **The castle . . . up** The castle is only at the point of surrender—it has not yet been handed over.
39 **She . . . lady** There is no lady living
43 **blood** the Wife is pale—supposedly from being persecuted, but actually from sexual passion (according to contemporary medical theories, the body's liquids needed to be maintained at steady levels for health).
44 **death** with the secondary meaning of orgasm, which she must 'bear', as at A2.1.80
49 **I suffer the like** I put up with the same thing. Leonella hastens to assure the Wife that she suffers the same pleasures or pains.
50 **Which . . . wisdom** In what direction? Would that be wise?
54–5 **my lord's he | That** it is my lord who

That gives him the house-freedom, all his boldness,
Keeps him o' purpose here to war with me.
LEONELLA
Now I hold wiser of my lord than so:
He knows the world. He would not be so idle.
WIFE
I speak sad truth to thee: I am not private
In mine own chamber, such his impudence is.
Nay, my repenting time is scarce blessed from him;
He will offend my prayers.
LEONELLA Out upon him!
I believe, madam, he's of no religion.
WIFE
He serves my lord, and that's enough for him,
And preys upon poor ladies like myself.
There's all the gentleman's devotion!
LEONELLA
Marry, the devil of hell give him his blessing!
WIFE
Pray watch the door, and suffer none to trouble us
Unless it be my lord.
LEONELLA [*aside*] 'Twas finely spoke, that—
My lord indeed is the most trouble to her.
Now must I show a piece of service here.
How do I spend my days? Life, shall I never
Get higher than a lady's doorkeeper?
I must be married, as my lady is, first,
And then my maid may do as much for me.
WIFE
O miserable time! Except my lord
Do wake in honourable pity to me
And rid this vicious gamester from his house
Whom I have checked so often, here I vow
I'll imitate my noble sister's fate,
Late mistress to the worthy Govianus,
And cast away my life as she did hers.
Enter Votarius to the door within
LEONELLA
Back! You're too forward, sir. There's no coming for you.
VOTARIUS
How, mistress Len, my lady's smock woman?
Am I no further in your duty yet?
LEONELLA
Duty? Look for't of them you keep under, sir.
VOTARIUS
You'll let me in?
LEONELLA Who would you speak withal?
VOTARIUS
With the best lady you make curtsy to.

That gives him the house-freedom, all his boldness,
Keeps him o' purpose here to war with me.
LEONELLA
Now I hold wiser of my lord than so:
He knows the world. He would not be so idle.
WIFE
I speak sad truth to thee: I am not private
In mine own chamber, such his impudence is.
Nay, my repenting time is scarce blessed from him;
He will offend my prayers.
LEONELLA Out upon him!
I believe, madam, he's of no religion.
WIFE
He serves my lord, and that's enough for him,
And preys upon poor ladies like myself.
There's all the gentleman's devotion!
LEONELLA
Marry, the devil of hell give him his blessing!
WIFE
Pray watch the door, and suffer none to trouble us
Unless it be my lord.
LEONELLA [*aside*] 'Twas finely spoke, that—
My lord indeed is the most trouble to her.
Now must I show a piece of service here.
How do I spend my days? Shall I never
Get higher than a lady's doorkeeper?
I must be married, as my lady is, first,
And then my maid may do as much for me.
WIFE
O miserable time! Except my lord
Do wake in honourable pity to me
And rid this vicious gamester from his house
Whom I have checked so often, here I vow
I'll imitate my noble sister's fate,
Late mistress to the worthy Govianus,
And cast away my life as she did hers.
Enter Votarius to the door within
LEONELLA
Back! You're too forward, sir. There's no coming for you.
VOTARIUS
How, mistress Len, my lady's smock woman?
Am I no further in your duty yet?
LEONELLA
Duty? Look for't of them you keep under, sir.
VOTARIUS
You'll let me in?
LEONELLA Who would you speak withal?
VOTARIUS
With the best lady you make curtsy to.

57 **Now...so** Now I think better of my lord than that.
58 **idle** silly, as at 4.4.42
59 **sad** serious, sober
66 **There's...devotion** That's all the prayers he makes (punning on prey/pray in the previous line, and also on the meaning of Votarius's name as 'devotee').
73 **doorkeeper** also, bawd
74–5 **I must...me** first I'll have to get married, as my lady is, and then my maid could do as much for me
76 **Except** unless
83 **coming** visiting, (sexual) access
84–5 **How...yet** What, mistress Len, who looks after my lady's underclothes? ('Smock woman' also suggests a sexual guardian—see 'smock sentinels', *Banquet*, 1.4.125.) Have I earned no more respect from you than this?
86 **them...under** i.e. your own servants (also, those under you in the act of sex)

LEONELLA
She will not speak with you.
VOTARIUS Have you her mind?
I scorn to take her answer of her broker.
[*He presses past Leonella*]
LEONELLA [*warning the Wife*]
Madam!
WIFE
What's there? How now, sir, what's your business?
We see your boldness plain.
VOTARIUS I came to see you, madam.
WIFE
Farewell, then; though 'twas impudence too much
When I was private.
VOTARIUS Madam!
WIFE Life, he was born
To beggar all my patience!
VOTARIUS I'm bold
Still to prefer my love.—Your woman hears me not.
[*He attempts to kiss her*]
WIFE
Where's modesty and honour? Have I not thrice
Answered thy lust?
LEONELLA [*aside*] By'r lady, I think oftener.
WIFE
And dar'st thou yet look with temptation on us?
Since nothing will prevail—come, death! Come,
vengeance!
I will forget the weakness of my kind,
And force thee from my chamber.
[*She seizes the sword and attacks Votarius*]
VOTARIUS How now, lady?
Ud's life, you prick me, madam!
WIFE [*aside to Votarius*] Prithee peace,
I will not hurt thee. [*Loudly*] Will you yet be gone, sir?
LEONELLA [*aside*]
He's upon going, I think.
VOTARIUS Madam!
Heart, you deal false with me! O, I feel it.
You're a most treacherous lady! This' thy glory?
My breast is all afire—O—
[*He dies*]
LEONELLA [*laughing*] Ha, ha, ha!
ANSELMUS [*coming from the closet*]
Ha! I believe her constancy too late,
Confirmed e'en in the blood of my best friend.
[*He seizes the sword to stab Leonella*]
Take thou my vengeance, thou bold perjurous strum-
pet,
That durst accuse thy virtuous lady falsely!
[*He*] *kills Leonella*

LEONELLA
She will not speak with you.
VOTARIUS Have you her mind?
I scorn to take her answer of her broker.
[*He presses past Leonella*]
LEONELLA [*warning the Wife*]
Madam!
WIFE
What's there? How now, sir, what's your business?
We see your boldness plain.
VOTARIUS I came to see you, madam.
WIFE
Farewell, then; though 'twas impudence too much
When I was private.
VOTARIUS Madam!
WIFE He was born
To beggar all my patience!
VOTARIUS I'm bold
Still to prefer my love.—Your woman hears me not.
[*He attempts to kiss her*]
WIFE
Where's modesty and honour? Have I not thrice
Answered thy lust?
LEONELLA [*aside*] By'r lady, I think oftener.
WIFE
And dar'st thou yet look with temptation on us?
Since nothing will prevail—come, death! Come,
vengeance!
I will forget the weakness of my kind,
And force thee from my chamber.
[*She seizes the sword and attacks Votarius*]
VOTARIUS How now, lady?
Ud's life, you prick me, madam!
WIFE [*aside to Votarius*] Prithee peace,
I will not hurt thee. [*Loudly*] Will you yet be gone, sir?
LEONELLA [*aside*]
He's upon going, I think.
VOTARIUS Madam!
You deal false with me! O, I feel it.
You're a most treacherous lady! This' thy glory?
My breast is all afire—O—
[*He dies*]
LEONELLA [*laughing*] Ha, ha, ha!
ANSELMUS [*coming from the closet*]
Ha! I believe her constancy too late,
Confirmed e'en in the blood of my best friend.
[*He seizes the sword to stab Leonella*]
Take thou my vengeance, thou bold perjurous strum-
pet,
That durst accuse thy virtuous lady falsely!
[*He*] *kills Leonella*

90 **broker** agent, intermediary
93–4 **'twas ... private** It was unacceptably rude of you when I was alone.
96 **prefer** put forward, offer
98 **Answered** responded to (the Wife means with a rebuke, Leonella means sexually)
103 **you prick me** you've stabbed me
105 **He's ... going** he's just about to go (i.e. die)
107 **This' thy glory** Is this your triumph? The poison, like fire in the blood, acts out the destructiveness of sexual passion (as in Hippolito's death from poisoned darts, *Women Beware*, 5.1.177–9, 186–7).

BELLARIUS
O deadly poison after a sweet banquet!
What make I here? I had forgot my heart.
I am an actor too, and never thought on't.
The blackness of this season cannot miss me.
[Bellarius descends to the main stage, draws his sword and challenges Anselmus]
Sirrah, you, lord!

WIFE *[aside]* Is he there? Welcome, ruin!

BELLARIUS
There is a life due to me in that bosom
For this poor gentlewoman.

ANSELMUS And art thou then receiver?
I'll pay thee largely, slave, for thy last scape!
They make a dangerous pass at one another. The Wife purposely runs between, and is killed by them both

WIFE *[aside]*
I come, Votarius!

ANSELMUS *[to Bellarius]*
Hold, if manhood guide thee!
[He kneels beside the Wife]
O, what has fury done?

BELLARIUS What has it done now?
Why, killed an honourable whore, that's all.

ANSELMUS
Villain, I'll seal that lie upon thy heart!
A constant lady!

BELLARIUS To the devil, as could be!
Heart, must I prick you forward? Either up
Or, sir, I'll take my chance. Thou couldst kill her
Without repenting, that deserved more pity,
And spend'st thy time and tears upon a quean—

ANSELMUS Slave!
[He rises. They fight, wounding one another fatally]

BELLARIUS
—That was deceived once in her own deceit,
As I am now! The poison I prepared
Upon that weapon for mine enemy's bosom
Is bold to take acquaintance of my blood too
And serves us both to make up death withal.

ANSELMUS
I ask no more of destiny but to fall

BELLARIUS
O deadly poison after a sweet banquet!
What make I here? I had forgot my heart.
I am an actor too, and never thought on't.
The blackness of this season cannot miss me.
Bellarius [descends to the main stage, draws his sword and challenges Anselmus]
Sirrah, you, lord!

WIFE *[aside]* Is he there? Welcome, ruin!

BELLARIUS
There is a life due to me in that bosom
For this poor gentlewoman.

ANSELMUS And art thou then receiver?
I'll pay thee largely, slave, for thy last scape!
They make a dangerous pass at one another. The Wife purposely runs between, and is killed by them both

WIFE *[aside]*
I come, Votarius!

ANSELMUS *[to Bellarius]*
Hold, if manhood guide thee!
[He kneels beside the Wife]
O, what has fury done?

BELLARIUS What has it done now?
Why, killed an honourable whore, that's all.

ANSELMUS
Villain, I'll seal that lie upon thy heart!
A constant lady!

BELLARIUS To the devil, as could be!
Must I prick you forward? Either up
Or, sir, I'll take my chance. Thou couldst kill her
Without repenting, that deserved more pity,
And spend'st thy time and tears upon a quean—

ANSELMUS Slave!
[He rises. They fight, wounding one another fatally]

BELLARIUS
—That was deceived once in her own deceit,
As I am now! The poison I prepared
Upon that weapon for mine enemy's bosom
Is bold to take acquaintance of my blood too
And serves us both to make up death withal.

ANSELMUS
I ask no more of destiny but to fall

114 **What...heart** What am I doing here? (this phrase is used by Bianca at the end of *Women Beware*, 5.1.247). I had forgotten my own feelings. Bellarius speaks these lines from the gallery ('here'), but descends immediately, challenging Anselmus at l. 117. As it normally took about eight lines for an actor to descend from the gallery (as at ll. 29–38), he may jump, swing or slide down onto the main stage (depending on the height of the gallery).

119–20 **And...scape** So you're going to call in my life, then (i.e. in payment for Leonella's)? I'll pay you back in full, scoundrel, for your previous offence (i.e. illegally entering my house).

121 **I come, Votarius** The Wife is (symbolically) slain between two men. As Bellarius suggestively puts it at l. A164, 'She ran upon two weapons' (swords/penises). Her last words suggest self-immolation for the accidental killing of Votarius, as well as her desire to join him. They seem to be said to herself or in an aside, since Anselmus does not apparently overhear them.

126–7 **must...chance** Must I goad you into fighting? Either get up, or I'll risk killing you where you are.

129 **quean** promiscuous woman

131–2 **That...now** That was once taken in by her own trick,—as I have been taken in by my own.

133 **mine enemy's** i.e. that of Votarius

134–5 **Is...withal** (The poison) is saucily familiar with my blood, also, and will suffice to bring about both our deaths (i.e. his and that of Votarius, since Anselmus dies from Bellarius's sword, which has not been poisoned).

Close by the chaste side of my virtuous mistress.
If all the treasure of my weeping strength
Be left so wealthy but to purchase that,
I have the dear wish of a great man's spirit.
[He drags himself towards the Wife's body]
Yet favour me—[*reaching her*] O yet I thank thee, fate.
I expire cheerfully and give death a smile.
Anselmus dies

BELLARIUS
O rage! I pity now mine enemy's flesh.
Enter Govianus with servants

GOVIANUS
Where should he be?

FIRST SERVANT My lady, sir, will tell you.
She's in her chamber here.

SECOND SERVANT [*looking about*]
O, my lord!

GOVIANUS Peace!
My honourable brother, madam, all!
So many dreadful deeds and not one tongue
Left to proclaim 'em?

BELLARIUS Yes. Hear, if a voice
Some minute long may satisfy your ear;
I've that time allowed it.

GOVIANUS 'Tis enough.
Bestow it quickly ere death snatch it from thee.

BELLARIUS
That lord, your brother, made his friend Votarius
To tempt his lady. She was won to lust,
The act revealed here by her serving woman.
But that wise, close adulteress, stored with art,
To prey upon the weakness of that lord,
Dissembled a great rage upon her love,
And indeed killed him; which so won her husband,
He slew this right discoverer in his fury,
Who, being my mistress, I was moved in heart
To take some pains with him, and he's paid me for't.
As for the cunning lady, I commend her:
She performed that which never woman tried,
She ran upon two weapons, and so died.
Now you have all, I hope I shall sleep quiet.
[He] dies

Close by the chaste side of my virtuous mistress.
If all the treasure of my weeping strength
Be left so wealthy but to purchase that,
I have the dear wish of a great man's spirit.
[He drags himself towards the Wife's body]
Yet favour me—[*reaching her*] O yet I thank thee, fate.
I expire cheerfully and give death a smile.
[Anselmus collapses]

BELLARIUS
O rage! I pity now mine enemy's flesh.
Enter Govianus with servants

GOVIANUS
Where should he be?

FIRST SERVANT My lady, sir, will tell you.
She's in her chamber here.

SECOND SERVANT [*looking about*]
O, my lord!

GOVIANUS Peace!
My honourable brother, madam, all!
So many dreadful deeds and not one tongue
Left to proclaim 'em?

BELLARIUS Yes. Hear, if a voice
Some minute long may satisfy your ear;
I've that time allowed it.

GOVIANUS 'Tis enough.
Bestow it quickly ere death snatch it from thee.

BELLARIUS
That lord, your brother, made his friend Votarius
To tempt his lady. She was won to lust,
The act revealed here by her serving woman.
But that wise, close adulteress, stored with art,
To prey upon the weakness of that lord,
Dissembled a great rage upon her love,
And indeed killed him; which so won her husband,
He slew this right discoverer in his fury,
Who, being my mistress, I was moved in heart
To take some pains with him, and he's paid me for't.
As for the cunning lady, I commend her:
She performed that which never woman tried,
She ran upon our weapons, and so died.
Now you have all, I hope I shall sleep quiet.
[He] dies

138–40 **If . . . spirit** If whatever's left of my strength, as I bleed, is only enough to buy my death (beside my mistress), I have gained the dearest wish of my great spirit.

143 **O rage!** He feels the burning of the poison, and momentarily pities Votarius.

155 **close** secret

157 **Dissembled . . . love** pretended to be furiously angry with her lover

159 **right discoverer** person who exposed the truth (i.e. Leonella)

161–4 **To . . . died** to take some trouble over him, and he has repaid me for it. As for the crafty (also, sexy) lady, I congratulate her: she did something no woman has ever attempted before: she threw herself upon two weapons, and so killed herself (Bellarius suggests that the Wife deliberately set out to achieve such a consummation).

B166–79 **O thunder . . . lust** In this additional passage, Anselmus survives long enough to learn from the dying Bellarius that his Wife had, in fact, betrayed him, and despairs.

B168–9 **I . . . me** Bellarius's words burn Anselmus inwardly, as the action of the poison had consumed the others. They condemn him to hell, both because they make him burn with anger (as if he were already there), and also because he would reject heaven itself to avoid meeting his Wife there, as he explains at ll. B175–7.

B171 **believing** trusting

B173 **grow beggars** are emptied of blood
sue beg, pray

B177 **sup with torments** i.e. in hell

B179 **"The . . . lust"** This epigram links women's lust to the serpent that persuaded Eve to disobey God by eating the apple, thus bringing desire, death, and misery into the world ('Now, the serpent was more subtil than any beast of the field . . .', Genesis 3:1). Even at the point of death, Anselmus remains self-deceived since he cannot admit his own part in his Wife's fall.

GOVIANUS
Is death so long a-coming to mankind,
It must be met halfways? 'Las, the full time
Is, to eternity, but a minute, a [breath].
Was that so long to stay? O cruel speed!
There's few men pay their debts before their day;
If they be ready at their time, 'tis well,
And but a few that are so. What strange haste
Was made among these people! My heart weeps for't.

[*To the servants*] Go, bear those bodies to a place more comely.
[*The bodies are carried out*]
[*To Anselmus*] Brother, I came for thy advice, but I

Find thee so ill a counsellor to thyself
That I repent my pains, and depart sighing.—
The body of my love is still at court.
I am not well to think on't. The poor spirit
Was with me once again about it, troth,
And I can put it off no more for shame,
Though I desire to have it haunt me still
And never to give over, 'tis so pleasing.
I must to court. I've plighted my faith to't.
'T'as opened me the way to the revenge.
Tyrant, I'll run thee on a dangerous shelf,
Though I be forced to fly this land myself! *Exit*

5.2 [*The throne is set out*]
Enter Tyrant with attendants

TYRANT
In vain my spirit wrestles with my blood,
Affection will be mistress here on earth.
The house is hers, the soul is but a tenant.
I ha' tasked myself but with the abstinence
Of one poor hour, yet cannot conquer that.
I cannot keep from sight of her so long.

ANSELMUS
O thunder that awakes me e'en from death,
And makes me curse my confidence with cold lips!
I feel his words in flames about my soul.
He's more than killed me.
GOVIANUS Brother!
ANSELMUS I repent the smile
That I bestowed on destiny! A whore!
[*He throws the Wife's body from him*]
I fling thee thus from my believing breast
With all the strength I have. My rage is great,
Although my veins grow beggars. Now I sue
To die far from thee. May we never meet!
Were my soul bid to joy's eternal banquet
And were assured to find thee there a guest,
I'd sup with torments and refuse that feast!
O thou beguiler of man's easy trust,
"The serpent's wisdom is in women's lust!"
[*He*] *dies*
GOVIANUS [*to the servants*]
Go, bear those bodies to a place more comely.
[*The bodies are carried out*]
[*To the body of Anselmus*] Brother, I came for thy advice, but I
Find thee so ill a counsellor to thyself
That I repent my pains, and depart sighing.—
The body of my love is still at court.
I am not well to think on't. The poor spirit
Was with me once again about it, troth,
And I can put it off no more for shame,
Though I desire to have it haunt me still
And never to give over, 'tis so pleasing.
I must to court. I've plighted my faith to't.
'T'as opened me the way to the revenge.
And I must through. *Exit*

5.2 [*The throne is set out*]
Enter Tyrant with attendants

TYRANT
In vain my spirit wrestles with my blood,
Affection will be mistress here on earth.
The house is hers, the soul is but a tenant.
I ha' tasked myself but with the abstinence
Of one poor hour, yet cannot conquer that.
I cannot keep from sight of her so long.

A166–7 **Is…halfways** Is death so slow to arrive for men that it must be met halfway? (Govianus voices the common man's reaction to the violence that has cut short the lives of five people.)

A170–3 **There's…people** Few men pay their debts (i.e. give up their lives) before they fall due; if they are ready to do so when called upon, that's good, but even then, only a few are. What a strange hurry these people were in.

A179/B185 **I am…on't** It makes me ill to think of it.

A180/B186 **about it** concerning that (i.e. her body having been taken to the court)

A184/B190 **plighted my faith** given my word

A186 **I'll…shelf** I'll drive you onto dangerous rocks.

B192 **I must through** I must go through with it. As the closing line of a scene, this recalls Maximus's words at the end of act 3 of Fletcher's *Tragedy of Valentinian*: 'Give me a certain ruin, I must through it' (3.3.170).

5.2.1–5 **In…that** My soul is wrestling unsuccessfully against my body: passion must rule here on earth. She owns the house (i.e. the body, as at 4.3.114); the soul is no more than a lodger. I have set myself to abstain (i.e. from seeing her) for a single hour, yet I cannot achieve even that (compare 2.3.3).

I starve mine eye too much. [*To an attendant*] Go,
bring her forth,
As we have caused her body to be decked
In all the glorious riches of our palace.
[*Exit attendant*]
Our mind has felt a famine for the time;
All comfort has been dear and scarce with us.
[*Enter soldiers with the Lady*]
The times are altered since. Strike on, sweet harmony!
[*Music plays*]
A braver world comes toward us.

They bring the body in a chair, dressed up in black velvet which sets out the paleness of the hands and face, and a fair chain of pearl across her breast and the crucifix above it. The Tyrant stands silent awhile, letting the music play, beckoning the soldiers that bring her in to make obeisance to her, and he himself makes a low honour to the body and kisses the hand.

A Song within, in voices

O what is beauty that's so much adorèd?
A flatt'ring glass that cozens her beholders:
One night of death makes it look pale and horrid;
The dainty preserv'd flesh, how soon it moulders.
To love it living, it bewitcheth many,
But after life is seldom heard of any.

FIRST SOLDIER [*aside*]
By this hand, mere idolatry! I make curtsy
To my damnation. I have learned so much,
Though I could never know the meaning yet
Of all my Latin prayers, nor ne'er sought for't.

TYRANT [*to the Lady's body*]
How pleasing art thou to us even in death!
I love thee yet, above all women living,
And shall do sev'n year hence.
I can see nothing to be mended in thee
But the too constant paleness of thy cheek.
I'd give the kingdom but to purchase there
The breadth of a red rose in natural colour,
And think it the best bargain
That ever king made yet; but fate's my hindrance,
And I must only rest content with art,
And that I'll have in spite on't!—[*To Second Soldier*] Is
he come, sir?

SECOND SOLDIER
Who, my lord?

I starve mine eye too much. [*To an attendant*] Go,
bring her forth,
As we have caused her body to be decked
In all the glorious riches of our palace.
[*Exit attendant*]
Our mind has felt a famine for the time;
All comfort has been dear and scarce with us.
Enter soldiers with the Lady
The times are altered since. Strike on, sweet harmony!
Music [*plays*]
A braver world comes toward us.

They bring the body in a chair, dressed up in black velvet which sets out the paleness of the hands and face, and a fair chain of pearl across her breast and the crucifix above it. The Tyrant stands silent awhile, letting the music play, beckoning the soldiers that bring her in to make obeisance to her, and he himself makes a low honour to the body and kisses the hand.

A Song within, in voices

O what is beauty that's so much adorèd?
A flatt'ring glass that cozens her beholders:
One night of death makes it look pale and horrid;
The dainty preserv'd flesh, how soon it moulders.
To love it living, it bewitcheth many,
But after life is seldom heard of any.

TYRANT [*to the Lady's body*]
How pleasing art thou to us even in death!
I love thee yet, above all women living,

I can see nothing to be mended in thee
But the too constant paleness of thy cheek.
I'd give the kingdom but to purchase there
The breadth of a red rose in natural colour,

But fate is my hinderer,
And I must only rest content with art,
And that I'll have in spite on't!—[*To Second Soldier*] Is
he come, sir?

SECOND SOLDIER Who, my lord?

10–11 **Our . . . us** My mind felt starved during that time (i.e. of her absence); any comfort seemed expensive and hard to come by.

13 **braver** brighter, better

13.1 ***the body in a chair*** probably a dummy (or else another actor), since the Lady's ghost enters at l. A153.1/B128.1 and speaks at l. A164/B139

13.2 ***sets out*** sets off

13.7 ***honour*** a bow (a distinctively Middletonian sense of the word)

13.9 ***in voices*** with different voices taking different parts. Sung offstage, the words of this madrigal emphasize physical decay, thus commenting ironically on the Tyrant's ceremony, although he seems unconscious of them. Polyphonic singing was characteristic of Catholic services.

A20–3 **By . . . for't** The first soldier finds the ceremony idolatrous or even Roman Catholic, as his reference to Latin prayers suggests (Anglican prayers were said in English). Protestants in any case considered Catholics idolatrous.

A26 **And . . . hence** Like Herod, who kept Mariamne's body embalmed for seven years (see 4.3.117).

A30/B25 **The breadth** as much colour (as . . .)

A32 **fate's my hindrance**; B26 **fate is my hinderer** fate (in the form of death) will prevent me

A33–4/B27–8 **I . . . on't** I shall have to be satisfied with mere artifice, and that I'll have, in spite of fate.

TYRANT Dull!—The fellow that we sent
For a court schoolmaster, a picture drawer,
A ladies' forenoon tutor. Is he come, sir?
FIRST SOLDIER
Not yet returned, my lord.
TYRANT The fool belike
Makes his choice carefully, for so we charged him,
To fit our close deeds with some private hand.
[*To the Lady*] It is no shame for thee, most silent mistress,
To stand in need of art,
When youth and all thy warm friends has forsook thee.
Women alive are glad to seek her friendship
To make up the fair number of their graces,
Or else the reck'ning would fall short sometimes,
And servants would look out for better wages.
Enter Third Soldier with Govianus [disguised as a painter]
SECOND SOLDIER
He's come, my lord.
TYRANT Depart then.
[*Exeunt First and Second Soldiers and attendants*]
Is that he?
THIRD SOLDIER The privat'st I could get, my lord.
GOVIANUS [*aside*]
O heav'n, marry patience to my spirit!
Give me a sober fury, I beseech thee,
A rage that may not overcharge my blood
And do myself most hurt! 'Tis strange to me
To see thee here at court, and gone from hence.
Didst thou make haste to leave the world for this?
And kept in the worst corner!
O who dares play with destiny but he
That wears security so thick upon him,
The thought of death and hell cannot pierce through!
TYRANT [*to Third Soldier*]
'Twas circumspectly carried. Leave us, go.
[*Exit Third Soldier*]
[*To Govianus*] Be nearer, sir: thou'rt much commended to us.
GOVIANUS
It is the hand, my lord, commends the workman.
TYRANT
Thou speak'st both modesty and truth in that.
We need that art that thou art master of.
GOVIANUS
My king is master both of that and me.

TYRANT Dull!—
The fellow that we sent for a picture drawer,
A ladies' forenoon tutor. Is he come, sir?
FIRST SOLDIER
Not yet returned, my lord.
TYRANT The fool belike
Makes his choice carefully, for so we charged him.
Where is he?
Enter Third Soldier with Govianus [disguised as a painter]
SECOND SOLDIER
He's come, my lord.
TYRANT Depart then.
[*Exeunt First and Second Soldiers and attendants*]
Is that he?
THIRD SOLDIER
The privat'st I could get, my lord.
GOVIANUS [*aside*]
O heav'n, marry patience to my spirit!
Give me a sober fury, I beseech thee,
A rage that may not overcharge my blood
And do myself most hurt! 'Tis strange to me
To see thee here at court, and gone from hence.
Didst thou make haste to leave the world for this?
O who dares play with destiny but he
That wears security so thick upon him,
The thought of death and hell cannot pierce through!
TYRANT [*to Third Soldier*]
'Twas circumspectly carried. Leave us, go.
[*Exit Third Soldier*]
[*To Govianus*] Be nearer, sir: thou'rt much commended to us.
GOVIANUS
It is the hand, my lord, commends the workman.
TYRANT
Thou speak'st both modesty and truth in that.
We need that art that thou art master of.
GOVIANUS
My king is master both of that and me.

A35/B30 **Dull** Stupid
A36/B31 **a picture drawer** a portrait painter
A37/B32 **ladies'...tutor** Court ladies supposedly spent their mornings painting their faces, or having them painted.
A40 **fit...deeds** suit our secret activities
A44–7 **Women...wages** Living women are happy to seek the help of art to make up the full quantity of their attractions, otherwise their sum total would sometimes fall short, and their lovers would look elsewhere for better rewards.
A51/B38 **sober** restrained, controlled
A56 **corner** secret or concealed place, perhaps for sexual activity, or for forbidden religious practices
A58/B44 **security** over-confidence—according to Calvinist theology, sinners were often impervious to the fear of eternal punishment

TYRANT
Look on yon face and tell me what it wants.
GOVIANUS
Which? That, sir?
TYRANT
That. What wants it?
GOVIANUS
Troth, my lord,
Some thousand years' sleep and a marble pillow.
TYRANT
What's that? [*Aside*] Observe it still. All the best arts
Hath the most fools and drunkards to their masters.
[*To Govianus*] Thy apprehension has too gross a film
To be employed at court. What colour wants she?
GOVIANUS
By my troth, all, sir. I see none she has,
Nor none she cares for.
TYRANT [*aside*]
I am overmatched here.
GOVIANUS
A lower chamber with less noise were kindlier
For her, poor woman, whatsoe'er she was.
TYRANT
But how if we be pleased to have it thus
And thou well hired to do what we command?
Is not your work for money?
GOVIANUS
Yes, my lord.
I would not trust at court, an I could choose.
TYRANT
Let but thy art hide death upon her face
That now looks fearfully on us, and but strive
To give our eye delight in that pale part
Which draws so many pities from these springs,
And thy reward for't shall outlast thy end,
And reach to thy friend's fortunes, and his friend.
GOVIANUS
Say you so, my lord? I'll work out my heart, then,
But I'll show art enough.
TYRANT
About it, then.
[*Aside*] I never wished so seriously for health
After long sickness.
GOVIANUS [*aside*]
A religious trembling shakes me by the hand
And bids me put by such unhallowed business,
But revenge calls for't, and it must go forward.
'Tis time the spirit of my love took rest.
Poor soul, 'tis weary, much abused and toiled.

TYRANT
Look on yon face and tell me what it wants.
GOVIANUS
Which? That, sir?
TYRANT
That. What wants it?
GOVIANUS
Troth, my lord,
Some thousand years' sleep and a marble pillow.
TYRANT
What's that? [*Aside*] Observe it still. All the best arts
Hath the most fools and drunkards to their masters.
[*To Govianus*] Thy apprehension has too gross a film
To be employed at court. What colour wants she?
GOVIANUS
By my troth, all, sir. I see none she has,
Nor none she cares for.
TYRANT [*aside*]
I am overmatched here.
GOVIANUS
A lower chamber with less noise were kindlier
For her, poor woman, whatsoe'er she was.
TYRANT
But how if we be pleased to have it thus
And thou well hired to do what we command?
Is not your work for money?
GOVIANUS
Yes, my lord.
I would not trust but few, an I could choose.
TYRANT
Let but thy art hide death upon her face
That now looks fearfully on us, and but strive
To give our eye delight in that pale part
Which draws so many pities from these springs,
And thy reward for't shall outlast thy end,
And reach to thy friend's fortunes, and his friend.
GOVIANUS
Say you so, my lord? I'll work out my heart, then,
But I'll show art enough.
TYRANT
About it, then.
[*Aside*] I never wished so seriously for health
After long sickness.
GOVIANUS [*aside*]
A religious trembling shakes me by the hand
And bids me put by such unhallowed business,
But revenge calls for't, and it must go forward.
'Tis time the spirit of my love took rest.
Poor soul, 'tis weary, much abused and toiled.

A66/B52 **wants** lacks
A68/B54 **thousand . . . sleep** sleep of the dead until the judgement day
A70/B56 **to** for
A71/B57 **Thy . . . film** Your understanding has too thick a skin over it.
A74/B60 **overmatched** outdone (in repartee), or out of my depth
A75/B61 **lower chamber** lower room, i.e. a grave
A78/B64 **hired** rewarded
A80 **I . . . choose** I would not give credit at court, if I had the choice. The Tyrant reminds Govianus that he is an employee, but Govianus (mis)understands him to mean 'Don't you work for ready money?' Since aristocrats could not be arrested for debt at this period, tradesmen were reluctant to grant credit.
A81/B67 **hide death** ironic: Govianus's art hides death in a sense that the Tyrant does not anticipate
A84/B70 **pities . . . springs** tears from these eyes
A85–6/B71–2 **And thy . . . friend** and your reward for this shall extend beyond your death, to include your friends and theirs
A87–8/B73–4 **I'll . . . enough** I'll work as hard as I can (also, fulfil my purpose), then, and show all the art you could wish for.
A90/B76 **After . . . sickness** i.e. as I have wished for this (perhaps recalling A3.1.235–41)
A92/B78 **put . . . business** give up such an unholy task

[He paints the Lady's face]

TYRANT *[aside]*

Could I now send for one to renew heat
Within her bosom, that were a fine workman!
I should but too much love him, but, alas,
'Tis as unpossible for living fire
To take hold there,
As for dead ashes to burn back again
Into those hard tough bodies whence they fell.
Life is removed from her, now, as the warmth
Of the bright sun from us when it makes winter,
And kills with unkind coldness—so is't yonder.
An everlasting frost hangs now upon her,
And, as in such a season men will force
A heat into their bloods with exercise
In spite of extreme weather, so shall we
By art force beauty on yon lady's face,
Though death sit frowning on't a storm of hail
To beat it off. Our pleasure shall prevail.

GOVIANUS *[finishing]*
My lord!

TYRANT Hast done so soon?

GOVIANUS That's as your grace
Gives approbation.

[He holds the Lady's head up for the Tyrant to see]

TYRANT O, she lives again!
She'll presently speak to me!

[The body sags]

Keep her up,
I'll have her swoon no more, there's treachery in't.

[Govianus straightens the Lady's body]

Does she not feel warm to thee?

GOVIANUS Very little, sir.

TYRANT
The heat wants cherishing, then. Our arms and lips
Shall labour life into her. Wake, sweet mistress,
'Tis I that call thee at the door of life!

[He kisses her]

Ha!
I talk so long to death, I'm sick myself.
Methinks an evil scent still follows me.

GOVIANUS
Maybe 'tis nothing but the colour, sir,
That I laid on.

TYRANT Is that so strong?

GOVIANUS Yes, faith, sir.
'Twas the best poison I could get for money.

[He reveals himself]

TYRANT
Govianus!

GOVIANUS O, thou sacrilegious villain,

[He paints the Lady's face]

TYRANT *[aside]*

Could I now send for one to renew heat
Within her bosom, that were a fine workman!
I should but too much love him, but, alas,
'Tis as unpossible for living fire
To take hold there,
As for dead ashes to burn back again
Into those hard tough bodies whence they fell.
Life is removed from her, now, as the warmth
Of the bright sun from us when it makes winter,
And kills with unkind coldness—so is't yonder.
An everlasting frost hangs now upon her,
And, as in such a season men will force
A heat into their bloods with exercise
In spite of extreme weather, so shall we
By art force beauty on yon lady's face,
Though death sit frowning on't a storm of hail
To beat it off. Our pleasure shall prevail.

GOVIANUS *[finishing]*
My lord!

TYRANT Hast done so soon?

GOVIANUS That's as your grace
Gives approbation.

[He holds the Lady's head up for the Tyrant to see]

TYRANT O, she lives again!
She'll presently speak to me!

[The body sags]

Keep her up,
I'll have her swoon no more, there's treachery in't.

[Govianus straightens the Lady's body]

Does she not feel warm to thee?

GOVIANUS Very little, sir.

TYRANT
The heat wants cherishing, then. Our arms and lips
Shall labour life into her. Wake, sweet mistress,
'Tis I that call thee at the door of life!

[He kisses her]

Ha!
I talk so long to death, I'm sick myself.
Methinks an evil scent still follows me.

GOVIANUS
Maybe 'tis nothing but the colour, sir,
That I laid on.

TYRANT Is that so strong?

GOVIANUS Yes, faith, sir.
'Twas the best poison I could get for money.

[He reveals himself]

A98/B84 **I . . . him** I should love him all too well

A102/B88 **those . . . bodies** i.e. trees, or perhaps coals

A104/B90 **from us** i.e. is removed from us

A111–12/B97–8 **Though . . . off** even if death were to sit and frown so that a hailstorm washed it off

A114/B100 **approbation** your approval

A115/B101 **up** i.e. propped up. The body's limpness seems to the Tyrant a form of disobedience ('treachery'—though the real treachery is that of Govianus).

A125/B111 **so strong** i.e. in smell

A127 **O . . . villain** Govianus denounces the Tyrant's sin as unparalleled, changing from the respectful 'you' to the scornful 'thou'.

Thou thief of rest, robber of monuments!
Cannot the body after funeral
Sleep in the grave for thee? Must it be raised
Only to please the wickedness of thine eye?
Does all things end with death and not thy lust?
Hast thou devised a new way to damnation
More dreadful than the soul of any sin
Did ever pass yet between earth and hell?
Dost strive to be particularly plagued
Above all ghosts beside? Is thy pride such
Thou scorn'st a partner in thy torments too?

TYRANT
What fury gave thee boldness to attempt
This deed, for which I'll doom thee with a death
Beyond the Frenchmen's tortures!

GOVIANUS I smile at thee.
Draw all the death that ever mankind suffered
Unto one head to help thine own invention,
And make my end as rare as this thy sin
And full as fearful to the eyes of women,
My spirit shall fly singing to his lodging
In midst of that rough weather. Doom me, tyrant!
Had I feared death, I'd never appeared noble
To seal this act upon me which e'en honours me
Unto my mistress' spirit—it loves me for't.
I told my heart 'twould prove destruction to't,
Who, hearing 'twas for her, charged me to do't.

TYRANT
Thy glories shall be shortened! Who's within, there?
Enter the Ghost in the same form as the Lady is dressed in the chair
I called not thee, thou enemy to firmness,
Mortality's earthquake.

GOVIANUS Welcome to mine eyes
As is the dayspring from the morning's womb
Unto that wretch whose nights are tedious.
As liberty to captives, health to labourers,
And life still to old people, never weary on't,
So welcome art thou to me. The deed's done,
Thou queen of spirits. He has his end upon him.
Thy body shall return to rise again,
For thy abuser falls, and has no power
To vex thee further now.

SPIRIT My truest love,
Live ever honoured here, and blest above. [*Exit*]

TYRANT
O, if there be a hell for flesh and spirit,

TYRANT Govianus!
What fury gave thee boldness to attempt
This deed, for which I'll doom thee with a death
Beyond th'extremest tortures!

GOVIANUS I smile at thee.
Draw all the death that ever mankind suffered
Unto one head to help thine own invention,
And make my end as rare as this thy sin
And full as fearful to the eyes of women,
My spirit shall fly singing to his lodging
In midst of that rough weather. Doom me, tyrant!
Had I feared death, I'd never appeared noble
To seal this act upon me which e'en honours me
Unto my mistress' spirit—it loves me for't.
I told my heart 'twould prove destruction to't,
Who, hearing 'twas for her, charged me to do't.

TYRANT
Thy glories shall be shortened! Who's within, there?
Enter the Ghost in the same form as the Lady is dressed in the chair
I called not thee, thou enemy to firmness,
Mortality's earthquake.

GOVIANUS Welcome to mine eyes
As is the dayspring from the morning's womb
Unto that wretch whose nights are tedious.
As liberty to captives, health to labourers,
And life still to old people, never weary on't,
So welcome art thou to me. The deed's done,
Thou queen of spirits. He has his end upon him.
Thy body shall return to rise again,
For thy abuser falls, and has no power
To vex thee further.

SPIRIT My truest love,
Live ever honoured here, and blest above. [*Exit*]

TYRANT
O, if there be a hell for flesh and spirit,

A130 **for thee** because of you
A137 **ghosts beside** other (damned) spirits
A137–8 **Is . . . too?** Is your pride so great that you cannot bear anyone to endure equal suffering in hell?
A141 **beyond the Frenchmen's tortures** i.e. worse than—the execution of François Ravaillac, assassin of King Henri IV in May 1610, was intended as a spectacular warning: after torture, he was torn apart by horses.
A143/B118 **Unto one head** together
A146/B121 **lodging** i.e. in heaven
A147/B122 **Doom** condemn
A148–50/B123–5 **Had . . . spirit** Had I feared death, I would not have come forward nobly to perform this act myself, which makes me honoured in the eyes of my lady's spirit.
A152/B127 **Who** i.e. my heart
A154–5/B129–30 **firmness . . . earthquake** the Lady's ghost makes the living shake (as an earthquake would) with fear
A156/B131 **the dayspring . . . womb** the birth of the morning (dayspring is dawn)
A161/B136 **He . . . him** He's dying (compare *Changeling*, 2.2.136, and the previous line with 2.2.143–4)
A162/B137 **to rise again** i.e. at the last judgement, when it was believed that all bodies would be resurrected

'Tis built within this bosom! My lords, treason!
Enter [Memphonius and] Nobles

GOVIANUS
Now, death, I'm for thee: welcome!

TYRANT
Your king's poisoned!

MEMPHONIUS
The King of heav'n be praised for't!

TYRANT
Lay hold on him,
On Govianus.

MEMPHONIUS
E'en with the best loves
And truest hearts that ever subjects owed.

TYRANT
How's that? I charge you both, lay hands on him!

MEMPHONIUS
Look you, my lord, your will shall be obeyed.
[The Nobles lay their hands on Govianus in homage.]
Enter Helvetius
Here comes another. We'll have his hand, too.

HELVETIUS
You shall have both mine, if that work go forward,
Beside my voice and knee.
[He lays his hands on Govianus]

TYRANT
Helvetius?
Then my destruction was confirmed amongst 'em,
Premeditation wrought it.
[The Nobles kneel to Govianus]
O, my torments!

ALL *[rising]*
Live Govianus long our virtuous king!

TYRANT
That thunder strikes me dead!
[He dies]

GOVIANUS
I cannot better
Reward my joys than with astonished silence,
For all the wealth of words is not of power
To make up thanks for you, my honoured lords.
I'm like a man plucked up from many waters
That never looked for help, and am here placed
Upon this cheerful mountain where prosperity
Shoots forth her richest beam.

MEMPHONIUS
Long injured lord,
The tyranny of his actions grew so weighty,
His life so vicious—

HELVETIUS
To which this is witness,

'Tis built within this bosom! My lords, treason!
Enter [Memphonius and] Nobles

GOVIANUS
Now, death, I'm for thee: welcome!

TYRANT
I am poisoned!

MEMPHONIUS
The King of heav'n be praised for't!

TYRANT
Lay hold on him,
On Govianus.

MEMPHONIUS
E'en with the best loves
And truest hearts that ever subjects owed.

TYRANT
How's that? I charge you all, lay hands on him!

MEMPHONIUS
Look you, my lord, your will shall be obeyed.
[The Nobles lay their hands on Govianus in homage]

ALL *[rising]*
Live Govianus long our virtuous king!
A flourish

TYRANT
That thunder strikes me dead!
[He dies]

A168/B143 **for thee** i.e. ready for thee. Govianus is expecting to be put to death, so the Nobles' reaction takes him by surprise.

A169/B144 **Lay hold on him** 'Seize him'. Memphonius deliberately misinterprets his words to mean 'lay hands on him in homage', here and at l. A172/B148.

A173.3 ***Enter Helvetius*** Helvetius's final appearance, though prepared for by the additional passage at B4.2a, was cut in the final production.

A175 **both mine** i.e. my hands. This moment recalls A2.1.154.1/B2.1.115.1, where the kneeling Helvetius asked Govianus for his blessing; this time it is his turn to confer gifts on Govianus.

A177 **Then...'em** The Tyrant mistakenly concludes that his death was the result of a conspiracy between Govianus and the Nobles.

A180/B150 **thunder** i.e. the shout in the previous line (but perhaps also suggesting God's punishment, as at B5.1.166)

A181 **reward** respond to

A183 **make up** compose, put together (adequate thanks)

A184–7 **plucked...beam** In Psalm 18:16–17, the speaker is 'drawn out of many waters' and 'delivered from my strong enemy'; mountain and sunshine figure worldly success, e.g. at A1.1.144/B1.1.125, A214–15/B191–2, and appear together in *No Wit*, 6.254–7.

[*Pointing to the Lady's body*]
Monster in sin, this the disquieted body
Of my too resolute child in honour's war.

MEMPHONIUS
—That he became as hateful to our minds—

HELVETIUS
—As death's unwelcome to a house of riches,
Or what can more express it.

GOVIANUS
Well, he's gone,
And all the kingdom's evils perish with him!
And since the body of that virtuous lady
Is taken from her rest, in memory
Of her admirèd mistress, 'tis our will
It receive honour dead, as it took part
With us in all afflictions when it lived.
Here place her in this throne, crown her our queen,
The first and last that ever we make ours,
Her constancy strikes so much firmness in us.
[*The Lady's body is placed on the throne and crowned*]
That honour done, let her be solemnly borne
Unto the house of peace from whence she came
As queen of silence.
The Spirit [*of the Lady*] *enters again and stays to go out with the body, as it were attending it*
O welcome, blessed spirit,
Thou need'st not mistrust me; I have a care
As jealous as thine own. We'll see it done
And not believe report. Our zeal is such,
We cannot reverence chastity too much.
Lead on.
I would those ladies that fill honour's rooms
Might all be borne so honest to their tombs.
[*Exeunt, carrying the bodies of the Lady and the Tyrant*]
Recorders or other solemn music plays them out
[*The throne is withdrawn*]
Finit Actus Quintus

GOVIANUS
Well, he's gone,
And all the kingdom's evils perish with him!
And since the body of that virtuous lady
Is taken from her rest, in memory
Of her admirèd mistress, 'tis our will
It receive honour dead, as it took part
With us in all afflictions when it lived.
The Spirit [*of the Lady*] *enters again and stays to go out with the body, as it were attending it*
O welcome, blessed spirit,
Thou need'st not mistrust me; I have a care
As jealous as thine own. We'll see it done
And not believe report. Our zeal is such,
We cannot reverence chastity too much.
Lead on.
I would those ladies that fill honour's rooms
Might all be borne so virtuous to their tombs.
[*Exeunt, carrying the bodies of the Lady and the Tyrant*]
Recorders or other solemn music plays them out
[*The throne is withdrawn*]
Finit Actus Quintus

A194 **Or ... it** compare 4.1.129

A197–8/B153–4 **in ... mistress** The crowning of the Lady is to be performed 'in memory' of his mistress's soul, thus distinguishing it from the Tyrant's worship of her body. This distinction may be intended to recall the Protestant revision of the act of communion, to be taken not 'as' but 'in remembrance' of Christ's body (see Introduction, 838).

A202–3 **and ... us** Govianus will not marry again, so impressed has he been by his Lady's constancy.

A208/B159 **jealous** watchful, careful

A209–10/B160–1 **Our ... much** Compare *Truth*: 'Her goodnesses are such, | We cannot honour her and her house too much' (457–8); and, less closely, *Revenger* 5.2.7–8.

A212–13/B163–4 **I ... tombs** The final couplet is addressed to court ladies, whose lax morals have been a recurrent theme of the play—'honour's rooms' are also the 'lord's rooms' (i.e. boxes) at the theatre. The suggestion that 'honourable ladies' should also be 'honest' (i.e. chaste) was toned down by the censor.

THE PARTS

Adult Males

The TYRANT (436 lines): Anselmus *or* Votarius *or* Bellarius; Fellows; Servant of Lady; Servants of Anselmus

GOVIANUS (344 lines): none

VOTARIUS (329 lines): Tyrant *or* Helvetius *or* Memphonius *or* Sophonirus; Servant of Lady; Fellows; Soldiers *or* Nobles

ANSELMUS (169 lines): Tyrant *or* Helvetius *or* Memphonius *or* Sophonirus; Servant of Lady; Fellows; Soldiers *or* Nobles

HELVETIUS (136 lines): Anselmus *or* Votarius *or* Bellarius; Fellows; Servants of Anselmus; Soldiers (if distinct from Guard)

BELLARIUS (77 lines): Tyrant *or* Helvetius *or* Memphonius *or* Sophonirus; Servant of Lady; Fellows; Soldiers *or* Nobles

SOPHONIRUS (72 lines): Anselmus *or* Votarius *or* Bellarius; Servants of Anselmus; Soldiers

FIRST SOLDIER (45 lines): (if distinct from Guard) Helvetius *or* Sophonirus; Anselmus *or* Votarius*or* Bellarius; servant of Lady; servants of Anselmus; Nobles

MEMPHONIUS (25 lines): Anselmus *or* Votarius *or* Bellarius; Servant of Lady; Fellows; Servants of Anselmus

FIRST FELLOW (19 lines): Tyrant *or* Helvetius *or* Memphonius; Anselmus *or* Votarius *or* Bellarius; Servant of Lady; Servants of Anselmus; Soldiers *or* Nobles

SECOND SOLDIER (18 lines): same as First Soldier

SERVANT of Lady (15 lines): Tyrant *or* Memphonius; Anselmus *or* Votarius *or* Bellarius; Servants of Anselmus; Fellows; Soldiers *or* Nobles

SECOND FELLOW (12 lines): same as First Fellow

Boys

The WIFE (237 lines): The Lady *or* page of Govianus

LEONELLA (169 lines): The Lady *or* page of Govianus

The LADY (168 lines): The Wife *or* Leonella

PAGE of Govianus (1 line): The Wife *or* Leonella

In the performance version, Helvetius's part at 5.2 has been cut altogether, which may indicate that he was played by a particular character actor, rather than being doubled. Allowing for rapid costume changes, it would have been technically possible for the Lady to double as the Wife, Leonella as the page, and for Sophonirus, Memphonius and the Tyrant to play Anselmus, Votarius and Bellarius, so that as few as 7 actors would have been required, plus walk-on parts. The two soldiers and/or fellows would have been played by clowns.

A CHASTE MAID IN CHEAPSIDE

Edited by Linda Woodbridge

Among the greatest of Middleton's city comedies, *A Chaste Maid in Cheapside* is a blistering satire whose relentless sexual jests lend a farcical atmosphere; but this can darken to unveil bleak vistas: with Sir Walter's collapse and the Allwits' defection the 'farcical surface... buckle[s], exposing the authentic horror of *The Changeling* and *Women Beware Women*' (R. B. Parker). Farce serves the cause of 'horror': in a superficial world of materialism, sensuality, self-serving, and cheap intrigue, horror lies in recognizing that this ugly surface *is* the world: there is nothing underneath. Life's farcicality, unlike its tragedy, is offset not even by human dignity; such recognitions are savage. Yet *Chaste Maid*'s very savagery crackles with vitality and a spirit of play.

The romantic plot is primarily sexual (though—compared to the rest of the play—refreshingly non-commercial). Touchstone Junior first speaks of his love in appetitive terms ('I must hasten it, | Or else peak o' famine; her blood's mine'), and addresses Moll first in unromantic prose (1.1.145–6, 150–5). 'Who can imagine a Berlioz or a Tchaikovsky writing a Touchstone Junior and Moll Yellowhammer overture?' demands G. R. Hibbard. (Though one *might* imagine songs written for them by Cole Porter or Kurt Weill.) Shakespearean comedy's joyful promise of fruition is here translated into a harsh 'nowadays'; though Middleton is obsessively interested in fertility, conception often proves disastrous, and not one of the play's babies is legitimate (Arthur Marotti). At the wedding, fruition is not mentioned. Though Ruby Chatterji finds family values affirmed in the emphasis on family life—birth, christening, education, and marrying of children—Joanne Altieri notes the play's exposure of kinship relations as economic relations. Satiric touches undermine the play's Aristophanic celebration of sex as a priapic elemental force: Touchwood Senior's keeping fools to which to marry his pregnant wenches is a quite unmythic family planning.

The funeral scene has been condemned as Beaumont-and-Fletcher-style cheap theatricality, and defended as a legacy of the *commedia dell'arte*, as an echo of fertility ritual's rebirths, or as parody of contemporary plays' extravagant theatricality. The abrupt rising of 'corpses' from coffins could be staged as a comical popping-up, like jacks-in-the-box. This scene is punctuated by unison utterances by everyone on stage; the first, 'Ne'er more pity!', sounds like a congregational response, but the third, 'Alive, sir? O sweet, dear couple!' might well be delivered by the assembled cast in a self-consciously camp style, as might the longest united declaration, 'Never was hour so filled with joy and wonder' (5.4.21, 30, 53). E. A. J. Honigmann discusses ways to make such simultaneous utterance more realistic on stage; but in this scene a frankly non-realistic delivery might be highly effective.

There are several 'humours' characters, each governed by one hyperbolic trait—Touchwood Senior's tall-tale virility, Allwit's preening wittoldry, the Kixes' fighting and reconciling. The protagonist is Cheapside life. The play combines densely specified Jacobean London rejoicing in sophisticated urban gamesmanship with figures and action from Roman comedy (the outwitted old father, the witty servant) and from folk tradition. From folk tale come the childless couple, numskull brother, clever wench (both the Wench with the child and Susan), the motif of the biter bit, and above all the tricksters. Touchwood Junior tricks Yellowhammer with a ring; Allwit and the Wench trick the Promoters; Sir Walter tricks Tim into marrying a 'whore'; Touchwood Senior tricks Sir Oliver with a potion; a series of tricks spirit Moll away. Aptly for a world of trickery and false appearance, over seventy speeches are delivered as asides. Surprise and reversal of expectation abound. Touchwood Senior's sober encomium to companionate marriage is followed by his confessing he has got seven women pregnant in three weeks. The Wench's pitiful 'thou hast undone me' yields to her revealing that she accuses various men of fathering her infant(s), and she abandons her baby. Yellowhammer's shock at hearing of Sir Walter's turpitude yields to his remarks on his own bastard. Early reversals undercut seemingly virtuous characters; late-play repentances and changes of heart continue the campaign of surprise—though in late play, too, comes the sudden revelation of cold ruthlessness underlying Allwit's wife's bovine complacency.

Mecca of tricksters, London springs to life, with its wharfs, steeples, guildhalls, gutters. Middleton began writing Lord Mayor's shows the year *Chaste Maid* was first acted; to *The Triumphs of Truth*, *Chaste Maid* is almost an anti-pageant, exposing London at its worst. As Gail Paster argues, civic pageants and city comedy exemplify *laus* (praise) and *vituperatio* (blame), idealization in the one just as hyperbolic as cynicism in the other (*Idea*). The city's moral status is slippery: the comedies' exposés of city wickedness shade off into celebration of city sophistication. Middleton avoids the city-bashing of pastoral writers to whom the countryside is a repository of simplicity and virtue: his Wench and Welsh gentlewoman are as corrupt and street-wise as the canniest Londoners.

Street-smartness is itself a primary value, and scorn is heaped on its converse, university education.

The play offers a textbook example of Gayle Rubin's 'Traffic in Women'. In a nexus of money and sex, Allwit exchanges his wife for material comforts; Sir Walter values Moll for her dowry; Lady Kix's pregnancy has cash value. Like other misers of both gold and women (Shakespeare's Shylock, Spenser's Malbecco), Yellowhammer locks up his daughter 'as carefully as my gold', and equates elopement with theft, with daughter-stealing (3.1.41–3, 1.1.207). London was already one of the world's great commercial cities; Heywood's *If You Know Not Me, You Know Nobody, Part 2* (1605) renders mythic the founding of the Royal Exchange. Yet there is something fishy about *Chaste Maid*'s financial world. Though commercial and sexual value operated on a gold standard—a chaste maiden was proverbially 'a girl worth gold'—the opening scene in a goldsmith's shop reveals a world of shifting and shifty value. Moll's love affair involves a commercial transaction over a ring, and is juxtaposed with a transaction involving a gold chain. Though goldsmiths sell, for money, objects fashioned from gold, here a gentleman tries to sell a goldsmith already-fashioned jewellery for money. That his first business in the play is assessing jewellery to be melted down gives Yellowhammer the air less of a respectable artisan than of a pawnbroker or even a fence. This erosion of the play's gold standard (abetted by talk of counterfeiting) may reflect on Moll's chastity too. The shopkeeper's formula 'What is't you lack?' (1.1.100) is apt for a consumer society—not having everything is construed as lack; but this gentleman lacks not goods but money. In a play in which much is consumed, the consumer society creates not wealth but lack. The absence from the play of those city-comedy favourites, prostitutes, bawds, and usurers, alerts us to the fact that it locates its marketed sex not in the streets but within marriage, while the complement of marketed sex, usurers' grasping materialism, here resides within the respectable milieu of shopkeepers and tradesmen.

The early modern shift to a money-based from a land-based economy habituated the mind to abstraction, a disappearance of the material that is like consumption. The gentleman values his chain at 100 pounds, residually a measure of weight; Yellowhammer offers 100 marks, a currency whose value was set by the government. In inscription-value money, as in language, abstract signs represent material reality (Marc Shell, Jean-Joseph Goux). *Chaste Maid* associates deceptive words with counterfeit coins: 'Has no attorney's clerk been here o'late | And changed his half-crown piece his mother sent him, | Or rather cozened you with a gilded twopence, | To bring the word in fashion?' (1.1.30–3). The many sexual puns are a sort of counterfeiting—a respectable word turns out to have a filthy meaning, like a gilded tuppence. Like Freud, the play associates money with sexuality: money, sex, and language are weirdly interchangeable. Sir Walter transmits English to his mistress through intercourse, like a venereal disease, and also turns her into gold (1.1.105–7); Tim labours to *beget* an epitaph (5.2.22); a man is to 'utter all' on his wedding night (5.4.48)—'utter' could mean to speak, to ejaculate sexually, to sell in the market, or to pass counterfeit money. 'Metaphors are words exchanged for other words' (Allen Hoey), and the play's similes often represent monetary exchange. The Welsh counterfeit virgin's fortune 'shine[s] like [her] bright trade', the simile exchanging 'fortune' for prostitution; Moll, 'like a mermaid', may be 'sold to fishwives' (1.1.108; 4.4.30–1).

Of one of Moll's several threats to die, Maudline scoffs, 'You that have tricks can counterfeit' (4.4.26); acting a part was a counterfeit coining. John Vernon's theory that similar mental operations underpin accepting money (as the equivalent of labour or goods) and accepting a realistic fiction as empirical reality works well here. Dense local reference creates 'realism'; but it takes a mentality habituated to accepting money as a signifier to find 'realistic' this outrageous plot, these extravagant caricatures. Whorehound's name specifies his character; yet meaning, transparent to the audience, is opaque to the characters, an impression of realism paid for in counterfeit coin. In the funeral scene, the play slips its mask, metatheatrically trumpeting its own extravagant artifice; here 'play' as acting and 'play' as game intersect. The playwright has been playing with us. An audience that believes in money will believe in anything. The final trick is on us, for finding in the play a realistic London.

England's grand market-place, London lives by exchange. Yellowhammer, making a ring, is one of only a few characters who perform work, or add labour value to an object; the porter and watermen ply their trade, but it is conveyance, not production: this is a world of middlemen, not producers. Allwit has quit work and lives by exchanging his wife; the Welsh gentlewoman exchanges her body as a mistress and later a wife. The gentry live off inheritance. Here is no green world, no contact with a world where food, cloth, metal are produced. And the market-place was changing, from an open area of communal life to a set of private shops, the commercial equivalent of the increasingly interiorized abstracting mind, unlike the more community-oriented medieval personality. This play about antisocial selfishness opens in a private shop, and satirizes both Puritans and acquisitive bourgeoisie. The Puritan ideal of knowing God by 'inner light', which helped interiorize the personality, risked a tendency to selfishness, to disregard of community and even family. The language of material exchange structured even spiritual life: Sir Walter repents that he has 'exchanged [his] soul' for sexual pleasure (5.1.81). The selfish greed of the ideal capitalist citizen is Cheapside's foremost trait.

The exchange system included brokered marriages. A Moll/Sir Walter match would give a merchant family gentility and a gentleman money. Tim's marriage is supposed to give a bourgeois family land. The Civil War was only a generation off, and much class tension simmers in Middleton's plays. In *Chaste Maid* citizens acquire gentlemen's possessions (the Allwits keep the booty that has helped to bankrupt Sir Walter) and a lewd knight consorts with a citizen's wife. Allwit thinks merchants live largely at the expense of 'prodigal heirs' (1.2.44). Servants, too, figure in class tensions: Allwit's and Sir Oliver's servants satirize their masters. Sometimes lower classes speak for the common decency their 'betters' neglect: the watermen call Maudline 'cruel'; Susan, 'made of pity', helps the lovers (3.3.29). But the money-mindedness and self-interest infecting various classes in the play erode class distinctions. And the play itself was commercial, part of a lucrative entertainment industry; *Chaste Maid*'s language/money equation points to the drama's own embeddedness in the market (see Douglas Bruster).

Sexual profligacy, part of the popular stereotype of gentlemen, does not disqualify Sir Walter or the 'decayed gentleman' Touchwood Senior from gentility in characters' eyes. Allwit's wittoldry, however, threatens to drop him out of the respectable middle class: 'he's but one pip above a servingman' (1.2.67–8). In a patriarchal society, a husband's abdication of sexual rights was the most contemptible of failings; our own marital climate, less patriarchal, may obscure for us how anti-ideological is Allwit's behaviour. The ubiquitous Renaissance cuckold jokes remind us how deep ran concerns about patriarchal authority and familial legitimacy—seriously disrupted by the Allwits and Kixes.

In the Renaissance, water imagery conventionally attended concupiscible passions—lust, gluttony, acquisitiveness (as in Spenser's *Faerie Queene*, book 2). The prominence of the latter passions in *Chaste Maid* makes logical its association of concupiscence with liquids. As Gail Paster shows, the play's permeable females drink too much, talk loosely, cry copiously, are sexually loose, and wet themselves ('Leaky Vessels'). The ideal woman was a sealed container, letting no drink or semen in, no tears, talk, or urine out. One index of Moll's chastity is that, like a 'good' woman in patriarchal ideology, she speaks little: when upset she cries 'O death'; when happy she murmurs 'I am silent with delight' (5.4.49). (Even the contemptuous term 'baggage', seven times applied to her, suggests a container.) Renaissance men were to go out to work, women to work in the house, reflecting the container metaphor; men were to make money, women to conserve through household thrift. (Women who worked in shops—often in the same premises as their homes—are a frequent source of male sexual anxiety in city comedies.) Paster thinks the pervasive images of female leakiness reflect cultural anxiety about women's potential for disrupting the protocapitalist system through spending rather than conserving. Male sexuality too is expressed in liquids: Touchwood Senior's 'water' or semen, or the name 'Walter'—pronounced 'Water'—for a lewd gentleman. In the usual way of gender ideology, female liquidity represents leakiness, while male liquidity spells potency.

That the lovers' break for freedom leads naturally to the river is a hint that London mirrors the human body. The Thames is the city's 'master-vein' which 'shoots from the heart' (3.1.16): 'blood' (that is, lust) naturally seeks it. Escape (from a household, from restraint) leads to lower ground and flowing water, associated with sex and with urine and excrement: Puddle Wharf, where horses left puddles, and Dung Wharf, where garbage was loaded on to barges, are to the city what urethra and anus are to the body. Yellowhammer tries to make his house a sealed-up vagina; Allwit's house in its fecundity and gluttony is womb and mouth. Though called 'the heart of the city' (1.1.101–2), Cheapside, home to grocers and butchers, is more the mouth of London: gustatory and sexual consumption proceed unchecked even in Lent.

This Lenten play is set in a meat market. 1613, when the play was first acted, saw one of the strictest Lents ever: the harvest had failed and meat was severely restricted. Yet a spirit of pre-Lent carnival pervades the play, recalling Bruegel's painting *The Battle of Carnival and Lent*. In *Chaste Maid*, Carnival seems to be winning. Mikhail Bakhtin shows how in carnival's topsy-turvydom, lower-body functions—eating, sex, urination, excretion—overwhelm the upper body's emotional, spiritual, and intellectual concerns. The play's main emotional tie, between the lovers, is openly sexual. Advocates of spiritual life, Puritans, are seen tippling, pilfering food, and lusting, and a parson leers 'I'll not be long | A-clapping you together' (3.1.8–9). Intellectual life is reduced to Tim and his tutor, a move which uncrowns the university. The outwitting of the Promoters who enforce Lenten laws is a carnivalesque subversion of obnoxious authority, as is the inversion wherein servants speak for common decency. Language is topsy-turvy: learned, cerebral Latin is translated into Anglo-Saxon monosyllables belonging to the lower body: *parentibus* becomes 'a pair of boots'; *fertur* becomes 'farts' (1.1.71, 4.1.114–16). The frank talk of sex, eating, excreting is also carnivalesque; improprieties are 'unofficial elements of speech, ... liberated from norms, hierarchies, and prohibitions of established idiom' (Bakhtin); as Susan Wells notes, satirists like Middleton 'were claiming a similar right to free speech'. Carnival expressed class tensions; but it had also traditionally comprised a festive world where a community celebrated together, and Middleton's invoking it exposes poignantly the breakdown of communality in this savagely self-centred society.

Meat-smuggling, conspicuous consumption at the baptism, gold jewellery, Allwit's orgasmic inventories of his goods—all paint brilliantly a consumer society, which finally consumes even people. Women are 'mutton'. Puritan brethren are 'consumed' (3.2.48). And a whiff of cannibalism attends the baby smuggled under meat, a prophetic glimpse of Swift's world, where a baby born poor might as well be eaten as starve. For all its scorching satire, the play's values are hard to pinpoint. No character 'sets a moral standard' (David Richman). Not even Moll: she bears a criminal name, is not put off by her lover's filthy talk, keeps trying to elope; and one can hardly serve as the play's moral centre who speaks so few lines—a total of forty-seven in the play, less than a third of the lines even of the witless Tim. Only four of Moll's speeches are more than one line long. This title figure is sketchily characterized, and though silence was linked to chastity, she could easily be staged as a sulky teenager or even an oversexed bimbo. People triumph at the end 'not because they are good but because they are clever intriguers' (Parker). 'Only Sir Walter is thoroughly penitent, and only Sir Walter is thoroughly crushed' (Alexander Leggatt); the scapegoating of Sir Walter, who siphons off the others' guilt, screams out the absence of poetic justice. Stephen Wigler sees Allwit/Touchwood Senior and Whorehound as Jungian 'splits', with Allwit/Touchwood the infantile self, given creature comforts and taking no responsibility for children fathered, and Whorehound the adult self which (however lewd) accepts family responsibility. This being so, the outcome conspicuously fails to valorize adult values: sympathetic figures 'live as if there were no tomorrow'; Sir Walter, who 'provide[s] carefully for the next day', is annihilated. Adultery is rewarded: for Lady Kix's adultery, the Kixes receive what they wanted: a baby, an inheritance, a reputation as a man for Sir Oliver. The lack of a moral centre, the 'starless ensemble character' of the action (Altieri), the reversals which keep us off balance, foster a decentredness congenial to our post-modern climate.

The play's treatment of women is mixed. Some speakers who paint women as commodities, property, food, as extravagant, sexually loose, leaky, gluttonous, or garrulous are being satirized for their attitudes, but the women's behaviour allows some charges to stick. The christening party is a fine example of the 'gossips' meeting' genre, a traditional male-authored vehicle for antifeminist comment, as is the schooling of a young woman by an older, with frank talk of men and sex, which opens the play (Woodbridge). The allusion to cosmetics' disgusting ingredients (3.2.53–4) belongs to an ancient misogynistic topos. Partly because literature lacked similar topoi for criticizing the male sex, the vices and follies of individual male characters tend not to be generalized to the male sex as a whole; generalizations about women at 1.1.36, 3.2.62–3, 3.2.203, and 5.4.15–16 find no counterpart in generalizations about males. Education was closed to most women, and Latin a male preserve; but Latinless women (Maudline, the Welsh gentlewoman) are still scorned. Moll can be bought and sold in marriage by parents who own her, but no one criticizes patriarchy; it may be 'not the system going wrong here but Moll's despicably bad parents'. We see nothing of Allwit's wife's feelings about her prostituted state, and the text 'makes us regret that Allwit is not more of a patriarchal male' (Ingrid Hotz-Davies). On the positive side, the play has an extraordinary number of female characters—twenty-one out of fifty-four or fifty-five. As is very rare in Shakespeare, a woman speaks the opening lines. Unlike the contemporary *Triumphs of Truth* which opens with an idealized Mother London, *Chaste Maid* is hard on mothers (Maudline, Allwit's wife, Lady Kix, the Wench), but at least (unlike many Shakespeare plays) it *has* mothers. In a play valuing street-smartness, women are among the most successful tricksters: the Wench, Susan, the Welsh gentlewoman, even (at last) Moll.

Notions of masculinity are unstable. Allwit abdicates conventional masculinity in not locking up his wife or exhibiting patriarchal dynastic concern. Such potential feminism is presented as an erosion of masculinity, as is his 'cotqueanish', unmanly interest in domestic furnishings; yet the character's sheer theatrical appeal subverts any easy pronouncements about patriarchy. Though Allwit's neglect of jealousy may undermine his masculinity, Sir Walter's rigorous jealousy does not make him a model male, nor does his sexual potency, which is presented as mere lewdness, though Touchwood Senior's priapism is treated with good-humoured indulgence, combining with his trickery to produce a near-magical figure of male potency. Manly Touchwood Senior is bereft of worldly goods, while those most prosperous are deficient in conventional masculinity—Yellowhammer the outwitted father, Allwit the wittol/cotquean, Sir Oliver the impotent. Critical of his society's materialism, Middleton did not define masculinity in terms of material success. Nor of violence: the one instance of physical aggression—the duel—ends with both parties severely wounded and nothing settled in the way of respective masculinity. Though women are mocked for ignorance, Tim's foolishness and the irrelevance of Latin disputation to practical life undermine intellectual prowess as a bulwark of masculinity. The one context where formation of masculine identity could have been explored, Tim's coming-of-age, treats the issue flippantly. And to the extent that a patriarchy depends on certainty of paternity, in Cheapside the state totters.

In a world lacking manual labour, sex role distinctions are diminished. Living by exchange, trickery, and inheritance rather than by productive labour destabilizes gender roles. Antifeminism and uncertainty about masculinity are both symptoms of that potentially fruitful (though locally uncomfortable) instability.

Reflecting fluid boundaries of social class, the play's versification effaces the common distinction in which lower orders speak prose. Allwit's servants, the Kixes' maid, the Wet Nurse, Wench, Watermen, even the Promoters speak verse. The verse/prose boundary is fluid too, with prose heavily rhythmic while verse is angular and unmetrical, with irregular syllable counts, and with many anapaests and feminine endings. The racy, colloquial effect resembles the 'strong lines' of contemporary John Donne. Despite its jaunty, prosy air, *Chaste Maid* is Middleton's only city comedy mainly in verse.

Exploring the play's intricate structure, Richard Levin notes four sexual triangles of two men and one woman: in the Touchwood Junior/Moll/Sir Walter triangle, the elder Yellowhammers labour to prevent a marriage and fail, but later accept it; in the Tim/Welsh gentlewoman/Sir Walter triangle, they promote a marriage and succeed, but later regret it. (Moll's dowry of £2,000 in gold symbolizes her virtue; the Welsh gentlewoman's imaginary two thousand runts, her vacuum of virtue. Moll sings a piteous, sentimental song, the Welsh gentlewoman a bawdy one.)

The Allwits/Sir Walter triangle and the Kixes/Touchwood Senior triangle involve a long-married couple and cuckolding man. The Kixes have been married seven years with no child; Sir Walter has kept Allwit's wife for seven years, with seven children. The first marriage displays true affection despite scrapping; the second is sordid, a business arrangement. (Levin's scheme neglects the Touchwood Seniors/Wench triangle.) The brilliant dovetailing of five plots is a *tour de force* even in an age revelling in multiple plots, yet 'the play never sprawls under the weight of its abundance' (Samuel Schoenbaum). An adaptation of ancient 'ring composition' can be glimpsed in the parallel between the first and last scenes, between 2.1 and 3.3, and elsewhere. The play also twins scenes: one illegitimate baby elaborately christened, another ingeniously abandoned; Allwit and Touchwood Senior both uttering soliloquies praising the married state in circumstances undercutting the praise; hypocritical promoters drooling over the flesh they confiscate, hypocritical Puritans professing spirituality while succumbing to animal appetites.

There are no definite sources but several close analogues (see R. C. Bald). The fertility-potion plot recalls Machiavelli's *Mandragola* and Andrea Calmo's *La Potione*. Allwit resembles the wittol in Mateo Aleman's *Guzman de Alfarache*, and his soliloquy echoes (at one point verbatim) Thomas Campion's *Observations in the Art of English Poesie*. The christening scenes may be indebted to *The Bachelor's Banquet*, a translation of the antifeminist *Le Quinze joies de mariage*, although lore of guzzling gossips was widespread. The Wench's baby trick may echo an event reported in an anonymous pamphlet of 1613, though such tricks (often involving country wenches duping shrewd cockneys) are common in ballads. The lamb/baby trick, the couple impoverished by too many children, the juxtaposition of tricksters with a central Christian festival, the alliance of a married couple (the Allwits) for trickery, recall the Wakefield cycle's *Second Shepherd's Play*; the guild plays' volatile mix of religious sobriety, socio-political shrewdness, and merry hi-jinks may have contributed to the tone of Middleton's city comedies. It is fitting that *The Second Shepherd's Play*, the first English double-plot play, has some relationship to one of the best English multiple-plot plays, *Chaste Maid*.

The play was first acted at the Swan Theatre by Lady Elizabeth's Men, probably augmented (to handle the many female roles) by the Queen's Revels boys, for whom Middleton had written earlier city comedies. The action and language of *Chaste Maid* undercut Alfred Harbage's theory of the uplifting influence of public theatre audiences. After its Jacobean performances, the full play was not staged again (to our knowledge) until 1938, perhaps because too bawdy, but the bawdy later twentieth century has seen many revivals, the majority at universities. (The revenge of Tim?) The first modern professional revival, William Gaskill's at the Royal Court Theatre in London in 1966, was variously reviewed as a justly neglected 'filthy farce' and as a 'bawdy, realistic, and brilliantly directed comedy of Jacobean London' (Parker). *Chaste Maid* has been produced oftener than any Middleton play except *The Changeling* and *The Revenger's Tragedy* (Marilyn Roberts). Modern productions often cut the promoters and many topical references; but those retaining the topical have found audiences responsive to the densely realized urban world, however unfamiliar the place-names. The play will have a stage future as long as audiences can respond to wit, trickery, brilliant plotting, infectious cynicism, and sheer vitality. It still bids us, in Maudline's words, 'Draw near and taste the welcome of the city'.

SEE ALSO

Music: *Companion*, 145 ('Weep eyes, break heart'), 149 ('Cupid is Venus' only joy')
Textual introduction and apparatus: *Companion*, 1011
Authorship and date: *Companion*, 373

A Chaste Maid in Cheapside

[for Lady Elizabeth's Men and the Children of the Queen's Revels at The Swan]

THE NAMES OF THE PRINCIPAL PERSONS

Master YELLOWHAMMER, a goldsmith
MAUDLINE, his wife
TIM, their son
MOLL, their daughter
TUTOR to Tim
SIR WALTER Whorehound, a suitor to Moll
SIR OLIVER Kix }
His wife, LADY Kix } kin to Sir Walter
Master Jack ALLWIT
His WIFE, whom Sir Walter keeps
WELSH GENTLEWOMAN, Sir Walter's whore
WAT }
NICK } his bastards
DAVY Dahumma, his man
TOUCHWOOD SENIOR, a decayed gentleman
His WIFE
TOUCHWOOD JUNIOR, his brother, another suitor to Moll
SUSAN, maid to Yellowhammer
Two PROMOTERS
Nine SERVANTS, two to Allwit, one to a comfit-maker, four to Kix, two to Sir Walter
A PORTER
A GENTLEMAN with a chain
A WENCH, former sexual partner of Touchwood Senior
Her baby
A MAID to the Kixes
A DRY NURSE to Allwit's Wife's baby
A WET NURSE to Allwit's Wife's baby
Allwit's Wife's baby
Two MEN, with meat in baskets
Two PURITAN women
A NURSE
Midwife
Five GOSSIPS
A PARSON
Three or four WATERMEN, one named Sam

1.1 *[Incipit] Actus Primus*

Enter Maudline and Moll, a shop being discovered

MAUDLINE Have you played over all your old lessons o' the virginals?

MOLL Yes.

MAUDLINE Yes? You are a dull maid o' late; methinks you had need have somewhat to quicken your green sickness. Do you weep? A husband. Had not such a piece of flesh been ordained, what had us wives been good for? To make salads, or else cried up and down for samphire. To see the difference of these seasons! When I was of your youth, I was lightsome, and quick, two years before I was married. You, fit for a knight's bed! Drowsy-browed, dull-eyed, drossy-sprited. I hold my life you have forgot your dancing. When was the dancer with you?

MOLL
The last week.

Title Possible pun on 'chaste': (*a*) sexually pure; (*b*) chased (Moll is pursued by two suitors and—in three elopement attempts—by her parents; with a possible suggestion of prostitutes 'chased' behind carts as a punishment). The echo effect between 'chaste maid' and 'Cheapside' sets the one against the other, suggesting that Cheapside is a difficult place in which to stay chaste. The title may well be meant to sound oxymoronic, like *Honest Whore*. Cheapside was the market district, the word coming from the Anglo-Saxon *ceap* meaning 'market'.

1.1.0.2 ***Maudline*** Derived from pictures of the weeping Mary Magdalene (a reformed prostitute), the name suggested tearful sentimentality and a shady past.

Moll pet form of Mary. Though 'Mary' brings to mind the Virgin, Moll was a traditional name for a prostitute or criminal's companion (see 2.2.69).

discovered revealed

2 **virginals** small, harpsichord-like instrument, with a suggestion of 'virgin', or chaste maid

5 **quicken** bring life to; suggests pregnancy

5–6 **green sickness** anemia in young women; unfocused sexual desire

8 **make salads** become salads (associated with impropriety because highly seasoned; also, women without men are like green salads without meat)

cried up and down shouted by sellers up and down the street

9 **samphire** herb provoking urine and desire for meat

seasons times, ages

10 **lightsome** graceful, merry; with a suggestion of 'sexually easy'

quick lively, ready to act; with a suggestion of 'pregnant'

12 **drossy-sprited** scummy-spirited

13 **dancing** Though dancing and musicianship were genteel accomplishments, teachers of dancing and music often had sex with their pupils in popular tales and plays; 'dancing' was slang for sexual intercourse.

MAUDLINE Last week! When I was of your bord,
He missed me not a night; I was kept at it;
I took delight to learn, and he to teach me;
Pretty brown gentleman, he took pleasure in my
company;
But you are dull, nothing comes nimbly from you,
You dance like a plumber's daughter, and deserve
Two thousand pound in lead to your marriage,
And not in goldsmith's ware.

Enter Yellowhammer

YELLOWHAMMER Now, what's the din betwixt mother and daughter, ha?

MAUDLINE Faith, small; telling your daughter Mary of her errors.

YELLOWHAMMER
Errors? Nay, the city cannot hold you, wife,
But you must needs fetch words from Westminster.
I ha' done, i'faith!—
Has no attorney's clerk been here o'late
And changed his half-crown piece his mother sent
him,
Or rather cozened you with a gilded twopence,
To bring the word in fashion for her faults
Or cracks in duty and obedience?
Term 'em e'en so, sweet wife.
As there is no woman made without a flaw,
Your purest lawns have frays, and cambrics bracks.

MAUDLINE
But 'tis a husband solders up all cracks.

MOLL
What, is he come, sir?

YELLOWHAMMER Sir Walter's come:
He was met at Holborn bridge, and in his company
A proper fair young gentlewoman, which I guess
By her red hair and other rank descriptions
To be his landed niece brought out of Wales,
Which Tim our son, the Cambridge boy, must marry.
'Tis a match of Sir Walter's own making,
To bind us to him and our heirs for ever.

MAUDLINE
We are honoured then, if this baggage would be
humble
And kiss him with devotion when he enters.
I cannot get her for my life
To instruct her hand thus, before and after—
Which a knight will look for—before and after.
I have told her still, 'tis the waving of a woman
Does often move a man and prevails strongly.
But, sweet, ha' you sent to Cambridge?
Has Tim word on't?

YELLOWHAMMER Had word just the day after, when you sent him the silver spoon to eat his broth in the hall amongst the gentlemen commoners.

MAUDLINE O, 'twas timely.

Enter Porter

YELLOWHAMMER How now?

PORTER
A letter from a gentleman in Cambridge.

15–18 **When ... company** The whole description of tutelage is sexually suggestive.

15 **bord** bore, calibre (with indecent implication); condition

18 **brown** dark-skinned or tanned, or brunette. Possibly suggests an Italian dancing master, drawing on stereotypes of lascivious Italians.

21 **to your marriage** a reference to the dowry ('to' means 'for')

22 **goldsmith's ware** i.e., gold

22.1 ***Yellowhammer*** (*a*) slang for a gold coin; (*b*) contemptuous term for a jealous husband (here extended to a protective father). He plays the conventional role of the *senex iratus*, angry old man who opposes his child's marital choice in favour of another suitor. Making him a goldsmith may be revenge—a money-lending goldsmith took Middleton to court four years before the play was first acted.

27 **Errors** To Yellowhammer a word with the aura of the law courts with their writs of error, or perhaps of chivalric romance, seems out of place in Goldsmith's Row.
the city The city mentioned so often in Jacobean comedy was both London and the realm of commercial enterprise as opposed to the country, the court, the church, or the university; the city was both a geographical location and a state of mind.
hold contain; also, keep from speaking

28 **must needs** feel driven to
Westminster the law court district

31 **half-crown piece** French crowns were in circulation in England, as well as English crowns and half crowns; the crown was worth five shillings.

32 **cozened** cheated
twopence silver coin worth two pence. The half-crown piece would have been worth about 15 times as much, and, since the twopence was much smaller, only a fool would have mistaken even a gilded half-crown for a twopence.

33 **the word** i.e., 'errors'. The clerk palms off counterfeit words as if they were of the mother tongue, as he fobs off a counterfeit coin as a gold piece given him by his mother. Attorneys are seen as purveyors of deceptive language or hifalutin jargon.

37 **Your ... frays** proverbial
lawns pieces of fine linen, resembling cambric
frays frayed or worn away places
cambrics fine white linens, originally made at Cambray in Flanders
bracks flaws in cloth

38 **solders up all cracks** mends all character flaws, with a sexual innuendo. Here, as often in the play, women are leaky containers.

40 **Holborn bridge** crossing the Fleet ditch on the main road from Wales into London via Newgate

42 **red hair** apparently a sign of Welshness; could also suggest sexual looseness
rank descriptions signifiers of high social standing; with a suggestion of rankness or lustfulness

44 **Tim** sometimes a term of abuse

47 **baggage** impertinent wench, good-for-nothing woman (referring to Moll)

52 **waving** with an affected gesture, perhaps demure or coy face fanning; suggestion of changing capriciously, said in this period to be a feminine flirting tactic

58 **gentlemen commoners** undergraduates whose wealth entitled them to dine apart from poorer students (they also wore different academic dress and paid higher fees). At Cambridge these were actually called 'pensioners'—Middleton's use of the Oxford term may recall his own student days at Oxford, an affiliation which helps account for his making witless Tim a student at Oxford's rival university.

61 **letter** the first of an unusually large number of stage properties in the play

YELLOWHAMMER
O, one of Hobson's porters: thou art welcome!
I told thee Maud, we should hear from Tim. [*He reads*]
Amantissimis carissimisque ambobus parentibus patri et matri.

MAUDLINE What's the matter?

YELLOWHAMMER
Nay, by my troth, I know not; ask not me:
He's grown too verbal, this learning is a great witch.

MAUDLINE
Pray, let me see it; I was wont to understand him.
Amantissimis carissimis: he has sent the carrier's man, he says; *ambobus parentibus*: for a pair of boots; *Patri et matri*: pay the porter or it makes no matter.

PORTER Yes, by my faith, mistress! There's no true construction in that; I have took a great deal of pains and come from the Bell sweating. Let me come to't, for I was a scholar forty years ago. 'Tis thus, I warrant you: *Matri*: it makes no matter; *ambobus parentibus*: for a pair of boots; *patri*: pay the porter: *amantissimis carissimis*: he's the carrier's man, and his name is Sims. And there he says true, forsooth; my name is Sims indeed. I have not forgot all my learning. A money matter; I thought I should hit on't.

YELLOWHAMMER Go, thou art an old fox! [*He gives him money*] There's a tester for thee.

PORTER If I see your worship at Goose Fair, I have a dish of birds for you.

YELLOWHAMMER Why, dost dwell at Bow?

PORTER All my lifetime, sir; I could ever say boo to a goose! Farewell to your worship. *Exit*

YELLOWHAMMER A merry porter!

MAUDLINE How can he choose but be so, coming with Cambridge letters from our son Tim?

YELLOWHAMMER What's here? [*He reads*] *Maximus diligo?* Faith, I must to my learned counsel with this gear, 'twill ne'er be discerned else.

MAUDLINE
Go to my cousin, then, at Inns of Court.

YELLOWHAMMER
Fie, they are all for French; they speak no Latin.

MAUDLINE
The parson then will do it.

Enter a Gentleman with a chain

YELLOWHAMMER Nay, he disclaims it,
Calls Latin 'papistry'; he will not deal with it.
What is't you lack, gentleman?

GENTLEMAN Pray, weigh this chain.

[*Yellowhammer weighs chain*]

Enter Sir Walter Whorehound, Welsh Gentlewoman, and Davy Dahumma

SIR WALTER
Now, wench, thou art welcome to the heart
Of the city of London.

WELSH GENTLEWOMAN *Duw cato chwi.*

SIR WALTER
You can thank me in English, if you list.

WELSH GENTLEWOMAN
I can, sir, simply.

62 **Hobson's** Cambridge carrier, or hauling and message company. Hobson's porters were comic types in the jest book 'The Pleasant Conceits of Old Hobson'.
64–5 ***Amantissimis ... matri*** 'to mother and father, both my most loving and beloved parents' (Latin)
66 **What's the matter?** what does this mean? or, what is wrong?
68 **verbal** verbose
witch bewitcher. To Yellowhammer, the Latin sounds like an incantation.
69 **Pray** I pray thee; i.e., please
was wont to used to
70 **man** employee
72 **matter** sense
73–4 **true construction** accurate translation
75 **the Bell** an inn frequented by Cambridge messengers
come to't have a try at translating it
82 **hit on't** understand it
84 **tester** sixpence
85–7 **Goose Fair ... Bow** a fair at London suburb Stratford-le-Bow featuring young geese; 'goose' also meant fool or whore, and 'bow' could mean 'pudendum'. The Porter's saying 'boo to a goose' puns on 'Bow'; 'boo' was probably pronounced 'bo'.
85–6 **dish of birds** a serving of loose women
88 **ever** always
say boo to a goose proverbial; 'boo' means to shout at or shoo away
89 **worship** form of address in deference to social superior
93 ***Maximus diligo*** Tim's error for either the Latin *Maxime diligo*, 'I love very greatly', or *maxima diligo*, 'I choose the greatest'
94 **counsel** attorney
gear business
95 **discerned** made sense of
96 **Inns of Court** where lawyers were educated in London
97 **Fie** mild exclamation of disapproval or disagreement
French Inns of Court students used law-French; also, hints at French pox (syphilis)
99 **papistry** hostile term for Roman Catholicism, with its Latin mass
100 **What ... lack** shopkeeper's formula, similar to 'May I help you?'
weigh this chain Gentlemen often wore gold chains, and often (owing to their dicing, wenching, and extravagant tailoring) had to sell them to stay afloat financially, an emblem of the gentry's loss of wealth and power to merchant-class citizens like Yellowhammer.
100.2 ***Sir Walter Whorehound*** 'Walter', related to 'wallow', suggests gross delight in sensuality. It can also mean 'overthrow', which hints at the character's final comeuppance. Pronounced 'water', it ties in with the play's pervasive imagery of liquids. 'Whorehound' means a chaser after whores, but 'water horehound' was also a plant that grew in moist places—its connection with deceptive practices is appropriate to the character.
100.3 ***Davy Dahumma*** 'Dahumma' is a phonetic spelling of the Welsh *dewch yma*, 'come hither'; 'man' means manservant.
101 **wench** a term of affection which, because of its implications of lower social class and of intimacy, Sir Walter does not address to the Welsh Gentlewoman in front of those who know nothing of their relationship. Sir Walter and the Welsh Gentlewoman are conversing apart, unheard by the Yellowhammer family.
101–2 **heart ... London** Cheapside lay in the heart of the city. That this is said while a gold chain is being weighed suggests that London has a heart of gold, in the sense that trade is the essence of the City.
102 ***Duw ... chwi*** God be with you (Welsh)
103 **list** like

SIR WALTER 'Twill serve to pass, wench;
'Twas strange that I should lie with thee so often
To leave thee without English; that were unnatural.
I bring thee up to turn thee into gold, wench,
And make thy fortune shine like your bright trade;
A goldsmith's shop sets out a city maid.
Davy Dahumma, not a word!

DAVY Mum, mum, sir.

SIR WALTER [*to the Welsh Gentlewoman*]
Here you must pass for a pure virgin.

DAVY [*aside*] Pure Welsh virgin!
She lost her maidenhead in Brecknockshire.

SIR WALTER
I hear you mumble, Davy.

DAVY I have teeth, sir;
I need not mumble yet this forty years.

SIR WALTER [*aside*]
The knave bites plaguily!

YELLOWHAMMER [*to Gentleman*]
What's your price, sir?

GENTLEMAN A hundred pound, sir.

YELLOWHAMMER
A hundred marks the utmost; 'tis not for me else.
What, Sir Walter Whorehound? [*Exit Gentleman*]

MOLL O death! *Exit*

MAUDLINE Why, daughter!
Faith, the baggage!
[*To Sir Walter*] A bashful girl, sir; these young things are shamefaced;
Besides, you have a presence, sweet Sir Walter,
Able to daunt a maid brought up i' the city:

Enter Moll

A brave court-spirit makes our virgins quiver
And kiss with trembling thighs. Yet see, she comes, sir.

SIR WALTER [*to Moll*]
Why, how now, pretty mistress? Now I have caught you.
What, can you injure so your time to stray
Thus from your faithful servant?

YELLOWHAMMER
Pish, stop your words, good knight—'twill make her blush else—
Which sound too high for the daughters of the freedom.
'Honour' and 'faithful servant'! They are compliments
For the worthies of Whitehall or Greenwich;
E'en plain, sufficient, subsidy words serves us, sir.
And is this gentlewoman your worthy niece?

SIR WALTER
You may be bold with her on these terms; 'tis she, sir,
Heir to some nineteen mountains.

YELLOWHAMMER Bless us all!
You overwhelm me, sir, with love and riches.

SIR WALTER
And all as high as Paul's.

DAVY [*aside*] Here's work, i'faith!

SIR WALTER How sayest thou, Davy?

DAVY
Higher, sir, by far; you cannot see the top of 'em.

YELLOWHAMMER
What, man! Maudline, salute this gentlewoman,
Our daughter if things hit right.

Enter Touchwood Junior

TOUCHWOOD JUNIOR [*aside*]
My knight, with a brace of footmen,

105–6 **'Twas . . . English** i.e., it would be strange if I had slept with you so often and left you without knowing English

107 **turn . . . gold** recalls Rumpelstiltskin's turning straw into gold. The play's talk of 'gold' more often than 'money' has a folk-tale resonance.

108 **your** may be impersonal, i.e., 'one's', thus referring to any lucrative trade; or may be personal, referring to her trade as 'whore'

109 **A goldsmith's . . . maid** serves as a foil to, heightening her attractiveness. May mean that as fiancée of a goldsmith's son the Welsh Gentlewoman will be 'set out' in the city, or may refer to Moll, whose city life has given her advantages over the Welsh Gentlewoman; in either case, 'sets out' suggests wares displayed for sale.

110 **Mum** i.e., I will keep silent

111 **pass for a pure virgin** Phrasing appropriate to supposed pure gold, this injunction gestures toward the play's counterfeiting motif.

113 **Brecknockshire** county in Wales

116 **plaguily** vexatiously

118 **marks** a mark was two-thirds of a pound

119 **O death!** Why Moll cries 'O death!' and exits is unclear. The scene could be played so that she overhears Sir Walter's private conversation with the Welsh Gentlewoman which her father is too distracted by customers to hear; or she could suffer revulsion against the appearance or demeanor of her husband-to-be, or simply be upset at his arrival because she is already in love with Touchwood Junior. Why she re-enters voluntarily four lines later is also obscure.

121 **shamefaced** shy; modest

124 **court-spirit** one accustomed to life at court

128 **your faithful servant** Sir Walter speaks the conventional language of courtly love; Jacobean comedy, however, regularly debases key terms of courtly love so that 'servant' comes to mean 'illicit lover'.

129 **Pish** expression of impatience

130 **the freedom** those licensed to practise trade in London

131 **'Honour'** Sir Walter has not actually used this word.

132 **worthies** persons of note or standing
Whitehall . . . Greenwich royal palaces

133 **subsidy** fit for the bourgeois world of material goods
serves are good enough for. Middleton often uses singular verbs with plural nouns.

136 **mountains** In Elizabethan stereotype, Wales was nearly all mountains; possible quibble on 'mountings'.

138 **as high as Paul's** i.e., Saint Paul's Cathedral; proverbial

141 **salute** greet, often with a kiss

142 **hit** work out

142.1 ***Touchwood Junior*** One meaning of 'touchwood' was a passionate, impulsive person. Both Touchwoods' names suggest the expression 'touch wood', living by luck.

143 **brace** two (usually applied to game birds)

Is come, and brought up his ewe-mutton
To find a ram at London; I must hasten it,
Or else peak o' famine; her blood's mine,
And that's the surest. Well, knight, that choice spoil
Is only kept for me.
[*He whispers to Moll from behind*]

MOLL Sir?

TOUCHWOOD JUNIOR Turn not to me till thou mayst lawfully; it but whets my stomach, which is too sharp-set already. [*Giving her a paper*] Read that note carefully; keep me from suspicion still, nor know my zeal but in thy heart. Read, and send but thy liking in three words; I'll be at hand to take it.

YELLOWHAMMER [*to Sir Walter*] O, Tim, sir, Tim!
A poor plain boy, an university man;
Proceeds next Lent to a bachelor of art:
He will be called Sir Yellowhammer then
Over all Cambridge, and that's half a knight.

MAUDLINE Please you, draw near and taste the welcome of the city, sir.

YELLOWHAMMER
Come, good Sir Walter, and your virtuous niece here.

SIR WALTER
'Tis manners to take kindness.

YELLOWHAMMER Lead 'em in, wife.

SIR WALTER
Your company, sir?

YELLOWHAMMER I'll give't you instantly.
[*Exeunt Maudline, Sir Walter, Davy, and the Welsh Gentlewoman*]

TOUCHWOOD JUNIOR [*aside*]
How strangely busy is the devil and riches!
Poor soul, kept in too hard, her mother's eye
Is cruel toward her, being kind to him.
'Twere a good mirth now to set him a-work
To make her wedding ring; I must about it:
Rather than the gain should fall to a stranger,
'Twas honesty in me to enrich my father.

YELLOWHAMMER [*aside*]
The girl is wondrous peevish, I fear nothing
But that she's taken with some other love,
Then all's quite dashed: that must be narrowly looked to,
We cannot be too wary in our children.
[*To Touchwood Junior*] What is't you lack?

TOUCHWOOD JUNIOR [*aside to Moll*]
O, nothing now; all that I wish is present.
[*To Yellowhammer*] I would have a wedding ring made for a gentlewoman
With all speed that may be.

YELLOWHAMMER Of what weight, sir?

TOUCHWOOD JUNIOR Of some half ounce;
Stand fair and comely with the spark of a diamond.
Sir, 'twere pity to lose the least grace.

YELLOWHAMMER
Pray, let's see it.
[*He takes diamond from Touchwood Junior*]
Indeed, sir, 'tis a pure one.

TOUCHWOOD JUNIOR
So is the mistress.

YELLOWHAMMER
Have you the wideness of her finger, sir?

TOUCHWOOD JUNIOR
Yes, sure, I think I have her measure about me.
Good faith, 'tis down; I cannot show't you,
I must pull too many things out to be certain.
Let me see: long, and slender, and neatly jointed;
Just such another gentlewoman that's your daughter, sir.

YELLOWHAMMER
And, therefore, sir, no gentlewoman.

TOUCHWOOD JUNIOR
I protest I never saw two maids handed more alike;
I'll ne'er seek farther, if you'll give me leave, sir.

YELLOWHAMMER
If you dare venture by her finger, sir.

144 **ewe-mutton** Jacobean comedy frequently refers to sexually-available women in terms of meat, 'mutton' applying especially to aging women with much sexual experience. The play's language repeatedly connects illicit sexuality with illicit meat-eating during Lent.
145 **hasten it** hurry
146 **peak** waste away
her blood's mine i.e., she is as full of sexual desire for me as I am for her; referring to Moll, not the Welsh Gentlewoman of whom he has just been speaking
147 **that's the surest** i.e., the best assurance that Moll will prefer me to Sir Walter
choice spoil prized acquisition or plunder, i.e., Moll
150–1 **Turn...lawfully** i.e., do not acknowledge our relationship until we are betrothed or married
151 **stomach** sexual appetite
sharp-set aroused
152 ***paper*** perhaps a love letter or details of an elopement plot
154 **liking** (*a*) consent; (*b*) expression of sexual desire
158 **Proceeds...to** receives a degree as
next Lent Since Tim is called a bachelor at 3.2.123 and 3.2.134, Act One must occur before Lent; Lent is first mentioned at 2.1.108.
159 **Sir Yellowhammer** The title 'Sir' acquired merely through taking a university degree was used with the surname only, hence making one 'half a knight'.
161 **Please you** if it pleases you
taste the welcome an invitation to come into the Yellowhammers' private chambers for refreshment. They would have lived in the same building as the shop.
164 **take kindness** accept hospitality
168 **him** i.e., Sir Walter
169 **him** i.e., Yellowhammer
172 **'Twas** it would be
father father-in-law-to-be
183 **Stand** i.e., standing
spark a small jewel
187 **measure** size, with bawdy innuendo
188 **down** deep in my pocket; suggestion of 'flaccid'
191 **that's** i.e., as
192 **no gentlewoman** Moll is of the merchant class; Yellowhammer may be displaying a humility that would be good for business, or may be warning off the gentleman by implying 'don't flirt with my daughter—she isn't of your social class'.
195 **venture** risk, in a commercial sense

TOUCHWOOD JUNIOR Ay, and I'll 'bide all loss, sir.

YELLOWHAMMER
Say you so, sir? Let's see hither, girl.

TOUCHWOOD JUNIOR
Shall I make bold with your finger, gentlewoman?

MOLL
Your pleasure, sir.
[*He tries the ring on Moll's finger*]

TOUCHWOOD JUNIOR
That fits her to a hair, sir.

YELLOWHAMMER What's your posy now, sir?

TOUCHWOOD JUNIOR
Mass, that's true: posy? I'faith, e'en thus, sir:
'Love that's wise
Blinds parents' eyes.'

YELLOWHAMMER
How, how! If I may speak without offence, sir,
I hold my life—

TOUCHWOOD JUNIOR
What, sir?

YELLOWHAMMER Go to; you'll pardon me?

TOUCHWOOD JUNIOR
Pardon you? Ay, sir.

YELLOWHAMMER Will you, i'faith?

TOUCHWOOD JUNIOR Yes, faith, I will.

YELLOWHAMMER
You'll steal away some man's daughter: am I near you?
Do you turn aside? You gentlemen are mad wags!
I wonder things can be so warily carried,
And parents blinded so; but they're served right
That have two eyes and wear so dull a sight.

TOUCHWOOD JUNIOR [*aside*] Thy doom take hold of thee.

YELLOWHAMMER
Tomorrow noon shall show your ring well done.

TOUCHWOOD JUNIOR
Being so, 'tis soon. Thanks, [*to Moll*] and your leave, sweet gentlewoman.
Exit

MOLL Sir, you are welcome.
[*Aside*] O, were I made of wishes, I went with thee.

YELLOWHAMMER
Come now, we'll see how the rules go within.

MOLL [*aside*]
That robs my joy; there I lose all I win. *Exeunt*

Enter Davy and Allwit severally I.2

DAVY [*aside*]
Honesty wash my eyes! I have spied a wittol.

ALLWIT
What, Davy Dahumma? Welcome from North Wales,
I'faith; and is Sir Walter come?

DAVY New come to town, sir.

ALLWIT
In to the maids, sweet Davy, and give order
His chamber be made ready instantly.
My wife's as great as she can wallow, Davy,
And longs for nothing but pickled cucumbers
And his coming; and now she shall ha't, boy.

DAVY She's sure of them, sir.

ALLWIT
Thy very sight will hold my wife in pleasure
Till the knight come himself. Go in, in, in Davy.
Exit [*Davy*]
The founder's come to town. I am like a man
Finding a table furnished to his hand,

196 **'bide** pay, if he should be wrong about the size
197 **hither** here
198 **make bold** be bold, by holding her finger
199 **to a hair** to a tee; with bawdy suggestion of pubic hair
200 **posy** verse motto inscribed inside a ring
201 **Mass** by the mass (oath). 'Mass' for the eucharistic service, denounced by Reformation Protestants as a relic of papistry, survived by habit in oaths.
203 **Blinds...eyes** Language of blindness and incomprehension pervades the play, related to its themes of proneness to trickery and of moral blindness.
205 **hold my life** i.e., I'll wager that
Go to come on
207 **am I near you?** do I guess your secret? (with an unintended irony in 'near': Yellowhammer himself is the man whose daughter is to be stolen away; possible unintended suggestion of 'nearly related', which they will ultimately become)
208 **wags** mischievous youths
213–14 **Tomorrow...soon** possible allusion to proverb 'Soon enough if well enough'
216 **went** would go
217 **rules** revels
I.2.0.1 ***Allwit*** all-knowing, full of wit; transposition of 'wittol', a willing cuckold
severally separately
1 **Honesty...eyes** i.e., may clean thinking clarify my vision (he ironically attributes his identification of Allwit as a wittol to his own filthy mind). Though as Sir Walter's man, Davy knows about Allwit, the secret seems otherwise well-kept; those who believe that no material comforts could compensate for the contempt in which a wittol is held ignore the fact that (at least until Allwit tips off Yellowhammer in 4.1) no one in Cheapside knows about Allwit's cuckoldry.
wittol a willing cuckold
6 **great** far advanced in pregnancy
wallow walk rollingly, like a sow wallowing in mud
7 **pickled cucumbers** Pregnancy's exotic cravings were a common theme of gynecological works and of satires on women such as *Le Quinze Joies de Mariage*, which often mention women's desire for dainty delicacies. That 'longs' refers to both cucumbers and Sir Walter's coming is one of the play's conflations of sex and food. Cucumbers are notably phallic.
9 **She's...them** either she is sure of both the pickled cucumbers and Sir Walter's arrival, or (if the actor emphasizes 'them') she is sure of the cucumbers but Sir Walter's coming (in a sexual sense) is a matter of doubt
12 **founder's** a founder is normally one who founds a charitable institution with funds to maintain it perpetually; here, one who maintains Allwit's household
13 **Finding...furnished** allusion to Psalm 23, line 5: 'Thou dost prepare a table before me' (Geneva)
to his hand near at hand

As mine is still to me, prays for the founder:
'Bless the right worshipful the good founder's life.'
I thank him, he's maintained my house this ten years,
Not only keeps my wife, but a keeps me
And all my family. I am at his table;
He gets me all my children, and pays the nurse
Monthly or weekly; puts me to nothing,
Rent, nor church-duties, not so much as the scavenger:
The happiest state that ever man was born to!
I walk out in a morning; come to breakfast,
Find excellent cheer; a good fire in winter;
Look in my coal-house about midsummer eve,
That's full, five or six chaldron new laid up;
Look in my backyard, I shall find a steeple
Made up with Kentish faggots, which o'erlooks
The water-house and the windmills: I say nothing,
But smile and pin the door. When she lies in,
As now she's even upon the point of grunting,
A lady lies not in like her; there's her embossings,
Embroid'rings, spanglings, and I know not what,
As if she lay with all the gaudy-shops
In Gresham's Burse about her; then her restoratives,
Able to set up a young pothecary,
And richly stock the foreman of a drug-shop;
Her sugar by whole loaves, her wines by runlets.
I see these things, but like a happy man
I pay for none at all; yet fools think 's mine;
I have the name, and in his gold I shine;
And where some merchants would in soul kiss hell
To buy a paradise for their wives, and dye
Their conscience in the bloods of prodigal heirs
To deck their night-piece, yet all this being done,
Eaten with jealousy to the inmost bone—
As what affliction nature more constrains
Than feed the wife plump for another's veins?—
These torments stand I freed of; I am as clear
From jealousy of a wife as from the charge.
O, two miraculous blessings! 'Tis the knight
Hath took that labour all out of my hands.
I may sit still and play; he's jealous for me,
Watches her steps, sets spies. I live at ease;
He has both the cost and torment: when the strings
Of his heart frets, I feed, laugh, or sing:
[*Singing*] *La dildo, dildo la dildo, la dildo dildo de dildo.*

Enter two Servants

FIRST SERVANT
What, has he got a singing in his head now?

15 **Bless ... life** 'God bless the founder' was proverbial.

16 **house** The play repeatedly exploits different meanings of this word—home, lineage, bloodlines, family, business establishment, brothel—for ironic effect; the word's biblical resonance (as in 'the house of David') adds to the irony.
ten years The duration of the arrangement is said to be ten years here and at 2.3.8, but twice said to be seven years (3.2.66–9, 4.1.229).

17 **a** he

19 **gets** begets

21 **church-duties ... scavenger** Church dues were paid with money or parish work; scavengers oversaw pavement repair, street cleaning, and repair of chimneys and furnaces; Sir Walter has paid in cash, relieving Allwit of parish work.

25 **midsummer eve** day before Midsummer Day, June 24, one of the four quarter days. That the winter's coal is laid up this early indicates Sir Walter's zealousness toward his illegitimate family, or perhaps merely his efficiency.

26 **chaldron** cauldron (32 bushels, or 198 to 238 cubic feet); five or six chaldron would provide enough to burn a bushel a day for half a year. A reference in Pepys's diary to the delivery of 10 chaldron of coal suggests that the amount is not necessarily hyperbolic, though Pepys would have had a large house, and in any case overstatement would fit in with the steeple-high firewood and wine in huge casks.

28 **Kentish faggots** firewood from the county of Kent
o'erlooks is higher than

29 **water-house** a new pump-house; or perhaps a reservoir built by goldsmith Hugh Myddelton, opened in 1613, the year *Chaste Maid* was first performed
windmills several were patented and erected at about this time, some for pumping water into private houses

30 **pin** bolt
lies in is confined for childbirth

32 **A lady ... her** The dainty tastes and extravagant demands of wives in the weeks before and after childbirth, the 'lying in' period, were a staple of Renaissance antifeminist satire.
embossings embossed ornaments

33 **spanglings** bits of glittering metal decorating fabrics

34 **gaudy-shops** boutiques

35 **Gresham's Burse** a kind of shopping mall, a covered walk lined with stalls featuring clothes and trinkets, on the south side of the Royal Exchange
restoratives foods, cordials or medicines to restore health or strength

36 **set up** set up in business
pothecary apothecary, druggist

37 **foreman** May allude to Simon Forman and the scandalous Essex divorce case with its drugs and accusations of impotence; see *Masque of Cupids*.

38 **loaves** a 'sugar loaf' was refined sugar moulded into a loaf or cone
runlets casks of varying sizes, up to 18.5 gallons

42 **would ... hell** would (figuratively) sell their souls to the devil; possible suggestion of witches' supposed practice of kissing the Devil's anus

43–4 **dye ... heirs** have upon their conscience the sin of having helped ruin prodigal heirs by selling them expensive wares

45 **night-piece** insulting term for wife or other sexual companion

47 **nature more constrains** more violates nature

48 **feed ... veins** 'Veins' is a synecdoche for a body in the throes of lust, envisioned as hot blood pulsing wildly; 'feed' paints lust as cannibalism, a wife fattened to be served at another's table.

52 **labour ... hands** A husband's duties, such as sex and jealousy, were sometimes regarded as drudgery.

54 **live at ease** Allwit's famous soliloquy parodies praises of the Golden Age, a classless utopia where all are fed abundantly without needing to work: closely contemporary with *Chaste Maid*, *The Tempest*'s Golden Age set piece imagines 'all men idle' and abundance produced 'without sweat or endeavour', a vision that a Middletonesque bystander glosses 'all idle: whores and knaves' (2.1.160–72).

55–6 **strings ... frets** the heart was thought to have strings, which could fray from emotional turmoil

57 **dildo** (*a*) a meaningless word in ballad refrains; (*b*) an artificial penis

58 **singing in his head** possible reference to headache caused by cuckold's horns

SECOND SERVANT
Now 's out of work, he falls to making dildoes.

ALLWIT
Now, sirs, Sir Walter's come.

FIRST SERVANT Is our master come?

ALLWIT
Your master! What am I?

FIRST SERVANT Do not you know, sir?

ALLWIT Pray, am not I your master?

FIRST SERVANT
O, you are but our mistress' husband.

ALLWIT *Ergo*, knave, your master.

Enter Sir Walter and Davy. [*Allwit removes his hat.*]

FIRST SERVANT
Negatur argumentum.—Here comes Sir Walter.
[*Aside to Second Servant*] Now a stands bare as well as we; make the most of him, he's but one pip above a servingman, and so much his horns make him.

SIR WALTER [*to Allwit*]
How dost, Jack?

ALLWIT Proud of your worship's health, sir.

SIR WALTER
How does your wife?

ALLWIT E'en after your own making, sir;
She's a tumbler i'faith; the nose and belly meets.

SIR WALTER They'll part in time again.

ALLWIT
At the good hour they will, an please your worship.

SIR WALTER [*to First Servant*] Here, sirrah, pull off my boots.—[*To Allwit*] Put on, put on, Jack.

ALLWIT I thank your kind worship, sir.

SIR WALTER Slippers! [*Second Servant brings slippers*] Heart, you are sleepy!

ALLWIT [*aside*] The game begins already.

SIR WALTER Pish! Put on, Jack.

ALLWIT [*aside, putting on his hat*] Now I must do it, or he'll be as angry now, as if I had put it on at first bidding. 'Tis but observing; 'tis but observing a man's humour once, and he may ha' him by the nose all his life.

SIR WALTER [*to First Servant*]
What entertainment has lain open here?
No strangers in my absence?

FIRST SERVANT Sure, sir, not any.

ALLWIT [*aside*]
His jealousy begins. Am not I happy now
That can laugh inward whilst his marrow melts?

SIR WALTER
How do you satisfy me?

FIRST SERVANT Good, sir, be patient.

SIR WALTER
For two months' absence I'll be satisfied.

FIRST SERVANT
No living creature entered.

SIR WALTER Entered? Come, swear!

FIRST SERVANT
You will not hear me out, sir.

SIR WALTER Yes, I'll hear't out, sir.

FIRST SERVANT
Sir, he can tell, himself.

SIR WALTER Heart, he can tell!
Do you think I'll trust him?—as a usurer
With forfeited lordships. Him? O monstrous injury!
Believe him? Can the devil speak ill of darkness?
[*To Allwit*] What can you say, sir?

ALLWIT Of my soul and conscience, sir, she's a wife as honest of her body to me, as any lord's proud lady can be.

SIR WALTER
Yet, by your leave, I heard you were once off'ring
To go to bed to her.

ALLWIT No, I protest, sir!

59 **out of work** (*a*) out of work; (*b*) sexually inactive

61–3 **What am I? . . . husband** recalls King Lear's demanding of a servant 'Who am I?' and being impertinently answered, 'My lady's father' (1.4.76–7 [Folio])

64 ***Ergo*** therefore (Latin)

65 ***Negatur argumentum*** the argument is denied (Latin)

66 **a** he
stands bare with his hat removed, a mark of respect for Sir Walter (hats were worn indoors in this period)

67 **pip** the mark on dice or playing cards; hence, a very small degree

68 **horns** the (figurative) insignia of a cuckold

69 **How dost** how do you do
Proud pleased, glad

70 **after . . . making** as you have fashioned her, with suggestion of 'making' meaning 'mating'

71 **tumbler** (*a*) acrobat (nose meeting belly requires contortions); (*b*) copulator
nose . . . meets proverbial description of pregnancy

73 **good hour** most auspicious time
an if it

74 **sirrah** term of address to male servants or boys, contemptuously expressing authority

75 **Put on** Allwit is still standing hatless.

77–9 **Heart . . . already** Sir Walter may be musingly addressing himself, to let the others know he is ready for bed, which prompts Allwit to observe that the game of sex with his wife is beginning; or Sir Walter may be upbraiding the servant for 'sleepy' or slow service in bringing the slippers, a prelude to his testy interrogation of the servants, in which case the 'game' is jealousy. ('Heart' is an exclamation of surprise.)

83 **humour** disposition, temperament

84 **by the nose** under his influence; proverbial

85 **lain open** Sir Walter's diction in this passage—'lain open', 'entered'—plays upon a common Renaissance identification of a woman's body with a house, which can be locked up but may also be illicitly entered.

88 **marrow** seat of animal vitality; love proverbially melted the marrow

92 **out . . . out** the first 'out' means 'to the end of my statement', the second 'the true story' (as in 'the truth will out')

93 **he** i.e., Allwit

94–5 **usurer . . . lordships** moneylender who has foreclosed on aristocratic property for non-repayment of loans. The passage may mean 'as I will trust a usurer not to foreclose on aristocratic property if given a chance'.

99 **honest** chaste

SIR WALTER
Heart, if you do, you shall take all. I'll marry.
ALLWIT O, I beseech you, sir!
SIR WALTER [*aside*]
That wakes the slave, and keeps his flesh in awe.
ALLWIT [*aside*]
I'll stop that gap where'er I find it open.
I have poisoned his hopes in marriage already—
Some old rich widows and some landed virgins,
Enter two children, [Wat and Nick]
And I'll fall to work still before I'll lose him,
He's yet too sweet to part from.
WAT [*to Allwit*] Good e'en, father.
ALLWIT
Ha, villain, peace.
NICK Good e'en, father.
ALLWIT Peace, bastard! [*aside*] Should he hear 'em! [*Aloud*] These are two foolish children, they do not know the gentleman that sits there.
SIR WALTER O, Wat! How dost, Nick? Go to school, ply your books, boys, ha?
ALLWIT [*aside to boys*] Where's your legs, whoresons? [*Aside*] They should kneel indeed, if they could say their prayers.
SIR WALTER [*aside*] Let me see, stay;
How shall I dispose of these two brats now
When I am married? For they must not mingle
Amongst my children that I get in wedlock;
'Twill make foul work, that, and raise many storms.
I'll bind Wat prentice to a goldsmith—my father Yellowhammer, as fit as can be! Nick with some vintner; good, goldsmith and vintner; there will be wine in bowls, i'faith.
Enter Allwit's Wife
WIFE Sweet knight,
Welcome! I have all my longings now in town;
Now, welcome the good hour.
SIR WALTER How cheers my mistress?
WIFE
Made lightsome e'en by him that made me heavy.
SIR WALTER
Methinks she shows gallantly, like a moon at full, sir.
ALLWIT True, and if she bear a male child, there's the man in the moon, sir.
SIR WALTER
'Tis but the boy in the moon yet, goodman calf.
ALLWIT
There was a man, the boy had never been there else.
SIR WALTER
It shall be yours, sir.
ALLWIT No, by my troth, I'll swear
It's none of mine. Let him that got it keep it!
[*Aside*] Thus do I rid myself of fear,
Lie soft, sleep hard, drink wine, and eat good cheer.
[*Exeunt*]
Finis Actus Primus

[*Incipit*] *Actus Secundus* 2.1
Enter Touchwood Senior and his Wife
WIFE
'Twill be so tedious, sir, to live from you,
But that necessity must be obeyed.
TOUCHWOOD SENIOR
I would it might not, wife. The tediousness
Will be the most part mine, that understand
The blessings I have in thee; so to part,
That drives the torment to a knowing heart,
But as thou say'st, we must give way to need,
And live awhile asunder; our desires
Are both too fruitful for our barren fortunes.
How adverse runs the destiny of some creatures:
Some only can get riches and no children,

105 **slave** contemptible fellow
106 **gap** i.e., the possibility of Sir Walter's marrying. Given adjacent imagery of openings, 'gap' is also sexually suggestive.
108.1 ***Wat*** (*a*) short for Walter; (*b*) a hare
Nick In the sense 'notch' perhaps suggests a notch on the belt of Sir Walter's sexual conquests.
115 **ply** work at
117 **Where's your legs** i.e., why aren't you bowing or kneeling? (Children knelt before their parents.)
whoresons Allwit's calling the boys 'bastard' and 'whoresons' raises the question of whether they know they are not his children, in which case he has committed the despicable act of implicating young children in the household's immoral arrangements; his thus addressing them if they think he is really their father is not very attractive behaviour either.
118–19 **if…prayers** i.e., Sir Walter should be considered their God
122 **mingle** intermix with, be acknowledged as heirs on an equal footing with
124 **storms** disputes, probably over property and equitable treatment
125 **prentice** apprentice. Since apprentices lived in their master's households, Sir Walter is imagining the cruel situation of forcing his illegitimate son to live as an apprentice in the very household where his legitimate offspring will have the status of grandchildren.
128.1 ***Allwit's Wife*** The fact that Allwit's wife, Lady Kix, and Touchwood Senior's wife are designated in the list of the 'Principal Persons' and elsewhere in the text only as 'his wife' is one instance among many in the play of wives being considered mere objects. Of the play's dozen wives, only Maudline Yellowhammer is given a first name.
130 **longings** desires. The word was especially used for pregnancy's cravings.
132 **lightsome** light-hearted, happy
heavy pregnant, with a paradoxical play on another meaning, 'sad'
136 **calf** dolt; suggestion of 'mooncalf'—natural idiot or aborted foetus
137 **There…else** i.e., there must have been a man, or else there could be no boy
138 **It…yours** Sir Walter may mean that Allwit wins the prize for this wit duel; Allwit takes him to mean that the child will pass as his legitimate heir.
139 **Let…keep it** proverbial
141 **good cheer** plentiful food
2.1.0.2 ***Touchwood Senior*** Touchwood was tinder used to ignite the touchhole of a musket, with a sexual implication.
1 **from** separated from
2 **necessity…obeyed** proverbial
5 **blessings** (*a*) happiness; (*b*) offspring
6 **knowing** i.e., savouring marital bliss; 'know' also meant to have sex with

We only can get children and no riches.
Then 'tis the prudent'st part to check our wills
And, till our state rise, make our bloods lie still.
Life, every year a child, and some years two—
Besides drinkings abroad, that's never reckoned;
This gear will not hold out.

WIFE
Sir, for a time
I'll take the courtesy of my uncle's house,
If you be pleased to like on't, till prosperity
Look with a friendly eye upon our states.

TOUCHWOOD SENIOR
Honest wife, I thank thee. I ne'er knew
The perfect treasure thou brought'st with thee more
Than at this instant minute. A man's happy
When he's at poorest that has matched his soul
As rightly as his body. Had I married
A sensual fool now, as 'tis hard to 'scape it
'Mongst gentlewomen of our time, she would ha' hanged
About my neck, and never left her hold
Till she had kissed me into wanton businesses,
Which at the waking of my better judgement
I should have cursed most bitterly,
And laid a thicker vengeance on my act
Than misery of the birth—which were enough
If it were born to greatness, whereas mine
Is sure of beggary, though it were got in wine.
Fullness of joy showeth the goodness in thee;
Thou art a matchless wife: farewell, my joy.

WIFE
I shall not want your sight?

TOUCHWOOD SENIOR
I'll see thee often,
Talk in mirth, and play at kisses with thee,
Anything, wench, but what may beget beggars;
There I give o'er the set, throw down the cards,
And dare not take them up.

WIFE
Your will be mine, sir.
Exit

TOUCHWOOD SENIOR
This does not only make her honesty perfect,
But her discretion, and approves her judgement.
Had her desires been wanton, they'd been blameless
In being lawful ever, but of all creatures
I hold that wife a most unmatchèd treasure
Than can unto her fortunes fix her pleasure
And not unto her blood. This is like wedlock;
The feast of marriage is not lust but love
And care of the estate; when I please blood,
Merely I sin and suck out others'; then
'Tis many a wise man's fault, but of all men
I am the most unfortunate in that game
That ever pleased both genders: I ne'er played yet
Under a bastard: the poor wenches curse me
To the pit where'er I come; they were ne'er served so,
But used to have more words than one to a bargain.
I have such a fatal finger in such business
I must forth with't, chiefly for country wenches,
For every harvest I shall hinder hay-making:

13 **check** curb
wills sexual desires
14 **state** financial condition
bloods sexual passions
15 **Life** God's life (oath)
16 **drinkings abroad** cost of drinking or dining out, with a suggestion of sexual encounters with other women
17 **gear** business; with a suggestion of 'genitals'
19 **like on't** approve it
20 **states** situations
23 **instant** present
32–3 **And . . . birth** i.e., he would make himself more miserable by cursing himself than the ensuing child would be made miserable by poverty; or, cursing would be an even greater penalty to him than the birth of the child would
33 **misery . . . birth** The Renaissance commonplace that humans are born into misery comes from Christianity (original sin) and from classical Greek authors.
33–5 **which . . . beggary** i.e., the birth of a child would be sad enough if it were born into wealth, whereas my child is certain to be poor
35 **got in wine** conceived while the parents were drunk (possible allusion to proverb 'let him drink, and forget his poverty'; perhaps alludes to a superstition that children begotten by drunken parents would grow up to be rich)
37 **matchless** peerless; also, possibly, husbandless
38 **want** lack
40 **Anything . . . beggars** His sexual 'fast' is counterpoised against Lenten food fasting in the play, the former being about as rigorous as the latter.
wench here, simply an affectionate term with no suggestion of rusticity or lower class
41 **give . . . set** give up the game (of sex); game imagery pervades the play
43–63 Touchwood Senior's soliloquy is balanced against Allwit's soliloquy in the preceding scene; both men relinquish their sex lives with their wives; both praise the married state in circumstances undercutting that praise.
44 **approves** confirms
49 **like wedlock** what wedlock should ideally be
50–1 **The feast . . . estate** for similar sentiments, see *No Wit* 9.214–5 and *Women Beware* 1.3.22–35, 41–49
52 **Merely . . . others'** i.e., I commit an absolute sin and harm other people ('others'' means 'other people's sins')
55–6 **ne'er . . . bastard** i.e., never had sex without producing at least one bastard. The image is perhaps from card-playing—to have a bastard is to be left with a card that scores against one.
57 **the pit** Hell; suggestion of pudendum
57–8 **ne'er . . . bargain** i.e., the maids are not used to conceiving after only one sexual encounter. To 'have more words than one to a bargain' is proverbial.
59 **fatal** (*a*) doomed by destiny; (*b*) deadly, ruinous
finger contribution, influence (figurative); with a suggestion of a sexually potent penis
61 **hinder hay-making** i.e., the pregnant country wenches cannot help with the harvest

Enter a Wench with a child

I had no less than seven lay in last progress
Within three weeks of one another's time.

WENCH
O, snap-hance, have I found you?

TOUCHWOOD SENIOR
How snap-hance?

WENCH [*showing him the baby*]
Do you see your workmanship?
Nay, turn not from it, nor offer to escape; for if you do,
I'll cry it through the streets and follow you.
Your name may well be called Touchwood, a pox on you!
You do but touch and take; thou has undone me;
I was a maid before, I can bring a certificate for it
From both the churchwardens.

TOUCHWOOD SENIOR
I'll have the parson's hand too, or I'll not yield to't.

WENCH Thou shalt have more, thou villain! Nothing grieves me but Ellen, my poor cousin in Derbyshire; thou hast cracked her marriage quite; she'll have a bout with thee.

TOUCHWOOD SENIOR
Faith, when she will, I'll have a bout with her!

WENCH A law bout, sir, I mean.

TOUCHWOOD SENIOR
True, lawyers use such bouts as other men do.
An if that be all thy grief, I'll tender her a husband.
I keep of purpose two or three gulls in pickle
To eat such mutton with, and she shall choose one.
Do but in courtesy, faith, wench, excuse me
Of this half yard of flesh, in which I think it wants
A nail or two.

WENCH
No, thou shalt find, villain,
It hath right shape and all the nails it should have.

TOUCHWOOD SENIOR
Faith, I am poor. Do a charitable deed, wench;
I am a younger brother and have nothing.

WENCH
Nothing! Thou hast too much, thou lying villain,
Unless thou wert more thankful.

TOUCHWOOD SENIOR
I have no dwelling;
I brake up house but this morning. Pray thee, pity me;
I am a good fellow, faith, have been too kind
To people of your gender; if I ha't
Without my belly, none of your sex shall want it.
[*Aside*] That word has been of force to move a woman.
[*To her*] There's tricks enough to rid thy hand on't, wench:
Some rich man's porch, tomorrow before day,
Or else anon i' the evening; twenty devices.
[*He gives her money*] Here's all I have, i'faith, take purse and all;
[*Aside*] And would I were rid of all the ware i' the shop so!

WENCH
Where I find manly dealings, I am pitiful:
This shall not trouble you.

TOUCHWOOD SENIOR
And I protest, wench, the next I'll keep myself.

WENCH Soft, let it be got first!

61.1 *Wench* A wench was a rustic or working-class girl, often regarded as sexually 'easy' and sometimes as witty and resourceful.

62 **lay in** were confined for childbirth
progress The monarch and members of Court went on a royal tour of England in July or August; they were lavishly entertained and courtiers often wreaked havoc on the local population; Touchwood Senior's impregnation of seven women parallels Sir Walter's fathering seven children by Allwit's wife.

64 **snap-hance** (*a*) bandit; (*b*) the flintlock or cock which ignites 'touchwood' or tinder in the touchhole (suggestion of pudendum) of a gun

69 **touch and take** speedily lay hands on; proverbial; with a suggestion of speedy impregnation
undone ruined my reputation and marital prospects

70 **certificate** a warrant of good conduct required of all those who moved out of their own parish; notoriously unreliable

71 **churchwardens** lay officers who helped parishioners

72 **parson's hand** the parson's signature, proving the maid's chastity

75 **cracked** broken

76 **bout** she means a law suit; but he interprets 'bout' as a sexual encounter

80 **An if** if

81 **of purpose** on purpose
gulls fools
in pickle (*a*) stored up, like pickled food; (*b*) in tubs for treating syphilis. Possibly recalls the pickled cucumbers with which Sir Walter is associated (1.2.7), obliquely suggesting that he, like the gulls, is being used.

82 **mutton** whore

84 **half yard of flesh** the baby

84–5 **wants...two** (*a*) is short of a half yard by a nail (measure of 2 1/2 inches) or two; (*b*) lacks some nails (children of syphilitics sometimes lacked finger- or toenails)

88 **younger brother** By the custom of primogeniture, in which the first-born son was heir to his father's title and estate, younger male children had little material wealth. Touchwood may be lying to the wench, since 'Touchwood Senior' suggests that he is the eldest son.

89–90 **Thou...thankful** She seems to mean that he will have 'too much' in that she will make him take the baby, unless he proves more grateful ('thankful') by giving her money.

91 **brake up house** parted from my family

92 **good fellow** good-hearted womanizer

94 **Without my belly** outside my belly; i.e., any food not actually eaten already; with sexual innuendo
want lack

95 **That...woman** i.e., that pose as a benefactor of the female sex has worked with women before

96 **There's...on't** i.e., there are many ways to rid yourself of a baby

98 **anon** at once
devices schemes

100 **ware...shop** Middleton's characters often use 'ware' to mean sexually available woman, casting women as shop goods in a consumer world.

101 **manly dealings** sardonic reference to his pay-off
pitiful pitying

104 **Soft** mild exclamation, similar to 'Wait a minute!'
got begotten

[*Aside*] This is the fifth; if e'er I venture more,
Where I now go for a maid, may I ride for a whore.
Exit

TOUCHWOOD SENIOR
What shift she'll make now with this piece of flesh
In this strict time of Lent, I cannot imagine;
Flesh dare not peep abroad now. I have known
This city now above this seven years,
But, I protest, in better state of government
I never knew it yet, nor ever heard of.
There has been more religious wholesome laws
In the half circle of a year erected
For common good, than memory ever knew of,

Enter Sir Oliver Kix and his Lady

Setting apart corruption of promoters,
And other poisonous officers that infect
And with a venomous breath taint every goodness.

LADY
O, that e'er I was begot, or bred, or born!

SIR OLIVER
Be content, sweet wife.

TOUCHWOOD SENIOR [*aside*]
What's here to do, now?
I hold my life she's in deep passion
For the imprisonment of veal and mutton
Now kept in garrets; weeps for some calf's head now.
Methinks her husband's head might serve with bacon.

Enter Touchwood Junior

LADY [*to Sir Oliver*] Hist!

SIR OLIVER Patience, sweet wife.

[*They walk aside*]

TOUCHWOOD JUNIOR
Brother, I have sought you strangely.

TOUCHWOOD SENIOR
Why, what's the business?

TOUCHWOOD JUNIOR
With all speed thou canst, procure a licence for me.

TOUCHWOOD SENIOR How, a licence?

TOUCHWOOD JUNIOR
Cud's foot, she's lost else! I shall miss her ever.

TOUCHWOOD SENIOR [*giving money*]
Nay, sure, thou shalt not miss so fair a mark
For thirteen shillings fourpence.

TOUCHWOOD JUNIOR
Thanks by hundreds!
Exit

SIR OLIVER [*to Lady Kix*]
Nay, pray thee, cease; I'll be at more cost yet,
Thou know'st we are rich enough.

LADY
All but in blessings,
And there the beggar goes beyond us. O, O, O!
To be seven years a wife and not a child,
O, not a child!

SIR OLIVER
Sweet wife, have patience.

LADY
Can any woman have a greater cut?

SIR OLIVER
I know 'tis great, but what of that, wife?
I cannot do withal; there's things making,
By thine own doctor's advice, at pothecaries':
I spare for nothing, wife, no, if the price
Were forty marks a spoonful;

105 **the fifth** her fifth child out of wedlock, or perhaps the fifth man she has accused of fathering this baby

105–6 **if e'er ... whore** i.e., if I pull this stunt again, I may no longer pass as a maid, but may be known as a whore. 'Ride' suggests the sex act and may also suggest a whore's punishment of being carted through the streets; or she may be anticipating not having to walk ('go') but being able to ride in a carriage, from her gains through prostitution.

107 **shift** evasive device
piece of flesh the infant. His conflation of the infant with a piece of Lent-forbidden meat foreshadows the 'shift' she will actually practise.

108 **strict ... Lent** From 1608 onwards acts which forbade the killing and eating of meat during Lent were more strictly enforced, and in 1613 laws were passed against even ill people and pregnant women having meat during Lent. Playwrights were not warmly-disposed toward Lent in the best of times, since theatres were often closed during Lent.

113 **religious wholesome laws** Lenten laws; Touchwood Senior's defence of these laws, unless ironic, may have aimed at mollifying King James, promulgator of Lenten prohibitions—James's daughter was the acting company's sponsor; a nearly identical phrase, used non-ironically, occurs in *The Triumphs of Truth*, 1613, 142

115.1 ***Sir Oliver Kix*** an oxymoronic name: 'Oliver' means 'fruitful', but a kix is a dry, hollow plant stalk, and hence a dried-up, sapless person. It is also the English name for cicuta, an anaphrodisiac medication that could prevent sexual maturation.

116 **Setting apart** except for
promoters informers. In 1613 the Privy Council appointed 'messengers' to spy out abuses of the Lenten regulations.

120 **What's ... do** i.e., what's all this about?

121 **I ... life** i.e., I would wager my life that
passion sorrow

123 **garrets** Butchers who wanted to evade Lenten laws sometimes operated secretly in attic rooms (cf. 2.2.91–2).
calf's head literally, meat; figuratively, fool. Touchwood Senior thinks that Lady Kix is upset about the lack of meat in Lent—he does not yet realize that this is not the sort of flesh she is longing for.

124 **husband's head** suggests that Sir Oliver has a calf's head or is a fool

125 **Hist!** silence! (She wishes not to be overheard by Touchwood Junior, who is entering; the Kixes have not noticed being overheard by Touchwood Senior.)

127 **strangely** urgently

128 **licence** A marriage licence from the bishop was necessary for a marriage that took place outside a church or chapel or for which banns had not been called.

130 **Cud's foot** by God's foot (oath)
miss her ever lose her forever

131 ***giving money*** shows he was lying when he told the Wench, shortly before, that he was giving her all his money (2.1.99)
mark (*a*) archery target (with suggestion of target as pudendum); the target image involves a pun on 'miss', which in the previous line meant 'lose' and here means 'fail to hit'; (*b*) thirteen shillings and fourpence, or two-thirds of a pound; the cost of a marriage licence

138 **cut** (*a*) misfortune; (*b*) pudendum. Since 'cut' can also refer to gelding, this could also apply to Sir Oliver.

140 **cannot do withal** cannot help it; or, cannot copulate

141 **pothecaries** apothecaries, druggists

I'd give a thousand pound to purchase fruitfulness:
[*Exit Touchwood Senior*]
'Tis but 'bating so many good works
In the erecting of bridewells and spittlehouses,
And so fetch it up again; for, having none,
I mean to make good deeds my children.

LADY
Give me but those good deeds, and I'll find children.

SIR OLIVER
Hang thee, thou hast had too many!

LADY
Thou li'st, brevity!

SIR OLIVER
O, horrible! Dar'st thou call me 'brevity'?
Dar'st thou be so short with me?

LADY
Thou deservest worse.
Think but upon the goodly lands and livings
That's kept back through want on't.

SIR OLIVER
Talk not on't, pray thee;
Thou'lt make me play the woman and weep too.

LADY
'Tis our dry barrenness puffs up Sir Walter;
None gets by your not-getting but that knight;
He's made by th' means, and fats his fortunes shortly
In a great dowry with a goldsmith's daughter.

SIR OLIVER They may all be deceivèd;
Be but you patient, wife.

LADY
I have suffered a long time.

SIR OLIVER
Suffer thy heart out, a pox suffer thee!

LADY
Nay, thee, thou desertless slave!

SIR OLIVER Come, come, I ha' done;
You'll to the gossiping of Master Allwit's child?

LADY Yes, to my much joy!
Everyone gets before me; there's my sister
Was married but at Barthol'mew-eve last,
And she can have two children at a birth:
O, one of them, one of them, would ha' served my
turn.

SIR OLIVER
Sorrow consume thee, thou art still crossing me,
And know'st my nature—
Enter a Maid

MAID
O, mistress! [*Aside*] Weeping or railing,
That's our house harmony!

LADY
What say'st, Jug?

MAID
The sweetest news!

LADY
What is't, wench?

MAID Throw down your doctors' drugs:
They're all but heretics; I bring certain remedy
That has been taught and proved and never failed.

SIR OLIVER
O that, that, that or nothing!

MAID
There's a gentleman,
I haply have his name too, that has got
Nine children by one water that he useth:
It never misses; they come so fast upon him,
He was fain to give it over.

LADY
His name, sweet Jug?

MAID
One Master Touchwood, a fine gentleman,
But run behindhand much with getting children.

SIR OLIVER
Is't possible?

MAID
Why sir, he'll undertake,
Using that water, within fifteen year,
For all your wealth, to make you a poor man,
You shall so swarm with children.

SIR OLIVER
I'll venture that, i'faith.

LADY
That shall you, husband.

MAID
But I must tell you first, he's very dear.

144.1 *Exit Touchwood Senior* COTES does not direct Touchwood Senior to exit here, but the plot seems to demand it. Touchwood, after remaining onstage long enough to overhear the Kixes' plight, exits for long enough to enlist the maid in his scheme; otherwise, the maid would be acting on her own initiative, unlikely since the miraculous 'water' she reports is actually Touchwood Senior's fabrication, tailored to this situation.

145–6 **'Tis ... spittlehouses** i.e., to finance fertility treatments, I would only have to reduce my spending on charities—the building of bridewells (workhouses for the poor, and houses of correction for prostitutes) and spittlehouses (leper houses, and hospitals for treating venereal diseases)

147 **fetch ... again** (*a*) raise money for fertility treatments; (*b*) regain sexual potency

147–8 **for, having ... my children** i.e., I will compensate for having no children by being a philanthropist

149 **good deeds** sexual acts

150 **too many** too many sexual encounters
brevity (*a*) shortness of penis, sexual inadequacy; (*b*) possible reference to the stature of a boy actor (With so many boys necessary to play the female parts, one of them could have been doubled into this part.)

152 **short** rude; with a pun on 'brevity'

153–4 **Think ... on't** i.e., think about the property that will go elsewhere (to Sir Walter Whorehound) because of your heirlessness. Some estate has been entailed so that the property passes to Sir Walter if the Kixes have no children.

155 **play the woman** behave like a woman

157 **gets** makes money
not-getting failure to impregnate

158 **by th' means** i.e., by their infertility
fats increases

162 **pox** venereal disease

163 **desertless** undeserving

165 **gossiping** christening or christening feast

168 **Barthol'mew-eve** August 23. Since it is now not even Mid-Lent Sunday (cf. 2.2.182), the twins were probably conceived out of wedlock.

170 **served my turn** suited my purposes

171 **crossing** agitating

174 **Jug** a common substitute for 'Joan', a generic name for maid-servants

176 **heretics** i.e., doctors are to medicine what heretics are to religion—purveyors of falsehood

179 **haply** (*a*) happen to; (*b*) fortunately

180 **water** (*a*) liquid medicine; (*b*) semen; a frequent Middleton double entendre

182 **fain** glad

184 **run behindhand** fallen into debt

190 **dear** expensive

SIR OLIVER
No matter; what serves wealth for?
LADY
True, sweet husband.
SIR OLIVER
There's land to come. Put case his water stands me
In some five hundred pound a pint,
'Twill fetch a thousand, and a kersen soul.
I'll about it.
LADY
And that's worth all, sweet husband.
Exeunt

2.2 *Enter Allwit*
ALLWIT
I'll go bid gossips presently myself.
That's all the work I'll do; nor need I stir,
But that it is my pleasure to walk forth
And air myself a little: I am tied to nothing
In this business; what I do is merely recreation,
Not constraint.
Here's running to and fro—nurse upon nurse,
Three charwomen, besides maids and neighbours' children!
Fie, what a trouble have I rid my hands on;
It makes me sweat to think on't.
Enter Sir Walter Whorehound
SIR WALTER
How now, Jack?
ALLWIT
I am going to bid gossips for your worship's child, sir;
A goodly girl, i'faith, give you joy on her!
She looks as if she had two thousand pound to her portion,
And run away with a tailor; a fine plump black-eyed slut:
Under correction, sir,
I take delight to see her.—Nurse!
Enter Dry Nurse
DRY NURSE
Do you call, sir?
ALLWIT
I call not you, I call the wet nurse hither.
Exit [Dry Nurse]
Give me the wet nurse!—
Enter Wet Nurse [with baby]
Ay, 'tis thou;
Come hither, come hither!
Let's see her once again; I cannot choose
But buss her thrice an hour.
WET NURSE
You may be proud on't sir;
'Tis the best piece of work that e'er you did.
ALLWIT
Think'st thou so, nurse? What sayest to Wat and Nick?
WET NURSE
They're pretty children both, but here's a wench
Will be a knocker.
ALLWIT [*fondling the baby*]
Pup!—Say'st thou me so? Pup! Little countess!
Faith, sir, I thank your worship for this girl
Ten thousand times and upward.
SIR WALTER
I am glad I have her for you, sir.
ALLWIT Here, take her in, nurse; wipe her, and give her spoon-meat.
WET NURSE
Wipe your mouth, sir.
Exit [with baby]
ALLWIT
And now, about these gossips.
SIR WALTER
Get but two; I'll stand for one myself.
ALLWIT To your own child, sir?
SIR WALTER
The better policy, it prevents suspicion;
'Tis good to play with rumour at all weapons.
ALLWIT
Troth, I commend your care, sir; 'tis a thing
That I should ne'er have thought on.
SIR WALTER [*aside*]
The more slave!

192 **Put case** suppose
192–3 **stands me | In** costs me
194 **fetch a thousand** bring in a thousand pounds (as part of the inheritance the birth of a child would bring them)
kersen Christian or christened
2.2.1 **bid** summon
gossips god-parents at a baptism; also, a woman's female friends invited to be present at a birth and/or christening party
presently immediately
9 **rid...on** rid myself of
10 **How now** i.e., how is it with you?
13 **to her portion** as her dowry
14 **run...tailor** it looks (judging from the extravagant christening clothes) as though she had has run away with a tailor
slut girl (playful, not seriously implying sluttishness)
15 **Under correction** if I may presume to say so (deferential phrase)
16.1 ***Dry Nurse*** a nurse who tended, but did not breastfeed, an infant
17 **I...you** Rejection of the Dry Nurse after she speaks only four words gives this character little purpose in the play, except that preference to the Wet Nurse continues the play's pervasive imagery of liquids; and the presence of two nurses in the household underlines the Allwits' extravagance.
wet nurse a nurse hired by wealthy families to breastfeed an infant
21 **buss** kiss
on't of it
25 **knocker** (*a*) a beauty; (*b*) notable copulator
26 **Pup** a favourite all-purpose exclamation with Middleton
countess possible reference to the extravagant lying in of the Countess of Salisbury; may be a bawdy pun, 'cuntess'
28 **upward** more
31 **spoon-meat** puréed food
32 **Wipe your mouth** i.e., you speak like a fool or slobberer—possibly for making a fool of himself by cooing over the baby
33 **Get...myself** A child normally had three godparents; besides the obvious hypocrisy of Sir Walter's attempt to conceal his paternity, this may be a reference to the Puritan practice of standing as godparents to their own children.
stand for serve as
35 **policy** devious strategy
36 **play...at** fight against rumour with
37 **Troth** by my troth (mild oath)

When man turns base, out goes his soul's pure flame,
The fat of ease o'erthrows the eyes of shame.

ALLWIT
I am studying who to get for godmother
Suitable to your worship. Now I ha' thought on't.

SIR WALTER
I'll ease you of that care, and please myself in't.
[*Aside*] My love, the goldsmith's daughter: if I send,
Her father will command her.—Davy Dahumma!

Enter Davy

ALLWIT
I'll fit your worship then with a male partner.

SIR WALTER What is he?

ALLWIT
A kind, proper gentleman, brother to Master Touchwood.

SIR WALTER
I know Touchwood: has he a brother living?

ALLWIT A neat bachelor.

SIR WALTER
Now we know him, we'll make shift with him:
Dispatch, the time draws near.—Come hither, Davy.

Exit [*with Davy*]

ALLWIT
In troth, I pity him, he ne'er stands still.
Poor knight, what pains he takes; sends this way one,
That way another; has not an hour's leisure:
I would not have thy toil for all thy pleasure.

Enter two Promoters

[*Aside*] Ha, how now? What are these that stand so close
At the street-corner, pricking up their ears
And snuffing up their noses, like rich men's dogs
When the first course goes in? By the mass, promoters!
'Tis so, I hold my life; and planted there
To arrest the dead corpses of poor calves and sheep,
Like ravenous creditors, that will not suffer
The bodies of their poor departed debtors
To go to th' grave, but e'en in death to vex
And stay the corpse with bills of Middlesex.
This Lent will fat the whoresons up with sweetbreads,
And lard their whores with lamb-stones; what their golls
Can clutch goes presently to their Molls and Dolls:
The bawds will be so fat with what they earn,
Their chins will hang like udders by Easter-eve
And, being stroked, will give the milk of witches.
How did the mongrels hear my wife lies in?
Well, I may baffle 'em gallantly. [*To them*] By your favour, gentlemen,
I am a stranger both unto the city
And to her carnal strictness.

FIRST PROMOTER Good; your will, sir?

ALLWIT
Pray, tell me where one dwells that kills this Lent?

FIRST PROMOTER
How, kills? [*Aside to Second Promoter*] Come hither, Dick; a bird, a bird!

SECOND PROMOTER [*to Allwit*]
What is't that you would have?

ALLWIT Faith, any flesh;
But I long especially for veal and green-sauce.

SECOND PROMOTER [*aside*] Green-goose, you shall be sauced.

ALLWIT
I have half a scornful stomach, no fish will be admitted.

FIRST PROMOTER Not this Lent, sir?

ALLWIT
Lent? What cares colon here for Lent?

FIRST PROMOTER You say well, sir:
Good reason that the colon of a gentleman—
As you were lately pleased to term your worship, sir—
Should be fulfilled with answerable food
To sharpen blood, delight health, and tickle nature.
Were you directed hither to this street, sir?

41 **studying** considering
46 **male partner** One godparent was of the same sex as the baby, the others of the opposite sex.
50 **neat** elegant
51 **make shift** be content
52 **Dispatch** get on with it
57 **close** hidden
58 **pricking ... ears** listening intently
59 **snuffing up** sniffing with
60 **first ... in** when a meal's first course is served
63 **suffer** allow
66 **bills of Middlesex** dubious method of extending the jurisdiction of the King's Bench outside of Middlesex, the county containing Westminster and part of London. A writ was issued allowing an arrest on bogus charges within Middlesex; if the defendent was not in Middlesex, the bill could be extended outside the county. Allwit jokingly pushes this legal abuse to its extreme: the grave.
67–8 **sweetbreads ... lamb-stones** the pancreas and testicles of a lamb, believed to be aphrodisiacs
68 **lard** fatten
golls hands
69 **Molls and Dolls** loose women consorting with criminals
70 **bawds** female pimps
71 **chins ... udders** a double chin was considered the hallmark of a bawd
Easter-eve i.e., the close of Lent
72 **milk of witches** Witches were believed to have an extra teat in an unusal place on the body (here, the chin), and to suckle the devil and familiar spirits.
73 **mongrels** derogatory reference to promoters, who often hung about the house of a pregnant women, counting on her cravings to tempt her into breaking the law
74 **baffle** hoodwink
76 **carnal strictness** prohibition on meat-eating; with bawdy innuendo
your will i.e., what do you want?
77 **kills this Lent** i.e., breaks the Lenten meat laws
78 **bird** victim (slang)
80 **veal and green-sauce** veal with vinegar sauce; metaphorically, 'to get what one deserves' or 'to be cheated'. Allwit purposely uses the provocative phrase, to help hoodwink the Promoters.
81 **Green-goose** (*a*) young goose made into pies for the goose fair at Bow; (*b*) cuckold or fool
sauced forced to pay dearly
82 **half a scornful** rather a choosy
84 **colon** gut; appetite
88 **fulfilled** satisfied
answerable suitable

ALLWIT
That I was, ay, marry.
SECOND PROMOTER And the butcher, belike,
Should kill and sell close in some upper room?
ALLWIT
Some apple-loft, as I take it, or a coal-house;
I know not which, i'faith.
SECOND PROMOTER Either will serve:
This butcher shall kiss Newgate, 'less he turn up
The bottom of the pocket of his apron.
You go to seek him?
ALLWIT Where you shall not find him:
I'll buy, walk by your noses with my flesh,
Sheep-biting mongrels, hand-basket freebooters!
My wife lies in. A *foutre* for promoters! *Exit*
FIRST PROMOTER
That shall not serve your turn.—What a rogue's this!
How cunningly he came over us.
Enter a Man with meat in a basket
SECOND PROMOTER Hush't, stand close!
MAN
I have 'scaped well thus far; they say the knaves
Are wondrous hot and busy.
FIRST PROMOTER By your leave, sir,
We must see what you have under your cloak there.
MAN
Have! I have nothing.
FIRST PROMOTER No? Do you tell us that?
What makes this lump stick out then? We must see, sir.
MAN What will you see, sir? A pair of sheets and two of my wife's foul smocks going to the washers?
SECOND PROMOTER O, we love that sight well! You cannot please us better.
[*He pulls meat out of basket*]
What, do you gull us? Call you these shirts and smocks?
MAN Now, a pox choke you!
You have cozened me and five of my wife's kindred
Of a good dinner; we must make it up now
With herrings and milk-pottage. *Exit*
FIRST PROMOTER 'Tis all veal.
SECOND PROMOTER All veal? Pox, the worse luck! I promised faithfully to send this morning a fat quarter of lamb to a kind gentlewoman in Turnbull Street that longs; and how I'm crossed!
FIRST PROMOTER Let's share this, and see what hap comes next then.
Enter another [Man] with a basket
SECOND PROMOTER
Agreed. Stand close again: another booty.
What's he?
FIRST PROMOTER
Sir, by your favour.
SECOND MAN Meaning me, sir?
FIRST PROMOTER
Good Master Oliver? Cry thee mercy, i'faith!
What hast thou there?
SECOND MAN
A rack of mutton, sir, and half a lamb;
You know my mistress' diet.
FIRST PROMOTER
Go, go, we see thee not; away, keep close!—
[*To Second Promoter*] Heart, let him pass! Thou'lt never have the wit
To know our benefactors. [*Exit Second Man*]
SECOND PROMOTER I have forgot him.
FIRST PROMOTER
'Tis Master Beggarland's man, the wealthy merchant
That is in fee with us.
SECOND PROMOTER Now I have a feeling of him.
FIRST PROMOTER
You know he purchased the whole Lent together,
Gave us ten groats a-piece on Ash Wednesday.
SECOND PROMOTER
True, true.

91 **marry** exclamation like 'indeed'; originally from the Virgin Mary
belike likely
92 **Should kill** i.e., was rumoured to kill
close surreptitiously
93 **apple-loft** a dark, cool place for storing apples; good for covert butchering
95 **kiss Newgate** go to prison. One of the gates in London's ancient wall, Newgate was London's main prison.
95–6 **turn... apron** pay a bribe
99 **Sheep-biting** slang for 'whoring'
hand-basket freebooters pirates of baskets or shopping bags of passers-by
100 ***foutre*** fuck (French)
101 **That... turn** i.e., that excuse will not do. Allwit thinks that since his wife 'lies in', she will be allowed meat during Lent, but the 1613 Lenten laws denied pregnant women the usual exemption.
102 **How... us** How Allwit eludes the Promoters, despite the fact that his trump card 'my wife lies in' is negated by the changed Lenten law, is obscure, as is the precise nature of the trick by which he 'baffles' them. It could be played as if in the false security of his misunderstanding of the law, he simply skips boldly off, while the Promoters do a double take, realizing they have not been swift enough to catch him and do not know his name.
103 **knaves** the Promoters
104 **wondrous** amazingly
hot keen
109 **foul** dirty
112 **gull** fool
116 **milk-pottage** milk broth
119 **Turnbull Street** Turnmill Street, a haunt of prostitutes and thieves. The 'gentlewoman' is probably a whore.
longs has the cravings of pregnancy
120 **crossed** thwarted
121 **hap** chance occurrence
127 **rack** neck, considered a delicacy suitable for invalids
131 **benefactors** those who bribe the Promoters
132 **Master Beggarland's** The name suggests that the merchant has got rich through beggaring the profligate heirs of landowners through providing them with extravagant goods.
133 **is... with** i.e., has bribed
have a feeling seem to remember
134 **purchased... together** bought immunity for the whole of Lent
135 **groats** coins worth fourpence; by 1600 used for any small sum

Enter a Wench with a basket, and a child in it under a loin of mutton

FIRST PROMOTER
A wench.

SECOND PROMOTER Why, then, stand close indeed.

WENCH [*aside*]
Women had need of wit, if they'll shift here,
And she that hath wit may shift anywhere.

FIRST PROMOTER
Look, look! Poor fool, she has left the rump uncovered too,
More to betray her. This is like a murd'rer
That will outface the deed with a bloody band.

SECOND PROMOTER What time of the year is't, sister?

WENCH
O, sweet gentlemen, I am a poor servant,
Let me go.

FIRST PROMOTER
You shall, wench, but this must stay with us.

WENCH O, you undo me, sir!
'Tis for a wealthy gentlewoman that takes physic, sir;
The doctor does allow my mistress mutton.
O, as you tender the dear life of a gentlewoman!
I'll bring my master to you; he shall show you
A true authority from the higher powers,
And I'll run every foot.

SECOND PROMOTER Well, leave your basket then,
And run and spare not.

WENCH Will you swear then to me
To keep it till I come?

FIRST PROMOTER Now by this light I will.

WENCH
What say you, gentleman?

SECOND PROMOTER What a strange wench 'tis!
Would we might perish else.

WENCH Nay, then I run, sir.
Exit, [*leaving the basket*]

FIRST PROMOTER
And ne'er return, I hope.

SECOND PROMOTER A politic baggage!
She makes us swear to keep it:
I prithee look what market she hath made.

FIRST PROMOTER
Imprimis, sir, a good fat loin of mutton.
What comes next under this cloth? Now for a quarter
Of lamb.

SECOND PROMOTER
Now for a shoulder of mutton.

FIRST PROMOTER Done!

SECOND PROMOTER
Why, done, sir!

FIRST PROMOTER
By the mass, I feel I have lost;
'Tis of more weight, i'faith.

SECOND PROMOTER Some loin of veal?

FIRST PROMOTER
No, faith, here's a lamb's head,
I feel that plainly; why, I'll yet win my wager.
[*He takes out baby*]

SECOND PROMOTER
Ha?

FIRST PROMOTER
'Swounds, what's here?

SECOND PROMOTER A child!

FIRST PROMOTER
A pox of all dissembling cunning whores!

SECOND PROMOTER
Here's an unlucky breakfast!

FIRST PROMOTER What shall 's do?

SECOND PROMOTER
The quean made us swear to keep it too.

FIRST PROMOTER
We might leave it else.

SECOND PROMOTER Villainous strange!
Life, had she none to gull but poor promoters
That watch hard for a living?

FIRST PROMOTER
Half our gettings must run in sugar-sops
And nurses' wages now, besides many a pound of soap
And tallow; we have need to get loins of mutton still,
To save suet to change for candles.

SECOND PROMOTER
Nothing mads me but this was a lamb's head with you;

137–8 **shift...shift** (*a*) make a living by one's own devices; (*b*) employ evasions, live by fraud
141 **outface...band** pretend innocence even though his collar or cuff is blood-stained
147 **physic** medicine
151 **true authority** In 1613, even the sick needed a special licence to buy meat in Lent.
154 **by this light** oath similar to 'by God's light'
157 **politic baggage** crafty strumpet; may say more than he knows in suggesting the tricky nature of the actual baggage or basket
159 **market** purchase
160 ***Imprimis*** a word introducing a list of items (Latin)
161–2 **Now...lamb** i.e., I'll wager that there is a quarter of lamb under this cloth
162 **Done!** the wager is agreed to
166.1 **baby** The discovery of a baby where a lamb was expected recalls the discovery of a sheep where a baby was expected in *The Second Shepherd's Play*. The trick is funny in context (the Promoters so richly deserve their comeuppance), but not far from sober reality: in early modern times between 10 and 40 per cent of urban children were abandoned, mostly out of poverty.
167 **'Swounds** God's wounds (oath)
170 **quean** whore
174 **sugar-sops** bread soaked in sugar water, to be given to the baby
176 **tallow** animal fat for making cheap candles
177 **candles** Candles, made of tallow and suet, are required because the baby will need night-time care.
178–9 **Nothing...felt it** i.e., nothing annoys me so much as to think that you, who felt the baby, still thought it was a lamb's head

You felt it! She has made calves' heads of us.

FIRST PROMOTER Prithee, no more on't.
There's time to get it up; it is not come
To Mid-Lent Sunday yet.

SECOND PROMOTER
I am so angry, I'll watch no more today.

FIRST PROMOTER
Faith, nor I neither.

SECOND PROMOTER Why then, I'll make a motion.

FIRST PROMOTER Well, what is't?

SECOND PROMOTER
Let's e'en go to the Checker at Queenhithe,
And roast the loin of mutton till young flood;
Then send the child to Brentford. [*Exeunt*]

2.3 *Enter Allwit in one of Sir Walter's suits, and Davy trussing him*

ALLWIT
'Tis a busy day at our house, Davy.

DAVY
Always the kers'ning day, sir.

ALLWIT Truss, truss me, Davy.

DAVY [*aside*] No matter an you were hanged, sir.

ALLWIT How does this suit fit me, Davy?

DAVY Excellent neatly; my master's things were ever fit for you, sir, e'en to a hair, you know.

ALLWIT Thou hast hit it right, Davy,
We ever jumped in one this ten years, Davy,
So well said.

Enter a Servant with a box

What art thou?

SERVANT Your comfit-maker's man, sir.

ALLWIT
O, sweet youth, in to the nurse quick,
Quick, 'tis time, i'faith;
Your mistress will be here?

SERVANT She was setting forth, sir.
[*Exit*]

Enter two Puritans

ALLWIT Here comes our gossips now; O, I shall have such kissing work today!—Sweet Mistress Underman, welcome, i'faith.

FIRST PURITAN
Give you joy of your fine girl, sir!
Grant that her education may be pure
And become one of the faithful.

ALLWIT
Thanks to your sisterly wishes, Mistress Underman.

SECOND PURITAN
Are any of the brethren's wives yet come?

ALLWIT
There are some wives within, and some at home.

FIRST PURITAN
Verily, thanks, sir. *Exeunt* [*Puritans*]

ALLWIT Verily, you are an ass, forsooth:
I must fit all these times, or there's no music.

Enter two Gossips

Here comes a friendly and familiar pair:
Now I like these wenches well.

FIRST GOSSIP How dost, sirrah?

ALLWIT
Faith, well, I thank you, neighbour, and how dost thou?

SECOND GOSSIP
Want nothing but such getting, sir, as thine.

ALLWIT
My gettings, wench? They are poor.

FIRST GOSSIP Fie, that thou'lt say so!
Th'ast as fine children as a man can get.

181 **get it up** make up the loss
182 **Mid-Lent Sunday** the fourth Sunday in Lent, March 17 in 1613
186 **Checker** an inn with the sign of a chessboard
Queenhithe a quay on the north bank of the Thames, west of Southwark Bridge, where fishing boats came in with the Lenten catch
187 **young flood** when the tide begins to flow upriver; Brentford is upriver from the city
188 **Brentford** a Middlesex town, eight miles upstream from London; a favourite place for assignations and for putting children out to nurse
2.3.0.2 ***trussing*** tying the 'points' or laces of hose or breeches to the doublet
2 **kers'ning** christening
3 **an** if
hanged a secondary meaning of 'trussed'
5 **things...fit** the relationship between the men makes sexual innuendo likely
6 **e'en to a hair** (*a*) exactly; (*b*) even to Allwit's wife's pubic hair; (*c*) pun on 'heir'?; cf. 1.1.199
8 **jumped in one** (*a*) agreed exactly; (*b*) enjoyed the same woman. Suggests that Sir Walter may have been right in suspecting Allwit of sleeping with his own wife (1.2.101–2).
9 **comfit-maker's** confectioner's
12.2 ***Puritans*** insulting term for Protestant reformers demanding purification of the English Church
13 **gossips** in the sense of female attendants of christenings and christening parties, rather than in the sense of godparents
14 **Underman** Her name suggests sexual profligacy. Partly because they were opposed to stage plays on moral grounds, Puritans were relentlessly satirized as hypocrites and sensualists in Jacobean drama; Middleton's satire on contemporary vices suggests that he agreed with many Puritan beliefs—what he consistently satirizes is not religious reform movements but ultra-holiness and hypocrisy.
18 **become** suit
20 **brethren's** male Puritans's
22 **Verily** Allwit mocks the Puritan's 'scriptural' style of speech
forsooth in truth
23 **I...music** (*a*) I must keep to the beat of all these rhythms ('times' in a musical sense) or I will produce social disharmony; (*b*) I must conform with the affectations of these times ('these times' in the sense of 'nowadays') or there will be no harmonious living. With his customary sail-trimming, Allwit says what the Puritans want to hear as he says what Sir Walter wants to hear.
27 **Want...thine** i.e., I lack nothing but your good luck in child-begetting
28 **gettings...poor** He is either deceptively speaking the truth (he has begotten no children), knowing it will be taken for modesty, or (if Sir Walter was right in suspecting him of sleeping with Allwit's wife) lying to prevent word getting back to Sir Walter that he *is* the father of his own children.

DAVY [*aside*]
Ay, as a man can get, and that's my master.
ALLWIT
They are pretty foolish things, put to making in minutes;
I ne'er stand long about 'em. Will you walk in, wenches?
[*Exeunt Gossips*]
Enter Touchwood Junior and Moll
TOUCHWOOD JUNIOR
The happiest meeting that our souls could wish for!
Here's the ring ready; I am beholden
Unto your father's haste, he's kept his hour.
MOLL
He never kept it better.
Enter Sir Walter Whorehound
TOUCHWOOD JUNIOR Back, be silent.
SIR WALTER
Mistress and partner, I will put you both
Into one cup.
[*He drinks their health*]
DAVY [*aside*] Into one cup! Most proper:
A fitting compliment for a goldsmith's daughter.
ALLWIT [*to Sir Walter*]
Yes, sir, that's he must be your worship's partner
In this day's business, Master Touchwood's brother.
SIR WALTER
I embrace your acquaintance, sir.
TOUCHWOOD JUNIOR It vows your service, sir.
SIR WALTER
It's near high time. Come, Master Allwit.
ALLWIT Ready, sir.
SIR WALTER [*to Touchwood Junior*]
Will't please you walk?
TOUCHWOOD JUNIOR Sir, I obey your time. *Exeunt*

2.4 *Enter* [*at one door*] *Midwife with the child,* [*Maudline, the two Puritans,*] *and the* [*five*] *Gossips, to the kers'ning*
[*Exit at another door Midwife with the child*]
FIRST GOSSIP [*offering precedence*]
Good Mistress Yellowhammer.
MAUDLINE In faith, I will not.
FIRST GOSSIP
Indeed, it shall be yours.
MAUDLINE I have sworn, i'faith.
FIRST GOSSIP I'll stand still then.
MAUDLINE
So will you let the child go without company,
And make me forsworn.
FIRST GOSSIP You are such another creature.
SECOND GOSSIP Before me? I pray come down a little.
THIRD GOSSIP Not a whit; I hope I know my place.
SECOND GOSSIP Your place? Great wonder, sure! Are you any better than a comfit-maker's wife?
THIRD GOSSIP And that's as good at all times as a pothecary's.
SECOND GOSSIP Ye lie! Yet I forbear you too.
FIRST PURITAN
Come, sweet sister; we go in unity, and show
The fruits of peace, like children of the spirit.
SECOND PURITAN I love lowliness.
FOURTH GOSSIP
True, so say I: though they strive more,
There comes as proud behind as goes before.
FIFTH GOSSIP Every inch, i'faith. *Exeunt*
Finis Actus Secundus

3.1 [*Incipit*] *Actus Tertius*
Enter Touchwood Junior and a Parson
TOUCHWOOD JUNIOR
O sir, if ever you felt the force of love,
Pity it in me!
PARSON Yes, though I ne'er was married, sir,
I have felt the force of love from good men's daughters,
And some that will be maids yet three years hence.
Have you got a licence?
TOUCHWOOD JUNIOR Here, 'tis ready, sir.
PARSON That's well.
TOUCHWOOD JUNIOR
The ring and all things perfect. She'll steal hither.
PARSON
She shall be welcome, sir; I'll not be long

31 **put to making** conceived
32 **stand long** (*a*) waste much time; (*b*) remain erect very long
33 **happiest meeting** The fact that a courting couple must seize on any pretext even to see each other is a measure of how thoroughgoing was a merchant-class patriarch's surveillance over his daughters.
37–8 **put...cup** i.e., I will pledge you both in a single toast. Since a couple drank from a single loving-cup after the betrothal ceremony, Sir Walter's words are unconsciously ironic.
42 **It vows your service** i.e., knowing you prompts me to promise to serve you
43 **high time** the appropriate time
44 **obey your time** i.e., follow your lead (a musical image)
2.4.1–19 **Good...i'faith** the christening party make a fuss about social precedence
6 **You...creature** light-hearted retort to an accuser; proverbial
7–13 **Before...too** The Second Gossip, an apothecary's wife ('As proud as an apothecary' was proverbial) thinks she is socially superior to the Third, a comfit-maker's wife.
7 **come down a little** be socially humbler
16 **I love lowliness** satirical portrait of a Puritan taking pride in the affectation of humility
18 **There...before** i.e., a person in high estate may be humble and a person of mean condition proud (proverbial). The meaning 'proud' as sexually excited is perhaps taken up in the next line.
3.1.4 **some...hence** including some that are still actually virgins, or will go on pretending to be virgins for at least another three years (at which time they will perhaps reach marriageable age)

A-clapping you together.

Enter Moll and Touchwood Senior

TOUCHWOOD JUNIOR O, here she's come, sir.

PARSON
What's he?

TOUCHWOOD JUNIOR
My honest brother.

TOUCHWOOD SENIOR Quick, make haste, sirs!

MOLL
You must dispatch with all the speed you can,
For I shall be missed straight; I made hard shift
For this small time I have.

PARSON Then I'll not linger.
Place that ring upon her finger:
This the finger plays the part,
Whose master-vein shoots from the heart.

[*Touchwood Junior puts ring on Moll's finger*]

Now join hands—

Enter Yellowhammer and Sir Walter

YELLOWHAMMER Which I will sever,
And so ne'er again meet, never!

MOLL
O, we are betrayed!

TOUCHWOOD JUNIOR Hard fate!

SIR WALTER I am struck with wonder.

YELLOWHAMMER
Was this the politic fetch, thou mystical baggage,
Thou disobedient strumpet! [*To Sir Walter*] And were you
So wise to send for her to such an end?

SIR WALTER
Now I disclaim the end; you'll make me mad.

YELLOWHAMMER [*to Touchwood Junior*]
And what are you, sir?

TOUCHWOOD JUNIOR An you cannot see
With those two glasses, put on a pair more.

YELLOWHAMMER
I dreamed of anger still!—Here, take your ring, sir.

[*He pulls ring off Moll's finger*]

Ha, this? Life, 'tis the same! Abominable!
Did not I sell this ring?

TOUCHWOOD JUNIOR
I think you did; you received money for't.

YELLOWHAMMER Heart, hark you, knight,
Here's no inconscionable villainy:
Set me a-work to make the wedding ring,
And come with an intent to steal my daughter.
Did ever runaway match it?

SIR WALTER [*to Touchwood Senior*]
This' your brother, sir?

TOUCHWOOD SENIOR He can tell that as well as I.

YELLOWHAMMER
The very posy mocks me to my face:
'Love that's wise
Blinds parents' eyes'!
I thank your wisdom, sir, for blinding of us;
We have good hope to recover our sight shortly;
In the mean time I will lock up this baggage
As carefully as my gold: she shall see
As little sun, if a close room or so
Can keep her from the light on't.

MOLL O, sweet father,
For love's sake, pity me!

YELLOWHAMMER Away!

MOLL [*to Touchwood Junior*] Farewell, sir,
All content bless thee, and take this for comfort:
Though violence keep me, thou canst lose me never,
I am ever thine although we part for ever.

YELLOWHAMMER
Ay, we shall part you, minx. *Exit* [*with Moll*]

SIR WALTER [*to Touchwood Junior*]
Your acquaintance, sir,
Came very lately, yet it came too soon;
I must hereafter know you for no friend,
But one that I must shun like pestilence
Or the disease of lust.

TOUCHWOOD JUNIOR Like enough, sir; you ha' ta'en me at the worst time for words that e'er ye picked out: faith, do not wrong me, sir. *Exit* [*with Parson*]

9 **A-clapping you together** joining your hands, marrying you (with a sexual suggestion)
12 **straight** right away
made . . . shift managed, with difficulty
13–17 **Then . . . hands** Doggerel verse substitutes for the Prayer Book wedding ceremony which would have been dangerous to echo onstage. The Parson continues this doggerel at 5.4.35 exactly where he leaves off here.
15–16 **This . . . heart** An artery was popularly believed to run directly from the heart to the third finger of the left hand.
17 **join hands** 'handfasting', the legally binding part of the marriage ceremony, is here interrupted
20 **politic fetch** cunning trick
mystical secret
21 **strumpet** prostitute. In this patriarchal society, disobedience to one's father is easily conflated with sexual looseness, reflecting also the theory that one kind of vice led quickly and inevitably to others.
22 **end** purpose
23 **disclaim the end** deny that my asking her to be a godparent was aimed at this purpose (her elopement)
24 **An** if
26 **dreamed . . . still** kept dreaming about anger (perhaps prophetically, the night before this occurrence)
27 **'tis the same** i.e., the ring Yellowhammer made for Touchwood Junior
31 **no inconscionable** (*a*) very lacking in conscience (employing the double negative as an emphatic); or (*b*) not unconscious
34 **Did . . . it?** i.e., did any runaway ever equal this villainy?
This' i.e., this is
43 **close** locked
50 **lately** recently
52 **pestilence** plague
53 **disease of lust** (*a*) lust considered as a disease; (*b*) venereal disease resulting from lust
54–5 **ta'en . . . out** i.e., for rendering a man at a loss for words, the situation in which you have caught me is the worst possible
56 **do . . . me** i.e., I am not so bad as the present situation makes me appear

TOUCHWOOD SENIOR
Look after him, and spare not: there he walks
That never yet receivèd baffling: you're blest
More than e'er I knew; go, take your rest. *Exit*

SIR WALTER
I pardon you, you are both losers. *Exit*

3.2 *A bed thrust out upon the stage, Allwit's Wife in it. Enter all the Gossips,* [*the Puritans, Maudline, Lady Kix, and Nurse with child. Low stools set out.*]

FIRST GOSSIP [*to Allwit's Wife*]
How is't, woman? We have brought you home
A kersen soul.

WIFE Ay, I thank your pains.

FIRST PURITAN
And, verily, well kersened i' the right way,
Without idolatry or superstition,
After the pure manner of Amsterdam.

WIFE
Sit down, good neighbours.—Nurse!

NURSE At hand, forsooth.

WIFE
Look they have all low stools.

NURSE They have, forsooth.

SECOND GOSSIP
Bring the child hither, nurse.—How say you now,
Gossip, is't not a chopping girl? So like the father.

THIRD GOSSIP
As if it had been spit out of his mouth!
Eyed, nosed, and browed as like a girl can be,
Only indeed it has the mother's mouth.

SECOND GOSSIP
The mother's mouth up and down, up and down!

THIRD GOSSIP
'Tis a large child; she's but a little woman.

FIRST PURITAN
No, believe me, a very spiny creature, but all heart;
Well mettled, like the faithful, to endure
Her tribulation here and raise up seed.

SECOND GOSSIP
She had a sore labour on't, I warrant you;
You can tell, neighbour.

THIRD GOSSIP O, she had great speed;
We were afraid once, but she made us all
Have joyful hearts again; 'tis a good soul, i'faith;
The midwife found her a most cheerful daughter.

FIRST PURITAN
'Tis the spirit; the sisters are all like her.
Enter Sir Walter with two spoons and plate, and Allwit

SECOND GOSSIP
O, here comes the chief gossip, neighbours.
[*Exit Nurse with child*]

SIR WALTER
The fatness of your wishes to you all, ladies.

THIRD GOSSIP
O, dear, sweet gentleman, what fine words he has:
'The fatness of our wishes'!

SECOND GOSSIP Calls us all 'ladies'!

FOURTH GOSSIP
I promise you, a fine gentleman and a courteous.

SECOND GOSSIP
Methinks her husband shows like a clown to him.

THIRD GOSSIP I would not care what clown my husband were too, so I had such fine children.

SECOND GOSSIP She's all fine children, gossip.

THIRD GOSSIP Ay, and see how fast they come.

FIRST PURITAN
Children are blessings, if they be got with zeal
By the brethren, as I have five at home.

57 **Look after him** watch out for him
58 **baffling** disgrace. This jousting term for the defeat or humiliation of an unworthy knight foreshadows the duel at 4.4.61–72; but its lofty chivalric connotations are undercut by the fact that Allwit uses the same word for his trick on the Promoters (2.2.74).
58–9 **you're ... knew** you are luckier than anyone I've known (i.e., to escape with your life)
60 **I ... losers** possible allusion to the proverb 'Give losers leave to speak'. Sir Walter's game image suggests that as one of life's winners he can afford to pardon the losers; his last lines (at 5.1.151) will reverse this boast.
3.2.2 **kersen** Christian or christened
3 **kersened** christened
5 **Amsterdam** a haven for Puritans and other religious dissenters. This remark, and the Puritans at the christening, may suggest that the Allwits have Puritan leanings, though Allwit mocks the excesses of the play's two doctrinaire Puritans.
8 **hither** here
9 **chopping** strapping
10 **spit ... mouth** proverbial. The baby's likeness to Allwit may be (*a*) a polite christening cliché; or (*b*) an intimation that Allwit is actually the father. Campion's portrait of a wittol, on which Middleton seems to have drawn, stresses that the wittol 'cuckolds' the man who keeps the wittol's wife.
13 **up and down** exactly
15 **spiny** lean
16 **mettled** spirited, with possible suggestion of 'tipsy'
the faithful Puritans (in their own parlance)
16–17 **endure ... here** Earthly life was called a tribulation to be endured as preparation for eternal life.
17 **raise up seed** produce and raise offspring
18 **sore ... on't** difficult labour
warrant assure
19 **You can tell** The eyewitness reports of the labour and birth show that Allwit's wife has followed the common custom of giving birth in the company of a group of women friends.
great speed good success
23 **the spirit** (*a*) the Holy Spirit; (*b*) alcohol
23.1 ***spoons*** a common christening gift
plate gold or silver ware
25 **fatness** fullness; suggestion of over-indulgence
27 **Calls ... 'ladies'** 'Lady' denoted aristocracy or gentry, appropriate to Sir Walter's class and to Lady Kix but an inflated compliment to the middle-class women at the christening.
29 **shows ... to** appears like a country bumpkin by comparison with
32 **She's** she has
34 **Children are blessings** proverbial
zeal religious enthusiasm, with suggestion of sexual gusto

SIR WALTER [*to Allwit's Wife*]
The worst is past, I hope now, lady.
WIFE So I hope too, good sir.
ALLWIT [*aside*]
Why, then, so hope I too for company;
I have nothing to do else.
SIR WALTER [*giving cup and spoons*]
A poor remembrance, lady,
To the love of the babe; I pray, accept of it.
WIFE O, you are at too much charge, sir!
SECOND GOSSIP
Look, look! What has he given her? What is't, gossip?
THIRD GOSSIP
Now, by my faith, a fair high standing-cup
And two great 'postle-spoons, one of them gilt.
FIRST PURITAN
Sure that was Judas then with the red beard.
SECOND PURITAN
I would not feed my daughter with that spoon
For all the world, for fear of colouring her hair;
Red hair the brethren like not, it consumes them much:
'Tis not the sisters' colour.
Enter Nurse with comfits and wine
ALLWIT
Well said, nurse;
About, about with them amongst the gossips!
[*Aside*] Now out comes all the tasselled handkerchiefs,
They are spread abroad between their knees already;
Now in goes the long fingers that are washed
Some thrice a day in urine; my wife uses it.
Now we shall have such pocketing: see how
They lurch at the lower end!
FIRST PURITAN
Come hither, nurse.
ALLWIT [*aside*]
Again? She has taken twice already.
FIRST PURITAN [*taking comfits*]
I had forgot a sister's child that's sick.
ALLWIT [*aside*] A pox! It seems your purity loves sweet things well that puts in thrice together.
Had this been all my cost now, I had been beggared;
These women have no consciences at sweetmeats,
Where'er they come; see an they have not culled out
All the long plums too, they have left nothing here
But short wriggle-tail comfits, not worth mouthing.
No mar'l I heard a citizen complain once
That his wife's belly only broke his back;
Mine had been all in fitters seven years since,
But for this worthy knight,
That with a prop upholds my wife and me,
And all my estate buried in Bucklersbury.
WIFE [*pledging them*]
Here, Mistress Yellowhammer and neighbours,
To you all that have taken pains with me,
All the good wives at once!
[*Nurse goes around pouring wine*]
FIRST PURITAN
I'll answer for them.
They wish all health and strength,
And that you may courageously go forward

38 **for company** in order to be sociable, with suggestion of sexual company; another example of Allwit's obsequious agreement with everything Sir Walter says
40 **accept of** accept
41 **you ... charge** i.e., you have spent too much money
43 **standing-cup** stemmed goblet
44 **'postle-spoons** silver spoons with an apostle portrayed on the handle; though a common christening gift, the spoons are considered idolatrous by the Puritans
gilt silver covered with gold
45 **Judas ... beard** The disciple who betrayed Christ was traditionally depicted with red hair, linked with lechery (note that the Welsh Gentlewoman has red hair). If the First Puritan is right about the identity of the apostle on the spoon, Judas seems an odd choice for a gift decoration, but apt enough considering all the betrayals in the play.
48 **consumes** eats them up (with anger, or lust)
49 **sisters** female Puritans
49.1 ***Enter Nurse ... wine*** From here on, the scene becomes a stock portrayal of female carousing, gormandizing, and gossiping at a christening party, found in many male-authored Renaissance antifeminist writings.
comfits sweets
49 **Well said** well done
51 **tasselled handkerchiefs** fashionably large, ornamental handkerchiefs with tassles at the corners
54 **urine** used as a cleansing or cosmetic lotion. The disgusting ingredients of cosmetics were a staple of antifeminist satire.
55 **pocketing** smuggling home of sweets
56 **lurch** filch
lower end far end of the table, with bawdy innuendo
59 **A pox** oath, equivalent to cursing the Puritan sister with venereal disease
62 **no ... sweetmeats** The notion of Puritan gluttony may have arisen from Puritan opposition to Lenten and Friday fasting, which Puritans saw as popish.
sweetmeats goodies preserved in sugar
63 **an** if
64 **plums** sugar plums. Their choosing the long sweets in preference to the short is phallically suggestive.
65 **short ... mouthing** suggestion of short phallus and oral sex; 'wriggle-tail' seems to describe a twisted sweet, but is also sexually suggestive. (Freudian readings make much of the play's oral and uro-genital fixations as suggesting infantile gratification.)
66 **No mar'l** no marvel; i.e., it is no wonder
67 **his ... back** (*a*) her gluttony, and pregnancies necessitating expensive, gluttonous christening parties, made him overwork to support her; (*b*) her demands for sex taxed his virility
only alone
68 **Mine had been** my back would have been
fitters small pieces
seven years see note to 1.2.16. In addition to Sir Walter's seven-year support of the Allwits, Touchwood Senior has lived in London for over seven years, the Kixes have been married and childless for seven years, and two sets of seven children are mentioned; the ubiquity of the number seven may suggest the Renaissance theory of seven-year cycles or climacterics, hinting that this materialistic society is at the end of a cycle, on the verge of regeneration.
since ago
70 **prop** financial support, with phallic suggestion
71 **Bucklersbury** street running south from Cheapside, occupied by grocers and apothecaries. Without Sir Walter, Allwit would have given these shopkeepers all his money for catering christenings.

To perform the like, and many such,
Like a true sister, with motherly bearing.
[*She drinks*]

ALLWIT [*aside*]
Now the cups troll about to wet the gossips' whistles.
It pours down, i'faith; they never think of payment.

FIRST PURITAN Fill again, nurse.
[*She drinks*]

ALLWIT [*aside*]
Now, bless thee, two at once! I'll stay no longer;
It would kill me an if I paid for't.—
[*To Sir Walter*] Will it please you to walk down and
leave the women?

SIR WALTER
With all my heart, Jack.

ALLWIT Troth, I cannot blame you.

SIR WALTER
Sit you all merry, ladies.

ALL GOSSIPS Thank your worship, sir.

FIRST PURITAN Thank your worship, sir.

ALLWIT [*aside*]
A pox twice tipple ye, you are last and lowest!
Exit [*with Sir Walter*]

FIRST PURITAN
Bring hither that same cup, nurse; I would fain
Drive away this—hup!—antichristian grief.
[*She drinks*]

THIRD GOSSIP
See, gossip, an she lies not in like a countess.
Would I had such a husband for my daughter!

FOURTH GOSSIP
Is not she toward marriage?

THIRD GOSSIP O no, sweet gossip!

FOURTH GOSSIP
Why, she's nineteen!

THIRD GOSSIP Ay, that she was last Lammas,
But she has a fault, gossip, a secret fault.

FOURTH GOSSIP
A fault? What is't?

THIRD GOSSIP I'll tell you when I have drunk.
[*She drinks. Exit Nurse*]

FOURTH GOSSIP [*aside*]
Wine can do that, I see, that friendship cannot.

THIRD GOSSIP
And now I'll tell you, gossip; she's too free.

FOURTH GOSSIP
Too free?

THIRD GOSSIP
O ay, she cannot lie dry in her bed.

FOURTH GOSSIP
What, and nineteen?

THIRD GOSSIP 'Tis as I tell you, gossip.
[*Enter Nurse*]

MAUDLINE
Speak with me, nurse? Who is't?

NURSE A gentleman
From Cambridge; I think it be your son, forsooth.

MAUDLINE
'Tis my son Tim, i'faith; prithee, call him up
Among the women, 'twill embolden him well,
[*Exit Nurse*]
For he wants nothing but audacity.
'Would the Welsh gentlewoman at home were here
now.

LADY Is your son come, forsooth?

MAUDLINE Yes, from the university, forsooth.

LADY 'Tis great joy on ye.

MAUDLINE There's a great marriage towards for him.

LADY
A marriage?

MAUDLINE Yes, sure, a huge heir in Wales
At least to nineteen mountains,
Besides her goods and cattle.

77 **perform . . . such** have many more successful childbirths
79 **troll** circulate
80 **of payment** i.e., of how much all this costs. It is ironic that Allwit the wife-renter is offended by the gossips' trivial failings, and that he who pays for nothing complains of the expense of the celebration; it is possible, though, to see Allwit here as a choric spokesman for patriarchal values, horrified that women, who are supposed to conserve, are extravagantly spending, a moral lapse paralleling their bladder incontinence.
84–5 **Will . . . Jack** a good example of male homosocial bonding fostered in opposition to female camaraderie, portrayed as disgusting
88 **tipple** (*a*) intoxicate; (*b*) descend on you as payment for your drunkenness; (*c*) topple, cause to fall down
last and lowest the Puritans sisters' wish for lowliness and insistence on low stools is now transmuted into the likelihood of their lying in a drunken stupor on the floor; possible ironic twist of proverb 'last but not least'
90 **hup** hiccup
91 **an she lies not** i. e., doesn't she lie
countess another possible reference to the extravagant lying in of the Countess of Salisbury
93 **toward marriage** about the age to be married
94 **Lammas** August 1, church harvest festival
95 **secret fault** That the gossip declares the fault secret and then immediately divulges it exemplifies the Renaissance stereotype that women cannot keep a secret; tippling exacerbated this fault in many satiric scenes of the period. Since the ideal chaste woman was seen as a sealed container, the 'bad' woman suffered varieties of leakiness: bibulousness, talkativeness, sexual profligacy, bladder incontinence.
97 **Wine . . . cannot** i.e., wine can produce intimacy that even friendship cannot produce; possible reference to proverb 'In wine there is truth' or 'What soberness conceals drunkenness reveals'
99 **cannot . . . bed** is a bed-wetter (another reference to women's physical incontinence, thought to reflect moral incontinence)
105 **wants** lacks
110 **towards** in the offing
111 **huge heir** heir to huge estates
112 **At least to** to at least
113 **cattle** (*a*) her two thousand runts; (*b*) chattel as wealth, property

Enter [Nurse with] Tim

TIM O, I'm betrayed! *Exit*

MAUDLINE
What, gone again? Run after him, good nurse;
[Exit Nurse]
He's so bashful; that's the spoil of youth.
In the university they're kept still to men,
And ne'er trained up to women's company.

LADY
'Tis a great spoil of youth, indeed.

Enter Nurse and Tim

NURSE
Your mother will have it so.

MAUDLINE Why son, why Tim!
What, must I rise and fetch you? For shame, son!

TIM
Mother, you do entreat like a freshwoman;
'Tis against the laws of the university
For any that has answered under bachelor
To thrust 'mongst married wives.

MAUDLINE Come, we'll excuse you here.

TIM
Call up my tutor, mother, and I care not.

MAUDLINE
What, is your tutor come? Have you brought him up?

TIM
I ha' not brought him up, he stands at door:
Negatur. There's logic to begin with you, mother.

MAUDLINE
Run, call the gentleman, nurse; he's my son's tutor.
[Exit Nurse]
[To Tim] Here, eat some plums.

TIM
Come I from Cambridge, and offer me six plums!

MAUDLINE Why, how now, Tim?
Will not your old tricks yet be left?

TIM Served like a child,
When I have answered under bachelor!

MAUDLINE
You'll never lin till I make your tutor whip you;
You know how I served you once at the free-school
In Paul's church-yard?

TIM O monstrous absurdity!
Ne'er was the like in Cambridge since my time;
Life, whip a bachelor! You'd be laughed at soundly;
Let not my tutor hear you!
'Twould be a jest through the whole university.
No more words, mother.

Enter Tutor

MAUDLINE Is this your tutor, Tim?

TUTOR
Yes, surely, lady, I am the man that brought him
In league with logic and read the Dunces to him.

TIM That did he, mother, but now I have 'em all in my own pate, and can as well read 'em to others.

TUTOR
That can he, mistress, for they flow naturally from him.

MAUDLINE *[to Tutor]*
I'm the more beholden to your pains, sir.

TUTOR
Non ideo sane.

MAUDLINE True, he was an idiot indeed,
When he went out of London, but now he's well mended.
Did you receive the two goose-pies I sent you?

TUTOR
And ate them heartily, thanks to your worship.

MAUDLINE *[to Gossips]* 'Tis my son Tim; I pray, bid him welcome, gentlewomen.

TIM 'Tim'? Hark you: 'Timotheus', Mother, 'Timotheus'.

MAUDLINE How? Shall I deny your name? 'Timotheus', quoth he. Faith, there's a name! 'Tis my son Tim, forsooth.

I'm betrayed Tim seems to have walked unwittingly into the scene of drunken gossiping.

115 **spoil** ruination

116–17 **In...company** a commonplace

116 **still to** always with

121 **freshwoman** female equivalent of 'freshman', a first-year university student (an absurdity since women never attended university); possible play on 'fresh' as sexually impudent

123 **answered...bachelor** achieved the standing of 'bachelor'

124 **thrust** with sexual innuendo

125–7 **up...up** Maudline seems to mean 'up from London', but Tim thinks she means 'upstairs'.

128 ***Negatur*** it is denied; portion of the Latin formula for denying an opponent's argument in an academic debate

131 **plums** perhaps a babyish food, unfitting for a university man; but 'plum' also had slang meaning 'pudendum'

133 **Will not...left** i.e., don't you retain any of the habits and likings of your childhood?

135 **lin** cease; i.e., stop being insubordinate to her

whip Students could be whipped by their tutors, but this was rare once they had reached adult age (about 18) and had taken their B.A. Whipping was considered such a disgrace that a year before *Chaste Maid* was first acted, the son of the Bishop of Bristol killed himself to avoid being whipped.

136 **served** treated; i.e., whipped or had him whipped for disobedience

free-school St Paul's School, founded by John Colet for poor scholars

144 **Dunces** 'schoolmen', the disciples of John Duns Scotus (1265?–1308?). When these scholastic philosophers were attacked by sixteenth-century humanists and reformers, the term came to mean 'blockhead', or 'pedant'.

146 **pate** head

147 **naturally** (*a*) spontaneously; (*b*) half-wittedly

149 ***Non ideo sane*** 'not for that reason indeed' (Latin); common tag in academic disputation. Maudline takes '*ideo*' for 'idiot'.

155 **Timotheus** Latinization of 'Tim'; spoofs the affectations of university learning, where published scholars often Latinized their names

156 **Shall I deny your name?** ironic echo of Revelation 3:8 (Geneva): 'Thou...hast kept my word, and hast not denied my name'

LADY You're welcome, Master Tim.

She kisses Tim

TIM [*aside to Tutor*] O this is horrible, she wets as she kisses! Your handkerchief, sweet tutor, to wipe them off as fast as they come on.

SECOND GOSSIP Welcome from Cambridge.

She kisses Tim

TIM [*aside to Tutor*] This is intolerable! This woman has a villainous sweet breath, did she not stink of comfits. Help me, sweet tutor, or I shall rub my lips off.

TUTOR I'll go kiss the lower end the whilst.

TIM Perhaps that's the sweeter, and we shall dispatch the sooner.

FIRST PURITAN Let me come next. Welcome from the wellspring of discipline that waters all the brethren.

[*She*] *reels and falls*

TIM Hoist, I beseech thee!

THIRD GOSSIP O bless the woman!—Mistress Underman!

FIRST PURITAN 'Tis but the common affliction of the faithful; We must embrace our falls.

TIM [*aside to tutor*] I'm glad I 'scaped it; it was some rotten kiss, sure, it dropped down before it came at me.

Enter Allwit and Davy

ALLWIT [*aside*] Here's a noise! Not parted yet?
Heyday, a looking glass! They have drunk so hard in plate
That some of them had need of other vessels.
[*Aloud*] Yonder's the bravest show!

ALL GOSSIPS Where, where, sir?

ALLWIT
Come along presently by the Pissing-Conduit
With two brave drums and a standard bearer.

ALL GOSSIPS O, brave!

TIM Come, tutor! *Exit* [*with Tutor*]

ALL GOSSIPS [*to Allwit's Wife*] Farewell, sweet gossip.

Exeunt [*Gossips*]

WIFE I thank you all for your pains.

FIRST PURITAN Feed and grow strong.

Exeunt [*Maudline, Lady Kix, and Puritans; the bed, with Allwit's Wife in it, is withdrawn*]

ALLWIT [*calling after the Puritans*]
You had more need to sleep than eat;
Go take a nap with some of the brethren, go,
And rise up a well-edified, boldified sister!
O here's a day of toil well passed o'er,
Able to make a citizen hare-mad!
How hot they have made the rooms with their thick bums!
Dost not feel it, Davy?

DAVY Monstrous strong, sir.

ALLWIT What's here under the stools?

DAVY
Nothing but wet, sir, some wine spilt here belike.

ALLWIT Is't no worse, think'st thou?
Fair needlework stools cost nothing with them, Davy.

DAVY [*aside*]
Nor you neither, i'faith.

ALLWIT Look how they have laid them,
E'en as they lie themselves, with their heels up!
How they have shuffled up the rushes too, Davy,
With their short figging little shuttle-cork heels!
These women can let nothing stand as they find it.
But what's the secret thou'st about to tell me,
My honest Davy?

DAVY If you should disclose it, sir—

ALLWIT
Life, rip my belly up to the throat then, Davy.

DAVY My master's upon marriage.

165 **sweet breath ... comfits** i.e., the scent of comfits overwhelms the alcohol on her breath. 'Kissing comfits' were taken like breath mints.

167 **lower end** those at the bottom end of the table
the whilst meanwhile

168 **that's the sweeter** Tim seems to think that 'the lower end' means 'the lower end of the women'.

171 **wellspring of discipline** Contemporary Cambridge was strongly Puritan; Tim's attending there is one of the indications that the Yellowhammers have Puritan tendencies.
waters spiritually nourishes, with a suggestion of urination (especially after 'lower end' in 3.2.167)
brethren Puritan brothers

172 **Hoist** lift up. This could be played so that she falls on top of Tim, which would lend piquancy to the ensuing line, which shows that it is Mistress Underman who has fallen on top of a man.

175 **embrace our falls** accept our moral (and sexual) lapses; a travesty of Calvin's doctrine that humans must humbly accept their fallen state

179 **Heyday** expression of surprise
looking glass (*a*) mirror in which the gossips can view their behaviour; (*b*) chamber-pot
in plate i.e., in the silver-plated vessels used for the christening party

180 **other vessels** chamber pots

181 **bravest** most magnificent

182 **presently** immediately
Pissing-Conduit a channel in Cheapside, close to the Royal Exchange, whose name has obvious resonance with the gossips' condition; since Allwit's house overlooks the Conduit, it must be located in the Stocks meat market

183 **two ... bearer** The phallic description of this procession rouses the gossips' enthusiasm; and it helps Allwit decoy them out of the house before they have a chance to drink any more.
brave splendid

187 **Feed** eat heartily

192 **hare-mad** as mad as a hare, which becomes wilder around breeding season—'as mad as a hare' was proverbial; possible pun on 'hair' as in pubic hair

193 **bums** (*a*) bumbasts, padding; (*b*) rumps

198 **needlework stools** stools with expensive embroidered covers (a current fashion)
cost ... them are not valued by them, because they did not pay for them

201 **rushes** green rushes were strewn on the floors of homes, in place of carpets

202 **short ... heels** a loose woman was said to be short-heeled because she fell over backwards easily; 'shortheels' was slang for 'tart'
figging worthless
shuttle-cork heels punning alteration of 'shuttle-cock', a slang term for whores (since shuttle-cocks bounce back and forth from player to player). Cork heels, much in fashion, were also associated with sexual profligacy.

203 **stand** (*a*) remain; (*b*) stay erect, in a sexual innuendo

204 **thou'st** thou wast

206 **then** i.e., if I tell

ALLWIT
Marriage, Davy? Send me to hanging rather!
DAVY [*aside*]
I have stung him.
ALLWIT
When, where? What is she, Davy?
DAVY
E'en the same was gossip, and gave the spoon.
ALLWIT
I have no time to stay, nor scarce can speak.
I'll stop those wheels, or all the work will break.
Exit
DAVY
I knew 'twould prick. Thus do I fashion still
All mine own ends by him and his rank toil.
'Tis my desire to keep him still from marriage.
Being his poor nearest kinsman, I may fare
The better at his death; there my hopes build,
Since my Lady Kix is dry and hath no child. *Exit*

3.3 *Enter both the Touchwoods*

TOUCHWOOD JUNIOR
Y'are in the happiest way to enrich yourself
And pleasure me, brother, as man's feet can tread in;
For though she be locked up, her vow is fixed only to me;
Then time shall never grieve me, for by that vow
E'en absent I enjoy her, assuredly confirmed that none
Else shall, which will make tedious years seem gameful
To me. In the mean space, lose you no time, sweet brother;
You have the means to strike at this knight's fortunes
And lay him level with his bankrupt merit;
Get but his wife with child, perch at tree-top
And shake the golden fruit into her lap;
About it, before she weep herself to a dry ground
And whine out all her goodness.
TOUCHWOOD SENIOR
Prithee, cease;
I find a too much aptness in my blood
For such a business without provocation;
You might' well spared this banquet of eryngoes,
Artichokes, potatoes, and your buttered crab:
They were fitter kept for your own wedding dinner.
TOUCHWOOD JUNIOR
Nay, an you'll follow my suit and save my purse too,
Fortune dotes on me: he's in happy case
Finds such an honest friend i' the Common Pleas.
TOUCHWOOD SENIOR
Life, what makes thee so merry? Thou hast no cause
That I could hear of lately since thy crosses,
Unless there be news come with new additions.
TOUCHWOOD JUNIOR
Why, there thou hast it right: I look for her
This evening, brother.
TOUCHWOOD SENIOR
How's that? Look for her?
TOUCHWOOD JUNIOR
I will deliver you of the wonder straight, brother:
By the firm secrecy and kind assistance
Of a good wench i' the house who, made of pity,
Weighing the case her own, she's led through gutters,
Strange hidden ways, which none but love could find
Or ha' the heart to venture; I expect her
Where you would little think.
TOUCHWOOD SENIOR
I care not where,
So she be safe, and yours.
TOUCHWOOD JUNIOR
Hope tells me so;
But from your love and time my peace must grow.
Exit

208 **hanging** allusion to proverb 'Weddings and hangings go by destiny'
210 **gave the spoon** Moll was not actually present at the spoon-giving (see 3.2.23–49), which is odd since she was one of the baby's godparents; perhaps we are to assume that after the foiled elopement in 3.1, she was either not in a partying mood, had no wish to participate in a ceremony with the other godparent (Sir Walter), or had been grounded by her father. 'Gave the spoon' might indicate she had literally or metaphorically 'signed the card' accompanying the gift, or simply that as a godparent she was a spoon-giver, a kind of defining epithet like 'treasure-giver' to an Anglo-Saxon king.
211–12 **speak . . . break** a common rhyme (both rhymed with 'cake')
212 **wheels** plots, machinations
214 **him** i.e., Allwit
rank (*a*) sweaty; (*b*) corrupt
215 **him** i.e., Sir Walter
217–18 **build . . . child** probably a rhyme
218 **dry** barren
3.3.6 **gameful** joyful
7 **space** time
8 **this knight's** i.e., Sir Walter's
9 **lay . . . merit** make his financial fortunes as bankrupt as is his moral worth
10 **his wife** i.e., Lady Kix
perch . . . tree-top the image is that of a harvester shaking down fruit into the apron of his helper below
11 **golden fruit** golden apples guarded by the Greek nymphs, the Hesperides; a symbol of sexual delight
12 **About it** get on with it
weep . . . ground turn herself into a barren field through weeping out all her natural moisture; continues the play's imagery of wetness and dryness
13 **Prithee** I pray thee; please
16 **might'** might have
16–17 **eryngoes . . . crab** delicacies, considered aphrodisiacs (eryngoes are candied sea-holly root); metaphorically, Touchwood Senior's erotically-charged language, which has an aphrodisiac effect
19 **an** if
21 **i' . . . Pleas** i.e., when in need; literally, in the Court of Common Pleas at Westminster, where civil cases were heard. Ties in with other legal language ('suit', 'case') to cast Touchwood Senior as his brother's legal advocate.
23 **crosses** setbacks
24 **new additions** (*a*) fresh information; (*b*) increases to your fortune
25 **look for** expect
30 **Weighing . . . own** i.e., considering Moll's situation as if it were her own; possible quibble on 'case' as pudendum
she's led she has led the way
gutters house gutters; Moll escapes over the roofs (cf. 4.1.273)
32 **ha'** have

TOUCHWOOD SENIOR
You know the worst then, brother.—Now to my Kix,
The barren he and she; they're i' the next room;
But to say which of their two humours hold them
Now at this instant, I cannot say truly.

SIR OLIVER (*to his lady, within*) Thou liest, barrenness!

TOUCHWOOD SENIOR
O, is't that time of day? Give you joy of your tongue,
There's nothing else good in you. This their life
The whole day, from eyes open to eyes shut,
Kissing or scolding, and then must be made friends;
Then rail the second part of the first fit out,
And then be pleased again, no man knows which way:
Fall out like giants and fall in like children;
Their fruit can witness as much.

Enter Sir Oliver Kix and his Lady

SIR OLIVER 'Tis thy fault.

LADY
Mine, drought and coldness?

SIR OLIVER Thine; 'tis thou art barren.

LADY
I barren? O life, that I durst but speak now
In mine own justice, in mine own right! I barren?
'Twas otherways with me when I was at court;
I was ne'er called so till I was married.

SIR OLIVER
I'll be divorced.

LADY Be hanged! I need not wish it;
That will come too soon to thee: I may say
'Marriage and hanging goes by destiny',
For all the goodness I can find in't yet.

SIR OLIVER
I'll give up house, and keep some fruitful whore,
Like an old bachelor, in a tradesman's chamber;
She and her children shall have all.

LADY Where be they?

TOUCHWOOD SENIOR Pray, cease;
When there are friendlier courses took for you
To get and multiply within your house
At your own proper costs, in spite of censure,
Methinks an honest peace might be established.

SIR OLIVER
What, with her? Never.

TOUCHWOOD SENIOR Sweet sir—

SIR OLIVER You work all in vain.

LADY
Then he doth all like thee.

TOUCHWOOD SENIOR Let me entreat, sir—

SIR OLIVER
Singleness confound her! I took her with one smock.

LADY
But, indeed, you came not so single
When you came from shipboard.

SIR OLIVER [*aside*] Heart, she bit sore there!—
[*To Touchwood Senior*] Prithee, make 's friends.

TOUCHWOOD SENIOR [*aside*]
Is't come to that? The peal begins to cease.

SIR OLIVER [*to Lady Kix*]
I'll sell all at an outcry!

LADY Do thy worst, slave!—
[*To Touchwood Senior*] Good sweet sir, bring us into love again.

TOUCHWOOD SENIOR [*aside*]
Some would think this impossible to compass.—
[*To them*] Pray, let this storm fly over.

SIR OLIVER
Good sir, pardon me; I'm master of this house,
Which I'll sell presently; I'll clap up bills this evening.

TOUCHWOOD SENIOR Lady! Friends! Come!

LADY
If e'er ye loved woman, talk not on't, sir.
What, friends with him! Good faith, do you think I'm mad?
With one that's scarce the hinder quarter of a man?

SIR OLIVER
Thou art nothing of a woman.

LADY Would I were less than nothing!

36 **know the worst** allusion to the proverb 'To know the worst is good'. He may mean that his brother's fortunes, having touched bottom, are bound to be on the way up.
37 **i'** in
38 **two humours** two moods, loving and fighting
41 **Give** i.e., God give
45 **fit** (*a*) section of a poem or song; (*b*) paroxysm of rage
47 **Fall out** quarrel; the notion of giants falling out may allude to the war of the Titans
fall in (*a*) make up; (*b*) have sexual intercourse; they make up 'like children', without fully consummated sex, as their lack of issue demonstrates
48 **fruit** offspring, or lack thereof
52 **'Twas...court** i.e., (*a*) I was never insulted at court, where people are more polite than you are; (*b*) I was never called barren at court because there I was sexually loose
54 **divorced** Divorce, possible only for a very few, necessitated an individual act of Parliament; barrenness would not be sufficient grounds for divorce, but Sir Oliver might plead non-consummation, or complain of the profligacy at court to which Lady Kix may just have confessed.
56 **'Marriage...destiny'** See note to 3.2.208.
59 **in a tradesman's chamber** i.e., living in lodgings
60 **Where be they?** i.e., you have yet to prove you can father a child
64 **proper** personal
in...censure (*a*) in spite of your mutual recrimination; or (*b*) averting the criticism of your neighbours (for your childlessness)
68 **Singleness** i.e., the divorced state
I...smock i.e., she had very little property when I married her; possible allusion to the well-known tale of patient Griselde
69 **not so single** unaccompanied, with the implication that he was lousy, had venereal disease, had brought a 'smock' (loose woman) with him, or came direct from a relationship with a sailor
71 **'s** us
72 **peal** volley of sound
73 **outcry** auction
75 **compass** accomplish
78 **presently** immediately
clap up bills i.e., hastily post advertisements for the auction
82 **scarce...man** i.e., not a complete man sexually

[She] weeps

SIR OLIVER
Nay, prithee, what dost mean?

LADY
I cannot please you.

SIR OLIVER
I'faith, thou art a good soul; he lies that says it;
[Kissing her]
Buss, buss, pretty rogue.

LADY
You care not for me.

TOUCHWOOD SENIOR *[aside]*
Can any man tell now which way they came in?
By this light, I'll be hanged then!

SIR OLIVER
Is the drink come?

TOUCHWOOD SENIOR *(aside)*
Here's a little vial of almond milk,
That stood me in some threepence.

SIR OLIVER
I hope to see thee, wench, within these few years,
Circled with children, pranking up a girl,
And putting jewels in their little ears;
Fine sport, i'faith!

LADY
Ay, had you been ought, husband,
It had been done ere this time.

SIR OLIVER
Had I been ought! Hang thee! Hadst thou been ought!
But a cross thing I ever found thee.

LADY
Thou art a grub to say so.

SIR OLIVER
A pox on thee!

TOUCHWOOD SENIOR *[aside]*
By this light, they are out again at the same door,
And no man can tell which way! *[To Sir Oliver]*
Come, here's your drink, sir.

SIR OLIVER
I will not take it now, sir,
An I were sure to get three boys ere midnight.

LADY
Why, there thou show'st now of what breed thou com'st,
To hinder generation. O thou villain,
That knows how crookedly the world goes with us
For want of heirs, yet put by all good fortune.

SIR OLIVER
Hang, strumpet! I will take it now in spite.

TOUCHWOOD SENIOR
Then you must ride upon't five hours.
[He gives vial to Sir Oliver]

SIR OLIVER
I mean so. Within there!
Enter a Servant

SERVANT
Sir?

SIR OLIVER
Saddle the white mare.
[Exit Servant]
I'll take a whore along and ride to Ware.

LADY
Ride to the devil!

SIR OLIVER
I'll plague you every way.
Look ye, do you see?
[He] drinks
'Tis gone.

LADY
A pox go with it!

SIR OLIVER Ay, curse and spare not now.

TOUCHWOOD SENIOR
Stir up and down, sir, you must not stand.

SIR OLIVER Nay, I'm not given to standing.

TOUCHWOOD SENIOR So much the better, sir, for the [ ].

SIR OLIVER
I never could stand long in one place yet;
I learned it of my father, ever figient.
How if I crossed this, sir?
[He] capers

TOUCHWOOD SENIOR O passing good, sir, and would show well a-horseback; when you come to your inn, if you leaped over a joint-stool or two, 'twere not amiss; *(Aside)*—although you brake your neck, sir.

SIR OLIVER *[capering]* What say you to a table thus high, sir?

TOUCHWOOD SENIOR Nothing better, sir; *[Aside]*—if it be furnished with good victuals. *[To him]* You remember how the bargain runs about this business?

85 **he . . . it** i.e., whoever says you cannot please me is lying
86 **buss** kiss
87 **Can . . . in** i.e., one would never know from the present sweet concord that the couple came in fighting a few minutes ago
89 **almond milk** drink made from sweet blanched almonds
90 **stood me in** cost me
92 **pranking up** dressing up
93 **jewels . . . ears** both sexes wore earrings until about 1660
94 **had . . . ought** i.e., if you had been anything in the way of a man
95 **ere** before
98 **grub** dwarfish, unmannerly fellow
102 **An** even if
106 **put by** neglect
108 **ride upon't** go horseback riding after taking it, with possible sexual innuendo, especially since he threatens to 'take a whore along' (3.3.110)
109 **mean so** intend to
Within there i.e., you! inside! (a demand that a servant come out and attend him)
white mare perhaps hints at the proverb 'He that has a white horse and a fair wife never lacks trouble'
110 **Ware** a Hertfordshire town, some 20 miles north of London, famous for amorous meetings. A Ware inn had a famous bed nearly 11 feet square, now in a museum.
114 **Stir** move
115 **standing** (*a*) keeping still; (*b*) staying sexually erect
117 **[ ]** One or two words, probably obscenities, are omitted; compare similar omissions, possibly the result of censorship, at 4.1.228, 4.1.232, 4.1.263.
119 **figient** fidgety
120 **crossed this** i.e, jumped over this—probably a joint-stool (see 3.3.123)
123 **joint-stool** a two-foot high wooden stool, assembled by a joiner. References to stool leaping, something of a fashionable pastime, are usually disparaging.
124 **brake** broke

SIR OLIVER [*capering about the stage all the while*] Or else I had a bad head: you must receive, sir, four hundred pounds of me at four several payments: one hundred pound now in hand.

TOUCHWOOD SENIOR Right, that I have, sir.

SIR OLIVER
Another hundred when my wife is quick;
The third when she's brought a-bed; and the last hundred
When the child cries, for if it should be still-born,
It doth no good, sir.

TOUCHWOOD SENIOR
All this even still: a little faster, sir.

SIR OLIVER [*still capering*] Not a whit, sir;
I'm in an excellent pace for any physic.

Enter a Servant

SERVANT
Your white mare's ready.

SIR OLIVER [*still capering*] I shall up presently.

[*Exit Servant*]

[*To Lady Kix*] One kiss, and farewell. [*He kisses her*]

LADY Thou shalt have two, love.

SIR OLIVER
Expect me about three. *Exit,* [*capering*]

LADY With all my heart, sweet.

TOUCHWOOD SENIOR [*aside*]
By this light, they have forgot their anger since,
And are as far in again as e'er they were.
Which way the devil came they? Heart, I saw 'em not,
Their ways are beyond finding out. [*To Lady Kix*] Come, sweet lady.

LADY How must I take mine, sir?

TOUCHWOOD SENIOR
Clean contrary; yours must be taken lying.

LADY
A-bed, sir?

TOUCHWOOD SENIOR
A-bed, or where you will for your own ease,
Your coach will serve.

LADY The physic must needs please.

Exeunt

Finis Actus Tertius

4.1 [*Incipit*] *Actus Quartus*

Enter Tim and Tutor

TIM *Negatur argumentum,* tutor.

TUTOR *Probo tibi,* pupil, *stultus non est animal rationale.*

TIM *Falleris sane.*

TUTOR *Quaeso ut taceas: probo tibi—*

TIM *Quomodo probas, domine?*

TUTOR *Stultus non habet rationem, ergo non est animal rationale.*

TIM *Sic argumentaris, domine: stultus non habet rationem, ergo non est animal rationale. Negatur argumentum* again, tutor.

TUTOR *Argumentum iterum probo tibi, domine: qui non participat de ratione, nullo modo potest vocari rationalibus*; but *stultus non participat de ratione, ergo stultus nullo modo potest dicere rationalis.*

TIM *Participat.*

TUTOR *Sic disputas: qui participat, quomodo participat?*

TIM *Ut homo, probabo tibi in syllogismo.*

TUTOR *Hunc proba.*

131 **bad head** poor memory; possible (unintended) reference to cuckold's horns

131–8 **you . . . sir** So pervasive are the habits of money and exchange that even a gentleman like Sir Oliver has the bourgeois knack of writing watertight contracts.

131–2 **four hundred pounds** Since Sir Oliver earlier was willing to spend £500 for Touchwood's fertility cure (2.1.192–4), and Touchwood Senior has to invest only threepence and some of his bodily fluids, both get a bargain.

135 **quick** pregnant

139 **even** just
faster Sir Oliver is still jumping to activate the potion

140 **whit** bit

141 **physic** medicine

142 **up** get mounted, with the usual sexual innuendo

145 **anger since** previous anger

147 **Which . . . they** i.e., one cannot keep track of their mood shifts

148 **Their . . . out** ironic echo of Romans 11:33 (Geneva): 'O the deepness of the riches, both of the wisdom, and knowledge of God! How unsearchable are his judgements, and his ways past finding out!'

150 **Clean contrary** in an exactly opposite way

152 **coach will serve** Many Renaissance writings allude to ladies copulating in their coaches.
must needs is bound to

4.1.1–20 Latin disputation was the major teaching method in Renaissance universities. The argument here, on a common topic, relies on both parties accepting the traditional definition of a human as a 'rational animal or creature' (*animal rationale*). Parker translates the dialogue as follows:

TIM Your proof is denied, tutor.

TUTOR I demonstrate it to you, pupil, a fool is not a rational creature.

TIM You will certainly fail.

TUTOR I beg you to be silent: I prove it to you—

TIM How do you prove it, sir?

TUTOR A fool has not the power of reason, therefore he is not a rational creature.

TIM Thus you argue, sir: a fool has not the power of reason, therefore he is not a rational creature. Your argument is denied again, tutor.

TUTOR Again I demonstrate the proof, sir: he who does not share the power of reason, in no wise can be termed rational; but a fool does not share the power of reason, therefore a fool in no wise can be said to be rational.

TIM He does share it.

TUTOR So you argue: who shares it, how does he share it?

TIM As a man: I will prove it to you by a syllogism.

TUTOR Prove this.

TIM Thus I prove it, sir: a fool is a man just as you and I are; a man is a rational creature, just so a fool is a rational creature.

12 ***rationalibus*** the Tutor's mistake for *rationalis*

14 ***dicere*** the Tutor's mistake for *dici*

TIM *Sic probo domine: stultus est homo sicut tu et ego sumus; homo est animal rationale, sicut stultus est animal rationale.*

Enter Maudline

MAUDLINE Here's nothing but disputing all the day long with 'em!

TUTOR *Sic disputas: stultus est homo sicut tu et ego sumus; homo est animal rationale, sicut stultus est animal rationale.*

MAUDLINE
Your reasons are both good, whate'er they be;
Pray, give them o'er; faith, you'll tire yourselves;
What's the matter between you?

TIM
Nothing but reasoning about a fool, mother.

MAUDLINE About a fool, son? Alas, what need you trouble your heads about that? None of us all but knows what a fool is.

TIM Why, what's a fool, mother? I come to you now.

MAUDLINE Why, one that's marrièd before he has wit.

TIM 'Tis pretty, i'faith, and well guessed of a woman never brought up at the university; but bring forth what fool you will, mother, I'll prove him to be as reasonable a creature as myself or my tutor here.

MAUDLINE
Fie, 'tis impossible.

TUTOR Nay, he shall do't, forsooth.

TIM 'Tis the easiest thing to prove a fool by logic;
By logic I'll prove anything.

MAUDLINE What, thou wilt not!

TIM I'll prove a whore to be an honest woman.

MAUDLINE Nay, by my faith, she must prove that herself,
Or logic will never do't.

TIM 'Twill do't, I tell you.

MAUDLINE Some in this street would give a thousand pounds
That you could prove their wives so.

TIM Faith, I can,
And all their daughters too, though they had three bastards.
When comes your tailor hither?

MAUDLINE Why, what of him?

TIM By logic I'll prove him to be a man,
Let him come when he will.

MAUDLINE [*to Tutor*] How hard at first was learning to him! Truly, sir, I thought he would never a took the Latin tongue. How many accidences do you think he wore out ere he came to his grammar?

TUTOR
Some three or four.

MAUDLINE Believe me, sir, some four-and-thirty.

TIM Pish, I made haberdines of 'em in church porches.

MAUDLINE He was eight years in his grammar, and stuck horribly at a foolish place there called *ass in praesenti.*

TIM Pox, I have it here now. [*He points to his forehead*]

MAUDLINE He so shamed me once before an honest gentleman that knew me when I was a maid.

TIM These women must have all out!

MAUDLINE '*Quid est grammatica?*' says the gentleman to him—I shall remember by a sweet, sweet token—but nothing could he answer.

TUTOR How now, pupil, ha? *Quid est grammatica?*

TIM *Grammatica*? Ha, ha, ha!

MAUDLINE Nay, do not laugh, son, but let me hear you say it now: there was one word went so prettily off the gentleman's tongue, I shall remember it the longest day of my life.

TUTOR Come, *quid est grammatica?*

TIM Are you not ashamed, tutor? *Grammatica*: why, *recte scribendi atque loquendi ars*, sir-reverence of my mother.

MAUDLINE That was it, i'faith! Why now, son, I see you are a deep scholar. And, Master Tutor, a word I pray. [*Aside to Tutor*] Let us withdraw a little into my husband's chamber. I'll send in the North-Wales gentlewoman to

23–4 **TUTOR** 'So you contend: a fool is a man just as you and I are; a man is a rational creature, just so a fool is a rational creature'. (Middleton repeats the Latin to make sure his audience grasps the joke: Tim and the Tutor are fools.)

27 **matter** issue

32 **I . . . now** I pose the question to you (disputation term)

33 **one . . . wit** a proverb that foreshadows the fate of the foolish Tim

34 **pretty** i.e., a clever argument

39 **prove a fool** (*a*) construct an argument proving fools rational; (*b*) turn out to be a fool oneself. (Tim is presumably oblivious to the second meaning.)

41 **honest** chaste, faithful to one man

49–50 **tailor . . . man** Tailors were frequently regarded as unmanly, probably because sewing was deemed 'feminine'; hence the proverb 'Nine tailors make but one man' and the nursery rhyme 'Four-and-twenty tailors | Went to kill a snail'.

53 **a took** have taken; i. e., mastered

54 **accidences** books of rules for Latin inflexions

55 **grammar** books of rules for syntax

57 **haberdines** dried salt cod; possibly a reference to a lost game similar to the modern children's game 'kippers'

59 ***ass in praesenti*** a phrase, meaning 'as in the present tense', occurring at the beginning of the 'verb' section of a famous Latin grammar text; the 'ass/arse' pun was frequent

62 **knew . . . maid** 'knew' was a biblical euphemism for 'had sex with'; 'maid' could mean either 'virgin' or 'unmarried woman'. Maudline's pronouncement seems unintentionally suggestive.

63 **must . . . out** i.e., must tell everything; with a sexual suggestion

64 ***Quid est grammatica*** what is grammar? (Latin)

65 **sweet token** the 'one word [that] went so prettily off the gentleman's tongue' (4.1.70–1)

71–2 **longest . . . life** for the rest of my life .

73–5 ***quid . . . ars*** what is grammar? . . . the art of writing and speaking correctly (Latin); from the beginning of a standard grammar book of the period

74 **Are . . . ashamed** i.e., 'aren't you ashamed to ask me such an easy question?', or (more likely, given his apology in the next sentence), 'Aren't you ashamed to ask me a question that will produce an answer like "arse"?'

75 **sir-reverence** corruption of 'saving your reverence' or *salve reverentia*, a formula similar to the modern 'pardon my French'

76 **That was it** i.e., the word '*ars*' was the 'sweet, sweet token' or 'one word' that her gentleman friend used to say (cf. 4.1.70)

him, she looks for wooing. I'll put together both and lock the door.

TUTOR
I give great approbation to your conclusion.
Exeunt [Maudline and Tutor]

TIM I mar'l what this gentlewoman should be that I should have in marriage. She's a stranger to me.
I wonder what my parents mean, i'faith,
To match me with a stranger so,
A maid that's neither kith nor kin to me.
Life, do they think I have no more care of my body than to lie with one that I ne'er knew, a mere stranger, one that ne'er went to school with me neither, nor ever play-fellows together?
They're mightily o'erseen in't, methinks.
They say she has mountains to her marriage;
She's full of cattle, some two thousand runts:
Now what the meaning of these runts should be,
My tutor cannot tell me.
I have looked in Rider's *Dictionary* for the letter R, and there I can hear no tidings of these runts neither; unless they should be Romford hogs, I know them not.
Enter Welsh Gentlewoman
And here she comes. If I know what to say to her now in the way of marriage, I'm no graduate.
Methinks, i'faith, 'tis boldly done of her
To come into my chamber, being but a stranger;
She shall not say I'm so proud yet but I'll speak to her; marry, as I will order it, she shall take no hold of my words, I'll warrant her.
[The Welsh Gentlewoman curtsies]
She looks and makes a cursy!—*[To her] Salve tu quoque, puella pulcherrima; quid vis nescio nec sane curo,*—Tully's own phrase to a heart!

WELSH GENTLEWOMAN *[aside]*
I know not what he means: a suitor quoth a?
I hold my life he understands no English.

TIM *Fertur, me hercule, tu virgo, Wallia ut opibus abundis maximis.*

WELSH GENTLEWOMAN *[aside]* What's this *fertur* and *abundundis?* He mocks me sure, and calls me a bundle of farts.

TIM *[aside]* I have no Latin word now for their runts; I'll make some shift or other: *[To her] Iterum dico, opibus abundis maximis montibus et fontibus et, ut ita dicam, rontibus; attamen vero homunculus ego sum natura simul et arte baccalaureus, lecto profecto non paratus.*

WELSH GENTLEWOMAN *[aside]*
This is most strange; maybe he can speak Welsh.
[To him] A fedrwch chwi Cymraeg? [Aside] Er duw, cog fo gennyf?

TIM *[aside] Cog foggin?* I scorn to cog with her; I'll tell her so too, in a word near her own language; *[To her] Ego non cogo.*

WELSH GENTLEWOMAN *Rhyw gosyn a chwigyn ar ôl bod yn cerdedd am dro.*

TIM *[aside]* By my faith, she's a good scholar, I see that already: She has the tongues plain; I hold my life she has travelled. What will folks say? 'There goes the learned couple'! Faith, if the truth were known she hath proceeded!
Enter Maudline

MAUDLINE How now, how speeds your business?

TIM *[aside]* I'm glad my mother's come to part us.

MAUDLINE *[to the Welsh Gentlewoman]* How do you agree, forsooth?

WELSH GENTLEWOMAN
As well as e'er we did before we met.

MAUDLINE How's that?

WELSH GENTLEWOMAN
You put me to a man I understand not;
Your son's no Englishman, methinks.

83 **mar'l** wonder
87 **neither . . . kin** neither neighbour nor relative
92 **o'erseen** imprudent
93 **to her marriage** i.e., as dowry
94 **runts** a breed of small cattle, common in Wales and the Scottish Highlands
97 **Rider's *Dictionary*** a Latin/English, English/Latin dictionary by John Rider first published in 1589, and the subject of a law case in 1613
99 **Romford hogs** 12 miles north-east of London, Romford was famous for markets, especially its Tuesday hog market; also a favourite place for amorous trysts
107 **cursy** curtsy
107–8 ***Salve . . . curo*** save you too, most beautiful young woman; what you want I do not know, nor truly do I care (Latin)
108 **Tully's** Cicero, whose prose served as a stylistic model for Renaissance writers; students were taught to imitate him
109 **to a heart** exactly, as if by heart
110 **quoth a** says he; i.e., 'indeed'
112–13 ***Fertur . . . maximis*** it is said—by Hercules!—virgin, that you abound with great wealth in Wales (Latin)
112 ***abundis*** Tim's error for *abundas*; see also 4.1.119
114–16 ***fertur* . . . farts** The 'er' in *fertur* may have been pronounced 'ar'.
118 **shift** contrivance, approximation
118–21 ***Iterum . . . paratus*** 'Again, I say, you abound in great riches, in mountains and fountains and, as I may call them, in "runts" [inventing the Latin-sounding *rontibus*]; yet, truly, I am a little man by nature and at the same time a bachelor by training, really not prepared for the marriage bed.' Tim's claim to be a 'homunculus' and the earlier emphasis on Sir Oliver's 'shortness' (3.3.98) may indicate the presence of boy actors from the Queen's Revels. A 'homunculus', in medical theory, was a fully-formed proto-human present in sperm; thus Tim's strained Latin suggests sexuality at the very moment he is insisting that he is not prepared for bed.
123 ***A fedrwch . . . Cymraeg?*** do you speak Welsh?
Er . . . gennyf for God's sake, is he pretending with me?
124 **cog** cheat, or have sex with
125–6 ***Ego non cogo*** I won't come together with you (Latin); *cogo* puns on 'cog' in 4.1.124
127–8 ***Rhyw . . . dro*** some cheese and whey after taking a walk. Cheese and whey were considered the staple diet of the Welsh.
131 **has travelled** with unintended suggestion of 'has travailed', or been in labour; also suggests 'has got around sexually'
133 **proceeded** taken a degree (cf. 1.1.158), with a suggestion again of sexual 'travelling'
134 **speeds** fares
136 **agree** get along together

MAUDLINE No Englishman?
Bless my boy, and born i' the heart of London!

WELSH GENTLEWOMAN
I ha' been long enough in the chamber with him,
And I find neither Welsh nor English in him.

MAUDLINE
Why, Tim, how have you used the gentlewoman?

TIM
As well as a man might do, mother, in modest Latin.

MAUDLINE
Latin, fool?

TIM And she recoiled in Hebrew.

MAUDLINE
In Hebrew, fool? 'Tis Welsh!

TIM All comes to one, mother.

MAUDLINE
She can speak English too.

TIM Who told me so much?
Heart, an she can speak English, I'll clap to her.
I thought you'd marry me to a stranger.

MAUDLINE [*to the Welsh Gentlewoman*]
You must forgive him: he's so inured to Latin,
He and his tutor, that he hath quite forgot
To use the Protestant tongue.

WELSH GENTLEWOMAN 'Tis quickly pardoned, forsooth.

MAUDLINE Tim, make amends and kiss her. [*To the Welsh Gentlewoman*] He makes towards you, forsooth.

[*Tim kisses the Welsh Gentlewoman*]

TIM O, delicious! One may discover her country by her kissing; 'tis a true saying: 'There's nothing tastes so sweet as your Welsh mutton.'—[*To the Welsh Gentlewoman*] It was reported you could sing.

MAUDLINE
O, rarely, Tim, the sweetest British songs.

TIM
And 'tis my mind, I swear, before I marry,
I would see all my wife's good parts at once,
To view how rich I were.

MAUDLINE Thou shalt hear sweet music, Tim.
[*To the Welsh Gentlewoman*] Pray, forsooth.

Music and Song

WELSH GENTLEWOMAN
Cupid is Venus' only joy,
But he is a wanton boy,
A very, very wanton boy;
He shoots at ladies' naked breasts,
He is the cause of most men's crests,—
I mean upon the forehead,
Invisible but horrid;
'Twas he first thought upon the way
To keep a lady's lips in play.

Why should not Venus chide her son
For the pranks that he hath done,
The wanton pranks that he hath done?
He shoots his fiery darts so thick,
They hurt poor ladies to the quick,
Ay me, with cruel wounding!
His darts are so confounding,
That life and sense would soon decay
But that he keeps their lips in play.

Can there be any part of bliss,
In a quickly fleeting kiss,
A quickly, quickly fleeting kiss?
To one's pleasure leisures are but waste,
The slowest kiss makes too much haste,
[ ]
And lose it ere we find it.
The pleasing sport they only know
That close above and close below.

TIM
I would not change my wife for a kingdom;
I can do somewhat too in my own lodging.

Enter Yellowhammer, and Allwit [in disguise]

YELLOWHAMMER
Why, well said, Tim! The bells go merrily;

145 **used** treated
147 **recoiled** retorted
148 **All ... one** i.e., it's all the same
150 **clap** clasp hands on the marriage contract, or stick close to. Since Tim often speaks more truly than he knows, the meaning 'to catch gonorrhea from' may also be hinted at.
151 **stranger** foreigner
154 **Protestant tongue** i.e., vernacular English rather than 'Catholic' Latin
157 **makes towards** approaches
158 **country** (*a*) her country of origin, Wales; (*b*) her 'country' sexual proclivities as in 'country matters'; (*c*) possible sexual innuendo of 'cunt'
160 **mutton** Welsh mutton was famous, but 'mutton' also meant 'whore'
161 **sing** with sexual innuendo (to 'sing' was to copulate)
162 **rarely** exceptionally well
British i.e., Welsh
164 **good parts** accomplishments, with bawdy innuendo
166.1 ***Music and Song*** Songs were often used to characterize Welsh nationality; this song, inappropriately in English, may have replaced an original Welsh song in the printed version, or in performances where no Welsh singer was available. See also *Masque of Cupids*, p. 1027, and *Dissemblers* 1.4.89–99; for a musical setting see *Companion*, p. 149.
167 **Cupid** Roman god of love, son of Venus; shoots arrows into his victims, causing them to fall in love
Venus Roman goddess of Love
171 **crests** (*a*) erections (implied and then rejected by the next line); (*b*) cuckolds' horns (coyly established as the 'true' meaning of 'crests' at 4.1.172)
172 **forehead** pronounced to rhyme with 'horrid'
175 **lips in play** through kissing (with a suggestion of labia)
180 **quick** tenderest part, with bawdy implication
182 **darts** In literature, arrow wounds often had sexual implications, and the 'dart of love' was the penis.
188 **To ... waste** intermissions in pleasure are a waste of time
191 **we ... find it** A line seems to have dropped out before or after this line, to judge from the rhyme scheme.
193 **close ... below** unite both upper and lower bodies
195 **I ... too** an understated sexual boast
in ... lodging (*a*) on my own account; (*b*) in the privacy of my nuptial lodging
196 **bells go merrily** i.e., everything is going well

I love such peals o' life. Wife, lead them in a while;
Here's a strange gentleman desires private conference.
Exeunt [Maudline, the Welsh Gentlewoman, and Tim]
[*To Allwit*] You're welcome, sir, the more for your name's sake,
Good Master Yellowhammer; I love my name well:
And which o' the Yellowhammers take you descent from,
If I may be so bold with you, which, I pray?

ALLWIT
The Yellowhammers in Oxfordshire near Abingdon.

YELLOWHAMMER
And those are the best Yellowhammers, and truest bred;
I came from thence myself, though now a citizen.
I'll be bold with you; you are most welcome.

ALLWIT
I hope the zeal I bring with me shall deserve it.

YELLOWHAMMER
I hope no less: what is your will, sir?

ALLWIT
I understand, by rumours, you have a daughter,
Which my bold love shall henceforth title 'cousin'.

YELLOWHAMMER I thank you for her, sir.

ALLWIT
I heard of her virtues and other confirmed graces.

YELLOWHAMMER A plaguy girl, sir!

ALLWIT
Fame sets her out with richer ornaments
Than you are pleased to boast of; 'tis done modestly:
I hear she's towards marriage.

YELLOWHAMMER You hear truth, sir.

ALLWIT
And with a knight in town, Sir Walter Whorehound.

YELLOWHAMMER
The very same, sir.

ALLWIT I am the sorrier for't.

YELLOWHAMMER The sorrier? Why, cousin?

ALLWIT
'Tis not too far past, is't? It may yet be recalled?

YELLOWHAMMER Recalled? Why, good sir?

ALLWIT
Resolve me in that point, ye shall hear from me.

YELLOWHAMMER
There's no contract passed.

ALLWIT I am very joyful, sir.

YELLOWHAMMER But he's the man must bed her.

ALLWIT
By no means, coz; she's quite undone then,
And you'll curse the time that e'er you made the match;
He's an arrant whoremaster, consumes his time and state,
[ ]
Whom in my knowledge he hath kept this seven years;
Nay, coz, another man's wife too.

YELLOWHAMMER O, abominable!

ALLWIT
Maintains the whole house, apparels the husband,
Pays servants' wages, not so much but [ ]

YELLOWHAMMER
Worse and worse! And doth the husband know this?

ALLWIT
Knows? Ay, and glad he may, too, 'tis his living,
As other trades thrive—butchers by selling flesh,
Poulters by vending conies, or the like, coz.

YELLOWHAMMER
What an incomparable wittol's this!

ALLWIT
Tush, what cares he for that? Believe me, coz,
No more than I do.

YELLOWHAMMER What a base slave is that!

ALLWIT
All's one to him; he feeds and takes his ease,
Was ne'er the man that ever broke his sleep
To get a child yet, by his own confession,
And yet his wife has seven.

YELLOWHAMMER What, by Sir Walter?

ALLWIT
Sir Walter's like to keep 'em and maintain 'em
In excellent fashion; he dares do no less, sir.

YELLOWHAMMER
Life, has he children too?

197 **peals o' life** life imagined as ringing like a bell with pulsating sexuality
198 **strange** unknown
199 **more ... sake** Allwit pretends to be Yellowhammer's distant cousin.
203 **Abingdon** actually the county town of Berkshire, five miles south of Oxford
204 **best Yellowhammers** The boasting about the name may reflect the fact that two medieval Yellowhammers were Lord Mayors of London.
205 **thence** there
citizen member of the London middle classes, including merchants, shopkeepers, well-off craftsmen, and some others (a fluid category)
211 **for her** on her behalf
212 **confirmed** firmly established
213 **plaguy** troublesome
216 **towards marriage** about to be married
220 **recalled** called off
222 **Resolve ... me** i.e., satisfy me on that question and then I'll continue
223 **contract** marriage agreement; it was legally very difficult to get out of such an agreement once formalized
225 **coz** familiar form of 'cousin'
228 **[ ]** A line seems to be missing here, the gist of which may be something like 'with a woman in this neighbourhood'.
232 another truncated and perhaps censored part-line, represented (as elsewhere) by a long dash in COTES
236 **Poulters** poulterers (poultry dealers), with suggestion of 'pimps'; another reference to the sale of women as food to be consumed.
vending conies selling rabbits, with suggestion of whores

ALLWIT Children! Boys thus high,
In their Cato and Corderius.
YELLOWHAMMER
What? You jest, sir!
ALLWIT Why, one can make a verse
And is now at Eton College.
YELLOWHAMMER
O, this news has cut into my heart, coz.
ALLWIT
It had eaten nearer, if it had not been prevented:
One Allwit's wife.
YELLOWHAMMER Allwit? Foot, I have heard of him;
He had a girl kersened lately?
ALLWIT Ay, that work
Did cost the knight above a hundred mark.
YELLOWHAMMER
I'll mark him for a knave and villain for't.
A thousand thanks and blessings! I have done with him.
ALLWIT [*aside*]
Ha, ha, ha! This knight will stick by my ribs still;
I shall not lose him yet; no wife will come;
Where'er he woos, I find him still at home. Ha, ha!
Exit
YELLOWHAMMER
Well, grant all this, say now his deeds are black,
Pray, what serves marriage but to call him back?
I have kept a whore myself, and had a bastard
By Mistress Anne, in *anno* [ ]
I care not who knows it; he's now a jolly fellow,
He's been twice warden. So may his fruit be;
They were but base begot, and so was he.
The knight is rich, he shall be my son-in-law.
No matter, so the whore he keeps be wholesome—
My daughter takes no hurt then. So let them wed;
I'll have him sweat well ere they go to bed.
Enter Maudline
MAUDLINE
O, husband, husband!
YELLOWHAMMER How now, Maudline?
MAUDLINE
We are all undone! She's gone, she's gone!
YELLOWHAMMER
Again? Death! Which way?
MAUDLINE Over the houses.
Lay the waterside; she's gone for ever, else.
YELLOWHAMMER O vent'rous baggage! *Exeunt*

4.2

Enter Tim and Tutor
TIM
Thieves, thieves! My sister's stol'n! Some thief hath got her:
O, how miraculously did my father's plate 'scape!
'Twas all left out, tutor.
TUTOR Is't possible?
TIM
Besides three chains of pearl and a box of coral.
My sister's gone. Let's look at Trig Stairs for her.
My mother's gone to lay the common stairs
At Puddle Wharf; and at the dock below
Stands my poor silly father. Run, sweet tutor, run!
Exeunt

4.3

Enter both the Touchwoods
TOUCHWOOD SENIOR
I had been taken, brother, by eight sergeants,

247 **Cato and Corderius** authors of two popular moralizing schoolbooks favoured by Puritans
249 **Eton College** school patronized by the gentle classes, 23 miles west of London; composing Latin verses was a common school exercise. Allwit seems to be lying about this son, who is nowhere else mentioned.
251 **prevented** anticipated
252 **Foot** short for 'Christ's foot' (oath)
254 **the knight** i.e., Sir Walter
above more than
hundred mark over 66 pounds
257 **stick...ribs** i.e., stay very close
261 **what...marriage** what is marriage good for. The idea that the love of a good woman could reform the wildest of men was current in Middleton's time.
call him back reform him
263 ***anno*** in the year (Latin)
[ ] The date may have been left blank for the actor to fill in the date the play was performed.
264 **he's** i.e., the bastard son
265 **warden** (*a*) member of the governing body of a city trade guild; (*b*) a kind of pear, hence the play on 'fruit'
his fruit Yellowhammer's bastard's offspring
266 **They...he** i.e., Yellowhammer's bastard son's children will prove to be illegitimately sired, like their father
267 **knight is rich** a reminder that positing a marital exchange of bourgeois money for the prestige of a gentleman's title is too simple: Touchwood Junior is a gentleman, but that is not enough—Yellowhammer wants gentility *and* money.
268 **wholesome** free of the pox
270 **sweat** be treated in a steam tub for venereal disease
273 **Over the houses** i.e., across the rooftops
274 **Lay** set watch on
275 **vent'rous baggage** bold girl
4.2.2 **plate** silver-plated ornaments. Tim's automatic placing of his sister in the same category as the family silver is another instance of daughters' being considered material property; but that such attitudes are attributed to a complete fool suggests that they are being satirized rather than unthinkingly accepted.
5–7 **Trig Stairs...dock below** embarkation points on the Thames; since 'trig' also meant coxcomb, the association with Tim is suitable
6 **common** public
7 **Puddle Wharf** originally so called because a man called Puddle kept a wharf there, but later because horses watered there and created puddles on the wharf; ties in with other urine imagery in the play
below downstream, perhaps at Dung Wharf, where the city refuse was loaded on to barges
8 **silly** innocent
4.3.1 **had been taken** would have been arrested
sergeants sheriff's officers

But for the honest watermen; I am bound to them;
They are the most requiteful'st people living,
For as they get their means by gentlemen,
They are still the forwardest to help gentlemen.
You heard how one 'scaped out of the Blackfriars,
But a while since, from two or three varlets
Came into the house with all their rapiers drawn,
As if they'd dance the sword-dance on the stage,
With candles in their hands, like chandlers' ghosts,
Whilst the poor gentleman so pursued and bandied
Was by an honest pair of oars safely landed.

TOUCHWOOD JUNIOR
I love them with my heart for't.

Enter three or four Watermen

FIRST WATERMAN Your first man, sir.

SECOND WATERMAN
Shall I carry you gentlemen with a pair of oars?

TOUCHWOOD SENIOR These be the honest fellows.
Take one pair and leave the rest for her.

TOUCHWOOD JUNIOR
Barn Elms.

TOUCHWOOD SENIOR
No more, brother.

FIRST WATERMAN Your first man.

SECOND WATERMAN Shall I carry your worship?

TOUCHWOOD JUNIOR
Go. *[Exit Touchwood Senior with First Waterman]*
And you honest watermen that stay,
Here's a French crown for you: *[He gives him money]*
There comes a maid with all speed to take water,
Row her lustily to Barn Elms after me.

SECOND WATERMAN
To Barn Elms, good, sir.—Make ready the boat, Sam;
We'll wait below. *Exeunt [Watermen]*

Enter Moll

TOUCHWOOD JUNIOR
What made you stay so long?

MOLL
I found the way more dangerous than I looked for.

TOUCHWOOD JUNIOR
Away, quick! There's a boat waits for you;
And I'll take water at Paul's-wharf and overtake you.

MOLL
Good sir, do; we cannot be too safe. *[Exeunt]*

Enter Sir Walter, Yellowhammer, Tim, and Tutor 4.4

SIR WALTER
Life! Call you this close keeping?

YELLOWHAMMER She was kept
Under a double lock.

SIR WALTER A double devil!

TIM
That's a buff sergeant, tutor; he'll ne'er wear out.

YELLOWHAMMER How would you have women locked?

TIM
With padlocks, father; the Venetian uses it;
My tutor reads it.

SIR WALTER
Heart, if she were so locked up, how got she out?

YELLOWHAMMER
There was a little hole looked into the gutter;
But who would have dreamed of that?

SIR WALTER A wiser man would.

2 **watermen** boatmen, running a taxi service on the Thames

3 **requiteful'st** most eager to return favours. The praise lavished on watermen reflects the symbiotic relationship between them and Bankside theatres. Early in 1614, John Taylor the watermen's poet and advocate emphasized the importance of water taxis to bankside theatres. When in 1614 the watermen petitioned the Privy Council to limit theatrical activity on the near side of the river so as to maintain their business on the bankside, His Majesty's Players' counter-petition declared, 'We might as justly remove the Exchange... to the Bank-side', the comparison with the Royal Exchange underlining the fact that theatre was big business, every bit as implicated in the money game as any of *Chaste Maid*'s grasping commercialists.

6 **Blackfriars** indoor, candle-lit private theatre, used by the King's Men 1608–42; it stood by a landing-stage on the Thames, close to Touchwood Junior's embarkation point, west of Puddle Wharf. The episode has not been traced, but to report it on the stage of the Swan was to denigrate a rival theatre, on the wrong side of the river in the watermen's view, as a rowdy, dangerous place.

7 **But a while since** not long ago
varlets low rascals

9 **sword-dance** ancient fertility-promoting dance, still practised in Middleton's time, mainly in the countryside

10 **candles** the ruffians carry candles to pursue a victim in the dark theatre
chandlers candle-makers. Since stage ghosts often carried distinctive symbols, chandlers' ghosts would carry candles.

12 **pair of oars** i.e., a waterman
landed brought to shore.

13 **Your first man** the waterman's trade cry, meaning 'I'm first in the queue'

17 **Barn Elms** a favourite lovers' resort
No more i.e., farewell

20 **French crown** French silver coin accepted as equivalent to the English five-shilling piece

21 **take water** to embark on the river, with possible suggestion of water as semen, as in 2.1.180

22 **lustily** vigorously, with possible sexual innuendo

27 **Paul's-wharf** between Puddle Wharf and Trig Stairs

28 **we... safe** It seems odd that Moll and Touchstone Junior should part now; they seem to think this will render them less liable to detection.

4.4.1 **close keeping** locking (Moll) up securely

2 **double devil** i.e., it took a double devil to escape from double locks—a reference to Moll, or perhaps Touchwood Junior

3 **buff sergeant** arresting officer, whose doggedness was often compared to his jerkin's durable ox-hide ('buff') leather. Tim may be saying that a buff sergeant is as hard-wearing as a double lock, or as persistent as a double devil.

5 **With padlocks... Venetian** Venetians were believed to keep control of women by chastity belts; many contemporary writings portray Italian women as closely locked up compared to freer English women.

6 **reads** has read about, or advises

8 **looked** that opened

TIM He says true, father; a wise man for love will seek every hole; my tutor knows it.

TUTOR *Verum poeta dicit.*

TIM *Dicit Virgilius*, father.

YELLOWHAMMER Prithee, talk of thy jills somewhere else, she's played the jill with me. Where's your wise mother now?

TIM Run mad, I think; I thought she would have drowned herself. She would not stay for oars but took a smelt-boat; sure, I think she be gone a-fishing for her!

YELLOWHAMMER
She'll catch a goodly dish of gudgeons now,
Will serve us all to supper.

Enter Maudline drawing Moll by the hair, [*wet*] *and Watermen*

MAUDLINE
I'll tug thee home by the hair.

FIRST WATERMAN
Good mistress, spare her!

MAUDLINE
Tend your own business.

SECOND WATERMAN
You are a cruel mother.

Exeunt [*Watermen*]

MOLL O, my heart dies!

MAUDLINE
I'll make thee an example for all the neighbours' daughters.

MOLL
Farewell, life!

MAUDLINE
You that have tricks can counterfeit.

YELLOWHAMMER
Hold, hold, Maudline.

MAUDLINE
I have brought your jewel by the hair.

YELLOWHAMMER
She's here, knight.

SIR WALTER
Forbear, or I'll grow worse.

TIM Look on her, tutor; she hath brought her from the water like a mermaid; she's but half my sister now, as far as the flesh goes, the rest may be sold to fishwives.

MAUDLINE
Dissembling, cunning baggage!

YELLOWHAMMER
Impudent strumpet!

SIR WALTER
Either give over, both, or I'll give over!—
[*To Moll*] Why have you used me thus, unkind mistress?
Wherein have I deserved?

YELLOWHAMMER
You talk too fondly, sir:
We'll take another course and prevent all;
We might have done't long since; we'll lose no time now,
Nor trust to't any longer. Tomorrow morn,
As early as sunrise we'll have you joined.

MOLL
O, bring me death tonight, love-pitying fates;
Let me not see tomorrow up upon the world.

YELLOWHAMMER
Are you content, sir? Till then she shall be watched!

MAUDLINE Baggage, you shall! *Exit* [*with Moll*]

TIM Why, father, my tutor and I will both watch in armour. [*Exit Yellowhammer*]

TUTOR How shall we do for weapons?

TIM Take you no care for that. If need be I can send for conquering metal, tutor, ne'er lost day yet. 'Tis but at Westminster; I am acquainted with him that keeps the monuments; I can borrow Harry the Fifth's sword. 'Twill serve us both to watch with. *Exit* [*with Tutor*]

SIR WALTER
I never was so near my wish as this chance
Makes me: ere tomorrow noon
I shall receive two thousand pound in gold
And a sweet maidenhead worth forty.

Enter Touchwood Junior with a Waterman

TOUCHWOOD JUNIOR O, thy news splits me!

10–11 **seek every hole** with bawdy innuendo; perhaps a lewd paraphrase of Ovid's *Ars Amatoria*, II.243–6. Tim comically misattributes it to lofty Virgil.
12 ***Verum . . . dicit*** the poet speaks the truth (Latin)
13 ***Dicit Virgilius*** Virgil says so (Latin)
14 **jills** loose women. Ignorant of Latin, Yellowhammer takes 'Virgilius' for a reference to 'jills'.
15 **played the jill** played a nasty trick; variation of 'play the Jack'
18 **stay** wait
18–19 **smelt-boat** a boat for fishing smelt, a small fish—poor folks' fare; a notably undignified mode of pursuit
20 **gudgeons** small fish used as bait; 'to gape for a gudgeon' meant to be deceived or be gullible
21 **serve . . . to supper** i.e., Maudline's behaviour will make them all look foolish; 'to' means 'for'
23 **Tend** mind
26 **You . . . counterfeit** i.e., you who are cunning can easily feign despair
27 **jewel** i.e., daughter
28 **Forbear . . . worse** i.e., stop pulling her by the hair or I'll feel even worse than I do
29–30 **from the water** Presumably Maudline has dragged Moll overboard from her water taxi into the smelt boat.
30 **mermaid** with overtones of the word's slang meaning, 'whore'
31 **fishwives** female fish-sellers, with overtones of the word's slang meaning, 'pimps'
33 **give over . . . give over** i.e., stop berating your daughter or I'll back out of the marriage
35 **fondly** foolishly
38 **trust to't** i.e., trust Moll's obedience to their wishes
39 **joined** married
44–5 **watch in armour** an absurdly misplaced reference to the chivalric custom of an armed knight keeping a solitary all-night vigil in a chapel as spiritual preparation for a quest; 'in armour' also meant 'emboldened by drinking'
47 **Take . . . for** don't worry about
48 **ne'er . . . yet** that never yet lost a battle
49 **Westminster** Westminster Abbey
49–50 **him . . . monuments** master of the monuments, official guide to the tombs of famous English kings and queens in Westminster Abbey
50 **Harry the Fifth's sword** an error or an idle boast: Henry V's armour had been stolen
55 **forty** i.e., forty thousand (one hopes)
56 **splits** tears apart

WATERMAN
Half drowned! She cruelly tugged her by the hair,
Forced her disgracefully, not like a mother.
TOUCHWOOD JUNIOR Enough! Leave me, like my joys.
Exit Waterman
Sir, saw you not a wretched maid pass this way?
Heart, villain, is it thou?
SIR WALTER Yes, slave, 'tis I!
Both draw and fight
TOUCHWOOD JUNIOR
I must break through thee, then; there is no stop
That checks my tongue and all my hopeful fortunes,
That breast excepted, and I must have way.
SIR WALTER
Sir, I believe 'twill hold your life in play.
[He wounds Touchwood Junior]
TOUCHWOOD JUNIOR *[recovering and fighting again]*
Sir, you'll gain the heart in my breast at first?
SIR WALTER
There is no dealing, then? Think on the dowry
For two thousand pounds.
TOUCHWOOD JUNIOR O, now 'tis quit, sir.
[He wounds Sir Walter]
SIR WALTER
And being of even hand, I'll play no longer.
TOUCHWOOD JUNIOR
No longer, slave?
SIR WALTER I have certain things to think on
Before I dare go further. *[Exit]*
TOUCHWOOD JUNIOR But one bout?
I'll follow thee to death, but ha't out. *Exit*
Finis Actus Quartus

5.1 *[Incipit] Actus Quintus*
Enter Allwit, his Wife, and Davy Dahumma

WIFE
A misery of a house!
ALLWIT What shall become of us?
DAVY
I think his wound be mortal.
ALLWIT Think'st thou so, Davy?
Then am I mortal too, but a dead man, Davy.
This is no world for me whene'er he goes;
I must e'en truss up all and after him, Davy—
A sheet with two knots, and away!
Enter Sir Walter, led in hurt [by two of his Servants]
DAVY O, see, sir,
How faint he goes! Two of my fellows lead him.
WIFE *[swooning]* O me!
ALLWIT
Heyday, my wife's laid down too! Here's like to be
A good house kept, when we are altogether down.
Take pains with her, good Davy, cheer her up there.
Let me come to his worship, let me come.
[Exeunt two Servants]
SIR WALTER
Touch me not, villain! My wound aches at thee,
Thou poison to my heart!
ALLWIT *[aside]* He raves already,
His senses are quite gone, he knows me not.—
[To him] Look up, an't like your worship; heave those eyes,
Call me to mind; is your remembrance left?
Look in my face: who am I, an't like your worship?
SIR WALTER
If anything be worse than slave or villain,
Thou art the man!
ALLWIT Alas, his poor worship's weakness!
He will begin to know me by little and little.
SIR WALTER
No devil can be like thee.
ALLWIT Ah, poor gentleman,
Methinks the pain that thou endurest—
SIR WALTER
Thou know'st me to be wicked, for thy baseness
Kept the eyes open still on all my sins;
None knew the dear account my soul stood charged with
So well as thou, yet, like hell's flattering angel,
Wouldst never tell me on't, let'st me go on,
And join with death in sleep; that if I had not waked
Now by chance, even by a stranger's pity,
I had everlastingly slept out all hope
Of grace and mercy.
ALLWIT Now he is worse and worse.

57 **by the hair** Modest, chaste women wore their hair bound up, a symbol of bodily containment; wearing the hair loose onstage conventionally represented recent rape or mental derangement, which is one reason Maudline's dragging Moll by the hair is so shocking to bystanders. The stage picture prepares the audience for Moll's seeming mental distraction in 5.2.
62 **stop** impediment
63 **checks my tongue** i.e., robs me of the power to make my marriage vows
64 **That...excepted** i.e., except Sir Walter
have way triumph over him
65 **'twill...play** i.e., the desire to win Moll away from me will mean working hard to defend your life
66 **at first** at once
67 **dealing** coming to terms (Sir Walter is offering to share the dowry)
68 **quit** paid back (wound for wound)
69 **even hand** on equal terms (a gaming term)
70 **certain...on** possible anticipation of his religious qualms
72 **ha't out** see this through to a conclusion
5.1.2 **his** Sir Walter's
3 **but** nothing but
5 **truss up** wrap in a shroud
after go after
6 **sheet...knots** i.e., a shroud, knotted at head and foot
16 **an't like** if it pleases
17 **is...left** is your memory intact?
25 **Kept...open** The play's blindness/sight imagery culminates in this scene.
still always
26 **dear** costly
27 **hell's...angel** Satan

[*Allwit's Wife revives from her swoon*] Wife, to him, wife; thou wast wont to do good on him.

WIFE
How is't with you, sir?

SIR WALTER Not as with you,
Thou loathsome strumpet! Some good pitying man
Remove my sins out of my sight a little;
I tremble to behold her, she keeps back
All comfort while she stays. Is this a time,
Unconscionable woman, to see thee?
Art thou so cruel to the peace of man
Not to give liberty now? The devil himself
Shows a far fairer reverence and respect
To goodness than thyself; he dares not do this,
But parts in time of penitence, hides his face;
When man withdraws from him, he leaves the place.
Hast thou less manners and more impudence
Than thy instructor? Prithee show thy modesty,
If the least grain be left, and get thee from me.
Thou shouldst be rather locked many rooms hence
From the poor miserable sight of me,
If either love or grace had part in thee.

WIFE [*weeping*]
He is lost for ever!

ALLWIT Run, sweet Davy, quickly,
And fetch the children hither; sight of them
Will make him cheerful straight. [*Exit Davy*]

SIR WALTER [*to Allwit's Wife*] O death! Is this
A place for you to weep? What tears are those?
Get you away with them! I shall fare the worse
As long as they are a-weeping. They work against me;
There's nothing but thy appetite in that sorrow—
Thou weep'st for lust. I feel it in the slackness
Of comforts coming toward me.
I was well till thou began'st to undo me.
This shows like the fruitless sorrow of a careless mother
That brings her son with dalliance to the gallows
And then stands by and weeps to see him suffer.

Enter Davy with the children [*Nick, Wat, and the baby girl*]

DAVY
There are the children, sir; an't like your worship,
Your last fine girl—in troth, she smiles.
Look, look, in faith, sir.

SIR WALTER
O, my vengeance! Let me for ever hide my cursed face
From sight of those that darkens all my hopes,
And stands between me and the sight of heaven!
Who sees me now, her too and those so near me,
May rightly say I am o'ergrown with sin.
O, how my offences wrestle with my repentance!
It hath scarce breath;
Still my adulterous guilt hovers aloft,
And with her black wings beats down all my prayers
Ere they be halfway up. What's he knows now
How long I have to live? O, what comes then?
My taste grows bitter; the round world all gall now;
Her pleasing pleasures now hath poisoned me,
Which I exchanged my soul for.
Make way a hundred sighs at once for me!

ALLWIT
Speak to him, Nick.

NICK I dare not, I am afraid.

ALLWIT
Tell him he hurts his wounds, Wat, with making moan.

SIR WALTER Wretched, death of seven.

ALLWIT
Come, let's be talking somewhat to keep him alive.
Ah, sirrah Wat, and did my lord bestow that jewel on thee
For an epistle thou mad'st in Latin?
Thou art a good forward boy, there's great joy on thee.

SIR WALTER
O sorrow!

ALLWIT [*aside*]
Heart, will nothing comfort him?
If he be so far gone, 'tis time to moan.
[*To him*] Here's pen and ink and paper, and all things ready;
Will't please your worship for to make your will?

SIR WALTER
My will? Yes, yes, what else? Who writes apace now?

ALLWIT
That can your man Davy, an't like your worship,
A fair, fast, legible hand.

SIR WALTER Set it down then:
[*Davy writes*]
Imprimis, I bequeath to yonder wittol

33 **do good on** (*a*) have a beneficial effect on; (*b*) copulate with
36 **sins** Allwit's wife has come to embody for him all his sins.
39 **Unconscionable** without conscience
47 **instructor** i.e., Satan
58–9 **There's . . . for lust** i.e., you are crying only because my death will leave you sexually frustrated
61 **I . . . me** Though true repentance meant self knowledge and acceptance of personal responsibility for sin, he blames his misconduct solely on the Allwits.
63 **with dalliance** through over-indulgence. This image, a parody of the Virgin Mary weeping at the foot of the cross, grants the son no responsibility for his own crime, as Sir Walter himself accepts no responsibility.
68 **my vengeance** the children represent God's vengeance
77 **halfway up** i.e., to heaven
What's he who is he who
79 **gall** bitter substance
82 **Make way** prepare
85 **death of seven** Sir Walter's children by Allwit's wife. His death will leave them unprovided for.
86 **somewhat** a little
87 **my lord** 'My lord' is an inappropriate form of address for a knight like Sir Walter; Allwit may mean some dignitary at a ceremonial occasion at Wat's school.
89 **forward** high-achieving
94 **apace** quickly

Three times his weight in curses.
ALLWIT
How!
SIR WALTER
All plagues of body and mind.
ALLWIT
Write them not down, Davy.
DAVY It is his will; I must.
SIR WALTER Together also
With such a sickness ten days ere his death.
ALLWIT [*aside*]
There's a sweet legacy! I am almost choked with't.
SIR WALTER
Next I bequeath to that foul whore his wife
All barrenness of joy, a drought of virtue,
And dearth of all repentance; for her end,
The common misery of an English strumpet,
In French and Dutch; beholding ere she dies
Confusion of her brats before her eyes,
And never shed a tear for it.
Enter a Servant [of Sir Walter's]
FIRST SERVANT Where's the knight?
O sir, the gentleman you wounded is newly departed!
SIR WALTER Dead? Lift, lift! Who helps me?
ALLWIT
Let the law lift you now, that must have all;
I have done lifting on you, and my wife too.
FIRST SERVANT [*to Sir Walter*]
You were best lock yourself close.
ALLWIT [*to Sir Walter*] Not in my house, sir,
I'll harbour no such persons as men-slayers;
Lock yourself where you will.
SIR WALTER What's this?
WIFE Why, husband!
ALLWIT
I know what I do, wife.
WIFE [*aside to Allwit*] You cannot tell yet;
For having killed the man in his defence,
Neither his life nor estate will be touched, husband.
ALLWIT
Away, wife! Hear a fool! His lands will hang him.
SIR WALTER
Am I denied a chamber?—[*To Mistress Allwit*] What
say you, forsooth?
WIFE
Alas, sir, I am one that would have all well
But must obey my husband.—[*To Allwit*] Prithee, love,
Let the poor gentleman stay, being so sore wounded:
There's a close chamber at one end of the garret
We never use; let him have that I prithee.
ALLWIT
We never use? You forget sickness then,
And physic times; is't not a place of easement?
Enter a [second] Servant [of Sir Walter's]
SIR WALTER
O death! Do I hear this with part
Of former life in me?—What's the news now?
SECOND SERVANT
Troth, worse and worse; you're like to lose your land,
If the law save your life, sir, or the surgeon.
ALLWIT [*aside to Allwit's Wife*]
Hark you there, wife.
SIR WALTER Why, how, sir?
SECOND SERVANT
Sir Oliver Kix's wife is new quickened;
That child undoes you sir.
SIR WALTER All ill at once!
ALLWIT
I wonder what he makes here with his consorts?
Cannot our house be private to ourselves
But we must have such guests? [*To Servants*] I pray,
depart, sirs,
And take your murderer along with you.
Good he were apprehended ere he go,
He's killed some honest gentleman. Send for officers!
SIR WALTER
I'll soon save you that labour.
ALLWIT I must tell you, sir,
You have been somewhat bolder in my house
Than I could well like of; I suffered you
Till it stuck here at my heart; I tell you truly
I thought you had been familiar with my wife once.
WIFE
With me? I'll see him hanged first. I defy him,

108 **French and Dutch** venereal diseases. Syphilis was called 'the French pox'; a 'Dutch widow' was a prostitute.
109 **Confusion** i.e., incestuous intercourse
112–13 **Lift...lift** Sir Walter means 'lift me up' (physically); Allwit means 'arrest'.
113 **law...all** i.e., the law will seize Sir Walter's possessions since he has killed Touchstone Junior
114 **lifting** (*a*) helping; (*b*) robbing; (*c*) (in the case of Allwit's wife) arousing sexually
on of
115 **were best** had better
close tightly, in hiding
121 **Hear a fool** i.e., listen to the fool talking
His...him i.e., since Sir Walter's lands will be forfeited to the Crown if he is convicted, the Crown will be sure to find him guilty and hang him
126 **close chamber** privy
129 **physic times** times of illness
place of easement privy
135 **new quickened** newly pregnant
136 **undoes you** i.e., a Kix heir will do Sir Walter out of the inheritance
ill evil, bad luck
137 **makes** does
consorts companions (i.e., Davy and the two servants)
142 **officers** officers of the watch
143 **save...labour** i.e., by dying
147 **been familiar** had sexual relations with, or at least flirted with

And all such gentlemen in the like extremity.

SIR WALTER
If ever eyes were open, these are they.
Gamesters, farewell, I have nothing left to play.
Exit [with his two Servants]

ALLWIT
And therefore get you gone, sir.

DAVY
Of all wittols
Be thou the head!—[*To Allwit's Wife*] Thou, the grand
whore of spittles!
Exit

ALLWIT
So, since he's like now to be rid of all,
I am right glad I am so well rid of him.

WIFE
I knew he durst not stay when you named officers.

ALLWIT That stopped his spirits straight.
What shall we do now, wife?

WIFE
As we were wont to do.

ALLWIT
We are richly furnished wife, with household stuff.

WIFE Let's let out lodgings then,
And take a house in the Strand.

ALLWIT
In troth, a match, wench:
We are simply stocked with cloth-of-tissue cushions
To furnish out bay-windows; pish, what not that's
quaint
And costly, from the top to the bottom?
Life, for furniture, we may lodge a countess!
There's a close-stool of tawny velvet too,
Now I think on't, wife.

WIFE
There's that should be, sir;
Your nose must be in everything!

ALLWIT
I have done, wench;
And let this stand in every gallant's chamber:
'There's no gamester like a politic sinner,
For whoe'er games, the box is sure a winner.'
Exeunt

Enter Yellowhammer and his wife [Maudline] 5.2

MAUDLINE
O husband, husband, she will die, she will die!
There is no sign but death.

YELLOWHAMMER
'Twill be our shame then.

MAUDLINE
O, how she's changed in compass of an hour!

YELLOWHAMMER
Ah, my poor girl! Good faith, thou wert too cruel
To drag her by the hair.

MAUDLINE
You would have done as much, sir,
To curb her of her humour.

YELLOWHAMMER
'Tis curbed sweetly! She catched her bane o'th' water.
Enter Tim

MAUDLINE How now, Tim?

TIM
Faith, busy, mother, about an epitaph
Upon my sister's death.

MAUDLINE
Death! She is not dead, I hope?

TIM
No, but she means to be, and that's as good,
And when a thing's done, 'tis done; you taught me
that, mother.

YELLOWHAMMER What is your tutor doing?

149 **extremity** degree
150 **If... they** Sir Walter's devastated shock when Allwit's wife defies him shows up an oddly credulous and sentimental streak: he has been buying her sexual favours, but seems to have believed her protestations of affection.
151 **Gamesters** (*a*) gamblers; (*b*) lechers. Sir Walter's final abandonment of his sexual and financial games echoes Touchwood's Senior's impulse (at 2.1.41) to give up the card game of sex.
153 **spittles** hospitals; suggests a whore's connection with disease
156 **durst** dared
158 **were wont to** used to
160 **let out** rent out their present lodgings
161 **Strand** A fashionable residential area, but (in the oddly-assorted mix typical of early modern London) also notorious for courtesans. The conversation about a well-furnished house, following the Allwit's agreement that they will now support themselves as they used to (presumably before Sir Walter's advent), suggests that they are planning to establish a fashionable brothel. In one of the play's many surprise turns, not only is a seemingly-respectable citizen an amateur brothel-keeper to his wife, but the couple were formerly *professional* brothel-keepers—another link between bourgeois marriage and prostitution.
a match formula for concluding an agreement
162 **simply** absolutely
cloth-of-tissue fabric with gold and silver thread
163 **bay-windows** jutting-out windows, good for advertising wares, such as prostitutes in the new Allwit brothel. The bay window was theatrical short-hand for a brothel.
quaint costly, fashionable, with a possible suggestion of 'queinte' or pudendum
164 **from... bottom** with bawdy innuendo
165 **lodge a countess** perhaps another reference to the Countess of Salisbury, with a possible suggestion of 'cuntess'
166 **close-stool** commode, chamber pot
167 **There's... be** i.e., there's everything one could wish
168 **nose... everything** A man who took too much interest in household matters (sometimes called a 'cotqueen') was an object of scorn; here the image of a man putting his nose in a chamber pot is even more unflattering.
169 **let... chamber** i.e., let this saying appear in the male customers' rooms in the brothel
170 **politic** crafty
171 **games** plays games, including sexual ones
box the percentage taken by the house. In a reversal of the initial impression that Allwit is being ignominiously used by Sir Walter, Allwit now sees himself as proprietor of a gaming house, and 'the house' always has a better chance of winning that any individual gambler like Sir Walter; his image recalls Sir Walter's last words earlier in the scene—those of a defeated gambler.
5.2.1 **she** Moll
3 **in compass of** in the space of
6 **curb... humour** i.e., prevent her from eloping
7 **bane** death (cf. the modern expression 'catch one's death of a cold')
9 **epitaph** It was customary to decorate the hearse and later the tomb with a few words about the dead person.
11 **means** intends

TIM
Making one too, in principal pure Latin
Culled out of Ovid his *de Tristibus*.

YELLOWHAMMER
How does your sister look? Is she not changed?

TIM
Changed? Gold into white money was never so changed
As is my sister's colour into paleness.
Enter Moll

YELLOWHAMMER
O, here she's brought; see how she looks like death!

TIM
Looks she like death, and ne'er a word made yet?
I must go beat my brains against a bed-post
And get before my tutor. [*Exit*]

YELLOWHAMMER [*to Moll*] Speak, how dost thou?

MOLL
I hope I shall be well, for I am as sick at heart
As I can be.

YELLOWHAMMER
'Las my poor girl!
The doctor's making a most sovereign drink for thee,
The worst ingredients dissolved pearl and amber;
We spare no cost, girl.

MOLL
Your love comes too late,
Yet timely thanks reward it. What is comfort,
When the poor patient's heart is past relief?
It is no doctor's art can cure my grief.

YELLOWHAMMER All is cast away then.
Prithee look upon me cheerfully.

MAUDLINE [*to Moll*]
Sing but a strain or two, thou wilt not think
How 'twill revive thy spirits: strive with thy fit,
Prithee, sweet Moll.

MOLL You shall have my good will, Mother.

MAUDLINE Why, well said, wench.
The Song

MOLL
Weep eyes, break heart,
My love and I must part.
Cruel fates true love do soonest sever:
O, I shall see thee never, never, never!
O, happy is the maid whose life takes end
Ere it knows parent's frown or loss of friend.
Weep eyes, break heart,
My love and I must part.
Enter Touchwood Senior with a letter

MAUDLINE
O, I could die with music!—Well sung, girl.

MOLL If you call it so, it was.

YELLOWHAMMER
She plays the swan and sings herself to death.

TOUCHWOOD SENIOR By your leave, sir.

YELLOWHAMMER
What are you, sir? Or what's your business, pray?

TOUCHWOOD SENIOR
I may be now admitted, though the brother
Of him your hate pursued; it spreads no further.
Your malice sets in death, does it not, sir?

YELLOWHAMMER
In death?

TOUCHWOOD SENIOR
He's dead: 'twas a dear love to him,
It cost him but his life, that was all, sir;
He paid enough, poor gentleman, for his love.

YELLOWHAMMER [*aside*]
There's all our ill removed, if she were well now.—
[*To Touchwood Senior*] Impute not, sir, his end to any hate
That sprung from us; he had a fair wound brought that.

TOUCHWOOD SENIOR
That helped him forward, I must needs confess;
But the restraint of love, and your unkindness,
Those were the wounds that from his heart drew blood;
But being past help, let words forget it too.
Scarcely three minutes ere his eye-lids closed
And took eternal leave of this world's light,
He wrote this letter, which by oath he bound me
To give to her own hands; that's all my business.

YELLOWHAMMER
You may perform it then; there she sits.

TOUCHWOOD SENIOR
O, with a following look!

YELLOWHAMMER Ay, trust me, sir,

14 **principal** choice
15 **Ovid his** Ovid's
de Tristibus a collection of dolorous poetry, popular as a textbook in grammar schools
17 **white** silver
20 **ne'er ... yet** i.e., not a word of her epitaph yet composed
21 **beat my brains** concentrate hard. (Tim's adding 'against a bed-post' makes the cliché comically literal.)
22 **get** beget (an epitaph)
23 **well** possible allusion to the proverb 'the dead are well'
25 **sovereign drink** potent remedy
26 **worst** least expensive
pearl and amber costly ingredients often used in restorative medicines
30 **grief** (*a*) sickness; (*b*) distress
31 **All ... then** i.e., I have wasted my money on the pearl and amber medicine
33–4 **Sing ... spirits** Music was considered therapeutic.
34 **strive ... fit** (*a*) struggle against your condition ('fit' as a symptom of illness); (*b*) put up a fight by singing a strain ('fit' as part of a song)
36 **You ... will** i.e., I'll do my best
37.1 ***The Song*** Laments by and about dying virgins or betrothed young women were popular in contemporary ballads; cf. also Ophelia's death in *Hamlet*. For a musical setting see *Companion*, p. 145.
48 **swan ... death** The swan proverbially sang before death; possible reference to Swan playhouse in which *Chaste Maid* was acted, which was shortly to close.
53 **sets** goes down like the sun
54 **dear** expensive
57 **ill** trouble
69 **following** i.e., she seems about to follow Touchwood Junior in death

I think she'll follow him quickly.
TOUCHWOOD SENIOR Here's some gold
He willed me to distribute faithfully
Amongst your servants.
[He gives money to servants]
YELLOWHAMMER 'Las, what doth he mean, sir?
TOUCHWOOD SENIOR [*to Moll*]
How cheer you, mistress?
MOLL I must learn of you, sir.
TOUCHWOOD SENIOR [*giving letter to Moll*]
Here's a letter from a friend of yours;
And where that fails in satisfaction,
I have a sad tongue ready to supply.
MOLL How does he, ere I look on't?
TOUCHWOOD SENIOR
Seldom better; he's a contented health now.
MOLL
I am most glad on't.
[She reads]
MAUDLINE [*to Touchwood Senior*]
Dead, sir?
YELLOWHAMMER
He is. [*Aside*] Now, wife, let's but get the girl
Upon her legs again, and to church roundly with her.
MOLL
O, sick to death he tells me! How does he after this?
TOUCHWOOD SENIOR
Faith, feels no pain at all: he's dead, sweet mistress.
MOLL [*swooning*]
Peace close mine eyes!
YELLOWHAMMER The girl! Look to the girl, wife!
MAUDLINE
Moll, daughter, sweet girl, speak! Look but once up,
Thou shalt have all the wishes of thy heart
That wealth can purchase!
YELLOWHAMMER
O, she's gone for ever! That letter broke her heart.
TOUCHWOOD SENIOR
As good now, then, as let her lie in torment
And then break it.
Enter Susan
MAUDLINE
O Susan, she thou loved'st so dear is gone!
SUSAN
O sweet maid!
TOUCHWOOD SENIOR
This is she that helped her still.—
I've a reward here for thee.
[He gives Susan money]
YELLOWHAMMER Take her in,
Remove her from our sight, our shame and sorrow.
TOUCHWOOD SENIOR
Stay, let me help thee; 'tis the last cold kindness
I can perform for my sweet brother's sake.
[Exeunt Touchwood Senior, Susan, and Servants, carrying Moll]
YELLOWHAMMER
All the whole street will hate us, and the world
Point me out cruel. It is our best course, wife,
After we have given order for the funeral,
To absent ourselves till she be laid in ground.
MAUDLINE Where shall we spend that time?
YELLOWHAMMER
I'll tell thee where, wench: go to some private church
And marry Tim to the rich Brecknock gentlewoman.
MAUDLINE Mass, a match!
We'll not lose all at once, somewhat we'll catch.
Exeunt

Enter Sir Oliver and [four] Servants 5.3
SIR OLIVER
Ho, my wife's quickened; I am a man for ever!
I think I have bestirred my stumps, i'faith.
Run, get your fellows all together instantly,
Then to the parish church and ring the bells.
FIRST SERVANT
It shall be done, sir. *[Exit]*

73 **How ... you** i.e., how do you feel?
I ... you i.e., I won't know how I feel until you give me the letter (and perhaps tell me more of Touchwood Junior)
77 **How does he** how is he? Since Moll was onstage when Touchwood Senior announced 'He's dead' (5.2.54), her asking after his health may indicate distracted wits, or a state of what grief therapists now call denial.
78 **he's ... now** a common phrase meaning 'he is well because he is in Heaven'
79 **glad on't** happy to hear it
81 **to church** to marry Sir Walter
roundly promptly
92 **still** always
93 **reward** payment for helping with Moll's attempted elopement, or perhaps money up front to ensure Susan's help with the present plan
96.1–2 ***Exeunt ... Moll*** The hand is quicker than the eye: what seems the carrying of a dead body off the stage is actually the third attempt to steal Moll from her parents.
102 **private church** a secluded church, or perhaps a private chapel where licensed marriages could be celebrated without the publicity of a parish church
103 **marry ... gentlewoman** The Yellowhammers plan to cash in on Sir Walter's half of their business arrangement—the Welsh heiress—even though he has been cut out of their half—Moll and the dowry.
104 **a match** (*a*) formula for concluding an agreement; (*b*) a marriage. Agreeing to this scheme for salvaging something after Moll's death, Maudline uses exactly the words with which Allwit, in the last scene, assented to his wife's scheme for cutting their losses after jettisoning Sir Walter: 'A match' (5.1.161).
105 **somewhat** at least a little
5.3.2 **bestirred my stumps** bustled about on my legs, with bawdy innuendo
3 **fellows** fellow servants
4–7 **ring ... night** Churchbells were rung and bonfires lit to announce important events; as the servant's response shows, this would have been a monstrously inflated reaction to begetting a baby. As Stow records, the London poor used to be treated with food and drink by the rich at summer festival 'bonfires', but this custom had lapsed by Middleton's time. Invoking this old symbol of charitable neighbourliness highlights the grasping selfishness of the present.

SIR OLIVER [*to Second Servant*]
Upon my love
I charge you, villain, that you make a bonfire
Before the door at night.

SECOND SERVANT A bonfire, sir?

SIR OLIVER
A thwacking one, I charge you.

SECOND SERVANT [*aside*] This is monstrous!
[*Exit*]

SIR OLIVER [*to Third Servant*]
Run, tell a hundred pound out for the gentleman
That gave my wife the drink, the first thing you do.

THIRD SERVANT
A hundred pounds, sir?

SIR OLIVER A bargain! As our joy grows,
We must remember still from whence it flows,
Or else we prove ungrateful multipliers.
[*Exit Third Servant*]
The child is coming and the land comes after;
The news of this will make a poor Sir Walter.
I have struck it home i'faith!

FOURTH SERVANT That you have, marry, sir;
But will not your worship go to the funeral
Of both these lovers?

SIR OLIVER Both? Go both together?

FOURTH SERVANT
Ay, sir, the gentleman's brother will have it so;
'Twill be the pitifulest sight. There's such running,
Such rumours, and such throngs, a pair of lovers
Had never more spectators, more men's pities,
Or women's wet eyes.

SIR OLIVER My wife helps the number then?

FOURTH SERVANT
There's such drawing out of handkerchiefs;
And those that have no handkerchiefs, lift up aprons.

SIR OLIVER
Her parents may have joyful hearts at this!
I would not have my cruelty so talked on,
To any child of mine, for a monopoly.

FOURTH SERVANT I believe you, sir.
'Tis cast so too that both their coffins meet,
Which will be lamentable.

SIR OLIVER Come, we'll see't. *Exeunt*

Recorders dolefully playing; enter at one door 5.4
the coffin of the Gentleman, [*Touchwood Junior*], *solemnly decked, his sword upon it, attended by many in black* [*including Sir Oliver Kix, Allwit, and a Parson,*] *his brother* [*Touchwood Senior*] *being the chief mourner; at the other door the coffin of the virgin* [*Moll*], *with a garland of flowers, with epitaphs pinned on't, attended by maids and women* [*including Lady Kix, Allwit's Wife, and Susan*]. *Then set them down one right over-against the other. While all the company seem to weep and mourn, there is a sad song in the music-room*

TOUCHWOOD SENIOR
Never could death boast of a richer prize
From the first parent; let the world bring forth
A pair of truer hearts. To speak but truth
Of this departed gentleman, in a brother
Might, by hard censure, be called flattery,
Which makes me rather silent in his right
Than so to be delivered to the thoughts
Of any envious hearer, starved in virtue,
And therefore pining to hear others thrive;
But for this maid, whom Envy cannot hurt
With all her poisons, having left to ages
The true, chaste monument of her living name,
Which no time can deface, I say of her
The full truth freely, without fear of censure:
What nature could there shine that might redeem
Perfection home to woman, but in her

6 **villain** here, an affectionately bullying term for the servant
8 **thwacking** huge
9 **tell** count
13 **multipliers** (*a*) breeders; (*b*) false coiners, reflecting the play's counterfeiting theme
14–15 **after ... Walter** Since contemporary pronunciation dropped the 'f' from 'after' and the 'l' from 'Walter', 'after' rhymes with 'Walter'.
16 **struck it home** copulated successfully (in duelling, to 'strike it home' was to give a winning blow)
18 **both these lovers** Moll and Touchwood Junior
23 **helps the number** increases the size of the congregation at the funeral
28 **monopoly** right, granted by the crown, to trade exclusively in some commodity. The abuse of monopolies, very lucrative for the patentees, was notorious in the first decade of the seventeenth century.
30 **cast** arranged
5.4.0.1–13 Conspicuous by their absence at Moll's funeral are her parents; they may have absented themselves to avoid their neighbours' hate (see 5.2.97), but Touchwood Senior may have deliberately excluded them as part of his plot.
0.1 ***Recorders*** the most common Jacobean wind instrument, often mentioned in plays
0.6 ***chief mourner*** Funeral processions were rigidly hierarchical, ordering the mourners by social class and family standing; the contrast between these carefully-distinguished social statuses and the levelling uniformity of black attire (5.4.0.4) enacts the tragic tension between the human wish to master death through ritual and the stark physical fact of death, which levels all classes.
0.11 ***over-against*** alongside
0.12 ***seem to ... mourn*** Stage directions occasionally use 'seem to' simply to indicate that the actors are acting, but several onstage here have a motive merely to *pretend* mourning.
0.13 ***music-room*** room occupied by the theatre's musicians, probably a gallery above the main stage
2 **From ... parent** i.e., since the time of Adam
let the world i.e., I challenge the world to
7 **delivered** made vulnerable to
8 **starved** lacking
9 **pining ... thrive** enviously wasting away at hearing others praised
11 **her** Envy's
15–16 **What ... woman** i.e., whatever natural goodness could exist to redeem womankind from the sin of Eve, restoring Woman to perfection, shone fully in Moll

Was fully glorious? Beauty set in goodness
Speaks what she was that jewel so infixed,
There was no want of anything of life
To make these virtuous precedents man and wife.

ALLWIT
Great pity of their deaths!

ALL
Ne'er more pity!

LADY
It makes a hundred weeping eyes, sweet gossip.

TOUCHWOOD SENIOR
I cannot think there's anyone amongst you
In this full fair assembly, maid, man, or wife,
Whose heart would not have sprung with joy and gladness
To have seen their marriage day.

ALL
It would have made a thousand joyful hearts.

TOUCHWOOD SENIOR [*to Touchwood Junior and Moll*]
Up, then, apace and take your fortunes,
Make these joyful hearts; here's none but friends.
[*Moll and Touchwood Junior rise out of their coffins*]

ALL
Alive, sir? O sweet, dear couple!

TOUCHWOOD SENIOR
Nay, do not hinder 'em now, stand from about 'em.
If she be caught again, and lose this time,
I'll ne'er plot further for 'em, nor this honest chambermaid
That helped all at a push.

TOUCHWOOD JUNIOR [*to Parson*]
Good sir, apace!

PARSON
Hands join now, but hearts for ever,
Which no parents' mood shall sever:
[*To Touchwood Junior*] You shall forsake all widows, wives, and maids;
[*To Moll*] You, lords, knights, gentlemen, and men of trades;
And if in haste any article misses,
Go interline it with a brace of kisses.

TOUCHWOOD SENIOR
Here's a thing trolled nimbly.—Give you joy, brother!
Were't not better thou shouldst have her
Than the maid should die?

WIFE
To you, sweet mistress bride.

ALL
Joy, joy to you both.

TOUCHWOOD SENIOR Here be your wedding sheets you brought along with you; you may both go to bed when you please to.

TOUCHWOOD JUNIOR
My joy wants utterance.

TOUCHWOOD SENIOR
Utter all at night then, brother.

MOLL I am silent with delight.

TOUCHWOOD SENIOR
Sister, delight will silence any woman,
But you'll find your tongue again among maidservants,
Now you keep house, sister.

ALL
Never was hour so filled with joy and wonder.

TOUCHWOOD SENIOR
To tell you the full story of this chambermaid,
And of her kindness in this business to us,
'Twould ask an hour's discourse; in brief, 'twas she

18 **Speaks** shows
infixed firmly fixed
19 **want** lack
20 **virtuous precedents** exemplars of virtue
22 **gossip** The word recalls the christening party, suggesting a counterposing of two rites of passage, christening and funeral, one welcoming new life, the other commemorating death.
24 **full fair** very handsome; a slightly archaic turn of phrase suggesting chivalric romance
28 **apace** quickly
29.1–2 ***Moll...coffins*** If (as many think) this 'resurrection' is parodic, there was plenty to parody: R. S. Forsythe lists no fewer than 132 English Renaissance plays which include the 'resurrection' of a character supposed dead. Resurrection from coffins for marriage was a staple of the *commedia dell' arte*.
31 **from about** away from
33–4 **I'll...push** This revelation reminds us that it was Touchwood Senior and Susan who carried Moll off after her swoon in 5.2, thus retroactively raising the possibility that the swoon and even her desperate illness were a trick, belonging to that female strategy common in Renaissance writing, feigned illness.
34 **at a push** when things were most critical; 'push' also meant 'copulate'
35 **Hands join** cf. 3.1.13–17. This verse bears no resemblance to an actual marriage service, but it was impermissible to enact a church ceremony on stage.
36 **mood** anger
37 **widows, wives, and maids** the traditional three estates of womankind
38 **You...trades** Since 'forsake' implies giving up what one has possessed, the line suggests that the 'chaste maid' has in the past enjoyed lord, knights, gentlemen, and men of trades—hardly an orthodox pronouncement for a clergyman performing a wedding.
39 **article** legally binding part of the ceremony
misses The diction implies that the clergyman has hastily fired a volley of legal articles at the couple, hoping some will hit their target—again, the ceremony hardly has an aura of sanctity.
40 **interline** write in (legal term)
41 **trolled** uttered rapidly
44 **To...bride** The occasion's holiness is further eroded by the toast to the bride's being offered by that travesty of wifeliness, Allwit's wife.
45 **wedding sheets** the coffin shrouds; light-hearted reversal of a common trope identifying wedding sheets with shrouds. Fascinated by similarity of symbols in the rituals closing tragedy (funerals) and comedy (weddings), Renaissance writers anticipated Arnold Van Gennep's thesis that all rites of passage share one repertoire of symbols.
48 **wants** craves
Utter (*a*) speak; (*b*) ejaculate sexually; (*c*) pass counterfeit money
51 **find...maidservants** i.e., once among your maidservants you will gossip a good deal. (Reflects the stereotype of women's talkativeness, especially with other women.)
52 **keep house** are the mistress of your own household
56 **ask** require

That wrought it to this purpose cunningly.

ALL
We shall all love her for't.
Enter Yellowhammer and his wife, [Maudline]

ALLWIT
See who comes here now!

TOUCHWOOD SENIOR
A storm, a storm, but we are sheltered for it.

YELLOWHAMMER
I will prevent you all and mock you thus,
You and your expectations: I stand happy
Both in your lives and your hearts' combination!

TOUCHWOOD SENIOR
Here's a strange day again!

YELLOWHAMMER
The knight's proved villain—
All's come out now—his niece an arrant baggage.
My poor boy Tim is cast away this morning,
Even before breakfast, married a whore
Next to his heart.

ALL
A whore?

YELLOWHAMMER
His 'niece', forsooth!

ALLWIT [*aside to his wife*]
I think we rid our hands in good time of him.

WIFE
I knew he was past the best when I gave him over.
[*To Yellowhammer*] What is become of him, pray, sir?

YELLOWHAMMER
Who, the knight?
He lies i'th' knight's ward. [*To Lady Kix*] Now your belly, lady,
Begins to blossom, there's no peace for him,
His creditors are so greedy.

SIR OLIVER [*to Touchwood Senior*]
Master Touchwood, hear'st thou this news?
I am so endeared to thee for my wife's fruitfulness
That I charge you both, your wife and thee,
To live no more asunder for the world's frowns.
I have purse, and bed, and board for you.
Be not afraid to go to your business roundly;
Get children, and I'll keep them.

TOUCHWOOD SENIOR
Say you so, sir?

SIR OLIVER
Prove me with three at a birth, an thou dar'st now.

TOUCHWOOD SENIOR
Take heed how you dare a man, while you live, sir,
That has good skill at his weapon.
Enter Tim and Welsh Gentlewoman, [and Tutor]

SIR OLIVER
Foot, I dare you, sir!

YELLOWHAMMER
Look, gentlemen, if ever you say the picture
Of the unfortunate marriage, yonder 'tis.

WELSH GENTLEWOMAN
Nay, good sweet Tim—

TIM
Come from the university
To marry a whore in London, with my tutor too!
O tempora! O mors!

TUTOR Prithee, Tim, be patient!

TIM I bought a jade at Cambridge;
I'll let her out to execution, tutor,
For eighteen pence a day, or Brentford horse-races,
She'll serve to carry seven miles out of town well.
Where be these mountains? I was promised mountains,
But there's such a mist, I can see none of 'em.
What are become of those two thousand runts?
Let's have a bout with them in the mean time;
A vengeance runt thee!

MAUDLINE
Good, sweet Tim, have patience.

TIM
Flectere si nequeo superos, Acheronta movebo, mother.

MAUDLINE
I think you have married her in logic, Tim.
You told me once by logic you would prove
A whore an honest woman; prove her so, Tim,
And take her for thy labour.

TIM
Troth, I thank you:

57 **wrought...purpose** brought about this successful conclusion

58.1 ***Enter Yellowhammer*** The Yellowhammers' entrance jolts us into realizing why the clergyman was rushing: despite the crowd onstage, this is an elopement—Moll has finally been spirited away from her parents. That Yellowhammer betrays no surprise that the lovers are alive is in keeping with the play's self-consciously unrealistic mode—he appears suddenly and blusters every time the couple is about to elope, like the Demon King in a pantomime.

60 **prevent** anticipate. He at first speaks in the old blustering manner, but soon reveals that he means to explode not the lovers' expectations of marriage but everyone's expectations that he will go on playing the heavy father.

63 **The knight's** Sir Walter's

64 **his niece** the Welsh Gentlewoman

67 **Next...heart** (*a*) closest to his affections; (*b*) on an empty stomach

71 **knight's ward** second-class accommodation in a London debtor's prison

79 **roundly** thoroughly, with a suggestion of pregnancy

80 **Get...keep them** Sir Oliver means that Touchwood Senior should beget children upon Touchwood Senior's wife, but the audience is bound to suspect that Lady Kix will be involved as well; the closing scenario with the Touchwoods and Kixes disarmingly resembles the earlier scenario with the Allwits and Sir Walter.

81 **Prove** test
an if

84–5 **Look...'tis** With the outwitting of the social-climbing Yellowhammers, city scheming comes full cycle: citizens' aspirations to gentlemanly status expose them to predation by sharpers like themselves.

84 **say** saw

88 ***O tempora...mors!*** The allusion is to Cicero's *Catiline*, which however reads *mores*, and thus means 'O times, O manners!', i.e., what is the world coming to? Tim's misquotation yields 'O time! O death!'

90 **jade** (*a*) broken-down horse; (*b*) whore. (He means that he bought a nag at Cambridge and therefore doesn't need another one.)

91 **to execution** for hire; Tim plans to act as his wife's pander

92 **Brentford** a favourite spot for assignations and for horseracing. See also note to 2.2.188.

94 **promised mountains** Tim takes literally the proverbial 'to promise mountains'.

98 **runt** berate

99 ***Flectere...movebo*** If I cannot move the gods, I will appeal to hell (Latin; from Virgil's *Aeneid*)

103 **for thy labour** (*a*) for your pains; (*b*) for your sexual effort

I grant you I may prove another man's wife so,
But not mine own.

MAUDLINE There's no remedy now, Tim;
You must prove her so as well as you may.

TIM
Why then, my tutor and I will about her
As well as we can.
Uxor non est meretrix, ergo falleris.

WELSH GENTLEWOMAN
Sir, if your logic cannot prove me honest,
There's a thing called marriage, and that makes me
honest.

MAUDLINE
O, there's a trick beyond your logic, Tim.

TIM I perceive then a woman may be honest according to the English print, when she is a whore in the Latin; so much for marriage and logic! I'll love her for her wit, I'll pick out my runts there; and for my mountains, I'll mount upon [ ]

YELLOWHAMMER So Fortune seldom deals two marriages
With one hand, and both lucky. The best is,
One feast will serve them both! Marry, for room,
I'll have the dinner kept in Goldsmiths' Hall,
To which, kind gallants, I invite you all. [*Exeunt*]

Finis

THE PARTS

Adult Males

ALLWIT (375 lines): porter *or* gentleman with a chain; [first or second Kix servant]; [second man with a basket]; [second waterman] *or* [third waterman] *or* [fourth waterman]

TOUCHWOOD SENIOR (265 lines): comfit-maker's servant; one of the Walter servants; porter *or* gentleman with a chain; one of the promoters *or* one of the men with meat in a basket

YELLOWHAMMER (231 lines): comfit-maker's servant; one of the promoters *or* one of the men with meat in a basket

SIR WALTER (198 lines): any Kix servant; comfit-maker's servant; [one of the men with meat in a basket]

TIM (184 lines): one of the Allwit servants; one of the Walter servants; porter *or* gentleman with a chain; one of the promoters *or* one of the men with meat in a basket *or* comfit-maker's servant; [any Kix servant]

SIR OLIVER (122 lines): porter *or* gentleman with a chain *or* Sir Walter *or* Davy *or* one of the Allwit servants; (Sir Walter *or* Davy *or* an Allwit servant); one of the promoters *or* one of the men with meat in a basket; (a promoter *or* comfit-maker's servant *or* Davy); one of the Walter servants *or* any waterman; (waterman *or* Sir Walter *or* Davy *or* a Walter servant)

TOUCHWOOD JUNIOR (117 lines): one of the Allwit servants; comfit-maker's servant; one of the promoters *or* one of the men with meat in a basket; [porter]; [first Kix servant] *or* [second Kix servant]

FIRST PROMOTER (60 lines): any but Allwit, Sir Walter, Davy, Second Promoter, first or second man with meat in a basket, comfitmaker's servant

SECOND PROMOTER (43 lines): any but Allwit, Sir Walter, Davy, First Promoter, first or second man with meat in a basket, comfitmaker's servant

DAVY (39 lines): any Kix servant *or* Sir Oliver *or* Touchwood Senior *or* parson; (parson *or* third Kix servant *or* fourth Kix servant); [one of the men with meat in a basket]; [any waterman]; (waterman *or* Touchwood Senior)

TUTOR (27 lines): any Kix servant; one of the Walter servants; porter *or* gentleman with a chain; one of the promoters *or* one of the men with meat in a basket; one of the Allwit servants *or* comfit-maker's servant

PARSON (19 lines): any but Touchwood Junior, Sir Oliver, Allwit, Touchwood Senior, Yellowhammer, Tim, tutor, Sir Walter, third or fourth Kix servant

PORTER (15 lines): any but Yellowhammer, gentleman with a chain, Davy, Sir Walter

Allwit's FIRST SERVANT (1.2; 13 lines): any but Allwit, Allwit's Second Servant, Davy, Sir Walter, Touchwood Senior

First MAN with meat in basket (2.2; 9 lines): any but Allwit, Sir Walter, promoters, second man with meat in a basket

FIRST WATERMAN (5 lines): any but Tim, tutor, Touchwood Junior, Touchwood Senior, other watermen, Sir Walter, Yellowhammer, Allwit, Davy, either Walter servant

SECOND WATERMAN (5 lines): any but Tim, tutor, Touchwood Junior, Touchwood Senior, other watermen, Sir

107 **about** i.e., work on, with bawdy innuendo

109 ***Uxor... falleris*** a wife is not a whore; therefore you utter a fallacy (Latin)

113–14 **honest... Latin** The Latin *meretrix*, 'whore', sounds like 'merry tricks'; a common joke.

114 **print** spelling; or perhaps edition

117 **[ ]** The line may have been censored for indecency ('cunts' to chime with 'runts' in the previous line?), or left open to be filled in by a lewd gesture, or cut short by Yellowhammer.

120 **One feast... both** Businessman to the end, Yellowhammer is pleased to get two weddings for the price of one.
for room to have enough room

121 **Goldsmiths' Hall** an imposing guild hall north of Cheapside

Walter, Yellowhammer, Davy, either Walter servant

Kix's FOURTH SERVANT (5.3; 13 lines): any but Touchwood Senior, Sir Oliver, other Kix servants, Tim, tutor, Yellowhammer, Allwit, parson

Allwit's SECOND SERVANT (1.2; 3 lines): any but Allwit, Allwit's First Servant, Davy, Sir Walter, Touchwood Senior

Walter's FIRST SERVANT (5.1; 3 lines): any but second Walter servant, Allwit, Davy, Sir Walter, Touchwood Junior, First waterman, Yellowhammer, Tim, tutor

SECOND MAN with meat in basket (2.2; 3 lines): any but Allwit, Sir Walter, promoters, first man with meat in a basket

Kix's FIRST SERVANT (3.3, 5.3; 2 lines): any but Touchwood Senior, Sir Oliver, other Kix servants, Tim, tutor, Yellowhammer, Allwit, parson

Kix's SECOND SERVANT (5.3; 2 lines): any but Touchwood Senior, Sir Oliver, other Kix servants, Tim, tutor, Yellowhammer, Allwit, parson

Walter's SECOND SERVANT (5.1; 2 lines): any but first Walter servant, Allwit, Davy, Sir Walter, Touchwood Junior, First waterman, Yellowhammer, Tim, tutor

GENTLEMAN with a chain (2 lines): any but porter, Yellowhammer, Davy, Sir Walter, Touchwood Junior

Comfit-maker's SERVANT (2.3; 2 lines): any but Allwit, Davy, promoters

Kix's THIRD SERVANT (5.3; 1 line): any but Touchwood Senior, Sir Oliver, other Kix servants, Tim, tutor, Yellowhammer, Allwit, parson

THIRD WATERMAN (no lines): any but Tim, tutor, Touchwood Junior, Touchwood Senior, other watermen, Sir Walter, Yellowhammer, Davy, either Walter servant

FOURTH WATERMAN (no lines): any but Tim, tutor, Touchwood Junior, Touchwood Senior, other watermen, Sir Walter, Yellowhammer, Davy, either Walter servant

Boys

MAUDLINE (187 lines): Kix maid; wet nurse; Wench *or* Touchwood Senior's wife; [Nick *or* Wat]; (Nick *or* Wat *or* Touchwood Senior's wife)

LADY Kix (70 lines): any but Maudline, Moll, Welsh Gentlewoman, Mistress Allwit, the puritans, the gossips, Kix maid, dry nurse, nurse, Susan

MOLL (48 lines): any but Maudline, Welsh gentlewoman, Mistress Allwit, Lady Kix, Susan

WELSH GENTLEWOMAN (47 lines): any but Maudline, Moll, Mistress Allwit, Lady Kix, Susan

WIFE (Mistress Allwit; 37 lines): midwife; Touchwood Senior's wife *or* Wench; Kix maid *or* wet nurse

WENCH (37 lines): any but Touchwood Senior's wife, Lady Kix

FIRST PURITAN (32 lines): Kix maid *or* wet nurse; Moll *or* Welsh gentlewoman *or* Susan; Wat *or* Nick *or* Touchwood Senior's wife; Wench (*or* Touchwood Senior's wife)

THIRD GOSSIP (28 lines): any but Maudline, Mistress Allwit, Lady Kix, dry nurse, the puritans, other gossips, nurse, midwife

Kix MAID (18 lines): any but Lady Kix, dry nurse, wet nurse

SECOND GOSSIP (16 lines): any but Maudline, Mistress Allwit, Lady Kix, dry nurse, the puritans, other gossips, nurse, midwife

FIRST GOSSIP (9 lines): any but Maudline, Mistress Allwit, Lady Kix, dry nurse, the puritans, other gossips, nurse, midwife

FOURTH GOSSIP (9 lines): any but Maudline, Mistress Allwit, Lady Kix, dry nurse, the puritans, other gossips, nurse, midwife

Touchwood Senior's WIFE (8 lines): any but Mistress Allwit, Wat, Nick, Wench

SECOND PURITAN (6 lines): Kix maid *or* wet nurse; Moll *or* Welsh gentlewoman *or* Susan; Wat *or* Nick *or* Touchwood Senior's wife; Wench (*or* Touchwood Senior's wife)

WET NURSE (5 lines): any but dry nurse

NURSE (5 lines): any but Maudline, Mistress Allwit, Lady Kix, the puritans, the gossips

NICK (2 lines): any but Wat, Maudline, Mistress Allwit, Touchwood Senior's wife

WAT (1 line): any but Nick, Maudline, Mistress Allwit, Touchwood Senior's wife

SUSAN (1 line): any but Maudline, Moll, Mistress Allwit, Lady Kix, Welsh gentlewoman

DRY NURSE (1 line): any but Maudline, Mistress Allwit, Lady Kix, wet nurse, the puritans, the gossips

FIFTH GOSSIP (1 line): any but Maudline, Mistress Allwit, Lady Kix, dry nurse, the puritans, other gossips, nurse, midwife

MIDWIFE (no lines): any but Maudline, the puritans, the gossips

Two Possible Sexual Dissidents:

1. As a young university graduate, Tim might conceivably be played by a boy, in which case these are the doubling possibilities: nurse; midwife, Wat *or* Nick *or* Touchwood Senior's wife *or* Wench; Kix maid *or* dry nurse *or* wet nurse.
2. R. B. Parker suggests that Sir Oliver Kix might have been played by a boy, citing a reference to his short stature; I might add that Oliver's sexual impotence could have suggested casting him as a boy rather than a man, for the sake of the high voice, etc. If Sir Oliver were played by a boy, here are the doubling possibilities: nurse; midwife; Wat *or* Nick *or* Touchwood Senior's wife; dry nurse *or* wet nurse *or* any of the gossips; nurse (*or* gossip).

THE MANNER OF HIS LORDSHIP'S ENTERTAINMENT

Edited by David M. Bergeron

THE speaker instructs the 'clerk of the work': 'reach me the book to show | How many arts from such a labour flow' (63–4). Although referring to the successful completion of the New River, the speaker could just as readily be referring to Middleton's 1613 'book', the one that contains, in its expanded issue, the texts of both *The Triumphs of Truth* and *The Manner of his Lordship's Entertainment on Michaelmas Day... At that most Famous and Admired Work of the Running Stream*. That book reveals the arts that flowed from Middleton's dramatic efforts in behalf of civic occasions in 1613. Although the two texts stand alone bibliographically, they both come from Middleton's pen, they praise two other men named Middleton (Myddelton), and they celebrate events held within a month of each other.

The New River was a forty-mile-long canal that brought water from Chadwell and the Amwell spring north of London to Islington. For the official opening, Middleton wrote this brief entertainment to honour Sir Hugh Myddelton, Goldsmith. On Michaelmas Day 1613, the day on which Sir Hugh's brother Thomas was officially elected the new mayor, some aldermen and other authorities of the city gathered at the cistern in Islington into which the river emptied. Today a statue of Hugh Myddelton, dating from 1862, stands on Islington Green in London to celebrate the New River project.

Several things stand out about this brief pageant. First, a dramatist might be called upon to offer entertainments for a surprising array of events. This New River pageant, clearly not a Lord Mayor's show, nevertheless responds to a civic occasion associated with the city. Second, Middleton knows how he is supposed to respond; he knows how to please the city fathers.

Middleton uses the word 'perfection' three times in the opening thirty-two lines of the text; he defines it as 'the crown of all inventions' (12). The speaker, who represents all the labourers who have worked on the project, says: 'Long have we laboured, long desired and prayed | For this great work's perfection' (35–6). Middleton intends 'perfection' to mean both successful 'completion' of the project and this project's 'flawless, faultless' character. Perfection 'makes the conquest' (22), Middleton writes earlier. The speaker later asserts: 'perfection draws | Favour from princes' (53–4). Middleton might have added that perfection, as in this pageant entertainment, draws favour from the citizenry as well. This pageant 'perfects' the New River because it becomes the last event to complete the celebration of a new era in the city's life: a desirable and ample source of water.

Sir Hugh Myddelton

With the early twenty-first century convenience of running water in most homes in developed countries, we have to remind ourselves of the difficulty of obtaining a ready supply of fresh, safe water in Middleton's London. With largely unfettered growth, London faced mounting problems of sanitation, pestilence, and danger of fire. Finding an inexpensive and reliable source of water became increasingly crucial. All across Europe cities struggled with this problem, knowing that their safety and future development depended on water.

Just how crucial water might be in the city's life may be revealed by the organization of John Stow's *Survey of London* (1598). When he begins to describe London, Stow starts with the wall around the city. But he next moves to the sources of fresh water that serve the city: the fountains, wells, springs, conduits, and the River Thames. A city, no matter how securely situated within a wall, cannot survive without water. At some length, then, Stow recounts the various sources of water and how those sources have changed over the centuries. The city's water supply had evolved over the course of some four hundred years. The water brought in from springs in the surrounding areas by means of leaded pipes had become inadequate. Water from the Thames had to be pumped into the city, and it became polluted because of sewage dumped into the river. Time and again Stow emphasizes the unparalleled importance of water.

The idea of bringing water into London from the northern outreaches dates back to the Elizabethan period. After many futile starts Hugh Myddelton finally stepped forward to rescue what seemed to be a doomed project. He signed the first agreement with the city on 21 April 1609 and a new one on 28 March 1611. Work had begun in earnest in 1609. Dozens of people became actively involved in the project, and a number made financial investments. But eventually it took the efforts of James I to save the project from its financial problems. On 2 May 1612 representatives of the King and Myddelton drew up a formal indenture. The basic agreement called for James to contribute half the expenditure, past as well as future. Probably the pageant speaker has this in mind when he says: 'That every week' the labourers 'had their royal pay' (78). In any event, many people, including the King and Myddelton, bore the cost for the new river.

The text's portrait of Hugh Myddelton combines a certain amount of fiction with an accurate view of his involvement in the project. The title-page asserts that the project was 'the sole invention, cost, and industry of that worthy Master Hugh Myddelton... for the general good of the city' (9–11). The speaker says that the project, 'a work so rare, | Only by one man's industry, cost, and care | Is brought to blest effect' (43–5). No warranted stretch of imagination could lead one to conclude that Hugh Myddelton's *sole* cost and effort led to the successful completion of the New River. Indeed, the speaker in the pageant embodies *all* the workers who have actually constructed the canal. That speaker also claims: 'His only aim the city's general good' (46). Doubtless Sir Hugh intended to meet one of the city's needs, but he also sought to make money.

Early in the text the poet refers to 'the warlike music of drums and trumpets' on this festive occasion and makes the analogy: 'there is no labour that man undertakes but hath a war within itself' (22–3). 'Onsets of malice, calumnies, and slanders' help define the battle that Hugh Myddelton faced. The speaker cites the five years' expense, 'the infinite ways | Of malice, envy, false suggestions' (40–1), and the 'many unjust complaints' (47) that have 'oft caused restraints' (48). The historical record confirms that Myddelton faced considerable opposition from landowners and some members of Parliament. Their warlike opposition cost the project a work stoppage of twenty-two months at one point. Middleton the poet puts a rough and realistic edge on what otherwise functions as an idealized celebration.

Later seventeenth-century reports somewhat muddy the waters of the New River. In his *Brief Lives* John Aubrey (1626–97) offers a bleak portrait of Hugh Myddelton, as one who stole ideas from others and profited from them. Aubrey credits William Ingelbert with being 'the first Inventor or Projector of bringing the water from Ware to London'. But Sir Hugh 'got the profit and also the Credit of that most useful Invention, for which there ought to have been erected a Statue for the memory of this poor-man from the City of London'. Instead, Sir Hugh's picture hangs in Goldsmiths' Hall, and Ingelbert has been reduced to one 'in a poor Rug-gown like an Alms-man'. What an appalling and journalistically appealing story Aubrey provides. Unfortunately for his sake, it has little basis in fact. True, Ingelbert did enter negotiations with the city, but he dropped out of the picture early on and therefore made no contribution to the successful completion of the project. Aubrey's perspective confirms continuing slander about Hugh Myddelton. Thomas Fuller in *The Worthies of England* (1662) offers an assessment that more nearly resembles Thomas Middleton's: 'how meritorious a work did this worthy man perform, who, to quench the thirst of thousands in the populous city of London fetched water on his own cost, more than twenty-four miles, encountering all the way with an army of oppositions'. All evidence to the contrary, writers insist on giving Sir Hugh sole credit for financing the new river. Somehow this must appeal to an entrepreneurial spirit that they wish to foster; perhaps it reflects ideas of emerging capitalism with its emphasis on individual risk. In any event, sometimes truth apparently takes a back seat to fiction-making.

One of the finest contemporary accounts appears in Anthony Munday's continuation (1618) of Stow's *Survey of London*. Munday insists on firsthand knowledge: 'I myself (by favour of the Gentlemen) did divers times ride to see it, and diligently observed, that admirable Art, pains and industry were bestowed for the passage of it.' Munday repeats the by now familiar story of the river's completion 'by the only care, cost and liberal expences of one Worthy Man, master Hugh Myddelton'. And he rehearses the story of the opposition that Myddelton overcame. Munday has gone to some trouble to include this four-page account in the *Survey*. At the bottom of the first page appears this printed note: 'Let this halfe sheete be plac'd betweene Folio 20. and 21.' This account seems to be a later addition after the pagination had already been worked out: this section has its own signature designation.

Munday's report of the New River also includes Middleton's pageant. Munday faithfully provides the events on Michaelmas Day, such as the gathering at the cistern in Islington, and includes the speech. With only two slight word changes Munday repeats the speech as found in Middleton's text. Munday writes, without revealing his source: 'The Speech at the Cistern, according as it was delivered to me.' Given the accuracy of this printing of the speech, one has to assume that Munday has his eye on Middleton's text. In any event, the 1618 *Survey* breathes new life into the New River entertainment; the final edition of the *Survey* (1633) also contains the story and speech of Middleton's entertainment.

Middleton's speaker argues that Hugh Myddelton's example may give 'Courage to some that may hereafter live | To practise deeds of goodness and of fame, | And cheerfully light their actions by his name' (60–2). But not only does this example offer courage to future virtuous action; it also instructs and informs the poet's view of himself. Middleton admires this Sir Hugh who has survived the onslaughts of 'malice, calumnies, and slanders'. Middleton would write in the Epistle Dedicatory of *The Triumphs of Truth* that he himself had suffered 'oppositions of malice, ignorance, and envy'. The poet therefore forges a link between himself and the successful Hugh Myddelton, just as he would closely identify himself with the mayor Thomas Myddelton in the other pageant text in the 1613 book. The writer hopes that his 'invention' will participate in the perfection of the New River, as he also in his self-fashioning identifies with political and financial leaders who have overcome adversity.

SEE ALSO

Textual introduction and apparatus: *Companion*, 629
Authorship and date: *Companion*, 375
General introduction to the civic entertainments: this volume, 968

The Manner of his Lordship's Entertainment

The manner of his Lordship's Entertainment on Michaelmas day last, being the day of his honourable election, together with the worthy Sir John Swinnerton, Knight, then Lord Mayor, the learned and judicious, Sir Henry Montagu, Master Recorder, and many of the right worshipful the Aldermen of the City of London.

At that most famous and admired work of the running stream from Amwell Head, into the cistern near Islington, being the sole invention, cost, and industry of that worthy Master Hugh Myddelton of London, Goldsmith, for the general good of the city.

Perfection, which is the crown of all inventions, swelling now high with happy welcomes to all the glad well-wishers of her admired maturity, the father and master of this famous work, expressing thereby both his thankfulness to heaven and his zeal to the City of London, in true joy of heart to see his time, travails, and expenses so successively greeted, thus gives entertainment to that honourable assembly.

At their first appearing, the warlike music of drums and trumpets liberally beats the air, sounds as proper as in battle, for there is no labour that man undertakes but hath a war within itself, and perfection makes the conquest; and no few or mean onsets of malice, calumnies, and slanders, hath this resolved gentleman borne off, before his labours were invested with victory, as in this following speech to those honourable auditors then placed upon the mount is more at large related.

A troop of labourers, to the number of threescore or upwards, all in green caps alike, bearing in their hands the symbols of their several employments in so great a business, with drums before them, marching twice or thrice about the cistern, orderly present themselves before the mount, and after their obeisance:

THE SPEECH

Long have we laboured, long desired and prayed
For this great work's perfection, and by th'aid
Of heaven and good men's wishes 'tis at length
Happily conquered by cost, art, and strength.
And after five years' dear expense in days,
Travail, and pains, besides the infinite ways
Of malice, envy, false suggestiöns,
Able to daunt the spirits of mighty ones
In wealth and courage, this, a work so rare,
Only by one man's industry, cost, and care
Is brought to blest effect, so much withstood,
His only aim the city's general good;
And where before many unjust complaints,
Enviously seated, hath oft caused restraints,
Stops, and great crosses, to our master's charge
And the work's hindrance; favour now at large
Spreads itself open to him, and commends
To admiration both his pains and ends,

2 **Michaelmas day** feast of St Michael, 29 September
3 **John Swinnerton** Merchant Taylor, elected mayor in 1612, honoured by Thomas Dekker's Lord Mayor's pageant, *Troia-Nova Triumphans*
5 **Henry Montagu** Recorder of the City of London, elected in May 1603; spoke in *Magnificent Entertainment* (ll. 1603–18); became Chief Justice of the King's Bench
8 **Amwell Head** Amwell springs located in Hertfordshire
9 **Islington** in the 17th century a country village on the northern edge of London; now part of London
invention Middleton typically implies both the action of inventing and the thing invented, the product
10 **Hugh Myddelton** (1560–1631); Goldsmith, brother of the mayor Thomas Myddelton; Member of Parliament several times for Denbigh
25 **resolved gentleman** Hugh Myddelton

The king's most gracious love: perfection draws
Favour from princes, and from all applause.
Then, worthy magistrates, to whose content,
Next to the state, all this great care was bent,
And for the public good, which grace requires,
Your loves and furtherance chiefly he desires,
To cherish these proceedings, which may give
Courage to some that may hereafter live
To practise deeds of goodness and of fame,
And cheerfully light their actions by his name.
Clerk of the work, reach me the book to show
How many arts from such a labour flow.

These lines following are read in the clerk's book:

First, here's the overseer, this tried man
An ancient soldier and an artisan;
The clerk; next him mathematician;
The master of the timber-work takes place
Next after these; the measurer in like case;
Bricklayer and engineer; and after those
The borer and the pavior; then it shows
The labourers next; keeper of Amwell-head;
The walkers last: so all their names are read;
Yet these but parcels of six hundred more
That at one time have been employed before;
Yet these in sight and all the rest will say,
That every week they had their royal pay.

The speech goes on.

Now for the fruits then: flow forth precious spring,
So long and dearly sought for, and now bring
Comfort to all that love thee; loudly sing,
And with thy crystal murmurs struck together,
Bid all thy true well-wishers welcome hither.

At which words the flood-gate opens, the stream let in into the cistern, drums and trumpets giving it triumphant welcomes; and, for the close of this their honourable entertainment, a peal of chambers.

FINIS.

53 ***king's*** King James I
67 ***ancient soldier*** standard bearer; also, experienced, venerable soldier
70 ***measurer*** one who takes measurements
72 ***borer*** one who bores, drills
pavior one who lays pavement
74 ***walkers*** an officer of the New River company who has charge of a 'walk' or section of the bank (*OED*)
78 ***royal pay*** refers to the monetary support of King James, who helped pay for the project
88 **peal of chambers** small piece of ordnance used to fire salutes

THE TRIUMPHS OF TRUTH

Edited by David M. Bergeron

WHY do so many critics, even at the beginning of the twenty-first century, typically cross to the other side of the street when they see a civic pageant approaching? Possibly because they share the assumptions implied or stated by a number of writers spanning several centuries who seem to have taken seriously Prospero's reference to 'insubstantial pageants'. For example, George Chapman in the Epistle Dedicatory, addressed to Robert Carr, of the translation of Homer's *Odyssey* (1614) refers specifically and unkindly to Middleton's first Lord Mayor's show, *The Triumphs of Truth*, when he writes: 'Why then is Fiction, to this end, so hateful to our true Ignorants? Or why should a poor Chronicler of a Lord Mayor's naked *Truth*, (that peradventure will last his year) include more worth with our modern wizards, than *Homer* for his naked *Ulysses*, clad in eternal Fiction?' Chapman continues by sneering at those writers who 'ride the ambling Muse' and 'Whose Raptures are in every Pageant seen'.

Chapman, the poet who has translated Homer, disdains those who dabble in pageants, for those with 'popular' taste. He refers disparagingly to Middleton as a 'poor chronicler'—as opposed to a true poet, one assumes. He contrasts the 'eternal fiction' of Homer with the ephemeral nature of a Lord Mayor's show—that peradventure will last a year. Ironically, Chapman helps confer permanence on Middleton's effort by this very reference, which appears unaltered again in the 1616 edition of Chapman's Homer. Chapman voices his contempt for the 'true Ignorants' and 'modern wizards' who do not share his superior judgement. More than two centuries after Chapman, J. B. Heath in a history of the Grocers' guild, who sponsored the 1613 pageant, writes that the pageants 'seem to have afforded great delight to the rude and uncultivated understandings of those for whose entertainment they were intended'. Even as Chapman and Heath register their uncomprehending annoyance that pageants have captured the public imagination, they inadvertently testify to the impact of such street entertainments.

In a generally sympathetic article on Middleton's pageants R. C. Bald nevertheless writes in the 1930s that any 'serious achievement in these shows was prevented not merely by the prescribed themes but by the fact that it was impossible to regard the show as a whole'. This bleak assessment depends upon unduly confident assumptions. Bald presumes—what cannot be proven—that someone 'prescribed' the themes for pageant writers, and that 'serious' artistic achievement is incompatible with 'prescribed themes'. This position embraces a romantic ideology about the relationship of patron and artist. When Bald complains about the difficulty of being able to regard 'the show as a whole', he raises the familiar argument of *unity*. Ideas about unity, derived in part from the totalizing concepts of New Criticism, do not fit pageants. In any case, we can 'regard the show as a whole' through the texts that survive. The event may be scattered, but the text is bound.

With any dramatic text of this early period we ponder its possible relationship to actual performance. Speeches and stage directions provide clues but not the whole event. Middleton's pageant texts do not pretend to give us only the dramatic event itself; instead, we encounter a textual performance that extends in several directions beyond mere representation of theatrical performance. Looking at the three extant texts of Elizabethan Lord Mayor's shows by George Peele (1585, 1591) and Thomas Nelson (1590), we perceive them as models of simplicity. They contain only the speeches and a few stage directions, but no prefatory material, no elaboration, no description, no marginalia—nothing else. By contrast, the Jacobean texts pursue copiousness, starting with Anthony Munday's *The Triumphs of Reunited Britannia* (1605) and certainly including Thomas Dekker's *Troia-Nova Triumphans* (1612). Middleton builds on the expanding pageant text. Clearly he intends his texts for *readers*; they become commemorative books that both capture the event and add to it. They assume an expository and narrative function that sets them apart from the typical dramatic text. Middleton's 1613 text also includes the musical score for the song sung early in the inaugural morning, the first time that a pageant text has contained such musical notation. The music appears at the end of the text, clearly intended for a reader and not trying to duplicate its place in the performance. As readers, we must abandon an overly narrow concern for unity and instead succumb to the pleasures of digressions, descriptions, and discourses on sometimes arcane topics. We experience the pageant text as an event itself, resembling but differing from the show.

Middleton begins the text of *The Triumphs of Truth* with a formal dedication to the new mayor, as he does all of his pageant texts. (Before Middleton only Dekker's 1612 text has such prefatory matter.) Not yet commonplace in dramatic texts, these dedications add to the sense of this document as a book. The 1613 dedication to the new mayor, also named Thomas Middleton (Myddelton), is Middleton's longest; he refers to the mayor's earlier life and notes their common name. A decidedly religious tone permeates this dedication; this tone may reflect Sir Thomas Myddelton's avowed Puritanism. In the text

Sir Thomas Myddelton

proper Middleton begins by discussing the quality of the mayor's reception into London and then moves to comment on his own experience with the Grocers, 'the wardens and committees, men of much understanding, industry, and carefulness, little weighing the greatness of expense, so the cost might purchase perfection' (72–5). Middleton adds: 'If any shall imagine that I set fairer colours upon their deserts than they upon themselves, let them but read and conceive' (78–80).

The personal pronouns 'I' and 'you' that recur in *Truth* and in Middleton's other pageant texts imply a dialogue with a reader, not an attempt to reproduce only the event. Describing the procession to St Paul's Churchyard, Middleton points to the appearance of five islands, 'those dumb glories that I spake of before upon the water' (391–2). Earlier he instructs the reader: 'If you hearken to Zeal...after his holy anger is passed against Error and his crew, he will give it you in better terms' (338–40). In the text of *Triumphs of Truth*, Middleton assumes the persona of a writer who speaks the truth. If we think that he exaggerates the virtue of the guild, then we need only 'read and conceive'—a wonderfully disingenuous position for Middleton, who in fact provides the principal means by which to judge his accuracy.

Middleton pauses at the end to recognize the contributions of Humphrey Nichols, John Grinkin, and Anthony Munday—the first such acknowledgements in a pageant text. Again, this information takes us beyond a report of the dramatic show. He adds: 'I now conclude, holding it a more learned discretion to cease of myself than to have Time cut me off rudely: and now let him strike at his pleasure' (790–4). No longer a conversation with a reader, this statement suggests Middleton's having a conversation with himself. In and through the text he now participates in the allegorical fiction that he had created for the pageant. Regularly Middleton reminds us that pageant texts exist as a special breed: dramatic texts that fulfil a wide array of functions, including but not restricted to providing the speeches and other apparatus of dramatic performance.

More than his Jacobean counterparts, Middleton uses his texts also to defend his 'art'. In the Epistle Dedicatory, Middleton suggests that he has overcome 'all oppositions of malice, ignorance, and envy' (37) and can now 'do service' to the mayor's fame: 'and my pen only to be employed in these bounteous and honourable triumphs, being but shadows to those eternal glories that stand ready for deservers' (40–3). In the opening lines of the text proper, Middleton hopes that 'the streams of art... equal those of bounty' (60–1). He laments the failure of 'the impudent common writer' to achieve such artistic desires: 'it would heartily grieve any understanding spirit to behold many times so glorious a fire in bounty and goodness offering to match itself with freezing art' (63–7). Whatever specific writers or events Middleton may allude to (and the criticism is deliberately, functionally, ambiguous), he has staked his own claim on the fire of art. This art must match the 'state and magnificence' of the Lord Mayor's inauguration. At the end of the text, he returns to the subject, referring to the 'art' of Nichols and the 'proper beauties' of workmanship, 'most artfully and faithfully performed by John Grinkin' (783–6). The artisans match the high artistic standards that Middleton has set for himself even as they construct the 'body' of the pageant. 'Art' as a word can be applied, comfortably, both to literary works of a poet and to the work of the city's trades and craftsmen.

Before the text, came the event it describes; and before that event, came the institution of mayoralty in London and the development of pageant entertainments to honour the new mayor. King John allowed the establishment of the elective office of mayor in London; Henry fitz Ailwin, who had been appointed mayor in 1189, became the first elected mayor in 1208. As part of the arrangements for this new office the King insisted that the new mayor annually take his oath of office, administered by one of the king's officials, at the Exchequer in the royal government offices in Westminster. The mayor came from the ranks of the aldermen; and they typically derived from one of the twelve principal, or livery, companies of London, which by 1538 had settled into a fixed order of prestige: Mercers, Grocers, Drapers, Fishmongers, Goldsmiths, Skinners, Merchant Taylors, Haberdashers, Salters, Ironmongers, Vintners, and Clothworkers.

The section on 'Temporal Government' in John Stow's *The Survey of London* (1598) provides a contemporary account of the procedures for electing the mayor and a guide to the ritual of his inauguration. Formally elected on Michaelmas Day (29 September), the new mayor took the oath of office on 29 October, the day after St Simon and St Jude's Day. Stow notes that the aldermen greet the new mayor at eight o'clock in the morning and escort him to the Guildhall, the seat of city government. From there the entourage goes to the river and takes barges upriver to Westminster where the mayor takes the oath. Entertainment may occur on this river journey. The party then returns downstream to the City of London. In the 1613 text, Middleton shows the procession beginning from the Guildhall, going by river to Westminster, then returning to London at Baynard's Castle, moving by land to St Paul's Cathedral, on to Cheapside, through St Lawrence Lane to the Guildhall, back to St Paul's for religious services, and finally to the mayor's home. Abbreviated versions of this traditional route govern all of Middleton's pageants. Unlike the great London royal entry pageants for Elizabeth I and James I which moved from the Tower westward through the City toward Westminster, the mayoral procession moved west to east. The mayor encountered tableaux and speeches along the way; indeed, as in the 1613 pageant, some of the devices followed the mayor in procession. The report from the Russian ambassador Aleksei Ziuzin, who was present for this pageant, underscores the importance of this ceremony, saying at one point: 'except for the King's coronation there is no other such great ceremony in England'. (Ziuzin's complete account is printed in this edition following the text of the pageant.) Not only did the mayor's representatives urge the ambassador's attendance, so did James I, according to the account. The ambassadorial dispatch (printed in this edition following the pageant's text) captures much of the spectacle, including the river procession, and emphasizes the participation by many different groups in the entertainment, including children who carried various constructed animals. The whole city, according to the ambassador, watched the festivities.

A mayor, a day, and a festive occasion do not inevitably lead to drama. By the beginning of the fifteenth century the London guilds became responsible for setting the Midsummer Watch on 24 and 29 June. By 1504, the pageant entertainment included a procession and dramatic representations mainly of biblical and religious subjects. But these shows decline because the guilds' attention shifts to the inaugural day of the new mayor. Henry Machyn provides in 1553 the first report of a Lord Mayor's show, although guild records indicate a pageant as early as 1535. Guild records in 1561 provide the first speeches for a Lord Mayor's Show; the first surviving printed text preserves George Peele's pageant of 1585 and also underscores the growing involvement of well-known writers and dramatists with these pageants. Peele's *Descensus Astraeae* (1591), although the last extant text of an Elizabethan mayoral show, is the first to have a distinct, specific title. In the hands of Munday, Dekker, and Middleton the Jacobean Lord Mayor's show gains a complexity unknown in the previous reign.

How do these dramatists fit into the guilds' plans and negotiations? As with medieval drama, the guilds assessed their membership in order to finance street pageants; therefore, an unbroken line of guild support of drama runs from the fourteenth century to the end of the seventeenth. Fortunately, guild records provide sufficient documentation for the planning and expenditures. The Grocers' Court Books reveal unusually early deliberations on 5 February 1613 about preparations for a mayoral pageant, surveying the need for banners, streamers, and other ornaments 'set in readiness in convenient time in honour of the next worthy Magistrate that shall be chosen out of this Company'. (The Grocers had not sponsored a pageant for a mayor from their ranks since 1598.) Also in February the Master, Wardens, and others gave consideration to a 'Device or project in writing set down' by Anthony Munday. Not unlike dramatists submitting plots to Henslowe for plays in public theatres, Munday, Middleton, and others offered a proposal to be considered by the appropriate authorities in the guild. If chosen, the dramatist would then negotiate the specific services that he would perform. Records in 1613 indicate that Munday received the gross sum of £149 for his 'device', providing apparel, securing players, and arranging transportation. Middleton got £40 'for the ordering overseeing and writing of the whole Device'.

Other records from March, June, and July 1613 reveal the workings of various committees planning the pageant. The records of April 1614 tally the various expenditures, including £4 to the printer Nicholas Okes for printing the text, probably the usual run of 500 copies for pageants as shown in other guild records. John Grinkin, the artificer, received £310 for the construction of all the pageant devices—the ship, chariots, five islands, and all the carpentry work, painting, and fireworks. The total cost of nearly £1,300 makes this show the most expensive such pageant; the average cost, based on available records, of a Lord Mayor's show in the early Stuart period comes to slightly over £700. The exceptionally early planning and generous expenditure suggest that the Grocers intended to outstrip recent pageants; this zeal may lay behind Middleton's criticism of the 'freezing art' of his predecessors.

Thus *The Triumphs of Truth* came into existence. Defying Chapman's assessment, it has lasted beyond its year. Whenever critics discuss mayoral pageants, they inevitably focus on *Truth*, as evident in the work of Gail Kern Paster, Muriel Bradbrook, Sheila Williams, Glynne Wickham, Theodore Leinwand, and David Bergeron. A. A. Bromham indeed explores the topical, political context of 1613 and its relevance to the pageant. Unlike other mayoral pageants, it even has a performance history. The Lord Mayor's celebration of 1913 purported to be a reproduction of Middleton's show; but in fact it did not resemble the earlier pageant, although it included representations of Thomas Myddelton (the new mayor) and Hugh Myddelton (his brother). A giant also represented the New River. On 2 May 1988, the Corporation of London presented 'The Lord Mayor of London's Jacobean Thames Pageant', consisting of several barges that moved along the Thames, all inspired by Middleton's *Triumphs of Truth*. Reflecting late twentieth-century reality, this 1988 show occurred 'in association with Thames Television' and served as a charity event for the 1988 ITV Telethon. A media and charity occasion, it had no real connection to the office of mayor or other traditional civic events; it became an excuse for spectacle. Nevertheless, the planners of this pageant did pay attention to Middleton's text and presented many of the figures from the 1613 show, such as London, Truth, Time, Truth's Angel, and Zeal. (Of course, they also added Roman soldiers and Roman handmaidens, possibly because they look good from barges.)

The artistic achievement of this pageant derives from Middleton's successful solution to the problem of how to represent the struggle between truth and error. Middleton approaches this conflict from several directions, relying on an implicit system of correspondences that enables the poet to connect moral ideas and historical persons to his fiction. The created characters make manifest the ideas that Middleton seeks to convey. Middleton also through the construction of his text underscores the battle between truth and error. For example, in the opening thirty-six lines of the text proper he twice makes rhetorical moves that hinge on this conflict. He first establishes the idea that no place receives a new mayor in such state and magnificence as London does: 'This being then infallible' (54). Error opposes this certainty by providing inadequate art for such an occasion, offering instead 'miserable want' and 'freezing art, sitting in darkness'—the place of error (62–7). Middleton begins line 69: 'But to speak truth'. If any imagine that the dramatist exaggerates the spectacle, 'their own understandings will light them to the acknowledgement of their errors' (80–2). Such rhetorical conflict makes sense, of course, only to a reader.

The representation of London in the performance heightens the tension between truth and error. Middleton presents the figure as a woman, 'a reverend mother', with long white hair and wearing 'on her head a model of steeples and turrets' (119–21). Middleton deliberately emphasizes the feminine gender so that he may pursue the metaphor of the city as caring mother. A female London links immediately to Truth, which always appears as feminine. Had he wanted, the dramatist might have named the pageant 'The Triumphs of London', reflecting the prominence of this character who speaks significantly more lines than any other. London exists in at least two ways in the pageant: as present reality and as representation. Middleton exploits this fiction–reality axis, common in most civic pageants. That is, London appears as a fictionalized, female character and as an obvious reality in the very streets where the performance takes place. Spectators looking at London also see London around them. The representation functions as a synecdoche of the city itself, resembling but obviously differing from the actual city.

In the opening speech London emphasizes her maternal connection to the mayor: 'I am thy mother' (131). Since she addresses the real mayor Thomas Myddelton, she thereby underscores the blurred boundary between fiction and reality. This speech (ll. 126–94) strikes us immediately because much of it forgoes the familiar rhymed couplets used by most pageant dramatists. In moral terms London sketches the difference between truth and error, as the speech moves from past actions to present and future imperatives. London asserts that the mayor's soul contains 'The sacred lights of divine fear and knowledge' (134), gained from this caring mother who has 'Set wholesome and religious laws' (142) before him and who has cheered his youth with 'the faith, the love, the zealous fires' (154). London boldly says: 'thou'st all from me' (159). These virtues derive from and embody truth. But error also exists in 'sons' who have been disobedient, who refrain 'from doing grace and service' (168) to London, a city that may also contain 'pollution, | Sin, and uncleanness' (188–9), the result of error. London closes with this benediction: 'My blessing be upon thee, son and lord, | And on my sons all that obey my word' (193–4). To obey London's 'word' means in effect to obey the Word of Truth. The words of London reinforce a moral struggle between truth and error; London joins this war as the pageant allegorizes a battle for the mayor's soul. This battle gains specific visual representation at London's Triumphant Mount, the last major device, located near the Little Conduit in Cheapside. London, surrounded by allegorical virtues, drives away the shroud that covers the mount, a darkness caused by Error.

Middleton dramatizes the Truth–Error conflict by choosing to personify such figures and to provide a 'naïve allegory' of their struggle. A psychomachian battle takes place simultaneously in the streets and in the mind of the mayor, who participates both in the fiction and in the real world of his inauguration. The representation of Truth and Error as characters depends on an allegorical frame of mind and on emblematic and iconographical techniques. Such techniques can be found in emblem books, which emerged on the European continent in the sixteenth century. Andrea Alciati's *Emblematum* (1531) and Cesare Ripa's *Iconologia* (1593) became particularly influential, existing in several editions and translations. Two important English emblem books depend on the Italian models: Geffrey Whitney's *A Choice of Emblemes* (1586), the first English emblem book, and Henry Peacham's *Minerva Britanna* (1612). Whether the dramatist knew these books directly matters less than his appropriation of their methods. Emblems typically contain three parts: motto, picture, and verses that pull the parts together. The tableaux that constitute *The Triumphs of Truth* resemble movable emblems, ones the audience could recognize.

Emblems participate in iconographical traditions, received ways in which certain mythological and allegorical figures should be represented. Middleton adapts and rehearses that which he inherited. Therefore he describes Truth who sits in a chariot 'in a close garment of white satin, which makes her appear thin and naked' (324–5), a dove over her head and serpents under her feet 'in that she treads down all subtlety and fraud' (331–2), a 'sun in her right hand' (335), 'on her breast a pure round crystal, showing the brightness of her thoughts and actions' (333–5). Zeal, the speaker, says: 'Nor by the naked plainness of her weeds | Judge thou her worth, no burnished gloss Truth needs' (348–9). But Zeal continues to offer a 'burnished gloss' for the benefit of the spectators, just as Middleton's text assists the reader in comprehending the symbolic value of Truth's properties. With slight variation Middleton's Truth could have walked off the pages of Peacham's *Minerva Britanna* and into the pageant. On page 134 of the emblem book Truth appears, naked, holding a sunburst in her right hand and a palm branch in her left and also a book, while her right foot rests on a globe—details that Peacham probably took from Ripa. Serpents form the decorative border for the emblem. Clearly Peacham's picture represents the 'triumphs of truth'. The verses interpret the symbolism of the emblem, much as Zeal's speech does in the pageant.

Middleton represents the quality Error in vivid terms as he sits in a chariot near St Paul's, 'his garment of ash-colour silk, his head rolled in a cloud, over which stands an owl, a mole on one shoulder, a bat on the other, all symbols of blind ignorance and darkness, mists hanging at his eyes' (245–9). This emblematic representation heightens the contrast with Truth. Envy accompanies Error, 'eating of a human heart, ... attired in red silk, ... her left pap bare, where a snake fastens' (250–2). This gruesome image could derive from a similar portrait in Whitney's and other emblem books or from Dekker's representation in the 1612 pageant. Interestingly, in Middleton's allegory the mayor and his retinue encounter Error before Truth, which may reflect Middleton's view of the post-lapsarian world. Such a sequence also underscores the importance of the figure London as the initial embodiment of truth.

For sheer seductive power nothing surpasses Error's first speech (255–318). If Error cannot look very attractive, he can certainly sound enticing. In effect, Error turns upside down the world articulated by London earlier in the pageant, at first by a kind of poetic imitation of London's speech. Like London, Error first avoids the typical pattern of rhymed couplets. If representation depends in part on resemblance, then Error first resembles London, but with a profound difference. If we heard only the opening few lines of Error's speech, we would hear a seemingly benign voice, like London's. Error says: 'Art come? O welcome, my triumphant lord, | My glory's sweetheart! how many millions | Of happy wishes hath my love told out | For this desirèd minute' (255–8). Error does not sound so bad.

But this disingenuous quality gives way to Error's true intent: to be false. The son of darkness adopts the imagery of light. With the mayor's arrival, Error claims now to be 'all of light, | Of fire, of joy, pleasure runs nimbly through me' (261–2). 'Power' becomes the operative word for Error as he adumbrates a programme for exercising power and gaining wealth, the seductive charms of high office. By line 270, 'And let thy will and appetite sway the sword', there can be no doubt about Error's purpose. The final movement of Error's speech concentrates on the 'evils' of Truth, her narrow, single, austere way of life, while Error offers pleasure and delight. Error notes that 'e'en in this throng' (302) of spectators he could find many 'children'. With some irony Error makes his final assertion: 'This of thy life I'll make the golden year' (317). But 'golden' for Error can only refer to material accumulation, whereas London has earlier urged, 'disdain all titles | Purchased with coin' (177–8). Middleton has succeeded in giving Error considerable dramatic interest.

The representation of truth and error takes another twist in the appearance of a King of Moors, his queen, and attendants. Moors had appeared in early sixteenth-century Midsummer Shows and in the 1585 Lord Mayor's show. The pageant's sponsoring guild, the Grocers, had joined with the East India Company to expand their trade—hence another reason to include the Moor. The Moorish king confronts directly the issue of his colour: 'does my complexion draw | So many Christian eyes that never saw | A king so black before?' (413–14). He connects his appearance with assumptions made about him: 'I being a Moor, then, in opinion's lightness, | As far from sanctity as my face from whiteness' (423–4). Beneath that dark exterior resides a transformed soul: 'Truth in my soul sets up the light of grace' (430). Having once pursued error in false religion ('And though in days of error I did run', 431), the king through the work of English merchants has been 'brought to the true Christian faith' (440). The power of truth, embodied in the English traders, had 'power to convert infidels' (442). Even the ship on which he has allegedly travelled and which has no pilot has safely brought him to the streets of London, 'Only by Truth steered, as our souls must be' (454). Dismayed at this show of piety, Error cries out: 'What, have my sweet-faced devils forsook me too?' (464). Error forsaken and Truth embraced: the pageant's essential programme for salvation.

Symbolic landscape functions also to represent the pageant's essential battle. The power of Error shrouds London's Triumphant Mount only to have it transformed again by Truth. This alteration occurs several times, suggesting, as Truth herself points out, the necessity of vigilance. Finally, Zeal, 'his head circled with strange fires' (769), seeks permission from Truth to destroy Error's chariot. He cries out: 'Then here's to the destruction of that seat; | There's nothing seen of thee but fire shall eat' (777–8). The text describes what then happens: 'At which a flame shoots from the head of Zeal, which, fastening upon that chariot of Error, sets it on fire, and all the beasts that are joined to it' (779–81). What a spectacular finish to the conflict between Truth and Error. But it is more than spectacle: Error's burned chariot 'being a figure or type of his lordship's justice on all wicked offenders in the time of his government' (789–90).

Sir Thomas Myddelton the mayor must have been justly pleased by the art of Mr Thomas Middleton the poet. From the playwright's pen has come this entertainment that pales only if compared to 'those eternal glories that stand ready for deservers'. The bounty of the Grocers has met its match in Middleton's art, which has produced not 'idle relish' but rather 'bounteous and honourable triumphs'. The glowing ashes of Error's chariot testify to the complete victory of Truth and to the imaginative zeal by which the poet has approached his task: no freezing art here. In 1613 Thomas Middleton helped set the standard by which to judge Lord Mayor's shows.

SEE ALSO

Ziuzin's account: 977
Music: *Companion*, 147
Textual introduction and apparatus: *Companion*, 627
Authorship and date: *Companion*, 375

The Triumphs of Truth

A solemnity unparalleled for cost, art, and magnificence at the confirmation and establishment of that worthy and true nobly-minded gentleman, Sir Thomas Myddelton, Knight, in the honourable office of His Majesty's lieutenant, the Lord Mayor of the thrice-famous City of London.

Taking beginning at his lordship's going and proceeding after his return from receiving the oath of mayoralty at Westminster, on the morrow next after Simon and Jude's day, October 29, 1613.

All the shows, pageants, chariots, morning, noon, and night triumphs.

Directed, written, and redeemed into form, from the ignorance of some former times, and their common writer, by Thomas Middleton.

The Epistle Dedicatory

To the great expectation of virtue and goodness, and most worthy of all those costs and honours which the noble Fellowship and Society of Grocers and general love of the whole City in full-heaped bounties bestow upon him, the truly generous and judicious Sir Thomas Myddelton, Knight, Lord Mayor of the honourable City of London

As often as we shall fix our thoughts upon the Almighty Providence, so often they return to our capacities laden with admiration, either from the divine works of his mercy or those incomprehensible of his justice. But here to instance only his omnipotent mercy, it being the health and preservation of all his works, and first, not only in raising, but also in preserving your lordship from many great and incident dangers, especially in foreign countries in the time of your youth and travels; and now, with safety, love, and triumph, to establish you in this year's honour, crowning the perfection of your days, and the gravity of your life, with power, respect, and reverence. Next, in that myself, though unworthy, being of one name with your lordship, notwithstanding all oppositions of malice, ignorance, and envy, should thus happily live, protected by part of that mercy—as if one fate did prosperously cleave to one name—now to do service to your fame and worthiness, and my pen only to be employed in these bounteous and honourable triumphs, being but shadows to those eternal glories that stand ready for deservers; to which I commend the deserts of your justice, remaining ever,

To your lordship, in the best of my observance,
Thomas Middleton

The Triumphs of Truth

Search all chronicles, histories, records, in what language or letter soever; let the inquisitive man waste the dear treasures of his time and eyesight, he shall conclude his life only in this certainty, that there is no subject upon earth received into the place of his government with the like state and magnificence as is the Lord Mayor of the City of London. This being then infallible, like the mistress of our triumphs, and not to be denied of any, how careful ought those gentlemen to be, to whose discretion and judgement the weight and charge of such a business is entirely referred and committed by the whole society, to have all things correspondent to that generous and noble freeness of cost and liberality; the streams of art to equal those

1 **unparalleled for cost** At a cost of £1300 this is the most expensive Lord Mayor's Show.

4 **Thomas Myddelton** became Mayor of London in October 1613, served until October 1614; had been Sheriff in 1603–4; served as Member of Parliament several different times; admitted to the Grocers company in 1583; died in 1631

10 **Simon and Jude's day** 28 October, the feast day of St Simon and St Jude

30–1 **in foreign countries** a possible reference to the mayor's youth spent in Antwerp

56 **gentlemen** members of the Grocers company

of bounty; a knowledge that may take the true height of such an honourable solemnity; the miserable want of both which, in the impudent common writer, hath often forced from me much pity and sorrow; and it would heartily grieve any understanding spirit to behold many times so glorious a fire in bounty and goodness offering to match itself with freezing art, sitting in darkness, with the candle out, looking like the picture of Black Monday.

But to speak truth, which many beside myself can affirm upon knowledge, a care that hath been seldom equalled and not easily imitated hath been faithfully shown in the whole course of this business, both by the wardens and committees, men of much understanding, industry, and carefulness, little weighing the greatness of expense, so the cost might purchase perfection, so fervent hath been their desire to excel in that, which is a learned and virtuous ambition, and so unfeignedly pure the loves and affections of the whole company to his lordship. If any shall imagine that I set fairer colours upon their deserts than they upon themselves, let them but read and conceive, and their own understandings will light them to the acknowledgement of their errors. First, they may here behold love and bounty opening with the morning, earlier than some of former years, ready at the first appearing of his lordship to give his ear a taste of the day's succeeding glory; and thus the form of it presents itself.

At Soper-Lane end a senate-house erected, upon which musicians sit playing, and more to quicken time, a sweet voice married to these words:

THE SONG

Mother of many honourable sons,
Think not the glass too slowly runs
That in Time's hand is set,
Because thy worthy son appears not yet:
Lady, be pleased, the hour grows on,
Thy joy will be complete anon;
Thou shalt behold
The man enrolled
In honour's books, whom virtue raises;
Love-circled round,
His triumphs crowned
With all good wishes, prayers, and praises.

What greater comfort to a mother's heart,
Than to behold her son's desert
Go hand in hand with love,
Respect, and honour, blessings from above?
It is of power all griefs to kill,
And with a flood of joy to fill
Thy agèd eyes,
To see him rise
With glory decked, where expectation,
Grace, truth, and fame,
Met in his name,
Attends his honour's confirmation.

After this sweet air hath liberally spent itself, at the first appearing of the Lord Mayor from Guildhall in the morning, a trumpet placed upon that scaffold sounds forth his welcome; then, after a strain or two of music, a grave feminine shape presents itself from behind a silk curtain, representing London, attired like a reverend mother, a long white hair naturally flowing on either side of her; on her head a model of steeples and turrets; her habit crimson silk, near to the honourable garment of the city; her left hand holding a key of gold: who, after a comely grace, equally mixed with comfort and reverence, sends from her lips this motherly salutation.

THE SPEECH OF LONDON

Honour and joy salute thee; I am raised
In comfort and in love to see thee, glad
And happy in thy blessings; nor esteem
My words the less 'cause I a woman speak,
A woman's counsel is not always weak.
I am thy mother; at that name I know
Thy heart does reverence to me, as becomes
A son of honour, in whose soul burns clear
The sacred lights of divine fear and knowledge;
I know that at this instant all the works
Of motherly love in me, shown to thy youth,
When it was soft and helpless, are summed up
In thy most grateful mind: thou well rememb'rest
All my dear pains and care; with what affection
I cherish thee in my bosom, watchful still
Over thy ways;
Set wholesome and religious laws before
The footsteps of thy youth; showed thee the way
That led thee to the glory of this day.
To which, with tears of the most fruitful joy
That ever mother shed, I welcome thee.
O, I could be content to take my part
Out of felicity only in weeping,
Thy presence and this day is so dear to me.
Look on my age, my honourable son,
And then begin to think upon thy office;
See how on each side of me hang the cares
Which I bestowed on thee, in silver hairs;
And now the faith, the love, the zealous fires
With which I cheered thy youth, my age requires.
The duty of a mother I have shown,
Through all the rites of pure affectiön,
In care, in government, in wealth, in honour,

68 **Black Monday** Easter Monday. Nineteenth-century editors assumed that Middleton was referring disparagingly to Anthony Munday, but this assumption seems unfounded.

72–3 **wardens and committees** organizational structure of the Grocers company

87 **Soper-Lane** street in London now called Queen Street, running south from Cheapside to Southwark Bridge, so called for the soapmakers who lived there

senate-house a structure resembling a meeting place for a senate

90 THE SONG For the music to this song, see *Companion*, 147.

Mother . . . sons i.e., London

115 **Guildhall** civic hall for the governing bodies of the City of London

Brought thee to what thou art, thou'st all from me;
Then what thou shouldst be I expect from thee.
Now to thy charge, thy government, thy cares,
Thy mother in her age submits her years:
And though—to my abundant grief I speak it,
Which now o'erflows my joy—some sons I have
Thankless, unkind, and disobedient,
Rewarding all my bounties with neglect,
And will of purpose wilfully retire
Themselves from doing grace and service to me,
When they've got all they can, or hope for, from me,
The thankfulness in which thy life doth move
Did ever promise fairer fruits of love,
And now they show themselves; yet they have all
My blessing with them, so the world shall see
'Tis their unkindness, no defect in me.
But go thou forward, my thrice-honoured son,
In ways of goodness; glory is best won
When merit brings it home; disdain all titles
Purchased with coin, of honour take thou hold
By thy desert; let others buy't with gold;
Fix thy most serious thought upon the weight
Thou go'st to undergo, 'tis the just government
Of this famed city, me, whom nations call
Their brightest eye; then with what care and fear
Ought I to be o'erseen, to be kept clear?
Spots in deformèd faces are scarce noted,
Fair cheeks are stained if ne'er so little blotted.
Seest thou this key of gold? It shows thy charge.
This place is the king's chamber; all pollution,
Sin, and uncleanness must be locked out here,
And be kept sweet with sanctity, faith, and fear:
I see grace takes effect: heaven's joy upon her.
'Tis rare when virtue opes the gate to honour.
My blessing be upon thee, son and lord,
And on my sons all that obey my word.

Then making her honour, as before, the waits of the city there in service, his lordship and the worthy company are led forward toward the waterside, where you shall find the river decked in the richest glory to receive him; upon whose crystal bosom stand five islands, artfully garnished with all manner of Indian fruit trees, drugs, spiceries, and the like; the middle island with a fair castle especially beautified.

But making haste to return to the city again, where triumph waits in more splendour and magnificence, the first then that attends to receive his lordship off the water at Baynard's Castle is Truth's Angel on horseback, his raiment of white silk powdered with stars of gold, on his head a crown of gold, a trumpeter before him on horseback, and Zeal, the champion of Truth, in a garment of flame-coloured silk, with a bright hair on his head, from which shoot fire-beams, following close after him, mounted alike, his right hand holding a flaming scourge, intimating thereby that as he is the manifester of Truth, he is likewise the chastiser of Ignorance and Error.

THE SALUTATION OF THE ANGEL

I have within mine eye my blessèd charge:
Hail, friend of Truth; safety and joy attends thee.
I am Truth's Angel, by my mistress sent
To guard and guide thee. When thou took'st thy oath,
I stood on thy right hand, though to thy eye
In visible form I did not then appear;
Ask but thy soul, 'twill tell thee I stood near;
And 'twas a time to take care of thee then,
At such a marriage before heaven and men,
Thy faith being wed to honour; close behind thee
Stood Error's minister that still sought to blind thee,
And wrap his subtle mists about thy oath,
To hide it from the nakedness of troth,
Which is Truth's purest glory; but my light,
Still as it shone, expelled her blackest spite;
His mists fled by, yet all I could devise
Could hardly keep them from some people's eyes,
But thine they flew from: thy care's but begun,
Wake on, the victory is not half yet won;
Thou wilt be still assaulted, thou shalt meet
With many dangers that in voice seem sweet,
And ways most pleasant to a worldling's eye;
My mistress has but one, but that leads high.
To yon triumphant city follow me,
Keep thou to Truth, eternity keeps to thee.

ZEAL

On boldly, man of honour; thou shalt win.
I am Truth's champion, Zeal, the scourge of sin.

The trumpet then sounding, the Angel and Zeal rank themselves just before his lordship and conduct him to Paul's-Chain, where in the south yard Error in a chariot with his infernal ministers attends to assault him, his garment of ash-colour silk, his head rolled in a cloud, over which stands an owl, a mole on one shoulder, a bat on the other, all symbols of blind ignorance and darkness, mists hanging at his eyes. Close before him rides Envy, his champion, eating of a human heart, mounted on a rhinoceros, attired in red silk, suitable to the bloodiness of her manners; her left pap bare, where a snake fastens; her arms half naked, holding in her right hand a dart tincted in blood.

THE GREETING OF ERROR

Art come? O welcome, my triumphant lord,
My glory's sweetheart! how many millions
Of happy wishes hath my love told out

188 ***king's chamber*** the familiar idea that London is the king's special chamber
195 **waits** wind instrumentalists, musicians
200 **Indian** from East India
206 **Baynard's Castle** site of an ancient castle close to where Blackfriars bridge crosses the Thames; stairs led up from the river into the city
227 ***troth*** promise, covenant
244 **Paul's-Chain** a lane running south from the southside of St Paul's Cathedral precinct
254 **tincted** coloured
257 ***told*** counted

For this desirèd minute. I was dead
Till I enjoyed thy presence; I saw nothing,
A blindness thicker than idolatry
Clove to my eyeballs; now I am all of light,
Of fire, of joy, pleasure runs nimbly through me;
Let's join together both in state and triumph,
And down with beggarly and friendless virtue,
That hath so long impoverished this fair city;
My beasts shall trample on her naked breast,
Under my chariot wheels her bones lie pressed,
She ne'er shall rise again. Great power this day
Is given into thy hand; make use on't, lord,
And let thy will and appetite sway the sword;
Down with them all now whom thy heart envies,
Let not thy conscience come into thine eyes
This twelvemonth, if thou lov'st revenge or gain;
I'll teach thee to cast mists to blind the plain
And simple eye of man; he shall not know't,
Nor see thy wrath when 'tis upon his throat;
All shall be carried with such art and wit,
That what thy lust acts shall be counted fit:
Then for attendants that may best observe thee,
I'll pick out sergeants of my band to serve thee;
Here's Gluttony and Sloth, two precious slaves,
Will tell thee more than a whole herd of knaves;
The worth of every office to a hair,
And who bids most, and how the markets are,
Let them alone to smell; and, for a need,
They'll bring thee in bribes for measures and light bread;
Keep thy eye winking and thy hand wide ope,
Then thou shalt know what wealth is, and the scope
Of rich authority; ho, 'tis sweet and dear.
Make use of time then, thou'st but one poor year,
And that will quickly slide, then be not nice:
Both power and profit cleaves to my advice;
And what's he locks his ear from those sweet charms,
Or runs not to meet gain with wide-stretched arms?
There is a poor, thin, threadbare thing called Truth,
I give thee warning of her; if she speak,
Stop both thine ears close; most professions break
That ever dealt with her; an unlucky thing,
She's almost sworn to nothing. I can bring
A thousand of our parish, besides queans,
That ne'er knew what Truth meant, nor ever means.
Some I could cull out here, e'en in this throng,
If I would show my children, and how strong
I were in faction. 'Las, poor simple stray.
She's all her lifetime finding out one way;
Sh'as but one foolish way, straight on, right forward,
And yet she makes a toil on't, and goes on
With care and fear, forsooth, when I can run
Over a hundred with delight and pleasure,
Back-ways and by-ways, and fetch in my treasure
After the wishes of my heart, by shifts,
Deceits, and sleights: and I'll give thee those gifts;
I'll show thee all my corners yet untold,
The very nooks where beldams hide their gold,
In hollow walls and chimneys, where the sun
Never yet shone, nor Truth came ever near:
This of thy life I'll make the golden year;
Follow me then.

ENVY

Learn now to scorn thy inferiors, those most love thee,
And wish to eat their hearts that sit above thee.

Zeal, stirred up with divine indignation at the impudence of these hell-hounds, both forceth their retirement and makes way for the chariot wherein Truth his mistress sits in a close garment of white satin, which makes her appear thin and naked, figuring thereby her simplicity and nearness of heart to those that embrace her; a robe of white silk cast over it, filled with the eyes of eagles, showing her deep insight and height of wisdom; over her thrice-sanctified head a milk-white dove, and on each shoulder one, the sacred emblems of purity, meekness, and innocency; under her feet serpents, in that she treads down all subtlety and fraud; her forehead empaled with a diadem of stars, the witness of her eternal descent; on her breast a pure round crystal, showing the brightness of her thoughts and actions; a sun in her right hand, than which nothing is truer; a fan, filled all with stars, in her left, with which she parts darkness and strikes away the vapours of ignorance. If you hearken to Zeal, her champion, after his holy anger is passed against Error and his crew, he will give it you in better terms, or at least more smoothly and pleasingly.

THE SPEECH OF ZEAL

Bold furies, back, or with this scourge of fire,
Whence sparkles out religious chaste desire,
I'll whip you down to darkness: this a place
Worthy my mistress; her eternal grace
Be the full object to feast all these eyes,
But thine the first; he that feeds here is wise.
Nor by the naked plainness of her weeds
Judge thou her worth, no burnished gloss Truth needs;
That crown of stars shows her descent from heaven;
That robe of white, filled all with eagles' eyes,
Her piercing sight through hidden mysteries;
Those milk-white doves her spotless innocence;
Those serpents at her feet her victory shows
Over deceit and guile, her rankest foes;
And by that crystal mirror at her breast
The clearness of her conscience is expressed;
And showing that her deeds all darkness shun,
Her right hand holds Truth's symbol, the bright sun;
A fan of stars she in the other twists,

286 ***measures*** a vessel of standard capacity for dealing out fixed quantities of grain
291 ***nice*** overly scrupulous or stupid
299 ***sworn to nothing*** i.e., she offers no promises, unlike Error
300 ***queans*** strumpets, harlots
304 ***'Las*** alas
314 ***beldams*** aged women, hags, witches
324 **close garment** close-fitting
344 ***this*** i.e., this is

The King of Moors on a leopard; from a manuscript drawing for Anthony Munday's Lord Mayor's Show for 1616, as reproduced in a nineteenth-century edition of the pageant for the Fishmongers.

With which she chaseth away Error's mists:
And now she makes to thee her so even grace,
For to her rich and poor look with one face.

THE WORDS OF TRUTH

Man, raised by faith and love, upon whose head
Honour sits fresh, let not thy heart be led,
In ignorant ways of insolence and pride,
From her that to this day hath been thy guide;
I never showed thee yet more paths than one,
And thou hast found sufficient that alone
To bring thee hither; then go forward still,
And having most power, first subject thy will;
Give the first fruits of justice to thyself.
Then dost thou wisely govern, though that elf
Of sin and darkness, still opposing me,
Counsels thy appetite to master thee.
But call to mind what brought thee to this day.
Was falsehood, cruelty, or revenge the way?
Thy lust or pleasures? people's curse or hate?
These were no ways could raise thee to this state,
The ignorant must acknowledge; if then from me,
Which no ill dare deny or sin control,
Forsake me not, that can advance thy soul:
I see a blessèd yielding in thy eye;
Thou'rt mine; lead on, thy name shall never die.

These words ended, they all set forward, this chariot of Truth and her celestial handmaids, the Graces and Virtues, taking place next before his lordship; Zeal and the Angel before that, the chariot of Error following as near as it can get; all passing on till they come into Paul's Churchyard, where stand ready the five islands, those dumb glories that I spake of before upon the water: upon the heighth of these five islands sit five persons, representing the Five Senses: *Visus*, *Auditus*, *Tactus*, *Gustus*, *Olfactus*, or Seeing, Hearing, Touching, Tasting, Smelling; at their feet their proper emblems: *aquila*, *cervus*, *araneus*, *simia*, *canis*; an eagle, a hart, a spider, an ape, a dog.

No sooner can your eyes take leave of these, but they may suddenly espy a strange ship making toward, and

386–7 **Graces and Virtues** familiar Renaissance idea of the Three Graces and the four Cardinal Virtues

390 **Paul's Churchyard** churchyard at the east end of St Paul's Cathedral precinct

that which may raise greater astonishment, it having neither sailor nor pilot, only upon a white silk streamer these two words set in letters of gold, *Veritate gubernor*: I am steered by Truth. The persons that are contained within this little vessel are only four: a king of the Moors, his queen, and two attendants of their own colour; the rest of their followers people the castle that stands in the middle island, of which company two or three on the top appears to sight. This king seeming much astonished at the many eyes of such a multitude, utters his thoughts in these words.

THE SPEECH OF THAT KING

I see amazement set upon the faces
Of these white people, wond'rings and strange gazes;
Is it at me? does my complexion draw
So many Christian eyes that never saw
A king so black before? no, now I see
Their entire object, they're all meant to thee,
Grave city-governor, my queen and I
Well honoured with the glances that pass by.
I must confess many wild thoughts may rise,
Opinions, common murmurs, and fixed eyes,
At my so strange arrival in a land
Where true religion and her temples stand.
I being a Moor, then, in opinion's lightness,
As far from sanctity as my face from whiteness;
But I forgive the judgings of th'unwise,
Whose censures ever quicken in their eyes,
Only begot of outward form and show.
And I think meet to let such censurers know,
However darkness dwells upon my face,
Truth in my soul sets up the light of grace;
And though in days of error I did run
To give all adoration to the sun,
The moon, and stars, nay, creatures base and poor,
Now only their Creator I adore.
My queen and people all, at one time won
By the religious conversatïon
Of English merchants, factors, travellers,
Whose truth did with our spirits hold commerce,
As their affairs with us; following their path,
We all were brought to the true Christian faith.
Such benefit in good example dwells,
It oft hath power to convert infidels;
Nor could our desires rest till we were led
Unto this place, where those good spirits were bred;
And see how we arrived in blessèd time
To do that mistress service, in the prime
Of these her spotless triumphs, and t'attend
That honourable man, her late-sworn friend.
If any wonder at the safe arrive
Of this small vessel, which all weathers drive
According to their rages, where appears
Nor mariner nor pilot, armed 'gainst fears,
Know this came hither from man's guidance free,
Only by Truth steered, as our souls must be.
And see where one of her fair temples stands;
Do reverence, Moors, bow low, and kiss your hands:
Behold, our queen.

QUEEN

Her goodnesses are such,
We cannot honour her and her house too much.

All in the ship and those in the castle bowing their bodies to the temple of St Paul; but Error smiling, betwixt scorn and anger to see such a devout humility take hold of that complexion, breaks into these.

ERROR

What, have my sweet-faced devils forsook me too?
Nay, then, my charms will have enough to do.

But Time, sitting by the frame of Truth his daughter's chariot, attired agreeable to his condition, with his hour-glass, wings, and scythe, knowing best himself when it is fittest to speak, goes forward in this manner.

TIME

This Time hath brought t'effect, for on thy day
Nothing but Truth and Virtue shall display
Their virgin ensigns; Infidelity,
Barbarism, and Guile, shall in deep darkness lie.
O, I could ever stand still thus and gaze;
Never turn glass again, wish no more days,
So this might ever last; pity the light
Of this rich glory must be cased in night.
But Time must on; I go; 'tis so decreed,
To bless my daughter Truth and all her seed
With joys immortal, triumphs never-ending.
And as her hand lifts me, to thy ascending
May it be always ready, worthy son,
To hasten which my hours shall quickly run.
Seest thou yon place? thither I'll weekly bring thee, St Paul's Cross
Where Truth's celestial harmony thou shalt hear;
To which I charge thee bend a serious ear.
Lead on, Time's swift attendants.

Then the five islands pass along into Cheapside, the ship next after them; the chariot of Truth still before his lordship, and that of Error still chased before it, where their eyes meet with another more subtle object, planting itself close by the Little Conduit, which may bear this character: the true form and fashion of a mount triumphant, but the beauty and glory thereof overspread with a thick, sulphurous darkness, it being a fog or mist raised from Error, enviously to blemish that place

404 **Moors** Presumably Middleton refers to residents of the East Indies, especially given the Grocers' connection to the East India company.

437 ***factors*** one who buys or sells on behalf of another; also, one of the third class of East India Company's servants (*OED*)

461 **St Paul** St Paul's Cathedral

484.n **St Paul's Cross** located on north side of St Paul's, a platform from which sermons were delivered

488 **Cheapside** chief commercial street in the City of London running east from St Paul's

492 **Little Conduit** water source located in the middle of the roadway of Cheapside

which bears the title of London's Triumphant Mount, the chief grace and lustre of the whole triumph. At the four corners sit four monsters, Error's disciples, on whom hangs part of the mist for their clothing, holding in their hands little thick clubs, coloured like their garments; the names of these four monsters, Barbarism, Ignorance, Impudence, Falsehood; who, at the near approaching of Truth's chariot, are seen a little to tremble, whilst her deity gives life to these words.

TRUTH

What's here? the mist of Error? dare his spite
Stain this Triumphant Mount, where our delight
Hath been divinely fixed so many ages?
Dare darkness now breathe forth her insolent rages,
And hang in pois'nous vapours o'er the place
From whence we received love, and returned grace?
I see if Truth a while but turn her eyes,
Thick are the mists that o'er fair cities rise:
We did expect to receive welcome here
From no deformed shapes, but divine and clear;
Instead of monsters that this place attends,
To meet with goodness and her glorious friends;
Nor can they so forget me to be far.
I know there stands no other envious bar
But that foul cloud to darken this bright day,
Which with this fan of stars I'll chase away.
Vanish, infectious fog, that I may see
This city's grace, that takes her light from me.
Vanish, give way.

At this her powerful command, the cloud suddenly rises and changes into a bright-spreading canopy, stuck thick with stars and beams of gold shooting forth round about it, the mount appearing then most rich in beauty and glory, the four monsters falling flat at the foot of the hill, that grave, feminine shape, figuring London, sitting in greatest honour. Next above her, in the most eminent place, sits Religion, the model of a fair temple on her head and a burning lamp in her hand, the proper emblems of her sanctity, watchfulness, and zeal; on her right hand sits Liberality, her head circled with a wreath of gold, in her hand a cornucopia, or horn of abundance, out of which rusheth a seeming flood of gold, but no way flowing to prodigality; for, as the sea is governed by the moon, so is that wealthy river by her eye, for bounty must be led by judgement; and hence is artfully derived the only difference between prodigality and bounty: the one deals her gifts with open eyes, the other blindfold: on her left side sits Perfect Love, his proper seat being nearest the heart, wearing upon his head a wreath of white and red roses mingled together, the ancient witness of peace, love, and union, wherein consists the happiness of this land, his right hand holding a sphere, where in a circle of gold is contained all the twelve companies' arms, and therefore called the Sphere of True Brotherhood, or *Annulus Amoris*, the Ring of Love. Upon his left hand stand two billing turtles, expressing thereby the happy condition of mutual love and society: on either side of this mount are displayed the charitable and religious works of London—especially the worthy company of Grocers—in giving maintenance to scholars, soldiers, widows, orphans, and the like, where are placed one of each number: and on the two heights sit Knowledge and Modesty, Knowledge wearing a crown of stars, in her hand a perspective glass, betokening both her high judgement and deep insight; the brow of Modesty circled with a wreath all of red roses, expressing her bashfulness and blushings, in her hand a crimson banner filled with silver stars, figuring the white purity of her shamefastness; her cheeks not red with shame or guilt but with virgin fear and honour. At the back of this Triumphant Mount, Chastity, Fame, Simplicity, Meekness, have their seats; Chastity wearing on her head a garland of white roses, in her hand a white silk banner filled with stars of gold, expressing the eternity of her unspotted pureness: Fame next under her, on her head a crown of silver, and a silver trumpet in her hand, showing both her brightness and shrillness: Simplicity with a milk-white dove upon her head; and Meekness with a garland of mingled flowers, in her hand a white silk banner with a red cross, a lamb at her feet, by which both their conditions are sufficiently expressed. The mount thus made glorious by the power of Truth, and the mist expelled, London thus speaks.

LONDON

Thick scales of darkness in a moment's space
Are fell from both mine eyes; I see the face
Of all my friends about me now most clearly,
Religion's sisters, whom I honour dearly.
O, I behold the work; it comes from thee,
Illustrious patroness, thou that mad'st me see
In days of blindest ignorance; when this light
Was e'en extinguished, thou redeem'st my sight.
Then to thy charge, with reverence, I commend
That worthy son of mine, thy virtuous friend,
Whom on my love and blessing I require
To observe thee faithfully, and his desire
To imitate thy will, and there lie bounded;
For power's a dangerous sea, which must be sounded
With truth and justice, or man soon runs on
'Gainst rocks and shelves to dissolutïon.
Then, that thou mayst the difference ever know
'Twixt Truth and Error, a few words shall show:
The many ways that to blind Error slide
Are in the entrance broad, hell-mouth is wide;
But when man enters far, he finds it then
Close, dark, and straight, for hell returns no men:
But the one sacred way which Truth directs,
Only at entrance man's affection checks,

545 **white and red roses** refers to the houses of York and Lancaster

548 **twelve companies'** the twelve principal guilds of London

551 **turtles** turtle doves

558 **perspective glass** optical instrument

And is there strict alone; to which place throngs
All world's afflictions, calumnies, and wrongs.
But having passed those, then thou find'st a way
In breadth whole heaven, in length eternal day;
Then, following Truth, she brings thee to that way:
But first observe what works she here requires,
Religion, knowledge, sanctity, chaste desires;
Then charity, which bounty must express
To scholars, soldiers, widows, fatherless:
These have been still my works, they must be thine;
Honour and action must together shine,
Or the best part's eclipsed: behold but this,
Thy very crest shows bounty, here 'tis put;
Thou giv'st the open hand, keep it not shut,
But to the needy or deserving spirit
Let it spread wide, and heaven enrols that merit.
Do these and prove my hopeful, worthy son;
Yet nothing's spoke but needfully must be done:
And so lead forward.

At which words the whole triumph moves, in his richest glory, toward the Cross in Cheap; at which place Error, full of wrath and malice to see his mist so chased away, falls into this fury.

ERROR

Heart of all the fiends in hell!
Could her beggarly power expel
Such a thick and poisonous mist
Which I set Envy's snakes to twist.
Up, monsters; was her feeble frown
Of force to strike my officers down?
Barbarism, Impudence, Lies, Ignorance,
All your hell-bred heads advance,
And once again with rotten darkness shroud
This Mount Triumphant: drop down, sulphurous cloud.

At which the mist falls again and hangs over all the beauty of the mount, not a person of glory seen, only the four monsters gather courage again and take their seats, advancing their clubs above their heads; which no sooner perceived, but Truth in her chariot, making near to the place, willing still to rescue her friends and servants from the powers of Ignorance and Darkness, makes use of these words.

TRUTH

Dare yet the works of ugliness appear
'Gainst this day's brightness, and see us so near?
How bold is sin and hell, that yet it dare
Rise against us; but know, perdition's heir,
'Tis idle to contend against our power.
Vanish again, foul mist, from honour's bower.

Then the cloud dispersing itself again, and all the mount appearing glorious, it passeth so on to the Standard, about which place, by elaborate action from Error, it falls again, and goes so darkened till it comes to St Lawrence Lane end, where, by the former words by Truth uttered being again chased away, London thus gratefully requites her goodness.

LONDON

Eternity's bright sister, by whose light
Error's infectious works still fly my sight,
Receive thy servant's thanks. Now, Perfect Love,
Whose right hand holds a sphere wherein do move
Twelve blest societies, whose beloved increase
Styles it the ring of brotherhood, faith, and peace,
From thy harmonious lips let them all taste
The golden counsel that makes health long last.

Perfect Love then standing up, holding in his right hand a sphere, on the other, two billing turtles, gives these words.

PERFECT LOVE

First, then, I banish from this feast of joy
All excess, epicurism, both which destroy
The healths of soul and body; no such guest
Ought to be welcome to this reverend feast,
Where Truth is mistress; who's admitted here
Must come for virtue's love more than for cheer.
These two white turtles may example give
How perfect joy and brotherhood should live;
And they from whom grave order is expected,
Of rude excess must never be detected.
This is the counsel which that lady calls
Golden advice, for by it no man falls:
He that desires days healthful, sound, and blest,
Let moderate judgement serve him at his feast.
And so lead on; may perfect brotherhood shine
Still in this sphere, and honour still in thine.

This speech so ended, his lordship and the companies pass on to Guildhall; and at their returning back, these triumphs attend to bring his lordship toward St Paul's church, there to perform those yearly ceremonial rites which ancient and grave order hath determined; Error by the way still busy and in action to draw darkness often upon that Mount of Triumph, which by Truth is as often dispersed. Then all returning homewards full of beauty and brightness, this mount and the chariot of Truth both placed near to the entrance of his lordship's gate near Leadenhall, London, the lady of that mount, first gives utterance to these words.

LONDON

Before the day sprang from the morning's womb
I rose, my care was earlier than the light,
Nor would it rest till I now brought thee home,
Marrying to one joy both thy day and night;

622 **Cross in Cheap** opposite Wood Street in Cheapside
650 **Standard** square pillar in Cheapside, also a water conduit
652 **St Lawrence Lane** narrow street running north from Cheapside, named for the church of St Lawrence Jewry at its north end
667 ***epicurism*** philosophy of pleasure derived from Epicurus
692 **Leadenhall** originally built in the 15th century; by Middleton's time had become a market, located at the intersection of Gracechurch street and Cornhill

Nor can we call this night, if our eyes count
The glorious beams that dance about this mount;
Sure, did not custom guide 'em, men would say
Two noons were seen together in one day,
The splendour is so piercing: Triumph seems
As if it sparkled, and to men's esteems
Threw forth his thanks, wrapped up in golden flames,
As if he would give light to read their names,
That were at cost this day to make him shine,
And be as free in thanks as they in coin.
But see, Time checks me, and his scythe stands ready
To cut all off; no state on earth is steady;
Therefore, grave son, the time that is to come
Bestow on Truth; and so thou'rt welcome home.

Time, standing up in Truth's chariot, seeming to make an offer with his scythe to cut off the glories of the day, growing near now to the season of rest and sleep, his daughter Truth thus meekly stays his hand.

TRUTH
Father, desist a while, till I send forth
A few words to our friend, that man of worth.
The power that heaven, love, and the city's choice,
Have all conferred on thee with mutual voice,
As it is great, reverend, and honourable,
Meet it with equal goodness, strive t'excel
Thy former self; as thy command exceeds
Thy last year's state, so let new acts, old deeds;
And as great men in riches and in birth,
Heightening their bloods and joining earth to earth,
Bestow their best hours and most serious cares
In choosing out fit matches for their heirs,
So never give thou over day or hour,
Till with a virtue thou hast matched this power;
For what is greatness if not joined with grace?
Like one of high blood that hath married base.
Who seeks authority with an ignorant eye,
Is like a man seeks out his enemy;
For where before his follies were not spread,
Or his corruptions, then they're clearly read
E'en by the eyes of all men; 'tis so pure
A crystal of itself, it will endure
No poison of oppression, bribes, hired law,
But 'twill appear soon in some crack or flaw:
Howe'er men soothe their hopes with popular breath,
If not in life, they'll find that crack in death.
I was not made to fawn or stroke sin smooth;
Be wise and hear me, then, that cannot soothe:
I have set thee high now; be so in example,
Made thee a pinnacle in honour's temple,
Fixing ten thousand eyes upon thy brow.
There is no hiding of thy actions now,
They must abide the light and imitate me,
Or be thrown down to fire where errors be.
Nor only with these words thy ear I feed,
But give those part that shall in time succeed,
To thee in present, and to them to come,
That Truth may bring you all with honour home
To these your gates, and to those, after these,
Of which your own good actions keep the keys.
Then, as the loves of thy society
Hath flowed in bounties on this day and thee,
Counting all cost too little for true art,
Doubling rewards there where they found desert,
In thankfulness, justice, and virtuous care,
Perfect their hopes; those thy requitals are.
With fatherly respect embrace 'em all,
Faith in thy heart and plenty in thy hall,
Love in thy walks, but justice in thy state,
Zeal in thy chamber, bounty at thy gate:
And so to thee and these a blessèd night;
To thee, fair City, peace, my grace and light.

Trumpets sounding triumphantly, Zeal, the champion of Truth, on horseback, his head circled with strange fires, appears to his mistress, and thus speaks.

ZEAL
See yonder, lady, Error's chariot stands,
Braving the power of your incensed commands,
Emboldened by the privilege of night
And her black faction; yet to crown his spite,
Which I'll confound, I burn in divine wrath.

TRUTH
Strike, then; I give thee leave to shoot it forth.

ZEAL
Then here's to the destruction of that seat;
There's nothing seen of thee but fire shall eat.

At which a flame shoots from the head of Zeal, which, fastening upon that chariot of Error, sets it on fire, and all the beasts that are joined to it.

The firework being made by master Humphrey Nichols, a man excellent in his art; and the whole work and body of the triumph, with all the proper beauties of the workmanship, most artfully and faithfully performed by John Grinkin; and those furnished with apparel and porters by Anthony Munday, gentleman.

This proud seat of Error lying now only glowing in embers—being a figure or type of his lordship's justice on all wicked offenders in the time of his government—I now conclude, holding it a more learned discretion to cease of myself than to have Time cut me off rudely: and now let him strike at his pleasure.

FINIS.

706–7 ***shine...coin*** a perfect rhyme
761 ***requitals*** recompense or reward
782 **Humphrey Nichols** No other reference to him can be found.
786 **John Grinkin** artificer first involved in a Lord Mayor's Show in 1604; also assisted with pageants in 1609, 1610, 1611, 1618, and 1620
787 **Anthony Munday** (1560–1633) prolific playwright, translator, poet, pamphlet writer, pageant writer, and historian. Wrote the first extant Jacobean Lord Mayor's Show, *The Triumphes of Reunited Britannia* (1605). His frequent association with Middleton gives the lie to the nineteenth-century idea that he and Middleton were angry rivals.

An Account by Aleksei Ziuzin

Text edited by Maija Jansson and Nikolai Rogozhin, and translated by Paul Bushkovitch

And the ambassador [Ziuzin] said to Sir Lewis: 'We hear the royal order that you have for us that your Sovereign King, James, shows his fraternal love and friendship to our Great Sovereign Tsar and Grand Duke Mikhail Fyodorovich, Autocrat of all Russia, to his Tsar's Majesty, that he wants to come to London for us soon. And at this we, seeing fraternal love and strong friendship between them, the Great Sovereigns, rejoice and expect to see the royal eyes. And in so far as your sovereign King James has ordered, showing his favour to us, that you ask about our health and food, we are grateful for his royal favour and until now we are in honour with him, your sovereign, and satisfied about everything. And in so far as Sir Thomas, the son of Thomas Smith, has come to us according to the royal command, and with him the King's gentlemen, and has told us the same thing as the royal order that we now hear from you, that we are to go to see your ceremony according to the royal command, the installation of the Lord Mayor, we have told Sir Thomas that until we have been with your sovereign King James, until we have seen his eyes, it is not possible for us to go to see your ceremony. And we tell you the same thing, Sir Lewis, that to the honour of his royal Majesty we will be with him, your sovereign, and we will see his eyes before [we see] your City and country ceremonies. This is our first business.'

And Sir Lewis said to the ambassadors: 'For your Great Sovereign, his Tsar's Majesty our Sovereign King James, wanting to see his Tsar's fraternal love and friendship to himself, and showing his favour to you, the ambassadors, even though he was not finished with his royal affairs, and leaving them, he is coming to London for you and wants to see you soon and to receive you honourably. And he has ordered you with care that you should see what happens in this state because another such ceremony will not happen while you are here. And you are not to disobey our sovereign nor to anger him, but to go and watch.' And having said this Sir Lewis left the ambassadors.

On October 29th, at the first hour of the day, conductor Sir Thomas, the son of Thomas, and his brother, Sir Richard, and four royal gentlemen and the merchants John Merrick and William Russell, (that William [who] comes to the Moscow state with John) came to the ambassadors at their lodgings. And Sir Thomas and his associates said to the ambassadors: 'So that you might obey the order of our sovereign, King James, and see the royal ceremony, the installation of the Lord Mayor, the royal coaches are with us ready for you, and it is time for you to go. And I am telling you this, taking care of the Sovereign's affairs, so that you should definitely not disobey the royal order and by this anger our sovereign, and so that you should not make any interference in his measures of state.'

And John Merrick said to the ambassadors properly: 'Just as is the case of his direct service to the Great Sovereign, his Tsar's Majesty, I tell you that our sovereign

The newly elected Tsar Michael of Russia, the first of the Romanovs, sought to increase political ties to England and to gain financial assistance. Therefore, he decided to send an ambassador to England in 1613, hoping thereby also to secure his legitimacy in the eyes of other European sovereigns. Ambassador Aleksei Ivanovich Ziuzin left Russia in August 1613, accompanied by another ship of English merchants. They finally reached England after an agonizing two months at sea. They arrived in London on 26 October but did not gain audience with King James until 7 November (he had been hunting at Royston in Hertfordshire). The Ambassador returned to Russia in early summer 1614 and filed this report then. The text comes from *England and the North: The Russian Embassy of 1613–1614*, edited by Maija Jansson and Nikolai Rogozhin, translated by Paul Bushkovitch (Philadelphia: American Philosophical Society, 1994), pp. 161–164.

Sir Thomas Smith explained to the Russian entourage on 28 October what they might expect to see at the Lord Mayor's Show the next day: the mayor 'is to ride from his house to the royal palace and, having been in the palace for a while as the ceremony requires, he is to ride back home through the city on horseback and by water on the river Thames in ships and boats. And there is a great salute from muskets and from all sorts of artillery. And the previous Lord Mayor who sat out his year before him rides with him, and the old Lord Mayors who were judges beforehand. And now those people, knights and aldermen, elected people who will in the future be Lord Mayors, and many other people of various ranks, accompany him; and the whole City watches. And except for the King's coronation there is no other such great ceremony in England' (p. 159).

1 **Sir Lewis** Lewis Lewkenor, first to be appointed to the newly created office of Master of Ceremonies

14 **Sir Thomas** Thomas Smith, member of the Haberdashers and Skinners, governor of the East India Company; had been sent by King James to Boris Godunov in June 1604.

42 **John Merrick** Merchant who had travelled to Russia earlier and sailed back to England in a ship that accompanied the Russian Ambassador's ship; in June 1614 James made Merrick the English Ambassador to Russia.
William Russell Member of the East India Company; in 1612, director of the Company of Merchants of London, also a member of the Muscovy Company. He, too, went to Russia and travelled back to England in 1613.

47 **royal ceremony** As is often the case in the Russian Ambassador's report, there is some confusion about titles and protocol.

King James, the son of Andrew, orders you with care and you should definitely not disobey in this matter.'

And the ambassadors did not dare to disobey the King's orders and, so that they would not by that harm the affairs of his Tsar's Majesty and not anger the King, they went to see their ceremony. And the ambassadors sat in the coaches in the great place and on the sides in the coach with Aleksei Ivanovich [Ziuzin], at the door, sat the conductor, Sir Thomas, and the royal gentlemen, and the merchant John Merrick. And with the Secretary with Aleksei in the coach near the doors sat Sir Richard, and the gentlemen, and the merchant William Russell. And the undersecretary and the translator sat in a separate coach. And the ambassadors' servants also rode in coaches, and when the ambassadors came to the yard and entered the building, at that time there were no people at the yard besides the conductors who came with the ambassadors and a few local servants in the rooms to arrange things. And they placed for the ambassadors fine places, chairs and tables, they honoured the ambassadors. And at the same time the Lord Mayor went up the river Thames to the royal palace and he sat in a ship, and it was a decorated ship, small, painted in all sorts of various colours. And it was rowed by oars. Under the ship were made boats, and on the ship, as is the case with a straight ship, the lower decks had windows and in these windows were rowers on both sides. And with him sat the previous Lord Mayor who had been Lord Mayor for the year before, and other people of rank. And before the ship and behind and on the sides, over the whole river, sailed on many boats, the King's gentlemen, and knights, and aldermen, and merchants, and traders, and the bodyguard of the King's court, and all sorts of people of the land in bright costume. And there were banners and great decorated royal flags and many others. And the King's trumpeters trumpeted, and they beat the drums and they played on litavra and there were all sorts of various instruments. And they fired a great salute from the ship in which the Lord Mayor sailed and from other ships which were there and from big boats and from the City wall. And from all the small boats there was a great shooting of muskets.

And when the Lord Mayor came to the royal palace where the King lives with the Queen and the Prince, at that time there was a great salute at the royal palace. And when the Lord Mayor had been at the palace for a short time he went back through the City riding on stallions and argamaks. And before him walked the bodyguards of the King's court, about one hundred and fifty men in bright clothes with gilded partisans, two by two, and after them walked the merchants and traders organized by livery companies and between them rode the King's trumpeters and drummers in decorated dress on royal horses and trumpeted while riding and played the drums and litavri. And all sorts of players walked and carried big royal banners and flags, bright coloured, wide and long. And after them other men, walking, carried on themselves wooden [models of] towns, worked and painted. And in the [model] towns were churches and on the towers and along the wall were constructed guns, and on the steeples of the churches and on the city ladder sat old and young people and boys and girls in bright dresses. And on them were masks like human faces and like all sorts of animals. And they carried two [model] places from the royal coronation ceremony like a dais, or platform, with high decorated steps on four sides and on the top and on the places sat one person in each place as if from the royal ceremony, and around on all sides, above, and below, sat small girls and boys and here they carried a variety of great beasts: elephants, and unicorns, and lions and camels, and boars, and other animals. And each one was made as if it was real. And there was a small decorated ship and all the people who carried it were draped from all sides to the ground. And around them went people in masks with palms, and they carried palms with fireworks, and they threw from them sparkling fire on both sides because of the great press of people, that they might give way. And before them and behind them went soldiers, and on both sides, turning quickly and waving swords and sabres so that people would get out of the way. And after, rode many of the King's gentlemen and behind them, last before the Lord Mayor, rode the knights who had been Lord Mayors before, in decorated clothing and wearing gold chains.

And with the Lord Mayor rode side by side, at his left hand, the Lord Mayor whom he was replacing, and behind them rode the aldermen, elected people who would be Lord

57 **Andrew** The name 'Henry' was unknown in Russian; the name 'Andrew' became a transliteration for the name Henry.

67 **Secretary** Aleksei Vitovtov

71–2 **the yard** at the palace in Whitehall

77 **Lord Mayor** Thomas Myddelton, Grocer

77–8 **river Thames** the description that follows adds information not available in Middleton's text

83–4 **previous Lord Mayor** Sir John Swinnerton, who had issued an order on 22 October requesting that the livery companies provide members to accompany the aldermen to greet the Russian Ambassador at Tower Wharf upon his arrival into London.

93 **litavra** kettle drums

103 **argamaks** name for Central Asian saddle horse

105 **gilded partisans** long-handled spears used as a leading staff, borne as halberds by civic and other guards (*OED*)

106–27 **walked the merchants... as if it was real** These details find no exact parallel in Middleton's text; the ambassador and his party must be located near the beginning of the procession once it returns to the City. The ambassador captures much of the spectacle as an eyewitness account. Certainly guild records contain expenses for items that do not appear in Middleton's text, such as expenditures for whifflers, staves, torches, javelins, and halberds.

127–8 **small decorated ship** It is possible that this became the ship used for the King of Moors.

130 **palms with fireworks** This is a common technique for moving the crowds so that the procession can pass through. The Grocers' records show a payment to John Grinkin for making a number of the devices and also money for 'greenmen, devils, and fireworks', all presumably used to help control the crowds.

Mayors in the future. And many people, men, women, and children—the whole City—watched this ceremony. And at the ambassadors' windows there were curtains and shutters, and when the Lord Mayor had passed, the ambassadors returned to their lodgings. And the conductors, Sir Thomas, the son of Thomas Smith, with his brother, Sir Richard, and with the royal gentlemen, and with those who were with them at first, and the merchant, John Merrick, accompanied the ambassadors to their lodgings.

WIT AT SEVERAL WEAPONS

Edited by Michael Dobson

Wit at Several Weapons is the first play Middleton co-wrote with William Rowley, and its combination of fluent and inventive comic plotting with incisive and fantastical dialogue makes it abundantly clear that from its inception the partnership brought out the best in both playwrights. Its status as the first fruit of this celebrated collaboration, however, has been obscured for most of four centuries by the circumstances of its publication: the play was not printed until 1647, when it appeared in the Royalist publisher Humphrey Moseley's grand folio volume of plays attributed to Francis Beaumont and John Fletcher, and from then until the late nineteenth century it was read and reprinted as part of the Beaumont and Fletcher canon. Only with the advent of sophisticated and reliable statistical tests for authorship in the later twentieth century (which have decisively confirmed the instincts of several Victorian scholars of the play) has *Wit at Several Weapons* been definitively re-established as the work of Middleton and Rowley.

It is possible that the play was published in the Beaumont and Fletcher folio because Middleton and Rowley were rewriting a play first composed by Fletcher, but if this is the case their revision was so thorough as to relegate this hypothetical Fletcherian first draft to the status of a mere source (the only specific source conjectured or known for the play). Its two central plots, on both of which the two writers worked closely together, are very much in the mode of the city comedy at which Middleton was already supremely accomplished. Both deal with the perilous intersections of family and money, one with an inheritance and the other with a marriage settlement. In the first, the Old Knight, Sir Perfidious Oldcraft—a rich city businessman whose career (by his own proud testimony) has progressed from pimping through the defrauding of orphans to the proposed embezzlement of two-thirds of his niece's dowry—threatens to disinherit his son Wittypate on the grounds that Wittypate must likewise rise in the world by his own 'wit', only to find himself made the next victim of the ruthless catalogue of frauds upon which Wittypate is in fact already embarked. In the interlocking counterpart to this plot, the Old Knight's unnamed Niece, at first jokingly presented by her uncle with the malcontented wit Cunningame by way of 'antemasque' to her real intended husband (his brainless but wealthy patron Sir Gregory Fop), falls in love with the penniless Cunningame, and each camouflages a passion for the other (and tests the seriousness of the other's interest) by flirting successively with a whole progression of bewildered rivals before arranging, with Wittypate's assistance, an elopement from a masque.

Whether these two dramatic situations were invented by Middleton and Rowley or derived from an idea by Fletcher, their elaboration in *Wit at Several Weapons* as it stands bears the unmistakable marks of both Middleton and Rowley at their most characteristic, and its cast list includes some of their most distinctive creations. The impoverished Lady Ruinous Gentry, for example (a rueful and reluctant assistant in Wittypate's Oedipal swindles), granted the bitter self-knowledge of a tragic heroine even while accepting a farcical cross-dressed role in a bogus highway robbery, is sheer Middleton, from our first glimpse of her onwards:

SERVANT
Nay, Lady—
LADY Put me not in mind on't, prithee;
You cannot do a greater wrong to women;
For in our wants 'tis the most chief affliction
To have that name remembered; 'tis a title
That misery mocks us by, and the world's malice.
Scorn and contempt has not wherewith to work
On humble callings: they are safe, and lie
Level with pity still, and pale distress
Is no great stranger to 'em; but when Fortune
Looks with a stormy face on our conditions,
We find affliction work, and envy pastime,
And our worst enemy then, that most abuses us,
Is that we are called by, 'Lady'. [*Exit Servant*]
O my spirit,
Will nothing make thee humble? I am well,
methinks,
And can live quiet with my fate sometimes,
Until I look into the world again ... (2.1.1–16)

Similarly, at the opposite end of the play's social and generic spectrum is a part every bit as characteristic of Rowley: the Clown, 'Pompey Doodle, *a clown, Sir Gregory's man, a piece of puff-paste, like his master*', as the List of Persons added to the play in 1679 aptly describes him. This character is easily recognizable as one of an illustrious succession of fat and fatuous fools written by Rowley for performance by himself—not least by his endearingly imaginative stupidity. Sent into raptures of garbled courtly love when the Niece makes feigned advances to him in order to excite Cunningame's jealousy, the Clown exchanges his servant's livery for the gaudy costume of a gallant, and he spends much of the second half of the play loitering on the northern fringes of London entertaining ever more picturesque delusions of grandeur:

> ...but now you talk of fobbing, I wonder the lady sends not for me, according to promise? I ha' kept out o' town these two days, o' purpose to be sent for; I'm almost starved with walking...Pray, do me the part and office of a gentleman; if you chance to meet a footman by the way, in orange-tawny ribbons, running before an empty coach, with a buzzard i'th' poop on't, direct him and his horses toward the New River by Islington; there they shall have me, looking upon the pipes and whistling. (4.1.345–8, 357–62)

Quite apart from its comedy, the Clown's plaintive and topical interest in the New River water-supply project (shared at some level by much of the play, which abounds in references to the area affected by its construction—Islington, Clerkenwell, St Pancras, Highgate) incidentally provides some of our best evidence for the dating of *Wit at Several Weapons*, which almost certainly belongs to 1613, the year of the New River's completion; Middleton, of course, celebrated this event in *The Manner of his Lordship's Entertainment*, and the Clown's at times disparaging comments may represent a quiet in-joke by Rowley. In any case this dating of the play, coupled with Rowley's likely creation of the role of the Clown in its first production, makes it probable that *Wit at Several Weapons* was originally written for Prince Charles's Men, with whom Rowley was closely associated as player, poet, and manager; the same company would stage Middleton and Rowley's next extant collaboration, *A Fair Quarrel*, some two or three years later.

Beyond this plausible assignation of the play to Prince Charles's Men, however, tantalizingly little is known of its stage history before the closing of the theatres in 1642. It was certainly popular enough to be still in the live repertory some six or seven years after its première, when its title (albeit abbreviated by later damage) appears at the top of a fragmentary list of plays jotted down on scrap paper by the Master of the Revels (a list which also includes two subsequent Middleton and Rowley comedies, *A Fair Quarrel* and *The Old Law*); but whether this note either recorded or resulted in a performance of the play at Court is not known. After this the play vanishes from the written record until its misattributed publication in 1647. It would not be performed again until 1709, when the actor/playwright (and later Poet Laureate) Colley Cibber updated its diction for early eighteenth-century consumption and produced it at Drury Lane under the title *The Rival Fools: or, Wit, at several Weapons*. Largely negligible as a response to the play, this wholly prose adaptation offered few of the attractions of its original save the presence of an actor/writer particularly skilled in 'puff-paste' roles, Cibber himself, in the role of the Clown (here rechristened Samuel Simple, a symptomatic come-down from Rowley's preposterous Pompey Doodle): it ran for five nights in 1709, scraped a bare two when Cibber revived it in 1722, and was last seen abbreviated to an after-piece for a solitary performance at the Haymarket in 1774. Since then, although regularly praised in the nineteenth century as containing some of the most striking passages in the Beaumont and Fletcher canon (featuring extensively, for example, in Horace Guilford's 1834 anthology of *Beauties of Beaumont and Fletcher*), *Wit at Several Weapons* has been generally neglected except by attribution specialists, its theatrical and critical history alike a story of spectacularly missed opportunity.

The kinds of authorship-preoccupied scrutiny to which the play *has* been subjected, however, have revealed much which can enhance an appreciation of its often unsettling comic procedures; in particular, by highlighting the patterns of substitution and redoubling around which Middleton and Rowley built their respective and answering shares of the text. The three most exhaustive and trustworthy authorship studies to date (by Cyrus Hoy, David Lake, and MacDonald P. Jackson) are in full agreement as to which playwright was primarily responsible for which sections of the text, and their conclusions amply support a reading of the play as a virtuouso fantasia on exchange and displacement, with Middleton and Rowley both collaborating and vying with one another to produce ever more comic and extreme variations on the themes of the two plots introduced in its first scene.

The mainsprings of both plots (the father–son conflict between the Old Knight and Wittypate, and the initially triangular love intrigue between the Niece, Cunningame, and Sir Gregory Fop) are wound in Middleton's 1.1, which not only introduces the play's chief lines of intrigue but establishes the characteristic pattern of inventive excess by which both will be elaborated. By the end of 1.1, for example, Middleton has not only set up the play's love triangle but has already begun to extend it, adding a fourth player when Cunningame opens his fraudulent courtship of the Niece's Guardianess. Rowley's 1.2 develops a corresponding variation on the inheritance plot, with Wittypate's outcast wit doubled and redoubled by his accomplice Priscian's impersonation of a starving scholar and their colleague Sir Ruinous Gentry's performance as an impoverished veteran ('what, arms and arts both go a-begging?', exclaims the deceived Old Knight, 1.2.119–20). It finishes with Wittypate electing a scapegoat to undergo his father's displeasure, as the three cheats plan their elaborate mischief against Wittypate's unworldly cousin, the Cambridge cleric Credulous. Middleton's haunting 2.1 furthers these plans, introducing Lady Ruinous Gentry, before Rowley's 2.2 and 2.3 complicate the love-plot to a still greater degree by introducing another suitor for the Niece in Sir Gregory's servant the Clown, and another niece to compete for Cunningame in the person of the Guardianess's ward Mirabell. Once Rowley's 2.4 has dramatized the fake highway robbery in which Wittypate embroils Credulous, Middleton takes over the writing for the whole of the third and fourth acts, where the substitutions and swappings of both plots extend to take in a whole catalogue of objects; false money exchanged for real as the Old Knight is compelled to buy Credulous out of his fictitious arrest, love-tokens exchanged between the Niece and Cunningame using Sir Gregory as an unwitting go-between, and, at the extreme of the process in 4.3, a dressmaker's dummy substituted for Mirabell and courted by Cunningame in a final bid to expose the Niece's jealousy and thus her affection. The writing of Act 5 is principally Rowley's (although it includes many 'composite' passages in which Middleton's participation is visible), and in resolving both plots it pushes their preoccupations still further. In 5.1 parts of two bodies are hilariously interchanged as Sir Gregory's hands undergo a betrothal ceremony with Mirabell from beneath Cunningame's gown, and 5.2 disguises and exchanges practically the entire cast in a masked dance at Lady Ruinous's mansion, from which the Niece and Cunningame elope while the Old Knight is detained to pay a musicians' bill for a hundred pounds from that 'consort of thieves' (5.2.128), Priscian and Sir Ruinous.

From this brilliantly and energetically pursued exercise in high farce, however, a surprisingly dark and disturbing play emerges. With characteristic Middletonian irony, the struggle between the Old Knight and his son proves to have no ethical dimension whatsoever—at its conclusion Wittypate's viciously unfilial extortions are rewarded as evidence of his proper filial loyalty to a merciless economic individualism—and even the play's romance plot functions on the purely predatory rationale expounded in the Old Knight's shocking introductory lecture. Cunningame and the Niece alike manœuvre ruthlessly for the position of cheat and just as ruthlessly nominate others for the position of dupe, their affinity founded on a shared willingness to exploit the emotions of others in their own interests; the discourse of romantic love is in this play reserved for the Clown, a mock-heroic loser who arrives back from the New River for the play's conclusion too late to be paired off with anybody. Such gulls, apparently, exist solely to provide meals for the play's knaves, often in a virtually cannibalistic sense. When Sir Gregory sees Priscian and Sir Ruinous in their roles as overqualified beggars, his first impulse is to eat them so as to acquire their qualities (1.2.137–42), but it is he who is ultimately fed as a lucratively nourishing broth by Cunningame to Mirabell (4.1.194–9); Wittypate practically salivates as he describes to Credulous how naïve university graduates are eaten for breakfast by London wits as if they were poached eggs (4.1.124–36). When not reduced to the status of food, the play's victims are perpetually metamorphosing into other inanimate objects: the Niece's first response to Sir Gregory is to liken him to a puppet (1.1.189), and as far as Cunningame is concerned, as he cynically plans to marry him off to another character who proves interchangeable with a lifeless effigy, both he and Mirabell are so much cast-off millinery (4.1.227), Sir Gregory the offspring of mere fabric:

> Some petticoat begot him, I'll be whipped else,
> Engend'ring with an old pair of paned hose
> Lying in some hot chamber o'er the kitchen;
> Very steam bred him... (4.1.288–91)

With people being taken for clothes and clothes for people on all sides (a dummy turned into a woman by the addition of Mirabell's hat and the Niece's scarf, a false beard creating fictitious identities for Wittypate, Priscian, and Sir Ruinous in turn, a male costume depriving the dispossessed Lady Ruinous even of her Ladyship), *Wit at Several Weapons* depicts a world which for all its comedy can look very alarming indeed, where the distinctions not just between people but between people and their possessions are perpetually under threat, and where the 'wit weapons' of the play's title may materialize, as they do at 5.2.92, as all too literal pistols. While it is true that this sinister side of the play is more often visible in Middleton's predominantly verse scenes than in Rowley's largely prose ones, the overwhelming impression given by the play is of a comedy whose components, however varied, work according to the same symbolic logic. Like much farce, *Wit at Several Weapons* touches not only on the comic results of economic exchange slipping over into affective relations but on the blind, remorseless solipsism of desire itself (as in the beautiful serenade at the centre of the play, 3.1.46–60, praising the superiority of erotic dreams to any waking reality), and the play's culminating dramatic image, appropriately, in the substantially composite 5.2, is the change of partners at a masked ball, danced in the house of a ruined lady to the music of a consort of thieves.

SEE ALSO

Music and dance: *Companion*, 148
Textual introduction and apparatus: *Companion*, 1062
Authorship and date: *Companion*, 375
The Manner of his Lordship's Entertainment, 959
Other Middleton–Rowley works: *Quarrel*, 1209; *Old Law*, 1331; *Tennis*, 1405; *Changeling*, 1632; *Gypsy*, 1723

WILLIAM ROWLEY and THOMAS MIDDLETON

Wit at Several Weapons

[*for Prince Charles's Men*]

THE PERSONS REPRESENTED IN THE PLAY

Sir Perfidious Oldcraft, an OLD KNIGHT, a great admirer of wit
WITTYPATE Oldcraft, his father's own son
SIR GREGORY Fop, a witless lord of land
CUNNINGAME, a discreet gentleman, Sir Gregory's comrade and supplanter
SIR RUINOUS Gentry, a decayed knight
PRISCIAN, a poor scholar. two sharking companions
Pompey Doodle, a CLOWN, Sir Gregory's man, a piece of puff-paste, like his master
Mr CREDULOUS, nephew to Sir Perfidious, a shallow-brained scholar
BOY, a singer
SERVANT to Sir and Lady Ruinous Gentry
SERVANT to Sir Perfidious Oldcraft
Two SERVANTS at a tavern

NIECE to Sir Perfidious, a rich and witty heir
LADY Ruinous, wife to Sir Ruinous
GUARDIANESS to Sir Perfidious's Niece, an old doting crone
MIRABELL, the Guardianess's niece

1.1 *Enter Sir Perfidious Oldcraft, an old knight, and Wittypate, his son*

WITTYPATE
Sir, I'm no boy, I'm deep in one-and-twenty,
The second year's approaching.
OLD KNIGHT A fine time
For a youth to live by his wits, then, I should think,
If e'er he mean to make account of any.
WITTYPATE Wits, sir?
OLD KNIGHT
Ay, wits, sir; if it be so strange to thee,
I'm sorry I spent that time to get a fool,
I might have employed my pains a great deal better.
Thou know'st all that I have I ha' got by my wits,
And yet to see how urgent thou art too;
It grieves me thou art so degenerate
To trouble me for means; I never offered it
My parents from a schoolboy; past nineteen once
(See what these times are grown to!), before twenty
I rushed into the world, which is indeed
Much like the art of swimming; he that will attain to't
Must fall plump, and duck himself at first,
And that will make him hardy and adventurous,
And not stand putting in one foot, and shiver,
And then draw t'other after, like a quake-buttock;
Well he may make a paddler i' the world,
From hand to mouth, but never a brave swimmer,
Borne up by th' chin, as I bore up myself
With my strong industry that never failed me;
For he that lies borne up with patrimonies
Looks like a long great ass that swims with bladders:
Come but one prick of adverse fortune to him
He sinks, because he never tried to swim,
When wit plays with the billows that choked him.
WITTYPATE
Why, is it not a fashion for a father, sir,
Out of his yearly thousands to allow
His only son a competent brace of hundreds,
Or such a toy?
OLD KNIGHT Yes, if he mean to spoil him
Or mar his wits he may, but never I.
This is my humour, sir, which you'll find constant;
I love wit so well, because I lived by't,
That I'll give no man power out of my means to hurt it,
And that's a kind of gratitude to my raiser,

1.1 composed primarily by Middleton
2 **second year's** of Wittypate's majority
7 **get** beget
10 **urgent** insistent
17 **plump** 'with a sudden drop or fall into the water' (*OED*)
20 **quake-buttock** coward
26 **bladders** inflated animal bladders used as aids to buoyancy
29 **When . . . him** while those who have wit sport on the waves that overwhelmed him
32 **competent** possibly used in the obsolete sense of 'no more than adequate'

Which great ones oft forget. I admire much
This age's dullness. When I scarce writ man,
The first degree that e'er I took in thriving,
I lay intelligencer close for wenching,
Could give this lord or knight a true certificate
Of all the maidenheads extant; how many lay
'Mongst chambermaids, how many 'mongst Exchange wenches
(Though never many there, I must confess,
They have a trick to utter ware so fast);
I knew which lady had a mind to fall,
Which gentlewoman new divorced, which tradesman breaking,
The price of every sinner to a hair,
And where to raise each price; which were the termers
That would give velvet petticoats, tissue gowns,
Which pieces, angels, suppers, and half-crowns:
I knew how to match and make my market,
Could give intelligence where the pox lay ledger,
And then to see the lechers shift a point,
'Twas sport and profit too; how they would shun
Their adored mistress' chambers, and run fearfully
Like rats from burning houses! So brought I
My clients o' the game still safe together,
And noble gamesters loved me, and I felt it:
Give me a man that lives by his wits, say I,
And never left a groat, there's the true gallant.
When I grew somewhat pursy, I grew then
In men's opinions too, and confidences;
They put things called executorships upon me,
The charge of orphans, little senseless creatures,
Whom in their childhoods I bound forth to feltmakers,
To make 'em lose and work away their gentry,
Disguise their tender natures with hard custom,
So wrought 'em out in time: there I risse ungently;
Nor do I fear to discourse this unto thee,
I'm armed at all points against treachery.
I hold my humour firm; if I can see thee thrive by thy wits while I live, I shall have the more courage to trust thee with my lands when I die; if not, the next best wit I can hear of carries 'em: for since in my time and knowledge so many rich children of the City conclude in beggary, I'd rather make a wise stranger my executor than a foolish son my heir, and to have my lands called after my wit, thou after my name; and that's my nature.

WITTYPATE [*aside*]
'Tis a strange harsh one; must I still shift then?
I come, brave cheats, once to my trade again,
And I'll ply't harder now than e'er I did for't—
You'll part with nothing then, sir?

OLD KNIGHT
Not a jot, sir.

WITTYPATE
If I should ask you blessing ere I go, sir,
I think you would not give't me.

OLD KNIGHT
Let me but hear thou liv'st by thy wits once,
Thou shalt have anything; thou'rt none of mine else,
Then why should I take care for thee?

WITTYPATE
Thank your bounty.
Exit

OLD KNIGHT
So wealth love me, and long life, I beseech it,
As I do love the man that lives by his wits,
He comes so near my nature. I'm grown old now,
And e'en arrived at my last cheat, I fear me,
But 'twill make shift to bury me, by daylight too,
And discharge all my legacies, 'tis so wealthy,
And never trouble any interest money.
I've yet a niece to wed, over whose steps
I have placed a trusty watchful guardianess
For fear some poor earl steal her ('t has been threatened)
To redeem mortgaged land, but he shall miss on't;
To prevent which, I have sought out a match for her;
Fop of Fop Hall he writes himself (I take it,
The ancient'st Fop in England), with whom I'm privately
Compounded for the third part of her portion.
Enter Sir Gregory and Cunningame
An she seems pleased, so—two parts rest with me.
He's come.—Sir Gregory, welcome; what's he, sir?

SIR GREGORY
Young Cunningame, a Norfolk gentleman,

45 **Exchange wenches** shopgirls employed in the boutiques of the Royal Exchange, the bourse at Cornhill in the City
47 **utter** sell
49 **breaking** going bankrupt
51 **termers** visitors in London to transact legal affairs (during the four law terms, when the courts were in session)
52 **tissue** the most expensive and prestigious dress fabric then available
53 **pieces** gold coins worth £1
angels coins, first minted in 1465, worth around ten shillings each in 1613
55 **lay ledger** was in residence or conducting a siege
56 **shift a point** A point was a lace used for attaching the codpiece, and the doublet, to the hose: hence 'to truss one's points' was the Jacobean equivalent of 'to do up one's flies'. 'Point', however, could also mean the tip of the penis, so this phrase might best be paraphrased as 'get their codpieces out of there'.
63 **groat** silver coin worth fourpence
64 **pursy** wealthy (having a full purse), with a secondary sense of 'plump'
68 **bound forth** apprenticed
71 **risse** rose
82 **shift** make do with living by tricks
95 **make shift** manage
by daylight Although nocturnal funerals were becoming fashionable in the 1610s, the practice was still chiefly associated with paupers and lazars.
97 **interest money** capital the Old Knight has loaned out at interest as a usurer (a practice regarded as sinful and unclean)
104–5 **with whom . . . portion** with whom I have privately negotiated to pay only a third of her dowry
105.1 ***Cunningame*** The name of the character described by the cast list as '*a discreet gentleman, Sir Gregory's comrade and supplanter*' obviously puns on 'cunning game', but it is worth noting that this was a perfectly ordinary contemporary spelling of the surname now rendered as 'Cunningham'.
106 **An** If

One that has lived upon the Fops, my kindred,
Ever since my remembrance; he's a wit indeed,
And we all strive to have him—nay, 'tis certain
Some of our name has gone to law for him;
Now 'tis my turn to keep him, and indeed
He's plaguy chargeable, as all your wits are,
But I will give him over when I list,
I ha' used wits so before.

OLD KNIGHT I hope when you're married, sir, you'll shake him off.

SIR GREGORY Why, what do you take me to be, old father-i'-law that shall be? Do you think I'll have any of the wits hang upon me after I am married once? None of my kindred ever had before me. But where's this niece? Is't a fashion in London to marry a woman and never see her?

OLD KNIGHT
Excuse the niceness, sir; that care's your friend;
Perhaps had she been seen, you had never seen her;
There's many a spent thing called 'An't like your honour'
That lies in wait for her; at first snap, she's a countess,
Drawn with six mares through Fleet Street, and a coachman
Sitting bare-headed to their Flanders buttocks.
[*Aside*] This whets him on.

SIR GREGORY Pray, let's clap up the business, sir.
I long to see her; are you sure you have her?
Is she not there already? Hark, O hark!

OLD KNIGHT
How now, what's that, sir?

SIR GREGORY Every caroach goes by
Goes e'en to th' heart of me.

OLD KNIGHT I'll have that doubt eased, sir,
Instantly eased, Sir Gregory: and now I think on't,
A toy comes i' my mind, seeing your friend there;
We'll have a little sport, give you but way to't,
And put a trick upon her. I love wit preciously!
You shall not be seen yet: we'll stale your friend first,
If't please but him to stand for the antemasque.

SIR GREGORY
Puh, he shall stand for anything: why, his supper
Lies i' my breeches here; I'll make him fast else.

OLD KNIGHT
Then come you forth more unexpectedly,
The masque itself, a thousand-a-year jointure:
The cloud, your friend, will be then drawn away,
And only you the beauty of the play.

SIR GREGORY
For red and black I'll put down all your fullers;
Let but your niece bring white, and we have three colours.

Exit

OLD KNIGHT
I'm given to understand you are a wit, sir.

CUNNINGAME
I'm one that fortune shows small favour to, sir.

OLD KNIGHT
Why, there you conclude it, whether you will or no, sir;
To tell you truth, I'm taken with a wit.

CUNNINGAME
Fowlers catch woodcocks so; let not them know so much.

OLD KNIGHT [*aside*]
A pestilence mazzard, a Duke Humphrey spark,
He'd rather lose his dinner than his jest—
I say, I love a wit the best of all things.

114 **chargeable** expensive, with a pun on legal charge, referring back to l. 112

119–20 **father-i'-law** used loosely but appropriately, since the Old Knight exercises paternal control over the Niece as her legal guardian

120–2 **Do you think . . . before me**. Literally Sir Gregory is assuring the Old Knight that, like other members of his family before him, he will not support 'wits' such as Cunningame as members of his household after his marriage, but his words carry a punning sense of which he is unaware, namely that he, in the traditional manner of Fops, will be witless as a husband.

127 **spent** ruined, bankrupt
'An't like your honour' if it pleases your honour, a phrase regarded as characteristic of the flattery given to aristocrats by their servants

129 **six mares** a coach and six would of course have been an ostentatious luxury, appropriate to a newly-ennobled bride
Fleet Street the chief thoroughfare from the mercantile City to the socially superior West End

130 **Flanders** at the time celebrated for its expensive horses

134 **caroach** carriage, luxury coach for urban use

137 **toy** fancy, whim

140 **stale** use as a lure or decoy

141 **antemasque** grotesque, burlesque interlude to precede and set off the main action of a Court masque

143 **i' my breeches** i.e. in my pocket

145 **jointure** marriage arrangement by which property would be held for the joint use of husband and wife for life (and generally entailed for the wife in the event of widowhood)

146 **cloud . . . away** divine revelations from behind mechanical clouds were a commonplace motif in contemporary masques

148–9 **For . . . colours** 'an obscure passage . . . Perhaps Sir Gregory is . . . dressed in a red and black suit of clothes. The white probably symbolizes sexual purity . . . Perhaps too some reference back to masques, or some specific masque drawing its effect from the striking use of colours, is intended' (Sharp)

148 **fullers** workers in the textile industry who beat or trod cloth so as to clean or thicken it

153 **taken with** (*a*) fond of (as the Old Knight intends) (*b*) duped by (as Cunningame punningly takes it)

155 **A pestilence mazzard** a plaguy head, i.e. this man's brain is a nuisance
Duke Humphrey spark Humphrey, Duke of Gloucester was mistakenly believed to be buried in the promenade of St Paul's, known as Duke Humphrey's Walk, where penurious gallants and wits ('sparks') would take shelter and loiter while their more fortunate fellow-citizens dined: hence the phrase 'to dine with Duke Humphrey', to which the Old Knight alludes, meaning to go hungry. Oldcraft thus labels Cunningame as penniless, a wit and a malcontent.

CUNNINGAME
Always except yourself.
OLD KNIGHT [*aside*] He's gi'n't me twice now,
All with a breath, I thank him! But that I love a wit
I should be heartily angry.
Enter Niece and Guardianess
Cuds, my niece!—
You know the business with her?
CUNNINGAME With a woman?
'Tis e'en the very same it was, I'm sure,
Five thousand years ago; no fool can miss it.
OLD KNIGHT
This is the gentleman I promised, niece,
To present to your affection.
CUNNINGAME [*aside*] 'Ware that arrow!
OLD KNIGHT
Deliver me the truth now of your liking.
CUNNINGAME [*aside*]
I'm spoiled already; that such poor lean game
Should be found out as I am!
OLD KNIGHT Go, set to her, sir. [*Aside*] Ha, ha, ha!
CUNNINGAME
How noble is this virtue in you, lady;
Your eye may seem to commit thousand slaughters
On your dull servants, which, truly tasted,
Conclude all in comforts.
OLD KNIGHT [*aside*] Puh.
NIECE
It rather shows what a true worth can make,
Such as yours is.
OLD KNIGHT [*aside*]
And that's not worth a groat.—
How like you him, niece?
NIECE It shall appear how well, sir.
I humbly thank you for him. [*Kisses Cunningame*]
OLD KNIGHT [*aside*]
Ha? ha, good gullery! he does it well, i'faith;
'Light, as if he meant to purchase lip-land there.—
Hold, hold! Bear off, I say! 'Slid, your part hangs too long.
CUNNINGAME [*aside*] My joys are mockeries.
NIECE
You've both expressed a worthy care and love, sir:
Had mine own eye been set at liberty
To make a public choice (believe my truth, sir),
It could not ha' done better for my heart
Than your good providence has.
OLD KNIGHT You will say so, then?
Alas, sweet niece, all this is but the scabbard;
Now I draw forth the weapon.
NIECE How?
OLD KNIGHT Sir Gregory,
Approach, thou lad of thousands!
Enter Sir Gregory
SIR GREGORY Who calls me?
NIECE [*aside*]
What motion's this? the model of Nineveh?
OLD KNIGHT
Accost her daintily now, let me advise thee.
SIR GREGORY
I was advised to bestow dainty cost on you.
NIECE
You were ill advised; back, and take better counsel.
You may have good for an angel: the least cost
You can bestow upon a woman, sir,
Trebles ten counsellors' fees; in lady-ware
You're over head and ears ere you be aware.
Faith, keep a bachelor still, and go to bowls, sir,
Follow your mistress there, and prick and save, sir,
For other mistresses will make you a slave, sir.

158 **He's gi'n't** He has given it
160 **Cuds** one of Middleton's favourite exclamations, a contraction of 'God save me'
165 **'Ware** beware of. 'Cunningame might refer here to Cupid's arrow, but his next two speeches take up the idea of the Niece's gaze shooting down her suitors. Presumably, then, the arrow darts from the Niece's eye rather than from Eros's bow' (Sharp)
167 **poor lean game** referring both to his defencelessness against the Niece's attractions and his position of impoverished powerlessness in relation to the Old Knight and Sir Gregory, of whose practical joke he has already become a victim (with a pun on his name)
169–72 **How... comforts** 'The Niece is more willing to be approached than her initial glare might indicate' (Sharp). The 'virtue' on which Cunningame remarks might equally be a friendly approach towards him by the Niece
173–4 **It... yours is** this behaviour simply reflects my sense of your genuine merits
178 **'Light** a mild oath (God's light)
lip-land playing on 'Lapland'
179 **'Slid** another mild oath (God's lid)
your part hangs too long you are taking your role too far (with a pun on sexual excitement)
188 **lad of thousands** (*a*) lad out of thousands (compare 'one in a million') (*b*) lad worth thousands of pounds
189 **motion's** puppet's (perhaps also with the sense of 'proposal')
the model of Nineveh a popular fairground puppet-show telling the story of Jonah and the whale, mentioned by Jonson in *Every Man out of His Humour* (1599) and *Bartholomew Fair* (1615); generically, a bathetic contrast to the masque in which Sir Gregory imagines himself to be starring. The Niece may cite this puppet-play in particular for the sake of the pun on 'ninny'
190–1 **Accost... on you** Sir Gregory fails to understand the word 'accost'; compare Shakespeare's Sir Andrew Aguecheek, *Twelfth Night*, 1.3.46–56
193–6 **You... aware** You might just be worth an angel (ten shillings), but the least amount you would have to give a woman [in order to compensate her for your personal deficiencies] would be the equivalent of thirty lawyers' fees; you are already head over heels in debt when it comes to the things desired by women before you even know it.
198 **mistress... save** The mistress is the small white ball at which bowls are aimed (the modern 'jack'); 'prick' and 'save' are also terms from bowls, meaning to deflect and to block. Middleton puns on the same three terms in *No Wit/Help like a Woman's*, 6.82–3.

SIR GREGORY
So, so, I have my liripoop already.
OLD KNIGHT
Why, how now, niece? This is the man, I tell you.
NIECE
He? Hang him, sir! I know you do but mock;
This is the man, you would say.
OLD KNIGHT [*aside*]
The devil rides, I think.
CUNNINGAME [*aside*] I must use cunning here.
OLD KNIGHT
Make me not mad; use him with all respect;
This is the man, I swear.
NIECE [*aside*] Would you could persuade me to that!—
Alas, you cannot go beyond me, Uncle!
You carry a jest well, I must confess,
For a man of your years, but—
OLD KNIGHT I'm wrought beside myself.
CUNNINGAME [*to the Guardianess*]
I never beheld comeliness till this minute.
GUARDIANESS
O good sweet sir, pray, offer not these words
To an old gentlewoman.
NIECE Sir!
CUNNINGAME Away, fifteen!
Here's fifty-one exceeds thee.
NIECE What's the business?
CUNNINGAME
Give me these motherly creatures! Come, ne'er smother it;
I know you are a teeming woman yet.
GUARDIANESS
Troth, a young gentleman might do much, I think, sir,
CUNNINGAME Go to, then!
GUARDIANESS
And I should play my part, or I were ingrateful.
NIECE
Can you so soon neglect me?
CUNNINGAME Hence, I'm busy.
OLD KNIGHT [*aside*]
This cross point came in luckily.—Impudent baggage,
Hang from the gentleman; art thou not ashamed
To be a widow's hindrance?
CUNNINGAME Are you angry, sir?
OLD KNIGHT
You're welcome; pray, court on. I shall desire
Your honest wise acquaintance. [*To Niece*] Vex me not,
After my care and pains to find a match for thee,
Lest I confine thy life to some out-chamber,
Where thou shalt waste the sweetness of thy youth
Like a consuming light in her own socket,
And not allowed a male creature about thee;
A very monkey thy necessity
Shall prize at a thousand pound, a chimney-sweeper
At fifteen hundred.
NIECE But are you serious, uncle?
OLD KNIGHT
Serious.
NIECE
Pray, let me look upon the gentleman
With more heed; then I did but hum him over,
In haste, good faith, as lawyers chancery sheets;
Beshrew my blood, a tolerable man,
Now I distinctly read him.
SIR GREGORY [*hums*] Hum, hum, hum.
NIECE
Say he be black, he's of a very good pitch;
Well ankled; two good confident calves; they look
As if they would not shrink at the ninth child;
The redness i'th' face, why, that's in fashion,
Most of your high bloods have it, sign of greatness, marry;
'Tis to be taken down, too, with May butter,
I'll send to my lady Spend-tail for her medicine.
SIR GREGORY [*hums*]
Lum te dum, dum, dum, de dum.
NIECE
He's qualified too, believe me.
SIR GREGORY
Lum te dum, de dum, de dum.
NIECE
Where was my judgement?
SIR GREGORY
Lum te dum, dum, dum, te dum, te dum.

200 **liripoop** lesson or part to be learned by heart; Sir Gregory has both received his sermon and been assigned his role
204 **The devil rides** from the proverb 'the devil rides upon a fiddlestick', meaning 'here's a fine commotion'
215 **teeming** fertile
220 **cross point** dance step in the contrary direction
226 **out-chamber** outhouse (away from all the other members of the household)
228 **socket** of a candlestick
235 **hum him over** glance quickly and superficially over him
236 **chancery sheets** briefs for the Lord Chancellor's court
239 **pitch** punningly suggesting Sir Gregory has an unappealingly pitch-dark complexion while ostensibly praising his height or build
240 **two...calves** 'From Cunningame's later remarks at 3.1.285–7 which cite Sir Gregory as an example of "thin gentlemen" with "small trapstick legs" it would seem that the Niece's flattery is heavily ironic' (Sharp)
243 **high bloods** (*a*) those of aristocratic birth (*b*) those exhibiting sexual arousal
244 **May butter** Sharp quotes the 1637 edition of Gervase Markham's *English Housewife*, 199: 'If during the month of May before you salt your butter you save a lump thereof, and put it into a vessel, and so set it into the sun the space of that month, you shall find it exceeding sovereign and medicinable for wounds, strains, aches and suchlike grievances'
245 **Spend-tail** the name implies promiscuity, following on from the sexual innuendo of 'high bloods' being 'taken down'

NIECE
Perfection's covered mess!

SIR GREGORY
Lum te dum, te dum, te dum.

NIECE [*aside*]
It smokes apparently.—Pardon, sweet sir,
The error of my sex.

OLD KNIGHT
Why, well said, niece.
Upon submission, you must pardon her now, sir.

SIR GREGORY
I'll do't by course; do you think I'm an ass, knight?
Here's first my hand; now't goes to the seal office.
[*Kisses her*].

OLD KNIGHT
Formally finished. [*To Cunningame and Guardianess*]
How goes this suit forward?

CUNNINGAME
I'm taking measure of the widow's mind, sir;
I hope to fit her heart.

GUARDIANESS
Who would have dreamt
Of a young morsel now? Things come in minutes.

SIR GREGORY
Trust him not, widow, he's a younger brother,
He'll swear and lie; believe me, he's worth nothing.

GUARDIANESS
He brings more content to a woman with that noth-ing
Than he that brings his thousands without any thing,
We have precedents for that amongst great ladies.

OLD KNIGHT
Come, come; no language now shall be in fashion
But your love-phrase, the bell to procreation. *Exeunt*

Enter Sir Ruinous, Wittypate, and Priscian, [sharing out money] 1.2

WITTYPATE Pox, there's nothing puts me besides my wits, but this fourth, this lay illiterate share, there's no conscience in't.

SIR RUINOUS Sir, it has ever been so where I have practised, and must be still where I am; nor has it been undeserved at the year's end, and shuffle the almanac together, vacations and term-times one with another—though I say't, my wife is a woman of a good spirit—then it is no lay share.

PRISCIAN Faith, for this five year, *ego possum probare*, I have had a hungry penurious share with 'em, and she has had as much as I always.

WITTYPATE Present or not present?

PRISCIAN *Residens aut non residens, per fidem.*

WITTYPATE And what precedent's this for me? Because your *hic et haec turpis* and *qui mihi discipulus* brains (that never got anything but by accidence and uncertainty) did allow it, therefore I must, that have grounded conclusions of wit, hereditary rules from my father to get by?

SIR RUINOUS Sir, be compendious; either take or refuse; I will bate no token of my wife's share: make even the last reckonings, and either so unite or here divide company.

PRISCIAN A good resolution, *profecto*: let every man beg his own way, and happy man be his dole.

251 **Perfection's covered mess** a covered mess was a 'made dish' served under a cover as one of the high points of a feast, hence the phrase means something like 'a delicious masterpiece'

253 **It smokes apparently** my deception is obviously working

259–60 **I'm . . . heart** punning on the Old Knight's use of the term 'suit'

265 **thing** with a sexual quibble

268 **bell** perhaps with the additional sense of 'mating call', as used of stags

1.2 Composed primarily by Rowley

0.1 ***Sir Ruinous . . . Priscian*** Sir Ruinous and Priscian are described as '*two sharking companions*' by the cast list, i.e. predatory rogues, cony-catchers. Priscian is named after the author (*fl. c.*AD 500) of the important Latin grammar *Institiones Gramaticae*, probably via the phrase 'to break Priscian's head', meaning 'to use incorrect Latin'.

2 **fourth** Sir Ruinous insists that the proceeds of the trio's previous exploit be split four ways, one share going to Lady Ruinous even though she did not participate in it.

lay non-practising

illiterate i.e. ignorant, non-speaking (and thus unearned)

6–7 **shuffle . . . another** i.e. average out the takings over the whole year to accommodate both the vacations and the (more lucrative) law terms (when London was full of wealthy litigants)

10 ***ego possum probare*** I can witness or demonstrate

14 ***Residens . . . fidem*** Present or absent, by my faith

15 **precedent's** playing on the sound of '*residens*'

16 ***hic . . . discipulus*** approximately, 'this dishonest male and female' (referring to Sir Ruinous) and 'who to me would be a pupil' (referring to the pedantic Priscian): both phrases derive from the standard Latin primer used by Renaissance schoolboys, William Lilly and John Colet's *A Short Introduction of Grammar* (1549), which gives 'Hic & Haec Parens' as its first example of the two genders, and concludes with a poem, '*Ad suos discipulos*' ('To his students'), the first words of which are '*Qui mihi discipulus*'

17 **accidence** the aspect of Latin grammar concerned with inflexions, here used as a pun on 'accidents'

18 **grounded** securely based

19 **conclusions** Wittypate is again playing with the terminology of Latin grammar, choosing the word 'conclusions' because of its linguistic sense of 'word endings, inflexions': he uses the word 'rules' similarly later in the sentence

20 **get** i.e. obtain money

21 **be compendious** be brief, i.e. come to the point

22 **bate** deduct

22–3 **make even the last reckonings** (let's) settle up our outstanding accounts (on that basis, i.e. with a whole quarter share for Lady Ruinous)

25 ***profecto*** indeed

26 **happy man be his dole** proverbial phrase meaning, approximately, 'the best of luck to the winner'

WITTYPATE Well, here's your double share and single brains. [*Giving money to Sir Ruinous*] *Pol, aedepol*, here's toward a *castor, ecastor* for you. [*Giving money to Priscian*] I will endure it a fortnight longer, but by these just five ends—

PRISCIAN Take heed, five's odd; put both hands together, or severally they are all odd unjust ends.

WITTYPATE *Medius fidius*, hold your tongue! I depose you from half a share presently else; I will make you a participle, and decline you; now you understand me: be you a quiet conjunction amongst the undeclined; you and your Latin ends shall go shift, *solus cum solo* together, else; and then if ever they get ends of gold and silver enough to serve that gerundine maw of yours, that without *do* will end in *di* and *dum* instantly—

Enter Old Knight and Sir Gregory

SIR RUINOUS Enough, enough, here comes company; we lose five shares in wrangling about one.

WITTYPATE My father! Put on, Priscian. He has Latin fragments too, but I fear him not. I'll case my face with a little more hair, and relieve. [*Retires, and puts on a false beard*]

OLD KNIGHT
Tush, nephew! I'll call you so, for if there be
No other obstacles than those you speak of,
They are but powder charges without pellets;
You may safely front 'em, and warrant your own danger.

SIR GREGORY No other that I can perceive, i'faith, sir, for I put her to't, and felt her as far as I could, and the strongest repulse was, she said she would have a little soldier in me, that, if need were, I should defend her reputation.

OLD KNIGHT
And surely, sir, that is a principle
Amongst your principal ladies: they require
Valour either in a friend or a husband.

SIR GREGORY And I allow their requests, i'faith, as well as any woman's heart can desire: if I knew where to get valour, I would as willingly entertain it as any man that blows.

OLD KNIGHT 'Breathes', 'breathes', sir; that's the sweeter phrase.

SIR GREGORY 'Blows' for a soldier, i'faith, sir; and I'm in practice that way.

OLD KNIGHT For a soldier, I grant it.

SIR GREGORY 'Slid, I'll swallow some bullets, and good round ones too, but I'll have a little soldier in me.

SIR RUINOUS [*aside to Priscian*] Will you on and beg, or steal and be hanged?

SIR GREGORY And some scholar she would have me besides.

OLD KNIGHT Tush, that shall be no bar; 'tis a quality in a gentleman, but of the least question.

PRISCIAN *Salvete, domini benignissimi, munificentissimi*!

OLD KNIGHT *Salvete dicis ad nos? Jubeo te salvere.* Nay, sir, we have Latin, and other metal in us too. [*To Sir Gregory*] Sir, you shall see me talk with this fellow now.

SIR GREGORY I could find in my heart to talk with him too, if I could understand him.

PRISCIAN *Charissimi doctissimique domini, ex abundantia charitatis vestrae estote propitii in me juvenem miserum, pauperem, et omni consolatione exulem.*

OLD KNIGHT A pretty scholar, by my faith, sir: but I'll to him again.

SIR GREGORY Does he beg or steal in this language, can you tell, sir? He may take away my good name from me, and I ne'er the wiser.

28 ***Pol, aedepol*** another nickname for Priscian drawn from Lilly and Colet's *Short Introduction of Grammar*, taken from its section 'Of the Adverb': 'Some be of Swearing: as Pol, aedepol, hercle, medius fidius . . .'. The literal sense is 'Pollux, by Pollux'.

28–9 **here's . . . you** *Castor, ecastor* means 'Castor, by Castor', but the exact point of Wittypate's invocation of the other heavenly twin here, apart from its echoing of '*Pol, aedepol*', has never been satisfactorily explained. Dyce rather dubiously records a friend's suggestion that it puns on the cant term 'caster', cloak, so that Wittypate is recommending that Priscian might spend his share on a cloak: Turner, on the strength of a 1565 translation of 'ecastor' as 'By my fay, used only of women' (in Thomas Cooper's *Thesaurus Linguæ Romanæ & Britannicæ*), glosses the line as 'here's something toward the price of a woman for you', presumably on the assumption that any obscure joke *must* be bawdy. It seems unlikely that either explanation would persuade a modern director not to cut the line.

30–1 **by . . . ends** 'i.e. by the fingers of this hand, or, in the modern vernacular, "by this bunch of fives"' (Sharp)

32 **odd** 'i.e. an odd number. Some of the puns in this scene are rather desperate in quality' (Sharp)

33 **severally** separately

34 ***Medius fidius*** most certainly. Wittypate is again mocking Priscian by quoting *A Short Introduction of Grammar* at him: see note on l. 28, above

36–7 **participle . . . undeclined** a further battery of grammatical terms

38 **ends** word-endings, inflexions
solus cum solo literally 'alone with alone'

39–40 **ends . . . silver** 'i.e. broken pieces of gold and silver' (Dyce)

40 **gerundine** 'Possibly this might be a misprint . . . for "gerundive", but equally it might be a nonce word invented by Wittypate to imply "gerund-spouting" or "gerund-loving"' (Sharp)

41 ***do . . . dum*** gerundive endings, perhaps once more from Lilly and Colet (who refer to 'certain voices called Gerunds ending in di, do, and dum'), with puns on 'do', 'die' and 'dumb'

43 **five shares** Sir Ruinous may be echoing 'five ends' at l. 30, but he surely means 'four': 'unless Wittypate also claims a double share, I do not understand Ruinous's arithmetic' (Sharp)

44 **Put on** Go to it

66 **'Blows' . . . soldier** punning on the pugilistic sense of 'blows'

76 ***Salvete . . . munificentissimi*** Greetings, most generous, most munificent sir

77 ***Salvete . . . salvere*** Are you speaking your greetings to us? I greet you in return

77–8 **Nay . . . too** punning on 'latten', an alloy resembling brass, and 'mettle'

82–4 ***Charissimi . . . exulem*** Most gracious and learned sir, from your state of charitable abundance look favourably on me, a young man in misery and poverty, exiled from all consolation

OLD KNIGHT He begs, he begs, sir.

PRISCIAN *Ecce, ecce, in oculis lachrymarum flumen, in ore fames sitisque; ignis in vultu, pudor et impudentia; in omni parte necessitas et indigentia.*

OLD KNIGHT *Audi tu, bonus socius; tu es scholasticus, sic intelligo; ego faciam argumentum.*—Mark now, sir, now I fetch him up.

SIR GREGORY I have been fetched up a hundred times for this, yet I could never learn half so much.

OLD KNIGHT *Audi, et responde; hoc est argumentum: nomen est nomen; ergo, quod est tibi nomen? Responde nunc, responde argumentum meum.*—Have I not put him to't, sir?

SIR GREGORY Yes, sir, I think so.

WITTYPATE [*aside to Sir Ruinous*] Step in; the rascal is put out of his penned speech, and he can go no farther.

OLD KNIGHT *Cur non respondes?*

PRISCIAN *O domine, tanta mea est miseria*—

WITTYPATE So, he's almost in again.

PRISCIAN —*ut nocte mecum pernoctet egestas, luce quotidie paupertas habitet.*

OLD KNIGHT *Sed quod est tibi nomen, et quis dedit? Responde argumentum.*

PRISCIAN Hem, hem.

WITTYPATE He's dry, he hems; on, quickly!

SIR RUINOUS [*coming forward*] Courteous gentlemen, if the brow of a military face may not be offensive to your generous eyeballs, let his wounds speak better than his words for some branch or small sprig of charity to be planted upon this poor barren soil of a soldier.

OLD KNIGHT How now! What, arms and arts both go a-begging?

SIR RUINOUS Such is the post-progress of cold Charity nowadays, who, for heat to her frigid limbs, passes in so swift a motion that two at the least had need be to stay her.

SIR GREGORY Sir, let's reward 'em, I pray you, and be gone. If any quarrel should arise amongst us, I am able to answer neither of them; his iron and steel tongue is as hard as the t'other's Latin one.

OLD KNIGHT Stay, stay, sir; I will talk a little with him first. Let me alone with both; I will try whether they live by their wits or no, for such a man I love.—And what, you both beg together, then?

PRISCIAN *Conjunctis manibus profecto, domine.*

SIR RUINOUS With equal fortunes, equal distribution; there's not the breadth of a sword's point uneven in our division.

SIR GREGORY What two qualities are here cast away upon two poor fellows! If a man had 'em that could maintain 'em, what a double man were that! If these two fellows might be bought, and sodden, and boiled to a jelly, and eaten fasting every morning, I do not think but a man should find strange things in his stomach.

OLD KNIGHT Come, sir, join your charity with mine, and we'll make up a couple of pence betwixt us.

SIR GREGORY If a man could have a pennyworth for his penny, I would bestow more money with 'em.

WITTYPATE [*coming forward*] Save you, gentlemen! how now? What, are you encountered here? What fellows are these?

OLD KNIGHT Faith, sir, here's Mars and Mercury, a pair of poor planets, it seems, that Jupiter has turned out to live by their wits; and we are e'en about a little spark of charity to kindle 'em a new fire.

WITTYPATE Stay, pray you, stay, sir; you may abuse your charity, nay, make that goodness in you no better than a vice: so many deceivers walk in these shadows

91–3 ***Ecce...indigentia*** Behold, behold, in my eyes a river of tears, in my mouth hunger and thirst; in my countenance a fire of shame at my shamelessness [in begging]; in every part of me necessity and indigence. (Throughout this scene, Priscian's Latin is as clumsy as Wittypate's taunts from *A Short Introduction of Grammar* might lead us to expect, and proves to have been learned parrot-fashion from a prepared script: see 1.1.105.1–1.1.106).

94–5 ***Audi...argumentum*** Listen, good friend; you are a scholar, so I understand; I will set you an argument. (The Old Knight's Latin, however, is even more basic than Priscian's.)

99–101 ***Audi...meum*** Listen and reply; this is the argument: a name is a name; and so, what is your name? Reply now, reply to my argument

105 ***Cur...respondes?*** Why do you not reply?

106 ***O...miseria*** O sir, such is my distress... (In response to the Old Knight's interrogation, Priscian is only able to revert to his pre-rehearsed begging routine.)

108–9 ***ut...habitet***...that through the hours of darkness destitution lodges with me, and through the hours of light every day poverty stays with me

110–11 ***Sed...argumentum*** But what is your name, and who will vouchsafe it? Reply to the argument

112 **Hem, hem** conventional sound of throat-clearing, by which Priscian may be deliberately signalling to his colleagues that he has 'dried'

116–17 **his wounds...his words** The wounds are those about to be claimed by Sir Ruinous in his character of a veteran soldier, the words those which Priscian has already spoken in his character of a poor scholar. Sir Ruinous adopts the elaborately figured, slightly bombastic language regarded as proper to a Renaissance soldier.

121 **post-progress** hurried movement or procession

124 **stay** detain, stop

128 **Latin** punning once more on 'latten': see ll. 77–8

133 ***Conjunctis...domine*** With hands united, indeed, sir

138 **maintain** afford to support

141 **fasting** on an empty stomach

142 **stomach** Sir Gregory is presumably thinking in particular of Sir Ruinous's assumed military virtues here, since the stomach was thought to be the seat of courage

145 **pennyworth** of Priscian's learning and Sir Ruinous's valour

148 **are you encountered here?** have you been accosted here?

150 **Mercury** appropriately, a deity associated with trickery as well as with study

151–2 **Jupiter...wits** 'We need not search for this incident in classical mythology. The Old Knight makes of Jupiter, chief of the gods, exactly the same sort of harsh, but wit-loving head of household as himself' (Sharp)

156 **shadows** disguises, stage costumes

nowadays that certainly your bounties were better spilt than reserved to so lewd and vicious uses.—Which is he that professes the soldier?

SIR RUINOUS He that professes his own profession, sir, and the dangerous life he hath led in it this pair of half-score years.

WITTYPATE In what services have you been, sir?

SIR RUINOUS The first that fleshed me a soldier, sir, was that great battle of Alcazar in Barbary, where the noble English Stukeley fell, and where that royal Portugal, Sebastian, ended his untimely days.

WITTYPATE Are you sure Sebastian died there?

SIR RUINOUS Faith, sir, there was some other rumour hopped amongst us that he, wounded, escaped, and touched on his native shore again, where, finding his country at home more distressed by the invasion of the Spaniard than his loss abroad, forsook it, still supporting a miserable and unfortunate life, which where he ended is yet uncertain.

WITTYPATE By my faith, sir, he speaks the nearest fame of truth in this.

SIR RUINOUS Since, sir, I served in France, the Low Countries, lastly at that memorable skirmish at Nieuport; where the forward and bold Scot there spent his life so freely, that from every single heart that there fell came home from his resolution a double honour to his country.

WITTYPATE This should be no counterfeit, sir.

OLD KNIGHT I do not think he is, sir.

WITTYPATE But, sir, methinks you do not show the marks of a soldier: could you so freely scape, that you brought home no scars to be your chronicle?

SIR RUINOUS Sir, I have wounds, and many; but in those parts where nature and humanity bids me shame to publish.

WITTYPATE A good soldier cannot want those badges.

SIR GREGORY Now am not I of your mind in that; for I hold him the best soldier that scapes best: always at a cock-fencing I give him the best that has the fewest knocks.

WITTYPATE Nay, I'll have a bout with your scholar too.—To ask you why you should be poor, yet richly learned, were no question, at least you can easily answer it; but whether you have learning enough to deserve to be poor or no (since poverty is commonly the meed of learning), is yet to be tried. You have the languages? I mean the chief, as the Hebrew, Syriac, Greek, Latin, *et caetera?*

PRISCIAN *Aliquantulum, non totaliter, domine.*

OLD KNIGHT The Latin I have sufficiently tried him in, and I promise you, sir, he is very well grounded.

WITTYPATE I will prove him in some of the rest.—*Tois miois fatherois iste coxcomboy?*

PRISCIAN *Kay yonkeron nigitton oy fouleroi asinisoy.*

WITTYPATE *Cheateron ton biton?*

PRISCIAN *Tous pollous strikerous, angelo to peeso.*

WITTYPATE Certainly, sir, a very excellent scholar in the Greek.

OLD KNIGHT I do note a wondrous readiness in him.

SIR GREGORY I do wonder how the Trojans could hold out ten years' siege, as 'tis reported, against the Greeks; if Achilles spoke but this tongue, I do not think but he might have shaken down the walls in a seventh-night, and ne'er troubled the wooden horse.

WITTYPATE I will try him so far as I can in the Syriac.—*Kircom bragmen, shag a dou ma dell mathou.*

161 **pair of half-score** elaborate military banter for 'a score', i.e. twenty

164–7 **The first...days** Sir Ruinous's recollections of his fictitious military career are of a distinctly hackneyed variety: the famous battle in which king Sebastian of Portugal perished in his attempt to win Morocco for Christianity, fought in 1578, was well known to playgoers from George Peele's drama *The Battle of Alcazar* (1594), while the career of the notorious English pirate and aventurer Thomas Stukeley, who also died there, had been made the subject of the anonymous play *Captain Thomas Stukeley* (1596; printed 1605).

169–75 **Faith...uncertain** Sebastian left no legal heir, and after his death at Alcazar Philip II of Spain was able to take control of Portugal, although rumours of Sebastian's survival persisted throughout Europe for many years

179 **skirmish at Nieuport** perhaps the most famous encounter of the Dutch civil wars, the Battle of Nieuport (2 July 1600), in which Protestant forces under Prince Maurice of Nassau, assisted by English and Scots troops commanded by Sir Edward Cecil and Sir Francis Vere, defeated Prince Albert of Spain

180–3 **the forward...country** The Scottish vanguard at Nieuport was cut off by the Spanish from the remainder of the army and massacred, achieving legendary status as a result. The story of this rare Protestant victory was so well-known in England that Sir Ruinous's ability to recount it constitutes a remarkably slender proof of his military experience, making Wittypate's success in persuading the Old Knight otherwise especially comic.

189–91 **Sir...publish** with an innuendo on the marks of venereal disease, taken up covertly by Wittypate's response

194 **scapes** escapes

195 **cock-fencing** cockfight. Sir Gregory obtusely fails to see that Sir Ruinous's lack of visible wounds actually does invalidate his story

201 **meed** reward. The learned have always been spectacularly underpaid, especially in England.

203 **Syriac** Cyrillic, i.e. Russian. It is probable that the dialogue from here through l. 227–8 was contributed to the scene by Middleton, who delighted in such scenes of fraudulent linguistic expertise.

205 ***Aliquantulum...domine*** Somewhat, not completely, sir

208–12 ***Tois...peeso*** The 'Greek' spoken by Wittypate and Priscian is magnificently spurious, consisting largely of English words given vaguely Greek-sounding endings: it is just possible to discern the sense of the conversation as, approximately, 'Is my father a coxcomb?—...(?)...fool, ass (?)—Shall we cheat him, bite him (in the cant sense of "cheat")?—...(?)...we can strike (coin) angels and pieces (from him)'. Compare the fraudulent Greek spoken by Idle in *Puritan* (4.2.108).

215 **wondrous readiness** due, as the Old Knight fails to realize, to careful rehearsal

219 **seventh-night** week

222–6 ***Kircom...nagothi*** this 'Syriac' is of course every bit as bogus as the preceding Greek

PRISCIAN *Hashagath rabgabash shobos onoriadka.*

WITTYPATE *Colpack rubasca, gnawerthem shigshag.*

PRISCIAN *Napshamothem ribshe bongomosh lashemech nagothi.*

WITTYPATE Gentlemen, I have done: any man that can, go further; I confess myself at a nonplus.

SIR GREGORY Faith, not I, sir; I was at my farthest in my natural language; I was never double-tongued, I thank my hard fortune.

WITTYPATE Well, gentlemen, 'tis pity,—[*To Priscian and Sir Ruinous*] Walk further off a little, my friends—I say, 'tis pity such fellows, so endowed, so qualified with the gifts of nature and arts, yet should have such a scarcity of Fortune's benefits: we must blame our iron-hearted age for it.

OLD KNIGHT 'Tis pity, indeed, and our pity shall speak a little for 'em: come, sir; here's my groat.

WITTYPATE A groat, sir? O, fie! Give nothing rather! 'Twere better you railed on 'em for begging, and so quit yourself. I am a poor gentleman, that have little but my wits to live on—

OLD KNIGHT Troth, and I love you the better, sir.

WITTYPATE —yet I'll begin a better example than so. [*To Priscian and Sir Ruinous, throwing them a purse*] Here, fellows, there's between you! Take purse and all, and I would it were heavier for your sakes! There's a pair of angels to guide you to your lodgings, a poor gentleman's good will.

PRISCIAN *Gratias, maximas gratias, benignissime domine*!

OLD KNIGHT This is an ill example for us, sir; I would this bountiful gentleman had not come this way today!

SIR GREGORY Pox, we must not shame ourselves now, sir. I'll give as much as that gentleman, though I never be soldier or scholar while I live.—Here, friends, [*throwing a gold coin to Sir Ruinous and Priscian*] there's a piece that if he were divided would make a pair of angels for me too, in the love I bear to the sword and the tongues.

OLD KNIGHT My largess shall be equal too, [*throwing them another gold coin*] and much good do you!—[*Aside*] This bounty is a little abatement of my wit, though, I feel that.

SIR RUINOUS May soldiers ever defend such charities!

PRISCIAN And scholars pray for their increase!

OLD KNIGHT [*to Wittypate*] Fare you well, sir: these fellows may pray for you; you have made the scholar's commons exceed today. And a word with you, sir; you said you lived by your wits; if you use this bounty, you'll beggar your wits, believe it.

WITTYPATE O, sir, I hope to increase 'em by it; this seed never wants his harvest. Fare you well, sir. *Exit*

SIR GREGORY [*aside*] I think a man were as good meet with a reasonable thief as an unreasonable beggar sometimes; I could find in my heart to beg half mine back again. [*To Priscian and Sir Ruinous*]—Can you change my piece, my friends?

PRISCIAN *Tempora mutantur, et nos mutamur in illis.*

SIR GREGORY My gold is turned into Latin.

Re-enter Wittypate

WITTYPATE Look you, good fellows, here's one round shilling more, that lay concealed.

OLD KNIGHT Sir, away! We shall be drawn farther into damage else.

SIR GREGORY A pox of the fool! He live by his wits? If his wits leave him any money but what he begs or steals very shortly, I'll be hanged for him.

Exeunt Old Knight and Sir Gregory

SIR RUINOUS This breakfast-parcel was well fetched off, i'faith.

WITTYPATE Tush, a by-blow for mirth; we must have better purchase. We want a fourth for another project that I have ripened.

SIR RUINOUS My wife; she shares, and can deserve it.

WITTYPATE She can change her shape, and be masculine?

SIR RUINOUS 'Tis one of the freest conditions: she fears not the crack of a pistol; she dares say 'Stand!' to a grazier.

PRISCIAN *Probatum fuit profecto, domine.*

WITTYPATE Good: then you, sir, [*To Priscian*] Bacchus Apollo, shall be dispatched with her share and some counters to meet us tomorrow, at a certain place and time appointed, in the masculine gender. My father has a nephew, and I an own cousin, coming up from the university, whom he loves most indulgently—easy Master Credulous Oldcraft (for you know what your mere academic is). Your carrier never misses his hour.

230 **double-tongued** bilingual

249 **pair of angels** The two coins Wittypate claims are in the purse would together be worth about £1, a sum sixty times larger than the groat initially offered by the Old Knight.

251 ***Gratias ... domine*** Thanks, the greatest thanks, most generous sir

257 **piece** coin worth £1, twice as much as an angel

267–8 **scholar's commons** daily allowance of food provided for university students (generally bread and cheese)

271 **seed** Wittypate's apparent investment in Priscian and Sir Ruinous has of course been precisely that, seed money, which has already reaped its harvest

278 ***Tempora ... illis*** Times change and we change with them: perhaps the most clichéd of all Latin tags

279 **Latin** another pun on 'latten': Sir Gregory's gold has been alchemically transformed into base metal

287 **breakfast-parcel** sum of money with which to pay for breakfast

289 **by-blow** trifling achievement

294 **'Tis** i.e. she is (or has)

295 **'Stand!'** stereotypical command of a highwayman to his prey
grazier one who fattens cattle and brings them to market, a proverbial target for highwaymen and footpads when on the way home with the proceeds

296 ***Probatum ... domine*** This has indeed been proven, sir

297–8 **Bacchus Apollo** Wittypate again calls Priscian by a nickname drawn from *A Short Introduction of Grammar*, this time from Lilly's poem '*Carmen de nominum generibus*', the second line of which includes the phrase 'Ut sunt divorum, Mars, Bacchus, Apollo'.

302 **easy** gullible

304 **Your ... hour** The punctuality of the Cambridge university carrier Thomas Hobson (*c*.1544–1631), who ferried students and baggage to and from London, was legendary; see Milton's two facetious epitaphs, printed in *Poems* (1645).

He must not be robbed, because he has but little to lose, but he must join with us in a device that I have, that shall rob my father of a hundred pieces, and thank me to be rid on't. For there's the ambition of my wit: to live upon his professed wit, that has turned me out to live by my wits.

PRISCIAN *Cum hirundinis alis tibi regratulor*.

WITTYPATE A male habit, a bag of a hundred weight, though it be counters (for my alchemy shall turn 'em into gold of my father's); the hour, the place, the action shall be at large set down: and, father, you shall know that I put my portion to use, that you have given me to live by;

And, to confirm yourself in me renate,
I hope you'll find my wit's legitimate. *Exeunt*

2.1 *Enter Lady Ruinous and Servant*

SERVANT
Nay, Lady—

LADY Put me not in mind on't, prithee;
You cannot do a greater wrong to women;
For in our wants 'tis the most chief affliction
To have that name remembered; 'tis a title
That misery mocks us by, and the world's malice.
Scorn and contempt has not wherewith to work
On humble callings: they are safe, and lie
Level with pity still, and pale distress
Is no great stranger to 'em; but when Fortune
Looks with a stormy face on our conditions,
We find affliction work, and envy pastime,
And our worst enemy then, that most abuses us,
Is that we are called by, 'Lady'. [*Exit Servant*]
O my spirit,
Will nothing make thee humble? I am well, methinks,
And can live quiet with my fate sometimes,
Until I look into the world again:
Then I begin to rave at my stars' bitterness,
To see how many muckhills placed above me,
Peasants and droils, caroaches full of dunghills,
Whose very birth stinks in a generous nostril,
Glistering by night like glow-worms through the high-streets,
Hurried by torchlight in the footmen's hands,
That show like running fire-drakes through the city:
And I put to my shifts and wits to live,
Nay, sometimes danger too, on foot, on horseback,
And earn my supper manfully ere I get it;
Many a meal I have purchased at that rate,
Enter Priscian [disguised with a beard]
Fed with a wound upon me, stamped at midnight.
Ha! what are you?

PRISCIAN (*pulls off his beard*)
Now you may tell yourself, lady.

LADY O, Master Priscian; what's the project?
For you ne'er come without one.

PRISCIAN First, your husband,
Sir Ruinous Gentry, greets you with best wishes,
And here has sent you your full share by me
In five cheats and two robberies.

LADY And what comes it to?

PRISCIAN
Near upon thirteen pound.

LADY A goodly share!
'Twill put a lady scarce in philip-and-cheyney
With three small bugle laces, like a chambermaid:
Here's precious lifting!

PRISCIAN 'Las, you must consider, lady,
'Tis but young term; attorneys ha' small doings yet;
Then highway-lawyers, they must needs ha' little.
We've had no great good luck, to speak troth, beauty,
Since your stout ladyship parted from's at Highgate:
But there's a fair hope now for a present hundred;
Here's man's apparel; your horse stands at door.

LADY
And what's the virtuous plot now?

PRISCIAN Marry, lady,
You, like a brave young gallant, must be robbed.

LADY
I robbed?

PRISCIAN Nay, then—

LADY Well, well, go on; let's hear, sir.

PRISCIAN
Here's a sealed bag of a hundred, which indeed
Are counters all, only some sixteen groats
Of white money i'the mouth on't.

LADY So: what saddle have I?

PRISCIAN
Monsieur Laroon's, the Frenchman's.

LADY That again!
You know so well it is not for my stride,

311 ***Cum . . . regratulor*** Coming back as the swallow
318 **renate** reborn
2.1 composed by Middleton
18 **muckhills** i.e. persons bred in farmyards (compare 'dunghills', 2.1.19)
19 **droils** common drudges
23 **fire-drakes** fireworks in the shape of dragons which propelled themselves along wires
26 **manfully** with the additional sense of 'in male attire'
28 **stamped** marked, inflicted
36 **philip-and-cheyney** a relatively inexpensive dress fabric
37 **bugle** a dark-coloured tubular bead made of glass
40 **highway-lawyers** highway robbers
42 **Highgate** increasingly fashionable settlement on high ground five miles north of the City, where the northward road's passage through a tollgate into open countryside provided a suitable venue for highway robberies
49–50 **sixteen . . . white money** 'white money' meant silver coins (such as the groat)
51–4 **Monsieur Laroon's . . . Scotch one** 'Evidently the saddles have been stolen, and some badinage about the comparative sexual capacities of Frenchmen and Scots[men] definitely seems intended . . .' (Sharp)

How oft have I complained on't?
PRISCIAN
You may have Jockey's then, the little Scotch one.
You must dispatch.
LADY I'll soon be ready, sir,
Before you ha' shifted saddles. *Exit Priscian*
Many women
Have their wealth flow to 'em; I was made, I see,
To help my fortune, not my fortune me. *Exit*

2.2 *Enter Cunningame*

CUNNINGAME
My ways are goblin-led, and the night-elf
Still draws me from my home, yet I follow;
Sure 'tis not altogether fabulous,
Such hags do get dominion of our tongues,
So soon as we speak, the enchantment binds.
I have dissembled such a trouble on me
As my best wits can hardly clear again.
Piping through this old reed, the guardianess,
With purpose that my harmony shall reach
And please the lady's ear, she stops below
And echoes back my love unto my lips,
Persuaded by most violent arguments
Of self-love in herself, I am so self-fool
To dote upon her hundred-wrinkled face.
I could beggar her to accept the gifts
She would throw upon me; 'twere charity;
But for pity's sake I will be a niggard
And undo her, refusing to take from her.
Enter Guardianess
I'm haunted again: if it take not now,
I'll break the spell.
GUARDIANESS Sweet Cunningame, welcome!
What, a whole day absent? Birds that build nests
Have care to keep 'em.
CUNNINGAME That's granted,
But not continually to sit upon 'em,
'Less in the youngling season; else they desire
To fly abroad and recreate their labours,
Then they return with fresher appetite
To work again.
GUARDIANESS Well, well, you have built a nest
That will stand all storms; you need not mistrust
A weather-wrack; and one day it may be
The youngling season, too; then, I hope,
You'll ne'er fly out of sight.
CUNNINGAME [*aside*] There will be pains,
I see, to shake this burr off.—And, sweetest,
Prithee, how fares thy charge? Has my good friend
Sir Gregory the countenance of a lover?
GUARDIANESS
No, by my troth, not in my mind; methinks,
Setting his worship aside, he looks like a fool.
CUNNINGAME
Nay, i'faith, ne'er divide his worship from him
For that small matter; fool and worship are
No such strangers nowadays. But my meaning is,
Has he thy lady's countenance of love?
Looks she like a welcome on him? Plainly,
Have they as good hope of one another
As, Cupid bless us, we have?
GUARDIANESS Troth, I know not;
I can perceive no forwardness in my charge;
But I protest I wish the knight the better
For your sake, bird.
CUNNINGAME
Why, thanks, sweet bird, and with my heart I wish
That he had as strong and likely hope of her
As thou hast of me.
GUARDIANESS Well, he's like to speed
Ne'er the worse for that good wish, and I'll tell you, bird,
(For secrets are not to be kept betwixt us two),
My charge thinks well of you.
CUNNINGAME Of me? For what?
GUARDIANESS
For my sake, I mean so; I have heard her
A hundred times say, since her uncle gave her
The first bob about you, that she'd do somewhat
For my sake, if things went well together:
We have spoke of doors and bolts, and things, and things—
Go to, I'll tell you all! But you'll find some
Advancement for my sake, I do believe.
CUNNINGAME
Faith, be not sparing, tell me.
GUARDIANESS By my lady,
You shall pardon me for that; 'twere a shame
If men should hear all that women speak behind
Their backs sometimes.
CUNNINGAME You must give me leave yet
At least to give her thanks.
GUARDIANESS Nor that neither;
She must not take a notice of my blabbing.
It is sufficient you shall give me thanks,

2.2 primarily composed, along with the remainder of act 2, by Rowley
1–5 **My . . . binds** Cunningame attributes his spontaneous idea of feigning to court the Guardianess in place of the Niece to the sort of magic by which goblins and elves were popularly supposed to lead benighted travellers astray
16–18 **'twere . . . her** it would be charitable (to accept the Guardianess's gifts), but out of pity I will be stingy (with my acceptance) and thus undo her by not taking them (instead of bankrupting her by doing so)
19–20 **if . . . spell** if my plan of wooing the Niece via the feigned wooing of the Guardianess doesn't succeed this time, I'll disabuse the Guardianess
24 **'Less** unless, except
else otherwise, at other times
54–5 **gave . . . bob** 'to give someone the bob' meant 'to make a fool of them' or 'play a trick on them'
57 **We . . . things** The conversation here sparingly reported has clearly been full of sexual innuendo
58 **Go . . . all!** i.e. get away, I'll be betraying all my secrets to you at this rate

For 'tis for my sake if she be bountiful:
She loves me, and loves you too for my sake.

CUNNINGAME
How shall I, knowing this, but be ingrate
Not to repay her with my dearest duty?

GUARDIANESS
Ay, but you must not know it; if you tell
All that I open to you, you'll shame us both:
Afar off you may kiss your hand, blush, or so,
But I'll allow no nearer conference.

CUNNINGAME
Whoop! you'll be jealous, I perceive now.

GUARDIANESS Jealous?
Why, there is no true love without it, bird,
I must be jealous of thee; but for her
(Were it within my duty to my master),
I durst trust her with the strongest tempter,
And I dare swear her now as pure a virgin
As e'er was welcomed to a marriage bed:
If thoughts may be untainted, hers are so.

CUNNINGAME
And where's the cause of your fear, then?

GUARDIANESS Well, well,
When things are past and the wedding torches
Lighted at matches, to kindle better fire,
Then I'll tell you more.

CUNNINGAME Come, come, I see further
That if we were married, you'd be jealous.

GUARDIANESS
I protest, I should a little, but not of her:
It is the married woman (if you mark it),
And not the maid, that longs; the appetite
Follows the first taste; when we have relished
We wish cloying; the taste once pleased before,
Then our desire is whetted on to more.
But I reveal too much to you, i'faith, bird.

CUNNINGAME
Not a whit, faith, bird, betwixt you and I;
I am beholding for bettering of my knowledge.

GUARDIANESS
Nay, you shall know more of me, if you'll be ruled;
But make not things common.

Enter Niece and Clown [*the latter giving her a ruff*]

CUNNINGAME Ud'so, your lady.

GUARDIANESS
Ay, 'tis no matter, she'll like well of this;
Our familiarity is her content.

NIECE This present from Sir Gregory?

CLOWN From my master, the worshipful right Sir Gregory Fop.

NIECE
A ruff? And what might be his high conceit
In sending of a ruff?

CLOWN I think he had two conceits in it, forsooth, too high, too low; ruff-high, because as the ruff does embrace your neck all day, so does he desire to throw his knightly arms.

NIECE
But then I leave him off o' nights.

CLOWN Why, then he is ruff-low, a ruffian, a bold adventurous errant to do any rough service for his lady.

NIECE
A witty and unhappy conceit! (*Toward Cunningame*)—
Does he mean
As he seems to say unto that reverence?
He does woo her, sure.

CLOWN To tell you truth, lady, his conceit was far better than I have blazed it yet.

NIECE Do you think so, sir?

CLOWN Nay, I know it, forsooth, for it was two days ere he compassed it, to find a fitting present for your ladyship: he was sending once a very fine puppy to you.

NIECE And that he would have brought himself.

CLOWN So he would, indeed, but then he altered his device, and sent this ruff, requesting withal, that whensoever it is foul, you with your own hands would bestow the starching of it.

NIECE (*toward Cunningame*)
Else she woos him: now his eyes shoot this way.—
And what was the reason for that, sir?

CLOWN There lies his main conceit, lady; 'For', says he, 'in so doing she cannot choose but in the starching to clap it often between her hands, and so she gives a great liking and applause to my present; whereas if I should send a puppy she ever calls it to her with "hist, hiss, hiss", which is a fearful disgrace.' He drew the device from a play at the Bull t'other day.

NIECE
Ay, marry, sir, this was a rich conceit, indeed.

85 **fire** with its secondary sense of 'passion'
96 **beholding** beholden to you
98.1 ***Clown*** The Clown, Pompey Doodle, is described by the cast list as '*a piece of puff-paste* [puff pastry], *like his master*', so it may be that there is something foppish about his clothes even before his transformation into a gallant later in the play.
98 **Ud'so** contraction of 'God save me'
104 **conceit** conception, fanciful underlying idea
106–7 **too high, too low** an expression which has greatly puzzled editors, although Sharp and Turner are in general agreement that of Sir Gregory's two conceits the first is 'too high' (in the sense of excited, the ruff about the neck signifying an embrace) and the second too low (too vulgar)
107–12 **ruff-high . . . lady** The puzzlement continues here, with some editors following Weber in suspecting an obscure pun derived from cardplaying (since 'ruff' could mean 'trump'), and Turner opting squarely for obscenity, pointing out that 'ruff' could mean 'pudendum' and 'rob the ruffian' could mean 'copulate'. That the 'lower' of the conceits is salacious, ll. 110–12, seems certain.
113 **unhappy** 'i.e. mischievous, waggish' (Dyce), although, as Sharp observes, the modern sense may also be present
120 **compassed** achieved
135 **the Bull** the Red Bull Theatre in Clerkenwell (near the Barbican), noted for its rowdiness

CLOWN
And far-fetched; therefore good for you, lady.
GUARDIANESS How now, which way look you, bird?
CUNNINGAME At the fool, bird; shall I not look at the fool?
GUARDIANESS At the fool, and I here? What need that?
Pray, look this way.
NIECE [*aside*]
I'll fit him aptly; either I'll awake
His wits (if he have any) or force him
To appear (as yet I cannot think him)
Without any.—Sirrah, tell me one thing true
That I shall ask you now: was this device
Your master's own? I doubt his wit in it;
He's not so ingenious.
CLOWN His own, I assure you, madam.
NIECE Nay, you must not lie.
CLOWN Not with a lady? I'd rather lie with you than lie with my master, by your leave, in such a case as this.
GUARDIANESS
Yet again your eye?
CUNNINGAME The fool makes mirth, i'faith,
I would hear some.
GUARDIANESS Come, you shall hear none but me.
NIECE
Come hither, friend; nay, come nearer me; did
Thy master send thee to me? He may be wise,
But did not show it much in that; men sometimes
May wrong themselves unawares, when they least
think on't:
Was Vulcan ever so unwise to send Mars
To be his spokesman, when he went a-wooing?
Send thee! Heigh-ho, a pretty rolling eye—
CLOWN I can turn up the white and the black too, an need be, forsooth.
NIECE Why, here's an amorous nose.
CLOWN You see the worst of my nose, forsooth.
NIECE A cheek!
How I could pat it now in dalliance!
A pair of lips—O, that we were uneyed!—
I could suck sugar from 'em. What a beard's here!
When will the knight thy master have such a stamp
Of manhood on his face? Nay, do not blush.
CLOWN
'Tis nothing but my flesh and blood that rises so.
CUNNINGAME Death, she courts the fool!
GUARDIANESS
Away, away! 'Tis sport; do not mind it.
NIECE
Give me thy hand; come, be familiar:
Ay, here's a promising palm; what a soft
Handful of pleasure's here! Here's down compared
With flocks and quilted straw; thy knight's fingers
Are lean mattress-rubbers to these feathers:
I prithee, let me lean my cheek upon't;
What a soft pillow's here!
CLOWN Hum, umh, hu, hum!
NIECE
Why, there's a courage in that lively passion.
Measure thee all o'er, there's not a limb
But has his full proportion: it is my voice,
There's no compare betwixt the knight and thee;
The goodlier man by half,
At once, now I see thee all over.
CLOWN If you had seen me swim t'other day on my back, you would have said you had seen: there was two chambermaids that saw me, and my legs by chance were tangled in the flags, and when they saw how I was hanged, they cried out, 'O, help the man for fear he be drowned!'
NIECE
They could do no less in pity. Come, thine arm;
We'll walk together.
CUNNINGAME
Blindness of love and women! why, she dotes
Upon the fool.
GUARDIANESS What's that to you? Mind her not.
CUNNINGAME
Away, you burr!
GUARDIANESS How's that?
CUNNINGAME
Hang off, flesh-hook! Fasten thine itchy clasp
On some dry toadstool, that will kindle with thee,
And burn together.
GUARDIANESS O, abominable!
Why, do you not love me?
CUNNINGAME No; never did.
I took thee down a little way to enforce
A vomit from my offended stomach; now

137 **far-fetched** alluding to the proverb 'far-fetched and dear bought is good for ladies' (i.e. women like exotic and expensive gifts)
151–2 **I'd . . . this** with a sexual quibble
159–60 **Was . . . a-wooing** Venus was of course unfaithful to her husband Vulcan with Mars
162–3 **I . . . forsooth** The Clown misunderstands the Niece's praise of his 'rolling' (i.e. sensually languorous) eye, boasting that he can perform the childish trick of rolling up his pupils until they become invisible.
165 **You . . . forsooth** The compliment to the Clown's nose might be received with similar ineptitude if he were to wipe it apologetically on this line.
179 **mattress-rubbers** rough mattress covers
191 **flags** irises
192 **hanged** The Clown ostensibly means 'suspended', but with a punning boast of his sexual endowment (compare the modern colloquialism 'well hung').
199 **flesh-hook** literally, a utensil for lifting meat from a stewpot: Cunningame's insult thus implies that the Guardianess belongs in the kitchen, as well as accusing her of excessive carnality
200 **dry toadstool** At this date the word 'toadstool' could be used to refer to mushrooms in general (rather than simply inedible or poisonous varieties), so Cunningame may well be continuing the stew metaphor he begins with 'flesh-hook', suggesting that the wrinkled flesh of an old, dry mushroom would be more appropriate for the Guardianess to draw out of the pot than his own.
kindle with thee take fire from you (i.e. from your inordinate sexual heat)

Thou'rt up again, I loathe thee filthily.

GUARDIANESS
O, villain!

CUNNINGAME
Why, dost thou not see a sight
Would make a man abjure the sight of women?

NIECE Ha, ha, ha! He's vexed. Ha, ha, ha!

CLOWN Ha, ha, ha!

NIECE Why dost thou laugh?

CLOWN Because thou laugh'st; nothing else, i'faith.

CUNNINGAME [*aside*]
She has but mocked my folly; else she finds not
The bosom of my purpose: some other way
Must make me know. I'll try her, and may chance quit
The fine dexterity of her lady-wit. *Exit*

NIECE
Yes, in troth, I laughed to think of thy master;
Now, what would he think if he knew this?

CLOWN By my troth, I laugh at him too: faith, sirrah, he's but a fool, to say the truth, though I say't that should not say't.

NIECE
Yes, thou shouldst say truth, and I believe thee.
Well, for this time we'll part: you perceive something;
Our tongues betray our hearts, there's our weakness,
But pray be silent.

CLOWN
As mouse in cheese, or goose in hay, i'faith.
[*Guardianess approaches them*]

NIECE Look, we are cut off: there's my hand where my lips would be.

CLOWN I'll wink, and think 'em thy lips. Farewell. *Exit*

NIECE
Now, guardianess, I need not ask where you have been.

GUARDIANESS
O, lady, never was woman so abused.
[*Re-enter Clown*]

CLOWN Dost thou hear, lady sweetheart? I had forgot to tell thee: if you will, I will come back in the evening.

NIECE
By no means; come not till I send for you.

CLOWN If there be any need (you may think of things when I am gone), I may be conveyed into your chamber. I'll lie under the bed while midnight or so, or you shall put me up in one of your little boxes; I can creep in at a small hole.

NIECE These are things I dare not venture; I charge you on my love, never come till I send for you.

CLOWN *Verbum insapienti*; 'tis enough to the wise: nor I think it is not fit the knight should know anything yet.

NIECE
By no means; pray you, go now; we are suspected.

CLOWN For the things that are past, let us use our secrets.

NIECE
Now I'll make a firm trial of your love;
As you love me, not a word more at this time,
Not a syllable; 'tis the seal of love; take heed.

CLOWN Hum, hum, hum, hum—
Exit, humming 'Loath to depart'

NIECE
So, this pleasant trouble's gone.—Now, guardianess;
What, your eyes easing your heart? The cause, woman?

GUARDIANESS
The cause is false man, madam: O, lady,
I have been gulled in a shining carbuncle,
A very glow-worm, that I thought had fire in't,
And 'tis as cold as ice.

NIECE
And justly served;
Wouldst thou once think that such an early spring
Would dote upon thine autumn?

GUARDIANESS
O, had you heard him
But protest!

NIECE
I would not have believed him.
Thou might'st have perceived how I mocked thy folly
In wanton imitation with the fool.
Go, weep the sin of thy credulity,
Not of thy loss, for it was never thine,
And it is gain to miss it. Wert thou so dull?
Nay, yet thou'rt stupid and uncapable:
Why, thou wert but the bait to fish with, not
The prey; the stale to catch another bird with.

GUARDIANESS
Indeed, he called me 'bird'.

NIECE
Yet thou perceiv'st not:
It is your niece he loves; wouldst thou be made
A stalking jade? 'Tis she, examine it.
[*Aside*] I'll hurry all awry, and tread my path

214 **quit** requite
225 **As...hay** 'Silent, of course, only because they are busily eating' (Sharp); both phrases are proverbial
234–7 Sharp notes that 'chamber', 'box' and 'hole' were all used as slang terms for the female pudenda.
236 **while** until
241 ***Verbum insapienti*** literally 'a word to the unwise', the Clown's misquotation of the proverb '*verbum sat sapienti*', 'a word is enough to the wise'
248.1 ***'Loath to depart'*** a popular song of valediction, the tune of which the Clown hums so as to express his reluctance to leave without disobeying the Niece's command; for the music, see *Companion*, p. 148
252 **gulled** deceived
carbuncle garnet or ruby
265 **stale** decoy
268 **stalking jade** A stalking horse was a real or artificial horse behind which a hunter could approach to within firing range of birds: the Niece chooses the term 'jade' for 'horse' because of its use as a disrespectful term for a woman, particularly an older woman.
269–71 **I'll...bouts** 'The general sense is clear, despite the peculiar phrasing. The Niece will arrive at her target (Cunningame) by a circuitous route intended to shake off the Old Knight and the Guardianess and, indeed, to test Cunningame himself' (Sharp)

Over unbeaten grounds; go level to the mark,
But by circular bouts. Rare things are pleasing,
And rare's but seldom in the simple sense,
But has her emphasis with eminence. *Exit*

GUARDIANESS My niece? She the rival of my abuse?
My flesh and blood wrong me? I'll aunt her for't.

Enter Mirabell

O, opportunity, thou blessest me!—
Now, gentlewoman, are you parted so soon?
Where's your friend, I pray? your Cunningame?

MIRABELL
What say you, aunt?

GUARDIANESS Come, come, your Cunningame.
I am not blind with age yet, nor deaf.

MIRABELL [*aside*]
Dumb I am sure you are not.—What, ail you, aunt?
Are you not well?

GUARDIANESS
No, nor sick, nor mad, nor in my wits, nor sleeping,
Nor waking, nor nothing, nor anything:
I know not what I am, nor what I am not.

MIRABELL
Mercy cover us! What do you mean, aunt?

GUARDIANESS
I mean to be revenged.

MIRABELL On whom?

GUARDIANESS On thee,
Baggage!

MIRABELL
Revenge should follow injury,
Which never reached so far as thought in me
Towards you, aunt.

GUARDIANESS Your cunning, minion,
Nor your Cunningame, can either blind me:
The gentle beggar loves you.

MIRABELL Beseech you,
Let me stay your error. I begin to hear,
And shake off my amazement: if you think
That ever any passage treating love
Hath been betwixt us yet commenced, any
Silent eye-glance that might but sparkle fire,
So much as brother and sister might meet with,
The lip-salute so much as strangers might
Take a farewell with, the commixèd hands,
Nay, but the least thought of the least of these,
In troth, you wrong your bosom: by that truth
Which I think yet you durst be bail for in me
If it were offered ye, I am as free
As all this protestation.

GUARDIANESS May I believe this?

MIRABELL
If ever you'll believe truth. Why, I thought
He had spake love to you; and if his heart
Prompted his tongue, sure I did hear so much.

GUARDIANESS
O, falsest man! Ixion's plague fell on me:
Never by woman such a masculine cloud,
So airy and so subtle, was embraced.

MIRABELL
By no cause in me, by my life, dear aunt.

GUARDIANESS
I believe you: then help in my revenge,
And you shall do't, or lose my love forever.
I'll have him quitted at his equal weapon:
Thou art young; follow him, bait his desires
With all the engines of a woman's wit,
Stretch modesty even to the highest pitch;
He cannot freeze at such a flaming beauty;
And when thou hast him by the amorous gills,
Think on my vengeance, choke up his desires,
Then let his banquetings be Tantalism:
Let thy disdain spurn the dissembler out.
O, I should climb my stars, and sit above,
To see him burn to ashes in his love.

MIRABELL
This will be a strange task, aunt, and an unwilling labour;
Yet, in your injunction, I am a servant to't.

GUARDIANESS Thou'lt undertake't?

MIRABELL
Yes; let the success commend itself hereafter.

GUARDIANESS
Effect it, girl; my substance is thy store;
Nothing but want of will makes woman poor.

Exeunt

Enter Sir Gregory and Clown 2.3

SIR GREGORY
Why, Pompey, thou art not stark mad, art thou?
Wilt thou not tell me how my lady does?

CLOWN Your lady?

SIR GREGORY Did she receive the thing that I sent her kindly, or no?

CLOWN The thing that you sent her, knight, by the thing that you sent, was for the thing's sake that was sent to carry the thing that you sent, very kindly received. First,

271–3 **Rare...eminence** 'Another cryptic utterance... She would appear to mean that although a rare thing (such as Cunningame) comes infrequently, its unusual excellence makes it of elevated importance' (Sharp)

290 **minion** hussy

304–5 **free...protestation** 'i.e. Mirabell is as free of guilt as the Guardianess is free with her accusations' (Sharp)

309 **Ixion's plague** In Greek legend Ixion fell in love with Hera, but his attempt to seduce her was frustrated when she substituted a cloud for herself

315 **quitted** requited

317 **engines** inventions, devices

322 **Tantalism** Tantalus was punished in Hades for betraying the secrets of the Greek gods by being stood up to his neck in water which receded each time he bent to drink it, beneath branches of fruit which withdrew each time he reached up to harvest them.

327 **injunction** 'authoritative order. Presumably Mirabell is the Guardianess's legal ward' (Sharp)

there is your indenture, [*handing over a paper*] now go seek you a servant; secondly, you are a knight; thirdly and lastly, I am mine own man; and fourthly, fare you well.

SIR GREGORY
Why, Pompey, prithee, let me speak with thee.
[*Aside*] I'll lay my life some hare has crossed him.

CLOWN Knight, if you be a knight, so keep you; as for the lady, who shall say that she is not a fair lady, a sweet lady, an honest and a virtuous lady, I will say he is a base fellow, a blab of his tongue, and I will make him eat these fingers' ends.

SIR GREGORY Why, here's nobody says so, Pompey.

CLOWN Whatsoever things have passed between the lady and the other party, whom I will not name at this time, I say she is virtuous and honest, and I will maintain it as long as I can maintain myself with bread and water.

SIR GREGORY Why, I know nobody thinks otherwise.

CLOWN Any man that does but think it in my hearing, I will make him think on't while he has a thought in his bosom; shall we say that kindnesses from ladies are common, or that favours and protestations are things of no moment betwixt parties and parties? I say still, whatsoever has been betwixt the lady and the party which I will not name, that she is honest, and shall be honest, whatsoever she does by day or by night, by light or by darkness, with cut and long tail.

SIR GREGORY Why, I say she is honest.

CLOWN Is she honest? In what sense do you say she is honest, knight?

SIR GREGORY If I could not find in my heart to throw my dagger at thy head, hilts and all, I'm an ass, and no gentleman!

CLOWN Throw your dagger at me! Do not, knight, I give you fair warning; 'tis but cast away if you do, for you shall have no other words of me. The lady is an honest lady, whatsoever reports may go of sports and toys, and thoughts, and words, and deeds, betwixt her and the party which I will not name. This I give you to understand: that another man may have as good an eye, as amorous a nose, as fair a stamped beard, and be as proper a man as a knight (I name no parties); a servingman may be as good as a Sir, a Pompey as a Gregory, a Doodle as a Fop; so servingman Pompey Doodle may be respected as well with ladies (though I name no parties) as Sir Gregory Fop; so farewell. *Exit*

SIR GREGORY If the fellow be not out of his wits, then will I never have any more wit while I live; either the sight of the lady has gastered him, or else he's drunk, or else he walks in his sleep, or else he's a fool, or a knave, or both; one of the three I'm sure 'tis. Yet, now I think on't, she has not used me so kindly as her uncle promised me she should: but that's all one, he says I shall have her, and I dare take his word for the best horse I have, and that's a weightier thing than a lady, I'm sure on't. *Exit*

Enter Lady Ruinous (as a man, [with a money-bag]), with Wittypate, Sir Ruinous, Priscian and Credulous [all with their faces disguised by scarves], who are binding and robbing her; Credulous finds the bag 2.4

LADY
Nay, I am your own, 'tis in your pleasure
How you'll deal with me; yet I would entreat
You will not make that which is bad enough
Worse than it need be, by a second ill,
When it can render you no second profit;
If it be coin you seek, you have your prey,
All my store, I vow (and it weighs a hundred);
My life, or any hurt you give my body,
Can enrich you no more.

WITTYPATE
You may pursue.

LADY
As I am a gentleman, I never will—

WITTYPATE
Only, we'll bind you to quiet behaviour
Till you call out for bail, and on th'other
Side of the hedge leave you; but keep the peace
Till we be out of hearing, for by that
We shall be out of danger; if we come back,
We come with a mischief.

LADY
You need not fear me.

PRISCIAN Come, we'll bestow you then.

Exeunt Priscian and Sir Ruinous, with Lady Ruinous

2.3.9 **indenture** the legal contract binding the Clown to his master, which he seems to think he can cancel simply by thus handing back his copy

14 **some hare has crossed him** 'A hare crossing a person's way was supposed to disorder his senses' (Dyce)

19 **these fingers' ends** these knuckles, i.e. my fist

34 **cut and long tail** from the proverbial phrase 'come cut and long tail', referring to all the varieties of horses or dogs (those with docked and those with uncut tails) and meaning 'no matter who or what is concerned', here with bawdy innuendoes on 'cut' (female genitalia) and 'tail' (male genitalia)

48 **stamped beard** as Sharp points out, the Clown's inaccurate recollection of the Niece's flattery ('such a stamp | Of manhood', 2.2.170–1)

56 **gastered** shocked out of his wits, flabbergasted

2.4.11–12 **Only . . . bail** Wittypate puns on the legal sense of 'bind', and imagines Lady Ruinous's cries to be released as requests for bail from imprisonment

WITTYPATE Why, law you, sir, is not this a swifter revenue than *sic probos*, *ergos* and *igiturs* can bring in? Why, is not this one of your syllogisms in Barbara, *Omne utile est honestum?*

CREDULOUS
Well, sir, a little more of this acquaintance
Will make me know you fully: I protest
You have (at first sight) made me conscious
Of such a deed my dreams ne'er prompted; yet
I could almost have wished rather ye'd robbed me
Of my cloak (for my purse, 'tis a scholar's)
Than to have made me a robber; I had rather
Have answered three difficult questions
Than this one, as easy as yet it seems.

WITTYPATE
Tush, you shall never come to further answer for't;
Can you confess your penurious uncle,
In his full face of love, to be so strict
A niggard to your commons that you are fain
To size your belly out with shoulder fees,
With rumps and kidneys, and cues of single beer,
And yet make dainty to feed more daintily
At this easier rate? Fie, Master Credulous,
I blush for you.

CREDULOUS This is a truth undeniable.

WITTYPATE
Why, go to, then; I hope I know your uncle;
How does he use his son, nearer than you?

CREDULOUS
Faith, like his jade, upon the bare commons,
Turned out to pick his living as he can get it.

WITTYPATE
He would have been glad to have shared in such
A purchase, and thanked his good fortune too;

Re-enter Sir Ruinous and Priscian

But mum, no more.—Is all safe, bullies?

SIR RUINOUS Secure.
The gentleman thinks him most happy in his loss,
With his safe life and limbs, and redoubles
His first vow, as he is a gentleman,
Never to pursue us.

WITTYPATE Well, away then;
Disperse, you with master Credulous, who still
Shall bear the purchase; Priscian and I
Will take some other course. You know our meeting;
At the Three Cups in Saint Giles, with this proviso
(For 'tis a law with us), that nothing be opened
Till all be present. The loser says a hundred,
And it can weigh no less.

SIR RUINOUS Come, sir, we'll be your guide.

CREDULOUS
My honesty, which till now was never forfeited,
All shall be close till our meeting.

Exeunt Credulous and Sir Ruinous

WITTYPATE Tush, I believe't,
And then all shall out. Where's the thief that's robbed?

Enter Lady Ruinous

LADY
Here, Master Oldcraft; all follows now.

WITTYPATE
'Twas neatly done, wench; now to turn that bag
Of counterfeits to current pieces, *et actum est.*

LADY
You are the chemist; we'll blow the fire still,
If you can mingle the ingredients.

WITTYPATE
I will not miss a cause, a quantity, a dram.
You know the place?

PRISCIAN I have told her that, sir.

WITTYPATE
Good. Turn Ruinous to be a constable
(I'm sure we want not beards of all sorts, from
The worshipful magistrate to the under-watchman).
Because we must have no danger of life,
But a cleanly cheat, attach Credulous

18–59 As Turner points out, Credulous's subsequent recollections at 4.1.111–12 suggest that Wittypate ought perhaps to light up a pipe during this dialogue.

18 **law you, sir** a favourite interjection of Middleton's, possibly signalling his collaboration in a scene otherwise dominated by Rowley

19 ***sic . . . igiturs*** terms from the Latin rhetoric and logic by which contemporary university syllabi were dominated, literally 'Thus-I-proves, therefores and thens'

20 **Barbara** the first word of a mnemonic by which scholars remembered the different figures and moods of the syllogism ('*Barbara, celarent, darii, ferioque prioris*')

20–1 ***Omne . . . honestum*** All that is profitable is virtuous (which is of course not actually a syllogism at all, but simply a single proposition)

32 **penurious** miserly, grudging

34 **commons** see note on 1.2.266–8

35 **size your belly out** fill your belly up (with a pun on 'sizing', a Cambridge term for a helping of drink or food from the buttery)
shoulder fees shoulder bones of beef from which the meat had already been removed, good only for broth

36 **cues** miniscule servings (another university word, from the 'q' entered in college accounts for a quarter-farthing's worth of beer or bread)
single beer small beer, the wateriest grade

37 **make dainty** show fastidiousness

42 **jade** old horse
bare commons thin communal pasture, with a pun on the university sense employed at l. 34

46 **bullies** a bluff term for 'good fellows'

54 **Three Cups in Saint Giles** 'The Three Cups' was a common tavern sign, perhaps chosen here in allusion to the street game in which the operator, usually dishonest, placed a pea or ball under one of three cups, switched them quickly about, and then invited spectators to gamble as to which of the three concealed it. This would sort well with the tavern's location, since the parish of Saint Giles (just north-west of Covent Garden) was a notorious haunt of beggars and thieves: perhaps appropriately it now contains Foyle's bookshop, the Centre Point office development and the guitar shops of Denmark Street.

58 **My honesty** i.e. by my honesty

63 ***et actum est*** and it is done

64 **chemist** alchemist

66 **cause** chemical agent
dram small measurement of liquid

72 **attach** arrest

(The cause is plain, the theft found about him),
Then fall I in, in his own cousin's shape
By mere accident, where, finding him distressed,
I with some difficulty must fetch him off
With promise that his uncle shall shut up all
With double restitution. Master constable Ruinous
His mouth shall be stopped; you, Mistress Rob-thief,
Shall have your share of what we can gull my father
of;
Is't plain enough?

LADY
As plain a cozenage as can be, faith.

WITTYPATE
Father, I come again; and again when this is
Past, too, father; one will beget another;
I'd be loath to leave your posterity barren:
You were best to come to composition, father,
Two hundred pieces yearly allow me yet,
It will be cheaper, father, than my wit;
For I will cheat none but you, dear father. *Exeunt*

❀

3.1 *Enter Old Knight and Sir Gregory*

OLD KNIGHT
Why, now you take the course, Sir Gregory Fop:
I could enforce her an I list, but love
That's gently won is a man's own for ever.
Have you prepared good music?

SIR GREGORY As fine a noise, uncle,
As heart can wish.

OLD KNIGHT Why, that's done like a suitor;
They must be wooed a hundred several ways,
Before you obtain the right way in a woman:
'Tis an odd creature, full of creeks and windings,
The serpent has not more; for sh'as all his,
And then her own beside came in by her mother.

SIR GREGORY
A fearful portion for a man to venture on.

OLD KNIGHT
But the way found once by the wits of men,
There is no creature lies so tame again.

SIR GREGORY
I promise you, not a house-rabbit, sir.

OLD KNIGHT
No sucker on 'em all.

SIR GREGORY What a thing's that?
They're pretty fools, I warrant, when they're tame
As a man can lay his lips to.

OLD KNIGHT How were you bred, sir?
Did you never make a fool of a tenant's daughter?

SIR GREGORY
Never, i'faith; they ha' made some fools for me,
And brought 'em many a time under their aprons.

OLD KNIGHT
They could not show you the way plainlier, I think,
To make a fool again.

SIR GREGORY There's fools enough, sir,
'Less they were wiser.

OLD KNIGHT This is wondrous rare!
Come you to London with a maidenhead, knight?
A gentleman of your rank ride with a cloak-bag?
Never an hostess by the way to leave it with,
Nor tapster's sister, nor head ostler's wife?
What, nobody?

SIR GREGORY Well mocked, old wit-monger:
I keep it for your niece.

OLD KNIGHT
Do not say so, for shame, she'll laugh at thee;
A wife ne'er looks for't; 'tis a bachelor's penny,
He may give't to a beggar-wench i'th' progress time,
And never called to account for't. *Exit*

SIR GREGORY Would I'd known so much,
I could ha' stopped a beggar's mouth by th' way,
Enter Boy
That railed upon me 'cause I'd give her nothing.—
What, are they come?

BOY And placed directly, sir,
Under her window.

SIR GREGORY What may I call you, gentleman?

BOY
A poor servant to the viol; I'm the voice, sir.

SIR GREGORY In good time, Master Voice.

78–9 **Ruinous | His** Ruinous's
86 **composition** compromise
3.1 composed primarily by Middleton
1 **course** i.e. right course of action
2 **an I list** if I wished
8 **creeks and windings** crooked devices and tricks
9 **sh'as** she has
10 **her mother** Eve
11 **portion** dowry
14 **house-rabbit** domestic rabbit
15 **sucker** young (suckling) rabbit
15–17 **What...to** The stress must be laid very heavily on the dubious 'I warrant', as it is otherwise not clear how the Old Knight deduces the sexual inexperience on which he comments in his next speech. Colley Cibber's 1709 adaptation *The Rival Fools* solves this problem by simply altering Sir Gregory's line to 'O, dear! ah! I warrant 'em they're pretty soft Fools when their Clothes are off.'
18 **make a fool of** (*a*) seduce (*b*) beget a bastard ('fool') upon
19 **fools** sweet puddings made of stewed fruit puréed with cream
22 **make a fool** in the sense of 'conceive a bastard'
25 **cloak-bag** an encumbrance which someone of Sir Gregory's status would normally get rid of to one of his servants (like, the Old Knight suggests, his virginity)
27 **tapster's** tavern servant employed to serve drinks
ostler's stableman
32 **progress time** when crowds gathered to watch a royal procession
34 **could...mouth** with an obscene quibble of which Sir Gregory is probably unconscious
36 **they** the (offstage) musicians who accompany the Boy's song
38 **viol** the six-stringed ancestor of the violin
39 **Master Voice** Sir Gregory mistakes the Boy's description of his part in the music for a surname

BOY
Indeed, good time does get the mastery.
SIR GREGORY What countryman, Master Voice?
BOY
Sir, born at Ely; we all set up in E-la,
But our house commonly breaks in Rutlandshire.
SIR GREGORY
A shrewd place, by my faith, it may well break your voice,
It breaks many a man's back. Come, set to your business.
BOY (*sings*)
Fain would I wake you, sweet, but fear
I should invite you to worse cheer;
In your dreams you cannot fare
Meaner than music; no compare;
None of your slumbers are compiled
Under the pleasure makes a child;
Your day-delights so well compact,
That what you think turns all to act:
I'd wish my life no better play,
Your dream by night, your thought by day.
Wake gently, wake,
Part softly from your dreams;
The morning flies
To your fair eyes,
To take her special beams.
SIR GREGORY
I hear her up; here, Master Voice,
Pay you the instruments; save what you can
Enter Niece, above
To keep you when you're cracked. *Exit Boy*
NIECE Who should this be
That I'm so much beholding to for sweetness?
[*Aside*] Pray Heaven it happens right.
SIR GREGORY Good morrow, mistress.
NIECE
An ill day and a thousand come upon thee!
SIR GREGORY
'Light, that's six hundred more than any almanac has.
NIECE
Comes it from thee? It is the mangiest music
That ever woman heard.
SIR GREGORY Nay, say not so, lady,
There's not an itch about 'em.
NIECE I could curse
My attentive powers for giving entrance to't;
There is no boldness like the impudence
That's locked in a fool's blood; how durst you do this?
In conscience, I abused you as sufficiently
As woman could a man; insatiate coxcomb,
The mocks and spiteful language I have given thee
Would, o' my life, ha' served ten reasonable men,
And rise contented too, and left enough for their friends.
You glutton at abuses, never satisfied!
I am persuaded thou devour'st more flouts
Than all thy body's worth, and still a-hungered!
A mischief of that maw; prithee, seek elsewhere;
In troth, I am weary of abusing thee;
Get thee a fresh mistress, thou't make work enough;
I do not think there's scorn enough in town
To serve thy turn; take the court-ladies in,
And all their women to 'em, that exceed 'em.
SIR GREGORY
Is this in earnest, lady?
NIECE O, unsatiable!
Dost thou count all this but an earnest yet?
I'd thought I'd paid thee all the whole sum, trust me;
Thou't beggar my derision utterly
If thou stay'st longer; I shall want a laugh:
If I knew where to borrow a contempt
Would hold thee tack, stay and be hanged thou should'st then;
But thou'st no conscience now to extort hate from me
When one has spent all she can make upon thee.
Must I begin to pay thee hire again
After I've rid thee twice? Faith, 'tis unreasonable.
SIR GREGORY
Say you so? I'll know that presently. *Exit*
NIECE Now he runs
To fetch my uncle to this musty bargain;
But I have better ware always at hand,
And lay by this still when he comes to cheapen.
Enter Cunningame [*below*]
CUNNINGAME
I met the music now, yet cannot learn

42 **E-la** the highest note in the Renaissance scale (or 'gamut'), corresponding to modern top E, punning on 'Ely'
43 **But . . . Rutlandshire** Rutlandshire, where the Boy claims the 'Voice family' usually fail, is on the route between Ely and London. The punning sense of this line is of course 'but voices usually break at puberty' (rutting time).
47 **cheer** 'fare', 'welcome' or 'state of mind'
49 **no compare** no comparison
50–1 **None . . . child** None of your dreams are made up of anything less than orgasm
52 **compact** composed, distilled
63 **when you're cracked** when your voice breaks
71 **attentive powers** senses
77 **served** (*a*) been sufficient for (*b*) provided adequate servings of (as at a banquet, a sense the Niece pursues in her next line)
84 **thou't** thou wilt
87 **women** serving women or maids (who excel their mistresses in contempt)
89 **earnest** The Niece punningly takes Sir Gregory's question as to whether she is serious as an enquiry as to whether her insults to date have been merely a down-payment.
91 **Thou't** thou wilt
94 **tack** fixed, fast
95 **thou'st** thou hast
98 **rid** sacked, fired
101 **musty** stale, mouldy, perhaps with an additional punning sense of 'compulsory', as at 5.2.86
103 **lay by** set aside
cheapen bargain (here literally 'woo')
104 **the music** the band of musicians

What entertainment he received from her.

NIECE [*aside*]
There's somebody set already, I must to't, I see.—
Well, well, Sir Gregory,

CUNNINGAME [*aside*] Ha, Sir Gregory?

NIECE
Where'er you come you may well boast your conquest.

CUNNINGAME [*aside*]
She's lost, i'faith; enough; has Fortune then
Remembered her great boy? She seldom fails 'em.

NIECE
He was the unlikeliest man at first, methought,
To have my love; we never met but wrangled.

CUNNINGAME [*aside*]
A pox upon that wrangling, say I still,
I never knew it fail yet, where'er't came;
It never comes but, like a storm of hail,
'Tis sure to bring fine weather at the tail on't;
There's not one match 'mongst twenty made without it;
It fights i'th' tongue, but sure to agree i'th' haunches.

NIECE
That man that should ha' told me, when time was,
I should ha' had him, had been laughed at piteously,
But see how things will change!

CUNNINGAME (*aside*) Here's a heart feels it!
O the deceitful promises of love!
What trust should a man put i'th' lip of woman?
She kissed me with that strength, as if she'd meant
To ha' set the fair print of her soul upon me.

NIECE
I would ha' sworn 'twould ne'er ha' been a match once.

CUNNINGAME [*aside*]
I'll hear no more; I'm mad to hear so much.
Why should I aim my thoughts at better fortunes
Than younger brothers have? That's a maid with nothing,
Or some old soap-boiler's widow, without teeth;
There waits my fortune for me; seek no farther. *Exit*

Enter Old Knight and Sir Gregory

OLD KNIGHT
You tell me things, Sir Gregory, that cannot be;
She will not, nor she dares not.

SIR GREGORY Would I were whipped, then.

NIECE [*above, as if to herself*]
I'll make as little show of love, Sir Gregory,
As ever woman did; you shall not know
You have my heart a good while.

OLD KNIGHT Heard you that?

NIECE
Man will insult so soon, 'tis his condition;
'Tis good to keep him off as long as we can;
I've much ado, I swear; and love i'th' end
Will have his course. Let maids do what they can,
They are but frail things till they end in man.

OLD KNIGHT
What say you to this, sir?

SIR GREGORY This is somewhat handsome.

NIECE
And by that little wrangling that I feigned,
Now I shall try how constant his love is,
Although't went sore against my heart to chide him.

SIR GREGORY
Alas, poor gentlewoman!

OLD KNIGHT Now you're sure of truth,
You hear her own thoughts speak.

SIR GREGORY They speak, indeed.

OLD KNIGHT
Go, you're a brainless cox, a toy, a fop
(I'll go no farther than your name, Sir Gregory,
I'll right myself there); were you from this place
You should perceive I'm heartily angry with you;
Offer to sow strife 'twixt my niece and I?—
Good morrow, niece, good morrow.

NIECE Many fair ones to you, sir.

OLD KNIGHT [*aside, to Sir Gregory*]
Go, you're a coxcomb!—How dost, niece, this morning?—
[*Aside to Sir Gregory*] An idle, shallow fool—Slept'st thou well, girl?—
[*Aside to Sir Gregory*] Fortune may very well provide thee lordships,
For honesty has left thee little manners.

SIR GREGORY [*aside*]
How am I banged o' both sides!

OLD KNIGHT Abuse kindness!—
Wilt take the air today, niece?

NIECE When you please, sir,
There stands the heir behind you I must take.
[*Aside*] Which I'd as lieve take as take him, I swear.

OLD KNIGHT [*aside to Sir Gregory*]
La you, do you hear't continued to your teeth now?
A pox of all such Gregories! what a hand
Have I with you!

Niece lets fall her scarf

SIR GREGORY No more, i'feck, I ha' done, sir.—
Lady, your scarf's fall'n down.

NIECE 'Tis but your luck, sir,

106 **set** stationed (as a spy). It is not clear here whether the Niece recognizes Cunningame and deliberately sets out to make him jealous, or whether she believes she is deceiving the Old Knight, via an informer, about her opinion of Sir Gregory.

110 **great boy** fool, simpleton

137 **insult** in the sense of 'exalt arrogantly over (a defeated adversary)'
condition nature, disposition

148 **cox** simpleton
toy i.e. trifle

158 **manners** punning on 'manors'

161–2 **There . . . swear** 'Stated baldly, the Niece would as soon accept a fart from the Old Knight ("the air behind you") as Sir Gregory ("the heir behind you")' (Sharp)

163 **La you** a meaningless interjection
to your teeth i.e. to your face

165 **i'feck** in faith

And does presage the mistress must fall shortly;
You may wear it, an you please.

OLD KNIGHT There's a trick for you.
You're parlously beloved; you should complain!

SIR GREGORY Yes, when I complain, sir,
Then do your worst; there I'll deceive you, sir.

OLD KNIGHT
You are a dolt; and so I leave you, sir. *Exit*

SIR GREGORY
Ah, sirrah mistress, were you caught, i'faith?
We overheard you all; I must not know
I have your heart; take heed o' that, I pray.
I knew some scarf would come.

NIECE [*aside*] He's quite gone, sure.—
Ah, you base coxcomb, could'st thou come again?
And so abused as thou wast?

SIR GREGORY How?

NIECE 'Twould ha' killed
A sensible man; he would ha' gone to his chamber
And broke his heart by this time.

SIR GREGORY Thank you heartily.

NIECE
Or fixed a naked rapier in a wall,
Like him that earned his knighthood ere he had it,
And then, refused, upon't ran up to th'hilts.

SIR GREGORY
Yes, let him run for me; I was never brought up to't,
I never professed running i' my life.

NIECE
What art thou made on? Thou tough, villainous vermin,
Will nothing destroy thee?

SIR GREGORY Yes, yes, assure yourself,
Unkind words may do much.

NIECE Why, dost thou want 'em?
I've e'en consumed my spleen to help thee to 'em;
Tell me what sort of words they be would speed thee,
I'll see what I can do yet.

SIR GREGORY I'm much beholding to you,
You're willing to bestow huge pains upon me.

NIECE
I should account nothing too much to rid thee.

SIR GREGORY
I wonder you'd not offer to destroy me
All the while your uncle was here.

NIECE
Why, there thou betray'st thy house; we of the Oldcrafts
Were born to more wit than so.

SIR GREGORY I wear your favour here.

NIECE
Would it might rot thy arm off. If thou knewst
With what contempt thou hast it, what heart's bitterness,
How many cunning curses came along with it,
Thou'dst quake to handle it.

SIR GREGORY A pox, take't again then!
[*Aside*] Who'd be thus plagued of all hands?

NIECE No, wear't still,
But long, I hope, thou shalt not. 'Tis but cast
Upon thee purposely to serve another
That has more right to't, as in some countries they convey
Their treasure upon asses to their friends;
If mine be but so wise and apprehensive
As my opinion gives him to my heart,
It stays not long on thy desertless arm.
I'll make thee ere I ha' done not dare to wear
Any thing of mine, although I give't freely;
Kiss it you may, and make what show you can,
But sure you carry't to a worthier man.
And so good morrow to you. [*Exit*]

SIR GREGORY Hu hum, ha hum.
I ha'n't the spirit now to dash my brains out,
Nor the audacity to kill myself,
But I could cry my heart out, that's as good,
For so't be out, no matter which way it comes.
If I can die with a fillip, or depart
At hot-cockles, what's that to any man,
If there be so much death that serves my turn there?
Everyone knows the state of his own body:
No carrion kills a kite, but then again
There's cheese will choke a daw. Time I were dead, i'faith,
If I knew which way without hurt or danger.

169 **parlously** perilously (used here simply as an intensifier, akin to the modern colloquial usage of 'terribly')
176 **scarf** in the sense of some salving bandage or sling for his own wounded heart
181–3 **Or . . . th'hilts** If this is an allusion to a real incident, it has not been identified
190 **speed** dispatch, kill
193 **rid** get rid of, dismiss
196 **house** family, i.e. Sir Gregory is showing that he is a Fop
202 **of all hands** on all sides, by everybody
207 **apprehensive** perceptive
219 **fillip** flicking blow administered with one finger
220 **hot-cockles** a game resembling blind man's buff, in which a kneeling player with eyes covered tries to guess which other player is administering playful blows from behind
223 **No . . . kite** a proverbial phrase generally used in the sense 'a shameless person is invulnerable to shame', more common in the form 'No carrion poisons a crow.' The kite, a bird of prey now confined to a few valleys in Wales, was a common scavenger in the streets of Jacobean London.
224 **There's . . . daw** apparently a contrary proverb, meaning 'everyone has some vulnerable point or Achilles' heel': for the notion of jackdaws as vulnerable to choking (with cheese?), cf. Shakespeare, *Much Ado About Nothing*, 2.3.241–3, 'just so much as you may take upon a knife's point and choke a daw withal'. This piece of obscure avian lore is additionally appropriate here since the jackdaw was regarded as a foolish bird, and hence 'daw' was slang for 'idiot'.

I am a maiden knight, and cannot look
Upon a naked weapon with any modesty,
Else 'twould go hard with me: and to complain
To Sir Perfidious the old knight again
Were to be more abused; perhaps he would beat me
well,
But ne'er believe me;

Enter Cunningame

And few men die o' beating, that were lost too.
O, here's my friend, I'll make my moan to him.

CUNNINGAME
I cannot tear her memory from my heart,
That treads mine down. Was ever man so fooled
That professed wit?

SIR GREGORY O, Cunningame.

CUNNINGAME Sir Gregory,
The choice, the victor, the town's happy man!

SIR GREGORY
'Sniggs, what dost mean? Come I to thee for comfort
And dost abuse me too?

CUNNINGAME Abuse you? How, sir?
With justifying your fortune and your joys?

SIR GREGORY
Pray, hold your hand, sir, I've been bobbed enough:
You come with a new way now, strike me merrily,
But when a man's sore beaten o' both sides already,
Then the least tap in jest goes to the guts on him.
Wilt ha' the truth? I'm made the rankest ass
That ere was born to lordships.

CUNNINGAME What? No, sir.

SIR GREGORY
I had not thought my body could 'a' yielded
All those foul scurvy names that she has called me;
I wonder whence she fetched 'em?

CUNNINGAME Is this credible?

SIR GREGORY
She pinned this scarf upon me afore her uncle,
But, his back turned, she cursed me so for wearing
on't,
The very brawn of mine arm has ached ever since,
Yet in a manner forced me to wear't still,
But hoped I should not long; if good luck serve
I should meet one that has more wit and worth
Should take it from me; 'twas but lent to me,
And sent to him for a token.

CUNNINGAME [*aside*] I conceit it.—
I know the man
That lies in wait for't: part with it, by all means,
In any case; you are waylaid about it.

SIR GREGORY
How, sir, waylaid?

CUNNINGAME Pox of a scarf, say I,
I prize my friend's life 'bove a million on 'em;
You shall be ruled, sir, I know more than you.

SIR GREGORY
If you know more than I, let me be rid on't;
'Las, 'tis not for my wearing, so she told me.

CUNNINGAME
No, no, give me't; the knave shall miss his purpose,
And you shall live.

SIR GREGORY I would, as long as I could, sir.

CUNNINGAME
No more replies, you shall, I'll prevent this;
Pompey shall march without it.

SIR GREGORY What, is't he?
My man that was?

CUNNINGAME Call him your deadly enemy;
You give him too fair a name, you deal too nobly,
He bears a bloody mind; a cruel foe, sir,
I care not if he heard me.

SIR GREGORY But do you hear, sir?
Can 't sound with reason she should affect him?

CUNNINGAME
Do you talk of reason? I never thought to have heard
Such a word come from you; reason in love?
Would you give that no doctor could e'er give?
Has not a deputy married his cook-maid?
An alderman's widow one that was her turn-broach?
Nay, has not a great lady brought her stable
Into her chamber, lay with her horsekeeper?

SIR GREGORY
Did ever love play such jade's tricks, sir?

CUNNINGAME O, thousands, thousands.
Beware a sturdy clown e'er while you live, sir.
'Tis like a housewifery in most shires about us;
You shall ha' farmers' widows wed thin gentlemen

226 **maiden knight** one who has never fought (with a pun on the sexual sense, too, which continues through the next line)

232 **that were lost too** that would be wasted too (since the Old Knight's beating would not prove fatal)

235 **That treads mine down** It is not clear whether 'mine' refers to Cunningame's memory or his heart, or whether 'That' refers back to 'her memory' or 'my heart', but in any case Cunningame feels trampled down by his perpetual recollection of the Niece.

238 **'Sniggs** God's nigs (a mild and meaningless oath)

240 **justifying** proclaiming as just

241 **bobbed** both in the sense of 'mocked' and that of 'beaten'

250 **pinned** used loosely in the sense of 'fastened'

257 **conceit** apprehend, get the idea of

260 **you...it** there is an ambush set for you on its account

268 **prevent** intercept

278–81 **Has not...horsekeeper?** if these are specific allusions, rather than simply drawn from the general archive of folklore, they have never been conclusively identified

279 **turn-broach** kitchen servant employed to turn a spit

282 **jade's tricks** punning on the equestrian nature of Cunningame's last example, since the phrase could refer to wilful or perverse behaviour on the part of either women or horses

283 **clown** peasant, rustic servant

284 **a housewifery** a policy of domestic economy

Much like yourself, but put 'em to no stress,
What work can they do with small trapstick legs?
They keep clowns to stop gaps, and drive in pegs,
A drudgery fit for hinds. E'en back again, sir,
You're safest at returning.

SIR GREGORY Think you so, sir?

CUNNINGAME
But how came this clown to be called Pompey first?

SIR GREGORY
Pish, one goodman Caesar, a pump-maker, christened him;
'Pompey' he writes himself, but his right name's 'Pumpey',
And stunk, too, when I had him; now he's crank.

CUNNINGAME
I'm glad I know so much to quell his pride, sir;
Walk you still that way. [*Aside*] I'll make use of this
To resolve all my doubts, and place this favour
On some new mistress, only for a try;
And if it meet my thoughts, I'll swear 'tis I. *Exit*

SIR GREGORY
Is Pompey grown so malapert? so frampold?
The only cutter about ladies' honours,
Enter Old Knight
And his blade soonest out?

OLD KNIGHT Now, what's the news, sir?

SIR GREGORY [*aside*]
I dare not say but good.—O, excellent good, sir.

OLD KNIGHT
I hope now you're resolved she loves you, knight?

SIR GREGORY
Cuds me, what else, sir? That's not to do now.

OLD KNIGHT
You would not think how desperately you angered me
When you belied her goodness; O, you vexed me
Even to a palsy.

SIR GREGORY What a thing was that, sir!
Enter Niece

NIECE [*aside*] 'Tis, that 'tis!
As I have hope of sweetness, the scarf's gone:
Worthy wise friend, I dote upon thy cunning!
We two shall be well matched; our issue male, sure,
Will be born counsellors; is't possible?
Thou shalt have another token out of hand for't;
Nay, since the way's found, pity thou should'st want, i'faith.—
O, my best joy and dearest!

OLD KNIGHT Well said, niece;
So violent fore your uncle? What will you do
In secret then?

SIR GREGORY [*aside*]
Marry, call me slave and rascal.

NIECE
Your scarf—the scarf I gave you—

OLD KNIGHT Mass, that's true, niece,
I ne'er thought upon that; the scarf she gave you, sir?
What, dumb? No answer from you? The scarf!

SIR GREGORY
I was waylaid about it, my life threatened:
Life's life, scarf's but a scarf, and so I parted from't.

NIECE
Unfortunate woman! My first favour too?

OLD KNIGHT
Will you be still an ass? No reconcilement
'Twixt you and wit? Are you so far fallen out
You'll never come together? I tell you true,
I'm very lousily ashamed on you,
That's the worst shame that can be.
[*Aside*] Thus baiting on him, now his heart's hooked in,
I'll make him, ere I ha' done, take her with nothing.
I love a man that lives by his wits, o' life!—
Nay, leave, sweet niece, 'tis but a scarf, let it go.

NIECE
The going of it never grieves me, sir.
It is the manner, the manner—

SIR GREGORY [*aside*]
O, dissembling marmoset! If I durst speak,
Or could be believed when I speak, what a tale
Could I tell, to make hair stand upright now!

NIECE
Nay, sir, at your request you shall perceive, uncle,
With what renewing love I forgive this.—
[*Giving a ring to Sir Gregory*] Here's a fair diamond, sir; I'll try how long
You can keep that.

SIR GREGORY [*aside to Niece*]
Not very long, you know't too,
Like a cunning witch as you are.

287 **trapstick** a stick about six inches long and two inches thick, tapering from the middle to both ends, used in the child's ball game of tip-cat (favoured by the Ward in *Women Beware*)
288 **stop . . . pegs** the sexual sense is obvious
289 **hinds** peasants, farm labourers
292 **Caesar** as incongruously illustrious a name as Pompey, and of course closely associated with it, since Julius Caesar briefly co-ruled the Roman empire with Pompey the Great before the outbreak of the civil wars between them which concluded with Caesar's victory at Pharsalus in 48 BC
pump-maker Sharp glosses this term as meaning 'shoemaker', suggesting that the association of the Clown with footwear is appropriate since he is a footman, but the Clown is nowhere referred to as such, and the subsequent pun on 'crank' makes it more likely that goodman Caesar was genuinely a manufacturer of pumping equipment
294 **And stunk** 'The joke, such as it is, turns on *pump* as "to fart"' (Turner)
crank arrogant, cocky (with another pun on 'pump')
298 **try** trial
299 **'tis I** i.e. that I am the one she intends
300 **malapert** impertinent
frampold sour-tempered, peevish
301 **cutter** 'swaggerer, ruffler' (Dyce)
302 **blade** with a sexual pun for 'penis'
304 **resolved** convinced
332 **o' life** as my life
336 **marmoset** a type of small monkey considered to be lecherous

NIECE (*aside to Sir Gregory*)
You're best let him ha' that too.
SIR GREGORY [*aside to Niece*]
So I were, I think, there were no living else,
I thank you, as you have handled the matter.
SIR GREGORY
Why, this is musical now, and Tuesday next
Shall tune your instruments; that's the day set.
NIECE
A match, good uncle.
OLD KNIGHT Sir, you hear me too?
SIR GREGORY O, very well; I'm for you.
NIECE [*to Sir Gregory*]
Whate'er you hear, you know my mind.
Exeunt Old Knight and Niece

SIR GREGORY Ay, a pox on't, too well! If I do not wonder how we two shall come together, I'm a bear-whelp. He talks of Tuesday next as familiarly as if we loved one another, but 'tis as unlikely to me as 'twas seven year before I saw her. I shall try his cunning: it may be he has a way was never yet thought on, and it had need to be such a one, for all that I can think on will never do't. I look to have this diamond taken from me very speedily; therefore I'll take it off o' my finger, for if it be seen, I shall be waylaid for that too. *Exit*

4.1 *Enter Old Knight and Wittypate*
OLD KNIGHT
O torture! torture! Thou carriest a sting i' thy tail;
Thou never brought'st good news i' thy life yet,
And that's an ill quality, leave it when thou wilt.
WITTYPATE
Why, you receive a blessing the wrong way, sir,
Call you not this good news? To save at once, sir,
Your credit and your kinsman's life together?
Would it not vex your peace, and gall your worth,
T'have one of your name hanged?
OLD KNIGHT Peace, no such words, boy.
WITTYPATE
Be thankful for the blessing of prevention, then.
OLD KNIGHT Lemme see,
There was none hanged out of our house since Brute,
I ha' searched both Stow and Holinshed.
WITTYPATE O, sir.
OLD KNIGHT
I'll see what *Polychronicon* says anon, too.
WITTYPATE
'Twas a miraculous fortune that I heard on't.
OLD KNIGHT
I would thou'dst never heard on't.
WITTYPATE That's true too,
So it had ne'er been done. To see the luck on't!
He was e'en brought to Justice Aurum's threshold:
There had flown forth a mittimus straight for Newgate,
And note the fortune too; sessions o' Thursday,
Jury culled out o' Friday, judgement o' Saturday,
Dungeon o' Sunday, Tyburn o' Monday.
Misery's quotidian ague, when't begins once,
Every day pulls him, till he pull his last.
OLD KNIGHT
No more, I say, 'tis an ill theme. Where left you him?
WITTYPATE
He's i'th' constable's hands below i'th' hall, sir,
Poor gentleman, and his accuser with him.
OLD KNIGHT What's he?
WITTYPATE
A judge's son, 'tis thought; so much the worse, too,
He'll hang his enemy, and't shall cost him nothing;
That's a great privilege.
OLD KNIGHT Within, there!
Enter Servant
SERVANT Sir?
OLD KNIGHT
Call up the folks i'th' hall. [*Exit Servant*]
I had such hope on him
For a scholar too, a thing thou ne'er wast fit for,
Therefore erected all my joys in him;

4.1 composed primarily, along with the remainder of act 4, by Middleton

11 **Brute** the legendary great-grandson of Aeneas supposed to have founded Britain

12 **Stow** the historian and geographer John Stow (*c.*1525–1605); the reference here is to his *Annals, or a General Chronicle of England from Brute until the Present Year of Christ 1580* (1580)
Holinshed Raphael Holinshed, compiler of *The Chronicles of England, Scotland, and Ireland* (1577, 1587)

13 ***Polychronicon*** a Latin history of the universe composed *c.*1360 by the English monk Ranulph Higden (who appears in *Hengist*), translated into English by John Trevisa in 1387 and most recently reprinted in 1527

17 **Aurum's** The name of course means 'gold', suggesting an amenability to bribes

18 **mittimus** warrant for someone's detention prior to trial
Newgate London's most important prison, on the site of the present-day Old Bailey

20 **culled out** picked out, chosen. Since Credulous's trial might begin on the first day of the sessions, the Thursday, however, it is possible that the first edition's 'cul'd' is an error for 'cal'd', i.e. 'called', and that Friday would be the day on which the jury considered their verdict rather than the day on which they were selected.

21 **Tyburn** London's chief gallows, situated at the meeting of the main westward road towards Oxford (now Oxford Street) and the Tyburn stream, the site of the present-day Marble Arch

22 **quotidian ague** disease from which the sufferer endured a fresh spasm every day

23 **pull his last** takes his last breath

Got a Welsh benefice in reversion for him,
Dean of Cardigan; has his grace already,
He can marry and bury, yet ne'er a hair on's face,
Enter Credulous, Sir Ruinous (as a constable) and Lady Ruinous (as a man)
Like a French vicar: and does he bring such fruits
To town with him? A thief at his first lighting?—
O, good e'en to you.

WITTYPATE
Nay, sweet sir, you're so vexed now, you'll grieve him,
And hurt yourself.

OLD KNIGHT
Away! I'll hear no counsel.—
[*To Credulous*] Come you but once in seven year to your uncle,
And at that time must you be brought home too,
And by a constable?

WITTYPATE
O, speak low, sir,
Remember your own credit; you profess
You love a man o' wit; begin at home, sir,
Express it i' yourself.

LADY
Nay, master constable,
Show yourself a wise man, 'gainst your nature too.

SIR RUINOUS
Sir, no dish-porridgement; we have brought home
As good men as ye.

OLD KNIGHT [*aside*]
Out, a North Britain constable! That tongue
Will publish all, it speaks so broad already.—
Are you the gentleman?

LADY
The unfortunate one, sir,
That fell into the power of merciless thieves,
Whereof this fellow (whom I'd call your kinsman
As little as I could, for the fair reverence
I owe to fame and years) was the prime villain.

OLD KNIGHT
A wicked prime.

WITTYPATE
Nay, not so loud, sweet father.

LADY
The rest are fled, but I shall meet with 'em;
Hang one of 'em I will certain, I ha' swore it,
And 'twas my luck to light upon this first.

OLD KNIGHT
A Cambridge man for this? These your degrees, sir?
Nine years at university for this fellowship?

WITTYPATE
Take your voice lower, dear sir.

OLD KNIGHT
What's your loss, sir?

LADY
That which offends me to repeat; the money's whole, sir,
'Tis i' the constable's hands there, a sealed hundred,
But I will not receive it.

OLD KNIGHT
No? Not the money, sir,
Having confessed 'tis all?

LADY
'Tis all the money, sir,
But 'tis not all I lost, for when they bound me
They took a diamond hung at my shirt string
Which fear of life made me forget to hide,
It being the sparkling witness of a contract
'Twixt a great lawyer's daughter and myself.

WITTYPATE
I told you what he was.—What does the diamond
Concern my cousin, sir?

LADY
No more did the money,
But he shall answer all now.

WITTYPATE
There's your conscience,
It shows from whence you sprung.

LADY
Sprung? I had leapt a thief
Had I leapt some of your alliance.

WITTYPATE
Slave!

LADY
You prevent me still.

OLD KNIGHT
'Slid, son, are you mad?

LADY Come, come; I'll take a legal course.

OLD KNIGHT
Will you undo us all?—What's your demand, sir?—
Now we're in's danger too.

LADY
A hundred mark, sir,
I will not bate a doit.

33 **Welsh benefice** evidence of the Old Knight's stinginess even to his favourite, since Welsh benefices were notoriously unrewarding (indeed we later learn that this one is worth only £10 a year, at 5.2.322). 'For what it may be worth, playing cards for money was one of a number of unbecoming practices resorted to by Welsh clergymen to eke out a living' (Turner)
in reversion for him reserved for him to take over on the death of the present incumbent

34 **has his grace already** has already been ordained

35–6 **yet ne'er... French vicar** Catholic clerics were encouraged to remain clean-shaven: the Anglican Credulous is so young that he has as yet no beard to shave

48 **dish-porridgement** 'disparagement', pronounced in the Scots accent which is part of Sir Ruinous's disguise and with which the 'porridge' is deliberately in keeping

50 **North Britain** i.e. Scottish; a topical circumlocution given James I's continuing attempts to negotiate a complete political and legal union between Scotland and England

51 **speaks so broad** punning on the senses of speaking in a thick accent and speaking abroad, spreading tales at large

57 **prime** here in the sense of youth, the springtime of life

62 **this fellowship** the company of the constable, punning on the university sense of the term

71 **contract** engagement

76–7 **I had... alliance** 'Leapt' here means copulated with, i.e. married: Wittypate's insult to the ancestors of Credulous's 'victim' provokes 'him' to point out the undesirability of marrying into Wittypate's disgraced family

77 **some of your alliance** some to whom you are related

78 **prevent** anticipate

81 **in's danger** in his danger, at risk from him
A hundred mark A mark was worth two-thirds of a pound, i.e. 13*s.* 4*d.*; a hundred marks is equal to £66 13*s.* 4*d.* (rounded up by the Old Knight to £67 at l. 90).

82 **bate** go without, lower my price by
doit the smallest and least valuable of all coins

WITTYPATE A hundred rascals!
LADY
Sir, find 'em out in your own blood, and take 'em.
WITTYPATE
Go, take your course, follow the law, and spare not.
OLD KNIGHT [*aside to Wittypate*]
Does fury make you drunk? Know you what you say?
WITTYPATE A hundred dogs' dungs! Do your worst.
OLD KNIGHT You do, I'm sure; who's loud now?
WITTYPATE
What, his own asking?
OLD KNIGHT Not in such a case?
WITTYPATE
You shall have but threescore pound, spite o' your teeth,
I'll see you hanged first.
OLD KNIGHT And what's seven pound more, man,
That all this coil's about?—Stay.—I say he shall ha't.
WITTYPATE
It is your own, you may do what you please with it;
Pardon my zeal, I would ha' saved you money;
Give him all his own asking?
OLD KNIGHT What's that to you, sir?
Be sparing of your own. Teach me to pinch
In such a case as this? Go, go, live by your wits, go.
WITTYPATE
I practise all I can.
OLD KNIGHT Follow you me, sir,
And master constable, come from the knave,
And be a witness of a full recompense.
WITTYPATE [*aside to Old Knight*]
Pray, stop the constable's mouth, whate'er you do, sir.
OLD KNIGHT
Yet again? As if I meant not to do that myself
Without your counsel?—As for you, precious kinsman,
Your first year's fruits in Wales shall go to rack for this.
You lie not in my house, I'll pack you out,
And pay for your lodging rather.
Exeunt Old Knight, Ruinous and Lady Ruinous
WITTYPATE O fie, cousin,
These are ill courses; you a scholar, too!
CREDULOUS
I was drawn into't most unfortunately
By filthy debauched company.
WITTYPATE Ay, ay, ay,
'Tis even the spoil of all our youth in England;
What, were they gentlemen?
CREDULOUS Faith, so like, some on 'em,
They were e'en the worse again.
WITTYPATE Hum.
CREDULOUS Great tobacco whiffers,
They would go near to rob with a pipe in their mouths.
WITTYPATE What? No!
CREDULOUS
Faith, leave it, cousin, because my rascals use it.
WITTYPATE
So they do meat and drink: must worthy gentlemen
Refrain their food for that? An honest man
May eat of the same pig some parson dines with;
A lawyer and a fool feed of one woodcock,
Yet one ne'er the simpler, t'other ne'er the wiser.
'Tis not meat, drink, or smoke, dish, cup, or pipe
Cooperates to the making of a knave;
'Tis the condition makes a slave a slave.
There's London philosophy for you. I tell you, cousin,
You cannot be too cautelous, nice, or dainty
In your society here, especially
When you come raw from the university
Before the world has hardened you a little;
For as a buttered loaf is a scholar's breakfast there,
So a poached scholar is a cheater's dinner here.
I ha' known seven of 'em supped up at a meal.
CREDULOUS
Why a poached scholar?
WITTYPATE 'Cause he pours himself forth,
And all his secrets, at the first acquaintance,
Never so crafty to be eaten i'th' shell,
But is outstripped of all he has at first,
And goes down glib; he's swallowed with sharp wit,
'Stead of wine vinegar.
CREDULOUS I shall think, cousin,
O' your poached scholar while I live.
Enter Servant
SERVANT Master Credulous,
Your uncle wills you to forbear the house;
You must with me, I'm charged to see you placed
In some new lodging about Thieving Lane;
What the conceit's, I know not, but commands you
To be seen here no more, till you hear further.
CREDULOUS
Here's a strange welcome, sir.
WITTYPATE This is the world, cousin,

83 **find 'em ... blood** find them among your own family
89 **spite o' your teeth** in despite of you, in flat defiance of you
91 **coil's** noise, fuss, squabble
100 **stop the constable's mouth** bribe the constable to silence
114 **leave it** Turner plausibly suggests, on the strength of this request, that Wittypate should produce and light his own pipe at some earlier stage in this passage of dialogue, perhaps on his previous line
122 **condition** nature, disposition
124 **cautelous** circumspect
nice, or dainty choosy or fastidious
135 **glib** easily, smoothly
140 **Thieving Lane** a shabby street in Westminster, chosen by the Old Knight for its opprobrious name
141 **What the conceit's** What the idea or whim is

When a man's fame's once poisoned. Fare thee well, lad.
Exeunt Credulous and Servant
This is the happiest cheat I e'er claimed share in:
It has a twofold fortune; gets me coin,
And puts him out of grace that stood between me,
My father's Cambridge jewel, much suspected
To be his heir; now there's a bar in's hopes.
Enter Sir Ruinous and Lady Ruinous, [*with a purse*]

SIR RUINOUS
It chinks, make haste!

LADY
The Goat at Smithfield Pens.

WITTYPATE
Zo, zo, zufficient.
[*Exeunt Sir Ruinous and Lady Ruinous*]
Enter Cunningame
Master Cunningame!
I never have ill luck when I meet a wit.

CUNNINGAME
A wit's better to meet than to follow then,
For I ha' none so good I can commend yet;
But commonly men unfortunate to themselves
Are luckiest to their friends, and so may I be.

WITTYPATE
I run o'er so much worth going but in haste from you,
All my deliberate friendship cannot equal.

CUNNINGAME
'Tis but to show that you can place sometimes
Your modesty atop of all your virtues.
Exit Wittypate
This gentleman may pleasure me yet again.
Enter Mirabell [*behind*]
I am so haunted with this broad-brimmed hat
Of the last progress block, with the young hatband,
Made for a sucking devil of two year old,
I know not where to turn myself.

MIRABELL
Sir!

CUNNINGAME
More torture?

MIRABELL
'Tis rumoured that you love me.

CUNNINGAME
O' my troth, gentlewoman,
Rumour's as false a knave as ever pissed then,
Pray tell him so from me; I cannot feign
With a sweet gentlewoman, I must deal downright.

MIRABELL
I heard, though, you dissembled with my aunt, sir,
And that makes me more confident.

CUNNINGAME [*aside*]
There's no falsehood
But pays us our own some way.—I confess
I feigned with her ('twas for a weightier purpose),
But not with thee, I swear.

MIRABELL
Nor I with you, then,
Although my aunt enjoined me to dissemble
To right her spleen. I love you faithfully.

CUNNINGAME [*aside*]
'Light, this is worse than 'twas.

MIRABELL
I find such worth in you
I cannot, nay, I dare not dally with you
For fear the flame consume me.

CUNNINGAME [*aside*]
Here's fresh trouble,
This drives me to my conscience, for 'tis foul
To injure one that deals directly with me.

MIRABELL
I crave but such a truth from your love, sir,
As mine brings you, and that's proportionable.

CUNNINGAME [*aside*]
A good geometrician, 'shrew my heart.—
Why, are you out o' your wits, pretty plump gentlewoman,
You talk so desperately? 'Tis a great happiness
Love has made one on's wiser than another;
We should be both cast away else:
Yet I love gratitude; I must requite you,
I shall be sick else, but to give you me,
A thing you must not take, if you mean to live
(For, o' my troth, I hardly can myself),

147 **between me** i.e. between me and my father's fortune

150 **The Goat** a widespread tavern sign, perhaps selected because of the association between goats and devilry; no other reference to an inn bearing this name in Smithfield is recorded **Smithfield Pens** Smithfield Market, London's principal livestock market, whose taverns, full of money-laden buyers and sellers of horses and cattle, attracted pickpockets and cheats of all kinds: the area was popularly known as 'Ruffian's Hall'

151 **Zo, zo, zufficient** Wittypate jokingly imitates Sir Ruinous's fake Scots accent

151–61 **Master Cunningame . . . again** This short passage of dialogue, which provides the first indication that Wittypate and Cunningame are acquainted but otherwise does not materially assist the play's narrative, has clearly been added at a late stage of revision to join two previously unconnected scenes: until this point the setting has clearly been within the Old Knight's house, but from here to the end of the act it is apparently in a public street.

162–5 **haunted . . . myself** In this slightly confused passage Cunningame for a second time associates the unwanted attentions of a woman with black magic (see 2.1.19), thinking of Mirabell at l. 162 as 'an evil spirit in a broad-brimmed hat' and at l. 164 as 'a currently harmless but potentially dangerous familiar' (Turner).

162–3 **this broad-brimmed . . . block** 'The *block* of a hat is the form upon which it is made, and hence the fashion of it in general. From the text it would seem that new fashions were frequently invented and sported at a progress of the monarch through the kingdom' (Weber). Broad-brimmed hats were regarded as 'mannish' wear for women, marking them as dangerously liable to take sexual initiatives (as Mirabell does here).

163 **young hatband** Turner points out that Mirabell appears to have given her out-of-fashion hat a new ('young') band to bring it up to date

164 **sucking devil . . . old** alluding to the proverb 'as innocent as a devil of two years old'

167 **as false . . . pissed** a familiar collocation, here, as Sharp observes, with a pun on the 'pst' sound of whispered gossip

176 **To right her spleen** to avenge her anger

183 **proportionable** commensurate

No wise physician will prescribe me for you.
Alas, your state is weak; you had need of cordials,
Some rich electuary, made of a son and heir,
An elder brother in a cullis, whole:
'Tmust be some wealthy Gregory, boiled to a jelly,
That must restore you to the state of new gowns,
French ruffs, and mutable headtires.

MIRABELL
But where is he, sir?
One that's so rich will ne'er wed me with nothing.

CUNNINGAME
Then see thy conscience and thy wit together;
Wouldst thou have me, then, that has nothing neither?
What say you to Fop Gregory the First yonder?
Will you acknowledge your time amply recompensed,
Full satisfaction upon love's record,
Without any more suit, if I combine you?

MIRABELL
Yes, by this honest kiss. [*Kisses him*]

CUNNINGAME
You're a wise client
To pay your fee beforehand; but all do so.
You know the worst already; that's the best too.

MIRABELL
I know he's a fool.

CUNNINGAME
You're shrewdly hurt, then;
This is your comfort: your great wisest women
Pick their first husband still out of that house,
And some will have 'em to choose, if they bury twenty.

MIRABELL
I'm of their minds that like him for a first husband,
To run youth's race with him, 'tis very pleasant,
But when I'm old I'd always wish a wiser.

CUNNINGAME
You may have me by that time. For this first business,
Rest upon my performance.

MIRABELL
With all thankfulness.

CUNNINGAME
I have a project you must aid me in too.

MIRABELL
You bind me to all lawful action, sir.

CUNNINGAME [*giving the Niece's scarf*]
Pray, wear this scarf about you.

MIRABELL
I conjecture now.

CUNNINGAME
There's a Court principle for't; one office must help another;
As, for example, for your cast o' manchets out o'th' pantry
I'll allow you a goose out o'th' kitchen.

MIRABELL
'Tis very sociably done, sir. Farewell, Performance,
I shall be bold to call you so.

CUNNINGAME
Do, sweet Confidence.
[*Exit Mirabell*]
If I can match my two broad-brimmed hats—
Enter Sir Gregory
'Tis he, I know the maggot by his head;
Now shall I learn news of him.—My precious chief!

SIR GREGORY
I have been seeking for you i'th' bowling green,
Enquired at Nettleton's and Anthony's ordinary,
'T has vexed me to the heart. Look, I've a diamond here,
And it cannot find a master.

CUNNINGAME
No? That's hard, i'faith.

SIR GREGORY
It does belong to somebody: a pox on him,
I would he had it; does but trouble me,
And she that sent it is so waspish too
There's no returning to her till't be gone.

CUNNINGAME [*aside*]
O ho!—[*Inspecting diamond*] Ah, sirrah, are you come?

SIR GREGORY
What's that, friend?

CUNNINGAME
Do you note that corner sparkle?

SIR GREGORY
Which? which? Which, sir?

CUNNINGAME
At the west end o' the collet.

SIR GREGORY
O, I see't now.

CUNNINGAME
'Tis an apparent mark: this is the stone, sir,
That so much blood is threatened to be shed for.

SIR GREGORY
I pray?

194 **cordials** medicines
195 **electuary** paste made of a medicinal powder crushed in honey or syrup
196 **cullis** strong broth with which to nourish an invalid
199 **French ruffs** an expensive form of ruff, deeper and less starched than the usual English variety
mutable headtires changeable head-attire, ample millinery (in contrast to the monotony of Mirabell's apparently unique current hat)
203 **Fop Gregory the First** a play on 'Pope Gregory the First'
207–8 **You're...beforehand** spoken ironically. Cunningame thinks it folly to pay in advance for services one has not yet received, although, as his next words acknowledge, the legal profession compels all its clients to do so.
210 **shrewdly** severely. 'In the context, "knowingly" seems also intended' (Sharp)
223 **cast o' manchets** serving of white bread rolls or small loaves
227–8 **If...head** 'This is the first reference in the text to Sir Gregory's wearing a broad-brimmed hat, but perhaps it is part of his foppish costume from his first entry in Act 1' (Sharp)
230 **bowling green** Given the play's numerous other references to the area just north-west of the City (St Pancras, Finsbury, Islington), this may be a reference to the popular bowling green at Clerkenwell, now commemorated in the name of Bowling Green Lane (EC1).
231 **Nettleton's and Anthony's ordinary** eating places now known only from this fleeting reference. An ordinary was a tavern or eating house serving a single 'dish of the day'
240 **collet** the part of a piece of jewellery's setting visible around the stone

CUNNINGAME
A tun, at least.
SIR GREGORY They must not find't
I' me, then; they must go where 'tis to be had.
CUNNINGAME
'Tis well it came to my hands first, Sir Gregory;
I know where this must go. [*Pockets diamond*]
SIR GREGORY Am I discharged on't?
CUNNINGAME
My life for yours now! (*Draws*)
SIR GREGORY What now?
CUNNINGAME 'Tis discretion, sir;
I'll stand upon my guard all the while I ha't.
SIR GREGORY
Troth, thou tak'st too much danger on thee still
To preserve me alive.
CUNNINGAME 'Tis a friend's duty, sir:
Nay, by a toy that I have late thought upon,
I'll undertake to get your mistress for you.
SIR GREGORY
Thou wilt not! Wilt?
CUNNINGAME Contract her by a trick, sir,
When she least thinks on't.
SIR GREGORY There's the right way to't,
For if she think on't once, she'll never do it.
CUNNINGAME
She does abuse you still, then?
SIR GREGORY A pox! Damnably,
Every time worse than other: yet her uncle
Thinks the day holds o' Tuesday; say it did, sir,
She's so familiarly used to call me 'rascal',
She'll quite forget to wed me by my own name,
And then that marriage cannot hold in law, you know.
CUNNINGAME
Will you leave all to me?
SIR GREGORY Who should I leave it to?
CUNNINGAME
'Tis our luck to love nieces; I love a niece too.
SIR GREGORY
I would you did, i'faith.
CUNNINGAME But mine's a kind wretch.
SIR GREGORY
Ay, marry, sir, I would mine were so too.
CUNNINGAME
No 'rascal' comes in her mouth.
SIR GREGORY Troth, and mine
Has little else in hers.
CUNNINGAME Mine sends me tokens
All the world knows not on.
SIR GREGORY Mine gives me tokens too,
Very fine tokens, but I dare not wear 'em.
CUNNINGAME
Mine's kind in secret.
SIR GREGORY And there mine's a hell-cat.
CUNNINGAME
We have a day set, too.
SIR GREGORY 'Slid, so have we, man,
But there's no sign of ever coming together.
CUNNINGAME
Tell thee who 'tis; the old woman's niece.
SIR GREGORY Is't she?
CUNNINGAME
I would your luck had been no worse for mildness.
But, mum, no words on't to your lady.
SIR GREGORY Foh!
CUNNINGAME
No blabbing, as you love me.
SIR GREGORY None of our blood
Were ever babblers.
CUNNINGAME [*giving a letter*]
Prithee, convey this letter to her,
But at any hand, let not your mistress see't.
SIR GREGORY
Yet again, sir?
CUNNINGAME There's a jewel in't;
The very art would make her dote upon't.
SIR GREGORY Say you so?
[*Aside*] And she shall see't for that trick only.
CUNNINGAME
Remember but your mistress, and all's well.
SIR GREGORY
Nay, if I do not, hang me. *Exit*
CUNNINGAME I believe you.
This is the only way to return a token:
I know he'll do't now, 'cause he's charged to'th' contrary.
He's the nearest kin to a woman, of a thing
Made without substance, that a man can find again.
Some petticoat begot him, I'll be whipped else,
Engend'ring with an old pair of paned hose
Lying in some hot chamber o'er the kitchen;
Very steam bred him.
He never grew where *rem in re* e'er came;
The generation of a hundred such
Cannot make a man stand in a white sheet,
For 'tis no act in law; nor can a constable
Pick out a bawdy business for Bridewell in't.

243 **tun** a type of barrel
244 **I' me** in me
251 **toy** device, trick
273 **Tell thee** I'll tell thee
289 **paned hose** 'breeches made of different coloured strips or panels, old-fashioned by the early seventeenth century' (Turner)
292 ***rem in re*** literally 'with the thing in the other thing': legal Latin phrase for sexual penetration
294 **stand in a white sheet** before the rest of the congregation, the ecclesiastical penance for fornication
296 **Bridewell** a prison mainly devoted to the punishment of female sexual offenders such as fornicators (and prostitutes): the original Bridewell was located at the mouth of the Fleet River close to Blackfriars, but by Middleton's time there were also two similar jails bearing the same name, one at Westminster and one at Clerkenwell

A lamentable case.
He's got with a man's urine, like a mandrake.
Enter Clown, as a gallant
How now? Ha! What prodigious bravery's this?
A most preposterous gallant; the doublet sits
As if it mocked the breeches.

CLOWN Save you, sir.

CUNNINGAME [*aside*]
He's put his tongue in the fine suit of words too.

CLOWN
How does the party?

CUNNINGAME [*aside*] Takes me for a scrivener.—
Which of the parties?

CLOWN Hum! Simplicity betide thee!
I would fain hear of the party; I would be loath to go
Further with her; honour is not a thing to be dallied withal,
No more is reputation, no, nor fame, I take it; I must not
Have her wronged when I'm abroad; my party is not
To be compelled with any party in an oblique way;
'Tis very dangerous to deal with women;
May prove a lady too, but shall be nameless,
I'll bite my tongue out ere it prove a traitor.

CUNNINGAME
Upon my life, I know her.

CLOWN Not by me;
Know what you can, talk a whole day with me,
You're ne'er the wiser; she comes not from these lips.

CUNNINGAME The old knight's niece.

CLOWN [*aside*]
'Slid, he has got her! Pox of his heart that told him!
Can nothing be kept secret?—Let me entreat you
To use her name as little as you can, though.

CUNNINGAME
'Twill be small pleasure, sir, to use her name.

CLOWN
I had intelligence, in my solemn walks
'Twixt Paddington and Pancridge, of a scarf
Sent for a token, and a jewel followed,
But I acknowledge not the receipt of any;
Howe'er 'tis carriéd, believe me, sir,
Upon my reputation, I received none.

CUNNINGAME
What, neither scarf nor jewel?

CLOWN 'Twould be seen
Somewhere about me, you may well think that;
I have an arm for a scarf, as others have,
An ear to hang a jewel, too, and that's more
Than some men have, my betters a great deal.
I must have restitution, where'er it lights.

CUNNINGAME
And reason good.

CLOWN For all these tokens, sir,
Pass i' my name.

CUNNINGAME It cannot otherwise be.

CLOWN
'Sent to a worthy friend.'

CUNNINGAME Ay, that's to thee.

CLOWN
I'm wronged under that title.

CUNNINGAME I dare swear thou art:
'Tis nothing but Sir Gregory's circumvention,
His envious spite; when thou'rt at Paddington
He meets the gifts at Pancridge.

CLOWN Ah, false knight!
False both to honour and the law of arms!

CUNNINGAME
What wilt thou say if I be revenged for thee,
Thou sit as witness?

CLOWN I should laugh in state then.

CUNNINGAME I'll fob him; here's my hand.

CLOWN I should be as glad as any man alive to see him well fobbed, sir; but now you talk of fobbing, I wonder the lady sends not for me, according to promise? I ha' kept out o' town these two days, o' purpose to be sent for; I am almost starved with walking.

CUNNINGAME Walking gets men a stomach.

CLOWN 'Tis most true, sir; I may speak it by experience, for I ha' got a stomach six times, and lost it again, as

298 **got with** begotten by
mandrake a poisonous, potentially narcotic plant whose man-shaped root inspired much folklore, of which this line provides, as Sharp observes, a comparatively tame example

299 **bravery's** finery's

300–1 **doublet ... breeches** Although usually of a different material, the doublet was supposed to match the remainder of the costume: the Clown's evidently does not.

303 **scrivener** clerk employed to transcribe or draw up legal documents

305–10 **I ... women** The Clown's curious, semi-poetic utterance—appropriately couched in wildly irregular verse—garbles legal terminology with dim recollections of the chivalric code of courtly love.

320 **'Twill ... name** i.e. compared to the pleasure of using her person

321 **intelligence** The source of the Clown's information is never explained, the transparency of the play's plotting in this regard perhaps providing a deliberate joke in itself.

322 **Paddington** at this time a rural hamlet, three miles west and about one to the north of the City, not far beyond Tyburn
Pancridge The large parish of St Pancras, around two miles east of Paddington, stretched as far north as Highgate and as far south as Gray's Inn, bordering on Islington to the east and Clerkenwell to the south-west: it was at this time sparsely populated and known as a haunt of thieves and other criminals, with a particular reputation as a venue for illicit marriages.

339–40 **Ah ... arms** further incongruous fragments of chivalry

343 **fob** dupe

344–5 The Clown's lapse back into prose at this point (the preceding dialogue being his only sustained verse in the play) probably signals that Rowley took over the writing from here to the Clown's exit at l. 361–2.

often as a traveller from Chelsea shall lose the sight of Paul's and get it again.

CUNNINGAME Go to her, man.

CLOWN Not for a million. Infringe my oath? There's a toy called a vow has passed between us, a poor trifle, sir. Pray, do me the part and office of a gentleman; if you chance to meet a footman by the way, in orange-tawny ribbons, running before an empty coach, with a buzzard i'th' poop on't, direct him and his horses toward the New River by Islington; there they shall have me, looking upon the pipes and whistling.

CUNNINGAME
A very good note. *Exit Clown*
This love makes us all monkeys.
But to my work: scarf first! And now a diamond!
These
Should be sure signs of her affection's truth;
Yet I'll go forward with my surer proof. *Exit*

4.2 *Enter Niece and Sir Gregory*

NIECE
Is't possible?

SIR GREGORY
Nay, here's his letter too;
There's a fine jewel in't, therefore I brought it to you.

NIECE
You tedious mongrel! Is't not enough
To grace thee, to receive this from thy hand,
A thing that makes me almost sick to do,
But you must talk too?

SIR GREGORY
I ha' done.

NIECE
Fall back;
Yet backer, backer yet: you unmannerly puppy,
Do you not see I'm going about to read it?

SIR GREGORY [*aside*]
Nay, these are golden days, now I stay by't;
She was wont not to endure me in her sight at all.
The world mends, I see that.

NIECE
What an ambiguous superscription's here,—
'To the best of nieces'.
Why, that title may be mine, and more than hers.
Sure, I much wrong the neatness of his art;
'Tis certain sent to me, and, to requite
My cunning in the carriage of my tokens,
Used the same fop for his.

SIR GREGORY [*aside*]
She nodded now to me; 'twill come in time.

NIECE What's here?
An entire ruby, cut into a heart,
And this the word: *Istud amoris opus*.

SIR GREGORY Yes, yes;
I've heard him say that love is the best stone-cutter.

NIECE
Why, thou saucy issue of some travelling sow-gelder,
What makes love in thy mouth? Is it a thing
That ever will concern thee? I do wonder
How thou dar'st think on't. Hast thou ever hope
To come i'the same room where lovers are
And scape unbrained with one of their velvet slippers?

SIR GREGORY [*aside*]
Love tricks break out, I see.—An you talk of slippers once,
'Tis not far off to bedtime.

NIECE
Is it possible
Thou canst laugh yet? I would ha' undertook
To ha' killed a spider with less venom far
Than I have spit at thee.

SIR GREGORY
You must conceive,
A knight's another manner o' piece of flesh.

NIECE
Back, owl's-face.

OLD KNIGHT (*within*)
Do, do.

NIECE (*aside*)
'Tis my uncle's voice, that.—
Why keep you so far off, Sir Gregory?
Are you afraid, sir, to come near your mistress?

SIR GREGORY [*aside*]
Is the proud heart come down? I looked for this still.

NIECE [*aside*]
He comes not this way yet.—Away, you dog-whelp!
Would you offer to come near me, though I said so?
I'll make you understand my mind in time:
You run in greedily, like a hound to his breakfast,

352–3 **Chelsea ... Paul's** Chelsea was at this time another separate village, a good four or five miles upriver from the West End proper. The old St Paul's Cathedral, considerably larger and taller than its post-Great Fire successor, was easily the most prominent building in the City (despite the destruction of its immense steeple by lightning in 1561), but would only be intermittently visible from the Chelsea road because of the meanderings of the Thames, which the route followed.

358–9 **footman ... ribbons** 'Orange-tawny' was a particularly ostentatious colour for servants' liveries

359 **buzzard** at this time regarded as an ignoble, scavenging bird, little better than a kite: presumably a comic mistake on the Clown's part for a heraldic eagle

360 **i'th' poop** at the stern, on the back. Whether the Clown is seriously expecting such an expensive messenger or confides these fantastical details with an air of mystery in the hopes of impressing Cunningame is not clear

360–1 **the New River by Islington** The New River, constructed between 1609 and 1613, brought water nearly forty miles from Ware in Hertfordshire to a system of reservoirs in Islington (and finally the Round Pond, Clerkenwell), from which it was piped to the City: its inauguration is celebrated by *His Lordship's Entertainment* and *Truth*.

4.2.9 **stay by't** persevere

12 **superscription's** the address on the letter

14 **hers** i.e. Mirabell's

22 ***Istud amoris opus*** A labour of love, for you

24 **I've ... stone-cutter** 'Sir Gregory's knowledge of Latin seems to have improved somewhat since 1.2' (Sharp)

25 **sow-gelder** punningly taking up Sir Gregory's 'stone-cutter'

26 **What ... mouth?** i.e. what is the word 'love' doing in your talk?

31 **An** If

That chops in head and all, to beguile his fellows.
I'm to be eaten, sir, with grace and leisure,
Behaviour and discourse, things that ne'er trouble you:
After I have pelted you sufficiently
I trow you will learn more manners.

SIR GREGORY [*aside*] I'm wondering still
When we two shall come together; Tuesday's at hand,
But I'm as far off as I was at first, I swear.

Enter Guardianess

GUARDIANESS [*aside*]
Now, Cunningame, I'll be revenged at large.—
Lady, what was but all this while suspicion
Is truth full blown now; my niece wears your scarf.

NIECE Ha!

GUARDIANESS
Do but follow me; I'll place you instantly
Where you shall see her courted by Cunningame.

NIECE [*aside*]
I go with greediness: we long for things
That break our hearts sometimes; there's pleasure's misery.

Exeunt Niece and Guardianess

SIR GREGORY
Where are those gadflies going? To some junket now:
That same old humble-bee toles the young one forth
To sweetmeats after kind. Let 'em look to't
The thing you wot on be not missed or gone;
I bring a maidenhead, and I look for one. *Exit*

4.3 *Enter Cunningame, in discourse with a masked gentlewoman in a broad hat and scarfed, and Niece at another door*

CUNNINGAME
Yes, yes.

NIECE [*aside*]
Too manifest now; the scarf and all.

CUNNINGAME
It cannot be: you're such a fearful soul.

NIECE [*aside*]
I'll give her cause of fear e'er I part from her.

CUNNINGAME
Will you say so? Is't not your aunt's desire too?

NIECE [*aside*]
What a dissembling crone's that! She'll forswear't now.

CUNNINGAME [*aside*]
I see my project takes; yonder's the grace on't.

NIECE [*aside*]
Who would put confidence in wit again?
I'm plagued for my ambition, to desire
A wise man for a husband, and I see
Fate will not have us go beyond our stint;
We are allowed but one dish, and that's woodcock;
It keeps up wit to make us friends and servants of,
And thinks anything's good enough to make us husbands.
O, that whore's hat o' thine, o' the riding block,
A shade for lecherous kisses!

CUNNINGAME Make you doubt on't?
Is not my love of force?

NIECE [*coming forward*] Yes, me it forces
To tear that sorcerous strumpet from th'embraces!

CUNNINGAME
Lady?

NIECE
O, thou hast wronged the exquisit'st love—

CUNNINGAME
What mean you, lady?

NIECE Mine; you'll answer for't.

CUNNINGAME
Alas, what seek you?

NIECE Sir, mine own, with loss.

CUNNINGAME
You shall.

NIECE I never made so hard a bargain.

CUNNINGAME
Sweet lady!

NIECE Unjust man, let my wrath reach her,
As you owe virtue duty. [*Cunningame falls*] Your cause trips you.
Now, minion, you shall feel what love's rage is,
Before you taste the pleasure.—Smile you, false sir?

CUNNINGAME
How can I choose, to see what pains you take
Upon a thing will never thank you for't?

45 **chops in** barges in
beguile cheat (of their shares of the food)

47 **Behaviour and discourse** Politeness and conversation

60 **gadflies** biting insects which cause cattle to rush frenetically about: used here in a transferred sense, likening the two women's behaviour to that of gadfly-bitten cows (as in the expression 'to gad about', meaning to have a frantically busy social life)
junket a sweet pudding made from curds and whey; hence a feast or party

61 **humble-bee** bumblebee, presumably a reference to the Guardianess's shape as well as her figurative sweet tooth
toles entices

62 **sweetmeats after kind** literally the sweet foods appropriate to their natures, but since 'kind' could also mean the urge to procreate the figurative sense is 'sexual pleasure'

63 **The thing you wot on** 'you know what', in this case the Niece's hymen

4.3.11 **woodcock** a proverbially stupid edible bird, hence the term could simply mean 'a fool'

12 **It** Fate
friends and servants lovers and admirers (after marriage)

14 **o' the riding block** see 4.1.163

17 **th'embraces** thy embraces

23 **Your cause trips you** i.e. the injustice of your cause trips you

NIECE
How?
[*Cunningame turns 'Mirabell', which proves to be a puppet so dressed*]

CUNNINGAME
See what things you women be, lady,
When clothes are taken for the best part of you!
This was to show you, when you think I love you not,
How you're deceived still; there the moral lies.
'Twas a trap set to catch you, and the only bait
To take a lady nibbling is fine clothes.
Now I dare boldly thank you for your love;
I'm pretty well resolved in't by this fit,
For a jealous ague always ushers it.

NIECE
Now blessings still maintain this wit of thine,
And I've an excellent fortune coming in thee;
Bring nothing else, I charge thee.

CUNNINGAME
Not a groat, I warrant ye.

NIECE
Thou shalt be worthily welcome; take my faith for't,
Next opportunity shall make us one.

CUNNINGAME
The old gentlewoman has fooled her revenge sweetly.

NIECE
'Las, 'tis her part; she knows her place so well yonder;
Always when women jump upon threescore,
Love shoves 'em from the chamber to the door.

CUNNINGAME Thou art a precious she-wit. *Exeunt*

❁

5.1 *Enter Cunningame at one door; Wittypate, Sir Ruinous, Lady Ruinous, and Priscian at the other*

CUNNINGAME
Friend, met in the harvest of our designs;
Not a thought but's busy.

WITTYPATE
I knew it, man,
And that made me provide these needful reapers,
Hooks, rakers, gleaners; we'll sing it home
With a melodious hornpipe. This is the bond:
That as we further in your great affair
You'll suffer us to glean, pick up for crumbs;
And if we snatch a handful from the sheaf
You will not look a churl on's.

CUNNINGAME
Friend, we'll share
The sheaves of gold; only the love-acre
Shall be peculiar.

WITTYPATE
Much good do you, sir.
[*To Sir Ruinous and Priscian*] Away, you know your way and your stay; get you the music ready, while we prepare the dancers.

SIR RUINOUS We are a consort of ourselves.

PRISCIAN And can strike up lustily.

WITTYPATE You must bring Sir Fop.

CUNNINGAME That's perfect enough.

SIR RUINOUS
Bring all the fops you can, the more the better fare,
So the proverb runs backwards.
Exeunt Sir Ruinous and Priscian

LADY
I'll bring the ladies.
Exit

WITTYPATE
Do so first, and then the fops will follow;
I must to my father; he must make one.
Enter two servants, with a banquet

CUNNINGAME
While I dispatch a business with the knight,
And I go with you. *Exit Wittypate*
—Well said, I thank you.
This small banquet will furnish our few guests
With taste and state enough. One reach my gown;
The action craves it rather than the weather.
[*Exit Second Servant*]

28.2 ***puppet*** a life-sized lay figure (of a type used by dressmakers), masked to conceal anything of its wooden face not hidden beneath the broad brim of Mirabell's hat (which is probably introduced into the play solely for the purposes of this scene)

35 **resolved in't** convinced of it

44 **jump upon** arrive at or get near to

45 **from the chamber ... door** with an allusion to the supposedly typical career trajectory of a prostitute, finishing her working life as a door-keeper or pander

5.1 Act 5 is primarily Rowley's, but it is full of 'composite' writing in which verbal mannerisms of both playwrights are visible, and is probably the section of the play on which they collaborated most closely

4 **Hooks** reaping hooks

7 **crumbs** here meaning 'grains'

9 **look a churl on's** take a miserly attitude towards us, with a pun on 'churl' as 'rustic', appropriate to the agricultural context

10 **the love-acre** the field or sphere of love, i.e. the Niece (as opposed to the 'knave's acre', the field of cheating; 'to return by Knave's Acre' was a proverbial phrase meaning 'to return empty-handed, as if cheated on the way home')

11 **peculiar** private, reserved for a single owner

13 **your stay** where you are to wait

20 **the proverb runs backwards** The proverb in question is 'The more the merrier, the fewer the better fare'; the reverse is now the case, Sir Ruinous suggests, because the larger the number of victims who can be brought to their 'party' the better their fare (i.e. the larger their shares of the booty) will be.

22 **make one** be one of those present

22.1 ***Enter two servants, with a banquet*** In Renaissance usage, the banquet was a dessert course after supper, consisting of sweetmeats and fruit. It is not made clear whose servants these are: Cunningame is too poor to have a household of his own, so presumably we are to infer that this scene takes place in a private room at a tavern.

24 **Well said** i.e. well done

FIRST SERVANT
There's one stays to speak with you, sir.
CUNNINGAME What is he?
FIRST SERVANT
Faith, I know not what, sir; a fool, I think,
That some broker's shop has made half a gentleman;
Has the name of a Worthy, too.
CUNNINGAME Pompey, is't not?
FIRST SERVANT That's he, sir.
CUNNINGAME
Alas, poor fellow. Prithee, enter him.
He will need too, he shall serve for a witness.

Enter Second Servant, with a gown

O, gramercy. If my friend Sir Gregory comes,
You know him, entertain him kindly.

[*Exit Second Servant*]

Enter Clown

O, Master Pompey, how is't, man?

CLOWN 'Snails! I'm almost starved with love, and cold, and one thing or other. Has not my lady sent for me yet?

CUNNINGAME Not that I hear; sure some unfriendly messenger is employed betwixt you.

CLOWN I was ne'er so cold in my life. In my conscience, I have been seven mile in length, along the New River: I have seen a hundred sticklebacks; I do not think but there's gudgeons, too; 'twill ne'er be a true water.

CUNNINGAME Why think you so?

CLOWN I warrant you, I told a thousand miller's thumbs in it.
I'll make a little bold with your sweetmeats.

CUNNINGAME And welcome, Pompey.

CLOWN 'Tis a strange thing, I have no taste in anything.

CUNNINGAME O, that's love, that distastes anything but itself.

CLOWN 'Tis worse than cheese in that point. May not a man break his word with a lady? I could find in my heart and my hose too.

CUNNINGAME By no means, sir; that breaks all the laws of love.

CLOWN Well, I'll ne'er pass my word without my deed to lady, while I live, again. I would fain recover my taste.

CUNNINGAME Well, I have news to tell you.

CLOWN Good news, sir?

CUNNINGAME Happy news: I help you away with a rival, your master, bestowed—

CLOWN Where, for this plum's sake?

CUNNINGAME Nay, listen me.

CLOWN I warrant you, sir, I have two ears to one mouth, I hear more than I eat; I'd ne'er row by Queenhithe while I lived else.

CUNNINGAME I have a wife for him, and thou shalt witness the contract.

CLOWN The old one, I hope; 'tis not the lady?

CUNNINGAME Choke him first! 'Tis one which thou shalt see; see him, see him deceived, see the deceit; only the injunction is, you shall smile with modesty.

CLOWN I'll simper, i'faith, as cold as I am yet. The old one, I hope!

Re-enter Second Servant

SECOND SERVANT Sir, here's Sir Gregory. [*Exit*]

CUNNINGAME Ud'so, shelter, shelter; if you be seen, all's ravelled out again. Stand there private, and you'll find the very opportunity to call you forth, and place you at the table.—

[*Clown withdraws*]. *Enter Sir Gregory*

You are welcome, sir. This banquet will serve, when it is crowned with such a dainty as you expect, and must have.

SIR GREGORY Tush, these sweetmeats are but sauce to that. Well, if there be any honesty or true word in a dream, she's mine own, nay, and changed extremely, not the same woman.

CUNNINGAME Who? Not the lady?

SIR GREGORY No, not to me: the edge of her tongue is taken off, gives me very good words; turned upside-down to me, and we live as quietly as two tortoises, if she hold on as she began in my dream.

CUNNINGAME Nay, if love send forth such predictions, you are bound to believe 'em. (*Soft music*) There's the watch-

31 **name of a Worthy** the Nine Worthies were nine great men, three from the Bible, three from the classics and three from romance, supposed to be the greatest heroes of all time: see *Heroes*
34 **He will need** he will be needed
38 **'Snails** His nails (an oath referring to the nails used in the Crucifixion)
44 **New River** see 4.1.360–1
45 **sticklebacks** a species of small fish
46 **gudgeons** another species of small fish, easily caught and often used as live bait for perch or pike; hence, figuratively, either deceitful baits or gullible simpletons
true i.e. fresh, drinkable, with a pun on the sense of 'honest'. The Clown's pessimism about the New River is in marked contrast to the attitude expressed in *His Lordship's Entertainment*, against which Rowley may be offering a deliberate in-joke here.
48 **miller's thumbs** small fishes about two inches long, their facetious name alluding to the proverbial dishonesty of millers, who were traditionally supposed to use their thumbs to depress the scales when weighing out the amount of flour to be handed over (so that the farmer received a smaller quantity of flour than he had brought of grain); hence the Clown's punning suspicion that the water will never be 'true'
50 **I'll . . . sweetmeats** The Clown eats diligently from this point until at least l. 145–6
53 **distastes** takes away the flavour of
60 **without my deed** i.e. before consummation
66 **this plum's** which presumably the Clown has just picked up to eat
69 **Queenhithe** a quay on the north side of the Thames between London Bridge and Blackfriars (directly opposite the Bankside theatres), on which fishmongers cried their wares: the Clown would be detained there indefinitely if he ate all the food he heard about
73 **The old one** the Guardianess

word of her coming; to your practised part now; if you hit it, *æquus Cupido nobis.* (*Both go into the gown*)

SIR GREGORY I will warrant you, sir, I will give arms to your gentry; look you forward to your business, I am an eye behind you. Place her in that chair, and let me alone to grope her out.

[*Clown comes forward, and sits at the banquet*]

CUNNINGAME Silence!—

Enter Mirabell

Lady, your sweet presence illustrates
This homely roof, and as coarse entertainment;
But where affections are both host and guest
They cannot meet unkindly. Please you sit;
Your something long stay made me unmannerly
To place before you; you know this friend here,
He's my guest, and more especially
That this our meeting might not be too single,
Without a witness to't.

MIRABELL
I came not unresolved, sir,
And when our hands are clasped in that firm faith
Which I expect from you, fame shall be bold
To speak the loudest on't.

[*Sir Gregory reaches out his hand from under the gown and clasps hers*]

O, you grasp me
Somewhat too hard, friend.

CUNNINGAME
That's love's eager will;
I'll touch it gentlier. (*Kisses her hand*)

MIRABELL
That's too low in you,
'Less it be doubly recompensed in me. (*She kisses* [*Sir Gregory's*] *hand*)

CLOWN [*aside*]
Puh, I must stop my mouth, I shall be choked else.

CUNNINGAME
Come, we'll not play and trifle with delays;
We met to join these hands, and willingly
I cannot leave it till confirmation.

MIRABELL
One word first, how does your friend, kind Sir Gregory?

CUNNINGAME
Why do you mention him? You love him not?

MIRABELL
I shall love you the less if you say so, sir;
In troth, I love him, but 'tis you deceive him.
This flattering hand of yours does rob him now,
Now you steal his right from him; and I know
I shall have hate for't, his hate extremely.

CUNNINGAME
Why, I thought you had not come so weakly armed;
Upon my life, the knight will love you for't,
Exceedingly love you, forever love you.

MIRABELL
Ay, you'll persuade me so.

CUNNINGAME
Why, he's my friend,
And wishes me a fortune equal with him;
I know, and dare speak it for him.

MIRABELL
O, this hand
Betrays him. You might remember him in some
Courtesy yet, at least.

CUNNINGAME
I thank your help in't;
Here's to his health, where'er he be. [*Drinks*]

MIRABELL
I'll pledge it, were it against my health. [*Drinks*]

CLOWN [*aside*] O, o! My heart hops after twelve mile a day upon a good return. Now could I walk three hundred mile afoot, and laugh forwards and backwards.

MIRABELL
You'll take the knight's health, sir?

CLOWN Yes, yes, forsooth.— [*Aside*] O, my sides! Such a banquet once a week would make me grow fat in a fortnight.

CUNNINGAME
Well, now to close our meeting with the close
Of mutual hands and hearts, thus I begin:

[*Sir Gregory's hand takes Mirabell's again*]

Here in Heaven's eye, and all love's sacred powers
(Which in my prayers stand propitious),
I knit this holy handfast, and with this hand
The heart that owes this hand, ever binding

99 ***æquus Cupido nobis*** Cupid deals justly with us

Both go into the gown Sir Gregory must stand or half-crouch under the gown behind Cunningame, who holds his arms concealed by his sides while Sir Gregory reaches his own around him and out through the sleeves. Previous editors have imagined Cunningame sitting in Sir Gregory's lap, but this would make some of the remaining action in the scene extremely awkward.

100–1 **arms to your gentry** Sir Gregory puns that he is ennobling Cunningame by lending him his arms (in the heraldic sense as well as the literal)

105 **illustrates** beautifies

110 **To place before you** to seat your fellow guest at the table before your arrival

114–16 **And . . . on't** A 'handfast' exchange of betrothal vows before one or more witnesses was regarded as legally binding; although the vows were more important in law than the clasping of hands which accompanied them, the custom provides the cue for the elaborate comic references to hands and comic pieces of stage business involving them which continue from here to l. 168.

119 **'Less** Unless

141 **after twelve mile a day** at a rate of twelve miles a day (an allusion, according to Turner, to the comedian Will Kemp's famous nine-days' jig from London to Norwich in 1600, which covered the ground at about this speed). The Clown's amusement has more than cured his earlier exhaustion from walking seven miles along the New River (5.1.43–4).

141–2 **upon a good return** for a good price (possibly, as Sharp suggests, such another jest as this)

143 **forwards and backwards** all the way and all the way back

152 **owes** owns

By force of this initiating contract
Both heart and hand in love, faith, loyalty,
Estate, or what to them belongs, in all the dues,
Rights, and honours of a faithful husband;
And this firm vow henceforth till death to stand
Irrevocable, sealed both with heart and hand.

MIRABELL
Which thus I second; but, O, Sir Gregory!

CUNNINGAME
Again? This interposition's ill, believe me.

MIRABELL
Here in Heaven's eye, and all love's sacred powers,
I knit this holy handfast, and with this hand
The heart that owes this hand, ever binding
Both heart and hand in love, honour, loyalty,
Estate, or what to them belongs, in all the dues,
Rights, and duties of a true faithful wife;
And this firm vow henceforth till death to stand
Irrevocable, sealed both with heart and hand.

SIR GREGORY A full agreement on both parts.

CUNNINGAME Ay, here's witness of that.

SIR GREGORY [*emerging from the gown*] Nay, I have overreached you, lady, and that's much, for any knight in England to overreach a lady.

MIRABELL
I rejoice in my deceit; I am a lady now,
I thank you, sir.

CLOWN Good morrow, Lady Fop.

SIR GREGORY 'Snails, I'm gulled, made a worshipful ass! This is not my lady.

CUNNINGAME
But it is, sir, and true as your dream told you
That your lady was become another woman.

SIR GREGORY I'll have another lady, sir, if there were no more ladies in London! Blind-man's buff is an unlawful game.

CUNNINGAME
Come, down on your knees first, and thank your stars.

SIR GREGORY A fire of my stars! I may thank you, I think.

CUNNINGAME
So you may pray for me, and honour me,
That have preserved you from a lasting torment
For a perpetual comfort; did you call me friend?

SIR GREGORY I pray pardon me for that; I did miscall you, I confess.

CUNNINGAME
And should I, receiving such a thankful name,
Abuse it in the act? Should I see my friend
Baffled, disgraced, without any reverence
To your title, to be called 'slave', 'rascal'?
Nay, cursed to your face, fooled, scorned, beaten down
With a woman's peevish hate, yet I should stand
And suffer you to be lost, cast away?
I would have seen you buried quick first,
Your spurs of knighthood to have wanted rowels
And to be kicked from your heels. 'Slave', 'rascal'?
Hear this tongue.

MIRABELL
My dearest love, sweet knight, my lord, my husband.

CUNNINGAME
So; this is not 'slave' and 'rascal', then.

MIRABELL
What shall your eye command, but shall be done
In all the duties of a loyal wife?

CUNNINGAME Good, good.
Are not curses fitter for you? Were't not better
Your head were broke with the handle of a fan,
Or your nose bored with a silver bodkin?

MIRABELL
Why, I will be a servant in your lady.

CUNNINGAME
Pox, but you shall not!—[*To Sir Gregory*] She's too good for you.—
[*To Mirabell*] This contract shall be a nullity. I'll break't off,
And see you better bestowed.

SIR GREGORY 'Slid, but you shall not, sir! She's mine own, and I am hers, and we are one another's lawfully, and let me see him that will take her away by the civil law. If you be my friend, keep you so; if you have done me a good turn, do not hit me i'th' teeth with't, that's not the part of a friend.

CUNNINGAME If you be content—

SIR GREGORY Content? I was never in better contention in my life. I'll not change her for both the Exchanges, New or the Old.—Come, kiss me boldly.

[*Sir Gregory and Mirabell kiss*]

CLOWN Give you joy, sir!

SIR GREGORY O sir, I thank you as much as though I did. You are beloved of ladies; you see we are glad

153 **initiating contract** As Turner points out, the ceremony performed here constitutes a spousal *de præsenti*, the beginning of the process of being married rather than its completion; at the conclusion of such a betrothal the parties still had to go through the marriage service in church and consummate before the marriage was fully established (although the parties here perform these last two stages in reverse order; see ll. 245–8). However, if after a spousal *de præsenti* either party married someone else, that subsequent marriage would be dissolved as unlawful.

166 **duties** In becoming a wife, Mirabell acquires 'duties' in contrast to her husband's 'honours', 156

181–2 **Blind-man's . . . game** Sir Gregory recognizes that the betrothal is not legally binding due to his deception as to the identity of the bride

197 **quick** alive

198 **rowels** the spiked discs at the ends of a pair of spurs

214–15 **we are . . . law** Sir Gregory changes his mind about the legality of the proceedings

220 **contention** 'Presumably a malapropism. Sir Gregory means "contentment"' (Sharp)

221 **both the Exchanges** The Royal Exchange at Cornhill dated from 1567; its rival the New Exchange in the Strand had opened in 1609.

225 **we** Sir Gregory grandly uses the royal first person plural

of under-women.

CLOWN Ladies? Let not ladies be disgraced: you are as it were a married man, and have a family, and for the party's sake that was unnamed before, being peascod time, I am appeased; yet I would wish you make a ruler of your tongue.

CUNNINGAME
Nay, no dissension here, I must bar that.
[*To Sir Gregory*] And this, friend, I entreat you, and be advised:
Let this private contract be yet concealed,
And still support a seeming face of love
Unto the lady. Mark how it avails you
And quits all her scorns: her uncle is now hot
In pursuit of the match, and will enforce her
Bend her proud stomach, that she shall proffer
Herself to you, which when you have flouted
And laughed your fill at, you shall scorn her off
With all your disgraces trebled upon her,
For there the pride of all her heart will bow,
When you shall foot her from you, not she you.

SIR GREGORY Good, i'faith, I'll continue it: I'd fain laugh at the old fellow too, for he has abused me as scurvily as his niece.—My knighthood's upon the spur: we'll go to bed, and then to church as fast as we can.

Exeunt Sir Gregory and Mirabell

CLOWN I do wonder I do not hear of the lady yet.

CUNNINGAME The good minute may come sooner than you are aware of; I do not think but 'twill ere night yet, as near as 'tis.

CLOWN Well, I will go walk by the New River in that meditation; I am o'er shoes, I'm sure, upon the dry bank. This gullery of my master will keep me company this two hours too; if love were not an enemy to laughter I should drive away the time well enough. You know my walk, sir: if she sends, I shall be found angling, for I will try what I can catch for luck sake, I will fish fair for't.
O knight, that thou should'st be gulled so! Ha, ha! it does me good at heart,
But O, lady, thou tak'st down my merry part. *Exit*

Enter Wittypate

WITTYPATE
Friend!

CUNNINGAME
Here, friend.

WITTYPATE All's afoot, and will go smooth away;
The woman has conquered the women, they are gone,
Which I have already complained to my father,
Suggesting that Sir Gregory is fall'n off
From his charge, for neglects and ill usage,
And that he is most violently bent
On Gentry's wife (whom I have called a widow),
And that without most sudden prevention
He will be married to her.

CUNNINGAME Foot, all this is wrong!
This wings his pursuit, and will be before me;
I am lost for ever. [*Leaving*]

WITTYPATE No, stay, you shall not go
But with my father: on my wit let it lie;
You shall appear a friendly assistant
To help in all affairs, and in execution
Help yourself only.

CUNNINGAME Would my belief were strong
In this assurance!

WITTYPATE You shall credit it,
And my wit shall be your slave if it deceive you.

Enter Old Knight

My father—

OLD KNIGHT
O sir, you are well met; where's the knight, your friend?

CUNNINGAME Sir, I think your son has told you—

WITTYPATE
Shall I stand to tell't again? I tell you, he loves,
But not my kinswoman: her base usage,
And your slack performance, which he accuses most
Indeed, has turned the knight's heart upside down.

OLD KNIGHT
I'll curb her for't: can he be but recovered
He shall have her, and she shall be dutiful,
And love him as a wife too.

CUNNINGAME With that condition, sir,
I dare recall him were he entered the church,
So much interest of love I assure in him.

OLD KNIGHT
Sir, it shall be no loss to you if you do.

WITTYPATE
Ay, but these are words still; will not the deeds be wanting
At the recovery, if it should be again?

OLD KNIGHT
Why, here, fool, I am provided: [*showing a purse*] five hundred in earnest
Of the thousands in her dower. But were they married once,
I'd cut him short enough; that's my agreement.

WITTYPATE
Ay, now I perceive some purpose in you, father.

227–8 **as it were** see note to l. 153 above
229–30 **peascod . . . appeased** clearly with a pun on 'peascod' and 'appeased'; the Clown is letting Sir Gregory off on the grounds either that it is literally the time of year when peas are harvested, or in the figurative sense that Sir Gregory is young
237 **quits** requites
247 **My . . . upon the spur** with a sexual quibble
247–8 **we'll . . . can** see note to l. 153 above
254–5 **o'er shoes . . . dry bank** alluding to the phrase 'over shoes in love'
272 **Foot** by Christ's foot
273 **and will be before me** i.e. and the Old Knight will get to the Niece before Cunningame can
296–7 **five hundred . . . dower** The Old Knight hopes to buy back Sir Gregory as a nephew-in-law by paying him an advance on the Niece's dowry

OLD KNIGHT
But wherefore is she then stol'n out of doors
To him?
WITTYPATE
To him? O, fie upon your error!
She has another object, believe it, sir.
OLD KNIGHT I never could perceive it.
CUNNINGAME
I did, sir, and to her shame I should speak it,
To my own sorrow I saw it; dalliance,
Nay, dotage, with a very clown, a fool.
OLD KNIGHT
Wit and wantonness, nothing else, nothing else.
She love a fool? She'll sooner make a fool
Of a wise man.
CUNNINGAME Ay, my friend complains so.
Sir Gregory says flatly she makes a fool of him,
And these bold circumstances are approved;
Favours have been sent by him, yet he ignorant
Whither to carry 'em; they have been understood
And taken from him; certain, sir, there is
An unsuspected fellow lies concealed,
What or where'er he is; these slight neglects
Could not be of a knight else.
OLD KNIGHT Well, sir, you
Have promised (if we recover him unmarried)
To salve all these old bruises?
CUNNINGAME I'll do my best, sir.
OLD KNIGHT
I shall thank you costly, sir, and kindly too.
WITTYPATE
Will you talk away the time here, sir, and come
Behind all your purposes?
OLD KNIGHT Away, good sir!
WITTYPATE
Then stay a little, good sir, for my advice.
Why, father, are you broke, your wit beggared,
Or are you at your wit's end, or out of
Love with wit? No trick of wit to surprise
Those designs, but with open hue and cry
For all the world to talk on? This is strange;
You were not wont to slubber a project so.
OLD KNIGHT
Can you help at a pinch now, show yourself
My son? Go to, I leave this to your wit,
Because I'll make a proof on't.
WITTYPATE 'Tis thus, then:
I have had late intelligence they are now
Buxom as Bacchus' frows, revelling, dancing,
Telling the music's numbers with their feet,
Awaiting the meeting of premonished friends,
That's questionless, little dreading you.
Now, sir, with a dextrous trick indeed, sudden
And sufficient, were well to enter on 'em
As something like the abstract of a masque.
What though few persons? If best for our purpose
That commends the project.
OLD KNIGHT This takes up time.
WITTYPATE
Not at all; I can presently furnish
With loose disguises that shall fit that scene.
OLD KNIGHT
Why, what wants then?
WITTYPATE Nothing but charge of music;
That must be paid, you know.
OLD KNIGHT
That shall be my charges; I'll pay the music,
Whate'er it cost.
WITTYPATE And that shall be all your charge.
Now on, I like it, there will be wit in't, father.
Exeunt Wittypate and Old Knight
CUNNINGAME
I will neither distrust his wit nor friendship;
Yet if his master-brain should be o'erthrown,
My resolution now shall seize mine own. *Exit*

5.2

Enter Niece, Lady Ruinous, Guardianess, Sir Ruinous, and Priscian, [the latter pair] with instruments, masked

LADY
Nay, let's have music; let that sweet breath, at least,
Give us her airy welcome; 'twill be the best,
I fear, this ruined receptacle will yield,
But that most freely.
NIECE [*aside to Lady Ruinous*]
My welcome follows me,
Else I am ill come hither; you assure me still
Master Cunningame will be here, and that it was
His kind entreaty that wished me meet him?
LADY
Else let me be that shame unto my sex
That all belief may fly 'em.
NIECE Continue still
The knight's name unto my guardianess,

307 **wantonness** sportiveness, playfulness
313 **understood** recognized through inside information
329 **slubber** spoil or bungle
334 **Buxom** merry, lively
Bacchus' frows 'Frow' is the English form of 'frau', a woman; 'Bacchus' frows' are thus Mænads or Bacchantes, the orgiastic priestesses of the wine-god Bacchus
335 **Telling . . . feet** The dancing party Wittypate describes takes place at the home of Sir and Lady Ruinous; see 5.2.1–4
336 **premonished** forewarned, tipped off
5.2 The opening passage of this scene, recognizably providing a glimpse of the Lady Ruinous of Middleton's 2.1, is probably Middleton's alone, although elsewhere Rowley seems to have done the bulk of the writing in this scene
0.3 ***instruments*** violins or viols; see l. 86, where the musicians are referred to as 'fiddlers'
1–4 Lady Ruinous's command is obeyed, and music plays throughout the ensuing dialogue (see l. 38), unless the 'musicians' busy themselves with setting or tuning up and do not start to play until after Sir Ruinous's speech at ll. 14–15 (which, however, he might perhaps deliver while playing). The actors playing Priscian and Sir Ruinous must be capable either of playing the violin or of miming to an offstage consort.

She expects no other.
LADY —He will, he will, assure you
Lady, Sir Gregory will be here, and suddenly;
This music fore-ran him; is't not so, consorts?

SIR RUINOUS Yes, lady; he stays on some device to bring along, such a labour he was busy in; some witty device.

NIECE 'Twill be long ere he come then, for wit's a great labour to him.

GUARDIANESS Well, well, you'll agree better one day.

NIECE Scarce two, I think.

GUARDIANESS
Such a mock-beggar suit of clothes as led me
Into the fool's pair-o'-dice, with deuce ace,
He that would make me Mistress Cun, Cun, Cunny
(He's quite out of my mind, but I shall ne'er
Forget him while I have a hole in my head),
Such a one I think would please you better, though
He did abuse you.

LADY Fie, speak well of him now,
Your niece has quitted him.

GUARDIANESS I hope she has,
Else she loses me for ever; but for Sir Gregory,
Would he were come; I shall ill answer this
Unto your uncle else.

NIECE You know 'tis his pleasure
I should keep him company.

GUARDIANESS Ay, and should be your own
If you did well too. Lord, I do wonder
At the niceness of you ladies nowadays.
They must have husbands with so much wit, forsooth.
Worship and wealth were both wont to be in
Better request, I'm sure; I cannot tell,
But they get ne'er the wiser children, that I see.

LADY
La, la, la, la, sol. This music breathes in vain:
Methinks 'tis dull to let it move alone,
Let's have a female motion; 'tis in private,
And we'll grace't ourselves, however it deserves.

NIECE
What say you, guardianess?

GUARDIANESS 'Las, I'm weary with the walk;
My jaunting days are done.

LADY
Come, come, we'll fetch her in by course, or else
She shall pay the music.

GUARDIANESS
Nay, I'll have a little for my money, then.
[They put on masks, and] dance. A cornet sounds

LADY
Hark! Upon my life, the knight. [*Aside to Niece*] 'Tis your friend,
This was the warning-piece of his approach.
Enter Old Knight, Wittypate and Cunningame, masked, who take [the three women] to dance

LADY [*to her partner, the Old Knight*] Ha? No words but mum? Well then, we shall need no counsel-keeping.

NIECE [*to her partner, Cunningame*] Cunningame?

CUNNINGAME Yes: fear nothing.

NIECE Fear? Why do you tell me of it?

CUNNINGAME Your uncle's here.

NIECE Ay me!

CUNNINGAME Peace!

OLD KNIGHT [*aside to Wittypate*] We have caught 'em.

WITTYPATE Thank my wit, father.

GUARDIANESS [*aside to Niece*] Which is the knight, think you?

NIECE
I know not; he will be found when he speaks;
No mask can disguise his tongue.

WITTYPATE [*aside to Old Knight*] Are you charged?

OLD KNIGHT Are you awake?

WITTYPATE I'm answered in a question.

CUNNINGAME [*to Niece*]
Next change we meet, we loose our hands no more.

NIECE
Are you prepared to tie 'em?

CUNNINGAME Yes.
[*To Guardianess, imitating Sir Gregory's voice*] You must go with me.

GUARDIANESS Whither, sir? Not from my charge, believe me.

CUNNINGAME She goes along.

NIECE [*aside to Cunningame*] Will you venture, and my uncle here?

14 **device** witty and fanciful idea, conceit
20 **mock-beggar** misleadingly wealthy-looking
21 **pair-o'-dice** hackneyed pun on 'paradise' **deuce ace** here, 'nothing'; worthless throw of the dice giving a two ('deuce') with one die and a one ('ace') with the other
22–4 **Cun, Cun ... head** the obvious obscenity of 'Cunny' is taken up by the 'hole' at l. 24; 'I shall never forget him while I have a hole in my head' ostensibly means 'I shall never forget him all my life (while I still have a mouth to breathe by)', but punningly suggests 'I shall be reminded of him whenever I think of a vagina'. Sharp suggests the player would pause lewdly after the word 'hole'.
38 **La ... sol** Lady Ruinous sings along with the music
44 **by course** in due course
46.1 ***cornet*** at this time, a wooden rather than brass instrument, with finger holes rather than valves
50 **counsel-keeping** secrecy. 'In a masqued ball the identities of the dancers were meant to be kept secret until unmasking time. Often this involved conspiracy between participants who had, in fact, recognized each other' (Sharp)
63 **charged** supplied with money (akin to the modern slang usage of 'loaded')
66 **Next change we meet** Appropriately to the entire Niece-Cunningame plot of the play, the dance involves the repeated exchange of partners. A 'change' is a finite phase or passage of a set dance.

CUNNINGAME His stay's prepared for.
Exeunt Cunningame and Niece
GUARDIANESS 'Tis the knight, sure; I'll follow. *Exit*
[*Music continues, then stops*]
OLD KNIGHT How now, the music tired before us?
SIR RUINOUS Yes, sir, we must be paid now.
WITTYPATE O, that's your charge, father.
OLD KNIGHT
But stay, where are our wanton ladies gone?
Son, where are they?
WITTYPATE Only changed the room in a change, that's all, sure.
OLD KNIGHT
I'll make 'em all sure else, and then return to you.
SIR RUINOUS
You must pay for your music first, sir.
OLD KNIGHT Must?
Are there musty fiddlers? Are beggars choosers now?
Ha! Why, Wittypate, son, where am I?
WITTYPATE
You were dancing e'en now, in good measure, sir,
Is your health miscarried since? What ail you, sir?
OLD KNIGHT
Death, I may be gulled to my face! Where's my niece?
What are you?
LADY [*unmasking*] None of your niece, sir.
[*Sir Ruinous and Priscian produce pistols*]
OLD KNIGHT
How now! Have you loud instruments too? I'll hear
No more, I thank you. What have I done, trow,
To bring these fears about me? Son, where am I?
WITTYPATE
Not where you should be, sir; you should be paying
For your music, and you are in a maze.
OLD KNIGHT
O, is't so? Put up, put up, I pray you;
Here's a crown for you.
LADY Pish, a crown?
SIR RUINOUS *and* PRISCIAN Ha, ha, ha! A crown!
OLD KNIGHT
Which way do you laugh? I have seen a crown
Has made a consort laugh heartily.
WITTYPATE Father,
To tell you truth, these are no ordinary
Musicians; they expect a bounty
Above their punctual desert.
OLD KNIGHT
A pox on your punks, and their deserts too!
Am I not cheated all this while, think you?
Is not your pate in this?
WITTYPATE If you be cheated,
You are not to be indicted for your own goods:
Here you trifle time, to market your bounty
And make it base, when it must needs be free
For aught I can perceive.
OLD KNIGHT Will you know the lowest price, sir?
WITTYPATE That I will, sir, with all my heart.
[*Wittypate talks apart to Sir Ruinous, Lady Ruinous and Priscian*]
OLD KNIGHT
Unless I was discovered, and they now fled
Home again for fear, I am absolutely beguiled,
That's the best can be hoped for.
WITTYPATE Faith, 'tis somewhat too dear yet, gentlemen.
SIR RUINOUS There's not a denier to be bated, sir.
OLD KNIGHT Now, sir, how dear is it?
WITTYPATE Bate but the t'other ten pound?
PRISCIAN Not a bawbee, sir.
OLD KNIGHT How? Bate ten pound? What's the whole sum, then?
WITTYPATE
Faith, sir, a hundred pound; with much ado
I got fifty bated, and faith, father, to say truth,
'Tis reasonable for men of their fashion.
OLD KNIGHT
La, la, la, down a hundred pound? La, la, la!
You are a consort of thieves, are you not?
WITTYPATE
No, musicians, sir, I told you before.
OLD KNIGHT Fiddle faddle!
Is't not a robbery? a plain robbery?
WITTYPATE No,
No, no, by no means, father; you have received
For your money, nay, and that you cannot give back;
'Tis somewhat dear, I confess, but who can help it?
If they had been agreed with beforehand...
'Twas ill forgotten.
OLD KNIGHT
And how many shares have you in this? I see
My force; case up your instruments; I yield.
Here, as robbed and taken from me, I deliver it. [*Gives money*]

75 **His stay's prepared for** i.e. arrangements have been made to detain him
82 **Only changed the room in a change** only danced into another room, according to the pattern of the dance
86 **musty** mouldy or stale; used here in a punning sense to mean 'coercive, imperious'
94 **trow** think, i.e. 'do you think' or 'am I to think'
97 **in a maze** i.e. amazed, confused
99 **crown** coin worth five shillings
100 **Which...laugh?** i.e. 'whether in jest or earnest' (Sympson)
104 **Above their punctual desert** i.e. beyond what they have technically earned
105 **punks** whores, punning on 'punctual'
108 **indicted** held to account
109–11 **Here...perceive** You are wasting time haggling over your generosity and thus devaluing it, when as far as I can see you have no choice but to give freely
112 **Will you know** i.e. will you find out
118 **denier** coin worth a tenth of a penny
121 **bawbee** halfpenny
127 **La...la** Sharp notes the similarity to Lady Ruinous's singing at l. 38, and suggests that the Old Knight sings his indignation to the tune to which he has just been dancing
130 **Fiddle faddle** dismissive exclamation, appropriately chosen for its musical reference
135 **If...beforehand** if you had negotiated the price in advance

WITTYPATE
No, sir; you have performed your promise now,
Which was to pay the charge of music; that's all.

OLD KNIGHT
I have heard no music, I have received none, sir.
There's none to be found in me nor about me.

WITTYPATE
Why, sir, here's witness against you; you have danced,
And he that dances acknowledges a receipt
Of music.

OLD KNIGHT I deny that, sir, look you, I can dance without music, [*dances*] do you see, sir? and I can sing without it too: [*sings*] You are a consort of thieves!—Do you hear what I do?

WITTYPATE Pray you, take heed, sir; if you do move the music again it may cost you as much more.

OLD KNIGHT Hold, hold, I'll depart quietly; I need not bid you farewell, I think now, so long as that hundred pound lasts with you. [*Aside*] Ha, ha, am I snapped, i'faith?

Enter Guardianess

GUARDIANESS O, Sir Perfidious!

OLD KNIGHT Ay, ay, some howling another while; music's too damnable dear.

GUARDIANESS O, sir, my heartstrings are broke! If I can but live to tell you the tale I care not: your niece, my charge, is—

OLD KNIGHT What, is she sick?

GUARDIANESS No, no, sir, she's lustily well married.

OLD KNIGHT To whom?

GUARDIANESS O, to that cunning dissembler, Cunningame.

OLD KNIGHT I'll hang the priest first! What was he?

GUARDIANESS Your kinsman, sir, that has the Welsh benefice.

OLD KNIGHT I saved him from the gallows to that end! Good! Is there any more?

GUARDIANESS And Sir Gregory is married too.

OLD KNIGHT To my niece too, I hope, and then I may hang her.

GUARDIANESS No, sir, to my niece, thank Cupid, and that's all that's likely to recover me; she's Lady Fop now, and I am one of her aunts, I thank my promotion.

Enter Credulous, Cunningame, Niece, Sir Gregory and Mirabell

CREDULOUS I have performed your behest, sir.

OLD KNIGHT What have you performed, sir?

WITTYPATE Faith, sir, I must excuse my cousin in this act, if you can excuse yourself for making him a priest (there's the most difficult answer): I put this practice on him as from your desire. A truth, a truth, father.

CREDULOUS I protest, sir, he tells you truth; he moved me to't in your name.

OLD KNIGHT I protest, sir, he told you a lie in my name, and were you so easy, Master Credulous, to believe him?

CREDULOUS If a man should not believe his cousin, sir, whom should he believe?

OLD KNIGHT
Good-e'en to you, good Master Cousin Cunningame,
And your fair bride, my cousin Cunningame too!
And how do you, Sir Gregory, with your fair lady?

SIR GREGORY A little better than you would have had me, I thank you, sir: the days of 'puppy' and 'slave' and 'rascal' are pretty well blown over now. I know crabs from verjuice, I have tried both: an thou'dst give me thy niece for nothing, I'd not have her.

CUNNINGAME I think so, Sir Gregory, for my sake you would not.

SIR GREGORY I would thou had'st scaped her too, and then she had died of the green-sickness. Know this, that I did marry in spite, and I will kiss my lady in spite, and love her in spite, and beget children of her in spite, and when I die they shall have my lands in spite. This was my resolution, and now 'tis out.

NIECE
How spiteful are you now, Sir Gregory!
Why, look you, I can love my dearest husband
With all the honours, duties, sweet embraces,
That can be thrown upon a loving man.

SIR GREGORY Pox, this is afore your uncle's face, but behind his back, in private, you'll show him another tale.

CUNNINGAME You see, sir, now the irrecoverable state of all these things before you. Come out of your muse: they have been but wit weapons; you were wont to love the play.

Enter Clown

OLD KNIGHT Let me alone in my muse a little, sir; I will wake to you anon.

CUNNINGAME [*to Niece*] Ud'so, your friend Pompey: how will you answer him?

NIECE Very well, if you'll but second it and help me.

CLOWN I do hear strange stories; are ladies things obnoxious?

NIECE
O, the dissembling, falsest wretch is come!

151 **move** i.e. to start playing again
153–5 **I need not . . . with you** i.e. since they will fare extremely well on all this money, while it lasts
155 **snapped** snapped up, caught, cheated
158 **some howling another while** i.e. let's have some howling for a change
173–4 **hang her** for bigamy, which had been made a capital offence in 1603
182 **practice** 'artful contrivance, stratagem' (Dyce)
190 **Master Cousin Cunningame** 'Cousin' is here used in its general sense of 'kinsman' (in this instance, 'nephew-in-law'), and with a pun on Cunningame's mastery of cozenage
195–6 **crabs from verjuice** Crabs are small, bitter apples, used for making a sweet purée called verjuice.
201 **green-sickness** an anaemic disease of young women, supposedly caused by unfulfilled sexual desire and curable by marriage
214–15 **wit weapons . . . play** 'Play' here puns on Wittypate's virtual quotation of the title of the play in which he is appearing

CUNNINGAME How now, lady?

NIECE

Let me come to him, and instead of love
Let me have revenge!

WITTYPATE Pray you now, will you first examine whether he be guilty or no?

NIECE He cannot be excused.—
How many messengers, thou perjured man,
Hast thou returned with vows and oaths that thou
Wouldst follow, and never till this unhappy hour
Could I set eye of thee, since thy false eye
Drew my heart to it? O, I could tear thee now,
Instead of soft embraces, pray give me leave—

WITTYPATE Faith, this was ill done of you sir, if you promised otherwise.

CLOWN By this hand, never any messenger came at me since the first time I came into her company; that a man should be wronged thus!

NIECE

Did not I send thee scarves and diamonds?
And thou returned'st me letters, one with a false
heart in't.

WITTYPATE

O, fie! To receive favours, return falsehoods,
And hold a lady in hand—

CLOWN Will you believe me, sir? If ever I received diamonds or scarf, or sent any letter to her, would this sword might ne'er go through me.

WITTYPATE Some bad messengers have gone between you, then.

NIECE

Take him from my sight, if I shall see tomorrow.

WITTYPATE

Pray you, forbear the place; this discontent
May impair her health much.

CLOWN Foot, if a man had been in any fault, 'twould ne'er have grieved him, sir, if you'll believe.

WITTYPATE

Nay, nay, protest no more, I do believe you,
But you see how the lady is wronged by't:
She has cast away herself, it is to be feared,
Against her uncle's will, nay, any consent,
But out of a mere neglect and spite to herself,
Married suddenly without any advice.

CLOWN Why, who can help it? If she be cast away she may thank herself; she might have gone further and fared worse; I could do no more than I could do. 'Twas her own pleasure to command me that I should not come till I was sent for, I had been with her every minute of an hour else.

WITTYPATE Truly, I believe you.

CLOWN Night and day she might have commanded me, and that she knew well enough; I said as much to her, between her and I; yet I protest she's as honest a lady for my part, that I'd say if she would see me hanged. If she be cast away I cannot help it; she might have stayed to have spoke with a man.

WITTYPATE Well, 'twas a hard miss on both parts.

CLOWN So 'twas; I was within one of her, for all this cross luck; I was sure I was between the knight and home.

NIECE Not gone yet? O, my heart! None regard my health?

WITTYPATE Good sir, forbear her sight a while, you hear how ill she brooks it.

CLOWN Foolish woman, to overthrow her fortunes so; I shall think the worse of a lady's wit while I live for't. Pox, I could almost cry for anger. If she should miscarry now 'twould touch my conscience a little, and who knows what love and conceit may do? What would people say as I go along? 'There goes he that the lady died for love on'. I am sure to hear on't i'th' streets. I shall weep beforehand; foolish woman, I do grieve more for thee now than I did love thee before. Well, go thy ways, wouldst thou spare thy husband's head and break thine own heart, if thou hadst any wit? I would some other had been the cause of thy undoing: I shall be twitted i'th' teeth with't, I'm sure of that, foolish lady. *Exit*

NIECE

So, so, this trouble's well shook off.—Uncle, how d'ee?
There's a dowry due, sir.

CUNNINGAME We have agreed it, sweetest,
And find your uncle fully recovered, kind
To both of us.

NIECE To all the rest, I hope.

OLD KNIGHT

Never to thee,—nor thee, easy cousin Credulous.
Was your wit so raw?

CREDULOUS Faith, yours, sir, so long seasoned,
Has been faulty too and very much to blame,
Speaking it with reverence, uncle.

SIR GREGORY Yes, faith, sir; you have paid as dear for your time as any man here.

WITTYPATE Ay, sir, and I'll reckon it to him. *Imprimis*, the first preface-cheat of a pair of pieces to the beggars; you remember that? I was the example to your bounty there; I spake Greek and Syriac, sir; you understand me now. Next, the robbery put upon your indulgent cousin: which indeed was no robbery, no constable, no justice, no thief, but all cheaters; there was a hundred mark, mark you that. Lastly, this memorable hundred pounds'

244 **hold a lady in hand** lead a lady on

247 **ne'er** The Clown confusedly swears by a wish that he should be killed with his own sword, rather than that he should not be.

272–3 **she might . . . man** i.e. she might have postponed her marriage until after we had spoken together

284 **conceit** here 'imagination'

289–90 **wouldst thou . . . heart** would you break your heart by refraining from cuckolding your husband with me?

294 **how d'ee** how do ye, how are you

304 ***Imprimis*** Firstly (as used in accounts)

307–8 **understand me now** in the double sense of retrospectively understanding the situation, and now being able to understand Wittypate (since he is speaking English)

308 **cousin** used loosely to mean any relative outside the immediate family, as at 5.2.190; here 'nephew'

worth of music: this was but cheats and wit too, and for the assistance of this gentleman to my cousin (for which I am to have a fee). That was a little practice of my wit, too, father. Will you come to composition yet, father?

CUNNINGAME Yes, faith, sir, do; two hundred a year will be easier than so much weekly. I do not think he's barren, if he should be put to't again.

OLD KNIGHT
Why, this was the day I looked for; thou shalt have't,
And the next cheat makes it up three hundred.
[*To Credulous*] Live thou upon thy ten pound vicarage,
Thou get'st not a penny more; here's thy full
Hire now.

CREDULOUS
I thank you, sir.

WITTYPATE
Why, there was the sum of all my wit, father:
To shove him out of your favour, which I feared
Would have disinherited me.

OLD KNIGHT Most certain it had,
Had not thy wit recovered it. Is there any here
That had a hand with thee?

WITTYPATE Yes, all these, sir.

OLD KNIGHT
Nephew, part a hundred pound amongst 'em,
I'll repay it. Wealth love me as I love wit!
When I die
I'll build an almshouse for decayèd wits.

SIR GREGORY I'll entertain one in my lifetime. [*To Priscian*] Scholar, you shall be my chaplain: I have the gift of twenty benefices, simple as I am here.

PRISCIAN Thanks, my great patron.

CUNNINGAME [*to Sir Ruinous*] Sir, your gentry and your name shall both be raised as high as my fortunes can reach 'em, for your friend's sake.

WITTYPATE Something will be in my present power, the future more. You shall share with me.

SIR RUINOUS *and* LADY Thanks, worthy gentlemen.

NIECE [*to Sir Gregory*] Sir, I would beg one thing of you.

SIR GREGORY You can beg nothing of me.

WITTYPATE O sir, if she begs, there's your power over her.

SIR GREGORY She has begged me for a fool already, but 'tis no matter; I have begged her for a lady that she might have been; that's one for another.

WITTYPATE Nay, but if she beg—

SIR GREGORY Let her beg again, then.

NIECE That your man Pompey's coat may come over his ears back again; I would not he should be lost for my sake.

SIR GREGORY Well, 'tis not granted, for mine own sake.

MIRABELL I'll entreat it, sir.

SIR GREGORY
Why, then, 'tis granted for your sake.

OLD KNIGHT Come, come,
Down with all weapons now, 'tis music time,
So it be purchased at an easy rate.
Some have received the knocks, some given the hits;
An all concludes in love, there's happy wits. *Exeunt*

THE PARTS

Adult Males

CUNNINGAME (511 lines): any servant(s) except First or Second
OLD KNIGHT (460 lines): any servant except the Old Knight's
WITTYPATE (425 lines): Lady Ruinous's servant
SIR GREGORY (390 lines): any servant(s) except First or Second
CLOWN (239 lines): any servant(s) except First or Second
SIR RUINOUS (72 lines)
PRISCIAN (58 lines): any servant(s) except Lady Ruinous's
CREDULOUS (34 lines): any servant(s) except the Old Knight's
Old Knight's SERVANT (4.1; 7 lines): any servant(s)
FIRST SERVANT (5.1; 5 lines): any servant(s) except Second
SECOND SERVANT (5.1; 1 line): any servant(s) except First
Lady Ruinous's SERVANT (2.1; 1 line): any servant(s)

Boys

NIECE (377 lines)
GUARDIANESS (169 lines)
LADY RUINOUS (115 lines)
MIRABELL (88 lines): Boy
BOY (21 lines): Mirabell

315 **composition** compromise, peace terms
318 **barren** of further ideas
331 **repay it** i.e. pay it over again (since the Old Knight has already paid them £100 for their music)
347 **begged me for a fool** 'An allusion to the applications made for the guardianship of fools: under a writ in the old common law, if a man is proved *pursus idiota*, the custody of his person and the profits of his lands may be granted by the King to some subject who has interest enough to obtain them. These wardships were sometimes sold' (Dyce)
352 **coat** servant's livery
359 **So it** So long as it

MASQUE OF CUPIDS

Introduced by M. T. Jones-Davies and Ton Hoenselaars, text edited and annotated by John Jowett

MIDDLETON'S *Masque of Cupids* is not extant, except for two songs that have been plausibly identified as parts of the lost text. Modified versions of one song appear in *More Dissemblers Besides Women* (1.4) and *A Chaste Maid in Cheapside* (4.1), and an alternative version of part of the other song appears in *The Witch* (2.1). The symbolic, spectacular effects in *Women, Beware Women*, with its several pages acting as destructive Cupids in the concluding masque, would also appear to reflect the influence of Middleton's earlier *Masque of Cupids*.

Occasion

Masque of Cupids was written and performed as part of the festivities organized around the wedding on 26 December 1613 of James I's favourite Robert Carr (or Ker, in Scottish), Earl of Somerset, and Frances Howard (daughter of Thomas Howard, Earl of Suffolk). This wedding had been preceded by most unorthodox divorce proceedings, and the events of the 1613/14 Christmas season excited no less interest.

With the king's mediation, Frances Howard had married Robert Devereux, third Earl of Essex, in 1606. The marriage was an attempt to reconcile the Devereux family with the Howard family, which had been instrumental in bringing the second Earl of Essex to the block in 1601. The bride was only thirteen years old, the bridegroom fourteen. The marriage was not consummated. Following the wedding Essex left for the Continent, while Howard went to live at court. Frances Howard grew up to become not only a great beauty but also a flirtatious young woman who may have tried, in vain, to become Prince Henry's mistress. Her great-uncle Henry Howard, Earl of Northampton, probably brought her and Carr together. The pro-Catholic Howards found themselves jeopardized by a court faction with strong puritan leanings, including Sir Thomas Egerton (Lord Ellesmere), Archbishop George Abbot, and William Herbert, third Earl of Pembroke; under the circumstances, it would certainly have suited the Earl of Northampton, a formidable politician, to have the king's favourite develop, through Frances, an attachment to the Howards. Carr succumbed to the temptations of the young Countess, who relied on Dr Simon Forman's sorcery. Private meetings between the lovers were arranged through Mrs Anne Turner, who had introduced the fashion of yellow starch in England—to which Middleton alludes in *The Widow* (5.1.54). Mrs Turner had premises for the lovers in Paternoster Row and at Hammersmith. The Court turned a blind eye. To write to Howard, Carr relied on his unofficial mentor Sir Thomas Overbury (the character writer, and former Oxford classmate of Middleton). Although Overbury belonged to the anti-Howard faction, he assisted his influential friend Carr in composing love letters to Frances Howard.

In December 1609, Essex back from the Continent claimed his rights as a husband. Only when compelled by her father did the Countess agree to live with Essex at Chartley. For three years, she tried to keep him from intercourse with her, calling on Dr Forman for drugs to secure her husband's impotence.

Carr's influence was growing. He had been knighted and made Gentleman of the Bedchamber in 1607. A year later, he had received Sir Walter Ralegh's Sherborne Estate, to which in 1610 were added the estates of Lord Maxwell. On 25 March 1611 he became Viscount Rochester, and the first Scot in the English House of Lords. He was soon made a Knight of the Garter. When Robert Cecil, Earl of Salisbury, died in May 1612, Carr joined the Privy Council. He became, with each new honour, an ever more desirable match.

By the end of 1612, a divorce was sought on the grounds of nullity. The annulment was supported by both Frances Howard and her husband. Northampton and Carr approached the king on the divorce, and found a willing ear. As the news spread, so did speculation about the adulterous ties between Howard and Carr. In February of the following year, it was rumoured that Howard had used the services of one Mary Woods to kill Essex, and in April, this 'scandal and slander' as John Chamberlain put it, led Frances Howard's father to consider stopping the divorce proceedings (I, 444–45). Overbury urged Carr to leave Howard and wrote *The Wife* as a marriage guide. His tactful advice soon gave way to open resentment, and with a quarrel in the Privy Gallery at Whitehall, during which Overbury called the Countess a 'base' woman, the friendship came to an end.

On 21 April 1613, Overbury, having repeatedly refused several foreign embassies, was committed to the Tower. Carr's role in this imprisonment remains unclear. To obtain easy access to the prisoner, Northampton had Sir Gervase Elwes appointed Lieutenant of the Tower on 6 May. Meanwhile, Howard plotted to have Richard Weston, her old *postillion d'amour*, made keeper of Overbury. Through him, she schemed, assisted by Mrs Turner, to poison the prisoner.

On 16 May, James assigned a number of Commissioners to try the divorce case in preparation of the marriage of Howard and Carr. The aim was to establish the Earl's impotence and Howard's virginity. Essex claimed that he had not slept with his wife. Still, he was unwilling to admit total impotence, as this would deprive him of any hope ever to marry again. He admitted that he was '*maleficiatus* only *ad illam*', or, in the words of Thomas Howard, that he 'had no ink in his pen' only where Howard was concerned. Her virginity had to be tried: as Chamberlain reports, 'ancient Ladies and midwives expert in those matters' inspected her. Since the Countess wore a veil on the occasion, rumour had it that her cousin Katherine Fines, or a daughter of Sir Thomas Monson, had substituted for her. The proceedings became a topic for gossip as did the rumours about the affair between Frances Howard and Carr. On 10 June, John Chamberlain wrote to Sir Ralph Winwood that he was stupefied that the Countess should have seen Carr 'three hours together within these two days'. Several weeks later, he wrote that 'The world speaks liberally that my Lord of Rochester and she be in love one with another.'

The Commissioners reached a stalemate in July 1613. The question arose if Essex had been bewitched. Archbishop Abbot told the king that *maleficium* could not be proved in the Church Fathers, but James, with his own *Daemonology* in hand, considered it a valid reason to grant the divorce. As it became evident that the Commissioners were equally divided in opinion, an impatient James appointed two additional members—the Bishops of Winchester and Rochester—who, as expected, swayed the balance. On 25 September, the Essex marriage was declared void, and at James's command the verdict was pronounced without any arguments or reasons. The news that on 14 September Sir Thomas Overbury had died in the Tower went nearly unnoticed.

The marriage took place on St Stephen's Day, 1613. For those who, like Chamberlain, remembered Howard's union with Essex in 1606, this was an intriguing event. The king was present on both occasions, and the venue was the same, the Chapel Royal. Moreover, Dr Montague, Bishop of Bath and Wells, who officiated in 1613, had also married Howard to Essex in 1606.

Epithalamiasts

Many material presents were bestowed on the new couple, but also poems, epithalamiums and masques. The marriage, which was thoroughly unpopular in the public eye, proved a delicate rhetorical subject to which each writer responded with more or less appropriate tactics.

George Chapman's mythological fable of Perseus and Andromeda, a virgin tied to a rock and miraculously released from a monster—drawn from Natale Conti—is an allegory of the Earl of Somerset's 'rescue' of Frances Howard from her ill-fated marriage with Essex. *Andromeda Liberata* starts as a warning to the Earl of Somerset and the Countess against scandal and gossip. The quotation from Petronius on the title-page leaves one in little doubt: '*Nihil a veritate nec virtute remotius quam vulgaris opinio*' ['Nothing is more remote from truth and virtue than common opinion']. To the happy couple is promised 'so renowned a progeny | As earth shall envy', and that 'to the last times of the world' (ll. 532–7). The song of praise ends on a cosmic vision when bridegroom and bride will be rapt to heaven and transformed into constellations.

Yet a few tactless allusions in *Andromeda Liberata* got Chapman into trouble. His observations that Andromeda was 'Bound to a barren rock' (l. 143), and that 'he no less a homicide is held, | That man to be born lets' (ll. 491–2), read like thinly veiled allusions to Essex's impotence. No wonder Chapman was to find himself in disgrace with the Essex faction.

John Donne was confronted with the same paradoxical circumstances as the other poets. But he was also under financial pressure to compose an epithalamium to procure Somerset's patronage. The poet's wit attempts to reconcile the claims of sexuality with social conventions, perhaps nowhere better than in lines 87–90:

Our little Cupid hath sued Livery,
        And is no more in his minority,
He is admitted now into that breast
        Where the King's counsels and his secrets rest.

Here, Cupid is the wise god of adult love. Thus, indirectly, the respectability of the newly-married couple is defended, since they are not the victims of Venus' childish son who shoots his darts at random. This is an allusion to Howard's former union with Essex, which had been a marriage of children. Donne cleverly interweaves compliments and criticisms. The refrains referring to the lovers' inflaming eyes, while insisting on their indivisible union, also allude to their illicit passion. And the pattern of the poem, made up of eleven stanzas, each consisting of eleven lines, stresses its ambiguity, with the pervasive presence of sin, as shown by Augustine in *The City of God*: 'the number eleven, passing ten as it does, stands for trespassing against the law, and consequently for sin' (IV, 535).

When Donne brings his nuptial song to the Court, he is full of the 'common' joy (l. 232). In the masques, this sense of community is increased. Thomas Campion's *Masque of Squires*, which was danced in the Banqueting Room at Whitehall on 26 December 1613, offers the royal family 'The fruit of Peace and Joy [...] in a perpetual spring'. Here 'false opinion' also interferes as Error with her fiendish associates, Rumour, Curiosity, and Credulity, provoke the confusion of a storm, an antimasque that may have been inspired by the *Ballet of the Winds* (Florence, 1608). Peace and Joy can only be restored by the benevolence of Bel-Anna, who will dissolve the evil charms. Thus Campion, with his diplomatic compliment to the Queen (who had originally expressed her disagreement with the Somerset/Howard match), aims at shifting attention to the royal family as the object of praise. The masque is a tribute to the King, the Queen, and Prince Charles, their 'triple majesty'.

As part of the season's festivities, the king would have a masque 'performed by some gentlemen of his own servants that are good dancers'. This was Ben Jonson's *Irish Masque at Court*, a gentlemen's masque that Chamberlain described as 'a medley mask of five

English and five Scots (which are called the high dancers)'. Jonson's contribution reads like a parody of Campion's masque in the Anglo-Irish jargon that, like all dialect imitation, would normally be expected to raise a laugh. Four Irish footmen arriving at the English court will speak to King 'Yamish'. But 'the villanous vild Irish sheas' have destroyed their fine clothes and they dance the main dance in Irish mantles (ll. 73–4). Only through the king's wonderful intervention could they be transformed into new-born creatures—a tale of metamorphosis like Campion's masque.

Jonson's *Challenge at Tilt* spread over two nights. The *Challenge* was offered on 27 December 1613, and the answering *Tilt* was played on 1 January 1614. The device presented in *Challenge at Tilt* is of special interest in connection with Middleton's *Masque of Cupids*. Jonson's is also a masque about Cupids—two rival Cupids acting as pages. One of these is the husband's page, who is slightly taller than the wife's. Yet each claims precedence, asserting that he is the true Cupid. The wife's page unashamedly hints at his service as he waited on the bride into 'the nuptial chamber', transforming her into 'the throne of love', with roses on her cheeks and kisses on her lips, and mentions Venus' girdle about her that the bridegroom was to untie (ll. 42–44). The husband's page summarizes, not without a few smutty allusions, what in an epithalamium like Donne's was referred to as 'the bridegroom's coming'. Jonson here stresses the communal sense of sexual license that, within the privileged society to which *The Tilt* was addressed, tended to make the newly-weds not morally abnormal, but rather socially normative. The public character of the celebration is stressed as the second Cupid, who now enters first, descending from his chariot, addresses the ladies in the audience, threatening to chastise them by 'whipping [their] rebellious farthingales, with [his] bow-string' (ll. 108–9). After the spectacle of the two Cupids' champions—ten against ten—has ended the contention, a new kind of tilting is recommended: 'to meet lips for lances' and 'crack kisses instead of staves' (ll. 184–85). Hymen then expounds the myth of Eros and his brother Anteros, whose quarrel is not 'who is the true love', but 'who loves most' (ll. 215–16). This is symbolized by a palm that the two Cupids will divide between them. Hymen is the victory of reciprocal affection.

For a conclusion of the Christmas festivities and of the solemnities and magnificences in honour of the Somerset marriage, the *Masque of Flowers* (prepared in three weeks) was presented by some gentlemen of Gray's Inn at the Court of Whitehall in the Banqueting House on Twelfth Night 1614, eleven nights after the wedding. As a joint masque of the four Inns of Court could not be arranged, Sir Francis Bacon encouraged the 'Grayans' to offer a most sumptuous spectacle—paying all expenses himself—which, as Chamberlain remarks, stood him 'in above £2000'. It may have been an opportunity for Bacon to express his gratitude to the king and to Somerset, who in October 1613 had been instrumental in promoting him to the Attorney-Generalship.

Thus, from Chapman's poem to Bacon's masque we can see diverse strategies at work: advice to protect the newly-weds against envy and gossip (Chapman); excuses for the poet's absence from court (Donne); a shift of attention to the royal family (Campion); vindication of the couple (*Challenge at Tilt*); and, finally, with Bacon's discretion, no reference at all to the moral implications of the marriage.

Considering the different tactics adopted by contemporary poets, how might Middleton have tried to respond to the delicate moral problem that also faced him when he was commissioned at short notice to write a masque for the same occasion? As he demonstrated in his civic pageantry, Middleton was capable of celebrating idealized virtues, and of overlooking the weaknesses of the human individuals who should have embodied those virtues. If he experienced some ambivalence regarding the morality of the Somerset wedding, he might have resolved it as an ironist who saw the harmony of love threatened by the wanton pranks of his antemasque Eros. Was not *Ironia* for him, as it is described in *The World Tossed at Tennis*, like a needle 'That with one eye looks two ways at once' (l. 125)? Just such an irony informs the two Middleton songs.

Masque of Cupids

The *Masque of Cupids* was performed at the Merchant Taylors' Hall, Threadneedle Street, on Tuesday, 4 January 1614. On 31 December 1613, 'The Lord Mayor was sent to by the King, to entertain this new married couple, with their friends and followers; but he making an excuse that his house was too little to receive them, it was not accepted, but word sent back that he might command the biggest hall in the town: whereupon calling a council, it was resolved,' says Chamberlain, 'to do it at the charge of the City in the Merchant Taylors' Hall upon four days' warning'. On the last day of the year, therefore, a meeting of knights and aldermen was called to 'advise and consider how and in what manner the entertainement [was to be] given, and what solemnities, sports, and triumphs [...] prepared for the great honour of the feast; and to give speedy direction for the effecting thereof' (Nichols, III, 731). Sir Thomas Myddelton, the Lord Mayor, was well known to the dramatist who had written *The Triumphs of Truth* on the occasion of Sir Thomas's inauguration two months before, and also another entertainment that autumn in honour of the Lord Mayor's brother Hugh. This association may explain the choice of our Middleton to write his *Masque of Cupids*.

As Chamberlain put it, the ceremony preceding the feast at the Merchant Taylors' Hall was itself already tantamount to a pageant: 'thither they went yesternight about six o'clock, through Cheapside all by torchlight, accompanied by the father and mother of the bride, and all the lords and ladies about the court. The men were well mounted and richly arrayed, making a goodly show; the women, all in coaches'. At the Hall, 'the Lord Mayor and

Aldermen of London, in their scarlet robes, entertained them with hearty welcome, and feasted them with all magnificence'. Following speeches and music, 'all the meat was served to the table by choice citizens of comeliest personage, in their gowns of rich foins, selected out of the twelve honourable companies'. After supper and a wassail followed 'two several pleasant masques, and a play', 'other pleasant dances' and a 'princely banquet'. There remains no trace of these other elements of the evening's entertainment; the poet was paid for other shows, which could include speeches and songs, like those later collected in *Honourable Entertainments*. The guests did not return to Whitehall until 3 o'clock in the morning (Nichols, II, 732).

Evidence for the involvement of 'Thomas Middleton, gent.' (also called 'Mr. Middleton, Poet') is provided by the proceedings of the Court of Aldermen. That document also establishes the title: although modern scholars usually describe the entertainment as a 'Masque of Cupid', the last word is clearly plural in the original manuscript.

That plural makes it likely that *Masque of Cupids* was directly inspired by Jonson's *The Challenge at Tilt* of 27 December 1613, with its first introduction into the English masque tradition of two Cupids named Eros and Anteros. This would not be the only instance of conscious intertextuality in the Somerset wedding masques: Campion's *Masque of Squires*, performed on 26 December 1613, was mocked three days later by Jonson in *The Irish Masque*.

The Common Hall of the Merchant Taylors was ideally suited for theatrical production. It had seen performances by the Westminster boys in the mid-sixteenth century, and when the Company opened the Merchant Taylors' School in 1561, its first headmaster Richard Mulcaster perpetuated the tradition with his pupils, until boys' plays there were stopped in 1574 (Chambers, II, 75). Later Stuart performances included 'A military show and sham battle by the gentlemen of the Artillery Garden' in October 1619 (Chambers, IV, 112), and, on 13 February 1634, James Shirley's *The Triumph of Peace* (Bentley, V, 1157–58).

The physical Hall was, according to a contemporary account, 'of stone, and of such bigness that it passes all the Halls in London for beauty and comeliness' (Clode). The Common Hall was approximately 82 feet in length, 43 feet in width, and 43 feet in height. Although in 1614 the sumptuous Common Hall had not yet been tiled, it was glazed. Its extravagance and size excepted, the interior of the Hall was of a traditional kind, having its dais at one end (east), facing the screen with a door on either side and a Minstrel's Gallery over it. Like the dais, the sides of the Hall were matted and boarded, leaving the centre or 'Marsh' for 'the display of pageants'. On public occasions, like the annual festival of the Merchant Taylors' patron saint, St John, nine vast pieces of arras, presumably representing the life of the saint, served to conceal and adorn the bare walls, excepting the screen. If the nine tapestries, with their total surface of 230 square

Interior of Merchant Taylors' Hall, *c.*1850.

yards (covering the three walls to a height of twelve feet) were indeed taken from their protective bagging to adorn the walls on 4 January 1614, the Christian subject matter provided an intriguing blend (if not altogether unfamiliar in Middleton's other work) with the classical mythology to which the title of the masque alludes. Given the evidence of Shirley's *The Triumph of Peace*, flying machinery may well have been available at the Hall in the 1610s. If Middleton used it for the *Masque of Cupids*, this would make it likely that he incorporated elements of the wedding entertainment into *More Dissemblers Besides Women*.

Cupid and Cupids

In John Fletcher's *The Elder Brother* (1625?), Eustace asks for a masque to celebrate his marriage, to which Egremont acquiesces with the remark: ''Tis not half an hour's work; | A Cupid and a fiddle, and the thing's done' (2.2). His words indicate the proverbial status of Cupid in a wedding masque. In court entertainments, the god of love continued the glorious career he had known in Renaissance poetry, whether in Petrarch's *Triumphus Cupidinis* or in Spenser's *Faerie Queene*, whose 'mask of Cupid' exhibited 'the wingèd god himself [...] riding on a lion ravenous' (III.xii.22). With his *Masque of Cupids*, Middleton followed the widespread custom, which made of Cupid(s) the central persona (or personae) of such aristocratic triumphs.

The nature and attributes of this figure of love owe much to the popularity of Plato in the fifteenth and sixteenth centuries. Plato's Pausanias speaks of two Aphrodites, the celestial Ourania and the popular Pandemos; and as there are two Aphrodites, there must be two figures of Eros. Plato's two Aphrodites became the twin Venuses of the Neoplatonists: the celestial Venus and the terrestrial

Venus. Each was attended by a corresponding Eros or Amor: *Amor divinus* and *Amor vulgaris*.

Henceforth, the poets would play with the two loves, Eros and his brother Anteros, and the rivalry between *Amor profano* and *Amor sacro*. Whereas the classical Anteros had stood for mutual love (*anti* = in return), they would sometimes choose the other sense (*anti* = against), implying an idea of contention. In *A Challenge at Tilt* (1614), as in *Love's Welcome at Bolsover* (1634), Jonson enhances the tradition by introducing Eros and his rival brother Anteros, and Middleton is likely to have adopted or perhaps mocked this device in the *Masque of Cupids*.

It is true that this neoplatonic ideology is more obviously present in Jonson's erudite entertainment than in the works of Middleton, which remain much closer to the native literary tradition. And yet, neoplatonism was part of the intellectual context in which both authors worked. And that Middleton should toy with the two figures of Eros and Anteros as they had just appeared in *A Challenge at Tilt* seems no impossibility; but his artistic approach would reveal a different stance from Jonson's, a stance on the side of irony, and even raillery.

Alternatively, Middleton's *Masque of Cupids* may have represented several Cupids. As early as 1594, in *The Tragedy of Dido, Queen of Carthage* by Marlowe and Nashe, Dido evokes 'ten thousand Cupids [that] hover in the air | And fan it in Aeneas' lovely face'. And there were the multiple decorative *putti* in baroque art. Multiple Cupids appear in *Hymenæi* where 'a thousand several-coloured loves [...] hop about the nuptial-room' (370). In Jonson's *Masque of Beauty* (1608), the ascent to the throne of harmony was covered with 'a multitude of Cupids', and in Campion's *Lords' Masque* (1612/13), in order not to 'wrong the Night | Of her Hymenaean right; | A thousand Cupids call away, | Fearing the approaching day'.

Cupid is a literary and theatrical as well as a visual figure, eliciting a wide variety of responses. Thus in *The Tragedy of Dido*, Cupid obeys his mother Venus, who orders him to turn to Ascanius's shape. In what is here printed as the first song, Cupid is described with his mother Venus. This is a Renaissance commonplace—witness the 1615 inventory of the Earl of Somerset, listing large panels representing Venus and Cupid. It suggests that Venus could well have been a character in *Masque of Cupids*.

Ladies are mentioned three times in one Middleton song, and women once in the other; this strongly suggests the presence of women, and probably specifically ladies, in the masque. And in fact, Middleton likes to have Cupid introduce masques of ladies—as happens in the second scene of *Timon of Athens* (a Middleton scene), at the time of the banquet, and in *The Nice Valour* where the Cupid character, a Lady disguised, leads in six ladies as masquers (2.1). That Cupid is mentioned again in the epilogue as 'Cupid in's petticoat'. In *A Chaste Maid in Cheapside*, *More Dissemblers Besides Women*, and *The Witch*, the altered versions of the two songs are sung by a woman. In *More Dissemblers*, Cupid also addresses several ladies referred to as 'fair beauties' (1.3.86). And we do not forget that Middleton's later Inns-of-Court *Masque of Heroes* was again to be presented 'as an entertainment for many worthy ladies'.

Whether or not Venus and other ladies were characters in the masque, Cupid certainly was. Cupid had different genealogies with the Neoplatonists, but his functions and attributes seldom change. In the first song, Cupid is a waggish boy, the exemplary archer who 'doth bend with his bow and enamour[s] with his arrow', as Richard Mulcaster describes him in his *Positions* (ch. 26, 101). The playful tone of the song recalls an extant fragment of *The Hunting of Cupid* by George Peele:

What thing is love? for (well I wot) love is a thing.
It is a prick; it is a sting;
It is a pretty pretty thing;
It is a fire; it is a coal
Whose flame creeps in at ev'ry hole.

The initial question of the song's second stanza—'Why should not Venus chide her son?'—is reminiscent of Titian's 'Education of Cupid': here it seems that blind Cupid will not be permitted to cause any more mischief with his bow and arrows. Middleton's quick rhythm, with the repetition of echoing words ('wanton boy', 'A very very wanton boy', 'wanton pranks'; 'fiery darts | his darts'), and the repeated last two lines of each stanza, with a quibble on 'lips' (*labia*) and the allusion to the cuckold's horn ('men's crests'), intensify the satirical tone that fits the antimasque or foil preceding the main masque. The pun on 'crests' with the sense of 'blazons' could have been an allusion to Somerset's newly acquired earldom. This also explains the line that follows, with its self-conscious 'I mean', intended to cancel any ambiguous reading. Yet, the reading that remains could easily refer to Essex's cuckoldry. This thesis can only be upheld if the song belonged to the antimasque—or 'antemasque', as Middleton would write—and was followed by the main masque in which any seedy detail would be resolved into an image of mutual love.

The second song opens on a cynical note, associating Cupid with commerce. Its next stanza looks back nostalgically to the days when lust between men and women was natural. The attitude to Cupid here recalls the song in Sir Philip Sidney's *Old Arcadia* sung by the love-hating shepherd named Dicus:

Poor painters oft with silly poets join
To fill the world with strange but vain conceits,
One brings the stuff, the other stamps the coin,
Which breeds naught else but glosses of deceits.
Thus painters Cupid paint, thus poets do,
A naked god, blind, young, with arrows two. (58)

Read in this way, the first and the second song are one another's counterparts. In the first, Cupid is an extremely bawdy presence, though also cynical like Shakespeare's Pandarus. The second song evokes the unspoiled time when the dart was made of flesh, and men did not disguise their sexual appetites with the fiction that Cupid made them do it. We cannot be certain if this contrast corresponds to the structure of the original masque, or tries to capture something of the scandal around the wedding for which it was produced.

Love is a 'speaking picture' in the collections of emblems, from Andrea Alciati to the representatives of the genre in England: Geffrey Whitney or Henry Peacham. Different emblems show Cupid carrying a torch (for the ardour of love) or thunder (a sign of power), taming lions or holding a fish in one hand and a flower in the other to show that he has power 'on sea and land' (Alciati, Whitney). He is stung by bees to signify that we often 'pluck a nettle for a rose' (Whitney). For Peacham he is stronger than Hercules, and Cupid dwells 'where he lists | Be it a palace or a simple shed'. To the influence on masques of the emblematists' imagery was added that of the Italian humanist Piero Valeriano's hieroglyphs: a good instance is 'the palm tree', which in Jonson's *Love's Triumph through Callipolis* (1631) is the hieroglyph of marriage (l. 211).

The major sources of dramatists and masque inventors were provided by the Italian mythographers and their compendia dealing with the ancient gods. Boccaccio's *Genealogia deorum gentilium* had been known in England since the fifteenth century, and is still quoted by Robert Burton when, in his *Anatomy of Melancholy*, he discusses the origins of love. There were three other great Italian manuals. In Lilio Gregorio Giraldi's *De deis gentium varia et multiplex historia* (1548), Cupid is multiple 'because loves of things are diverse'. Vincenzo Cartari's *Le Imagine colla Spozione degli dei* (1556) depicts Cupid as a single god and then as the personification of mere human desires (*multiplices cupidines*). He also pictures the struggle of naked Eros and Anteros for the palm. Natale Conti's *Mythologiae sive Explicationis fabularum libri decem* (1568), distinguishes between the abuse of Cupid and Cupid himself, 'whose force is the primal attraction that fashioned the Universe from Chaos' (an idea later developed by Bacon). These manuals were used by scholars, poets, and painters alike. And, at the end of the sixteenth century, Cesare Ripa's *Iconologia*—'Opera [...] non meno utile che necessaria a Poeti, Pittori, Scultori, & altri per rappresentare le Virtu, Vitii, Affeti et Passioni humane'—was published in Italy. It is an immense repertoire of Renaissance symbolism which was to become a mine of information for the masque inventors. Like Jonson, Middleton, though less erudite, would turn to Ripa's work for his symbolic characters as well as Valeriano's *Hieroglyphica* or Alciati's commentaries, and the humanists' compendia.

Cupid being the most frequently represented character in masques, many legends, roles, and anecdotes associated with him will colour his many-faceted figure. Eros appears accompanied by Desire (*Masque of Beauty*), with Games, Laughter, Sports and Delights (*Time Vindicated*). He is the run-away after whom Aphrodite raises the hue and cry (*Masque of Haddington*). Eros is bound captive (*Love Freed from Ignorance and Folly*), or he is the blind archer, with his 'bewitching philters' and 'alluring baits' that will be banished by Diana in Robert White's *Cupid's Banishment* (1617), where the victory of Chastity repeats Petrarch's *Triumphus Pudicitiae* that follows his *Triumphus Cupidinis*. Elsewhere we watch him in contest with Plutus, the god of money, who is also painted blind, Impostor Mammon, 'who has stolen Love's ensigns' (Jonson's *Love Restored*, ll. 174–75). We note an allusion to the myth of Pores and Penia: 'The father Plenty is; the mother, Want' (*Love's Triumph through Callipolis*, l. 58). 'Rebellious he' disobeys Venus, who punishes him by forcing his arms away (*Chloridia*), which explains why Inigo Jones's design of Cupid is inscribed 'without bow or quiver' (Jones-Davies). Cupid is above all such an efficient dramatic figure that Venus would 'let him out for the week to the King's players': 'they have need of him'—one more tribute to his invaluable favour with the public (Jonson's *Christmas His Masque*, 1616, 441–42). The wanton boy of Middleton's bawdy song is also Venus' wanton son of *Lovers Made Men* (1617), 'fashioned to tilt with ladies' lips', and reappears in Philip Massinger's *The Bondman* (1.1.50–52):

a raw young fellow,
One never trained in arms, but rather fashioned
To tilt with ladies' lips than crack a lance.

Since Cupid could not be represented naked in English plays and masques, he nearly always appeared disguised as a page. Alternatively, the illusion of nakedness was suggested by sartorial means, as in Francis Beaumont's *Masque of the Inner Temple and Gray's Inn* (1613), where a stage direction reads: 'Enter foure *Cupids* from each side of the Boscage [= grove], attired in flame coloured Taffita close to their bodie like naked Boyes' (132). Middleton elsewhere had a preference for the former solution, most notably in *More Dissemblers Besides Women* where the revised version of the song is sung by a woman disguised as a page. However, in the more private setting of the *Masque of Cupids* performance, the pretence of nudity would have been appropriate to the more sexually adventurous culture of the Jacobean court. And Thomas Carew's *Coelum Brittannicum* (1634), a masque praising the moral reformation that Charles I had brought about, seems to imply that Cupid had been performed naked in the Jacobean court. Among the sanctions that Jove will impose on his own kingdom, in imitation of Charles, is that 'Cupid must go no more so scandalously naked, but is enjoined to make him breeches, though of his mother's petticoats' (159).

The scandalous future of the marriage so royally celebrated at the Merchant Taylors' Hall on 1 January 1614 is narrated elsewhere in this volume. (See the Critical Introduction to *The Witch*, 1124.) Given the scandals before and scandals after the Somerset wedding, it may be no accident that the full text of Middleton's *Masque of Cupids* was never printed, no accident that Middleton cannibalized and recycled elsewhere anything that seemed theatrically salvageable. Even Jonson, when he came to include his *Irish Masque* in the 1616 edition of his *Works*, removed any mention of the occasion for which it was written. However happy Middleton may have been to receive a commission from his new patrons in the London government, he may have felt no great desire to publicize his part in this business.

SEE ALSO

Music: *Companion*, 149 ('Cupid is Venus' only joy'), 151 ('Cupid is an idle toy')
Textual introduction and apparatus: *Companion*, 630
Authorship and date: *Companion*, 377
Related works: *Timon*, 467; *Chaste Maid*, 907; *More Dissemblers*, 1034; *Witch*, 1124; *Women Beware*, 1488; *Nice Valour*, 1679

Two Songs from '*Masque of Cupids*'

1 [*First*] *Song*

Cupid is Venus' only joy,
But he is a wanton boy,
A very, very wanton boy.
He shoots at ladies' naked breasts;
He is the cause of most men's crests—
  I mean upon the forehead,
  Invisible but horrid.
'Twas he first thought upon the way
To keep a lady's lips in play.

Why should not Venus chide her son
For the tricks that he hath done,
The wanton tricks that he hath done?
He shoots his fiery darts so thick
They wound poor ladies to the quick,
  Ay me, with cruel wounding.
  His darts are so confounding
That life and strength would soon decay,
But that it keeps their lips in play.

[*Second Song*] 2

Cupid is an idle toy.
Never was there such a boy.
If there were, let any show
Or his quiver or his bow
Or a wound by him they got
Or a broken arrow-shot.
Money, money makes us bow.
There is no other Cupid now.

Whilst the world continued good
People loved for flesh and blood.
Men about them bore the dart
That would catch a woman's heart.
Women likewise, great and small,
With a pretty thing they call
Cunny, cunny, won the men,
And this was all the Cupid then.

These songs are likely to have been taken from the lost *Masque of Cupids*. They survive in later music manuscripts. The first of them is the basis for songs in *Chaste Maid*, at 4.1.167–93, and *Dissemblers*, at 1.4.89–99.

1.1 **only joy** as said of a parent's sole child, Cupid being the son of Venus, but with a sexual equivocation

2 **wanton** lewd, skittish, unrestrained

4 **He shoots** Refers to the traditional depiction of Cupid with a bow and arrow.

ladies' naked breasts Perhaps refers to the fashion for court ladies to wear diaphanous or transparent coverings over their breasts, as exampled in court masques, some of which represented Cupids.

breasts The non-erotic sense is 'hearts'.

5 **crests** (*a*) the cuckold's horns (*b*) erections (the sense denied)

9 **lips** with a quibble on the labia of the vulva

13–18 **He...play** There is a sustained undercurrent of allusion to sexual penetration.

15–16 **wounding...confounding** Compare Pandarus's bawdy song in Shakespeare's *Troilus and Cressida* (3.1) with its rhyme on 'wound' and 'confound'.

17 **strength** more often an attribute of male sexual performance, here transferred to the female

18 **it** refers back to 'wounding'

2.1 **idle** foolish

toy primarily 'piece of nonsense, joke', the claim being that Cupid doesn't exist. Also knick-knack, friskiness, sexual caress, (female) sexual organ. Perhaps also 'frivolous tune', referring to the song of Cupid itself.

4 **Or** either

quiver the case for Cupid's arrows, but also, equivocally, 'vagina'

bow equivocally, 'penis'

5 **wound** Refers to the wound of Cupid's arrow, the penetrated vagina, and loss of chastity or good reputation

6 **arrow-shot** Probably 'arrow-shaft', altered for rhyme. Otherwise the flight of an arrow, 'broken' in that it has hit its target, hence the wound of broken flesh.

9–10 **Whilst...blood** A provocative variation of the Christian idea of prelapsarian innocence, combined with the classical myth of the Golden Age, in which there were no metals, money, or violence.

11–12 **the dart...heart** i.e. (*a*) Cupid's arrow, (*b*) the penis

15 **Cunny** cunt

MORE DISSEMBLERS BESIDES WOMEN

Edited by John Jowett

More Dissemblers takes a quizzical look at the persistence of desire in a court world where romantic and sexual love have been subordinated to religion. It explores the inexorable clash between love and religion as manifested in two views of life, two styles of speech and behaviour. For the godly the heart of the state is defined as a religious cloister. The libidinous seek to redefine it as a sexual market-place.

The play belonged to the repertoire of the King's Men. Though the date of first performance has variously been conjectured as 1614, *c.*1615, or 1619, the earliest year is perhaps in balance more likely. Subsequently, on 17 October 1623, Sir Henry Herbert, the new Master of the Revels, issued a new licence. The King's Men, having presumably revived the play at the Blackfriars theatre, staged it at court on 6 January 1624, as we know from Herbert's note in his office-book: 'Upon Twelfth Night, the masque being put off, *More Dissemblers Besides Women*, by the King's company, the Prince only being there. At Whitehall.' The masque in question, Jonson's *Neptune's Triumph*, had been designed to celebrate as a triumph of Protestant diplomacy Prince Charles's and the Duke of Buckingham's return to London empty-handed after the negotiations in Madrid for a betrothal between Charles and the Spanish Infanta had broken down. *Neptune's Triumph* had to be 'put off' to avoid a diplomatic wrangle involving the Spanish ambassador. As a substitute *More Dissemblers* is perhaps not anodyne. The Gypsy scene, in which a fool has his palm read and is tricked of his money, might now have served to recall another Jonson masque, *The Gypsies Metamorphosed* (1621), in which Buckingham played the 'Patrico', or First Gypsy, who read King James's palm. The Gypsy scene as a whole can scarcely have been introduced for the court performance, as it is intrinsic to the rest of the play's action and so cannot have been a late addition, but it could possibly have been revised for the court performance. Whether revised or not, the scene could scarcely have failed to be topical to the court occasion. The play as a whole could have acquired further new significance because it deals with the fortunate breakdown of a match that involves a head of state (as Charles was destined to become) and is based on a compromising infatuation (such as Charles initially conceived towards the Infanta). At the revival, the final affirmation of the Duchess's celibacy might well have acquired new political overtones of national independence and uncompromised Protestant virtue. Middleton was shortly to write his strongly anti-Spanish *Game at Chess.*

Herbert's note adds the first recorded criticism of *More Dissemblers*: 'The worst play that e'er I saw'. Such denunciations of plays were not uncommon in the seventeenth century. As similar comments in the diary of Samuel Pepys suggest, they can reflect on the production or on the social occasion, and in this case there may have been disgruntlement over the cancelled masque. *More Dissemblers* held its place in the King's Men's repertoire, for as late as 1641 it was protected along with other of the company's plays against unauthorized publication, and in 1669 it was one of the plays allotted to Thomas Killigrew as 'formerly acted at the Blackfriars and now allowed of to his Majesty's Servants at the New Theatre'. The Restoration apparently lost interest, except in the Gypsy scenes, which were plagiarized in John Leanerd's comedy *The Rambling Justice*, acted at Drury Lane in 1678. *More Dissemblers* is not known to have been revived until a student production at the University of Toronto in 1970.

The play first reached a reading public in 1657, a year before Oliver Cromwell's death. Humphrey Moseley, a major Interregnum publisher of pre-1642 drama, brought the play out in an octavo volume with *Women, Beware Women*, under the joint title *Two New Plays.* He probably regarded the pair and *No Wit/Help like a Woman's*, which he published in the same year, as a coherent group. The collocated titles, setting forth a common theme in women, characterize them as witty, dissembling, and dangerous, and so suggest ways in which women might compensate for their traditionally subordinate role. Each title marks out a distinct stage between male approval and apprehension.

The title-page declares *More Dissemblers* a comedy, thus complementing the tragedy *Women, Beware Women.* Despite the obvious differences in tone and genre, there are some points of contact between these plays. Both develop the theme of sexual betrayal in an Italianate setting. They share the figure of a moralizing Cardinal (though the temporizing hypocrisy of the churchman in *More Dissemblers* largely disappears in *Women, Beware Women*). There are similarites too of dramatic technique. In particular, each play has a set-piece scene in which a woman, standing at a window, is led towards sexual involvement with the man at the centre of a state procession over the main stage below; each makes ironic use of a Cupid or Cupids in its masque scene; and each of these scenes is unusually elaborate in its staging. The Duchess in *More Dissemblers* attempts but fails to use her ducal authority to obtain sexual gratification; the Duke in *Women, Beware Women* by threatening violence succeeds in such a project. And there seem to be glances at the title of *More Dissemblers* in *Women, Beware Women* at 4.2.157–8 and 184–5.

More Dissemblers itself glances back to John Webster's tragedy *The Duchess of Malfi*, which similarly concerns the dilemma of a widowed Italian duchess who has to choose between chastity and the urgings of the heart. Middleton may also have encountered Hans Holbein's striking portrait of Christina, Duchess of Milan, a young widow whom Henry VIII briefly contemplated as a bride. The portrait was commissioned to give Henry an idea of Christina's appearance; the potentially lecherous gaze of Henry and Merry England is answered with calm reserve and self-assurance. The play's Duchess of Milan is likewise a young widow who considers coming out of mourning to remarry but finally remains in widowhood. The portrait constitutes a possible visual 'source' for some of the play's materials. It is especially tantalizing in the absence of any known full narrative or dramatic source, though the theme of the widow who cannot uphold her vows against remarriage goes back at least as far as Petronius.

In early modern England, a widow inheriting her husband's estate might find herself in a position of unusual power and autonomy, and yet discover that she was hemmed in by the advice or imperatives of the men best placed to substitute for her dead husband's authority. When the widow inherits nothing less than a duchy, the stability of the state itself is at issue. Middleton's Duchess is a figure of compromised political power and endangered moral authority. A Protestant audience might have mistrusted the principle that a widow should maintain vows of chastity for being too close to the Catholic ideals of celibate priesthood and conventual chastity. To Calvin, vows of continence were wrong, and to the English Protestant reformer William Tyndale they might even be blasphemous. The Duchess's resolution is at first upheld by a Cardinal whose addiction to ritual and inclination to sanctify the Duchess might seem analogous to Catholic traits. And his principles collapse on their first and only test. On the other hand both Moll in *Roaring Girl* and the White Queen's Pawn in *Game at Chess* demand approbation when they finally affirm their celibacy, and the Pawn's preserved chastity is a victory for the Protestant cause. Lisa Geller (1991) notes of the Duchess that 'Her self-imposed vow—subject to the approval of neither father nor husband—has a stature and a validity that her earlier vow could not command.'

The Cardinal's scheme to fortify the Duchess's heroic chastity by exposing her to the temptations of man is riddled with folly and self-interest. The Duchess is brought into contact with subjects who are volatile and divided, and she becomes the social high-point in a circle of sexual pursuit. Most of the links in this circle are set in place during the early scenes. The play begins with Lactantio hearing an off-stage song from the Duchess's lodgings in praise of her celibate widowhood. This opening might be thought of as a window-scene without a visible female window-character: the song marks out her absence both as an object of display and as a participant in the social world. It is soon confirmed that the Duchess and Lactantio stand for the play's opposed principles of chastity and lust. In 1.2, the character disguised as an unnamed Page reveals herself as Lactantio's pregnant former mistress, who, like Aurelia, seeks to claim him as her husband. Then Aurelia's father, after exploding *her* brief disguise as a man, hands her over to his choice of a prospective husband. The latter, the Governor of the Fort, acts in his official role by imprisoning her. Such is the world of convoluted and unedifying sexual relationships that the Duchess enters when, accepting the Cardinal's challenge, she abandons her cloistered isolation so as to wage a 'harder fight' in the sight of men.

The military imagery is appropriate, for her first public act is to grace with her presence the triumphal return of General Andrugio from the wars—and her private response is to fall in love with him. The now tangled plot is given a formal and emblematic summary as the action, with gratuitously assured indifference to plausibility, becomes masque-like. Necessarily, and as elsewhere in Middleton, the socially cohesive Platonic harmonies of the masque are inverted. The spectacle is split into a series of separate sub-actions played out on the main stage (the procession), the upper acting space (the Duchess's window, where she now appears in public view), and in flight (a descent from the 'heavens' of a 'Cupid', who was probably played by the singing boy-actor who also appeared as the 'Page'). Even the events on the main stage are radically divided between the General's public welcome and his private dismay at returning to find his beloved Aurelia lost to him. In the mean time, the Duchess's feelings, like Andrugio's, are running counter to her official role in the welcome. The fragmented staging provides a visual metaphor for these emotional disparities as the figure of Cupid, suspended from above as in flight, mischievously appropriates the formal procession to his own ends. Love is victor over both War and Chastity, and the state occasion becomes a masque of Cupid.

In another emblematic piece of theatre in 2.1 the Duchess attempts to recuperate the vows made to her dying husband, re-enacting them with the Cardinal playing her husband. But their force has been lost; at the crucial moment she interposes: 'I can go no further'. If this seems to be a break from a pious artificial self that is no longer tenable, it paradoxically marks her entry into another state of dissembling. She guesses that self-interest will prevail over the Cardinal's moral dismay, and so she pretends love for his nephew Lactantio. Her guess is right; in 2.2, the Cardinal admits, 'I love his good as dearly as her vow', with disconcertingly rapid slippage on the words *love*, *good*, and *dearly*. When the Duchess sees Lactantio in private (3.2) the mutual seduction he anticipates rapidly turns to convoluted intrigue, as the Duchess persuades Lactantio to write a bawdy and self-defaming letter of seduction supposedly from Andrugio to her. In this passage the pen becomes explicitly phallic. More precisely, the penis is rewritten as the pen, seen as an instrument of duplicitous trickery and sexual wordplay. Sexual punning, like duplicity, is endemic to the play, and seeks to underwrite every utterance with the language of the body. In practice, however, consummation is repeatedly deferred, and the sexual humour remains based on sexual frustration. In a play where the intrigue will lead nowhere, the forged bawdy epistle is a summary emblem of the language-splitting intrinsic to punning and dissembling. Obscenity and disguise are driven by sexual impulse; but in the event the object of desire, like the pun's object of signification, proves elusive.

Andrugio is arrested by Lactantio so that Lactantio can deliver him into the Duchess's hands, but Andrugio maintains his loyalty to Aurelia. This prompts the Duchess to realize her error and renew her vows of chastity. The complexities of the plot entail slight movements, and are easily if arbitrarily resolved. But the play's strength lies elsewhere, in the witty continuities it threads between morality, authority, and language. These ideas are given dramatic articulation in two highly theatrical episodes towards the end of the play.

Aurelia's literal imprisonment by her father's choice of husband, the Governor of the Fort, offers an extreme and scathingly humorous image of patriarchal authority, but the outcome is a turn towards carnival. When she escapes, Aurelia seeks out a roving Gypsy band that seems to promise anarchic liberty. Lactantio's servant Dondolo takes the same course, to evade the humiliations of service. There is a glance here at the alleged 'conversion' of English rogues to Gypsyism, as described, for example in William Harrison's *Description of Britain* (1577), and as targeted in an Act of Parliament of 1596 that made vagabonds of those 'wandering and pretending themselves to be Egyptians' (see Dale B. J. Randall, 1975). But Aurelia and Dondolo seek an alternative commonwealth rather than a guise for villainy.

In Chapter 8 of *English Villainies Discovered by Lantern and Candlelight* (1608) Thomas Dekker describes Gypsies as dissolute vagabonds, whilst admitting into his account an element of the comic grotesque:

> They are a people more scattered than Jews and more hated—beggarly in apparel, barbarous in condition, beastly in behaviour, and bloody if they meet advantage... Their apparel is odd and fantastic, though it be never so full of rents. The men wear scarfs of calico or any other base stuff, hanging their bodies like morris-dancers with bells and other toys... The woman as ridiculously attire themselves and, like one that plays the rogue on a stage, wear rags and patched filthy mantles uppermost when the under-garments are handsome and in fashion... These barns are the beds of incests, whoredoms, adulteries and of all other black and deadly damned impieties... Upon days of pastime and liberty they spread themselves in small companies amongst the villages and, when young maids and bachelors—yea, sometimes old doting fools that should be beaten to this world of villainies and forewarn others—do flock about them, they then profess skill in palmistry and forsooth can tell fortunes. Which for the most part are infallibly true, by reason that they work upon rules which are grounded upon certainty: for one of them will tell you that you shall shortly have some evil luck fall upon you and, within half an hour after, you shall find your pocket picked or your purse cut.

Middleton's version of Gypsydom is more tolerant. Yet he was surely familiar with Dekker's hostile account, for *Lantern and Candlelight* appears to have informed the play's Gypsy language. The cant, or rather the sprinkling of cant upon sheer nonsense, stands at a further stage than the pun in the disintegration of lawful and determinate language, and so contributes to Middleton's almost celebratory treatment of the Gypsies. *More Dissemblers* anticipates *The Gyspies Metamorphosed* in playing down the criminality attributed to Gypsies to the extent that thefts, drunkenness, and libertinism are presented as reprehensible but gamesome fun. The spirit is not far removed from that found in the broadside ballad 'The Brave English Gypsy' (printed and published before 1626), in which 'English Gypsies all live free, | And love and live most jovially', boasting that 'Wheresoe'er we come, we find, | For one that hates, an hundred kind'.

Any prospect of utopian linguistic and moral anarchy is, however, short-lived. Though they offer an existence outside the law, the Gypsies reproduce, in caricature, the ritual, discipline, and authority of church and state. A comic ceremony of anointing Dondolo's face with pig-fat and soot parodies the Catholic ritual of marking the forehead with ash on Ash Wednesday (fittingly, as the play identifies Gypsies with Egyptians, and Protestant polemic identified Old-Testament Egyptians with Roman Catholics). Dondolo's and Aurelia's expectations of a libertarian convert's life amongst the Gypsies remain unfulfilled. Dondolo is robbed; Aurelia finds herself the 'doxy' to the inanely un-Gypsyfied Dondolo.

That is one parabola by which the play reaches towards its conclusion. Despite the shift back from the antithetical Gypsy highway to the thetic and enclosed court, there is a logic whereby the Gypsy episode leads coherently to the penultimate scene, in which the secretly pregnant 'Page' is unmasked. Here is another route, sadistic and farcical, by which the wayward individual returns to social reality. The 'Page', whom the audience has yet to see dressed as a woman, finds herself pushed into vocal gymnastics by her music teacher, then forced by her dancing master to practise leaping dance movements. These stresses send her into labour. In Castiglione's *The Courtier* there is a cautionary remark against women indulging in 'manly exercises' such as 'swift and violent tricks' in dancing or singing, or playing music with 'hard and often divisions'. Sexual identity itself is threatened by such activities. In *More Dissemblers* the extremes of the exercises are supposed to train the 'Page' into manhood, but the effeminacy of the teachers suggests rather that singing and dancing are androgynous arts. The attempt to make the 'Page' more manly, or at least more pagely, achieves the opposite. Middleton was probably familiar with a case related by Montaigne in his essay 'Of the Force of Imagination' of an erstwhile woman who, 'upon a time, leaping, and straining himself to overleap another, he wot not how, but where before he was a woman, he suddenly felt the instrument of a man to come out of him', and thereafter remained a man. In contrast with this woman turned man, Middleton's effeminate 'man' produces a baby. As so often in Middleton, the physical body reproves and betrays the person's moral failings. But the return to a safely gendered and moralized reality is only achieved by passing through a dizzying collapse of apparent gender identity. This scene offers a startling example of the darker, almost manic edge to the play's humour.

There can be no true reconciliation between the defining, contrasted, but oddly contiguous obsessions of chastity and lust. Chastity yields no ground; the Duchess finally turns her back on Andrugio and renews her vows. Marriage, where it proceeds, has more to do with punishment than reward, and, most of all, is the instrument of social and moral regulation. Aurelia and then Lactantio are both 'plagued justly' by being denied their first choice of partner. These are uneasy resolutions for a play advertised as a comedy. What logic is at work? On the one hand, a cloistered spiritual and secular élite has been threatened with a loss of its identity and sense of merit. On the other hand, a self-sufficient world of frivolous behaviour finally accepts without reverence or surprise the consequences exacted by law and nature. These are potentially autonomous worlds forced into reluctant but necessary mutual recognition. The Duchess comes to acknowledge her own propensity to lust and her overdependence on the Cardinal's and the Lords' dissembling piety; she comes to know at first hand the consanguinity of duchess, cardinal, and knave. In the last scene she exercises government over her people for the first time, and with a directness that was not before possible. Yet she is addressing only the men that have threatened her state of chastity and the women whose chastity they have taken; she is about to retreat from all this. The state of moral siege will resume, and the end of the play is the end of a communication that had scarcely begun. Some things have been shaken out during the action; others remain hidden in a text that seems intriguingly burdened with its political and apolitical unconscious.

SEE ALSO

Music: *Companion*, 149
Textual introduction and apparatus: *Companion*, 1131
Authorship and date: *Companion*, 378

More Dissemblers Besides Women

[*for the King's Men*]

THE ACTORS' NAMES

DUCHESS of Milan, a widow
CELIA, her waiting-gentlewoman
LORD CARDINAL of Milan
LACTANTIO, his nephew
DONDOLO, Lactantio's man-servant
ANDRUGIO, General of Milan
AURELIA, mistress formerly to Andrugio, now to Lactantio
Aurelia's FATHER
GOVERNOR of the Fort, suitor to Aurelia
Lactantio's former mistress disguised as a PAGE

LORDS of Milan
A CUPID
CAPTAIN of the Gypsies
Other GYPSIES
CROTCHET, a singing master
CINQUEPACE, a dancing master
USHER to Cinquepace

SERVANTS
Officers of the Guard

More Dissemblers besides Women.

1.1 *Incipit Actus Primus*

Enter Lactantio

Song, music [within]

To be chaste is woman's glory,
'Tis her fame and honour's story.
Here sits she, in funeral weeds,
Only bright in virtuous deeds.
Come and read her life and praise,
That singing weeps, and sighing plays.

Enter Aurelia and servant

LACTANTIO [*to Aurelia*]
Welcome, soul's music! I have been listening here
To melancholy strains from the Duchess' lodgings—
That strange great widow that has vowed so stiffly
Never to know love's heat in a second husband;
And she has kept the fort most valiantly,
To th' wonder of her sex, this seven years' day,
And that's no sorry trial. A month's constancy
Is held a virtue in a city widow;
And are they excelled by so much more i'th' court?
My faith, a rare example for our wives!
Heaven's blessing of her heart for't, poor soul!
She'd need have somewhat to comfort her.
What wouldst thou do, faith now,
If I were dead, suppose I were thy husband?—
As shortly I will be, and that's as good.
Speak freely an thou lov'st me.

AURELIA
Alas, sir,
I should not have the leisure to make vows,
For, dying presently, I should be dead
Before you were laid out.

LACTANTIO
Now fie upon thee for a hasty dier,
Wouldst thou not see me buried?

AURELIA
Talk not on't, sir,
These many years, unless you take delight
To see me swoon or make a ghost of me.

LACTANTIO
Alas, poor soul! I'll kiss thee into colour.
Canst thou paint pale so quickly? I perceive then
Thou'dst go beyond the Duchess in her vow:
Thou'dst die indeed. What's he?

AURELIA
Be settled, sir.
Spend neither doubt nor fear upon that fellow.
Health cannot be more trusty to man's life
Than he to my necessities in love.

LACTANTIO
I take him of thy word, and praise his face.
Though he look scurvily, I will think hereafter
That honesty may walk with fire in's nose
As well as brave desert in broken clothes.
But for thy further safety I've provided
A shape that at first sight will start thy modesty
And make thee blush perhaps; but 'twill away
After a qualm or two. Virginity
Has been put often to those shifts before thee
Upon extremities. A little boldness
Cannot be called immodesty, especially
When there's no means without it for our safeties.
Thou knowest my uncle the Lord Cardinal
Wears so severe an eye, so strict and holy,
It not endures the sight of womankind
About his lodgings.
Hardly a matron of fourscore's admitted.
Though she be worn to gums, she comes not there
To mumble matins. All his admiration
Is placed upon the Duchess. He likes her
Because she keeps her vow and likes not any.
So does he love that man, above his book,
That loves no woman. For my fortune's sake then—
For I am like to be his only heir—
I must dissemble, and appear as fair
To his opinion as the brow of piety,
As void of all impureness as an altar.
Thine ear.

[*He whispers*]

That, and we are safe.

AURELIA
You make me blush, sir.

LACTANTIO
'Tis but a star shot from a beauteous cheek.

1.1.0.2 ***Lactantio*** The name perhaps glances ironically at the Christian apologist Lactantius.

2 **honour's** fame for chastity's
story historical narrative (especially of a virtuous or celebrated person)

3 **weeds** clothes

7 **soul's music** Lactantio's soul is touched by Aurelia rather than the song celebrating chastity.

9 **great** (in both rank and virtue)

11 **kept the fort** i.e. defended her chastity

12 **this seven years' day** seven years as of today

13 **sorry** petty

13–16 **A... wives** Citizens' morality was often considered superior to that of the licentious court.

16 **our wives** Lactantio may be mocking citizen speech ('the wives of us citizens'). Alternatively, 'Milan's citizen-wives'.

17 **Heaven's... for't** Proverbial.

18 **She'd... her** Refers to the music.

24 **presently** instantly

26 **hasty dier** Probably quibbles on *death* as a euphemism for orgasm.

28 **These many** i.e. for many

29 **make... me** (*a*) make me ghostly pale (*b*) make me die

31 **paint pale** turn pale. *Paint* is literally 'colour the face with cosmetics'.

33 **die** (punning on *dye*)
indeed in reality. The Duchess is figuratively 'dead' to men.
settled calm

34 **that fellow** (the servant)

37 **of** on

38 **scurvily** (*a*) rudely (*b*) infected with scurvy, scabby (anticipating 'fire in's nose') (*c*) *scurvy*, contemptible

39 **fire** inflammation

40 **brave... clothes** Suggests the figure of the poverty-stricken discharged soldier, such as Andrugio pretends to be in 2.3.
brave valorous (but playing on the sense 'showily dressed')
broken Might also apply to 'brave desert' himself, and to inflamed skin.

42 **shape** Both 'disguise' and 'theatrical role'.
start startle

44 **Virginity** i.e. the appearance of it

45 **shifts** (*a*) stratagems (*b*) changes of clothing

54 **worn to gums** with the innuendo 'sexually worn out'

62 **brow of** expression worn by

65 **star** shooting star

It blazes beauty's bounty, and hurts nothing.
AURELIA The power of love commands me.
LACTANTIO
I shall wither in comforts till I see thee.
Exeunt [Lactantio at one door,
Aurelia and servant at another]

1.2 *Enter two or three Lords, and [they discover] the*
Lord Cardinal in his closet, [seated with his books]

LORD CARDINAL
My lords, I have work for you. When you have hours
Free from the cares of state, bestow your eyes
Upon those abstracts of the Duchess' virtues,
My study's ornaments. I make her constancy
The holy mistress of my contemplation.
Whole volumes have I writ in zealous praise
Of her eternal vow. I have no power
To suffer virtue to go thinly clad,
I that have ever been in youth an old man
To pleasures and to women,
And could never love but pity 'em
And all their momentary frantic follies.
[*Rising*] Here I stand up in admiratïon,
And bow to the chaste health of our great Duchess,
Kissing her constant name. O my fair lords,
When we find grace confirmed, especially
In a creature that's so doubtful as a woman,
We're spirit-ravished; men of our probation
Feel the spheres' music playing in their souls.
So long, unto the eternizing of her sex,
She's kept her vow, so strictly, and as chaste
As everlasting life is kept for virtue
E'en from the sight of men; to make her oath
As uncorrupt as th'honour of a virgin,
That must be strict in thought, or else that title,
Like one of frailty's ruins, shrinks to dust;
No longer she's a virgin than she's just.
FIRST LORD
Chaste, sir? The truth and justice of her vow
To her deceased lord's able to make poor
Man's treasury of praises. But, methinks,
She that has no temptation set before her,
Her virtue has no conquest. Then would her con-
stancy
Shine in the brightest goodness of her glory
If she would give admittance, see and be seen,
And yet resist and conquer. There were argument
For angels; 'twould outreach the life of praise
Set in mortality's shortness. [*Aside*] I speak this
Not for religion, but for love of her
Whom I wish less religious and more loving;
But I fear she's too constant, that's her fault.
But 'tis so rare few of her sex are took with't,
And that makes some amends.
LORD CARDINAL
You have put my zeal into a way, my lord,
I shall not be at peace till I make perfect.
I'll make her victory harder. 'Tis my crown
When I bring grace to great'st perfectïon;
And I dare trust that daughter with a world,
None but her vow and she. I know she wears
A constancy will not deceive my praises,
A faith so noble. She that once knows heaven
Need put in no security for her truth.
I dare believe her face, use all the art,
Temptation, witcheries, sleights, and subtleties
You temporal lords and all your means can practise.
SECOND LORD
My lord, not any, we.
LORD CARDINAL Her resolute goodness
Shall as a rock stand firm, and send the sins
That beat against it
Into the bosom of the owners, weeping.
THIRD LORD
We wish her virtues so.
LORD CARDINAL O, give me pardon,
I have lost myself in her upon my friends.
Your charitable censures I beseech.
So dear her white fame is to my soul's love,
'Tis an affliction but to hear it questioned.

66 **blazes** (*a*) causes to blaze (*b*) blazons, proclaims
nothing not at all
1.2.0.1 ***discover*** reveal by drawing back curtains
3 **abstracts** summary accounts, distillations
4 **study's ornaments** i.e. the books, both as accessories to contemplation (as in church ornaments) and as gracious embellishments of the '*closet*' where he studies
5 **mistress** guiding influence, personified as a woman; female object of devotion
8 **thinly clad** (figurative for 'poor, *unrewarded*'; here 'bare of praise')
14 **chaste health** health of the chastity
17 **doubtful** giving cause for apprehensions
18 **spirit-ravished** transported in spirit
probation religious discipline
19 **the spheres' music** i.e. the imagined divine music of harmony between the celestial 'spheres' or orbs
21–3 **as...men** The analogy is with the remoteness of everlasting life from mortal experience, with play on *men* as humans and as males.
23 **E'en from** (*a*) away from even (with the emphasis on *sight*), or (*b*) completely away from
24 **th'honour** the virginity, maidenhead
27 **just** righteous
31–2 **She...conquest** Montaigne commented that 'Of Stoic and Epicurean philosophers, I say, there are divers who have judged that it was not sufficient to have the mind well placed, well ordered, and well disposed to virtue...it was very requisite to seek for occasions whereby a man might come to the trial of it', citing Seneca: 'Virtue provoked adds much to itself' ('Of Cruelty'). Compare also the proverb 'She's chaste whom none will have'.
34 **see and be seen** Proverbial.
35 **argument** subject of discourse
43 **a way** such a way
44 **make perfect** fully accomplish
47 **daughter** i.e. daughter of *grace* (a biblical usage)
50 **so** as
51 **put...security** (*a*) deposit no forfeitable pledge (*b*) require no physical protection
52 **face** outward appearance
56 **as...firm** Proverbial.
58 **weeping** Qualifies *owners*.
60 **lost...upon** i.e. become absorbed with her at the expense of

She's my religious triumph.
If you desire a belief rightly to her,
Think she can never waver, then you're sure.
She has a fixèd heart, it cannot err.
He kills my hopes of woman that doubts her.

FIRST LORD
No more, my lord, 'tis fixed.

LORD CARDINAL
Believe my judgement.
I never praise in vain, nor ever spent
Opinion idly, or lost hopes of any
Where I once placed it. Welcome as my joys
Now you all part believers of her virtue.

ALL LORDS
We are the same most firmly.

LORD CARDINAL
Good opinion
In others rèward you, and all your actions.
[Exeunt Lords]
Who's near us?
Enter a Servant

SERVANT
My lord.

LORD CARDINAL
Call our nephew. *[Exit Servant]*
There's a work too
That for blood's sake I labour to make perfect,
And it comes on with joy. He's but a youth,
To speak of years, yet I dare venture him
To old men's goodnesses and gravities
For his strict manners, and win glory by him;
And for the chasteness of his continence,
Which is a rare grace in the spring of man,
He does excel the youth of all our time;
Which gift of his, more than affinity,
Draws my affection in great plenty to him.
The company of a woman is as fearful to him
As death to guilty men. I've seen him blush
When but a maid was named. I'm proud of him,
Heaven be not angry for't. He's near of kin
In disposition to me. I shall do much for him
In lifetime, but in death I shall do all.
There he will find my love. He's yet too young
In years to rise in state, but his good parts
Will bring him in the sooner.
Enter Lactantio with a book
Here he comes.—
What, at thy meditation? Half in heaven?

LACTANTIO
The better half, my lord. My mind's there still;
And when the heart's above, the body walks here
But like an idle serving-man below,
Gaping and waiting for his master's coming.

LORD CARDINAL
What man in age could bring forth graver thoughts?

LACTANTIO
He that lives fourscore years is but like one
That stays here for a friend. When death comes, then
Away he goes, and is ne'er seen again.
I wonder at the young men of our days,
That they can dote on pleasure, or what 'tis
They give that title to, unless in mockage.
There's nothing I can find upon the earth
Worthy the name of pleasure, unless't be
To laugh at folly, which indeed good charity
Should rather pity. But of all the frenzies
That follow flesh and blood, O reverend uncle,
The most ridiculous is to fawn on women.
There's no excuse for that. 'Tis such a madness
There is no cure set down for't. No physician
Ever spent hour about it, for they guessed
'Twas all in vain when they first loved themselves,
And never since durst practise. Cry '*Hei mihi*',
That's all the help they have for't. I had rather meet
A witch far north than a fine fool in love;
The sight would less afflict me. But for modesty,
And your grave presence that learns men respect,
I should fall foul in words upon fond man
That can forget his excellence and honour—
His serious meditations being the end
Of his creation, to learn well to die—
And live a prisoner to a woman's eye.
Can there be greater thraldom, greater folly?

LORD CARDINAL *[aside]*
In making him my heir, I make good works,
And they give wealth a blessing; where, on the contrary,
What curses does he heap upon his soul
That leaves his riches to a riotous young man,
To be consumed on surfeits, pride, and harlots!
Peace be upon that spirit whose life provides
A quiet rest for mine.

67 **fixèd** firmly resolved, attached to its object (in contrast to *err*, literally 'wander')
72 **Welcome** Also 'well come'.
76 **near** in attendance on
77 **for blood's sake** i.e. because he is a blood-relative
79 **To speak of years** by the measure of his age
80 **To** against
81 **manners** moral conduct
82 **continence** Puns on *countenance*.
83 **spring** i.e. youth
85 **affinity** kinship
89 **but a maid was** a maid was but
91 **disposition** temperament
92 **do all** i.e. bequeath everything
95 **bring him in** establish him
97 **still** constantly
99 **idle** unoccupied
100 **Gaping** (*a*) open-mouthed, yawning (*b*) eagerly longing
107 **mockage** mockery
116 **spent** wasted
guessed rightly conjectured
118 **Hei mihi** In Ovid's *Metamorphoses* I. 523, Phoebus' cry of despair at his powerlessness against love. He laments: 'Of physic and of surgery I found the arts for need, | The power of every herb and plant doth of my gift proceed; | Now *woe is me* [in Latin, *hei mihi*], that ne'er a herb can heal the hurt of love, | And that the arts that others help their lord doth helpless prove' (trans. Arthur Golding, 1567).
120 **A witch far north** Alludes probably to the Lancashire witches executed at Lancaster Castle in August 1612.
122 **learns** teaches
123 **fond** (*a*) foolish (*b*) doting
132 **riotous** dissolute

Enter Page, with a letter

LACTANTIO How now, the news?

PAGE
A letter, sir, brought by a gentleman
That lately came from Rome.

LACTANTIO [*aside*] That's she, she's come.
I fear not to admit her in his presence;
There is the like already. I'm writ chaste
In my grave uncle's thoughts, and honest meanings
Think all men's like their own. [*Aside to the Page*]
Thou look'st so pale.
What ail'st thou here o'late?

PAGE I doubt I have cause, sir.

LACTANTIO
Why, what's the news?

PAGE I fear, sir, I'm with child.

LACTANTIO
With child? Peace, peace, speak low!

PAGE 'Twill prove, I fear, so.

LACTANTIO
Beshrew my heart for that! [*Aloud to the Page*] Desire
the gentleman
To walk a turn or two.

LORD CARDINAL What gentleman?

LACTANTIO
One lately come from Rome, my lord, in credit
With Lord Vincentio; so the letter speaks him.

LORD CARDINAL
Admit him, my kind boy. [*Exit Page*]
The prettiest servant
That ever man was blest with! 'Tis so meek,
So good and gentle, 'twas the best alms-deed
That e'er you did to keep him. I have oft took him
Weeping alone, poor boy, at the remembrance
Of his lost friends, which, as he says, the sea
Swallowed with all their substance.

LACTANTIO 'Tis a truth, sir,
Has cost the poor boy many a feeling tear,
And me some too, for company. In such pity
I always spend my part.

Enter Aurelia, like a gentleman

Here comes the gentleman.

LORD CARDINAL
Welcome to Milan, sir. How is the health
Of Lord Vincentio?

AURELIA May it please your grace,
I left it well and happy, and I hope
The same blest fortune keeps it.

LORD CARDINAL I hear you're near him.

AURELIA One of his chamber, my lord.

LACTANTIO [*aside*]
I'd ne'er wish one of her condition nearer
Than to be one of mine.

LORD CARDINAL Your news is pleasing.
Whilst you remain in Milan, I request you
To know the welcome of no house but ours.

AURELIA
Thanks to your Grace.

LORD CARDINAL I'll leave you to confer.
I'll to the Duchess, and labour her perfection. *Exit*

LACTANTIO
Then thus begins our conference: I arrest thee
In Cupid's name. Deliver up your weapon.
It is not for your wearing, Venus knows it.
Here's a fit thing indeed, nay, hangers and all!
Away with 'em, out upon 'em, things of trouble,
And out of use with you. Now you're my prisoner,
And till you swear you love me, all and only,
You part not from mine arms.

AURELIA I swear it willingly.

LACTANTIO
And that you do renounce the General's love
That heretofore laid claim to you.

AURELIA My heart bids me,
You need not teach me that. My eye ne'er knew
A perfect choice till it stood blest with you.
There's yet a rival whom you little dream of.
Tax me with him, and I'll swear too I hate him.
I'll thrust 'em both together in one oath,
And send 'em to some pair of waiting-women
To solder up their credits.

LACTANTIO Prithee, what's he?
Another yet? For laughter' sake, discover him.

AURELIA
The Governor of the Fort.

LACTANTIO That old dried neat's-tongue?

AURELIA
A gentleman after my father's relish.

Enter [Aurelia's] Father and Governor [of the Fort]

FATHER
By your kind favours, gentlemen.

139 **the like** i.e. the Page (another woman disguised as a man)
142 **doubt** suspect
145 **Beshrew** curse
148 **speaks** testifies
152 **took** found
154 **friends** relatives, family
155 **substance** possessions, wealth
158 **spend my part** With a quibble suggesting 'employ my penis', or 'discharge my semen'.
163 **near him** i.e. a trusted member of his household
164 **One of his chamber** an attendant of his private rooms. Lactantio turns the phrase to mean 'one of his bed-partners'.
165 **her condition** Insinuates Aurelia is a whore.
nearer more closely related
172 **weapon** i.e. sword (as worn by men, with a phallic innuendo)
174 **thing** Quibbles on the euphemism for 'penis'.
hangers straps from which the sword hangs (and so, quibblingly, 'testicles')
176 **out of use** useless (with a sexual pun on *use* as 'copulation')
184 **Tax** censure, accuse
187 **solder up** repair, as with solder (with a suggestion of sexual union)
credits reputations
189 **dried neat's-tongue** Suggests a shrivelled shape; *neat* is 'ox'.
190 **after** in accordance with
relish taste. Picks up on *neat's tongue* as a kind of food.

AURELIA [*aside to Lactantio*] O, my father!
We are both betrayed.
LACTANTIO Peace, you may prove too fearful.—
To whom your business, sir?
FATHER To the Lord Cardinal,
If it would please yourself or that young gentleman
To grace me with admittance.
LACTANTIO I will see, sir.
The gentleman's a stranger, new come o'er.
He understands you not.
[*To Aurelia*] *Lofftro veen, tant umbro, hoff tufftee, locumber shaw.*
AURELIA *Quisquimken, sapadlaman*, fool-urchin, old *astrata.*
FATHER Nay, an that be the language we can speak't too:
strumpetikin, bold *harlotum, queaninisma, whoremongeria.*
Shame to thy sex, and sorrow to thy father.
Is this a shape for reputatïon
And modesty to mask in? Thou too cunning
For credulous goodness!
Did not a reverent respect and honour
That's due unto the sanctimonious peace
Of this lord's house restrain my voice and anger
And teach it soft humility, I would lift
Both your disgraces to the height of grief
That you have raised in me; but, to shame you,
I will not cast a blemish upon virtue.
Call that your happiness, and the dearest, too,
That such a bold attempt could ever boast of.
We'll see if a strong fort can hold you now.—
Take her, sir, to you.
GOVERNOR [*to Aurelia*] How have I deserved
The strangeness of this hour?
FATHER Talk not so tamely.
[*To Lactantio*] For you, sir, thank the reverence of this place,
Or your hypocrisy I had put out of grace,
I had, i'faith. If ever I can fit you,
Expect to hear from me.
Exeunt [*Father, Governor, and Aurelia*]
LACTANTIO I thank you, sir;
The cough o'th' lungs requite you. I could curse him
Into diseases by whole dozens now;
But one's enough to beggar him, if he light
Upon a wise physician. 'Tis a labour
To keep those little wits I have about me.
Still did I dream that villain would betray her;
I'll never trust slave with a parboiled nose again.
I must devise some trick to excuse her absence
Now to my uncle too. There is no mischief
But brings one villainy or other still
E'en close at heels on't. I'm pained at heart.
If ever there were hope of me to die
For love, 'tis now; I never felt such gripings.
If I can scape this climacterical year,
Women, ne'er trust me, though you hear me swear.
Kept with him in the fort! Why, there's no hope
Of ever meeting now; my way's not thither.
Love bless us with some means to get together,
And I'll pay all the old reck'nings. *Exit*

Enter Duchess, above, and Celia 1.3

DUCHESS
What a contented rest rewards my mind
For faithfulness! I give it constancy,
And it returns me peace. How happily
Might woman live, methinks, confined within
The knowledge of one husband!
What comes of more rather proclaims desire
Prince of affections than religious love,
Brings frailty and our weakness into question
'Mongst our male enemies, makes widows' tears
Rather the cup of laughter than of pity.
What credit can our sorrows have with men,
When in some month's space they turn light again,
Feast, dance, and go in colours? If my vow
Were yet to make, I would not sleep without it,
Or make a faith as perfect to myself
In resolution as a vow would come to,
And do as much right so to constancy
As strictness could require; for 'tis our goodness
And not our strength that does it. I am armed now
'Gainst all deserts in man, be't valour, wisdom,
Courtesy, comeliness, nay, truth itself,
Which seldom keeps him company. I commend

196 **new come o'er** Quibbles on the sense 'recently mounted sexually'.
200 **fool-urchin** *Urchin* was variously 'hedgehog', 'goblin', or 'hunchback'.
202 ***queaninisma*** Based on *quean*, 'prostitute'.
205 **mask in** disguise themselves in (perhaps suggesting a masquerade or court entertainment)
208 **sanctimonious** sacred, holy (without any suggestion of pretence)
220 **grace** (*a*) i.e. its seeming grace (*b*) favour
221 **fit** fittingly punish
228 **that villain** (presumably the scurvy-looking Servant of 1.1)
229 **parboiled** over-boiled, overheated (i.e. inflamed). The *nose* has a phallic connotation.
231–3 **There...on't** From the proverbs 'One misfortune comes on the neck of another' and 'Every sin brings in another'.
232 **other still** yet another, yet others
235 **gripings** (*a*) gripping pains (*b*) afflictions
236 **climacterical** critical to health or fortune
1.3.6 **What comes of more** i.e. (*a*) what knowledge comes of more husbands, or (*b*) what comes of more knowledge
8 **question** discussion, scrutiny
10 **cup** As of wine drunk to mark a shared sentiment; also as in the biblical image of the overflowing cup of sorrow, etc.
12 **month's** The usual period of mourning was a year.
turn light (*a*) start wearing light-coloured clothing (*b*) become light-hearted, lascivious
13 **colours** coloured garments (as distinct from mourning black)
14 **make** be made
without it i.e. until it had been made
15 **faith** pledge
19 **not our strength** Based on the proverbs 'flesh is frail' and 'all women may be won'.
20 **deserts** good qualities, merits
21 **truth** righteousness, faithfulness

The virtues highly, as I do an instrument
When the case hangs by th' wall; but man himself
Never comes near my heart.

Enter Lord Cardinal, [above]

LORD CARDINAL
The blessing of perfection to your thoughts, lady,
For I'm resolved they are good ones.

DUCHESS Honour of greatness,
Friend to my vow, and father to my fame,
Welcome, as peace to temples.

LORD CARDINAL I bring war.

DUCHESS
How, sir?

LORD CARDINAL
A harder fight. If now you conquer,
You crown my praises double.

DUCHESS What's your aim, sir?

LORD CARDINAL
To astonish sin and all her tempting evils,
And make your goodness shine more glorious.
When your fair noble vow showed you the way
To excellence in virtue, to keep back
The fears that might discourage you at first,
Pitying your strength, it showed you not the worst.
'Tis not enough for tapers to burn bright;
But to be seen, so to lend others light,
Yet not impair themselves, their flame as pure
As when it shined in secret. So t'abide
Temptations is the soul's flame truly tried.
I have an ambition, but a virtuous one:
I would have nothing want to your perfection.

DUCHESS
Is there a doubt found yet? Is it so hard
For woman to recover, with all diligence
And a true fasting faith from sensual pleasure,
What many of her sex has so long lost?
Can you believe that any sight of man,
Held he the worth of millions in one spirit,
Had power to alter me?

LORD CARDINAL No; there's my hope,
My credit, and my triumph.

DUCHESS I'll no more
Keep strictly private, since the glory on't
Is but a virtue questioned. I'll come forth
And show myself to all. The world shall witness
That, like the sun, my constancy can look
On earth's corruptions, and shine clear itself.

LORD CARDINAL
Hold conquest now, and I have all my wishes.

Cornetts and a shout within

DUCHESS
The meaning of that sudden shout, my lord?

LORD CARDINAL
Signor Andrugio, general of the field,
Successful in his fortunes, is arrived,
And met by all the gallant hopes of Milan,
Welcomed with laurel wreaths and hymns of praises.
Vouchsafe but you to give him the first grace, madam,
Of your so long hid presence, he has then
All honours that can bless victorious man.

DUCHESS
You shall prevail, grave sir. *[Exit Lord Cardinal]*

Enter Andrugio, attended with the nobility and state, [wreathed with bays] like a victor. [Amongst the nobility is Lactantio, in black and yellow.] [The Duchess and Celia stand in view above].

Song, music

ALL THE NOBILITY
Laurel is a victor's due,
I give it you,
I give it you.
Thy name with praise,
Thy brow with bays,
We circle round.
All men rejoice
With cheerful voice,
To see thee like a conqueror crowned.

A [winged] Cupid, [with a bow,] descending, sings this

CUPID
I am a little conqueror, too.
For wreaths of bays
There's arms of cross,
And that's my due.
I give the flaming heart,
It is my crest,
And by the mother's side
The weeping eye,
The sighing breast.
It is not power in you, fair beauties.
If I command love, 'tis your duties.

He ascends.

23–4 **an ... wall** i.e. a musical instrument when it is in its case, hanging unused on the wall. With a glance at the bawdy senses of *instrument* and *case* as the female sex organs.
25 **comes ... heart** In the continued metaphor of a musical instrument, suggests (*a*) the moving qualities of music and (*b*) the playing of an instrument such as a lute, which is held close to the chest.
27 **Honour of greatness** i.e. one who does honour to his power and eminence
32 **astonish** stun, dismay
38–9 **'Tis ... light** From Christ's parable (Matthew 5:15, Mark 4:21, Luke 8:16 and 11:33).
40 **Yet ... themselves** In contrast with the candle that proverbially 'lights others and consumes itself'.
44 **want to** lack in
52 **credit** belief
56–7 **like ... itself** From the proverb, 'The sun is never the worse for shining on a dunghill'.
58 **Hold conquest** let conquest remain secure
58.1 ***Cornetts*** wind instruments capable of great brilliance
62 **hopes** men in whom hope is placed
64 **Vouchsafe but you** if only you deign
67.2 ***state*** persons of rank
76.1–2 ***A ... this*** The Cupid would have been suspended aloft from the stage-roof (the 'heavens'). See Introduction.
79 **arms of cross** crossed or folded arms (a posture indicating sadness)
82 **crest** heraldic device above shield and helmet in a coat of arms
83 **by ... side** inherited from the mother

During these songs, Andrugio peruses a letter delivered him by a Lord, and then [the welcome] closes with this song below

ALL THE NOBILITY

Welcome, welcome, son of fame!
Honour triumphs in thy name.

Exeunt in state [Andrugio and all the nobility except the Lord who delivered the letter]

LORD

Alas, poor gentleman! I brought him news
That like a cloud spread over all his glories.
When he missed her whom his eye greedily sought for,
His welcome seemed so poor he took no joy in't;
But when he found her by her father forced
To the old Governor's love, and kept so strictly,
A coldness struck his heart. There is no state
So firmly happy but feels envy's might.
I know Lactantio, nephew to the Cardinal,
Hates him as deeply as a rich man death;
And yet his welcome showed as fair and friendly
As his that wore the truest love to him;
When in his wishes he could drink his blood,
And make his heart the sweetness of his food. *Exit*

CELIA Madam, madam!

DUCHESS

Beshrew thy heart, dost thou not see me busy?
You show your manners.

CELIA In the name of goodness,
What ails my lady?

DUCHESS I confess I'm mortal.
There's no defending on't. 'Tis cruel flattery
To make a lady believe otherways.
Is not this flesh? Can you drive heat from fire?
So may you love from this. For love and death
Are brothers in this kingdom; only death
Comes by the mother's side, and that's the surest.
That General is wondrous fortunate:
Has won another field since, and a victory
That credits all the rest. He may more boast on't
Than of a thousand conquests. I am lost,
Utterly lost. Where are my women now?
Alas, what help's in them, what strength have they?
I call to a weak guard when I call them.
In rescuing me they'd be themselves o'ercome.
When I that professed war am overthrown,
What hope's in them then that ne'er stirred from home?
My faith is gone for ever;
My reputation with the Cardinal,
My fame, my praise, my liberty, my peace
Changed for a restless passion. O hard spite
To lose my seven years' victory at one sight! *Exeunt*

Enter Dondolo and the Page, with a shirt 1.4

PAGE I prithee, Dondolo, take this shirt, and air it a little against my master rises. I'd rather do anything than do't, i'faith.

DONDOLO O monstrous, horrible, terrible, intolerable! Are not you big enough to air a shirt? Were it a smock now, you lickerish page, you'd be hanged ere you'd part from't. If thou dost not prove as arrant a smell-smock as any the town affords in a term-time, I'll lose my judgement in wenching.

PAGE Pish! Here, Dondolo, prithee take it.

DONDOLO It's no more but up and ride with you then? All my generation were beadles and officers; and do you think I'm so easily entreated? You shall find a harder piece of work, boy, than you imagine, to get anything from my hands. I will not disgenerate so much from the nature of my kindred. You must bribe me one way or other if you look to have anything done, or else you may do't yourself. 'Twas just my father's humour when he bore office. You know my mind, page: the song, the song. I must either have the song you sung to my master last night when he went to bed, or I'll not do a stitch of service for you from one week's end to the other. As I am a gentleman, you shall brush cloaks, make clean spurs, pull off strait boots, although in the tugging you chance to fall and hazard the breaking of your little buttocks. I'll take no more pity of your marrowbones than a butcher's dog of a rump of beef.

95 **kept** confined
102 **he** i.e. Lactantio
110 **flesh** (proverbially frail)
110–13 **Can...surest** The drift is that love can only be separated from the body by consigning it to death.
110 **Can...fire** Proverbially, 'The fire is never without heat'.
111–12 **love...kingdom** From the biblically-derived proverb 'Love is strong as death' (Song of Solomon 8:6).
112 **this kingdom** i.e. the body
112–13 **only...side** Alludes to Eve's primary responsibility for original sin and its consequence, death.
113 **that's the surest** *The mother's side* is proverbially *surest* (as the father may not be known), but also *death* is proverbially sure.
115 **field** battle
since i.e. since his other, military, victories
116 **credits** does credit to
117 **am lost** (*a*) am given over to the enemy (*b*) have lost my way (*c*) am damned
124 **My faith** (*a*) faith others have in me (*b*) my faithfulness (*c*) my religious belief
1.4.0.1 ***Dondolo*** Meaning 'a shallow-pate, a silly gull' (Florio), and perhaps also a wanderer.
2 **against** ready for when
6 **lickerish** lecherous
7 **smell-smock** skirt-chaser
8 **term-time** (when young men studying at the Inns of Court were resident in London)
11 **It's...ride** Proverbial. Implies a casual or dismissive attitude in the Page; with a sexual innuendo.
12 **generation** family
beadles low-ranking parish constables
15 **disgenerate** Dondolo's error for *degenerate*.
20–30 **I must...boots-haling** The lines are riddled with variously specific homosexual innuendos. In particular, *singing* can refer to fellatio.
23 **As...gentleman** Dondolo apparently is not.
24 **strait** narrow, tight-fitting
27 **marrowbones** i.e. large thigh bones (the top of which are under the buttocks)

Nay, ka me, ka thee. If you will ease the melancholy of my mind with singing, I will deliver you from the calamity of boots-haling.

PAGE Alas, you know I cannot sing.

DONDOLO Take heed; you may speak at such an hour that your voice may be clean taken away from you. I have known many a good gentlewoman say so much as you say now, and have presently gone to bed and lay speechless. 'Tis not good to jest, as old Chaucer was wont to say, that broad famous English poet. Cannot you sing, say you? O, that a boy should so keep cut with his mother and be given to dissembling!

PAGE
Faith, to your knowledge in't, ill may seem well;
But as I hope in comforts, I've no skill.

DONDOLO A pox of skill; give me plain simple cunning. Why should not singing be as well got without skill as the getting of children? You shall have the arrant'st fool do as much there as the wisest coxcomb of 'em all, let 'em have all the help of doctors put to 'em, both the directions of physicians and the erections of pothecaries. You shall have a plain hobnailed country fellow marrying some dairy wench tumble out two of a year, and sometimes three, by'r Lady, as the crop falls out; and your nice puling physicking gentlefolks some one in nine years, and hardly then a whole one as it should be; the wanting of some apricock or something loses a member on him, or quite spoils it. Come, will you sing, that I may warm the shirt? By this light, he shall put it on cold for me else.

PAGE A song or two I learnt with hearing gentlewomen practise themselves.

DONDOLO Come, you are so modest, now, 'tis pity that thou wast ever bred to be thrust through a pair of canions; thou wouldst have made a pretty, foolish waiting-woman, but for one thing. Wilt sing?

PAGE As well as I can, Dondolo.

DONDOLO Give me the shirt then; I'll warm't as well I can, too.

[*He takes it*]

Why, look, you whoreson coxcomb, this is a smock.

PAGE
No, 'tis my master's shirt.

DONDOLO
Why, that's true too;
Who knows not that? Why, 'tis the fashion, fool.
All your young gallants here of late wear smocks,
Those without beards especially.

PAGE Why, what's the reason, sir?

DONDOLO Marry, very great reason in't. A young gallant lying abed with his wench, if the constable should chance to come up and search, being both in smocks, they'd be taken for sisters, and I hope a constable dare go no further. And as for the knowing of their heads, that's well enough too; for I know many young gentlemen wear longer hair than their mistresses.

PAGE
'Tis a hot world the whilst.

DONDOLO
Nay, that's most certain,
and a most witty age of a bald one for all languages.
You've many daughters so well brought up they speak
French naturally at fifteen, and they are turned to the
Spanish and Italian half a year after.

PAGE That's like learning the grammar first and the accidence after, they go backward so.

DONDOLO
The fitter for the Italian. Thou'st no wit, boy;
Hadst had a tutor, he'd have taught thee that.
Come, come, that I may be gone, boy.

Song, music

PAGE
Cupid is Venus' only joy,
But he's a wanton boy,
A very, very wanton boy.
He shoots at ladies' naked breasts;

28 **ka me, ka thee** if you scratch my back, I'll scratch yours. *Ka*, a corruption of *claw*, was used only in this proverbial expression.

32–3 **you...you** Alludes to the voice breaking in male adolescence (particularly dangerous for boy actors).

34–5 **much...now** Presumably the Page has put on a hoarse voice.

36 **jest** (*a*) trifle (as Dondolo accuses the Page); (*b*) make jokes

38–9 **keep cut with** take after, assume the same shape as. *Cut* is 'style of clothing', and also, unintendedly, 'cunt' (implying that the boy has a girl's sexual organs).

41 **comforts** i.e. divine grace

44 **arrant'st** most out-and-out

45–6 **the...all** Perhaps glances at the French King Henri IV's description of King James as 'the wisest fool in Christendom'.

45 **coxcomb** fool (literally 'fool's hat')

47 **erections** Probably used only for the phallic quibble.

48 **pothecaries** apothecaries, druggists

49 **tumble out** i.e. cause children to tumble out
of in

50 **by'r Lady** Short for 'by our Lady', an oath by the Virgin Mary.

50–1 **falls out** chances, happens

51 **nice** delicate
puling (*a*) whining (*b*) sickly
physicking medicine-taking

53 **wanting** lack
apricock apricot (quibbling on *cock*, 'penis', and referring to the pregnant women's craving for the fruit)

55 **By this light** an oath by the sun

56 **for me** as far as I'm concerned

61 **canions** legs of breeches (literally ornamental rolls around the ends of them)
foolish probably an endearment

62 **thing** euphemistic for male or female genitals

79 **hot** lustful
the whilst these days

80 **witty** clever, crafty
of for
bald (*a*) plain, crude (in speech) (*b*) hairless (baldness being an effect of both *age* and syphilis, variously referred to as the French, Spanish, or Italian pox)
for in

82–3 **they...after** Implies variety of sexual experience, as well as its consequence in disease.

85 **accidence** first principles of grammar
go backward i.e. learn backwards (quibbling in Dondolo's reply on 'have sexual intercourse from behind', as was associated with Italians)

87 **that** Either the fact or the practice.

88.1 *Song* The first seven and last two lines make the first stanza of the song in *Chaste Maid* 4.1.167. For a musical setting, see *Companion*, p. 149.
music The Page probably plays an instrument such as a lute.

92 **shoots** fires arrows

He is the cause of most men's crests—
I mean upon the forehead,
Invisible, but horrid.
Of the short velvet mask he was deviser,
That wives may kiss, the husbands ne'er the wiser.
'Twas he first thought upon the way
To keep a lady's lips in play.

DONDOLO O, rich, ravishing, rare, and enticing! Well, go thy ways for as sweet a breasted page as ever lay at his master's feet in a truckle-bed.

PAGE You'll hie you in straight, Dondolo?

DONDOLO I'll not miss you. *Exit [Page]*
This smockified shirt, or shirted smock,
I will go toast. Let me see what's o'clock.
I must to th' castle straight to see his love,
Either by hook or crook. My master, storming,
Sent me last night, but I'll be gone this morning.
Exit

Finis Actus Primus

2.1 *Incipit Actus Secundus*
Enter Duchess and Celia

DUCHESS
Seek out the lightest colours can be got,
The youthfull'st dressings; tawny is too sad.
I am not thirty yet, I have wronged my time
To go so long in black, like a petitioner.
See that the powder that I use about me
Be rich in cassia.

CELIA [*leaving*] Here's a sudden change.

DUCHESS [*aside*]
O, I'm undone, in faith!—Stay, art thou certain
Lactantio, nephew to the Cardinal, was present
In the late entertainment of the General?

CELIA
Upon my reputation with your excellence,
These eyes beheld him. He came foremost, madam.
'Twas he in black and yellow.

DUCHESS
Nay, 'tis no matter, either for himself
Or for the affectation of his colours,
So you be sure he was there.

CELIA As sure as sight
Can discern man from man, madam.

DUCHESS It suffices.
Exit [Celia]
O, an ill cause had need of many helps,
Much art, and many friends, ay, and those mighty,
Or else it sets in shame. A faith once lost
Requires great cunning ere't be entertained
Into the breast of a belief again.
There's no condition so unfortunate,
Poor, miserable, to any creature given,
As hers that breaks in vow; she breaks with heaven.
[She weeps.] Enter Lord Cardinal

LORD CARDINAL
Increase of health, and a redoubled courage
To chastity's great soldier! What, so sad, madam?—
The memory of her seven years' deceasèd lord
Springs yet into her eyes, as fresh and full
As at the seventh hour after his departure.
What a perpetual fountain is her virtue!—
Too much to afflict yourself with ancient sorrow
Is not so strictly for your strength required.
Your vow is charge enough, believe me 'tis, madam;
You need no weightier task.

DUCHESS Religious sir,
You heard the last words of my dying lord.

LORD CARDINAL
Which I shall ne'er forget.

DUCHESS May I entreat
Your goodness but to speak 'em over to me
As near as memory can befriend your utterance,
That I may think a while I stand in presence
Of my departing husband?

LORD CARDINAL What's your meaning
In this, most virtuous madam?

DUCHESS 'Tis a courtesy
I stand in need of, sir, at this time specially.
Urge it no further yet. As it proves to me,
You shall hear from me; only I desire it
Effectually from you, sir; that's my request.

LORD CARDINAL
I wonder, yet I'll spare to question farther.
You shall have your desire.

DUCHESS I thank you, sir.
A blessing come along with't.

93 **crests** (*a*) erect penises (the sense denied) (*b*) cuckold's horns (as excrescences on the head and emblematic device)
96 **short velvet mask** (covering the eyes and cheeks but not the mouth; worn by ladies particularly at court entertainments)
99 **lips** Quibbles on 'vulvas'.
100–1 **go thy ways for** off you go, being
101 **breasted** Refers to the lungs as used in singing, but the Page is also breasted as a woman.
102 **truckle-bed** low bed that could be pushed on its castors under a larger one
103 **hie you** hasten
104 **miss** fail
107 **his** i.e. Lactantio's
108 **by . . . crook** Proverbial.
2.1.1 **lightest** (*a*) palest and brightest (*b*) most frivolous and wanton
4 **petitioner** plaintiff
6 **cassia** perfume from the fragrant plant cassia
9 **late** recent
19 **sets** like the sun, whose reddening suggests blushes of *shame*
30 **fountain** spring. Refers both to the Duchess's tears and to her self-renewing *virtue*.
32 **your strength** i.e. a woman of your limited strength
40 **meaning** intention, purpose
45 **Effectually** earnestly, ardently (postdates *OED*'s last citation, 1578)

LORD CARDINAL
'You see, my lords, what all earth's glory is,
Rightly defined in me: uncertain breath,
A dream of threescore years to the long sleeper,
To most not half the time. Beware ambition;
Heaven is not reached with pride, but with submis-
sion.
And you, Lord Cardinal, labour to perfect
Good purposes begun; be what you seem,
Steadfast and uncorrupt, your actions noble,
Your goodness simple, without gain of art,
And not in vesture holier than in heart.—
But 'tis a pain more than the pangs of death
To think that we must part, fellows of life.
Thou richness of my joys, kind and dear princess,
Death had no sting but for our separation;
'Twould come more calmer than an ev'ning's peace
That brings on rest to labours. Thou art so precious
I should depart in everlasting envy
Unto the man that ever should enjoy thee.
O, a new torment strikes his force into me
When I but think on't; I am racked and torn.
Pity me in thy virtues.'

DUCHESS 'My loved lord,
Let your confirmed opinion of my life,
My love, my faithful love, seal an assurance
Of quiet to your spirit, that no forgetfulness
Can cast a sleep so deadly on my senses
To draw my affections to a second liking.'

LORD CARDINAL
''T 'as ever been thy promise, and the spring
Of my great love to thee. For once to marry
Is honourable in woman, and her ignorance
Stands for a virtue, coming new and fresh.
But second marriage shows desires in flesh;
Thence lust and heat and common custom grows.
But she's part virgin who but one man knows.
I here expect a work of thy great faith
At my last parting. I can crave no more,
And with thy vow I rest myself for ever;
My soul and it shall fly to heaven together.
Seal to my spirit that quiet satisfaction,
And I go hence in peace.'

DUCHESS 'Then here I vow, never—'

LORD CARDINAL
Why, madam!

DUCHESS I can go no further.

LORD CARDINAL What,
Have you forgot your vow?

DUCHESS I have, too certainly.

LORD CARDINAL
Your vow? That cannot be; it follows now
Just where I left.

DUCHESS My frailty gets before it.
Nothing prevails but ill.

LORD CARDINAL What, ail you, madam?

DUCHESS
Sir, I'm in love.

LORD CARDINAL O all you powers of chastity,
Look to this woman! Let her not faint now
For honour of yourselves. If she be lost
I know not where to seek my hope in woman.
Madam, O madam!

DUCHESS My desires are sickened
Beyond recovery of good counsel, sir.

LORD CARDINAL
What mischief owed a malice to the sex,
To work this spiteful ill? Better the man
Had never known creation than to live
Th'unlucky ruin of so fair a temple.
Yet think upon your vow, revive in faith;
Those are eternal things. What are all pleasures,
Flatteries of men, and follies upon earth,
To your most excellent goodness? O, she's dead,
Stark cold to any virtuous claim within her.
What now is heat is sin's. Have I approved
Your constancy for this, called your faith noble,
Writ volumes of your victories and virtues?
I have undone my judgement, lost my praises,
Blemished the truth of my opinïon.
Give me the man, that I may pour him out
To all contempt and curses.

49 **earth's glory** Recalls 1 Corinthians 15:40, 'the glory of the earthly' (in contrast with heavenly glory).
55 **be...seem** Proverbial.
57 **simple** (*a*) artless (*b*) pure, unmixed with other qualities
60 **fellows** companions, spouses
of during
62 **Death had no sting** 'O death, where is thy sting' (1 Corinthians 15:55)
had would have had
67 **his** its
68 **racked** tortured by stretching on the rack
72 **forgetfulness** (both of her husband and of her moral being)
73 **deadly** (*a*) death-like (*b*) mortally sinful
76–7 **once...woman** Varies the biblical 'Marriage is honourable among all' (Hebrews, 13:4).
78 **for** as
80 **common custom** i.e. promiscuous and unsanctified habits
81 **she's...knows** Restates the Protestant doctrine that marital fidelity is a form of chastity.
82 **a...faith** 'Even so, faith, if it hath no works, is dead in itself' (James 2:17). Contrast the Duchess's 'true fasting faith from sensual pleasure' (1.2.47). Protestant doctrine emphasized the priority of faith over good works.
86 **quiet satisfaction** peace-bringing release from uncertainty. *Satisfaction* is perhaps also 'fulfilment of obligation'.
89 **forgot** The Cardinal refers to the words; the Duchess refers to disregarding their import.
98 **of** by
99 **mischief** worker of mischief
the sex the female sex
101 **known creation** i.e. been born
102 **Th'unlucky** The harmful, malicious
ruin cause of ruin
temple i.e. human soul. The word in its literal sense appropriately implies a sacrilege.
106 **To** compared with
107 **virtuous claim** claim to virtue
108 **heat** (previously of zeal for virtue, now of lust)
approved confirmed, commended
111 **undone** ruined, discredited
113 **Give me** identify to me
pour him out expose him

DUCHESS The man's innocent,
Full of desert and grace; his name, Lactantio.
LORD CARDINAL How?
DUCHESS Your nephew.
LORD CARDINAL My nephew!
DUCHESS
Beshrew the sight of him! He lives not, sir,
That could have conquered me, himself excepted.
LORD CARDINAL
He that I loved so dearly, does he wear
Such killing poison in his eye to sanctity?
He has undone himself for ever by't,
Has lost a friend of me, and a more sure one.
Farewell, all natural pity. Though my affection
Could hardly spare him from my sight an hour,
I'll lose him now eternally, and strive
To live without him. He shall straight to Rome.
DUCHESS
Not if you love my health or life, my lord.
LORD CARDINAL
This day he shall set forth.
DUCHESS Dispatch me rather.
LORD CARDINAL
I'll send him far enough.
DUCHESS Send me to death first.
LORD CARDINAL
No basilisk that strikes dead pure affection
With venomous eye lives under my protection. *Exit*
DUCHESS
Now my condition's worse than e'er 'twas yet.
My cunning takes not with him. He's broke through
The net that with all art was set for him,
And left the snarer here herself entangled
With her own toils. O, what are we, poor souls,
When our dissembling fails us? Surely creatures
As full of want as any nation can be
That scarce have food to keep bare life about 'em.
Had this but took effect, what a fair way
Had I made for my love to th' General,
And cut off all suspect, all reprehension!
My hopes are killed i'th' blossom. *Exit*

2.2 *Enter Lord Cardinal*

LORD CARDINAL Let me think upon't,
Set holy anger by a while; there's time
Allowed for natural argument. 'Tis she
That loves my nephew, she that loves, loves first.
What cause have I to lay a blame on him then?
He's in no fault in this. Say 'twas his fortune
At the free entertainment of the General,
'Mongst others the deserts and hopes of Milan,
To come into her sight, where's th'offence yet?
What sin was that in him? Man's sight and presence
Are free to public view. She might as well
Have fixed her heart's love then upon some other.
I would 't had lighted anywhere but there!—
Yet I may err to wish't, since it appears
The hand of heaven that only picked him out,
To rèward virtue in him by this fortune.
And through affection I'm half conquered now.
I love his good as dearly as her vow—
Yet there my credit lives in works and praises.
I never found a harder fight within me
Since zeal first taught me war. Say I should labour
To quench this love?—And so quench life and all,
As by all likelihood it would prove her death.
For it must needs be granted she affects him
As dearly as the power of love can force,
Since her vow awes her not, that was her saint.
What right could that be to religïon
To be her end, and dispossess my kinsman?
No, I will bear, in pity to her heart;
The rest commend to fortune and my art. *Exit*

2.3 *Enter Father, Governor, Aurelia, and Andrugio disguised [as a poor soldier]*

GOVERNOR
I like him passing well.
FATHER He's a tall fellow.
ANDRUGIO [*aside*]
A couple of tall wits!—I have seen some service, sir.
GOVERNOR
Nay, so it seems by thy discourse, good fellow.
ANDRUGIO [*aside*]
'Good-fellow': calls me thief familiarly.—
I could show many marks of resolution,
But modesty could wish 'em rather hidden.
I fetched home three and twenty wounds together
In one set battle, where I was defeated
At the same time of the third part of my nose;

119 **He lives not** no man lives
122 **Such . . . eye** Alludes to the basilisk, a legendary reptile whose look was fatal; compare ll. 132–4.
124 **a more sure one** (i.e. God)
125 **natural pity** compassion arising from kinship
127 **eternally** The banishment resembles damnation.
130 **Dispatch** kill (with a quibble on 'send')
132 **basilisk** See note to l. 122.
137–8 **left . . . toils** Proverbial.
138 **we** Either human beings generally, or, as in the play's title, women.
145 **killed i'th' blossom** Proverbial.
2.2.3 **natural argument** arguing the case as a relative
7 **free** magnamimous
8 **others** others of
15 **only picked him** picked only him
19 **works** good works
24 **affects** loves
26 **saint** i.e. object of personal devotion and source of strength
29 **bear** tolerate. Compare Romans 15:1: 'We which are strong ought to bear the infirmities of the weak, and not please ourselves'.
2.3.0.2 ***disguised . . . soldier*** A concluded military campaign deposited poor, unemployed, and injured ex-soldiers onto the streets.
1, 2 **tall** brave, fine (ironic in l. 2)
2 **service** military service
4 **Good-fellow** thief
5 **marks** (*a*) signs (*b*) scars
8 **was defeated** lost possession

But, meeting with a skilful surgëon,
Took order for my snuffling.

GOVERNOR And a nose
Well healed is counted a good cure in these days.
It saves many a man's honesty, which else
Is quickly drawn into suspicïon.
This night shall bring you acquainted with your
charge;
In the mean time you and your valour's welcome.
Would we had more store of you, although they come
With fewer marks about 'em.

FATHER So wish I, sir.

Exeunt Father and Governor

ANDRUGIO [*aside*]
I was about to call her, and she stays
Of her own gift, as if she knew my mind.
Certain she knows me not, not possible.

AURELIA [*aside*]
What if I left my token and my letter
With this strange fellow, so to be conveyed
Without suspicion to Lactantio's servant?
Not so, I'll trust no freshman with such secrets.
His ignorance may mistake, and give't to one
That may belong to th' General, for I know
He sets some spies about me; but all he gets
Shall not be worth his pains. I would Lactantio
Would seek some means to free me from this place.
'Tis prisonment enough to be a maid;
But to be mewed up too, that case is hard,
As if a toy were kept by a double guard.

ANDRUGIO [*aside*]
Away she steals again, not minding me.
'Twas not at me she offered.—Hark you, gentlewo-
man.

AURELIA
With me, sir?

ANDRUGIO I could call you by your name,
But gentle's the best attribute to woman.

AURELIA
Andrugio! O, as welcome to my lips
As morning dew to roses! My first love!

ANDRUGIO
Why, have you more then?

AURELIA What a word was there!
More than thyself what woman could desire,
If reason had a part of her creation?
For loving you, you see, sir, I'm a prisoner;
There's all the cause they have against me, sir;
A happy persecution, I so count on't.
If anything be done to me for your sake,
'Tis pleasing to me.

ANDRUGIO Are you not abused,
Either through force or by your own consent?
Hold you your honour perfect and unstained?
Are you the same still that at my departure
My honest thoughts maintained you to my heart?

AURELIA
The same, most just.

ANDRUGIO Swear't.

AURELIA By my hope of fruitfulness,
Love, and agreement, the three joys of marriage.

ANDRUGIO
I am confirmed, and in requital on't
Ere long expect your freedom.

AURELIA O, you flatter me!
It is a wrong to make a wretch too happy,
So suddenly upon afflictïon.
Beshrew me if I be not sick upon't.
'Tis like a surfeit after a great feast.
My freedom, said you?

ANDRUGIO Does't o'ercome you so?

AURELIA
Temptation never overcame a sinner
More pleasingly than this sweet news my heart.
Here's secret joy can witness, I am proud on't.

ANDRUGIO
Violence I will not use, I come a friend,
'Twere madness to force that which wit can end.

AURELIA
Most virtuously delivered.

ANDRUGIO Thou art in raptures.

AURELIA
My love, my love.

11 **order** measures
13–14 **It...suspicïon** Alludes to destruction of the nasal bones through syphilis.
17 **store** supply
although even if
20 **Of her own gift** as a favour freely given
25 **freshman** (*a*) newcomer (*b*) matriculating student (hence 'His ignorance')
27 **belong to** be in the service of
31–3 **'Tis...guard** Plays on the idea that the maidenhead locks out sexual penetration. In the analogy of l. 33, the second guard might be a chastity-belt.
32 **mewed** cooped
case (*a*) situation (*b*) cage (also quibbling on 'vagina')
33 **toy** trinket, plaything (alluding to the female sexual organs)
35 **offered** showed intention to address
40 **What...there** i.e. what an idea
42 **had...creation** was an ingredient in her making
45 **happy persecution** Compare 2 Corinthians 12:10, 'Therefore I take pleasure in infirmities, in reproaches, in necessities, in persecutions, in distresses, for Christ's sake'.
47 **abused** dishonoured
52 **just** (*a*) exactly (*b*) honourably
52–3 **By...marriage** Based on God's three 'causes' for instituting marriage in the opening address of the marriage service in the Book of Common Prayer: 'One was the procreation of children... Secondly it was ordained for a remedy against sin and to avoid fornication... Thirdly for the mutual society, help, and comfort that the one ought to have of the other'.
52 **fruitfulness** fertility, child-bearing
53 **agreement** harmony
54 **confirmed** assured, convinced
55 **flatter me** tempt me with pleasing ideas
57 **So...afflictïon** Qualifies *wretch*.
upon after
59 **surfeit** sickness with overeating
63 **proud** elated, pleased
64 **a friend** (to the Governor)
65 **wit** cunning

ANDRUGIO [*aside*] 'Most virtuously delivered'!
Spoke like the sister of a puritan midwife.—
Will you embrace the means that I have thought on
With all the speed you can?
AURELIA Sir, anything;
You cannot name't too dangerous or too homely.
ANDRUGIO
Fie, you overact your happiness,
You drive slight things to wonders.
AURELIA Blame me not, sir;
You know not my affection.
ANDRUGIO Will you hear me?
There are a sect of pilf'ring juggling people
The vulgar tongue call Gypsies.
AURELIA True, the same, sir;
I saw the like this morning. Say no more, sir,
I apprehend you fully.
ANDRUGIO What, you do not!
AURELIA
No? Hark you, sir.
[*She whispers*]
ANDRUGIO Now by this light, 'tis true.
Sure if you prove as quick as your conceit
You'll be an exc'llent breeder.
AURELIA
I should do reason, by the mother's side, sir,
If fortune do her part, in a good getter.
ANDRUGIO
That's not to do now, sweet: the man stands near thee.
AURELIA
Long may he stand most fortunately, sir,
Whom her kind goodness has appointed for me.
ANDRUGIO
A while I'll take my leave to avoid suspicion.
AURELIA
I do commend your course. Good sir, forget me not.
ANDRUGIO
All comforts sooner.
AURELIA Liberty is sweet, sir.
ANDRUGIO
I know there's nothing sweeter, next to love—
But health itself, which is the prince of life.
AURELIA
Your knowledge raise you, sir.
ANDRUGIO Farewell till evening.
Exit
AURELIA
And after that, farewell, sweet sir, for ever.
A good kind gentleman to serve our turn with,
But not for lasting. I have chose a stuff
Will wear out two of him, and one finer too.
I like not him that has two mistresses,
War and his sweet-heart; he can ne'er please both.
And war's a soaker; she's no friend to us;
Turns a man home sometimes to his mistress
Some forty ounces poorer than he went,
All his discourse out of the book of surgery,
Cerecloth and salve, and lies you all in tents
Like your camp-vict'lers. Out upon't, I smile
To think how I have fitted him with an office!
His love takes pains to bring our loves together,
Much like your man that labours to get treasure
To keep his wife high for another's pleasure. *Exit*
Finis Actus Secundus

Incipit Actus Tertius 3.1
Enter Lactantio and Page
PAGE
Think of your shame, and mine.
LACTANTIO I prithee, peace.
Thou art th'unfortunat'st piece of taking business
That ever man repented when day peeped.
I'll ne'er keep such a piece of touchwood again,
An I were rid of thee once. Well fare those
That never shamed their master! I have had such,
And I may live to see the time again,
I do not doubt on't.
PAGE If my too much kindness

68 **Spoke ... midwife** Puns on 'delivered' as applied to assisting childbirth, and takes 'virtuously' as typical of puritan diction.
71 **homely** (*a*) unassuming (*b*) rough
76 **vulgar tongue** common people
80 **quick** prompt (with the quibble 'easily made *quick* with child')
conceit understanding (punning on 'conception')
82 **do reason** be satisfactory
the mother's side i.e. characteristics inherited from the mother
83 **in** in being
getter begetter
84 **That's ... now** i.e. fortune's part (providing a male partner) doesn't any longer need to be done
85 **stand** Quibbles on the 'standing' of the erect penis.
86 **her** (i.e. fortune's)
89 **Liberty is sweet** Proverbial.
90 **next to** compared with
love (proverbially sweet in the beginning but sour in the ending)
91 **health ... life** Perhaps suggested by the proverb 'health is great riches'.
92 **raise** advance (with a possible phallic quibble)
95 **stuff** material
97 **I ... mistresses** Ironic, as she likes Lactantio.
99 **soaker** exhauster
101 **poorer** i.e. lighter
103 **Cerecloth** cloth used as plaster in surgery
salve ointment
tents (*a*) lint dressings (*b*) camping tents
104 **camp-vict'lers** victuallers, suppliers
Out upon't Expresses repugnancy.
105 **fitted** supplied
office post, employment
108 **high** wealthy (perhaps also 'sexually excited', but the sense is not in *OED*)
3.1.2 **taking business** Both words imply sexual transaction. *Taking* is also 'conceiving with child', on the analogy of *touchwood* taking fire.
3 **when day peeped** i.e. the next morning
4 **touchwood** kindling wood
5 **Well fare those** may those prosper

Receive your anger only for reward,
The harder is my fortune. I must tell you, sir,
To stir your care up to preventïon—
Misfortunes must be told as well as blessings—
When I left all my friends in Mantua
For your love's sake alone, then with strange oaths
You promised present marriage.

LACTANTIO 'With strange oaths', quoth a?
They're not so strange to me. I have sworn the same things,
I am sure, forty times over; not so little.
I may be perfect in 'em, for my standing.

PAGE
You see 'tis high time now, sir.

LACTANTIO Yes, yes, yes.
Marriage is nothing with you, a toy till death.
If I should marry all those I have promised,
'Twould make one vicar hoarse ere he could dispatch us.
[*The Page stands apart and weeps*]
I must devise some shift. When she grows big
Those masculine hose will shortly prove too little.
What if she were conveyed to Nurse's house—
A good, sure old wench, and she'd love the child well
Because she suckled the father. No ill course,
By my mortality; I may hit worse.
Enter Dondolo
Now, Dondolo, the news?

DONDOLO The news?

LACTANTIO How does she?

DONDOLO
Soft, soft, sir, you think 'tis nothing to get news
Out o'th' castle? I was there.

LACTANTIO Well, sir?

DONDOLO As you know,
A merry fellow may pass anywhere.

LACTANTIO So, sir?

DONDOLO
Never in better fooling in my life.

LACTANTIO What's this to th' purpose?

DONDOLO Nay, 'twas nothing to th' purpose, that's certain.

LACTANTIO
How wretched this slave makes me! Didst not see her?

DONDOLO
I saw her.

LACTANTIO
Well, what said she, then?

DONDOLO Not a word, sir.

LACTANTIO
How, not a word?

DONDOLO Proves her the better maid,
For virgins should be seen more than they're heard.

LACTANTIO
Exceeding good, sir; you are no sweet villain.

DONDOLO
No, faith, sir, for you keep me in foul linen.

LACTANTIO
Turned scurvy rhymer, are you?

DONDOLO Not scurvy neither,
Though I be somewhat itchy in the profession.
If you could hear me out with patïence,
I know her mind as well as if I were in her belly.

LACTANTIO
Thou saidst e'en now she never spake a word.

DONDOLO
But she gave certain signs, and that's as good.

LACTANTIO
Canst thou conceive by signs?

DONDOLO O, passing well, sir,
E'en from an infant; did you ne'er know that?
I was the happiest child in all our country;
I was born of a dumb woman.

LACTANTIO How?

DONDOLO Stark dumb, sir. My father had a rare bargain of her, a rich pennyworth. There would have been but too much money given for her. A Justice of Peace was about her, but my father, being then constable, carried her before him.

LACTANTIO
Well, since we are entered into these dumb-shows,
What were the signs she gave you?

DONDOLO Many and good, sir.
Imprimis, she first gaped; but that, I guessed,
Was done for want of air 'cause she's kept close;
But had she been abroad and gaped as much,
'T had been another case. Then cast she up

11 **preventïon** action to anticipate what will happen
13 **friends** relatives, family
15 **present** immediate
18 **may** may well, ought to
perfect expert
for for the sake of
standing (*a*) reputation with the Lord Cardinal (*b*) erections
19 **high** Quibbles on *standing*: what stands has height.
22 **dispatch** marry (but also suggesting 'bury'; compare l. 20)
23 **shift** trick, expedient
24 **hose** close-fitting breeches
28 **hit** hit upon, think of
worse Rhymes with 'course'.
35 **What's . . . purpose** Proverbial.
40 **virgins . . . heard** Varies the proverbial 'Maidens should be seen and not heard'.
41 **sweet villain** A term of endearment. Dondolo takes *sweet* as 'sweet-smelling'.
43 **scurvy** Lactantio uses the word figuratively: 'lousy, rotten'. Dondolo takes it literally.
44 **the profession** (of rhymer)
46 **I . . . belly** Proverbial.
49 **conceive** understand
passing surpassingly
51 **happiest** most fortunate
54–5 **My . . . her** Proverbially, 'silence is the best ornament of a woman'.
56 **Peace** Plays on the sense 'silence'.
57–8 **carried . . . him** won her before he did (quibbling on 'brought her to be tried before him')
59 **dumb-shows** Alludes to set pieces of theatrical mime.
61 ***Imprimis*** in the first place
62 **close** confined
63 **abroad** at large, out of doors
64 **'T had . . . case** i.e. it would have been a sexual come-on
64–5 **cast . . . winked** Another sexual come-on, but Dondolo absurdly understands a mime indicating sunset.

Her pretty eye and winked; the word me thought was then
'Come not till twitter light'.
Next, thus her fingers went, as who should say,
'I'd fain have a hole broke to scape away.'
Then looked upon her watch, and twice she nodded,
As who should say, 'The hour will come, sweetheart,
That I shall make two noddies of my keepers.'

LACTANTIO
A third of thee. Is this your mother tongue?
My hopes are much the wiser for this language!
There is no such curse in love to an arrant ass.

DONDOLO
O yes, sir, yes, an arrant whore's far worse.
You ne'er lin
Railing on me from one week's end to another.
But you can keep a little titmouse page there,
That's good for nothing but to carry toothpicks,
Put up your pipe, or so; that's all he's good for.
He cannot make him ready as he should do;
I am fain to truss his points ev'ry morning.
Yet the proud scornful ape, when all the lodgings
Were taken up with strangers th'other night,
He would not suffer me to come to bed to him,
But kicked and pricked and pinched me like an urchin.
There's no good quality in him. O' my conscience,
I think he scarce knows how to stride a horse.
I saw him with a little hunting nag
But thus high t'other day, and he was fain to lead him
To a high rail and get up like a butter-wench.
There's no good fellowship in this dandiprat,
This dive-dapper, as is in other pages.
They'd go a-swimming with me familiarly
I'th' heat of summer, and clap what-you-call-'ems;
But I could never get that little monkey
Yet to put off his breeches.
A tender, puling, nice, chitty-faced squall 'tis.

LACTANTIO
Is this the good you do me? His love's wretched
And most distressed that must make use of fools.

DONDOLO [*aside*]
'Fool' to my face still! That's unreasonable.
I will be a knave one day for this trick, or it shall cost me a fall, though it be from a gibbet—
It has been many a proper man's last leap.
Nay, sure I'll be quite out of the precincts of a fool if I live but two days to an end.
I will turn Gypsy presently,
And that's the highway to the daintiest knave
That ever mother's son took journey to.
O, those dear Gypsies,
They live the merriest lives, eat sweet stol'n hens
Plucked over pales or hedges by a twitch;
They are ne'er without a plump and lovely goose,
Or beautiful sow-pig.
Those things I saw with mine own eyes today.
They call those vanities and trifling pilf'ries,
But if a privy search were made amongst 'em
They should find other manner of ware about 'em:
Cups, rings, and silver spoons, by'r Lady, bracelets,
Pearl necklaces, and chains of gold sometimes.
They are the wittiest thieves. I'll stay no longer,
But e'en go look what I can steal now presently,
And so begin to bring myself acquainted with 'em.
Exit

LACTANTIO
Nothing I fear so much as, in this time
Of my dull absence, her first love, the General,
Will wind himself into her affection
By secret gifts and letters; there's the mischief.
I have no enemy like him. Though my policy
Dissembled him a welcome, no man's hate
Can stick more close unto a loathed disease
Than mine to him.

66 **twitter light** twilight
67 **thus** Dondolo presumably makes a circle with the thumb and forefinger of one hand, passing a finger of the other hand through it. The sexual innuendo is taken up in 'a hole broke', l. 68.
as who should say as if to say
69 **watch** The hands and dial of a watch were considered sexually suggestive.
71 **noddies** idiots (punning on *nodded*)
72 **mother** (*a*) native (*b*) mother's
74 **to** compared with
76 **lin** cease
79–80 **to ... pipe** Toothpicks and pipe were fashionable, and small.
80 **Put ... pipe** Meant literally ('put away your pipe'), but playing on the set expression meaning 'shut up', and on *pipe* as slang for 'penis'.
82 **fain** obliged
truss his points pull his laces tight and tie them (in particular, those attaching the hose to the doublet)
85 **come ... him** It was common for servants, etc., of the same sex to share a bed.
86 **urchin** (*a*) hedgehog (hence 'pricked') (*b*) goblin, spirit (hence 'pinched')
89 **hunting nag** pony
91 **rail** fence
like a butter-wench i.e. by climbing up from the fence
92 **dandiprat** contemptibly small person (from the name of a small coin)
93 **dive-dapper** dabchick (as a particularly small water-fowl)
95 **what-you-call-'ems** Apparently a clapping game whose name Dondolo forgets or avoids as indecent.
98 **puling** sickly
nice fastidious
chitty-faced (*a*) pinch-faced, or (*b*) baby-faced
squall (*a*) small, insignificant person; (*b*) girl
101 **unreasonable** (*a*) unfair (*b*) irrational (like a fool)
102 **for this trick** in return for treating me like this
103 **fall** (*a*) throw (as in wrestling) (*b*) drop (as in hanging)
105 **of a** of being a
107 **presently** at once
108 **highway** (both figurative 'route' and the road of travelling people)
to i.e. to becoming
112 **pales** fences
twitch tug, snatch
116 **pilf'ries** petty thefts
121 **wittiest** cunningest
126 **wind** insinuate

Enter Lord Cardinal

LORD CARDINAL
What ails this pretty boy to weep so often?
Tell me the cause, child. How his eyes stand full!
Beshrew you, nephew, you're too bitter to him.
He is so soft th'unkindness of a word
Melts him into a woman. 'Las, poor boy,
Thou shalt not serve him longer. 'Twere great pity
That thou shouldst wait upon an angry master.
I have promised thee to one will make much of thee,
And hold thy weak youth in most dear respect.

PAGE
O, I beseech your grace, that I may serve
No master else.

LORD CARDINAL
Thou shalt not. Mine's a mistress,
The greatest mistress in all Milan, boy:
The Duchess' self.

PAGE Nor her, nor any.

LORD CARDINAL Cease, boy,
Thou knowest not thine own happiness, through
fondness,
And therefore must be learnt. Go dry thine eyes.

PAGE
This rather is the way to make 'em moister. *Exit*

LORD CARDINAL
Now nephew, nephew.

LACTANTIO O, you've snatched my spirit, sir,
From the divinest meditation
That ever made soul happy.

LORD CARDINAL [*aside*] I am afraid
I shall have as much toil to bring him on now
As I had pains to keep her off from him.—
I have thought it fit, nephew, considering
The present barrenness of our name and house
(The only famine of succeeding honour)
To move the ripeness of your time to marriage.

LACTANTIO
How, sir, to marriage?

LORD CARDINAL Yes, to a fruitful life.
We must not all be strict; so generation
Would lose her right. Thou'rt young; 'tis my desire
To see thee bestowed happily in my lifetime.

LACTANTIO
Does your grace well remember who I am
When you speak this?

LORD CARDINAL Yes, very perfectly;
You're a young man, full in the grace of life,
And made to do love credit; proper, handsome,
And for affection pregnant.

LACTANTIO I beseech you, sir,
Take off your praises rather than bestow 'em
Upon so frail a use. Alas, you know, sir,
I know not what love is, or what you speak of.
If woman be amongst it, I shall swoon. Take her
away,
For contemplation's sake. Most serious uncle,
Name no such thing to me.

LORD CARDINAL Come, come, you're fond.
Prove but so strict and obstinate in age,
And you are well to pass. There's honest love
Allowed you now for recreation.
The years will come when all delights must leave you;
Stick close to virtue then. In the mean time
There's honourable joys to keep youth company;
And if death take you there, dying no adulterer,
You're out of his eternal reach, defy him.
List hither, come to me, and with great thankfulness
Welcome thy fortunes. 'Tis the Duchess loves thee.

LACTANTIO
The Duchess!

LORD CARDINAL
Dotes on thee, will die for thee
Unless she may enjoy thee.

LACTANTIO She must die then.

LORD CARDINAL How?

LACTANTIO
Alas, do you think she ever means to do't, sir?
I'll sooner believe all a woman speaks
Than that she'll die for love. She has a vow, my lord,
That will keep life in her.

LORD CARDINAL Believe me, then,
That should have bounteous interest in thy faith,
She's thine, and not her vow's.

LACTANTIO The more my sorrow,
My toil, and my destruction. [*Aside*] My blood dances.

141–2 **I...else** 'No man can serve two masters' (Matthew 6:24). More particularly, the 'Page', being pregnant by Lactantio, might avoid having to *serve* another master likewise.

145 **fondness** foolishness (also, ironically, 'love', for Lactantio)

151 **bring him on** induce him

155 **famine** i.e. the dirth caused by *barrenness*, as when a crop fails, and threatening extinction

of succeeding honour i.e. to prevent honour being passed on

156 **move** urge

ripeness of your time Perhaps based on Revelation 14:15: 'the time is come to reap, for the harvest of the earth is ripe'.

157–9 **Yes...right** Recalls God's injunction to 'be fruitful and multiply' (Genesis 1:22, 28; King James version); but in biblical terms a *fruitful life* would more usually be productive in the service of God.

158 **generation** reproduction of offspring

164 **proper** good-looking, worthy

165 **pregnant** apt. Lactantio might take up the sense 'with child' in *use*.

167 **use** (with hints at 'sexual use' and 'profit from investment')

171 **fond** foolish

174 **recreation** (also 're-creation')

178 **there** i.e. in those joys

179 **defy** you defy

180 **List** (*a*) deserve, chose (*b*) listen (*c*) lean (as of a ship)

185 **I'll...speaks** Women were proverbially considered changeable and duplicitous.

187 **keep life in her** i.e. preserve her soul

188 **interest** spiritual concern (but also 'financial stake')

LORD CARDINAL
And though that bashful maiden virtue in thee,
That never held familiar league with woman,
Binds fast all pity to her heart that loves thee,
Let me prevail. My counsel stands up to thee;
Embrace it as the fullness of thy fortunes,
As if all blessings upon earth were closed
Within one happiness; for such another
Whole life could never meet with. Go and present
Your service and your love; but, on your hopes,
Do it religiously. [*Aside*] What need I doubt him,
Whom chastity locks up?

LACTANTIO [*aside*] O envy,
Hadst thou no other means to come by virtue
But by such treachery? The Duchess' love!
Thou wouldst be sure to aim it high enough;
Thou knew'st full well 'twas no prevailing else.—
Sir, what your will commands, mine shall fulfil.
I'll teach my heart in all t'obey your will.

LORD CARDINAL
A thing you shall not lose by.
Enter Lords
Here come the lords.
Go follow you the course that I advised you.
The comfort of thy presence is expected.
Away with speed to court; she languishes
For one dear sight of thee. For life's sake, haste.
You lose my favour if you let her perish.

LACTANTIO [*aside*]
And art thou come, brave fortune, the reward
Of neat hypocrisy, that ever booked it,
Or turned up transitory white o'th' eye
After the feminine rapture? Duchess and I
Were a fit match can be denied of no man:
The best dissembler lights on the best woman.
'Twere sin to part us. *Exit*

LORD CARDINAL
You lights of state, truth's friends, much honoured lords,
Faithful admirers of our Duchess' virtues,
And firm believers: it appears as plain
As knowledge to the eyes of industry
That neither private motion, which holds counsel
Often with woman's frailty and her blood,
Nor public sight, the lightning of temptations
Which from the eye strikes sparks into the bosom
And sets whole hearts on fire, hath power to raise
A heat in her 'bove that which feeds chaste life
And gives that cherishing means. She's the same still,
And seems so seriously employed in soul
As if she could not tend to cast an eye
Upon deserts so low as those in man.
It merits famous memory, I confess.
Yet many times, when I behold her youth
And think upon the lost hopes of posterity,
Succession, and the royal fruits of beauty,
All by the rashness of one vow made desperate,
It goes so near my heart I feel it painful,
And wakes me into pity oftentimes,
When others sleep unmoved.

FIRST LORD I speak it faithfully,
For 'tis poor fame to boast of a disease:
Your grace has not endured that pain alone;
'T 'as been a grief of mine; but where's the remedy?

LORD CARDINAL
True, there your lordship spake enough in little.
There's nothing to be hoped for but repulses.
She's not to seek for armour against love
That has bid battle to his powers so long.
He that should try her now had need come strong,
And with more force than his own arguments,
Or he may part disgraced, being put to flight.
That soldier's tough has been in seven years' fight;
Her vow's invincible. For you must grant this:
If those desires trained up in flesh and blood
To war continually 'gainst good intents
Prove all too weak for her, having advantage
Both of her sex and her unskilfulness
At a spiritual weapon, wanting knowledge
To manage resolution, and yet win,
What force can a poor argument bring in?
The books that I have published in her praise
Commend her constancy, and that's fame-worthy;
But if you read me o'er with eyes of enemies,
You cannot justly and with honour tax me
That I dissuade her life from marriage there.
Now heaven and fruitfulness forbid, not I.
She may be constant there; and the hard war
Of chastity is held a virtuous strife
As rare in marriage as in single life,

192 **familiar** intimate
193 **Binds fast** firmly restrains
194 **stands up to** withstands, does not retreat from
199 **on** at peril of
201 **envy** malice, evil
202 **come by** get at
204 **aim...enough** *treachery* is seen as an arrow aimed *high* to reach a *high* (morally impeccable, socially elevated) target
215 **neat** (*a*) cleverly contrived (*b*) unadulterated
booked it devoted himself to books (not in *OED*)
216 **turned...eye** (a momentary gesture of piety)
217 **After...rapture** i.e. in response to female intoxication in love; or in imitation of female ecstatic virtue
Duchess and I i.e. That the Duchess and I
224 **the...industry** i.e. diligent eyes
225 **motion** impulse, desire (also 'proposals', as appropriate to *holds counsel*)
226 **blood** fleshly nature, vitality, desires
227 **public sight** seeing the public world
229 **sets...fire** Proverbial.
238 **royal fruits** Recalls Jacob predictively blessing his sons: 'he shall yield royal dainties...Joseph is a fruitful bough' (Genesis 49:20–22; King James version)
239 **desperate** without hope
248 **She's not to** she need not
258–9 **unskilfulness...weapon** i.e. lack of spiritual training
260 **manage** bring about; train up (as of a horse)

Nay, by some writers, rarer. Hear their reasons,
And you'll approve 'em fairly. She that's single,
Either in maid or widow, oftentimes
The fear of shame more than the fear of heaven
Keeps chaste and constant. When the tempest comes
She knows she has no shelter for her sin;
It must endure the weathers of all censure.
Nothing but sea and air that poor barque feels;
When she in wedlock is like a safe vessel
That lies at anchor. Come what weathers can,
She has her harbour. At her great unlading
Much may be stol'n, and little missed; the master
Thinks himself rich enough with what he has,
And holds content by that. How think you now,
lords?
If she that might offend safe does not err,
What's chaste in others is most rare in her.

SECOND LORD
What wisdom but approves it?

FIRST LORD
But, my lord,
This should be told to her it concerns most;
Pity such good things should be spoke and lost.

LORD CARDINAL
That were the way to lose 'em utterly.
You quite forget her vow. Yet, now I think on't,
What is that vow? 'Twas but a thing enforced,
Was it not, lords?

FIRST LORD
Merely compelled, indeed.

LORD CARDINAL
Only to please the Duke; and forcèd virtue
Fails in her merit, there's no crown prepared for't.
What have we done, my lords? I fear we have sinned
In too much strictness to uphold her in't,
In cherishing her will; for woman's goodness
Takes counsel of that first, and then determines.
She cannot truly be called constant now
If she persèvere; rather obstinate,
The vow appearing forcèd, as it proves
Tried by our purer thoughts. The grace and triumph
Of all her victories are but idle glories,
She wilful, and we enemies to succession.
I will not take rest till I tell her soul
As freely as I talk to those I keep.

ALL LORDS
And we'll all second you, my lord.

LORD CARDINAL
Agreed.
We'll knit such knots of arguments so fast
All wit in her shall not undo in haste.

SECOND LORD
Nay, sure, I think all we shall be too hard for her,
Else she's a huge wild creature.

FIRST LORD [*aside*]
If we win
And she yield marriage, then will I strike in. *Exeunt*

Enter Duchess and Celia 3.2

DUCHESS
Thou tell'st me happy things, if they be certain,
To bring my wishes about wondrous strangely.
Lactantio, nephew to the Cardinal,
The General's secret enemy?

CELIA
Most true, madam.
I had it from a gentleman, my kinsman,
That knows the best part of Lactantio's bosom.

DUCHESS
It happens passing fortunately, to save
Employment in another. He will 'come now
A necessary property. He may thank
The need and use we have of him for his welcome.
Knocks within
Now who's that knocks?

CELIA
Madam, 'tis he, with speed.
I thought he had brought his horse to th' chamber
door,
He made such haste and noise.

DUCHESS
Admit him, prithee,
And have a care your heart be true and secret.

CELIA
Take life away from't when it fails you, madam.

DUCHESS
Enough, I know thee wise. *Exit* [*Celia*]
Enter Lactantio, [*hastily*]
He comes with haste indeed.—Are you come now, sir?
You should have stayed yet longer, and have found
me
Dead, to requite your haste.

LACTANTIO
Love bless you better, madam.

DUCHESS
Must I bid welcome to the man undoes me,
The cause of my vow's breach, my honour's enemy,
One that does all the mischief to my fame,
And mocks my seven years' conquest with his name?
This is a force of love was never felt.
But I'll not grudge at fortune; I will take
Captivity cheerfully. Here, seize upon me;
And if thy heart can be so pitiless
To chain me up for ever in those arms,
I'll take it mildly, ay, and thank my stars;
For we're all subject to the chance of wars.

LACTANTIO
We are so, yet take comfort, vanquished Duchess.

274 **shame** dishonour (specifically, pregnancy)
278 **barque** boat
282 **master** (*a*) ship's owner (*b*) husband
289 **lost** Rhymes with *most*.
293 **Merely** entirely
294 **forcèd virtue** Suggests an ironically inappropriate comparison with rape.
295 **crown** garland of victory
303 **purer** purified
307 **those I keep** my servants
310 **haste** Rhymes with *fast*.
312 **a … creature** Suggests that the *knots*, l. 309, are of ropes that will capture her.
313 **strike in** (with a sexual innuendo)
3.2.6 **bosom** thoughts and feelings
8 **'come** become
9 **property** tool
30 **the … wars** Proverbially, 'The chance of war is uncertain'.

I'll use you like an honourable prisoner;
You shall be entreated. Day shall be
Free for all sports to you, the night for me.
That's all I challenge, all the rest is thine;
And, for your fare, 't shall be no worse than mine.

DUCHESS
Nay, then I'm heartily pleasant, and as merry
As one that owes no malice, and that's well, sir.
You cannot say so much for your part, can you?

LACTANTIO
Faith, all that I owe is to one man, madam,
And so can few men say. Marry, that malice
Wears no dead flesh about it, 'tis a stinger.

DUCHESS
What is he that shall dare to be your enemy,
Having our friendship, if he be a servant
And subject to our law?

LACTANTIO Yes, trust me, madam.
Of a vile fellow, I hold him a true subject.
There's many arrant knaves that are good subjects,
Some for their livings' sakes, some for their lives',
That will, unseen, eat men, and drink their wives.

DUCHESS
They are as much in fault that know such people
And yet conceal 'em from the whips of justice.
For love's sake give me in your foe betimes,
Before he vex you further. I will order him
To your heart's wishes, load him with disgraces,
That your revenge shall rather pity him
Than wish more weight upon him.

LACTANTIO Say you so, madam?
[*Aside*] Here's a blest hour, that feeds both love and hate;
Then take thy time, brave malice.—Virtuous princess,
The only enemy that my vengeance points to
Lives in Andrugio.

DUCHESS What, the General?

LACTANTIO
That's the man, madam.

DUCHESS Are you serious, sir?

LACTANTIO
As at my prayers.

DUCHESS We meet happily, then,
In both our wishes. He's the only man
My will has had a longing to disgrace,
For divers capital contempts. My memory
Shall call 'em all together now. Nay, sir,
I'll bring his faith in war now into question,
And his late conference with th'enemy.

LACTANTIO
By'r Lady, a shrewd business, and a dangerous.
[*Aside*] Signor, your neck's a-cracking.

DUCHESS Stay, stay, sir.
Take pen and ink.

LACTANTIO Here's both, and paper, madam.

DUCHESS
I'll take him in a fine trap.

LACTANTIO That were exc'llent.

DUCHESS
A letter so writ would abuse him strangely.

LACTANTIO
Good madam, let me understand your mind,
And then take you no care for his abusing;
I serve for nothing else. I can write fast and fair
Most true orthography, and observe my stops.

DUCHESS Stay, stay a while,
You do not know his hand?

LACTANTIO A bastard Roman,
Much like mine own. I could go near it, madam.

DUCHESS
Marry, and shall.

LACTANTIO We were once great together,
And writ Spanish epistles one to another,
To exercise the language.

DUCHESS Did you so?
It shall be a bold letter of temptation
With his name to't, as writ and sent to me.

LACTANTIO
Can be no better, lady. Stick there, madam,
And never seek further.

DUCHESS Begin thus: 'Fair Duchess', say.
We must use flattery if we imitate man;
'Twill ne'er be thought his pen else.

LACTANTIO 'Most fair Duchess'.

DUCHESS
What need you have put in 'most'? Yet since 'tis in,
Let't e'en go on. Few women would find fault with't.
We all love to be best, but seldom mend.
Go on, sir.

LACTANTIO
'Most fair Duchess!' Here's an admiration point.

34 **sports** diversions
35 **challenge** lay claim to
37 **pleasant** merry
38 **owes** owns, has
malice (such as a prisoner might feel)
44 **Having our friendship** Applies to *you*.
servant (as in 'servant of state', referring to Andrugio's position as General)
46 **Of** for
48 **for their lives'** i.e. for the sake of saving their lives
49 **eat** Proverbially used to indicate oppression, destruction, or exploitation.
drink Implies 'sexually consume'.
52 **give me in** deliver to me
betimes soon
53 **order** dispose of, punish
58 **time** opportunity
65 **divers** several (and varying)
capital (*a*) major (*b*) punishable with death
69 **shrewd** mischievous, evil
73 **abuse** disgrace
75 **his abusing** disgracing him
77 **observe my stops** punctuate correctly
79 **bastard** impure
Roman i.e. with round and bold letters (with a glance at Roman Catholicism, taken up in *Spanish*, l. 82)
80 **go near** imitate
81 **Marry, and shall** Proverbial.
great together good friends
92 **mend** improve
94 **admiration point** exclamation mark (playing on the *admiration* in 'Most fair Duchess')

DUCHESS
'The rèport of your vow shall not fear me—'
LACTANTIO 'Fear me:'—two stops at 'fear me'.
DUCHESS
'I know you're but a woman—'
LACTANTIO 'But a woman,'—
A comma at 'woman'.
DUCHESS
'And what a woman is a wise man knows.'
LACTANTIO 'Wise man knows.'—A full prick there.
DUCHESS
'Perhaps my condition may seem blunt to you—'
LACTANTIO
'Blunt to you,'—a comma here again.
DUCHESS
'But no man's love can be more sharp set—'
LACTANTIO 'Sharp set:'
There a colon, for colon is sharp set oftentimes.
DUCHESS 'And I know
Desires in both sexes have skill at that weapon.'
LACTANTIO
'Skill at that weapon.'—A full prick here, at 'weapon'.
DUCHESS
So, that will be enough. Subscribe it thus, now:
'One that vows service
To your affections, Signor such-a-one'.
LACTANTIO
'Signor Andrugio, G.'. That stands for 'General'.
DUCHESS [*aside*]
And you shall stand for goosecap.—Give me that;
Betake you to your business speedily, sir.
We give you full authority from our person,
In right of reputation, truth, and honour,
To take a strong guard, and attach his body;
That done, to bring him presently before us.
Then we know what to do.
LACTANTIO My hate finds wings.
Man's spirit flies swift to all revengeful things. *Exit*
DUCHESS
Why, here's the happiness of my desires,
The means safe, unsuspected, far from thought.
His state is like the world's condition right,
Greedy of gain, either by fraud or stealth;
And whilst one toils, another gets the wealth. *Exit*
Finis Actus Tertius

Incipit Actus Quartus 4.1
Enter Andrugio
ANDRUGIO
Now, Fortune, show thyself the friend of love.
Make her way plain and safe; cast all their eyes
That guard the castle
Into a thicker blindness than thine own,
Darker than ignorance or idolatry,
That in that shape my love may pass unknown,
And by her freedom set my comforts free.
This is the place appointed for our meeting.
Yet comes she not. I am coveteous of her sight.
That Gypsy habit alters her so far
From knowledge that our purpose cannot err.
She might have been here now by this time, largely,
And much to spare. I would not miss her now
In this plight for the loss of a year's joy.
She's ignorant of this house, nor knows she where
Or which way to bestow herself, through fear.
Enter Lactantio, with a guard
LACTANTIO
Close with him, gentlemen.—In the Duchess' name
We do attach your body.
ANDRUGIO How, my body!
What means this rudeness?
LACTANTIO You add to your offences
Calling that rudeness that is fair command,
Immaculate justice, and the Duchess' pleasure.
ANDRUGIO
Signor Lactantio! O, are you the speaker?
LACTANTIO
I am what I am made.
ANDRUGIO Show me my crime.
LACTANTIO
I fear you'll have too many shown you, sir.
ANDRUGIO
The father of untruths possess thy spirit,
As he commands thy tongue. [*Aside*] I defy fear,
But in my love; it only settles there.
LACTANTIO
Bring him along.
ANDRUGIO Let law's severest brow
Bend at my deeds, my innocence shall rise
A shame to thee and all my enemies.

95 **rèport** reputation
96 **two stops** a colon. *Stops* also suggests physical hesitation.
98 **comma** Its shape is suggestive of a limp penis.
100 **full prick** full stop (quibbling on 'erect penis')
101 **condition** behaviour
103 **sharp set** (as with a keen appetite or an erect penis)
104 **colon** (the punctuation mark; but also 'gut', hence 'appetite')
107 **weapon** (quibblingly, 'penis')
112 **stand for goosecap** be reckoned an idiot
116 **attach** arrest
117 **presently** immediately
122 **right** exactly
4.1.4 **Into…own** Fortune was often portrayed as blind.
6 **that shape** that disguise (referring to Gypsies' dark skin and supposed religious *ignorance*)
11 **knowledge** recognition, notice
12 **largely** easily. Not so defined in *OED*; but Aurelia has had *large*, 'generous, ample', time.
14 **plight** engagement (or possibly 'state of mind')
25 **The father of untruths** i.e. the devil
27 **there** (rhymes with *fear*)
28 **Let** even if
29 **Bend** frown, scowl
30 **enemies** (rhymes with *rise*)

LACTANTIO
You're much the happier man.
ANDRUGIO [*aside*] O my hard crosses!—
Grant me the third part of one hour's stay.
LACTANTIO
Sir, not a minute.
ANDRUGIO [*aside*] O, she's lost!
LACTANTIO
Away. *Exeunt*

4.2 *Enter Aurelia, like a Gypsy*

AURELIA
I'm happily escaped. Not one pursues me;
This shape's too cunning for 'em. All the sport was
The porter would needs know his fortune of me
As I passed by him. 'Twas such a plunge to me,
I knew not how to bear myself. At last
I did resolve of somewhat: looked in's hand,
Then shook my head, bade him make much on's eyes,
He would lose his sight clean, long before he dies.
And so away went I; he lost the sight of me quickly. I told him his fortune truer for nothing than some of my complexion that would have cozened him of his money.
This is the place of meeting. Where's this man now
That has took all this care and pains for nothing?
The use of him is at the last cast now.
Shall only bring me to my former face again,
And see me somewhat cleanlier, at his cost,
And then farewell Andrugio. When I am handsome
I'm for another straight. I wonder, troth,
That he would miss me thus. I could have took
Many occasions besides this to have left him.
I'm not in want; he need not give me any.
A woman's will has still enough to spare
To help her friends, an need be. What, not yet?
What will become of me in this shape then?
If I know where to go I'm no dissembler;
And I'll not lose my part in woman so,
For such a trifle to forswear myself.
But comes he not indeed?
Enter Dondolo
DONDOLO
O exc'llent! By this light, here's one of them. I thank my stars. I learnt that phrase in the Half Moon Tavern.—By your leave, good Gypsy, I pray how far off is your company?
AURELIA [*aside*]
O happiness! This is the merry fellow
My love Signor Lactantio takes delight in.
I'll send him away speedily with the news
Of my so strange and fortunate escape,
And he'll provide my safety at an instant.—
My friend, thou serv'st Signor Lactantio.
DONDOLO Who, I serve? Gypsy, I scorn your motion. An if the rest of your company give me no better words, I will hinder 'em the stealing of more pullen than fifty poulterers were ever worth, and prove a heavier enemy to all their pig booties; they shall travel like Jews, that hate swine's flesh, and never get a sow by th' ear all their lifetime. I serve Lactantio? I scorn to serve anybody, I am more Gypsy-minded than so. Though my face look of a Christian colour, if my belly were ripped up you shall find my heart as black as any patch about you. The truth is, I am as arrant a thief as the proudest of your company, I'll except none. I am run away from my master in the state of a fool, and till I be a perfect knave I never mean to return again.
AURELIA [*aside*]
I'm ne'er the happier for this fortune now.
It did but mock me.
DONDOLO Here they come! Here they come!
Enter a company of Gypsies, men and women, with booties of hens and ducks, etc., singing.
Music; song
CAPTAIN
Come, my dainty doxies,
My dells, my dells most dear.
We have neither house nor land,
Yet never want good cheer.
ALL GYPSIES
We never want good cheer.
CAPTAIN
We take no care for candle-rents.
SECOND GYPSY
We lie.

31 **crosses** thwartings, obstacles
4.2.0.1 *like a Gypsy* See Introduction.
2 **shape's** disguise's
4 **plunge** danger, crisis, dilemma
7 **make much on's** make the most of his
8 **clean** completely
10–11 **my complexion** Aurelia has darkened her skin.
14 **at the last cast** Proverbial.
cast throw of dice. Aurelia's use of Andrugio to help her escape is a gambling game in which she is a cheat.
15 **Shall** he shall
16 **cleanlier** more cleanly dressed (perhaps also 'looking more innocent')
18 **straight** at once
21 **any** i.e. any occasion
22 **will** (*a*) wilfulness (*b*) bequest (*c*) lust (with *friends* specifically 'lovers')
still always
26 **part in** (*a*) share in being (*b*) role as
30–1 **Half Moon Tavern** Fitting to learn a phrase about stars there.
39 **motion** suggestion
41 **pullen** hens
44 **get . . . ear** Plays on the proverbial expression 'have a sow by the right ear', i.e. get things right.
47 **a Christian colour** i.e. pale (as most Christians were Europeans). White was associated with both innocence and cowardice.
48 **black** Quibbles on darkness of complexion and inclination to wickedness.
55.1 *Gypsies* See Introduction.
56 **doxies** Gypsy cant for women who, according to alleged custom, might have intercourse with any of the group's men.
57 **dells** young wenches, virgins
59 **want** lack
61 **candle-rents** rents for house-property (so called because they diminished in time as the property deteriorated)

THIRD GYPSY
We snort.

CAPTAIN
We sport in tents;
Then rouse betimes, and steal our dinners.
Our store is never taken
Without pigs, hens, or bacon,
And that's good meat for sinners.
At wakes and fairs we cozen
Poor country folks by dozen.
If one have money, he disburses;
Whilst some tell fortunes, some pick purses.
Rather than be out of use,
We'll steal garters, hose, or shoes,
Boots, or spurs with jingling rowels,
Shirts or napkins, smocks or towels.
Come live with us, come live with us,
All you that love your eases.
He that's a Gypsy
May be drunk or tipsy
At what hour he pleases.

ALL GYPSIES
We laugh, we quaff, we roar, we scuffle,
We cheat, we drab, we filch, we shuffle.

DONDOLO O sweet!
They dèserve to be hanged for ravishing of me.

AURELIA [*aside*]
What will become of me if I seem fearful now,
Or offer sudden flight? Then I betray myself.
I must do neither.

CAPTAIN
Ousabel, camcheateroon,
Pusscatelion, house-drows.

SECOND GYPSY
Rumbos stragadelion
Alla piss-kitch in sows-clows.
O, O!

DONDOLO *Piss-kitch in house-clout*! I shall ne'er keep a good tongue in my head till I get this language.

CAPTAIN
Umbra fill kevolliden, magro-pye.

DONDOLO He calls her maggot o' pie.

AURELIA
I love your language well, but understand it not.

CAPTAIN Ha!

AURELIA
I am but lately turned to your profession,
Yet from my youth I ever loved it dearly,
But never could attain to't. Steal I can;
It was a thing I ever was brought up to.
My father was a miller, and my mother
A tailor's widow.

DONDOLO She's a thief on both sides.

CAPTAIN [*to Aurelia*]
Give me thy hand. Thou art no bastard born;
We have not a more true-bred thief amongst us.

ALL GYPSIES Not any, captain.

DONDOLO I pray take me into some grace amongst you too, for though I claim no goodness from my parents to help me forward into your society, I had two uncles that were both hanged for robberies, if that will serve your turn, and a brave cut-purse to my cousin-german. If kindred will be taken, I am as near a kin to a thief as any of you that had fathers and mothers.

CAPTAIN
What is it thou requirest, noble cousin?

DONDOLO Cousin! Nay, an we be so near a kin already now we are sober, we shall be sworn brothers when we are drunk. The naked truth is, sir, I would be made a Gypsy as fast as you could devise.

CAPTAIN A Gypsy!

DONDOLO Ay, with all the speed you can, sir. The very sight of those stol'n hens eggs me forward horribly.

CAPTAIN Here's dainty ducks, too, boy.

DONDOLO I see 'em but too well. I would they were all rotten-roasted, and stuffed with onions.

CAPTAIN
Lov'st thou the common food of Egypt, onions?

DONDOLO Ay, and garlic too. I have smelt out many a knave by't; but I could never smell mine own breath yet, and that's many a man's fault—he can smell out a knave in another sometimes three yards off, yet, his nose standing so nigh his mouth, he can never smell out himself.

CAPTAIN
A pregnant Gypsy.

ALL GYPSIES A most witty sinner.

62 **snort** snore
63 **rouse betimes** wake up early
64 **taken** found
66 **sinners** i.e. the Gypsies as thieves, and as unconverted heathens (alluding again to pig as an animal not eaten by faithful Jews, here analagous to Christians)
67 **wakes** village festivals
71 **use** (*a*) practise (*b*) employment
81 **drab** mix with harlots, fornicate
83 **ravishing** delighting (quibbling on 'raping', hence *They deserve to be hanged*)
87–8 ***camcheateroon*...*house-drows*** Nonsense with meaningful words embedded in it. These and other such words are modelled on Gypsy cant: words such as *mendelion* (overcoat) *dewse-a-vill* (the country), and *cannikin* (plague).
90 ***piss-kitch in*** *Kitch in* is perhaps *kitchin*, cant for 'child'.
92 ***house-clout*** Dondolo confuses nonsense *house-drows* and the previous *sows-clows*. *House-clout* is 'house-cloth' (for mopping up, presumably of *piss*).
92–3 **keep...head** i.e. speak properly (quibbling on *tongue* as 'language'). From the proverb 'To have a tongue in one's head'.
95 **maggot o' pie** magpie. A variant of the usual form *maggot-pie*.
102–3 **My...sides** Millers and tailors were both proverbially thieves.
104 **bastard born** As implied by Aurelia's account of her parentage.
111 **to** as
cousin-german first cousin
112 **taken** accepted
117 **naked truth** Proverbial.
121 **eggs** urges (with the obvious pun)
124 **rotten-roasted** roasted when gamy
125 **Egypt** i.e. the Gypsies (supposed to originate in Egypt, from which their name derives)
126 **smelt out** Quibbles on the figurative sense (proverbial for 'detected') and the literal.
132 **pregnant** quick-witted, promising

CAPTAIN
Stretch forth thy hand, coz. Art thou fortunate?

DONDOLO How, fortunate? Nay, I cannot tell that myself. Wherefore do I come to you but to learn that? I have sometimes found money in old shoes, but if I had not stol'n more than I have found, I had had but a scurvy thin-cheeked fortune on't.

CAPTAIN [*studying Dondolo's palm*] Here's a fair table.

DONDOLO Ay, so has many a man that has given over housekeeping: a fair table when there's neither cloth nor meat upon't.

CAPTAIN
What a brave line of life's here, look you, Gypsies.

DONDOLO
I have known as brave a line end in a halter.

CAPTAIN [*stealing Dondolo's money*]
But thou art born to precious fortune.

DONDOLO The devil I am!

CAPTAIN *Bette, Bucketto.*

DONDOLO How, to beat bucks?

CAPTAIN *Stealee Bacono.*

DONDOLO O, to steal bacon, that's the better fortune o'th' two indeed.

CAPTAIN
Thou wilt be shortly Captain of the Gypsies.

DONDOLO
I would you'd make me corporal i'th' mean time,
Or standard-bearer to the women's regiment.

CAPTAIN
Much may be done for love.

DONDOLO Nay, here's some money.
I know an office comes not all for love.—
A pox of your lime-twigs, you have't all already.

CAPTAIN
It lies but here in cache for thine own use, boy.

DONDOLO Nay, an't lie there once I shall hardly come to the fing'ring on't in haste. Yet make me an apt scholar, and I care not. Teach me but so much Gypsy to steal as much more from another, and the devil do you good of that.

CAPTAIN
Thou shalt have all thy heart requires.
First, here's a girl for thy desires.
[*He presents Aurelia to Dondolo*]
This doxy fresh, this new-come dell,
Shall lie by thy sweet side and swell.
Get me Gypsies brave and tawny,
With cheek full plump and hip full brawny.
Look you prove industrious dealers
To serve the commonwealth with stealers,
That th'unhoused race of fortune-tellers
May never fail to cheat town-dwellers,
Or to our universal grief
Leave country fairs without a thief.
This is all you have to do,
Save ev'ry hour a filch or two,
Be it money, cloth or pullen.
When the ev'ning's brow looks sullen,
Lose no time, for then 'tis precious.
Let your sleights be fine, facetious;
Which hoping you'll observe, to try thee,
With rusty bacon thus I Gypsify thee.
[*He marks Dondolo's face with rusty bacon*]

DONDOLO
Do you use to do't with bacon?

CAPTAIN Evermore.

DONDOLO By this light, the rats will take me now for some hog's cheek, and eat up my face when I am asleep. I shall have ne'er a bit left by tomorrow morning; and lying open mouthed, as I use to do, I shall look for all the world like a mousetrap baited with bacon.

CAPTAIN
Why, here's a face like thine, so done,
Only grained in by the sun, and this, and these.

DONDOLO Faith, then there's a company of bacon-faces of you, and I am one now to make up the number. We are a kind of conscionable people, and 'twere well thought upon for to steal bacon and black our faces with't: 'tis like one that commits sin, and writes his faults in his forehead.

135–6 **I . . . shoes** Fairies were superstitiously supposed to reward good servants by leaving money in their shoes.
139 **table** the quadrangle formed by principal lines in the hand. The first of a series of palmistry terms. Dondolo takes *table* as the furniture, and the food served on it.
140 **given over** abandoned
141 **housekeeping** hospitality (or 'managing his household')
142 **meat** food
143 **brave** fine
line of life's (*a*) the line of life of the palm (*b*) pedigree, family. Dondolo takes *line* as the hangman's rope.
146 **The devil I am** Proverbial.
148 **beat bucks** dry loads of washing by beating them
153 **corporal** (punning on *corporeal*)
154 **standard-bearer** (with a phallic joke in *standard*)
women's regiment Alludes to John Knox's *The First Blast of the Trumpet against the Monstrous Regiment of Women* (1558). In Knox, *regiment* is 'rule'.
157 **lime-twigs** twigs smeared with birdlime for catching birds; hence the fingers of thieves
158 **cache** hidden storage (punning on *cash*)
162–3 **the . . . that** Proverbial.
167 **swell** (with pregnancy)
168 **Get** beget
171 **the commonwealth** the 'nation' or collective well-being of the Gypsies (also, ironically, of society at large)
175 **thief** theft
181 **facetious** sprightly, polished. Rhymes with *precious*.
182 **try thee** set you apart
183 **With . . . thee** Dekker reports vagabonds tattooing marks by pricking or razing the skin then rubbing in 'burnt paper, piss, and gunpowder' (*O per se O*). See also Introduction.
rusty rancid
184 **use to** regularly
192 **bacon-faces** The usual, figurative, sense on which Dondolo puns is 'fat-faces'.
194 **conscionable** conscientious
195–7 **'tis . . . forehead** Proverbially, one's faults are (or are not) written in one's forehead.

CAPTAIN Wit, whither wilt thou?

DONDOLO Marry, to the next pocket I can come at, and if it be a gentleman's I wish a whole quarter's rent in't. Is this my 'in dock, out nettle'? What's Gypsy for her?

CAPTAIN
Your doxy she.

DONDOLO O, right. Are you my doxy, sirrah?

AURELIA
I'll be thy doxy and thy dell.
With thee I'll live, for thee I'll steal.
From fair to fair, from wake to wake,
I'll ramble still for thy sweet sake.

DONDOLO O dainty fine doxy! She speaks the language as familiarly already as if she'd been begot of a canter. I pray, captain, what's Gypsy for the hind quarter of a woman?

CAPTAIN *Nosario.*

DONDOLO *Nosario.* Why, what's Gypsy for my nose then?

CAPTAIN Why, *arsinio.*

DONDOLO *Arsinio*? Faith, methinks you might have devised a sweeter word for't.

Enter Father and Governor

CAPTAIN
Stop, stop; fresh booties, gentlefolks,
Signoros, cavallario, folkadelio.

SECOND GYPSY *Lagnambrol a tumbrel.*

DONDOLO How? Give me one word amongst you, that I may be doing too.

AURELIA [*aside*]
Yonder they are again. O guiltiness,
Thou putt'st more trembling fear into a maid
Than the first wedding night. Take courage, wench;
Thy face cannot betray thee with a blush now.

FATHER [*to the Governor*]
Which way she took her flight, sir, none can guess,
Or how she scaped.

GOVERNOR Out at some window, certainly.

FATHER
O, 'tis a bold daring baggage!

GOVERNOR See, good fortune, sir,
The Gypsies; they're the cunning'st people living.

FATHER
They cunning? what a confidence have you, sir!
No wise man's faith was ever set in fortunes.

GOVERNOR
You are the wilful'st man against all learning still.
I will be hanged now if I hear not news
Of her amongst this company.

FATHER
You are a gentleman of the flatt'ring'st hopes
That e'er lost woman yet.

GOVERNOR [*to Aurelia*] Come hither, Gypsy.

AURELIA [*aside*]
Luck now, or I'm undone.—What says my master?
Bless me with a silver cross,
And I will tell you all your loss.

GOVERNOR
Lo you there, sir: 'all my loss', at first word too.
There is no cunning in these Gypsies now?

FATHER
Sure I'll hear more of this.

GOVERNOR [*to Aurelia*] Here's silver for you.

AURELIA
Now attend your fortune's story.
You loved a maid.

GOVERNOR Right.

AURELIA She never loved you.
You shall find my words are true.

GOVERNOR
Mass, I am afraid so.

AURELIA You were about
To keep her in, but could not do't.
Alas the while, she would not stay.
The cough o'th' lungs blew her away.
And, which is worse, you'll be so crossed
You'll never find the thing that's lost.
Yet oftentimes your sight will fear her;
She'll be near you, and yet you ne'er the nearer.
Let her go, and be the gladder;
She'd but shame you, if you had her.
Ten counsellors could never school her.
She's so wild, you could not rule her.

GOVERNOR
In troth I am of thy mind, yet I'd fain find her.

AURELIA
Soonest then, when you least mind her;
But if you mean to take her tripping,
Make but haste; she's now a-shipping.

198 **Wit...thou** Proverbial phrase addressed to someone talking too much or foolishly. Dondolo takes it literally.

201 **in dock, out nettle** Originally chanted when a dock-leaf was rubbed on the skin to relieve nettle-sting. Proverbial for changeability, but here suggesting the 'in' and 'out' of both copulation and thieving. *Dock* is prompted by the word Dondolo is searching for, *doxy*.

202 **sirrah** Often jocularly applied to women.

203–6 **I'll...sake** In the manner of a reply to Marlowe's pastoral lyric 'The Passionate Shepherd to his Love', which begins 'Come live with me, and be my love'. There were several imitations and replies.

208 **canter** user of thieves' or Gypsies' cant; vagabond

213 ***arsinio*** Quibbling on *arse*. An appropriate 'Gypsy' word as a recollection of Arsinoe, Queen of Egypt.

215 **sweeter** sweeter-smelling

217 ***cavallario*** (suggesting 'cavalier, gentleman')

218 ***Lagnambrol a tumbrel*** (perhaps disguising *amble* and *tumble*, 'act as decoy')

227 **baggage** strumpet, good-for-nothing

237 **cross** coin (with a cross stamped on it)

245 **Mass** by the Mass
about busy, contriving

248 **cough o'th' lungs** (a trait of old men such as the Governor)

249 **crossed** thwarted

252 **ne'er the nearer** Proverbial.

260 **a-shipping** boarding ship (also, quibblingly, 'loading herself with freight', i.e. stealing)

GOVERNOR
I ever dreamed so much.
FATHER Hie to the quay!
We'll mar your voyage; you shall brook no sea.
Exeunt Father and Governor

CAPTAIN
Cheateroon, high gulleroon.
DONDOLO
Filcheroon, purse-fulleroon.
I can say somewhat too.
ALL GYPSIES Excellent Gypsy, witty rare doxy.
DONDOLO I would not change my dell for a dozen of black bell-wethers.
CAPTAIN
Our wealth swells high, my boys.
DONDOLO
Our wealth swells high, my boys.
CAPTAIN
Let every Gypsy
Dance with his doxy,
And then drink, drink for joy.
DONDOLO
Let every Gypsy
Dance with his doxy,
And then drink, drink for joy.
ALL GYPSIES
And then drink, drink for joy.
Exeunt with a strange wild-fashioned dance to the oboes or cornetts

4.3 *Enter Duchess, Lord Cardinal, and other Lords*
LORD CARDINAL
That which is merely called a will in woman,
I cannot always title it with a virtue.
DUCHESS
O good sir, spare me.
LORD CARDINAL Spare yourself, good madam.
Extremest justice is not so severe
To great offenders as your own forced strictness
To beauty, youth and time. You'll answer for't.
DUCHESS
Sir, settle your own peace; let me make mine.
LORD CARDINAL
But here's a heart must pity it. When it thinks on't,
I find compassion, though the smart be yours.
FIRST LORD
None here but does the like.
SECOND LORD Believe it, madam,
You have much wronged your time.
FIRST LORD Nay, let your grace
But think upon the barrenness of succession.
SECOND LORD
Nay, more, a vow enforced.
DUCHESS What, do you all
Forsake me then, and take part with yon man?
Not one friend have I left? Do they all fight
Under th'inglorious banner of his censure,
Serve under his opinion?
LORD CARDINAL So will all, madam,
Whose judgements can but taste a rightful cause.
I look for more force yet; nay, your own women
Will shortly rise against you when they know
The war to be so just and honourable
As marriage is. You cannot name that woman
Will not come ready armed for such a cause.
Can chastity be any whit impaired
By that which makes it perfect? Answer, madam.
Do you profess constancy, and yet live alone?
How can that hold? You're constant, then, to none.
That's a dead virtue. Goodness must have practice,
Or else it ceases. Then is woman said
To be love-chaste knowing but one man's bed—
A mighty virtue. Beside, fruitfulness
Is part of the salvation of your sex;
And the true use of wedlock's time and space
Is woman's exercise for faith and grace.
DUCHESS
O, what have you done, my lord?
LORD CARDINAL Laid the way plain
To knowledge of yourself and your creation;
Unbound a forcèd vow that was but knit
By the strange jealousy of your dying lord,
Sinful i'th' fast'ning.
DUCHESS All the powers of constancy
Will curse you for this deed.
LORD CARDINAL You speak in pain, madam,
And so I take your words like one in sickness
That rails at his best friend. I know a change
Of disposition has a violent working
In all of us; 'tis fit it should have time
And counsel with itself. May you be fruitful, madam,
In all the blessings of an honoured love.
FIRST LORD
In all your wishes fortunate, [*aside*] and I
The chief of 'em myself.
LORD CARDINAL Peace be at your heart, lady.

261 **I...much** Dreams were supposed to be capable of showing distant or future events.
262 **brook** endure
263 ***gulleroon*** (based on *guller*, which is synonymous with *cheater*)
268 **bell-wethers** Castrated rams that led flocks of sheep, so-called because they carried a bell round their necks.
4.3.9 **smart** affliction
11 **wronged your time** (*a*) misspent your time; or (*b*) wronged your youth
19 **force** military forces
21–2 **so...is** See note to 2.1.76–7.
28–9 **That's...ceases** From the proverb 'Virtue must be practised, not praised'.
31–2 **fruitfulness...sex** (referring to the Protestant doctrine that motherhood was a woman's Christian duty)
34 **exercise** practice of virtue (perhaps also with reference to the sense 'military training')
36 **your creation** i.e. the specific nature and purpose of your being in the world

FIRST LORD And love, say I.

LORD CARDINAL
We'll leave good thoughts now to bring in themselves.
Exeunt Lord Cardinal and Lords

DUCHESS
O, there's no art like a religious cunning!
It carries away all things smooth before it.
How subtlely has his wit dealt with the lords,
To fetch in their persuasions to a business
That stands in need of none, yields of itself,
As most we women do when we seem farthest!
But little thinks the Cardinal he's requited
After the same proportion of deceit
As he sets down for others.
Enter Page
O, here's the pretty boy he preferred to me.
I never saw a meeker, gentler youth
Yet made for man's beginning. How unfit
Was that poor fool to be Lactantio's page!
He would have spoiled him quite, in one year utterly;
There had been no hope of him. Come hither, child,
I have forgot thy name.

PAGE Antonio, madam.

DUCHESS
Antonio! So thou told'st me. I must chide thee:
Why didst thou weep when thou cam'st first to serve
me?

PAGE
At the distrust of mine own merits, madam,
Knowing I was not born to those deserts
To please so great a mistress.

DUCHESS 'Las, poor boy,
That's nothing in thee but thy modest fear,
Which makes amends faster than thou canst err.
It shall be my care to have him well brought up
As a youth apt for good things. Celia!
[*Enter Celia*]

CELIA Madam.

DUCHESS
Has he bestowed his hour today for music?

CELIA
Yes, he has, madam.

DUCHESS How do you find his voice?

CELIA
A pretty, womanish, faint, sprawling voice, madam;
But 'twill grow strong in time if he take care
To keep it, when he has it, from fond exercises.

DUCHESS
Give order to the dancing-schoolmaster
Observe an hour with him.

CELIA It shall be done, lady.
He is well made for dancing, thick i'th' chest, madam.
He will turn long and strongly.

DUCHESS
He shall not be behind a quality
That aptness in him or our cost can purchase;
And see he lose no time.

CELIA I'll take that order, madam.

PAGE [*aside*]
Singing and dancing! 'Las, my case is worse.
I rather need a midwife and a nurse.
Exeunt Celia and Page

DUCHESS
Lactantio, my procurer, not returned yet?
His malice I have fitted with an office
Which he takes pleasure to discharge with rigour.
Enter General [*Andrugio*], *Lactantio, and the guard*
He comes, and with him my heart's conqueror.
My pleasing thraldom's near.

ANDRUGIO [*to Lactantio*] Not know the cause?

LACTANTIO
Yes, you shall soon do that now, to the ruin
Of your neck-part, or some nine years' imprisonment.
You meet with mercy an you scape with that—
Beside your lands all begged and seized upon—
That's admirable favour. Here's the Duchess.

DUCHESS [*to Andrugio*]
O sir, you're welcome.

LACTANTIO [*aside*] Marry, bless me still
From such a welcome.

DUCHESS You are hard to come by,
It seems, sir, by the guilt of your long stay.

ANDRUGIO
My guilt, good madam?

DUCHESS Sure you'd much ado
To take him, had you not? Speak truth, Lactantio,
And leave all favour: were you not in danger?

LACTANTIO
Faith, something near it, madam. He grew head-
strong,
Furious and fierce; but 'tis not my condition
To speak the worst things of mine enemy, madam;
Therein I hold mine honour. But had fury
Burst into all the violent storms that ever

51 **bring in** adduce, introduce
53 **smooth** smoothly
55 **fetch in** (*a*) gain as supporters (*b*) take in, deceive
56 **of itself** of its own accord
57 **most** most of
61 **preferred** introduced, recommended
63 **for man's beginning** to begin to be a man
64 **fool** (here an endearment)
70 **the distrust of** i.e. my mistrust in
71–2 **those deserts | To** such deserving merits as to
81 **when he has it** (referring to the Page's reluctance or inability to sing)
fond foolish
83 **Observe** regularly to spend
85 **strongly** strong
86 **behind** slow to develop
88 **that order** that responsibility, measures for that
89 **case** situation (also 'womb')
92 **fitted** fittingly supplied (perhaps also 'fittingly punished')
95 **cause** accusation
99 **begged** begged for (by the likes of Lactantio himself, as reward for service to the Duchess)
103 **stay** delay in coming
106 **leave** set aside
favour lenient mitigation
108 **condition** character

Played over anger in tempestuous man,
I would have brought him to your grace's presence,
Dead or alive.

DUCHESS [*to Andrugio*]
You would not, sir?

ANDRUGIO
What pride
Of pampered blood has mounted up this puckfist?
If any way, uncounselled of my judgement,
My ignorance has stepped into some error,
Which I could heart'ly curse, and so brought on me
Your great displeasure, let me feel my sin
In the full weight of justice, virtuous madam,
And let it wake me throughly. But, chaste lady,
Out of the bounty of your grace, permit not
This perfumed parcel of curled powdered hair
To cast me in the poor relish of his censure.

DUCHESS
It shall not need, good sir; we are ourself
Of power sufficient to judge you, ne'er doubt it, sir.—
Withdraw, Lactantio; carefully place your guard
I'th' next room.

LACTANTIO [*to Andrugio*]
You'll but fare the worse.
You see your niceness spoils you. You'll go nigh now
To feel your sin indeed.

ANDRUGIO
Hell-mouth be with thee!
Exeunt Lactantio and guard
Was ever malice seen yet to gape wider
For man's misfortunes?

DUCHESS
First, sir, I should think
You could not be so impudent to deny
What your own knowledge proves to you.

ANDRUGIO That were a sin, madam,
More gross than flattery spent upon a villain.

DUCHESS
Your own confession dooms you, sir.

ANDRUGIO
Why, madam?

DUCHESS
Do not you know I made a serious vow
At my lord's death never to marry more?

ANDRUGIO
That's a truth, madam, I'm a witness to.

DUCHESS
Is't so, sir? You'll be taken presently;
This man needs no accuser. Knowing so much,
How durst you then attempt so bold a business
As to solicit me, so strictly settled,
With tempting letters and loose lines of love?

ANDRUGIO
Who, I do't, madam?

DUCHESS
Sure the man will shortly
Deny he lives, although he walk and breathe.

ANDRUGIO
Better destruction snatch me quick from sight
Of human eyes than I should sin so boldly.

DUCHESS
'Twas well I kept it then from rage or fire,
For my truth's credit. Look you, sir.
[*She gives him the letter*]
Read out.
You know the hand and name.

ANDRUGIO
Andrugio!

DUCHESS
An if such things be fit the world shall judge.

ANDRUGIO Madam—

DUCHESS
Pish, that's not so; it begins otherwise.
Pray look again, sir. How you'd slight your knowledge!

ANDRUGIO
By all the reputation I late won—

DUCHESS
Nay, an you dare not read, sir, I am gone.

ANDRUGIO
Read? 'Most fair Duchess!'

DUCHESS
O, have you found it now?
There's a sweet flatt'ring phrase for a beginning.
You thought, belike, that would o'ercome me.

ANDRUGIO I, madam?

DUCHESS Nay, on, sir; you are slothful.

ANDRUGIO
'The rèport of your vow shall not fear me—'

DUCHESS
No? Are you so resolute? 'Tis well for you, sir.

ANDRUGIO
'I know you're but a woman—'

DUCHESS
Well, what then, sir?

ANDRUGIO
'And what a woman is a wise man knows.'

DUCHESS
Let him know what he can, he's glad to get us.

ANDRUGIO
'Perhaps my condition may seem blunt to you—'

DUCHESS
Well; we find no fault with your bluntness.

ANDRUGIO 'But no man's love can be more sharp set—'

DUCHESS Ay, there's good stuff now.

ANDRUGIO 'And I know
Desires in both sexes have skill at that weapon.'

DUCHESS 'Weapon'! You begin like a flatterer, and end like a fencer.
Are these fit lines now to be sent to us?

ANDRUGIO
Now by the honour of a man, his truth, madam,
My name's abused.

DUCHESS
Fie, fie, deny your hand?

112 **over** as an effect of
115 **mounted up** elevated, raised in influence
puckfist literally 'puffball'; hence 'braggart'
123 **parcel** piece, quantity
124 **relish** tinge, small quantity
129 **niceness** fastidiousness
141 **presently** immediately
156 **How . . . knowledge** Illiteracy, though widespread, might not be expected in a general.

I will not deny mine; here, take it freely, sir,
And with it my true constant heart for ever.
I never disgraced man that sought my favour.

ANDRUGIO
What mean you, madam?

DUCHESS
To requite you, sir.
By courtesy I hold my reputation,
And you shall taste it. Sir, in as plain truth
As the old time walked in when love was simple
And knew no art nor guile, I affect you.
My heart has made her choice. I love you, sir,
Above my vow. The frown that met you first
Wore not the livery of anger, sir,
But of deep policy. I made your enemy
The instrument for all; there you may praise me,
And 'twill not be ill given.

ANDRUGIO [*aside*]
Here's a strange language!
The constancy of love bless me from learning on't,
Although ambition would soon teach it others.—
Madam, the service of whole life is yours; but—

DUCHESS
Enough; thou'rt mine for ever.—Within there!

Enter Lactantio and the guard

LACTANTIO
Madam.

DUCHESS
Lay hands upon him; bear him hence;
See he be kept close prisoner in our palace.
[*Aside to Andrugio*] The time's not yet ripe for our nuptial solace.

Exit

LACTANTIO
This you could clear yourself?

ANDRUGIO [*aside*]
There's a voice that wearies me
More than mine own distractions.

LACTANTIO
You are innocent?

ANDRUGIO [*aside*]
I have not a time idle enough from passion
To give this devil an answer. O, she's lost!
Cursed be that love by which a better's crossed!
There my heart's settled. [*Exit with the guard*]

LACTANTIO
How is he disgraced,
And I advanced in love! Faith, he that can
Wish more to his enemy is a spiteful man,
And worthy to be punished. *Exit*

Finis Actus Quartus

❁

Incipit Actus Quintus 5.1

Enter Page, [carrying music-books,] Celia, and Crotchet

CELIA [*to Crotchet*]
Sir, I'm of that opinion. Being kept hard to't,
In troth I think he'll take his prick-song well.

CROTCHET
G sol-re-ut! You guess not right, i'faith.
Mistress, you'll find you're in an error straight.—
Come on, sir, lay the books down. [*To Celia*] You shall see now.

[*Crotchet and Celia talk apart*]

PAGE [*aside*]
Would I'd an honest caudle next my heart!
Let whos' would 'sol fa'; I'd give them my part.
In troth, methinks I have a great longing in me
To bite a piece of the musician's nose off.
But I'll rather lose my longing
Than spoil the poor man's singing.
The very tip will serve my turn, methinks.
If I could get it, that he might well spare;
His nose is of the longest. [*Laying down the books*] O, my back!

CROTCHET [*to Celia*]
You shall hear that.—Rehearse your gamut, boy.

PAGE [*aside*]
Who'd be thus toiled for love, and want the joy?

CROTCHET
Why, when? Begin, sir. I must stay your leisure?

PAGE [*singing*]
Gam ut, A re, B mi, C fa, D sol—

CROTCHET
E la: aloft, above the clouds, my boy.

184 **courtesy** common allowance (as distinct from inherent right)
185 **taste** (*a*) test (*b*) savour, enjoy (because her *reputation* will prove ill-founded)
truth (seen as a garment)
186 **the old time** the distant past (idealized as a golden age without artifice)
187 **affect** love
195 **others** to other persons (or possibly 'otherwise')
200 **solace** comfort (also 'sport, entertainment')
202 **distractions** bewilderment
203 **passion** strong feeling, sorrow
205 **a better's** i.e. the love of someone more powerful is
206 **There** in that
settled certain, resolved
5.1.0.3 *Crotchet* The music-teacher is named after the musical note; *crotchet* is also 'whimsical fancy'.
2 **take** learn (and see next note)
prick-song song, performed from written music (with a quibble on *prick* as 'penis', pertinent as the Page secretly does not have one)
3 **G sol-re-ut** Crotchet's exclamation is, in his manner, a nonce-word based on the musical letter G and its equivalent in the hexachord system. The hexachord scale (ut, re, mi, fa, sol, la), used for teaching singing, could be based on ut as C, F, or G, making G sol, re, or ut.
6 **caudle** restorative warm drink of thin gruel with sweetened and spiced wine or ale
7 **whos'** whoso, whoever
would who would
8–9 **I . . . off** Perhaps an absurd case of food-craving during pregnancy, and/or an allusion to a Court brawl of 1613 in which a piece of nose was reportedly bitten off. The nose is also phallic; only a sex-change could save the Page. Crotchet might wear a pointed stage nose.
10 **lose my longing** Proverbial.
15 **gamut** musical scale. Literally 'gamma' (G) and 'ut' (first note in any hexachord)
16 **want** lack
17 **when** (exclamation of impatience)
stay await
18 **Gam ut** See note to l. 15. The expression is here used to indicate a particular musical note; *Gam* indicating the pitch and *ut* its position in the scale. Similarly with 'A re', etc.

PAGE
It must be a better note than 'E la', sir,
That brings musicians thither; they're too hasty,
The most part of 'em, to take such a journey,
And must needs fall by th' way.

CROTCHET How many clefs be there?

PAGE
One clef, sir.

CROTCHET O intolerable heretic
To voice and music! Do you know but one clef?

PAGE
No more, indeed, one, sir; [*aside*] and at this time
I know too much of that.

CROTCHET How many notes be there?

PAGE
Eight, sir. [*Aside*] I fear me I shall find nine shortly,
To my great shame and sorrow. O, my stomach!

CROTCHET
Will you repeat your notes, then? I must sol-fa you.
Why, when, sir?

PAGE A large, a long, a breve, a semibreve, a minim, a crotchet, a quaver, a semiquaver.

CROTCHET
O, have you found the way?

PAGE Never trust me
If I have not lost my wind with naming of 'em.

CROTCHET
Come, boy, your mind's upon some other thing now.
Set to your song.

PAGE [*aside*] Was ever wench so punished?

CROTCHET
Ut. Come, begin.

PAGE [*singing*] Ut, re, mi, fa, sol, la.

Here the Page and Crotchet sing prick-song

CROTCHET Keep time, you foolish boy!

[*They sing again*]

How like you this, madonna?

CELIA Pretty.
He will do well in time, being kept under.

CROTCHET
I'll make his ears sore and his knuckles ache else.

CELIA
And that's the way to bring a boy to goodness, sir.

CROTCHET
There's many now waxed proper gentlemen
Whom I have nipped i'th' ear, wench, that's my comfort.—
Come, sing me over the last song I taught you.
You're perfect in that, sure. Look you keep time well,

[*He offers to beat the Page*]

Or here I'll notch your faults up. Sol, sol, begin, boy.

Music. Song [*sung by the Page*]

CELIA [*to Crotchet*] So, you've done well, sir.

Enter Cinquepace the dancer

Here comes the dancing-master now; you're discharged.

CINQUEPACE
O, Signor Crotchet, O!

CROTCHET A minim rest,
Two clefs, and a semibreve! In the name
Of Alamire, what's the matter, sir?

CINQUEPACE
The horriblest disaster that ever disgraced
The lofty cunning of a dancer.

CROTCHET B fa, B mi!
Heaven forbid, man!

CINQUEPACE O, oo, the most cruel fortune!

CROTCHET
That semiquaver is no friend to you,
That I must tell you. 'Tis not for a dancer
To put his voice so hard to't; every workman
Must use his own tools, sir. D la-sol, man, dilate
The matter to me.

CINQUEPACE Faith, riding upon my foot-cloth, as I use to do, coming through a crowd, by chance I let fall my fiddle.

CROTCHET D sol-re! Your fiddle, sir?

CINQUEPACE O, that such an instrument should be made to betray a poor gentleman! Nay, which is more lamentable, whose luck should it be to take up this unfortunate

20 **note** Puns on the senses 'characteristic feature', 'way of doing things' (as in *change one's note*,) and 'reputation'; with a probable quibble on the circle and upright stem of a written musical note as suggesting the male sex organs.

21–3 **they're . . . way** The sexual *double entendre* is that musicians are hasty lovers who detumesce (*fall by th' way*) too soon.

23 **clefs** In her answer, the Page puns on *clefts*, in the sense 'vulvas'.

27 **notes** musical notes. But the ninth of l. 28 is (*a*) the cries of the expected baby (*b*) attention, stigma, notoriety.

31 **when** (as in l. 17)

32–3 **A . . . semiquaver** The *notes* seem to retain a phallic connotation. The original sense of *breve* was 'brief'. *Quaver* suggests 'tremble, quiver'.

32 **large** musical note (equivalent to two or three 'longs')
long (equivalent to two or three breves)

34 **found the way** worked it out, learnt it

38.1 ***Here . . . prick-song*** The song is clearly a learner's piece which elaborates on the six-note scale.

40 **madonna** my lady

42 **being** i.e. if he is
under under control

45 **waxed** grown, become

49 **Or . . . up** a threat of corporal punishment

50.1 ***Cinquepace*** Named after the lively dance.

54 **Alamire** (the note A below middle C, being la, mi, or re in the various hexachords; here perhaps punning on *Allah*)

56 **cunning** skill

B fa, B mi B flat: fa on the F hexachord, and B natural, mi on the G hexachord; here used as a nonsense exclamation

58 **That semiquaver** i.e. Cinquepace's 'O, oo' (punning on *quaver* as 'tremulousness')

60–1 **every . . . tools** Varies the proverb 'What is a workman without his tools?'

61 **D la-sol** D as on the F and G hexachords
dilate tell at length

63 **foot-cloth** richly ornamented cloth laid over a horse's back and hanging to the ground (a mark of dignity and state)
use to habitually

65 **fiddle** Cinquepace's foot-cloth implies higher rank than appropriate; in contrast the fiddle might suggest a humble itinerent musician. There is also a phallic innuendo, as in *Roaring Girl* 4.20–4.

66 **sol-re** re: D on the C hexachord

fiddle but a barber's prentice, who cried out presently, according to his nature, 'You trim gentleman on horse-back, you've lost your fiddle, your worship's fiddle!' Seeing me upon my foot-cloth, the mannerly coxcomb could say no less. But away rid I, sir, put my horse to a coranto pace, and left my fiddle behind me.

CROTCHET D la-sol-re!

CINQUEPACE Ay; was't not a strange fortune? An excellent treble viol, by my troth, 'twas my master's when I was but a pumper—that is, a puller-on of gentlemen's pumps.

CROTCHET C, C sol-fa. I knew you then, sir.

CINQUEPACE But I make no question but I shall hear on't shortly at one broker's or another, for I know the barber will scorse it away for some old cithern.

CROTCHET E la-mi, my life for yours on that, sir. I must to my other scholars, my hour calls me away. I leave you to your practise. Fa-sol-la. Fare you well, sir.

CINQUEPACE The lavoltas of a merry heart be with you, sir; and a merry heart makes a good singing man.

Exit [*Crotchet with his books*]

A man may love to hear himself talk when he carries pith in's mouth.—*Metereza* Celia!

CELIA Signor Cinquepace, the welcom'st gentleman alive of a dancer!
This is the youth. He can do little yet;
His prick-song very poorly. He is one
Must have it put into him; somewhat dull, sir.

CINQUEPACE
As you are all at first. You know 'twas long
Ere you could learn your doubles.

CELIA
Ay, that's true, sir,
But I can tickle't now. [*Dancing*] Fa-la-la (*etc.*)
Lo you, how like you me now, sir?

CINQUEPACE Marry, pray for the founder; here he stands. Long may he live to receive quartr'ages, go brave, and pay his mercer wondrous duly—ay, and his jealous laundress, that for the love she bears him starches yellow, poor soul; my own flesh knows I wrong her not. Come, *Metereza*, once more shake your great hips and your little heels, since you begin to fall in of yourself, and dance over the end of the coranto I taught you last night.

CELIA The tune's clear out of my head, sir.

CINQUEPACE A pox of my little usher! How long he stays, too, with the second part of the former fiddle! Come, I'll sol-fa it i'th' mean time. Fa-la-la-la (*etc.*)

[*Celia dances*]

Perfectly excellent. I will make you fit to dance with the best Christian gentleman in Europe, and keep time with him for his heart, ere I give you over.

CELIA Nay, I know I shall do well, sir, and I am somewhat proud on't; but 'twas my mother's fault when she danced with the Duke of Florence.

CINQUEPACE Why, you'll never dance well, while you live, if you be not proud. I know that by myself. I may teach my heart out if you have not the grace to follow me.

CELIA I warrant you for that, sir.

CINQUEPACE
Gentlewomen that are good scholars will come
As near their masters as they can. I have known some
Lie with 'em for their better understanding.
I speak not this to draw you on, forsooth.
Use your pleasure. If you come you're welcome;
You shall see a fine lodging, a dish of comfits,
Music, and sweet linen.

CELIA
And trust me, sir, no woman can wish more in this world,
Unless it be ten pound i'th' chamber window,
Laid ready in good gold against she rises.

CINQUEPACE
Those things are got in a morning, wench, with me.

CELIA
Indeed, I hold the morning the best time of getting.
So says my sister; she's a lawyer's wife, sir,

73 **coxcomb** conceited fool
75 **coranto** a dance with a running step
78 **treble viol** (the equivalent in art music of the violin, which was traditionally associated with popular music)
79 **pumper** (a nonce-word)
81 **C** (punning on Italian *si*, 'yes')
sol-fa C on the F and G hexachords
82 **on't** i.e. of the fiddle
83–4 **the... cithern** Citherns, lute-like instruments, were commonly kept in barbers' shops for customers to play.
84 **scorse** barter
85 **la-mi** mi: third note on the hexachord
my... yours Proverbial.
87 **Fa-sol-la** a musical farewell
88 **lavoltas** high bounds. The lavolta was a vigorous dance with such steps.
90 **A... talk** Proverbial.
91 ***Metereza*** mistress (pseudo-Italian)
96 **put into him** (with the quibble on *prick*)
dull obtuse, slow to learn
98 **doubles** a kind of dancing step; with a quibble on sexual doubling
99 **tickle't** do it ticklingly
101 **pray... founder** Proverbial.
the founder i.e. Cinquepace himself, founder of Celia's dancing skills
102 **quartr'ages** quarterly fees
brave finely dressed
105 **yellow** the colour of jealousy
107 **fall... yourself** begin of your own accord
111 **stays** delays
112 **second part** replacement (using music terminology for the second playing part in a piece of music)
former (*a*) formerly possessed (*b*) aforesaid (*c*) preferred (*d*) taking the first musical part
116 **heart** well-being, strength of spirit. As throughout, dancing has a sexual undertone.
give you over give up on you, quit teaching you
118 **'twas** i.e. pride was
fault mistake, undoing
121 **proud** spirited
121–2 **teach... out** Probably varies the proverbial 'eat one's heart out'.
123 **warrant you for** guarantee you're right about
124–5 **come | As near** (*a*) i.e. learn to dance as much like (*b*) approach as close to (and perhaps (*c*) come to orgasm as near)
128 **Use your pleasure** do what you want (but also suggesting 'use your ability to make pleasure')
133 **against** ready for when
134 **got** (*a*) earned (*b*) begot (the sense Celia takes)
with me (*a*) by me (*b*) from me

And should know what belongs to cases best.
A fitter time for this; I must not talk
Too long of women's matters before boys.
He's very raw. You must take pains with him;
It is the Duchess' mind it should be so.
She loves him well, I tell you. *Exit*

CINQUEPACE How, love him?
He's too little for any woman's love i'th' town, by three handfuls. I wonder of a great woman she's no more wit, i'faith. One of my pitch were somewhat tolerable.

Enter Usher, [*with a viol*]

O, are you come? Who would be thus plagued with a dandiprat usher? How many kicks do you deserve, in conscience?

USHER
Your horse is safe, sir.

CINQUEPACE Now I talked of kicking,
'Twas well remembered. Is not the footcloth stol'n yet?

USHER
More by good hap than any cunning, sir.
Would any gentleman but you get a tailor's son to walk his horse, in this dear time of black velvet?

CINQUEPACE
Troth, thou say'st true. Thy care has got thy pardon.
I'll venture so no more. [*To the Page*] Come, my young scholar,
I am ready for you now.

PAGE [*aside*] Alas, 'twill kill me!
I'm even as full of qualms as heart can bear.
How shall I do to hold up?—Alas, sir,
I can dance nothing but, ill-favouredly,
A strain or two of passemeasures galliard.

CINQUEPACE
Marry, you're forwarder than I conceived you.
A toward stripling. Enter him, Nicholao,
For the fool's bashful, as they are all at first
Till they be once well entered.

USHER Passemeasures, sir?

CINQUEPACE
Ay, sir, I hope you hear me. Mark him now, boy.

[*The Usher plays the viol, entering the Page into a*] *dance*

Ha, well done, exc'llent boys! Dainty fine springals,
The glory of Dancers' Hall—if they had any.
And of all professions they had most need of one,
For room to practise in; yet they have none.
O times! O manners! you have very little.
Why should the leaden-heeled plumber have his hall,
And the light-footed dancer none at all?
But *fortune de la guerre*, things must be.
We're born to teach in back-houses and nooks,
Garrets sometimes, where't rains upon our books.—
Come on, sir, are you ready? First your honour.

PAGE [*aside*]
I'll wish no foe a greater cross upon her.

[*The Page curtsies*]

CINQUEPACE Curtsy, heyday! Run to him, Nicholao! By this light, he will shame me; he makes curtsy like a chamber-maid.

USHER Why, what do you mean, page? Are you mad? Did you ever see a boy begin a dance and make curtsy like a wench before?

PAGE
Troth, I was thinking of another thing,
And quite forgot myself. I pray forgive me, sir.

CINQUEPACE Come, make amends then now with a good leg, and dance it sprightly.

[*The Page makes a leg*]

What a beastly leg has he made there now! 'Twould vex one's heart out. Now begin, boy.

[*He plays a cinquepace on the viol, and the Page dances with close knees*]

O, O, O, O! (*etc.*) Open thy knees, wider, wider, wider, wider! Did you ever see a boy dance clenched up? He needs a pick-lock. Out upon thee for an arrant ass, an arrant ass! I shall lose my credit by thee, a pest'lence on thee! [*To the Usher*] Here, boy, hold the viol; let

137 **belongs** appertains
cases (*a*) legal cases (*b*) women's internal sexual organs (perhaps also (*c*) window-cases, i.e. window-frames)
141 **mind** intention
143–4 **three handfuls** (i.e. three 'hands', four-inch measurements used especially to reckon the height of horses; perhaps also, quibblingly, the male sex organs are 'handfuls')
144 **great** (*a*) eminent, powerful (*b*) large
145 **pitch** (*a*) rank (*b*) height
145.1 *Usher* assistant teacher
147 **dandiprat** contemptibly small person
147–8 **in conscience** rightly, in truth
150 **yet** though
153 **dear time of** time of expensive
155 **venture** risk
158 **hold up** keep going
159 **ill-favouredly** unpleasingly, badly
160 **strain** musical phrase, tune
passemeasures (a slow variety of the galliard dance)
161 **forwarder** more advanced
conceived thought
162 **toward** ready, forward
Enter him i.e. play the music for him to begin dancing
163 **fool's** (a term of endearment)
164 **entered** begun (with a sexual equivocation)
166 **Dainty** excellent, delightful
springals youths
167 **Hall** i.e. guildhall
170 **O times! O manners!** Translates Cicero's lament, 'O tempora, O mores'.
manners (*a*) customs, usages (seen as degenerate) (*b*) good ways (of which the times *have very little*)
171 **Why...hall** The Plumbers were an influential merchant company, though at the time Middleton wrote they merely rented a hall. A new Plumbers' Hall may have been projected.
leaden-heeled i.e. heavy-footed. *Plumber* derives from Latin *plumbum*, 'lead'.
173 ***fortune de la guerre*** fortune of war (French). Here a stoical acceptance of how things work out, as in the proverb 'The chance of war is uncertain'.
things must be Proverbial.
176 **honour** bow (or curtsey)
184 **another thing** something else (quibbling on *thing* as 'sexual organ')
187 **leg** obeissance made by drawing back one leg and bending the other
189 **vex...out** Varies the proverb 'eat one's heart out'.
192 **Out upon thee** exclamation of impatience with her
193 **credit** reputation

me come to him. I shall get more disgrace by this little monkey now than by all the ladies that ever I taught.

[*The Usher plays the viol*]

[*To the Page*] Come on, sir, now; cast thy leg out from thee, lift it up aloft, boy. A pox, his knees are soldered together, they're sewed together. Canst not stride? O, I could eat thee up, I could eat thee up, and begin upon thy hinder quarter, thy hinder quarter. I shall never teach this boy without a screw; his knees must be opened with a vice, or there's no good to be done upon him.—Who taught you to dance, boy?

PAGE
It is but little, sir, that I can do.

CINQUEPACE No; I'll be sworn for you.

PAGE
And that Signor Lactantio taught me, sir.

CINQUEPACE
Signor Lactantio was an arrant coxcomb,
And fit to teach none but white-baker's children
To knead their knees together. You can turn above
ground, boy?

PAGE
Not I, sir. [*Aside*] My turn's rather underground.

CINQUEPACE
We'll see what you can do. I love to try
What's in my scholars, the first hour I teach them.
Show him a close trick now, Nicholao.

[*The Usher makes a leaping turn*]

Ha, dainty stripling! Come, boy.

PAGE 'Las, not I, sir.
I am not for lofty tricks, indeed I am not, sir.

CINQUEPACE
How! Such another word, down goes your hose, boy.

PAGE [*aside*]
Alas, 'tis time for me to do anything then.

[*The Page offers to leap, and falls*]

CINQUEPACE
Heyday, he's down! Is this your lofty trick, boy?

USHER
O master, the boy swoons. He's dead, I fear me.

CINQUEPACE
Dead! I ne'er knew one die with a lofty trick before.—
Up, sirrah, up.

PAGE A midwife, run for a midwife!

CINQUEPACE
A midwife? By this light, the boy's with child!
A miracle! Some woman is the father.
The world's turned upside down. Sure if men breed
Women must get; one never could do both yet.
No marv'l you danced close-knee'd the cinquepace.
Put up my fiddle; here's a stranger case.

Exit Cinquepace, [*supporting the*] *Page*

USHER
That 'tis, I'll swear; 'twill make the Duchess wonder.
I fear me 'twill bring dancing out of request,
And hinder our profession for a time.
Your women that are closely got with child
Will put themselves clean out of exercise,
And will not venture now for fear of meeting
Their shames in a coranto, specially
If they be near their time. Well, in my knowledge,
If that should happen we are sure to lose
Many a good waiting-woman that's now over-shoes.
Alas the while! *Exit*

5.2

Enter the Duchess and Celia

DUCHESS
Thou tell'st me things are enemies to reason.
I cannot get my faith to entertain 'em,
And I hope ne'er shall.

CELIA 'Tis too true, madam.

DUCHESS
I say 'tis false. 'Twere better thou'dst been dumb
Than spoke a truth s'unpleasing; thou shalt get
But little praise by't. He whom we affect
To place his love upon so base a creature?

CELIA
Nay, ugliness itself—you'd say so, madam,
If you but saw her once—a strolling Gypsy.
No Christian that is born a hind could love her;
She's the sun's masterpiece for tawniness;
Yet have I seen Andrugio's arms about her,
Perceived his hollow whisp'rings in her ear,
His joys at meeting her.

DUCHESS What joy could that be?

CELIA
Such, madam, I have seldom seen it equalled.
He kissed her with that greediness of affection
As if her lips had been as red as yours.
I looked still when he would be black in mouth,
Like boys with eating hedgeberries. Nay, more,
madam;
He bribed one of his keepers with ten ducats
To find her out amongst a flight of Gypsies.

198 **soldered** pronounced 'sowdered', anticipating *sowed*
206 **No** (agreeing with the negative of *but little*)
208 **coxcomb** (with a possible pun on *cock* as 'penis')
209 **white-baker's** a baker of white bread's
210 **turn above ground** execute a turn whilst in the air
211 **turn's** movement's **underground** hidden (antedates *OED*'s first citation, 1677)
214 **close** secret
217 **hose** breeches
225 **The . . . down** Proverbial for an inversion of natural order.
228 **case** (*a*) situation (*b*) violin-case (*c*) womb
232 **closely** secretly
235 **coranto** a dance with a running step
238 **over-shoes** Proverbial for 'gone too far' (literally, stepped into water or mud that has gone over the shoes)
5.2.2 **I . . . 'em** i.e. I can't believe them
6 **we** I (the 'royal' plural)
10 **hind** rustic servant
18 **looked . . . be** kept expecting to see him **black in mouth** Proverbial.
19 **hedgeberries** blackberries
20 **ducats** gold or silver coins
21 **flight** roving band (not in *OED*, but on the analogy of a flight of birds)

DUCHESS
I'll have that keeper hanged—and you, for malice.
She cannot be so bad as you report
Whom he so firmly loves. You're false in much,
And I will have you tried. Go fetch her to us.
Exit Celia
He cannot be himself and appear guilty
Of such gross folly; has an eye of judgement,
And that will overlook him. This wench fails
In understanding service. She must home,
Live at her house i'th' country; she decays
In beauty and discretion.
Enter Celia, and Aurelia, [like a Gypsy]
Who hast brought there?

CELIA
This is she, madam.

DUCHESS
Youth and whiteness bless me!
It is not possible. He talked sensibly
Within this hour; this cannot be. How does he?
I fear me my restraint has made him mad.

CELIA
His health is perfect, madam.

DUCHESS
You are perfect
In falsehood still; he's certainly distracted.
Though I'd be loath to foul my words upon her,
She looks so beastly, yet I'll ask the question.
Are you beloved, sweet face, of Andrugio?

AURELIA
Yes, showrly, mistress, he done love me
'Bove all the girls that shine above me.
Full often has he sweetly kissed me,
And wept as often when he missed me;
Swore he was to marry none
But me alone.

DUCHESS
Out on thee, marry thee?—Away with her.
Clear mine eyes of her.—
A curate that has got his place by simony,
Is not half black enough to marry thee. *Exit Aurelia*
Surely the man's far spent, howe'er he carries it.
He's without question mad; but I ne'er knew
Man bear it better before company.
The love of woman wears so thick a blindness
It sees no fault but only man's unkindness;
And that's so gross it may be felt. Here, Celia,
[She gives Celia a token of her warrant]
Take this; with speed command Andrugio to us,
And his guard from him.

CELIA
It shall straight be done, madam.
Exit

DUCHESS
I'll look into his carriage more judiciously
When I next get him. A wrong done to beauty
Is greater than an injury done to love,
And we'll less pardon it; for had it been
A creature whose perfection had outshined me,
It had been honourable judgement in him,
And to my peace a noble satisfaction;
But as it is, 'tis monstrous above folly!
Look he be mad indeed, and throughly gone,
Or he pays dearly for't. 'Tis not
The ordinary madness of a gentleman
That shall excuse him here. He'd better lose
His wits eternally than lose my grace.
So strange is the condition of his fall,
He's safe in nothing but in loss of all.
Enter Andrugio [and Celia]
He comes. Now by the fruits of all my hopes,
A man that has his wits cannot look better.
It likes me well enough. There's life in's eye,
And civil health in's cheek; he stands with judgement,
And bears his body well. What ails this man?
Sure I durst venture him 'mongst a thousand ladies,
Let 'em shoot all their scoffs—which makes none laugh
But their own waiting-women, and they dare do no otherwise.
Come nearer, sir. I pray keep further off,
Now I remember you.

ANDRUGIO
What new trick's in this now?

DUCHESS
How long have you been mad, sir?

ANDRUGIO
Mad? A great time, lady:
Since I first knew I should not sin, yet sinned;
That's now some thirty years, by'r Lady, upwards.

DUCHESS [*aside*]
This man speaks reason wondrous feelingly,
Enough to teach the rudest soul good manners.—
You cannot be excused with lightness now,
Or frantic fits; you're able to instruct, sir,
And be a light to men. If you have errors
They be not ignorant in you, but wilful,
And in that state I seize on 'em. Did I
Bring thee acquainted lately with my heart?
And when thou thought'st a storm of anger took thee,
It in a moment cleared up all to love,
To the abusing of thy spiteful enemy

25 **tried** tested
28 **overlook** watch over
33 **sensibly** rationally
35 **fear me** am afraid
36 **perfect** unimpaired (but in the Duchess's reply, 'expert')
41 **showrly** (mock-rustic pronunciation of *surely*)
done does (rustic)
49 **A . . . simony** i.e. a man both black in his attire and morally 'black' or sinful
51 **spent** ruined (mentally)
carries it behaves
59 **carriage** behaviour
67 **Look he** he had better
throughly thoroughly
76 **likes** pleases
77 **civil** well-governed
78 **What ails this man?** Implies that surely nothing ails him.
87 **feelingly** (*a*) understandingly (*b*) effectively in provoking feelings
89 **lightness** lightheadedness
97 **abusing** deception, maltreatment, disgrace

That sought to fix his malice upon thee;
And couldst thou so requite me?

ANDRUGIO
How, good madam?

DUCHESS
To wrong all worth in man, to deal so basely
Upon contempt itself, disdain, and loathsomeness—
A thing whose face through ugliness frights children,
A straggling Gypsy!

ANDRUGIO
See how you may err, madam,
Through wrongful information. By my hopes
Of truth and mercy, there is no such love
Bestowed upon a creature so unworthy.

DUCHESS
No? Then you cannot fly me.—Fetch her back;
[*Exit Celia*]
And though the sight of her displease mine eye
Worse than th'offensiv'st object earth and nature
Can present to us, yet, for truth's probation,
We will endure't contentfully.
Enter Celia, and Aurelia, [like herself]
What now,
Art thou returned without her?

ANDRUGIO
No, madam. This is she my peace dwells in.
If here be either baseness of descent,
Rudeness of manners, or deformity
In face or fashion, I have lost, I'll yield it.
Tax me severely, madam.

DUCHESS [*to Celia*]
How thou stand'st,
As dumb as the salt-pillar! Where's this Gypsy?
[*Celia brings Aurelia forward, and shows the Gypsy clothes Aurelia was wearing*]
What, no! I cannot blame thee then for silence.
Now I'm confounded too, and take part with thee.

AURELIA [*kneeling*]
Your pardon and your pity, virtuous madam.
Cruel restraint, joined with the power of love,
Taught me that art; in that disguise I scaped
The hardness of my fortunes. You that see
What love's force is, good madam, pity me.

ANDRUGIO [*kneeling*]
Your grace has ever been the friend of truth;
And here 'tis set before you.

DUCHESS
I confess
I have no wrong at all; she's younger, fairer.
He has not now dishonoured me in choice.
I much commend his noble care and judgement.
'Twas a just cross, led in by a temptation,
For offering but to part from my dear vow,
And I'll embrace it cheerfully.—Rise both.
The joys of faithful marriage bless your souls.
I will not part you.

ANDRUGIO [*rising*]
Virtue's crown be yours, madam.
Enter Lactantio

AURELIA [*aside*]
O, there appears the life of all my wishes.—
Is your grace pleased, out of your bounteous goodness
To a poor virgin's comforts, I shall freely
Enjoy whom my heart loves?

DUCHESS
Our word is past,
Enjoy without disturbance.

AURELIA [*rising*]
There, Lactantio.
Spread thy arms open wide, to welcome her
That has wrought all this means to rest in thee.

ANDRUGIO Death of my joys! How's this?

LACTANTIO
Prithee away, fond fool. Hast no shame in thee?
Thou'rt bold and ignorant, whate'er thou art.

AURELIA
Whate'er I am? Do not you know me then?

LACTANTIO
Yes, for some waiting-vessel; but the times
Are changed with me, if you'd the grace to know 'em.
I looked for more respect; I am not spoke withal
After this rate, I tell you. Learn hereafter
To know what belongs to me. You shall see
All the court teach you shortly. Farewell, Manners.

DUCHESS [*aside*]
I'll mark the event of this.
[*She whispers to Celia. Exit Celia*]

AURELIA [*aside*]
I've undone myself
Two ways at once: lost a great deal of time,
And now I am like to lose more. O my fortune!
I was nineteen yesterday, and partly vowed
To have a child by twenty, if not twain.
To see how maids are crossed! But I'm plagued justly;
And she that makes a fool of her first love,
Let her ne'er look to prosper. [*To Andrugio*] Sir.

ANDRUGIO
O falsehood!

AURELIA
Have you forgiveness in you? There's more hope of me
Than of a maid that never yet offended.

ANDRUGIO
Make me your property?

AURELIA
I'll promise you

100–1 **deal . . . Upon** have dealings . . . with
103 **straggling** roving
107 **fly me** i.e. prevent me from finding you guilty
110 **probation** proof
117 **Tax** censure
118 **As . . . salt-pillar** alluding to the transformation of Lot's wife to a pillar of salt when she looked back on the destruction of Sodom and Gomorrah, Genesis 19:26
120 **take part with thee** i.e. join you in silence (also, perhaps, 'take sides with you')
131 **cross** prevention, thwarting
147 **waiting-vessel** (dismissive for 'attendant'; *vessel* is also a contemptuous term for women, seen as receptacles)
147–8 **the . . . me** From the proverb 'Times change, and we with them'.
150 **After** according to, in
rate (*a*) style (*b*) estimation, value
151 **belongs** appertains
152 **Manners** (as Lactantio sarcastically calls Aurelia)
153 **mark** If Celia leaves here, *mark* is 'put my mark on'; otherwise it is 'observe'.
event outcome
163 **property** i.e. object to be disposed with at will, instrument

I'll never make you worse; and, sir, you know
There are worse things for women to make men.
But by my hope of children, and all lawful,
I'll be as true for ever to your bed
As she in thought or deed that never erred.

ANDRUGIO
I'll once believe a woman, be it but to strengthen
Weak faith in other men. I have a love
That covers all thy faults.
Enter Lord Cardinal and the Lords

LORD CARDINAL [*aside to Lactantio*]
Nephew, prepare thyself
With meekness and thanksgiving to receive
Thy reverend fortune. Amongst all the lords,
Her close affection now makes choice of thee.

LACTANTIO [*aside*]
Alas, I'm not to learn to know that now.
Where could she make choice here if I were missing?
'Twould trouble the whole state, and puzzle 'em all,
To find out such another.

LORD CARDINAL
'Tis high time, madam,
If your grace please, to make election now.
Behold, they are all assembled.

DUCHESS
What election?
You speak things strange to me, sir.

LORD CARDINAL
How, good madam?

DUCHESS
Give me your meaning plainly, like a father.
You are too religious, sir, to deal in riddles.

LORD CARDINAL
Is there a plainer way than leads to marriage,
madam,
And the man set before you?

DUCHESS
O blasphemy
To sanctimonious faith! Comes it from you, sir?—
An ill example. Know you what you speak,
Or who you are? Is not my vow in place?
How dare you be so bold, sir! Say a woman
Were tempt with a temptation, must you presently
Take all th'advantage on't?

LORD CARDINAL
Is this in earnest, madam?

DUCHESS
Heaven pardon you if you do not think so, sir;
You've much to answer for. But I will leave you;
Return I humbly now from whence I fell.
All you blest powers that register the vows
Of virgins and chaste matrons, look on me
With eyes of mercy; seal forgiveness to me
By signs of inward peace; and, to be surer
That I will never fail your good hopes of me,
I bind myself more strictly. All my riches
I'll speedily commend to holy uses,
This temple unto some religious sanctuary,
Where all my time to come I will allow
For fruitful thoughts; so knit I up my vow.

LACTANTIO
This 'tis to hawk at eagles. Pox of pride;
It lays a man i'th' mire still, like a jade
That has too many tricks and ne'er a good one.
I must gape high! I'm in a sweet case now.
I was sure of one, and now I have lost her too.

DUCHESS [*to the Lord Cardinal*]
I know, my lord, all that great studious care
Is for your kinsman; he's provided for
According to his merits.

LORD CARDINAL
How's that, good madam?

DUCHESS
Upon the firmness of my faith, it's true, sir.
[*Enter Celia, and the former Page, like herself, with an infant*]
See, here's the gentlewoman; the match was made
Near forty weeks ago. He knows the time, sir,
Better than I can tell him, and the poor gentlewoman
Better than he. But being religious, sir, and fearing
you,
He durst not own her for his wife till now,
Only contracted with her in man's apparel,
For the more modesty, because he was bashful,
And never could endure the sight of woman
For fear that you should see her. This was he
Chose for my love; this page preferred to me.

LACTANTIO
I'm paid with mine own money.

LORD CARDINAL
Dare hypocrisy,
For fear of vengeance, sit so close to virtue?
Steal'st thou a holy vestment from religion,
To clothe forbidden lust with? Th'open villain
Goes before thee to mercy, and his penitency
Is blest with a more sweet and quick return.
I utterly disclaim all blood in thee.
I'll sooner make a parricide my heir
Than such a monster.—O forgive me, madam!
Th'apprehension of the wrong to you
Has a sin's weight at it. I forget all charity
When I but think upon him.

DUCHESS
Nay, my lord,
At our request, since we are pleased to pardon,
And send remission to all former errors

165 **worse things** (such as cuckolds)
174 **close** (*a*) secret (*b*) emotionally close
175 **I'm not to** I don't need to
177 **puzzle** confound
185 **And the man** the man being
190 **tempt** tempted
presently immediately
202 **This temple** i.e. the Duchess's body
205 **pride** quibbling on the sense 'sexual arousal'
206 **It ... mire** From the proverb 'To lie in the mire'.
jade contemptuous term for a horse; hence also 'worn-out trollop'
207 **tricks** quibbling on the sense 'sexual devices'
208 **I must** ironic: 'just like me to have to'
high upwards (at someone of 'high' rank)
sweet case fine situation
219 **contracted with** betrothed
223 **Chose** chosen
preferred he preferred
224 **I'm ... money** Proverbial.
229 **quick** (*a*) fast (*b*) living, fruitful

Which conscionable justice now sets right,
From you we expect patience. He's had punishment
Enough in his false hopes; trust me he has, sir;
They have requited his dissembling largely.
And to erect your falling goodness to him,
We'll begin first ourself. Ten thousand ducats
The gentlewoman shall bring out of our treasure
To make her dowry.

LORD CARDINAL None has the true way
Of overcoming anger with meek virtue
Like your compassionate grace.

LACTANTIO Curse of this fortune!
This 'tis to meddle with taking stuff, whose belly cannot be confined in a waistband. [*To the Page*] Pray, what have you done with the breeches? We shall have need of 'em shortly. An we get children so fast they are too good to be cast away. My son and heir need not scorn to wear what his mother has left off. I had my fortune told me by a Gypsy seven years ago; she said then I should be the spoil of many a maid, and at seven years' end marry a quean for my labour; which falls out wicked and true.

DUCHESS [*to the Lord Cardinal*]
We all have faults; look not so much on his.
Who lives i'th' world that never did amiss?—
For you, Aurelia, I commend your choice.
You've one after our heart. And though your father
Be not in presence, we'll assure his voice.
Doubt not his liking, his o'erjoying rather.
[*To Lactantio*] You, sir, embrace your own; 'tis your full due.
No page serves me more that once dwells with you.
O, they that search out man's intents shall find
There's more dissemblers than of womenkind.

Exeunt

Finis

THE PARTS

Men

LORD CARDINAL (471 lines): Crotchet *or* Cinquepace
LACTANTIO (344 lines): Servant, a Gypsy; Crotchet *or* Cinquepace
DONDOLO (271 lines): Andrugio, Servant; Crotchet *or* Cinquepace
ANDRUGIO (148 lines): Servant; Donolo or a Gypsy; Crotchet *or* Cinquepace
CINQUEPACE (5.1 only; 123 lines): any but Crotchet
CAPTAIN of Gypsies (4.2 only; 77 lines): any but Dondolo, Father, Governor, Cardinal, Lords
Two or three LORDS (56 lines): Father or Governor; Crotchet *or* Cinquepace
CROTCHET (5.1 only; 40 lines): any but Cinquepace
FATHER (38 lines): A Lord or Servant; Crotchet *or* Cinquepace
GOVERNOR (26 lines): A Lord or Servant; Crotchet *or* Cinquepace
Two other GYPSIES (4.2 only; 13 lines): any but Dondolo, Father, Governor, Cardinal, Lords
SERVANT (1.2 only; 1 line): any but Cardinal, Lords

Boys

DUCHESS (495 lines): None
AURELIA (211 lines): Cupid, Usher
PAGE (93 lines): Cupid
CELIA (74 lines): None
USHER (5.1 only; 20 lines): any but Page, Duchess, Celia
CUPID (1.3 only; 11 lines): any but Duchess, Celia

Most crowded scene: 5.2 (10 characters)

244 **treasure** treasury
248 **taking** kindling, taking with child (also 'alluring, captivating')
253 **left off** stopped wearing
256 **quean** prostitute. The Gypsy's prophecy equivocated between *quean* and *queen*.
256–7 **wicked and true** i.e. true in its bad interpretation
258 **We all have faults** Proverbial.
261 **after our heart** in accordance with our affection

THE WIDOW

Text edited and introduced by Gary Taylor, annotated by Michael Warren and Gary Taylor

'To make you gay', the prologue says of this play, 'Is all th'ambition 't has'. The title-page of the first edition, printed in 1652, describes the text as 'A COMEDY', and our responses to the particulars of *The Widow* are inevitably entangled in our attitudes to Comedy generally. But in limiting the play's artistic ambition to merrymaking, its prologue implicitly rejects the classical critical standard most famously articulated by Horace: *Omne tulit punctum, qui miscuit utile dulci*—that is (as Ben Jonson translated it), the best poems offer readers 'Sweet mixed with sour', combining 'doctrine and delight'. From Horace to Freud, from formalism to feminism, critics of comedy have sought to find in it a significance beyond pleasure.

Pleasure *The Widow* has supplied. The play was, its title-page asserts, '*acted with great applause*' by the King's Men at the Blackfriars Theatre; apparently revived in the 1630s, it was the first of Middleton's plays separately published, with his name under the title, after the closing of the theatres; the actor Alexander Gough, who had probably played one of the women's parts in the 1630s, in his preface favourably compared 'this lively piece' to the great dead works of antiquity; after the Restoration, it was often revived, attracting the attendance of Samuel Pepys, John Evelyn, and Charles II; the popular song at 3.1.22–37 was recycled in at least two other plays. In the eighteenth century *The Widow* was selected for Robert Dodsley's first anthology of *Old Plays*, and remained one of the few works of Middleton regularly reprinted and available before Dyce's edition of 1840; late in the nineteenth century, Swinburne celebrated the 'fluency and facility' of 'this brilliant play', and Havelock Ellis included it among the ten plays selected for the popular Mermaid edition—which did not find room for *Michaelmas Term, A Mad World, My Masters*, or *A Game at Chess*.

In the twentieth century, by contrast, *The Widow* became almost invisible—never anthologized; often ignored even in books devoted to Middleton; rarely mentioned in critical essays, and then only in the indifferent haste of surveys of some topic, like Paula Berggren's of cross-dressing.

This invisibility belongs, in part, to the more general neglect of what Inga-Stina Ewbank calls 'The Middle of Middleton'. But *The Widow* has also suffered, more particularly, from the expectation that Middleton's comedies should always be city comedies. Within the literary canon, 'minor' writers supplement 'major' writers by providing specimens of a particular tone or manner: 'Fletcherian tragicomedy', 'Lylyean court comedy', 'Jonsonian humours comedy'. Likewise, Middleton's career has been falsely divided into two tones—early 'city comedy' and late 'Jacobean tragedy'—which define the protocols for reading him; critics have not known how to read texts which do not fit those protocols.

The Widow is not a city comedy, though its sources gave it every encouragement to become one. In the second tale of the second day of Boccaccio's *Decameron*, a man is robbed and stripped by his travelling companions; like Ansaldo, he walks to the home of a 'beautiful and comely' 'young lady', who is immediately attracted to him; within twenty-four hours, the man is married. But in Boccaccio the victim is 'a merchant', travelling with other 'merchants like himself', and the young lady lives in a walled town. Middleton's Ansaldo, by contrast, is no merchant, and the house which receives him is located in the woods. In the third tale of the third day, a gentlewoman, like Philippa, communicates her erotic interest in a handsome young man by complaining to a third party of the gentleman's (entirely fictitious) unwelcome advances; the third party rebukes the gentleman, who in turn correctly interprets the woman's indirect instructions. But in Boccaccio this story takes place 'in our own city (more full of craft and deceit, than love or faithful dealing)', and the gentlewoman, though 'descended of very great parentage', is 'married to an artisan, a clothier or draper', whom she disdained 'because he was a tradesman'. By contrast, Middleton's Philippa is married to a country Justice of the Peace, urban class rivalries play no part in her attempted liaison with Francisco, and the whole play takes place, not in 'our own city' but on the Adriatic coast near Istria.

As the thief Latrocinio says, 'Hang him that has but one way to his trade!' (4.2.29). Middleton knew more than one way to write comedy, and here he deliberately avoided the sharp tonality and relentless speed of a young man's city comedy; here, instead, a mature virtuoso is using the entire keyboard. Ellis described *The Widow* as a play 'always bright and alert, with no jarring discord to spoil its joyous humanity', written in Middleton's 'most delightful style of romantic comedy'; its 'unalloyed cheerfulness' gives us a 'glimpse of a large and sunny world'.

If that does not sound much like the Middleton of modern criticism, it is because modern criticism has tended to celebrate the satire but ignore the romance in Middleton's work (Sousa). Ellis goes to the opposite extreme; but he does point to something pertinent about the play's tone. In Boccaccio, the robbed merchant is abandoned by his own servant; the woman who welcomes him is a nobleman's kept mistress; the gentlewoman in the other tale adulterously satisfies, in the end, her 'sensual appetite'. In

The Widow, by contrast, no infidelity is consummated, no woman is reduced to a sexual property, no servant betrays a master. No one is married off to a whore, or stripped of all their possessions, or taken away to be whipped. Even the *commedia dell'arte* thieves are full of music, pity, and wit. The worst wished on anyone in this play is to 'be stoned to death with pipkins' (5.1.137).

Likewise, the character for whom the play is named differs strikingly from the standard widows of city comedy and misogynist satire. As Jennifer Panek observes, Middleton was more interested in widows than any playwright of his time, and he 'offers an alternative to the common and degrading belief than a woman's passion controlled her reason.' Unlike her namesake in John Dickenson's tale *Fair Valeria of London* (1598), Middleton's Valeria does not keep a stable of young male whores to service her lust. She does not remarry with indecent haste; she has no children from her first marriage, to suffer in her second; the estate she has inherited seems not to be the fruit of immoral profiteering. Like Moll in *The Roaring Girl*, Valeria is a smart, capable, experienced woman who knows her own mind, is determined not to be dominated, and can see through the men around her. But unlike Moll, Valeria has a plausible and honest economic basis for her independence—the only basis for real independence most women could have hoped for. In early modern London, as Vivien Brodsky has demonstrated, 'more than half of all marriages lasted ten years or less'. Middleton's own grandmother, mother, sister, and wife all outlived a husband. Most widows were poor, but one like Valeria—a 'rich widow', and relatively young—was uniquely positioned to control her own destiny.

Also unlike Moll, Valeria—like most women, and even most widows, in Middleton's time and ours—wants a mate. Because this is a comedy, she gets the mate she wants. Ricardo is, physically and theatrically, the most attractive man around. Admittedly, from the outset he is interested in Valeria's wealth. When 'a young gentleman' is 'spent', he naturally seeks 'to have a rich widow set him up again' (1.2.2–4). Middleton announces from the outset the conventionality of the Valeria/Ricardo plot; indeed, the very title would have promised Jacobean playgoers a story in which a prodigal young man courts and conquers a well-endowed widow. Elizabeth Hanson argues that the popularity of this plot reflected a changing attitude toward the acquisition of wealth, which was often allegorized as a woman: *regina Pecunia*, Lady Money, Lady Treasure, Lady Lucre, Middleton's own Lady Goldenfleece, the rich widow in *No Wit*. Such plays hover between allegory and realism, and their male protagonists embody capitalism's new ethic of acquisition, what Hanson calls 'a desire for money that could be neither satisfied by nor subordinated to sanctioned social roles'. Ricardo is a man on the make, a distant but still recognizable ancestor of the Horatio Alger hero, Ragged Dick, who starts the play with nothing and ends with everything. What gets Ricardo everything is sheer determination, masculine energy, opportunism, 'wit'. In this new psychological model, which created and/or reflected the new economy, desire for money and desire for a woman were really the same thing. Desire is desire is desire. Ricardo leaves us in no doubt of his physical desire for the 'sweet' widow, and her cunning resistance only captivates him the more: 'I have a greater mind to her now than e'er I had' (2.2.46–7). In the play's final speech he declares 'I'm as hungry of my widow | As you can be upon your maid', just before he exits to enjoy 'My widow and my meat'.

Money and meat are not very romantic accessories for a mate. But Middleton insists that romance can only be real, that comedy can only be convincing, by remaining practical. Raphael Seligmann has called attention to the fact that Capo d'Istria sits at the very edge, then as now, of the Western European world, geographically close to the setting of *Twelfth Night*—but imaginatively we are a long way from Shakespeare's Illyria. Lyly, Shakespeare, and Fletcher use the distant geography of romance to legitimate a marvellous suspension of the rules of daily life: comedy is made possible by the problem-dissolving powers of identical twins, gods and goddesses, magic potions, and resurrections from the dead. Middleton instead translates the proper names of romance back into the vernacular common places of an 'all here' (5.1.453) in a lucid 'now at this present' (3.2.108).

Consequently, the play is consistently unsentimental about the economic and sexual realities of marriage. For the First Suitor, 'Marrying for love' is a recipe for filling the commonwealth with 'beggars'; for the Second, it guarantees a life of violent misery ('He'll give her a black eye within these three days, | Beat half her teeth out by Allhallowtide'); Valeria herself acknowledges that 'Want on both sides makes all affection cold' (5.1.340–63). If lack of funds can cripple a marriage, so can lack of fun. Valeria's sister-in-law Philippa is so anxious to commit adultery precisely because her eighty-year-old husband cannot satisfy her physically.

Evelyn described *The Widow* as 'a lewd play'. Certainly, its characters are lewd enough. Everyone's language is frank and physical, and Ricardo claims to have had a thousand women—half of them other men's wives. Francisco begins the action trying to commit adultery with a woman married to a man of his own father's generation, who was his father's good friend; the appeal of this illicit union is, in part, incestuous, and its consummation is prevented, at the last moment, when Francisco thinks he sees the ghost of his dead father blocking his entrance to Philippa's gate. Philippa herself, having solicited Francisco unsuccessfully, immediately transfers her erotic attention to Ansaldo. She first sees him dressed in her husband's clothes, and finds the conjunction particularly arousing: 'here's my husband young again!' (3.3.69). Later, she disguises Ansaldo as a woman, and fantasizes about having him, dressed as her waiting woman, 'lay night by night with her in way of comfort' (5.1.88–93). The

Second Suitor, too old for sex, now enjoys instead 'no other venery but vexation' (4.1.25).

In all these conjugations, desire is inscribed in a grammar of substitution and transgression. Ricardo, trying to teach his friend Francisco how to seduce a woman, gives Francisco the woman's part; Ricardo then becomes so engrossed in the game of overcoming Francisco's feminine resistance that, in the end, he assaults her/him physically, using kisses 'to stop all your mouths', and has to be pulled off by a third man, who wakes him from his 'fairest dream' (1.2.115–48). Desire is aroused, not by biological genitalia, but by the mere performance of gender. Gender is theatre. Hence, when Ansaldo is dressed as a woman, he not only attracts Philippa, who imagines having sex with a man dressed in her husband's or her woman's clothes; he also attracts Francisco, who believes he is a real woman. Philippa finds this vengefully amusing, and urges Ansaldo to play the woman's part for all it's worth, in order to maximize the embarrassment of Francisco: the joke culminates in 'one man married to another!' (5.1.409).

But Middleton, finally, takes the joke even further than Philippa intended. Ansaldo, it turns out, actually *is* a woman, Marcia—a discovery apparently meant to be as surprising to the audience as to Philippa and Violetta. Middleton was not the first dramatist to conceal so long a character's gender from the audience: Ben Jonson had done so, at least for Latinless spectators, in *Epicoene*. But in Jonson that last-minute discovery is the result of a cruel practical joke, a discovery which dissolves a marriage and strips away theatrical pretence, showing us that a supposedly 'female' character is actually being played by a boy actor. In Middleton's play, Jonson's world is turned upside down: the discovery *undoes* a cruel practical joke, it *enables* a marriage, and it *insists* upon pretence, by revealing that a supposedly male character is 'actually' female. Of course, since even 'actual' females were played by male actors, Middleton's conclusion remains ambiguous, as Jonson's does not; spectators can leave a performance still arguing and asking about Ansaldo's 'real' gender. The play can leave us feeling that, like Ricardo in his 'dream', we cannot really tell the difference between men and women—that, indeed, there may be no essential difference, beyond performance. 'I can do that', Ansaldo declares (5.1.249), realizing and relishing his own potential: a deceptively simple but deliciously comic moment, as the 2001 Georgia Shakespeare Festival public reading of the play demonstrated.

Middleton's play celebrates what Jonson's play fears, the collapse of sexual distinction in a merry-go-round of substitutions. *The Widow* tears down the walls of gender, showing that those walls are made, mostly, of mere clothes, or of actions which can be put on and off as easily as clothes. We are initiated, here, into a world of absolute play. Francisco begins the action by pretending to want a warrant; Philippa pretends to receive a letter and pretends to be outraged by it; Ricardo turns a pretended exchange of vows into a binding contract. The pretences and disguises of lovers and suitors are doubled by those of the thieves. Indeed, the thieves may have been doubled by the same players who played the male romantic leads. 'How round the world goes', the robbers/lovers/players sing, 'And everything that's in it' (3.1.114–15).

This playground of lawless egalitarian circulation is, of course, the world of festival, the font of Rabelaisian comedy (according to Mikhail Bakhtin) and of Shakespearean comedy too (according to C. L. Barber and François Laroque). Its prologue calls *The Widow* 'a sport only for Christmas', and whether or not the play was written for performance at Christmas, the comparison itself reveals something about the tone of the play. The twelve days of Christmas were celebrated with songs (like the five in *The Widow*, and the four sung between its acts), feasts (like that which waits off-stage in the final scene), and plays (like *The Widow* itself). The longest and merriest of the holidays combined birth and death, looking backward at the grotesque old year (Brandino, Martino, the two suitors) and forward to the erotic young year (Francisco, Ricardo, Ansaldo, Violetta). And in the most outrageous of transgressive substitutions, it exalted a Lord of Misrule or Christmas Prince, replacing reverence with ridicule. At a time when Justices of the Peace were 'the most influential class of men in England' (G. M. Trevelyan) and 'rulers of the countryside' (J. H. Gleason), Brandino is a venerable wealthy JP, but he has his pocket picked, his eyes washed with urine, his robes of office mocked, stolen, and cut up into a hundred pieces; his opinions oscillate with all the dignified integrity of a teetertotter; he unwittingly delivers instructions for his own cuckolding. Martino, his loyal pet clerk, begins the play dreaming of buttocks, and is later farcically relieved of teeth and purse simultaneously.

Of course, Christmas takes place in a winter world, and so does *The Widow*, both literally (1.1.173, etc.) and figuratively. There are 'few portmanteaus stirring' (4.2.22); business, of every kind, is at an ebb. There is real physical pain here: 'I that feel it think it somewhat', Brandino insists (4.2.191). Real emotional pain too: Violetta reminds Philippa that 'I have grief enough of mine own to tend, mistress' (5.1.40). The Second Suitor viciously compounds complacency ('I have enough') and capriciousness ('and I will have my humour'). Philippa ends the play, as she began it, trapped in an unsatisfying marriage with an impotent old buffoon; Violetta, having offered herself and her inheritance to Ricardo, is publicly rejected; our jolly band of thieves and impostors is in jail.

Nevertheless, out of such materials *The Widow* constructs the possibility of celebration. Like Christmas, like Christianity more generally, the play offers believers a comedy about love, about true and false cures, about the forgiveness of debts, about the inadequacy of law. Brandino is a judge; the play begins with the writing of an arrest warrant, ends with the arrest of thieves, and in between is saturated with legal language and practice, with a sense of the complicated exploitive process of judicature (Taylor 1994). Even lovers are put on 'trial': Philippa tests Francisco and Ansaldo, Valeria tests Ricardo and the other suitors. And while the characters are judging each other, we are judging them. They (we) are all imperfect: 'The best have their mistakings' (4.2.205). As C. John Sommerville has noted, this sense that inadequacy is not an individual failing, but a universal condition, was the foundation of Puritan humour, a new 'facetiousness' characterized above all by 'self-mockery' and 'self-effacement'.

No one here deserves to be saved. But they are saved, nevertheless: Ricardo by 'a strange miraculous courtesy' (2.2.104), Francisco 'most miraculously' (3.2.101). As Lancelot Andrewes observed, 'there is no *joy* in the world to the *joy* of a man *saved*'. The comic principle behind *The Widow* is not poetic justice, but poetic grace. John Donne's Christmas sermons are more helpful in understanding such a comedy than Horace or Jonson—not because Donne's sermons influenced Middleton, but because they articulate widely shared beliefs about the grounds for celebration in a fallen world. We might think, looking at Ricardo the practised or Francisco the novitiate adulterer, 'that it is impossible God should have mercy upon such a man' (Donne, iv.297). But they are saved from their own bad intentions '*quia complacuit*, merely in the good pleasure of God' (iv.291). This is the flip side of Calvinism: if damnation is arbitrarily predestined, so is salvation. Only grace can save us, but grace can save *any of us*. God has enough, and God will have his humour.

Preachers encouraged their congregations 'to call to mind God's occasional mercies to them—such mercies as a regenerate man will call mercies, though a natural man would call them accidents, or occurrences, or contingencies' (vi.171). Aristotle and Horace had banished improbable accidents from the drama, but no one could banish them from life, and *The Widow* is unembarrassed, indeed insistent, about the importance of mere chance to comedy. The word *luck* is echoed three times within the first twelve lines of dialogue, and fourteen times in the play as a whole; *fortune*, *misfortune*, and *unfortunate* are spoken 33 times; both sets of words occur in *The Widow* more often than in any other work in the Middleton canon. In the play's language and structure, happiness is something that happens by happenstance, haply. This is a rags-to-riches story in which no one *earns* anything: rich happens.

Early modern Protestants were fascinated by accidents, seeing in them, not evidence of chaos, but what Thomas Beard called *The Theatre of God's Judgements*. In Middleton's theatre, at the very centre of his play, in its longest speech, Francisco sees Ansaldo stripped to his shirt, and mistakes him for the ghost of his own father (3.2.85–119). By this improbable accident or occurrence or contingency, Francisco is diverted from adultery, and can later declare 'I wear no guilty blush upon my cheek | For a sin stamped last midnight' (5.1.127–8). Francisco's encounter is what Thomas Wilson, in his *Christian Dictionary* (1612), would have called Fortune or Chance, words used for 'such things as, in regard of our foresight, happen accidentally to us', or which 'fall out beside our purpose, and whereof we can give no reason'. But Wilson reminded his readers that 'in respect of God, who knoweth all things, and ordereth them most wisely to just and due ends, there is no chance nor fortune'. Likewise, Donne tells his audience of 'The adulterer, whose eye waits for the twilight, goes forth, and casts his eyes upon forbidden houses, and would enter', but then he 'sees a *Lord have mercy upon us* upon the door; this is an occasional mercy', because by this sign God reminds the adulterer that 'his lustful loins' will carry him 'to everlasting perdition' (vi.171).

This moment of apparently accidental revelation is, by Donne's definition, Christmas itself: 'every manifestation of Christ to the world, to the Church, to a particular soul, is an Epiphany, a Christmas-day' (vii.279). Whereas Barber sees festive comedy moving 'through release to clarification', Donne and Middleton trace a movement from clarification to release.

The play encourages an attention to the effects of chance, the limits of will, the interplay of fortune and nature, but it does not force Calvinism upon us, any more than it forces us to interpret the Ricardo/Valeria plot as an allegory of capitalism. Herbert Jack Heller rightly insists that Francisco's crisis of conscience dramatically enacts a classic conversion narrative familiar to every early modern Christian. But we may also see Francisco's pivotal retreat as yet another comic example of how easily this would-be lover is discouraged—which no doubt explains why, to the amazement of his neighbours, 'he has his maidenhead yet' (5.1.242). Middleton's ambidextrous sport is epitomized in a sentence of Valeria's first speech:

He that likes me not now, as heaven made me,
I will never hazard hell to do him a pleasure,
Nor lie every night like a woodcock in paste
To please some gaudy goose i'th' morning.
(2.1.15–18)

Divine and mundane explanations, hell and geese, stand shoulder to shoulder, and the action makes sense whichever we privilege. Christmas is a secular as well as a sacred festival, and in early modern Europe it was observed, not as a time when small impacted families retreat into private domesticity, but as the most openly communal occasion of the year, celebrating a togethering of friendship, kinship and sinship, an imperfect but possible human warmth against the world's chill. So—in the community of a theatre—does this play. 'I hope 'twill make you laugh.'

SEE ALSO

Music: *Companion*, 152
Textual introduction and apparatus: *Companion*, 1084
Authorship and date: *Companion*, 379

The Widow: A Comedy

[for the King's Men at The Blackfriars]

THE PERSONS OF THE PLAY

BRANDINO, a fat old Justice of the Peace
MARTINO, his old clerk
PHILIPPA, Valeria's sister, Brandino's handsome young second wife
VIOLETTA, Philippa's unmarried waiting woman

VALERIA, a rich widow
Two old men, SUITORS to Valeria
RICARDO, a handsome gentleman, in debt, suitor to Valeria
FRANCISCO, a handsome curly-haired twenty-one-year-old gentleman, Ricardo's friend

ATTILIO, another gentleman, friend to Francisco and Ricardo

ANSALDO, a handsome youth

LATROCINIO, leader of a band of thieves
OCCULTO, SILVIO, STRATIO, FIDUCIO — his confederates

Officers
Servants

Prologue *Enter Prologue*

A sport only for Christmas is the play
This hour presents t' you. To make you gay
Is all th'ambition 't has, and fullest aim
(Bent at your smiles) to win itself a name.
And if your edge be not quite taken off,
Wearied with sports, I hope 'twill make you laugh.

[*Exit*]

Incipit Actus 1 1.1

Table and standish. Enter Signor Martino (an old justice's clerk) and Francisco [a young gentleman]

FRANCISCO Martino?

MARTINO Signor Francisco? You're the luckiest gentleman to meet or see first in a morning; I never saw you yet but I was sure of money within less than half an hour.

This commentary pays particular attention to 'complex' words: idioms, sometimes apparently simple, which carried a central or compound significance in early modern culture. See for instance 'gentleman' (1.1.0.3). An index to the complex words appears on p. 1123.

Prologue.1 sport here (*a*) a pleasant pastime; recreation; diversion; but also elsewhere (*b*) sexual pleasure. The first, innocent sense obtains also at 5.1.246 and 5.1.364. However, the word is used more ambiguously at Prologue.6, 5.1.176, and 5.1.410, and with a specific sense of sexual pleasure by Francisco at 2.2.3 and by Violetta at 3.2.46.

2 **hour** occasion

3–4 **fullest aim ... name** the furthest extent of its aim, having your smiles as the target aimed at, is to gain itself fame (the metaphor 'bent' is from archery)

5 **edge** sword's sharpness; by extension ardour, liking, appetite

taken off blunted; carried away, removed

6 **sports** festive pastimes, especially associated with the Christmas season; but the preceding words suggest that the audience may be weary from sexual activity

1.1.0.2 ***standish*** a stand containing inks, pens, and other writing materials and accessories

Martino Italian: 'Martino, taken for a man's bum or arse' (Florio). The name encourages an emphasis on buttocks in the actor's appearance or performance.

0.3 **gentleman** a person of a distinct social rank; Francisco is the social superior of Martino, who is described later as looking 'half like a gentleman' (5.1.187). In the rural hierarchy, within which this play takes place, *gentlemen* were members of the gentry, ranked below knights and esquires but above yeomen; their wealth was based on land, the cultivation of their estates, and profitable marriage. As gentry they sought to maintain their way of life and to advance socially by increasing their family power and wealth. Early modern society was complicated by the overlapping and competition of two systems of hierarchy, a status system based on birth (epitomized by 'gentlemen'), and a class system based on wealth (which might be accumulated by persons who had inherited no status at all). Young gentry were notorious for wasting their patrimony: the 'poor indebted gentleman' (1.2.49) Ricardo has sold his land and plans to restore his fortune by marrying a rich widow (1.2.14–25). However, older gentlemen pursued wealth similarly: the two suitors who are Ricardo's rivals for Valeria withdraw their interest in her when she declares that she has given all she has to her brother-in-law (5.1.298–332); Brandino regards himself as cheated when Valeria destroys the 'deed of gift' (5.1.379–86). Marcia has run away because her father wanted to marry her to an old 'wealthy gentleman' (2.1.165); he accepts Francisco as a prospective husband for her since he comes 'of a noble family', although he regards him as 'somewhat spent' (5.1.421–2); Brandino describes Francisco to her as 'worth ten thousand dollars' (5.1.174).

FRANCISCO I bring you the same luck still.

MARTINO What? You do not! I hope, sir, you are not come for another warrant?

FRANCISCO Yes, faith, for another warrant.

MARTINO Why, there's my dream come out then. I never dreamed of a buttock but I was sure to have money for a warrant. It is the luckiest part of all the body to me. Let every man speak as he finds. Now your usurer is of opinion that to dream of the devil is your wealthier dream, and I think if a man dream of that part that brings many to the devil, 'tis as good, and has all one smatch indeed. For if one be the flesh, th'other's the broth. So 'tis in all his members, an we mark it. If gluttony be the meat, lechery is the porridge: they're both boiled together, and we clerks will have our modicum too, though it conclude in the twopenny chop.

[*Francisco does not mark Martino's speech*]

Why, sir, Signor Francisco?

FRANCISCO [*aside*] 'Twas her voice sure,
Or my soul takes delight to think it was,
And makes a sound like hers.

MARTINO Sir, I beseech you.

FRANCISCO
It is the prettiest contrived building, this.
What posy's that, I prithee?

MARTINO Which, sir? that
Under the great brass squirt?

FRANCISCO Ay, that, sir, that.

MARTINO
'From fire, from water, and all things amiss
Deliver the house of an honest justice.'

FRANCISCO There's like to be a good house kept then, when fire and water's forbidden to come into the kitchen.
[*Aside*] Not yet a sight of her? This hour's unfortunate.—
And what's that yonder, prithee?—[*Aside*] O love's famine,
There's no affliction like thee.—Ay, I hear you, sir.

MARTINO
You're quicker-eared than I then: you hear me
Before I heard myself.

FRANCISCO A gift in friendship;
Some call it an instinct.

MARTINO It may be;
Th'other's the sweeter phrase though. Look you, sir:
Mine own wit this, and 'tis as true as turtle.
'A goose quill and a clerk,
a constable and a lantern
Brings many a bawd from coach to cart,
and many a thief to one turn.'

FRANCISCO That 'one turn' helped you well.

MARTINO It's helped me to money indeed for many a warrant. I am forty dollars the better for that one turn; an 'twould come off quicker, 'twere ne'er a whit the worse for me. But indeed when thieves are taken, and break away twice or thrice one after another, there's

5 **luck** On the concept of chance, see the Introduction, and notes on *will* (1.1.79), *happy* (1.1.133), and *fortune* (1.1.185, 1.2.4, 34).

7 **warrant** a writ or order issued by some executive authority, empowering an officer to make an arrest, seizure, etc.

10 **have money** Martino must charge Francisco for the legal document.

11 **luckiest... body** See 1.1.2.

12 **your** a (hypothetical use)

13–14 **usurer... wealthier dream** Since usury is considered sinful, to dream of the devil would be considered profitable by the usurer.

15 **part... devil** usually the genitals, but Martino is more interested in the buttock than the crotch

16–17 **one... flesh, th'other's... broth** if the devil is the flesh, then the buttock is the prepared extract or reduced form of the devil

16 **smatch** taste, smack, flavour

17 **members** parts of the body

18 **porridge** pottage or soup made by stirring vegetables, herbs, or meat, often thickened with pot-barley or other farinaceous addition; possibly a pun on 'partridge', meaning 'whore'

20 **modicum** small quantity or portion of food or the like, but also used of a person, especially a woman (compare 'piece, bit')

20–1 **twopenny chop** chopped meat in broth; the context of gluttony is pervasive, and 'twopenny chop' may be an extension of *modicum* in once more presenting a sexual reference: *chop* = 'a fissure, cleft, or crack'

22 **'Twas... sure** (The audience may or may not hear Philippa's voice offstage.)

24 **And makes... hers** His soul responds in harmony with hers.

25 **contrived** ingeniously or artfully planned

26 **posy** a motto or short inscription (often metrical, and usually in patterned or formal language)

27 **squirt** a tubular instrument by which water may be squirted, used as a fire extinguisher

32 **unfortunate** not favoured by fortune; inopportune; compare Martino's emphasis on luck (1.1.2–4)

36–7 **A gift... instinct** Francisco explains his anticipation in conversation as an instance of telepathy among friends rather than his distraction by the thought of Philippa.

37 **instinct** innate propensity (in animate or inanimate things)

38 **Th'other's** the phrase 'A gift in friendship', which sounds sweeter than *instinct* (which includes the word 'stink').
sweeter The word *sweet, -er, -est* appears 49 times in the play; it is the common adjective of approval and is used regularly in compliments before nouns referring to persons (*widow*, *gentleman*, etc.). Among the favourite adjectives in verse of the period.

39 **turtle** turtle-dove, a bird proverbial for its fidelity

42 **Brings** The singular verb with plural subject is not uncommon; see also 1.1.49, where the phenomenon is not noted.
coach to cart prosperity to punishment. In the Jacobean period luxury coaches became increasingly popular among the well-to-do. They also offered opportunities for illicit sexual assignations: in *Owl* (1618) they are described as 'running bawdy-houses' (361). Carts were used for conveying convicts to the gallows, and for the public exposure and chastisement of offenders, esp. lewd women.

43 **thief** initiating a disquisition on thieves, which has no connection to the play's plot until much later: see 3.1.0.3.
turn hanging. (Stealing thirteen pence or more was punishable by hanging.)

44 **helped you well** (by giving you a rhyme for your poem)

46 **dollars** The English name for the German *thaler*, a large silver coin; in the succeeding lines Martino wishes for more frequent hangings, but speaks happily of gains from thieves' escapes which lead him to issue more warrants and so bring in money.

my gains; then goes out more warrants to fetch 'em again. One fine nimble villain may be worth a man ten dollars in and out, o' that fashion. I love such a one with my heart; ay, and will help him to 'scape, too, an I can. Hear you me that? I'll have him in at all times at a month's warning. Nay, say I let him run like a summer nag all the vacation—see you these blanks? I'll send him but one of these bridles, and bring him in at Michaelmas with a vengeance. Nothing kills my heart, but when one of 'em dies, sir. Then there's no hope of more money. I had rather lose at all times two of my best kindred than an excellent thief; for he's a gentleman I'm more beholden to.

FRANCISCO

You betray your mystery too much, sir. [*Aside*] Yet no
comfort?
'Tis but her sight that I waste precious time for,
For more I cannot hope for, she's so strict;
Yet that I cannot have.

MARTINO I'm ready now, signor.
Here are blank warrants of all dispositions.
Give me but the name and nature of your malefactor,
and I'll bestow him according to his merits.

FRANCISCO [*aside*]

This only is th'excuse that bears me out
And keeps off impudency and suspicion
From my too frequent coming. What name now
Shall I think on, and not to wrong the house?
This coxcomb will be prating.—One Astilio;
His offence, wilful murder.

52 **in and out** (of jail)

55–6 **run like a summer nag** have the freedom of movement of an unemployed horse at pasture

56 **vacation** a part of the year during which the law courts were closed
blanks warrants

58 **Michaelmas** the feast of St Michael, 29 September; Michaelmas Term, beginning on 9 October, was the autumn session of the law courts in London
with a vengeance (an intensifier; here, 'with alacrity')

62 **beholden** indebted

63 **mystery** occupation, skill, craft, trade, art. The word derives from Medieval Latin *misterium*—a form of *ministerium* (service, employment)—by confusion with *mysterium* (mystery)—a word associated with both religious truth and hidden or secret secular truth; it was probably also confused with *maistrie* (mastery). Thus the mystery was not just a trade or skill but rather a special province of protected knowledge. It is that which Francisco conceives Martino as betraying.
comfort a favourite Middleton word. Here it means only 'relief from mental torment', the pleasure it would give Francisco to see Philippa, whose presence he anxiously anticipates. It can also indicate more literal physical relief (like that which Latrocinio promises his patients in 4.2) or explicitly sexual satisfaction (like that which a bedmate provides at 5.1.91). But *comfort* can also mean 'spiritual solace', as at *Solomon* 3.12 ('Heaven is their haven, comfort their reward') and *Two Gates* 48.I.c ('for the comfort of sinners'). Much of the play's action turns upon the confused relation between the sexual and spiritual senses of the word—as in Ricardo's ambiguous oath, 'let me never hope for comfort' (2.1.42).

65 **strict** virtuous, proper, stern in matters of conscience or morality

66 **I'm ready now** (to respond to Francisco's request of 1.1.6–8)

67 **dispositions** (*a*) kinds, characters (*b*) legal decisions (*c*) the act of disposing of a person (as to custody by a warrant); (*d*) the mental constitution or temperament of an individual, a sense associated with *nature* in the next line

68 **nature** the character or essential quality of a person, here with the sense of the criminal quality, thus leading to the idea of his *merits* determining where he shall be bestowed. *Nature* is a word with such multiple uses that it underlies all areas of human culture, primarily as that which is prior to or unaffected by subsequent cultural modification. In Christian thought concerning the quality of the human being it implies the state existing before the advent of God's grace (without which humans are not capable of acts of goodness), defined by Thomas Wilson as (*a*) 'our state by birth, being born into the world corrupt and sinful' and (*b*) 'sensuality'. Thus although Martino's use here may be commonplace, it reflects in its connection with *malefactor* the play's sense of the essentially depraved actions of humans that are socially regulated by legal institutions and spiritually brought to good ends by a force outside them, specifically at *Christmas* (Prologue.1).

69 **bestow** place, dispose of

70 **bears me out** gives me justification

74 **coxcomb** conceited fool (after the name for the cap worn by a professional fool, which was like a cock's comb in shape and colour)
prating chattering
Astilio Francisco's invention of this name is confusing in the light of the presence in the play of a character named Attilio.

75–80 **wilful . . . Are you wilful?** Martino's question is apparently addressed to the supposed murderer, whose warrant he is writing; but it is also relevant to Francisco. The root noun *will* can refer to determination and to sexual desire: Francisco lustfully pursues Philippa, despite worldly obstacles and spiritual sanctions. Likewise, the struggle between Ricardo and Valeria turns upon the meanings of the repeated 'will' in 2.1.63–93 ('an you will', 'have your will', 'wilful'); the validity of the contract—contested because of the 'wilful' stubbornness of both parties—depends upon whether she vowed willingly (*voluntate*, 4.1.12). All these senses are united by conscious intention and premeditated desire, which Protestant theologians found troubling, because it was difficult to reconcile predestination with personal volition. The resulting theological debates presupposed a binary distinction between 'God's will' and 'man's will', which virtually ensured that 'man's will' was characterized negatively. 'Simply to will anything is of nature, but to will well is of grace—our will being free in respect of sinful acts, but bound in respect of good works, till it be set free by Christ' (Wilson). In the play, wilfulness characterizes murder, sexual desire, legal wrangling, and theft. Here, it is a disembodied 'wilfulness' which (comically) incenses Martino. For those who believed that the human will, as a faculty of mind, was almost inevitably misguided, salvation depended upon an acceptance of the unexpected and unwilled—what the play characterizes as 'fortune' or 'luck'. Nevertheless, a person's response to such moments of grace might be characterized as an act of will, and a will to godliness might itself be a sign of God's grace. Hence William Perkins, for instance, asked 'how far forth the will worketh in the receiving of grace?' The Calvinist preoccupation with 'will' made it a central category for understanding, not only the fate of persons [narrative], but the organization of souls [character]. Thus, Brandino has no will of his own, being easily persuaded to change his opinion; the Second Suitor, by contrast, refuses to be dissuaded from his 'humour' (see 2.1.175).

MARTINO Wilful murder? O, I love o' life to have such a fellow come under my fingers. Like a beggar that's long a-taking leave of a fat louse, I'm loath to part with him; I must look upon him over and over first. Are you wilful? I'faith, I'll be as wilful as you then.

Enter Philippa and Violetta at a window

PHILIPPA
Martino!

MARTINO
Mistress?

PHILIPPA Make haste; your master's going.

MARTINO I'm but about a wilful murder, forsooth. I'll dispatch that presently.

[*Martino writes*]

PHILIPPA [*to Francisco*]
Good morrow, sir. [*Aside*] O that I durst say more.

[*Exeunt Philippa and Violetta from the window*]

FRANCISCO [*aside*]
'Tis gone again, since. Such are all life's pleasures—
No sooner known, but lost; he that enjoys 'em
The length of life has but a longer dream;
He wakes to this i'th' end, and sees all nothing.

[*Enter Philippa above*]

PHILIPPA
He cannot see me now. I'll mark him better
Before I be too rash. Sweetly composed he is.
Now as he stands, he's worth a woman's love
That loves only for shape, as most on's do.
But I must have him wise as well as proper.
He comes not in my books else, and indeed
I have thought upon a course to try his wit. Violetta!

[*Enter Violetta above*]

VIOLETTA Mistress?

PHILIPPA Yonder's the gentleman again.

VIOLETTA O, sweet mistress,
Pray give me leave to see him.

PHILIPPA Nay, take heed.
Open not the window, an you love me.

VIOLETTA
No, I've the view of his whole body here, mistress,
At this poor little slit. O, enough, enough.
In troth, 'tis a fine outside.

PHILIPPA I see that.

VIOLETTA He's curled his hair most judiciously well.

PHILIPPA Ay, there's thy love now: it begins in barbarism. She buys a goose with feathers, that loves a gentleman for's hair; she may be cozened to her face, wench. Away, he takes his leave. Reach me that letter hither. Quick, quick, wench!

[*Violetta hands the letter to Philippa, who drops it as the men talk below*]

MARTINO [*to Francisco*] Nay, look upon't, and spare not. Everyone cannot get that kind of warrant from me, signor. Do you see this prick i'th' bottom? It betokens power and speed. It is a privy mark, that runs betwixt the constables and my master. Those that cannot read, when they see this, know 'tis for lechery or murder; and this being away, the warrant comes gelded and insufficient.

FRANCISCO
I thank you, sir.

MARTINO Look you, all these are *nihils*,
They want the punction.

FRANCISCO Yes, I see they do, sir.
There's for thy pains.—[*Aside*] Mine must go
unrewarded.

76 **love o' life** love dearly

77 **under my fingers** into my clutches, in my control

80.1 ***at a window*** a window located on an upper part of the stage; Philippa and Violetta are conceived as at a window here and at 1.1.88.1.

83 **presently** immediately

85 **'Tis** his vision of Philippa is
since now, already

88.1 ***above*** another location at the upper level in which Philippa cannot be seen (see 1.1.100)

90 **rash** hasty
composed fashioned, framed

92 **on's** of us

93 **proper** handsome

94 **books** favour

95 **try** test experimentally; examine judicially; in both these senses related to *trial*. When applied to persons, both *try* and *trial* posit an interior reality which a misleading surface may conceal; the trial is a procedure for determining the true nature of a thing (a metallic ore, for instance) or a person. Philippa tries Francisco, and later Ansaldo; Francisco claims to have made 'friendly trial' of Philippa (1.2.233); Ricardo tries Francisco's performance of 'ladyship' (1.2.114); Valeria promises to 'make great trial' of any man she would marry (2.1.22), and when in distress tries the First Suitor's 'goodness' (2.1.152), etc. In Christian theology, God similarly 'tries' persons, in order to reveal their true nature. See 'prove' (3.3.52, 5.1.382).
wit intelligence and ingenuity. Although the word *wit* derives from Old English *wit* or *gewit* (mind, reason, intelligence—thus the five wits and the capacity to lose one's wits; see 3.3.11, 17), it develops early a capacity to stand for the distinctive quality of an individual mind. Just as important is the development of the sense associated with cleverness, ability, and ingenuity. Philippa here is testing not just Francisco's intelligence but the sprightliness of his invention in a challenging situation. See also 3.1.59, 3.3.3, 8, 47, 75.

95.1 ***above*** See 1.1.88.1.

100 **Open ... window** The scene is conceived as Philippa and Violetta looking through a window, either partially opened or with a shutter; note at 102 'this poor little slit', a narrow opening.

104 **judiciously** prudently (an arch or affected use)

105 **barbarism** (*a*) unsophisticated behaviour (Philippa criticizes Violetta's praise of Francisco), but also (*b*) a pun, 'the work of the barber'

112 **prick** (*a*) a dot or hole, but also (*b*) a penis; sexual puns are frequent in the rest of Martino's speech.
betokens denotes, signifies

113 **privy** secret

116 **away** absent
gelded castrated (an image often used of authoritative texts that had been altered illegitimately). It refers explicitly to removal of the testicles, the source of male seed; here, a document that has been 'gelded' is 'insufficient' for 'lechery'.

118 ***nihils*** nothings (Latin), powerless things; 'thing' = sexual organ, thus 'no-things' = geldings

119 **punction** the act of pricking

120–1 **unrewarded ... regarded** a rhyme

The better love, the worse by fate regarded. *Exit*

MARTINO Well, go thy ways for the sweetest customer that ever penman was blessed withal.—Now will he come for another tomorrow again. If he hold on this course, he will leave never a knave i'th' town within this twelvemonth. No matter, I shall be rich enough by that time.

PHILIPPA [*above*] Martino!

MARTINO Say you, forsooth?

PHILIPPA
What paper's that the gentleman let fall there?

MARTINO Paper? [*Aside*] 'Tis the warrant, I hope. If it be, I'll hide it, and make him pay for't again. No, pox; 'tis not so happy.

PHILIPPA What is't, sirrah?

MARTINO 'Tis nothing but a letter, forsooth.

PHILIPPA Is that nothing?

MARTINO Nothing in respect of a warrant, mistress.

PHILIPPA A letter? Why, it's been many a man's undoing, sir.

MARTINO So has a warrant, an you go to that, mistress.

PHILIPPA
Read but the superscription, and away with't.
Alas, it may concern the gentleman nearly.

MARTINO
Why, mistress, this letter is at home already.

PHILIPPA
At home? How mean you, sir?

MARTINO You shall hear, mistress.
[*Reads*] 'To the deserving'st of all her sex, and most worthy of his best respect and love, Mrs Philippa Brandino.'

[*He gives her the letter*]

PHILIPPA How, sir, to me?

MARTINO To you, mistress.

PHILIPPA
Run, as thou lov'st my honour and thy life.
Call him again. I'll not endure this injury.
But stay; stay, now I think on't. 'Tis my credit.
I'll have your master's counsel. Ah, base fellow,
To leave his loose lines thus! 'Tis even as much
As a poor honest gentlewoman's undoing,
Had I not a grave wiseman to my husband—
And thou, a vigilant varlet, to admit
Thou car'st not whom.

MARTINO 'Las, 'tis my office, mistress.
You know you have a kirtle every year,
And 'tis within two months of the time now.
The velvet's coming over. Pray be milder.
A man that has a place must take money of anybody.
Please you to throw me down but half a dollar, and I'll make you a warrant for him now; that's all I care for him.

PHILIPPA
Well, look you be clear now from this foul conspiracy
Against mine honour, or your master's love to you,
That makes you stout, shall not maintain you here.
It shall not; trust to't. *Exit*

MARTINO This is strange to me now.
Dare she do this, and but eight weeks to New Year's tide?

122 **go thy ways for** off you go, for you are
customer client, but also slang for prostitute

123 **withal** with

133 **happy** fortunate, lucky; the word derives from the idea of *hap* or good fortune, and not until the 16th century did it become associated with inner contentment (as at 1.2.225) and with fitness to circumstances, or an aptitude for getting done what the circumstances require (as at 5.1.94). It recurs frequently in *The Widow*, as do the related words *fortune* and *luck*. The play is notable for the characters' experience of chance and coincidence unrelated to their own apparent determinations and of reward unjustified by their actions; it has a 'happy' ending despite their wrong ambitions. (See Introduction.)

137 **in respect of** in comparison with

138–40 **letter . . . warrant** (perhaps alluding to the fate of those involved in the scandalous Overbury murder trials of 1615–16)

138 **undoing** cause of ruin

141 **superscription** the direction or head of a letter
away with't put it away

142 **nearly** particularly, intimately

149–50 **you . . . thou** Martino addresses his mistress Philippa formally and politely as *you*, and she answers him, her subordinate, with the informal and familiar *thou*.

151 **injury** insult, affront. From Latin *iniuria* (wrong, hurt, detriment), the word enters English as a wrong inflicted or suffered. It also encompasses hurtful language, slander, or calumny. The sense of physical injury was current but not primary. See also at 1.2.143, 5.1.45, and 5.1.194.

152 **credit** honour, reputation

154 **loose** (*a*) not tied up; (*b*) unchaste
lines message, writing

155 **honest** virtuous, chaste, faithful in marriage. Philippa represents herself as a chaste wife, vulnerable to slander and fearful for her reputation. The word enters English from French *honeste* (Latin *honestus*, respectable, decent, honourable) and has the initial sense of 'held in honour, respectable'. But by Middleton's day its general sense 'of good moral character, virtuous' had developed a specific application for women relating to sexual virtue, i.e., complete sexual abstinence or fidelity to a spouse. Throughout the play honest/honesty operates within this gendered context, except at 5.1.365 where the Second Suitor, challenging Valeria's 'honesty', is testing the sincerity of her affection for Ricardo. See also *honour* as a gendered term at 3.2.94 and 3.3.48.
undoing cause of ruin

156 **wiseman** (ironic) a simpleton

157 **varlet** knave, rogue, rascal

159 **kirtle** a woman's gown or skirt

161 **coming over** from France, the source of such velvet; at this point the language assumes an English setting

162 **place** a position of responsibility

168 **stout** defiant, rebellious

170 **eight . . . tide** Compare 1.1.160; Martino suggests that she is risking her New Year's present by attacking him.

A man that had his blood as hot as hers now
Would fit her with French velvet. I'll go near it.
Enter Brandino (the justice) and Philippa

PHILIPPA
If this be a wrong to modest reputation
Be you the censurer, sir, that are the master
Both of your fame and mine.

BRANDINO Signor Francisco?
I'll make him fly the land.

MARTINO That will be hard, sir.
I think he be not so well feathered, master;
He's spent the best part of his patrimony.

PHILIPPA
Hark of his bold confederate.

BRANDINO There thou'rt bitter,
And I must chide thee now.

PHILIPPA What should I think, sir?
He comes to your man for warrants.

BRANDINO There it goes then.—
Come hither, knave. Comes he to you for warrants?

MARTINO Why, what of that, sir?
You know I give no warrants to make cuckolds.
That comes by fortune and by nature, sir.

BRANDINO
True, that comes by fortune and by nature, wife.
Why dost thou wrong this man?

MARTINO He needs no warrant, master, that goes about such business. A cuckold-maker carries always his warrant about him.

BRANDINO [*to Philippa*]
La, has he answered well now? to the full?
What cause hast thou t'abuse him?

PHILIPPA Hear me out, I pray.
Through his admittance, he's had opportunity
To come into the house and court me bodily.

BRANDINO [*to Martino*]
Sirrah, you're foul again methinks.

MARTINO Who, I, sir?

BRANDINO
You gave this man admittance into th'house.

MARTINO
That's true, sir. You never gave me any order yet
To write my warrants i'th' street.

BRANDINO [*to Philippa*] Why, sure thou tak'st delight
To wrong this fellow, wife. Ha?—'cause I love him.

PHILIPPA
Pray see the fruits, see what he's left behind here.
Be angry where you should be. There's few wives
Would do as I do.

BRANDINO Nay, I'll say that for thee.
I ne'er found thee but honest.

PHILIPPA She's a beast

171 **blood...hot** violence of passion. The *blood* was one of the four 'cardinal humours' of the human body, fluids that determined mental and physical health (see *humour* 2.1.175); its predominance in the human constitution maintained a 'sanguine' disposition. Here it is used in the sense of the seat of emotion and passion in humans, and particularly in association with anger and sexual desire, both of which are relevant here (*hot... blood*). Martino perceives Philippa as angry, but speaks about male revenge against her in terms of sexual violence, thus combining the concepts of lust and anger; he is, however, unaware of the sexual desire that is Philippa's motivation.

172 **fit...velvet** provide her with the velvet that is 'coming over' (1.1.161) from France; however the context suggests sexual humour, and 'French' is frequently associated with nouns to do with syphilis.
I'll go near it I'll consider it; I'll hint at it.

172.1 ***Brandino*** Italian, 'brandire, to brandish a sword. Also to smug or trim up' (Florio); an ironic name for an eighty-year-old husband of a young wife. He is also apparently quite fat (4.2.103–4) and moves very slowly (2.2.119–20).

174 **censurer** judge; Philippa is assuring Brandino that he has charge of her reputation as well as his own.

176 **fly the land** go into exile

177 **well feathered** prosperous; Martino is picking up on the metaphor of flying

178 **patrimony** inheritance

180 **chide** scold, rebuke severely

185 **by fortune and by nature** the two sources of gifts to humans, the first of benefits granted during life, the second of qualities born in the individual. Fortune and Nature are usually contrasted (as in the debate at *As You Like It* 1.2.30–53); Martino's phrasing suggests that the two are in some sense not opposed but identical, and in Calvinist theology they were easily conflated, since God was thought to be the source of both, and the apparent accidents which occur during a life were just as predetermined as the characteristics inherited at birth. Moreover, cuckoldry is not usually considered a benefit; it would normally be attributed to 'misfortune' or 'ill fortune', and the idea that it comes 'by fortune' implies that great wealth (another sense of 'fortune') inevitably leads to cuckoldry. In city comedy, successful merchants are often cuckolds, as though there were an inverse relation between economic and sexual potency; more generally, wealth has often enabled older men to acquire pretty young wives, and in comic tradition such wives are almost invariably unfaithful. Their unfaithfulness comes 'by nature' either (ideologically) because women are regarded as naturally lecherous, or (literally) because 'nature' is slang for the genitals.

189 **business** Martino puns on two senses of *business*: (*a*) legal or commercial activity, and (*b*) sexual intercourse. The two senses are fused in much of the action of the play, since the wooing of Valeria by Ricardo and the two suitors is dominated by concern for financial profit, and Francisco's pursuit of Philippa is conducted under the guise of legal activity. Though the word is occasionally used in the first sense alone in the play, it frequently appears in sexual puns; see 2.1.103, 2.2.18, 38, 40, 101, and especially Francisco's uses at 3.2.62, 74, and 94.

190 **warrant** in commenting on the 'illegality' of cuckoldry, Martino gives *warrant* a double meaning: (*a*) instrument of authority, and (*b*) penis.

191 **to the full** completely, satisfactorily (with double entendre: 'all the way' or 'all the way in')

193 **his...he's** Martino's...Francisco is

194 **bodily** in person, but with the physical association

195 **foul** wicked

200 **fruits** consequences; the word has a moral charge as the inevitable consequence of the quality of life or actions: see Matthew 7:18–19, and *Two Gates* 35.II.c ('idolatry and the fruits thereof')

203 **honest** truthful, but also chaste; see 1.1.155

That ever was found otherways.

BRANDINO Read, Martino.
Mine eyes are sore already, and such business
Would put 'em out quite.

MARTINO [*reads*] 'Fair, dear and incomparable mistress—'

BRANDINO
O, every letter draws a tooth, methinks.

MARTINO [*aside*]
And it leads mine to wat'ring.

PHILIPPA Here's no villainy?

MARTINO [*reads*] 'My love being so violent, and the opportunity so precious in your husband's absence tonight, who as I understand takes a journey this morning—'

BRANDINO
O plot of villainy!

PHILIPPA Am I honest, think you, sir?

BRANDINO
Exactly honest, perfectly improved.—
On, on, Martino.

MARTINO [*reads*] 'I will make bold, dear mistress, though your chastity has given me many a repulse, to wait the sweet blessings of this long desired opportunity at the back gate between nine and ten this night.'

BRANDINO
I feel this Inns o' Court man in my temples.

MARTINO [*reads*] 'Where if your affection be pleased to receive me, you receive the faithfullest that ever vowed service to woman: Francisco.'

BRANDINO
I will make Francisco smart for't.

PHILIPPA
Show him the letter. Let him know you know him;
That will torment him. All your other courses
Are nothing, sir, to that; that breaks his heart.

BRANDINO
The strings shall not hold long then. Come, Martino.

Exeunt Brandino and Martino

PHILIPPA
Now, if Francisco have any wit at all,
He comes at night; if not, he never shall. *Exit*

Enter [three gentlemen:] Francisco and Ricardo and Attilio 1.2

RICARDO Nay, mark; mark it, Francisco. It was the naturalest courtesy that ever was ordained: a young gentleman being spent, to have a rich widow set him up again. To see how Fortune has provided for all mortality's ruins: your college for your old standing scholar, your hospital for your lame creeping soldier, your bawd for your mangled roarer, your open house for your beggar, and your widow for your gentleman. Ha, Francisco?

FRANCISCO
Ay, sir, you may be merry; you're in hope
Of a rich widow.

RICARDO And why shouldst not thou be in hope of another, if there were any spirit in thee? Thou art as likely a

204 **was found** He takes her to mean 'turned out to be' but she means 'was discovered to be'.
205 **sore** painful, inflamed
208 **draws a tooth** causes suffering
209 **And . . . wat'ring** makes him salivate with titillation
213 **honest** chaste
214 **improved** cultivated, cultured
217 **chastity** Philippa is a married woman, not a virgin, but *chastity* means 'an abstinence and forbearing, not from marriage, but from all strange and roving lusts about the desire of sex' (Wilson).
218–19 **at the back gate** (alluding, by *double entendre*, to anal intercourse)
220 **Inns o' Court man** law student
temples The cuckold's horns grew from his temples; but there is also a pun on the names of two Inns of Court, the Inner Temple and the Middle Temple.
221 **affection** love
223 **service** (*a*) devotion to the beloved's wellbeing, but also (*b*) sexual activity as the male's performance for the female; the double sense suggests always the complexity of human desire. Here it is Philippa who uses the pun in the letter that she constructs to attract Francisco's desire to *serve* her. The word functions differently when Marcia/Ansaldo uses it to Philippa; s/he plays the naïve role of dedicated courtier to Philippa, who understands instead the complexity that she invests the term with in this first scene; see 3.3.100 and 3.3.111.
228 **The strings** his heartstrings
229 **wit** intelligence, ingenuity
230 **at night** tonight
1.2.2 **courtesy** courteous or generous act. In its broadest sense 'courtesy' is the elaborate code of behaviour that distinguishes the person of gentle rank; 'naturalest courtesy' is an oxymoron since by contrast to 'nature' it is the 'art' of conduct. It is 'courtesy' in the form of generosity that Ansaldo receives from Philippa, and in the form of gracious conduct that attracts Philippa to Ansaldo; see 3.3.61, 3.3.71, 3.3.92, 3.3.97, 3.3.119, and 3.3.126.
ordained arranged, destined
3 **spent** bankrupt (but also 'sexually emptied')
3–4 **set him up** (*a*) restore his financial credit (*b*) give him an erection
4 **Fortune** Early texts do not orthographically distinguish the abstract concept of chance from the personified 'deity' worshipped by sinners (*Solomon* 2.21) and pagans (*Hengist* 1.2.0.1), who emblematically 'Stood reeling on a rolling stone' (*Ghost* 296), carrying 'a silver wheel' (*Industry* 92) or 'a golden round full of lots' (*Hengist* 1.2.0.2). Fortune was always female, and her operations were often attributed to personal affection: 'Fortune dotes on me' (*Chaste Maid* 3.3.20). Ricardo associates Fortune with a rich widow, who will bestow her gifts on him; in an inverse economy, only those who have lost or given up their fortunes will be cared for by Fortune. In the plot, Ricardo's fortune, and his chance to regain the material fortune he has squandered, depend upon the affections of a rich widow.
5 **standing** perpetual (perhaps sexually erect)
7 **bawd** either madam (as financial provider) or pimp (as alternative profession)
mangled hacked, mutilated (perhaps castrated)
roarer a bully or reveller; a wild young man

fellow as any is in the company. I'll be hanged now if I do not hit the true cause of thy sadness—and confess truly, i'faith: thou hast some land unsold yet, I hold my life.

FRANCISCO Marry, I hope so, sir.

RICARDO A pox on't! Have I found it? 'Slight, away with't with all speed, man. I was never merry at heart while I had a foot. Why, man, Fortune never minds us till we are left alone to ourselves. For what need she take care for them that do nothing but take care for themselves? Why, dost think, if I had kept my lands still, I should ever have looked after a rich widow? Alas, I should have married some poor young maid, got five-and-twenty children, and undone myself.

FRANCISCO I protest, sir, I should not have the face, though, to come to a rich widow with nothing.

RICARDO
Why, art thou so simple as thou mak'st thyself?
Dost think, i'faith,
I come to a rich widow with no thing?

FRANCISCO
I mean, with state not answerable to hers.

RICARDO
Why, there's the fortune, man, that I talked on.
She knows all this, and yet I am welcome to her.

FRANCISCO
Ay, that's strange, sir.

RICARDO Nay, more to pierce thy hard heart—
And make thee sell thy land, if thou'st any grace:
She has, 'mongst others, two substantial suitors.
One (in good time be't spoke) I owe much money to;
She knows this too, and yet I'm welcome to her.
Nor dares the unconscionable rascal trouble me.
She's told him thus: those that profess love to her
Shall have the liberty to come and go—
Or else get him gone first. She knows not yet
Where fortune may bestow her; she's her gift;
Therefore to all will show a kind respect.

FRANCISCO
Why, this is like a woman. I ha' no luck in't.

RICARDO
And, as at a sheriff's table—O, blest custom!—
A poor indebted gentleman may dine,
Feed well, and without fear, and depart so,
So to her lips fearless I come and go.

FRANCISCO
You may well boast; you're much the happier man, sir.

RICARDO
So you would be, an you would sell your land, sir.

FRANCISCO
I have heard the circumstance of your sweet fortunes;
Prithee give ear to my unlucky tale now.

RICARDO
That's an ill hearing. But come on for once, sir.

FRANCISCO
I never yet loved but one woman.

RICARDO
Right, I begun so too, but I have loved
A thousand since.

FRANCISCO
Pray, hear me, sir. But this is a man's wife.

RICARDO
So has five hundred of my thousand been.

14 **the company** our social circle (but also suggesting 'this band of actors'—the first of several theatrical allusions in this scene)

16 **land unsold** Ricardo suggests that Francisco is sad because property is a burdensome responsibility, and ties up cash.

18 **Marry** a mild interjection used by a broad range of characters in the play; originally an invocation of the name of the Virgin Mary, it had lost that significance by this time

19 **'Slight** by God's light (a strong oath). The oaths in this play show the observance of the *Act to Restrain Abuses of Players* (1606), which forbade actors to 'jestingly or prophanely speak or use the holy Name of God or of Christ Jesus, or of the Holy Ghost or of the Trinity.' See also Ricardo's similar contracted oaths *Life* (2.1.93, 2.2.107), *'Od's light* (2.2.62), *Heart* (2.2.95). The most frequent oath in the play is the mild *faith/ i'faith*, which occurs on forty occasions. Note also *heaven* as an avoidance of the name of God at 2.1.12, 2.1.15, 2.1.21, 2.2.116, 5.1.195, 5.1.415, 5.1.430.

25 **looked after** sought out

27 **undone myself** ruined my life, not ruined my finances

28 **face** effrontery, nerve, gall

29 **nothing** no money

30 **mak'st thyself** appear to be

32 **no thing** Ricardo exposes Francisco's verbal innocence by joking on thing = penis.

33 **state** position in the world, especially in relation to prosperity in wealth or property
answerable comparable or corresponding to

34 **fortune** good luck, blessing; although Ricardo has earlier spoken of *Fortune* in the sense of the goddess he here uses the word in its more commonplace sense of the consequences of her generosity. See 1.2.4.

35 **She** the widow

37 **grace** good sense; a word often with strong theological significance as God's gift that enables humans to do virtuous acts, but here reduced to a purely secular sense in the context of Ricardo's mockery of penitential language ('*to pierce thy hard heart*').

39 **in good time** by good fortune; or right away

45 **her gift** Fortune's gift; however, it could mean that she is her own to give in the context of what fortune brings.

46 **kind** natural, gracious. The word is of Old English origin, and the early senses of its noun form relate to birth and origin, to birthright and 'character or quality derived from birth or native constitution.' The adjective originally was used for 'natural, in various senses'—'in accordance with the nature of things, appropriate, by birth'—and was extended to further positive senses, such as 'well bred' (see 5.1.172 'came of a good kind') and, as usually in this play, 'naturally well disposed, having a benevolent nature, generous, courteous' (*OED* a. 5). (See also 'unkindly', 2.2.145.)

51 **fearless** without trepidation

52 **happier** more fortunate, more blessed. (The issue is not inner contentment but the benevolence of external forces.)

56 **an ill hearing** unpleasant to hear

FRANCISCO
Nay, see an you'll regard me!
RICARDO No? You see I do;
I bring you an example in for everything.
FRANCISCO
This man's wife—
RICARDO So you said.
FRANCISCO Seems very strict.
RICARDO Ha!—hm.
FRANCISCO
Do you laugh at that?
RICARDO 'Seems very strict', you said.
I hear you, man. I'faith, you are so jealous still.
FRANCISCO But why should that make you laugh?
RICARDO
Because she *seems* so. You're such another!
FRANCISCO
Nay, sir, I think she *is*.
RICARDO You cannot tell then?
FRANCISCO
I dare not ask the question, I protest,
For fear of a repulse; which, yet not having,
My mind's the quieter, and I live in hope still.
RICARDO Ha!—hm.
[*To Attilio*] This 'tis to be a landed man.—Come, I perceive
I must show you a little of my fortune, and instruct you.
Not ask the question?
FRANCISCO Methought still she frowned, sir.
RICARDO
Why, that's the cause, fool, that she looked so scurvily.
Come, come, make me your woman; you'll ne'er do't else.
I'll show you her condition presently.
I perceive you must begin like a young vaulter, and get up at horse-tail, before you get into the saddle. Have you the boldness to utter your mind to me now, being but in hose and doublet? I think if I should put on a farthingale, thou wouldst never have the heart to do't.
FRANCISCO
Perhaps I should not then for laughing at you, sir.
RICARDO In the mean time I fear I shall laugh at thee without one.
FRANCISCO
Nay, you must think, friend, I dare speak to a woman.
RICARDO You shall pardon me for that, friend; I will not think it, till I see't.
FRANCISCO
Why, you shall, then. I shall be glad to learn, too,
Of one so deep as you are.
RICARDO So you may, sir.
[*To Attilio*] Now 'tis my best course to look mildly; I
Shall put him out at first, else.
FRANCISCO A word, sweet lady.
RICARDO [*as a woman*]
With me, sir? Say your pleasure.
FRANCISCO O Ricardo,
Thou art too good to be a woman long.
RICARDO
Do not find fault with this, for fear I prove
Too scornful; be content when you're well used.
FRANCISCO
You say well, sir.—Lady, I have loved you long.
RICARDO [*as a woman*] 'Tis a good hearing, sir.

62 **see . . . me** look how you don't listen to me
64 **strict** virtuous, chaste
67 **jealous** fearful, doubtful
69 **such another!** such an innocent (see Dent A250)
70 **tell** discern, perceive
77 **Not . . . question** (don't tell me you) could not even speak to her directly
78 **scurvily** sourly
80 **condition** nature, character, quality. The word derives from French *condicion* after Latin *condicion-em*, 'an agreement or compact', but in Latin the word had already the senses 'situation, position, rank, circumstances, nature, manner'. In English it develops a complex of senses related to modes or states of being; here Ricardo protests that he will show (act out for) Francisco her true character as he understands it. See also the uses at 4.2.74 and 5.1.307 and 310.
presently right now
81–2 **vaulter . . . saddle** the stages of mounting a horse, but here with sexual joke: leaping or vaulting into the saddle is an idiom for copulation
84 **hose and doublet** men's clothes
85 **farthingale** women's clothes; a hooped petticoat
87–8 **laugh . . . one** Seeing a male *not* in female clothes would not normally be laughable, but it might be so if the male in question normally cross-dressed. This is one of several moments in the scene which would make better sense if the actor playing Francisco had, until recently, played female roles: see 1.2.111.
92–3 **I . . . are** (like a young actor, taking lessons from a more experienced one)
93 **deep** learned, experienced
95 **put him out** disconcert him, put him off; specifically, make an actor forget his lines
lady female equivalent of 'lord' (a word not used of any of the male characters), indicating a status usually higher than 'gentlewoman'. This is the first occurrence of the word in the play; it occurs eight times in 1.2.95–149, perhaps prompted by association with 'the scornful lady' (see note at 1.2.103).
96 **Say your pleasure** What do you want? The word *pleasure* always has a latent complexity. Used in phrases such as this it expresses the formal courteous sense of providing a person with what s/he wishes; however, there is the secondary risk that the respondent's desire may be of a kind that is beyond the courteous, and may be unwelcome or threatening. In the cross-gendered role-playing of this scene the formal phrase assumes a strong erotic potential. Note further uses at 1.1.85; 1.2.105; 2.2.1; 2.2.78; 2.2.109; and of *pleasant* at 3.2.108.
101 **'Tis a good hearing** That's good to hear

[*To Attilio*] If he be not out now, I'll be hanged.

FRANCISCO
You play a scornful woman? I perceive, Ricardo, you have not been used to 'em. Why, I'll come in at my pleasure with you. Alas, 'tis nothing for a man to talk when a woman gives way to't. One shall seldom meet with a lady so kind as thou played'st her.

RICARDO Not altogether, perhaps. He that draws their pictures must flatter 'em a little; they'll look he that plays 'em should do't a great deal then.

FRANCISCO
Come, come, I'll play the woman; that I'm used to.
I see you ne'er wore shoe that pinched you yet;
All your things comes on easy.

RICARDO Say you so, sir?
I'll try your ladyship, faith.—Lady, well met.

FRANCISCO [*as a woman*] I do not think so, sir.

RICARDO
A scornful gom!—and at the first dash, too.
My widow never gave me such an answer.
I'll to you again, sir.—
Fairest of creatures, I do love thee infinitely.

FRANCISCO [*as a woman*] There's nobody bids you, sir.

RICARDO Pox on thee! Thou art the beastliest, crossest baggage that ever man met withal. But I'll see thee hanged, sweet lady, ere I be daunted with this. Why, thou'rt too awkward, sirrah.

FRANCISCO [*as a woman*] Hang thee, base fellow.

RICARDO [*To Attilio*]
Now by this light, he thinks he does't indeed.
Nay then, have at your plum-tree! Faith, I'll not be foiled.—
Though you seem to be careless, madam, as you have enough wherewithal to be, yet I do, must, and will love you.

FRANCISCO [*as a woman*] Sir, if you begin to be rude, I'll call my woman.

RICARDO [*to Attilio*] What a pestilent quean's this! I shall have much ado with her, I see that.
—Tell me as you're a woman, lady, what
Serve kisses for? But to stop all your mouths.
[*He makes to kiss Francisco*]

FRANCISCO Hold, hold, Ricardo!

RICARDO Disgrace me, widow?
[*Ricardo throws Francisco down*]

FRANCISCO Art mad? I'm Francisco.

ATTILIO Signor Ricardo, up, up!
[*Attilio pulls Ricardo off Francisco*]

RICARDO Who is't? Francisco?

FRANCISCO Francisco, quoth a! What, are you mad, sir?

RICARDO A bots on thee! Thou dost not know what injury thou hast done me. I was i'th' fairest dream. This is your way now, an you can follow it.

FRANCISCO 'Tis a strange way, methinks.

RICARDO
Learn you to play a woman not so scornfully, then,
For I am like the actor that you spoke on:
I must have the part that overcomes the lady.
I never like the play, else.—Now your friendship,
But to assist a subtle trick I ha' thought on,

103 **scornful woman** with 'scornful' at 99, perhaps alluding to Beaumont and Fletcher's most popular play, *The Scornful Lady* (1613); perhaps the actor playing Francisco originally played the part of the title character in that play.

104–5 **come in at my pleasure** visit as I please; but the erotic suggestion of sexual penetration and pleasure is present.

109 **look** expect

111 **I'll . . . used to** depending on whether there is a strong pause after 'woman', this could mean either (*a*) I'll act like the woman with whom I am familiar, or (*b*) I'll act the part of a woman; I'm accustomed to doing that. The first sense could refer to Philippa, or to a female role the actor now playing Francisco was famous for playing in the past ('the scornful lady'). The second sense would suggest that Francisco has never asserted himself in a manly fashion, or that the actor is a 'juvenile romantic lead' who has, until recently, played female roles for the company. Dick Robinson (formerly a boy actor playing women's parts) may have first performed the part of Francisco. Robinson seems to have played the 'young gallant' Wittipol in Jonson's *The Devil is an Ass* (probably first performed in late 1616); Jonson's play calls attention to Robinson's acting, and his transition from playing young women to playing young men.
play the woman (*a*) behave in an effeminate fashion (*b*) act the role of a woman in a play

112 **shoe that pinched** a woman's small shoe

113 **things** genitals, in this case female, rendering the previous line bawdy

116 **gom** godmother; an old woman
at the first dash at the first stroke or blow (*OED* sb1.2), immediately

124 **awkward** perverse, disagreeable
sirrah ordinary form of address to inferiors, used to women as well as men

127 **plum-tree** female genitals. 'Have at your plumb-tree' in the same sense occurs in Thomas Nashe's *Have with you to Saffron Walden* (1596).

128 **careless** unconcerned, not caring

133 **quean's** a bold, impudent, or ill-behaved woman

134 **much ado** (perhaps alluding to Shakespeare's popular play *Much Ado about Nothing*, famous for Beatrice's scornful retorts to the young gallant Benedick—an allusion irresistible if the Ricardo-actor had played Benedick against the Francisco-actor's Beatrice)

136 **all your mouths** (*a*) the mouths of all women (*b*) all a woman's orifices

138 **Disgrace** treat me with disfavour, or dismiss from favour

143 **A bots on thee** an expression of execration; 'bots' is a disease of cattle

148 **actor** Francisco has not mentioned an actor, but the audience will easily assume an earlier unstaged part of their conversation; in any case, this is probably a reference (which the audience could be expected to recognize) to the kinds of roles normally played by the actor playing Ricardo; it also promises a happy ending.

149 **part** (*a*) role in the play; (*b*) sexual organ

150 **play** (*a*) playhouse performance; (*b*) sexual adventure
Now your friendship now let me have your support as a friend

And the rich widow's mine within these three hours.

ATTILIO *and* FRANCISCO
We should be proud of that, sir.

RICARDO List to me then.
I'll place you two (I can do't handsomely,
I know the house so well) to hear the conference
'Twixt her and I. She's a most affable one;
Her words will give advantage, and I'll urge 'em
To the kind proof, to catch her in a contract.
Then shall you both step in as witnesses
And take her in the snare.

FRANCISCO But do you love her?
And then 'twill prosper.

RICARDO By this hand, I do—
Not for her wealth, but for her person too.

FRANCISCO
It shall be done then.

RICARDO But stay, stay, Francisco.
Where shall we meet with thee some two hours hence now?

FRANCISCO
Why, hark you, sir.
[*He whispers to Ricardo*]

RICARDO Enough. Command my life;
Get me the widow, I'll get thee the wife.
Exeunt Ricardo and Attilio

FRANCISCO
O that's now with me past hope. Yet I must love her.
I would I could not do't.
Enter Brandino and Martino [*aloof*]

MARTINO Yonder's the villain, master.

BRANDINO Francisco? I am happy.

MARTINO Let's both draw, master,
For there's nobody with him.—Stay, stay, master.
Do not you draw till I be ready too.
Let's draw just both together, and keep e'en.

BRANDINO
What an we killed him now, before he saw us?

MARTINO
No, then he will hardly see to read the letter.

BRANDINO
That's true. Good counsel, marry.

MARTINO Marry, thus much, sir:
you may kill him lawfully, all the while he's a-reading on't, as an Anabaptist may lie with a brother's wife all the while he's asleep.

BRANDINO
He turns, he looks.—Come on, sir, you, Francisco!
I loved your father well, but you're a villain.
He loved me well too, but you love my wife, sir.
After whom take you that? I will not say
Your mother played false.

FRANCISCO No, sir, you were not best.

BRANDINO
But I will say, in spite of thee, my wife's honest.

MARTINO
And I, my mistress.

FRANCISCO You may; I'll give you leave.

BRANDINO
Leave or leave not, there!
[*He gives Francisco the letter*]
She defies you, sir.
Keep your adulterous sheet to wind you in,
Or cover your forbidden parts at least,
For fear you want one. Many a lecher may
That sins in cambric now.

MARTINO And in lawn too, master.

BRANDINO [*to Francisco*] Nay, read and tremble, sir.
[*Brandino and Martino talk apart, while Francisco reads*]

MARTINO Now shall I do't, master? I see a piece of an open seam in his shirt: shall I run him in there? for my sword has ne'er a point.

BRANDINO No, let him foam awhile.

MARTINO If your sword be no better than mine, we shall not kill him by daylight; we had need have a lantern.

152 **three hours** (He expects to put his plan into practice immediately. But this reference may also be to actual playing time: literally, in less than three hours of performance, he will have won the widow)
156 **'Twixt her and I** 'The inflections of Personal Pronouns are frequently neglected or misused' (Abbott)
affable civil and courteous in conversation
157 **urge** press forcibly
158 **kind** natural; see 1.2.46
proof good outcome or result
contract legal agreement, here specifically to marry
160 **snare** an animal trap in the form of a noose
162 **Not…too** (contradictory, since 'too' acknowledges that her wealth *is* part of her attraction)
person her being, her *self*; Ricardo's use of the word protests that he loves her both as an individual moral being and as a physical body
167 **O…her** either (*a*) 'I have no hope of marrying her (because she's already married), but I must have sex with her' or (*b*) 'I have no hope of consummation, but I can't help desiring her'
170 **happy** fortunate
177 **marry** to be sure
179 **Anabaptist** an early term for 'Baptists', but loosely used of dissenters from the Church of England; as extremists in religion they were portrayed as unconventional in belief and sexual practice.
brother's co-religionist's (but also suggesting incest)
189 **adulterous sheet** 'lewd piece of paper', but suggesting 'sheet on a bed in which adultery has been committed'. No fornication has occurred, but *adultery* could mean 'all manner of uncleanness about desire of sex' (Wilson), including presumably masturbation associated with adulterous fantasy.
to wind you in to serve as a burial sheet
191 **want** lack
may i.e., lack one in the future
192 **cambric** a fine white linen, originally made at Cambray in Flanders
193 **lawn** a kind of fine linen resembling cambric
197 **ne'er a** no
199–200 **If your sword…daylight** i.e., it will take a long time
200–2 **lantern…lant-horns…horns** The old form 'lanthorn' made possible a pun on the horns of the cuckold.

BRANDINO
Talk not of lant-horns. He's a sturdy lecher.
He would make the horns fly about my ears.
FRANCISCO [*aside*]
I apprehend thee. Admirable woman!
Which to love best I know not: thy wit or beauty.
BRANDINO [*to Francisco*]
Now sir, have you well viewed your bastard there,
Got of your lustful brain? Give you joy on't.
FRANCISCO
I thank you, sir, although you speak in jest.
I must confess I sent your wife this letter
And often courted her, tempted and urged her.
BRANDINO Did you so, sir?
Then first, before I kill thee, I forewarn thee my house.
MARTINO And I, before I kill thee, forewarn thee my office.
Die tomorrow next, thou never get'st warrant of me more, for love or money.
FRANCISCO
Remember but again from whence I came, sir,
And then I know you cannot think amiss of me.
BRANDINO
How's this?
MARTINO Pray hear him; it may grow to a peace.—
[*Aside*] For master, though we have carried the business nobly, we are not altogether so valiant as we should be.
BRANDINO [*aside to Martino*]
Peace. Thou sayst true in that.—What is't you'd say, sir?
FRANCISCO
Was not my father (quietness be with him)
And you sworn brothers?
BRANDINO Why, right, that's it urges me.
FRANCISCO
And could you have a thought that I could wrong you
As far as the deed goes?
BRANDINO You took the course, sir.
FRANCISCO
To make you happy, an you rightly weighed it.
MARTINO [*to Brandino*]
Troth, I'll put up at all adventures, master.
It comes off very fair yet.
FRANCISCO [*to Brandino*] You, in years,
Married a young maid. What does the world judge, think you?
MARTINO [*to Brandino*] By'r Lady, master, knavishly enough, I warrant you.
I should do so myself.
FRANCISCO [*to Brandino*]
Now, to damp slander
And all her envious and suspicious brood,
I made this friendly trïal of her constancy,
Being son to him you loved; that now confirmed,
I might advance my sword against the world
In her most fair defence, which joys my spirit.
MARTINO [*to Brandino*]
O master, let me weep, while you embrace him.
BRANDINO
Francisco, is thy father's soul in thee?
Lives he here still? What, will he show himself
In his male seed to me? Give me thy hand.
Methinks it feels now like thy father's to me.
Prithee forgive me.
MARTINO [*to Francisco*]
And me too, prithee.
BRANDINO [*to Francisco*]
Come to my house; thy father never missed it.
MARTINO [*to Francisco*]
Fetch now as many warrants as you please, sir,
And welcome too.
FRANCISCO To see how soon man's goodness
May be abused.
BRANDINO But now I know thy intent,
Welcome to all that I have.
FRANCISCO Sir, I take it.
A gift so given, hang him that would forsake it. *Exit*
BRANDINO
Martino, I applaud my fortune and thy counsel.
MARTINO
You never have ill fortune when you follow it.
Here was things carried now in the true nature of a quiet *duello*;
A great strife ended without the rough soldier or the *punto bello*.
And now you may take your journey.
BRANDINO Thou art my glee, Martino. *Exeunt*

❁

2.1
Incipit Actus 2
Enter Valeria (the widow) and a servant
VALERIA
Servellio!

203 **apprehend thee** understand her trick; see 3.2.4
Admirable exciting wonder; the word was stronger than in modern use.
205 **bastard** the letter, regarded as the illegitimate issue of his brain, conceived in an 'adulterous sheet'; also a handwriting of mixed letter forms
211 **forewarn** prohibit, but here with the sense 'forbid to enter'
222 **urges** provokes to anger
224 **deed** sexual intercourse
226 **put up** put away his weapon
at all adventures anyway, whatever the consequence
227 **in years** old
231 **damp** extinguish, stifle
243 **missed it** failed to visit it
251 ***duello*** duel
252 ***punto bello*** fine thrust. (These words of Italian fencing jargon are an editorial conjecture, to fill out the metre and supply the rhyme; at this point the quarto has a dash.)
254 **glee** joy
2.1.0.2 ***Valeria*** Italian, 'Valere... to be worth, to be of value, Also to be much or greatly esteemed...' (Florio)

SERVANT Mistress?

VALERIA If that fellow come again,
Answer him without me. I'll not speak with him.

SERVANT
He in the nutmeg-coloured band, forsooth?

VALERIA
Ay, that spiced coxcomb, sir. [*Exit Servant*]
Never may I marry again
If his right worshipful idolatrous face
Be not most fearfully painted; so hope comfort me,
I might perceive it peel in many places,
And under's eye lay a betraying foulness,
As maids sweep dust o'th' house all to one corner.
It showed me enough there, prodigious pride
That cannot but fall scornfully. I'm a woman,
Yet I praise heaven I never had th'ambition
To go about to mend a better workman.
She ever shames herself i'th' end that does it.
He that likes me not now, as heaven made me,
I will never hazard hell to do him a pleasure,
Nor lie every night like a woodcock in paste
To please some gaudy goose i'th' morning.
A wise man likes that best that is itself,
Not that which only seems, though it look fairer.
Heaven send me one that loves me, and I'm happy—
Of whom I'll make great trïal ere I have him,
Though I speak all men fair and promise sweetly.
I learn that of my suitors; 'tis their own,
Therefore injustice 'twere to keep it from 'em.

Enter Ricardo

RICARDO And so, as I said, sweet widow—

VALERIA Do you begin where you left, sir?

RICARDO I always desire, when I come to a widow, to begin i'th' middle of a sentence, for I presume she has a bad memory of a woman that cannot remember what goes before.

VALERIA
Stay, stay, sir. Let me look upon you well.
Are not you painted too?

RICARDO How, painted, widow?

VALERIA
Not 'painted widow'; I do not use it, trust me, sir.

RICARDO
That makes me love thee.

VALERIA I mean 'painted gentleman',
Or if you please to give him a greater style, sir.
Blame me not, sir. It's a dangerous age, I tell you;
Poor simple-dealing women had need look about 'em.

RICARDO
But is there such a fellow in the world, widow,
As you are pleased to talk on?

VALERIA Nay, here lately, sir.

RICARDO Here? A pox! I think I smell him. 'Tis vermilion sure. Ha? Oil of ben! Do but show him me, widow, and let me never hope for comfort if I do not immediately geld him and grind his face upon one o'th' stones.

VALERIA Suffices you've expressed me your love and valour and manly hate against that unmanly pride. But sir, I'll save you that labour; he never comes within my door again.

RICARDO I'll love your door the better while I know't, widow. A pair of such brothers were fitter for posts without-door indeed, to make a show at a new-chosen magistrate's gate, than to be used in a woman's chamber. No, sweet widow, having me, you've the truth of a man.
All that you see of me is full mine own,
And what you see, or not see, shall be yours.

3 **band** the neckband or collar of a shirt
4 **spiced** delicate, over-refined; Valeria plays upon 'nutmeg'
5 **right worshipful** a mocking acknowledgement of the unnamed suitor's rank
idolatrous worshipping false beauty, i.e., his own
6 **fearfully** inducing fear, but used as modern 'awfully', or 'terribly'
painted wearing cosmetics; Valeria jests on the association of painted idols in 'idolatrous'
10 **prodigious** monstrous
11 **scornfully** in a way that will attract scorn
13 **mend . . . workman** improve on the work of God, the 'better workman'
17 **woodcock** (*a*) a bird; (*b*) a gullible person, a fool
paste (*a*) a pastry shell in which a woodcock would be cooked; (*b*) almond paste, used for whitening the skin
18 **gaudy** glaringly showy
goose a foolish person
24 **their own** i.e., the art of speaking fair and promising sweetly
30–1 **what goes before** (*a*) what happened in her former marriage; (*b*) what happened or was said at their last meeting; (*c*) a penis
36 **greater style** more elevated title than 'gentleman' (such as 'knight', 'marquis', 'earl', etc.). Many Jacobean courtiers were 'painted', but it would be 'dangerous' for Valeria—or the actor, or playwright—to say so.
38 **simple-dealing** honest, candid
40 **on** of
41 **vermilion** cinnabar or red crystalline mercuric sulphide used as a cosmetic
42 **Oil of ben** oil obtained from the ben-nut (the winged seed of the horse-radish tree)
43 **comfort** i.e., spiritual or sexual
44 **stones** testicles (imagined as grindstones, used for sharpening knives, etc.)
49 **door** (*a*) house; (*b*) genitals
50–1 **posts without-door** wooden posts that stood outside the doors of sheriffs or magistrates, and that were repainted with each new office-holder

I ever hated to be beholden to art, or to borrow anything but money.

Francisco and Attilio [*enter and*] *stand unseen*

VALERIA
True, and that you never use to pay again.

RICARDO What matter is't? If you be pleased to do't for me,
I hold it as good.

VALERIA O, soft you, sir, I pray.

RICARDO Why, i'faith, you may, an you will.

VALERIA I know that, sir.

RICARDO Troth, and I would have my will then, if I were as you. There's few women else but has.

VALERIA
But since I cannot have't in all, signor,
I care not to have't in anything.

RICARDO
Why, you may have't in all, an you will, widow.

VALERIA
Pish! I would have one that loves me for myself, sir,
Not for my wealth—and that I cannot have.

RICARDO
What say you to him that does the thing you wish for?

VALERIA
Why, here's my hand, I'll marry none but him then.

RICARDO
Your hand and faith?

VALERIA My hand and faith.

[*They clasp hands*]

RICARDO 'Tis I, then.

VALERIA
I shall be glad on't, trust me; 'shrew my heart, else.

RICARDO A match!

Francisco and Attilio [*come forward*]

FRANCISCO
Give you joy, sweet widow!

ATTILIO Joy to you both!

VALERIA How?

RICARDO
Nay, there's no starting now. I have you fast, widow.—
You're witness, gentlemen.

FRANCISCO *and* ATTILIO We'll be deposed on't.

VALERIA
Am I betrayed to this then? Then I see
'Tis for my wealth. A woman's wealth's her traitor.

RICARDO
'Tis for love chiefly, I protest, sweet widow,
I count wealth but a fiddle to make us merry.

VALERIA
Hence!

RICARDO
Why, thou'rt mine.

VALERIA I do renounce it utterly.

RICARDO
Have I not hand and faith?

VALERIA Sir, take your course.

RICARDO
With all my heart: ten courses, an you will, widow.

VALERIA
Sir, sir, I'm not so gamesome as you think me.
I'll stand you out by law.

RICARDO
By law? O cruel merciless woman,
To talk of law, and know I have no money.

VALERIA
I will consume myself to the last stamp
Before thou get'st me.

RICARDO Life, I'll be as wilful then too.
I'll rob all the carriers in Christendom
But I'll have thee, and find my lawyers money.
I scorn to get thee under *forma pauperis*;

57 **art** artifice, modification of the 'natural'. The word appears in *The Widow* with three different meanings. Deriving from the Latin *art-em*, skill, it entered the English language with this meaning (as Latrocinio employs it at 4.2.51–3), and was used in education in the phrase the *liberal arts*, those modes of knowledge that make a free person. However, the nature of the skill and the attitude to that skill led to various specializations of meaning. Here it is used in the sense in which it is opposed to nature: *art* is the human skill in ornamenting or modifying nature (often, as here, with some sense of corrupting primal purity). At 3.1.42, where Latrocinio says to Ansaldo that 'Art should be rewarded. You must pay your music, sir', he is using the word as the distinctive term for music (belonging to that class of experiences that are now called *art*), but with a secondary meaning of cunning in crime, because he has just used his song to introduce the idea of robbery. At 4.2.62, 4.2.118, and 5.1.68 Latrocinio in his disguise is called the 'man of art'; the advertised sense is of wisdom and learning, specifically mysterious healing power, but the sense 'con artist' is also ironically present. (The same term is used of Subtle in Jonson's *The Alchemist*.) Valeria makes 'trial' (see 1.1.95) of men in order to distinguish their 'art' from their 'nature' (1.1.185).

59 **again** back

66 **has** i.e., has her will

76 **match** by leading Valeria into offering him her 'hand and faith' in the presence of (unseen) witnesses, Ricardo has tricked her into a marriage contract (*sponsalia per verba de praesenti*)

79 **starting** escaping (*OED* v.6)
fast securely

80 **be deposed** swear a deposition

86 **take your course** (*a*) leave immediately; (*b*) pursue your legal suit

87 **courses** (*a*) courses of a meal; (*b*) sexual bouts

88 **gamesome** merry, playful

89 **stand you out** resist you, hold out against you

90 **law . . . merciless** As in the commonplaces of Protestant doctrine, Ricardo opposes law (represented by the Old Testament, which condemns men to punishment for the sins they will inevitably commit) and mercy (represented by the New Testament, which promises them undeserved grace). Compare *Two Gates* Preface.35–8 ('that law was a curst *judge* and ready to condemn. But the King of *heaven* being as full of mercy as of justice, abated the edge of the axe').

92 **stamp** coin

96 ***forma pauperis*** in the form of a poor person, Latin legal term; 'one allowed, on account of poverty, to sue or defend in a court of law, without paying costs'

I have too proud a heart, and love thee better.

VALERIA [*to Francisco and Attilio*]
As for you gentlemen, I'll take course against you.
You came into my house without my leave;
Your practices are cunning and deceitful;
I know you not, and I hope law will right me.

RICARDO
It is sufficient that your husband knows 'em.
'Tis not your business to know every man;
An honest wife contents herself with one.

VALERIA
You know what you shall trust to. Pray depart, sir,
And take your rude confederates along with you
Or I will send for those shall force your absence.
I'm glad I found your purpose out so soon.
How quickly may poor women be undone!

RICARDO Lose thee? By this hand, I'll see fifteen counsellors first, though I undo a hundred poor men for 'em, and I'll make 'em yaul one another deaf, but I'll have thee.

VALERIA
Me?

RICARDO
Thee.

VALERIA Ay, fret thy heart out. *Exit Ricardo*

FRANCISCO Were I he now
I'd see thee starve for man before I had thee.

VALERIA
Pray counsel him to that, sir, and I'll pay you well.

FRANCISCO Pay me? Pay your next husband.

VALERIA
Do not scorn't, gallant. A worse woman than I
Has paid a better man than you.
[*Exeunt Francisco and Attilio*]

Enter two old suitors

FIRST SUITOR
Why, how now, sweet widow?

VALERIA Oh, kind gentlemen,
I am so abused here.

AMBO Abused?

[*The suitors draw their swords*]

VALERIA
What will you do, sirs? Put up your weapons.

SECOND SUITOR Nay, they're not so easily drawn, that I must tell you. Mine has not been out this three years. Marry, in your cause, widow, 'twould not be long a-drawing. Abused? By whom, widow?

VALERIA Nay, by a beggar.

SECOND SUITOR A beggar? I'll have him whipped then, and sent to the house of correction.

VALERIA Ricardo, sir.

SECOND SUITOR Ricardo? Nay, by th' mass, he's a gentleman beggar; he'll be hanged before he be whipped. Why, you'll give me leave to clap him up, I hope?

VALERIA
'Tis too good for him. That's the thing he would have;
He would be clapped up whether I would or no,
methinks.
Placed two of his companions privately,
Unknown to me, on purpose to entrap me
In my kind answers, and at last stole from me
That which I fear will put me to some trouble,
A kind of verbal courtesy, which his witnesses
And he forsooth call by the name of contract.

FIRST SUITOR
O politic villain!

VALERIA But I am resolved, gentlemen,
If the whole power of my estate can cast him,
He never shall obtain me.

SECOND SUITOR Hold you there, widow.
Well fare your heart for that, i'faith.

FIRST SUITOR Stay, stay, stay.—
You broke no gold between you?

VALERIA We broke nothing, sir.

FIRST SUITOR
Nor drunk to one another?

VALERIA Not a drop, sir.

FIRST SUITOR
You're sure of this you speak?

VALERIA Most certain, sir.

98 **take course** pursue legal action
103 **know** (*a*) be acquainted with (*b*) have sexual intercourse with
105 **trust to** put confidence in
108–9 **soon . . . undone** a rhyme
111 **undo** ruin
112 **yaul** shout
116 **Pay your next husband** (i.e. you will have to buy a husband)
121 AMBO both
122 **weapons** swords, but the Second Suitor puns on 'weapon' as 'penis'
129 **house of correction** a prison designed to reform its occupants
132 **hanged . . . whipped** Ricardo's rank as a gentleman will protect him from whipping
133 **clap him up** imprison him with no delay
135 **clapped up** married
138 **kind** courteous, appropriately civil; see 1.2.46
140 **courtesy** gesture of respect, as in 'curtsy' (see 1.2.2), but here with a special legal sense: 'a tenure by which a husband, after his wife's death, holds certain kinds of property which she has inherited, the conditions varying with the nature of the property' (*OED* sb. 4)
141 **contract** a legal commitment of marriage as at 2.1.76; Valeria will challenge Ricardo's claim to her on the ground that her 'kind of verbal courtesy' was not an expression of a will to marry
142 **politic** crafty, cunning; the word enters the language in the 15th century in the sense of 'pertaining to a citizen' and thence to a state; but in the 16th century it develops a sinister sense and is associated with craft and deceit, the activities of a *villain*, particularly in the context of English perceptions of Machiavelli's thought.
143 **cast** defeat in an action of law
144 **Hold you there** Be steadfast in that
146 **broke no gold** to break gold was a pledge of constancy in betrothals and symbolized sharing wealth; see 2.1.155–6
nothing i.e. 'no maidenhead, either'

FIRST SUITOR
Be of good comfort, wench. I'll undertake then
At mine own charge to overthrow him for thee.

VALERIA
O do but that, sir, and you bind me to you.
Here shall I try your goodness. I'm but a woman
And, alas, ignorant in law businesses.
I'll bear the charge most willingly.

FIRST SUITOR Not a penny.
Thy love will reward me.

VALERIA And where love must be,
It is all but one purse, now I think on't.

FIRST SUITOR
All comes to one, sweet widow.

SECOND SUITOR [*aside*] Are you so forward?

FIRST SUITOR
I know his mates, Attilio and Francisco.
I'll get out process and attach 'em all.
We'll begin first with them.

VALERIA I like that, strangely.

FIRST SUITOR
I have a daughter run away, I thank her;
I'll be a scourge to all youth for her sake.
Some of 'em has got her up.

VALERIA Your daughter?
What, sir? Marcia?

FIRST SUITOR Ay, a shaker marry her!
I would have wed her to a wealthy gentleman
No older than myself; she was like to be
Shrewdly hurt, widow.

VALERIA It was too happy for her.

FIRST SUITOR I'm of thy mind.
Farewell, sweet widow. I'll about this straight.
I'll have 'em all three put into one writ,
And so save charges.

VALERIA How I love your providence!

Exit First Suitor

SECOND SUITOR [*aside*]
Is my nose bored? I'll cross ye both for this,
Although it cost me as much o'th' other side.
I have enough, and I will have my humour.
I may get out of her what may undo her too.—
Hark you, sweet widow. You must now take heed
You be of a sure ground; he'll overthrow you else.

VALERIA
Marry, fair hope forbid!

SECOND SUITOR That will he,
Marry, lemme see, lemme see.—Pray, how far passed it
Between you and Ricardo?

VALERIA Farther, sir,
Than I would now it had; but I hope well yet.

SECOND SUITOR
Pray, let me hear't. I've a shrewd guess o'th' law.

VALERIA
Faith, sir, I rashly gave my hand and faith
To marry none but him.

SECOND SUITOR Indeed?

VALERIA Ay, trust me, sir.

SECOND SUITOR
I'm very glad on't. I'm another witness,
And he shall have you now.

VALERIA What said you, sir?

SECOND SUITOR
He shall not want money in an honest cause, widow.
I know I have enough, and I will have my humour.

VALERIA
Are all the world betrayers?

149 **wench** a familiar form of address used to a wife, daughter, sweetheart, or servant (see also 3.2.6, 5.1.167, and 5.1.462)
151 **bind me to you** earn my gratitude and loyalty; but the First Suitor may understand a promise of marriage
152 **try** put to the test
159 **process** 'the mandate, summons, or writ by which a person or thing is brought into court for litigation' (*OED* sb. 7b)
attach arrest
160 **strangely** either (*a*) extremely or (*b*) strange to say
163 **got her up** (*a*) driven her from cover, as birds or animals in hunting; (*b*) (perhaps) made her pregnant
164 **shaker** (*a*) disreputable person (*b*) boaster (*c*) fever
167 **Shrewdly hurt** severely misused (spoken sarcastically)
168 **happy** fortunate
172 **providence** care, thrift
173 **Is my nose bored?** Am I being cheated?
cross thwart. 'Every grievous or painful thing sent by God, either to our minds or bodies . . . is the general cross common to all men' (Wilson). But such a *cross* is paradoxically a blessing in that it tests the virtue of the person. In the context of trial and proof in the play (see 1.1.95) the frustrations that characters such as Ricardo, Valeria, Francisco, and Marcia/Ansaldo undergo are fortunate in their outcomes. See 3.2.60, 66, 99, 3.3.60, and 5.1.66.
174 **o'th' other side** to work in opposition
175 **have my humour** have whatever I want. *Humour* is fancy, whim, caprice, impulse. The word comes into English via French from Latin *umor* or *humor* meaning dampness or moisture, but it develops a technical sense in medieval and early modern English in respect especially to the 'cardinal humours', 'the four chief fluids of the body (blood, phlegm, choler, and melancholy or black choler), by the relative proportions of which a person's physical or mental qualities and dispositions were held to be determined' (*OED* sb. 2b). The purely medical sense is present in 'hydropic humour' (4.2.91). From this technical use arose the sense of personal humour, the distinctive quality or temperament of the individual. However, by about 1550 it developed the sense employed by the Second Suitor repeatedly in this play: 'A particular disposition, inclination, or liking, *esp.* one having no apparent ground or reason' (*OED* sb. 6). Indeed, his repetition of the phrase itself constitutes a humour, and the First Suitor takes him at his word when he commands him to 'Follow your humour out' (2.2.167). This is the sense in the titles of Jonson's *Every Man in His Humour* and *Every Man out of His Humour*. In practice, a *humour* is clearly related to personal *will* and *wilfulness* (see 1.1.79–80), but its medical root emphasizes the purely material, fleshly origin of such behaviour.

SECOND SUITOR Pish, pish, widow.
You've borne me in hand this three months, and now fobbed me.
I've known the time when I could please a woman.
I'll not be laughed at now. When I'm crossed, I'm a tiger.
I have enough, and I will have my humour.

VALERIA
This only shows your malice to me, sir.
The world knows you ha' small reason to help him,
So much in your debt already.

SECOND SUITOR Therefore I do't.
I have no way but that to help myself.
Though I lose you, I will not lose all, widow.
He marrying you, as I will follow't for him,
I'll make you pay his debts, or lie without him.

VALERIA
I looked for this from you.

SECOND SUITOR I ha' not deceived you then.
Exit Valeria
Fret, vex, and chafe; I'm obstinate where I take.
I'll seek him out and cheer him up against her.
I ha' no charge at all, no child of mine own
But two I got once of a scouring woman,
And they're both well provided for, they're i'th' Hospital.
I have ten thousand pound to bury me,
And I will have my humour. *Exit*

2.2 *Enter Francisco*

FRANCISCO
A man must have a time to serve his pleasure
As well as his dear friend. I'm forced to steal from 'em
To get this night of sport for mine own use.
What says her amiable witty letter here?
''Twixt nine and ten'. Now 'tis 'twixt six and seven.
As fit as can be: he that follows lechery
Leaves all at six and seven, and so do I methinks.
Sun sets at eight; it's 'bove an hour high yet.
Some fifteen mile have I before I reach her,
But I've an excellent horse, and a good gallop
Helps man as much as a provoking banquet.
Enter First Suitor with officers

FIRST SUITOR
Here's one of 'em. Begin with him first, officers.

OFFICER [*to Francisco*]
By virtue of this writ, we attach your body, sir.
[*Officers seize Francisco*]

FRANCISCO
My body? Life, for what?

FIRST SUITOR Hold him fast, officers.

OFFICER
The least of us can do't, now his sword's off, sir.
We have a trick of hanging upon gentlemen;
We never lose a man.

FRANCISCO O treacherous fortune!
Why, what's the cause?

FIRST SUITOR The widow's business, sir.
I hope you know me?

FRANCISCO For a busy coxcomb
This fifteen year, I take it.

FIRST SUITOR O you're mad, sir.
Simple though you make me, I stand for the widow.

FRANCISCO
She's simply stood for, then. What's this to me, sir,
Or she, or you, or any of these flesh-hooks?

FIRST SUITOR
You're like to find good bail before you leave us
Or lie till the suit's tried.

FRANCISCO O my love's misery!

FIRST SUITOR
I'm put in trust to follow't, and I'll do't
With all severity. Build upon that, sir.
Enter Ricardo and Attilio [aloof]

FRANCISCO
How I could curse myself!

RICARDO [*to Attilio*] Look, here's Francisco.
Will you believe me, now you see his qualities?

ATTILIO
'Tis strange to me.

RICARDO I tell you, 'tis his fashion.
He never stole away in's life from me
But still I found him in such scurvy company.
[*Ricardo and Attilio come forward*]
A pox on thee, Francisco! Wilt never leave thy old tricks?
Are these lousy companions for thee?

FRANCISCO [*warning them*] Pish, pish, pish!

FIRST SUITOR
Here they be all three now: 'pprehend 'em, officers.

191 **borne me in hand** kept me in expectation, deluded
fobbed cheated
200 **follow't** pursue the business to its conclusion
201 **lie without him** sleep alone; the Second Suitor will imprison him for debt.
203 **take** seize my prey; (perhaps) infect
206 **scouring** cleaning
207 **Hospital** orphanage; the audience would probably have thought of Christ's Hospital in London
2.2.1 **serve his pleasure** do what he wishes, but also satisfy his desires
3 **sport** sexual pleasure
7 **at six and seven** in confusion
10–11 **a good . . . banquet** the horse ride stirs sexual appetite as much as a sensuous banquet
11 **provoking** arousing
13 **attach** arrest
19 **busy** officious, meddlesome
21 **stand for** represent
22 **simply** (*a*) easily; (*b*) by a simpleton
23 **these flesh-hooks** the officers
24 **You're like to** You may expect to
25 **lie** in custody
26 **put in trust** obliged
27 **Build** depend
29 **qualities** personal or moral character
32 **still** always
scurvy contemptible
34 **lousy** mean (literally, infected with lice)

[*Officers seize Ricardo and Attilio*]

RICARDO What's this?

FRANCISCO
I gave you warning enough to make away.
I'm in for the widow's business; so are you now.

RICARDO What, all three in a noose? This is like a widow's business indeed.

FIRST SUITOR
She's catched you, gentlemen, as you catched her.
[*To Ricardo*] The widow means now to begin with you, sir.

RICARDO
I thank her heartily; she's taught me wit—
for had I been any but an ass, I should ha' begun with her indeed. By this light, the widow's a notable housewife, she bestirs herself. I have a greater mind to her now than e'er I had. I cannot go to prison for one I love better, I protest; that's one good comfort.—
And what are you, I pray, sir, for a coxcomb?

FIRST SUITOR
It seems you know me by your anger, sir.

RICARDO
I've a near guess at you, sir.

FIRST SUITOR Guess what you please, sir.
I'm he ordained to trounce you, and indeed
I am the man must carry her.

RICARDO Ay, to me.
But I'll swear she's a beast, an she carry thee.

FIRST SUITOR
Come, where's your bail, sir? Quickly, or away.

RICARDO
Sir, I'm held wrongfully. My bail's taken already.

FIRST SUITOR Where is't, sir, where?

RICARDO
Here they be both. Pox on you, they were taken
Before I'd need of 'em.—An you be honest,
Officers, let's bail one another;
For by this hand, I do not know who will else.—

Enter Second Suitor

'Od's light, is he come too? I'm in for midnight then.
I shall never find the way out again.
My debts, my debts! I'm like to die i'th' Hole now.

FIRST SUITOR [*to Second Suitor*]
We have him fast, old signor, and his consorts.
Now you may lay action on action on him.

SECOND SUITOR
That may I, sir, i'faith.

FIRST SUITOR And I'd not spare him, sir.

SECOND SUITOR
Know you me, officers?

OFFICER Your bounteous worship, sir.

RICARDO [*aside*] I know the rascal so well, I dare not look upon him.

SECOND SUITOR [*to officers*]
Upon my worth, deliver me that gentleman.

FRANCISCO
Which gentleman?

SECOND SUITOR Not you, sir; you're too hasty.—
[*To Attilio*] No, not you neither, sir; pray, stay your time.

RICARDO [*aside*]
There's all but I now, and I dare not think he means me.

SECOND SUITOR [*to officers*]
Deliver me Ricardo.

RICARDO [*aside*] O sure he lies,
Or else I do not hear well.

OFFICER Signor Ricardo.

RICARDO
Well, what's the matter?

OFFICER You may go. Who lets you?
It is his worship's pleasure, sir, to bail you.

RICARDO
Bail me?

SECOND SUITOR
I will. Ay, sir, look in my face, man.
Thou'st a good cause. Thou'lt pay me when thou'rt able?

RICARDO
Ay, every penny, as I am a gentleman.

SECOND SUITOR
No matter if thou dost not; then, I'll make thee,
And that's as good at all times.

FIRST SUITOR But I pray, sir,
You go against the hair there.

37 **make away** escape
38 **I'm in** (custody)
for on account of
39 **in a noose** trapped
39–40 **widow's business** being trapped in marriage (but also implying that three men are needed to satisfy the sexual appetite of a widow)
44 **begun** initiated sexual intercourse
46 **housewife** a woman who manages her household with skill and thrift
49 **what . . . coxcomb?** what sort of a fool are you?
52 **trounce** get the better of, defeat
53 **carry** win as a prize, but Ricardo's 'Ay, to me' takes it as 'convey'
54 **carry** bear his weight in sexual intercourse
56 **taken** Ricardo puns on the meanings 'received' and 'arrested' in respect of 'bail' as both money and the person providing the money
62 **'Od's light** by God's light
for midnight until midnight; figuratively 'forever'
64 **debts** Ricardo is literally in debt, but his expectation of death in bondage may also have figurative meanings: sin 'is called a debt, because for sin we do owe unto the justice of God eternal death' (Wilson), and 'in [Christ] alone all debts are paid' (*Two Gates* Preface.108–9).
Hole a prison cell, but also 'the name of one of the worst apartments in the Counter prison in Wood Street, London' (*OED* sb. 2b)
66 **lay action . . . on him** bring multiple charges against him
73 **stay your time** remain for your allotted time
77 **lets** prevents, obstructs
78 **pleasure** desire, but also the gracious act of the superior that needs no explanation, a secular grace
84 **against the hair** contrary to the natural way; against the grain

SECOND SUITOR Against the widow, you mean, sir.
Why, 'tis my purpose truly, and against you too.
I saw your politic combinatïon;
I was thrust out between you. Here stands one
Shall do as much for you, and he stands rightest.
His cause is strong and fair, nor shall he want
Money or means or friends, but he shall have her.
I've enough, and I will have my humour.

FIRST SUITOR
Hang thee! I have a purse as good as thine.

RICARDO [*aside*]
I think they're much alike; they're rich knaves both.—
'Heart, an I take you railing at my patron, sir,
I'll cramp your joints.

SECOND SUITOR Let him alone, sweet honey.
I thank thee for thy love, though.

RICARDO [*aside*] This is wonderful.

FRANCISCO O Ricardo!
'Tis seven, struck in my pocket. I lose time now.

RICARDO
What sayst, Francisco?

FRANCISCO I ha' mighty business
That I ne'er thought on. Get me bailed; I'm spoiled else.

RICARDO
Why, you know, 'tis such a strange miraculous courtesy
I dare not be too forward to ask more of him,
For fear he repent this and turn me in again.

FRANCISCO
Do somewhat, an you love me.

RICARDO I'll make trial, faith.—
May't please you, sir.—Life, if I should spoil all now!

SECOND SUITOR
What sayst, Ricardo?

RICARDO Only a thing by th' way, sir;
Use your own pleasure.

SECOND SUITOR That I like well from thee.

RICARDO
'Twere good, an those two gentlemen were bailed too;
They're both my witnesses.

SECOND SUITOR They're well, they're well.
An they were bailed, we know not where to find 'em.
Let 'em go to prison; they'll be forthcoming the better.
I have enough, and I will have my humour.

RICARDO [*aside*]
I knew there was no more good to be done upon him.
'Tis well I've this; heav'n knows I never looked for't.

FRANCISCO
What plaguy luck had I to be ensnared thus!

OFFICER
O patience.

Enter Brandino and Martino

FRANCISCO Pox o' your comfortable ignorance!

BRANDINO
Martino, we ride slow.

MARTINO But we ride sure, sir.
Your hasty riders often come short home, master.

BRANDINO
Bless this fair company!

FRANCISCO [*aside*] Here he's again too.
I am both shamed and crossed.

BRANDINO Seest thou who's yonder,
Martino?

MARTINO
We ride slow, I'll be sworn now, master.

BRANDINO
How now, Francisco! Art thou got before me?

FRANCISCO
Yes, thank my fortune, I am got before you.

BRANDINO
What? No! In hold?

RICARDO Ay, o' my troth. Poor gentleman!
Your worship, sir, may do a good deed to bail him.

BRANDINO Why do not you do't then?

MARTINO [*to Ricardo*] La you, sir, now!
My master has that honesty
He's loath to take a good deed from you, sir.

RICARDO
I'll tell you why: I cannot. Else I would, sir.

[*Ricardo and Brandino talk apart*]

FRANCISCO [*aside*]
Luck, I beseech thee!—If he should be wrought
To bail me now, to go to his own wife,
'Twere happiness beyond expressïon.

BRANDINO [*to Ricardo*]
A matter but of controversy?

87 **politic** crafty, cunning (see 2.1.142)
combinatïon conspiracy
89 **rightest** with most justice
95 **'Heart** by God's heart
96 **cramp your joints** make your joints stiff and painful (by beating you)
honey term of endearment—a characteristic verbal tic of the Second Suitor, who as his 'patron' has a relation to Ricardo comparable to James I's relations with his favourites Somerset and Buckingham, whom he addressed with similarly erotic pet-names and epithets.
100 **struck in my pocket** Francisco has a chiming watch in his pocket.
102 **spoiled** ruined
106 **make trial** try
faith in faith
109 **Use your own pleasure** if it please you; but Second Suitor interprets the phrase as a sexual invitation
111 **well** all right
113 **forthcoming** available in the future
117 **plaguy** disagreeable
ensnared trapped
118 **Pox o'** a curse upon
119 **slow . . . sure** Martino plays on the proverb 'slow but sure'.
120 **come short home** (*a*) return without bringing back all that they need—their haste causing forgetfulness or inefficiency (*b*) ejaculate prematurely
124 **Art thou got before me?** Have you got ahead of me?
125 **got before you** brought before you (as an accused man before a judge)
126 **In hold** in custody
133 **wrought** persuaded, convinced
136 **controversy** civil dispute; Ricardo is assuring Brandino that Francisco is not arrested for a crime.

RICARDO
That's all; trust me, sir.
BRANDINO
Francisco shall ne'er lie for't. He's my friend
And I will bail him.
MARTINO
He's your secret friend, master:
Think upon that.
BRANDINO
Give him his liberty, officers.
Upon my peril, he shall be forthcoming.
FRANCISCO
How I am bound to you!
FIRST SUITOR [*to Brandino*]
Know you whom you cross, sir?
'Tis at your sister's suit; be well advised, sir.
BRANDINO
How, at my sister's suit?—Take him again, then.
FRANCISCO
Why, sir, do you refuse me?
BRANDINO
I'll not hear thee.
RICARDO
This is unkindly done, sir.
FIRST SUITOR
'Tis wisely done, sir.
SECOND SUITOR
Well shot, foul malice.
FIRST SUITOR
Flattery stinks worse, sir.
RICARDO
You'll never leave till I make you stink as bad, sir.
FRANCISCO
O Martino, have I this for my late kindness?
MARTINO
Alas, poor gentleman! Dost complain to me?
Thou shalt not fare the worse for't.—Hark you,
master.
Your sister's suit, said you?
BRANDINO
Ay, sir, my wife's sister.
MARTINO
And shall that daunt you, master? Think again.
Why, were't your mother's suit—your mother's suit,
Mark what I say—the dearest suit of all suits,
You're bound in conscience, sir, to bail this gentle-
man.
BRANDINO
Yea, am I so? How prov'st thou that, Martino?
MARTINO
Have you forgot so soon what he did lately?
Has he not tried your wife to your hand, master,
To cut the throat of slander and suspicion?
And can you do too much for such a man?
Shall it be said I serve an ingrateful master?
BRANDINO
Never, Martino. I will bail him now,
An 'twere at my wife's suit.
FRANCISCO [*aside*]
'Tis like to be so.
MARTINO
And I his friend, to follow your example, master.
FRANCISCO
Precious Martino!
FIRST SUITOR [*to Brandino*]
You've done wondrous well, sir.
Your sister shall give you thanks.
RICARDO [*to Second Suitor*]
This makes him mad, sir.
SECOND SUITOR
We'll follow't now to th' proof.
FIRST SUITOR
Follow your humour out.
The widow shall find friends.
SECOND SUITOR
And so shall he, sir,
Money and means.
RICARDO [*to First Suitor*]
Hear you me that, old huddle?
[*Exit First Suitor, with officers*]
SECOND SUITOR
Mind him not. Follow me, and I'll supply thee.
Thou shalt give all thy lawyers double fees.
I've buried money enough to bury me,
And I will have my humour.
Exit [*Second Suitor, with Ricardo and Attilio*]
BRANDINO
Fare thee well once again, my dear Francisco.
I prithee, use my house.
FRANCISCO
It is my purpose, sir.
BRANDINO
Nay, you must do't then. Though I am old, I'm free.
Exit
MARTINO
And when you want a warrant, come to me. *Exit*
FRANCISCO
That will be shortly now, within this few hours.
This fell out strangely happy. Now to horse.
I shall be nighted, but an hour or two
Never breaks square in love. He comes in time
That comes at all; absence is all love's crime. *Exit*

137 **lie** (in jail)
138 **secret friend** (Martino reminds Brandino that Francisco has recently acted confidentially and trustworthily in testing Philippa's chastity)
140 **forthcoming** ready to appear when required; but also freed from custody
142 **sister's** sister-in-law (see 2.2.151)
145 **unkindly** ungenerously, unnaturally (see 1.2.46)
146 **Well shot** an applauding exclamation when a shooter hits the mark
148 **kindness** generosity
158 **to your hand** without exertion on your part
163 **An 'twere . . . suit** even if it were her suit (to imprison him)
'Tis like to be so it's likely to be her suit (to relieve him)
164 **And I his friend** (Martino bails Attilio.)
167 **to th' proof** to the court hearing
169 **huddle** a miserly old person
170 **supply** provide for
176 **free** generous, ready to give. The word derives from Old English, in which its primary sense was 'not in bondage to another'; it developed two main paths of meaning, the first associated with looseness and absence of restriction, the second with nobility of birth or character, whence the sense of generosity and magnanimity that Brandino invokes here.
179 **happy** fortunately
180 **nighted** overtaken by night
181 **breaks square** does no harm, does not matter
182 **all love's crime** the only crime in love

3.1 *Incipit Actus 3*

Enter Occulto, Silvio, and two or three other thieves

OCCULTO
Come, come, let's watch th'event on yonder hill.
If he need help, we can relieve him suddenly.

SILVIO
Ay, and with safety too, the hill being watched, sir.

OCCULTO
Have you the blue coats and the beards?

SILVIO
They're here, sir.

OCCULTO
Come, come away, then. A fine cock-shoot evening.

Exit [Occulto, with other thieves]

Enter Latrocinio (the chief thief) and Ansaldo

LATROCINIO [*singing*]
Kuck before and kuck behind, *etc.*

ANSALDO
Troth, you're the merriest and delightful'st company, sir,
That ever traveller was blessed withal.
I praise my fortune that I overtook you, sir.

LATROCINIO
Pish, I've a hundred of 'em.

ANSALDO
And believe me, sir,
I'm infinitely taken with such things.

LATROCINIO
I see there's music in you. You kept time, methought,
Pretty and handsomely with your little hand there.

ANSALDO
It only shows desire but, troth, no skill, sir.

LATROCINIO
Well, while our horses walk down yonder hill, sir,
I'll have another for you.

ANSALDO
It rids way pleasantly.

LATROCINIO
Lemme see now. One confounds another, sir.
You've heard this certainly: [*sings*] Come, my dainty doxies.

ANSALDO
O that's all the country over, sir.
There's scarce a gentlewoman but has that pricked.

LATROCINIO
Well, here comes one I'm sure you never heard then.

[*He sings a*] *song*

I keep my horse, I keep my whore,
I take no rents, yet am not poor.
I travel all the land about
And yet was born to ne'er a foot.
With partridge plump, with woodcock fine,
I do at midnight often dine,
And if my whore be not in case
My hostess' daughter takes her place.
The maids sit up and watch their turns;
If I stay long the tapster mourns;
The cook-maid has no mind to sin,
Though tempted by the chamberl'in.
But when I knock, O how they bustle!
The ostler yawns, the geldings justle.

3.1.0.2 ***Occulto*** Italian, 'hidden, concealed, secret, close' (Florio)

Silvio 'of the woods' (from Latin *silva*, a wood; not in Florio)

0.3 ***thieves*** People who make a living by stealing from others—like the thieves eulogized by Martino earlier (1.1.43–62)—permeate the play's social world: the miller is a thief (4.2.39–44), as is the tailor (4.2.40–5), and the play's medical practitioners are (literally) thieves (4.2). All economic activity can be understood as theft, in so far as it operates, not through fair exchange within carefully constructed rules (under the medieval guild system), but through improvisation and deception (increasingly, under emergent capitalism). The thief is therefore located at the centre of a system of circulation, 'the sequence of the world' (*Five Gallants* 3.1.135), which runs from usury to prostitution, innkeeping, farming, and the court (3.1.115–22). Moreover, theft is often associated with lechery, a woman's body being regarded as a man's possession, which another man may steal. Hence Tarquin for raping Lucrece is called 'a Roman thief' (*Ghost* 275), and when Moll elopes the Yellowhammers exclaim 'Some thief hath got her' (*Chaste Maid* 4.2.1); 'adulterous thefts' (*Women Beware* 4.3.36) and 'a stolen ... kiss' (*Hengist* 1.2.13) may lead to the conception of a bastard child, who steals into the world illegitimately, 'the thief of nature' (*Revenger* 1.2.159). Combining larceny and lechery, theft epitomizes unregenerate humanity, from Adam and Eve's theft of the apple to the two thieves crucified on either side of Christ. Thus, when Middleton's characters think of the ten commandments, it is the seventh ('Thou shalt not steal') which comes to mind: *Puritan* 1.4.126–44, *Five Gallants* 3.4.109, *Measure* 1.2.10.

1 **th'event** the result

2 **relieve** (*a*) provide comfort; (*b*) take his possessions

3 **the hill being watched** (*a*) provided with watchers (themselves); (*b*) guarded by a watch

4 **blue coats ... beards** their disguise; blue coats were worn by servants

5 **cock-shoot** a broad way or glade in a wood, through which woodcocks etc might dart or 'shoot' so as to be caught by nets stretched across the opening; thus here a fine evening to catch foolish birds, i.e. unsuspecting travellers

5.2 ***Latrocinio*** Italian, 'larceny, theft, stealing' (Florio)

6 **Kuck ... behind** a refrain from a (lost) song

Kuck void excrement (but also probably suggesting 'cock' = penis)

before in front

9 **overtook** caught up with

11 **infinitely** exceedingly

16 **rids way** passes the time on the journey

17 **confounds** becomes confused with

18 **Come, my dainty doxies** For the full text of this song, see *Dissemblers* 4.2.56–81.

doxies whores, but also 'gypsy sweethearts'

20 **pricked** noted down or marked; but also with sexual puns on 'country' and 'prick'

22 **I keep my horse** For a musical setting, see *Companion*, p. 152.

28 **not in case** not in good physical condition, i.e. menstruating; case = female genitals

30 **watch their turns** take turns to be on duty (?)

33 **chamberl'in** waiter

If maid but sleep, O how they curse her!
And all this comes of 'Deliver your purse, sir!'
[*He draws a weapon*]

ANSALDO How, sir?

LATROCINIO
Few words. Quickly, come, deliver your purse, sir.

ANSALDO
You're not that kind of gentleman, I hope, sir,
To sing me out of my money.

LATROCINIO 'Tis most fit
Art should be rewarded. You must pay your music, sir,
Where'er you come.

ANSALDO But not at your own carving.

LATROCINIO
Nor am I common in't. Come, come, your purse, sir.

ANSALDO
Say it should prove th'undoing of a gentleman?

LATROCINIO Why, sir, do you look for more conscience in us than in usurers? Young gentleman, you've small reason for that, i'faith.

ANSALDO [*giving his purse*]
There 'tis, and all I have, and—so truth comfort me—
All I know where to have.

LATROCINIO Sir, that's not written
In my belief yet. Search. 'Tis a fine evening;
Your horse can take no harm. I must have more, sir.

ANSALDO
May my hopes perish if you have not all, sir,
And more I know than your compassionate charity
Would keep from me, if you but felt my wants.

LATROCINIO
Search, and that speedily. If I take you in hand,
You'll find me rough. Methinks men should be ruled
When they're so kindly spoke to. Fie upon't!

ANSALDO [*aside*]
Good fortune and my wit assist me then!
A thing I took in haste, and never thought on't.—
Look, sir, I've searched; here's all that I can find,
[*He shows a pistol*]
And you're so covetous, you will have all, you say,
And I'm content you shall, being kindly spoke to.

LATROCINIO
A pox o' that young devil of a handful long!
That's frayed many a tall thief from a rich purchase.

ANSALDO
This and my money, sir, keeps company.
Where one goes, th'other must. Assure your soul
They vowed never to part.

LATROCINIO Hold, I beseech you, sir.

ANSALDO
You rob a prisoner's box, an you rob me, sir.

LATROCINIO [*giving back the purse*]
There 'tis again.

ANSALDO I knew 'twould never prosper with you.
Fie, rob a younger brother? O take heed, sir.
'Tis against nature, that. Perhaps your father
Was one, sir, or your uncle; It should seem so
By the small means was left you, and less manners.
Go, keep you still before me. And do you hear me?
To pass away the time to the next town,
I charge you, sir, sing all your songs for nothing.

LATROCINIO
O horrible punishment!
[*He sings*] *a song*
Enter Stratio [*disguised as a servant*]

STRATIO Honest gentleman—

ANSALDO
How now, what art thou?

STRATIO Stand you in need of help?
I made all haste I could. My master charged me,
A knight of worship. He saw you first assaulted
From top of yonder hill.

ANSALDO Thanks, honest friend.

LATROCINIO [*aside*]
I taste this trick already. *Exit*

STRATIO Look, he's gone, sir.
Shall he be stopped? What is he?

ANSALDO Let him go, sir.
He can rejoice in nothing; that's the comfort.

STRATIO
You have your purse still then?

ANSALDO Ay, thanks fair fortune
And this grim handful.

STRATIO We were all so 'fraid o' you.
How my good lady cried, 'O help the gentleman!'
'Tis a good woman, that. But you're too mild, sir.
You should ha' marked him for a villain, faith,
Before he'd gone, having so sound a means, too.

37 **'Deliver . . . sir!'** the highwayman's challenge
39 **Few words** 'Few words and many deeds' (proverb)
42 **Art** his skill in singing, but also his cunning in deceiving Ansaldo; see 2.1.57
music musicians
43 **at your own carving** as you please
44 **common** ordinary, commonplace
in't in singing
50 **All . . . have** all I am aware of having anywhere
50–1 **that's . . . belief** I am not persuaded of that
56 **take you in hand** Latrocinio's threat of violence comes in a phrase whose standard meaning is 'to assume responsibility for someone'.
59 **wit** quickness of invention
64 **young devil . . . long** the pistol
65 **frayed** frightened
tall bold
purchase booty, prize
69 **prisoner's box** the box let down by the prisoner through the prison-grating, to receive money or food from the charitable
71 **younger brother** proverbially poor, since the oldest son traditionally inherited the family estate
78.2 ***Stratio*** Italian, 'torture, torment, rough handling, ill usage' (Florio)
81 **worship** renown
83 **taste** perceive, recognize
86 **thanks** thanks to
87 **grim handful** the pistol
o' you for your wellbeing
90 **marked** with a wound

ANSALDO
Why, there's the jest, man. He had once my purse—
STRATIO
O villain! Would you let him 'scape unmassacred?
ANSALDO
Nay, hear me, sir. I made him yield it straight again
And—so hope bless me!—with an uncharged pistol.
STRATIO
Troth, I should laugh at that.
ANSALDO It was discharged, sir,
Before I meddled with't.
STRATIO I'm glad to hear't.
[*He threatens Ansaldo*]
ANSALDO
Why, how now, what's your will?
STRATIO Ho! Latrocinio, Occulto, Silvio!
Enter Latrocinio and the rest: Occulto, Silvio, Fiducio
LATROCINIO [*to Ansaldo*] What, are you caught, sir?
STRATIO The pistol cannot speak.
LATROCINIO He was too young.
I ever thought he could not, yet I feared him.
ANSALDO
You've found out ways too merciless to betray
Under the veil of friendship and of charity.
LATROCINIO
Away, sirs! Bear him in to th' next copse and strip him.
STRATIO Brandino's copse, the Justice?
LATROCINIO Best of all, sir, a man of law. A spider lies unsuspected in the corner of a buckram bag, man.
ANSALDO
What seek you, sirs? Take all, and use no cruelty.
LATROCINIO You shall have songs enough.
ALL THIEVES [*singing a*] *song*
How round the world goes
And everything that's in it.
The tides of gold and silver
Ebb and flow in a minute.
From the usurer to his sons,
There a current swiftly runs;
From the sons to queans in chief,
From the gallant to the thief,
From the thief unto his host,
From the host to husbandmen,
From the country to the court,
And so comes to use again.
How round the world goes
And everything that's in it.
The tides of gold and silver
Ebb and flow in a minute. *Exeunt*

Enter Philippa and Violetta above at the window 3.2
PHILIPPA
What time of night is't?
VIOLETTA Time of night do you call't?
It's so late, 'tis almost early, mistress.
PHILIPPA
Fie on him! There's no looking for him, then.
Why, sure this gentleman apprehends me not.
VIOLETTA
'Tis happy then you're rid of such a fool, mistress.
PHILIPPA
Nay sure, wench, if he find me not out in this,
Which were a beaten path to any wiseman,
I'll never trust him with my reputation.
Therefore I made this trial of his wit.
If he cannot conceive what's good for himself,

95 **uncharged** unloaded
97 **meddled** concerned myself
98.2 ***Fiducio*** Italian, 'Fiducia, trust, faith, confidence' (Florio)
108 **buckram bag** a lawyer's bag; buckram is a kind of coarse linen or cloth stiffened with gum or paste
111 **round the world goes** In the new Copernican astronomy, the earth was not fixed at the centre of the universe, but a globe which rotated on its axis, and revolved around the sun.
112 **And...it** An increasingly globalized economy brought commodities to London from the Americas, Africa, and Asia.
113–14 **The tides...minute** money comes and goes quickly and endlessly (like the tides on which ships left and returned to the port of London, on transoceanic commercial voyages).
114 **minute** A subdivision of time increasingly significant to urban Protestant populations: personal timepieces, though still expensive, became for the first time reasonably reliable, enabling a new discipline of business practices, scientific observation, and personal behaviour. Kepler declared, in Middleton's lifetime, that 'the universe...is similar to a clock'.
115 **usurer** moneylender (an increasingly important figure, in an emergent capitalist economy). The sons of men who had hoarded money in their lifetime were often portrayed as lecherous prodigals; the progress described here in 115–17 also occurs in *Microcynicon*.
117 **queans** whores (see also 1.2.133)
in chief in the chief or highest position
118 **gallant** fashionable woman (*OED* sb.1.b), but used here as a synonym for 'quean'.
120 **husbandmen** farmers (who would be paid by the host, for supplying him with produce for his inn or tavern, and who would in turn pay rents to the lord of their estates, thereby passing the money from 'country' to 'court')
122 **use** usury (thus completing the circle, returning to the usurer). The Jacobean court was heavily in debt; much of the money courtiers collected from their country estates went to pay off interest on loans. But 'use' also has less technical senses: money in circulation is being 'used', rather than sitting idle, and the particular economy imagined in this song involves, in part, sexual employment (also called 'use').
3.2.4 **apprehends me not** does not understand me, does not get the point of the letter. The word derives from Latin *apprehendere*, to seize. In English it is used both in the sense of physical seizing, as in arrests, and of mental grasping, as in learning. In the latter strain it includes the idea of understanding mentally, and also that of being sensible of something or somebody. Philippa here despairs (*a*) of Francisco's *wit*, although he has indeed understood her message perfectly (see 1.2.203); (*b*) of his attention, since he has not appeared, and (*c*) of being seized physically by him.
6 **find...out** (*a*) does not understand my intention; (*b*) does not discover what I'm like
7 **a beaten path** obvious

He will worse understand what's good for me.

VIOLETTA
But suppose, mistress, as it may be likely,
He never saw your letter.

PHILIPPA
How thou plyest me
With suppositions! Why, I tell thee, wench,
'Tis equally as impossible for my husband
To keep it from him as to be young again,
Or as his first wife knew him, which he brags on
For bearing children by him.

VIOLETTA
There's no remedy then.
I must conclude Francisco is an ass.

PHILIPPA
I would my letter, wench, were here again.
I'd know him wiser ere I sent him one,
And travel some five year first.

VIOLETTA
So he'd need, methinks,
To understand the words. Methinks the words
Themselves should make him do't, had he but the perceiverance
Of a cock-sparrow, that will come at 'Philip!',
And can nor write nor read, poor fool. This coxcomb,
He can do both, and your name's but Philippa,
And yet to see if he can come when's called!

PHILIPPA
He never shall be called again for me, sirrah.
Well, as hard as the world goes, we'll have a song, wench;
We'll not sit up for nothing.

VIOLETTA
That's poor comfort, though.

PHILIPPA
Better than any's brought, for aught I see yet.
So set to your lute.
[*They sing a*] *song*

[PHILIPPA]
If in this question I propound to thee
Be any, any choice,
Let me have thy voice.

[VIOLETTA]
You shall most free.

[PHILIPPA]
Which hadst thou rather be
If thou mightst choose thy life:
A fool's, a fool's mistress
Or an old man's wife?

[VIOLETTA]
The choice is hard; I know not which is best.
One ill you're bound to, and I think that's least.

[PHILIPPA]
But being not bound, my dearest sweet,
I could shake off the other.

[VIOLETTA]
Then, as you lose your sport by one,
You lose your name by t'other.

[PHILIPPA]
You counsel well, but love refuses
What good counsel often chooses.
[*They remain above, unseen*]
Enter Ansaldo in his shirt [*below*]

ANSALDO
I ha' got myself unbound yet. Merciless villains!
I never felt such hardness since life dwelt in me.
'Tis for my sins. That light in yonder window—
That was my only comfort in the woods,
Which oft the trembling of a leaf would lose me—
Has brought me thus far; yet I cannot hope
For succour in this plight: the world's so pitiless,
And everyone will fear or doubt me now.
To knock will be too bold; I'll to the gate
And listen if I can hear any stirring.
Enter Francisco [*aloof*]

FRANCISCO [*aside*]
Was ever man so crossed?—No, 'tis but sweat, sure,
Or the dew dropping from the leaves above me;
I thought 't'ad bled again. These wenching businesses
Are strange unlucky things and fatal fooleries;
No mar'l so many gallants die ere thirty.
'Tis able to vex out a man's heart in five year,
The crosses that belong to't: first, arrested—
That set me back two mangy hours at least;
Yet that's a thing my heat could have forgiv'n,
Because arresting, in what kind soever,
Is a most gentleman-like affliction.
But here, within a mile o'th' town, forsooth,
And two mile off this place, when a man's oath
Might ha' been taken for his own security,
And his thoughts brisk and set upon the business,
To light upon a roguy flight of thieves—

13 **plyest** importune
16 **it** the letter
22 **travel some five year first** grow up from the experience of five years travelling. (Philippa is impatient with Francisco's apparent failure to respond to her invitation.)
24 **perceiverance** perception, understanding
25 **'Philip!'** a common name for sparrows
33 **set to** direct your attention to
34–48 PHILIPPA...PHILIPPA The 1653 edition attributes the lines of the song simply to speakers '1' and '2'; the distribution adopted here might be reversed.
37 **free** readily
43 **One ill** being an old man's wife
45 **shake off the other** be rid of the fool
46 **sport** sexual pleasure
47 **name** reputation (either as a chaste wife because the fool reveals the relationship to others, or as an intelligent woman because she has a fool for a lover)
49.2 ***shirt*** a long white shirt, like a nightshirt, which might be worn by a man or a woman (see 3.3.29), and which in the theatre was the usual costume for representing a ghost or apparition
50 **yet** nevertheless
54 **would lose me** would cause me to lose
57 **doubt** suspect
60 **crossed** thwarted
65 **vex out** wear out with frustration
66 **crosses** frustrations, thwartings
68 **heat** (*a*) excess bodily temperature, caused by physical exertion (*b*) emotional intensity (*c*) sexual excitement
72 **off** distant from
75 **roguy** roguish, dishonest
flight flock (usually of birds)

Pox on 'em! Here's the length of one of their whittles.
But one of my dear rascals I pursued so
The jail has him, and he shall bring out's fellows.
Had ever young man's love such crooked fortune?
I'm glad I'm so near yet. The surgeon bade me too
Have a great care. I shall never think of that now.

ANSALDO [*aside*]
One of the thieves come back again? I'll stand close.
He dares not wrong me now, so near the house,
And call in vain 'tis, till I see him offer't.

FRANCISCO [*aside*]
Life, what should that be? A prodigious thing
Stands just as I should enter, in that shape too
Which always appears terrible.
Whate'er it be, it is made strong against me
By my ill purpose. For 'tis man's own sin
That puts an armour upon all his evils
And gives them strength to strike him. Were it less
Than what it is, my guilt would make it serve.
A wicked man's own shadow has distracted him.
Were this a business now to save an honour,
As 'tis to spoil one, I would pass this then,
Stuck all hell's horrors i' thee; now I dare not.
Why may't not be the spirit of my father
That loved this man so well, whom I make haste
Now to abuse? And I have been crossed about it
Most fearfully hitherto, if I well think on't,
'Scaped death but lately too, nay most miraculously.
And what does fond man venture all these ills for,
That may so sweetly rest in honest peace?
For that which, being obtained, [
] is as he was
To his own sense, but removed nearer still
To death eternal. What delight has man
Now at this present for his pleasant sin
Of yesterday's committing? 'Las, 'tis vanished,
And nothing but the sting remains within him.
The kind man bailed me too. I will not do't now,
An 'twere but only that. How blest were man,
Might he but have his end appear still to him,
That he might read his actions i'th' event?
'Twould make him write true, though he never
meant.
Whose check soe'er thou art, father's or friend's
Or enemy's, I thank thee. Peace requite thee.—
Light, and the lighter mistress, both farewell.
He keeps his promise best that breaks with hell. *Exit*

ANSALDO
He's gone to call the rest, and makes all speed.
I'll knock, whate'er befalls, to please my fears,
For no compassion can be less than theirs.
[*Ansaldo knocks*]

PHILIPPA
He's come, he's come.—O, are you come at last, sir?
Make little noise.—Away, he'll knock again else.
[*Exeunt above*]

ANSALDO
I should have been at Istria, by daybreak too;
Near to Valeria's house, the wealthy widow's,
There waits one purposely to do me good.
What will become of me?
Enter Violetta [*below*]

VIOLETTA
O you're a sweet gallant. This, your hour?

76 **whittles** large knives; a reference to his wound(?)
77 **dear rascals** a pun on 'rascal', a young or inferior deer (*OED* sb.4.b)
78 **bring out's** produce his
80 **yet** nevertheless
82 **close** concealed
84 **call in vain 'tis** it would be pointless to call for help
offer't offer wrong, attack or rob
85 **prodigious** ominous
86–7 **that shape . . . terrible** (Ansaldo out of doors at night dressed in just a shirt appears to Francisco to be an apparition.)
90 **armour** One meaning of *armour* was 'those strong and powerful lusts of sin, whereby Satan conquereth natural men, and holdeth them fast under his banner and dominion' (Wilson).
92 **serve** fulfil the function of an ominous warning, or simply overcome him
93 **distracted him** driven him insane
94–5 **to save . . . one** to preserve a woman's chastity as it is in fact to defile one
96 **Stuck . . . i' thee** even if all hell's horrors were bristling on you
98 **loved . . . well** Brandino was a great friend of Francisco's father (see 1.2.221–43)
99 **crossed about it** thwarted in pursuit of it
101 **miraculously** (In this crisis of conscience Francisco interprets all events as examples of miraculous intervention. See Introduction.)
102 **fond** (*a*) foolish (*b*) enamoured
104–5 There appears to be a gap in the text here. We can only guess at the missing words; perhaps something like 'favours the beggar | With a minute's dream; who, waked,'.
108 **Now at this present** right now, by contrast to yesterday when the sin was committed (but also implying 'at this moment, here in the theatre', as in *Revenger* 2.2.136–43, 157–8, etc.)
pleasant that gives pleasure, in this context to be rejected as a false corrupt desire
110 **sting** the acute pain of guilty conscience
111 **The kind man** Brandino; kind = generous, natural (see 1.2.46); in his crisis of conscience Francisco has a new view of Brandino.
112 **An . . . that** if only for that reason (Brandino's bailing of him)
113 **end** death
still always
114 **read** recognize the true nature of
event outcome
115 **'Twould . . . meant** i.e., it would make him act honestly even if he had not set out to
116 **check** rebuke, corrective
118 **Light . . . lighter mistress** the light that Ansaldo saw (3.2.52); Philippa as unchaste (*lighter*)
119 **breaks with** breaks (his promise) to, breaks off (relations) with
125 **Istria** the sole reference in the text to the location of the action; Istria is a peninsula in the northern Adriatic, the northern part of which is now in Slovenia, the rest Croatia. It was governed at the time by Venice—hence the play's Italian names and idioms. Though the source stories in Boccaccio's *Decameron*, 2.2 and 3.3, apparently take place in Italy, there is no reference to a specific location.

Give me your hand. Come, come, sir, follow me.
I'll bring you to light presently. Softly, softly, sir.
Exeunt

3.3 *Enter Philippa below*

PHILIPPA
I should ha' given him up to all my thoughts
The dullest young man, if he had not found it.
So short of apprehension and so witless,
He were not fit for woman's fellowship.
I've been at cost too for a banquet for him.
Why, 'twould ha' killed my heart, and most especially
To think that man should ha' no more conceit.
I should ha' thought the worse on's wit forever,
And blamed mine own for too much forwardness.
Enter Violetta

VIOLETTA
O mistress, mistress!

PHILIPPA How now, what's the news?

VIOLETTA
O I was out of my wits for a minute and a half.

PHILIPPA Ha?

VIOLETTA They are scarce settled yet, mistress.

PHILIPPA What's the matter?

VIOLETTA Do you ask that seriously?
Did you not hear me squeak?

PHILIPPA How? Sure thou art
Out of thy wits indeed.

VIOLETTA O, I'm well now,
To what I was, mistress.

PHILIPPA Why, where's the gentleman?

VIOLETTA
The gentleman's forthcoming, and a lovely one,
But not Francisco.

PHILIPPA What sayst? not Francisco?

VIOLETTA
Pish, he's a coxcomb. Think not on him, mistress.

PHILIPPA What's all this?

VIOLETTA
I've often heard you say ye'd rather have
A wise man in his shirt than a fool feathered,
And now Fortune has sent you one, a sweet young gentleman,
Robbed e'en to nothing but what first he brought with him.
The slaves had stripped him to th' very shirt, mistress.
I think it was a shirt; I know not well,
For gallants wear both nowadays.

PHILIPPA This is strange.

VIOLETTA
But for a face, a hand, and as much skin
As I durst look upon, he's a most sweet one.
Francisco is a child of Egypt to him.
I could not but in pity to th' poor gentleman
Fetch him down one of my old master's suits.

PHILIPPA 'Twas charitably done.

VIOLETTA
You'd say, mistress, if you had seen him as I did.
Sweet youth! I'll be sworn, mistress, he's the loveliest,
Proper'st young gentleman, and so you'll say yourself,
If my master's clothes do not spoil him; that's all the fear now.
I would 't'ad been your luck to have seen him
Without 'em, but for scaring on you.

PHILIPPA
Go, prithee fetch him in whom thou commend'st so.
Exit Violetta
Since fortune sends him, surely we'll make much on him;
And better he deserves our love and welcome
Than the respectless fellow 'twas prepared for.
Yet if he please mine eye never so happily
I will have trïal of his wit and faith
Before I make him partner with my honour.
'Twas just Francisco's case, and he deceived me.
I'll take more heed o'th' next for't. Perhaps now

131 **light** Compare the light that guided Ansaldo to the house initially (3.2.52), and the beauty and 'lightness' of Philippa (3.2.118), who expects Ansaldo to be Francisco.
3.3.1 **given . . . thoughts** considered him
2 **found it** i.e., understood the implied message in the letter she sent to him through her husband
3 **apprehension** understanding; see 3.2.4.
witless (*a*) senseless, without ingenuity or prudence (*b*) without physical sensation—associated with possible sexual innuendoes in *short* (with a small penis), *dullest* (not easily aroused), and *fit* (just right for snug intercourse)
5 **banquet** either a sumptuous entertainment or an exquisite dessert; whichever, rich food was thought to stimulate sexual appetites
7 **conceit** understanding. The word derives from 'conceive' and initially has the sense of an idea or thought, something conceived; but it develops the sense of the capacity for having ideas or thoughts. The sense 'esteem' and 'self-esteem' were current at the time of the play, but here the word seems more to be associated with imaginative intelligence and capacity for judgement.
8 **wit** intelligence; Philippa desires acuteness of social perception and invention. See 3.3.3.
9 **forwardness** boldness
11, 17 **out of . . . wits** mad
11 **minute** See 3.1.114.
18 **To** compared with
21 **Pish** an exclamation of rejection or contempt
24 **feathered** fully dressed with an expensive feather in his hat, hence wealthy
26 **what first . . . him** an allusion to being born naked
29 **both** shirts and smocks (conventionally men's and women's clothes respectively, but the second decade of the 17th century witnessed a brief flourishing of unisex fashions, with women wearing styles previously limited to men, and vice versa)
32 **child of Egypt** dark-complexioned like a gypsy or an Egyptian, and therefore less attractive within the conventional values of the time (but also, a sinner, contrasted with 'the chosen people, the elect' who escaped from Egypt into Israel)
38 **Proper'st** handsomest
41 **but for scaring on you** except that you would have been scared. (Violetta mocks Philippa's sexual interest in young men.)
45 **respectless** discourteous
46 **if he . . . happily** however attractive I happen to find him
47 **wit** intelligence; see 3.3.8
48 **honour** reputation for chastity

To furnish his distress he will appear
Full of fair promising courtship; but I'll prove him then
For a next meeting, when he needs me not,
And see what he performs then when the storm
Of his so rude misfortunes is blown over
And he himself again. A distressed man's flatteries
Are like vows made in drink, or bonds in prison:
There's poor assurance in 'em. When he's from me
And in's own pow'r, then I shall see his love.

Enter Ansaldo [in Brandino's clothes] and Violetta

Mass, here he comes.

[*Ansaldo and Violetta talk apart*]

ANSALDO Never was star-crossed gentleman
More happy in a courteous virgin's love
Than I in yours.

VIOLETTA I'm sorry they're no better for you.
I wished 'em handsomer and more in fashion,
But truly, sir, our house affords it not.
There is a suit of our clerk's hangs i'th' garret,
But that's far worse than this, if I may judge
With modesty of men's matters.

ANSALDO I deserve not this,
Dear and kind gentlewoman. Is yon your mistress?

PHILIPPA
Why, trust me, here's my husband young again!—
It is no sin to welcome you, sweet gentleman.

ANSALDO
I am so much indebted, courteous lady,
To the unmatchèd charity of your house,
My thanks are such poor things they would but shame me.

[*Philippa and Violetta talk apart*]

PHILIPPA
Beshrew thy heart for bringing o' him! I fear me
I have found wit enough already in him.
If I could truly but resolve myself
My husband was thus handsome at nineteen,
Troth, I should think the better of him at fourscore now.

VIOLETTA
Nay, mistress, what would he be, were he in fashion—
A hempen curse on those that put him out on't!—
That now appears so handsome and so comely, in clothes
Able to make a man an unbeliever
And good for nothing but for shift or so
If a man chance to fall i'th' ditch with better?
This is the best that ever I marked in 'em.
A man may make him ready in such clothes
Without a candle.

PHILIPPA Ay, for shame of himself, wench.

VIOLETTA
My master does it oft in winter mornings
And never sees himself till he be ready.

PHILIPPA
No, nor then neither, as he should do, wench.—
I am sorry, gentle sir, we cannot show you
A courtesy in all points answerable
To your undoubted worth. Your name I crave, sir.

ANSALDO
Ansaldo, lady.

PHILIPPA 'Tis a noble name, sir.

ANSALDO
The most unfortunate now.

VIOLETTA So do I think, truly,
As long as that suit's on.

PHILIPPA The most unfitting
And unprovidest, sir, of all our courtesies,
I do presume, is that you've passed already.
Your pardon but for that, and we're encouraged.

ANSALDO
My faithful service, lady.

PHILIPPA Please you, sir,
To taste the next, a poor slight banquet, for sure I think you were
Unluckily prevented of your supper, sir.

ANSALDO
My fortune makes me more than amends, lady,
In your sweet kindness, which (so nobly shown to me)
It makes me bold to speak my occasions to you.
I am this morning, that with clearness now
So cheerfully hastens me, to meet a friend
Upon my state's establishing, and the place

51 **furnish** embellish, render more attractive
52 **prove** make trial of. See *try*, 1.1.95.
55 **rude** harsh
57 **bonds** covenants, agreements
58 **from** away from
60 **star-crossed** ill-fated
62 **they're** the clothes are
64 **house** perhaps with the sense 'playhouse' (*OED* 4g: from Latin *domus*). Here, the theatrical sense would add a joke about the company's wardrobe; see also 5.1.213 and 5.1.272.
67 **matters** (with a flirting innuendo on the sense 'genitals')
74 **Beshrew** curse
75 **wit** hardly 'intelligence, ingenuity', since Ansaldo has shown neither yet; rather Philippa has found in Ansaldo a sexually attractive person able to replace Francisco and so uses *wit* ironically as a convenient term for her desire
76 **resolve** convince
80 **A hempen curse on those** may they be hanged
out on't out of fashion
82 **Able...unbeliever** clothes not fit for a Christian. If (proverbially) 'clothes make the man', then these clothes are so atrocious that they could turn a Christian into a pagan.
83 **for shift** for want of something better; as makeshift
85 **marked** observed, saw
86 **make him ready** dress himself
96 **unfitting** unbecoming (punning on 'poorly fitting')
97 **unprovidest** unprepared
100 **service** See 1.1.223.
101 **banquet** the meal prepared for Francisco; see 3.3.5
102 **prevented of** deprived of
105 **occasions** business affairs
108 **Upon** about
state's financial affairs

Ten mile from hence. O I am forced unwillingly
To crave your leave for't; which done, I return
In service plentiful.

PHILIPPA Is't so important?

ANSALDO
If I should fail, as much as my undoing.

PHILIPPA
I think too well of you to undo you, sir,
Upon this small acquaintance.

ANSALDO My great happiness.

PHILIPPA
But when should I be sure of you here again, sir?

ANSALDO
As fast as speed can possibly return me.

PHILIPPA You will not fail?

ANSALDO
May never wish go well with me then!

PHILIPPA [*giving him money*]
There's to bear charges, sir.

ANSALDO Courtesy dwells in you.
I brought my horse up with me from the woods;
That's all the good they left me, 'gainst their wills too.
May your kind breast never want comfort, lady,
But still supplied as liberally as you give.

PHILIPPA
Farewell, sir, and be faithful.

ANSALDO Time shall prove me.
Exit

PHILIPPA
In my opinion now, this young man's likeliest
To keep his word. He's modest, wise, and courteous.
He has the language of an honest soul in him.
A woman's reputation may lie safe there.
I'm much deceived else. H'as a faithful eye,
If it be well observed.

VIOLETTA [*calling*] Good speed be with thee, sir!—
He puts him to't, i'faith.

PHILIPPA Violetta.

VIOLETTA Mistress?

PHILIPPA
Alas, what have we done, wench?

VIOLETTA What's the matter, mistress?

PHILIPPA
Run, run, call him again. He must stay, tell him,
Though it be upon's undoing. We're undone else.
Your master's clothes, they're known the country
over.

VIOLETTA
Now by this light that's true, and well remembered.
But there's no calling of him; he's out of sight now.

PHILIPPA
O what will people think?

VIOLETTA What can they think, mistress?
The gentleman has the worst on't. Were I he now
I'd make this ten mile forty mile about
Before I'd ride through any market town with 'em.

PHILIPPA
Will he be careful, think'st?

VIOLETTA My life for yours, mistress.

PHILIPPA
I shall long mightily to see him again.

VIOLETTA
And so shall I; I shall ne'er laugh till then. *Exeunt*

Incipit Actus 4 4.1
Enter Ricardo and Second Suitor at one door, and Valeria and First Suitor at another door. [*Ricardo and Second Suitor talk apart*]

RICARDO
It goes well hitherto, my sweet protector.

SECOND SUITOR
Ay, and shall still to th'end, to th'end, my honey.
Wherefore have I enough, but to have't go well, sir?
[*Valeria and First Suitor talk apart*]

FIRST SUITOR
My whole state on't: thou overthrow'st him, widow.

VALERIA
I hope well still, sir.

FIRST SUITOR Hope? Be certain, wench.
I make no question now but thou art mine,
As sure as if I had thee in thy night-gear.

VALERIA
By'r Lady, that I doubt, sir.

FIRST SUITOR O, 'tis clear, wench,
By one thing that I marked.

VALERIA What's that, good sweet sir?

FIRST SUITOR
A thing that never failed me.

VALERIA Good sir, what?

109 **Ten mile** Ansaldo presumably intends to keep his rendezvous at Istria, near Valeria's house (3.2.125–7). His sense of the distance may be vague: elsewhere, Francisco (soon after leaving Valeria's) speaks of being fifteen miles from Brandino's house (2.2.9), and Brandino speaks of Violetta riding fifteen miles for a meeting with Valeria and Ricardo (4.1.124). However, it is not clear exactly where 2.2 or 4.1 takes place. Brandino's house is a mile from town, and two miles from where the thieves attacked Francisco and Ansaldo (3.2.71–2). The play takes place in an area where everyone knows everyone else, with a small 'market town' (3.3.141), highways, and apparently isolated houses owned by wealthy gentry; it resembles an English county.

119 **bear charges** pay your expenses

122 **kind** naturally charitable

131 **puts him to't** rides his horse hard (which Violetta perceives as a sign of virility)

135 **country** countryside, county

143 **mightily** greatly

4.1.4 **state** estate

7 **night-gear** night clothes

FIRST SUITOR
I heard our counsellor speak a word of comfort:
Invita voluntate. Ha! That's he, wench,
The word of words, the precious chief, i'faith.

VALERIA
Invita voluntate. What's the meaning, sir?

FIRST SUITOR
Nay, there I leave you. But assure you thus much,
I never heard him speak that word i' my life
But the cause went on's side; that I marked ever.
[*Ricardo and Second Suitor talk apart*]

SECOND SUITOR
Do, do, and spare not! Thou wouldst talk with her?

RICARDO
Yes, with your leave and liking.

SECOND SUITOR Do, my adoption,
My chosen child. An thou hold'st so obedient,
Sure thou wilt live, and cozen all my kindred.

RICARDO
A child's part in your love, that's my ambition, sir.

SECOND SUITOR
Go and deserve it then. Please me well now.
I love wrangling, o' life, boy; there's my delight.
I have no other venery but vexation;
That's all my honey now. Smartly now to her!
I've enough, and I will have my humour.

RICARDO
This need not ha' been, widow.

VALERIA You say right, sir.
No, nor your treachery, your close conspiracy
Against me for my wealth need not ha' been neither.

RICARDO
I had you fairly. I scorn treachery
To your woman that I never meant to marry,
Much more to you whom I reserved for wife.

VALERIA How, wife?

RICARDO
Ay, wife, wife, widow. Be not ashamed on't;
It's the best calling ever woman came to,
And all your grace indeed, brag as you list.

SECOND SUITOR Ha ha!

VALERIA
I grant you, sir—but not to be *your* wife.

FIRST SUITOR
O O!

RICARDO
Not mine? I think 'tis the best bargain
That e'er thou mad'st i' thy life, or ever shall again,
When my head's laid—but that's not yet this
threescore year.
Let's talk of nearer matters.

VALERIA You're as near, sir,
As e'er you're like to be, if law can right me.

RICARDO
Now, before conscience, you're a wilful housewife.

VALERIA How!

RICARDO
Ay, and I fear you spend my goods lavishly.

VALERIA
Your goods?

RICARDO I shall miss much, I doubt me,
When I come to look over the inventory.

VALERIA
I'll give you my word you shall, sir.

RICARDO Look to't, widow.
A night may come will call you to account for't.

VALERIA
O, if you had me now, sir, in this heat,
I do but think how you'd be revenged on me.

RICARDO
Ay, may I perish else, if I would not get
Three children at a birth, an I could o' thee.

12 ***Invita voluntate*** with an unwilling willingness (Latin); at 4.1.15–17 the First Suitor is unable to explain to Valeria what the words mean, but they are explicitly relevant to the legal issue at hand, whether Valeria willingly entered into a contract with Ricardo.

15 **there I leave you** in that I can't help you

19 **adoption** Wilson defines adoption as 'The purpose of God eternally decreeing to make some his children ... to take him for a son, who was a child of wrath by nature'. This theological sense connects divine election with the secular sense of a 'chosen child'.

20 **hold'st** remain

21 **cozen all my kindred** cheat his relations out of any inheritance (the First Suitor has just addressed him as 'my adoption | My chosen child'), with pun on 'cozen/cousin'

22 **A child's part ... ambition** (*a*) I would like to receive love from you as your child; (*b*) I would like to inherit a portion appropriate to a loved child.

24 **wrangling** contentious dispute
o' life dearly

25 **venery** sexual pleasure

26 **honey** sexual pleasure

29 **close** secret

31–3 **I scorn ... wife** Ricardo declares his honourable approach to his wooing, asserting that he would not deceive the waiting woman in order to gain access to her, and especially would not deceive the woman he wishes to marry.

36 **calling** station in life. Although the word derives the sense of naming or appellation (*OED* sb 4) from the idea of the action of greeting, the word developed a special religious sense as the 'summons, invitation, or impulse of God to salvation or to his service', and by extension therefore the position, estate, or station in life to which God has called a person (*OED* cites 1 Corinthians 7:20 in this connection: 'Let every man abide in the calling wherein he was called'). Thus though the word can mean an occupation or trade, it nevertheless may retain an aspect of Godly sanction. Ricardo's use implies the sanctified nature of the wifely role.

37 **all your grace** the particular source of grace for women

42 **When my head's laid** when I die

43 **nearer** more personal, immediate
matters (punning on 'genitals')

44 **right me** redress my injuries

45 **wilful** independent, determined to have her way
housewife (*a*) a woman who manages a household (*b*) hussy, slut

51 **account** (punning on 'a cunt')

52 **heat** eagerness, (sexual) passion

FIRST SUITOR [*to Second Suitor*]
Take off your youngster there.
SECOND SUITOR Take off your widow first.
He shall have the last word; I pay for't dearly.—
To her again, sweet boy; that side's the weaker.
I have enough, and I will have my humour.
Enter Brandino and Martino. [*Ricardo and Second Suitor stand apart*]
VALERIA
O brother, see, I'm up to th'ears in law here.
[*She shows him many legal papers*]
Look, copy upon copy.
BRANDINO
'Twere grief enough if a man did but hear on't,
But I'm in pain to see't.
VALERIA What, sore eyes still, brother?
BRANDINO
Worse and worse, sister. The old woman's water
Does me no good.
VALERIA Why, it's helped many, sir.
BRANDINO It helps not me, I'm sure.
MARTINO O! O!
VALERIA What, ails Martino too?
MARTINO O! O! the toothache, the toothache!
BRANDINO
Ah, poor worm! This he endures for me now.
There beats not a more mutual pulse of passion
In a kind husband when his wife breeds child
Than in Martino. I ha' marked it ever.
He breeds all my pains in's teeth still—and, to quite me,
It is his eye-tooth too.
MARTINO Ay, ay, ay, ay!
VALERIA
Where did I hear late of a skilful fellow,
Good for all kind of maladies? True, true, sir,
His flag hangs out in town here, i'th' Cross Inn,
With admirable cures of all conditions.
It shows him a great travelling and learned empiric.
BRANDINO
We'll both to him, Martino.
VALERIA Hark you, brother.
Perhaps you may prevail, as one indifferent.
FIRST SUITOR
Ay, about that, sweet widow.
VALERIA True. Speak low, sir.
BRANDINO
Well, what's the business? Say, say.
VALERIA Marry, this, brother.
Call the young man aside, from the old wolf there,
And whisper in his ear 'a thousand dollars'—
If he will vanish, and let fall the suit,
And never put's to no more cost and trouble.
FIRST SUITOR
Say me those words, good sir; I'll make 'em worth
A chain of gold to you at your sister's wedding.
Enter Violetta
BRANDINO
I shall do much for that.
[*Brandino whispers to Ricardo, apart*]
VALERIA Welcome, sweetheart.
Thou com'st most happily. I'm bold to send for thee
To make a purpose good.
VIOLETTA I take delight forsooth
In any such employment.
FIRST SUITOR Good wench, trust me.
[*Valeria and Second Suitor whisper to Violetta, apart*]
RICARDO [*to Brandino*]
How, sir, let fall the suit? Life, I'll go naked first.
BRANDINO
A thousand dollars, sir: think upon them.
RICARDO
Why, they're but a thousand dollars, when they're thought on.
BRANDINO
A good round sum.
RICARDO A good round widow's better.
There's meat and money too. I have been bought
Out of my lands and yielded, but (sir) scorn
To be bought out of my affectïon.
BRANDINO
Why, here's e'en just my university spirit.
I prized a piece of red deer above gold then.
RICARDO [*aside*]
My patron would be mad, an he should hear on't.
MARTINO
I pray, what's good, sir, for a wicked tooth?
RICARDO
Hanged, drawn, and quart'ring. Is't a hollow one?

56 **Take off** lead or draw away
64 **old woman's** 'wise woman's', healer's
water curative liquid, perhaps urine, which was used as a remedy for sore eyes
69 **toothache** since devoted husbands were believed to suffer toothache in sympathy with their wives' labour pains, Martino, the dedicated clerk, responds similarly to his master's distress
74 **still** always
quite requite, match, correspond precisely with
78 **flag** sign
80 **empiric** physician; specifically one who 'relies solely upon observation and experiment'
82 **indifferent** impartial
88 **never...no more** the double negative is an emphatic negative, not a positive
92 **happily** fortunately; the emphasis is on the benevolence of chance, not her or his pleasure
93 **make a purpose good** bring a project to a successful conclusion
95 **suit** Ricardo puns on the legal term and the item of clothing to assert his financial investment in his success at law
99 **meat** woman as sexual body
102 **university spirit** undergraduate recklessness
103 **red deer** female flesh
105 **wicked** painful, harmful
106 **Hanged, drawn, and quart'ring** the torture and death meted out to traitors are associated with the drawing of a tooth and its hanging on a thread after extraction

MARTINO
Ay, 'tis a hollow one.
RICARDO
Then take the powder
Of a burnt warrant, mixed with oil of felon.
MARTINO
Why, sure you mock me.
RICARDO
Troth, I think I do, sir.
SECOND SUITOR
Come hither, honey. What's the news in whispers?
[Ricardo and Second Suitor whisper apart]
BRANDINO *[to Valeria]*
He will not be bought out.
VALERIA
No? That's strange, brother.
Pray take a little pains about this project then,
And try what that effects.
BRANDINO
I like this better.
[Brandino approaches Ricardo and Second Suitor]
Look you, sweet gentles, see what I produce here
For amity's sake and peace, to end all controversy:
This gentlewoman—my charge, left by her friends,
Whom for her person and her portïon
I could bestow most richly; but in pity
To her affection, which lies bent at you, sir,
I am content to yield to her desire.
RICARDO
At me?
BRANDINO
But for this jar, 't'ad ne'er been offered.
I bring you flesh and money, a rich heir
And a maid too—and that's a thing worth thanks, sir;
Nay, one that has rid fifteen mile this morning
For your love only.
SECOND SUITOR *[to Ricardo]*
Honey, hearken after her.
Being rich, I can have all my money there,
Ease my purse well, and never wage law further.
I have enough, yet I will have my humour.
RICARDO *[to Violetta]*
Do you love me, forsooth?
VIOLETTA
O infinitely!
RICARDO
I do not ask thee, that I meant to have thee,
But only to know what came in thy head to love me.
VIOLETTA
My time was come, sir; that's all I can say.
RICARDO
'Las, poor fool! Where didst thou love me first, prithee?
VIOLETTA
In happy hour be't spoke, out at a window, sir.
RICARDO
A window? Prithee clap it to, and call it in again.
What was I doing then, should make thee love me?
VIOLETTA
Twirling your band-string—which, methought, became you
So generously well.
RICARDO
'Twas a good quality to choose a husband for.
That love was likely to be tied in matrimony
that begun in a band-string. Yet I ha' known as much come to pass ere now upon a tassel. Fare you well, sister. I may be cozened in a maid; I cannot, in a widow.
SECOND SUITOR
Art thou come home again? Stick'st thou there still?
I will defend thee still then.
FIRST SUITOR
Sir, your malice
Will have enough on't.
SECOND SUITOR
I will have my humour.
FIRST SUITOR
Beggary will prove the sponge.
SECOND SUITOR
Sponge i' thy gaskins,
Thy galligaskins there!
RICARDO
Ha! Brave protector!
BRANDINO
I thought 'twould come to open wars again.
Let 'em agree as they will. Two testy fops!
I'll have a care of mine eyes.
MARTINO
I, of my chops.
Exeunt [severally]

Enter Latrocinio and Occulto 4.2
LATROCINIO
Away, out with the banner! Send's good luck today!
A banner of cures and diseases hung out
OCCULTO
I warrant you. Your name's spread, sir, for an empiric.
There's an old mason troubled with the stone
Has sent to you this morning for your counsel;
He would have ease, fain.

116 **gentlewoman** Violetta, whom Brandino offers to marry to Ricardo
117 **portïon** dowry
121 **jar** discord, dispute
123 **maid** Brandino stresses her virginity
135 **clap it to ... it** shut the window ... love
137 **band-string** a string for fastening a collar or 'band'; at 4.1.141 Ricardo puns on the band/bond of marriage
142 **tassel** (*a*) a decorative ornament on clothing; (*b*) perhaps a pun on 'tussle'
143 **sister** this form of address disavows sexual interest
144 **come home again** returned to where you started
147 **Beggary ... sponge** poverty (as a result of losing the lawsuit) will dry up your capacity for indulging your whims; humour derives from the word for moisture (see note to 2.1.175)
gaskins breeches
148 **galligaskins** wide or loose breeches
Brave excellent, worthy
150 **testy** short-tempered
fops fools
151 **chops** jaws, mouth
4.2.1 **Away** get on with it
2 **Your name's spread** (*a*) his reputation has been published; (*b*) his name is spread out on the banner
empiric physician; see 4.1.80.
3 **stone** a kidney stone, with a pun on the mason's occupation
5 **fain** gladly

LATROCINIO Marry, I cannot blame him, sir.
But how he will come by't? There lies the question.

OCCULTO
You must do somewhat, sir, for he's swoll'n most piteously;
Has urine in him now was brewed last March.

LATROCINIO 'Twill be rich gear for dyers.

OCCULTO I would 'twere come to that, sir.

LATROCINIO Lemme see.
I'll send him a whole musketcharge of gunpowder.

OCCULTO
Gunpowder? What, sir, to break the stone?

LATROCINIO Ay, by my faith, sir.
It is the likeliest thing I know to do't.
I'm sure it breaks stone walls and castles down;
I see no reason, but 't should break the stone.

OCCULTO
Nay, use your pleasure, sir.

LATROCINIO Troth, if that do not
I ha' nothing else that will.

OCCULTO I know that too.

LATROCINIO
Why then thou'rt a coxcomb to make question on't.
Go call in all the rest. I have employment for them.
[*Exit Occulto*]
When the highways grow thin with travellers
And few portmanteaus stirring (as all trades
Have their dead time, we see—thievery poor takings,
And lechery cold doings, and so forwards still),
Then do I take my inn, and those curmudgeons
Whose purses I can never get abroad,
I take 'em at more ease here i' my chamber,
And make 'em come to me. It's more state-like too.
Hang him that has but one way to his trade!
He's like a mouth that eats but on one side
And half-cozens his belly, 'specially
If he dine among shavers and both-handed feeders.
Stratio, Silvio, and Fiducio!
Enter all the rest [*of the thieves*]*: Silvio, Stratio, Fiducio*
I will have none left out. There's parts for you.

SILVIO
For us? Pray, let's have 'em.

LATROCINIO Change yourselves
With all speed possible into several shapes
Far from your own, as: you, a farmer, sir;
A grazier, you; and you may be a miller.

FIDUCIO
O no, a miller comes too near a thief;
That may spoil all again.

LATROCINIO Some country tailor then.

FIDUCIO
That's near enough, by'r Lady; yet I'll venture that.
The miller's a white devil; he wears his theft
Like innocence in badges most apparently
Upon his nose, sometimes between his lips;
The tailor, modestly, between his legs.

LATROCINIO
Why, pray, do you present that modest thief then.
And hark you for the purpose.

SILVIO 'Twill improve you, sir.

LATROCINIO
'Twill get believers, believe that, my masters,
Repute and confidence, and make all things clearer.
When you see any come, repair you to me
As samples of my skill. There are few arts
But have their shadows, sirs, to set 'em off;
Then where the art itself is but a shadow,
What need is there, my friends? Make haste, away, sirs!
Exeunt [*Stratio, Silvio, and Fiducio*]

7 **somewhat** something
9 **rich...dyers** valuable material for dyers to use in their processes
22 **portmanteaus** travelling bags for clothes
24 **doings** copulation
and so forwards and so forth
25 **take my inn** take up residence (*OED* sb.2.a)
curmudgeons miserly or churlish persons
26 **abroad** out of doors
27 **here** Since this speech is addressed to the audience, the actor may be referring to the theatre itself: in *Mad World* and *Hengist* Middleton equates actors with thieves.
28 **state-like** stately. In the increasingly corrupt Jacobean patronage system, well-connected courtiers profited handsomely by letting clients and suitors 'come to them' in their 'chambers', giving them gifts and bribes in exchange for offices, patents, and monopolies.
31 **half-cozens** half-cheats
32 **shavers** swindlers. More literally, a clean-shaved man can eat faster than a bearded one, because he needn't worry about getting food in his beard.
34 **parts** jobs; theatrical roles
36 **shapes** theatrical roles or costumes
39–40 **miller...tailor** both traditionally regarded as thieves
39 **comes too near** is too like in qualities
42 **white devil** For the Reformation origins of this image of hypocrisy, see long commentary note at *Game* ('Early') 3.214. Here, 'white' plays on the literal sense (he is covered with flour).
theft what he has stolen, flour
43 **badges** distinguishing marks
apparently manifestly
45 **tailor...legs** the tailor puts the stolen material into his own breeches; also tailor = penis
46 **present** act the part of
47 **hark...purpose** (The action is not clear here; Latrocinio does something, or whispers something, which will contribute to Fiducio's impersonation of a tailor.)
improve make you appear more prosperous, of higher social rank (This may also be a comment on whatever Latrocinio has just done.)
51 **samples** illustrations, examples, of his capacity to effect cures
51–3 **There...shadow** nearly every skill exploits mysteries to enhance its power; but when the skill is itself a complete illusion or trick...(see 2.1.57). The shadow is the dark background against which the art is highlighted. The use of *shadow* here may refer to the association of actors with shadows; see 'If we shadows have offended', *A Midsummer Night's Dream* Epilogue.1.

Enter Occulto [disguised]

OCCULTO
Where are you, sir?

LATROCINIO Not far, man. What's the news?

OCCULTO
The old Justice, sir, whom we robbed once by moonlight,
And bound his man and he in haycock time
With a rope made of horsemeat, and in pity
Left their mares by 'em, which I think ere midnight
Did eat their hay-bound masters both at liberty—

LATROCINIO
Life, what of him, man?

OCCULTO He's inquiring earnestly
For the great man of art—indeed, for you, sir.
Therefore withdraw, sweet sir. Make yourself dainty now,
And that's three parts of any profession.

LATROCINIO
I have enough on't. *Exit*

Enter Ansaldo [in old Brandino's clothes]

OCCULTO *[aside]* How now, what thing's this?
Now by this light, *The Second Part o'th' Justice,*
'Newly revived'—with never a hair on's face.
It should be the first rather, by his smoothness;
But I ha' known *The First Part* written last.
'Tis he, or let me perish—the young gentleman
We robbed and stripped! But I am far from knowledge now.

ANSALDO
One word, I pray, sir.

OCCULTO With me, gentle sir?

ANSALDO
Was there not lately seen about these parts, sir,
A knot of fellows, whose conditïons
Are privily suspected?

OCCULTO Why do you ask, sir?

ANSALDO
There was a poor young gentleman robbed last night.

OCCULTO
Robbed?

ANSALDO
Stripped of all, i'faith.

OCCULTO O beastly rascals!
'Las, what was he?

ANSALDO Look o' me, and know him, sir.

OCCULTO
Hard-hearted villains! Strip? Troth, when I saw you
Methought those clothes were never made for you, sir.

ANSALDO
Want made me glad o' 'em.

OCCULTO Send you better fortunes, sir!—
[Aside] That we may have a bout with you once again.

ANSALDO
I thank you for your wish of love, kind sir.

OCCULTO
'Tis with my heart, i'faith. New store of coin
And better clothes be with you!

ANSALDO There's some honest yet
And charitably minded. How, what's here to do?
(*Reads*) 'Here within this place is cured
All the griefs that were e'er endured.'—
Now there thou liest. I endured one last night
Thou canst not cure this morning. A strange promiser.—
'Palsy, gout, hydropic humour,
Breath that stinks beyond perfumer,
Fistula *in ano*, ulcer, mègrum,
Or what disease soe'er beleag'r 'em,
Stone, rupture, squinancy, impostume,
Yet too dear it shall not cost 'em.'—
That's conscionably said, i'faith.—
'In brief, you cannot, I assure you,
Be unsound so fast as I can cure you.'—
By'r Lady, you shall pardon me; I'll not try't, sir.
[Exit Occulto]

Enter Brandino and Martino [aloof]

BRANDINO
Martino, is not yon my hinder parts?

MARTINO
Yes, and your fore parts too, sir.

BRANDINO I trow so.

57 **haycock time** harvest time; a haycock is 'a conical heap of hay in a field' (*OED*)
58 **rope ... horsemeat** The next two lines show that they were bound with ropes of hay, 'hay-bound'
62 **man of art** wise man (see 2.1.57)
63 **dainty** impressive in appearance
64 **three parts** three-quarters
65 **have enough on't** understand well
67 **'Newly revived'** (a cliché of theatrical advertising). Ansaldo appears like a theatrical sequel in the life of Brandino, whose clothes he wears; in his youthfulness Ansaldo looks like a reborn Brandino
69 ***The First* ... last** Occulto refers to new plays that present material anterior to the events portrayed in a prior work ('prequels'); he suggests that Ansaldo's youth creates such an experience.
71 **But ... knowledge now** Occulto must pretend ignorance of Ansaldo's identity.
74 **knot** group or band
conditïons behaviour, morals (see 1.2.80)
75 **privily** secretly
82 **bout** 'go, turn', contest, opportunity to overcome (with sexual suggestion)
88 **griefs** (*a*) misfortunes; (*b*) sicknesses
91 **Palsy** shaking
hydropic humour condition of being swollen with retained fluid
93 **Fistula** a pipelike ulcer
in ano in the anus (Latin)
mègrum headache, migraine
94 **beleag'r** surround, beset
95 **Stone** kidney stone
squinancy quinsy
impostume abscess
97 **conscionably** in good faith
99 **unsound so fast** so very unhealthy
101–2 **hinder parts ... fore parts** they spot Ansaldo wearing Brandino's clothes; in 103–4, where the references are physical, Brandino's failure to see his fore parts suggests that he has always been too fat to see his genitals

I never saw my hind parts in my life else,
No, nor my fore ones neither.—What are you, sir?
Are you a justice, pray?

ANSALDO
A justice? No, truly.

BRANDINO
How came this suit to you then?

ANSALDO
How, this suit?
Why, must he needs be a Justice, sir, that wears it?

BRANDINO
You'll find it so. 'Twas made for nobody else.
I paid for't.

ANSALDO [*aside*]
O strange fortune! I have undone
The charitable woman.

BRANDINO
He'll be gone.
Martino, hold him fast. I'll call for aid.

ANSALDO
Hold me? O curse of fate!
[*Ansaldo strikes Martino on the face*]

MARTINO
O master, master!

BRANDINO
What ails, Martino?

MARTINO
In my conscïence
He's beat out the wrong tooth. I feel it now,
Three degrees off.

BRANDINO [*to Ansaldo*]
O slave! spoiled a fine penman.

ANSALDO
He lacked good manners, though. Lay hands o' me?
I scorn all the deserts that belong to't.
Enter Latrocinio [disguised as an empiric]

LATROCINIO
Why, how now? What's the broil?

BRANDINO
The man of art
I take you, sir, to be.

LATROCINIO
I'm the professer
Of those slight cures you read of in the banner.

BRANDINO
Our business was to you, most skilful sir,
But in the way to you, right worshipful,
I met a thief.

LATROCINIO
A thief?

BRANDINO
With my clothes on, sir.
Let but the hose be searched, I'll pawn my life
There's yet the tailor's bill in one o'th' pockets
And a white thimble that I found i' moonlight.—
Thou saw'st me when I put it in, Martino.

MARTINO Oy, oy.

BRANDINO
O, he's spoiled the worthiest clerk that e'er drew warrant here.

LATROCINIO [*to Ansaldo*]
Sir, you're a stranger, but I must deal plain with you.
That suit of clothes must needs come oddly to you.

ANSALDO [*aside*]
I dare not say which way; that's my affliction.

LATROCINIO
Is not your worship's name Signor Brandino, sir?

BRANDINO
It has been so these threescore year and upwards.

LATROCINIO
I heard there was a robbery done last night
Near to your house.

ANSALDO
You heard a truth then, sir,
And I the man was robbed.

LATROCINIO
Ah, that's too gross.
Send him away for fear of farther mischief.
I do not like him; he's a cunning knave.

BRANDINO
I want but aid.

LATROCINIO
Within there!
Enter [Occulto and] two or three servants

BRANDINO
Seize upon
That impudent thief!

ANSALDO
Then hear me speak.

BRANDINO
Away!
I'll neither hear thee speak, nor wear those clothes again.
To prison with the varlet!

ANSALDO
How am I punished!

BRANDINO
I'll make thee bring out all before I leave thee.
Exit [servants] with Ansaldo

LATROCINIO
You've took an excellent course with this bold villain, sir.

BRANDINO
I am sworn for service to the commonwealth, sir.
Enter Stratio, Silvio, and Fiducio [disguised as a farmer, a grazier, and a tailor]
What are these, learnèd sir?

LATROCINIO
O, they're my patients.—
Good morrow, Gout, Rupture, and Palsy.

STRATIO
'Tis farewell gout almost, I thank your worship.

LATROCINIO
What? No, you cannot part so soon, I hope?
You came but lately to me.

STRATIO
But most happily.
I can go near to leap, sir.

LATROCINIO
What, you cannot?
[*Stratio leaps*]
Away, I say! Take heed. Be not too vent'rous, though.

103 **else** otherwise, under other circumstances
117 **deserts...to't** the consequences of striking Martino (?), or the respect due to Martino's skill as a penman (?)
118 **broil** disturbance
128 **Oy, oy** cries of pain (?)
132 **affliction** distress
137 **gross** evident
144 **bring out** produce, utter (*OED* bring, vb.21.c)
146 **service** as a Justice of the Peace
150 **part** depart (because cured)
151 **happily** fortunately, advantageously
152 **go near to** almost

I've had you but three days, remember that.

STRATIO
Those three are better than three hundred, sir.
[*Stratio leaps*]

LATROCINIO
Yet again?

STRATIO Ease takes pleasure to be known, sir.
[*Exit*]

LATROCINIO [*to Silvio*]
You with the rupture there, *hernia in scrotum*,
Pray let me see your space this morning. Walk, sir.
[*Silvio walks in a bow-legged manner*]
I'll take your distance straight. 'Twas 'F.O.' yesterday.
Ah, sirrah, here's a simple alteration,
Secundo gradu, you're 'F.U.' already.
Here's a most happy change. Be of good comfort, sir.
Your knees are come within three inches now
Of one another; by tomorrow noon
I'll make 'em kiss and jostle.

SILVIO Bless your worship!
[*Exit*]

BRANDINO
You have a hundred pray'rs in a morning, sir.

LATROCINIO
Faith, we have a few to pass away the day with.—
Tailor, you had a stitch.

FIDUCIO O, good your worship,
I have had none since Easter. Were I rid
But of this whoreson palsy, I were happy.
I cannot thread my needle.

LATROCINIO No, that's hard.
I never marked so much.

FIDUCIO It comes by fits, sir.

LATROCINIO
'Las, poor man!—What would your worship say now
To see me help this fellow at an instant?

BRANDINO
And make him firm from shaking?

LATROCINIO As a steeple,
From the disease on't.

BRANDINO 'Tis to me miraculous.

LATROCINIO [*to Fiducio*]
You, with your whoremaster disease, come hither.
Here, take me this round glass, and hold it steadfast.
Yet more, sir; yet, I say! So.

BRANDINO Admirable!

LATROCINIO
Go, live, and thread thy needle. [*Exit Fiducio*]

BRANDINO Here, Martino.—
'Las, poor fool, his mouth is full of praises
And cannot utter 'em.

LATROCINIO No? What's the malady?

BRANDINO
The fury of a tooth.

LATROCINIO A tooth? Ha ha!
I thought 't'ad been some gangrene, fistula,
Cancer, or ramex.

BRANDINO No, it's enough as 'tis, sir.

LATROCINIO
My man shall ease that straight.—Sit you down there, sir.
[*Martino sits*]
[*To Occulto*] Take the tooth, sirrah, daintily, insensibly.—
But what's your worship's malady? That's for me, sir.

BRANDINO
Marry, pray look you, sir: your worship's counsel
About mine eyes.

LATROCINIO Sore eyes? That's nothing too, sir.

BRANDINO
By'r Lady, I that feel it think it somewhat.

LATROCINIO
Have you no convulsions? pricking achës, sir?
Ruptures or apostemates?

BRANDINO No, by my faith, sir,
Nor do I desire to have 'em.

LATROCINIO Those are cures;
There do I win my fame, sir.—Quickly, sirrah,
Reach me the eye-cup hither.—Do you make water well, sir?

BRANDINO I'm all well there.

LATROCINIO You feel no grief i'th' kidney?

BRANDINO Sound, sound, sound, sir.

LATROCINIO
O, here's a breath, sir, I must talk withal
One of these mornings.

BRANDINO There I think, i'faith,
I am to blame indeed, and my wife's words

156 **Ease . . . known** happiness wants to make itself known to others
158 **space** The '*hernia in scrotum*' prevents Silvio from walking with a natural space between his legs.
159 **take your distance** measure the 'space'
159–61 **'F.O.' . . . 'F.U.'** an indication that Silvio's condition has improved sufficiently for him to bring his legs closer together. The meaning (if any) of these abbreviations is not clear: 'eff' (as a euphemism for *fuck*) is not recorded until the twentieth century.
160 **simple** clear
161 ***Secundo gradu*** in the second degree (Latin)
168 **stitch** a sharp pain; a pun on the tailor's trade
170 **whoreson** damned
171 **hard** either (*a*) a severe case or (*b*) unfortunate
175–6 **steeple . . . on't** as a steeple, since he will be free of the disease
177 **whoremaster disease** palsy was perceived as a consequence of syphilis
180 **live** (*a*) live your life; (*b*) make your living
185 **ramex** rupture, hernia
187 **daintily** deftly
insensibly imperceptibly
193 **apostemates** large deep-seated abscesses
198 **grief** pain
200 **breath** bad breath, but quibbling on 'speech'
talk withal treat
202 **wife's words** (Philippa has presumably complained about Brandino's bad breath, and predicted that others would notice it.)

Are come to pass, sir.
[*Occulto draws a tooth from Martino*]
MARTINO O, O! 'Tis not that, 'tis not that!
It is the next beyond it: there, there, there.
OCCULTO
The best have their mistakings. Now I'll fit you, sir.
BRANDINO [*to Latrocinio*]
What's that, sweet sir, that comforts with his coolness?
LATROCINIO
O, sovereign gear. Wink hard, and keep it in, sir.
[*While he applies the eye-cup, he picks Brandino's pocket*]
MARTINO O, O, O!
OCCULTO
Nay, here he goes. One twitch more and he comes, sir.
[*While he draws a tooth, he picks Martino's pocket*]
MARTINO
Auh, ho.
OCCULTO Spit out. I told you he was gone, sir.
BRANDINO
How cheers Martino?
MARTINO O, I can answer you now, master.
I feel great ease, sir.
BRANDINO So do I, Martino.
MARTINO
I'm rid of a sore burden, for my part, master,
Of a scald little one.
LATROCINIO [*to Brandino*]
Please but your worship now
To take three drops of the rich water with you,
I'll undertake your man shall cure you, sir,
At twice i' your own chamber.
BRANDINO Shall he so, sir?
LATROCINIO
I will uphold him in't.
MARTINO Then will I do't, sir.
LATROCINIO
How lively your man's now!
MARTINO O, I'm so light, methinks,
Over what e'er I was!
BRANDINO [*to Latrocinio*]
What is't contents your worship?
LATROCINIO
E'en what your worship please. I am not mercenary.
BRANDINO
My purse is gone, Martino!
LATROCINIO How, your purse, sir?
BRANDINO
'Tis gone, i'faith. I've been among some rascals.
MARTINO And that's a thing
I ever gave you warning of, master. You care not
What company you run into.
BRANDINO
Lend me some money. Chide me anon, I prithee.
A pox on 'em for vipers! They ha' sucked blood o' me.
MARTINO
O master!
BRANDINO
How now, man?
MARTINO My purse is gone too.
BRANDINO How?
I'll never take warning more of thee while I live then.
Thou art an hypocrite, and art not fit
To give good counsel to thy master, that
Canst not keep from ill company thyself.
LATROCINIO
This is most strange, sir. Both your purses gone?
MARTINO
Sir, I'd my hand on mine when I came in.
LATROCINIO
Are you but sure of that? O would you were!
MARTINO
As I'm of ease.
LATROCINIO Then they're both gone one way;
Be that your comfort.
BRANDINO Ay, but what way's that, sir?
LATROCINIO
That close knave in your clothes has got 'em both.
'Tis well you've clapped him fast.
BRANDINO Why, that's impossible.
LATROCINIO
O, tell not me, sir. I ha' known purses gone
And the thief stand and look one full i'th' face,
As I may do your worship and your man now.
MARTINO
Nay, that's most certain, master.
BRANDINO I will make
That rascal in my clothes answer all this then
And all the robberies that have been done
Since the moon changed. Get you home first, Martino,
And know if any of my wife's things are missing,
Or any more of mine. Tell her he's taken,
And by that token he has took both our purses.
[*He gives Martino a token*]
MARTINO
That's an ill token, master.
BRANDINO That's all one, sir.

205 **fit you** treat you, sort you out
206 **his** its
207 **sovereign** excellent
gear treatment, remedy
214 **scald** contemptible
215 **rich** of great worth
217 **At twice** on a second occasion, at a later time
218 **uphold** give him assistance
219 **light** (*a*) merry, but also (*b*) of little substance (since without his knowledge he has been robbed)
220 **Over** beyond what (*OED prep.* 9b)
227 **anon** later
237 **of ease** free from pain
240 **clapped** confined
250 **token** some object (unidentified) that appears to be distasteful or unsatisfactory; Martino calls it an *ill token* in the next line

She must have that or nothing, for I'm sure
The rascal has left nothing else for a token.
Begone! Make haste again, and meet me part o'th'
way.

MARTINO I'll hang the villain
An 'twere for nothing but the souse he gave me.
Exit

BRANDINO
Sir, I depart ashamed of my requital,
And leave this seal ring with you as a pledge
Of further thankfulness.

LATROCINIO No, I beseech you, sir.

BRANDINO
Indeed you shall, sir.

LATROCINIO O, your worship's word, sir.
[*Brandino gives him the ring*]

BRANDINO
You shall have my word too, for a rare gentleman
As e'er I met withal.

LATROCINIO Clear sight be with you, sir!
Exit Brandino
—If conduit-water and my hostess' milk,
That comes with the ninth child now, may afford it.
[*Enter Stratio, Silvio, and Fiducio*]
Life, I feared none but thee, my villainous tooth-
drawer.

OCCULTO
There was no fear of me. I've often told you
I was bound prentice to a barber once,
But ran away i'th' second year.

LATROCINIO Ay, marry,
That made thee give a pull at the wrong tooth,
And me afraid of thee.—What have we there, sirs?

OCCULTO
Some threescore dollars i' the master's purse
And sixteen in the clerk's, a silver seal,
Two or three amber beads, and four blank warrants.

LATROCINIO
Warrants? Where be they? The best news came yet.
Mass, here's his hand, and here's his seal, I thank
him.
This comes most luckily. One of our fellows
Was took last night; we'll set him first at liberty,
And other good boys after him—and if he
In th'old Justice's suit, whom we robbed lately,
Will come off roundly, we'll set him free too.

OCCULTO
That were a good deed, faith; we may in pity.

LATROCINIO
There's nothing done merely for pity nowadays;
Money or ware must help too.
Song in parts

THIEVES
Give me fortune, give me health,
Give me freedom, I'll get wealth.
Who complains his fate's amiss
When he has the wide world his?
He that has the devil in fee
Can have but all, and so have we.
Give us fortune, give us health,
Give us freedom, we'll get wealth.
In every hamlet, town and city,
He has lands, that was born witty. *Exeunt*

Incipit Actus 5 5.1
Enter Philippa and Violetta

PHILIPPA
How well this gentleman keeps his promise too!
Sure there's no trust in man.

VIOLETTA They're all Franciscos.
That's my opinion, mistress. Fools, or false ones.
He might have had the honesty yet, i'faith,
To send my master's clothes home.

PHILIPPA Ay, those clothes.

VIOLETTA
Colliers come by the door ev'ry day, mistress.
Nay, this is market-day too: poulterers, butchers,
They would have lain most daintily in a pannier
And kept veal from the wind.

PHILIPPA Those clothes much trouble me.

VIOLETTA
Faith, an he were a gentleman, as he seemed to be,
They would trouble him too, I think.
Methinks he should have small desire to keep 'em.

PHILIPPA
Faith, and less pride to wear 'em, I should think,
wench,
Unless he kept 'em as a testimony

254 **again** back
256 **souse** heavy blow
257 **requital** (lack of) payment for services
263 **conduit-water** water from the conduit, the source of public supply; with the hostess' breast milk it made up the eye-wash
265 **villainous** devilishly skilled (ironic praise)
267 **barber** Barbers originally practised dentistry and surgery.
268 **second year** (a full apprenticeship lasted for seven)
273 **amber beads** Amber has various associations: it has been a symbol of immortality, and in the 17th century was advanced as a universal cure. However, with respect to Martino it may be relevant that amber 'was used as an amulet to attract lovers' (*OED* sub. 4); 'beads made of amber preserved the wearer against rheumatism, toothache' and many other complaints (Budge), and Camillus Leonardus records among its other properties that 'it fastens teeth that are loosened' (*Speculum Lapidum*, 1502).
278 **good boys** fellow criminals
280 **come off** pay up
roundly promptly
282 **merely** just, solely
283.1 ***Song in parts*** a song for several voice-parts in simple harmony
288 **devil in fee** has retained the devil as his servant (or lawyer)
5.1.6 **Colliers** coal-merchants
8 **They** the clothes; Violetta says that they could have been returned by trades-people, using them as rags

For after-times, to show what misery
He passed in his young days, and then weep over 'em.

VIOLETTA Weep, mistress?
Nay, sure, methinks he should not weep for laughing.

Enter Martino

PHILIPPA [*aside to Violetta*]
Martino? O, we're spoiled, wench. Are they come then?

MARTINO Mistress, be of good cheer. I have excellent news for you. Comfort your heart. What have you to breakfast, mistress?
You shall have all again, I warrant you.

PHILIPPA [*aside*]
What says he, wench?

VIOLETTA [*aside*] I'm loath to understand him.

MARTINO
Give me a note of all your things, sweet mistress.
You shall not lose a hair. Take't of my word.
We have him safe enough.

PHILIPPA [*aside*] O 'las, sweet wench,
This man talks fearfully.

VIOLETTA [*aside*] And I know not what yet;
That's the worst, mistress.

MARTINO Can you tell me, pray,
Whether the rascal has broke ope my desk or no?
There's a fine little barrel of pome-citrons
Would have served me this seven year—O, and my fig-cheese!
The fig of everlasting obloquy
Go with him if he have eat it! I'll make haste;
He cannot eat it all yet. He was taken, mistress,
Grossly and beastly—how do you think, i'faith?

PHILIPPA
I know not, sir.

MARTINO Troth, in my master's clothes.
Would any thief but a beast been taken so?

PHILIPPA [*aside*] Wench, wench.

VIOLETTA [*aside*]
I have grief enough of mine own to tend, mistress.

PHILIPPA [*to Martino*]
Did he confess the robbery?

MARTINO O no, no, mistress.
He's a young cunning rascal; he confessed nothing.
While we were examining on him, he took away
My master's purse and mine, but confessed nothing still.

PHILIPPA [*aside*]
That's but some slanderous injury raised against him.—
Came not your master with you?

MARTINO No, sweet mistress,
I must make haste and meet him. Pray, dispatch me then.

PHILIPPA
I have looked over all with special heedfulness.
There's nothing missed, I can assure you, sir,
But that suit of your master's.

MARTINO I'm right glad on't.
That suit would hang him. Yet I would not have him
Hanged in that suit, though; it will disgrace
My master's fashion for ever, and make it as hateful
As yellow bands. *Exit*

PHILIPPA
O, what shall's do, wench?

VIOLETTA 'Tis no marvel, mistress,
The poor young gentleman could not keep his promise.

PHILIPPA
Alas, sweet man, he's confessed nothing yet, wench.

VIOLETTA
That shows his constancy and love to you, mistress.
But you must do't, of force; there is no help for't.
The truth can neither shame nor hurt you much.
Let 'em make what they can on't; 'twere sin and pity, i'faith,
To cast away so sweet a gentleman
For such a pair of infidel hose and doublet.
I would not hang a Jew for a whole wardrobe on 'em.

PHILIPPA
Thou sayst true, wench.

Enter Ansaldo [in old Brandino's clothes]

VIOLETTA O O, they're come again, mistress.

PHILIPPA
Signor Ansaldo?

ANSALDO The same—mightily crossed, lady,
But, past hope, freed again by a doctor's means,
A man of art; I know not justly what, indeed,
But pity and the fortunate gold you gave me
Wrought my release between 'em.

20–2 **Mistress ... mistress?** Martino does not mention Brandino's token; there could be silent theatrical business associated with it—for instance, he could deliver the distasteful object to Philippa, without explanation, while saying 'I have excellent news for you'.

28 **fearfully** in a manner to excite fear; he appears crazy to them

31 **pome-citrons** citrus fruit; lemons and limes were often covered by this category.

32 **fig-cheese** a conserve of figs, having the consistency of cheese or the form of cheese

33–4 **The fig ... | Go with** a curse upon ... (The fig was an abusive gesture made by putting the thumb between two closed fingers or into one's mouth.)

34 **have** (subjunctive form)
eat eaten; a form of the past participle now relatively rare, pronounced 'et'

45 **injury** calumny

54 **yellow bands** a fashion for collars and ruffs stiffened with yellow starch, reputedly introduced to the court by Mrs Anne Turner, who was ordered to wear them at her execution in 1615 for her part in the murder of Sir Thomas Overbury

55 **shall's** must we

59 **of force** of necessity

64 **Jew** (here regarded as the most contemptible of persons; antisemitism was widespread, and officially encouraged)

65 **they're** the doublet and hose

66 **crossed** thwarted

67 **past hope** beyond what one would hope
doctor's a man of learning's

68 **art** special skill in healing (see 2.1.57)

PHILIPPA Met you not
My husband's man?

ANSALDO I took such strange ways, lady,
I hardly met a creature.

PHILIPPA O, most welcome!

VIOLETTA
But how shall we bestow him now we have him, mistress?

PHILIPPA
Alas, that's true.

VIOLETTA Martino may come back again.

PHILIPPA
Step you into that little chamber—speedily, sir—
And dress him up in one of my gowns and headtires.
His youth will well endure it.

VIOLETTA That will be admirable.

PHILIPPA
Nay, do't, do't quickly then, and cut that suit
Into a hundred pieces, that it may never be known again.

VIOLETTA
A hundred? Nay, ten thousand at the least, mistress,
For if there be a piece of that suit left
as big as my nail, the deed will come out. 'Tis worse than a murder; I fear 'twill never be hid.

PHILIPPA
Away! Do your endeavour, and dispatch, wench.

Exeunt Violetta and Ansaldo

I've thought upon a way of certain safety,
And I may keep him while I have him too,
Without suspicion now. I've heard o'th' like.
A gentleman, that for a lady's love
Was thought six months her woman, tended on her
In her own garments, and (she being a widow)
Lay night by night with her in way of comfort;
Marry, in conclusion match they did together.
Would I'd a copy of the same conclusion.

Enter Brandino with a writing

He's come himself now. If thou be'st a happy wench,
Be fortunate in thy speed. I'll delay time
With all the means I can.—O, welcome sir.

BRANDINO
I'll speak to you anon, wife, and kiss you shortly.
I'm very busy yet.—[*Reads*] 'Cocksey-down, Memberry,
Her manor house at Welldun.'

PHILIPPA What's that, good sir?

BRANDINO
The widow's, your sweet sister's, deed of gift.
She's made all her estate over to me, wench.
She'll be too hard for 'em all.—And now come buss me.
Good luck after thieves' handsel.

PHILIPPA O, 'tis happy, sir,
You have him fast.

BRANDINO I ha' laid him safe enough, wench.

PHILIPPA
I was so lost in joy at the report on't
I quite forgot one thing to tell Martino.

BRANDINO
What's that, sweet blood?

PHILIPPA He and his villains, sir,
Robbed a sweet gentlewoman last night.

BRANDINO
A gentlewoman?

PHILIPPA Nay, most uncivilly,
And basely stripped her, sir.

BRANDINO O, barbarous slaves!

PHILIPPA
I was e'en fain—for womanhood's sake,
Alas, and charity's—to receive her in
And clothe her poor wants in a suit of mine.

BRANDINO
'Twas most religiously done. I long for her.
Who have I brought to see thee, think'st thou, woman?

PHILIPPA
Nay, sir, I know not.

BRANDINO Guess, I prithee heartily.
An enemy of thine.

PHILIPPA That I hope you have not, sir.

BRANDINO
But all was done in jest; he cries thee mercy.
Francisco, sirrah.

PHILIPPA O, I think not on him.

BRANDINO
That letter was but writ to try thy constancy.
He confessed all to me.

PHILIPPA Joy on him, sir.

Enter Francisco

So far am I from malice, look you, sir:—
Welcome, sweet signor. But I'll never trust you, sir.

76 **headtires** headdresses
77 **His youth . . . endure it** His youth will enable him to pass for a woman.
80–3 **Nay . . . hid** (Proverbially, 'murder will out'.)
82 **nail** finger-nail
84 **your endeavour** all you can, your best
92 **match** marry
93 **Would I'd . . . conclusion** I wish I might enjoy the same conclusion.
94–6 **He's . . . can** (perhaps stage-whispered to Violetta, offstage; or spoken aside, thinking of Violetta)
94–5 **If . . . speed** If you are favoured by fortune ('happy'), may you be fortunate in being quick; speed = (*a*) success, (*b*) quickness
98–9 **'Cocksey-down, Memberry . . . Welldun.'** sexual puns: cock, member, well-fucked
102 **hard** shrewd, obdurate
buss kiss
103 **after thieves' handsel** after a first experience of thieves; handsel = first experience. Dent records a use in 1609 of the proverb 'Thieves handsell is alwaies naught' (Dent, T122.11).
107 **sweet blood** Brandino's endearment stresses Philippa's attractiveness and youthful health; he ignores the association of *blood* and sexual desire.
111 **fain** obliged
114 **long for** sympathize with
118 **cries thee mercy** asks pardon of you

BRANDINO
Faith, I'm beholden to thee, wife, for this.
FRANCISCO [*aside*]
Methinks I enter now this house with joy,
Sweet peace, and quietness of consciënce.
I wear no guilty blush upon my cheek
For a sin stamped last midnight; I can talk now
With that kind man, and not abuse him inwardly
With any scornful thought made of his shame.
What a sweet being is an honest mind.
It speaks peace to itself and all mankind.
Enter Martino
BRANDINO
Martino.
MARTINO
Master?
BRANDINO There's another robbery done, sirrah,
By the same party.
MARTINO What? Your worship mocks,
Under correction.
PHILIPPA I forgot to tell thee
He robbed a lovely gentlewoman.
MARTINO O pagan!
This fellow will be stoned to death with pipkins.
Your women in the suburbs will so maul him
With broken cruses and pitchers without ears
He will ne'er die alive; that's my opinion.
Enter Ansaldo [*dressed as a gentlewoman*], *and Violetta*
PHILIPPA
Look you, your judgements, gentlemen—yours especially,
Signor Francisco, whose mere object now
Is woman, at these years; that's the eye-saint, I know,
Amongst young gallants.—Husband, you have a glimpse too;
You offer half an eye, as old as you are.
BRANDINO
By'r Lady, better, wench: an eye and a half, I trow.
I should be sorry else.
PHILIPPA What think you now, sirs?
Is't not a goodly manly gentlewoman?
BRANDINO Beshrew my heart else, wife.—
Pray, soft a little, signor. You're but my guest, remember;
I'm master of the house; I'll have the first buss.
PHILIPPA
But husband, 'tis the courtesy of all places
To give a stranger ever the first bit.
BRANDINO In woodcock or so, but there's no heed to be taken in mutton; we commonly fall so roundly to that, we forget ourselves.—
I'm sorry for thy fortune, but thou'rt welcome, lady.
[*Brandino kisses Ansaldo*]
MARTINO [*aside*]
My master kisses as I've heard a hackney man
Cheer up his mare: chap, chap.
BRANDINO [*to Ansaldo*] I have him fast, lady,
And he shall lie by't close.
ANSALDO You cannot do me
A greater pleasure, sir.
BRANDINO I'm happily glad on't.
FRANCISCO [*aside*]
Methinks there's somewhat whispers in my soul
This is the hour I must begin my acquaintance
With honest love, and banish all loose thoughts.
My fate speaks to me from the modest eye
Of yon sweet gentlewoman.
[*Francisco kisses Ansaldo. Philippa and Violetta talk apart*]
PHILIPPA Wench, wench!
VIOLETTA Pish, hold in your breath, mistress.
If you be seen to laugh, you spoil all presently.
I keep it in with all the might I have—puh!
ANSALDO [*to Brandino*]
Pray, what young gentleman's that, sir?
BRANDINO An honest boy, i'faith,
And came of a good kind. Dost like him, lady?
I would thou hadst him, an thou be'st not promised;
He's worth ten thousand dollars.
VIOLETTA By this light, mistress,
My master will go near to make a match anon.

128 **stamped** perpetrated; the metaphor is from striking an impression into something, as in minting a coin, and may be associated with conceiving a child (the 'sin').
129 **inwardly** in private thought
135 **Under correction** if you'll pardon my saying so; a deferential gesture after the possibly indiscreet remark that preceded it
137 **pipkins** small earthenware pots
138 **women in the suburbs** (including prostitutes; the 'suburbs' were the prime location of the brothels in London)
139 **cruses** small earthen vessels for liquids; pots, jars, or bottles
ears handles
140 **ne'er die alive** he will be dead before he can be executed (unintentionally absurd)
142 **mere** sole
143 **eye-saint** object of the eye's veneration
148 **manly** independent, courageous; but the pun is obvious
150 **signor** addressed to Francisco, who has taken the initiative with regard to the 'gentlewoman'
153 **bit** morsel to eat
154–5 **woodcock...mutton** small birds... joints of lamb; but Brandino is talking idiomatically: woodcock = fool, mutton = prostitutes, or at least women regarded as sexual beings
155 **fall so roundly to** eat so ravenously
159 **him** the thief, who is in fact Ansaldo, whom Brandino may at this moment still be holding
160 **lie by't close** lie securely in prison (but permitting an unintended sexual pun on 'lie beside Philippa in bed')
162 **somewhat** something
169 **presently** immediately
172 **good kind** good descent, good family

Methinks I dream of admirable sport, mistress.

PHILIPPA
Peace, thou art a drab.

BRANDINO Come hither now, Francisco.
I've known the time I've had a better stomach;
Now I can dine with looking upon meat.

FRANCISCO [*to Ansaldo*]
That face deserved a better fortune, lady,
Than last night's rudeness showed.

ANSALDO We cannot be
Our choosers, sir, in our own destiny.

FRANCISCO [*aside*]
I return better pleased than when I went.

MARTINO [*to Ansaldo*]
And could that beastly imp rob you, forsooth?

ANSALDO Most true, forsooth.
I will not altogether, sir, disgrace you,
Because you look half like a gentleman.

MARTINO
And that's the mother's half.

ANSALDO There's my hand for you.

MARTINO
I swear you could not give me anything
I love better. A hand gets me my living.
O sweet lemon-peel!
[*Martino kisses Ansaldo's hand*]

FRANCISCO [*to Ansaldo*]
May I request a modest word or two, lady,
In private with you?

ANSALDO With me, sir?

FRANCISCO
To make it sure from all suspect of injury
Or unbeseeming privacy, which heaven knows
Is not my aim now, I'll entreat this gentleman
For an ear-witness unto all our conference.

ANSALDO
Why, so, I am content, sir.

BRANDINO So am I, lady.
Exeunt Francisco and Ansaldo

MARTINO O master, here's a rare bedfellow for my mistress tonight—for you know we must both out of town again.

BRANDINO That's true, Martino.

MARTINO
I do but think how they'll lie telling of tales together,
The prettiliest.

BRANDINO The prettiliest, indeed.

MARTINO Their tongues will never
Lin wagging, master.

BRANDINO Never, Martino, never.
Exeunt Brandino [at one door, following Francisco and Ansaldo], and Martino [at another door]

PHILIPPA Take heed you be not heard.

VIOLETTA I fear you most, mistress.

PHILIPPA Me, fool?—Ha ha!

VIOLETTA
Why, look you, mistress; faith, you're faulty—ha ha!

PHILIPPA
Well said, i'faith. Where lies the fault now, gossip?

VIOLETTA
O for a husband! I shall burst with laughing else.
This house is able to spoil any maid.

PHILIPPA
I'll be revenged now soundly of Francisco
For failing me when time was.

176 **admirable** wonderful, surprising
sport The innocent sense of jest and the sexual sense of intercourse are both present as Violetta contemplates what she believes to be Francisco's betrothal to a man; see also 5.1.410.

177 **drab** prostitute, but here (by extension) a talkative person

178 **stomach** appetite (for food, but here with sexual association)

182 **destiny** Ansaldo's response to Francisco may be an artful and diplomatic reply from a person in double disguise, but it also relates to Francisco's emphasis at their meeting on *fate* (165, 234), *fortune* (180), and *ordained* (233, 254), and to the workings of predestination in the resolution of the play.

183 **I...went** I am happier returning to this house than I was leaving it (ironically connecting his happiness now with his distress in 3.3—both caused, without his realizing it, by the same person, Ansaldo)

184 **imp** a child of the devil

188 **mother's half** proverbially, 'The mother's side is the surer side'. Martino affirms his rank while jesting about his paternity; specifically, he implies a liaison between an upper-class woman and a lower-class man.

190–1 **hand...lemon-peel** Martino praises a hand because he earns his living by his hand; he compares hers to lemon-peel because with his passion for lemons it is extravagant praise.

194 **suspect** suspicion
injury wrongful act

195 **unbeseeming** inappropriate

196 **this gentleman** Brandino, who leaves the stage at 206.1; his exit is delayed by Martino, who presumably pulls him aside on his way out

206 **Lin** cease

208 **fear you** am afraid for you

210 **faulty** to blame, naughty

211 **fault** (*a*) sin (*b*) woman's genitals, considered as a crack or flaw in the body. The physical and moral senses often intertwine, as in 'love covers faults' (*Trick* 2.1.51; *Dissemblers* 5.2.171). Ansaldo, as a man, would not have the 'fault' which Francisco expects. This sense also leads to Violetta's following wish for a husband: as Maud says in relation to the 'faults or cracks' of her daughter, ''tis a husband solders up all cracks' (*Chaste Maid* 1.1.30–8). Within this system of correspondences a woman's vagina and mouth were easily twinned: an infant daughter has 'the mother's mouth, up and down' (*Chaste Maid* 3.2.13), for instance, and Helkiah Crooke relates anecdotal evidence of the physiological interchangeability, in women, of the two orifices (p. 254). Volubility (an open mouth) could therefore be taken as a sign of sexual incontinence (an open 'fault'). Violetta must find a husband, or she will 'burst with laughing': a husband, by stopping up one orifice, will thereby enable greater control of the other.

213 **house** perhaps in the secondary sense 'playhouse': many contemporary critics alleged that a visit to the public theatres was 'able to spoil any maid'. See 3.3.64.

214 **revenged** (by manipulating Francisco into marrying a man)

VIOLETTA Are you there, mistress?
I thought you would not forget that, however. A good turn disappointed is ever the last thing that a woman forgives. She'll scarce do't when she's speechless. Nay, though she hold up her whole hand for all other injuries, she'll forgive that but with one finger.

PHILIPPA
I'll vex his heart as much as he mocked mine.

VIOLETTA
But that may mar your hopes too, if our gentlewoman
Be known to be a man.

PHILIPPA Not as I'll work it.
I would not lose this sweet revenge, methinks,
For a whole fortnight of the old man's absence,
Which is the sweetest benefit next to this.

Enter Ansaldo [dressed as a gentlewoman]

Why, how now, sir, what course take you for laughing?
We are undone for one.

ANSALDO Faith, with great pain
Stifle it and keep it in. I ha' no receipt for't.
But pray, in sadness say: what is the gentleman?
I never knew his like for tedious urgings.
He will receive no answer.

PHILIPPA Would he would not, sir.

ANSALDO
Says I'm ordained for him, merely for him,
And that his wiving fate speaks in me to him;
Will force on me a jointure speedily
Of some seven thousand dollars.

PHILIPPA Would thou hadst 'em, sir!
I know he can, an he will.

ANSALDO For wonder's pity,
What is this gentleman?

PHILIPPA Faith, shall I tell you, sir?
One that would make an excellent honest husband
For her that's a just maid at one-and-twenty,
For on my conscience he has his maidenhead yet.

ANSALDO
Fie, out upon him, beast!

PHILIPPA Sir, if you love me,
Give way but to one thing I shall request of you.

ANSALDO
Your courtesies, you know, may lay commands on me.

PHILIPPA
Then, at his next solicitings, let a consent
Seem to come from you. 'Twill make noble sport, sir.
We'll get jointure and all—but you must bear
Yourself most affable to all his purposes.

ANSALDO
I can do that.

PHILIPPA Ay, and take heed of laughing.

ANSALDO
I've bide the worst of that already, lady.

Enter Francisco

PHILIPPA
Peace, set your countenance then, for here he comes.

FRANCISCO
There is no middle continent in this passion.
I feel it since; it must be love or death;
It was ordained for one.

PHILIPPA [*taking him aside*]
Signor Francisco,
I'm sorry 'twas your fortune in my house, sir,
To have so violent a stroke come to you.
The gentlewoman's a stranger; pray be counselled, sir,
Till you hear further of her friends and portion.

FRANCISCO
'Tis only but her love that I desire;
She comes most rich in that.

PHILIPPA But be advised, though.
I think she's a rich heir, but see the proof, sir,
Before you make her such a generous jointure.

FRANCISCO
'Tis mine, and I will do't.

PHILIPPA She shall be yours too,
If I may rule her then.

FRANCISCO You speak all sweetness.

PHILIPPA
She likes your person well; I tell you so much,
But take no note I said so.

FRANCISCO Not a word.

PHILIPPA [*to Ansaldo*]
Come, lady, come. The gentleman's deserftul,

215 **Are you there, mistress?** Is that what you're thinking about?
216 **however** whatever happened in the mean time
216–17 **A good turn** a favour, but possibly also with a sexual sense: 'turn' = 'bout of sex'
218–20 **speechless…finger** Violetta refers to the practice of asking a speechless dying person to respond to questions by making hand signals; the 'injury' or insult of sexual disappointment produces the most grudging forgiveness.
227 **course** plan of action, remedy
for laughing to prevent laughing
228 **undone for** in trouble for the lack of
229 **receipt** remedy
230 **sadness** seriousness
233 **merely** solely
235 **jointure** 'A sole estate limited to the wife, being "a competent livelihood of freehold for the wife of lands and tenements, to take upon the death of the husband for the life of the wife at least" (Coke upon Littleton, 36b)' (*OED*)
241 **maidenhead** used of male virginity as well as female
242 **out upon** a phrase of rejection
250 **bide** endured, survived
252 **continent** a containing area or space; Francisco protests that there are only extreme states available to him.
253 **since** from then till now
254 **one** a person
256 **stroke** blow (as a metaphor for love; but it could also be used as a metaphor for fornication, of the kind which Philippa *had* wanted Francisco to experience in her house)
258 **portion** dowry
259 **only but** solely
265 **person** appearance, physical presence
267 **deserftul** deserving

And, o' my conscience, honest.
ANSALDO Blame me not.
I am a maid, and fearful.
FRANCISCO Never truth
Came perfecter from man.
PHILIPPA Give her a lip-taste,
Enter Brandino
That she herself may praise it.
[*Francisco kisses Ansaldo*]
BRANDINO Yea, a match, i'faith!
[*Exeunt Francisco, Ansaldo, Philippa, and Violetta*]
My house is lucky for 'em.
[*Enter Martino*]
Now, Martino?
MARTINO
Master, the widow has the day.
BRANDINO The day?
MARTINO
She's overthrown my youngster.
BRANDINO Precious tidings!
Clap down four woodcocks more.
MARTINO They're all at hand, sir.
BRANDINO
What, both her adversaries too?
MARTINO They're come, sir.
BRANDINO
Go bid the cook serve in two geese in a dish.
MARTINO
I like your conceit, master, beyond utterance. [*Exit*]
Enter Valeria, Ricardo, and two Suitors
BRANDINO
Welcome, sweet sister. Which is the man must have you?
I'd welcome nobody else.
FIRST SUITOR Come to me then, sir.
BRANDINO
Are you he, faith, my chain of gold? I'm glad on't.
VALERIA [*to Ricardo*]
I wonder you can have the face to follow me,
That have so prosecuted things against me.
But I ha' resolved myself, 'tis done to spite me.
RICARDO [*tearing his hair*]
O dearth of truth!
SECOND SUITOR Nay, do not spoil thy hair.
Hold, hold I say. I'll get thee a widow somewhere.
RICARDO
If hand and faith be nothing for a contract,
What shall man hope?
SECOND SUITOR 'Twas wont to be enough, honey,
When there was honest meaning amongst widows;
But since your bribes came in, 'tis not allowed
A contract without gifts to bind it fast.
Everything now must have a feeling first.—
Do I come near you, widow?
VALERIA No, indeed, sir,
Nor ever shall, I hope.—And for your comfort, sir,
That sought all means t'entrap me for my wealth,
Had law unfortunately put you upon me
You had lost your labour, all your aim and hopes, sir.
Here stands the honest gentleman my brother
To whom I've made a deed of gift of all.
BRANDINO
Ay, that she has, i'faith. I thank her, gentlemen.
Look you here, sirs.
[*He shows a writing*]
VALERIA I must not look for pleasures
That give more grief, if they prove false or fail us,
Than ever they gave joy.
FIRST SUITOR Ha' you served me so, widow?
SECOND SUITOR [*to Ricardo*]
I'm glad thou hast her not. Laugh at him, honey. Ha Ha!
VALERIA
I must take one that loves me for myself.
Here's an old gentleman looks not after wealth
But virtue, manners, and conditïons.
FIRST SUITOR
Yes, by my faith. I must have lordships too, widow.
VALERIA How, sir?
FIRST SUITOR
Your manners, virtue, and conditions, widow,
Are pretty things within doors; I like well on 'em.
But I must have somewhat without, 'lying or being
In the tenure, or occupatïon,
Of Master such-a-one'—ha? Those are fine things indeed.
VALERIA
Why, sir, you swore to me it was for love.
FIRST SUITOR
True, but there's two words to a bargain ever
All the world over, and if love be one
I'm sure money's the other. 'Tis no bargain else.
Pardon me, I must dine as well as sup, widow.
VALERIA
Cry mercy, I mistook you all this while, sir.
It was this ancient gentleman, indeed,

272 **house** perhaps in the secondary sense 'playhouse': marriages take place with great frequency in the theatre. See 3.3.64.
274 **She's overthrown** she is victorious over **my youngster** Ricardo (as at 4.1.56)
275 **Clap down** set [the table] with
278 **conceit** idea
281 **chain of gold** (promised by the First Suitor at 4.1.90)
282 **face** nerve, gall
290 **bribes** (see 4.2.28)
292 **feeling** material base
293 **Do I come near you** does what I say affect you
303 **served** treated
307 **conditïons** qualities of character (see 1.2.80)
308 **lordships** estates
312–14 **'lying...such-a-one'** The First Suitor talks of land in the forms of hypothetical legal documents.
316 **there's...bargain** The proverb 'Two words to a bargain' suggests that agreement is the essence of a bargain, but the First Suitor thinks in terms of love and money in marriage.

Whom I crave pardon on.
SECOND SUITOR What of me, widow?
VALERIA
Alas, I have wronged you, sir. 'Twas you that swore
You loved me for myself.
SECOND SUITOR By my troth, but I did not.
Come, father not your lies upon me, widow.
I, love you for yourself?—Spit at me, gentlemen,
If ever I'd such a thought.—Fetch me in, widow;
You'll find your reach too short.
VALERIA Why, you have enough, you say.
SECOND SUITOR Ay, but I will have
My humour too; you never think of that.
They're coach-horses; they go together still.
VALERIA
Whom should a widow trust? I'll swear 'twas one of
you
That made me believe so.—Mass, think 'twas you, sir,
Now I remember me.
RICARDO I swore too much
To be believed so little.
VALERIA Was it you then?
Beshrew my heart for wronging of you.
RICARDO Welcome, blessing.
Are you mine faithfully now?
VALERIA As love can make one.
FIRST SUITOR
Why, this fills the commonwealth so full of beggars,
Marrying for love—which none of mine shall do.
VALERIA [*to Ricardo*]
But now I think on't, we must part again, sir.
RICARDO
Again?
VALERIA
You're in debt; and I, in doubt of all,
Left myself nothing too. We must not hold;
Want on both sides makes all affection cold.
I shall not keep you from that gentleman.
You'll be his more than mine, an when he list
He'll make you lie from me in some sour prison.
Then let him take you now for altogether, sir,
For he that's mine shall be all mine, or nothing.
RICARDO
I never felt the evil of my debts
Till this afflicting minute.
SECOND SUITOR [*aside*] I'll be mad
Once in my days; I have enough to cure me,
And I will have my humour. They're now but
Desperate debts again; I ne'er look for 'em,
And ever since I knew what malice was
I always held it sweeter to sow mischief
Than to reap money; 'tis the finer pleasure.
I'll give him in his bonds, as 'twere in pity,
To make the match, and bring 'em both to beggary.
Then will they ne'er agree; that's a sure point.
He'll give her a black eye within these three days,
Beat half her teeth out by Allhallowtide,
And break the little household-stuff they have
With throwing at one another. O sweet sport!—
Come, widow, come. I'll try your honesty.
Here to my honey you've made many proffers;
I fear they're all but tricks.—
[*He shows writings*]
Here are his debts, gentlemen.
How I came by 'em, I know best myself.—
Take him before us faithfully for your husband,
And he shall tear 'em all before your face, widow.
VALERIA
Else may all faith refuse me.
SECOND SUITOR [*to Ricardo*] Tear 'em, honey.
'Tis firm in law, a consideration given.
[*Ricardo tears the papers*]
What, with thy teeth? Thou'lt shortly tear her so.
That's all my hope. Thou'dst never had 'em else.
I've enough, and I will have my humour.
RICARDO
I'm now at liberty, widow.
VALERIA I'll be so too,
And then I come to thee.—Give me this from you,
brother.
[*She takes the writing from Brandino*]
BRANDINO Hold, sister, sister!
VALERIA [*to Ricardo*]
Look you, the deed of gift, sir. I'm as free.
He that has me, has all—and thou art he.
BOTH SUITORS
How's that?
VALERIA You're bobbed; 'twas but a deed in trust.—
And all to prove thee, whom I have found most just.
BRANDINO
I'm bobbed among the rest too. I'd have sworn
'T'ad been a thing for me and my heirs for ever.
If I'd but got it up to the black box above
It had been past redemption.
FIRST SUITOR How am I cheated!

322 **on** from
327 **Fetch me in** cheat me
332 **still** always
340 **none of mine** no relative of mine
343 **hold** maintain our attachment, remain devoted
345 **gentleman** the Second Suitor, to whom Ricardo owes money
346 **list** desires (subjunctive form)
348 **for altogether** for all time to come
352 **cure** take care of
354 **Desperate debts** bad debts, unrecoverable
358 **give . . . in** hand back, return
362 **Allhallowtide** 1 November
372 **'Tis . . . given** The cancelling of the bonds is legally valid, because the First Suitor has been given something, a 'consideration' (Valeria's oath to marry Ricardo), in exchange for their value.
381 **bobbed** cheated, deceived
deed in trust not a gift in perpetuity
382 **prove** test

SECOND SUITOR [*to Ricardo*]
I hope you'll have the conscience now to pay me, sir.

RICARDO
O wicked man, sower of strife and envy,
Open not thy lips.

SECOND SUITOR How? How's this?

RICARDO
Thou hast no charge at all, no child of thine own
But two thou got'st once of a scouring-woman,
And they are both well provided for, they're i'th' hospital.
Thou hast ten thousand pound to bury thee;
Hang thyself when thou wilt. A slave go with thee!

SECOND SUITOR
I'm gone. My goodness comes all out together.
I have enough, but I have not my humour. [*Exit*]

Enter Violetta

VIOLETTA
O master, gentlemen, and you, sweet widow—
I think you are no forwarder, yet I know not:
If ever you be sure to laugh again,
Now is the time.

VALERIA Why, what's the matter, wench?

VIOLETTA Ha ha ha!

BRANDINO Speak, speak!

VIOLETTA Ha! a marriage, a marriage—I cannot tell't for laughing. Ha ha!

BRANDINO
A marriage? Do you make that a laughing matter?

VIOLETTA
Ha! Ay, and you'll make it so, when you know all.

Enter Francisco, and Ansaldo [dressed as a gentlewoman, followed by Philippa]

Here they come!
Here they come, one man married to another!

VALERIA
How, man to man?

VIOLETTA Ay, man to man, i'faith.
There'll be good sport at night to bring 'em both to bed.
Do you see 'em now? Ha ha ha!

FIRST SUITOR [*to Ansaldo*] My daughter Marcia!

ANSALDO
O my father! Your love and pardon, sir.

VALERIA 'Tis she indeed, gentlemen.

ANSALDO [*to First Suitor*] I have been disobedient, I confess,
Unto your mind, and heaven has punished me
With much affliction since I fled your sight;
But, finding reconcilement from above
In peace of heart, the next (I hope) 's your love.

FIRST SUITOR
I cannot but forgive thee, now I see thee.
Thou fled'st a happy fortune of an old man,
But Francisco's of a noble family,
Though he be somewhat spent.

FRANCISCO I loved her not, sir,
As she was yours (for I protest I knew't not)
But for herself, sir, and her own deservings—
Which, had you been as foul as you've been spiteful,
I should have loved in her.

FIRST SUITOR Well, hold your prating, sir;
You're not like to lose by't.

PHILIPPA
O Violetta, who shall laugh at us now?

VIOLETTA
The child unborn, mistress.

ANSALDO [*to Philippa*] Be good.

FRANCISCO [*to Philippa*] Be honest.

ANSALDO [*to Philippa*]
Heav'n will not let you sin, an you'd be careful.

FRANCISCO [*to Philippa*]
What means it sends to help you, think and mend.
You're as much bound as we to praise that friend.

PHILIPPA
I am so, and I will so.

ANSALDO [*to Violetta*] Marry you speedily.
Children tame you; you'll die like a wild beast else.

VIOLETTA
Ay, by my troth, should I. I've much ado
To forbear laughing now; more's my hard fortune.

Enter Martino

MARTINO
O master, mistress, and you gentles all,
To horse, to horse! presently, if you mean
To do your country any service.

BRANDINO
Art not ashamed, Martino, to talk of horsing
So openly before young married couples thus?

MARTINO
It does concern the commonwealth, and me,
And you, master, and all: the thieves are taken.

ANSALDO
What sayst, Martino?

MARTINO La, here's commonwealth's-men!—
The man of art, master, that cupped your eyes,
Is proved an arrant rascal; and his man

388 **strife and envy** Ricardo's moral rebuke is an echo of Philippians 1:15, 'Some indeed preach Christ even of envy and strife; and some of good will', and also of James 3:14, 'But if ye have bitter envying and strife in your hearts ...'

390–3 **Thou ... thee** Ricardo recalls the Second Suitor's speech at 2.1.205–8.

390 **charge** financial responsibilities

395 **comes ... out** comes to an end

398 **forwarder** closer (to marriage, or resolution of your disputes)

411 **Marcia** Italian, 'Martiale, a Martial-man, a Martialist' (Florio)

422 **somewhat spent** At 1.1.178 Martino says that 'He's spent the best part of his patrimony'.

425 **foul** poor

426 **prating** idle chatter

429 **The child unborn** posterity
honest chaste

431 **mend** reform yourself

440 **horsing** copulating; a term for the stallion's action in mating with the mare

444 **commonwealth's-men** good citizens; Martino is ironic

446 **arrant** notorious, manifest

That drew my tooth, an excellent purse-drawer.
I felt no pain in that; it went insensibly.
Such notable villainies confessed!

BRANDINO
Stop there, sir.
We'll have time for them.—Come, gentlefolks,
Take a slight meal with us; but the best cheer
Is perfect joy, and that we wish all here.

RICARDO
Stay, stay, sir.—I'm as hungry of my widow
As you can be upon your maid, believe it,
But we must come to our desires in order.
There's duties to be paid, ere we go further.—
[*Ricardo addresses the Epilogue to the audience*]
He that, without your likings, leaves this place,
Is like one falls to meat and forgets grace,
And that's not handsome, trust me, no.
Our rights being paid, and your loves understood,
My widow and my meat then does me good.
—I ha' no money, wench; I told thee true.
For my report—pray, let her hear't from you.
Exeunt

THE PARTS

Adult Males

RICARDO (317 lines): Silvio *or* Stratio *or* Fiducio [*or* Latrocinio *or* Occulto]; any servant
MARTINO (287 lines): Servellio
BRANDINO (275 lines): Servellio
FRANCISCO (264 lines): any servant; any one thief
LATROCINIO (191 lines): Francisco *or* Attilio *or* an officer [*or* Ricardo *or* a suitor]; Servellio
SECOND SUITOR (152 lines): Silvio *or* Stratio *or* Fiducio [*or* Latrocinio *or* Occulto]; any servant
FIRST SUITOR (102 lines): Silvio *or* Stratio *or* Fiducio [*or* Latrocinio *or* Occulto]; any servant
OCCULTO (52 lines): Francisco *or* Attilio *or* an officer [*or* Ricardo *or* a suitor]; Servellio
STRATIO (24 lines): Francisco *or* Attilio *or* an officer [*or* Ricardo *or* a suitor]; Servellio
FIDUCIO (12 lines): Francisco *or* Attilio *or* an officer [*or* Ricardo *or* a suitor]; Servellio
OFFICER (9 lines): any servant; any one thief
PROLOGUE (6 lines): anyone but Martino *or* Francisco
SILVIO (5 lines): Francisco *or* Attilio *or* an officer [*or* Ricardo *or* a suitor]; Servellio
ATTILIO (3 lines): Servellio; any one thief *or* Ansaldo *or* servants in 4.2

Youths

ANSALDO (185 lines): Attilio

Boys

PHILIPPA (300 lines)
VALERIA (204 lines)
VIOLETTA (164 lines)

Most crowded scene: 5.1 (10 speaking parts)

INDEX OF COMPLEX WORDS

448 **insensibly** without any feeling
456 **duties to be paid** obligations to be met (to a social superior: the audience is here being treated as though it were a lord or monarch); taxes to be paid (when importing goods: hence 'ere we go further')
457 **likings** approval, and so by extension applause
460 **rights** duties; also a pun on 'rites', the ritual of the performance and the ritual of marriage
paid performed, discharged
461 **meat** food, generally (not specifically animal flesh), alluding to the 'meal' just promised, but also to the fact that plays were performed in the late afternoon, and that actors and spectators would have had their evening meal soon afterward.
462 **I** (both Ricardo, and the actor playing him)
wench Valeria
463 **my** (appropriating the audience's applause for the whole cast as approval of the actor/character Ricardo)
report reputation, deserving

THE WITCH

Edited by Marion O'Connor

A Page, a Knight, a Viscount and an Earl
Did lately marry with an English girl—
A maid, a wife, a widow, and a whore.
Whoever saw so cross a match before?

THE solution to this Jacobean riddle, of which various versions were widely circulated in manuscript, is a notorious narrative. That narrative, and the form of the riddle itself, provide a solution to many of the more puzzling features of *The Witch*, Middleton's drama of a maid, a wife, a widow, and a whore—plus more than one witch.

Robert Carr began his courtly progress in Edinburgh, as page to the Earl of Dunbar. Having come to England and attracted the attention of King James I, Carr was knighted in 1607, made Viscount Rochester and then Knight of the Garter in 1611, and created Earl of Somerset in 1612. At the end of 1613 he married Frances Howard, who had been married to Robert Devereux, the Earl of Essex, early in 1606. Where royal utterance was the source of three of the four names assigned Carr in the riddle, legal pronouncements account for the same proportion of hers. Her claim to be called a maid had been upheld in June of 1613 after inspection by a panel of seven of her matronly peers and two midwives, their verdict of '*virgo incorrupta*' being indispensable to secure the annulment of her marriage to Essex. Pronounced on 25 September 1613, the episcopal commissioners' judgement in favour of the plaintiff was closely preceded by an event whereof the outcome would bring her and her second husband to the dock as defendants in a murder case. On 14 September 1613 Sir Thomas Overbury, whose close association with Carr had soured over the royal favourite's liaison with Howard, died in the Tower after four months' imprisonment there. Within two years, Howard's great-uncle, Henry Howard, the Earl of Northampton, died; George Villiers displaced Somerset at the centre of James's attentions; and ugly rumours were actualized as due process of law. Somerset and his Countess were accused of having procured Overbury's poisoning and eventual murder. Trial was delayed by her pregnancy (their daughter, Anne, being born early in December of 1615), and by the legal necessity of securing the conviction of their agents before prosecuting the couple as accessories before the fact. At their respective trials late in May of 1616, she pleaded guilty, while he (in the teeth of royal attempts to get him to follow his wife's lead) insisted upon his innocence. Both were convicted and condemned to death, but neither followed their agents to the block, for both received royal pardons. Her pardon came within two months, but his was not sealed until 1624. For years, then, his status as a man attainted of a felony meant that he was '*civiliter mortuus*'—dead in civil law—and she was thus, in legal fiction, a widow. In fact, she predeceased him, dying in 1632 while he survived until 1645. At the time of her death, when she was probably not quite forty years old, Frances Howard Devereux Carr had been labelled whore for half her lifetime. On this label the different versions of the riddle concur: where they vary is in the abusiveness of the terms enchained to that conclusion. The line 'A maid, a wife, a widow and a whore' in one manuscript miscellany of verse appears in another as 'A maid, a wife, a countess and a whore' and in still another as 'A wife, a witch, a murderer and a whore'.

Frances Howard's name was linked with witchcraft long before she was tried for murder. In the spring of 1613, as rumours arose of her alienation from Devereux and her association with Carr, John Chamberlain reported the latest gossip:

> There was speech of a divorce to be prosecuted this term 'twixt the earl of Essex and his lady... but there happened an accident that hath altered the case, for she having sought out a certain wise woman had much conference with her, and she after the nature of such creatures drawing much money from her, at last cozened her of a jewel of great value, for the which being apprehended and clapped up, she accuses the Lady of divers strange questions and projects, and in conclusion that she dealt with her for the making away of her Lord (as aiming at another mark) upon which scandal and slander the Lord Chamberlain [Frances Howard's father, Thomas, Earl of Suffolk] and his friends think it not fit to proceed with the divorce. (Letter to Sir Ralph Winwood, [6 May 1613])

A 'wise wo/man' or 'cunning wo/man' being deemed equivalent to a witch in orthodox Jacobean demonology, merely to consult such a person was risky. Being rumoured to have sought such murderous and adulterous assistance as Frances Howard was said to have asked was scandalous indeed. And when the nullity proceedings got under way, the question of witchcraft came up again. The grounds on which the annulment was eventually granted were 'that the Earl of Essex, for some secret, incurable, binding impediment, did never carnally know, or was or is able carnally to know the lady Frances Howard'. The reason proposed by the Earl for his selective impotence was simply that, having once loved her, he had ceased to do so. Treatises upon witchcraft, however, offered more exotic explanations: selective impotence could be ascribed to *maleficium versus hanc*, an evil spell affecting a man's sexual relations with one particular woman. It was as such that the Devereux/Howard conjugal relations were debated between George Abbot, Archbishop of Canterbury and an opponent of the annulment, and King James I, its prime mover as well as the author of a *Demonologie* (1597).

While the published records of the 1613 annulment bear no trace of speculation as to the human perpetrators of the *maleficium* hypothesized by the King, in the published records of the 1615–16 trials Frances Howard's name is linked with witchcraft upon various victims. It was claimed that (with her agent Anne Turner, a physician's widow) the Countess had often had resort to Simon Forman 'that by force of magic, he should procure the now Earl of Somerset, then Viscount Rochester, to love her'. Mrs Turner confessed 'that Dr Savories was used in succession after Forman and practised many sorceries upon the Earl of Essex's person'. Another agent, the apothecary and druggist James Franklin, confessed even more than he was charged with: not only had he provided the seven different poisons administered to Overbury, but 'then he wrought the love between Rochester and [the countess] . . . and was to have £200 to continue their loves until the[ir] marriage'. Franklin's confession implied an excuse beyond price: the Countess, he said, 'was able to bewitch any man'. With women, however, she had been less successfully bewitching, even when abetted by the professionals: a memorandum to the King concerning the charges against Somerset included the claim 'that the countess laboured Forman and Gresham, the conjurors, to enforce the queen by witchcraft to favour the countess'.

Between this narrative and all three plots of *The Witch* the correspondences are startling. Notably, in the first plot to be unfolded in the course of the play, Sebastian procures from the witch a spell rendering Antonio selectively impotent in relation to Isabella. For this first plot, *The Atheist's Tragedy* (1611), ascribed to Cyril Tourneur, is a likely, although not an absolutely certain, source. Where the Charlemont/Castabella/Rousard relationship in *The Atheist's Tragedy* diverges from the Sebastian/Isabella/Antonio relationship in *The Witch*, the differences go in the direction of the Carr/Howard/Devereux relationship and suggest that if Middleton was indeed reshaping a plot from Tourneur's play, he was recasting it in the mould of the contemporary scandal. The express desire of Isabella for maternity and the involvement of the bride's powerful uncle in her matrimonial ventures, for example, both correspond to matters well known in the Howard/Devereux marriage and its annulment. The second plot is dominated by a figure whose name (Francisca, homophonous with Frances Carr), age (sixteen, the age of the Countess when Essex returned from France and attempted to consummate their marriage), disposition, and sexual morals link her with the popular image of Frances Howard. Francisca has a brother whose angry intervention in his sister's sexual entanglements aligns with the public quarrel (which only royal intervention stopped short of a duel) between the Countess's brother Henry and Essex. Francisca is pregnant, as the Countess both actually was when the murder trials began in the autumn of 1615, and also was rumoured to be again at the end of the following year. For this second plot of *The Witch*, no literary source has been identified. There is, however, a marked correspondence between some stage business assigned to Francisca and a visual image circulated of Frances. At 2.3.31–7 the character's gratuitous comments upon her own appearance require her to be contemplating herself in a mirror, a gesture most easily achieved if her costume follows the Jacobean fashion of wearing a decorated mirror as an ornament: it is in such a pose and with such a bauble that the Countess was quite recognizably represented in a broadsheet entitled *Mistress Turner's Farewell to All Women* (reproduced above, p. 45). The third plot—the Duchess's revenge upon her consort and her attempt to dispose of her agent—probably derives from a narrative of early Lombardy as retold, from the chronicle of Paul the Deacon, by Niccolò Machiavelli in his *Florentine History*, of which an English translation had been published in 1595. This narrative of ultramontane sex and skullduggery was held to be instructively like the scandal around Overbury's death: both stories figure in a Jacobean preacher's 1616 catalogue of cases proving that 'if we mark the dealings of God with murderers, it will appear that very seldom, or never, they 'scape unpunished, but by one means or other, he finds them out and meets with them, though it be by suffering them to murder themselves' (Tuke). Here again, dramatizing this exemplum from the *Florentine History* as the third plot in *The Witch*, Middleton made adjustments which improve the fit between the narrative and contemporary facts. The Duchess's resort to a witch for poison, for example, is a point which does not appear in the source but was well publicized at the Countess's trials. Such, too, is the Duchess's insistence on her own sexual propriety even as she acknowledges herself to be a murderess:

Blood I am guilty of
But not adultery, not the breach of honour.
(5.3.102–3)

The Duke's final speech, fulsomely thanking

heaven for such a wife,
Who though her intent sinned, yet she makes amends
With grief and honour, virtue's noblest ends
(5.3.131–3)

corresponds to the praise which the *prosecution*, in the person of the Attorney General, Sir Francis Bacon, accorded the Countess (pale, tearful, and very fetching in black) for her penitence, femininity, and ancestry. The conclusion of her trial was outrageous: Lord Ellesmere, acting as Lord High Steward, virtually assured the Countess of a royal pardon with the same breath—indeed, in the middle of the same grammatical sentence—as he pronounced legal sentence of death upon her. The conclusion of *The Witch* is analogously outrageous: to attempt to explain all the unexpected revelations and reversals solely as tragicomic conventions, or even yet as parodies of those conventions, is to overburden generic expectations.

The contemporary references in *The Witch* are altogether too insistent and too elaborate to be either accidental or incidental. Middleton's dispersal of them across three plots may have ensured that no single figure or configuration would run the risk of being cited as a representation of the crimes of his social superiors. That they are nonetheless to be seen, ensemble, as just such a representation is secured by the presence of the witch of the title. It is not that the witch brings the plots together in some formal unity of the sort that twentieth-century criticism so often, and inappropriately, foisted upon Renaissance dramaturgy. The witch has no direct involvement in one plot, the second, for neither Francisca nor her partner Aberzanes has any resort to her. In the other two plots Hecate is active but finally otiose. The love-charm which she gives Almachildes to use on the waiting woman Amoretta at first appears impressively powerful: having once served its limited dramatic purpose as the occasion of an entertaining turn (sexual attraction On/Off), however, the charm works only as a dupe, misleading both Almachildes about the waiting woman and also the audience about her mistress. The poisons which the witch gives the Duchess so that Almachildes may meet 'a sudden and a subtle' death (5.2.2) turn out in the next and last scene either not to have worked or perhaps not even to have been ingested: they have been forgotten. The spell which the witch puts on Antonio does the detumescent trick all right; but then, after having gone to such lengths to preserve Isabella's virginity for his own purposes, Sebastian turns squeamish about violating it with a rape. That he subsequently gets what he wants is no thanks to the witch but rather to 'a fearful, unexpected accident' (5.3.25).

In no plot of *The Witch* do the activities of the witch and her coven of companions determine the outcome nor even affect the actions of the human figures. The courtiers who consult her are neither her victims nor her converts but rather simply her clients. That they are neither harmed nor corrupted by their encounters with witchcraft is a flat violation of the rules of demonology as articulated in Elizabethan and Jacobean treatises on the subject. Almachildes, for example, should be shown as sexually subjugated to the witch: she has, she lustfully gloats, 'had him thrice in incubus already' (1.2.197), an anterior relationship which ought to ensure his enthralment. Almachildes, however, is shown to be buying her charm-making services with marzipan, an exchange which occasions no more than a few sexually innuendoed lines (1.2.220–3) and some mildly ribald stage business with a wet handkerchief. Nor does Almachildes's acceptance of the dinner to which the witch invites him and which she conjures up, complete with Cat and Fiddle, put him in any greater jeopardy than a hungry hangover. Conspicuously ineffectual in their plot relations to the courtiers, the witch and her colleagues appear almost innocent alongside them. For all her talk of incest and infanticide, the coven is not shown to be performing anything more noxious than their aerial song and dance routine. Within the fiction of *The Witch*, it is in the court that vices are enacted, and it is by the courtiers that crimes are committed, with ultimate impunity.

The witch, then, proves useless within the dramatic fiction, but she nevertheless serves to point up the contemporary significance of that fiction by bringing its several strands together around a single figure, Frances Howard. The name of the witch, a name emphasized from the first of the three scenes in which she appears, is Hecate. Although she is a mortal being with only three years left to run on her 120-year lifespan (1.2.64–71), the witch bears the name of a classical divinity. It is important to notice which one, for Hecate was no simple patroness of black arts. Basing their understanding mainly on literary texts of late classical antiquity, Renaissance mythographers of the late sixteenth and early seventeenth centuries construed Hecate as part of a trinity and usually referred to her with epithets advertising her threesomeness. In Virgil's *Aeneid*, for example, Dido offers pyreside prayers to assorted underworld deities, including 'three-bodied Hecate, three faces of the virgin Diana [*tergeminam... Hecaten, tria virginis ora Dianae*]' (IV.511), a line cited by Ben Jonson in his note to the lines in which his Dame addresses Hecate as 'thou three-formed star... to whose triple name... Thus we incline, once, twice and thrice the same' (*The Masque of Queens*, 1609). In thus requiring his witches to bow three times to a tri-form deity, Jonson gets some theatrical mileage out of an epithet so recognizably familiar that no name need be attached to it. Jonson's understanding of Hecate was available in the standard Renaissance mythographies of Natalis Comes [Natale Conti] and Vicenzo Cartari and in their English-language derivatives:

> She is also called *Hecate*. ἑχατόν signifieth an hundred: which simple & determinate number, is put for an infinite or great number: meaning, that the Moon hath many and infinite operations in and over these inferior bodies. She had three faces, called for that *Trivia*, *Triformis*, and *Tergemina*. For, in heaven she is called *Luna*, in the woods *Diana*, under the earth *Hecate*, or *Proserpina*. That of these three faces, which was on the right side, was the face and head of a horse, figuring the swiftness of the Moon in ending her revolution. The left was of a dog, noting that when she hideth herself from us she is then *Proserpina* with her hellish hound: the middle was of a boar, signifying her jurisdiction in fields and forests. (Fraunce)

Other mythographers were less interested in the zoology of Hecate's three heads than in their solid geometry. Spatial

Two views of a bronze statuette of Hecate, made in Padua *c.*1520.

necessity requires a three-headed goddess to be imagined as facing in three different directions:

> This Hecate the ancients worshipped and adored as she that had the guard and keeping of all crossways, and such lanes as in the end concurred and conjoined themselves in one, and for that cause they depictured her with three heads... And it is said, that Orpheus ascribed unto her such faces, meaning to declare thereby the divers and sundry aspects which we oftentimes may discern to be in the Moon, and that her virtues and effects are powerful and working, not only in the heavens where she is called Luna, and on the earth where she is known by the name of Diana, but also extend down even to the bowels of Erebus, where she is called Hecate and Proserpina. (Lynche)

The title character of *The Witch*, then, has been given the name of a multiform and multivalent deity. Diana/Artemis, Luna/Selene, and Proserpina/Hecate all constitute a single goddess. Like the string of apparently incompatible names in every version of the riddle, the divine names all designate a single 'she'. The presiding presence of Hecate in *The Witch* brings the contemporary references together as representations of that same 'she', Frances Howard Devereux Carr, and labels her not just witch but also whore. The pronunciation of the name 'Hecate' in *The Witch* is disyllabic and its mere utterance carries a sexual innuendo, 'cat' being early modern slang for 'whore'. The Countess had already been more immediately insulted with the feline epithet: in at least two of the sometimes astonishingly obtuse letters which Overbury sent from the Tower to Carr, she is cited as the 'Catopard'.

At the same time, moreover, the particular name by which this triform goddess is called invokes her as the patroness of a particular aspect of female sexuality—Diana/Artemis is associated with virginity, Luna/Selene with maternity, and Proserpina/Hecate with sterility. These phases correspond to the sexual/social placement of the principal female characters in *The Witch*: the youthful and nubile Francisca, the newly-wed Isabella, and the mature Duchess. (Amoretta is functionally a cipher—necessary, but necessary only in relation to another character, the Duchess, whose name she shares [2.2.106] and as whose woman she is designated by the original list of *dramatis personae.*) Francisca, Isabella, and the Duchess form a configuration which repeats the sequence in the first version of the riddle quoted above: a maid, a wife, a widow. However, none of these ladies actually meets the terms of sexual conduct defining the social category to which she is assigned. Francisca the sixteen-year-old mother is no maiden. Isabella, promised in marriage to one man and bound in an unconsummated marriage with another, is no wife. The Duchess, having (as only the final moments of the play make clear) failed to kill her husband, is no widow. And even when she thinks the Duke to be dead, the Duchess is no figure of mourning and abstinence but rather a sexual predator. In *The Witch*—again as in the riddle—the maid, the wife, and the widow exist merely by sleights of language. Indeed, among the female characters in the play, only Hecate and Florida are entitled to the names by which they are known—witch and whore.

The fact that the other female characters do not meet the job descriptions for their respective titles points to the play's preoccupation with the problem of determining a woman's moral worth and her social status solely with respect to her sexual relations with men. To Anglo-American sensibilities of the twenty-first century, this is perhaps above all an issue of equity. To earlier centuries it has sometimes, and in some places, been a question of epistemology. The epistemological problem lies in the unverifiability of those all-determining relations: what are the true and certain indicators of sexual experience in women? Even witchcraft, the Jacobean definition of which centred on so private and interior an event as a secret pact between human and devil, had its relatively sure signs. Such evidence was important because the issue of witchcraft in the period was a matter not just of theological disputation but also of legal procedure; and it was primarily to the latter that Reginald Scot objected in *The Discoverie of Witchcraft* (1584), Middleton's principal source for his witch scenes. The devil was believed to leave his marks upon his follower's body and/or to desensitize patches of it: once discovered and tested, such marks and patches constituted presumptive evidence of the diabolical pact hypothesized as their cause. But objective evidence of sexual activity was harder to secure. Sexual activity does not always leave its marks upon a female body; and even when it does, such marks can sometimes be concealed. Francisca manages to hide a pregnancy, and Frances Howard was thought to have faked a virginity test. Furthermore, and more unsettlingly, male observation of females for signs of sexual activity is subject to Heisenberg's uncertainty principle, the conditions of observation affecting the data. Faced with both Florida the experienced courtesan and Gaspero the obliging (nudge-wink) manservant, Sebastian evinces less confidence in his own accuracy as judge of the woman than of the man:

I know that face
To be a strumpet's, or mine eye is envious
And would fain wish it so where I would have it.
I fail if the condition of this fellow
Wears not about it a strong scent of baseness.
(3.2.15–19)

The Witch was probably written in the middle of 1616, after the convictions of Frances Howard and Robert Carr for their parts in the murder of Thomas Overbury and amid other coded outcries against the King's protection of the couple from the full penalty of the law. Middleton's text survives in a single manuscript which a professional scrivener prepared some imprecisely 'long' time after the play was presented in, conjecturally, the latter months of 1616 and some time before Middleton died in 1627. It was not printed during Middleton's lifetime, nor for another century and a half thereafter. So topical a dramatic text has a short theatrical shelf-life. The stage history of *The Witch* begins in a cloud of ambiguity and promptly disappears into a void. No professional production is known to have occurred subsequent to its first performance(s), of which tantalizingly little is known. The manuscript subtitles *The Witch* as having been 'long since acted by his Majesty's Servants at the Blackfriars'. The spectacular staging needs of the witch scenes would have been particularly well served by the theatrical resources which the King's Men commanded at the Blackfriars. Middleton's dedicatory epistle, however, clearly indicates that the play had in some sense failed: 'I have...recovered into my hands (though not without much difficulty) this (ignorantly-ill-fated) labour of mine.' The parentheses tease. What difficulty beset Middleton's recovery of his dramatic labour? It is unclear whether the ill fate was a matter of theatrical failure or of political suppression, and it is correspondingly unclear whether unappreciative audiences are being accused of ignorance or Middleton is (implausibly and belatedly) excusing himself on grounds of ignorance. His next sentence, however, hints at the latter alternatives: 'Witches are (*ipso facto*) by the law condemned, & that only (I think) hath made her lie so long in an imprisoned obscurity.' The organizing conceit of this dedication, the verbal elision between a text entitled *The Witch* and a woman labelled a witch, points the reader back to the realm of riddles.

SEE ALSO

Music and dance: *Companion*, 151 ('In a maiden time professed'), 153 ('Come away'), 158, 160 (dances)

Textual introduction and apparatus: *Companion*, 995

Authorship and date: *Companion*, 382

The Witch

[*for the King's Men at The Blackfriars*]

THE PERSONS

DUKE
LORD GOVERNOR [of Ravenna]
SEBASTIAN, contracted to Isabella
FERNANDO, his friend
ANTONIO, husband to Isabella
ABERZANES, a gent[leman] neither honest, wise, nor valiant
ALMACHILDES, a fantastical gentleman
GASPERO & HERMIO } servants to Antonio
FIRESTONE, the clown and Hecate's son
DUCHESS
ISABELLA, niece to the [lord] governor
FRANCISCA, Antonio's sister
AMORETTA, the Duchess's woman
FLORIDA, a courtesan
HECATE, the chief witch
STADLIN [&] HOPPO } witches
[GENTLEMAN in 2.1]
[STABLEBOY]
[OLD WOMAN]
[Malkin, a spirit like a CAT]
Other Witches, [Spirits], [Watermen] & Servants } mutes

Epistle *To the truly worthy and generously affected*
Thomas Holmes, Esquire

Noble Sir,

As a true testimony of my ready inclination to your service, I have (merely upon a taste of your desire) recovered into my hands (though not without much difficulty) this (ignorantly ill-fated) labour of mine. Witches are (*ipso facto*) by the law condemned, and that only (I think) hath made her lie so long in an imprisoned obscurity. For your sake alone she hath thus far conjured herself abroad and bears no other charms about her but what may tend to your recreation, nor no other spell but to possess you with a belief that as she, so he that first taught her to enchant, will always be

Your devoted
Tho: Middleton.

[*Incipit*] *Actus Primus* 1.1
Enter Sebastian and Fernando

SEBASTIAN
My three years spent in war has now undone
My peace for ever.

FERNANDO Good, be patient, sir.

SEBASTIAN
She is my wife by contract before heaven
And all the angels, sir.

FERNANDO I do believe you,
But where's the remedy now? You see she's gone:
Another has possession.

SEBASTIAN There's the torment.

FERNANDO
This day, being the first of your return,
Unluckily proves the first too of her fast'ning.

This commentary devotes particular attention to Middleton's sources, especially in relation to witchcraft.

Persons.8 **fantastical** (*a*) capricious (*b*) foppishly attired

12 **clown** buffoon part

Epistle.5–6 **Witches . . . condemned** Under a 1563 statute (5 Eliz.I.c.16), first convictions of witchcraft carried the death penalty only when the criminal had caused another's death. However, a 1604 statute (1 Jac.I.c.12) both extended the definition of witchcraft to cover activities (such as graverobbing) ignored by the Elizabethan statute and also lowered the level of damage which carried the death penalty even for first convictions.

1.1.3–4 **wife . . . angels** Sebastian and Isabella have exchanged marriage vows without public ceremony and sacerdotal supervision. Such contracts were forbidden but also recognized as morally and legally binding. See 4.2.3–20, where it is also revealed that Fernando had been a witness to the lovers' exchange of vows.

Her uncle, sir, the Governor of Ravenna,
Holding a good opinion of the bridegroom,
As he's fair-spoken, sir, and wondrous mild—

SEBASTIAN
There goes the devil in a sheepskin!

FERNANDO
—with all speed
Clapped it up suddenly. I cannot think, sure,
That the maid over-loves him; though, being married
Perhaps (for her own credit) now she intends
Performance of an honest duteous wife.

SEBASTIAN
Sir, I've a world of business. Question nothing:
You will but lose your labour. 'Tis not fit
For any—hardly mine own secrecy—
To know what I intend. I take my leave, sir.
I find such strange employments in myself
That unless death pity me and lay me down,
I shall not sleep these seven years: that's the least, sir.
Exit

FERNANDO
That sorrow's dangerous can abide no counsel:
'Tis like a wound past cure. Wrongs done to love
Strike the heart deeply: none can truly judge on't
But the poor sensible sufferer, whom it racks
With unbelievèd pains which men in health
That enjoy love, not possibly can act—
Nay, not so much as think. In troth I pity him!
His sighs drink life blood in this time of feasting.
[*Noises off*]
A banquet towards too? Not yet hath riot
Played out her last scene? At such entertainments still
Forgetfulness obeys and surfeit governs.
Here's marriage sweetly honoured in gorged stomachs
And overflowing cups.
Enter Gaspero and Servant

GASPERO
Where is she, sirrah?

SERVANT
Not far off.

GASPERO
Prithee, where? Go fetch her hither.
[*Exit Servant*]
[*Aside*] I'll rid him away straight. [*To Fernando*] The Duke's now risen, sir.

FERNANDO
I am a joyful man to hear it, sir.
It seems he's drunk the less, though I think he
That has the least, he's certainly enough.
Exit

GASPERO
I have observed this fellow all the feast time.
He hath not pledged one cup but looked most wickedly
Upon good malaga, flies to the black jack still
And sticks to small drink like a water rat.
Enter Florida
O, here she comes. Alas, the poor whore weeps!
'Tis not for grace now: all the world must judge.
It is for spleen and madness 'gainst this marriage.
I do but think how she could beat the vicar now,
Scratch the man horribly that gave the woman,
The woman worst of all, if she durst do it.—
Why, how now, mistress, this weeping needs not, for though
My master marry for his reputatïon,
He means to keep you too.

FLORIDA
How, sir?

GASPERO
He doth indeed.
He swore't to me last night. Are you so simple
—And have been five years traded—as to think
One woman would serve him? Fie, not an empress!
Why, he'll be sick o'th' wife within ten nights,
Or never trust my judgement.

FLORIDA
Will he, think'st thou?

GASPERO
Will he?

FLORIDA
I find thee still so comfortable!
Beshrew my heart, if I knew how to miss thee!

9 **Ravenna** port on the Adriatic coast of Italy and the scene of part of the narrative which is the source for the ducal plot of *The Witch*: see note to 1.1.110–43 below

12 **the devil in a sheepskin** an amalgamation of two proverbs derived from the New Testament: (*a*) 'The Devil can transform himself into an angel of light' (Tilley D231) from Corinthians 11:14; and (*b*) 'A wolf in a sheepskin' (Tilley W614) from Matthew 7:15

27 **sensible** emotionally sensitive

29 **act** simulate

30 **troth** truth

32 **banquet** dessert course of fruit, sweetmeats, etc., for which guests remove to a room other than that in which the meal has been served. Fernando's line thus both explains the offstage noises which cue it and also heralds the approach of the wedding party.
riot debauchery, extravagance

34 **surfeit** excessive indulgence in food and drink

36 **sirrah** term of address used to men or boys expressing contempt, reprimand or assumption of authority on the part of its speaker

42 **fellow** Having swiftly realized his intention (announced at l. 38) to clear the scene of Fernando, Gaspero proceeds to refer to him, a social superior whom in person he addresses as 'Sir', as 'fellow'. The condescension of the reference continues Gaspero's self-characterization as manipulative and impudent.

43 **pledged** toasted

44 **malaga** Spanish white wine, named for the southern port of Malaga, which exported it
black jack tarred leather jug for beer

45 **small** weak, low in alcohol

46–7 **weeps . . . not for grace** At her first entrance in tears of chagrin, Florida is mockingly contrasted with the New Testament woman of ill repute (Luke 7:36–50) whose tears were the visible signs of her repentance and divine grace.

54 **keep** maintain for bedservice. The cost of maintaining Florida is given by Gaspero at 2.1.21.

56 **traded** i.e., as a prostitute

60 **comfortable** comforting, giving of solace. (The comfort which Florida here evokes, like the 'kindness' which she proceeds to invite in l. 61, is sexual.)

61 **miss** do without

They talk of gentlemen, perfumers, and such things:
Give me the kindness of the master's man
In my distress, say I.

GASPERO
'Tis your great love, forsooth.
Please you withdraw yourself to yon private parlour.
I'll send you ven'son, custard, parsnip pie.
For banqueting stuff—as suckets, jellies, syrups—
I will bring in myself.

FLORIDA
I'll take 'em kindly, sir. *Exit*

GASPERO
She's your grand strumpet's complement to a tittle.
'Tis a fair building. It had need: it has
Just at this time some one-and-twenty inmates.
But half of 'em are young merchants: they'll depart
shortly.
They take but rooms for summer and away they
When't grows foul weather. Marry, then come the
termers,
And commonly they're well booted for all seasons.

Enter Almachildes and Amoretta

But, peace! No more! The guests are coming in.

ALMACHILDES
The fates have blessed me: have I met you privately?

AMORETTA
Why, sir? Why, Almachildes?

ALMACHILDES
Not a kiss.

AMORETTA
I'll call aloud, i'faith.

ALMACHILDES
I'll stop your mouth.

AMORETTA
Upon my love to reputatïon,
I'll tell the Duchess once more.

ALMACHILDES
'Tis the way
To make her laugh a little.

AMORETTA
She'll not think
That you dare use a maid of honour thus.

ALMACHILDES
Amsterdam swallow thee for a Puritan
And Geneva cast thee up again like she that sunk
At Charing Cross and rose again at Queenhithe!

AMORETTA
Ay, these are the holy fruits of the sweet vine, sir.
[*Exit*]

ALMACHILDES
Sweet venery be with thee, and I at the tail
Of my wish! I am a little headstrong, and so
Are most of the company. I will to the witches.
They say they have charms and tricks to make
A wench fall backwards, and lead a man herself
To a country-house some mile out of the town,
Like a fire-drake: there be such whoreson kind girls
And such bawdy witches, and I'll try conclusions.
[*Exit through one door*]

Enter [*through other door*] *Duke, Duchess, Lord Governor, Antonio, Isabella and Francisca* [*with Servants bearing a banquet*]

DUKE
A banquet yet? Why surely, my Lord Governor,
Bacchus could never boast of a day till now
To spread his power, and make his glory known.

DUCHESS
Sir, you've done nobly. Though in modesty
You keep it from us, know we understand so much
All this day's cost: 'tis your great love bestows

62 **perfumers** (*a*) those employed to fumigate or perfume rooms (*b*) those engaged in making or selling perfumes
63 **master's man** gentleman's servant, valet
65 **parlour** (*a*) intimate dining room, apart from the great hall, (*b*) female genitalia. The innuendo anticipates the architectural conceit which Gaspero develops at ll. 70–5.
66 **ven'son** venison, table meat from wild animal (usually deer) killed by hunting
67 **For** (*a*) with respect to (*b*) instead of. The initial preposition creates a syntactical ambiguity which sustains the innuendo of the speech: Gaspero proposes both to bring in and to be the sweet course.
suckets succades, sweetmeats of fruit which has been candied or preserved in syrup. In this context, the utterance of the word carries an easily audible innuendo.
68 **take** (*a*) receive, accept (*b*) admit to sexual intercourse
kindly (*a*) as a kindness (*b*) fittingly
69 **grand strumpet's complement** that which goes to complete the courtesan: hence, the set of personal accomplishments or qualities appropriate to her
to a tittle to the smallest particular
74 **termers** those who—in order to conduct legal business, to study at the Inns of Court, or to pursue amusements, intrigues or dishonest practices—came to London for the law terms, the periods when the courts were in session
75 **booted** equipped for riding, with an innuendo on 'riding' as 'sexual intercourse'
84–5 **Amsterdam . . . Geneva** centres of radical Protestantism, these Continental cities gave refuge to successive generations of English religious exiles
85–6 **she that . . . Queenhithe** Queen Elinor, wife of King Edward I. Legend held this to have been the punishment she brought upon herself by falsely swearing her innocence of a murder which she had committed. In linking the geography of this legend with Amsterdam and Geneva, Almachildes implies the usual anti-Puritan accusation of moral hypocrisy.
87 **holy** Drawing attention to his inebriation, Amoretta bounces the charge of excessive religiosity back at her challenger.
88–9 **Sweet . . . wish** Almachildes wishes sexual pleasure for Amoretta, and then a share in that pleasure for himself.
89 **headstrong** drunk
90 **I will to the witches** The first mention of witches in the play both associates them with illicit sexual activity and also coincides with the first appearance of the court party.
92 **fall backwards** lie on her back, as the passive partner in the 'missionary position' for sexual intercourse
93 **country-house** (punning on 'cunt'). See also 3.2.193.
94 **fire-drake** will-o-th'-wisp
95 **try conclusions** experiment, see what will come of it
97 **Bacchus** classical Greek god of wine
99–104 **Sir, you've done nobly . . . 'tis rightly** To the Duchess's interpretation of his magnificence as a compliment to his niece, the Lord Governor replies that it is to be construed as a tribute to goodness and to the Duchess herself. Their exchange of courtly compliments is harshly terminated by the Duke's mid-line announcement of his barbaric business with the skull-cup.

In honour of the bride, your virtuous niece.
LORD GOVERNOR
In love to goodness, and your presence, madam!
So understood, 'tis rightly.
DUKE
Now will I
Have a strange health after all these.
LORD GOVERNOR
What's that, my lord?
DUKE
A health in a strange cup; and't shall go round.
LORD GOVERNOR
Your grace need not doubt that, sir, having seen
So many pledged already. This fair company
Cannot shrink now for one, so it end there.
DUKE
It shall, for all ends here:
[*He produces a skull set as a cup*]
here's a full period.
LORD GOVERNOR
A skull, my lord?
DUKE
Call it a soldier's cup, man.
LORD GOVERNOR
Fie, how you fright the women!
DUKE
I have sworn
It shall go round, excepting only you, sir,
For your late sickness, and the bride herself,
Whose health it is.
[*He drinks*]
ISABELLA
Marry, I thank heaven for that.
DUKE
Our duchess, I know, will pledge too, though the cup
Was once her father's head, which, as a trophy,
We'll keep till death, in memory of that conquest.
He was the greatest foe our steel e'er struck at,
And he was bravely slain. Then took we thee
Into our bosom's love. Thou madest the peace
For all thy country, thou, that beauty did.
We're dearer than a father, are we not?
DUCHESS
Yes, sir, by much.
DUKE
And we shall find that straight.
ANTONIO
That's an ill bride-cup for a marriage-day.
I do not like the fate on't.
LORD GOVERNOR
Good my lord,
The duchess looks pale. Let her not pledge you there.
DUKE
Pale?
DUCHESS
Sir, not I!
[*She takes the cup and drinks*]
DUKE
See how your lordship fails now.
The rose's not fresher, nor the sun at rising
More comfortably pleasing.
DUCHESS [*To Antonio*]
Sir, to you,
The lord of this day's honour.
[*She presents cup to him*]
ANTONIO
All first moving
From your grace, madam, and the duke's great favour!
[*He drinks*]
Sister, it must.
[*He presents cup to Francisca*]
FRANCISCA [*aside*]
This's the worst fright that could come
To a concealed great belly. I'm with child,
And this will bring it out, or make me come
Some seven weeks sooner than we maidens reckon.
[*She drinks, then presents cup to Almachildes*]
DUCHESS [*aside*]
Did ever cruel, barbarous act match this?
Twice hath his surfeits brought my father's memory
Thus spitefully and scornfully to mine eyes,
And I'll endure't no more. 'Tis in my heart since:
I'll be revenged, as far as death can lead me.
ALMACHILDES
Am I the last man, then? I may deserve
To be first one day.
[*He drinks*]
LORD GOVERNOR
Sir, it's gone round now.
DUKE
The round? An excellent way to train up soldiers.
Where's bride and bridegroom?
ANTONIO
At your happy service.
DUKE
A boy tonight at least: I charge you look to't,
Or I'll renounce you for industrious subjects.

109 **so** provided that

110–43 **It shall . . . now** Book I of Thomas Bedingfield's translation (1595) of Niccolò Machiavelli's *Istorie fiorentine* (1525) is the source of this incident: 'The kingdom [of the Longobards] being come to *Alboino* a man courageous & cruel, they passed the river *Danubio*, and fought with *Comundo* . . . and overthrew him in *Pannonia*, which he then possessed. *Alboino* . . . happened to take prisoner the daughter of *Comundo*, called *Rosmunda*, married her, and thereby became Lord of *Pannonia*. Then moved by the cruelty of his nature, he made a cup of her father's head, whereof in memory of the victory) [punctuation *sic*] he used to drink. But then called into *Italy* . . . he celebrated a solemn feast in *Verona*, whereat, being by drinking much, become very merry, and seeing the skull of *Comundo* full of wine, he caused the same to be presented to the Queen *Rosmunda*, who sat over against him at the table (saying unto her, with so loud a voice that euery one might hear him) that she should now at this feast drink with her father: which speech pierced the Lady to the Heart, and she forthwith determined to revenge the same.'

110 **full period** complete stop, terminus—to drinking, to predication, to life

125 **bride-cup** cup or bowl handed round at a wedding

126 **fate on't** (*a*) what will come of it (*b*) what it portends

128 **fails** mistakes

133 **it must** you have no choice

134 **concealed great belly** secretly pregnant woman

135 **bring it out** reveal the fact of pregnancy

135–6 **make . . . reckon** induce labour perilously early

144 **round** (*a*) military watchman's circuit of the garrison which he is guarding (*b*) of alcoholic drink

147 **for** as

ANTONIO
Your grace speaks like a worthy and tried soldier.
Exeunt [all but Gaspero]

GASPERO
And you'll do well, for one that ne'er tossed pike, sir.
Exit

1.2 *Enter Hecate with properties and habits fitting [including a baby, serpents and snakes]*

HECATE
Titty and Tiffin, Suckin
And Pidgin, Liard and Robin!
White spirits, black spirits, grey spirits, red spirits!
Devil-toad, devil-ram, devil-cat and devil-dam!
Why, Hoppo and Stadlin, Hellwain and Puckle?

STADLIN [*within*]
Here, sweating at the vessel.

HECATE
Boil it well.

HOPPO [*within*]
It gallops now.

HECATE
Are the flames blue enough
Or shall I use a little seeton more?

STADLIN [*within*]
The nips of fairies upon maids' white hips
Are not more perfect azure.

HECATE
Tend it carefully.
Send Stadlin to me with a brazen dish
That I may fall to work upon these serpents
And squeeze 'em ready for the second hour.
Why, when?
[*Enter Stadlin with brass dish*]

STADLIN
Here's Stadlin, and the dish.

HECATE [*handing over baby*]
There, take this unbaptizèd brat.

149 **tossed pike** brandished (*a*) weapon of the ordinary infantryman (*b*) penis. Silent since the middle of the scene, Gaspero closes it with a sneer at the military and sexual competence of his master Antonio, who has just complimented the Duke on the same points of machismo.

1.2.0.1 ***properties . . . fitting*** Some indication of what constituted 'properties and habits fitting' for witches on a Jacobean stage can be found in Ben Jonson's account of the anti-masque of eleven witches in his 1609 *Masque of Queens*. They were, he writes, 'all differently attired: some with rats on their head, some on their shoulders; others with ointment pots at their girdles; all with spindles, timbrels, rattles or other venefical instruments, making a confused noise, with strange gestures. The device of their attire was Master [Inigo] Jones his . . . Only I prescribed them their properties of vipers, snakes, bones, herbs, roots and other ensigns of their magic, out of the authority of ancient and late writers.'

0.2 **[*including . . . snakes*]** The dialogue requires Hecate, at this her first appearance in *The Witch*, to be equipped with serpents (l. 12) and a human infant (l. 15). The baby is quickly handed over to Stadlin and carried offstage (a transfer which anticipates the disposal of Aberzanes and Francisca's offspring at 2.3.1–4). The serpents are squeezed into the brazen dish which the dialogue requires Stadlin to bring on at l. 14 and Firestone to carry off at l. 101. (See Hecate's instructions to Firestone at ll. 63, 78, and 99.) Their skins remain onstage until Sebastian removes them at l. 178. Middleton's deft care in deploying these stage properties is a pointer to their importance. Within the iconographical language available to his dramaturgy, snakes and serpents tend to be encoded with wickedness. For important example, in Cesare Ripa's *Iconologia* (1593), the standard Renaissance handbook devoted to the iconography of moral concepts, snakes generally appear as the appurtenances of the more extreme moral evils—heresy, sin (in general), false religion, and enmity to God.

1–4 **Titty . . . devil-dam** Hecate's first lines in the play come from Chapter 33 of *A Discourse of diuels and spirits* which Reginald Scot appended to *The Discoverie of Witchcraft* (1584): 'Now, how *Brian Darcy's* he spirits and she spirits, Titty and Tiffin, Suckin and Pidgin, Liard and Robin, &c: his white spirits and black spirits, grey spirits and red spirits, devil toad and devil lamb, devil's cat and devil's dam . . . can stand consonant with the word of GOD . . . , let heaven and earth judge. In the mean time, let any man with good consideration peruse that book published by *W.W.* . . . .' The title of the book published by *W.W.* (in 1582) is *A true and just Record of the Information, Examination and Confession of all the witches, taken at S. Oses in the county of Essex*. This account, and the St Osyth witchhunt which it records, were principally the work of an Essex Justice of the Peace, Brian Darcy. Scot, who personally observed some of the St Osyth trials, evidently (and rightly) despised Darcy's investigative methods and juridical proceedings as grotesque violations of due process of law. The book published by *W.W.* parades detail after detail of Darcy's findings: particularly preoccupied with witches' familiars, he records the name, species, colour, sex, and maleficent activity of each familiar that he can discover, and finally he even tabulates the data by accused witch. Thus, 'Ursley Kemp had four spirits, their names Titty a he like a grey Cat, Jack a he like a black Cat, Pidgin a she, like a black Toad, and Tiffin a she, like a white Lamb. The he's were to plague to death and the she's to punish with bodily harm, and to destroy cattle.'

4 **Devil-toad, devil-ram, devil-cat** venefical familiars
devil-dam proverbial (Tilley D225)

5 **Hoppo and Stadlin** Middleton's source for these names was probably another passage from *The Discoverie of Witchcraft* in which Scot contemptuously reports the findings of witch-hunters: 'It is constantly affirmed [by James Sprenger and Heinrich Kremer] in *M[alleus] Mal[ificarum]* [1486] that *Stafus* . . . had a disciple called *Hoppo*, who made *Stadlin* witch, and could all when they list invisibly transfer the third part of their neighbours' dung, hay, corn, etcetera, into their own ground, make hail, tempests, and floods, with thunder and lightning; and kill children, cattle, etcetera, reveal things hidden, and many other tricks' (XII, 5).
Hellwain and Puckle Both names appear in the incantation which Middleton fillets from Scot and assigns to Hecate at 1.2.102–6. (See note below.)

6 **vessel** cauldron

7 **gallops** boils (the earliest occurrence recorded for this sense by *OED*)

8 **seeton** This substance has yet to be identified.

13 **the second hour** the witching hour, when the moon rises and witches take to the sky. See also 1.2.34. With advance preparations for the witches' flight underway throughout this scene, audience expectations are thereby heightened for their next, and more spectacular, appearance onstage.

15–18 **unbaptizèd . . . air** In *The Discoverie of Witchcraft* (III, 1), Scot summarizes demonologists' accounts of the susceptibility of unchristened babies to being snatched, alive or dead, by witches for use in transvection ointments: 'if there be any children unbaptized . . . then the

Boil it well. Preserve the fat:
You know 'tis precious to transfèr
Our 'nointed flesh into the air
In moonlit nights, o'er steeple-tops,
Mountains, and pine-trees, that like pricks or stops
Seem to our height: high towers and roofs of princes
Like wrinkles in the earth. Whole provinces
Appear to our sight then, e'en leek
A russet mole upon some lady's cheek,
When hundred leagues in air we feast, and sing,
Dance, kiss, and coll, use every thing.
What young man can we wish, to pleasure us
But we enjoy him in an incubus?
Thou know'st it, Stadlin?

STADLIN
Usually that's done.

HECATE
Last night thou got'st the Mayor of Whelpley's son:
I knew him by his black cloak, lined with yellow.
I think thou'st spoiled the youth: he's but seventeen.
I'll have him the next mounting. Away, in!
Go feed the vessel for the second hour.

STADLIN
Where be the magical herbs?

HECATE
They're down his throat,
His mouth crammed full, his ears and nostrils stuffed.
I thrust in *eleoselinum* lately,
Aconitum, frondes populeas, and soot—
You may see that, he looks so black i'th' mouth—
Then *sium, acorum vulgare* too,
Pentaphyllon, the blood of a flitter-mouse,
Solanum somniferum et oleum.

STADLIN
Then there's all, Hecate?

HECATE
Is the heart of wax

witches may and do catch them from their mothers' sides in the night, or out of their cradles, or otherwise kill them with their ceremonies; and after burial steal them out of their graves, and seeth them in a cauldron, until their flesh be made potable. Of the thickest whereof they make ointments, whereby they ride in the aire.' The sixth of the eleven hags who comprise the coven in Jonson's *Masque of Queens* boasts of having 'Killed an infant to have his fat' (163).

20 **pricks . . . stops** small marks of punctuation

23 **leek** like (archaic)

24 **russet** reddish-brown

25–8 **we feast . . . enjoy him** After the second of the recipes which are quoted below (note to 1.2.37–42) from Scot's *Discoverie of Witchcraft* (x, 8), comes an account of the effects perceived by users of transvection ointment: 'By this means . . . in a moonlight night they seem to be carried in the aire, to feasting, singing, dancing, kissing, culling, and other acts of venery, with such youths as they love and desire most'.

26 **coll** hug, fondle in the arms
use every thing (*a*) copulate with everything (*b*) engage in those 'other acts of venery' which Scot (as quoted above in the note to 1.2.25–8) leaves to the imagination

28 **incubus** devil (or witch) disguised in a(nother) corporeal form in order to engage in sexual intercourse with a human being. Strict demonological usage distinguishes 'incubus' (disguise as male partner, assumed to be active and prone) from 'succubus' (disguise as female partner, assumed to be passive and supine). In Zacharie Jones's 1605 translation of part of Pierre Le Loyer's *Livre des Spectres*, incubi are defined as: 'a kind of Deuils, or Spirits, in the form of men, whose delight is in lasciviousness, and are as wanton and lecherous as Goats . . . And their nature is . . . to desire to ravish and force women, and in the night time to go into their bed, and to oppress them, striving to have carnal company with them. The like do those Spirits which are called *Succubs*, which are devils passive, as the former active, and taking the form of women, do seek to enjoy their pleasure of men.'

30 **Whelpley's** Denoting a south-east Wiltshire village which has vanished since the seventeenth century, the place-name still connotes both the contempt of the speaker and the age and inclinations of her victim.

31 **black cloak, lined with yellow** The gratuitous precision of this detail of reported costume invites interpretation. While colour conventions (linking black to evil and yellow to love) provide one possibility, it is more probably a reference to Anne Turner. At her execution for the murder of Thomas Overbury, she wore black, as did the executioner; and both (at the macabre command of Lord Chief Justice Coke) also wore linen/lace treated with the yellow starch which she had made fashionable.

33 **mounting** (*a*) aerially, in flight with the coven (*b*) sexually, as an incubus

37–42 ***eleoselinum . . . oleum*** Save for the pungent reminder of the effects of soot, this list comes *verbatim* from two different recipes for transvection ointment which Scot reports in *The Discoverie of Witchcraft* (x, 8):

> Rx. The fat of young children, and seeth it with water in a brazen vessel, reserving the thickest of that which remaineth boiled in the bottom, which they lay up and keep, until occasion serveth to use it. They put hereunto *Eleoselinum, Aconitum, Frondes populeas,* and Soot.
>
> *Another recipe to the same purpose.*
> Rx. *Sium, acarum vulgare, pentaphyllon,* the blood of a flittermouse, *solanum somniferum, & oleum.* They stamp all these together, and then they rub all parts of their bodies exceedingly, till they look red, and be very hot, so as the pores may be opened, and their flesh soluble and loose. They join herewithal either fat, or oil instead thereof, that the force of the ointment may the rather pierce inwardly, and so be more effectual.

37 ***eleoselinum*** smallage, a wild species of parsley

38 ***Aconitum*** genus of poison plant, of which the common European species is popularly known as 'wolfs bane' or 'monkshood'
frondes populeas poplar leaves

40 ***sium*** sion, an aquatic plant, formerly also known as 'bellrags' and 'laver'
acorum vulgare a kind of reed, the root of which was used medicinally

41 ***Pentaphyllon*** cinquefoil, so called because the leaves of this genus of plant are composed of five leaflets
flitter-mouse bat

42 ***Solanum somniferum*** deadly (or sleeping) nightshade
et oleum 'and oil': where the first of the recipes quoted above begins with the fat of young children, the second does not specify what sort of fat or oil is to be used to bind the ointment

43–4 **heart of wax . . . needles** In *The Discoverie of Witchcraft* (xii, 16) Scot gives various versions of '*A charme teaching how to hurt whom you list with images of wax, &c.*' and tells of a recent Kentish case involving a fraudulent accusation, complete with fabricated evidence, of witchcraft wrought by means of a wax heart stuck full of needles.

Stuck full of magic needles?
STADLIN 'Tis done, Hecate.
HECATE
And is the farmer's picture, and his wife's,
Laid down to th' fire yet?
STADLIN They're a-roasting, both, too.
[*Exit Stadlin, with baby*]
HECATE Good:
Then their marrows are a-melting subtly
And three months' sickness sucks up life in 'em.
They denied me often flour, barm and milk,
Goose-grease and tar, when I ne'er hurt their charmings,
Their brewlocks, nor their batches, nor forespoke
Any of their breedings.
[*Squeezing snakes and serpents into brass dish, she sets aside their skins*]
Now I'll be meet with 'em.
Seven of their young pigs I've bewitched already
Of the last litter, nine ducklings, thirteen goslings,
And a hog fell lame last Sunday after evensong too.
And mark how their sheep prosper, or what sope
Each milk-kine gives to th' pail. I'll send those snakes
Shall milk 'em all beforehand: the dew'd-skirted dairy-wenches
Shall stroke dry dugs for this, and go home cursing.
I'll mar their syllabubs, and frothy feastings
Under cows' bellies with the parish youths.
Where's Firestone? Our son Firestone?
Enter Firestone
FIRESTONE Here am I, mother.
HECATE
Take in this brazen dish full of dear ware.
Thou shalt have all when I die, and that will be
E'en just at twelve o'clock at night, come three year.
FIRESTONE And may you not have one o'clock into th' dozen, mother?
HECATE No.
FIRESTONE Your spirits are then more unconscionable than bakers. You'll have lived then, mother, six-score years to the hundred; and methinks after six-score years, the devil might give you a cast, for he's a fruiterer too, and has been from the beginning: the first apple that e'er was eaten came through his fingers. The costermonger's, then, I hold to be the ancientest trade, though some would have the tailor pricked down before him.
HECATE
Go, and take heed you shed not by the way!
The hour must have her portion. 'Tis dear syrup:
Each charmèd drop is able to confound
A family consisting of nineteen
Or one-and-twenty feeders.
FIRESTONE Marry, here's stuff indeed!
[*Aside*] 'Dear syrup', call you it? A little thing
Would make me give you a dram on't, in a posset,
And cut you three years shorter.
HECATE Thou'rt now
About some villainy?
FIRESTONE Not I, forsooth.
[*Aside*] Truly the devil's in her, I think! How one villainy smells out another straight! There's no knavery but is nosed like a dog, and can smell out a dog's meaning. [*To Hecate*] Mother, I pray give me leave to ramble abroad tonight, with the nightmare, for I have a great mind to overlay a fat parson's daughter.
HECATE
And who shall lie with me, then?

49–52 **They denied ... breedings** Most of the lurid activities which Hecate claims for herself ultimately derive, via Scot's *Discoverie of Witchcraft*, from Continental demonological treatises. The narrative of petty crime and retribution in this speech, however, is closer to contemporary English pamphlets reporting particular cases of witchcraft in provincial communities. Hecate bears a grudge because her begging for basic foodstuffs had been refused on a farm where she had not previously meddled with the butter-making, brewing, baking, and breeding. Essential to rural economy, these processes abounded in occasions of error: when things went wrong, accusations of witchcraft offered an explanation of natural disaster as well as a venting of emotions onto liminal figures whose survival depended on communal charity.

49 **barm** yeast

50 **charmings** variant form of 'churnings'

51 **brewlocks** brewings. (The second syllable is a rare survival, one not noted in the *OED*, of an Anglo-Saxon suffix meaning 'activity'. More technical glosses have been suggested but context demands the general sense.)

56 **sope** small amount of drink

57 **milk-kine** milk-cow

63 **dear ware** precious product—i.e., the venom or juice of those serpents upon which the speaker undertook (at 1.2.12–14) to 'fall to work ... and squeeze 'em ready for the second hour'.

69 **unconscionable** extortionate, harsh

70 **six-score** 120: Hecate is therefore 117 years old. At 1.2.32 the Mayor of Whelpley's son was reported to have been 17, while at 2.1.121 it will be said that Francisca has not yet attained that age.

71 **to the hundred** Firestone implies that Hecate has been living on borrowed time since her 100th birthday.

72 **cast** chance, playing on faint homophony with 'cost[ard]' (apple)

72–4 **he's a fruiterer ... fingers** In the Old Testament (Genesis 2 and 3), a serpent successfully tempts Eve (and through her, Adam) to disobey God's command not to eat the fruit of the tree of knowledge of good and evil. Christian exegetical tradition has always construed the serpent as the devil; and iconographic convention has long represented the fruit as an apple.

75 **costermonger's** a costermonger is a fruiterer or apple seller; often used contemptuously

76 **pricked down** play on several senses of 'prick': (*a*) mark, tick (*b*) awl, bodkin (*c*) penis

78 **shed** spill (the serpent venom imagined to be the contents of the brazen vessel)

79 **her portion** the part allotted to it

83–4 **A little ... make me** It wouldn't take much to make me

91 **nightmare** spirit or monster supposed to settle on people when they are asleep at night, and produce a sense of suffocation by its weight. Nightmare is to nocturnal terror as incubus or succubus is to nocturnal pleasure.

FIRESTONE The great cat
For one night, mother: 'tis but a night!
Make shift with him for once.

HECATE You're a kind son;
But 'tis the nature of you all, I see that.
You had rather hunt after strange women still
Than lie with your own mothers. Get thee gone.
Sweat thy six ounces out about the vessel,
And thou shalt play at midnight: the nightmare
Shall call thee when it walks.

FIRESTONE Thanks, most sweet mother.
Exit [*with brass dish*]

Enter Sebastian

HECATE [*conjuring*] Urchins, Elves, Hags, Satyrs, Pans, Fauns, Silens, Kit-with-the-Candlestick, Tritons, Centaurs, dwarves, Imps, the Spoorne, the Mare, the Man i'th' Oak, the Hellwain, the Fire-Drake, the Puckle! *A-Ab-Hur-Hus*!
[*She sinks into a trance*]

SEBASTIAN
Heaven knows with what unwillingness and hate
I enter this damned place. But such extremes
Of wrongs in love fight 'gainst religious knowledge
That were I led by this disease to deaths
As numberless as creatures that must die
I could not shun the way. I know what 'tis
To pity madmen now: they're wretched things
That ever were created, if they be
Of woman's making, and her faithless vows.
I fear they're now a-kissing: what's o'clock.?
'Tis now but supper-time, but night will come;
And all new-married couples make short suppers.
[*To Hecate*] Whate'er thou art, I have no spare time to fear thee:
My horrors are so strong and great already
That thou seem'st nothing. Up and laze not!
Hadst thou my business, thou couldst ne'er sit so.
'Twould firk thee into air, a thousand mile
Beyond thy ointments. I would I were read
So much in thy black power as mine own griefs.
I'm in great need of help: will't give me any?

HECATE
Thy boldness takes me bravely. We're all sworn
To sweat for such a spirit. See, I regard thee:
I rise, and bid thee welcome. What's thy wish now?

SEBASTIAN
O, my heart swells with't. I must take breath first.

HECATE
Is't to confound some enemy on the seas?
It may be done tonight. Stadlin's within:
She raises all your sudden ruinous storms
That shipwreck barques, and tears up growing oaks,
Flies over houses, and takes *Anno Domini*
Out of a rich man's chimney. (A sweet place for't!
He would be hanged ere he would set his own years there.
They must be chambered in a five-pound picture,
A green silk curtain drawn before the eyes on't,
His rotten-diseased years.) Or dost thou envy
The fat prosperity of any neighbour?
I'll call forth Hoppo, and her incantation
Can straight destroy the young of all his cattle,

93 **The great cat** Hecate's familiar, who makes a brief appearance at the end of this scene and then a spectacular entrance into a later one, where (3.3.60) he is given the name 'Malkin'

102–5 **Urchins ... Puckle** Another *verbatim* borrowing from Scot's *Discoverie of Witchcraft* (VII, 15): 'But in our childhood our mothers maids ... have so fraied vs with bull beggars, spirits, witches, urchins, elves, hags, fairies, satyrs, pans, fauns, sylens, kit with the cansticke, tritons, centaurs, dwarfes, giants, imps, calcars, conjurors, nymphs, changelings, *Incubus*, Robin good-fellow, the spoorne, the mare, the man in the oak, the hell wain, the firedrake, the puckle, Tom thumb, hob goblin, Tom tumbler, boneles, and such other bugs, that we are afraid of our own shadowes.' This roll call of folk demons includes two names—Kit-with-the-Candlestick and Man i'th' Oak—for which *OED* cites no other occurrences than Scot and Middleton.

102 **Satyrs** woodland gods or demons, in form partly human and partly bestial

103 **Silens** sileni, members of a species of satyr
Kit-with-the-Candlestick jack-o-lantern

104 **Spoorne** species of spectre or phantom

104–5 **Man i'th' Oak** spirit supposed to inhabit an oak

105 **Hellwain** phantom wagon seen in the sky at night
Puckle a kind of bugbear. Etymologically and mythologically close to 'Puck'—in popular superstition, an evil, malicious, or mischievous spirit or demon who from the sixteenth century was also called 'Robin Goodfellow' and 'Hobgoblin'.

106 ***A-Ab-Hur-Hus*** In *The Discoverie of Witchcraft* (XII, 14) Scot recounts charms 'for all diseases and griefs, specially for such as bad physicians and surgeons know not how to cure', and '*A ab hur hus, &c.*' is among the charms against toothache. Whether or not Middleton expected his audiences to recognize Hecate's exclamation as a dental cure, he could have counted on their hearing the homophony with 'whorehouse'.

110 **disease** uneasiness

116 **what's o'clock** what's the time

123 **firk** drive

125 **So** As

128 **regard** look at, gaze upon

132–3 **Stadlin's ... storms** See note to 1.2.5.

135 ***Anno Domini*** here designates a date carved or inscribed into the fabric of a building to record the year of its construction. The sites usually being durable as well as public—chimneys and fireplaces, lintels and arches—the removal of such a memorial implies the destruction of the entire building.

136 **A sweet place for't** Ironic: literally meaning 'in the year of Our Lord' and indicating that time is being tallied from the birth of Christ, the phrase *Anno Domini* deserves a more honourable and/or hallowed site than a rich man's chimney.

137–40 **He ... years** Often recording the age of the sitter, Tudor and Stuart portraits were frequently hung in long galleries designed for purposes of domestic display.

138 **chambered** enclosed, confined
five-pound Although £5 was a substantial sum in 1616, it probably was not a very high price to pay for a portrait.

139 **green silk curtain** Portraits were hung with curtains across them: the practice is represented by the first dumb show in 2.2 of John Webster's *White Devil*.

142–6 **Hoppo ... own ground** See note to 1.2.5.

Blast vineyards, orchards, meadows, or in one night
Transport his dung, hay, corn, by ricks, whole stacks,
Into thine own ground.

SEBASTIAN This would come most richly now
To many a country grazier; but my envy
Lies not so low as cattle, corn or vines.
'Twill trouble your best powers to give me ease.

HECATE
Is it to starve up generatïon?
To strike a barrenness in man or woman?

SEBASTIAN Hah?

HECATE
'Hah?'! Did you feel me there? I knew your grief.

SEBASTIAN
Can there be such things done?

HECATE Are these the skins
Of serpents? These of snakes?
[*She produces them*]

SEBASTIAN I see they are.

HECATE
So sure into what house these are conveyed,
Knit with these charmèd and retentive knots,
Neither the man begets nor woman breeds,
No, nor performs the least desires of wedlock
Being then a mutual duty. I could give thee
Chirocineta, adincantida,
Archimedon, marmaritin, calicia,
Which I could sort to villainous barren ends
But this leads the same way. More I could instance—
As the same needles thrust into their pillows
That sews and socks up dead men in their sheets,
A privy gristle of a man that hangs
After sunset—good, excellent. Yet all's there, sir.
[*She gives him the skins*]

SEBASTIAN
You could not do a man that special kindness
To part 'em utterly now? Could you do that?

HECATE
No. Time must do't. We cannot disjoin wedlock:
'Tis of heaven's fast'ning. Well may we raise jars,
Jealousies, strifes and heart-burning disagreements,
Like a thick scurf o'er life, as did our master
Upon that patient miracle; but the work itself
Our power cannot disjoint.

SEBASTIAN I depart happy
In what I have, then, being constrained to this,
And grant, you greater powers that dispose men,
That I may never need this hag again.
Exit [*with skins*]

HECATE
I know he loves me not, nor there's no hope on't.
'Tis for the love of mischief I do this;
And that we're sworn to—the first oath we take.
[*Enter Firestone*]

FIRESTONE
O, mother, mother!

HECATE What's the news with thee now?

FIRESTONE There's the bravest young gentleman within, and the fineliest drunk. I thought he would have fall'n into the vessel! He stumbled at a pipkin of child's grease, reeled against Stadlin, overthrew her, and in the tumbling cast struck up old Puckle's heels with her clothes over her ears.

HECATE Hey-day!

FIRESTONE I was fain to throw the cat upon her to save her honesty, and all little enough. I cried out still, 'I pray, be covered!'
See where he comes now, mother!
Enter Almachildes

ALMACHILDES Call you these witches?
They be tumblers, methinks, very flat tumblers.

HECATE [*Aside*]
'Tis Almachildes! Fresh blood stirs in me—
The man that I have lusted to enjoy!

147 **grazier** one who feeds cattle for the market

153–4 **Are these ... snakes?** Here, as later with the Duchess at 5.2.13–32, Hecate dismisses doubts by posing a rhetorical question and then overwhelming her client with a parade of claims as extreme as they are derivative.

159–61 **I could give thee ... *calicia*** The menu is a classical one derived from Scot's *Discoverie of Witchcraft* (VI, 3): '*Pythagoras* and *Democritus* give us the names of a great many magical herbs and stones, whereof now, both the virtue, and the things themselves also are unknown: as *Marmaritin*, whereby spirits might be raised: *Archimedon*, which would make one bewray in his sleep, all the secrets in his heart: *Adincantida, Calicia,* ... *Chirocineta, &c*: which had all their several virtues, or rather poisons. But all these now are worn out of knowledge: marry in their stead we have hog's turd and chervil, as the only thing whereby our witches worke miracles.'

163–7 **More ... sunset** For this part of Hecate's self-advertisement to Sebastian and again for her exchange with Firestone at 1.2.205–10, Middleton uses items from a catalogue in Scot's *Discoverie of Witchcraft* (VI, 7): 'The toys which are said to procure love ... are these: the hair growing in the nethermost part of a wolf's tail, a wolf's yard [= penis], a little fish called *Remora*, the brain of a cat, of a newt, or of a lizard: the bone of a green frog, the flesh thereof being consumed with pismires or ants; ... the garments of the dead, candles that burn before a dead corpse, and needles wherewith dead bodies are sewn or socked into their sheets: and diverse other things, which for the reverence of the reader, and in respect of the unclean speech to be used in the description thereof, I omit.'

173–4 **Like ... miracle** alluding to one of the diabolically inflicted (but divinely authorized) sufferings of Job. In *The Discoverie of Witchcraft* (V, 8) Scot pays extended attention to this Old Testament narrative.

185 **pipkin** small earthenware pot or pan, used chiefly in cookery

185–6 **child's grease** See note to 1.2.5.

187 **tumbling cast** somersault

189 **Hey-day** an exclamation denoting gaiety

194 **flat tumblers** (*a*) incompetent acrobats (*b*) downright muddlers. There is a sexual innuendo on 'tumblers'.

I have had him thrice in incubus already.
ALMACHILDES
Is your name Goody Hag?
HECATE 'Tis anything.
Call me the horrid'st and unhallowed'st things
That life and nature trembles at, for thee
I'll be the same. Thou com'st for a love-charm now?
ALMACHILDES
Why, thou'rt a witch, I think.
HECATE Thou shalt have choice
Of twenty, wet or dry.
ALMACHILDES Nay, let's have dry ones.
HECATE
If thou wilt use't by way of cup and potion,
I'll give thee a remora shall bewitch her straight.
ALMACHILDES
A remora? What's that?
HECATE A little suckstone:
Some call it a sea-lamprey, a small fish.
ALMACHILDES And must't be buttered?
HECATE
The bones of a green frog, too—wondrous precious,
The flesh consumed by pismires.
ALMACHILDES Pismires? Give me a chamber-pot.
FIRESTONE [*aside*]
You shall see him go nigh to be so unmannerly,
He'll make water before my mother, anon.
ALMACHILDES
And now you talk of frogs, I have somewhat here.
I come not empty-pocketed from a banquet:
I learned that of my haberdasher's wife.
[Pulling a wet handkerchief from his pocket, he unfolds it to reveal the contents]
Look, Goody Witch, there's a toad in marzipan for you.
HECATE
O sir, you've fitted me!
ALMACHILDES And here's a spawn or two
Of the same paddock-brood too, for your son.
FIRESTONE
I thank your worship, sir. How comes your handkerchief
So sweetly thus berayed? Sure, 'tis wet sucket, sir!
ALMACHILDES
'Tis nothing but the syrup the toad spit.
Take all, I pray thee.
HECATE This was kindly done, sir,
And you shall sup with me tonight for this.
ALMACHILDES
How? Sup with thee? Dost think I'll eat fried rats
And pickled spiders?
HECATE No, I can command, sir,
The best meat i'th' whole province for my friends,
And reverently served in, too.
ALMACHILDES How?
HECATE In good fashion.
ALMACHILDES
Let me but see that, and I'll sup with you.
She conjures, and enter [Malkin,] a Cat (playing on a fiddle) and Spirits (with meat)
The Cat and Fiddle? An excellent ordinary!
You had a devil once, in a fox-skin?
HECATE
O, I have him still! Come walk with me, sir!
Exeunt [all but Firestone]

FIRESTONE How apt and ready is a drunkard now to reel to the devil! Well, I'll even in and see how he eats, and I'll be hanged if I be not the fatter of the twain with laughing at him. *Exit*

Finis Actus Primi

[Incipit] Actus Secundus 2.1
Enter Antonio and Gaspero

GASPERO
Good sir, whence springs this sadness? Trust me, sir.
You look not like a man was married yesterday.
There could come no ill tidings since last night
To cause that discontent. I was wont to know all
Before you had a wife, sir. You ne'er found me
Without those parts of manhood—trust and service.
ANTONIO
I will not tell thee this.

198 **Goody** Goodwife. This polite title for a married woman of lower class forms an oxymoron when it is prefixed to 'Hag' or, as at 1.2.217, to 'Witch'.
anything Frequently named by the other witches and Firestone, Hecate remains anonymous to her human clients. Namelessness is next to godlessness in this play, as it is in *Macbeth* (4.1.64).
205 **remora** sucking fish, also called 'echeneis'
206 **suckstone** remora
207 **sea-lamprey** lamprey eel, species of a genus of fish which resemble eels in shape and in lack of scales and which have sucker-like mouths. Hecate's identification of the remora as a lamprey may be a taxonomic error, but it establishes the sexual innuendo of the exchange. Compare John Webster's *Duchess of Malfi*: 'Women like that part which, like the lamprey, | Hath ne'er a bone in't' (1.1.336–7).
a small fish Scot is dismissive of the reported use of the remora as an aphrodisiac charm: see the quotation from *The Discoverie of Witchcraft* (VI, 7) in the note to 1.2.163–7 above. Elsewhere in *The Discoverie of Witchcraft* (XIII, 4), however, Scot is much less doubtful of claims that the remora—'a little fish being but half a foot long'—is able to halt any ship to which it attaches itself.
210 **pismires** ants. The inebriated Almachildes hears only the first syllable. On the charm, see the note to 1.2.163–7 above.
215–16 **empty-pocketed ... wife** as a vendor of small items pertaining to dress, a haberdasher (like a pedlar) wore garments with many pockets
219 **paddock-brood** family of toads
221 **berayed** dirtied, stained
wet sucket syrup: see note to 1.1.67
230 **ordinary** eating-house or tavern where public meals are provided at a fixed price
235 **fatter of the twain** because Almachildes will not actually be eating anything: see note to 2.2.7–8
2.1.6 **parts** attributes

GASPERO Not your true servant, sir?
ANTONIO
True? You'll all flout according to your talent,
The best a man can keep of you; and a hell 'tis
For masters to pay wages to be laughed at.
Give order that two cocks be boiled to jelly.
GASPERO
How? Two cocks boiled to jelly?
ANTONIO
Fetch half an ounce of pearl. *Exit*
GASPERO This is a cullis
For a consumption; and I hope one night
Has not brought you to need the cook already,
And some part of the goldsmith. What, two trades
In four-and-twenty hours'—and less—time?
Pray heaven the surgeon and the 'pothecary
Keep out, and then 'tis well. You'd better fortune
(As far as I see) with your strumpet-sojourner,
Your little four-nobles-a-week. I ne'er knew you
Eat one panada all the time you've kept her.
And is't in one night, now, come up to two-cock-broth?
I wonder at the alteration strangely.
Enter Francisca
FRANCISCA
Good morrow, Gasper.
GASPERO Your hearty wishes, mistress,
And your sweet dreams come upon you.
FRANCISCA What's that, sir?
GASPERO
In a good husband—that's my real meaning.
FRANCISCA
Saw you my brother lately?
GASPERO Yes.
FRANCISCA I met him now
As sad (methought) as grief could make a man:
Know you the cause?
GASPERO Not I! I know nothing
But half an ounce of pearl, and kitchen business
Which I will see performed with all fidelity.
I'll break my trust in nothing, not in porridge, I.
Exit
FRANCISCA
I have the hardest fortune, I think,
Of a hundred gentlewomen!
Some can make merry with a friend seven year
And nothing seen: as perfect a maid still
(To the world's knowledge) as she came from rocking.
But 'twas my luck, at the first hour (forsooth)
To prove too fruitful. Sure, I'm near my time.
I'm yet but a young scholar: I may fail
In my account, but certainly I do not.
These bastards come upon poor venturing gentlewomen
Ten to one faster than your legitimate children.
If I had been married, I'll be hanged
If I had been with child so soon now.
When they are once husbands, they'll be whipped
Ere they take such pains as a friend will do.
To come by water to the back door at midnight,
There stay perhaps an hour in all weathers
With a pair of reeking watermen,
Laden with bottles of wine, chewets,
And currant-custards (I may curse those egg-pies!
They are meat that help forward too fast!):
This hath been usual with me night by night
(Honesty forgive me!) when my brother
Has been dreaming of no such junkets.
Yet he hath fared the better for my sake,
Though he little think for what, nor must he ever.

8 **flout** recite with sarcastic purpose
11 **cocks...jelly** chicken broth, to be taken as a cure for impotence
13 **half an ounce of pearl** an expensive aphrodisiac. Regarded as restorative (see Tilley P166), pearl appears on the list of pharmaceutical simples needed for recipes in the *Pharmacopoeia Londinensis* (1618), the apothecaries' standard reference book. Within Jacobean drama, the ingestion of pearl signals extravagance, and (an apothecary's ounce being 1/12th of an apothecary's pound) Antonio is calling for a considerable quantity.
cullis strong broth used to nourish invalids
14 **consumption** wasting disease. Gaspero is interpreting Antonio's self-prescribed cures for impotence as treatments for venereal disease. In Thomas Vicary's *The English mans treasure* (1613), a thirty-day diet of chicken boiled with borage is recommended 'for the French poxe'.
15–18 **the cook...the surgeon and the 'pothecary** In *A Short & Profitable Treatise, touching the cure of the disease called* (*Morbus Gallicus*) (1579, revised 1585 and 1596), the Elizabethan surgeon [medical practitioner] William Clowes outlined the treatment of syphilis by (i) diet (ii) evacuation—bloodletting, purges and sweating, the last produced by—(iii) unction with ointments.
20 **strumpet-sojourner** sojourner: guest, visitor
21 **four-nobles-a-week** noble: gold coin then worth 6*s*. 8*d*. [33*p*.] At £1.32 a week, Florida's maintenance was not an insignificant sum on any 1616 price index, but the medicinal diet ordered by Antonio would be costlier still.
22 **panada** bread boiled in water and flavoured
27 **real** sincere, honest
33 **porridge** potage, thick soup (see ll. 11–12)
43 **venturing** (*a*) risk-taking (*b*) sexually wanton
47–53 **When...currant-custards** Francisca's account of her friend's nightly visitations situates its speaker as a prostitute whose client comes by boat across the Thames to her Southwark brothel and brings with him the victuals which brothel-keepers were not allowed to sell. A number of the Jacobean aristocratic palaces in the Strand, on the north side of the Thames, were also accessible 'by water to the back door'.
51 **reeking** steaming, vapour-breathing
watermen boatmen
52 **chewets** dishes cooked from various forms of meat or fish, chopped fine and seasoned
53 **currant-custards** open pies containing currants covered with a mixture of milk and eggs, sweetened, seasoned and baked
curse...egg-pies i.e., on account of the aphrodisiac powers attributed to them
54 **meat** food
57 **junkets** (*a*) confections (*b*) merrymakings accompanied with feasting

My friend promised me to provide safely for me,
And devise a means to save my credit here i'th' house.
My brother sure would kill me if he knew't,
And powder up my friend, and all his kindred,
For an East Indian voyage.

Enter Isabella

ISABELLA
Alone, sister?

FRANCISCA [*aside*]
No, there's another with me, though you see't not.
[*To Isabella*] 'Morrow, sweet sister! How have you slept tonight?

ISABELLA
More than I thought I should: I've had good rest.

FRANCISCA
I'm glad to hear't.

ISABELLA
Sister, methinks you are too long alone
And lose much good time, sociable and honest.
I'm for the married life: I must praise that now.

FRANCISCA
I cannot blame you, sister, to commend it.
You have happened well, no doubt, on a kind husband,
And that's not every woman's fortune, sister.
You know if he were any but my brother
My praises should not leave him yet so soon.

ISABELLA
I must acknowledge, sister, that my life
Is happily blessed with him: he is no gamester
That ever I could find or hear of yet,
Nor midnight surfeiter. He does intend
To leave tobacco too.

FRANCISCA
Why, here's a husband!

ISABELLA
He saw it did offend me and swore freely
He'd ne'er take pleasure in a toy again
That should displease me: some knights' wives in town
Will have great hope, upon his reformation,
To bring their husbands' breaths into th'old fashion
And make 'em kiss like Christians, not like pagans.

FRANCISCA
I promise you, sister, 'twill be a worthy work
To put down all these pipers: 'tis great pity
There should not be a statute against them
As against fiddlers.

ISABELLA
These good offices
If you'd a husband, you might exercise
To th' good o'th' commonwealth, and do much profit.
Beside it is a comfort to a woman
T'have children, sister—a great blessing certainly.

FRANCISCA
They will come fast enough.

ISABELLA
Not so fast neither,
As they're still welcome to an honest woman.

FRANCISCA [*aside*]
How near she comes to me! I protest she grates
My very skin.

ISABELLA
Were I conceived with child,
Beshrew my heart, I should be so proud on't!

FRANCISCA
That's natural: pride is a kind of swelling.
[*Aside*] And yet I've small cause to be proud of mine.

ISABELLA
You are no good companion for a wife.
Get you a husband, prithee, sister, do,
That I may ask your counsel now and then.
'Twill mend your discourse much: you maids know nothing.

FRANCISCA
No, we are fools; [*aside*] but commonly we prove
Quicker mothers than you that have husbands.
I'm sure I shall else: I may speak for one!

Enter Antonio

ANTONIO [*aside*]
I will not look upon her: I'll pass by
And make as though I see her not.

ISABELLA
Why, sir.
Pray, your opinion, by the way, with leave, sir,
I'm counselling your sister here to marry.

ANTONIO
To marry? Soft, the priest is not at leisure yet!
Some five year hence!—Would you fain marry, sister?

FRANCISCA
I have no such hunger to't, sir, for I think
I've a good bit that well may stay my stomach
As well as any that broke fast a sinner.

ANTONIO [*to Isabella*]
Though she seem tall of growth, she's short in years

63 **powder up** preserve with salt or spice
78 **happily** (*a*) felicitously (*b*) perchance. See also 4.3.20.
gamester (*a*) gambler (*b*) fornicator
83 **toy** (*a*) trifle, folly (*b*) amorous sport
84 **some knights' wives** many ladies (an allusion to King James I's sales of knighthoods)
in town in London (during legal terms—see 1.1.74)
89 **pipers** (*a*) pipe-smokers with a pun on (*b*) strolling musicians who play on pipes
90–1 **statute... against fiddlers** Minstrels (along with 'fencers, bearwards, [and] common players of interludes') were among the entertainers banned by successive Tudor and Stuart laws against vagabonds. The law in force during Middleton's professional lifetime was *An Act for Punishment of Rogues, Vagabonds and Sturdy Beggars* (39 Elizabeth 1.c.4 & 5; 1 James 1.c.7; and 7 James 1.c.4).
91 **offices** services
94 **Beside** Moreover
107 **fools** (*a*) simpletons, ignoramuses (*b*) dupes, victims (*c*) darlings. ('Fool-sticker' = slang 'penis'.)
108 **Quicker** as adverb modifying 'we prove'—(*a*) more quickly; as adjective modifying 'mothers'—(*b*) more intelligent (*c*) at stage of pregnancy when foetal movement becomes perceptible
109 **else** if it is not believed
117 **bit** (*a*) portion (in life) (*b*) morsel (referring to unborn child)
118 **any... sinner** (*a*) any human being (all being presumed sinners) (*b*) anyone 'the morning after' sexual activity

Of some that seem much lower.—How old, sister?
Not seventeen, for a yard of lawn!

FRANCISCA Not yet, sir.

ANTONIO [*to Isabella*] I told you so.

FRANCISCA [*aside*]
I would he'd laid a wager of old shirts rather!
I shall have more need of them shortly; and yet
A yard of lawn will serve for a christ'ning cloth.
I have use for everything, as my case stands.

ISABELLA
I care not if I try my voice this morning;
But I have got a cold, sir, by your means.

ANTONIO
I'll strive to mend that fault.

ISABELLA I thank you, sir.

Song

In a maiden time professed,
Then we say that life is best.
Tasting once the married life,
Then we only praise the wife.
There's but one state more to try
Which makes women laugh or cry:
Widow, widow, of these three,
The middle's best, and that give me.

ANTONIO [*kissing her*]
There's thy reward.

ISABELLA I will not grumble, sir,
Like some musician: if more come, 'tis welcome.

FRANCISCA [*aside*]
Such tricks has made me do all that I've done.
Your kissing married folks spoils all the maids
That ever live i'th' house with 'em.

Enter Aberzanes [with watermen carrying provisions]

O, here he comes
With his bags, and bottles: he was born
To lead poor watermen, and I.

ABERZANES
Go, fellows, into th' larder: let the bakemeats
Be sorted by themselves.

ANTONIO Why, sir!

ABERZANES
Look the canary bottles be well stopped:
The three of claret shall be drunk at dinner.

[*Exeunt watermen*]

ANTONIO
My good sir, you're too plenteous of these courtesies,
Indeed you are! Forbear 'em, I beseech ye!
I know no merit in me, but poor love,
And a true friend's well-wishing, that can cause
This kindness in excess. [*Aside*] I'th' state that I am
I shall go near to kick this fellow shortly
And send him downstairs with his bag and baggage.
Why comes he now I'm married? There's the point!
[*To Aberzanes*] I pray, forbear these things.

ABERZANES Alas, you know, sir,
These idle toys, which you call courtesies,
They cost me nothing but my servants' travail.
One office must be kind, sir, to another:
You know the fashion. What, the gentlewoman
Your sister's sad, methinks.

ANTONIO I know no cause she has.

FRANCISCA [*aside*]
Nor shall you, by my good will.

[*Still aside, to Aberzanes*]

What do you mean, sir?
Shall I stay here, to shame myself and you?
The time may be tonight, for aught you know.

ABERZANES
Peace, there's means wrought, I tell thee.

121 **yard of lawn** Lawn is a fine linen fabric resembling cambric. A single yard of it would be, like Francisca's age, no great length.

125 **I shall ... shortly** Old shirts would be useful in childbirth because they can serve as absorbent and clean cloths.

126 **christ'ning cloth** chrisom: a white head-cloth or garment put on a baby before its anointing in a Christian baptismal ceremony and customarily returned by the mother at her churching (see 3.2.114)

127 **have use for everything** (*a*) can put anything to good use (*b*) am sexually available to any man
case (*a*) situation (*b*) vagina

129 **got a cold ... means** Ostensibly apologizing for her singing voice and covertly complaining of sexual frustration, Isabella chides Antonio for both conditions.

131–8 **In a maiden time ... that give me** Isabella's song is a metadramatic tally of the female figures at the centre of each of the three plots of *The Witch*. In its immediate dramatic situation, it is both a covert rebuke to Antonio for his impotence and also an allusion to Frances Howard's divorce from Robert Devereux, in which her claim to virginity was crucial. And it may also be an echo from the celebrations surrounding her subsequent marriage. In two seventeenth-century song manuscripts, this song appears with a musical setting by John Wilson and two further (and bawdier) verses, reproduced in the Textual Notes and in this edition's text of *Masque of Cupids*; for the music, see *Companion*, p. 151.

143.1–2 ***with ... provisions*** With such a display, Aberzanes at his first appearance in the play is visibly a figure of Gluttony.

143–9 **here he comes ... at dinner** Aberzanes's arrival at Antonio's house recapitulates his visitations to Francisca as the 'friend' described at 2.1.46–53. On both occasions his baggage and behaviour are not appropriate for a guest, but, rather, suggest a customer at a Southwark brothel. Antonio's exclamation at l. 157—'Why comes he now I'm married? There's the point!'—implies the speaker's own experience of sexual transactions in which Aberzanes has figured.

145 **To lead ... and I** Francisca draws audience attention both to what Aberzanes literally does (leading in a gaggle of heavily laden watermen) onstage as she speaks and to what he has figuratively done (leading her astray) on other occasions in which watermen have figured.

146 **larder** room in which meat and other provisions are stored
bakemeats pies

147 **sorted** arranged

148 **canary** light sweet wine from the Canary Islands

160 **travail** labour

161 **office** (*a*) office-holder (*b*) service. Antonio's implication in an economy of courtly office was noted by Francisca at ll. 56–9.

FRANCISCA Ay, sir, when?

Enter Sebastian [in disguise] and Gentleman

ANTONIO
How now? what's he?

ISABELLA O, this is the man, sir,
I entertained this morning for my service:
Please you to give your liking.

ANTONIO Yes, he's welcome:
I like him not amiss.—Thou wouldst speak business,
Wouldst thou not?

SEBASTIAN Yes, may it please you, sir.
There is a gentleman from the northern parts
Hath brought a letter, as it seems, in haste.

ANTONIO
From whom?

GENTLEMAN Your bonny lady mother, sir.

[He presents letter]

ANTONIO
You're kindly welcome, sir: how doth she?

GENTLEMAN
I left her healt' varray well, sir.

ANTONIO [*reading letter aloud*] 'I pray send your sister down with all speed to me. I hope it will prove much for her good, in the way of her preferment. Fail me not, I desire you, son; nor let any excuse of hers withhold her. I have sent, ready furnished, horse and man for her.'

ABERZANES [*aside, to Francisca*]
Now, have I thought upon you?

FRANCISCA Peace, good sir!
You're worthy of a kindness another time.

ANTONIO
Her will shall be obeyed. Sister, prepare yourself.
You must down with all speed.

FRANCISCA [*aside*] I know down I must,
And good speed send me.

ANTONIO 'Tis our mother's pleasure.

FRANCISCA
Good sir, write back again, and certify her
I'm at my heart's wish here. I'm with my friends
And can be but well: say.

ANTONIO You shall pardon me, sister:
I hold it no wise part to contradict her,
Nor would I counsel you to't.

FRANCISCA 'Tis so uncouth
Living i'th' country, now I'm used to th' city,
That I shall ne'er endure't.

ABERZANES Perhaps, forsooth,
'Tis not her meaning you shall live there long.
I do not think but after a month or so
You'll be sent up again: that's my conceit.
However, let her have her will.

ANTONIO Ay, good sir,
Great reason 'tis she should.

ISABELLA I am sorry, sister,
'Tis our hard fortune, thus to part so soon.

FRANCISCA
The sorrow will be mine.

ANTONIO [*to Gentleman*] Please you walk in, sir,
We'll have one health into those Northern parts
[*Aside*] Though I be sick at heart.

ABERZANES Ay, sir, a deep one,
[*To Francisca*] Which you shall pledge too.

Exeunt [Antonio, Isabella and Gentleman]

FRANCISCA You shall pardon me:
I have pledged one too deep already, sir.

ABERZANES
Peace! All's provided for: thy wine's laid in,
Sugar and spice: the place not ten mile hence.
What cause have maids now to complain of men
When a farmhouse can make all right again?

Exeunt [Aberzanes and Francisca]

SEBASTIAN
It takes: he's no content. How well she bears it yet!
Hardly myself can find so much from her,
That am acquainted with the cold disease.
O, honesty's a rare wealth in a woman:
It knows no want—at least, will express none,
Not in a look. Yet I'm not th'roughly happy:
His ill does me no good. Well may it keep me
From open rage and madness for a time,
But I feel heart's grief in the same place, still.
What makes the greatest torment 'mongst lost souls?
'Tis not so much the horror of their pains
(Though they be infinite) as the loss of joys.
It is that deprivation is the mother
Of all the groans in hell; and here on earth
Of all the red sighs in the hearts of lovers.
Still she's not mine, that can be no man's else
Till I be nothing, if religïon
Have the same strength for me as 't has for others.

168 **what's he?** The question is fair, as well as dramaturgically useful: there has been no previous indication that Sebastian would disguise himself, let alone seek service in Antonio's household. The pseudonym 'Celio' will not be introduced until 4.2.112.

175 **bonny** 'The northern parts' from which the gentleman is said to have come are here signalled as northern Britain, not Italy. His message being false, the Scottish accent indicated for his two half-lines could be played as flagrantly phony. The more outrageous the accent sounds, the more it mocks the Scottish courtiers around King James I, notably Robert Carr.

177 **healt' varray** phonetic approximation of 'health very' in Jacobean stage Scottish.

178 **down** away from the capital, into the country

186 **down...down** double ellipsis: go down (into the country)... lie down (in childbirth)

188 **certify** assure

197 **up** back to the capital
conceit opinion

205 **pledged** (*a*) toasted (*b*) conceived

212 **cold disease** sexual starvation

219–21 **What makes...loss of joys** Christian teaching construes damnation as eternal separation from God.

224 **red** hot, burning

226 **religïon** devotion, fidelity

Holy vows, witness that our souls were married.
Enter Gaspero and Lord Governor

GASPERO
Where are you, sir? Come, pray give your attendance.
Here's my lord governor come.

LORD GOVERNOR Where's our new kindred?
Not stirring yet, I think?

GASPERO Yes, my good lord.
Please you walk near?

LORD GOVERNOR Come, gentlemen: we'll enter.

SEBASTIAN [*aside*]
I've done't upon a breach: this's a less venture.
[*Exeunt*]

2.2 *Enter Almachildes*

ALMACHILDES
What a mad toy took me, to sup with witches!
Fie of all drunken humours! By this hand,
I could beat myself when I think on't.
And the rascals made me good cheer too
And to my understanding then
Eat some of every dish and spoiled the rest.
But coming to my lodging, I remember,
I was as hungry as a tired foot-post.
What's this? O, 'tis the charm her hagship gave me
For my duchess' obstinate woman, wound about
A threepenny silk ribbon, of three colours.
'*Necte tribus nodis ternos Amoretta colores*'
—Amoretta! Why, there's her name indeed!—
'*Necte, Amoretta*'—Again! Two bouts!—
'*Nodo et Veneris, dic vincula necte.*'
Nay, if veneries be one, I'm sure there's no dead flesh in't.
If I should undertake to cònstrue this now
I should make a fine piece of work of it,
For few young gallants are given to good construction
Of any thing (hardly of their best friends' wives,
Sisters or nieces). Let me see what I can do now.
'*Necte tribus nodis*'—'Nick of the tribe of noddies'—
'*Ternos colores*'—that makes 'turned colours'—
'*Nodo et Veneris*'—'goes to his venery like a noddy'—
'*Dic vincula*'—'with Dick the vintner's boy'!
Here were a sweet charm now, if this were the meaning on't, and very likely to overcome an honourable gentlewoman! The whoreson old hellcat would have given me the brain of a cat once, in my handkerchief—I bade her make sauce with't, with a vengeance—and a little bone in the nethermost part of a wolf's tail—I bade her pick her teeth with't, with a pest'lence.
Nay, this is somewhat cleanly yet, and handsome,
A coloured ribbon! A fair gentle charm!
A man may give't his sister, his brother's wife
Ordinarily.
Enter Amoretta
See, here she comes, luckily.

AMORETTA
Blessed powers, what secret sin have I committed
That still you send this punishment upon me?

ALMACHILDES
'Tis but a gentle punishment, so take it.
[*Embracing and fondling her, he slips the charm into the bodice of her dress*]

AMORETTA
Why, sir, what mean you? Will you ravish me?

ALMACHILDES
What, in the gallery? And the sun peep in?
There's fitter time and place! [*Aside*] 'Tis in her bosom now.

AMORETTA
Go, you're the rudest thing e'er came at court.

ALMACHILDES
Well, well, I hope you'll tell me another tale
Ere you be two hours older. A rude thing?

233 **upon a breach** in battle

2.2.8 **I was as hungry** In *The Discoverie of Witchcraft* (III, 2), Scot drily notes that after the witches' necromantic feasts, 'at their return home they are like to starve for hunger'.
foot-post letter-carrier or messenger who travels on foot

12–15 ***Necte tribus . . . vincula necte*** The source of the charm is Virgil's Eighth Eclogue: *Necte tribus nodis ternos, Amarylli, colores;* | *Necte, Amarylli, modo et 'Veneris', dic, 'vincula necto.'* ('Twine three colour[ed ribbon]s in three knots, Amaryllis; | Just twine [them], Amaryllis, and say, "I twine the chains of Venus."') Although not as egregiously incompetent as Almachildes's English translation, the Latin quotation is flawed—notably in the replacement of *modo* by *nodo* (which Almachildes renders as 'noddy'). Thanks to this error in transmission, Middleton's intermediate source for the Virgilian charm has been identified as Zacharie Jones's 1605 English translation of part of Pierre Le Loyer's *Livre des Spectres*. The final word in the quotation is also a mistake, but one not found in the intermediate source: the replacement of Virgil's present indicative *necto* with the imperative *necte*. This may be Crane's slip rather than Middleton's substitution; but the specification of a threepenny ribbon suggests some determination to weave triplets into the passage, and the Latin error gives the charm a third *necte*. It also makes the charm end on the word with which it has begun: such linguistic loops are characteristic of charms and riddles, to which Scot pays recurrent attention in *The Discoverie of Witchcraft* (VII, 4; XIII, 11).

14 **bouts** (*a*) attempts, casts (*b*) boughts [= knots]

15–16 ***Veneris* . . . veneries** Mistranslating the Latin genitive singular form meaning 'of Venus' as 'venery', Almachildes plays on different senses of the English word: (*a*) sexual pleasure (*b*) hunting

17 **cònstrue** translate orally, word/phrase for word/phrase

19 **construction** (*a*) translation from another language (*b*) interpretation of behaviour

22 **noddies** fools, simpletons

28 **hellcat** witch. *OED* gives this as its first occurrence and suggests derivation from 'Hecate'.

29–31 **brain of a cat . . . wolf's tail** See 1.2.163–7.

36 **Ordinarily** in conformity with established custom

43 **rudest** most uncouth or unrefined

I'll make you eat your word. I'll make all split else.
Exit

AMORETTA
Nay, now I think on't better, I'm to blame too.
There's not a sweeter gentleman in court,
Nobly descended too, and dances well.
Beshrew my heart, I'll take him when there's time.
He will be catched up quickly! The Duchess says
She's some employment for him, and has sworn me
To use my best art in't. Life of my joys,
There were good stuff! I will not trust her with him.
I'll call him back again: he must not keep
Out of my sight so long—I shall go mad then.

Enter Duchess

DUCHESS [*aside*]
He lives not now to see tomorrow spent,
If this means take effect, as there's no hardness in't.
Last night he played his horrid game again,
Came to my bedside at the full of midnight,
And in his hand that fatal fearful cup,
Waked me, and forced me pledge him, to my trembling
And my dead father's scorn. That wounds my sight
That his remembrance should be raised in spite;
But either his confusion, or mine, ends it.—
O, Amoretta, hast thou met him yet?
Speak, wench, hast done that for me?

AMORETTA
What, good madam?

DUCHESS
Destruction of my hopes, dost ask that now?
Didst thou not swear to me, out of thy hate
To Almachildes, thou'dst dissemble him
A loving entertainment, and a meeting
Where I should work my will?

AMORETTA
Good madam, pardon me!
A loving entertainment I do protest
Myself to give him—[*Aside*] with all speed I can too!—
But as I'm yet a maid, a perfect one,
As the old time was wont to afford, when
There was few tricks, and little cunning stirring,
I can dissemble none that will serve your turn.
He must have e'en a right one, and a plain one.

DUCHESS
Thou mak'st me doubt thy health: speak, art thou well?

AMORETTA
O, never better—[*Aside*] if he would make haste
And come back quickly! He stays now too long.

[*The charm falls from Amoretta's dress to the floor*]

DUCHESS
I'm quite lost in this woman! What's that fell
Out of her bosom now? Some love-token?

[*Duchess picks up the charm*]

AMORETTA
Nay, I'll say that for him: he's the uncivil'st gentleman
And every way desertless.

DUCHESS
Who's that now
She discommends so fast?

AMORETTA
I could not love him, madam,
Of any man in court!

DUCHESS
What's he now, prithee?

AMORETTA
Who should it be but Almachildes, madam?
I never hated man so deeply yet.

DUCHESS
As Almachildes?

AMORETTA
I am sick, good madam,
When I but hear him named.

DUCHESS
How is this possible?
But now thou saidst thou lov'dst him, and didst raise him
'Bove all the court, in praises.

AMORETTA
How great people
May speak their pleasure, madam! But surely I
Should think the worse of my tongue while I lived then.

DUCHESS
No longer have I patience to forbear thee,
Thou that retain'st an envious soul to goodness.
He is a gentleman deserves as much
As ever Fortune yet bestowed on man,
The glory and prime lustre of our court.
Nor can there any but ourself be worthy of him
And take you notice of that now from me,
Say you have warning on't: if you did love him,
You must not now.

AMORETTA
Let your grace never fear it.

DUCHESS
Thy name is Amoretta, as ours is:
It's made me love and trust thee.

AMORETTA
And my faithfulness
Has appeared well i'th' proof still, has't not, madam?

DUCHESS
But if't fail now, 'tis nothing.

58 **hardness** (*a*) cruelty (in the Duchess's purposed effect), or (*b*) difficulty (in the means adopted to secure that end)

65 **confusion** overthrow, destruction

76 **the old time** the Golden Age. Ostensibly Amoretta evokes a mythical time of strict sexual discipline, when maidens in name were in fact virgins intact. Her protestations, however, are remarkably resonant with the last verse of 'In a Maiden Time Professed', Isabella's song in the previous scene, as it survives in two seventeenth-century song manuscripts. As celebrated in that verse, the mythical past was a time of sexual liberty. See note to 2.1.131–8 and Textual Notes.

99–100 **He is . . . on man** an ambivalent assessment

102 **ourself** The Duchess occasionally affects the royal 'we': see 2.2.106, 3.1.26, 3.1.56.

106 **as ours is** Coming immediately after her praise of Almachildes at lines 99–105, the Duchess's announcement of her own Christian name makes it appear that the charm, which she holds and will carry offstage, has worked on her.

AMORETTA Then it shall not.
I know he will not be long from flutt'ring
About this place, now he's had a sight of me;
And I'll perform in all that I vowed, madam, faith-
fully.

DUCHESS
Then am I blessed both in revenge and love;
And thou shalt taste the sweetness. *Exit*

AMORETTA What your aims be
I list not to enquire: all I desire
Is to preserve a competent honesty
Both for mine own and his use that shall have me,
Whose luck soe'er it be.
Enter Almachildes
O, he's returned already!
I knew he would not fail.

ALMACHILDES It works by this time,
Or the devil's in't, I think: I'll never trust witch else,
Nor sup with 'em this twelve month.

AMORETTA I must soothe him now,
And 'tis great pain to do't against one's stomach.

ALMACHILDES
Now, Amoretta?

AMORETTA Now you're welcome, sir,
If you'd come always thus.

ALMACHILDES O, am I so?
Is the case altered since?

AMORETTA If you'd be ruled,
And know your times, 'twere somewhat, a great
comfort.
'Las, I could be as loving and as venturous
As any woman—we're all flesh and blood, man—
If you could play the game out modestly
And not betray your hand: I must have care, sir.
You know I have a marriage time to come,
And that's for life. Your best folks will be merry
But look to the main chance—that's reputation—
And then do what they list.

ALMACHILDES Wilt hear my oath?
By the sweet health of youth, I will be careful
And never prate on't, nor like a cunning snarer
Make thy clipped name the bird to call in others.

AMORETTA
Well, yielding then to such conditïons
As my poor bashfulness shall require from you,
I shall yield shortly after.

ALMACHILDES I'll consent to 'em
And may thy sweet humility be a pattern
For all proud women living.

AMORETTA They're beholding to you.
Exeunt

Enter Aberzanes and an old woman [*with baby*] 2.3

ABERZANES
So, so: away with him! I love to get 'em
But not to keep 'em. Dost thou know the house?

OLD WOMAN
No matter for the house—I know the porch.

ABERZANES
There's sixpence more for that.
[*He hands her a coin*]
Away! Keep close!
[*Exit Old Woman, with baby*]
My tailor told me he sent away a maidservant
Well ballast of all sides, within these nine days—
His wife ne'er dreamed on't—gave the drab ten pound
And she ne'er troubles him. A common fashion,
He told me 'twas, to rid away a scape,
And I have sent him this for't. I remember
A friend of mine once served a prating tradesman
Just on this fashion, to a hair, in troth!
'Tis a good ease to a man: you can swell a maid up
And rid her for ten pound. There's the purse back
again
Whate'er becomes of your money, or your maid.
This comes of bragging, now. It's well for the boy,
too:
He'll get an excellent trade by't, and on Sundays
Go like a gentleman that has pawned his rapier.
He need not care what countryman his father was,
Nor what his mother was, when he was gotten.
The boy will do well, certain! Give him grace
To have a quick hand and convey things cleanly:
'Twill be his own another day.
Enter Francisca [*with a mirror*]
O, well said!
Art almost furnished? There's such a toil always
To set a woman to horse, a mighty trouble.
The letter came to your brother's hands, I know,
On Thursday last by noon: you were expected there
Yesterday night.

FRANCISCA It makes the better, sir.

116 **competent** suitable, adequate
125 **case** (*a*) situation (*b*) vagina
132–3 **Your best folks . . . reputation** (possibly a reference to Frances Howard)
137 **clipped name** mutilated reputation. The metaphor is of a bird, its wing-feathers trimmed to render it incapable of flight, being used as decoy to trap other birds. Homophony between 'clipped' and 'cleped' [= called] is also in play.
2.3.6 **ballast** burdened (by pregnancy)
7 **drab** slut
9 **scape** bastard
14 **purse** slang for both 'vagina' and 'scrotum'
18 **rapier** (sartorial sign of gentlemanly status)
22 **quick hand** skill, dexterity
convey . . . cleanly (*a*) manage smoothly (*b*) steal imperceptibly
23 **'Twill . . . day** proverbial (Tilley M628)
well said! The range of interpretations admitted by this bland half-line makes it a good example of the making of dramatic meaning in theatrical performance. The gloss 'fittingly spoken!' makes the exclamation Aberzanes's applause of his own utterance. The gloss 'well done!' could refer either to Aberzanes's contrivance or to Francisca's appearance. If the exclamation is addressed to her, it implies that her attire is noteworthy.
25 **set . . . to horse** (*a*) get on horseback (for a journey) (*b*) ride in sexual intercourse

ABERZANES
We must take heed we ride through all the puddles
'Twixt this and that now, that your safeguard there
May be most probably dabbled.

FRANCISCA [*looking at her reflection in mirror*]
Alas, sir!
I never marked till now—I hate myself—
How monstrous thin I look.

ABERZANES Not monstrous neither!
A little sharp i'th' nose, like a country woodcock.

FRANCISCA
Fie, fie, how pale I am! I shall betray myself!
I would you'd box me well and handsomely
To get me into colour.

ABERZANES Not I, pardon me.
That let a husband do, when he has married you.
A friend at court will never offer that.
Come, how much spice and sugar have you left now
At this poor one month's voyage?

FRANCISCA Sure, not much, sir.
I think some quarter of a pound of sugar
And half an ounce of spice.

ABERZANES Here's no sweet charge!
And there was thirty pound good weight and true,
Beside what my man stole when't was a-weighing—
And that was three pound more. I'll speak wi' th' least.
The Rhenish wine, is't all run out in caudels too?

FRANCISCA
Do you ask that, sir? 'Tis of a week's departure!
You see what 'tis now, to get children, sir.
[*Enter Stableboy*]

STABLEBOY
Your mares are ready, both, sir.

ABERZANES Come, we'll up then.
Youth, give my sister a straight wand: there's two pence.

STABLEBOY
I'll give her a fine whip, sir.

ABERZANES No, no, no!
[*Aside*] Though we have both deserved it.

STABLEBOY Here's a new one.

ABERZANES
Prithee talk to us of no whips, good boy:
My heart aches when I see 'em. Let's away. *Exeunt*

Finis Actus Secundi

[*Incipit*] *Actus Tertius* 3.1

Enter Duchess, leading Almachildes blindfold [*with scarves*]

ALMACHILDES
This's you that was a maid? How are you born
To deceive men? I'd thought to have married you:
I had been finely handled, had I not?
I'll say that man is wise ever hereafter
That tries his wife beforehand: 'tis no marvel
You should profess such bashfulness, to blind one,
As if you durst not look a man i'th' face,
Your modesty would blush so. Why do you not run
And tell the Duchess now? Go! You should tell all!
Let her know this too—why, here's the plague now!—
'Tis hard at first to win 'em: when they're gotten,
There's no way to be rid on 'em. They stick
To a man like birdlime. My oath's out:
Will you release me? I'll release myself else.

DUCHESS
Nay, sure I'll bring you to your sight again.
[*She removes his blindfold*]
Say, thou must either die, or kill the Duke—
For one of them thou must do.

ALMACHILDES How, good madam?

30 **safeguard** overskirt worn to protect a woman's dress from mud

31 **probably dabbled** i.e., spattered with enough mud to suggest a journey down to London from 'Northern parts'

33–5 **How monstrous . . . pale I am** Contemplating her own reflection in a hand-mirror, an elaborately-dressed Francisca becomes a stage icon, an image that can be variously decoded by different texts. She is recognizably an analogue of the image of Frances Howard circulated in a broadsheet response to the Overbury trials (see 45). She is also (like that image titled 'Lady Pride') cast in the figure of Vanity. And in Ripa's *Iconologia* she meets the principal specifications for 'LASCIVIA . . . [LUST. A richly dressed young woman, she holds in her left hand a mirror in which she studies herself attentively (and) with the right she keeps beautifying her face . . .]'

34 **woodcock** (*a*) long-billed bird which is easily snared, whence (*b*) simpleton, gull (*c*) prostitute (*d*) tailor

36 **box** slap (and thereby redden) my face

43 **sweet** (*a*) saccharine (*b*) easy
charge (*a*) weight (*b*) expense

46 **speak wi' th' least** estimate conservatively

47 **Rhenish** from the Rhineland
caudels warm drinks which were mixed from gruel, wine, sugar and spice and used for invalids and women in childbed

3.1.1–2 **How . . . To deceive men** An abbreviated allusion to a misogynistic proverb ('Women naturally deceive, weep, and spin' [Tilley W716]) which is itself a translation from a medieval Latin jingle ('Fallere, flere, nere tria sunt haec in muliere').

3 **finely** cunningly
handled made use of

13 **birdlime** viscous sticky substance made from bark of holly and used for catching small birds
out finished

16 **either die, or kill the Duke** The options, and the bed-trick which enforces them, come from Bedingfield's translation of Machiavelli's *Istorie fiorentine*: 'Knowing that *Almachilde* (a valiant young gentleman of *Lombardi* loved a maiden of hers, of whom he obtained to lie with her, and the Queen being privy to that consent, did herself tarry in the place of their meeting, which being without light, *Almachilde* came thither, and supposing to have lien with the maiden, enjoyed the Queen her mistress, which done, the Queen discovered herself and said unto him, that it was in his power to kill *Alboino*, and possess her with her kingdom forever; but if he refused so to do, she would procure that *Alboino* should kill him, as one that had abused his wife. To this motion . . . *Almachilde* consented.'

DUCHESS
Thou hast thy choice, and to that purpose, sir,
I've given thee knowledge now of what thou hast,
And what thou must do, to be worthy on't.
You must not think to come by such a fortune
Without desert: that were unreasonable.
He that's not born to honour must not look
To have it come with ease to him: he must win't.
Take but into thine actions, wit and courage:
That's all we ask of thee. But if through weakness
Of a poor spirit thou deniest me this,
Think but how thou shalt die, as I'll work means for't,
No murderer ever like thee, for I purpose
To call this subtle, sinful snare of mine
An act of force from thee. Thou'rt proud, and youthful:
I shall be believed. Besides, thy wantoness
Is at this hour in question 'mongst our women—
Which will make ill for thee.

ALMACHILDES I had hard chance
To light upon this pleasure, that's so costly!
'Tis not content with what a man can do
And give him breath, but seeks to have that too.

DUCHESS
Well, take thy choice.

ALMACHILDES I see no choice in't, madam,
For 'tis all death, methinks.

DUCHESS Thou'st an ill sight, then,
Of a young man! 'Tis death if thou refuse it,
And say my zeal has warned thee. But consenting
'Twill be new life, great honour, and my love
Which in perpetual bands I'll fasten to thee.

ALMACHILDES
How, madam?

DUCHESS I'll do't religiously,
Make thee my husband. May I lose all sense
Of pleasure in life else, and be more miserable
Than ever creature was: for nothing lives
But has a joy in somewhat.

ALMACHILDES Then by all
The hopeful fortunes of a young man's rising
I will perform it, madam.

DUCHESS [*kissing him*] There's a pledge then
Of a duchess' love for thee. And now trust me
For thy most happy safety. I will choose
That time, shall never hurt thee. When a man
Shows resolution, and there's worth in him,
I'll have a care of him. Part now for this time,
But still be near about us till thou canst
Be nearer, that's ourself.

ALMACHILDES And that I'll venture hard for.

DUCHESS Good speed to thee. *Exeunt* [*severally*]

Enter Gaspero and Florida 3.2

FLORIDA Prithee be careful of me, very careful now.

GASPERO I warrant you. He that cannot be careful of a quean can be careful of nobody. 'Tis every man's humour, that: I should ne'er look to a wife half so handsomely.

FLORIDA
O, softly, sweet sir! Should your mistress meet me now,
In her own house, I were undone for ever.

GASPERO
Never fear her. She's at her pricksong close:
There's all the joy she has, or takes delight in.
Look, here's the garden key! My master gave't me,
And willed me to be careful: doubt not you on't.

FLORIDA [*seizing key*]
Your master is a noble, complete gentleman,
And does a woman all the right that may be.
[*Exit, with key*]

Enter Sebastian, [*passing Florida*]

SEBASTIAN
How now? What's she?

GASPERO A kind of doubtful creature—
I'll tell thee more anon. [*Exit, pursuing Florida*]

SEBASTIAN I know that face
To be a strumpet's, or mine eye is envious
And would fain wish it so, where I would have it.
I fail if the condition of this fellow
Wears not about it a strong scent of baseness.
I saw her once before here, five days since 'tis,
And the same wary panderous diligence
Was then bestowed on her. She came altered then,

31 **act of force** rape
proud amorous, lustful
33 **in question** discussed
36 **'Tis** The abbreviated pronoun refers to 'pleasure' in l. 34.
do perform sexually
37 **breath** (*a*) post-coital rest (*b*) life
39 **ill sight** bad vision
40 **Of** For
44 **religiously** etymological play upon the derivation of this adverb from the Latin verb *religare*—'to bind'
49 **rising** (both socially and sexually)
57 **venture** (*a*) risk oneself (*b*) copulate
3.2.3 **quean** whore
4 **humour** inclination
5 **handsomely** courteously
8 **pricksong** written (as opposed to memorized) vocal music, with quibble on 'prick' [= penis]
close shut up, in private
10 **here's the garden key** No particular plot function is established either for this key, or for the key which Sebastian will give to Florida at 4.2.33–6, or for the one which Francisca will produce at 4.3.20. On all three occasions, possession of a key operates as a stage signal, a clear indication of access and thus a strong implication of intimacy.
14 **doubtful** of questionable character
16 **envious** malicious
18 **condition** moral character, nature
21 **panderous** characteristic of a pander, pimp or procuress
22 **altered** (*a*) changed (*b*) thirsty

And more inclining to the city-tuck.
Whom should this piece of transformation visit
After the common courtesy of frailty
In our house here? Surely not any servant—
They are not kept so lusty, she so low.
I'm at a strange stand: love and luck assist me.
The truth I shall win from him by false play.

Enter Gaspero

He's now returned. Well, sir, as you were saying—
Go forward with your tale!

GASPERO
What? I know nothing.

SEBASTIAN
The gentlewoman.

GASPERO
She's gone out at backdoor now.

SEBASTIAN
Then farewell she, and you, if that be all.

GASPERO
Come, come: thou shalt have more. I have no power
To lock myself up from thee.

SEBASTIAN
So methinks.

GASPERO
You shall not think—trust me, sir—you shall not!
Your ear: she's one o'th' falling family,
A quean my master keeps. She lies at Rutney's.

SEBASTIAN
Is't possible? I thought I had seen her somewhere.

GASPERO
I tell you truth sincerely. She's been thrice here
By stealth within these ten days, and departed still
With pleasure and with thanks, sir, 'tis her luck.
Surely I think, if ever there were man
Bewitched in this world, 'tis my master, sirrah.

SEBASTIAN
Think'st thou so, Gaspero?

GASPERO
O, sir, too apparent!

SEBASTIAN [*aside*]
This may prove happy. 'Tis the likeliest means
That Fortune yet e'er showed me.

Enter Isabella

ISABELLA
You're both here now,
And strangers newly lighted! Where's your attend-
ance?

SEBASTIAN [*aside*]
I know what makes you waspish. A pox on't—
She'll every day be angry now at nothing.

Exeunt [*Gaspero and Sebastian*]

ISABELLA
I'll call her stranger ever in my heart!
She's killed the name of sister, through base lust,
And fled to shifts. O, how a brother's good thoughts
May be beguiled in woman! Here's a letter,
Found in her absence, reports strangely of her
And speaks her impudence. She's undone herself—
I could not hold from weeping when I read it!—
Abused her brother's house and his good confidence!
'Twas done not like herself: I blame her much,
But if she can but keep it from his knowledge
I will not grieve him first: it shall not come
By my means to his heart.

Enter Gaspero

Now, sir, the news?

GASPERO
You called 'em strangers: 'tis my master's sister,
madam!

ISABELLA
O, is't so? She's welcome. Who's come with her?

GASPERO
I see none but Aberzanes. [*Exit*]

ISABELLA
He's enough
To bring a woman to confusïon
More than a wiser man, or a far greater.
A letter came last week to her brother's hands
To make way for her coming up again
After her shame was lightened; and she writ there,
The gentleman her mother wished her to,
Taking a violent surfeit at a wedding,
Died ere she came to see him. What strange cunning
Sin helps a woman to!

Enter Aberzanes and Francisca

Here she comes now.
Sister, you're welcome home again.

23 **city-tuck** urban fashion
24 **piece** person in whom an activity is exemplified
transformation metamorphosis, action of changing in form, shape or appearance. Both substantives in 'piece of transformation' carry insulting implications, 'piece' implying contempt and 'transformation' implying 'corruption'. Inasmuch as it is condemnatory, the phrase is also an inadvertent verdict on its speaker, Sebastian, who has himself assumed a disguise in order to alter his identity. In the wider context of early modern demonological literature, moreover, the phrase is heavily significant: venefical and diabolical shape-changing greatly interested the writers of such treatises and of their sources.
25 **After . . . frailty** in accordance with the conventions of prostitution
27 **They . . . low** They [the servants] are not so pleasurably maintained, nor is she [a courtesan] so far down the the social scale [as to service servants]
28 **at a strange stand** extremely perplexed
31 **Go forward with your tale** Even Gaspero deserves a better pun than this half-line.
37 **one o'th' falling family** a prostitute
38 **Rutney's** The establishment has not been identified and may be purely fictive, invented for the innuendo on 'rut' [= period of sexual excitement in male animals]
44 **Bewitched** (*a*) under a necromantic spell (*b*) sexually fascinated. The speaker uses the participle in its second, figurative sense. Unaware of Hecate's charm against Antonio, he is ignorant that the primary sense also obtains, let alone that his interlocutor has procured the spell. The irony of the line is compounded by its conclusion in a patronizing term of address: see note to 1.1.36.
48 **lighted** alighted (from horseback), dismounted
49 **waspish** irascible
53 **shifts** (*a*) subterfuges, with quibble on (*b*) chemises, smocks
55 **strangely** surprisingly
56 **impudence** shamelessness
66 **confusïon** ruin
72 **surfeit** sickness caused by intemperance

FRANCISCA Thanks, sweet sister.
ISABELLA
You've had good speed.
FRANCISCA [*aside*] What says she?—I have made
All the best speed I could.
ISABELLA I well believe you.—
Sir, we're all much beholding to your kindness.
ABERZANES
My service ever, madam, to a gentlewoman.
I took a bonny mare I keep and met her
Some ten mile out of town—eleven, I think.
[*He prompts Francisca*]
'Twas at the stump I met you, I remember,
At bottom of the hill.
FRANCISCA 'Twas thereabout, sir.
ABERZANES
Full eleven, then, by the rod, if they were measured.
ISABELLA [*To Francisca*]
You look ill, methinks. Have you been sick of late?—
'Troth, very bleak, doth she not? How think you, sir?
ABERZANES
No, no, a little sharp with riding: she's rid sore.
FRANCISCA
I ever look lean after a journey, sister.
One shall do, that has travailed, travailed hard.
ABERZANES
Till evening, I commend you to yourselves, ladies.
Exit
ISABELLA [*Aside*]
And that's best trusting to, if you were hanged.—
You're well acquainted with his hand went out now?
FRANCISCA His hand?
ISABELLA
I speak of nothing else.
[*She produces a letter*]
I think 'tis there.
Please you to look upon't, and when you've done,
If you did weep, it could not be amiss—
A sign you could say grace after a full meal.
You had not need look paler, yet you do.
'Twas ill done to abuse yourself, and us,
To wrong so good a brother and the thoughts
That we both held of you. I did doubt you much
Before our marriage day, but then my strangeness
And better hope still kept me off from speaking.
Yet may you find a kind and peaceful sister of me,
If you desist here and shake hands with folly—
Which you've more cause to do, than I to wish you.
As truly as I bear a love to goodness,
Your brother knows not yet on't, nor shall ever
For my part, so you leave his company.
But if I find you impudent in sinning,
I will not keep't an hour—nay, prove your enemy,
And you know who will aid me. As you've goodness,
You may make use of this:
[*She throws down the letter*]
I'll leave it with you. *Exit*
FRANCISCA
Here's a sweet churching after a woman's labour,
And a fine 'Give-you-joy'!
[*She snatches up the letter*]
Why, where the devil
Lay you to be found out? The sudden hurry
Of hast'ning to prevent shame, brought shame forth.
That's still the curse of all lascivious stuff:
Misdeeds could never yet be wary enough!
Now must I stand in fear of every look—
Nay, tremble at a whisper. She can keep it secret?
—That's very likely!—and a woman too?
I'm sure I could not do't, and I am made
As well as she can be for any purpose.
'Twould never stay with me two days—I've cast it—
The third would be a terrible sick day with me,
Not possible to bear it. Should I then
Trust to her strength in't, that lies every night
Whispering the day's news in a husband's ear?
No, and I have thought upon the means. Blessed
Fortune!
I must be quit with her in the same fashion
Or else 'tis nothing. There's no way like it,
To bring her honesty into question cunningly.
My brother will believe small likelihoods
Coming from me, too. I, lying now i'th' house,
May work things to my will, beyond conceit too.
Disgrace her first, her tale will ne'er be heard:
I learned that counsel first of a sound guard.
I do suspect Gasper, my brother's squire there,
Had some hand in this mischief, for he's cunning,

76 **good speed** (*a*) success (*b*) swiftness
78 **kindness** (*a*) benificence (*b*) sexual favours
79 **service** (*a*) respect, duty (*b*) sexual attention
80 **mare** (*a*) female horse, with quibble on extended sense as (*b*) woman (one held in contempt)
82 **stump** (*a*) trunk of a tree (*b*) post, pillar (*c*) penis
84 **rod** (*a*) unit of linear measure equivalent to 16 1/2 feet (*b*) penis
86 **'Troth** In truth
bleak pale
87 **sharp** peaked, thin
89 **travailed** Punning on the homophony between 'travel' [= journey] and 'travail' [= labour in childbirth]
92 **hand** (*a*) handwriting (*b*) touch
102 **strangeness** unfamiliarity
105 **shake hands with** bid farewell to
109 **so** provided that
110 **impudent** shameless
114 **churching** a woman's first public appearance at church after childbirth, for a ceremony of thanksgiving. Francisca's metaphor casts Isabella in the role of cleric praying over a recently delivered woman.
119 **Misdeeds . . . enough** Rhyme draws attention to this line and distinguishes it as a *sententia*, a rhetorical statement of proverbial wisdom.
125 **cast** tried, attempted
136 **conceit** imagination
138 **first of a sound guard** (*a*) as best precaution (*b*) originally from a trusty protector
139 **squire** (*a*) personal servant (*b*) pimp

And I perhaps may fit him.
Enter Antonio

ANTONIO Your sister told me
You were come: thou'rt welcome.

FRANCISCA
Where is she?

ANTONIO Who? My wife?

FRANCISCA Ay, sir.

ANTONIO Within.

FRANCISCA
Not within hearing, think you?

ANTONIO Within hearing?
What's thy conceit in that? Why shak'st thy head so?
And look'st so pale and poorly?

FRANCISCA I'm a fool indeed
To take such grief for others—for your fortune, sir.

ANTONIO
My fortune? Worse things yet? Farewell life then!

FRANCISCA
I fear you're much deceived, sir, in this woman.

ANTONIO
Who? In my wife? Speak low. Come hither, softly, sister.

FRANCISCA
I love her as a woman you made choice of,
But when she wrongs you, natural love is touched, brother,
And that will speak, you know.

ANTONIO I trust it will.

FRANCISCA
I held a shrewd suspicion of her lightness
At first, when I went down, which made me haste the sooner;
But more, to make amends, at my return now
I found apparent signs.

ANTONIO Apparent, say'st thou?

FRANCISCA
Ay, and of base lust too: that makes th'affliction.
[*She holds up the letter*]

ANTONIO
There has been villainy wrought upon me then:
'Tis too plain now.

FRANCISCA Happy are they, I say still,
That have their sisters living i'th' house with 'em,
Their mothers, or some kindred: a great comfort
To all poor married men. It is not possible
A young wife can abuse a husband then:
'Tis found straight. But swear secrecy to this, brother.

ANTONIO
To this, and all thou wilt have.

FRANCISCA Then this follows, sir.
[*She whispers in his ear*]

ANTONIO
I praise thy counsel well: I'll put't in use straight.
See where she comes herself.
Enter Isabella
[*Exit Francisca*]
Kind, honest lady,
I must now borrow a whole fortnight's leave of thee.

ISABELLA How, sir? A fortnight?

ANTONIO
It may be but ten days: I know not yet.
'Tis business for the state, and't must be done.

ISABELLA
I wish good speed to't then.

ANTONIO Why, that was well spoke.
I'll take but a footboy: I need no more.
The rest I'll leave at home, to do you service.

ISABELLA
Use your own pleasure, sir.

ANTONIO Till my return
You'll be good company, my sister and you.

ISABELLA
We shall make shift, sir.

ANTONIO I'm glad now she's come,
And so the wishes of my love to both. *Exit*

ISABELLA
And our good prayers with you, sir.
Enter Sebastian

SEBASTIAN [*aside*] Now my fortune.—
By your kind favour, madam.

ISABELLA With me, sir?

SEBASTIAN
The words shall not be many; but the faithfulness
And true respect that is included in 'em
Is worthy your attention and may put upon me
The fair repute of a just, honest servant.

ISABELLA
What's here to do, sir, there's such great preparation toward?

SEBASTIAN
In brief, that goodness in you is abused, madam.
You have the married life, but 'tis a strumpet
That has the joy on't, and the fruitfulness:
There goes away your comfort.

ISABELLA How? A strumpet?

SEBASTIAN
Of five years' cost, and upwards: a dear mischief,
As they are all of 'em. His fortnight's journey
Is to that country, if it be not rudeness

141 **fit** requite
145 **conceit** meaning
146 **look'st so pale and poorly** Offering yet another interpretation of Francisca's pallor and thinness, Antonio here instantiates the play's preoccupation with women's bodies as sets of signs which invite, but baffle, interpretation.
152 **natural** familial, blood-related
154 **shrewd** ominous, coming near the truth
lightness wantonness
157 **apparent** manifest, palpable
174 **footboy** boy-attendant, page-boy
175 **do you service** (*a*) give you assistance (*b*) pay you sexual attention
189 **fruitfulness** fecundity, fertility in offspring
191 **Of...upwards** maintained for over five years
193 **country** punning (again) on 'cunt'

To speak the truth: I have found it all out, madam.

ISABELLA
Thou'st found out thine own ruin, for to my knowledge
Thou dost belie him basely: I dare swear
He's a gentleman as free from that folly
As ever took religious life upon him.

SEBASTIAN
Be not too confident to your own abuse, madam:
Since I have begun the truth, neither your frowns,
The only curses that I have on earth
(Because my means depends upon your service),
Nor all the execration of man's fury
Shall put me off. Though I be poor, I'm honest,
And too just in this business. I perceive now,
Too much respect and faithfulness to ladies
May be a wrong to servants.

ISABELLA
Art thou yet
So impudent to stand in't?

SEBASTIAN
Are you yet so cold, madam,
In the belief on't? There my wonder's fixed.
Having such blessed health and youth about you,
Which makes the injury mighty.

ISABELLA
Why, I tell thee
It were too great a fortune for thy lowness
To find out such a thing: thou dost not look
As if thou'rt made for't. By the precious sweets of love,
I would give half my wealth for such a bargain
And think 'twere bought too cheap. Thou canst not guess
Thy means, and happiness, should I find this true.
First, I'd prefer thee to the lord my uncle.
He's governor of Ravenna: all the advancements
I'th' kingdom flows from him. What need I boast that
Which common fame can teach thee?

SEBASTIAN
Then thus, madam:
Since I presume now on your height of spirit
And your regard to your own youth, and fruitfulness,
Which every woman naturally loves and covets,
Accept but of my labour in directions.
You shall both find your wrongs, which you may right
At your own pleasure, yet not missed tonight
Here in the house neither. None shall take notice
Of any absence in you, as I have thought on't.

ISABELLA
Do this, and take my praise and thanks for ever.

SEBASTIAN
As I deserve, I wish 'em, and will serve you. *Exeunt*

3.3

Enter Hecate, Hoppo and Stadlin [through one door] and Firestone [with basket, through the other, unnoticed]

HECATE
The moon's a gallant: see how brisk she rides!

STADLIN
Here's a rich evening, Hecate.

HECATE
Ay, is't not, wenches,
To take a journey of five thousand mile?

HOPPO
Ours will be more tonight.

HECATE
O, 'twill be precious.
Heard you the owl yet?

STADLIN
Briefly in the copse,
As we came through now.

HECATE
'Tis high time for us then.

STADLIN
There was a bat hung at my lips three times
As we came through the woods, and drank her fill.
Old Puckle saw her.

HECATE
You are fortunate still.
The very screech-owl lights upon your shoulder
And woos you, like a pigeon. Are you furnished?
Have you your ointments?

STADLIN
All.

HECATE
Prepare to flight then:
I'll overtake you swiftly.

STADLIN
Hie thee, Hecate.
We shall be up betimes.

HECATE
I'll reach you quickly.
[*Exeunt Stadlin and Hoppo*]

FIRESTONE [*aside*] They're all going a-birding tonight. They talk of fowls i'th'air, that fly by day: I'm sure they'll be a company of foul sluts there tonight. If we have not mortality after it, I'll be hanged, for they are able to putrefy it, to infect a whole region. She spies me now.

HECATE What, Firestone, our sweet son?

FIRESTONE A little sweeter than some of you, or a dunghill were too good for me.

HECATE
How much hast here?

FIRESTONE
Nineteen, and all brave plump ones,

194 **I have found it all out** Antonio having announced his fortnight's journey only two dozen lines earlier, Sebastian's knowledge of his master's intentions has perplexed some editors. Perhaps Francisca has told the servants of Antonio's travel plans. The problem is unlikely to be perceived in performance.
208 **stand** persevere
218 **prefer** recommend
219–20 **all the advancements ... from him** Otiose within the dramatic fiction, the boast draws attention to familiar facts outside it: in the first half of James I's reign, Frances Howard's great-uncle had been the source of all advancements in the newly united kingdom.
3.3.1 **gallant** fine lady, fashionably attired beauty
brisk smartly dressed
9 **still** ever, always
15 **a-birding** flying
18 **mortality** death
23 **Nineteen ... ones** Firestone does not specify what he is counting. The actor playing him could probably make an empty basket pass for one crammed with necromantic ware, but some plump snakes could be dangling out from among eggs and greens.

Besides six lizards and three serpentine eggs.

HECATE

Dear and sweet boy! What herbs hast thou?

FIRESTONE

I have some *Mar Martin* and *mandragon*.

HECATE

Marmaritin, and *mandragora*, thou wouldst say.
Here's *panax* too: I thank thee.

FIRESTONE

My pan aches, I am sure,
With kneeling down to cut 'em.

HECATE

And *selago*!
Hedge-hyssop too: how near he goes my cuttings!
Were they all cropped by moonlight?

FIRESTONE

Every blade of 'em.
Or I am a moon-calf, mother.

HECATE

Hie thee home with 'em.
Look well to the house tonight: I am for aloft.

FIRESTONE

Aloft, quoth you? [*Aside*] I would you would break your neck once,
That I might have all quickly!—Hark, hark, mother!
They are above the steeple already, flying
Over your head with a noise of musicians.

HECATE

They are there indeed: Help, help me! I'm too late else.

Song

VOICES [*from off-stage or above*]

Come away, come away!
Hecate, Hecate, O come away!

HECATE

I come, I come, I come, I come
With all the speed I may,
With all the speed I may.
Where's Stadlin?

VOICE [*from off-stage or above*]

Here.

HECATE

Where's Puckle?

VOICE [*from off-stage or above*]

Here.
And Hoppo too, and Hellwain too.
We lack but you, we lack but you.
Come away, make up the count.

HECATE

I will but 'noint, and then I mount.

A spirit like a cat descends

VOICE [*from off-stage or above*]

There's one comes down to fetch his dues:
A kiss, a coll, a sip of blood—
And why thou stay'st so long

[CAT]

I muse, I muse

VOICE [*from off-stage or above*]

Since the air's so sweet and good.

HECATE [*to Cat*]

O, art thou come?

[CAT]

What news, what news?

[HECATE]

All goes still to our delight:

VOICE [*from off-stage or above*]

Either come, or else

[CAT]

Refuse, refuse.

HECATE

Now I am furnished for the flight.

FIRESTONE [*aside*] Hark, hark, the cat sings a brave treble in her own language.

HECATE (*going up* [*with Cat*])

Now I go, now I fly,
Malkin, my sweet spirit, and I.
O, what a dainty pleasure 'tis

27 ***Marmaritin*** See note to 1.2.159–61. Giving no other occurrence of the word, the *OED* links it to the Latin *marmaritis*. Lewis and Short define this as a plant that grows in marble quarries and identify it with Pliny's *aglaophotis*. The species thus appears to be known only to classical zoology. Its name here serves to occasion Firestone's recasting it as '*Mar Martin*'. His mistake may allude to *Mar Martine*, a pamphlet published in the Martin Marprelate controversy of the 1580s.

mandragora mandrake, used as narcotic or soporific drug

28 ***panax*** genus of plants, to some of which medicinal virtues are attributed: hence, 'panacea'.

pan head, skull (brain-pan)

29 ***selago*** club-moss

30 **Hedge-hyssop** species of figwort, formerly noted for medicinal qualities

31 **cropped by moonlight** Firestone's horticultural habits come from Zacharie Jones's 1605 translation of part of Pierre Le Loyer's *Livre des Spectres*: '*Virgil* doth recite ... ceremonies which the Sorcerers used in gathering of their herbs ... as to cut them in the night time by the light of the Moonshine with a hook of brass, which maketh me also to remember certain observations of the Magicians and Sorcerers in times past, in cutting of their herb *Elleborus*, *Mandragoras*, and the herb *Panaceum* ... and those also of the *Druids* ... who used, without any knife or iron, to pluck the herb which they called *Selago*.'

32 **moon-calf** absent-minded person who gazes at the moon

37 **noise** company, band

38.1 ***Song*** In the MS of *The Witch* this song is distinguished by layout and an italic hand, but its distribution among singers is not very clear. Hecate's parts are headed '*Hec*'; others are marked 'in ye aire' (twice) or '*above*'; and still others are not assigned at all. The song also survives in two manuscript copies of a setting believed to have been composed by Robert Johnson (*c.*1582–1633), a lutenist associated with the King's Men. These manuscripts do not divide the melody among different voices. See Textual Notes; for the music, see *Companion*, p. 153.

57–8 **the cat ... own language** If these lines are taken to refer to Malkin, the 'spirit like a cat' that has descended at l. 48, then Malkin must sing at least some of the unattributed lines. A feline miaouw would suit the vowel sounds in 'muse', 'news' and 'refuse', and the effect would be exaggerated by the high notes by which these words are distinguished in Robert Johnson's setting of the song. Firestone's aside could, however, be made to refer to Hecate. The witch has sung the line immediately preceding her son's spoken comment on the singing; the pronominal reference of his aside more certainly applies to her than to Malkin, who is gendered masculine (see 1.2.95); and the disyllabic pronunciation of her name throughout the play brings it into homophony with 'the cat'. If the aside is taken to refer to Hecate, then her singing voice should be remarkable—perhaps for dissonance.

To ride in the air
When the moon shines fair
And sing and dance and toy and kiss!
Over woods, high rocks and mountains,
Over seas, our mistress' fountains,
Over steeple towers and turrets,
We fly by night 'mongst troops of spirits.

[ALL] [*from off-stage or above*]
No ring of bells, to our ears sounds;
No howls of wolves, no yelps of hounds.
No, not the noise of waters' breach
Or cannon's throat, our height can reach.
[*Exeunt all but Firestone*]

FIRESTONE Well, mother, I thank your kindness: you must be gamboling i'th'air, and leave me to walk here like a fool, and a mortal. *Exit*

Finis Actus Tertii

4.1 [*Incipit*] *Actus Quartus*
Enter Almachildes

ALMACHILDES Though the Fates have endued me with a pretty kind of lightness, that I can laugh at the world in a corner on't, and can make myself merry on fasting-nights to rub out a supper (which were a precious quality in a young formal student), yet let the world know there is some difference betwixt my jovial condition and the lunary state of madness. I am not quite out of my wits: I know a bawd from an aqua vitae shop, a strumpet from wildfire, and a beadle from brimstone. Now shall I try the honesty of a great woman soundly: she reckoning the duke's made away, I'll be hanged if I be not the next now. If I trust her as she's a woman, let one of her long hairs wind about my heart and be the end of me (which were a piteous lamentable tragedy, and might be entitled *A Fair Warning for all Hair-Bracelets*).
Already there's an insurrectïon
Among the people: they are up in arms
Not out of any reason but their wills,
Which are in them their saints. Sweating and swear-
ing
(Out of their zeal to rudeness) that no stranger
(As they term her) shall govern over them,
They say they'll raise a duke among themselves first.
Enter Duchess

DUCHESS
O Almachildes, I perceive already
Our loves are born to crosses! We're beset
By multitudes and—which is worse—I fear me
Unfriended too of any. My chief care
Is for thy sweet youth's safety.

ALMACHILDES [*aside*] He that believes you not
Goes the right way to heaven, o' my conscience.

DUCHESS
There is no trusting of 'em! They are all as barren
In pity as in faith: he that puts confidence
In them, dies openly to the sight of all men,
Not with his friends and neighbours in peace private,
But as his shame, so his cold farewell is,
Public and full of noise. But keep you close, sir,
Not seen of any, till I see the way
Plain for your safety. I expect the coming
Of the Lord Governor, whom I will flatter
With fair entreaties to appease their wildness
And before him take a great grief upon me
For the Duke's death, his strange and sudden loss;
And when a quiet comes, expect thy joys.

ALMACHILDES [*aside*]
I do expect now to be made away
'Twixt this and Tuesday night: if I live Wednesday,
Say I have been careful and shunned spoonmeat.
Exit

64 **toy** (*a*) frisk about (*b*) flirt
66 **our mistress' fountains** The seas, like the witches, are controlled by the moon (which the opening lines of this scene have personified as a fashionable lady).
71 **waters' breach** water-break, an irruption of water
4.1.1 **endued** supplied
2 **pretty** fine, agreeable
lightness high spirits
4 **rub out** omit, miss
5 **formal** regular, complete
9 **aqua vitae** alcoholic spirits distilled from wine
wildfire erysipelas, a febrile inflammation which produces deep red eruptions in the skin and spreads easily
10 **beadle** parish constable
brimstone inflammable sulphur, by extension hellfire. Almachildes catalogues pairs of commonly linked, but separable, entities.
15 **piteous lamentable tragedy** Using old-fashioned dramatic terms and form, Almachildes evokes his own demise as the fall of a great man.
15–16 ***A Fair Warning for all Hair-Bracelets*** An allusion to *A Warning for Fair Women* (1599), an exemplary tragedy of wifely adultery.
17–23 **Already...first** In Bedingfield's translation of Machiavelli's *Istorie fiorentine*, the insurrection carries somewhat more narrative weight than it does in the plot here: 'After the murder performed, [Almachilde] finding that he could not according to his expectation enjoy the kingdom, and fearing to be slain of the *Lombards* for the love they bare to *Alboino*, the Queen and he...fled to *Longino* at *Ravenna*, who honourably there received them.'
20 **their saints** i.e., their objects of devotion
25 **crosses** thwartings
45 **spoonmeat** soft or liquid food suitable for invalids. The apothecary convicted of murder in the Overbury case was charged with having laced broths and jellies with poisons over a period of months in which the victim's health degenerated.

DUCHESS
This fellow lives too long after the deed!
I'm weary of his sight: he must die quickly
Or I've small hope of safety. My great aim's
At the Lord Governor's love: he is a spirit
Can sway and countenance. These obey and crouch.
My guiltiness had need of such a master
That with a beck can suppress multitudes
And dim misdeeds with radiance of his glory,
Not to be seen with dazzled popular eyes.
And here behold him come.

Enter Lord Governor [and Servant]

LORD GOVERNOR [*to Servant*] Return back to 'em:
Say we desire 'em to be friends of peace
Till they hear farther from us. [*Exit Servant*]

DUCHESS O my lord,
I fly unto the pity of your nobleness,
The grievèd'st lady that was e'er beset
With storms of sorrows or wild rage of people.
Never was woman's grief for loss of lord
Dearer than mine to me.

LORD GOVERNOR There's no right done
To him now, madam, by wrong done to yourself:
Your own good wisdom may instruct you so far.
And for the people's tumult (which oft grows
From liberty or rankness of long peace),
I'll labour to restrain, as I've begun, madam.

DUCHESS
My thanks and pray'rs shall ne'er forget you, sir,
And, in time to come, my love.

LORD GOVERNOR Your love, sweet madam!
You make my joys too happy! I did covet
To be the fortunate man that blessing visits,
Which I'll esteem the crown and full reward
Of service present and deserts to come.
It is a happiness I'll be bold to sue for
When I have set a calm upon these spirits
That now are up for ruin.

DUCHESS Sir, my wishes
Are so well met in yours, so fairly answered
And nobly recompensed, it makes me suffer
In those extremes that few have ever felt,
To hold two passions in one heart at once
Of gladness, and of sorrow.

LORD GOVERNOR Then, as the olive
Is the meek ensign of fair, fruitful peace,
So is this kiss, of yours.
[*He kisses her*]

DUCHESS Love's power be with you, sir!

LORD GOVERNOR [*aside*]
How she's betrayed her! May I breathe no longer
Than to do virtue service, and bring forth
The fruits of noble thoughts, honest and loyal.
This will be worth th'observing, and I'll do't. *Exit*

DUCHESS
What a sure happiness confirms joy to me
Now, in the times of my most imminent dangers!
I looked for ruin, and increase of honour
Meets me auspiciously! But my hopes are clogged now
With an unworthy weight: there's the misfortune.
What course shall I take now with this young man,
For he must be no hindrance? I have thought on't!
I'll take some witch's counsel for his end—
That will be sur'st! Mischief is mischief's friend. *Exit*

Enter Sebastian and Fernando 4.2

SEBASTIAN
If ever you knew force of love in life, sir,
Give to mine pity!

FERNANDO You do ill to doubt me.

SEBASTIAN
I could make bold with no friend seemlier
Than with yourself, because you were in presence
At our vow-making.

FERNANDO I'm a witness to't.

SEBASTIAN
Then you best understand of all men living
This is no wrong I offer, no abuse
Either to faith or friendship, for we're registered
Husband and wife in heaven, though there wants that
Which often keeps licentious man in awe
From starting from their wedlocks—the knot public.
'Tis in our souls knit fast, and how more precious
The soul is than the body, so much judge
The sacred and celestial tie within us
More than the outward form, which calls but witness
Here upon earth to what is done in heaven.
Though I must needs confess the least is honourable,
As an ambassador sent from a king
Has honour by the employment, yet there's greater
Dwells in the king that sent him: so in this.

FERNANDO
I approve all you speak and will appear to you
A faithful, pitying friend.

Enter Florida

SEBASTIAN [*apart to Fernando*]
Look, there is she, sir—
One good for nothing but to make use of,

46–50 **This fellow ... and crouch** This development is much altered from Bedingfield's translation of Machiavelli's *Istorie fiorentine*: '*Longino* hoped that time would well serve him ... to become King of *Lombardy* and all *Italy*. And conferring his intent with the Queen, persuaded her to kill *Almachilde*, and take him for her husband: she accepted ... preparing a cup of wine poisoned, and with her one hand she offered the same to *Almachilde* ... he having drunk half the wine, and ... mistrusting the poison, enforced *Rosmunda* to drink the rest, whereof both the one and the other within few hours died, and *Longino* bereft of his expectation to become King.'

62 **Dearer** more earnest, more heartfelt

65 **for** as for

81–2 **the olive ... peace** See Genesis 8:11.

91 **clogged** encumbered, obstructed

4.2.22–7 **she ... her** Although they may confuse a reader, the pronominal references of these lines would not pose problems in performance.

22–4 **she ... One ... her** Florida

And I'm constrained to employ her to make all things
Plain, easy and probable, for when she comes
And finds one here that claims him—[*aside*] as I've taught
Both this to do't and he to compound with her—
'Twill stir belief the more of such a business.

FERNANDO
I praise the carriage well.

SEBASTIAN [*to Florida*] Hark you, sweet mistress:
I shall do you a simple turn in this,
For, she disgraced thus, you are up in favour
Forever with her husband.

FLORIDA That's my hope, sir.
I would not take the pains else. Have you the keys
Of the garden-side, that I may get betimes in,
Softly, and take her lodging?

SEBASTIAN Yes, I have thought upon you:
Here be the keys.

FLORIDA [*seizing keys*] Marry, and thanks, sweet sir!
Set me a work so still.

SEBASTIAN [*aside*] Your joys are false ones.
You're like to lie alone. You'll be deceived
Of the bedfellow you look for, else my purpose
Were in an ill case. He's on his fortnight's journey:
You'll find cold comfort there. A dream will be
Even the best market you can make tonight.
[*To Florida*] She'll not be long now. You may lose no time, neither.
If she but take you at the door, 'tis enough.
When a suspect doth catch once, it burns mainly.
There may you end your business, and as cunningly
As if you were i'th' chamber, if you please
To use but the same art.

FLORIDA What need you urge that
Which comes so naturally I cannot miss on't?
What makes the devil so greedy of a soul
But 'cause he's lost his own, to all joys lost?
So 'tis our trade to set snares for other women
'Cause we were once caught ourselves. [*Exit*]

SEBASTIAN A sweet allusion!
Hell and a whore, it seems, are partners then,
In one ambition. Yet thou'rt here deceived now:
Thou canst set none to hurt or wrong her honour.
It rather makes it perfect. [*To Fernando*] Best of friends
That ever love's extremities were blessed with,
I feed mine arms with thee and call my peace
The offspring of thy friendship. I will think
This night my wedding-night, and with a joy
As reverend as religion can make man's
I will embrace this blessing: honest actions
Are laws unto themselves, and that good fear
Which is on others forced, grows kindly there.

FERNANDO
Hark, hark! One knocks: away, sir! 'Tis she certainly.
It sounds much like a woman's jealous 'larum.

[*Exit Sebastian through one door*]

Enter Isabella [*through the other door*]

ISABELLA
By your leave, sir.

FERNANDO You're welcome, gentlewoman.

ISABELLA
Our ladyship then stands us in no stead now.
One word in private, sir—
[*She whispers in his ear*]

FERNANDO No, surely, forsooth!
There is no such here: you've mistook the house.

ISABELLA
O, sir, that have I not! Excuse me there,
I come not with such ignorance: think not so, sir.
'Twas told me at the ent'ring of your house here
By one that knows him too well.

FERNANDO Who should that be?

ISABELLA
Nay, sir, betraying is not my profession;
But here I know he is, and I presume
He would give me admittance, if he knew on't,
As one on's nearest friends.

FERNANDO You're not his wife, forsooth?

ISABELLA
Yes, by my faith, am I.

FERNANDO Cry you mercy then, lady!

ISABELLA
She goes here by the name on's wife: good stuff!
But the bold strumpet never told me that.

FERNANDO
We are so oft deceived that let out lodgings,
We know not whom to trust. 'Tis such a world!

25 **she** Isabella
26 **one** Florida
him Antonio
27 **this** Florida
he Fernando
compound agree
her Florida
29 **carriage** management. Sebastian's plans appear less praiseworthy than Fernando's acuity in apprehending them. With the connivance of Florida and Fernando, Sebastian is contriving to trick Isabella into bed and there deflower her. The bed in question is Florida's in her lodgings at a house belonging to Fernando. Florida vacates her chamber here so that Isabella can be lured into it (and Sebastian's embraces) and so that she herself can take over Isabella's chamber (and husband) in Antonio's house. On her way out of Fernando's house, Florida is to encounter Isabella and let the lady know of Antonio's familiarity with the place and his intimacy with Florida's person. Fernando, who is acting as brothel-keeper, is to back up Florida's claims, which are expected to alienate Isabella from her husband.
34 **garden-side** garden entrance
betimes in good time
35 **take . . . lodging** occupy her chamber
45 **suspect** suspicion
mainly vigorously
53 **allusion** likening
65 **kindly** naturally
68 **gentlewoman** a woman of good birth or breeding but without titled rank. Addressing Isabella thus is part of Fernando's pretence that he does not recognize her, an 'error' for which he apologizes at l. 80.
79 **on's** of his

There are so many odd tricks nowadays
Put upon housekeepers.

ISABELLA Why? Do you think I'd wrong
You or the reputation of your house?
Pray show me the way to him.

FERNANDO He's asleep, lady,
The curtains drawn about him.

ISABELLA Well, well, sir,
I'll have that care I'll not dis-ease him much.
Tread you but lightly. O, of what gross falsehood
Is man's heart made of? Had my first love lived,
And returned safe, he would have been a light
To all men's actions, his faith shined so bright.

Exeunt [Fernando and Isabella through one door]

Enter Sebastian [through the other door]

SEBASTIAN
I cannot so deceive her: 'twere too sinful.
There's more religion in my love than so.
It is not treacherous lust that gives content
T'an honest mind: and this could prove no better.
Were it in me a part of manly justice,
That have sought strange, hard means to keep her chaste
To her first vow, and I t'abuse her first?
Better I never knew what comfort were
In woman's love, than wickedly to know it!
What could the falsehood of one night avail him
That must enjoy for ever, or he's lost?
'Tis the way rather to draw hate upon me:
For, known, 'tis as impossible she should love me
As youth in health to dote upon a grief,
Or one that's robbed, and bound, t'affect the thief!
No, he that would soul's sacred comfort win
Must burn in pure love, like a seraphin.

Enter Isabella

ISABELLA
Celio?

SEBASTIAN
Sweet madam?

ISABELLA Thou'st deluded me:
There's nobody.

SEBASTIAN How? I wonder he would miss, madam,
Having appointed too! 'Twere a strange goodness
If heaven should turn his heart now, by the way.

ISABELLA
O, never, Celio!

SEBASTIAN Yes, I've known the like.
Man is not at his own disposing, madam.
The blessed powers have provided better for him,
Or he were miserable. He may come yet:
'Tis early, madam. If you would be pleased
To embrace my counsel, you should see this night over,
Since you've bestowed this pains.

ISABELLA I intend so.

SEBASTIAN *[aside]*
That strumpet would be found, else she should go.
I curse the time now, I did e'er make use
Of such a plague: sin knows not what it does.

Exeunt

Enter Francisca [above,] in her chamber 4.3

FRANCISCA
'Tis now my brother's time, even much about it,
For though he dissembled a whole fortnight's absence,
He comes again tonight: 'twas so agreed
Before he went. I must bestir my wits now
To catch this sister of mine and bring her name
To some disgrace first, to preserve mine own.
There's profit in that cunning: she cast off
My company betimes tonight by tricks and sleights,
And I was well contented. I am resolved
There's no hate lost between us, for I know
She does not love me now but painfully,
Like one that's forced to smile upon a grief
To bring some purpose forward; and I'll pay her
In her own metal. They're now all at rest,
And Gasper there, and all—

[Snoring noises off]

List!—Fast asleep!
He cries it hither. I must dis-ease you straight, sir.
For the maidservants and the girls o'th' house,
I spiced them lately with a drowsy posset:
They will not hear in haste.

[Knocking noises off]

My brother's come!
O, where's this key now for him?

[She produces key]

Here 'tis, happily!
But I must wake him first. Why, Gasper! Gasper!

Enter Gaspero [undressed, below]

GASPERO
What a pox gasp you for?

FRANCISCA Now I'll throw't down.

[She drops key onto stage behind him]

GASPERO
Who's that called me now? Somebody called, 'Gasper!'

FRANCISCA
O, up, as thou'rt an honest fellow, Gasper!

GASPERO
I shall not rise tonight, then. What's the matter?

86 **housekeepers** (*a*) householders, possibly with an innuendo as (*b*) brothel-keepers
90 **dis-ease** disturb
109 **t'affect** to fancy
111 **seraphin** seraphim, the highest of the nine orders of angels
115 **by the way** en route
121 **see this night over** stay overnight
123 **else** otherwise
4.3.11 **but** except, other than
14 **metal** coin
16 **cries it** proclaims it [sleep]
21.1 **[*undressed*]** Gaspero's entrance here, undressed, anticipates Aberzanes's entrance, untrussed, in the next scene.
25 **not rise** (*a*) not get out of bed (because he is not honest) (*b*) not have an erection (because he has to get out of bed)

Who's that? Young mistress?
FRANCISCA Ay! Up, up, sweet Gasper!
My sister hath both knocked and called this hour,
And not a maid will stir.
GASPERO They'll stir enough sometimes.
[*Noises off*]
FRANCISCA
Hark, hark again! Gasper! O, run, run, prithee!
GASPERO
Give me leave to clothe myself.
FRANCISCA Stand'st upon clothing
In an extremity?
[*Noises off*]
Hark, hark again!
She may be dead ere thou com'st. O, in quickly!
[*Exit Gaspero*]
He's gone. He cannot choose but be took now
Or met in his return: that will be enough.
Enter Antonio [armed, above]
Brother? Here, take this light.
[*She takes torch from wall and hands it to him*]
ANTONIO My careful sister!
[*Exit above*]
FRANCISCA [*calling after him*]
Look first in his own lodging, ere you enter.
[*Enter Antonio below, torch in hand, to discover key on stage floor*]
ANTONIO
O abused confidence! Here's nothing of him
But what betrays him more.
FRANCISCA Then 'tis too true, brother!
ANTONIO
I'll make base lust a terrible example:
No villainy e'er paid dearer.
[*He draws his sword*]
FRANCISCA Help! Hold, sir!
ANTONIO
I'm deaf to all humanity! [*Exit. Noises off*]
FRANCISCA List, list:
A strange and sudden silence after all!
I trust he's spoiled 'em both! Too dear a happiness!
O, how I tremble between doubts and joys!
[*Enter Antonio below*]
ANTONIO
There perish both! Down to the house of falsehood,
Where perjurous wedlock weeps! O, perjurous woman!
She'd took the innocence of sleep upon her
At my approach, and would not see me come—
As if she'd lain there, like a harmless soul
And never dreamed of mischief. What's all this now?
I feel no ease: the burden's not yet off
So long as th'abuse sticks in my knowledge.
O, 'tis a pain of hell to know one's shame!
Had it been hid, and done, it'd been done happy,
For he that's ignorant lives long, and merry.
FRANCISCA [*Aside*]
I shall know all now.—Brother!
ANTONIO Come down quickly,
For I must kill thee too!
FRANCISCA Me?
ANTONIO Stay not long
If thou desir'st to die with little pain.
Make haste, I'd wish thee, and come willingly:
If I be forced to come, I shall be cruel
Above a man to thee.
FRANCISCA Why, sir, my brother?
ANTONIO
Talk to thy soul, if thou wilt talk at all.
To me thou'rt lost forever.
FRANCISCA This is fearful in you
Beyond all reason, brother. Would you thus
Reward me for my care and truth shown to you?
ANTONIO
A curse upon 'em both, and thee for company!
'Tis that too diligent thankless care of thine
Makes me a murderer, and that ruinous truth
That lights me to the knowledge of my shame.
Hadst thou been secret, then had I been happy
And had a hope (like man) of joys to come.
Now here I stand, a stain to my creation
And, which is heavier than all torments to me,
Ha' understanding of this base adultery
And that thou toldst me first, which thou deserv'st
Death worthily for.
FRANCISCA If that be the worst, hold, sir!
Hold, brother! I can ease your knowledge straight.
By my soul's hopes, I can! There's no such thing.
ANTONIO
How?
FRANCISCA
Bless me but with life, I'll tell you all.
Your bed was never wronged.
ANTONIO What, never wronged?
FRANCISCA
I ask but mercy, as I deal with truth now.
'Twas only my deceit, my plot and cunning
To bring disgrace upon her, by that means
To keep mine own hid, which none knew but she.
To speak troth: I'd a child by Aberzanes, sir.
ANTONIO
How? Aberzanes?

28 **stir** (*a*) awaken (*b*) arouse sexual desire
35 **careful** painstaking
39–41 **I'll make... all humanity** Threatening to make an example of lust, Antonio makes himself into an emblem of another deadly sin—wrath. With bared sword in one hand and burning torch in the other, he is equipped as the figure of Wrath in Ripa's *Iconologia*: 'IRA... [she will hold a naked sword in her right hand, and in the left she will have a burning torch... The naked sword signifies that Wrath quickly seizes steel and embarks upon vengeance. The burning torch is the wrathful man's heart, which continually burns and consumes itself.]'
39 **terrible** terrifying
43 **spoiled** destroyed
46 **perjurous... perjurous** characterized by perjury... forworn, guilty of perjury
61 **Above a man** inhumanly

FRANCISCA And my mother's letter
Was counterfeited, to get time and place
For my delivery.

ANTONIO O, my wrath's redoubled!

FRANCISCA
At my return, she could speak all my folly
And blamed me with good counsel. I, for fear
It should be made known, thus rewarded her,
Wrought you into suspicion without cause
And at your coming raised up Gasper suddenly,
Sent him but in before you, by a falsehood,
Which (to your kindled jealousy) I knew
Would add enough. What's now confessed is true.

ANTONIO
The more I hear, the worse it fares with me.
I've killed 'em now for nothing: yet the shame
Follows my blood still. Once more, come down.
Look you, my sword goes up.
[He sheathes his sword]
Call Hermio to me,
Let the new man alone: he'll wake too soon
To find his mistress dead, and lose a service.
[Exit Francisca above]
Already the day breaks upon my guilt.
I must be brief and sudden. Hermio!
Enter Hermio

HERMIO
Sir.

ANTONIO
Run, knock up Aberzanes speedily.
Say I desire his company this morning:
To yonder horse-race, tell him. That will fetch him.
O, hark you, by the way—
[He whispers in his ear]

HERMIO Yes, sir.

ANTONIO Use speed now,
Or I will ne'er use thee more, and perhaps
I speak in a right hour. My grief o'erflows:
I must in private go and vent my woes.
Exeunt [severally]

Finis Actus Quarti

5.1 *[Incipit] Actus Quintus*
Enter Antonio and Aberzanes, [his clothing in disarray]

ANTONIO
You are welcome, sir.

ABERZANES I think I'm worthy on't,
For look you, sir, I come untrussed, in troth.

ANTONIO *[aside]*
The more's the pity (honester men go to't!)
That slaves should 'scape it.—What blade have you got there?

ABERZANES Nay, I know not that, sir. I am not acquainted greatly with the blade. I am sure 'tis a good scabbard, and that satisfies me.

ANTONIO
'Tis long enough indeed, if that be good.

ABERZANES
I love to wear a long weapon: 'tis a thing
Commendable.

ANTONIO I pray draw it, sir.

ABERZANES
It is not to be drawn.

ANTONIO Not to be drawn?

ABERZANES
I do not care to see't. To tell you troth, sir,
'Tis only a holiday thing, to wear by a man's side.

ANTONIO
Draw it, or I'll rip thee down from neck to navel,
Though there's small glory in't.

ABERZANES Are you in earnest, sir?

ANTONIO
I'll tell thee that anon.

ABERZANES Why, what's the matter, sir?

ANTONIO
What a base misery is this in life now!
This slave had so much daring courage in him
To act a sin, would shame whole generations;
But hath not so much honest strength about him
To draw a sword, in way of satisfaction.
This shows thy great guilt, that thou dar'st not fight.

ABERZANES
Yes, I dare fight, sir, in an honest cause.

ANTONIO
Why, come then, slave! Thou'st made my sister a whore!

ABERZANES
Prove that an honest cause and I'll be hanged.

ANTONIO
So many starting-holes? Can I light no way?
Go to, you shall have your wish: all honest play.
Come forth, thou fruitful wickedness, thou seed
Of Shame and Murder.
[Enter Francisca]
Take to thee in wedlock
Baseness and Cowardice, a fit match for thee.
Come, sir, along with me.
[He leads him by the hand]

ABERZANES 'Las, what to do?

105 **knock up** arouse by knocking at the door
110 **I speak in a right hour** i.e., my threat is timely
5.1.1 **You are welcome** Antonio's greeting initiates fifteen lines of *double-entendre* in which the secondary sense eludes Aberzanes.
2 **untrussed** (*a*) without having tied up the laces (called 'points') attaching the top of his breeches to his doublet (*b*) not hanged
4 **it** i.e., hanging
blade (*a*) weapon (*b*) penis
6 **scabbard** (*a*) sheath (*b*) vagina
13 **holiday** trifling, frivolous
26 **starting-holes** means of evasion
light strike
27 **play** (*a*) proceeding (*b*) sexual sport
28 **seed** cause

I am too young to take a wife, in troth.

ANTONIO
But old enough to take a strumpet, though.
You'd fain get all your children beforehand
And marry when you've done: that's a strange course, sir.
This woman I bestow on thee:
[*He joins their hands*]
What dost thou say?

ABERZANES
I would I had such another to bestow on you, sir.

ANTONIO
Uncharitable slave, dog, coward as thou art
To wish a plague so great as thine to any!

ABERZANES
To my friend, sir, where I think I may be bold.

ANTONIO
Down, and do't solemnly.
[*He forces them to kneel*]
Contract yourselves
With truth, and zeal, or ne'er rise up again.
I will not have her die i'th' state of strumpet,
Though she took pride to live one. Hermio, the wine!
[*Enter Hermio*]

HERMIO
'Tis here, sir. [*Aside*] 'Troth, I wonder at some things,
But I'll keep honest.
[*He serves wine to Antonio*]

ANTONIO
So: here's to you both now,
[*He drinks*]
And to your joys, if't be your luck to find 'em.
I tell you, you must weep hard if you do.
[*He gives wine cup to Aberzanes and Francisca*]
Divide it 'twixt you both: you shall not need
A strong bill of divorcement after that
If you mislike your bargain.
[*They drink*]
Go, get in now:
Kneel and pray heartily to get forgiveness
Of those two souls whose bodies thou hast murdered.
[*Exeunt Aberzanes and Francisca*]
Spread, subtle poison. Now my shame in her
Will die when I die: there's some comfort yet.
I do but think how each man's punishment
Proves still a kind of justice to himself.
I was the man that told this innocent gentlewoman,
Whom I did falsely wed and falsely kill,
That he that was her husband first, by contract,
Was slain i'th' field, and he's known yet to live.
So did I cruelly beguile her heart—
For which I'm well rewarded. So is Gasper,
Who, to befriend my love, swore fearful oaths
He saw the last breath fly from him. I see now
'Tis a thing dreadful t'abuse holy vows
And falls most weighty.

HERMIO
Take comfort, sir:
You're guilty of no death. They're only hurt,
And that not mortally.

ANTONIO
Thou breath'st untruths.
Enter Gaspero, [*wounded*]

HERMIO
Speak, Gasper, for me then.

GASPERO
Your unjust rage, sir
Has hurt me without cause

ANTONIO
'Tis changed to grief for't.
How fares my wife?

GASPERO
No doubt, sir, she fares well,
For she ne'er felt your fury. The poor sinner
That hath this seven year kept herself sound for you,
'Tis your luck to bring her into th' surgeon's hands now.

ANTONIO
Florida?

GASPERO
She: I know no other, sir.
You were ne'er at charge yet, but with one light horse.

ANTONIO
Why, where's your lady? Where's my wife tonight then?

GASPERO
Nay, ask not me, sir: your struck doe within
Tells a strange tale of her.

ANTONIO
This is unsufferable.
Never had man such means to make him mad!
O, that the poison would but spare my life
Till I had found her out!

HERMIO
Your wish is granted, sir.
Upon the faithfulness of a pitying servant
I gave you none at all. My heart was kinder.
Let not conceit abuse you: you're as healthful—
For any drug—as life yet ever found you.

ANTONIO
Why, here's a happiness, wipes off mighty sorrows!
The benefit of ever-pleasing service
Bless thy profession!
Enter Lord Governor
O my worthy lord,
I've an ill bargain: never man had worse.
The woman that (unworthy) wears your blood
To countenance sin in her, your niece—she's false.

50 **bill of divorcement** written petition for annulment of marriage. (Probably an allusion to Frances Howard's divorce proceedings against Robert Devereux.)
58 **this innocent gentlewoman** i.e., Isabella
59 **falsely . . . falsely** treacherously . . . erroneously
74 **seven year** Estimates vary: see 1.1.56 and 3.2.191.
sound healthy, free of (venereal) disease
77 **at charge . . . with** (*a*) financially responsible for (*b*) sexually effective with
light horse courtesan. *OED* gives no other instance of usage in this sense.
79 **struck** stricken, wounded
86 **conceit** imagination, fancy
87 **For** In respect of
drug poison

LORD GOVERNOR
False?
ANTONIO
Impudent, adulterous!
LORD GOVERNOR
You're too loud
And grow too bold too, with her virtuous meekness.
Enter Florida, [wounded]
Who dare accuse her?
FLORIDA
Here's one dare and can.
She lies this night with Celio, her own servant,
The place Fernando's house.
LORD GOVERNOR
Thou dost amaze us!
ANTONIO
Why, here's but lust translated from one baseness
Into another: here I thought to have caught 'em
But lighted wrong, by false intelligence,
And made me hurt the innocent. But now
I'll make my revenge dreadfuller than a tempest.
An army should not stop me, or a sea
Divide 'em from my revenge. *Exit*
LORD GOVERNOR
I'll not speak
To have her spared, if she be base and guilty.
If otherwise, heaven will not see her wronged:
I need not take care for her. Let that woman
Be carefully looked to, both for health, and sureness.
It is not that mistaken wound thou wear'st
Shall be thy privilege.
FLORIDA
You cannot torture me
Worse than the surgeon does, so long I care not.
[*Exeunt Florida and Gaspero*]
LORD GOVERNOR
If she be adulterous, I will never trust
Virtues in women: they're but veils for lust. *Exit*
HERMIO
To what a lasting ruin mischief runs!
I had thought I had well and happily ended all
In keeping back the poison, and new rage now
Spreads a worse venom. My poor lady grieves me!
'Tis strange to me that her sweet seeming virtues
Should be so meanly overtook with Celio,
A servant. 'Tis not possible.
Enter Isabella and Sebastian
ISABELLA
Good morrow, Hermio!
My sister stirring yet?
HERMIO
How? Stirring, forsooth!
Here has been simple stirring. Are you not hurt,
Madam? Pray speak: we have a surgeon ready.
ISABELLA
How a surgeon?
HERMIO
Hath been at work these five hours.
ISABELLA
How he talks!
HERMIO
Did you not meet my master?
ISABELLA
How your master? Why, came he home tonight?
HERMIO
Then know you nothing. Madam, please you
But walk in, you shall hear strange business.
ISABELLA [*to Sebastian*]
I'm much beholding to your truth now, am I not?
You've served me fair: my credit's stained for ever.
Exeunt [Isabella and Hermio]
SEBASTIAN
This is the wicked'st fortune that e'er blew!
We're both undone, for nothing: there's no way
Flatters recovery now. The thing's so gross
Her disgrace grieves me more than a life's loss. *Exit*

5.2

Enter Duchess, Hecate, Firestone [with necromantic equipment, including a cauldron]

HECATE
What death is't you desire for Almachildes?
DUCHESS
A sudden and a subtle.
HECATE
Then I have fitted you.
Here lie the gifts of both sudden and subtle.
His picture, made in wax and gently molten
By a blue fire kindled with dead men's eyes,
Will waste him by degrees.
DUCHESS
In what time, prithee?
HECATE
Perhaps in a moon's progress.
DUCHESS
What, a month?
Out upon pictures, if they be so tedious!
Give me things with some life.
HECATE
Then seek no farther.
DUCHESS
This must be done with speed, dispatched this night
If it may possibly.
HECATE
I have it for you!
Here's that will do't. Stay but perfection's time,
And that's not five hours hence.
DUCHESS
Canst thou do this?
HECATE Can I?
DUCHESS I mean, so closely!
HECATE So closely, do you mean too?
DUCHESS So artfully, so cunningly!
HECATE
Worse and worse! Doubts and incredulities—
They make me mad! Let scrupulous greatness know:

109 **sureness** security
111 **privilege** protection from arrest
120 **meanly** basely
overtook caught
122 **stirring** awake, up and about
123 **stirring** commotion, uproar
134 **Flatters recovery** fosters hopes of recovery
5.2.2 **fitted** supplied, furnished
3 **gifts** powers
8 **tedious** dilatory, slow
12 **perfection's** completion's
15 **closely** quickly (an extension of sense, from spatial to temporal proximity)
19 **scrupulous** distrustful

Cum volui ripis ipsis mirantibus amnes
In fontes redieri suos concussaque sisto,
Stantia concutio, cantu freta nubila pello,
Nubilaque induco ventos, abigoque vocoque,
Viperias rumpo verbis, et carmine fauces
Vivaque saxa, sua convulsaque robora terra,
Et silvas moveo, jubeoque tremiscere montes
Et mugire solum, manesque exire sepulchris.
Teque luna traho. Can you doubt me then, daughter?
That can make mountains tremble, miles of woods walk,
Whole earth's foundation bellow, and the spirits
Of the entombed to burst out from their marbles,
Nay, draw yon moon to my involved designs?

FIRESTONE I know as well as can be when my mother's mad and our great cat angry, for one spits French then, and th'other spits Latin.

DUCHESS
I did not doubt you, mother.

HECATE
No? What did you?
My power's so firm, it is not to be questioned.

DUCHESS
Forgive what's past; and now I know th'offensiveness
That vexes art, I'll shun th'occasion ever.

HECATE
Leave all to me and my five sisters, daughter.
It shall be cònveyed in at owlet time,
Take you no care. My spirits know their moments.
Raven or screech-owl never fly by th' door
But they call in, I thank 'em, and they lose not by't.
I give 'em barley soaked in infants' blood:
They shall have *semina cum sanguine*,
Their gorge crammed full, if they come once to our house.
We are no niggard. [*Exit Duchess*]

FIRESTONE They fare but too well when they come hither: they eat up as much t'other night as would have made me a good conscionable pudding.

HECATE
Give me some lizard's brain, quickly, Firestone!
Where's Grannam Stadlin, and all the rest o'th' sisters?

FIRESTONE All at hand, forsooth.

HECATE
Give me *marmaritin*, some bear-breach. When?

FIRESTONE
Here's bear-breach and lizard's brain, forsooth.

HECATE Into the vessel.
And fetch three ounces of the red-haired girl
I killed last midnight.

FIRESTONE
Whereabouts, sweet mother?

HECATE
Hip. Hip or flank. Where is the *Acopus*?

FIRESTONE
You shall have *Acopus*, forsooth.

HECATE
Stir, stir about, whilst I begin the charm.

A Charm Song: about a vessel

Black spirits and white, red spirits and grey,
Mingle, mingle, mingle, you that mingle may.
Titty, Tiffin, keep it stiff in.
Fire-drake, Pucky, make it lucky.
Liard, Robin, you must bob in.
Round, around, around, about, about,
All ill come running in, all good keep out.

[*Enter Witches*]

[STADLIN]
Here's the blood of a bat.

HECATE
Put in that, O put in that.

[HOPPO]
Here's libbard's bane.

HECATE
Put in again.

[STADLIN]
The juice of toad, the oil of adder.

20–8 ***Cum volui . . . luna traho*** In Book VII of Ovid's *Metamorphoses*, Medea, abandoned by Jason, speaks these lines within a vengeful prayer to the gods of the groves and the night. The Ovidian passage is quoted and translated in Scot's *Discoverie of Witchcraft* (XII, 7), near the beginning of the first of a series of chapters on charms.

31 **marbles** sepulchres. (The word translates *sepulchris* of l. 27.)

32 **involved** (*a*) complicated (*b*) covert

34 **spits French** a jibe at French vowel sounds as resembling feline noises. Malkin's 'French' accent has been heard at 3.3.51, 3.3.53, and 3.3.55.

39 **shun th'occasion** avoid giving cause [for offence]

40 **five sisters** This line is the only indication of the size of Hecate's coven. However, with no other witches onstage to be tallied at this point, the line need not be construed as a firm census. Stadlin and Hoppo are the only 'sisters' required to speak, and to be spoken to.

46 ***semina cum sanguine*** grain with blood

51 **conscionable** fair

52 **lizard's brain** See the list of venefical aphrodisiacs quoted from Scot's *Discoverie of Witchcraft* (VI, 7) in the note to 1.2.163–7.

53 **Grannam** grandam, old woman

55 **bear-breach** species of herbaceous plant of the genus *Acanthus*. Its popular names—bear-breach, brank-ursine, bear's foot—are thought to refer to the shagginess and shape of the leaf.

60 ***Acopus*** *Anagyros* or bean trefoil, a bushy shrub used medicinally in childbirth

62 **Stir, stir about** Hecate's command suggests that Firestone stir the contents of the cauldron, at least initially. He may move away from it to find the ingredient which he produces at l. 77.

62.1 ***Charm Song*** Like the song at 3.3.39–55, this song is invoked, by title only, in the text of *Macbeth* as printed in the Shakespearean First Folio (1623). For this song, however, no musical setting is known to have survived, and it is possible that the charm was chanted. The final exchange between Hecate and Firestone at ll. 84–8 can be construed as evidence that music only begins there, at the end of the scene, with the witches' dance. (See note to 5.2.88.1.)

about a vessel The subtitle of the charm song requires its singer(s) to go around the cauldron.

63–7 **Black spirits . . . Robin** See notes to 1.2.1–5 and 1.2.105–1.2.106.1.

72 **libbard's bane** leopardsbane, a plant of the genus *Doronicum*. Among the witches in Jonson's *Masque of Queens*, Hag 9, the herbalist, 'ha' been plucking, plants among, | Hemlock, henbane, adder's tongue, | Nightshade, moonwort, libbard's bane' (ll. 174–77).

[HOPPO]
Those will make the younker madder.

HECATE
Put in. There's all, and rid the stench.

FIRESTONE
Nay, here's three ounces of the red-haired wench.

ALL
Round, around, around, about, about,
All ill come running in, all good keep out.
[*End Song*]

HECATE
So, so, enough. Into the vessel with it:
There, 't hath the true perfection. I am so light
At any mischief! There's no villainy
But is a tune, methinks.

FIRESTONE [*Aside*] A tune! 'Tis to the tune of damnation then, I warrant you, and that song hath a villainous burden.

HECATE
Come, my sweet sisters. Let the air strike our tune
Whilst we show reverence to yon peeping moon.
Here they dance the Witches' Dance and exeunt

5.3 *Enter Lord Governor, Isabella, [Sebastian], Florida [bandaged], Francisca, Aberzanes, Gaspero [bandaged], [Servants]*

ISABELLA
My lord, I have given you nothing but the truth
Of a most plain and innocent intent.
My wrongs being so apparent in this woman,
A creature that robs wedlock of all comfort
Where'er she fastens, I could do no less
But seek means privately to shame his folly.
No farther reached my malice, and it glads me
That none but my base injurer is found
To be my false accuser.

LORD GOVERNOR This is strange
That he should give the wrongs, yet seek revenge.
[*To Sebastian*] But sirrah, you! You are accused here doubly:
First, by your lady, for a false intelligence
That caused her absence, which much hurts her name
Though her intents were blameless; next, by this woman
For an adulterous design and plot
Practised between you to entrap her honour
Whilst she, for her hire, should enjoy her husband.
Your answer!

SEBASTIAN Part of this is truth, my lord,
To which I'm guilty, in a rash intent,
But clear in act, and she most clear in both,
Not sanctity more spotless.
[*Enter Hermio*]

HERMIO O my Lord!

LORD GOVERNOR
What news breaks there?

HERMIO Of strange destructïon!
Here stands the lady that within this hour
Was made a widow.

LORD GOVERNOR How?

HERMIO Your niece, my lord!
A fearful, unexpected accident
Brought death to meet his fury; for my lord
Ent'ring Fernando's house like a rash tempest
Which nothing heeds but its own violent rage,
Blinded with wrath and jealousy, which scorn guides,
From a false trapdoor fell into a depth—
Exceeds a temple's height—which takes into it
Part of the dungeon that falls threescore fathom
Under the castle.

LORD GOVERNOR O you seed of lust,
Wrongs and revenges wrongful, with what terrors
You do present yourselves to wretched man
When his soul least expects you!

ISABELLA I forgive him
All his wrongs now, and sign it with my pity.

FLORIDA
O my sweet servant!
[*She swoons*]

LORD GOVERNOR Look to yon light mistress.

GASPERO
She's in a swoon, my lord.

75 **younker** fashionable young man. The charm is to be used on Almachildes, who at 4.1.5 has characterized himself as young.

85 **that song** i.e., 'damnation'

86 **burden** (*a*) bass accompaniment to melodic line (*b*) refrain. If Firestone carries off the cauldron on this line, then there will be further wordplay on (*c*) weight, load.

88.1 ***the Witches' Dance*** The venefical anti-masque to Jonson's *Masque of Queenes* was bracketed by dancing: his eleven hags danced immediately before they first spoke, and then again immediately before they disappeared. Jonson's account of their first dance pronounces it 'an usual ceremony at their convents, or meetings, where sometimes also they are visored and masked'. His account of the second dance is rather more helpful for a reconstruction of the Witches' Dance in Middleton's play. After casting spells for nearly 100 lines of Jonsonian verse, 'with a strange and sudden music they fell into a magical dance full of preposterous change and gesticulation, but most applying to their property, who at their meetings do all things contrary to the custom of men, dancing back to back and hip to hip, their hands joined, and making their circles backward, to the left hand, with strange fantastic motions of their heads and bodies.' In a note to this account Jonson records that his hags were armed with brooms: Middleton's witches may also have been equipped with them. For the music, see *Companion*, p. 158.

5.3.12 **intelligence** communication, information

14 **this woman** Florida

16–17 **her . . . she . . . her . . . her** Isabella's . . . Florida . . . Florida's . . . Isabella's

20 **clear** innocent

32 **fathom** unit of linear measure equivalent to 6 feet. That Fernando's house should include a shaft reaching a depth of 360 feet is sufficiently remarkable to invite an allegorical reading of this architectural feature as hell-mouth.

LORD GOVERNOR Convey her hence!
It is a sight would grieve a modest eye
To see a strumpet's soul sink into passion
For him that was the husband of another.—
[Exeunt Servants, supporting Florida]
Yet all this clears not you.
[Sebastian removes his disguise]

SEBASTIAN Thanks to heaven
That I am now of age to clear myself then!

LORD GOVERNOR
Sebastian?

SEBASTIAN
The same, much wronged, sir!

ISABELLA Am I certain
Of what mine eye takes joy to look upon?

SEBASTIAN
Your service cannot alter me from knowledge
I am your servant ever.

LORD GOVERNOR Welcome to life, sir!—
Gasper, thou swor'st his death.

GASPERO I did indeed, my lord,
And have been since well paid for't: one forsworn
mouth
Hath got me two or three more here.

SEBASTIAN I was dead, sir,
Both to my joys and all men's understanding,
Till this my hour of life: for 'twas my fortune
To make the first of my return to Urbin
A witness to that marriage—since which time
I have walked beneath myself and all my comforts,
Like one on earth whose joys are laid above;
And though it had been offence small in me
To enjoy mine own, I left her pure and free.

LORD GOVERNOR
The greater and more sacred is thy blessing,
For where heaven's bounty holy groundwork finds,
'Tis like a sea encompassing chaste minds.
Enter Duchess

HERMIO
The Duchess comes, my lord.

LORD GOVERNOR Be you then all witnesses
Of an intent most horrid.

DUCHESS *[Aside]* One poor night
Ends Almachildes now.
Better his meaner fortunes wept than ours
That took the true height of a prince's spirit
To match unto their greatness: such lives as his
Were only meant to break the force of fate
Ere it came at us, and receive the venom.
'Tis but a usual friendship for a mistress
To lose some forty years' life in hopeful time
And hazard an eternal soul for ever,
As young as he has done, and more desertful.

LORD GOVERNOR Madam.

DUCHESS My lord.

LORD GOVERNOR
This is the hour that I've so long desired:
The tumult's full appeased. Now may we both
Exchange embraces with a fortunate arm
And practise to make love knots, thus—
[The body of the] Duke is discovered

DUCHESS My lord!

LORD GOVERNOR
Thus, lustful woman and bold murd'ress, thus!
Blessed powers, to make my loyalty and truth so
happy!
Look thee, thou shame of greatness! Stain of honour,
Behold thy work, and weep before thy death
If thou be'st blessed with sorrow and a conscience,
Which is a gift from heaven and seldom knocks
At any murderer's breast with sounds of comfort.
See this, thy worthy and unequalled piece,
A fair encouragement for another husband!

DUCHESS
Bestow me upon death, sir. I am guilty
And of a cruelty above my cause.
His injury was too low for my revenge.
Perform a justice that may light all others
To noble actions. Life is hateful to me,
Beholding my dead lord. Make us an one
In death, whom marriage made one of two living
Till cursèd fury parted us. My lord,
I covet to be like him.

LORD GOVERNOR No, my sword
Shall never stain the virgin brightness on't
With blood of an adult'ress.

DUCHESS There, my lord,
I dare my accuser and defy the world,
Death, shame and torment. Blood I am guilty of
But not adultery, not the breach of honour.

LORD GOVERNOR
No? Come forth, Almachildes!
Enter Almachildes

DUCHESS Almachildes!
Hath Time brought him about to save himself
By my destruction? I am justly doomed.

LORD GOVERNOR *[to Almachildes]* Do you know this woman?

ALMACHILDES I have known her better, sir, than at this time.

LORD GOVERNOR But she defies you there.

44 **of age** old enough
51 **two or three more** i.e., wounds
54 **Urbin** Urbino. Having headed the play with '*The Scene Ravenna*' (a city altogether distinct, although not very distant, from Urbino), the manuscript probably records an error here. In Bedingfield's translation of Machiavelli's *Istorie fiorentine*, Urbino is mentioned two pages after the narrative which was Middleton's source for the Duchess/Almachildes plot.
80.1 ***discovered*** revealed (presumably in a curtained-off space, such as an inner stage, which the Lord Governor uncovers with a single gesture)
95 **Make us an one** unite us
107 **know** (carnally)

ALMACHILDES That's the common trick of them all.

DUCHESS
Nay, since I am touched so near, before my death, then,
In right of honour's innocence, I am bold
To call heaven, and my woman here, to witness.
Enter Amoretta
My lord, let her speak truth, or may she perish.

AMORETTA
Then, sir, by all the hopes of a maid's comfort
Either in faithful service or blessed marriage,
The woman that his blinded folly knew
Was only a hired strumpet, a professor
Of lust and impudence, which here is ready
To approve what I have spoken.

ALMACHILDES A common strumpet!
This comes of scarves: I'll never more wear
An haberdasher's shop before mine eyes again.

LORD GOVERNOR
My sword is proud thou art lightened of that sin.
Die, then, a murd'ress only.
[Duke revives]

DUKE Live a duchess,
Better than ever loved, embraced and honoured!

DUCHESS
My lord?

DUKE Nay, since in honour thou canst justly rise,
Vanish all wrongs: thy former practice dies.
I thank thee, Almachildes, for my life;
This lord, for truth; and heaven, for such a wife,
Who, though her intent sinned, yet she makes amends
With grief and honour, virtue's noblest ends.
What grieved you then shall never more offend you:
Your father's skull with honour we'll inter
And give the peace due to the sepulchre.
And in all times, may this day ever prove
A day of triumph, joy and honest love. *Exeunt*
Finis Actus Quinti

THE PARTS

ABERZANES (97 lines): Fernando *or* Servant (1.1); Cat

ALMACHILDES (155 lines): Gentleman (2.1)

AMORETTA (80 lines): Gentleman (2.1); Old Woman *or* Stableboy (*or* Hecate *or* Stadlin *or* Firestone *or* Hoppo); Cat *or* Hecate (*or* Stableboy) *or* Stadlin (*or* Stableboy) *or* Firestone (*or* Stableboy) *or* Hoppo (*or* Stableboy)

ANTONIO (216 lines): Old Woman *or* Stableboy (*or* Stadlin *or* Firestone *or* Hoppo); Stadlin (*or* Stableboy) *or* Firestone (*or* Stableboy) *or* Hoppo (*or* Stableboy) *or* Cat; [Fernando]

CAT (3 lines): Fernando *or* Servant (1.1) *or* Florida (*or* Duke *or* Lord Governor *or* Isabella *or* Francisca); Duke (or Florida) *or* Lord Governor (*or* Florida) *or* Isabella (*or* Florida) *or* Francisca (*or* Florida); Old Woman *or* Stableboy

DUCHESS (192 lines): Gentleman (2.1); [Servant (1.1)]; [Florida]; [Cat]

DUKE (42 lines): Gentleman (2.1); Stableboy (*or* Stadlin *or* Firestone *or* Hoppo); Stadlin (*or* Stableboy) *or* Firestone (*or* Stableboy) *or* Hoppo (*or* Stableboy) *or* Cat; [Fernando]

FERNANDO (49 lines): Stableboy (*or* Hecate *or* Stadlin *or* Firestone *or* Hoppo); Hecate (*or* Stableboy) *or* Stadlin (*or* Stableboy) *or* Firestone (*or* Stableboy) *or* Hoppo (*or* Stableboy) *or* Cat; Hermio *or* [Aberzanes] *or* [Lord Governor] *or* [Duke] *or* [Francisca]

FIRESTONE (83 lines): Antonio *or* Gentleman (2.1); Stableboy

FLORIDA (31 lines): Gentleman (2.1); Old Woman *or* Stableboy; Cat

FRANCISCA (227 lines): Fernando; Servant (1.1); [Cat]

GASPERO (114 lines): Stableboy *or* Old Woman

GENTLEMAN (2.1; 2 lines): any but Sebastian, Gaspero, Lord Governor, Antonio, Isabella, Francisa, Aberzanes

HECATE (263 lines): Old Woman (*or* Amoretta); Fernando (*or* Amoretta)

HERMIO (42 lines): Fernando; Stableboy (*or* Hecate *or* Stadlin *or* Firestone *or* Hoppo); Hecate (*or* Stableboy) *or* Stadlin (*or* Stableboy) *or* Firestone (*or* Stableboy) *or* Hoppo (*or* Stableboy) *or* Cat

HOPPO (4 lines): Fernando; Antonio; Amoretta *or* Duke *or* Hermio

ISABELLA (178 lines): Old Woman *or* Stableboy; Cat

LORD GOVERNOR (104 lines): Fernando; Cat; Old Woman *or* Stableboy

OLD WOMAN (1 line): any but Amoretta, Almachildes, Aberzanes, Francisca, Stableboy

SEBASTIAN (245 lines): Old Woman *or* Stableboy

STABLEBOY (3 lines): any but Aberzanes, Almachildes, Duchess, Francisca, Old Woman

STADLIN (20 lines): Fernando *or* Servant (1.1); Amoretta; [Duke]; [Florida]

Most crowded scene: 5.3: 12 (+ 2 mute servants)

111 **common trick** usual practice
119 **professor** one who makes a profession of, a professional

THE TRAGEDY OF MACBETH: A GENETIC TEXT

Text edited by Gary Taylor, introduced by Inga-Stina Ewbank

IN including *The Tragedy of Macbeth* in an edition of *The Collected Works of Thomas Middleton* the intention is not to dispute the fact that the greater part of this play, by far, was written by William Shakespeare. On the other hand, the consensus of editorial and critical opinion, since the Clarendon edition of 1869, is that there are non-Shakespearean interpolations in the first printed text of *Macbeth*, the 1623 Folio; and recent scholarship points unmistakably to Middleton as the author of these. The Folio text calls for the performance of two songs, referred to only by their opening phrases, '*Come away, come away, &c.*' (3.5.36.1) and '*Blacke Spirits, &c.*' (4.1.43.1), which can be found in full in Middleton's tragicomedy *The Witch*; the text of both is printed, with minor variants, in the 1674 edition of William Davenant's *Macbeth*, which is clearly based on a prompt copy of Shakespeare's play. Middleton's hand can also be seen in the Hecate material framing these songs, in 3.5 and 4.1. Gary Taylor concludes that Middleton wrote about eleven per cent of the adapted text, and Stephen Orgel notes that in performance the added songs 'would have been accompanied by dances, which means that in the theatre these scenes took a good deal longer than they do on the page'. Middleton may also be responsible for cutting one quarter or more of the original. The cuts cannot be recovered, of course, but this edition typographically distinguishes material probably altered or added by Middleton. *Macbeth* is presented here, then, as part of both the Shakespeare and the Middleton canon, to be read and seen if not at the intersection of the two canons at least at a point where one touches the other rather more than tangentially.

The interpolations have on the whole had a bad press: disapproved of by editors, ignored by critics, and almost invariably cut by modern theatre directors although, as Brooke points out, they 'form the core of the operatic development of the play which held the stage' until the twentieth century (53). In the Restoration, Davenant's staging of *Macbeth* delighted Samuel Pepys with its 'variety of dancing and music' (19 April 1667), and to eighteenth- and nineteenth-century audiences *Macbeth* was a play of spectacle and music—indeed Verdi's opera (1847) was based on, and not a far cry from, contemporary London stage versions. Twentieth-century distaste for the Hecate scenes is part of a more general purism, the theatrical equivalent of the scholarly search for authenticity, for the 'original' play. If *Macbeth* is seen as Shakespeare's play, with the stress on 'Shakespeare's' rather than on 'play', then it is also natural to see Middleton's additions as contaminating a text 'owned' by Shakespeare. For all our knowledge of Renaissance stage practice, we find it easier to approach a play text in terms of the imaginative coherence imposed on it by an individual mind than as the record of stage performances. We know that in the Elizabethan and Jacobean theatre the company, not the author, owned the text, and that in a play kept in active repertory cuts, revisions, and additions would be made to suit particular performances—at court, for example, or in the provinces—or to adapt the play to changing theatre conditions or popular taste. Title-pages of printed texts often proudly claim 'new additions'. We know that Shakespeare, as not only playwright but also actor and shareholder in his company, would have had more control than most authors over the performing texts of his plays, at least until he left the theatre, in or about 1613; but also that even at the height of his professional power he regarded collaboration as normal. So, of course, did Middleton, who wrote alone, in collaboration, and as an adapter, and for several companies, including the King's Men. Both would have been baffled by the terms, still fundamental to much thinking about Renaissance drama, in which Henrik Ibsen in 1883 defended his 'ownership' of a play that reviewers had found derivative, by insisting that 'that which makes a work of art the spiritual property of its originator is that he has imprinted on it the stamp of his own personality'.

In the playhouse the additions to *Macbeth* clearly proved their worth, and Heminges and Condell were proud to include in the Folio an augmented and altered text of *Macbeth*, although it could not possibly have been entirely Shakespeare's 'spiritual property' and may well have two personalities imprinted on it. A further comparison with Ibsen may be to the point. Once he had gained recognition as a playwright, Ibsen preserved the manuscript drafts of his plays with a care which suggests that he wanted posterity to see and study them as underlying the printed corpus, pointing the difference from, and the way to, the final, authoritative version in which each phrase and each structural unit had reached its definitive form. For *Macbeth* we have only the Folio text, and the way to it, through revisions, cuts, and additions, must remain conjectural. This is not the place to rehearse all the many conjectures that have been made, ever since Clark and Wright (1869) assigned 300 lines of *Macbeth* to Middleton. But R. V. Holdsworth's work on Middleton's collaboration with Shakespeare must be mentioned, as he has demonstrated remarkably convincing signs of Middleton's hand—the idiosyncratic stage direction '*Enter . . . meeting . . .*' (1.2 and 3.5) and other verbal characteristics—not only in the Hec-

Three weïrd sisters meet the mounted Macbeth and Banquo; from Holinshed, *Historie of Scotlande* (1577)

ate passages but also at a number of other points in the text. It seems possible that Middleton was responsible both for cuts which produced the famous brevity and tightness of the extant text and for additions which either merely bridge such cuts or, as with the Hecate scenes, bring in his own material for reuse. Such recycling is a typically Middletonian practice. Thus, for example, he reuses a song from *Masque of Cupids* in *More Dissemblers Besides Women*, and a song from *Dissemblers* in *The Widow*; both plays were written in the period when he is most likely to have been revising *Macbeth* (about 1616).

In order to see how the text of *Macbeth* relates to Middleton's as well as Shakespeare's canon it is necessary to review briefly the relation between this play and *The Witch*, since the same songs appear in both plays and the Hecate passages are inextricably connected with the songs. Because Hecate shares responses with singers who have plot parts in *The Witch*, the songs are almost bound to have been originally written for that play. The likelihood on which the following discussion is built is that some time after Shakespeare's retirement from the theatre Middleton made additions to a text of *Macbeth* which already had the weïrd sisters and a cauldron scene (4.1); that he interpolated the two songs and a dance from the 'ignorantly-ill-fated' *Witch* which, probably written in 1616, had fallen foul of the censor; and that, in order to motivate the appearance of Hecate in these, he added the rest of what is now 3.5 and some lines in 4.1 (39–43; 143–50). The result was to give the play a new dimension of theatrical magic. Middleton may well have seen himself as both underscoring Shakespeare's intentions in the play and adding his own stamp by local subversions of those intentions.

To support and develop this point some re-tracing of the road to the Folio text is necessary. The play was first performed in 1606–7; and, whether or not its first performance was before James I, there is little doubt that the 'weïrd sisters' owe something to the King's interest in witchcraft. Ben Jonson capitalized on that interest in the spectacular antimasque of witches which he devised for his *Masque of Queens*, performed at court on 2 February

Three bearded witches meet the horseless Macbeth and Banquo; from a 1901 edition of Mary Lamb's *Tales from Shakespeare*

1609 and printed soon thereafter. It is possible that in a first version of *Macbeth* the weïrd sisters were nothing like the 'secret black and midnight hags' we now know. The creatures who Banquo thinks 'should be women | and yet your beards forbid me to interpret | that you are so' (1.3.42–4), summon up the gender ambivalence of an early modern play like *The Roaring Girl* or of a postmodern image like the Dutch artist Charlotte Schleiffert's 'Bearded Women Make Great Leaders'. It does not seem to have anything in common with Simon Forman's account of the performance of *Macbeth* that he saw at the Globe on 20 April 1611, which refers to Macbeth's encounter with 'three women fairies or nymphs'. Holinshed, in telling of Macbeth, has the phrase 'some nymphs or fairies' as well as a woodcut representing three quite un-haglike ladies in medieval costume. Forman's own interest in the occult, as well as Holinshed's reference to Macbeth's later trust in the words of 'certain wizards' and the prophecies of 'a certain witch', makes it oddly significant that Forman's account has nothing corresponding to *Macbeth* 4.1, perhaps because as originally written the scene was much less impressive than it had become by 1623.

Yet Shakespeare's imagination was powerfully engaged with the 'charm of powerful trouble' that brews in 4.1.

There is some overlap of *materia magica* between Jonson's and Shakespeare's witches, but the Jonsonian hell-broth remains verbal only, whereas in *Macbeth* a cauldron is producing a real, nasty stew surreally compacted of social and moral evil:

finger of birth-strangled babe
ditch-delivered by a drab
make the gruel thick and slab

At the same time Shakespeare integrates the cauldron scene with Macbeth's descent into a hell of his own making. The king bursts in on the witches' ritual with his chaos-defying demand to know his future; and in response they stage for him a show that is so structured as to repeat in a different theatrical mode the ironies of the banquet scene (3.4). The banquet, intended to be a formal occasion in celebration of Macbeth's kingship, collapses into shambles because of the repeated appearance of the ghost of Banquo. The witches' show has its own far more spectacular formality. Macbeth is equivocally assured of his future in a perverse version of a royal entertainment. The witches act as choric presenters; and thunder substitutes for music. It is ironically appropriate that Macbeth should refer to his royal self, in this stage configuration, as 'our high-placed Macbeth' 4.1.115. It is ironic, too, that when the witches, directors of the show, want it to end on Macbeth's belief that he 'shall live the lease of nature, pay his breath | To time and mortal custom', it is his own insistence on being 'satisfied' that provokes the climax: the cauldron sinks and oboes announce '*A show of eight kings, the last with a glass in his hand*'.

On stage, this looks like an inversion of the fundamental gesture of the Stuart court masque which lodges all past, present, and future virtue in the king. In *The Masque of Queens* the twelve witches of the antimasque threaten to bring chaos but vanish to a loud blast of music as the scene changes to the House of Fame displaying the twelve queens. Eleven of them are 'of times long gone'; the twelfth is 'Bel-Anna' (Queen Anne) who possesses all the virtues for which the others were famed but of course ultimately 'Confesseth all the lustre of her merit: | To you, most royal and most happy king' (407–8). In *Macbeth* the witches remain in charge; and in the procession of kings, staged to 'show his eyes and grieve his heart', Macbeth's past and present crimes are seen to control his future 'to th' crack of doom'. Judgement is passed on Macbeth from the point of view of the audience's present as the eighth king holds up the magic mirror in which Macbeth sees 'many more', some carrying 'twofold balls and treble sceptres'—as did the ninth Stuart monarch, James VI of Scotland, who was also James I of England and Wales.

The direction in which Shakespeare had taken *Macbeth* would have seemed congenial to Middleton who, from the beginning to the end of his career, excelled in the ironic use of conventional dramatic devices. He could write 'straight' pageants, but he could also use pageant and masque material to ironic ends, from *Your Five Gallants* to *Women, Beware Women*. As he added music, song, and dance to *Macbeth*, he resolutely introduced Hecate as a formal presenter of such material. Her two appearances are framed by self-reflexive references to the 'art' of the witch scenes. When she first enters, in a clap of thunder, it is to rebuke the three witches for trafficking with Macbeth without calling on her to 'show the glory of our art' (3.5.9)—a nudge to the text for not making enough, theatrically, of the witch world. With the 'Come away' scene the audience is then shown that 'glory'. In 4.1 her last few lines (assuming that they are meant to be hers) almost amount to putting quotation marks around the interpolated passages:

come sisters cheer we up his sprites
and show the best of our delights
I'll charm the air to give a sound
while you perform your antic round
that this great king may kindly say
our duties did his welcome pay (4.1.145–50)

Within the fiction of the play the idea of cheering Macbeth up in this fashion is as ironic as that of Dr Faustus taking pleasure in the pageant of the Seven Deadly Sins. Un-Shakespearean as these lines may seem, Middleton makes their irony structurally cohesive, for the 'welcome' for 'this great king' recalls the elaborate welcoming ceremony in the banquet scene, where the 'hearty welcome' that Macbeth offers his guests is only one of four uses of the word in some thirty lines (3.4.2, 5, 7, 34)—a ceremony interrupted first by the First Murderer and then by the first unwelcome visit of Banquo's ghost, whose second visit disrupts the Lords' drinking 'our duties and the pledge'. But the thrust of Hecate's lines goes beyond the dramatic fiction, to self-referential theatricality. As the ultimate irony, the last two lines could well be commemorating, as has been often suggested, an actual performance before James I—the king who could not make up his mind about witchcraft, but enjoyed 'shows'.

It has also often been suggested that the music and choreography of the witches' dance at 4.1.150 were those used in the antimasque of *The Masque of Queens* (Brooke; Cutts). If so, we have Jonson's account of how, to the sound of 'a strange and sudden music', the dance was executed, 'full of preposterous change, and gesticulation', the witches doing 'all things contrary to the custom of men, dancing back to back, hip to hip, their hands joined, and making their circles backward, to the left hand, with strange fantastic motions of their heads and bodies'; the dance ended when 'on the sudden was heard a sound of loud music, as if many instruments had given one blast', at which point 'the hags... quite vanished' (327–336). If there was a sameness, it would be lost on an audience at the Globe, though effective at a court performance. But whether transposed directly from Jonson's masque or from 5.2 of *The Witch*, in its *Macbeth* context the dance both completes the pattern of an un-royal entertainment for Macbeth and asserts the witches' freedom. Macbeth, whose 'society' (3.4.3) was seen to disintegrate in the banquet scene, here stands 'amazedly', utterly alone and frozen into immobility, while in glaring visual contrast the 'sisters' join hands to affirm their community in an 'antic round'. There is a world elsewhere, to which Macbeth has no access, but which the theatre audience glimpses through the enactment of the witches' literally marvellous freedom. The dancing witches in *The Masque of Queens* are routed as the scene changes to the main masque, and later they appear bound before the queens' chariots. The witches in *Macbeth* dance and vanish freely, as in *The Witch*, leaving the stage to Macbeth for a speech which is the antithesis of the way the traditional masque ends, as for example in *Oberon* (361–68), with the wish that this glorious moment last forever: 'Let this pernicious hour | Stand aye accursèd in the calendar' (4.1.151–2).

What the introduction of the song and dance in 4.1 achieves, while building on the framework laid down by Shakespeare, is to make the scene less focused on the moral self-destruction of Macbeth and to shift the emphasis on to the witches as being in command, free and unbounded. In introducing the song 'Black spirits and white', headed in the manuscript of *The Witch* 'A Charm Song: about a Vessel', Middleton might be thought simply to be adding more of the same to the cauldron scene and the weïrd sisters' 'Round about the cauldron go'. But this is not so. The music for the song has not survived, but the text reads, as Brooke points out, 'like a singing game such as children play, leading to a girl claiming her own choice of boy' (229). Whether or not it draws on a traditional rhyme, or even ballad, the effect is to lift the scene towards gaiety as it moves from the three weïrd sisters' oppressive rhythms—'double double toil and trouble'—to a choric jingle, 'Round around around about about | all ill come running in all good keep out', in which words like 'good' and 'ill' are merely counters. In *The Witch*, where this song follows a sinister visit to Hecate by the Duchess who wants a means to quickly do away with a tool villain, the lift into an a-moral world is identified by Hecate at the end of the song: 'I am so light | At any mischief! There's no villainy | But is a tune, methinks' (5.2.81–3).

This 'light'-ness, literally realized by flying machinery and mimetically rendered in song, is also a quality Middleton transposes from *The Witch* into the scene which became 3.5 of *Macbeth*. As plot goes, its only function is to prepare for the meeting 'at the pit of Acheron', but it must have been a theatrical highlight at the Globe or Blackfriars. The sudden shift, as we move from the oppressive ending of 3.4 and Macbeth's descent into his 'strange and self-abuse', is not merely one of tone; it offers the audience the kind of contrast which only the theatre can produce: magic made 'real' as a way to an alternative, literally marvellous world. 'Come away come away' is not simply a song; it is a kind of proto-operatic scene in which Hecate, while anointing herself for transvection, engages in a sung dialogue with voices in the air and with a thoroughly embodied 'spirit like a cat' who descends and with whom she ascends. Rising, she sings to celebrate her freedom and the joys of flight 'when the moon shines fair', and the chorus of voices above repeat her triumphant last four lines:

> no ring of bells to our ears sounds
> no howls of wolves no yelps of hounds
> no not the noise of waters breach
> or cannons' throat our height can reach (3.5.68–71)

These words evoke an ethos far from the weïrd sisters' 'fair is foul and foul is fair', and a world opposed to Macbeth's world of darkness, tolling bells and howling wolves. The words were probably set to music by Robert Johnson, who composed for the King's Men as well as for court masques; and Raphael Seligmann who has analysed the score and the way it is adapted to the text finds in it 'irreverent allusions to liturgical and courtly musical tradition'. Clearly, there is neither verbally nor musically anything grotesque or threatening about this song; the triumphant negatives that define 'our height' are a contrast to, not a deepening of, the evil in Macbeth's world. In Shakespeare's thematic structure the only such contrast is the loyal world of England under Edward the Confessor who—like James I—touches for King's Evil (4.3.142–60). The 'come away' interlude is subversive in an un-Shakespearean way in so far as it enacts an alternative not of benevolent monarchy but of positive, joyful anarchy and so makes the play as a whole that much less royalist. It is as though Middleton should have dropped an Autolycus, or even a Falstaff, into the morally determined world of Macbeth—but then the analogy itself suggests that he might not have seen his interpolation as wholly un-Shakespearean.

Nor might he have seen himself as doing anything wholly untypical in terms of his own aesthetics. Incorporating into *Macbeth* parts of *The Witch* meant returning them to a play which had acted as a sounding board for *The Witch*. I use this image, rather than 'source', for while Jacobean plays are generally full of more or less conscious echoes of each other, Middleton has a way—particularly pronounced in the tragicomedies he was writing in this period—of using intertextuality with a difference: of drawing on audiences' reminiscence of another play or plays (Ewbank, 1991). The manuscript of *The Witch* tells us that it had been 'long since acted by His Majesty's seruants at the Blackfriars'; Middleton wrote it to be performed by actors whom the audience would also have seen in *Macbeth*—an audience who could hardly help seeing one witch play as an alternative to the other. *The Witch* supplied a fictive world in which the words and deeds of 'these juggling fiends' can be both laughed and marvelled at, and where there is always a way out for the human characters. At the same time the play can be seen to be sceptical about its own tragicomic resolution, as Middleton questions the very conventions he uses. The bed-trick, for example, is shown up for what it is—a facile way of turning tragedy into comedy—by the bathetic moral drawn by Almachildes when the final scene reveals the last in the series of deceptions played on him, and on the audience: 'This comes of scarves: I'll never more wear | An haberdasher's shop before mine eyes again' (5.3.123–4). The plot twists of the denouement are so resolutely abrupt as to draw attention to their own artifice. Everything ends happily, but only as long as morality is brushed under the carpet—or covered by a scarf. The audience of *The Witch* was hardly allowed to forget the tragic alternative to the tragicomedy.

In *Macbeth*, for all that Macbeth implores 'seeling night' to 'scarf up the tender eye of pitiful day' (3.2.47–8), there is no way of blinding oneself to the logic of the deed and its consequences—of being 'the deed's creature' as Middleton was to call it in *The Changeling*. Middleton's interpolations do not turn the play into a tragicomedy or radically change its overall moral structure. The lightness of being of the witches in the interpolated passages introduces a note of subversive freedom; but in the end the logic of doom closes in on Macbeth all the more relentlessly for these glimpses of spirits who do not merely equivocate but simply don't care—who, unlike human beings, have access to a world elsewhere.

This is where the other function of Middleton's Hecate becomes operative. As we have seen, she is a metatheatrical device, but she also represents, in her long speech in 3.5, an attempt to bridge two worlds. She is not the dramatic character of *The Witch*, with her libido and her son, Firestone—the play's chief comic part, who appears in all the witch scenes as a sneering deflater of magic and its accoutrements. Nor does she have the divinity or convey the universal horror implied in Macbeth's vision of evil when 'Witchcraft celebrates | Pale Hecate's offerings' (2.1.51–2). Middleton is not, in her speech, trying to write Shakespearean lines, as modern directors have been known to do. He is translating Hecate into his own theatre language. In a sense she becomes a figure who, like characters in his comedies or the Cardinal in *Women, Beware Women*, rises out of the turmoil of the action to moralize it; but the moral register and terms here are her own. This kind of translation—into a pragmatic syntax and a discourse relying on the literal force of a plain vocabulary—results in presenting Macbeth as 'a wayward son | spiteful and wrathful who as others do | loves for his own ends not for you'. Hecate's preview, then, of 4.1 where the spirits 'by the strength of their illusion | shall draw him on to his confusion', becomes:

> he shall spurn fate scorn death and bear
> his hopes 'bove wisdom grace and fear

To anyone who treasures the metaphorical density of *Macbeth* (and who does not?) this may seem nugatory: verbally too thin, morally too simple. But if we see the lines in the full context of what Middleton was trying to do—making Hecate the presenter of a kind of Triumph of Truth more spectacular than anything the weïrd sisters were capable of—then they are not so much a loss as pointers to a new kind of gain: a dimension in which theatricality itself—the 'illusion' enacted by Hecate and her witches—adds a measure to Macbeth's tragedy.

Some forty lines into the cauldron scene, Hecate arrives to cheer the proceedings:

> O well done I commend your pains
> and everyone shall share i'th'gains

The second of her lines has a meta-textual potential which points us back to what the additions meant in the playhouse. There is no account book to record payment to Middleton for 'additions in *Macbeth*'. What we can be sure of in reading the augmented *Macbeth* is that the 'gains' were those of the company and its sharers—as well as its audiences.

SEE ALSO

Music and dance: *Companion*, 153 ('Come away'), 158, 160 (dances)
Textual introduction and apparatus: *Companion*, 690
Authorship and date: *Companion*, 383
Other Middleton–Shakespeare works: *Timon*, 467; *Measure*, 1542

WILLIAM SHAKESPEARE, adapted by THOMAS MIDDLETON

The Tragedy of Macbeth

[for the King's Men at the Blackfriars]

1.1 *Sc. 1* ***1.1***
incipit actus primus
thunder and lightning
enter three weïrd sisters ***witches***

FIRST
when shall we three meet again
in thunder lightning or in rain

SECOND
when the hurly burly's done
when the battle's lost and won

THIRD
that will be ere set of sun

FIRST
where the place

SECOND
upon the heath

THIRD
there to meet with Macbeth
[a cat mews within]

FIRST
I come Greymalkin
[a toad croaks within]

SECOND
Paddock calls
[an owl shrieks within]

THIRD
anon

ALL
fair is foul and foul is fair
hover through the fog and filthy air *exeunt*

1.2 *Sc. 2* ***1.2***
alarum within enter King Malcolm Donalbain
Lennox with attendants

[ ]
the merciless Macdonald
worthy to be a rebel for to that
the multiplying villainies of nature
do swarm upon him from the western isles
of kerns and galloglasses is supplied
and fortune on his damnèd quarrel smiling
showed like a rebel's whore
[ ]
[Enter]
[ ]
for brave Macbeth well he deserves that name
disdaining fortune with his brandished steel
which smoked with bloody executïon
like valour's minïon carved out his passage
[ ]

Adaptation. Passages apparently added or rewritten by Middleton are printed in bold type; passages apparently deleted or intended for deletion are printed in grey; transposed passages are printed in grey where Shakespeare probably placed them, and in bold where Middleton apparently moved them. For detailed explanations of the evidence for Middleton's alterations to Shakespeare's original, see 'Canon and Chronology', *Companion* 383.

Punctuation. This edition removes all punctuation and all capitalization at the beginning of sentences or verse lines. The punctuation in the text first printed in 1623 bears little, if any, relation to the authors' intentions; it reflects the preferences of different compositors and scribes. Neither playwright capitalized the beginnings of sentences or verse lines. This completely unpunctuated text lets readers decide for themselves how to interpret the words. For a more detailed discussion of the original text and the decision not to punctuate this edition, see 'Textual Introduction', *Companion* 690. For Middleton's punctuation, see *A Game at Chesse: An Early Form*.

Commentary. Glossarial commentaries, like punctuation, make interpretive choices about which meanings are appropriate and which are not. This commentary to *Macbeth* is limited to clarifying aspects of the process of adaptation signalled typographically in the text.

Title ***Blackfriars*** The indoor theatre (where the King's Men began performing in 1608 or 1609) certainly had machinery for elaborate 'flying' scenes, like 3.5, added by Middleton.

1.1.0.1 *Sc. 1* *Macbeth* was originally written for the Globe, *c.*1606, where there were no act intervals. The text was adapted for the later theatrical convention of five acts separated by musical intervals.

0.4 ***witches*** Middleton's major adaptation was to transform into witches the three characters who are identified as 'weïrd sisters' in Shakespeare's chief historical source and in passages clearly written by Shakespeare.

7.1–1.1.8 ***a cat*** ... **anon** probably added as part of the process of identifying Shakespeare's 'weïrd sisters' as witches

10 **hover through** This suggests that the witches are flying, a spectacular effect also used in 3.5; the sisters do not fly in Shakespeare's source. Shakespeare might have had the sisters 'drink the ... air', as in *Tempest* 5.1.102 and *Timon* 1.84.

1.2 Middleton apparently abbreviated Shakespeare's more extended original battle sequence, transposing some material and providing transitional phrases of his own. The original battle sequence might have been much more extensively dramatized, like those in *Troilus and Cressida*, *Antony and Cleopatra*, or *Coriolanus*.

KING
O valiant cousin worthy gentleman
[ ]
as whence the sun 'gins his reflectïon
shipwrecking storms and direful thunders strike
[ ]
Enter ***meeting a bleeding captain***
KING
what bloody man is that he can report
as seemeth by his plight of the revolt
the newest state
MALCOLM this is the sergeant
who like a good and hardy soldier fought
'gainst my captivity hail brave friend
say to the king the knowledge of the broil
as thou didst leave it
CAPTAIN **doubtful it stood**
as two spent swimmers that do cling together
and choke their art the merciless Macdonald
worthy to be a rebel for to that
the multiplying villainies of nature
do swarm upon him from the western isles
of kerns and galloglasses is supplied
and fortune on his damnèd quarrel smiling
showed like a rebel's whore but all's too weak
for brave Macbeth well he deserves that name
disdaining fortune with his brandished steel
which smoked with bloody executïon
like valour's minion
carved out his passage till he faced the slave
which ne'er shook hands nor bade farewell to him
till he unseamed him from the nave to th' chops
and fixed his head upon our battlements
KING
O valiant cousin worthy gentleman
CAPTAIN
as whence the sun 'gins his reflectïon
shipwrecking storms and direful thunders strike
so from that spring whence comfort seemed to come
discomfort swells mark king of Scotland mark
no sooner justice had with valour armed
compelled these skipping kerns to trust their heels
but the Norwegian lord surveying vantage
with furbished arms and new supplies of men
began a fresh assault
KING
dismayed not this our captains Macbeth and Banquo
CAPTAIN
yes as sparrows eagles or the hare the lion
if I say sooth I must report they were
as cannons overcharged with double cracks
so they doubly redoubled strokes upon the foe
except they meant to bathe in reeking wounds
or memorize another Golgotha
I cannot tell
but I am faint my gashes cry for help
KING
so well thy words become thee as thy wounds
they smack of honour both go get him surgeons
[*exit captain with attendants*]
enter Ross and Angus
who comes here
MALCOLM the worthy thane of Ross
LENNOX
what haste looks through his eyes so should he look
that seems to speak things strange
ROSS God save the king
KING
whence cam'st thou worthy thane
ROSS from Fife great king
where the Norwegian banners flout the sky
and fan our people cold [
]
Norway himself with numbers terrible
assisted by that most disloyal traitor
the thane of Cawdor began a dismal conflict
till that Bellona's bridegroom lapped in proof
confronted him with self comparisons
point against point rebellious arm 'gainst arm
curbing his lavish spirit and to conclude
the victory fell on us
KING great happiness
ROSS that now
Sweno the Norways' king craves composition
nor would we deign him burial of his men
till he disbursëd at Saint Colum's Inch
ten thousand dollars to our general use
KING
no more that thane of Cawdor shall deceive
our bosom interest go pronounce his present death
and with his former title greet Macbeth
ROSS I'll see it done
KING
what he hath lost noble Macbeth hath won
exeunt [*severally*]

Sc. 3 **1.3** 1.3
thunder enter the three weïrd sisters ***witches***
FIRST
where hast thou been sister
SECOND
killing swine

44.2 ***and Angus*** probably a remnant of the original, more expansive version of the scene, in which Angus took part

50–2 **cold [ ] Norway** Here and elsewhere, square brackets indicate places where we conjecture that a passage of indeterminate length and content may have been cut. We have not tried to identify all the metrical or grammatical gaps in the text which might have been caused by cutting; many cuts would have left no traces at all.

1.3.1–27 FIRST ... **come** This passage may originally have been part of 4.1; without it, the sisters are initially ambiguous.

THIRD **sister where thou**
FIRST
a sailor's wife had chestnuts in her lap
and munched and munched and munched give me quoth I
aroint thee witch the rump-fed runnion cries
her husband's to Aleppo gone master o'th' Tiger
but in a sieve I'll thither sail
and like a rat without a tail
I'll do I'll do and I'll do
SECOND
I'll give thee a wind
FIRST
thou'rt kind
THIRD
and I another
FIRST
I myself have all the other
and the very ports they blow
all the quarters that they know
i'th' shipman's card
I'll drain him dry as hay
sleep shall neither night nor day
hang upon his penthouse lid
he shall live a man forbid
weary se'en-nights nine times nine
shall he dwindle peak and pine
though his barque cannot be lost
yet it shall be tempest-tossed
look what I have
SECOND **show me show me**
FIRST
here I have a pilot's thumb
wrecked as homeward he did come
drum within
THIRD
a drum a drum
Macbeth doth come
ALL [*dancing in a ring*]
the weïrd sisters hand in hand
posters of the sea and land
thus do go about about
thrice to thine and thrice to mine
and thrice again to make up nine
peace the charm's wound up

enter Macbeth and Banquo [*on horseback*]
MACBETH
so foul and fair a day I have not seen
BANQUO
how far is't called to Forres what are these
fairies or nymphs **so withered and** so wild in their attire
that look not like th'inhabitants o'th' earth
and yet are on't live you or are you aught
that man may question you seem to understand me
by each at once her chappy finger laying
upon her skinny lips **you should be women**
and yet your beards forbid me to interpret
that you are so
MACBETH speak if you can what are you
FIRST
all hail Macbeth hail to thee thane of Glamis
SECOND
all hail Macbeth hail to thee thane of Cawdor
THIRD
all hail Macbeth that shalt be king hereafter
BANQUO
good sir why do you start and seem to fear
things that do sound so fair i'th' name of truth
are ye fantastical or that indeed
which outwardly ye show my noble partner
you greet with present grace and great prediction
of noble having and of royal hope
that he seems rapt withal to me you speak not
if you can look into the seeds of time
and say which grain will grow and which will not
speak then to me who neither beg nor fear
your favours nor your hate
FIRST hail
SECOND hail
THIRD hail
FIRST
lesser than Macbeth and greater
SECOND
not so happy yet much happier
THIRD
thou shalt get kings though thou be none
so all hail Macbeth and Banquo
FIRST
Banquo and Macbeth all hail
MACBETH
stay you imperfect speakers tell me more

30 ***dancing*** For music that may have been used, see *Companion*, p. 158.

35.1 [*on horseback*] The 1611 spectator's account specifies that they entered this scene 'riding'. That may indicate dialogue (talking about horses offstage), but probably refers to the actual appearance of a horse or horses in the theatre, perhaps riding through the yard toward the stage. *Alarum for London* (1599?) and *The Late Lancashire Witches* (1634), both performed at the Globe, require a horse. Indoor theatres did not attempt such effects. Removing the horse(s) probably also removed an unknown amount of dialogue.

38–45 **so withered . . . are so** A spectator at a performance of *MacBeth* at the Globe in 1611 described the weïrd sisters in this scene as 'three women fairies or nymphs', a characterization that fits their presentation as 'nymphs or fairies' in Shakespeare's historical sources. The original text might well have contained something like the phrase found in Shakespeare's source. The Middletonian words and phrases in this speech transform the three figures who could be played by adult male actors, rather than boys.

42–3 **chappy . . . skinny** These negative adjectives might be Middleton's rather than Shakespeare's.

by Sinel's death I know I am thane of Glamis
but how of Cawdor the thane of Cawdor lives
a prosperous gentleman and to be king
stands not within the prospect of belief
no more than to be Cawdor say from whence
you owe this strange intelligence or why
upon this blasted heath you stop our way
with such prophetic greeting speak I charge you
witches vanish

BANQUO
the earth hath bubbles as the water has
and these are of them whither are they vanished

MACBETH
into the air and what seemed corporal
melted as breath into the wind would they had stayed

BANQUO
were such things here as we do speak about
or have we eaten on the insane root
that takes the reason prisoner

MACBETH
your children shall be kings

BANQUO
you shall be king

MACBETH
and thane of Cawdor too went it not so

BANQUO
to th' selfsame tune and words who's here
enter Ross and Angus

ROSS
the king hath happily received Macbeth
the news of thy success and when he reads
thy personal venture in the rebels' fight
his wonders and his praises do contend
which should be thine or his silenced with that
in viewing o'er the rest o'th' selfsame day
he finds thee in the stout Norwegian ranks
nothing afeard of what thyself didst make
strange images of death as thick as hail
came post with post and every one did bear
thy praises in his kingdom's great defence
and poured them down before him

ANGUS
we are sent
to give thee from our royal master thanks
only to herald thee into his sight
not pay thee

ROSS
and for an earnest of a greater honour
he bade me from him call thee thane of Cawdor
in which addition hail most worthy thane
for it is thine

BANQUO
what can the devil speak true

MACBETH
the thane of Cawdor lives why do you dress me
in borrowed robes

ANGUS
who was the thane lives yet
but under heavy judgement bears that life
which he deserves to lose whether he was combined
with those of Norway or did line the rebel
with hidden help and vantage or that with both
he laboured in his country's wrack I know not
but treasons capital confessed and proved
have overthrown him

MACBETH
Glamis and thane of Cawdor
the greatest is behind thanks for your pains
do you not hope your children shall be kings
when those that gave to me the thane of Cawdor
promised no less to them

BANQUO
that trusted home
might yet enkindle you unto the crown
besides the thane of Cawdor but 'tis strange
and oftentimes to win us to our harm
the instruments of darkness tell us truths
win us with honest trifles to betray's
in deepest consequence cousins a word I pray you

MACBETH two truths are told
as happy prologues to the swelling act
of the imperial theme I thank you gentlemen
this supernatural soliciting
cannot be ill cannot be good if ill
why hath it given me earnest of success
commencing in a truth I am thane of Cawdor
if good why do I yield to that suggestion
whose horrid image doth unfix my hair
and make my seated heart knock at my ribs
against the use of nature present fears
are less than horrible imaginings
my thought whose murder yet is but fantastical
shakes so my single state of man that function
is smothered in surmise and nothing is
but what is not

BANQUO
look how our partner's rapt

MACBETH
if chance will have me king why chance may crown
me
without my stir

BANQUO
new honours come upon him
like our strange garments cleave not to their mould
but with the aid of use

MACBETH
come what come may
time and the hour runs through the roughest day

BANQUO
worthy Macbeth we stay upon your leisure

MACBETH
give me your favour my dull brain was wrought
with things forgotten kind gentlemen your pains
are registered where every day I turn
the leaf to read them let us toward the king
think upon what hath chanced and at more time
the interim having weighed it let us speak
our free hearts each to other

BANQUO very gladly

MACBETH till then enough come friends *exeunt*

1.4 *Sc. 4* 1.4

flourish enter King Lennox Malcolm Donalbain and attendants

KING

is execution done on Cawdor or are not
those in commission yet returned

MALCOLM

my liege
they are not yet come back but I have spoke
with one that saw him die who did report
that very frankly he confessed his treasons
implored your highness pardon and set forth
a deep repentance nothing in his life
became him like the leaving it he died
as one that had been studied in his death
to throw away the dearest thing he owed
as 'twere a careless trifle

KING

there's no art
to find the mind's construction in the face
he was a gentleman on whom I built
an absolute trust

enter Macbeth Banquo Ross and Angus

O worthiest cousin
the sin of my ingratitude even now
was heavy on me thou art so far before
that swiftest wing of recompense is slow
to overtake thee would thou hadst less deserved
that the proportion both of thanks and payment
might have been mine only I have left to say
more is thy due than more than all can pay

MACBETH

the service and the loyalty I owe
in doing pays itself your highness' part
is to receive our duties and our duties
are to your throne and state children and servants
which do but what they should by doing everything
safe toward your love and honour

KING

welcome hither
I have begun to plant thee and will labour
to make thee full of growing noble Banquo
that hast no less deserved nor must be known
no less to have done so let me enfold thee
and hold thee to my heart

BANQUO

there if I grow
the harvest is your own

KING

my plenteous joys
wanton in fullness seek to hide themselves
in drops of sorrow sons kinsmen thanes
and you whose places are the nearest know
we will establish our estate upon
our eldest Malcolm whom we name hereafter
the prince of Cumberland which honour must
not unaccompanied invest him only
but signs of nobleness like stars shall shine
on all deservers from hence to Inverness
and bind us further to you

MACBETH

the rest is labour which is not used for you
I'll be myself the harbinger and make joyful
the hearing of my wife with your approach
so humbly take my leave

KING

my worthy Cawdor

MACBETH

the prince of Cumberland that is a step
on which I must fall down or else o'erleap
for in my way it lies stars hide your fires
let not light see my black and deep desires
the eye wink at the hand yet let that be
which the eye fears when it is done to see *exit*

KING

true worthy Banquo he is full so valiant
and in his commendations I am fed
it is a banquet to me let's after him
whose care is gone before to bid us welcome
it is a peerless kinsman *flourish exeunt*

Sc. 5 1.5 1.5

enter Macbeth's wife alone with a letter

LADY they met me in the day of success and I have learned by the perfect'st report they have more in them than mortal knowledge when I burned in desire to question them further they made themselves air into which they vanished whiles I stood rapt in the wonder of it came missives from the king who all-hailed me thane of Cawdor by which title before these weïrd sisters saluted me and referred me to the coming on of time with hail king that shalt be this have I thought good to deliver thee my dearest partner of greatness that thou mightst not lose the dues of rejoicing by being ignorant of what greatness is promised thee lay it to thy heart and farewell

Glamis thou art and Cawdor and shalt be
what thou art promised yet do I fear thy nature
it is too full o'th' milk of human kindness
to catch the nearest way thou wouldst be great
art not without ambition but without
the illness should attend it what thou wouldst highly
that wouldst thou holily wouldst not play false
and yet wouldst wrongly win thou'dst have great Glamis
that which cries thus thou must do if thou have it
and that which rather thou dost fear to do
than wishest should be undone hie thee hither
that I may pour my spirits in thine ear
and chastise with the valour of my tongue
all that impedes thee from the golden round
which fate and metaphysical aid doth seem
to have thee crowned withal

enter messenger

what is your tidings

MESSENGER

the king comes here tonight

LADY

thou'rt mad to say it
is not thy master with him who were't so
would have informed for preparatïon

MESSENGER

so please you it is true our thane is coming

one of my fellows had the speed of him
who almost dead for breath had scarcely more
than would make up his message

LADY
give him tending
he brings great news *exit messenger*
the raven himself is hoarse
that croaks the fatal entërance of Duncan
under my battlements come you spirits
that tend on mortal thoughts unsex me here
and fill me from the crown to the toe topfull
of direst cruelty make thick my blood
stop up th'access and passage to remorse
that no compunctious visitings of nature
shake my fell purpose nor keep peace between
th'effect and it come to my woman's breasts
and take my milk for gall you murd'ring ministers
wherever in your sightless substances
you wait on nature's mischief come thick night
and pall thee in the dunnest smoke of hell
that my keen knife see not the wound it makes
nor heaven peep through the blanket of the dark
to cry hold hold

enter Macbeth

great Glamis worthy Cawdor
greater than both by the all-hail hereafter
thy letters have transported me beyond
this ignorant present and I feel now
the future in the instant

MACBETH
my dearest love
Duncan comes here tonight

LADY
and when goes hence

MACBETH
tomorrow as he purposes

LADY
O never
shall sun that morrow see
your face my thane is as a book where men
may read strange matters to beguile the time
look like the time bear welcome in your eye
your hand your tongue look like the innocent flower
but be the serpent under't he that's coming
must be provided for and you shall put
this night's great business into my dispatch
which shall to all our nights and days to come
give solely sovereign sway and masterdom

MACBETH
we will speak further

LADY
only look up clear
to alter favour ever is to fear
leave all the rest to me *exeunt*

1.6 *Sc. 6* **1.6**

oboes and torches enter King Malcolm Donalbain Banquo Lennox Macduff Ross Angus and attendants

KING
this castle hath a pleasant seat the air
nimbly and sweetly recommends itself
unto our gentle senses

BANQUO
this guest of summer
the temple-haunting martlet does approve
by his loved masonry that the heavens' breath
smells wooingly here no jutty frieze
buttress nor coign of vantage but this bird
hath made his pendant bed and procreant cradle
where they must breed and haunt I have observed
the air is delicate

enter Lady

KING
see see our honoured hostess
the love that follows us sometime is our trouble
which still we thank as love herein I teach you
how you shall bid God 'ield us for your pains
and thank us for your trouble

LADY
all our service
in every point twice done and then done double
were poor and single business to contend
against those honours deep and broad wherewith
your majesty loads our house for those of old
and the late dignities heaped up to them
we rest your hermits

KING
where's the thane of Cawdor
we coursed him at the heels and had a purpose
to be his purveyor but he rides well
and his great love sharp as his spur hath holp him
to his home before us fair and noble hostess
we are your guest tonight

LADY
your servants ever
have theirs themselves and what is theirs in count
to make their audit at your highness' pleasure
still to return your own

KING
give me your hand
conduct me to mine host we love him highly
and shall continue our graces towards him
by your leave hostess *exeunt*

Sc. 7 **1.7** 1.7

oboes torches enter a sewer and divers servants with dishes and service over the stage then enter Macbeth

MACBETH
if it were done when 'tis done then 'twere well
it were done quickly if th'assassination
could trammel up the consequence and catch
with his surcease success that but this blow
might be the be-all and the end-all here
but here upon this bank and shoal of time
we'd jump the life to come but in these cases
we still have judgement here that we but teach
bloody instructions which being taught return
to plague th'inventor this even-handed justice
commends th'ingredience of our poisoned chalice
to our own lips he's here in double trust
first as I am his kinsman and his subject
strong both against the deed then as his host
who should against his murderer shut the door
not bear the knife myself besides this Duncan
hath borne his faculties so meek hath been

so clear in his great office that his virtues
will plead like angels trumpet-tongued against
the deep damnation of his taking off
and pity like a naked new-born babe
striding the blast or heavens cherubin horsed
upon the sightless couriers of the air
shall blow the horrid deed in every eye
that tears shall drown the wind I have no spur
to prick the sides of my intent but only
vaulting ambition which o'erleaps itself
and falls on th'other

enter Lady

how now what news

LADY
he has almost supped why have you left the chamber

MACBETH
hath he asked for me

LADY
know you not he has

MACBETH
we will proceed no further in this business
he hath honoured me of late and I have bought
golden opinions from all sorts of people
which would be worn now in their newest gloss
not cast aside so soon

LADY
was the hope drunk
wherein you dressed yourself hath it slept since
and wakes it now to look so green and pale
at what it did so freely from this time
such I account thy love art thou afeard
to be the same in thine own act and valour
as thou art in desire wouldst thou have that
which thou esteem'st the ornament of life
and live a coward in thine own esteem
letting I dare not wait upon I would
like the poor cat i'th' adage

MACBETH
prithee peace
I dare do all that may become a man
who dares do more is none

LADY
what beast was't then
that made you break this enterprise to me
when you durst do it then you were a man
and to be more than what you were you would
be so much more the man nor time nor place
did then adhere and yet you would make both
they have made themselves and that their fitness now
does unmake you I have given suck and know
how tender 'tis to love the babe that milks me
I would while it was smiling in my face
have plucked my nipple from his boneless gums
and dashed the brains out had I so sworn
as you have done to this

MACBETH
if we should fail

LADY
we fail
but screw your courage to the sticking place
and we'll not fail when Duncan is asleep
whereto the rather shall his day's hard journey
soundly invite him his two chamberlains
will I with wine and wassail so convince
that memory the warder of the brain
shall be a fume and the receipt of reason
a limbeck only when in swinish sleep
their drenchëd natures lie as in a death
what cannot you and I perform upon
th'unguarded Duncan what not put upon
his spongy officers who shall bear the guilt
of our great quell

MACBETH
bring forth men children only
for thy undaunted mettle should compose
nothing but males will it not be received
when we have marked with blood those sleepy two
of his own chamber and used their very daggers
that they have done't

LADY
who dares receive it other
as we shall make our griefs and clamour roar
upon his death

MACBETH
I am settled and bend up
each corporal agent to this terrible feat
away and mock the time with fairest show
false face must hide what the false heart doth know

exeunt

❁

Sc. 8 ***2.1*** **2.1**

incipit actus secundus

enter Banquo and Fleance with a torch before him

BANQUO how goes the night boy

FLEANCE
the moon is down I have not heard the clock

BANQUO
and she goes down at twelve

FLEANCE
I take't 'tis later sir

BANQUO
hold take my sword there's husbandry in heaven
their candles are all out take thee that too
a heavy summons lies like lead upon me
and yet I would not sleep merciful powers
restrain in me the cursèd thoughts that nature
gives way to in repose

enter Macbeth and a servant with a torch

give me my sword who's there

MACBETH a friend

BANQUO
what sir not yet at rest the king's a-bed
he hath been in unusual pleasure and
sent forth great largesse to your offices
this diämond he greets your wife withal
by th' name of most kind hostess and shut up
in measureless content

MACBETH
being unprepared
our will became the servant to defect
which else should free have wrought

BANQUO
all's well
I dreamt last night of the three weïrd sisters
to you they have showed some truth

MACBETH
I think not of them

yet when we can entreat an hour to serve
we would spend it in some words upon that business
if you would grant the time

BANQUO at your kind'st leisure

MACBETH
if you shall cleave to my consent when 'tis
it shall make honour for you

BANQUO so I lose none
in seeking to augment it but still keep
my bosom franchised and allegiance clear
I shall be counselled

MACBETH good repose the while

BANQUO thanks sir the like to you

exit Banquo [with Fleance]

MACBETH
go bid thy mistress when my drink is ready
she strike upon the bell get thee to bed *exit servant*
is this a dagger which I see before me
the handle toward my hand come let me clutch thee
I have thee not and yet I see thee still
art thou not fatal vision sensible
to feeling as to sight or art thou but
a dagger of the mind a false creation
proceeding from the heat oppressèd brain
I see thee yet in form as palpable
as this which now I draw
thou marshall'st me the way that I was going
and such an instrument I was to use
mine eyes are made the fools o'th'other senses
or else worth all the rest I see thee still
and on thy blade and dudgeon gouts of blood
which was not so before there's no such thing
it is the bloody business which informs
thus to mine eyes now o'er the one half world
nature seems dead and wicked dreams abuse
the curtained sleep witchcraft celebrates
pale Hecate's offerings and withered murder
alarumed by his sentinel the wolf
whose howl's his watch thus with his stealthy pace
with Tarquin's ravishing strides towards his design
moves like a ghost thou sure and firm-set earth
hear not my steps which way they walk for fear
thy very stones prate of my whereabout
and take the present horror from the time
which now suits with it whiles I threat he lives
words to the heat of deeds too cold breath gives

a bell rings

I go and it is done the bell invites me
hear it not Duncan for it is a knell
that summons thee to heaven or to hell *exit*

2.2 *Sc. 9* **2.2**

enter Lady

LADY
that which hath made them drunk hath made me bold
what hath quenched them hath given me fire

[an owl shrieks within]

hark peace
it was the owl that shrieked the fatal bellman
which gives the stern'st good-night he is about it
the doors are open and the surfeited grooms
do mock their charge with snores I have drugged their possets
that death and nature do contend about them
whether they live or die

enter Macbeth [above]

MACBETH who's there what ho *[exit]*

LADY
alack I am afraid they have awaked
and 'tis not done th'attempt and not the deed
confounds us hark I laid their daggers ready
he could not miss 'em had he not resembled
my father as he slept I had done't

[enter Macbeth below]

my husband

MACBETH
I have done the deed didst thou not hear a noise

LADY
I heard the owl scream and the crickets cry
did not you speak

MACBETH when

LADY now

MACBETH as I descended

LADY
ay

MACBETH
hark who lies i'th' second chamber

LADY
Donalbain

MACBETH this is a sorry sight

LADY
a foolish thought to say a sorry sight

MACBETH
there's one did laugh in's sleep and one cried murder
that they did wake each other I stood and heard them
but they did say their prayers and addressed them
again to sleep

LADY there are two lodged together

MACBETH
one cried God bless us and amen the other
as they had seen me with these hangman's hands
list'ning their fear I could not say amen
when they did say God bless us

LADY
consider it not so deeply

MACBETH
but wherefore could not I pronounce amen
I had most need of blessing and amen
stuck in my throat

LADY these deeds must not be thought
after these ways so it will make us mad

MACBETH
methought I heard a voice cry sleep no more
Macbeth does murder sleep the innocent sleep

sleep that knits up the ravelled sleeve of care
the death of each day's life sore labour's bath
balm of hurt minds great nature's second course
chief nourisher in life's feast

LADY
what do you mean

MACBETH
still it cried sleep no more to all the house
Glamis hath murdered sleep and therefore Cawdor
shall sleep no more Macbeth shall sleep no more

LADY
who was it that thus cried why worthy thane
you do unbend your noble strength to think
so brain-sickly of things go get some water
and wash this filthy witness from your hand
why did you bring these daggers from the place
they must lie there go carry them and smear
the sleepy grooms with blood

MACBETH
I'll go no more
I am afraid to think what I have done
look on't again I dare not

LADY
infirm of purpose
give me the daggers the sleeping and the dead
are but as pictures 'tis the eye of childhood
that fears a painted devil if he do bleed
I'll gild the faces of the grooms withal
for it must seem their guilt *exit*

knock within

MACBETH
whence is that knocking
how is't with me when every noise appals me
what hands are here ha they pluck out mine eyes
will all great Neptune's ocean wash this blood
clean from my hand no this my hand will rather
the multitudinous seas incarnadine
making the green one red

enter Lady

LADY
my hands are of your colour but I shame
to wear a heart so white

knock [within]

I hear a knocking
at the south entry retire we to our chamber
a little water clears us of this deed
how easy is it then your constancy
hath left you unattended

knock [within]

hark more knocking
get on your nightgown lest occasion call us
and show us to be watchers be not lost
so poorly in your thoughts

MACBETH
to know my deed 'twere best not know myself

knock [within]

wake Duncan with thy knocking I would thou couldst

exeunt

Sc. 10 **2.3** **2.3**

enter a porter
knocking within

PORTER here's a knocking indeed if a man were porter of hell gate he should have old turning the key

knock [within]

knock knock knock who's there i'th' name of Beelzebub here's a farmer that hanged himself on th'expectation of plenty come in time hanger have napkins enough about you here you'll sweat for't

knock [within]

knock knock who's there in th'other devil's name faith here's an equivocator that could swear in both the scales against either scale who committed treason enough for God's sake yet could not equivocate to heaven O come in equivocator

knock [within]

knock knock knock who's there faith here's an English tailor come hither for stealing out of a French hose come in tailor here you may roast your goose

knock [within]

knock knock never at quiet what are you but this place is too cold for hell I'll devil-porter it no further I had thought to have let in some of all professions that go the primrose way to th'everlasting bonfire

knock [within]

anon anon

[he opens the gate]

I pray you remember the porter

enter Macduff and Lennox

MACDUFF
was it so late friend ere you went to bed
that you do lie so late

PORTER faith sir we were carousing till the second cock and drink sir is a great provoker of three things

MACDUFF
what three things does drink especially provoke

PORTER marry sir nose-painting sleep and urine lechery sir it provokes and unprovokes it provokes the desire but it takes away the performance therefore much drink may be said to be an equivocator with lechery it makes him and it mars him it sets him on and it takes him off it persuades him and disheartens him makes him stand to and not stand to in conclusion equivocates him in a sleep and giving him the lie leaves him

MACDUFF
I believe drink gave thee the lie last night

PORTER that it did sir i' the very throat on me but I requited him for his lie and I think being too strong for him though he took up my legs sometime yet I made a shift to cast him

MACDUFF is thy master stirring

enter Macbeth

our knocking has awaked him here he comes

[exit porter]

LENNOX
good morrow noble sir
MACBETH good morrow both
MACDUFF
is the king stirring worthy thane
MACBETH not yet
MACDUFF
he did command me to call timely on him
I have almost slipped the hour
MACBETH I'll bring you to him
MACDUFF
I know this is a joyful trouble to you
but yet 'tis one
MACBETH
the labour we delight in physics pain
this is the door
MACDUFF I'll make so bold to call
for 'tis my limited service *exit Macduff*
LENNOX
goes the king hence today
MACBETH he does he did appoint so
LENNOX
the night has been unruly where we lay
our chimneys were blown down and as they say
lamentings heard i'th'air strange screams of death
and prophesying with accents terrible
of dire combustion and confused events
new-hatched to th' woeful time the òbscure bird
clamoured the livelong night some say the earth
was feverous and did shake
MACBETH 'twas a rough night
LENNOX
my young remembrance cannot parallel
a fellow to it
enter Macduff
MACDUFF O horror horror horror
tongue nor heart cannot conceive nor name thee
MACBETH *and* LENNOX what's the matter
MACDUFF
confusion now hath made his masterpiece
most sacrilegious murder hath broke ope
the Lord's anointed temple and stole thence
the life o'th' building
MACBETH what is't you say the life
LENNOX mean you his majesty
MACDUFF
approach the chamber and destroy your sight
with a new Gorgon do not bid me speak
see and then speak yourselves
exeunt Macbeth and Lennox
awake awake
ring the alarum bell murder and treason
Banquo and Donalbain Malcolm awake
shake off this downy sleep death's counterfeit
and look on death itself up up and see
the great doom's image Malcolm Banquo
as from your graves rise up and walk like sprites
to countenance this horror
bell rings enter Lady
LADY what's the business
that such a hideous trumpet calls to parley
the sleepers of the house speak speak
MACDUFF O gentle lady
'tis not for you to hear what I can speak
the repetition in a woman's ear
would murder as it fell
enter Banquo
O Banquo Banquo
our royal master's murdered
LADY woe alas
what in our house
BANQUO too cruel anywhere
dear Duff I prithee contradict thyself
and say it is not so
enter Macbeth Lennox and Ross
MACBETH
had I but died an hour before this chance
I had lived a blessed time for from this instant
there's nothing serious in mortality
all is but toys renown and grace is dead
the wine of life is drawn and the mere lees
is left this vault to brag of
enter Malcolm and Donalbain
DONALBAIN what is amiss
MACBETH you are and do not know't
the spring the head the fountain of your blood
is stopped the very source of it is stopped
MACDUFF
your royal father's murdered
MALCOLM O by whom
LENNOX
those of his chamber as it seemed had done't
their hands and faces were all badged with blood
so were their daggers which unwiped we found
upon their pillows they stared and were distracted
no man's life was to be trusted with them
MACBETH
O yet I do repent me of my fury
that I did kill them
MACDUFF wherefore did you so
MACBETH
who can be wise amazed temp'rate and furious
loyal and neutral in a moment no man
th'expedition of my violent love
outran the pauser reason here lay Duncan
his silver skin laced with his golden blood
and his gashed stabs looked like a breach in nature
for ruin's wasteful entrance there the murderers
steeped in the colours of their trade their daggers
unmannerly breeched with gore who could refrain

2.3.87.1 ***and Ross*** probably a remnant of the original, more expansive version of the scene.

that had a heart to love and in that heart
courage to make's love known

LADY
help me hence ho

MACDUFF
look to the lady

MALCOLM
why do we hold our tongues
that most may claim this argument for ours

DONALBAIN
what should be spoken here where our fate
hid in an auger hole may rush and seize us
let's away our tears are not yet brewed

MALCOLM
nor our strong sorrow
upon the foot of motion

BANQUO
look to the lady
[*exit Lady attended*]
and when we have our naked frailties hid
that suffer in exposure let us meet
and question this most bloody piece of work
to know it further fears and scruples shake us
in the great hand of God I stand and thence
against the undivulged pretence I fight
of treasonous malice

MACDUFF
and so do I

ALL
so all

MACBETH
let's briefly put on manly readiness
and meet i'th' hall together

ALL
well contented
exeunt [*all but Malcolm and Donalbain*]

MALCOLM
what will you do let's not consort with them
to show an unfelt sorrow is an office
which the false man does easy I'll to England

DONALBAIN
to Ireland I our separated fortune
shall keep us both the safer where we are
there's daggers in men's smiles the nea'er in blood
the nearer bloody

MALCOLM
this murderous shaft that's shot
hath not yet lighted and our safest way
is to avoid the aim therefore to horse
and let us not be dainty of leave-taking
but shift away there's warrant in that theft
which steals itself when there's no mercy left *exeunt*

2.4 *Sc. 11* **2.4**

enter Ross with an old man

OLD MAN
threescore and ten I can remember well
within the volume of which time I have seen
hours dreadful and things strange but this sore night
hath trifled former knowings

ROSS
ha good father
thou seest the heavens as troubled with man's act
threatens his bloody stage by th' clock 'tis day
and yet dark night strangles the travelling lamp
is't night's predominance or the day's shame
that darkness does the face of earth entomb
when living light should kiss it

OLD MAN
'tis unnatural
even like the deed that's done on Tuesday last
a falcon tow'ring in her pride of place
was by a mousing owl hawked at and killed

ROSS
and Duncan's horses a thing most strange and certain
beauteous and swift the minions of their race
turned wild in nature broke their stalls flung out
contending 'gainst obedience as they would
make war with mankind

OLD MAN
'tis said they ate each other

ROSS
they did so to th'amazement of mine eyes
that looked upon't
enter Macduff
here comes the good Macduff
how goes the world sir now

MACDUFF
why see you not

ROSS
is't known who did this more than bloody deed

MACDUFF
those that Macbeth hath slain

ROSS
alas the day
what good could they pretend

MACDUFF
they were suborned
Malcolm and Donalbain the king's two sons
are stol'n away and fled which puts upon them
suspicion of the deed

ROSS
'gainst nature still
thriftless ambition that will raven up
thine own life's means then 'tis most like
the sovereignty will fall upon Macbeth

MACDUFF
he is already named and gone to Scone
to be invested

ROSS where is Duncan's body

MACDUFF carried to Colmekill
the sacred storehouse of his predecessors
and guardian of their bones

ROSS
will you to Scone

MACDUFF
no cousin I'll to Fife

ROSS
well I will thither

MACDUFF
well may you see things well done there adieu
lest our old robes sit easier than our new

ROSS farewell father

117, 122 **look to the lady** The repetition of this phrase suggests that the intervening lines by Malcolm and Donalbain may have been added; if so, they were probably transferred from another scene of the original, since the writing seems clearly to be Shakespeare's.

OLD MAN
God's benison go with you and with those
that would make good of bad and friends of foes
exeunt omnes [severally]

3.1 *Sc. 12* ***3.1***
incipit actus tertius
enter Banquo

BANQUO
thou hast it now king Cawdor Glamis all
as the weïrd women promised and I fear
thou played'st most foully for't yet it was said
it should not stand in thy posterity
but that myself should be the root and father
of many kings if there come truth from them
as upon thee Macbeth their speeches shine
why by the verities on thee made good
may they not be my oracles as well
and set me up in hope but hush no more
sennet sounded enter Macbeth as king Lady [as queen] Lennox Ross lords and attendants

MACBETH
here's our chief guest

LADY
if he had been forgotten
it had been as a gap in our great feast
and all-thing unbecoming

MACBETH
tonight we hold a solemn supper sir
and I'll request your presence

BANQUO
let your highness
command upon me to the which my duties
are with a most indissoluble tie
for ever knit

MACBETH ride you this afternoon

BANQUO ay my good lord

MACBETH
we should have else desired your good advice
which still hath been both grave and prosperous
in this day's council but we'll talk tomorrow
is't far you ride

BANQUO
as far my lord as will fill up the time
'twixt this and supper go not my horse the better
I must become a borrower of the night
for a dark hour or twain

MACBETH fail not our feast

BANQUO my lord I will not

MACBETH
we hear our bloody cousins are bestowed
in England and in Ireland not confessing
their cruel parricide filling their hearers
with strange invention but of that tomorrow
when therewithal we shall have cause of state
craving us jointly hie you to horse adieu
till you return at night goes Fleance with you

BANQUO
ay my good lord our time does call upon's

MACBETH
I wish your horses swift and sure of foot
and so I do commend you to their backs
farewell *exit Banquo*
let every man be master of his time
till seven at night to make society
the sweeter welcome we will keep ourself
till supper time alone while then God be with you
exeunt [all but Macbeth and a servant]
sirrah a word attend those men our pleasure

SERVANT
they are my lord without the palace gate

MACBETH
bring them before us *exit servant*
to be thus is nothing
but to be safely thus our fears in Banquo
stick deep and in his royalty of nature
reigns that which would be feared 'tis much he dares
and to that dauntless temper of his mind
he hath a wisdom that doth guide his valour
to act in safety there is none but he
whose being I do fear and under him
my genius is rebuked as it is said
Mark Antony's was by Caesar he chid the sisters
when first they put the name of king upon me
and bade them speak to him then prophet-like
they hailed him father to a line of kings
upon my head they placed a fruitless crown
and put a barren sceptre in my grip
thence to be wrenched with an unlineal hand
no son of mine succeeding if't be so
for Banquo's issue have I filed my mind
for them the gracious Duncan have I murdered
put rancours in the vessel of my peace
only for them and mine eternal jewel
given to the common enemy of man
to make them kings the seeds of Banquo kings
rather than so come fate into the list
and champion me to th'utterance who's there
enter servant and two murderers
now go to the door and stay there till we call
exit servant
was it not yesterday we spoke together

MURDERERS
it was so please your highness

MACBETH
well then now
have you considered of my speeches know
that it was he in the times past which held you
so under fortune which you thought had been
our innocent self this I made good to you
in our last conference passed in probation with you
how you were borne in hand how crossed the instruments
who wrought with them and all things else that might
to half a soul and to a notion crazed

say thus did Banquo
FIRST MURDERER you made it known to us
MACBETH
I did so and went further which is now
our point of second meeting do you find
your patience so predominant in your nature
that you can let this go are you so gospelled
to pray for this good man and for his issue
whose heavy hand hath bowed you to the grave
and beggared yours for ever
FIRST MURDERER we are men my liege
MACBETH
ay in the catalogue ye go for men
as hounds and greyhounds mongrels spaniels curs
shoughs water rugs and demi-wolves are clept
all by the name of dogs the valued file
distinguishes the swift the slow the subtle
the housekeeper the hunter every one
according to the gift which bounteous nature
hath in him closed whereby he does receive
particular addition from the bill
that writes them all alike and so of men
now if you have a station in the file
not i'th' worst rank of manhood say't
and I will put that business in your bosoms
whose execution takes your enemy off
grapples you to the heart and love of us
who wear our health but sickly in his life
which in his death were perfect
SECOND MURDERER I am one my liege
whom the vile blows and buffets of the world
hath so incensed that I am reckless what
I do to spite the world
FIRST MURDERER and I another
so weary with disasters tugged with fortune
that I would set my life on any chance
to mend it or be rid on't
MACBETH both of you
know Banquo was your enemy
MURDERERS true my lord
MACBETH
so is he mine and in such bloody distance
that every minute of his being thrusts
against my near'st of life and though I could
with barefaced power sweep him from my sight
and bid my will avouch it yet I must not
for certain friends that are both his and mine
whose loves I may not drop but wail his fall
who I myself struck down and thence it is
that I to your assistance do make love
masking the business from the common eye
for sundry weighty reasons
SECOND MURDERER we shall my lord
perform what you command us
FIRST MURDERER though our lives
MACBETH
your spirits shine through you within this hour at most
I will advise you where to plant yourselves
acquaint you with the perfect spy o'th' time
the moment on't for't must be done tonight
and something from the palace always thought
that I require a clearness and with him
to leave no rubs nor botches in the work
Fleance his son that keeps him company
whose absence is no less material to me
than is his father's must embrace the fate
of that dark hour resolve yourselves apart
I'll come to you anon
MURDERERS we are resolved my lord
MACBETH
I'll call upon you straight abide within
[*exeunt murderers*]
it is concluded Banquo thy soul's flight
if it find heaven must find it out tonight [*exit*]

Sc. 13 ***3.2*** 3.2

enter Macbeth's Lady and a servant

LADY is Banquo gone from court
SERVANT
ay madam but returns again tonight
LADY
say to the king I would attend his leisure
for a few words
SERVANT madam I will *exit*
LADY naught's had all's spent
where our desire is got without content
'tis safer to be that which we destroy
than by destruction dwell in doubtful joy
enter Macbeth
how now my lord why do you keep alone
of sorriest fancies your companions making
using those thoughts which should indeed have died
with them they think on things without all remedy
should be without regard what's done is done
MACBETH
we have scorched the snake not killed it
she'll close and be herself whilst our poor malice
remains in danger of her former tooth
but let the frame of things disjoint both the worlds suffer
ere we will eat our meal in fear and sleep
in the affliction of these terrible dreams
that shake us nightly better be with the dead
whom we to gain our peace have sent to peace
than on the torture of the mind to lie
in restless ecstasy Duncan is in his grave
after life's fitful fever he sleeps well
treason has done his worst nor steel nor poison
malice domestic foreign levy nothing
can touch him further
LADY come on gentle my lord
sleek o'er your rugged looks be bright and jovial
among your guests tonight
MACBETH so shall I love
and so I pray be you let your remembrance

apply to Banquo present him eminence
both with eye and tongue unsafe the while that we
must lave our honours in these flattering streams
and make our faces visors to our hearts
disguising what they are

LADY you must leave this

MACBETH
O full of scorpions is my mind dear wife
thou know'st that Banquo and his Fleance lives

LADY
but in them nature's copy's not eterne

MACBETH
there's comfort yet they are assailable
then be thou jocund ere the bat hath flown
his cloistered flight ere to black Hecate's summons
the shard-born beetle with his drowsy hums
hath rung night's yawning peal there shall be done
a deed of dreadful note

LADY what's to be done

MACBETH
be innocent of the knowledge dearest chuck
till thou applaud the deed come seeling night
scarf up the tender eye of pitiful day
and with thy bloody and invisible hand
cancel and tear to pieces that great bond
which keeps me pale light thickens and the crow
makes wing to th' rooky wood
good things of day begin to droop and drowse
whiles night's black agents to their preys do rouse
thou marvell'st at my words but hold thee still
things bad begun make strong themselves by ill
so prithee go with me *exeunt*

3·3 *Sc. 14* ***3·3***

enter three murderers

FIRST MURDERER
but who did bid thee join with us

THIRD MURDERER Macbeth

SECOND MURDERER
he needs not our mistrust since he delivers
our offices and what we have to do
to the direction just

FIRST MURDERER then stand with us
the west yet glimmers with some streaks of day
now spurs the lated traveller apace
to gain the timely inn and near approaches
the subject of our watch

THIRD MURDERER hark I hear horses

BANQUO (*within*)
give us a light there ho

SECOND MURDERER then 'tis he the rest
that are within the note of expectation
already are i'th' court

FIRST MURDERER his horses go about

THIRD MURDERER
almost a mile but he does usually
so all men do from hence to th' palace gate
make it their walk

enter Banquo and Fleance with a torch

SECOND MURDERER a light a light

THIRD MURDERER 'tis he

FIRST MURDERER stand to't

BANQUO
it will be rain tonight

FIRST MURDERER let it come down

[*first murderer strikes out the torch the others attack Banquo*]

BANQUO
O treachery fly good Fleance fly fly fly
thou mayst revenge O slave [*he dies exit Fleance*]

THIRD MURDERER who did strike out the light

FIRST MURDERER was't not the way

THIRD MURDERER
there's but one down the son is fled

SECOND MURDERER
we have lost best half of our affair

FIRST MURDERER
well let's away and say how much is done

exeunt [*with Banquo's body*]

Sc. 15 ***3·4*** 3·4

banquet prepared enter Macbeth Lady Ross Lennox lords and attendants [*Lady sits*]

MACBETH
you know your own degrees sit down at first and last
the hearty welcome

LORDS thanks to your majesty

[*they sit*]

MACBETH
ourself will mingle with society
and play the humble host our hostess keeps her state
but in best time we will require her welcome

LADY
pronounce it for me sir to all our friends
for my heart speaks they are welcome

enter first murderer [*to the door*]

MACBETH
see they encounter thee with their hearts' thanks
both sides are even here I'll sit i'th' midst
be large in mirth anon we'll drink a measure
the table round

[*Macbeth talks apart to first murderer*]

there's blood upon thy face

FIRST MURDERER 'tis Banquo's then

MACBETH
'tis better thee without than he within
is he dispatched

FIRST MURDERER
my lord his throat is cut that I did for him

MACBETH
thou art the best o'th' cutthroats yet he's good
that did the like for Fleance if thou didst it
thou art the nonpareil

FIRST MURDERER most royal sir

Fleance is scaped

MACBETH
then comes my fit again I had else been perfect
whole as the marble founded as the rock
as broad and general as the casing air
but now I am cabined cribbed confined bound in
to saucy doubts and fears but Banquo's safe

FIRST MURDERER
ay my good lord safe in a ditch he bides
with twenty trenchèd gashes on his head
the least a death to nature

MACBETH thanks for that
there the grown serpent lies the worm that's fled
hath nature that in time will venom breed
no teeth for th' present get thee gone tomorrow
we'll hear ourselves again *exit first murderer*

LADY my royal lord
you do not give the cheer the feast is sold
that is not often vouched while 'tis a-making
'tis given with welcome to feed were best at home
from thence the sauce to meat is ceremony
meeting were bare without it

enter the ghost of Banquo and sits in Macbeth's place

MACBETH sweet remembrancer
now good digestion wait on appetite
and health on both

LENNOX may't please your highness sit

MACBETH
here had we now our country's honour roofed
were the graced person of our Banquo present
who may I rather challenge for unkindness
than pity for mischance

ROSS his absence sir
lays blame upon his promise please't your highness
to grace us with your royal company

MACBETH
the table's full

LENNOX here is a place reserved sir

MACBETH where

LENNOX
here my good lord what is't that moves your highness

MACBETH
which of you have done this

LORDS what my good lord

MACBETH
thou canst not say I did it never shake
thy gory locks at me

ROSS [*rising*]
gentlemen rise his highness is not well

LADY [*rising*]
sit worthy friends my lord is often thus
and hath been from his youth pray you keep seat
the fit is momentary upon a thought
he will again be well if much you note him
you shall offend him and extend his passion
feed and regard him not

[*she speaks apart with Macbeth*]
are you a man

MACBETH
ay and a bold one that dare look on that
which might appal the devil

LADY O proper stuff
this is the very painting of your fear
this is the air-drawn dagger which you said
led you to Duncan O these flaws and starts
impostors to true fear would well become
a woman's story at a winter's fire
authòrized by her grandam shame itself
why do you make such faces when all's done
you look but on a stool

MACBETH
prithee see there behold look lo how say you
why what care I if thou canst nod speak too
if charnel houses and our graves must send
those that we bury back our monuments
shall be the maws of kites [*exit ghost*]

LADY what quite unmanned in folly

MACBETH
if I stand here I saw him

LADY fie for shame

MACBETH
blood hath been shed ere now i'th'olden time
ere human statute purged the gentle weal
ay and since too murders have been performed
too terrible for the ear the time has been
that when the brains were out the man would die
and there an end but now they rise again
with twenty mortal murders on their crowns
and push us from our stools this is more strange
than such a murder is

LADY my worthy lord
your noble friends do lack you

MACBETH I do forget
do not muse at me my most worthy friends
I have a strange infirmity which is nothing
to those that know me come love and health to all
then I'll sit down give me some wine fill full

enter ghost

I drink to th' general joy of the whole table
and to our dear friend Banquo whom we miss
would he were here to all and him we thirst
and all to all

LORDS our duties and the pledge

[*they drink*]

MACBETH
avaunt and quit my sight let the earth hide thee
thy bones are marrowless thy blood is cold
thou hast no speculation in those eyes
which thou dost glare with

LADY think of this good peers
but as a thing of custom 'tis no other
only it spoils the pleasure of the time

MACBETH what man dare I dare
approach thou like the rugged Russian bear

the armed rhinoceros or th'Hyrcan tiger
take any shape but that and my firm nerves
shall never tremble or be alive again
and dare me to the desert with thy sword
if trembling I inhabit then protest me
the baby of a girl hence horrible shadow
unreal mock'ry hence [*exit ghost*]
why so being gone
I am a man again pray you sit still

LADY
you have displaced the mirth broke the good meeting
with most admired disorder

MACBETH can such things be
and overcome us like a summer's cloud
without our special wonder you make me strange
even to the disposition that I owe
when now I think you can behold such sights
and keep the natural ruby of your cheeks
when mine is blanched with fear

ROSS what sights my lord

LADY
I pray you speak not he grows worse and worse
question enrages him at once good night
stand not upon the order of your going
but go at once

LENNOX good night and better health
attend his majesty

LADY a kind good-night to all *exit lords*

MACBETH
it will have blood they say blood will have blood
stones have been known to move and trees to speak
augurs and understood relations have
by maggot pies and choughs and rooks brought forth
the secret'st man of blood what is the night

LADY
almost at odds with morning which is which

MACBETH
how sayst thou that Macduff denies his person
at our great bidding

LADY did you send to him sir

MACBETH
I hear it by the way but I will send
there's not a one of them but in his house
I keep a servant fee'd I will tomorrow
and betimes I will to the weïrd sisters
more shall they speak for now I am bent to know
by the worst means the worst for mine own good
all causes shall give way I am in blood
stepped in so far that should I wade no more
returning were as tedious as go o'er
strange things I have in head that will to hand
which must be acted ere they may be scanned

LADY
you lack the season of all natures sleep

MACBETH
come we'll to sleep my strange and self abuse
is the initiate fear that wants hard use
we are yet but young in deed *exeunt*

thunder enter the three witches meeting Hecate 3.5

FIRST WITCH
why how now Hecate you look angerly

HECATE
have I not reason beldams as you are
saucy and overbold how did you dare
to trade and traffic with Macbeth
in riddles and affairs of death
and I the mistress of your charms
the close contriver of all harms
was never called to bear my part
or show the glory of our art
and which is worse all you have done
hath been but for a wayward son
spiteful and wrathful who as others do
loves for his own ends not for you
but make amends now get you gone
and at the pit of Acheron
meet me i'th' morning thither he
will come to know his destiny
your vessels and your spells provide
your charms and everything beside
I am for th'air this night I'll spend
unto a dismal and a fatal end
great business must be wrought ere noon
upon the corner of the moon
there hangs a vap'rous drop profound
I'll catch it ere it come to ground
and that distilled by magic sleights
shall raise such artificial sprites
as by the strength of their illusion
shall draw him on to his confusion
he shall spurn fate scorn death and bear
his hopes 'bove wisdom grace and fear
and you all know security
is mortals' chiefest enemy
***music and a song* [*by other witches*]**

[SINGING WITCHES] [*singing within*]
Hecate Hecate Hecate O come away come away
[*a cloud appears carrying a spirit like a cat*]

HECATE
hark I am called my little spirit see
sits in a foggy cloud and stays for me
the song

[FOURTH WITCH] (*in the air within*)
come away come away Hecate Hecate
O come away

3.5 A new scene, written entirely by Middleton, introducing Hecate and expanding the play's supernatural dimension. For the song see also *The Witch* 3.3.39–72; an edition of the music appears in the *Companion*, p. 153. For the theatrical and critical significance of this addition see Critical Introduction.

HECATE
I come I come I come I come
with all the speed I may
with all the speed I may
where's Stadlin
[FIFTH WITCH] (*in the air within*)
here
HECATE where's Puckle
[SIXTH WITCH] (*in the air within*) here
and Hoppo too and Hellwain too
[FOURTH WITCH] (*in the air within*)
we lack but you we lack but you
come away make up the count
HECATE
I will but 'noint and then I mount
I will but 'noint and then I mount
a spirit like a cat descends [*the other three witches appear above*]
[FOURTH WITCH] (*above*)
here comes one down to fetch his dues
a kiss a coll a sip of blood
and why thou stay'st so long
[CAT] I muse I muse
[FOURTH WITCH]
since the air's so sweet and good
[HECATE]
O art thou come
[CAT] what news what news
[FIFTH WITCH]
all goes still to our delight
either come or else
[CAT] refuse refuse
HECATE
now I am furnished for the flight
Hecate and the cat go up
now I go and now I fly
Malkin my sweet spirit and I
O what a dainty pleasure's this
to ride in the air
when the moon shines fair
and feast and dance and toy and kiss
over woods high rocks and mountains
over seas our mistress fountains
over steeples towers and turrets
we fly by night 'mongst troops of spirits
no ring of bells to our ears sounds
no howls of wolves nor yelps of hounds
no nor the noise of waters' breach
or cannon's throat our height can reach
[*exeunt Hecate and the cat into the heavens*]
[SINGING WITCHES] (*above*)
no ring of bells to our ears sounds
no howls of wolves nor yelps of hounds
no nor the noise of waters' breach
or cannon's throat our height can reach
[*exeunt singing witches*]
FIRST WITCH
come let's make haste she'll soon be back again
exeunt

Sc. 16 **3.6** 3.6
enter Lennox and another lord

LENNOX
my former speeches have but hit your thoughts
which can interpret farther only I say
things have been strangely borne the gracious Duncan
was pitied of Macbeth marry he was dead
and the right valiant Banquo walked too late
whom you may say if't please you Fleance killed
for Fleance fled men must not walk too late
who cannot want the thought how monstërous
it was for Malcolm and for Donalbain
to kill their gracious father damnèd fact
how it did grieve Macbeth did he not straight
in pious rage the two delinquents tear
that were the slaves of drink and thralls of sleep
was not that nobly done ay and wisely too
for 'twould have angered any heart alive
to hear the men deny't so that I say
he has borne all things well and I do think
that had he Duncan's sons under his key
as an't please heaven he shall not they should find
what 'twere to kill a father so should Fleance
but peace for from broad words and 'cause he failed
his presence at the tyrant's feast I hear
Macduff lives in disgrace sir can you tell
where he bestows himself
LORD the son of Duncan
from whom this tyrant holds the due of birth
lives in the English court and is received
of the most pious Edward with such grace
that the malevolence of fortune nothing
takes from his high respect thither Macduff
is gone to pray the holy king upon his aid
to wake Northumberland and warlike Siward
that by the help of these with him above
to ratify the work we may again
give to our tables meat sleep to our nights
free from our feasts and banquets bloody knives
do faithful homage and receive free honours
all which we pine for now and this report
hath so exasperate their king that he
prepares for some attempt of war
LENNOX [
]
LORD sent he to Macduff

3.6.23–23p sir . . . war apparently intended for deletion, as part of the adaptation's diminution of the role of the Catholic saint, England's King Edward the Confessor. The speech prefixes after the cut are confused.

LORD **LENNOX**
he did and with an absolute sir not I
the cloudy messenger turns me his back
and hums as who should say you'll rue the time
that clogs me with this answer
LENNOX **LORD** and that well might
advise him to a caution t'hold what distance
his wisdom can provide
LENNOX some holy angel
fly to the court of England and unfold
his message ere he come that a swift blessing
may soon return to this our suffering country
under a hand accursed
LORD I'll send my prayers with him
exeunt

❁

4.1 *Sc. 17* ***4.1***
incipit actus quartus
[a cauldron] ***thunder***
enter the three *weïrd sisters* ***witches***

FIRST
thrice the brinded cat hath mewed
SECOND
thrice and once the hedge-pig whined
THIRD
Harpier cries 'tis time 'tis time
FIRST
where hast thou been sister
SECOND
killing swine
THIRD sister where thou
FIRST
a sailor's wife had chestnuts in her lap
and munched and munched and munched give me
quoth I
aroint thee witch the rump-fed runnion cries
her husband's to Aleppo gone master o'th' Tiger
but in a sieve I'll thither sail
and like a rat without a tail
I'll do I'll do and I'll do
SECOND
I'll give thee a wind
FIRST
thou'rt kind
THIRD
and I another
FIRST
I myself have all the other
and the very ports they blow
all the quarters that they know
i'th' shipman's card
I'll drain him dry as hay
sleep shall neither night nor day
hang upon his penthouse lid
he shall live a man forbid
weary se'en-nights nine times nine
shall he dwindle peak and pine
though his barque cannot be lost
yet it shall be tempest-tossed
look what I have
SECOND show me show me
FIRST
here I have a pilot's thumb
wrecked as homeward he did come
[SECOND]
[ ]
[THIRD]
[ ]
FIRST
round about the cauldron go
in the poisoned entrails throw
toad that under cold stone
days and nights has thirty-one
sweltered venom sleeping got
boil thou first i'th' charmèd pot
ALL
double double toil and trouble
fire burn and cauldron bubble
SECOND
fillet of a fenny snake
in the cauldron boil and bake
eye of newt and toe of frog
wool of bat and tongue of dog
adder's fork and blind-worm's sting
lizard's leg and owlet's wing
for a charm of pow'rful trouble
like a hell-broth boil and bubble
ALL
double double toil and trouble
fire burn and cauldron bubble
THIRD
scale of dragon tooth of wolf
witch's mummy maw and gulf
of the ravined salt-sea shark
root of hemlock digged i'th' dark
liver of blaspheming Jew
gall of goat and slips of yew
slivered in the moon's eclipse
nose of Turk and Tartar's lips
finger of birth-strangled babe
ditch-delivered by a drab
make the gruel thick and slab

30–3.6.30.4 LENNOX some ... accursed A continuation of the cut at 23–23p.

4.1.3a–aa FIRST where ... come These lines fit the post-murder atmosphere of 4.1 better than the 'fairies and nymphs' of 1.3. Middleton might have moved them to the earlier scene in order to make room for Hecate, the charm song, and the apparitions here.

3ab–ac [SECOND] ... [ ] A transitional passage appears to be lost, with lines spoken by one or two of the other weïrd sisters, or all three together (perhaps the choral 'Double, double ...'?)

add thereto a tiger's chaudron
for th'ingredience of our cauldron

ALL
double double toil and trouble
fire burn and cauldron bubble

SECOND
cool it with a baboon's blood
then the charm is firm and good

enter Hecate and the other three witches

HECATE
O well done I commend your pains
and everyone shall share i'th' gains
and now about the cauldron sing
like elves and fairies in a ring
enchanting all that you put in

music and a charm song about a vessel

black spirits and white red spirits and grey
mingle mingle mingle you that mingle may
Titty Tiffin keep it stiff in
Fire-Drake Puckey make it lucky
Liard Robin you must bob in

[ALL]
round around around about about
all ill come running in all good keep out

[FOURTH WITCH]
here's the blood of a bat

HECATE
put in that O put in that

[FIFTH WITCH]
here's leopard's bane

HECATE
put in a grain

[FOURTH WITCH]
the juice of toad the oil of adder
those will make the charm grow madder

[FIFTH WITCH]
put in there's all and rid the stench

[HECATE]
nay here's three ounces of a red-haired wench

[ALL]
round around around about about
all ill come running in all good keep out

SECOND
by the pricking of my thumbs
something wicked this way comes

[*knock within*]

open locks
whoever knocks

enter Macbeth

MACBETH
how now you secret black and midnight hags
what is't you do

ALL BUT MACBETH
a deed without a name

MACBETH
I conjure you by that which you profess
howe'er you come to know it answer me
though you untie the winds and let them fight
against the churches though the yeasty waves
confound and swallow navigation up
though bladed corn be lodged and trees blown down
though castles topple on their warders' heads
though palaces and pyramids do slope
their heads to their foundations though the treasure
of nature's germens tumble all together
even till destruction sicken answer me
to what I ask you

FIRST
speak

SECOND
demand

THIRD
we'll answer

MACBETH
[ ]

HECATE
say if thou'dst rather hear it from our mouths
or from our masters

MACBETH
call 'em let me see 'em

HECATE
pour in sow's blood that hath eaten
her nine farrow grease that's sweaten
from the murderers' gibbet throw
into the flame

[ALL BUT MACBETH]
come high or low
thy self and office deftly show

thunder first apparition an armed head

MACBETH
tell me thou unknown power

HECATE
he knows thy thought
hear his speech but say thou naught

FIRST APPARITION
Macbeth Macbeth Macbeth beware Macduff
beware the thane of Fife **dismiss me enough**

he descends

MACBETH
time thou anticipat'st my dread exploits
the castle of Macduff I will surprise
seize upon Fife give to th'edge o'th' sword
his wife his babes and all unfortunate souls

38.1–4.1.60 ***enter*...out** Another expansion of the supernatural dimension, like the addition of 3.5. For the song see also *The Witch* 5.2.63–79 and *Companion*, p. 158.

38.1 ***the other three witches*** that is, the three singing witches in 3.5, presumably played by boy actors

78a–4.1.107 MACBETH ...APPARITION Middleton apparently added the apparitions, who speak prophecies originally spoken by the three weïrd sisters. This involved some transposition and rewriting of Shakespeare's lines. Macbeth's questions, promised in lines 68–78, were apparently cut as part of this addition.

81–5 **pour...show** probably transposed from its original position at 122a–e, introducing the show of eight kings

89a–e time...line Middleton used these lines in a soliloquy for Macbeth at the end of the scene.

that trace him in his line [
]
whate'er thou art for thy good caution thanks
thou hast harped my fear aright **but one word more**

HECATE
he will not be commanded here's another
more potent than the first
thunder second apparition a bloody child

SECOND APPARITION Macbeth Macbeth Macbeth

MACBETH had I three ears I'd hear thee

SECOND APPARITION
be bloody bold and resolute laugh to scorn
the pow'r of man for none of woman born
shall harm Macbeth
descends

MACBETH
then live Macduff what need I fear of thee
but yet I'll make assurance double sure
and take a bond of fate thou shalt not live
that I may tell pale-hearted fear it lies
and sleep in spite of thunder
thunder third apparition a child crowned with a tree in his hand
what is this
that rises like the issue of a king
and wears upon his baby brow the round
and top of sovereignty

[ALL BUT MACBETH] **listen but speak not to't**

THIRD APPARITION
be lion-mettled proud and take no care
who chafes who frets or where conspirers are
Macbeth shall never vanquished be until
great Birnam Wood to high Dunsinane Hill
shall come against him
descend

MACBETH that will never be
who can impress the forest bid the tree
unfix his earth-bound root sweet bodements good
rebellious dead rise never till the wood
of Birnam rise and our high-placed Macbeth
shall live the lease of nature pay his breath
to time and mortal custom yet my heart
throbs to know one thing tell me if your art
can tell so much shall Banquo's issue ever
reign in this kingdom

[ALL BUT MACBETH] seek to know no more

MACBETH
I will be satisfied deny me this
and an eternal curse fall on you let me know

FIRST
pour in sow's blood that hath eaten
her nine farrow grease that's sweaten
from the murderers' gibbet throw
into the flame

[ALL BUT MACBETH]
come high or low
thy self and office deftly show
[*the cauldron sinks*]

MACBETH
why sinks that cauldron
oboes
and what noise is this

FIRST show

SECOND show

THIRD show

[ALL BUT MACBETH]
show his eyes and grieve his heart
come like shadows so depart *the witches vanish*
a show of eight kings the last with a glass in his hand ***and Banquo***

MACBETH
thou art too like the spirit of Banquo down
thy crown does sear mine eyeballs and thy hair
thou other gold-bound brow is like the first
a third is like the former filthy hags
why do you show me this a fourth start eyes
what will the line stretch out to th' crack of doom
another yet a seventh what is this
that rises like the issue of a king
and wears upon his baby brow the round
and top of sovereignty I'll see no more
and yet the eighth appears who bears a glass
which shows me many more and some I see
that twofold balls and treble sceptres carry
horrible sight now I see 'tis true
for the blood-baltered Banquo smiles upon me
and points at them for his what is this so

HECATE
ay sir all this is so but why
stands Macbeth thus amazedly
come sisters cheer we up his sprites
and show the best of our delights
I'll charm the air to give a sound
while you perform your antic round
that this great king may kindly say
our duties did his welcome pay
music the witches dance and vanish [*with Hecate*]

MACBETH
where are they gone let this pernicious hour
stand aye accursèd in the calendar
come in without there

128.2 ***and Banquo*** added by Middleton, linking this scene backward to 3.4

135–6 **what...sovereignty** This passage probably referred originally to the grandfather of James I, the seventh Stuart king of Scotland, who was crowned when he was 'one year, five months, and ten days old'. Shakespeare's lines, written to refer to the Stuart lineage, might have been transferred to refer to the third apparition.

143–4.1.150.1 **HECATE...*vanish*** The added witches' dance may have been based on that in Ben Jonson's *Masque of Queens*; see *Companion*, p. 158.

153–61 **come...lord** This exchange replaces the information reported in the passage apparently deleted from 3.6.

enter Lennox

LENNOX **what's your grace's will**

MACBETH
saw you the weïrd sisters

LENNOX **no my lord**

MACBETH
came they not by you

LENNOX **no indeed my lord**

MACBETH
infected be the air whereon they ride
and damned all those that trust them *exit*
I did hear
the galloping of horse who was't came by

LENNOX
'tis two or three my lord that bring you word
Macduff is fled to England

MACBETH **fled to England**

LENNOX **ay my good lord**

MACBETH
time thou anticipat'st my dread exploits
the flighty purpose never is o'ertook
unless the deed go with it from this moment
the very firstlings of my heart shall be
the firstlings of my hand and even now
to crown my thoughts with acts be it thought and done
the castle of Macduff I will surprise
seize upon Fife give to th'edge o'th' sword
his wife his babes and all unfortunate souls
that trace him in his line no boasting like a fool
this deed I'll do before this purpose cool
but no more sights where are these gentlemen
come bring me where they are *exeunt*

4.2 *Sc. 18* **4.2**

enter Macduff's wife her son and Ross

WIFE
what had he done to make him fly the land

ROSS
you must have patience madam

WIFE he had none
his flight was madness when our actions do not
our fears do make us traitors

ROSS you know not
whether it was his wisdom or his fear

WIFE
wisdom to leave his wife to leave his babes
his mansion and his titles in a place
from whence himself does fly he loves us not
he wants the natural touch for the poor wren
the most diminutive of birds will fight
her young ones in her nest against the owl
all is the fear and nothing is the love
as little is the wisdom where the flight
so runs against all reason

ROSS my dearest coz
I pray you school yourself but for your husband
he is noble wise judicious and best knows
the fits o'th' season I dare not speak much further
but cruel are the times when we are traitors
and do not know ourselves when we hold rumour
from what we fear yet know not what we fear
but float upon a wild and violent sea
each way and none I take my leave of you
shall not be long but I'll be here again
things at the worst will cease or else climb upward
to what they were before my pretty cousin
blessing upon you

WIFE
fathered he is and yet he's fatherless

ROSS
I am so much a fool should I stay longer
it would be my disgrace and your discomfort
I take my leave at once *exit*

WIFE sirrah your father's dead
and what will you do now how will you live

SON
as birds do mother

WIFE what with worms and flies

SON
with what I get I mean and so do they

WIFE
poor bird thou'dst never fear the net nor lime
the pitfall nor the gin

SON
why should I mother poor birds they are not set for
my father is not dead for all your saying

WIFE
yes he is dead
how wilt thou do for a father

SON **nay how will you do for a husband**

WIFE **why I can buy me twenty at any market**

SON **then you'll buy 'em to sell again**

WIFE **thou speak'st with all thy wit and yet i'faith with wit enough for thee**

SON **was my father a traitor mother**

WIFE **ay that he was**

SON **what is a traitor**

WIFE **why one that swears and lies**

SON **and be all traitors that do so**

162–74 **time . . . are** This soliloquy—mostly Middleton's, but incorporating some Shakespearean lines apparently transferred from earlier in the scene—with the preceding dialogue gives the boy actors time for a costume change, to reappear as Macduff's wife and son.

4.2.39, 59 **how wilt thou do for a father** The repetition of the same phrase by the same character, and the change from verse to prose, suggest that the intervening material has been added; stylistically the prose resembles Middleton, and the added material seems to allude to the Overbury scandal of 1616 (with its perjury, hangings of some but not all of the guilty, related accusations of treason, issues of remarriage, and survival of a mother/wife after her husband had been condemned to death). For the political context see *Witch*.

WIFE everyone that does so is a traitor and must be hanged
SON and must they all be hanged that swear and lie
WIFE every one
SON who must hang them
WIFE why the honest men
SON then the liars and swearers are fools for there are liars and swearers enough to beat the honest men and hang up them
WIFE now God help thee poor monkey
but how wilt thou do for a father
SON
If he were dead you'd weep for him if you would not
it were a good sign that I should quickly
have a new father
WIFE poor prattler how thou talk'st
enter a messenger
MESSENGER
bless you fair dame I am not to you known
though in your state of honour I am perfect
I doubt some danger does approach you nearly
if you will take a homely man's advice
be not found here hence with your little ones
to fright you thus methinks I am too savage
to do worse to you were fell cruelty
which is too nigh your person heaven preserve you
I dare abide no longer *exit messenger*
WIFE whither should I fly
I have done no harm but I remember now
I am in this earthly world where to do harm
is often laudable to do good sometime
accounted dangerous folly why then alas
do I put up that womanly defence
to say I have done no harm
enter murderers
what are these faces
A MURDERER where is your husband
WIFE
I hope in no place so unsanctified
where such as thou mayst find him
A MURDERER he's a traitor
SON
thou liest thou shag-haired villain
A MURDERER what you egg
young fry of treachery
SON he has killed me mother
run away I pray you
exit [*Wife*] *crying murder* [*murderers exit following her taking son's body*]

4·3 *Sc. 19* **4.3**
enter Malcolm and Macduff
MALCOLM
let us seek out some desolate shade and there
weep our sad bosoms empty
MACDUFF let us rather
hold fast the mortal sword and like good men
bestride our downfall birthdom each new morn
new widows howl new orphans cry new sorrows
strike heaven on the face that it resounds
as if it felt with Scotland and yelled out
like syllable of dolour
MALCOLM what I believe I'll wail
what know believe and what I can redress
as I shall find the time to friend I will
what you have spoke it may be so perchance
this tyrant whose sole name blisters our tongues
was once thought honest you have loved him well
he hath not touched you yet I am young but something
you may discern of him through me and wisdom
to offer up a weak poor innocent lamb
t'appease an angry God
MACDUFF I am not treacherous
MALCOLM but Macbeth is
a good and virtuous nature may recoil
in an imperial charge but I shall crave your pardon
that which you are my thoughts cannot transpose
angels are bright still though the brightest fell
though all things foul would wear the brows of grace
yet grace must still look so
MACDUFF I have lost my hopes
MALCOLM
perchance even there where I did find my doubts
why in that rawness left you wife and child
those precious motives those strong knots of love
without leave-taking I pray you
let not my jealousies be your dishonours
but mine own safeties you may be rightly just
whatever I shall think
MACDUFF bleed bleed poor country
great tyranny lay thou thy basis sure
for goodness dare not check thee wear thou thy wrongs
the title is affeered fare thee well lord
I would not be the villain that thou think'st
for the whole space that's in the tyrant's grasp
and the rich east to boot
MALCOLM be not offended
I speak not as in absolute fear of you
I think our country sinks beneath the yoke
it weeps it bleeds and each new day a gash
is added to her wounds I think withal
there would be hands uplifted in my right
and here from gracious England have I offer
of goodly thousands but for all this
when I shall tread upon the tyrant's head
or wear it on my sword yet my poor country
shall have more vices than it had before
more suffer and more sundry ways than ever
by him that shall succeed

58 **now God . . . monkey** This phrase may have been intended for deletion, in connection with the addition; it is clearly Shakespeare's.

MACDUFF what should he be
MALCOLM
it is myself I mean in whom I know
all the particulars of vice so grafted
that when they shall be opened black Macbeth
will seem as pure as snow and the poor state
esteem him as a lamb being compared
with my confineless harms
MACDUFF not in the legions
of horrid hell can come a devil more damned
in evils to top Macbeth
MALCOLM I grant him bloody
luxurious avaricious false deceitful
sullen malicious smacking of every sin
that has a name but there's no bottom none
in my voluptuousness your wives your daughters
your matrons and your maids could not fill up
the cistern of my lust and my desire
all continent impediments would o'erbear
that did oppose my will better Macbeth
than such an one to reign
MACDUFF boundless intemperance
in nature is a tyranny it hath been
th'untimely emptying of the happy throne
and fall of many kings but fear not yet
to take upon you what is yours you may
convey your pleasures in a spacious plenty
and yet seem cold the time you may so hoodwink
we have willing dames enough there cannot be
that vulture in you to devour so many
as will to greatness dedicate themselves
finding it so inclined
MALCOLM with this there grows
in my most ill-composed affection such
a staunchless avarice that were I king
I should cut off the nobles for their lands
desire his jewels and this other's house
and my more having would be as a sauce
to make me hunger more that I should forge
quarrels unjust against the good and loyal
destroying them for wealth
MACDUFF this avarice
sticks deeper grows with more pernicious root
than summer-seeming lust and it hath been
the sword of our slain kings yet do not fear
Scotland hath foisons to fill up your will
of your mere own all these are portable
with other graces weighed
MALCOLM
but I have none the king-becoming graces
as justice verity temp'rance stableness
bounty perseverance mercy lowliness
devotion patience courage fortitude
I have no relish of them but abound
in the division of each several crime
acting it many ways nay had I power I should
pour the sweet milk of concord into hell
uproar the universal peace confound
all unity on earth
MACDUFF O Scotland Scotland
MALCOLM
if such a one be fit to govern speak
I am as I have spoken
MACDUFF fit to govern
no not to live O nation miserable
with an untitled tyrant bloody-sceptered
when shalt thou see thy wholesome days again
since that the truest issue of thy throne
by his own interdiction stands accused
and does blaspheme his breed thy royal father
was a most sainted king the queen that bore thee
oft'ner upon her knees than on her feet
died every day she lived fare thee well
these evils thou repeat'st upon thyself
hath banished me from Scotland O my breast
thy hope ends here
MALCOLM Macduff this noble passion
child of integrity hath from my soul
wiped the black scruples reconciled my thoughts
to thy good truth and honour devilish Macbeth
by many of these trains hath sought to win me
into his power and modest wisdom plucks me
from over-credulous haste but God above
deal between thee and me for even now
I put myself to thy direction and
unspeak mine own detraction here abjure
the taints and blames I laid upon myself
for strangers to my nature I am yet
unknown to woman never was forsworn
scarcely have coveted what was mine own
at no time broke my faith would not betray
the devil to his fellow and delight
no less in truth than life my first false speaking
was this upon myself what I am truly
is thine and my poor country's to command
whither indeed before thy here approach
old Siward with ten thousand warlike men
already at a point was setting forth
now we'll together and the chance of goodness
be like our warranted quarrel why are you silent
MACDUFF
such welcome and unwelcome things at once
'tis hard to reconcile
enter a doctor
MALCOLM
well more anon **comes the king forth I pray you**
DOCTOR
ay sir there are a crew of wretched souls

4.3.141–60 **comes . . . grace** probably replacing, as reported speech rather than dialogue, a longer sequence in which the holy King Edward appeared and performed a miracle on stage. See the conjectural reconstruction at 4.3.242a–ab.

that stay his cure their malady convinces
the great essay of art but at his touch
such sanctity hath heaven given his hand
they presently amend

MALCOLM
I thank you doctor ***exit doctor***

MACDUFF
what's the disease he means

MALCOLM
'tis called the evil
a most miraculous work in this good king
which often since my here remain in England
I have seen him do how he solicits heaven
himself best knows but strangely visited people
all swoll'n and ulcerous pitiful to the eye
the mere despair of surgery he cures
hanging a golden stamp about their necks
put on with holy prayers and 'tis spoken
to the succeeding royalty he leaves
the healing benediction with this strange virtue
he hath a heavenly gift of prophecy
and sundry blessings hang about his throne
that speak him full of grace

enter Ross

MACDUFF
see who comes here

MALCOLM
my countryman but yet I know him not

MACDUFF
my ever gentle cousin welcome hither

MALCOLM
I know him now good God betimes remove
the means that makes us strangers

ROSS
sir amen

MACDUFF
stands Scotland where it did

ROSS
alas poor country
almost afraid to know itself it cannot
be called our mother but our grave where nothing
but who knows nothing is once seen to smile
where sighs and groans and shrieks that rend the air
are made not marked where violent sorrow seems
a modern ecstasy the dead man's knell
is there scarce asked for who and good men's lives
expire before the flowers in their caps
dying or ere they sicken

MACDUFF
O relation
too nice and yet too true

MALCOLM
what's the newest grief

ROSS
that of an hour's age doth hiss the speaker
each minute teems a new one

MACDUFF
how does my wife

ROSS
why well

MACDUFF
and all my children

ROSS
well too

MACDUFF
the tyrant has not battered at their peace

ROSS
no they were well at peace when I did leave 'em

MACDUFF
be not a niggard of your speech how goes't

ROSS
when I came hither to transport the tidings
which I have heavily borne there ran a rumour
of many worthy fellows that were out
which was to my belief witnessed the rather
for that I saw the tyrant's power afoot
now is the time of help your eye in Scotland
would create soldiers make our women fight
to doff their dire distresses

MALCOLM
be't their comfort
we are coming thither gracious England hath
lent us good Siward and ten thousand men
an older and a better soldier none
that Christendom gives out

ROSS
would I could answer
this comfort with the like but I have words
that would be howled out in the desert air
where hearing should not latch them

MACDUFF
what concern they
the general cause or is it a fee-grief
due to some single breast

ROSS
no mind that's honest
but in it shares some woe though the main part
pertains to you alone

MACDUFF
if it be mine
keep it not from me quickly let me have it

ROSS
let not your ears despise my tongue for ever
which shall possess them with the heaviest sound
that ever yet they heard

MACDUFF
hm I guess at it

ROSS
your castle is surprised your wife and babes
savagely slaughtered to relate the manner
were on the quarry of these murdered deer
to add the death of you

MALCOLM
merciful heaven
what man ne'er pull your hat upon your brows
give sorrow words the grief that does not speak
whispers the o'erfraught heart and bids it break

MACDUFF
my children too

ROSS
wife children servants all
that could be found

MACDUFF
and I must be from thence
my wife killed too

ROSS
I have said

MALCOLM
be comforted
let's make us med'cines of our great revenge

190–3 **gracious . . . out** perhaps transferred from the deleted later scene.

to cure this deadly grief
MACDUFF
he has no children all my pretty ones
did you say all O hell-kite all
what all my pretty chickens and their dam
at one fell swoop
MALCOLM dispute it like a man
MACDUFF I shall do so
but I must also feel it as a man
I cannot but remember such things were
that were most precious to me did heaven look on
and would not take their part sinful Macduff
they were all struck for thee naught that I am
not for their own demerits but for mine
fell slaughter on their souls heaven rest them now
MALCOLM
be this the whetstone of your sword let grief
convert to anger blunt not the heart enrage it
MACDUFF
O I could play the woman with mine eyes
and braggart with my tongue but gentle heavens
cut short all intermission front to front
bring thou this fiend of Scotland and myself
within my sword's length set him if he scape
heaven forgive him too
MALCOLM this tune goes manly
come go we to the king our power is ready
our lack is nothing but our leave Macbeth
is ripe for shaking and the powers above
put on their instruments receive what cheer you may
the night is long that never finds the day ***exeunt***
come go we to the king
[Flourish]
comes the king forth 242a
[Enter at one door as many poor people as may be, and kneel]
[ROSS]
[sir what are these]
[MALCOLM] a crew of wretched souls 242b
that stay his cure their malady convinces 242c

242a–ab come … day This is a rough, minimal, and conjectural reconstruction, using elements that Middleton may have re-used and transposed to other parts of the scene, of what might have been the climax of Shakespeare's scene, the appearance of the holy English king, blessing the Scots resistance and formally lending them his general and soldiers. King Edward's role may have been much larger in the original script. The 1611 observer referred to him as 'Edward the Confessor', which suggests that phrase was spoken in performance; otherwise, there were many English kings named 'Edward'. Shakespeare took the account of Young Siward's death from the account of the reign of Edward the Confessor in Holinshed's *Chronicles*, which also provided other information that Shakespeare might have used in material that Middleton cut. Something that would have interested Shakespeare's patron King James (an avid hunter) was the information that 'The pleasure that [King Edward] took chiefly in this world for refreshing of his wits, consisted only in hawking and hunting, which exercises he daily used'. Another point emphasized by Holinshed, and potentially relevant to the way Shakespeare typically dramatized history, was the fact that 'King Edward put away the Queen his wife' and 'forbore to have fleshly pleasure with her'. His rigorous control of his wife would have contrasted with Lady Macbeth's excessive influence over her husband. Other details are directly relevant to the action in this scene. As an explanation for appointing others to lead an army, Holinshed records, 'age would not give him leave to execute the same by his own hand and force of body'; elsewhere he notes that Edward had 'white hair, both head and beard'. This would have created an obvious parallel with Duncan. The costuming of Edward, in this or an earlier deleted scene, might have been suggested by Holinshed's note that 'In diet and apparel he was spare and nothing sumptuous'. Shakespeare and other Londoners could have seen the shrine of Edward the Confessor in Westminster Abbey, 'which he had in his life time royally repaired, after such a stately sort as few churches in those days were like thereunto within this realm' (Holinshed); this information might have been used if Westminster Abbey were identified as the location of this conjectured lost scene, a setting which would have made it more interesting for London audiences. The same sentence that was the basis for Shakespeare's account of Edward's touching for the king's evil also records that 'As hath been thought he was inspired with the gift of prophecy'. Holinshed then gives a detailed account of his final prophecy, beginning 'Oh Lord God almighty, if this be not a vain fantastical illusion, but a true vision which I have seen, grant me space to utter the same unto these that stand here present'. The prophecy Holinshed records concerns the Norman invasion of England, which would hardly have suited Shakespeare's purposes; more relevant to Shakespeare and King James in 1606 would have been the fact that Edward, as King of England, was invited to intervene in Scotland (militarily and successfully) and that 'all the savage people of Wales [were] reduced into the form of good order under the subjection of King Edward' (Holinshed). Edward thus anticipated the uniting of the three kingdoms effected by James I, and in the play he might well have predicted a future peaceful and prosperous union. Like James, Edward 'abhorred wars and shedding of blood' (something that could have been mentioned parenthetically, by him or someone else), and it would be appropriate for him to predict that the unfortunately necessary warfare of the play's final scenes would lead, eventually, to the peace of James I, a future Scots King entering England to balance the English army about to enter the play's Scotland. Such a prophecy would have been politically topical, and welcomed by the patron of the King's Men, in 1606, when King James was again pressing his proposals for a full legal union of the two kingdoms; but those proposals were definitively rejected by Parliament in 1608, and therefore would have become increasingly problematic as the years passed (and especially after James terminated the abortive Parliament of 1614). Middleton may also have been uncomfortable with the celebration of a Catholic saint, especially if his appearance here were accompanied by any kind of religious ritual (which would have made the scene theatrically more compelling, but ideologically more objectionable). The Catholic polemicist Robert Parsons had called attention, in a pamphlet published in 1606, to the 'Obedience of King Edward the Confessor to the Popes of Rome in his time', and although Shakespeare probably would not have included that detail, it is the kind of thing that made Edward a problematic figure for many Protestants.

242d the great essay of art but at his touch
242e such sanctity hath heaven given his hand
242f they presently amend

[Solemn music. Enter at the other door Saint Edward the Confessor with Siward and monks. He touches the sufferers and hangs a golden chain about their necks and they arise healed and exeunt]

MACDUFF
what's the disease he [cures]
242g MALCOLM 'tis called the evil
242h a most miraculous work in this good king
242i which often since my here remain in England
242j I have seen him do how he solicits heaven
242k himself best knows but strangely visited people
242l all swoll'n and ulcerous pitiful to the eye
242m the mere despair of surgery he cures
242n hanging a golden stamp about their necks
242o put on with holy prayers and 'tis spoken
242p to the succeeding royalty he leaves
242q the healing benediction with this strange virtue
242r he hath a heavenly gift of prophecy
242s and sundry blessings hang about his throne
that speak him full of grace
242t [KING EDWARD] [
242u] good Siward
242v an older and a better soldier none
that Christendom gives out
242w [SIWARD] [is your] power ready
[MALCOLM]
our lack is nothing but our leave
242x [KING EDWARD] Macbeth
242y is ripe for shaking and the powers above
242z put on their instruments [
242aa] receive what cheer you may
242ab the night is long that never finds the day *exeunt*

5.1 *Sc. 20* **5.1**

incipit actus quintus

enter a doctor of physic and a waiting gentlewoman

DOCTOR I have two nights watched with you but can perceive no truth in your report when was it she last walked

GENTLEWOMAN since his majesty went into the field I have seen her rise from her bed throw her nightgown upon her unlock her closet take forth paper fold it write upon't read it afterwards seal it and again return to bed yet all this while in a most fast sleep

DOCTOR a great perturbation in nature to receive at once the benefit of sleep and do the effects of watching in this slumb'ry agitation besides her walking and other actual performances what at any time have you heard her say

GENTLEWOMAN that sir which I will not report after her

DOCTOR you may to me and 'tis most meet you should

GENTLEWOMAN neither to you nor anyone having no witness to confirm my speech

enter lady with a taper

lo you here she comes this is her very guise and upon my life fast asleep observe her stand close

DOCTOR how came she by that light

GENTLEWOMAN why it stood by her she has light by her continually 'tis her command

DOCTOR you see her eyes are open

GENTLEWOMAN ay but their sense are shut

DOCTOR what is it she does now look how she rubs her hands

GENTLEWOMAN it is an accustomed action with her to seem thus washing her hands I have known her continue in this a quarter of an hour

LADY yet here's a spot

DOCTOR hark she speaks I will set down what comes from her to satisfy my remembrance the more strongly

LADY out damned spot out I say one two why then 'tis time to do't hell is murky fie my lord fie a soldier and afeard what need we fear who knows it when none can call our power to account yet who would have thought the old man to have had so much blood in him

DOCTOR do you mark that

LADY the thane of Fife had a wife where is she now what will these hands ne'er be clean no more o' that my lord no more o' that you mar all with this starting

DOCTOR go to go to you have known what you should not

GENTLEWOMAN she has spoke what she should not I am sure of that heaven knows what she has known

LADY here's the smell of the blood still all the perfumes of Arabia will not sweeten this little hand O O O

DOCTOR what a sigh is there the heart is sorely charged

GENTLEWOMAN I would not have such a heart in my bosom for the dignity of the whole body

DOCTOR well well well

GENTLEWOMAN pray God it be sir

DOCTOR this disease is beyond my practice yet I have known those which have walked in their sleep who have died holily in their beds

LADY wash your hands put on your nightgown look not so pale I tell you yet again Banquo's buried he cannot come out on's grave

DOCTOR even so

LADY to bed to bed there's knocking at the gate come come come come give me your hand what's done cannot be undone to bed to bed to bed *exit*

DOCTOR will she go now to bed

GENTLEWOMAN directly

DOCTOR
foul whisp'rings are abroad unnatural deeds
do breed unnatural troubles infected minds
to their deaf pillows will discharge their secrets
more needs she the divine than the physician
God God forgive us all look after her
remove from her the means of all annoyance

and still keep eyes upon her so good night
my mind she has mated and amazed my sight
I think but dare not speak

GENTLEWOMAN good night good doctor

exeunt

5.2 *Sc. 21* **5.2**

drum and colours enter Menteith Caithness Angus Lennox soldiers

MENTEITH
the English pow'r is near led on by Malcolm
his uncle Siward and the good Macduff
revenges burn in them for their dear causes
would to the bleeding and the grim alarm
excite the mortified man

ANGUS near Birnam Wood
shall we well meet them that way are they coming

CAITHNESS
who knows if Donalbain be with his brother

LENNOX
for certain sir he is not I have a file
of all the gentry there is Siward's son
and many unrough youths that even now
protest their first of manhood

MENTEITH what does the tyrant

CAITHNESS
great Dunsinane he strongly fortifies
some say he's mad others that lesser hate him
do call it valiant fury but for certain
he cannot buckle his distempered cause
within the belt of rule

ANGUS now does he feel
his secret murders sticking on his hands
now minutely revolts upbraid his faith-breach
those he commands move only in command
nothing in love now does he feel his title
hang loose about him like a giant's robe
upon a dwarfish thief

MENTEITH who then shall blame
his pestered senses to recoil and start
when all that is within him does condemn
itself for being there

CAITHNESS well march we on
to give obedience where 'tis truly owed
meet we the med'cine of the sickly weal
and with him pour we in our country's purge
each drop of us

LENNOX or so much as it needs
to dew the sovereign flower and drown the weeds
make we our march towards Birnam

exeunt marching

5.3 *Sc. 22* **5.3**

enter Macbeth doctor and attendants

MACBETH
bring me no more reports let them fly all
till Birnam Wood remove to Dunsinane
I cannot taint with fear what's the boy Malcolm
was he not born of woman the spirits that know
all mortal consequences have pronounced me thus
fear not Macbeth no man that's born of woman
shall e'er have power upon thee then fly false thanes
and mingle with the English epicures
the mind I sway by and the heart I bear
shall never sag with doubt nor shake with fear

enter servant

the devil damn thee black thou cream-faced loon
where gott'st thou that goose look

SERVANT there is ten thousand

MACBETH geese villain

SERVANT soldiers sir

MACBETH
go prick thy face and over-red thy fear
thou lily-livered boy what soldiers patch
death of thy soul those linen cheeks of thine
are counsellors to fear what soldiers whey-face

SERVANT the English force so please you

MACBETH
take thy face hence [*exit servant*]
Seyton I am sick at heart
when I behold Seyton I say this push
will cheer me ever or disseat me now
I have lived long enough my May of life
is fall'n into the sere the yellow leaf
and that which should accompany old age
as honour love obedience troops of friends
I must not look to have but in their stead
curses not loud but deep mouth-honour breath
which the poor heart would fain deny and dare not
Seyton

enter Seyton

SEYTON
what's your gracious pleasure

MACBETH what news more

SEYTON
all is confirmed my lord which was reported

MACBETH
I'll fight till from my bones my flesh be hacked
give me my armour

SEYTON 'tis not needed yet

MACBETH I'll put it on
send out more horses skirr the country round
hang those that talk of fear give me mine armour
how does your patient doctor

DOCTOR not so sick my lord
as she is troubled with thick-coming fancies
that keep her from her rest

MACBETH cure her of that
canst thou not minister to a mind diseased
pluck from the memory a rooted sorrow
raze out the written troubles of the brain
and with some sweet oblivious antidote
cleanse the fraught bosom of that perilous stuff
which weighs upon the heart

DOCTOR therein the patient
must minister to himself

MACBETH
throw physic to the dogs I'll none of it
come put mine armour on give me my staff
Seyton send out doctor the thanes fly from me
come sir dispatch if thou couldst doctor cast
the water of my land find her disease
and purge it to a sound and pristine health
I would applaud thee to the very echo
that should applaud again pull't off I say
what rhubarb senna or what purgative drug
would scour these English hence hear'st thou of them

DOCTOR
ay my good lord your royal preparation
makes us hear something

MACBETH
bring it after me
I will not be afraid of death and bane
till Birnam forest come to Dunsinane

DOCTOR
were I from Dunsinane away and clear
profit again should hardly draw me here
exeunt

5·4

Sc. 23 **5·4**

drum and colours enter Malcolm Siward Macduff Siward's son Menteith Caithness Angus and soldiers marching

MALCOLM
cousins I hope the days are near at hand
that chambers will be safe

MENTEITH
we doubt it nothing

SIWARD
what wood is this before us

MENTEITH
the wood of Birnam

MALCOLM
let every soldier hew him down a bough
and bear't before him thereby shall we shadow
the numbers of our host and make discovery
err in report of us

A SOLDIER
it shall be done

SIWARD
we learn no other but the confident tyrant
keeps still in Dunsinane and will endure
our setting down before't

MALCOLM
'tis his main hope
for where there is advantage to be gained
both more and less have given him the revolt
and none serve with him but constrainèd things
whose hearts are absent too

MACDUFF
let our just censures
attend the true event and put we on
industrious soldiership

SIWARD
the time approaches
that will with due decision make us know
what we shall say we have and what we owe
thoughts speculative their unsure hopes relate
but certain issue strokes must arbitrate
towards which advance the war
exeunt marching

5·5

Sc. 24 **5·5**

enter Macbeth Seyton and soldiers with drum and colours

MACBETH
hang out our banners on the outward walls
the cry is still they come our castle's strength
will laugh a siege to scorn here let them lie
till famine and the ague eat them up
were they not forced with those that should be ours
we might have met them dareful beard to beard
and beat them backward home
a cry within of women
what is that noise

SEYTON
it is the cry of women my good lord
[*exit*]

MACBETH
I have almost forgot the taste of fears
the time has been my senses would have cooled
to hear a night-shriek and my fell of hair
would at a dismal treatise rouse and stir
as life were in't I have supped full with horrors
direness familiar to my slaughterous thoughts
cannot once start me
[*enter Seyton*]
wherefore was that cry

SEYTON
the queen my lord is dead

MACBETH
she should have died hereafter
there would have been a time for such a word
tomorrow and tomorrow and tomorrow
creeps in this petty pace from day to day
to the last syllable of recorded time
and all our yesterdays have lighted fools
the way to dusty death out out brief candle
life's but a walking shadow a poor player
that struts and frets his hour upon the stage
and then is heard no more it is a tale
told by an idiot full of sound and fury
signifying nothing
enter a messenger
thou com'st to use
thy tongue thy story quickly

MESSENGER
gracious my lord
I should report that which I say I saw
but know not how to do't

MACBETH
well say sir

MESSENGER
as I did stand my watch upon the hill
I looked toward Birnam and anon methought
the wood began to move

MACBETH
liar and slave

MESSENGER
let me endure your wrath if't be not so
within this three mile may you see it coming
I say a moving grove

MACBETH
if thou speak'st false
upon the next tree shall thou hang alive
till famine cling thee if thy speech be sooth

I care not if thou dost for me as much
I pall in resolution and begin
to doubt th'equivocation of the fiend
that lies like truth fear not till Birnam Wood
do come to Dunsinane and now a wood
comes toward Dunsinane arm arm and out
if this which he avouches does appear
there is nor flying hence nor tarrying here
I 'gin to be aweary of the sun
and wish th'estate o'th' world were now undone
ring the alarum bell
[*alarums*]
blow wind come wrack
at least we'll die with harness on our back *exeunt*

5.6 Sc. 25 **5.6**
drum and colours enter Malcolm Siward Macduff and their army with boughs

MALCOLM
now near enough your leafy screens throw down
and show like those you are
[*they throw down the boughs*]
you worthy uncle
shall with my cousin your right noble son
lead our first battle worthy Macduff and we
shall take upon's what else remains to do
according to our order

SIWARD fare you well
do we but find the tyrant's power tonight
let us be beaten if we cannot fight

MACDUFF
make all our trumpets speak give them all breath
those clamorous harbingers of blood and death
exeunt alarums continued

5.7 Sc. 26 **5.7**
enter Macbeth

MACBETH
they have tied me to a stake I cannot fly
but bear-like I must fight the course what's he
that was not born of woman such a one
am I to fear or none
enter young Siward

YOUNG SIWARD what is thy name

MACBETH thou'lt be afraid to hear it

YOUNG SIWARD
no though thou call'st thyself a hotter name
than any is in hell

MACBETH my name's Macbeth

YOUNG SIWARD
the devil himself could not pronounce a title
more hateful to mine ear

MACBETH no nor more fearful

YOUNG SIWARD
thou liest abhorrèd tyrant with my sword
I'll prove the lie thou speak'st
fight and young Siward slain

MACBETH thou wast born of woman
but swords I smile at weapons laugh to scorn
brandished by man that's of a woman born
exit [*with the body*]

5.8 Sc. 27 **5.8**
alarums enter Macduff

MACDUFF
that way the noise is tyrant show thy face
if thou be'st slain and with no stroke of mine
my wife and children's ghosts will haunt me still
I cannot strike at wretched kerns whose arms
are hired to bear their staves either thou Macbeth
or else my sword with an unbattered edge
I sheathe again undeeded there thou shouldst be
by this great clatter one of greatest note
seems bruited let me find him fortune
and more I beg not *exit alarums*

5.9 Sc. 28 **5.9**
enter Malcolm and Siward

SIWARD
this way my lord the castle's gently rendered
the tyrant's people on both sides do fight
the noble thanes do bravely in the war
the day almost itself professes yours
and little is to do

MALCOLM we have met with foes
that strike beside us

SIWARD enter sir the castle *exeunt alarum*

5.10 Sc. 29 **5.10**
enter Macbeth

MACBETH
why should I play the Roman fool and die
on mine own sword whiles I see lives the gashes
do better upon them
enter Macduff

MACDUFF turn hell-hound turn

MACBETH
of all men else I have avoided thee
but get thee back my soul is too much charged
with blood of thine already

MACDUFF I have no words
my voice is in my sword thou bloodier villain
than terms can give thee out
fight alarum

MACBETH thou losest labour
as easy mayst thou the intrenchant air
with thy keen sword impress as make me bleed
let fall thy blade on vulnerable crests
I bear a charmèd life which must not yield
to one of woman born

MACDUFF despair thy charm
and let the angel whom thou still hast served
tell thee Macduff was from his mother's womb
untimely ripped

MACBETH
accursèd be that tongue that tells me so

for it hath cowed my better part of man
and be these juggling fiends no more believed
that palter with us in a double sense
that keep the word of promise to our ear
and break it to our hope I'll not fight with thee

MACDUFF then yield thee coward
and live to be the show and gaze o'th' time
we'll have thee as our rarer monsters are
painted upon a pole and underwrit
here may you see the tyrant

MACBETH I will not yield
to kiss the ground before young Malcolm's feet
and to be baited with the rabble's curse
though Birnam Wood be come to Dunsinane
and thou opposed being of no woman born
yet I will try the last before my body
I throw my warlike shield lay on Macduff
and damned be him that first cries hold enough

exeunt fighting alarums

***enter fighting and Macbeth slain* [*exit Macduff with body*]**

5.11 *Sc. 30* **5.11**

retreat and flourish enter with drum and colours Malcolm Siward Ross thanes and soldiers

MALCOLM
I would the friends we miss were safe arrived

SIWARD
some must go off and yet by these I see
so great a day as this is cheaply bought

MALCOLM
Macduff is missing and your noble son

ROSS
your son my lord has paid a soldier's debt
he only lived but till he was a man
the which no sooner had his prowess confirmed
in the unshrinking station where he fought
but like a man he died

SIWARD then he is dead

ROSS
ay and brought off the field your cause of sorrow
must not be measured by his worth for then
it hath no end

SIWARD had he his hurts before

ROSS
ay on the front

SIWARD why then God's soldier be he
had I as many sons as I have hairs
I would not wish them to a fairer death
and so his knell is knolled

MALCOLM he's worth more sorrow
and that I'll spend for him

SIWARD he's worth no more
they say he parted well and paid his score
and so God be with him here comes newer comfort

enter Macduff with Macbeth's head

MACDUFF
hail king for so thou art behold where stands
th'usurpers cursèd head the time is free
I see thee compassed with thy kingdom's pearl
that speak my salutation in their minds
whose voices I desire aloud with mine
hail king of Scotland

ALL BUT MALCOLM hail king of Scotland

flourish

MALCOLM
we shall not spend a large expense of time
before we reckon with your several loves
and make us even with you my thanes and kinsmen
henceforth be earls the first that ever Scotland
in such an honour named what's more to do
which would be planted newly with the time
as calling home our exiled friends abroad
that fled the snares of watchful tyranny
producing forth the cruel ministers
of this dead butcher and his fiend-like queen
who as 'tis thought by self and violent hands
took off her life this and what needful else
that calls upon us by the grace of grace
we will perform in measure time and place
so thanks to all at once and to each one
whom we invite to see us crowned at Scone

flourish exeunt omnes

5.10.34.2 ***enter...slain*** either an addition, creating suspense before some spectacular special effect for Macbeth's death, or an indication that an intervening scene has been cut. Compare *Changeling* 3.1.10.2: '*Exeunt at one door and enter at the other.*'

THE PARTS

Adult Males

MACBETH (711 lines): Captain; messenger (1.5); messenger (4.2); **English Doctor**

MALCOLM (231 lines): messenger (1.5); Porter; any servant; any murderer; Lord; [**first three witches**] *or* **First Apparition**; messenger (4.2); [Old Man; Seyton *or* Scottish Doctor]

MACDUFF (178 lines): messenger (1.5); Lord; any murderer; messenger (4.2); **first three witches** *or* **First Apparition**

ROSS (136 lines): any messenger; Porter; servant (3.2); Lord; Scottish Doctor *or* Seyton; Young Siward; [**first three Witches**; Captain; English Doctor; Second *or* Third Murderer]; **First Apparition**

BANQUO (110 lines): *any but* Macbeth, Witches, Ross, Angus, Duncan, Lennox, Malcolm, Donalbain, Macduff, any murderer

KING (69 lines): any messenger; Porter; Old Man; any servant; any murderer; Lord; **First Apparition**; English Doctor; Menteith *or* Caithness *or* Siward *or* Young Siward; Seyton *or* Scottish Doctor (*or* Servant (5.3))

LENNOX (69 lines): any messenger; any servant; Seyton *or* Siward *or* Young Siward; [Old Man; Second *or* Third Murderer; Scottish Doctor (*or* Seyton); **first three Witches**]; **First Apparition; English Doctor**

FIRST WITCH (47 lines): *any but* other witches, Macbeth, Banquo, [King, Malcolm, Donalbain, Lennox, Captain, Ross, Lord]

SCOTTISH DOCTOR (42 lines): *any but* Macbeth, Seyton, servant (5.3) [Menteith, Caithness, Angus, Lennox, Malcolm, Macduff, Siward, Young Siward]

PORTER (34 lines) *any but* Macduff, Lennox, Macbeth

CAPTAIN (1 scene; 34 lines): *any but* King, Malcolm, Donalbain, Lennox, [Ross, first three Witches]

SIWARD (31 lines): *any but* Menteith, Caithness, Angus, Malcolm, Siward's son, Macduff, [Macbeth *or* Scottish Doctor *or* Seyton]

SECOND WITCH (27 lines): *any but* other witches, Macbeth, Banquo, [King, Malcolm, Donalbain, Lennox, Captain, Ross, Lord]

THIRD WITCH (27 lines): *any but* other witches, Macbeth, Banquo, [King, Malcolm, Donalbain, Lennox, Captain, Ross, Lord]

FIRST MURDERER (25 lines): *any but* servant (3.1), Macbeth, Second Murderer, Third Murderer, Banquo, Ross, Lennox [servant (3.2)]

ANGUS (21 lines): *any but* Macbeth, Banquo, King, Malcolm, Lennox, Donalbain, Ross, Macduff, Menteith, Caithness, Siward, Young Siward, [Scottish Doctor, Seyton, messenger (5.5)]

SECOND MURDERER (14 lines): *any but* servant (3.1), Macbeth, First Murderer, Third Murderer, Banquo, [Ross, Lennox, servant (3.2)]

MENTEITH (12 lines): *any but* Caithness, Angus, Lennox, Malcolm, Siward, Siward's son, Macduff, [Macbeth *or* Scottish Doctor *or* Seyton]

CAITHNESS (11 lines): *any but* Menteith, Angus, Lennox, Malcolm, Siward, Siward's son, Macduff, [Macbeth *or* Scottish Doctor *or* Seyton]

OLD MAN (1 scene, 11 lines): *any but* Ross, Macduff, [Malcolm, Donalbain]

MESSENGER (4.2: 9 lines): *any but* [Murderers]

MESSENGER (5.5: 9 lines): *any but* Macbeth, Seyton, [Malcolm, Siward, Macduff]

Parts The 1623 edition of *Macbeth* does not contain a list of dramatis personae, and we have not included an editorial list, for the same reason we have omitted a glossarial commentary. Every list of dramatis personae makes arbitrary choices about the sequence of persons and the description of each, and thus prejudices a reader's response to the playwrights' script. For a history of dramatis personae lists, see 'The Order of Persons' (*Companion*, 31). We include this list of parts because it illuminates the process of adaptation. This list differs from those elsewhere in the edition by the use of bold font (to indicate roles that belong only to the adaptation) and grey font (to indicate parts that belong only to the original).

0.1 *Adult Males* The adaptation requires 10 named speaking adult males for the transition between 5.3 and 5.4 (Macbeth, Doctor, Seyton, Malcolm, Siward, Macduff, Young Siward, Menteith, Caithness, Angus) plus Macbeth's unnamed attendants (in 5.3) and the unnamed soldiers (in 5.4). If we assume two attendants and two soldiers, the total of 14 men is the same as that required for 4.1.

1 MACBETH was originally played by Richard Burbage, who was still acting at the probable time of the adaptation. The part was changed only in the cue for the first speech, in a few speeches and cues in 4.1, and a final silent entry.

10 ROSS is not named in stage directions between 4.3 and 5.11, though he would naturally belong to the army from England in 5.4 and 5.6; this suggests that the actor doubled the Scottish Doctor or Seyton.

14 BANQUO was altered in the adaptation only in the very first speech and in an added stage direction at the very end of the part. For addition of a mute final entrance by an existing character, compare Juliet in *Measure for Measure*.

17 KING The very beginning of Duncan's role may have been abridged; this is also true of other secondary Scottish lords.

21 LENNOX This part was adapted by rearrangement and cutting in 3.6 and an addition in 4.1; it may also have been affected by abridgement of the initial battle scene(s). It might have been played, in either version, by a hired man.

25 FIRST WITCH was originally the First Weïrd Sister, played in 1606 by a boy actor, who would no longer have been a boy in 1616. The adaptation made it an adult part, which therefore completely changed its doubling possibilities. (All this also applies to Second Witch and Third Witch.)

32 CAPTAIN This one-page part was apparently rewritten.

34 SIWARD The beginning of this part was probably cut.

46 ANGUS This role, probably played by a hired man, seems to have been abridged.

DONALBAIN (8 lines): *any but* King, Malcolm, Lennox, Captain, Ross, Macbeth, Macduff, Banquo, Angus, [old man, **first three Witches**]

THIRD MURDERER (1 scene; 8 lines): *any but* First and Second Murderer, Banquo, [Macbeth, Ross, Lennox]

YOUNG SIWARD (7 lines): *any but* Menteith, Caithness, Angus, Malcolm, Siward, Macduff, Macbeth, [Scottish Doctor *or* Seyton]

SEYTON (5 lines): *any but* Macbeth, Scottish Doctor, messenger (5.5), [servant (5.3), Menteith, Caithness, Angus, Malcolm, Siward, Young Siward, Macduff]

LORD (one scene, 5 lines) *any but* Lennox *or* **first three witches**

ENGLISH DOCTOR (1 scene, 5 lines): *any but* Malcolm, Macduff, [Ross]

MESSENGER (1.5: 5 lines): *anyone*

SERVANT (3.1–3.2: 3 lines): *any but* [Macbeth, First and Second Murderer]

SERVANT (5.3: 3 lines): *any but* Macbeth, Scottish Doctor, [Seyton]

FIRST APPARITION (2 lines): *any but* Macbeth

KING EDWARD (one scene): *any but* Malcolm, Macduff, Ross, Siward, English Doctor

Boys

LADY (253 lines): wife *or* son; [Fleance]; **any singing witch** *or* **Cat; Second Apparition** *or* **Third Apparition** (*or* **any singing witch**); any weïrd sister

HECATE (88 lines): Fleance; Gentlewoman; wife *or* son

FIRST WEÏRD SISTER (49 lines): Lady, Wife *or* Son, Gentlewoman, Fleance

WIFE (40 lines): *any boy part but* Son

THIRD WEÏRD SISTER (32 lines): Lady, Wife *or* Son, Gentlewoman, Fleance

SECOND WEÏRD SISTER (31 lines): Lady, Wife *or* Son, Gentlewoman, Fleance

GENTLEWOMAN (23 lines): *any boy part but* Lady

SON (20 lines): *any boy part but* Wife

FOURTH WITCH (11 lines): Lady; Fleance; Gentlewoman; wife *or* son

FIFTH WITCH (5 lines): Lady; Fleance; Gentlewoman; wife *or* son

THIRD APPARITION (5 lines): *any but* Hecate, singing witches

SECOND APPARITION (4 lines): *any but* Hecate, singing witches

CAT (3 lines): Lady; Fleance; Gentlewoman; **Second Apparition** *or* **Third Apparition**; wife *or* son

SIXTH WITCH (2 lines): Lady; Fleance; Gentlewoman; wife *or* son

FLEANCE (2 lines): *any boy part but* Lady (?)

Most crowded scene: **4.1** (6 boys, 5 adults, 9 adult mutes)

75 LORD This one-scene part originally was larger (21 lines), and could have been doubled with any adult male roles but Lennox and Macbeth.

77 **ENGLISH DOCTOR** His lines were originally probably spoken by Malcolm, later in the same scene (4.3).

85 KING EDWARD This deleted part may have been more substantial than the minimal reconstruction offered here.

86.1 *Boys* The adaptation requires at least six boys (in 4.1), including five with good singing voices (for 3.5), and it would have required eight or nine boys if the three Weïrd Sisters had not been transformed into bearded adult Witches. The original script apparently required only three speaking boys (and none who could sing); the three Weïrd Sisters could easily have doubled Wife, Son, Gentlewoman, and Fleance, without requiring any doubling for Lady.

93 WIFE This one-scene part was expanded by 8 lines in the adaptation.

99 SON Half of the lines in this small one-scene part were added in the adaptation.

112 **4.1** The original scene would probably have required 3 boys, 1 adult, 7 adult mutes, and 1 boy mute.

CIVITATIS AMOR

Edited by David M. Bergeron

MIDDLETON demonstrates in *Civitatis Amor* that he can also write for a royal occasion, here the investiture of the sixteen-year-old Prince Charles as Prince of Wales. James I may have felt some urgency about endowing Charles with greater stature, especially if we consider the situation of the royal family in 1616. Prince Henry, the great hope of many Englishmen, especially militant Protestants, had died in November 1612 after a brief but rather gruesome illness (probably typhoid fever). In February 1613, Princess Elizabeth, the only royal daughter, married the German prince Frederick, Elector Palatine, and left England. When Middleton writes of Charles's 'rare proofs of promising heroical virtues' (22–3), he merely echoes what had been said of the popular Henry. In contrast to the glorious moment in 1610 when the entire royal family gathered for Henry's investiture, in 1616 only one of the three Stuart children remained, and only one of the two royal parents appeared. Queen Anne did not attend the public festivities in 1616 because the memory of Prince Henry remained too recent and painful for her, according to the letter-writer John Chamberlain. By contrast, in Howes's continuation of Stow's *Chronicles* (1631) we find a reference to the pageant's 'pleasant trophies and ingenious devices', more striking than 'ever was at any former Creation of any Prince of Wales'. But the Venetian Ambassador in London noted the diminished quality of the festivities.

Records of the Corporation of London indicate that the city spent £323 for the pageant entertainment on 31 October in a pattern of financial arrangements that resembles how the guilds sponsored Lord Mayor's shows. Middleton provided two scenes, one when the Prince and his party arrived by the river at Chelsea and the other at Whitehall. Both give prominence to the idea of peace: a reflection of James I's motto *Beati pacifici*, made clear again in the publication of his *Works* earlier in 1616.

Middleton creates an imaginative poetic encounter between allegorical figures and Prince Charles. At Chelsea a figure representing London, 'sitting upon a sea-unicorn with six Tritons sounding before her' (46–7), greets and speaks to Charles, as does the mythological figure Neptune. Mythology, allegory, and reality converge at Chelsea. Middleton personifies London; but she also appears in the persons of the mayor, aldermen, and others who fill barges brought along the Thames from the City of London. Mythologized, the River Thames obviously exists in fact. The whole entertainment, taking place on the river, underscores its importance in civic, commercial, and cultural life. Stow in his *Survey of London* (1603) calls the Thames 'the most famous river of this island', noting its origins in Oxfordshire and how it comes 'with a marvellous quiet course to London, and thence breaketh into the French ocean'. It serves the 'great commodity of Travellers, by which all kinds of Merchandise be easily conveyed to London, the principal store house, and Staple of all commodities within this Realm'. Michael Drayton begins a sonnet in his *Idea* sequence: 'Our floods' queen, Thames, for ships and swans is crowned.' Middleton crowns the river with a royal entertainment. Neptune addresses Thamesis, noting her fame 'to all those | That must observe thy precious tides' (58–9). Waving his silver mace, Neptune calls for silence on the river. Middleton calls for recognition of the river and the occasion.

Style and theme account in part for Middleton's accomplishment in London's remarkable thirty-line speech, which begins: 'Treasure of hope, and jewel of mankind' (74). Interestingly, the allegorical figures never address Charles by name, in contrast to the 1610 investiture pageant, which regularly named Prince Henry. Middleton instead resorts to metaphors in London's speech: 'treasure of hope', 'glory of our days', 'hope of these', and 'joy of after ages'. These metaphors accumulate with a kind of biblical resonance, as they mystify the occasion and idealize the prince. Such discourse elevates the prince's status: 'lift our loves up with his fame' (102).

Middleton skilfully weaves into London's speech the twin themes of peace and hope. These ideas become allegorical figures in the Whitehall part of the pageant as it actualizes London's speech, making manifest what has been but an idea. London also indicates that she functions as synecdoche: 'The loves of many thousands speak in me' (77). On the banks of the Thames at Chelsea she gathers up the life of the city, embodying and representing it.

Stuart political ideology and mythology appear in London's speech in the emphasis on the peaceful succession and peaceful reign of James I. London connects England's current condition—'Richer no kingdom's peace did ever see' (75)—to the peacemaker king. London adds: 'What a fair glorious peace for many years, | Has sung her sweet calms to the hearts of men' (94–5). Convinced of Charles's virtue, London foresees the continuation of a peaceful dynasty. At this hour, peace 'begins her hymns again' (97). In 1616 the country might justly celebrate peace.

London, Neptune, and their companions move on to Whitehall where they encounter 'the figures of two sacred deities, Hope and Peace' (109). Middleton describes Hope as 'leaning her breast upon a silver anchor, attended with four virgins all in white, having silver oars in their hands' (115–17). In addressing the allegorical figures, London urges Hope to 'behold the fullness of thy good' (111) and Peace to see 'the glory of thy song' (114). These qualities appear in Prince Charles, but they have yet to be dramatically realized. Middleton anticipates such fulfilment in the Whitehall scene.

Hope's response takes the extraordinary form of a sonnet, the only one in Jacobean pageants. Hope begins: 'Fair and most famous city, thou hast waked me | From the sad slumber of disconsolate fear' (118–19). If we remove the word 'city', then we could be in the presence of innumerable sonnets that focus on the 'fair' qualities of the beloved, reflecting Petrarchan influence. Sonnet 81 of Spenser's *Amoretti*, for example, contains five lines that begin with the word 'fair', all pointing to the idea of beauty. In a pageant entitled *Civitatis Amor*, we cannot be surprised to find Middleton's love sonnet, one in which the 'music' of London's 'voice' (120) awakens Hope. The idea of hope also runs as a constant thread through Elizabethan sonnet sequences. By the second quatrain Hope has moved from disconsolate fear to certainty: 'Now has my anchor her firm hold again' (122). As the procession of barges and the Prince has moved along the Thames, it has arrived securely at, first, Chelsea and then Whitehall. Coming to Whitehall, the royal palace, prompts Hope to assert: 'This is the place that I'll cast anchor in' (126). From city to court: the movement of the sonnet corresponds to the movement of the pageant. The couplet closes the sonnet with prayerful intention, as the speaker anticipates securing 'this happy shore' (130). The slightly irregular metre and the caesura in the last line add force to the idea: 'Till all be changed, never to alter more' (131). After long storms and tempests, the speaker in Spenser's Sonnet 63 of *Amoretti* has a vision: 'Fair soil it seems from far, and fraught with store.' Arriving at this happy shore, the poet asserts: 'All sorrows short that gain eternal bliss.' Middleton's Hope shares this view: till change be no more.

The city's love for Charles finds its final expression in the song of Peace, who sits 'on a dolphin, with her sacred choir' (132). Only 'such a prince, and such a day' (144) can satisfy expectations. Again, Charles exists in various metaphors: 'spring of joy and peace' (134), 'glory of life' (146). In a double metaphor Peace likens the spectators ('the many thousand faces', 137) to an 'amorous flood' (138) that becomes in turn 'like a moving wood, | Usurping all her crystal spaces' (139–40). 'Amorous flood' describes the pageant: movement along a river characterized by a loving display of entertainment. Middleton himself has usurped the blank spaces along the route at Chelsea and Whitehall and filled them with pageantry.

In an unusual development this entertainment of 31 October shared barges from the Lord Mayor's show, performed on 29 October, producing a wonderful mixture of royal and city interests. The Fishmongers sponsored the mayoral pageant, *Chrysanaleia: The Golden Fishing*, written by Anthony Munday. Their records for 11 November indicate that the Master of the King's Barges came and desired payment 'for the making... and furnishing of two barges for carrying of the mermen and mermaids by water and for barge hire at the Lord Mayor's presentment and at the meeting of the prince on the day of his instalment'. Munday's pageant included a fishing boat (in honour of the company) and barges for conveying a dolphin and mermen and mermaids. The boat Munday named the 'Fishmongers *Esperanza*, or *Hope of London*', making a connection between London and Hope that Middleton pursues two days later for Charles's arrival. Doubtless the close proximity of time for the two events (itself rare) and the city's involvement in both led to cooperation.

Two disproportionate parts make up the text of *Civitatis Amor*, for which the title-page does not indicate an author. Instead, Middleton's name appears on l. 147, at the end of the show at Whitehall. This has led editors to doubt whether the remainder of the text—an extended description of the actual investiture of Charles—should be attributed to Middleton. The description derives from the anonymous *The Order and Solemnity of the Creation of the High and Mighty Prince Henry... Prince of Wales* (1610). Middleton or his publisher simply used this earlier text, changing the names to reflect the 1616 investiture. In 1610 two separate texts record the ceremonies: *The Order and Solemnity* and Anthony Munday's *London's Love to Royal Prince Henry*, which describes the pageant for which Munday received payment. *Civitatis Amor* in effect collapses two texts into one: pageant and investiture, neatly packaged in one quarto.

Civitatis Amor begins: 'His Majesty, as well to show the bounty of his affection towards his royal son, as to settle in the hearts of his loving subjects a lively impression of his kingly care for continuance of the happy and peaceable government of his land in his issue and posterity...' (14–18). Middleton capturing James I's love for Charles and the decision to have this ceremony? No: Middleton copying almost verbatim from the 1610 *Order and Solemnity*. The 1616 text describes the barges of London's guilds 'richly decked with banners, streamers, and ensigns, and sundry sorts of loud-sounding instruments aptly placed amongst them' (35–8). This does not necessarily describe the 1616 occasion because it comes verbatim from the 1610 text. One can multiply examples. All of this material appears *before* Middleton's name on l. 147. If Middleton can so easily and obviously adapt the 1610 text at this moment in his own, then he might well have been responsible for the rest of *Civitatis Amor*, beyond the entertainment at Chelsea and Whitehall.

The remainder of *Civitatis Amor* focuses on and recounts the ceremonies for the Knights of the Bath on Saturday, 2 November; the investiture service for Charles on Monday, 4 November; and the running at the ring on Wednesday, 6 November, by fourteen noblemen. The writer records the involvement of gentlemen of the Inns of Court in some of the festivities, 'whose names, for their worthiness, I commend to fame' (206–7). After a brief report of running at the ring, the text adds: 'I should have set a period, but that the Knights of the Bath, being a principal part and ornament of this sacred triumph, I cannot pass them over without some remembrance' (243–6). We might assume that the 'I' refers to Thomas Middleton, but even the 'I' comes from the 1610 *Order and Solemnity*. Because we do not know the identity of the author of the 1610 text, we find ourselves in the presence of a floating 'I', unattached to certain identity. The 'I' of *Civitatis Amor* usurps the 'I' of the 1610 text, just as Prince Charles usurps the place of Prince Henry in truth and in text. The 'author' erases one, creating a crystal space, and inscribes another.

SEE ALSO

Textual introduction and apparatus: *Companion*, 632
Authorship and date: *Companion*, 398
General introduction to the civic entertainments: this volume, 963

Civitatis Amor

The City's Love

An entertainment by water, at Chelsea, and Whitehall. At the joyful receiving of that illustrious hope of Great Britain, the High and Mighty Charles, to be created Prince of Wales, Duke of Cornwall, Earl of Chester, etc.

Together with the ample order and solemnity of his Highness' creation, as it was celebrated in his Majesty's palace of Whitehall on Monday, the fourth of November 1616.

As also the ceremonies of that ancient and honourable Order of the Knights of the Bath; and all the triumphs shown in honour of his Royal creation.

The Ample Order and Solemnity of Prince Charles his Creation

His Majesty, as well to show the bounty of his affection towards his royal son, as to settle in the hearts of his loving subjects a lively impression of his kingly care for continuance of the happy and peaceable government of his land in his issue and posterity, having determined to invest his princely Highness with those titles and solemnities which the former princes of this realm have usually been adorned; it seemed fittest, both in regard of his Highness' years, showing the rare proofs of promising heroical virtues, and also that it would be a gladness most grateful and acceptable to the commonwealth, to have the solemnities thereof royally performed: to the effecting of which, the Lord Mayor and Aldermen of the City of London, with the several companies, honourably furnished and appointed, and marshalled in fair and comely order, both by the care and industry of Master Nicholas Leate, citizen and merchant of London, and one of the chief captains for the city; as also by the well-observed and deserving pains of Master Thomas Sparro, water-bailiff, made for that day marshal for the water-triumphs, were ready attending, with a great train and costly entertainment, to receive his Highness at Chelsea, their barges richly decked with banners, streamers, and ensigns, and sundry sorts of loud-sounding instruments aptly placed amongst them. And for his Grace's first entertainment, which was near Chelsea, a personage figuring London, sitting upon a sea-unicorn, with six Tritons sounding before her, accompanied both with Neptune and the two rivers Thamesis and Dee, at his first appearing speaks as followeth.

The City's Love. The Entertainment by Water at Chelsea and Whitehall

At Chelsea

A personage figuring London, sitting upon a sea-unicorn, with six Tritons sounding before her, accompanied thither with Neptune, and the two rivers Thamesis and Dee, at the first appearing of the Prince speaks as followeth:

LONDON

Neptune, since thou hast been at all this pains,
Not only with thy Tritons to supply me,
But art thyself come from thy utmost mains
To feast upon that joy that's now so nigh me,
To make our loves the better understood,
Silence thy wat'ry subject, this small flood.

Neptune gives action toward Thamesis and speaks.

NEPTUNE

By the timely ebbs and flows,

1 **Chelsea** western area of London on north bank of Thames
Whitehall area of royal palace and government buildings in Westminster
3 **Charles** Born in 1600 in Scotland, Charles was the youngest child of King James I and Queen Anne. His elder brother Henry had died in 1612.
16 **impression** copy
18 **issue** progeny, children
27 **companies** guilds
32 **water-bailiff** enforces shipping regulations
41 **Thamesis** poetic name of the river Thames
Dee river in western England, flowing through Wales
52 ***mains*** high sea, open ocean

That make thee famous to all those
That must observe thy precious tides
That issue from our wealthy sides,
Not a murmur, not a sound,
That may this lady's voice confound.
And, Tritons, who by our commanding power
Attend upon the glory of this hour,
To do it service and the city grace,
Be silent till we wave our silver mace.

LONDON

And you, our honoured sons, whose loyalty,
Service, and zeal, shall be expressed of me,
Let not your loving, over-greedy noise
Beguile you of the sweetness of your joys.
My wish has took effect, for ne'er was known
A greater joy and a more silent one.

Then turning to the Prince, thus speaks.

Treasure of hope, and jewel of mankind,
Richer no kingdom's peace did ever see;
Adorned in titles, but much more in mind,
The loves of many thousands speak in me,
Who from that blessing of our peaceful store,
Thy royal father, hast received most free,
Honours that wooed thy virtues long before,
And ere thy time were capable of thee;
Thou whose most early goodness, fixed in youth,
Does promise comfort to the length of time;
As we on earth measure heaven's works by truth,
And things which natural reason cannot climb:
So, when we look into the virtuous aim
Of thy divine addiction, we may deem,
By rules of grace and principles of fame,
What worth will be, now in so high esteem,
And so betimes pursued; which thought upon,
Never more cause this land had to rejoice;
But chiefly I, the city, that has known
More of this good than any, and more choice.
What a fair glorious peace for many years,
Has sung her sweet calms to the hearts of men,
Enriched our homes, extinguished foreign fears,
And at this hour begins her hymns again.
Live long and happy, glory of our days,
And thy sweet time marked with all fair presages,
Since heaven is pleased in thy blest life to raise
The hope of these, and joy of after ages.
Sound, Tritons; lift our loves up with his fame,
Proclaimed as far as honour has a name.

NEPTUNE

Sound on.

The Entertainment at Whitehall

This personage, figuring London, with the six Tritons sounding before, Neptune, and the two rivers, being arrived at Whitehall, where attend the Prince's landing the figures of two sacred deities, Hope and Peace, thus speaks.

LONDON

Hope, now behold the fullness of thy good,
Which thy sick comforts have expected long.
And thou, sweet Peace, the harmony of this flood,
Look up, and see the glory of thy song.

Hope, leaning her breast upon a silver anchor, attended with four virgins all in white, having silver oars in their hands, thus answers.

HOPE

Fair and most famous city, thou hast waked me
From the sad slumber of disconsolate fear,
Which at the music of thy voice forsaked me,
And now begin to see my comforts clear.
Now has my anchor her firm hold again.
And in my blest and calm security
The expectations of all faithful men
Have their full fruits, being satisfied in me.
This is the place that I'll cast anchor in,
This, honour's haven, the king's royal court;
Here will I fasten all my joys again,
Where all deservers and deserts resort:
And may I never change this happy shore
Till all be changed, never to alter more.

Then Peace, sitting on a dolphin, with her sacred choir, sings this song following.

THE SONG OF PEACE

Welcome, O welcome, spring of joy and peace,
Born to be honoured and to give increase
To those that wait upon thy graces;
Behold the many thousand faces
That make this amorous flood
Look like a moving wood,
Usurping all her crystal spaces;
'Mongst which the City's love is first,
Whose expectation's sacred thirst
Nothing truly could allay
But such a prince, and such a day.
Welcome, O welcome, all fair joys attend thee,
Glory of life, to safety we commend thee.

Tho. Middleton

Prince Charles his Creation

The day's triumph ended, to the great honour of the city and content of his Highness, who, out of the goodness of his love, gave the Lord Mayor and Aldermen many thanks.

On Monday following, the lords and peers of the realm being all assembled at Whitehall, his Highness then proceeded in this manner to his creation.

First went the trumpets, then the heralds and officers of arms in their rich coats; next followed the Knights of

87 ***divine addiction*** bent or leaning toward religious matters

115 **Hope . . . anchor** The allegorical figure of Hope is typically represented with an anchor.

143 ***allay*** temper or abate

the Bath, being six-and-twenty in number, apparelled in long robes of purple satin, lined with white taffeta; then Sir William Segar, knight, alias Garter principal King of Arms, bearing the letters patents; the Earl of Sussex the purple robes; the train borne by the Earl of Huntington, the sword by the Earl of Rutland, the ring by the Earl of Derby, the rod by the Earl of Shrewsbury, the cap and coronet by the Duke of Lennox, lord steward. His princely Highness, supported by the Earls of Suffolk and Nottingham, came bareheaded, and so entered the great hall, where the King was set in his royal throne, and the whole state of the realm in their order.

The Prince made low obeisance to his Majesty three times; and after the third time, when he was come near to the King, he kneeled down on a rich pillow or cushion, whilst Sir Ralph Winwood, principal secretary, read his letters patents: then his Majesty, at the reading of the words of investment, put the robes upon him, and girded on the sword, invested him with the rod and ring, and set the cap and coronet on his head. With which ceremony the creation being accomplished, the King arose, and went up to dinner; but the Prince, with his lords, dined in the hall, and was served with great state and magnificence, accompanied at his table with divers great lords, as the Earl of Suffolk, lord treasurer; the Earl of Arundel, lord marshal; the Earl of Nottingham, lord admiral; the Duke of Lennox, lord steward; the Earl of Pembroke, lord chamberlain; the Earls of Shrewsbury, Derby, Rutland, and Sussex; the Prince sitting in a chair at the upper end, and the rest in distance about four yards from him, one over against another, in their degrees; all which were those that were employed in several offices of honour about his royal creation.

At another table, in the same room, on the left hand of the Prince, sat the Knights of the Bath, all on one side, and had likewise great service and attendance. About the midst of dinner, Sir William Segar, knight, alias Garter principal King of Arms, with the rest of the King's Heralds and Pursuivants of Arms, approached the Prince's table, and with a loud and audible voice proclaimed the King's style in Latin, French, and English, thrice; and the Prince's, in like manner, twice: then the trumpets sounding, the second course came in. And dinner done, that day's solemnity ceased.

At night, to crown it with more heroical honour, forty worthy gentlemen of the noble societies of Inns of Court, being ten of each house, every one appointed, in way of honourable combat, to break three staves, three swords, and exchange ten blows apiece, whose names, for their worthiness, I commend to fame, began thus each to encounter other. And not to wrong the sacred antiquity of any of the houses, their names are here set down in the same order as they were presented to his Majesty; viz. of the Middle Temple—Master Strowd, Master Izord. Gray's Inn—Master Courthop, Master Calton. Lincoln's Inn—Master Skinner, Master Windham. Inner Temple—Master Crow, Master Vernon. Middle Temple—Master Argent, Master Glascock. Gray's Inn—Master Wadding, Master St John. Lincoln's Inn—Master Griffin, Master Fletcher. Inner Temple—Master Parsons, Master Brocke. Middle Temple—Master Bentley, senior, Master Peere. Gray's Inn—Master Selwyn, Master Paston. Lincoln's Inn—Master Selwyn, Master Clinch. Inner Temple—Master Chetwood, Master Smalman. Middle Temple—Master Bentley, junior, Master Bridges. Gray's Inn—Master Covert, Master Fulkes. Lincoln's Inn—Master Jones, Master Googe. Inner Temple—Master Wilde, Master Chave. Middle Temple—Master Wansted, Master Goodyeere. Gray's Inn—Master Burton, Master Bennet. Lincoln's Inn—Master Hitchcock, Master Nevill. Inner Temple—Master Littleton, Master Trever.

On Wednesday, the sixth day of November, to give greater lustre and honour to this triumph and solemnity, in the presence of the King, Queen, Prince, and lords, fourteen right honourable and noble personages, whose names hereafter follow, graced this day's magnificence with running at the ring; viz. The Duke of Lennox, lord steward. Earl of Pembroke, lord chamberlain. Earl of Rutland. Earl of Dorset. Earl of Montgomery. Viscount Villiers. Lord Clifford. Lord Walden. Lord Mordaunt. Sir Thomas Howard. Sir Robert Rich. Sir Gilbert Gerrard. Sir William Cavendish. Sir Henry Rich.

Having thus briefly described the manner of his Highness' creation, with the honourable service shown to the solemnity both by the lords and gentlemen of the Inns of Court, I should have set a period, but that the Knights of the Bath, being a principal part and ornament of this sacred triumph, I cannot pass them over without some remembrance: therefore thus much out of the note of directions, from some of the principal officers of arms, and some observation of credit concerning the order and ceremonies of the knighthood.

The lords and other that were to receive the honourable Order of the Bath repaired on Saturday, the second of November, to the Parliament House at Westminster, and there in the afternoon heard evening prayer, observing

161 **letters patents** an open letter or document here certifying membership in the Order of the Bath

182 **Earl of Suffolk** Thomas Howard, born 1561, son of Thomas Howard
Earl of Arundel Thomas Howard, son of Philip Howard, born 1586

183 **Earl of Nottingham** Charles Howard, Lord Admiral

184 **Duke of Lennox** Ludovic Stuart, son of Esmé Stuart, an early favourite of King James VI of Scotland who became King James I of England
Earl of Pembroke William Herbert

185–6 **Earls of Shrewsbury...Sussex** Earl of Shrewsbury, Edward Talbot; Earl of Derby, William Stanley; Earl of Rutland, Francis Manners; Earl of Sussex, Robert Radcliffe

196 **Pursuivants** heraldic officers of the College of Arms

205 **staves** sticks of wood

236 **Earl of Dorset** Richard Sackville, son of Robert
Earl of Montgomery Philip Herbert, brother of William

236–7 **Viscount Villiers** George Villiers, eventually Duke of Buckingham

no other ceremony at that time, but only the heralds going before them in their ordinary habits from thence to King Henry the Seventh's chapel at Westminster, there to begin their warfare, as if they would employ their service for God especially; from whence, after service ended, they returned into the chamber they were to sup in. Their supper was prepared all at one table, and all sat upon one side of the same, every man having an escutcheon of his arms placed over his head, and certain of the King's officers being appointed to attend them. In this manner, having taken their repast, several beds were made ready for their lodging in another room hard by, after the same manner, all on one side; their beds were pallets with coverings, testers, or canopies of red say, but they used no curtains.

The Knights in the meanwhile were withdrawn into the bathing chamber, which was the next room to that which they supped in; where for each of them was provided a several bathing-tub, which was lined both within and without with white linen, and covered with red say; wherein, after they have said their prayers and commended themselves to God, they bathe themselves, that thereby they might be put in mind to be pure in body and soul from thenceforth; and after the bath, they betook themselves to their rest.

Early the next morning they were awakened with music, and at their uprising invested in their hermits' habits, which was a gown of grey cloth, girded close, and a hood of the same, and a linen coif underneath, and an handkerchief hanging at his girdle, cloth stockings soled with leather, but no shoes; and thus apparelled, their esquires governors, with the heralds wearing the coats of arms, and sundry sorts of wind instruments before them, they proceeded from their lodging, the meanest in order foremost, as the night before, until they came to the chapel, where, after service ended, their oath was ministered unto them by the Earl of Arundel, lord marshal, and the Earl of Pembroke, lord chamberlain, in a solemn and ceremonious manner, all of them standing forth before their stalls, and at their coming out making low reverence towards the altar, by which the commissioners sat. Then were they brought up by the heralds by two at once, the chiefest first, and so the rest, till all successively had received their oath, which in effect was this: that above all things they should seek the honour of God, and maintenance of true religion; love their sovereign; serve their country; help maidens, widows, and orphans; and, to the utmost of their power, cause equity and justice to be observed.

This day, whilst they were yet in the chapel, wine and sweetmeats were brought them, and they departed to their chamber to be disrobed of their hermits' weeds, and were revested in robes of crimson taffeta, implying they should be martial men, the robes lined with white sarsenet, in token of sincerity, having white hats on their heads with white feathers, white boots on their legs, and white gloves tied unto the strings of their mantles; all which performed, they mount on horseback, the saddle of black leather, the arson white, stirrup-leathers black gilt, the pectoral of black leather, with a cross pattee of silver thereon, and without a crupper, the bridle likewise black, with a cross pattee on the forehead or frontlet; each knight between his two esquires well apparelled, his footman attending, and his page riding before him, carrying his sword, with the hilts upward, in a white leather belt without buckles or studs, and his spurs hanging thereon.

In this order ranked, every man according to his degree, the best or chiefest first, they rode fair and softly towards the court, the trumpets sounding, and the heralds all the way riding before them. Being come to the King's hall, the Marshal meets them, who is to have their horses, or else 100 shillings in money for his fee: then, conducted by the heralds and others appointed for that purpose, his Majesty, sitting under his cloth of estate, gave to them their knighthood in this manner:

First, the principal lord that is to receive the order comes, led by his two esquires, and his page before him bearing his sword and spurs, and kneeleth down before his majesty; the lord chamberlain takes the sword of the page and delivers it to the King, who puts the belt over the neck of the knight, aslope his breast, placing the sword under his left arm; the second nobleman of the chief about the King puts on his spurs, the right spur first; and so is the ceremony performed. In this sort Lord Maltravers, son and heir to the Earl of Arundel, lord marshal, which was the principal of this number, being first created, the rest were all consequently knighted alike. And when the solemnity thereof was fully finished, they all returned in order as they came, saving some small difference, in that the youngest or meanest knight went now foremost, and their pages behind them.

Coming back to the Parliament House, their dinner was ready prepared, in the same room, and after the fashion as their supper was the night before; but being set, they were not to taste of anything that stood before them, but, with a modest carriage and graceful abstinence, to refrain; divers kinds of sweet music sounding the while; and after a convenient time of sitting, to arise and withdraw themselves, leaving the table so furnished to their esquires and pages.

About five of the clock in the afternoon they rode again to court, to hear service in the King's chapel, keeping the

261 **escutcheon** shield
265 **hard by** close by
267 **testers** canopy over bed
say cloth of fine texture, sometimes partly of silk
282 **coif** close-fitting cap
285 **esquires** attendants to knights, carried knights' shields
307 **sarsenet** fine, soft silk material
312 **arson** saddle bow
pectoral ornamental cloth worn on breast
313 **pattee** an expanded, open cross
314 **crupper** leather strap buckled to back of saddle
334 **aslope** aslant
345 **Parliament House** meeting place of Parliament in Westminster Palace

same order they did at their return from thence in the morning, every knight riding between his two esquires, and his page following him. At their entrance into the chapel, the heralds conducting them, they make a solemn reverence, the youngest knight beginning, the rest orderly ensuing; and so one after another take their standing before their stalls, where all being placed, the eldest knight maketh a second reverence, which is followed to the youngest; and then all ascend into their stalls, and take their accustomed places.

Service then beginneth, and is very solemnly celebrated with singing of divers anthems to the organs; and when the time of their offertory is come, the youngest knights are summoned forth of their stalls by the heralds, doing reverence first within their stalls, and again after they are descended, which is likewise imitated by all the rest; and being all thus come forth, standing before their stalls as at first, the two eldest knights, with their swords in their hands, are brought up by the heralds to the altar, where they offer their swords, and the dean receives them, of whom they presently redeem them with an angel in gold, and then come down to their former places, whilst two other are led up in like manner. The ceremony performed and service ended, they depart again in such order as they came, with accustomed reverence. At the chapel door, as they came forth, they were encountered by the King's master cook, who stood there with his white apron and sleeves, and a chopping knife in his hand, and challenged their spurs, which were likewise redeemed with a noble in money, threatening them, nevertheless, that if they proved not true and loyal to the King, his lord and master, it must be his office to hew them from their heels.

On Monday morning they all met together nigh at the court, where, in a private room appointed for them, they were clothed in long robes of purple satin, with hoods of the same, all lined and edged about with white taffeta; and thus apparelled, they gave their attendance upon the Prince at his creation, and dined that day in his presence, at a sideboard, as is already declared.

The Names of such Lords and Gentlemen as were made Knights of the Bath, in honour of his Highness' Creation

James Lord Maltravers, son and heir to the Earl of Arundel.

Algernon Lord Percy, son and heir to the Earl of Northumberland.

James Lord Wriothesley, son to the Earl of Southampton.

Edward Lord Clinton, son to the Earl of Lincoln.

Edward Lord Beauchamp, grandchild to the Earl of Hertford.

Lord Berkeley.

Lord Mordaunt.

Sir Alexander Erskine, son to the Viscount Fenton.

Sir Henry Howard, second son to the Earl of Arundel.

Sir Robert Howard, fourth son to the Earl of Suffolk.

Sir Edward Sackville, brother to the Earl of Dorset.

Sir William Howard, fifth son to the Earl of Suffolk.

Sir Edward Howard, sixth son to the Earl of Suffolk.

Sir Montague Bertie, eldest son to the Lord Willoughby of Eresby.

Sir William Stourton, son to the Lord Stourton.

Sir Henry Parker, son to the Lord Mounteagle.

Sir Dudley North, eldest son to the Lord North.

Sir Spencer Compton, son and heir to Lord Compton.

Sir William Spencer, son to the Lord Spencer.

Sir William Seymour, brother to the Lord Beauchamp.

Sir Rowland St John, third son to the Lord St John.

Sir John Cavendish, second son to the Lord Cavendish.

Sir Thomas Nevill, grandchild to the Lord Abergavenny.

Sir John Roper, grandchild to the Lord Tenham.

Sir John North, brother to the Lord North.

Sir Henry Carey, son to Sir Robert Carey.

And for an honourable conclusion of the King's royal grace and bounty shown to this solemnity, his Majesty created Thomas Lord Ellesmere, lord chancellor of England, Viscount Brackley; the Lord Knolles, Viscount Wallingford; Sir Philip Stanhope, Lord Stanhope of Shelford in Nottinghamshire.

These being created on Thursday the seventh of November, the Lord Chancellor Viscount Brackley being led out of the council chamber into the privy gallery by the Earl of Montgomery and Viscount Villiers, the Viscount Wallingford, by the Earl of Suffolk, Lord Treasurer and the Viscount Lisle, the Lord Stanhope, by the Lord Danvers and the Lord Carew, etc.

FINIS.

362 **stalls** choir stalls
376 **angel** gold coin
384 **noble** gold coin, first minted in reign of Edward III

A FAIR QUARREL

Edited by Suzanne Gossett

A Faire Quarrell.

As it was Acted before the King and diuers times publikely by the Prince his Highnes Seruants.

Written By *Thomas Midleton* and *William Rowley.* Gent.

Printed at London for *I. T.* and are to bee sold at Christ Church Gate. 1617.

A Fair Quarrel, though written collaboratively by Middleton and Rowley, built on three plots, and echoing other plays by Middleton and his contemporaries, is a cohesive, powerful, and original tragicomedy. The main theme is traditionally said to be honour, which for Captain Ager, disparagingly called 'son of a whore' by his Colonel, is embodied in his military standing and his family's purity; for Jane Russell, secretly married and pregnant, is identified with female chastity; and for Chough, Jane's foolish Cornish suitor, is the 'reputation of gallantry' earned by holding his own in 'roaring' contests with the riff-raff of London. Richard Levin and Roger Holdsworth have demonstrated how these parallels are carried into the structure, with each plot—if one includes the added scene between Chough and the Irish pander Captain Albo—constructed around a quarrel between men about a woman's virtue. Yet the more general interest of *A Fair Quarrel* lies in its exploration of the morality of absolutes, and its sceptical view of both the duelling field and the field of male-female relations.

The story of Captain Ager was apparently invented by the authors, though it recalls Thomas Heywood's *A Woman Killed With Kindness*, whose title plot concerns woman's adultery and family honour and the second plot two friends who quarrel and duel to disastrous effect, until the rift is cured by the exchange of a sister. Captain Ager's anguished uncertainty about the chastity of his mother resonates with Middleton's repeated depiction of sexual distrust between the generations, seen as early as *The Phoenix* and at its most violent in *The Revenger's Tragedy*.

Ager, barely twenty and still a 'boy' to his Colonel, with whom he has an intense bond both filial and homosocial, cannot bring himself to defend his mother's honour without further reassurances about her fidelity. His insecurity is based not on her behaviour, which has been exemplary, but on profound psychological discomfort about male dependence upon women:

who lives
That can assure the truth of his conception,
More than a mother's carriage makes it hopeful?
And is't not miserable valour then
That man should hazard all upon things doubtful?
(2.1.14–18)

It is his lack of faith, however, that corrupts his mother's sincerity. Her immediate reaction when he probes for the truth of the phrase, 'son of a whore', is in straightforward contrast to his hesitations: striking him, she shouts, 'Thou liest!' (2.1.86). Her son has failed to respond to the Colonel's insult by 'giving the lie', the usual procedure for clearing an accusation and provoking a challenge. Lady Ager has no such qualms until she realizes that she may lose her only child, perhaps after losing another—her brother says that 'she has no daughter now. | It follows all the love must come to him [Ager]' (1.1.34–5)—and so she invents an imaginary lapse, just enough to assure the 'untruth' of the Captain's conception. She is thus the first of the play's women to choose loyalty to another over self, abandoning an abstract commitment to truth for the immediate goal of saving her son. Selfishly, Ager ignores her feelings and concentrates on his own pain, petulantly asking: 'O, were you so unhappy to be false, | Both to yourself and me? But to me chiefly' (2.1.194–5). He nevertheless lacks the courage to refuse to go to the duelling field, and there he gives speeches against duelling—'Why should man, | For a poor hasty syllable or two ... Chain all the hopes and riches of his soul | To the revenge of that, die lost forever?' (3.1.81–5)—that ring hollow once his fury is unleashed by the Colonel's second accusation, of cowardice.

Despite requisite admiration for military prowess, *A Fair Quarrel* shares the anti-duelling attitudes of *The Peacemaker*, written not long after. Ager's seconds represent all that is wrong with private warfare. They prod him to the duel, use undignified language ('Pox on him, I could eat his buttock baked, methinks', 3.1.107), flaunt the shallowness of their knowledge ('An absolute *punto*, hey!' ''Twas a *passado*, sir', 3.1.155), and are indifferent to religious scruples. When Ager claims to come with 'Peace, constant amity, and calm forgiveness, | The weather of a Christian and a friend', one mutters, 'Give me a valiant Turk, though not worth tenpence, rather' (3.1.71–3). Only when Ager wounds the Colonel, apparently mortally, do they acknowledge that such slaughter might require justification. In contrast, the wound brings the Colonel to recognize that he has pursued his own ruin by following a code that drives men to fight regardless of the righteousness of their cause. In his repentance he, like Lady Ager, abandons his unwavering commitment to a principle found meaningless and inhumane.

Modern criticism of the play began with Charles Lamb, who in 1808 anthologized Ager's confrontation with his mother, as well as the duelling scene, and praised this plot's 'delicacy of perception in questions of right and wrong'. Subsequent analysis has concentrated on the moral quandaries facing Captain Ager and his mother. There are signs that Jacobean audiences, instead, particularly enjoyed the farcical scenes. The first edition exists in two issues, both published in 1617; the second contains an additional scene (4.4) in which Chough and his man Trimtram practise what they have learned in the roaring school (4.1). Apparently Rowley—who probably played Chough, one of his typical fat-clown roles, himself—prepared the extra scene in time for it to be inserted in the remaining copies of the original issue. The cancel title leaf tempts buyers with 'new additions of Mr. Chough's and Trimtram's Roaring, and the Bawd's Song'. In the additional material Meg, the bawd, praises the 'new play', where the 'finest players' use the 'handsomest narrow-mouthed names' for 'gentlewomen of our quality'. These 'names', absurd insults for women which the Cornishmen study methodically, remained popular enough to be quoted metatheatrically almost a decade later in Rowley and Webster's *A Cure for a Cuckold* (1624–5).

Once we notice the play's focus on female sexuality, the story of Jane Russell's secret marriage comes to seem increasingly central. Indeed, the history of Jane's trials forms less a sub-plot than a balancing point, an attainable ideal, between the 'roaring' about women at the heart of the plots on either side. (The similarity of these plots would be accentuated if, as the names suggest, the parts of Captain Ager the hero and Captain Albo the pander were doubled.) Throughout *A Fair Quarrel* women of all social classes are expected to yield to the desires of their male kin. Lady Ager has no authority to prevent her son from duelling; the Colonel's Sister is willed along with other gifts to the Captain; Jane Russell is to be wed at her father's bidding to a fool who thinks marriage is a form of wrestling; and Anne, the Physician's sister, describes herself as 'his creature' and excuses herself for abetting his sexual blackmail of Jane because 'Who lives commanded must obey his keeper' (3.2.147). These women are made subservient by law, social custom, economics, and biology.

A Fair Quarrel is unusually explicit in its depiction of power relations between brothers and sisters. Middleton and Rowley concentrate not on the psychosexual but on the social and economic consequences of the authority that, in the absence of fathers, brothers exercised over their unmarried sisters. This authority was conventionally demonstrated, as it is by the Colonel, through a brother's control of his sister's marriage. Much rarer on stage was a figure like Anne, for whom marriage is not mentioned, who was historically likely to be an ageing spinster economically dependent on her brother, and who, most surprising of all, openly articulates dislike of her sibling. Even widows like Lady Ager expected to take direction from their brothers, so it is not surprising that the play begins with a brief meeting between Russell and his sister the Lady (Gossett, 1992).

Both Lady Ager and the Colonel's Sister accept the patriarchal ideal that their responsibilities are to male relatives rather than to themselves. Faced with a dying brother's demand that she 'tender both herself and all these enfeoffments to ... my late enemy, Captain Ager' (4.2.67–9), moved by an appeal that she not grudge peace to his soul, the Sister agrees to perform 'What by your will you have enjoined me to, | Though the world never show me joy again' (4.2.112–13). Similarly, Lady Ager willingly slanders her own honour to preserve her son. These decisions are made from a perspective that values personal relations more than general moral imperatives. Yet Middleton reminds us that women's choices are neither unconstrained nor reciprocated. The Colonel's plea to his sister includes reminders of his economic power and his misogyny—'Am I content, | Having much kindred, yet to give thee all ... And canst thou prove so thankless to my bounty .... O, wretched is the man | That builds the last hopes of his saving comforts | Upon a woman's charity!' (4.2.87–98). Lady Ager asserts that out of maternal affection she did something that 'were my own life's safety put upon't | I'd rather die than do't'. Nevertheless, she complains, her son still hazarded himself; ''Twas but unkindly done' (4.3.36–9). The pun on 'unkind', both inconsiderate and indifferent to the 'great tie of blood' (2.1.103), emphasizes the difference between male and female attitudes towards their mutual obligations.

Yet despite homilies of obedience and injunctions to silence, women in Middleton's London, a world of saltpetre men, unemployed soldiers, roaring boys and whores and materialistic fathers, were neither entirely helpless nor truly yielding. Russell himself half recognizes this. He attempts to soothe Jane by promising that her foolish suitor is:

> A thing that will be ruled, and thou shalt rule.
> Consider of your sex's general aim,
> That domination is a woman's heaven. (2.2.195–7)

Jane never acknowledges such intentions, but she and the other women use wit and psychological pressure to contest male control. The story of a young woman blackmailed by the physician who has secretly delivered her baby is based on the fifth tale in the fourth decade of Giambattista Cinzio Giraldi's *Gli Ecatommiti* (The Hundred Tales). Yet Jane Russell's character is much stronger than her Italian predecessor's, and her pregnancy is, surprisingly, less problematic.

The scene in which the Physician attempts to extract sexual favours from Jane is one of the play's most intense. Offered payment, he refuses monetary compensation because 'in our loving donatives to others | Man's virtue best consists'; instead he asks ambiguously for 'love', suggesting, no doubt with appropriate gestures, that 'our meanings are better understood | Than shifted to the tongue'. Only slowly does Jane fathom the Physician's intentions, but then she furiously accuses him, in an appropriately medical metaphor, of having 'Skinned o'er a green wound to breed an ulcer'. Unimpressed, he reminds her pointedly of woman's vulnerability and objectification by men: 'You've a good face now, but 'twill grow rugged; | Ere you grow old, old men will despise you' (3.2.126–7).

Jane, however, has two weapons of resistance. The first is female solidarity. Anne, sent to second her brother's demand for 'this act of woman' (3.2.148), vacillates briefly as she considers the Physician's power to destroy Jane's reputation, but ultimately 'speaks her soul' and urges the frightened and angry girl to resist. Later Anne will take revenge for her own oppression by testifying that her brother is mad. Jane is also assisted by a positive attitude towards fertility which, though in apparent conflict with the idealization of female chastity, frequently appears in the plays of Middleton and Rowley. The physical aspects of pregnancy may be carnivalesque, as they are in *A Chaste Maid in Cheapside* or *More Dissemblers Besides Women*, but they are seldom associated, as sometimes in Shakespeare, with death. The Physician himself, giving the baby to the Dutch nurse, asserts that children are 'above the quantity of price.... we are made | Immortal one by other' (3.2.6–12). A similar attitude emerges in Russell's unperturbed reaction to news of Jane's motherhood:

> Well, wipe thine eyes, I'm a grandfather then.
> If all bastards were banished, the City would be thin
> In the thickest term-time. (5.1.249–51)

While exaggerated, Russell's statement reflects the actualities of Jacobean life, when many brides were pregnant and, despite church disapproval, intercourse between betrothed couples was frequently tolerated. Jane, who tells Anne in her first confession that ''Tis no black swan I show you: these spots stick | Upon the face of many go for maids' (2.2.76–7), is not terrified by the threat of doing public penance in a sheet (5.1.28–30). She and Fitzallen have a *de praesenti* marriage, and penances in such cases were often reduced to confession before a group of fellow parishioners (Hayne).

The play's tragicomic tone is sustained by the seriousness of its events and the intensity of its central scenes. The Colonel's brush with death, the Captain's anguish, Lady Ager's dilemma, and Jane's confrontation with the Physician are all persuasively moving. Yet potential tragedy in *A Fair Quarrel* is kept in check as the plots repeatedly swerve away from personal disaster: the Colonel recovers, Captain Ager becomes instantly infatuated with the Colonel's Sister, Jane succeeds in resisting the Physician and her father and marrying Fitzallen. Tragedy is also contained by the joyous concatenation of languages: the Surgeon's jargon, the Nurse's mingled Dutch and English, the duellists' Italian, the whores' bawdy, and the nonsense of the roaring school. Finally, the clowns, Chough and his sidekick Trimtram, are a fully comic routine.

Yet even Chough's roaring scenes reiterate the contest for authority between the sexes. In 4.4 Priss warns Captain Albo of his 'penance' should he fail to defend them valiantly, and Meg reminds him of the painful consequences when 'I and my Amazons stripped you as naked as an Indian' (4.4.39–40). The key insults Chough and Trimtram learn are 'thy sister is a bronsterops', 'thy sister is a fructifer', and 'thy mother is a callicut, a panagron, a duplar and a sindicus' (4.1.112–31). The last parodies the Colonel's hollow accusation of Captain Ager; the other insults emphasize the commodification of sisters throughout. Chough is not pure fool when he asks Captain Albo, 'Is this thy sister?...I say she is a bronsterops, and this is a fucus' (4.4.65–8). The pimp determines the sexual and economic lives of Meg and Priss just as the Physician and Colonel do for their sisters; the difference between a 'fructifer' and a woman of status praised for her potential fruitfulness (5.1.432–3) quickly blurs. On all social levels, affection and family bonds easily reduce to sex and material dependence.

A Fair Quarrel was composed jointly by Middleton and Rowley, with Middleton writing 1.1.1–93, 1.1.394–425, 2.1, 3.1, 3.3, 4.2, 4.3, and 5.1.393–448. The attributions are uncertain only for the opening and closing of the first act and the end of the last, where there is not enough material to allow full statistical analysis of linguistic differences. Yet Middleton's participation in these scenes fits the general impression that the two authors worked closely together to create this intricately unified play. Middleton introduces Russell, Lady Ager, Captain Ager, and the Colonel, and writes the powerful scenes between Ager, his mother, and the Colonel; Rowley is responsible for Jane's history, the roaring scenes, and the confrontation between the Colonel and Captain Ager that builds to the provocative insult. If Rowley later wrote 4.4 alone, he nevertheless integrated it tightly into the rest of the play. In the overall structure the major plots are united by the sibling relationship between Russell and Lady Ager, which was neither artificial in early seventeenth-century London, where rich men's daughters were wives of choice among the impoverished nobility, nor arbitrary in a play which thematizes the relationship between brothers and sisters.

A Fair Quarrel demonstrates how shared attitudes and authorship may blur distinctions and create mutual influence between collaborators. Rowley's section of the first act recalls the final scene of *The Patient Man and the Honest Whore*. The treatment of sexuality in *No Wit/Help like a Woman's*—a play that includes a mother who lies to save her son, a foolish suitor encouraged for his money, a secretly married, pregnant young woman, a father consoled because he hopes 'to be a grandfather yet by 'em' (1.248), and Dutch characters—apparently lies behind Rowley's sections of *A Fair Quarrel*. On the other hand, the greatest scene in *The Changeling*, in which Beatrice-Joanna slowly realizes what compensation De Flores expects for murdering Alonzo de Piracquo, is modelled on the confrontation between Jane and the Physician. This time the model is by Rowley, the elaboration by Middleton.

The date of *A Fair Quarrel* lies between 1612, the year of Peter Lowe's *A Discourse of the Whole Art of Surgery*, which Middleton consulted for the professional jargon of the Surgeon, and the play's publication in 1617. The apparent influence of the roaring scenes in Jonson's *Bartholomew Fair*, performed in October 1614, narrows the time further. In all likelihood the play was composed in 1615–16, in which years roaring boys, the invasion of private property to search for saltpetre, and duels were all troublesome. Since the second issue, which includes the additional scene, is also dated 1617, the extra material must have been written within a year or two, perhaps for a revival. There is no obvious explanation for the prompt publication of this popular play: Rowley wrote the dedication to Robert Gray and was the leader of Prince Charles's Men, who first played it 'before the King and divers times publicly'.

A Fair Quarrel was probably performed at the Red Bull (Gurr), though if it appeared before 1617 it may have been first staged at the Hope on the Bankside (Bentley, *Jacobean Stage*). In 1979 it was revived for the first time since the Restoration at the National Theatre in London. An acute reviewer praised its 'revelation of the busy domestic actuality of London under James I' and its depiction of 'individuals stuffed with complex motives and unconscious hypocrisies' (Barber, 1979). If we add praise for its linguistic variety, its psychological acuteness, its sympathy for women, and its dramatic intensity, we explain its continuing appeal over the centuries.

SEE ALSO

Textual introduction and apparatus: *Companion*, 633
Authorship and date: *Companion*, 398
Other Middleton–Rowley works: *Weapons*, 980; *Old Law*, 1331; *Tennis*, 1405; *Changeling*, 1632; *Gypsy*, 1723

WILLIAM ROWLEY and THOMAS MIDDLETON

A Fair Quarrel

[*for Prince Charles's Men*]

THE PERSONS OF THE PLAY

RUSSELL, a rich citizen
JANE, his daughter and heir
FITZALLEN, a gentleman, lover of Jane
CHOUGH, a simple Cornish gentleman of great estate, suitor to Jane
TRIMTRAM, his man
LADY Ager, Russell's sister
CAPTAIN Ager, her son
Two FRIENDS OF THE CAPTAIN
The COLONEL, kinsman of Fitzallen and Ager's superior officer
The Colonel's SISTER, a virtuous gentlewoman
COLONEL'S FIRST FRIEND, keeper of a Roaring School
COLONEL'S SECOND FRIEND
Two SERGEANTS, disguised as Saltpetre men
PHYSICIAN
ANNE, the Physician's sister
Dutch NURSE
SURGEON
USHER of the Roaring School
VAPOUR, a whiffler or tobacco-man
ROARER
CAPTAIN ALBO, an Irish pander
Meg, a BAWD
Priss, a WHORE
SERVANT TO RUSSELL
Two SERVANTS TO LADY AGER

Epistle *To the nobly disposed, virtuous, and faithful-breasted Robert Grey Esquire, one of the grooms of his Highness's bedchamber, his poor well-willer wishes his best wishes.*

Hic et supra.

Worthy sir, this is but a play, and a play is but a butt, against which many shoot many arrows of envy. 'Tis the weaker part, and how much more noble shall it be in you to defend it, yet if it be (as some philosophers have left behind 'em) that this megacosm, this great world, is no more than a stage where everyone must act his part, you shall of necessity have many part-takers, some long, some short, some indifferent, all some, while indeed the players themselves have the least part of it. For I know few that have lands, which are a part of the world, and therefore no grounded men. But howsoever they serve for mutes, happily they must wear good clothes for attendance. Yet all have exits and must all be stripped in the tiring-house (viz., the grave), for none must carry anything out of the stock. You see, sir, I write as I speak, and I speak as I am, and that's excuse enough for me. I did not mean to write an epistle of praise to you, it looks so like a thing I know you love not, flattery, which you exceedingly hate actively, and unpleasingly accept passively. Indeed I meant to tell you your own, that is, that this child of the muses is yours. Whoever begat it, 'tis laid to your charge, and for aught I know you must father and keep it too, if it please you. I hope you shall not be ashamed of it neither, for it has been seen, though I say it, in good companies, and many have said it is a handsome, pretty-spoken infant. Now be your own judge, at your leisure look on it, at your pleasure laugh at it, and if you be sorry it is no better you may be glad it is no bigger.

Yours ever,
William Rowley.

1.1 *Incipit Actus Primus*
Enter Master Russell solus

RUSSELL
It must be all my care; there's all my love,
And that pulls on the t'other. Had I been left
In a son behind me, while I had been here
He should have shifted as I did before him,
Lived on the freeborn portion of his wit.
But a daughter, and that an only one, O,
We cannot be too careful o'er, too tender;
'Tis such a brittle niceness, a mere cupboard of glasses,
The least shake breaks or cracks 'em. All my aim is
To cast her upon riches, that's the thing
We rich men call perfection, for the world
Can perfect naught without it. 'Tis not neatness,
Either in handsome wit or handsome outside,
With which one gentleman, far in debt, has courted her,
Which boldness he shall rue. He thinks me blind
And ignorant; I have let him play a long time,
Seemed to believe his worth, which I know nothing.
He may perhaps laugh at my easy confidence,
Which closely I requite upon his fondness,
For this hour snaps him, and before his mistress,
His saint, forsooth, which he inscribes my girl,
He shall be rudely taken and disgraced.
The trick will prove an everlasting scarecrow
To fright poor gallants from our rich men's daughters.
Enter the Lady Ager with two servants
Sister! I've such a joy to make you a welcome of;
Better you never tasted.

LADY
Good sir, spare it not.

RUSSELL
Colonel's come, and your son Captain Ager.

LADY
My son!
She weeps

RUSSELL
I know your eye would be first served;
That's the soul's taster still for grief or joy.

LADY
O, if a mother's dear suit may prevail with him,
From England he shall never part again.

RUSSELL
No question he'll be ruled, and grant you that.

Epistle.0.2 **Robert Grey Esquire** Grey was a Scottish soldier who became one of the Grooms of the Bedchamber to Charles, Duke of York, by 1609, the same year that Rowley joined the Duke of York's men; *Ager* may be an anagram of *Grey*. ***his Highness's*** Charles, who became Prince of Wales on 4 November 1616
0.4 ***Hic et supra*** now as formerly
1 **butt** a mark for archery practice
5 **megacosm** macrocosm, cosmos
12 **happily** punning on haply/happily, by chance and cheerfully
13 **tiring-house** theatrical dressing room
14–15 **none...stock** Henslowe imposed a fine on actors for violating the rule against carrying off theatre property.
19 **unpleasingly** without pleasure
21 **the muses** Greek deities of the arts
21–2 **to your charge** (*a*) blamed upon you (*b*) a financial burden upon you
1.1.1–93 attributed to Middleton
2 **t'other** variation of other
4 **shifted** contrived, managed
8 **niceness** delicacy
17 **worth** wealth
20 **snaps him** catches him
21 **which he inscribes** as he calls
29 **taster** servant who tastes food to assure its wholesomeness

LADY
I'll bring all my desires to that request.
Exeunt Lady Ager and her servants
RUSSELL
Affectionate sister, she has no daughter now.
It follows all the love must come to him,
And he has a worth deserves it, were it dearer.
Enter a Friend of the Colonel's and another of Captain Ager's
COLONEL'S FIRST FRIEND
I must not give way to't.
RUSSELL What's here to question?
COLONEL'S FIRST FRIEND
Compare young Captain Ager with the Colonel!
CAPTAIN'S FIRST FRIEND
Young? Why, do you make youth stand for an imputation?
That which you now produce for his disgrace
Infers his nobleness, that being young
Should have an anger more inclined to wisdom
And moderation than the Colonel,
A virtue as rare as chastity in youth.
And let the cause be good (conscience in him
Which ever crowns his acts, and is indeed
Valour's prosperity) he dares then as much
As ever made him famous that you plead for.
COLONEL'S FIRST FRIEND
Then I forbear too long.
CAPTAIN'S FIRST FRIEND His worth for me!
[*They draw and fight*]
RUSSELL
Here's noble youths! Belike some wench has crossed 'em,
And now they know not what to do with their blood.
Enter the Colonel and Captain Ager
COLONEL
How now!
CAPTAIN Hold, hold! What's the incitement?
COLONEL
So serious at your game? Come, come, the quarrel?
COLONEL'S FIRST FRIEND
Nothing, good faith, sir.
COLONEL Nothing, and you bleed?
COLONEL'S FIRST FRIEND
Bleed, where? Pish, a little scratch by chance, sir.
COLONEL
What need this niceness, when you know so well
That I must know these things, and truly know 'em?
Your daintiness makes me but more impatient,
This strange concealment frets me.
COLONEL'S FIRST FRIEND
Words did pass, which I was bound to answer,
As my opinion and love instructed me,
And should I take in general fame into 'em,
I think I should commit no error in't.
COLONEL
What words, sir, and of whom?
COLONEL'S FIRST FRIEND This gentleman
Paralleled Captain Ager's worth with yours.
COLONEL
With mine!
COLONEL'S FIRST FRIEND
It was a thing I could not listen to
With any patience.
CAPTAIN What should ail you, sir?
There was little wrong done to your friend i'that.
COLONEL
How, little wrong to me!
CAPTAIN I said so, friend,
And I suppose that you'll esteem it so.
COLONEL
Comparisons?
CAPTAIN Why sir, 'twixt friend and friend
There is so even and level a degree
It will admit of no superlative.
COLONEL
Not in terms of manhood?
RUSSELL Nay, gentlemen—
COLONEL
Good sir, give me leave. In terms of manhood
What can you dispute more questionable?
You are a captain, sir, I give you all your due.
CAPTAIN
And you are a colonel, a title
Which may include within it many captains.
Yet, sir, but throwing by those titular shadows,
Which add no substance to the men themselves,
And take them uncompounded, man and man,
They may be so with fair equality.
COLONEL
You're a boy, sir.
CAPTAIN And you have a beard, sir.
Virginity and marriage are both worthy,
And the positive purity there are some
Have made the nobler.
COLONEL How now!
RUSSELL Nay, good sir.
CAPTAIN
I shrink not. He that goes the foremost
May be o'ertaken.
COLONEL Death, how am I weighed?
CAPTAIN
In an even balance, sir; a beard put in
Gives but a small advantage. Man and man

38 **Captain** commander of a company of about 200 soldiers
Colonel commander of a regiment
41 **Infers** implies
45 **conscience in him** as demanded by his conscience
62 **take in general fame into 'em** include reputation, as well as opinion and love
80 **titular shadows** mere titles, as opposed to substance (1.1.81)
86 **positive purity** absolute chastity, i.e. virginity. The Captain does not accept the argument that marital fidelity is a form of chastity equal to virginity.

And lift the scales.
COLONEL Patience shall be my curse
If it ride me further.
RUSSELL How now, gallants?
Believe me then, I must give aim no longer.
Can words beget swords and bring 'em forth, ha?
Come, they are abortive propagations:
Hide 'em, for shame! I had thought soldiers
Had been musical, would not strike out of time
But to the consort of drum, trumps, and fife.
'Tis madman-like to dance without music,
And most unpleasing shows to the beholders,
A Lydian ditty to a Doric note.
Friends embrace with steel hands? Fie, it meets too hard,
I must have those encounters here debarred.
COLONEL
Shall I lose here what I have safe brought home
Through many dangers?
CAPTAIN What's that, sir?
COLONEL My fame,
Life of the life, my reputation.
Death! I am squared and measured out, my heights,
Depths, breadth, all my dimensions taken.
Sure I have yet beyond your astrolabe
A spirit unbounded.
CAPTAIN Sir, you might weigh—
RUSSELL
Tush, all this is weighing fire, vain and fruitless.
The further it runs into argument
The further plunged. Beseech you, no more on't.
I have a little claim, sir, in your blood,
As near as the brother to your mother;
If that may serve for power to move your quiet,
The rest I shall make up with courtesy
And an uncle's love.
CAPTAIN I have done, sir, but—
RUSSELL
But! I'll have no more shooting at these butts.
COLONEL
We'll to pricks when he please.
RUSSELL You rove all still.
Sir, I have no motive proof to digest
Your raisèd choler back into temperate blood,
But if you'll make mine age a counsellor,
As all ages have hitherto allowed it—
Wisdom in men grows up as years increase—
You shall make me blessed in making peace
And do your judgement right.
COLONEL In peace at home
Grey hairs are senators, but to determine
Soldiers and their actions—
Enter Fitzallen and Jane
RUSSELL 'Tis peace here, sir,
And see, here comes a happy interim.
Here enters now a scene of loving arms.
This couple will not quarrel so.
COLONEL'S FIRST FRIEND [*to the Colonel*] Be advised, sir;
This gentleman, Fitzallen, is your kinsman;
You may o'erthrow his long-laboured fortunes
With one angry minute. 'Tis a rich churl
And this his sole inheritrix. Blast not
His hopes with this tempest.
COLONEL It shall calm me.
All the town's conjurors and their demons
Could not have laid my spirit so.
FITZALLEN Worthy coz,
I gratulate your fair return to peace.
Your swift fame was at home long before you.
COLONEL
It meets, I hope, your happy fortunes here,
And I am glad in't. I must salute your joys, coz,
With a soldier's encounter.
The Colonel kisses Jane
FITZALLEN Worthy Captain Ager,
I hope my kinsman shortly—
RUSSELL [*aside*] You must come short indeed,
Or the length of my device will be ill shrunk.
[*To Fitzallen*] Why now it shows finely, I'll tell you, sir—
Sir, nay, son, I know i'th' end 'twill be so—
FITZALLEN
I hope so, sir.
RUSSELL Hope? Nay 'tis past all hope, son.
Here has been such a stormy encounter
Betwixt my cousin captain and this brave colonel,
About I know not what, nothing indeed,
Competitions, degrees, and comparatives
Of soldiership, but this smooth passage
Of love has calmed it all. Come, I'll have't sound.
Let me see your hearts combined in your hands,
And then I will believe the league is good.
It shall be the grape's if we drink any blood.
COLONEL
I have no anger, sir.

93–393 attributed to Rowley
94 **give aim** assist the discussion to continue in this direction
98 **strike out of time** (*a*) miss a musical beat; (*b*) fight in a civilian setting
99 **consort** musical group
102 **Lydian ditty** a song in one of the Greek modes, characterized as soft and sweet **Doric note** music in the Doric mode, characterized by simplicity
104 **debarred** prohibited
110 **astrolabe** an astronomical instrument for taking altitudes
114 **plunged** more deeply involved
121 **pricks** a pun, on (*a*) the centre of the target; (*b*) sword; and (*c*) penis
122–3 **motive proof to digest ... blood** One of the four humours, choler was formed in the liver and caused anger; Russell has no argument certain to dissolve the choler back to blood.
123 **choler** anger
131 **interim** interlude
137 **inheritrix** female heir
140 **laid** quieted
141 **gratulate** congratulate
152 **cousin** used loosely of any relative. Ager is Russell's nephew.

CAPTAIN I have had none,
My blood has not yet rose to a quarrel,
Nor have you had cause.
COLONEL No cause of quarrel!
Death, if my father should tell me so—
RUSSELL Again!
FITZALLEN
Good sir, for my sake—
COLONEL Faith, I have done, coz.
You do too hastily believe mine anger,
And yet to say diminuting valour
In a soldier is no cause of quarrel—
RUSSELL
Nay, then, I'll remove the cause to kill the effect.
[*To Ager*] Kinsman, I'll press you to't, if either love
Or consanguinity may move you to't,
I must disarm you though you are a soldier.
Pray grant me your weapon, it shall be safe
At your regress from my house.
[*Ager gives his sword to Russell*]
Now I know
No words can move this noble soldier's sword
To a man undefenced so. We shall parle
And safely make all perfect friends again.
COLONEL
To show my will, sir, accept mine to you:
As good not wear it as not dare to use it.
[*The Colonel gives Russell his sword*]
COLONEL'S FIRST FRIEND
Nay then, sir, we will be all exampled.
We'll have no arms here now but lovers' arms.
[*Colonel's First Friend gives Russell his sword*]
CAPTAIN'S FIRST FRIEND
No seconds must begin a quarrel. Take mine, sir.
[*Captain's First Friend gives Russell his sword*]
RUSSELL
Why, law, what a fine sunshine's here! These clouds
My breath has blown into another climate.
I'll be your armourers, they are not pawned.
[*Aside*] These were the fish that I did angle for;
I have caught 'em finely. Now for my trick.
My project's lusty and will hit the nick.
Exit with weapons
COLONEL
What, is't a match, beauty? I would now have
Alliance with my worthy Captain Ager
To knit our loves the faster; here's witness
Enough if you confirm it now.
JANE Sir, my voice
Was long since given; since that I gave my hand.
COLONEL
Would you had sealed too.
JANE (*aside*) That wish comes too late,
For I too soon fear my delivery.
[*To the Colonel*] My father's hand sticks yet, sir, you may now
Challenge a lawful interest in his.
He took your hand from your enragèd blood
And gave it freely to your opposite,
My cousin Ager. Methinks you should claim from him,
In the less quality of calmer blood,
To join the hands of two divided friends,
Even these two that would offer willingly
Their own embrace.
CAPTAIN'S FIRST FRIEND
Troth, she instructs you well,
Colonel, and you shall do a lover's part
Worth one brave act of valour.
COLONEL Why, I did
Misdoubt no scruple. Is there doubt in it?
FITZALLEN
Faith, sir, delays, which at the least are doubts.
But here's a constant resolution fixed,
Which we wish willingly he would accord to.
COLONEL
Tush, he shall do't, I will not be denied,
He owes me so much in the recompense
Of my reconcilement. Captain Ager,
You will take our parts against your uncle
In this quarrel?
CAPTAIN I shall do my best, sir,
Two denials shall not repulse me. I love
Your worthy kinsman and wish him mine, I know
He doubts it not.
COLONEL See, he's returned.
Enter Russell and a Servant
RUSSELL [*aside to Servant*] Your cue,
Be sure you keep it, 'twill be spoken quickly.
Therefore watch it. [*Exit Servant*]
COLONEL Let's set on him all at once.
OMNES
Sir, we have a suit to you.
RUSSELL What, all at once?
OMNES All, all, i'faith, sir.

166 **diminuting** belittling
170 **consanguinity** blood relationship
173 **regress** withdrawal
175 **parle** confer
187 **hit the nick** reach my goal
190–1 **witness...now** A valid *de presenti* marriage required a verbal agreement in the presence of witnesses.
191–3 **voice...hand...sealed** The comments here and at 2.2.86–7 and 5.1.369–71 reflect the complex state of Elizabethan marriage arrangements. By giving her voice Jane presumably agreed to a *de futuro* marriage; this became a *de praesenti* marriage by handfasting, creating the 'jugal knot' that heaven witnessed (2.2.86). The marriage has been consummated ('sealed') but there has been no church ceremony. Jane also puns that she is sealed or marked by her sexual activity.
194 **delivery** (*a*) formal transfer of a deed (*b*) childbirth
206 **Misdoubt no scruple** not anticipate any objection
220 **Omnes** all together

RUSSELL
One speaker may yet deliver. Say, say,
I shall not dare to stand out against so many.

COLONEL
Faith, sir, here's a brabbling matter hangs on demur,
I make the motion for all without a fee.
Pray you, let it be ended this term.

RUSSELL Ha, ha, ha!
(*Aside*) That's the rascal's cue, and he has missed it.
[*To the Colonel*] What is it? What is it, sir?

COLONEL Why sir, here's a man,
And here's a woman; you're scholar good enough.
Put 'em together and tell me what it spells.

RUSSELL Ha, ha, ha!
[*Aside*] There's his cue once again.

Enter Servant

O, he's come, humh.

SERVANT [*aside*]
My master laughs, that's his cue to mischief.

COLONEL
What say you, sir?

SERVANT Sir—

RUSSELL Ha? What say you, sir?

SERVANT
Sir, there's a couple desire speedily to speak with you.

RUSSELL
A couple, sir? Of what, hounds or horses?

SERVANT
Men, sir, gentlemen or yeomen, I know not which,
But thc one sure they are.

RUSSELL
Hast thou no other description of them?

SERVANT They come with commission, they say, sir, to taste of your earth; if they like it, they'll turn it into gunpowder.

RUSSELL
O, they are saltpetremen, before me,
And they bring commission: the King's power indeed!
They must have entrance, but the knaves will be bribed.
There's all the hope we have in officers.
They were too dangerous in a commonwealth
But that they will be very well corrupted.
Necessary varlets.

SERVANT
Shall I enter in, sir?

RUSSELL By all fair means, sir,
And with all speed, sir, give 'em very good words
To save my ground unravished, unbroke up.

[*Exit Servant*]

Mine's yet a virgin earth: the worm hath not been seen
To wriggle in her chaste bowels, and I'd be loath
A gunpowder fellow should deflower her now.

COLONEL
Our suit is yet delayed by this means, sir.

RUSSELL
Alas, I cannot help it. These fellows gone
(As I hope I shall dispatch 'em quickly)
A few articles shall conclude your suit.
Who? Master Fitzallen? The only man
That my adoption aims at.

COLONEL There's good hope then.

Enter two Sergeants in disguise

FIRST SERGEANT Save you, sir.

RUSSELL
You are welcome, sir, for aught I know yet.

SECOND SERGEANT
We come to take a view and taste of your ground, sir.

RUSSELL
I had rather feed you with better meat,
Gentlemen, but do your pleasures, pray.

FIRST SERGEANT
This is our pleasures: [*To Fitzallen*] we arrest you, sir,
In the King's name.

FITZALLEN Ha! At whose suit?

RUSSELL How's that?

COLONEL
Our weapons, good sir, furnish us.

JANE Ay me!

RUSSELL
Stay, stay, gentlemen, let's inquire the cause.
It may be but a trifle, a small debt
Shall need no rescue here.

SECOND SERGEANT Sir, betwixt three creditors, Master Leech, Master Swallow, and Master Bonesuck, the debts are a thousand pounds.

RUSSELL
A thousand pounds? Beshrew me, a good man's substance.

COLONEL
Good sir, our weapons! We'll teach these varlets
To walk in their own parti-coloured coats,
That they may be distinguished from honest men.

FIRST SERGEANT
Sir, attempt no rescue, he's our prisoner.
You'll make the danger worse by violence.

COLONEL
A plague upon your gunpowder treason!
Ye quick-damned varlets,

224 **brabbling... demur** A minor but disputed question awaits resolution; demur is from *demurrer*, a legal objection.
225–6 **motion... fee... term** The Colonel, acting as a lawyer without payment, applies for a decision during the present legal session.
237 **gentlemen** a man with financial independence from labour, though not a nobleman
yeomen a freeholder or farmer
243 **saltpetremen** officers appointed to find saltpetre for the production of gunpowder. Saltpetremen had the right to enter private premises to search for the material.
250 **enter in** the officers, understood
261 **adoption** acceptance as a relation
278 **parti-coloured** multicoloured
282 **gunpowder treason** the Gunpowder Plot to blow up the king and parliament, 5 November 1605

Is this your saltpetre proving, your tasting earth?
Would you might never feed better, nor none
Of your catchpole tribe. [*To Russell*] Our weapons, good sir,
We'll yet deliver him.

RUSSELL
Pardon me, sir,
I dare not suffer rescue here, at least
Not be so great an accessory
As to furnish you. Had you had your weapons,
But to see the ill fate on't! [*Aside*] My fine trick, i'faith.
Let beggars beware to love rich men's daughters,
I'll teach 'em the new morris, I learned it
Myself of another careful father.

FITZALLEN
May I not be bailed?

SECOND SERGEANT
Yes, but not with swords.

COLONEL
Slaves, here are sufficient men.

FIRST SERGEANT
Ay, i'th' field,
But not in the city, sir. If this gentleman
Will be one, we'll easily admit the second.

RUSSELL
Who, I, sir? Pray pardon me, I am wronged,
Very much wronged in this, I must needs speak it.
Sir, you have not dealt like an honest lover
With me nor my child. Here you boast to me
Of a great revenue, a large substance
Wherein you would endow and state my daughter.
Had I missed this, my opinion yet
Thought you a frugal man, to understand
The sure wards against all necessities,
Boldly to defend your wife and family,
To walk unmuffled, dreadless of these flesh-hooks,
Even in the daringest streets through all the city.
But now I find you a loose prodigal,
A large unthrift. A whole thousand pound?
Come from him, girl, his inside is not sound.

FITZALLEN
Sir, I am wronged. These are malicious plots
Of some obscure enemies that I have.
These debts are none of mine.

RUSSELL
Ay, all say so.
Perhaps you stand engaged for other men:
If so you do, you must then call't your own.
The like arrearage do I run into
Should I bail you. But I have vowed against it,
And I will keep my vows, that's religious.

FITZALLEN
All this is nothing so, sir.

RUSSELL
Nothing so?
By my faith it is, sir, my vows are firm.

FITZALLEN
I neither owe these debts, nor engaged for others.

RUSSELL
The easier is your liberty regained.
These appear proofs to me.

COLONEL
Liberty, sir?
I hope you'll not see him go to prison.

RUSSELL
I do not mean to bear him company
So far, but I'll see him out of my doors.
O sir, let him go to prison, 'tis a school
To tame wild bloods. He'll be much better for't.

COLONEL
Better for lying in prison?

RUSSELL
In prison.
Believe it, many an honest man lies in prison,
Else all the keepers are knaves; they told me so themselves.

COLONEL
Sir, I do now suspect you have betrayed him
And us, to cause us to be weaponless.
If it be so, you're a blood-sucking churl,
One that was born in a great frost, when charity
Could not stir a finger, and you shall die
In heat of a burning fever i'th' dog-days,
To begin your hell to you. I have said your grace for you,
Now get you to supper as soon as you can.
Pluto, the master of the house, is set already.

CAPTAIN
Sir, you do wrong mine uncle.

COLONEL
Pox on your uncle
And all his kin, if my kinsman mingle
No blood with him.

CAPTAIN
You're a foul-mouthed fellow.

COLONEL
Foul-mouthed I will be, thou'rt the son of a whore.

CAPTAIN
Ha! Whore! Plagues and furies! I'll thrust that back
Or pluck thy heart out after. Son of a whore?

COLONEL
On thy life I'll prove it.

CAPTAIN
Death, I am naked!
Uncle, I'll give you my left hand for my sword
To arm my right with. O, this fire will flame me
Into present ashes.

COLONEL
Sir, give us weapons.

286 **catchpole** contemptuous term for a petty officer, especially one who arrests for debt
293 **morris** country dance
304 **state** instate
307 **wards** defences
309 **flesh-hooks** hooks for removing meat from a pot, here, metaphorically, the sergeants who seize Fitzallen. In *Quiet Life* there is a sergeant named Fleshhook.
310 **daringest** most dangerous
319 **arrearage** indebtedness
338 **great frost** During the Great Frost of 1606–7 the Thames froze for six weeks.
340 **dog-days** the hottest part of the year, from late July to early August
343 **Pluto** god of the underworld
347 **son of a whore** the standard phrase used to provoke a challenge from the person insulted, normally understood to be without literal significance
350 **naked** without a weapon

We ask our own, you will not rob us of them?

RUSSELL

No sir, but still restrain your furies here.
At my door I'll give you them, nor, at this time,
My nephew's. A time will better suit you,
And I must tell you, sir, you have spoke swords,
And 'gainst the law of arms poisoned the blades
And with them wounded the reputation
Of an unblemished woman. Would you were out of
my doors!

COLONEL

Pox on your doors, and let it run all your house o'er!
Give me my sword.

CAPTAIN We shall meet, Colonel?

COLONEL

Yes, better provided. To spur thee more
I do repeat my words, son of a whore!

Exit with his Friend

CAPTAIN'S FIRST FRIEND

Come, sir, 'tis no worse than 'twas, you can do
nothing now.

Exit Captain and his Friend

RUSSELL

No, I'll bar him now, away with that beggar. *Exit*

JANE [*giving money to First Sergeant*]

Good sir, let this persuade you for two minutes stay.
At this price I know you can wait all day.

FIRST SERGEANT

You know the remora that stays our ship always.

JANE

Your ship sinks many when this hold lets go.
O my Fitzallen, what is to be done?

FITZALLEN

To be still thine is all my part to be,
Whether in freedom or captivity.

JANE

But art thou so engaged as this pretends?

FITZALLEN

By heav'n, sweet Jane, 'tis all a hellish plot.
Your cruel-smiling father all this while
Has candied o'er a bitter pill for me,
Thinking by my remove to plant some other,
And then let go his fangs.

JANE Plant some other?
Thou hast too firmly stamped me for thine own
Ever to be rased out. I am not current
In any other's hand; I fear too soon
I shall discover it.

FITZALLEN Let come the worst,
Bind but this knot with an unloosèd line,
I will be still thine own.

JANE And I'll be thine.

FIRST SERGEANT

My watch has gone two minutes, master.

FITZALLEN

It shall not be renewed. I go, sir. Farewell.

JANE

Farewell. We both are prisoned, though not together,
But here's the difference in our luckless chance:
I fear mine own, wish thy deliverance.

FITZALLEN

Our hearts shall hourly visit, I'll send to thee.
Then 'tis no prison where the mind is free.

Exit with Officers

Enter Russell

RUSSELL

So, let him go. Now wench, I bring thee joys,
A fair sunshine after this angry storm.
It was my policy to remove this beggar.
What, shall rich men wed their only daughters
To two fair suits of clothes, and perhaps yet
The poor tailor is unpaid? No, no, my girl,
I have a lad of thousands coming in.
Suppose he have more wealth than wit to guide it,
Why, there's thy gains, thou keep'st the keys of all,
Disposest all, and, for generation,
Man does most seldom stamp 'em from the brain:
Wise men begets fools, and fools are the fathers
To many wise children. *Hysteron proteron*,
A great scholar may beget an idiot,
And from the plough-tail may come a great scholar.
Nay, they are frequent propagations.

JANE

I am not well, sir.

RUSSELL Ha! Not well, my girl?
Thou shalt have a physician then,
The best that gold can fetch upon his footcloth.
Thou know'st my tender pity to thee ever.
Want nothing that thy wishes can instruct thee
To call for. Fore me, and thou look'st half ill indeed.
But I'll bring one within a day to thee
Shall rouse thee up, for he's come up already:
One Master Chough, a Cornish gentleman.
H'as as much land of his own fee-simple

363 **meet** in combat
370 **remora** a sucking fish believed capable of stopping the ship to which it attaches itself
375 **pretends** claims
379 **remove** removal
381–3 **stamped ... rased out ... current ... hand** Jane describes herself as a coin bearing the permanent imprint of a monarch, useless in any other realm. The metaphor includes a series of sexual puns on conception and pregnancy.
385 **Bind** strengthen
unloosèd unloosened
394–425 attributed to Middleton
402 **keep'st the keys of all** control all the household possessions, kept locked in chests and pantries
403 **generation** begetting of children
406 ***Hysteron proteron*** by inversion of the natural order of things
409 **propagations** offspring
412 **footcloth** ornamental cloth placed over the back of a horse and hanging down on each side; a sign of dignity
417 **come up** to London
418 **Chough** a nickname for the Cornish crow or *Fregillus Graculus*, a bird with red bill and legs common in Cornwall
Cornish from Cornwall, the extreme south-west of England
419 **fee-simple** full ownership

As a crow can fly over in half a day,
And now I think on't, at the Crow at Aldgate
His lodging is. He shall so stir thee up!
Come, come, be cheered, think of thy preferment.
Honour and attendance, these will bring thee health,
And the way to 'em is to climb by wealth. *Exeunt*

Finis Actus Primus

2.1 *Incipit Actus Secundus*

Enter Captain Ager

CAPTAIN The son of a whore?
There is not such another murd'ring piece
In all the stock of calumny: it kills
At one report two reputations,
A mother's and a son's. If it were possible
That souls could fight after the bodies fell,
This were a quarrel for 'em. He should be one indeed
That never heard of heaven's joys or hell's torments
To fight this out. I am too full of conscience,
Knowledge, and patience to give justice to't,
So careful of my eternity, which consists
Of upright actions, that unless I knew
It were a truth I stood for, any coward
Might make my breast his foot-pace. And who lives
That can assure the truth of his conception
More than a mother's carriage makes it hopeful?
And is't not miserable valour then
That man should hazard all upon things doubtful?
O, there's the cruelty of my foe's advantage!
Could but my soul resolve my cause were just,
Earth's mountain nor sea's surge should hide him from me;
E'en to hell's threshold would I follow him
And see the slanderer in before I left him.
But as it is it fears me, and I never
Appeared too conscionably just till now.
My good opinion of her life and virtues
Bids me go on, and fain would I be ruled by't;
But when my judgement tells me she's but woman,
Whose frailty let in death to all mankind,
My valour shrinks at that. Certain she's good:
There only wants but my assurance in't
And all things then were perfect. How I thirst for't!
Here comes the only she that could resolve,
But 'tis too vile a question to demand indeed.

Enter the Lady Ager

LADY
Son, I've a suit to you.

CAPTAIN [*aside*] That may do well.
[*To Lady Ager*] To me, good madam? You're most sure to speed in't,
Be't i'my power to grant it.

LADY 'Tis my love
Makes the request, that you would never part
From England more.

CAPTAIN With all my heart 'tis granted;
[*Aside*] I'm sure I'm i'th' way never to part from't.

LADY
Where left you your dear friend, the Colonel?

CAPTAIN
O, the dear Colonel, I should meet him soon.

LADY
O, fail him not then, he's a gentleman
The fame and reputation of your time
Is much engaged to.

CAPTAIN Yes, and you knew all, mother.

LADY
I thought I'd known so much of his fair goodness
More could not have been looked for.

CAPTAIN O, yes, yes, madam,
And this his last exceeded all the rest.

LADY
For gratitude's sake let me know this, I prithee.

CAPTAIN
Then thus, and I desire your censure freely
Whether it appeared not a strange noble kindness in him.

LADY
Trust me, I long to hear't.

CAPTAIN You know he's hasty,
That by the way.

LADY So are the best conditions;
Your father was the like.

CAPTAIN [*aside*] I begin now
To doubt me more. Why am not I so too then?
Blood follows blood through forty generations,
And I've a slow-paced wrath. A shrewd dilemma!

LADY
Well, as you were saying, sir.

CAPTAIN Marry thus, good madam.
There was in company a foul-mouthed villain—stay, stay,
Who should I liken him to that you have seen—
He comes so near one that I would not match him with,
Faith, just o' the Colonel's pitch. He's ne'er the worse man:
Usurers have been compared to magistrates,
Extortioners to lawyers and the like,
But they all prove ne'er the worse men for that.

421 **Crow** Inns were identified by names; Sugden suggests that the Crow in Aldgate was the same as the Pye Inn in Aldgate High Street.
2.1.1–250 attributed to Middleton
2 **murd'ring piece** a small cannon or mortar
4 **report** (*a*) detonation (*b*) declaration
14 **foot-pace** place to put the feet, mat
16 **carriage** behaviour
24 **fears me** frightens me
25 **conscionably** conscientiously
29 **Whose...mankind** a reference to Eve
50 **censure** judgement
53 **conditions** dispositions, temperaments
62 **pitch** height, both physical and metaphorical

LADY
That's bad enough, they need not.
CAPTAIN
This rude fellow,
A shame to all humanity or manners,
Breathes from the rottenness of his gall and malice
The foulest stain that ever man's fame blemished,
Part of which fell upon your honour, madam,
Which heightened my affliction.
LADY
Mine? My honour, sir?
CAPTAIN
The Colonel soon enraged, as he's all touchwood,
Takes fire before me, makes the quarrel his,
Appoints the field. My wrath could not be heard
His was so high-pitched, so gloriously mounted.
Now what's the friendly fear that fights within me:
Should his brave noble fury undertake
A cause that were unjust in our defence,
And so to lose him everlastingly
In that dark depth where all bad quarrels sink,
Never to rise again. What pity 'twere
First to die here and never to die there.
LADY
Why, what's the quarrel, speak, sir, that should raise
Such fearful doubt, my honour bearing part on't?
The words, whate'er they were.
CAPTAIN
Son of a whore.
LADY Thou liest!
She strikes him
And were my love ten thousand times more to thee,
Which is as much now as e'er mother's was,
So thou shouldst feel my anger. Dost thou call
That quarrel doubtful? Where are all my merits?
Not one stand up to tell this man his error?
Thou might'st as well bring the sun's truth in question
As thy birth or my honour.
CAPTAIN
Now blessings crown you for't,
It is the joyfullest blow that e'er flesh felt.
LADY
Nay stay, stay, sir, thou art not left so soon.
This is no question to be slighted off,
And at your pleasure closed up fair again
As though you'd never touched it. No, honour doubted
Is honour deeply wounded, and it rages
More than a common smart, being of thy making.
For thee to fear my truth, it kills my comfort.
Where should fame seek for her reward, when he
That is her own by the great tie of blood
Is farthest off in bounty? O poor goodness,
That only pay'st thyself with thy own works,
For nothing else looks towards thee. Tell me, pray,
Which of my loving cares dost thou requite
With this vile thought? Which of my prayers or wishes?
Many thou owest me for. This seven year hast thou known me
A widow, only married to my vow.
That's no small witness of my faith and love
To him that in life was thy honoured father,
And live I now to know that good mistrusted?
CAPTAIN
No, 't shall appear that my belief is cheerful,
For never was a mother's reputation
Noblier defended. 'Tis my joy and pride
I have a firm to bestow upon it.
LADY
What's that you said, sir?
CAPTAIN
'Twere too bold and soon yet
To crave forgiveness of you. I will earn it first;
Dead or alive, I know I shall enjoy it.
LADY
What's all this, sir?
CAPTAIN
My joy's beyond expression;
I do but think how wretched I had been
Were this another's quarrel and not mine.
LADY
Why, is it yours?
CAPTAIN
Mine! Think me not so miserable
Not to be mine. Then were I worse than abject,
More to be loathed than vileness or sin's dunghill.
Nor did I fear your goodness, faithful madam,
But came with greedy joy to be confirmed in't,
To give the nobler onset. Then shines valour,
And admiration from her fixed sphere draws,
When it comes burnished with a righteous cause,
Without which I'm ten fathoms under coward
That now am ten degrees above a man,
Which is but one of virtue's easiest wonders.
LADY
But pray, stay; all this while I understood you
The Colonel was the man.
CAPTAIN
Yes, he's the man,
The man of injury, reproach, and slander,
Which I must turn into his soul again.
LADY
The Colonel do't! That's strange.
CAPTAIN
The villain did it;
That's not so strange. Your blessing and your leave.
LADY
Come, come, you shall not go.
CAPTAIN
Not go! Were death
Sent now to summon me to my eternity,
I'd put him off an hour. Why, the whole world
Has not chains strong enough to bind me from it.
The strongest is my reverence to you,

72 **touchwood** tinder
101 **fear my truth** be uncertain about my fidelity
110 **to my vow** probably a vow never to remarry, like that taken by the Duchess in *Dissemblers*, but possibly her original marriage vow
117 **firm** signature or sign, here, the mark from his sword

Which if you force upon me in this case
I must be forced to break it.
LADY Stay, I say.
CAPTAIN
In anything command me but in this, madam.
LADY [*aside*]
'Las, I shall lose him! [*To Ager*] You'll hear me first.
CAPTAIN
At my return I will.
LADY You'll never hear me more, then.
CAPTAIN How?
LADY Come back, I say.
You may well think there's cause I call so often.
CAPTAIN
Ha, cause! What cause?
LADY So much, you must not go.
CAPTAIN How?
LADY You must not go.
CAPTAIN
Must not! Why?
LADY I know a reason for it,
Which I could wish you'd yield to, and not know.
If not, it must come forth. Faith, do not know,
And yet obey my will.
CAPTAIN Why, I desire
To know no other than the cause I have,
Nor should you wish it if you take your injury,
For one more great I know the world includes not.
LADY
Yes, one that makes this nothing. Yet be ruled,
And if you understand not, seek no further.
CAPTAIN
I must, for this is nothing.
LADY Then take all,
And if amongst it you receive that secret
That will offend you, though you condemn me
Yet blame yourself a little, for perhaps
I would have made my reputation sound
Upon another's hazard with less pity,
But upon yours I dare not.
CAPTAIN How?
LADY I dare not.
'Twas your own seeking, this.
CAPTAIN If you mean evilly,
I cannot understand you, nor for all the riches
This life has, would I.
LADY Would you never might.
CAPTAIN
Why, your goodness, that I joy to fight for.
LADY
In that you neither right your joy nor me.
CAPTAIN
What an ill orator has virtue got here?
Why, shall I dare to think it a thing possible
That you were ever false?
LADY O, fearfully!
As much as you come to.
CAPTAIN O silence, cover me!
I've felt a deadlier wound than man can give me.
False?
LADY
I was betrayed to a most sinful hour
By a corrupted soul I put in trust once,
A kinswoman.
CAPTAIN Where is she? Let me pay her.
LADY
O, dead long since.
CAPTAIN Nay, then sh'as all her wages.
False! Do not say't, for honour's goodness do not,
You never could be so. He I called father
Deserved you at your best, when youth and merit
Could boast at highest in you. You'd no grace
Or virtue that he matched not, no delight
That you invented but he sent it crowned
To your full wishing soul.
LADY That heaps my guiltiness.
CAPTAIN
O, were you so unhappy to be false,
Both to yourself and me? But to me chiefly.
What a day's hope is here lost, and with it
The joys of a just cause. Had you but thought
On such a noble quarrel, you'd ha' died
Ere you'd ha' yielded, for the sin's hate first,
Next for the shame of this hour's cowardice.
Cursed be the heat that lost me such a cause,
A work that I was made for. Quench, my spirit,
And out with honour's flaming lights within thee!
Be dark and dead to all respects of manhood;
I never shall have use of valour more.
Put off your vow for shame: why should you hoard up
Such justice for a barren widowhood
That was so injurious to the faith of wedlock?
Exit Lady Ager
I should be dead, for all my life's work's ended:
I dare not fight a stroke now, nor engage
The noble resolution of my friends:
That were more vile.
Enter two Friends of Captain Ager's
They're here! Kill me, my shame,
I am not for the fellowship of honour.
CAPTAIN'S FIRST FRIEND
Captain! Fie, come sir, we have been seeking for you
Very late today. This was not wont to be.
Your enemy's i'th' field.
CAPTAIN Truth enters cheerfully.
CAPTAIN'S SECOND FRIEND
Good faith, sir, you've a royal quarrel on't.

181 **As much . . . to** My infidelity brought about your birth.
185 **pay her** kill her

CAPTAIN
Yes, in some other country, Spain or Italy,
It would be held so.

CAPTAIN'S FIRST FRIEND
How, and is't not here so?

CAPTAIN
'Tis not so contumeliously received
In these parts, an you mark it.

CAPTAIN'S FIRST FRIEND Not in these?
Why, prithee, what is more, or can be?

CAPTAIN Yes,
That ordinary commotioner, the lie,
Is father of most quarrels in this climate,
And held here capital, and you go to that.

CAPTAIN'S SECOND FRIEND
But sir, I hope you will not go to that,
Or change your own for it. Son of a whore!
Why, there's the lie down to posterity,
The lie to birth, the lie to honesty.
Why would you cozen yourself so and beguile
So brave a cause, manhood's best masterpiece?
Do you ever hope for one so brave again?

CAPTAIN
Consider then the man, Colonel,
Exactly worthy, absolutely noble,
However spleen and rage abuses him,
And 'tis not well nor manly to pursue
A man's infirmity.

CAPTAIN'S FIRST FRIEND
O miracle!
So hopeful, valiant, and complete a captain
Possessed with a tame devil! Come out, thou spoilest
The most improved young soldier of seven kingdoms,
Made captain at nineteen, which was deserved
The year before, but honour comes behind still.
Come out, I say, this was not wont to be.
That spirit never stood in need of provocation,
Nor shall it now. Away, sir.

CAPTAIN Urge me not.

CAPTAIN'S FIRST FRIEND
By manhood's reverend honour, but we must.

CAPTAIN
I will not fight a stroke.

CAPTAIN'S FIRST FRIEND O blasphemy
To sacred valour!

CAPTAIN Lead me where you list.

CAPTAIN'S FIRST FRIEND
Pardon this traitorous slumber, clogged with evils;
Give captains rather wives than such tame devils.
Exeunt

Enter Physician and Jane 2.2

PHYSICIAN
Nay, mistress, you must not be covered to me.
The patient must ope to the physician
All her dearest sorrows: art is blinded else,
And cannot show her mystical effects.

JANE
Can art be so dim-sighted, learnèd sir?
I did not think her so incapacious.
You train me, as I guess, like a conjuror,
One of our fine oraculous wizards,
Who from the help of his examinant,
By the near guess of his suspicion
Appoints out the thief by the marks he tells him.
Have you no skill in physiognomy?
What colour, says your coat, is my disease?
I am unmarried, and it cannot be yellow;
If it be maiden green, you cannot miss it.

PHYSICIAN
I cannot see that vacuum in your blood.
But gentlewoman, if you love yourself,
Love my advice, be free and plain with me.
Where lies your grief?

JANE Where lies my grief indeed?
I cannot tell the truth where my grief lies,
But my joy's imprisoned.

PHYSICIAN This is mystical.

JANE
Lord, what plain questions you make problems of!
Your art is such a regular highway
That put you out of it and you are lost.
My heart is imprisoned in my body, sir,
There's all my joy, and my sorrow too
Lies very near it.

PHYSICIAN They are bad adjuncts:
Your joy and grief, lying so near together,
Can propagate no happy issue. Remove
The one, and let it be the worst, your grief,
If you'll propose the best unto your joy.

JANE
Why, now comes your skill. What physic for it?

220 **contumeliously** disgracefully, dishonourably
223 **commotioner** one who stirs up tumult or rebellion
225 **capital** deadly
and you go to that if you go that far
230 **beguile** cheat, disappoint
231 **brave** worthy
235 **spleen** hot or proud temper
239 **Come out** addressed to the 'tame devil', as in an exorcism
240 **improved** cultivated, with additional sense of approved
242 **comes behind still** always comes late
2.2.1–240 attributed to Rowley
1 **covered to me** secretive
2 **ope** open
6 **incapacious** deficient in mental capacity
7 **train me** lure me on
8 **oraculous** apparently infallible or authoritative, like an oracle
9 **examinant** one being examined
11 **Appoints out** points out
12 **physiognomy** the art of judging character from the features of the face
13 **coat** profession
14 **yellow** as the colour of jealousy
15 **green** referring to green sickness or chlorosis, anemic disease affecting young women around the age of puberty

PHYSICIAN
Now I have found you out. You are in love.

JANE
I think I am. What's your appliance now?
Can all your Paracelsian mixtures cure it?
'T must be a surgeon of the civil law,
I fear, that must cure me.

PHYSICIAN
Gentlewoman,
If you knew well my heart you would not be
So circular. The very common name
Of physician might reprove your niceness.
We are as secret as your confessors
And as firm obliged; 'tis a fine like death
For us to blab.

JANE
I will trust you. Yet, sir,
I had rather do it by attorney to you;
I else have blushes that will stop my tongue.
Have you no friend so friendly as yourself
Of mine own sex, to whom I might impart
My sorrows to you at the second hand?

PHYSICIAN
Why, law, there I hit you! And be confirmed
I'll give you such a bosom counsellor
That your own tongue shall be sooner false to you.
Make yourself unready and be naked to her.
I'll fetch her presently. *Exit*

JANE
I must reveal:
My shame will else take tongue and speak before me.
'Tis a necessity impulsive drives me.
O my hard fate! But my more hard father,
That father of my fate. A father, said I?
What a strange paradox I run into:
I must accuse two fathers of my fate
And fault, a reciprocal generation.
The father of my fault would have repaired
His faulty issue, but my fate's father hinders it:
Then fate and fault, wherever I begin
I must blame both, and yet 'twas love did sin.

Enter Physician and Anne his sister

PHYSICIAN
Look you, mistress, here's your closet. Put in
What you please, you ever keep the key of it.

JANE
Let me speak private, sir.

PHYSICIAN
With all my heart.
I will be more than mine ears' length from you.
[*He retires*]

JANE
You hold some endeared place with this gentleman.

ANNE
He's my brother, forsooth, I his creature.
He does command me any lawful office
Either in act or counsel.

JANE
I must not doubt you.
Your brother has protested secrecy
And strengthened me in you. I must lay ope
A guilty sorrow to you: I am with child.
'Tis no black swan I show you: these spots stick
Upon the face of many go for maids.
I that had face enough to do the deed
Cannot want tongue to speak it, but 'tis to you,
Whom I accept my helper.

ANNE
Mistress, 'tis locked
Within a castle that's invincible.
It is too late to wish it were undone.

JANE
I have scarce a wish within myself so strong,
For understand me, 'tis not all so ill
As you may yet conceit it. This deed was done
When heaven had witness to the jugal knot;
Only the barren ceremony wants,
Which by an adverse father is abridged.

ANNE
Would my pity could help you.

JANE
Your counsel may.
My father yet shoots widest from my sorrow
And with a care indulgent, seeing me changed
From what I was, sends for your good brother
To find my grief and practice remedy.
You know it, give it him, but if a fourth
Be added to this counsel, I will say
You're worse than you can call me at the worst,
At this advantage of my reputation.

ANNE
I will revive a reputation
That women long has lost: I'll keep counsel.
I'll only now oblige my teeth to you,
And they shall bite the blabber if it offer
To breathe on an offending syllable.

35 **Paracelsian** characteristic of Paracelsus, celebrated Swiss physician and philosopher (1490–1541)
36 **surgeon of the civil law** Punning on sergeant of the [civil] law. Jane needs legal assistance to free Fitzallen as well as medical help.
39 **circular** indirect
42 **firm obliged** firmly bound
44 **by attorney** through an agent
52 **Make yourself unready** undress; metaphorically, expose yourself
54 **take tongue . . . before me** The baby will be born and heard.
55 **impulsive** compulsory
59 **two fathers** Fitzallen is father of her fault, and Russell is father of her fate.
65 **closet** cabinet, private repository of valuables
70 **creature** one activated by the will of another
73 **protested** promised
74 **strengthened me in you** urged me to have faith in you
76 **black swan** rarity
78 **face** impudence
85 **conceit** imagine
86–7 **heaven . . . jugal . . . ceremony wants** See note to 1.1.191–3.
88 **abridged** blocked
97 **At this advantage . . . reputation** to take advantage to damage my reputation
100 **oblige my teeth to you** engage my teeth to maintain the silence you desire

JANE
I trust you, go, whisper. Here comes my father.
Enter Russell, Chough, and Trimtram

RUSSELL
Sir, you are welcome, more and most welcome,
All the degrees of welcome, thrice welcome, sir.

CHOUGH
Is this your daughter, sir?

RUSSELL Mine only joy, sir.

CHOUGH I'll show her the Cornish hug, sir.
[*He kisses Jane*]
I have kissed you now, sweetheart, and I never do any kindness to my friends, but I use to hit 'em in the teeth with it presently.

TRIMTRAM My name is Trimtram, forsooth; look, what my master does, I use to do the like.
[*He attempts to kiss Anne*]

ANNE You are deceived, sir, I am not this gentlewoman's servant, to make your courtesy equal.
[*She withdraws and whispers to Physician*]

CHOUGH You do not know me, mistress.

JANE
No indeed. [*Aside*] I doubt I shall learn too soon.

CHOUGH My name is Chough, a Cornish gentleman. My man's mine own countryman too, i'faith. I warrant you took us for some of the small islanders.

JANE
I did indeed, between the Scotch and Irish.

CHOUGH Red-shanks? I thought so, by my truth. No, truly, we are right Cornish diamonds.

TRIMTRAM Yes, we cut out quarrels and break glasses where we go.

PHYSICIAN [*to Anne*]
If it be hidden from her father, yet
His ignorance understands well his knowledge,
For this I guess to be some rich coxcomb
He'd put upon his daughter.

ANNE That's plainly so.

PHYSICIAN
Then only she's beholden to our help
For the close delivery of her burden,
Else all's o'erthrown.

ANNE And pray be faithful in that, sir.

PHYSICIAN
Tush, we physicians are the truest
Alchemists, that from the ore and dross of sin
Can new distill a maidenhead again.

RUSSELL
How do you like her, sir?

CHOUGH Troth, I do like her, sir, in the way of comparison to anything that a man would desire. I am as high as the Mount in love with her already, and that's as far as I can go by land, but I hope to go further by water with her one day.

RUSSELL
I tell you, sir, she has lost some colour
By wrestling with a peevish sickness now of late.

CHOUGH Wrestle? Nay, and she love wrestling, I'll teach her a trick to overthrow any peevish sickness in London, what e'er it be.

RUSSELL
Well, she had a rich beauty, though I say't,
Nor is it lost; a little thing repairs it.

CHOUGH She shall command the best thing that I have in Middlesex, i'faith.

RUSSELL
Well, sir, talk with her, give her a relish
Of your good liking to her. You shall have time
And free access to finish what you now begin.

JANE [*aside*]
What means my father? My love's unjust restraint,
My shame were it published, both together
Could not afflict me like this odious fool.
Now I see why he hated my Fitzallen.

CHOUGH Sweet lady, your father says you are a wrestler. If you love that sport, I love you the better. I'faith, I love it as well as I love my meat after supper, 'tis indeed meat, drink, and cloth to me.

JANE
Methinks it should tear your clothes, sir.

CHOUGH Not a rag, i'faith. Trimtram, hold my cloak. I'll wrestle a fall with you now; I'll show you a trick that you never saw in your life.

JANE
O good sir, forbear, I am no wrestler.

PHYSICIAN [*coming forward*]
Good sir, take heed, you'll hurt the gentlewoman.

CHOUGH I will not catch beneath the waist, believe it. I know fair play.

JANE
'Tis no woman's exercise in London, sir.

CHOUGH I'll ne'er believe that. The hug and the lock between man and woman, with a fair fall, is as sweet

107 **Cornish hug** a hold in Cornish wrestling where each contestant grasps the other's clothing
109 **hit 'em in the teeth** reproach them with it
119 **small islanders** inhabitants of the Hebrides off the west coast of Scotland and thus between the Scotch and the Irish
121 **Red-shanks** Celtic inhabitants of the Scottish highlands and Ireland
122 **Cornish diamonds** quartz crystals, a byword for fraudulence
123 **quarrels** (*a*) diamond-shaped panes of glass; (*b*) causes of complaint
127 **coxcomb** fool
130 **close** secret
138 **Mount** St Michael's Mount, a small island in Mount's Bay at Land's End, the westernmost tip of Cornwall
139 **go further by water** have sexual relations with
143 **Wrestle . . . wrestling** Throughout this passage wrestle has a secondary meaning of 'participate in a love bout'.
148–9 **the best thing that I have in Middlesex** a sexual pun
150 **relish** taste
170 **hug . . . lock** wrestling holds, with bawdy pun

an exercise for the body as you'll desire in a summer's evening.

PHYSICIAN
Sir, the gentlewoman is not well.

CHOUGH
It may be you are a physician, sir.

PHYSICIAN 'Tis so, sir.

CHOUGH I say then, and I'll stand to't, three ounces of wrestling with two hips, a yard of a green gown put together in the inturn, is as good a medicine for the green sickness as ever breathed.

TRIMTRAM Come, sir, take your cloak again. I see here will be ne'er a match.

JANE [*aside*] A match? I'd rather be matched from a musket's mouth and shot unto my death.

CHOUGH I'll wrestle with any man for a good supper.

TRIMTRAM Ay, marry, sir, I'll take your part there, catch that catch may.

PHYSICIAN [*to Russell*]
Sir, she is willing to't. There at my house
She shall be private and near to my attendance.
I know you not mistrust my faithful care.
I shall return her soon and perfectly.

RUSSELL
Take your charge, sir. Go with this gentleman, Jane,
But prithee look well this way ere thou goest.
[*Aside to Jane*] 'Tis a rich simplicity of great estate,
A thing that will be ruled, and thou shalt rule.
Consider of your sex's general aim,
That domination is a woman's heaven.

JANE
I'll think on't, sir.

RUSSELL [*to Chough*]
My daughter is retiring, sir.

CHOUGH I will part at Dartmouth with her, sir.
[*He kisses Jane*]
O, that thou didst but love wrestling, I would give any man three foils on that condition.

TRIMTRAM There's three sorts of men that would thank you for 'em, either cutlers, fencers, or players.

RUSSELL
Sir, as I began I end, wondrous welcome.
Exeunt Russell, Jane, Physician, Anne

TRIMTRAM What, will you go to school today? You are entered you know, and your quarterage runs on.

CHOUGH What? To the roaring school? Pox on't, 'tis such a damnable noise I shall never attain it neither. I do wonder they have never a wrestling school. That were worth twenty of your fencing or dancing schools.

TRIMTRAM Well, you must learn to roar here in London, you'll never proceed in the reputation of gallantry else.

CHOUGH How long has roaring been an exercise, thinkest thou, Trimtram?

TRIMTRAM Ever since guns came up: the first was your roaring Meg.

CHOUGH Meg? Then 'twas a woman was the first roarer.

TRIMTRAM Ay, afire of her touch-hole, that cost many a proper man's life since that time; and then the lions, they learned it from the guns, living so near 'em; then it was heard to the Bankside, and the bears they began to roar; then the boys got it, and so ever since there have been a company of roaring boys.

CHOUGH And how long will it last, thinkest thou?

TRIMTRAM As long as the water runs under London Bridge, or watermen at Westminster stairs.

CHOUGH Well, I will begin to roar too, since it is in fashion. O Corineus, this was not in thy time, I should have heard on't by the tradition of mine ancestors (for I'm sure there were Choughs in thy days) if it had been so. When Hercules and thou wert on the Olympic mount together, then was wrestling in request.

TRIMTRAM Ay, and that mount is now the Mount in Cornwall. Corineus brought it thither under one of his arms, they say.

CHOUGH O Corineus my predecessor, that I had but lived in those days to see thee wrestle! On that condition I had died seven year ago.

TRIMTRAM Nay, it should have been a dozen at least, i'faith, on that condition. *Exeunt*

Finis Actus Secundus

179 **inturn** in wrestling, the act of putting a leg between the thighs of an opponent and lifting him up
183 **matched** married; lit with a match
199 **Dartmouth** on the south coast of Devon, with pun on a kiss
200 **give** allow as a handicap
201 **foils** (*a*) in wrestling, throws not resulting in a fall; (*b*) sheets of metal for a cutler or knife-maker; (*c*) light fencing weapons
206 **quarterage** quarterly payment
207 **roaring school** a place to learn bullying and riotous conduct
211 **to roar** to behave in a noisy, boisterous manner
216 **roaring Meg** originally a great gun in Edinburgh Castle, Mons Meg; hence, any large piece of ordnance
217 **a woman was the first roarer** because 'roaring Meg' also refers to Long Meg of Westminster, a roaring girl like Moll Frith in *Roaring Girl*
218 **touch-hole** a hole in the breech of a fire-arm, through which the charge is ignited; with sexual innuendo
219 **proper** handsome
lions kept in the Tower of London
221 **Bankside . . . bears** On the Bankside or south side of the Thames river there were brothels, theatres, and bear-baiting grounds. The Hope Theatre, built 1613–14, alternated playing and bear-baiting.
226 **watermen at Westminster stairs** Ferrymen for hire on the Thames waited for fares at stairways connecting the shore with landing stages on the river. Westminster stairs was at the foot of Old Palace Yard.
228 **Corineus** Legendary Trojan hero who came to Britain with Brutus and ruled over Cornwall
231 **Hercules . . . Olympic mount** According to tradition, Corineus founded wrestling in Cornwall, but Chough jumbles Greek and Cornish mythology.

3.1 *Incipit Actus Tertius*
Enter Captain Ager with his two Friends

CAPTAIN
Well, your wills now?

CAPTAIN'S FIRST FRIEND
Our wills? Our loves, our duties
To honoured fortitude. What wills have we
But our desires to nobleness and merit,
Valour's advancement, and the sacred rectitude
Due to a valorous cause?

CAPTAIN
O, that's not mine.

CAPTAIN'S SECOND FRIEND
War has his court of justice, that's the field,
Where all cases of manhood are determined,
And your case is no mean one.

CAPTAIN
True, then 'twere virtuous;
But mine is in extremes, foul and unjust.
Well, now you've got me hither, you're as far
To seek in your desire as at first minute,
For by the strength and honour of a vow
I will not lift a finger in this quarrel.

CAPTAIN'S FIRST FRIEND
How? Not in this? Be not so rash a sinner.
Why sir, do you ever hope to fight again?
Then take heed on't, you must never look for that.
Why, the universal stock of the world's injury
Will be too poor to find a quarrel for you.
Give up your right and title to desert, sir;
If you fail virtue here, she needs you not
All your time after. Let her take this wrong
And never presume then to serve her more.
Bid farewell to the integrity of arms,
And let that honourable name of soldier
Fall from you like a shivered wreath of laurel,
By thunder struck from a desertless forehead
That wears another's right by usurpation.
Good Captain, do not wilfully cast away
At one hour all the fame your life has won.
This is your native seat, here you should seek
Most to preserve it; or, if you will dote
So much on life, poor life, which in respect
Of life in honour is but death and darkness,
That you will prove neglectful of yourself,
Which is to me too fearful to imagine,
Yet for that virtuous lady's cause, your mother,
Her reputation, dear to nobleness
As grace to penitence, whose fair memory
E'en crowns fame in your issue—for that blessedness
Give not this ill place, but in spite of hell
And all her base fears, be exactly valiant.

CAPTAIN
O, O, O!

CAPTAIN'S SECOND FRIEND
Why, well said, there's fair hope in that.
Another such a one.

CAPTAIN
Came they in thousands
'Tis all against you.

CAPTAIN'S FIRST FRIEND
Then poor friendless merit
Heaven be good to thee. Thy professor leaves thee;
Enter the Colonel and his two Friends
He's come. Do you but draw, we'll fight it for you.

CAPTAIN
I know too much to grant that.

CAPTAIN'S FIRST FRIEND
O dead manhood!
Had ever such a cause so faint a servant?
Shame brand me if I do not suffer for him.

COLONEL
I've heard, sir, you've been guilty of much boasting
For your brave earliness at such a meeting.
You've lost the glory of that way this morning:
I was the first today.

CAPTAIN
So were you ever
In my respect, sir.

CAPTAIN'S FIRST FRIEND
O most base præludium!

CAPTAIN
I never thought on victory, our mistress,
With greater reverence than I have your worth,
Nor ever loved her better.

CAPTAIN'S FIRST FRIEND [*aside to Captain's Second Friend*]
'Slight, I could knock
His brains about his heels, methinks.

CAPTAIN'S SECOND FRIEND
Peace, prithee peace!

CAPTAIN
Success in you has been my absolute joy,
And when I have wished content, I have wished your
friendship.

CAPTAIN'S FIRST FRIEND
Stay, let me but run him through the tongue a little.
There's lawyer's blood in't, you shall see foul gear
straight.

CAPTAIN'S SECOND FRIEND
Come, you are as mad now as he's cowardous.

COLONEL
I came not hither, sir, for an encomium.

CAPTAIN'S FIRST FRIEND
No, the more coxcomb he, that claws the head
Of your vainglory with't.

COLONEL
I came provided
For storms and tempests and the foulest season
That ever rage let forth or blew in wildness
From the incensèd prison of man's blood.

3.1.1–184 attributed to Middleton
25 **wreath of laurel** traditional sign of the victor
45 **professor** announced follower
54 **præludium** prelude or introduction
62 **foul gear** corrupt matter, pus
64 **encomium** formal expression of praise
65 **claws the head** scratches, soothes

CAPTAIN
'Tis otherwise with me. I come with mildness,
Peace, constant amity, and calm forgiveness,
The weather of a Christian and a friend.

CAPTAIN'S FIRST FRIEND
Give me a valiant Turk, though not worth tenpence,
rather.

CAPTAIN
Yet, sir, the world will judge the injury mine,
Insufferable mine, mine beyond injury.
Thousands have made a less wrong reach to hell,
Ay, and rejoiced in his most endless vengeance
(A miserable triumph, though a just one).
But when I call to memory our long friendship
Methinks it cannot be too great a wrong
That then I should not pardon. Why should man,
For a poor hasty syllable or two,
(And vented only in forgetful fury),
Chain all the hopes and riches of his soul
To the revenge of that, die lost for ever?
For he that makes his last peace with his Maker
In anger, anger is his peace eternally.
He must expect the same return again
Whose venture is deceitful. Must he not, sir?

COLONEL
I see what I must do: fairly put up again;
For here'll be nothing done, I perceive that.

CAPTAIN
What shall be done in such a worthless business
But to be sorry and to be forgiven?
You, sir, to bring repentance, and I pardon.

COLONEL
I bring repentance, sir?

CAPTAIN If it be too much
To say repentance, call it what you please, sir.
Choose your own word. I know you're sorry for't,
And that's as good.

COLONEL
I sorry? By fame's honour, I am wronged!
Do you seek for peace and draw the quarrel larger?

CAPTAIN
Then 'tis I'm sorry that I thought you so.

CAPTAIN'S FIRST FRIEND
A captain? I could gnaw his title off.

CAPTAIN
Nor is it any misbecoming virtue, sir,
In the best manliness to repent a wrong,
Which made me bold with you.

CAPTAIN'S FIRST FRIEND I could cuff his head off.

CAPTAIN'S SECOND FRIEND Nay, pish.

CAPTAIN'S FIRST FRIEND
Pox on him, I could eat his buttock baked, methinks.

COLONEL [*to his sword*]
So, once again take thou thy peaceful rest then,
But as I put thee up I must proclaim
This captain here, both to his friends and mine,
That only came to see fair valour righted,
A base submissive coward. So I leave him.

The Colonel offers to go away

CAPTAIN
O, heaven has pitied my excessive patience
And sent me a cause. Now I have a cause!
A coward I was never. Come you back, sir.

COLONEL
How?

CAPTAIN
You left a coward here?

COLONEL Yes, sir, with you.

CAPTAIN
'Tis such base metal, sir, 'twill not be taken;
It must home again with you.

CAPTAIN'S SECOND FRIEND Should this be true now?

CAPTAIN'S FIRST FRIEND
Impossible! Coward do more than bastard?

COLONEL
I prithee mock me not. Take heed you do not,
For if I draw once more I shall grow terrible,
And rage will force me do what will grieve honour.

CAPTAIN Ha, ha, ha.

COLONEL
He smiles; dare it be he? What think you, gentlemen?
Your judgements, shall I not be cozened in him?
This cannot be the man! Why, he was bookish,
Made an invective lately against fighting—
A thing, in troth, that moved a little with me—
Put up a fouler contumely far
Than thousand cowards came to and grew thankful.

CAPTAIN
Blessèd remembrance in time of need!
I'd lost my honour else.

CAPTAIN'S SECOND FRIEND
Do you note his joy?

CAPTAIN
I never felt a more severe necessity,
Then came thy excellent pity. Not yet ready?
Have you such confidence in my just manhood
That you dare so long trust me, and yet tempt me
Beyond the toleration of man's virtue?
Why, would you be more cruel than your injury?
Do you first take pride to wrong me and then think
me
Not worth your fury? Do not use me so;
I shall deceive you then. Sir, either draw,
And that not slightingly, but with the care

73 **Turk . . . tenpence** A target in the figure of a Turk was set up as an easy mark in fields of archery.

88–9 **return . . . venture** interest . . . commercial undertaking or investment

90 **put up** sheathe my sword

107 **Pox on him** The pox usually meant plague or syphilis; the phrase was commonly used as an imprecation.

117 **base metal** like a coin not made of silver or gold, with pun on mettle

125 **cozened** fooled

127 **invective** denunciation

129 **contumely** insult

142 **slightingly** disdainfully

Of your best preservation, with that watchfulness
As you'd defend yourself from circular fire,
Your sin's rage, or her lord. This will require it,
Or you'll be too soon lost. For I've an anger
Has gathered mighty strength against you, mighty;
Yet you shall find it honest to the last,
Noble and fair.

COLONEL I'll venture't once again,
And if't be but as true as it is wondrous,
I shall have that I come for. Your leave, gentlemen.
[*They fight*]

CAPTAIN'S FIRST FRIEND
If he should do't indeed, and deceive's all now!
Stay, by this hand he offers, fights, i'faith,
Fights! By this light he fights, sir!

CAPTAIN'S SECOND FRIEND So methinks, sir.

CAPTAIN'S FIRST FRIEND
An absolute *punto*, hey!

CAPTAIN'S SECOND FRIEND
'Twas a *passado*, sir.

CAPTAIN'S FIRST FRIEND
Why, let it pass, and 'twas, I'm sure, 'twas somewhat.
What's that now?

CAPTAIN'S SECOND FRIEND
That's a *punto*.

CAPTAIN'S FIRST FRIEND O, go to, then,
I knew 'twas not far off. What a world's this?
Is coward a more stirring meat than bastard, my masters?
Put in more eggs, for shame, when you get children,
And make it true court custard. Ho! I honour thee.
[*The Colonel falls*]
'Tis right and fair, and he that breathes against it,
He breathes against the justice of a man,
And man to cut him off, 'tis no injustice.
Thanks, thanks, for this most unexpected nobleness.

CAPTAIN
Truth never fails her servant, sir, nor leaves him
With the day's shame upon him.

CAPTAIN'S FIRST FRIEND Thou'st redeemed
Thy worth to the same height 'twas first esteemed.
Exeunt Captain and his Friends

COLONEL'S FIRST FRIEND
Alas, how is it, sir? Give us some hope
Of your stay with us; let your spirit be seen
Above your fortune. The best fortitude
Has been of fate ill-friended. Now force your empire
And reign above your blood spite of dejection,
Reduce the monarchy of your abler mind,
Let not flesh straiten it.

COLONEL O, just heaven has found me
And turned the stings of my too hasty injuries
Into my own blood. I pursued my ruin
And urged him past the patience of an angel.
Could man's revenge extend beyond man's life,
This would ha' waked it. If this flame will light me
But till I see my sister, 'tis a kind one;
More I expect not from it. Noble deserver!
Farewell, most valiant and most wronged of men;
Do but forgive me, and I am victor then.
Exit, led by his Friends

Enter Physician, Jane, Anne, Dutch Nurse with the child 3.2

PHYSICIAN
Sweet Fro, to your most indulgent care
Take this my heart's joy. I must not tell you
The value of this jewel in my bosom.

NURSE
Dat you may vell, sir, der can niet forstoore you.

PHYSICIAN
Indeed I cannot tell you. You know, Nurse,
These are above the quantity of price.
Where is the glory of the goodliest trees
But in the fruit and branches? The old stock
Must decay, and sprigs, scions such as these,
Must become new stocks from us, to glory
In their fruitful issue. So we are made
Immortal one by other.

NURSE You spreke a most lieben fader, and ick sall do de best of tender nurses to dis infant, my pretty frokin.

144 **circular fire** fire on all sides
145 **her lord** Satan
153 **offers** attempts
155 ***punto*** a stroke with the point of the sword
passado a forward thrust with the sword, one foot being advanced at the same time
157 **go to** a contemptuous concession
159 **coward ... bastard** Is it more provoking to be called coward than bastard?
159–61 **bastard ... more eggs ... court custard** Bastard is a sweet wine. Eggs are needed to make it into a court, that is, impressive, custard, though the metaphor is not entirely clear. Custard also puns on coward.
160 **get** beget
171 **fortune** chance; fate
173 **spite** despite
174 **Reduce** bring back, recall
175 **straiten** restrict freedom or power
180 **this flame** his remaining spirit of life
3.2.0.1 ***Dutch Nurse*** Dutch in this period referred to the language and inhabitants of the Low Countries and Germany, now distinguished as Dutch and German.
1–175 attributed to Rowley
1 **Fro** lady, from the Dutch *vrouwe*
4 **vell** well. The Nurse mixes mispronounced English words with her Dutch.
der can niet forstoore you He (the baby) cannot understand you, from *verstaen*, understand. Consequently, the Nurse implies, the Physician may freely praise the baby in its presence.
6 **These** i.e., children
above ... price beyond what can be valued in money
9 **scions** new shoots
13 **spreke** speak; Hexham *spreecken*
lieben fader loving father, in a mixture of German and Dutch
ick I
13–14 **de best** *De* is the masculine article in Dutch, but the Nurse probably just mispronounces 'the'.
14 **frokin** little girl, a diminutive from Dutch *vrouwe*

PHYSICIAN
I know you will be loving. Here, sweet friend,
He gives the Nurse money
Here's earnest of a large sum of love and coin
To quit your tender care.

JANE I have some reason, too,
To purchase your dear care unto this infant.
She gives the Nurse money

NURSE You be de witness of de baptism, dat is, as you spreken, de godimother, ick vell forstoor it so.

JANE (*aside*)
Yes, I am the bad mother, if it be offence.

ANNE I must be a little kind, too.
She gives the Nurse money

NURSE Much tanks to you all. Dis child is much beloven, and ick sall see much care over it.

PHYSICIAN
Farewell. Good sister, show her the way forth.
I shall often visit you, kind Nurse.

NURSE You sall be velcome. *Exeunt Anne and Nurse*

JANE
O sir, what a friend have I found in you!
Where my poor power shall stay in the requital
Yourself must from your fair condition
Make up in mere acceptance of my will.

PHYSICIAN
O, pray you, urge it not. We are not born
For ourselves only—self-love is a sin—
But in our loving donatives to others
Man's virtue best consists. Love all begets;
Without, all are adulterate and counterfeit.

JANE
Your boundless love I cannot satisfy
But with a mental memory of your virtues.
Yet let me not engage your cost withal;
Beseech you then, take restitution
Of pains and bounty which you have disbursed
For your poor debtor.

PHYSICIAN You will not offer it;
Do not esteem my love so mercenary
To be the hire of coin. Sure, I shall think
You do not hold so worthily of me
As I wish to deserve.

JANE Not recompense!
Then you will beggar me with too much credit.
Is't not sufficient you preserve my name,
Which I had forfeited to shame and scorn;
Cover my vices with a veil of love;
Defend and keep me from a father's rage,
Whose love yet infinite, not knowing this,
Might, knowing, turn a hate as infinite?
Sure he would throw me ever from his blessings
And cast his curses on me. Yes, further,
Your secrecy keeps me in the state of woman,
For else what husband would choose me his wife,
Knowing the honour of a bride were lost?
I cannot number half the good you do me
In the concealed retention of my sin.
Then make me not worse than I was before
In my ingratitude, good sir.

PHYSICIAN Again!
I shall repent my love, if you'll so call't,
To be made such a hackney. Give me coin?
I had as leave you gave me poison, lady,
For I have art and antidotes 'gainst that;
I might take that, but this I will refuse.

JANE
Well, you then teach me how I may requite you
In some small quantity.

PHYSICIAN (*aside*) 'Twas that I looked for.
Yes, I will tell you, lady, a full quittance,
And how you may become my creditress.

JANE
I beseech you, do, sir.

PHYSICIAN Indeed I will, lady.
Not in coin, mistress, for silver, though white,
Yet it draws black lines. It shall not rule my palm,
There to mark forth his base corruption.
Pay me again in the same quality
That I to you tendered, that's love for love.
Can you love me, lady? You have confessed
My love to you.

JANE Most amply.

PHYSICIAN Why, faith then,
Pay me back that way.

JANE How do you mean, sir?

PHYSICIAN
Tush, our meanings are better understood
Than shifted to the tongue; it brings along
A little blabbing blood into our cheeks
That shames us when we speak.

JANE I understand you not.

PHYSICIAN
Fie, you do, make not yourself ignorant
In what you know; you have ta'en forth the lesson
That I would read to you.

JANE Sure then, I need not
Read it again, sir.

PHYSICIAN Yes, it makes perfect.
You know the way unto Achilles' spear;

16 **earnest** money paid as an instalment
17 **quit** requite, repay
20 **spreken** speak, from *spreecken*
godimother The Nurse's mispronunciation of godmother permits Jane's punning self-accusation.
ick vell forstoor I well understand, from *verstaen*, as at 3.2.4
29 **stay** halt or be insufficient
34 **donatives** gifts
38 **with a mental memory** by remembering
39 **engage your cost** involve you in expenses
47 **beggar . . . credit** make me poor because I owe too much
56 **state of woman** esteemed as a virgin
60 **concealed retention** secret concealment
64 **hackney** one who does servile work for hire
70 **quittance** recompense or repayment
73–4 **silver . . . lines** proverbial, Tilley S459
89 **Achilles' spear** which traditionally both wounds and cures, with phallic pun

If that hurt you, I have the cure, you see.

JANE
Come, you're a good man, I do perceive you:
You put a trial to me. I thank you.
You're my just confessor, and believe me,
I'll have no further penance for this sin.
Convert a year unto a lasting ever,
And call't Apollo's smile, 'twas once, then never.

PHYSICIAN
Pray you, mistake me not, indeed I love you.

JANE
In deed, what deed?

PHYSICIAN
The deed that you have done.

JANE
I cannot believe you.

PHYSICIAN
Believe the deed then.
[*He offers to kiss her*]

JANE
Away, you're a blackamoor! You love me?
I hate you for your love. Are you the man
That in your painted outside seemed so white?
O, you're a foul dissembling hypocrite.
You saved me from a thief that yourself might rob me,
Skinned o'er a green wound to breed an ulcer.
Is this the practice of your physic college?

PHYSICIAN
Have you yet uttered all your niceness forth?
If you have more, vent it. Certes I think
Your first grant was not yielded with less pain.
If 'twere, you have your price, yield it again.

JANE
Pray you tell me, sir—I asked it before—,
Is it a practice 'mongst you physicians?

PHYSICIAN
Tush, that's a secret. We cast all waters;
Should I reveal, you would mistrust my counsel.
The lawyer and physician here agrees:
To women clients they give back their fees.
And is not that kindness?

JANE
This for thy love!
She spits
Out, outside of a man, thou cinnamon tree,
That but thy bark hast nothing good about thee!
The unicorn is hunted for his horn,
The rest is left for carrion. Thou false man,
Th'ast fished with silver hooks and golden baits,
But I'll avoid all thy deceiving sleights.

PHYSICIAN
Do what you list, I will do something too;
Remember yet what I have done for you.
You've a good face now, but 'twill grow rugged;
Ere you grow old, old men will despise you.
Think on your grandam Helen, the fairest queen:
When in a new glass she spied her old face
She smiling wept to think upon the change.
Take your time, you're crazed, you're an apple fallen
From the tree; if you be kept long, you'll rot.
Study your answer well. Yet I love you.
If you refuse I have a hand above you. *Exit*

JANE
Poison thyself, thou foul empoisoner:
Of thine own practic drink the theory.
What a white devil have I met withal!
What shall I do? What do! is't a question?
Nor shame, nor hate, nor fear, nor lust, nor force
(Now being too bad) shall ever make me worse.
Enter Anne
What have we here, a second spirit?

ANNE
Mistress,
I am sent to you.

JANE
Is your message good?

ANNE
As you receive it. My brother sent me
And you know he loves you.

JANE
I heard say so,
But 'twas a false report.

ANNE
Pray pardon me, I must do my message:
Who lives commanded must obey his keeper.
I must persuade you to this act of woman.

JANE
Woman! Of strumpet.

ANNE
Indeed of strumpet.
He takes you at advantage of your fall,
Seeing you down before.

JANE
Curse on his fainèd smiles.

ANNE
He's my brother, mistress, and a curse on you
If e'er you bless him with that cursèd deed.
Hang him, poison him! He held out a rose
To draw the yielding sense, which come to hand
He shifts, and gives a canker.

JANE
You speak well yet.

ANNE
Ay, but mistress, now I consider it,

96 **Apollo's smile** from the Latin proverb *semel in anno ridet Apollo*, Apollo smiles once a year, Tilley Y15
100 **blackamoor** a dark-skinned African
105 **Skinned** covered
green recent and unhealed
106 **physic college** medical society. The Royal College of Physicians was founded 1518.
107 **niceness** coyness
108 **Certes** certainly
109 **Your first grant** your first sexual yielding
113 **cast all waters** literally, diagnose disease by the inspection of urine; figuratively, deal with everyone
118–19 **outside . . . thee** Metaphorically, the Physician looks better than he is.
128 **Helen** Helen of Troy
131 **crazed** (*a*) impaired, ruined; (*b*) cracked (no longer a virgin); (*c*) driven mad
136 **practic** practice
137 **white devil** moral hypocrite
147 **keeper** guardian
151 **down before** already down
156 **canker** dog-rose, an inferior kind of rose

Your reputation lies at his mercy;
Your fault dwells in his breast. Say he throw it out,
It will be known; how are you then undone?
Think on't, your good name; and they are not to be
sold
In every market. A good name's dear,
And indeed more esteemed than our actions
By which we should deserve it.

JANE
Ay me, most wretched!

ANNE
What, do you shrink at that?
Would you not wear one spot upon your face
To keep your whole body from a leprosy,
Though it were undiscovered ever? Hang him,
Fear him not! Horseleeches suck out his corrupt
blood;
Draw you none from him, 'less it be pure and good.

JANE
Do you speak your soul?

ANNE
By my soul do I.

JANE
Then yet I have a friend. But thus exhort me,
And I have still a column to support me.

ANNE
One fault heaven soon forgives, and 'tis on earth
forgot;
The moon herself is not without one spot. *Exeunt*

3.3 *Enter the Lady Ager, meeting one of her servants*

LADY
Now, sir, where is he? Speak, why comes he not?
I sent you for him. Bless this fellow's senses,
What has he seen? A soul nine hours entranced,
Hovering 'twixt hell and heaven, could not wake
ghastlier.
Enter another Servant
Not yet return an answer? [*To Second Servant*] What
say you, sir?
Where is he?

SECOND SERVANT
Gone!

LADY
What say'st thou?

SECOND SERVANT
He is gone, madam,
But as we heard, unwillingly he went
As ever blood enforced.

LADY
Went? Whither went he?

SECOND SERVANT
Madam, I fear I ha' said too much already.

LADY
These men are both agreed. Speak, whither went he?

SECOND SERVANT
Why to—I would you'd think the rest yourself,
madam.

LADY
Meek patience bless me!

SECOND SERVANT
To the field.

FIRST SERVANT
To fight, madam.

LADY
To fight!

FIRST SERVANT
There came two urging gentlemen
That called themselves his seconds, both so powerful
As 'tis reported they prevailed with him
With little labour.

LADY
O, he's lost, he's gone!
For all my pains, he's gone. Two meeting torrents
Are not so merciless as their two rages:
He never comes again. Wretched affection,
Have I belied my faith? Injured my goodness?
Slandered my honour for his preservation,
Having but only him, and yet no happier?
'Tis then a judgement plain, truth's angry with me,
In that I would abuse her sacred whiteness
For any worldly temporal respect.
Forgive me, then, thou glorious woman's virtue,
Admired where'er thy habitation is,
Especially in us weak ones. O, forgive me,
For 'tis thy vengeance this. To belie truth,
Which is so hardly ours, with such pain purchased,
Fastings and prayers, continence and care,
Misery must needs ensue. Let him not die
In that unchaste belief of his false birth
And my disgrace. Whatever angel guides him,
May this request be with my tears obtained:
Let his soul know my honour is unstained.
Run, seek, away! *Exeunt Servants*
If there be any hope
Let me not lose him yet. When I think on him,
His dearness and his worth, it earns me more:
They that know riches tremble to be poor.
My passion is not every woman's sorrow:
She must be truly honest feels my grief,

159 **Your . . . breast** He knows about your (sexual) slip.

169 **Horseleeches** Leeches were used medicinally to bleed patients; horseleeches were larger than the ones usually employed.

3.3.1–44 attributed to Middleton

3–4 **A soul nine hours entranced, | Hovering 'twixt hell and heaven** a soul neither alive nor dead, in limbo. Sampson claims that because nine is three times three it is a mystical number.

In 4.2.50–2 the Colonel says he has been lord of a more happy conquest in the nine hours since he was wounded than in the nine years before.

7–8 **unwillingly . . . enforced** (*a*) Ager's unwillingness was like that of blood being forced to run. (*b*) Though unwilling, Ager was forced by his blood relationship to go.

19 **He never comes** He will never come.

22 **happier** more fortunate

26 **woman's virtue** truth, especially glorious in women or 'weak ones' (3.3.28), since it is often identified with their chastity

30 **so hardly** with such difficulty

33 **unchaste belief** belief in my unchastity

39 **earns me** affects me with poignant grief

And only known to one. If such there be,
They know the sorrow that oppresseth me. *Exit*

Finis Actus Tertius

❁

4.1 *Incipit Actus Quartus*

Enter Colonel's First Friend, Usher, Roarer with Chough and Trimtram

COLONEL'S FIRST FRIEND Truth, sir, I must needs blame you for a truant, having but one lesson read to you, and neglect so soon. Fie, I must see you once a day at least.

CHOUGH Would I were whipped, tutor, if it were not 'long of my man Trimtram here.

TRIMTRAM Who, of me?

CHOUGH [*aside to Trimtram*] Take't upon thee, Trim, I'll give thee five shillings, as I am a gentleman.

TRIMTRAM I'll see you whipped first. Well, I will, too. [*To Colonel's First Friend*] Faith, sir, I saw he was not perfect, and I was loath he should come before to shame himself.

COLONEL'S FIRST FRIEND How! Shame, sir? Is it a shame for scholars to learn? Sir, there are great scholars that are but slenderly read in our profession. Sir, first it must be economical, then ecumenical. Shame not to practice in the house how to perform in the field. The nail that is driven takes a little hold at the first stroke, but more at the second, and more at the third, but when 'tis home to the head, then 'tis firm.

CHOUGH Faith, I have been driving it home to the head this two days.

TRIMTRAM I helped to hammer it in as well as I could too, sir.

COLONEL'S FIRST FRIEND Well, sir, I will hear you rehearse anon. Meantime peruse the exemplary of my bills, and tell me in what language I shall roar a lecture to you, or I'll read to you the mathematical science of roaring.

CHOUGH Is it mathematical?

COLONEL'S FIRST FRIEND O, sir, does not the winds roar? the sea roar? the welkin roar? Indeed, most things do roar by nature, and is not the knowledge of these things mathematical?

CHOUGH Pray proceed, sir.

COLONEL'S FIRST FRIEND (*reads his bill*) 'The names of the languages, the Sclavonian, Parthamenian, Barmeothian, Tyburnian, Wappinganian, or the modern Londonian. Any man or woman that is desirous to roar in any of these languages, in a week they shall be perfect, if they will take pains. So let 'em repair into Holborn to the sign of the cheat-loaf.'

CHOUGH Now your bill speaks of that, I was wondering a good while at your sign. The loaf looks very like bread, i'faith, but why is it called the cheat-loaf?

COLONEL'S FIRST FRIEND This house was sometimes a baker's, sir, that served the court, where the bread is called cheat.

TRIMTRAM Ay, ay, 'twas a baker that cheated the court with bread.

COLONEL'S FIRST FRIEND Well, sir, choose your languages, and your lectures shall be read, between my usher and myself, for your better instruction, provided your conditions be performed in the premises beforesaid.

CHOUGH Look you, sir, there's twenty pound in hand, and twenty more I am to pay when I am allowed a sufficient roarer.

[*He gives Colonel's First Friend money*]

COLONEL'S FIRST FRIEND You speak in good earnest, sir.

CHOUGH Yes, faith, do I. Trimtram shall be my witness.

TRIMTRAM Yes indeed, sir, twenty pound is very good earnest.

USHER Sir, one thing I must tell you belongs to my place. You are the youngest scholar, and till another comes under you, there is a certain garnish belongs to the school. For in our practice we grow to a quarrel. Then there must be wine ready to make all friends, for that's the end of roaring, 'tis valiant but harmless, and this charge is yours.

CHOUGH With all my heart, i'faith, and I like it the better because no blood comes on it. Who shall fetch?

ROARER I'll be your spaniel, sir.

---

43 **known to one** having had sexual experience with only one person
4.1.0.2 **Usher** assistant teacher
1–255 attributed to Rowley
4 **Would I were whipped** let me be whipped
4–5 **'long of** because of
11 **come before** come earlier
15 **but slenderly read** have small knowledge
16 **economical, then ecumenical** private before universal. The Colonel's Friend's language is inflated and inexact.
17–20 **nail … head** a variant of the proverb, to drive the nail to the head, Tilley N15
25 **rehearse** repeat his lesson
26 **exemplary** exemplar, copy
bills generally, documents, but here handbills
28 **mathematical** exact
31 **welkin** the sky, the upper atmosphere
36–8 **Sclavonian, Parthamenian, Barmeothian, Tyburnian, Wappinganian … Londonian** nonce words combining adjectives derived from places around the world—S[c]lavonian is the language of the Slavs or Russians, Parthamenian is derived from Parthia, an ancient kingdom of western Asia—with others derived from places familiar in Jacobean England. Tyburn was the site of a gallows where felons were hanged; Wapping, on the north bank of the Thames, was the usual place of execution for pirates. Barmeothian may come from Bermudas, the name given a notorious quarter of London.
40 **Holborn** one of the main thoroughfares of London, running from the Old Bailey to Drury Lane through a quarter of lawyers, taverns, booksellers, and gardens of dubious repute
41 **sign of the cheat-loaf** Inns were identified by their signs; this would once have been a baker's shop.
cheat-loaf a loaf of coarse wheat bread
53 **conditions … beforesaid** you pay as previously agreed
59–60 **very good earnest** (*a*) very serious (*b*) a satisfactory instalment payment
63 **under you** younger than you, after you
garnish money extorted from a new prisoner for drink
69 **fetch** fetch it
70 **I'll be your spaniel** Spaniels were considered notably fawning.

COLONEL'S FIRST FRIEND Bid Vapour bring some tobacco, too.

CHOUGH Do, and here's money for't.

[*He offers money to Roarer*]

USHER No, you shall not, let me see the money.

[*He takes the money*]

So, I'll keep it, and discharge him after the combat.

Exit Roarer

For your practice sake you and your man shall roar him out on't (for indeed you must pay your debts so, for that's one of the main ends of roaring), and when you have left him in a chafe, then I'll qualify the rascal.

CHOUGH Content, i'faith. Trim, we'll roar the rusty rascal out of his tobacco.

TRIMTRAM Ay, and he had the best craccus in London.

COLONEL'S FIRST FRIEND Observe, sir, we could now roar in the Sclavonian language, but this practice hath been a little sublime, some hair's breadth or so above your caput. I take it for your use and understanding both, it were fitter for you to taste the modern assault, only the Londonian roar.

CHOUGH I'faith, sir, that's for my purpose, for I shall use all my roaring here in London. In Cornwall we are all for wrestling, and I do not mean to travel over sea to roar there.

COLONEL'S FIRST FRIEND Observe, then, sir, but it were necessary you took forth your tables to note the most difficult points for the better assistance of your memory.

CHOUGH Nay, sir, my man and I keep two tables.

TRIMTRAM Ay, sir, and as many trenchers, cat's meat and dog's meat enough.

COLONEL'S FIRST FRIEND Note, sir: Dost thou confront my cyclops?

USHER With a briarean brousted.

CHOUGH [*writing*] Cyclops.

TRIMTRAM [*writing*] Briarean.

COLONEL'S FIRST FRIEND I know thee and thy lineal pedigree.

USHER It is collateral, as Brutus and Posthumus.

TRIMTRAM [*writing*] Brutus.

CHOUGH [*writing*] Posthumus.

COLONEL'S FIRST FRIEND False as the face of Hecate. Thy sister is a—

USHER What is my sister, centaur?

COLONEL'S FIRST FRIEND I say thy sister is a bronsterops.

USHER A bronsterops!

CHOUGH Tutor, tutor, ere you go any further, tell me the English of that. What is a bronsterops, pray?

COLONEL'S FIRST FRIEND A bronsterops is in English a hippocrene.

CHOUGH A hippocrene. Note it, Trim. I love to understand the English as I go.

TRIMTRAM What's the English of hippocrene?

CHOUGH Why, bronsterops.

USHER Thou dost obtrect my flesh and blood.

COLONEL'S FIRST FRIEND Again I denounce, thy sister is a fructifer.

CHOUGH What's that, tutor?

COLONEL'S FIRST FRIEND That is in English a fucus or a minotaur.

CHOUGH [*writing*] A minotaur.

TRIMTRAM [*writing*] A fucus.

USHER I say thy mother is a callicut, a panagron, a duplar and a sindicus.

COLONEL'S FIRST FRIEND Dislocate thy bladud.

USHER Bladud shall conjure, if his demons once appear.

Enter Roarer with wine and Vapour with tobacco

COLONEL'S FIRST FRIEND Advance thy respondency.

CHOUGH Nay, good gentlemen, do not fall out. A cup of wine quickly, Trimtram!

USHER [*drawing his sword*] See, my steel hath a glister.

CHOUGH Pray wipe him and put him up again, good Usher.

USHER Sir, at your request I pull down the flag of defiance.

COLONEL'S FIRST FRIEND Give me a bowl of wine. My fury shall be quenched. Here, Usher.

[*He drinks*]

USHER I pledge thee in good friendship.

75 **discharge** pay
79 **in a chafe** in a rage
qualify appease
80 **rusty** lacking polish
82 **craccus** a kind of tobacco
85 **sublime** exalted
86 **caput** head (Latin)
94 **tables** writing tablets
97 **trenchers** plates
100 **cyclops** one-eyed giant of Greek mythology
101 **briarean** of Briareus, a hundred-handed monster of Greek mythology
brousted uncertain; perhaps a variation of roasted
104–5 **lineal pedigree** direct line of descent
106 **collateral** descended of the same stock, but in a different line
Brutus and Posthumus Silvius Posthumus was the father of Brutus, the legendary founder of Rome.
109 **Hecate** a goddess of the infernal regions and of witchcraft
111 **centaur** a mythological creature, half man and half horse
112 **bronsterops** procuress or bawd. The *OED* citation, in the form *bronstrops*, which also appears in ELD, is from *A Fair Quarrel*. The word may be formed from the names of two Cyclops, Brontes and Steropes.
117 **hippocrene** a fountain on Mount Helicon sacred to the muses; here another term for a sexually loose woman, perhaps combining hippo and quean
122 **obtrect** disparage
123 **denounce** proclaim
124 **fructifer** nonce word meaning a whore, from Latin *fructifer*, bearing fruit
126 **fucus** nonce word meaning a painted woman, with pun on 'fuck us'. Fucus was a cosmetic for the face.
127 **minotaur** a monster with the body of a man and the head of a bull
130 **callicut** from callet, strumpet, with pun on 'cunt'
panagron Greek for fishing net, and thus full of holes
duplar double, implying unfaithfulness
131 **sindicus** Latin for advocate, with no obvious relevance
132 **Dislocate thy bladud** unsheathe your blade, i.e. sword. Bladud was a legendary British king addicted to necromancy.
133 **conjure** bring about as by magic
134 **respondency** answer; here, his sword
137 **glister** gleam, with pun on glyster or clyster, enema

[*He drinks*]

CHOUGH I like the conclusion of roaring very well, i'faith.

TRIMTRAM It has an excellent conclusion indeed, if the wine be good, always provided.

COLONEL'S FIRST FRIEND O, the wine must be always provided, be sure of that.

USHER Else you spoil the conclusion, and that, you know, crowns all.

CHOUGH 'Tis much like wrestling, i'faith, for we shake hands ere we begin. Now that's to avoid the law, for then if he throw him a furlough into the ground, he cannot recover himself upon him, because 'twas done in cold friendship.

COLONEL'S FIRST FRIEND I believe you, sir.

CHOUGH And then we drink afterwards, just in this fashion. Wrestling and roaring are as like as can be, i'faith, even like long sword and half pike.

COLONEL'S FIRST FRIEND Nay, they are reciprocal, if you mark it, for as there is a great roaring at wrestling, so there is a kind of wrestling and contention at roaring.

CHOUGH True, i'faith, for I have heard 'em roar from the Six Windmills to Islington. Those have been great falls then.

COLONEL'S FIRST FRIEND Come, now a brief rehearsal of your other day's lesson, betwixt your man and you, and then for today we break up school.

CHOUGH Come, Trimtram. If I be out, tutor, I'll be bold to look in my tables, because I doubt I am scarce perfect.

COLONEL'S FIRST FRIEND Well, well, I will not see small faults.

CHOUGH [*to Trimtram*] The wall!

TRIMTRAM The wall of me? To thy kennel, spaniel!

CHOUGH Wilt thou not yield precedency?

TRIMTRAM To thee? I know thee and thy brood.

CHOUGH Know'st thou my brood? I know thy brood too: thou art a rook.

TRIMTRAM The nearer akin to the Choughs.

CHOUGH The rooks akin to the Choughs?

COLONEL'S FIRST FRIEND Very well maintained.

CHOUGH Dungcrower, thou liest.

TRIMTRAM Lie! Enucleate the kernel of thy scabbard.

CHOUGH Now if I durst draw my sword, 'twere valiant, i'faith.

COLONEL'S FIRST FRIEND Draw, draw, howsoever.

CHOUGH Have some wine ready to make us friends, I pray you.

TRIMTRAM Chough, I will make thee fly and roar.

CHOUGH I will roar if thou strikest me.

COLONEL'S FIRST FRIEND So, 'tis enough, now conclude in wine. I see you will prove an excellent practitioner. Wondrous well performed on both sides.

CHOUGH Here, Trimtram, I drink to thee.

[*He drinks*]

TRIMTRAM I'll pledge you in good friendship.

[*He drinks*]

Enter a Servant

SERVANT Is there not one Master Chough here?

USHER This is the gentleman, sir.

SERVANT My master, sir, your elected father-in-law, desires speedily to speak with you.

CHOUGH Friend, I will follow thee. I would thou hadst come a little sooner, thou shouldst have seen roaring sport, i'faith.

SERVANT Sir, I'll return that you are following.

CHOUGH Do so. *Exit Servant*

I'll tell thee, tutor, I am to marry shortly, but I will defer it a while till I can roar perfectly, that I may get the upper hand of my wife on the wedding day. 'T must be done at first or never.

COLONEL'S FIRST FRIEND 'Twill serve you to good use in that, sir.

CHOUGH How likest thou this, whiffler?

VAPOUR Very valiantly, i'faith, sir.

CHOUGH Tush, thou shalt see more by and by.

VAPOUR I can stay no longer indeed, sir. Who pays me for my tobacco?

CHOUGH How, pay for tobacco? Away, ye sooty-mouthed piper, you rusty piece of Martlemas bacon, away!

TRIMTRAM Let me give him a mark for't.

CHOUGH No, Trimtram, do not strike him, we'll only roar out a curse upon him.

TRIMTRAM Well, do you begin then.

148–9 **conclusion . . . all** the end crowns all, proverbial, Tilley E116

152 **he throw him** Chough is describing a typical case, not specific individuals.

153 **recover himself upon him** sue him successfully

158 **long sword and half pike** a sword with a long cutting blade and a small pike with a shaft half the length of the full-sized one. These weapons are not the same but are more similar than the regular forms.

163 **Six Windmills** There were three windmills in Finsbury Field in the time of Stow's survey (1598), and six by 1658.

Islington a suburb north of London

165 **rehearsal** repetition

168 **If I be out** if I forget

169 **I doubt** I suspect

172 **The wall!** I claim the wall side of the street, that is, the cleanest place to walk.

175 **brood** (*a*) family (contemptuous); (*b*) hatch of birds

177 **rook** (*a*) crow; (*b*) fool, simpleton

178 **Choughs** (*a*) small crows, jackdaws; (*b*) redlegged Cornish crows; (*c*) chatterers

181 **Dungcrower** a rooster or other noisy bird

182 **Enucleate the kernel . . . scabbard** extract your sword from its sheathe

197 **elected** chosen

202 **return** report

210 **whiffler** (*a*) attendant who clears the way for a procession; (*b*) swaggerer

215–16 **sooty-mouthed piper** one who smokes tobacco through a pipe, blackening his mouth with smoke

216 **rusty** rancid

Martlemas bacon bacon from cattle slaughtered on November 11, Martinmas or the Feast of St Martin, and put aside for the winter

217 **mark** (*a*) 12*s*. 4*d* in money; (*b*) visible trace

CHOUGH May thy roll rot, and thy pudding drop in pieces, being sophisticated with filthy urine.

TRIMTRAM May sergeants dwell on either side of thee, to fright away thy twopenny customers.

CHOUGH And for thy penny ones, let them suck thee dry.

TRIMTRAM When thou art dead, mayst thou have no other sheets to be buried in but mouldy tobacco leaves.

CHOUGH And no strewings to stick thy carcass but the bitter stalks.

TRIMTRAM Thy mourners all greasy tapsters—

CHOUGH With foul tobacco pipes in their hats instead of rotten rosemary. And last of all, may my man and I live to see all this performed and to piss reeking even upon thy grave.

TRIMTRAM And last of all for me, let this epitaph be remembered over thee.

'Here coldly now within is laid to rot
A man that yesterday was piping hot.
Some say he died by pudding, some by prick,
Others by roll and ball, some leaf, all stick
Fast in censure, yet think it strange and rare
He lived by smoke, yet died for want of air.
But then the surgeon said when he beheld him,
It was the burning of his pipe that killed him.'

CHOUGH So, are you paid now, whiffler?

VAPOUR All this is but smoke out of a stinking pipe.

CHOUGH So, so, pay him now, Usher.

[Usher gives money to Vapour]

COLONEL'S FIRST FRIEND Do not henceforth neglect your schooling, Master Chough.

CHOUGH Call me rook if I do, tutor.

TRIMTRAM And me raven, though my name be Trimtram.

CHOUGH Farewell, tutor.

TRIMTRAM Farewell, Usher.

[Exeunt Chough and Trimtram]

COLONEL'S FIRST FRIEND

Thus when the drum's unbraced and trumpet cease,
Soldiers must get pay for to live in peace. *Exeunt*

4.2

[The Colonel discovered in bed, with his two Friends watching him.] Enter the Colonel's Sister, meeting the Surgeon

SISTER

O my most worthy brother, thy hard fate 'twas—
Come hither, honest surgeon, and deal faithfully
With a distressèd virgin. What hope is there?

SURGEON Hope? Chillis was 'scaped miraculously, lady.

SISTER What's that, sir?

SURGEON Cava vena. I care but little for his wound i'th oesophag, not thus much, [*snapping his fingers*] trust me, but when they come to diaphragma once, the small intestines, or the spinal medull, or i'th' roots of the emunctories of the noble parts, then straight I fear a syncope, the flanks retiring towards the back, the urine bloody, the excrements purulent, and the dolour pricking or pungent.

SISTER

Alas, I'm ne'er the better for this answer.

SURGEON Now I must tell you his principal dolour lies i'th region of the liver, and there's both inflammation and turmafaction feared. Marry, I made him a quadrangular plumation, where I used sanguis draconis, by my faith, with powders incarnative, which I tempered with oil of hypericon, and other liquors mundificative.

SISTER

Pox o' your mundies figatives, I would they were all fired.

SURGEON But I purpose, lady, to make another experiment at next dressing with a sarcotrick medicament, made

221 **roll** a quantity of tobacco leaves rolled up in a cylinder, with sexual innuendo **pudding** tobacco in a compressed form, with sexual innuendo
223 **sergeants** arresting officers
228 **strewings** flowers and leaves scattered on a grave
230 **tapsters** men who draw beer for the customers in a tavern
232 **rotten rosemary** Rosemary was traditionally strewn at funerals as well as weddings.
238 **piping hot** punning on the smoker's pipe
239 **prick** (*a*) a small roll of tobacco; (*b*) penis
240 **roll and ball**... **leaf**... **stick** presentations of tobacco
254 **unbraced** with relaxed tension
4.2.0.1 **discovered** The bed may be thrust out, or a curtain pulled back.
0.3 **Surgeon** one who practises the art of healing by manual operation. Unlike physicians, surgeons dealt particularly with wounds and fractures.
1–4.3.124 attributed to Middleton
4–6 **Chillis**... **Cava vena** terms for the *vena cava*, the vein that goes to the liver
7 **oesophag** oesophagus, gullet
8 **diaphragma** diaphragm, midriff
9 **spinal medull** spinal marrow, spinal cord
9–10 **roots of the emunctories of the noble parts** Emunctories are the excretory ducts of the body; Lowe says 'in our bodies there are three noble parts, whereby we are governed, and without them can do nothing, as the brains, the heart, and the liver' (312).
11 **syncope** heart attack **flanks** sides
12 **purulent** discharging pus, putrid **dolour** pain
13 **pungent** sharp
17 **turmafaction** tumefaction, swelling
17–18 **quadrangular plumation** Plumations are little pieces of cloth cut into a variety of shapes for bandages; these are square.
18 **sanguis draconis** dragon's blood, a bright red gum or resin exuded upon the fruit of a palm
19 **incarnative** promoting the growth of flesh in a wound
19–20 **oil of hypericon** a drug prepared from the herb hypericum or St John's-wort
20 **liquors mundificative** cleansing medicines
21 **mundies figatives** The sister's dismissal of the medical jargon puns on fig, a contemptuous sexual gesture (the finger).
23 **sarcotrick** from sarcotic, inducing the growth of flesh, healing **medicament** medicine

of iris of Florence. Thus, mastic, calaphena, opopanax, sacrocolla—

SISTER Sacro-halter!
What comfort is i'this to a poor gentlewoman?
Pray tell me in plain terms what you think of him.

SURGEON Marry, in plain terms I know not what to say to him. The wound, I can assure you, inclines to paralism, and I find his body cacochymic. Being then in fear of fever and inflammation, I nourish him altogether with viands refrigerative and give for potion the juice of sanicola, dissolved with water cerefolium. I could do no more, Lady, if his best guiguimos were dissevered. *Exit*

SISTER
What thankless pains does the tongue often take
To make the whole man most ridiculous.
I come to him for comfort, and he tires me
Worse than my sorrow. What a precious good
May be delivered sweetly in few words,
And what a mount of nothing has he cast forth.
[*She approaches the bed*]
Alas, his strength decays! How cheer you, sir,
My honoured brother?

COLONEL In soul, never better.
I feel an excellent health there, such a stoutness!
My invisible enemy flies me. Seeing me armed
With penitence and forgiveness, they fall backward,
Whether through admiration, not imagining
There were such armoury in a soldier's soul
As pardon and repentance, or through power
Of ghostly valour. But I have been lord
Of a more happy conquest in nine hours now
Than in nine years before. O, kind lieutenants,
This is the only war we should provide for,
Where he that forgives largest and sighs strongest
Is a tried soldier, a true man indeed,
And wins the best field, makes his own heart bleed.
Read the last part of that will, sir.

COLONEL'S FIRST FRIEND (*reads*) 'I also require at the hands of my most beloved sister, whom I make full executrix, the disposure of my body in burial at St Martin's i'th' field, and to cause to be distributed to the poor of the same parish, forty mark, and to the hospital of maimed soldiers, a hundred. Lastly, I give and bequeath to my kind, dear, and virtuous sister the full possession of my present estate in riches, whether it be in lands, leases, money, goods, plate, jewels, or what kind soever, upon this condition following: that she forthwith tender both herself and all these enfeoffments to that noble captain, my late enemy, Captain Ager.'

SISTER How, sir?

COLONEL
Read it again, sir, let her hear it plain.

SISTER
Pray spare your pains, sir, 'tis too plain already.
Good sir, how do you, is your memory perfect?
This will makes question of you. I bestowed
So much grief and compassion o' your wound,
I never looked into your senses' epilepsy.
The sickness and infirmity of your judgement
Is to be doubted now, more than your body's.
Why, is your love no dearer to me, sir,
Than to dispose me so upon the man
Whose fury is your body's present torment,
The author of your danger, one I hate
Beyond the bounds of malice? Do you not feel
His wrath upon you? I beseech you, sir,
Alter that cruel article.

COLONEL Cruel, sister?
Forgive me, natural love, I must offend thee,
Speaking to this woman. Am I content,
Having much kindred, yet to give thee all,
Because in thee I'd raise my means to goodness,
And canst thou prove so thankless to my bounty
To grudge my soul her peace? Is my intent
To leave her rich, whose only desire is
To send me poorer into the next world
Than ever usurer went, or politic statist?
Is it so burdensome for thee to love
Where I forgive? O, wretched is the man
That builds the last hopes of his saving comforts

24 **iris of Florence** white iris
mastic gum or resin from the tree *Pistacia Lentiscus*
calaphena in Lowe, colaphonie, resin distilled from turpentine
opopanax a gum resin obtained from the root of *Opopanax Chironium*; also the juice obtained from lovage
25 **sacrocolla** sarcocolla, a gum-resin. The mistake is in Lowe.
26 **Sacro-halter** The sister's pun suggests her annoyance, and is based on the proverb, 'after the collar comes a halter', Tilley C513.
30 **paralism** paralysis
31 **cacochymic** containing unhealthy humours or fluids
33 **viands refrigerative** cooling foods
34 **sanicola** sanicle, a plant
cerefolium chervil, a salad herb
35 **guiguimos** presumably an error for *gingylmus*, a hinge-like joint, though the earliest *OED* citation is 1657
dissevered divided, separated
44 **stoutness** firmness, valour
45–6 **invisible enemy . . . they** The enemy are the devils who lie in wait for mankind to fall; through 4.2.50 the metaphor is of a battle in which the Colonel is spiritually armed against a hostile host.
47 **Whether through admiration** either by surprise
50 **ghostly valour** spiritual courage
51 **happy** fortunate
55 **tried** tested
59 **executrix** a woman appointed by a testator to implement his will
60–1 **St Martin's i'th' field** now St Martin-in-the-fields, a well-known church and parish in London
67–8 **tender . . . herself** offer herself in marriage. With some exceptions, the law gave whatever possessions a woman had upon marriage to her husband.
68 **enfeoffments** deeds of possession
69 **late** recent
73 **perfect** sound or sane
78 **doubted** feared
82 **danger** risk (of death)
86 **natural love** love based in nature, usually of relatives
89 **raise my means to goodness** increase my means of doing good
91 **grudge** begrudge
94 **usurer** one who takes excessive interest on loans
politic statist shrewd politician

Upon a woman's charity! He's most miserable;
If it were possible, her obstinate will
Will pull him down in his midway to heaven.
I've wronged that worthy man past recompense,
And in my anger robbed him of fair fame,
And thou the fairest restitution art
My life could yield him. If I knew a fairer,
I'd set thee by and thy unwilling goodness,
And never make my sacred peace of thee.
But there's the cruelty of a fate debarred:
Thou art the last, and all, and thou art hard.

SISTER
Let your grieved heart hold better thoughts of me.
I will not prove so, sir, but since you enforce it
With such a strength of passion, I'll perform
What by your will you have enjoined me to,
Though the world never show me joy again.

COLONEL
O, this may be fair cunning for the time,
To put me off knowing I hold not long,
And when I look to have my joys accomplished
I shall find no such things. That were vile cozenage
And not to be repented.

SISTER
By all the blessedness
Truth and a good life looks for, I will do't, sir.

COLONEL
Comforts reward you for't whene'er you grieve;
I know if you dare swear I may believe. *Exeunt*

4.3 *Enter Captain Ager*

CAPTAIN
No sooner have I entrance i'this house now
But all my joy falls from me, which was wont
To be the sanctuary of my comforts.
Methought I loved it with a reverent gladness,
As holy men do consecrated temples,
For the saint's sake, which I believed my mother,
But proved a false faith since, a fearful heresy.
O, who'd erect th'assurance of his joys
Upon a woman's goodness, whose best virtue
Is to commit unseen and highest secrecy
To hide but her own sin? There's their perfection.
And if she be so good, which many fail of, too,
When these are bad how wondrous ill are they?
What comfort is't to fight, win this day's fame,
When all my after days are lamps of shame?

Enter the Lady Ager

LADY
Blessings be firm to me, he's come, 'tis he!
A surgeon speedily!

CAPTAIN
A surgeon! Why, madam?

LADY
Perhaps you'll say 'tis but a little wound;
Good to prevent a danger. Quick, a surgeon!

CAPTAIN Why, madam—

LADY
Ay, ay, that's all the fault of valiant men,
They'll not be known o' their hurts till they're past help,
And then too late they wish for't.

CAPTAIN
Will you hear me?

LADY
'Tis no disparagement to confess a wound;
I'm glad, sir, 'tis no worse. A surgeon quickly!

CAPTAIN
Madam—

LADY
Come, come, sir, a wound's honourable,
And never shames the wearer.

CAPTAIN
By the justice
I owe to honour, I came off untouched.

LADY
I'd rather believe that.

CAPTAIN
You believe truth so.

LADY
My tears prevail then. Welcome, welcome, sir,
As peace and mercy to one new departed.
Why would you go, though, and deceive me so,
When my abundant love took all the course
That might be to prevent it? I did that
For my affection's sake—goodness forgive me for't—
That were my own life's safety put upon't
I'd rather die than do't. Think how you used me then,
And yet would you go and hazard yourself too?
'Twas but unkindly done.

CAPTAIN
What's all this, madam?

LADY
See then how rash you were, and short in wisdom.
Why, wrong my faith I did, slandered my constancy,
Belied my truth. That which few mothers will
Or fewer can, I did, out of true fear
And loving care, only to keep thee here.

CAPTAIN
I doubt I am too quick of apprehension now,
And that's a general fault when we hear joyfully.
With the desire of longing for't, I ask it:
Why, were you never false?

LADY
May death come to me
Before repentance then.

107 **debarred** closed off
112 **will** (*a*) desire; (*b*) last testament
115 **hold not long** will not live much longer
116 **accomplished** carried out
117 **cozenage** trickery
4.3.2–3 **which was wont | To be** the house usually was
3 **sanctuary** (*a*) holy place; (*b*) place of refuge
7 **proved a false ... fearful heresy** Since she has proven false, my belief in the holiness of the house is a dangerous heresy.
10 **commit unseen** sin in secret
12 **And ... too** if she is nevertheless virtuous to a degree that many do not attain
19 **Good to prevent a danger** It is good to guard against possible risk.
33–4 **took all the course | That might be** did everything possible
34 **did that** i.e., lied about my fidelity
39 **unkindly** (*a*) ungenerously; (*b*) against the ties of kindred
45 **doubt ... apprehension** fear ... understanding

CAPTAIN I heard it plain, sure.
Not false at all?
LADY By the reward of truth,
I never knew that deed that claims the name on't.
CAPTAIN
May then that glorious reward you swore by
Be never failing to you; all the blessings
That you have given me since obedient custom
Taught me to kneel and ask 'em, are not valuable
With this immaculate blessing of your truth.
This is the palm to victory,
The crown for all deserts past and to come.
Let 'em be numberless, they are rewarded,
Already they're rewarded. Bless this frame,
I feel it much too weak to bear the joy on't.
[*He kneels*]
LADY Rise, sir.
CAPTAIN O, pardon me—
I cannot honour you too much, too long.
I kneel not only to a mother now,
But to a woman that was never false.
You're dear, and you're good, too, ay, think o' that.
What reverence does she merit? 'Tis fit such
Should be distinguished from the prostrate sex,
And what distinction properer can be shown
Than honour done to her that keeps her own?
LADY
Come, sir, I'll have you rise.
CAPTAIN To do a deed then
He rises
That shall forever raise me. O, my glory!
Why this, this is the quarrel that I looked for,
The t'other but a shift to hold time play.
You sacred ministers of preservation,
For heaven's sake send him life
And with it mighty health, and such a strength
May equal but the cause. I wish no foul things;
If life but glow in him he shall know instantly
That I'm resolved to call him to account for't.
LADY
Why, hark you, sir—
CAPTAIN I bind you by your honour, madam,
You speak no hindrance to't. Take heed, you ought not.
LADY
What an unhappiness have I in goodness;
'Tis ever my desire to intend well
But have no fortunate way in't. For all this,
Deserve I yet no better of you
But to be grieved again? Are you not well,
With honest gain of fame with safety purchased?
Will you needs tempt a ruin that avoids you? *Exit*
CAPTAIN
No, you've prevailed; things of this nature sprung
When they use action must use little tongue.
Enter a Servant
Now, sir, the news?
SERVANT Sir, there's a gentlewoman
Desires some conference with you.
CAPTAIN How, with me?
A gentlewoman? what is she?
SERVANT Her attendant
Delivered her to be the Colonel's sister. [*Exit*]
CAPTAIN
O, for a storm then! 'Las, poor virtuous gentlewoman,
I will endure her violence with much pity.
She comes to ease her heart, good noble soul;
'Tis e'en a charity to release the burden.
Were not that remedy ordained for women
Their hearts would never hold three years together.
And here she comes, I never marked so much of her.
Enter the Colonel's Sister
That face can be the mistress of no anger
But I might very well endure a month, methinks.
I am the man. Speak, lady, I'll stand fair.
SISTER
And I'm enjoined by vow to fall thus low
She kneels
And from the dying hand of a repentant
Offer for expiation of wrongs done you
Myself, and with myself all that was his,
Which upon that condition was made mine,
Being his soul's wish to depart absolute man:
In life a soldier, death a Christian.
CAPTAIN
O, heaven has touched him nobly! How it shames
My virtue's slow perfection! Rise, dear brightness,
I forget manners, too; up, matchless sweetness.
SISTER
I must not, sir, there is not in my vow
That liberty. I must be received first,
Or all denied; if either, I am free.
CAPTAIN
He must be without soul should deny thee,
And with that reverence I receive the gift
As it was sent me.
[*He raises her*]
Worthy Colonel,
H'as such a conquering way i'th' blest things,
Whoever overcomes, he only wins. *Exeunt*

55–6 **are not ... With** cannot be compared in value with
69 **prostrate sex** submissive sex, i.e. women
71 **her own** i.e. honour
75 **shift** an expedient forced by circumstances
90 **Will you needs tempt a ruin** Must you put yourself in the way of danger.
91 **you've prevailed** As the Captain intends to fight again, this is ironic; he will base his action on what she has told him, rather than on her desire that he remain in peace.
107 **I'm ... vow** I have sworn
112 **absolute** perfect

4.4 VOICE (*within*)
Hem!

Enter Captain Albo, a Bawd, and a Whore

BAWD Hark of these hard-hearted bloodhounds. These butchers are e'en as merciless as their dogs, they knock down a woman's fame e'en as it walks the streets by 'em.

WHORE And the Captain here, that should defend us, walks by like John-of-the-apple-loft.

CAPTAIN ALBO What for interjections, Priss? *Hem, Evax, Vah*! Let the carnifexes scour their throats, thou knowest there is a curse hangs over their bloody heads: this year there shall be more butchers' pricks burnt than of all trades besides.

BAWD I do wonder how thou camest to be a captain.

CAPTAIN ALBO As thou camest to be a bawd, Meg, and Priss to be a whore, everyone by their deserts.

BAWD Bawd and whore? Out, you unprofitable rascal, hast not thou been at the new play yet, to teach thee better manners? Truly they say they are the finest players, and good speakers of gentlewomen of our quality. Bawd and whore is not mentioned amongst 'em, but the handsomest narrow-mouthed names they have for us, that some of them may serve as well for a lady as for one of our occupation.

WHORE Prithee, patroness, let's go see a piece of that play. If we shall have good words for our money, 'tis as much as we can deserve, i'faith.

BAWD I doubt 'tis too late now, but another time, servant.

CAPTAIN ALBO Let's go now, sweet face. I am acquainted with one of the pantomimics: the bulchins will use the Irish captain with respect, and you two shall be boxed amongst the better sort.

WHORE Sirrah, Captain Albo, I doubt you are but white-livered. Look that you defend us valiantly, you know your penance else. Patroness, you remember how you used him once?

BAWD Ay, servant, and I shall never forget it till I use him so again. Do you remember, Captain?

CAPTAIN ALBO Mum, Meg, I will not hear on't now.

BAWD How I and my Amazons stripped you as naked as an Indian—

CAPTAIN ALBO Why, Meg!

BAWD And then how I bound you to the good behaviour in the open fields.

WHORE And then you strewed oats upon his hoppers—

CAPTAIN ALBO Prithee, sweet face—

WHORE And then brought your ducks to nibble upon him, you remember?

CAPTAIN ALBO O, the remembrance tortures me again. No more, good sweet face.

BAWD Well, lead on, sir. But hark a little.

Enter Chough and Trimtram

CHOUGH Didst thou bargain for the bladders with the butcher, Trim?

TRIMTRAM Ay, sir, I have 'em here. I'll practise to swim, too, sir, and then I may roar with the water at London Bridge. He that roars by land and by water both is the perfect roarer.

CHOUGH Well, I'll venture to swim too. If my father-in-law gives me a good dowry with his daughter, I shall hold up my head well enough.

TRIMTRAM Peace, sir, here's practice for our roaring, here's a centaur and two hippocrenes.

CHOUGH Offer the jostle, Trim.

Trimtram jostles the Captain

CAPTAIN ALBO Ha! What meanest thou by that?

TRIMTRAM I mean to confront thee, cyclops.

CHOUGH I'll tell thee what a means. Is this thy sister?

CAPTAIN ALBO How then, sir?

CHOUGH Why then, I say she is a bronsterops, and this is a fucus.

WHORE No indeed, sir, we are both fucusses.

CAPTAIN ALBO Art thou military? Art thou a soldier?

CHOUGH A soldier? No, I scorn to be so poor. I am a roarer.

CAPTAIN ALBO A roarer?

TRIMTRAM Ay, sir, two roarers.

CAPTAIN ALBO Know then, my freshwater friends, that I am a captain.

CHOUGH What, and have but two to serve under you?

CAPTAIN ALBO I am now retiring the field.

TRIMTRAM You may see that by his bag and baggage.

CHOUGH Deliver up thy panagron to me.

TRIMTRAM And give me thy sindicus.

CAPTAIN ALBO Deliver?

BAWD I pray you, Captain, be contented, the gentlemen seem to give us very good words.

CHOUGH Good words? Ay, if you could understand 'em, the words cost twenty pound.

BAWD What is your pleasure, gentlemen?

4.4.1–237 attributed to Rowley

2 **Hark of** listen to
bloodhounds here, butchers

7 **John-of-the-apple-loft** Apple-loft was a slang term for brothel, as apple-squire (4.4.121) was for pimp.

8 **What for interjections** Pay no attention to exclamations (referring to the offstage voice calling Hem! at 4.4.1).

8–9 ***Hem, Evax, Vah*** Latin interjections

9 **carnifexes** butchers

11 **butchers' pricks** skewers, with bawdy second sense

17 **new play** *A Fair Quarrel*, first produced without this scene

21 **narrow-mouthed** literally, having a small mouth; here, metaphorical, polite

24 **patroness** The whore is the dependent of the bawd, who finds her work.

27 **I doubt** I fear

29 **pantomimics** actors
bulchins bull-calves, used as a term of contempt

30 **boxed** seated in a box or private room on the side of the stage

32–3 **white-livered** cowardly

39 **my Amazons** the prostitutes in her employ

42 **bound you to the good behaviour** constrained you to good conduct, as if with legal authority

44 **hoppers** hips

62 **the jostle** collision, push

64 **confront** oppose
cyclops in Greek mythology, giant with one eye who forged thunderbolts for Zeus

74 **freshwater friends** because they have not crossed the sea as soldiers

77 **retiring the field** retreating from the field of battle

79 **panagron** see 4.1.130

80 **sindicus** see 4.1.131

CHOUGH I would enucleate my fructifer.

WHORE What says he, patroness?

BAWD He would enoculate; I understand the gentleman very pithily.

CAPTAIN ALBO Speak, are you gentle or plebeian? Can you give arms?

CHOUGH Arms? Ay, sir, you shall feel our arms presently.

TRIMTRAM 'Sault you the women, I'll pepper him till he stinks again. I perceive what countryman he is; let me alone with him.

CAPTAIN ALBO Darest thou charge a captain?

TRIMTRAM Yes, and discharge upon him, too.

[*Trimtram turns his back to the Captain*]

CAPTAIN ALBO Foh, 'tis poison to my country, the slave has eaten pippins! O, shoot no more, turn both thy broadsides rather than thy poop! 'Tis foul play: my country breeds no poison. I yield, the great O'Toole shall yield on these conditions.

CHOUGH I have given one of 'em a fair fall, Trim.

TRIMTRAM Then thus far we bring home conquest. Follow me, Captain, the cyclops doth command.

CHOUGH Follow me, tweaks, the centaur doth command.

BAWD Anything, sweet gentlemen. Will't please you to lead to the tavern where we'll make all friends?

TRIMTRAM Why, now you come to the conclusion.

CHOUGH Stay, Trim; I have heard your tweaks are like your mermaids: they have sweet voices to entice the passengers. Let's have a song, and then we'll set 'em at liberty.

TRIMTRAM In the commendation of roaring, not else, sir.

CHOUGH Ay, in the commendation of roaring.

BAWD The best we can, gentlemen.

Sing Bawd

Then here thou shalt resign
Both captain and commander;
That name was never thine,
But apple-squire and pander.
And henceforth will we grant
In pillage or in moneys,
In clothing or provant,
Whate'er we get by conies.
With a hone, a hone, a hone,
No cheaters nor decoys
Shall have a share, but alone
The bravest roaring boys.

Whate'er we get by gulls,
Of country or of city,
Old flat-caps or young heirs,
Or lawyers' clerks so witty,
By sailors newly landed,
To put in for fresh waters,
By wandering gander-mooners,
Or muffled late night-walkers.
With a, etc.

Whate'er we get by strangers,
The Scotch, the Dutch, or Irish,
Or to come nearer home,
By masters of the parish.
It is concluded thus,
By all and every wench,
To take of all their coins
And pay 'em back in French.
With a, etc.

CHOUGH Melodious minotaur!

TRIMTRAM Harmonious hippocrene!

CHOUGH Sweet-breasted bronsterops!

TRIMTRAM Most tuneable tweak!

CHOUGH Delicious duplar!

TRIMTRAM Putrefactious panagron!

CHOUGH Calumnious callicut!

TRIMTRAM And most singular sindicus!

BAWD We shall never be able to deserve these good words at your hands, gentlemen.

CAPTAIN ALBO Shake golls with the captain, he shall be thy valiant friend.

CHOUGH Not yet, Captain, we must make an end of our roaring first.

87–9 **enucleate . . . fructifer . . . enoculate** Chough would lay open his whore, in a sexual sense. But the bawd hears enoculate, with a pun on knockers.

90 **pithily** speaking with few and significant words

91–2 **gentle . . . arms?** well-born, with the right to bear arms, or base

93 **Arms . . . arms** armorial bearings. Chough, however, understands limbs or weapons

94 **'Sault you** you attack
pepper (*a*) pelt with missiles; (*b*) make pungent

98 **discharge** (*a*) shoot at; (*b*) break wind

99 **poison to my country** Irishmen were supposed to be especially sensitive to flatulence.

100 **pippins** apples

101 **broadsides** side of a ship, here, metaphorically, the side of a man
poop (*a*) afterpart of a ship; (*b*) rump, posteriors of a man

102 **country . . . poison** According to legend, St Patrick freed Ireland of snakes.
O'Toole Arthur Severus O'Toole was a notorious Irish captain in London.

104 **fair fall** wrestling term for being thrown on one's back by one's opponent, with bawdy second sense

112–13 **mermaids . . . passengers** Mermaids are imaginary creatures with the head of a woman and the body of a fish, frequently confused, as here, with sirens, sea-songstresses that charm sailors with their music and lead them to their deaths. Sirens are half woman and half bird.

118–19 **resign . . . commander** give up being Captain or Commander

121 **apple-squire** pimp
pander go-between

123 **pillage** booty, spoil

124 **provant** an allowance of food, especially for soldiers

125 **conies** dupes, gulls. Conies are rabbits, supposed to be stupid.

126 **hone** nonsense syllable

129 **roaring boys** roisterers and bullies about London

132 **flat-caps** London citizens or apprentices, who wore round caps with a low, flat crown

136 **gander-mooners** husbands during the month after their wives give birth; hence, married men who go to whores

137 **muffled** wrapped up and hidden

146 **French** the French disease, i.e., the pox, syphilis

148–55 **minotaur . . . sindicus** see 4.1.112–31 and notes

158 **golls** hands

TRIMTRAM We'll serve 'em as we did the tobacco man: lay a curse upon 'em. Marry, we'll lay it on gently, because they have used us so kindly, and then we'll shake golls together.

WHORE As gently as you can, sweet gentlemen.

CHOUGH For thee, O pander, mayst thou trudge till the damned soles of thy boots fleet into dirt, but never rise into air.

TRIMTRAM Next, mayst thou fleet so long from place to place, till thou beest kicked out of Fleet Street.

CHOUGH As thou hast lived by bad flesh, so rotten mutton be thy bane.

TRIMTRAM When thou art dead, may twenty whores follow thee, that thou mayst go a squire to thy grave.

CAPTAIN ALBO Enough for me, sweet faces, let me sleep in my grave.

CHOUGH For thee, old sindicus, may I see thee ride in a caroche with two wheels and drawn with one horse.

TRIMTRAM Ten beadles running by, instead of footmen.

CHOUGH With every one a whip, 'stead of an Irish dart.

TRIMTRAM Forty barbers' basins sounding before instead of trumpets.

BAWD This will be comely indeed, sweet gentlemen roarers.

TRIMTRAM Thy ruff starched yellow with rotten eggs.

CHOUGH And mayst thou then be drawn from Holborn to Hounslow Heath.

TRIMTRAM And then be burnt to Colebrook for destroying of Maidenhead.

BAWD I will study to deserve this kindness at your hands, gentlemen.

CHOUGH Now for thee, little fucus, mayst thou first serve out thy time as a tweak, and then become a bronsterops as she is.

TRIMTRAM Mayst thou have a reasonable good spring, for thou art like to have many dangerous foul falls.

CHOUGH Mayst thou have two ruffs torn in one week.

TRIMTRAM May spiders only weave thy cobweb lawn.

CHOUGH Mayst thou set up in Rogue Lane.

TRIMTRAM Live till thou stinkest in Garden Alleys.

CHOUGH And die sweetly in Tower Ditch.

WHORE I thank you for that, good sir roarer.

CHOUGH Come, shall we go now, Trim? My father-in-law stays for me all this while.

TRIMTRAM Nay, I'll serve 'em as we did the tobacco man: I'll bury 'em altogether, and give 'em an epitaph.

CHOUGH All together, Trim? Why then the epitaph will be accessory to the sin.

TRIMTRAM Alas, he has kept the door all his lifetime, for pity let 'em lie together in their graves.

CAPTAIN ALBO E'en as thou wilt, Trim, and I thank you, too, sir.

TRIMTRAM
He that the reason would know, let him hark,
Why these three were buried near Marybone Park;
These three were a pander, a bawd, and a whore,
That sucked many dry to the bones before.
Will you know how they lived? Here't may be read,
The Low Countries did ever find 'em bread.
They lived by Flushing, by Sluys, and the Groyne,
Sickened in France, and died under the Line.
Three letters at last commended 'em hither,
But the hangman broke one in putting together.
P. was the first, who cries out for a pardon.
O. craves his book, yet could not read such a hard one.
An X. was the last, which in conjunction
Was broke by Brandon, and here's the conclusion:
By three trees, three letters; these three, pander, bawd, whore,
Now stink below ground, stunk long above before.

CHOUGH So, now we have done with you, remember roaring boys.

TRIMTRAM Farewell centaur.

CHOUGH Farewell bronsterops.

168 **fleet** dissolve, disintegrate

171 **Fleet Street** Fleet Street extended from Ludgate Hill to Temple Bar; it contained taverns, tobacconists, and booksellers, and abutted the Inns of Court and the houses of the nobility along the Strand.

172 **mutton** slang for a prostitute

179 **caroche** a stately town carriage. But Chough describes the kind of cart used to convey bawds for whipping.

180 **beadles** minor parish officers, one of whose duties was whipping offenders

181 **Irish dart** a weapon carried by Irish footmen

185 **ruff...eggs** a starched linen neckpiece, arranged in horizontal flutings, popular under Elizabeth and James. Yellow ruffs were made notorious by Mrs Ann Turner, a laundress executed for assisting Lady Frances Howard in murdering Sir Thomas Overbury.

186 **Holborn** a major thoroughfare running from the Old Bailey to Drury Lane and used for the public carting and flogging of criminals

187 **Hounslow Heath** a heath next to the town of Hounslow in Middlesex, 11 miles west of London. The heath was notorious for highway robberies; executed felons were hung in chains there.

188 **Colebrook** or Colnbrook, a village some 5 miles east of Windsor, with pun on coal meaning (*a*) ashes and (*b*) bawd

189 **Maidenhead** see 5.1.181

198 **cobweb lawn** very fine transparent linen

199 **Rogue Lane** nickname for Shire Lane, which had a disreputable character

200 **Garden Alleys** alleys behind various gardens where prostitutes plied their trade

201 **Tower Ditch** the moat around the Tower of London

207–8 **epitaph...sin** Because men and women will lie in the grave together, the epitaph will participate in sexual misconduct.

214 **Marybone Park** near Tyburn; now part of Regent's Park

218 **Low Countries** the Netherlands and Belgium, with bawdy pun

219 **Flushing** Vlissingen, town in the south-west Netherlands, with bawdy pun on spurting, drawing off liquid from
Sluys a fortified town in Holland, with pun on sluice, to cause to flow out (metaphorically, to copulate)
the Groyne Groningen, a fortified city in Friesland, with bawdy pun

220 **the Line** the equator

224 **O. craves...hard one** a reference to the the 'neck verse', a Latin verse printed in black letter (usually the beginning of the fifty-first psalm) set before a condemned prisoner claiming benefit of clergy. If he could read the verse he would escape execution. O finds the offered verse too difficult.

226 **Brandon** Sir William Brandon, the Elizabethan hangman

TRIMTRAM Farewell fucus. *Exeunt Chough and Trimtram*

CAPTAIN ALBO Well, Meg, I will learn to roar and still maintain the name of captain over these lanceprisados.

BAWD If thou dost not, mayst thou be buried under the roaring curse. *Exeunt*

Finis Actus Quartus

5.1

Incipit Actus Quintus

Enter Physician and Jane [dressed] as a Bride

PHYSICIAN
Will you be obstinate?

JANE
Torment me not,
Thou ling'ring executioner to death,
Greatest disease to nature, that striv'st by art
To make men long a-dying. Your practice is
Upon men's bodies. As men pull roses
For their own relish but to kill the flower,
So you maintain your lives by others' deaths.
What eat you then but carrion?

PHYSICIAN
Fie, bitterness!
Y'ad need to candy o'er your tongue a little,
Your words will hardly be digested else.

JANE
You can give yourself a vomit to return 'em
If they offend your stomach.

PHYSICIAN
Hear my vow.
You are to be married today.

JANE
A second torment,
Worse than the first, 'cause unavoidable.
I would I could as soon annihilate
My father's will in that as forbid thy lust.

PHYSICIAN
If you then tender an unwilling hand
Meet it with revenge: marry a cuckold.

JANE
If thou wilt marry me, I'll make that vow
And give my body for satisfaction
To him that should enjoy me for his wife.

PHYSICIAN
Go to, I'll mar your marriage.

JANE
Do, plague me so.
I'll rather bear the brand of all that's passed
In capital characters upon my brow
Than think to be thy whore, or marry him.

PHYSICIAN
I will defame thee ever.

JANE
Spare me not.

PHYSICIAN I will produce thy bastard,
Bring thee to public penance.

JANE
No matter, I care not:
I shall then have a clean sheet. I'll wear twenty
Rather than one defiled with thee.

PHYSICIAN
Look for revenge.

JANE
Pursue it fully then. [*Aside*] Out of his hate
I shall pursue, I hope, a loathèd fate. *Exit*

PHYSICIAN
Am I rejected, all my baits nibbled off,
And not the fish caught? I'll trouble the whole stream
And choke it in the mud; since hooks not take,
I'll throw in nets that shall or kill or break.

Enter Trimtram with rosemary

This is the bridegroom's man.—Hark, sir, a word.

TRIMTRAM
'Tis a busy day, sir, nor I need no physic.
You see I scour about my business.

PHYSICIAN Pray you a word, sir.
Your master is to be married today?

TRIMTRAM Else all this rosemary's lost.

PHYSICIAN I would speak with your master, sir.

TRIMTRAM My master, sir, is to be married this morning, and cannot be within while soon at night.

PHYSICIAN
If you will do your master the best service
That e'er you did him; if he shall not curse
Your negligence hereafter, slacking it;
If he shall bless me for the dearest friend
That ever his acquaintance met withal:
Let me speak with him ere he go to church.

TRIMTRAM A right physician, you would have none go to the church nor churchyard till you send them thither! Well, if death do not spare you yourselves, he deals hardly with you, for you are better benefactors and send more to him than all diseases besides.

CHOUGH (*within*) What, Trimtram, Trimtram!

TRIMTRAM I come, sir! Hark you, you may hear him. He's upon the spur and would fain mount the saddle of matrimony, but if I can I'll persuade him to come to you.

PHYSICIAN
Pray you do, sir. *Exit Trimtram*
I'll teach all peevish niceness
To beware the strong advantage of revenge.

Enter Chough

CHOUGH
Who's that would speak with me?

235 **lanceprisados** lance-corporals, low-grade non-commissioned officers
5.1.1–392 attributed to Rowley
2 **ling'ring executioner to death** one who aggravates the death sentence by dragging it out
6 **but to kill** but in the process kill
9 **candy o'er** sweeten
18 **cuckold** husband of an unfaithful wife
24 **capital characters upon my brow** as if branded
28 **public penance** typically, standing in a sheet in a public place as a sign of repentance and shame
36.1 **rosemary** symbol of wedding
38 **physic** medicine
39 **scour** move hastily
45 **while** until
48 **slacking it** for omitting it
50 **withal** with
52 **right** true
59 **upon the spur** in the utmost haste
59–60 **saddle of matrimony** continuing the metaphor of riding, with sexual sense
62 **peevish niceness** obstinate coyness
63 **advantage** superior position

PHYSICIAN None but a friend, sir:
I would speak with you.

CHOUGH Why sir, and I dare speak with any man under the universe. Can you roar, sir?

PHYSICIAN No, i'faith, sir.
I come to tell you mildly for your good,
If you please to hear me. You are upon marriage?

CHOUGH
No, sir, I am towards it, but not upon it yet.

PHYSICIAN Do you know what you do?

CHOUGH Yes sir, I have practised what to do before now, I would be ashamed to be married else. I have seen a bronsterops in my time, and a hippocrene, and a tweak, too.

PHYSICIAN
Take fair heed, sir. The wife that you would marry
Is not fit for you.

CHOUGH Why, sir, have you tried her?

PHYSICIAN
Not I, believe it, sir, but believe withal
She has been tried.

CHOUGH
Why, sir, is she a fructifer? or a fucus?

PHYSICIAN
All that I speak, sir, is in love to you.
Your bride that may be has not that portion
That a bride should have.

CHOUGH
Why sir, she has a thousand and a better penny.

PHYSICIAN
I do not speak of rubbish, dross, and ore,
But the refinèd metal, honour, sir.

CHOUGH What she wants in honour shall be made up in worship, sir. Money will purchase both.

PHYSICIAN
To be plain with you, she's naught.

Physician draws his sword

CHOUGH If thou canst not roar thou'rt a dead man. My bride naught?

PHYSICIAN
Sir, I do not fear you that way. What I speak
My life shall maintain. I say she's naught.

CHOUGH Dost thou not fear me?

PHYSICIAN Indeed I do not, sir.

CHOUGH I'll never draw upon thee while I live for that trick. Put up and speak freely.

PHYSICIAN [*sheathing his sword*]
Your intended bride is a whore, that's freely, sir.

CHOUGH Yes, faith, a whore's free enough, an she hath a conscience. Is she a whore? Foot, I warrant she has the pox then.

PHYSICIAN
Worse, the plague; 'tis more incurable.

CHOUGH A plaguy whore? A pox on her, I'll none of her.

PHYSICIAN
Mine accusation shall have firm evidence.
I will produce an unavoided witness,
A bastard of her bearing.

CHOUGH A bastard? 'Snails, there's great suspicion she's a whore then. I'll wrestle a fall with her father for putting this trick upon me, as I am a gentleman.

PHYSICIAN
Good sir, mistake me not. I do not speak
To break the contract of united hearts.
I will not pull that curse upon my head,
To separate the husband and the wife.
But this in love I thought fit to reveal,
As the due office betwixt man and man,
That you might not be ignorant of your ills.
Consider now of my premonishment
As yourself shall please.

CHOUGH I'll burn all the rosemary to sweeten the house, for in my conscience 'tis infected. Has she drunk bastard? If she would piss me wine vinegar now nine times a day I'd never have her, and I thank you too.

Enter Trimtram

TRIMTRAM Come, will you come away, sir? They have all rosemary and stay for you to lead the way.

CHOUGH I'll not be married today, Trimtram. Hast e'er an almanac about thee? This is the nineteenth of August, look what day of the month 'tis.

[*Trimtram*] *looks in an almanac*

TRIMTRAM 'Tis twenty-nine indeed, sir.

CHOUGH What's the word? What says Bretnor?

TRIMTRAM The word is, sir, 'There's a hole in her coat.'

CHOUGH I thought so. The physician agrees with him. I'll not marry today.

TRIMTRAM I pray you, sir, there will be charges for new rosemary else. This will be withered by tomorrow.

CHOUGH Make a bonfire on't to sweeten Rosemary Lane. Prithee, Trim, entreat my father-in-law that might have been to come and speak with me.

70–1 **upon marriage . . . upon it** about to marry. Chough takes the phrase in a sexual sense.
75 **bronsterops . . . hippocrene . . . tweak** see above, 4.1.112, 116–17. Tweak was another slang word for a prostitute.
79–81 **tried . . . tried** (*a*) tested; (*b*) tried out (sexually) (*c*) made to suffer
82 **fructifer . . . fucus** see above, 4.1.124, 126
84 **portion** (*a*) dowry; (*b*) virginity
87 **dross** scum thrown off while melting metals
90 **worship** respect
91 **naught** immoral, worthless
101, 141 **an** if
102–3 **the pox** syphilis
107 **unavoided** unavoidable, certain
119 **premonishment** forewarning
122 **in my conscience** upon my word
drunk bastard (*a*) consumed a sweet Spanish wine; (*b*) produced a child out of wedlock
131 **word** phrase or motto for the day
Bretnor Thomas Bretnor, author of a series of almanacs. See *Owl* for a satirical example.
137 **Rosemary Lane** now Royal Mint Street, running from the Minories to Leman Street. Occupied by old clothes shops, it was an abode of whores and thieves.

TRIMTRAM The bride cries already, and looks t'other way. An you be so backward, too, we shall have a fine arseward wedding on't. *Exit*

CHOUGH You'll stand to your words, sir?

PHYSICIAN I'll not fly the house, sir.
When you have need, call me to evidence. *Exit*

CHOUGH If you'll prove she has borne a bastard, I'll stand to't she's a whore.

Enter Russell and Trimtram

RUSSELL
Why, how now, son, what causeth these delays?
All stay for your leading.

CHOUGH
Came I from the Mount to be confronted?

RUSSELL How's that, sir?

CHOUGH Canst thou roar, old man?

RUSSELL Roar? How mean you, sir?

CHOUGH Why then, I'll tell thee plainly: thy daughter is a bronsterops.

RUSSELL A bronsterop? What's that, sir?

TRIMTRAM
Sir, if she be so she is a hippocrene.

CHOUGH Nay worse, she is a fructifer.

TRIMTRAM Nay then, she is a fucus, a minotaur, and a tweak.

RUSSELL
Pray you, speak to my understanding, sir.

CHOUGH If thou wilt have it in plain terms, she is a callicut and a panagron.

TRIMTRAM
Nay then, she is a duplar and a sindicus.

RUSSELL Good sir, speak English to me.

CHOUGH All this is Cornish to thee. I say thy daughter has drunk bastard in her time.

RUSSELL
Bastard! You do not mean to make her a whore?

CHOUGH Yes, but I do. If she make a fool of me, I'll ne'er make her my wife till she have her maidenhead again.

RUSSELL
A whore? I do defy this calumny.

CHOUGH Dost thou? I defy thee then.

TRIMTRAM Do you, sir? Then I defy thee too. Fight with us both at once in this quarrel if thou darest.

CHOUGH I could have had a whore at Plymouth.

TRIMTRAM Ay, or at Penryn.

CHOUGH Ay, or under the Mount.

TRIMTRAM Or as you came, at Yeovil.

CHOUGH Or at Hockey Hole in Somersetshire.

TRIMTRAM Or at the hanging stones in Wiltshire.

CHOUGH Or at Maidenhead in Berkshire. And did I come in by Maidenhead to go out by Staines? O, that man, woman, or child would wrestle with me for a pound of patience!

RUSSELL
Some thief has put in poison at your ears
To steal the good name of my child from me.
Or if it be a malice of your own,
Be sure I will enforce a proof from you.

CHOUGH He's a goose and a woodcock that says I will not prove any word that I speak.

TRIMTRAM Ay, either goose or woodcock; he shall, sir, with any man.

CHOUGH [*calls*] Phy-si-ci-an, *mauz avez* Physician.

RUSSELL Is he the author?

[*Enter Physician*]

PHYSICIAN
Sir, with much sorrow for your sorrow's sake
I must deliver this most certain truth:
Your daughter is an honour-stainèd bride,
Indeed she is the mother to a child
Before the lawful wife unto a husband.

CHOUGH Law, that's worse than I told thee. I said she had borne a bastard, and he says she was the mother on't, too.

RUSSELL
I'm yet an infidel against all this,
And will believe the sun is made of brass,
The stars of amber—

CHOUGH And the moon of a Holland cheese—

RUSSELL
Rather than this impossibility.
O, here she comes.

141–2 **backward ... arseward wedding** (*a*) If Chough turns his back, as Jane has done, they will be 'arseward' to each other. (*b*) Chough's unwillingness to go forward with the wedding may suggest he is instead interested in anal intercourse.

149 **All stay for your leading** Everyone is waiting for you to lead the way.

150 **confronted** forced to face a hostile situation. Chough, however, seems to mean affronted, insulted.

156 **bronsterop** Russell does not quite catch the word the first time.

168–70 **make her a whore ... make a fool of me ... make her my wife** Russell means that Chough does not intend to call her a whore, but Chough understands the phrase as *make her into* a whore, and continues this sense of *make* in the succeeding phrases.

171 **calumny** a damaging false charge, slander

175 **Plymouth** on the south coast of England in Devon, east of Cornwall

176 **Penryn** in Cornwall at the head of a branch of Falmouth harbour

177 **under the Mount** near St Michael's Mount

178 **Yeovil** in Somerset (with pun on evil)

179 **Hockey Hole in Somersetshire** Wookey Hole, near Wells, was on Chough's route to London; there were two places called Hockley in the Hole, one in London, the other in Bedfordshire.

180 **hanging stones in Wiltshire** Stonehenge

181 **Maidenhead in Berkshire** Maidenhead is at the east end of Berkshire, near London.

182 **in by Maidenhead to go out by Staines** Staines is a town in Middlesex, 17 miles west of London; the sequence punningly suggests defloration.

188 **enforce a proof** force you to prove

189 **goose and a woodcock** Both birds were symbols of foolishness.

193 **mauz avez** Usually glossed as Rowley's attempts at Cornish, the phrase also suggests the French *mauvez*, wicked.

201 **on't** of it

203 **infidel** unbeliever

Enter Jane and Anne

Nay, come, daughter, stand at the bar of shame.
Either now quit thyself or kill me ever.
Your marriage day is spoiled if all be true.

JANE
A happy misery. Who's my accuser?

PHYSICIAN
I am, that knows it true I speak.

CHOUGH Yes, and I'm his witness.

TRIMTRAM And I.

CHOUGH And I again.

TRIMTRAM
And I again, too. There's four, that's enough I hope.

RUSSELL
How can you witness, sir, that nothing know
But what you have received from his report?

CHOUGH Must we not believe our physicians? Pray you, think I know as much as every fool does.

TRIMTRAM
Let me be Trimtram. I pray you too, sir.

JANE
Sir, if this bad man have laid a blemish
On my white name, he is a most false one,
Defaming me for the just denial
Of his foul lust. [*To Physician*] Nay, now you shall be known, sir.

ANNE
Sir, I'm his sister and do better know him
Than all of you. Give not too much belief
To his wild words. He's oftentimes mad, sir.

PHYSICIAN
I thank you, good sister.

ANNE Are you not mad
To do this office? Fie upon your malice!

PHYSICIAN
I'll presently produce both nurse and child,
Whose very eyes shall call her mother before it speaks.
[*Exit*]

CHOUGH Ha, ha, ha, ha! By my troth, I'd spend a shilling on that condition to hear that. I think in my conscience I shall take the physician in a lie. If the child call her mother before it can speak I'll never wrestle while I live again.

TRIMTRAM It must be a she child if it do, sir, and those speak the soonest of any living creatures, they say.

CHOUGH Bow wow, a dog will bark a month sooner, he's a very puppy else.

RUSSELL [*aside to Jane*]
Come, tell truth 'twixt ourselves, here's none but friends.
One spot a father's love will soon wipe off.
The truth, and then try my love abundant.
I'll cover it with all the care I have
And yet, perhaps, make up a marriage day.

JANE
Then it's true, sir, I have a child.

RUSSELL Hast thou?
Well, wipe thine eyes, I'm a grandfather then.
If all bastards were banished, the City would be thin
In the thickest term-time. Well, now, let me alone,
I'll try my wits for thee. Richard, Francis, Andrew!
None of my knaves within?

Enter his Servant

SERVANT
Here's one of 'em. Sir, the guests come in apace.

RUSSELL
Do they, Dick? Let 'em have wine and sugar,
We'll be for 'em presently. But hark, Dick.

[*He whispers*]

CHOUGH I long to hear this child speak, i'faith, Trim. I would this foolish physician would come once.

TRIMTRAM If it calls her mother, I hope it shall never call you father.

CHOUGH No, and it do I'll whip it, i'faith, and give thee leave to whip me.

RUSSELL Run on thy best legs, Dick.

SERVANT I'll be here in a twinkling, sir. *Exit*

Enter Physician, Nurse, with the Child

PHYSICIAN
Now gentlemen, believe your eyes if not my tongue.
[*To Jane*] Do not you call this your child?

CHOUGH Phew, that's not the point. You promised us the child should call her mother. If it does this month, I'll ne'er go to the roaring school again.

RUSSELL Whose child is this, Nurse?

NURSE
Dis gentleman's, so he to me reden.

She points to the Physician

CHOUGH 'Snails, she's the physician's bronsterops, Trim.

TRIMTRAM His fucus, his very tweak, i'faith.

CHOUGH A glister in his teeth, let him take her, with a purgation to him.

RUSSELL
'Tis as your sister said: you are stark mad, sir,
This much confirms it. You have defamed

209 **bar** as in a court
210 **quit thyself** clear thyself of the charge
222 **Let me be Trimtram** Let me be known as Trimtram, rather than as a fool like Chough.
224 **white** pure
233 **call her mother** identify her as its mother
251 **term-time** when the law courts were in session and many people came to London
let me alone give me a chance
253 **knaves** servants
254 **apace** swiftly
256 **for 'em** with them, ready for them
271 **me reden** told me, from Middle Dutch *reden, redenen*, to reason or speak. Based on the Physician's statement that the baby is his 'heart's joy' (3.2.2), the Nurse believes he is the child's father.
272 **'Snails** exclamation, God's nails
274 **glister** enema
277–80 **defamed . . . bastard** Russell threatens the physician with legal action in an ecclesiastical court for defamation, as well as with the civil punishment he will receive for fornication and the fine for support of his child.

Mine honest daughter. I'll have you punished for't,
Besides the civil penance of your sin
And keeping of your bastard.

PHYSICIAN This is fine.
All your wit and wealth must not thus carry it.

RUSSELL Sir Chough, a word with you.

CHOUGH I'll not have her, i'faith, sir. If Trimtram will have her, an he will, let him.

TRIMTRAM Who, I, sir? I scorn it. If you'll have her, I'll have her too; I'll do as you do, and no otherwise.

RUSSELL
I do not mean't so either. This only, sir:
That whatsoe'er you've seen, you would be silent.
Hinder not my child of another husband
Though you forsake her.

CHOUGH I'll not speak a word, i'faith.

RUSSELL As you are a gentleman.

CHOUGH
By these basket-hilts, as I am a youth,
A gentleman, a roarer.

RUSSELL Charm your man, I beseech you, too.

CHOUGH I warrant you, sir, he shall do nothing but what I do before him.

Enter Servant with Fitzallen

RUSSELL
I shall most dearly thank you. O, are you come?
Welcome, son-in-law. This was beyond your hope.
We old men have pretty conceits sometimes:
Your wedding day's prepared, and this is it.
How think you of it?

FITZALLEN As of the joyfullest
That ever welcomed me. You show yourself now
A pattern to all kind fathers. My sweetest Jane!

RUSSELL
Your captivity I meant but as sauce
Unto your wedding dinner. Now, I'm sure,
'Tis far more welcome in this short restraint
Than had it freely come.

FITZALLEN A thousandfold.

JANE I like this well.

CHOUGH [*aside to Trimtram*] I have not the heart to see this gentleman gulled so. I will reveal, I make it mine own case. 'Tis a foul case.

TRIMTRAM Remember you have sworn by your hilts.

CHOUGH I'll break my hilts rather than conceal. I have a trick. Do thou follow me. I will reveal it and yet not speak it neither.

TRIMTRAM 'Tis my duty to follow you, sir.

CHOUGH (*sings*)
Take heed in time, O man, unto thy head.

TRIMTRAM (*sings*)
All is not gold that glistereth in bed.

RUSSELL Why, sir? Why, sir?

CHOUGH [*sings*]
Look to't, I say, thy bride's a bronsterops.

TRIMTRAM [*sings*]
And knows the thing that men wear in their slops.

FITZALLEN How's this, sir?

CHOUGH [*sings*]
A hippocrene, a tweak, for and a fucus.

TRIMTRAM [*sings*]
Let not fond love with foretops so rebuke us.

RUSSELL Good sir!

CHOUGH [*sings*]
Behold a baby of this maid's begetting.

TRIMTRAM [*sings*]
A deed of darkness after the sun-setting.

RUSSELL Your oath, sir!

CHOUGH [*sings*]
I swear and sing, thy bride has taken physic.

TRIMTRAM [*sings*]
This was the doctor cured her of that phthisic.

CHOUGH [*sings*]
If you'll believe me I will say no more.

TRIMTRAM [*sings*]
Thy bride's a tweak, as we do say that roar.

CHOUGH
Bear witness, gentlemen, I have not spoke a word:
My hilts are whole still.

FITZALLEN
This is a sweet epithalamium
Unto the marriage bed, a musical
Harmonious Io! Sir, you've wronged me,
And basely wronged me. Was this your cunning fetch,
To fetch me out of prison, forever
To marry me unto a strumpet?

RUSSELL None of those words, good sir.
'Tis but a fault, and 'tis a sweet one, too.

283–4 **will have her, an he will** if he will have her
293 **basket-hilts** hilts provided with a metal defence for the swordsman's hand
300 **pretty conceits** clever fancies, tricks
311 **gulled** fooled
311–12 **I make it mine own case** I imagine this were happening to me.
312 **foul case** (*a*) dirty situation; (*b*) impure vagina; (*c*) taken from the wrong case of printer's type
318 **unto thy head** lest thou have horns on thy head, i.e. be a cuckold
319 **All is not gold that glistereth** proverbial, Tilley A146
322 **knows** is sexually familiar with
slops wide baggy breeches or hose
324 **for and** apparently added for the rhythm
325 **foretops** the top of the head, here suggesting horns and cuckoldry
330 **taken physic** received medicine, especially purges; here with ironic reference to the birth of the baby
331 **phthisic** wasting disease of the lungs
336 **epithalamium** wedding song
338 **Io!** a Greek and Latin exclamation of joy, frequent in epithalamia
339–40 **fetch ... fetch** (*a*) contrivance, trick; (*b*) bring

Come, sir, your means is short: lengthen your fortunes
With a fair proffer. I'll put a thousand pieces
Into the scale to help her to weigh it up
Above the first dowry.

FITZALLEN Ha? You say well.
Shame may be bought out at a dear rate.
A thousand pieces added to her dowry?

RUSSELL
There's five hundred of 'em to make the bargain.
[*He gives Fitzallen money*]
I have worthy guests coming and would not delude 'em.
Say, speak like a son to me.
[*Jane and Fitzallen kneel*]

FITZALLEN Your blessing, sir,
We are both yours. Witness, gentlemen,
These must be made up a thousand pieces,
Added to a first thousand for her dowry,
To father that child.

PHYSICIAN O, is it out now?

CHOUGH
For t'other thousand I'll do't myself yet.

TRIMTRAM Or I, if my master will.

FITZALLEN [*rising with Jane*]
The bargain's made, sir. I have the tender
And possession both, and will keep my purchase.

CHOUGH Take her e'en to you with all her movables, I'll wear my bachelor's buttons still.

TRIMTRAM So will I, i'faith; they are the best flowers in any man's garden, next to heartsease.

FITZALLEN [*taking the child*]
This is as welcome as the other, sir,
And both as the best bliss that e'er on earth
I shall enjoy. Sir, this is mine own child,
You could not have found out a fitter father;
Nor is it basely bred, as you imagine,
For we were wedded by the hand of heaven
Ere this work was begun.

CHOUGH At Pancridge, I'll lay my life on't.

TRIMTRAM I'll lay my life on't too, 'twas there.

FITZALLEN
Somewhere it was, sir.

RUSSELL Was't so i'faith, son?

JANE
And that I must have revealed to you, sir,
Ere I had gone to church with this fair groom.
[*Pointing to the Physician*] But thank this gentleman, he prevented me.
I am much bound unto your malice, sir.

PHYSICIAN
I am ashamed.

JANE Shame to amendment then.

RUSSELL
Now get you together for a couple of cunning ones.
But son, a word. The latter thousand pieces
Is now more than bargain.

FITZALLEN No, by my faith, sir.
Here's witness enough on't, 'must serve to pay my fees.
Imprisonment is costly.

CHOUGH By my troth, the old man has gulled himself finely.
Well, sir, I'll bid myself a guest, though not a groom.
I'll dine and dance and roar at the wedding for all this.

TRIMTRAM So will I, sir, if my master does.

RUSSELL
Well sir, you are welcome. But now, no more words on't
Till we be set at dinner, for there will mirth
Be the most useful for digestion.
See, my best guests are coming.
Enter Captain Ager, Surgeon, Lady Ager, the Colonel's Sister, Captain Ager's two Friends

CAPTAIN Recovered, sayst thou?

SURGEON May I be excluded quite out of Surgeon's Hall else. Marry, I must tell you the wound was fain to be twice corroded, 'twas a plain gastrolophe, and a deep one, but I closed the lips on't with bandages and sutures, which is a kind conjunction of the parts separated against the course of nature.

CAPTAIN Well, sir, he is well.

SURGEON I feared him, I assure you, Captain. Before the suture in the belly it grew almost to a convulsion, and there was like to be a bloody issue from the hollow vessels of the kidneys.

344 **means is short** resources are slender
345 **proffer** offer
346–7 **Into the scale ... dowry** He will put an extra thousand pieces into one side of the scale to make Jane heavier, with implied contrast to light, i.e. sexually promiscuous.
348 **dear** expensive
354 **made up a thousand pieces** brought up to a thousand pieces
359 **tender** formal offer, usually of money
360 **possession** (*a*) monetary ownership; (*b*) sexual knowledge of
purchase that which is obtained, winnings
361 **movables** personal property
362–4 **bachelor's buttons ... heartsease** flowers, usually buttercups and pansies, with secondary meanings based on the names
365 **the other** Jane, but it could also mean the money
370 **wedded by the hand of heaven** in a private contract of marriage; see note to 1.1.191–3
372 **Pancridge** St Pancras, a large parish in London. St Pancras church was often used for hasty and irregular marriages.
377 **he prevented me** His actions anticipated mine.
382 **more than bargain** more than was agreed
383–4 **fees ... costly** Prisoners had to pay their own upkeep.
393–448 attributed to Middleton
394 **Surgeon's Hall** Barber-Surgeon's Hall in Monkswell Street
else otherwise
395–6 **twice corroded** worn away
396 **gastrolophe** Lowe mentions a suture used in the belly, called gastroraphie; the term is applied here to the wound itself.
401 **feared him** feared for him
403 **issue** discharge

CAPTAIN (*giving him money*)
There's that to thank thy news and thy art together.
SURGEON And if your worship at any time stand in need of incision, if it be your fortune to light into my hands, I'll give you the best. [*Exit*]
CAPTAIN
Uncle, the noble Colonel's recovered.
RUSSELL Recovered!
Then honour is not dead in all parts, coz.
Enter the Colonel with his two Friends
CAPTAIN'S FIRST FRIEND Behold him yonder, sir.
CAPTAIN [*aside*]
My much unworthiness is now found out.
Thou'st not a face to fit it.
COLONEL'S FIRST FRIEND Sir, yonder's Captain Ager.
COLONEL
O lieutenant, the wrong I have done his fame
Puts me to silence. Shame so confounds me
That I dare not see him.
CAPTAIN
I never knew how poor my deserts were
Till he appeared. No way to give requital?
[*He gives Captain's First Friend the will*]
Here, shame me lastingly, do't with his own.
Return this to him, tell him I have riches
In that abundance in his sister's love
These come but to oppress me and confound
All my deservings everlastingly.
I never shall requite my wealth in her, say.
How soon from virtue and an honoured spirit
May man receive what he may never merit!
[*Captain's First Friend takes will to the Colonel*]
COLONEL
This comes most happily to express me better,
For since this will was made there fell to me
The manor of Fitzdale; give him that too.
[*He writes on the will*]
He's like to have charge, there's fair hope
Of my sister's fruitfulness. For me,
I never mean to change my mistress,
And war is able to maintain her servant.
CAPTAIN'S FIRST FRIEND [*returning will to Ager*]
Read there, a fair increase, sir, by my faith!
He hath sent it back, sir, with new additions.
CAPTAIN
How miserable he makes me. This enforces me
To break through all the passages of shame
And headlong fall—
COLONEL Into my arms, dear worthy!
[*They embrace*]
CAPTAIN You have a goodness
Has put me past my answers. You may speak
What you please now, I must be silent ever.
COLONEL
This day has shown me joy's unvalued treasure.
I would not change this brotherhood with a monarch,
Into which blessed alliance sacred heaven
Has placed my kinsman and given him his ends.
Fair be that quarrel makes such happy friends.
Exeunt omnes

Finis Actus Quintus

THE PARTS

Adult Males

CAPTAIN Ager (403 lines): Lady Ager's Second Servant; Captain Albo; Usher *or* Roarer *or* Vapour

RUSSELL (322 lines): Captain Albo; Usher *or* Roarer *or* Vapour

CHOUGH (319 lines): Lady Ager's First Servant *or* Lady Ager's Second Servant; First Sergeant *or* Second Sergeant

The COLONEL (211 lines): Captain Albo; Lady Ager's First Servant *or* Lady Ager's Second Servant; Usher *or* Roarer *or* Vapour

PHYSICIAN (205 lines): Captain Albo; Lady Ager's First Servant *or* Lady Ager's Second Servant; First Sergeant *or* Second Sergeant; Usher *or* Roarer *or* Vapour

TRIMTRAM (193 lines): Lady Ager's First Servant *or* Lady Ager's Second Servant; First Sergeant *or* Second Sergeant

COLONEL'S FIRST FRIEND (125 lines): Captain Albo; [Lady Ager's First Servant *or* Lady Ager's Second Servant]

CAPTAIN'S FIRST FRIEND (107 lines): Captain Albo; Usher *or* Roarer *or* Vapour; [Lady Ager's First Servant *or* Lady Ager's Second Servant]

420 **No way to give requital** no way to pay him back
422–3 **riches | In that abundance** such great riches
426 **requite my wealth in her** repay the riches I find in her
429 **happily** fortunately
431 **give him that too** Legally, as soon as they are married the Captain will have full control of the Sister's property. By returning the will to the Colonel the Captain starts a contest in generosity between the men. Since the Colonel's intent is to enrich the Captain, he sends the will back, with the additional gift, directly to him.
432 **like to have charge** likely to have expenses

FITZALLEN (62 lines): Captain Albo; Lady Ager's First Servant *or* Lady Ager's Second Servant; Usher *or* Roarer *or* Vapour

CAPTAIN ALBO (4.4; 40 lines): any but Chough or Trimtram

SURGEON (39 lines): Captain Albo; Lady Ager's First Servant *or* Lady Ager's Second Servant; First Sergeant *or* Second Sergeant; Usher *or* Roarer *or* Vapour

USHER (4.1; 27 lines): any but Chough, Trimtram, Colonel's First Friend, Russell's Servant, Roarer, Vapour

CAPTAIN'S SECOND FRIEND (21 lines): Captain Albo; Lady Ager's First Servant *or* Lady Ager's Second Servant; First Sergeant *or* Second Sergeant; Usher *or* Roarer *or* Vapour

Russell's SERVANT (19 lines): Captain Albo; Lady Ager's First Servant *or* Lady Ager's Second Servant; First Sergeant *or* Second Sergeant

FIRST SERGEANT (1.1; 10 lines): any but Captain Ager, Russell, Colonel, Fitzallen, Colonel's First Friend, Captain's First Friend, Second Sergeant

Lady Ager's SECOND SERVANT (7 lines): any but Russell, Lady Ager's First Servant

Lady Ager's FIRST SERVANT (5 lines): any but Russell, Captain Ager, Lady Ager's Second Servant

SECOND SERGEANT (1.1; 5 lines): any but Captain Ager, Russell, Colonel, Fitzallen, Colonel's First Friend, Captain's First Friend, First Sergeant

VAPOUR (4.1; 4 lines): any but Chough, Trimtram, Colonel's First Friend, Russell's Servant, Usher, Roarer

ROARER (4.1; 1 line): any but Chough, Trimtram, Colonel's First Friend, Russell's Servant, Usher, Vapour

COLONEL'S SECOND FRIEND (no lines): Captain Albo; Lady Ager's First Servant *or* Lady Ager's Second Servant; First Sergeant *or* Second Sergeant; Usher *or* Roarer *or* Vapour

Boys

JANE (229 lines): Bawd *or* Whore

LADY Ager (171 lines): Bawd *or* Whore

BAWD (4.4; 66 lines): Lady Ager *or* Jane *or* Anne *or* Nurse *or* Colonel's Sister

ANNE (54 lines): Bawd *or* Whore

Colonel's SISTER (49 lines): Bawd *or* Whore

WHORE (4.4; 16 lines): Lady Ager *or* Jane *or* Anne *or* Nurse *or* Colonel's Sister

NURSE (9 lines): Bawd *or* Whore

Most crowded scene: 5.1, 17 characters

THE TRIUMPHS OF HONOUR AND INDUSTRY

Text edited by David M. Bergeron, annotated and introduced by Kate D. Levin

> LOOKING below us onto the street we saw a huge mass of people, surging like the sea, moving here and there in search of places to watch or rest—which proved impossible because of the constant press of newcomers. It was a chaotic mixture: dotards; insolent youths and children, especially of that race of apprentices I mentioned earlier; berriboned serving wenches; lower class women with their children in their arms: all were there to see the beautiful show. We saw few carriages about, and fewer horsemen... because the insolence of the crowd is extreme.

The report of Orazio Busino, chaplain to the Venetian Ambassador, provides vivid descriptions of the audiences for the pageant celebrating the installation of George Bolles, Grocer, as London's Lord Mayor on 29 October 1617. In addition to the crowds roiling through the streets and hanging out of windows, Busino talks about the spectators who are paying for the show, the guildmembers whose authority and influence make the city 'more like a republic of merchants than anything else'. The day's spectacle had to entertain 'the crowd' and affirm 'the republic'; Thomas Middleton's *The Triumphs of Honour and Industry*, printed in a single edition of 500 copies by Nicholas Okes, is a canny effort to do both. It takes a distinct position in the debate about the form and purpose of such entertainments, a debate that erupted periodically in the texts of civic pageants and court masques throughout the Stuart era.

The basic conflict was over the question of audience: who were these performances for? What were spectators likely to understand? What was the relationship between the audiences for court and city entertainments—and between the entertainments themselves? The honour of 'ordering, overseeing and writing' the 1617 pageant was a lucrative one. The pageant cost £882, of which Middleton received £282 to cover his own fee as well as the salaries of a range of actors and artisans. Anthony Munday got a generous consolation prize of £5 for 'his pains in drawing a project for this business'. The other contestant was Middleton's frequent collaborator Thomas Dekker, who was paid £4 'for the like'. The competition between these writers was more than a commercial one; they represent very different artistic approaches to the questions outlined above.

Middleton and Dekker are on one side of the convoluted debate about the audience—and by extension, the aesthetic value—of civic entertainments. Dekker, in his text of the 1612 pageant *Troia-Nova Triumphans*, defines two kinds of spectators and validates the different abilities of both groups to respond: 'Princes' behold triumphs 'with delight; common people with admiration'. *Honour and Industry* shares this encompassing view of its audience. The elaborate iconography invites aristocratic 'delight', while the breezy, ebullient narrative encourages and welcomes popular 'admiration'.

Ben Jonson represents a very different point of view. Although he removed himself from the milieu of civic pageantry by cultivating the position of house dramatist to James I, a position cemented in 1616 with a royal pension, Jonson always seemed to be looking over his shoulder for potential gatecrashers. In a masque text from 1609, Jonson describes his clientele as having 'enquiring eyes' and 'quick ears'; a world of difference from 'those sluggish ones of porters, and mechanics, that must be bored through, at every act, with narrations'. Although Jonson would have been appalled by the comparison, Anthony Munday was in many ways his counterpart in the world of 'porters and mechanics'. Skewered by Jonson in *The Case is Altered* (*c.*1600) as Antonio Balladino, the 'pageant poet' specializing in stale conceits, Munday was nonetheless as ubiquitous in serving the livery companies as Jonson was in writing for the court. Between 1602 and 1616, Munday was chosen to compose or help produce at least nine Lord Mayor's pageants (to Middleton's one).

The dramaturgy and written description of a Munday pageant is consistent over the years. He creates a succession of 'inventions', from which one figure emerges as a kind of narrator or presenter. At some point toward the end of the pageant this figure explains to the Lord Mayor and his entourage the iconography of all the devices they have seen—the 'narration' that so disgusted Jonson. Munday's pamphlets similarly segregate performance and explication. He describes all the inventions in the first part of each text, giving lengthy and painstakingly learned derivations for his themes. The speeches are listed in the second part of each pamphlet. Munday's tone is monochromatically earnest, and his texts teem with scholarly justifications and marginal glosses, as if aspiring to the solidity and profundity of a Jonsonian entertainment. That aspiration is explicit at the close of *Metropolis-coronata* (1615), when Munday describes the final procession 'as if it had been a royal masque, prepared for the marriage of an immortal deity, as in the like nature we hold the Lord Mayor, to be this day solemnly married to London's supreme dignity, by representing the awful authority of sovereign majesty'.

Where Munday in the texts of his city entertainments strives to emulate a 'higher' tone associated with the court, Middleton in *The Triumphs of Honour and Industry* works to frame a mode of civic rhetoric that is neither craven nor pedantic. Unlike Munday, Middleton's prose commandeers attention through its integration of narration and performance. Readers are told to look, listen, imagine, by a narrator who often seems distracted in his eagerness to show us the best bits. 'The first invention', the Indians 'at work in an island of growing spices', is typographically announced with its own heading. Its successor, however, simply rolls into view in the following paragraph. This chariot features India, 'the seat of merchandise', and several emblematic companions. Middleton starts to sketch out the significance of the device but interrupts himself, telling us, 'if you give attention to Industry that now sets forward to speak, it will be yours more exactly'.

Industry finishes her encomium to the virtues and rewards of hard work by introducing the next device, the 'Pageant of Nations', but the narrator again intervenes, backtracking to give us a more detailed description of the props and costumes of the mercantile values peopling the chariot, 'that you may take the better note of their adornments': India's wedge of gold, Perfection's crown, and so forth. Only then are we reminded of Industry's closing lines, as 'the Pageant of Several Nations, which is purposely planted near the sound of the words, moves with a kind of affectionate joy' into the procession. Eventually, all but panting, the narrator confesses, 'I arrive now at that part of triumph which my desire ever hastened to come to, this Castle of Fame or Honour, which Industry brings her sons unto in their reverend ages.' Here, the narrator does not merely describe the emblematic participants, he takes us by the hand and points: 'If you look upon Truth first, you shall find her properly expressed'.

Throughout, the narrator is wry, hard-working, supremely confident of his own worth, and, by implication, the worth of the occasion and the honorand. This persona holds right up to the pamphlet's final lines. Honour's last speech is set down, the artisans responsible for the devices are thanked, and we are told, 'The season cuts me off; and after this day's trouble, I am as willing to take my rest.'

The various 'inventions' are composed with an eye toward their effect in performance, and can be 'admired' by audience members not stationed near enough to hear the words. The Island of Spices needs only to be seen; Busino admired the 'grace and many varied gestures' that marked the children's dancing. The speeches themselves are relatively brief and provide ample opportunity for expository pantomime: Industry gesturing with her prop, a large, golden, Cupid-topped sphere; Justice reprimanding Reward in front of an open seat in the Castle of Honour. Middleton has not just written a lecture on the ethics of high government office or a guided tour of the pageant's iconography; dramatic action, however rudimentary, is embedded in the material.

One 'invention', the Pageant of Nations, constitutes an act of genuine theatrical daring. According to Industry, the pageant represents 'several nations where commerce abounds', producing 'a stream of amity and peace'. London's interest in—and profound ambivalence toward—cultural exotics would most likely have rendered these appropriately costumed foreigners far more 'readable' to the crowd than the 'six celestial figures' accompanying them on the pageant wagon. Busino's eyewitness account of *Honour and Industry* suggests the emblematic significance of national dress for xenophobic Londoners:

> Foreigners in London are little liked, not to say hated, so those who are wise take care to dress in the English style or that of France, which has been adopted by the court, and make themselves understood by signs whenever they can avoid speaking, and so they avoid mishaps. Only the Spanish nation choose the prerogative of dressing in their own fashion, and are therefore easily recognized and mortally hated.

The Venetian goes on to report a brawl along the pageant route in which the crowd, incited by a woman wielding a bunch of greens, mobbed a gentleman believed to be connected with the Spanish embassy.

Spain and France, twin objects of England's secret admiration and obsessive fears, come in for special treatment in *Honour and Industry*. Hysterical talk of imminent invasion—by Catholicism, by a second armada—boomed alongside trade with both countries. Rumours proliferated identifying members of James's inner circle as spies in the pay of the Spanish Ambassador, Gondomar; at the same time, the English appetite for Spanish imports like sugar and wine burgeoned. A pamphlet from 1615 bemoans the 'pretty mystery' of trade with Spain: 'though the gain scarce provideth for the merchants' livelihood, yet the commodities make the land merry'. France, with its Catholic seminaries swallowing up recusant English youth, was a constant object of English paranoia. For several years now the English had followed with fascination and horror a series of embassies between James I and the royal families of France and Spain to negotiate for the marriage of Prince Charles to an (unavoidably) Catholic princess of either house. In the weeks leading up to the performance of *Honour and Industry*, court circles were abuzz with news of the latest exploded conspiracy: a Milanese Jesuit had claimed that powerful French and Spanish factions were plotting to kidnap His Majesty and Prince Charles, incite a Catholic uprising, invade England, and present the conquered kingdom as a dowry for the marriage of the second Princess of Spain to the Duke of Orleans.

Middleton, as a playwright, must have been acutely aware of the range of possible audience responses to his featured players in the Pageant of Nations. His Spaniard and Frenchman, dressed to the life, are 'not content with a silent joy, like the rest of the nations'; rather, they 'have a thirst to utter their gladness'. The pageant text records (and translates) their speeches of congratulations and well-wishing: flattering to the Grocers, unimpeachably bland to court auditors, riotous—in performance—to the crowd. Busino confirms Middleton's theatrical acumen, reporting that the Spaniard 'kept kissing his hands, right and left, but especially to the Spanish Ambassador, who was a short distance from us, in such a wise as to elicit roars of laughter from the multitude'.

Presumably this invention was part of the proposal that won Middleton the pageant-writing job. On paper, it must have appealed to the Grocers in their capacity as traders working to encourage and even protect commerce with 'strangers'. The implication that London's merchants warranted diplomatic greetings independent from those delivered to the King would also have been gratifying. New links between court and City were being forged by the success of London's overseas trading ventures. Several important noblemen were admitted to the freedom of the East India Company in 1614; in 1617 the opportunity to invest in the Company's Second Joint-Stock produced something of a stampede on the part of astute courtiers. And yet *The Triumphs of Honour and Industry* does not try to assert the City's status by adopting an élite or exclusive stance. Instead, the pageant is an effort to negotiate a distinct civic voice and dramaturgical method through which to address its several audiences: the merchants, the multitude, and the monarchy.

SEE ALSO

Textual introduction and apparatus: *Companion*, 643
Authorship and date: *Companion*, 400
General introduction to the civic entertainments: this volume, 968
Busino's account: this volume, 1264
'On Sir George Bolles': this volume, 1890

The Triumphs of Honour and Industry

A solemnity performed through the City at confirmation and establishment of the right honourable George Bolles in the office of His Majesty's lieutenant, the Lord Mayor of the famous City of London.

Taking beginning at his lordship's going, and proceeding after his return from receiving the oath of mayoralty at Westminster on the morrow next after Simon and Jude's day, October 29, 1617.

The commentary for *The Triumphs of Honour and Industry* and for the eyewitness account of it that follows are efforts to detail the economics of civic pageantry, and to suggest the matrix of commercial, social and political forces that shaped this form of theatre.

Currencies. The relationship of different denominations of currency during this period is straightforward: 12 pennies or pence (12*d.*) equalled one shilling (1*s.*), and 20 shillings (20*s.*) made up £1. A mark was worth two-thirds of £1 (or 13*s.* and 4*d.*—or 160*d.*).

Values. The sums quoted below cannot be interpreted by means of a formula converting Jacobean currency into present-day values; such mathematics would give no sense of the vast differences in commodities and culture. A brief listing of prices and incomes should, however, help the reader evaluate the costs associated with Lord Mayor's shows. Between 1610 and 1620, a successful skilled worker in the construction trades (a journeyman mason or carpenter) might earn £18–20 a year. The Bishop of London's revenues totalled £1400 in 1604; a decade later the vicar of St Lawrence Jewry and similarly placed parish rectors could earn £60 annually. In 1612 the Earl of Salisbury's landed income was £7,313. Around 1619, a baker's average expenses included 2*s.* 4*d.* a week to feed each of his children, 10*s.* a week for his own and his wife's meals, 12*s.* a week for wood, 8*d.* a week for water, and £30 a year for rent. His journeymen received weekly salaries of 2*s.* 6*d.* (£6. 10*s.* a year); his maidservants were paid 10*d.* a week (slightly over £2 annually). In 1607 eggs were 10 for 4*d*; complaints were registered in 1615 over the high price of butter: 8*d.* a pound. Alehouses were to sell a quart of the strongest beer for 1*d.*; a quart of 'small' beer cost halfpenny. The price of a horse ranged from £1 for an 'old nag' to £15 for a superior animal. The standard amount of 'common cloth' for an adult garment, 4 1/2 yards, cost £4. 13*s.* 4*d.* in 1617; a pair of shoes cost 2*s.* 8*d.* The baker's staggering annual expenditure of £20 on clothing for himself, his wife, and two apprentices is thus far from extravagant. Public theatre admission prices ranged from a penny for standing room to 6*d.* for the best accommodations. At a private theatre such as the Blackfriars, 6*d.* was the minimum charge; a box by the stage cost 2*s.* 6*d.*

5 **beginning at his lordship's going** Middleton's text in fact begins *after* Bolles has returned by water from Westminster, and is travelling through London's streets. By the time of *Honour and Industry*, the usual route, after disembarking at Baynard's Castle, was to St Paul's Churchyard and from there along Cheapside to Guildhall. Pageant devices were stationed at intervals in the streets or in courtyards, and each one was carried as part of the procession after the Lord Mayor had stopped to watch and hear. After feasting at Guildhall, the Lord Mayor was escorted back to St Paul's for religious services. The pageant devices were then regrouped for the delivery of one last speech upon his return to his house in the evening.

6 **receiving the oath** According to Munday's 1618 continuation of Stow, the new Lord Mayor, accompanied by his predecessor and the Aldermen, arrive at Westminster, whereupon they 'put on their cloaks within the palace, and go round about . . . making divers courtesies in the Hall, passing up to the Exchequer' where the actual swearing-in takes place. 'After the oath taken in the Exchequer, they descend down again, and go first to the King's Bench, then to the [Court of] Common Pleas, and putting off their cloaks, go about the King's Tomb in Westminster Abbey' before returning by barge to the City.

The Tryumphs of Honour and Induſtry.

The Epistle Dedicatory

To the worthy deserver of all the costs and triumphs which the noble society of Grocers in bounteous measure bestow on him, the right honourable George Bolles, Lord Mayor

10–11 **all the costs . . . in bounteous measure bestow** The scrupulously detailed budget in the account book kept by wardens of the Grocers' Company 'concerning matters of Triumph' for 1617 records a total of £884. 12*s.* 10*d.* collected for the pageant, which cost £882. 18*s.* 11*d.*, leaving a surplus of £1. 13*s.* 11*d.* This 'bounteous measure' was tithed from the wealthier members of the Grocers' yeomanry—all those who had obtained the 'freedom' of the Company allowing them to engage in trade (see note to 11–12 below regarding the 'freedom'). The majority of the yeomanry, aside from journeymen who were free of the Company but not independent shopkeepers, were retail grocers. Approximately 140 members of the Company (perhaps 20 per cent of the total membership) were recruited to serve as members of the livery, an élite group from which the guild's executive leadership—its master, wardens, and the 20–25 person Court of Assistants—was chosen. Initial entrance into the livery was usually as a 'bachelor', either in 'budge' (wearing a gown faced with sheepskin on special occasions), or—denoting greater wealth—in 'foynes' (a gown faced with marten fur). Members of the livery were asked to contribute at a higher rate than the yeomanry toward triumphs such as Lord Mayor's pageants. For *Honour and Industry*, the 'bachelors in budge' were assessed £4 each; 42 of them contributed £162. 4*s.* The 'bachelors in foynes' were dunned £6; £393 was raised from 69 members of this group. The sums raised in both of these categories are not evenly divisible by the amounts requested: one bachelor in budge came up with a mere £2. 4*s* rather than the full £4, and three bachelors in foynes offered £5 instead of the £6 requested. These reduced payments may be evidence of the relatively straitened financial circumstances in which successful merchants occasionally found themselves. But if some members of the livery endured reversals of fortune, others wilfully refused to contribute. In response to this lack of fraternal spirit, the Grocers in 1617 paid £4 to one William Atkins, 'the Lord Mayor's officer, for pains by him taken about such brothers of this Company as were disobedient and refused to pay as they were assessed'. (See note to *Busino* 28–9 for other refusals to undertake guild and civic responsibilities.) In addition to members of the livery, 53 'special contributors', a category of wealthy yeomen who were not serving as bachelors, made contributions in differing amounts, ranging from £3 to £8, adding up to £258. 2*s.* 8*d.* Another 47 yeomen, also not liverymen, made donations from 10*s* to £2 as 'general contributors', totalling £71. 6*s.* 2*d.*

The cost of Lord Mayor's shows is frequently alluded to in pageant texts, usually as a tribute to the power and prosperity of the guilds able to raise such enormous sums from their members. Nonetheless, these huge outlays apparently occasioned some unease, as registered in Thomas Dekker's text for the 1612 show by his paradoxical language asserting that 'a sumptuous thriftiness in these civil ceremonies manag[es] all'. But for Dekker, the political advantages to be won by a 'sumptuous' display justify the expense. Indeed, using language reminiscent of pageant 'devices', he implies that conspicuous consumption is itself an aesthetic category for determining the success of these shows: 'the chairs of magistrates ought to be adorned, and to shine like the chariot which carries the sun . . . as well to dazzle and amaze the common eye, as to make it learn that there is some excellent and extraordinary arm from heaven thrust down to exalt a superior man, that thereby the gazer may be drawn to more obedience and admiration'.

12 **George Bolles** (1538–1621) Bolles, with his network of family connections, range of investments, and steady progress through the Grocers' Company ranks, in many respects typifies the active and successful guildsman of his age. His father-in-law, John Harte (d. 1604), had been Lord Mayor (1589–90), a Member of Parliament from London (1592–3, 1597–8), one of the principal founders and a governor of the East India Company, an investor in the Levant and Muscovy Companies, and a Grocer; at least one of Bolles's brothers-in-law and a son-in-law were also members of the Grocers' Company. Bolles subscribed £1,000 jointly with Harte at the East India Company's formation in 1599 and is named in the Company's first charter, issued in 1600. Bolles subsequently adventured £400 in the Company's third voyage (1607) and £550 in the forth (1608), and was a committee member of the Company in 1602–7 and 1610–11. Other trade-related investments included the Virginia Company (1609), the North-West Passage Company of 1612, and the Muscovy Company (1620). Bolles was not, however, a 'mere merchant'—a term for those who engaged personally and exclusively in foreign enterprise. Instead, he invested capital in joint-stock companies whose officers and employees conducted the actual trading overseas. Nor were Bolles's business interests limited to the grocery trade. The 'freedom of the City', achieved through membership in one of London's guilds, allowed its possessor to undertake any line of commerce and was a prerequisite for holding public office. Bolles's primary occupation appears to have been the domestic grocery trade, perhaps in London, certainly in the provinces, but by the 1590s he was the main supplier of general commodities—including though not limited to foodstuffs—to Hull and King's Lynn. He may have shared this business with his father-in-law, who left Bolles his 'great warehouse' at his death in 1604. Bolles started assuming responsibilities within the Grocers' Company just as his active involvement in trading began to taper off. He was admitted to the Grocers' Court of Assistants in 1598, became a Warden of the Company in 1599, a Master of the Company in 1606, an Alderman of the City in 1607, and served as Sheriff in 1608–9 before becoming Lord Mayor.

Bolles is associated with an anecdote that reflects the often prickly relations between City and Court during these years. Shortly after publication of the *Book of Sports* in May, 1618, James I, apparently intent on (literally) driving home its message, had his carriages clatter through London's streets on a Sunday during church services. Bolles, exercising his authority as Mayor, commanded that the carriages be stopped. Infuriated, the king is said to have issued an official warrant for his carriages, exclaiming, 'He thought there had been no more kings in England but himself.' Bolles obeyed the warrant, apparently informing the king, 'Whilst it was in my power, I did my duty; but that being taken away by a higher power, it is my duty to obey.' See the epitaph by Middleton, 'On Sir George Bolles' for a character summary emphasizing his civic responsibility and generosity.

Anthony Munday's continuation of Stow's *Survey* (1618) is dedicated to Bolles, Lord Mayor at its publication, and also to the Recorder of London and 'all the knights and Aldermen' of the City. Munday, himself a member of the Drapers' Company, apparently presented the augmented *Survey* to all the major guilds. The Skinners', Goldsmiths' and Merchant Taylors' accounts record 'gratuities' (ranging from 11*s.* to 22*s.*) to Munday for the volume.

Lord Mayor London's Lord Mayor was chosen annually from among the senior

of the famous City of London.

Right Honourable,

Out of the slightest labours and employments there may that virtue sometimes arise that may enlighten the best part of man, nor have these kind of triumphs an idle relish, especially if they be artfully accomplished; under such an esteemed slightness may often lurk that fire that may shame the best perfection. For instance, what greater means for the imitation of virtue and nobleness can anywhere present itself with more alacrity to the beholder than the memorable fames of those worthies in the castle, manifested by their escutcheons of arms, the only symbols of honour and antiquity. The honourable seat that is reserved, all men have hope that your justice and goodness will exactly merit, to the honour of which I commend your lordship's virtues, remaining

At your honour's service,

T. M.

The Triumphs of Honour and Industry

It hath been twice my fortune in short time to have employment for this noble society, where I have always met with men of much understanding, and no less bounty; to

Aldermen; as of 1622, an Alderman was required to have assets worth at least 10,000 marks (£6,666). (See also ll. 28–9 of the *Busino Account* and note for the costs of public office—and some consequences of those costs.)

20 **shame . . . perfection** outdo the best of things (as opposed to Middleton's pageant, which he calls the slightest of things)

24 **escutcheons** shields

26 **reserved** held for Bolles alone to occupy as its duly elected occupant. Middleton's pageant supplies a literal chair or 'seat of honour' (190) as part of the Castle of Fame.

32 **twice . . . time** Middleton had also written *The Triumphs of Truth* for the Grocers in 1613. For that pageant, however, his responsibilities were limited to 'the ordering overseeing and writing of the whole device and also for the apparelling the personage in the pageant', for which he was paid £40. Anthony Munday had been an essential (and much better paid) collaborator, receiving £149 for 'the device of the pageant and other shows, and for the apparelling and finding of all the personages in the said shows (excepting the pageant) and also for the portage and carriage both by land and water'. (See the *Busino Account*, note to l. 192, regarding the terms 'device' and 'pageant'.) By 1617, Middleton was fully entrusted with producing, in addition to writing, the show. He was paid £282 not just 'for the ordering, overseeing and writing of the whole device', but also as a kind of general contractor 'for the making of the Pageant of Nations, the Island, the Indian Chariot, the Castle of Fame, trimming the Ship, with all the several beasts which drew them, and for all the carpenter's work, painting, gilding and garnishing of them, with all other things necessary for the apparelling and finding of all the personages in the said shows, and for all the portage and carriage, both by land and by water, for the lighters for the show by water, for painting of a banner of the Lord Mayor's arms, and also in full for the greenmen, devils and fireworks'.

34–5 **to whom cost appears but as a shadow** While the £882 paid out for *Honour and Industry* did not equal the £1,295 lavished on the previous Grocers' pageant (*The Triumphs of Truth*, 1613), the 1617 spectacle was among the more costly Lord Mayor's shows during this period. The Merchant Taylors spent £747. 2*s*. 10*d*. in 1602, but their Court Books make clear that this is an extraordinary sum meant to satisfy the 'greater expectation now looked from our Company than ordinary, by reason we have been free so long from the same charge, having not had a Mayor of our company sithence . . . thirty and three years at the least'. A scant decade later, the Company raised £978. 12*s*. 11*d*. for Thomas Dekker's 1612 extravaganza, *Troia-Nova Triumphans*. The thrifty Ironmongers spent a mere £205. 15*s*. 11*d*. in 1609; the £523. 11*s*. 9*d*. spent on their 1618 show was much closer to the average cost of £700 for Jacobean and Caroline pageants. That the guilds undertook expenditures on civic pageantry in something of a competitive spirit is evident from Anthony Munday's thinly veiled apology for the shortcomings of the 1609 Ironmongers' show: 'And let me tell you, did their number hold level with other Societies, or carry correspondency in the best helping matter, their bounty should hardly have gone behind the best.'

The other locus of theatrical conspicuous consumption was King James's court. As with Lord Mayor's pageants, the designers/producers of these spectacles received much larger payments than the writers, and it is difficult to determine if this difference reflects the relative value placed on these different services, or the expenses involved in purchasing the necessary materials and labour. *Oberon, the Fairy Prince*, performed by Prince Henry at Court in 1611, cost £1,087. 6*s*. 10*d*., of which Ben Jonson received £40 for his work with designer Inigo Jones, who was paid at least £390. Composer Alphonso Ferrabosco received £20. Extant accounts record payments of approximately £1000 (the total expenditure was rumoured to be £1500) for *The Lords' Masque*, staged at Court in honour of Princess Elizabeth's marriage in 1613. Jones received upwards of £370—although some of this seems to have been for two other masques also performed as part of the nuptial celebrations—while Thomas Campion, as 'poet', received £66. Jonson's annual pension bestowed by James I in 1616 was for an amount similar to Campion's fee: 100 marks (£66) for services 'done and to be done', including the writing of masques. In 1617, £750 was spent for two performances of Jonson and Jones's *The Vision of Delight*, featuring the newly-made Earl of Buckingham, with additional payment of £100 to be divided among the twelve French musicians who performed in this and other holiday entertainments for the King. By 1618, word at Court was that straitened royal finances had forced the Queen to cancel a planned masque of ladies and caused the King to allocate £4,000 of a loan from Middelburg and Dutch East India merchants for Jonson and Jones's *Pleasure Reconciled to Virtue*. Also performed twice, this masque celebrated the investiture of Prince Charles as Prince of Wales. Detailed accounts survive for the costumes of Prince Charles and two companions: these three masquing suits alone cost £249.

whom cost appears but as a shadow, so there be fullness of content in the performance of the solemnity; which that the world may judge of, for whose pleasure and satisfaction custom hath yearly framed it (but chiefly for the honour of the City), it begins to present itself, not without form and order, which is required in the meanest employment.

The first invention

A company of Indians, attired according to the true nature of their country, seeming for the most part naked, are set at work in an island of growing spices: some planting nutmeg trees, some other spice trees of all kinds; some gathering the fruits, some making up bags of pepper; every one severally employed. These Indians are all active youths, who, ceasing in their labours, dance about the trees, both to give content to themselves and the spectators.

After this show of dancing Indians in the island follows triumphantly a rich personage presenting India, the seat of merchandise. This India sits on the top of an illustrious chariot; on the one side of her sits Traffic or Merchandise, on the other side, Industry, both fitted and adorned according to the property of their natures: Industry holding a golden ball in her hand, upon which stands a Cupid, signifying that Industry gets both wealth and love, and, with her associate Traffic or Merchandise, who holds a globe in her hand, knits love and peace amongst all nations. To the better expressing of which, if you give attention to Industry that now sets forward to speak, it will be yours more exactly.

THE SPEECH OF INDUSTRY IN THE CHARIOT

I was jealous of the shadowing of my grace,
But that I know this is my time and place.
Where has not Industry a noble friend?
In this assembly even the best extend
Their grace and love to me, joyed or amazed:
Who of true fame possessed, but I have raised,
And after added honours to his days.
For Industry is the life-blood of praise:
To rise without me is to steal to glory;
And who so abject to leave such a story?
It is as clear as light, as bright as truth,
Fame waits their age, whom Industry their youth.
Behold this ball of gold, upon which stands
A golden Cupid, wrought with curious hands;
The mighty power of Industry it shows,
That gets both wealth and love, which overflows
With such a stream of amity and peace,
Not only to itself adding increase,

35–6 **so there be fullness of content** Middleton seems to be playing on two senses of the word 'content': the one implying satisfaction and the one referring to what is contained in a work. 'Fullness of content' was occasionally a matter of dispute. Anthony Munday was brought before the Ironmongers in early November, 1609, to hear their objections to the performance of *Camp-bell*, that year's effort. Problems included 'that the children were not instructed their speeches which was a special judgement of the consideration, then that the music and singing were wanting, the apparel most of it old and borrowed, with other defects'. Munday had the temerity to ask for a £5 increase in his fee 'in regard of his speeches made for the water', but the Ironmongers were unbending: 'in respect he performed not his speeches on land, nor the rest of his contracted service, the Company were not to go beyond their bargain'.

43 **Indians** honours the connection of the Grocers to the East India Company; Bolles and his father-in-law were important members of both (see note to 11–12 above). The East India Company, chartered in 1600, was a phenomenal financial success for many of its investors and for the Crown, which benefitted from customs and imposts on the East India trade. In 1621, for example, Crown revenues from these sources were said to exceed £20,000. Indeed, the Company's dynamism made it vulnerable to royal interference around the time of *Honour and Industry*'s performance. The long-established Merchant Adventurers were just beginning to recover from King James's suspension of their charter between 1614 and early 1617 in favour of the disastrous Cokayne project. Undaunted, James seems to have had a related idea of intervening in East Indian trade. By early November of 1617, he had granted a patent to his 'Right trusty and well-beloved cousin and councellor' Sir James Cunningham for the establishment of a Scottish East India Company, to compete directly with the established company. Protests from the English East India merchants caused the patent to be withdrawn by March of 1618, but only on the condition that the Company reimburse Cunningham and his associates for the hypothetical profits they had foregone; the King then demanded a loan of £20,000 for the royal treasury.

48 **pepper** a reference to the Grocers' original name, the Guild or Fraternity of Pepperers, whose existence is first recorded in 1180. The Guild traded drugs, spices and other commodities in large quantities. By the 1370s, merchants selling 'engrossed' goods were members of 'the Company of Grocers'.

49 **youths** Most of the figures on the pageant wagons in Lord Mayor's shows were played by children, and there is no evidence to suggest that the main figures in *Honour and Industry*, including the members of the Pageant of Nations (see l. 96 ff. below), were an exception (see note to l. 244–5 below). This practice was not without its problems, and adult actors seem to have taken on increased responsibilities at least in Munday's pageants. In *Camp-bell*, the 1609 effort for which he was sternly reprimanded by the sponsoring Ironmongers (see note to l. 35 above), Munday explains that he has chosen to have two key roles played by adults in part because 'the weak voices of so many Children, which such shows as this do urgently require, for personating each device, in a crowd of such noise and uncivil turmoil, are not any way able to be understood'.

56 **Industry** Middleton's 'Industry' is very different from Dekker's in his 1612 show, *Troia-Nova Triumphans*. There, Industry is figured 'in the shape of an old country-man, bearing on his shoulder a spade, as the emblem of labour'.

59 **gets** both 'aquires' and 'begets'

65 **jealous** Industry here refers to the 'shadowing of my grace' by the more centrally placed and spectacularly dressed India. This assignment of an extra-emblematic motivation—the implication, even, of rudimentary dramatic conflict—is typical of Middleton's efforts to give the stock figures of civic pageantry distinct voices and even personalities.

78 **with** by

The arms of Sir George Bolles.

But several nations where commérce abounds
Taste the harmonious peace so sweetly sounds;
For instance, let your gracious eye be fixed
Upon a joy true, though so strangely mixed.

And that you may take the better note of their adornments, India, whose seat is the most eminent, for her expression holds in her hand a wedge of gold; Traffic, her associate, a globe; Industry, a fair golden ball in her hand, upon which stands a golden Cupid; Fortune expressed with a silver wheel; Success holding a painted ship in a haven; Wealth, a golden key where her heart lies; Virtue bearing for her manifestation a silver shield; Grace holding in her hand a book; Perfection, a crown of gold.

At which words, the Pageant of Several Nations, which is purposely planted near the sound of the words, moves with a kind of affectionate joy, both at the honour of the day's triumph and the prosperity of Love, which by the virtue of Traffic is likely ever to continue. And for a good omen of the everlasting continuance of it, on the top of this curious and triumphant pageant shoots up a laurel tree, the leaves spotted with gold, about which sit six celestial figures, presenting Peace, Prosperity, Love, Unity, Plenty, and Fidelity: Peace holding a branch of palm; Prosperity, a laurel; Love, two joined hands; Unity, two turtles; Plenty holding fruits; Fidelity, a silver anchor. But before I entered so far, I should have showed you the zeal and love of the Frenchman and Spaniard, which now I hope will not appear unseasonably: who, not content with a silent joy, like the rest of the nations, have a thirst to utter their gladness, though understood of a small number; which is this:

THE SHORT SPEECH DELIVERED BY THE FRENCHMAN IN FRENCH

La multitude m'ayant monté sur ce haut lieu pour contempler le glorieux triomphe de cette journée, je vois qu'en quelque sorte la noble dignité de la très honorable Société des Grociers y est représentée, dont me jouissant par-dessous tous, je leur souhaite et à Monseigneur le Maire le comble de toutes nobles et heureuses fortunes.

THE SAME IN ENGLISH *It is my joy chiefly (and I stand for thousands) to see the glory of this triumphant day, which in some measure requites the noble worthiness of the honourable Society of Grocers, to whom and to my Lord Mayor I wish all good successes.*

This Frenchman no sooner sets a period to his speech, but the Spaniard, in zeal as virtuous as he, utters himself to the purpose of these words:

86 **strangely** 'strange' had the sense of 'unusual' or 'uncommon'; 'stranger' was also synonymous with 'foreigner' during this period

92 **wheel** In emblem books, the changeable nature of Fortune is routinely symbolized by a wheel. While in this particular case Middleton is following the standard iconography, models for his pageant figures and their symbolic accessories cannot always be found in the emblem literature of his day.

95 **book** In association with Grace, the book here most likely represents divine truth. Books are also used in emblems to signify secular wisdom.

crown of gold Crowns appear in emblems that depict divine as well as temporal authority.

103 **laurel** a sign for triumph or lasting fame

106 **palm** also used to represent triumph

107 **turtles** turtle doves. Often a reference to married love, turtle doves are appropriate here in association with the figure of Unity.

anchor An anchor is most often used in emblems depicting Hope, but also appears in representations of religious faith.

112–13 **understood . . . number** This suggests that in performance, the speeches of the Frenchman and Spaniard were not followed by the English translations Middleton supplied in his pamphlet. The pamphlet itself was printed by Nicholas Okes, who received £4 from the Grocers for printing 500 copies—the customary number of copies at the usual price for these commemorative publications. Only a handful are entered in the Stationers' Register (*Honour and Industry* is not among them), and it is unclear whether the pamphlets were consistently intended for sale to the general public or primarily for distribution among the members of the Lord Mayor's guild. A somewhat specialized audience for this and other such pageant texts is implied by their tendency to assume a reader's familiarity with the overall shape and geography of the shows. For example, although Middleton's fee included compensation for many aspects of the spectacle on the Thames accompanying Bolles's passage to and from Westminster for his oath-taking, the text of *Honour and Industry* contains almost nothing about this part of the day's festivities—presumably because no speeches were written for delivery on the water. By comparison, in the *Busino Account* the flotilla on the river is described at length as an essential part of the celebration. (See note to l. 32–3 for the responsibilities covered by Middleton's fee.)

127 **utters** delivers

The arms of the Grocers.

THE SPANIARD'S SPEECH IN SPANISH *Ninguna de todas estas naciones conciben mayor y verdadera alegría en este triunfante y glorioso día que yo, no, ninguna de todas ellas, porque ahora que me parece, que son tan ricas, es señal que los de mi nación en tratando con ellas recibirán mayor provecho de ellas, a mi señor Don Mayor todas buenas y dichosas fortunas, y a los de la honrada Compañía de Especieros dichosos deseos, y así Dios guarde a mi señor Don Mayor, y ruego a Dios que todo el año siguiente, puede ser tan dichoso como esta entrada suya, a la dignidad de su Señoría, guarde Dios a su Señoría.*

THE SAME IN ENGLISH *None of all these nations conceive more true joy at this triumphant day than myself: to my Lord Mayor all fair and noble fortunes, and to the worthy Society of Grocers all happy wishes; and I pray heaven that all the year following may be as happy and successful as this first entrance to your dignity.*

This expression of their joy and love having spent itself, I know you cannot part contented without their several inscriptions: now the favour and help must be in you to conceive our breadth and limits, and not to think we can in these customary bounds comprehend all the nations, but so many as shall serve to give content to the understander, which thus produce themselves:

An Englishman, a Frenchman, an Irishman, a Span-

148 **inscriptions** An inscription was a written legend or description, often inscribed on the thing it explicated. Here, Middleton seems to be combining this meaning with the tradition, lapsed by 1617, of having pageant devices bear written labels. In 1575, William Smyth had described a 'pageant of triumph richly decked, whereupon by certain figures and writings, (partly touching the name of the said mayor) some matter touching Justice, and the office of a magistrate is represented'.

149–51 **not to think we can . . . comprehend all the nations** Middleton's Pageant of Nations does in fact exclude the Dutch, with whom England had long-standing trade relations. Middleton had used a Dutchman and his son—and parodied the Dutch language—in *No Wit* (1611); the omission from a pageant glorifying London's mercantile power was not due to oversight or unfamiliarity. England's natural allies and co-religionists on the continent had, paradoxically, become ferocious competitors in the sphere of foreign trade in the first decades of the seventeenth century. The growth of hostilities between the English and Dutch East India Companies during this period would have been of particular concern to the Grocers. As early as 1610, the Dutch had proposed a union of the two Companies, but, as one letter to the English Ambassador in Holland attests, the proposal was not looked on with favour: 'we fear that in case of joining, if it be on equal terms, the art and industry of their people will wear out ours'. Hostilities between the two merchant groups erupted into open warfare during 1618–19, and reached their severest crisis—at least in the English popular imagination—with the notorious murder of English merchants by the Dutch in the 1624 'Massacre of Amboyna'.

153 **a Frenchman** Trade with France for commodities including cloth and wine was steady throughout this period. A brief effort was made in 1611 to regulate trade with France by establishing a French Company; aside from its charter, this entity left few records.

an Irishman The performer dressed as an Irishman is presumably included to acknowledge the Grocers' membership in the Irish Society. In the aftermath of rebellion by a number of powerful Roman Catholics in the province of Ulster, King James offered the City of London the opportunity to resettle the seized lands. 'Motives and Reasons to induce the City of London to undertake Plantation in the North of Ireland', issued by the Privy Council, was delivered to the Lord Mayor in 1609; he in turn asked each of the major guilds to nominate representatives to a committee charged with considering the undertaking. The 'motives' included the hope that these plantations would 'furnish the City of London yearly with manifold provision' and that these 'colonies may be a means to utter infinite commodities from London to furnish the whole north of Ireland and Isles of Scotland'. After deliberating, the City helped form the Irish Society with a subscription of £20,000, of which the Grocers contributed £1,748. The actual division of lands did not take place for a number of years; the Grocers received final details of their allotment on 12 February 1617.

153–4 **a Spaniard** Trade with Spain was unregulated, except for the formation of Spanish Companies from 1577–85 and 1604–6. The peace treaty of 1604 between England and Spain touched off enormous growth in trade between the two countries, with the balance weighted unfavourably for the English. Traders were relatively ineffectual in selling English-made goods but imported large amounts of Spanish wares such as sugar, tobacco and wines.

iard, a Turk, a Jew, a Dane, a Polander, a Barbarian, a Russian or Muscovian.

This fully expressed, I arrive now at that part of triumph which my desire ever hastened to come to, this Castle of Fame or Honour, which Industry brings her sons unto in their reverend ages.

In the front of this Castle, Reward and Justice, decked in bright robes, keep a seat between them for him to whom the day's honour is dedicated, showing how many worthy sons of the City and of the same society have by their truth, desert, and industry come to the like honour before him; where on a sudden is shown divers of the same right worshipful Society of Grocers, manifested both by their good government in their times, as also by their escutcheons of arms, as an example and encouragement to all virtuous and industrious deservers in time to come. And in honour of antiquity is shown that ancient and memorable worthy of the Grocers' company, Andrew Bockrill, who was mayor of London the sixteenth year of Henry the Third, 1231, and continued so mayor seven years together.

Likewise, for the greater honour of the company, is also shown in this Castle of Fame the noble Allen de la Zouche, grocer, who was mayor of London the two-and-fiftieth year of the same Henry the Third, which Allen de la Zouche, for his good government in the time of his mayoralty, was by the said King Henry the Third made both a baron of this realm and Lord Chief Justice of England; also that famous worthy, Sir Thomas Knolles, grocer, twice mayor of this honourable city, which Sir

154 **a Turk** The development of English Levantine trade in the late 1500s exemplifies the interrelationships between London's political and economic élites. The Levant Company, chartered in 1592, was an amalgam of the Turkey and Venice Companies. Of the twelve members issued the Turkey Company's original patent in 1581, eight were or subsequently became Aldermen of the City of London, seven were Lord Mayors, and four served as MPs from the City of London. John Harte, George Bolles's father-in-law, was among these founding twelve. In 1592, the Turkey Company joined with the only slightly-less formidable leadership of the Venice Company to form the Levant Company. A select group of twenty additional merchants were, upon payment of £130, allowed to join the original fifty-three persons granted the patent for this new enterprise. Among the monopolies included in this grant was the right to establish and make exclusive use of an overland trade route to the Far East. The leading members of the Levant Company (again including John Harte) instead formed the East India Company, which received its first charter in 1600. Meanwhile, the Levant Company, which had changed from a joint-stock (a company funded by a range of investors but whose activities were directed by a small governing committee) to a regulated company (whose members individually engaged in trade), continued to enjoy royal favour. In 1615, the Crown went so far as to make it illegal for any merchandise to be imported into England from the Levant except directly, and in English shipping. Competition from foreign merchants, or from English entrepreneurs working overland routes, was effectively eliminated.
a Jew Jews served as middlemen in both the Barbary and Levant trades. Physical descriptions were available in accounts by English travellers abroad, such as George Sandy's observations about Turkish Jews in his *A Relation of a Journey begun An: Dom: 1610*, published in 1615: 'Their undergarments, differing little from the Turks' in fashion, are of purple cloth; over that they wear gowns of the same colour, with large wide sleeves, and clasped beneath the chin, without band or collar: on their heads high brimless caps of purple, which they move at no time in their salutations. They shave their heads all over... it being their ancient fashion'.
a Dane, a Polander The Eastland Company, incorporated in 1579, was a regulated company, offering its members a monopoly on trade of English merchandise with Denmark and Poland. The Danes controlled access to the Baltic Sea of all foreign shipping, exacting a variety of tolls on the value of goods being shipped. The King of Denmark, Christian IV, was brother of James I's Queen Anne; commerce between the two countries was occasionally shaped by this royal family connection. Poland was a significant source of grain imported into England, particularly during the second decade of the seventeenth century. In addition, Poles were generally thought to use more spices on their meat than other European nationals, making the country a market for the resale of commodities imported into England from India.
a Barbarian The entire northern coast of Africa was referred to as 'Barbary' during this period, but Middleton's 'Barbarian' most likely acknowleges England's commerce with Morocco. Established in the 1550s, this trade was a major source of grocery goods such as sugar and dates. A regulated company, created largely at the insistence of the Earl of Leicester, was chartered for twelve years from 1585 to 1597, and unregulated trade resumed thereafter.

154–5 **a Russian or Muscovian** Chartered in 1555, the Russia Company helped to pioneer the joint-stock principal of commercial organization, although it was trading as a regulated company by the mid-1620s, shortly after George Bolles's investment (see note on 'a Turk' at l. 154 above for 'joint-stock' vs. 'regulated'). Russia's relevance to the grocery trade included its market for English re-exports such as wine and spices; Russia also provided some spices, primarily from Persia, for English consumers. The first Russian ambassador to England, Osep Napea, arrived in 1557 under the auspices of the nascent Russia Company. Napea and his entourage were feted by the Lord Mayor, aldermen, and members of the Company for almost a month before being received at court by King Philip and Queen Mary. The Company continued to play an important role in diplomatic relations between England and Russia. For example, the Company paid at least £1,376 toward the expenses of Sir Richard Lee's embassy on behalf of Queen Elizabeth I to the Tsar in 1600. The week after the performance of *Honour and Industry*, the Company hosted an ambassador from Russia, who arrived with an entourage of seventy-five people as well as gifts of white hawks and live sables for James I. At the ambassador's departure in June, 1618, he was understood to take with him a loan of £50,000 from the Company, made 'not merely with the hope of obtaining privileges advantageous for their traffic, but also the monopoly of the Russian trade, to the utter exclusion of the Dutch'.

157–8 **Castle of Fame or Honour** Middleton's lack of specificity here—Fame or Honour—is interesting. He certainly does not mean for them to be synonymous, as they are given distinct personifications—and distinct genders—later in the pageant: Fame is 'not without her silver trumpet' (229), Honour is 'manifested by a fair star in his hand' (232).

Thomas begun at his own charge that famous building of Guildhall in London, and other memorable works both in this city and in his own company; so much worthiness being the lustre of this castle, and ought indeed to be the imitation of the beholder.

My lord no sooner approaches, but Reward, a partner with Justice in keeping that seat of honour, as overjoyed at the sight of him, appears too free and forward in the resignation.

REWARD

Welcome to Fame's bright Castle; take thy place:
This seat's reserved to do thy virtue's grace.

JUSTICE

True, but not yet to be possessed. Hear me:
Justice must flow through him before that be;
Great works of grace must be required and done
Before the honour of this seat be won.
A whole year's reverend care in righting wrongs,
And guarding innocence from malicious tongues,
Must be employed in virtue's sacred right
Before this place be filled: 'tis no mean fight
That wins this palm; truth, and a virtuous care
Of the oppressèd, those the loadstones are
That will 'gainst envy's power draw him forth
To take this merit in this seat of worth,
Where all the memorable worthies shine
In works of brightness able to refine
All the beholders' minds, and strike new fire
To kindle an industrious desire
To imitate their actions and their fame,
Which to this Castle adds that glorious name.
Wherefore, Reward, free as the air or light,
There must be merit, or our work's not right.

REWARD

If there were any error, 'twas my love;
And if it be a fault to be too free,
Reward commits but once such heresy.
Howe'er, I know your worth will so extend,
Your fame will fill this seat at twelve months' end.

About this Castle of Fame are placed many honourable figures, as Truth, Antiquity, Harmony, Fame, Desert, Good Works; on the top of the Castle, Honour, Religion, Piety, Commiseration: the works of those whose memories shine in this Castle.

If you look upon Truth first, you shall find her properly expressed, holding in her right hand a sun, in the other a fan of stars; Antiquity with a scroll in her hand, as keeper of Honour's records; Harmony holding a golden lute, and Fame not without her silver trumpet; for Desert, 'tis glorious through her own brightness, but holds nothing; Good Works expressed with a college or hospital. On the top of the Castle, Honour manifested by a fair star in his hand; Religion with a temple on her head; Piety with an altar; Commiseration with a melting or burning heart. And, not to have our speakers forgotten, Reward and Justice, with whom we entered this part of Triumph, Reward holding a wreath of gold ready for a deserver, and Justice furnished with her sword and balance.

185 **Guildhall** civic hall for the governing bodies of the City of London

191–2 **too free . . . resignation** Reward too easily relinquishes the seat to the new Lord Mayor, according to Justice in the speech that follows.

225 **Truth** Compare the representation of Truth in the 1613 pageant.

231 **Good Works . . . college or hospital** London's guilds contributed to the foundation and maintenance of a number of educational institutions, and the Lord Mayor, Court of Aldermen and Common Council were responsible for the upkeep of the City's four royal hospitals: St Bartholomew's, Bethlehem, Christ's, and St Thomas's. Four beadles from each of the four hospitals marched in the procession in blue coats; in 1617 the Grocers paid 'diverse tailors' 14*d* for each coat. In addition, the beadles from each hospital received 12*d* each 'for their dinners and attendance in this service done'—in addition to 'long caps and ribbons'.

240 **Paul's Churchyard** churchyard at the east end of St Paul's Cathedral. The Grocers' paid 10*s*. 'for taking up of the spurs at Paul's and for setting them again and for paving and gravel'. 'Spurs' were cylindrical stones set at the corner of buildings or archways to protect against damage by wheeled traffic. Presumably they were removed and then reset to accommodate the anticipated crowds. Another piece of evidence that property along the pageant route was modified for the day's celebration is the payment of £1. 14*s*. 6*d*. to the 'city carpenter, for pulling down divers signs and setting them up again'.
Cheapside chief commercial street running east from St Paul's. The churchwardens of St Peter's, located along the pageant route on Cheapside, received 3*s*. 4*d*. for allowing the waits of the City, a group of wind-instrumentalists maintained by the municipality, to be stationed there while providing musical accompaniment for the procession. The waits themselves were paid £2. 13*s*. 4*d*. for five days of 'service' in connection with the Lord Mayor's inaugural.

241–2 **that gave delight upon the water** This is Middleton's only allusion within the text of *Honour and Industry* to the elaborate water-borne procession that took place prior to the events that he does narrate. While Middleton's pageant does not feature speeches delivered as part of a 'water show', a practice begun by George Peele in his pageant of 1591 and continued sporadically over the years, 'both castle and island' now gathered before the Lord Mayor had begun the day's festivities transported by boat as part of the flotilla on the Thames. Middleton's fee included arranging for water transport as well as 'lighters for the show by water' for the actual performance, but the Grocers paid a separate sum of 2*s*. 6*d*. for 'going by water at several times to see the work made ready' prior to the big day. The inaugural ceremony's logistical complexities are suggested by the payment of 13*s*. to 'several watermen for carrying of the whifflers', young freemen serving as armed attendants, and 'divers' members of the Court of Assistants and liverymen, 'to and from Westminster'. Presumably, Bolles paid for his own transportation, as there is no sum assigned for the usual rental of a barge for the new Lord Mayor. The Grocers' Accounts do, however, record payment of £1. 10*s*. for the hire of a barge to carry various members to the separate oath-taking ceremonies at Westminster of Robert Johnson, a grocer, as one of London's two Sheriffs. It was customary for the mayor-elect to choose one of the Sheriffs, usually from his own guild; Johnson was selected by Bolles to serve during his Mayoral term. The other

All this service is performed before the feast, some in Paul's Churchyard, some in Cheapside; at which place the whole triumph meets, both castle and island, that gave delight upon the water. And now, as duty binds me, I commend my lord and his right honourable guests to the solemn pleasure of the feast, from whence, I presume, all epicurism is banished; for where Honour is master of the feast, Moderation and Gravity are always attendants.

The feast being ended at Guildhall, my lord (as yearly custom invites him) goes accompanied with the triumph towards St Paul's, to perform the noble and reverend ceremonies which divine antiquity virtuously ordained, and is no less than faithfully observed, which is no mean lustre to the City. Holy service and ceremonies accomplished, he returns by torchlight to his own house, the whole triumph placed in comely order before him; and at the entrance of his gate, Honour, a glorious person, from the top of the castle gives life to these following words.

HONOUR

There is no human glory or renown,
But have their evening and their sure sun-setting,
Which shows that we should upward seek our crown
And make but use of time for our hope's bettering.

Sheriff was elected by London's Common Council (see the *Busino Account*, notes to ll. 28–9 and 236).

244 **the feast** Stow's *Survey* of 1603 records the tradition, dating back at least to the reign of Henry VIII, that London's 60 guilds were represented at the 'Mayor's feast' by their wardens and a stated number of Company members, ranging from 17 for the venerable Mercers to one for lesser guilds like the Coopers. These guests—several hundred of them—were joined by members of the nobility, ambassadors, and other worthies. The Grocers' accounts do not record the cost of this feast for 1617; the banquet was traditionally paid for by the new Lord Mayor and Sheriffs. The Grocers did pay the keeper of Guildhall 12*s.* to have the 'Mercers' hangings' carried to and from the Guildhall, hung up and taken down, and for the necessary timber and hooks. These 'hangings' were presumably the result of the bequest of £73. 6*s.* 8*d.* 'for a hanging of tapestry to serve for principal days in the Guildhall' by Nicholas Alwyn, a Mercer and Lord Mayor in 1499. The Grocers also paid George Newball, Keeper of Blackwell Hall, £2 'for the use of his house for the children' during the feast, and the porters of the Hall received 10*s.* for 'looking to the pageant and other shows whilst the children were at dinner' (see note to l. 49 above regarding child performers). Blackwell or Bakewell Hall, used as a cloth market in Stow's time, was adjacent to the Guildhall. In addition, the Company picked up the tab for the breakfast shared by the bachelors and other participants in the day's festivities 'at the Ship behind Old Fish Street', conveniently located near the pageant route (which they would be expected to line) from Baynard's Castle to St Paul's Churchyard. Mr Abell, a vintner, received £27. 8*s.* 9*d.* 'for all manner of charges'. Another entry suggests that these shows provided an opportunity for expense-account socializing: committee members involved in supervising various aspects of the pageant, along with the Company Wardens, consumed £25. 16*s.* worth of 'dinners and potations . . . in the hall as elsewhere during the time of their sitting about these businesses'.

presume The pageant text, along with the public, waits patiently outside the doors during the feast and the services at St Paul's which follow. Munday's continuation of Stow, however, gives a glimpse into the hierarchical, ritualized private part of the public celebration at Guildhall: 'the new Lord Mayor with two of the ancientest Aldermen, Master Recorder and the Sheriffs, go up to the lords' table to bid them welcome, and likewise all the other guests there: and from thence to the Lady Mayoress' table: and so come forth to the gentlewomen's table, and to the judges; and from thence he goeth into the Chamberlain's Office, where he dineth. But the old Lord [Mayor], at their first entering into the Hall, goeth up directly to the high table of the hustings, and there keepeth the state for that feast. After the Hall is almost served the seconds, then the new Lord Mayor goeth with Master Recorder, and those other aldermen that dined with him, to bid the old Lord [Mayor], and all the guests in the Hall welcome.'

245 **epicurism** excess in eating; see *Triumphs of Truth* 666. The 'moderation and gravity' which Middleton ascribed to the proceedings would have been in sharp contrast to the behaviour of guests at court masques. Orazio Busino, observer of Court as well as City entertainments, described the scene that followed Prince Charles's performance in Jonson and Jones's *Pleasure Reconciled to Virtue* (1618): 'His majesty . . . glanced round the table and departed, and at once like so many harpies the company fell on their prey. The table was almost entirely covered with sweetmeats, with all kinds of sugar confections . . . The meal was served in bowls or plates of glass; the first assault threw the table to the ground, and the crash of glass platters reminded me exactly of the windows breaking in a great midsummer storm.'

253 **torchlight** 49 dozen 'large staff torches' cost £36. 15*s.* The Company also paid £5. 8*s.* 3*d.* for ten-and-half dozen 'small torches' and five-and-a-half dozen 'links' 'to light the pageant and other shows from Leadenhall over night to Carter Lane and other places appointed'. Leadenhall, used variously as a market for cloth and a storage facility for grain, also had a role in civic pageantry. According to a petition of 1519, 'if any triumph or nobleness were to be done, or showed by the commonality of the city for the honour of our sovereign lord the King, and realm, and for the worship of the said City, the said Leadenhall is most meet and convenient place to prepare and order the said triumph therein, and from thence to issue forth to the places therefore appointed'. Carter Lane, one street away from St Paul's, appears to have been the location where pageant wagons were stored the night before a Lord Mayor's show. For the 1613 pageant written by Middleton, Anthony Munday received an additional £3. 13*s.* 4*d.* over his £149 producer's fee for 'the clearing of all charges for the standing of the pageant etc. at the Bell in Carter Lane'.

254 **placed in comely order** 'Ordering' the pageant throughout the day was a major concern; failure to do so could have dire consequences for the production. In his 1615 pageant text, Munday is apparently explaining some organizational glitches in transferring the pageants from water to land when he bemoans 'the time being so short, and our preparation requiring such decency in order: yet much abused by neglect in marshalling, and hurried away with too impudent hastiness'. The various pageant devices had to be kept in order; so did Company members and participating dignitaries. And the pageant route itself had to be kept clear of people so that the whole cumbersome procession could circulate in a timely way. For *Honour and Industry*, the Grocers paid £5 to George Bell 'for himself and 10 others for the ushering, marshalling and making way for the whole Company on the day, they furnishing themselves with all things necessary'. (See also the *Busino Account*, l. 157 ff. and notes.)

So, to be truly mindful of our own
Is to perform all parts of good in one.
The close of this triumphant day is come,
And Honour stays to bid you welcome home.
All I desire for my grace and good
Is but to be remembered in your blood,
With honour to accomplish the fair time,
Which power hath put into your hands. A crime
As great as ever came into sin's band
I do entitle a too-sparing hand:
Nothing deads honour more than to behold
Plenty cooped up, and bounty faint and cold,
Which ought to be the free life of the year;
For bounty 'twas ordained to make that clear,
Which is the light of goodness and of fame,
And puts by honour from the cloud of shame.
Great cost and love hath nobly been bestowed
Upon thy triumph, which this day hath showed.
Embrace 'em in thy heart, till times afford
Fuller expression; in one absolute word,
All the content that ever made man blest,
This triumph done, make a triumphant breast.

No sooner the speech is ended but the triumph is dissolved, and not possible to 'scape the hands of the defacer; things that, for their quaintness (I dare so far commend them), have not been usually seen through the City; the credit of which workmanship I must justly lay upon the deserts of Master Rowland Bucket, chief master of the work; yet

269–71 **A crime...too-sparing hand** This kind of rhetoric, encouraging the Lord Mayor's generosity, is a frequent refrain in these pageants. The Lord Mayor was responsible for securing and storing grain for distribution to the City's poor in time of dearth, and the pageants' constant appeals for 'bounty' may reflect this larger corporate duty. Individual philanthropy was also a hallmark of the successful tradesman. Here again, Bolles is exemplary. His will includes bequests of £50 to Christ's Hospital, £20 to St Bartholomew's, £20 to aid prisoners, and £19 for poor relief. He was also generous to the Grocers, leaving £30 for plate, £33 for a commemorative dinner, and £50 for the Company's general use. The generosity of Bolles's father-in-law was more spectacular: among his many bequests John Harte left £112 to London's hospitals, £733 to found a grammar school in Yorkshire, and, along with at least one identifiably Puritan London magnate, £30 towards the purchase of books and £600 as endowment for the newly-established Sidney Sussex College at Cambridge.

284–94 These closing credits contain information about Middleton's collaborators that presumably was not communicated to the pageant's audience. Like the translations provided in the pamphlet for the speeches of the Spaniard and Frenchman (see note to l. 112 above), this is a difference between the text and performance of *Honour and Industry*.

285 **the hands of the defacer** Pageant producers were occasionally reimbursed for items 'defaced' in the course of the day's activities. In 1616 Anthony Munday applied to the Fishmongers for an additional £10 over his fee for a number of reasons including the 'spoiling [of] the silk coats which the halberdiers did wear'; he was 'content thankfully to accept' a little over half that amount. Accounts for the 1617 show indicate the Grocers' concern that the 'triumph' be preserved as carefully as possible. The Company's beadle received 12*s.* 9*d.* 'for candles and for bringing in of the pageants after the show to the hall'; another 11*s.* were disbursed 'to certain workmen for setting up the beasts in the pageant-chamber over the entry in the hall'. An order in the Goldsmiths' records from 1611 suggests that the display, or at least storage, of these scenic elements at livery company halls was a common practice: 'the leopards, unicorns, and mermaids of the pageants standing in the gallery next the hall shall be taken down and laid in some other place...because it is intended that provision of armour shall be made and set up there'. In addition to looking after the 'triumph', the Grocers took some care to clean up the city streets: 11*s.* were paid 'for carrying away the rubbish at Leadenhall'—where the pageant elements were prepared—'and taking down the partitions there'.

286 **quaintness** ingeniously designed; skilfully made; elaborate

287 **seen through the City** The hiring of porters to carry the various pageants through the streets was one of the responsibilities to be covered out of Middleton's £282 fee. The Grocers allotted an additional £1. 10*s.* to be divided among eight of these men in 'gratuity' for their services; 5*s.* was paid to 'Thomas Hunt, porter, being hurt in the service'.

289 **Rowland Bucket** Munday thanks 'the exact and skilful painter Rowland Bucket' at the end of the text for the 1614 Lord Mayor's Show, *Himatia-Polcos*. It seems that Bucket did not, however, work exclusively on civic projects or for guild-related clients. Indeed, a sampling of his known employments indicates numerous points of contact between London's different social élites. Bucket received £7. 5*s.* in connection with the 1620 Accession Day tilt. For building six chariots for *The Triumph of Peace* (1634), a lavish masque sponsored by the Inns of Court, Bucket was paid £272. 17*s.*; Inigo Jones received £200 for scenery and James Shirley got the generous sum of £120 for writing the text. Bucket was also employed with some frequency by the Earl of Salisbury. One project undertaken for this last patron was overtly hostile to the City's interests. Bucket participated in the interior decoration of the New Exchange, developed beginning in 1607 as a commercial centre by the Earl outside the City walls along the increasingly fashionable Strand. The building had sparked an outcry from City merchants who feared that 'if such a work be erected, the situation of the place...being near unto the Court of Whitehall in the midst of the nobility and where much of the gentry lodge... will have such advantages' that the Royal Exchange already extant within the City will be rendered 'of no use for salesmen at all'. Undaunted by the City's protests, Salisbury proceeded with his plan and commissioned Ben Jonson and Inigo Jones to prepare an entertainment, costing £179, to greet James I and his family, all of whom attended the opening of the building on April 11, 1609. Jonson's text for this most unusual entertainment—a court-sponsored celebration promoting commerce in London—affirms the appeal to his élite audience of exotic items from faraway places. However, the tradesmen importing and selling such goods are portrayed with implicit scepticism. A merchant displaying his wondrous inventory to the august audience is as much charlatan as wizard, and he bluntly describes his competitors 'about the town' as stocking their shelves with counterfeit goods and 'trash'. London citizens are unambiguous figures of fun: another character ridicules their ignorant curiosity about the construction of the New Exchange by describing at length the 'quotidian torture that I have endured...from my great cousin the multitude'.

not forgetting the faithful care and industry of my well approved friend, Master Henry Wilde, and Master Jacob Challoner, partners in the business.

The season cuts me off; and after this day's trouble I am as willing to take my rest.

FINIS.

291 **Henry Wilde** painter, cited in the Haberdashers' Minutes for his contribution to that guild's 1604 Lord Mayor's Show

291–2 **Jacob Challoner** painter, cited in *Honour and Industry*'s accounts for painting or repairing a range of banners, streamers, and shields. A sampling of his services and their cost: 'for a great square banner of the Prince's arms within the sunbeams of gold', £7; for mending the Company's banner, 5*s*.; for 'the new painting and gilding of 10 trumpet banners at 4*s*. a piece', £2; for mending '24 trumpet banners', £1. 4*s*.; 'for painting and gilding of 2 long pennants of the Lord Mayor's arms on callico', £2. 13*s*. 4*d*.; 'for painting and gilding of 8 other pennants on callico with the arms of the City, Company, England, and Scotland', £8. Challoner and two companions were also involved in the actual pageant: they received 13*s*. 4*d*. 'for the ordering, marshalling, and setting forth of the banners, streamers, and other silk works and for looking to them and for their pains all that day'. The Grocers were concerned that Challoner, along with other non-guildmembers essential to the pageant's success, be distinctively costumed: £1. 1*s*. 4*d* was spent on 16 ells of taffeta 'for scarves for the fencers, marshals and Jacob Challoner'.

Orazio Busino's Eyewitness Account of The Triumphs of Honour and Industry

Translated and annotated by Kate D. Levin

Public solemnity in the manner of a triumph for the City of London's chief magistrate, known as 'my Lord Mayor', held for the enjoyment of the populace shortly after his election.

For a good understanding of this supreme judicial office, you need to know that in addition to the absolute power of His Majesty the King, there exists in London a head of that city's government. The city itself is more like a republic of merchants than anything else: idlers are banished, and noblemen and foreigners are excluded from its government. All the houses on the major streets, with the exception of a few mansions, are shops of a variety of tradesmen, and each house has its own sign or trademark like an inn. Anyone who wants to attain the eminent position of the Lord Mayorship must start in youth by working for seven years, bareheaded, in the shop of a tradesman whose business he wants to learn, just to acquire the title 'apprentice'. Then he can open his own shop, and with earnings from trade or other good fortune, increase his capital to the sum of 200,000 ducats—at which point he is eligible for this august office. First, though, he has to have served as sheriff, which is to say as a kind of criminal magistrate, and also as an alderman, which is like a senator. Hundreds of such children exist in this little world of London, and, because it costs so much and a new person must be chosen each year, anyone of them might be elected to the office. Moreover, anyone with a clear head flees the opportunity

Title Orazio Busino Busino was chaplain to Pietro Contarini, appointed the Venetian ambassador to England in 1617. Accompanied by Busino, Contarini arrived in England in October of that year. His chief commission was to enlist England's support for Venice against Spanish-sanctioned (and funded) efforts to invade and annex the Venetian republic. Busino's obvious and ardent anti-Spanish sentiments have much to do with that country's predatory attitude towards his own. This eyewitness account of *The Triumphs of Honour and Industry* is not an official dispatch; it does not have the status of a diplomatic *relazione*. Instead, Busino's observations about English personalities and customs were written for the enjoyment of Contarini's brothers back home. In late 1618 Busino left England with Contarini, who had been appointed his country's ambassador to Spain.

1 **triumph** The classical Roman triumphal entry honouring military victories was revived in fifteenth-century Italy to welcome important visitors (usually royal or noble) and celebrate major civic and religious festivals. The defining feature of these triumphs was the use of elaborate chariots representing historical or allegorical scenes. Middleton's use of 'triumph' in the titles of most of his Lord Mayor's pageants plays on this sense of the word as a lavish continental form of entertainment associated with the wealthy and powerful. Busino's description of *Honour and Industry* as being 'in the style of a triumph' affirms the Grocers' own aspirations for the event: the expenditures for 1617 are described in the wardens' account book as 'concerning matters of Triumph'.

10–11 **noblemen . . . government** Only those who had earned the 'freedom of the City' were eligible for election to one of the City's governing bodies (see *Industry* 12, note regarding the 'freedom').

16–18 **seven years . . . the title 'apprentice'** In fact, the title for youths *during* those seven years of work was 'apprentice'.

16 **bareheaded** an indication of subservience

20–1 **200,000 ducats** £50,000; one ducat was worth 5*s*. Although fortunes of this size were not unheard of among London's élite, Busino exaggerates in asserting that this amount was prerequisite for selection as Lord Mayor (see note to 28–9 below, and *Industry* 12, note).

28–9 **flees . . . enormous** The financial burdens of the mayoralty on its incumbent had historically been substantial. A petition from 1535 asking that the households of the Lord Mayor and Sheriffs be combined 'at an expense of not less than £1600' was an early, but by no means the only, effort to scale back the costs of these positions. An Act of Common Council passed in 1555, again attempting to redress the problem, acknowledged that 'almost all good Citizens fly and refuse to serve'. At the time of *Honour and Industry*'s composition, the Lord Mayor's expenses, in addition to numerous acts of public generosity, included the food, lodging and most of the liveries of an official household consisting of thirty or so functionaries. The cost of feeding such a household, in addition to the Lord Mayor's own family, was by itself enormous. Upon the death in office of Lord Mayor Thomas Skinner in 1596, the Court of Aldermen allotted £10 to be distributed among his official retinue as reimbursement for meals that had not been provided in the relatively brief interim before the installation of the new Lord Mayor. The price of acquiring a suitable dwelling could also be astronomical. Sir James Pemberton, Lord Mayor in 1610–11, spent £4000–5000 on this alone. London's Common Council helped to defray the Lord Mayor's housekeeping expenses in different ways over the years. For example, during a period in the 1580s the Council switched from annual donations of 4 tuns of wine (one tun equalled 252 gallons) to payments of £40. The Council also allocated substantial sums for 'decorations'. Individual guilds were apparently expected to help member Lord Mayors establish their households. George Bolles seems to have spared his colleagues this burden, since Grocers' Company accounts record £2 'paid and given in benevolence to certain officers of the Lord Mayor's house, in

because the expenditure is so enormous as the position requires hosting elaborate public festivals for an entire year. The Lord Mayor is set up as monarch by the twelve heads of companies of very picked men, extremely wealthy and experienced, and within these twelve are placed and subordinated another sixty companies comprising all the mechanical arts, however humble. On public occasions company members wear gowns reaching the ground, with slight differences which will be described at another time so as not to postpone recounting the style used on the day of the triumph for the new Lord Mayor, which took place on November 8. His Excellency received a private invitation to see the first part of the triumph, the water show, which features ships, galleons, brigantines, large boats and barges as long as a galley. This all takes place on the River Thames, beginning near the Lord Mayor's house and heading toward the King's palace or court, where he swears his oath of fealty. The incumbent made his progress with the greatest possible pomp he could devise, always alluding to his line of trade with huge expenditure, which in truth exceeds that of a petty or medium duke. At a very early hour His Excellency arrived at the house of a nobleman with a fine and commodious view from a dock on the Thames. This river flows the length of the City like our Grand Canal in Venice, but the width is like that of the Giudecca Canal. We watched as a large flotilla, including the big vessels already mentioned, made an appearance accompanied by innumerable small boats of sightseers—like the gondolas that swarm around the Bucintoro. The ships were very beautifully decorated, their balustrades festooned with various paintings, huge banners and an infinite number of pennants. Accompanied by thundering

regard his Lordship took no money of the bachelors'.

Not surprisingly, financial ruin was an occasional consequence of office. Richard Martin, who served as sheriff for a year (1581–82) and as mayor for parts of two terms (1589, 1594), spent £7000 on these offices; in 1602 he was removed from the Court of Aldermen 'on account of his unfitting demeanour and carriage'—euphemisms, as it turns out, for his poverty and imprisonment for debt. His colleagues had apparently given him 1,000 marks (£667) as a condition of his resignation from office, which he then refused to do. In 1621, Sir Francis Jones's 'failing' was the talk of London. According to the indefatigable letter writer John Chamberlain, Jones, 'the night before he should have accompanied his successor to Westminster did *sgombrare*, conveying all of worth out of his house, and himself with his wife into some secret corner in the country, where ever since he has played least in sight. He is one of the farmers [of the customs] and always esteemed a man of great wealth. Howsoever it falls out that... many men [are] like to lose great sums by him.'

The office of Lord Mayor was only one among several positions that prominent Londoners sought to avoid. Individuals selected as Aldermen frequently paid fines averaging £500 rather than undertake the more costly duties of office. The merchant Sir Thomas Myddelton, the subject of *The Triumphs of Truth* (1613), agreed to serve as Alderman upon his election in 1603 only after being imprisoned in Newgate for refusing either to take office or pay a fine. Myddelton's confinement took place even though James I petitioned for his release on the grounds that his position as Surveyor of Customs exempted him from 'private service'. The acceptance of fines in lieu of service seems to have caused particular difficulty in filling the office of Sheriff. In 1613, twelve persons were elected and refused to serve; 1614 saw eleven refusals. This breakdown of civic-mindedness—or increase in cost-consciousness—on the part of London's guildmembers is registered in Munday's 1614 pageant text, *Himatia-poleos, The Triumphs of Old Drapery*. In an outburst of fraternal pride, Munday, himself a draper, notes that 'when many solemn meetings have been made in the Guildhall, for election of a Sheriff by common consent, and as many refusals still happening day by day...; yet when no one would undergo the office and charge, a draper has done it, worthily and willingly'. Even the guilds themselves had to threaten members with stiff fines for refusing to be elevated to the next—and more costly—rung of membership. The Merchant Taylors' 1613 ordinances charged members unwilling to serve as Wardens £50.

31–4 **twelve heads... sixty companies** The Lord Mayor was chosen annually from London's Court of Aldermen, all of whose members belonged to a craft guild, or company. The twelve largest and wealthiest of these companies—the Mercers, Grocers, Drapers, Fishmongers, Goldsmiths, Skinners, Merchant Taylors, Haberdashers, Salters, Ironmongers, Vintners, and Clothworkers—supplied the vast majority of Aldermen throughout this period. The near-monopoly of the larger guilds on elective positions is partially due to the tradition, almost always observed, whereby members of the sixty or so smaller guilds obtained membership in one of the twelve 'great' companies upon election as Aldermen. Translation to membership in one of the twelve companies was an absolute requirement upon election to the Lord Mayorship.

40 **November 8** Busino is using the Gregorian calendar, adopted by Roman Catholic countries in 1582 at the behest of Pope Gregory XIII. Until 1752 England remained on the Julian calendar, which, in 1617, was ten days behind the Gregorian. By English calculations, the Lord Mayor's pageant took place on October 29.

45–6 **palace... fealty** i.e. Westminster (see *Industry* 6, note)

48 **line of trade** i.e. the grocery trade

57 **Bucintoro** The Bucintoro (ship of gold) was an elaborately decorated barge used by the Doge of Venice for the annual enactment of Venice's 'marriage with the sea'. This rite, performed as part of Ascension Day festivities, included the throwing of a golden wedding band into the waters around the Lido. The Englishman Thomas Coryate, who visited Venice in 1608, described the Bucintoro as 'a thing of marvellous worth, the richest galley of all the world; for it cost one hundred thousand crowns which is thirty thousand pound sterling. A work so exceeding glorious that I never heard or read of the like in any place of the world, these only excepted, viz: that of Cleopatra, which she so exceeding sumptuously adorned with cables of silk and other passing beautiful ornaments; and those that the Emperor Caligula built with timber of cedar and poops and sterns of ivory.' With a surge of patriotism, Coryate adds, 'lastly that most incomparable and peerless ship of our gracious Prince called the Prince Royal... doth by many degrees surpass this Bucintoro of Venice, and any ship else (I believe) in Christendom.'

Leathersellers, depicted in the 1604 charter of their company.

canon and fireworks, a very numerous and well-appointed group of musicians sang and played on fifes, drums, and other instruments. They were rowed swiftly upriver with the swelling tide, to the constant peal of firing ordnance. We saw the aforementioned barges carrying stages highly decorated with various devices, which later served as triumphal cars on the city's main thoroughfare. When the fleet arrived at a certain point it received a booming salute from the sakers, and a greater one when the Lord Mayor disembarked at the dock near the court of Parliament where, as I have said, he takes his oath before the appointed judges. Amazed by all this, we then went to the house of a respected goldsmith on the main street in the most beautiful part of the city, where we had been assigned windows from which to see more of the show. While the procession was being ordered we gazed up and down the street. The houses have many high vantage points and all the façades are entirely of windows, glazed from one side to the other. They were filled with the handsomest faces, like so many beautiful paintings, with varied headtires and rich clothing of every colour, including silver and gold. Two lone ugly faces marred the charming view—and I say this apart from our natural loathing of the nation—two Spaniards: badly dressed, emaciated, with sunken eyes, ugly as ogres. We couldn't avoid catching glimpses of them from time to time as we gazed at the nearby English ladies who, by comparison, were all the more radiant. Looking below us onto to the street we saw a huge mass of people, surging like the sea, moving here and there in search of places to watch or rest—which proved impossible because of the constant press of newcomers. It was a chaotic mixture: dotards; insolent youths and children, especially of that race of apprentices I mentioned earlier; beribboned serving wenches; lower-class women with their children in their arms: all were there to see the beautiful show. We saw few carriages about, and fewer horsemen; only a few carrying ladies to watch the procession from the houses of close friends or relatives on the street, because the insolence of the crowd is extreme. They swing up onto the back of carriages, and if one of the drivers turns on them with his whip, they jump to the ground and hurl stinking mud at him. We saw them dirty the beautiful livery of a coachman in exactly this way; one must have patience. No one unsheathes a sword in these great tumults: everything resolves itself with kicks and punches and muddy faces. A perpetual shower of firecrackers rained from the windows onto the seething crowd, popping mischievously under everyone's clothes and faces and between their legs. The children fight with each other to collect the squibs off the ground once they are extinguished. Looking up again

64–5 **firing ordnance** John Kellocke was paid £32. 10*s*. 'for the whole charge of the . . . [barge] and a galley, and for his service with men, shot, powder, cassocks, colours and all other necessaries for them.'

69 **salute from the sakers** Sakers were small cannon. Robert Bevis Connor received £31 'for the charge of six score chambers, twice shot off'.

73–4 **main street . . . city** Goldsmiths' Row, a stretch of properties in Cheapside controlled by the Goldsmiths' Company and leased to members of that guild, like Busino's host. Stow described the Row as 'the most beautiful frame of fair houses and shops that be within the walls of London, or elsewhere in England', and one foreign visitor was impressed by the 'great treasures and vast amount of money [which] may be seen here'. From their window in the Row, the Venetian party would have had an excellent view of the pageant's progress along Cheapside to Guildhall. It seems from his account that Busino does not actually see one of the devices performed for the Lord Mayor; rather, he is describing the entire procession in motion. Nonetheless, it is clear that the actors, dancers, and musicians on each pageant wagon continue to perform as they move through the streets.

75 **assigned windows** It usually fell to the King's Master of Ceremonies to find suitable vantage points for visiting diplomats who wished to see the procession through Cheapside. A fee of £3 was expected by householders for the use of their windows when the ambassadors themselves paid. When the King paid, as he often did for 'extraordinary' ambassadors (foreign emissaries of the highest rank sent on specific, usually short-term missions), the rate was £5.

at windows farther down the street, we saw various young men mingling with lovely damsels and, in our naïvete, we thought that these were brothers or husbands for the protection of each young lady. We were told, however, that, to the contrary, these men were their servants, which is to say in plain language, their lovers and favourites, granted great intimacy and many liberties. Foreigners in London are little liked, not to say hated, so those who are wise take care to dress in the English style or that of France, which has been adopted by the court, and make themselves understood by signs whenever they can avoid speaking, and so they avoid mishaps. Only the Spanish nation choose the prerogative of dressing in their own fashion, and are therefore easily recognized and mortally hated. Some of us saw a wretched woman enraged against a man thought to belong to the Catholic Ambassador's household. She aroused the crowd to persecute him, leading the way by striking him with a bunch of greens while calling him 'Spanish rogue'. And although he was already dressed very finely, his clothes were further embroidered in a nasty manner with a kind of soft, fetid mud found at all times in such quantity that this city would better be called '*Lorda*' than '*Londra*'. And if the don hadn't saved himself in a shop, they would certainly have torn out his eyes. So much are the haughty Spaniards detested that they are considered harpies in this country; it seems to me that they are not as well known elsewhere. The companies of gownsmen now began to appear. Their purpose was merely to line the sides of the streets, but they were accompanied by footmen and other officers to protect them from the press of the crowd. Their gowns were like doctoral robes, or like those of the Doge, with sleeves very wide from the shoulders and lined with various materials like plush, velvet, marten, feathers, a beautiful kind of badger, and also sable. These gownsmen were members of the apothecaries' guild from which the present Lord Mayor derives. Several different marching groups numbering over a thousand all together wore a kind of pouch over the left shoulder, half of red cloth and half of black, in the shape I've sketched in the margin. Other gownsmen wore long robes and pouches of red damask; these members were younger than the first and had to wait at table during the banquet. Others wore gowns with all red shoulders; still others wore small stoles at their throats. To assist the proceedings and clear a pathway in the street, a constable on horseback, with a gold chain around his neck and two footmen in livery, weaved up and down; he was so large and plump that, we

113–18 **in our naïvete ... liberties** Note that the Italians, stock figures of lascivious immorality in the plays of Middleton and his contemporaries, are shocked by the behaviour of these English ladies and their gallants.

128 **Catholic Ambassador's** This ostensibly peculiar reference to a Spanish diplomat as *the* 'Catholic Ambassador'—Busino was himself a Catholic chaplain of the Catholic Ambassador from Venice—is understandable in light of the Venetian Republic's long history of challenges to papal authority. As recently as 1606, the pope had excommunicated the Venetian government and interdicted its territories for failing to exempt Catholic clergymen from civil laws and church property from taxation. However, despite enormous pressure brought to bear on the Republic, the papal interdict completely failed to curb Venice's ideological independence and was revoked in less than a year, following a series of face-saving manœuevres by a papal envoy. In calling Spain's ambassador 'the Catholic Ambassador', Busino registers Venetian hostility towards Spain for its powerful support of papal orthodoxy.

134 ***Lorda*** filth
Londra London

145–6 **various materials ... sable** The garments worn by those in the procession were part of a sartorial code that distinguished levels of guild and civic office (see *Industry* 10–11, note). An order from 1562 stipulates that bachelors of the Grocers Company should not 'wear any kinds of furs in their gowns, but only foynes', or marten, 'and budge', or sheepskin. The use of velvet in their gowns is carefully restricted, and they are prohibited 'any unreasonable ruffs in their shirts, but only black and white; their doublets to be of black satin, and they with coats or jackets of satin or damask, and of no other colour'. By contrast, the Wardens are 'to wear russet satin in their doublets'. At various events during the year London's Aldermen wore their violet or scarlet gowns, 'lined' or 'furred' depending on the season, often in combination with similarly coloured cloaks. The Lord Mayor's installation called for the 'scarlet gown, furred'. Aldermen who had 'passed the chair' or served as Lord Mayor were entitled to wear 'grey amis'—hoods of grey fur (probably badger)—while Alderman who had not yet been Mayor could wear 'calabre' or squirrel fur.

147 **apothecaries' guild** In identifying Bolles as an apothecary, not a grocer, Busino touches on a controversy then at its apogee. Apothecaries had long been part of the Grocers' company, which had jurisdiction over the sale of drugs. However, increasing complaints about the quality of pharmaceuticals and the competence of those administering them led King James to take a personal interest in the Apothecaries' 1614 petition for a separate charter. Despite vociferous protests by the Grocers, the charter was granted on December 6, 1617.

150–2 **pouch ... in the margin** Busino is describing a vestige of medieval guild livery. According to Stow, this garment is 'a memory of the hoods of old time ... made in colours according to ... [the companies'] gowns, which were of two colours, as red and blue or red and purple ... ; but now of late time they have used their gowns to be all of one colour, and those of the saddest, but their hoods being made the one half of the same cloth their gowns be of, the other half remaineth red as of old time.'

154 **wait at table** A group of bachelors acted as the Lord Mayor's serving gentlemen on feast days throughout the year.

157 **constable** The Grocers paid £4 to Roger Walrond, 'marshal of this city ... in respect of his service and attendance with his men on the day'. Walrond seems to have been in charge of more general matters of crowd control, while George Bell and his ten assistants (see *Industry* 241–2, note) were primarily concerned with ordering the pageant and Company members. In addition, whifflers, young freemen of the Company, helped to clear the way and keep back the crowds. The Grocers purchased '24 dozen of white staves' for £4. 17*s*. 8*d*. to be distributed among 'the whifflers, the marshals and their men', and the porters charged with carrying the pageant and attending the Company at Guildhall.

The arms of the East India Company.

agreed without hesitation, he was of the genuine porcine race of Bacchus. A number of robust youths and men also managed to clear the way with their fencing swords, which they brandished about with much dexterity; but as soon as one part of the street was freed of people, the crowd closed in on another. Some men masked as wild giants strode through the crowd with wheels and fireballs, hurling sparks here and there at the bodies and faces of the multitude, but to no avail in making a wide and clear route for the procession. The first stages which appeared were harnessed to hippogriffs, each one ridden by a child dressed in silk livery; others followed with lions, camels, and other equally large animals, laden with bales from which the children threw various confections to the crowd. These animals were yoked by silk cords and pulled the triumphal cars. The first car represented a very beautiful wood with fruit atop its trees, peopled by children dressed like Indians, with long hair on their heads and tinted faces, as if naked, with a little apron from which hung plumes, or more exactly red and variously coloured bird feathers. In addition, there were two pastoral figures with fifes, one dressed head to foot in red feathers and the other wrapped in a tiger skin, as if they were man and wife. They played very well in the Indian manner as the children danced with much grace and many varied gestures, using their entire bodies—hands, head, and feet—turning in good measure around the trees, changing from one position to the next in a way that amazed everybody. After that followed other large and handsome stages, one of which represented, as far as I could understand, the Indians' religion of the sun above a grouping of various other figures. Another stage

161–2 **robust youths . . . swords** Payment of £7 was made to 'John Bradshaw, fencer, for himself and 18 fellow flourishers with long swords for their service'. (See *Industry* 291–2, note, regarding the distinctive dress of fencers and marshals.)

166–7 **wild giants . . . fireballs** The use of 'giants' or 'greenmen' hurling firecrackers into the crowd was a time-honoured method of clearing a pathway for the oncoming procession. Part of Middleton's fee in 1617 included the hiring of 'greenmen, devils, and fire works'. The efforts of one of these individuals seems to have been particularly appreciated: the Grocers paid 11*s*. 'in benevolence to the fireman or greenman over and above his agreement'.

170–2 **hippogriffs . . . camels** Busino is describing the griffins and camels, featured in the Grocers' Company coat of arms, which were a regular part of company-sponsored pageants. 'Hippogriffs' were not, however, mere griffins. Memorable features of Ariosto's epic romance *Orlando Furioso*, hippogriffs had the body and legs of a horse. Busino's choice of words thus indicates something about his familiarity with Italian literature; it also suggests that the fantastic animals referred to here were almost always in fact cloth, lath and plaster constructions costuming more mundane beasts—usually horses—which were frequently used to pull pageant wagons through the streets. Alternatively, pageant devices sometimes included animal statuary carrying performers (see the 'King of the Moors' illustration for *Triumphs of Truth*, p. 972).

173 **various confections** The Grocers spent £5. 7*s*. 8*d*. for '50 sugar loaves, 36 pounds of nutmegs, 24 pounds of dates, and 114 pounds of ginger, which were thrown about the streets by those which sat on the griffins and camels'.

177 **dressed like Indians** While these Indians are definitely meant to represent inhabitants of the 'East Indies', their resemblance to North American Indians may reflect the confusion and lack of specificity associated with the term 'Indian' during this period. In the 1614 edition of *Purchas, His Pilgrimage*, Samuel Purchas explains that 'The name of India is now applied to all far distant countries, not in the extreme limits of Asia alone; but even to whole America, through the error of Columbus and his fellows; who at their first arrival in the western world, thought that they had met with Ophir and the Indian regions of the east.'

190 **Indians' religion of the sun** This is probably a misreading of the second device Middleton describes: India seated on the chariot with Industry at her side, holding a golden ball. The sun was believed to be the object of religious devotion by the 'Indians' of North America as well as those encountered in the East India trade. George Chapman and Inigo Jones's *The Memorable Masque*, staged at Court as part of the 1613 nuptial celebrations for Princess Elizabeth and the Elector Palatine, had featured 'the Phoebades', a group of sun-worshipping 'Virginians'.

carried a very beautiful castle; another was a fine ship, apparently returning from the Indies with cargo and crew aboard. Other stages carried the figures of Trade, and the nations which traffic with the Indies. Among these, a Spaniard was perfectly impersonated, the gestures of his nation expertly mimicked, with small black mustachios, hat and cape after the Spanish fashion, a ruff at the throat and little palm-length muffs on his hands. He was continually blowing kisses to the onlookers; but to the Spanish Ambassador, who was a short distance from us, he did it to such a superlative degree that the entire crowd roared with laughter. After this triumphant fleet the Archbishop of Canterbury appeared on horseback, which is to say the Pope of England. He was on the right, the country's principal baron was on his left, and before them marched forty gentlemen on foot wearing gold chains around their necks. There were mace-bearers, footmen, and other officers wearing coats of black velvet with the rose, the imprese of the kingdom, richly embroidered on the back in gold and silk. Then followed in pairs the earls, marquises and other lords and treasurers of the realm. After that came various banners, including one especially large one with its panels smoothed, carried by four or six men who supported the staff with other staves attached to it; others carried the long tail of this banner. It really was a splendid spectacle. All these banners bore the insignia of the Lord Mayor's company; all the other companies have different banners of their own. Following this came fifty old men in liveries of long peacock blue gowns with red caps and sleeves, each holding a javelin. At night these same men carry torches to the Lord Mayor's doorway. After these came a big man wearing a red hat, large as a basket, and holding a very beautiful gilded rapier. He was followed closely by two little children, immaculately dressed, each carrying a small staff topped with flowers. Finally we saw his Excellency the Lord Mayor, on a barded horse, in a red gown and chain of gold around his neck, over which was a large order like the Fleece, given in earlier times by a king to a Lord Mayor for having uncovered a conspiracy and killed the oppressor. This order is all of gold with a very large and precious jewel. Fifteen or twenty aldermen then followed on horseback all dressed in red gowns like the Lord Mayor's; those with gold chains around their necks had previously held that

192 **fine ship** The 'Ship', featured prominently in the pageant's accounts, is not specifically mentioned in Middleton's text. A ship appears in a great number of Lord Mayor's shows, and it has been suggested that such standard or subsidiary features (along with lions and camels) were originally referred to as 'devices' while the term 'pageant' was reserved for especially elaborate inventions or those specific to a particular show or occasion. Since Middleton has not given the ship's occupants any speeches in *Industry*, he does not feel compelled to describe it. This explanation would seem to be supported by the reference to tradition in the Grocers' accounts regarding the musicians aboard the ship: they 'were present in the show according to the accustomed manner'. These musicians included thirty-two of his Majesty's Trumpeters and 'a boy to sound in the ship'; the group received a lump sum of £26, while the Sergeant Trumpeter got a separate fee of 11*s*. Another child, 'a little boy which played on the drum in the ship', received 12*s*.; he too was contracted for as part of a professional adult group, who would appear to be the same ones described in lines 61–3 of Busino's account. These '8 drums and 4 fifes', supplying their own costumes of 'black hats, white doublets, black hose and white stockings and with scarves according to the colour' of the Grocer's Company, collectively received £12. 11*s*.

200–1 **the Spanish Ambassador** Don Diego Sarmiento de Acuña, known as Count Gondomar, the inspiration for the Black Knight in *A Game at Chess*.

213 **various banners** Under the heading 'mercery wares for banners and other things' the Grocers' accounts record payment of £6. 12*s*. for '7 yards of crimson damask', £8 for '20 ells of taffeta sarsenet, at 8*s*. per ell', and £10. 16*s*. 11*d*. for '59 dozen of crimson and white ribbon of all sorts' (see also *Industry* 291–2, note).

214–16 **four or six men...others** Sixteen 'poor men', recipients of the Company's alms, were paid 5*s*. each 'for their service in carrying of the streamers, banners, and other things, in respect they had no coats'. Ten others 'of the said banner and streamer bearers which had coats' got 1*s*. each 'for their dinners'.

215 **other staves** 'Two new banner staves' were purchased for 8*s*.

220 **peacock blue gowns** The livery worn by these 'fifty old men'—also almsmen—was apparently the same as that worn by the banner and streamer bearers. The Grocers paid £159. 4*s*. 6*d*. 'to divers clothworkers' for '18 azure coloured cloths for the poor men's gowns', and this fabric was used to make '124 gowns, after 12*d*. a piece'—a total of £6. 4*s*. paid 'to divers tailors'.

220–1 **red caps and sleeves** Thomas Hinkman, 'capper', received £18. 3*d*. for '10 dozen of round caps, and 5 dozen and 3 long caps'. Roger Clarke, a mercer, received £10 for '10 pieces of crimson mochado to make sleeves for the poor men, and to face the beadles', streamer- and banner-bearers' coats'. The mochado, a kind of silk, was then turned over to 'divers tailors' to make '124 pair of sleeves, at 2*d*. a piece' (a total of £1. 8*d*.).

221 **javelin** The Grocers paid £1. 13*s*. 4*d*. for 'the hire of 124 javelins'.

223–4 **big man...rapier** The Mayor's Swordbearer and head of his official household.

228 **barded** armoured

chain of gold Presumably the 'rich collar of gold, to be worn by the Mayor', given to the City of London by Sir John Allen, a Mercer and Lord Mayor in 1525 and 1535.

229 **the Fleece** A reference to the ornament worn by the knights of the Golden Fleece, an order of knighthood associated with the Catholic faith, instituted at Bruge in 1430 by Philip the Good, duke of Burgundy.

230–1 **a Lord Mayor...oppressor** Busino here is referring to that paragon of civic heroism, Sir William Walworth, a Lord Mayor and fishmonger whose slaying of Wat Tyler in 1381 saved the kingdom for Richard II. Munday's 1616 pageant, *Chrysanaleia: The Golden Fishing*, features the awakening of Walworth from his tomb to address his distant successor as Lord Mayor.

office. Last in line on horseback were the two sheriffs, dressed in slightly different red gowns, with small gold chains around their necks. These two have been chosen to administer justice in London for the present year as officials of this Lord Mayor. All of this fine company were to enjoy the bounty, and they were followed by an endless troop of scavengers, sticking like a tail to the procession, all of whom also expect to participate in the very sumptuous feast that begins today and continues with open doors for an entire year. Let this serve as a close for the illustrious gentlemen so as not to be as protracted as the long itinerary already described; making them most humble reverence and thanks.

236 **two sheriffs** The Lord Mayor's appointee was Robert Johnson, a grocer; the Sheriff elected by the Common Council (often referred to as election 'by common consent') was William Halliday, a mercer. Halliday had refused the shrievalty in 1614, the same year he became a Committee member of the East India Company. He was a governor of that Company from 1621–24 (see note to 28–9 above for refusals of civic office, and *Industry* 241–2, note, regarding the selection of sheriffs).

245 **open doors…entire year** The munificent hospitality of London's Lord Mayor impressed a number of foreigners. Paul Hentzner of Brandenburg, travelling through England in 1598, noted that during 'the year of his magistracy' the Lord Mayor 'is obliged to live so magnificently that foreigner or native, without any expense, is free, if he can find a chair empty, to dine at his table, where there is always the greatest plenty.' In fact, the City's generosity to foreign notables was often under orders from the Crown. In addition to feasting important visitors, the Lord Mayor was periodically directed to obtain, and occasionally pay for, housing for foreign diplomats. The difficulties of such a task can be inferred from the Privy Council's letter of January 9, 1617, requiring the Lord Mayor to 'take present order for some fair and convenient house…within the city' for the French ambassador, 'and to cause the same to be furnished with hangings, bedding, and all other furniture necessary for such a purpose. And if perhaps you cannot find room sufficient in any one house for the lodging of all his company, which we conjecture may require some eighteen or twenty beds…, you shall in that case do well to take up so many lodgings in some good houses near adjoining to the place where the ambassador shall be, as shall serve the turn.'

246 **illustrious gentlemen** The brothers of Busino's patron; see note to Title above.

THE OWL'S ALMANAC

Edited by Neil Rhodes

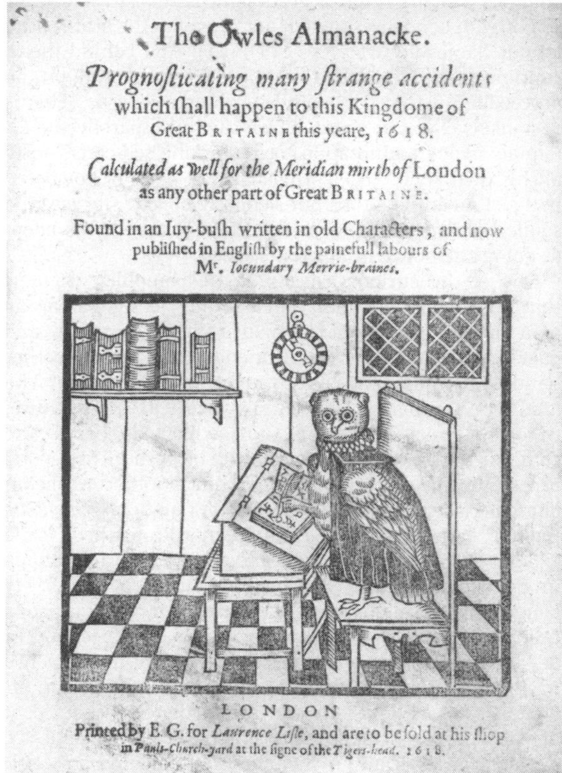

The Owles Almanacke.

Prognoſticating many ſtrange accidents which ſhall happen to this Kingdome of Great BRITAINE this yeare, 1618.

Calculated as well for the Meridian mirth of London as any other part of Great BRITAINE.

Found in an Iuy-buſh written in old Characters, and now publiſhed in Engliſh by the painefull labours of Mr. *Iocundary Merrie-braines.*

LONDON

Printed by E. G. for *Laurence Liſle*, and are to be ſold at his ſhop in *Pauls-Church-yard* at the ſigne of the *Tigers-head.* 1618.

THE almanac, with its prognostication of forthcoming events, has an ancient pedigree. Edmund in *The Tragedy of King Lear* is sarcastic about his father's belief in dire astrological predictions, and the Fool, who offers his own burlesque of such fateful documents, tells us that he is living before the time of Merlin. If we are willing to accept the Fool's chronology then these must be the earliest prognostication and mock-prognostication recorded in Britain. At the other end of the spectrum, if you want to be ahead of next year's events you can buy a copy of *Old Moore's Almanack* in the UK or *The Farmer's Almanac* in the US from your local newsagent or railway bookstall. So while almanacs are among the most topical, socially specific, and ephemeral of all publications, the almanac itself seems timeless.

The Owl's Almanac (1618) is the most elaborate and also the cleverest parody of the early printed almanac. These publications were enormously popular in the late sixteenth and early seventeenth centuries, as we can see from the fact that the Stationers' Company closely guarded the patent privilege for almanacs (as for bibles) because there was so much and such predictable demand, and the Owl stitches together a ludicrous sampler of their most familiar features: the law terms, the 'computation of time' (a sort of countdown of major events from Adam and Eve to the present which survives in the modern *Timetables of History*), tide predictions, the anatomy or astrological man, rules for health and profit, lists of the major fairs and highways, and finally, that indispensable calendar of 'good' and 'bad' days in the forthcoming year. The principal sources for the Owl's mockery are almanacs by Edward Pond (1609) and Thomas Bretnor (1617), two of the most prolific prognosticators in the Jacobean period and solemn exponents of the astrologer's art. Pond, for example, gives a laborious account of how to tell time by the moon, which is parodied in the Owl's opaque do-it-yourself instructions for assembling a moon-clock, while Bretnor's computation of time is redesigned by the Owl to include such notable events as the appearance of a dancing horse on the top of St Paul's. (A version of the moon-clock, incidentally, reappeared in 1757 as 'a striking sun-dial' in Benjamin Franklin's comic almanac, *Poor Richard.*) But perhaps the most distinctive feature of the Owl's parody is that it extends to the style as well as the substance of the serious almanac. In Sir Thomas Overbury's character of an almanac-maker we are told that 'The verses in his book have a worse pace than ever had Rochester hackney: for his prose, 'tis dappled with inkhorn terms ...' (*A Wife*, 1614), and these ponderous neologisms are reproduced—or rather reactivated—in the bizarre verbal inventiveness of *The Owl's Almanac*. Another feature which the Owl pounces upon is Bretnor's liking for laconic catchphrases, presumably intended to suggest sibylline gravity but which have more the flavour of Christmas-cracker mottoes. Some of the elaborate marginalia, which are such a striking feature of Middleton's text, parody these, but others reflect the practice of almanac owners jotting down their own observations on the blank pages opposite the calendars; hence the fatuous marginal glosses from the Owl such as 'Terrible doings' (644.n) or 'No such women now' (612.n). The parody in *The Owl's Almanac* is certainly comprehensive when even the readers of almanacs are not spared.

The Owl's other main source is Dekker's *The Raven's Almanac* (1609), a mock-prognostication which the Owl directly addresses in a prefatory epistle to the Raven. Dekker himself was originally identified as the Owl, but this cannot be the case: he is hardly likely to have written a letter to himself and, besides, there are many stylistic aspects of the work which are beyond his range. Modern bibliographies acknowledge that *The Owl's Almanac* is not by Dekker. The author was, however, certainly part of Dekker's circle, and new research has made a strong case for Middleton's authorship: we now know that Middleton wrote *Plato's Cap* (1604), another mock-almanac which he put out in the same year as the brilliant Nasheian pastiche, *The Black Book*, and almanac parody crops up frequently in his dramatic work. In *A Yorkshire Tragedy*, Sam is 'the true picture of a common servingman' because he has an almanac in his pocket (1.28–9); in *The Puritan Widow* Pieboard's almanac is given a sarcastic going-over (3.5.239 ff.); in *The Roaring Girl* Laxton refers to an almanac 'calculated for the meridian of cooks' wives' (3.47–8); in *Anything for a Quiet Life* the barber-surgeon Sweetball is guided by his almanac (3.2.158–62); and in *No Wit/Help like a Woman's* Weatherwise allows his entire life to be governed by his almanac's directions. Chough's foolishness is confirmed by his reliance on Bretnor in *A Fair Quarrel* (5.1.131), and, most significantly, within months of the publication of *The Owl's Almanac* Middleton staged an almanac parody in *Masque of Heroes*, presided over by a Doctor Almanac and with characters representing Good Days and Bad Days appearing in the antemasque.

But perhaps the strongest pointer to Middleton's authorship of *The Owl's Almanac* is its stylistic virtuosity, which derives from Nashe's extraordinary experiments in comic prose technique during the 1590s. (In fact, Nashe refers to '*The Owl's Almanac* which Pasquil hath undertaken to write' in two of his anti-Marprelate tracts, but no connection has been established between that and the present work.) A number of writers attempted to emulate Nashe's prose style, but Middleton was the only one to do so with real success (see Rhodes 1980). There is a eulogy to Nashe in *The Ant and the Nightingale* (1604), and in *The Black Book* Middleton writes a sequel to *Pierce Penniless* which manages to reproduce many of the hallmarks of Nashe's style: an intrusive authorial persona, electric rhetorical shifts, comic-grotesque physicality and, above all, a sense of pace, dexterity, and metaphoric flair. These are also the characteristics which make *The Owl's Almanac* as lively as any comic prose pamphlet of the Jacobean period. Most texts of this kind are consciously *written* documents and betray signs of a certain stylistic rigor mortis. By contrast, what preserves the Owl's vitality is his ability, like Nashe's, to mimic the rhetorical strategies of the stand-up comic in an oral rather than a written mode of discourse. This is why, when introducing Aquarius in the zodiacal line-up, the Owl explains that he will tell us his story 'admirably, though he be illiterate and unlearned' (1057–8), and this is why at various points the text seems to be theatrically conceived. There is audience presence: 'Nay, but there be more tormentors of my kind coming. Draw the curtains of your eyes and see' (1082–4), and there is digressive patter: 'In good faith, 'tis strange, my masters, to my sense: a couple of fishes (I'll tell you their names as they fall better into my knowledge) come leaping over the fallows like pepper in a mortar...' (1086–9). There is a variety of characters: witness the appearance of the mincing, petulant twins after the 'ram-headed oration' of Aries and the 'bull-headed oration' of Taurus, or the sudden intrusion of the fine lady in the prognostication for chandlers: 'Fah! What a gross light is this! In truth, Sir Timothy, it condenses the wit and stupefies the brain; pray let our flames be wax...' (2119–21). And behind them, running the show, is the Owl himself, commenting on the proceedings with such pointless observations as 'This is very likely' (824.n; these, as we saw, also parody the almanac owner's annotation) or remarking self-consciously on his own style: 'The spring is like a piece of powdered beef...I mean when 'tis but slenderly boiled...or else the simile holds not' (1309–15). Certainly, the Owl is adept at doing the police in different voices.

One of the curious aspects of the pamphlet, then, is that it is on the one hand an elaborately designed parody of a printed document, in which the typography and page layout have a comic function, and on the other hand something that is very much a performance. The first aspect provides Middleton's text with a structure, a set of limits and forms, into which he pours and contains the free-floating verbal play of Nashe. The second aspect, however, serves to underline another Nasheian characteristic, which is the rapid fluctuation in stylistic register. We are told, for instance, that Prometheus loved 'a pretty damosel that dwelt under the immortal canopy in this cold horizon, which made his virgin in frosty congealing mornings look like Vespasian, as if she had been wringing at a hard stool' (540–5). The sudden, deflating switch from the lyrical opening of the sentence to the picture of a Roman emperor straining on his chamber-pot is hilarious, and immediately reminiscent of Nashe (face-wrinkling metaphors also happen to be a Nasheian speciality). Switches of this kind are not, however, confined to a lowering of tone. In a remarkable passage on the origin of the human heart, the Owl describes how it was pumped into action by fear: 'the poor heart with very thought of the terrifying beast drives itself with a continual systole and diastole, like the clack of a mill or a sun-sucked leaf chained to a spider's twine. Yet I have not read that before that time it ever stirred' (875–9). This is imaginative writing of real quality. The physiological terms, which it is surprising to find being used as early as 1618, are suddenly translated into metaphors which capture brilliantly the clatter of the palpitations, driven as if under the pressure of escape, and at the same time the delicacy and fragility of the vital organ, the parched and chained leaf imaging the prison of mortality. This is not only imaginatively crafted, but sensitive.

Throughout *The Owl's Almanac* there is experimentation in the Nasheian mode, and it is the metaphorical scatter which gives the text its distinctive verbal texture.

This may take the form of compound coinages such as 'ghost-groping' (948) for Pluto, god of the underworld, or 'cranny-lighted' (1738) for the dimly lit corners of the haberdasher's workshop; and this kind of formulation can also serve for metonymic epithets in such inventions as 'marrow-melting luminists' (chandlers, or candlemakers) and 'pale-bodied blazers' (candles) (2135–6). There is a fair number of more pedantic coinages, the 'inkhornisms' which, according to Overbury, 'dappled' the pages of the serious almanac ('dimidiate', 460; 'saxifies', 1079; 'inaulated', 1672; 'labecutable', 1748). There are grotesque but ingenious similes, as in the picture of Cancer, 'like a waterman in a boat, his arse toward the place to which he was going; he looked like a piece of Hebrew spelled the wrong way' (787–90), and there is in general a suppleness in the language of the text which makes it responsive to the physical characteristics of its subjects: Capricorn, for example, is described as 'falling flat and flexible on his knees' (1012), a picture which captures precisely the goat's emblematic posture.

Concentrating upon the Owl's stylistic inventiveness helps us to establish the probable authorship of the pamphlet, and it also suggests why it is so successful as a parody. But does this text have any context or content? Is it simply a clever display of word-spinning? The 'contents' are indeed labelled as such at the start, and these are necessarily determined to a large extent by the contents of actual almanacs. There are, however, two original sequences in *The Owl's Almanac* which together account for well over half of the complete text: the story of Prometheus and the signs of the zodiac, and the set of prognostications for the London livery companies, the 'fundamental trades'. The Prometheus story is a fantastic concoction based upon the picture of astrological man which prefaced many almanacs. This shows a naked human body surrounded by the signs of the zodiac, with pointers from each sign to the part of the body which it governs. There are famous examples of the picture from the medieval period and later, but by the early seventeenth century the astrological man had become something of a figure of fun, as Dekker indicates at the start of *The Raven's Almanac*: 'At the beginning of every almanac it is the fashion to have the body of a man drawn as you see, and not only baited, but bitten and shot at by wild beasts and monsters . . . he stands as if he had been some notorious malefactor, and being stripped stark naked to go to execution'. He then compares the figure to an 'anatomy', i.e. a gallows corpse carved up by the barber-surgeons in the interests of medical science. Dekker's grim joke provides the Owl with a starting point for an elaborate aetiological fantasy or explanation of causes: what is the origin of the zodiac, and where do the parts of the body come from? (Spoof aetiologies, incidentally, are another Nasheian feature.) The Owl contends that it all begins with Prometheus's theft of fire from the gods. So far from this being a welcome piece of new technology for terrestrial life, it turns out to be a calamity for many creatures. Fire provides the means by which Aries the ram is sheared of his fleece, Virgo polluted by the tobacco smoke of young gallants, and Capricorn the goat stigmatized as lecherous (as a result of Prometheus's kindling of sexual heat); even Aquarius bears a grudge against him on the grounds that the widespread use of fire has depleted his resources of water. So Prometheus is chained to a stake in the Caucasus and, spurred on by a punitive Jupiter, the creatures proceed in turn to bite, head-butt, sting, shoot, and generally torment their wretched victim. Various parts of the body originate from these attacks (the navel, for instance, is created by Virgo's hurling a red-hot spit at Prometheus's belly), and when the ceremony is complete Jupiter places his instruments of revenge in the sky as the zodiac.

This focus on the human body and its various members and organs supplies the Owl with a fund of the kind of comic-grotesque metaphor that we associate with Nashe, but the way in which Prometheus is presented as a victim is much more typical of Middleton. As we have seen, one of the most remarkable passages in the text is the depiction of the terror-stricken heart, and underlying the comedy of the zodiac sequence is a view from the scaffold. Prometheus 'stands shivering and shaking like a condemned caitiff that attends the fatal stroke' (651–3); he is turned into the subhuman 'like an Indian (in New Spain), stood there exposed as a fair mark for any man's fury' (660–1); and human/animal roles are reversed when he is baited at the stake by Taurus the bull. Jupiter, the author of these torments, is ambiguously presented. At one point he refers, Prospero-like, to 'the nurture of my sceptre' (866) which can limit 'boundless savageness', but in the Taurus section we are told how glad he is to see justice 'so nobly and stoutly executed on a villain' (719–20). That sounds very much like Middletonian irony. And, interestingly, in the later section on the disposition of the planets for the year, Jupiter reappears as a pseudonym for King James in a political moral about Europe, and then stands metonymically to represent kings in general. There is perhaps a hint of a Shelleyan rebel Prometheus in *The Owl's Almanac*.

The immediate context, however, for the Owl's handling of the Prometheus story is the Ovidian theme of the end of the Golden Age and loss of innocence. The arrival of fire on earth is a tragedy, but here principally for Prometheus himself as he stands exposed to the excoriating justice of Jupiter, and the theatricality of the text is reinforced by the fact that the entire sequence is designed in terms of the scaffold as sadistic spectacle. The scene of punishment has an audience, 'troupes and multitudes of all kinds . . . spreading themselves either as actors or spectators in this rueful tragedy' (1122–6). Following this sequence the Owl moves on to 'a lecture upon the four quarters, with what particular diseases hang upon every quarter' (1355–6), and then to floods and famines. The metaphor of the anatomy, or executed traitor, is extended to 'the body of the year', and so the Owl rather neatly links his tale of Prometheus to the almanac calendar itself. At this point the text changes direction—'The string of sorrow is now tuned to a merry note. Diseases, drownings, dearths and other dreary tragedies, get you from the stage' (1455–7)—and we move into the comic set of predictions for the London livery companies. Here, the timeless aspects of the almanac represented in the Owl's reworking of Ovidian myth are replaced by the topical and socially specific: this is London, this is 1618.

What also happens in the last major section of the text is that we see a return of the Golden Age. After the miseries attributed to and inflicted upon Prometheus, the London tradesmen are promised a year of milk and honey, a bonanza. Labourers will buy velvet neck-pieces from the mercers, and servants will break their masters' plate to the benefit of goldsmiths; doctors will prescribe wine from the vintners, an epidemic of rust will provide work for armourers and property developers will boost the profits of carpenters. Throughout this section there is a sense of an economy going into overdrive, as raw materials are turned into a cornucopia of saleable commodities in the way that Lorna Hutson has described in *Thomas Nashe in Context*. Moreover, the hectic economic activity feeds into the comic prose style, with the tradesmen conceived in terms of their own materials and products, and the products acquiring human characteristics in a riot of anthropomorphism. Pewter is a soft-natured gentleman; money will choke the throats of misers' purses; leaning buildings bow to the Lord Mayor; and tottering houses have their ribs painted. This section of *The Owl's Almanac* shows us an urban society at work, and in doing so emphasizes the materiality of the almanac and its parodic offspring. The almanac is concerned with time and tide, the phases of the moon and the rotation of the seasons, but it is also concerned with the body and with the fabric of economic and social life. What *The Owl's Almanac* ultimately gives us, in the range and vivacity of its parody, is a rich, comic panorama of Jacobean life, and in particular of the life of Middleton's London.

SEE ALSO

Textual introduction and apparatus: *Companion*, 641
Authorship and date: *Companion*, 400

The Owl's Almanac

Prognosticating many strange accidents
which shall happen to this kingdom of
Great Britain this year 1618. Calculated as
well for the meridian mirth of London
as any other part of Great Britain. Found in
an ivy bush written in old characters and
now published in English by the painful
labours of Mr Jocundary Merry-brains.

To the right worshipful and generous-minded gentleman, Sir Timothy Thornhill, Knight

Sir,

Is it not strange that an owl should write an almanac? Yet why not, as well as a crow to speak Latin to Caesar? And why not an owl prognosticate wonders which are sure to happen this year, as for astrological wizards to shoot threating calendars out of their ink-pots at the world, and yet when they hit, their fillips hurt nothing? Lies are as well acquainted with astronomers as oaths are with soldiers, or as owing money is familiar to courtiers, but Madge Owlet fetches her predictions out of an upper room in heaven where never any common star-catcher was garreted before. Had I a bird of paradise I should gladly send her flying to you, and therefore I hope that your acceptance of this owl (though she be none of mine, but hiding her broad face under my eaves by chance) will keep petty, idle birds from wondering about her. I wish every year you are to live to begin and end with you as merrily as this prognostication takes her aim to make you, and that I may cease to be when I give over from being

Devoted ever at your worship's disposing,

L. L.

The Contents of this Work

1. An epistle of the Owl to a certain Raven, an almanac-maker
2. The beginnings and endings of the four terms in the year
3. Annual computations of time
4. The beginning and ending of the year
5. English tides
6. Computation diurnal and astrological
7. A moon-clock
8. The anatomy of man's body governed by the twelve signs

Title several features of the illustrated title-page parody the title-page of the 1616 edition of *Doctor Faustus*, notably the sphere of destiny on the wall

6 **ivy bush** 'To look like an owl in an ivy-bush' is a proverbial expression.

21 **Madge Owlet** nickname for the barn-owl

23 **garreted** lodged in an attic

34 **L. L.** Laurence Lyle, the publisher

36 **Raven** Thomas Dekker, author of *The Raven's Almanac* 1609 (see Introduction)

9. The signs of the zodiac
10. How the signs came to be hung up in the zodiac
11. A general calendar for the common motion of the moon in all the months of the year
12. The disposition of the planets for this year
13. Rules for health and profit
14. The four quarters of the year with the diseases incident to each of them
15. General diseases to reign this year
16 Inundations and most strange overflowings of waters
17. Of a dearth
18. A brief and merry prognostication presaging good fortunes to a set of fundamental trades:

Viz.

1. Mercers
2. Grocers
3. Drapers
4. Fishmongers
5. Goldsmiths
6. Skinners
7. Tailors
8. Haberdashers
9. Salters
10. Ironmongers
11. Vintners
12. Clothworkers
13. Dyers
14. Brewers
15. Leathersellers
16. Pewterers
17. Barber-Surgeons
18. Armourers
19. Bakers
20. Chandlers
21. Girdlers
22. Cutlers
23. Saddlers
24. Butchers
25. Carpenters
26. Shoemakers
27. Painters

19. Fairs in England
20. The highways
21. Good and bad days

The Owl's epistle to the Raven

Brother Raven, I did ever envy the happiness of other birds when I saw them freely enjoying woods, fields, parks, forests, cities, kingdoms, and all that the moving canopy of heaven can cover, as their proper cages to sing in all the day, drawing thereby audience to their bewitching music-lectures, when poor I (having more knowledge, except in song, than the proudest of them) durst never or seldom gad abroad in the light. But when I heard and beheld yourself a student in the mathematics, and by jumbling together a hotch-potch of calculations to be counted an astronomer and to paste up your name on every post in the title of a book called *The Raven's Almanac*, I did then more vex than ever before.

I confess you are a bird of larger wing than I am, goodlier is your proportion, piercing are your eyes, your colour so amiable that women take a pride to have hair black as a raven's; dreadful is your voice, bloody your beak, and your talons full of terror. But let your bosom be open, and then (as in some great statesmen who carry an outward-glorious show) nothing is to be found but ugliness, treachery and rapacity. But if it shall be no dishonour for me to stand on the tiptoes of mine own commendations, I would then against your ominous croaking thus far prefer my wakeful hooting that I have ever been held a predooming bird, but (besides that) an emblem of wisdom, and so sacred among the Athenians that they carried the reverence of my picture stamped upon their money.

Now (Brother Raven) as in this point I spitefully make comparisons with you, as proving myself not one to whom you may cry 'Hail fellow well met', so will I in these my Ptolemaical predictions discover to the world such wonders from the planetary regions that not only thou, but all other birds (daring to pry into the privy chamber of heaven) shall pluck in their heads (as I do until twilight) with shame, and never offer more to pester Paul's Churchyard with their trivial prognostications. I have been this year in progress with the moon, riding on the dog which the man in the moon leads, whose bush of thorns he lent me instead of a fan to keep off the wind, whilst he himself ran along by me as my footman. Much skill learned I of the moon, for she is a great light to almanac-makers, albeit in show she seem but a cold friend to them, and much mad talk had I with that lunatical fellow (the squire of her body). The twelve houses of the sun lay higher up into the country, so that, by reason my sight hath ever been bad, I had no great stomach to mount up thither, because I know the sun (who could never endure me) would have spied both a mote

61 **fundamental trades** i.e. the city livery companies
82 **Chandlers** candlemakers
121 **predooming** pronouncing the sentence beforehand (coinage)
129 **Ptolemaical** Ptolemy was the ancient astronomer whose theory that the sun and planets revolved around a stationary earth held until the seventeenth century.
135 **Paul's Churchyard** centre of the London book trade
136 **in progress** (alludes to a state journey by the monarch)
144 **squire of her body** personal attendant; pimp
149–50 **mote . . . beam** a splinter and a log, a small and a large fault; see Matthew 7:3

in mine eye and a beam too. Here I caught stars faster than a cat will kill flies, of which store I shot some down to help those that write almanacs for London. Some of the twelve signs (which like cast garments, being worn to pieces, were thrown by into an odd corner) I clapped close under my wings, and now they are to be seen hanging in the middle of Cheapside, for there's the Ram, the Bull, the Crab, Capricorn, etc. Only the young wench (called Virgo) would by no means sit in any shop in that street, because so many gallants lie over the stalls courting every handsome woman there, that the maid was afraid to have lost her head in the company. Thus with weary wing travelled I, but being now come back from the court of the moon (who is not much unlike me, having a great broad platter face as mine is), listen to the wonders which I bring with me. So hooting and whooping a silence to your Ravenship, I prognosticate myself, yours for a strange almanac for a whole year,

The Owl

The beginnings and endings of the four terms in the year

Hilary Term

Hilary term is the merriest term of all four. It begins in hope to the lawyer to have good doings, and ends in despair to the client that he shall not be dispatched this term.

It hath four returns.

1 The first return, the lawyer comes up with an empty cap-case.

2 The second return, the client comes up with a full cap-case.

3 The third return, all the client's money is in the lawyer's cap-case.

4 The fourth return, nothing but lawyers' papers stuff client's cap-case.

Easter term

Easter term comes in all in green, with the spring (like a puny clerk) waiting upon him, and would be as merry as Hilary but that puritans pluck down profane and high-perching maypoles.

It begins with *pax vobis* and ends with *pox vobis*.

It hath five returns.

1 The first return, the client hopes well.

2 The second return, the attorney heartens him well.

3 The third return, the client lays it on well.

The fourth return, he prays and pays well. 4

The fifth return, the attorney laughs well. 5

Trinity term

Trinity term is a very hot fellow, yet in regard he is but short lived (for he is born the ninth of June and departs the twenty-eighth of July) he doth no great good to the lawyer, nor great hurt to the client.

It begins in one of the King's courts at Westminster Hall and ends in one of the prisons about London.

It hath four returns.

And those returns are like the four quarters of a decreasing or waning moon.

The first return, the rich plaintiff with corpulent, bacon-fed guts rides puffing up to London with a purse warmly lined, and that's the full moon—during which fullness he far outshines the defendant and gives great light to the lawyers, though in the end they light him when his own torch burns no longer. 1

The second return, the lamentably-complaining defendant comes up too, being more in the wane than the other (nay, perhaps altogether out both of the wain, horses and oxen) and yet his purse not three quarters full neither. 2

The third return, what with counsellors, attorneys, clerks and other ministers of justice, the plaintiff's purse is scarce half full, which he empties every day (as he melts his grease) with trudging from court to court only to undo his poor adversary. 3

The fourth return, there is a judgement gotten against the defendant, and now his heart and cause being both overthrown together, his spirits are so darkened with black clouds of sorrow that he seems utterly eclipsed until the first quarter of a new moon, which will not show her horns until next term. 4

Michaelmas term

Michaelmas term comes in with his nose dropping and a pipe of lighted tobacco puffing out of his mouth to dry up the rheum, for he's but a snivelling companion. You shall seldom see him but daubed up to the hams with dirt and rain, and commonly, to make amends for that, a pint of mulled sack is his morning's draught. It begins with a shivering to five hundred that are termers, but ends in a burning fever, for Westminster and

157 **Cheapside** main commercial street in the City of London
157–8 **Ram...Capricorn** shop and inn signs
160–1 **lie over the stalls** have lodgings over the shops
162 **head** (pun on maidenhead)
173 ***terms*** Bretnor's dates for the law terms in his almanac for 1617 seem impossibly short and the Owl gives different dates for Trinity (see ll. 200–1); broadly speaking, Hilary is January–February; Easter, April–May; Trinity, June–July; Michaelmas, October–December
178 ***returns*** the days on which the sheriff reports back to the courts on the results of writs issued by them
180 **cap-case** brief-case
191 ***pax vobis*** peace unto you (Latin)
204–5 **Westminster Hall** the old hall of the Palace of Westminster where the law courts were held
215 **light him** relieve him of his money
220 **wain** cart
242 **termers** those who go to London in term for business at a court of law

London are too hot for four hundred of those five hundred to tarry by it.

It hath eight returns.

1 The first return, an Essex yeoman hath a goose goes gaggling into his neighbour's barn.

2 The second return, he that owns that barn wrings off the neck of this goose.

3 The third return, the goose's master ambles up to the term to a man of law, drawing out his purse as he drivels out his speech and scrapes with his hobnails for counsel how to sue in the goose's name.

4 The fourth return, he that assaulted and battered the goose gallops up too and thrashes out his silver about that goose too.

5 The fifth return, the matter comes to trial.

So that:
- The goose is plucked — there's the jury.
- The goose is roasted with delicate sauce — there's the verdict.
- The lawyer eats the goose — there's a judgement entered—
- and gives the feathers to stick the other two coxcombs — execution upon that judgement.

6 The sixth return, the lawyer persuades his client it was no goose, but a gander. To it again they go.

7 The seventh return, the two Essex calves have sucked each other dry and have neither goose nor gander.

8 The eighth return, they go home like a couple of tame geese when their feathers are plucked, and are passing good friends.

Star Chamber days

There are Star Chamber days in all these four terms, for the council of heaven (with the King in all his glory) sits to censure the riots of the mighty on earth oppressing the poor, the fatherless and widow, and by the royal authority of that most honourable court to guard innocence and weakness from the malice and tyranny of bloody-minded creditors, whose pleas are never heard before so high an assembly of judges.

A memorial of the time sithence some strange and remarkable accidents until this year 1617

First lie

Since the first lie was told is (as I remember) 5565 years: and that was by all computation in Adam's time, but now in these days men and women lie downright. } 5565

2

Since the burning of Paul's steeple many fiery faces have heated the city, but especially some catchpoles' red noses have set five hundred a-sweating coming by the Counter gate. But since the burning at Winchester (at which time no small number of geese were both plucked and powdered) many heads ache to this day to remember it, albeit it be now about twelve or thirteen years past. } 12

Winchester Geese

3 First snuffing tobacco

Since the first making of noses chimneys, with smoking men's faces as if they were bacon and baking dried neats' tongues in their mouths. } 32

4 Printing of presses

Some almanacs talk that printing hath been in England not above 156 years, but I find in an old worm-eaten cabalistical author that sheets have been printed in this kingdom above a 1000 years before that time. } 100

5 Tailors' stitches

Tailors have been troubled with stitches ever since yards came up to measure women's petticoats, and that is at least ago years: } 5000

6 Lemons

Oranges came from Seville into England above a 100 years past, but we had great store of lemons long before. } 100

7 Hot waters

Since hot waters caused bad livers in London and her suburbs is not much above 15 or 16 years, but they never burnt out the bottom of men's purses so much until Ralph Savage gave them phlegethontical brewings and horrible necromantical names. } 16

275 **Essex calves** fools; also a nickname for Essex men
281 **Star Chamber** in Westminster Hall; a notoriously tyrannical court dealing with crown interests, abolished 1640
290 ***sithence*** since
293–365 **5565 years . . . morning** following Bretnor's almanacs (see Introduction)
297 **Paul's steeple** destroyed by lightning on 4 June 1561
299 **catchpoles** officers who arrest for debt, bailiffs
301 **Counter** there were two debtors' prisons of this name, one in Poultry and the other in Wood Street, Cheapside
302–7 **Winchester . . . years past** referring to the movement of the London law sessions to Winchester during the plague of 1603–4; Londoners who fled to Winchester were 'burned' by high prices for lodging and food. For a full account, see *News from Gravesend.*
303.n ***Winchester Geese*** Winchester goose was a slang term for sexually transmitted disease.
304 **powdered** salted or pickled
310–11 **neats' tongues** ox tongues
315 **cabalistical** dealing with the esoteric or mystic
319 **yards** (pun on penis)
330 **phlegethontical** Phlegethon was a fiery river in the underworld

8 *Dancing and pumps* Dancing was in England long before the Conquest, but pumps have been used in London within 60 years or thereabouts. } 60

9 *Bottle-ale and roaring boys* Since bottle-ale came puffing into England, and thereby troubled the country with terrible winds, all the put-gallies serving brew-houses near the Thames are weeping witnesses, but whether puffing and roaring boys were before that time, look into the calendar of Newgate and there 'tis recorded.

Since the horrible dance to Norwich.—14

Since the arrival of Monsieur Nobody.—11

Since that old and loyal soldier George Stone of the Bear-garden died. } 8

Since the dancing horse stood on the top of Paul's whilst a number of asses stood braying below. } 17

Rich men's earthquakes The general earthquake in rich men's consciences hath no certain time when it shall be, but the earthquake and cold shivering in poor men's bodies is now every day, and charity cold herself she knows not how to comfort them.

Since the German fencer cudgelled most of our English fencers, now about a month past.

Yellow bands Since yellow bands and saffroned chaperons came up is not above two years past, but since citizens' wives fitted their husbands with yellow *Yellow hose* hose is not within the memory of man.

Since close coaches were made running bawdy-houses, yesterday.

Since swearing and forswearing cried 'What do you lack' in London, no longer ago than this very morning.

The beginning and ending of the year as also of the world

Year begins The year begins with me when I have money in my purse, which with a good suit on my back, a fair gelding under me, and a gilt rapier by my side makes it complete.

The year begins with some gallants when they cry ''Swounds, drawers, ye rogues', and is near expiration when they ask in a low voice, 'What's to pay?'

The year ends with me when my silver is melted and my elbows are ragged. *Year ends*

In the interim of these two extremes it is indifferent current.

The world begins with a young man when he new sets up for himself, and ends with him when his wife sets up for herself.

The world begins with an old man when every day his bags fill, and that he can drink half a pint of sack off at a draught and cry 'hm!' after it, and the world ends with him when he begins to dote on a young wench. *World begins and ends*

English tides

High water above London Bridge when the prentices there dwelling pluck up buckets full to the top of the house to serve their kitchens, and low water when people go over the Thames dry shod. *High water*

High water at London Bridge when the tide is come in, low water when 'tis gone out.

High water at all havens when their mouths swill in so much that they cast it out again. *Havens*

And high water with all rivers when bridges, and they meeting the bridges, are glad to stand up to the middle to save themselves. *Bridges*

High water in schoolboys' eyes after the fearful sentence of 'Take him up', and in women's when either they cry for anger or are maudlin drunk. *Schoolboys. Women*

It flows with good fellows when their cups are full and their brains swim, and it ebbs at the postern when the physic works and the body purgeth backward. *Drunkards*

It's high water at Westminster Hall when porters are fee'd by lawyers to ride a pick-pack on them instead of mules and so to turn them into asses, and wonderful low water when the stream of quicksilver hath his current stopped up. *Lawyers*

Computation diurnal and astrological

Golden number is any number of golden angels or other coin of the same metal. It is this year with me two for the golden number; next year I hope it will be more. *Golden number*

Epact is a comprehension of the teeth of the moon, for look into her mouth with the watching candle of astronomical skill and by the soundness *Epact*

338 **put-gallies** receptacles for raising water from wells
340 **roaring boys** riotous youths
341 **calendar of Newgate** record of the inmates of Newgate prison, issued as a publication from 1773
343 **dance to Norwich** Will Kemp, the clown, danced from London to Norwich for a wager in February 1600; *Kemp's Nine Days' Wonder* was published in April. (The Owl is inaccurate about the date.)
344 **Monsieur Nobody** reference to the anonymous play *Nobody and Somebody* (1606)
345–6 **George Stone** famous bear used for baiting
347 **dancing horse** appeared on St Paul's in February 1601; the horse was the much-mentioned Morocco, a curtal owned by Banks.
355 **German fencer** mentioned in Rowley's *Noble Soldier*, 2.1 ('Shall I be that German fencer and beat all the knocking boys before me?') and *Roaring Girl.*
357 **yellow bands** the fashion of wearing yellow bands was introduced by the infamous Mrs Turner, who wore them at the gallows in November 1615
chaperons hoods or caps worn by ladies
373 **drawers** tavern waiters
385 **sack** fortified white wine
389–90 **prentices** apprentices
395 **havens** harbours
401 **'Take him up'** i.e. to be whipped
402 **maudlin** tearful, sentimental
405 **postern** back-door; also the anus
408 **pick-pack** pick-a-back, piggy-back
417 **Epact** the number of days that constitutes the excess of the solar over the lunar year of twelve months

of her gum-pales you shall know how old her great belly is.

Circle of the sun

The circle of the sun is bigger than any town bushel, yea though you allow unto it London water-measure. A sieve cannot hold it, for the beams peep out at every little hole.

Roman indiction

The Roman indiction this year is that we eat no flesh on Fridays and that none feed upon Saturdays unless he have victuals.

Dominical letter L

The dominical letter 'L' with a dash over it signifies either a lord or a pound, the one sometimes being more welcome to an almanac-maker than the other.

Shrove Tuesday falls on that day on which the prentices plucked down the Cockpit, and on which they did always use to rifle Madam Leak's house at the upper end of Shoreditch.

Ash Wednesday on a Wednesday.

Good Friday the Friday before Easter.

And this year Holy Thursday (which I never wonder at) will fall upon a Thursday.

Easter day, my grandam says, she never knew but on a Sunday, and I say as much for Whitsunday.

And now listen to a double-ribbed distichon of an old author.

Old rhymes to remember times

Christmas (as I remember)
Is ever in December,
And May the first of the row,
St John after Steven,
The day after even,
Believe me, I say it so.

A moon-clock, or a rule to know the hour of the night by the moon

An excellent moon-dial, but that the dial is too big to carry in a man's pocket

Take a pair of iron tongues; pitch them straddling over a kennel; then fasten a wagon-wheel to the diameter of the tongues; which done, mark what spoke doth cast the shadow of the moon into the sink directly between the bestriders; from which, count the spokes till you come right opposite to the shadow, then dimidiate or part in two equal parts that number, divide it by 3, multiply it by 7, from which extract the number of the epact and the *remanet* will be the just hour of the night. To show a platform were idle when the precept is so plain.

The anatomy of man's body

1. Aries, the ram, governs the head: men whose wives have light heels are called ram-headed cuckolds.

2. Taurus, the bull, governs the neck and throat: for stiff-necked fellows are roaring boys and dead their tools often in Turnbull Street.

3. Gemini, the twins, govern the arms and shoulders: so thieves go to the sessions two by two, arm in arm, shoulder to shoulder.

4. Cancer, the crab, governs the stomach: and reason, for a crab well buttered is excellent meat.

5. Leo, the lion, governs the heart: he that hath not the heart of a lion hath the head of an ox.

6. Virgo, the virgin, governs bowels and belly and makes both cry 'O!' if they meddle too much with her government.

7. Libra, the balance, governs the loins, for much double-dealing is done in those quarters.

8. Scorpio, the scorpion, governs the secret parts, for those sting pockily.

9. Sagittarius, the archer, governs the thighs, for between them is the sweetest shooting.

10. Capricornus, the goat, governs the knees, for a man lecherous as a goat is brought upon his knees.

11. Aquarius, the water-bearer, governs the legs; he hath a staff to help, too, and all little enough sometimes when he carries drink and water both.

12. Pisces, the fishes, govern the feet, for let a man come out of any tavern in Fish Street drunk, it is so slippery with fish-water that down he comes and lies like a heap of stinking gubbins.

If these twelve be not able to govern man's unruly body, then let the twelve companies of London have him to their halls and whip him. But to prove that these are strong enough to hold him, you may by the verses following perceive that the sun of these twelve makes himself a girdle in the zodiac.

The signs of the zodiac

Signs

The ram, the bull, twins, crab, the lion hot,
Virgin, scales, scorpion, he which archer hight,
The goat, and bearer of the water pot,
A brace of fishes—with heavenly light

424 **water-measure** a kind of measurement formerly used for coal, salt, fruit, etc., sold on board vessels in port or on the river
426 **Roman indiction** a fiscal period of fifteen years instituted by Emperor Constantine; a specified year in the recurring period of fifteen years
429 **dominical letter** the letter used to denote the Sundays in a particular year
434 **the Cockpit** the Cockpit theatre was sacked by the apprentices on Shrove Tuesday, 1617.
435 **Madam Leak's** keeper of a brothel
444 **distichon** two lines of rhyming verse
455 **kennel** gutter
460 **dimidiate** divide in half (coinage)
463 ***remanet*** the remainder (Latin)
464 **platform** plan
472 **dead their tools** blunt (pun); take the edge off their lust
Turnbull Street otherwise Turnmill Street, a red-light area of Clerkenwell, north London
474 **sessions** law sessions, trials
486 **sting pockily** hurt with the pox, i.e., syphilis
499 **gubbins** fragments, especially of fish
501 **companies** twelve premier city livery companies or guilds
509 ***hight*** is called

These sum the dozen of those stars in sky
Which lend bright Cynthia such variety.

The first induction of the zodiac

The zodiac, which begged his name of living creatures (for all the cullizans in it except one, which is of no great weight neither, drew their pedigree from the idea of some excellent animal) took his original thus.

How the zodiac took his original

When Jupiter reigned in the sky, and the fry of the gods in the zodiac circle, Prometheus, that melancholic artisan, casting down from the earth's ceiling a compassionate eye on mankind, who at that time had no other fire than that of love, (which was Cupid's,) and that of anger, (which is the heat of Nemesis,) commiserated man's cold comfort and vowed when time served to pull opportunity by the nose and pleasure man with that artificious pantechnon which in worth far transcended that peerless pearl of Antony's lady.

Man at first without the use of fire

Prometheus the thief that first stole fire

What might move him to divulge this treasure out of the exchequer of heaven, I know not. Some think it was a swelling desire that possessed him, thinking to eternize his fame and make his name immortal by bestowing this rare gift upon mortals.

Others imagine that this Prometheus was wound into the love (and not unlikely, for your semi-saints and demi-deities were ever liable to Cupid's archery) of a pretty damosel that dwelt under the immortal canopy in this cold horizon, which made his virgin in frosty congealing mornings look like Vespasian, as if she had been wringing at a hard stool, and that for her sake he became so liberal to the earth's inhabitants.

Armourers had first use of fire

Howsoever, whether this or that was his instigation, occasion being tossed in his way he bestowed this hot benefit on man, imparting it first unto Pyrodes, an excellent armourer.

The means how he came by it is not certainly known. Some think that he himself by his deep-searching wit first invented the manner how to dash it out of the igniferous flint.

First fire from a flint

In his right hand a shivering flint he locks,
Which 'gainst another in his left he knocks
So up and down that from the coldest stone
At every stroke small fiery sparkles shone,
Which withered, Daphne with her leaves doth feed,
This was our fire's ('tis thought) both root and seed.

Prometheus robbed Vulcan's forge of fire

Others imagine he got this knowledge by coming into Mulciber's shop (which stands at the foot of brimstone-bubbling Etna) and secretly peeping over the old farrier's shoulder as he was striking fire. But the most received opinion is that he played the thief and stole it either out of Vulcan's forge (as some would have it) or rather *e coelo* out of Jove's treasury, as most imagine. Howsoever, he bestowed it on man, flat against Jove's will and pleasure, who was much enraged at this his action.

Why Jove was angry seeing men to use fire

And surely there was just cause of Jove's displeasure, for it is thought that at that time as many damned mischiefs thronged into the world with fire as there did fantastical fooleries with Monsieur into England. Then pranked Dame *Poena et Pecunia* (money and misery), bags and beggary, the very heart and head of infelicity. Then came craft into the world with his pages, Sinon, Davus, Geta, Parasitus (the fawn), and goodman Dolus (Doctor Deceit), who for his antiquity might bear arms as big as Charles's Wain. Then came posting in (on a piebald cut) Simony (see money), Bribery, Humorism, Malice, all the whelps of Acheron, all the weeds of the infernal banks, with pale-faced Incontinence and giddy-brained Intemperance, the two swiftest coach-horses of hell.

Fire the breeder of mischief

The Brazen Age

About this very time landed *Deterior Aetas* (the ill-favoured-faced beldam) and calendared herself into the earth's almanac, a cunning, a coying and purloining sorceress at whose tail marched in most stinking ranks all the sores, mischiefs

513 ***Cynthia*** the moon, e.g. the night sky
516 **cullizans** corruption of cognizance; badge or sign
520 **fry** offspring
526 **Nemesis** goddess of retribution
529 **pantechnon** all-purpose technological aid (coinage)
530–1 **Antony's lady** Cleopatra
543 **Vespasian** Roman emperor, AD 69–79, reputed to have died while trying to excrete
549 **Pyrodes** the discoverer of the art of kindling fire
558 ***Daphne*** nymph who was saved from rape by Apollo by being changed into a laurel tree
561 **Mulciber's** another name for Vulcan, god of fire and metal-work
562 **Etna** volcano in Sicily
566 ***e coelo*** from the heavens (Latin)
575 **Monsieur** the Duke of Anjou, one of Elizabeth I's suitors, arrived in England in October, 1581
pranked disported themselves
578 **Sinon** Greek soldier who persuaded the Trojans to admit the wooden horse into Troy
Davus the cunning slave in Terence's play *Andria*
579 **Geta** brother of Caracalla. Became Caesar in AD 198. Assassinated by his brother in 212.
581 **Charles's Wain** the Plough constellation
582 **piebald cut** a black and white horse
Simony (see money) buying or selling of ecclesiastical preferment. (A facetious etymology: see = bishopric.)
583 **Humorism** whimsical, capricious or obsessional behaviour
Acheron one of the rivers of the underworld
587 ***Deterior Aetas*** weaker age (Latin)
588 **beldam** hag
589 **coying** coaxing, wheedling

and state-imposthumes that covered their damned heads with *Pasquil's Madcap*, or else were minced and boiled together in *Madcap's Gallimaufry*. Now issued in from the rearward Madam Vice or old Iniquity, with a lath dagger painted according to the fashion of an old Vice in a comedy, with a head of many colours as showing her subtlety, and at her back two punks that were her chambermaids, the one called Too Little, the other Too Much, and these two had like quicksilver eaten the world's goodness to the heart.

Omne nimium vertitur in vitium

In a left wing of this army of Barathrum were skirmishing more sins than ever *The Bellman of London* or *Lanthorn and Candlelight* did ever muster up together.

Two books written by T. D.

For before these barrels of mischief were set abroad every old man was a piece of reverend coin on which the very face of goodness was engraven, and every sprig of youth was a laurel branch which all the year long grew green and smelt sweet of innocency. Women were those creatures that were fairer within than without, wooing men to love them for their virtues, and not one of that name did then sound *woe-man*. Maids had that title from modesty, marriage was the merry-age, a child playing with a dog the emblem of simplicity; every man's life was his chronicle to following times, and in every leaf was Honesty and Fidelity in texted letters. A Golden Age was this, yet without gold, where every commonwealth was more (if more might be) than Sir Thomas More's never-enough-praised Utopian.

A figure of the Golden Age

No such women now

No maids, puppies and children do so still

Sir Thomas More his Utopia

Jove, the reputed admiral of the air's ocean, billowing his brows with disdain and fury, cracking a cloud at every bended wrinkle and thumping out a thunder at every frown, his face flashing fire and his looks menacing storms, stood still as if mortality had seen Medusa stamped on the ground, as if Cato had seen a swaggerer, vowed with a thousand Stygian oaths that Prometheus should repent him of his bold attempt and audacious profusion in communicating that Jovial flame which would in time set the whole world in combustion. Forthwith flies there a voice which summons his winged herald Mercury, to whom the fire-stealer is delivered in charge to be conveyed to Vulcan, the master of the heavenly ferrary or Jove's iron works, to be chained to the top of the cold Caucasus. Mercury presently made proclamation (with an iron voice out of his star-threating turret) that all creatures who thought themselves endamaged by this fire-work of Prometheus should instantly present themselves before him and wreak their baleful ire on him at their pleasure. On frosty-fronted Caucasus, that cold mountain, (at Jove's command) was this Prometheus lodged, shackled to a stake with chains which Vulcan had hammered out for that unruly hell-hound, the wide-throated porter of Erebus (Cerberus), where to this hour he stands shivering and shaking like a condemned caitiff that attends the fatal stroke to sever his headpiece from his fear-frozen carcass, or like a schoolboy doomed with that fatal *solve ligulas* (or 'untruss'). Even so he stood till the sound of the writhen horn had famoused his act far and near with the liberty of inflicting penalties, *viz.* how that all the world was licensed to whet the spears of anger to spit him who, like an Indian (in New Spain), stood there exposed as a fair mark for any man's fury.

Jove in a pelting chase

Prometheus, look to your coxcomb.

Jove's pursuivant called for

Terrible doings

The thief taken

Hell's porter and a prison porter cousins as I take it

Aries: the ram

The first tilter that ran against him was Aries the crooked-horned-winding ram; off left he his grazing and thus began he his indictment.

Calling to mind the prejudice that this fire-filcher had done him, how that now such craft had sunk into the brains of man, such rape and

A ram-headed oration

592 **state-imposthumes** corruption or insurrections in the State
593 ***Pasquil's Madcap*** Pasquil was a satirical persona, adopted by Nashe in his anti-Marprelate pamphlets, derived from the statue in Rome to which lampoons were pinned. This and *Madcap's Gallimaufry* are probably the titles of satirical pamphlets, now lost.
594 ***Gallimaufry*** hodge-podge
596 **lath dagger** wooden dagger carried by the Vice in the Morality plays
597 **Vice** a mischief-making character in the Morality plays; stage jester
599 **punks** prostitutes
600.n ***Omne … vitium*** all excess becomes a vice (Latin)
603.n ***T. D.*** Thomas Dekker
603 **Barathrum** a deep pit at Athens into which criminals condemned to death were thrown
604–5 ***The Bellman … Candlelight*** pamphlets published in 1608 and 1609 respectively exposing the characters and practices of the London underworld
615 ***woe-man*** popular false etymology
620 **texted** in fine, large handwriting
621.n ***Utopia*** More's work was first published in Latin in 1516 and translated into English by Ralph Robinson in 1551.
629 **Medusa** one of the three Gorgons, mythological female monsters with snakes for hair
630 **Cato** Cato the Younger, 95–46 BC, Roman statesman, general and Stoic philosopher; opponent of Catiline and Caesar
631 **Stygian** inviolable, like the oath by the Styx which the gods themselves feared to break
633 **profusion** lavish gift
637.n ***pursuivant*** herald, messenger
639 **ferrary** blacksmiths' shop (from Latin)
642 **turret** see the herald in the turret in De Witt's drawing of the Swan theatre (1596), p. 80
650 **Erebus** the underworld
652 **caitiff** prisoner
655 ***solve ligulas*** undo your laces (Latin), i.e. for whipping by the schoolmaster
656 **writhen** twisted
660 **New Spain** a Spanish viceroyalty of the 16th to 19th centuries comprising Mexico, Central America, the south-western U.S. and the Spanish West Indies. Members of the native population were sometimes used for target practice.
664 **off left he** i.e. he left off
666.n ***ram-headed*** thick-witted

avarice into his heart, that poor rams could no more sleep in their golden fleeces; whereas before that time their woollen coats were never in fear or danger of cutting out by the cruelty of fire-moulded metal, their tender lambs were never taken from their uberous sides, their blood was never 'tainted in the parliament of wolves, nor had the fox that crafty noddle of his own to play the bloodsucker amongst their flocks. This tale being bleated out and heard, this cornuted husband of the sheep's heads fetching a feeze backward (like the Roman ram, to push forward with the more violent and villainous force) ran with all his horniferous strength at the poor fire-felon and stroke his brow-butters full in Prometheus's forehead that the very print remaineth in his front, and doth still in some of his race to this day; yea, such was the violence of the blow that it hath caused a wrinkled brow in all his progeny.

A sweet parliament

O brave ram!

These horn-heads are terrible fellows

Jove stood by in a cloud beholding the courage of the ram, which after he had applauded with his pleasing looks, he placed him on the chained head to vex his pate forever as the head-sign at which hung his fury.

Rewards for revenge

Taurus: the bull

But casting his eye aside, behold came Taurus up the hill with roaring throat, sweating like a bull as he was, bellowing out on behalf of all his beastly kindred that by Prometheus's means his soul and body was brought in danger. For the invention of the scythe which mowed down the grass from his hungry paunch, the iron chain that restrained his grinders from hewing up the blades, were by the help of fire first framed. Nay, the butcher had all the instruments of death from this theft of his. The goad that spurs his slowness forward, and the boldness of man that durst encounter such a mass of flesh, first fetched their original from this act of his.

'Ware the bull. Bull's oration

These speeches with a bull-beef countenance being uttered (for he was like Ajax, more warrior than orator), he ran at this bellows-maker (whose filching was the first inventor of kindling fire) with such a roaring and bellowing violence that, goring his thievish neck, he almost doubly nailed it to the stake.

A Paris Garden bull could have done no more

Jove clapped the bull on the flanks (as a bear-ward doth the bull at Paris Garden in a great day of baiting) and was glad to see justice (whose sword is put into the hands of fools and coxcombs upon earth) to be so nobly and stoutly executed on a villain by a creature merely irrational.

Jove a stickler

Gemini: the twins

Yea, the thunder-darting god laughs so loud that the echo of that noise even shook the palaces celestial, but before the wrinkles of his cheeks were made smooth again, Jove fed his eyes with the sight of two twins (called Gemini) hand-in-hand approaching this condemned miscreant. The tears fell in sweet showers from their eyes, sometimes trickling down their tender cheeks, anon those balls of light swimming only in circles of water like two islands encompassed about with a pair of rivers. So stood they gazing and grieving to behold that arch-pirate, their tormented enemy, whose punishment in heart they wished to be doubled as were their bodies.

Room for two fencers

Destiny had given them more woes than words, but nature was so good a schoolmistress to them that they could without book rehearse their own misfortunes. 'Who thou art', quoth the Gemini with feeble voices, 'we cannot tell; known only art thou unto us as a fatal tree upon which grows all our miseries. Thou didst first reveal the use of fire to man, teaching him since how to feed and foster it continually, and by that mystery opened to him the way to our undoing. It was thy wit and work to set the world at wars by the fire of dissension and the burning coals of ambition, and to that end smiths, gun-makers, spear-makers and suchlike hard-handed fellows have been a long time thy slaves and prentices, night and day hammering from the murd'rous anvil knives, poniards, stilettoes, swords, bills, pole-axes, cannons, culverins, sakers, muskets, petronels and pistols, to feed whose insatiable, sulphurous and devouring, fire-spitting mouths that black meal of hell (gunpowder) hath likewise been invented. It was long of thee that our parents were slain, that our states were overthrown and all misfortunes fell upon us. Two we are to one, yet our force is but small and the stroke of our revenge but feeble. Yet to prove that there is spleen even in

Good boys!

Sea-coal of Newcastle a good benefactor to this

Armourers had never been a company else

That's odds

674 **uberous** supplying plenty of milk or nourishment
676 **noddle** head
678 **cornuted** horned
679 **fetching a feeze** taking a short run before jumping
680 **Roman ram** battering ram
682 **horniferous** horn-bearing (coinage)
709 **Ajax** Greek hero of the Trojan war who killed himself in rage when Achilles's armour was given to Odysseus
716 **Paris Garden** bear-baiting arena on the south side of the river near the theatres
742.n ***Sea-coal*** often explained as coal brought by sea from Newcastle to London, but originally jet, or coal from the sea as opposed to charcoal
752 **poniards** daggers
753 **culverins** cannons
sakers small cannons
754 **petronels** large pistols used especially by horse-soldiers
757 **long of** on account of

Habet et musca splenem

poor flies, and to show a love to our parents, we will in scorn of thee bestride thy shoulders, and there with the horrid noise of our wrongs so lug thee by the ears with our nails, and so torment thy hearing, that thou shalt wish to be burnt in ten thousand bonfires for filching that handful of fire from heaven, rather than be tortured by two such cruel hangmen as we shall prove to thee.'

Prometheus made an ass to carry two apes

This threatened sentence took place: upon his shoulders they mounted, Prometheus both patient and speechless, enduring their bawling exclamations whose scolding day and night grew to be so loud, and the barking so intolerable, that the head of man and his ears laid their noddles together, taking counsel of the brain how to prevent the shaking down and utter ruin of the capital building by such an everlasting, roaring thunder; and thereupon found out no better means to stop such breaches than by clammy wax just at the wickets of the ears, whose little key-holes being so choked up, the horror of their sounds could not pierce too far; so that ever since, the head (being the body's hive) doth by certain bee-workings of the brain convey wax to the cells of hearing.

How wax crept into the ears

Cancer: the crab

A sour-faced crab

Next came Cancer like a waterman in a boat, his arse toward the place to which he was going; he looked like a piece of Hebrew spelled the wrong way, or like a rope-maker who as he gets his living doth go (like a corpse carried to church) with his heels forwards, or, if you will, like a witch who says her prayers backwards; just in that manner marched Signor Cornuto Cancer with the crab-tree face, *testudineo gradu*, crawling with his tail before him. He was very desirous to mend his pace (not daring to swear, for fear his claws should catch no fish) but, protesting he would give all his palaces of dead horse-heads, and cared not who buttered his lecherous guts with eggs and muscadine, and so eat him, upon condition he might but give that termagant Prometheus but three pinches; not upon any legitimate spleen in the world, but only that he would not like a snail pluck in his horns in such a combat, where the ram, bull and a couple of Jack Sprat boys had laid about them so like fencers. The revenge was as common as the law, or as the blows of a spital whore (hot and dangerous), and therefore like the ass in the fable that would needs be so lusty at legs as to lend the lion a brace of kicks and to play at spurn-point with him, so would the crab have a bout with Don Fire-Drake. But the ass played his jade's tricks when Coeur-de-Lion lay half dead in his belly, scarce having one tooth in his head because age, being his barber, had plucked all out, and so Monsieur Cancro was the more hot upon his enemy because he had him bound to the peace.

O cruel crab

Age a terrible tooth-drawer

Or it may be he was thus sour the rather because Prometheus looked like a fisher (as he hung) with a long drivelling beard, who was wont to scare such crabbed companions out of their rocky and mossy dens; or else because fishermen, by help of that felon's skill in fire-works, got both anchors to hold their peter-boats and little hooks to choke harmless fishes, with other engines to destroy the poor inhabitants of the ocean.

This is very likely

Hinc illae lachrimae!

Howsoever or whatsoever it was which boiled within him, but Cancer crawled up to Prometheus his linked ribs, where he fell so to pinch his stomach that all his chamber of melancholy (I mean the milt) was in a dogged and sullen, scurvy puffing, so that the poor scab was as splenetic as the Cappadocian bawd in Plautus. '*Habet et musca splenem*', quoth Jove, 'Cancer can be choleric and my little crab crawl on his belly, but he will bite his enemy'.

Crabs are windy meat for the stomach

Leo: the lion

But O! on a sudden the belly-bitten thief yells out, roars and bandies up curses able to crack the clouds asunder, yelping with loud-yawning throat like a prisoner in Ludgate, or the gratemen in the begging room of the King's Bench common jail when they do but smell the breath of four Flanders mares whurrying near them in a caroche. All his body grew cold with fear, his shoulders shook like an aspen and his heart quaked like a half-dead eel upon a hot gridiron; and what was it but Leo came flinging up the hill, bearing his head

Either of which bawl extremely

Enter Lion

762 **flies** boys hired to help the pressman
762.n ***Habet...splenem*** even the fly has a spleen (Latin)
764 **lug** pull violently (a term used in bear-baiting)
780 **wickets** small doors or gates
789 **Hebrew** written from right to left
795 **crab-tree** crooked, knotted
testudineo gradu in the manner (literally 'step') of a tortoise (Latin); quoted from Plautus, *Aulularia*
801 **muscadine** musk-scented wine
802 **termagant** imaginary deity of violent character
806 **Jack Sprat** i.e. skinny
808 **spital** hospital, poor-house
810 **ass in the fable** Aesop's fable of 'The Mighty Fallen'; also in Aristotle, *Politics*, III, 13
812 **spurn-point** an old game, possibly similar to hopscotch
813 **Fire-Drake** a fiery dragon of Germanic myth
814 **jade's tricks** the tricks of an ill-tempered horse
825 **peter-boats** small, decked fishing boats on the Thames
826.n ***Hinc illae lachrimae*** hence those tears (Latin)
832 **milt** the spleen in mammals
834 **Cappadocian bawd** Cappadox in Plautus, *Curculio*
834–5 ***Habet...splenem*** see l. 762.n
842 **Ludgate** prison west of St Paul's Cathedral
gratemen jailers
843 **King's Bench** jail for poor prisoners in Southwark

as high as the last foot of Horace his first song, his fiery-trembling mane being proudly erected and his tail retorted on his back, as chafing his ridge-bone to provoke his courage, complaining of the man's act and the fruit of his act (fire and sword); the one with his flame dismays his valour, the other with his lustre terrifies his prey-coveting thoughts more than the fearful crowing of the watchful chanticleer. Then, giving his speech a treble plaudit, with three round roars he skips to the heart of the object, and had wholly sent it into his seldom full or never satisfied throat, had not Jove sent a thunder of retreat unto him out of hand. 'Lofty Lion', said Jove, 'I will thee clasp thy jaws and shut the portal of that vorant grave which makes whole towns look pale, till the nurture of my sceptre shall have limited thy boundless savageness:

The addressing of the lion to the combat

Well roared, lion

When that thou shalt espy this pilferer's heart
To slack his motion and to rest as still,
Then shalt thou prey upon that resting part,
Till when remain morigerat to our will.'*

Jove can make verses too

*Obedient**

Fast under his left arm stands this greedy lion, expecting with wide-gaping mouth the sedency and tired motion of his life's fountain, at whose fearful vigilancy the poor heart with very thought of the terrifying beast drives itself with a continual systole and diastole, like the clack of a mill or a sun-sucked leaf chained to a spider's twine. Yet I have not read that before that time it ever stirred.

The lion swore to have a leg or an arm

Virgo: the maid

But, methinks, fuming fury should not smoke out of virgins' entrails when they have so many petticoats to smother it. Such tendrils of Venus' grove should not harbour a shadow of revenge. Yea, but look here where Virgo comes pacing up the hill, as fast as a hangman up a ladder at the hope of a good suit, or at least as fast as her busk will give her leave. Well, to be as brief as an ape's tail, she had no sooner got up the hill but she begins to chide out these causes of her direful approach to tongue-tied Prometheus, knocking her fists as the custom of shrews is, where at length her frowns vented this foam: 'Now, thou pilled, pilfering knave, thou maleficious rascal, was the mumps of thy brain swollen so big that they must needs break out into flames, and bring such a smoke into the world that has infected all our youngsters' breath? Thou hast taught men (thou captivated cur) to kindle that quenchless fire of tobacco (O my bodkin! I'll dig out his eyes) in which thou hast robbed me of my greatest pleasure. Let a fresh bachelor in his new clothes come but towards me with intent to draw breath at my lips, why, I smell my youth before I come at him. And if he offer me the courtesy I turn him away with a "foh!, you smell (save reverence) of tobacco". If I walk in the streets and chance to come down Bucklersbury, O, how the whole orb of air is infected with this fume, which so much alters my complexion that if I should not view my visage every hour of the day in the glass, I durst be sworn that I should not know myself. But the worst of all is that this Promethean smoke melts off the complexion from our coloured cheeks as fast as we lay it on. I cannot forbear, the spoil of that faculty spurs me forward.' And forthwith sent she a red-hot spit (as valorously as ever Tomyris struck off Cyrus' head) into the midst of his belly, that you might well say that Prometheus was no hypocrite, for you might easily see into him. Jove of pity, or rather of envy, healed the wound, as strengthening the offender for further vengeance, but the scar of the wound remains in human portraiture, which we call the navel.

A hot whore

A woman is violent in revenge

Now for a fit of scolding

Thou for my money

Women hate tobacco

She loved kissing

Tobacco a Promethean smoke

A painted punk yet goes for a maid

O whore!

Libra: the balance

Libra, she that followed Virgo (as fast as her apron-strings would give her leave), came creeping through the supporters of the press, and being almost breathless with taking such wide strides, in short language laid open her case and courted Jove for revenge: 'You know, attendants all, the wrongs that I have endured since the firing of the world. My mistress Equity (whose emblem I am) hath hid her face since fraud set up her banners, and weeps in obscure corners to see deceit brandish the square of upright dealing. I that before was the equal hand of justice am now no more Libra for scales, but Libra for pounds. Nay, further, our tradesmen use me in weighing such beastly, stinking stuff, and that so unjustly, that I can no longer endure it. Wherefore, great Jove, fasten me to this lubber's loins that I may ever stick by his ribs to put him in mind of his unequal

A good lawyer, she opens her own case

This is a chambermaid to justice

Chandlers, a bob for you

850 **last foot of Horace** *Odes*, I.i.36 (*Sublimi feriam sidera vertice*, 'with my exalted head I shall strike the stars')
858 **chanticleer** cock
859 **plaudit** a round of applause
859.n ***Well roared, lion*** quoting *Midsummer Night's Dream* 5.1.260
862 **retreat** i.e. the signal for retreat
864 **vorant** devouring (coinage)
873 **sedency** sluggishness (coinage)
877 **systole and diastole** rhythmic contraction and dilation of the heart
887 **busk** corset
894 **pilled** literally, bald, shaven; here, miserable, beggarly
maleficious witchcraft-using
895 **mumps** disease characterized by inflammation and swelling
900 **bodkin** needle
906 **foh!** an expression of disgust
908 **Bucklersbury** street near Cheapside, noted for herb and spice merchants
917–18 **Tomyris . . . Cyrus** Cyrus, the founder of the Persian empire, was killed in battle by Tomyris, a queen of the Massagetae, in 529 BC.
939.n ***bob*** a shilling; five pence in modern coinage
942 **lubber's** lout's

Lex talionis

dealing.' Prometheus's reins being sore affrighted at the sight of such a misshapen creature, like a heartless hound fell a-running away, and had not Jove stopped their race, he might have died of that disease and resigned his spirit to ghost-groping Pluto.

Scorpio: the scorpion

Not long after came Scorpio, alleging that by the virtue of this attracting fire men had learned to cure his body-biting sting and sought out devices to entrap his person and to convert his corpse into a liquid oil (most sovereign against empoisonings). More than this, that in derision of his name, Prometheus the great artificer had made a scourge for his apprentice's delinquency and called it a scorpion, for which injuries he enviously skipped up to his genitals, murdering that place, lest Prometheus should beget some more audacious boldings of his venturous nature.

Whips indeed bite sore

He lies stone dead

Sagittarius: the archer

Sagittarius the bowman (Robin Hood's great grandsire) stood aiming at this fettered wretch, ready to let fly at him, had not the proceeding (*indicta causa*) hindered him; whereupon he produceth that this salamander-breeder had brought so many books and subtleties into the world, and so stained all the livers on the earth with craft and foxism, that whereas before he could have slain a soul at every errand he had sent his feather-cheeked lackey, now his bolts make many a vain voyage and return empty. The buck, as soon as he spies these limb-slicing shafts, erecteth his front and ears and paceth into the thicket where he is warded from the dart of death. 'Thus is the use of my intended arrow defeated; yea, of the shafts themselves this Prometheus labours to delude me, for when the world had no other heat than *ardorem solis* (the heavens' heat) every hedge and quickset, every knot and turb of trees, was able to yield quiver-shafts sufficient choice and variety; now whole woods and forests can scarce fit me with a pair to my liking. All the arborean and arbustian army are so suddenly dried up and turned to colour as pale as ashes at the very sight of this Promethean fire; yea (even to this hour) if a collier or an iron-grinder pass but by a young and tender grove in autumn, you shall see within a handful of days after all the humid sap of those burning branches fled within the rind and sunk under the ground (like a moor-hen at the sight of a spaniel), as dreading by a secret antipathy those two wood-wasting tyrants. Stand aside', said the shooter, 'I'll venture this at a haunch of his, though all the woods in Arabia fail me in yielding such another. I'll lame him first, afterwards (as my passion shall move me) I'll rage farther, have at his thigh.' Away flies the arrow, buzzing in the air, as singing in his greedy voyage for joy of his wished prey. After follows Sagittarius, viewing how his hungry arrow drunk up the traitor's tainted blood.

Foxism

Birds may sing merrily at this news

The buck too crafty for a bow

Sunshine the first heat man warmed his hands at

Now his bolt flies

Capricornus: the goat

No sooner was this brunt over, but lo another calamity: Capricornus the Sophy-bearded goat came frisking in as if he would have capered over the Alps; his chinny dependant was bedewed with his pearled sweat that issued from his head with too much haste, which so tired him that, falling flat and flexible on his knees, he thus gan say: 'Since this fire-founder Prometheus incensed the whole course of nature by his damned inventions, lust and lechery, the buds of heat and ardour have dispersed themselves through all the ranks of breathing creatures. My grey-bearded sire well calculating the event of this mischief would ever charge his sons and daughters to beware of those force-enfeebling companions (the children of heat), declaring to us by way of items (as he went grazing down the hill) the aptness and inclination of our bodies that way. I (for mine own part) thought myself sufficiently instructed against these hot-spurs, but having them occasionately tossed in my way, I resisted (like Ovid's Corinna) as though I would not join. And suddenly my spirits were so strongly addicted to the sinful act (so strangely framed to the venom of venery) that even now already I am become the odious signature and emblem of unchastity. Yea, when men would decipher to the world a man that is lodged in lust, in one word (by way of metaphor) they term him a goat. Neither is this the utmost of my grief or of the scathe that this fire brood hath done me, for he hath so searched and wrought upon my body that

More anger yet

Now the goat's beard begins to wag

Hairy bodies lecherous

Grata est vis ipsa

Goats emblems of lust

944.n ***Lex talionis*** the law of retaliation, an eye for an eye (Latin)
944 **reins** the region of the kidneys
967 ***indicta causa*** his case not put (Latin)
971 **foxism** craftiness (coinage)
982 **quickset** hedge or thicket
turb clump of trees
986 **arbustian** of shrubs (coinage)
1006 **brunt** charge, violent attack
1007 **Sophy-bearded** Sophy: the Shah of Persia
1009 **chinny dependant** beard
1021 **items** maxims, words of advice
1025 **occasionately** in a manner brought about by some occasion or secondary cause
1026 **Ovid's Corinna** the Roman poet's mistress who offered token resistance in *Amores*, I, v
1026.n ***Grata est vis ipsa*** Force herself is attractive (Latin)
1035 **scathe** harm

Goats subject to agues, quails to the falling sickness. Gout, of goat

I am continually vexed with the spirit-spending ague, as the quail with the falling sickness, or else ever buckled and bended in the knees with the joint-tormenting gout (which I think borrowed his name of goat), as now I am whilst kneeling I tell this story, so that Damage herself calls upon me to sacrifice in wrath to her sister Nemesis, and (as I intend) this wagoner of lust shall rue my malevolent mood before he and I depart. His knees, which I trow are within my reach, for I will proportion his penance to the quality of his offence, shall be the object of my baneful butchery. O! ever will I pray that the gonagra may possess his hams and the sciatica his hips eternally.'

Aquarius: the water-bearer

The rage of fire

Water-bearers are sore emptiers of full tankards

But opinion might persuade me that of all men alive Aquarius the water-porter should not fume at fiery Prometheus so much, since old Oceanus the senior sea god would lovingly call him his endeared friend. Yea, but Aquarius has excellent reason for it and will tell it as admirably, though he be illiterate and unlearned: 'For', saith he, 'in times past when fire was kept underboard like a prisoner and dwelt far from our houses like the antipodes, every conduit might flow his circle, every fountain run his dripling race without molest. But now, since fire is grown superlative and breathes naught but devastations and incendiaries, since it hath got the knack of translating houses into bonfires (for envious neighbours to warm themselves by), making them lofty torches as though they would outface the moon, the pipes of our aquary conveyance have been so drawn, the channels of springs so sucked, that I can sound my tankard like an empty cask and look into the bottom, but see not a drop of water. And, assuredly, were all the waters of Europe sunk down into their kennels, yet would I lave this thief with this relic of water in my tankard, and send it into his shoes with an army of imprecations that it might prove like the Ethiopian well in the daytime or the Sicilian river in the night, or (at least) like the English fount that saxifies wood and turns it into rigid stone; that his supporters might be congealed and his legs condensed into glassy ice, that boys might slide his shins to shatters. Nay, but there be more tormentors of my kind coming. Draw the curtains of your eyes and see.'

Pisces: the fishes

It may be they are two otters

Fire-stealer. Why the fishes govern the feet

In good faith, 'tis strange, my masters, to my sense: a couple of fishes (I'll tell you their names as they fall better into my knowledge) come leaping over the fallows like pepper in a mortar, as though Revenge had sent them on her errand. The company turned their heads back jointly at the voice of that news like a steeple weathercock at the landing of another wind. Well, not many skips spent but fortune led them to this *Igni-fur*, and being seated low by nature they covet no higher than his feet (a lesson for ambitiosoes), which by this time were drowned in water that ran from the waterman's pitcher (sufficient life-room for these two sworn brothers) where, engraving some few signs and characters in the plain visage of the water (for fishes are the mutest creatures alive), the beholders might gather thus much.

An oration writ in water

Yarmouth herrings complain much of this

Thus use the fishmongers when they blow their nails

'Fire (which this tyrant to fishes hath invented against us of the moister orb) hath so instructed the fish-chasers in the art of framing bearded hooks and such inevitable baits of faithless forgery, that the hare lives not in more fear of the hound than we of these traitorous, enticing (I may call them Italian) salads. And, alas, when our captivated corpses are yielded to those scale-hunters, then begins the Tamburlaine-Ignis to broil our bark and carbonado our well-compacted limbs. In heat has this hunter offended, but we will torment him in another kind. O, let our frosten nature benumb the passages of his veins, and let no blood of warmth have recourse to these forward feet that led this wretch into this woe, whiles that our tenter-teeth, armed with envy's points, nibble on his toes and vex his corns and kibes.'

Jove, thus seeing the delinquent perplexed in every part, shoring up his eyelids above the snow-topped Caucasus (where were met whole troupes and multitudes of all kinds, except some drops of mechanicals and a spoonful of old women that

1038 **quail . . . sickness** In the Old Testament when the Israelites were fed up with manna God made quails fall out of the sky so that they could eat meat; see Numbers 11:31.

1049 **gonagra** gout in the knee (first citation in *OED*, 1657)

1060–1 **antipodes** the opposite side of the world

1062 **dripling** a formation combining 'dripping' and 'dribbling' (coinage)

1074 **lave** wash

1078 **Sicilian river** Arethusa, a nymph who was desired by the river-god Alpheus and who was turned into a fountain at Syracuse. Alpheus, flowing under the sea, was united with the fountain. It was believed in antiquity that there was a real connection with the river, whose source was in Arcadia, and the spring.

1079 **English fount** reference to Mother Shipton's well in Knaresborough, North Yorkshire
saxifies turns to stone

1089 **fallows** ploughed fields

1096 **ambitiosoes** Ambitioso is the name of the Duchess's eldest son in *Revenger*.

1109 **Italian) salads** diabolically tempting morsels

1111 **Tamburlaine-Ignis** the tyrant fire; Tamburlaine was the Asiatic conqueror dramatized by Marlowe

1112.n ***Yarmouth*** Norfolk fishing port eulogized by Thomas Nashe in *Lenten Stuff* (1599)

1112 **carbonado** barbecue

1118 **tenter-teeth** hooked teeth (coinage)

1119 **kibes** chilblains

1122 **troupes** (suggests a company of actors)

1124 **mechanicals** artisans or labourers

were snivelling o'er the fire, spreading themselves either as actors or spectators in this rueful tragedy) hoisted up these his instruments of revenge that took arms on them against this traitor Prometheus (whom he left standing still) into the greater plain of heaven called *coelum stellatum* (the star-coated sky) where he placed them every one in his order of revolution and dignity of desert, composing of their bodies twelve special signs. And because they were so far seated from the regiment of human constitution, Jove thought it good that they should apply their power to the Lady Moon, and she should convey the virtue of their constellations into man's body as being nearer and better acquainted with the same: so that, ever since, the empress of the lower world sojourning in their palaces hath a more forcible operation in our bodies' constitution; that though Prometheus and his offspring be distant from their corporal domination, yet by their infusive quality (as it were by an unknown sympathy) he is still pliable to their sidereal regiment. The bleeding sores Jove sent Aesculapius his physician to cure, Vulcan (his armourer) to enfranchise and set him at liberty, and Mercury his page to bid him void the hall. Prometheus roused himself up (as though he had slept on Avernus' bank or had pulled a twig of lotus tree), gat him to his earthly tent, weighed the order of the matter well, Jove's proceeding and his offence, and wore out the rest of his life in some better ease and content. And now has my pen (like a wandering planet) run through the circle of the zodiac. Let your favour assist his next journey or 'tis like to be eclipsed.

That's to say, the twelve signs

The moon conveys the virtue of these constellations into our bodies

All sublunary bodies guided by the moon

A general calendar for the common motion of the moon in all the months of the year

○ Full moon in misers' purses on payment day. With landlords at Michaelmas and Our Lady day. With beggars when they are trussed full. With women when they have great bellies. With the Moon Tavern in Aldersgate Street when there's no room in any room.

☾ Last quarter with thieves at Newgate two or three days after the sessions. With sick persons when the bell rings out for them. With my almanac when 'tis put under pie-crust.

● New moon when the good wife sets her cheese together or when the tailor broacheth a new fashion.

☽ First quarter when my hostess vents her new vessel and I clap two pots on my new score.

The disposition of the planets for this year

Lady *Luna*, queen of variety and mistress of alteration, shall domineer in the minds of women more than in all the world besides (the sea excepted). Her two handmaids (Change and Novelty) shall something infatuate religious cares, but the sap of her tree (Apishness) shall colour the whole court, city and country. And God shield the university.

Luna

Women more lunatic than men

Change, Novelty, Apishness, three good girls

Mercury, the god of cozenage (as the poets term him), ducks with the sun like a dog with a mallard and follows his train like an apple-squire, but so muffled in his cloak and so hooded in his knavery that a man can hardly find him, for all the candle is so near him. He shall reign in fairs and markets more than in the sky, in tradesmen's shops more than in his orb, in the minds of fetching companions more than in his sphere. Buying and selling will be as good as a pair of stilts for him to walk his stations on, and chopping and changing better than a brace of arms to hold him up.

Mercury

Cutpurses pray for him

Venus is likely to be retrograde, falling backward under the earth after sunset: somewhat short-heeled (an ordinary fault in a hackney), I fear me she will prove combust with some of the rest after once or twice conjunction.

Venus

Burnt as many of her train are

Sol sits in the midst like a diamond in a ring or a centre in a circle, that all the other dim-sighted stars are the lighter for him. His nature can hardly be imitated, 'tis so difficult to be impartially liberal. He is likely to enlighten more eyes than understandings and to heat more bodies with warmth than minds with zeal, yet he that gazeth on him too much may hap be purblind and he that pisseth against him may be counted a fool for his labour.

Sol

I believe it

Zeal is not so hot

Mars will take horse at the armourer's shop and never leave riding till he fall in the amorous lap (Venus and he sympathize so well together). His chiefest news is a common guest with us, that domestical sedition will be no foreigner.

Mars

Soldiers are whoremasters

1135 **regiment** regulation, government
1146 **sidereal** of the stars
1151 **Avernus** sulphurous lake in Italy, regarded as the entrance to hell
1152 **lotus** leaf of narcotic properties described in Homer, *Odyssey*, IX
1162 **Our Lady day** 25 March, the feast of the Annunciation of the Virgin Mary
1163 **trussed** tied up
1165 **Aldersgate** leading to the north gate of the City
1170 **pie-crust** popular joke about books being torn up and used to line pastry dishes
1174 **vents** pours from
1175 **score** slate recording consumption of drink on credit
1181 **infatuate** reduce to foolishness
1184 **cozenage** trickery
1186–7 **apple-squire** pimp
1192 **fetching companions** tricksters
1200 **combust** burnt up, as it were, by the sun
1201 **conjunction** proximity of the planets; pun on sexual intercourse
1209 **purblind** short-sighted, partially blind

Jupiter

A moral

Jupiter tells me his like for ambition will easily be found, but not a compare for celestial regiment. Those that will love as he did will not be so kind to their loves as he was. Jupiter bore Europa on his shoulders to show that our governors should sustain Europe's kingdoms. Jupiter himself was once sufficient to bear Europa on his shoulders: God grant that all our Jupiters be able to bear up Europe against her strong enemy, the Turk.

Saturn

Let such repair to Moll Cut-purse

A tribus ad centum

More fools they

No matter

Saturn, the father of melancholy, is like to domineer in the minds of those that have lost purse and money, that have made an ill match and could find in their hearts to hang themselves. In maids likewise that are tympanized before their time and in boys that are sullen. In those that have lost at lotteries and in some that watch out their money. In poets when they are scurvily rewarded or paid, and in players when for their bad acts they are scurvily hissed.

Predictions for this year

1. More blazing stars will be on the morrow after Simon and Jude's day next in Cheapside than were seen at the conquest of Julius at Rome.

2. More Charles's Wains in London highway than in the high down of heaven.

3. More planets among scholars' opinions than fixed stars.

4. More quaking agues in cold complexions than in the earth.

5. More shall dine with Duke Humphrey than sup with the man i'th' moon.

6. More battles fought in the fields than in the clouds.

7. More satin and velvet will be taken up upon trust and 'God damn me's' than shall be paid for in seven years after.

8. More boxes on the ear shall be given at Billingsgate with a good hand and a heart than shall willingly be taken.

9. It is to be feared that divers noblemen will run the city quite through and through, being drawn so to do by the devilish, headstrong whurry of their coach-horses.

10. More stinking breaths will be begotten by tobacco this year than children.

11. If the singing men of the chapel of Paul's and of Windsor meet this year together in any one of the court cellars, I set it down infallibly as fate some hogshead or other must that day be knocked soundly.

12. More plucking of men by the cloak and elbows in Birchin Lane than clapping men o' the shoulder at the Counter gates.

Some wise Justice of the Peace, that sits not upon the bench for nothing, avert these ills and clap up these threating mischiefs in the close prison of obscurity by the vociferous doom of his inexorable *mittimus*.

Rules for health and profit

Purging

Purge when you come from a gluttonous feast within some hour after the cramming of your guts, but if your body be foul, the joiners of Southwark can tell you how you may have the best stools.

Blood-letting

Let blood when you have a pig to be killed and long to see it come in piping hot.

Libbing

Lib or geld cattle when you see them begin to be too stone-hearted.

Vomits

Evacuate by vomit when The Sun in New Fish Street draws excellent French wines that leap up in your face.

Timber

Fell timber and wood when you are to build or want a good fire.

Corn

Reap corn never till 'tis ripe, and rather than want money, away with it to market as fast as ye can.

Hair

Cut hair if it be too long or that the head is lousy, or when you are to go before a shaving justice lest he cut it for you.

The quarters of the year

WINTER

Winter a mess of mustard

The winter this year will be as like a mess of mustard as may be: cold and moist, of a phlegmatic complexion, only hot in the nose by virtue of the frost-nip, but the best is an you clap a piece of bread to your snout you shall find present remedy.

Diseases incident to this quarter

Winter diseases

Are hunger (a sore disease and very dangerous to the maw). Laziness with her three daughters,

1220 **Europa** princess raped by Jupiter in the form of a bull
1227.n ***Moll Cutpurse*** notorious woman thief, dramatized in *Roaring Girl*
1230 **tympanized** swollen; i.e. pregnant
1231.n ***A tribus ad centum*** from three to a hundred (Latin)
1238 **Simon and Jude's day** 28 October
1239 **conquest of Julius** Caesar's assassination
1246 **dine with Duke Humphrey** The supposed tomb of Humphey, Duke of Gloucester, in St Paul's Cathedral was a rendezvous during the dinner hour for gallants and others trying to escape arrest for debt.
1254 **Billingsgate** fish market east of London Bridge, formerly London's principal dock
1265 **hogshead** large cask for storing drink
1268 **Birchin Lane** otherwise Birchovers Lane, off Lombard Street in the City; haunt of second-hand clothes dealers.
1269 **Counter gates** see note to l. 301–2
1274 ***mittimus*** warrant for arrest
1279 **Southwark** on the south side of the river; theatre land
1283 **Lib** castrate
1285–6 **The Sun in New Fish Street** tavern mentioned by Weatherwise in *No Wit*; New Fish Street, off Eastcheap in the City, was also known as Bridge Street
1294–5 **shaving justice** hanging judge
1298 **mess** dish

1. Crouching in the chimney corner, 2. Lying a bed, 3. Kibed heels.

SPRING

Spring a piece of powdered beef

The spring is like a piece of powdered beef that is new skipped out of purgatory: of nature hot and moist (paralleled to the sanguine complexion), I mean when 'tis but slenderly boiled so that the blood may flash through the crashers (this were enough now to make a good stomach bark) or else the simile holds not. And surely there will be very good agreement betwixt powdered beef and the spring, that falling so justly in Lent. Nay, Taurus himself (the sign where the sun dwells in the height of the spring) shall domineer in this quarter as lively as in a butcher's shop.

Diseases incident to this quarter

Spring diseases

Are crawling things, being lobsters, wriggling eels and other fish to weak and watery stomachs, and fasting days to good stomachs.

SUMMER

Summer a marrow-bone

Summer will be like the beef's marrow-bone (sweet and sweaty), smacking of the taste of the doublet collar. Of a fretting complexion being called summer, *quasi* 'sun-more', because the sun is more powerful then than at other seasons.

Diseases incident to this quarter

Summer diseases

Diseases that now land are dry throats and wet backs. For the first, the first part of Cancer (the sign which Sol sets foot in at the beginning of this quarter) is very sovereign, but the latter must be beholden to the launderer. Choleric humours will rage now in a man's body more than in his picture, and a cross word may chance to cost many a servant a cracked crown, which though it will not be taken at the goldsmith's, yet must it be taken to the surgeon's.

AUTUMN, *or Foli-lapse (fall of the leaf)*

Fall of the leaf the pewter dish

The harvest quarter is like in my judgement (that I may go no farther than my mess of meat) to the pewter dish it is put in (according to his natural operation cold and dry), as opposite to the flesh that lies in it as Cato and Catiline.

Diseases

Autumnian diseases

a H

b Griping

That invest themselves into men's bodies are gluttonous surfeits, uphoarding of corn, raising of rents and arresting of debtors, the eighth letter[a] in men's joints, the old wives' vice[b] in young folk's bellies.

And thus have I anatomized the whole body of the year and read a lecture upon the four quarters, with what particular diseases hang upon every quarter, but the body of the year being great, gross and subject to much corruption, his breath striking all sorts of people (as being infectious) poisons them in general. And these are other diseases which I find will be reigning.

General diseases to reign this year

More hospitals must be built if this world hold

Many young wenches will be subject to the falling sickness, cramps with pitiless convulsion will hold fast the strings of misers' purses, giddiness and staggers threaten draymen, porters, tapsters, carmen, and shoemakers upon Mondays. Swellings both in men and women, and some women greatly vexed with pushes, but every prison horribly tormented with scabs. All the fiddlers that play upon wind instruments shall in cold, nipping mornings have fistulas in their fingers. The toothache will vex young children at first breeding of them, and young people that are to pluck teeth out will be ready to run mad. Comfit-makers' wives shall cry out to have a hollow tooth stopped, and waiting gentlewomen never lie still till it be drawn. Some carbuncles will be found among goldsmiths, but they not very hotly reigning.

Fistula a pipe

Inundations and most strange overflowings of waters

Never did the stars stuff an almanac with more prodigious births of nature than this year is to bring forth. Sins of men grow thicker than the hair-bushes on the head, and having filled bodies (as by the former hospital bed roll appears) with maladies, mark how the very element of water (as if heaven had drunk up a second deluge to drown all) spreads abroad his dankish and showery wings.

Widows drowned in tears

For widows that have buried 5 or 6 husbands before are likely this year at the burial of the last to weep out so much water as may serve to wash another wedding smock, but that joy hath dried up both the conduits of their eyes.

Rich heirs not an eye to see with

So will rich heirs and executors wear mourning garments and have onions in one hand, but branches of heartsease in the other.

These waters do less hurt than the Thames doth at Billingsgate in men's cellars

The Lord Mayor's cauldrons, brass pots, kettles, chafers, skillets etc. will have their waters and broths flow up so high in his kitchen chimney, till they gallop so fast that they shall (in spite of all scummers) run over, whilst all the fat runs

1307 **Kibed** chapped or chilblained
1313 **flash through the crashers** squirt through the teeth
1327 **doublet** close-fitting body-garment
1347 **Cato and Catiline** See note to l. 630. Catiline, ?108–62 BC, organized an unsuccessful conspiracy to seize power in Rome.
1351.n *H* ache (pun)
1366 **draymen** brewers' drivers
tapsters barmen
1367 **carmen** carters, carriers
1369 **pushes** pimples, boils
1372 **fistulas** long, pipe-like ulcers
1375 **Comfit-makers** makers of sweets
1378 **carbuncles** inflammations similar to boils
1397 **heartsease** the pansy
1399 **chafers** cooking vessels
skillets three-footed saucepans
1402 **scummers** shallow ladles for removing scum

into the fire. Hot waters threaten so to overflow the stomachs of frozen-blooded bawds and dried up panderesses till they lie drowned, being dead drunk, that roaring boys shall take their hackney mares out of the stable, put them into coaches and ride them to Ware for nothing but their provender.

Terrible doings at Ware

Romney Marsh, by all signs and tokens, will meet with such an inundation of waters this winter that, the summer following, oxen shall go up to the knees and sheep up to the bellies in grass—a fatal manger to fatten fools at, for they feed themselves plump, and no sooner fed full but they go to the pot.

What beasts are oxen to do this

If all the jailers in and about London should this year shake off the fetters of mortality, the learned astrologians are of opinion that all the cellars and tap-houses of prisons would be drowned in strong beer and ale, which from the eyes of barrels should gush out for extreme sorrow.

This will be a woeful day

Of a dearth

Are there more horrors yet? Yes, yes, every mischief hath his twin, and no calamity was ever born alone. What can follow diseases but inundations of waters, which are tears? And after deep floods dearth must of consequence play the servingman.

Wenches and mischiefs are ever breeding

Infinite numbers, therefore, of sheep, calves, and oxen shall this year die so that people will be in danger to be better fed than taught. The blood of these innocents will dye red a shambles, and most merciless cutting of throats shall there be in Eastcheap. A thousand lambs shall be carried to the stocks and three times that number lose their lives at Smithfield Bars, some of them in that butcherous massacre being driven up into Whitecross Street.

Tragedies at none of the playhouses

Our constables carry geese thither

Beef will be sold so dear that a hundred pound will not be taken in Cheapside for a stone, nor in any other market 19*s.* 6*d.* be taken for a pound. Against Simon and Jude's day such a dearth and death of poultry that all the cooks in London shall sit up day and night to make coffins to bury them in.

What will the price be, with a mess of mustard too

Guildhall smokes for this

Bread (by the scarcity of true weights) will be so little this year that many a baker will rather stand on the pillory and have his batch marked with O (a goose eye, the memento of a pillory) than to give every loaf his just bigness.

Pillories. Baker, your hole for nine pence

Pheasant, partridge and quails will be very dainty this year, but woodcocks shall fly up and down the city.

Stultorum plena sunt omnia

A brief and merry prognostication, presaging good fortunes to a set of fundamental trades

The string of sorrow is now tuned to a merry note. Diseases, drownings, dearths and other dreary tragedians, get you from the stage, and now let a company of jovial citizens have a fit of mirth to make them laugh a little.

Mercers

You that fold up angels' hues and attire your walls with Indian coats, never link your souls to your shins, nor look as desperate as a piece of rash for the matter. For this year shall old plain lads that never went farther than the leatherseller for their habits mount to your shops, wrap themselves in your royal weeds and scorn to dine thrice in a suit. Old Euclioes and old Corydons shall persuade Chremes, and all three swear it in silk and sweat it in satin.

Brave doings for mercers

The world in a new coat

Bespeak new shop books in Papernoster Row, inquire for them of a one hundred quire, make a new counter on the other side, for such a cluster of dash-thrifts and scatter-goods are coming up out of all shires that your shops will swarm again. I could tell you (were it not needless) what a volume of velvet ladies' trains will devour, and of which piles, and what a bundle of silk of Seres will be trussed up in gentlemen's wardrobes.

But not paid for

Long summers will discard the draper, when every tender soul must have a stuff gown, for cloth is too stubborn. Punks are now no more regarded than withered pinks, unless the head wears a saffroned chaperon and the back a loose gown of light-coloured silk. Not so much as Madam Fill-the-pot (mine hostess) but must have a changeable

All Westminster can witness this

1405 **panderesses** bawds, procuresses
1407 **mares** prostitutes
1408 **Ware** in Hertfordshire; famous for the Great Bed of Ware
1409 **Romney Marsh** in Kent
1433 **Eastcheap** location of the butchers' shops
1435 **Smithfield Bars** wooden barrier marking the western boundary of the City; site of the main cattle market
1437 **Whitecross Street** running north of the City from Cripplegate to Old Street
1439 **stone** a measure of weight, usually equal to fourteen pounds
1440 **19*s.* 6*d.*** nineteen shillings and sixpence; six pence short of a pound in old money
1443 **coffins** pastry cases
1444.n ***Guildhall*** built *c.*1440 in what is now called Gresham Street; seat of civic government for the City of London
1447 **O** brand to indicate short measure; also suggesting a bruised eye
1451 **woodcocks** simpletons, dupes
1452.n ***Stultorum . . . omnia*** the world is full of fools (Latin)
1460 ***Mercers*** dealers in fabrics, the premier city livery company; the other companies appear in order of seniority
1463 **rash** a smooth textile fabric made of silk or worsted
1468 **Euclioes** referring to the miser in Plautus, *Aulularia*
Corydons Corydon was a generic proper name for a shepherd in classical pastoral
1469 **Chremes** an old miser in several plays of Terence
1471 **Papernoster Row** i.e. Paternoster Row, by St Paul's; home of the printers and booksellers
1472 **quire** a gathering of leaves in a book
1478 **Seres** name of a people anciently inhabiting some part of Eastern Asia, probably China, whose country was believed to be the original home of silk
1481 **stuff gown** gown made of textile fabric

silk forepart, and every country lass a taffeta apron, for linen is wear for milkmaids, perpetuana is for pedants and attorneys' clerks, and durance would be thought an excellent wear in some virgins' petticoats. Every plain Ploddall will have a velvet neck-piece, and every old bawd will have her heels guarded with sparks of satin. Every fool will clothe himself with rash in all his actions, and every fantastical ass will be in a fustian fume at this my prognostication, but *odi profanum vulgus*.

Grocers

Grocers

Never look as pale as your sugarloaves, you cinnamonian gingibers, for that your spices groan in their bags like a pig in a wallet, I can tell you there are ten thousand sour countenances that hope all to be sweetened by the grocer. Nay, all the scolds' tongues in the country that were wont to rail so bitterly must be bathed (as it is decreed by the authority of their husbands) in the oil of your ware, that is, in the syrup of sugar. For your hotter spices, why, they'll fly quickly; abundance of choleric complexions will never be without hot mouths, and you yourselves know that everybody will take pepper in the nose before he hath a casket to put it in. All the children in the world (if they be like me) will have a sweet tooth in their head, the first that grows out of their gums. Yea, and your own prentices will jerk a clod of currants currently down their throats, and it may be, pocket up an injury as big as a pound of sugar to welcome a friend in a tavern.

Grocery ware good physic for scolds

Old folks shall take my lady's part
that often use this speech:
I love the grocer next my heart,
the skinner next my breech.

Every old-trot will wrap up a race to heat her cold stomach.

The gentle nurse to still her baby's cry
Will hasten to your shops, your plums to buy.

Not so much as the cobbler but he shall have a plum pie as black as his wax he slimes his thread with, so well stuffed that the grocer shall quick-smother the butcher, and weak, waterish stomachs (as tender as basin custards) shall not break a piece of flesh without Spanish trappings.

Christmas comes but once a year

Boon companions shall purse up a nutmeg to muster with a black-pot and a toast, and he that will drink a cup of mulled sack must needs lay up a crust of ginger. Raisins will be much asked for, especially in an action of injury, and he that hath none of the moon must come to you for some of the sun. Your starch will be in great request for stiffening, and your blue will keep a band clean a whole seven-night. If you please, I can help you to those will take your tobacco freely, and rather than fail, our scullion hath got such a use he cannot make clean a pair of boots without it; tobacco makes him spit, and this is the reason why the shoe-clouts look so pale in respect of the inside of a tobacco-pipe: it fears a drowning.

I believe you

Tobacco keeps boots clean

Drapers

Now you, Master Drapers, that harbour the minds as well as the mantles of sheep, droop your fronts like a piece of well basted cloth, for gentlemen shall put more cloth in their hose now than ever they did, and tailors ask more lining than ever they had. You shall not need to fear the second birth of those French gascoignes, nor the base retire of bases, when a cloak or horseman's coat is more comely. Good husbands will have a cloth gown to sit by the fire in and whip off a measure of ale, and all our wives that smell of housewifery must have their winter weeds from the draper. An ordinary cloth shall lose the nap within a month after it kissed the back, and a good shower of rain shall wash off the wool of a new cloak. White frieze will turn the warm fashion because 'twill say well against the cold wind, and frizado the country ministers will buy up to make them cassocks because 'tis warm and comely. Your yard is like to be as short as ever it was, and you shall have many days as dark as twilight. But the main is this: there is a lean spindle-shank that looks as if he had eat never a bit of meat since the creation will speak to you for a thousand black; he will help you to sell them and you need not see him, Monsieur *Mors*, Domine Death, that peeps over

Tailors have a hell for that purpose

Death a friend to drapers

1487 **forepart** covering for the breast or stomacher
taffeta a kind of silk fabric
1488 **perpetuana** hard-wearing woollen fabric
1489 **durance** stout, durable cloth
1491 **Ploddall** plodder
1493 **guarded** ornamented, trimmed
1495 **fustian** coarse cloth
1496 ***odi profanum vulgus*** I hate the common crowd (Latin); Horace, *Odes*, III.i.1
1499 **cinnamonian** referring to the spice (coinage)
gingibers gingers
1500 **wallet** sack
1514 **jerk** throw suddenly
1522 **old-trot** old woman
race root of ginger
1533 **black-pot** a beer-mug
1535 **Raisins** reasons (pun)
1537–8 **moon . . . sun** silver and gold coins, see l. 1621
1539 **blue** blue pigment used for laundering whites
1545 **shoe-clouts** shoe cloths
1550 **basted** stitched
1552.n ***hell*** hole in the floor of the shop for the tailor's scraps and cuttings
1554 **gascoignes** or gaskins; a kind of breech or hose (also a native of Gascony in France, notorious for braggarts)
1555 **bases** a brocaded skirt appended to the doublet
1560 **nap** the pile of threads or fibres on a fabric
1563–4 **frieze . . . frizado** a kind of coarse woollen cloth and its finer version
1566 **cassocks** long cloaks worn by clergymen
1569 **spindle-shank** a person with long, thin legs

the merchant's shoulder whilst he casts up his gains and sums up his hundreds. He has pinched a number of them by the arms and has given some a pluck by the shoulders. He has set some old ones in Charon's boat with one foot, and another in their beds, but when he wasteth they must all attend him. It is a merry world with you when many mourn, and the more wet eyes the more dry clothes.

Some men's misery is other's mirth

Fishmongers

Fishmongers

I promise to you, you soldiers under happy herring, that there shall be great store of fishmongers this year. For all the butcher curseth our fasting days, yet shall your gettings be good, and if he grudge that you should be permitted to sell all the year, and his shop shut up in Quadragesima, you shall tell him that Lent is the fishmonger's harvest, though it be the butcher's spring. You need not fear the defect of water, for a cold morn shall wring it out of your nose and you take it not off with your sleeve. A codshead will be an ordinary dish, or a dish at an ordinary, and a red sprat a good breakfast for a prentice. Stockfish and onions will be a dish for Dutchmen, and a side of ling will make a double brace of servingmen's beards wag. The kindreds of Rufus that frequent the grape will metamorphose their noses into rochet, and he that has no facing may feed upon his cousin greenfish. Every maid will be in love with fish, and old men will make much of hearing. In fine, the fishmonger shall be more beholden to one recusant than all the puritans in a city.

Codsheads are picking meat all the year long

Goldsmiths

Goldsmiths

Goods ill got worse spent

Proface, you goldsmiths, harken to my news, and I'll make your hearts jog like a quicksilver jelly with laughing. This year shall great minerals of gold and silver burst out of misers' coffers, and their heirs shall play their pelf away at span-counter. What though the golden age be worn out, yet the golden art shall flourish still, and though no mines of the earth appear to us, yet earthly minds will be plenty. Every Jack will have a jewel in his ear that he may defy the pillory with the better grace, and many elder brothers shall study alchemy to concoct the gold their friends left them. Jolly travellers, hot-shots that mean to breathe in beyond-sea air, shall come to you to metamorphose their moon into your sun, their shillings into sovereigns, to clap them close in their coffers and so geld England of her gold, and posters to fairs shall court ducats to beguile thieves and lessen their carriage.

Silver into gold, good alchemy

On St George's day you may put out a thousand chains to grass on men's shoulders, and you know what the citizens will give for one to welcome his majesty to London.

A blue coat without a cullizan will be like haberdine without mustard. Every kitchen-maid will have a marriage ring as an emblem of her good man's love, and the youths of the parish will offer gold at a bridal, the metal's purity being a signet of the bride's virginity.

Negligent servants will crack their masters' plate lest it last too long, and a little fall will make a salt look like Grantham steeple with his cap to the alehouse.

Fine wives will have a goldsmith's shop on their livery cupboards though their husbands stand up to the chin in the mercer's rolls, and five thousand will have silver in the mouth when they have none in the purse.

Wives' pride undo husbands

Gallant ladies will have silver stools for fear of pollution, and every malkin will have a silver bodkin to rouse a bird in the hair-bush.

Every busy wooer will present a costly necklace to his lovely joy, and not a pin that came not through your fingers. Gossips at christ'nings shall help you away with many spoons, and New Year's gifts (to leave out bribes) are able to make you rich. There shall be more gilding now than honest dealing, and gentlemen's spurs shall speak false Latin: they shall jingle as if they were all silver to the heel when they are lead at the heart.

Many church doors shall be opened with silver keys lest the locks be thought baser than the bell metal, and that which you thought not of, most men might climb the ladder of promotion by silver steps. And after all this 'twill be good fishing with a silver hook.

Silver keys open any doors

1574 **casts** counts
1578 **Charon's** Charon: ferryman who brought the dead across the Styx to the underworld
1589 **Quadragesima** the forty days of Lent
1595 **ordinary** set meal at a tavern
sprat a small sea-fish
1599 **Rufus** a ruddy-faced person
1600 **rochet** the red gurnard (fish)
1601 **facing** complexion
greenfish fresh, unsalted fish, esp. cod
1603 **hearing** herring (pun)
1604 **recusant** somebody who refused to attend services of the Church of England, esp. a Roman Catholic
1607 ***Proface*** an expression of welcome or good wishes at a meal (from Latin)
1611 **pelf** money
1611–12 **span-counter** boys' game, similar to marbles
1618 **concoct** to bring metals to their perfect state by heat (alchemical term)
1624 **posters** messengers, carriers of news
1626 **St George's day** 23 April
1630 **cullizan** see l. 516
1631 **haberdine** salt cod
1638 **salt** salt-cellar
Grantham steeple in Lincolnshire
1641 **livery cupboards** sideboards from which food is served
1642 **rolls** account books
1646 **malkin** servant, lower-class woman

Skinners

Skinners

Old wives, you pelleters, that are as gripple of the world as a man shot overboard of a rope, shall line their coats with your softest furs lest they forfeit their voice to the cold. Your badge shall be worn in ruddy braggadocian's countenance, for modesty shall hang down the head like a twig with a pompion at it. Our citizens must have their destructions from the skinners or else they'll confound their order, and inaulated punies must have a silver hair for their capes or else Littleton will not know them.

Pedlars good benefactors to skinners

The trotting pedlar shall summon up to your shops an army of cony skins, and pick them out of the country kitchens for points, pins, and all to enrich you. Every simpering Sib and coy Katherine shall round a muff before her as a case for her nose, or a den for her fingers in frost-biting weather, and every oyster-wife's throat shall be furred with marry-muffs when cold complexions will be content to warm their fingers in a meaner fire. Your trade must needs hold, for every tipsitaptrapolonian will maintain an excellent good facing. But you must not, when you espy a hard-favoured gentleman with a bugled cheek or a chin like a visor, pace down your row with cry, 'Will you buy a good face, will you buy a good face, sir?' 'Twill make him hereafter go five miles about rather than grace your street any more with that face he has, as bad as 'tis.

Tailors

Tailors

Tailors pray for new fashions

I presage, you limb-trimmers, a shipful of new fashions shall sail into our coasts out of the Isle Lunatic, and you dapper lances shall make at the footman's armour so valiantly that they shall pierce it in a hundred places. Your snippers never looked so bright as they are this year, and your goose shall be counted the valiantest lad in a country, for that he can make so many drapers shrink. I foretell a great rot amongst the present fashions: they shall change as fast as the moon for her heart; for mine own part, I never loved them since my horse died of them. 'Tis like to prove a very windy spring, and by that means many Venetians will be blasted out behind; everyone rub one till the world is out at the elbows, and they that use wrestling must needs to the tailor. Every schoolboy that plays the truant should not want a jerkin, and he that learns more knavery than virtue should have a breech or two. An ocean of indentures will not serve you for measures, and as much thread as would compass the world will be stitched up in a twelve month.

Birchen breeches a good wearing for boys

Rich men will be ashamed hereafter to transport their hose so often to the botchers for fear they purchase creepers. Neither will there be any more such old miserrimoes that when they hear one knock at the door will clap on their gown (their sloven's cover) lest their patched rags appear to the world; I know you shall take measure of them for a new suit first. Finally, a long waist will be much in request if you can frame it, because a short body is obnoxious to a stinking breath, the mouth and tail are too nigh.

Haberdashers

Haberdashers

Never indenture your foreheads so ruefully, you bonny bonnetonists, for you see the fashion of steeple crowns (a sore waster of felts) is already past. There is an ambassador making for England now so fraught with quaint humoralities and attireable sesquipedalities that he will set all the noses of your now worn bonnets utterly out of joint. But, do you hear me, never doubt of the fashion of your blocks for all this; rather, when a swad-swained gentleman shall amount into your cranny-lighted shops and call for a hat of the courtier's block, exonerate your press, out with a Spaniardo and clap it on his coxcomb, and swear an oath as long as your tongue, 'This hat is excellently blocked, sir'.

The courtier's block

Fools' caps

For the state of your trade, your fools' caps will this summer fly all from your stalls that stuck

1664 **pelleters** dealers in hides and furs
gripple gripping, tenacious
1668 **braggadocian's** boaster, swaggerer
1670 **pompion** pumpkin
1672 **inaulated** admitted to halls; here, the inns of court (coinage, from Latin *aulum*)
punies novices, freshmen
1673 **Littleton** possibly Sir Thomas Littleton (1402–81), author of the standard work on English property law. However, the phrase 'or else Littleton will not know them' seems to suggest a superior person who will not acknowledge the Inns of Court freshmen if they are not properly dressed. Edward, later Lord Littleton was an Inner Temple lawyer who was called to the bar in 1617; he became a Bencher of his Inn, an MP and Chief Justice for North Wales. Middleton wrote *Heroes* for the Inner Temple in 1619.
1676 **cony** rabbit
1677 **points** fasteners for tying doublet to hose; often used as a type of something of small value
1682 **marry-muffs** cheap textile fabrics
1687 **bugled** covered in blackheads
1688 **visor** mask
1695–6 **Isle Lunatic** an imaginary place
1696 **lances** lancers, i.e. users of needles
1698 **snippers** scissors
1711 **jerkin** pun on 'jerking', i.e. whipping
1711.n ***Birchen breeches*** the birch was used for whipping
1717 **botchers** menders
1718 **creepers** lice
1719 **miserrimoes** miserable types (coinage)
1729 **bonnetonists** makers of headgear (coinage)
1730 **steeple crowns** hats with very tall crowns
1732 **humoralities** extravagant fashions (coinage)
1733 **sesquipedalities** literally things a foot and a half in length; here, extravagant headgear
1736 **blocks** moulds for hats
1737 **swad-swained** coinage made up from 'swad' and 'swain', both meaning country bumpkin
amount climb up (i.e. to the attic)
1739 **exonerate** unload
1740 **Spaniardo** a style of hat
coxcomb jocularly, the head

there this seven year, to keep the wit of addle pates from freezing, and many old boys shall drink till their caps crack. White hats will take slur quickly, for their colour is labecutable, and pure black shall moulder to dirt, for that was burnt on the block.

Citizens' wives shall shift their taffetas often, for that the low portals knap them out at the crown, and all my black sisters must get them broader brims, for these will not hide their forehead faults. A shower of rain shall put a pasteboard out of square and order, and a little drop will cockle your silk as rising for revenge if it come from the gutter. Five hundred virgins shall be married in their velvet pot-lids, and but ten millions of blowzes in their felt stool-pans. O, how many brides will measure their brain on their wedding eve in your shop, and he that roofs not his wife under one of your shelters on his marriage day shall be trussed up in wool and sent into Burgundy.

Brides

Prentices shall wear no more caps, for it makes them look like costards, and he that fronts it with straw must be content also to lie in straw. But the best friend to men of your mould will be mannerly courtesy and obsequious compliments. Two friends shall not pass in the street without an interchange of vails, nor old men see Cardinal candle cast his eye upon the table without reverence to his charity. As for those of your name that are conversant with small wares, they shall fly out of your shops like foul words out of a thankless person.

Prentices' flat-caps

Cardinal candle

Salters

Salters

And as for you, Master Salters, you'll flourish this year, for white herrings, a hot summer, and fresh beef shall stand as stiffly under you as any three legs under the bright trifoot in the world. All the brewers have sworn by the pearly cognizance that Barleycorn gives his pages in their faces that there shall be no more broom foisted into the vat instead of your hops. Fatal cords will be busily set on work and hempen caudles will be common physic for desperate persons. Mice and rats will gnaw the goodwife's yarn, and hands and feet shall rub out her linen, so that need will make her trot to your worships for flax and tow, and thrift will make her set her maid to the distaff. Musicians will be counted scrapers and crowders if they buy not some of your rosin, and had not our sow cast her farrow it should have gone hard, but we would have had some of it to unhair a fat pig. Ships will leak and they be not lined with your pitch. In a word, the wheel and the brewer, the shepherd and the mariner, will make you now or never.

White herring, hot summer, fresh beef—the three pillars of salters

Ironmongers

Iron-mongers

You that draw your line from the loins of Ironside, you shall have harder doings than ever you had since your hammer told his master what his trade was, and I think a hard world is that which you desire. Such an iron age is now on foot, and such a crew of copper consciences, that to sheath a blade in a man's corpse will be counted voluntary valour, and a hard heart will be thought a good spirit, steel to the back. Opulent, rich clunch-fists shall lie in as much fear of the pilferer as a buck of the wood-knife, and to prevent the purloiner they shall gird the ribs of their chests with girths of your iron, and lace the belly of their money-tombs with laces of your weaving.

A hard world with iron-mongers

He's mad that lays up gold of Ophir
In a wooden linèd coffer.

Boys are as like to break glass windows as ever they were, and that will make men speak for your wires; and thieves are as like to break prison, and that will make the jailer sue for your iron to bolt them. A warming pan will be counted excellent physic for a featherbed, and an iron cradle very good authority to hold up sea-coal. My gossip Gooseling must needs have a fair pair of andirons to garnish her hall against her belly's abed, and all the wives in the parish shall beg as much of their sweethearts at midnight. All the hobbinolls of the country shall arm their high shoes with your metal to encounter with London stones, and there shall be so much scratching between Susan Scold-out and Tib Tattle-basket that I am persuaded the single combat will make you sell all your nails.

Vintners

Vintners

A cask full of comfort for you, crimson-nosed vintners, that quilt your guests' apparel with the best bombast. You shall not need to take much care for those fellows that war so long under the colours of sack and sugar in the rearward, that

1747 **slur** thin mud
1748 **labecutable** easily stained (coinage, from Latin *labes*)
1755 **cockle** cause to pucker or crease
1758 **blowzes** beggar women
1759 **stool-pans** chamber-pots
1765 **costards** large apples
1770 **vails** gratuities; pun on veils and *vales*, i.e. greetings (Latin)
1781 **pearly cognizance** the sign of pearl barley
1783 **broom** a yellow shrub
1785–6 **caudles . . . desperate persons** ropes for suicides to hang themselves with
1789 **tow** the fibre of flax, hemp or jute prepared for spinning
1790 **distaff** a staff used for spinning wool or flax
1791 **crowders** fiddlers who play to a crowd
1792 **rosin** distillation of oil of turpentine used to lubricate the strings of a fiddler's bow
1799 **Ironside** nickname of Edmund II of England
1807 **clunch-fists** misers
1813 ***Ophir*** place mentioned in the Old Testament where fine gold was obtained; see Job 22:24
1822 **andirons** ornamental iron supports positioned on either side of the fireplace
1825 **hobbinolls** rustics who wear hobnail boots
1834 **bombast** stuffing; here, wine

now they are like to make an uproar and cast up their accounts after the shot. Never fear any foul play in this case, for when Sergeant Grape has arrested any of these Sim Suck-spigots of an action of liberty, then shall Gaffer Giddy hale them to prison, where *Somnus* the jailer shall shackle their hams till the fume of Bacchus his anger be over, and then you may save their credits and your own with a grace. This year, all the Catos in the world that never used wine but physic shall take it down at their diet as lively as Tricongius, and all our abstemious youths at the sight of *Qui medice vivit misere vivit* shall turn pure swash and visit your taverns at midnight. Many physicians shall set it down as an aphorism that a cup of wine (as the fellow said of butter) shall be good for anything: old wine excellent for old men. It shall inspire more wit into the scholar's brain than all the muses can from their fountains, make a lawyer's tongue resound like a mill-clack, and enrich a courtier with a nest of compliments. It shall make a clown step into the fashion, a beggar take the wall of a gentleman, and a coward go into the field with a fencing German. *Nunquam nisi potus ad arma*, never fight but when thou art foxed, shall be the soldier's motto; *arcana recludit*, wine untwines hidden mysteries, shall be the poet's posy, and a cup of hippocras shall be the best stomacher for a sweet heart. The benefit of a good stomach shall be the grape's attribute, the exiler of melancholy shall be the title of the vintner's hogshead, and the reviving of the fly-blown blood in old men shall be Lyaeus his honour. Divers friends shall meet jump at a tavern that were almost worn out of memory; then must a quart of wine play the ambassador to renew the league of friendship between them. Sack and claret are like to rise in your houses if the party's stomach be not sound, and sobriety's light shall be clean extinguished with your liquor.

Giddy, the constable

Praise of wine

Hippocras stomachers

Clothworkers

Were't not for two weathers your trade would be down, the first from the sheepfold, the last from the sun, but both shall succeed well if rot and the rain cross not my calendar and prove your bane.

Clothworkers

Two sorts of weathers uphold clothworkers

Tush, Master Furbushers, the moth will set you a-work as long as the ram shall have a warm coat, and dusty laziness shall send ware to your shops. As long as winter shall be fronted with frost, flatterers shall claw their prodigal patrons like your currying cards, and envious varlets will stick on men's coats to prick their proceedings like a burr. A cozening nip shall sheep-shear a cony of his coin, and poor men may be sure to be pressed to the quick. Many a chuff will steal a nap by the fireside, and many a crafty mate will raise wool out of a hired, bare coat.

Dyers

And for you, dyers, your colours shall be washed off this year better than ever they were; your dye shall be so slightly grounded, yet as well beloved as ever they have been, men shall be so light-minded. A good blast of wind shall blow away a sea-water green, and a forty miles journey will banish a garden violet; purple in grain shall challenge a ruby nose, and a brown blue a tobacconist's inside. Maiden's blush shall be counterfeitly worn, and gall-imbrued green shall be a colour for a malicious pine-soul. Pursuers of the aspen-quaking buck shall image the grass to resemble forestry; mourners shall count your sable hues, your ebon backs to imitate night, woe, and death, and divines your cerulean sky to put them in mind of their embassady. Every creature shall have his several colours, and not so much as the russet coats that were wont to be worn on ploughmen's backs as they came from the lamb's limbs, but they shall this year have a lick at your dye pan. In a word, sick men and dyers shall be dying all the year long.

Dyers

A true maiden's blush, a colour hard to be found

Dying all the year long

Brewers

All Royston fields, brewers, shall be barley this year, you nectar-boiling brewers, and the best part of my garden shall be hops, and all to support the user of good liquor. A thousand brace of black jacks shall duck to the malt vat like the friar to the pope, and a whole army of rosin cans shall anatomize the corpse of Barleycorn, and all to enrich the patron of good potation.

Brewers

1842 **Somnus** sleep (Latin)
1843 **Bacchus** god of wine
1845 **Catos** see l. 630
1846 **but physic** except as medicine
1847 **Tricongius** lit. 'Threebottler' (Latin *congius* was about six pints in our measure)
1848–9 ***Qui . . . vivit*** he who lives under doctor's order lives miserably
1849 **swash** swagger, swaggerer
1856 **mill-clack** the clapper of a mill
1860 **fencing German** see l. 355
1861 **foxed** drunk
1863 **posy** motto used as signature by courtly poets
1864 **hippocras** wine flavoured with spices; so called because it was filtered through a conical bag known as Hippocrates' sleeve
1869 **Lyaeus** another name for Bacchus
jump by chance
1877 **weathers** pun on wethers, i.e. castrated rams
1879 **rot** liver disease of sheep
1886 **currying cards** instruments for combing out the fibres in cloth
1888 **nip** cutpurse
cony dupe
1890 **chuff** churlish miser
1902 **Maiden's blush** a delicate pink colour
1904 **pine-soul** envious person? (coinage)
1908 **cerulean** of a deep blue colour
1909 **embassady** a combination of 'embassy' and 'embassade' (coinage)
1917 **Royston** town in Hertfordshire, ten miles south of Cambridge
1921 **black jacks** jugs for beer

Fill your barrels full with heart of oak and flower of the field, then will they untruss a hoop and lask like a squirt, so shall the maids' faucets fly from the taphole, and this will make them trot to the fountain of liquid liquor again.

Alms and ale have not one entertainment

Every market town shall be better furnished with houses for ale than for alms, and that village shall be counted a dunghill of puritans where there is never a tapstering of bene-bouse. Small beer shall be for diet-keepers, but strong twang shall prove as good as bagpudding (meat, and drink, and cloth). The best medicine for the fleas will be a cup of merry-go-down, and the only help to clap the door upon sorrow and shut him out will be a draught of March beer.

Cares are drowned in cups

The merry physician's counsel to an odd patient of his shall be the very pitch of Paracelsians' diet: the first draught will wash a man's liver, the second increase his blood, and the third satisfies his thirst. And all the world knows what a countryman's bond is:

Good wax

A pot of ale still the assurance doth hatch,
And serves for the scrivener to bind up the match.

The water in Netherland will taste of the brack, and most of those Flemings would taste of our English beer. Harvest men will be as dry as the Arabian sand, and a dozen of hay-tossers will quickly toss down a bung of moisture. Salt meat will be a great dish if it come to the board in a charger, and that will draw down liquor. Red herring will prove a prologue to a hungry fast, and that will work for the brewer. Monsieur Domingo, knight of the malt-hoop, has enacted against sippers and sparrowinchers, but those that take off their life by *quantus* shall be dubbed on a barrel head.

New dubbing

There will be one in a parish shall piss as much against the wall in a year as half his neighbours spend in three. Other of your customers shall carry as much as your horse, but those that drink in an empty cup may chance to have sore lips for their labour.

Leathersellers

Leathersellers

You that clothe your shops with cattle's coats, be not all a mort as dumb as your hides, for all our park vermin are like to fall into paste and our bucks' heads into pots to pleasure your faculty and wardrobe your shelves. A buff jerkin shall be a lordly wear and a pair of buskins a preservative against the gout. All tradesmen that occupy with the leathern apron shall sue unto you, so that your vocation may be called the forepart of most mechanicals, and many cutpurses shall nip those foreparts to make you vend your leather.

Cutpurses loving to leathersellers

Our boys in Lent shall put off and scrape to your worships for a metal to course their tops, and most of the world will turn Adam and Eve and put on mortality. The owners of our country will be new-belted against Christmas, and the plough-joggers of our town must smell of your counter at Easter. To conclude, ample indentures, large copies, and drumheads will metamorphose your skins, an you will let them.

Pewterers

Pewterers

From great and gorgeous swilling, you pewter Johns, issueth a world of leaking, and I know every man will purchase a piss-pot to prevent the colic, or else he must spout out at the window, and that may prove perilous to the urine if the descent be violent. At fairs and marts young married wives must look out for their vessels, and all the year shall Francis Truge wear your buttons' metal before him. Many a good bit shall be turned in your platters, and many a mouth shall pronounce (when the feast comes marching in the pewterers' livery) that you are the upholders of all good cheer. Basins and ewers shall revive into the fashion, as a pewter standish proves profitable for a scribe; 'twill be somewhat chargeable in the melting, but foist in the leaden lubber and it will pay your painstaking. Sea-coal fire this year shall melt a million of dishes, and the negligence of servants shall put many a pot in the pillory, for pewter shall be the softest natured gentleman, he shall sink at every blow and take thought inwardly at every knock. In sum, a pewter pot of ale with a toast in his belly will quench a man's

This is most true

1927 **lask** to become loose in the bowels; to purge
squirt an attack of diarrhoea
1933 **bene-bouse** cant term for good drink
Small beer weak beer
1934 **twang** presumably strong ale or beer; the closest definition in *OED* is something with a nasty taste
1936–7 **merry-go-down** strong ale
1939 **March beer** beer brewed in March was supposed to be the best
1941 **Paracelsians** followers of Paracelsus, the sixteenth century Swiss physician and alchemist who had challenged the doctrine of the four humours
1946 ***scrivener*** professional scribe
1951 **bung** cask
1953 **charger** large dish
1956 **malt-hoop** measure of liquor
1957 **sparrowinchers** small drinkers (coinage)
1958 ***quantus*** yardstick, rule (Latin)
dubbed knighted
1967 **all a mort** a dialect phrase used as an intensive; one of Bretnor's catchphrases
1969 **faculty** means, resources
1971 **buskins** knee-length boots
1972 **occupy** (probably a pun: to have sexual intercourse)
1978 **course** whip, drive
1980 **mortality** i.e. animal skins
1981 **plough-joggers** ploughmen
1993 **vessels** probably a sexual pun
1995 **bit** money
1999 **ewers** water jugs
2000 **standish** inkstand
2002 **foist in** introduce surreptitiously
lubber lout

thirst better than a silver tankard with nothing in it.

Barber-Surgeons

Barber-Surgeons

Bragging prizes

Neapolitan incomes

Cracked crowns beget silver crowns

You cunning cutbeards, never let your stomachs quail to suck your living out of festered sores, for *lucri bonus est odor*, silver has a sweet sound; ask Vespasian the emperor else. For your comfort a proud match at football shall send many a lame soldier to your tent, and a fiery fray in Smithfield shall bring many a bloody companion to your shop. The fencing schools will serve to keep your hand in ure, but the bragging prizes, a hundred pound to a pig's turd, will put chink into your purses. The French something shall line your squirrel skins brim-full, and stretch the strings and so thoroughly choke their throats that they shall speak no more than an oven's mouth rampired. O, the income that is Neapolitan shall bring in a hot summer to you; an it were not for tobacco, which is a preventer, I think surgeons would be the only purchasers in London. Joints shall be ill-knit, and gentles shall cut their fingers; sanguine complexions shall swarm, and letting of blood will be common. But the spider shall intercept something of you again. He shall be phlebotomist to the fly if she come in his net, and the fleas must be let blood at midsummer for God-a-mercy. Tavern quarrels shall find you Sunday fare all the Sundays in the year, and lazy ignavoes that sit still and putrify like a mud-sink shall fall into your hands for felons. And this shall attire you from Good Friday to Maundy Thursday: curst and crabbed masters shall send many a cracked crown to your cure, and the toothache shall find you beef for your house your lifetime. Young beards shall pullulate and multiply like a willow, if worm bark them not; howsoever, shaving will be good to make a down spout. The picke-devant (I presage) will be the cut, and a pair of muchatoes that will fence for the face shall be the tantara flash sea-coal. Fume shall besmudge our neatoes that they shall go to the barber's ball oftener than to church, and every nice bachelor shall entreat a lick with the barber's apron and a dash with his rosebud to smell odoriferous in his mistress's nostrils.

Armourers

Armourers

Hares in helmets

The foresaid surgeon and Vulcanian crease-fist sacrifice alike for quarrels, but *bellum, bellum*, war, war, would fit the armourer's hand better than a pair of gloves of twenty pound. Yet in pranking peace the canker and rust, taking the armourer's part, so bedent the soldier's livery that men must seek unto this ward-part for amendment, or else prepare their purse for fresh ones. But I take it I speak it to the encouragement of this brood of Mulciber, who framed a child's shield and Aeneas his armour, that within a while *arma virumque cano* will be the world's posy. Men's bodies are but of earthly mould, but their minds taste of fiery fury: a little word will kindle war, and the Spaniard's self-conceit must have its issue. It is comfort enough for you that sweat in the wardrobe of war to foretell that men shall be proud, for pride is such a manly mother that Juno-like she can beget Mars without a father. Armour of proof will be in great request at the tilt, and fearful frogs will down with their dust for good breast-plates. A helmet will be an excellent wear for him that has little wit, and a gauntlet a good guard for a tender-fingered combatant.

Bakers

Bakers

Christmas loaves

Nurses this year, you little-fisted bakers, shall crumb their infants' milk with your white bread out of all measure, and a white crust shall make no more teeth bleed to fright little ones from the love of it. Though daily delvers mumble on a brown crust all the year, yet they shall sweeten their chaps with a white loaf at Christmas, and though the vulgar shall browse on your bran as cheaper in the purse, yet most will desire your loaves like your bolters as whiter in the hand. Besides, the physician will tell you that is hard of digestion, when this will nourish out of all

2012 ***Barber-Surgeons*** Barbers and surgeons formed a united company in 1540; the barbers' surgical work was restricted to bleeding and dentistry.
2015 ***lucri ... odor*** literally, the smell of profit is good (Latin)
2016 **Vespasian** see l. 543–4
2021 **ure** operation, action
2023 **French something** sexually transmitted disease
2024 **squirrel skins** purses
2026 **rampired** fortified
2027.n **Neapolitan** i.e. syphilitic
2034 **phlebotomist** surgeon who bleeds patients
2038 **ignavoes** idlers (coinage, from Latin *ignavus*)
2041 **Maundy Thursday** the Thursday before Easter
curst bad-tempered
2045 **pullulate** sprout
2045–6 **worm bark them** figurative reference to hair loss as a symptom of sexually transmitted disease
2047 **picke-devant** short beard trimmed to a point
2048 **muchatoes** moustaches
2049 **tantara** brash, brassy (imitating the sound of a trumpet)
flash showy
2050 **sea-coal** i.e. jet-black; see l. 742.n
neatoes dapper gentlemen (coinage)
2057 **crease-fist** clench-fist? (coinage)
2060 **pranking** showily dressed
2067–8 ***arma virumque cano*** I sing of arms and men (Latin), the first words of Virgil's *Aeneid*
2075 **Juno-like** Juno was queen of the gods and wife of Jupiter
2077 **frogs** general term of abuse; or possibly a reference to Aesop's fable of King Log
2079 **gauntlet** armoured glove
2086 **delvers** diggers, labourers
mumble chew toothlessly
2089 **browse** feed
2091 **bolters** cloths used for sifting

exclamation. Poor men shall not have money enough to bargain with the meal-man, and that will make them take it of you by the penny. And those that will be wealthy shall have no skill to heat an oven, and that will set your boys awork to carry it to their doors.

White puddings

White puddings shall grate upon many a loaf, and soppets in white broth shall drown many a dozen. 'Twill be thought the traveller's antidote to let his tongue play at tennis with a crust before he drink, and as good physic as any in Galen, *stomachum concludere sicco*, to truss up the stomach with a dry bit.

A crust good physic

Shoemakers shall lose their predominant armour, of a barrel of beer to a halfpenny loaf, and tailors shall be patterns and precedents to sober men, a bushel of wheat to a tankard of beer, lest they cut their fingers when they are whittled. Lastly, bread shall be concluded the better nourisher, and beer but a puffer; bread shall show itself the honest binder, good loose-livers, when liquor shall be known but a loose fellow, and thus farewell Master Baker.

Beer a puffer. Bread a nourisher

Chandlers

Chandlers

Fine ladies that set by their scents, you lampwrights, will make such a face at the sight of a tallow-chandler as if their holiday ruff were on fire: 'Fah! What a gross light is this! In truth, Sir Timothy, it condenses the wit and stupefies the brain; pray let our flames be wax', and this will make the waxer shrug and say this gear will cotton one day. It is like to prove a very dark winter (except Lady *Luna* borrow her face), and you know it is hard borrowing of faces (though hypocrites might spare their counterfeit ones), and torches will be another star in the street. Besides, every knock at a post will dash out a rib, and then where dwells the taperer? Tailors shall spend searing candles beyond your thoughts by reason of the abundance of extravagant stuffs that shall act on their shop-stage, and virtuous virgins must have a wax candle with them to the nocturnal lectures, yea verily. But, O, the long nights that shall devour your pale-bodied blazers (you marrow-melting luminists), and the windy chinks that shall lave out the candle with the great wick. How many thieves, think you, will steal into the tallow and play prodigal with the workman's light, and how many good husbands will card it all night by the help of your faculty?

Tailors help chandlers

Puritans love virgin wax

Chandlers make ill husbands

I would not have you look as if you were grinding mustard, and took thought for the utterance. I tell you, salt fish and powdered beef will make your quern fly about like a windmill in a tempest. The butcher must sell you his tallow at a reasonable rate for fear of the rats in the winter, and the summer heat shall melt it off from his stall into the kennel, and there's for your buying. Honest men will be as scarce as none-fingered and unsophisticated tobacco, and knaves (you know) must have good store of soap to scour their shirts, or they will never be clean. Many cast volumes will fall into your employment, your doing will be so great, but forbear, I pray you, to wrap your halfpenny wares in these leaves of mine.

Honest men as scant as good tobacco

Girdlers

Girdlers

Now, you waist-circulating girdlers, you that are the best in our age for tutors and guardians, you can keep men in compass better than all the counsel of love or the authority of law can do. The time-trodden proverb will doubtless stretch himself on his startups again, *male cincti, male sancti*, ungirt, unblessed, and that will make men seek for the girdler's blessing to avoid some unfortunate curse, and those that be made *Praecincti* (as Sulla said Caesar was) shall be counted shrewd underminers of the commonwealth. Licentious and loose living will be as much abandoned as may be, and when a man is well girt he shall think himself far warmer, which will be as good as an orator to persuade men to the cincturer. Great gashimargoes shall prove wiser than geese and who are light in the middle, 'cause they wear no girdles, and shall gird in their paunches for fear they run about the house; and fine waists shall make much of a girdle to keep their bodies in fashion.

Ungirt, unblessed

Cutlers

Cutlers

Now, you cutlers, how many shavers will be sharp set, trow ye? He that claps him down at a board without a little sword in his sheath may chance to rise a-hungered, or be set upon with the gentlewoman: 'What, sir, have you never a knife, then cut my finger'. Old men shall make as much of a knife as of one of their best teeth, and your good housewife shall so love Signor Coltello she will not suffer him to be absent from her side. The highways will prove peremptory and therefore a

Signor Coltello

2100 **soppets** small pieces of bread (only citation in *OED*, 1664)
2104 **Galen** Greek physician, anatomist and physiologist, AD ?130–?200; he codified existing medical knowledge and his authority continued until the seventeenth century.
2110 **whittled** drunk
2116 **set by** set store by, value
2118 **tallow-chandler** who made his candles with animal fat rather than wax
2122–3 **this gear will cotton** this matter will go on successfully; a Bretnor catchphrase
2124 ***Luna*** the moon (Latin)
2130 **searing** burning
2134 **lectures** puritan sermons
2140 **card it** play at cards; pun on the preparation of wool for spinning
2145 **quern** hand-mill
2150 **none-fingered** unshredded?
2153 **cast volumes** old books
2163 **startups** rustic shoes
2166 ***Praecincti*** belted, girdled (Latin)
Sulla Roman general and dictator, 138–78 BC; introduced reforms to strengthen the power of the Senate
2172 **cincturer** belt-maker, girdler (coinage)
2172–3 **gashimargoes** fat people? (coinage)
2186.n **Coltello** knife (Italian)
2188 **peremptory** deadly

weapon will be a good companion, and the thief that ruins the country lad will let him ride like a free man an he but swear and discourse to him of his irons. The soldier that lies on the bare ground ready to be congealed with cold shall think his side very warm if he have the cutler by him, and he that delights in blunt metal may cut his foreman's throat with a packsaddle.

Butchers

Butchers

A hungry year, you carnal carvers, I know you shall have, for the conjunction of heat and moisture (in the kitchen of digesture) foretells no less, and he that hath no stomach to his work, or not a piece of a heart to meet a man in the field, shall have as good a stomach to his provant as a starved bristleback to his waste, or a crop-eared courser to his mill-bruised beans. Woolner (that cannon of gluttony) shall revive again, and those that lived by love and feed upon the air shall fall to their victuals and furbish their trenchers. A piece of powdered beef will make a man as strong as a cable, and a target of veal will be as good to defend a sick body from dying as a dead crow to defend our corn from the living. Pottage that will fur the ribs (an inch thick) are mere restorative, and the best fast-killer in a morning will be one of your marrow bones. Mutton will be like a ripe medlar, or a false lover rotten at the liver, but never pine at the spleen, for it smells of the blood-pot. Keep your own counsel, set a smooth face and a round face upon it, and then there is never a steward that sharks in your shambles will smell out the putrefaction. The tanners will prevent the worst and ply you with pledges aforehand for your hides, but keep not back the horns in any case, for that's ominous. Furriers and glovers will put money into your hands as warm as wool for your sheepskins, but for the love of a chitterling see you hold your beasts' entrails at a clean price and make the tripewives pay sweetly for them, or I protest in the presence of a hog's countenance I'll never feed more on them. The country farmers' wives will swap with you quickly for their calves, because they draw away their milk and mar their good markets, and the graziers will send you their big-boned beeves upon trust if you pay them largely and keep your day truly.

Woolner the great eater

Targets of veal are excellent weapons

Furriers and glovers the butcher prays for

Saddlers

Saddlers

I shall never beat it into your brains, you horse-ridge cushioners, what care men in general will take for soft saddles, lest their shrewish wives get the vantage of the proverb ('twas Socrates' speech when he was in jail) 'He loves not his wife that loves not his tail'. Coaches are like to have a downfall this year if the horses be frantic at a side of a ditch, and penny-fathers will say 'tis fond to be vexed with a brace of jades when one is sufficient to tire a man. Dirty passes shall so bespot the complexion of a velvet saddle that if your prentices were horses they would break their halters with laughing, and the dusty canker so spoil the silkman that he must be brushed till he be bald again. A voider for those fellows that will ride flat-breeched on a swain's panel, I do not think that you shall take one man (that hath but a dream of wealth) in that trick of clownery this year. Why, I tell you, every substantial webbe in a parish that hath a seat of his own in his church shall buttock a saddle and adorn his prancer with your stately trappings, and Jockie that rode on his courser (hair to hair) shall suddenly leap into his tuftaffety. Horses will be headstrong as unnurtured lobcocks and snap their bridles in pieces as fast as hops. The powerful provender shall make them swell in the belly like a sullen girl in the cheek, or a wench after toying, and that will crack girts apace. But, for conclusion, divers women shall saddle their poor husbands' backs and make plain ninny-hammers of noddies, and the Lenten-faced usurer shall bridle our prodigal spend-alls most miserably.

Jockie a gentleman now

Women saddle men

Carpenters

Carpenters

You human harbour-raisers, you are the only householders in these days of do-no-good, for were it not that you held up the house without by your faculty, it might well fall down within for want of hospitality. Well, there be abundance of rotten doors in London, and they must all fall into your

Hospitality dwells nowhere

2200 **digesture** the process of digesting
2204 **bristleback** pig (not recorded in *OED* as a noun)
2205 **courser** horse
2205.n **Woolner** Richard Woolner, of Windsor, was a notorious glutton who, after safely digesting iron, glass, and oyster shells, 'by eating a raw eel was overmastered'.
2208 **trenchers** flat pieces of wood on which food was served; plates or platters
2210 **target** shield
target joint of meat, usually lamb, consisting of neck and breast
2212 **Pottage** thick soup
2216 **medlar** fruit eaten when decayed to a soft, pulpy state
2220 **sharks** pilfers
shambles abattoir, slaughterhouse
2226 **chitterling** the smaller intestine of the pig
2228 **tripewives** women who prepared and sold offal
2240 **Socrates** Athenian philosopher, ?470–399 BC, condemned to death for impiety and the corruption of youth
2244 **penny-fathers** misers, skinflints
2251 **voider** a basket for removing rubbish, scraps of food etc.
2252 **panel** a piece of cloth placed under the saddle
2255 **webbe** weaver
2258.n **Jockie** type of a common lad
2260 **tuftaffety** tufted silk fabric
2261 **lobcocks** simpletons
2264 **toying** amorous play
2265 **girts** saddle-belt
2267 **ninny-hammers** simpletons
noddies simpletons

chimneys shortly, for we must not look for another Orpheus to build a city with his harmony; our musicians will never do the like to that Theban. I tell you, many overleaning buildings will lack a little of your help, yet some of them that bow to my Lord Mayor when he rides by their front, and lean into the streets as though they would shake him by the hand or look the farther after him, may stand as they do to teach aproned slovens agility in the knee. 'As the bed's head rises', quoth he that was wont to lay his bags there, 'our houses must stand, and as I store up my wealth I will story up my chambers'.

Two poor people of whom Ovid writes

'Away', quoth Monsieur Prodigo, 'with these base cottages of Philemon and Baucis, my generous blood cannot brook such a degenerous lodging. Down with wood, and up with my older oaks; stone is too damp, and brick is too cold.' All this tickles the carpenter. I would be loth to tell him too much of his joy, lest with his laughing he fall from his building and mar the fashion of his perpendicular. You shall not need to see the topgallant, the tiler, for he'll leave many a crack in the crown of a house for his own commodity, and that will make timber rot like a muckhill. And you know that the decay of a commonwealth is first in the state, the defect of my body first in my head, and the ruin of a house first in the roof. Finally, many things will be exceedingly out of order, and there will be much use of your line, rule and square.

Shoemakers

Shoemakers

Gentlemen put into the shoemaker's stocks

You'll laugh till you stink again, you shoemakers, to hear yourselves called eternal constables, and that (without control) you can cast the best gentleman in the land into your stocks only upon his suspicion that he would have a fine foot, or means not to tread in his old steps. I protest, I think you are able to make a greater fleet in a rainy day than the King of Spain in his whole age, for all his fleeting. This is in your shops an excellent memento (make but use of it) of your mortality. Wet weather will be as good as a purgation for dry leather, and boys' spurn-point will grate out shoes as fast as a cook can bread. Our sirs that want shoes must trash out their boots, and if they be in love with the fire tonight they must be in league with you tomorrow. Those that would be taken for gentlewomen must sue for shoes that creak like a frog, but our shrewd dames will have dumb bottoms that they may rush upon their maids as 'twere out of an ambush. As long as hats and shoes shall be slipped on with horns your trade shall be extant, and as long as you clap the fur to tender virgins' soles you shall maintain the name of the gentle craft.

Hats and shoes pulled on with horns

Painters

Painters

You beauty-shadowers that rob the rainbow of her colours and disrobe the golden garden of her orient spots and flowers, your craft shall have his spring all the year and your art his flourish all your life. The parasite that gives the dug to humour shall paint it in soothing to his patron, the light lover in phrasing to his mistress, and the undermining cony-catcher in compliments to his cony. The impotent debtor shall paint it in protesting to his creditor, the fetching salesman in praising to the buyer, and all the world besides shall paint their bosom carriage with hypocrisy. Alas, men are so frosty-natured that they cannot be thawed but by viewing the colours of the playing satyrs and the coupling nymphs behind the curtains. Heaven's smith with the sky's fair one (chaste Lucrece) and her foe in a chamber, the banished Dardan and his fere in a cave: this puts life into the beholder's corpse and coin into the painter's calf-skin. While he lays colours on the table, they gild his fist, and while he makes shadows for them, he himself may sit in the sunshine. The ribs of tottering houses must be coated with a new paint against the christening of the next child, and a thin wall would have a painter's skin to shroud him from the blast of Boreas. A coloured clout will set the stamp of decorum on a rotten partition, and a pretty picture will hide a hole in a hall out of all question. My Lord Mayor's posts must needs be trimmed against he takes his oath, and the vintner's lattices must have a new blush, and all these will make you suck your pencils to the bone. O, but our sweet-faced gentlewomen will keep your profession in great request; our lack-looks and barren-beauties will uphold it forever, when the old bawd like a green apple parched in an oven, or the Italian colourist with his new-cast

Excellent painting

2278 **Orpheus** in myth, a poet and musician whose song had a civilizing power
2291 **Philemon and Baucis** a poor old couple who offered hospitality to the disguised Jupiter and Mercury; see Ovid's *Metamorphoses* VIII
2292 **degenerous** fallen from ancestral virtue or excellence
2299 **topgallant** sail on the topmast of a ship
2300 **commodity** benefit, profit
2320 **spurn-point** children's game, perhaps similar to hopscotch
grate out wear out
2322 **trash out** spoil by tramping through mud
2326–7 **dumb bottoms** noiseless soles
2341 **cony-catcher** cheat, trickster
2348–9 **Heaven's smith** Vulcan
2349 **Lucrece** legendary Roman woman who killed herself after being raped by a son of Tarquin the proud; subject of *Ghost of Lucrece*
2350 **banished Dardan** Dardanus was the founder of the Trojan race; used here to refer to Aeneas after his flight from Troy
2351 **fere** partner, i.e. Dido
2352 **calf-skin** purse
2359 **Boreas** the north wind
2362–3 **posts . . . trimmed** posts used for fixing proclamations were newly painted when a magistrate or mayor came into office

face, shall present this good complexion. Why then, to painting speedily.

When nature's birth appeareth lame,
To aid with art I count no shame.
But the smoke of my lungs will melt the vermilion, and then more work for the painter.

The winding up of the clue

Thus have you here the zephyral and spring part of your destinies. 'Twere a task beyond all time to suffer any wagon wheel to press every land's end. Only if you pardon this precursion, it may so happen that as I have here chattered of your vernal age, so I may hereafter tell you of your winter blasts, of the rigorous tempests that shall beat the blossoms from your blooming plants. But for this time I desist.

So, tradesmen, fare you well.

Yet before we shake hands at parting, let us, as country chapmen going from their inns in a morning, give one another the *Basileu* on horseback with a cup of white wine and sugar, if it be summer. But now I remember, it being the fall of the leaf and trees beginning to stand like tattered rogues half-naked, a cup of mulled sack and ginger is better for the stomach. Take this, therefore, next your heart. I know that to catch riches in a net you fish in all the wealthy streams of the world besides the broad sea, but is it not more safe for you to angle standing on land, and what land is more peaceable than your own? And upon your own where shall you meet less foul dealings than at fairs? To the fairest of fairs I wish you, therefore, to turn your horses' heads. Many fairs are in England, and (being wenching fellows as you are) I think not but you have set up your standings and opened booths in all or the best of them. But my prognostication speaks of other fairs to which, if travelling, your purses be ever the warmer lined. Stand wondering no more at the ill-faced Owl, but say she hath a piercing eye to catch mice in such corners. And so in the name of Minerva (patroness of handicrafts) set forward, for now I proclaim my fairs.

Fairs in England

A fare at Westminster Bridge every forenoon of all the four terms in the year, and in the afternoons of the same days a fare at Temple Stairs. And these fares (no bawdy booths in them) are kept in wherries.

A fare on the Bankside when the playhouses have twopenny tenants dwelling in them.

A fare at Blackfriars when any gentleman coming to the place desires to be a landed man.

A fare is sure to be at Coldharbour when a fresh, delicate whore lies there *cum privilegio*.

Bartholomew Fair begins ever on the 24 of August, but Bartlemew-babies are held in London (in men's arms) all the year long.

A fair at Cuckold's Haven every St Luke's day, but all that pass that way have not gilded horns as (then) the Haven has.

A fair kept heretofore at Beggar's Bush is this year removed and held in the prisons about London, and in some of the streets of the City too.

A fair of horses at Ripon in Yorkshire this year, and every year a fair of asses at Leighton Buzzard.

A fair of sows on Michaelmas day at Blockley in Worcestershire, but your best pigs and fattest pork are at Our Lady fair in Southwark.

A fair at Romford for hogs every Tuesday in the week, but your fairest headed oxen are fed in London.

A fair wench is to be seen every morning in some shop in Cheapside, and in summer afternoons the self-same fair opens her booth at one of the garden houses about Bunhill.

A fair pair of gallows is kept at Tyburn from year's end to year's end, and the like fare (but not

2375 ***vermilion*** cosmetic, i.e. rouge
2376 **clue** a ball of thread used to guide someone through a maze
2377 **zephyral** mildly breezy
2380 **precursion** prognostication (first citation in *OED* as a noun, 1701)
2388 **chapmen** itinerant traders
2389 ***Basileu*** 'your majesty'? (there is no record of this as a greeting in *OED*)
2393 **tattered** ragged
2411 **Minerva** better known as goddess of wisdom
2416 **Temple Stairs** landing place on the river for the Inns of Court
2418 **wherries** light rowing-boats used to carry passengers and goods
2419 **Bankside** on the south side of the river; theatre land
2421 **Blackfriars** site of the most important private theatre in London; landing place east of the Fleet river
2423 **Coldharbour** tenements near London Bridge, popularly regarded as a place of sanctuary; also a place where marriages could be expedited
2424 ***cum privilegio*** reserved for you; royal patent (Latin)
2425 **Bartholomew Fair** famous Smithfield fair, represented in Ben Jonson's play (1614)
2426 **Bartlemew-babies** dolls or puppets
2428 **Cuckold's Haven** proverbial
St Luke's day 18 October, proverbially associated with Cuckold's Haven
2431 **Beggar's Bush** a bush under which a begger finds shelter; William Harrison records a fair at Beggar's Bush near Rye on Bartholomew Day in his *Description of England* (1577), III, xv
2434 **Ripon** cathedral city; Harrison records a horse fair at Ripon on Holyrood day, 14 September
2435 **Leighton Buzzard** town in Bedfordshire
2436 **Michaelmas day** 29 September, the feast of St Michael
2438 **Our Lady fair** the other great London fair, south of the river
2439 **Romford** town in Essex
2445 **garden houses** used for sexual encounters
Bunhill Bunhill fields, north of London near Finsbury, where archery matches and artillery practice were held
2446 **Tyburn** the chief place of execution, west of London

so much resort of chapmen and crack-ropes to it) is at St Thomas à Waterings.

The highways of England: how they lie,
and how to travel from one place to another

Now because there are no fairs but they are kept in some certain places, and that no place can be gone unto but by knowledge of the ways, I have therefore chalked out here some of the most notorious ways in the kingdom for the benefit of galled-toe travellers thereby the sooner to come to their inns, *viz.*

The way between York and London is just so many miles as between London and York. It hath divers times been ridden in a day, so that by my geometrical dimensions I find it but a day's journey, yet the postmasters of the North swear 'tis a great deal more.

The way between Charing Cross, and not a cross to be found scarce in one purse for twenty that passes by, is to be tried by many a gallant's pocket with yellow band, feather pendant-regardant and cloak lined with velvet, and therefore here I spare to speak of so poor a thing.

The way between the two Counters in London may be travelled in as short time as one of the varlets there ventures his soul for money, and that's much about quarter of an hour, or half at most.

The way to prove the taking of any purse (be it never so full), and to stand in that quarrel even to the death, is to go first to Newgate and then to Tyburn.

The way to be an arrant ass is to be a mere university scholar.

The highway to Bedlam is first to set forth at Westminster Hall and there to be undone in four or five terms by corrupted lawyers.

Between stark drunk and reasonable sober is much about four hours sleeping, but some that have travelled those overflowing countries say 'tis sometimes more.

The way to heaven is to walk with a good conscience; he that rides without it goes vilely out of the way, and ten to one if ever he gets thither.

The way to hell is clean the contrary way to heaven; the one turns o' the right hand, t'other on the left.

Good days

1. Not one whore in all Westminster.
3. Not one knave in Long Lane.
4. Three catchpoles cast into the Thames.
8. All that walk in Paul's dine today.
10. Nobody hangs in Barbican.
14. Attorneys get no money.
15. Not a bribe taken this term.
17. My husband is gone a-ducking.
18. Bob for eels now or never.
20. A cony for nothing.
23. One hole for nine pence.
26. Turnbull Street full of puritans.
28. The scrivencr i'th' pillory.
30. Room for the baker.

Bad days

2. Quarter sessions.
5. Farewell and be hanged.
6. The doorkeepers steal.
7. Globe afire.
9. Cockpit plucked down.
11. The play is hissed at.
12. My wife is out of her letters and falls to joining.
13. Not a woodcock to be had for love or money.
16. The chambermaid is bedridden.
19. He hunts close, yet has lost his hare.
21. I can read my husband's name in his little boy's hornbook.
22. My maid is poisoned with a pudding.
24. His evidence is burnt, yet the seals saved.
25. A cuckold by Westminster clock, and that goes true.
27. You are peppered.
29. Ale-tapwives in loose gowns.
31. None of the Guard drunk.

These thirty-one Good and Bad days may wait as pages upon all the months of the year, and the rather because our bad days are still more in number than our good ones (as here they are). Also, because where the days are bad, none can be worse than these, and where they happen to be good, few better than these.

FINIS

2448 **crack-ropes** rogues
2449 **St Thomas à Waterings** watering place in Southwark for Canterbury pilgrims; site of a gallows erected in 1593
2465 **Charing Cross** in Westminster
2468–9 **pendant-regardant** heraldic term; regardant = looking backward
2471 **the two Counters** prisons: one in the Poultry, the other in Wood Street, Cheapside
2482 **Bedlam** Bethlehem Hospital on Bishopsgate, the asylum for the insane
2497 **Long Lane** in Smithfield. 'This lane is now lately builded on both the sides with tenements for brokers, tipplers [i.e. tavern-keepers], and suchlike' (John Stow, *A Survey of London*, II, 28).
2499 **Paul's** see note to l. 1246
2500 **Nobody . . . Barbican** probably a reference to the bookseller Trundle's sign in Cripplegate
2513 **doorkeepers** pimps
2514 **Globe afire** the Globe theatre burned down on 29 June 1613
2515 **Cockpit** see note to l. 434
2523 **hornbook** a paper containing the alphabet and protected by a transparent plate of horn, mounted on a wooden tablet with a handle, used to teach children the alphabet

THE PEACEMAKER; OR, GREAT BRITAIN'S BLESSING

Text edited and annotated by Paul Mulholland, introduced by Susan Dwyer Amussen

WHAT does violence mean in early modern society? And what does it mean to be a peacemaker? These are the questions addressed by Thomas Middleton in *The Peacemaker*. In doing so, Middleton sheds light on central conflicts in early Stuart society. For the modern reader, the pamphlet raises many questions, as the range of subjects it addresses makes it appear disjointed and somewhat incoherent. Although its sentiments represent conventional pieties, and in the condemnation of duelling government policy, the links between ideas are not obvious. Why, for instance, is there an extended section on drunkenness and other vices in a pamphlet on peace? These peculiarities—and the significance of *The Peacemaker*—can best be understood by placing it in the context of a debate about the nature of masculinity as defined through morality and violence that was part of the early Stuart campaign for the reformation of manners.

The Peacemaker, which was licensed for publication by the King, was published anonymously; its royal privilege and the address of the Epistle 'To all Our true-loving and peace-embracing subjects' (l. 11) led to its attribution to James I in both the British Library and Short Title Catalogues. Perhaps because of its quasi-official status, it rapidly went through five editions—faster than any other work of Middleton in his lifetime.

The Peacemaker celebrates James I's contribution to European peace, but was licensed on 19 July 1618, more than a month after news had reached England of the events in Prague that led to the outbreak of the Thirty Years War and when the threat of war was evident. It also celebrated the 'loving union' of England and Scotland—although formal union, much to James's chagrin, had actually been rejected by Parliament some years earlier. Finally, the attack on drunkenness as a disturber of peace is published under the protection—and possibly at the request—of a King notorious for excess and debauchery: ''tis drunkenness that leads now' (l. 229) could be a political, as well as a moral lament. Such ironies suggest that we would do well to try to understand the larger context in which *The Peacemaker* was written.

One of the most striking aspects of *The Peacemaker* for the modern reader is the range of topics that are raised. The paean to James I's abilities as a peacemaker in the international realm is conventional, and is what we would expect from a pamphlet with this title. James was well known for his commitment to peace, and was proud of his diplomatic efforts for peace. The use of James's biblical motto, '*beati pacifici*', at the end of the last eight paragraphs of the first section (ll. 61–118) emphasizes this familiar aspect of peacemaking. The second section (ll. 119–224), which acknowledges the difficulties of establishing peace, as well as its benefits—in the expansion of trade and the encouragement of justice, charity, and religion—begins to shift the focus to the domestic implications of international peace. The attention Middleton pays to the economic benefits of peace is not unique, and certainly not surprising given Middleton's knowledge of London merchants. More surprisingly, the domestic implications of peace yield to the threats to domestic peace.

In the context of the analogical thinking so common in early modern England, which I have discussed elsewhere, the shift from the international to the domestic (both national and familial) is entirely predictable. Yet the third and fourth sections of the pamphlet shift the discussion to a personal level, insisting that peace is based on a series of decisions made by individuals on a daily basis. The linking of personal behaviour to international peace is a reminder that the separation of politics from other social issues is a division that we create, but that Middleton and his contemporaries would not recognize. More than half the pamphlet (60 per cent) focuses not on peacemaking in the international arena, but on the evils of duelling and the sins—particularly drinking—that disrupt domestic peace. These disruptions of the peace of the soul and the community are, for Middleton, the real threats to peace.

Middleton's reflection on the nature of manhood begins in the third section (ll. 225–358), with its discussion of the impact of drunkenness and other vices. There was extensive preaching against the evils of drink in the early seventeenth century, and many commentators shared Middleton's view that drunkenness was epidemic. Such ideas were almost inevitable in a society where beer and ale were the primary forms of liquid refreshment. They were simultaneously sources of carbohydrates and calories, and were also considered stimulants.

We often assume that warnings about the decline of morals and the spread of sin merely reflect moral panic. In this case, there was at least some basis in fact for the concern. Alcohol consumption probably did increase in the late sixteenth and early seventeenth centuries. Peter Clark has shown that there was a significant rise in the numbers of alehouses in this period. There were certainly a lot of them: in the City of London alone in 1657 there were more than nine hundred licensed alehouses, or one licensed alehousekeeper for every sixteen houses; in addition, the more socially exclusive taverns and inns catered to the élite. At the same time, during the sixteenth century there was a gradual transformation of brewing, with old-fashioned ale being replaced by beer. Because the equipment for brewing beer was more expensive than that for brewing ale, this encouraged the commercialization of brewing, particularly in the towns and cities. Beer not only kept far longer than ale, but was also usually more alcoholic. In addition, in London the prosperous could drink wine at the many inns and taverns that served the city, and a growing group of distillers provided a range of (extremely potent) spirits for consumption. Thus drink with an increasing alcoholic content was more easily available to all ranks of English society at a time when poverty and social dislocation may have increased the demand for it—as well as for other products, like tobacco, which were thought to be stimulants.

While beer and ale were often consumed at home, drunkenness was associated with alehouses; any discussion of drunkenness, then, inevitably reflects not only on diet, but also on patterns of hospitality and recreation. Like most attacks on drunkenness at the time, Middleton's does not argue for teetotalism, but for restraint. Elizabeth Foyster has shown that drinking without becoming drunk was a critical dimension of constructing manhood. This emphasis on restraint and self-control is the starting point of Middleton's development of an alternative model of manhood, particularly for prosperous young men. Manhood in early modern England, as I have recently argued, was closely connected with both conviviality and violence. As a result of the late age at marriage, much socializing by young people was in single-sex groups, and for men at least these groups usually met in alehouses. As Keith Wrightson has shown, alehouses were natural centres of sociability, in part because in winter their fires made them one of the warmest places around. But they also served as common space where those from different households, especially servants, could gather.

Middleton's redefinition of manhood defines drunkenness itself as unmanly. The imagery of this section repeatedly assumes an equation between true manliness and virtue, while sin corrupted both true manhood and true womanhood. The man who is drunk is 'unmanned', while drunkenness itself is a 'sick and unwholesome harlot' (261–2, 292). Here manhood is linked to self-control and autonomy. Such a definition built on existing political concepts which identified real adulthood with economic independence. What Middleton has added is the idea that manhood depends not just on independence, but on sobriety. Abandoning oneself to drink is a way of losing one's independence.

Middleton does not challenge the centrality of the alehouse or other drinking centres as social institutions. Instead, he redefines appropriate behaviour in the alehouse. In his approach to this necessarily contentious subject, Middleton sought to disconnect popular conceptions of manhood from excessive drinking. It is this which ties the attack on drunkenness to peacemaking. As I have argued elsewhere, the conviviality of the alehouse involved not just drinking, but participation in various semi-ritual combats, whether brawls (for the lower orders) or duels. Both were fought for a variety of reasons—to teach an opponent a lesson, to defend one's reputation, or to make a point in an argument. Middleton argues that resort to such violence was encouraged by excessive drinking. The fourth section of *The Peacemaker* (ll. 359–669) begins with a criticism of quarrels in general, but soon narrows the focus to the bloodshed caused by duels. His attack on duelling forms the second part of Middleton's redefinition of manhood.

As V. G. Kiernan has shown, there was great concern with duels at this time. James I had published several proclamations against duels—first prohibiting the publication of news of duels in 1613, then effectively prohibiting them by banning challenges in 1614. Duels, like other fights, had an ambiguous place in the culture of early modern England. They were judged according to the same standards as all other forms of violence. First, they were supposed to be justified: violence should not be random. Second, they should be limited in impact, with a consequence equal to the offence. Finally, they should not be carried out in anger, but thoughtfully and purposefully. The chances of death in any quarrel depended to a great extent on the use of weapons, which were present by definition in duels. Duels were most likely to offend early modern viewers by the incommensurability of the consequence (death) to the offence—often a relatively trivial insult. Middleton makes much of the possibility of death, insisting that the reasons that most men fought duels did not deserve death, and that in fighting, the participants abrogated to themselves the role of God.

Middleton's attack on duels goes further, however, taking on central social values, especially those relating to reputation. Although this section displays Middleton's classical education through its frequent use of Seneca, the issues were central in English society. The 'wise man' whose behaviour is to be emulated, who 'cares [not] how many darts of malice or contumely are shot against him' (384–5) was rare. Unlike most others in Jacobean society, he was not overly sensitive to reputation. He is, in a sense, a new man, who really believes that God will exact vengeance from those who have harmed him. Yet in early modern England, as I and other recent scholars—including Martin Ingram and J. A. Sharpe—have shown, reputation was central at all social levels. Reputation governed how others responded to you, where one was placed, the roles one could play in society, and much more. Its implications were not just social, but financial—as suggested by the use of the word 'credit' to describe reputation as well as solvency. As a result, almost everyone was jealous of their reputations: they defended them not only with duels, but with numerous lawsuits. In so far as law is the continuation of a fight by other means, it was a satisfactory substitute for a duel or other violent confrontation; if there was any success in the campaign against duels, it may be indicated by the vast increase in litigation that occurred in the sixteenth and seventeenth centuries.

Reputation was shaped by many different components, some of which were extremely sensitive to words spoken by others. Although wealth was an important component of reputation it did not alone ensure the excellence of one's reputation. Rather, the propertied (from the gentry to merchants and shopkeepers as well as yeoman farmers) were assumed to be of good character; they were responsible for the governance of their communities. That presumption could be undermined by anything from excessive drunkenness, to disorderly sexual behaviour, to blatant dishonesty. To allow the allegation of any such behaviour to go unanswered would be to allow people to assume it were true, especially because reputation was based on the opinion of 'people of credit and estimation'—or what people said about you. Middleton argues, however, that reputation was more effectively protected by wise, cautious, and judicious behaviour than by resort to arms.

Middleton's argument required not only a redefinition of the basis of reputation, but of the place of duelling in English society. Violence was a familiar feature of early modern English society, but it was not always accepted. The duel—with its specialized weapons, its elaborate codes and rituals—was a form of the brawl. The ability and willingness to fight was often considered a sign of manliness. The attraction of the duel, however, was its association with the upper class. After all, not everyone could learn to fight with a rapier. Skill was expected to distinguish the true aristocrat from the parvenu. Yet the lines of division in English society were not so clear that such distinctions could be made easily. Although the case which occasioned *The Charge of Sir Francis Bacon Knight* (1614)—on which Middleton based some of his discussion—involved one man called a 'gentleman', and the other 'Esquire', Bacon clearly thought little of them. 'I could have wished that I had met with some greater persons, as a subject for your censure'; it is appropriate for 'the dog to be beaten before the lion'; and finally, 'I should think (my Lords) that men of birth and quality will leave the practice, when it begins to be vilified, and come so low as to barbers surgeons and butchers, and such base mechanical persons.' Middleton develops this theme, suggesting that duelling is not a sign of courage and honour, but shame and dishonour; but while Bacon located the source of the shame in the status of others who fought duels, Middleton located it in the morality of the duel itself.

Duels were enmeshed in concepts of class and masculinity—in particular the manhood of young gentlemen. It is indicative of Middleton's audience that he focuses on duels, rather than the more common—and plebeian—brawl. The argument that Middleton makes against duels serves to separate the manhood of the élite from that of the lower classes of society: not only is Middleton silent on the subject of fights that do not qualify as duels, but his definition of a wise man is effectively reserved for those—at various social levels—who are confident of their position in society: they are the ones who do not need to pay excessive attention to petty slights. For those whose position is more tenuous, or who are trying to define their place in society, such restraint is difficult. The focus on self-restraint and self-control are part of an attempt to redefine the nature of aristocratic and gentle manhood. They are not unique; indeed the advice literature of the church had for a long time argued that true manhood was *not* violent.

In the context of the redefinition of manhood, *The Peacemaker* is best read as a contribution to the campaign for the 'reformation of manners' in the early seventeenth century. This campaign, usually associated with Puritans, sought to impose higher standards of personal morality on society; it emphasized self-restraint in many forms. This campaign, as described by Keith Wrightson and David Underdown, included intense concern with drinking, reflected in repeated campaigns against alehouses as sources of disorder, crime, and sin. Personal morality was emphasized in the context of proper adherence to gender roles—both in attacks on assertive women and on men who failed to uphold proper (as defined by the reformers) standards of manhood. The campaign for the reformation of manners was carried out by Puritans in the broadest sense of the word—people who wanted religion to represent a more serious commitment to personal moral improvement. The reformation of manners sought to impose stricter standards of behaviour on the (morally) unregenerate masses, and it had support throughout society. This support was, however, concentrated among the 'middling sort'—yeomen, merchants, and craftsmen, whose lives were more likely to conform in any case to its expectations. In the process of trying to create a single moral standard, the campaign divided society profoundly.

Middleton associates the reformation of manners with a reformation of manhood through the connections drawn between drinking and duelling, and underscores the cultural and social divisions it implies. A reformation of manners inevitably leads to cultural polarization, as it distinguishes between those who behave 'properly' and those who do not. But Middleton's shift from all quarrels to duels illuminates the process by which the distinction between the moral and the immoral came to mirror the social polarization of English society in the early seventeenth century. When duelling is accepted as a way of settling disagreements between élite young men, their relationship to violence is distinguished from that of less prosperous young men only by weapons and ritual. While the weapons contribute to the potential for bloodshed that Middleton so laments, they do not remove young men from violence. When the duel is rejected, however, the relationship of élite men to violence is radically different from that of other young men. Those who accept the duel can understand the brawl; those who reject the duel cannot. By proposing to change the relationship of some, but not all, men to violence, Middleton's focus on duels makes this polarization one based more on status than morality. In this way, Middleton contributes to the process of differentiating manhoods—of creating different meanings for manhood in different social groups. The cultural gap between the godly and the unregenerate has become one between the élite and the rest.

It is in the context of reinventing manhood that the inclusion of a long discussion of drunkenness is necessary in *The Peacemaker*: the self-control necessary for avoiding duels depended on the self-control—more commonly sought—that avoided drunkenness. In addition, the unmanliness of drunkenness, and its association with duelling, made it easier to make the reformation of manhood a central aspect of the reformation of manners. Middleton understood, as did his contemporaries, that all forms of violence were connected; a society which prepared its sons for war would train them to duel. To argue for a world of peace, where trade, industry, and agriculture flourished, involved redefining what was important, what was valued in society. And it involved creating, in many ways, a new man. That this was always the goal of the godly made the discourse familiar. Middleton's use of these commonplace ideas reveals the profound transformation of society sought in the reformation of manners.

SEE ALSO

Textual introduction and apparatus: *Companion*, 648
Authorship and date: *Companion*, 402

The Peacemaker

Or, Great Britain's Blessing

Framed for the continuance of that mighty happiness wherein this Kingdom excels many Empires;

Showing the Idleness of a Quarrelling Reputation, wherein consists neither Manhood nor Wisdom;

Necessary for all Magistrates, Officers of Peace, Masters of Families, for the conformation of Youth, and for all his Majesty's most true and faithful Subjects:

To the general avoiding of all Contention and Bloodshedding.

Cum Privilegio.

To all Our true-loving and peace-embracing subjects

The glory of all virtues is action; the crown of all acts, perfection; the perfection of all things, peace and union. It is the riches of our beings, the reward of our sufferings, the music on our deathbeds. Never had so great a treasure so poor a purchaser, for man hath the offer of it. The God of Peace sent it, the Lamb of Peace brought it, the Spirit of Peace confirmed it, and We still seek to preserve it. With what power then may the good purpose of this work arrive at the hearts of all faithful Christians? And with what cheerfulness and freeness ought it to be embraced of all Our loving subjects, having so many glorious seals of honour, power, and virtue to strengthen it? All that is required of Us from you is a faithful and hearty welcome, and that bestowed upon man's best and dearest friend, either in life or death. For peace that hath been a stranger to you is now become a sister, a dear and natural sister; and to your holiest loves, We recommend her.

This commentary pays special attention to the work's sources. For further background on versions of the Bible used by Middleton, see the commentary to *Two Gates*, p. 683.

Title **Great Britain's** In 1604 James I was proclaimed 'King of Great Britain', the first English monarch to be so styled.

3 **Quarrelling Reputation** (1) contentious disputing of the validity of a reputation; (2) finding fault with a reputation

6 **Families** households (including servants)

11 ***Our*** The royal plural here and elsewhere together with the royal coat of arms in type ornaments that accompany the early editions is apparently part of a strategy aimed at giving the impression that the epistle, if not the whole pamphlet, was the work of the king. Two of the ornaments are reproduced in our text; an alternative version of the second is printed in the *Companion*. The earliest state of this forme contains the phrase 'By the King'—an error possibly deriving from tactics employed to suggest royal authorship.

12 **glory . . . action** i.e. in making virtues manifest

13 **union** unity, concord

14 **It** peace

15 **music . . . deathbeds** Cf. 'music at the close', Shakespeare, *Richard II* 2.1.12.

16–17 **God . . . Lamb . . . Spirit** in reference to the Trinity

19 **work** action (i.e. of sending, bringing, and confirming)

22 **seals** pledges

27 **sister** possibly drawing on conventional iconographic representations of Peace as a sister of Justice

The Peace-maker.

The Peacemaker

The book itself in glory of its name
Is proud to tell from whence the subject came.

Peace be to you. I greet you in the blessing of a *God*, the salutation of an *Apostle*, and the motto of a *King*. My subject hath her being in heaven, her theory in holy writ, and her practice in England, *insula pacis*: the Land of Peace, under the King of Peace.

Like Noah's dove, she was sent out to seek a resting place to see if the whole world were not yet covered with the perpetual deluge of *blood* and *enmity*, and only here she found the *olive leaf*. Hitherto hath she been pilot to the *ark*, and here it first touched shore. Here now it hath remained full fifteen years, I am proud to report it.

Rejoice, O England, with thine espoused Scotland, and let thy handmaid Ireland joy with thee. Let all thy servant *islands* be glad; yea, let in strangers to behold and taste thy blessings.

The disturbed French seek succour with thee; the troubled Dutch fly to thy confines; the Italian leaves his hotter climate. These and many more all seek shelter under the sweet shadow of thine *olive branches*.

O London, blessed mistress of this happy Britain, build new thy gates: there's *peace* ent'ring at them. The God of *Peace* hath sent this *peace* of God. O, ever love her that she may never leave thee: salute her and invite her. Let Whitehall, fit emblem for her purity, be her chief palace, and let it say, *Ades, alma salus*.

Peace and *contention* lie here on earth as trading factors for life and death.

Who desires not to have traffic with life? Who, weary of life, but would die to live?

Peace is the passage from life to life; come then to the factory of *peace*, thou that desirest to have life: behold the substitute of *peace* on earth, displaying the flag of *peace*, *Beati pacifici*.

Let *contention* enjoy, without joy, large empires; here we enjoy, with all joy, our happy *sanctuary*. It was born with him; he brought it with him after five-and-thirty years' increase, and here hath multiplied it to fifty with us. O blessed *jubilee*, let it be celebrated with all joy and cheerfulness, and all sing *Beati pacifici*.

And are not the labours blessed with the workman? England and Scotland (though not malicious enemies, yet churlish neighbours) are reconciled, feast, love, live, and die together, are indeed no more neither what they were, but a new thing betwixt them, more firm and near in their

32 **Peace . . . you** a salutation in Gen. 43:23 and Christ's words to the disciples after the resurrection as recorded in Luke 24:36 and John 20:19, 20, 26

32–3 ***God . . . Apostle . . . King*** The text is unusual in italicizing many such common nouns.

33 **salutation . . . *Apostle*** many of the Apostle Paul's epistles begin with the salutation, 'Grace be with you, and peace from God our Father, and from the Lord Jesus Christ' (Geneva–Tomson)
motto . . . *King* i.e. *Beati pacifici*, blessed are the peacemakers (Latin), Matt. 5:9, the motto of James I

35 ***insula pacis*** island of peace (Latin)

37 **Noah's dove** Gen. 8:8

40 ***olive leaf*** Gen. 8:11; the *olive* is also an emblem of peace.

42 **fifteen years** i.e. the length of the reign of James I since becoming king of England

43 **espoused Scotland** i.e. by virtue of James's uniting of England and Scotland under his rule

44 **handmaid** perhaps a figurative use of the naval sense of a vessel employed to attend on larger ships

44–5 **servant *islands*** presumably in reference to islands under English rule such as Jersey and Guernsey

45 **let in strangers** either as visitors or immigrants

47 **disturbed French** possibly in allusion to the turmoil generated by the assassination of Henri IV in 1610

48 **troubled Dutch** The final years of the Twelve Years' Truce between Spain and the Dutch United Provinces (1609–21) were akin to a cold-war period during which the Dutch were making preparations for renewed hostilities; Dutch enclaves and interests elsewhere in Europe were also under threat.
Italian James I was advised in 1609 to found a college for Italian refugees in England, casualties of political and religious skirmishes among independent Italian and neighbouring states.

51 **happy** blessed; fortunate

51–2 **build new thy gates** The 1618 edition of Stow's *Survey of London* draws attention to the recent 'new building' of two of London's gates: Aldgate and Aldersgate.

53 ***peace*** with a pun on 'piece'

55 **Whitehall** the palace of the kings of England from Henry VIII to William III, situated on the north bank of the Thames near Westminster Bridge; the reference plays on the suitability of 'white' as an emblem of purity.

56 ***Ades, alma salus*** Come, kindly salvation (Latin); possibly derived from Statius, *Thebaid*, 10.611: '*venit alma salus*', kindly salvation comes.

57 **factors** agents

60 **but** that

62 **factory** workshop; trading station

63 **substitute** deputy

64 ***Beati pacifici*** Blessed are the peacemakers (Latin), Matt. 5:9

66 **sanctuary** refuge, shelter

67 **him** 'the substitute of peace on earth', i.e. James I

67–8 **five-and-thirty . . . increase** the reference is presumably to James I's age at his accession to the English throne in 1603, but the reckoning is faulty: he was born 19 June 1566 and so was 36 when Elizabeth I died.

68 **fifty** as with the preceding reference, at least one year out of line with James I's age in 1618

69 ***jubilee*** fiftieth anniversary; among the significances of the Biblical Year of Jubilee was the proclamation of liberty to all the inhabitants of the land (Lev. 25:9–10)

72–3 **England . . . reconciled** The political union of the English and Scottish monarchies that resulted from James becoming king of England significantly reduced tensions between the two nations.

loving union than ever divided in their hearty unkindness; and now both say with one tongue, *Beati pacifici*.

Ireland, that rebellious outlaw, that so many years cried blood and death (filling her marish grounds with massacres, affording many preys of slaughtered bodies to her ravenous wolves, and in their wombs keeping the brutish obsequies), would know no lord, but grew more stubborn in her chastisement till this white ensign was displayed; then she came running with this hallowed text in her mouth: *Beati pacifici*.

Spain, that great and long-lasting opposite, betwixt whom and England the ocean ran with blood not many years before, nor ever truced her crimson effusion: their merchants on either side trafficked in blood, their Indian ingots brought home in blood (a commerce too cruel for Christian kingdoms), yet now shake hands in friendly amity and speak our blessing with us, *Beati pacifici*.

Nay, what Christian kingdom that knows the blessing of *peace* has not desired and tasted this our blessing from us? Come they not hither as to the fountain from whence it springs? Here sits Solomon, and hither come the *tribes* for judgements. O happy moderator, blessed father, not father of thy country alone, but father of all thy neighbour countries about thee. Spain and her withstanding provinces (long bruised on both sides) thou hast set at peace, turning their bloody leaguers to leagues of friendship. Do not those children now live to bless thee (who had else been buried in their parents' wombs) and say, *Beati pacifici?*

Denmark and Suecia, Suecia and Poland, Cleves and Brandenburg: have not these and many more come to this oracle of *peace* and received their dooms from it? If the members of a natural body by concord assist one another, if the politic members of a kingdom help one another, and by it support itself, why shall not the monarchal bodies of many kingdoms be one mutual Christendom, if still they sing this blessed lesson taught them, *Beati pacifici?*

Let England then, the seat of our Solomon, rejoice in her happy government, yea, her government of governments; and she that can set peace with others, let her, at least, enjoy it herself. Let us love peace, and be at peace in love. We live in *Beth-salem*, the house of *Peace*; then let us ever sing this song of peace, *Beati pacifici*.

Detraction snarls and tempts fair Peace to show
The plenty of her fruits and how they grow.

Detraction to Peace

Sed ubi fructus? Where are all these rich and opulent blessings that this tender white-robed Peace hath brought with her? *Ætas parentum peior avis*, etc. Our *grandfathers*, for the most part, were honester men than our *fathers*, our *fathers* better than we, and our *children* are like enough to

76 **hearty** bold; zealous
78 **Ireland... outlaw** in allusion to the rebellious posture of the Irish tribal chieftains, and possibly Tyrone and Tyrconnell in particular, who despite submission to the English crown in 1603 continued to wield their accustomed authority until 1607
79 **marish** marshy
81–2 **in their wombs... obsequies** in their bellies observing the savage funeral rites
83 **white ensign** i.e. as a token of peaceful or friendly intention; possibly in reference to James's efforts to establish himself as Ireland's sovereign lord, thereby supplanting the authority of the tribal chiefs, and his proclamation that the Irish were his 'free, natural and immediate subjects'; also included might be allusion to the plantation of Ulster that followed the departure of Tyrone and Tyrconnell, which aimed by the redistribution of land to set up a new order.
84 **hallowed** with a pun on the senses 'sanctified' and 'shouted'
87 **ocean... blood** i.e. in reference to the Spanish Armada of 1588 and other naval battles in Elizabeth's reign
88 **truced** put an end to
88–9 **their... side** presumably Spanish merchants on either side of the Atlantic, since they *now shake hands in friendly amity... with us*
89 **trafficked** traded
89–90 **Indian ingots** i.e. precious metals from the West Indies and South America
90 **brought home in blood** presumably in allusion to Spanish atrocities in the New World
91–2 **shake hands... amity** James concluded a peace with Spain in August 1604
96 **Solomon** In wisdom and as a peace-maker Solomon (the name means 'peace-making' or 'man of peace') had a particular appeal for James I, which is reflected both in his own writings and those of his contemporaries.
97 ***tribes*** classes or divisions of persons; possibly with a play through the Latin form of James (*Jacobus*) on the twelve tribes descended from Jacob
98 **father** Cf. James's insistence on himself as father of all his subjects; also Solomon as the father of David (and James was also blessed as a father of an heir, Charles)
100 **withstanding** opposing or offering resistance
provinces in reference to the United Provinces, the seven northern provinces of the Netherlands allied by the Union of Utrecht (1579); with the support of France and England the Netherlands forced Spain to agree to the Twelve Years' Truce that ran from 1609 to 1621
101 **leaguers** laagers, military camps
102 **children** carrying on the image of James as father; cf. Solomon and his children
105 **Denmark... Poland** King James intervened in a diplomatic capacity to defuse tensions between Denmark (King Kristian IV was his brother-in-law) and Sweden (*Suecia*, Latin) in the Treaty of Knäred, 21 Jan. 1613, after the War of Kalmar; and in Nov. 1613, in conjunction with the Dutch, he mediated between Sweden and Poland, whose King Sigismund III was a pretender to the throne of Sweden, in an attempt to achieve a lasting armistice or truce.
105–6 **Cleves and Brandenburg** The crisis over succession that arose from the death in 1609 of the childless Catholic Duke of Cleves, Jülich, and Berg, three strategically and economically valuable duchies situated along the lower Rhine, produced various claimants and political entanglements. James favoured the protestant Elector of Brandenburg and contributed to a resolution of sorts in arranging the Treaty of Xanten in 1614.
107 **dooms** judgements, sentences
112 **lesson** with a pun on the senses 'musical exercise or performance' and 'matter to be learned'
117 ***Beth-salem*** house of peace (Hebrew)
119 ***Detraction*** disparagement, calumny (here, the voice of nostalgia for Elizabeth's reign)
121 ***Sed ubi fructus?*** But where are the fruits? (Latin); untraced
123 ***Ætas... avis*** Our parents' age, worse than our grandsires' (Latin; Horace, *Odes*, III.6.46)

be worse than ourselves. Does *Peace* keep a palace where *charity* may warm herself?

Peace answers

Shame, murmurer, hadst thou rather with the forgetful Israelites go back to the flesh-pots of Egypt, bought with blows and burdens, than eat *manna* in the way to Canaan?

Dost thou thirst here? 'Tis for want of *sacrifice* to him that should refresh thee then.

Thy grandfather prayed for this that thou enjoyest, and though he had it not himself, yet prepared it as a blessing on thee. The sun that daily shines on thee, thou letst it pass with a careless and neglective eye; but were it hid from thee the change of a *moon*, thou wouldst then welcome it with all alacrity and cheerfulness.

Were blows more bountiful to thee? Did blood yield thee benefit? War afford thee wealth? Didst thou make that thine own by violence which was another's by right? It may be the *handmaid* was fruitful and the mistress barren, but Sarah has now brought forth, and in her seed are the blessings come.

Hagar is despised, *Peace* hath conceived, and smiling Isaac hath left us Jacob, a new Israel, a prince of God, a man that hath prevailed with God to plant his peace with us.

The trading merchant finds it, who daily plows the sea, and as daily reaps the harvest of his labours. What wants England that the world can enrich her with? Tyre sends in her purples, India her spices, Afric her gold, Muscovy her costly skins of beasts, all her neighbour countries their best traffic, and all purchased by friendly commerce, not, as before, by savage cruelty.

The fearless trades and handicraft men sing away their labours all day, having no note drowned with either noise of drum or cannon, and sleep with *peace* at night.

The frolic countryman opens the fruitful earth and crops his plenty from her fertile bosom; nay, even his toiling beasts are trapped with bells, who taste in their labours the harmony of peace with their awful governors.

The *magistrate*, constantly draws his sword of justice on offenders, not o'erawed by party-headed contentions.

The kingdom's beauty, the *nobility*, who were wont to be strangers in their native country, leading the ranks of blood and death against their enemies, have now no enemy, but keep their practice amongst themselves to pastime with (*nonne hæc meminisse voluptas?*). And now, more sweet and holy, are pillars at home, that were enforced to be prodigies abroad; all being by a heavenly *metamorphosis* trans-shaped to become the becoming branches of the great *olive tree* of *peace*. And doth not *Charity* dwell here with *Peace*? O blind detraction. Has not in foretimes unwilling necessity erected two *hospitals*? And now most free and willing *Charity* hath, in augmentation of her glory, raised twenty *almshouses*; yea, so many for one, and give her true testimony.

Nay, has she not done the great wonder? Built some churches, repaired many, and still her hand is dealing? Is not the sum of all, *Religion*, established by her? Are not the *flesh-eating* fires quenched, and our faggots converted

128 **murmurer** one who complains against constituted authority; in reference to Exod. 16:2

128–9 **forgetful...Egypt** in reference to Exod. 16:3

130 **Canaan** the land of promise

131 **thirst** in allusion to the thirst of the children of Israel after departing the wilderness of Sin (Exod. 17:2–3)

136 **neglective** neglectful

137 **the change of a *moon*** a month

142 **mistress barren** Queen Elizabeth, who ruled during the wars with Spain in the time of Middleton's father and grandfather, was childless; James had three children.

143 **Sarah** wife of Abraham; barren for ninety years, she at last gave birth to Isaac.

145 **Hagar** Egyptian handmaid of Sarah; while Sarah was barren she offered her maid, Hagar, as a concubine to Abraham and Hagar bore him Ishmael (Gen. 16). ***Peace* hath conceived** In addition to figurative senses, Elizabeth, Electress Palatine, daughter of James I, had given birth to her second son 24 December 1617 and was pregnant with her first daughter, Elizabeth, in the spring of 1618.

146 **Jacob** son of Isaac, but also in reference to James I, playing on the Latin form of his name, *Jacobus*

147 **prevailed with God** in allusion to Jacob's wrestling with God in the form of a man; when Jacob prevailed, his opponent conferred on him the blessing of changing Jacob's name to Israel (Gen. 32:24–8)

150 **wants** lacks; desires

151–3 **Tyre...beasts** in allusion to expanded trade resulting largely from expeditions on the part of the Muscovy (Russia), Levant, and East India Companies especially after 1609

151–2 **Tyre...purples** Tyre was famous for its scarlet or purple dye extracted from local shellfish.

152 **India her spices** Possibly in reference to the East Indies, which were famous for spices. **Afric** Africa was believed to have rich gold mines. **Muscovy** Russia

154 **traffic** goods, merchandise

159 **frolic** merry; free

161 **trapped** adorned

162 **awful** profoundly respectful

163 **constantly** resolutely, faithfully

164 **party-headed** partisan

166 **strangers...country** i.e. because they were abroad marshalling forces against the country's enemies

168–9 **pastime** amuse themselves

169 ***nonne...voluptas*** Surely it is a pleasure to remember these things? (Latin); possibly adapted from Ovid, *Heroides*, 18.55: '*namque est meminisse voluptas*', for the memory has a charm for me.

170 **pillars** persons who are the main supporters of the state

171 **prodigies** persons whose deeds excite wonder

172 **trans-shaped** changed in form, transformed

175 **two *hospitals*** Possibly in reference to St Thomas's in Southwark and St Bartholomew's in West Smithfield, two of London's five main hospitals, which cared for 'the poor by casualty' including wounded soldiers, decayed housekeepers, and those visited with grievous disease, according to the 1633 edition of Stow's *Survey of London*.

177 **twenty *almshouses*** In 1618 several members of the Fishmongers' Company erected, at their own expense, 22 almshouses in the parish of St Mary's, Newington, where Middleton lived; King James named them 'St Peter's Hospital'.

to gentler uses? O, but those cornfields must never be without some *tares* until the general *harvest*: Israel must not at once destroy all the inhabitants of the Land of Promise, but by little and little, lest they boast and say, it was our strength and not the Lord's hand that did it.

Nor shall our *peace* in her young plantation enjoy so full and perfect a tranquillity, but that there will be with us contentious Canaanites, seditious Jebusites, crafty Gibeonites, drunken Amorites, and arrogant Anakims.

Envy shall stand between and hold two brothers of either hand of her; *sectarists* and *schismatics* shall break the *peace* of God, wound the mother of *peace* (the Church), and bind together false brotherhoods to dissipate the unity and bonds of *peace*.

Law shall wrangle with her; *Ebriety* and Drink shall strike her, *Pride* and *Ambition* shall seek to overthrow her; yea, even her oily and most dangerous enemy, *Hypocrisy*, shall get within to strangle her; yet still shall she stand, and reign, and conquer. *Invidiam pax prosternet.* She shall mount to *heaven* and throw her enemies as low as *hell*, where *peace* shall never come.

Envy shall gnaw her own entrails, *Schism* shall perish, *Law* shall be silent, *Drunkenness* shall burst itself, *Pride* shall be humbled in her own habitation, and hollow-hearted *Hypocrisy* shall find no *peace*.

Ubi deorum numen prætenditur sceleribus, subit animum timor (Flamin. Consul.). Where the majesty of God is made a colour for mischief, a fear comes into that breast: his *peace* shall be tremblings and doubts and horrors; his heart shall then faint that told him before, like heart-stealing Absalom in his father's gates, thy cause was good, when it was not so. Or like the false and foolish prophets that told the people it was *pax, pax*, peace, peace, when it was no peace (Ezek. 13:10).

The walls were daubed with untempered mortar, and they shall fall, yet still shall *Truth* have *Peace*, and the *Peacemaker* shall preserve the truth; they shall dwell together and live together. The heavenly Soldiers have sung it; the Father hath sent it; the Son hath brought it; the blessed Dove shall preserve it, ever comfort us with it; our anointed hath received it; we do enjoy it, and see it plentiful in Israel.

Peace takes a view of such as do molest
And kindle most unquiet in her breast.

Put up the *bell-bearer* first, then all the flock will follow. *Pride* has lost her place, or comes behind for her greater state; 'tis *Drunkenness* that leads now—and mark the *herd* that troop after her. *Lust* follows close, *Contention* at her sleeve. *Emulation* on t'other side; *Envy* keeps the scent like a bloodhound; *Revenge* and *Murder* come coupled together.

The smaller-headed *beasts* are unseen yet, as *Breach of Friendship*, unlocking hearty secrets, *Slander*, *Oaths* and *Blasphemies*, fearful *Invocations* (all which custom hath driven so far distant from the *soul's eye*, as the moon from the *ocular sight*, whose body overbulks the *Earth's* large

183–4 **O, but . . . *harvest*** in reference to the parable of the tares, Matt. 13:24–39; Geneva–Tomson glosses the passage: 'Christ showeth in another parable of the evil seed mixed with the good that the Church shall never be free and quit from offences, both in doctrine and manners, until the day appointed for the restoring of all things do come, and therefore the faithful have to arm themselves with patience and constancy.'

190–1 **Canaanites . . . Anakims** Peoples who inhabited Canaan, the land of promise, previous to and concurrently with the Israelites, and deemed worldly and unsanctified enemies of the true people of God. Only the epithet 'crafty' appears to have particular relevance to the people named. The Gibeonites tricked the Israelites into making a treaty with the city of Gibeon (Josh. 9).

193 ***sectarists*** zealous members of a sect
schismatics those who promote schism or disunity

197 ***Ebriety*** drunkenness

201 ***Invidiam . . . prosternet*** Peace will overthrow envy (Latin); untraced

204 ***Envy* . . . entrails** a common emblematic representation of Envy; cf. Middleton's contribution to *Magnificent Entertainment*, 2152–3

205 ***Drunkenness*** James I issued a number of proclamations aimed at reducing the incidence of drunkenness in the early years of his reign (despite his own addiction to alcohol); in *A Counterblast to Tobacco* he called drunkenness 'the root of all sins'.

208–9 ***Ubi . . . timor*** Livy 39.16.7; translated in the following line

209 **Flamin. Consul.** The quoted passage comes not from Livy's account of the consulship of Gaius Flaminius and M. Aemilius Lepidus (187 BC) but from that of his successors, Spurius Postumius Albinus and Quintus Marcius Philippus.

210 **colour** pretext

212–14 **heart-stealing Absalom . . . not so** in reference to Absalom's conspiracy to usurp David's throne; II Sam. 15:2 (Geneva): 'And Absalom rose up early, and stood hard by the entering in of the gate . . .'; 15:3: 'Then Absalom said unto him, See, thy matters are good and righteous, but there is no man deputed of the king to hear thee' and 15:6: 'And on this manner did Absalom to all Israel, that came to the king for judgement: so Absalom stole the hearts of the men of Israel.'

217–18 **The walls . . . fall** adapted from Ezek. 13:10–11 (Geneva): 'And therefore, because they have deceived my people, saying, Peace, and there was no peace: and one built up a wall, and behold, the others daubed it with untempered mortar, Say unto them which daub it with untempered mortar, that it shall fall . . .'

217 **daubed** coated, covered

220 **heavenly Soldiers** i.e. angels

220–1 **heavenly Soldiers . . . sung it** in reference to Luke 2:13–14 (Geneva–Tomson), with lyrics cited at ll. 642–3. Geneva–Tomson glosses 'a multitude of heavenly soldiers' (Luke 2:13): 'Whole armies of angels, which compass the majesty of God round about, as it were soldiers'.

222 **Dove** Spirit of God (in completion of the Trinity)

223 **our anointed** i.e. King James

227 **Put up** rouse; accuse; enclose
bell-bearer the leading sheep of a flock from the neck of which hangs a bell

233 **as** namely

235–6 **custom . . . *eye*** in oblique allusion to St. Augustine's '*Consuetudo peccati tollit sensum peccandi*': the custom of sinning takes away the feeling of sin

236–8 **moon . . . *centre*** apparently in reference to the belief that the moon was larger than the earth, found, for example, in Pliny, *Natural History*, II.viii.49; *the earth's large centre* would accordingly refer to the earth's size and position at the centre of the universe

237 ***ocular sight*** physical vision (as opposed to rational or spiritual observation, the *soul's eye*)
overbulks exceeds in size

centre, yet seems as little as her *figure* taken on the tavern sign, where these brutish orgies are *celebrated*), *Abuse of Time*, *Riot*, *Prodigality*, and lineal-succeeding *Poverty*. All these are *Peace*'s professed *Enemies*, her domestic foes, who, unless this fore-battle be repulsed and suppressed in the first assault, the rest will follow, though to their own *perdition*.

Non ignota refero, these are no wonders with us. There may be *monsters* among them, but too familiar with our *acquaintance*. Examine the *ringleader*: *Drunkenness* is no *stranger* in the world; she came in with the earth's first general *curse*, and he that 'scaped that *inundation* of *waters* tasted the deluge of *wine*. *Shame* fell on him, and his *curse* to *posterity*. Noah tasted one, and Ham felt the other. Lot had his portion in her: there *Drunkenness* begat *Incest* (an *unnatural issue* of a *brutish mother*) and her succession, two wicked *generations*, Moab and Ammon. *Drunkenness* played the part of a *headsman* with Holofernes, stooping his neck to the weak arm of a *woman*; and he that stopped the *waters* of Bethulia from others had so much of his own *wine* as made him senseless of either *wine* or *water* ever after.

Alexander inter epulas Clitum carissimum transfodit: the friend hath sprinkled his wine-bowls with the dear *blood* of his friend. O brutish sacrifice! O man unmanned! O absent man! Where, out of thyself, dost thou remain while this fiend possesseth thee? But why do we seek *antiquities* for proof of a practice so present with us? Had Israel any sin that England hath missed? Was Noah drunk, one of the ark, and one of the eight reeling there? It is eight to one that seven of eight do stagger here, if not the whole vessel. It was a shame to one then, but custom hath made it no shame for all now. Did Lot commit incest with his own daughters? Could we not wish *Drunkenness* to excuse us now? Does not *Lust*, her hellish handmaid, challenge this weapon hers? The example was too soon found, and yet too late to remember. O, would that had been the first, and that we might never know a second. *Nec linguam nec manum continet ebrius*, how many bosomed counsels have been vomited out of the mouth of a drunkard, though to the ruin and destruction of his former friend?

O insania voluntaria! O wilful madness of man, to depress and quench out all thy faculties of reason with this puddle *Drunkenness*! Thou, that armed in thine own lordly fortitudes, canst reach the stars, measure the earth's large globe, search and understand the sea's profound *abyss*, yet in this sottish ignorance canst not find the depth of thine own stomach. The Jews' old proverb hath carried his full sense quite through Christendom: *chomets ben yayin*. Wine must needs acknowledge itself the parent of vinegar, meaning that a good father may have a different and saucy son. But we have from him the daughter of a worse hair: this common strumpet, *Drunkenness*, whom almost all sorts do sleep with—not *vinum ægrum*, but *ægrotum*, is our issue, a sick and unwholesome harlot; yet hath spread herself into large offsprings, in most lineal and natural children, as *Lust*, *Envy*, *Revenge*, *Murder*, etc., all impious and turbulent peacebreakers.

O *Peace*! Shall we not fear thy longer abode with us if we embrace thee with no better love? How many loving friends have broke that diamond of amity (whose pieces once dissevered can never be reconciled) for the embrace

239 **where** i.e. in a tavern
celebrated with a play on the *celebration* of eucharist
240 **lineal-succeeding** in the direct line of succession
242 **fore-battle** advance battalion; advance engagement
245 ***Non ignota refero*** I do not report strange matters (Latin); untraced
251 **Noah ... other** in reference to Ham's discovery of his father, Noah, naked in a state of drunkenness; in the Geneva Bible Ham's derisive and contemptuous report of his father's state to his brothers Shem and Japheth brought about Noah's curse on Ham's posterity, Gen. 9:20–5
251–2 **Lot ... *Incest*** in allusion to Lot's daughters plying their father with wine in preparation for incestuous union to preserve his seed, Gen. 19:32–8
253 ***issue*** offspring
254 **Moab and Ammon** sons of Lot by his daughters; Ammon is more commonly referred to as Ben-ammi, Gen. 19:38
255 **Holofernes** The Assyrian King Nebuchadnezzar's chief general who, after laying siege to the Israelites at Bethulia, was beguiled by the charms of Judith. When he succumbed to drink in anticipation of her submission to him, she cut off his head; Jth. 2:4–13:20.
260 ***Alexander ... transfodit*** Alexander stabbed Clitus, his dearest friend, at a banquet (Latin); a slightly modified version of Seneca, *Epistle* 83.19 or *Of Anger* III.17.1.
262 **brutish sacrifice** in contrast to the Christian sacrifice (which also involves wine and blood)
man unmanned Alexander (an epitome of manhood) deprived of manly attributes; also contrasting with the paradox of Christ's incarnation
262–3 **absent man** i.e. in reference to the disappearance of the drunkard's rational faculties and loss of self-control; also in contrast to 'present God' of Christian sacrament
266–7 **one ... reeling there** The *eight* who survived the flood consisted of Noah, his three sons (Ham, Shem, and Japheth), and their respective wives; only one of this number succumbed to drink (Noah).
272 **challenge** claim
274 **late** recent; delayed
275–6 ***Nec ... ebrius*** The drunkard restrains neither tongue nor hand (Latin); adapted from Seneca, *Epistle* 83.20
279 ***O insania voluntaria*** O condition of insanity purposely assumed (Latin); probably adapted from Seneca, *Epistle* 83.18
284–5 **canst not ... stomach** i.e. his stomach is bottomless
286 ***chomets ben yayin*** vinegar, son of wine (Hebrew); derived from *The Babylonian Talmud. Seder Neziḳin. Baba Meẓiʿa*, fol. 83b, which remained untranslated into Latin until later in the century and did not appear in English until the late nineteenth century. A citation in some as yet unidentified work seems the likeliest source.
289 **saucy** with a pun on the senses 'highly seasoned, piquant' and 'insolent'
290 **hair** kind, nature
291 ***vinum ægrum ... ægrotum*** sour wine ... diseased (Latin); untraced
293 **spread** dispersed
296 **fear** doubt

of a lascivious courtesan whose arms are like the iron idol that crushed the cursed sacrifices in pieces?

Envy! O what does that *ulcus animæ* amongst us? That Etna in a man that continually burns itself, *intus et extra,* within and without; that, like the *cantharides* found feeding on the fairest and flourishing roses, so *Envy* is ever opposed against the most sweet, noble, flourishing, and peaceful blossoms. Were she as rare as the comparison, I could call her *phoenix,* and wish that this day she would burn herself and leave her ashes issueless.

Revenge! Whence have we borrowed thee? O Salmoneus' terror: shall we play with thunder and lightning, and follow thy precipitated fate? Shall we snatch the sword (the peculiar sword) from the Almighty hand? Have we received wrongs on earth? Consider then if we have done no wrongs to heaven. If we stand guilty there (as, *quis non?*), do we then revenge? No, we stand disobedient and repugnant to our own just punishments. We have a milder Sister given in her stead: *Justice*, the arbiter of our injuries. But *Vengeance* is God's alone, which no man ought to take in hand, but as delivered from his hand; nor so to imitate his Majesty and Greatness that does it not but by authority, and in the way and path of his goodness.

Murder! O Cain-created sin! Cursed catastrophe of all the rest! This is *summum opus*: here is the full point and end of the labour. All the precedent travellers are here at home, the end hazarding the endless end: fearful spectacle! Here is capital sacrilege, the temple of a *holy spirit* robbed and ruined. Here is treason in the highest degree: the workmanship and image of the *Creator* defaced. Unhappy passive, but more, and most of all, unhappy active! Thou that dost murder dost first deface Him in thyself, then in thy brother. God is the God of *Peace*, of *Mercy*, *Meekness*, *Long Suffering*, and *Loving Kindness*: all these hast thou expulsed from thyself and lost thy shape with them; there is neither *Peace*, *Mercy*, *Meekness*, *Sufferance*, nor *Love* in thee. Then in thy brother thou destroyest them. His blood is *vox clamans*; and he is enforced in death from the many mouths of his wounds to cry out for revenge. But is heaven far off, and will not that move us? Look upon the deed then with natural *pity* (or a *conscience*, which is as inseparable as thy soul, that shall not leave thee living). Behold a brother weeping over his brother, a distracted mother tearing her hair and rending her heart for her child's loss, a friend with tears embalming his dear friend's body, a raving father ready to send his soul after his son, yea, perhaps his only son, his name and posterity destroyed with him. Then brothers, friends, mothers, fathers, all their curses to be thrown on thee. Are heaven and earth both dull motives to thee? O, beware the third place: let hell affright thee, and let thy *conscience* describe it to thee.

I return to that which I would wish thee never to pass—and then thou canst not come to the unblessed discovery of it—and its paths, before recited, that lead thee to it: *Peace*. Stay and abide with her and thou shalt never know her enemies, God's enemies, and thine own enemies. Let them that seek peace, find peace, enjoy peace, and have their souls laid up in eternal peace.

Of wise men I discourse, by injuries never shaken.
What reputation is, I show: a thing so long mistaken.

In this small particle consists the ground of all quarrels whatsoever, either by suspecting false things, or by aggravating small things. Now how far these two are from the ways of a wise man, and how ill-becoming, reason makes manifest, for suspicion and aggravation are the offsprings of passion, and a wise man is free from passion.

Nor can there be a greater argument of defect and despair of merit in man than suspicion; and mark her

300–1 **iron idol . . . pieces** The passage is reminiscent of several Biblical elements: the image that had legs of iron and broke all that opposed it in pieces, Dan. 2:32 ff., the stone cut without hands that destroyed the image, Dan. 2:34 and 45, and the whore of Babylon, Rev. 17.
302 ***ulcus animæ*** ulcer of the spirit (Latin); untraced
303–4 ***intus et extra*** inside and outside (Latin); untraced
304 ***cantharides*** properly an insect commonly called Spanish fly, but probably used here, as often in early writers, for 'aphides'
308 ***phoenix*** the fabled bird, of which only one existed at any time, that lived 500 or 600 years in the Arabian desert, was consumed by flame, and then rose anew from its own ashes
310–11 **Salmoneus' terror** Arrogantly boasting that he was greater than Zeus, Salmoneus drove through his city a chariot fitted with noise-making devices and threw torches into the air to simulate thunder and lightning. Zeus destroyed his city and hurled him into Tartarus with a thunderbolt; derived from the accounts by Diodorus Siculus 4.68 and Apollodorus, 1.9.7–8.
312 **precipitated** violently cast down
312–13 **sword . . . hand** i.e. the sword of justice; Geneva–Tomson glosses Matt. 26:51: 'They take the sword to whom the Lord hath not given it, that is to say, they which use the sword, and are not called to it.'
313 **peculiar** own particular
315–16 ***quis non?*** who [does] not? (Latin); untraced
317–18 **milder Sister** Justice (Dike) was the sister of Peace (Eirene) and Discipline (Eunomia), who together were referred to as the Horae. They were sisters also of the three fates (Moirai), who may be confused or mixed here with the avenging furies (Erinyes).
319 ***Vengeance . . .* alone** Deut. 32:35
323 **Cain-created** Gen. 4:8
323–4 **catastrophe . . . rest** disastrous end or conclusion of the sequence embracing Drunkenness, Envy, Revenge
324 ***summum opus*** the highest part of the work (Latin); untraced
325 **precedent travellers** i.e. as Pride, Drunkenness, Envy, Revenge
326 **end . . . endless end** conclusion (or death) risking eternal damnation
330 **passive . . . active** 'suffering action brought about by external agency' (e.g. as the victim of some action) as opposed to 'originating or exerting action upon others' (e.g. as the perpetrator of murder)
337 ***vox clamans*** a voice crying (Latin); untraced
342 **living** i.e. while you are alive
343 **distracted** mentally deranged
361 **particle** i.e. reputation
362 **suspecting** imagining something to be evil, false, or undesirable on slight or no grounds

nutriment, what strange food passion hath provided for it. It feeds upon false things, for indeed, true things are not to be suspected. And how just the punishment meets with the offence: in erring from the truth, it hath falsehood for a reward. But *in peiora ruunt omnia*, the worse devil is behind.

The aggravation of small things, when a spark shall grow to a flaming beacon, a word to a wound, the lie to a life; when every man will be the master of his own revenge, presuming to give law to themselves, and in rage to right their own wrongs, at which time the sword is extorted out of the hand of magistracy, contrary to the sacred ordinance of the Almighty.

Now the wise and understanding man is not subject or exposed to any of these injuries whatsoever; neither cares he how many darts of malice or contumely are shot against him, since he knows that he cannot be pierced. Even as there are certain hard stones which iron cannot enter; and the adamant will neither be cut, filed, nor beaten to powder, but abateth the edge of those instruments that are applied unto it; and as there are certain things which cannot be consumed with fire, but continue their hardness and habitude amidst the flames; and as the rocks that are fixed in the heart of the sea break the waves and retain no impression of the storms that have assailed them; so the heart of a wise man is solid, and hath gathered such invincible force that he stands as secure from injury as those insensible substances I made mention of. Not that injuries are not offered him, but that he admits them not, so highly raised above all the attaints of worldly wrongs that all their violences shall be frustrate before a wise man be offended. Even as arrows or bullets that are shot into the air mount higher than our sight, but they fall back again without touching heaven; and as celestial things are not subject to human hands; and they that overturn temples do no way hurt the godhead to whom they are consecrated; so, whatsoever injuries are attempted against a wise man return without effect, and are to him but as cold or heat, rain or hail, the weather of the world.

And for words of contumely, it is held so small, and so slight an injury as no wise man complains or revengeth himself for it: therefore, neither do the laws themselves pre-fix any penalty thereunto, not imagining that they would ever be burdensome. *Quis enim phrenetico medicus irascitur?* For what physician is angry with a lunatic person? Who will interpret a sick man's reproaches to the worst, that is vexed of a fever? Why, the same affection hath a wise man toward all men as the physician hath toward his sick patients: not offended to hear their outrages, he looks upon them as upon intemperate sick men, therefore is not angry with them if during their

370–1 **true things . . . suspected** genuine things are not disposed to be imagined guilty or false

373 ***in peiora ruunt omnia*** all things fall quickly into ruin in worse states (Latin); untraced

380 **extorted** wrested

382–97 **Now . . . mention of** probably derived from Thomas Lodge's translation of Seneca's *Works* (1614), *Of the Constancy of a Wise Man*, 3.5: 'I say then that a wise man is not subject or exposed to any injury whatsoever; neither careth he how many darts are shot against him since he knoweth that he cannot be pierced. Even as there are certain hard stones which iron cannot enter; and the adamant will neither be cut, filed, or beat to powder, but abateth the edge of these tools that are applied unto it; as there are certain things which cannot be consumed by fire, but continue their hardness and habitude amidst the flames; and even as the rocks that are fixed in the heart of the sea break the waves and, although they have been assaulted and beat upon many infinite times, retain no impression of the storms that have assailed them; even so the heart of a wise man is solid, and hath gathered such force that he is as secure from injury as those I made mention of.'

384 **contumely** reproachful treatment, disgrace

387 **adamant** very hard mineral identified with diamond

391 **habitude** constitution, essential character

397–402 **Not that . . . heaven** translation of Seneca, *Constancy*, 4.1, with some resemblances to Lodge: 'What then, is there no man that will attempt to do injury to a wise man? Yes, he will attempt, but he shall not attain unto him; for he is so highly raised above all the attaints of worldly things that there is no violence whatsoever that can aim his attempts so high . . . All their endeavours shall be frustrate before a wise man be offended, even as arrows and bullets that are shot into the air mount more high than our sight, but they fall back again without touching heaven.'

398 **attaints** blows; stains

402–6 **and as . . . effect** translation of Seneca, *Constancy*, 4.2 with some resemblances to Lodge: 'Even as celestial things are not subject to human hands, and they that overturn temples and melt down images do no ways hurt the deity, so whatsoever is attempted either crabbedly, immodestly, or proudly against a wise man is done in vain.'

406–8 **and are . . . world** translation of Seneca, *Constancy*, 9.1, which reads in Lodge: 'He therefore endureth all these misfortunes as he would abide the rigour of the winter, rains, heats, and other accidents . . .', possibly conflated with the marginal commentary: '*All injuries to a wise man are but as cold and heat, rain and sickness.*'

412 **pre-fix** fix or appoint beforehand

413–14 ***Quis . . . irascitur*** translated in following line (Latin); Seneca, *Constancy*, 13.1

414–24 **For what . . . insolencies** derived from Lodge's translation of Seneca, *Constancy*, 13.1–2: '. . . for what physician is angry with a lunatic person? Who will interpret a sick man's reproaches to the worst that is vexed with a fever, and is forbidden to drink cold water? The same affection hath a wise man towards all men as the physician hath towards his sick patients, who disdaineth not to handle their privities if they have need of remedy, nor to see their urines and excrements, nor to hear the outrages which fear maketh them to utter. The wise man knoweth that all these which jet in their gowns, or are apparelled in purple, who, although they are well coloured and fair, are sick and diseased, whom in no other sort he looketh upon but as intemperate sick men. Therefore is he not angry with them if during their sickness they have been so bold as to speak injuriously against him who would heal them; and as he setteth light by all their honours, so tormenteth he himself as little with their despite and insolencies.'

sickness they have been so bold as to speak injuriously against him. And as he sets light by all their words of honour, so torments he himself as little with all their despite and insolencies. For he that is displeased for an injury that is done him will likewise be glad to be honoured at his hands that did it, which a wise man is free from. For he that revenges a contumely honours him that did it in taking it so much to heart and respecting it.

Art thou angry with thy superior? Alas, death is at hand, which shall make us equals. Dost thou wish him with whom thou art displeased any more than death? Although thou attemptest nothing against him, he shall be sure of that. Thou losest thy labour then in offering to do that which will be done without thee.

We laugh, saith the wisest of philosophers, in beholding the conflict of the bull and bear when they are tied one to another, which after they have tired one another, the butcher attends for them both to drive them to the slaughterhouse. The like do we. We challenge him that is coupled with us: brother or friend, we charge him on every side; meanwhile both the conqueror and conquered are near unto their ruin. Rather let us finish that little remainder of our life in quiet and peace that our end may be a pleasure to no man.

Thou wishest a man's death! And there is always but a little difference betwixt the day of thy desire and the affliction of the sufferer.

Whilst we are therefore amongst men, let us embrace humanity, be dreadful and dangerous to no man. Let us contemn injuries and contumelies, for but looking back we may behold death presently attending us.

Pisistratus, that lived a tyrant in Athens, being for his cruelty mocked and reproved by a drunken man, answered that he was no more angry with him than if a blindfold fellow, having his eyes bound up, should run upon him.

Another said to his friend, 'I prithee, chastise my servant with strokes because I am angry,' intimating thus much: that a servant ought not to fall into his power that is not master of himself.

But now the compounding of quarrels is grown to a trade. And as a most worthy father of law and equity

424 **despite** contempt, scorn

424–8 **For he ... respecting it** possibly adapted from Lodge's translation of Seneca, *Constancy*, 13.5: '... now if but once he embase himself so far as either he be moved with injury or contumely, he can never be secure; but security is the proper good of a wise man. Neither will he endure that by revenging the contumely that is offered him [lest] he honour him that did the same; for it must needs be that he whosoever is displeased for an injury that is done him will likewise be glad to be honoured at his hands.'

429 **Art ... superior** adapted from Seneca, *Of Anger*, III.43.1, possibly derived from Lodge's translation: '... who is so bitter and troublesome to his superiors? Why fretteth thou at thy servant? Thy lord? Thy king? Why art thou angry with thy client?'

429–30 **Alas ... equals** possibly derived from Lodge's translation of Seneca, *Of Anger*, III.43.1: 'Bear with him a little: behold, death is at hand which shall make us equals.'

430–4 **Dost thou ... without thee** from Lodge's translation of Seneca, *Of Anger*, III.43.3: 'Dost thou wish him with whom thou art displeased any more than death? Although thou sayest nothing to him, he shall die; thou losest thy labour, thou wilt do that which will be done.'

435–44 **We laugh ... no man** from Lodge's translation of Seneca, *Of Anger*, III.43.2, which includes 'We were wont to laugh' (not in Seneca): 'We were wont to laugh, in beholding the combats which are performed on the sands in the morning, to mark the conflict of the bull and bear when they are tied one to another, which, after they have tired one another, the butcher attendeth for them both to drive them to the slaughterhouse. The like to do we. We challenge him that is coupled with us, we charge him on every side; meanwhile both the conquered and the conqueror are near unto their ruin. Rather let us finish that little remainder of our life in quiet and peace, and let not our death be a pleasure to any man.'

445–51 **Thou wishest ... attending us** probably adapted from Lodge's translation of Seneca, *Of Anger*, III.43.4–5: 'Dost thou wish him with whom thou art displeased any more than death? ... there is but a very little difference betwixt the day of thy desire until the punishment which such a one shall endure ... Whilst we are amongst men let us embrace humanity, let us be dreadful or dangerous to no man; let us contemn detriments, injuries, slanders, and garboils, and with great minds suffer short incommodities, whilst we look behind us, as they say, and turn ourselves: behold, death doth presently attend us.'

450 **contemn** despise

452–6 **Pisistratus ... upon him** probably derived from Lodge's translation of Seneca, *Of Anger*, III.11.4: 'It is reported that Pisistratus, a tyrant in Athens, when as a certain drunken man that sat at banquet with him had spoken many things against his cruelty (and there wanted not some who would have executed whatsoever he should have commanded, and one man on this side and another on the other laboured to enkindle his displeasure) that he took all things patiently, and answered those that provoked him after this manner, that he was no more angry with him than if a blindfold fellow having his eyes tied up should run upon him.'

457–60 **Another ... himself** derived from Lodge's translation of *Of Anger*, III.12.7, which specifies Plato as the angered party and Speusippus as his friend: '... and notwithstanding because his servant had committed some fault that was worthy punishment, he said unto Speusippus, "I pray thee chastise my servant with strokes because I am angry." He beateth him not for that which another had beaten him: "I am angry," said he, "I shall do more than I should. I will do it more willingly. Let not this servant be in his power that is not master of himself."'

461 **compounding** settling

462 **trade** (1) occupation, business; (2) habitual course of action

father of law and equity i.e. Sir Francis Bacon, in 1618 named Chancellor; the court of chancery elevated *equity* over precedent

speaks, there be some counsel learned of *duels* that teach young gentlemen when they are beforehand and when behindhand, and thereby incense and incite them to the *duel*, and make an art of it: the spur and incitement, false and erroneous imagination of honour and credit, when most commonly those golden hopes end in a halter.

That folly and vainglory should cast so thick a mist before the eye of gentry! To fix their aim and only end upon reputation, and end most lamentably without it; nay, farthest from it: first to hazard the eternal death of their souls, and the surviving bodies to die the death of a cutpurse.

A miserable effect and most horrid resolution when young men, full of towardness and hope, such as the poets call *auroræ filii*, the sons of the morning, in whom the sweet expectation and comfort of their friends consists, shall be cast away and ruined for ever in so vain a business.

But much more is it to be deplored when so much noble and gentle blood shall be spilt upon such follies which, adventured in honourable service, were able to make the fortune of a day and to change the fortune of a kingdom.

It is evident then how desperate an evil this is which troubles peace, disfurnishes war, brings sudden calamity upon private men, peril upon the state, and contempt upon the law.

They pretend above all things to regard honour, yet chiefly seek the dishonour of God and of justice, and, which is worse than madness in those men, that adventuring to leave this life in anger, presume to press into the next (to the supper of the Lamb, which is all Peace and Love) without Peace, Love, or Charity. O, that gentlemen would learn to esteem themselves at a just price! How dearly they are bought, how most precious their redemption!

The root of this offence is stubborn—for it despiseth death, which is the utmost of all temporal punishments—and had need of the severity used in France, where the man-slayers, though gentlemen of great quality, are hanged with their wounds bleeding, lest a natural death should prevent the example of justice.

This punctuality of reputation is no better than a bewitching sorcery that enchants the spirits of young men, like the smoke of fashion, that witch *tobacco*, which hath quite blown away the smoke of hospitality, and turned the chimneys of their forefathers into the noses of their children. And by all computation (if computation may be kept for folly), I think the vapour of the one and the vainglory of the other came into England much upon a voyage, and hath kept as close together as the report follows the powder.

463–6 **there . . . of it** taken with minor changes from *The Charge of Sir Francis Bacon, Knight, His Majesty's Attorney General, Touching Duels, upon an Information in the Star Chamber against Priest and Wright* (1614), sigs. D4^{v}–E1: 'Nay, I hear there be some counsel learned of duels that tell young men when they are beforehand and when they are otherwise, and thereby incense and incite them to the duel, and make an art of it.'

466–8 **the spur . . . halter** Cf. Bacon, *The Charge*, E1: 'I hope I shall meet with some of them too, and I am sure, my lords, this course of preventing duels in nipping them in the bud is fuller of clemency and providence than the suffering them to go on, and hanging men with their wounds bleeding, as they did in France.'

468 **halter** i.e. on the gallows

475–80 **A miserable . . . business** taken in slightly altered form from Bacon, *The Charge*, B1^{v}–B2: 'Again, my lords, it is a miserable effect when young men full of towardness and hope, such as the poets call *auroræ filii*, sons of the morning, in whom the expectation and comfort of their friends consisteth, shall be cast away and destroyed in such a vain manner.'

477 ***auroræ filii*** translated in the following phrase; Virgil, *Aeneid* I.751, where the reference is to Memnon, the son of Aurora, who was slain by Achilles

481–4 **But much . . . kingdom** derived from Bacon, *The Charge*, B2: '. . . but much more it is to be deplored when so much noble and gentle blood shall be spilt upon such follies, as, if it were adventured in the field in service of the king and realm, were able to make the fortune of a day, and to change the fortune of a kingdom'.

481–2 **noble and gentle** i.e. of the nobility and gentry

483–4 **make . . . day** win a battle

485–8 **It is . . . law** derived from Bacon, *The Charge*, B2: 'So as your lordships see what a desperate evil this is: it troubleth peace, it disfurnisheth war, it bringeth calamity upon private men, peril upon the state, and contempt upon the law.'

491–4 **that adventuring . . . Charity** essentially from Henry Howard, Earl of Northampton's (but published anonymously), *A Publication of His Majesty's Edict* (1613), p. 11: '. . . that adventuring to leave this life in passion, presume to press in the next, to the supper of the lamb without charity . . .'

496 **bought** procured, obtained

497 **redemption** ransom, the price of their deliverance (i.e. their lives)

498–9 **The root . . . punishments** taken in slightly modified form from Bacon, *The Charge*, C1^{v}: '. . . the root of this offence is stubborn, for it despiseth death, which is the utmost of punishments . . .'

500–3 **severity . . . justice** adapted from Bacon, *The Charge*, C1^{v}: 'And yet the late severity in France was more, where by a kind of martial law established by ordinance of the king and parliament, the party that had slain another was presently had to the gibbet, in so much as gentlemen of great quality were hanged, their wounds bleeding, lest a natural death should prevent the example of justice.'

504 **punctuality** punctiliousness

506–9 **witch *tobacco* . . . children** possibly a nod to James I's *A Counterblast to Tobacco* (1604)

511 **upon** in consequence of

512 **voyage** a possible allusion to Sir Walter Ralegh, a conspicuous patron of tobacco. Mistrusted by James I and imprisoned in the Tower from 1603 to 1616, Ralegh emblematized for James military heroism—largely anti-Spanish—associated with Elizabeth's reign and now out of favour. He was arrested soon after his return in June 1618 from his final, disastrous voyage to the New World and subsequently beheaded. **report** i.e. the sound of a gunshot

513 **powder** gunpowder (i.e. the ignition of the powder)

For when, but in the latterness of these times, hath so much private and domestic blood been shed? Like the three Jewish brothers in that perplexed history of Jerusalem, who, wanting enemies, still flew upon themselves. So these malicious, unthankful spirits, fattened with the abundant blessings of a mellifluous peace, disgorge themselves upon their Christian brothers, like those that surfeit upon too much honey.

And well may this vainglory, or opinion of reputation, be called a satanical illusion and apparition of honour against religion, law, moral virtue, and against all the honourable precedents and examples of the best times and valiantest nations. For hereby have gentlemen lost the true knowledge and understanding of fortitude and valour. For true fortitude distinguisheth of the grounds of quarrels whether they be just; and not only so, but whether they be worthy; and sets a better value upon men's lives than to bestow them idly—which are not so to be trifled away, but offered up and sacrificed to honourable services, public merits, good causes, and noble adventures.

And behold here thy folly: thou attemptest a way freely to lose thy soul eternally, but not thy reputation. Fool that thou art, in offering to save that which indeed is nothing, thou losest all! For reputation is but another man's opinion, and opinion is no substance for thee to consist of. For how canst thou consist of a thing that is without thee? Which may be any man's at an instant as well as thine; and when thou hast it, it is but a breath. And of what certainty or permanence is it when they must die that give it thee?

Perhaps because some have said that fame hath a perpetuity, thou hasten'st to lose thy soul to provide for thy name. How much thou deceivest thyself! Why, it is no more than the echo of a glory, for as an echo no longer resounds than it is fed with a voice, no longer does fame sound forth man's praises than it is supplied and cherished with deservings. For when thy noise ceases in itself, it will quickly cease the noise of thee. However, at the farthest a general dissolution will come when fame, that is next to nothing now, shall have no being then at all.

Happy is then the wise and understanding spirit. For, though he be injured, he can lose nothing thereby, neither his fame nor reputation, for a wise man entertains nothing that is subject to loss. Fortune takes nothing but what she hath given. She gives not virtue, nor wisdom; therefore cannot take that away.

The more thou thinkest upon reputation, the farther off thou art from all contention, unless custom in ignorance or wilfulness in nature make thee throw an abuse upon the word. For what is reputation but consideration? A diligent weighing, considering, and revolving in the mind? And that is quite opposite to rashness: truth will shame thee if thou confess not so much.

There can be then no reputation in rashness; that is manifest. And what are quarrels but the fruits of rashness? There can be then no reputation in quarrels.

And as it is consideration, it were dreadful to think that any man in the state of his best counsel and advisedness should attempt to destroy the image of his Creator in the life of his Christian brother. And therefore divinely have our human laws bent their hate and punishments against the abhorred act committed in cold blood, which is as wilful an opposition against man's life (considering what he does) as blasphemy against the Word of Truth, the conscience knowing it offends of set purpose (the only sin against the Holy Ghost). And as the body of every true Christian is said to be the Temple of the Holy Ghost (1 Cor. 3:16), what does the accursed man-slayer but in the blood of his brother destroys the temple, as the blasphemer wounds the Lord of the Temple?

Behold then, not without a face of horror, the miserable condition the sons of this age run into. All they venture for

516–17 **three Jewish . . . themselves** Presumably in allusion to the self-destructive strife among three rival Jewish factions led respectively by Eleazar, John, and Simon that broke out within Jerusalem during peaceful intervals in the Romans' siege of the city, set out in an account by Thomas Nashe in *Christ's Tears Over Jerusalem* derived from Josephus, *The Jewish War*.

516 **perplexed** complicated, intricate

519 **mellifluous** playing on the etymological meaning: 'honey-flowing'

522 **opinion** favourable estimate, esteem

523–6 **satanical . . . nations** from Bacon, *The Charge*, B2^{v}: '. . . and a kind of satanical illusion and apparition of honour; against religion, against law, against moral virtue, and against the precedents and examples of the best times and valiantest nations . . .'

526–33 **For hereby . . . adventures** from Bacon, *The Charge*, B3–B3^{v}: '. . . men have almost lost the true notion and understanding of fortitude and valour. For fortitude distinguisheth of the grounds of quarrels, whether they be just; and not only so, but whether they be worthy; and setteth a better price upon men's lives than to bestow them idly. Nay, it is weakness and disesteem of a man's self to put a man's life upon such ledger performances. A man's life is not to be trifled away, it is to be offered up and sacrificed to honourable services, public merits, good causes, and noble adventures.'

540 **without** outside of

554–9 **Happy . . . away** probably adapted from Lodge's translation of Seneca, *Constancy*, 5.3–4: 'Injury hath this intent to harm some man. But wisdom leaveth no place for evil: for there is no evil for her but vice, which cannot enter there where virtue and honesty dwell; and therefore injury doth not affect a wise man: for if injury be the sufferance of some evil, and a wise man cannot suffer evil, there is no evil that appertaineth to a wise man. Every injury is a diminution of him to whom it is offered, and no man may receive any injury without some detriment either in honour, body, or in goods, but a wise man can lose nothing. He hath all his good enclosed in himself. He no ways putteth confidence in fortune; he entirely possesseth his riches, contenting himself with virtue, which hath no need of accidental things, and therefore may neither increase nor decrease. For having attained to the height, there is no place for increase. Fortune taketh away nothing but that which she hath given; she giveth not virtue, and therefore cannot take it away'.

556 **entertains** cherishes

577–9 **blasphemy . . . Holy Ghost** in reference to Matt. 12:31–2, Mark 3:28–9, or Luke 12:10

is to bring the bloodiness of their action into the compass of Honour—as if Honour consisted in destruction. Now what impossibility follows that labour even the weakest may conjecture. For Honour is the rumour of a beautiful and virtuous action which redoundeth from our souls to the view of the world, and by reflection into ourselves, bringing to us a testimony of that which others believe of us, which turns to a great peace and contentment of mind—blessings which were never yet found in a bloodshedder, let his cause be never so glorious. And where there is no *Peace*, all other benefits have a cessation. It is the only health of thy soul; and that once lost, thy soul sickens immediately, even to death, and can no more taste or relish a joy after than a sick man's palate his nutriment.

Is not this then a delusion of Honour? Nay, can there be anything more delusive? Alas, when it is at the greatest height of human glory, it is of a small and slender efficacy, uncertain, a stranger, and as it were separated in the air from him that is honoured. For it does not only not enter into him, nor is inward and essential unto him, but it does not so much as touch him. A poor and miserable purchase at the best for so great and eternal a hazard!

Flatter not thy soul then to her everlasting ruin in thinking reputation consists in bloodshedding. *Sanguis clamat*, as the Almighty speaks in the letter of his own law. Blood cries, and with a louder voice to Heaven than thy fame can sound on Earth. Rumour's ten thousand tongues are hoarse to that. They compass but some nook or angle of the World; the other reaches from the field to Heaven.

'The voice of thy brother's blood crieth unto me from the earth' (Gen. 4:10). And no sooner the Cry comes but the Curse follows in the very next words: 'Now therefore thou art cursed from the earth, which hath opened her mouth to receive thy brother's blood from thy hand.' And immediately in the next, 'A vagabond and a runagate shalt thou be on the earth', which shows the horror of the guilty conscience, which, after the deed done, would fain fly from itself: a distraction which follows all the children of wrath unto this day.

Well may peace then have the excellency of her glorious name advanced above all titles and inscriptions: and so much the rather in that it pleaseth the Almighty Creator himself to be called the God of Peace, and the Author (1 Cor. 14:33), nay, Love itself, delighting in the name (1 John 4:16): 'God is love, and he that dwelleth in love, dwelleth in God, and God in him.' And (1 Thess. 5:23), 'Now the very God of Peace sanctify you throughout, etc.' Christ the Saviour of the World, the Lamb of Peace (John 1:29): 'Behold, the Lamb of God, which taketh away the sins of the world.' There is Peace made in taking sin away, which is the only fuel of Wrath. And (Eph. 2:14), 'Christ is our Peace, which hath made of both, one, and hath broken the stop of the partition wall.'

Moreover, the heavenly Soldiers at the birth of Christ, praising God, said, 'Glory be to God, in the high Heavens, and Peace in Earth, and toward men, good will.'

And as his most blessed nativity was the Fountain of Peace, there wanted not the fruits that sprang from that sacred Fountain in his departure (John 14:27): 'Peace I leave with you; my peace I give unto you. Let not your heart be troubled, nor fear.' Let not your heart, speaking to many, because all his ought to be of one heart, which is a work of Peace.

And not leaving, but in the same evangelist (John 14:16), 'I will pray my Father, and he shall give you another Comforter, that he may abide with you for ever': intimating thereby the eternal Peace of Soul and Conscience by the coming of the Holy Ghost, calling him in the words immediately following (John 14:17), 'Even the Spirit of Truth,' (John 14:26) 'whom the Father will send in my name'. He comes all Peace, and in the name of Peace, of Christ our Saviour.

And to add more glory to the name of *Peace*, behold how the incomprehensible Godhead desires to be comprehended all into Unity, Trinity in Unity, which shows that Unity is the Conserver, Sustainer, and Comprehender of all things, both in Heaven and Earth.

Thou, therefore, that in the madness of thy blood attemptest to destroy Unity, thou seekest to destroy that which Heaven and Earth is sustained by. Most miserable of creatures, thy soul hath but one supporter, and in the tempest of thy fury thou overturnest that and all.

Peace enters here in arms and overthrows
By force of her own strength her strongest foes.

And first behold her contending with her most honourable enemy, even he that with better authority may slay his ten thousand than any other his thousand, ay, his hundred, yea, one single life (either the haughty *challenge*,

588 **weakest** feeblest intellect
609 **Flatter** deceive with false hopes
610–11 ***Sanguis clamat*** blood cries out (Latin); cited in *A Publication of His Majesty's Edict*, I1; probably derived from Gen. 4:10, quoted at ll. 617–18
613–14 **Rumour's ... tongues** Rumour was conventionally emblematized as a figure adorned with many tongues and eyes.
637 **sins** Various versions of the Bible read 'sin'; but Geneva–Tomson glosses the passage: 'That is, that root of sins, to wit, our corruption, and so consequently the fruits of sin, which are commonly called in the plural number, sins.'
638–40 **Christ ... partition wall** essentially drawn from Geneva–Tomson
640 **broken ... partition wall** The gloss in Geneva–Tomson reads: 'As by the ceremonies and worship appointed by the Law, the Jews were divided from the Gentiles, so now Christ, having broken down the partition wall, joineth them both together, both in himself, and betwixt themselves, and to God.'
the stop piece that keeps a part fixed in its place
partition wall internal wall dividing one room or portion of a building from another
641 **heavenly Soldiers** See ll. 220–1 and note.
642–3 **Glory ... will** Luke 2:14 (Geneva–Tomson)
646–8 **Peace ... fear** Geneva–Tomson
661–2 **comprehended** included, contained

the curious *duel*, or the blood-thirsty *revenge*): to wit, *War* itself, sometimes a principal arrow shot from the heavenly Bow of Justice, a forced Arbiter betwixt different Kingdoms, and often proves the dear Moderator. Yet this great Soldier, with all his attributes of Fame and Honour, falls far short of our high-throned Empress, *Peace*.

Mark how the philosopher hath ordered this battle and given the colonies to both these great commanders: *Pacem cum omnibus habebis, bellum cum vitiis*. Have peace with all the world, only war with thy sins. *Melior et tutior est certa pax quam incerta victoria*: for more safe and noble is a certain peace than a doubtful victory, with all his honours attending.

But let us believe no cowardly philosophers; let him that in his hand holds both, and from his hand sends both, be the Judge betwixt us.

When was war sent as a blessing, or peace as a punishment? Let his judges judge our cause (Judg. 5:8): 'They chose new gods, then was war in the gates.' Here is an Offence and here is a Punishment: Idolatry and War.

Again, 'They turn to the Lord, and the land had Peace forty years.' Here is Penitence, and here is the Blessing: Serving God, and Peace.

If then the General of Blood and Death, even War itself, be a prodigy, a curse, and not a blessing, what shall his base imitator be? What Honour shall the challenger lay challenge to? What blood shall the Revenger dare to shed? Or what Fame shall the schoolmaster of duels achieve, with all his vainglorious and punctual orders of firsts and seconds, lengths of weapons, distances of place, heights of grounds, equalities of wind and sun? O wicked Ashkelon and her suburbs, let them be taken and destroyed together. Why do we quarrel? What is the end of the fairest War? To enjoy Peace. See how the servant labours for the mistress, and foolish they that enjoy their inheritance, yet know it not: thriftless gamesters to play for their own money.

Is thy night quiet, and sweet with Peace? Embrace her in the day and keep her continually. If thou letst blood into thy bosom in the day, Peace will not stay with thee at night. Peace wears no parti-coloured coat, no mixed scarlet and white, but white in her purity; nor fat nor blood must be eaten in the *Peace-offering* (Lev. 3). Now ascend Abarim and climb up to the Mountain of Nebo, and see some part of the Land of Promise, whither this blessed Peace shall lead thee, if she be thy conduct: but be sure to look upwards, and then thou canst not fear the depth beneath thee.

Behold the Father (the God of Peace), the Son (the Lamb of Peace), the blessed Spirit (the Dove of Peace), the Angels (Servants and Ministers to this power of Peace); infinites and all rejoicing at one soul's entrance into Peace.

Behold the new Jerusalem, *Kiriath-salem*, the City of Peace. That which was militant and troubled in the wilderness (the Church), behold it there triumphant in ever-blessed Peace. That Peace, which as it is unintelligible, so is it most unutterable.

Then, if we desire to be inhabitants in this Land of Promise and Peace, observe our entrance. We have yet two mountains to pass over Jordan by: Gerizim and Ebal; and the twelve tribes placed on each side, both to bless or curse us:

676 **curious** fastidious; skilful

683 **colonies** territories (i.e. the matters under contention between Peace and War)

683–4 ***Pacem . . . vitiis*** translated in the following line (Latin). This apophthegm occurs in two classical sources: *De Institutione Morum*, 34, uncertainly attributed to Seneca, and Publilius Syrus, *Sententiae*, 45, both of which share wordings that differ slightly from *Peacemaker*'s: '*Pacem cum hominibus habebis, bellum cum vitiis*' (have peace with men, war with your sins). The Latin Vulgate Bible, Rom. 12:18, may have influenced the cited reading: '*cum omnibus hominibus pacem habentes*' (have peace with all men).

685–6 ***Melior . . . victoria*** adapted from Livy 30.30.19: '*Melior tutiorque est certa pax quam sperata victoria*', better and safer is certain peace than a hoped-for victory (Latin). This oft-quoted aphorism appears in adapted form in James I's Speech to Parliament of 19 March 1604: 'a secure and honourable warre must be preferred to an vnsecure and dishonourable Peace', p. 134.

696–7 **They . . . years** presumably based on Judg. 5:31, but Judg. 3:11 or 8:28 are candidates. Various versions of the Bible read 'rest' in place of 'Peace'.

700 **prodigy** something extraordinary, abnormal; a wonder, marvel

701 **challenger** claimant

702 **challenge** claim

704 **punctual** punctilious

705–6 **firsts . . . sun** in reference to various points, strict observance of which was stipulated by the code of duelling

705 **firsts** principal parties in a duel
seconds those who act as representatives of the principals in a duel
lengths of weapons the challenged party was generally presented with a stick prescribing the length of sword to be used

707 **Ashkelon** Philistine city the destruction of which is foretold by several prophets, e.g. Jer. 47:5–7
her suburbs in reference to outlying localities characterized by licentiousness (probably inspired by the model of London)

708–9 **What . . . Peace** possibly in allusion to the Latin epigram, '*pax quæritur bello*', peace is sought by war

709 **servant** war

710 **mistress** Elizabeth I

710–11 **foolish . . . know it not** an echo of the position set out at ll. 133–8; the end of Elizabethan military campaigns was peace, which has been duly passed on to the heirs of the previous reign (though some are foolishly blind to this)

712 **for their own money** i.e. in placing the principal at risk

716 **parti-coloured** partly of one colour, partly of another

717–18 **nor fat . . . *Peace-offering*** Lev. 3:17

719 **Abarim** a range of mountains of Moab, east of and facing Jordan opposite Jericho
Nebo the highest mountain in the Abarim range from which Moses viewed the promised land, Deut. 32:49

726 **infinites** exceedingly large numbers

728 ***Kiriath-salem*** city of peace (Hebrew)

735 **Gerizim . . . Ebal** the mountain of blessings in Ephraim and mountain of curses in Samaria respectively, designated by Moses to ensure adherence to the law before crossing Jordan into the promised land: Deut. 11:29, 27:12–26

<table>
<tr>
<td>EBAL
Pride
Malice
Ambition
Schismatical
Contentions
Revenge
Impiety</td>
<td>Here we have our choice, and we are ever going on in this passage.
O, let us pass by Gerizim, the Mount of Blessings, the right hand and the right hill.
Turn thy back to Ebal, but let none of her curses fall upon thee.</td>
<td>GERIZIM
Humility
Mercy
Charity
Faith

Peace
Piety</td>
</tr>
</table>

Be thou strong or weak, thou mayst with more ease bear six on thy right hand than one on thy left.

Pride is a great weight, able to overthrow the strongest man. *Malice*, a ponderous load, turning thy sleeps to unquiet slumbers, and even there haunting thee in restless dreams. *Ambition*, a mountain itself, to sink thee. *Schism*, a spirit and conscience troubler. *Revenge*, an impostume of blood—which, broken once, strangles thee with thine own corruption. *Impiety*, a cloud and mist of darkness, turning thee from thy way.

Whenas on the other side, how light and easily mayst thou bear about thee *Humility*? How sweet a companion is *Mercy*? How loving a fellowship is *Charity*? How sure a friend is *Faith*? How nourishing a cordial is *Peace*? How bright a lamp is *Piety*? And then, how glorious a reward is *Eternity*, and *Peace* in *Eternity*?

Now let us bind ourselves to the Peace, put in security for our good behaviours. Let our souls be bound for our bodies, our bodies for our souls, and let each come in at the general sessions (to save his bail), where we shall find a merciful Judge. If there we can answer, 'We have not broke his Peace,' our bonds shall be cancelled. As we have kept the Peace, we shall be rewarded with Peace, and kept in Eternal Peace. *Amen.*

FINIS.

748 **right . . . left** The textual arrangement places the curses on the left or sinister side and the blessings on the right; in setting the text confronting the choice between the curses and blessings the layout symbolically represents the crossing of Jordan.

753 **impostume** festering sore, abscess

757 **Whenas** whereas

763–4 **put in . . . behaviours** i.e. as securing our 'good behaviour', our appearance in court at a specified time, or performance of some undertaking

766 **general sessions** a court held four times a year, otherwise known as 'quarter sessions'

MASQUE OF HEROES; OR, THE INNER TEMPLE MASQUE

Text edited and annotated by Jerzy Limon, introduced by James Knowles

'A right Christmas' as celebrated in Jonson's *Christmas His Masque* (1616) featured Christmas and his 'children' Misrule, Carol, Minced Pie, Gambol, Post and Pair, New Year's Gift, Mumming, Wassail, Offering, and Baby Cake, who entertained the company with songs and dances. Such amusements and delicacies typified a seventeenth-century aristocratic Christmas when the festivities might include singing, dancing, gift-giving, feasting, and various forms of sanctioned festive misrule, all designed to foster social harmony. In London, many of the City institutions and guilds, but also the Inns of Court, vied with the aristocracy in the magnificence—and sometimes riotousness—of their seasonal celebrations. Indeed, such competition occasionally became explicit so that Middleton's *Masque of Heroes; or, The Inner Temple Masque* (performed sometime between 6th January and 2nd February 1619) amidst its seasonal compliments also emulated another Christmas masque, Jonson's *Pleasure Reconciled to Virtue* (1618).

Masque of Heroes combines a lively debate between traditional figures such as Doctor Almanac (a stock comic character), New Year, and the irrepressible, rotund Plumporridge (a seasonal food), with a masque proper and social dancing. Middleton's prefatory verses emphasize the occasion's 'mirth', gracefully acknowledging the hospitality and commensality of the Inner Temple which the masque itself displayed. Such 'mirth' was 'found free' (7), that is both 'noble' and 'generous', although 'free' might encompass the elements of festive licence, levity, and sociability that the masque also displays. These qualities, nobility, liberality, and festivity, serve well as a self-characterization of the Inns of Court which, although primarily legal institutions, functioned as a third university for England. At the Inner Temple cultural education supplemented the legal tuition which might launch a career in the judiciary, administration, or even at court. Masques constituted an important part of this milieu.

Indeed, masques made ideal Christmas entertainments since the structure of antimasque followed by masque and then revels provided the guests with comedy (in the antimasque performed by professional actors), a graceful ordered vision of hope for the future which commended the society (danced by the members of the inn), and finally participatory dances (the revels). These elements, combining festivity, hospitality, and generosity, permeate *Heroes*, notably in the extant antimasque music 'The New Year's Gift' (see *Companion*, p. 161), which conveys the significance of the entertainment as a demonstration of the 'free' ethos of the inn and its guests. The presentation of gifts exemplifies hope for the new year, and symbolizes the social and political cohesion of the audience, as spectators and participants in the masque.

Formally, *Heroes* falls into three main sections. The 'ante-masques' contain dialogue between Doctor Almanac, Fasting Day, Plumporridge, and New Year, about the death of the old year and the decline of Master Kersmas, diagnosed by Doctor Almanac in his patient's water (57–62, 91–2). The discussions are enlivened by the animosity between 'plump and lusty' Plumporridge (literally embodying festivity) and the Fasting Day who has been 'out of service' (44) since the beginning of Christmas. Aided by Doctor Almanac and Time, the New Year fits all the differently tempered days (ranging from the disturbed days through the good, bad, and indifferent days) into New Year's 'service' (household) (155, 179). Each group of days then performs a separate 'antemasque' rounded off with an antic dance. In the second segment of *Heroes* dance, music, and formal speeches predominate, with the masque of Nine Worthies, introduced by Harmony, while the entertainment closes with the revels as the masquers select dancing partners from the audience.

Festivity provides one of the masque's central themes as Middleton's prefatory verses claim: 'I only made the time they sat to see | Serve for the mirth itself' (6–7). Yet Christmas, like other traditional calendar feasts, had become a site of religious dissension, as Puritans like John Stubbes emphasized how

> more mischief is that time committed than in all the year besides. What masking and mumming—whereby robbery, whoredom, murder and what not is committed? What dicing and carding, what eating and drinking, what banqueting and feasting is then used, more than in all the year besides, to the great dishonour of God and impoverishing of the realm. (Durston)

Alexander Leighton complained in 1625 that Christ*mas* recalled Catholic idolatry, as 'the Popes of Rome solemnized their festivals and jubilees with all sorts of plays and sports for recreation, and to delight the people with such fooleries'. For James VI and I, however, these 'fooleries' constituted 'lawful recreations' which he defended in his *Declaration of Sports* (1618): 'For when shall the common people have leave to exercise, if not upon the Sundays and holidays?'

Debates over the legitimacy and degree of festivity and events surrounding the *Declaration of Sports* provide important contexts for *Heroes*. The *Declaration* had been sparked by the King's discovery, during a royal progress through Lancashire, that Puritan ministers had forbidden any Sunday recreations; the King then ordered a relaxation of Sunday observances. He allowed not only sabbatarian games but also popular ceremonials such as Whitsun Ales and May poles, and obliquely the *Declaration* also defended Anglican ritual, another target of the Puritans. This recently publicized controversy may explain why Fasting Day considers Lancashire for employment, presumably amongst its stricter brethren (165).

Such issues merged into court politics since the King also constantly sought to persuade his gentry to diminish their court attendance and continue the tradition of country residence, the foundation of Jacobean political and social control through the gentry's role as local representatives of the monarch. Simultaneously, however, the King struggled to curb the extravagance of the court and reduce royal expenditure. Many of James's leading courtiers—notably James Hay, Earl of Carlisle—practised conspicuous consumption, not only in magnificent festivals (sometimes graced with their own masques, such as Jonson's *Lovers Made Men* [1617]) but also in the form of the ante-supper, a sumptuous banquet set before the guests, only to be whipped away untouched. Conspicuous consumption vied with non-consumption as symbols of aristocratic opulence, and critical satires circulated against the monarch's 'merry boys with masks and toys' (Malone MS 25).

Throughout, *Heroes* engages with these wider discussions of the politics of festivity and hospitality. Jonson's *Pleasure Reconciled to Virtue* (1618) opposes the 'vicious hospitality' (Marcus) of Comus, the walking belly, with the virtuous Hercules, and rejects puritan parsimony (allegorized in the figure of Antaeus and his pygmies). The masque envisions James as Hesperus and England as his Hesperides, an ideal image of pastoral hospitality and moderation, bountiful yet temperate. Contemporaneously, the anonymous *Coleorton Masque* contrasted the commensality of Leicestershire and its old families, the 'good fellows in this corner of the country' (67–8), with the current parsimony, mocked by the buttery spirit Bob:

> Puck, housekeeping is a rag of Rome—'tis abolished. All good fellowship, called feasting, is turned to a dish of Bibles. The country mirth and pastime, that's... dead and buried... This new sect, in sincerity, 'tis a dry one... (29–35)

The audience, members of the Hastings and Devereux families, typified 'great houses... o'th'old way' (34) who, combining ancient aristocracy and Protestantism, were at odds with the court's arriviste favourites. In 1621 Middleton contributed to the debate in another Christmas entertainment, where Severity and Levity argue over the proper celebration of the season (*Honourable Entertainments*, 7).

Questions about the function and propriety of festivity and hospitality permeate *Heroes*. Thus Fasting Day laments his exclusion from the calendar, the 'only man in place' being Plumporridge:

> I have been out of service all this Kersmas;
> Nobody minds Fasting Day;
> I have scarce been thought upon o' Friday nights;
> And because Kersmas this year fell upon't
> The Fridays have been ever since so proud
> They scorn my company... (44–9)

Neglected by even his closest kin, Fasting Day sees his sworn adversary Plumporridge thrive, 'sure of welcome... like one of the great porridge tubs, going to the Counter' (66–7). Plumporridge's only concern is the sickening of his Master Kersmas, although Fasting Day longs for the end of Christmas and the austere start to the new year.

When New Year actually arrives he recognizes Fasting Day as one of his father's old retainers and although Doctor Almanac denigrates the 'unseasonable coxcomb' (155), Fasting Day defends himself on grounds that his economy made New Year's ancestors rich through parsimony. To reconcile the two principles of fasting and festival New Year agrees to welcome Fasting Day into his household, but not until Candlemas Eve:

> Thou shalt not all be lost, nor for vainglory
> Greedily welcomed; we'll begin with virtue.
> As we may hold with't, that does virtue right.
> (180–2)

Later, Doctor Almanac, acting as physician to the calendar politic, under instruction from New Year and aided by Time, allots each of the festival and fast days 'their places due by custom' (204). This location of each of the feasts and fasts in their correct place and time provides an image of the rightful place of both celebration and penance and envisages the harmony possible in the formation of New Year's household.

Parallels with *Pleasure Reconciled* weave throughout the masque, in the balance of festal days and in the implicit defence of the calendrical rituals. Plumporridge and Comus are clearly related figures and, indeed, the resolution of the *Heroes* ends with a similar vision of Virtue. Yet although the themes of the two entertainments are similar their treatments vary, for whereas Jonson relies upon classical and to some extent abstract ideas, Middleton draws upon the popular culture of the almanacs, folk plays (for Doctor Almanac), and upon the shared culture of calendrical ritual. Plumporridge, an altogether more prepossessing and humorous figure than Jonson's classical Comus, emerges from the traditions of Christmas games, the popular pastimes antithetical to Jonsonian erudition. Most importantly, the agent of resolution lies in the providential pattern of the calendrical cycle rather than royal power:

> The goodness of thy thought
> This blessèd work hath wrought,
> Time shall be reconciled.
> Thy spring shall in all sweets abound,
> Thy summer shall be clear and sound,

Thy autumn swell the barn and loft
With corn and fruits, ripe, sweet and soft,
And in thy winter, when all go,
Thou shalt depart as white as snow. (284–92)

This vernacular pastoral vision contrasts with the royalist Hesperides, an opposition which can again be traced in Middleton's *Honourable Entertainments* where civic pastoral for the Spittle sermon stands against the classicized courtly pastoral in Jonson's *Pan's Anniversary* (1621).

The 'antemasques' of *Heroes* substitute providential for monarchical power, while the masque offers a vision of active heroism that further diverges from the celebration of courtly virtue and royal authority in *Pleasure Reconciled*. Both masques end with a vision of virtue enabled by Harmony but the virtues offered differ, for whilst the 'masked knights' of Jonson's masque practise a self-contained, almost personal virtue, Middleton presents an activist, communal heroism. In *Heroes* virtue is defined as 'heroic glory' (316) which tends to the 'human good' (301), personified not in anonymous courtier-knights but in the Nine Worthies.

Although during their fleeting entry in *Heroes* the Nine Worthies remain silent, some of the implications of these familiar figures can be traced from their reappearance in *The World Tossed at Tennis* where they are introduced at length, with emphasis placed upon the Old Testament figures (especially Judas Maccabaeus and King David—both suitably Protestant exemplars), and upon the three Christians, all as military figures. The Worthies symbolize a fame to be aspired to and exemplify how 'Men strive to know too much, too little do' (308). In *Heroes* Harmony comments that the heroes

...all descend to have their worth
Shine to imitation forth;
And by their motion, light and love,
To show how after-times should move! (303–6)

Their manifestation will 'Raise merit from his ancient slumber' (318).

While such compliments are traditional to the masque whatever its origin or playing space, the particular date, location, and political context all lend a special resonance to the sentiments. In the 'polycentric world' (Smuts) of Jacobean élite culture the Inns of Court (like the London and provincial homes of the greater nobles) functioned as privileged sites of political debate, where the full variety of political viewpoints might find expression. The Inner Temple, for instance, had a distinct Protestant ethos, with several pro-puritan benchers (senior members), and this religious bias may have shaped attitudes, especially towards fellow Protestants in Bohemia and the Palatinate (modern Germany). In 1613 the Inns of Court had taken a significant role in celebrations for the marriage between Princess Elizabeth and Frederick, Elector Palatine when the Inner Temple had staged Beaumont's *Masque of the Inner Temple and Gray's Inn* at Whitehall. During the Bohemian crisis, the Inns of Court shared the national enthusiasm for military intervention, a climate that may be glimpsed in a sermon from the Temple Church minister, Abraham Gibson, whose *Christiana-Polemica, or a Preparative to War* (1619) advocated militarized Protestantism. It may be that even the choice of performers for *Heroes*, Prince Charles's Men, reflects a similar political stance.

The Bohemian crisis arose in 1618 when the kingdom, with its largely Protestant population, revolted against Ferdinand of Styria, and wholesale war with the Catholic Hapsburg powers threatened. The Bohemians appealed to the wider Protestant community. In late 1618 the Dutch Commissioners urged James to intervene, and although in January 1619 the King ostentatiously refused to quarrel with Spain, he came under increasing pressure, not least from some sections of the Privy Council and from Buckingham and Prince Charles, to respond. This pressure only increased with the arrival in January 1619 of the Bohemian representative Achatius, Baron zu Dohna. Thus the forward-looking tone of *Masque of Heroes* not only suits the new year but speculates about future need for heroic virtue in the face of Catholic threat: 'how after-times *should* move' (306: my italics).

Contemporary responses are encapsulated in one of James's own poems about the comet that appeared in 1618, and which many interpreted as an apocalyptic signal germane to the Palatine:

You men of Britain, wherefore gaze you so,
Upon an angry star...?
Oh, be so happy, then, while time does last
As to remember, Doomsday is not past,
And misinterpret not the vain conceit
The character you see on heaven's gate,
Which though it bring the world some news from fate
The letter's such as no man can translate.
And for to guess at God Almighty's mind
Were such a thing might cozen all mankind.
Wherefore I wish the curious man to keep
His rash imagination till he sleep:
Then let him dream of famine, plague and war,
And think the match with Spain has caused this star.
Or let them think that if their prince, my minion,
Will shortly change, or (which is worse) religion...

The excitement the crisis generated amongst Protestants who at last saw the opportunity for alliance against the Antichrist can be gauged in Sir Henry Wotton's comment from October 1618: 'the actions in Bohemia give us leave to be wanton'. Whilst the King explicitly denied such expectations ('remember Doomsday is not past'), the foreign policy crisis permitted Protestants to interpret events apocalyptically, and Middleton's use of such undertones in this masque may indicate the ideological position of the text.

In contrast, *Pleasure Reconciled to Virtue*, written shortly before the crisis erupted, still extolled the vision of peaceable Britain and domestic virtue. Its depiction of James as Hesperus 'the brightest star' (172) who shines across the 'Atlantic seas' (173) may celebrate glorious isolation over continental involvement. The *Coleorton Masque*, written from outside the immediate royal circle, prefers Spenserian echoes and internationalist Protestantism: military heroism 'Atlas-like uphold[s] all lands' and 'Keep[s] the world [so] it does not run | To the old confusïon' (163–5). Situated in a more ambivalent location on the periphery, neither totally within the court orbit nor in country-based exile, Middleton's *Heroes* adopts the mean: it proposes the need for military heroism as the main form of virtue, but as yet only as a future possibility.

The subject matter and approach both show how *Heroes* partakes in the political debates of 1619, with different emphases from those found in court entertainments, and such divergences also invest the formal elements of the text as *Heroes* challenges Jonsonian models. Throughout its existence the Jonsonian masque had its critics, especially Samuel Daniel and Thomas Campion (two of the losers in the patronage battle with Jonson), but after 1618 it came under increasing pressure—from the politics of the Palatine crisis which made its pacific classicism increasingly redundant, and from internal forces, partly generated by the increasing dominance of Buckingham and his family, and also the emergence of a new, bitter factional politics around foreign policy questions.

By 1618 even Jonson had to recognize the internal contradictions in the form, riven between praise and the counsel he claimed to present. *Pleasure Reconciled* exemplifies such tensions, since on one hand it embodies the panegyric ideal, 'royal education' (201), whilst its actual circumstances, when the restive monarch interrupted the masque and contemporary commentators dismissed the text as dull and indecorous, demonstrates how ideal and reality often clashed. 'Royal education' suggests, slightly contradictorily, that the monarchy both offers but also needs education, and the issue of whether any of the exhortations embedded in the masque are heeded, remains unanswered. Later, Jonson's 'An Epistle to a Friend, to Persuade Him to the Wars' excoriates the flattery surrounding court grandees and depicts the poet 'hoarse with praising' so that his 'voice' (perhaps message as well as medium) is beyond 'recovery' (151, 154).

In this climate Middleton offers a reformation, or rewriting, of the Jonsonian masque, much as envisaged by Daniel, a technique prefigured in his revisionist civic pageant *The Triumphs of Truth*, which was 'redeemed into form' (13). Whereas *Pleasure Reconciled* depicts the instant dissolution of antimasque disorder by the appearance of magical royal order, *Heroes* dramatizes another pattern whereby the antimasque forces are not expelled but absorbed into the proper order. Thus Fasting Day and all the different days are placed in New Year's household and allotted their place in the calendar, and the opposites of feast and penitence are 'reconciled' through the agency of Time (286). Even when faced with the disagreements of Plumporridge and Fasting Day, Doctor Almanac still appeals to 'friendship, friendship' (80) as proper to the time. Whereas the reconciliation of *Pleasure Reconciled* can only be achieved in the initial banishment of opposing forces, Middleton's masque seeks to gather the opposites together into a constructive tension symbolized in the ideal of Harmony.

Middleton repeats this strategy in the reconciliation of Levity and Severity in the *Honourable Entertainments*, in the integration of Mean and Base in the choruses of *An Invention*, and in *World Tossed at Tennis*, which dramatizes a series of newfound fellowships and collaborations as an alternative to the divisive patterns propounded by the Jonsonian masque. These occasional works emphasize the key ideal of harmony which encompasses all oppositions, and includes the monarchy only as *primus inter pares*. Here Middleton's habit of spelling 'antemasques' with an 'e' may well be significant, since the oppositions of his masque are not absolute antitheses but simply precursors, connected by the sequence of action and time to what follows upon them. Such formal eclecticism and the integration of different materials belongs to a structure which places less emphasis upon the transformation of the scene by a mystical vision of power and authority. Thus the 'antemasques' of *Heroes* belong to the overall pattern of the year, just as much as does the hope for virtuous heroism. Doctor Almanac links the two elements when he suggests that the 'low births and natures' (267) of the antemasques have cheered New Year and stand as portents of the happiness and blessedness predicted by his 'secret in astrology' (271) and which Harmony then displays in the form of the Worthies. Almanac says of this juncture that 'The minute, nay, the point of time's arrived' (277), thus marking the auspiciousness of the moment and the year that will reconcile all factions in a vision of active virtue which will unite the nation.

This insistence connects the auspiciousness of the new year, its hopes for the future, and echoes more overtly political apocalypticism that depicted this as the moment for war against Antichrist. The transformation enacted in the masque, from current world to future heroic ideal and from old to new year, from the old man to the new man, also contains further Protestant nuances. Like *Pleasure Reconciled*, Middleton's masque provides an image of 'lawful recreations'—though whereas Jonson locates these in courtly ceremonial, Middleton finds them in popular culture. Moreover, the recreation offered by the vision of inspired military heroism may allude to another Protestant sense of recreation: the duty of each true Christian to 're-create' him or herself every day. To cast off the old year and welcome the new not only enacts a transformation of foreign policy, it also defines a Pauline spiritual metamorphosis for individuals and for the nation. Here Middleton reappropriates the debate over festivity and propriety, rewriting it within Protestant discourse as a 'lawful' but also literal 're-creation', not simply authorized by the monarch, but invested with spiritual authority. In complex ways Middleton fulfils his promise to make the 'time' serve for the 'mirth' of his masque, but the mirth is the permitted pleasure that accompanies the metamorphosis of the world at Christmas, a 'mirth' that stems from the hope that providence brings in a new law and new world, where battle against the Antichrist will be joined.

SEE ALSO

Music and dance: *Companion*, 161 (entrance of New Year), 162 (first antemasque), 163 (second antemasque), 164 (entrance of masquers), 164 (their dance), 164 (their exit)
Textual introduction and apparatus: *Companion*, 646
Authorship and date: *Companion*, 404

Masque of Heroes

Or, The Inner Temple Masque

Presented as an entertainment for many worthy ladies
by gentlemen of the same ancient and noble house.

The Masque.

This nothing owes to any tale or story,
With which some writer pieces up a glory;
I only made the time they sat to see
Serve for the mirth itself, which was found free
And herein fortunate (that's counted good)
Being made for ladies, ladies understood.

T.M.

The Parts	*The Speakers*
DOCTOR ALMANAC	Joseph Taylor
PLUMPORRIDGE	William Rowley
A FASTING DAY	John Newton
NEW YEAR	Hugh Atwell
TIME	William Carpenter
HARMONY	A Boy

Two Antemasques

In the first, six Dancers
1. *Candlemas Day*
2. *Shrove Tuesday*
3. *Lent*
4. *Ill May Day*
5. *Midsummer-Eve*
6. *The First Dog Day*

The second Antemasque, presented by eight Boys
Good Days—3.
Bad Days—3.
Indifferent Days—2.

The Masque itself receiving its illustration from nine of the Gentlemen of the House.

The Inner Temple Masque.

Enter Doctor Almanac coming from the funeral of December, or the Old Year

DOCTOR ALMANAC
I have seen the old year fairly buried,
Good gentleman he was, but toward his end
Full of diseases: he kept no good diet,
He loved a wench in June (which we count vile),
And got the latter end of May with child.
That was his fault, and many an old year smells on't.
[*Enter Fasting Day*]
How now? Who's this? Oh, one o'th' Fasting Days
That followed him to his grave; I know
Him by his gauntness, his thin chitterlings;
He would undo a tripe-wife. Fasting Day,
Why art so heavy?

FASTING DAY Oh, sweet Doctor Almanac,
I have lost a dear old master. Beside, Sir,

11 ***The Speakers*** These were professional actors, not the gentlemen-masquers of l. 31.
12 **Joseph Taylor** actor; early in 1619 became a King's man and is known to have performed many of the roles created by Burbage who died in that year.
13 **William Rowley** actor and playwright. His typical role was that of a fat clown.
14 **John Newton** the actor who played the lean clown to Rowley's fat clown.
15 **Hugh Atwell** actor. Rowley's elegy suggests that he was a 'little man'.
16 **William Carpenter** one of the Prince's actors
18 ***Antemasques*** one of the structural elements of masques, usually consisting of 'rude' or allegorical characters, often involving dancing. Earlier masques usually had one antemasque, which preceded the main masque, but later it became common for the masques to have several antemasques.
30 ***The Masque itself*** the final discovery of masked gentlemen was considered the most important element of the performance; see 292.1–3.
31 ***House*** The Inner Temple
31.2 ***Doctor Almanac*** almanacs were written by students and practitioners in astronomy or astrology, or by physicians
35 **He loved a wench in June** echoes Tilley J102: 'In June, July, and August, wife, I know thee not'; also S422: 'Who marries between sickle and scythe will never thrive'
39 **That . . . grave** i.e. followed the Old Year of ll. 32–7
40 **gauntness** abnormally slim as from hunger
chitterlings (ironic) intestines
41 **tripe-wife** term of abuse
42 **heavy** serious, grieved

I have been out of service all this Kersmas;
Nobody minds Fasting Day;
I have scarce been thought upon o' Friday nights;
And because Kersmas this year fell upon't
The Fridays have been ever since so proud
They scorn my company; the butchers' boys
At Temple-Bar set their great dogs upon me,
I dare not walk abroad, nor be seen yet:
The very poulters' girls throw rotten eggs at me,
Nay, Fish Street loves me, e'en but from teeth outward,
The nearest kin I have looks shy upon me,
As if't had forgot me. I met Plumporridge now,
My big-swollen enemy: he's plump and lusty,
The only man in place. Sweet Master Doctor,
Prefer me to the New Year, you can do't.

DOCTOR ALMANAC
When can I do't, sir? You must stay till Lent.

FASTING DAY
Till Lent? You kill my heart, sweet Master Doctor.
Thrust me into Candlemas Eve, I do beseech you.

DOCTOR ALMANAC Away, Candlemas Eve will never bear thee i' these days; 'tis so frampold, the Puritans will never yield to't.

Enter Plumporridge

FASTING DAY
Why, they're fat enough.

DOCTOR ALMANAC Here comes Plumporridge.

FASTING DAY Ay, he's sure of welcome; methinks he moves like one of the great porridge tubs, going to the Counter.

PLUMPORRIDGE Oh, killing cruel sight, yonder's a Fasting Day: a lean spiny rascal with a dog in's belly; his very bowels bark with hunger. Avaunt, thy breath stinks; I do not love to meet thee fasting; thou art nothing but wind, thy stomach's full of farts, as if they had lost their way, and thou made with the wrong end upward, like a Dutch maw that discharges still into the mouth!

FASTING DAY Why thou whoreson breakfast, dinner, nuntions, supper and bever, cellar, hall, kitchen, and wet-larder!

PLUMPORRIDGE
Sweet Master Doctor, look quickly upon his water,
That I may break the urinal about his pate.

[*He offers a urinal to Doctor Almanac*]

DOCTOR ALMANAC
Nay, friendship, friendship!

PLUMPORRIDGE Never, Master Doctor,
With any Fasting Day, persuade me not.
Nor anything belongs to Ember week.
And if I take against a thing, I'm stomachfull;
I was born an Anabaptist, a fell foe
To fish and Fridays; pig's my absolute sweetheart.
And shall I wrong my love, and cleave to saltfish?
Commit adultery with an egg and butter?

DOCTOR ALMANAC
Well, setting this apart, whose water's this, sir?

PLUMPORRIDGE
Oh, thereby hangs a tail, my Master Kermas's.
It is his water, sir, he's drawing on.

DOCTOR ALMANAC Kersmas? Why let me see,
I saw him very lusty o' Twelfth Night.

PLUMPORRIDGE
Ay, that's true, sir, but then he took his bane
With choosing king and queen;
He's made his will already, here's the copy.

DOCTOR ALMANAC And what has he given away? Let me see, Plumbroth.

[*Doctor Almanac takes the will from Plumporridge*]

PLUMPORRIDGE He could not give away much, sir, his children have so consumed him beforehand.

DOCTOR ALMANAC (*reading*) The last will and testament of Kersmas, irrevocable. *Imprimis*: I give and bequeath to my second son In-and-In, his perpetual lodging i'the King's Bench, and his ordinary out of the basket.

44 **Kersmas** corruption of Christmas
47 **fell upon't** (as it did in 1618)
50 **Temple-Bar** Butcher Row was just outside Temple Bar on the north side of the Strand.
51 **abroad** out-of-doors
53 **Fish Street** the main fish market in London
55 **Plumporridge** porridge containing prunes, raisins, currants, etc; a favourite Christmas dish
58 **Prefer me** recommend me
63 **frampold** pert, saucy
the Puritans (known for their strict observance of fasting)
65 **fat enough** (Puritans were often accused of hypocrisy)
67 **Counter** (a prison)
69 **spiny** slender
73 **wrong end upward** i.e., he 'farts' out of his mouth, instead of his anus
74 **Dutch maw** Dutch stomach (?); the Dutch were often the object of ridicule, but the meaning of this phrase remains obscure.
75–6 **nuntions** snacks between meals
76 **bever** drinking, or, a small snack between meals
82 **Ember week** the name of the four weeks of fasting and prayer appointed by the Church to be observed respectively in the four seasons of the year. Since 1095 Ember days have been the Wednesday, Friday, and Saturday next following (1) the first Sunday of Lent (2) Whit Sunday (3) Holy Cross Day (14th September) (4) St Lucia's Day (13th December).
83 **stomachfull** obstinate, hostile
85 **fish and Fridays** Friday was a fish day on religious grounds, but Saturday was a statutory fish day, that is, a day on which meat-eating was forbidden by an Act of Parliament.
pig's (alluding to the Puritan fondness for pork)
87 **egg and butter** traditional food for fasting days
89 **tail** conclusion, termination (*OED* 4b); with a bawdy innuendo
90 **drawing on** dying
92 **Twelfth Night** (traditional climax of the Christmas festivities)
93 **took his bane** caught his death
94 **choosing king and queen** (traditional entertainment during Twelfth-tide)
102 **In-and-In** a game at dice
103 **King's Bench** prison
basket (in which broken meat and bread from the sheriffs' table was carried to poorer prisoners)

PLUMPORRIDGE A sweet allowance for a second brother.

DOCTOR ALMANAC Item, I give to my youngest sons Gleek and Primavista the full consuming of nights and days and wives and children, together with one secret gift, that is, never to give over while they have a penny.

PLUMPORRIDGE And if e'er they do, I'll be hanged.

DOCTOR ALMANAC For the possession of all my lands, manors, manor houses, I leave them full and wholly to my eldest son, Noddie, whom during his minority I commit to the custody of a pair of knaves and one-and-thirty.

PLUMPORRIDGE There's knaves enough o' conscience to cozen one fool.

DOCTOR ALMANAC Item, I give to my eldest daughter, Tickle-me-quickly, and to her sister My-lady's-hole, free leave to shift for themselves either in court, city, or country.

PLUMPORRIDGE We thank him heartily.

DOCTOR ALMANAC Item, I leave to their old aunt, My-sow-has-pigged, a litter of courtesans to breed up for Shrovetide.

PLUMPORRIDGE They will be good ware in Lent, when flesh is forbid by proclamation.

DOCTOR ALMANAC Item, I give to my nephew Gambols, commonly called by the name of Kersmas Gambols, all my cattle, horse and mare, but let him shoe 'em himself.

PLUMPORRIDGE I ha' seen him shoe the mare forty times over.

DOCTOR ALMANAC Also, I bequeath to my cousin-german Wassail-bowl, born of Dutch Parents, the privilege of a free denizen, that is, to be drunk with Scotch ale or English beer; and lastly, I have given by word of mouth to poor Blind Man's Buff, a flap with a foxtail.

PLUMPORRIDGE
Ay, so he's given 'em all, for ought I see.
But now what think you of his water, sir?

DOCTOR ALMANAC
Well, he may linger out till Candlemas,
But ne'er recover it.

FASTING DAY Would he were gone once!
I should be more respected.

Enter New Year [dancing]

DOCTOR ALMANAC Here's New Year!

PLUMPORRIDGE
I have ne'er a gift to give him; I'll be gone. *[Exit]*

DOCTOR ALMANAC
Mirth and a healthful time fill all your days.
Look freshly, sir.

NEW YEAR I cannot, Master Doctor.
My father's death sets the spring backward i' me.
For joy and comfort yet, I'm now between
Sorrow and joy, the winter and the spring,
And as time gathers freshness in its season,
No doubt affects will be subdued with reason.

DOCTOR ALMANAC
You've a brave mind to work on; use my rules
And you shall cut a caper in November,
When other years, your grandfathers, lay bed-rid.

NEW YEAR
What's he, that looks so piteously, and shakes so?

DOCTOR ALMANAC
A Fasting Day.

NEW YEAR How's that?

DOCTOR ALMANAC A foolish Fasting Day,
An unseasonable coxcomb, seeks now for a service;
He's hunted up and down, h'as been at court,
And the long porter broke his head across there;
He had rather see the devil, for this he says:
He ne'er grew up so tall with Fasting Days.
I would not for the price of all my almanacs
The guard had took him there, they would ha' beat out

105 **Gleek** a game at cards
106 **Primavista** a game at cards
108 **give over** give over gambling
112 **Noddie** a game at cards
113 **knaves** jacks
113–14 **one-and-thirty** a game at cards
116 **cozen** cheat, dupe
118 **Tickle-me-quickly** a game at cards
My-lady's-hole a game at cards
122–3 **My-sow-has-pigged** a game at cards
125–6 **They will . . . proclamation** an annual proclamation was issued against the eating of flesh (during Lent).
128 **Kersmas Gambols** During Twelfth Night festivities students also appear to have amused themselves electing 'King of the Bean' whoever came upon a dried bean concealed in his portion of cake. Henry Bourne mentions this custom, calling it 'Christmas gambol' (p. 153).
129 **mare . . . shoe 'em himself** 'Shoeing the mare' was a boisterous Christmas sport. One of the players was chosen to be the wild mare, and others chased him about the room with the object of shoeing him. Tilley records the proverb 'To ride (shoe) the wild mare'.
132 **cousin-german** near relation
133 **Wassail-bowl** spiced ale used in Twelfth Night and Christmas-Eve celebrations; alludes to the custom of drinking healths on those occasions
Dutch Parents Dutchmen's drinking was proverbial: 'The Dutchmen drinks pure wine in the morning, at noon wine without water, in the evening as it comes from the butt' (Tilley D656).
136 **Blind Man's Buff** a game in which one player is blindfolded, and tries to catch and identify any one of the others, who, on their part, push him about, and make sport with him
a flap with a foxtail a contemptuous dismissal. A foxtail was one of the badges of the fool.
139 **Candlemas** falls on the 2nd of February; the 'vulgar' often prolonged Christmas festivities beyond Twelfth Night until Candlemas.
142 **a gift to give him** (Presents were given not on Christmas day but on the New Year's.)
149 **affects** affections
155 **coxcomb** a jester's cap; hence a metonym for a fool
157 **long porter** an allusion to one Walter Parsons of Staffordshire, of whom Thomas Fuller reported that 'he grew so tall in stature that a hole was made for him in the Ground to stand therein up to his knees, so to make him adequate with his Fellow-work-men [in a smithy]. He afterwards was Porter to King James' (*Worthies*, 48).

His brains with bombards. I bade him stay till Lent
And now he whimpers he would to Rome forsooth,
That's his last refuge, but would try a while
How well he should be used in Lancashire.

NEW YEAR He was my father's servant,
That he was, sir.

DOCTOR ALMANAC 'Tis here upon recòrd.

FASTING DAY
I served him honestly, and cost him little.

DOCTOR ALMANAC
Ay, I'll be sworn for that.

FASTING DAY Those were the times, sir,
That made your predecessors rich, and able
To lay up more for you, and since poor Fasting Days
Were not made reckoning on, the pampered flesh
Has played the knave; maids have had fuller bellies;
Those meals that once were sav'd, have stirr'd and
leapt,
And begot bastards, and they must be kept.
Better keep Fasting Days, yourself may tell ye,
And for the profit of purse, back and belly!

DOCTOR ALMANAC
I never yet heard truth better whined out.

NEW YEAR
Thou shalt not all be lost, nor for vainglory
Greedily welcomed; we'll begin with virtue.
As we may hold with't, that does virtue right.
Set him down, sir, for Candlemas Eve at night.

FASTING DAY
Well, better late than never.
This is my comfort, I shall come to make
All the fat rogues go to bed supperless,
Get dinners where they can. *[Exit]*

[Enter Time]

NEW YEAR How now? What's he?

DOCTOR ALMANAC 'Tis old Time, sir, that belonged
To all your predecessors.

NEW YEAR Oh, I honour
That reverend figure; may I ever think
How precious thou'rt in youth, how rarely
Redeemed in age.

TIME Observe, you have Time's service.
There's all in brief.

Enter the first antemasque

NEW YEAR Ha? Doctor? What are these?

TIME
The rabble that I pity, these I have served too,
But few or none have ever observed me,
Amongst this dissolute rout. Candlemas-Day!
I'm sorry to see him so ill associated!

DOCTOR ALMANAC
Why that's his cause of coming to complain,
Because Shrove Tuesday this year dwells so near him.
But 'tis his place, he cannot be removed.
You must be patient, Candlemas, and brook it.
This rabble, sir, Shrove Tuesday, hungry Lent,
Ill May Day, Midsummer Eve, and the first Dog Day,
Come to receive their places due by custom,
And that they build upon.

NEW YEAR Give 'em their charge,
And then admit 'em.

DOCTOR ALMANAC I will do't incony.
Stand forth Shrove Tuesday, one o' the silenced
bricklayers;
'Tis in your charge to pull down bawdy-houses,
To set your tribe a-work, cause spoil in Shoreditch
And make a dangerous leak there, deface Turnbull,

162 **bombards** wide leathern drinking vessels

163 **Rome** fasting was more closely observed in Catholic countries than in Protestant ones

165 **Lancashire** Fuller noted that in the western part of Lancashire people were 'Popishly affected', hence 'many Papists, and Jesuits have been born and bred in this County' (*Worthies*, 105).

173 **pampered** over fed

174 **fuller bellies** i.e. became pregnant. A full belly was also associated with foolishness: 'A fat belly does not engender a Subtle wit' (Tilley B293), or 'A Belly full of gluttony will never study willingly' (B285).

176 **kept** supported

194 **rabble** disorderly people

196 **rout** disorderly or disreputable crowd

199 **Shrove Tuesday... near him** Candlemas fell on the day before St Blaise's Day, 3rd of February, which was, traditionally the earliest possible day for Shrove Tuesday. Lent follows the latter. Shrove Tuesday was the traditional day for often violent misrule—hence Candlemas's complaint.

202 **Shrove Tuesday** allusively meaning 'a time of merriment'

203 **Ill May Day** so called in allusion to the rising of the apprentices on the 1st of May 1517 against foreigners and aliens. **Midsummer Eve** one of the festive days notorious for drinking and misrule **Dog Day** the day about the time of the heliacal rising of the Dog-star (i.e. Sirius), noted from ancient time as the hottest and most unwholesome period of the year; in current almanacs dog days are said to begin on 3 July and end 11 August.

206 **incony** (*a*) happily (*b*) rarely, skilfully

207 **silenced bricklayers** Possibly an allusion to Ben Jonson, who was the son of a bricklayer and an apprentice himself, especially if we take into account his 'tribe' of l. 209. 'The tribe of Ben' was the contemporary name for a group of poets who were Jonson's followers. Also playing on 'silenced ministers' = Puritans forbidden to preach.

208 **pull down bawdy-houses** Many writers record the custom of London apprentices' revelry on Shrove Tuesday, including their attacks on brothels and theatres, as if they wanted to clean the city of all the 'dirt' before Lent.

209 **tribe** (see note to l. 207 above) **Shoreditch** This parish in London had the worst reputation as a haunt of loose women and bad characters in general.

210 **leak** possibly an allusion to Mrs Leak who kept a bawdy-house in Shoreditch and is mentioned as being attacked by prentices in *Owl's Almanac* 434. The riot took place on Shrove Tuesday, 1617, and many apprentices were arrested, along with Mrs Leak. **Turnbull** one of the most disreputable streets in London, a haunt of thieves and prostitutes.

And tickle Codpiece Row, ruin the Cockpit:
The poor players ne'er thrived in't, o' my conscience
Some quean pissed upon the first brick.
For you, lean Lent, be sure you utter first
Your rotten herrings and keep up your best
Till they be rotten, then there's no deceit
When they be all alike. You, Ill May Day,
Be as unruly a rascal as you may
To stir up Deputy Double Diligence
That comes perking forth with halberds;
And for you, Midsummer Eve, that watches warmest,
Be but sufficiently drunk, and you're well harnessed;
You, Dog Day!

DOG DAY Wow!

DOCTOR ALMANAC A churlish maund'ring rogue!
You must both beg and rob, curse and collogue;
In cooler nights the barn with doxies fill,
In harvest lie in haycock with your Jill.
They have all their charge.

NEW YEAR You have gi'n't at the wrong end.

DOCTOR ALMANAC
To bid 'em sin's the way to make 'em mend,
For what they are forbid, they run to headlong.
I ha' cast their inclinations. Now, your service,
To draw fresh blood into your master's cheeks, slaves!

The first dance and first antemasque, consisting of these six rude ones

Exeunt [antemasquers and Time]

NEW YEAR
What scornful looks the abusive villains threw
Upon the reverend form and face of Time!
Methought it appeared sorry, and went angry.

DOCTOR ALMANAC
'Tis still your servant.

[Enter second antemasque]

NEW YEAR How now? What are these?

DOCTOR ALMANAC
These are your Good Days, and your Bad Days, sir;
Those your Indifferent Days, nor good nor bad.

NEW YEAR
But is here all?

DOCTOR ALMANAC
A wonder there's so many.
How broke those loose? Every one stops their passage
And makes inquiry after 'em:
This farmer will not cast his seed i'th' ground
Before he look in Bretnor; there he finds
Some word which he hugs happily, as 'Ply the box',
'Make hay betimes', 'It falls into thy mouth'.
A punctual lady will not paint, forsooth,
Upon his critical days, 'twill not hold well,
Nor a nice city-wedlock eat fresh herring
Nor periwinkles,
Although she long for both, if the word be that day
'Gape after gudgeons', or some fishing phrase.
A scrivener's wife will not entreat the money-master
That lies i'th' house and gets her husband's children
To furnish a poor gentleman's extremes
If she find 'Nihil in a bag' that morning;
And so of thousand follies, these suffice
To show you Good, Bad, and Indifferent Days,
And all have their inscriptions—here's 'Cock-a-Hoop',
This 'The gear cottons', and this 'Faint heart never'—
These, noted black for badness, 'Rods in piss';
This 'Post for puddings', this 'Put up thy pipes',
These black and white indifferently, inclining
To both their natures, 'Neither full nor fasting',
'In dock out nettle'.—Now to your motion,
Black knaves and white knaves, and you parcel-rascals,
Two hypocritical, parti-coloured varlets,
That play o' both hands.

211 **Codpiece Row** a court in Westminster notorious as a haunt of prostitutes
ruin the Cockpit The Cockpit (or the Phoenix) was one of the public playhouses. It was sacked by apprentices on Shrove Tuesday 1617, a fact recorded by many writers, and also mentioned in *Owl's Almanac* 433 and 2514.
213 **quean** prostitute
219 **Deputy** a deputy alderman in the City's Common Council
220 **perking forth** insolently
halberds weapon consisting of a sharp-edged blade ending in a point and spearhead mounted on a handle five to seven feet long.
222 **harnessed** in armour
223 **Wow!** Woof!
churlish rude, rough
maund'ring whining like a beggar
224 **collogue** conspire
225 **doxies** whores
226 **Jill** wench
236 **Good Days...Bad Days** every almanac included a list of 'good' and 'bad' days in a given month.
242 **Bretnor** Thomas Bretnor was the famous almanac-maker; his works often include many agricultural hints.
243 **word** motto
Ply the box wield vigorously
245 **paint** use make-up
246 **his** i.e. Bretnor's
247 **city-wedlock** wife of a citizen of London
248 **periwinkles** common European mollusc
250 **Gape after gudgeons** proverbial; 'gudgeon' is a small fresh water fish much used for bait, hence to 'gape after gudgeons' means figuratively 'something swallowed greedily or credulously' (see Tilley G473)
251 **A scrivener's wife** A scrivener was a scribe, a notary or one who received money to place out at interest. Scriveners had a bad reputation, as in Tilley U28: 'A Usurer is one that puts his money to the unnatural act of generation, and the scrivener is his bawd'.
252 **gets her husband's children** (as in *Chaste Maid*)
253 **extremes** life's final phase
254 **Nihil** Latin for 'nothing', hence a trifle of no value
257 **Cock-a-Hoop** to drink without stint; reckless enjoyment
258 **The gear cottons** the matter goes on successfully
259 **Rods in piss** punishment in store
260 **Post for puddings** proverbial, meaning 'to hurry' (Tilley P629)
Put up thy pipes proverbial, meaning 'to make an end and be gone, to desist' (Tilley P345).
263 **In dock out nettle** This phrase was originally a charm uttered to cure nettle stings by dock leaves and later became a proverbial expression for changeableness and inconstancy (Tilley D421–2).
264 **parcel-rascals** partly rascals
265 **varlets** knaves
266 **play o' both hands** cheat (Tilley H115)

Here the second dance, and last antemasque: eight boys, habited according to their former characters. The three Good Days, attired all in white garments, sitting close to their bodies, their inscriptions on their breasts: on the first 'Cock-a-hoop'; on the second 'The gear cottons'; on the third 'Faint heart never'. The three Bad Days all in black garments, their faces black, and their inscriptions: on the first 'Rods in piss'; on the second 'Post for puddings'; on the third 'Put up thy pipes'. The Indifferent Days in garments half white, half black, their faces seamed with that parti-colour, and their inscriptions: the first 'Neither full nor fasting'; the second 'In dock out nettle'.

These having purchased a smile from the cheeks of many a beauty by their ridiculous figures, vanish, proud of that treasure

DOCTOR ALMANAC [*to New Year*]
I see these pleasures of low births and natures
Add little freshness to your cheeks; I pity you,
And can no longer now conceal from you
Your happy omen. Sir, blessings draw near you,
I will disclose a secret in astrology
By the sweet industry of Harmony,
Your white and glorious friend;
Ev'n very deities have conspired to grace
Your fair inauguration; here I find it,
'Tis clear in art,
The minute, nay, the point of time's arrived;
Methinks the blessings touch you, now they're felt, sir.

At which loud music heard, the first cloud vanishing, Harmony is discovered with her sacred choir.

The first song

HARMONY [*singing*]
New Year, New Year! hark, hearken to me!
I am sent down
To crown
Thy wishes with me!
Thy fair desires in virtue's court are filed.
The goodness of thy thought,
This blessèd work hath wrought,
Time shall be reconciled.
Thy spring shall in all sweets abound,
Thy summer shall be clear and sound,
Thy autumn swell the barn and loft
With corn and fruits, ripe, sweet and soft,
And in thy winter, when all go,
Thou shalt depart as white as snow.

Then a second cloud vanishing, the Masquers themselves discovered, sitting in arches of clouds, being nine in number, heroes deified for their virtues.

The song goes on

[HARMONY] [*singing*]
Behold, behold, hark, hearken to me!
Glories come down
To crown
Thy wishes with me:
Bright heroes in lasting honour sphered,
Virtue's eternal spring,
By making Time their king,
See, they're beyond Time reared.
Yet in their love to human good,
In which estate themselves once stood,
They all descend to have their worth
Shine to imitation forth;
And by their motion, light and love,
To show how after-times should move!

Then the Masquers descend [and] set to their first dance.

The second song

HARMONY [*singing*]
Move on, move on, be still the same,
You beauteous sons of brightness,
You add to honour, spirit and flame,
To virtue, grace and whiteness.

You whose every little motion
May learn strictness more devotion,
Every pace of that high worth
It treads a fair example forth,
Quickens a virtue, makes a story,
To your own heroic glory;
May your three-times-thrice blest number
Raise merit from his ancient slumber!

Move on, move on, be still the same,
You beauteous sons of brightness,
You add to honour, spirit and flame,
To virtue, grace and whiteness.

Then they order themselves for their second dance, after which

266.12–13 ***seamed . . . parti-colour*** decorated with lines in a variety of colours

273 **white** beloved

278.2 ***discovered*** a sudden discovery of allegorical figures, often accompanied by a change of scenery, is characteristic for all masques.

283 **virtue's court** (where the performance is taking place)

292.1–2 ***Masquers . . . discovered*** (the discovery of the masquers was the culminating moment of every masque)

292.3–4 ***heroes deified for their virtues*** since there are nine 'heroes', we may associate them with the 'nine Worthies', especially because their 'worth' is mentioned in l. 314. The nine Worthies include three Jews (Joshua, David, and Judas Maccabaeus), three Gentiles (Hector, Alexander, and Julius Caesar), and three Christians (Arthur, Charlemagne, and Godfrey of Bouillon).

297 **sphered** there were also nine spheres in the Ptolemaic heavens.

306.1–2 ***the Masquers . . . dance*** (the final moment of every masque)

The third song

HARMONY [*singing*]

See, whither fate hath led you, lamps of honour,
For goodness brings her own reward upon her;
Look, turn your eyes, and then conclude, commending,
And say you have lost no worth by your descending.
Behold a heaven about you, spheres more plenty,
There, for one Luna, here shines ten
And for one Venus, twenty;
Then heroes, double both your fame and light,
Each choose his star, and full adorn this night.

At which the Masquers make choice of their ladies, and dance.

Time [*enters*], *thus closing all*

TIME

The morning grey
Bids come away;
Every lady should begin
To take her chamber, for the stars are in.

Then making his honour to the ladies

Live long the miracles of times and years
Till with those heroes you sit fixed in spheres.

[*Exeunt*]

Finis

328 **Luna** personification of the Moon
329 **Venus** goddess of beauty and love; here, the paragon of beauty.
331.1–2 ***At which...dance*** (every masque concluded with a dance of the masquers with the partners drawn from the audience)
335.1 ***honour*** bow

AN/THE OLD LAW

Edited by Jeffrey Masten

Honour thy father* and thy mother....
*By the which is meant all that have authority over us.

—Exodus 20:12 and its gloss, *The Geneva Bible* (1570)

IMAGINE a culture—a culture at once strikingly like early modern England and at the same time apparently ancient and distant from it—that passes a law mandating the execution of old people when they reach a given age. This is the unusual proposition with which *Old Law* begins—though, as the play makes clear, this proposition and the response to it are unusual for reasons other than those we might expect today.

Old Law is a tragicomedy of euthanasia. If this description seems an oxymoron, it is also, as we will see, a redundancy; an exploration of both terms illuminates the play. Philip Sidney called tragicomedy a 'mongrel' genre; John Fletcher (who collaborated with Beaumont, Massinger, Rowley, Shakespeare, and others) wrote, less disparagingly, that

> A tragicomedy is not so called in respect of mirth and killing, but in respect it wants deaths, which is enough to make it no tragedy, yet brings some near it, which is enough to make it no comedy (which must be a representation of familiar people with such kind of trouble as no life be questioned), so that a god is as lawful in this as in a tragedy, and mean people as in a comedy.

Though labelled an 'Excellent Comedy' in the first printed edition (1656), *Old Law* nonetheless meets a number of Fletcher's tragicomic criteria: no god makes an appearance, but the play mixes in its three related plots characters ranging from the lower-class Clown, Wife, and Wench (Fletcher's 'mean people') to a Duke and his courtiers. The play brings some so 'near' death that everyone (including the audience) assumes they have died, and, in the play's climactic trial scene, others are in danger of being sentenced to death for their 'capital' crimes against the state (5.1.143).

In fact, the play out-goes Fletcher's definition in its mixing of tragedy and comedy, for it insistently brings together 'mirth and killing'. Epire's law that executes all men at the age of eighty and women at the age of sixty produces a series of comic scenes and jokes about the death of the aged. The scene in which the Clown persuades the Clerk to antedate his wife's birthday in the parish registry is one of the funniest in the play (at the same time that it is, from a number of other perspectives, one of the most outrageous). Jokes themselves are said to be fatal, and death produces laughter: 'An't be a laughing business,' says the young courtier Simonides, 'Put it to me; I'm one of the best in Europe. | My father died last too; I have the most cause' (3.2.3–5).

Two ceremonies staged in the play are amalgamations that 'match hornpipes and funerals', to use Sidney's metaphor for tragicomedy's ostensibly inappropriate mixing. (This metaphor is literalized several times in the course of a play closely attuned to kinds of music.) Staging his father's funeral prematurely so that he can hide him from the Old Law, Cleanthes leads a joyful funeral ('We'll seem to weep, and seem to joy withal, | That death so gently has prevented you | The law's sharp rigour' [1.1.470–2]), and the Duke remarks of this mournful festivity, 'I never saw a corse so joyfully followed.... Was ever such a contrariety seen | In natural courses yet, nay, professed openly?' (2.1.156, 161–2). The Clown's procession in the final scene—which he intends as the simultaneous funeral of his first wife and the marriage of his second—recalls Cleanthes's earlier spectacle, as well as other tragicomic mixtures of marriages and funerals, like those in the first and last scenes of Fletcher and Shakespeare's *The Two Noble Kinsmen* (1613). The Clown theorizes this 'contrariety' for the Duke:

> As the destiny of the day falls out, my lord, one [wife] goes out to wedding; another goes to hanging. And your grace in the due consideration shall find 'em much alike: the one hath the ring upon her finger; the other a halter about her neck. 'I take thee, Beatrice', says the bridegroom; 'I take thee, Agatha', says the hangman, and both say together, 'to have and to hold till death do part us'. (5.1.387–94)

That much of the humour surrounding this mixture is at the near-fatal expense of old women is, like the gendered difference of twenty years in the law itself, something to which we will need to return.

The legislation of euthanasia (the Old Law for the killing of old people) is the play's 'improbable hypothesis'—to use the term a more recent critic of tragicomedy, Eugene Waith, cites as characteristic of the genre. And yet, as twentieth-century debates over euthanasia and suicide suggest, what is 'improbable' is relative to cultural context; the improbability of euthanasia in the context of seventeenth-century English culture (and its meaning as a proposal for social reform) differs in important ways from its improbability and its possible meanings in later Anglo-American culture.

What I am calling 'euthanasia' in *Old Law* is not the early (and etymological) notion of euthanasia—that is, from the Greek, 'good death', a term often used to denote an easy, usually self-inflicted death, as described, for example, in Montaigne's essay 'A Custom of the Isle of Cea' (trans. 1603), or in Thomas More's *Utopia* (1516). This 'euthanasia' might be considered literally redundant in the context of tragicomedy, where all deaths turn out to be good, or rather not to be deaths in the conventional sense at all. Nor is what I've called 'euthanasia' the more recent (post-nineteenth-century) practice usually glossed today as 'mercy killing'. The euthanasia of *Old Law*, in fact, more closely resembles fascist social engineering—the extermination of what Nazi ideology called 'lives unworthy of life'—than these other meanings; 'euthanasia' is 'good death' in the play only from the particular vantage point of 'the care and good of the commonwealth', to quote the law (1.1.128–9).

Historical changes in the terms and discourses surrounding the killing of old people are at issue here; indeed, what may be most shocking to a modern reader of *Old Law* is the way in which resistance to the Old Law enacted in Epire is not staged in the terms we may have come to expect in the late twentieth century, amid controversies over abortion and medically assisted suicide. In the play, discussion of and resistance to a law that arbitrarily kills certain members of society deemed non-functioning is *not* framed in the now familiar vocabulary of inherent rights—the individual's right to life, or to death, or to self-determination. Anthony Trollope's controversial 1882 novel *The Fixed Period*, which rewrites the play as an ironic first-person narrative, illustrates the magnitude of this epistemic shift.

The play's opening scene—between Simonides (the greedy young courtier who approves of the law), Cleanthes (the young courtier who opposes it), and two mercenary lawyers—makes clear that the law will be contested among Epire's sons, not those most fatally affected by the legislation. To the extent that the play depicts condemned characters resisting the law in something like a post-Enlightenment discourse of self-determination, the characters who espouse such a view are comically denigrated. The Clown's Wife, Agatha (shortened to 'Ag', which in the Clown's dialect sounds like 'hag'), is ridiculed for her desire to live out even the full life-span allowed by law, after the Clown has succeeded in antedating her birthdate; Lisander, in his attempts to rejuvenate his appearance and behaviour, is made ludicrous—if not quite as ridiculous as the young courtiers with whom he competes. In contrast, all of the characters of the older generation whom the play constructs as worthy go willingly, almost cheerfully, off to death. Creon, Simonides's father, initially resists the law on the grounds that he has faithfully served a state that now discards him, but a few moments later, appearing before the Duke, he mouths the words of the law back to its legislator:

'Tis just I die indeed, my lord, for I confess
I'm troublesome to life now, and the state
Can hope for nothing worthy from me now,
Either in force or counsel. (2.1.87–90)

Though she has additional years to live under the law, Creon's wife, Antigona, accepts her own death as part of his, and her later resistance to the law, before the Duke, is a plea on behalf of Creon, not herself. In the face of Creon's own willingness to die, she articulates her opposition in terms of his ability still to serve the state, linked explicitly to his worthiness as a father: 'He is not lost in judgement . . . | His very household laws prescribed at home by him | Are able to conform seven Christian kingdoms | They are so wise and virtuous' (2.1.98, 2.1.101–3).

As these lines begin to suggest, opposition to the law in this play is based *not* in a rhetoric of self-determination, but instead in the discourse of early modern patriarchalism. Creon's 'household laws prescribed at home' are also laws 'able to conform seven Christian kingdoms'; they recapitulate (in a language familiar to subjects versed in James I's words and works) a connection between the governance of families and of nations. Further, these laws are, significantly, written on a 'table' (tablet) and are linked in this scene to the ten commandments (2.1.119). The Old Law—Epire's new law for the killing of old people—is thus resisted here and elsewhere in the play on the basis of an older law on which the play's title puns: the law of the Old Testament (i.e., the Hebrew Bible), as received and reinscribed through its early-modern patriarchalist interpretation.

Old Law recalls, at a number of points, the ten commandments of Exodus 20 and catalogues the ways in which the play's old law results in transgressions of the older Mosaic laws—the various incidents of attempted adultery, of coveting a neighbour's wife and/as property, of murder by changing a wife's birthdate in the church register, etc. But the play's primary concern is the fifth commandment (central to the theory and practice of patriarchalism) to 'Honour thy father and thy mother.' In seventeenth-century England, there was a frequent slippage between the commandment's citation of both father *and* mother and patriarchalism's insistence on the importance of fathers alone. This is an effacement enacted in the play: when Creon is sent to his death after Antigona's unsuccessful plea, she simply disappears until the end of the play, and, in the plot detailing Cleanthes's resistance to the law, there is no mother to complicate the play's focus on the father. Whether in Antigona's emphasis on Creon's exemplary household government or in Cleanthes's concealment of his father Leonides, the resistance to the euthanasia law is based upon the law's failure to honour the father and (more incidentally) the mother; at the same time, opposition is voiced not by the person whose death is subject to law, but by the children (and, in the case of Antigona, the dutiful wife). As in our own time, then, euthanasia is contested, but on very different terms.

The ending of the play might seem simply to restore a fully patriarchalist status quo, with its validation of filial piety, its new law replacing the old, its privileging of the good son Cleanthes and punishing of the prodigal Simonides. And yet, in exploring the relation of family values and political governance so central to seventeenth-century political theory, the play discloses—whether intentionally or not—manifold fractures within this system. This is particularly the case in the concluding trial scene, which addresses a central contradiction in patriarchalist discourse. If, as James I argued in *The True Law of Free Monarchies* (a text first published in 1598, widely circulated in the early years of his reign in England, and included in his 1616 collected *Works*), 'the King towards his people is rightly compared to a father of children, and to a head of a body composed of divers members', then which father—the royal or the household father—requires the highest obedience? Like the Geneva Bible quoted above, *GOD and the King* (the 1615 pamphlet published and studied at James's command) attempts to settle this question in its gloss on the fifth commandment: '*honour thy Father and thy Mother*: where as we are required to honour the *Father* of private families, so much more the *Father* of our Country and the whole kingdom.' But for *Old Law* (probably first written and performed within a few years of these publications) the question remains open to contestation: can a father of what *GOD and the King* calls a 'private family' be simultaneously a head and a member of a body? Which is the head here, and which the member?

Cleanthes's trial focuses on precisely this question, and the sentence Simonides hands down confronts the issue explicitly:

Cleanthes, there is none can be
A good son and a bad subject, for if princes
Be called the peoples' fathers, then the subjects
Are all his sons, and he that flouts the prince
Doth disobey his father; there you're gone. (5.1.197–201)

Yet even here in the most straightforward statement of a patriarchal-absolutist stance, the plural 'princes' may begin to overwhelm the subsequent emphasis on singular authority. How many princes, how many peoples, how many fathers are there? These are questions for the editor as well as the reader (as the notes to the play suggest, these activities are often indistinguishable), for the earliest printed text of the play has no apostrophe in 'peoples'. Though the play may seem in the end to resolve such issues (the political and familial fathers turn out, in the tragicomic ending, not to have been opposed after all), the play has raised the possibility of fracture, has staged the adjudication of a theory the king himself understood as self-evident. Cleanthes's trial, we might say, takes place in the space between the Geneva Bible's statement of the fifth commandment and its authoritarian gloss in the margin. There are other moments of resistance marked in the notes to the play (for example, the question of whether a husband is more closely identified with his wife or father), and readers will undoubtedly locate others.

This is not to say that the play had these particular meanings for all its audiences; my notes to the text attempt to demonstrate the multiple valences of the play's language, meanings that may have been heard or read by some spectators or readers, though not by others. Indeed, the existence of two slightly different titles for the play in the seventeenth century—*An Old Law*, *The Old Law*—may suggest the variability with which audience members or readers may have seen in the play 'an' indefinite law (or one among several possible), and 'the' law (the definitive dictum, nevertheless potentially replaceable by 'the' [or 'a'?] new one). (On the variant titles, see *Canon and Chronology*.)

Further, the play may have signified in very different ways late in 1618 or in 1619 (when it was written by Middleton, Rowley, and possibly Thomas Heywood, and first performed, probably by Prince Charles's Men at either the Red Bull or the Cockpit); and then in the 1630s, when it may have been revived (and possibly revised at this point by Heywood, if he was not a part of the initial collaboration); and yet again in 1656, when it was published, after the theatres had been closed for more than a decade. (Though readers or audiences hardly need unravel the play's collaborative texture to experience its comedy and power—and, as I have argued elsewhere, there are potentially serious methodological problems, from a historicist perspective, in doing so—recent critics interested in attributing the play's authorship have agreed that Middleton probably wrote scenes 2.2, 3.2, and 4.2, and that Rowley wrote all or parts of 4.1 and 5.1. Although Philip Massinger is associated with the play on its first printed title-page, Gary Taylor has recently argued strongly for Heywood as the writer of the first half of the final act, 5.1.1–347; his argument simultaneously casts significant doubt on Massinger's participation at any point in the play's writing.)

During the 1640s and 1650s, the play's political vocabulary—its juxtaposition of terms including *prince*, *senate*, *parliament*, *republic*, and *commonwealth*—would have been particularly charged, as would the patriarchalist discourse explored above after the beheading of James I's son in 1649. (According to the 1656 title-page, the play was at some point performed for 'the King and Queen', probably Charles I and Henrietta Maria.) In other words, although a version of the play we now read was probably first composed in the second decade of the seventeenth-century, it continued to be revised and reinterpreted for at least forty years; like many plays of the period that were printed long after early performances, *Old Law* may have been revised for a revival in the interim (see 4.1.89, 5.1.347.1–4). Further, the compositors who set the type for the 1656 text may have changed or augmented, intentionally or not, the political valences of the play. As the notes attempt to detail, an analysis of some issues treated above may rest on whether a reader or editor accepts or rearranges the speech headings assigned by the 1656 text (particularly in Act 5), and on what might have been considered 'characteristic' of characters at a given historical moment (see for example 5.1.267, 5.1.270).

Old Law thus dynamically participates in the culture of its era(s), reflecting and rewriting that culture in multiple ways. The play's most important source might be said to be the ten commandments (though they are never quoted in the play itself), along with the many sermons, proclamations, political-theoretical texts (by James I and others), and biblical marginalia that produced the fifth commandment in particular as political theory and social practice. While the play seems for the Cleanthes plot to rewrite in particular a story transmitted from the medieval *Historia septum sapientum* and to draw on a tale retold from Giambattista Cinzio Giraldi's *Gli Ecatommiti* (1565) in Barnaby Rich's *Farewell to Military Profession* (1581) for the plot of the Clown's two wives, *Old Law* is also widely allusive, agglutinative, and revisionary in a way that defies any simple understanding of 'source'. The play satirizes Renaissance courtiers, lawyers, and legal discourse (Middleton's participation in legal wrangling over his filial inheritance may itself function as a 'source', especially in the first and last scenes), and the play seems to address James I (or advise his son) about reforming a court perceived as excessively young, fashionable, and effeminate. The play draws obliquely on a Montaigne essay (noted above) for its mention of some character-names and the setting. Other character names (for example, Hippolita) connect the play to a range of others in the period. The play apparently reworks or parodies lines from George Peele's now-lost play *The Turkish Mahamet and Hyrin the Fair Greek* (1581–94) and from Thomas Kyd's *The Spanish Tragedy* (1592), which in the Clown's parodic revision produces yet another complicated moment of tragicomic mixing (5.1.500–3).

Add to this list the play's broad classical attentiveness: its resurrecting of names from *Antigonê*, Sophocles's tragedy of social resistance (available in Latin translation by 1581); its use of Thomas North's translation of Plutarch's *Lives* (1579); and Cleanthes's recounting, to the patricidal young judges, of Aeneas's escape from burning Troy carrying his father—a passionate aria that puts the old text of Virgil's *Aeneid* in the service of the Old Testament. There is, finally, the play's closing reference to Plato's *Cratylus* at 5.1.618, an allusion that (just at the moment the law seems firmly re-rooted in 'natural' law

Emblem of Aeneas fleeing Troy, '*Pietas filiorum in parentes*', from Geffrey Whitney, *A Choice of Emblemes* (1586).

and the Old Testament) asks whether the foundation of law lies in convention or nature, and calls into question the very ideas of stability and authenticity in language. (In what might almost seem a Pynchonesque message to twentieth-century readers of a modernized text, the *Cratylus* also argues the impossibility of establishing stable spellings and meanings of old words.) Here we may again find a linking of classical, theoretical seriousness and 'mirth'; seemingly like the Platonic dialogue, the Clown laments, near the end of the play: 'I am not the first by forty that has been undone by the law; *'tis but a folly to stand upon terms*' (5.1.535–7, my emphasis). The form in which the allusion to the *Cratylus* arrives on stage—the character-revelation that produces the allusion—might itself be taken as a joke or as something altogether more serious: mirth or killing? Both?

SEE ALSO

Music and dance: *Companion*, 166
Textual introduction and apparatus: *Companion*, 1123
Authorship and date: *Companion*, 405
Other Middleton–Rowley works: *Weapons*, 980; *Quarrel*, 1209; *Tennis*, 1405; *Changeling*, 1632; *Gypsy*, 1723

WILLIAM ROWLEY, THOMAS MIDDLETON, and THOMAS HEYWOOD

An / *The* } *Old Law*

Or, A New Way to Please You

[*for Prince Charles's Men (at the Red Bull?)*]

Commentary 'To interpret a text is not to give it a (more or less justified, more or less free) meaning, but on the contrary to appreciate what *plural* constitutes it.... this text is a galaxy of signifiers, not a structure of signifieds; it has no beginning; it is reversible; we gain access to it by several entrances, none of which can be authoritatively declared to be the main one...' (Roland Barthes, *S/Z* 5).

Like all commentaries, this column of running commentary interprets the play even as it ostensibly clarifies or 'glosses' (3.2.219) it. This commentary in particular attempts to activate some of the 'plural' meanings of *Old Law* available to audiences and readers in the seventeenth century. The plurality of meanings cited in this column are the result of a number of factors; often these are difficult fully to distinguish in any given instance:

1) *linguistic plurality*, the fact that early modern English pronunciation, spelling, and punctuation lacked (though its speakers did not necessarily think of it as lacking) the standardization of modern English; also, the possibility of words having one meaning in general usage and another in a more specialized area of the language (for example, legal discourse); 2) *intentional plurality*, often called 'quibbles' or 'puns', wit attributed to characters like the Clown, and intended by the playwrights; 3) *collaborative plurality*, the production of plural meanings through the interventions of players or bookholders (prompters) in the theatre, or the printers in the printing house (doubled stage directions, omitted words, inverted pieces of type, etc.); 4) *aural plurality*, the fact the different audience members might have heard different or multiple meanings during the playing of this text on stage.

While this edition provides a version of *Old Law* that can be read as reconstructing a performance of a play, the commentary nevertheless insists on the multiple interventions the editorial process makes in the text in order to *produce* such an experience for the reader. For readers of both the text and the commentary column, reading cannot be merely, as Barthes writes, 'a parasitical act, the reactive complement of writing which we endow with all the glamour of creation and anteriority.' Rather, '[i]t is a form of work...I write my reading...' (*S/Z* 10). See *gloss* (3.2.219).

For these reasons, then, this commentary departs from the general protocol of this edition by including both commentary and the textual notes detailing changes (emendations) and modernizations made in the text; textual notes ordinarily appear in the *Companion*. Commentary notes refer to the first printed edition of *Old Law* (dated 1656) as BELL (for Jane Bell, who printed it). Other editors mentioned here include: COXETER (1761), MASON (1779), GIFFORD (1805), COLERIDGE (1839/40), DYCE (1840), BULLEN (1885), SHAW (1982), and TAYLOR (in consultation on the present edition). (Notes also occasionally mention specific copies of BELL stored at particular libraries; these are referenced as: FOLGER, HOUGHTON1, HOUGHTON2, HUNTINGTON, LCP, NEWBERRY, WILLIAMS.) Full bibliographical references for all editions appear in the *Companion*.

Title ***An Old Law/The Old Law*** The title appeared in two forms in the seventeenth century (see below), both of which raise some questions. Does *The Old Law* refer to the law for the killing of old people as described in the first scene? the law(s) of the 'Old Testament' (i.e., the Hebrew Bible), especially the fifth commandment ('honour thy father and thy mother')? Does the 'old' law suggest that there will be a new law, later on? If so, will it correspond to the New Testament? Or will it function as the parodic opposite of the New Testament—as the Old Law of 1.1 functions in relation to the Old Testament? If there is 'an' old law, might there be any number of others, or a young law?

Or, A New Way to Please You An alternative title for the play, or a subtitle? (Does this title substitute for *Old Law*, or does it supplement it?) In which of its senses will an old law be pleasing? Does this title promise a 'new way' that will replace the old law? Or does this phrase simply promise an innovation in dramatic repertoire? How is this title related to other 'pleasing' titles and subtitles—e.g. *As You Like It*, or *Twelfth Night, or What You Will*? Is the subtitle, possibly added for publication in 1656, a play on Massinger's play entitled *A New Way to Pay Old Debts* (published 1633)?

The Old Law; or, A New Way to Please You BELL (THE *Excellent Comedy, called* THE OLD LAW: OR A new way to pleafe you.); An ould Lawe REVELS; The Old Law. A Comedy COXETER. On the variant titles, see Taylor, '"The Old Law" or "An Old Law"?' On the play's genre, see Critical Introduction.

THE OLD LAW:

Persons This list is an editorial construction for this edition. BELL's list (transcribed in the *Companion*, p. 1127) was almost certainly prepared by someone unfamiliar with the details of the play (perhaps the publisher) some time after the play was acted, especially since it includes some significant errors of description. A seventeenth-century theatre audience would not have possessed a list of the play's persons, and the emergence of such lists (increasingly, they accompanied printed plays in the seventeenth century) is the product of the practice of reading, rather than (or in addition to) seeing plays. (See Gary Taylor's essay 'The Order of Persons' in the *Companion*, p. 31.) A list of 'persons' may give the impression that the play's characters pre-exist the performance that in fact constitutes them—that they have essences, pasts, futures, thoughts, motives, or even stable titles ('Executioner') or relationships ('Wife') separate from the performance/text. This list follows BELL's in not divulging some characters' names until they are addressed on stage or 'discovered' later in the play. Specific commentary on particular names appears at the moment of a character's first entrance or naming in the play itself.

16 LISANDER Although BELL suggests he is Cleanthes's 'uncle', the play itself does not specify the relation of Lisander to Cleanthes more closely than 'coz' (kinsman).

19 DANCER dancing teacher

PERSONS OF THE PLAY

SIMONIDES } 2 courtiers
CLEANTHES }

FIRST LAWYER
SECOND LAWYER

CREON, father to Simonides
ANTIGONA, mother to Simonides and wife to Creon
BUTLER }
BAILIFF }
TAILOR }
COOK } servants to Creon
COACHMAN }
FOOTMAN }
Old women, wives to Creon's servants

HIPPOLITA, wife to Cleanthes
LEONIDES, father to Cleanthes

LISANDER, husband to Eugenia and kinsman to Cleanthes
EUGENIA, wife to Lisander and mother to Parthenia
PARTHENIA, daughter to Lisander and Eugenia
DANCER
Servants to Lisander

DUKE of Epire
FIRST COURTIER
SECOND COURTIER
THIRD COURTIER
EXECUTIONER
FIRST GUARD
SECOND GUARD
FIRST OFFICER
Officers

CLOWN
Clown's WIFE
WENCH

CLERK

DRAWER

Musicians
Old men

1.1.0.1 *Incipit Actus Primus* THIS EDITION; Act. I. Scen. I. BELL

1 **Is ... sir** Unless otherwise noted, partial verse lines depicted in THIS EDITION as completing or continuing a verse line begun by another character were set in BELL as separate lines of type.

4 **conceive** understand

Incipit Actus Primus 1.1
Enter Simonides and two Lawyers

SIMONIDES
Is the law firm, sir?
FIRST LAWYER The law—what more firm, sir,
More powerful, forcible, or more permanent?
SIMONIDES By my troth, sir,
I partly do believe it; conceive, sir,

You have indirectly answerèd my question.
I did not doubt the fundamental grounds
Of law in general for the most solid,
But this particular law that me concerns
Now at the present, if that be firm and strong,
And powerful, and forcible, and permanent.
I am a young man that has an old father.

SECOND LAWYER Nothing more strong, sir;
It is *secundum statutum principis*
Confirmatum cum voce senatus,
Et voce reipublicæ, nay, *consummatum*
Et exemplificatum. Is it not in force
When divers have already tasted it
And paid their lives for penalty?

SIMONIDES 'Tis true,
My father must be next; this day completes
Full fourscore years upon him.

SECOND LAWYER He's here then
Sub pœna statuti, hence I can tell him,
Truer than all the physicians in the world,
He cannot live out tomorrow; this is
The most certain climacterical year,
'Tis past all danger, for there's no 'scaping it.
What age is your mother, sir?

SIMONIDES Faith, near her days too,
Wants some two of threescore.

FIRST LAWYER So, she'll drop away
One of these days too; here's a good age now
For those that have old parents, and rich inheritance.

SIMONIDES
And sir, 'tis profitable for others too:
Are there not fellows that lie bedrid in their offices
That younger men would walk lustily in,
Churchmen, that even the second infancy
Hath silenced, yet hath spun out their lives so long
That many pregnant and ingenious spirits
Have languished in their hoped reversïons
And died upon the thought, and by your leave, sir,
Have you not places filled up in the law
By some grave senators that you imagine
Have held them long enough, and such spirits as you,
Were they removed, would leap into their dignities?

FIRST LAWYER
Dic quibus in terris et eris mihi magnus Apollo.

SIMONIDES
But tell me, faith, your fair opinïon:
Is't not a sound and necessary law,
This by the Duke enacted?

FIRST LAWYER Never did Greece
(Our ancient seat of brave philosophers)
'Mongst all her *nomothetai* and lawgivers,
Not when she flourished in her sevenfold sages,
Whose living memory can never die,
Produce a law more grave and necessary.

SIMONIDES
I'm of that mind too.

SECOND LAWYER I will maintain, sir,
Draco's oligarchy, that the government

13–16 ***secundum . . . exemplificatum*** 'according to the Prince's statutes, confirmed with the voice of the senate, and the voice of the republic, nay, perfected and put into practice.'
14 ***senatus*** MASON; *senatum* BELL
15 ***reipublicæ*** BELL (*republicæ*)
17 **divers** several, many, a variety (often used in legal and scriptural contexts)
21 ***Sub pœna statuti*** 'under the penalty of the law'
24 **climacterical year** an especially critical, dangerous, or fatal stage of life. The ages 81 and 63 were considered 'grand climacterics', making them especially critical.
25 **'scaping** escaping
35 **pregnant** resourceful, ready
36 **hoped** expected
reversïons inheritances; *reversion*: the right to succeed to, or occupy, an estate after the death of its owner (legal term). Here and elsewhere, THIS EDITION occasionally adds diacritical marks not in BELL to assist readers with a possible scansion of a verse line.
42 ***Dic . . . Apollo*** 'Tell me how, and you will be as great as Apollo to me.' The line is adapted from Virgil's third *Eclogue*, translated in 1589 by Abraham Fleming as: 'tell me in what ground . . . and thou shalt be Apollo great to mee.'
47 **'Mongst** amongst
nomothetai BELL (Nomotheta); this modernization follows *OCD*'s rendering from Greek. In ancient Athens, this committee of lawmakers drafted or revised laws.
51–70 **I will . . . shame** The speech is a catalogue of famous lawmakers, reformers, and legal theorists of ancient Greece.
51 **maintain** support, defend; carry on a law case
52 **Draco's** Draco is traditionally credited with introducing the first Athenian laws to be set down in writing (*c.*620 BCE); the laws, including those for homicide, were known for their severe penalties.

Of community reducèd into few
Framed a fair state. Solon's *Creocopides*,
That cut off poor men's debts to their rich creditors,
Was good and charitable (but not full allowed);
His *seisachtheia* did reform that error,
His honourable senate of *Areopagitæ*.
Lycurgus was more loose, and gave too free
And licentious reins unto his discipline,
As that a young woman in her husband's weakness
Might choose her able friend to propagate,
That so the commonwealth might be supplied
With hope of lusty spirits. Plato did err,
And so did Aristotle, allowing
Lewd and luxurious limits to their laws;
But now our Epire, our Epire's Evander,
Our noble and wise prince, has hit the law
That all our predecessive students
Have missed unto their shame.

Enter Cleanthes

SIMONIDES Forbear the praise, sir;
'Tis in itself most pleasing. Cleanthes,
O lad, here's a spring for young plants to flourish!
The old trees must down kept the sun from us;
We shall rise now, boy.

CLEANTHES Whither, sir, I pray?
To the bleak air of storms among those trees
Which we had shelter from.

SIMONIDES Yes—from our growth,
Our sap and livelihood, and from our fruit.
What, 'tis not jubilee with thee yet, I think,
Thou look'st so sad on't. How old's thy father?

CLEANTHES
Jubilee, no indeed, 'tis a bad year with me.

SIMONIDES
Prithee, how old's thy father? Then I can tell thee.

CLEANTHES
I know not how to answer you, Simonides.
He is too old being now exposed
Unto the rigour of a cruel edict,
And yet not old enough by many years,
'Cause I'd not see him go an hour before me.

SIMONIDES
These very passions I speak to my father.
Come, come, here's none but friends here; we may speak
Our insides freely. These are lawyers, man,
And shall be counsellors shortly.

CLEANTHES They shall be now, sir,
And shall have large fees if they'll undertake
To help a good cause, for it wants assistance;
Bad ones (I know) they can insist upon.

FIRST LAWYER
O sir, we must undertake of both parts,
But the good we have most good in.

CLEANTHES Pray you, say
How do you allow of this strange edict?

FIRST LAWYER
Secundum justitiam, by my faith, sir,

54 **Solon's** One of the 'sevenfold sages' of ancient Greece (and a metaphor for wise legislator in the Renaissance), Solon was an Athenian statesman who reformed laws and government during a crisis that arose because of the severe conditions of serfdom (*c.*600 BCE). His *seisachtheia* (1.1.57, literally, a 'shaking off of burdens') cancelled debts, released peasants from serfdom and slavery, and forbade money-borrowing that considered persons as security for the debt. According to Thomas North's 1579 translation of Plutarch's *Lives of the Noble Grecians and Romans*, Solon's friends were known as '*Greocopides*, "cutters of detts"'. Solon also repealed Draco's laws, except those against homicide.
Creocopides THIS EDITION; Crecopedi BELL; *chreokopia* GIFFORD. From context, BELL's term seems to mean *chreokopia*, the cancelling of debts under Solon. However, BELL's spelling (Crecopedi) seems to be an attempt to render the term not for the process, but for persons who cancelled their debts (*chreokopides*), which North's Plutarch spells '*Greocopides*' (see previous note.) The confusion may indicate that Second Lawyer does not fully understand the precedents he cites. The spelling in this edition imagines that BELL (and potentially the hypothetical manuscript that was its copy) followed North's form, but corrected the initial letter.

57 ***seisachtheia*** MASON (Seisactheia); *Sisaithie* BELL. Modernization follows *OCD*. See l. 54.

58 ***Areopagitæ*** members of a judicial council (the Areopagus) reformed by Solon

59 **Lycurgus** legendary legislator credited with creating a social system and laws for Sparta (*c.*900 BCE). North's translation of Plutarch says of Lycurgus's marital rules: 'a man was not to be blamed, being stepped [= advanced] in yeres, and having a young wife, if seeing a fayer young man that liked him [= pleased him], and knowen with all to be of a gentle nature, he brought him home to get his wife with childe.... Lycurgus did not like that children should be private to any men, but that they should be common to the common weale'.

61 **woman** BELL; wife TAYLOR *conj.* (spelled 'wiue')

64–5 **Plato...Aristotle** referring to the systems of social organization proposed in Plato's *Republic* and Aristotle's *Politics*

66 **luxurious** lecherous; excessive
limits extents

67 **Epire** Epirus, a region of north-west Greece, considered backward in ancient times, and isolated geographically, culturally, and linguistically from the rest of Greece (see 5.1.618–21)

69 **predecessive** preceding (meaning earlier in history and perhaps earlier in this speech). This term, which is only known to appear in this play, may be a parody of legal language.

74 **Whither** BELL (Whether)

78 **jubilee** occasion of joyful celebration; in the Old Testament (the Hebrew Bible) and Jewish history, the celebration of a year of Jubilee every fifty years included the freeing of slaves and the reversion of property to its earlier owners.

83 **He is** GIFFORD; Hees is BELL

97 ***Secundum justitiam*** 'according to the law'

The happiest edict that ever was in Epire.

CLEANTHES

What, to kill innocents, sir? It cannot be;
It is no rule in justice there to punish.

FIRST LAWYER O sir,
You understand a conscience, but not law.

CLEANTHES

Why, sir, is there so main a difference?

FIRST LAWYER

You'll never be good lawyer, if you understand not that.

CLEANTHES

I think then 'tis the best to be a bad one.

FIRST LAWYER

Why, sir, the very letter and the sense both
Do both o'erthrow you in this statute,
Which that speaks, that every man living to
Fourscore years, and women to threescore, shall then
Be cut off as fruitless to the republic,
And law shall finish what nature lingered at.

CLEANTHES

And this suit shall soon be dispatched in law.

FIRST LAWYER

It is so plain it can have no demur;
The church-book overthrows it.

CLEANTHES And so it does;
The church-book overthrows it if you read it well.

FIRST LAWYER

Still you run from the law into error.
You say it takes the lives of innocents;
I say no, and so says common reason:
What man lives to fourscore and women to three
That can die innocent?

CLEANTHES A fine lawful evasion.
Good sir, rehearse the full statute to me.

SIMONIDES

Fie, that's too tedious, you have already
The full sum in the brief relatïon.

CLEANTHES

Sir, 'mongst many words may be found contradictions,
And these men dare sue and wrangle with a statute;
If they can pick a quarrel with some error—

SECOND LAWYER Listen sir, I'll gather it as brief as I can for you. [*Reads*] '*Anno primo Evandri*, be it (for the care and good of the commonwealth, for divers necessary reasons that we shall urge) thus peremptorily enacted'—

CLEANTHES

A fair pretence, if the reasons foul it not.

SECOND LAWYER [*reads*] 'That all men living in our dominions of Epire in their decayed nature to the age of fourscore, or women to the age of threescore, shall on the same day be instantly put to death, by those means and instruments that a former proclamation had (to this purpose) through our said territories dispersed.'

CLEANTHES

There was no women in this senate, certain.

103 **is** COXETER; ls BELL. The difference between *i* and *l* is obviously slight; in lightly printed copies of BELL, the difference is undetectable, and readers probably would not have interpreted this as a moment requiring intervention.

main great

106–7 **both ... both** It is difficult for a reader to differentiate the exaggerations of the lawyer's language from the possibility of an extra word (the first *both*?) in BELL. In l. 108, 'Which that' (as an archaic construction meaning 'which') may work similarly.

107 **o'erthrow** The first use of this and related terms that link the way in which the old people are executed (2.1.132–6) and the social and political consequences of this action (the overturning of 'proper' hierarchies, the world upside-down). See 1.1.114–15, 1.1.482, 4.2.196, 5.1.216.

113 **demur** delay, doubt, hesitation; in legal terminology, a *demurrer* was an objection that delayed the proceedings: 'a kind of pawse upon a point of difficultie in any action', John Cowell, *The Interpreter* (1637)

114 **church-book** the parish registry that records dates of christenings, marriages, burials, and thus the ages of parishioners. In the next line, however, Cleanthes uses the term to mean 'bible'.

119 **women** BELL; woman TAYLOR *conj.*

127 **gather** collect, bring together

128 ***Anno primo Evandri*** 'the first year of Evander's reign'

129 **commonwealth** 1) public welfare (in this case BELL's two-word spelling, *common wealth*, is more appropriate); 2) the group of people making up a nation or state; 3) a republic governed by the people; 4) the term used specifically to designate the English form of government at the time this play was first published (1656)

divers several; various

130 **peremptorily** decisively, conclusively; in a way that precludes debate or objection (legal term)

131 **pretence** aim or purpose (not necessarily hypocritical) (*OED*)

138 **women** BELL. Since *was* could be used as a plural verb, the commonplace emendation to *woman* (COXETER) is unnecessary. Readers of some copies (particularly FOLGER and LCP) would have confronted a blotch in place of the second vowel and might have interpreted this graphic shape as either word.

FIRST LAWYER [*reads*] 'That these men, being past their bearing arms, to aid and defend their country, past their manhood and livelihood, to propagate any further issue to their posterity, and as well past their counsels (which overgrown gravity is now run into dotage), to assist their country, to whom in common reason nothing should be so wearisome as their own lives, as it may be supposed is tedious to their successive heirs, whose times are spent in the good of their country, yet wanting the means to maintain it, and are like to grow old before their inheritance (born to them) come to their necessary use; for the which are the women, for that they never were defence to their country, never by counsel admitted to the assist of government of their country, only necessary to the propagation of posterity, and now at the age of threescore to be past that good, and all their goodness: it is thought fit, then, a quarter abated from the more worthy member, to be put to death as is before recited, provided that, for the just and impartial execution of this our statute, the example shall first begin in and about our court, which ourself will see carefully performed, and not for a full month following extend any further into our dominions. Dated the sixth of the second month, at our palace royal in Epire.'

CLEANTHES
A fine edict, and very fairly gilded.
And is there no scruple in all these words
To demur the law upon occasion?

SIMONIDES
Pox, 'tis an unnecessary inquisition;
Prithee, set him not about it.

SECOND LAWYER [*to Cleanthes*] Troth, none, sir,
It is so evident and plain a case
There is no succour for the defendant.

CLEANTHES
Possible? Can nothing help in a good case?

FIRST LAWYER
Faith, sir, I do think there may be a hole
Which would protract delay, if not remedy.

CLEANTHES
Why, there's some comfort in that, good sir; speak it.

FIRST LAWYER
Nay, you must pardon me for that, sir.

SIMONIDES Prithee, do not,
It may ope a wound to many sons and heirs
That may die after it.

CLEANTHES [*to First Lawyer*]
Come, sir, I know how to make you speak;
[*He gives him money*]
will this do't?

FIRST LAWYER
I will afford you my opinion, sir.

CLEANTHES [*to Second Lawyer*]
Pray you, repeat the literal words, expressly
The time of death.

SIMONIDES
'Tis an unnecessary question; prithee, let it alone.

139–63 Since it is largely impossible to differentiate between deliberately labyrinthine prose that parodies legal language and errors in the text, I have taken a middle road in this speech, repunctuating it (as with the rest of the play) to make it legible to a modern reader, but leaving the words largely as they are in BELL—modernizing their spellings, but not rewriting the passage, as many previous editors have. The point or effect of the speech may have been that 'the old law' does not (within either a grammatical or a certain moral paradigm) make complete sense. See ll. 106–7.

141 **livelihood** BELL; likelihood GIFFORD

142 **counsels** ability to give advice. BELL's spelling (*councells*) might also be modernized as *councils*, especially since *counsel* is rarely plural. The modernization of BELL's spelling *Counsell* is more interpretively significant at l. 152, where it could mean: 'never admitted, by advice of counsel'; or 'never permitted to serve as counsel'; or 'never admitted by council' (a deliberative body).

143 **which** BELL; for MASON; whose GIFFORD

146 **it . . . is** BELL; they may be supposed COXETER; it may be supposed, [they are] SHAW

148 **yet** nevertheless; still
means BELL; Mean MASON

149 **born to them** theirs by birth, with a pun on *borne* (carried)

150 **for the which are** BELL; for the which they are adjudged to death MASON; [be condemned to die]: for GIFFORD; for BULLEN; [and they be condemned to death.] For SHAW

151 **never were defence** BELL; were never a Defence MASON; were never defence SHAW

152 **the . . . government** BELL; assist in the Government COXETER; the assist[ance] of [the] government DYCE

154 **to be past** BELL; being MASON; past GIFFORD; they be past BULLEN; be past SHAW

155 **fit** COXETER; flt BELL
then BELL; for them MASON; *not in* GIFFORD

156 **member** BELL; Members MASON. *Member* = part of the body politic, the commonwealth.
to be BELL; that they be GIFFORD; they be DYCE

161 **further** COXETER; furrher BELL

164 **fairly gilded** adorned with beautiful words; covered over with decoration that conceals defects; possibly also with a suggestion of gold/money (*guilders*) and of lawyers as a group (*guild*)—all readings suggested by BELL's spelling *guilded*

167 **Pox** an exclamation of impatience; literally, a disease

176 **ope** open

180 **expressly** in plain terms; in particular

SECOND LAWYER
Hear his opinion; 'twill be fruitless, sir.
[*Reads*] 'That man at the age of fourscore, and women
at threescore shall the same day be put to death.'
FIRST LAWYER
Thus, I help the man to twenty-one years more—
CLEANTHES That were a fair addition.
FIRST LAWYER
Mark it, sir: we say man is not at age
Till he be one-and-twenty; before, his infancy
And adolescency; nor (by that addition)
Fourscore he cannot be till a hundred and one.
SIMONIDES O poor evasion!
He's fourscore years old, sir—
FIRST LAWYER That helps more, sir:
He begins to be old at fifty, so at fourscore
He's but thirty years old, so believe it, sir,
He may be twenty years in declination
And so long may a man linger and live by't.
SIMONIDES
The worst hope of safety that e'er I heard.
Give him his fee again; 'tis not worth two *deniers*.
FIRST LAWYER There's no law for restitution of fees, sir.
Enter Creon and Antigona
CLEANTHES
No, no, sir, I meant it lost when 'twas given.
SIMONIDES No more, good sir;
Here are ears unnecessary for your doctrine.
FIRST LAWYER
I have spoke out my fee and I have done, sir.
SIMONIDES
O my dear father!
CREON Tush, meet me not in exclaims;
I understand the worst and hope no better.
A fine law; if this hold, white heads will be cheap,
And many watchmen's places will be vacant.
Forty of 'em I know my seniörs,
That did due deeds of darkness too—their country
Has watched 'em a good turn for't, and ta'en 'em
Napping now. The fewer hospitals will serve too;
Many may be used for stews and brothels,
And those people will never trouble 'em to fourscore.
ANTIGONA
Can you play and sport with sorrow, sir?
CREON
Sorrow for what, Antigona? For my life?
My sorrow's I have kept it so long well
With bringing it up unto so ill an end.
I might have gently lost it in my cradle,
Before my nerves and ligaments grew strong
To bind it faster to me.
SIMONIDES [*aside*] For mine own sake,
I should have been sorry for that.
CREON In my youth
I was a soldier; no coward in my age,
I never turned my back upon my foe.
I have felt nature's winters' sicknesses,
Yet ever kept a lively sap in me

184–5 **man ... threescore** The law's twenty-year difference in the execution age of men and women may reflect a similar difference encoded in an Elizabethan statute regulating labour, which freed women over 40 and men over 60 from compulsory agricultural work ('Statute of Artificers' 5 Eliz c. 4 (1562), sections 5 and 17).

190 **nor** BELL; now MASON. The final letter is legible only in some copies (FOLGER, WILLIAMS); the indistinctly printed word might have been read as *not* in other copies.

197 **declination** decline

198 **by't** BELL (bit). *by't* = by it (i.e., by this interpretation of the law). A modernization first adopted by DYCE, though suggested by COXETER (by it). Other possible readings for BELL's 'linger and live bit'—a line without end punctuation:
And so long may a man linger and live [a] bit.
And so long may a man linger and live bit [by bit]—
[*Simonides interrupts*]
And so long may a man linger and live bit. [i.e., stung by death, but not yet dead]

200 ***deniers*** BELL (deneers). Coins of little value (one-twelfth of a French *sou*); a term sometimes used in English to translate the Latin monetary term *denarius*

201.1 ***Enter Creon and Antigona*** The names recall (not altogether sensically in this context) the tyrant king and resistant heroine of Sophocles's tragedy *Antigone*.
Creon BELL (HOUGHTON2, HUNTINGTON); Cre on BELL (HOUGHTON1, FOLGER, WILLIAMS, LCP, NEWBERRY). Unlike another press variant identified in these notes (2.1.96), but like letters that seem to fail to print throughout BELL at various points in various copies (see 4.1.148), this variant cannot necessarily be ascribed to deliberate alteration of the text during the process of printing. BELL's intra- and inter-word spacing is often unusual, even when considered within the broad range of early modern spelling and typesetting practices.

204 **ears unnecessary for** ears that need not hear

206 **Tush** an exclamation of impatient contempt
in exclaims with exclamations

210–13 **Forty ... now** I know forty men older than me who did required service (like watchmen) defending their country, which has returned the favour by executing them in their old age.

211 **due** BELL; do COXETER
too—their country MASON; ~‸~~ BELL

212 **ta'en** taken

214 **stews** whore-houses; hot baths

218 **sorrow's** BELL (sorrowes); sorrowe's NEWBERRY (added handwritten apostrophe)

219 **unto** BELL; to TAYLOR *conj.*

222 **aside** Since at this point Simonides seems still to be disguising his attempt to hustle his father off to death, I have placed an 'aside' in the text. But BELL does not indicate lines spoken 'aside', and they must always be read in the text column as an interpretive act by the editor. Whether a reader accepts that interpretation may depend on how brazenly he/she understands Simonides to be acting toward his parents at this point in the play; what it is appropriate to say aloud to one's parent in Renaissance culture might be said to be the subject matter of the play as a whole. For other ambiguous instances of 'asides', see 2.1.108, 3.2.266–8, 4.2.132.

226 **winters' sicknesses** BELL (winters ſickneſſes); Winter's ~ COXETER; Winters, ~ MASON *conj.*; winter-sicknesses BULLEN *conj.*; winter sicknesses SHAW

To greet the cheerful spring of health again.
Dangers on horseback, on foot, by water,
I have 'scaped to this day, and yet this day,
Without all help of casual accidents,
Is only deadly to me, 'cause it numbers
Fourscore years to me. Where's the fault now?
I cannot blame time, nature, nor my stars,
Nor aught but tyranny; even kings themselves
Have sometimes tasted an even fate with me:
He that has been a soldier all his days
And stood in personal opposition
'Gainst darts and arrows, the extremes of heat,
And pinching cold, has treacherously at home
In his securèd quiet by a villain's hand
[ ]
Am basely lost in my star's ignorance,
And so must I die by a tyrant's sword.

FIRST LAWYER
O say not so, sir; it is by the law!

CREON
And what's that, sir, but the sword of tyranny,
When it is brandished against innocent lives?
I'm now upon my deathbed, sir, and 'tis fit
I should unbosom my free conscïence
And show the faith I die in: I do believe
'Tis tyranny that takes my life.

SIMONIDES [*aside*] Would it were gone
By one means or other. What a long day
Will this be ere night!

CREON Simonides.

SIMONIDES
Here, sit—([*breaks off*], *weeping*)

CREON Wherefore dost thou weep?

CLEANTHES [*aside*]
'Cause you make no more haste to your end.

SIMONIDES
How can you question nature so unjustly?
I had a grandfather, and then had not you
True filial tears for him?

CLEANTHES [*aside*] Hypocrite,
A disease of drought dry up all pity from him
That can dissemble pity with wet eyes!

CREON
Be good unto your mother, Simonides;
She must be now your care.

ANTIGONA To what end, sir?
The bell of this sharp edict tolls for me
As it rings out for you; I'll be as ready
With one hour's stay to go along with you.

CREON
Thou must not, woman; there are years behind
Before thou canst set forward in this voyage,
And Nature sure will now be kind to all:
She has a quarrel in't, a cruel law
Seeks to prevent her; she'll therefore fight in't
And draw out life even to her longest thread.
Thou art scarce fifty-five.

ANTIGONA So many morrows,
Those five remaining years I'll turn to days,
To hours, or minutes for thy company;
'Tis fit that you and I, being man and wife,
Should walk together arm-in-arm.

SIMONIDES [*aside*]
I hope they'll go together—I would they would,
i'faith,
Then would her thirds be saved too. [*To Creon*] The
day goes away, sir.

CREON
Why, wouldst thou have me gone, Simonides?

SIMONIDES
O my heart, would you have me gone before you, sir?
You give me such a deadly wound—

CLEANTHES [*aside*] Fine rascal.

SIMONIDES
Blemish my duty so with such a question!
Sir, I would haste me to the Duke for mercy;
He that's above the law may mitigate
The rigour of the law. How a good meaning
May be corrupted by misconstruction!

CREON
Thou corrupt'st mine; I did not think thou mean'st so.

CLEANTHES [*aside*] You were in the more error.

SIMONIDES The words wounded me.

CLEANTHES [*aside*] 'Twas pity thou died'st not on't.

235–41 **kings...hand** These lines may allude to the assassination in 1610 of King Henri IV of France, a famous life-long soldier stabbed to death in a Paris street.

237–44 **He...sword** Either a line (or more) is missing in BELL between 'hand' and 'Am' (as here), or Creon changes pronouns in the midst of this speech, moving from an abstract, third-person description of his situation to an explicitly personal conclusion at 243. A number of other interventions (noted below) have been suggested as a way of making sense of BELL's shift in grammatical person.

240 **has** BELL; dies COXETER

241–3 **hand...Am** THIS EDITION; hand | Am BELL

243 **Am** BELL; I'm COXETER; Been GIFFORD+
my BELL; his GIFFORD+
star's ignorance ignorance of my fate (as dictated by the stars); state's ignorance TAYLOR *conj.*

254 **Here, sit—([*breaks off*], *weeping*)** THIS EDITION; Heer fit —— —— weeping. BELL; Here, Sir [*weeping.* COXETER; Here, sir,—weeping. GIFFORD; Here [I] sit, weeping. SHAW. PRICE argues that (as in the 1623 quarto of *The Duke of Milan*) 'the compositor has in places left blanks for words he could not decipher...' (123). THIS EDITION interprets BELL's unusual punctuation as suggesting that 'weeping' is a marginal stage direction rather than part of Simonides's speech. Alternatively, the entire line in BELL might be read as a stage direction for the actor playing Simonides. See note to 3.2.173.

272 **morrows** days after today; mornings

278 **thirds** the third of a deceased husband's personal property that was inherited by his widow (legal term)

287 **mean'st** BELL (meaneft)

SIMONIDES
I have been ransacking the helps of law,
Conferring with these learnèd advocates;
If any scruple, cause, or wrested sense
Could have been found out to preserve your life,
It had been bought (though with your full estate),
Your life's so precious to me, but there is none.

FIRST LAWYER
Sir, we have canvassed it from top to toe,
Turned it upside down, threw her on her side,
Nay, opened and dissected all her entrails,
Yet can find none; there's nothing to be hoped
But the Duke's mercy.

SIMONIDES [*aside*] I know the hope of that;
He did not make the law for that purpose.

CREON
Then to his hopeless mercy last I go;
I have so many precedents before me,
I must call it hopeless. Antigona,
See me delivered up unto my deathsman,
And then we'll part; five years hence I'll look for thee.

SIMONIDES [*aside*]
I hope she'll not stay so long behind you.

CREON
Do not bate him an hour by grief and sorrow;
Since there's a day prefixèd, haste it not.
Suppose me sick, Antigona; dying now,
Any disease thou wilt may be my end,
Or when death's slow to come, say tyrants send.
Exeunt [*Creon and Antigona*]

SIMONIDES
Cleanthes, if you want money tomorrow use me;
I'll trust you while your father's dead.
Exeunt [*Simonides and Lawyers*]

CLEANTHES Why here's a villain
Able to corrupt a thousand by example.
Does the kind root bleed out his livelihood
In parent distribution to his branches,
Adorning them with all his glorious fruits,
Proud that his pride is seen when he's unseen?
And must not gratitude descend again
To comfort his old limbs in fruitless winter?
Improvident, at least partial, Nature—
Weak woman in this kind—who in thy last
Teeming still forgets the former, ever making
The burden of thy last throes the dearest
Darling. O, yet, in noble man reform it,
And make us better than those vegetives
Whose souls die within 'em! Nature, as thou art old,
If love and justice be not dead in thee,
Make some the pattern of thy piety,
Lest all do turn unnaturally against thee,
And thou be blamed for our oblivions
And brutish reluctations.
Enter Leonides and Hippolita
Ay, here's the ground
Whereon my filial faculties must build
An edifice of honour or of shame
To all mankind.

HIPPOLITA [*to Leonides*]
You must avoid it, sir,

291 **ransacking** examining thoroughly, making a detailed search; plundering, damaging, destroying

293 **cause** case, legal action; fact (legal term)

297–301 The law's transformation here from a neuter body to a female one may have served to remind an audience of the asymmetrical gendering of the law itself, also formulated in the language of the body ('member', l. 156). This figurative description of the law's dissection also resonates with depictions of dissection in Renaissance anatomical treatises, like the title-page of Andreas Vesalius, *De humani corporis fabrica libri* (1543).

304 **precedents** previous cases, examples (legal term); fore-runners (i.e. those already executed). BELL spells 'presidents'; though we now distinguish these words, they were spelled interchangeably, which may suggest the way in which precedents were thought to preside. Advising Prince Charles to follow the example of his father (King James) in 1616, James Montagu wrote: 'Neither doeth the Honour of a good Sonne consist in any thing more, then in immitating the good *Presidents* of a good Father....' (James I, *Workes*).

309 **bate** subtract, lessen (abate); as a legal term, *abate* could mean: to put an end to a legal action, to render a writ null and void. In this context, audiences might have heard a suggestion (not altogether sensical) of the legal term *abatement*, the intrusion of someone without inheritance rights onto lands before the proper heir's possession of them.
him the Executioner (l. 306) or Simonides

313 **tyrants send** In the theatre, an audience might have heard 'tyrants end'.

315 **while** until

317 **bleed out** bleed forth, but perhaps also with a suggestion of 'exhaust' (an unusual usage)

318 **parent** parental. *Parent* was only rarely used as an adjective, in the phrases *heir parent* and *parent heir*, uses clearly related to this passage.

323–7 **Improvident...Darling** One possible paraphrase of this difficult sentence: Nature, you are not forward-looking (provident) in always seeming to favour youth (what you have produced most recently) over age. See 1.1.443.

324 **Weak woman in this kind** weak, like a woman, in this way
last BELL; latest TAYLOR *conj.*

326 **burden** BELL (burthen)
last throes latest labour-pains, possibly with a suggestion of death-throes (especially since *last* is repeated)

328 **vegetives** vegetables or plants, 'capable of growth and development but devoid of sensation and thought' (*OED*)

331 **pattern** BELL's spelling is *patern*, and, in a speech arguing for 'parent distribution' from father to son, it is worth noting that the word we now spell *pattern* was not fully differentiated from its root *patron* (and the related term *paternal*) until 1700. *Patron* could mean an advocate or defender. Describing to Prince Charles the collected *Workes* of his father King James, Montagu wrote: 'Let these *Workes*, therefore, most gracious *Prince*, lie before you as a Patterne; you cannot haue a better...' (a4).

333 **oblivions** things forgotten; forgetfulness

334 **brutish** beastly, non-human
reluctations struggles against, or resistances to something (the 'turnings against' of 1.1.332)

334.1 ***Hippolita*** a queen of the Amazons, later conquered and married to Theseus

If there be any love within yourself.
This is far more than fate of a lost game
That another venture may restore again;
It is your life which you should not subject
To any cruelty if you can preserve it.

CLEANTHES
O dearest woman, thou hast now doubled
A thousand times thy nuptial dowry to me.
Why, she whose love is but derived from me
Is got before me in my debted duty!

HIPPOLITA
Are you thinking such a resolution, sir?

CLEANTHES
Sweetest Hippolita, what love taught thee
To be so forward in so good a cause?

HIPPOLITA
Mine own pity, sir, did first instruct me,
And then your love and power did both command me.

CLEANTHES
They were all blessèd angels to direct thee,
And take their counsel. [*To Leonides*] How do you fare, sir?

LEONIDES
Never better, Cleanthes; I have conceived
Such a new joy within this old bosom,
As I did never think would there have entered.

CLEANTHES
Joy call you it? Alas, 'tis sorrow, sir,
The worst of sorrows, sorrow unto death.

LEONIDES
Death? What's that, Cleanthes? I thought not on't;
I was in contemplation of this woman.
'Tis all thy comfort, son; thou hast in her
A treasure unvaluable; keep her safe.
When I die, sure 'twill be a gentle death,
For I will die with wonder of her virtues—
Nothing else shall dissolve me.

CLEANTHES
'Twere much better, sir,
Could you prevent their malice.

LEONIDES
I'll prevent 'em,
And die the way I told thee: in the wonder
Of this good woman. I tell thee, there's few men
Have such a child; I must thank thee for her.
That the stronger tie of wedlock should do more
Than Nature in her nearest ligaments
Of blood and propagation! I should ne'er
Have begot such a daughter of my own.
A daughter-in-law! Law were above nature
Were there more such children.

CLEANTHES
This admiration
Helps nothing to your safety; think of that, sir.

LEONIDES
Had you heard her, Cleanthes, but labour
In the search of means to save my forfeit life,
And knew the wise and sound preservations
That she found out, you would redouble all
My wonder in your love to her.

CLEANTHES
The thought,
The very thought claims all that from me,
And she's now possessed of it. But good sir,
If you have aught received from her advice,
Let's follow it, or else let's better think,
And take the surest course.

LEONIDES
I'll tell thee one:
She counsels me to fly my severe country,
Turn all into treasure, and there build up
My decaying fortunes in a safer soil,
Where Epire's law cannot claim me.

CLEANTHES
And sir,
I apprehend it as a safest course
And may be easily accomplishèd;
Let us be all most expeditïous.
Every country where we breathe will be our own,
Or better soil. Heaven is the roof of all,
And now, as Epire's situate by this law,
There is 'twixt us and heaven a dark eclipse.

HIPPOLITA
O then avoid it, sir; these sad events
Follow those black predictions.

LEONIDES
I prithee peace.
I do allow thy love, Hippolita,
But must not follow it as counsel, child;
I must not shame my country for the law.
This country here hath bred me, brought me up,
And shall I now refuse a grave in her?
I'm in my second infancy, and children
Ne'er sleep so sweetly in their nurse's cradle
As in their natural mother's.

340 **venture** endeavour, with the suggestion of risk-taking. For more on this important word, see 3.1.177.

343 **now doubled** BELL; doubled now TAYLOR *conj.*

345 **derived** See 1.1.458–63.

362 **unvaluable** invaluable, priceless

370 **stronger** BELL. TAYLOR suggests 'stranger', since wedlock connects one to 'strangers', which paradoxically 'do[es] more' than the nearest natural connection.

374–5 **daughter-in-law . . . children** Leonides's emphasis on 'law' is a prime instance of the play's frequent comparison of the law with what is perceived to be natural. For one definition of *natural* in the play, see Cleanthes's speech, 1.1.317–34.

378 **forfeit life** Leonides's life, given up (forfeited) in compliance with the Old Law. The legal term *forfeiture* signified 'the effect of transgressing a penall law, rather than the transgression itself' (Cowell, *The Interpreter*, 1637). Since *fet* was a past participle of *fetch*, BELL's spelling *forfet* may carry the additional resonance of *fore-fet* (fetched ahead of its time).

379 **preservations** means of preserving (*OED*); preservatives TAYLOR *conj.*

380 **found** COXETER; fouud BELL. The inversion of *n/u* occurs occasionally in this text, most significantly at 5.1.57.

396 **situate by** situated, placed in relation to

407–9 **natural mother's . . . her** Again emphasizing that the law violates what is represented as 'natural' by Hippolita and Cleanthes, and hearkening back to Cleanthes's presentation of a reproductive, female Nature (1.1.323–7).

HIPPOLITA Ay, but sir,
She is unnatural; then the stepmother
Is to be preferred before her.

LEONIDES Tush, she shall
Allow it me despite of her entrails!
Why, do you think how far from judgement 'tis
That I should travel forth to seek a grave
That is already digged for me at home—
Nay, perhaps find it in my way to seek it?
How have I then sought a repentant sorrow?
For your dear loves, how have I banished you
From your country ever with my base attempt?
How have I beggared you in wasting that
Which only for your sakes I bred together—
Buried my name in Epire, which I built
Upon this frame to live forever in?
What a base coward shall I be to fly
From that enemy which every minute meets me!
And thousand odds he had not long vanquished me
Before this hour of battle! Fly my death?
I will not be so false unto your states,
Nor fainting to the man that's yet in me:
I'll meet him bravely; I cannot (this knowing) fear
That when I am gone hence I shall be there.
Come, I have days of preparation left.

CLEANTHES Good sir, hear me.
I have a genius that has prompted me,
And I have almost formed it into words—
'Tis done, pray you observe 'em: I can conceal you
And yet not leave your country.

LEONIDES Tush, it cannot be
Without a certain peril on's all.

CLEANTHES
Danger must be hazarded rather than accept
A sure destruction. You have a lodge, sir,
So far remote from way of passengers
That seldom any mortal eye does greet with it,
And, yes, so sweetly situate with thickets
Built with such cunning labyrinths within,
As if the provident heavens, foreseeing cruelty,
Had bid you frame it to this purpose only.

LEONIDES
Fie, fie—'tis dangerous, and treason too,
To abuse the law!

HIPPOLITA 'Tis holy care, sir,
Of your dear life, which is your own to keep,
But not your own to lose, either in will
Or negligence.

CLEANTHES Call you it treason, sir?
I had been, then, a traitor unto you,
Had I forgot this. Beseech you accept of it;
It is secure, and a duty to yourself.

LEONIDES
What a coward will you make me!

CLEANTHES You mistake—
'Tis noble courage: now you fight with death,

410 **entrails** thought to be the location of emotions

414–23 Since exclamation points and question marks are sometimes used in ways that seem interchangeable in BELL, it is possible to read a number of the questions in this speech as exclamations.

415 **have I** i.e., will I have

417 **with my base attempt** Given BELL's lack of punctuation, it is not clear whether this phrase belongs with the question that precedes or follows it. BELL reads 'From your Country ever with my base attempt'; the editorial question mark inserted at the end of this line might instead be inserted after 'ever'. This intervention might seem extreme (because it places a question mark in the middle of an unpunctuated line), but punctuation of the kind a modern reader would expect is often scarce or absent in BELL.

426 **your states** 1) governments in general; 2) the government of Epire specifically (its authorities, its nobles, or its ruling assembly, the 'estates of the realm', elsewhere in the play called a 'senate' and a 'parliament' [1.1.138]); 3) Cleanthes and Hippolyta's welfare; and 4) more specifically, the legal term for Cleanthes and Hippolyta's right or title to property or 'estates', about which Leonides has just spoken at ll. 418–19. Interpreting this word need not be a choice of any one definition; since the appropriate conduct of the state and the family are closely linked in the play (and in early modern English culture generally), the word may carry these meanings simultaneously.

428–9 **I...there** Knowing this, I can't/won't allow myself to fear that when I am dead I'll be in a foreign country.

432 **genius** Several meanings are applicable here, in ways that may significantly complicate an understanding of Cleanthes as a 'character'. In a classical meaning that extends to the present, *genius* signified the god or spirit that accompanied each person through life 'to govern his fortunes and determine his character' (*OED*). Later there developed, in the words of a 1614 text, the 'tradition of two Genii [geniuses], which attend euery man, one good, the other euill' (*Purchas his Pilgrimage*). At about the same time, the word also began to mean the 'characteristic disposition' of a person—what we might call 'personality', but with the significant reminder that the genius is figured (as it is here) as Other, an entity originating *outside* the person in question. In a way that may be important to an interpretation of the later part of the play, then, Cleanthes here says that he has a spirit (good? bad?) that arrives at the plan he proceeds to outline, a spirit that 'prompts' him from the outside. (Importantly, *genius* did not begin to mean superabundant creativity or intelligence until well after the writing and publication of this play—in the mid-eighteenth century).

436 **on's** on us

438 **lodge** a secluded house in a forest that serves as a temporary retreat

439 **passengers** travellers, passersby

441 **yes** indeed. Possibly an error for 'yet' (= furthermore, besides).
yes BELL; yet COXETER
situate with situated with, placed among

443 **provident** foreseeing

445 **treason** The choice established here—between treason to one's country and treason to one's father—is central to the play, for it distinguishes two things that were often said to go together in early modern English culture. See 5.1.198–201.

446–9 **'Tis...negligence** The line cites the Christian (Augustinian) prohibition against suicide, whether active or passive.

446 **holy** This spelling (BELL's) was used at least through the sixteenth century to signify the words we now distinguish as *holy* and *wholly*.

And yield not to him till you stoop under him.

LEONIDES
This must needs open to discovery,
And then what torture follows?

CLEANTHES
By what means, sir?
Why, there's but one body in all this counsel,
Which cannot betray itself. We two are one—
One soul, one body, one heart, that think all one
thought—
And yet we two are not completely one;
But as I have derived myself from you,
Who shall betray us where there is no second?

HIPPOLITA
You must not mistrust my faith, though my sex
Plead weak and frailty for me.

LEONIDES
O, I dare not!
But where's the means that must make answer for
me?
I cannot be lost without a full account,
And what must pay that reckoning?

CLEANTHES
O sir, we will
Keep solemn obits for your funeral;
We'll seem to weep, and seem to joy withal,
That death so gently has prevented you
The law's sharp rigour, and this no mortal ear
Shall participate the knowledge of.

LEONIDES Ha, ha, ha!
This will be a sportive fine demur,
If the error be not found.

CLEANTHES
Pray, doubt of none;
Your company and best provisïon
Must be no further furnished than by us,
And in the interim your solitude
May converse with heaven, and fairly prepare
Which was too violent and raging
Thrown headlong on you.

LEONIDES
Still, there are some doubts
Of the discovery, yet I do allow't.

HIPPOLITA
Will you not mention now the cost and charge
Which will be in your keeping?

LEONIDES
That will be somewhat
Which you might save too.

CLEANTHES
With his will against him,
What foe is more to man than man himself?
Are you resolved, sir?

LEONIDES
I am, Cleanthes.
If by this means I do get a reprieve
And cozen death awhile, when he shall come
Armed in his own power to give the blow,
I'll smile upon him then, and laughing go. *Exeunt*

Finis Actus Primus

Incipit Actus Secundus 2.1
Enter Duke, three Courtiers, and Executioner

DUKE Executioner.

EXECUTIONER
My lord.

457 **torture** torture (in the modern sense); executioner, torturer. BELL's spelling *tortor* was one possible seventeenth-century spelling of *torture*; *tortor*'s additional meaning of executioner is relevant here, especially since a character named Executioner appears in the scene that 'follows'. Both spellings suggest the legal discourse of 'tort'—the perceived wrongness (etymologically, the 'twisted' nature) of this particular law.

458–63 **one body...second** It is not entirely clear which 'two' are 'one' in this speech—Leonides and Cleanthes, or Cleanthes and Hippolita. The speech initially seems directed at Leonides, suggesting the commonplace that the son was a true and perfect copy of his father, a 'second-self' as Prince Charles was said to be in relation to King James I (*Workes*). Yet the end of the speech, turning to Cleanthes's derivation from his father, suggests that he had been initially referring to Hippolita, with whom he is (in the words of Genesis 2:24, quoted frequently in the period) 'one flesh'. In l. 461, *we two* may again refer to Leonides. The complicated mathematics of the speech may thus reveal an important fracture in the discourse of the family in early modern England: with which 'one body' is the son 'one flesh', the father or the wife? These questions of identity are further complicated here by l. 462's apparently missing 'I' (added here).

460 **one body, one heart** BELL; one heart, one body TAYLOR *conj.*

462 **as I** MASON; ~‸ BELL

465 **weak** weakness. The meaning is clear; the usage is unusual. The difficult syntax may result from a play on 'plead guilty'; most editions substitute *weakness*, though doing so disrupts the iambic metre. TAYLOR conjectures that *weak and* may be an error for *weakend* (weakened).

weak and frailty BELL. MASON's emendation (weak and frailly) seems unsupported by *OED*, which lists no adverbial uses of *weak*; GIFFORD's (Weakness and frailty), adopted by all subsequent editions, disrupts the fairly regular metre in this passage, without any real benefit in meaning. See previous note.

467 **account** 1) explanation; or 2) arithmetical or financial reckoning (the next line plays on this meaning). *Account/accompt* (BELL's spelling) were interchangeable in the period, and both could designate a legal term: 'Accompt is a writ, and it lieth where a bayliffe or a Receiver to any Lord or other man, which ought to render accompt, will not give his account' (John Rastell, *The exposicians of the termes of the lawes*, 1618).

account BELL (accompt)

469 **obits** rites

473 **participate** partake, share

475 **sportive** playful

demur delay. See 1.1.113.

481 **Which** BELL; What TAYLOR *conj. Which* = that which (i.e. Leonides's eventual death)

482 **headlong** hastily, recklessly; head-first (head fore-most, or down-most)—a meaning that gestures again toward the mode of execution (described in the next scene) and its cultural resonances of the world upside-down (see 1.1.107).

492.1 ***Primus*** BELL (*Primi*)

2.1.0.1 ***Incipit Actus Secundus*** THIS EDITION; Act. II. Scen. I. BELL

DUKE How did old Diocles take his death?

EXECUTIONER
As weeping brides receive their joys at night, my lord:
With trembling yet with patience.

DUKE Why, 'twas well.

FIRST COURTIER
Nay, I knew my father would do well, my lord,
Whene'er he came to die; I'd that opinion of him,
Which made me the more willing to part from him.
He was not fit to live i'th' world indeed
Any time these ten years, my lord.
But I would not say so much.

DUKE No, you did not well in't,
For he that's all spent is ripe for death at all hours,
And does but trifle time out.

FIRST COURTIER Troth, my lord,
I would I had known your mind nine years ago.

DUKE
Our law is fourscore years, because we judge
Dotage complete then, as unfruitfulness
In women at threescore. Marry, if the son
Can within compass bring good solid proofs
Of his own father's weakness and unfitness
To live or sway the living, though he want five
Or ten years of his number, that's not it,
His defect makes him fourscore, and 'tis fit
He dies when he deserves, for every act
Is in effect then, when the cause is ripe.

SECOND COURTIER An admirable prince—how rarely he talks! O that we'd known this, lads! What a time did we endure in twopenny commons! And in boots twice vamped!

FIRST COURTIER Now we have two pair a week, and yet not thankful. 'Twill be a fine world for them sirs that come after us.

SECOND COURTIER
Ay, an they knew't.

FIRST COURTIER Peace, let them never know't.

THIRD COURTIER
A pox, there be young heirs will soon smell't out.

SECOND COURTIER
'Twill come to 'em by instinct, man.—May your grace
Never be old, you stand so well for youth.

DUKE
Why, now methinks our court looks like a spring,
Sweet, fresh, and fashionable, now the old weeds are gone.

FIRST COURTIER
'Tis as a court should be: gloss and good clothes, my lord, no matter for merit, and herein your law proves a provident act, my lord, when men pass not the palsy of their tongues, nor colour in their cheeks.

DUKE But women by that law should live long, for they're ne'er past it.

FIRST COURTIER
It will have heats, though, when they see the painting
Go an inch deep i'th' wrinkle, and take up
A box more than their gossips. But for men, my lord,

2 **Diocles** a resonant name from antiquity; three men of this name seem especially relevant here, all of whom lived around 400 BCE: 1) a Syracusan democrat and legislator, 2) an Athenian comic poet, 3) a physician, contemporary of Aristotle.
11 **ripe** ready
17 **compass** limits (or perhaps: the established time)
20 **that's not it** who's not at the age limit. TAYLOR suggests emending to 'that's no wit', meaning: 1) 'that's no whit' (it makes no difference whether he's 70 or 75); 2) 'that has no wit' (he that is 70 or 75 has no wit).
23 **when...ripe** when the purpose or end of the law has been reached
cause purpose; case, suit (legal term)
26 **twopenny commons** cheap accommodations
27 **vamped** patched
29 **them sirs** those courtiers. 'Them' sounds incorrect to modern ears but was not in the seventeenth century. Another possible modernization of BELL: ''Twill be a fine world for them, sirs, that come after us.'
31 **an** if. BELL's spelling (and) could mean both 'and' (the conjunction) and 'if'; throughout THIS EDITION, 'and' has been modernized to 'an' to distinguish these for a modern reader.
FIRST COURTIER COXETER; 2.*Cou.* BELL. In BELL, this and the preceding speech appear on the same line and are each assigned to the Second Courtier. This textual error may suggest the way in which the courtiers were readable as indistinguishable (at least by the compositor who typeset this scene); compare Rosencrantz and Guildenstern in *Hamlet*, and the silence/disappearance of Third Courtier after the next line, his only speech in the play. See 5.1.3, 5.1.139–40.
43 **have heats** produce intense feelings (anger, passions, excitement)
painting cosmetics
44–5 **take...box** buy or possess themselves of a box (of cosmetics)
45 **gossips** friends; but also with the derogatory sense of 'gossipers'

That should be the sole bravery of a palace,
To walk with hollow eyes and long white beards
(As if a prince dwelt in a land of goats),
With clothes as if they sat upon their backs on purpose
To arraign a fashion and condemn't to exile,
Their pockets in their sleeves, as if they laid
Their ear to avarice and heard the devil whisper!
Now ours lie downward here close to the flank,
Right spending pockets as a son's should be
That lives i'th' fashion, where our diseased fathers—
Wood with the sciatica and aches—
Brought up your paned hose first, which ladies laughed at,
Giving no reverence to the place (lies ruined);
They love a doublet that's three hours a-buttoning,
And sits so close makes a man groan again,
And his soul mutter half a day; yet these are those
That carry sway and worth, pricked up in clothes.
Why should we fear our rising?

DUKE
You but wrong
Our kindness and your own deserts to doubt on't.
Has not our law made you rich before your time?
Our countenance then can make you honourable.

FIRST COURTIER
We'll spare for no cost, sir, to appear worthy.

DUKE
Why, you're i'th' noble way, then, for the most
Are but appearers; worth itself, it is lost,
And bravery stands for't.

Enter Creon, Antigona, and Simonides

FIRST COURTIER
Look, look who comes here!
I smell death, and another courtier,
Simonides.

SECOND COURTIER
Sim!

SIMONIDES [*aside to Courtiers*]
Push! I'm not for you yet;
Your company's too costly. After the old man's
Dispatched I shall have time to talk with you.
I shall come into the fashion, ye shall see too,
After a day or two; in the mean time,
I am not for your company.

DUKE
Old Creon, you have been expected long.
Sure you're above fourscore.

SIMONIDES
Upon my life,
Not four-and-twenty hours, my lord; I searched
The church-book yesterday. Does your grace think
I'd let my father wrong the law, my lord?
'Twere pity o' my life then. No, your act
Shall not receive a minute's wrong by him
While I live, sir, and he's so just himself too,
I know he would not offer't. Here he stands.

CREON
'Tis just I die indeed, my lord, for I confess
I'm troublesome to life now, and the state
Can hope for nothing worthy from me now,

46 **bravery** splendour, finery (clothing)
55 **where** BELL; whereas MASON. MASON's meaning is clear without the emendation.
diseased BELL's spelling ('diseased') may suggest three syllables.
56 **Wood** BELL (Would), a modernization conjectured by MASON
Wood with crazy with the pain of
sciatica a painful disease affecting nerves of the leg and especially the hip
57 **paned hose** breeches or hose made of multicoloured strips of cloth; punning, perhaps, on *pained*
paned BELL (paind)
58 **Giving . . . ruined** 1) the paned hose don't flatter the figure (of the old men), which lies ruined in any case; 2) the laughing ladies give no reverence to the status of the old men, whose bodies are in ruins; 3) by wearing paned hose, the old men don't show proper respect for the palace (the place), which the courtier sees as ruined by their habits of dress.
60 **sits** BELL (fits), which some readers (including SHAW) may have interpreted as *fits*
61 **mutter** grumble. But, given the printing of BELL at precisely this point (in all copies consulted a small ink blot appears precisely over the first vowel in what is here taken to be BELL's *mutter*), the word might be *matter*. And since 'soule' could be spelled 'sole' (and possibly *vice versa*), the reading might be, or might have been taken to be, 'sole matter'. This meaning is perhaps clearer than 'soul mutter' (for it is unclear why the soul and not its usual antithesis the body would mutter in these binding garments); thus: the doublet that requires three hours to button becomes a man's only activity (sole matter) half the day. Whether *mutter* or *matter* was pronounced on stage, audiences might have heard *soul* or *sole*.
69 **itself, it is lost** BELL (it ſelfe it is loſt). The repetition may serve for emphasis; in the context of an otherwise metrically regular passage, the second 'it' might also be construed as a printer's error (an incorrect repetition) to be eliminated.
70 **bravery** See 2.1.46. In the mouth of the Duke, the word may carry both positive and (in retrospect, at the end of the play) negative connotations.
72 **Sim** The courtiers' nickname for Simonides has a number of other meanings and resonances in the context of the play. 'Sim Subtle' was a nickname for a crafty or devious person in the late sixteenth century. *Sim* may also suggest *similarity* (i.e., Simonides's likeness with the courtiers, from whom he is attempting to differentiate himself at this point). Compare the son named Sim Quomodo in *Michaelmas Term*.
Push an exclamation of impatience (like *Pish* at 3.2.188)
81 **church-book** See 1.1.114; this line carries the irony that Simonides has apparently not read the book's (i.e., the Bible's) injunction to 'Honour thy father and thy mother' (Exodus 20:12).
86 **not** COXETER; no BELL. This change might be a simple modernization; *OED* cites possible seventeenth-century evidence of *no* meaning 'not' (see adv.1, 1.α), though it notes that these may be 'misprints', which of course is precisely what we are using *OED* to adjudicate here.

Either in force or counsel. I've o' late
Employed myself quite from the world, and he that once
Begins to serve his maker faithfully
Can never serve a worldly prince well after.
'Tis clean another way.

ANTIGONA [*to the Duke*] O give not confidence
To all he speaks, my lord, in his own injury!
His preparation only for the next world
Makes him talk wildly to his wrong of this.
He is not lost in judgement—

SIMONIDES [*aside*] She spoils all again.

ANTIGONA [*to the Duke*]
Deserving any way for state employment.

SIMONIDES Mother—

ANTIGONA [*to the Duke*]
His very household laws prescribed at home by him
Are able to conform seven Christian kingdoms
They are so wise and virtuous.

SIMONIDES Mother, I say—

ANTIGONA [*to the Duke*]
I know your laws extend not to desert, sir,
But to unnecessary years, and, my lord,
His are not such: though they show white, they're worthy,
Judicious, able, and religïous.

SIMONIDES [*aside to Antigona*]
I'll help you to a courtier of nineteen, Mother.

ANTIGONA
Away, unnatural!

SIMONIDES [*aside*] Then I am no fool, I'm sure,
For to be natural at such a time
Were a fool's part indeed.

ANTIGONA [*to the Duke*] Your grace's pity, sir,
And 'tis but fit and just.

CREON [*to the Duke*] The law, my lord,
And that's the justest way.

SIMONIDES Well said, father, i'faith.
Thou wert ever juster than my mother still.

DUKE [*to Simonides*]
Come hither, sir.

SIMONIDES My lord.

DUKE What are those orders?

ANTIGONA Worth observation, sir,
So please you hear them read.

SIMONIDES
The woman speaks she knows not what, my lord.
He make a law? Poor man, he bought a table indeed,
Only to learn to die by't. There's the business now,
[*He shows his father's table and gives it to the Duke*]
Wherein there are some precepts for a son too—
How he should learn to live—but I ne'er looked upon't,
For when he's dead I shall live well enough,
And keep a better table than that, I trow.

DUKE
And is that all, sir?

90 **o' late** BELL (alate). Of late, lately

91 **world** Translating Montaigne's essay on voluntary suicide, John Florio writes: 'a man doth also sometimes desire death, in hope of a greater good. I desire (saith Saint Paul) to be out of this world, that I may be with Iesus Christ.... Cleombrotus Ambraciota...was so possessed with a desire and longing for an after-life, that without other occasion or more adoe, he went and headlong cast himselfe into the sea' ('A custome of the Ile of Cea', [1603]).

94 **clean** entirely (adv.). But *clean* might also be read as an adj. ('Things are pure in the other world'); in Renaissance translations of Old Testament law, *clean* often means 'undefiled' or 'undefiling'.

96 **preparation** BELL (HOUGHTON1, HOUGHTON2, HUNTINGTON, NEWBERRY); prepartion BELL (FOLGER, WILLIAMS, LCP). This is the only press variant that can be confidently identified as such; see also 1.1.201.1.

97 **talk...this** BELL's lack of punctuation produces several meanings: 1) Creon's preparation for heaven makes him talk wildly of this secular world, to the detriment (wrong) of his own life/survival. In this version, commas can be imagined around 'to his wrong'. 2) Creon's preparation for heaven makes him talk wildly, treating this world unjustly (wronging this world).
wrong harm, injury or damage (legal term)

102 **seven Christian kingdoms** England, Scotland, Wales, Ireland, France, Spain, and Italy

108 ***[aside to Antigona]*** On *asides*, see 1.1.222–3.

115 **orders** the 'household laws' of l. 101, with the added civic and moral ideology this word often conveyed: 'As the good Housholder ought to set his house in order,...so ought a good Magistrate to order a Cittie and Common-weale.... Order is the due disposing of al things' (*The Mirrovr of Policie*, 1599).

119 **table** writing tablet, but with the added sense (alluded to throughout this exchange) of the ten commandments of Exodus 20, known as 'the first and second tables'. For example, James I decried 'all the impieties and sins that can be devised against both the first and second Table' (*His Maiesties Speach*, 1605).

120.1–2 ***[He...Duke]*** When BELL's stage directions include props or descriptions of onstage action, it is usually at the point of a character's entrance, which may explain why there is no descriptive direction here. My addition thus is one hypothesis of what might have taken place on stage.

121 **precepts** Simonides dismisses the popular genre of 'precepts' transmitted from a father to a son about to undertake travel (a situation revised here); see, for example, Polonius's 'few precepts' (*Hamlet* 1.3).
too BELL (to)

124 **keep a better table** punning on 'dining table'; i.e., maintain a more lavish lifestyle

127 **cheese-trenchers** plate or platter on which cheese was cut and served; 'trencher' thus resonates with 'household laws' and 'table'/tablet (above) and signals Simonides's debasement of his father's 'orders' and by association the ten commandments. Short verses were sometimes painted 'vpon the backe sides of our fruite trenchers of wood' (*The Arte of English Poesie*, 1589).

128 **runnet** rennet, a 'mass of curdled milk found in the stomach of an unweaned calf or other animal', used in cheesemaking to curdle milk (*OED*). In the next line, the joke continues with 'calves' maws'.

131 **Agent** person who acts for, does the work of, another; also a legal term

133 **Before surfeit with** before it is surfeited with (exceeds the limits of); already surfeited with (in which case, *before-surfeit* works as a compound, like *before-mentioned* or *before-named*).

134 **promontory** a cliff jutting out over the sea

135 **sea** Again, the English version of Montaigne's essays includes a striking parallel to this passage: 'from the top of an high-steepy rocke, appointed for that purpose, [the old people] cast themselves headlong into the Sea'. On *headlong*, see 1.1.482. These executions are an age-reversal of the execution in Lycurgus's Sparta of unfit children, who were 'throwen in a deepe pyt of water' because it was thought that 'it was neither good for the childe, nor yet for the common weale, that it should live, considering from his birthe he was not well made, nor geven to be stronge, healthfull, nor lustie of bodie all his life longe' (North, *Plutarch's Lives*). On Lycurgus, see 1.1.59–64.

139 **cast down** punning on 1) the mode of execution; 2) the demolition of a building; 3) 'downcast' (= dejected); and chiefly, 4) lying down to have sex

140 **an** if

141.1 [***Exeunt Antigona and Executioner with Creon***] THIS EDITION; *not in* BELL. COLERIDGE provides separate exits for Creon (after 2.1.135–6) and Antigona (after 2.1.143).

143 **You've** BELL (Yave)

145 **hold you talk** have conversation with you

146 **suit** lawsuit; suit of clothes (following line)

146.1 ***Recorders*** A flute-like wind instrument often associated with funerals and other solemn ceremonies in Renaissance drama (see, for example, *Chaste Maid* 5.4.0.1). Significantly, recorders will recur in the complement to this scene (5.1.251.1–2).

Recorders . . . off THIS EDITION; *Recorders* BELL (in the margin of 2.1.146); *Recorders within* GIFFORD (after 2.1.149); *Recorders* [*sound from above*] SHAW. It is possible that this marginal reference to recorders is one of the 'anticipatory stage directions' that occur frequently later in BELL—that is, a promptbook annotation that instructed the musicians to be prepared to play/enter in a few lines.

147 **form** beauty, handsomeness; body; mode of behaviour

148 **else** otherwise; if not

with a mischief with a vengeance

150.1–2 ***Recorders . . . musicians*** THIS EDITION; *Recorders. Enter* | Cleanthes & Hi-|polita *with a hearſ* BELL (in the margin of ll. 150–2). BELL clearly indicates that music of recorders is to sound; whether (as imagined here) the musicians entered as part of the procession is not clear. (Compare the stage direction at 5.1.347.1–4.)

150.2 **hearse** the corpse; the coffin; the pall over the corpse; and/or the carriage used to transport the corpse at a funeral

153 **habited** dressed; 'suitable' in the next line plays on this.

156 **corse** BELL (Coarſe). Body (corpse); or way of action (course). BELL's spelling could signify the nouns *corse*, *corpse*, and *course*, as well as the adjective *coarse*; early modern English did not differentiate (in spelling or pronunciation) among what we think of as separate words. The spelling provided here both signals the most prominent meaning in the text at this point and reminds the reader who speaks or hears the line that 'course' (a way of action, proceeding, or behaviour) is also a possible meaning: the Duke has never seen a corpse accompanied so joyfully, and/or he has never seen a funeral conducted in such a joyful way (course).

SIMONIDES All I vow, my lord,
Save a few running admonitiöns
Upon cheese-trenchers, as, 'Take heed of whoring, shun it;
'Tis like a cheese too strong of the runnet',
And such calves' maws of wit and admonition
Good to catch mice with, but not sons and heirs—
They're not so easily caught.

DUKE [*to Executioner*] Agent for death.

EXECUTIONER
Your will, my lord?

DUKE Take hence that pile of years,
Before surfeit with unprofitable age,
And with the rest from the high promontory
Cast him into the sea.

CREON 'Tis noble justice.

ANTIGONA 'Tis cursèd tyranny.

SIMONIDES [*aside*] Peace, take heed, Mother; you have but a short time to be cast down yourself, and let a young courtier do't, an you be wise, in the mean time.

ANTIGONA Hence, slave!

[*Exeunt Antigona and Executioner with Creon*]

SIMONIDES Well, seven-and-fifty,
You've but three years to scold, then comes your payment.

FIRST COURTIER Simonides.

SIMONIDES
Push, I am not brave enough to hold you talk yet.
Give a man time; I have a suit a-making.

Recorders [*begin to play within, as afar off*]

SECOND COURTIER
We love thy form first; brave clothes will come, man.

SIMONIDES
I'll make 'em come else with a mischief to 'em,
As other gallants do that have less left 'em.

DUKE
Hark! Whence those sounds? What's that?

Recorders [*still*]. *Enter Cleanthes and Hippolita* [*in joyful attire*] *with a hearse* [*and musicians*]

FIRST COURTIER Some funeral
It seems, my lord, and young Cleanthes follows.

DUKE
Cleanthes?

SECOND COURTIER
'Tis, my lord, and in the place
Of a chief mourner too, but strangely habited.

DUKE
Yet suitable to his behaviour, mark it.
He comes all the way smiling; do you observe't?
I never saw a corse so joyfully followed.

161 **contrariety** discordance; diametrical opposition. 'Contrarietie is when our talke standeth by contrary wordes or sentences together' (Wilson, *The Art of Rhetorique* 1585). Cleanthes's following speeches exemplify this rhetorical figure.
162 **natural courses** This phrase continues and complicates the non-differentiation of the set of words discussed at 2.1.156. BELL's spelling ('naturall courses') seems at first to refer to 'the way things (courses) naturally proceed' and then (given the descriptions that follow) to a live 'natural corse', the body of Cleanthes. On *natural*, see 1.1.374–5, 1.1.317–34, 1.1.407–9.
164 **handkerchief** BELL (handkercher)
t'other the other; BELL (tother)
166 **apparently** openly, visibly
173 **That** COXETER; Thae BELL
179 **blacks** black clothing, for mourning; also, funeral draperies, and a 'mute or hired mourner at a funeral' (*OED*), a meaning more prominent when the word is repeated two lines later
180 **orient** brilliant, radiant (like the sun, which rises in the east/Orient)
182 **to't** to it; the sense of the sentence has shifted, with *it* seeming to refer not to 'blacks' (plural) but to the colour (singular)
187 **sables** black mourning clothes
188 **gaudy-hearted** gaudy: showy, ornate (excessively); possibly also with a suggestion of 'joyful' (the Latin etymology). Though Cleanthes's speech seems to be built on the opposition of exterior, theatrical displays of mourning *versus* interior, authentic emotion, Cleanthes's use of 'gaudy' may engage both sides of the opposition here: these lines describe both a 'showy' theatrical façade and a heart that is also 'gaudy' (joyful? excessive? showy? deceitful?).
190 **entirely merry** BELL spells 'intirely', which may suggest more fully than the modernized word a pun on clothing ('attire' and 'tire'). Thus, 'in/tirely merry' might also sound like 'merry in clothes'.
195 **on't** of it
197 **performed** here and in the Duke's reply, a reminder of the theatricality of the staged funeral
202 **revènue** income from property
206 **Duke in sight** MASON *conj.*, GIFFORD; dim ſight BELL; dim Sight COXETER. THIS EDITION follows MASON's emendation, with the hypothesis that the manuscript copy for BELL read 'D. in sight' (where 'D.' is an abbreviation for 'duke' and 'in' was misread by the compositor as 'im'). D (*conj.* in MASON) would retain 'dim sight', explaining that Cleanthes is 'happy that he could shed a Tear' during the fake funeral.

Light colours and light cheeks! Who should this be?
'Tis a thing worth resolving.

SIMONIDES One belike
That doth participate in this our present joy.

DUKE
Cleanthes.

CLEANTHES
O, my lord—

DUKE He laughed outright now.
Was ever such a contrariety seen
In natural courses yet, nay, professed openly?

FIRST COURTIER
I ha' known a widow laugh closely, my lord,
Under her handkerchief, when t'other part
Of her old face has wept, like rain in sunshine,
But all the face to laugh apparently
Was never seen yet.

SIMONIDES Yes, mine did once.

CLEANTHES
'Tis of a heavy time the joyfull'st day
That ever son was born to.

DUKE How can that be?

CLEANTHES
I joy to make it plain: my father's dead.

DUKE
Dead!

SECOND COURTIER
Old Leonides?

CLEANTHES In his last month, dead;
He beguiled cruel law the sweetliest
That ever age was blessed to.
It grieves me that a tear should fall upon't,
Being a thing so joyful, but his memory
Will work it out, I see. When his poor heart broke,
I did not so much but leapt for joy,
So mountingly I touched the stars, methought.
I would not hear of blacks, I was so light,
But chose a colour orient, like my mind,
For blacks are often such dissembling mourners,
There is no credit given to't, it has lost
All reputation by false sons and widows.
Now I would have men know what I resemble,
A truth indeed, 'tis joy clad like a joy,
Which is more honest than a cunning grief
That's only faced with sables for a show,
But gaudy-hearted. When I saw death come
So ready to deceive you, sir, forgive me,
I could not choose but be entirely merry,
And yet to see now of a sudden
Naming but Death, I show myself a mortal,
That's never constant to one passion long.
I wonder whence that tear came when I smiled;
In the production on't, sorrow's a thief,
That can when joy looks on steal forth a grief.
But gracious leave, my lord; when I have performed
My last poor duty to my father's bones,
I shall return your servant.

DUKE Well, perform it.
The law is satisfied; they can but die,
And by his death, Cleanthes, you gain well,
A rich and fair revènue.
Flourish. [*Exeunt Duke, Courtiers, and Executioner*]

SIMONIDES I would I had e'en another father, condition he did the like.

CLEANTHES [*aside*]
I have passed it bravely; now how blessed was I
To have the Duke in sight, now 'tis confirmed,
Past fear or doubts confirmed.—On, on, I say,
He that brought me to man I bring to clay.
[*Exeunt Cleanthes and Hippolita, with hearse and Recorders*]

SIMONIDES
I'm wrapped now in a contemplatiön,
Even at the very sight of yonder hearse;
I do but think what a fine thing 'tis now
To live and follow some seven uncles thus,
As many cousin-germans, and such people
That will leave legacies. A pox, I'd see 'em hanged else
ere I'd follow one of them, and they could find the way.
Now I've enough to begin to be horrible covetous.

Enter Butler, Tailor, Bailiff, Cook, Coachman, and Footman

BUTLER
We come to know your worship's pleasure, sir,
Having long served your father, how your good will
Stands towards our entertainment.

SIMONIDES
Not a jot, i'faith:
My father wore cheap garments; he might do't.
I shall have all my clothes come home tomorrow;
They will eat up all you, an there were more of you, sirs,
To keep you six at livery and still munching.

TAILOR
Why, I'm a tailor; you've most need of me, sir.

SIMONIDES
Thou mad'st my father's clothes, that I confess,
But what son and heir will have his father's tailor
Unless he have a mind to be well laughed at?
Thou'st been so used to wide, long-side things that when I come to truss I shall have the waist of my doublet lie upon my buttocks—a sweet sight.

BUTLER I, a butler.

SIMONIDES There's least need of thee, fellow; I shall ne'er drink at home, I shall be so drunk abroad.

BUTLER But a cup of small beer will do well next morning, sir.

SIMONIDES I grant you, but what need I keep so big a knave for a cup of small beer?

COOK Butler, you have your answer; marry, sir, a cook I know your mastership cannot be without.

SIMONIDES The more ass art thou to think so, for what should I do with a mountebank, no drink in my house? The banishing the butler might have been a warning for thee, unless thou mean'st to choke me.

COOK I'th' mean time you have choked me, methinks.

BAILIFF
These are superfluous vanities indeed,
And so accounted of in these days, sir,
But then, your bailiff, to receive your rents—

SIMONIDES I prithee, hold thy tongue, fellow; I shall take a course to spend 'em faster than thou canst reckon 'em. 'Tis not the rents must serve my turn, unless I mean to be laughed at; if a man should be seen out of slash-me, let him ne'er look to be a right gallant! But sirrah, with whom is your business?

COACHMAN Your good mastership.

SIMONIDES [*to Coachman and Footman*]
You have stood silent all this while, like men
That know their strengths i' these days. None of you
Can want employment; you can win me wagers,
Footman, in running races.

FOOTMAN
I dare boast it, sir.

SIMONIDES
And when my bets are all come in and store,
Then, coachman, you can hurry me to my whore.

COACHMAN
I'll firk 'em into foam else.

SIMONIDES
Speaks brave matter,
And I'll firk some too, or't shall cost hot water.

[*Exeunt Simonides, Coachman, and Footman*]

209 **wrapped** BELL (wrapt)
wrapped . . . contemplatiön absorbed in meditation or thought (also with a mock-religious sense)

213 **cousin-germans** first cousins; relatives

214 **legacies** bequests

215 **and . . . way** and they could find the way to burial themselves. Possibly *and* should be read as *an* (= if): 'if they could find the way to die'.

216 **covetous** The text gestures toward another of the 'old laws', the tenth commandment: 'Thou shalt not couet thy neighbours house, nether shalt thou couet thy neighbours wife, nor his man seruant, nor his maid, nor his oxe, nor his asse, nether any thing that is thy neighbours' (Exodus 20:17, Geneva Bible).

216.1 ***Bailiff*** BELL (Bayly). A lord's agent, who managed his estate and collected his rents. Elsewhere BELL spells 'Bayliff' and 'Bayliffe', in directions and in dialogue. *OED* records *bailie* as a separate though obsolete word.

219 **entertainment** employment; also pay for service

225 **mad'st** BELL (madeft)

228 **long-side things** long and sweeping garments

229 **truss** tie the laces that joined the doublet and hose

234 **small** weak

241 **mountebank** pretender, con-man

251 **out of slash-me** out of fashion. Probably a reference to garments with slits that exposed linings of contrasting colour; the practice was called 'new fashioned' in 1615 (*OED*).

256 **i' these days** Because BELL's commas can sometimes be read not as pauses (in the modern way) but as emphasizing what comes after, it is not clear in which direction this phrase reads: it may belong with the preceding or following sentence.

256–8 **you . . . races** The line probably refers to a famous event of 1618, in which wagers were placed on a race run by footmen. A letter written 10 April 1618 reports a popular 'race of two footmen from St Albans to Clerkenwell; the one [footman] an Englishman, belonging lately to the Countess of Bedford, but now to the king; the other an Irish youth, that lost the day, and I know not how much money laid on his head' (Maxwell 144). The race drew huge crowds (including the king).

259 **store** (adv.) abundantly

261 **firk** whip; with the suggestion of *frig*/*frike* (= fuck) in Simonides's reply
Speaks (he) speaks

262 **cost hot water** cause (someone) trouble

COOK Why, here's an age to make a cook a ruffin, and scald the devil indeed, do strange mad things, make mutton pasties of dogs' flesh, bake snakes for lamprey-pies, and cats for conies.

BUTLER Come, will you be ruled by a butler's advice once? For we must make up our fortunes somewhere now, as the case stands. Let's e'en therefore go seek out widows of nine-and-fifty an we can; that's within a year of their deaths, and so we shall be sure to be quickly rid of 'em, for a year's enough of conscience to be troubled with a wife for any man living.

COOK Oracle butler, oracle butler! He puts down all the doctors o'th' name. *Exeunt*

2.2 *Enter Eugenia and Parthenia [at separate doors]*

EUGENIA
Parthenia.

PARTHENIA
Mother.

EUGENIA [*aside*] I shall be troubled
This six months with an old clog; would the law
Had been cut one year shorter!

PARTHENIA Did you call, forsooth?

EUGENIA
Yes, you must make some spoon-meat for your father,
And warm three night-caps for him. [*Exit Parthenia*]
Out upon't!
The mere conceit turns a young woman's stomach!
His slippers must be warmed in August too,
And his gown girt to him in the very dog-days
When every mastiff lolls out's tongue for heat.
Would not this vex a beauty of nineteen now?
Alas, I shall be tumbling in cold baths now,
Under each armpit a fine bean-flour bag
To screw out whiteness when I list,
And some seven of the prop'rest men i'th' dukedom,
Making a banquet ready i'th' next room for me,
Where he that gets the first kiss is envied
And stands upon his guard a fortnight after.
This is a life for nineteen, but 'tis justice,
For old men, whose great acts stand in their minds
And nothing in their bodies, do ne'er think
A woman young enough for their desire,
And we young wenches that have mother wits
And love to marry muck first, and man after,
Do never think old men are old enough
That we may soon be rid on 'em—there's our quit-
tance.
I have waited for the happy hour this two year,
And if death be so unkind still to let him live,
All that time I am lost.

Enter Courtiers [fashionably dressed]

FIRST COURTIER
Young lady.

SECOND COURTIER
O sweet precious bud of beauty!—
Troth, she smells over all the house, methinks.

FIRST COURTIER
The sweet-brier's but a counterfeit to her—
It does exceed you only in the prickle,
But that it shall not long, if you'll be ruled, lady.

EUGENIA
What means this sudden visitation, gentlemen?
So passing well performed, too! Who's your milliner?

FIRST COURTIER
Love and thy beauty, widow.

EUGENIA Widow, sir?

FIRST COURTIER
'Tis sure and that's as good. In troth, we're suitors;
We come a-wooing, wench—plain dealing's best.

263 **ruffin** 1) the ruff, a fish (playing on the speaker's occupation); 2) slang for the Devil (next line); and 3) ruffian (villain, criminal, with a connotation of low social-class), of which *ruffin* is a period spelling. MASON and all later editions change to 'Ruffian'; losing this play of meaning.

265 **bake** COXETER; backe BELL. That *OED* does not cite BELL's spelling as a form of *bake* may suggest the limits of *OED* as a guide to modernization.
lamprey-pies pies made with an eel-like fish

266 **conies** rabbits. BELL's spelling 'Cunnies' suggests the Renaissance pronunciation, and a pun on *cunt* is possible here, especially with the phallic 'snakes' and 'lamprey' in the same line.

272 **of conscience** in fairness, reasonably (but with the larger irony that such a plan would usually be said to go against conscience)

274–5 **Oracle butler . . . name** referring to Dr William Butler, a renowned and eccentric physician (1535–1618). Butler famously treated royalty—Prince Henry in 1612, King James in 1614. *Oracle* here may function as an imperative verb, or as part of a compound noun.

2.2.1 **Parthenia** (from the Greek: virgin, maiden)
Mother step-mother. (Eugenia implies below that she is nineteen and has been married only two years.)

2 **This** these
clog like a ball-and-chain, a heavy piece of wood tied to a person or animal to prevent its escape; an encumbrance

3 **forsooth** truly

4 **spoon-meat** soft food for babies or invalids

5 **Out upon't** Fie upon it

8 **girt to** wrapped around, fastened to
dog-days the hottest days of the year

9 **out's** out his/its

11 **shall be** should be; ought to be. Modern idiom would seem to require *should* (and most editions emend), but this may be a possible usage of *shall* in the period (see *OED* II.2, 4, 8, and 11a). The usage here is in a sense poised on the line between 'shall be' (will in the future, when Lisander dies) and 'should be' (ought to be).

12 **bean-flour bag** The specific use of this cosmetic in this context is not clear; bean-flour was sometimes used for colouring the hair white (see Webster, *The Devil's Law-Case* 4.2.290).
bean-flour BELL (beane flower)

13 **screw out** draw out (*OED*)

17 **stands** The first of this scene's many jokes about penises, erections, and impotence; see below at ll. 20 (no/thing = no penis), 32, 133–4, and 158–68.

23 **muck** money

25 **quittance** release, reward

28.1 *Enter Courtiers* On the apparent disappearance of the Third Courtier, see 2.1.31.

32 **prickle** thorn, but also *prick* (penis)

35 **performed** BELL; perfum'd COXETER

37 **we're** BELL (w'are)

EUGENIA
A-wooing? What, before my husband's dead?

SECOND COURTIER
Let's lose no time. Six months will have an end, you know;
I know't by all the bonds that e'er I made yet.

EUGENIA
That's a sure knowledge, but it holds not here, sir.

FIRST COURTIER
Do not you know the craft of your young tumblers—that you wed an old man, you think upon another husband as you are marrying of him? We, knowing your thoughts, made bold to see you.

Enter Simonides [fashionably dressed and] Coachman

EUGENIA [*aside*] How wondrous right he speaks! 'Twas my thought indeed.

SIMONIDES By your leave, sweet widow, do you lack any gallants?

EUGENIA [*aside*] Widow again! 'Tis a comfort to be called so.

FIRST COURTIER
Who's this—Simonides?

SECOND COURTIER Brave Sim, i'faith.

SIMONIDES Coachman.

COACHMAN Sir.

SIMONIDES
Have an especial care of my new mares.
They say, sweet widow, he that loves a horse well
Must needs love a widow well. When dies thy husband?
Is't not July next?

EUGENIA O you're too hot, sir!
Pray, cool yourself and take September with you.

SIMONIDES
September! O, I was but two bows wide.

FIRST COURTIER Master Simonides.

SIMONIDES
I can entreat you gallants; I'm in fashion too.

Enter Lisander

LISANDER
Ha! Whence this herd of folly? What are you?

SIMONIDES
Well-willers to your wife. Pray tend your book, sir,
We have nothing to say to you; you may go die,
For here be those in place that can supply.

LISANDER
What's thy wild business here?

SIMONIDES Old man, I'll tell thee:
I come to beg the reversion of thy wife;
I think these gallants be of my mind too.
But thou art but a dead man; therefore what should a man do talking with thee? Come, widow, stand to your tackling.

LISANDER Impious bloodhounds.

SIMONIDES Let the ghost talk, ne'er mind him.

LISANDER Shames of nature.

SIMONIDES
Alas, poor ghost, consider what the man is.

LISANDER
Monsters unnatural, you that have been covetous
Of your own fathers' deaths, gape ye for mine now?
Cannot a poor old man, that now can reckon
E'en all the hours he has to live, live quiet
For such wild beasts as these, that neither hold
A certainty of good within themselves,
But scatter others' comforts that are ripened
For holy uses? Is hot youth so hasty
It will not give an old man leave to die
And leave a widow first, but will make one,
The husband looking on? May your destructions
Come all in hasty figures to your souls,
Your wealth depart in haste, to overtake
Your honesties, that died when you were infants!
May your male seed be hasty spendthrifts too!
Your daughters hasty sinners and diseased
Ere they be thought at years to welcome misery,
And may you never know what leisure is
But at repentance! I am too uncharitable,
Too foul; I must go cleanse myself with prayers.
These are the plagues of fondness to old men;
We're punished home with what we dote upon. *Exit*

SIMONIDES
So so, the ghost is vanished now; your answer, lady.

41 **e'er** BELL (ere)
43 **tumblers** acrobats; hunting dogs that distract their prey with tumbling; people having sex
43–4 **tumblers— | that you wed** BELL (Tumblers? | That you wed); Tumblers? You that wed MASON; tumblers? That when you wed GIFFORD
44 **that** When (when that). (See *OED that*, II.6b.)
61 **two bows wide** two bow-lengths away
62 **Master** BELL (Mr.)
63 **entreat you gallants** BELL's lack of punctuation (replicated in this text) allows several possibilities: 1) I can entreat you, gallants (I can handle you); 2) I can entreat, you gallants (I can negotiate [a marriage]).
65 **Pray tend your book** lack of punctuation allows either of two possibilities: 1) I pray you, tend your book; 2) Pray to God; tend your book (bible, or church register).
69 **reversion** right to inherit or occupy (usually, an estate). See 1.1.36.
72–3 **stand to your tackling** hold your ground (without the modern sense of football tackling)
78 **covetous** alluding to the tenth commandment (2.1.216)
82 **For** From
82–4 **neither ... But** do not ... and instead
89 **hasty figures** 1) at a premature age (*figure* = number), as the next scene illustrates; 2) premature or hastily prepared horoscopes
91 **honesties** truthfulness; chastity
99 **home** to the utmost; but also suggesting: at home, at the core/centre
100 **now;** Again BELL's punctuation would allow *now* to read in either direction: as in the text here, or, 'the ghost is vanished; now your answer, lady'. See 2.1.255–7.

EUGENIA
Excuse me, gentlemen, 'twere as much impudence
In me to give you a kind answer yet,
As madness to produce a churlish one.
I could say now, come a month hence, sweet gentle-
men,
Or two or three, or when you will indeed,
But I say no such thing, I set no time,
Nor is it mannerly to deny any;
I'll carry an even hand to all the world.
Let other women make what haste they will,
What's that to me? But I profess unfeignedly,
I'll have my husband dead before I marry;
Ne'er look for other answer at my hands, gentlemen.

SIMONIDES
Would he were hanged, for my part looks for other.

EUGENIA
I'm at a word.

SIMONIDES And I'm at a blow then;
I'll lay you o'th' lips and leave you.
[Simonides kisses her]

FIRST COURTIER Well struck, Sim.

SIMONIDES
He that dares say he'll mend it, I'll strike him.

FIRST COURTIER
He would betray himself to be a botcher
That goes about to mend it.

EUGENIA Gentlemen,
You know my mind, I bar you not my house,
But if you choose out hours more seasonably,
You may have entertainment.
Enter Parthenia

SIMONIDES
What will she do hereafter when she is a widow,
Keeps open house already?
Exeunt [Simonides, Coachman, and Courtiers]

EUGENIA How now, girl?

PARTHENIA
Those feathered fools that hither took their flight
Have grieved my father much.

EUGENIA Speak well of youth, wench,
While thou'st a day to live; 'tis youth must make
thee,
And when youth fails, wise women will make it,
But always take age first to make thee rich.
That was my counsel ever, and then youth
Will make thee sport enough all thy life after.
'Tis time's policy, wench. What is't to bide
A little hardness for a pair of years or so—
A man whose only strength lies in his breath,
Weakness in all parts else, thy bedfellow
A cough o'th' lungs, or say, a whining matter—
Then shake off chains, and dance all thy life after?

PARTHENIA
Everyone to their liking, but I say
An honest man's worth all, be he young or grey.
Enter Hippolita
Yonder's my cousin. *[Exit]*

103 **churlish** rude

110 **unfeignedly** straightforwardly. But modernizing BELL's spelling 'unfainedly' may erase the suggestion of 'unfain' and thus 'reluctantly'.

113 **my ... other** 'I look for another answer', possibly with a bawdy play on Eugenia's 'hands' (body parts), in which case Simonides (or Simonides's 'part' [= penis?]) suggests an interest in other 'parts' of Eugenia.

114 **I'm at a word** That's all I have to say. Simonides's response alludes to the commonplace, 'to move from words to blows'.

117 **botcher** MASON; brother BELL. A tailor who patches and makes repairs (playing on 'mend it'). BELL's 'betray himselfe to be a brother', emended here, might be readable as: 'go against his solidarity with us', though this is not a typical use of *betray*.

122 **she is** COXETER; sh is BELL. The frequency of non-printing letters in copies of BELL makes it possible that in an unconsulted or now-missing copy, the text reads 'sheis'.

126 **thou'st** BELL (th'aft)

129 **my counsel ever** Not, however, her counsel at the beginning of this scene, 2.2.5–28.

135 **whining** THIS EDITION; wheening BELL; whening COXETER; wheezing MASON+. Since none of the other proposed emendations seems especially persuasive, THIS EDITION adopts *whining* as a near-spelling of BELL's *wheening* (see *OED whining*, vbl. n., and *whine* v.).

whining matter whimpering body. *Matter* may also signify a bodily discharge. One heretofore unexplored emendation is 'whining mammet', a phrase used in *Romeo and Juliet* (3.5.184). *Mammet* (= puppet, ugly figure) is a term of derision, and, in Massinger's *The Picture*, is used in connection with age (rather than youth, as in *Romeo and Juliet*): '*Sophia*. Are they handsome women? | *Vbaldo*. Fie noe, course mammets, and whats worse they are old to, | Some fifty, some threescore ...' (3.6.58–60). TAYLOR conjectures 'matten' (matin), which might in context mean 'a whining morning song'.

135–6 **matter— ... after?** It is not unusual for BELL to lack question-marks in sentences that would now require them. Indeed, the whole issue of what constitutes 'a sentence' is put into question by early modern punctuation practice in general, and by BELL's scarcity of end-stops and abundance of commas and semicolons in particular. Here, as elsewhere, the question is: where do sentences, or other syntactic units, begin and end? Another punctuation possibility for this 'sentence', then, is: 'matter? | Then shake off chains, and dance all thy life after!'

EUGENIA Art, I must use thee now.
Dissembling is the best help for a virtue
That ever woman had; it saves their credit often.
[*She seems to weep*]

HIPPOLITA How now, cousin,
What, weeping?

EUGENIA Can you blame me, when the time
Of my dear love and husband now draws on?
I study funeral tears against the day
I must be a sad widow.

HIPPOLITA
In troth, Eugenia, I have cause to weep too,
But when I visit, I come comfortably,
And look to be so quited. Yet more sobbing?

EUGENIA
O, the greatest part of your affliction's past;
The worst of mine's to come. I have one to die;
Your husband's father is dead, and fixed in his
Eternal peace, past the sharp tyrannous blow.

HIPPOLITA
You must use patience, coz.

EUGENIA Tell me of patience.

HIPPOLITA
You have example for't in me and many.

EUGENIA
Yours was a father-in-law, but mine a husband.
O, for a woman that could love and live
With an old man! Mine is a jewel, cousin,
So quietly he lies by one, so still—

HIPPOLITA [*aside*]
Alas! I have a secret lodged within me
Which now will out, in pity I can't hold.

EUGENIA
One that will not disturb me in my sleep
After a whole month together, 'less it be
With those diseases age is subject to,
As achës, coughs, and pains, and these (heaven
knows)
Against his will too. He's the quietest man,
Especially in bed.

HIPPOLITA Be comforted.

EUGENIA How can I, lady?
None knows the terror of an husband's loss
But they that fear to lose him.

HIPPOLITA [*aside*]
Fain would I keep it in, but 'twill not be;
She is my kinswoman, and I'm pitiful.
I must impart a good, if I know't once,
To them that stand in need on't. I'm like one
Loves not to banquet with a joy alone;
My friends must partake too. [*To Eugenia*] Prithee
cease, cousin.
If your love be so boundless—which is rare
In a young woman in these days, I tell you,
To one so much past service as your husband—
There is a way to beguile law, and help you;
My husband found it out first.

EUGENIA O sweet cousin!

141 **woman...their credit** Eugenia speaks of women as if she were not one herself; audiences may have heard this line as a gesture toward the play's mode of production: a boy would have acted ('dissembled') this role.

141.1 **[*She seems to weep*]** The lack of stage direction in BELL is an example of directions to Renaissance actors being encoded within the words of their speeches, rather than dictated by a separate stage direction. In supplying a stage direction, as I have here, the question is whether to foreground Eugenia's 'dissembling'; another version might read simply: [*She weeps*].

142 **cousin** relative, cousin. BELL uses the spelling 'cozen' throughout this scene; as a verb, *cozen* meant 'to trick or deceive', and was thought in the period to be related to the word we now spell 'cousin'. This scene illustrates the conjunction of meanings, with a cozening cousin, Eugenia.

148 **comfortably** comfortingly

149 **quited** requited, repaid

154 **coz** cousin

158 **With** COXETER; Wi h BELL. Context clearly suggests *With*, but all copies consulted have a space in the position of the presumptive *t*.

160 **lodged** (punning on the location of the secret)

163 **'less** unless

175 **on't** of it

179 **In** COXETER; n BELL; all consulted copies have an initial space at the beginning of this line. In FOLGER, an initial I has been written in; the date of this and other corrections in FOLGER has not been determined.

182 **O sweet cousin** BELL's 'Oh sweet Cozen!' is a reminder of the multiple cozenings occurring here: Hippolita and Cleanthes's cozening of the law, and Eugenia's pretended sympathy with Hippolita's family values.

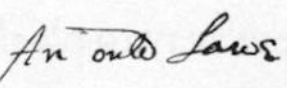

184 **order** arrange
191 **dainty** pleasant
199–200 *Exit* | EUGENIA ... **me** The question of whether Hippolita hears Eugenia's line is interpretively significant. BELL's placement of 'exit' directions is not always precise in a modern sense but may suggest that Hippolita exits before Eugenia speaks the line; nevertheless, it is possible that Hippolita hears it. The line could signify in several ways, and in any event could remind an audience that Eugenia is throughout characterized as never to be trusted.
202–3 **conceal? ... funeral? ... husband?** THIS EDITION renders BELL's commas as question marks; they could as easily be exclamation points (signifying what Eugenia might see as the ludicrousness of Hippolita's suggestions).
204 **'Las** Alas. BELL's spelling (Laffe) could be modernized as 'Lass' (girl), perhaps signaling that Eugenia thinks Hippolita is naïve.
207 **prick the man down** mark the chosen man on the list; but also engaging the sexual sense of *prick* (2.2.32), which then resonates with *do* (= have sex).
208 **him** Lisander
208.1 *Secundus* BELL *Secnndi*
3.1.0.1 *Incipit Actus Tertius* THIS EDITION; Act. III. Scen. I. BELL
0.2 *Enter Clown and Clerk [with the church-book]* THIS EDITION; *Enter the Clown and Clark.* BELL THIS EDITION routinely deletes definite articles before character names; BELL's usage is not consistent.
church-book See 1.1.114.
3 **wot on** know of
4 **be covered** put your hat back on (after it has been removed as a sign of respect). In the next lines, Clerk and Clown argue over who has the lower social standing; to replace one's hat first would be to acknowledge one's higher class position.
6 **remember yourself** 1) recall your social status; 2) put your hat back on ('remembering one's courtesy' = 'be covered'); 3) remind yourself
7 **small** minor (but perhaps playing on the height of the actor)
10 **great** socially important (but perhaps playing on the obesity of the Clown, possibly played by William Rowley)

HIPPOLITA
You may conceal him, and give out his death
Within the time, order his funeral too.
We had it so for ours, I praise heaven for't,
And he's alive and safe.
EUGENIA
O blessèd coz,
How thou reviv'st me!
HIPPOLITA
We daily see
The good old man, and feed him twice a day.
Methinks it is the sweetest joy to cherish him
That ever life yet showed me.
EUGENIA
So should I think
A dainty thing to nurse an old man well.
HIPPOLITA
And then we have his prayers and daily blessing,
And we two live so lovingly upon't,
His son and I, and so contentedly,
You cannot think unless you tasted on't.
EUGENIA
No, I warrant you. O loving cousin,
What a great sorrow hast thou eased me of!
A thousand thanks go with thee.
HIPPOLITA
I have a suit to you:
I must not have you weep when I am gone. *Exit*
EUGENIA
No, if I do, ne'er trust me. Easy fool,
Thou hast put thyself into my power forever;
Take heed of ang'ring of me. I conceal?
I feign a funeral? I keep my husband?
'Las, I have been thinking any time these two years
I have kept him too long already.
I'll go count o'er my suitors, that's my business,
And prick the man down; I ha' six months to do't,
But could dispatch him in one, were I put to't. *Exit*
Finis Actus Secundus

Incipit Actus Tertius 3.1
Enter Clown and Clerk [with the church-book]

CLOWN You have searched o'er the parish chronicle, sir?
CLERK Yes, sir, I have found out the true age and date of the party you wot on.
CLOWN Pray you be covered, sir.
CLERK When you have showed me the way, sir.
CLOWN O sir, remember yourself, you are a clerk.
CLERK A small clerk, sir.
CLOWN Likely to be the wiser man, sir, for your greatest clerks are not always so, as 'tis reported.
CLERK You are a great man in the parish, sir.
CLOWN I understand myself so much the better, sir, for all the best in the parish pay duties to the clerk, and I would owe you none, sir.
CLERK Since you'll have it so, I'll be the first to hide my head.
[Clerk puts on his hat]

16 **cap-case** bag, box, case; with pun on cap (= hat)
20 **dial** sun-dial, clock, or other timepiece (referring to the church-book)
21 **You... witness** To say that the church-book says something is to require no further proof or authority. (*Ipse dixit* = 'he said it'.)
24 **Agatha** (from the Greek for 'good')
29 **Bollux** a nonsense word that sounds like *ballocks* (testicles), *bullocks* (castrated bulls), and Bullokar (next note)
30 **orthography** spelling (literally 'right writing'); punning on the subject and author of William Bullokar's *Booke at large, for the Amendment of Orthographie* (1580), which advocated a new standardized, phonetic spelling system for English, to replace the 'old' conventions. (The lines may thus also associate spelling reform with the legal reform referenced by the play's title and the rewriting of dates in this scene; on spelling reform and languages, see 5.1.618.) The lines may also reference a hard-word dictionary published by Bullokar's son John, *An English Expositor* (1616, 1621), which is also concerned with 'true orthography'.
32 **Pollux... Castor** in Greek and Roman mythology, twin brothers and inseparable companions. 'Castor' perhaps puns on 'cast her' (= throw her down); see l. 66.
33 ***anno*** BELL (*an.*)
33–4 **1540...'99** In contrast to the apparent ancient Greek setting of the larger play, the Clown's plot mixes a classical Greek setting (ll. 91–2) with what would have been the recent past for the play's audience. The years 1540 and 1599 may have been chosen for ease with which an audience could follow the subtraction.
39 **deduct it** trace it out
51 **indifferent** impartially (but also suggesting 'not particularly')
54 **you... all** (a clerk's duty at church-services)
58 **above your duty** beyond your regular duties as clerk; in excess of the usual fee for your services (in which case one might add a stage-direction: *Clown gives the Clerk money*).
59 **e'en** BELL (in). Elsewhere, *in* is a possible spelling of *e'en* (*even*); COXETER and all later editions interpret as the modern word *in* and delete.
61 **sexton** church sexton (in charge of tolling the bells)
63 **conceit** conceive, understand
63–4 **jack... clock-house** a mechanical figure on the outside of a clock that strikes a bell (referring here to the sexton)
64 **hand of the dial** 1) hand of the clock (i.e., time); 2) handwriting in the church-book (see l. 20)
66 **cast a figure** write a number; but the usual meaning of this phrase (which Clerk responds to) is to calculate a horoscope. Additional meanings relevant to the ensuing scene: 1) condemn a person (in law, *cast* = to defeat in a suit, to declare guilty, to condemn); 2) set aside a figure (a number or a person); 3) estimate a number or amount.
71 **cipher** zero

CLOWN [*putting on his hat*] Mine is a cap-case. Now to our business in your hand: good luck, I hope. I long to be resolved.

CLERK
Look you, sir, this is that cannot deceive you,
This is the dial that goes ever true;
You may say '*ipse dixit*' upon this witness,
And 'tis good in law too.

CLOWN Pray you, let's hear what it speaks.

CLERK Mark, sir: [*reading from the church-book*] 'Agatha the daughter of Pollux', this is your wife's name, and the name of her father, 'born'—

CLOWN Whose daughter, say you?

CLERK The daughter of Pollux.

CLOWN I take it his name was Bollux.

CLERK 'Pollux', the orthography, I assure you, sir; the word is corrupted else.

CLOWN Well, on, sir: 'of Pollux'—now come on Castor.

CLERK [*continues reading*] 'Born in *anno* 1540', and now 'tis '99. By this infallible record, sir, (let me see) she is now just fifty-nine and wants but one.

CLOWN I am sorry she wants so much.

CLERK Why, sir? Alas, 'tis nothing, 'tis but so many months, so many weeks, so many—

CLOWN Do not deduct it to days, 'twill be the more tedious, and to measure it by hour-glasses were intolerable.

CLERK Do not think on it, sir; half the time goes away in sleep, 'tis half the year in nights.

CLOWN O, you mistake me, neighbour, I am loath to leave the good old woman. If she were gone now, it would not grieve me, for what is a year, alas, but a ling'ring torment? And were it not better she were out of her pain? 'T'must needs be a grief to us both.

CLERK I would I knew how to ease you, neighbour.

CLOWN You speak kindly, truly, and if you say but 'amen' to it, which is a word that I know you are perfect in, it might be done. Clerks are the most indifferent honest men, for to the marriage of your enemy, or the burial of your friend, the curses or the blessings to you are all one—you say 'amen' to all.

CLERK With a better will to the one than the other, neighbour, but I shall be glad to say 'amen' to anything might do you a pleasure.

CLOWN There is first something above your duty; now I would have you set forward the clock a little, e'en to help the old woman out of her pain.

CLERK I will speak to the sexton for that, but the day will go ne'er the faster for that.

CLOWN O neighbour, you do not conceit me; not the jack of the clock-house, the hand of the dial I mean. Come, I know you, being a great clerk, cannot choose but have the art to cast a figure.

CLERK Never indeed, neighbour, I never had the judgement to cast a figure.

CLOWN I'll show you on the back side of your book.
[*He writes*]
Look you, what figure's this?

CLERK Four with a cipher—that's forty.

CLOWN So, forty.

[He writes]

What's this now?

CLERK The cipher is turned into nine by adding the tail, which makes forty-nine.

CLOWN Very well understood.

[He writes]

What is't now?

CLERK The four is turned into three—'tis now thirty-nine.

CLOWN Very well understood. And can you do this again?

CLERK O easily, sir.

CLOWN A wager of that; let me see the place of my wife's age again.

CLERK Look you, sir, 'tis here: 1540.

CLOWN Forty drachmas, you do not turn that forty into thirty-nine.

CLERK A match with you.

CLOWN Done, and you shall keep stakes yourself; [*giving him money*] there they are.

CLERK A firm match. But stay, sir, now I consider it, I shall add a year to your wife's age. Let me see, [*reads*] '*Skirophorion* the seventeenth', and now 'tis *Hekatombaion* the eleventh. If I alter this, your wife will have but a month to live by the law.

CLOWN That's all one, sir; either do it or pay me my wager.

CLERK Will you lose your wife before you lose your wager?

CLOWN A man may get two wives before half so much money by 'em. Will you do't?

CLERK I hope you will conceal me, for 'tis flat corruption.

CLOWN Nay, sir, I would have you keep counsel, for I lose my money by't and should be laughed at for my labour, if it should be known.

CLERK Well sir,

[He writes]

there, 'tis done, as perfect thirty-nine as can be found in black and white. But mum, sir, there's danger in this figure-casting.

CLOWN Ay, sir, I know that better men than you have been thrown over the bar for as little. The best is, you can be but thrown out of the belfry.

Enter Cook, Tailor, Bailiff, and Butler

CLERK Lock close—here comes company. Asses have ears as well as pitchers.

COOK [*to Clown*] O Gnothoes, how is't? Here's a trick of discarded cards of us; we were ranked with coats as long as our old master lived.

CLOWN And is this, then, the end of serving-men?

COOK Yes, faith, this is the end of serving-men; a wise man were better serve one God than all the men in the world.

CLOWN 'Twas well-spoke of a cook. And are all fall'n into fasting-days and ember-weeks, that cooks are out of use?

81 **wife's** Early modern English did not differentiate *wives* (singular possessive, now spelled 'wife's') from *wives* (plural), except by context. Thus, throughout this scene, BELL spells (and the actor probably would have pronounced) this word as 'wives'. Though the meaning of any given occurrence of 'wives' is not ambiguous, in a larger sense, the scene is about Clown's refusal to distinguish morally between having singular or plural wives.

84 **drachmas** silver coins of ancient Greece. See also 4.1.54.

86 **A match with you** It's a bet. Perhaps with a pun on *match* = marriage compact, especially at l. 187.

91 ***Skirophorion*** MASON (Scirophorion); Scirophon BELL

91–2 ***Skirophorion*...*Hekatombaion*** Month names in the ancient Athenian calendar. Perhaps the month names are used for their effect as classical signifiers and are not meant to correspond to calculable dates. Alternatively, part of the humour of the scene, at least for educated audience members, may be that the Clerk's calculations are wrong: Skirophorion is the last month of the calendar, and Hekatombaion the first (beginning just after the summer solstice).

91 **seventeenth** BELL (17.)

92 ***Hekatombaion*** MASON (Hecatombaion); Hecatomcaon BELL **eleventh** BELL (II.)

98 **corruption** The line, and the passage that follows (109–40), may refer to the corruption scandal in the Royal Navy, brought to light in the 1618 reform commission report. This context seems especially apt, since corruption was in part associated with unaccountable clerks, and one of the reforms instituted included the reduction in the number of officers' servants (Peck, *Court Patronage and Corruption*).

105 **figure-casting** See ll. 65–6.

107 **thrown over the bar** disbarred (from practising law), imprisoned; punning on *cast* (ll. 103–5)

108 **thrown...belfry** The line may refer to the 'defenestration of Prague': in May 1618, three noble Catholic officials were thrown out the windows of Prague castle by a band of Protestant nobles. As a crucial event in Catholic/Protestant European politics and the start of what became the Thirty Years War, the event attracted much attention in England.

108.1 ***Enter...Butler*** Creon's servants had earlier appeared in livery (uniforms provided by a master to mark his servants distinctively); here, as Cook notes at ll. 111–12, they appear without their livery coats.

109 **Lock close** shut the book tightly; don't disclose this transaction

109–10 **Asses...pitchers** alluding to the proverb, 'little pitchers [i.e. children] have wide ears.'

111 **Gnothoes** BELL. Clown's name derives from the Greek verb 'to know'; pronounced onstage (probably without an initial *g*), it might have sounded like its opposite (the Greek word for 'bastard' or 'false', *nothos*) or, to the English-speaking audience, 'no-toes'. The name is also legible as an allusion to Gnatho, a sycophantic character in the Roman Terence's play *Eunuchus*, available in Nicholas Udall's 1533/34 popular Latin textbook translation (seven subsequent reprints, the last in 1581). All editions after MASON silently alter Clown's name to *Gnotho* throughout. Whatever clarification of meaning is intended as a result of this alteration, BELL unmistakably gives a final *s* in all thirteen occurrences, spelling 'Gnothos' (twice) or 'Gnothoes' (11 times).

111–12 **trick...coats** The language of playing-cards is used to play on the servants' loss of their livery uniforms (see 3.1.108.1); *coats* = coat-cards = face-cards, cards of the highest rank.

114 **And...serving-men** The line is said by the nineteenth-century editors of the play to allude to an old ballad (Gifford, Bullen).

118 **well-spoke** BELL (well spak)

119 **ember-weeks** periods of church-appointed fasting and prayer (one during each of the four seasons)

121 **lists** strips of cloth

121–2 **if this world hold** Because BELL has only commas in this speech, the 'if' clause can modify in the other direction as well: 'All tailors will be cut into lists and shreds; if this world hold, we shall grow both out of request.'

127 **long of** attributable to

128 **publican** Roman tax-collector (often used derogatorily)

130 **seam-rent... piece** torn apart at the seams
cracked... piece completely ruined (*piece* = piece of cloth and of land). The speech uses terms common to the language of both tailors and bailiffs.

150 **laid by** 1) placed a bet on, gambled on 2) set aside 3) had sex with

151 **old** BELL; old enough GIFFORD. If BELL's line is not strictly parallel, it is entirely intelligible and therefore does not require the emendation made by GIFFORD and all later editions.

153 **stock** 1) line of descent, genealogy 2) fund of money 3) sum of money to invest, principal 4) property that produces income 5) dowry for a daughter, endowment for a son 6) a term from 'Bookkeeping by Double Entry' (*OED*), relevant to Clown's double-entry wager with Clerk. Perhaps also suggesting 'the town-stocks', a mode of punishment. Given Clerk's obliviousness earlier in the scene, it is not clear that the text characterizes him as 'realizing' or 'intending' all of these meanings, which are nevertheless available to the audience.

154 **today** BELL (to day); to a Day COXETER. BELL's reading makes sense, but since its spacing of words/letters is highly irregular, even for a seventeenth-century printed text, there might also have been an omission. The servants' response in the next line may suggest that the text should read 'to a day', or 'to the day'.

155 **OMNES** all the servants. The speech raises a theatrical problem: how would this unison speech be spoken on stage? (Is this only a question for a modern, 'realist' theatre?)

167.1–3 **[*Cook... apart*]** Here and at ll. 189.1, 204.1, and 222, the stage-directions are one interpretation of action suggested by, but not made explicit in, BELL.

168–70 **bailiff... behind... bum** An elaborate sodomy joke on *bum*. A 'bumbailiff' was a bailiff of the lowest kind; bailiffs were said to be at the backs of—'behind' or 'in the bum of'—debtors.

TAILOR And all tailors will be cut into lists and shreds, if this world hold; we shall grow both out of request.

BUTLER And why not butlers as well as tailors; if they can go naked, let 'em neither eat nor drink.

CLERK That's strange, methinks, a lord should turn away his tailor of all men, and how dost thou, tailor?

TAILOR I do so-so, but indeed all our wants are long of this publican, my lord's bailiff, for had he been rent-gatherer still, our places had held together still, that are now seam-rent, nay, cracked in the whole piece.

BAILIFF Sir, if my lord had not sold his lands that claim his rents, I should still have been the rent-gatherer.

COOK The truth is, except the coachman and the footman, all serving-men are out of request.

CLOWN Nay, say not so, for you were never in more request than now, for requesting is but a kind of begging, for when you say, 'I beseech your worship's charity', 'tis all one if you say, 'I request it', and in that kind of requesting, I am sure serving-men were never in more request.

COOK Troth, he says true. Well, let that pass, we are upon a better adventure. I see, Gnothoes, you have been before us; we came to deal with this merchant for some commodities.

CLERK With me, sir? Anything that I can.

BUTLER Nay, we have looked out our wives already; marry, to you we come to know the prices, that is, to know their ages, for so much reverence we bear to age, that the more aged, they shall be the more dear to us.

TAILOR The truth is, every man has laid by his widow, so they be lame enough, blind enough, and old, 'tis good enough.

CLERK I keep the town stock; if you can but name 'em, I can tell their ages today.

OMNES We can tell their fortunes to an hour then.

CLERK Only you must pay for turning of the leaves.

COOK O bountifully, come mine first!

BUTLER The butler before the cook while you live; there's few that eat before they drink in a morning.

TAILOR Nay, then the tailor puts in his needle of priority, for men do clothe themselves before they either drink or eat.

BAILIFF I will strive for no place; the longer ere I marry my wife, the older she will be, and nearer her end and my ends.

CLERK I will serve you all, gentlemen, if you will have patience.

[*Cook, Butler, and Tailor turn the leaves of the church-book with Clerk; Clown and Bailiff speak apart*]

CLOWN I commend your modesty, sir; you are a bailiff, whose place is to come behind other men, as it were in the bum of all the rest.

BAILIFF So sir, and you were about this business too, seeking out for a widow?

CLOWN Alack no, sir, I am a married man, and have those cares upon me that you would fain run into.

BAILIFF What, an old rich wife? Any man in this age desires such a care.

CLOWN Troth, sir, I'll put a venter with you if you will; I have a lusty old quean to my wife, sound of wind and limb, yet I'll give out to take three for one, at the marriage of my second wife.

BAILIFF Ay, sir, but how near is she to the law?

CLOWN Take that at hazard, sir; there must be time, you know, to get a new. Unsight, unseen, I take three to one.

BAILIFF Two to one I'll give, if she have but two teeth in her head.

CLOWN [*giving him money*] A match, there's five drachmas for ten at my next wife.

BAILIFF A match.

[*They rejoin the others*]

COOK I shall be fitted bravely—fifty-eight and upwards, 'tis but a year and a half, and I may chance make friends, and beg a year of the Duke.

BUTLER Hey, boys, I am made Sir Butler! My wife that shall be wants but two months of her time; it shall be one ere I marry her, and then the next will be a honeymoon.

TAILOR I outstrip you all; I shall have but six weeks of Lent, if I get my widow, and then comes eating-tide plump and gorgeous.

CLOWN This tailor will be a man if ever there were any.

BAILIFF [*to Clerk*] Now comes my turn, I hope, Goodman *Finis*, you that are still at the end of all with a 'so be it'. [*To Cook, Butler, and Tailor*] Well now, sirs, do you venter there as I have done, and I'll venter here after you; good luck, I beseech thee.

[*Bailiff and Clerk speak apart from the rest*]

CLERK Amen, sir.

BAILIFF That deserves a fee already.

[*He gives him money*]

There 'tis, please me and have a better.

CLERK Amen, sir.

COOK [*to Clown*] How, two for one at your next wife? Is the old one living?

CLOWN You have a fair match; I offer you no foul one. If death make not haste to call her, she'll make none to go to him.

BUTLER I know her, she's a lusty woman, I'll take the venter.

CLOWN [*giving him money*] There's five drachmas for ten at my next wife.

BUTLER A bargain.

COOK Nay then, we'll be all merchants; give me.

TAILOR And me.

[*Clown gives Cook and Tailor money*]

BUTLER What, has the bailiff sped?

BAILIFF [*rejoining the others*] I am content, but none of you shall know my happiness.

CLERK As well as any of you all, believe it, sir.

BAILIFF O clerk, you are to speak last always.

CLERK I'll remember't hereafter, sir. You have done with me, gentlemen?

177 **venter** This word is perhaps the pivotal term of the Clown's plot, with several meanings played upon in the scenes that follow: 1) wager, commercial speculation, venture; 2) one of two or more wives who produce offspring for the same man (legal term), as in this usage by jurist Edward Coke: 'a man hath issue [of] a sonne and a daughter by one venter, & a son by another ve[n]ter....' (*Institvtes of the Lawes of England*, 1628); 3) the womb (from the French for 'stomach'); 4) a mother. Most editors modernize *venter* to *venture* (since it was one possible spelling), but to do so erases the other meanings of *venter* that are highly relevant to a scene in which Clown attempts to arrange for a quick second marriage. Throughout Clown's scenes, the equating of commercial speculation and wives produces much of the play's humour—at the expense (so to speak) of women. All other editions silently alter BELL's *venter* to *venture*, with the resulting erasure of relevant meanings discussed above. BELL is remarkably consistent in its use of *venter* (15 occurrences); *venture* occurs only twice, in an instance where the meaning signified by the modern word *venture* seems most appropriate (Hippolita's speech at 1.1.340) and at 5.1.491.

178 **quean** woman (term of abuse); whore

179–80 **I'll... wife** 'I announce three-to-one odds that I can marry a second wife.'

179 **give out** announce, proclaim

183 **Unsight, unseen** sight unseen

190 **fitted bravely** well situated, well provided for

197–8 **eating-tide... gorgeous** punning on *Eastertide*, which follows Lent (a time of fasting); *gorgeous* = sumptuous, brilliantly coloured, with the resonance of *gorge* (= eat greedily)

199 **tailor... man** alluding to several proverbs: 'the tailor makes the man' and 'three tailors make a man'.

200–1 **Goodman *Finis*** Mr. End. From here to Clerk's exit, speeches allude to the fact that clerks had the last word (*amen* = so be it) at services and kept the church-book, which foretells the *finis* of various old people.

203 **here after** BELL (heereafter)

221 **sped** met with success

Enter Wife

OMNES For this time, honest register.

CLERK Fare you well then; if you do, I'll cry 'amen' to't. *Exit*

COOK Look you, sir, is not this your wife?

CLOWN My first wife, sir.

BUTLER Nay then we have made a good match on't; if she have no froward disease, the woman may live this dozen years by her age.

TAILOR I'm afraid she's broken-winded, she holds silence so long.

COOK We'll now leave our venter to the event; I must a-wooing.

BUTLER I'll but buy me a new dagger and overtake you.

BAILIFF So we must all, for he that goes a-wooing to a widow without a weapon will never get her.

Exeunt [Cook, Tailor, Bailiff, and Butler]

CLOWN O wife, wife!

WIFE What ail you, man, you speak so passionately?

CLOWN 'Tis for thy sake, sweet wife. Who would think so lusty an old woman, with reasonable good teeth, and her tongue in as perfect use as ever it was, should be so near her time? But the Fates will have it so.

WIFE What's the matter, man? You do amaze me.

CLOWN Thou art not sick neither, I warrant thee.

WIFE Not that I know of, sure.

CLOWN What pity 'tis, a woman should be so near her end, and yet not sick.

WIFE
Near her end, man? Tush, I can guess at that.
I have years good yet of life in the remainder;
I want two yet, at least, of the full number,
Then the law, I know, craves impotent and useless,
And not the able women.

CLOWN Ay, alas, I see thou hast been repairing time as well as thou couldst; the old wrinkles are well filled up, but the vermilion is seen too thick, too thick, and I read what's written in thy forehead; it agrees with the church-book.

WIFE Have you sought my age, man? And I prithee, how is it?

CLOWN I shall but discomfort thee.

WIFE Not at all, man; when there's no remedy, I will go, though unwillingly.

CLOWN 1539 just. It agrees with the book; you have about a year to prepare yourself.

WIFE Out, alas, I hope there's more than so, but do you not think a reprieve might be gotten for half a score? An 'twere but five year, I would not care. An able woman, methinks, were to be pitied.

CLOWN Ay, to be pitied, but not helped; no hope of that, for indeed women have so blemished their own reputations nowadays, that it is thought the law will meet them at fifty very shortly.

WIFE Marry, the heavens forbid!

CLOWN There's so many of you that when you are old become witches; some profess physic, and kill good subjects faster than a burning fever; and then schoolmistresses of the sweet sin, which commonly we call bawds—innumerable of that sort. For these and such causes 'tis thought they shall not live above fifty.

WIFE Ay, man, but this hurts not the good old women.

CLOWN I'faith, you are so like one another, that a man cannot distinguish 'em now. Were I an old woman, I would desire to go before my time, and offer myself willingly two or three years before. O, those are brave women and worthy to be commended of all men in the world, that when their husbands die, they run to be burnt to death with 'em. There's honour and credit; give me half a dozen such wives.

WIFE Ay, if her husband were dead before, 'twere a reasonable request. If you were dead, I could be content to be so.

CLOWN Fie, that's not likely, for thou hadst two husbands before me.

WIFE Thou wouldst not have me die, wouldst thou, husband?

CLOWN No, I do not speak to that purpose, but I say what credit it were for me and thee, if thou wouldst; then thou shouldst never be suspected for a witch, a physician, a bawd, or any of those things, and then how daintily should I mourn for thee, how bravely should I see thee buried. When, alas, if he goes before, it cannot choose but be a great grief to him to think he has not seen his wife well buried. There be such virtuous women in the world, but too few, too few who desire to die seven years before their time with all their hearts.

228 OMNES See l. 155.

233 **froward** difficult to deal with, unfavourable (thus, incurable); perhaps with a pun on *forward* (= advanced). BELL provides only commas in this speech; again, the 'if' clause could read in either direction.

235 **broken-winded** out of breath; more specifically, an incurable respiratory disease in horses; possibly with a resonance of *break wind* (= belch or fart)

241.1 ***Exeunt Cook, Tailor, Bailiff, and Butler*** THIS EDITION; *Exeunt*. BELL (in the margin of 244)

243 **What ail you, man, you** What's the matter, that you

247 **Fates** three mythological goddesses in charge of human destinies

260 **vermilion** scarlet cosmetic

263–4 **how is it?** (a plausible question, in a culture where people often did not keep track of their age or celebrate birthdays)

268 **just** precisely

271 **An** If (see 2.1.31).

280 **profess physic** practise medicine

283 **bawds** procuresses, madames, pimps

297–8 **thou . . . me** Modern social historians suggest that 'throughout the early modern period females preserved a lead over males in their capacity to survive to age 65' (Pelling).

305 **bravely** One of several minor irregularities in BELL's catchwords; page 35/F2 catchword is *ly*, and 36/F2v begins with *lie*. Other irregular catchwords: 19/D2 *Dnke*, 20/D2v *Du.*; 47/G4 whether, 48/G4v Whether; 61/I3 *Duke.*, 62/I3v *Duk.*; 72/K4v Til, 73/L1 Till; 73/L1 *Creo.*, 74/L1v *Creon.*

WIFE I have not the heart to be of that mind. But indeed, husband, I think you would have me gone.

CLOWN No, alas, I speak but for your good and your credit, for when a woman may die quickly, why should she go to law for her death? Alack, I need not wish thee gone, for thou hast but a short time to stay with me; you do not know how near 'tis. It must out—you have but a month to live by the law.

WIFE Out, alas!

CLOWN Nay, scarce so much.

WIFE O, O, O, my heart!

[She] swoons)

CLOWN Ay, so, if thou wouldst go away quietly, 'twere sweetly done and like a kind wife. Lie but a little longer and the bell shall toll for thee.

WIFE *[reviving]* O my heart, but a month to live!

CLOWN *[aside]* Alas, why wouldst thou come back again for a month? I'll throw her down again. *[To Wife]* O woman, 'tis not three weeks, I think a fortnight is the most.

WIFE Nay, then, I am gone already.

[She] swoons

CLOWN I would make haste to the sexton now, but I'm afraid the tolling of the bell will wake her again. If she be so wise as to go now—she stirs again, there's two lives of the nine gone.

WIFE *[reviving]* O, wouldst not thou help to recover me, husband?

CLOWN Alas, I could not find in my heart to hold thee by thy nose,
Or box thy cheeks; it goes against my conscience.

WIFE
I will not be thus frighted to my death;
I'll search the church record. A fortnight—
'Tis too little, of conscience; I cannot be so near.
O time, if thou beest kind, lend me but a year. *Exit*

CLOWN What a spite's this, that a man cannot persuade his wife to die in any time with her good will. I have another bespoke already; though a piece of old beef will serve to breakfast, yet a man would be glad of a chicken to supper. The clerk, I hope, understands no Hebrew, and cannot write backward what he hath writ forward already, and then I am well enough:
'Tis but a month at most, if that were gone,
My venter comes in with her two for one,
'Tis use enough, o' conscience, for a broker if he had a conscience. *Exit*

Enter Eugenia at one door; Simonides, Courtiers at the other 3.2

EUGENIA
Gentlemen courtiers.

FIRST COURTIER
All your servants vowed, lady.
O I shall kill myself with infinite laughter!
Will nobody take my part?

SIMONIDES
An't be a laughing business,
Put it to me; I'm one of the best in Europe.
My father died last too; I have the most cause.

EUGENIA
You ha' picked out such a time, sweet gentlemen,
To make your spleen a banquet.

SIMONIDES
O, the jest, lady!
I have a jaw stands ready for't, I'll gape
Halfway and meet it.

EUGENIA
My old husband,
That cannot say his prayers out for jealousy
And madness at your coming first to woo me—

SIMONIDES Well said.

FIRST COURTIER Go on.

SECOND COURTIER On, on.

EUGENIA
Takes counsel with the secrets of all art
To make himself youthful again.

SIMONIDES
How, youthful? Ha, ha, ha!

EUGENIA
A man of forty-five he would fain seem to be
Or scarce so much if he might have his will indeed.

SIMONIDES
Ay, but his white hairs, they'll betray his hoariness.

EUGENIA
Why, there you are wide; he's not the man you take him for,
Nay will you know him when you see him again,
There will be five to one laid upon that.

FIRST COURTIER
How?

EUGENIA
Nay, you did well to laugh faintly there;
I promise you, I think he'll outlive me now,
And deceive law and all.

313 **credit** reputation

314 **quickly** with a paradoxical pun (*quick* = alive)

326 ***aside*** The first as well as the third sentence of this speech might be spoken within the hearing of the reviving Wife, though the second is not.

331 **sexton** church official whose duty it was to ring bells and dig graves

344 **spite's** annoyance is

345 **die** (with a possible play on 'have an orgasm')
in BELL; e'en TAYLOR *conj.* See l. 59–60.

348–9 **Hebrew . . . backward** Hebrew is written from right to left.

353–4 **o' conscience . . . a conscience** BELL (a ~ . . . a ~)
conscience . . . conscience Clown plays on the relative meaninglessness of the mild exclamation *o' conscience* (see 2.1.271–2).

353 **broker** MASON; brother BELL. *Broker* = 1) middleman who transacts business for a fee, 'use' 2) hired matchmaker 3) pander, pimp.

3.2.7 **make . . . banquet** indulge yourself in merriment. The spleen was considered the location of laughter.

17 **would fain** is desirous; with a suggestion of *feign* (2.2.110)

21 **Nay** Never. Emendation to *nor* (COXETER and most other editions) is unnecessary.

SIMONIDES Marry, gout forbid.

EUGENIA
You little think he was at fencing-school
At four o'clock this morning.

SIMONIDES How, at fencing-school?

EUGENIA
Else give no trust to woman.

SIMONIDES By this light
I do not like him then; he's like to live
Longer than I, for he may kill me first now.

EUGENIA
His dancer now came in as I met you.

FIRST COURTIER
His dancer too!

EUGENIA They observe turns and hours with him;
The great French rider will be here at ten
With his curveting horse.

SECOND COURTIER These notwithstanding,
His hair and wrinkles will betray his age.

EUGENIA
I'm sure his head and beard as he has ordered it
Looks not past fifty now; he'll bring't to forty
Within these four days, for nine times an hour, at
least,
He takes a black lead comb and kembs it over.
Three quarters of his beard is under fifty;
There's but a little tuft of fourscore left,

Enter Lisander [aloof off]

All of one side, which will be black by Monday,
And to approve my truth, see where he comes?
Laugh softly, gentlemen, and look upon him.

SIMONIDES
Now by this hand, he's almost black i'th' mouth
indeed.

FIRST COURTIER He should die shortly then.

SIMONIDES
Marry, methinks he dies too fast already,
For he was all white but a week ago.

FIRST COURTIER
O, this same cony-white takes an excellent black
Too soon; a mischief on't!

SECOND COURTIER He will beguile us all
If that little tuft northward turn black too.

EUGENIA
Nay, sir, I wonder 'tis so long a-turning.

SIMONIDES
Maybe some fairy's child held forth at midnight
Has pissed upon that side.

FIRST COURTIER Is this the beard?

LISANDER [*to himself*]
Ah, sirrah, my young boys, I shall be for you—
This little mangy tuft takes up more time
Than all the beard beside. Come you a-wooing
And I alive and lusty? You shall find
An alteration, jack-boys; I have a spirit yet,
(And I could match my hair to't; there's the fault)
And can do offices of youth yet lightly.
At least I will do though it pain me a little.

25 **gout forbid** 'God forbid' is an obvious meaning here, but, given that it was illegal (beginning with the 1606 'Act to Restrain Abuses of Players') to 'jestingly or profanely speak or use the name of God' on stage, BELL's spelling ('gowt') may also suggest, for us, the difficulty of determining how or why such an instance of multiple meanings is produced in the text: is this a joke, with the appearance of intentionality on Simonides's part—his substitution of a disease for *God* in a familiar phrase? Or is it, in a different way, a joke for playwrights, actors, and/or audiences aware of the censorship law—a phrase that sounds like 'God forbid', but is not?

31 **dancer** dancing teacher

32 **observe turns and hours** take hourly turns

34 **curveting** leaping

39 **comb and kembs** BELL (Combe and kembs). BELL (as well as *OED*) differentiates these words, which mean the same thing; modernizing *kembs* to *combs* would introduce a repetition that is not in BELL.

41.1 [*aloof off*] (the others on stage observe him unseen)

42 **black by Monday** (playing on 'Black Monday', the Monday that followed Easter and thought to be particularly unlucky)

45 **black i'th' mouth** as opposed to black *around* the mouth (the dyed beard), perhaps with a joke on being black in the mouth as a sign of death

47 **dies** Modernizing a homonym like *dies/dyes* requires an editor to decide which meaning seems more prevalent at the point the word appears; thus, l. 46 is *die* (pass away), while this line might become *dyes* (colours). But deciding which signification a character 'means' (or might mean, were he a person and not a collection of letters on a page, or collection of prescripted movements and sounds on a stage) is a complex operation. As one reads/hears l. 47, *dies* is appropriate; only when one proceeds to l. 48 does *dyes* seem the more prominent meaning.

49 **cony-white** rabbit-white
takes absorbs

50 **beguile** COXETER; beguild BELL. *Beguile* = fool, cheat. BELL's 'beguild' (with its possible associations of *gild/begild*, 'to cover with gold') may have arisen from all the puns on colouring in this passage.

53 **held forth** displayed (?). Possibly BELL's *held* should be emended to *haled* (TAYLOR *conj.*), meaning that the child has been hauled out (kidnapped) like a fairy's changeling.

55 **for you** ready for you

59 **jack-boys** boys employed in menial labour, especially stable boys. Lisander's language is full of terms referring to horses and riding: *mangy* (l. 56), *tits* (l. 64), *jade* and *wrench* (ll. 94–5).

64 **court-tits** tits: small horses; also, derogatory term for young women (but probably without the modern slang sense of 'breasts'). Without further evidence, it is impossible to know whether this term was typically applied to young men (this line is *OED*'s only example), or whether, instead, this is a context in which young men are being portrayed as effeminate. In contrast to the modern stereotype that links effeminacy and homosexuality, effeminacy in the Renaissance was often said to result from ostensibly excessive contact with women.

65 **tomboys'** As with *tits*, it is unclear whether this term is being used as it may have been normatively gendered (*tomboy* = boisterous boy), or used of women (*tomboy* = 'inappropriately' boisterous woman) but transferred onto the courtiers in an effeminizing way; most of the evidence available from the period suggests the term was usually applied to women.

tricks pranks; deceits; ways of acting (probably suggesting sexual acts)

70 **'Slight** God's light (a mild oath)

72 **ginny** BELL; grinny MASON; grinning GIFFORD. BELL's spelling may signify some or all of the following: 1) *guinea*, short for *guinea-fowl* (turkey) or *guinea-hen* (female turkey, and slang for prostitute), perhaps referring to its distinctive call; 2) *jenny*, woman (also applied to effeminate men); 3) *ginny*, seductive, ensnaring (from *gin* = ingenuity); possibly 4) *jennet*, a small horse (referring to its neighing).

75 **Pup!** the sound of the outburst

77 **one-and-twenty** BELL; twenty-one TAYLOR *conj.* If written as a figure in the manuscript (as in, for example, manuscripts of *Game*), the number might have been translated into words either way, and TAYLOR's conjecture is more metrically regular.

79 **codlings** 1) small cod-fish 2) variety of apple 3) scrotum 4) derogatory slang for a 'raw youth' (*OED*)

parboiled overcooked, thoroughly boiled

80 **Cupid's scalding-house** perhaps a brothel; more likely, a sweating tub (an ostensible cure for venereal disease)

82 DANCER COXETER; *Dauc.* BELL

86 **horse-trick** continuing Lisander's use of language related to horses, with an extended play on 'to horse' = for a stallion to 'cover' (= copulate with) a mare, especially at l. 87.

92 **My life for yours** I'm sure

93 **by my viol** an oath, referring to a 'viol' (musical instrument) or perhaps 'vial' (vessel, possibly with religious overtones deriving from Rev. 15:7). BELL's spelling (Vioil) could signify both words, but an oath using either term is unusual. If *viol*, perhaps the Dancer uses a musical instrument to accompany his pupil.

94 **jade** inferior horse; also derogatorily applied to women (= hussy). 'Played the jade' and 'wrench i'th' back' thus imply injury resulting from sexual overexertion. *Wrench* was also applied to injuries in horses.

Shall not a man for a little foolish age
Enjoy his wife to himself? Must young court-tits
Play tomboys' tricks with her, and he live, ha?
I have blood that will not bear't, yet I confess
I should be at my prayers. But where's the dancer
 there?

Enter Dancer

DANCER Here, sir.

LISANDER
Come, come, come, one trick a day, and I shall soon
Recover all again.

EUGENIA [*apart*] 'Slight, an you laugh too loud,
We are all discovered, gentlemen.

SIMONIDES
And I have a scurvy ginny laugh o' mine own
Will spoil all, I'm afraid.

EUGENIA Marry, take heed, sir.

SIMONIDES
Nay, an I should be hanged, I can't leave it—

[*He bursts out laughing*]

Pup! There 'tis—

EUGENIA Peace, O peace!

LISANDER [*to Dancer*] Come, I am ready, sir.
I hear the church-book's lost where I was born too,
And that shall set me back one-and-twenty years.
There is no little comfort left in that
And my three court codlings that look parboiled,
As if they came from Cupid's scalding-house.

SIMONIDES
He means me specially, I hold my life.

DANCER
What trick will your old worship learn this morning,
 sir?

LISANDER
Marry, a trick—if thou couldst teach a man
To keep his wife to himself, I'd fain learn that.

DANCER
That's a hard trick for an old man specially.
The horse-trick comes the nearest.

LISANDER Thou sayst true, i'faith;
They must be horsed indeed, else there's no keeping
 on 'em
And horse-play at fourscore is not so ready.

DANCER
Look you, here's your worship's horse-trick, sir.

[*He dances the step*]

LISANDER Nay, say not so,
'Tis none of mine; I fall down horse and man,
If I but offer at it.

DANCER My life for yours, sir.

LISANDER
Sayst thou me so?

[*He dances the step*]

DANCER Well offered, by my viol, sir.

LISANDER
A pox of this horse-trick, 't'as played the jade with me
And given me a wrench i'th' back.

DANCER
Now here's your inturn, and your trick above ground.
[*He dances another step*]
LISANDER
Prithee no more, unless thou hast a mind
To lay me underground; one of these tricks
Is enough in the morning.
DANCER For your galliard, sir,
You are complete enough, ay, and may challenge
The proudest coxcomb of 'em all, I'll stand to't.
LISANDER
Faith, and I've other weapons for the rest too,
I have prepared for 'em, if e'er I take
My Gregories here again.
SIMONIDES O, I shall burst;
I can hold out no longer.
[*He laughs*]
EUGENIA He spoils all.
LISANDER [*noting them*]
The devil and his grinners—are you come?
Bring forth the weapons, we shall find you play,
All feats of youth too, jack-boys, feats of youth,
And these the weapons: drinking, fencing, dancing—
Your own roadways, you glister-pipes. I'm old, you
say—
Yes, parlous old, kids, an you mark me well.
This beard cannot get children, you lank suck-eggs,
Unless such weasels come from court to help us?
We will get our own brats, you lecherous dogbolts!
Enter [*Servants*] *with glasses* [*and foils*]
Well said, down with 'em. Now we shall see your
spirits.
What, dwindle you already?
SECOND COURTIER I have no quality.
SIMONIDES
Nor I, unless drinking may be reckoned
For one.
FIRST COURTIER Why Sim, it shall.
LISANDER Come, dare you choose your weapon now?
FIRST COURTIER
I, dancing, sir, an you will be so hasty.
LISANDER
We're for you, sir.
SECOND COURTIER Fencing, I.
LISANDER We'll answer you too.
SIMONIDES
I'm for drinking your wet weapon there.
LISANDER
That wet one has cost many a princock's life,
And I will send it through you with a powder.
SIMONIDES
Let't come with a pox—I care not, so't be drink.
[*Aside*] I hope my guts will hold, and that's e'en all
A gentleman can look for of such trillibubs.
LISANDER
Play the first weapon, come strike, strike I say!
Yes, yes, you shall be first, I'll observe court rules:

96 **inturn** possibly a term from wrestling: placing a leg between an opponent's thighs and lifting (thus continuing the sexual meanings)
99 **galliard** a lively dance in triple time
101 **coxcomb** fool
104 **Gregories** The term probably plays on the name of Gregory Brandon, the famous London hangman during the reign of James I and Charles I, popularly known as 'Gregory'. Lisander's 'Gregories' thus means 'hangmen, men who are trying to kill me before my time'; it may also refer to both Brandon and his son Richard, who succeeded him shortly before 1640 and was known as 'Young Gregory'. PRICE conjectures a misreading of *Gregues* (= galligaskins, breeches); another possibility is *Gregorians* (= a type of wig).
106 **grinners** 'grinning' signified more ominously at the time, often emphasizing the showing of teeth.
109 **weapons** BELL (wapons)
110 **own roadways** usual activities
glister-pipes a term that may combine *clyster-pipes* (enema tubes, sometimes spelled 'glister') and an allusion to the courtiers' elaborate, brilliant (glistering) mode of dress
111 **parlous** perilously; very
112 **lank suck-eggs** thin (hungry) avaricious people, with reference to weasels (l. 113), said to suck eggs
114 **dogbolts** wretches
114.1 ***Enter...glasses*** BELL's stage-directions are often in the right margin of the page, opposite several lines (here, lines corresponding to 3.2.114). Thus, placing them within the linear flow of the speeches of the text 'proper' entails an inexact estimation of what might have happened on stage.
115 **Well said** Lisander either compliments himself on his insulting rhetoric, or thanks the servants (= 'well done').
down with 'em put down the drinks and foils; down the drinks
116 **quality** skill, talent
124 **princock's** conceited young man's
princock's BELL (princox)
125 **powder** medicine, drug (punning on 'gunpowder')
126 **Let't** BELL (Let). Modernization conj. TAYLOR.
128 **trillibubs** entrails

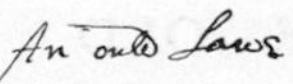

[*Music for*] *a galliard, 'La Migniard'*
Always the worst goes foremost—so 'twill prove I
  hope.
  [*First Courtier dances*]
So sir, you've spit your poison, now come I.
[*Aside*] Now forty years, go backward and assist me,
Fall from me half my age but for three minutes,
That I may feel no crick; I will put fair for't,
Although I hazard twenty sciaticas.
  [*He dances a galliard*]
So, I have hit you.

FIRST COURTIER You've done well, i'faith, sir.

LISANDER
If you confess it well, 'tis excellent,
And I have hit you soundly. I am warm now,
The second weapon instantly.

SECOND COURTIER What, so quick, sir?
Will you not allow yourself a breathing time?

LISANDER
I've breath enough at all times, Lucifer's musk-cod,
To give your perfumed worship three venies.
A sound old man puts his thrust better home
Than a spiced young man. There I—
  [*Lisander begins the fencing match*]

SECOND COURTIER Then have at you, fourscore.

LISANDER
You lie twenty, I hope, and you shall find it.
  [*They fight; Lisander gives the first hit*]

SIMONIDES [*aside*]
I'm glad I missed this weapon; I had had an eye
Popped out ere this time, or my two butter-teeth
Thrust down my throat instead of a flap-dragon.

LISANDER [*giving the second hit*]
There's two, pent-weezle.

DANCER Excellently touched, sir.

SECOND COURTIER
Had ever man such luck? Speak your opinion, gentlemen.

SIMONIDES
Methinks your luck's good that your eyes are in still;
Mine would have dropped out like a pig's half-roasted.

LISANDER
There wants a third,
  [*He gives the third hit*]
  and there 'tis again.

SECOND COURTIER The devil has steeled him.

EUGENIA What a strong fiend is jealousy!

LISANDER You're dispatched, bear-whelp.

SIMONIDES
Now comes my weapon in.

LISANDER Here, toadstool, here—
'Tis you and I must play these three wet venies.

SIMONIDES
Venies in Venice glasses, let 'em come;
They'll bruise no flesh, I'm sure, nor break no bones.

SECOND COURTIER Yet you may drink your eyes out, sir.

130.1 ***'La Migniard'*** BELL (La-|mi niard). The name of a dance-tune, also cited in Richard Brome's *The New Academy, Or The New Exchange* (written *c.*1635, published 1659), where it appears in a list of courantes (distinguished from a list of galliards). For the music, see *Companion*, p. 166.
Migniard dainty, delicate; a French word that entered English around 1600 and is related to *mignon* and *minion.* To those familiar with the tune of this name, the music may have transmitted a gendered message, further emphasizing the effeminacy of the courtiers (see ll. 64–5). James I advised his son: 'In your language be plaine, honest, naturall, comelie, cleane, short, and sentencious: eschewing . . . mignarde & effœminate tearmes' (*Basilikon Doron* [1603]).

133 **go** COXETER; ago BELL

135 **put fair** make a good attempt

136 **sciaticas** attacks of sciatica (2.1.56)

137 **hit you** scored against you (in the language of fencing that pervades the scene)

142 **musk-cod** the bag that contains musk in some animals; here, roughly: 'perfumed devil'

143 **venies** hits or thrusts in fencing

147 **lie twenty** 'miss my age by twenty'; but also Lisander's identification of Second Courtier's age as 'twenty' (responding to Second Courtier's accusation 'fourscore')

148 **had had** THIS EDITION (Taylor); had BELL; I'd had GIFFORD. TAYLOR notes that grammar, metre, and the possibility of easy scribal or compositor misreading argue for this emendation; BELL may nevertheless be intelligible.

149 **butter-teeth** front teeth

150 **flap-dragon** raisin, in a game in which raisins are caught with the mouth out of burning brandy

151 **pent-weezle** COXETER (pentweezle); pentwizle BELL. *Pent-weezle* = blocked windpipe (resonating with 'throat' in the previous line); penned weasel. (BELL's *wizle* corresponds to no recorded early spelling of either *weezle* or *weasel.*)

158 **bear-whelp** cub

160 **you and I** MASON; with you and I BELL; with you I SHAW
wet venies Lisander applies fencing language to drinking.

161 **Venies** THIS EDITION; Vennis BELL; Venue COXETER; Venues GIFFORD. BELL's 'Vennis' is a contemporary spelling of *Venice*, not *venies*, and therefore an emendation.
Venice glasses delicate drinking glasses for which Venice was famous

SIMONIDES Ay, but that's nothing; then they go voluntarily. I do not love to have 'em thrust out whether they will or no.

LISANDER Here's your first weapon, duck's meat.
[*He drinks the first glass*]

SIMONIDES How, a Dutch what-you-call-'em,
'Stead of a German falchion? A shrewd weapon,
And of all things, hard to be taken down,
Yet down it must.
[*He drinks*]
I have a nose goes into't;
I shall drink double, I think.

FIRST COURTIER The sooner off, Sim.

LISANDER
I'll pay you speedily—with a trick
I learned once amongst drunkards; here's half-pike.
[*He drinks the second glass*]

SIMONIDES
Half-pike comes well, after Dutch what-you-call-'em;
They'd never be asunder by their good will.

FIRST COURTIER
Well pulled of an old fellow.

LISANDER O, but your fellows
Pull better at a rope.

FIRST COURTIER There's a hair, Sim,
In that glass.

SIMONIDES
An't be as long as a halter, down it goes;
No hair shall cross me.
[*He drinks the second glass*]

LISANDER
I make you stink worse than your polecats do.
Here's long sword, your last weapon.
[*He drinks the third glass*]

SIMONIDES No more weapons.

FIRST COURTIER
Why, how now, Sim? Bear up, thou sham'st us all
else.

SIMONIDES
Light, I shall shame you worse an I stay longer.
I ha' got the scotomy in my head already,
The whimsy—you all turn round, do not you dance,
gallants?

SECOND COURTIER
Pish, what's all this? Why, Sim, look, the last veny.

SIMONIDES
No more venies goes down here, for these two
Are coming up again.

SECOND COURTIER Out! The disgrace of drinkers!

SIMONIDES Yes, 'twill out,
Do you smell nothing yet?

FIRST COURTIER Smell?

SIMONIDES Farewell quickly then;
It will do if I stay. *Exit*

FIRST COURTIER A foil go with thee.

LISANDER
What, shall we put down youth at her own virtues?
Beat folly in her own ground wondrous much?

167 **duck's meat** a plant that covers the surface of still water (another apparently nonsensical insult)

168 **Dutch what-you-call-'em** Probably a reference to a specific kind of weapon associated with the Dutch; some possibilities are *halberd* and *handspike* (especially given the play on *half-pike* at l. 175) and *bill* (a type of weapon, here playing on *duck's*). The chain of puns on *Dutch* is apparently triggered by *duck's* in the previous line; the word *Dutch* continued, into the seventeenth century, to refer to people and things we now distinguish as *Dutch* or *deutch* (*German*), though by 1600 English had begun to differentiate these countries, languages, and peoples. The Dutch were ostensibly heavy drinkers.

169 **falchion** a curved broad sword

173 **speedily—with a trick** MASON (long dash); ſpeedily——— with a trick BELL. Long dashes seem to signify interrupted or curtailed speeches elsewhere in BELL (at the equivalent of 3.1.38, 3.2.306, 4.2.59). THIS EDITION interprets the dashes as a pause in Lisander's speech, perhaps to prepare his drinking 'trick'. Other editions have read the dashes as marking space for an actor's improvisation of expletives, or expletives that could not be printed (GIFFORD). This might seem unlikely, since BELL copiously inscribes Lisander's other insults, but TAYLOR notes that the other insults are not profane; 'if the original here was profane, or politically objectionable, it might have been struck out, and the other insults left intact'. See l. 25 above.

174 **learned** BELL (learnt)
half-pike a shorter version of the pike, a shaft with a sharp pointed head

175 **Half-pike . . . what-you-call-'em** See l. 168.

177 **pulled of** drunk for

178 **Pull better at a rope** hang better

181 **hair** (with pun on *heir*)

182 **polecats** animals related to skunks, known for their smell; slang for 'prostitute'

185 **Light** God's light (an oath)
an if

186 **scotomy** GIFFORD; Scotony BELL. *Scotomy* = scotoma, 'dizziness accompanied by dimness of sight' (*OED*)

187 **whimsy** whim, fantastical idea; dizziness

189 **venies goes** Should this verb agree? How might one distinguish between a grammatical error on the part of the writer(s) (at a point in the history of English when verb agreement was not as strictly maintained), a textual error, or a drunken character's syntactical difficulties?

194 **foil** disgrace (with a pun on the weapon)

195 LISANDER COXETER (*Lysan.*); *Life.* BELL. The final letter is unclear in all copies consulted (possibly *c*); BELL's usual speech prefix for Lisander is *Lif.*

Why, may not we be held as full sufficient
To love our own wives then, get our own children,
And live in free peace till we be dissolved?
For such spring butterflies that are gaudy-winged,
(But no more substance than those shamble-flies
Which butchers' boys snap between sleep and waking)
Come but to crush you once; you are all but maggots,
For all your beamy outsides.

Enter Cleanthes

EUGENIA [*to Courtiers*] Here's Cleanthes;
He comes to chide. Let him alone a little;
Our cause will be revenged. Look, look, his face
Is set for stormy weather. Do but mark
How the clouds gather in't; 'twill pour down straight.

CLEANTHES [*to Lisander*]
Methinks I partly know you; that's my grief.
Could you not all be lost that had been handsome?
But to be known at all, 'tis more than shameful.
Why, was not your name wont to be Lisander?

LISANDER 'Tis so still, coz.

CLEANTHES
Judgement, defer thy coming, else this man's miserable.

EUGENIA [*to Courtiers*]
I told you there would be a shower anon.

SECOND COURTIER We'll in and hide our noddles.

Exeunt Courtiers and Eugenia

CLEANTHES
What devil brought this colour to your mind,
Which since your childhood I ne'er saw you wear?
You were ever of an innocent gloss
Since I was ripe for knowledge, and would you lose it
And change the livery of saints and angels
For this mixed monstrousness, to force a ground
That has been so long hallowed like a temple
To bring forth fruits of earth now, and turn back
To the wild cries of lust, and the complexion
Of sin in act, lost and long since repented?
Would you begin a work ne'er yet attempted,
To pull time backward?
See what your wife will do. Are your wits perfect?

LISANDER My wits?

CLEANTHES
I like it ten times worse, for 't'ad been safer
Now to be mad, and more excusable.
I hear you dance again and do strange follies.

LISANDER
I must confess I have been put to some, coz.

CLEANTHES
And yet you are not mad? Pray say not so:
Give me that comfort of you that you are mad,
That I may think you are at worst, for if
You are not mad, I then must guess you have
The first of some disease was never heard of,
Which may be worse than madness, and more fearful.
You'd weep to see yourself else, and your care
To pray would quickly turn you white again.
I had a father, had he lived his month out

198 **get** beget, father
199 **dissolved** deceased
200 **gaudy-winged** See 2.1.188.
201 **shamble-flies** flies in a butcher's stall or slaughterhouse. *Shamble* may also imply 'ill-formed'.
203 **you . . . you** i.e., one . . . they
204 **beamy** radiant
210 **Could . . . handsome?** Could you (who had been handsome) not be entirely unrecognizable? Possibly BELL's line should be repunctuated 'Could you not all be lost? That had been handsome—'; *handsome* would then have its historically older meaning of 'proper, appropriate', rather than 'attractive'.
216 **noddles** heads
219 **gloss** exterior; perhaps with the added resonance of a marginal comment (like this one) that explains or annotates a 'text', in this case Lisander's earlier virtue. In both senses, the word often had sinister connotations: in the first, of a cover-up; in the second, of a *gloze*, a devious argument or explanation. Thus, *innocent gloss* may (whether intentionally or not) carry a whiff of oxymoron.
221 **livery . . . angels** i.e., white
224 **back** COXETER; black BELL. The emendation makes better syntactic sense of the phrase 'turn back | To . . . the complexion | Of sin in act'; at the same time, the substitution sacrifices BELL's resonant play on colours. (If BELL's 'turn black' was pronounced on stage, audiences might still have heard the resonance of the idiom 'turn back'.)
226 **act** action; a sex act
228 **pull time backward** attempted, in fact, at ll. 133–4
229 **See . . . do** Notice what your wife is doing (as a result of your behaviour)

253–3.2.254.1 *Exit Lisander... Enter Eugenia* See 3.2.114.1.
265 **stickest** pierces; or remains fixed
266–8 The question of whether Cleanthes's speeches here are 'asides' is again significant; see 1.1.222–3. Given that he describes Eugenia as 'fast asleep' (l. 261), it may have been theatrically effective to treat all the lines as spoken aloud; in such a scenario, Cleanthes acts *as if* he is not speaking these lines to Eugenia, but speaks them within her hearing for [what he perceives to be] her benefit. See also ll. 259–61.
274 **gone backward** See ll. 133–4, 228.
288 **Have** who have
297 **stronger master** i.e., the devil
298 **Bless** protect, save
299 **impudently common** shamelessly promiscuous. *Common woman* was a term for prostitute—i.e. a woman said to be shared 'in common' by multiple men, like a piece of land (a *common*). *Impudently*) is closely related to *pudendum* (= vulva).
301 **fit** punish
303 **I can 'sure** The edited version here interprets BELL's 'I can sure' as 'I can assure that...'; another possibility would read 'sure' as 'certainly, surely':

He that attempts to take away my pleasure,
I'll take away his joy, and I can, sure.
His concealed father pays for't...

307 **He's** BELL (Has), a modernization suggested by GIFFORD (He has)
a bout BELL (about)
Since now
308 **flirt** a quick blow or tap; a stroke of wit

But to ha' seen this most prodigious folly,
There needed not the law to have cut him off:
The sight of this had proved his executioner,
And broke his heart. He would have held it equal
Done to a sanctuary, for what is age
But the holy place of life, chapel of ease
For all men's wearied miseries? And to rob
That of her ornament, it is accursed,
As from a priest to steal a holy vestment,
Ay, and convert it to a sinful covering. *Exit Lisander*
I see 't'as done him good; blessing go with it,
Enter Eugenia
Such as may make him pure again.

EUGENIA
'Twas bravely touched, i'faith, sir.

CLEANTHES
O, you're welcome.

EUGENIA
Exceedingly well handled.

CLEANTHES
'Tis to you I come;
He fell but i' my way.

EUGENIA
You marked his beard, cousin.

CLEANTHES
Mark me.

EUGENIA Did you ever see a hair so changed?

CLEANTHES [*aside*]
I must be forced to wake her loudly too;
The devil has rocked her so fast asleep.—Strumpet.

EUGENIA Do you call, sir?

CLEANTHES
Whore.

EUGENIA
How do you, sir?

CLEANTHES
Be I ne'er so well,
I must be sick of thee. Thou'rt a disease
That stickest to th' heart, as all such women are.

EUGENIA
What ails our kindred?

CLEANTHES [*aside*] Bless me, she sleeps still.
What a dead modesty is i' this woman!—
Will never blush again? Look on thy work
But with a Christian eye: 'twould turn thy heart
Into a shower of blood to be the cause
Of that old man's destruction—think upon't—
Ruin eternally! For through thy loose follies
Heaven has found him a faint servant lately;
His goodness has gone backward and engendered
With his old sins again, has lost his prayers
And all the tears that were companions with 'em,
And—like a blindfold man, giddy and blinded,
Thinking he goes right on still, swerves but one foot
And turns to the same place where he set out—
So, he that took his farewell of the world
And cast the joys behind him out of sight,
Summed up his hours, made even with time and men,
Is now in heart arrived at youth again,
All by thy wildness. Thy too hasty lust
Has driven him to this strong apostasy.
Immodesty like thine was never equalled;
I've heard of women (shall I call 'em so)
Have welcomed suitors ere the corpse were cold,
But thou, thy husband living—thou art too bold.

EUGENIA
Well, have you done now, sir?

CLEANTHES
Look, look, she smiles yet.

EUGENIA
All this is nothing to a mind resolved.
Ask any woman that; she'll tell you so much.
You have only shown a pretty saucy wit,
Which I shall not forget, nor to requite it.
You shall hear from me shortly.

CLEANTHES
Shameless woman,
I take my counsel from thee—'tis too honest—
And leave thee wholly to thy stronger master.
Bless the sex of thee from thee, that's my prayer.
Were all like thee, so impudently common,
No man would be found to wed a woman. *Exit*

EUGENIA I'll fit you gloriously;
He that attempts to take away my pleasure,
I'll take away his joy, and I can 'sure
His concealed father pays for't. I'll e'en tell
Him that I mean to make my husband next,
Enter Simonides
And he shall tell the Duke—mass, here he comes.

SIMONIDES
He's had a bout with me too.

EUGENIA
What? No! Since, sir?

SIMONIDES
A flirt, a little flirt; he called me strange names,

309 **quit** repay (2.2.149)
315.1 ***Tertius*** BELL (*Tertii*)
4.1.0.1 ***Incipit Actus Quartus*** THIS EDITION; Act. IV. Scen. I. BELL
1 **gentlemen** COXETER; Gentlmen BELL
draw (with a pun on his occupation)
5 ***De clare*** clary wine, a mixture of wine, honey, and spices
6 **bullies** friends, good-fellows (without the modern sense of intimidation)
8 **two** BELL (too)
9 **basted** moistened (continuing the jokes in culinary language), but with a sexual meaning as well
11 **stuck her with rosemary** Meat was stuck with the herb rosemary as a flavoring; rosemary was also used as an ornament at both weddings and funerals (see ll. 33–5). 'Stuck her' suggests sexual penetration.
14 **fly-blown** tainted (with deposits of flies' eggs)
15 **Put her off** get rid of her
21 **Palermo** a kind of wine from Palermo, Sicily
22 **lick-spigot** insulting name for a tapster
23 ***Ad imum*** to the last
36 **account** See 1.1.467.
43 **wire-drawers** i.e., string-players. Lines 42–50 play upon the intersections in the vocabularies of music and drinking.
46 **sack-butts** casks of white wine; also a common musical instrument, now obsolete (a bass trumpet with a slide like a trombone)
48 **theirs** MASON; their BELL
cittern- and gittern-heads citterns and gitterns were guitar-like stringed instruments, often with a 'grotesquely-carved head' (*OED*)
51 **fool** BELL (foole). *fool* = play the fool. All other editions emend unnecessarily to *foot*.
52 **Siren** in Greek mythology, one of a group of monsters, part-bird, part-woman, who lured sailors to their deaths with enchanting singing (*Odyssey* 12)
53 **Hiren** slang for seductive woman, harlot (synonymous with *Siren*). The passage references a frequently quoted line ('have we not Hiren here?') probably from a now-lost play associated with George Peele, *The Turkish Mahamet and Hyrin the fair Greek* (c.1594). This story was also kept in circulation by William Barksted's 1611 narrative poem *Hiren: or The faire Greeke*.

But I ne'er minded him.
EUGENIA You shall quit him, sir,
When he as little minds you.
SIMONIDES I like that well.
I love to be revenged when no one thinks of me.
There's little danger that way.
EUGENIA This is it, then.
He you shall strike; your stroke shall be profound,
And yet your foe not guess who gave the wound.
SIMONIDES
O' my troth, I love to give such wounds. *Exeunt*
Finis Actus Tertius

❁

4.1 *Incipit Actus Quartus*
Enter Clown, Butler, Bailiff, Tailor, Cook, Drawer, Wench

DRAWER Welcome, gentlemen, will you not draw near? Will you drink at door, gentlemen?
BUTLER O, the summer air's best!
DRAWER What wine will please you drink, gentlemen?
BUTLER *De clare*, sirrah. [*Exit Drawer*]
CLOWN What, you're all sped already, bullies?
COOK My widow's o'th' spit and half ready, lad; a turn or two more and I have done with her.
CLOWN Then, cook, I hope you have basted her before this time.
COOK And stuck her with rosemary too, to sweeten her; she was tainted ere she came to my hands. What an old piece of flesh of fifty-nine, eleven months, and upwards! She must needs be fly-blown.
CLOWN Put her off, put her off, though you lose by her; the weather's hot.
COOK Why, Drawer!
Enter Drawer
DRAWER By and by—here, gentlemen, here's the quintessence of Greece; the sages never drunk better grape.
COOK Sir, the mad Greeks of this age can taste their Palermo as well as the sage Greeks did before 'em. Fill, lick-spigot.
DRAWER *Ad imum*, sir.
CLOWN My friends, I must doubly invite you all, the fifth of the next month, to the funeral of my first wife, and to the marriage of my second, my two-to-one. This is she.
COOK I hope some of us will be ready for the funeral of our wives by that time, to go with thee. But shall they be both of a day?
CLOWN O, best of all, sir! Where sorrow and joy meet together, one will help away with another the better. Besides, there will be charges saved too; the same rosemary that serves for the funeral will serve for the wedding.
BUTLER How long do you make account to be a widower, sir?
CLOWN Some half an hour—long enough, o' conscience. Come, come, let's have some agility! Is there no music in the house?
DRAWER Yes, sir, here are sweet wire-drawers in the house.
COOK O, that makes them and you seldom part; you are wine-drawers, and they wire-drawers.
TAILOR And both govern by the pegs too.
CLOWN And you have pipes in your consort too.
DRAWER And sack-butts too, sir.
BUTLER But the heads of your instruments differ; yours are hogsheads, theirs cittern- and gittern-heads.
BAILIFF All wooden heads; there they meet again.
COOK Bid 'em strike up; we'll have a dance. [*Exit Drawer*] Gnothoes, come, thou shalt fool it too.
CLOWN No dancing with me; we have Siren here.
COOK Siren? 'Twas Hiren the fair Greek, man.

54 **drachmas** BELL (Drachmes); Drachms COXETER. Here and in 3.1, BELL employs the spellings 'drachmaes' and 'drachmes' without distinction (three occurrences each), though this scene consistently capitalizes. In the next three lines, *drachmas* refers to 1) a Greek coin (3.1.84); 2) a small amount of liquor *drachm* (pronounced and sometimes spelled *dram*); and/or 3) the unit of weight on which both of these were based (thus resonating with the puns on measurement that follow). The words were largely interchangeable, and either pronunciation may have been employed on stage in this scene.

62 **Helen of Greece** Helen, married to Menelaus of Sparta, later abducted by Paris of Troy, triggering the Trojan War

66 **shorter** COXETER; ſhorer BELL

69 **an ell** 1) unit of measurement (45 inches) 2) 'a Nell'

yard 36 inches; also, a standard word for 'penis'

70–2 **There ... Cressida** Women thought promiscuous or unchaste were described as 'light'; moving from length to weight in his jokes on measurements, the clown is weighing the relative chastity of two famous women of antiquity.

70 **Cressid** Trojan woman in love with Troilus, during the siege of Troy

71 **Troy weight** the standard system of weights for precious metals, in which a pound = 12 ounces

avoirdupois BELL (haberdepoyſe). A system of weights, in which a pound = 16 ounces. BELL's spelling may suggest 'haver of poise', punning on *have/held* and on *poise*, meaning balanced between two things (in this case, men).

76 **plaster of Paris** common white plaster, playing on Paris, Helen's seducer; 'plasters' were also bandages used to place medicine on a wound, and thus to 'stop holes'—with a joke about sexual penetration

80–1 **I ... both** The line resonates with the staging practices in early performances; men and boys would have played the women's parts.

81 **visors** BELL (vizards); Wizards MASON. *visors/vizards* = masks. Most editors substitute *wizards*, suggesting that Drawer is corrected by Cook and then excused by Butler, but the speech can be read as it stands in BELL, giving the sense that Drawer tentatively proposes a term, which Cook confirms and Butler then plays on.

86.1 ***Enter ... masks*** MASON (*subst.*); *Old women.* BELL (in the margin of 4.1.85–4.1.86.1).

88.1–4.1.91.2 ***Musicians ... Wench*** BELL's stage direction here is detailed; at the same time, BELL does not fully distinguish lines spoken, speech headings, and stage directions at the right margins of speeches. The version in the text column, then, is one possible interpretation of BELL; in an attempt to render what may have transpired on stage, it re-orders the relation of some stage directions and speeches. BELL reads:

> *Draw.* They deſire to enter amongſt any merry company of
> Gentlemen good fel'owes for a ſtraine or too. *Old women.*
> *Cook.* Weel ſtrain our ſelves with em ſay, let em come *Gnothoes:*
> now for the honour of *Epire.* *Dance.*
> *She* dancing with me, we have *Siren* heere.
> *The* Dance *of old women maskt, then offer to take the men, they a-*
> *gree all but* Gnothoes; *he ſits with his Wench after they Whiſper.*
> *Cook.* I ſo kind then every one his Wench to his ſeverall room:
> *Gnothoes* we are all provided now as you are *Exeunt* each with
> *Clo.* I ſhall have two it ſeemes away I have his wife *maskt*
> *Siren* heere already *Gnothoes* wife unmaskt.

88.1 ***Musicians ... dance*** THIS EDITION (Taylor); *Dance.* BELL (in margin following 4.1.88). THIS EDITION interprets BELL's marginal direction as a cue for the music (as might have been the case in a promptbook); previous editions have treated *Dance* as a duplication of the direction that follows.

88.3 ***take*** dance with

Clown THIS EDITION; *not in* BELL

89 CLOWN COXETER (*Gno.*); *Gnothoes*: BELL (in the margin after 4.1.87). In BELL the speech itself has no speech heading; editors interpret the word *Gnothoes* at the right of 4.1.87 as a misplaced speech heading. If this is correct, it is the only time BELL uses Clown's name as a speech heading (though *Gnothoes* does appear in the stage direction). See next note.

She ... here. THIS EDITION. BELL places this line of speech before the stage direction; THIS EDITION places it in the middle of the stage direction, so that it supplies a text for Clown's refusal to dance. If (as hypothesized in the previous note), the marginal *Gnothoes* is a speech heading, this line of speech may have appeared marginally, as an addition in the manuscript copy for BELL.

She Clown's Wife (masked)

We have Siren here See ll. 52, 92, 102–3.

CLOWN Five drachmas of that! I say Siren the fair Greek, and so are all fair Greeks.

COOK A match—five drachmas her name was Hiren.

CLOWN Siren's name was Siren, for five drachmas.

COOK 'Tis done.

TAILOR Take heed what you do, Gnothoes.

CLOWN Do not I know our own countrywomen Siren and Nell of Greece, two of the fairest Greeks that ever were?

COOK That Nell was Helen of Greece too.

CLOWN As long as she tarried with her husband she was Ellen, but after she came to Troy she was Nell of Troy, or Bonny Nell, whether you will or no.

TAILOR Why, did she grow shorter when she came to Troy?

CLOWN She grew longer, if you mark the story. When she grew to be an ell, she was deeper than any yard of Troy could reach by a quarter. There was Cressid was Troy weight, and Nell was avoirdupois; she held more by four ounces than Cressida.

BAILIFF They say she caused many wounds to be given in Troy.

CLOWN True, she was wounded there herself, and cured again by plaster of Paris, and ever since, that has been used to stop holes with.

Enter Drawer

DRAWER Gentlemen, if you be disposed to be merry, the music is ready to strike up, and here's a consort of mad Greeks. I know not whether they be men or women, or between both; they have—what you call 'em? visors?—on their faces.

COOK Visors, goodman lick-spigot.

BUTLER If they be wise women, they may be wizards too.

DRAWER They desire to enter amongst any merry company of gentlemen good-fellows for a strain or two.

[*Enter*] *old women* [*and Wife, in masks*]

COOK We'll strain ourselves with 'em, say; let 'em come now, for the honour of Epire!

[*Musicians within play a*] *dance*

The dance of old women masked, then [*they*] *offer to take the men; they agree, all but* [*the Clown*] *Gnothoes*

CLOWN She dancing with me? We have Siren here.

He sits with his Wench after they whisper

COOK Ay, so kind, then every one his wench to his several room. Gnothoes, we are all provided now as you are.

Exeunt each with his wife, manet Gnothoes' Wife, [*Clown, and Wench*]

CLOWN I shall have two, it seems. Away, I have Siren here already.

WIFE What, a mermaid?

CLOWN No, but a maid, horse-face.

[*Wife unmask*]

O, old woman, is it you?

WIFE Yes, 'tis I; all the rest have gulled themselves and taken their own wives, and shall know that they have done more than they can well answer. But I pray you, husband, what are you doing?

CLOWN Faith, thus should I do if thou wert dead, old Ag, and thou hast not long to live, I'm sure. We have Siren here.

WIFE Art thou so shameless whilst I am living to keep one under my nose?

CLOWN No, Ag, I do prize her far above thy nose; if thou wouldst lay me both thine eyes in my hand to boot, I'll not leave her. Art not ashamed to be seen in a tavern, and hast scarce a fortnight to live? O, old woman, what art thou? Must thou find no time to think of thy end?

WIFE O unkind villain.

CLOWN [*to Wench*] And then, sweetheart, thou shalt have two new gowns, and the best of this old, old woman's shall make thee raiments for the working days.

WIFE O, rascal, dost thou quarter my clothes already too?

CLOWN [*to Wench*] Her ruffs will serve thee for nothing but to wash dishes, for thou shalt have nine of the new fashion.

WIFE Impudent villain! [*To Wench*] Shameless harlot!

CLOWN [*to Wench*] You may hear she never wore any but rails all her lifetime.

[*Wife attacks Wench; Clown restrains her*]

WIFE Let me come—I'll tear the strumpet from him.

CLOWN Dar'st thou call my wife 'strumpet'? Thou preterp-luperfect tense of a woman! I'll make thee do penance in the sheet thou shalt be buried in. Abuse my choice, my two-to-one!

WIFE
No, unkind villain, I'll deceive thee yet.
I have a reprieve for five years of life;
I am with child.

WENCH Cudso, Gnothoes, I'll not tarry so long. Five years—I may bury two husbands by that time.

CLOWN Alas, give the poor woman leave to talk. She with child? I with a puppy! As long as I have thee by me, she shall not be with child, I warrant thee.

WIFE The law and thou and all shall find I am with child.

CLOWN I'll take my corporal oath I begat it not, and then thou diest for adultery.

WIFE No matter, that will ask some time in the proof.

CLOWN O, you'd be stoned to death, would you? All old women would die o' that fashion with all their hearts, but the law shall overthrow you the t'other way first.

89.1 ***after they whisper*** Clown and Wench sit, after which they whisper; or they sit after they whisper. (The text seems to provide no further explanation for the whispering.)

91.1 ***manet*** remain (on stage)

91.2 ***Gnothoes' Wife*** BELL (*Gnothoes* wife)
Clown, and Wench GIFFORD (*subst.*); *not in* BELL.

94 **mermaid** prostitute; synonymous with *siren* (l. 52)

95.1 ***Wife unmask*** THIS EDITION (Taylor); wife unmaskt. BELL (in the margin opposite l. 93); *Takes off her mask.* GIFFORD (at l. 94). Clown's question, and particularly his interjection 'O', suggest that he has not recognized his wife until now. Alternatively, Clown's ability to dissimulate elsewhere in the text may suggest he *pretends* not to recognize his wife until now, in which case BELL's original placement of 'wife unmaskt' might be followed. Clown's term 'Horse-face' might refer either to his wife's face or to her mask; animal masks were common in the period. TAYLOR argues that there is no reason for Wife to remove her mask at the point where BELL marks the action, and he suggests that, given the amount of material apparently in the margin here, the compositor could have become confused: 'Exeunt... | Wife | Wife | unmaske' could easily have been interpreted as an erroneous duplication, part of a single sentence, which would encourage the (easy) misreading of a terminal 'e' as 't'.

101 **old Ag** the nickname for Agatha may sound like 'old hag'

115 **quarter my clothes** alluding to the division of Jesus of Nazareth's clothes at his crucifixion (John 19:23)

116 **ruffs** decorative collars

121 **rails** neckerchiefs, playing on *rail* (= use abusive language, harangue)

122 **him** BELL; thee TAYLOR *conj.*

123–4 **preterpluperfect tense** literally, 'beyond the pluperfect tense'; before the past, older than old

130 **Cudso** BELL (Cud fo). An exclamation related to *God's*

136 **corporal oath** an oath made while touching a sacred object (e.g. the Bible, the communion host)

139 **stoned** a mode of execution (for adultery, particularly in the Hebrew Bible and New Testament), with a play on *stones* as testicles; thus, perhaps, 'fucked to death', a sense underlined by *overthrow*. (See *cast down* at 2.1.139.)

141 **t'other** the other (a redundant idiom)

An oulde Lawe

WENCH Indeed, if it be so, I will not linger so long, Gnothoes.

CLOWN [*to Wife*] Away, away, some botcher has got it; 'tis but a chushion, I warrant thee. The old woman is 'loath to depart'; she never sung other tune in her life.

WENCH We will not have our noses bored with a chushion if it be so.

CLOWN [*to Wife*] Go, go thy ways, thou old almanac—at the twenty-eighth day of December e'en almost out-of-date! Down on thy knees, and make thee ready. Sell some of thy clothes to buy thee a death's-head, and put't upon thy middle finger; your least-considering bawds do so much. Be not thou worse, though thou art an old woman as she is. I am cloyed with old stock-fish; here's a young perch is sweeter meat by half. Prithee, die before thy day if thou canst, that thou mayst not be counted a witch.

WIFE No, thou art a witch and I'll prove it. I said I was with child; thou knewest no other but by sorcery; thou said'st it was a cushion and so it is; thou art a witch for't, I'll be sworn to't.

CLOWN Ha, ha, ha! I told thee 'twas a chushion. Go get thy sheet ready; we'll see thee buried as we go to church to be married. *Exeunt* [*Clown and Wench*]

WIFE Nay, I'll follow thee, and show myself a wife; I'll plague thee as long as I live with thee, and I'll bury some money before I die that my ghost may haunt thee afterward. *Exit*

4.2 *Enter Cleanthes*

CLEANTHES
What's that? O, nothing but the whispering wind
Breathes through yon churlish hawthorn, that grew
rude,
As if it chid the gentle breath that kissed it.
I cannot be too circumspect, too careful,
For in these woods lies hid all my life's treasure,
Which is too much ever to fear to lose,
Though it be never lost. And if our watchfulness
Ought to be wise and serious against a thief
That comes to steal our goods—things all without us,
That proves vexation often more than comfort—
How mighty ought our providence to be
To prevent those, if any such there were,
That come to rob our bosom of our joys,
That only makes poor man delight to live?
Pshaw, I'm too fearful. Fie, fie, who can hurt me?
But 'tis a general cowardice that shakes
The nerves of confidence; he that hides treasure
Imagines everyone thinks of that place,
When 'tis a thing least minded. Nay, let him change
The place continually; where'er it keeps,
There will the fear keep still. Yonder's the storehouse
Of all my comfort now,
Enter Hippolita
and see, it sends forth
A dear one, to me, precious chief of women.—
How does the good old soul? Has he fed well?

144 **botcher** a tailor who patches and makes repairs
got fathered

145 **chushion** BELL. Cushion, pillow; also, a simulated pregnancy. This spelling, unrecorded in *OED*, is retained because it may represent a dialect pronunciation; it appears three times (also at ll. 147 and 163, always attributed to Clown or Wench), in contrast to Wife's usage (l. 161).

146 **'loath to depart'** the name of a familiar tune. (See *Weapons* 2.2.248.1.)

147 **have our noses bored** be swindled

148 **if** Like many other less significant cases that could be cited, the appearance of this word only in some copies of BELL illustrates the difficulty of distinguishing between press variants and letters that do not print (or print as ink blotches) in BELL. HOUGHTON2 lacks the word entirely at the end of this line (p. 49/H1); FOLGER, LCP, and HOUGHTON1 have the hint of a letter but are otherwise illegible; WILLIAMS shows a clear *i* and a blotched *f*; HUNTINGTON clearly shows *if*.

150 **twenty-eighth** BELL (28.)
December While the play insists at certain points (the beginning of this scene, for example) on its Greek setting, there is a persistent multiculturalism in the play, a constant resurfacing of English terms and customs. Greek month-names are used earlier (3.1.91–2).

152–4 **death's-head...bawds** Bawds commonly wore rings with representations of skulls.

153 **put't** BELL (put). Modernization conj. TAYLOR.

155 **cloyed** overfed, satiated; encumbered
stock-fish cured, dried salt-water fish

156 **perch** freshwater fish; something to sit on (sexually)

158 **witch** (suggesting that old women were more likely to be accused of witchcraft)

165 *Exeunt* BELL (*Ex.*)

167–9 **bury...afterward** Ghosts were thought to haunt spots where they had buried treasure in life.

4.2.2 **yon** COXETER; you BELL. For other *u*/*n* inversions, see notes to 1.1.380, 5.1.57.

5 **life's** BELL (lives)

7 **Though** COXETER; *Hip.* Though BELL. In BELL, this line is preceded by *Hip.*, as if it begins a speech by Hippolita, but this is apparently one of BELL's many anticipatory stage directions, preparing for her entrance. Such directions appear throughout BELL, usually in the right margin, as does Hippolita's actual entrance direction at l. 22; they suggest that the text from which BELL was typeset was one that had been used in the theatre as a book-holder's copy, or 'promptbook'.

10 **proves** prove. Early modern English occasionally used third-person plural verbs ending in *-s*. See l. 14.

22.1 *Enter Hippolita* THIS EDITION; BELL (in the margin of 4.2.21–2); GIFFORD (after 4.2.22)

23 **dear one, to me** BELL reads: 'A deere one, to me, pretious chiefe of women' (which THIS EDITION follows), but there are several other possibilities of punctuation (and thus of meaning): 'A dear one to me, precious chief of women.' 'A dear one, to me precious chief of women.' And as direct address (since BELL ends the line with a comma): 'A dear one to me. Precious chief of women, | How does the good old soul?'

27 HIPPOLITA COXETER; *Eip.* BELL
31.1 *Enter Leonides* COXETER; *Ent.* Leonides. BELL (in the margin of 4.2.32, at the end of the first line of the speech given to him by editors)
32 LEONIDES COXETER; *not in* BELL. In BELL the speech continues as Hippolita's, after a line break, and a reader might initially have taken it as such.
34 CLEANTHES BELL. Most editions treat this as a continuation of the previous speech, reassigned to Leonides.
Lists of honour delights of honour. *Lists* = joy, desire, delight (archaic).
55.1 [*sounds…off*] THIS EDITION; *not in* BELL
58 **consort** partner (used with spouses, parents, associates, and thus possibly resonating with Cleanthes's earlier speech that fails to distinguish wife and father, 1.1.458–63).
59 HIPPOLITA COXETER; *H p* BELL. All copies consulted have a medial space in this speech heading.

HIPPOLITA
Beshrew me, sir, he made the heartiest meal today.
Much good may't do his health.
CLEANTHES A blessing on thee,
Both for thy news and wish.
HIPPOLITA His stomach, sir,
Is bettered wondrously since his concealment.
CLEANTHES
Heaven has a blessed work in't. Come, we're safe here;
I prithee call him forth, the air's much wholesomer.
HIPPOLITA Father!
Enter Leonides
LEONIDES
How sweetly sounds the voice of a good woman!
It is so seldom heard that when it speaks
It ravishes all senses.
CLEANTHES Lists of honour,
I've a joy weeps to see you, 'tis so full,
So fairly fruitful.
[*He kneels*]
I hope to see you often and return,
Loaden with blessings, still to pour on some,
I find 'em all in my contented peace,
And lose not one in thousands. They're dispersed
So gloriously I know not which are brightest.
I find 'em as angels are found, by legions:
First in the love and honesty of a wife,
Which is the first and chiefest of all temporal blessings;
Next in yourself, which is the hope and joy
Of all my actions, my affairs, my wishes;
And lastly, which crowns all, I find my soul
Crowned with the peace of 'em, th'eternal riches,
Man's only portion for his heavenly marriage.
LEONIDES
Rise: thou art all obedience, love and goodness.
[*Cleanthes rises*]
I dare say that which thousand fathers cannot,
And that's my precious comfort. Never son
Was in the way more of celestial rising;
Thou art so made of such ascending virtue
That all the pow'rs of hell cannot sink thee.
A horn [*sounds within, as afar off*]
CLEANTHES Ha.
LEONIDES
What was't disturbed my joy?
CLEANTHES Did you not hear,
As afar off?
LEONIDES What, my excellent consort?
CLEANTHES [*to Hippolita*] Nor you?
HIPPOLITA
I heard a—
A horn [*sounds within*]
CLEANTHES Hark, again.
LEONIDES Bless my joy,
What ails it on a sudden?
CLEANTHES Now, since lately—

LEONIDES
'Tis nothing but a symptom of thy care, man.
CLEANTHES
Alas, you do not hear well.
LEONIDES What was't, daughter?
HIPPOLITA
I heard a sound twice.
A horn [*sounds within*]
CLEANTHES Hark, louder and nearer.
In, for the precious good of virtue, quick, sir.
[*Exit Leonides, as a horn sounds still*]
Louder and nearer yet—at hand, at hand!
A hunting here? 'Tis strange, I never
Knew game followed in these woods before.
Enter Duke, Simonides, Courtiers, and Executioner
HIPPOLITA Now let 'em come and spare not.
CLEANTHES
Ha! 'Tis, is't not the Duke? Look sparingly.
HIPPOLITA
'Tis he, but what of that? Alas, take heed, sir,
Your care will overthrow us.
CLEANTHES Come, it shall not.
Let's set a pleasant face upon our fears,
Though our hearts shake with horror. Ha, ha, ha!
DUKE Hark!
CLEANTHES [*to Hippolita*] Prithee proceed,
I'm taken with these light things infinitely
Since the old man's decease. Ha, so they parted—ha,
ha, ha!
DUKE
Why, how should I believe this? Look, he's merry,
As if he had no such charge. One with that care
Could never be so; still he holds his temper,
And 'tis the same still with no difference
He brought his father's corpse to th' grave with;
He laughed thus then, you know.
FIRST COURTIER Ay, he may laugh, my lord;
That shows but how he glories in his cunning,
And perhaps done more to advance his wit,
Than to express affection to his father,
That only he has overreached the law.
SIMONIDES
He tells you right, my lord; his own cousin-german
Revealed it first to me, a free-tongued woman,
And very excellent at telling secrets.
DUKE
If a contempt can be so neatly carried,
It gives me cause of wonder.
SIMONIDES Troth, my lord,
'Twill prove a delicate cozening, I believe;
I'd have no scrivener offer to come near it.
DUKE
Cleanthes.
CLEANTHES
My loved lord.
DUKE [*aside*] Not moved a whit,
Constant to light'ning still.—'Tis strange to meet you
Upon a ground so unfrequented, sir.

64.1 ***Exit…still*** THIS EDITION; *not in* BELL. Other editions call for Leonides to exit at l. 65 or for Hippolita to exit with him and return at l. 67.1.
66 **hunting** hunt
76 **light** cheerful; frivolous
78 **merry** COXETER; merrry BELL
88 **cousin-german** COXETER; Cofen germen BELL
89 **me, a free-tongued woman** What modern grammar would call Simonides's 'misplaced modifier' is significant, and may effeminize him further.
91 **neatly carried** cleverly or dexterously enacted. To *carry* could mean: 1) to conduct one's body in a certain way; 2) to succeed ('carry the day'); 3) to bear a corpse to burial.
94 **scrivener** notary; professional copyist
96 **Constant to light'ning** continuing his light-heartedness
light'ning BELL (lightning); lightening COXETER; Lightness MASON+

101 **vicïous** bad, harmful, a vice (without the modern sense of violence); marred by a defect, illegal (legal term)
105 **proportion** i.e. of mirth and sadness
118 **it... fadge** something's happening. *fadge* = suit, succeed.
132 **[*apart to Cleanthes*]** Since the on-stage audience may be hearing (and is certainly interpreting) these exchanges between Cleanthes and Hippolita, they are not *asides* in the usual sense; see 1.1.222–3.
133 **Speak... sir** BELL's lack of commas allows for several meanings: 'speak something good, sir', or 'speak something, good sir'.

This does not fit your passion; you're for mirth
Or I mistake you much.

CLEANTHES
But finding it
Grow to a noted imperfection in me—
For anything too much is vicïous—
I come to these disconsolate walks, of purpose
Only to dull and take away the edge on't.
I ever had a greater zeal to sadness,
A natural proportion, I confess, my lord,
Before that cheerful accident fell out,
If I may call a father's funeral cheerful
Without wrong done to duty or my love.

DUKE
It seems, then, you take pleasure i' these walks, sir.

CLEANTHES
Contemplative content I do, my lord.
They bring into my mind oft meditations
So sweetly precïous, that in the parting
I find a shower of grace upon my cheeks,
They take their leave so feelingly—

DUKE
So, sir—

CLEANTHES
Which is a kind of grave delight, my lord.

DUKE
And I've small cause, Cleanthes, t'afford you
The least delight that has a name.

CLEANTHES
My lord.

SIMONIDES
Now it begins to fadge.

FIRST COURTIER
Peace, thou art so greedy, Sim.

DUKE
In your excess of joy you have expressed
Your rancour and contempt against my law.
Your smiles deserve fining; you've professed
Derision openly, e'en to my face,
Which might be death, a little more incensed.
You do not come for any freedom here,
But for a project of your own.
But all that's known to be contentful to thee
Shall in the use prove deadly; your life's mine
If ever thy presumption do but lead thee
Into these walks again—ay, or that woman.
I'll have 'em watched o' purpose.

FIRST COURTIER
Now, now, his colour ebbs and flows.

SIMONIDES
Mark hers too.

HIPPOLITA [*apart to Cleanthes*]
O, who shall bring food to the poor old man now?
Speak somewhat good, sir, or we're lost forever!

CLEANTHES [*apart to Hippolita*]
O, you did wondrous ill to call me again.
There are not words to help us. If I entreat,
'Tis found; that will betray us worse than silence.
Prithee, let heaven alone, and let's say nothing.

FIRST COURTIER [*to the Duke*]
You've struck 'em dumb, my lord.

SIMONIDES
Look how guilt looks.
I would not have that fear upon my flesh

To save ten fathers.
CLEANTHES [*apart to Hippolita*]
He is safe still, is he not?
HIPPOLITA [*apart to Cleanthes*]
O you do ill to doubt it.
CLEANTHES [*apart to Hippolita*]
Thou'rt all goodness.
SIMONIDES [*to the Duke*]
Now does your grace believe?
DUKE 'Tis too apparent.
Search, make a speedy search, for the imposture
Cannot be far off by the fear it sends.
CLEANTHES
Ha!
SIMONIDES
H'as the lapwing's cunning, I'm afraid, my lord,
That cries most when she's farthest from the nest.
CLEANTHES
O we're betrayed.
HIPPOLITA Betrayed, sir.
SIMONIDES See, my lord,
It comes out more and more still.
Exeunt Courtiers and Simonides
CLEANTHES Bloody thief,
Come from that place; 'tis sacred homicide,
'Tis not for thy adulterate hands to touch it.
HIPPOLITA
O miserable virtue, what distress
Art thou in at this minute?
CLEANTHES Help me, thunder,
For my power's lost. Angels, shoot plagues and help
me.
Why are these men in health and I so heart-sick?
Or why should nature have that power in me
To levy up a thousand bleeding sorrows
And not one comfort?—only makes me lie
Like the poor mockery of an earthquake here,
Panting with horror, and have not so much force
In all my vengeance to shake a villain off o' me.
Enter Courtiers, Simonides, Leonides
HIPPOLITA
Use him gently and heaven will love you for't.
CLEANTHES
Father, O Father, now I see thee full
In thy affection. Thou'rt a man of sorrow
But reverently becom'st it; that's my comfort.
Extremity was never better graced
Than with that look of thine. O, let me look still,
For I shall lose it; all my joy and strength
Is e'en eclipsed together.
[*He kneels before the Duke*]
I transgressed
Your law, my lord; let me receive the sting on't.
Be once just, sir, and let the offender die;
He's innocent in all, and I am guilty.
LEONIDES
Your grace knows when affection only speaks
Truth is not always there; his love would draw

145 **lapwing's** bird that protects its nest by leading intruders noisily away from it

149 **sacred** accursed (*OED* 6). Audiences might also have heard the contrary resonance of 'holy' (the usual sense).

163 **a man of sorrow** 'He is despised and reiected of men, a man of sorrows, and acquainted with griefe' (Isaiah 53:3, *Authorized Version*, 1611); in Christian readings, the passage was taken to prophesy the treatment of Jesus of Nazareth at the time of his trial and execution.

An undeserved misery on his youth,
And wrong a peace resolved, on both parts sinful.
'Tis I am guilty of my own concealment,
And like a worldly coward injured heaven
With fear to go to't; now I see my fault,
And am prepared with joy to suffer for't.

DUKE [*to Executioner*]
Go give him quick dispatch; let him see death,
[*To Cleanthes*] And your presumption, sir, shall come to judgement.

Exeunt [Duke, Courtiers, Simonides, and Executioner,] with Leonides

HIPPOLITA
He's going—O he's gone, sir.

CLEANTHES
Let me rise.

HIPPOLITA
Why do you not then, and follow?

CLEANTHES
I strive for't.
Is there no hand of pity that will ease me
And take this villain from my heart awhile?
[*He rises*]

HIPPOLITA
Alas, he's gone.

CLEANTHES
A worse supplies his place then,
A weight more pond'rous, I cannot follow.

HIPPOLITA
O misery of affliction.

CLEANTHES
They will stay
Till I can come; they must be so good ever,
Though they be ne'er so cruel.
My last leave must be taken, think o' that,
And this last blessing given; I will not lose
That for a thousand consorts.

HIPPOLITA
That hope's wretched.

CLEANTHES
The inutterable stings of fortune!
All griefs are to be borne, save this alone;
This like a headlong torrent overturns the frame of nature,
For he that gives us life first, as a father,
Locks all his natural sufferings in our blood too;
The sorrows that he feels are on our heads:
They are incorporate to us.

HIPPOLITA
Noble sir.

CLEANTHES
Let me behold thee well.

HIPPOLITA
Sir?

CLEANTHES
Thou shouldst be good,
Or thou'rt a dangerous substance to be lodged
So near the heart of man.

HIPPOLITA
What means this, dear sir?

CLEANTHES
To thy trust only was this blessèd secret
Kindly committed. 'Tis destroyed; thou seest
What follows to be thought on't.

HIPPOLITA
Miserable!
Why, here's th'unhappiness of woman still,
That having forfeited in old times their trust

174 **undeserved misery** BELL's spelling, 'undeservd misery', suggests a non-metrical pronunciation; the line could be spoken iambically with 'undeservèd mis'ry'.

185.1 ***He rises*** Cleanthes may rise here, or perhaps at ll. 188–9 or 194. BELL does not indicate his kneeling or rising; placing the stage direction here reads Hippolita's speech as meaning 'it's too late now anyway'.

192 **this** BELL; his COXETER

193 **consorts** friends, associates, perhaps Hippolita (see 58).

196 **headlong torrent overturns** referencing the mode of execution, the father as 'head', and the world upside-down; see 1.1.107, 1.1.482. BELL's metrically long line may echo Cleanthes's point here.

198 **blood too** BELL (·~, to). Most editions end the line with *blood*. See next note.

199 **on our heads** THIS EDITION; our heads BELL; our Heart's MASON; our heart's too GIFFORD

200 **incorporate to** embodied in, made a part of (1.1.458–63)

201 CLEANTHES COXETER (Clean.); *Cleaa.* BELL
thee MASON; him BELL. Strictly speaking, BELL's pronoun does not make sense, although (in this context of 'incorporate' emotions) it resonates with Cleanthes's inability here and elsewhere to distinguish fully his father, wife, and self.

208 **in . . . trust** a reference to Eve that links Hippolita to Eugenia's untrustworthiness (2.2.200, 3.2.28). The placing of Eugenia's entrance in BELL (marginally, next to Hippolita's couplet) focuses the couplet's commentary on Eugenia.

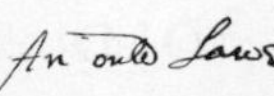

Enter Eugenia

Now makes their faiths suspected that are just.

CLEANTHES
What shall I say to all my sorrows, then,
That look for satisfaction?

EUGENIA Ha, ha, ha, cousin!

CLEANTHES
How ill dost thou become this time!

EUGENIA Ha, ha, ha!
Why that's but your opinion; a young wench
Becomes the time at all times.

CLEANTHES [ ]

EUGENIA
Now, coz, we're even; an you be remembered,
You left a strumpet and a whore at home with me,
And such fine field-bed words, which could not cost
you
Less than a father.

CLEANTHES Is it come that way?

EUGENIA Had you an uncle,
He should go the same way too.

CLEANTHES O eternity,
What monster is this fiend in labour with?

EUGENIA
An ass-colt with two heads; that's she and you.
I will not lose so glorious a revenge,
Not to be understood in't: I betrayed him,
And now we're even; you'd best keep you so.

CLEANTHES
Is there not poison yet enough to kill me?

HIPPOLITA
O sir, forgive me, it was I betrayed him.

CLEANTHES How?

HIPPOLITA I.

CLEANTHES
The fellow of my heart—'twill speed me then.

HIPPOLITA
Her tears that never wept, and mine own pity
E'en cozened me together, and stole from me
This secret, which fierce death should not have
purchased.

CLEANTHES
Nay then, we're at an end; all we are false ones,
And ought to suffer: I was false to wisdom
In trusting woman, thou wert false to faith
In uttering of the secret, [*to Eugenia*] and thou false
To goodness in deceiving such a pity.
We are all tainted someway, but thou worst,
And for thy infectious spots ought to die first.
[*Cleanthes draws his weapon*]

EUGENIA
Pray turn your weapon, sir, upon your mistress;
I come not so ill-friended. Rescue, servants!
Enter Simonides and Courtiers

CLEANTHES
Are you so whorishly provided?

214 CLEANTHES THIS EDITION; *not in* BELL. In BELL, there are two consecutive speeches assigned to *Eug.* (4.2.212–14, 4.2.214–18). Either a speech by Cleanthes has been omitted (the conjecture here), an extra speech heading has been inserted in a continuous speech, or a revised speech was added and the former version left undeleted (PRICE). There are other signs that the compositor may have been compressing text in the latter half of the last page of the gathering (H4^{v}) (the two parts of 4.2.218 are printed on a single line); the conjectured missing line may have been intended to be printed on the same line as 4.2.214. The relatively regular metrical context provides further evidence for a missing part-line.

217 **field-bed** portable bed for use outdoors (perhaps signifying promiscuity)

222 **in labour** working with; giving birth to

225 **betrayed** COXETER; betray BELL

226 **you'd** BELL (y'ad)

230 I *I* could also indicate the word *Ay*.

233 **cozened** On the homonyms *cozen/cousin*, see 2.2.142, 2.2.182.

240 **someway** BELL (some way). Somehow, in some way

242 **weapon** The first of the ensuing scene's many equations of weapon and penis (l. 245).

SIMONIDES
Yes, sir, she has more weapons at command than
one.
EUGENIA
Put forward, man, thou art most sure to have me.
SIMONIDES [*aside*]
I shall be surer if I keep behind though.
EUGENIA Now, servants, show your loves.
SIMONIDES [*aside*] I'll show my love too, afar off.
EUGENIA
I love to be so courted; woo me there.
SIMONIDES [*aside*]
I love to keep good weapons though ne'er fought;
I'm sharper set within than I am without.
[*Cleanthes and Courtiers fight*]
HIPPOLITA
O gentlemen! Cleanthes!
EUGENIA Fight! Upon him!
HIPPOLITA
Thy thirst of blood proclaims thee now a strumpet.
EUGENIA
'Tis dainty, next to procreation fitting;
I'd either be destroying men or getting.
Enter Officers
FIRST OFFICER
Forbear, on your allegiance, gentlemen.
He's the Duke's prisoner, and we seize upon him
To answer this contempt against the law.
CLEANTHES
I obey fate in all things.
HIPPOLITA Happy rescue!
SIMONIDES [*aside*] I would you'd seized upon him a minute sooner; 't'ad saved me a cut finger. I wonder how I came by't, for I never put my hand forth, I'm sure. I think my own sword did cut it, if truth were known, maybe the wire in the handle. I have lived these five-and-twenty years and never knew what colour my blood was before. I never durst eat oysters, nor cut peck loaves.
EUGENIA
You have shown your spirits, gentlemen,—[*to Simonides*] but you
Have cut your finger.
SIMONIDES Ay, the wedding-finger too, a pox on't.
FIRST COURTIER You'll prove a bawdy batchelor, Sim, to have a cut upon your finger, before you are married.
SIMONIDES I'll never draw sword again to have such a jest put upon me. *Exeunt*
Finis Actus Quartus

5.1

Incipit Actus Quintus
[*With the*] *sword and mace carried before them* [*by officers and guards*], *enter Simonides, and the Courtiers*
SIMONIDES [*to officers*]
Be ready with your prisoner; we'll sit instantly

252 **sharper set** more eager; more sexually desirous
256 **I'd** COXETER; 'de BELL. BELL has what appears to be an apostrophe or dot in initial position in the line. In FOLGER, a minim has been written in under the dot and an apostrophe added; the interpretation by this unknown reader is thus: 'i'de'.
getting conceiving; having sex
268 **peck loaves** loaves of bread made from a peck of flour
273 **cut** (with a pun on *cunt*)
275.1 ***Quartus*** BELL (*Quarti*)
5.1.0.1 ***Incipit Actus Quintus*** THIS EDITION; Act. V. Scen. I. BELL
0.2 **sword and mace** magistrates' symbols of office

And rise before 'leven, or when we please.
Shall we not, fellow judges?

FIRST *or* SECOND COURTIER 'Tis committed
All to our power, censure, and pleasure, now
The Duke hath made us chief lords of this sessions,
And we may speak by fits or sleep by turns.

SIMONIDES
Leave that to us, but, whatsoe'er we do,
The prisoner shall be sure to be condemned;
Sleeping or waking we are resolved on that
Before we set upon him.

SECOND COURTIER Make you question?
If not Cleanthes, and our enemy,
Nay, a concealer of his father, too,
A vile example in these days of youth—

SIMONIDES
If they were given to follow such examples,
But sure I think they are not; howsoe'er,
'Twas wickedly attempted, that's my judgement,
And it shall pass whilst I am in power to sit.
Never by prince were such young judges made,
But now the cause requires it, if you mark it:
He must make young or none, for all the old ones
Hereafter he hath sent a-fishing, and
My father's one, I humbly thank his highness.

Enter Eugenia

FIRST COURTIER Widow?

EUGENIA
You almost hit my name—no, gentlemen,
You come so wondrous near it I admire you
For your judgement.

SIMONIDES My wife that must be, she.

EUGENIA
My husband goes upon his last hour now.

FIRST COURTIER
On his last legs, I am sure.

EUGENIA September the seventeenth,
I will not bate an hour on't, and tomorrow
His latest hour's expired.

SECOND COURTIER Bring him to judgement.
The jury's panelled and the verdict given
Ere he appears; we have ta'en course for that—

SIMONIDES
And officers to attach the grey young man,
The youth of fourscore. Be of comfort, lady;
We shall no longer bosom January,
For that I will take order, and provide
For you a lusty April.

EUGENIA The month that ought indeed
To go before May.

FIRST COURTIER Do as we have said:
Take a strong guard and bring him into court,
Lady Eugenia; see this charge performed,
That having his life forfeited by the law
He may relieve his soul.

EUGENIA Willingly.
From shaven chins never came better justice
Than these ne'er touched by razor.

2 **And** COXETER; an BELL
'leven BELL (leaven); Eleven COXETER. Eleven, punning on *leaven* (yeast)

3 **fellow** MASON (Fellow-judges); follow BELL. While unlikely, BELL's reading might be retained by reading *follow* as 'punish, prosecute' (legal term).
FIRST *or* SECOND COURTIER THIS EDITION; *Cour.* BELL. Given BELL's ambiguous speech heading, either Courtier could have spoken the speech on stage; the Courtiers are indistinguishable from each other and, increasingly in the scene, from Simonides. Most editions give the speech to First Courtier.

5 **sessions** series of sittings of a court

10 **Before . . . him** An anticipatory stage direction in the margin of this line in BELL (not included here) instructs the actor playing Eugenia to prepare for his/her entrance. On anticipatory directions, see 4.2.7.
set upon attack, assail; but also 'sit upon' (the spellings overlap in the period), meaning 'decide his case'

11 **If** BELL; Is't TAYLOR *conj.*
our MASON; one BELL; an GIFFORD

17 **it shall pass** this judgement will be rendered (legal term)

20–1 **all . . . sent** He has (by his law) sent all the men who will be old in the future ('hereafter') to their deaths

21 **Hereafter** THIS EDITION; Her father BELL; Their fathers DYCE; *not in* COXETER (which begins the line 'He hath . . .')

23 **Widow** COXETER; Widdows BELL

29 **bate** delay (1.1.309)

32 **Ere** MASON; Ever BELL
ta'en BELL (tane)

35 **bosom January** protect the aged

35–8 **January . . . May** In Chaucer's 'Merchant's Tale', an old man named 'January' marries a young woman named 'May'.

37 **April.** Anticipatory stage direction: 'Lifander *and* Guardian' in the margin. PRICE views the distance between this anticipatory direction and the later entrance (at l. 83.1) as evidence of a revision that added new material (133). Alternatively, the direction might suggest that some or all of ll. 44–83 was cut (TAYLOR *conj.*).

44 **ne'er . . . razor** MASON *conj.*, GIFFORD; new tucht by reafon BELL.

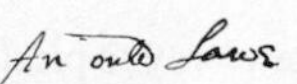

SIMONIDES What you do,
Do suddenly, we charge you, for we purpose
To make but a short sessions.
[*Exit Eugenia and a Guard*]

Enter Hippolita

A new business!

FIRST COURTIER
The fair Hippolita, now what's your suit?

HIPPOLITA
Alas, I know not how to style you yet;
To call you judges doth not suit your years,
Nor heads and brains show more antiquity,
Yet sway yourselves with equity and truth,
And I'll proclaim you reverent, and repeat:
'Once in my lifetime I have seen grave heads
Placed upon young men's shoulders.'

SECOND COURTIER Hark, she flouts us,
And thinks to make us monstrous.

HIPPOLITA Prove not so,
For yet methinks you bear the shapes of men,
Though nothing more than merely beauty feigns
To make you appear angels. But—if, crimson,
Your name and power with blood and cruelty
Suppress fair virtue and enlarge foul vice,
Both against heaven and nature draw your sword,
Make either will or humour turn the soul
Of your created greatness, and in that
Oppose all goodness—I must tell you, there
You're more than monstrous; in the very act,
You change yourself to devils.

FIRST COURTIER She's a witch;
Hark, she begins to conjure.

SIMONIDES Time, you see,
Is short; much business now on foot. Shall I
Give her her answer?

SECOND COURTIER None upon the bench
More learnedly can do it.

SIMONIDES Hee, hee, hem—then list:
I wonder at thine impudence, young huswife,
That thou dar'st plead for such a base offender.
Conceal a father past his time to die—
What son and heir would have done this but he?

FIRST COURTIER
I vow not I.

HIPPOLITA Because ye are parricides!
And how can comfort be derived from such
That pity not their fathers?

SECOND COURTIER
You are fresh and fair: practise young women's ends;
When husbands are distressed, provide them friends.

SIMONIDES
I'll set him forward for thee without fee;
Some wives would pay for such a courtesy.

HIPPOLITA
Times of amazement! What duty, goodness dwell?
I sought for charity, but knock at hell. *Exit*

47 **suit** COXETER; suits BELL

48 **style** name, address; *style of the court* = the manner of proceeding in a particular court (legal term)

50 **heads and brains** the hair of the head and the reasonings of the brain. GIFFORD's emendation makes for a tidy reading, but it does *make* that reading, and it raises the question of where, for an editor or reader of BELL, the line lies between editing the text and improving it in cases where it is already intelligible. Is the play's trope here a doubled metonymy ('heads' stands for 'hair', 'brains' stands for 'thoughts'), rather than supplementarity (two kinds of hair—heads and beards)?
brains BELL; beards GIFFORD+

52 **reverent** respectful; or, worthy of respect (reverend). BELL's spelling 'reverent' could be used for either meaning.

57 **beauty feigns** THIS EDITION; beautifeaus BELL. This emendation imagines that the text from which BELL was typeset read 'beauty feans', on the basis of the following evidence: *OED* gives *feane* as a possible sixteenth-century form of *feign*; BELL routinely collapses spacing between words; BELL occasionally inverts type, here *u* for *n* (see also 1.1.380). Some other emendations: beautiful COXETER; beauty serves GIFFORD; mercy beautifies BULLEN (for BELL's *meerly beautifeaus*).
feigns pretends

58–66 The syntax of this speech is difficult; this version of BELL's text interprets 'name and power' as the subject of an extended dependent clause beginning 'if'. In other words: 'If your name and power (crimson with blood and cruelty) does all these horrible things, you are worse than monsters and you change yourselves from angels to devils.'

60 **foul** THIS EDITION; of old BELL; old COXETER; bold GIFFORD. This emendation represents something as likely as GIFFORD's in relation to BELL's manuscript copy, and seems stronger on the grounds of the common antithesis *fair/foul*.

75 **parricides** murderers of parents or other close relatives

76 **derived** BELL (derived). BELL's spelling suggests trisyllabic pronunciation.

80 **for thee without fee** GIFFORD; fee thee | *without fee*. BELL ('*without fee*' appears in the right margin of the next line, as if a stage direction); without Fee COXETER. TAYLOR conjectures a misinterpreted proof correction.
fee legal fee; bribe

82 **What duty, goodness dwell** BELL (what duty goodness dwell); where doth goodness dwell BULLEN *conj.*, SHAW; where do your Goodness dwell MASON. Other editions that retain BELL here interpret this phrase as Hippolita's incomplete thought; this seems unlikely in a couplet, though *dwell* in the absolute sense proposed here (next note) is not an easy reading either.
dwell remain

84 SIMONIDES In contrast to its usual practice of abbreviating speech headings, BELL spells Simonides's full name before this speech.

86 **strives** BELL; strikes GIFFORD (*conj.*), BULLEN

91 **manumissions** releases from slavery

93 **feed on snakes** Eating snakes was thought to restore youth.

100 **elbow-healths** drinks (*health* = a toast drunk in someone's honour)

103 **peppered** MASON *conj.*, GIFFORD; prepard BELL. *Peppered* = trounced, ruined. The best case that might be made for BELL's *prepard* is that it reads ironically (i.e. 'I was almost cooked'); there might also be a resonance of *pared* (= cut, trimmed), a word closely related to *prepare*.

took Audience members might have heard here a pun on a kind of weapon; BELL's 'took' is a spelling of *tuck*, a slender, pointed, thrusting sword, often described as 'long' (and thus resembling the 'third veny' of the earlier contest).

104 **Long sword** THIS EDITION; Being ſwolne BELL; Longsword | Being swol'n MASON. BELL's verb ('had…took') seems to lack an object, supplied here. This emendation expands MASON's suggestion, interpreting BELL's 'Being swolne' as a compositor's misreading of a similar series of graphic shapes ('Long sword') in the hypothetical manuscript copy. The emendation makes sense of BELL's unidiomatic use of 'took' (otherwise unexplained) and completes Simonides's review of the 'weapons' in his earlier drinking contest with Lisander.

104.1–5.1.107 *A flourish*…**Lisander** In BELL the complicated passage spans a page break (pp. 61–62/I3–I3[v]) and reads:

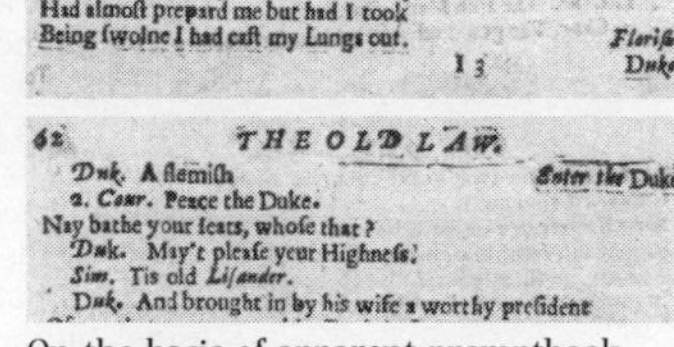

Had almoſt prepard me but had I took
Being ſwolne I had caſt my Lungs out. *Floriſh.* Duke.
I 3

62 THE OLD LAW.
Duk. A flemiſh *Enter the* Duke.
2. *Cour.* Peace the Duke.
Nay bathe your ſeats, whoſe that?
Duk. May't pleaſe your Highneſs,
Sim. Tis old *Liſander.*
Duk. And brought in by his wife a worthy preſident

On the basis of apparent promptbook annotations and anticipatory and doubled stage directions elsewhere in BELL, the hypothesis here is that the text from which BELL was typeset included two sets of stage directions, one in the right margin (Florish | Enter the Duke) and another in the body of the text (Duke. A Florish). If so, the editing process here simply eliminates one. (The misalignment in speech headings that seems to have resulted is discussed in notes below, ll. 105–7.) An alternative hypothesis, more difficult to explain in terms of hypothetical manuscript copy, might make a case for BELL's 'A flemish' as an intended part of Simonides's speech somehow displaced down one line and associated with the Duke's entrance. Hypothetically, as a description of the third veny ('but had I took | A Flemish', meaning 'a Flemish one', 'a Flemish veny'), the line would thus continue scene 3.2's punning on Dutch/German nationality (*Flemish* = 'Low Dutch'), drinking, and weapons ('fleming knives').

104.1 *A flourish* COXETER (Flourish.); *Duk.* A flemiſh BELL

105–8 For several lines, BELL's speech headings are out of alignment with the lines that would seem appropriate for these characters to speak (see photoquote above). The version here argues that the speech headings have simply been misplaced down one line.

106 DUKE COXETER; *not in* BELL, which continues the speech as assigned to Second Courtier. See note to l. 106–7.

take D (*conj.* in note to MASON), SHAW; bathe BELL; keep MASON *conj.*; back 't' GIFFORD

SIMONIDES COXETER; *Duk.* BELL; 2 Court. GIFFORD

108 **precedent** Spelled 'president' in BELL, the line may hint that Eugenia has (inappropriately, in one moral paradigm) 'presided' over her husband by turning him in; see 1.1.304.

Enter Eugenia, with Lisander [as a] prisoner, [and] a Guard

SIMONIDES
Eugenia, come.—Command a second guard
To bring Cleanthes in. We'll not sit long;
My stomach strives to dinner. [*Exit a Guard*]

EUGENIA
Now, servants—may a lady be so bold
To call your power so low?

SIMONIDES
A mistress may;
She can make all things low; then in that language
There can be no offence.

EUGENIA
The time's now come
Of manumissions; take him into bonds,
And I am then at freedom.

SECOND COURTIER
This the man?
He hath left of late to feed on snakes;
His beard's turned white again.

FIRST COURTIER
Is't possible these gouty legs danced lately,
And shattered in a galliard?

EUGENIA
Jealousy
And fear of death can work strange prodigies.

SECOND COURTIER
The nimble fencer this, that made me tear
And traverse 'bout the chamber?

SIMONIDES
Ay, and gave me
Those elbow-healths, the hangman take him for't!
They had almost fetched my heart out; the Dutch veny
I swallowed pretty well, but the half-pike
Had almost peppered me; but had I took
Long sword, I had cast my lungs out.

A flourish. Enter the Duke [and Executioner]

SECOND COURTIER Peace, the Duke.

DUKE
Nay, take your seats. Who's that?

SIMONIDES
May't please your highness,
'Tis old Lisander.

DUKE
And brought in by his wife: a worthy precedent
Of one that no way would offend the law,
And should not pass away without remark.
[*To Lisander*] You have been looked for long.

LISANDER
But never fit
To die till now, my lord; my sins and I
Have been but newly parted, much ado
I had to get them leave me, or be taught
That difficult lesson how to learn to die.
I never thought there had been such an act,
And 'tis the only discipline we are born for;
All studies as are are but as circular lines,
And death the centre where they must all meet.—
I now can look upon thee, erring woman,
And not be vexed with jealousy; on young men,
And no way envy their delicious health,

125–5.1.135.3 **And...*him*** This passage in BELL presents a cluster of editorial problems:

Sim. And know how to dispose him that my Liege
Hath been before determined, you confesse
Your selfe of full age.
Lis. Yes and prepard to inherit
Hip. Your place above—Duke—away to death with him
Sim. Of which the hangmans strength *Cleanthes Guard.*
Shall put him in possession, tis still guard
To take me willing and in mind to die.
And such are when the earth growes weary of them
Most fit for heaven, the Court shall make his Mittimus
And send him thither presently ith mean time.
Enter a Guard with Cleanthes, Hippollita *weeping after him.*

Though it is impossible to say why BELL's text takes this form, the reconstruction in the text column reflects the hypothesis that an anticipatory stage direction at the left margin of 5.1.127–30 in the manuscript copy for BELL was twice interpreted as part of the text: that is, 1) what BELL gives as a speech heading ('*Hip.*') may have been part of the marginal entry '*Cleanthes Guard*', since the three enter together a few lines later; and 2) the word *guard* at the end of the next line ('tis still guard') repeats the final word of the same direction. At the same time, a short speech of the Duke's, possibly in the margin of the copy, has been printed in the midst of these lines; see note to l. 128–9.

126 **determined** BELL (determined), which suggests four syllables.

128 SIMONIDES **Your** THIS EDITION (Taylor); *Hip.* Your BELL; *Eug.* Your COXETER+. All editions give the speech to Eugenia, though her name appears nowhere in this vicinity in BELL.

129 DUKE COXETER (after 5.1.135); Duke— BELL. BELL's 'Duke' is not clearly marked as a speech heading (see photoquote above), nor is there a clear place to situate it within the dialogue. COXETER and all later editions place the short speech after 'mean time' (l. 135); the version here interprets it as an interruption and maintains its location in BELL. Since the short speech appears at a moment when BELL may be confusing the text and marginal notations of its copy, the short speech may have been a later addition. Whenever or wherever it appeared in the hypothetical manuscript copy, the speech raises questions crucial to an interpretation of the Duke and his political agency. The Duke explicitly avoids intervention in this trial scene (see ll. 159–61), at least until l. 245. But he does pronounce a parallel execution order at 4.2.180.

131 **good** THIS EDITION; guard BELL; cared GIFFORD; grace TAYLOR *conj.* The emendation here hypothesizes that the compositor mistakenly substituted the similar word 'guard' from the anticipatory stage direction typeset in the previous line (right margin) of BELL. See photoquote above.

132 **'em** THIS EDITION (Taylor); me BELL. Without this emendation (which hypothesizes the transposition of two letters in BELL), the pronoun problem seems to require the rearrangement of several speech headings; most editions, following GIFFORD, assign ''Tis still...heaven' to Lisander and resume Simonides's speech with 'The court...'. COXETER and MASON simply delete ''Tis still...die'.

134 **mittimus** a warrant from the court sending a convict to prison (legal term)

Pleasure, and strength, all which were once mine own,
And mine must be theirs one day.
DUKE [*to Eugenia and judges*] You have tamed him.
SIMONIDES
And know how to dispose him; that, my liege,
Hath been before determined. [*To Lisander*] You confess
Yourself of full age?
LISANDER Yes, and prepared to inherit—
SIMONIDES Your place above—
DUKE [*to Executioner*] Away to death with him.
SIMONIDES Of which the hangman's strength
Shall put him in possession. 'Tis still good
To take 'em willing and in mind to die.
And such are, when the earth grows weary of them,
Most fit for heaven; the court shall make his mittimus
And send him thither presently.
[*Exit Lisander and Guard*]
I'th' mean time—
Enter a Guard with Cleanthes, Hippolita weeping after him
So, see, another person brought to the bar.
FIRST COURTIER The arch-malefactor.
SECOND COURTIER
The grand offender, the most refractory
To all good orders; 'tis Cleanthes, he—
SIMONIDES
That would have sons grave fathers ere their fathers
Be sent unto their graves.
DUKE There will be expectation
In your severe proceedings against him,
His act being so capital—
SIMONIDES Fearful and bloody;
Therefore we charge these women leave the court,
Lest they should sound to hear it.
EUGENIA I in expectation
Of a most happy freedom. *Exit*
HIPPOLITA I with the apprehension
Of a most sad and desolate widowhood. *Exit*

138 **offender** COXETER; offenders BELL. COXETER's emendation either captures the rhetorical spirit of the passage, or produces one. Alternatively, with the emendation in l. 139, BELL's sentence makes sense and could be modernized as follows: 'The grand offender's the most refractory | to all good orders. 'Tis Cleanthes....'
refractory rebellious, unyielding

139 **all** COXETER; call BELL

139–41 **'tis...graves** Simonides and the Courtiers often finish or continue each other's sentences; the collaborative quality of their discourse (the ways in which any given speech cannot be said to be 'characteristic' of a particular character) makes reassigning speeches necessarily tentative in cases where speech headings seem to be inappropriately attached. See l. 3. The issue of character exchangeability extends to Creon/Cleanthes (5.1.374–81), and, most significantly, to Cleanthes/Simonides/Courtiers (5.1.267).

142 **proceedings** COXETER; pooceedings BELL

143 **capital** BELL (Capitall). BELL's capitalization may inscribe an orthographic pun.

145 **sound** THIS EDITION; stand BELL; start MASON; swoon GIFFORD+. *sound* = faint. The emendation is supported by Eugenia's and Hippolita's swoonings at the reversal of the situation later in the scene (ll. 314.1 and 336.1, respectively); at l. 314.1, BELL uses the form 'sounds'. If this emendation is correct, the manuscript copy for BELL may have read 'swond' (TAYLOR *conj.*) or 'sound'. The only rationale for BELL's *stand* seems to be the meaning 'have the opportunity' (*OED*, v., 16c).

145, 146 **I** i.e., I ['leave the court']

FIRST COURTIER
We bring him to the bar.
SECOND COURTIER Hold up your hand, sir.
CLEANTHES
More reverence to the place than to the persons.
To the one, I offer up a palm
Of duty and obedience, showed as to heaven,
Imploring justice, which was never wanting
Upon that bench whilst there our fathers sat.
But unto you, my hand's contracted thus,
As threat'ning vengeance against murderers,
For they that kill in thought shed innocent blood.—
With pardon to your highness; too much passion
Made me forget your presence and the place
I now am called to.
DUKE All our majesty
And power we have to pardon or condemn
Is now conferred on them.
SIMONIDES [*to Cleanthes*] And these we'll use
Little to thine advantage.
CLEANTHES I expect it,
And as to these I look no mercy from,
And, much less, shame to intreat it, I thus now
Submit me to the emblems of your power—I mean
The sword and bench—but, my most reverend judges,
Ere you proceed to sentence, for I know
You have given me lost, will you resolve me one
thing?
FIRST COURTIER
So it be briefly questioned.
SECOND COURTIER Show your honour;
Day spends itself apace.
CLEANTHES My lords, it shall.
Resolve me, then: where are your filial tears,
Your mourning habits and sad hearts become,
That should attend your father's funeral?
Though the strick law—which I will not accuse,
Because a subject—snatched away their lives,
It doth not bar you to lament their deaths.
Or if you cannot spare one sad suspire,
It doth not bid you laugh them to their graves,
Lay subtle trains to antedate their years,
To be the sooner seized of their estates.
O time of age, where's that Aeneas now
Who, letting all his jewels to the flames,
Forgetting country, kindred, treasure, friends,
Fortunes, and all things save the name of son,
Which you so much forget—godlike Aeneas,
Who took his bedrid father on his back,
And with that sacred load (to him no burden)
Hewed out his way through blood, through fire,
Through even all the armèd streets of bright-burning
Troy,
Only to save a father?
SIMONIDES We have no leisure now
To hear lessons read from Virgil; we are past school,
And all this time thy judges.

150 **a palm** Many editions insert a word to complete this line metrically, noting the apparent error in the next line; GIFFORD, e.g., has '[spreading] palm'. But BELL's 'ſhowdu s' in the next line provides little help in supplementing a perceived deficit in this one.

151 **showed as** COXETER; ſhowdu s BELL; as GIFFORD; showed [th]us SHAW

153 **there** BELL (their)
our THIS EDITION (Taylor); own BELL. 'Owr' and 'owre' are possible spellings of *our* in the period; the emendation hypothesizes that the compositor exchanged two very similar words.

159 **our** COXETER; one BELL

163 **as...from** i.e., as to these judges, from [whom] I expect no mercy
from BELL; from them COXETER

164 **shame** THIS EDITION (Taylor); ſhowne BELL; mean GIFFORD+

165 **to** MASON; *not in* BELL. BELL's spacing between words is not uniform, and it may be significant that there is slightly more space between BELL's 'me' and 'the', possibly indicating that a word was thought missing, or fell out of the forme, though there is not room for two letters.

169 **honour** respect, high esteem (i.e. to the court). DYCE emends to 'humour'.

170 **shall** i.e., shall ['be briefly questioned']

171–2 **are...become** have...gone. (Modern English would say 'what has become of....')

173–97 For much of BELL's p. 64/I4^{v}, some of the types have apparently tilted themselves in the forme so that, in all copies consulted, many words and letters, especially in Cleanthes's speech on Aeneas, are printed at unusual angles. There is a less severe occurrence on BELL's p. 39/F4.

173 **father's funeral** BELL (fathers funerall). Editions have suggested a range of possibilities: Father's Funerals COXETER; fathers' funerals COLERIDGE; fathers' funeral SHAW.

174 **strick** swift, rapid (said of water, and thus resonating with the mode of execution); but also *strict* (inescapable, severe). BELL's spelling *strick* could be used for either word; all other editions modernize unnecessarily to *strict*, losing the resonance of the law's rapidity/haste/prematurity.

176 **you** MASON; them BELL

177 **suspire** sigh

179 **Lay subtle trains** create clever schemes, traps

180 **seized** BELL's spelling (ceaſ'd), a possible seventeenth-century spelling of *seized*, may nevertheless also carry the added resonance (not entirely intelligible syntactically) of 'stopped': the lives of the fathers have apparently ceased; the lives of the courtiers should cease (because of their actions); the courtiers should cease to inherit their fathers' estates, etc.

181 **Aeneas** This episode, in which Aeneas carries his father Anchises from Troy as it is being burned and conquered by the Greeks, is recounted in Book II of Virgil's *Aeneid*. Cleanthes's retelling effaces Aeneas's attention to his own son, whom he leads by the hand, and his wife, whom he returns to the burning city to find when she is left behind.

185 **godlike** COXETER; goe like BELL. The emendation (made in all editions except SHAW) is supported by the fact that Aeneas was the son of a goddess, and it addresses the problem of BELL's unusual syntax here. Nevertheless, a case could be made for retaining 'go like' in the sense of 'be guided by; follow the example of; conduct yourself as', or even 'walk, proceed (out of Troy) as' Aeneas did.

188–9 **Hewed...even** Following GIFFORD, several editions maintain BELL's third *through* at the end of l. 188 and add *arms*, since BELL's line seems to lack a syllable, in the midst of a speech that closely adheres to iambic pentameter. THIS EDITION relineates but does not add words to BELL's text.

SECOND COURTIER 'Tis fit
That we proceed to sentence.
FIRST COURTIER You are the mouth,
And now 'tis fit to open.
SIMONIDES Justice indeed
Should ever be close-eared, and open-mouthed;
That is, to hear him little, and speak much.
Lo, then, Cleanthes, there is none can be
A good son and a bad subject, for if princes
Be called the peoples' fathers, then the subjects
Are all his sons, and he that flouts the prince
Doth disobey his father; there you're gone.
FIRST COURTIER
And not to be recovered.
SIMONIDES And again—
SECOND COURTIER
If he be gone once call him not again.
SIMONIDES
I say: again, this act of thine expresses
A double disobedience: as our princes
Are fathers, so they are our sovereigns too,
And he that doth rebel against sovereignty
Doth commit treason in the height of degree,
And now thou art quite gone.
FIRST COURTIER Our brother in commission
Hath spoke his mind both learnedly and neatly,
And I can add but little; howsoever,
It shall send him packing.
He that begins a fault that wants example
Ought to be made example for the fault.
CLEANTHES
A fault? No longer can I hold myself
To hear vice upheld and virtue thrown down.
A fault, judge! Then I desire, where it lieth—
In those that are my judges or in me.
Heaven, stand on my side; pity, love and duty—
SIMONIDES
Where are they, sir, who sees them but yourself?
CLEANTHES Not you, and I am sure
You never had the gracious eyes to see them.
You think you arraign me, but I hope
To sentence you at the bar.
SECOND COURTIER That would show brave.
CLEANTHES
This were the judgement seat, we now would try
The heaviest crimes that ever made up
Unnaturalness in humanity.
You are found foul and guilty by a jury
Made of your fathers' curses, which have brought
Vengeance impending on you, and I now
Am forced to pronounce judgement on my judges.
The common laws of reason and of nature
Condemn you *ipso facto*; you are parricides,
And if you marry will beget the liar
Who, when you're grown to full maturity,
Will hurry you their fathers to their graves.
Like traitors, you take counsel from the living;
Of upright judgement you would rob the bench—

194–5 **Justice... open-mouthed** (rewriting the commonplace depiction of Justice as blind)

197 **Lo** BELL (Low)

198–201 **princes... father** 'The King towardes his people is rightly compared to a father of children, and to a head of a bodie composed of diuers members' (King James I, *The Trve Lawe of free Monarchies*, 1598, reprinted 1616). BELL reads 'peoples'; because early modern English orthography and pronunciation did not distinguish between singular and plural possessive, this could be either 'people's' or 'peoples''. The latter, chosen here, is in agreement with the plural 'princes' and 'fathers', under the assumption that in patriarchal discourse like James's one people could only have one father. The fluctuation between the singular and plural 'princes' of 198 and 200 is the crux of the political question the play wrestles with here: how many fathers/princes/authorities does one have? Is primary devotion owed to the political father, or the familial father? (See also the ambiguity of 'they', l. 206.)

199 **peoples'** BELL (peoples); People's MASON; people's GIFFORD+

201 **gone** undone, ruined

202 **recovered** This spelling (BELL's) would normally indicate a four-syllable pronunciation (as opposed to 'recover'd' or 'recoverd'), but the line works metrically with three. See l. 336 ('feared').

207 **against** BELL; 'gainst GIFFORD

220 BELL's unpunctuated line might be interpreted as two sentences: 'Where are they, sir? Who sees them but yourself?' See 2.2.135–6.

225 **This... seat** i.e., 'if this [the prisoner's bar or dock where I now stand] were the judges' bench'. To clarify this use of the subjunctive, COXETER emends to read: 'Were this the Judgment Seat,....'

we now would try THIS EDITION; we now BELL; we stand at now COXETER; we [k]now SHAW; were one to try now TAYLOR *conj.* (were one to trie now). THIS EDITION's conjecture, admittedly unsupported by any words present in BELL, has the advantages of 1) supplying an iambic foot to what may be an incomplete line, and 2) completing the sentence in a way that seems compatible with the context. Like TAYLOR's conjecture, THIS EDITION's reading could be explained by compositor eyeskip ('we nowe would trie').

232 **common laws** English common law (as opposed to more recent statutory law) was said to be based on established ancient principles of nature, God, and reason. *Old Law* was probably written and first performed at a time of great controversy over the primacy of common law; in November 1616, James I dismissed the prominent jurist Edward Coke from the King's Bench for his defence of common law.

233 ***ipso facto*** 'by the fact itself'

234 **liar** BELL (lyar); like MASON+. Though the singular noun is somewhat dissonant in relation to the plurals around it ('you', 'parricides', 'their'), the text has elsewhere not been consistent about this kind of agreement (compare ll. 198–201). Another possibility: 'liars'.

249–50 I…**effects** In the right margin opposite these two lines BELL has '*Recorders.* | *Old men.*' This may be an anticipatory stage direction (though it directly precedes the actual entrance direction), or it may have functioned simply to highlight for the book-holder an important music cue and entrance.

251.1–2 ***Music…appear*** This direction emends and fills out BELL's stage direction in the text and supplements it with material from the marginal notation (see note to ll. 249–50). BELL reads 'Mufick, Sons *and the old men appeare*' and thus seems to call for the appearance of additional 'sons' who do not elsewhere appear on stage in this scene. This seems unlikely (though not impossible) from the perspective of casting, and the Duke's pointed reuniting of 'lads' and fathers at l. 257 also suggests sons who are already on stage. The mixed font of BELL's stage direction may provide additional support for SHAW's emendation.

251.1 ***recorders*** See 2.1.146.1.
sounds SHAW; Sons BELL. See previous note.

252 **talks** BELL; walks TAYLOR *conj.*

254 **ill-entreated** ill-treated

257 **[*to…men*]** Alternatively, the Duke may speak this line jokingly to the young men onstage.

267 FIRST COURTIER THIS EDITION (following NEWBERRY [see below]); *Clean.* BELL. All other editions attribute the speech to Simonides; while such an attribution would support a certain view of the play (making the contrast of Simonides and Cleanthes pivotal at this climactic reversal), this edition construes ll. 265–9 as an exchange between the two Courtiers. This reading is supported by evidence of one apparently seventeenth-century reader's corrections in NEWBERRY; the reader has crossed out BELL's '*Clean.*', written in and crossed out 'Simon.', and written in a word ending in 'r:' (the page has been cropped). The surviving 'r' suggests the First Courtier. (See Masten, 'Family Values', and following notes.) In several senses BELL's attribution of the speech to Cleanthes seems utterly wrong: Cleanthes has already indicated that he's seen his father (ll. 252–6); the speech is prose, but he speaks verse elsewhere; the lines seem uncharacteristic of his portrayal thus far in the play as the archetypal Good Son. Yet, given his history of theatricality (his staging of his father's funeral before the Duke in 2.1) and his feigned performance of mixed emotions there ('We'll seem to weep, and seem to joy withal' [1.1.470]), the speech heading in BELL may be comprehensible in the terms of the play—though it radically destabilizes an earlier sense of Cleanthes's character (and/or perhaps our modern sense of 'character'). If Cleanthes does speak these lines, the play may be said to suggest that none of the sons resists the euthanasia law and the threat to filial piety it represents. Any reading of BELL here, then, always-already depends on one's interpretation of the play, and one's definition of 'characteristic' speech in a play that has already worked to undermine that definition. When is Cleanthes 'seeming'?

270 CLEANTHES NEWBERRY (Cle:) (handwritten marginal correction), COXETER; *Sim.* BELL. In NEWBERRY, a reader has circled and crossed out BELL's '*Sim.*' To continue the argument in the previous note: the assignment of that speech to Cleanthes may be only a temporary suggestion of doubt toward the character Cleanthes, for this speech, assigned in BELL to Simonides, seems to belong to Cleanthes, since its speaker asks to be returned to trial. It seems probable, then, that a performance would have reassigned these speeches as they appear 'corrected' in NEWBERRY and in THIS EDITION. But it is also possible that for at least one seventeenth-century compositor and probably a number of BELL's readers there was the possibility of another interpretation of the play. (In most of the other surviving copies of BELL, no change is made.) Here then is BELL's version of the passage, with the original assignments:

> 2. *Cour.* Is thy father amongſt them ?
> *Clean.* Oh a Pox I ſaw him the firſt thing I lookt on
> A live againe, ſlight I believe now a father
> Hath as many lives as a mother.
> *Sim.* Tis full as bleſſed as tis wonderfull
> Oh bring me back to the ſame law againe
>
> *THE OLD LAW.* 67
> I am fowler then all theſe, ceaſe on me Officers
> And bring me to new ſentence.
> *Clean.* Whats all this?
> A fault not to be pardoned
> Unnaturallneſs is but ſuns ſhaddow to it.

Experience and discretion snatched away
From the earth's face—turn all into disorder,
Imprison virtue and enfranchise vice,
And put the sword of justice into the hands
Of boys and madmen.

SIMONIDES Well, well, have you done, sir?

CLEANTHES
I have spoke my thoughts.

SIMONIDES Then I'll begin and end.

DUKE 'Tis time I now begin
Where your commission ends.
Cleanthes, you come from the bar.
Because I know you're severally disposed,
I here invite you to an object will
No doubt work in you contrary effects.
Music!

Music [*of*] *recorders sounds and the old men* [*including Leonides, Lisander, and Creon*] *appear*

CLEANTHES
Pray heaven, I dream not; sure he moves, talks
comfortably
As joy can wish a man. If he be changed
Far above from me, he is not ill-entreated;
His face doth promise fullness of content,
And glory hath a part in't.

LEONIDES O, my son.

DUKE [*to the old men*]
You that can claim acquaintance with these lads
Talk freely.

SIMONIDES I can see none there that's worth
One hand to you from me.

DUKE [*to Cleanthes*]
These are thy judges and, by their grave law,
I find thee clear, but these delinquents guilty.
You must change places, for 'tis so decreed,
Such just preeminence hath thy goodness gained,
Thou art the judge now; they, the men arraigned.

FIRST COURTIER Here's fine dancing, gentlemen.

SECOND COURTIER Is thy father amongst them?

FIRST COURTIER O, a pox! I saw him the first thing I looked on! Alive again—'slight, I believe now a father hath as many lives as a mother.

CLEANTHES
'Tis full as blessèd as 'tis wonderful!
O, bring me back to the same law again;
I am fouler than all these. Seize on me, officers,
And bring me to new sentence.

DUKE What's all this?

CLEANTHES
A fault not to be pardonèd;
Unnaturalness is but sun's shadow to it.

SIMONIDES
I am glad of that; I hope the case may alter
And I turn judge again.

DUKE Name your offence.

CLEANTHES
That I should be so vile
As once to think you cruel.

DUKE Is that all?
'Twas pardoned ere confessed. You that have sons,
If they be worthy, here may challenge them.

CREON
I should have one amongst them, had he had grace
To have retained that name.

SIMONIDES (*kneels*) I pray you, father—

CREON
That name, I know, hath been long since forgot.

SIMONIDES [*aside*] I find but small comfort in rememb'ring it now.

DUKE
Cleanthes, take your place with these grave fathers,
And read what in that table is inscribed.
[*He gives Cleanthes a table*]
Now set these at the bar,
And read, Cleanthes, to the dread and terror
Of disobedience and unnatural blood.
[*Simonides rises*]

CLEANTHES [*reading the table*] 'It is decreed by the grave and learned council of Epire that no son and heir shall be held capable of his inheritance at the age of one-and-twenty, unless he be at that time as mature in obedience, manners and goodness.'

SIMONIDES
Sure I shall never be at full age then,
Though I live to an hundred years, and that's nearer by twenty than the last statute allowed.

FIRST COURTIER A terrible act.

CLEANTHES [*reading*] 'Moreover is enacted, that all sons aforesaid, whom either this law or their own grace shall reduce into the true method of duty, virtue, and affection, relate their trial and approbation from Cleanthes, the son of Leonides'—from me, my lord?

DUKE
From none but you as fullest; proceed, sir.

CLEANTHES [*reading*] 'Whom, for his manifest virtues, we make such judge and censure of youth and the absolute reference of life and manners.'

SIMONIDES
This is a brave world! When a man should be
Selling land, he must be learning manners.
Is't not, my masters?
Enter Eugenia

EUGENIA
What's here to do? My suitors at the bar,
The old bawd shines again—O miserable!

273 DUKE NEWBERRY (Duk) (handwritten marginal correction), SHAW; *Clean.* BELL; Sim. COXETER. (See previous notes.)

274 CLEANTHES COXETER; *not in* BELL. In BELL, these lines continue a speech there assigned to Cleanthes, the first line of which is here reassigned to the Duke. (See previous note.)

281 **here may challenge them** COXETER; heare my ~ then BELL

282 CREON COXETER; *Cle.* BELL. BELL assigns both this speech and l. 284 to *Cle.* BELL's usual speech-heading abbreviations are *Clean.* for Cleanthes and *Cre.* for Creon. The first speech is more appropriate to Creon, though the second could be spoken by either man.

284 CREON COXETER; *Cle.* BELL. See previous note.

285 ***aside*** On *asides*, see 1.1.222–3.

287 **place** COXETER; places BELL
fathers COXETER; father BELL. Some copies of BELL have an unidentifiable mark—perhaps a broken piece of type—that can only be hypothesized to have been an *s*. In any other context within BELL, the mark would be taken as an accidential blotch or an apostrophe. None of the copies consulted has *s*.

288 **table** tablet (See 2.1.119.)

293 **council** council (as Parliament/Senate), or counsel (those who give advice) (1.1.142, 1.1.152)

295 **mature** MASON; nature BELL. While MASON's emendation seems more appropriate to the law's grammar and context, the word *nature* appears repeatedly in the play and is referenced only a few lines before, also in connection with obedience (l. 291–5.1.291.1). Though not self-evidently grammatical, *nature* may work in this context ('as nature' = 'as a person should naturally be') and may suggest at least one seventeenth-century reader's sense of the equivalence of the two terms in this context. That is, natural sons and mature ones will behave the same way in a patriarchal context.

301 CLEANTHES COXETER; *not in* BELL. In BELL the speech appears to continue the First Courtier's speech, but it is marked by beginning on a new line, and the speech later identifies itself with Cleanthes.

301–5 **Moreover ... Leonides** The syntax of the new law in BELL is either deliberately complicated in a way that does not seem to make syntactic sense or is not registered accurately in the printed text. (Intervening editorially at such an important point in the play might thus alter the politics of the play's outcome.) The emendations suggested to these lines in the notes below hypothesize that, in the midst of complicated legal syntax, BELL's compositor may have unnecessarily repeated several words, which, deleted here, make for a more coherent new law. Still, it is impossible to know whether the text was intended to read smoothly or is (again) imitating and perhaps parodying legal discourse (see 1.1.139–63). If the new law is 'better' than the old law within the moral scheme the play delineates, it might be expected not to be parodic in form.

302–3 **grace shall** COXETER (*subst.*); grace, whom it ſhall BELL; with it TAYLOR *conj.* All editions delete BELL's 'whom it'; see previous note.

304 **affection, relate** THIS EDITION; affection; and relate BELL; affection, [shall appear before us] and relate GIFFORD; affection appear before us and TAYLOR *conj.*
relate ... from receive the approval of
relate refer to (a legal term, probably used incorrectly)

314 **old bawd shines** the old man lives. *Bawd* could refer to a person of either sex who arranges sexual activity for another; here it may suggest that Eugenia is figuring *Lisander* as someone whose age has in effect procured her suitors/sexual partners (see scenes 2.2 and 3.2). See next note.
bawd BELL (baud); Bard COXETER; Beard D (*conj.* in note to MASON); band GIFFORD+. Alternatively, GIFFORD's 'band' (meaning 'group of old men') could be adopted, interpreting BELL's *baud* as a case of *u*/*n* type-inversion; see 1.1.380, 5.1.57. More extensive emendations of the line have been proposed: The old revived MASON *conj.*; The old bald sires DYCE *conj.*

318 **the** BELL; their MASON+. Sentences noting the legal status and responsibilities of 'the husband' in the abstract are standard legal discourse in the period. While MASON's emendation brings some of the sentence's numbers into agreement, no editor has opted to pursue this numerical logic to give their plural 'husbands' plural 'deaths'. The number of husbands is precisely what the law here seeks to regulate; thus, one editor's standardizing emendation may be another's opportunity to note instability in the law's rhetoric. The same can be said of the next word in BELL ('husbands'), where a modern edition must make a decision between a singular- or plural-possessive form of the word in this and the following line. On the apostrophe, see 3.1.81, 5.1.198–201.

330 **judged** COXETER; judge BELL

332 **judged** COXETER; judge BELL

332.1 ***Enter Hippolita*** In the right margin opposite lines 330–2, BELL has duplicate entrance directions for Hippolita: *Hippolita.* | *Enter Hip.*

333 **prevent** prepare you for (literally, 'come before'), with a theological meaning: provide spiritual guidance (usually said of God)

341 **May** FOLGER (handwritten marginal correction), COXETER; My BELL

346.1 ***still*** THIS EDITION; *not in* BELL

347.1–4 ***Enter...wedding*** THIS EDITION. This direction is the second of BELL's two extensive, consecutive stage directions describing this large entrance (see Stage Directions list), to which is added (from the first) the 'one carrying' the bridecake. BELL reads:

THE OLD LAW. 69
This day is all devout to liberty.
Clo. &c. *Enter Musick one carrying a Bridecake, the Clowne, the rest with them old Women.*

Enter Clowne, *and* Wench, *the rest with the old women, the* Clownes *wife, Musick, and a Bride Cake to the wedding.*

The second direction is adopted here because it is more fully descriptive, but it is important to note that the two directions present different orders for this procession, and thus each might emphasize a particular interpretation of the episode. Some reasons for BELL's doubling of this direction: 1) The direction was revised (with whatever interpretive intentions/effects) but the first version was not clearly deleted from the manuscript from which BELL was typeset; 2) More fancifully, the text from which BELL was set included the first large direction at the bottom of a page; since the timing and conduct of such a large entrance was clearly important in performance, the text reinscribed a near-duplicate version at the top of the following page, and, though no change of page is at issue in BELL, the compositors simply followed the duplication of the text that was their model. However it came about, this is not a textual 'problem'; it gives BELL's reader more, rather than less, information about the performance(s) of the play. BELL also includes here what may have been a book-holder's brief marginal notation (*Clo.* &c.) in the left margin of the first stage direction.

347.3 ***music*** musicians

348 **crowd on** press on; punning on *crowd* = fiddle

She [swoons]

DUKE
Read the law over to her; 'twill awake her.
'Tis one deserves small pity.

CLEANTHES [*reading*] 'Lastly, it is ordained that all such wives now whatsoever that shall design the husband's death to be soon rid of them and entertain suitors in their husbands' lifetime'—

SIMONIDES You had best read that a little louder, for, if anything, that will bring her to herself again, and find her tongue.

CLEANTHES [*reading*] 'Shall not presume, on the penalty of our heavy displeasure, to marry within ten years after'—

EUGENIA [*reviving*]
That law's too long by nine years and a half.
I'll take my death upon't; so shall most women.

CLEANTHES [*reading*] 'And those incontinent women so offending to be judged and censured by Hippolita, wife to Cleanthes.'

EUGENIA
Of all the rest, I'll not be judged by her.

Enter Hippolita

CLEANTHES
Ah, here she comes. Let me prevent thy joys,
Prevent them but in part, and hide the rest;
Thou hast not strength enough to bear them else.

HIPPOLITA
Leonides—

She faints

CLEANTHES
I feared it all this while.
I knew 'twas past thy power, Hippolita.
What contrariety is in women's blood?
One faints for spleen and anger; she, for grace.

DUKE
Of sons and wives we see the worst and best:
May future ages yield Hippolitas
Many, but few like thee, Eugenia.
Let no Simonides henceforth have a fame,
But all blessed sons live in Cleanthes' name.

Music [within]

Ha, what strange kind of melody was that?
Yet give it entrance whatsoe'er it be;

Music [still]

This day is all devout to liberty.

Enter Clown and Wench, the rest [—Cook, Butler, Tailor, Bailiff—] with the old women, the Clown's Wife, music, and one carrying a bridecake, to the wedding

CLOWN Fiddlers, crowd on, crowd on; let no man lay a block in your way. Crowd on, I say.

DUKE Stay the crowd awhile; let's know the reason of this jollity.

CLEANTHES [*to Clown*] Sirrah, do you know where you are?

CLOWN Yes, sir, I am here, now here, and now here again, sir.

LISANDER Your hat's too high-crowned, the Duke in presence.

CLOWN The Duke (as he is my sovereign) I do give him two crowns for it, and that's equal change all the world over. As I am lord of the day (being my marriage day the second) I do advance bonnet.—Crowd on afore!

LEONIDES Good sir, a few words if you'll vouchsafe 'em. Or will you be forced?

CLOWN Forced? I would the Duke himself would say so.

DUKE I think he dares, sir, and does: if you stay not, you shall be forced.

CLOWN I think so, my lord, and good reason too. Shall not I stay when your grace says I shall? I were unworthy to be a bridegroom in any part of your highness' dominions, then. Will it please you to taste of the wedlock courtesy?

DUKE
O, by no means, sir; you shall not deface
So fair an ornament for me.

CLOWN If your grace please to be cake-ated, say so.

CLEANTHES *or* CREON And which might be your fair bride, sir?

CLOWN [*showing Wench*] This is my two-for-one that must be *uxor uxoris*, the remedy *doloris*, and the very *syceum amoris*.

DUKE And hast thou any else?

CLOWN I have an older, my lord, for other uses.

CLEANTHES
My lord, I do observe a strange decorum here:
These that do lead this day of jollity
Do march with music and most mirthful cheeks;
Those that do follow, sad and woefully,
Nearer the haviour of a funeral
Than a wedding.

DUKE 'Tis true. Pray, expound that, sir.

CLOWN As the destiny of the day falls out, my lord, one goes out to wedding; another goes to hanging. And your grace in the due consideration shall find 'em much alike: the one hath the ring upon her finger; the other, a halter about her neck. 'I take thee, Beatrice', says the bridegroom; 'I take thee, Agatha', says the hangman, and both say together, 'to have and to hold till death do part us.'

DUKE This is not yet plain enough to my understanding.

CLOWN If further your grace examine it, you shall find I show myself a dutiful subject and obedient to the law—myself (with these, my good friends and your good subjects), our old wives, whose days are ripe and their lives forfeit to the law. Only myself, more forward than the rest, am already provided of my second choice.

DUKE
O, take heed sir; you'll run yourself into danger.
If the law finds you with two wives at once,
There's a shrewd præmunire.

CLOWN I have taken leave of the old, my lord; I have nothing to say to her. She's going to sea; your grace knows whither better than I do. She has a strong wind

358 **equal change** (punning on kinds of English coins: a sovereign [worth 10 or 11 shillings at the time of the play's first performances] was equal to two crowns [at 5 shillings apiece.])

360 **advance bonnet** (punning on raising his hat, moving forward, and advancing a sum of money [*bonnet* = crown])

370 **wedlock courtesy** wedding cake. *Courtesy* was also a legal term describing a man's right to hold certain kinds of property belonging to his wife after her death.

373 **cake-ated** BELL (cacated). *cake-ated* = served with cake (the only known use of this term), possibly with a pun on *cack* (= shit). The spelling of THIS EDITION departs from the editorial tradition (cakated) for the sake of aural intelligibility. There is no reason to accept *OED*'s spelling, since this is *OED*'s only citation, and it gets many details wrong in this instance.

374 CLEANTHES ***or*** CREON THIS EDITION; *Clo.* BELL; Duke. COXETER. In BELL, there are three consecutive speeches (ll. 373, 374–5, 376–8) attributed to *Clo.*, BELL's standard speech-prefix abbreviation for 'Clown'. This emendation argues that the prefix here is an error for *Cle.* or *Cre.*; compare ll. 282–4, 381. Alternatively, as COXETER suggests, the conversation might instead be imagined to remain entirely between Duke and Clown at this point.

376 **two-for-one** the odds of Clown's 'venter' with the servants, but suggesting the legal term *venter* itself (3.1.177)

377 ***uxor uxoris*** 'wife of wives'
doloris 'sadness'

377–8 ***syceum amoris*** probably 'fig of love', with a pun on *syceum/fig* (= vulva)

381 CLEANTHES BELL (*Cle.*). Elsewhere BELL's speech heading '*Cle.*' also seems to denote Creon (5.1.282), who might alternatively speak the speech. (See l. 374.) Especially (but not only) if spoken by Cleanthes, this speech resonates with his staging of Leonides's funeral earlier—itself a hybrid production of joy and sadness, observing 'a strange decorum'.

385 **haviour** manner, conduct

391 **Beatrice** (apparently Wench's given name)

404 **præmunire** penalty. Præmunire was the offence, originally, of prosecuting in a foreign court a suit that could be tried in England and, eventually, of maintaining or defending papal jurisdiction in England. Thus, though the law originated with Richard II, there may be a reference here to Henry VIII, whose split from the Roman church led to the second meaning of this term and was centred on the question of multiple wives. The play *All is True* (*Henry VIII*), which uses the term and was performed in 1613, had emphasized this.

407 **whither** BELL (whether). 'Whether' might also be a meaning here.

407–8 **strong wind...poop** 1) she's ready to set sail for execution. But there is also the strong sense of excretory puns here (*wind* = flatulence; *poop* = rear of a ship, also a tooting sound); thus, 2) she's breaking wind. (*Poop* probably does not carry the modern slang sense of 'faeces'.)

409 **disembogue** BELL (disemboge). 1) literally, come out of the mouth of a river into the sea (continuing the reference to execution); 2) discharge like a river (thus continuing the series of excretory puns); 3) a word suggesting *disembark* and *disembowel*

418 **venter** On *venter*'s multiple meanings, see 3.1.177.

422 **censure** sentence, judgement

426 **an** if

429 **paints** uses cosmetics

437 **edge-tool** implement with a sharp, cutting edge (e.g. a sword)

441 **if** COXETER; it BELL

442 **give ... ears** listen to him. But also playing on another form of punishment, in which a prisoner's ears were cut off.

444 **church-book** (with pun on *bible*)

with her; it stands full in her poop. When you please, let her disembogue.

COOK And the rest of her neighbours with her, whom we present to the satisfaction of your highness' law.

CLOWN And so we take our leaves and leave them to your highness.—Crowd on!

DUKE
Stay, stay, you are too forward. Will you marry,
And your wife yet living?

CLOWN Alas, she'll be dead before we can get to church, if your grace would set her in the way. I would dispatch her; I have a venter on't, which would return me, if your highness would make a little more haste, two for one.

DUKE [*to the judges*]
Come, my lords, we must sit again, here's a case
Craves a most serious censure.

COOK [*to the Clown and other servants*]
Now they shall be dispatched out of the way.

CLOWN
I would they were gone once; the time goes away.

DUKE
Which is the wife unto the forward bridegroom?

WIFE I am, an it please your grace.

DUKE
Trust me, a lusty woman, able-bodied,
And well-blooded cheeks.

CLOWN O, she paints, my lord; she was a chambermaid once, and learnt it of her lady.

DUKE
Sure, I think she cannot be so old.

WIFE
Truly, I think so too, an please your grace.

CLOWN Two-to-one with your grace of that; she's threescore by the book.

LEONIDES Peace, sirrah, you're too loud.

COOK Take heed, Gnothoes. If you move the Duke's patience, 'tis an edge-tool; but a word and a blow, he cuts off your head.

CLOWN Cut off my head? Away, ignorant! He knows it cost more in the hair; he does not use to cut off many such heads as mine. I will talk to him too; if he cut off my head, I'll give him my ears.—I say my wife is at full age for the law; the clerk shall take his oath, and the church-book shall be sworn too.

DUKE [*to the judges*] My lords, I leave this censure to you.

LEONIDES
Then, first, this fellow does deserve punishment
For offering up a lusty able woman
Which may do service to the commonwealth,
Where the law craves one impotent and useless.

CREON
Therefore, to be severely punishèd
For thus attempting a second marriage,
His wife yet living.

LISANDER Nay, to have it trebled,
That even the day and instant when he should mourn
As a kind husband to her funeral,

He leads a triumph to the scorn of it,
Which unseasonable joy ought to be punished
With all severity.

BUTLER The fiddles will be in a foul case too by and by.

LEONIDES
Nay, further, it seems he has a venter
Of two-for-one at his second marriage,
Which cannot be but a conspiracy
Against the former.

CLOWN A mess of wise old men.

LISANDER
Sirrah, what can you answer to all these?

CLOWN You're good old men and talk as age will give you leave. I would speak with the youthful Duke himself; he and I may speak of things that shall be thirty or forty years after you are dead and rotten. Alas, you are here today and gone to sea tomorrow.

DUKE
In troth, sir, then I must be plain with you:
The law that should take away your old wife from
you,
The which I do perceive was your desire,
Is void and frustrate, so for the rest.
There has been since another parliament
Has cut it off.

CLOWN I see your grace is disposed to be pleasant.

DUKE
Yes, you might perceive that; I had not else
Thus dallied with your follies.

CLOWN I'll talk further with your grace when I come back from church; in the mean time, you know what to do with the old women.

DUKE
Stay, sir, unless in the mean time you mean
I cause a gibbet to be set up in your way
And hang you at your return.

WIFE O gracious prince!

DUKE
Your old wives cannot die today by any
Law of mine; for aught I can say to 'em,
They may by a new edict bury you,
And then perhaps you pay a new fine too.

CLOWN This is fine indeed.

WIFE O gracious prince, may he live a hundred years more.

COOK Your venter is not like to come in today, Gnothoes.

CLOWN Give me the principal back.

COOK Nay, by my troth, we'll venter still, and I'm sure we have as ill a venter of it as you, for we have taken old wives of purpose, where that we had thought to have put away at this market, and now we cannot utter a pennyworth.

DUKE [*to Clown*]
Well, sirrah, you were best to discharge
Your new charge and take your old one to you.

CLOWN
O music, no music, but prove most doleful trumpets;
O bride, no bride, but thou mayst prove a strumpet;

455 **triumph** 1) the procession of a victorious commander and army through the streets of Rome after an important victory; 2) any public celebration, pageant.

458 **case** instrument case; legal case; pun on 'female genitals'

463 **mess** 1) a group of people (usually four) who dine together, especially judges and students at the Inns of Court; 2) a group of people or things; 3) a serving of food. *Mess* did not yet carry the modern sense of 'disorder'.

468–9 **here…tomorrow** BELL's spacing/spelling ('heere to day and gone to Sea to morrow') may alert a reader to some of the aural puns available here: the punning repetition of *to*; the expansion of the proverb ('here today, and gone tomorrow'); the possibility of hearing *sea* as *see* (going to sea to see the future).

473 **frustrate** invalid (legal term)—in the usage of a legal commentator, writing about wills: 'the later testament doth make frustrate the former' (Henrie Swinburn, *A Briefe Treatise of Testaments and Last Willes*, 1590).

474 **parliament** Lines 1.1.14 and 1.1.138 emphasize that the legislature of Epire is a 'senate'; the use of the more English term here emphasizes the play's topical connections to early seventeenth-century English culture and the way it speaks within seventeenth-century discourses of government. The relation of the parliament to the Duke as absolute ruler and national 'father' also re-plays aspects of English debates over the relative power of king and parliament at the time of the play.

483 **gibbet** gallows

491 **venter** BELL (venture). This is the only instance in which BELL uses the spelling 'venture' in the context of Clown's wagers; THIS EDITION 'modernizes' it to *venter* for the same reason that that spelling is retained elsewhere in the text—to keep in circulation its multiple meanings, which are clearly relevant here (see 3.1.177).

495 **where that** it being the case that; in view of the fact that

495–6 **where…and** BELL; that we had thought to have put away at this market, where TAYLOR *conj.* Given the inverted type in BELL (see following note), TAYLOR's conjecture is based on the possibility of a miscorrected proof page.

496 **put away** dispose of, sell
and COXETER; ʁnd BELL
utter sell

500–3 **O…gone** The speech comically rewrites Hieronimo's lament for his murdered son in Act 3 of *The Spanish Tragedy*:

> Oh eies, no eies, but fountains fraught with teares,
> Oh life, no life, but liuely fourme of death:
> Oh world, no world but masse of publique wrongs,
> Confusde and filde, with murder and misdeeds
> Oh sacred heauens....

First acted in 1592 and repeatedly published thereafter, this popular revenge tragedy was revised at least once (1602) and reprinted often (including an edition in 1618); it is one of the most frequently quoted and parodied plays in early modern English drama.

O venter, no venter, I have for one now none;
O wife, thy life is saved when I hoped 't'had been gone.—
Case up your fruitless strings, no penny, no wedding;—
Case up thy maidenhead, no priest, no bedding.
Avaunt, my venter; it can ne'er be restored,
Till Ag, my old wife, be thrown overboard.
Then come again, old Ag, since it must be so;
Let bride and venter with woeful music go.

COOK What for the bridecake, Gnothoes?

CLOWN
Let it be mouldy now 'tis out-of-season;
Let it grow out of date, current and reason;
Let it be chipped and chopped and given to chickens;
No more is got by that than William Dickins
Got by his wooden dishes.
Put up your plums, as fiddlers put up pipes;
The wedding dashed, the bridegroom weeps and wipes.
Fiddlers, farewell, and now, without perhaps,
Put up your fiddles as you put up scraps.

LISANDER This passion has given some satisfaction yet. My lord, I think you'll pardon him now, with all the rest, so they live honestly with the wives they have.

DUKE O, most freely; free pardon to all.

COOK Ay, we have deserved our pardons if we can live honestly with such reverend wives that have no motion in 'em but their tongues.

WIFE Heaven bless your grace; you're a just prince.

CLOWN All hopes dashed, the clerk's duty's lost, venter gone, my second wife divorced, and (which is worst) the old one come back again. Such voyages are made nowadays; I will weep, too, salt of one nose, besides these two fountains of fresh water. Your grace had been more kind to your young subjects; heaven bless and mend your laws, that they do not gull your poor countrymen in this fashion. But I am not the first by forty that has been undone by the law; 'tis but a folly to stand upon terms. I take my leave of your grace, as well as mine eyes will give me leave; I would they had been asleep in their beds when they opened 'em to see this day.—Come Ag, come Ag. [*Exeunt Clown and Wife*]

CREON [*to servants*] Were not you all my servants?

COOK During your life, as we thought, sir, but our young master turned us away.

CREON [*to Simonides*]
How headlong, villain, wert thou in thy ruin?

SIMONIDES I followed the fashion, sir, as other young men did; if you were as we thought you had been, we should ne'er have come for this, I warrant you. We did not feed after the old fashion on beef and mutton and suchlike.

CREON [*to servants*] Well, what damage or charge you have run yourselves into by marriage, I cannot help, nor deliver you from your wives; them you must keep. Yourselves shall again retain to me.

503 **hoped** COXETER+ (*subst.*); hope BELL

504 **no penny, no wedding** rewriting the commonplace saying, 'no penny, no paternoster', referring to priests' insisting on payment in return for services; thus: 'if you want something, you must pay for it'.

512 **grow ... reason** multiple puns: 1) on time (out-of-season, out-of-date, current); 2) on fruits (grow, date, raisin, and currant [BELL's spelling, not distinguished in the period from 'current']); 3) on unreasonableness (out of reason); 4) on money (currency)
current BELL (currant)

514 **William Dickins** A proverbial figure for someone who loses money in a transaction, Dickins was said to have bought five dishes for twopence and then to have sold six dishes for only a penny.

516 **plums** 1) plums in the modern sense; 2) dried grapes or raisins used in puddings and cakes

525 **reverend** old; but see 5.1.52

528 **duty's** fee's

530–1 **Such ... nowadays** i.e., voyages back from the (near) dead. The speech may also allude to Sir Walter Ralegh's return from his last, unsuccessful voyage in the spring of 1618.

531–2 **I ... water** BELL; *not in* COXETER

531 **too, salt** BELL (~‸~); two salt ones out DYCE
one THIS EDITION; our BELL; my GIFFORD. This emendation is supported by BELL's apparent interchanging of *one*/*our* elsewhere in this scene (ll. 11, 159) and adds a Clownish play on numbers.

532 **two ... water** eyes, but playing on the saltiness of tears by using *fresh* to mean 'new, recent' instead of 'unsalty'. See 5.1.561.

535 **countrymen in this fashion** BULLEN; Country men:faſhion BELL; Countrymen COXETER

537 **stand upon terms** 1) insist upon conditions (i.e., the terms of the old law); 2) to rely on or attach value to language; 3) to stand (literally) at the boundaries or limits. There is also the possible resonance of *term* as session of a law court.

546 **were** COXETER; have BELL; had hanged TAYLOR *conj.* (had hangd)

OMNES We thank your lordship for your love, and must thank ourselves for our bad bargains.

[Exeunt servants, wives, and wedding party]

DUKE

Cleanthes, you delay the power of law,
To be inflicted on these misgovernèd men,
That filial duty have so far transgressed.

CLEANTHES

My lord, I see a satisfactïon
Meeting the sentence, even preventing it,
Beating my words back in their utterance.
See, sir, there's salt sorrow bringing forth fresh
And new duties (as the sea propagates).

[Simonides and Courtiers kneel]

The elephants have found their joints too; why,
Here's humility able to bind up
The punishing hands of the severest masters,
Much more the gentle fathers.

SIMONIDES I had ne'er thought to have been brought so low as my knees again, but since there's no remedy, fathers, reverend fathers, as you ever hope to have good sons and heirs, a handful of pity. We confess we have deserved more than we are willing to receive at your hands, though sons can never deserve too much of their fathers, as shall appear afterwards.

CREON

And what way can you decline your feeding now?
You cannot retire to beeves and muttons, sure.

SIMONIDES Alas, sir, you see a good pattern for that; now we have laid by our high and lusty meats and are down to our marrowbones already.

CREON

Well, sir, rise to virtues; we'll bound you now.

[Simonides and Courtiers rise]

You that were too weak yourselves to govern,
By others shall be governèd.

LISANDER Cleanthes,
I meet your justice with reconcilement;
If there be tears of faith in woman's breast,
I have received a myriad which confirms me
To find a happy renovatïon.

CLEANTHES *[turning to Leonides]* Here's virtue's throne,
Which I'll embellish with my dearest jewels
Of love and faith, peace and affectïon.
This is the altar of my sacrifice,
Where daily my devoted knees shall bend.
Age-honoured shrine, time still so love you
That I so long may have you in mine eye,
Until my memory lose your beginning.—
For you, great prince, long may your fame survive,
Your justice and your wisdom never die,
Crown of your crown, the blessing of your land
Which you reach to her from your regent's hand.

LEONIDES

O Cleanthes, had you with us tasted
The entertainment of our retirement,
Feared and exclaimed on in your ignorance,
You might have sooner died upon the wonder

553 OMNES See 3.1.155.

558 **satisfactïon** 1) an act of compensation or amends (legal term); 2) an act of penance after confession; 3) in Christian theology, Christ's paying for the sins of the world

559 **Meeting... preventing it** encountering... coming before it. BELL's 'Meeting' was also a possible spelling of *meting* (= measuring, ascertaining, weighing a judgement). Since *mete* is also a legal term meaning 'boundaries', audiences might have heard *meting* as 'limiting' or 'diminishing' here. In any event, *meeting* probably modifies *satisfaction* rather than *I*, though, again, the elliptical syntax might have led audiences to hear Cleanthes expressing *his* satisfaction.

561 **salt sorrow** tears

562 **as the sea propagates** just as the sea expands; or, as the sea creates new life

563 **elephants... joints** Elephants were thought to lack knee-joints.

575 **beeves** plural of *beef*

577 **high and lusty** flavorful and hearty (with pun on *lust*)

578 **marrowbones** BELL (mary bones). *marrowbones* = animal bones containing marrow to be eaten (considered 'dainty' [*OED*]); knees

579 **bound you** make you leap up like a horse; limit you, set your boundaries

583–4 **If... myriad** The speech may refer to Eugenia's repentance or to Lisander's own.

597 **regent's** ruler's, probably without the more familiar sense of 'temporary or substitute ruler'

605 **Viands** food
607 **fantasies** imaginations, perceptions (probably without the sense of 'whim' or 'desire' now usually indicated by this spelling). BELL spells (phantafies).
614 **weeds** (punning on 'clothing')
616–17 **abuse...bosom** take into our confidence; misrepresent as a result of our secret
618 **Cratilus** The introduction of a new character with a highly resonant and allusive name at this late point in the play may prompt an audience to a retrospective revision of the play's action. Cratylus was the name of a philosopher (a contemporary of Socrates and teacher of Plato); in Plato's dialogue *Cratylus*, a discussion of the origins of names and naming, Cratylus argues that all names are naturally appropriate to the things they represent, while Hermogenes maintains that names are entirely the product of convention. There are a number of passages in the dialogue relevant to the play: Socrates's discussion of legislators (lawgivers) as the wise inventors of names; his discussion with Cratylus of the difference between numbers and names ('the number ten at once becomes other than ten if a unit be added or subtracted' [see 3.1]); his discussion of two identical objects, Cratylus and the image of Cratylus, and whether these have the same name. Much of the dialogue is occupied with Socrates's analyses of elaborate etymologies; he argues that letters have been added or subtracted from original terms to create the current versions of words, or he seems to add and subtract letters to make particular names conform with what he takes to be their essence. As such, in addition to its relevance to the play (the Clown's discussions of orthography [Bullox/Pollux, Hiren/Siren, Helen/ell/Ellen]), the introduction of Cratilus may serve as a cautionary note to the modernizing and emending editor who adds to and subtracts letters from an old text to produce a new version of the text (see also 3.1.30 and 5.1.131–6). Socrates's summary of the issue also resonates with Clown's warning not 'to stand upon terms' (5.1.536–7): 'no man of sense will...so far trust names or the givers of names as to be confident in any knowledge which condemns himself and other existences to an unhealthy state of reality.' The dialogue as a whole is concerned with the stability or instability of language and its ability to project the essence of a thing; on this, see particularly the note on *venter* (3.1.177) and, in general, all the notes above.
619–21 **travelled...languages** '[T]he one text is [an] entrance into a network with a thousand entrances; to take this entrance is to aim, ultimately, not at a legal structure of norms and departures, a narrative or poetic Law, but at a perspective (of fragments, of voices from other texts, other codes), whose vanishing point is nonetheless ceaselessly pushed back, mysteriously opened...' (Barthes, *S/Z* 12). Toward what languages, what voices, does this moment gesture?
622 **crown** crowning ornament; culmination
623 **set it high** 1) set the music at a high (and thus exaltant) pitch; 2) set the (metaphorical) crown high, in celebration; perhaps 3) set the following text to music.

Than any rage or passion for our loss.
A place at hand we were all strangers in,
So sphered about with music, such delights,
Viands, and attendance, and once a day
So cheerèd with a royal visitant,
That oft-times (waking) our unsteady fantasies
Would question whether we yet lived or no,
Or had possession of that paradise
Where angels be the guard.

DUKE
Enough, Leonides,
You go beyond the praise; we have our end
And all is ended well: we have now seen
The flowers and weeds that grew about our court.

SIMONIDES [*aside*] If these be weeds, I'm afraid I shall wear none so good again as long as my father lives.

DUKE
Only this gentleman we did abuse
With our own bosom; we seemed a tyrant
And he our instrument. Look, 'tis Cratilus,
Discover the Executioner
The man that you supposed had now been travelled,
Which we gave leave to learn to speak
And bring us foreign languages to Greece.
All's joyed, I see. Let music be the crown,
And set it high. The good needs fear no law;
It is his safety, and the bad man's awe.
[*Music. Exeunt omnes*]

Finis

THE TRIUMPHS OF LOVE AND ANTIQUITY

Text edited and annotated by David M. Bergeron, introduced by Lawrence Manley

The Triumphs of Love and Antiquity, Middleton's third mayoral pageant, was commissioned by the Company of Skinners following a competition in which 'Anthonie Mondaie, Thomas Middleton and Richard Grimston poette, all showed to the table their several plot for devices for the shows and pageant'. The third most expensive of Middleton's productions, costing £726, the show was the first in which major responsibility for the pageant-works was awarded to the naval carver Garret Christmas. Praised along with Robert Norman for his 'workmanship' at the end of Middleton's pamphlet, Christmas thereafter became the chief collaborator in all of Middleton's remaining mayoral shows and, with his sons, dominated the fabrication of the pageants until 1639.

Though in many respects typical of the shows Middleton wrote after his extraordinary 1613 debut, *The Triumphs of Love and Antiquity* is exceptional for its place in Middleton's career and for what it reveals about Middleton's ability to adapt his artistry to the exigencies of patronage and the demands of ceremonial occasion. The Lord Mayor whose inauguration the Skinners had commissioned Middleton to celebrate was Sir William Cokayne, one of the most notorious merchant-courtiers of the Jacobean period. A London Alderman and prominent Eastland trader who had made his fortune purveying victuals to the army in Ireland 1600–1603, Cokayne was the chief architect of the disastrous 'Cokayne Project', a scheme to replace England's traditional economic lifeline, the export by the Merchant Adventurers of unfinished woollen textiles to the Netherlands, with the direct delivery of home-finished cloth to markets throughout Northern Europe. While promising to employ domestic clothworkers, who had always objected to the Merchant Adventurers' unfinished exports, and to enhance customs revenues through direct competition with the Dutch clothing trade, the scheme was probably an attempt by interloping Eastland and Levant traders to wrest the lucrative textile monopoly from the Merchant Adventurers. While the project was initially opposed (by Robert Middleton, among others) in the 1614 Parliament and by leading Privy Counsellors, Cokayne and his syndicate managed, with the dismissal of Parliament and with the aid of bribes to Suffolk and Somerset, to win approval for a project that appealed both to the vanity of King James and to the search, by the Howard faction, for non-parliamentary sources of revenue. Following the revocation of the Merchant Adventurers' charter and the royal incorporation of the 'King's Merchants Adventurers of the New Trade of London', Cokayne earned his knighthood by feasting and bestowing lavish gifts on the monarch in his home in 1617.

By the time of this festive occasion, marked by a masque in which dyers, cloth dressers, and merchants from Hamburg were presented to the King and 'spoke such language as Ben Jonson put in their mouths', textile exports had plummeted, domestic producers were complaining of unsold inventories, and the English cloth trade had slipped into a depression that would last a decade. Sir Edward Coke, who had initially supported Cokayne's project, described its leaders as 'Projectors and Deluders of the State', and King James was said to have threatened Cokayne that 'if he had abused him by wrong information his four quarters should pay for it'.

With the return of the hated Merchant Adventurers to their monopoly, and with the further disruption of trade by war on the continent, the targets of blame were sufficiently numerous that Cokayne escaped retribution, 'better', as one contemporary noted, 'than could be wished'. Yet he was a man whose reputation had been damaged. When his London home and possessions were destroyed by fire in 1625, John Chamberlain wrote to Sir Dudley Carlton that he 'had seldom known a man less pitied,... and specially for that business of clothing (wherein all England hath and is like to suffer so much) which was his only plot and project, and procured him many a curse from poor people'. Coming on the heels of his failed project, Cokayne's elevation to the London mayoralty in 1619 was a crucial step in his rehabilitation. Middleton's pageant, written both 'to the service of his honour and honourable Society', was an important contribution to it.

The key device in Middleton's pageant is the figure of Love, who, from his opening announcement of 'the love of the city to his lordship' (34–5), to his closing speech on the circular, reciprocal nature of bounty and obligation, symbolizes the variety of bonds essential to the City's life—the amity of all citizens, the brotherhood of the Skinners' guild, the solicitude of officeholders, and the esteem that Middleton insists is due to their virtuous works. The pageant's underlying spousal tropes celebrate the inauguration of a whole series of relationships based on love: the moral 'match' between 'the city's general love' and the candidate's deserving (46); the political bond by which the mayor becomes 'the city's bridegroom' (440); the divine assurance that, all else failing, the mayor's 'good works' will 'wed thee to eternity' (52). As adapted to this particular occasion, however, the love that compensates the magistrate who 'Collects his spirits, redeems his hours with care' is understood as relieving more burdens than those of office. So is the assertion later on, in the Sanctuary of Fame, that Cokayne is now a 'worthy' ensconced among the former mayors and benefactors who distinguished the company of Skinners.

The three pageants that follow Love's opening speech—the Wilderness at Paul's Chain, the Sanctuary of Fame near the Little Conduit, and the Parliament of Honour at St Lawrence Lane end—form a pattern that, in keeping with both the citizen ethos and the syntagmatic nature of the triumph form, emphasizes secular causes and effects rather than the thaumaturgic mysteries associated with royal advents like that of James I. In Middleton's mayoral shows, as in those of his contemporaries, the rough and boisterous celebration of the mayor's return by river from Westminster, where he had taken his oath to the Crown, was a transitional event that marked a successful negotiation between political jurisdictions, and more broadly, between the dangers of the external world and the community's inner stability. The rite of arrival, moreover, provided the occasion for constructing narratives of arrival—myths, stories, and symbolic tableaux staging the historical passage from rude nature to urban culture, from the violence of pagan origins to the serenity of Christian community, from a barbarous past to a civilized present.

In *The Triumphs of Love and Antiquity*, this pattern begins with the presenter of the Wilderness, Orpheus, a figure associated throughout Renaissance mythography with the civilizing powers that, according to Thomas Lodge, made 'poets . . . the first raisers of cities'. A founder-hero who (in George Puttenham's words) brought 'savage people to a more civil and orderly life' and who (according to William Webbe) enabled them to 'keep company, make houses, and keep fellowship together', Orpheus had appeared in London mayoral shows as early as 1561. In Middleton's 1619 show, Orpheus and the Wilderness with beasts are skilfully adapted to compliment Cokayne's legendary eloquence (at Cokayne's funeral, John Donne recalled the King's observation that he had never heard a Londoner 'handle businesses more rationally, more pertinently, more eloquently, more persuasively') and to extol the patron Company of Skinners, to whose trade Middleton returns in his closing epigram on 'those beasts bearing fur, and now in use with the bountiful Society of Skinners' (446–7). The emphasis, however, picking up on the 'Graces' silver chimes' sounded in Love's opening speech (76), falls on the political theme of Orpheus' 'harmonious government' (160). The cock that appears over the head of Orpheus, an heraldic emblem of the Cokayne family, provides the basis for an allegory of the mayor's vigilance and power (165–84); it marks a transition from the animal kingdom to the ordered world of man. The orphic taming of the wilderness is a motif that runs throughout Middleton's show, from Orpheus' concluding tribute to the Stuart theme of union—extended to include 'the civilly instructed Irishman' (in 1610 Cokayne had become the first governor of the City of London's plantations in Londonderry and Coleraine)—to the last of the day's major pageants, which ends with mention of the fur-trimmed robes of state, produced by the Skinners, that adorn British kings 'when they consent/ To ride most glorious to high parliament' (269–70).

In passing from the Wilderness to the Sanctuary of Fame and the Parliament of Honour, then, the mayor's progress was meant to follow a path toward political consolidation and cultural perfection. The Sanctuary of Fame, in which Middleton extols London's twenty-six Aldermen and the worthy Skinners who have served the City's good, is represented as both a moral 'reward' for the 'cares in government' (211–13) first figured in Orpheus and as an historical step in the passage from a world 'that knows no laws' (158) into the security of local government and communal spirit. The pattern culminates in the Parliament of Honour, where, in passages borrowed heavily from John Stow's *Survey of London* (1598), the figure of Antiquity recalls (as was conventional) the Company's noble and royal patrons in order to celebrate the amity and mutual dependency between citizenry and gentry, commune and Crown, City and nation. Invoking the Skinners' ancient identity as the 'Fraternity of Corpus Christi', the guild that had sponsored the processions and performances in which medieval Londoners had celebrated their corporate life, Middleton's Parliament of Honour completes not only a narrative but a hierarchical image of the body politic. Upon the mayor's return from the Guildhall feast, when 'the whole triumph' was 'placed in comely and decent order before him' (405–6), London's citizenry would have witnessed passing before them the rising echelons of the social order, from the 'rude multitude' figured in the Wilderness (157), to the 'large benefactors and sweet governors' (223) of the urban community, to the chief of England's nobility and royalty. The whole movement is reinforced by a cycle of light imagery that extends from the vigilance of the heraldic cock, 'the morning's herald' (166), to the 'six-and-twenty bright-burning lamps' of London's magistrates (204–5), to the circular motion of 'the bright sun' (416) invoked in Love's closing speech.

In the Wilderness pageant, where the cock's timely vigilance is contrasted with the time-serving clocks that are irresponsibly turned back on 'revelling nights' at court (113–27), Middleton may be glancing not only at courtiers in general but at the first glimmerings of an anti-Buckingham sentiment. Six months after becoming mayor, Cokayne married his daughter to Charles, Baron Howard of Effingham, a minor scion of the Howard faction whose leaders, Nottingham and Suffolk, rivals to Buckingham, were brought down in the months preceding Cokayne's inauguration. Six weeks before the inauguration, moreover, Frederick the Elector, the King's son-in-law, had announced his acceptance of the Bohemian crown; in the incipient war-fever, sentiments ran high (on September 12 Archbishop Abbot called in a letter for 'ringing of bells, and making of bonfires in London' and for a campaign to 'tear the Whore and make her desolate'). By the time of the mayoral inauguration in late October, Buckingham was being blamed for the King's reluctance to commit himself to the Protestant cause in

Europe. The unusually heavy use, in Middleton's inaugural show, of the City Trained Bands, whose Lord-General Cokayne became with his inauguration, may reflect the City's eagerness, manifest later in Cokayne's mayoralty, to contribute to war with Spain.

In its topicality, *The Triumphs of Love and Antiquity* is thus adapted both to the current political scene and to Cokayne's complex place within it. At least three of the earliest of Middleton's *Honourable Entertainments* were written specifically for Cokayne during his mayoralty. Throughout these works, Middleton uses the Cokayne cock and the golden cock-shaped loving cups which Cokayne's father had bequeathed to the Company of Skinners without alluding to the fact that the Company had been forced to sue the son in order to obtain its legacy. In Middleton's mayoral show, the heraldic cock appears above the head of Orpheus, the archetypal figure of the civic poet. The presenters of all three pageants in the show—Orpheus, Example, and Antiquity—symbolize the attributes of eloquence that sustain the civic order. In view of his services to the City and to Cokayne, it is not surprising that in September 1620—the last month of Cokayne's mayoralty—Middleton became the first official Chronologer to the City of London, appointed to 'set down all memorable acts of this City...and for such other employments as this Court shall have occasion to use him in'.

SEE ALSO

Textual introduction and apparatus: *Companion*, 672
Authorship and date: *Companion*, 408
General introduction to the civic entertainments: this volume, 968
Other Middleton–Christmas works: *Aries*, 1586; *Virtue*, 1714; *Integrity*, 1766; *Prosperity*, 1901; lost pageant for Charles I, 1898

The Triumphs of Love and Antiquity

An honourable solemnity performed through the City, at the confirmation and establishment of the Right Honourable Sir William Cokayne, Knight, in the office of His Majesty's lieutenant, the Lord Mayor of the famous City of London.

Taking beginning in the morning at his lordship's going, and perfecting itself after his return from receiving the oath of mayoralty at Westminster, on the morrow after Simon and Jude's Day, October 29, 1619.

To the honour of him, to whom the noble Fraternity of Skinners, his worthy brothers, have dedicated their loves in costly triumphs, the Right Honourable, Sir William Cokayne, Knight, Lord Mayor of this renowned city, and Lord General of all the military forces

Love, triumph, honour, all the glorious graces,
This day holds in her gift; fixed eyes and faces
Apply themselves in joy all to your look:
In duty then, my service, and the book.

At your lordship's command,
Tho. Middleton.

The Triumphs of Love and Antiquity

If foreign nations have been struck with admiration at the form, state, and splendour of some yearly triumphs wherein art hath been but weakly imitated and most beggarly worded, there is fair hope that things where invention flourishes, clear art and her graceful proprieties should receive favour and encouragement from the content of the spectator, which, next to the service of his honour and honourable Society, is the principal reward it looks for; and not despairing of that common favour—which is often cast upon the undeserver, through the distress and misery of judgement—this takes delight to present itself.

And first, to begin early with the love of the city to his lordship, let me draw your attentions to his honour's entertainment upon the water, where expectation, big with the joy of the day, but beholding to free love for language and expression, thus salutes the great master of the day and triumph.

THE SPEECH TO ENTERTAIN HIS LORDSHIP UPON THE WATER.

LOVE

Honour and joy double their blessings on thee.
I, the day's love, the city's general love,
Salute thee in the sweetness of content;
All that behold me worthily may see
How full mine eye stands of the joy of thee;
The more, because I may with confidence say
Desert and love will be well matched today.
And herein the great'st pity will appear,
This match can last no longer than a year.

3 **William Cokayne** Sheriff, 1609–10; Alderman from 1609 until his death in 1626; member of Skinners from 1590; admitted of Gray's Inn, 1600

Yet let not that discourage thy good ways,
Men's loves will last to crown thy end of days;
If those should fail, which cannot easily die,
Thy good works wed thee to eternity.
Let not the shortness then of time dismay
The largeness of thy worth, gain every day;
So many years thou gain'st that some have lost;
For they that think their care is at great cost,
If they do any good in time so small,
They make their year but a poor day in all.
For, as a learnèd man will comprehend
In compass of his hour, doctrine so sound,
Which give another a whole year to mend,
He shall not equal upon any ground.
So the judicious, when he comes to bear
This powerful office, struck with divine fear,
Collects his spirits, redeems his hours with care,
Thinks of his charge and oath, what ties they are;
And with a virtuous resolution then
Works more good in one year than some in ten.
Nor is this spoken any to detract,
But all t'encourage to put truth in act.
Methinks I see oppression hang the head,
Falsehood and injury with their guilt struck dead,
At this triumphant hour; ill causes hide
Their leprous faces, daring not t'abide
The brightness of this day; and in mine ear
Methinks the Graces' silver chimes I hear.
Good wishes are at work now in each heart,
Throughout this sphere of brotherhood play their part;
Chiefly thy noble own fraternity,
As near in heart as they're in place to thee,
The ensigns of whose love bounty displays,
Yet esteems all their cost short of thy praise.
There will appear elected sons of war,
Which this fair city boasts of, for their care,
Strength, and experience, set in truth of heart,
All great and glorious masters in that art
Which gives to man his dignity, name, and seal,
Prepared to speak love in a noble peal,
Knowing two triumphs must on this day dwell,
For magistrate one, and one for colonel:
Return lord-general, that's the name of state
The soldier gives thee, peace the magistrate.
On then, great hope. Here that good care begins,
Which now earth's love and heaven's hereafter wins.

At his lordship's return from Westminster, those worthy gentlemen whose loves and worths were prepared before in the conclusion of the former speech by water, are now all ready to salute their lord-general with a noble volley at his lordship's landing; and in the best and most commendable form, answerable to the nobleness of their free love and service, take their march before his lordship, who, being so honourably conducted, meets the first triumph by land waiting his lordship's most wished arrival in Paul's Churchyard, near Paul's Chain, which is a Wilderness, most gracefully and artfully furnished with divers kinds of beasts bearing fur, proper to the fraternity; the presenter the musical Orpheus, great master both in poesy and harmony, who by his excellent music drew after him wild beasts, woods, and mountains; over his head an artificial cock, often made to crow and flutter with his wings. This Orpheus, at the approach of his lordship, gives life to these words.

THIS SPEECH DELIVERED BY ORPHEUS

Great lord, example is the crystal glass
By which wise magistracy sets his face,
Fits all his actions to their comeliest dress,
For there he sees honour and seemliness:
'Tis not like flattering glasses, those false books
Made to set age back in great courtiers' looks;
Like clocks on revelling nights, that ne'er go right,
Because the sports may yield more full delight;
But when they break off, then they find it late,
The time and truth appears: such is their state,
Whose death by flatteries is set back awhile,
But meets 'em in the midst of their safe smile.
Such horrors those forgetful things attend,
That only mind their ends, but not their end.
Leave them to their false trust; list thou to me.
Thy power is great, so let thy virtues be,
Thy care, thy watchfulness, which are but things
Remembered to thy praise; from thence it springs,
And not from fear of any want in thee.
For in this truth I may be comely free:
Never was man advanced yet waited on
With a more noble expectation:
That's a great work to perfect; and as those
That have in art a mast'ry can oppose
All comers, and come off with learnèd fame,
Yet think not scorn still of a scholar's name,
A title which they had in ignorant youth,
So he that deals in such a weight of truth
As th'execution of a magistrate's place,
Though never so exact in form and grace,
Both from his own worth and man's free applause,
Yet may be called a labourer in the cause,
And be thought good to be so, in true care
The labour being so glorious, just, and fair.
Behold, then, in a rough example here
The rude and thorny ways thy care must clear;
Such are the vices in a city sprung,
As are yon thickets that grow close and strong;

76 ***Graces'*** could be either the chimes of the mythological Graces or those of the Theological Graces: Faith, Hope, and Love

81 ***ensigns*** banners, flags

Such is oppression, coz'nage, bribes, false hires,
As are yon catching and entangling briers;
Such is gout-justice, that's delay in right,
Demurs in suits that are as clear as light.
Just such a wilderness is a commonwealth
That is undressed, unpruned, wild in her health;
And the rude multitude the beasts o'th' wood,
That know no laws, but only will and blood;
And yet, by fair example, musical grace,
Harmonious government of the man in place,
Of fair integrity and wisdom framed,
They stand as mine do, ravished, charmed, and tamed:
Every wise magistrate that governs thus,
May well be called a powerful Orpheus.
  Behold yon bird of state, the vigilant cock,
The morning's herald and the plowman's clock,
At whose shrill crow the very lion trembles,
The sturdiest prey-taker that here assembles;
How fitly does it match your name and power,
Fixed in that name now by this glorious hour,
At your just voice to shake the bold'st offence
And sturdiest sin that e'er had residence
In secure man, yet, with an equal eye,
Matching grave justice with fair clemency,
It being the property he chiefly shows,
To give wing-warning still before he crows,
To crow before he strike; by his clapped wing
To stir himself up first, which needful thing
Is every man's first duty; by his crow,
A gentle call or warning, which should flow
From every magistrate; before he extend
The stroke of justice, he should reprehend
And try the virtue of a powerful word,
If that prevail not, then the spur, the sword.
See, herein honours to his majesty
Are not forgotten, when I turn and see
The several countries, in those faces plain,
All owing fealty to one sovereign;
The noble English, the fair-thriving Scot,
Plain-hearted Welsh, the Frenchman bold and hot,
The civilly instructed Irishman,
And that kind savage the Virginian,
All lovingly assembled, e'en by fate,
This thy day's honour to congratulate.
On, then; and as your service fills this place,
So through the city do his lordship grace.

At which words this part of triumph moves onward and meets the full body of the show in the other Paul's Churchyard; then dispersing itself according to the ordering of the speeches following, one part, which is the Sanctuary of Fame, plants itself near the Little Conduit in Cheap; another, which hath the title of the Parliament of Honour, at St Lawrence Lane end. Upon the battlements of that beauteous Sanctuary, adorned with six-and-twenty bright-burning lamps, having allusion to the six-and-twenty aldermen—they being, for their justice, government, and example, the lights of the city—a grave personage, crowned with the title and inscription of Example, breathes forth these sounds.

EXAMPLE

From that rough wilderness, which did late present
The perplexed state and cares of government,
Which every painful magistrate must meet,
Here the reward stands for thee: a chief seat
In Fame's fair Sanctuary, where some of old,
Crowned with their troubles, now are here enrolled
In memory's sacred sweetness to all ages;
And so much the world's voice of thee presages.
  And these that sit for many, with their graces
Fresh as the buds of roses, though they sleep,
In thy Society had once high places,
Which in their good works they forever keep;
Life called 'em in their time honour's fair stars,
Large benefactors and sweet governors.
If here were not sufficient grace for merit,
Next object, I presume, will raise thy spirit.

In this masterpiece of art, Fame's illustrious Sanctuary, the memory of those worthies shine gloriously that have been both lord mayors of this city and noble benefactors and brothers of this worthy fraternity; to wit, Sir Henry Barton, Sir William Gregory, Sir Stephen Jennings, Sir Thomas Mirfen, Sir Andrew Judd, Sir Wolstan Dixie, Sir Stephen Slany, Sir Richard Saltonstall, and now the right honourable Sir William Cokayne.

That Sir Henry Barton, an honour to memory, was the first that, for the safety of travellers and strangers by night through the city, caused lights to be hung out from Allhallowtide to Candlemas; therefore, in this Sanctuary of Fame, where the beauty of good actions shine, he is most properly and worthily recorded. His lordship by this time gracefully conducted toward that Parliament of Honour, near St Lawrence Lane end, Antiquity, from its eminence, thus gloriously salutes him.

ANTIQUITY, IN THE PARLIAMENT OF HONOUR

Grave city-governor, so much honour do me,
Vouchsafe thy presence and thy patience to me,
And I'll reward that virtue with a story,
That shall to thy fraternity add glory;
Then to thy worth no mean part will arise,
That art ordained chief for that glorious prize.

151 ***coz'nage*** cheating, fraud
153 ***gout-justice*** justice that is halting or tardy
182 ***reprehend*** reprimand, rebuke
185 ***his majesty*** King James I
229–30 **Henry Barton** mayor 1416 and again in 1428
230 **William Gregory** mayor, 1451
Stephen Jennings mayor, 1508
231 **Thomas Mirfen** mayor, 1518
Andrew Judd mayor, 1550
Wolstan Dixie mayor, 1585
232 **Stephen Slany** mayor, 1595
Richard Saltonstall mayor, 1597
237 **Allhallowtide** liturgical season of All Saints
Candlemas church festival on 2 February
244 ***Vouchsafe*** confer on, bestow

'Tis I that keep all the records of fame,
Mother of truths, Antiquity my name;
No year, month, day, or hour, that brings in place
Good works and noble, for the city's grace,
But I record, that after-times may see
What former were, and how they ought to be
Fruitful and thankful, in fair actions flowing,
To meet heaven's blessings, to which much is owing.
For instance, let all grateful eyes be placed
Upon this mount of royalty, by kings graced,
Queens, prince, dukes, nobles, more by numb'ring gained
Than can be in this narrow sphere contained;
Seven kings, five queens, only one prince alone,
Eight dukes, two earls, Plantagenets twenty-one;
All these of this fraternity made free,
Brothers and sisters of this company:
And see with what propriety the Fates
Have to this noble brotherhood knit such states;
For what society the whole city brings
Can with such ornaments adorn their kings,
Their only robes of state, when they consent
To ride most glorious to high parliament?
And mark in this their royal intent still;
For when it pleased the goodness of their will
To put the richest robes of their loves on
To the whole city, the most ever came
To this society, which records here prove,
Adorning their adorners with their love,
Which was a kingly equity.
Be careful then, great lord, to bring forth deeds
To match that honour that from hence proceeds.

At the close of which speech the whole triumph takes leave of his lordship for that time; and, till after the feast at Guildhall, rests from service. His lordship, accompanied with many noble personages; the honourable fellowship of ancient magistrates and aldermen of this city; the two new sheriffs, the one of his own fraternity (the complete Brotherhood of Skinners), the right worshipful Master Sheriff Dean, a very bountiful and worthy citizen; not forgetting the noble pains and loves of the heroic captains of the city, and gentlemen of the Artillery-garden, making, with two glorious ranks, a manly and majestic passage for their lord-general, his lordship, through Guildhall yard; and afterward their loves to his lordship resounding in a second noble volley.

Now, that all the honours before mentioned in that Parliament, or Mount of Royalty, may arrive at a clear and perfect manifestation, to prevent the over curious and inquisitive spirit, the names and times of those kings, queens, prince, dukes, and nobles, free of the honourable Fraternity of Skinners in London, shall here receive their proper illustrations.

Anno 1329. King Edward the Third, Plantagenet, by whom, in the first of his reign, this worthy society of Skinners was incorporate, he their first royal founder and brother: queen Philipa his wife, younger daughter of William Earl of Hainaut, the first royal sister; so gloriously virtuous that she is a rich ornament to memory; she both founded and endowed Queen's College in Oxford, to the continuing estate of which I myself wish all happiness; this queen at her death desired three courtesies, some of which are rare in these days. First, that her debts might be paid to the merchants; secondly, that her gifts to the church might be performed; thirdly, that the king, when he died, would at Westminster be interred with her.

Anno 1357. Edward Plantagenet, surnamed the Black Prince, son to Edward the Third, Prince of Wales, Duke of Guienne, Aquitaine, and Cornwall, Earl Palatine of Chester. In the battle of Poitiers in France, he, with 8000 English against 60,000 French, got the victory; took the king, Philip his son, seventeen earls, with divers other noble personages, prisoners.

King Richard the Second, Plantagenet. This king being the third royal brother of this honourable Company, and at that time the society consisting of two brotherhoods of Corpus Christi, the one at St Mary Spital, the other at St Mary Bethl'em without Bishopsgate, in the eighteenth of his reign granted them to make their two brotherhoods one, by the name of the Fraternity of Corpus Christi of Skinners, which worthy title shines at this day gloriously amongst 'em; and toward the end of this king's reign, 1396, a great feast was celebrated in Westminster Hall, where the lord mayor of this city sat as guest.

Anno 1381. Queen Anne, his wife, daughter to the Emperor Charles the Fourth, and sister to Emperor Wenceslaus, whose modesty then may make this age blush now, she being the first that taught women to ride sideling on horseback; but who it was that taught 'em to ride straddling, there is no records so immodest that can show me, only the impudent time and the open profession. This fair precedent of womanhood died at Sheen, now Richmond; for grief whereof King Richard her lord abandoned and defaced that goodly house.

Anno 1399. King Henry the Fourth, Plantagenet, surnamed Bullingbrooke, a fourth royal brother. In his time the famous Guildhall in London was erected, where the honourable courts of the city are kept, and this bounteous feast yearly celebrated. In the twelfth year of his reign the river Thames flowed thrice in one day.

262 ***Plantagenets*** familiar name for the ruling family of England, 1154–1485

289 **gentlemen... Artillery-garden** the Honourable Artillery company of the City of London, revitalized in 1610; the 'garden' or exercising ground for the company located between west side of Finsbury Square and Bunhill Row.

324 **St Mary Spital** Spitalfields, fields east of London which once belong to the Priory and Hospital of St Mary Spital, founded in 1197

324–5 **St Mary Bethl'em** Hospital of St Mary of Bethlehem, located in Bishopsgate ward, known as a lunatic hospital from 1547

Queen Joan, or Jane, Duchess of Brittany, late wife to John Duke of Brittany and daughter to the King of Navarre, another princely sister.

Anno 1412. King Henry the Fifth, Plantagenet, Prince of Wales, proclaimed Mayor and Regent of France. He won that famous victory on the French at the battle of Agincourt. Queen Catherine, his wife, daughter to Charles the Sixth, King of France.

King Henry the Sixth, Plantagenet, of the house of Lancaster.

King Edward the Fourth, Plantagenet, of the house of York. This king feasted the Lord Mayor, Richard Chawry, and the aldermen his brethren, with certain commoners in Waltham Forest: after dinner rode a-hunting with the king, who gave him plenty of venison, and sent to the lady mayoress and her sisters the aldermen's wives, two harts, six bucks, and a tun of wine, to make merry; and this noble feast was kept at Drapers' Hall.

Anno 1463. Queen Elizabeth Grey, his wife, daughter to Richard Woodville, Earl Rivers, and to the Duchess of Bedford; she was mother to the Lord Grey of Ruthen that in his time was Marquess Dorset.

King Richard the Third, brother to Edward the Fourth, Duke of Gloucester, and of the house of York.

Lionel Plantagenet, third son to the third Edward, Duke of Clarence and Earl of Ulster; Philipa his daughter and heir married Edward Mortimer, Earl of March, from whom the house of York descends.

Henry Plantagenet, grandchild to Edmond Crouchback, second son to Henry the Third.

Richard Plantagenet, father of Edward the Fourth, Duke of York and Albemarle, Earl of Cambridge, Rutland, March, Clare, and Ulster.

Thomas Plantagenet, second son of Henry the Fourth.

John Plantagenet, third son of Henry the Fourth; so noble a soldier and so great a terror to the French, that when Charles the Eighth was moved to deface his monument—being buried in Rouen—the king thus answered: Pray, let him rest in peace, being dead, of whom we were all afraid when he lived.

Humphrey Plantagenet, fourth son of Henry the Fourth.

John Holland, Duke of Exeter.

George Plantagenet, brother to Edward the Fourth.

Edmond Plantagenet, brother to Edward the Fourth.

Richard Neville, Earl of Salisbury and Warwick, called the Great Earl of Warwick.

John Cornwall Knight, Baron Fanhope.

The royal sum: Seven kings, five queens, one prince, seven dukes, one earl; twenty-one Plantagenets. Seven kings, five queens, one prince, eight dukes, two earls, one lord; twenty-four Skinners.

The feast ended at Guildhall, his lordship, as yearly custom invites it, goes, accompanied with the triumph before him, towards St Paul's, to perform the noble and reverend ceremonies which divine antiquity religiously ordained, and is no less than faithfully observed. Holy service and ceremonies accomplished, his lordship returns by torchlight to his own house, the whole triumph placed in comely and decent order before him: the Wilderness, the Sanctuary of Fame, adorned with lights, the Parliament of Honour, and the Triumphant Chariot of Love, with his graceful concomitants, the chariot drawn with two luzerns. Near to the entrance of his lordship's gate, Love, prepared with his welcome, thus salutes him.

LOVE

I was the first, grave lord, that welcomed thee
To this day's honour, and I spake it free,
Just as in every heart I found it placed,
And 'tis my turn again now to speak last;
For love is circular, like the bright sun,
And takes delight to end where it begun,
Though indeed never ending in true will,
But rather may be said beginning still,
As all great works are of celestial birth,
Of which love is the chief in heaven and earth.
To what blessed state then are thy fortunes come,
Since that both brought thee forth and brings thee home?
Now, as in common course, which clears things best,
There's no free gift but looks for thanks at least;
A love so bountiful, so free, so good,
From the whole city, from thy brotherhood—
That name I ought a while to dwell upon—
Expect some fair requital from the man
They've all so largely honoured: what's desired?
That which in conscience ought to be required;
O, thank 'em in thy justice, in thy care,
Zeal to right wrongs, works that are clear and fair,
And will become thy soul, whence virtue springs,
As those rich ornaments thy brother-kings.
And since we cannot separate love and care—
For where care is, a love must needs be there,
And care where love is, 'tis the man and wife,
Through every estate that's fixed in life;
You are by this the city's bridegroom proved,
And she stands wedded to her best beloved:
Then be, according to your morning vows,
A careful husband to a loving spouse;
And heaven give you great joy, both it and thee,
And to all those that shall match after ye.

361 **Waltham Forest** forest near the village of Waltham in Hertforshire, a few miles north of London
364 **tun** large barrel
410 **luzerns** lynx

The names of those beasts bearing fur, and now in use with the bountiful Society of Skinners, the most of which presented in the Wilderness, where Orpheus predominates

Ermine, foine, sables, martin, badger, bear,
Luzern, budge, otter, hipponesse, and hare,
Lamb, wolf, fox, leopard, mink, stot, miniver,
Raccoon, moashy, wolverine, caliber,
Squirrel, mole, cat, musk, civet, wild and tame,
Cony, white, yellow, black, must have a name,
The ounce, rowsgray, jennet, pampilion;
Of birds the vulture, bittern, ostrich, swan:
Some worn for ornament, and some for health,
All to the Skinners' art bring fame and wealth.

The service being thus faithfully performed, both to his lordship's honour and to the credit and content of his most generously bountiful society, the season commends all to silence; yet not without a little leave taken to reward art with the comely dues that belong unto it, which hath been so richly expressed in the body of the triumph with all the proper beauties of workmanship, that the city may, without injury to judgement, call it the masterpiece of her triumphs; the credit of which workmanship I must justly lay upon the deserts of master Garret Christmas and master Robert Norman, joined-partners in the performance.

FINIS.

449 **foine** animal of polecat or weasel kind
sables small carnivorous quadruped
martin possibly a kind of monkey
450 **budge** lamb's skin with wool dressed outward
hipponesse fur-bearing animal
451 **stot** a steer
miniver fur-bearing animal
452 **moashy** some kind of fur
caliber a type of squirrel
453 **musk** animal producing musk, usually the musk deer
civet in size and appearance between a fox and a weasel
454 **Cony** rabbit
455 **ounce** common lynx
rowsgray obscure (*OED* cites this example)
pampilion fur-bearing animal
456 **bittern** a bird smaller than a heron
469 **Garret Christmas** Christmas and his two sons were involved with the production of Lord Mayor's Shows from 1618 to 1639, twenty-one years. Garret Christmas (also known as Gerard Christmas) is first cited for his work with Munday in the 1618 Lord Mayor's Show, *Sidero-thriambos*. He works on all the subsequent shows by Middleton.
Robert Norman Norman served as artificer in the pageants of 1628, 1634, and 1635.

THE WORLD TOSSED AT TENNIS

Edited by C. E. McGee

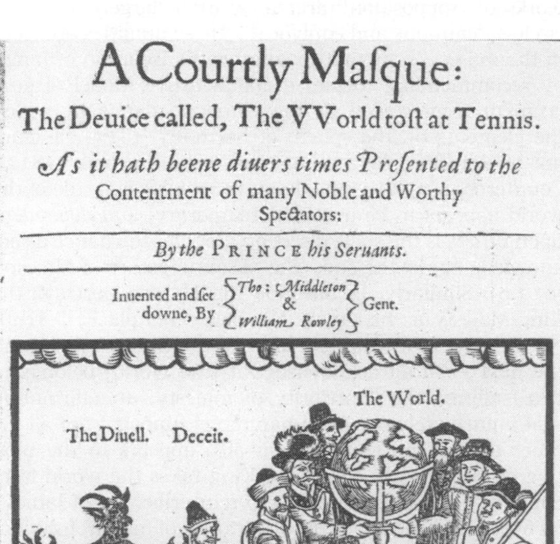

A Courtly Maſque:

The Deuice called, The VVorld toſt at Tennis.

As it hath beene diuers times Preſented to the Contentment of many Noble and Worthy Spectators:

By the PRINCE *his Seruants.*

Inuented and ſet downe, By *Tho: Middleton* & *William Rowley* Gent.

The World. The Diuell. Deceit.

London printed by *George Purſlowe*, and are to be ſold by at Chriſt Church Gate, 1620.

A Courtly Masque, further entitled *The World Tossed at Tennis*, should have been performed, probably early in 1620, at Denmark House in the presence of King James and Prince Charles. The King gave Denmark House to the Prince of Wales by a grant of 28 September 1619, thereby making him lord not only of Richmond and St James's but also of the palace of the late Queen Anne. To express his gratitude for this gift and to display his magnificence, newly enhanced by the King's generosity, Prince Charles set in motion preparations for an entertainment of James, the centrepiece of which was to be a courtly masque. Charles further established his prestige by summoning his own players, led by William Rowley, to take the major roles in the production, and Rowley, presumably, turned to his trusted collaborator, Thomas Middleton, for help with the masque. The intended performance at court was a splendid opportunity, offering the authors and actors a place of prominence before an audience full of potential patrons. However, the very forces that ennobled the occasion, the sponsorship of Charles and the presence of James, made it problematic—particularly at this time, when the King and the Prince were at odds over England's policy concerning Europe, 'the world' already being tossed by the Thirty Years War.

Writing early in 1620 under these historical conditions, Middleton and Rowley had to mediate between the scholarly pacifism of the King and the Protestant militancy of his son. Prince Charles favoured moral, financial, and military support of the claim to the crown of Bohemia staked by his brother-in-law, Frederick, the Elector Palatine. The Estates of Bohemia had chosen Frederick to be their king on 26 August 1619, after fifteen months of armed civil insurrection in which Protestant forces in Bohemia rebelled against their monarch, the Austrian Emperor, Matthias, and his cousin, the heir apparent to the throne of Bohemia, Ferdinand, Duke of Styria. Ferdinand, a staunch Roman Catholic, had persecuted cruelly the Protestants of Styria and, like other Habsburgs before him, had tried to subvert the elective monarchy of Bohemia by establishing a hereditary claim to it. Protestant insurgents in Bohemia could not accept the grim prospect of his succession, so that, having routed the Austrian forces and set up a provisional government in 1618, they formally deposed Ferdinand on 31 July 1619. When Frederick, the Elector Palatine, accepted the crown offered to him by the Bohemian Estates, he became the central figure in a momentous political and religious conflict, one in which he counted on the support of Protestant states such as England—especially England, where his father-in-law reigned.

King James, however, true to his motto, *Beati pacifici* ('Blessed are the peacemakers', Matthew 5:9), wanted to restore peace and order in Europe by negotiation and treaty. In particular, he hoped to protect England's *rapprochement* with a long-standing Catholic foe, Spain, and to confirm that alliance with the marriage of Prince Charles and the Spanish princess. For five months after learning that Frederick had accepted the Bohemian crown, James played the scholar's part; he studied Frederick's right to be 'King of Bohemia' and debated the question with Baron zu Dohna, Frederick's emissary in England. Evidence of the consequences of James's strategy, gathered together by S. R. Gardiner in *Letters and Other Documents Illustrating the Relations between England and Germany at the Commencement of the Thirty Years War*, appears in the dispatches of foreign ambassadors, who described the King as divided from the Prince, from his favourite, the Duke of Buckingham, from the Earl of Doncaster, England's special envoy to Europe, from the Privy Council—from 'in a word all good patriots' according to Sir Francis Nethersole. The diplomats regularly noted the inaction and isolation of King James; Venetian Girolamo Lando, though oversimplifying somewhat, is typical: 'The whole nation takes the same side, and all the kingdom declares its impatience of this prolonged irresolution. Nevertheless His Majesty takes advice from no one but himself. He gives out that he has not yet succeeded in understanding the arguments bearing upon the affair...' Faced with these tactics, 'the great men and nobility', according to the ambassador to the States General, Noel de Caron, 'will not stop till they have spurred and driven' the monarch to come to the aid of the Elector Palatine. *Tennis*, had it been performed at court, would have been part of this project.

To 'entangle' James in the Protestant cause, the masque not only celebrated the glorious war in Europe, but also tried to elicit from the King a public gesture of support for the enterprise. This ploy occurs at the very end, when the Scholar and the Soldier present their 'wish with reverence to this place, | For here't must be confirmed or 'tas no grace' (887–8). Here, as in other masques, characters in a fictive world reach into the world of the audience. Though well established in Tudor and Stuart entertainments, this strategy was risky, especially if that audience included the often impatient, unresponsive King James, for the closure of the entire show depended on the willingness of the monarch to play along, and, in the case of *Tennis*, publicly to support the Soldier's readiness to fight in Europe. There is little reason to think that James, who, according to the French ambassador reporting in March 1620, 'dislikes utterly all the proceedings in Bohemia', would have obliged.

Disinclined to be put in the awkward position required by the final speech of the masque, of having to endorse the Soldier's campaign as a condition for approving of the Scholar's hopeful acceptance of the Jacobean peace, King James may have scuttled the entertainment at Denmark House planned by Prince Charles. No evidence of a production of *Tennis* at court has been found, but the masque *was* performed, at the Prince's Arms (otherwise known as the Swan) and, according to the title-page, 'divers times...to the contentment of many noble and worthy spectators'. William Beeston, manager of the Cockpit in Drury Lane, evidently judged *Tennis* to be negotiable in the public theatres and maintained his right to '*The World*' until at least 1639. Presented in 1620 to a Swan audience—presumably made up in part of lords and gentry disappointed by the King's irresolute response to the Protestant cause in Europe and in part of Londoners like those who celebrated the coronation of the Elector Palatine with bonfires, raised money for his defence, and joined the forces levied to protect the Palatinate—*Tennis*'s militant Protestantism would have been welcome. At this venue, the final appeal would have been directed 'with reverence' (887) to the playgoers. Put in the King's position for the moment, the audience was empowered to confirm by their applause the Soldier's commitment to go 'over yonder to the most glorious wars' (878). But for this audience too the moment might have been awkward as their applause was co-opted in support of the Scholar's endeavours and James's peace.

In the ambiguity of this final engagement of its audiences, *Tennis* is, as Margot Heinemann has said of other works of '"opposition" drama' written 'largely for court circles', 'cautious and equivocal'. These qualities are clear in the masque's attempt to counter the isolation of James by recommending to him a collaborative model of government, represented in the climactic dance in which the elements of 'the sphere of harmony' (811)—including Majesty/the player-King—'all move mutually' (812). Counterpointing this final dance in which royal rule of the world appears to be unstable, temporary, and dependent upon others is the stage direction glossing the dance as acknowledging, in the end, 'the absolute power of Majesty' (813.6). Similarly, in one line the Flamen portrays the King/Majesty as his equal ('...here's his place, | Truth his defence, and majesty his grace' [816–17]), but in the next ('We all acknowledge it [the world] belongs to you') affirms the superiority of majesty, an affirmation that immediately receives unanimous support from all the other characters. Equivocation also appears in the plotting of the masque. When the King takes the world from Simplicity, the masque seems to reinscribe one of James's favourite arguments for the superiority of monarchs: since kings come first after the age of innocence, their priority establishes their pre-eminence. However, Jupiter provides an alternative interpretation of the sequence of events when he intervenes (a step he takes only this once) after the Land-Captain receives the world from the King. The priority of the King and his deference to the Land-Captain are necessary for teaching a different lesson (one implicitly critical of Buckingham's distribution of patronage), that meritorious service should be honoured above all, even by monarchs:

> This was the season when desert was stooped to,
> By greatness stooped to, and acknowledged greatest;
> But in thy time, now, desert stoops itself
> To every baseness and makes saints of shadows.
> (619–22)

Finally, as these lines also suggest, there are the contradictory representations of the present, of England in 1620. Like most masques, *Tennis* transmutes its vision of ideal governance into a mirror of the current regime. The monarchy of King James becomes 'the sphere of harmony' that dashes the hopes of the Devil and Deceit while renewing those of the Soldier and the Scholar. In Middleton's hands, however, the grand compliments expected of the finale are qualified ('*when* his glorious peace' [815]; italics mine) and conditional ('*if* it hold' [876]; italics mine). More important, the high praise of 'this glorious time' (862) with its 'most glorious wars' (878) and 'a most glorious peace' (880) counterpoint, but fail to offset, the sustained criticism of society throughout the masque. The Soldier and the Scholar, both unemployed (as were more and more of their professions during James's reign) complain about the conditions of their lives with wit and conviction; nor do the rebukes of Pallas or the railing of Jupiter refute their claims. Persisting in their quest simply for a living, for 'a competence' (203) not a fortune, the Soldier and the Scholar prompt Pallas and Jupiter to extend the critique of the present by voicing their own sense of how values have declined from the 'first and simple state | To the foul centre where it now abides' (412–13). Similarly, Time undercuts the force of the ideal embodied in the Nine Worthies by refocusing attention on the present and its abuses. If the compliments of Jacobean rule in the finale are not deliberately inadequate to the critique of Jacobean rule throughout the masque, then *Tennis* is clearly, strategically 'cautious and equivocal'.

In two crucial respects however, it is not cautious or equivocal at all. First, whereas most masques, particularly those of Ben Jonson, praise King James as the embodiment in the present of the edifying ideals of the show, *Tennis* gives Prince Charles that status. Pallas's 'complete man' (164) is he who partakes of both arms and arts, and Jupiter reaffirms this ideal in his parting instructions to the Soldier and the Scholar: 'Scholar and soldier must both be shut in one; | That makes the absolute and complete man' (870–1). James was not, by this criterion, absolute or complete; personally renowned for his scholarship, he is praised at the end of the masque for a peaceful regime conducive to learning. Nor are the Soldier and Scholar complete men, for though they support one another's endeavours, in the end each goes his own separate way. Nor is this ideal to be found in 'the sphere of harmony'; there learning, the Lawyer and the Flamen, is split off from valour, the Land-Captain and the Sea-Captain. With one possible comic exception, 'the son of Simplicity' (Epistle.25–6) who was raised among 'good scholars of all sorts' and 'did good and honest service beyond the small seas' (Epistle.12–14), Prince Charles is the only 'absolute and complete man', being by Jupiter's account not only the son of Minerva, goddess of arts, but also her 'valiant'st, hopefull'st son' (866). Coming from the Prince's Men on an occasion when the Prince was playing host to the King and court, such singular praise of Charles is understandable. At the same time, whether delivered at Denmark House or in the Swan, this prominence given to Charles, particularly the valiant Charles, implies support for his policies, specifically for the valorous exercise of arms in Europe.

Secondly, *Tennis* emphasizes throughout the value of mutuality and collaboration. In the main show-within-the-show, Jupiter's dramatized history of the governance of the world, Middleton pokes fun at land-captain and sea-captain, churchman and lawyer by deftly caricaturing the narrowness of each one's concerns as well as the peculiarity of his rhetoric and comportment. He dramatizes also the failure of each character's regime: none of these characters falls for the greedy, Deceitful schemes of their aides, but all of them, when given rule of the world, indulge their own predilections. Middleton's comic effects are crucial, for they expose the limitations of the characters as individuals, so as to set up the main political point of the show: good government depends upon the cooperation of the various professions. The achievement of 'the sphere of harmony' epitomizes a pattern of the masque. Unlike the Jonsonian masque in which the disorderly forces of the antimasque have to be banished before an edifying, mystical vision of the court can appear, *Tennis* dramatizes a series of reconciliations. Characters overcome anxiety, disaffection, or rivalry, in order to establish new forms of fellowship. The Induction opens with Richmond worrying about the need to compete with a new rival for the attention of Prince Charles, but meeting Denmark House, who appreciates Richmond's distinctive strengths, relieves Richmond's anxiety so that both houses can join with St James's in a fellowship of seasonable service to their lord. Likewise, the Starches, testy and abrasive at first, perform their dance after agreeing unanimously that 'The sin's not i' the colour, but the pride' (406). The world itself, tossed from character to character, finally settles in the hands of Majesty, surrounded and supported in 'partnership' (848) by Valour, Religion, and Law. And the stage business by the Soldier and the Scholar at the very end of the masque emphasizes their new alliance, as the two exchange good wishes, shake hands, and, like brothers, present one petition to the audience. Matching this image of common purpose at the end are several at the start of the work: the Prologue's maxim, 'No man is lifted but by other hands' (15); the dedication of the work to new partners in marriage; the title-page announcing the collaborative authorship of Middleton and Rowley. The main thrust of *Tennis* opposes any ruler who, like James in 1619–20, would take advice 'from no one but himself'.

It is difficult to exaggerate how unusual *Tennis* is as a masque. The antimasque/masque structure developed by Jonson hardly applies given the brevity of the Starches scene and their integration into the masque's dominant pattern of collaborations. Unlike Jonson, Middleton and Rowley *seem* indifferent to the unity of the work; on the contrary, to provide delight they delight in eclecticism—promising a show that is pastoral, comical, tragical, historical; delivering one that is all that and satirical to boot. Most odd, the authors invert the conventional masque structure by placing first, rather than last as usual, the one dance that might have been performed by courtiers, that of the Nine Worthies. Non-speaking roles suitable for aristocratic amateurs, the Worthies are ushered in ceremoniously and represent the masque's highest ideals. Dancing first, they define an ideal that is quickly judged to be admirable but now unattainable; as a result, instead of demonstrating an ideal transcendence of current corruption, they measure the extent of the current moral decline. Radically different in form from the Jonsonian masque, *Tennis* is also radically different in its politics. According to Martin Butler, Jonson's *Pan's Anniversary*, also written in 1620, 'sets out to counter the current expectations of a more aggressive position on European affairs and to restrain them within limits of deference to James's kingship'. Jonson may well have been writing against Middleton and Rowley. Like *Pan's Anniversary* as Butler perceives its wider significance, *The World Tossed at Tennis* 'marks a new and disturbing development in court culture under James I... [in] making a contribution (albeit a small one) to the developing polarizations of attitude that were to be so significant a feature of English politics in the coming decade'.

SEE ALSO

Textual introduction and apparatus: *Companion*, 667
Authorship and date: *Companion*, 408
Other Middleton–Rowley works: *Weapons*, 980; *Quarrel*, 1209; *Old Law*, 1331; *Changeling*, 1632; *Gypsy*, 1723

THOMAS MIDDLETON and WILLIAM ROWLEY

The World Tossed at Tennis

A Courtly Masque

[*for Prince Charles's Men at The Swan*]

THE FIGURES AND PERSONS PROPERLY RAISED FOR EMPLOYMENT THROUGH THE WHOLE MASQUE

First, three ancient and princely receptacles: RICHMOND, ST JAMES'S, DENMARK HOUSE

A SCHOLAR
A SOLDIER

PALLAS
JUPITER

The Nine WORTHIES [with the MUSES]
The first song and first dance

TIME, a plaintiff (but his grievances delivered courteously)

The five STARCHES: WHITE, BLUE, YELLOW, GREEN, and RED
The second dance

SIMPLICITY, the Intermedler
DECEIT, the Disguiser
The second song, sung by REAPERS

A KING
A LAND-CAPTAIN
A SEA-CAPTAIN
MARINERS

The third song and third dance

The FLAMEN
The LAWYER
The fourth and last dance: the DEVIL an Intermixer

Persons.0.1 FIGURES the allegorical characters as opposed to the divine and human personages
RAISED produced; possibly punning on 'reared'

1 **princely** magnificent and, in this case, owned by Prince Charles
receptacles places where people are received; the terminology is consistent with the representation of the palaces as female

9 **courteously** punning: politely; appropriately for the courts of law; respectfully of the king and the courtly audience

12 **Intermedler** intermediator among the several characters who appear in the last part of the masque

22 **Intermixer** suggesting that the Devil was more thoroughly involved in the final dance, more aggressively engaged in the pursuit of the world (and probably more vividly repulsed) than the description of the dance (813.1–11) indicates

Dedication *The Epistle Dedicatory*

To the truly noble, Charles, Lord Howard, Baron of Effingham, and to his virtuous and worthy lady, the Right Honourable Mary, Lady Effingham, eldest daughter of the truly generous and judicious Sir William Cokayne, Knight, Lord Mayor of this City, and Lord General of the Military Forces.

To whom more properly may art prefer
Works of this nature, which are high and rare,
Fit to delight a prince's eye and ear,
Than to the hands of such a worthy pair?
Imagine this, mixed with delight and state,
Being then an entertainment for the best,
Your noble nuptials comes to celebrate;
And though it fall short of the day and feast
Of your most sacred and united loves,
Let none say therefore it untimely moves.
It can, I hope, come out of season never,
To find your joys new, as at first, for ever.

Most respectfully devoted to both your honours,
Thomas Middleton

To the well-wishing, well-reading understander, well-understanding reader—Simplicity S. P. D. **Epistle**

After most hearty commendations, my kind and unknown friends, trusting in Phoebus your understandings are all in as good health as Simplicity's was at the writing hereof, this is to certify you further that this short and small treatise that follows, called *A Masque*, the device further entitled *The World Tossed at Tennis*—how it will be now tossed in the world I know not—a toy brought to the press rather by the printer than the poet, who requested an epistle for his pass to satisfy his perusers how hitherto he hath behaved himself. First for his conception, he was begot in Brentford, born on the Bankside of Helicon, brought up amongst noble, gentle, commons, and good

Dedication.0.1 ***Epistle Dedicatory*** Invoking the names of Cokayne and Howard, the dedication of the book of the masque points toward the policy of military engagement advanced by the masque. William Howard (1510–1573), created Baron Howard of Effingham in 1554, served as Lord High Admiral from 1553 to 1558. Charles Howard (born in 1536) was far more famous: Lord High Admiral from 1585 until he resigned the office early in 1619, he secured his renown by leading the English forces against the Spanish armada in 1588 and at the capture of Cadiz in 1596.

To his second son and namesake, Middleton dedicated *Tennis*. This Charles Howard (1579–1642), styled Baron Effingham following the death of his older brother (William) in 1615, had not distinguished himself in arms prior to the publication of the masque, but he would serve as Lord Lieutenant of Surrey from 1621 and as Vice-Admiral of Sussex from 1626 until his death. When asked for donations in support of the cause of the Palatinate (see the Critical Introduction, 1405), he offered to serve in person because he lacked the financial resources to back the war effort. Clearly, Middleton was trading on the strength of the Howard name, not on the achievements of the latest Baron Effingham, whom John Chamberlain disparaged as a man 'worne out in state, credit, years, and otherwise' (2:301).

Sir William Cokayne had more to do with land-captains than with sea-captains like the Howards, for he began as a purveyor to the English army in Ireland in 1598, provided that service again in 1603, and maintained substantial mercantile interests overseas. As Lord General of the Military Forces, Cokayne was, in effect, commander-in-chief; however, his impressive title belies the improvisational nature and the disorganization of the military forces, which the pacifistic policies of King James had seriously weakened. Not a standing army, these forces consisted of the garrisons for forts and the militia of boroughs. For more on Cokayne, see *Antiquity* and *Entertainments*.

3 **Mary** Chamberlain judged the young, handsome Mary Cokayne to be a prize wasted on Charles Howard, but Cokayne wanted prestigious matches for his daughters, five of whom married earls, one a viscount, and one a knight. Mary Cokayne was an important bridge to her father, Middleton's most reliable, generous patron in 1619–20. Middleton, using the dedication of *Tennis* to represent the masque book as a belated wedding gift, adds this entertainment to the others he had written for the service of the Lord Mayor.

5 **Lord Mayor** see *Antiquity* for Cokayne's lord mayor's show.

7 **prefer** recommend

8 **high** noble

9 **prince's** alluding to Prince Charles's original sponsorship of the masque

11 **state** stateliness; pomp

13 **nuptials** wedding

14 **fall short** arrive late, for the book of the masque was not published until July 1620

the day 22 April 1620

16 **untimely** inopportunely, being late

Epistle.0.2 ***S. P. D.*** abbreviation of *salutem plurimam dicit*; Simplicity extends many greetings

2 **Phoebus** Apollo as the sun god, whose patronage of eloquence and medicine seem particularly relevant here

4 **to certify** generally, assure; more precisely, to attest legally. It is typical of the epistle and productive of its comic tone that Simplicity never says what he sets out so forcefully to make certain. The one point that might need to be certified is that the printer rather than the poet desired the publication of the masque, but Simplicity gets distracted from that point by the title of the work, its possible reception, and its essential insignificance.

5 **treatise** a book dealing with a particular subject

device an invention or contrivance; the word was often used specifically to refer to the entire show set forth on a civic pageant

7 **tossed** bandied about; received, debated and assessed

toy insignificant thing

9 **epistle** covering letter

pass written permission

11 **Brentford** Brentford, a holiday resort and lovers' rendezvous about eight miles west of London; see *Michaelmas* 2.3.185. While 'Braine-ford', the spelling used in Purslowe's edition, may serve Simplicity's biographical purposes by implying high intelligence, the locale also suggests ironically his illegitimacy.

Bankside of Helicon a bankside was the ground sloping down to a body of water. Helicon, a mountain in Boetia sacred to Apollo and the muses, was the site of the fountain Hippocrene. Hence, the 'Bankside of Helicon' may refer to the margin of the waters of poetic inspiration flowing from Hippocrene. However, for Londoners the Bankside had less rarefied associations, for it was a suburb on the south side of the Thames, a site of stews, theatres, and baiting pits.

12 **noble, gentle, commons** bathos for comic effect; while 'noble' and 'gentle' suggest upper-class associates, 'commons' brings the poet down to his proper place in the social structure

scholars of all sorts, where, for his time, he did good and honest service beyond the small seas. He was fair-spoken, never accused of scurrilous or obscene language (a virtue not ever found in scenes of the like condition), of as honest meaning reputed as his words reported, neither too bitterly taxing nor too soothingly telling the world's broad abuses, moderately merry as sententiously serious, never condemned but for his brevity in speech, ever wishing his tale longer to be assured he would continue to so good a purpose. Having all these handsome qualities simply and no other compounded with knavery, there is great hope he shall pass still by the fair way of good report, persevering in those honest courses which may become the son of Simplicity, who, though he be now in a masque, yet is his face apparent enough. And so, loving cousins, having no news to send you at this time but that Deceit is entering upon you (whom I pray you have a care to avoid), and this notice I can give you of him: there are some six or eight pages before him, the Lawyer and the Devil behind him. In this care I leave you, not leaving to be,

Your kind and loving kinsman,
Simplicity

Prologus

This, our device, we do not call a play,
Because we break the stage's laws today
Of acts and scenes. Sometimes a comic strain
Hath hit delight home in the master vein—
Thalia's prize. Melpomene's sad style
Hath shook the tragic hand another while.
The muse of history hath caught your eyes,
And she that chants the pastoral psalteries.
We now lay claim to none, yet all present,
Seeking out pleasure to find your content.
You shall perceive by what comes first in sight,
It was intended for a royal night.
There's one hour's words, the rest in songs and
dances.
Lauds no man's own; no man himself advances.
No man is lifted but by other hands:
Say he could leap, he lights but where he stands.
Such is our fate: if good, much good may't do you;
If not, sorry, we'll lose our labours wi'you.

An Induction to the Masque,
prepared for his Majesty's entertainment at Denmark House

Enter Richmond and St James's

ST JAMES'S Why, Richmond, Richmond, why art so heavy?

RICHMOND I have reason enough for that, good sainted sister. Am I not built with stone—fair, large, and free stone—some part covered with lead too?

ST JAMES'S All this is but a light-headed understanding now. I mean, why so melancholy?—thou look'st mustily methinks.

RICHMOND
Do I so? and yet I dwell in sweeter air
Than you, sweet St James's. How three days'
Warming has spirited you! You have sometimes
Your vacations as other of your friends have,
If you call yourself to mind.

ST JAMES'S Thou never saw'st

14 **small seas** probably the English Channel, the North Sea, or the Irish Sea, as opposed to the Atlantic
15 **scurrilous** indecent
16 **scenes** situations
18 **taxing** criticizing
19 **sententiously** wisely, with the suggestion of some pomposity
22 **simply** without admixture, with simplicity, and as the offspring of Simplicity
23 **knavery** dishonesty
24 **pass ... report** be well reputed
25 **courses** activities
26 **masque** punning on mask
27 **cousins** kindred spirits
31 **behind** after
32 **leaving** ceasing
Prologue.2 **the stage's laws** alluding to the normative status of classical models for the division of plays into acts and scenes. The prominent place of Terence on the curriculum of schools so re-enforced this idea of dramatic structure that it might be taken to have the force of 'laws'.
3 **strain** passage
4 **master vein** as the dominant effect
5 **Thalia's** the muse of comedy's
Melpomene's the muse of tragedy's
sad serious
7 **muse of history** Clio
8 **pastoral** literature of idyllic country life, the muse of which was Euterpe
psalteries songs sung to a psaltery, an ancient stringed instrument
11 **by ... sight** the Induction welcoming King James
14 **Lauds no man's own** praises no individual himself
Induction.0.1 *Induction* formal introduction
1 **heavy** sad; but mistakenly taken in the literal sense ('weighty') by Richmond
3 **sister** because the Latin word for 'palace' (*regia*) was feminine, such buildings were conventionally represented as female
3–4 **free stone** freestone: a high quality, fine grained limestone. The impressive royal apartments of Richmond, rising three storeys beside the Thames, were faced with freestone. The gown of the character probably imitated stonework, as those of St James's and Denmark House did brickwork. Presumably each character, like London in *Truth*, wore a headpiece with the recognizable skyline of each castle.
4 **lead** the towers atop Richmond were 'crowned with leaden cupolas of picturesque profile'; see Colvin.
5 **light-headed** foolish; St James's choice of word plays off 'heavy' (1) and Richmond's reference to her uppermost parts.
6–7 **mustily** tainted by damp (*lit*); sullen (*fig*)
8 **sweeter air** given the lack of urban pollution
10 **Warming** by means of the fireplaces; part of making St James's ready to accommodate Prince Charles and his attendants
spirited enlivened
11 **vacations** periods of emptiness. The English court regularly moved from castle to castle to allow for sewage disposal, cleaning, and refurbishing.
friends other royal houses, e.g. Whitehall or Greenwich
12 **call yourself to mind** think of your own experience

My new gallery and my tennis-court, Richmond.
RICHMOND
No, but I heard of it, and from whence it came too.
ST JAMES'S
Why, from whence came it?
RICHMOND
Nay, lawfully derived, from the brickhills,
As thou didst thyself.
ST JAMES'S Thou breed'st crickets, I think,
And that will serve for the anagram to a critic.
Come, I know thy grief:
Thou fear'st that our late rival, Denmark House,
Will take from our regard, and we shall want
The noble presence of our princely master,
In his so frequent visitation,
Which we were wont so fully to enjoy.
RICHMOND
And is not that a cause of sorrow then?
ST JAMES'S
Rather a cause of joy, that we enjoy
So fair a fellowship. Denmark—why she's
A stately palace and majestical,
Ever of courtly breeding, but of late
Built up unto a royal height of state,
Rounded with noble prospects. By her side
The silver-footed Thamesis doth slide
As, though more faintly, Richmond, does by thee,
Enter Denmark House
Which I, denied to touch, can only see.
RICHMOND
Who's this?
ST JAMES'S 'Tis she herself, i'faith,
Comes with a courteous brow.
DENMARK HOUSE You're welcome, most nobly welcome.
ST JAMES'S
Hark you now, Richmond, did not I tell thee
'Twas a royal house?
DENMARK HOUSE Why, was there any doubt
Of our kind gratulation? I am proud
Only to be in fellowship with you,
Co-mate and servant to so great a master.
ST JAMES'S
That's Richmond's fear, thou'lt rob us both;
Thou hast such an enticing face of thine own.
DENMARK HOUSE
O let not that be any difference.
When we do serve, let us be ready for't;
And, called at his great pleasure, the round year
In her circumferent arms will fold us all
And give us all employment seasonable.
I am for colder hours, when the bleak air
Bites with an icy tooth. When summer has seared
And autumn, all discoloured, laid all fallow,
Pleasure taken house and dwells within doors,
Then shall my towers smoke and comely show;
But when again the fresher morn appears,
And the soft spring renews her velvet head,
St James's takes my blest inhabitants,

13 **gallery** covered passageway. The long gallery of St James's was newly wainscotted in 1609–10. Prince Charles's main addition to this palace was a two-storey buttery built in 1617–18; though classical in character and probably designed by Inigo Jones, this building does not seem to include a new gallery.
tennis-court shown between St James's Street and Pall Mall on Fairthorne and Newcourt's map (1643–47). If the tennis-court was new in 1620, Colvin may be wrong in concluding that it was 'probably of Tudor date'; on the other hand, this line may allude to a renovation of the tennis-court.

15 **whence** The King's Works Accounts (1616–17) note that the tennis-court built at Richmond for Prince Henry in 1610–12 was torn up, and the bricks were saved and cleaned for re-use. The discussion of the source of the tennis-court at St James's would be a nicer joke if the bricks from Richmond were used to make or to restore it.

16 **brickhills** hills rich with deposits of clay for making bricks; there were several such areas on the outskirts of London

18 **anagram** transposing letters: 'cricket' (or 'cricit') becomes 'critic', fault finder

20 **late** recent

21 **take...regard** detract from the esteem in which we are held

23 **visitation** periodic visit

24 **Which...enjoy** modifying 'presence'

28 **stately** dignified

29 **courtly breeding** Denmark House, originally Somerset House, was built between 1548 and 1551 by Edward Seymour, Duke of Somerset, Lord Protector of Edward VI. The palace served as the London residence of Princess Elizabeth during the reign of Queen Mary (1553–58). In 1604, James assigned Somerset House to Queen Anne, who initiated massive renovations and additions from 1609 until 1617, when Somerset House was renamed Denmark House in honour of Anne's Danish royal family.

30 **Built...state** This celebration of the restoration of the magnificence of Denmark House might not have been altogether pleasing to King James, for he had to pay for the construction. 'Taken in conjunction with the sums spent on furnishing and equipment it [the construction] constitutes Somerset House one of the most ruinously expensive enterprises of James I's reign' (Colvin).

31 **Rounded** finished off
prospects look-outs; Anne's building included a three-storey, stone gallery of arched openings fronting on the garden.

32 **silver-footed** shimmering
Thamesis the River Thames; see *Civitatis* for Thamesis as a character in a pageant

36 **courteous** respectful; not, as Richmond fears, arrogant
brow the forehead, as the seat of the facial expression of emotion (*OED*)

39 **Of...gratulation** that we [Denmark House] would be welcomed with kindness

43 **face** the face of the character and the façade of the building. Queen Anne made the main entrance to Denmark House more enticing when, in 1612–13, she restored the classical façade facing the Strand.

44 **difference** cause for disagreement

46 **his** Prince Charles's
round cyclical

47 **circumferent** encircling
fold embrace

48 **seasonable** suited to the seasons of the year

50 **seared** withered

51 **fallow** without crops

53 **comely show** appear properly attractive

55 **velvet head** an image of new growth: the soft, velvety covering both of the buds of some plants and of the antlers of deer as they develop

For she can better entertain them then
In larger bounds, in park, sports, delights, and grounds.
A third season yet, with the western oars,
Calls 'Up to Richmond!' when the high-heated year
Is in her solsticy; then she affords
More sweeter-breathing air, more bounds, more pleasures:
The hounds' loud music to the flying stag,
The feathered taloner to the falling bird,
The bowman's twelve score prick, even at the door,
And to these I could add a hundred more.
Then let not us strive which shall be his homes,
But strive to give him welcome when he comes.

RICHMOND
By my troth, he shall be welcome to Richmond
Whensoever he comes.

ST JAMES'S And to St James's, i'faith, at midnight.

DENMARK HOUSE
Meantime, 'tis fit I give him welcome hither.
But first, to you, my royal royal'st guest,
And I could wish your banquet were a feast;
Howe'er, your welcome is most bounteous,
Which, I beseech you, take as gracious.
To you, my owner, master, and my lord,
Let me the second unto you afford,
And then from you to all, for it is you
That gives indeed what I but seem to do.
I was from ruin raised by a fair hand,
A royal hand; in that state let me stand
For ever now. To bounty I was bred;
My cups full brimmed and my free tables spread
To hundreds daily, even without my door
I had an open hand unto the poor.
I know I shall so still; then shall their pray'rs
Pass by the porter's keys, climb up each stairs,
And knit and joint my new re-edified frames,
That I shall able be to keep your names
Unto eternity. Denmark House shall keep
Her high name now till time doth fall asleep
And be no more. Meantime, welcome, welcome,
Heartily welcome!—but chiefly you, great sir,
Whate'er lies in my power, command me all,
As freely as you were at your Whitehall. *Exeunt*

A Courtly Masque

Enter Soldier and Scholar

SCHOLAR Soldier, ta-ra-ra-ra-ra, how is't?—thou look'st as if thou hadst lost a field today.

SOLDIER No, but I have lost a day i'th' field. If you take me a maunding but where I am commanding, let 'em show me the house of correction.

SCHOLAR Why, thou wert not maunding, wert thou? There's martial danger in that, believe it.

SOLDIER No sir, but I was bold to show myself to some of my old and familiar acquaintance; but being disguised with my wants, there's nobody knew me.

SCHOLAR Faith, and that's the worst disguise a man can walk in. Thou wert better have appeared drunk in good clothes—much better. There's no superfluities shame a man, as to be over-brave, over-bold, over-swearing, over-lying, over-whoring; these add still to his repute. 'Tis the poor indigence, the want, the lank deficiency,

58 **bounds** boundaries
59 **western oars** Richmond being upstream, west of London
60 **'Up to Richmond!'** using the call of the watermen soliciting passengers
61 **solsticy** the summer solstice, when the sun is as far north as it can be from the equator
62 **bounds** spaciousness. In 1605, James formed a new park, 3 1/2 miles in circumference, north of Richmond. Given its several hunting lodges and the size of its parkland, Richmond was, according to Colvin, the fourth most expensive royal house to maintain.
63 **music** baying
64 **taloner** falcon; 'talent' was an early form of 'talon' (Dyce)
65 **twelve score prick** target set 240 yards away from the archers
even at the door conveniently located
67 **strive** compete against one another
69 **By my troth** truly
70 **midnight** a most inconvenient time for the Prince's arrival
72 **you** King James
73 **banquet** a light repast usually served after a masque
74 **welcome** the joy and goodwill toward the king
76 **you** Prince Charles
77 **the second** 'welcome' understood
afford extend
78–9 **you That gives** acknowledging Prince Charles's sponsorship of the entertainment. The same lines make explicit a conventional trope of manor house shows: the magnificence of the building and the munificence of the festivities bespeak the worthiness of the host.
80 **a fair hand** Queen Anne's
81 **in...stand** an indirect petition for financial support
82 **bounty** generosity
85 **I...poor** such charitable hospitality was by this time a commonplace of poems in praise of country houses; see Heal and Hibbard
86 **pray'rs** presumably prayers of thanksgiving
87 **porter's** doorkeeper's
88 **knit** connect firmly (*fig*)
joint fit together
re-edified re-built
frames framing: the supporting structure of a building
89 **names** the continued magnificence of a building secures the fame of its builders. King James might have balked at this claim, since Denmark House, by its name, aggrandizes not James or Charles, but Christian IV of Denmark and his sister, Anne.
95 **Whitehall** the main London residence of King James
1 **ta-ra-ra-ra-ra** imitating the marching sounds of drums
2 **field** battle
3 **field** battlefield
4 **maunding** begging
5 **house of correction** institution for detaining and punishing offenders
7 **martial** appertaining to someone in the military; punning on 'marshal', suggesting the danger of arrest and imprisonment for begging
9–10 **disguised with** concealed by; hence, revealing
10 **wants** needs
13 **superfluities** excesses
14 **over-brave** excessively gallant or handsomely dressed
15 **repute** reputation
16 **indigence** poverty
lank deficiency skinny neediness

as when a man cannot be brave, dares not be bold, is afraid to swear, wants maintenance for a lie and money to give a whore a supper—this is *pauper, cuius modicum non satis est*. Nay, he shall never be rich with begging neither, which is another wonder, because many beggars are rich.

SOLDIER O *canina facundia*!—this dog-eloquence of thine will make thee somewhat one day, scholar. Couldst thou turn but this prose into rhyme, there were a pitiful living to be picked out of it.

SCHOLAR I could make ballads for a need.

SOLDIER Very well, sir, and I'll warrant thee thou shalt never want subject to write of: one hangs himself today, another drowns himself tomorrow, a sergeant stabbed next day, here a pettifogger a'the pillory, a bawd in the cart's nose, and a pander in the tail. *Hic Mulier*, *Haec Vir*, fashions, fictions, felonies, fooleries—a hundred havens has the balladmonger to traffic at, and new ones still daily discovered.

SCHOLAR Prithee, soldier, no further this way. I participate more of Heraclitus than Democritus; I could rather weep the sins of the people than sing 'em.

SOLDIER Shall I set thee down a course to live?

SCHOLAR Faith, a coarse living I think must serve my turn. But why hast thou not found out thine own yet?

SOLDIER
Tush, that's resolved on—beg. When there's use for me,
I shall be brave again, hugged and beloved.
We are like winter garments, in the height
And hot blood of summer, put off, thrown by
For moth's meat, never so much as thought on
Till the drum strikes up storms again; and then,
'Come my well-lined soldier' (with valour,
Not velure) 'keep me warm. O, I love thee!'
We shall be trimmed and very well brushed then.
If we be faced with fur, 'tis tolerable,
For we may pillage then and steal our prey
And not be hanged for't, when the least fing'ring
In peaceful summer chokes us. A soldier,
At the best, is even but the forlorn hope
Unto his country, sent desperately out
And never more expected. If he come,
Peace's war perhaps, the law, providently
Has provided for him; some house or lands
May be suspensed in wrangling controversy
And he be hired to keep possession,
For there may be swords drawn; he may become
The abject second to some stinking bailiff.
O, let him serve the pox first, and die a gentleman.
Come, I know my ends, but would fain provide for thee.
Canst thou make?

SCHOLAR What, I have no handicraft, man.

SOLDIER
Cuckolds, make cuckolds, 'tis a pretty trade
In a peaceful city; 'tis women's work, man,
And they are good paymasters.

SCHOLAR I dare not.
'Tis a work of supererogation,

18 **maintenance** financial means
19–20 ***pauper . . . est*** the poor man, whose means are not enough
23 ***canina facundia*** dog-eloquence (*lit*); snippy, snarling rhetoric (*fig*)
26 **picked** pecked; metaphor emphasizing the poor income from poetry
27 **for a need** if necessary
28 **warrant** guarantee
31 **pettifogger** legal practitioner of lower status; one who uses unfair, quibbling methods
pillory stocks
bawd prostitute
32 **cart's** carts were used for transporting offenders to their punishment
pander pimp
Hic Mulier or, *The Man-Woman* (London, 1620); pamphlet (of which the title is deliberately incorrect in grammar) criticizing women for dressing and acting like men
32–3 ***Haec Vir*** or, *The Womanish-Man: Being an Answere to . . . 'Hic Mulier'* (London, 1620).
33 **felonies** serious crimes
34 **traffic at** do business in
37 **Heraclitus** 'the weeping philosopher' of Ephesus (*c.*500 BC) who understood the universe as an unceasing conflict of opposites
Democritus 'the laughing philosopher' of later antiquity (*c.*460–370 BC) who recommended cheerfulness as an ethical principle
40 **a coarse living** playing on the Soldier's 'course' (39), the Scholar complains about his prospects—unemployment and poverty. Such complaints were neither unusual nor unfounded. The number of students at Oxford and Cambridge rose sharply during the first two decades of the 17th century and, after a decline in the 1620s, reached a peak in the 1630s that would not be equalled until the 1820s. Unfortunately, there was no corresponding increase in the number of positions in the schools or the church for these scholars.
serve my turn meet my need
43 **brave** courageous and finely attired
49 **velure** a kind of velvet, punning on 'valour'
50 **trimmed** prepared for use
51 **faced** adorned with, as the collars and cuffs of military jackets often were
52 **pillage** plunder
53 **fing'ring** petty theft
55 **forlorn hope** doomed or hopeless hope; specifically, a band of soldiers picked out to lead the attack
58 **providently** with foresight
60 **suspensed** legally delayed
63 **abject** lowly
second assistant; representative of a principal in a duel
64 **O . . . gentleman** better to commit oneself to a disfiguring disease and die with one's integrity than to be reduced to being the 'abject second to some stinking bailiff.' 'Serve', as 'be employed by', ironically sets employment in opposition to remaining a gentleman; 'serve' may also connote 'endure' and 'dispense'.
65 **fain** willingly
66 **make** produce things
67 **Cuckolds** men whose wives have been unfaithful to them
70 **a work of supererogation** in Catholic moral theology, an act that is not just good but morally better, such as St Paul's teaching that to choose virginity is better than to choose matrimony. Part of the humour here comes from calling a sin a morally superior work.

And the church forbids it.

SOLDIER
Prithee, what's Latin for
A 'cuckold', scholar? I could never learn yet.

SCHOLAR
Faith, the Latins have no proper word for it
That ever I read. 'Homo', I take it, is the best,
Because it is a common name to all men.

SOLDIER
You're mad fellows, you scholars. I am persuaded
Were I a scholar now, I could not want.

SCHOLAR
Every man's most capable of his own grief.
A scholar said you?—why, there are none nowadays.
Were you a scholar, you'd be a singular fellow.

SOLDIER
How, no scholars! What's become of 'em all?

SCHOLAR
I'll make it proof from your experience.
A commander's a commander, captain, captain;
But, having no soldiers, where's the command?
Such are we: all doctors, no disciples now.
Every man's his own teacher; none learns of others.
You have not heard of our mechanic rabbis,
That shall dispute in their own tongues backward and forward
With all the learnèd fathers of the Jews.

SOLDIER
Mechanic rabbis!—what might those be?

SCHOLAR
I'll show you sir, and they are men are daily to be seen:
There's Rabbi Job, a venerable silk-weaver,
Jehu, a throwster dwelling i'th' Spitalfields;
There's Rabbi Abimelech, a learnèd cobbler;
Rabbi Lazarus, a superstitious tailor.
These shall hold up their shuttles, needles, awls,
Against the gravest Levite of the land,
And give no ground neither.

SOLDIER
That I believe;
They have no ground for any thing they do.

SCHOLAR
You understand right, and these men by practic
Have got the theory of all the arts
At their fingers' ends, and in that they'll live.
Howe'er they'll die I know not, for they change daily.

SOLDIER This is strange.
How come they to attain this knowledge?

SCHOLAR
As boys learn arithmetic, practise with counters
To reckon sums of silver, so with their tools
They come to grammar, logic, rhetoric,
And all the sciences; as, for example,
The devout weaver sits within his loom
And thus he makes a learnèd syllogism:
His woof the major and his warp the minor,
His shuttle then the brain, and firm conclusion
Makes him a piece of stuff that Aristotle,
Ramus, nor all the logicians can take a' pieces.

SOLDIER
This has some likelihood.

SCHOLAR
So likewise by
His deep instructive and his mystic tools,
The tailor comes to be rhetorical.
First on the spread velvet, satin, stuff, or cloth,
He chalks out a circumferent paraphrase,
That goes about the bush where the thief stands.

71 **the church** the Church of England; see Article XIV of the *Thirty-nine Articles* for a repudiation of works of supererogation as conducive to impiety and pride. Ironically, in rejecting supererogation, the church forbids not only the extreme of cuckoldry, but also its opposite, virginity

74 **Homo** man, or, as applied by the Scholar, everyman

74–5 **Homo . . . men** proverbial

77 **want** be needy

78 **capable of** susceptible to; typically wry humour

80 **singular** punning: (*a*) unusual; (*b*) one of a kind

85 **disciples** dedicated students

87 **mechanic** pertaining to manual work
rabbis in general, learned masters, but the term applied specifically to puritan sectaries, especially lay preachers (Heinemann)

88 **tongues** languages

92 **venerable** respectable

93 **throwster** one who twists silk fibres into raw silk or raw silk into thread
Spitalfields London suburb to the north-east; centre of the silk trade which James backed strongly

94 **cobbler** shoemaker

95 **superstitious** probably with a pun on 'stitch'

96 **shuttles** devices for weaving cloth
awls sharp pointed tool by which shoemakers made holes in leather

97 **gravest** authoritative
Levite one of the tribe of Levi; generally, a churchman

98 **give no ground** not retreat

99 **ground** basis

100 **practic** practice (of their trades)

102 **At their fingers' ends** because they work with their hands

106 **counters** devices for counting

107 **reckon** calculate

108 **grammar . . . rhetoric** the trivium, the lower division of the liberal arts of medieval schooling

109 **sciences** in addition to the trivium, the quadrivium: music, arithmetic, geometry, and astronomy

111 **syllogism** an argument consisting of two related propositions (the major premise and the minor premise) leading necessarily to a third proposition (the conclusion)

112 **woof** thread stretched across the width of a loom
warp thread stretched lengthwise, at right angle to the woof

114 **Aristotle** philosopher and logician of antiquity; along with Ramus, the most influential logicians in English schools in 1620

115 **Ramus** Peter Ramus, 16th-century philosopher, who developed an influential system of logic different from Aristotle's

117 **mystic** penetrating into spiritual mysteries; hyperbolic praise

119 **stuff** fabric

120 **chalks out** outlines
circumferent roundabout
paraphrase to retell in different words, and, in this case, to amplify

121 **That . . . stands** misses the point; proverbial

Then come his shears in shape of an *eclipsis*
And takes away the t'other's too long tail.
By his needle he understands *ironia*,
That with one eye looks two ways at once;
Metonymia ever at his fingers' ends;
Some call his piccadill *synecdoche*,
But I think rather that should be his yard,
Being but *pars pro toto*; and by metaphor
All know the cellarage under the shop-board
He calls his hell, not that it is a place
Of spirits' abode, but that from that abyss
Is no recovery or redemption
To any owner's hand, whatever falls.
I could run further, were't not tedious,
And place the stiff-toed cobbler in his form.
But let them mend themselves, for yet all's naught.
They now learn only never to be taught.

SOLDIER
Let them alone. How shall we learn to live?

SCHOLAR
Without book is most perfect, for with 'em
We shall hardly. Thou mayst keep a fence-school.
'Tis a noble science.

SOLDIER
I had rather be i'th' crown-office.
Thou mayst keep school too, and do good service,
To bring up children for the next age better.

SCHOLAR
'Tis a poor living that's picked out of boys' buttocks.

SOLDIER
'Tis somewhat better than the night-farmer yet.

Music. Pallas descends

Hark! What sounds are these?

SCHOLAR
Ha! there's somewhat more:
There is in sight a glorious presence,
A presence more than human.

SOLDIER
An amazing one, Scholar.
If ever thou couldst conjure, speak now.

SCHOLAR
In name of all the deities, what art thou?
Thy shine is more than sub-celestial;
'Tis at the least heavenly angelical.

PALLAS
A patroness unto ye both, ye ignorant
And undeserving favourites of my fame.
You are a soldier?

SOLDIER
Since these arms could wield arms,
I have professed it, brightest deity.

PALLAS
To thee I am Bellona.—You are a scholar?

SCHOLAR
In that poor pilgrimage, since I could go

122 **shears** large scissors
eclipsis figure of speech by which words needed to make sense are omitted or, in this instance, deleted or cut; punning on the clipping of scissors
123 **t'other's** the paraphrase's
tail punning on 'tale'
124 ***ironia*** figure of speech in which the literal meaning is opposite to the intended one; the first syllable punning on 'eye'
125 **one ... ways** the single hole of the needle has openings on its two sides
126 ***Metonymia*** figure of speech by which a quality or an adjunct is used to identify a thing; the third syllable punning perhaps on 'nim', 'to filch'.
at ... ends figuratively, ready at hand, or acquired by practical experience. For the tailor to have metonymy 'at his fingers' ends' may mean that he is well versed in rhetoric; or, taking the phrase literally, if a needle is understood to be at his finger tips, the line points to, metonymically, the needle trade
127 **piccadill** large, starched collar, usually reinforced with wire and adorned with a lace or perforated border, made by tailors
synecdoche figure of speech by which a part is used to refer to the whole, the piccadill being a thing characteristic of the tailor or a yard being a part of the whole piece of cloth needed to make a piece of clothing. The actor, by gesturing toward an imaginary collar about his neck, might set up a pun on the second syllable of 'synecdoche'.
128 **yard** measuring-stick
129 ***pars pro toto*** the part for the whole; with bawdy suggestiveness
130 **shop-board** platform at which tailors worked
131 **hell** place beneath the shop-board where tailors threw their scraps
132 **abode** dwelling-place
abyss a (the infernal) pit
133 **redemption** punning on salvation and buying back
134 **To ... hand** metonymic for the owner unable to grasp again for regain possession of the material
whatever falls preceding 'of' understood
136 **stiff-toed** alluding to the cobbler's last, inserted into a shoe when working on it
form the cobbler's seat, a long one without a back
137 **all's** punning on 'awl'
naught pointless
139 **live** choose how best to lead our lives
140 **Without ... perfect** with the additional quibbling sense: by memory is most expert
141 **hardly** after which 'live' (in the sense of 'to make a living') understood
fence-school fencing school; for Middleton's criticism of fencing schools, see *Quarrel*, and *Peacemaker* 461–8.
142 **science** field of knowledge
143 **crown-office** administrative offices of the Court of King's Bench
146 **poor living** On the status of the schoolmaster, see Richard Mulcaster: 'Our calling creeps low and hath pain for a companion, still thrust to the wall, though still confessed good' (quoted in Notestein). Notestein himself observes that the schoolmaster 'did about as well as the poorer country clergyman, but his calling had by no means the same prestige'.
picked ... buttocks by keeping them in their seats; alluding perhaps to corporal punishment and homosexual activity
147 **night-farmer** gong-farmer, a cleaner of privies
147.1 ***Pallas*** Minerva in Roman mythology; goddess of wisdom and warfare, she was normally portrayed wearing some armour and carrying her shield, on which the head of the Gorgon was depicted
descends probably by means of a mechanical device covered to look like a cloud
151 **conjure** communicate with spirits; a power represented as a product of learning, for example in Marlowe's *Doctor Faustus*, 1.3.1–20 or Shakespeare's *Hamlet*, 1.1.40.
153 **sub-celestial** beneath the heavens; earthly
155 **patroness** protector and advocate
ignorant mis-informed
159 **Bellona** goddess of war
160 **pilgrimage** journey, especially one made as an act of devotion
go walk

I hitherto have walked.
PALLAS
To thee I am Minerva,
Pallas to both, goddess of arts and arms,
Of arms and arts, for neither has precedence.
For he's the complete man partakes of both,
The soul of arts joined with the flesh of valour,
And he alone participates with me.
Thou art no soldier unless a scholar,
Nor thou a scholar unless a soldier.
You've noble breedings both, worthy foundations,
And will ye build up rotten battlements
On such fair groundsels?—that will ruin all.
Lay wisdom on thy valour, on thy wisdom valour,
For these are mutual coincidents.
What seeks the soldier?
SOLDIER
My maintenance.
PALLAS
Lay by thine arms and take the city then.
There's the full cup and can of maintenance.—
And your grief is want too?
SCHOLAR
I want all but grief.
PALLAS
No, you want most what most you do profess.
Where read you to be rich was happiest?
He had no bay from Phoebus nor from me
That e'er wrote so, no Minerva in him.
My priests have taught that poverty is safe,
Sweet, and secure, for nature gives man nothing
At his birth. When life and earth are wedded,
There's neither basin held nor dowry given;
At parting nor is any garner stored,
Wardrobe or warehouse kept for their return.
Wherefore shall, then, man count his myriads
Of gold and silver idols, since thrifty nature
Will nothing lend but she will have't again—
And life and labour for her interest?
My priests do teach: seek thou thyself within,
Make thy mind wealthy, thy knowing conscience,
And those shall keep thee company from hence.
Or would you wish to emulate the gods,
Live, as you may imagine, careless and free,
With joys and pleasures crowned, and those eternal?
This were to far exceed 'em, for while earth lasts,
The deities themselves abate their fullness,
Troubled with cries of ne'er contented man.
Man then to seek and find it?—all that hope
Fled when Pandora's fatal box flew ope.
SOLDIER
Divine lady, there's yet a competence
Which we come short of.
PALLAS
That may as well be caused
From your own negligence as our slow blessings;
But I'll prefer you to a greater power,
Even Jupiter himself, father and king of gods,
With whom I may well join in just complaint.
These latter ages have despoiled my fame.
Minerva's altars are all ruined now;
I had a long-adored Palladium,
Offerings and incense fuming on my shrine.
Rome held me dear, and old Troy gave me worship;
All Greece renowned me till the Ida prize
Joined me with wrathful Juno to destroy 'em,
For we are better ruined than profaned.
Now let the latter ages count the gains
They got by wanton Venus' sacrifice.
But I'll invoke great Jupiter.
SCHOLAR
Do, goddess,
And re-erect the ruins of thy fame,

163 **precedence** priority, hence superiority; see l. 374.4, and note to l. 499.1
166 **participates** has things in common with
169 **breedings** up-bringings
170 **battlements** uppermost parts of a wall; usually indented parapets
171 **groundsels** foundation timbers
173 **coincidents** correspondences in character
174 **maintenance** livelihood
176 **full cup** symbol of the physical means of support
can proverbial; see also Textual Notes
177 **want . . . want** first used in the sense of 'poverty'; secondly as 'need'
178 **want** lack
what . . . profess that is, scholarship, good scholarship, the lessons of which Pallas goes on to establish
179 **Where . . . happiest** the critique of the desire for wealth informs the masque, especially in the figure of Deceit who, in every role except that of a Ranger, tempts others with the world's wealth or plots to horde it; see ll. 502–4, 591–3, 655, 715–17, 809–10
180 **bay** a wreath of bay leaves symbolized the poet and the conqueror
Phoebus see note to Epistle.1–3
182 **poverty is safe** proverbial
184 **When . . . wedded** an image of birth, when the soul and body are conjoined
185 **basin** rich plate, customary as a wedding gift
held owned
dowry assets given with a wife
186 **parting** death
garner storehouse of grain
187 **Wardrobe** room or cupboard for clothes
warehouse place for storing goods
188 **myriads** countless numbers
191 **interest** profit earned on a loan
194 **those** that is, one's rich mind and well-informed conscience
keep thee company go with you
195 **emulate** strive to behave like
196 **careless** carefree
199 **abate** curtail
201 **it** divine fullness
that stressed, so as to clarify that hope alone remained in Pandora's box
202 **Pandora's fatal box** a beautiful box, given by Jove to Pandora (according to Hesiod, the first mortal woman who lived), containing a host of plagues that were released and made humans suffer
203 **competence** sufficient income
206 **prefer** recommend
208 **complaint** grievance
211 **Palladium** statue of Pallas; most famous was that at Troy
212 **fuming** smoking
214 **Ida prize** a golden apple, named after Mount Ida, the site where Pallas, Juno, and Venus met to be judged by Paris. When Paris chose Venus as the fairest, Pallas and Juno became allies in opposition to the Greeks.
215 **wrathful** furious
'em Greeks and Trojans, through war
216 **profaned** desecrated
218 **wanton** lascivious
sacrifice of Helen of Troy, whom Venus offered to Paris when he had to evaluate the beauty of the goddesses
219 **invoke** summon

For poesy can do it.

PALLAS Altitonant,
Imperial-crowned and thunder-armèd Jove,
Unfold thy fiery veil, the flaming robe
And superficies of thy better brightness;
Descend from thine orbicular chariot;
Listen the plaints of thy poor votaries.
'Tis Pallas calls, thy daughter, Jupiter,
Ta'en from thee by the Lemnian Mulciber,
A midwife god to the delivery
Of thy most sacred, fertile, teeming brain.

Music. Jupiter descends

Hark! These sounds proclaim his willing, sweet descent.
If not full blessings, expect some content.

JUPITER
What would our daughter?

PALLAS Just-judging Jove,
I mediate the suit of humble mortals,
By whose large sceptre all their fates are swayed,
Adverse or auspicious.

JUPITER 'Tis more than Jupiter
Can do to please 'em. Unsatisfied man
Has in his ends no end. Not hell's abyss
Is deeper gulfed than greedy avarice.
Ambition finds no mountain high enough
For his aspiring foot to stand upon.
One drinks out all his blessings into surfeits;
Another throws 'em out, as all were his,
And the gods bound for prodigal supply.
What is he lives content in any kind?
That long incensèd nature is now ready
To turn all back into the fruitless chaos.

PALLAS
These are two noble virtues, my dread sire,
Both arts and arms, well-wishers unto Pallas.

JUPITER
How can it be but they have both abused,
And would, for their ills, make our justice guilty?
Show them their shames, Minerva, what the young world
In her unstable youth did then produce.
She should grow graver now, more sage, more wise,
Know concord and the harmony of goodness;
But if her old age strike with harsher notes,
We may then think she is too old, and dotes.
Strike by white art, a theomantic power,
Magic divine, not the devil's horror
But the delicious music of the spheres.
The thrice three Worthies summon back to life.
There let 'em see what arts and arms commixed,
For they had both, did in the world's broad face—
Those that did propagate and beget their fames,
And for posterity left lasting names.

PALLAS
I shall, great Jupiter.

221 **poesy** poetry
Altitonant invoking Jove as 'thundering on high'
222 **Imperial-crowned** emperor
Jove or Jupiter; chief deity; sky-god; his characterization picks up the derivation of his name from the verb 'to shine'
223 **veil** covering; this suggests that the staging, included a discovery of Jupiter behind a brilliant fabric embellished with flames of cloth, perhaps a curtain or perhaps the character's robe. If this was the case, then the masque included a double revelation on the upper stage: first this one of Jupiter; then (266.1) that of the Muses and the Nine Worthies
224 **superficies** outer manifestation
225 **orbicular chariot** spherical vehicle
226 **votaries** devoted worshippers
228 **Lemnian Mulciber** in Greek mythology Vulcan; married to Pallas and banished to Lemnos by Jove
230 **teeming** bountiful
234 **mediate** intercede on behalf of
suit petition
235 **sceptre** rod of royal or imperial authority
fates futures
236 **Adverse** unfavourable
auspicious prosperous
241 **aspiring** climbing up; ambitious
242 **surfeits** excesses; illness and nausea caused by excessive indulgence
244 **bound** legally contracted
prodigal wastefully lavish
245 **kind** way
246 **incensèd** inflamed (with anger)
247 **fruitless** sterile
chaos the formless void of primordial matter
248 **dread** reverend
250 **abused** done wrong
251 **make . . . guilty** blame us for being just
252 **shames** deeds to make them feel ashamed
254 **graver** more serious and dignified
sage wise and grave
257 **dotes** is foolishly fond of
258 **white art** white magic, magic relying on manipulation of the powers of nature
theomantic divinely inspired
260 **music of the spheres** harmonious sounds produced by the motions of the planets and stars
262 **commixed** joined together
263 **in the world's broad face** in the wide world
264 **beget** sire; generate
265 **posterity** later generations
266.1 ***invocation*** chant summoning the muses

Music and this song as an invocation to the nine Muses, who, in the time, are discovered on the upper stage, placed by the Nine Worthies; and toward the conclusion [the Worthies] descend, each one led by a Muse, the most proper and pertinent to the person of the Worthy, as Terpsichore with David, Urania with Joshua, etc. After the song, Pallas describes them [the Worthies]; then [they] dance and exeunt

The First Song

Muses, usher in those states,
And amongst 'em choose your mates.
There wants not one, nor one to spare,
For thrice three both your numbers are.
Learning's mistress, fair Calliope,
Loud Euterpe, sweet Terpsichore,
Soft Thalia, sad Melpomene,
Pleasant Clio, large Erato,
High-aspiring-eyed Urania,
Honey-lingued Polyhymnia,
Leave awhile your Thespian springs
And usher in those more than kings.
We call them Worthies; 'tis their due
Though long time dead, still live by you.

Enter [the Muses, ushering in] the Nine Worthies, three after three, whom, as they enter, Pallas describes

PALLAS

These three were Hebrews:
This noble duke was he at whose command
Hyperion reined his fiery coursers in,
And fixèd stood over Mount Gilboa;

266.2 ***Muses*** originally, nymphs of the springs whose water inspired artists; later, goddesses of song and representatives of the various arts. The last of these roles is most pertinent to *Tennis* because the conjunction of Muses and Worthies constitutes an emblem of the combination of arts and arms. The Muses probably wore loose, light gowns, for, as Thomas Dekker said of the costumes of the Liberal Sciences in *Troia-Nova Triumphans* (1612), 'Knowledge should be *free*.' Gowns of different colours, distinctive headdresses, and properties identifying areas of expertise likely individuated the Muses, as they did in the Lord Mayor's Show of 1620, John Squire's *Tes Irenes Trophoea*: '...on the water was Pernassus Mount, whereon the Nine Muses sate; Clyo the first, suted in a gowne of purple taffaty, and studiously imploy'd in turning over bookes, shee being the Historicall Muse; Melpomene was attired in a black taffaty robe, her head deckt with cypress, and playing on a theorbo; Thalia, the Comic Muse, in a light changeable taffaty robe, and playing on a voyall; Euterpe, the Muse that first invented wind instruments, was richly apparelled, and play'd on a flute-recorder; Terpsichore on the lute; and the Geometrical Muse Erato with a scale and compass in her hand; the Heroicall Muse Calliope was shap'd in a tauny silke robe, and her temples girt with bayes; the heavenly Muse Urania, that invented astrologie, was deckt in a robe of azure taffaty semined with starres, on her head shee wore a coronet of starres, and her right hand supported a spheare; Polymneia, the inventress of rhetorique, assumed her place neerest to Apollo...' (Nichols, 4:621–2). For the properties associated with each Muse in classical lore, see the notes to 266.5, 266.6, 266.7. For a contemporary illustration of the Muses, see Folger MS V.b.232, ff. 146^{v}–150^{v}.

discovered revealed; see note to l. 223

266.3 ***Worthies*** probably wearing armour, the head gear of which may have individuated the characters, as it does to some degree in the pictures of the Worthies in Folger MS V.b.232, ff. 142–6. In this manuscript, for example, the style of the Greek helmet differs from that of the plumed Roman one, and David wears what appears to be a simple cloth hat whereas Godfrey of Boulogne has a helmet with a cross on the top. The Worthies may have been further individuated by crests on their costumes; for details of this possibility, see F. J. Furnivall's transcription of a poem on the Nine Worthies in BL MS. Harley 2259, f. 39^{v}.

266.5 ***pertinent*** the illustrative pairings noted by Rowley (266.6–9), that of David with Terpsichore (muse of music and dance; classical property: a lyre) and that of Joshua and Urania (muse of astronomy; property: a globe, and sometimes a staff for pointing out features of the globe) do not clearly establish the basis for aligning Muses with Worthies. Given the prominent role of Julius Caesar in tragedy and of Hector in epic poetry, the former would probably accompany Melpomene (muse of tragedy; properties: a wreath of ivy, the mask of tragedy, and sometimes a weapon), and the latter, Calliope (muse of epic; properties: a wax tablet and pencil, a closely rolled parchment, or, sometimes, a trumpet). More tentative are the following alignments: Arthur with Erato (muse of love poetry; properties: a crown of roses and myrtle and a small lyre) because of the crucial importance of love (and infidelity) to Camelot; Godfrey of Boulogne with Thalia (muse of comedy; properties: a wreath of ivy, the mask of comedy, and sometimes a shepherd's staff) because of the fame that his court earned for festivities; Alexander the Great with Clio (muse of history and philosophy; property: a half-opened scroll and laurel wreath) because Clio's symbol, the laurel wreath, was also appropriate to the world's greatest conqueror; Judas Maccabee with Euterpe (muse of pastoral poetry; property: horns, most often flute) because he represents a more primitive age; Charlemagne with Polyhymnia (muse of rhetoric; property: a veil) because he was a great law-giver.

266.6 ***Terpsichore*** muse of music and dance; traditionally depicted with a lyre

266.7 ***David*** writer of the psalms; see l. 287

Urania muse of astronomy; depicted carrying a globe and sometimes with a staff for pointing out details of the globe

Joshua made the sun and the moon stand still in order to triumph over the Amorites; see Joshua 10:12–14

267 **states** dignified personages

269 **There...spare** there are exactly the right number

272 **Loud** symbolized by horns

274 **large** generous, unrestrained

276 **Honey-lingued** sweet-spoken

277 **Thespian** the city of Thespiae was located at the foot of Mount Helicon, home of the Muses

280 **still live** preceding 'they' understood

280.2 ***three after three*** see Textual Introduction, *Companion*, 668

282 **This noble duke** Joshua; see 266.7–9 note

283 **Hyperion** sun-god

fiery coursers horses drawing the chariot of the sun

284 **Mount Gilboa** an error for Gibeon, one of the cities of the Amorites over which Joshua made the sun stand still

This Mattathias' son, the Maccabee,
Under whose arm no less than worthies fell;
This the most sweet and sacred psalmograph.
These, of another sort, of much less knowledge,
Little less valour: a Macedonian born,
Whom afterwards the world could scarcely bear
For his great weight in conquest; this Troy's best
soldier;
This Rome's first Caesar. These three of latter times,
And to the present more familiar:
Great Charles of France, and the brave Boulogne
duke,
And this is Britain's glory, kinged thirteen times.
You've fair aspects; more to express Jove's power,
Show you have motion for a jovial hour.
The Worthies dance and exeunt

JUPITER
Were not these precedents for all future ages?

SCHOLAR
But none attains their glories, King of Stars.
These are the fames are followed and pursued,
But never overtaken.

JUPITER The Fates below,
The gods' arms, are not shortened, nor do we shine
With fainter influence. Who conquers now
Makes it his tyrant's prize and not his honour's,
Abusing all the blessings of the gods.
Learnings and arts are theories, no practics;
To understand is all they study to.
Men strive to know too much, too little do.
Enter Time

SOLDIER
Plaints are not ours alone, great Jupiter.
See, Time himself comes weeping.

TIME Who has more cause?
Who more wronged than Time? Time passes all men
With a regardless eye at best. The worst
Expect him with a greedy appetite:
The landed lord looks for his quarter-day;
The big-bellied usurer for his teeming gold,
That brings him forth the child of interest—
He that, beyond the bounds of heaven's large blessing,
Hath made a fruitless creature to increase,
Dull, earthen minerals to propagate—
These only do expect and entertain me.
But being come, they bend their plodding heads,
And while they count their bags, they let me pass,
Yet instant wish me come about again.
Would Time deserve their thanks, or Jove their praise,
He must turn time only to quarter-days.
O, but my wrongs they are innumerable!
The lawyer drives me off from term to term,
Bids me—and I do't—bring forth my Alethe,
My poor child Truth; he sees and will not see her.
What I could manifest in one clear day
He still delays a cloudy jubilee.
The prodigal wastes and makes me sick with surfeits.
The drunkard, strong in wine, trips up my heels
And sets me topsy-turvy on my head,
Waking my silent passage in the night
With revels, noise, and thunder-clapping oaths,
And snoring on my bright meridian.
And when they think I pass too slowly by,
They have a new-found vapour to expel me—
They smoke me out. Ask 'em but why they do't,
And he that worst can speak, yet this can say:
'I take this whiff to drive the time away.'
O, but the worst of all, women do hate me.
I cannot set impression on their cheeks
With all my circular hours, days, months, and years,
But 'tis wiped off with gloss and pencilry.
Nothing so hateful as grey hairs and time—
Rather no hair at all! 'Tis sin's autumn now,
For those fair trees that were more fairer cropped

285 **Mattathias' son** Judas, one of the five sons of Mattathias who rebelled with his sons against the pagan abuses of Antiochus in 167 BC.
286 **Under...fell** platitudinous praise
287 **This** David
psalmograph writer of psalms
288 **less knowledge** less scholarly
289 **a Macedonian** Alexander the Great, born in ancient Macedonia
born quibbles on 'borne', given 'bear' in the next line
291 **this** Hector
292 **Rome's first Caesar** Julius Caesar
294 **Charles** Charlemagne
Boulogne duke Godfrey, Duke of Boulogne
295 **Britain's glory** Arthur
296 **aspects** physical features
297 **jovial** joyful, punning on 'Jove'
298 **precedents** previous examples
301 **Fates** Clotho, Lachesis, and Atropos: the three goddesses who determine the course of human life
306 **practics** applied sciences
308.1 ***Time*** in pageantry and in emblem books, Time is usually portrayed as an old man, with the identifying properties noted by Middleton in *Truth* 468: wings, a scythe, and an hour glass
309 **Plaints** complaints; grievances; lamentations
312 **regardless** unregarded, or indifferent; whereas the best care little about Time, the worst watch for it because it serves their materialistic purposes
314 **landed lord** landlord
quarter-day the day, one every three months, when rents were due
315 **usurer** moneylender, usually at excessive rates of interest
teeming procreative; breeding
319 **minerals** gold and silver
320 **entertain** welcome
321 **being come** modifying 'me', Time
plodding stolidly working
322 **bags** money-bags
323 **instant** immediately
327 **term** a period of the year appointed for the sitting of a court
328 **Alethe** Truth, daughter of Time
331 **jubilee** period of fifty years
332 **prodigal** spendthrift
337 **meridian** noon
339 **vapour** i.e. tobacco smoke
344 **set impression** leave a mark; print lines on the face
346 **gloss** a superficial lustre produced by make-up
pencilry painting
348 **no hair** alluding to the loss of hair because of syphilis
autumn time of the harvest
349 **more fairer cropped** more bountifully laden with a crop

Or they fall of themselves or will be lopped.
Even Time itself, to number all his griefs
Would waste himself unto his ending date.
How many would eternity wish here,
And that the sun, and time, and age, might stand,
And leave their annual distinction,
That nature were bed-rid, all motion sleep?
Time, having then such foes, has cause to weep.
Redress it Jupiter. *Exit Time*

JUPITER
I tell thee, glorious daughter, and you things
Shut up in wretchedness, the world knew once
His age of happiness. Blessed times owned him
Till those two ugly ills, Deceit and Pride,
Made it a perished substance. Pride brought in
Forgetfulness of goodness, merit, virtue,
And placed ridiculous officers in life—
Vainglory, fashion, humour, and such toys
That shame to be produced:
The frenzy of apparel that's run mad
And knows not where to settle, masculine painting,
And the five Starches, mocking the five senses.
All in their diff'rent and ridiculous colours,
Which, for their apish and fantastic follies,
I summon to make odious, and will fit 'em
With flames of their own colours.

Music striking up a light fantastic air, those five Starches afore summoned come dancing in, and, after a ridiculous strain, White Starch, challenging precedency, standing upon her right by antiquity, out of her just anger presents their pride to 'em. Those five Starches—White, Blue, Yellow, Green, and Red—all properly habited to express their affected colours

WHITE STARCH
What, no respect amongst you? must I wake you
In your forgetful duties? Jet before me?
Take place of me?—You rude, presumptuous gossips,
Pray, who am I?—not I the primitive starch?
You, blue-eyed *frauchen*, looks like fire and brimstone;
You, caudle-colour, much of the complexion
Of high Shrove-Tuesday batter, yellowhammer;
And you, my tansy-face, that shows like pride
Served up in sorrel sops, green-sickness baggage;
And last, thou Red Starch, that wear'st all thy blushes
Under thy cheeks, looks like a strangled moon-calf
With all thy blood settled about thy neck—
The ensign of thy shame, if thou hadst any.
Know I'm Starch Protestant, thou Starch Puritan,
With the blue nostril, whose tongue lies i' thy nose.

BLUE STARCH
Wicked interpretation!

350 **Or** either
lopped cut back; applied to hair, this image points toward venereal disease (a cause of hair falling out) or the cutting of hair (a fault for which women were castigated by James I)
355 **distinction** of the seasons
356 **motion** temporal movement
358 **Redress** set right
359 **things** disparaging reference to Time, the Soldier, and the Scholar
360 **wretchedness** misery
363 **it** happiness
365 **officers** people in positions of authority
366 **Vainglory** pretentiousness
fashion novelty
humour whimsy
toys insignificant things
367 **shame** are ashamed
368 **frenzy of** craziness about
369 **masculine painting** use of make-up by men
370 **mocking** generally, imitating; in this context, corresponding in number to
371 **colours** with the added sense of deceptive outward appearance; perhaps with a pun on 'collars', a feature of their costumes
372 **apish** foolishly imitative
fantastic grotesque
follies mischiefs
373 **odious** hateful
fit supply
374 **flames** suggesting bright, flamboyant colours in flame patterns; for similar costumes, see *The Lords' Masque* (1613) by Thomas Campion and Inigo Jones's designs for the same show. Presumably the colours of the Starches' costumes were deepened for theatrical effect, for the shades produced by coloured starches were quite pale; see Arnold.
374.1 ***fantastic*** fanciful
374.3 ***strain*** melody
challenging claiming
374.4 ***precedency*** see note to l. 163
antiquity seniority
374.7 ***habited*** costumed
374.8 ***affected*** pretended
376–7 **Jet . . . me** questions implying stage business, specifically the jockeying for position by the Starches
377 **presumptuous** uppity
gossips women who delight in idle chat
378 **not I** preceded by 'am' understood; the use of fragments is typical of volatile style of White Starch's speech
primitive original; given the later designation of White Starch as protestant and Blue Starch as puritan (388), this likely alludes to protestant argument about the 'primitive' church
379 **You** to Blue Starch
blue-eyed having dark circles under her eyes would be consistent with the satire
frauchen little woman; the foreign usage suggests that she is a Puritan exile from the continent
like fire and brimstone threatening; fierce
380 **caudle-colour** the colour of a thin gruel
381 **Shrove-Tuesday** the last Tuesday before Lent; pancake day
yellowhammer a species of yellow bird, regularly used as a term of contempt; see *Chaste Maid* 1.1.22.1
382 **tansy-face** *tansy*: a plant with dark green leaves and a very bitter aroma; small portions of the leaves were used to flavour tansy pudding and tansy cake, both of which were Easter fare
383 **sorrel sops** *Sorrel*: a reddish-brown perennial with green leaves served in salad or cooked; like tansy, the flavour was bitter. *Sops*: liquid in which bread is dipped before eating.
green-sickness a kind of anaemia, suffered mostly by young women and characterized by the development a light green tinge on the skin
baggage good-for-nothing
385 **Under thy cheeks** in the starched red collar 'about [her] neck' (386)
moon-calf a creature deformed at birth
387 **ensign** banner
388 **Starch** stiff, strict
389 **With . . . nostril** synecdoche for Blue Starch; the grotesqueness of this image and of the one that immediately follows jab satirically at the Puritans
whose . . . nose alluding to the nasal delivery of the 'humming prayers' of Puritans; 'lies' also carries pejorative associations with deceit and falsehood

YELLOW STARCH I have known
A white-faced hypocrite, Lady Sanctity.
A yellow ne'er came near her; and she's been
A citizen's wife too, starched like innocence,
But the devil's pranks not uglier. In her mind
Wears yellow, hugs it, if her husband's trade
Could bear it—there's the spite; but since she cannot
Wear her own linen yellow, yet she shows
Her love to't and makes him wear yellow hose.
I am as stiff i' my opinion
As any Starch amongst you.

GREEN STARCH I, as you.

RED STARCH And I as any.

BLUE STARCH I scorn to come behind.

YELLOW STARCH Then conclude thus:
When all men's several censures, all the arguments
The world can bring upon us, are applied,
The sin's not i' the colour, but the pride.

ALL
Oracle Yellow! *The Starches dance and exeunt*

JUPITER
These are the youngest daughters of Deceit,
With which the precious time of life's beguiled,
Fooled, and abused. I'll show you straight their father,
His shapes, his labours, that has vexed the world
From age to age, and tossed it from his first and simple state
To the foul centre where it now abides.
Look back but into times; here shall be shown
How many strange removes the world has known.

Music. Loud music sounding, Jupiter leaves his state and, to show the strange removes of the world, places the orb, whose figure it bears, in the midst of the stage, to whom Simplicity, by order of time has first access

Enter Simplicity

PALLAS
Who's this, great Jupiter?

JUPITER Simplicity,
He that had first possession, one that stumbled
Upon the world and never minded it.

SIMPLICITY Hah, hah! I'll go see how the world looks since I stepped aside from't, there's such heaving and shoving about it, such toiling and moiling. Now I stumbled upon't when I least thought on't.

Takes up the orb

'Uds me, 'tis altered of one side since I left it. Hah, there's a milkmaid got with child since, methinks. What, and a shepherd forsworn himself?—here's a foul corner. By this light, Subtlety has laid an egg too, and will go nigh to hatch a lawyer. This was well foreseen: I'll mar the fashion on't; so, the egg's broke, and 't has a yolk as black as buckram. What's here a' this side? O, a dainty world!—here's one a-sealing with his tooth, and, poor man, he has but one in all. I was afraid he would have left it upon the paper, he was so honestly earnest. [*A reaping song, as at a distance, within*] Here are the reapers singing. I'll lay mine ear to 'em.

Enter Deceit like a ranger

DECEIT [*aside*]
Yonder's Simplicity, whom I hate deadly;
H'as held the world too long. He's but a fool—
A toy will cozen him. If I once fasten on't,
I'll make it such a nursery for hell,
Planting black souls in't, it shall ne'er be fit
For Honesty to set her simples in.

SIMPLICITY [*aside*]
Whoop! here's the coz'ning'st rascal in a kingdom,
The master villain; has the thunder's property,
For if he come but near the harvest folks,

391 **white-faced** made-up; duplicitous
395 **Wears yellow** secretly longs to dress in clothes of that fashionable colour
396 **spite** irritating problem
398 **makes … hose** thereby ruling her husband and making a fool of him, like Malvolio in Shakespeare's *Twelfth Night*, 3.4; yellow hose were also a sign of a jealous husband
399 **stiff** firm, from starch
402 **scorn** proudly refuse
404 **censures** criticisms
407 **Oracle** source of revelation
408 **youngest daughters** see 'Critical Introduction' concerning London starch-makers
409 **beguiled** allured
410 **Fooled** made a fool of
straight directly
411 **shapes** external forms
vexed tossed about; hence, harassed and troubled
412 **simple state** condition of simplicity
414 **Look … times** an important directive, for it makes all that follows into a vision of the past, a history of the world
415 **removes** changes of conditions
415.1 ***Music*** though apparently redundant given the phrase that follows, the two references to music suggest the possibility of music building to the climax that cues Jupiter's action
415.2 ***state*** raised chair with a canopy, symbolic of power and magnificence; presumably, Jupiter descended from the upper stage on this throne
415.3 ***orb*** a globe, like that depicted on the title-page; the orb of royal regalia, a globe surmounted by a cross, would also be appropriate given Jove's introduction of this property and its final resting place with the King
whose figure a map of the world
415.4 ***stage*** suggesting performance on a raised platform both at the Swan and at Denmark House
415.4–5 ***by order of time*** the first (the age of innocence) comes first
417 **stumbled** discovered by chance, with a suggestion of the characteristic naïve clumsiness of Simplicity
418 **minded** took care of
421 **moiling** drudgery
423 **'Uds** God save
424 **got with child** pregnant
425 **forsworn** perjured
426 **Subtlety** craftiness
427 **will go nigh to** is just about to
428 **mar** destroy
fashion making
429 **buckram** coarse, stiffened cloth; specifically, a lawyer's bag
430 **dainty** delightful
a-sealing setting a seal on a document to authenticate it
434 **reapers** cutters of grain
434.1 ***ranger*** keeper of a forest or park
437 **toy** trifle
cozen dupe
438 **nursery** plot for developing young plants
440 **simples** medicinal herbs
442 **thunder's property** the power of a storm to spoil the harvest

His breath's so strong that he sours all their bottles. If he should but blow upon the world now, the stain would never get out again. I warrant, if he were ripped, one might find a swarm of usurers in his liver, a cluster of scriveners in his kidneys, and his very puddings stuffed with bailiffs.

DECEIT [*aside*]
I must speak fair to the fool.

SIMPLICITY [*aside*] He makes more near me.

DECEIT
'Las, who has put that load, that carriage,
On poor Simplicity? had they no mercy?
Pretty, kind, loving worm, come, let me help it.

SIMPLICITY Keep off, and leave your cogging. [*Aside*] Foh, how abominably he smells of controversies, schisms, and factions! Methinks I smell forty religions in him, and ne'er a good one. His eyes look like false lights, cozening trap-windows.

DECEIT
The world, sweetheart, is full of cares and troubles—
No match for thee. Thou art a tender thing,
A harmless, quiet thing, a gentle fool,
Fit for the fellowship of ewes and rams.
Go, take thine ease and pipe. Give me the burden,
The clog, the torment, the heartbreak, the world.
Here's for thee, lamb, a dainty oaten pipe.
[*Offers a pipe*]

SIMPLICITY Pox a' your pipe!—if I should dance after your pipe, I should soon dance to the devil.

DECEIT [*aside*]
I think some serpent sure has licked him over,
And given him only craft enough to keep,
And gone no further with him. All the rest
Is innocence about him, truth and bluntness.
I must seek other course, for I have learned
Of my infernal sire not to be lazy,
Faint, or discouraged at the tenth repulse.
Methinks that world Simplicity now hugs fast
Does look as if't should be Deceit's at last. *Exit*

SIMPLICITY So, so, I'm glad he's vanished. Methought I had much ado to keep myself from a smack of knavery, as long as he stood by me, for certainly villainy is infectious, and in the greater person the greater poison; as for example, he that gets but the itch of a citizen may take the scab of a courtier. [*The Reapers' Song, within*] Hark, the reapers begin to sing; they're come nearer methinks too.

The Reapers' Song

Happy times we live to see,
Whose master is Simplicity.
This is the age where blessings flow.
In joy we reap, in peace we sow.
We do good deeds without delay.
We promise and we keep our day.
We love for virtue, not for wealth.
We drink no healths, but all for health.
We sing, we dance, we pipe, we play;
Our work's continual holiday.
We live in poor contented sort,
Yet neither beg nor come at court. [*Exeunt*]

SIMPLICITY These reapers have the merriest lives. They have music to all they do; they'll sow with a tabor and get children with a pipe.

Enter King, after him Deceit [as a courtier]

DECEIT
Sir, he's a fool—the world belongs to you.

444 **bottles** trusses of hay
445 **blow** a mark of the corruptive power of Deceit, merely his breath produces an ineradicable stain
446 **warrant** guarantee
ripped torn open
447 **usurers** see note to l. 315
448 **scriveners** people who received money to invest for interest
puddings guts
449 **bailiffs** in this context, collectors of rent
451 **'Las** alas
carriage load
453 **help it** help you with it
454 **cogging** trickery aimed to cheat another
455 **schisms** hostile divisions, especially within religions
456 **factions** partisan groups, often with the additional sense of unscrupulousness in their activities
458 **trap-windows** hinged or sliding window, deceptive in that it falsified the intensity of the light emitted; see *Michaelmas* 1.2.88 for the same conjunction of this image and false light
460 **match** companion
461 **fool** an innocent, without any pejorative connotation
462 **ewes and rams** images of the pastoral world
463 **pipe** presumably an imperative: play your pipe (the simple wind instrument, a regular feature of shepherds in pastoral literature)
464 **clog** burden
466 **Pox a'** a pox on; imprecation emphatically rejecting the offered pipe
468 **serpent** source of worldly wisdom
licked him over shaped or educated him
469 **craft** intelligence
keep continue in the same state
473 **infernal sire** the Devil, father of Deceit; see James I, *Demonology* (Edinburgh, 1597), 1–5, for this conjunction of the demons and deceit
474 **Faint** dispirited
475 **fast** tightly
478 **smack** taste
knavery dishonesty
480 **in ... poison** villainy is pro-rated according to social rank
481–2 **he ... courtier** a person who contracts a minor skin disease, such as eczema, from a citizen may contract a more serious one, such as syphilis, from someone of higher rank
490 **day** appointed day for work or payment of rent
492 **healths** toasts
493 **pipe** to play music with a pipe (see note to l. 463)
495 **sort** conditions
496 **at** to; as Induction.32–5 suggests, the poor could expect some handouts from a great household
498 **tabor** small drum
499 **pipe** with a bawdy reference to the penis
499.1 ***King*** that the king enters first after Simplicity establishes the precedency of monarchy and, hence, its superiority to lawyers and churchmen. King James based his concept of monarchy on the notion that kings received their power from God and distributed responsibility to estates beneath them, lawyers and churchmen.

You're mighty in your worth and your command.
You know to govern, form, make laws, and take
Their sweet and precious penalties; it befits
A mightiness like yours. The world was made
For such a lord as you, so absolute
A mast'ry in all princely nobleness
As yourself is; but to lie useless now,
Rusty, or lazy, in a fool's pre-eminence,
It is not for a glorious worth to suffer.

KING
Thou'st said enough.

DECEIT [*aside*] Now my hope ripens fairly.

SIMPLICITY [*aside*]
Here's a brave, glist'ring thing looks me i' the face.
I know not what to say to't.

KING What's thy name?

SIMPLICITY
You may read it in my looks: Simplicity.

KING
What mak'st thou with so great a charge about thee?
Resign it up to me, and be my fool.

SIMPLICITY
Troth, that's the way to be your fool indeed;
But shall I have the privilege to fool freely?

KING
As ever folly had.
[*Simplicity gives the orb to the King*]

SIMPLICITY I'm glad I'm rid on't.

DECEIT
Pray, let me ease your majesty.

KING Thou? hence,
Base sycophant, insinuating hell-hound.
Lay not a finger on it, as thou lov'st
The state of thy whole body. All thy filthy
And rotten flatteries stink i' my remembrance,
And nothing is so loathsome as thy presence.

SIMPLICITY [*aside*]
Sure this will prove a good prince.

DECEIT [*aside*] Still repulsed?
I must find ground to thrive on. *Exit Deceit*

SIMPLICITY Pray, remember now
You had the world from me clean as a pick,
Only a little smutted a' one side
With a bastard got against it or such a toy,
No great corruption nor oppression in't,
No knavery, tricks, nor cozenage.

KING
Thou say'st true, fool, the world has a clear water.

SIMPLICITY Make as few laws as you can then to trouble it—the fewer the better—for always the more laws you make, the more knaves thrive by't; mark it when you will.

KING Thou'st counsel i' thee too.

SIMPLICITY
A little against knavery. I'm such an enemy to't
That it comes naturally from me to confound it.

KING
Look, what are those?

SIMPLICITY Tents, tents. That part o' the world
Shows like a fair, but, pray, take notice on't,
There's not a bawdy booth amongst 'em all.
You have 'em white and honest as I had 'em.
Look that your laundresses pollute 'em not.

KING
How pleasantly the countries lie about,
Of which we are sole lord. What's that i' the middle?

SIMPLICITY
Looks like a point you mean, a very prick?

KING
Ay, that, that.

SIMPLICITY 'Tis the beginning of Amsterdam. They say the first brick there was laid with fresh cheese and cream,

501 **worth** personal merit and financial well-being
command dominion over others
503 **penalties** fines
506 **nobleness** dignity; perhaps punning on the coin, 'noble', as a variation on the motif of money
508 **Rusty** unused and decaying
a fool's Simplicity's
pre-eminence rule
509 **suffer** be subjected to
511 **brave** see note to l. 14
glist'ring glittering; suggestive of the splendid costume of the King
512 **I...to't** given his lack of sophistication, Simplicity is tongue-tied in the face of greatness
514 **charge** burden (the globe)
515 **fool** jester
516 **fool** dupe
517 **to fool freely** to play the part of the licensed fool, that of a moral and social critic
519 **ease** disburden
520 **Base** morally low
sycophant parasite
insinuating wheedling
hell-hound dog of hell; fiend
521–2 **as...body** if you love your body whole rather than ripped apart
523 **stink** stench, a commonplace feature of the Devil
524 **loathsome** hateful
526 **thrive** prosper
527 **pick** pointed metal instrument, the shape of which prevents dirt from adhering
528 **smutted** smudged
529 **bastard** illegitimate child
got born
531 **tricks** deceitful practices
532 **clear water** clear urine, a sign of good health
533 **then** therefore
535 **by't** by the law
537 **counsel** prudent advice
539 **confound** overthrow
541 **pray** I entreat you
take notice on't observe it
542 **bawdy booth** stall trading in obscenity
544 **pollute 'em** stain or make dingy the tents
547 **prick** a sharp point, such as that made by the capital 'a' with which Amsterdam (549) begins. The bawdy joke counters the praise of the fair free of bawdry (thereby allowing no extreme to stand as absolute in value) and makes fun of the Amsterdam Puritans.
549–52 **They...fornication** ridiculing the prurience of Dutch Puritans

because mortar made of lime and hair was wicked and committed fornication.

Enter a Land-Captain, and Deceit as a soldier

KING
Peace, who are these approaching?

SIMPLICITY Blustering fellows: the first's a soldier; he looks just like March.

DECEIT
Captain, 'tis you that have the bloody sweats.
You venture life and limbs. 'Tis you that taste
The stings of thirst and hunger.

LAND-CAPTAIN There thou hast named
Afflictions sharper than the enemy's swords.

DECEIT
Yet lets another carry away the world,
Of which by right you are the only master,
Stand curts'ing for your pay at your return,
Perhaps with wooden legs, to every groom
That dares not look full right upon a sword
Nor upon any wound or slit of honour?

LAND-CAPTAIN
No more, I'll be myself. I that uphold
Countries and kingdoms, must I halt downright
And be propped up with part of mine own strength,
The least part too? Why, have not I the power
To make myself stand absolute of myself,
That keep up others?

KING How cheers
Our noble captain?

LAND-CAPTAIN Our own captain,
No more a hireling. Your great foe's at hand;
Seek your defence elsewhere, for mine shall fail you.
I'll not be fellow-yoked with death and danger
All my lifetime and have the world kept from me,
March in the heat of summer in a bath,
A furnace girt about me, and in that agony,
With so much fire within me, forced to wade
Through a cool river—practising in life
The very pains of hell, now scorched, now shivering—
To call diseases early into my bones
Before I've age enough to entertain 'em.
No, he that has desire to keep the world,
Let him e'en take the sore pains to defend it.

KING
Stay, man of merit, it belongs to thee.
[*He gives the orb to the Land-Captain*]
I cheerfully resign it. All my ambition
Is but the quiet calm of peaceful days
And that fair good, I know, thy arm will raise.

LAND-CAPTAIN
Though now an absolute master, yet to thee
Ever a faithful servant.

DECEIT Give't me, sir,
To lay up; I am your treasurer
In a poor kind. *Exit King*

LAND-CAPTAIN In a false kind, I grant thee.
How many vile complaints from time to time
Have been put up against thee? They have wearied
me
More than a battle sixteen hours a-fighting.
I've heard the raggèd regiment so curse thee,
I looked next day for leprosy upon thee
Or puffs of pestilence as big as wens,
When thou wouldst drop asunder, like a thing
Inwardly eaten, thy skin only whole.
Avaunt, defrauder of poor soldiers' rights;
Camp caterpillar, hence!—or I will send thee
To make their rage a breakfast.

DECEIT [*aside*] Is it possible?
Can I yet set no footing in the world?
I'm angry, but not weary. I'll hunt out still,
For, being Deceit, I bear the devil's name,
And he's known seldom to give o'er his game.
Exit Deceit

551 **lime and hair** elements of mortar mix; hair facilitated the binding capacity of the cement (lime)
552.1 ***Land-Captain*** officer in charge of a troop
soldier one of the rank and file who serves in the army for pay
554 **Blustering** boisterous
555 **like March** that is, blustery; punning perhaps on marching and Mars
556 **bloody sweats** sweat mingled with blood because of the physical exertions of battle. Deceit is also alluding sacrilegiously to the bloody sweat of Jesus in Gethsemane (Luke 22:44).
557 **venture** risk
560–5 **Yet... honour** Deceit's rhetoric changes with each role he plays; here, for example, from the fawning flattery of the monarch to the mild ridicule of the discrepancy between the Land-Captain's power and his servility
561 **right** deliberately confused with 'might' in Deceit's argument
562 **curts'ing** bowing
563 **groom** man-servant, with contempt here
564 **full right** directly
565 **slit of honour** honourable injury
567 **halt** limp
downright plainly
570 **absolute** self-sufficient
571 **cheers** feels, but presuming good feelings
572 **Our noble... Our own** repetition stresses the conflict between the characters; see also Lineation Notes
573 **hireling** servant working for wages
575 **fellow-yoked** joined with
577 **in a bath** bathed in sweat
578 **furnace... me** carrying equipment, the weight of which intensifies the heat and aggravates the sweaty labour
581 **scorched... shivering** characteristic extremism of hell
583 **entertain 'em** to receive diseases properly; with wry humour
589 **arm** strength and weaponry
592 **lay up** store
593 **In a poor kind** humble
597 **raggèd** poor and weary
599 **puffs** swellings
pestilence an epidemic; specifically, the plague
wens tumours
602 **Avaunt** get away
603 **caterpillar** parasite
604 **To... breakfast** to feed and satisfy their anger
605 **footing** secure foothold
608 **give o'er** quit

SIMPLICITY Troth, now the world begins to be in hucksters' handling. By this light, the booths are full of cutlers, and yonder's two or three queans going to victual the camp. Hah! would I were whipped, if yonder be not a parson's daughter with a soldier between her legs, bag and baggage.

SOLDIER
Now 'tis the soldier's time, great Jupiter;
Now give me leave to enter on my fortunes.
The world's our own.

JUPITER Stay, beguiled thing, this time
Is many ages discrepant from thine.
This was the season when desert was stooped to,
By greatness stooped to, and acknowledged greatest;
But in thy time, now, desert stoops itself
To every baseness and makes saints of shadows.
Be patient, and observe how times are wrought,
Till it comes down to thine, that rewards naught.

Chambers shot off. Enter a Sea-Captain, and Deceit as a purser

OMNES
Hah? what's the news?

SEA-CAPTAIN
Be ready if I call to give fire to the ordnance.

SIMPLICITY Bless us all, here's one spits fire as he comes. He will go nigh to mull the world with looking on it. How his eyes sparkle!

DECEIT
Shall the Land-Captain, sir, usurp your right?—
Yours, that try thousand dangers to his one:
Rocks, shelves, gulfs, quicksands, hundred hundred horrors,
That make the landmen tremble when they're told,
Besides the enemy's encounter.

SEA-CAPTAIN
Peace, Purser, no more; I'm vexed. I'm kindled.
You, Land-Captain, quick, deliver.

LAND-CAPTAIN
Proud salt-rover, thou hast the salutation of a thief.

SEA-CAPTAIN
Deliver, or I'll thunder thee a-pieces,
Make night within this hour, e'en at high noon,
Belched from the cannon. Dar'st expostulate
With me? my fury? What's thy merit, land-worm,
That mine not centuples?
Thy lazy marches and safe-footed battles
Are but like dangerous dreams to my encounters.
Why, every minute the deep gapes for me,
Beside the fiery throats of the loud fight.
When we go to't and our fell ordnance play,
'Tis like the figure of a latter day.
Let me but give the word, night begins now,
Thy breath and prize both beaten from thy body.
How dar'st thou be so slow? Not yet—then—

LAND-CAPTAIN Hold.

[He gives the orb to the Sea-Captain]

DECEIT *[aside]*
I knew 'twould come at last.

SEA-CAPTAIN *[to the Land-Captain]*
For this resign,
Part thou shalt have still, but the greatest mine.
Only to us belongs the golden sway.
Th'Indies load us; thou liv'st but by thy pay.

DECEIT
And shall your purser help you?

SEA-CAPTAIN No in sooth, sir,
Coward and coz'ner. How many sea-battles
Hast thou compounded to be cabled up?
Yet, when the fights were ended, who so ready
To cast sick soldiers and dismembered wretches
Overboard instantly?—crying 'Away
With things without arms!—'Tis an ugly sight.'
When, troth, thine own should have been off by right.
But thou lay'st safe within a wall of hemp,

609 **hucksters'** hawkers' or pedlars'; so handled, the world is likely to be roughly used
610 **cutlers** dealers in knives
611 **queans** harlots
victual provision, presumably with sexual treats
613–14 **bag and baggage** primarily, all the equipment of the soldiers individually and of the army collectively; in this context, with the bawdy connotations of scrotum and penis; possibly with a pun on 'baggage' in the sense of 'strumpet'
618 **discrepant** removed in time
619 **desert** merit
stooped to respected
620 **greatness** of blood; hence, the nobility
621 **stoops** declines
622 **makes . . . shadows** worships insubstantial things
623 **wrought** made
624 **naught** nothing
624.1 ***Chambers*** small cannons
Sea-Captain commander of a ship; a more prestigious officer than a land-captain in the British military forces
624.2 ***purser*** ship's officer in charge of money matters and provisions
626 **ordnance** cannons
627 **spits fire** speaks fiercely
628 **mull** warm up
630 **usurp** wrongfully claim
631 **try** undergo
634 **enemy's encounter** battles with the enemy
635 **vexed** stirred up; annoyed
636 **deliver** hand over the world
637 **salt-rover** seaman
salutation greeting (the command to deliver one's goods)
639 **Make night** darkening the sky with smoke from the cannons
640 **expostulate** debate
642 **centuples** multiplies by a hundred
644 **but** merely
645 **deep** sea
646 **fiery throats** openings of the cannons
647 **fell** fierce
play discharge
648 **figure** image
latter day one of the last, apocalyptic days
650 **prize** the world
651 **How . . . slow** the actors could make clear that the impatience of the Sea-Captain, not any tardiness on the part of the Land-Captain, informs this question
652 **resign** surrender
654 **golden sway** the power of wealth, enhanced by plunder
658 **compounded . . . up** gathered together to be tied up; i.e. how many sea-battles are in your tally?
663 **own** arms understood
664 **hemp** coil of rope

Telling the guns and numbering 'em with farting.
Leave me, and speedily. I'll have thee rammed
Into a culverin else, and thy rear flesh
Shot all into poached eggs.

DECEIT [*aside*] I will not leave yet:
Destruction plays in me such pleasant strains
That I would purchase it with any pains. *Exit Deceit*

SEA-CAPTAIN
The motion's worthy. [*To the Land Captain*] I will join with thee
Both to defend and enrich majesty.

SIMPLICITY
Hoyday! I can see nothing now for ships.
[*The Mariners' Song, within*]
Hark a' the mariners.

The Mariners' Song

Hey, the world's ours; we have got the time by chance.
Let us then carouse and sing, for the very house doth skip and dance
That we do now live in.
We have the merriest lives;
We have the fruitfull'st wives
Of all men.
We never yet came home,
But the first hour we come,
We find them all with child again.

A shout within; then, enter two Mariners with pipe and can, dancing severally by turns, for joy the world is come into their hands; then exeunt

SIMPLICITY What a crew of mad rascals are these? They're ready at every can to fall into the haddocks' mouths. The world begins to love lap now.

Enter a Flamen and Deceit like [*an aedituus*]

FLAMEN
Peace and the brightness of a holy love
Reflect their beauties on you.

SEA-CAPTAIN Who's this?

LAND-CAPTAIN
A reverend shape.

SEA-CAPTAIN Some scholar.

LAND-CAPTAIN A divine one.

SEA-CAPTAIN
He may be what he will for me, fellow-captain,
For I have seen no church these five-and-twenty years—
I mean, as people ought to see it, inwardly.

FLAMEN
I have a virtuous sorrow for you, sir,
And 'tis my special duty to weep for you;
For to enjoy one world as you do there,
And be forgetful of another, sir,
(O, of a better millions of degrees!)
It is a frailty and infirmity
That many tears must go for—all too little.
What is't to be the lord of many battles
And suffer to be overrun within you,
Abroad to conquer, and be slaves at home?
Remember there's a battle to be fought
Which will undo you if it be not thought.
And you must leave that world, leave it betimes,
That reformation may weep of the crimes.
There's no indulgent hand the world should hold,
But a strict grasp. For making sin so bold,
We should be careless of it, and not fond
Of things so held: there is the best command.

SEA-CAPTAIN
Grave sir, I give thy words their deserved honour,
And to thy sacred charge freely resign
All that my fortune and the age made mine.
[*He gives the orb to the Flamen*]

SIMPLICITY
If the world be not good now, 'twill ne'er be good;
There's no hope on't.

665 **Telling the guns** tallying the gun-shots
numbering counting
667 **culverin** large cannon
670 **with any pains** no matter how great the pains
671 **motion's** *motion*: the action of upbraiding and dismissing Deceit
673 **Hoyday** exclamation of surprise
675 **carouse** drink freely
678–82 **We...again** the song implies their wives are pregnant because of their infidelity
682.2 ***pipe*** boatswain's whistle
can metal pot, from which they drink liquor and on which they may bang out the beat for their dancing
severally individually
by turns one after the other
683 **crew** ship's crew and gang
684 **at every can** with every drink of liquor; as the dancers drink more they seem to Simplicity to be increasingly in danger of falling into the sea
685 **lap** liquor
685.1 ***Flamen*** priest of a particular deity in Roman antiquity; also religious leaders of heathen Britain, replaced by bishops after the conversion of the people to Christianity. The archaic usage, which is never used in the speeches, seems a literary extension of the caricature of the Flamen, a caricature effected in production by costume, comportment, and style of speech.
aedituus churchwarden, the parish official in charge of financial matters
686 **Peace** marking the shift from war to peace, from soldier to scholar
691 **inwardly** punning: 'from the inside' and 'spiritually'
693 **'tis...you** patronizing in his compassion
694 **one world** the physical one
695 **another** the spiritual one
696 **better** after which 'by' understood
703 **thought** kept in mind
704 **that world** the world of military conquest
betimes soon
705 **reformation** amendment
weep of regret or atone for sins, as a result of remembering
707–9 **For...held** the failure to be strict emboldens sin and demonstrates not genuine fondness of the world, but lack of care
708 **it** the world
fond loving and genuinely caring
711 **charge** custody

DECEIT [*aside*]
I have my wishes here. [*To the Flamen*] My sanctified patron,
I'll first fill all the chests i'th' vestry;
Then there's a secret vault for great men's legacies.

FLAMEN
Art not confounded yet? struck blind or crippled
For thy abusive thought, thou horrid hypocrite?
Are these the fruits of thy long orisons
Three hours together, of thy nine lectures weekly,
Thy swooning at the hearing of an oath,
Scarce to be fetched again? Away! depart!—
Thou white-faced devil, author of heresy,
Schisms, factions, controversies. Now I know thee
To be Deceit itself, wrought in by simony
To blow corruption upon sacred virtue.

DECEIT [*aside*]
I made myself sure here. Church fail me too?
I thought it mere impossible by all reason,
Since there's so large a bridge to walk upon
'Twixt negligence and superstition.
Where could one better piece up a full vice?
One service lazy, t'other over-nice,
There had been 'twixt 'em room enough for me.
I will take root or run through each degree.

Exit Deceit

SIMPLICITY Whoop, here's an alteration. By this hand, the ships are all turned to steeples, and the bells ring for joy, as if they would shake down the pinnacles. How!—the masons are at work yonder, the freemasons; I swear it's a free time for them. Hah!—there's one building of a chapel of ease. O, he's loath to take the pains to go to church. Why, will he have it in's house, when the proverb says, 'The devil's at home'? These great rich men must take their ease i' their inn. They'll walk you a long mile or two to get a stomach for their victuals, but not a piece of a furlong to get an appetite to their prayers.

Flourish. Enter King, a Lawyer, and Deceit as a pettifogger

LAWYER
No more, the case is clear.

SIMPLICITY 'Slid, who have we here?

LAWYER
He that pleads for the world must fall
To his business roundly. Most gracious
And illustrious prince, thus stands the case:
The world in Greek is *cosmos*, in Latin *mundus*,
In law-French *le monde*. We leave the Greek
And come to the law-French, or glide upon the Latin—
All's one business.
Then *unde mundus*? shall we come to that?
Nonne derivatur a munditia?
The word 'cleanness', *mundus, quasi mundus*, 'clean'.
And what can cleanse or mundify the world
Better than law, the clearer of all cases,
The sovereign pill or potion that expels
All poisonous, rotten, and infectious wrongs
From the vexed bosom of the commonwealth?
There's a familiar phrase implies thus much,
'I'll put you to your purgation'; that is,
The law shall cleanse you. Can the sick world then,
Tossed up and down from time to time, repose itself
In a physician's hand better improved?
Upon my life and reputation
In all the courts I come at, be assured
I'll make it clean.

SIMPLICITY Yes, clean away.
I warrant you, we shall ne'er see't again.

LAWYER
I grant my pills are bitter, ay, and costly,

715 **sanctified** holy
716 **vestry** room in the church for storing vestments and other valuables
717 **vault** safe
legacies bequests
720 **orisons** prayers
721 **lectures** a jab at Puritans, whose religious practice included lectures, at some times and in some places daily, on the Scriptures
722 **swooning** fainting because of hearing someone swear; clearly, an overreaction
723 **fetched** revived
724 **white-faced** deceptively innocent in outward appearance
heresy unorthodox teaching
726 **wrought in** worked in; punning on 'rotten'
simony the selling of ecclesiastical offices
727 **blow corruption upon** defame; remove the bloom from
729 **mere** simply
731 **negligence** laziness in ministry (see 733)
superstition over-nice ministry (see 733)
732 **piece up** put together
733 **over-nice** too fastidious
735 **degree** rank in the social hierarchy
738 **pinnacles** little ornamental turrets
739 **freemasons** society of skilled workers in stone
741 **chapel of ease** chapel built for people who live far from the parish church; developed pejoratively here
743 **The devil's at home** proverbial (Tilley D243)
744 **take their ease** make themselves comfortable
745 **get a stomach** work up an appetite
victuals food
746 **furlong** length of a furrow in a common field; approximately 220 yards
747.2 ***pettifogger*** one of the lower order of legal practitioners; also one who uses mean, deceitful practices
748 **case** legal suit
749 **pleads** speaks as an advocate to the court
750 **roundly** openly; playing on the spherical shape of the world
754 **glide upon** pass over smoothly
756 ***unde mundus?*** whence the world? *mundus* also means 'clean'
757 ***Nonne . . . munditia?*** is it not derived from 'cleanness'?
758 ***mundus, quasi mundus*** 'the world', just as 'clean'
759 **mundify** also in the specific medical sense, to purge the body or the blood of noxious matter
760 **clearer** eliminator
763 **vexed** distressed
766–8 **Can . . . improved** rhetorical question; given the medical metaphors for the activity of the law, the question implies that the world cannot be better off than in a lawyer's hand
767 **repose** settle
770 **courts** punning on law courts and royal courts

But their effects are rare, divine, and wholesome.
There's an *Excommunicate capiendo*,
Capias post K. and a *Ne exeat regno.*
I grant there's bitter *egrimony* in 'em
And *antimony*. I put money in all still,
And it works preciously. Who ejects injuries,
Makes 'em belch forth in vomit, but the law?
Who clears the widow's case, and after gets her
If she be wealthy, but the advocate?—Then, to conclude,
If you'll have *mundus, a mundo*, clean, firm,
Give him to me; I'll scour him every term.

FLAMEN

I part with't gladly; take't into thy trust.
[*He gives the orb to the Lawyer*]
So will it thrive as thy intent is just.

DECEIT

Pity your trampler, sir, your poor solicitor.

LAWYER

Thee!—infamy to our profession,
Which, without wrong to truth, next the divine one
Is the most grave and honourable function
That gives a kingdom blessed. But thou, the poison
Disease that grows close to the heart of law,
And mak'st rash censurers think the sound part perished;
Thou foul eclipse that, interposing equity
As the dark earth the moon, mak'st the world judge
That blackness and corruption have possessed
The silver shine of justice, when 'tis only
The smoke ascending from thy pois'nous ways:
Coz'nage, demurs, and fifteen term-delays.
Yet hold thee!—take the muck on't; that's thine own,
The devil and all. But the fair fame and honour
Of righteous actions, good men's prayers and wishes,
Which is that glorious portion of the world
The noble lawyer strives for, that thy bribery,
Thy double-handed grip, shall never reach to.
With fat and filthy gain thy lust may feast,
But poor men's curses beat thee from the rest.

DECEIT

I'll feed upon the muck on't; that awhile
Shall satisfy my longings. Wealth is known
The absolute step to all promotion.

KING

Let this be called the sphere of harmony,
In which, being met, let's all move mutually.

OMNES

Fair love is i'th' motion, kingly love.

In this last dance, as an ease to memory, all the former removes come close together: the Devil and Deceit aiming at the world, but the world remaining now in the Lawyer's possession. [*He*], *expressing his reverend and noble acknowledgement to the absolute power of Majesty, resigns it loyally to its royal government, Majesty to Valour, Valour to Law again, Law to Religion, Religion to Sovereignty, where it firmly and fairly settles; the Law confounding Deceit, and the Church the Devil*

FLAMEN

Times suffer changes, and the world has been
Vexed with removes, but when his glorious peace
Firmly and fairly settles, here's his place,

775 ***Excommunicate capiendo*** a writ for the arrest of someone excommunicated for forty days and for the detention of that person 'till he hath made agreement to holy Church for the contempt and wrong' (Rastell)

776 ***Capias post K*** perhaps *capias post calumnia*: a writ of arrest upon accusation ***Ne exeat regno*** writ forbidding someone to leave the kingdom

777 ***egrimony*** sorrow; punning on 'money'

778 ***antimony*** antinomy: a contradiction within a law or between two binding laws; the reversal of the 'n' and the 'm' may have been deliberate to obtain another pun on 'money'

779 **ejects** expels **injuries** injustices

783 ***mundus, a mundo*** the world, from clean: noting again the derivation of terms so as to reinforce the Lawyer's connection of them

784 **term** see note to l. 327

787 **trampler** one who gets about on foot; also with the more pejorative sense of one who treads harmfully upon others **solicitor** an advocate in a court of equity

788 **infamy** disgrace

789 **the divine one** the religious profession

791 **gives** produces

793 **censurers** critics **sound** healthy

794 **interposing** obstructing **equity** fairness

797 **silver shine** silver was the traditional colour of Diana, goddess of the moon; the lunar eclipse prevents the light of the moon from being seen

799 **Coz'nage** fraud **demurs** suspension of an action **fifteen term-delays** long postponement; sixteen term-delays would be four years

800 **muck** filth; in this context, money (see 808–10) **on't** on the world, which Deceit still has a hand on

802 **actions** legal suits

803 **portion** share distributed by law

805 **double-handed** two-handed, and duplicitous

811 **sphere** the globe and the group of characters

812 **mutually** interdependently

813.2 ***removes . . . together*** what action is called for is somewhat ambiguous: if 'removes' refers to the various changes in the condition of the world, changes embodied in the characters who hold it, 'come close together' may indicate that they gather more tightly around the orb to protect it from the threats of the Devil and Deceit; if 'removes' refers to the transfers of the globe from one character to another, as described in the lines that follow, then 'come close together' may point to a quicker series of transfers. These options are not mutually exclusive: speeding up the transfer of the world from character to character would depend upon getting the members of the group closer to one another. Accelerating the transfers would also serve 'as an ease to memory' by reproducing—in short, as it were—what took a longer time to present throughout the body of the masque.

813.3 ***aiming at*** threatening

813.7 ***Valour*** the Land-Captain and the Sea-Captain allied

814 **suffer** undergo

815 **his** the world's

Truth his defence, and majesty his grace.
We all acknowledge it belongs to you.

ALL
Only to you, sir.

They all deliver the world up to the King

FLAMEN
Regis ad exemplum totus componitur orbis—Which shows,
That if the world form itself by the king,
'Tis fit the former should command the thing.

DECEIT
This is no place for us.

DEVIL Depart! Away!
I thought all these had been corrupted evils,
No court of virtues, but a guard of devils.

Exeunt Deceit and the Devil

KING
How blest am I in subjects! Here are those
That make all kingdoms happy: worthy soldier,
Fair churchman, and thou, uncorrupted lawyer,
Virtue's great miracle, that hast redeemed
All justice from her ignominious name.

SIMPLICITY
You forget me, sir.

KING What, Simplicity!
Who thinks of virtue cannot forget thee.

SIMPLICITY Ay, marry, my masters, now it looks like a brave world indeed. How civilly those fair ladies go yonder; by this hand, they are neither trimmed, nor trussed, nor poniarded. Wonderment! O, yonder's a knot of fine-sharp-needle-bearded gallants, but that they wear stammel cloaks, methinks, instead of scarlet. 'Slid, what's he that carries out two custards now under the porter's long nose? O, he leaves a bottle of wine i'th' lodge, and all's pacified, cry mercy.

KING
Continue but thus watchful o'er yourselves,
That the great cunning enemies, Deceit
And his too mighty lord, beguile you not,
And you're the precious ornaments of state,
The glories of the world, fellows to virtues,
Masters of honest and well-purchased fortunes,
And I am fortunate in your partnership.
But if you ever make your hearts the houses
Of falsehood and corruption, ugliness itself
Will be a beauty to you, and less pointed at.
Spots in deformèd faces are scarce noted;
Fair cheeks are stained if ne'er so little blotted.

ALL
Ever the constant servants to great virtue.

KING
Her love inhabit you.

Exeunt [all except Jupiter, Pallas, Soldier, and Scholar]

JUPITER Now, sons of vexation,
Envy and discontent, what blame lay you
Upon these times now? Which does merit most
To be condemned, your dullness or the age?
If now you thrive not, Mercury shall proclaim
You're undeservers, and cry down your fame.
Be poor still, scholar, and thou, wretch despised,
If in this glorious time thou canst not prosper,
Upon whose breast noble employments sit,
By honour's hand in golden letters writ.
Nay, where the prince of nobleness himself
Proves our Minerva's valiant'st, hopefull'st son,
And early in his spring puts armour on,
Unite your worths, and make of two, one brother,
And be each one perfection to the other.
Scholar and soldier must both be shut in one;
That makes the absolute and complete man.
So now into the world, which, if hereafter
You ever tax of foul, ingrateful crimes,
Your dullness I must punish, not the times.

818 **you** in a performance before King James, the show might at this point have culminated with the presentation of the globe to James
820 ***Regis . . . orbis*** the whole world is ordered by the example of the king. James I quotes the same line at the outset of the second book ('Of a King's Duty in his Office') of *Basilikon Doron* (Edinburgh, 1599).
822 **former** he who forms it
829 **redeemed** rescued
830 **ignominious** shameful
833 **marry** by Mary
834 **civilly** with moderation
835 **trimmed** wearing hats or garments decorated with ribbons, lace, or other trimmings
836 **trussed** wearing garments drawn tightly around the body
poniarded wearing daggers, a fashion that James found particularly abhorrent in women
837 **knot** group
fine-sharp-needle-bearded a beard fashionably cut to form a sharp point at the bottom
gallants fine, fashionable gentlemen
838 **stammel** coarse wool, usually dyed red
scarlet symbolic of their pride and self-indulgence
841 **pacified** the apparent theft of custards is set right
cry mercy I beg your pardon
844 **lord** the Devil
845 **ornaments** attendants upon
state regal power
846 **fellows** allies
847–8 **fortunes . . . fortunate** polyptoton; playing on financial well-being, attractive personal prospects, and good luck
851 **less pointed at** because commonplace
855 **vexation** dissatisfaction
858 **dullness** foolishness
age times
859 **Mercury** god who broadcast the fame of people
860 **cry down** condemn
861 **thou** Soldier
862 **glorious time** alluding to the wars in Europe; see note to 878
863 **whose breast** that of the present time
863–4 **noble . . . writ** honourable opportunities present themselves
865 **the prince** Charles, Prince of Wales
867 **his spring** his youth
puts armour on for his first tilt, 24 March 1620 and again on 18 April
868 **worths** strengths
873 **tax** charge with

SOLDIER *and* SCHOLAR
Honour to mighty Jupiter.

Jupiter ascends [with Pallas]

SOLDIER
The world's in a good hand now, if it hold, brother.

SCHOLAR
I hope for many ages.

SOLDIER
Fare thee well then.
I'll over yonder to the most glorious wars
That e'er famed Christian kingdom.

SCHOLAR
And I'll settle
Here, in a land of a most glorious peace
That ever made joy fruitful, where the head
Of him that rules, to learning's fair renown,
Is doubly decked, with laurel and a crown,
And both most worthily.

SOLDIER
Give me thy hand;
Prosperity keep with thee.

SCHOLAR
And the glory
Of noble action bring white hairs upon thee.
Present our wish with reverence to this place,
For here't must be confirmed or 'tas no grace.

Exeunt severally

Epilogue

Epilogue

Gentlemen,
We must confess that we have vented ware
Not always vendible—masques are more rare
Than plays are common; at most but twice a year
In their most glorious shapes do they appear—
Which, if you please, accept. We'll keep in store
Our debted loves, and thus entreat you more:
Invert the proverb now, and suffer not
'That which is seldom seen, be soon forgot'.

Finis

THE PARTS

Adult Males

SIMPLICITY (127 lines): Prologue, Epilogue, Time
SCHOLAR (115 lines): Prologue, Epilogue
JUPITER (93 lines): Prologue, Epilogue
DECEIT (83 lines): Prologue, Epilogue, Time
SOLDIER (82 lines): Prologue, Epilogue
LAWYER (56 lines): Prologue, Epilogue, Time
TIME (49 lines): any but Scholar, Soldier, Jupiter
KING (46 lines): Prologue, Epilogue, Time
SEA-CAPTAIN (44 lines): Prologue, Epilogue, Time
FLAMEN (40 lines): Prologue, Epilogue, Time
LAND-CAPTAIN (40 lines): Prologue, Epilogue, Time
PROLOGUE (18 lines): any character
EPILOGUE (9 lines): any character
DEVIL (3 lines): Prologue, Epilogue, Time

Boys

PALLAS (113 lines): Richmond *or* St James's *or* Denmark House
DENMARK HOUSE (55 lines): Pallas
ST JAMES'S (31 lines): Pallas
RICHMOND (15 lines): Pallas

Dancers/Singers: Adult

WORTHIES (no lines): Mariners, Reapers

Dancers/Singers: Boys

MUSES (no lines): Starches

Most crowded scene: Finale—12 characters

Most crowded dance: Nine Worthies—22 characters (9 Muses [torchbearers rather than dancers?]; 9 Worthies; 4 actors)

876 **hold** last
878 **wars** in support of the claim made by Frederick, Elector Palatine, to the crown of Bohemia
879 **Christian** alluding to the way in which the wars were perceived, as a conflict of Protestantism and Catholicism
883 **laurel** symbolizing King James's achievements as a scholar
885–6 **And . . . thee** may you grow old in noble military enterprises
887 **this place** possibly the throne of Jupiter on high; more likely the throne of King James at Denmark House, or in the Swan theatre the audience
Epilogue.2 **vented** sold
ware goods
3 **vendible** marketable
4 **twice a year** the masques that graced state occasions were usually performed at Twelfth Night and at Shrovetide
6 **Which** 'ware' understood
6–7 **We'll . . . loves** we shall remember that we are in your debt
8 **suffer** allow

HONOURABLE ENTERTAINMENTS *and* AN INVENTION

Edited by Anthony Parr

On 29 April 1620 John Chamberlain wrote to Sir Dudley Carleton informing him of 'a great Commission come forth for the business of [St] Paul's, comprehending all the [Privy] Council . . . divers aldermen and other citizens'. A new determination to do something about the fabric of the long-neglected cathedral had been forged a month earlier, when the Lord Mayor Sir William Cokayne met James I at St Paul's and an agreement was reached about sharing the costs of repair. Chamberlain himself was a member of the Commission, and relates that after its first meeting on 22 April all its members 'were invited to dine that day with the Lord Mayor; but because I love not such confusion of company, I went not'. It is unclear from Chamberlain's laconic phrasing whether he disliked crowds or the mixing of social ranks, but he adds that he might have gone if he had known that Cokayne's daughter, who had been married that day to Charles Howard, son and heir of the Earl of Nottingham, was to be present. He concludes by offering a sour assessment of the match: 'I do not greatly allow my Lord Mayor's judgement, to purchase so poor honour with the price of his daughter, a handsome young woman (they say), and to bestow her on a man so worn out in state, credit, years and otherwise. But the match may prove reasonable indifferent, for as they can look for little or nothing of him but bare honour, so from her side they are to expect no great matter more than money.'

By excusing himself from dinner Chamberlain lost the opportunity to have his opinion softened by a skilful entertainment. Cokayne clearly decided to make the official occasion double as a wedding reception, perhaps hoping to impress his distinguished guests with this opportune match; and Middleton's preamble to the text of *Entertainment* 1 traces a process whereby the original in-house tribute to the Mayor and Aldermen (apparently given at two civic banquets on 17 and 18 April) became by the end of the week a sort of wedding masque played before a larger audience of notables. (The marriage was also the occasion of Middleton's dedication of *The World Tossed at Tennis*.) Cokayne may have felt not only that the glittering occasion demonstrated his fitness for aristocratic connections but also that the marriage would thereby gain some lustre amongst his peers in the city government, some of whom might have agreed with Chamberlain and a modern biographer that Howard was 'dim and dull', a poor successor to his famous father the former Lord Admiral. Middleton's piece, put to work in these different contexts, represents the adaptable, confident, outward-looking face of civic authority, refining social and political relations with the help of an elegant show.

The cultural rivalry between Whitehall and London in the early seventeenth century, evident in the way both the court masque and the Lord Mayor's pageant became increasingly lavish and spectacular events, is also visible in these intimate entertainments, which are in some ways more revealing of a civic ambition to match the ceremony of the court and of aristocratic great houses. We can glimpse something of the increasing provision for entertainment on formal occasions in the treatment of the city 'waits', or municipal musicians, in the Jacobean period. In 1604 the independent musicians of London petitioned successfully to be incorporated as a Company, and in the following year the waits appealed to the City for a pay rise, citing 'their continual daily and nightly services and small wage'; as a result their salary was almost doubled to £20 per year. By 1613 the consort used on such occasions—which had its own uniform of blue gown with red sleeves and caps, and a silver chain and badge of office—was probably ten or a dozen strong. Exact figures are not available, but we know that it employed a small band of wind and string players and both men and boy singers. What Middleton refers to as 'the City Music' (1.10.2–3) was in fact the only permanent group of its kind in London other than the King's Music and the cathedral choirs, and it clearly played a prominent part in all the indoor entertainments.

Middleton was presumably following the wishes of his employers (whose permission he needed to publish what he wrote for city functions) when in a number of small details he aligns his civic shows with the pomp and circumstance of courtly ritual. He informs us, for instance, that *Ent.* 3 took place at 'the Conduit Head near the Banqueting House', which for any reader of masque texts, then or now, would inevitably recall the Whitehall setting of court entertainments like those of Ben Jonson. In fact the reference is to the large house north of Oxford Street in what is now Stratford Place, where the city fathers dined once a year after visiting the springs at Tyburn; and it gains an extra piquancy from the fact that in 1620–1 there was no royal equivalent, since the Banqueting House in Whitehall had burned down in 1619 and Inigo Jones's replacement was not finished until 1622. In *Ent.* 4 Alderman Hamersley is grandly described as 'President of the noble Council of War' (he was in charge of the Artillery Company), and in the headnote to the opening piece Lord Mayor Cokayne is designated 'Lord General of the military forces', a title Middleton had already given him in his inaugural pageant, recognizing (and somewhat inflating) his authority over the city militia. But if the merchants who governed London sought to rival the opulence and refinement of Whitehall, this was because they wished to enhance their self-esteem and project a modern corporate image, and not because they saw themselves as being in opposition to royal authority.

The point needs to be made here because the supposed political sympathies of Middleton's employers have sometimes been used to advance the case for his own political radicalism. Margot Heinemann claims that 'it was pretty clearly as a protege of Parliamentary Puritans among the City oligarchs that Middleton entered on his City employments'; but if he routinely served puritan interests we might expect to find clearest evidence for it in these diverse entertainments, given the fact that they are addressed not (like the mayoral pageants) to a single Mayor or guild but to the city government in a variety of festive and workaday contexts. The men to whom Middleton dedicates his book comprise the Court of Aldermen, the senior governing body of the City of London. They were mostly wholesale merchants, many of them having interests in overseas trade through the Levant and East India Companies, and as Robert Brenner has most recently shown, their most intimate affiliation was with the Crown, which protected their corporate privileges in return for political and financial support. Many of these men were royal employees, then or later: Proby was active at court and a former governor of Ulster; Jones was a customs farmer; Ducy eventually became banker to Charles I. Men like Bolles were old gentry stock; he is one of eight ex-Lord Mayors and knights of the realm listed in the Dedication in strict order of seniority, as are the other Aldermen in the order in which they had held the post of Sheriff (and in which they would become Mayor, in the case of those destined to reach that office). This powerful oligarchy, proud of its long tradition of civic independence, inevitably had complex, often difficult relations with other political groups and interests, and it was no stranger to conflict with the Crown, usually over taxation; but amidst the shifting allegiances of this period the City's political enemies were generally to be found not in the royal government but in Parliament, which in the name of free trade regularly opposed merchant privileges and monopolies.

Middleton habitually views these matters from the City's point of view; but we may guess that he felt comfortable with his employers not for ideological reasons but because they reflected his own pragmatic attitude to self-betterment. Consider, for example, the battle over the Virginia Company that was going on while these pieces were being produced. About one-third of the named Aldermen were Adventurers in the company, a high proportion, arguably, given the extensive withdrawal by London merchants from investment in Virginia after the company was taken over by the gentry party of Sir Edwin Sandys in 1619. A leading light in the campaign to regain merchant control was Alderman Johnson, son-in-law of the city magnate Sir Thomas Smith; Hugh Hamersley and James Campbell were also declared opponents of the Sandys faction. But to achieve their ends the merchants formed an alliance with the Rich family, the colonizing aristocrats who had originally backed Sandys's efforts at colonial reform but had been alienated by his attempt to halt their own privateering activities. The merchants themselves had good reason to dislike privateers and had little taste for Robert Rich's overseas ventures (in which plunder and settlement were always closely related), but it suited their interests to make common cause with him on this occasion. And it is likely that Middleton, always an adaptable writer, would have been quick to appreciate that the civic virtues he praises so lavishly were founded upon a thoroughly practical grasp of commercial priorities.

He is also alert to the implications of the customs and practices that he commends, drawing out their particular significance for the time. Sometimes this means he has to tread carefully. *Ent.* 4, for instance, was devised against the background of another overseas crisis, the onset of the Thirty Years War in Europe, which led to calls for military preparedness at home. Sporadic efforts to revive military training for the citizenry had been made since 1613 (when a Spanish invasion had been expected), giving rise to a vogue for municipal artillery 'gardens' or parade grounds; but in 1617, the year before war broke out on the Continent, Thomas Adams lamented the lack of home defences ('O the madness of us Englishmen!') and counselled: 'You then that have the places of government in this honourable city, *offer willingly* your hands, your purses, yourselves to this noble exercise.' By 1620 the City had responded to the King's appeal for funds to defend the Palatinate by levying the individual livery companies; but the programme for military training was disrupted by bitter disputes over public use of the Artillery Garden and the captaincy of its Company; both matters were referred to the Privy Council. Middleton may be alluding to this in 4.25–6 and making the City's case that it should be allowed to run its own affairs (a claim backed by the antique pedigree given to its officers in 4.21–2). But citizens were absent from the Artillery Garden not just because of bureaucratic arguments but because they lacked (or so they claimed) the resources to train properly. On 3 October 1620, at about the time this speech was due to be given, the Court of Aldermen was petitioned to provide subsidies for those 'practising arms in the Artillery Garden', on the grounds that they were having to equip themselves and numbers had fallen by more than half in three years. The Aldermen, however, had already cancelled the muster for that year on 19 September (perhaps acknowledging the problem), so Middleton's speech was never heard.

If militia training was one of those instances where government demands popular initiative but fails to provide the means for it to flourish, Middleton's other examples of civic encouragement for projects and customs have a happier ring. The archery contests held at Bunhill near

Moorfields (*Ent.* 2) were a convenient opportunity to celebrate social solidarity and native tradition, for they represented an early example of the heritage industry at work. At the end of the sixteenth century John Stow had complained that 'the ancient daily exercises in the longbow by citizens of this city' are 'now almost clean left off and forsaken', despite the early Tudor statutes enforcing them that Middleton refers to in 2.9–10. But as the longbow ceased to be a significant weapon of war it became a cultural symbol, and the focus of attempts to counter the enclosure of common fields where archery was practised. These efforts spawned the numerous pageants and competitive shows held during the Jacobean period; one of the biggest was held on Mayday and was probably the 'shooting day' in question. (By the mid-1620s, and perhaps earlier, the Bunhill festivities included mock-battles and sieges, which Ben Jonson made fun of in his poem 'A Speech according to Horace'.) In 2.13–16 Middleton borrows from Roger Ascham's *Toxophilus* (1545) to underline the idea of archery as a distillation of English skill and nobility, and uses this to develop an elaborate analogy with wise government. (Much the same idea is embodied in the emblematic figure of Honour with his sheaf of arrows in *An Invention.*) The visit to the Conduit Head (*Ent.* 3) exploits similar associations and links them to practical social needs. The reservoirs in the Tyburn area (constructed in mediaeval times) supplied piped water to the Great Conduit in Eastcheap, and the annual autumn expedition to inspect this vital supply had become in the sixteenth century a ceremonial occasion marked by hunting and feasting. The visits lapsed with the opening in 1613 of Hugh Myddelton's New River project (to which the Nymph refers at 3.30–5); but in the intervening period any notion that the New River would solve all problems of supply seems to have yielded to more long-sighted estimates. Measures were enacted at this time for the 'conservancy' of the Thames, and the impact of London's rapidly growing population must have convinced the city fathers that the traditional visit to the Conduit Head should be revived to safeguard resources.

The pieces gathered in *Honourable Entertainments* do not belong to a single genre and cannot simply be distinguished as a group from pageants or court entertainments. Two of them (7 and 8) are full-fledged masques for Christmas and Easter respectively, though the simple structure of the latter, dominated by songs, seems to provoke Middleton into more theatrical use of its central character, Flora, in the two pieces that follow. In the first of these (*Ent.* 9) he also had a special commission to fulfil. Ten days before it was performed for the Privy Council, James I had come to the Guildhall to reprimand the city authorities for not punishing adequately some youths who had abused the Spanish ambassador in the street; and Flora's speech is an assiduous apology for the lapse, one which cunningly links James's visit to the idea of London as the *camera regis*, the King's 'chosen city' which is the 'chamber of his sweet security' (9.57–9). Flora reappears again 'in her bower' in *Ent.* 10, which promises to restore the bucolic mood of *Ent.* 8 but is immediately complicated by the antimasque device of Hyacinth's interruption ('Speak thrice together?'); so Flora must restate the theme of delegation and responsibility (10.25–30) before complete harmony can be achieved. Individually these final two items are no more than interludes, but on the page they combine with *Ent.* 8 to form an ambitious masque design. The indoor pieces (including *An Invention*) seem all to have been given at banquets, and several of these are basically theatricalized orations, adding the iconography of court masque (Comus, Flora, Gentleman Sewer, 'made dish') to a long tradition of public speechmaking on civic occasions. The outdoor events (2 and 3) have similar elements, but they also resemble moments both in royal entries (or 'progress' entertainments) and in mayoral pageants: the water-nymph who rises—oddly but poetically—'out of the ground' in *Ent.* 3 and Pallas on horseback greeting the Mayor in *Ent.* 4 each effect a quasi-spontaneous encounter which turns Cokayne and his Aldermen into silent players in a small drama.

The first two shows for Jones (*Ents.* 6 and 7) taken together read like a bourgeois version of Jonson's masque *Pleasure Reconcil'd to Virtue*, presented at court in 1618, which may have influenced Milton's *Masque at Ludlow Castle.* In his masque Jonson had made Comus into a Rabelaisian figure, the 'god of cheer, or the belly'; Middleton offers in *Ent.* 6 a more traditional portrait of the 'smooth youth of feasts', evoking the classical exemplar of the boy crowned with vine leaves, so that the serene explication of the Haberdashers' Arms is infused with rich festivity rather than challenged by Bacchic riot. But as he moves from one piece to the next Middleton once again opens up the prospect of a larger design. *Ent.* 7 sets Levity and Severity in opposition, the former a *voluptas* figure who turns a mirror on the revellers and challenges them to value excess and abandon, the latter a killjoy who urges them to see such behaviour as a disruptive antimasque. Their conflict is resolved by Temperance (the favoured attribute of the governor in numerous mayoral pageants), who brings about a richly orchestrated close to the piece. Yet her dismissal of both figures as unworthy of the company seems forced and over-simplified. A capacity for festive cheer is a mark of the public-spirited mayor (inscribed in popular mythology by Dekker's Simon Eyre in *The Shoemakers' Holiday*), while the figure of Severity is in the emblem-books the very type of the strong magistrate. Both qualities, admirable in themselves but capable of being abused, are stabilized and enriched by their interaction, pleasure reconciled to virtue. But despite having laid the foundations for this idea in *Ent.* 6 with the decorous figure of Comus, Middleton is apparently unwilling to develop its implications for his sober and conservative audience. The modest resources at his disposal—a couple of actors, musicians, a few props—were certainly better suited to a clear and elegant exposition of received ideas.

But we should be wary of reinscribing the notion that Middleton's civic entertainments are hackwork in the service of unimaginative employers. They are polished efforts perfectly tailored to their individual occasions, and if the governing idea in each seems simple, it is invariably deployed with grace and economy. Moreover, though Middleton's job is to flatter, he usually manages to avoid sounding servile. The pieces he wrote during the mayoralty of Sir William Cokayne (which must have helped to get Middleton the job of City Chronologer) frequently capitalize on the formidable reputation of this merchant prince by structuring the action around him, rather in the same way that the monarch is the focal point of a Jacobean masque. But he makes no attempt to do the same with Cokayne's successor, Sir Francis Jones, an altogether less impressive man who was known to be fiscally unreliable (he absconded on the last night of his term as Mayor). The tactical shift of emphasis can be seen in *Ents.* 5–6: in both Middleton uses the device of an elaborately sculptured pie to carry his theme, but after a mock-funeral for the end of Cokayne's mayoralty (embodied in an imaginative visual pun, since piecrust was often called a 'coffin') he takes the opportunity of Jones's inaugural dinner for the Haberdashers to exalt the Company rather than the man. This is perhaps a shrewd use of the principle of *laudando praecipere* or praising to stimulate self-improvement, prompting Jones to live up to the Haberdashers' example. The contrast between the two pieces was one available to readers of Middleton's text of *Honourable Entertainments*, confirming that the maker of shows for the city is alert to, and helps to clarify, the standards and principles by which a viable civic culture will be judged.

SEE ALSO

An Invention, 1446
Textual introduction and apparatus: *Companion*, 673
Authorship and date: *Companion*, 410

Honourable Entertainments

Dedication *To the Right Honourable Sir Francis Jones, knight, Lord Mayor of the City of London; the Right Worshipful Sir John Garrard, Sir Thomas Bennett, Sir Thomas Lowe, Sir Thomas Myddelton, Sir John Jolles, Sir John Leman, Sir George Bolles, Sir William Cokayne, knights and Aldermen; the truly generous and noble Heneage Finch, esquire, Master Recorder; Master Edward Barkham, Master Alexander Prescott, Master Peter Proby, Master Martin Lumley, Master William Gore, Master John Gore, Master Alan Cotton, Master Cuthbert Hackett, Master William Halliday, Master Robert Johnson, Master Richard Herne, Master Hugh Hamersley, Master Richard Dean, Master James Campbell, Aldermen; Master Edward Allen, Master Robert Ducy, Sheriffs and Aldermen*

All brethren-senators, precedents of religious and worthy actions, careful assistants in the state of so unmatched a government, and all of them being his worthy and honourable patrons, T.M. wisheth the fullness of that honour whose object is virtue and goodness.

Those things that have took joy at several feasts
To give you entertainment as the guests
They held most truly worthy, become now
Poor suitors to be entertained by you.
So were they from the first. Their suit is, then,
Once serving you, to be received again;
And you to equal justice are so true
You always cherish that which honours you.

Ever obedient in his studies, to the service of so complete a goodness,

Tho. Middleton.

Honourable Entertainments

On Monday and Tuesday in Easter Week, 1620, the first entertainment at the house of the right worthy Sir William Cokayne, then Lord Mayor, which on the Saturday following was fashioned into service for the Lords of his Majesty's most honourable Privy Council; upon which day that noble marriage was celebrated betwixt the Right Honourable Charles Lord Howard, Baron of Effingham, and Mary, eldest daughter of the said Sir William Cokayne, then Lord Mayor of London and Lord General of the military forces.

Dedication.5 *Cokayne* the most famous of the group of knights and former Lord Mayors listed in 1–5. He made a large fortune in the cloth trade, and was the first governor of Ulster and founder of Londonderry.

15 **brethren-senators** dignifying the city fathers by associating them with ancient Roman government: the first of several such references

20 **things** actors

23 **entertained** employed

1.7 **Charles...Effingham** the 41-year-old son of Thomas Howard, Earl of Nottingham and former Lord Admiral. He apparently inherited the barony before his father's death in 1624.

The cock-and-tortoise drinking cups.

Enter one habited like a Gentleman Sewer, bearing in his hand an artificial cock, conducted by the City Music towards the high table, a song giving notice of his entrance.

Song.

Room, room, make room
You friends to fame,
Officers of worth and name,
Make room, make room.
Behold the bird of state doth come,
Make room,
Clear the place,
O do it all the grace.
It is the king of birds whose chanting
And early morning crowing,
So quick and strongly flowing,
Does make the king of beasts lie panting.
How worthy then to be brought in with honour
That daunts the proudest in that humble manner.

The speech.

Two powers at strife about conceivèd wrong
To whom this bird should properly belong
Were reconciled by Harmony. First the sun
Called it his bird, 'cause still, when day began
To ope her modest eye, this creature then
Proclaims his glory to the world again.
Minerva next, goddess of arms and art,
Claimed it for hers, not without just desert,
He like the morning being the Muses' friend,
And then for courage, 'tis his life, his end.
Without wrong, then, those properties related,
To both he may be justly consecrated.
But, worthy lord, how properly to you
Whose place partakes of both. It is so true
An emblem of your worth, charge, power and state,
None noblier can express a magistrate.
For all that is, in this bird, quality
Is in you virtue, justice, industry.
What does his early morning note imply
But in you early care and vigilancy?
A duty that begets duty to you;
So virtue still pays and receives her due.
What does the striking of his wings import,
Ere to his neighbour he his sounds retort,
But the dear labours and incessant pains
Of a just magistrate, that e'en constrains
His nerves to give more virtue to his word
And beat in sense into the most absurd?
The sharpest is the easiest to apply,
For his quick spur law's sword doth signify:
The execution of your charge and place
To cut off all crimes that are bold and base.
'Virtues should be with kind embraces heaped,
But with a sword sin's harvest must be reaped.'

To the Aldermen.

My reverence next to you, to you that are
The fathers of this city, by whose care,
Wisdom and watchfulness the good cause thrives.
You that are lights and precedents in lives,
Noble examples, honours t'age and time,
This is the top which your good cares must climb.

10.1 *Sewer* attendant in charge of the banquet

10.2 *cock* one of a set of silver-gilt cups in the shape of a cock standing on a tortoise, with removable heads for drinking. They were made in 1605, a sum having been left to the Skinners by Cokayne's father for the purpose. See illustration.

31 **Minerva** She was the goddess of crafts and trade guilds in ancient Rome, but was also identified with the Greek goddess Pallas Athena and took over her martial characteristics.

43–4 **What...vigilancy?** recalling the cock of Aesculapius which 'doth teach his watching and his care | To visit oft his patients' (Whitney, 212).

50–1 **constrains...nerves** musters his resources

53–4 **sharpest...spur** The Skinners' cups (see illustration) show the cocks wearing the spurs which were attached to fighting birds.

'A ceaseless labour virtue hath imposed,
Upon all those whom honour hath enclosed.'
And such are you, selected from the rest.
Works then that are most choice become you best;
Place before all your actions and intents
The rare gifts of that bird, this but presents.
Behold the very shape and figure now
Serves for a noble welcome, turned into
A cup of bounty, and t'adorn the feast
Laden with love comes to each worthy guest.
And but observe the manner, there's in that
Freeness expressed, humility, yet state.
First you take off his head to taste his heart,
Which shows at this time power is laid apart
And bounty fills the place. Then he goes round
To show a welcome of an equal sound,
To everyone a free one through the board:
So plain he speaks the goodness of his lord.
Take then respectful notice through the hall
That here the noble health begins to all.

The Cock-cup then delivered by this Gentleman Sewer to the Lord Mayor, he beginning the health, a second song thus honouring it.

Second Song

The health's begun
In the bird of the sun.
Pledge it round, pledge it round,
With hearty welcome it comes crowned,
O pledge it round.
The ceremonies due,
Forget not as they were begun to you.
When you are drunk to, you're by duty led
First to kiss your hand, then take off the head.
You cannot miss it then,
To put it on and kiss it again.
The next to whom the health doth flow
It taught to honour your pledge so.
So round, round, round, round let it go,
As above, so below,
For bounty did intend it always so.

2 *The Second Entertainment*

At Bunhill, on the shooting day, another habited like an archer did thus greet the Lord Mayor and Aldermen after they were placed in their tent.

Why, this is nobly done, to come to grace
A sport so well becomes the time and place.
Old time made much on't, and it thought no praise
Too dear for't, nor no honour in those days.
Not only kings ordained laws to defend it
But shined the first examples to commend it;
In their own persons honoured it so far
A land of peace showed like a field of war.
But chiefly Henry, memory's fame, the Eighth,
And the sixth Edward, gave it worth and weight
By act and favour—not without desert,
It being the comeliest and the manliest art.
And whereas meaner crafts took their first form
From humble things, as twisting from a worm,
And weaving from the spider's limber frame,
Music and archery from Apollo came.
He calls himself great master of this sport
In whose bright name fair wisdom keeps her court.
Well may this instrument be first in fame
Above all others that have got a name
In war or peace, when Heaven itself doth show
'The covenant of mercy by a bow.'
And as each creature, nay, each senseless thing
Is made a glass to see Heaven's goodness in,
So, though this be a mere delight, a game,
Justice may see here something she may claim
Without wrong done to state, and call't her own,
Since the great'st power is oft through weakness known.
What are reproofs—with them I first begin—
But arrows shot against the breast of sin?
Who hits vice home and cleaves a wrong in twain,
So that it never comes too close again,
Shows not he noble archery? I'll pray ever
He may be followed, mended he can never.
And as a cunning bowman marks his ground
And from light things, which being tossed up, is found
Where the wind sits, for his advantage best,
Before he lets his arrow pass his breast,
So the grave magistrate, discreetly wise,
Makes use of light occasions that arise
To lead him on to weightier, winds a cause,
From things but weakly told much substance draws,
And will the state of truth exactly try
Before he let the shaft of judgement fly.
Then in this art there's virtue still expressed,
For every man desires here to be best.
Their aim is still perfection, to outreach
And go beyond each other, which does teach

70 **this**... **presents** of which this is only an image
76 **state** authority
92–7 **When**... **so** Elaborate toasting ceremonies were a feature of city banquets.
2.0.2 ***Bunhill*** fields adjoining Bunhill Row on the west side of the Artillery Garden, near Moorfields
9–11 **But**... **favour** Henry VIII passed two statutes (ratified by his successor) to enforce the practice of archery by all male citizens.
13–16 **And**... **came** adapted from *Toxophilus*, Roger Ascham's 1545 treatise on archery: 'mean crafts be first found out by men or beasts, as weaving by a spider, and such other: but high and commendable sciences by gods, as shooting and music by Apollo'.
22 **bow** rainbow
27 **state** the dignity of high office
35 **marks** observes
43 **exactly try** precisely assess

A noble strife in our more serious deeds,
Assuring glory to him best exceeds.
And where some sports seek corners for their shame
Daylight and open place commends this game;
Much like an honest cause, it appears bold
In public court for all eyes to behold.
To the Archers.
On then, Apollo's scholars, you ne'er found
Nobler spectators compassed in this ground.
To whom I wish, worthy their virtuous ways,
Peace to their hearts, long health and blessed days.

3 *The Third Entertainment*

Upon the renewing of the worthy and laudable custom of visiting the springs and conduit heads for the sweetness and health of the city, a visitation long discontinued.

A water-nymph, seeming to rise out of the ground by the conduit head near the Banqueting House, thus greets the honourable assembly.

Ha! Let me clear mine eyes. Methinks I see
Comforts approach as if they came to me.
I am not used to 'em; I ha' been long without.
How comes the virtue of the time about?
Has ancient custom yet a friend of weight?
So many? Rare! Goodness is waked o'late
Out of her long sleep, sure, that has lain still
Many a dear day charmed with neglect and will.
I thought I'd been forsaken, quite forsook,
For none, these seven years, has bestowed a look
Upon my wat'ry habitation here;
I mean of power, that ought to see me clear
For yon fair city's health, which sweetness bless
And virtue in full strength ever possess.
Well fare thy visitation, noble lord,
And this most grave assembly, that accord
In ways of charity and care with thee.
Joys visit you, as your loves visit me.
The water stands so full now in mine eyes
I cannot choose but weep, but the tears rise
From gladness, not from sorrow, for that's lost
Now I see you. Unkindness yet has cost
Many a dear drop since I beheld the face
Of the last magistrate in power and place.
I ha' done good service: 'tis no boasting part
In one forgot to speak her own desert.
I grant my kind and loving sisters, both
Chadwell and Amwell, have expressed no sloth
In their pipe-pilgrimage, but fairly proved
Most excellent servants, housed and well beloved;
And have, when hard necessity requires,
Given happy quench to many merciless fires.
Therefore am I neglected? An old friend?
The head, that to the heart o'th'city send
My best and clearest service, take delight
To be at hand, make your dames pure and white
Who for their civil neatness are proclaimed
Mirrors of women, through all kingdoms famed.
Can I be so forgot? And daily hear
The noise of water-bearers din your ear?
Those are my alms-folks, trotting in a ring,
And live upon the bounty of my spring,
Yet like dull worms that have no sense at all
Lick up the dews, ne'er look from whence they fall.
The head's not minded whence the goodness flows.
So with the world's condition right it goes.
'Blessings are swallowed with a greedy love,
But thanks fly slowly to yon place above'
From whence the ever-living waters spring
Which to your souls eternal comforts bring.
The dews of heaven fall on you; prosperous fates
Like fruitful rivers flow into your states.

The Fourth Entertainment 4

Upon discontinuance, and to excite them to practice, a speech intended for the general training. Being appointed for the Tuesday next ensuing the visitation of the springs; but upon some occasion the day deferred.

Pallas on horseback, on her helmet the figure of a cock, her proper crest, thus should have greeted the lord general the Lord Mayor Sir William Cokayne at his entrance into the field, the worthy colonels, the right generous Master Alderman Hamersley, President of the noble Council of War, for the martial garden; the captains, etc.

Why, here's my wish, the joy I live upon,
Wisdom and valour when both meet in one.
Now 'tis a field of honour, fame's true sphere;
Methinks I could eternally dwell here.
Why, here's perfection, 'tis a place for me,
Pallas delights in such community.
This bird of courage, enemy to fear,
Whose figure on my helmet now I wear—
And have done ever from my birth in heaven—
Is consecrate to me, as to thee given.
Our crest's alike, and fits both war and peace.
The virtues are valour and watchfulness,
And both shine clear now in thy present state,
Field-general and city-magistrate.

51–2 **And . . . game** alluding to the 'bowling allies and dicing houses' which John Stow complained were springing up as common fields were enclosed and built upon (*A Survey of London*, 1603).
3.1–3 **Upon . . . discontinued** See Introduction, p. 1431.
15 **of power** anyone in authority
27 **last magistrate** Sir John Swinnerton of the Merchant Taylors was Lord Mayor in 1612–3.
31 **Chadwell and Amwell** villages in Hertfordshire where were located the springs feeding Hugh Myddelton's New River project, opened in 1613
48 **minded** bothered
4.1–4 **Upon . . . deferred** See Introduction, p. 1432.
4.1–2 ***Pallas . . . crest*** In Ripa's *Iconologia* Minerva, Pallas's Roman counterpart, wears a helmet similarly adorned.
4.7 **martial garden** the Artillery Garden
15 **Our . . . alike** Cokayne's coat of arms featured three cocks.

As I from arts and arms derive my name,
So thou suppliest two offices with fame.
Why, here the ancient Roman honour dwells:
A praetor, general; senators, colonels;
Captains, grave citizens; so richly inspired
They can assist in council if required,
And set court causes in as fair a form
As they do men here without rage or storm.
Lieutenants, ensigners, sergeants of bands,
Of worthy citizens the army stands,
Each in his place deserving fair respect.
I can complain of nothing but neglect
That such a noble city's armed defence
Should be so seldom seen. I could dispense
With great occasions, but alas, whole years
To put off exercise gives cause of fears.
'In getting wealth all care should not be set,
But some in the defending what you get.'
There's few but have their providence so pure,
Blessed with a fair estate, to make it sure
By strength of writings, and in good men's hands
Putting their coin, secured by lives and lands.
This is the common fort to which all fly,
Every man labours for security.
But what's all this—I speak in truth's behalf—
If neither men, city, nor deeds be safe?
Where's now security of state? That day
When life stands neglectful of her house of clay,
A ruin which neglect of glorious arms
Has brought on many a kingdom, rocked with charms
Of lazy dullness by unpractised men
Fit for no service. I resolve you then:
This is security, if you'll rightly know,
And does secure that word which you call so.
Let not a small pecuniary expense
(Which is but drossy dotage) keep you hence;
You lose all that you save after that manner.
What is't to rise in riches, fall in honour?
Nay, to your safeties to commit self-treason
Which everything provides for, blessed with reason.
Let this grave lord's example, in its prime,
Who perfects all his actions with his time,
Makes even with the year to his fair fame,
Gives his accounts up with a glorious name
In field and court, move all men to discharge
Their manly offices and pains at large.
Let every year at least once in his round
See you like sons of honour tread this ground;
And heaven that both gives and secures just wealth
The city bless with safety, you with health.

The Fifth Entertainment **5**

At the house of Sir William Cokayne, upon Simon and Jude's Day following, being the last great feast of the magistrate's year, and the expiration of his praetorship.

One attired like a mourner enters after a made dish like a hearse stuck with sable bannerets; drums and trumpets expressing a mournful service.

The Speech.

Imagine now, each apprehensive guest,
The year departed. This his funeral feast;
I a chief mourner; this a sad pageant here,
Set with the orphan's sigh, the widow's tear.
All seem to mourn, as locked from their reliefs,
Till the new sun of justice dry their griefs.
And as there is no glorious thing that ends
But leaves a fame behind it that commends
Or disapproves the progress of his acts,
So in this epitaph sad truth contracts
A spacious story which, spread forth at large,
Might instruct all, built up for power and charge.

The Last Will and Testament of 1620 finishing for the city.

Imprimis, I *Annus* 1620 do bequeath to my successor '21 all my good wishes, pains, labours and reformations, to be nobly perfected by his endeavours and diligence.

Item, I make Justice my executor, and Wisdom my overseer, which is that honourable court which never failed yet to see justice performed.

Item, I give and bequeath to all the officers for legacies: truth, temperance, example of humility, and gentleness.

Lastly, I bequeath to the whole body of the beloved commonalty three inestimable jewels, love, meekness and loyalty, which are always the forerunners of a blessed prosperity; which Heaven grant they may everlasting enjoy.

The Epitaph.

Here ends a year that never misspent day,
Through fame's celestial signs made his own way,
By discreet judgement all his time still led
Which is the only sign governs the head.
Mercy to wants and bounty to desert,
The special sign that rules the noble heart.
A year of goodness and a year of right
In which the honest cause sued with delight.

22 **praetor** governing magistrate in republican Rome
24 **assist in council** act as royal advisers
25 **set** resolve, put in order
27 **ensigners** standard-bearers
35 **set** directed, concentrated
54 **is . . . dotage** only a miser would worry about
65 **every . . . once** When it suspended the muster for 1620 at which this speech would have been heard, the Court of Aldermen decreed that in future training would take place on 10 April.
5.1–2 **Simon . . . Day** October 28th, the last day of the mayoral year
3.1 **made dish** sculpted cakes or pies were a popular feature at banquets in this period
8 **locked from** denied
11 **fame** record
32 **fame's celestial signs** the zodiac

A year wherein nothing that's good was dull,
Began at moon's increase and ends at full.
Full cup, full welcome, adding the sun's gift
Who, nearer his declining, the more swift
In his illustrious course, more bright, more clear.
Such is the glorious setting of this year:
His beamy substance shines e'en through his shroud
As the fair sun shoots splendour through his cloud.
May every year succeeding this still have
No worse an epitaph to deck his grave.
And so my last farewell (this tear for me)
Wishing that many may conclude like thee.

6 *The Sixth Entertainment*

At the house of the Right Honourable Sir Francis Jones.

The first entertainment at his first great feast prepared to give welcome to his own noble fraternity, the Company of Haberdashers. The property to which this speech especially hath respect was a device like a made dish expressing two naked arms breaking through a cloud, supporting a wreath of laurel, being part of the Haberdashers' Arms.

The speech presented by a servant to Comus, the great sir of feasts.

Free love, full welcome, bounty fair and clear
E'en as it flows from Heaven, inhabit here,
And with your liberal virtues bless the year.
Make this thy palace, thou smooth youth of feasts,
Comus! And put joy into all the guests
That they may truly taste in fewest words
Th'abundant welcome yon kind lord affords
Especially to you above the rest,
Of all most worthy to be first and best.
You challenge two respects: in brotherhood, one
Which had desert enough, came it alone
Without a second virtue; but to add
Unto your worthiness, your love was clad
With honour, cost, and care; and how applied
The late triumphant day best testified,
Stands in no need of my applause and praise.
Your worth can of itself itself best raise.
So much for noble action in your right,
Which I presume his goodness will requite.
Now for himself—not far to wade or swim—
I borrow of your honours to fit him,
Which both preserves me in my first bounds still
And may agree best with his love and will.

Here the property is presented.

Behold in this rare symbol of renown
The emblem of all justice, and the crown
The fair reward for't, ever fresh and green,
Which imitates those joys eye hath not seen.
These arms, that for their nakedness resemble
E'en truth itself, no covering to dissemble
Nor shift for bribe, but open, plain and bare,
Shows men of power should keep their conscience fair.
And were their acts transparent, without veil,
Disguise or visor, and such never fail.
Observe this more, 'tis not one arm alone
That bears this laurel, but two joined in one:
Mercy and Justice, the two props of state,
They must be both fixed in the magistrate;
If wanting either, subject to much harm,
For he that has but one has but one arm.
Judge then the imperfection. Mark again:
They break both through a cloud, which instructs men
How they should place their reverence and their love,
Seeing all lawful power comes from above.
And as the laurel which is now your due—
Being due to honour, therefore most to you—
Fears no injurious weather the year brings,
But spite of storms looks ever green and springs
Apollo's tree which lightnings never blast,
So, honoured lord, should burning malice cast
Her pitchy fires at your triumphant state,
You are Apollo's tree, a magistrate
Which no foul gust of envy can offend,
Nor may it ever to your lordship's end.
Health and a noble courage bless your days.
To this your worthy brotherhood, fame and praise.

The Seventh Entertainment 7

At the house of the Right Honourable Sir Francis Jones, Lord Mayor, for the celebration of the joyful feast of Christmas last.

Levity, a person attired suitable to her condition, from a window unexpectedly thus greets the assembly in the midst of the feast.

LEVITY

Why, well said! Thus should Christmas be,
Lightsome, jocund, blithe and free.
Now it looks like bounty's palace
Where every cup has his full ballast.
Drown cares with juice that grapes have bled
And make Time's cheek look fresh and red.

6.2 **first . . . feast** Not the inaugural banquet for the incoming Lord Mayor, which was held at the Guildhall with all the Aldermen present, but a subsequent and more exclusive gathering, at which the Mayor's guild celebrates the honour of having one of its number elected.

8.1–2 ***Comus . . . feasts*** See Introduction, p. 1433.

18 **challenge . . . respects** deserve praise on two counts

23 **late . . . day** Comus's festive spirit has infused the inaugural banquet on 29th October as well as the present occasion.

27 **his** Jones's

41 **visor** mask

46 **wanting** lacking

56 **Apollo's tree** the laurel wreath

7.3.2 ***from a window*** on one side of the carved screen at the end of the hall which housed the musicians' balcony (cf. ll. 32–3).

Let nothing now but healths go round,
And no sooner off but crowned
With sparkling liquors, bounding up,
Quick in palate, as in cup.
To be heavy, to be dull
Is a fault so pitiful
We bar it from the course of reason.
Care must not peep abroad this season,
Nor a sad look dare appear
Within ten mile of Christmas cheer.
Sighs are banished ten leagues farther
Either cellar, hall or larder.
To be jovial then and blithe
Is truly to pay Christmas tithe,
And where free mirth is and impartial
Christmas there has made me marshal.

Severity from an opposite window as unexpectedly reproves her.

SEVERITY
Why, how now? Know you where you are? Rude thing,
Bold and unmannered licence, dare you bring
Your free speech hither, before me begin?
Who let this skittish thing of lightness in?
Some call the porter hither! Yet stay, stay,
I've power in words to chase this toy away.
I wonder that the music suffers thee
To come into their room!

LEVITY Why, nicety?

SEVERITY
Believe me, honest men (whate'er you be),
She's able to spoil all your harmony,
Corrupt your airs with lightness.

LEVITY O fie, fie,
How ill you blaze my coat, Severity!

SEVERITY
Is this a place for you? Can lightness here
Under the hazard of her shame appear?

LEVITY
Why, thou dull lumpish thing, void of all fashion,
Mirth's poison, enemy to recreation,
Thou melancholy wretch, so filled with spite
Thou eat'st thy heart when others take delight.
I must be merry, 'tis my nature—

SEVERITY
Fool!

LEVITY
Dull dogbolt!

SEVERITY Skit!

Enter below Temperance.

TEMPERANCE What, this a scolding school?
How now? So high got, and so loud withal?
Whose doing was't placed you two there to brawl?
Pray mark the assembly, look upon 'em well;
Think where you are, and let that rude thought quell
Your unbeseeming difference. 'Tis not here
As at a pit! Here's reverence, worth, and fear.

LEVITY
She says but right in that.

SEVERITY O Levity—

TEMPERANCE
No, nor you neither.

LEVITY You may be gone too!

TEMPERANCE
You're both extremes, therefore no place for you.
Lightness becomes not, nor severity:
It must be between both, and I am she.
Too light is bad, and too severe, as vile;
But both well-tempered makes the mixture mild.
As I stand now between you, so it makes
A perfect virtue up when it partakes
Of each, and comes no nearer than I do.
And virtue made, we have no need of you.
Vanish! Be gone.

SEVERITY I give place willingly
To you, but not to her.

They give place.

LEVITY Nor I to thee.

TEMPERANCE
Thus things should have their becoming grace,
For Temperance fits the reverence of this place.
Grave senators, in goodness still increased!
Long may you live to celebrate this feast,
This blessed season of true joy compiled
In which fair heaven and man were reconciled.
Music! Thou modest servant to this place,
Raise chaste delight to do this season grace.

A song, answered at several places

SINGER
Echo! Echo! By thy love once to Narcissus
I now conjure thee not to miss us,
But make thy sound
Upon the woods rebound
And mountains—
(*Echo*) And mountains
And to thy neighbouring sisters call—
(*Echo*) Sisters call
Lodged in cave or hollow wall.

25.1 ***Severity*** Presumably contrasted to Levity by being clad in formal attire. The emblem books interpret the figure as commanding regal awe, but this is not appropriate here.

37 **blaze my coat** paint my reputation

39 **Under . . . of** risking

45 **dogbolt** literally, a blunt arrow; a common insult

Skit tart. The word implies wantonness or frivolity.

49 **rude thought** stark realization

50 **difference** quarrel

51 **pit** i.e. a bear or bull-baiting

fear power to judge

64.1–7.64 ***They . . .* thee** Having formed a triangular image with Temperance between and below them (l. 59), the two disappear from their windows after Levity's retort.

72.1 ***several places*** different parts of the hall

73 **Echo . . . Narcissus** The nymph Echo fell in love with Narcissus and after being rejected by him wasted away to a voice.

And those resounding near fair fountains—
(*Echo*) Near fair fountains
Let 'em call to one another—
(*Echo*) To one another,
(*Second Echo*) one another
And one sister raise up t'other.
(*Echo*) Up t'other.
Let it go from me to you—
[*Echo*] From me to you,
[*Second Echo*] me to you
From you to them, be just and true.
(*Echo*) Just and true.
Never cease your voice's flight
Till you raise up chaste delight.
(*Echo*) Up chaste delight.

DELIGHT
Who calls me from my cave?

SINGER 'Twas I.
(*Echo*) 'Twas I, 'twas I.
This is no time in silence now to lie.

DELIGHT
Who, I?

SINGER O ay!
This is a season of all joy compiled
In which fair heaven and man were reconciled.
(*Echo*) Heaven and man were reconciled,
[*Second Echo*] reconciled.
Behold how many a worthy guest
Are met to celebrate this feast.

DELIGHT
I see it plain. O blame me then,
I ne'er will show such sloth again.
For whose delight am I now raised?

SINGER
O, for the city's.

DELIGHT How, for the city's?
(*Echo*) For the city's.
To fail a mistress so renowned it were a thousand pities.
(*Echo*) Thousand pities.

SINGER
Those are her honoured sons you now behold.

DELIGHT
Heaven bless them all with graces manifold.

TEMPERANCE (*to the music*) So!
'Tis thankfully accepted, you've expressed
Your service well and fully to this feast;
Adorned and honoured in each happy part
With those most reverend patrons to desert.

The close

Joy never fail your meetings; good success
All your endeavours and your fortunes bless.
Gladness of heart dwell ever in your breasts,
And peace of fair works bring you glorious rests.

The Eighth Entertainment 8

At the house of the Right Honourable Sir Francis Jones, Lord Mayor, for the solemn feast of Easter last, upon the times of that blessed and laudable custom of celebrating the memory of pious works in this city at Saint Mary Spital.

The Invention.
The four seasons of the year, spring, summer, autumn and winter, in a song into four parts divided call up Flora, the goddess of the spring, who in a bower decked with artificial flowers appears upon the musical invocation.

The song at several windows

SPRING
Flora, Flora!
We call thee here,

SUMMER We call thee here
From forth thy fragrant bower.

SPRING
Thou queen of every laughing flower
Appear!
Appear to us.

SUMMER To us appear,
Thou banquet of the year.

SPRING
Or if a name may be more sweet, more dear,
Hark, summer, hark!

SUMMER Mark, autumn, mark
How coughing winter mourns to see
This smiling hour.

WINTER Would it were nipped for me!
But soft, I feel no such decay
But I may live to kiss fair May,

90–1 Eld's punctuation suggests the intricacy of echoic effects.

97 **cave** probably a property placed in front of the screen

120 **desert** do justice to

8.4–5 **Saint... Spital** a former priory and hospital on the east side of Bishopsgate; after the Reformation sermons continued to be given there on the Monday and Tuesday in Easter Week from an outdoor pulpit in the churchyard. These were attended by the city fathers, who had been provided in 1594 with 'one fair builded house... to sit in, there to hear the sermons' (Stow); this was probably a covered three-sided structure. On both days the Aldermen and Sheriffs would breakfast and dine at the Mayor's house; the evening banquet is the same occasion celebrated in *Ent.* 1 and *An Invention*, and it seems usually to have been a sumptuous one. In 1617 senior courtiers and the Archbishop of Canterbury were invited, and the elaborate nature of Middleton's entertainment for 1621 may point to a similarly important guest-list on this occasion.

5.7 ***several*** different

6–20 **Flora... flowers** The seasons were probably marked out simply by the colour of their coats or headgear, but Winter has a more expressive role than the others and runs no risk of upstaging Flora, so he may have had a more elaborate costume like Inverno in *The Masque of Flowers* put on by Gray's Inn in 1613: 'an old man in a short gown of silk shag like withered grass all frosted and snowed over... with long white hair and beard hung with icicles'.

And in the morn and evening hours
Leave my cold sweats upon the flowers.

SPRING

Alas, poor mumps! At thy weak power
We laugh.
The sun will rise and take thy cold kiss off.
And now behold!

WINTER

O, O, O!

AUTUMN

He's struck cold
At Flora's first appearing;
Look! In a sound
Will drop to th' ground.
Help, help, help, he wants your cheering.

WINTER

O I confess,
Field-empëress,
The beauty of thy power amazes.
I am content to join
With those three friends of thine
And help to chant thy praises.

ALL

Now all the seasons of the year agree
To give, fair Flora, the prime place to thee.

Flora, rising in her bower, calls forth two of her servants.

FLORA

Where's Hyacinth, the boy Apollo loved
And turned into a flower?

HYACINTH

Here, queen of sweetness.

FLORA

Adonis! Thou that for thy beauteous chastity
Wert turned into the chastest of all flowers,
The close-enfolded rose—blown into blushes,
It is so maiden-modest!

ADONIS

What's thy pleasure,
Fair empress of sweet odours?

FLORA

Willing servants!
I have employment for you both, and speedy.

BOTH

We wait with much joy to receive the charge on't.

FLORA

Haste to the two assisting magistrates,
Those worthy city consuls.
Bear our sweet wishes to 'em, and speak joy
From us to both their feasts,
And to that part of their grave-worthy guests
Which here we miss today, though here be those
Whom we ought more especially to honour.
Say, though we cannot there ourself appear
Because we owe our greater service here,
Yet that they shall not fail of all their due
We send the wishes of our heart by you.

HYACINTH

Which shall be faithfully tendered.

FLORA

'Tis presumed.

[*Exeunt Hyacinth and Adonis*]

But to this fair assembly present now
I, and these yielding sweets all their heads bow
In honour of this feast; of the day, chief,
Made solemn by the works of your relief,
Your cares, your charities, the holy use
Of pious exercise, all which infuse
Blessings into your fortunes. You abound
In temporal things, 'cause blessèd fruits are found
Upon the stocks you graft on. Mark the increase:
You plant poor orphans in a ground of peace
And carefully provide; when fruit time comes,
You gather Heaven's joys for't in infinite sums.
This day you viewed the garden of those deeds
That bless the founders; and all those succeeds
In zeal and imitation. You saw there
Virtue's true paradise dressed with your care,
Your most religious care, and those blue sets
That are the city's bank of violets
That smells most sweet to heaven. Never cease then,
You worthy precedents for times and men,
Till charity spring, by your examples given,
As thick on earth as rewards stand in Heaven.
If there were sloth or faintness toward good works—
As blessed be heaven there is not—Time instructs
The season of the year. For as the ground
The heaviest and dull'st creature can be found,
Yet now begins both in her meads and bowers
To offer up her sacrifice in flowers,
How much more ought that earth with a soul blessed,
Which is of every of you here possessed,
To spring forth works of piety and love
To gratify those dews fall from above.
And as the humblest flower that ever grew
Has not his scent alone, but virtue too

21 **mumps** a common, rather patronizing endearment

27 **sound** faint

38 **Hyacinth** the beautiful youth in Greek myth who is loved by both Apollo and Zephyrus. The latter kills him out of jealousy, and from his blood springs the flower bearing his name.

40–2 **Adonis . . . rose** In Greek myth Adonis refuses Aphrodite's advances and, after he is killed by a wild boar, the rose springs from his blood.

47 **two . . . magistrates** the two Sheriffs for the year, Edward Allen and Robert Ducy, who are entertaining elsewhere. The command helps further to link this piece with the two that follow, since they were performed at the Sheriffs' homes.

48 **consuls** In republican Rome two consuls ruled annually.

68 **poor orphans** The city supported a number of orphanages; see next note.

69 **And carefully provide** referring to the children of Christ's Hospital in Newgate Street, who were also provided (see note to ll. 4–5) with 'a house . . . to sit in' at St Mary Spital to listen to the sermons.

75 **blue sets** The children of Christ's Hospital wore long blue coats and yellow stockings.

85 **meads** fields

92 **virtue** medicinal properties

Good for man's griefs, so 'tis not man's full fame
To have a Christian savour or a name,
An empty voice of charity and relief.
He must apply ease to his brother's grief:
'Faith is the scent and odour of the flower,
But work's the virtue that makes good the power.'
'Tis like the tincture of those robes you wear
In which clear vesture you to me appear
Like borders of fair roses, and worn high
Upon the city's forehead. That rich dye,
As it is reverend, honourable, grave,
So it is precious, wholesome; which doth crave
A double virtue at the wearer's hands:
Justice and mercy, by which goodness stands.
Thus honour still claims virtue for his due,
And may both ever lay just claim to you.
What? The four seasons of the year struck dumb?
I looked for a kind welcome now I'm come.

Second song by the four seasons, called the song of flowers.

SPRING
Welcome, O welcome, queen of sweetness,
Welcome in the noblest manner,
With all thy flowers, thy sweet-breathed maids of honour.

SUMMER
Flower gentle, I begin with thee.

AUTUMN
Fair flower of crystal, that's for me.

SPRING
Apples of love, there sweetness dwells.

WINTER
Puh! Give me Canterbury bells.

SPRING
Fair double-gold cups, griefs expelling,

SUMMER
Agnus Castus, all excelling,

AUTUMN
Venus' bath, the loveliest pride of June,

WINTER
Give me that flower called 'go to bed at noon'.

SPRING
Blessed thistle, famed for good,

SUMMER
Shepherd's pouch for staunching blood,

AUTUMN
Fair yellow knight-wort for a foul relapse,

WINTER
And lady's mantle, good for maidens' paps.

SPRING
Tuft hyacinth, that crowns the bower,
Called of some the virgin's flower;

WINTER
Take that for me, more good I feel
In ruffling robin and lark's heel.

SPRING
There is a sweet, unnamèd yet,
The root is white, the mark of pure delight,
Bearing his flowers fair and high,
The colour like a purple dye.

WINTER
What is the name 'tis blessed withal?

SPRING
Live-long; it so the shepherds call.

WINTER
Live-long? 'Tis virtue's promised due
And may it long remain with you,
Honoured patrons,
Virtuous matrons,
Whose lives and acts this city graces,
Daily striving
And reviving
Works worthy your renown and places.

FLORA
So y'are confirmed. From your harmonious closes
May sweetness drop as honeydew from roses.

Then turning to the Lord Mayor and Aldermen.

A blessèd health possess you, and a long,
That in this latter spring of your grave years
You may be green in virtues, and grow strong
In works of grace, which souls to heaven endears.

93 **full fame** best ambition
101 **Like...roses** Stow describes the Aldermen 'in their scarlets at the Spital in the holidays'.
114 **Flower gentle** *Amaranthus*, a plant with long-lasting spiky flowers, used as a coagulant
115 **Fair...crystal** probably flea-wort, *psyllium sempervirens*, an evergreen plant whose seeds were boiled to make a purgative
116 **Apples of love** *Poma amaris* or Golden Apple, a Mediterranean variety
117 **Canterbury bells** the Giant Bell-flower or throat-wort, used as a remedy for throat infections and mouth ulcers
118 **double-gold cups** crow-foot, wild flower used as a purgative
119 ***Agnus Castus*** bushy shrub known as the 'chaste tree' because it supposedly acted as an anaphrodisiac; also used as a remedy for various ills
120 **Venus' bath** wild teasel
121 **go...noon** Goat's-beard, whose flower opens only in the morning; the root boiled in wine 'assuageth the pain and pricking stitches of the sides' (Gerard)
123 **Shepherd's pouch** common weed, also known as shepherds' purse
124 **knight-wort** probably knight's pond-wort, an aquatic plant used to treat wounds and make poultices
125 **lady's mantle** Gerard says that when this wild flower (*Alchimilla*) is used to treat breasts that 'be too great or flaggy it maketh them lesser or harder'.
126 **Tuft hyacinth** *Clematis peregrina*, usually known as Virgin's bower
129 **ruffling robin** possibly 'Ragged Robin' or another winter-flowering plant **lark's heel** flowering shrub of the larkspur family
135 **Live-long** Orpine, an herbaceous plant known for its hardiness

Your good cares here, justice, and well spent hours
Crown you hereafter with eternal flowers.

Hyacinth and Adonis, sent forth by Flora to the two other feasts, thus sets off their employments.

The goddess Flora, empress of the spring,
Choosing this feast her flow'ry sojourning
Under the roof of the chief magistrate,
Whose power lays just claim to the greatest state,
Hath sent me forth, not meanest in her grace,
To breathe forth her sweet wishes to this place.
First to the master of this bounteous feast
To speak her joy; next, to each worthy guest.
And though she cannot now herself appear
Because she owes her greater service there,
Yet her heart's love to everyone I bring
To whom she's sent a present of the spring.

Then falls into the former speech of Flora, making use of her divine instructions

9 Here follows the worthy and noble entertainments of the lords of his Majesty's most honourable Privy Council, at the houses of the Lord Mayor and Sheriffs.

The Ninth Entertainment

The first entertainment upon Thursday in Easter week, being the fifth of April, 1621. And upon the sixteenth of the same month those persons of honour received their second noble welcome, in a free and generous entertainment at the house of the right worshipful Master Sheriff Allen.

Flora, the person used before, thus prepared for them.

FLORA

Am I so happy to be blessed again?
With these, the choice of many thousand men
For royal trust selected, and a care
That makes you sacred: may the world compare
A confidence with yours? From so complete
And excellent a master? Or so great
And free a love can any nation show
In subject to the sovereign than doth flow
From this most thankful city? Waves of love
E'en overwhelm each other as they move;
All striving to be first, they run in one
To th' ocean's breast (the King's affection).
And you of honour, that do oft appear
In presence of a majesty so clear,
So mighty in heaven's blessings, be so kind
To grace with words what he shall ever find—
And 'tis a glorious truth and well beseems
Places and persons of your fair esteems:—
Not all the kingdoms of the earth contain
A city freer to her sovereign,
More faithful and more careful. Observe here
His highness' excellent trial. Love and fear
Make up a subject's duty to his king,
As justice and sweet mercy makes up him.
So two-fold virtue two-fold duty cheers;
He knew their loves, now came and touched their fears
To try their temper. O blessed heaven, he found
It was the fear he looked for—had its ground
Upon religion, reverence, sweet respect.
Love looked not lovelier, nor divinelier decked.
Each reprehensive word he did impart
Flew and cleaved fast to their obedient heart.
'Twas fire within their bosom, 'could not rest
Till in some serious manner they'd expressed
Their duteous care; with all speed put in act
Their sovereign's sacred pleasure, to coact
Where manners failed, and force, as with a pill,
From humours rude the venom of the ill.
'A king's own admonition against crimes
Is physic to the body of the times.'
And herein did he imitate the highest
To whom it best becomes him to be nighest.
To chasten where he loves it is the seal
Of the Almighty's favour. He doth deal
So with his chosen: do not languish then,
Thou prince of cities, 'cause the king of men
Divinely did reprove thee; know 'tis love.
Thou art his chosen city, and wilt prove—
As thou hast ever been—faithful and free,
The chamber of his sweet security.
Then in a health of joy your hearts express
Whilst I breathe welcome to those noble guests.

The song of welcome, after which Flora closes the entertainment.

A trust of honour, and a noble care
Still to discharge that trust, keep your fames fair.
You have proceeded carefully; go on,
And a full praise crown your progression.

The last entertainment 10

Full as noble and worthy as the former, upon the Saturday ensuing, being the twenty-first of the same month, at the house of the equally generous and bounteous the right worshipful Master Sheriff Ducy.

Flora, this the third time, in her bower beginning to speak, interrupted by her two servants Hyacinth and Adonis.

FLORA

Good Heaven—

HYACINTH Fie, this is usurpation merely!
Speak thrice together? There's no right in this.

151.2 **sets off** discharge. Presumably the following speech was given at each of the Sheriffs' feasts, with Flora's blessing (146–51) repeated for the benefit of their 'grave-worthy guests' (51). The Sheriffs' houses may have been close enough to the Mayor's to allow the actors playing Hyacinth and Adonis in the main show to carry the message, and Adonis's speech in the last Entertainment (10.9–10) seems to assume this sort of continuity; but the idea is perhaps more charming than plausible.

9.47 **humours rude** unruly elements

FLORA
What's that?

ADONIS
I have the juster cause to take exceptions:
This is the place I served in, lately served in,
And by her own appointment my wrong's greatest.

FLORA
Here's a strange sudden boldness o' both sides o' me!

HYACINTH
Was't not sufficient grace for you to speak
At the chief magistrate's house, there where that
bower
Was first erected? But to shift your seat
From place to place, pull down and then set up—
I wonder how she 'scapes informers, trust me!

ADONIS
Believe me, so do I. She's favour shown her.

FLORA
So, this becomes you well!

HYACINTH
There's right in all things;
We might have kept our places as we held 'em.
There's little conscience in your dealing thus;
You might have left the lower books for us
For our poor service.

FLORA
Thus I answer you,
Taking my precedent from the just care
Of those clear lights of honour, shining fair
To their work's end. You see before your eyes
The trust that was committed to their wise
And discreet powers, for his Highness' use.
They put not off to others with excuse
Of weariness or pains. As they begun,
In their own noble persons see all done.
So, by their sweet example, I that am
Your queen and mistress and may rightly blame
And tax the boldness of your ruder blood,
I do not think or hold myself too good
In mine own person to commend their cares
That have so justly served their King in theirs.
Now, you pull in your heads.

BOTH
Pardon, sweet queen.

FLORA
Yet why should anger in my brow be seen?
They came but to show duty to the time.
Contention to do service was their crime,
That's no ill-looking fault; but 'tis still known,
'They that give honour love to do't alone.'
It brooks no partnership—to give this last
Duty her due as others before past,
Though it came now from men of meaner rank
Where wealth was ne'er known to o'erflow the bank
Like spring tides of the rich that swell more high.
Yet tak't for truth, it comes as cheerfully,
All smiling givers; and well may it come
With smooth and loving faces. The small sum
That they return is thousand times repaid
In peace and safety, besides sovereign aid
For each heart's grievance to its full content
By this high synod of the parliament,
Before whose fair, clear and unbribèd eyes,
When it appears, corruption sinks and dies.
Secure oppression once comes trembling thither;
'Stead of her hard heart, knocks her knees together.
This benefit is purchased, this reward
To which all coin is dross to be compared.

But the fair work's concluded on all parts.
Your care, which I place first of all deserts—
And it becomes it—'t has been nobly just.
You have discharged with honour your high trust.
The city's love I must remember next
And faithful duty, both devoutly mixed.
And, as the state of court sets last the best,
His boundless goodness not to be expressed,
That is your king and master, blessings fall
Upon his actions; honour on you all.

FINIS.

10.16 **I ... informers** insinuating that Flora keeps on the move like a criminal
21 **lower books** lesser occasions. This is not a slight to the Privy Council but a reference to their city hosts on this occasion, men 'of meaner rank' (45) than the Court of Aldermen.
43 **brooks** stands for
54 **high ... parliament** the Privy Council

An Invention

Performed for the service of the Right Honourable Edward Barkham, Lord Mayor of the City of London, at his lordship's entertainment of the Aldermen his brethren, and the honourable and worthy guests at his house assembled and feasted in the Easter holidays, 1622. Written by Thomas Middleton.

An Invention

A song in several parts, ushering toward the high table a personage in armour representing Honour, holding in his hand a sheaf of arrows

MEAN
A hall, a hall! Below, stand clear.
What, are you ready?

BASE
They appear.

MEAN
[ ] then
Present your duties to those men
Of worth and honour.

CHORUS
We rejoice
When so we spend art, hour and voice.

MEAN
Tell me, O tell me, what is he appears
So like a son of Fame, and bears
A sheaf of arrows, bound with silken bands?

BASE
'Tis Honour with two armèd hands
Showing the figure of his crest,
Who gives it and deserves it best.

MEAN
A braver emblem for the place
I ne'er beheld.

BASE
Nor for his race
A fitter symbol (without pride or spite)
Being armed at all points to do merit right.

MEAN
What word's that?

BASE
Diligentia
Fortunae Mater.

MEAN
This honoured day
Makes good that motto; 'tis expressed
Not in him only but in every guest.
I joy to see!

CHORUS
We joy to see
Your places and your works agree.

Finis the first song

Then Honour delivers this speech

Though in this martial habit I appear
I bring nor cause of doubt nor thought of fear.
'Tis only a way found to express best
The worthy figure of yond noble crest.
Nor barely to be shown is the intent
And scope of this time's service; more is meant.
There's use and application, whence arise
Profit and comfort to the grave and wise.
A nobler emblem of charge, power, and place,
Justice and valour, never yet did grace
A station more; a crest becomes the state
Of our best champion, a good magistrate.
Two armèd arms: to what may they allude
More properer than to truth and fortitude,
The armour of a Christian? To be strong
In a just cause then to these arms belong.
The sheaf of arrows: what do they imply
But shafts of justice 'gainst impiety?
Yet they must pass through a judicious hand,
For see, they're tied with mercy's silken band.
They must not inconsiderately be spent
But used like weapons of just punishment.
And as it is in course of combat known
'Tis not the property of one hand alone
Both to defend and offend at one time,
So let not one hand pass upon a crime—
The weight may fall too heavy; but take both
Mercy with justice, twins of equal growth.
Those carry a cause level through a land,
For no man shoots an arrow with one hand.
Believe we this: do envy what it can,
Religious conscience is an armèd man.
Another way to make it general—
For 'tis an emblem that concerns you all,
You of the honourable brotherhood
Knit all together for the city's good,
In whose grave wisdoms her fair strength doth stand:
You are the sheaf; the magistrate the band
Whose love is wound about you. Witness be
His bounty and his welcome, both most free.
And as this day you saw the golden sheaf
Of this blessed city's works in the relief
Of the poor fatherless, may you behold
That sheaf of glory that makes dross of gold,
Th'Almighty's arrows, on your enemies fall,
And heaven's armèd arms protect you all.

2 **Barkham** Middleton had previously written *The Sun in Aries* to mark the installation of Barkham, a Draper, as Lord Mayor in October 1621.

7 **A hall** Make way! Mean and Base are probably at the windows in the hall screen adjacent to the musicians' gallery (see note to *Entertainments* 7.3.2).

16 **two . . . hands** possibly carrying a sword in the other hand, but more likely referring to chain-mail coverings

23–4 ***Diligentia . . . Mater*** Diligence is the mother of Fortune: the motto on Markham's coat of arms, which is presumably displayed on the hall screen

28 **Your . . . agree** that your achievements are worthy of your rank

69–71 **as . . . fatherless** See note to *Entertainments* 8.4–5.

Second song

MEAN
Joy be ever at your feasts.
BASE
Bounty welcome all your guests.
CHORUS
That this city's honour may
Spread as far as morn shoots day.
MEAN
Fair your fortunes ever be
BASE
Plenty bless the land that's free.
CHORUS
That this city's honour may
Spread as far as morn shoots day.
MEAN
Health your powers with gladness fill
BASE
Justice be your armour still.
MEAN
Pious works the golden sheaf
BASE
Those arrows strike the wicked deaf.
MEAN
And dumb.
BASE
And lame.
CHORUS
So virtue may
Spread forth as far as morn shoots day.

Finis

76 **Bounty** The occasion may have been less sumptuous than usual, for when the King appealed to the City for funds towards the defence of the Palatinate, the Drapers were levied the sum of £387, which made them cut down on their feasts until 1623.

HENGIST, KING OF KENT; *or*, THE MAYOR OF QUEENBOROUGH

Edited by Grace Ioppolo

Who could expect such treason from the breast?
(4.4.65)

Hengist, King of Kent, or *The Mayor of Queenborough*, is a play about betrayal, both political and personal. The political tragedy of the end of Celtic and Roman Britain and the personal tragedies of Vortiger, his wife Castiza, his mistress Roxena, his ally Hengist, and his trusted confidant Hersus all result from 'foul devouring treachery' (4.4.120). Yet the tragedy lies not simply in the act of betrayal but in the characters' refusal to recognize that one act will beget others until the betrayer becomes the betrayed. The vicious sexual battery of Castiza and her public humiliation by her husband foreshadow the public humiliation and treachery her husband will soon suffer at the hands of Hengist. Vortiger's response to his political ally's shocking and unprovoked treachery during a peace parley—the cry 'Treason, treason!'—echoes *verbatim* the earlier response of his wife Castiza—'Treason, treason!'—when Vortiger shockingly and unprovokedly abducts and rapes her, but Vortiger does not recognize the irony.

Written between 1616 and 1620, *Hengist, King of Kent* or *The Mayor of Queenborough* occupies a central and essential place in the Middleton canon. Contemporary records suggest that it was one of the most popular plays of the Jacobean and Caroline eras—Simon the Mayor was so beloved a comic figure that the title 'Mayor of Queenborough' became a cultural tag for a foolish politician on and off the stage. But since its publication in 1661, the play has appeared in only a handful of eighteenth- and nineteenth-century collections, and the only modern edition, now out of print, is an unmodernized 1938 text derived from a transcription of one of its two scribal manuscripts.

Neglected editorially, the play has also been neglected critically. Usually called a 'lesser' tragedy, stigmatized as a curious and clashing mix of genres, and excused as an early or rehashed effort, the play has received little modern critical attention. Critics first attempted to validate the play's inconsistent form by assigning it to one genre: they classified the play as either a tragedy (but of whom, they wondered—Vortiger? Hersus? Hengist?) or a chronicle history play (yet, as these critics acknowledged, the play drops its interest in history after the first act), full of antiquated dumb shows. But Middleton's play mocks any attempt to give it a generic tag, because—as the 'players' demonstrate to Simon and his audience—the art of playing requires actors to serve as 'comedians, tragedians, tragicomedians, comi-tragedians, pastoralists, humorists, clownists, and satirists' (5.1.71–3). The drama is more fluid than any generic tag or category that tries to contain it. For Middleton, genres could be successfully blended; he knew that history is inherently bound to tragedy and tragedy to history, and to prove his point he had to look no farther than Holinshed's *Chronicles*, which prominently featured the story of Hengist's betrayal of Vortiger as the seminal event, both tragic and celebratory, in the establishment of Anglo-Saxon Britain.

If history could be interspersed with tragedy and comedy in the foundation of Hengist's England, it could also lay bare the cracking foundation of James I's England. In addition to dismissing the play's form, critics had apologized for its contents, terming them too archaic and remote to Jacobean audiences eager for the immediacy of more recent British history. Yet the story of Hengist was anything but distant or fictional to Middleton's audience. Hengist, the fifth-century warrior, was both famous and infamous as the king who brought the Saxons to England—forever altering the language, nationality, and political and social structures of the country. Historians (Bede, Nennius, Geoffrey of Monmouth, Wace, Layamon, Raynulph Higden, Fabyan, Grafton, Foxe, Camden, and William Lambarde, as well as Holinshed) had repeated and embellished his story, featuring it prominently at the beginning of the Saxon chapters in their works. Hengist entered the culture as a mythical figure responsible not only for the custom of 'wassail' and for the creation of Stonehenge but for the politically drastic division of the English kingdom into the heptarchies, the seven kingdoms, that would require hundreds of years of turmoil, war, and death to re-unite.

Even in James's age, historians had to continue to insist that (contrary to popular belief) 'England' was not a corruption of 'Hengist's land', but a reference to the land of the Angles. (Anthony Munday, dramatist turned historical chronicler, reiterated this point as late as 1605.) The exploits of Hengist had been celebrated for centuries in poetry (including *Beowulf, The Mirror for Magistrates* and *The Faerie Queene*) and drama (including the no longer extant 1597 'henges' play and its 1596 prequel 'valteger', whose costumes and properties Philip Henslowe partially financed). William Lambarde in his historical survey, *A Perambulation of Kent* (published in 1576, then expanded and reissued in 1596), gave specific directions on how to locate the ruins of Thong Castle, Hengist's Kentish fortress. Lambarde appears to have been the first historian to have named Hengist's daughter 'Roxena' (the others had called her 'Rowen' or 'Rowena'), suggesting that Middleton was one of the many readers of Lambarde's popular book. Middleton capitalizes on this historical immediacy by intertwining the story of mythical England with divisive contemporary political issues—including the financial collapse of the cloth industry, a threatened insurrection in Jersey, and the scandals surrounding Lady Frances Howard, notorious 'strumpet' and convicted murderer.

The 'decay' of the cloth trade resulted from the failure of the 'Cokayne Project', begun in 1614 by Alderman William Cokayne. The trade involved not just the Merchant Adventurers (the company licensed to deal in and export the product), but the Merchant Staplers (who acted as middlemen) and workmen and merchants from a series of interrelated textile industries—sheep graziers, fellmongers (sheepskin dealers), wool dealers, spinners, weavers, tailors, buttonmakers, and other clothiers and brokers. Also affected were those employed in the second most important non-agrarian industry, the leather trade, such as cattle graziers, tanners, and glovers. Cokayne proposed that all wool exported from England be dyed and dressed before leaving the country, rather than exported 'white' and then dyed and dressed in other cloth-producing or cloth-dyeing countries such as Holland and Germany; James agreed, convinced that the new enterprise would result in tremendously increased revenue.

But Cokayne and his allies had not anticipated that their own marketing incompetence—combined with the boycott of English wool instituted by Holland, Germany, and other countries which had previously served as staunch allies and business partners—would doom the Project to failure, plunging the country into economic depression by contributing to a temporary but dangerous decline in the supply of coin and an imbalance in trade that threatened other important industries such as farming and fishing. It took several years of political and economic manœuvring, and the cancellation of the Project, to rescue the country from bankruptcy, and although the English cloth trade began to revive in 1618, it was quickly depressed again from 1620–24 due to surpluses and the lingering effects of the Cokayne Project.

Middleton briefly alludes to this crisis in the petitioners' complaints to Constantius (1.3.87–117) about the 'enormity' of wool, the exorbitant price of land, and the near beggaring of the country. More generally, the Mayor of Queenborough plot is peopled by tanners, tailors, buttonmongers, glovers, fellmongers, and graziers, as well as that 'Puritan and fustian-weaver' Oliver (5.1.156), whose flax and cotton 'heretic' cloth—produced by those enemies of the Cokayne Project, Holland and Germany—becomes the scapegoat for Queenborough's ills. The Mayor of Queenborough plot can be seen as Middleton's send-up of local politics (as Margot Heinemann has argued), but it also deserves to be seen as a more complex condemnation of the economic crisis which would, for example, force the Clothiers of Gloucestershire to protest to the Privy Council in 1622 about

> their inability longer to maintain their workmen, much of their cloth being unsold, or in pawn. The people begin to steal, and many are starving; all trades are decayed, money very scarce, the whole county impoverished and unable to maintain their poor, by public stock, or any means except by their own trades; [they] entreat the unrestrained buying of cloth, that the clothiers may be able to continue their trade, and much misery be prevented.

In this period of economic gloom, Middleton dramatizes the triumph of Simon and his brethren, true English tradesmen, over Oliver, who conjures by Amsterdam but still has his fustian loom seized and broken by his fellow English citizens.

If in his farcical plot of the Mayor of Queenborough Middleton makes a national crisis into a petty quarrel, in his tragical story of Hengist, King of Kent he makes a petty quarrel into a national crisis. Middleton may be drawing on the lessons James I offered his son in *Basilikon Doron* (first printed in England in 1603). James there set out the principles of kingship in detail, warning 'especially, put never a foreigner in any principal office of estate: for that will never fail to stir up sedition and envy in the countrymen's hearts, both against you and him' (p. 69). This advice seems to be echoed in the warnings of Vortiger's subjects to reject the foreign, non-Christian Hengist and to deny him the powers of kingship which he dangerously appropriates. James faced such a crisis in a political power struggle among his Anglo-French appointed governors of the Isle of Jersey from 1616–1619 in which he had to intervene personally. The dispute arose from a series of arguments between John Peyton, governor of the island, and Jean Herault, its bailiff, when each accused the other of usurping the power of James, who had appointed them; each, however, then claimed some of this usurped power for himself. James ordered the creation of a Privy Council commission of inquiry into this matter in 1617 and forced the officials to appear before him and the Privy Council and reprimanded them. Herault was later jailed and then pardoned by James.

As *Hengist* shrewdly records political injustices that threatened the security and unity of the nation, even as they became more and more personal and petty, so too it anatomizes the most notorious scandal of the second decade of the seventeenth century, which began as intensely personal and private and soon captured the rapt attention of the entire nation. The scandals surrounding Frances Howard—for whose remarriage to the Earl of Somerset Middleton had written *Masque of Cupids*, and whose trial for the murder of Sir Thomas Overbury forms the backdrop to *The Witch*—are crucial to understanding *Hengist, King of Kent*. The play's women must be seen in the cultural framework created by these scandals, although Middleton exploits that framework rather than reinforcing it. In Roxena's masquerade as a virgin, including her self-imposed virginity test while privately acknowledging herself a whore, Middleton mocks the virginity test widely believed to have been faked by Frances Howard as part of the proceedings leading to annulment of her first marriage. In Roxena's poisoning of her stepson Vortiner, evidently with her husband's consent, Middleton recalls Frances's amateurish but ultimately successful efforts to have Overbury, an impediment to her union with Somerset, poisoned, possibly with her husband's consent. In Roxena's betrayal of Vortiger, Middleton offers a man of great power, like Somerset, brought down by his lust for a conniving and promiscuous 'strumpet', a man who did not expect such 'treason from the breast'.

Previous critics have treated *Hengist* as a moral fable on male sexuality but, as Thomas McAlindon has argued, Middleton locates the tragic experience mainly in women. Women are victimized by men who perceive themselves to be the victims of women. Middleton insisted on the strength of these women and on the weakness of these men. He counterposes the genuine virgin, Castiza (who is raped by her husband in disguise, publicly humiliated for her act of 'adultery', and then imprisoned as a whore), with the genuine whore Roxena (who connives with her lover Hersus to impersonate a virgin, convincing her new lover Vortiger of her virtue). When Vortiger discovers he has been cuckolded, he blames her and Hersus for his own evil behaviour—which began long before they entered his kingdom.

Rather than representing the stock character of the whore, as previous critics have suggested, Roxena demonstrates the cruel, destructive and ultimately fraudulent control that men assume they exert over the women. To dismiss Roxena as a whore figure, or as a simple representation of Frances Howard, is to ignore the dramatic power with which Middleton endowed her. Her speeches are shrewd, wise, and sophisticated; more importantly, Roxena gives the play its shape and centre in her lament:

> I pity all the fortunes of poor gentlewomen
> Now in mine own unhappiness; when we have given
> All that we have to men, what's their requital?
> An ill-faced jealousy, which resembles much
> The mistrustfulness of an insatiate thief
> That scarce believes he has all though he has stripped
> The true man naked, and left nothing on him
> But the hard cord that binds him: so are we
> First robbed and then left bound with jealousy.
> (3.1.44–52)

Ironically, as Roxena recognizes too well, men fall not because they expect betrayal by women, but because they do not expect betrayal by men. (The shrewd Hengist is the only male who grasps this fact.) As Roxena is all too aware, 'we can call | Nothing our own if they be deeds to come; | They are only ours when they are past and done' (3.1.11–13). Hersus concludes Roxena's inquiry in his later description to Vortiger of the perfect strategy by which to entrap the 'honest gentlewoman':

> I pity her now,
> Poor soul, she's enticed forth by her own sex
> To be betrayed to man, who in some garden house,
> Or remote walk, taking his lustful time,
> Binds darkness on her eyes, surprises her
> And having a coach ready, turns her in
> Hurrying her where he list for the sin's safety,
> Making a rape of honour without words. (3.1.165–72)

However, Hersus betrays no genuine pity in his words or in his actions later while abetting Vortiger in the secret abduction and rape of his own wife. For Hersus, all women are whores because all women will betray. Even though he has been Roxena's first and only lover, responsible for her 'cracked virginity', when Vortiger tries to make Roxena his 'mistress', Hersus threatens to expose her as a 'whore impost'rous' (2.4.235, 239).

For all of the play's characters, a woman is defined by the status of her sexuality; if she is sexually active, she is already a whore, and if she is not, she will be a whore soon enough. When Hersus blindfolds Castiza in 3.2 and torments her, insisting that he will rape her (in order to keep her from suspecting that it is Vortiger who will do so), he tries to convince her that she has provoked the rape because of her 'sin', her 'contempt of man, and he's a noble creature'. The ignoble Hersus continues his assault on Castiza with words (the rape will be done 'without words'), warning her that she is 'far from any pity', and denying that her love for her husband disproves her contempt, for 'you should love those you are not tied to love, | That's the right trial of a woman's charity'. Yet he decides, 'To strip my words as naked as my purpose, | I must and will enjoy you' (3.2.32–4, 40–1, 53–4). All his language in this scene, all his arguments and analogies, are borrowed from Roxena in 3.1. The bed-trick substitution by which Castiza is deceived exploits a common dramatic convention, but—as Marliss Desens has demonstrated—out of the forty-four Elizabethan and Jacobean plays with bed-tricks, only *Hengist, King of Kent* offers an act of marital rape, making the convention uniquely and intensely disturbing.

When Castiza gives her all to the man who rapes her, her requital will be not be sympathy and compassion but, as Roxena predicted in 3.1, jealousy, public humiliation, and betrayal. Castiza's first chastity test is imposed by Constantius in 1.3, when he twice has her assure him that she is never yet 'known to the will of man' (1.3.161). The second test is imposed by Vortiger in 4.2, when he repeatedly has her assure him that she has known the will of no man but himself. When he first asks her ladies-in-waiting to swear to their sexual fidelity, they equivocate; his wife will swear to the truth in her unknowingly ironic response—'The honour of your bed has been abused' (4.2.154), but only because she was 'ravished'. Castiza cannot bring herself to use the word 'rape' which Hersus had used so freely in 3.1. The only person willing to plead for her is Hengist (who understands the nature of betrayal), but he is silenced by Vortiger. At the same instant, Roxena is assured by Hersus that she can lie and swear herself a virgin because the English 'swear by that we worship not, | So you may swear your heart out, and ne'er hurt yourself' (4.2.173–4).

Middleton's *Hengist, King of Kent* or *The Mayor of Queenborough* encompasses kingdoms—whether that of Vortiger, Hengist, or even Simon—that connect the personal to the political through treachery. No one is safe from the betrayal of trust, not fathers, uncles, husbands, wives, sons, daughters, lovers, or friends. Castiza, used by her fiancé Vortiger as sexual bait to lure Constantius out of the monastery, will be more viciously used by her husband Vortiger as mere sexual matter when he rapes her in disguise. Vortiger, proclaimed king through his own deceitful manipulation of the people and the murder of the man he forced to precede him, will fall because of his own failure to recognize the deceit in his political ally Hengist. And like his wife, Vortiger will come to be a victim of his friends and lovers; in the final scene he attributes his corruption not to his own ambition but to his victimization by Roxena and Hersus (her lover and his friend). Ironically, only Simon the Mayor will reap the rewards that Vortiger had so firmly expected: Simon's marriage to the widow of his former employer brings him a joyful private union and a political base on which to rise to power; his election to mayor showers him with the private trust of his allies and the public permission to punish his enemies; and his friendship with Hengist strengthens his personal and political identity, allowing him to create a world which he commands without question.

In Hengist's rallying cry, 'Nemp your sexes!' ('Draw your knives!'), Middleton offers us the central lesson of *Hengist, King of Kent*: betray others in order to redeem yourself.

SEE ALSO

Textual introduction and apparatus: *Companion*, 1029
Authorship and date: *Companion*, 410

Hengist, King of Kent

Or, The Mayor of Queenborough

[*for the King's Men*]

THE PERSONS OF THE PLAY

VORTIGER, a British lord, later King of the Britons
HENGIST, a Saxon, King of Kent
HERSUS, a Saxon
ROXENA, a Saxon, daughter of Hengist
CASTIZA, wife of Vortiger
CONSTANTIUS, a monk, King of the Britons
AURELIUS AMBROSE, brother of Constantius
UTHER PENDRAGON, brother of Constantius and Aurelius
DEVONSHIRE, a lord, father of Castiza
STAFFORD, a lord, uncle of Castiza
VORTINER, a prince, son of Vortiger and Castiza
LUPUS, a monk
GERMANUS, a monk
RAYNULPH, monk of Chester, Chorus
SIMON, a tanner
OLIVER, a fustian-weaver
Three Graziers
GLOVER
BARBER
TAILOR
FELLMONGER
BUTTONMONGER
BRAZIER
COLLIER
AMINABAB, a clerk
Two Cheaters
CLOWN
Petitioners
Gentlemen
Two Ladies
Footman
Saxons
Soldiers
Lords
Captain of the Guard
Officers
Fortune

1.0 *Incipit Actus Primus*
Enter Raynulph, a monk, the presenter

RAYNULPH
What Raynulph, monk of Chester, can
Raise from his *Polycronicon*
That raises him as works do men
(To see light so long parted-with again),
That best may please this round fair ring
With sparkling judgements circled in
I shall produce; if all my power
Can win the grace of two poor hours
Well apaid I go to rest.
Ancient stories have been best:
Fashions that are now called new
Have been worn by more than you,
Elder times have used the same
Though these new ones get the name,
So in story what's now told
That takes not part with days of old?
Then to prove time's mutual glory
Join new times' love to old times' story. *Exit*

1.1 *Shout* [*within*]. *Enter Vortiger* [*holding a crown*]

VORTIGER
Will that wide-throated beast, the multitude,
Never lin bellowing? Courtiers are ill advised
When they first make such monsters.
What do they but make head against themselves by't?
How near was I to a sceptre and a crown!
Fair power was ever upon me, my desires
Were tasting glory, till this forkèd rabble
With their infectious acclamations
Poisoned my fortune. They will have none
As long as Constantine's three sons survive,
As if the vassals knew not how to obey
But in that line, like their professions
That all their lifetime hammer out one way,
Beaten into their pates with seven years'
Bondage. Well! Though I rise not king, I'll seek
The means to grow as close to one as policy can
And choke their expectations.

Enter Devonshire and Stafford

Now, kind lords,
In whose loves and wishes I am built
As high as human dignity can aspire,
Are yet those trunks, that have no other souls
But noise and ignorance, something more quiet?

DEVONSHIRE
Nor are they like to be, for aught we gather,
Their wills are up still, nothing will appease 'em,
Good speeches are but cast away upon 'em.

VORTIGER
Then since necessity and fate withstand me
I'll strive to enter at a stranger passage.
Your sudden aids and counsels, good my lords?

STAFFORD
They're ours no longer than they do you service.

Music. Enter certain monks [*including*] *Germanus* [*and Lupus*]; *Constantius being one, singing as at procession.* [*Enter also Aurelius and Uther*]

Song

MONKS
Boast not of high birth or blood
To be great is to be good,
Holy and religious things,
Those are vestures fit for kings.
By how much man in fame shines clearer,
He to heaven should draw the nearer;
He deserving best of praises
Whom virtue raises.
It is not state, it is not birth;
The way to heaven is grace on earth.
Sing to the temple, hymn so holy
Sin may blush to think on folly.

VORTIGER
Vessels of sanctity, be pleased awhile
To give attention to the public peace
Wherein heaven is served too, though not so purely.
Constantius, eldest son of Constantine,
We here seize on thee for the general good
And in thy right of birth.

CONSTANTIUS On me! For what, lords?

1.0.0.2 ***Raynulph*** Raynulph Higden, Benedictine monk (d. 1364) whose history, *Polychronicon*, includes the story of Hengist's invasion of England. Raphael Holinshed, whose *Chronicles* Middleton used as his main source for the play, also discusses Higden in his passages on Hengist.

2–3 **raise ... raises** puns on 'brings to life' and 'exalts'

5 **round fair ring** suggesting a public, outdoor theatre like the Globe; the title-page of HERRINGMAN lists the play as having been performed at '*Black-Fryars*', the King's Men's private, indoor theatre, thus the play may have moved between the two types of venues

8 **two poor hours** approximate time for theatre performance

1.1.2 **lin** cease

10 **Constantine's three sons** this story is given in Holinshed's *Chronicles*, Book 5

14–15 **seven years' | Bondage** the minimum term of apprenticeship

28.1–2 ***Germanus [and Lupus]*** Germanus (378?–448), a bishop of Auxere, was famous as an anti-Pelagian; he was accompanied by another bishop, Lupus, during his missionary travels through Britain.

VORTIGER
The kingdom's government.

CONSTANTIUS
O powers of blessedness,
Keep me from groaning downwards into earth again!
I hope I am further on my way than so; set forward.

VORTIGER
You must not.

CONSTANTIUS
How?

VORTIGER
I know your wisdom
Will light upon a way to pardon us
When you shall read in every Briton's brow
The urged necessity of the times.

CONSTANTIUS
What necessity
Can be i'th' world, but prayer and repentance,
And that business I am about.
[A] shout within

VORTIGER
Hark, afar off still,
We lose hazard much. Holy Germanus
And reverend Lupus, with all expedition
Set the crown on him.

CONSTANTIUS
No such mark of fortune comes near my head.

VORTIGER
My lord, we are forced to rule you.

CONSTANTIUS
Dare you receive heaven's light in at your eyelids
And offer violence to religion?
Take heed, the very beam let in to comfort you
May be the fire to burn you. On these knees
Hardened with zealous prayers, I entreat you,
Bring not my cares into the world again.
Think with how much unwillingness and anguish
A glorified soul departed from the body
Would to that loathsome jail return again;
With such great pain a well-subdued affection
Re-enters worldly business.

VORTIGER
Good my lord,
I know you cannot lodge so many virtues
But patience must be one. As low as earth
We beg the freeness of your own consent
Which else must be constrained, and time it were
Either agreed or forced. Speak, good my lord,
For you bind up more sin in this delay
Than thousand prayers can absolve again.

CONSTANTIUS
Were't but my death you should not kneel so long
for't.

VORTIGER
'Twill be the death of millions if you rise not,
And that betimes too: lend your helps, my lords,
For fear all come too late.

CONSTANTIUS
This is a cruelty
That peaceful man did never suffer yet,
To make me die again that was once dead
And begin all that ended long before.
Hold, Lupus and Germanus; you are lights
Of holiness and religion; can you offer
The thing that is not lawful? Stand not I
Clear from all temporal charge by my profession?

GERMANUS
Not when a time so violent calls upon you.
Who's born a prince is born a general peace,
Not his own only, heaven will look for him
In others' business, and require him there.
What is in you religious must be shown
In saving many more souls than your own.

CONSTANTIUS
Did not great Constantine, our noble father,
Deem me unfit for government and rule
And therefore praised me into this profession,
Which I have held strict and love it above glory?
Nor is there want in me; yourselves can witness,
Heaven has provided largely for your peace
And blest you with the lives of my two brothers.
Fix your obedience there, leave me a servant.

VORTIGER
You may even at this instant.
[Lupus and Germanus crown Constantius]

CONSTANTIUS
O this cruelty!

ALL
Long live Constantius, son of Constantine,
King of the Britons.
Flourish

AURELIUS
They have changed their tune already.

CONSTANTIUS
I feel want
And extreme poverty of joy within me.
The peace I had is parted 'mongst rude men;
To keep them quiet I have lost it all.
What can the kingdom gain by my undoing?
That riches is not blest, though it be mighty,
That's purchased with the spoil of any man,
Nor can the peace so filched ever thrive with 'em;
And if't be worthily held sacrilege
To rob a temple, 'tis no less offence
To ravish meditations from a soul,
The consecrated altar in a man,
And all their hopes will be beguiled in me.
I know no more the way to temporal rule
Than he that's born and has his year come to him
In a rough desert. Well may the weight kill me,
And that's the fairest good I look for from't.

VORTIGER
Not so, great king: here stoops a faithful servant
Would sooner perish under it with cheerfulness
Than your meek soul should feel the least oppression
Of ruder cares. Such common, coarse employments
Cast upon me, your subject, upon Vortiger.
I see you are not made for noise and pains,
Clamours of suitors, injuries and redresses,

56 **hazard** that which is at stake

Millions of rising actions with the sun,
Like laws, still ending and yet never done
Of power to turn a great man to the state
Of his insensible monument with o'er-watching.
To be oppressed is not required of you, my lord,
But only to be king. The broken sleeps
Let me take from you, sir; the toils and troubles,
All that is burdensome in authority,
Please you to lay't on me, and what is glorious
Receive it to your own brightness.

CONSTANTIUS Worthy Vortiger,
If 'twere not sin to grieve another's patience
With what we cannot tolerate ourselves,
How happy were I in thee, and thy charity!
There's nothing makes man feel his miseries
But knowledge only; reason that is placed
For man's director is his chief afflicter,
For though I cannot bear the weight myself,
I cannot have that barrenness of remorse
To see another groan under my burden.

VORTIGER [*aside*]
I'm quite blown up, a conscionable way.
There's even a trick of murdering in some pity.
The death of all my hopes I see already;
There was no other likelihood, for religion
Was never friend of mine yet.

CONSTANTIUS Holy partners
In strictest abst'nence, fastings and vigils,
Cruel necessity has forced me from you.
We part, I fear, forever, but in mind
I will be always here, here let me stay.

DEVONSHIRE My lord, you know the times.

CONSTANTIUS
Farewell blest souls. I fear I must offend;
He that draws tears from you takes your best friend.
Flourish. Exeunt all but Vortiger

VORTIGER
Can this great motion of ambition stand
Like wheels false wrought by an unskilful hand?
Then time stand thou too, let no hopes arrive
At their sweet wishfulness till mine set forward.
Would I could stay this existence, as I can
Thy glassy counterfeit, in hours of sand,
I'd keep thee turned down till my wishes rose,
Then we'd both rise together.
What several inclinations are in nature!
How much is he disquieted, and wears royalty
Disdainfully upon him like a curse,
Calls a fair crown the weight of his afflictions,
When here's a soul would sing under that burden!
Yet well recovered! I will seek all ways
To vex authority from him, I will weary him
As low as the condition of a hound
Before I give him over, and in all
Study what most may discontent his blood,
Making my mask my zeal to th' public good.
Not possible a richer policy
Can have conception in the thought of man.
Enter three Graziers

FIRST GRAZIER
An honourable life enclose your lordship.

VORTIGER
Now, what are you?

SECOND GRAZIER Graziers, an't like your lordship.

VORTIGER
So it should seem by your enclosures.
What's your affairs with me?

FIRST GRAZIER
We are your petitioners, my lord.

VORTIGER What? Depart!
Petitioners to me? You've well deserved
My grace and friendship. Have you not a ruler
After your own election? Hie to court,
Get near and close, be loud and bold enough,
You cannot choose but speed.

SECOND GRAZIER And that will do't;
We have throats wide enough, we'll put 'em to't.
Exeunt

Music. Dumb Show: Fortune is discovered upon an 1.2
altar, in her hand a golden round full of lots. Enter Hengist and Hersus with others; they draw lots and hang them up with joy; so all departs saving Hengist and Hersus, who kneel and embrace each other as partners in one fortune; to them enter Roxena, seeming to take her leave of Hengist, her father, but especially privately and warily of Hersus, her lover; she departs weeping, and Hengist and Hersus go to the door and bring in their soldiers with drum and colours, and so march forth
Enter Raynulph

RAYNULPH
When Germany was overgrown
With sons of peace too thickly sown,
Several guides were chosen then
By destined lots to lead out men,
And they whom fortune here withstands
Must prove their fates in other lands;
On these two captains fell that lot;

132 **Like . . . done** perhaps an allusion to Privy Council proclamations and ordinances which were to be in effect for a specified period but then continually renewed

183 **enclose** surround. This word also suggests 'monastic seclusion' as Vortiger has forced Constantius out of a monastery.

185 **enclosures** he puns here on their clothing, dirty and ragged from their professions of working their fenced-off land, i.e. their 'enclosures', as well as on their use of the word at l. 183. He uses 'enclose' again at 1.3.105 to suggest the same double meanings of 'fenced-off' and 'isolated'.

1.2.0.1–12 ***Dumb Show . . . forth*** This first dumb show, unlike the others in the play, involves characters who have not yet been introduced to the audience.

But that which must not be forgot
Was Roxena's cunning grief,
Who from the father like a thief
Hid her best and truest tears,
Which her lustful lover wears,
In many a stol'n and wary kiss
Unseen of father: that maids will do this
Yet highly scorn to be called strumpets too,
But what they lack on't I'll be judged by you.
Exit

1.3 *Enter Vortiger, Fellmonger, Buttonmonger,* [*First*] *Grazier,* [*Brazier, and other*] *Petitioners*

VORTIGER This way his majesty comes.
ALL Thank your good lordship.
VORTIGER When you hear yon door open—
FELLMONGER Very good, my lord.
VORTIGER
Be ready with your several suits, put forward.
GRAZIER
That's a thing every man does naturally, sir,
That's a suitor if he mean to speed.
VORTIGER
'Tis well you're so deep learned. Take no denials.
FELLMONGER No my good lord.
VORTIGER
Not any if you love the prosperity of your suits.
You mar all utterly and overthrow
Your fruitful hopes for ever if either
Fifth or sixth, nay tenth, repulse
Fasten upon your bashfulness.
BUTTONMONGER Say you so, my lord?
We can be troublesome an we list.
VORTIGER [*aside*] I know't,
I felt it but too late in the general sum
Of your rank brotherhood, which now I'll thank you for.
While this vexation is in play, I'll study
To raise a second, then a third to that,
One still to back another: I'll make quietness
As dear and precious to him as night's rest
To a man in suits in law; he shall be glad
To yield up power, if not, it shall be had. *Exit*

BUTTONMONGER Hark, I profess my heart was coming upward, I thought the door had opened.
GRAZIER Marry, would it had, sir.
BUTTONMONGER I have such a treacherous heart of mine own, 'twill throb at the very fall of a farthingale.
BRAZIER Not if it fall on the rushes.
BUTTONMONGER Yes, truly; if there be no light in the room I shall throb presently. The first time it took me, my wife was i'th' company; I remember the room was not half so light as this, but I'll be sworn I was a whole hour afinding on her.
BRAZIER By'r lady, you'd a long time of throbbing on't then.
BUTTONMONGER Still I felt men, but I could find no women, I thought they had been all sunk. I have made a vow for't, I'll never have a meeting by candlelight again.
GRAZIER Yes, sir, in lanthorns.
BUTTONMONGER Yes, sir, in lanthorns, but I'll never trust a naked candle again, tak't on my word.
GRAZIER Hark there, stand close, it opens now indeed.

Enter Constantius [*as king and*] *two Gentlemen*

BUTTONMONGER O majesty, what art thou! I'd give any man half my suit to deliver my petition now. 'Tis in the behalf of buttonmakers, and so it seems by my flesh.
CONSTANTIUS
Pray do not follow me, unless you do't
To wonder at my garments. There's no cause
I give you why you should; 'tis shame enough
Methinks for me to look upon myself;
It grieves me that more should. The other weeds
Became me better, but the lords are pleased
To force me to wear these, I would not else.
I pray be satisfied, I called you not.
Wonder of madness! Can you stand so idle
And know you must die?
FIRST GENTLEMAN We are all commanded, sir,
Besides it is our duty to your grace
To give attendance.
CONSTANTIUS What a wild thing's this?
We marvel though you tremble at death's name
When you'll not see the cause why you are cowards.
All our attendances are far too little
On our own selves, yet you'll give me attendance
Who looks to you the whilst, and so you vanish
Strangely and fearfully. For charity's sake
Make not my presence guilty of your sloth,
Withdraw, young men, and find you honest business.
SECOND GENTLEMAN
What hopes have we to rise by following him?
I'll give him over shortly.
FIRST GENTLEMAN He's too nice,
Too holy, for young gentlemen to follow

1.3.0.1 ***Fellmonger*** sheepskin dealer ***Buttonmonger*** button dealer
0.2 ***Brazier*** brass-worker
23 **a man in suits in law** a man involved in lawsuits
29 **fall of a farthingale** fall of a woman's petticoat (he introduces a bawdy pun here on his sexual arousal at the drop of a woman's petticoat)
30 **it...rushes** fall on the floor quietly (rush was used as a floor covering)
34 **light** by strict logic he means 'dark'
39 **sunk** sleeping in beds placed lower on the ground, with an unintentional pun on sunk as 'depraved'
41 **in lanthorns** lit by a candle contained in a lanthorn (i.e. lantern) rather than a 'naked' candle capable of dripping hot wax; 'in lanthorns' also puns on having 'horns', i.e. being cuckolded.
49 **my garments** Constantius has changed from monastic to royal clothing.
69 **nice** foolish

That have good faces and sweet running fortunes.
Exeunt Gentlemen

CONSTANTIUS
Eight hours a day in serious contemplation
Is but a bare allowance, no higher food
To the soul than bread and water to the body,
And that's but needful then, more would do better.

GRAZIER Let's all kneel together, 'twill move pity; I have been at begging a hundred suits.
[*The petitioners kneel*]

CONSTANTIUS
How happy am I in the sight of you!
Here are religious souls that lose no time.
With what devotion do they kneel to heaven
And seem to check me that am so remiss! [*Kneeling*]
I bring my zeal amongst you, holy men,
If I see any kneel, and I sit out,
That hour is not well served, methinks. Strict souls,
You have been of some order in your times?

GRAZIER Graziers and braziers some, and this a fellmonger.

BRAZIER Here's my petition.

BUTTONMONGER Mine an't like your grace.

GRAZIER Look upon mine, I am the longest suitor, I was undone seven years ago, my lord.

CONSTANTIUS
I have mocked my good hopes! Call you these petitions?
Why, there's no form of prayer amongst 'em all.

BUTTONMONGER
Yes, i'th' bottom there's some half a line
Prays for your majesty if you look on mine.

CONSTANTIUS
Make your request to heaven, not to me.

BUTTONMONGER 'Las, mine's a supplication for brass buttons, sir.

FELLMONGER There's a great enormity in wool, I beseech your grace consider't.

GRAZIER Pastures rise to twopence an acre, my lord, what will this world come too?

BRAZIER I do beseech your grace.

GRAZIER Good your grace.

CONSTANTIUS
O this is one of my afflictïons
That with the crown enclosed me; I must bear it.

GRAZIER
Your grace's answer to my supplication?

BRAZIER
To mine, my lord?

CONSTANTIUS No violent storm lasts ever,
That's all the comfort on't.

FELLMONGER Your highness's answer?

GRAZIER We are almost half undone, the country almost beggered.

BRAZIER See, see, he points to heaven as who should say there's enough there, but 'tis a great way thither. There's no good to be done here, I see that we may all spend our mouths like a company of hounds in the chase of a royal deer, and go home and fall to cold mutton bones when we have done.

BUTTONMONGER My wife will hang me, that's my destiny.
Exeunt [*all but Constantius*]

CONSTANTIUS
Thanks, heaven, 'tis over. We should never know rightly
The sweetness of a calm but for a tempest.
Here's a wished hour for contemplation now,
All still and silent, this is a true kingdom.

Enter Vortiger

VORTIGER
My lord.

CONSTANTIUS
Again?

VORTIGER Alas, this is but early
And gentle to the troops of businesses
That flock about authority, my lord.
You must forthwith settle your mind to marry.

CONSTANTIUS
To marry?

VORTIGER Suddenly; there's no pause given.
The people's wills are violent
And covetous of succession from your loins.

CONSTANTIUS
From me there can come none; a professed abstinence
Hath set a virgin seal upon my blood
And altered all the course. The heat I have
Is all enclosed within a zeal to virtue,
And that's not fit for earthly propagation.
Alas, I shall but forfeit all their hopes,
I'm a man made without desires, tell 'em.

VORTIGER
This gives no satisfaction to their wills, my lord,
I proved them with such words, but all were fruitless;
Their sturdy voices blew 'em into clouds.
A virgin of the highest subject's blood
They have picked out for your embrace, and sends her
Blest with their general wishes into fruitfulness.

81 **check** rebuke

85 **some order** Constantius uses 'order' to mean religious order but the petitioners take it as 'guild'.

98 **There's . . . wool** Middleton may be quoting from Holinshed here: 'It chanced also the same time, that there was great plenty of corn and store of fruit . . . these abuses and great enormities reigned not only in the temporality, but also in the spirituality and chief rulers in the same' (*Chronicles*). However, from 1613–22, the wool industry in England nearly collapsed due to the demands of the 'Cokayne Project' to control domestically all aspects of producing, weaving, dyeing, and dressing wool before exporting it to neighbouring countries.

111–12 **as who should say** as if to say

114–15 **hounds . . . deer** engage in futile action because royal deer could not be hunted

123 **to** compared with

137 **proved them** tried to persuade them with

See where she comes, my lord.
Enter Castiza
CONSTANTIUS I never felt
Unhappy hand of misery 'til this touch:
A patience I could find for all but this.
CASTIZA [*aside to Vortiger*] My lord, your vowed love ventures me but dangerously.
VORTIGER [*aside to Castiza*] 'Tis but to strengthen a vexation politicly.
CASTIZA [*aside to Vortiger*] That's an uncharitable practice, trust me, sir.
VORTIGER [*aside to Castiza*]
No more of that.
CASTIZA [*aside to Vortiger*]
But say he should affect me, sir,
How should I 'scape him then? I have but one faith, my lord,
And that you have already, our late contract's
A divine witness to't.
VORTIGER [*aside to Castiza*]
Leave it to me still,
I am not without shifting-rooms and helps
For all my projects I commit with you. *Exit*
CASTIZA [*aside*]
This' an ungodly way to come to honour,
I do not like't. I love lord Vortiger
But not these practices, they're too uncharitable.
CONSTANTIUS
Are you a virgin?
CASTIZA Never yet, my lord,
Known to the will of man.
CONSTANTIUS O blessed creature!
And does too much felicity make you surfeit?
Are you in soul assured there is a state
Prepared for you, for you, a glorious one
In midst of heaven, now in the state you stand,
And had you rather after much known misery,
Cares and hard labours mingled with a curse,
Throng but to th' door and hardly get a place there?
Think, has the world a folly like this madness?
Keep still that holy and immaculate fire,
You chaste lamp of eternity, 'tis a treasure
Too precious for death's moment to partake,
This twinkling of short life; disdain as much
To let mortality know you as stars
To kiss the pavements. You've a substance
As excellent as theirs; holding your pureness,
They look upon corruption as you do
But are stars still. Be you a virgin too.
CASTIZA [*aside*]
I'll never marry; what though my troth be engaged
To Vortiger? Forsaking all the world
I save it well and do my faith no wrong.
[*To Constantius*] You've mightily prevailed, great virtuous lord,
I'm bound eternally to praise your goodness.
I carry thoughts away as pure from man
As ever made a virgin's name immortal.
Enter Vortiger and Gentleman
CONSTANTIUS
I will do that for joy I never did
Nor ever will again. [*He kisses her;*] *exit Castiza*
GENTLEMAN My lord, he's taken.
VORTIGER
I'm sorry for't, I like not that so well,
They're somewhat too familiar for their time, methinks.
[*Aside*] This way of kissing is no course to vex him.
Why, I, that have a weaker faith and patience,
Could endure more than that coming from woman.
Dispatch and bring his answer speedily. *Exit*
GENTLEMAN
My lord, my gracious lord.
CONSTANTIUS Beshrew thy heart.
GENTLEMAN
They all attend your grace.
CONSTANTIUS I would not have 'em.
'Twould please me better an they'd all depart
And leave the court to me, or put me out
And take it to themselves.
GENTLEMAN
The noon is past, my lord, meat's upon the table.
CONSTANTIUS
Meat? Away, get from me, thy memory's diseased.
What saint's eve's this?
GENTLEMAN Saint Agatha, as I take it.
CONSTANTIUS
O is it so? I am not worthy to be
Served before her, and so return, I pray.
GENTLEMAN He'll starve the guard, an this be suffered. If we set court bellies by a monastery clock, he that breaks a fellow's pate now will scarce be able to crack a louse within this twelvemonth. [*Exit*]
CONSTANTIUS
Sure, 'tis forgetfulness and not man's will
That leads him forth into licentious ways.
Enter Vortiger, Devonshire and Stafford
He cannot certainly commit such errors
And think upon 'em truly as they are acting.
Why's abstinence ordained but for such seasons?
VORTIGER
My lord, you've pleased to put us to much pains,

142.1 ***Castiza*** In the chronicle sources, including Holinshed, this character is not named and is only later once named as Vortiger's 'wife' when he divorces her to marry Roxena. In naming her 'Castiza', Middleton makes use of a generic name deriving from 'castitas', the Latin word for 'chastity'. The name appears also in *Revenger* for the chaste female character.
155 **shifting-rooms and helps** practices of evasion
190 **vex** agitate
194 **Beshrew** make wretched
201 **Saint Agatha** Sicilian saint and martyr who was tortured to death for refusing to surrender her virginity

But we confess 'tis portion of our duties.
Will your grace please to walk? Dinner stays for you.

CONSTANTIUS
I have answered that already.

VORTIGER
But my lord,
We must not so yield to you, pardon me,
'Tis for the general good you must be ruled, sir.
Your health and life is dearer to us now.
Think where you are, at court, this is no monastery.

CONSTANTIUS
But sir, my conscience keeps still where it was;
I may not eat this day.

VORTIGER
We have sworn you shall, and plentifully too.
We must preserve you, sir, though you'll be wilful.
'Tis no slight condition to be a king.

CONSTANTIUS Would I were less than man.

VORTIGER
What, will you make the people rise, my lord,
In great despair of your continuance,
If you neglect the means that must sustain you?

CONSTANTIUS
I never eat on knees.

VORTIGER
But now you must;
It concerns others' healths that you take food.
You've changed your life, you may well change your mood.

CONSTANTIUS
This is beyond all cruelty!

VORTIGER
'Tis our care, my lord.
Exeunt

Finis Actus Primus

2.1 *Incipit Actus Secundus*
Music. Enter Vortiger and Castiza

CASTIZA
My lord, I am resolved, tempt me no further,
'Tis all to fruitless purpose.

VORTIGER
Are you well?

CASTIZA
Never so perfect in the truth of health
As at this instant.

VORTIGER
Then I doubt mine own, or that I am not waking.

CASTIZA
Would you were then, you'd praise my resolution.

VORTIGER
This is wondrous! Are you not mine by contract?

CASTIZA 'Tis most true, my lord,
And I'm better blest in't than I looked for;
In that I am confined in faith so strictly
I'm bound, my lord, to marry none but you,
You'll grant me that, and you I'll never marry.

VORTIGER
It draws into me violence and hazard,
I saw you kiss the king.

CASTIZA
I grant you so, sir,
Where could I take my leave of the world better?
I wronged not you; in that you will acknowledge
A king is the best part on't.

VORTIGER
O my passion!

CASTIZA
I see you somewhat yielding to infirmity, sir,
I take my leave.

VORTIGER
Why, 'tis not possible.

CASTIZA
The fault is in your faith; time I was gone
To give it better strengthening.

VORTIGER
Hark you, lady.

CASTIZA
Send your intent to the next monastery,
There you shall find my answer ever after,
And so with my last duty to your lordship,
For whose perfections I will pray as heartily
As for mine own. *Exit*

VORTIGER
How am I served in this?
I offer a vexation to the king,
He sends it home into my blood with vantage.
I'll put off time no longer. I have wrought him
Into most men's neglect, calling his zeal
A deep pride hallowed over, love of ease
More than devotion or the public benefit,
Which catches many men's beliefs. I am stronger too
In people's wishes, their affections point to me.
I lose much time and glory; that redeemed,
She that now flies returns with joy and wonder.
Greatness and woman's wish never keep asunder.
Exit

2.2 *Oboes. Dumb Show: enter two villains, enter to them Vortiger, seeming to solicit them; gives them gold, then swears them; exit Vortiger. Enter to them Constantius in private meditation, they rudely come to him, strike down his book and draw their swords upon him. He fairly spreads his arms, and yields to their furies; at which they seem to be overcome with pity, but looking on the gold, kill him as he turns his back, and hurry away his body. Enter Vortiger, Devonshire, Stafford in private conference. To them enter the murderers presenting the head to Vortiger; he seems to express much sorrow, and before the astonished lords makes officers lay hold on 'em, who, offering to come towards*

230 **on knees** (manuscript text); on eves (quarto text). During prayer (i.e. while kneeling in prayer on the eve of a holyday).

2.1.3 **truth of health** health in its true meaning, i.e. spiritual health

7 **mine by contract** i.e. they have a formal contract to marry

17 **passion** grief

2.2.0.6 ***fairly*** distinctly

Vortiger, are commanded to be hurried away as to execution. Then the lords, all seeming respect, crown Vortiger, then bring in Castiza, who seems to be brought in unwillingly, [*by*] *Devonshire and Stafford, who crown her and then give her to Vortiger, she going forth with him with a kind of a constrained consent. Then enter Aurelius and Uther, the two brothers, who, much astonished, seem to fly for their safety*
Enter Raynulph

RAYNULPH
When nothing could prevail to tire
The good king's patience, death had hire
In wicked strengths to take his life,
In whom a while there fell a strife,
Pity and fury, but the gold
Made pity faint and fury bold.
Then to Vortiger they bring
The head of that religious king,
Who feigning grief to clear his guilt
Makes the slaughterous blood be spilt.
Then crown they him, and force the maid,
That vowed a virgin life, to wed;
Such a strength great power extends,
It conquers fathers, kin, and friends;
And since fate's pleased to change her life
She proves as holy in a wife;
More to tell were to betray
What deeds in their own tongues must say;
Only this, the good king dead,
The brothers poor in safety fled. *Exit*

2.3 *Enter Vortiger* [*crowned. Enter*] *a Gentleman,* [*hastily*]

GENTLEMAN
My lord.
VORTIGER
I fear thy news will fetch a curse,
It comes with such a violence.
GENTLEMAN
The people are up in arms against you.
VORTIGER
O this dream of glory! I could wish
A sting into thee; there's no such felt in Hell
The fellow but to mine I feel now.
Sweet power, before I can have power to taste thee
Must I forever lose thee? What's the impostume
That swells 'em now?
GENTLEMAN The murder of Constantius.
Exit
VORTIGER
Ulcers of realms, they hated him alive,
Grew weary of the minute of his reign
Compared with some kings' time, and poisoned him
Often before he died in their black wishes,
Called him an evil of their own electing;
And is their ignorant zeal so fiery now
When all their thanks are cold? The mutable hearts
That move in their false breasts!
Shout
Provide me safety!
Hark, I hear ruin threaten me with a voice
That imitates thunder.
Enter Gentleman
GENTLEMAN Where's the king?
VORTIGER
Who takes him?
GENTLEMAN
Send peace to all your royal thoughts, my lord.
A fleet of valiant Saxons newly landed
Offer the truth of all their service to you.
VORTIGER
Saxons? My wishes! Let 'em have free entrance
And plenteous welcomes from all hearts that love us.
They never could come happier.
Enter Hengist, Hersus, [*with*] *drum and soldiers*
HENGIST
Health, power and victory to Vortiger!
VORTIGER
There can be no more wished to a king's pleasures
If all the languages earth speaks were ransacked.
Your names I know not, but so much good fortune
And warranted worth lightens your fair aspects,
I cannot but in arms of love enfold you.
HENGIST
The mistress of our births, hope-faithful Germany,
Calls me Hengistus and this Captain Hersus,
A man low built, but, sir, in acts of valour
Flame is not swifter. We are all, my lord,
The sons of Fortune, she has sent us forth
To thrive by the red sweat of our own merits;
And since after the rage of many a tempest
Our fate has cast us upon Britain's bounds,
We offer you the first fruits of our wounds.
VORTIGER
Which we shall dearly prize; the mean'st blood spent
Shall at wealth's fountain make his own content.
HENGIST
You double vigour in us then, my lord.
Pay is the soul of them that thrive by th' sword.
Exeunt

2.4 *Alarums and Skirmish; enter Vortiger and Gentleman*

GENTLEMAN
My lord, these Saxons bring a fortune with 'em
Stains any Roman success.
VORTIGER On, speak forward.
I will not take a moment from thy tidings.
GENTLEMAN
The main supporters of this insurrection
They have taken prisoners, and the rest so tame
They stoop to the least grace that flows from mercy.

2.3.8 **impostume** swelling, especially of pride

VORTIGER
Never came power guided with better stars
Than these men's fortitudes, yet are misbelievers.
'Tis to my reason wondrous.
Enter Hengist, Hersus, with drum [and] colours, [and] Soldiers leading Prisoners
You've given me such a first taste of your worth
'Twill never from my love. Sure when life's gone
The memory will follow my soul still,
Participating immortality with't;
And here's the misery of earth's limited glory:
There's not a way revealed to give you honour
Above the sum which your own praises give you.

HENGIST
Indeed, my lord, we hold, when all's summed up
That can be made for worth to be expressed,
The fame that a man wins himself is best;
That he may call his own. Honours put to him
Make him no more a man than his clothes do,
And as soon taken off; for as in warmth
The heat comes from the body, not the weeds,
So man's true fame must strike from his own deeds;
And since by this event which fortune speaks us
This land appears the fair predestined soil
Ordained for our good hap, we crave, my lord,
A little earth to thrive on, what you please,
Where we'll but keep a nursery of good spirits
To fight for you and yours.
Enter Simon with a hide

VORTIGER Sir, for our treasure,
'Tis open to your merits as our love,
But for you're strangers in religion chiefly,
Which is the greatest alienation can be
And breeds most factions in the bloods of men,
I must not grant you that.

HENGIST 'Sprecious, my lord,
I see a pattern: be it but so little
As yon poor hide will compass.

VORTIGER How, the hide?

HENGIST
Rather than nothing, sir.

VORTIGER Since you're so reasonable,
Take so much in the best part of our kingdom.

HENGIST
We thank your grace.
[*Exeunt Vortiger and Gentleman*]
Rivers from blushing springs
Have rise at first, and great from abject things.
Stay yonder fellow, he came luckily,
And he shall fare well for't, what e'er he be;
We'll thank our fortune in rewarding him.

HERSUS [*to Simon*] Stay, fellow.

SIMON How, 'fellow'? 'Tis more than you know whether I be your fellow or no, for I am sure you see me not whether I be your fellow or no, I am sure you see me not.

HERSUS Come, what's the price of your hide?

SIMON O unreasonable villain, he would buy the house o'er a man's head; I'll be sure now to make my bargain wisely, they may buy me out of my skin else. Whose hide would you have, mine or the beast's? There's little difference in their complexions. I think mine be the better o'th' twain; you shall see for your love and buy for your money. A pestilence on you all, how have you gulled me! You, buy an oxhide! You, buy a good calf's gather! They are all hungry soldiers, and I took 'em for shoemakers.

HENGIST Hold, fellow; prithee, hold: right a fool worldling that kicks at all good fortune. Whose man art thou?

SIMON I am a servant, yet I am a masterless man, sir.

HENGIST How? Prithee, how that now?

SIMON Very nimbly, sir. My master's dead and I serve my mistress. I am a masterless man, sir, she's now a widow, and I am the foreman of her tanpit.

HENGIST [*giving him gold*] Hold you, and thank your fortune, not your wit.

SIMON 'Faith, and I thank your bounty and not your wisdom, you are not troubled greatly with wit neither it seems. Now by this light, a nest of yellowhammers! What will become of me? If I can keep all these without hanging of myself, I am happier than a hundred of my neighbours. You shall have my skin into the bargain too, willingly, sir, then if I chance to die like a dog, the labour will be saved of fleaing. I'll undertake, sir, you shall have all the skins of our parish at this rate, man and woman's.

HENGIST Sirrah, give ear to me now. Take your hide and cut it all into the slenderest thongs that can bear strength to hold.

SIMON That were a jest indeed: go and spoil all the leather? Sin and pity, why, 'twould shoe half your army.

HENGIST Do't, I bid you.

2.4.13 **Participating** partaking of
27 **hap** fortune
30.1 ***Enter...hide*** Holinshed does not relate the story of Hengist's receipt of enough land as encompassed by the hide; however the story appears in Fabyan, and in Lambarde's *A Perambulation of Kent* thus: 'that among other devices (practised for their own establishment and security) they begged of King Vortiger so much land to fortify upon, as the hide of a beast (cut to thongs) might encompass, and that thereof the place should be called Thongcaster or Thwangcaster'. 'Simon, a tanner' is one of the companions of St Peter in Acts 9:43 and 10:6 and 32.
35 **'Sprecious** God's precious (an oath)
40 **blushing** modest
54–5 **There's...complexions** both have become brown with tanning
59 **gather** heart, liver and lungs
61 **a fool worldling** a foolish person devoted to the pleasures of the world
62 **kicks at** spurns
67 **foreman...tanpit** overseer of her business, as well as bawdy pun on being her lover
72 **yellowhammers** gold coins

SIMON What, cut it all in thongs? Hunch, this is like the vanity of your Roman gallants that cannot wear good suits but they must have 'em cut and slashed into gigots that the very crimson taffeta sits blushing at their follies. I would I might persuade you, sir, from the humour of cutting, 'tis but a kind of swaggering condition and nothing profitable. What, an't were but well pinked, 'twould last longer for a summer suit.

HENGIST What a gross lump of ignorance have I lighted on! I must be forced to beat my drift into him—look you to make you wiser than your parents. I have so much ground given me as this hide will compass, which, as it is, is nothing.

SIMON 'Nothing', quoth a! Why 'twill not keep a hog.

HENGIST Now, with the vantage cut into several parcels,
'twill stretch and make a liberal circuit.

SIMON A shame on your crafty hide! Is this your cunning? I have learned more knavery now than ever I shall shake off while I live. I'll go purchase lands by cows' tails, and undo the parish. Three good bulls' pizzles would set up a man forever. This is like a pin a day doubled to set up a haberdasher of small wares.

HENGIST [*to Hersus*]
Thus men as mean to thrive, as we must learn,
Captain, set in a foot at first.

SIMON A foot, do you call it? The devil's in that foot that takes up all this leather.

HENGIST Dispatch away and cut it carefully with all the advantage, sirrah.

SIMON You could never have lighted upon such a fellow captain to serve your turn. I have such a trick of stretching too, I learned it of a tanner's man that was hanged last sessions, that I'll warrant you I'll get you in a mile and a half more than you are aware of.

HENGIST Pray, serve me so as oft as you will, sir.

SIMON I'm casting about for nine acres to make you a garden plot out of one of the buttocks.

HENGIST 'Twill be a good soil for nosegays.

SIMON 'Twill be a good soil for cabbages, to stuff out the guts of your fellows there. *Exit* [*with the hide*]

HENGIST
You, sirs, go see it carefully performed.
[*Exeunt Soldiers with Prisoners*]
It is the first foundations of our fortunes
On Britain's earth and ought to be embraced
With a respect ne'er linked to adoration.
Methinks it sounds to me a fair assurance
Of large honours and hopes, does't not, Captain?

HERSUS
How many have begun with less at first
That have departed emperors from their bodies,
And left their carcasses as much in monument
As would erect a college.

HENGIST
There's the fruits
Of their religious shows too, to lie rotting
Under a million spent in gold and marble
When thousands left behind dies without shelter,
Having nor house nor food.

HERSUS
A precious charity!
But where shall we make choice of our ground,
Captain?

HENGIST
About the fruitful banks of uberous Kent,
A fat and olive soil, there we came in.
O Captain, he's given I know not what.

HERSUS Long may he give so.

HENGIST
I tell thee, sirrah, he that begged a field
Of fourscore acres for a garden plot,
'Twas pretty well, but he came short of this.

HERSUS
Send over for more Saxons.

HENGIST
With all speed, captain.

HERSUS
Especially for Roxena.

HENGIST
Who, my daughter?

HERSUS
That star of Germany, forget not her, sir,
She's a fair fortunate maid. [*Aside*] I shall betray
myself.
Fair is she and most fortunate may she be,
But in maid lost forever, my desire
Has been the close confusion of that name.
A treasure 'tis, able to make more thieves
Than cabinets set open to entice,
Which learns one theft that never knew the vice.

86 **Hunch** i.e. humph

87 **Roman gallants** overdressed men (the English frequently mocked the Italians' concern with fashion)

88 **gigots** small pieces; also possibly the analogy of a leg of mutton prepared for cooking with slashes through the fatty surface so as to expose the red flesh

90–1 **humour of cutting** puns on 'cutting' as slicing or slashing with a knife or sword and on bullying

92 **pinked** cut with holes or slashes as a form of ornamentation of a fabric

105 **pizzles** penises (used as whips)

106 **pin a day** 'A pin a day is a groat [a small amount] a year' (proverbial).

109 **Captain** Hengist addresses Hersus here but Simon assumes he's addressing him. See 2.4.115.

109, 110 **foot** puns on 'foot' as measure of distance and part of the body

117 **sessions** sessions of the peace, i.e. periodical sittings of the justices of the peace

120–1 **I'm . . . buttocks** scatological joke, hence the 'good soil for nosegays' to perfume the air at 2.4.122

123 **cabbages** He puns here on an alternate meaning of cabbages, 'shreds (or larger pieces) of cloth cut off by tailors in the process of cutting out cloths' (*OED*).

133 **as much in monument** in as grand a monument

140 **uberous** richly productive

141 **olive** green, i.e. fertile

152 **in maid** in maidenhood, also a reference to Hersus's having taken her 'maidenhead', i.e. her virginity

153 **close confusion** secret destruction

156 **learns** teaches

HENGIST
Some I'll dispatch with speed.
HERSUS
Do you forget not.
HENGIST
Marry, pray help my memory if I should.
HERSUS
Roxena, you remember.
HENGIST
What more, dear sir?
HERSUS
I see you need no help, your memory's clear, sir.
Shouts; flourish
HENGIST
Those sounds leapt from our army.
HERSUS
They were too cheerful to voice a bad event.
Enter Saxon Gentleman
HENGIST Now, sir, your news?
SAXON GENTLEMAN
Roxena the fair—
HENGIST
True, she shall be sent for.
SAXON GENTLEMAN
She's here.
HENGIST
What say'st?
SAXON GENTLEMAN
She's come, sir.
HERSUS [*aside*]
A new youth begins me o'er again.
SAXON GENTLEMAN [*to Hengist*] Followed you close, sir,
With such a zeal as daughter never equalled,
Exposed herself to all the merciless dangers
Set in mankind or fortune, not regarding
Aught but your sight.
HENGIST
Her love is infinite to me.
HERSUS [*aside*]
Most charitably censured; 'tis her cunning,
The love of her own lust, which makes a woman
Gallop downhill as fearless as a drunkard.
There's no true loadstone i'th' world but that;
It draws 'em through all storms, by sea or shame,
Life's loss is thought too small to pay that game.
SAXON GENTLEMAN
What follows more of her will take you strongly.
HENGIST
How?
SAXON GENTLEMAN
Nay, 'tis worth your wonder.
HENGIST
I thirst for't.
SAXON GENTLEMAN
Her heart-joy, ravished at your late success,
Being the early morning of your fortunes,
So prosperously now opening, at her coming
She takes a cup of gold, and midst the army,
Teaching her knee a current cheerfulness
Which well became her, drank a liberal health
To the King's joys and yours. The King in presence,
Who with her sight, but her behaviour chiefly,
Or chief I know not which, but one, or both,
But he's so far 'bove my expression caught,
'Twere art enough for one man's time and portion
To speak him and miss nothing.
HENGIST
This is astonishing!
HERSUS [*aside*]
O this ends bitter now, our close-hid flame
Will break out of my heart, I cannot keep it.
HENGIST
Gave you attention to this, Captain? How now, man?
HERSUS
A kind of grief about these times o'th' moon still.
I feel a pain like a convulsïon,
A cramp at heart, I know not what name fits it.
Flourish; cornett. Enter Vortiger, Roxena and attendants
HENGIST
Nor never seek one for't, let it go
Without a name; would all griefs were served so,
Our using of 'em mannerly makes 'em grow.
HERSUS
A love-knot already, arm-in-arm!
VORTIGER
What's he lays claim here?
HENGIST
In right of fatherhood
I challenge an obedient part, my lord.
VORTIGER
Take't and send back the rest.
HENGIST
What means your grace?
VORTIGER
You'll keep no more than what belongs to you, will you?
HENGIST
That's all, my lord, it all belongs to me yet,
I keep a husband's interest till he come,
Yet out of duty and respect of majesty
I send her back your servant.
VORTIGER
My mistress, sir, or nothing.
HENGIST
Come again?
I never thought to have lived to have heard so ill of thee.
VORTIGER
How, sir, so ill?
HENGIST
So beyond detestable!
To be an honest vassal is some calling,
Poor is the worst of that, shame comes not to't;
But 'mistress', that's the only common bait,
Fortune sits at all hours catching 'whore' with it
And plucks 'em up by clusters. There's my sword, my lord,
And if your strong desires aim at my blood,
Which runs too purely there, a nobler way

171 **censured** judged
174 **loadstone** magnet
182–5 **She ... presence** According to chronicle sources such as Holinshed, the custom of 'wassail' was introduced to England by Roxena and Hengist.
194 **grief** illness, but playing on 'sadness'
215 **hours** pun on 'whores'

Quench it in mine.
VORTIGER I ne'er took sword in vain.
Hengist, we here create thee Earl of Kent.
HERSUS [*aside*]
O that will do't, 'twill do't.
[*He faints*]
VORTIGER What ails our friend? Look to him.
ROXENA
O 'tis his epilepsy, I know it well,
I helped him once in Germany. Comes't again?
A virgin's right hand stroked upon his heart
Gives him ease straight, but't must be a pure virgin,
Or else it brings no comfort.
VORTIGER What a task
She puts upon herself unurged for purity!
The proof of this will bring love's rage upon me.
ROXENA [*aside to Hersus*]
O this would mad a woman, there's no plague
In love to indiscretion.
HERSUS [*aside to Roxena*]
Pish, this cures not.
ROXENA [*aside to Hersus*]
Dost think I'll ever wrong thee?
HERSUS [*aside to Roxena*] O most feelingly,
But I'll prevent it now, and break thy neck
With thine own cunning. Thou hast undertook
To give me help, to bring in royal credit
Thy cracked virginity, but I'll spoil all;
I will not stand on purpose, though I could,
But fall still to disgrace thee.
ROXENA [*aside to Hersus*] What, you will not?
HERSUS [*aside to Roxena*]
I have no other way to help myself,
For when thou'rt known to be a whore impost'rous
I shall be sure to keep thee.
ROXENA [*aside to Hersus*] O, sir, shame me not!
You've had what's precious; try my faith yet once more,
Undo me not at first in chaste opinion.
HERSUS [*aside to Roxena*]
All this art shall not make me find my legs.
ROXENA [*aside to Hersus*]
I prithee, wilt thou wilfully confound me?
HERSUS [*aside to Roxena*]
Well, I'm content for this time to recover
To save thy credit and bite in my pain,
But if thou ever fail'st me, I will fall,
And thou shalt never get me up again.
ROXENA [*aside to Hersus*]
Agreed 'twixt you and I, sir.
[*Hersus rises*]
[*To Vortiger*] See, my lord,
A poor maid's work. The man may pass for health now
Amongst the clearest bloods and whose are nicest.
VORTIGER
I have heard of women bring men on their knees
But few that ever restored 'em. How now, Captain?
HERSUS
My lord, methinks I could do things past man;
I am so renewed in vigour I long most
For violent exercise to take me down;
My joy's so high in blood, I am above frality.
VORTIGER
My lord of Kent?
HENGIST Your love's unworthy creature.
VORTIGER
Seest thou this fair chain? Think upon the means
To keep it linked forever.
HENGIST O my lord,
'Tis many degrees sundered from that hope,
Besides your grace has a young, virtuous queen.
VORTIGER
I say think on't, think on't!
HERSUS [*aside*] An this wind hold,
I shall even fall to my old disease again.
VORTIGER [*to Roxena*]
There's no fault in thee but to come so late,
All else is excellent; I chide none but fate.
Flourish; cornetts. Exeunt
Finis Actus Secundus

Incipit Actus Tertius 3.1
Enter Hersus and Roxena
ROXENA
I have no conceit now that you ever loved me,
But as lust held you for the time.
HERSUS So, so.
ROXENA
Do you pine at my advancement, sir?
HERSUS O barrenness
Of understanding, what a right love is this?
'Tis you that fall, I that am reprehended.
What height of honours, eminence and fortune
Should ravish me from you?
ROXENA
Who can tell that, sir? What's he can judge
Of a man's appetite, before he sees him eat?
Who knows the strength of any's constancy
That never yet was tempted? We can call
Nothing our own if they be deeds to come;
They are only ours when they are past and done.

230 **to** compared with
Pish exclamation of contempt or impatience
231 **feelingly** painfully to him, with sensual touches on her part
239 **impost'rous** false
251 **nicest** most fastidious
256 **take me down** specifically 'cause me to detumesce'; the whole speech is equivocal in this vein
266 **I chide...fate** i.e. 'I chide no one; it is entirely fate that does so'

How blest are you above your apprehension
If your desire would lend you so much patience
To examine the adventurous condition
Of our affections, which are full of hazard,
And draw in the times' goodness to defend us!
First, this bold course of ours can't last long,
Or never does in any without shame,
And that you know brings danger; and the greater
My father is in blood, as he's well risen,
The greater will the storm of his rage be
'Gainst his blood's wronging. I have cast for this,
'Tis not advancement that I love alone,
'Tis love of shelter to keep shame unknown.

HERSUS
O were I sure of thee, as 'tis impossible
There to be ever sure where there's no hold,
Your pregnant hopes should not be long arising.

ROXENA
By what assurance have you held me thus far
Which you found firm, despair you now in that?

HERSUS
True, that was good security for the time,
But admit a change of state. When you're advanced
You women have a French toy in your pride,
You make your friend come crouching, or perhaps
To bow i'th' hams the better, he is put
To compliment three hours with your chief gentlewo-
man,
Then perhaps not admitted—nay, nor never,
That's the more noble fashion. Forgetfulness,
'Tis the pleasing'st virtue anyone can have
That rises up from nothing, for by the same,
Forgetting all, they forget from whence they came:
An excellent property for oblivion.

ROXENA
I pity all the fortunes of poor gentlewomen
Now in mine own unhappiness; when we have given
All that we have to men, what's their requital?
An ill-faced jealousy, which resembles much
The mistrustfulness of an insatiate thief
That scarce believes he has all though he has stripped
The true man naked, and left nothing on him
But the hard cord that binds him: so are we
First robbed and then left bound with jealousy.
Sure, he that finds us now has a great purchase,
And well he gains that builds another's ruins!
Yet man, the only seed that's sown in envy,
Whom little would suffice as any creature
Either in food or pleasure, yet 'tis known
What would give ten enough contents not one.
A strong-diseased conceit may tell strange tales to you
And so abuse us both; take but th'opinion
Of common reason, and you'll find it impossible
That you should lose me in this king's advancement,
Who here's a usurper. As he has the kingdom,
So shall he have my love, by usurpation,
The right shall be in thee still. My ascension
To dignity is but to waft thee upward,
And all usurpers have a falling sickness,
They cannot keep up long.

HERSUS
May credulous man
Put all his confidence in so weak a bottom
And make a saving voyage?

ROXENA
Nay, as gainful as ever man yet made.

HERSUS
Go, take thy fortune, aspire with my consent,
So thy ambition will be sure to prosper.
Speak the fair certainty of Britain's queen
Home to thy wishes.

ROXENA
Speak in hope I may, but not in certainty.

HERSUS
I say in both, hope and be sure. I'll quickly
Rèmove her that stands between thy glory.

ROXENA Life is love!
If lost virginity can win such a day
I'll have no daughter but shall learn my way. *Exit*

HERSUS
'Twill be good work for him that first instructs 'em,
Maybe some son of mine, got by this woman too.
Man's scattered lust brings forth most strange events,
An 'twere but strictly thought on. How many brothers
Wantonly got, through ignorance of their births,
May match with their own sisters?
Enter Vortiger
[*Aside*] Peace, 'tis he,
Invention fail me not, 'tis a gallant's credit
To marry his whore bravely.

VORTIGER [*aside*] Have I power
Of life and death and cannot command ease
In mine own blood? After I was a king

3.1.14 **apprehension** understanding

22–4 **blood ... blood's** rank (an ironic sense, as it is properly a notion of rank as 'breeding, stock' and so should depend on birth) ... kin's

29 **pregnant** inventive and full of expectation, as well as 'with child'

44–68 **I ... long** This speech underwent revision between the play's original composition and the later version represented by the quarto text of the play. In 3.1.46, Roxena's query 'what's their requital' has been altered in the quarto text to 'what our requital', significantly changing the meaning of the rest of the speech. Also, her lines from 3.1.53 to the middle of 3.1.60 are marked for deletion in both of the manuscripts; these lines do not appear in the quarto text.

67–8 **And ... long** This has three levels of meaning: the political analogy of short-lived usurpation might apply literally to Vortiger; illicit affairs cannot be sustained (see ll. 19–26 where the same point is made with reference to Hersus himself); poaching lovers are poor performers.

69 **bottom** ship

70 **saving** profitable

72 **fortune** Hersus is punning on Roxena's use of 'fortunes' at l. 44.

89 **marry ... bravely** Bald notes that at least two other Middleton plays, *Trick* and *Chaste Maid*, portray a man attempting to bravely (or profitably) marry off his mistress.

I thought I never should have felt pain more,
That there had been a ceasing of all passions
And common stings which subjects use to feel
That were created with a patience fit
For all extremities. But such as we
Know not the way to suffer than to do't.
How most prepost'rous 'tis! What's all our greatness
If we that prescribe bounds to meaner men
Must not pass these ourselves? O most ridiculous!
This makes the vulgar merry to endure,
Knowing our state is strict, and less secure.
I'll break through custom. Why should not the mind,
The nobler part that's of us, be allowed
Change of affections, as our bodies are
Still change of food and raiment? I'll have't so.
All fashions appear strange at first production,
But this would be well followed. [*To Hersus*] O Captain!

HERSUS
My lord, I grieve for you, I scarce fetch breath
But a sigh hangs at end on't. This is no way,
If you'll give way to counsel.

VORTIGER
Set me right then,
And quickly, sir, or I shall curse thy charity
For lifting up my understanding to me
To show that I was wrong. Ignorance is safe,
I slept happily; if knowledge mend me not,
Thou hast committed a most cruel sin
To make me into judgement and then leave me.

HERSUS
I will not leave you so, sir, that were rudely.
First, you've a flame too open and too violent,
Which like blood guiltiness in an offender
Betrays him when none can. Out with it, sir,
Or let some cunning coverture be made
Before our practice enters; 'twill spoil all else.

VORTIGER
Why, look you, sir, I can be as calm as silence,
All the whiles music plays; strike on, sweet friend,
As mild and merry as the heart of ignorance;
I prithee take my temper. Has a virgin
A heat more modest?

HERSUS [*aside*]
He does well to ask me,
I could have told that once. [*To Vortiger*] Why here's a government!
There's not a sweeter amity in friendship
Than in this friendly league 'twixt you and health.

VORTIGER
Then since thou find'st me capable of happiness,
Instruct me with the practice.

HERSUS
What would you say, my lord,
If I ensnare her in an act of lust?

VORTIGER
O there were art to the life; but that's impossible,
I prithee flatter me no further with't;
Fie, so much sin as goes to make up that
Will ne'er prevail with her! Why, I tell thee, sir,
She's so sin-killing modest, that if only to
Move the question were enough adultery
To cause a separation, there's no gallant
So brassy-impudent durst undertake
The words that should belong to't.

HERSUS
Say you so, sir?
There's nothing made i'th' world, but has a way to't,
Though some be harder than the rest to find.
Yet one there is that's certain, and I think
I have took the course to light on't.

VORTIGER
O I pray for't.

HERSUS
I heard you lately say—from whence, my lord,
My practice received light first—that your queen
Still consecrates her time to contemplation,
Takes solitary walks.

VORTIGER
Nay, late and early, sir,
Commands her weak guard from her, which are but women
When 'tis at strongest.

HERSUS
I like all this well, my lord,
And now your grace shall know what net is used
In many places to catch modest women
Such as will never yield by prayers or gifts.
Now, there are some will catch up men as fast,
But those she-fowlers nothing concerns us;
Their birding is at windows, ours abroad,
Where ring-doves should be caught, that's married wives
Or chaste maids, what the appetite has a mind to.
'Tis practised often, therefore worth discovery
And may well fit the purpose.

VORTIGER
Make no pause then.

HERSUS
The honest gentlewoman, where e'er she be,
When nothing will prevail, I pity her now,
Poor soul, she's enticed forth by her own sex
To be betrayed to man, who in some garden house,
Or remote walk, taking his lustful time,
Binds darkness on her eyes, surprises her
And having a coach ready, turns her in,
Hurrying her where he list for the sin's safety,
Making a rape of honour without words;
And at the low ebb of his lust, perhaps
Some three days after, sends her coached again
To the same place, and, which would make most mad,

94 **use to** habitually
118 **rudely** rudely done
159 **Their . . . windows** i.e. their seductions take place at the window.
160 **ring-doves** plays on the species of dove and ring-wearing women
166–74 **she's . . . again** It is not clear whether Middleton is alluding to a genuine practice of the period or has invented it for the purposes of the drama.
167 **garden house** notorious as places of illicit sexual encounters
172 **without words** without speaking

She's spoiled of all, yet knows not where she was robbed.
Wise, dear, precious mischief!

VORTIGER Is this practised?

HERSUS
Too much, my lord, to be so little known,
A springe to catch a maidenhead after sunset,
Clip it and send it home again to th' city;
There 'twill be never perceived.

VORTIGER
My raptures want expression; I conceit
Enough to make me fortunate, and thee great.

HERSUS
I praised it then, my lord, I knew 'twould take.
Exeunt

3.2 *Enter Castiza, with a book, and two Ladies*

CASTIZA
Methinks you live strange lives! When I see't not
The less it grieves me; you know how to ease me then.
If you but knew how well I loved your absence,
You would bestow't upon me without asking.

FIRST LADY
Faith, for my part, were it no more for ceremony
Than 'tis for love, you should walk long enough
For my attendance; so think all my fellows,
Though they say nothing. Books in women's hands,
They are as much against the hair, methinks,
As to see men work stomachers and night-rails.
She that has the green-sickness and should follow her counsel
Would die like an ass and go to th' worms like a salad.
Not I, as long as such a creature as man is made;
She's a fool that will not know what he's good for.
Exeunt Ladies

CASTIZA
Though amongst life's elections, that of virgin
I speak noblest, yet't has pleased just heaven
To send me a contented blessedness
In this of marriage which I ever doubted.
I see the king's affection was a true one,
It lasts and holds out long. That's no mean virtue
In a commanding man, though in great fear
At first I was enforced to venture on't.
Enter Vortiger and Hersus disguised

VORTIGER [*aside to Hersus*]
All's happy clear and safe.

HERSUS [*aside to Vortiger*] The rest comes gently then.

VORTIGER [*aside to Hersus*]
Be sure you seize on her full sight at first,
For fear of my discovery.

HERSUS [*aside to Vortiger*] I'll not miss it.

VORTIGER
Now, fortune, and I am sped!
[*Hersus seizes and blindfolds Castiza from behind*]

CASTIZA O help, treason, treason!

HERSUS
Sirrah, how stand you? Prevent noise and clamour
Or death shall end thy service.

VORTIGER [*aside*] A sure cunning!

CASTIZA
O rescue!

HERSUS Dead her voice, away, make speed.
[*Hersus and Castiza*] *exeunt and enter again*

CASTIZA No help, no succour?

HERSUS
Louder yet? Extend your voice to the last rack,
You shall have leave now, you're far from any pity.

CASTIZA What's my sin?

HERSUS
Contempt of man, and he's a noble creature,
And takes it in ill part to be despised.

CASTIZA
I never despised any.

HERSUS No? You hold us
Unworthy to be loved, what call you that?

CASTIZA
I have a lord disproves you.

HERSUS Pish, your lord?
You're bound to love your lord, that's no thanks to you.
You should love those you are not tied to love,
That's the right trial of a woman's charity.

CASTIZA
I know not what you are nor what my fault is,
But if't be life you seek, whate'er you be,
Use no immodest words, and take it from me.
You kill me more in talking sinfully
Than acting cruelly. Be so far pitiful
To end me without words!

HERSUS Long may you live,
The wish of a good subject. 'Tis not life
That I thirst after, loyalty forbid
I should commit such treason. You mistake me,
I have no such bloody thought, only your love
Shall content me.

CASTIZA What said you, sir?

HERSUS Thus, thus, plainly,
To strip my words as naked as my purpose,
I must and will enjoy you.
[*Castiza faints*]
Gone already?

179 **springe** trap
180 **Clip** literally, to deflower; also plays on 'clip' as 'embrace' and clipping a bird's wings so it can't fly
3.2.10 **men ... night-rails** i.e. for men to sew women's decorative undergarments and dressing-gowns
11 **green-sickness** anemic disease of young girls, implying innocence about sexuality
29.1 **[Hersus] ... *again*** Hersus wants Castiza to think that she's been moved to another, isolated location.
38 **Pish** exclamation of contempt or impatience

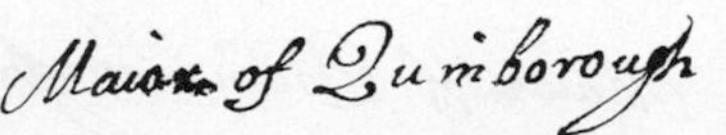

Look to her, bear her up, she goes apace.
I feared this still, and therefore came provided.
There's that will fetch life from a dying spark
And make it spread a furnace.
[He revives her]
She's well straight,
It kept a lord seven years alive together
In spite of nature, that he looked like one
Had leave to walk out of a grave to air himself
Yet still walked lord. Pish, let her go; she stands,
Upon my knowledge, or else she counterfeits,
I know the virtue.

CASTIZA
Never did sorrows in afflicted woman
Meet with such cruelty; such hard-hearted ways
Human invention never found before.
To call back life to live is but ill taken
Of some departing soul, then to force mine back
To an eternal act of death in lust,
What is it but most ex'crable?

HERSUS
So, so.
But this is from the business. List to me,
Here you are now far from all hope of friendship,
Save what you make in me; 'scape me you cannot,
Send your soul that assurance. That resolved on,
You know not who I am, nor never shall,
I need not fear you then. But give consent
Then with the faithfulness of a true friend,
I'll open myself to you, fall your servant,
As I do now in hope, proud of submission,
And seal the deed up with eternal secrecy.
Not death should pick it open, much less
King's authority or torture.

VORTIGER *[aside]* I admire him.

CASTIZA *[kneeling]*
O sir, whate'er you are, I teach my knee
Thus to requite you, be content to take only
My sight as ransom for mine honour,
And where you have but mocked mine eyes with
darkness
Pluck 'em out quite. All outward light of body
I'll spare most willingly, but take not from me
That which must guide me to another world
And leave me dark forever, fast without
That cursèd pleasure which would make two souls
Endure a famine everlastingly.

HERSUS *[aside]*
This almost moves.

VORTIGER *[aside]* By this light, he'll be taken.

HERSUS *[aside]*
I'll wrestle down all pity. *[To Castiza]* Will you
consent?

CASTIZA
I'll never be so guilty.

HERSUS Farewell words then.
You hear no more of me, but thus I seize thee.

CASTIZA
O if a power above be reverend in thee,
I bind thee by that name, by manhood, nobleness
And all the charms of honour.
Exeunt Vortiger, Castiza

HERSUS Here's one caught
For an example; never was poor lady
So mocked into false terror! With what anguish
She lies with her own lord! Now she could curse
All into barrenness and beguile herself by't.
Conceit's a powerful thing and is indeed
Placed as a palate to taste grief or love,
And as that relishes so we approve.
Hence it comes that our taste is so beguiled,
Changing pure blood for some that's mixed and soiled.
Exit

3.3

Enter Hengist

HENGIST
A fair and fortunate constellation reigned
When we set footing here; from his first gift
Which to a king's unbounded eyes seemed nothing—
The compass of a hide—I have erected
A strong and spacious castle, yet contained myself
Within my limits, without check or censure.
Thither with all the observance of a subject—
The liveliest witness of a grateful mind—
I purpose to invite him and his queen
And feast 'em nobly.
A noise [within]

BARBER *[within]* We will enter sir,
'Tis a state business of a twelve month long,
The choosing of a mayor.

HENGIST What noise is that?

TAILOR *[within]*
Sir, we must speak with the good Earl of Kent,
Though we were ne'er brought up to keep a door,
We are as honest, sir, as some that do.
Enter Gentleman

HENGIST
Now, what's the occasion of their clamours, sir?

GENTLEMAN
Please you, my lord, a company of townsmen
Are bent against all denials and resistance
To have speech with your lordship, and that you
Must end a difference, which none else can do.

HENGIST
Why then there's reason in their violence
Which I never looked for; let in first but one,

94 **be taken** moved to pity
105 **Conceit's** imagination, understanding
3.3.11 **a twelve month long** a government office with a tenure of twelve months
14 **keep a door** act as a porter or servant, with a secondary meaning of 'act as pander'

And as we relish him, the rest comes on.
Exit Gentleman
'Twere no safe wisdom in a rising man
To slight off such as these; nay rather these
Are the foundation of a lofty work;
We cannot build without them and stand sure.
He that first ascends up to a mountain's top
Must first begin at foot.
Enter Gentleman
Now, sir, who comes?

GENTLEMAN
They cannot yet agree, my lord, of that.

HENGIST How?

GENTLEMAN
They say 'tis worse now for 'em than ever 'twas before,
For where the difference stood but between two,
Upon this coming first they're at odds.
One says, sir, he shall lose his place at church by't,
Another, he'll not do his wife that wrong,
And by their good wills they would come all at first.
The strife continues in most heat, my lord,
Between a country barber and a tailor
Of the same town, and which your lordship names,
'Tis yielded by consent that one shall enter.

HENGIST
Here's no sweet toil, I'm glad they're grown so reasonable.
Call in the Barber; if the tale be long,
He'll cut it short, I trust, that's all the hope on't.
Enter Barber
Now, sir, are you the barber?

BARBER O most barbarous! A corrector of enormities in hair, my lord, a promoter of upper lips, or what your lordship in the neatness of your discretion shall vouchsafe to call it.

HENGIST Very good, I see this you have without book, but what's your business now?

BARBER Your lordship comes to a high point indeed, the business, sir, lies all about the head.

HENGIST That's work for you.

BARBER No, my good lord, there is a corporation, a kind of body, a body.

HENGIST
The Barber's out o'th body, let in the Tailor.
This 'tis to reach beyond your own profession:
When you let go your head, you lose your memory,
You have no business with the body.

BARBER Yes, sir, I am a barber-surgeon, I have had something to do with't in my time, my lord, and I was never so out o'th' body as I have been here of late. Send me good luck; I'll go marry some whore or other but I'll get in again.
Enter Tailor

HENGIST
Now, sir, a good discovery come from you
That we may know the inwards of the business.

TAILOR
I will rip the linings to your lordship
And show what stuff 'tis made on, for the body
Or corporation—

HENGIST
There the Barber left indeed.

TAILOR 'Tis pieced up of two factions.

HENGIST A patched town the whilst.

TAILOR
Nor can go through stitch, noble lord,
The collar is so great in the one party,
And as in linsey-woolsey wove together,
One piece makes several suits, so, upright Earl,
Our linsey-woolsey hearts makes all this coil.

HENGIST What's all this now?
Call in the rest; I'm ne'er the wiser, yet
I should commend my wit could I but guess
What this would come to.
[*Enter Glover, Buttonmonger and Brazier*]
Now, sirs, what are you?

GLOVER Sir-reverence of your lordship, I am a glover.

HENGIST What needs that then?

GLOVER Sometimes I deal with dog's leather, sir-reverence, all that while.

HENGIST Well, to the purpose, if there be any towards.

GLOVER I were an ass else, saving your lordship's pleasure. We have a body, but our town wants a hand, a hand of justice, a worshipful master mayor.

HENGIST This is well handed yet, a man may take some hold. You want a mayor?

GLOVER
Right, but there's two at fisticuffs about it, sir;
As I may say, at daggers' drawing, sir,
But that I cannot say, because they have none;
And you being Earl of Kent, the town does say
Your lordship's voice shall choose and part the fray.

34 **coming first** i.e. neither wants to be first in pressing his suit
35 **lose . . . by't** his place in a high-ranking pew
36 **he'll . . . wrong** subject her to the humiliation
46–65 **BARBER O . . . again** As Hengist realizes at ll. 57–8, the Barber is not a member of the Barber-Surgeon Company, indeed he seems to have been expelled from it (ll. 63–4), and so cannot lawfully practise, hence his circumlocutions (ll. 46–9) and his hope to marry into membership (ll. 64–5). But 'the corporation' would seem also to be the body of tradesmen offstage, as more limitedly at ll. 69–70.
46 **enormities** both 'misdeeds' and 'excesses'
50 **without book** without learning
61 **barber-surgeon** before 1461, barbers practised surgery and dentistry; after the Company of Barber-Surgeons was incorporated by Edward IV in 1461 (their title was altered to 'Company of Barbers and Surgeons' in Henry VIII's reign), barbers were restricted to the practice of dentistry.
74 **collar** pun on 'choler'
75 **linsey-woolsey** cloth woven from wool and flax (with a pun on its other meaning of 'nonsense')
82 **Sir-reverence** standard contraction of 'save your reverence'
88 **wants** lacks
92 **at fisticuffs** in a fistfight

HENGIST
This is strange work for me. Well, sir, what be they?

GLOVER
The one is a tanner.

HENGIST Fie, I shall be too partial,
I owe too much affection to that trade
To put it to my voice. What's his name?

GLOVER
Simon, sir.

HENGIST How, Simon too?

GLOVER
Nay 'tis but Simon one, sir, the very same Simon
That sold your lordship the hide.

HENGIST What say'st thou?

BARBER That's all his glory, sir. He got his master's widow by't presently after, a rich tanner's wife; she has set him up. He was her foreman a long time in her other husband's days.

HENGIST [*aside*]
Now let me perish in my first aspiring
If the pretty simplicity of his fortune
Does not most highly take me; 'tis a presage, methinks,
Of bright succeeding happiness to mine
When my fate's glow-worm casts forth such a shine.
[*To Tailor*] And what's the other that contends with him?

TAILOR
Marry, my noble lord, a fustian-weaver.

HENGIST
How, will he offer to compare with Simon?
He a fit match for him?

BARBER Hark, hark, my lord,
Here they come both now in a pelting chase
From the town house.

Enter [*Oliver followed by Simon*], *Fellmonger*, [*Collier and others*]

SIMON Before me? I scorn thee, thou wattle-faced, singed pig!

OLIVER Pig? I defy thee! My uncle was a Jew and scorned the motion.

SIMON
I list not brook thy vaunts. Compare with me?
Thou spindle of concupiscence, 'tis well known
Thy first wife was a flax-wench.

OLIVER But such a flax-wench
Would I might never want at my most need,
Nor any friend of mine. My neighbours knew her;
Thy wife was but a hempen halter to her.

SIMON
Use better words, I'll hang thee in my year else,
Let whos' will choose thee afterwards.

GLOVER Peace, for shame, quench your great spirits. Do you not see his lordship?

HENGIST What, Master Simonides?

SIMON Simonides? What a fine name he has made of Simon! There, he's an ass that calls me Simon again, I'm quite out of love with't.

HENGIST Give me thy hand, I love thee and thy fortunes, I like a man that thrives.

SIMON I took a widow, my lord, to be the best piece of ground to thrive on, and by my faith, there's a young Simonides like a green onion peeping up already.

HENGIST
Th'ast a good lucky hand.

SIMON I have somewhat, sir.

HENGIST
But why to me is this election offered?
The choosing of a mayor goes by most voices.

SIMON True, sir, but most of our townsmen are so hoarse with drinking there's ne'er a good voice amongst 'em all that are now here in this company.

HENGIST
Are you content both to put all to these then,
To whom I liberally resign my interest
To prevent censure?

SIMON I speak first, my lord.

OLIVER Though I speak last, I hope I am not least. If he will cast away a town-born child, they may, 'tis but dying forty years or so before my time.

HENGIST
I'll leave you to your choice awhile.

ALL Your good lordship.

Exit Hengist

SIMON Look you, neighbours: view us both well e'er you be too hasty, let Oliver the fustian-weaver stand as fair as I do, and the devil give him good on't.

OLIVER I do, thou upstart callimoother, I do. 'Tis well known to thee I have been twice ale-cunner, thou

106–7 **other husband's** previous husband's
112 **glow-worm** luminary, used contemptuously
114 **fustian-weaver** weaver who works in fustian, a cloth made of cotton and flax (with a pun on 'a maker of bombast', i.e. fustian)
118 **town house** town hall
119–20 **wattle-faced, singed pig** a scorched pig having a fleshy appendage hanging from the mouth
121–2 **My . . . motion** i.e. he did not eat pork
123 **list not** care not to
125 **flax-wench** a flax-worker, hence a common woman (here used insultingly as 'whore', a meaning Oliver does not recognize)
128 **hempen halter** halter made of hemp (with a pun on 'hangman's noose')
129 **in my year** during his year as mayor
134 **Simonides** Middleton appears to be punning on the name of Simonides of Ceos, a Greek lyric poet and scholar.
144 **by most voices** by the majority of verbal votes
159 **callimoother** (manuscript text); callimoocher (quarto text). *OED* cites this play as having the only occurrence of this word, and they define it as 'a raw cadger, a greenhorn'. However, the context suggests that the word means 'usurper'.
160 **ale-cunner** inspector of ale

mushrump, that shot up in one night with lying with thy mistress.

SIMON Faith, thou art such a spiny bald-rib, all the mistresses in the town would never get thee up.

OLIVER I scorn to rise by a woman as thou didst. My wife shall rise by me.

SIMON The better for some of thy neighbours when you are asleep.

GLOVER I pray cease of your communication, we can do nothing else.

[The townspeople confer]

OLIVER *[aside]* I gave that Barber a fustian suit, and twice redeemed his cittern, he may remember me.

SIMON *[aside]* I fear no false measure but in that Tailor; the Glover and the Buttonmonger are both cocksure; that Collier's eye I like not. Now they consult, the matter is a-brewing. Poor Jill, my wife, lies longing for this news, 'twill make her a glad mother.

ALL A Simon, a Simon, a Simon, a Simon!

SIMON My good people, I thank you all.

OLIVER Wretch that I am! Tanner, thou hast curried favour.

SIMON I, curry? I defy thy fustian fume!

OLIVER But I will prove a rebel all thy year and raise up the seven deadly sins against thee! *Exit*

SIMON The deadly sins will scorn to rise with thee an they have any breeding, as commonly they are well brought up, 'tis not for every scab to be acquainted with 'em. But, leaving scabs, to you, good neighbours, lo, I bend my speech, first to say more than a man can say, I hold it not so fit to be spoken; but to say what man ought to say, there I leave you also. I must confess that your loves have chosen a weak and unlearned man, that I can neither write nor read you all can witness, yet not altogether so unlearned but I could set my mark to a bond, if I would be so simple, an excellent token of government. Cheer you then, my hearts, you have done you know not what. There's a full point, you must all cough and hem now.

ALL Hem, hem, hem, cough.

SIMON Now, touching our common adversary, the fustian weaver, who threateneth he will raise the deadly sins amongst us, which as I take it are seven in number, let 'em come, our town's big enough to hold 'em, we will not much disgrace it. Besides, a deadly sin will lie in a narrow hole. But when they think themselves safest and the web of their iniquity woven, with the horse-strength of my justice I'll break the looms of their concupiscence; and let the weaver go seek his shuttle. Here you may hem again, if you'll do me the favour.

ALL Cough and hem.

SIMON Why, I thank you, and it shall not go unrewarded. Now for seven deadly sins: first for Pride which always sits uppermost and will be placed without a church-warden, being a sin that is not like to be chargeable for the parish, I slip it over and think it not worthy of punishment. Now you all know that Sloth does not anything—this place you see requires wisdom—how can a man in conscience punish that which does nothing? Envy, a poor lean creature that eats raw liver, perhaps it pines to see me chosen, and that makes me the fatter with laughing. If I punish Envy then I punish mine own carcass, a great sin against authority. Wrath, the less we say, the better 'tis; a scurvy desperate thing it is that commonly hangs itself and saves justice many a halter by't. Now for Covetousness and Gluttony, I'll tell you more when I come out of mine office, I shall have time to try what they are. I'll prove 'em soundly, and if I find Covetousness and Gluttony to be directly sins, I'll bury one i'th' bottom of a chest, and th'other i'th' end of my garden. But, sirs, for lechery, I mean to tickle that home, nay I'm resolved upon't, I will not leave one whore in all the town.

BARBER Some of your neighbours may go seek their wives i'th' country then.

SIMON Barber, be silent, I will cut thy comb else. To conclude, I will learn the villainies of all trades—mine own I know already. If there be any knavery in the baker, I will bolt it out, if in the brewer, I will taste him thoroughly, and then piss out his iniquity in his own sink-hole. In a word, I will knock out all enormities like a bullock, and send the hide to my fellow tanners.

ALL A Simonides, a true Simonides indeed.

Enter Hengist [with a book] and Roxena

HENGIST
How now, how goes your choice?

161 **mushrump** mushroom, with a pun on 'rump', meaning both 'buttocks' and 'upstart'

161–8 **shot...asleep** a series of puns on male sexual arousal (also applied to women at 3.3.165–6).

163 **bald-rib** lean or bony fellow, literally having a 'bald rib'

172 **redeemed his cittern** bought back the cittern, an 'instrument of the guitar kind, but strung with wire, and played with a plectrum or quill... commonly kept in barbers' shops for the use of the customers' (*OED*)

176–7 **Poor...mother** i.e. he jokes on cravings in pregnancy

182 **fustian fume** display of anger

186–7 **commonly...up** playing on the proverbial idea that the devil is a gentleman

187 **scab** low, mean, or scurvy fellow

197 **full point** full stop, end

198 **cough and hem** cough and clear their throats in agreement

205 **hole** pun on 'vagina'

208 **shuttle** weaver's instrument

213–14 **placed...church-warden** seated without the permission of the lay officer of the church responsible for seating parishioners

214–15 **chargeable for the parish** charged to the financial responsibilty of the parish

219 **eats raw liver** Envy is presumably seen as a bird of prey; there may also be a conflation with the punishment of Prometheus.

227 **prove** test, implying that he will 'indulge in' them

231 **tickle that home** beat it out of town, with a pun on using the whores before sending them all away

235 **cut thy comb** humiliate

238 **bolt** sift, separate

240 **sink-hole** (manuscript text); suck-hole (quarto text): hole used for foul matter

TAILOR Here's he, my lord.

SIMON You may prove I am the man, I am bold to take the upper hand of your lordship a little, I'll not lose an inch of mine honour.

HENGIST
Hold, sirs, there's some few crowns to mend your feast,
Because I like your choice.

BARBER
Joy bless your lordship, we'll drink your health with trumpets.

SIMON
I, with sack-butts,
That's the more solemn drinking for my state,
No malt this year shall fume into my pate.
Exeunt [all but Hengist and Roxena]

HENGIST
Continues still that fervour in his love?

ROXENA
Nay, with increase, my lord; the flame grows greater,
Though he has learned a better art of late
To set a screen before it.

HENGIST Canst speak low?
[They speak aside; Roxena exits, and Hengist sits upstage, reading a book]

Enter Vortiger and Hersus

HERSUS
Heard every word, my lord.

VORTIGER Plainly?

HERSUS Distinctly.
The course I took was dangerous but not failing,
For I conveyed myself behind the hangings,
Even first before her entrance.

VORTIGER 'Twas well ventured.

HERSUS
I had such a woman's first and second longing in me
To hear how she would bear her mocked abuse
After she was half returned to privacy,
I could have fasted out an ember-week
And never thought of hunger to have heard her.
She fetched three short turns, I shall ne'er forget 'em,
Like an imprisoned lark that offers still
Her wing at liberty and returns checked,
So would her soul fain have been gone, and even hung
Flittering upon the bars of poor mortality,
Whichever as it offered, drove her back again.
Then came your holy Lupus and Germanus.

VORTIGER
O, two holy confessors.

HERSUS At whose sight
I could perceive her fall upon her breast
And cruelly afflict herself with sorrow—
I never heard a sigh till I heard hers—
Who after her confession, pitying her,
Put her into a way of patience,
Which now she holds, to keep it hid from you.
There's all the pleasure that I took in't now
When I heard that my pains was well remembered.
So with applying comforts and relief
They have brought it low now to an easy grief,
But yet the taste is not quite gone.

Enter Castiza

VORTIGER
Still fortune sits bettering our invitation.

HERSUS
Here she comes.

CASTIZA [*aside*]
Yonder's my lord, O I'll return again.
Methinks I should not dare to look on him. *Exit*

HERSUS
She's gone again.

VORTIGER It works the kindlier, sir.
Go and call her back. *[Exit Hersus]*
She winds herself
Into the snare so prettily, 'tis a pleasure
To set toils for her.

[Enter Hersus with Castiza]

CASTIZA [*aside*] He may read my shame
Now in my blush.

VORTIGER Come, you're so linked to holiness
So taken up with contemplative desires,
That the world has you, yet enjoys you not;
You have been weeping too.

CASTIZA Not I, my lord.

VORTIGER
Trust me, I fear you have, you're much to blame
An you should yield so to passion without cause.
Is not there time enough for meditation,
Must it lay title to your health and beauty,
And draw them into time's consumption too?
'Tis too exacting for a holy faculty.
[He discovers Hengist, seemingly asleep]
My lord of Kent? I pray wake him, captain,
He reads himself asleep sure.

HERSUS My lord?

HENGIST Your pardon, sir.

VORTIGER
Nay, I'll take away your book, and bestow't here—
Lady, you that delight in virgin stories
And all chaste works, here's excellent reading for you.
Make of that book as raised men make of favour
Which they grow sick to part from—and now, my lord,

244 **I am the man** I am more manly
250 **sack-butts** casks of sack, a white wine (with a pun on the meaning 'trumpets')
252 **malt** beer brewed from barley
260 **her** Castiza's
261 **a woman's...second longing** cravings during pregnancy
264 **ember-week** a one week period encompassing three fast days
266 **fetched** performed
292 **toils** snares
298 **passion** grief

You that have so conceitedly gone beyond me
And made such large use of a slender gift,
Which we never minded, I commend your thrift,
And for your building's name shall to all ages
Carry the stamp and impress of your wit,
It shall be called Thong Castle.

HENGIST How, my lord?
Thong Castle! There your highness quits me kindly.

VORTIGER
'Tis fit art should be known by her right name.
You that can spread my gift, I'll spread your fame.

HENGIST
I thank your grace for that, sir.

VORTIGER And loved lord,
So well we do accept thy invitation,
With all speed we'll set forward.

HENGIST Your love honours me.
Music. Exeunt

Finis Actus Tertius

4.1 *Incipit Actus Quartus*
Enter Vortiger, Castiza, two Ladies, Roxena, Devonshire, Stafford at one door; Simon and his brethren [holding a scabbard and dagger], at the other

SIMON
Lo, I the Mayor of Queenborough town by name,
With all my brethren, saving one that's lame,
Are come as fast as fiery mill-horse gallops
To meet thy grace, thy queen and thy fair trollops.
For reason of our coming do not look,
It must be done, I found it i'th' town book,
And yet not I myself, I scorn to read,
I keep a clerk to do these jobs for need.
And now expect a rare conceit before Thong Castle, so thee,
Reach me the thing to give the king, the other too, I prithee;
[He takes the scabbard and dagger from the brethren]
Now here they be for queen and thee, the gifts all steel and leather,
But the conceit of mickle weight, and here they're come together;
To show two loves must join in one, our town presents to thee
This gilded scabbard to the queen, this dagger unto thee.

VORTIGER
Forbear your tedious and ridiculous duties,
I hate 'em as I do the rotten roots of you.
You inconstant rabble, I have felt your fits;
Sheath up your bounty with your iron wits
And get you gone.
Music. Exeunt King, Queen, Ladies, and Lords

SIMON
Look, sir, is his back turned?

ALL 'Tis, 'tis.

SIMON
Then bless the good Earl of Kent, say I.
I'll have this dagger turned into a pie
And eaten up for anger, every bite on't,
And when that pie is new cut up by some rare cunning pieman,
They shall all lamentably sing, 'Put up thy dagger, Simon'.
Exeunt

4.2 *Oboes. [Enter] the King and his train, met by Hengist and Hersus; they salute and exeunt, while the banquet is brought forth. Music plays. Enter Vortiger, [Hengist], Hersus, Devonshire, Stafford, Castiza, Roxena, and two Ladies [and attendants]*

HENGIST
A welcome, mighty lord, may appear costlier,
More full of talk and toil, show and conceit,
But one more stored with thankful love and truth
I forbid all the sons of men to boast of.

VORTIGER
Why, that's a welcome that implies
The building plain but substantial;
Methinks it looks as if it mocked all ruin
Save that great masterpiece of consummation,
The end of time, which must consume even ruin
And eat that into cinders.

HENGIST
There's no brass would last your praise, my lord,
'Twould last beyond it and shame our durablest metal.

VORTIGER *[aside to Hersus]*
Hersus!

HERSUS *[aside to Vortiger]*
My lord?

VORTIGER *[aside to Hersus]*
This is the time I have chosen, here's a full meeting,
And here will I disgrace her.

310 **conceitedly** ingeniously, wittily
312 **minded** intended
313 **for** so that
315 **Thong Castle** In 1576 Lambarde noted that 'the ditch and ruins of this old castle do yet appear at Tong Mill within one quarter of a mile of the parish church there, and about so much northward from the highway between London and Canterbury: where you may see the water drained from the Castleditch, to serve the corn mill' (*A Perambulation of Kent*).
4.1.3 **mill-horse gallops** Simon's foolish error, as a mill-horse would plod slowly
4 **trollops** Simon's error for 'ladies'; also perhaps a desperate rhyme-word
7 **scorn to read** he is, of course, illiterate, but he assumes the attitude of an aristocrat who might scorn to read
14 **gilded scabbard** unintended sexual implication that is particularly embarrassing in view of the rape of Castiza

HERSUS [*aside to Vortiger*] 'Twill be sharp, my lord.
VORTIGER [*aside to Hersus*]
O 'twill be best, sir.
HERSUS [*aside to Vortiger*]
Why here's the earl, her father.
VORTIGER [*aside to Hersus*]
And, ay, the lord, her uncle, that's the height on't,
Invited both, o' purpose to rise sick,
Full of shame's surfeit.
HERSUS [*aside to Vortiger*]
And that's shrewd, by'r lady,
It ever sticks close to the ribs of honour,
Great men are never sound men after it,
It leaves some ache or other in their names still
Which their posterity feels at every weather.
VORTIGER [*aside to Hersus*]
Mark but the least presentment of occasion
As such times yields enough, and then mark me.
HERSUS [*aside to Vortiger*]
My observance is all yours, you know't, my lord.
[*Aside*] What careful ways some take t'abuse themselves!
But as there be assurers of men's goods
'Gainst storm or pirates, which gives venturers courage,
So such there must be to make up man's theft,
Or there would be no woman venturer left.
See, now they find their seats. What a false knot
Of amity he ties about her arm,
Which rage must part! In marriage 'tis no wonder
Knots knit with kisses are oft broke with thunder.
Music
Music, then I have done; I always learn
To give my betters place.
VORTIGER Where's Captain Hersus?
HERSUS
My lord.
VORTIGER
Sit, sit, we'll have a health anon
To all good services.
HERSUS [*sitting*] They're poor in these days;
They had rather have the cup than the health, my lord.
I sit wrong now; he hears me not, and most great men
Are deaf on that side.
Song
[SINGER]
If in music were a power
To breathe a welcome to thy worth,
This should be the ravishing hour
To vent her spirit's treasure forth.
HERSUS
Welcome, o welcome, in that word alone.
She'd choose to dwell and draw all parts to one.
VORTIGER
My lord of Kent, I thank you for this welcome,
It came unthought of in the sweetest language
That ever my soul relished.
HENGIST You are pleased, my lord,
To raise my happiness from slight deservings
To show what power's in princes: not in us
Ought worthy, 'tis in you that makes us thus.
I'm chiefly sad, my lord, your queen's not merry.
VORTIGER
So honour bless me, he has found the way
To my grief strangely. [*To Castiza*] Is there no delight?
CASTIZA
My lord, I wish not any, nor is't needful,
I am as I was ever.
VORTIGER That's not so.
CASTIZA
How? O my fears!
VORTIGER [*to Devonshire*]
When she writ maid, my lord,
You knew her otherwise.
DEVONSHIRE To speak but truth,
I never knew her a great friend to mirth,
Nor taken much with any one delight,
Though there be many seemly and honourable
To give content to ladies without taxing.
VORTIGER [*drinking*]
My lord of Kent, this to thy full desert
Which intimates thy higher flow to honour.
HENGIST
Which like a river shall return service
To the great master-fountain.
VORTIGER [*to the Ladies*] Where's your lord,
I missed him not 'til now, Lady, and yours?
No marvel then we were so out o'th' way
Of all pleasant discourse, they are the keys
Of human music. Sure, at their nativities
Great nature signed a general patent to 'em,
To take up all the mirth in a whole kingdom.
What's their employment now?
FIRST LADY May't please your grace,
We never are so far acquainted with 'em;
Nothing we know but what they cannot keep,
That's even the fashion of 'em all, my lord.
VORTIGER
It seems you have great faith though in their constancy,
And they in yours, you dare so trust each other.
SECOND LADY
Hope well we do, my lord, we have reason for't,
Because they say brown men are honestest,
But she's a fool will swear for any colour.

4.2.19 **shrewd** nasty, unpleasant
31 **woman venturer** whore
60 **writ maid** was unmarried, with an ironic pun on when she was virginal
65 **taxing** tiring (or causing censure?)
83 **brown . . . honestest** proverbial

VORTIGER
They would for yours.
SECOND LADY 'Troth, 'tis a doubtful question,
And I'd be loath to put mine to't, my lord.
VORTIGER
Faith, dare you swear for yourselves? That's a plain motion.
SECOND LADY
My lord?
VORTIGER
You cannot deny that with honour,
And since 'tis urged, I'll put you to't, in troth.
FIRST LADY
May't please your grace?
VORTIGER 'Twill please me wondrous well,
And here's a book, mine never goes without one,
She's an example to you all for purity.
Come swear, I have sworn you shall, that you never knew
The will of any man besides your husband's.
SECOND LADY
I'll swear, my lord, as far as my remembrance.
VORTIGER
How? Your remembrance! That were strange.
FIRST LADY
Your grace, hearing our just excuses, will not say so.
VORTIGER
Well, what's your just excuse? You're ne'er without some.
FIRST LADY
I'm often taken with a sleep, my lord,
The loudest thunder cannot waken me,
Not if a cannon's burden were discharged
Close by mine ear. The more may be my wrong;
There can be no infirmity, my lord,
That's more excusable in any woman.
SECOND LADY
And I'm so troubled with the mother too,
I have often called in help, I know not whom,
Three at once has been too weak to keep me down.
VORTIGER
I perceive there's no fastening. [*To Castiza*] Well fair one then
That ne'er deceives faith's anchor of her hold,
Come at all seasons. Here, be thou the star
To guide those erring women: show the way
Which I will make 'em follow. Why dost start,
Draw back and look so pale?
CASTIZA My lord?
VORTIGER Come hither,
Nothing but take that oath, thou'lt take a thousand.
A thousand, poor! A million, nay as many
As there be angels registers of oaths.
Why, look there, over-holy fearful chastity,
That sins in nothing but in too much niceness!
I'll begin first and swear for thee myself:
I know thee a perfection so unstained,
So sure, so absolute, I will not pant on't
But catch time greedily. By all these blessings,
That blows truth into fruitfulness, and those curses
That with their barren breaths blast perjury,
Thou art as pure as sanctity's best shrine
From all man's mixture, but what's lawful mine.
CASTIZA [*aside*]
O heaven forgive him, he's forsworn himself!
VORTIGER
Come, 'tis but going now my way.
CASTIZA [*aside*] That's bad enough.
VORTIGER I have cleared all doubts, you see.
CASTIZA
Good my lord, spare me.
VORTIGER How? It grows later now than so,
For modesty's sake, make more speed this way.
CASTIZA
Pardon me, my lord, I cannot.
VORTIGER What?
CASTIZA I dare not.
VORTIGER
Fail all confidence in thy weak kind forever!
DEVONSHIRE Here's a storm
Able to make all of our name inhumid
And raise 'em from their sleeps of peace and fame
To set the honour of their bloods right here
Hundred years after; a perpetual motion
Has their true glory been from seed to seed,
And cannot be choked now with a poor grain
Of dust and earth. We that remain, my lord,
Her uncle and myself, wild in this tempest,
As ever robbed man's peace, will undertake
Upon lives' deprivation, lands and honour,
And make one ruin serve our joys and yours.
CASTIZA [*aside*]
Why here's a height of misery never reached yet!
I lose myself and others.
DEVONSHIRE You may see
How much we lay in balance with your goodness,
And had we more, it went, for we presume
You cannot be religious and so vile.
CASTIZA
As to forswear myself: 'tis true, my lord,
I will not add a voluntary sin
To a constrained one. I confess, great sir,
The honour of your bed has been abused.
VORTIGER
O beyond patience!
CASTIZA Give me hearing, sir,
But far from my consent: I was surprised
By villains and so ravished.

85 **'Troth** In truth
105 **the mother** hysteria
121 **pant on't** i.e. pretend to be short-winded and unable to 'catch time'
122 **catch time** seize the opportunity
126 **mixture** sexual intercourse
135 **inhumid** buried or laid in a grave

VORTIGER Hear you that, sirs?
O cunning texture to enclose adultery!
Mark but what subtle veil her sin puts on,
Religion brings her to confession first,
Then steps in art to sanctify that lust.
'Tis likely you could be surprised.

CASTIZA My lord!

VORTIGER
I'll hear no more. Our guard, seize on those lords.
[*Guards seize Castiza, Devonshire, and Stafford*]

DEVONSHIRE
We cannot perish now too fast, make speed
To swift destruction, he breathes most accursed
That lives so long to see his name die first.
Exeunt [*Guards with Devonshire and Stafford*]

HERSUS [*aside*]
Ha, ha, here's no dear villany!

HENGIST Let him entreat, sir,
That falls in saddest grief for this event,
Which ill begins the fortune of this building, my lord.

ROXENA [*aside to Hersus*]
What if he should cause me to swear too, Captain?
You know, sir, I'm as far to seek in honesty
As the best here can be; I should be shamed too.

HERSUS [*aside to Roxena*]
Why, fool, they swear by that we worship not,
So you may swear your heart out, and ne'er hurt yourself.

ROXENA [*aside to Hersus*]
That was well thought on, I'd quite lost myself.

VORTIGER [*to Hengist*]
You shall prevail in noble suits, my lord,
But this, this shames the speaker.

HERSUS [*aside*] I'll step in now,
Though it shall be to no purpose. [*To Vortiger*] Good my lord,
Think on your noble and most hopeful issue,
Lord Vortiner, the prince.

VORTIGER A bastard, sir.
O that his life were in my fury now!

CASTIZA
That injury stirs my soul to swear the truth
Of his conception. Here I take the book, my lord:
By all the glorified rewards of virtue
And prepared punishments for consents in sin,
A queen's hard sorrow never supplied a kingdom
With issue more legitimate than Vortiner.

VORTIGER
Pish, this takes not out the stain of present shame though.
To be once good is nothing when it ceases,
Continuance crowns desert, she can ne'er go
For perfect honest that's not always so.
[*Aside to Hersus*] Beshrew this needless urging of this oath!
'T has justified her somewhat.

HERSUS [*aside to Vortiger*] To small purpose, sir.

VORTIGER
Amongst so many women not one here
Dare swear a simple chastity? Here's an age
To propagate virtue in! Since I have began't,
I'll shame you altogether, and so leave you.
My lord of Kent!

HENGIST Your highness?

VORTIGER That's your daughter?

HENGIST
Yes, my good lord.

VORTIGER Though I'm your guest today,
And should be less austere to you or yours,
In this life pardon me, I will not spare her.

HENGIST
Then her own goodness friend her; here she comes, my lord.

VORTIGER
The tender reputation of a maid
Makes up your honour, or else nothing can,
The oath you take is not for truth to man
But to your own white soul, a mighty task.
What dare you do in this?

ROXENA My lord, as much
As chastity can put a woman to.
I ask no favour, and t'approve the purity
Of what my habit and my time professes,
As also to requite all courteous censure,
Here I take oath I am as free from man
As truth from death, or sanctity from stain.

VORTIGER
O thou treasure that ravishes the possessor!
I know not where to speed so well again,
I'll keep thee while I have thee. Here's fountain
To spring forth princes and the seed of kingdoms.
Away with that infection of great honour
And those her leprous pledges, by her poison
Blemished and spotted in their fames forever!
Here will restore succession with true peace
And of pure virgin's grace the poor increase.
Music. Exeunt [*all but Hersus*]

HERSUS
Ha, ha, he's well provided now, here struck my fortune!
With what an impudent confidence she swore honest,
Having the advantage of the oath. The mischiefs
That peoples a lost honour, O they're infinite!
For as at a small breach in town or castle
When one has entrance, a whole army follows;
In woman, so abusively once known,
Thousands of sins has passage made with one:

158 **texture** cloth fabric; also 'composed story'

160–1 **Religion . . . lust** perhaps recalling Protestant attacks on Catholicism.

175 **lost myself** given myself away; also damned myself (with ironic logic)

Voice comes with troops, and they that entertain
A mighty potentate must receive his train.
Methinks I should not hear from fortune next
Under an earldom now; she cannot spend
A night so idly but to make a lord
With ease, methinks, and play. The Earl Kent
Is calm and smooth, like a deep dangerous water,
He has some secret way, I know his blood,
The grave's not greedier, nor hell's lord more proud.
Somewhat will hap, for this astonishing choice
Strikes pale the kingdom at which I rejoice. *Exit*

4.3

Oboes. Dumb Show: enter Lupus, Germanus, Devonshire and Stafford leading Vortiner; they seat him in the throne and crown him king. Enter Vortiger in great passion and submission; they neglect him, then Roxena expressing great fury and discontent; they lead out Vortiner, and leave Vortiger and Roxena; she subborns two Saxons to murder Vortiner; they swear performance and secrecy and exeunt with Roxena. Then Vortiger, left alone, draws his sword and offers to run himself thereon; enter Hersus and prevents him, then the Lords enter again and exit Hersus. Then is brought in the body of Vortiner in a chair dead, they all in amazement and sorrow take Vortiger, and upon his submission, restore him, swearing him against the Saxons. Then enter Hengist with diverse Saxons, Vortiger and the rest, with their swords drawn, threaten their expulsion; whereat Hengist amazed sends one to entreat a peaceable parley, which seeming to be granted by laying down their weapons, exeunt severally

Enter Raynulph

RAYNULPH
Of pagan blood a queen being chose,
Roxena hight, the Britons rose,
And Vortiner they crownèd King,
But she soon poisoned that sweet spring;
Then to rule they did restore
Vortiger, and him they swore
Against the Saxons. They, constrained,
Begged peace-treaty, and obtained;
And now in numbers equally
Upon the plain near Salisbury,
A peaceful meeting they decreen
Like men of love, no weapon seen;
But Hengist that ambitious lord
Full of guile corrupts his word,
As the sequel too well proves;
On that your eyes, on us your loves. *Exit*

4.4

Enter Hengist, Gentleman, and Saxons

HENGIST
If we let slip this opportuneful hour,
Take leave of fortune, certainty, or thought
Of ever fixing, we are loose at root,
And the least storm may rend us from the bosom
Of this land's hopes forever. But, dear Saxons,
Fasten we now, and our unshaken firmness
Will assure after-ages.

GENTLEMAN We are resolved, my lord.

HENGIST
Observed you not how Vortiger the king,
Base in submission, threatened our expulsion,
His arm held up against us? Is't not time
To make our best preventions? What should check
me?
He's perfected that great work in our daughter,
And made her Queen, she can ascend no higher,
Nor can the incessant flow of his love-praises,
Which yet still sways, take from that height it raises.
She's sure enough. What rests then that but I
Make happy mine own hopes; and policy
Forbids no way, noble or treacherous ended,
What best effects is of her best commended.
Therefore be quick, dispatch. Here every man
Receive into the service of his vengeance
An instrument of steel, which will unseen
Lurk like the snake under the innocent shade
Of a spread summer's leaf; and as great substance
Blocks itself up into less room in gold
Than other metals, and less burdensome,
So in the other hand lies all confined
Full as much death as ever changed mankind.
'Tis all the same time that a small watch shows
As great church dials, and as have as those.
Take heart, the commons loves us: those removed
That are his nerves, our greatness stands improved.

GENTLEMAN
Give us the word, my lord, and we are perfect.

HENGIST
That's true, the word, I lose myself,
'*Nemp your sexes*', it shall be that.

GENTLEMAN Enough, sir, then we strike.

HENGIST
But the King's mine, take heed you touch not him.

GENTLEMAN
We shall not be at leisure, never fear't,
We shall have work enough of our own, my lord.

HENGIST
They come; calm looks but stormy souls possess you.

4.3.2 **hight** named
11 **decreen** decree, i.e. set up
4.4.18 **ended** in its ends?
33 **perfect** fully prepared
35 **'*Nemp your sexes*'** Draw your knives; the Old English form would be 'Nimath eowre seax' (*OED*). Holinshed uses the form '*Nempt your sexes*'.

Enter Vortiger and British Lords, [unarmed]

VORTIGER
We see you keep your word in all points firm.

HENGIST
No longer may we boast of so much breath
As goes to a word making than of care
In the preserving of it when 'tis made.

VORTIGER
You're in a virtuous way, my lord of Kent,
And since we're both sides well met like sons of peace,
All other arms laid by in sign of favour
If our conditions be embraced—

HENGIST Th'are, th'are.

VORTIGER
We'll use no other but these only here.
[*Vortiger and Hengist embrace*]

HENGIST
Nemp your sexes!
[*The Saxons draw their swords on the British Lords*]

BRITISH LORDS Treason, treason!

HENGIST Follow to th' heart,
My trusty Saxons, 'tis your liberty,
Your wealth and honour!
[*Hengist seizes Vortiger*]
Soft, you're mine, my lord.

VORTIGER
Take me not basely when all sense and strength
Lies bound up in amazement at this treachery.
What devil hath breathed this everlasting part
Of falsehood into thee?

HENGIST Let it suffice,
I have you and will hold you prisoner
As fast as death holds your best props in silence.
We know the hard conditions of our peace,
Slavery or diminution, which we hate
With a joint loathing: may all perish thus
That seek to subjugate or lessen us.

VORTIGER
O you strange nooks of guile and subtlety,
Where man so cuninngly lies hid from man!
Who could expect such treason from the breast,
Such thunder from your voice, or take your pride
To imitate the fair uncertainty
Of a bright day that teems the sudden'st storm
When the world least expects one? But of all,
I'll never trust fair sky in man again;
Their's the deceitful weather. Will you heap
More guilt upon you by detaining me,
Like a cup taken after a full surfeit,
Even in contempt of health and heaven together?
What seek you?

HENGIST Ransom for your liberty
As I shall like of, or you ne'er obtain't.

VORTIGER
Here's a most headstrong dangerous ambition.
Sow you the seeds of your aspiring hopes
In blood and treason, and must I pay for 'em?
Have not I raised you to this height?

HENGIST My lord,
A work of mine own merit, since you enforce it.

VORTIGER
There's even the general thanks of all aspirers.
When they have all the honours kingdoms can impart
They write above it still their own desert.

HENGIST
I have writ mine true, my lord.

VORTIGER That's all their sayings.
Have I not raised your daughter to Queen?

HENGIST
Why, y'have the harmony of your pleasure for't,
Y'have crowned your own desires, what's that to me?

VORTIGER
And what will crown yours, sirs?

HENGIST Faith, things of reason:
I demand Kent.

VORTIGER Why, y'have the earldom on't.

HENGIST
The kingdom on't I meant, without control,
The full possession.

VORTIGER This is strange in you.

HENGIST
It seems you're not acquainted with my blood yet
To call this strange.

VORTIGER Never was King of Kent yet
But who was general king.

HENGIST
I'll be the first then, everything has beginning.

VORTIGER No less title?

HENGIST
Not if you hope for liberty, my lord.
So dear a happiness would be wronged by slighting.

VORTIGER
Well, take't, I resign't.

HENGIST Why, I thank your grace.

VORTIGER
Is your great thirst sufficed yet?

HENGIST Faith, my lord,
There's yet behind a pair of teeming sisters,
Norfolk and Suffolk, and I have done with you.

VORTIGER
Y'have got a fearful thirst, my lord, of late,
Howe'er you came by't.

HENGIST It behoves me then
For my blood's health to seek all means to quench it.

VORTIGER
Them, too?

HENGIST There's nothing will be abated sir.

50 **heart** puns on 'hart', imitating a hunting cry

95 **general king** king of England

96 **everything has beginning** proverbial, as in 'Everything has an end'; also, less widespread, 'Everything has its seed'.

Put your assurance in't.

VORTIGER You have the advantage; he whom
Fate captivates must yield to all; take 'em.

HENGIST
And you your liberty and peace, my lord,
With our best love and wishes. Here's an hour
Begins us Saxons in wealth, fame and power.
[Exeunt all but Vortiger]

VORTIGER
Are these the noblest fruits and fairest requitals
From works of our own raising?
Methinks the murder of Constantius
Speaks to me in the voice on't, and the wrongs
Of our late Queen slipped both into one organ.
Here is no safety for me but what's most doubtful;
The rank rout love me not, and the strength I had
This foul devouring treachery has demolished.
Enter Hersus
Ambition, hell, mine own undoing lust,
And all the brood of plagues conspire against me.

HERSUS My lord, he dies
That says it but yourself, were't that thief-king
That has so boldly stol'n his honours from you,
A treason that wrings tears from honest manhood.

VORTIGER
So rich am I now in thy love and pity
I feel no loss at all. But we must part,
My queen and I, to Cambria.

HERSUS My lord,
And I not named that have vowed lasting service
To life's extremest minute to your fortunes?

VORTIGER
Is my ruined fate blest with so dear a friend?

HERSUS
My lord, not space in earth nor breadth in sea
Shall divide me from you.

VORTIGER O faithful treasure,
All my lost happiness is made up in thee! *Exit*

HERSUS
I'll follow you through the world to cuckold you,
That's my way now. Everyone has his toy
While he lives here; some men delight in building
A trick of Babel and will ne'er be left,
Some in consuming what was raised with toiling,
Hengist in getting honour, I in spoiling. *Exit*
Finis Actus Quartus

Incipit Actus Quintus 5.1
Enter Simon, [Aminadab, his] Clerk, Glover,
Fellmonger, Grazier, [and others].
Music

SIMON Is not that rebel Oliver, the fustian-weaver, that traitor to my year, 'prehended yet?

CLERK Not yet, so please your worship.

SIMON Not yet, say'st thou? How durst thou say 'not yet' and see me present, thou malapert clerk that's good for nothing but to write and read? Is his loom seized on?

CLERK Yes, an it like your worship, and sixteen yards of fustian.

SIMON Good, let a yard be saved to mend me between the legs, the rest cut in pieces and given to the poor. 'Tis heretic fustian and should be burnt indeed, but being worn threadbare, the shame will be as great. How think you neighbours?

GLOVER
Greater methinks the longer it is worn
Where being once burnt, it can be burned no more.

SIMON
True, wise and most senseless.
Enter Footman
How now, sirrah,
What's he approaching here in dusty pumps?

CLERK
A footman, sir, to the great King of Kent.

SIMON
The King of Kent? Shake him by the hand for me.
Footman, thou art welcome; lo, my deputy shakes
thee.
Come when my year's out and I'll do't myself.
An't 'twere a dog come from the King of Kent,
I keep those officers would shake him, I trow.
And what's the news with thee, well-stewed footman?

FOOTMAN
The King, my master—

SIMON Hah?

FOOTMAN With a few Saxons
Intend this night to make merry with you.

SIMON
Merry with me? I should be sorry else, fellow,
And take it in evil part, so tell Kent's king.
Why was I chosen mayor but that great men
Should make merry with me? There's a jest indeed.
Tell him I looked for't, and me much he wrongs
If he forget Simon that cut out his thongs.

FOOTMAN
I'll run with your worship's answer. *Exit*

119 **rout** common people
129 **Cambria** Latin name for Wales
139 **A trick of Babel** a visionary scheme, with an allusion to the Biblical tower of Babel ruined by God as punishment for over-reaching (as Vortiger's castle will be ruined with wildfire in 5.2)
5.1.9 **yard** phallic quibble
10–11 **'Tis heretic fustian** Traditionally, fustian was woven by Puritans, thus the cloth is heretical to Protestants such as Simon.
16 **senseless** Simon's error for 'sensible'
17 **dusty pumps** soiled shoes (pumps were a type of shoe worn by servants)
24 **well-stewed** drunken

SIMON That fellow will be roasted against supper, he's half enough already, his brows baste him. The King of Kent! The King of Christendom shall not be better welcome to me, for you must imagine now neighbours this is the time that Kent stands out of Christendom, for he that's King there now was never christened.

This for your more instruction I thought fit,
That when you're dead you may teach your children wit.

Clerk!

CLERK
At your worship's elbow.

SIMON I must turn you from the hall into the kitchen tonight. Give order that twelve pigs be roasted yellow, nine geese and some three larks for piddling-meat, but twenty woodcocks. I'll bid all my neighbours. Give charge the mutton come in all blood raw, that's infidel meat; the King of Kent's a pagan and must be served so. And let those officers that seldom or never go to Church bring't in, 'twill be well taken. Run. *[Exit Clerk]*

Come hither you now, take all the cushions down and thwack 'em soundly after my feast of millers, for their buttocks has left a peck of flour in 'em. Beat 'em carefully o'er a bolting-hutch, there'll be enough for a pan pudding as your dame will handle it. Then put fresh water into both the bough-pots, and burn a little juniper i'th' hall chimney. Like a beast as I was, I pissed out the fire last night and never thought of the King's coming.

[Enter Clerk]

How now, returned so quickly?

CLERK Please your worship, there's a certain company of players.

SIMON Hah, players?

CLERK Country comedians, interluders, sir, desires your worship's leave and favour to enact in the town hall.

SIMON I'th' town hall! 'Tis ten to one I never grant it. Call 'em before my worship. If my house will not serve their turn, I would fain see the proudest he lend a barn to 'em.

Enter [two] Cheaters, [a Clown, and others]

Now sirs, are you comedians?

SECOND CHEATER We are anything sir: comedians, tragedians, tragicomedians, comi-tragedians, pastoralists, humorists, clownists and satirists. We have 'em, sir, from the smile to the laugh, from the laugh to the handkerchief.

SIMON You are very strong i'th' wrists. And shall these good parts you're endowed withal be cast away among pedlars and malt-men?

FIRST CHEATER For want of better company, an't please your worship.

SIMON What think you of me, my masters? Have you audacity enough to play before so high a person? Will not my countenance daunt you? For if you play before me I shall often look at you, I give you that warning beforehand; take it not ill, my masters, I shall laugh at you, and truly when I'm least offended with you. My humour 'tis, but be not you abashed.

FIRST CHEATER Sir, we have played before a lord ere now, though we be country actors.

SIMON A lord? Ha, ha, you'll find it a harder thing to please a mayor.

FIRST CHEATER We have a play wherein we use a horse.

SIMON Fellows, you use no horseplay in my house, my rooms are rubbed; keep it for hackney men.

FIRST CHEATER We will not offer't to your worship, sir.

SIMON Give me a play without a beast, I charge you.

SECOND CHEATER That's hard without a cuckold or a drunkard.

SIMON O those beasts are often the best men i'th' parish and must not be kept out. But which is your merriest play now? That would I harken after.

SECOND CHEATER Why, your worship shall hear the names all o'er and take your choice.

SIMON And that's plain dealing, trust me. Come, begin, sir.

SECOND CHEATER *The Whirligig, The Whibble, Carwidgeon.*

SIMON Hey-day, what names are these?

SECOND CHEATER New names of late. *The Wild Goose Chase.*

SIMON I understand thee now.

SECOND CHEATER *Gull upon Gull.*

SIMON Why, this is somewhat plain yet.

SECOND CHEATER *Woodcock of our Side.*

35 **his brows baste him** i.e., he's perspiring

45 **piddling-meat** trifling or insignificant meat

46 **woodcocks** a type of bird much valued for its flavor, with an unintentional pun on woodcock as 'fool'

54 **bolting-hutch** hutch used to store sifted meal

56 **bough-pots** pots to hold boughs or flowers

70–1 **comedians . . . comedians** Simon uses the word to mean 'actors'; the Second Cheater uses it to mean 'players of comedy'

71–3 **We . . . satirists** Compare *Hamlet*, 2.2.396–9, 'the best actors in the world, either for tragedy, comedy, history, pastoral, pastoral-comical, historical-pastoral, tragical-historical, tragical-comical-historical-pastoral'.

78 **malt-men** men who make malt (beer)

91 **mayor** puns on 'mare'

94 **rubbed** polished by rubbing

hackney men men who keep or attend to a hackney horse or carriage

106 ***The Whirligig, The Whibble, Carwidgeon*** These play titles, which mean, respectively, 'whirling toy', 'quibble', and 'pun' ('Carwidgeon' is a variant on 'carriwitchet' for the sake of a pun on 'widgeon', the first bird joke) and those at 5.1.110, 5.1.112, and 5.1.114 are apparently nonsense titles used by the Cheaters to convince Simon of their repertory. No plays with these titles are extant.

108 ***The Wild Goose Chase*** punning allusion to Fletcher's play of the same name

110 ***Gull upon Gull*** a nonsense title that puns on 'gull' as fool

112 ***Woodcock of our Side*** A nonsense title that puns on 'woodcock' as fool; a work of this title is referred to by John Taylor the Water Poet in the preface to his *Sir Gregory Nonsense His News from No Place* of 1622.

SIMON Get you farther off then.

FIRST CHEATER *The Cheater and the Clown.*

SIMON Is that come up again? That was a play when I was prentice first.

SECOND CHEATER Ay, but the Cheater has learned more tricks since, sir, and gulls the Clown with new additions.

SIMON Then is Clown a coxcomb; which is he?

CLOWN I am the Clown, sir.

SIMON He's too fair to make the people laugh.

FIRST CHEATER Not as he may be dressed, sir.

SIMON Faith, dress him how you will, I'll give him that gift, he'll never look half scurvily enough. O, the clowns that I have seen in my time! The very peeping out of 'em would have made a young heir laugh if his father had lain a-dying. A man undone in law the day before, the saddest case that can be, might for his twopence have burst himself with laughing and ended all his miseries. Here was a merry world, my masters! Some talk of things of state, of puling stuff, there's nothing in a play to a clown's part, if he have the grace to hit on't, that's the thing indeed. The king shows well but he sets off the king.
But not the King of Kent, I mean not so.
The king I mean is one I do not know.

SECOND CHEATER
Your worship speaks with safety like a rich man,
And for your finding fault our hope is greater,
Neither with him the Clown, nor me the Cheater.

SIMON
Away then, shift, Clown, to thy motley crupper
We'll see 'em first, the King shall after supper.
Exeunt Cheaters [*and Clown*]

GLOVER I commend your worship's wisdom in that, Master Mayor.

SIMON Nay, 'tis a point of justice, an't be well examined, not to offer the king worse than I'll see myself, for a play may be dangerous, I have known a great man poisoned in a play.

GLOVER What, have you, Master Mayor?

SIMON But to what purpose, many times I know not.

FELLMONGER Methinks they should destroy one another so.

SIMON No, no, he that's poisoned is always made privy to it; that's one good order they have amongst 'em.
A shout within
What joyful throat is that, Aminadab? What is the meaning of this cry?

CLERK
The Rebel's ta'en.

SIMON
Oliver the Puritan?
Oliver is brought in

CLERK
Oliver, Puritan and fustian-weaver altogether.

SIMON
Fates, I thank you for this victorious day!
Bonfires of pease-straw burn, let the bells ring.

GLOVER
There's two amending, sir, you know they cannot.

SIMON
'Las, the tenor's broken; ring forth the treble,
I'm overcloyed with joy, welcome thou rebel.

OLIVER
I scorn thy welcome!

SIMON
Art thou yet so stout?
Wilt thou not stoop for grace? Then get thee out.

OLIVER
I was not born to stoop but to my loom;
That seized upon, my stooping days are doon.
In plain terms, if thou hast anything to say to me, send me away quickly. This is not biding place, I understand there's players in the house, dispatch me, I charge thee, in the name of all the brethren.

SIMON
Nay, now proud rebel, I will make thee stay,
And to thy greater torment see the play.

OLIVER
O Devil, I conjure thee by Amsterdam!

SIMON
Our word is past,
Justice may wink awhile but see at last.
The play begins; hold, stop him, stop him.
[*Trumpet*]

OLIVER O, O, that profane trumpet!

SIMON
Set him down there, I charge you, officers.

OLIVER
I'll hide mine ears, and stop mine eyes.

SIMON
Down with his golls, I charge you.

OLIVER
O tyranny! Revenge it, tribulation!

SIMON
For rebels there are many deaths, but sure the only way
To execute a Puritan is seeing of a play.

OLIVER
O, I shall swoon.

SIMON
But if thou dost, to fright thee

114 ***The Cheater and the Clown*** a nonsense title that, ironically sums up the play, or trick, being performed for Simon, who unwittingly plays the role of the Clown

126 **young heir laugh** the joke is that it would not take much for the young heir to laugh at this

130 **a merry world, my masters!** Middleton's pun on the title of his play, *A Mad World, My Masters*

131 **puling** crying

133–4 **he . . . king** i.e. the clown puts the King out of consideration

158 **Bonfires . . . ring** Royal events or anniversaries were marked with bonfires and bell-ringing.

169 **brethren** brothers, i.e. fellow citizens

172 **conjure** presumably both 'solemnly call upon' and 'command by incantation' (as a spirit)

Amsterdam centre for Puritan refugees

175 **profane trumpet** trumpets were played before and during play performances

178 **golls** hands

180–1 **the . . . play** Puritans considered plays sinful, thus Oliver thinks this play will cause his death and damnation.

A player's boy shall bring thee aqua vitae.

Enter First Cheater [*in costume*]

OLIVER
O, I'll not swoon at all for't, though I die.

SIMON
Peace, here's a rascal, list and edify.

FIRST CHEATER I say still he's an ass that cannot live by his wits.

SIMON What a bold rascal's this? He calls us all asses at first dash. Sure, none of us lives by our wits, neighbours, unless it be Oliver the Puritan.

OLIVER I scorn as much to live by my wits as the proudest on you all.

SIMON Why, you are are an ass for company, Oliver, and so hold your prating.

Enter Second Cheater [*in costume*]

SECOND CHEATER Fellows in arms, welcome! The news, the news?

SIMON 'Fellows in arms', quoth a? He may well call 'em fellows in ams for they are all out o'th' elbows.

FIRST CHEATER Be lively, my heart, be lively, the booty's in hand. He's but a fool of a yeoman's eldest son, he comes balanced on both sides, bully, he's going to pay rent with th'one pocket, and buy household stuff with th'other.

SECOND CHEATER 'And if this be his last day, my chuck, he shall forfeit his lease', quoth th'one pocket, 'and eat his meat i'th' old wooden platters', quoth th'other.

SIMON Faith, then he's not so wise as he ought to be, if he let such tatterdemalions get th'upper hand on him.

Enter Clown [*in costume*]

FIRST CHEATER He comes, he comes.

SECOND CHEATER Ay, but do you mark how he comes, small to our comfort, with both his hands in's pockets? How is't possible to pick a lock when the key's o'th' inside door?

SIMON Ay, here's the part now, neighbours, that carries away the play: if the clown miscarry, farewell my hopes forever, the play's spoiled.

CLOWN They say there's a foolish thing called cheaters abroad that will gull any yeoman's son of his purse, and laugh in's face like an Irishman. I would fain meet with one of those cheaters. I'm in as good state to be gulled now as ever I was in my life, for I have two purses at this time about me, and I'd fain be acquainted with that rascal that would but take one of 'em now.

SIMON Faith, thou mayst be acquainted with two or three that will do their good wills, I warrant you.

FIRST CHEATER
That way's too plain, too easy, I'm afraid.

SECOND CHEATER
Come, come, sir, your familiar cheats takes best,
They show like natural things and least suspected.
Give me a round shilling quickly.

FIRST CHEATER
'Twill but fetch one of his hands neither, if it take.

SECOND CHEATER
Thou art so covetous, let's have one at first, prithee.
There's time enough to fetch out th'other after.

[*The First Cheater gives him a coin*]

Thou liest, 'tis lawful money, current money.

They draw

FIRST CHEATER
Ay, so is copper in some country, country sir.

CLOWN
Here's a fray towards, but I'll hold my hands,
Let whos' will part 'em.

SECOND CHEATER Copper! I defy thee,
And now I shall disprove thee. Look you, sir,
Here comes an honest yeoman's son o'th' country,
A man of judgement.

[*The Cheaters doff their caps*]

CLOWN Pray be covered, sir, I have eggs in my cap and cannot put it off.

FIRST CHEATER [*to Second Cheater*]
Will you be tried by him?

SECOND CHEATER I am content, sir.

SIMON They look rather as if they would be tried next sessions.

FIRST CHEATER [*to the Clown*]
Pray give your judgement of this piece of coin, sir.

CLOWN Nay, an't be coin you strive about, let's see't, I love to handle money.

FIRST CHEATER
Look on't well, sir.

They pick [*the Clown's*] *pocket*

SECOND CHEATER Let him do his worst, sir.

CLOWN You'd need to wear cut cloths, gentlemen, you're both so choleric.

SECOND CHEATER
Nay, rub it and spare't not, sir.

CLOWN
Now by this silver, gentlemen, 'tis good money,
Would you'd a hundred of 'em.

SECOND CHEATER We hope well, sir. [*Aside to First Cheater*]

183 **aqua vitae** alcoholic spirits used to revive
198 **out o'th' elbows** wearing ragged clothes
200 **yeoman's** freeholding farmer's
201 **bully** a term of endearment
205–6 **eat . . . platters** a proverbial expression suggesting he will live in poverty
208 **tatterdemalions** persons in ragged clothing
235 **hold my hands** i.e. keep my hands in my pockets
244 **sessions** see note on 2.4.117
249–50 **You'd . . . choleric** Choler induces heat, and the ornamental cuts in the cloth would afford ventilation.

Th'other pocket now and we are made men.

Exeunt [First and Second Cheaters]

SIMON O neighbours, I begin to be sick to see this fool so cozened, I would make the case mine own.

CLOWN Still would I fain meet with this thing called cheaters.

SIMON A whoreson coxcomb, they have met with thee! I can endure him no longer with patience.

CLOWN O my rent, my whole year's rent!

SIMON A murrain on you, this makes us landlords stay so long without our money.

CLOWN The cheaters have been here.

SIMON A scurvy hobby-horse that could not leave his money with me, having such a charge about him. A pox on thee for an ass! Thou play a clown? I will commit thee for offering on't. Officer, away with him.

[An Officer seizes the Clown]

CLOWN With me? An't please your worship, 'twas my part.

SIMON But 'twas as foolish a part as ever thou played'st in thy life, and I'll make thee smoke for't. I'll teach thee to understand to play a clown, thou shalt know every man is not born to't, look thee. Away with him quickly, he'll have the other pocket, I hear him say't with mine own ears. See, he comes in another disguise to cheat thee again.

[Enter Second Cheater]

Exit [Officer with] Clown

SECOND CHEATER Pish, whither goes he now? He spoils all my part.

SIMON Come on, sir, let's see what your knaveship can do at me now.

He throws off his gown, discovering his doublet with a satin forepart and a canvas back

You must think now, rascal, you have no fool in hand, the fool I have committed for playing the part so like an ass.

SECOND CHEATER What's here to do?

GLOVER *[to Simon]* Fie, good sir, come away. Will your worship base yourself to play a clown?

SIMON Away, brother, 'tis not good to scorn anything, a man does not know what he may come to. Everyone knows his ending but not his beginning. Proceed, varlet, do thy worst, I defy thee.

SECOND CHEATER I beseech your worship, let's have our own clown. I know not how to go forward else.

SIMON Knave, play out thy part with me, or I'll lay thee by the fool all the days of thy life else. Why, how now, my masters, who's that laughed now? Cannot a man of worship play the clown a little for his pleasure but he must be laughed at? Do you know who I am? Is the King's Deputy of no better account amongst you? Was I chosen to be laughed at? Where's my clerk?

CLERK Here, an't please your worship.

SIMON Take a note of all those that laugh at me, that when I have done, I may commit 'em. Let me see who dares do't now, and now to you once again, Sir Cheater. Look you, here's my purse-strings; I defy you.

SECOND CHEATER Good sir, tempt me not, my part is so written that I should cheat your worship an you were my father.

SIMON I should have much joy to have such a rascal to my son.

SECOND CHEATER Therefore I beseech your worship pardon me, the part has more knavery than when your worship saw it at first, I assure you, you'll be deceived in't, sir, the new additions will take any man's purse in Kent or Christendom.

SIMON An thou canst take mine now, I'll give't thee freely; and do thy worst, I charge you, as thou'lt answer't.

SECOND CHEATER
I shall offend your worship.

SIMON Knave, do't quickly.

SECOND CHEATER Say you so? Then, there's for you and here's for me then.

[He] throws meal in [Simon's] face, takes his purse and exits

SIMON
O bless me neighbours, I am in a fog,
A cheater's fog, I can see nobody.

GLOVER Run, follow him, officers. *[Exit Clerk and Officers]*

SIMON Away, let him go, for he'll have all your purses and he come back. A pox of your new additions! They spoil all the plays that ever they come in! The old way had no such roguery in't, remember! Call you this a merry comedy when as a man's eyes are put out? Brother Honeysuckle?

GRAZIER What says your sweet worship?

SIMON I make you my deputy to rule the town 'til I can see again, which I hope will be within nine days at furthest. Nothing grieves me but that I hear Oliver the rebel laugh at me. A pox of your Puritan face, this will make you in love with plays ever hereafter, we shall not keep you from 'em now.

OLIVER In sincerity, I was never better pleased and edified at an exercise.

SIMON Neighbours, what colour is that rascal's dust he threw in my face?

GLOVER 'Tis meal, an't please your worship.

SIMON Meal, I'm glad on't; I'll hang the Miller for selling on't.

GLOVER Nay, ten to one the Cheater never bought it, he stole it certainly.

SIMON Why then, I'll hang the Cheater for stealing on't and the Miller for being out of the way when he did it.

FELLMONGER Ay, but your worship was in the fault yourself, you bade him do his worst.

SIMON His worst, that's true, but he has done his best, the rascal, for I know not how a villain could put out a man's eyes better, and leave 'em in's head, than he has done.

260 **coxcomb** fool's cap
263 **murrain** plague
272 **make thee smoke** give you a roasting
289–90 **Everyone . . . beginning** inverted proverb
329 **Honeysuckle** a term of endearment
338 **exercise** religious service

Enter Clerk

CLERK Where's my master's worship?

SIMON How now, Aminadab? I hear thee though I see thee not.

CLERK You're sure cozened, sir, they are all cheaters professed. They have stolen three spoons too, and the Clown took his heels with all celerity. They only take the name of country comedians to abuse simple people, with a printed play or two they bought at Canterbury last week for sixpence, and which is worst, they speak but what they list on't and fribble out the rest.

SIMON
Here's no abuse to th' commonwealth,
If a man could see to look into't.
But mark the cunning of these cheating slaves,
First they make justice blind, then play the knaves.

Enter Hengist

GLOVER 'Ods precious brother, the King of Kent's new lighted.

SIMON
The King of Kent? Where is he, where is he?
O, that I should live to this day, and yet not live to see
to bid him welcome!

HENGIST
Now where's Simonides, our friendly host?

SIMON
As blind as one that had been foxed a se'night.

HENGIST Why, how now, man?

SIMON
Faith, practising a clown's part for your grace,
I have practised both mine eyes out.

HENGIST
What need you practise that?

SIMON A man's never too old to learn: your grace will say so when you hear all the villainy. The truth 'tis, my lord, I meant to have been merry, and now 'tis my luck to weep water and oatmeal, but I shall see again at suppertime, I make no doubt on't.

Enter Gentleman

HENGIST
This is strange to me, sirs.

GENTLEMAN Arm, arm, my lord!

HENGIST
What's that?

GENTLEMAN With swiftest speed, if ever
You'll behold the queen, your daughter, alive again.

HENGIST
Roxena?

GENTLEMAN
They're besieged.
Aurelius Ambrose and his brother, Uther,
With numbers infinite in Britain's forces,
Beset their castle, and they cannot 'scape
Without your speedy succour.

HENGIST
For her safety I'll forget food and rest. Away!

SIMON I hope your grace will hear the jest afore you go.

HENGIST
The jest! Torment me not. Set forward.

SIMON I'll follow you to Wales with a dog and a bell, but I'll tell't you.

HENGIST Unreasonable folly! *Exit with Gentleman*

SIMON
'Tis sign of war when great ones disagree.
Look to the rebel well till I can see,
And when my sight's recovered, I'll have his eyes pulled
out for a fortnight.

OLIVER
Hang thee! Mine eyes? A deadly sin or two
Shall pluck 'em out first, that's my resolution.

Exeunt

5.2

Enter Aurelius and Uther with Soldiers

UTHER
My lord, the castle is so fortified.

AURELIUS
So fortified? Let wildfire ruin it,
That his destruction may appear to him
I'th' figure of heaven's wrath at the last day.
That murderer of our brother haste away.
I'll send my heart no peace till't be consumed.

[His men set fire to the castle]

[Enter] Vortiger [and] Hersus, on the walls

UTHER
There he appears again, behold, my lord.

AURELIUS
O, that the zealous fire on my soul's altar,
To the high birth of virtue consecrated,
Would fit me with a sighting now to blast him,
Even as I look upon him.

UTHER Good my lord,
Your anger is too noble and too precious
To waste it on guilt so foul as his.
Let ruin work her will.

VORTIGER Begirt all round?

HERSUS
All, all, my lord, 'tis folly to make doubt on't.
You question things that horror long agone
Resolved us on.

VORTIGER Give me leave, Hersus, though.

HERSUS
Do what you will, sir, question 'em again,
I'll tell 'em over to you.

VORTIGER
Not so, sir, I will not have 'em told again.

363 **fribble** stammer

368 **'Ods precious brother** God's precious brother (an oath)

374 **foxed** deluded

395 **with a dog and a bell** the proverbial companions of a blind beggar

5.2.2 **Let wildfire ruin it** This story appears in Holinshed's *Chronicles*. 'Wildfire' is a 'composition of highly inflammable substances readily ignited and very difficult to extinguish' (*OED*).

14 **Begirt** surrounded

HERSUS
It rests then.

VORTIGER
That's an ill word put in when thy heart knows
There is no rest at all, but torment making.

HERSUS
True, my heart finds it that sits weeping blood now
For poor Roxena's safety. You'll confess, my lord,
My love to you has brought me to this danger?
I could have lived like Hengist, King of Kent,
And London, York, Lincoln and Winchester
Under the power of my command: the portion
Of my most desert—it fell to't—enjoyed now
By lesser deservers.

VORTIGER Say you so, sir?
And you'll confess, since you begin confession—
A thing I should have died before I'd thought on—
I'm out of your love's debt, i'th' same condition.
You've marred the fashion of your affection utterly
In your own wicked counsel; there you paid me.
You could not but in conscience love me afterward,
You were bound to do't, as men in honesty
That vitiate virgins to give dowries to 'em.
My faith was pure before to faithful woman.

HERSUS
My lord, my counsel—

VORTIGER 'Tis the map now spread
That shows me all my miseries and discovers
Strange new-found ruin to me; all these objects
That in a dangerous ring circle my safety,
Are yours, and of your fashioning.

HERSUS
Death, mine? Extremity breeds the wildness of a desert
Into your soul, and since, you've lost your thankful-
ness,
Which is the noblest part in king or subject,
My counsel do't.

VORTIGER Why, I'll be judged by those
That knit death in their brows, and think me now
Not worthy the acception of a flattery.
Most of those faces smiled when I smiled once.
[*To Aurelius*] My lord.

UTHER Reply not, brother.

VORTIGER Seeds of scorn,
I mind you not; I speak to those alone
Whose force makes yours a power, which else were
none.
Show me the main food of your hate, my lords,
Which cannot be the murder of Constantius
That crawls in your revenges, for your love
Was violent long since that.

GENTLEMAN And had been still,
If from that pagan woman thou'dst slept free;
But when thou fled'st from heaven we fled from thee.

VORTIGER [*to Hersus*]
Was this your counsel now?

HERSUS Mine? 'Twas the counsel
Of your own lust and blood; your appetite knows it.

VORTIGER [*to Aurelius*]
May thunder strike me from these walls, my lord,
And leave me many leagues off from your eyes,
If this be not the man whose Stygian soul
Breathed forth that counsel to me, and sole plotter
Of all these false injurious disgraces
That have abused the virtuous patience
Of our religious Queen.

HERSUS A devil in madness!

VORTIGER
Upon whose life I swear there sticks no stain
But what's most wrongful, and where now she thinks
A rape dwells in her honour, only I
Her ravisher was, and his the policy.

AURELIUS
Inhuman practice!

VORTIGER Now you know the truth,
Will his death serve your fury?

HERSUS Mine? My death?

VORTIGER
Will't do't?

HERSUS What if it would?

VORTIGER Say, will it do't?

HERSUS
Say they should, say it would?

VORTIGER Why then, it must.

HERSUS
It must?

VORTIGER
It shall. Speak but the words, my lord,
He shall be yielded up.

HERSUS I, yielded up?
My lords, believe him not, he cannot do't.

VORTIGER Cannot?

HERSUS
'Tis but a false and base insinuation
For his own life, and like his late submission.

VORTIGER
O sting to honour, alive or dead thou goest
For that word's rudeness only.
[*He*] *stabs* [*Hersus*]

GENTLEMAN See, sin needs
No more destruction then it breeds
In its own bosom.

VORTIGER Such another brings him.

HERSUS
What, has thy wild rage stamped a wound upon me?
I'll send one to thy soul shall never heal for't.

VORTIGER
How, to my soul?

HERSUS It shall be thy master torment,

39 **vitiate** corrupt

Both for the pain and the everlastingness.
VORTIGER Ha, ha.
HERSUS
Dost laugh? Take leave on't, all eternity
Shall never see thee do so much again.
Know thou art a cuckold.
VORTIGER What?
HERSUS You change too soon, sir.
Roxena, whom thou'st raised to thine own ruin,
She was my whore in Germany.
VORTIGER Burst me open;
Your violence is whirlwinds!
HERSUS Hear me out first.
For her embrace, which yet my flesh sits warm in,
I was thy friend and follower.
VORTIGER Deafen me,
Thou most imperious noise that starts the world!
HERSUS
And to serve our lust, I practised with thee
Against thy virtuous queen.
VORTIGER
Bane to all comforts!
HERSUS Whose faithful sweetness,
Too precious for thy blood, I made thee change
For love's hypocrisy.
VORTIGER Insufferable!
HERSUS
Only to make my way to pleasure
Fearless, free and fluent.
VORTIGER Hell's trump is in that throat.
HERSUS
It shall sound shriller.
VORTIGER I'll dam it up with death first.
I am at thy heart, I hope.
HERSUS Hold out breath
And I shall find thee quickly.
[Vortiger and Hersus] stab each other [and continue fighting;] Roxena enters in fear
ROXENA O for succour!
Who's near me? Help me, save me, the flame follows me,
It's the figure of poor Vortiner the prince
Whose life I took by poison.
VORTIGER I'll tug out thy soul here.
HERSUS
Do, monster!
ROXENA Vortiger!
VORTIGER Monster!
ROXENA My lord!
VORTIGER
Slave!
ROXENA
Hersus, Hersus!
HERSUS Murderer!
ROXENA My lord!
VORTIGER
Toad pagan!
HERSUS Viper Christian!
ROXENA Hear me, help me!
My love, my lord, I'm scorched! What, all in blood?
O happy men, that ebb shows you're near falling.
Have you chose that way yourselves rather to die
By your own swords than feel fire's keener torment,
And will not kill me that most needs that pity?
Captain, my lord, send me some speedier death
And one less painful; I have a woman's sufferings.
O think upon't: go not away so easily
And leave the harder conflict to my weakness.
Most wretched, I'm not worth so much destruction
As would destroy me quickly, and turn back
I cannot. O 'tis here, my lord, 'tis here!
Hersus, look up, if not to succour me,
To see me yet consumed. O what is love
When life is not regarded?
VORTIGER *[to Hersus]*
What strength is left I'll fix upon thy throat.
HERSUS I have some force yet.
Both stab; Hersus falls [and dies]
ROXENA
No way to 'scape. Is this the end of glory,
Doubly beset with enemies' wrath and fire?
See, for an arm of lust, I'm now embraced
With one that will destroy me, where I read
The horror of dishonest actïons.
It waxes nearer now, rivers and fountains!
Guile and dissemblance! Tears were now a blessing.
It sucks away my breath! I cannot give
A curse to sin, and hear't out whilst I live.
O help, help, help!
She falls [into the flames and dies]
VORTIGER Burn, burn, now I can tend thee.
Take time with her in torments, call her life
Afar off to thee, dry up her strumpet blood
And hardly parch the skin, let one heat strangle her,
Another fetch her to her sense again,
And the worst pain be only her reviving.
Follow her eternally. Give her not o'er
But in a bitter shape. I shall be cold
Before thy rage reach me. O mystical harlot,
Thou hast thy full due! Whom lust crowned Queen before,
Flames crown her now for a triumphant whore,

110 **trump** trumpet
121 As in 3.1, Roxena's speech on the consequences for women of men's mistreatment of them has been cut; her lines beginning at l. 120 and ending after 'consumed' in l. 133 are marked for deletion in the manuscripts, and her lines beginning at the middle of l. 120 to 'my lord' in l. 131 do not appear in the quarto.
146 **now . . . thee** Vortiger implies he can take care of Roxena when they both reach hell.
149 **hardly** severely
154 **mystical** secret, unavowed (also 'mysterious' and 'allegorical embodiment of')

And that end crowns 'em all!
He falls [and dies]

AURELIUS Our peace is full now
In yon usurper's fall; nor have I known
A judgement meet more fearfully.
[*To a Soldier*] Here, take this ring, deliver the good Queen,
And those grave pledges of her injured honour,
Her worthy father and her noble uncle,
Too long too much abused, whose clear-eyed fames
I reverence with respect to holiness due,
A spotless name being sanctity now in few.
Enter Devonshire [and] Stafford, leading Hengist prisoner
How now, my lords, the meaning of these sounds?

HENGIST
The consumer has been there; she's gone, she's lost.
In glowing cinders lies all my joys,
The headlong fortune of my rash captivity
Strikes not so fierce a wound into my hopes
As thy dear loss.

AURELIUS Her father and her uncle!

GENTLEMAN
They are indeed, my lord.

AURELIUS Part of my wishes!
What fortunate power has prevented me,
And, ere my love came, brought 'em victory?

GENTLEMAN
My wonder sticks in Hengist, King of Kent.

DEVONSHIRE
My lord, to make that plain which now I see
Fixed in astonishment, the only name
Of your return and being brought such gladness
To this distracted kingdom that, to express
A thankfulness to heaven, it grew great
In charitable actions, from which goodness
We tasted liberty that lay engaged
Upon the innocence of woman's honour,
A kindness that even threatened to undo us;
And having newly but enjoyed the benefit
And fruits of our enlargement, 'twas our happiness
To intercept this monster of ambition,
Bred in these times of usurpatïon,
The rankness of whose insolence and treason
Grew to such height, 'twas armed to bid you battle,
Whom as our fames' redemption, on our knees
We present captive.

AURELIUS Had it needed reason,
You rightly came provided. What is he?

GENTLEMAN
My lord, that treacherous Hengist, King of Kent.

AURELIUS
I understand not your desert till now my lords.
Is this that German Saxon whose least thirst
Could not be satisfied under a province?

HENGIST
Had but my fate directed this bold arm
To thy life, the whole kingdom had been mine,
That was my hopes' great aim. I have a thirst
Could never have been full quenched under all,
The whole land must, or nothing.

AURELIUS A strange drought;
And what a little ground shall death now teach you
To be content withal!

HENGIST Why, let it then,
For none else can; you've named the only way.
When I'm content, it must be when I'm clay.

AURELIUS
My lords, the best requital yet we give you
Is a fair inward joy. Speak to your fame's
Glories unblemished, for the queen your daughter
Lives firm in honour, neither by consent
Or act or violence stained, as her grief judges.
'Twas her own lord abused her honest fear,
Whose ends shamed him only to make her clear.

DEVONSHIRE
Had your grace given a kingdom for a gift
It had not been so welcome.
Enter Castiza [and] a Gentleman

AURELIUS [*kneeling*]
Here she comes whose virtues I must reverence.

CASTIZA [*kneeling*]
O my lord, I kneel a wretched woman.

AURELIUS Arise with me,
Great in true joy and honour.
[*They rise*]

HENGIST This sight splits me,
It brings Roxena's ruin to my memory.

CASTIZA [*to Aurelius*]
My lord, it is too great a joy for life!

AURELIUS
'Tis truth and that, I know, you ever joyed in.
His end confessed it.

CASTIZA Are you returned, soul's comforts?

AURELIUS
Nay, to approve thy pureness to posterity,
The fruitful hopes of a fair peaceful kingdom
Here will I plant.

CASTIZA Too worthless are my merits.

AURELIUS
There speaks thy modesty and to the firmness of
Truth's plantation in this land forever,
Which always groans under some curse without it.
As I begin my rule with the destruction
Of this ambitious pagan, so shall all
With his adulterate faith distained and soiled
Either turn Christians, die, or live exiled.

167 **consumer** destroying fire
171 **her** i.e. Castiza's
214–34 DEVONSHIRE **Had . . . virtues** For a discussion of the dramatic impact of the revised ending of the play found in HERRINGMAN, see the Textual Introduction.

ALL
A blessing on those virtues. *Flourish. Exeunt*
Finis Actus Quintus

Epilogue *Enter Raynulph*

RAYNULPH
For story of truth compact
I chose these times, these men to act,
As careful now to make you glad
As this were the first day they played;
And though some that give none their due
Please to mistake 'em, do not you,
Whose censures have been ever kind.
We hope 'tis good, but if we find
Your grace and love by pleased signs understood,
We cease to hope, for then we know 'tis good. *Exit*
Music
Finis

Epilogue.9 by pleased signs understood i.e. through applause

WOMEN, BEWARE WOMEN: A TRAGEDY

Edited by John Jowett

SINCE Charles Lamb's favourable mention in *Specimens of English Dramatic Poets* (1808), *Women, Beware Women* has been central to Middleton's reputation as a major playwright. Appreciative criticism came long before stage revival, but a number of recent productions have confirmed that the play is a compelling stage work. Late twentieth-century sensibilities have responded positively to its precise, ironic, and intense concentration on sexuality in the field of power.

Thus, when the Royal Shakespeare Company staged the first modern production in 1962, in a ground-breaking studio production at the Arts Theatre, the London *Times* reviewer (5 July) wondered if 'squeamishness of taste' had previously kept the play off the boards, and Kenneth Tynan, reviewing in the *Observer* (8 July), saw its urgent significance to a period characterized in Philip Larkin's neatly exaggerated declaration that 'sexual intercourse was invented in 1963'. Granada Television might have noted such comments, for a televised performance was broadcast in 1965. The Traverse Theatre put on the first Scottish production for the Edinburgh Fringe Festival of 1968; it emphasized the play's austere and stylized qualities. The following year the RSC mounted a new full-scale production directed by Terry Hands. A chessboard set on which was placed a large statue of Venus emphasized the emblematic sexual manœuvrings. Bianca (Judi Dench) surrounded herself with a protective shell of apparent innocence, whilst Leantio (Richard Pasco), in contrast to Nicol Williamson's coarse and resentful proletarian of 1962, was exposed as a naïve victim out of his depths in Florentine sexual politics.

In 1986 the Royal Court Theatre staged an adaptation by Howard Barker. He described it in the playscript/programme as a piece of 'creative vandalism' in which a pared-down text of the first four acts was followed by a second part in modern idiom written entirely in Barker's own hand. Barker notes that in Middleton 'lust leads to the grave'; in his own version, which rejects the Cardinal's moralizations as a lie, 'desire alters perception', becoming a frenzy that leads towards political revolution. Kathleen McLuskie (1989) sees this chaotic and frank adaptation as confirming phallic power even as it demystifies it, and a theatrical riposte to Barker has come from Valerie Ellis, whose own adaptation for the American Repertory Theatre in Cambridge, Massachusetts, in 1991 responded to what she saw as the grotesque sexism of Barker's version. Meanwhile, the Birmingham Repertory Theatre had staged a revival of the Middleton play in 1989, and subsequently in 1995 Philip Prowse's production at the Glasgow Citizens' Theatre was played in modern dress on a set framed with skeletons.

When the RSC returned to the play in 2006, stylishly directed by Laurence Boswell, references to chess were present but muted. Costumes were predominantly Jacobean with inflections of post-punk. Careful blocking emphasized the physical distance between characters, a distance thrown into the vertical dimension when Bianca and Leantio's Mother appeared at a very high window. Age distances were strongly marked, with an immature Leantio looking young enough to be his old mother's grandson. Tim Pigott-Smith played a casually offhand but compelling Duke, and Penelope Wilton confirmed Livia as mainspring of the plot's manipulative cynicism.

Women, Beware Women finds no mention in records from before the Civil Wars, so information about early performances is confined to what can be inferred from the first printed edition of 1657. The men's parts might be performed by as few as seven adults. Middleton must have been especially confident in the strength of the envisaged company's boy actors, for few plays of the period have three more demanding female roles. The gamble seems to have paid off. The Calvinist poet and dramatist Nathaniel Richards in his commendatory verse in the 1657 edition claims to recall it being 'Acted in state, presented to the life', judging that 'Never came tragedy off with more applause'. If so, the applause was not renewed after 1660, despite the availability of a printed text. *Women, Beware Women* may have been too sociopolitically disturbing for Restoration tastes, and its stagecraft does not adapt readily to the proscenium-arch theatre. There are no recorded performances between 1642 and 1962.

The play maps out the progress of illicit desire in two thematically and structurally related plots. The events concerning Bianca come from Florentine history, and are close to the account in Celio Malespini's *Ducento Novelle* (1609), Part 2, novelle 84 and 85. Malespini's account ends with the murder of the character equivalent to Leantio, but an Italian manuscript continues the story to the death of Bianca and the Cardinal. A variation of this final episode is given in the unpublished manuscript chapters of Fynes Moryson's *Itinerary Containing his Ten Years' Travel* (completed 1619–20). Though Middleton may have consulted Moryson, his immediate source for the play's conclusion was probably an untraced manuscript. The Isabella plot derives from a French novella, *Histoire véritable des infortunées et tragiques amours d'Hypolite et d'Isabella, Napolitains* (1597). An English translation was published in 1628, after Middleton's death; Middleton may have seen the original French or a manuscript version of the translation. Middleton tightens up these source narratives and integrates them in a complicated way. His Hippolito and Livia have equivalents in both the sources; indeed Livia is based on no less than four characters. Middleton's conflation creates in Livia a complex and structurally central figure. She above all is the woman of whom others must 'beware'.

The title *Women, Beware Women* reflects on the debate between the castigators and defenders of women that took place in print and on stage during the middle and later Jacobean period. J. R. Mulryne, in his 1975 edition, heard in it an echo of words spoken by the character called Misogynous in the tragicomedy *Swetnam the Woman-hater Arraigned by Women* (performed in 1617–18 and published in 1620):

And Fortune, if thou be'st a deity,
Give me but opportunity that I
May all the follies of your sex declare,
That henceforth men of women may beware.

Middleton's title finds a still closer and hitherto unnoticed parallel in a ballad on the Overbury scandal (see *The Masque of Cupids*) called 'Mistress Turner's Farewell to all Women', which includes the admonition 'Women by me beware'. Here, in contrast with *Swetnam*, the address is to *women*, and *beware* has imperative force. In the illustrative woodcut Mistress Turner wears citizen garb that might be appropriate to Leantio's Mother, but her role as procuress and manipulator of sexual intrigue in the Overbury affair is closer to that of the play's other widow, Livia. Bianca might recall the woodcut's courtly 'Lady Pride', who is implied to be Frances Howard.

Comparison with the broadsheet ballad gives the play a precise orientation in relation to both anti-court and anti-woman satire. Richards thought that the play simply conformed to such models; he approved its presentation of 'drabs of state vexed' (sumptuous high-ranking whores provoked to anger). It is strange, then, that the initial scene of each plot establishes that all later female subterfuges have a base in male oppression. This is uncompromisingly clear in the case of Isabella, who faces an arranged marriage to the Ward. His and Sordido's desensitized physical grotesquerie is stranded in a society whose moral grotesquerie is glossed over by urbane worldliness. These two characters are funny to each other, embarrassing to all others. Despite the Ward's unsocialized sexuality and anti-woman rhetoric, Isabella's father Fabritio has chosen him to be her husband. There is satire here on the Court of Wards, an institution notorious for providing a source of royal revenue by farming out rich orphans. A guardian could reap a financial reward if his ward was married off before he reached maturity; he had invested in the ward and his stake was high. But marriages arranged for reasons of property were an object of more general criticism. The Ward gives flesh to a scenario in which marriage becomes a flawed institution orientated to the needs of those who dispose of wealth. Isabella's dowry can only buy her misery. When uncle Hippolito confesses his desire for his niece, Isabella's dilemmas deepen. She responds with horrified rejection, whilst parenthetically recognizing that pleasures are thereby denied: 'Though my joys fare the harder'. It takes Livia's lie that Isabella's uncle is no blood relative to make her openly acknowledge her physical attraction to him. Yet if she now thinks Hippolito is not her uncle, in social fact he must partly remain so, even to her.

For Isabella, marriage can become a mask for adultery. It is one way of coming to terms with her position as her father's disposable chattel, which is the fate Bianca has deliberately avoided. She has allowed herself to be 'stolen' from her family by her lover Leantio, but that romantic episode belongs to the past. The play opens more soberly with the newly married couple's return to Leantio's home, where he lives with his mother, who has the unusual privilege for a female character of speaking the play's first lines. Leantio is now confronted with translating sexual adventurism away from home into marital life within the physical bounds and psychopathology of everyday life. He must defer sensual pleasures, spending the week in commercial travelling so as to earn his living as a merchant's agent. His bourgeois values inform an alternatingly smug and anxious attitude to his gentlewomanly wife: she is a commodity, a jewel to be locked away from public sight. The habit of thought comes easily to him, but is reinforced by a fear of reprisals that might not be wholly fanciful: the English were aware of Italy as a place of violent and macabre family vengeance. To avoid such outcomes, Leantio constructs a marriage whose sensuality is hemmed in by possessiveness and guilt. As husband he imprisons the wife within the lustreless fabrics of middle-class existence.

Bianca, like Isabella, escapes from the patriarchal family only to become, eventually, mistress to a protective father substitute: in her case, the Duke of Florence. Livia uses Leantio's garrulous old mother as a means for drawing Bianca to her house; there Bianca is betrayed into the Duke's hands. Bianca is entrapped, threatened with violence, denied meaningful choice, restrained as she struggles ('strive not' says the Duke); she is raped (Gossett, 1984). Yet the emphasis on the event shifts even during its enactment from direct violence towards a subtler form of coercion whereby the violence is euphemized, as though the Duke did not understand the nature of consent. When he takes Bianca off-stage, he speaks of love, peace, and joy:

Should any doubt arise, let nothing trouble thee.
Put trust in our love for the managing
Of all to thy heart's peace. We'll walk together,
And show a thankful joy for both our fortunes.

Much of the episode is based on the techniques and language of political intrigue and diplomacy, as is emphasized in the emblematic commentary that emerges from the chess game played between Livia and the Mother below.

The threat of war has produced a capitulation, and now the Duke celebrates peace on his own terms. Bianca's final silence looks back to her equally cryptic silence in response to her 'purchase' by Leantio in the opening scene. As a response to threatened rape it is at sharp variance with that of Lucretia, whose technical consent under duress was sometimes cited to problematize her status as rape victim. Bianca's final silence forces the actor or reader to interpret what she fails verbally to express: at best 'a kind of constrained consent' (the words in the manuscript stage direction describing the dumb-show of Castiza's forced marriage in *Hengist* 2.2.0.17–22; the printed text says 'unwillingly'), or a dawning acceptance that an affair with the Duke might offer 'glory' as well as destruction; at worst the last resistance of the powerless.

The imagined offstage sex is over brutally soon (Daileader, 1998). When Bianca returns to the stage alone and altered, she expresses her horror at the moral corruption that has been forced on her in images of infectious mists and leprosy, whilst internalizing her entrapment as personal guilt. 'Sin and I'm acquainted' catches through personification the enigmatic conflict between sin seen as an otherly external agent (such as the Duke) and an inward state of being. Paradoxically it may seem, while castigating Guardiano for his role as procurer, she goes on to declare defiantly 'He likes the treason well, but hates the traitor'. The line marks a willed accommodation to her new situation that foreshadows her role in the rest of the play. Her lack of spontaneity is figured in the objectified, potentially regendered 'He', and the whole line is marked in the 1657 printed text as a sententia. As the previous line hints, it might be a 'politic' response to her new situation, advising Guardiano that she is able to accept a role as the Duke's mistress that will be dangerous to her betrayer. Yet that acceptance is without further regret; the private thoughts we hear are not of recrimination towards Guardiano or the Duke, but malice towards a Cardinal who first urges the Duke to abandon his courtesan and then tries to prevent their marriage. Gossett has urged that Middleton takes the misogynist view that she masochistically enjoys rape. But, especially seen in the context of a culture that habitually treated acknowledged victims of rape as dishonoured women, the speech we have been considering perhaps rather implies that she confronts an initially appalling prospect after her fate and her identity have been decided for her, and that she adapts to it. The Duke's ostentatious appreciation of her (unmatched by Leantio) and his provision of wealth both might reinforce her acceptance of the inevitable.

At all events her position as object and commodity is drastically redefined. Leantio feared Bianca's exchange value, and so feared and denied Bianca her social existence. She was his 'unvalued'st purchase': priceless, but also uniquely free from valuation, because unknown in Florence. When she is invited to the Duke's banquet, Leantio hides her in guilty darkness:

> You know, mother,
> At the end of the dark parlour there's a place
> So artificially contrived for a conveyance
> No search could ever find it. When my father
> Kept in for manslaughter, it was his sanctuary.
> There will I lock my life's best treasure up,
> Bianca.

Only a few moments later, the Duke publicly celebrates her brightness as his paramour:

> Methinks there is no spirit amongst us, gallants,
> But what divinely sparkles from the eyes
> Of bright Bianca; we sat all in darkness
> But for that splendour.

Her affair with the Duke has set her in another box of male cultural construction; this one is not a dark prison but a theatre where she is object of the gaze of others.

John Stachniewski (1990) has suggested that a Calvinist sensibility might enable Middleton to intimate what we would now call the unconscious mind. The seeds of repressed sinfulness can lie buried in the soul of the apparently upright being, so that corruption is an ironic maturation of self. Events engineered cynically by Livia bring that potential, lurking as repressed fantasy, into fulfilment. Yet if such an approach, applied to Bianca, suggestively adds psychological depth to the character, it does so at the expense of blaming the victim for her fate. Her momentary excitement when the Duke notices her during the ducal procession in 1.3 cannot determine that she willingly capitulates under duress. If Middleton is working with ideas of predestination, he is offering a hugely secularized revision of them. Bianca faces a combination of naked power and the constraint of ideological emplacement. She has the designation 'strumpet' written upon her as though it were somehow innate. Herein lies the stronger determinism, the court's power to shape lives and to taint souls.

The play opens upon a conspicuously secular world. Livia betrays both women into the hands of men, but within her own frankly cynical and amoral horizon of meaning she provides them with self-fulfilment and sexual comfort. For Livia, morality is a mere instrument of oppression, a convention to be exploited and overturned. She ranks amongst the 'atheists' of Jacobean drama: characters who deny that divine providence can be effectual, who attempt to put human affairs firmly in human hands. When Bianca harshly denounces her after the entrapment scene, Livia muses:

> 'Tis but a qualm of honour; 'twill away;
> A little bitter for the time, but lasts not.
> Sin tastes at the first draught like wormwood water,
> But drunk again, 'tis nectar ever after.

This, characteristically, reduces 'honour' to a fastidious stomach and 'Sin' to a taste impression. The joys of sin become quasi-religious ('nectar ever after') because they are only attained through suffering, and so sin assumes a perverse positive role in defining what has value. In this perspective it is a kindness to acquaint someone with sin, and Livia does not stint in doing so.

Livia was played as a terrifyingly inhuman figure in the RSC's 1962 production. She is the play's most powerful, enigmatic, and multifaceted dramatic role. Though her amorality is a matter of principle, she nonetheless takes delight in engineering other women's seductions and vicariously enjoys their pleasures. She claims to be an 'experienced widow' beyond love's foibles. As a manipulator, she is highly self-controlled, despite a hint of incest in her feelings for her brother Hippolito. But in Act 3 she succumbs to sudden and violent desire for Leantio, and surrenders her prized discretion. She offers to purchase his sexual favours, and he sees possibilities for evening the score with his wife. His cynical affair with Livia provides the trigger for an explosive undoing of all she has done, and so precipitates the revenge actions that are played out in the final scene.

Thus the first part of the play, up to the banquet scene (3.3), is based on Livia's amoral but constructive schemes; generically it is not too far removed from city comedy. The second part follows the consequences through to destruction and chaos. This generic shift towards tragedy introduces a second horizon of signification: the judgemental outlook articulated most forcefully by the Cardinal, who first speaks in 4.1. Criticism of the play's moral meaning, or lack of it, will focus on how effectively this new moralism supersedes the initial amorality associated with Livia, who loses ideological authority as she loses her grip on the play's action. Despite the hints of irony some critics find in Middleton's presentation of him, the Cardinal introduces an insistent note of Christian severity. His brother the Duke, previously the presiding figure in a satire against a sexually corrupt society, is now subject to momentary spiritual anguish. When he arranges Leantio's death in order to protect Bianca, marriage quickly follows; the Cardinal detects an astounding moral confusion, and it is hard to demur.

The Cardinal's prominence in the later scenes ensures that the spiritual hypocrisy he seeks to correct is firmly linked to the world of the court. The play enacts its own process of social mobility as it moves from the factor's dwelling to the aristocratic households of Livia and Guardiano, and so to the ducal court itself. Bianca and Leantio are refashioned by their lovers as spruce courtiers, and in a bitter exchange in 4.1 mock each other's sexually-purchased accoutrements. By the end of the play the Cardinal has emphasized the view that moral turpitude flows from the Duke downwards. *Women, Beware Women* cannot be seen as a programmatic anti-court satire without straitjacketing some of its complexities; it admits some fascination with the psychology of sexual corruption, and indeed treats the victims of passion with considerable sympathy. But the final contest between Bianca and the Cardinal allows a more condemnatory viewpoint, whereby religious censure and moral outrage have an inescapable political dimension. The play has become what Albert H. Tricomi (1989) calls an 'anatomy of court culture', and one way of reading it is as an articulation of anti-court grievances. Here the title's probable allusion to the Overbury scandal and the satire on wardship are equally relevant. Courtly power, supposedly directed to the common good, is seen as a vehicle to material and sensual gratification; courtly refinement is reduced to suave machination in the kingdom of lust. The final masque violently repudiates the Platonic idealizations of the Jacobean court masque, in which the court flattered itself in extravagant, high-minded entertainments. The scene resonates strongly with the often-expressed view that the court put on an outward show of finery and embraced a specious Platonism as a guise for sordid sexual transactions and secret acts of violence. In the play's court world, Bianca's first words after her entrapment, 'Now bless me from a blasting', are in vain; courtly advancement exacts the highest spiritual fee.

Middleton has created space for a view of political power that unremittingly strips illusions away. The play presents an image of the psychology of human behaviour that similarly denies sentiment or illusion, yet recognizes, especially in the case of Bianca, the force of human passions. It is in some ways misleading to call all this 'realism' or, in Lamb's admiring phrase, 'an immediate transcript from life', for the play is sometimes harshly caricatural, sometimes highly emblematic. The term 'realism' is, however, helpful in suggesting a style of depiction that can complicate stereotypical moral categories and demystify social processes. We may be reminded too of the play's careful observance of life's physical textures, and of the way characters speak almost obsessively of material value as if it were abstract value. In Middleton's Italy, though it is a country populated with strange vices, the human characters and social mores are disturbingly familiar. This is a class-conscious play, and Florence is Jacobean London writ large.

The dialogue is conducted with a naturalism alert to social nuance. Persistent sexual and spiritual consciousness in the undercurrents of language can be read equally for symbolic resonance and socio-historical truth to seventeenth-century life. Similarly, the techniques of characterization hover between an alienated sense of social life and emblematic counter-realism. Personal names, if given at all, are reserved for special purposes. Bianca's name appears only in Act 3, where it is an emotionally charged token of romantic and sexual contest between Leantio and the (unnamed) Duke. Similarly, Leantio is anonymous until Act 4, where he is the object of Livia's love and the Duke's enmity. Guardiano is not named at all (see note to 1.2.96). The audience is persistently denied the impression of easy familiarity afforded by personal names. In this respect the play on stage has a different texture from either the play as printed, replete with speech-prefixes and stage directions, or critical discussions such as the present one. The characters themselves normatively think of each other in terms of social roles and family relationships. Yet community and family are consistently ironized, and characters find their feelings dislocated from the object of those feelings and stranded in extended asides. Dialogue is instrumental, conflictual, insincere; established lovers are usually denied communication.

Even the most lifelike scenes are shaped by an artifice and theatricality that insistently estranges the impression of transcripted life. The limits of realism are most vividly defined in the play's often emblematic stagecraft. For instance, there are two processions of the Florentine state over the stage. The first is 'a yearly custom and solemnity | Religiously observed by th' Duke and state'. It excludes Bianca, who is the onlooker, but includes the Cardinal. The second procession shows Bianca at the Duke's side, but now the Cardinal is the outside figure; he breaks up the ceremony denouncing 'Religious honours done to sin'. The Cardinal embodies 'Religion'. Thus the entrapment scene is not unique in its emblematic dramaturgy.

Like a number of other commentators, Max Stafford-Clark, who inspired and directed Barker's adaptation, found Middleton's play marred by a last act that was 'unperformable and rather silly'. In the Citizens' Theatre production, the masque was replaced by successive descents through trapdoors to hell. Dorothy McMillan described the effect as 'hellish chic' (*Times Literary Supplement*, 17 February 1995), which, despite the alterations, is perhaps not far from the tone of the original text. Certainly the staging and orchestration of the final scene are complex, and exploit the full physical resources of the professional Jacobean stage. The masque represents the procedures of court masque, drawing on non-realistic traditions of drama that accommodate symbolic tableaux. It also depends on precedents in the revenge drama, not least for the convention of representing stylized but excessive retributions through the expedient device of court entertainment. Difficulties for modern theatrical practitioners are perhaps inevitable. But there are the questions of tone too. The revenges are emblematic witticisms, and amidst violent death the vein of humour refuses to dry. Tragedy competes with tragedy parodied; pity and horror compete with horrified laughter.

The effect of this final débâcle can be considered in relation to earlier scenes. As an ensemble portraying a state occasion, the masque recapitulates the banquet of 3.2, which similarly brought a major phase of the play to its logical close. But equally, the final scene, in its use of the upper acting space (but see commentary to 5.1.37.1–2), its division into separate stage groupings, and its emblematic qualities, recalls the game of chess in 2.2. Livia's control over the action of 2.2 is echoed in her control of the chess game. In 5.2 she presides over the masque, suspended from the heavens in the ironic role of Juno the marriage goddess; but by this time no character is able to take an overview of what is going on, much less control it. If both scenes work through high artifice, by the time of the final masque there is effectively no primary artificer (unless it be a vengeful God), for the plotters are many. Plurality, disharmony, and violent enmity invert the Platonic values intrinsic to masque, suggesting that the marriage it celebrates is itself a parody of holy matrimony. Even if one allows for the theatrical conventions at work, it remains possible to see the episode as attempting to represent something so anarchic as to be unrepresentable. Another critical but suggestive viewpoint is that the masque scene cannot adequately resolve conflicting interpretive and generic demands as, for example, between cynical realism and theological moralism. Both approaches recognize the play's ambitious complexity. But perhaps the scene's meaning, in relation to its audience, is spelled out most clearly by Hippolito:

DUKE
I have lost myself in this quite.
HIPPOLITO
My great lords, we are all confounded.

Women, Beware Women is an impressively stark and disturbing play. As in *King Lear*, the plots reinforce each other; each of the contrasted marriage-matches seals off the possibility of there being a happier alternative in its opposite. The language has a conversational surface that is firmly locked into a network of unremitting ironies. Characters speak of the immediate physical and emotional urge as if it were something of fundamental meaning. They are in the first instance trivial and mistaken in this, but ultimately they make themselves right in ways they fail to understand. In this way dramatic irony transports the everyday stuff of social comedy into a tragic world. The women are almost casually tricked into a deceptive sexual paradise; the paradise collapses into a disturbing but still ironized vision of earthly damnation. As she dies amongst strangers, Bianca, forgetting the Duke and Guardiano, blames women for it all—perhaps, in this at least, a woman of whom women should beware.

SEE ALSO

Textual introduction and apparatus: *Companion*, 1140
Authorship and date: *Companion*, 414

Women, Beware Women: A Tragedy

THE PERSONS OF THE PLAY

BIANCA Capella, a gentlewoman from Venice
LEANTIO, a factor, Bianca's husband
Leantio's MOTHER, a widow

Lady LIVIA, a widow
ISABELLA, Livia's niece
FABRITIO, Isabella's father and Livia's brother
HIPPOLITO, Isabella's uncle and Livia's brother

The WARD, a foolish rich young heir
SORDIDO, the Ward's man
GUARDIANO, the Ward's guardian

DUKE of Florence
The LORD CARDINAL, the Duke's brother
Two LADIES
A LORD
Two other Cardinals
States of Florence

One or two CITIZENS
A PRENTICE
Two or three BOYS

MESSENGER
SERVANTS
A PAGE

Other lords, ladies, and attendants

In the Masque:

HEBE
HYMEN
GANYMEDE
Two Nymphs
Two Pages as Cupids

1.1 *Incipit Actus Primus*
Enter Leantio, with Bianca and Mother. [*Bianca stands apart*]

MOTHER [*to Leantio*]
Thy sight was never yet more precious to me.
Welcome with all the affection of a mother
That comfort can express from natural love.
Since thy birth-joy, a mother's chiefest gladness
After she's undergone her curse of sorrows,
Thou wast not more dear to me than this hour
Presents thee to my heart. Welcome again.

LEANTIO [*aside*]
'Las, poor affectionate soul, how her joys speak to me!
I have observed it often, and I know it is
The fortune commonly of knavish children
To have the loving'st mothers.

MOTHER What's this gentlewoman?

LEANTIO
O, you have named the most unvalued'st purchase
That youth of man had ever knowledge of.
As often as I look upon that treasure
And know it to be mine—there lies the blessing—
It joys me that I ever was ordained
To have a being and to live 'mongst men;
Which is a fearful living, and a poor one,
Let a man truly think on't.
To have the toil and griefs of fourscore years
Put up in a white sheet, tied with two knots!
Methinks it should strike earthquakes in adulterers
When e'en the very sheets they commit sin in
May prove, for aught they know, all their last garments.
O, what a mark were there for women then!
But beauty able to content a conqueror
Whom earth could scarce content keeps me in compass.
I find no wish in me bent sinfully
To this man's sister or to that man's wife.

1.1.3 **comfort** source of comfort, source of delight
express elicit
natural i.e. maternal
5 **curse of sorrows** i.e. pain in childbirth, God's punishment of womankind for Eve's transgression: 'I will greatly increase thy sorrows' (Genesis 3:16).
12 **unvalued'st** priceless
purchase acquisition (bought or stolen)
13 **youth** (i.e. when a man might expect to *purchase* a wife, but not to enjoy riches)
20 **griefs** hardships, sufferings
21 **Put up** placed for safe keeping
sheet winding-sheet (and anticipating the bed-sheets of 23)
25 **mark** example
26–7 **a ... content** (alludes to Alexander the Great, supposed to have wept because the world had insufficient lands for him to conquer)
27 **earth** the world
in compass within bounds. Also a suggestion of the navigational compass, prompted by *earth* and taken up in *bent*, 'inclined, drawn': Leantio's compass-needle remains directed to Bianca.

In love's name, let 'em keep their honesties
And cleave to their own husbands; 'tis their duties.
Now when I go to church I can pray handsomely,
Not come like gallants only to see faces,
As if lust went to market still on Sundays.
I must confess I am guilty of one sin, mother,
More than I brought into the world with me,
But that I glory in. 'Tis theft, but noble
As ever greatness yet shot up withal.

MOTHER
How's that?

LEANTIO
Never to be repented, mother,
Though sin be death. I had died if I had not sinned.
And here's my masterpiece; do you now behold her.
Look on her well, she's mine. Look on her better.
Now say if't be not the best piece of theft
That ever was committed. And I have my pardon for't:
'Tis sealed from heaven by marriage.

MOTHER
Married to her!

LEANTIO
You must keep counsel, mother, I am undone else.
If it be known, I have lost her. Do but think now
What that loss is; life's but a trifle to't.
From Venice her consent and I have brought her,
From parents great in wealth, more now in rage;
But let storms spend their furies now we have got
A shelter o'er our quiet innocent loves.
We are contented. Little money she's brought me.
View but her face, you may see all her dowry,
Save that which lies locked up in hidden virtues
Like jewels kept in cabinets.

MOTHER
You're to blame,
If your obedience will give way to a check,
To wrong such a perfection.

LEANTIO
How?

MOTHER
Such a creature,
To draw her from her fortune, which no doubt
At the full time might have proved rich and noble!
You know not what you have done. My life can give you
But little helps, and my death lesser hopes;
And hitherto your own means has but made shift
To keep you single, and that hardly, too.
What ableness have you to do her right then
In maintenance fitting her birth and virtues?—
Which ev'ry woman of necessity looks for,
And most to go above it, not confined
By their conditions, virtues, bloods, or births,
But flowing to affections, wills and humours.

LEANTIO
Speak low, sweet mother. You are able to spoil as many
As come within the hearing. If it be not
Your fortune to mar all, I have much marvel.
I pray, do not you teach her to rebel,
When she's in a good way to obedience:
To rise with other women in commotion
Against their husbands for six gowns a year,
And so maintain their cause, when they're once up,
In all things else that require cost enough.
They are all of 'em a kind of spirits soon raised,
But not so soon laid, mother. As for example,
A woman's belly is got up in a trice;
A simple charge ere it be laid down again.
So ever in all their quarrels and their courses.
And, I'm a proud man, I hear nothing of 'em.
They're very still, I thank my happiness,
And sound asleep. Pray let not your tongue wake 'em.
If you can but rest quiet, she's contented
With all conditions that my fortunes bring her to:
To keep close as a wife that loves her husband,
To go after the rate of my ability,
Not the licentious swinge of her own will,
Like some of her old schoolfellows. She intends
To take out other works in a new sampler,

30 **honesties** chastities, marital fidelities
31 **cleave** The biblical term (Genesis 2:24, Matthew 19:5, etc.)
32 **handsomely** (*a*) fittingly, properly (*b*) elegantly
33–4 **Not...Sundays** (an abuse of church-going noted by various writers of the time)
36 **I...me** (referring to humanity's innate 'original sin' resulting from the Fall of Adam and Eve, as distinct from sins committed in life)
38 **shot up** rapidly flourished
40 **sin be death** (from Romans 6:23, 'The wages of sin is death')
41 **masterpiece** (*a*) masterly achievement (*b*) excelling art-object
43 **piece** (*a*) instance (*b*) article
46 **keep counsel** maintain secrecy
49 **Venice** (notorious for sexual license)
57 **check** rebuke (perhaps also suggesting the chess term, anticipating 2.2)
58 **perfection** perfect creature
63 **but made shift** barely managed
64 **keep** support
66 **virtues** good qualities
69 **conditions** social ranks
70 **to** according to. *Affections*, *wills*, and *humours* are seen as drawing a woman as the moon draws a tide.
affections inclinations
humours whims
76 **commotion** tumult, rebellion
78 **up** risen up, up in arms
80 **spirits** (*a*) animated people (*b*) ghosts, demons
raised (*a*) brought to rebellion (*b*) summoned (as of ghosts) (*c*) swollen up
81 **laid** (*a*) overthrown, humbled (*b*) put to rest (as of ghosts) (*c*) made flat
82 **got up** made to swell
83 **simple** minor (ironic); or 'unmitigated'
charge expense, responsibility
84 **courses** reprehensible conduct
90 **keep close** (*a*) stay shut up at home (*b*) stay near
91 **go...ability** walk at the speed I can manage (with a sexual connotation taken up in *licentious swinge*); hence 'live at a rate I can afford'
92 **swinge** (*a*) free scope, impulse, power; (*b*) copulation (see *OED*, *v.*1, 1e)
94 **take out** copy
sampler piece of embroidery serving as a pattern

And frame the fashion of an honest love
Which knows no wants, but, mocking poverty,
Brings forth more children, to make rich men wonder
At divine providence that feeds mouths of infants,
And sends them none to feed, but stuffs their rooms
With fruitful bags, their beds with barren wombs.
Good mother, make not you things worse than they are
Out of your too much openness, pray take heed on't,
Nor imitate the envy of old people
That strive to mar good sport because they are perfect.
I would have you more pitiful to youth,
Especially to your own flesh and blood.
I'll prove an excellent husband, here's my hand,
Lay in provision, follow my business roundly,
And make you a grandmother in forty weeks.
Go, pray salute her, bid her welcome cheerfully.

MOTHER
Gentlewoman, thus much is a debt of courtesy
Which fashionable strangers pay each other
At a kind meeting.
[*She kisses Bianca*]
Then there's more than one
Due to the knowledge I have of your nearness.
I am bold to come again, and now salute you
By th' name of daughter, which may challenge more
Than ordinary respect.
[*She kisses Bianca again*]

LEANTIO [*aside*] Why, this is well now,
And I think few mothers of threescore will mend it.

MOTHER
What I can bid you welcome to is mean,
But make it all your own. We are full of wants,
And cannot welcome worth.

LEANTIO [*aside*] Now this is scurvy,
And spake as if a woman lacked her teeth.
These old folks talk of nothing but defects,
Because they grow so full of 'em themselves.

BIANCA
Kind mother, there is nothing can be wanting
To her that does enjoy all her desires.
Heaven send a quiet peace with this man's love,
And I am as rich as virtue can be poor,
Which were enough, after the rate of mind,
To erect temples for content placed here.
I have forsook friends, fortunes, and my country,
And hourly I rejoice in't. Here's my friends,
And few is the good number. [*To Leantio*] Thy successes,
Howe'er they look, I will still name my fortunes.
Hopeful or spiteful, they shall all be welcome.
Who invites many guests has of all sorts,
As he that traffics much drinks of all fortunes,
Yet they must all be welcome and used well.
I'll call this place the place of my birth now,
And rightly, too, for here my love was born,
And that's the birth-day of a woman's joys.
You have not bid me welcome since I came.

LEANTIO
That I did, questionless.

BIANCA No, sure. How was't?
I have quite forgot it.

LEANTIO Thus.
[*He kisses her*]

BIANCA O sir, 'tis true.
Now I remember well. I have done thee wrong.
Pray take't again, sir.
[*She kisses him*]

LEANTIO How many of these wrongs
Could I put up in an hour, and turn up the glass
For twice as many more!

MOTHER
Will't please you to walk in, daughter?

BIANCA Thanks, sweet mother.
The voice of her that bare me is not more pleasing.
Exeunt Mother and Bianca

LEANTIO
Though my own care and my rich master's trust
Lay their commands both on my factorship,
This day and night I'll know no other business
But her, and her dear welcome. 'Tis a bitterness
To think upon tomorrow: that I must leave her
Still to the sweet hopes of the week's end;
That pleasure should be so restrained and curbed,
After the course of a rich workmaster
That never pays till Saturday night.

95 **frame** (*a*) devise (*b*) impose over the frame used to stretch the embroidery cloth
fashion (*a*) shape (*b*) current custom, taste
96–100 **mocking ... wombs** Alludes to the supposed fecundity of the poor and sterility of the rich.
100 **bags** (of money)
104 **perfect** i.e. without sexual misdemeanour
108 **business** (with a sexual connotation)
roundly thoroughly (with a quibble on the rounding of the belly in pregnancy)
113 **one** i.e. one kiss
114 **your nearness** i.e. our kinship
116 **challenge** lay claim to
118 **mend** improve on
121 **scurvy** shabby, worthless. Also refers to the disease, a symptom of which was loss of teeth (122), though toothlessness also suggests age (123–4).
128 **as ... poor** Virtue is proverbially its own reward.
129 **after ... mind** i.e. if the scale of value is one that measures the mind's inclinations
130 **for** in gratitude for
here i.e. (*a*) in Leantio's house (*b*) in Bianca's heart
131, 132 **friends** family
133 **few is the good number** The proverbial riposte to 'The more the merrier' is 'the fewer the better cheer'.
successes fortunes (good or bad)
137 **traffics** trades, travels to and fro
138 **used** treated
147 **put up** endure, store up
glass hour-glass
151 **my own care** (*a*) my conscientiousness (*b*) self-regard
152 **factorship** post of merchant's agent. Leantio's travels are presumably to negotiate and effect purchases.
158 **After the course** in accordance with the practice

Marry, it comes together in a round sum then,
And does more good, you'll say. O fair-eyed Florence,
Didst thou but know what a most matchless jewel
Thou now art mistress of, a pride would take thee
Able to shoot destruction through the bloods
Of all thy youthful sons. But 'tis great policy
To keep choice treasures in obscurest places.
Should we show thieves our wealth, 'twould make
'em bolder.
Temptation is a devil will not stick
To fasten upon a saint; take heed of that.
The jewel is cased up from all men's eyes.
Who could imagine now a gem were kept
Of that great value under this plain roof?
But how in times of absence? What assurance
Of this restraint then? Yes, yes, there's one with her.
Old mothers know the world; and such as these,
When sons lock chests, are good to look to keys.
Exit

I.2 *Enter Guardiano, Fabritio, and Livia*

GUARDIANO [*to Fabritio*]
What, has your daughter seen him yet? Know you
that?
FABRITIO
No matter, she shall love him.
GUARDIANO Nay, let's have fair play.
He has been now my ward some fifteen year,
And 'tis my purpose, as time calls upon me,
By custom seconded, and such moral virtues,
To tender him a wife. Now, sir, this wife
I'd fain elect out of a daughter of yours.
You see my meaning's fair. If now this daughter
So tendered—let me come to your own phrase, sir—
Should offer to refuse him, I were handselled.
[*Aside*] Thus am I fain to calculate all my words
For the meridian of a foolish old man,
To take his understanding.—What do you answer,
sir?
FABRITIO
I say still she shall love him.
GUARDIANO Yet again?
And shall she have no reason for this love?
FABRITIO
Why, do you think that women love with reason?
GUARDIANO [*aside*]
I perceive fools are not at all hours foolish,
No more than wise-men wise.
FABRITIO I had a wife;
She ran mad for me; she had no reason for't,
For aught I could perceive.—What think you, lady
sister?
GUARDIANO [*aside*] 'Twas a fit match, that,
Being both out of their wits.—A loving wife: it seemed
She strove to come as near you as she could.
FABRITIO
An if her daughter prove not mad for love too,
She takes not after her; nor after me,
If she prefer reason before my pleasure.—
You're an experienced widow, lady sister,
I pray let your opinion come amongst us.
LIVIA
I must offend you then, if truth will do't,
And take my niece's part, and call't injustice
To force her love to one she never saw.
Maids should both see and like; all little enough.
If they love truly after that, 'tis well.
Counting the time she takes one man, till death,
That's a hard task, I tell you; but one may
Enquire at three years' end amongst young wives,
And mark how the game goes.
FABRITIO Why, is not man
Tied to the same observance, lady sister,
And in one woman?
LIVIA 'Tis enough for him.
Besides, he tastes of many sundry dishes
That we poor wretches never lay our lips to,
As obedience, forsooth, subjection, duty, and such
kickshaws
All of our making, but served in to them;
And if we lick a finger then sometimes,
We are not to blame; your best cooks use it.
FABRITIO
Thou'rt a sweet lady, sister, and a witty.
LIVIA
A witty? O, the bud of commendation
Fit for a girl of sixteen. I am blown, man.
I should be wise by this time; and, for instance,
I have buried my two husbands in good fashion,
And never mean more to marry.

163 **pride** (*a*) self-esteem (*b*) sexual excitement
take strike with disease
164 **bloods** (*a*) life (*b*) sexual passions
165 **policy** calculated prudence
168 **stick** scruple
I.2.3–10 **He . . . handselled** Orphaned children of the nobility became Wards of Court; i.e. their estates were held by the Crown until they were 21. Wardship was farmed out by the Crown, with possible financial benefit to the guardian. Guardiano would benefit from the marriage by being relieved of the Ward, and would be able to exact a payment from his estate if the Ward refused the marriage. See Introduction.
5 **moral** (*a*) righteous (*b*) customary
10 **handselled** given an auspicious present (ironic)
12 **meridian** special capacities. A figurative extension of the astrological term, which informs *calculate* (11) and *take* (13; see note).
13 **take** capture, secure (quibbling on 'measure by scientific observation')
17 **fools . . . foolish** (proverbial)
23 **come as near** be as like (quibbling on physical proximity, and perhaps nearness of orgasm)
34 **Counting** (*a*) considering (*b*) summing up
37 **the game** (with a sexual innuendo)
42 **kickshaws** fancy dishes (from French *quelque chose*)
45 **your . . . it** From the proverb 'he is a poor cook that cannot lick his fingers'.
use practise
48 **am blown** have blossomed; have seen better days

GUARDIANO No? Why so, lady?

LIVIA
Because the third shall never bury me.
I think I am more than witty.—How think you, sir?

FABRITIO
I have paid often fees to a counsellor
Has had a weaker brain.

LIVIA Then I must tell you,
Your money was soon parted.

GUARDIANO [*to Fabritio*] Light her now, brother.

LIVIA
Where is my niece? Let her be sent for straight
If you have any hope 'twill prove a wedding.
'Tis fit, i'faith, she should have one sight of him,
And stop upon't, and not be joined in haste
As if they went to stock a new-found land.

FABRITIO
Look out her uncle and you're sure of her.
Those two are ne'er asunder. They've been heard
In argument at midnight; moonshine nights
Are noon-days with them; they walk out their sleeps,
Or rather at those hours appear like those
That walk in 'em, for so they did to me.
Look you, I told you truth. They're like a chain:
Draw but one link, all follows.

Enter Hippolito and Isabella the niece [*hand in hand*]

GUARDIANO O affinity,
What piece of excellent workmanship art thou!
'Tis work clean wrought, for there's no lust, but love, in't,
And that abundantly; when in stranger things
There is no love at all, but what lust brings.

FABRITIO [*to Isabella*]
On with your mask, for 'tis your part to see now,
And not be seen. Go to, make use of your time.
See what you mean to like; nay, and I charge you,
Like what you see. Do you hear me? There's no dallying;
The gentleman's almost twenty, and 'tis time
He were getting lawful heirs, and you a-breeding on 'em.

ISABELLA
Good father!

FABRITIO Tell not me of tongues and rumours.
You'll say the gentleman is somewhat simple;
The better for a husband, were you wise,
For those that marry fools live ladies' lives.
On with the mask; I'll hear no more. He's rich;
The fool's hid under bushels.

[*Isabella puts on her mask. The Ward is heard within*]

LIVIA Not so hid, neither;
But here's a foul great piece of him, methinks.
What will he be when he comes altogether?

Enter the Ward, with a trapstick, and Sordido, his man

WARD [*to Sordido*] Beat him?
I beat him out o'th' field with his own catstick,
Yet gave him the first hand.

SORDIDO O, strange!

WARD I did it.
Then he set jacks on me.

SORDIDO What, my ladies' tailor?

WARD
Ay, and I beat him, too.

SORDIDO Nay, that's no wonder;
He's used to beating.

WARD Nay, I tickled him
When I came once to my tippings.

SORDIDO Now you talk on 'em, there was a poulterer's wife made a great complaint of you last night to your guardianer, that you struck a bump in her child's head as big as an egg.

56 **Your . . . parted** Alludes to the proverb 'a fool and his money are soon parted'.
Light her (*a*) give her intellectual enlightenment (ironic: Fabritio has proved himself foolish); or (*b*) relieve, cheer her (urging Fabritio to cease defending loveless marriage)
brother (referring probably to the projected relationship of brother-in-law)
60 **stop** halt, pause
61 **As . . . land** An allusion to hasty marriages of intending colonists.
64 **argument** discussion
65 **walk out their sleeps** use up their hours of sleep by walking
66–7 **Or . . . 'em** Sleep-walking suggests unawareness of spiritual peril.
69 **affinity** kinship
71 **clean** (*a*) adroitly (*b*) chastely
72 **stranger things** unrelated creatures
74–5 **'tis . . . seen** Draws on the proverbs 'Maidens should be seen, and not heard' and 'see and be seen'; also refers to the custom where the man and woman would not see each other before the betrothal day.
79 **on** of
80 **tongues** gossip
85 **The . . . bushels** 'Neither do men light a candle and put it under a bushel, but on a candlestick' (Matthew 5:15).
bushels vessels used to measure eight gallons; hence 'large quantities (of money)'
85.1–2 ***The . . . within*** The exact staging is not clear. A loud flatulence seems suggested. Otherwise, the Ward might partially appear entering backwards.
86 **piece** (quibbling on the sense 'cask of liquor', which picks up on bushels, 85)
87.1 ***trapstick*** In the rustic game of 'cat' the trap-stick, or cat-stick, was a truncheon used to flick in the air and bat away the 'cat', an hourglass-shaped piece of wood.
88 **Beat** (*a*) defeated (*b*) cudgelled
90 **hand** stroke
91 **jacks** scoundrels. Sordido evidently hears 'Jaques', the tailor's name.
my ladies' tailor Either 'my ladies'-tailor' or 'my lady's tailor'. Tailors were notoriously effeminate and cowardly.
93 **tickled** (euphemistic for 'thrashed')
94 **When I came once** once I came
tippings smart tappings (as to flick the 'cat' in the air)
96 **guardianer** An unusual form, spoken only by the Ward and Sordido, intermediate between *guardian* and *Guardiano*; the latter is used in stage directions but never in dialogue.

WARD An egg may prove a chicken then in time: the poulterer's wife will get by't. When I am in game I am furious: came my mother's eyes in my way, I would not lose a fair end; no, were she alive but with one tooth in her head, I should venture the striking out of that. I think of nobody when I am in play, I am so earnest. Coads me, my guardianer!
Prithee, lay up my cat and catstick safe.

SORDIDO
Where, sir, i'th' chimney corner?

WARD
Chimney corner?

SORDIDO
Yes, sir, your cats are always safe i'th' chimney corner,
Unless they burn their coats.

WARD
Marry, that I am afraid on.

SORDIDO
Why, then I will bestow your cat i'th' gutter,
And there she's safe, I am sure.

WARD
If I but live
To keep a house, I'll make thee a great man,
If meat and drink can do't. I can stoop gallantly,
And pitch out, when I list; I'm dog at a hole.
I mar'l my guardianer does not seek a wife for me;
I protest I'll have a bout with the maids else,
Or contract myself at midnight to the larderwoman
In presence of a fool or a sack-posset.

GUARDIANO Ward!

WARD [*to Sordido*]
I feel myself after any exercise
Horribly prone. Let me but ride, I'm lusty.—
A cock-horse straight, i'faith.

GUARDIANO
Why, ward, I say!

WARD [*to Sordido*]
I'll forswear eating eggs in moonshine nights.
There's ne'er a one I eat but turns into a cock
In four-and-twenty hours. If my hot blood
Be not took down in time, sure 'twill crow shortly.

GUARDIANO
Do you hear, sir? Follow me; I must new school you.

WARD
School me? I scorn that now; I am past schooling.
I am not so base to learn to write and read;
I was born to better fortunes in my cradle.
Exit [*Guardiano, followed by Ward and Sordido*]

FABRITIO [*to Isabella*]
How do you like him, girl? This is your husband.
Like him or like him not, wench, you shall have him,
And you shall love him.

LIVIA
O, soft there, brother! Though you be a justice,
Your warrant cannot be served out of your liberty.
You may compel, out of the power of father,
Things merely harsh to a maid's flesh and blood;
But when you come to love, there the soil alters;
You're in another country, where your laws
Are no more set by than the cacklings
Of geese in Rome's great Capitol.

FABRITIO
Marry him she shall, then
Let her agree upon love afterwards. *Exit*

LIVIA
You speak now, brother, like an honest mortal
That walks upon th'earth with a staff:
You were up i'th' clouds before. You'd command love,
And so do most old folks that go without it.
[*Livia embraces Hippolito*]
My best and dearest brother, I could dwell here.
There is not such another seat on earth
Where all good parts better express themselves.

HIPPOLITO You'll make me blush anon.

99 **get** gain
in game (with a sexual innuendo)
101 **fair end** game promising a win
102 **venture** risk
104 **Coads me** (interjection of surprise)
106 **chimney corner** (quibbling on *chimney* as 'vagina')
107 **cats** Refers to the catstick as a phallic object; but also possibly suggests 'prostitutes'.
108 **Unless ... coats** (alluding to the burning effects of syphilis)
109–10 **I ... sure** Draws on the proverb 'they agree like two cats in the gutter'; *gutter* suggests the anus, as Sordido might indicate with a gesture of the 'cat'.
111 **great** (*a*) powerful (*b*) corpulent
112 **stoop** (*a*) crouch to *pitch out* the 'cat' (*b*) crouch in sexual intercourse (*c*) debase myself (*d*) follow a scent (anticipating *dog*)
113 **pitch out** (*a*) pitch the 'cat' (*b*) ejaculate
dog at Proverbial for 'adept'; here also suggests a dog sniffing and digging at an animal's burrow.
hole (with the innuendo 'vagina')
114 **mar'l** marvel
117 **In ... sack-posset** A witness was needed to make a verbal contract binding. *A fool or a sack-posset* would be conveniently at hand, and could be repudiated.
fool An idiot would not make a legal witness, but the context suggests also a custard or dish of whipped cream.
sack-posset hot milk curdled with white wine and flavoured with sugar and spices
120 **prone** eager (for a copulative *ride*)
121 **cock-horse** (*a*) hobby-horse (*b*) whore
straight immediately
122 **eating ... nights** Merges (*a*) eating eggs during moonlit nights with (*b*) eating eggs-in-moonshine (poached eggs with an onion sauce) at nights. Eggs were regarded as aphrodisiacs.
123 **cock** (*a*) male fowl (see 94–9) (*b*) erect penis
125 **took down** made to detumesce
crow ejaculate
129 **I ... cradle** A poorer man, or younger son, might need literacy to study for a career as clergyman, lawyer, etc.
134 **liberty** district within which a Justice of the Peace's warrant was valid
136 **merely** entirely
139 **set by** taken notice of
139–40 **the ... Capitol** Refers to the sacred geese whose cackling awoke the Romans during a night-time attack by the Gauls. The point might be that they are ignored not in Rome but in other countries, but the image is rather confused.
139 **cacklings** Pronounced 'cackëlings'.
142–4 **like ... before** i.e. like a typical old man who assumes the authority of a god come to earth
145.1 ***Livia embraces Hippolito*** Alternatively, Livia's *here*, 146, means in gazing at Hippolito.
147 **seat** residence, place
148 **parts** qualities
express manifest

LIVIA
'Tis but like saying grace before a feast then,
And that's most comely. Thou art all a feast,
And she that has thee a most happy guest.
Prithee, cheer up that niece with special counsel.
[*Exit*]

HIPPOLITO [*aside*]
I would 'twere fit to speak to her what I would, but
'Twas not a thing ordained. Heaven has forbid it,
And 'tis most meet that I should rather perish
Than the decree divine receive least blemish.
Feed inward, you my sorrows, make no noise,
Consume me silent, let me be stark dead
Ere the world know I'm sick. You see my honesty;
If you befriend me, so.

ISABELLA [*aside*] Marry a fool!
Can there be greater misery to a woman
That means to keep her days true to her husband
And know no other man? So virtue wills it.
Why, how can I obey and honour him,
But I must needs commit idolatry?
A fool is but the image of a man,
And that but ill-made neither. O, the heart-breakings
Of miserable maids where love's enforced!
The best condition is but bad enough:
When women have their choices, commonly
They do but buy their thraldoms, and bring great
portions
To men to keep 'em in subjectïon;
As if a fearful prisoner should bribe
The keeper to be good to him, yet lies in still,
And glad of a good usage, a good look
Sometimes. By'r Lady, no misery surmounts a wo-
man's.
Men buy their slaves, but women buy their masters.
Yet honesty and love makes all this happy
And, next to angels', the most blest estate.
That providence that has made ev'ry poison
Good for some use, and sets four warring elements
At peace in man, can make a harmony
In things that are most strange to human reason.
O, but this marriage!—What, are you sad too, uncle?
Faith, then there's a whole household down together.
Where shall I go to seek my comfort now
When my best friend's distressed? What is't afflicts
you, sir?

HIPPOLITO
Faith, nothing but one grief that will not leave me,
And now 'tis welcome. Ev'ry man has something
To bring him to his end, and this will serve—
Joined with your father's cruelty to you;
That helps it forward.

ISABELLA O, be cheered, sweet uncle!
How long has't been upon you? I ne'er spied it.
What a dull sight have I! How long, I pray, sir?

HIPPOLITO
Since I first saw you, niece, and left Bologna.

ISABELLA
And could you deal so unkindly with my heart
To keep it up so long hid from my pity?
Alas, how shall I trust your love hereafter?
Have we passed through so many arguments,
And missed of that still, the most needful one?
Walked out whole nights together in discourses,
And the main point forgot? We are to blame both.
This is an obstinate wilful forgetfulness,
And faulty on both parts. Let's lose no time now.
Begin, good uncle, you that feel't. What is it?

HIPPOLITO
You of all creatures, niece, must never hear on't.
'Tis not a thing ordained for you to know.

ISABELLA
Not I, sir? All my joys that word cuts off.
You made profession once you loved me best;
'Twas but profession.

HIPPOLITO Yes, I do't too truly,
And fear I shall be chid for't. Know the worst, then:
I love thee dearlier than an uncle can.

ISABELLA
Why, so you ever said, and I believed it.

HIPPOLITO [*aside*]
So simple is the goodness of her thoughts,
They understand not yet th'unhallowed language
Of a near sinner. I must yet be forced,
Though blushes be my venture, to come nearer.—
As a man loves his wife, so love I thee.

ISABELLA What's that?
Methought I heard ill news come toward me,
Which commonly we understand too soon,

150 **saying grace before** (*a*) saying thanksgiving before (*b*) speaking of gracious qualities in front of
151 **comely** agreeable, fitting
160–1 **You . . . so** (still addressed to his sorrows, hoping that they will kill him)
167 **image** outward semblance. The fool is like a man in the same way an idol is like a god: the *image* without the substance.
168 **neither** as well
172 **portions** dowries
175 **in** i.e. in prison
182 **warring elements** i.e. earth, air, fire, and water, seen as the constituents of all matter. Equivalent to the four 'humours', the kinds of temperament thought to be varyingly mixed in each person.
186 **down** (as with sickness)
196 **Bologna** (in Middleton's source, Hippolito's birthplace)
198 **keep it up** shut his *grief* away
200 **arguments** topics of conversation
211 **but profession** i.e. merely words
217 **near** (*a*) nearby (*b*) almost (*c*) closely related
218 **venture** peril, risk
nearer nearer to the point
221–3 **Methought . . . hearing** Developed from the proverb 'Ill news comes too soon'. Isabella refigures the *ill news* as something intuitively understood before it is heard. The intuitive hearing pre-empts the literal one.

Then over-quick at hearing. I'll prevent it,
Though my joys fare the harder. Welcome it?
It shall ne'er come so near mine ear again.
Farewell, all friendly solaces and discourses.
I'll learn to live without ye, for your dangers
Are greater than your comforts. What's become
Of truth in love if such we cannot trust,
When blood that should be love is mixed with lust?
Exit

HIPPOLITO
The worst can be but death, and let it come.
He that lives joyless, every day's his doom. *Exit*

1.3 *Enter Leantio, alone*

LEANTIO
Methinks I'm e'en as dull now at departure
As men observe great gallants the next day
After a revels; you shall see 'em look
Much of my fashion if you mark 'em well.
'Tis e'en a second hell to part from pleasure
When man has got a smack on't. As many holidays
Coming together makes your poor heads idle
A great while after, and are said to stick
Fast in their fingers' ends; e'en so does game
In a new-married couple: for the time
It spoils all thrift, and indeed lies abed
To invent all the new ways for great expenses.
Enter Bianca and Mother above
See an she be not got on purpose above now
Into the window to look after me.
I have no power to go now an I should be hanged.
Farewell, all business. I desire no more
Than I see yonder. Let the goods at quay
Look to themselves. Why should I toil my youth out?
It is but begging two or three year sooner,
And stay with her continually: is't a match?
O fie, what a religion have I leaped into!
Get out again, for shame. The man loves best
When his care's most; that shows his zeal to love.
Fondness is but the idiot to affection,
That plays hot-cockles with rich merchants' wives:
Good to make sport withal when the chest's full
And the long warehouse cracks. 'Tis time of day
For us to be more wise; 'tis early with us;
And if they lose the morning of their affairs
They commonly lose the best part of the day.
Those that are wealthy and have got enough,
'Tis after sunset with 'em; they may rest,
Grow fat with ease, banquet, and toy and play,
When such as I enter the heat o'th' day;
And I'll do't cheerfully.

BIANCA
I perceive, sir,
You're not gone yet. I have good hope you'll stay
now.

LEANTIO
Farewell; I must not.

BIANCA
Come, come, pray return.
Tomorrow, adding but a little care more,
Will dispatch all as well; believe me, 'twill, sir.

LEANTIO
I could well wish myself where you would have me;
But love that's wanton must be ruled a while
By that that's careful, or all goes to ruin.
As fitting is a government in love
As in a kingdom. Where 'tis all mere lust,
'Tis like an insurrection in the people
That, raised in self-will, wars against all reason;
But love that is respective for increase
Is like a good king that keeps all in peace.
Once more, farewell.

BIANCA
But this one night, I prithee.

LEANTIO
Alas, I'm in for twenty if I stay,
And then for forty more. I have such luck to flesh

223 **Then over-quick** and we are then too hasty
224 **Welcome it?** A consideration prompted by the thought of her *joys*, and immediately rejected.
230 **blood . . . lust** consanguineous love is mixed with the 'blood' of lust
1.3 The location is the street outside Leantio's house, whose frontage would have been represented by the stage's rear wall. The upper acting space above the stage represents a window. Leantio enters as it were from the house; the procession after 101 passes over the stage in front of it.
3 **revels** night of revelry. Can suggest specifically 'lovemaking'.
6 **smack** taste
7 **your poor heads** the heads of poor people
8–9 **stick . . . ends** i.e. make them slow and clumsy in their work
9 **game** (*a*) sexual play (*b*) holiday activities
11 **lies abed** (as the *game* does figuratively and the *couple* do literally)
12 **invent . . . expenses** (with the quibbling sense 'try novel sexual techniques that produce great emissions of semen')
19 **It is but** i.e. staying at home merely leads to
20 **match** agreement, deal
24 **Fondness** infatuation
the idiot to i.e. a mocking caricature as compared with the proper form of
25 **That** who
hot-cockles A rustic game in which one player, kneeling with his head in another's lap, has to guess the identity of others who strike his back. The imputation is of casual and promiscuous sex, and perhaps also performance of cunnilingus.
26–7 **when . . . cracks** The merchants themselves are busy accumulating wealth. Their warehouses are full to bursting; analogously the adulterer is turgid. *Chest* implies 'testicles' and *long warehouse* is the penis ready to emit semen (*crack*).
29–30 **if . . . day** Proverbial; compare 'Some work in the morning may trimly be done, that all the day after may hardly be won.'
29 **they** The impersonal 'one'. Leantio is thinking of himself, in contrast with 'Those that are wealthy' (31).
33 **toy** dally amorously
43–4 **As . . . kingdom** i.e. discretion in matters of love is as needful as political authority in a kingdom
44 **mere** utter
47 **respective for** considerate to, partial to
increase increase of wealth (with an ironic glance at 'procreation')
51 **to** with respect to
flesh (*a*) sensual appetites; sexual intercourse (*b*) animals

I never bought a horse but he bore double.
If I stay any longer, I shall turn
An everlasting spendthrift. As you love
To be maintained well, do not call me again,
For then I shall not care which end goes forward.
Again farewell to thee.

BIANCA [*weeping*] Since it must, farewell too.

Exit Leantio

MOTHER
Faith, daughter, you're to blame; you take the course
To make him an ill husband, troth you do;
And that disease is catching, I can tell you,
Ay, and soon taken by a young man's blood,
And that with little urging. Nay, fie, see now,
What cause have you to weep? Would I had no more,
That have lived threescore years: there were a cause,
An 'twere well thought on. Trust me, you're to blame.
His absence cannot last five days at utmost.
Why should those tears be fetched forth? Cannot love
Be e'en as well expressed in a good look,
But it must see her face still in a fountain?
It shows like a country maid dressing her head
By a dish of water. Come, 'tis an old custom
To weep for love.

Enter two or three Boys, and a Citizen or two with an Apprentice

BOYS
Now they come, now they come!

SECOND BOY The Duke!

THIRD BOY The state!

CITIZEN
How near, boy?

FIRST BOY I'th' next street, sir, hard at hand.

CITIZEN [*to his Apprentice*]
You, sirrah, get a standing for your mistress,
The best in all the city.

APPRENTICE I have't for her, sir.
'Twas a thing I provided for her overnight;
'Tis ready at her pleasure.

CITIZEN Fetch her to't, then.
Away, sir! [*Exit Apprentice*]

BIANCA What's the meaning of this hurry?
Can you tell, mother?

MOTHER What a memory
Have I! I see by that years come upon me.
Why, 'tis a yearly custom and solemnity,
Religiously observed by th' Duke and state,
To St Mark's Temple, the fifteenth of April.
See if my dull brains had not quite forgot it.
'Twas happily questioned of thee. I had gone down else,
Sat like a drone below, and never thought on't.
I would not to be ten years younger again
That you had lost the sight. Now you shall see
Our Duke, a goodly gentleman of his years.

BIANCA
Is he old then?

MOTHER About some fifty-five.

BIANCA
That's no great age in man; he's then at best
For wisdom and for judgement.

MOTHER The Lord Cardinal,
His noble brother—there's a comely gentleman,
And greater in devotion than in blood.

BIANCA
He's worthy to be marked.

MOTHER You shall behold
All our chief states of Florence. You came fortunately
Against this solemn day.

BIANCA I hope so always.

Music

MOTHER
I hear 'em near us now. Do you stand easily?

BIANCA
Exceeding well, good mother.

MOTHER Take this stool.

BIANCA
I need it not, I thank you.

MOTHER Use your will then.

Enter in great solemnity six knights, bare-headed, then two cardinals, and then the Lord Cardinal, then the Duke; after him the states of Florence by two and two; with variety of music and song.
[*They pass over the stage and*] *exeunt.*
[*Exeunt Citizens and Boys*]

MOTHER
How like you, daughter?

BIANCA 'Tis a noble state.
Methinks my soul could dwell upon the reverence
Of such a solemn and most worthy custom.
Did not the Duke look up? Methought he saw us.

52 **bore double** carried two riders. As applied to Bianca, might imply that she will bear children, or (by dramatic irony) that she will bear a second man in copulation.
56 **which...forward** what happens (proverbial). Leantio confuses business objectives with bodily 'ends' that might engage in sexual intercourse.
60 **that disease** (i.e. self-indulgence)
68 **e'en** just
69 **see...fountain** i.e. ensure that her face is always in a fountain of tears (but *see her face* anticipates the country maid's dish of water)
70 **shows like** has the appearance of
dressing arranging, tidying
71 **a dish of water** Used to reflect, as a simple mirror. Presumably love, by implication, produces dish-fuls of tears.
73 **state** nobility, rulers
75 **standing** place to stand (but the Apprentice's reply quibbles on 'erection of the penis')
78 **Fetch** (With the unintended bawdy 'arouse')
82 **solemnity** ceremonial procession (predates *OED*, 2b [1636])
86 **happily** fortunately
down downstairs
95 **blood** birth
98 **Against** in time for
99 **easily** comfortably
103 **reverence** solemnity

MOTHER
That's everyone's conceit that sees a duke:
If he look steadfastly, he looks straight at them,
When he perhaps, good careful gentleman,
Never minds any, but the look he casts
Is at his own intentions, and his object
Only the public good.

BIANCA Most likely so.

MOTHER
Come, come, we'll end this argument below. *Exeunt*
Finis Actus Primus

❁

2.1 *Incipit Actus Secundus*
Enter Hippolito, and Lady Livia the widow

LIVIA
A strange affection, brother. When I think on't,
I wonder how thou cam'st by't.

HIPPOLITO E'en as easily
As man comes by destruction, which oft-times
He wears in his own bosom.

LIVIA Is the world
So populous in women, and creation
So prodigal in beauty and so various,
Yet does love turn thy point to thine own blood?
'Tis somewhat too unkindly. Must thy eye
Dwell evilly on the fairness of thy kindred,
And seek not where it should? It is confined
Now in a narrower prison than was made for't.
It is allowed a stranger; and where bounty
Is made the great man's honour, 'tis ill husbandry
To spare, and servants shall have small thanks for't.
So he heaven's bounty seems to scorn and mock
That spares free means, and spends of his own stock.

HIPPOLITO
Never was man's misery so soon summed up,
Counting how truly.

LIVIA Nay, I love you so
That I shall venture much to keep a change from you
So fearful as this grief will bring upon you.
Faith, it even kills me when I see you faint
Under a reprehension; and I'll leave it,
Though I know nothing can be better for you.
Prithee, sweet brother, let not passion waste
The goodness of thy time and of thy fortune.
Thou keep'st the treasure of that life I love
As dearly as mine own; and if you think
My former words too bitter, which were ministered
By truth and zeal, 'tis but a hazarding
Of grace and virtue; and I can bring forth
As pleasant fruits as sensuality wishes
In all her teeming longings, this I can do.

HIPPOLITO
O, nothing that can make my wishes perfect!

LIVIA
I would that love of yours were pawned to't, brother,
And as soon lost that way as I could win.
Sir, I could give as shrewd a lift to chastity
As any she that wears a tongue in Florence.
She'd need be a good horse-woman, and sit fast,
Whom my strong argument could not fling at last.
Prithee, take courage, man. Though I should counsel
Another to despair, yet I am pitiful
To thy afflictions, and will venture hard—
I will not name for what; 'tis not handsome.
Find you the proof, and praise me.

HIPPOLITO Then I fear me
I shall not praise you in haste.

LIVIA This is the comfort:
You are not the first, brother, has attempted
Things more forbidden than this seems to be.
I'll minister all cordials now to you,
Because I'll cheer you up, sir.

HIPPOLITO I am past hope.

LIVIA
Love, thou shalt see me do a strange cure, then,
As e'er was wrought on a disease so mortal
And near akin to shame. When shall you see her?

HIPPOLITO
Never in comfort more.

LIVIA You're so impatient, too.

HIPPOLITO
Will you believe death? She's forsworn my company,
And sealed it with a blush.

LIVIA So, I perceive
All lies upon my hands then. Well, the more glory
When the work's finished.
Enter Servant
How now, sir, the news?

SERVANT
Madam, your niece, the virtuous Isabella,
Is lighted now to see you.

LIVIA [*to Hippolito*] That's great fortune.

106 **conceit** thought, fancy
108 **careful** full of care
112 **argument** debate on a particular subject
2.1.7 **point** (*a*) compass-needle (*b*) sword (with a phallic innuendo)
8 **unkindly** against family kind, unnatural
13 **honour** i.e. source of honour
16 **spares** (*a*) is niggardly of (*b*) avoids
free (*a*) freely given (*b*) innocent
spends ... stock (*a*) wastes his own resources (*b*) releases his sexual energies on his own family
17 **summed up** (*a*) summarized (*b*) counted up (responding to Livia's comments on *husbandry*)
18 **Counting** if one reckons
20 **grief** suffering
24 **passion** suffering
28 **ministered** prompted, administered (and dispensed like a medicine; see 48)
32 **her teeming longings** i.e. the longings she produces in swarms
33 **perfect** realized, satisfied
36 **shrewd** (*a*) hard, sharp (*b*) wicked
lift (*a*) attack (*b*) up-rearing (like a horse throwing its rider, anticipating 38–9)
37 **wears** has
43 **handsome** fitting
51 **mortal** (*a*) fatal (*b*) damnable
55 **sealed** confirmed. The blush is like red wax sealing a written oath.
59 **Is lighted** has descended from her coach

Sir, your stars bless you simply.—Lead her in.
Exit Servant

HIPPOLITO
What's this to me?

LIVIA
Your absence, gentle brother.
I must bestir my wits for you.

HIPPOLITO
Ay, to great purpose.
Exit

LIVIA
Beshrew you! Would I loved you not so well
I'll go to bed, and leave this deed undone.
I am the fondest where I once affect,
The carefull'st of their healths and of their ease, forsooth,
That I look still but slenderly to mine own.
I take a course to pity him so much now
That I have none left for modesty and myself.
This 'tis to grow so liberal! You've few sisters
That love their brothers' ease 'bove their own honesties;
But if you question my affectïons,
That will be found my fault.
Enter Isabella the niece
Niece, your love's welcome.
Alas, what draws that paleness to thy cheeks—
This enforced marriage towards?

ISABELLA
It helps, good aunt,
Amongst some other griefs; but those I'll keep
Locked up in modest silence, for they're sorrows
Would shame the tongue more than they grieve the thought.

LIVIA
Indeed the ward is simple.

ISABELLA
Simple? That were well.
Why, one might make good shift with such a husband;
But he's a fool entailed; he halts downright in't.

LIVIA
And, knowing this, I hope 'tis at your choice
To take or refuse, niece.

ISABELLA
You see it is not.
I loath him more than beauty can hate death,
Or age her spiteful neighbour.

LIVIA
Let't appear, then.

ISABELLA
How can I, being born with that obedience
That must submit unto a father's will?
If he command, I must of force consent.

LIVIA
Alas, poor soul! Be not offended, prithee,
If I set by the name of niece a while,
And bring in pity in a stranger fashion.
It lies here in this breast would cross this match.

ISABELLA
How, cross it, aunt?

LIVIA
Ay, and give thee more liberty
Than thou hast reason yet to apprehend.

ISABELLA
Sweet aunt, in goodness keep not hid from me
What may befriend my life.

LIVIA
Yes, yes, I must,
When I return to reputatïon,
And think upon the solemn vow I made
To your dead mother, my most loving sister.
As long as I have her memory 'twixt mine eyelids,
Look for no pity now.

ISABELLA
Kind, sweet, dear aunt!

LIVIA
No, 'twas a secret I have took special care of,
Delivered by your mother on her deathbed.
That's nine years now, and I'll not part from't yet;
Though ne'er was fitter time nor greater cause for't.

ISABELLA
As you desire the praises of a virgin—

LIVIA
Good sorrow! I would do thee any kindness
Not wronging secrecy or reputation.

ISABELLA
Neither of which, as I have hope of fruitfulness,
Shall receive wrong from me.

LIVIA
Nay, 'twould be your own wrong
As much as any's, should it come to that once.

ISABELLA
I need no better means to work persuasion then.

LIVIA
Let it suffice you may refuse this fool;
Or you may take him, as you see occasion
For your advantage—the best wits will do't.
You've liberty enough in your own will.
You cannot be enforced; there grows the flower,
If you could pick it out, makes whole life sweet to you.

60 **simply** absolutely
61 **Your absence** Not a response to Hippolito's question, but an instruction to depart.
64 **I'll** I'd
65 **fondest** (*a*) most affectionate (*b*) most foolish
66 **ease** Carries the specific sense 'sexual relief'.
67 **still** always
70 **liberal** (*a*) generous (*b*) unrestrained by prudence, licentious
73 **That ... fault** From the proverb 'Every men has his faults'.
75 **towards** about to take place
80 **make good shift** manage well
81 **entailed** with inalienable right to the title
halts downright in't (*a*) comes to an absolute full-stop at it (*b*) is utterly defective in it (*OED*, *halt*, *v.*1, 4)
85 **her spiteful neighbour** The image of an envious old woman living next door to a beauty implies that old age maliciously follows soon after beauty.
appear be made known
88 **of force** of necessity
91 **stranger** (*a*) previously unknown (*b*) appropriate to a non-relative
99 **sister** i.e. sister-in-law
107 **sorrow** (addressed to Isabella as sorrow personified)
109 **fruitfulness** fertility, children
111 **once** ever
117 **there** in that

That which you call your father's command's nothing;
Then your obedience must needs be as little.
If you can make shift here to taste your happiness,
Or pick out aught that likes you, much good do you.
You see your cheer; I'll make you no set dinner.

ISABELLA
And, trust me, I may starve for all the good
I can find yet in this. Sweet aunt, deal plainlier.

LIVIA
Say I should trust you now upon an oath,
And give you in a secret that would start you;
How am I sure of you in faith and silence?

ISABELLA
Equal assurance may I find in mercy
As you for that in me.

LIVIA
It shall suffice.
Then know, however custom has made good,
For reputation's sake, the names of niece
And aunt 'twixt you and I, we're nothing less.

ISABELLA
How's that?

LIVIA
I told you I should start your blood.
You are no more allied to any of us,
Save what the courtesy of opinion casts
Upon your mother's memory and your name,
Than the mer'st stranger is, or one begot
At Naples when the husband lies at Rome;
There's so much odds betwixt us. Since your knowledge
Wished more instruction, and I have your oath
In pledge for silence, it makes me talk the freelier.
Did never the report of that famed Spaniard,
Marquis of Coria, since your time was ripe
For understanding, fill your ear with wonder?

ISABELLA
Yes; what of him? I have heard his deeds of honour
Often related when we lived in Naples.

LIVIA
You heard the praises of your father then.

ISABELLA
My father!

LIVIA
That was he; but all the business
So carefully and so discreetly carried
That fame received no spot by't, not a blemish.
Your mother was so wary to her end,
None knew it but her conscience and her friend;
Till penitent confession made it mine,
And now my pity yours. It had been long else;
And I hope care and love alike in you,
Made good by oath, will see it take no wrong now.
How weak his commands now whom you call father!
How vain all his enforcements, your obedience!
And what a largeness in your will and liberty,
To take, or to reject, or to do both!—
For fools will serve to father wise men's children.
All this you've time to think on. O, my wench,
Nothing o'erthrows our sex but indiscretion!
We might do well else, of a brittle people,
As any under the great canopy.
I pray, forget not but to call me aunt still—
Take heed of that; it may be marked in time else—
But keep your thoughts to yourself, from all the world,
Kindred or dearest friend; nay, I entreat you,
From him that all this while you have called uncle;
And though you love him dearly, as I know
His dèserts claim as much e'en from a stranger,
Yet let not him know this, I prithee, do not.
As ever thou hast hope of second pity
If thou shouldst stand in need on't, do not do't.

ISABELLA
Believe my oath, I will not.

LIVIA
Why, well said!
[*Aside*] Who shows more craft t'undo a maidenhead,
I'll resign my part to her.

Enter Hippolito

She's thine own. Go. *Exit*

HIPPOLITO [*aside*]
Alas, fair flattery cannot cure my sorrows!

ISABELLA [*aside*]
Have I passed so much time in ignorance,
And never had the means to know myself
Till this blest hour, thanks to her virtuous pity
That brought it now to light? Would I had known it
But one day sooner! He had then received
In favours what, poor gentleman, he took
In bitter words: a slight and harsh reward
For one of his deserts.

HIPPOLITO [*aside*]
There seems to me now
More anger and distraction in her looks.
I'm gone; I'll not endure a second storm.

121 **make shift** contrive (and 'have a sexual affair')
here in this
122 **do you** may it do you
123 **cheer** (*a*) food offered as hospitality (*b*) cause for cheerfulness
127 **that** that which
start startle
129 **mercy** divine mercy
130 **As you** i.e. as much for you as
133 **nothing less** (*a*) anything rather than that (*b*) no less (picking up on the slang senses of *niece* as 'prostitute' and *aunt* as 'procuress')
134 **start your blood** (*a*) startle you (*b*) arouse you
137 **name** (*a*) surname (*b*) reputation
140 **odds** difference
143 **report** renown
144 **time** age
149 **business** (with a sexual connotation)
153 **friend** lover
160 **largeness** unrestrained liberty
164 **Nothing . . . indiscretion** Paraphrases the Latin tag '*Si non caste, tamen caute*'.
165 **of** for
brittle fragile, frail
166 **great canopy** sky, heavens
168 **marked** noticed
175 **second pity** i.e. another compassionate favour

The memory of the first is not past yet.

ISABELLA [*aside*]
Are you returned, you comforts of my life,
In this man's presence? I will keep you fast now,
And sooner part eternally from the world
Than my good joys in you.—Prithee, forgive me.
I did but chide in jest. The best loves use it
Sometimes; it sets an edge upon affection.
When we invite our best friends to a feast,
'Tis not all sweetmeats that we set before them;
There's somewhat sharp and salt, both to whet appetite
And make 'em taste their wine well. So methinks
After a friendly sharp and savoury chiding,
A kiss tastes wondrous well, and full o'th' grape.
[*She kisses him*]
How think'st thou: does't not?

HIPPOLITO
'Tis so excellent
I know not how to praise it, what to say to't.

ISABELLA
This marriage shall go forward.

HIPPOLITO
With the ward?
Are you in earnest?

ISABELLA
'Twould be ill for us else.

HIPPOLITO [*aside*]
For us? How means she that?

ISABELLA [*aside*]
Troth, I begin
To be so well, methinks, within this hour,
For all this match able to kill one's heart,
Nothing can pull me down now. Should my father
Provide a worse fool yet, which I should think
Were a hard thing to compass, I'd have him, either,
The worse the better; none can come amiss now
If he want wit enough. So discretion love me,
Desert and judgement, I have content sufficient.—
She that comes once to be a housekeeper
Must not look every day to fare well, sir,
Like a young waiting-gentlewoman in service;
For she feeds commonly as her lady does—
No good bit passes her but she gets a taste on't—
But when she comes to keep house for herself,
She's glad of some choice cates then once a week,
Or twice at most, and glad if she can get 'em.
So must affection learn to fare with thankfulness.
Pray make your love no stranger, sir; that's all—
[*Aside*] Though you be one yourself, and know not on't;
And I have sworn you must not. *Exit*

HIPPOLITO
This is beyond me!
Never came joys so unexpectedly
To meet desires in man. How came she thus?
What has she done to her? Can any tell?
'Tis beyond sorcery this, drugs, or love-powders:
Some art that has no name, sure, strange to me
Of all the wonders I e'er met withal
Throughout my ten years' travels. But I'm thankful for't.
This marriage now must of necessity forward.
It is the only veil wit can devise
To keep our acts hid from sin-piercing eyes. *Exit*

2.2

Enter Guardiano and Livia

LIVIA
How, sir, a gentlewoman, so young, so fair
As you set forth, spied from the widow's window?

GUARDIANO
She!

LIVIA
Our Sunday-dinner woman?

GUARDIANO
And Thursday-supper woman, the same still.
I know not how she came by her, but I'll swear
She's the prime gallant for a face in Florence;
And no doubt other parts follow their leader.
The Duke himself first spied her at the window;
Then in a rapture, as if admiration
Were poor when it were single, beckoned me,
And pointed to the wonder warily,
As one that feared she would draw in her splendour
Too soon if too much gazed at. I ne'er knew him
So infinitely taken with a woman;
Nor can I blame his appetite, or tax
His raptures of slight folly: she's a creature
Able to draw a state from serious business,
And make it their best piece to do her service.
What course shall we devise? He's spoke twice now.

LIVIA
Twice?

192 **comforts** sources of strength, succour, and delight
197 **sets ... affection** makes desire sharper (and gives it an erection)
198 **a feast** (a sexual metaphor)
211 **pull me down** make me ill
215 **So** if
215–16 **discretion ... judgement** The qualities are (*a*) those Isabella sees in Hippolito, hence Hippolito himself (*b*) abstractions (such as Fortune) whose favour Isabella seeks, so as to succeed in her *discretion* (both discriminating choice and discreet behaviour), obtain her *desert*, and be vindicated in her *judgement*.
217–25 **She ... thankfulness** Isabella seems to be excusing her previous hostility to Hippolito as an effect of her (impending) marriage.
217 **once** once and for all
housekeeper woman who runs a household (as analogous to a wife)
218 **fare** eat (as a metaphor for getting sexual gratification)
220 **commonly** (*a*) usually (*b*) as widely
223 **cates** delicacies
231 **she** (Livia)
233 **Some ... name** (and so more mysterious and terrible than a named one)
2.2.2 **set forth** describe
spied from i.e. spied looking from
3–4 **Our ... woman** The Mother either helped to prepare these meals or was invited as a lowly guest.
6 **gallant** handsome person (sometimes applied, as here, to a woman)
7 **their leader** (the face)
16 **slight folly** foolish triviality
17 **state** state council
18 **piece** piece of work

GUARDIANO
'Tis beyond your apprehension
How strangely that one look has catched his heart.
'Twould prove but too much worth in wealth and favour
To those should work his peace.

LIVIA
And if I do't not,
Or at least come as near it—if your art
Will take a little pains and second me—
As any wench in Florence of my standing,
I'll quite give o'er, and shut up shop in cunning.

GUARDIANO
'Tis for the Duke; and if I fail your purpose,
All means to come by riches or advancement
Miss me and skip me over.

LIVIA
Let the old woman then
Be sent for with all speed; then I'll begin.

GUARDIANO
A good conclusion follow, and a sweet one,
After this stale beginning with old ware.—
Within there!

Enter Servant

SERVANT
Sir, do you call?

GUARDIANO
Come near, list hither.

[*They talk apart*]

LIVIA
I long myself to see this absolute creature
That wins the heart of love and praise so much.

GUARDIANO
Go, sir, make haste.

LIVIA [*to the Servant*]
Say I entreat her company.
Do you hear, sir?

SERVANT
Yes, madam. *Exit*

LIVIA
That brings her quickly.

GUARDIANO
I would 'twere done. The Duke waits the good hour,
And I wait the good fortune that may spring from't.
I have had a lucky hand these fifteen year
At such court-passage with three dice in a dish.

Enter Fabritio

Signor Fabritio!

FABRITIO
O sir, I bring an alteration in my mouth now.

GUARDIANO [*aside to Livia*]
An alteration! No wise speech, I hope;
He means not to talk wisely, does he, trow?—
Good! What's the change, I pray, sir?

FABRITIO
A new change.

GUARDIANO
Another yet! Faith, there's enough already.

FABRITIO
My daughter loves him now.

GUARDIANO
What, does she, sir?

FABRITIO
Affects him beyond thought: who but the ward, forsooth?
No talk but of the ward; she would have him
To choose 'bove all the men she ever saw.
My will goes not so fast as her consent now;
Her duty gets before my command still.

GUARDIANO
Why then, sir, if you'll have me speak my thoughts,
I smell 'twill be a match.

FABRITIO
Ay, and a sweet young couple,
If I have any judgement.

GUARDIANO [*aside*]
Faith, that's little.—
Let her be sent tomorrow before noon,
And handsomely tricked up; for 'bout that time
I mean to bring her in and tender her to him.

FABRITIO
I warrant you for handsome. I will see
Her things laid ready, every one in order,
And have some part of her tricked up tonight.

GUARDIANO
Why, well said.

FABRITIO
'Twas a use her mother had
When she was invited to an early wedding.
She'd dress her head o'ernight, sponge up herself,
And give her neck three lathers—

GUARDIANO [*aside*]
Ne'er a halter?

FABRITIO
On with her chain of pearl, her ruby bracelets,
Lay ready all her tricks and jiggumbobs—

GUARDIANO
So must your daughter.

FABRITIO
I'll about it straight, sir. *Exit*

23 **work** bring about
29–30 **All . . . over** (subjunctive: '*may* all means . . .')
33 **stale** (*a*) past the prime of life (*b*) person, particularly a prostitute, used as bait to trap someone
ware (suggests a metaphor of trading; also applies jocularly to a woman, and to the sexual organs)
35 **absolute** perfect
42 **court-passage . . . dish** *Passage* is a dice game using *three dice in a dish*; one player throws until two doubles show, and wins if they add up to over ten. The implication of an intrigue involving three people, two of whom will be matched, is strengthened by *passage* as 'amorous exchange'.
44 **an . . . mouth** news of a changed attitude. Guardiano takes the phrase as 'a change in my speech'.
46 **trow** I wonder
48 **Another . . . already** Quibbles on the redundant *new*; and perhaps alludes to the New Change (i.e. financial exchange), opened in 1609 to supplement the Royal Exchange, and long considered superfluous.
54 **before** ahead of
56 **sweet** Picks up on the literal meaning of *smell*.
59, 63 **tricked up** decked out (and 'sexually aroused')
64 **use** custom
65 **early** (in the morning)
67 **lathers . . . halter** 'Lather' was a variant of *ladder*; hence the quibble on *halter*, 'noose'.
69 **tricks** ornaments (and possibly 'sexual know-how')
jiggumbobs knick-knacks

LIVIA
How he sweats in the foolish zeal of fatherhood,
After six ounces an hour, and seems
To toil as much as if his cares were wise ones!

GUARDIANO
You've let his folly blood in the right vein, lady.

LIVIA
And here comes his sweet son-in-law that shall be.
They're both allied in wit before the marriage;
What will they be hereafter, when they are nearer?
Yet they can go no further than the fool:
There's the world's end in both of 'em.

Enter the Ward and Sordido, one with a shuttlecock, the other a battledore

GUARDIANO [*to the Ward*] Now, young heir!

WARD
What's the next business after shuttlecock now?

GUARDIANO
Tomorrow you shall see the gentlewoman
Must be your wife.

WARD There's e'en another thing too
Must be kept up with a pair of battledores.
My wife! What can she do?

GUARDIANO
Nay, that's a question you should ask yourself, ward,
When you're alone together.

WARD That's as I list.
A wife's to be asked anywhere, I hope.
I'll ask her in a congregation if I have a mind to't, and so save a licence. [*To Sordido*] My guard'ner has no more wit than an herb-woman that sells away all her sweet-herbs and nosegays, and keeps a stinking breath for her own pottage.

SORDIDO
Let me be at the choosing of your beloved
If you desire a woman of good parts.

WARD Thou shalt, sweet Sordido.

SORDIDO I have a plaguy guess. Let me alone to see what she is; if I but look upon her cony-way, I know all the faults to a hair that you may refuse her for.

WARD
Dost thou? I prithee, let me hear 'em, Sordido.

SORDIDO
Well, mark 'em then. I have 'em all in rhyme.
The wife your guard'ner ought to tender
Should be pretty, straight, and slender;
Her hair not short, her foot not long,
Her hand not huge, nor too, too loud her tongue;
No pearl in eye, nor ruby in her nose,
No burn or cut but what the catalogue shows.
She must have teeth, and that no black ones,
And kiss most sweet when she does smack once.
Her skin must be both white and plumped,
Her body straight, not hopper-rumped,
Or wriggle sideways like a crab.
She must be neither slut nor drab,
Nor go too splay-foot with her shoes
To make her smock lick up the dews.
And two things more which I forgot to tell ye:
She neither must have bump in back nor belly.
These are the faults that will not make her pass.

WARD
And if I spy not these, I am a rank ass.

SORDIDO
Nay, more: by right, sir, you should see her naked,
For that's the ancient order.

WARD See her naked?
That were good sport, i'faith. I'll have the books
turned over,
And if I find 'her naked' on record
She shall not have a rag on. But stay, stay:
How if she should desire to see me so too?
I were in a sweet case then. Such foul skin!

SORDIDO
But you've a clean shirt, and that makes amends, sir.

72 **After** at the rate of

74 **let...vein** Literally, 'opened the correct vein to draw off blood tainted with his folly', as in the medical practice of letting blood. Quibbling on 'in the right vein' as colloquial for 'in the right way'.

78 **the fool** i.e. the position of being a fool

79 **the world's end** i.e. as far as it is possible to go

79.2 ***battledore*** racket

80 **business...shuttlecock** Both words have sexual innuendos.

82–3 **There's...battledores** Further sexual innuendos: *another thing* implies another (*shuttle*)*cock*; *kept up* is 'kept going' or 'kept erect'; the *pair of battledores* may imply the testes.

86 **list** please

88–9 **I'll...licence** Refers to asking the banns of marriage in church, without which a special licence was needed.

89, 100 **guard'ner** The form allows a pun on *gardener* that might be taken up in the references to herbs and pottage, and in *tender* (100) as 'tend'.

91–2 **keeps...pottage** Draws on proverbial 'keep your breath to cool your pottage' (thick soup); i.e. save your breath ((*a*) words (*b*) exhalation) for your own use.

94 **parts** (*a*) qualities (*b*) parts of the body

95 **a plaguy** (an intensifier, as in 'one hell of a')

96 **cony-way** i.e. rabbit burrow. *Cony* puns on *con* 'cunt', and also allows 'to a hair' ('exactly') to allude to pubic hair and pun on *hare*. The first printed edition of 1657 omits the obscenity, printing a long dash for *cony*.

100–16 **The...pass** Debases the medieval convention of the catalogue of female beauty.

104 **pearl...ruby** 'Cataract' and 'red pimple' respectively, with ironic reference to the jewels.

105 **burn** (probably alluding to venereal disease)
cut (quibbling on the sense 'cunt')

107 **smack** kiss loudly

109 **hopper-rumped** (perhaps suggesting the jerky movements of the grain-hopper of the time as well as its conical shape)

112 **go...with** walk...in

115 **belly** Its *bump* might be of fatness or pregnancy.

118 **see her naked** Sir Thomas More related an imaginary custom whereby either partner of a couple entering a marriage-match could be exhibited naked (*Utopia*, 1516).

124 **case** (*a*) situation (*b*) costume

WARD
I will not see her naked for that trick though. *Exit*

SORDIDO
Then take her with all faults, with her clothes on;
And they may hide a number with a bum-roll.
[*To Guardiano*] Faith, choosing of a wench in a huge farthingale
Is like the buying of ware under a great penthouse.
What, with the deceit of one,
And the false light of th'other—mark my speeches—
He may have a diseased wench in's bed,
And rotten stuff in's breeches. *Exit*

GUARDIANO
It may take handsomely.

LIVIA
I see small hindrance.

Enter Mother

How now, so soon returned?

GUARDIANO
She's come.

LIVIA
That's well.
Widow, come, come, I have a great quarrel to you.
Faith, I must chide you that you must be sent for!
You make yourself so strange, never come at us;
And yet so near a neighbour, and so unkind.
Troth, you're to blame. You cannot be more welcome
To any house in Florence, that I'll tell you.

MOTHER
My thanks must need acknowledge so much, madam.

LIVIA
How can you be so strange then? I sit here
Sometime whole days together without company
When business draws this gentleman from home,
And should be happy in society,
Which I so well affect, as that of yours.
I know you're alone too. Why should not we
Like two kind neighbours, then, supply the wants
Of one another, having tongue, discourse,
Experience in the world, and such kind helps
To laugh down time and meet age merrily?

MOTHER
Age, madam? You speak mirth: 'tis at my door,
But a long journey from your ladyship yet.

LIVIA
My faith, I'm nine-and-thirty, every stroke, wench;
And 'tis a general observatïon
'Mongst knights' wives or widows, we account
Ourselves then old when young men's eyes leave looking at's.
'Tis a true rule amongst us, and ne'er failed yet
In any but in one that I remember.
Indeed she had a friend at nine-and-forty.
Marry, she paid well for him, and in th'end
He kept a quean or two with her own money,
That robbed her of her plate, and cut her throat.

MOTHER
She had her punishment in this world, madam;
And a fair warning to all other women
That they live chaste at fifty.

LIVIA
Ay, or never, wench.
Come, now I have thy company I'll not part with't
Till after supper.

MOTHER
Yes, I must crave pardon, madam.

LIVIA
I swear you shall stay supper. We have no strangers, woman;
None but my sojourners and I, this gentleman
And the young heir his ward. You know our company.

MOTHER
Some other time I will make bold with you, madam.

GUARDIANO
Nay, pray stay, widow.

LIVIA
Faith, she shall not go.
Do you think I'll be forsworn?

[*Guardiano sets out*] *table and chess*

MOTHER
'Tis a great while
Till supper time; I'll take my leave then now, madam,
And come again i'th' evening, since your ladyship
Will have it so.

LIVIA
I'th' evening? By my troth, wench,
I'll keep you while I have you. You have great business, sure,
To sit alone at home! I wonder strangely
What pleasure you take in't. Were't to me, now,
I should be ever at one neighbour's house
Or other all day long. Having no charge,
Or none to chide you if you go or stay,
Who may live merrier, ay, or more at heartsease?
Come, we'll to chess or draughts. There are an hundred tricks
To drive out time till supper, never fear't, wench.

MOTHER
I'll but make one step home, and return straight, madam.

LIVIA
Come, I'll not trust you. You use more excuses
To your kind friends than ever I knew any.

126 **for that trick** on that account (or 'at the cost of her playing that trick')
128 **bum-roll** cushion worn around the hips, over which the woman's skirt hung
129 **farthingale** framework of hoops worn from the waist to extend the skirt outwards
130 **penthouse** annex (without external doors or windows)
132 **false** deceptive
134 **rotten...breeches** (*a*) breeches of rotten fabric (*b*) the effects of venereal disease inside his breeches
135 **take** take effect
139 **so strange** so much a stranger
150 **neighbours** Livia's diction is condescendingly citizen-like.
162 **friend** lover
164 **quean** prostitute
165 **plate** gold and silver ware
167 **a...women** Probably alludes to the play *A Warning for Fair Women*, 1599.
172 **sojourners** visiting guests
176 **forsworn** (see 171)
181 **strangely** exceedingly
187 **chess** (a game associated with sexual and political intrigue)

What business can you have, if you be sure
You've locked the doors?—and that being all you
have,
I know you're careful on't. One afternoon
So much to spend here? Say I should entreat you now
To lie a night or two, or a week, with me,
Or leave your own house for a month together?
It were a kindness that long neighbourhood
And friendship might well hope to prevail in.
Would you deny such a request? I'faith,
Speak truth, and freely.

MOTHER
I were then uncivil, madam.

LIVIA
Go too then, set your men. We'll have whole nights
Of mirth together ere we be much older, wench.

MOTHER [*aside*]
As good now tell her then, for she will know't.
I have always found her a most friendly lady.

LIVIA
Why, widow, where's your mind?

MOTHER
Troth, e'en at home, madam.
To tell you truth, I left a gentlewoman
E'en sitting all alone, which is uncomfortable,
Especially to young bloods.

LIVIA
Another excuse!

MOTHER
No; as I hope for health, madam, that's a truth.
Please you to send and see.

LIVIA
What gentlewoman? Pish!

MOTHER
Wife to my son, indeed—but not known, madam,
To any but yourself.

LIVIA
Now I beshrew you!
Could you be so unkind to her and me
To come and not bring her? Faith, 'tis not friendly.

MOTHER
I feared to be too bold.

LIVIA
Too bold? O, what's become
Of the true hearty love was wont to be
'Mongst neighbours in old time?

MOTHER
And she's a stranger, madam.

LIVIA
The more should be her welcome. When is courtesy
In better practice than when 'tis employed
In entertaining strangers? I could chide, i'faith.
Leave her behind, poor gentlewoman, alone too?
Make some amends, and send for her betimes; go.

MOTHER
Please you command one of your servants, madam.

LIVIA
Within there!

Enter Servant

SERVANT
Madam.

LIVIA
Attend the gentlewoman.

MOTHER
It must be carried wondrous privately
From my son's knowledge; he'll break out in storms
else.—
Hark you, sir.
[*She speaks apart to the Servant; then exit Servant*]

LIVIA [*to Guardiano*]
Now comes in the heat of your part.

GUARDIANO
True, I know it, lady; and if I be out,
May the Duke banish me from all employments,
Wanton or serious.

LIVIA
So, have you sent, widow?

MOTHER
Yes, madam; he's almost at home by this.

LIVIA
And, faith, let me entreat you that henceforward
All such unkind faults may be swept from friendship,
Which does but dim the lustre; and think thus much:
It is a wrong to me, that have ability
To bid friends welcome, when you keep 'em from me.
You cannot set greater dishonour near me,
For bounty is the credit and the glory
Of those that have enough. I see you're sorry,
And the good 'mends is made by't.

Enter Bianca and Servant

MOTHER
Here she's, madam.
[*Exit Servant*]

BIANCA [*aside*]
I wonder how she comes to send for me now?

LIVIA
Gentlewoman, you're most welcome, trust me, y'are,
As courtesy can make one, or respect
Due to the presence of you.

BIANCA
I give you thanks, lady.

LIVIA
I heard you were alone, and 't had appeared
An ill condition in me, though I knew you not
Nor ever saw you—yet humanity
Thinks every case her own—to have kept our com-
pany
Here from you, and left you all solitary.
I rather ventured upon boldness then
As the least fault, and wished your presence here—
A thing most happily motioned of that gentleman,
Whom I request you, for his care and pity,
To honour and reward with your acquaintance;
A gentleman that ladies' rights stands for,

202 **men** chessmen
208 **uncomfortable** cheerless
223 **betimes** forthwith, speedily
228 **heat** intense stage
part Guardiano understands the theatrical sense
229 **be out** forget my lines
232 **by this** by now
235 **Which does** i.e. the *faults* do
241 **'mends** amends
247 **condition** characteristic
248 **humanity** the humane in a person
253 **motioned of** suggested by
256 **stands** (with a phallic quibble)

That's his profession.
BIANCA 'Tis a noble one,
And honours my acquaintance.
GUARDIANO All my intentions
Are servants to such mistresses.
BIANCA 'Tis your modesty,
It seems, that makes your dèserts speak so low, sir.
LIVIA
Come, widow.
[*Livia and Mother sit to play at chess*]
[*To Bianca*] Look you, lady, here's our business.
Are we not well employed, think you?—an old quarrel
Between us that will never be at an end.
BIANCA
No, and methinks there's men enough to part you,
lady.
LIVIA
Ho, but they set us on! Let us come off
As well as we can, poor souls; men care no farther.
I pray sit down, forsooth, if you have the patience
To look on two weak and tedious gamesters.
GUARDIANO
Faith, madam, set these by till evening;
You'll have enough on't then. The gentlewoman,
Being a stranger, would take more delight
To see your rooms and pictures.
LIVIA Marry, good sir,
And well remembered. I beseech you, show 'em her;
That will beguile time well; pray heartily, do, sir;
I'll do as much for you. Here, take these keys.
Show her thc monument too—and that's a thing
Everyone sees not; you can witness that, widow.
MOTHER
And that's worth sight indeed, madam.
BIANCA Kind lady,
I fear I came to be a trouble to you—
LIVIA
O, nothing less, forsooth.
BIANCA And to this courteous gentleman
That wears a kindness in his breast so noble
And bounteous to the welcome of a stranger.
GUARDIANO
If you but give acceptance to my service,
You do the greatest grace and honour to me
That courtesy can merit.
BIANCA I were to blame else,
And out of fashion much. I pray you, lead, sir.
LIVIA
After a game or two we're for you gentlefolks.
[*She moves at chess*]
GUARDIANO
We wish no better seconds in society
Than your discourses, madam, and your partner's
there.
MOTHER
I thank your praise, I listened to you, sir;
Though when you spoke there came a paltry rook
Full in my way, and chokes up all my game.
Exeunt Guardiano and Bianca
LIVIA
Alas, poor widow, I shall be too hard for thee.
MOTHER
You're cunning at the game, I'll be sworn, madam.
LIVIA
It will be found so, ere I give you over.
She that can place her man well—
MOTHER As you do, madam.
LIVIA
As I shall, wench—can never lose her game.
[*Mother offers to move at chess*]
Nay, nay, the black king's mine.
MOTHER Cry you mercy, madam.
LIVIA
And this my queen.
MOTHER I see't now.
[*She moves at chess*]
LIVIA Here's a duke
Will strike a sure stroke for the game anon.
[*She moves at chess*]
Your pawn cannot come back to relieve itself.
MOTHER
I know that, madam.
[*She moves at chess*]
LIVIA You play well the whilst.
How she belies her skill! I hold two ducats
I give you check and mate to your white king—

257 **his profession** i.e. what he asserts and/or practices
258 **honours my acquaintance** bestows honour on my being acquainted with him
intentions endeavours
264 **men** (*a*) chessmen (between the players) (*b*) human men (who might separate fighters or make the women quarrel)
265 **set us on** (*a*) incite us to quarrel (*b*) sexually excite us
come off (*a*) retire from battle (*b*) achieve orgasm
276 **monument** statue
280 **nothing less** not at all
284 **grace and honour** (with a glance at the rewards expected from the Duke)
286 **out of fashion** lacking in polite behaviour
287 **we're for** we'll join
288 **seconds in society** i.e. encouragement to our social intercourse
291 **paltry** despicable
rook (the chess-piece)
292, 297 **game** (with the secondary sense, unintended by the Mother, 'sexual intrigue')
298 **the black king's mine** With an emblematic suggestion that Livia is evil. Compare 'your white king ... your saintish king' (304–5).
Cry you mercy beg your pardon
299 **duke** Another name for the *rook* or castle in chess, but also referring to the person of the Duke.
300 **strike ... game** Alludes to (*a*) the chess-game (*b*) the Duke's intrigue (*c*) thrusting in the *game* of copulation.
301 **Your ... itself** A rule of chess that also applies to Bianca's situation.
303 **hold** offer as a wager
304–5 **I ... there** See note on the *black king*, 298.

Simplicity itself—your saintish king there.
[*She moves at chess, taking a piece*]

MOTHER Well, ere now, lady,
I have seen the fall of subtlety.
[*She moves at chess, taking a piece*]
Jest on.

LIVIA
Ay, but simplicity receives two for one.
[*She moves at chess, taking a piece*]

MOTHER
What remedy but patience?
Enter, above, Guardiano and Bianca

BIANCA Trust me, sir,
Mine eye ne'er met with fairer ornaments.

GUARDIANO
Nay, livelier, I'm persuaded, neither Florence
Nor Venice can produce.

BIANCA Sir, my opinion
Takes your part highly.

GUARDIANO There's a better piece
Yet than all these.
Enter Duke, above, [*behind Bianca*]

BIANCA Not possible, sir!

GUARDIANO Believe it,
You'll say so when you see't. Turn but your eye now,
You're upon't presently. *Exit*
[*Bianca sees the Duke*]

BIANCA O, sir!

DUKE He's gone, beauty.
Pish, look not after him. He's but a vapour
That when the sun appears is seen no more.
[*He takes hold of her*]

BIANCA
O, treachery to honour!

DUKE Prithee, tremble not.
I feel thy breast shake like a turtle panting
Under a loving hand that makes much on't.
Why art so fearful? As I'm friend to brightness,
There's nothing but respect and honour near thee.
You know me, you have seen me; here's a heart
Can witness I have seen thee.

BIANCA The more's my danger.

DUKE
The more's thy happiness. Pish, strive not, sweet.
This strength were excellent employed in love now,
But here 'tis spent amiss. Strive not to seek
Thy liberty and keep me still in prison.
I'faith, you shall not out till I'm released now.
We'll be both freed together, or stay still by't;
So is captivity pleasant.

BIANCA O, my lord!

DUKE
I am not here in vain. Have but the leisure
To think on that, and thou'lt be soon resolved.
The lifting of thy voice is but like one
That does exalt his enemy, who, proving high,
Lays all the plots to confound him that raised him.
Take warning, I beseech thee. Thou seem'st to me
A creature so composed of gentleness
And delicate meekness, such as bless the faces
Of figures that are drawn for goddesses
And makes art proud to look upon her work,
I should be sorry the least force should lay
An unkind touch upon thee.

BIANCA O, my extremity!
My lord, what seek you?

DUKE Love.

BIANCA 'Tis gone already;
I have a husband.

DUKE That's a single comfort.
Take a friend to him.

BIANCA That's a double mischief,
Or else there's no religion.

DUKE Do not tremble
At fears of thine own making.

BIANCA Nor, great lord,
Make me not bold with death and deeds of ruin
Because they fear not you. Me they must fright;
Then am I best in health. Should thunder speak
And none regard it, it had lost the name,
And were as good be still. I'm not like those
That take their soundest sleeps in greatest tempests.
Then wake I most, the weather fearfullest,
And call for strength to virtue.

DUKE Sure I think
Thou know'st the way to please me. I affect
A passionate pleading 'bove an easy yielding,
But never pitied any—they deserve none—
That will not pity me. I can command—
Think upon that—yet if thou truly knewest
The infinite pleasure my affection takes
In gentle, fair entreatings, when love's businesses
Are carried courteously 'twixt heart and heart,
You'd make more haste to please me.

308 **simplicity ... one** (proverbial)
311 **livelier** (anticipating the living 'monument')
316 **presently** immediately
318 **the sun** (a common image for a prince)
320 **turtle** turtle-dove
322 **brightness** beauty
326 **happiness** good fortune
329 **in prison** Figurative for denial of sexual freedom, but Bianca is herself physically restrained by the Duke's arms ('you shall not out').
331 **still** (*a*) continually (*b*) motionless
by't i.e. in prison
336 **exalt** (*a*) praise, magnify (*b*) raise in power (*c*) raise physically (see previous note). Also glancing at exalting (i.e. *lifting*) the voice.
his enemy i.e. the man who turns out to be his enemy
proving high i.e. once in power
340 **such** (the *gentleness* and *meekness*)
341 **for** of
347 **friend** lover
to in addition to
350 **bold with** presumptuous towards
351 **fear** frighten
352 **Then** i.e. in being frightened at the right times
thunder (as a warning of tempests)
354 **still** quiet
357 **to** to maintain

BIANCA
Why should you seek, sir,
To take away that you can never give?

DUKE
But I give better in exchange: wealth, honour.
She that is fortunate in a duke's favour
Lights on a tree that bears all women's wishes.
If your own mother saw you pluck fruit there,
She would commend your wit and praise the time
Of your nativity. Take hold of glory.
Do not I know you've cast away your life
Upon necessities, means merely doubtful
To keep you in indifferent health and fashion—
A thing I heard too lately, and soon pitied—
And can you be so much your beauty's enemy
To kiss away a month or two in wedlock
And weep whole years in wants for ever after?
Come, play the wife, wench, and provide for ever.
Let storms come when they list, they find thee
sheltered.
Should any doubt arise, let nothing trouble thee.
Put trust in our love for the managing
Of all to thy heart's peace. We'll walk together,
And show a thankful joy for both our fortunes.

Exeunt Duke and Bianca from above

LIVIA
Did I not say my duke would fetch you over, widow?

MOTHER
I think you spoke in earnest when you said it,
madam.

LIVIA
And my black king makes all the haste he can, too.

MOTHER
Well, madam, we may meet with him in time yet.

LIVIA
I have given thee blind mate twice.

MOTHER
You may see, madam,
My eyes begin to fail.

LIVIA
I'll swear they do, wench.

Enter Guardiano [below]

GUARDIANO [*aside*]
I can but smile as often as I think on't.
How prettily the poor fool was beguiled,
How unexpectedly! It's a witty age.
Never were finer snares for women's honesties
Than are devised in these days; no spider's web
Made of a daintier thread than are now practised
To catch love's flesh-fly by the silver wing.
Yet to prepare her stomach by degrees
To Cupid's feast, because I saw 'twas queasy,
I showed her naked pictures by the way:
A bit to stay the appetite. Well, advancement,
I venture hard to find thee. If thou com'st
With a greater title set upon thy crest,
I'll take that first cross patiently, and wait
Until some other comes greater than that.
I'll endure all.

LIVIA
The game's e'en at the best now. You may see,
widow,
How all things draw to an end.

MOTHER
E'en so do I, madam.

LIVIA
I pray take some of your neighbours along with you.

MOTHER
They must be those are almost twice your years then,
If they be chose fit matches for my time, madam.

LIVIA
Has not my duke bestirred himself?

MOTHER
Yes, faith, madam;
He's done me all the mischief in this game.

LIVIA
He's showed himself in's kind.

MOTHER
'In's kind' call you it?
I may swear that.

370–1 **a...there** Recalls the serpent that induced Eve to eat the forbidden fruit of the Tree of Knowledge, Genesis, 3:1–6.

372–3 **praise...nativity** (as an auspicious time to be born)

375 **merely** entirely

381 **play the wife** i.e. (*a*) play the housewife, don't squander beauty but *provide for ever* (*b*) put yourself in the role of my wife (*c*) don't take being Leantio's wife too seriously, play the game

387–9 **Did...too** As an allusion to the betrayal of Bianca, Livia's *duke* is Hippolito, and her *black king* is the Duke.

387 **fetch you over** get the better of you

390 **meet with** (*a*) encounter in battle; or (*b*) be even with

391 **blind mate** Technically, a checkmate that the attacker claims as merely a check. Here it is the Mother who is blind, in the senses of being poorer at chess, oblivious to Bianca's entrapment, and, as she replies, literally poor-sighted. But Livia too has not actually seen the two traps sprung above that she has engineered. *Blind* also suggests 'secret, furtive' and implies spiritual blindness.

394 **fool** (more a term of pity than contempt)

399 **flesh-fly** blow-fly (specified for the sexual connotation of *flesh*)

400 **stomach** appetite

401 **queasy** (*a*) nauseous (*b*) fastidious

403 **bit** morsel
stay sustain, strengthen (with ironic reference to the usual sense in this situation, 'hold back, appease')

405 **title** inscription (the bearer's motto of his worth). The title in mind is presumably that of pandar.
crest device above the shield and helmet in a heraldic coat of arms. There is also probably a reference to cuckold's horns: Guardiano has abetted adultery.

406–8 **I'll...all** *Cross* and *endure* are ironic; Hippolito is pleased with himself.

406 **cross** thwarting (or perhaps a casually blasphemous use of the sense 'affliction borne for Christ's sake')

407 **some other** i.e. some other opportunity to gain a *title*

409–10 **The...end** (with a secondary allusion to the Duke and Bianca's *game*, reaching its sexual climax)

410 **E'en so do I** (referring to the approach of death)

411 **I...you** The imputation is apparently that the *neighbours* can be better spared from life than the Mother; numbers might increase her chance of survival.

413 **time** age

414 **bestirred** (with a sexual innuendo)

416 **in's kind** according to his nature (but he has been *un*kind to the Mother, hence her query)

LIVIA Yes, faith, and keep your oath.

GUARDIANO
Hark, list, there's somebody coming down; 'tis she.
Enter Bianca

BIANCA [*aside*]
Now bless me from a blasting! I saw that now
Fearful for any woman's eye to look on.
Infectious mists and mildews hang at's eyes.
The weather of a doomsday dwells upon him.
Yet since mine honour's leprous, why should I
Preserve that fair that caused the leprosy?
Come, poison all at once. [*Aside to Guardiano*] Thou in whose baseness
The bane of virtue broods, I'm bound in soul
Eternally to curse thy smooth browed treachery,
That wore the fair veil of a friendly welcome,
And I a stranger. Think upon't, 'tis worth it.
Murders piled up upon a guilty spirit
At his last breath will not lie heavier
Than this betraying act upon thy conscience.
Beware of off'ring the first-fruits to sin.
His weight is deadly who commits with strumpets
After they have been abased and made for use;
If they offend to th' death, as wise men know,
How much more they then that first made 'em so?
I give thee that to feed on. I'm made bold now,
I thank thy treachery. Sin and I'm acquainted,
No couple greater; and I'm like that great one
Who, making politic use of a base villain,
"He likes the treason well, but hates the traitor."
So I hate thee, slave.

GUARDIANO [*aside*] Well, so the Duke love me,
I fare not much amiss then. Two great feasts
Do seldom come together in one day;
We must not look for 'em.

BIANCA What, at it still, mother?

MOTHER
You see we sit by't. Are you so soon returned?

LIVIA [*aside*]
So lively and so cheerful: a good sign that.

MOTHER
You have not seen all since, sure?

BIANCA That have I, mother,
The monument and all. I'm so beholding
To this kind, honest, courteous gentleman
You'd little think it, mother; showed me all,
Had me from place to place, so fashionably.
The kindness of some people, how't exceeds!
Faith, I have seen that I little thought to see
I'th' morning when I rose.

MOTHER Nay, so I told you
Before you saw't, it would prove worth your sight.—
I give you great thanks for my daughter, sir,
And all your kindness towards her.

GUARDIANO O good widow,
Much good may't do her!—[*Aside*] forty weeks hence, i'faith.
Enter Servant

LIVIA
Now, sir.

SERVANT May't please you, madam, to walk in?
Supper's upon the table.

LIVIA Yes, we come. [*Exit Servant*]
Will't please you, gentlewoman?

BIANCA Thanks, virtuous lady.
[*Aside to her*] You're a damned bawd. [*Aloud*] I'll follow you, forsooth.
Pray take my mother in. [*Aside to her*] An old ass go with you.
[*Aloud*] This gentleman and I vow not to part.

LIVIA
Then get you both before.

BIANCA [*aside*] There lies his art.
Exeunt Guardiano and Bianca

LIVIA
Widow, I'll follow you. [*Exit Mother*]
Is't so: 'damned bawd'?
Are you so bitter? 'Tis but want of use.
Her tender modesty is sea-sick a little,
Being not accustomed to the breaking billow
Of woman's wavering faith, blown with temptations.
'Tis but a qualm of honour; 'twill away;
A little bitter for the time, but lasts not.
Sin tastes at the first draught like wormwood-water,
But, drunk again, 'tis nectar ever after. *Exit*
Finis Actus Secundus

419 **bless me** i.e. may I be protected
a blasting (*a*) calumny, infamy, ruin (*b*) blighting by the *Infectious mists and mildews* of 421. Perhaps also 'the curse of heaven' (compare *doomsday*, 422).
421 **mists** (thought to carry disease)
428 **veil** (probably punning on *vail*, salutation by doffing the hat)
433 **first-fruits** (alluding to Bianca herself, as newly married)
to sin (rather than to God, to whom first-fruits were customarily offered)
436 **they** (i.e. those who consort with strumpets)
437 **'em** (i.e. the strumpets themselves)
440 **greater** more intimate and friendly (also anticipating *great*, 'powerful')
that great one (probably referring to Machiavelli)
442 **He . . . traitor** Italicized in the original edition, to mark the line's function as a sententia.
443 **so** if
446 **look for** expect
449 **since** already (*OED*, *adv.*, 1c; sole example dated *c.*1553)
453 **Had** (quibbling on sexual possession)
467 **There lies his art** that's what he's skilful at (i.e. leading Bianca forward or astray)
469 **want of use** lack of practice
472 **wavering . . . temptations** (wordplay on *wave* and *tempests*)
475 **wormwood-water** (a drink prepared with the proverbially bitter herb wormwood)

3.1 *Incipit Actus Tertius*
Enter Mother

MOTHER
I would my son would either keep at home
Or I were in my grave.
She was but one day abroad, but ever since
She's grown so cutted there's no speaking to her.
Whether the sight of great cheer at my lady's
And such mean fare at home work discontent in her,
I know not; but I'm sure she's strangely altered.
I'll ne'er keep daughter-in-law i'th' house with me
Again if I had an hundred. When read I of any
That agreed long together, but she and her mother
Fell out in the first quarter?—nay, sometime
A grudging of a scolding the first week, by'r Lady.
So takes the new disease, methinks, in my house.
I'm weary of my part. There's nothing likes her.
I know not how to please her here o' late.
Enter Bianca
And here she comes.

BIANCA
This is the strangest house
For all defects as ever gentlewoman
Made shift withal to pass away her love in.
Why is there not a cushion-cloth of drawn-work,
Or some fair cut-work pinned up in my bedchamber,
A silver and gilt casting-bottle hung by't?
Nay, since I am content to be so kind to you
To spare you for a silver basin and ewer,
Which one of my fashion looks for of duty:
She's never offered under where she sleeps.

MOTHER
She talks of things here my whole state's not worth.

BIANCA
Never a green silk quilt is there i'th' house, mother,
To cast upon my bed?

MOTHER
No, by troth, is there,
Nor orange tawny neither.

BIANCA
Here's a house
For a young gentlewoman to be got with child in!

MOTHER
Yes, simple though you make it, there has been three
Got in a year in't, since you move me to't,
And all as sweet-faced children and as lovely
As you'll be mother of. I will not spare you:
What, cannot children be begot, think you,
Without gilt casting-bottles; yes, and as sweet ones?
The miller's daughter brings forth as white boys
As she that bathes herself with milk and bean-flour.
'Tis an old saying: one may keep good cheer
In a mean house; so may love affect
After the rate of princes in a cottage.

BIANCA
Troth, you speak wondrous well for your old house
here.
'Twill shortly fall down at your feet to thank you,
Or stoop when you go to bed, like a good child,
To ask you blessing. Must I live in want
Because my fortune matched me with your son?
Wives do not give away themselves to husbands
To the end to be quite cast away; they look
To be the better used and tendered, rather,
Higher respected, and maintained the richer.
They're well rewarded else for the free gift
Of their whole life to a husband! I ask less now
Than what I had at home when I was a maid,
And at my father's house kept short of that
Which a wife knows she must have—nay, and will,
Will, mother, if she be not a fool born.
And report went of me that I could wrangle
For what I wanted when I was two hours old;
And by that copy this land still I hold.
You hear me, mother. *Exit*

MOTHER
Ay, too plain, methinks;
And were I somewhat deafer when you spake,
'Twere ne'er a whit the worse for my quietness.
'Tis the most sudden'st, strangest alteration,
And the most subtlest, that e'er wit at threescore
Was puzzled to find out. I know no cause for't, but
She's no more like the gentlewoman at first
Than I am like her that ne'er lay with man yet;
And she's a very young thing, where'er she be.
When she first lighted here, I told her then
How mean she should find all things. She was
pleased, forsooth,
None better. I laid open all defects to her;
She was contented still. But the devil's in her,
Nothing contents her, now. Tonight my son
Promised to be at home. Would he were come once,

3.1.4 **cutted** curt
12 **grudging** (as of an approaching *disease*, 13). The sense 'grumbling', though it doesn't fit the sentence, anticipates *scolding*.
13 **takes** catches
the new disease (vogue term for any undiagnosed fever)
14 **likes** pleases
16–25 **This...sleeps** There is an undercurrent of bawdy carried in *Made shift* ('contrived for sexual purposes'), *drawn* ('sexually used or drained'), *cut-work* ('cunt'), *casting-bottle* ('penis').
18 **Made shift** managed
19 **cushion-cloth of drawn-work** ornamented cushion cover. The patterns of drawn-work were made by drawing out particular threads.
20 **cut-work** embroidered lace
21 **casting-bottle** bottle for sprinkling perfume
23 **To spare you for** not to expect from you
24 **looks for of duty** expects as due to her
25 **under** less
26 **state's** estate's
29 **orange tawny** brownish orange (a fashionable, courtly colour)
37 **white** (*a*) dear, darling (*b*) the colour of flour and milk
38 **bathes...bean-flour** (an epitome of luxury)
41 **After the rate of** on the same scale as
49 **tendered** cherished
59 **copy** transcribed document establishing security of tenure from a landlord. Bianca sees the verbal *report* of her success in wrangling as a document establishing her right to so continue.
62 **quietness** (*a*) peace of mind (*b*) enjoyment of silence
74 **once** finally

For I'm weary of my charge, and life too.
She'd be served all in silver, by her good will,
By night and day. She hates the name of pewterer
More than sick men the noise, or diseased bones
That quake at fall o'th' hammer, seeming to have
A fellow feeling with't at every blow.
What course shall I think on? She frets me so.
[*She stands apart.*] *Enter Leantio*

LEANTIO
How near am I now to a happiness
That earth exceeds not, not another like it!
The treasures of the deep are not so precious
As are the còncealed comforts of a man
Locked up in woman's love. I scent the air
Of blessings when I come but near the house.
What a delicious breath marriage sends forth!
The violet bed's not sweeter. Honest wedlock
Is like a banqueting-house built in a garden
On which the spring's chaste flowers take delight
To cast their modest odours; when base lust
With all her powders, paintings, and best pride
Is but a fair house built by a ditch side.
When I behold a glorious dangerous strumpet
Sparkling in beauty, and destruction too,
Both at a twinkling, I do liken straight
Her beautified body to a goodly temple
That's built on vaults where carcasses lie rotting;
And so by little and little I shrink back again,
And quench desire with a cool meditation.
And I'm as well, methinks.
[*Enter Bianca*]
Now for a welcome
Able to draw men's envies upon man;
A kiss now that will hang upon my lip
As sweet as morning dew upon a rose,
And full as long. After a five-days' fast
She'll be so greedy now, and cling about me,
I take care how I shall be rid of her.
And here't begins.

BIANCA
O, sir, you're welcome home.

MOTHER [*aside*]
O, is he come? I'm glad on't.

LEANTIO [*aside*]
Is that all?
Why this?—as dreadful now as sudden death
To some rich man that flatters all his sins
With promise of repentance when he's old,
And dies in the midway before he comes to't.—
Sure you're not well, Bianca! How dost, prithee?

BIANCA
I have been better than I am at this time.

LEANTIO
Alas, I thought so.

BIANCA
Nay, I have been worse, too,
Than now you see me, sir.

LEANTIO
I'm glad thou mend'st yet;
I feel my heart mend too. How came it to thee?
Has anything disliked thee in my absence?

BIANCA
No, certain; I have had the best content
That Florence can afford.

LEANTIO
Thou makest the best on't.—
Speak, mother, what's the cause? You must needs know.

MOTHER
Troth, I know none, son; let her speak herself—
[*Aside*] Unless it be the same gave Lucifer
A tumbling cast; that's pride.

BIANCA
Methinks this house stands nothing to my mind.
I'd have some pleasant lodging i'th' high street, sir;
Or if 'twere near the court, sir, that were much better.
'Tis a sweet recreation for a gentlewoman
To stand in a bay window and see gallants.

LEANTIO
Now I have another temper, a mere stranger
To that of yours, it seems. I should delight
To see none but yourself.

BIANCA
I praise not that.
Too fond is as unseemly as too churlish.
I would not have a husband of that proneness
To kiss me before company for a world.
Beside, 'tis tedious to see one thing still, sir,
Be it the best that ever heart affected.
Nay, were't yourself, whose love had power, you know,
To bring me from my friends, I would not stand thus
And gaze upon you always; troth, I could not, sir.
As good be blind and have no use of sight
As look on one thing still. What's the eye's treasure
But change of objects? You are learned, sir,

77 **pewterer** Cheaper vessels were made of pewter.
78 **the noise** (of the pewterer's hammering) **diseased** i.e. brittle and wasted with venereal disease
79 **quake** i.e. (*a*) tremble in fear (*b*) vibrate (anticipating the emotional and physical *fellow feeling*, 80)
90 **banqueting-house** garden house where snacks and delicacies were eaten (ironically, often a place of sexual assignation)
92 **when** whereas
93 **powders, paintings** i.e. cosmetics **pride** (*a*) ostentatious finery (*b*) sexual fervour (*c*) sinful self-regard
94 **a fair ... side** Houses stood close by London's City Ditch, virtually an open sewer.
98–9 **a ... rotting** One of many contemporary passages drawn from Matthew, 23:27, where Christ compares the hypocritical scribes and Pharisees to 'whited tombs, which appear beautiful outward, but are within full of dead men's bones and all filthiness'.
106 **full as long** Dew soon evaporates, but endures longer than most kisses, and might be thought to linger on the rose.
108 **take care** worry
120 **disliked** displeased
126 **tumbling cast** fall, throw (as in wrestling). With a sexual equivocation as applied to Bianca.
127 **nothing to my mind** not at all as I want it
135 **churlish** niggardly (also drawing on the literal meaning, 'peasant-like')
136 **proneness** (*a*) inclination (*b*) sexual fervour

And know I speak not ill. 'Tis full as virtuous
For woman's eye to look on several men
As for her heart, sir, to be fixed on one.

LEANTIO
Now thou com'st home to me. A kiss for that word.

BIANCA
No matter for a kiss, sir; let it pass.
'Tis but a toy; we'll not so much as mind it.
Let's talk of other business, and forget it.
What news now of the pirates? Any stirring?
Prithee, discourse a little.

MOTHER [*aside*] I am glad he's here yet
To see her tricks himself. I had lied monstrously
If I had told 'em first.

LEANTIO [*to Bianca*] Speak, what's the humour, sweet,
You make your lip so strange? This was not wont.

BIANCA
Is there no kindness betwixt man and wife
Unless they make a pigeon-house of friendship,
And be still billing? 'Tis the idlest fondness
That ever was invented, and 'tis pity
It's grown a fashion for poor gentlewomen.
There's many a disease kissed in a year by't,
And a French curtsey made to't. Alas, sir,
Think of the world, how we shall live. Grow serious;
We have been married a whole fortnight now.

LEANTIO
How, a whole fortnight? Why, is that so long?

BIANCA
'Tis time to leave off dalliance: 'tis a doctrine
Of your own teaching, if you be remembered,
And I was bound to obey it.

MOTHER [*aside*] Here's one fits him!
This was well catched, i'faith, son, like a fellow
That rids another country of a plague,
And brings it home with him to his own house.

Knock within

Who knocks?

LEANTIO Who's there now? Withdraw you, Bianca.
Thou art a gem no stranger's eye must see,
Howe'er thou please now to look dull on me.

Exit Bianca

Enter Messenger

You're welcome, sir. To whom your business, pray?

MESSENGER
To one I see not here now.

LEANTIO Who should that be, sir?

MESSENGER
A young gentlewoman I was sent to.

LEANTIO A young gentlewoman?

MESSENGER
Ay, sir, about sixteen. Why look you wildly, sir?

LEANTIO
At your strange error. You've mistook the house, sir.
There's none such here, I assure you.

MESSENGER I assure you, too,
The man that sent me cannot be mistook.

LEANTIO
Why, who is't sent you, sir?

MESSENGER The Duke.

LEANTIO The Duke?

MESSENGER
Yes; he entreats her company at a banquet
At Lady Livia's house.

LEANTIO Troth, shall I tell you, sir,
It is the most erroneous business
That e'er your honest pains was abused with.
I pray forgive me if I smile a little;
I cannot choose, i'faith, sir, at an error
So comical as this.—I mean no harm though.—
His grace has been most wondrous ill informed.
Pray so return it, sir. What should her name be?

MESSENGER
That I shall tell you straight, too: Bianca Capella.

LEANTIO
How, sir, Bianca? What do you call th'other?

MESSENGER
Capella. Sir, it seems you know no such then?

LEANTIO
Who should this be? I never heard o'th' name.

MESSENGER
Then 'tis a sure mistake.

LEANTIO What if you enquired
In the next street, sir? I saw gallants there,
In the new houses that are built of late.
Ten to one, there you find her.

MESSENGER Nay, no matter.
I will return the mistake, and seek no further.

LEANTIO
Use your own will and pleasure, sir; you're welcome.

Exit Messenger

What shall I think of first? Come forth, Bianca;
Thou art betrayed, I fear me.

Enter Bianca

BIANCA Betrayed? How, sir?

LEANTIO
The Duke knows thee—

BIANCA Knows me! How know you that, sir?

LEANTIO
Has got thy name.

BIANCA [*aside*] Ay, and my good name too;

154 **yet** i.e. despite his discomfiture
156 **humour** whim
160 **idlest** most foolish
fondness (*a*) silliness, timidity (*b*) affection
164 **French curtsey** (alluding to the supposed elaborate manners of the French, and to syphilis, the 'French disease')
170 **fits him** punishes him fittingly
184 **be mistook** make a mistake (and 'be misrecognized')
203 **mistake** i.e. allegation of a mistake
207 **knows** knows of (but in Bianca's reply, 'knows carnally')
208 **good name** reputation

That's worse o'th' twain.
LEANTIO How comes this work about?
BIANCA
How should the Duke know me? Can you guess,
mother?
MOTHER
Not I, with all my wits. Sure we kept house close.
LEANTIO
Kept close? Not all the locks in Italy
Can keep you women so. You have been gadding,
And ventured out at twilight to th' court green
yonder,
And met the gallant bowlers coming home—
Without your masks, too, both of you, I'll be hanged
else.
Thou hast been seen, Bianca, by some stranger;
Never excuse it.
BIANCA I'll not seek the way, sir.
Do you think you've married me to mew me up
Not to be seen? What would you make of me?
LEANTIO
A good wife, nothing else.
BIANCA Why, so are some
That are seen every day, else the devil take 'em.
LEANTIO
No more then; I believe all virtuous in thee
Without an argument. 'Twas but thy hard chance
To be seen somewhere; there lies all the mischief.
But I have devised a riddance.
MOTHER Now I can tell you, son,
The time and place.
LEANTIO When? Where?
MOTHER What wits have I!
When you last took your leave, if you remember,
You left us both at window.
LEANTIO Right, I know that.
MOTHER
And not the third part of an hour after,
The Duke passed by in a great solemnity
To St Mark's Temple; and, to my apprehension,
He looked up twice to th' window.
LEANTIO O, there quickened
The mischief of this hour!
BIANCA [*aside*] If you call't mischief;
It is a thing I fear I am conceived with.
LEANTIO [*to Mother*]
Looked he up twice, and could you take no warning?
MOTHER
Why, once may do as much harm, son, as a thou-
sand.
Do not you know one spark has fired an house
As well as a whole furnace?
LEANTIO My heart flames for't.
Yet let's be wise, and keep all smothered closely.
I have bethought a means. Is the door fast?
MOTHER
I locked it myself after him.
LEANTIO You know, mother,
At the end of the dark parlour there's a place
So artificially contrived for a conveyance
No search could ever find it. When my father
Kept in for manslaughter, it was his sanctuary.
There will I lock my life's best treasure up,
Bianca.
BIANCA
Would you keep me closer yet?
Have you the conscience? You're best e'en choke me
up, sir!
You make me fearful of your health and wits,
You cleave to such wild courses. What's the matter?
LEANTIO
Why, are you so insensible of your danger
To ask that now? The Duke himself has sent for you
To Lady Livia's, to a banquet, forsooth.
BIANCA
Now I beshrew you heartily! Has he so,
And you the man would never yet vouchsafe
To tell me on't till now? You show your loyalty
And honesty at once. And so, farewell, sir.
LEANTIO
Bianca, whither now?
BIANCA Why, to the Duke, sir.
You say he sent for me.
LEANTIO But thou dost not mean
To go, I hope.
BIANCA No: I shall prove unmannerly,
Rude, and uncivil, mad, and imitate you.
Come, mother, come. Follow his humour no longer.
We shall be all executed for treason shortly.
MOTHER
Not I, i'faith; I'll first obey the Duke,
And taste of a good banquet; I'm of thy mind.
I'll step but up and fetch two handkerchiefs

211 **kept house close** remained closely indoors
213 **gadding** wandering at large
215 **gallant bowlers** Bowling was a pastime for 'gallants'.
216 **masks** (worn by upper-class English women at entertainments, and by Italian women in public more generally)
219 **mew** coop
232 **apprehension** notice, knowledge
233 **quickened** Leantio uses metaphorically ('came to life'); Bianca takes literally ('became pregnant')
243 **parlour** side room, inner room
244 **artificially** skilfully
for a conveyance (*a*) for an underhand dealing (*b*) as a secret passage
246 **Kept in** remained indoors
for i.e. because of committing
249 **You're . . . up** you may as well suffocate me
254 **banquet** (either a large meal or a spread of sweetmeats and delicacies)
263 **Follow his humour** go along with his odd state of mind
267 **step but up** just go upstairs

To pocket up some sweetmeats, and o'ertake thee.
Exit

BIANCA [*aside*]
Why, here's an old wench would trot into a bawd now,
For some dry sucket or a colt in marzipan. *Exit*

LEANTIO
O thou the ripe time of man's misery, wedlock;
When all his thoughts, like overladen trees,
Crack with the fruits they bear, in cares, in jealousies.
O, that's a fruit that ripens hastily
After 'tis knit to marriage. It begins,
As soon as the sun shines upon the bride,
A little to show colour. Blessèd powers,
Whence comes this alteration? The distractions,
The fears and doubts it brings are numberless,
And yet the cause I know not. What a peace
Has he that never marries! If he knew
The benefit he enjoyed, or had the fortune
To come and speak with me, he should know then
The infinite wealth he had, and discern rightly
The greatness of his treasure by my loss.
Nay, what a quietness has he 'bove mine
That wears his youth out in a strumpet's arms,
And never spends more care upon a woman
Than at the time of lust; but walks away,
And if he find her dead at his return
His pity is soon done: he breaks a sigh
In many parts, and gives her but a piece on't.
But all the fears, shames, jealousies, costs, and troubles,
And still-renewed cares of a marriage bed
Live in the issue when the wife is dead.
Enter Messenger

MESSENGER
A good perfection to your thoughts.

LEANTIO
The news, sir?

MESSENGER
Though you were pleased of late to pin an error on me,
You must not shift another in your stead too:
The Duke has sent me for you.

LEANTIO
How, for me, sir?
[*Aside*] I see then 'tis my theft. We're both betrayed.
Well, I'm not the first has stol'n away a maid;
My countrymen have used it.—I'll along with you, sir.
Exeunt

A banquet prepared. Enter Guardiano and Ward 3.2

GUARDIANO
Take you especial note of such a gentlewoman.
She's here on purpose. I have invited her,
Her father, and her uncle to this banquet.
Mark her behaviour well; it does concern you;
And what her good parts are, as far as time
And place can modestly require a knowledge of,
Shall be laid open to your understanding.
You know I'm both your guardian and your uncle:
My care of you is double, ward and nephew,
And I'll express it here.

WARD
Faith, I should know her
Now by her mark among a thousand women.
A little, pretty, deft, and tidy thing, you say.

GUARDIANO Right.

WARD
With a lusty sprouting sprig in her hair.

GUARDIANO
Thou goest the right way still. Take one mark more:
Thou shalt ne'er find her hand out of her uncle's,
Or else his out of hers, if she be near him.
The love of kindred never yet stuck closer
Than theirs to one another. He that weds her
Marries her uncle's heart too.
Cornetts [*sound within*]

WARD
Say you so, sir?
Then I'll be asked i'th' church to both of them.

GUARDIANO
Fall back; here comes the Duke.

WARD
He brings a gentlewoman:
I should fall forward rather.
Enter Duke, Bianca, Fabritio, Hippolito, Livia, Mother, Isabella, and attendants

DUKE
Come, Bianca:
Of purpose sent into the world to show

268 **o'ertake** catch up with
269 **into** into being
270 **dry sucket** (sweetmeat made by allowing rosewater-flavoured syrup to solidify around fruit)
in made out of
marzipan sweet confection of ground almonds (pronounced as two syllables)
275 **knit** joined together (also suggesting the forming or setting of fruit)
288 **spends** (with a quibble on emission of semen)
294 **still-renewed** ever-renewed
296 **perfection** completion, outcome
298 **shift...stead** (*a*) substitute another person for you (*b*) contrive another trick to your advantage.
300 **'tis my theft** Leantio thinks Bianca's family has caught up with him by way of the Duke.
302 **used** often done
3.2.0.1 ***prepared*** i.e. set out on the stage
6 **require** search for
of of them
11 **mark** characteristic feature. *Mark* and *thing* (12) quibble on 'vulva', anticipating 13.
14 **lusty** (*a*) large (*b*) vigorous(ly) (*c*) lustful(ly)
sprig (*a*) sprig-like ornament (*b*) rod (phallic; ironically anticipating 15–20)
hair (with a suggestion of 'pubic hair')
21 **asked** (as at 2.2.88–9)
22 **Fall back** make way. Deliberately or stupidly misunderstood by the Ward in the literal sense.
a gentlewoman Probably refers to Isabella (compare 1–3), but the Ward might have seen the Duke entering with Bianca.
23 **fall forward** (in sexual embrace)
23.2 ***Isabella*** Livia might be looking after the Mother and Isabella; but, if the list of names does not reflect theatrical practice, Isabella would more plausibly appear with Fabritio and Hippolito.

Perfection once in woman; I'll believe
Henceforward they have every one a soul too,
'Gainst all the uncourteous opinions
That man's uncivil rudeness ever held of 'em.
Glory of Florence, light into mine arms!
Enter Leantio

BIANCA
Yon comes a grudging man will chide you, sir.
The storm is now in's heart, and would get nearer
And fall here if it durst; it pours down yonder.

DUKE
If that be he, the weather shall soon clear.
List, and I'll tell thee how.
[*He whispers in her ear*]

LEANTIO [*aside*] A-kissing too?
I see 'tis plain lust now, adultery boldened.
What will it prove anon when 'tis stuffed full
Of wine and sweetmeats, being so impudent fasting?

DUKE
We have heard of your good parts, sir, which we honour
With our embrace and love.
[*Leantio kneels*]
Is not the captainship
Of Ruinse citadel, since the late deceased,
Supplied by any yet?

GENTLEMAN By none, my lord.

DUKE [*to Leantio*]
Take it, the place is yours then; and as faithfulness
And dèsert grows, our favour shall grow with't.
Rise now the captain of our fort at Ruinse.

LEANTIO [*rising*]
The service of whole life give your grace thanks.

DUKE
Come, sit, Bianca.
[*They sit. Leantio stands apart*]

LEANTIO [*aside*] This is some good yet,
And more than e'er I looked for. A fine bit
To stay a cuckold's stomach! All preferment
That springs from sin and lust, it shoots up quickly,
As gardeners' crops do in the rotten'st grounds.
So is all means raised from base prostitution
E'en like a sallet growing upon a dunghill.
I'm like a thing that never was yet heard of:
Half merry and half mad, much like a fellow
That eats his meat with a good appetite,
And wears a plague-sore that would fright a country;
Or rather like the barren, hardened ass
That feeds on thistles till he bleeds again;
And such is the condition of my misery.

LIVIA
Is that your son, widow?

MOTHER Yes; did your ladyship
Never know that till now?

LIVIA No, trust me, did I;
[*Aside*] Nor ever truly felt the power of love
And pity to a man till now I knew him.
I have enough to buy me my desires,
And yet to spare; that's one good comfort. [*To Leantio*]
Hark you!
Pray let me speak with you, sir, before you go.

LEANTIO
With me, lady? You shall; I am at your service.—
What will she say now, trow? More goodness yet?

WARD
I see her now, I'm sure. The ape's so little
I shall scarce feel her. I have seen almost
As tall as she sold in the fair for tenpence.
See how she simpers it, as if marmalade
Would not melt in her mouth. She might have the kindness, i'faith,
To send me a gilded bull from her own trencher,
A ram, a goat, or somewhat to be nibbling.
These women, when they come to sweet things once
They forget all their friends, they grow so greedy—
Nay, oftentimes their husbands.

DUKE Here's a health now, gallants,
To the best beauty at this day in Florence.

BIANCA
Whoe'er she be, she shall not go unpledged, sir.

DUKE
Nay, you're excused for this.

BIANCA Who, I, my lord?

DUKE
Yes, by the law of Bacchus. Plead your benefit;
You are not bound to pledge your own health, lady.

BIANCA
That's a good way, my lord, to keep me dry.

DUKE
Nay, then I will not offend Venus so much.
Let Bacchus seek his 'mends in another court.
Here's to thyself, Bianca.

26 **they** i.e. women. The view that women had no souls remained current in misogynist rhetoric.
37 **impudent** shameless
40 **Ruinse** Probably an Anglicization of 'Ruinate', a place near a fort on the walls of Florence whose name means 'ruinous'.
41 **Supplied** filled
47 **bit** morsel
51 **means** (*a*) opportunity (*b*) wealth (with a suggestion of 'all that is lowly')
52 **sallet** salad vegetable
55 **meat** food
57–8 **the . . . again** (with a glance at the proverb 'the ass loaded with gold still eats thistles')
57 **barren** poor, useless, stupid
71 **sold . . . tenpence** (referring to either apes or dolls)
72 **marmalade** jam (not necessarily of citrus fruits)
74 **gilded bull** One of the marzipan shapes. The bull, ram, and goat all suggest lechery.
trencher wooden plate
77–8 **They . . . husbands** The Duke's *health* (78–9) affirms the relevance to Bianca.
77 **friends** relatives
82 **Plead your benefit** Usually refers to the clergy's or peerage's benefits of exemption.
85 **Venus** (associated with warmth and moistness)
86 **'mends** amends
court (*a*) court of law (*b*) prince's court

BIANCA Nothing comes
More welcome to that name than your grace.
[*They drink*]

LEANTIO [*aside*] So, so.
Here stands the poor thief now that stole the treasure,
And he's not thought on. Ours is near kin now
To a twin misery born into the world:
First the hard-conscienced worldling, he hoards wealth up;
Then comes the next, and he feasts all upon't.
One's damned for getting, th'other for spending on't.
O equal justice, thou hast met my sin
With a full weight. I'm rightly now oppressed.
All her friends' heavy hearts lie in my breast.

DUKE
Methinks there is no spirit amongst us, gallants,
But what divinely sparkles from the eyes
Of bright Bianca; we sat all in darkness
But for that splendour. Who was't told us lately
Of a match-making rite, a marriage tender?

GUARDIANO
'Twas I, my lord.

DUKE 'Twas you indeed. Where is she?

GUARDIANO
This is the gentlewoman.

FABRITIO My lord, my daughter.

DUKE
Why, here's some stirring yet.

FABRITIO She's a dear child to me.

DUKE
That must needs be; you say she is your daughter.

FABRITIO
Nay, my good lord, dear to my purse, I mean,
Beside my person; I ne'er reckoned that.
She has the full qualities of a gentlewoman.
I have brought her up to music, dancing, what not
That may commend her sex and stir her husband.

DUKE
And which is he now?

GUARDIANO This young heir, my lord.

DUKE
What is he brought up to?

HIPPOLITO To cat-and-trap.

GUARDIANO
My lord, he's a great ward, wealthy, but simple.
His parts consist in acres.

DUKE O, wise-acres.

GUARDIANO
You've spoke him in a word, sir.

BIANCA 'Las, poor gentlewoman,
She's ill bestead, unless she's dealt the wiselier
And laid in more provision for her youth.
Fools will not keep in summer.

LEANTIO [*aside*] No, nor such wives
From whores in winter.

DUKE [*to Fabritio*] Yea, the voice too, sir?

FABRITIO
Ay, and a sweet breast too, my lord, I hope,
Or I have cast away my money wisely!
She took her pricksong earlier, my lord,
Than any of her kindred ever did.
A rare child, though I say't—but I'd not have
The baggage hear so much; 'twould make her swell straight;
And maids of all things must not be puffed up.

DUKE
Let's turn us to a better banquet then,
For music bids the soul of man to a feast,
And that's indeed a noble entertainment
Worthy Bianca's self. [*To Bianca*] You shall perceive, beauty,
Our Florentine damsels are not brought up idlely.

BIANCA
They're wiser of themselves, it seems, my lord,
And can take gifts when goodness offers 'em.
Music

LEANTIO [*aside*]
True, and damnation has taught you that wisdom;
You can take gifts too. O, that music mocks me!

LIVIA [*aside*]
I am as dumb to any language now,
But love's, as one that never learned to speak.
I am not yet so old but he may think of me.
My own fault I have been idle a long time;
But I'll begin the week and paint tomorrow,
So follow my true labour day by day.

88 **that name** i.e. Bianca herself
91 **Ours** i.e. the lot of me and those like me
96 **equal** impartial
97 **oppressed** (drawing on the literal sense 'pressed down, crushed')
98 **friends'** relatives'
101 **sat** should have sat
106 **stirring** excitement
109 **reckoned that** included that in my reckoning
112 **stir** sexually excite
114 **cat-and-trap** (the game the Ward played in 1.2)
115 **great** (*a*) eminent in wealth (*b*) grown up (*OED*, *adj.* 7)
116 **parts** (*a*) accomplishment, qualities (*b*) possessions
120 **Fools...keep** (*a*) cream dishes will not stay fresh; hence (*b*) idiots have no sexual endurance
121 **From** i.e. *keep* from becoming
whores (perhaps quibbling on *hoar*, 'frost' or 'mold')
the voice (i.e. Isabella's)
122 **breast** singing voice (but see 155–60)
123 **wisely** (ironic for 'foolishly')
124 **pricksong** singing from written music, without improvisation (quibbling on *prick*, 'penis', anticipating 127–8)
127 **baggage** (expression of worthlessness; at worst 'whore'; here perhaps 'little good-for-nothing')
127–8 **swell...puffed up** (*a*) with pride (*b*) with child
130 **bids** invites
134 **of themselves** innately
135 **take gifts** i.e. acquire talents. Leantio quibbles on *gifts* as (*a*) presents (*b*) what is given, and the physical endowments used, in sexual intercourse.
135.1 *Music* Played on strings (see 154–5). Either Isabella plays a lute type of instrument, or the Duke's musicians play viols.
142 **begin the week** i.e. start afresh
paint (with cosmetics)
143 **true labour** vocation

I never thrived so well as when I used it.

ISABELLA (*sings*)
What harder chance can fall to woman
Who was born to cleave to some man
Than to bestow her time, youth, beauty,
Life's observance, honour, duty,
On a thing for no use good
But to make physic work, or blood
Force fresh in an old lady's cheek? She that would be
Mother of fools, let her compound with me.

WARD [*speaking during the song*] Here's a tune indeed! Pish, I had rather hear one ballad sung i'th' nose now of the lamentable drowning of fat sheep and oxen, than all these simpering tunes played upon catsguts and sung by little kitlings.

FABRITIO [*to the Duke*]
How like you her breast now, my lord?

BIANCA [*aside*] Her breast?
He talks as if his daughter had given suck
Before she were married—as her betters have.
The next he praises, sure, will be her nipples.

DUKE [*to Fabritio*]
Methinks now, such a voice to such a husband
Is like a jewel of unvalued worth
Hung at a fool's ear.

FABRITIO May it please your grace
To give her leave to show another quality?

DUKE
Marry, as many good ones as you will, sir;
The more, the better welcome.

LEANTIO [*aside*] But the less,
The better practised. That's soul's black indeed
That cannot commend virtue; but who keeps it?
The extortioner will say to a sick beggar
'Heaven comfort thee!', though he give none himself.
This good is common.

FABRITIO [*to Guardiano*]
Will it please you now, sir,
To entreat your ward to take her by the hand,
And lead her in a dance before the Duke?

GUARDIANO
That will I, sir; 'tis needful.—Hark you, nephew.

FABRITIO
Nay, you shall see, young heir, what you've for your money,
Without fraud or imposture.

WARD Dance with her?
Not I, sweet guardianer; do not urge my heart to't;
'Tis clean against my blood. Dance with a stranger?
Let whos' will do't; I'll not begin first with her.

HIPPOLITO [*aside*]
No, fear't not, fool; she's took a better order.

GUARDIANO
Why, who shall take her then?

WARD Some other gentleman.
Look, here's her uncle, a fine-timbered reveller;
Perhaps he knows the manner of her dancing too.
I'll have him do't before me—I have sworn, guardianer—
Then may I learn the better.

GUARDIANO Thou'lt be an ass still.

WARD
Ay, all that 'uncle' shall not fool me out.
Pish, I stick closer to myself than so.

GUARDIANO [*to Hippolito*]
I must entreat you, sir, to take your niece
And dance with her. My ward's a little wilful;
He would have you show him the way.

HIPPOLITO Me, sir?
He shall command it at all hours; pray tell him so.

GUARDIANO
I thank you for him; he has not wit himself, sir.

HIPPOLITO [*aside to Isabella*]
Come, my life's peace. [*Aside*] I have a strange office on't here.
'Tis some man's luck to keep the joys he likes
Concealed for his own bosom, but my fortune
To set 'em out now for another's liking,
Like the mad misery of necessitous man
That parts from his good horse with many praises,
And goes on foot himself. Need must be obeyed
In every action; it mars man and maid.

Music. [*Hippolito and Isabella*] *dance, making honours to the Duke and curtsey to themselves both before and after*

DUKE [*speaking during the dance*]
Signor Fabritio, you're a happy father.
Your cares and pains are fortunate, you see.
Your cost bears noble fruits.—Hippolito, thanks.

FABRITIO
Here's some amends for all my charges yet.
She wins both prick and praise where'er she comes.

DUKE
How lik'st, Bianca?

148 **observance** dutiful service
150–1 **to ... cheek** (examples of a fool's use as an amusing figure)
150 **physic** medicine (specifically laxative, which might work better when assisted by laughter)
152 **compound** come to an agreement
154 **i'th' nose** nasally
157 **kitlings** kittens
158 **breast** singing voice (but Bianca takes as 'bosom')
162 **to** as against
163 **unvalued** priceless
169 **keeps** practises
177 **Dance** With the bawdy innuendo 'copulate'.
179 **blood** inclination (also suggesting 'sexual desire')
180 **whos'** whoso
181 **took a better order** made better arrangements
182 **take** (with a suggestion of 'take sexually')
183 **fine-timbered** well-built
185 **before** (*a*) in advance of (*b*) in front of
187 **out** out of my resolve
188 **myself** i.e. my (*a*) resolutions (*b*) self-interest (*c*) foolishness
199 **parts from** i.e. sells
201 **mars** (*a*) hinders (*b*) distresses (*c*) ruins
201.2 ***honours*** bows
206 **both prick and praise** praise for excellence (quibbling on *prick*, 'penis')

BIANCA All things well, my lord,
But this poor gentlewoman's fortune, that's the worst.

DUKE
There is no doubt, Bianca, she'll find leisure
To make that good enough: he's rich and simple.

BIANCA
She has the better hope o'th' upper hand indeed,
Which women strive for most.

GUARDIANO [*to the Ward*] Do't when I bid you, sir.

WARD
I'll venture but a hornpipe with her, guardianer,
Or some such married man's dance.

GUARDIANO Well, venture something, sir.

WARD
I have rhyme for what I do.

GUARDIANO But little reason, I think.

WARD
Plain men dance the measures; the cinquapace, the gay;
Cuckolds dance the hornpipe, and farmers dance the hay;
Your soldiers dance the round, and maidens that grow big;
Your drunkards the canaries, your whore and bawd the jig.
Here's your eight kind of dancers. He that finds the ninth, let him pay the minstrels.
[*He offers to dance with Isabella*]

DUKE
O, here he appears once in his own person.
I thought he would have married her by attorney,
And lain with her so too.

BIANCA Nay, my kind lord,
There's very seldom any found so foolish
To give away his part there.

LEANTIO [*aside*] Bitter scoff;
Yet I must do't. With what a cruel pride
The glory of her sin strikes by my afflictions!
Music. Ward and Isabella dance; he ridiculously imitates Hippolito

DUKE [*speaking during the dance*]
This thing will make shift, sirs, to make a husband,
For aught I see in him. How think'st, Bianca?

BIANCA
Faith, an ill-favoured shift, my lord, methinks.
If he would take some voyage when he's married,
Dangerous, or long enough, and scarce be seen
Once in nine year together, a wife then
Might make indifferent shift to be content with him.

DUKE
A kiss; that wit deserves to be made much on.
[*They kiss*]
Come, our caroche!

GUARDIANO Stands ready for your grace.

DUKE
My thanks to all your loves. Come, fair Bianca.
We have took special care of you, and provided
Your lodging near us now.

BIANCA Your love is great, my lord.

DUKE
Once more, our thanks to all.

OMNES All blest honours guard you!
Cornetts flourish. Exeunt all but Leantio and Livia

LEANTIO [*aside*]
O, hast thou left me then, Bianca, utterly?
Bianca! Now I miss thee, O, return,
And save the faith of woman! I ne'er felt
The loss of thee till now. 'Tis an affliction
Of greater weight than youth was made to bear,
As if a punishment of after-life
Were fall'n upon man here. So new it is
To flesh and blood, so strange, so insupportable
A torment, e'en mistook as if a body
Whose death were drowning must needs therefore suffer it
In scalding oil.

LIVIA Sweet sir!

LEANTIO [*aside*] As long as mine eye saw thee,
I half enjoyed thee.

LIVIA Sir?

LEANTIO [*aside*] Canst thou forget
The dear pains my love took, how it has watched
Whole nights together in all weathers for thee,
Yet stood in heart more merry than the tempests
That sung about mine ears—like dangerous flatterers
That can set all their mischief to sweet tunes—
And then received thee from thy father's window
Into these arms at midnight, when we embraced
As if we had been statues only made for't,
To show art's life, so silent were our comforts,
And kissed as if our lips had grown together?

LIVIA [*aside*]
This makes me madder to enjoy him now.

213 **hornpipe** a vigorous dance usually for one dancer (with a quibble on the cuckold's horns)
216 **the measures** a slow and stately dance
cinquapace a lively dance
217 **hay** a country dance, like a reel (with a pun on the grass-crop)
218 **round** danced in a circle. Puns on the military *round*, 'inspection of sentinels', and on the roundness of pregnancy.
219 **canaries** (*a*) a lively Spanish dance (*b*) sweet white wine (both thought to originate from the Canary Islands)
jig (associated with lewdness)
220–1 **the ninth** (presumably copulation)
221 **minstrels** itinerant musicians who would play for a fee to gatherings in inns, etc.
222 **once** for once
223 **by attorney** by proxy
229 **make shift** (*a*) try hard, manage with difficulty (*b*) go through a comic performance. Bianca takes *shift* as 'set of clothes' in 231, then *make shift* as 'manage with difficulty' in 235.
231 **ill-favoured** offensive; i.e. smelly
237 **caroche** stately coach
262 **show art's life** i.e. demonstrate the lifelike qualities of art (because the *statues* are actually living)

LEANTIO
Canst thou forget all this, and better joys
That we met after this, which then new kisses
Took pride to praise?

LIVIA [*aside*] I shall grow madder yet.—Sir.

LEANTIO [*aside*]
This cannot be but of some close bawd's working.—
Cry mercy, lady. What would you say to me?
My sorrow makes me so unmannerly,
So comfort bless me, I had quite forgot you.

LIVIA
Nothing but e'en in pity to that passion
Would give your grief good counsel.

LEANTIO Marry, and welcome, lady.
It never could come better.

LIVIA Then first, sir,
To make away all your good thoughts at once of her,
Know most assurèdly she is a strumpet.

LEANTIO
Ha: 'most assurèdly'! Speak not a thing
So vile so certainly; leave it more doubtful.

LIVIA
Then I must leave all truth, and spare my knowledge;
A sin which I too lately found and wept for.

LEANTIO
Found you it?

LIVIA Ay, with wet eyes.

LEANTIO O, perjurious friendship!

LIVIA
You missed your fortunes when you met with her, sir.
Young gentlemen that only love for beauty,
They love not wisely. Such a marriage rather
Proves the destruction of affectïon.
It brings on want, and want's the key of whoredom.
I think you'd small means with her.

LEANTIO O, not any, lady.

LIVIA
Alas, poor gentleman! What, meant'st thou, sir,
Quite to undo thyself with thine own kind heart?
Thou art too good and pitiful to woman.
Marry, sir, thank thy stars for this blest fortune
That rids the summer of thy youth so well
From many beggars that had lain a-sunning
In thy beams only else, till thou hadst wasted
The whole days of thy life in heat and labour.
What would you say now to a creature found
As pitiful to you, and, as it were,
E'en sent on purpose from the whole sex general
To requite all that kindness you have shown to't?

LEANTIO
What's that, madam?

LIVIA Nay, a gentlewoman, and one able
To reward good things, ay, and bears a conscience
to't.
Couldst thou love such a one that, blow all fortunes,
Would never see thee want,
Nay, more, maintain thee to thine enemies' envy?—
And shalt not spend a care for't, stir a thought,
Nor break a sleep unless love's music waked thee;
No storm of fortune should. Look upon me,
And know that woman.

LEANTIO O my life's wealth, Bianca!

LIVIA
Still with her name? Will nothing wear it out?
That deep sigh went but for a strumpet, sir.

LEANTIO
It can go for no other that loves me.

LIVIA [*aside*]
He's vexed in mind; I came too soon to him.
Where's my discretion now, my skill, my judgement?
I'm cunning in all arts but my own love.
'Tis as unseasonable to tempt him now,
So soon, as a widow to be courted
Following her husband's corpse, or to make bargain
By the graveside, and take a young man there.
Her strange departure stands like a hearse yet
Before his eyes, which time will take down shortly.
Exit

LEANTIO
Is she my wife till death, yet no more mine?
That's a hard measure. Then what's marriage good
for?
Methinks by right I should not now be living,
And then 'twere all well. What a happiness
Had I been made of had I never seen her;
For nothing makes man's loss grievous to him
But knowledge of the worth of what he loses,
For what he never had he never misses.
She's gone for ever, utterly. There is
As much redemption of a soul from hell
As a fair woman's body from his palace.
Why should my love last longer than her truth?
What is there good in woman to be loved
When only that which makes her so has left her?
I cannot love her now but I must like
Her sin, and my own shame too, and be guilty

268 **This** i.e. Bianca's desertion to the Duke
close furtive
269 **Cry mercy** I beg your pardon
271 **So...me** as I may be blessed with comfort (an asseveration)
275 **make away** put an end to
280 **found** i.e. discovered in myself (the *sin* of leaving truth, ironically referring, unknown to Leantio, to her betrayal of Bianca). Alternatively 'discovered in Bianca', referring back to 276.
293 **beggars** (Leantio's children)
298 **general** collectively
302 **blow all fortunes** i.e. whatever fortunes blow (anticipating *storm of fortune*, 311)
312 **vexed** tormented
319 **hearse** temporary but elaborate framework placed over a coffin before burial, bearing candles, banners, epitaphs, etc.
322 **measure** (*a*) treatment (*b*) restriction
326–7 **For...loses** (drawing on the idea that the sense of loss is the greatest torment of the damned, as in *Witch* 2.1.219–23)
330 **As...hell** Proverbially there is no redemption from hell.
335 **but I must like** i.e. unless I like
336–7 **be...her** i.e. share the guilt of committing adultery with her (by condoning it)

Of law's breach with her, and mine own abusing;
All which were monstrous. Then my safest course
For health of mind and body is to turn
My heart and hate her, most extremely hate her.
I have no other way. Those virtuous powers
Which were chaste witnesses of both our troths
Can witness she breaks first. And I'm rewarded
With captainship o'th' fort—a place of credit,
I must confess, but poor. My factorship
Shall not exchange means with't. He that died last in't,
He was no drunkard, yet he died a beggar,
For all his thrift. Besides, the place not fits me;
It suits my resolution, not my breeding.

Enter Livia

LIVIA [*aside*]
I have tried all ways I can, and have not power
To keep from sight of him.—How are you now, sir?

LEANTIO
I feel a better ease, madam.

LIVIA
Thanks to blessedness.
You will do well, I warrant you, fear it not, sir,
Join but your own good will to't. He's not wise
That loves his pain or sickness, or grows fond
Of a disease whose property is to vex him
And spitefully drink his blood up. Out upon't, sir,
Youth knows no greater loss. I pray let's walk, sir.
You never saw the beauty of my house yet,
Nor how abundantly fortune has blessed me
In worldly treasure. Trust me, I have enough, sir,
To make my friend a rich man in my life,
A great man at my death; yourself will say so.
If you want anything and spare to speak,
Troth, I'll condemn you for a wilful man, sir.

LEANTIO
Why, sure this can be but the flattery of some dream.

LIVIA [*kissing him*]
Now by this kiss, my love, my soul and riches,
'Tis all true substance.
Come, you shall see my wealth. Take what you list.
The gallanter you go, the more you please me.
I will allow you too your page and footman,
Your racehorses, or any various pleasure
Exercised youth delights in; but to me
Only, sir, wear your heart of constant stuff.
Do but you love enough, I'll give enough.

LEANTIO
Troth then, I'll love enough, and take enough.

LIVIA Then we are both pleased enough. *Exeunt*

Enter Guardiano and Isabella at one door, and the Ward and Sordido at another 3.3

GUARDIANO
Now, nephew, here's the gentlewoman again.

WARD
Mass, here she's come again. Mark her now, Sordido.

GUARDIANO
This is the maid my love and care has chose
Out for your wife, and so I tender her to you.
Yourself has been eyewitness of some qualities
That speak a courtly breeding and are costly.
I bring you both to talk together now.
'Tis time you grew familiar in your tongues.
Tomorrow you join hands, and one ring ties you,
And one bed holds you, if you like the choice.
Her father and her friends are i'th' next room,
And stay to see the contract ere they part;
Therefore dispatch, good ward; be sweet and short.
Like her or like her not; there's but two ways,
And one your body, th'other your purse, pays.

WARD
I warrant you, guardianer, I'll not stand all day thrumming,
But quickly shoot my bolt at your next coming.

GUARDIANO
Well said. Good fortune in your birding then.

WARD I never missed mark yet. [*Exit Guardiano*]

SORDIDO
Troth, I think, master, if the truth were known,
You never shot at any but the kitchen wench,
And that was a she-woodcock, a mere innocent
That was oft lost and cried at eight-and-twenty.

WARD
No more of that meat, Sordido. Here's eggs o'th' spit now;
We must turn gingerly. Draw out the catalogue
Of all the faults of women.

339–40 **turn**...**and hate her** From Psalms, 105:25: 'He turned their heart to hate his people'.
345–6 **My**...**with't** i.e. the *captainship* will not provide an income equal to Leantio's *factorship*
348 **place** office
349 **resolution** i.e. determined animosity
not my breeding Leantio is no soldier.
354 **Join** if you join
356 **vex** afflict
362 **friend** lover
374 **constant stuff** (as opposed to *changeable stuff*, glossy silk which changes hue when seen from different angles)
3.3.12 **contract** agreement of terms for the marriage
15 **one**...**pays** The cost is in lost pleasure to the body if the Ward does not like her, or financial expense if he does.
16 **thrumming** idly fidgetting (with a quibble on 'copulating', anticipated in *stand* as 'stay erect')
17 **shoot my bolt** i.e. let loose my tongue, give my decision. Proverbially 'a fool's bolt is soon shot'; i.e. he is quick to speak and exhaust his little wisdom. Also refers to hasty ejaculation.
18 **birding** chasing women. Literally 'fowling', taking up *bolt* as 'bird-bolt', the blunt-headed arrow used by fowlers.
19 **mark** target (hence also 'vulva')
22 **she-woodcock** (*a*) the bird (*b*) simpleton
innocent half-wit
23 **cried** called for by the town crier (perhaps also 'wept')
24 **eggs o'th' spit** (proverbial for something that needs careful handling, as the dish needed careful cooking)
25 **turn** i.e. turn the *spit*. The Ward probably turns Isabella; compare 36.

SORDIDO How, all the faults? Have you so little reason to think so much paper will lie in my breeches? Why, ten carts will not carry it if you set down but the bawds. All the faults? Pray let's be content with a few of 'em; an if they were less you would find 'em enough, I warrant you. Look you, sir.

[*They pry at Isabella*]

ISABELLA [*aside*]
But that I have th'advantage of the fool
As much as woman's heart can wish and joy at,
What an infernal torment 'twere to be
Thus bought and sold, and turned and pried into, when, alas,
The worst bit is too good for him! And the comfort is
He's but a cater's place on't, and provides
All for another's table. Yet how curious
The ass is!—like some nice professor on't
That buys up all the daintiest food i'th' markets,
And seldom licks his lips after a taste on't.

SORDIDO
Now to her, now you've scanned all her parts over.

WARD
But at what end shall I begin now, Sordido?

SORDIDO O, ever at a woman's lip. While you live, sir, do you ask that question?

WARD Methinks, Sordido, she's but a crabbed face to begin with.

SORDIDO A crabbed face? That will save money.

WARD How, save money, Sordido?

SORDIDO Ay, sir; for, having a crabbed face of her own, she'll eat the less verjuice with her mutton; 'twill save verjuice at year's end, sir.

WARD
Nay, an your jests begin to be saucy once,
I'll make you eat your meat without mustard.

SORDIDO
And that in some kind is a punishment.

WARD Gentlewoman, they say 'tis your pleasure to be my wife, and you shall know shortly whether it be mine or no to be your husband; and thereupon thus I first enter upon you.

[*He kisses her*]

[*Aside*] O, most delicious scent! Methinks it tasted as if a man had stepped into a comfit-maker's shop to let a cart go by all the while I kissed her.—It is reported, gentlewoman, you'll run mad for me if you have me not.

ISABELLA
I should be in great danger of my wits, sir,
For being so forward—[*Aside*] should this ass kick backward now.

WARD
Alas, poor soul! And is that hair your own?

ISABELLA
Mine own, yes, sure, sir, I owe nothing for't.

WARD 'Tis a good hearing; I shall have the less to pay when I have married you. [*To Sordido*] Look, does her eyes stand well?

SORDIDO They cannot stand better
Than in her head, I think. Where would you have them?
And for her nose, 'tis of a very good last.

WARD I have known as good as that has not lasted a year though.

SORDIDO That's in the using of a thing. Will not any strong bridge fall down in time if we do nothing but beat at the bottom? A nose of buff would not last always, sir, especially if it came into th' camp once.

WARD But, Sordido, how shall we do to make her laugh, that I may see what teeth she has? For I'll not bate her a tooth, nor take a black one into th' bargain.

SORDIDO Why, do but you talk with her; you cannot choose but one time or other make her laugh, sir.

29 **set down** write down
bawds (who might be punished by being displayed to public view in a cart)
38 **cater's** purchaser of household provisions
40 **nice professor** fastidious devotee
42 **after** for
45 **lip** (ambiguous: might indicate 'vulva')
51–3 **for...sir** *Crabbed* suggests 'crab-apple', whose juice (*verjuice*) was used as apple sauce.
54 **saucy** (*a*) impudent (*b*) pertaining to sauce (a legitimate usage)
55 **meat without mustard** Picks up on *saucy*, and echoes the proverb 'after meat, mustard' (applied to wise words after the event).
56 **And...punishment** The point is that the punishment is slight. Evidently alludes to a passage in Nashe's *Pierce Penniless* (1592), in which 'a mad ruffian on a time, being in danger of shipwreck by a tempest' makes the 'desperate jest' of vowing, if he is saved, 'never to eat haberdine [dried cod] more whilst I live'. After the storm abates, he adds: 'Not without mustard, good Lord, not without mustard'. Nashe comments, 'as though it had been the greatest torment in the world to have eaten haberdine without mustard' (*Works*, ed. McKerrow, I.171).
59–60 **enter upon** begin to deal with (also, 'assume possession of' and 'begin an attack upon')
62 **comfit-maker's** *comfit*: a fruit and ginger sweetmeat
67 **forward** (*a*) pert, eager (*b*) close
kick backward i.e. refuse the marriage
68 **is...own** Wig-wearing was often considered a vice, and might be to conceal baldness as an effect of venereal disease. The boy-actor playing Isabella would in fact be wearing a wig.
69 **Mine...for't** (taking *your own* as 'legally possessed')
70 **a good hearing** good to hear it
75 **nose** Acquires the innuendo 'sexual organs'.
last i.e. shape. Literally, the cobbler's last on which shoes were shaped. The Ward takes as 'duration'.
76–81 **I...once** Venereal disease caused the nose-bones to collapse.
78 **using of a thing** Quibbles on 'sexual using of genitals'.
79 **bridge** (*a*) road-bridge (*b*) nose-bridge; hence (*c*) pubis
beat i.e. (*a*) erode (*b*) copulate
80 **buff** hard-wearing leather of which soldier's tunics were made
81 **camp** soldiers' camp
83 **bate** deduct (from the expected total)

WARD It shall go hard, but I will. [*To Isabella*] Pray, what qualities have you beside singing and dancing? Can you play at shittlecock, forsooth?

ISABELLA
Ay, and at stool-ball too, sir; I have great luck at it.

WARD Why, can you catch a ball well?

ISABELLA
I have catched two in my lap at one game.

WARD
What, have you, woman? I must have you learn
To play at trap too; then you're full and whole.

ISABELLA
Anything that you please to bring me up to
I shall take pains to practise.

WARD 'Twill not do, Sordido; we shall never get her mouth opened wide enough.

SORDIDO No sir? That's strange! Then here's a trick for your learning.

He yawns. [*Isabella yawns, covering her mouth with a handkerchief*]

Look now, look now; quick, quick there!

WARD
Pox of that scurvy mannerly trick with handkerchief!
It hindered me a little, but I am satisfied.
When a fair woman gapes and stops her mouth so,
It shows like a cloth stopple in a cream-pot.
I have fair hope of her teeth now, Sordido.

SORDIDO
Why then, you've all well, sir. For aught I see,
She's right and straight enough now as she stands.
They'll commonly lie crooked; that's no matter; wise gamesters
Never find fault with that; let 'em lie still so.

WARD I'd fain mark how she goes, and then I have all. For of all creatures I cannot abide a splay-footed woman. She's an unlucky thing to meet in a morning! Her heels keep together so as if she were beginning an Irish dance still, and the wriggling of her bum playing the tune to't. But I have bethought a cleanly shift to find it. Dab down as you see me, and peep of one side when her back's toward you. I'll show you the way.

SORDIDO
And you shall find me apt enough to peeping.
I have been one of them has seen mad sights
Under your scaffolds.

WARD [*to Isabella*]
Will it please you walk, forsooth,
A turn or two by yourself? You are so pleasing to me
I take delight to view you on both sides.

ISABELLA
I shall be glad to fetch a walk to your love, sir.
'Twill get affection a good stomach, sir—
[*Aside*] Which I had need have, to fall to such coarse victuals.

[*She walks about. The Ward ducks down to peep at her legs*]

WARD [*aside*]
Now go thy ways for a clean-treading wench
As ever man in modesty peeped under.

[*Sordido ducks down*]

SORDIDO [*aside*]
I see the sweetest sight to please my master.
Never went Frenchman righter upon ropes
Than she on Florentine rushes.

WARD [*to Isabella*] 'Tis enough, forsooth.

ISABELLA
And how do you like me now, sir?

WARD
Faith, so well
I never mean to part with thee, sweetheart,
Under some sixteen children, and all boys.

ISABELLA
You'll be at simple pains if you prove kind
And breed 'em all in your teeth.

WARD
Nay, by my faith,
What serves your belly for? 'Twould make my cheeks
Look like blown bagpipes.

Enter Guardiano

GUARDIANO
How now, ward and nephew,
Gentlewoman and niece? Speak, is it so, or not?

WARD
'Tis so; we are both agreed, sir.

GUARDIANO
In to your kindred then.
There's friends and wine and music waits to welcome you.

WARD
Then I'll be drunk for joy.

89 **shittlecock** A form of the word 'shuttlecock' in which here *shit* anticipates *stool*, and *cock* anticipates *ball*.
90 **stool-ball** A sort of indoor cricket, played mainly by women, using a stool as the wickets. See previous note.
92 **I . . . game** The suggestion of sexual gymnastics is developed in the Ward's reply.
95 **bring me up to** train me in
105 **stopple** plug
109 **lie crooked** (*a*) sleep in a crooked posture (*b*) are unfaithful in bed
gamesters (in copulation)
110 **still** always
111 **goes** walks
113 **unlucky . . . morning** (because splay-footed women were often thought to be witches)
116 **cleanly shift** clever trick
Dab dip, duck
121 **your scaffolds** (not possessive: 'scaffolds as you know them')
scaffolds platforms for theatre stages, public executions etc., or for spectators to view processions
125 **fetch** perform
to your love according to your desire
126 **stomach** appetite
128 **clean-treading** neatly-walking
131 **Frenchman** (referring to French rope-walkers)
132 **rushes** (spread on floors, especially for formal occasions, and on the theatre stage)
136 **simple** unqualified (punning on 'foolish')
kind affectionate (punning on 'in character')
137 **breed . . . teeth** Alludes to the superstition that an affectionate father had toothache while his wife was pregnant; but the Ward takes the expression literally.

SORDIDO And I for company.
I cannot break my nose in a better action. *Exeunt*
Finis Actus Tertius

4.1 *Incipit Actus Quartus*
Enter Bianca, attended by two Ladies

BIANCA
How goes your watches, ladies? What's o'clock now?
FIRST LADY
By mine, full nine.
SECOND LADY By mine, a quarter past.
FIRST LADY
I set mine by St Mark's.
SECOND LADY St Antony's,
They say, goes truer.
FIRST LADY That's but your opinion, madam,
Because you love a gentleman o'th' name.
SECOND LADY
He's a true gentleman then.
FIRST LADY So may he be
That comes to me tonight, for aught you know.
BIANCA
I'll end this strife straight: I set mine by the sun.
I love to set by th' best; one shall not then
Be troubled to set often.
SECOND LADY You do wisely in't.
BIANCA
If I should set my watch, as some girls do,
By every clock i'th' town, 'twould ne'er go true;
And too much turning of the dial's point,
Or tamp'ring with the spring, might in small time
Spoil the whole work too. Here it wants of nine now.
FIRST LADY
It does indeed, forsooth. Mine's nearest truth yet.
SECOND LADY
Yet I have found her lying with an advocate, which showed
Like two false clocks together in one parish.
BIANCA
So now I thank you, ladies; I desire
A while to be alone.
FIRST LADY And I am nobody,
Methinks, unless I have one or other with me.
Faith, my desire and hers will ne'er be sisters.
Exeunt Ladies
BIANCA
How strangely woman's fortune comes about!
This was the farthest way to come to me,
All would have judged that knew me born in Venice,
And there with many jealous eyes brought up
That never thought they had me sure enough
But when they were upon me. Yet my hap
To meet it here, so far off from my birthplace,
My friends, or kindred! 'Tis not good, in sadness,
To keep a maid so strict in her young days.
Restraint breeds wand'ring thoughts, as many fasting days
A great desire to see flesh stirring again.
I'll ne'er use any girl of mine so strictly.
Howe'er they're kept, their fortunes find 'em out;
I see't in me. If they be got in court
I'll never forbid 'em the country, nor the court
Though they be born i'th' country. They will come to't,
And fetch their falls a thousand mile about,
Where one would little think on't.
Enter Leantio [richly attired]
LEANTIO [*aside*]
I long to see how my despiser looks
Now she's come here to court. These are her lodgings.
She's simply now advanced. I took her out
Of no such window, I remember, first;
That was a great deal lower, and less carved.
BIANCA
How now, what silkworm's this, i'th' name of pride?
What, is it he?
LEANTIO [*bowing*]
A bow i'th' hams to your greatness.
You must have now three legs, I take it, must you not?
BIANCA
Then I must take another; I shall want else
The service I should have; you have but two there.
LEANTIO
You're richly placed.
BIANCA Methinks you're wondrous brave, sir.

144 **break...action** i.e. suffer in a better cause. Bawdily, 'break my erection in a better bout of copulation'.
4.1.1 **watches** Watches were expensive and items of display. Women often wore them on chains around the waist, which assists the sexual innuendo 'pudenda'. The church clocks are phallic. Watches had to be regularly set by public clocks as they were less accurate.
8 **the sun** Implies the Duke.
13 **dial's point** Implies the penis in the vagina.
14 **spring** Implies 'clitoris'.
15 **whole work** Puns on *hole-work*.
wants of is before
18 **two false clocks** i.e. the sexually dishonest lady and the generally dishonest advocate
together i.e. giving the same time. Most people would depend on public clocks to know the time.
20–1 **I...me** (drawing on the proverb 'one is no number')
30 **sadness** seriousness
33 **stirring** Emphasizes the sexual connotation of *flesh*.
36 **got** begotten
39 **fetch** reach
a...about by a roundabout course of a thousand miles
43 **simply** unqualifiedly
46 **silkworm's** Said contemptuously of someone ostentatiously wearing silk.
47 **i'th' hams** from the waist
48 **three legs** (*a*) three bows (*b*) the two limbs and the 'third leg', the penis
49 **take another** (*a*) receive another bow (*b*) have an affair with another man
want lack
50 **service** (*a*) courtly deference (*b*) service of copulation
51 **brave** finely dressed

LEANTIO
A sumptuous lodging.
BIANCA
You've an excellent suit there.
LEANTIO
A chair of velvet.
BIANCA
Is your cloak lined through, sir?
LEANTIO
You're very stately here.
BIANCA
Faith, something proud, sir.
LEANTIO
Stay, stay, let's see your cloth-of-silver slippers.
BIANCA
Who's your shoemaker? He's made you a neat boot.
LEANTIO Will you have a pair?
The Duke will lend you spurs.
BIANCA
Yes, when I ride.
LEANTIO
'Tis a brave life you lead.
BIANCA
I could ne'er see you
In such good clothes in my time.
LEANTIO
In your time?
BIANCA Sure I think, sir,
We both thrive best asunder.
LEANTIO
You're a whore.
BIANCA
Fear nothing, sir.
LEANTIO
An impudent, spiteful strumpet.
BIANCA
O, sir, you give me thanks for your captainship.
I thought you had forgot all your good manners.
LEANTIO [*showing her a letter*]
And to spite thee as much, look there, there read,
Vex, gnaw; thou shalt find there I am not love-
starved.
The world was never yet so cold or pitiless
But there was ever still more charity found out
Than at one proud fool's door, and 'twere hard, faith,
If I could not pass that. Read, to thy shame, there.
A cheerful and a beauteous benefactor, too,
As e'er erected the good works of love.

BIANCA [*aside*] Lady Livia!
Is't possible? Her worship was my pand'ress.
She dote, and send, and give, and all to him?
Why, here's a bawd plagued home!—You're simply
happy, sir;
Yet I'll not envy you.
LEANTIO
No, court-saint, not thou!
You keep some friend of a new fashion.
There's no harm in your devil; he's a suckling;
But he will breed teeth shortly, will he not?
BIANCA
Take heed you play not, then, too long with him.
LEANTIO
Yes, and the great one too. I shall find time
To play a hot religious bout with some of you,
And perhaps drive you and your course of sins
To their eternal kennels. I speak softly now—
'Tis manners in a noble woman's lodgings,
An I well knew all my degrees of duty—
But come I to your everlasting parting once,
Thunder shall seem soft music to that tempest.
BIANCA
'Twas said last week there would be change of
weather,
When the moon hung so, and belike you heard it.
LEANTIO
Why, here's sin made, and ne'er a conscience put
to't;
A monster with all forehead and no eyes.
Why do I talk to thee of sense or virtue,
That art as dark as death? And as much madness
To set light before thee as to lead blind folks
To see the monuments, which they may smell as soon
As they behold; marry, oft-times their heads,
For want of light, may feel the hardness of 'em.
So shall thy blind pride my revenge and anger,
That canst not see it now; and it may fall
At such an hour when thou least seest of all.
So to an ignorance darker than thy womb
I leave thy perjured soul. A plague will come. *Exit*

53 **through** throughout
54 **proud** splendid
58 **lend you spurs** With the innuendo 'apply the spurs to you' (i.e. excite you sexually), which Bianca takes up in her reply.
63 **Fear nothing** don't fear for that (sarcastically polite)
71 **pass** go beyond
72 **cheerful** welcoming, hospitable
73 **erected...love** (combines an image of a charitably-bequested building with a phallic innuendo)
77 **plagued home** A forceful way of saying 'fittingly punished'.
79 **friend** lover
80 **he's a suckling** Perhaps alludes to the belief that witches suckled their familiar spirits.
81 **breed teeth** cut his teeth
83 **the great one** i.e. the game for the highest stakes
84 **hot religious bout** With an incongruous sexual reference. The exact nature of the threat is unclear, but as Leantio derives his confidence in affrontery from his own affair with Livia, his claim to the moral high-ground is insecure.
85 **course** pack (as of hounds hunting hares). Also glancing at 'progress through successive stages', 'habit', and 'prescribed series of prayers' (ironic; compare *religious*).
86 **eternal kennels** (i.e. of damnation)
89 **come I** if I come
your everlasting parting (of Bianca and the Duke, or of Bianca from life; in either case the meaning is 'your death')
91–2 **'Twas...it** Takes up Leantio's metaphorical *thunder* and *tempest* as if casual chat about the weather. Perhaps also refers to the 'horned' moon, emblematic of a cuckold.
92 **hung** i.e. hung in the sky as it did
93 **made** created
put added
94 **forehead** assurance, impudence. Compare Jeremiah, 3:3, 'thou hadst a whore's forehead, thou wouldst not be ashamed'.
eyes (of *conscience*, as in many biblical usages)
95 **sense** i.e. sight
98 **monuments** (objects both visually impressive and morally edifying)
100 **feel the hardness of** i.e. bump into
103 **when...all** i.e. of greatest sinfulness
105 **plague** calamitous divine punishment

BIANCA
Get you gone first, and then I fear no greater;
Nor thee will I fear long. I'll have this sauciness
Soon banished from these lodgings, and the rooms
Perfumed well after the corrupt air it leaves.
His breath has made me almost sick, in troth.
A poor, base start-up! Life! Because he's got
Fair clothes by foul means, comes to rail, and show 'em.
Enter the Duke
DUKE
Who's that?
BIANCA
Cry you mercy, sir.
DUKE
Prithee, who's that?
BIANCA
The former thing, my lord, to whom you gave
The captainship. He eats his meat with grudging still.
DUKE
Still!
BIANCA
He comes vaunting here of his new love,
And the new clothes she gave him. Lady Livia,
Who but she now his mistress?
DUKE
Lady Livia?
Be sure of what you say.
BIANCA
He showed me her name, sir,
In perfumed paper, her vows, her letter,
With an intent to spite me. So his heart said,
And his threats made it good; they were as spiteful
As ever malice uttered, and as dangerous
Should his hand follow the copy.
DUKE
But that must not.
Do not vex your mind. Prithee, to bed, go.
All shall be well and quiet.
BIANCA
I love peace, sir.
DUKE
And so do all that love. Take you no care for't;
It shall be still provided to your hand. *Exit Bianca*
Who's near us there?
Enter Messenger
MESSENGER
My lord.
DUKE
Seek out Hippolito,
Brother to Lady Livia, with all speed.
MESSENGER
He was the last man I saw, my lord.
DUKE
Make haste.
Exit Messenger
He is a blood soon stirred; and as he's quick
To apprehend a wrong, he's bold and sudden
In bringing forth a ruin. I know likewise
The reputation of his sister's honour's
As dear to him as life-blood to his heart.
Beside, I'll flatter him with a goodness to her
Which I now thought on—but ne'er meant to practise
Because I know her base—and that wind drives him.
The ulcerous reputation feels the poise
Of lightest wrongs, as sores are vexed with flies.
Enter Hippolito
He comes.—Hippolito, welcome.
HIPPOLITO
My loved lord.
DUKE
How does that lusty widow, thy kind sister?
Is she not sped yet of a second husband?
A bed-fellow she has; I ask not that;
I know she's sped of him.
HIPPOLITO
Of him, my lord?
DUKE
Yes, of a bed-fellow. Is the news so strange to you?
HIPPOLITO
I hope 'tis so to all.
DUKE
I wish it were, sir;
But 'tis confessed too fast her ignorant pleasures,
Only by lust instructed, have received
Into their services an impudent boaster:
One that does raise his glory from her shame
And tells the midday sun what's done in darkness;
Yet, blinded with her appetite, wastes her wealth,
Buys her disgraces at a dearer rate
Than bounteous housekeepers purchase their honour.
Nothing sads me so much as that in love
To thee and to thy blood I had picked out
A worthy match for her, the great Vincentio,
High in our favour and in all men's thoughts.
HIPPOLITO
O thou destruction of all happy fortunes,
Unsated blood! Know you the name, my lord,
Of her abuser?
DUKE
One Leantio.
HIPPOLITO
He's a factor.
DUKE
He ne'er made so brave a voyage,
By his own talk.
HIPPOLITO
The poor old widow's son.
I humbly take my leave.

106 **greater** i.e. greater *plague* (in the weakened sense 'nuisance')
108–9 **the...leaves** Refers to the practise of fumigating rooms with aromatic smoke, supposedly to rid them of plague infection.
110 **breath** (*a*) exhaled air (*b*) speech
111 **start-up** upstart
124 **Should...copy** i.e. should his deeds follow the example set in his words. Literally, *copy* is the 'copy book' used to teach penmanship.
128 **provided to your hand** i.e. given you
132 **blood** man of spirit
137 **goodness** beneficial intention
138 **now** just now
139 **that wind drives him** The image is of a sailing ship.
140 **poise** weight, pressure
144 **Is...of** has she not yet succeeded in obtaining
second A minor inconsistency with 1.2.50.
146 **sped** obtained her desire
152 **raise...shame** A half-realized horticultural image; compare 3.2.48–52.
156 **honour** reputation, social standing
162 **blood** sexual appetite
164 **voyage** Harks back to Leantio's venturings in trade, figuring Livia as a rich cargo. Compare his description of Bianca as an *unvalued'st purchase* (1.1.12).

DUKE [*aside*] I see 'tis done.—
Give her good counsel, make her see her error.
I know she'll hearken to you.

HIPPOLITO Yes, my lord,
I make no doubt, as I shall take the course,
Which she shall never know till it be acted;
And when she wakes to honour, then she'll thank me for't.
I'll imitate the pities of old surgeons
To this lost limb, who ere they show their art
Cast one asleep, then cut the diseased part.
So, out of love to her I pity most,
She shall not feel him going till he's lost.
Then she'll commend the cure. *Exit*

DUKE The great cure's past;
I count this done already. His wrath's sure,
And speaks an injury deep. Farewell, Leantio.
This place will never hear thee murmur more.

Enter Lord Cardinal, attended [*with Servants bearing lights*]

Our noble brother, welcome!

LORD CARDINAL [*to Servants*] Set those lights down;
Depart till you be called. [*Exeunt Servants*]

DUKE [*aside*] There's serious business
Fixed in his look; nay, it inclines a little
To the dark colour of a discontentment.—
Brother, what is't commands your eye so powerfully?
Speak; you seem lost.

LORD CARDINAL The thing I look on seems so:
To my eyes, lost for ever.

DUKE You look on me.

LORD CARDINAL
What a grief 'tis to a religious feeling
To think a man should have a friend so goodly,
So wise, so noble, nay, a duke, a brother,
And all this certainly damned!

DUKE How?

LORD CARDINAL 'Tis no wonder
If your great sin can do't. Dare you look up,
For thinking of a vengeance? Dare you sleep,
For fear of never waking but to death,
And dedicate unto a strumpet's love
The strength of your affections, zeal, and health?
Here you stand now; can you assure your pleasures
You shall once more enjoy her, but once more?
Alas, you cannot. What a misery 'tis then
To be more certain of eternal death
Than of a next embrace! Nay, shall I show you
How more unfortunate you stand in sin
Than the love-private man? All his offences,
Like enclosed grounds, keep but about himself,
And seldom stretch beyond his own soul's bounds;
And when a man grows miserable, 'tis some comfort
When he's no further charged than with himself;
'Tis a sweet ease to wretchedness. But, great man,
Every sin thou commit'st shows like a flame
Upon a mountain: 'tis seen far about,
And with a big wind made of popular breath
The sparkles fly through cities; here one takes,
Another catches there, and in short time
Waste all to cinders. But remember still
What burnt the valleys first came from the hill.
Every offence draws his particular pain,
But 'tis example proves the great man's bane.
The sins of mean men lie like scattered parcels
Of an unperfect bill; but when such fall,
Then comes example, and that sums up all.
And this your reason grants: if men of good lives,
Who by their virtuous actions stir up others
To noble and religious imitation,
Receive the greater glory after death—
As sin must needs confess—what may they feel
In height of torments and in weight of vengeance,
Not only they themselves not doing well,
But sets a light up to show men to hell?

DUKE
If you have done, I have. No more, sweet brother.

LORD CARDINAL
I know time spent in goodness is too tedious.
This had not been a moment's space in lust now.
How dare you venture on eternal pain,
That cannot bear a minute's reprehension?
Methinks you should endure to hear that talked of
Which you so strive to suffer. O my brother!
What were you if you were taken now?
My heart weeps blood to think on't. 'Tis a work
Of infinite mercy you can never merit
That yet you are not death-struck, no, not yet.
I dare not stay you long, for fear you should not
Have time enough allowed you to repent in.
There's but this wall betwixt you and destruction
When you're at strongest, and but poor thin clay.
Think upon't, brother. Can you come so near it
For a fair strumpet's love, and fall into
A torment that knows neither end nor bottom
For beauty but the deepness of a skin,

177 **great cure's** major surgery. *Cure* is also 'charge, care, duty'.
180 **murmur** mutter anger, complain
186 **lost** enraptured (but in the Cardinal's reply, 'damned')
203 **love-private** private in lovemaking
209–10 **a . . . mountain** (such as a signal beacon)
214 **Waste all** i.e. 'they waste all' or 'all wastes'
216 **his** its
pain punishment
217 **example** setting the example
218 **parcels** separate items
219 **unperfect** not totalled up
such i.e. great men
225 **sin** i.e. even sin, the sinful themselves
228 **sets** i.e. their example setting
233 **reprehension** rebuke
236 **taken** (by death)
242 **this wall** (the Duke's body; see following note)
243 **clay** Continues the *wall* metaphor. In biblical phraseology man is made from clay, to which he returns on death.

And that not of their own neither? Is she a thing
Whom sickness dare not visit, or age look on,
Or death resist? Does the worm shun her grave?
If not—as your soul knows it—why should lust
Bring man to lasting pain, for rotten dust?

DUKE
Brother of spotless honour, let me weep
The first of my repentance in thy bosom,
And show the blest fruits of a thankful spirit;
And if I e'er keep woman more, unlawfully,
May I want penitence at my greatest need—
And wise men know there is no barren place
Threatens more famine than a dearth in grace.

LORD CARDINAL
Why, here's a conversion is at this time, brother,
Sung for a hymn in heaven, and at this instant
The powers of darkness' groan makes all hell sorry.
First I praise heaven; then in my work I glory.—
Who's there attends without?

Enter Servants

SERVANTS My lord.

LORD CARDINAL
Take up those lights. There was a thicker darkness
When they came first. The peace of a fair soul
Keep with my noble brother.

DUKE Joys be with you, sir.

Exit Cardinal, with Servants [bearing lights]

She lies alone tonight for't, and must still,
Though it be hard to conquer; but I have vowed
Never to know her as a strumpet more,
And I must save my oath. If fury fail not,
Her husband dies tonight, or at the most
Lives not to see the morning spent tomorrow.
Then will I make her lawfully mine own,
Without this sin and horror. Now I'm chidden
For what I shall enjoy then unforbidden;
And I'll not freeze in stoves. 'Tis but a while.
Live like a hopeful bridegroom, chaste from flesh,
And pleasure then will seem new, fair, and fresh.

Exit

4.2

Enter Hippolito

HIPPOLITO
The morning so far wasted, yet his baseness
So impudent? See if the very sun do not blush at him!
Dare he do thus much, and know me alive?
Put case one must be vicious, as I know myself
Monstrously guilty: there's a blind time made for't.
He might use only that; 'twere conscionable.
Art, silence, closeness, subtlety, and darkness
Are fit for such a business; but there's no pity
To be bestowed on an apparent sinner,
An impudent daylight lecher. The great zeal
I bear to her advancement in this match
With Lord Vincentio, as the Duke has wrought it
To the perpetual honour of our house,
Puts fire into my blood to purge the air
Of this corruption, fear it spread too far
And poison the whole hopes of this fair fortune.
I love her good so dearly that no brother
Shall venture farther for a sister's glory
Than I for her preferment.

Enter Leantio and a Page

LEANTIO [*aside*] Once again
I'll see that glist'ring whore, shines like a serpent
Now the court sun's upon her.—Page!

PAGE Anon, sir.

LEANTIO [*aside*]
I'll go in state too.—See the coach be ready.
I'll hurry away presently. [*Exit Page*]

HIPPOLITO Yes, you shall hurry,
And the devil after you.

[*He strikes him*]

Take that at setting forth.

[*He draws his sword*]

Now, an you'll draw, we are upon equal terms, sir.
Thou took'st advantage of my name in honour
Upon my sister. I ne'er saw the stroke
Come till I found my reputation bleeding,
And therefore count it I no sin to valour
To serve thy lust so. Now we are of even hand,
Take your best course against me. You must die.

LEANTIO [*aside*]
How close sticks envy to man's happiness!
When I was poor, and little cared for life,
I had no such means offered me to die;
No man's wrath minded me.

[*He draws his sword*]

Slave, I turn this to thee,
To call thee to account for a wound lately
Of a base stamp upon me.

HIPPOLITO 'Twas most fit

---

248 **And...neither** (because produced by cosmetics)
252 **lasting** everlasting
rotten dust (all that will remain of the strumpet after death)
254 **first** (suggesting *first-fruits*, an idea developed in 255)
257 **want** lack
260–1 **here's...heaven** Compare Luke, 15:10, 'There is joy in the presence of the angels of God for one sinner that coverteth'.
262 **sorry** woeful, wretched
266 **fair** unsullied
277 **freeze in stoves** i.e. be sexually continent in places suited to lechery. *Stoves* is probably 'hot air or vapour baths', and may, like *stew*, have suggested 'brothel'.
4.2.4 **Put case** suppose
vicious full of vice
5 **blind** i.e. dark
7 **Art** cunning
closeness secrecy
9 **apparent** manifest
15 **fear** for fear
20 **shines** who shines
21 **court sun's** i.e. the Duke's
23 **presently** at once
27 **stroke** (of the penis as well as the sword)
30 **of even hand** on equal terms
37 **stamp** impression, character. Suggests the stamping of an illegitimate impression on a coin.

For a base metal. Come and fetch one now
More noble then, for I will use thee fairer
Than thou hast done thine own soul, or our honour.
[They fight. Hippolito wounds Leantio, who falls]
And there I think 'tis for thee.

VOICES WITHIN Help, help! O, part 'em!

LEANTIO
False wife! I feel now thou'st prayed heartily for me.
Rise, strumpet, by my fall; thy lust may reign now.
My heart-string and the marriage knot that tied thee
Breaks both together.
[He groans and dies]

HIPPOLITO There I heard the sound on't,
And never liked string better.

Enter Livia [at one door], Guardiano, Isabella, Ward, and Sordido [at another]

LIVIA 'Tis my brother.
Are you hurt, sir?

HIPPOLITO Not anything.

LIVIA Blessèd fortune!
Shift for thyself. What is he thou hast killed?

HIPPOLITO
Our honour's enemy.

GUARDIANO Know you this man, lady?

LIVIA
Leantio! My love's joy! *[To Hippolito]* Wounds stick upon thee
As deadly as thy sins. Art thou not hurt?
The devil take that fortune! And he dead!
Drop plagues into thy bowels without voice,
Secret and fearful.—Run for officers.
Let him be apprehended with all speed,
For fear he scape away. Lay hands on him;
We cannot be too sure; 'tis wilful murder.
You do heaven's vengeance, and the law just service.
You know him not as I do; he's a villain
As monstrous as a prodigy, and as dreadful.

HIPPOLITO
Will you but entertain a noble patience
Till you but hear the reason, worthy sister?

LIVIA
The reason! That's a jest hell falls a-laughing at.
Is there a reason found for the destruction
Of our more lawful loves, and was there none
To kill the black lust 'twixt thy niece and thee
That has kept close so long?

GUARDIANO How's that, good madam?

LIVIA
Too true, sir. There she stands; let her deny't.
The deed cries shortly in the midwife's arms,
Unless the parents' sins strike it stillborn;
And if you be not deaf and ignorant,
You'll hear strange notes ere long.—Look upon me, wench!
'Twas I betrayed thy honour subtlely to him
Under a false tale. It lights upon me now.—
His arm has paid me home upon thy breast,
My sweet beloved Leantio!

GUARDIANO Was my judgement
And care in choice so dev'lishly abused,
So beyond shamefully? All the world will grin at me.

WARD O Sordido, Sordido, I'm damned, I'm damned!

SORDIDO Damned? Why, sir?

WARD One of the wicked—dost not see't?—a cuckold, a plain reprobate cuckold.

SORDIDO Nay, an you be damned for that be of good cheer, sir; you've gallant company of all professions. I'll have a wife next Sunday too, because I'll along with you myself.

WARD That will be some comfort yet.

LIVIA *[to Guardiano]*
You, sir, that bear your load of injuries
As I of sorrows, lend me your grieved strength
To this sad burden, who in life wore actions:
Flames were not nimbler. We will talk of things
May have the luck to break our hearts together.

GUARDIANO
I'll list to nothing but revenge and anger,
Whose counsels I will follow.

Exeunt Livia and Guardiano [bearing Leantio's body]

SORDIDO A wife, quoth a?
Here's a sweet plum-tree of your guard'ner's grafting!

WARD Nay, there's a worse name belongs to this fruit yet, an you could hit on't, a more open one; for he that marries a whore looks like a fellow bound all his lifetime to a medlar-tree—and that's good stuff: 'tis no sooner ripe but it looks rotten; and so do some queans at nineteen. A pox on't, I thought there was some knavery abroach, for something stirred in her belly the first night I lay with her.

38 **metal** Continues the coin image; also *mettle*, 'spirit'.
one i.e. a wound
44 **heart-string** Thought to brace and sustain the heart.
46 **string** Quibbles on the music of a stringed instrument.
50 **Wounds stick** (subjunctive: 'may wounds stick'; similarly *Drop plagues*, 53)
53 **voice** noise
60 **prodigy** deformed infant, whose birth was regarded as unnatural and a portent of evil
65 **more lawful** (than Hippolito's)
67 **close** secret, hidden
72 **strange notes** (of the infant's cries)
85 **a wife next Sunday** Proverbially, 'Who will have a handsome wife, let him choose her upon Saturday and not upon Sunday'. Women dressed up for church on Sunday; compare 1.1.34.
90 **wore** displayed
92 **to break** of breaking
95 **plum-tree** *Plum* alludes to the pudenda.
guard'ner's guardian's (punning on *gardener's*)
97 **open** Alludes to *open-arse*, the scurrilous name for the medlar fruit, so called because of the obvious 'eye' between the fruit lobes.
99 **medlar-tree** See previous note. The fruit was not ripe for eating until rotten and was therefore a common image for sexual degeneracy in women. *Rotten* (100) suggests infestation with venereal disease.
100 **queans** whores
102 **abroach** begun, afoot (and 'had broached her')

SORDIDO What, what, sir!

WARD This is she brought up so courtly, can sing and dance—and tumble too, methinks. I'll never marry wife again that has so many qualities.

SORDIDO Indeed, they are seldom good, master; for likely when they are taught so many, they will have one trick more of their own finding out. Well, give me a wench but with one good quality, to lie with none but her husband, and that's bringing up enough for any woman breathing.

WARD This was the fault when she was tendered to me. You never looked to this.

SORDIDO Alas, how would you have me see through a great farthingale, sir? I cannot peep through a millstone, or in the going to see what's done i'th' bottom.

WARD
Her father praised her breast; she'd the voice, forsooth.
I marvelled she sung so small, indeed, being no maid.
Now I perceive there's a young chorister in her belly.
This breeds a singing in my head, I'm sure.

SORDIDO 'Tis but the tune of your wife's cinquapace, danced in a feather bed. Faith, go lie down, master—but take heed your horns do not make holes in the pillow-beres. *[The Ward begins to leave]* I would not batter brows with him for a hogshead of angels; he would prick my skull as full of holes as a scrivener's sandbox. *Exeunt Ward and Sordido*

ISABELLA *[aside]*
Was ever maid so cruelly beguiled,
To the confusion of life, soul, and honour,
All of one woman's murd'ring? I'd fain bring
Her name no nearer to my blood than woman,
And 'tis too much of that. O shame and horror!
In that small distance from yon man to me
Lies sin enough to make a whole world perish.—
'Tis time we parted, sir, and left the sight
Of one another; nothing can be worse
To hurt repentance, for our very eyes
Are far more poisonous to religion
Than basilisks to them. If any goodness
Rest in you, hope of comforts, fear of judgements,
My request is I ne'er may see you more;
And so I turn me from you everlastingly,
So is my hope to miss you. *[Aside]* But for her,
That durst so dally with a sin so dangerous
And lay a snare so spitefully for my youth,
If the least means but favour my revenge
That I may practise the like cruel cunning
Upon her life as she has on mine honour,
I'll act it without pity.

HIPPOLITO *[aside]* Here's a care
Of reputation, and a sister's fortune
Sweetly rewarded by her! Would a silence
As great as that which keeps among the graves
Had everlastingly chained up her tongue!
My love to her has made mine miserable.

Enter Guardiano and Livia

GUARDIANO *[aside to Livia]*
If you can but dissemble your heart's griefs now,
Be but a woman so far.

LIVIA *[aside to Guardiano]*
Peace; I'll strive, sir.

GUARDIANO *[aside to Livia]*
As I can wear my injuries in a smile,
Here's an occasion offered that gives anger
Both liberty and safety to perform
Things worth the fire it holds, without the fear
Of danger or of law; for mischiefs acted
Under the privilege of a marriage-triumph
At the Duke's hasty nuptials will be thought
Things merely accidental, all 's by chance,
Not got of their own natures.

LIVIA *[aside to Hippolito]* I conceive you, sir,
Even to a longing for performance on't;
And here behold some fruits.
[She kneels to Hippolito and Isabella]
Forgive me both.
What I am now returned to, sense and judgement,
Is not the same rage and distractïon
Presented lately to you. That rude form
Is gone for ever. I am now myself,
That speaks all peace and friendship, and these tears
Are the true springs of hearty penitent sorrow
For those foul wrongs which my forgetful fury
Slandered your virtues with. This gentleman
Is well resolved now.

GUARDIANO I was never otherways.

106 **tumble** (*a*) dance with contortions, perform acrobatics (*b*) copulate
110 **trick** sexual device
117 **I...millstone** From the proverb 'I can see as far into a millstone as another man', the point being the impossibility of doing so.
118 **going** (*a*) the millstone's turning (*b*) Isabella's walking in 3.3 (*c*) copulative 'grinding'
to see 'To' is redundant to the sense.
i'th' bottom (*a*) underneath (*b*) in the anal/genital area. Also alludes to the expression 'search to the bottom', i.e. get to the heart of a matter.
120 **small** gently, softly
being no maid (something not actually known to the Ward at the time)
122 **a...head** the headache caused by cuckold's *horns*, 125
123 **cinquapace** (a lively dance)
126 **pillow-beres** pillow-cases
127 **hogshead** large barrel
128 **angels** gold coins
129 **sandbox** box with perforated top used for sprinkling sand to blot wet ink
131 **confusion** destruction
133 **blood** family, kinship
134 **'tis...that** i.e. Livia is too full of the vices of women
141 **basilisks** (in classical legend, reptiles whose glance was fatal)
145 **miss** avoid
164 **marriage-triumph** *triumph*: lavish spectacle
166 **'s** as
167 **conceive** understand (with *fruits* suggesting wordplay on 'become pregnant')
176 **For** as for
forgetful heedless
178 **resolved** satisfied, reassured

I knew, alas, 'twas but your anger spake it,
And I ne'er thought on't more.

HIPPOLITO Pray rise, good sister.

[*She rises*]

ISABELLA [*aside*]
Here's e'en as sweet amends made for a wrong now
As one that gives a wound and pays the surgeon:
All the smart's nothing, the great loss of blood,
Or time of hind'rance. Well, I had a mother;
I can dissemble too.—What wrongs have slipped
Through anger's ignorance, aunt, my heart forgives.

GUARDIANO [*Aside*]
Why, this' tuneful now!

HIPPOLITO And what I did, sister,
Was all for honour's cause, which time to come
Will approve to you.

LIVIA Being awaked to goodness,
I understand so much, sir, and praise now
The fortune of your arm, and of your safety;
For by his death you've rid me of a sin
As costly as e'er woman doted on.
'T has pleased the Duke so well too that, behold, sir,

[*She gives him a letter*]

He's sent you here your pardon, which I kissed
With most affectionate comfort. When 'twas brought,
Then was my fit just passed; it came so well, methought,
To glad my heart.

HIPPOLITO I see his grace thinks on me.

LIVIA
There's no talk now but of the preparation
For the great marriage.

HIPPOLITO Does he marry her then?

LIVIA
With all speed, suddenly, as fast as cost
Can be laid on with many thousand hands.
This gentleman and I had once a purpose
To have honoured the first marriage of the Duke
With an invention of his own. 'Twas ready,
The pains well past, most of the charge bestowed on't;
Then came the death of your good mother, niece,
And turned the glory of it all to black.
'Tis a device would fit these times so well too:
Art's treasury not better. If you'll join,
It shall be done; the cost shall all be mine.

HIPPOLITO
You've my voice first; 'twill well approve my thankfulness
For the Duke's love and favour.

LIVIA What say you, niece?

ISABELLA
I am content to make one.

GUARDIANO The plot's full then.
[*To Livia*] Your pages, madam, will make shift for Cupids.

LIVIA
That will they, sir.

GUARDIANO You'll play your old part still.

LIVIA
What, is't good? Troth, I have e'en forgot it.

GUARDIANO
Why, Juno Pronuba, the marriage goddess.

LIVIA
'Tis right indeed.

GUARDIANO [*to Isabella*]
And you shall play the nymph
That offers sacrifice to appease her wrath.

ISABELLA
Sacrifice, good sir?

LIVIA Must I be appeased then?

GUARDIANO
That's as you list yourself, as you see cause.

LIVIA
Methinks 'twould show the more state in her deity
To be incensed.

ISABELLA 'Twould; but my sacrifice
Shall take a course to appease you, or I'll fail in't—
[*Aside*] And teach a sinful bawd to play a goddess.

GUARDIANO [*to Hippolito*]
For our parts, we'll not be ambitious, sir.
Please you walk in and see the project drawn,
Then take your choice.

HIPPOLITO I weigh not, so I have one.

Exeunt all but Livia

LIVIA
How much ado have I to restrain fury
From breaking into curses! O, how painful 'tis
To keep great sorrow smothered! Sure I think
'Tis harder to dissemble grief than love.
Leantio, here the weight of thy loss lies,
Which nothing but destruction can suffice. *Exit*

184 **hind'rance** injury, incapacity
187 **this'** this is
189 **approve** demonstrate, confirm
197 **came so** thus came
205 **invention... own** theatrical entertainment he devised himself
206 **charge** expense
212 **voice** vote, support
214 **make one** be included
plot's *plot*: outline of the dramatic action (a document on which actors' names might be noted)
215 **make shift for** improvise as
218 **Juno** (sister and wife of Jove; patroness of marriage, also an archetype of the jealous wife)
Pronuba presiding over marriage (one of several names indicating Juno's special attributes)
224 **incensed** enraged (punning on 'perfumed with incense', as 'Juno' is in 5.2)
227 **For our parts** (*a*) for our roles (*b*) as for us
228 **project drawn** Refers to the *plot* (214) and perhaps also designs for scenery and costumes.
229 **weigh not** don't mind
so so long as
233 **dissemble** disguise, pretend not to have
234 **here** Presumably Livia gestures to her heart.

4.3

Oboes. Enter in great state the Duke and Bianca, richly attired, with lords, cardinals, ladies, and other attendants. They pass solemnly over. Enter Lord Cardinal in a rage, seeming to break off the ceremony

LORD CARDINAL
Cease, cease! Religious honours done to sin
Disparage virtue's reverence, and will pull
Heaven's thunder upon Florence. Holy ceremonies
Were made for sacred uses, not for sinful.
Are these the fruits of your repentance, brother?
Better it had been you had never sorrowed
Than to abuse the benefit and return
To worse than where sin left you.
Vowed you then never to keep strumpet more;
And are you now so swift in your desires
To knit your honours and your life fast to her?
Is not sin sure enough to wretched man,
But he must bind himself in chains to't? Worse:
Must marriage, that immaculate robe of honour
That renders virtue glorious, fair, and fruitful
To her great master, be now made the garment
Of leprosy and foulness? Is this penitence
To sanctify hot lust? What is it otherways
Than worship done to devils? Is this the best
Amends that sin can make after her riots,
As if a drunkard, to appease heaven's wrath,
Should offer up his surfeit for a sacrifice?
If that be comely, then lust's offerings are
On wedlock's sacred altar.

DUKE
Here you're bitter
Without cause, brother. What I vowed, I keep
As safe as you your conscience, and this needs not.
I taste more wrath in't than I do religion,
And envy more than goodness. The path now
I tread is honest, leads to lawful love
Which virtue, in her strictness, would not check.
I vowed no more to keep a sensual woman.
'Tis done: I mean to make a lawful wife of her.

LORD CARDINAL
He that taught you that craft,
Call him not master long; he will undo you.
Grow not too cunning for your soul, good brother.
Is it enough to use adulterous thefts
And then take sanctuary in marriage?
I grant, so long as an offender keeps
Close in a privileged temple, his life's safe;
But if he ever venture to come out,
And so be taken, then he surely dies for't.
So now you're safe; but when you leave this body,
Man's only privileged temple upon earth
In which the guilty soul takes sanctuary,
Then you'll perceive what wrongs chaste vows endure
When lust usurps the bed that should be pure.

BIANCA
Sir, I have read you over all this while
In silence, and I find great knowledge in you,
And severe learning; yet 'mongst all your virtues
I see not charity written, which some call
The first-born of religion, and I wonder
I cannot see't in yours. Believe it, sir,
There is no virtue can be sooner missed
Or later welcomed; it begins the rest,
And sets 'em all in order. Heaven and angels
Take great delight in a converted sinner;
Why should you then, a servant and professor,
Differ so much from them? If every woman
That commits evil should be therefore kept
Back in desires of goodness, how should virtue
Be known and honoured? From a man that's blind
To take a burning taper 'tis no wrong,
He never misses it; but to take light
From one that sees, that's injury and spite.
Pray, whether is religion better served:
When lives that are licentious are made honest,
Than when they still run through a sinful blood?
'Tis nothing virtue's temples to deface;
But build the ruins, there's a work of grace.

DUKE
I kiss thee for that spirit. Thou hast praised thy wit
A modest way.—On, on, there! *Oboes*

LORD CARDINAL
Lust is bold,
And will have vengeance speak ere't be controlled.
Exeunt

Finis Actus Quartus

4.3.2 **Disparage** degrade
3 **Florence** i.e. (*a*) the city (*b*) the Duke
16 **her great master** i.e. God
22 **surfeit** (*a*) transgression (*b*) vomit
26 **needs not** is unnecessary
28 **envy** malice
33 **He** i.e. the devil
35 **for** for the good of
36 **use adulterous thefts** i.e. habitually steal the pleasures of adultery. Recalls Leantio's description of Bianca's seduction from her parents as a theft, 1.1.37, etc.
39 **privileged** (with right of sanctuary)
49 **severe** (*a*) censurious (*b*) grave
49–55 **yet...order** Alludes to 1 Corinthians, 13:13, 'And now abideth faith, hope, charity, these three; but the greatest of these is charity' (King James Bible; Geneva has 'love' for 'charity'). In Protestant thinking, however, charity and good works proceed from faith, which is more important for salvation than works.
54 **later** more belatedly
begins brings into existence
57 **servant** (of God)
professor professed Christian
65 **whether** in which of the two
67 **Than** 'Or' is logically required.
68 **nothing** i.e. no effort
deface destroy
69 **build** rebuild

❁

5.1 *Incipit Actus Quintus*
[An altar set forth for the masque.]
Enter Guardiano [with a caltrop] and Ward

GUARDIANO
Speak, hast thou any sense of thy abuse?
Dost thou know what wrong's done thee?

WARD
I were an ass else.
I cannot wash my face but I am feeling on't.

GUARDIANO
Here, take this caltrop, then convey it secretly
Into the place I showed you. Look you, sir,
This is the trapdoor to't.

WARD I know that of old, uncle, since the last triumph. Here rose up a devil with one eye, I remember, with a company of fireworks at's tail.

GUARDIANO
Prithee leave squibbing now. Mark me, and fail not;
But when thou hear'st me give a stamp, down with't;
The villain's caught then.

WARD
If I miss you, hang me.
I love to catch a villain, and your stamp shall go current, I warrant you. But how shall I rise up and let him down too, all at one hole? That will be a horrible puzzle. You know I have a part in't; I play Slander.

GUARDIANO
True, but never make you ready for't.

WARD No? My clothes are bought and all, and a foul fiend's head with a long contumelious tongue i'th' chaps on't, a very fit shape for Slander i'th' out-parishes.

GUARDIANO
It shall not come so far; thou understand'st it not.

WARD
O, O!

GUARDIANO
He shall lie deep enough ere that time,
And stick first upon those.

WARD
Now I conceive you, guardianer.

GUARDIANO
Away; list to the privy stamp, that's all thy part.

WARD Stamp my horns in a mortar if I miss you, and give the powder in white wine to sick cuckolds, a very present remedy for the headache.
Exit [through the trapdoor, with the caltrop]

GUARDIANO
If this should any way miscarry now,
As, if the fool be nimble enough, 'tis certain,
The pages that present the swift-winged Cupids
Are taught to hit him with their shafts of love—
Fitting his part—which I have cunningly poisoned.
He cannot scape my fury; and those ills
Will be laid all on fortune, not our wills,
That's all the sport on't. For who will imagine
That at the celebration of this night
Any mischance that haps can flow from spite? *Exit*
Flourish. Enter, above, Duke, Bianca, Lord Cardinal, Fabritio, and other cardinals, lords, and ladies, in state

DUKE
Now our fair duchess, your delight shall witness
How you're beloved and honoured. All the glories
Bestowed upon the gladness of this night
Are done for your bright sake.

BIANCA
I am the more
In debt, my lord, to loves and courtesies
That offer up themselves so bounteously
To do me honoured grace without my merit.

DUKE
A goodness set in greatness, how it sparkles
Afar off like pure diamonds set in gold!
[*To Bianca and Lord Cardinal*] How perfect my desires were might I witness
But a fair noble peace 'twixt your two spirits!
The reconcilement would be more sweet to me
Than longer life to him that fears to die.
Good sir!

LORD CARDINAL
I profess peace, and am content.

DUKE
I'll see the seal upon't, and then 'tis firm.

LORD CARDINAL
You shall have all your wish.

5.1.0.3 ***caltrop*** (an instrument of war with four metal spikes arranged so that one always projects upwards)
3 **feeling on't** (*a*) sensing the *wrong* done me (*b*) i.e. touching the cuckold's horns
6 **trapdoor** A usual feature of Jacobean stages. The space below the stage was symbolically associated with hell, as it was in *the last triumph*.
8 **devil with one eye** The imagined pageant figure has a phallic innuendo.
10 **squibbing** (*a*) making witty comments (*b*) letting off squibs
11 **with't** i.e. with the trapdoor
13 **stamp** (*a*) stamp of the foot (*b*) impression on coin, coinage (hence *go current*)
14–15 **how . . . hole** (with a sexual innuendo)
19 **contumelious** insolent
20 **out-parishes** suburbs (as places of scandal-mongering or of play-acting)
21 **so far** (in the performance)
23 **those** i.e. the caltrop's spikes
24 **privy** secret
25–6 **Stamp . . . cuckolds** Horn was considered an antidote for poison; wine was often used as a base for medicines.
25 **Stamp** grind to a powder
27 **present** instant
29 **As** even though
'tis certain (to succeed)
30 **present** act
32 **his part** (of lovesick shepherd)
37.1 ***above*** The main part of the stage is reserved for the main action of the masque. The number of people is exceptionally large for the upper gallery, and the masquers must be able to pass cups to their audience; a dais or raised platform may have been put in place before 5.1, though Leslie Thomson (*Studies in English Literature, 1500–1900* 26 (1986), 331–43) has defended the use of the upper acting area.
44 **To . . . merit** Alludes to the Protestant doctrine that God's grace does not depend on the recipient's *merit*.
47 **perfect** fully contented

[*He kisses Bianca*]

DUKE
I have all indeed now.

BIANCA [*aside*]
But I have made surer work. This shall not blind me.
He that begins so early to reprove,
Quickly rid him, or look for little love.
Beware a brother's envy; he's next heir too.
Cardinal, you die this night; the plot's laid surely.
In time of sports death may steal in securely.
Then 'tis least thought on.
For he that's most religious, holy friend,
Does not at all hours think upon his end.
He has his times of frailty, and his thoughts
Their transportations too through flesh and blood,
For all his zeal, his learning, and his light,
As well as we, poor souls, that sin by night.

[*Fabritio gives Duke a paper*]

DUKE
What's this, Fabritio?

FABRITIO
Marry, my lord, the model
Of what's presented.

DUKE
O, we thank their loves.—
Sweet duchess, take your seat; list to the argument.

[*They sit, and he*] *reads*

'There is a nymph that haunts the woods and springs,
In love with two at once, and they with her.
Equal it runs; but, to decide these things,
The cause to mighty Juno they refer,
She being the marriage goddess. The two lovers,
They offer sighs, the nymph a sacrifice,
All to please Juno, who by signs discovers
How the event shall be. So that strife dies.
Then springs a second, for the man refused
Grows discontent and, out of love abused,
He raises Slander up, like a black fiend,
To disgrace th'other, which pays him i'th' end.'

BIANCA
In troth, my lord, a pretty, pleasing argument,
And fits th'occasion well. Envy and Slander
Are things soon raised against two faithful lovers;
But comfort is, they are not long unrewarded.

Music

DUKE
This music shows they're upon entrance now.

BIANCA [*aside*]
Then enter all my wishes.

Enter [below] Hymen in yellow, Ganymede in a blue robe powdered with stars, and Hebe in a white robe with golden stars, with covered cups in their hands. They dance a short dance, then, bowing to the Duke, etc., Hymen speaks

HYMEN [*giving Bianca a cup*]
To thee, fair bride, Hymen offers up
Of nuptial joys this the celestial cup.
Taste it, and thou shalt ever find
Love in thy bed, peace in thy mind.

BIANCA
We'll taste you sure; 'twere pity to disgrace
So pretty a beginning.

[*She drinks*]

DUKE
'Twas spoke nobly.

GANYMEDE
Two cups of nectar have we begged from Jove.
Hebe, give that to innocence, I this to love.

[*He gives Duke a cup, and Hebe gives Lord Cardinal a cup*]

Take heed of stumbling more; look to your way;
Remember still the Via Lactea.

[*The Duke and Lord Cardinal drink*]

HEBE
Well, Ganymede, you have more faults, though not so known.
I spilt one cup, but you have filched many a one.

HYMEN
No more; forbear. For Hymen's heart
In love we met, and so let's part. *Exeunt masquers*

DUKE
But soft: here's no such persons in the argument
As these three, Hymen, Hebe, Ganymede.
The actors that this model here discovers
Are only four, Juno, a nymph, two lovers.

BIANCA
This is some antemasque, belike, my lord,

64 **transportations** travellings
too i.e. like ours
65 **light** spiritual enlightenment
67 **model** summary
69 **argument** outline of the plot
76 **discovers** reveals
77 **event** outcome
81 **which pays him** Either raising Slander chastizes (*pays*) *th'other*, or *th'other* chastizes him for doing so.
85 **unrewarded** unpunished (for raising Envy and Slander)
87.1–5.1.101 ***Enter*...*masquers*** This unexpected *antemasque* has been arranged by Bianca, in order to poison the Lord Cardinal.
87.1 ***Hymen*** God of marriage. Yellow is the colour he traditionally wears.
Ganymede Zeus (Jove) was prompted by homoerotic desire to carry him off to be his cupbearer.
87.2 ***powdered*** sprinkled
Hebe (daughter of Zeus)
96–7 **Take...Lactea** Alludes to a myth about the formation of the Milky Way (*Via Lactea*) in which Hebe stumbled on a star and spilt the wine or milk that she was carrying in her cup.
98–9 **Well...one** Ganymede's drunkenness accounts for confusion between the cups.
99 **spilt** Perhaps jocular for 'drank'.
106 **antemasque** An episode (usually comic) before the main masque.

To entertain time. Now my peace is perfect,
Let sports come on apace. Now is their time, my lord.
Music
Hark you, you hear from 'em!
Enter [below] two dressed like nymphs, bearing two tapers lighted; then Isabella, dressed with flowers and garlands, bearing a censer with fire in it.

DUKE
The nymph indeed.
They set the censer and tapers on Juno's altar, with much reverence, this ditty being sung in parts:

[ISABELLA *and the* NYMPHS]
Juno, nuptial goddess,
Thou that rul'st o'er coupled bodies,
Ti'st man to woman never to forsake her,
Thou only powerful marriage-maker,
Pity this amazed affection.
I love both, and both love me;
Nor know I where to give rejection,
My heart likes so equally,
Till thou set'st right my peace of life
And with thy power conclude this strife.

ISABELLA
Now with my thanks depart you to the springs,
I to these wells of love. [*Exeunt nymphs*]
Thou sacred goddess
And queen of nuptials, daughter to great Saturn,
Sister and wife to Jove, imperial Juno,
Pity this passionate conflict in my breast,
This tedious war 'twixt two affectïons.
Crown one with victory, and my heart's at peace.
Enter [below] Hippolito and Guardiano, like shepherds

HIPPOLITO
Make me that happy man, thou mighty goddess.

GUARDIANO
But I live most in hope if truest love
Merit the greatest comfort.

ISABELLA
I love both
With such an even and fair affectïon,
I know not which to speak for, which to wish for,
Till thou, great arbitress 'twixt lovers' hearts,
By thy auspicious grace design the man;
Which pity I implore.

HIPPOLITO *and* GUARDIANO
We all implore it.
Livia descends, like Juno [with her pages like two winged Cupids holding bows and arrows]

ISABELLA
And after sighs, contrition's truest odours,
I offer to thy powerful deity
This precious incense. May it ascend peacefully.
[*Incense ascends from the censer*]
[*Aside*] And if it keep true touch, my good aunt Juno,
'Twill try your immortality er't be long.
I fear you'll never get so nigh heaven again
When you're once down.

LIVIA
Though you and your affections
Seem all as dark to our illustrious brightness
As night's inheritance, hell, we pity you,
And your requests are granted. You ask signs;
They shall be given you. We'll be gracious to you.
He of those twain which we determine for you
Love's arrows shall wound twice. The later wound
Betokens love in age; for so are all
Whose love continues firmly all their lifetime
Twice wounded at their marriage, else affection
Dies when youth ends. [*Aside*] This savour overcomes me.—
Now, for a sign of wealth and golden days,
Bright-eyed prosperity which all couples love,
Ay, and makes love, take that.

107 **entertain** pleasantly occupy
my peace is perfect *Peace* is a key word for Bianca: see 1.1.127 (her first speech), 2.2.385, 4.1.126, and 5.1.48. Can be understood here variously as the *peace* of mind Bianca anticipates from the Lord Cardinal's death, or the amity she has supposedly established with him (compare *perfect*, 47); also as a *piece* of drama and act of villainy, the antemasque itself. Perhaps too the drama of her life is complete and her *peace* or lack of it after death has been determined.
perfect perfected, complete
109.6–7 **in parts** i.e. with each singer taking a separate harmonic line. Isabella presumably takes the leading part.
114 **amazed** bewildered
120 **the springs** (the Nymphs' dwelling-place)
121 **wells** sources, fountains. The literal *springs* of 120 become an image of the lovesick shepherds, or a reference to Juno's altar.
125 **tedious** laborious, drawn-out
133 **design** indicate
134.1 ***descends*** i.e. is lowered in a chariot from the 'heavens' in the stage's roof so as to hang suspended above the stage
like Juno Her identity is established by feathers (176) and perhaps figures of peacocks, birds sacred to Juno. She carries a flaming arrow that she is to throw at Isabella, and possibly has above her head a device representing the region of fire of medieval cosmology.
134.1–2 ***with . . . arrows*** The staging is uncertain: the original text provides neither entry nor exit for the Cupids. As they are sons of Juno's rival Venus and symbols of illicit love, they are incongruous attendants on the marriage goddess, highlighting the irony of Livia's playing the role.
138 **keep true touch** (*a*) acts faithfully (*b*) proves a true touchstone
142 **to** compared with
151 **savour** smell (of incense)
152 **for** as

[She throws flaming gold upon Isabella's lap]
Our brother Jove
Never denies us of his burning treasure,
T'express bounty.
Isabella falls and dies

DUKE
She falls down upon't.
What's the conceit of that?

FABRITIO
As overjoyed, belike.
Too much prosperity overjoys us all,
And she has her lapful, it seems, my lord.

DUKE
This swerves a little from the argument though.
Look you, my lords.

GUARDIANO *[aside]*
All's fast. Now comes my part to toll him hither;
Then with a stamp given he's dispatched as cunningly.

HIPPOLITO
Stark dead. O, treachery! Cruelly made away!
[He strikes the floor in grief. The trapdoor opens, and Guardiano falls through]
How's that?

FABRITIO
Look, there's one of the lovers dropped away too.

DUKE
Why, sure this plot's drawn false; here's no such thing.

LIVIA
O, I am sick to th' death. Let me down quickly.
This fume is deadly. O, 't has poisoned me!
[She is let down to the stage, with the Cupids]
My subtlety is sped: her art has quitted me;
My own ambition pulls me down to ruin. *[She dies]*

HIPPOLITO *[to Isabella]*
Nay, then I kiss thy cold lips, and applaud
This thy revenge in death.
Cupids shoot [at Hippolito]

FABRITIO
Look, Juno's down too.
What makes she there? Her pride should keep aloft.
She was wont to scorn the earth in other shows.
Methinks her peacock feathers are much pulled.

HIPPOLITO
O, death runs through my blood, in a wild flame too.
Plague of those Cupids! Some lay hold on 'em.
Let 'em not scape; they have spoiled me. The shaft's deadly.

DUKE
I have lost myself in this quite.

HIPPOLITO
My great lords, we are all confounded.

DUKE
How?

HIPPOLITO
Dead; and I worse.

FABRITIO
Dead? My girl dead? I hope
My sister Juno has not served me so.

HIPPOLITO
Lust and forgetfulness has been amongst us,
And we are brought to nothing. Some blest charity
Lend me the speeding pity of his sword
To quench this fire in blood. Leantio's death
Has brought all this upon us—now I taste it—
And made us lay plots to confound each other.
The event so proves it; and man's understanding
Is riper at his fall than all his lifetime.
[Pointing to Livia] She, in a madness for her lover's death,
Revealed a fearful lust in our near bloods,
For which I am punished dreadfully and unlooked for;
Proved her own ruin too. Vengeance met vengeance
Like a set match, as if the plagues of sin
Had been agreed to meet here all together.
But how her fawning partner fell I reach not,
Unless caught by some springe of his own setting;
For, on my pain, he never dreamed of dying.
The plot was all his own, and he had cunning
Enough to save himself; but 'tis the property

154.1 ***flaming gold*** This and some other staging details come from a manuscript note in a copy of the 1657 edition. The reference to *golden days* (152) and Isabella's lapful of *prosperity* (158), taken with Livia's suggestion that the *burning treasure* (155) is borrowed from Jove, suggests that the effect is of a golden shaft of lightning or a shower of gold (see note to 159). An ornamented arrow or short spear might deliver the poison most effectively, and might be suitably phallic.

155 **burning** Refers to the flames represented, and to the burning effects of the poison.

157 **conceit** significance

159 **she has her lapful** Apparently the *flaming gold* strikes Isabella in the lap. This suggests to Fabritio an analogy with Jupiter's rape of Danae in a shower of gold.

160 **argument** plot summary

162 **fast** firmly in place
toll him lure him (also 'ring his death-bell')
hither i.e. to the trapdoor

164 **Stark ... away** Spoken of Isabella.

170 **is sped** has succeeded (ironic)
quitted requited

173.1 ***Cupids shoot*** As an ironized emblem of love this effectively coincides with Hippolito's embrace of Isabella.

174 **makes she** is she doing

175 **other shows** Alludes to masques with Juno such as Jonson's *Hymenaei* (1606) and the masque in Shakespeare's *The Tempest* (1610–11 onwards).

176 **peacock feathers** See note to 134.1.

179 **spoiled** destroyed

180 **I ... quite** The Duke is still trying to match the action with the written *argument*.

182 **worse** i.e. in agony from the poison

184 **forgetfulness** moral obliviousness

185 **we ... nothing** Recalls Jeremiah, 10:24, 'O lord, correct me; but with judgement, not in thine anger, lest thou bring me to nothing'.

186 **speeding** hastening

188 **taste it** 'Taste death' is biblical.

190 **event** outcome

193 **near** closely related

194 **unlooked for** unexpectedly

195 **Proved** *She* proved

196 **set** prearranged
match (*a*) conspiracy to rob (the primary sense) (*b*) contest. *Meet* (197) accordingly suggests (*a*) gather, or (*b*) encounter as opponents.

198 **reach** understand

199 **springe** snare

200 **on my pain** Refers to damnation or the effect of the poison.

Of guilty deeds to draw your wise men downward;
Therefore the wonder ceases.—O, this torment!

DUKE
Our guard below there!
Enter a Lord [*below*] *with a guard* [*bearing halberds*]

LORD [*to Hippolito*] My lord.

HIPPOLITO [*aside*] Run and meet death then,
And cut off time and pain.
[*He runs upon a halberd, and dies*]

LORD [*to the Duke*] Behold, my lord.
He's run his breast upon a weapon's point.

DUKE
Upon the first night of our nuptial honours,
Destruction play her triumph, and great mischiefs
Masque in expected pleasures! 'Tis prodigious;
They're things most fearfully ominous; I like 'em not.
Remove these ruined bodies from our eyes.
[*The Lord and guard exeunt with the bodies*]

BIANCA [*aside, looking on Lord Cardinal*]
Not yet? No change? When falls he to the earth?
[*Enter a Lord, above*]

LORD [*giving Duke a paper*]
Please but your excellence to peruse that paper,
Which is a brief confession from the heart
Of him that fell first, ere his soul departed;
And there the darkness of these deeds speaks plainly.
'Tis the full scope, the manner, and intent.
His ward, that ignorantly let him down,
Fear put to present flight at the voice of him.

BIANCA [*aside*] Nor yet?

DUKE [*to Lord Cardinal*]
Read, read; for I am lost in sight and strength.

LORD CARDINAL
My noble brother!

BIANCA O, the curse of wretchedness!
My deadly hand is fall'n upon my lord.
Destruction take me to thee!—Give me way.
The pains and plagues of a lost soul upon him
That hinders me a moment.

DUKE
My heart swells bigger yet. Help here; break't ope.
My breast flies open next. [*He dies*]

BIANCA O, with the poison
That was prepared for thee, thee, Cardinal.
'Twas meant for thee.

LORD CARDINAL Poor prince!

BIANCA Accursèd error!
[*To Duke*] Give me thy last breath, thou infected bosom,
And wrap two spirits in one poisoned vapour.
[*She kisses him*]
Thus, thus reward thy murderer, and turn death
Into a parting kiss. My soul stands ready at my lips,
E'en vexed to stay one minute after thee.

LORD CARDINAL
The greatest sorrow and astonishment
That ever struck the general peace of Florence
Dwells in this hour.

BIANCA So my desires are satisfied:
I feel death's power within me.
Thou hast prevailed in something, cursèd poison,
Though thy chief force was spent in my lord's bosom.
But my deformity in spirit's more foul;
A blemished face best fits a leprous soul.
What make I here? These are all strangers to me,
Not known but by their malice now thou'rt gone;
Nor do I seek their pities.
[*She drinks from the poisoned cup*]

LORD CARDINAL O, restrain
Her ignorant wilful hand!

BIANCA Now do; 'tis done.
Leantio, now I feel the breach of marriage
At my heart-breaking. O, the deadly snares
That women set for women, without pity
Either to soul or honour! Learn by me
To know your foes. In this belief I die:
Like our own sex we have no enemy, no enemy.

LORD [*to Lord Cardinal*] See, my lord,
What shift she's made to be her own destruction.

BIANCA
Pride, greatness, honours, beauty, youth, ambition,
You must all down together, there's no help for't.
Yet this my gladness is, that I remove
Tasting the same death in a cup of love. [*She dies*]

LORD CARDINAL
Sin, what thou art these ruins show too piteously.
Two kings on one throne cannot sit together,
But one must needs down, for his title's wrong;
So where lust reigns, that prince cannot reign long.
Exeunt [*with the bodies*]

Finis

209 **triumph** (*a*) theatrical spectacle (*b*) celebration of victory (*c*) trump card
210 **prodigious** monstrous, ill-omened
216 **him that fell first** (Guardiano)
218 **scope** end in view
219 **let him down** (through the trapdoor)
223 **wretchedness** wickedness (both evil acts that misfire and the state of evil that leads to damnation)
228 **My . . . bigger** The blood was thought to swell up the heart at death.
239 **astonishment** shock, dismay
243 **in something** to some extent
246 **A blemished face** Bianca's face may be disfigured by the poison, or she may here scratch her face with her nails. Alternatively, Bianca claims that an unblemished face matched with a leprous soul, such as her own, is the greater deformity.
leprous Compare the application to Bianca at 2.2.423–4 and 4.3.17.
256 **no enemy** The repetition of these words might trail off into death or be spoken emphatically.
261 **remove** depart, die
264 **Two . . . together** From Seneca, *Thyestes*, 444, 'non capit regnum duos' (a throne will not hold two kings); possibly proverbial.
266 **that prince** i.e. the prince of that state

Women beware Women.

THE PARTS

Men

LEANTIO (504 lines): Citizen; Lord Cardinal (*or* Servant *or* Hymen *or* Lord), Hymen (*or* Lord Cardinal), Lord (*or* Lord Cardinal), Servant (*or* Lord Cardinal)

DUKE (271 lines): Sordido

GUARDIANO (244 lines): Hymen, Lord, [Messenger]

WARD (205 lines): Citizen, Servant, Hymen, Lord, [Messenger]

HIPPOLITO (180 lines): Hymen

LORD CARDINAL (130 lines): Messenger; Leantio *or* Sordido

SORDIDO (113 lines): Duke (*or* Lord Cardinal *or* Citizen *or* Servant *or* Messenger), Lord Cardinal (*or* Duke *or* Citizen *or* Servant), Citizen (*or* Duke *or* Lord Cardinal), Messenger (*or* Duke), Servant (*or* Duke *or* Lord Cardinal)

FABRITIO (98 lines): Messenger, [Servant]

MESSENGER (19 lines): any but Leantio, Duke, Hippolito, [Guardiano, Ward]

LORD (12 lines; 5.1): any but Duke, Lord Cardinal, Fabritio, Hippolito, Guardiano

SERVANT (7 lines): Citizen, Hymen, Lord; Leantio *or* Messenger; Ward [*or* Sordido]

HYMEN (6 lines; 5.1): any but Duke, Lord Cardinal, Fabritio, Hippolito, Guardiano

CITIZEN (5 lines; 1.3): any but Duke, Lord Cardinal

Boys

LIVIA (581 lines): a Lady, Ganymede, Hebe, Page; a Boy *or* Apprentice

BIANCA (421 lines): Page

MOTHER (226 lines): a Lady, Page, Ganymede, Hebe

ISABELLA (215 lines): a Lady, Page; a Boy *or* Apprentice

FIRST LADY (10 lines; 4.1): any but Bianca, other Lady

SECOND LADY (7 lines; 4.1): any but Bianca, other Lady

GANYMEDE (4 lines; 5.1): any but Bianca, Hebe, Isabella

APPRENTICE (3 lines; 1.3): any but Mother, Bianca, Boys

HEBE (2 lines; 5.1): any but Bianca, Ganymede, Isabella

FIRST BOY (1 line; 1.3): any but Mother, Bianca, Apprentice, other Boys

SECOND BOY (1 line; 1.3): any but Mother, Bianca, Apprentice, other Boys

THIRD BOY (1 line; 1.3): any but Mother, Bianca, Apprentice, other Boys

PAGE (1 line; 4.2): any but Livia, Isabella

Fabritio, Hippolito, and Guardiano probably appear among the knights and nobility in 1.3.

Most crowded scene: 5.1, excluding its opening episode: 12 characters (+ 2? cardinals, 2? lords, 2? ladies, all mute, with mute nymphs, and Cupids able to double with Hebe and Ganymede)

MEASURE FOR MEASURE: A GENETIC TEXT

Edited by John Jowett

Measure for Measure must have been first written and performed in 1603–4. On St Stephen's Night, 26 December 1604, the King's Men staged, according to the Revels office accounts, 'a play called *Measure for Measure*' by 'Shaxberd' as part of the Christmas festivities at the Whitehall Banqueting Hall. *Measure* first appeared in the Shakespeare First Folio of 1623 (JAGGARD). Its credentials as a Shakespeare play are sound. However, it seems clear that the 1623 text had undergone adaptation by Middleton. The present edition is accordingly designed to highlight Middleton's contribution.

Even before the hand of a reviser other than Shakespeare becomes an issue, there are grounds for asserting that *Measure* was revived no earlier than in the last years of Shakespeare's professional career. The purity of diction is implausible for a Shakespeare play of 1603–4, particularly one such as *Measure* that insistently intertwines the passionate and the scurrilous. Asseverations that do exist repeatedly use phrases that look like unShakespearean substitutions for Shakespearean oaths. The play has almost certainly been expurgated of oaths at some time after the 1606 Act of Parliament to restrain abuses of players had made blasphemy on stage illegal. JAGGARD's act divisions suggest a later date still. They are unlikely to have been present in the original playbook, which would have been written for performance without act-intervals, as was usual when the King's Men first brought a play to the stage. Act-breaks would have been needed for any production after about 1609, when the King's Men began to play at the Blackfriars and to observe the hall theatre convention of act-intervals. On both counts, the text printed in 1623 would seem to derive (indirectly) from a manuscript prepared for a revival.

The dating of this event can be pushed markedly later than 1609. The one and only song in *Measure*, 'Take, O take those lips away', happens to be positioned immediately after one of the act-breaks. This lyric also occurs, with a second stanza, in the Fletcherian tragedy *Rollo, Duke of Normandy* (1617–20; also known as *The Bloody Brother*). Every indication is that the song originated in *Rollo*. The song fits the context of *Rollo* considerably better than that of *Measure*, and, as the two stanzas were influenced by a common source, the Latin lyric '*Ad Lydiam*', it can reasonably be inferred that they were written as a single piece. Accordingly, the song must have been introduced into *Measure* for the occasion of a revival staged several years after Shakespeare's death.

Before the introduction of 'Take, O take those lips away' into *Measure*, the Duke's passage through the city in the eventual Act 3 would lead directly to his meeting with Isabella at the moated grange after the song episode in the eventual Act 4. This conclusion seems inevitable unless an episode was deleted to make way for the new act-break and song. In either case, it seems that both sides of the act-break were affected by the alterations. The Duke's soliloquy 'He who the sword of heaven will bear', a moralizing summary written in sententious rhyming couplets, is well suited to its function at the end of JAGGARD's Act 3. In contrast, the six-line soliloquy 'O place and greatness' which in JAGGARD stands as the time allotted for Isabella to explain her plight to Mariana and put to her, without offence, the difficult proposal that she should substitute for Isabella as Angelo's sexual partner in the walled garden, has struck many critics as grotesquely short measure. It is further suspect because it is obscurely if at all relevant to its immediate context. This situation seems to have arisen because in the adaptation the two soliloquies were transposed. The longer one, previously in 4.1, could now produce an effective close to the act, matching the strong new opening to the fourth act with its interpolated song.

A short piece of dialogue forms a bridge between the song and Mariana's exit to leave the Duke and Isabella on stage (4.1.7–25). The technique hereabouts of reshaping extant text and adding minimal and merely functional new writing is a reminder that a posthumous revival is an enterprise of a fundamentally different complexion from dramatic authorship.

But a longer passage at the beginning of 1.2 is a more straightforward and sustained piece of composition for the adaptation. It can be dated with some confidence to a time after the composition of *Rollo*, so providing an independent affirmation that the play was adapted posthumously, and the case for Middleton's authorship of the passage is particularly strong. In JAGGARD, the first 79 lines of 1.2 marked in the present text as an interpolation and the episode after it marked as a cancel are printed as a continuous sequence. This causes a duplication. First Mistress Overdone delivers the news of Claudio's arrest for getting Juliet with child, then, suddenly ignorant of the situation, she prompts Pompey to deliver the same news to her. The sequence might be attributed to Shakespeare's oversight (though a rather puzzling one), or to a result of his revision, were it not that the opening episode includes a striking cluster of grammatical and lexical features that would not be expected in a Shakespeare text. It is Middleton who favours the linguistic forms that mark this passage out from the rest of the play and from Shakespeare's usage more generally: 'has' (as against 'hath'), 'whilst' (as against 'while'), 'ay' (as against 'yes'), and 'between' (as against 'betwixt'). Together, these preferences not only distinguish Middleton from Shakespeare, but favour him against other possible candidates for a revision of a King's Men play such as Philip Massinger, John Webster, and John Fletcher. Furthermore, whereas only four relatively unremarkable words in the passage are found in Shakespeare's works but not Middleton's, an impressive array of individual words, distinctive phrases, and idiosyncratic turns of thought can be paralleled in Middleton but not Shakespeare. Finally, as described below, the passage is peculiarly rich in topical references; these are conspicuously awkward in relation to the play's date of original composition, but point strongly to 1621, a time when Shakespeare had been dead for several years, but Middleton remained an active dramatist. It seems, then, that Middleton wrote a passage to replace the original opening of the scene.

There are, then, two major alterations that, on account of a range of different but converging signals, can be assigned to a 1621 adaptation. Other changes made at the same time may be harder to detect, yet if adaptation affected two passages it could potentially affect others as well. And indeed it probably did so. With varying degrees of probability, a number of other changes can be identified.

First, and most certainly, the revision evidently accentuated the role of Juliet. This was achieved simply by bringing her onstage in two scenes. She is mentioned in 1.2, but she says nothing and is not referred to in any way that supposes her presence. Virtually the same situation happens again in Act 5. Notes to the stage directions for Juliet's first and final entries in the adapted manuscript would have allowed her to appear in both scenes as a silent moral comment, a visible reminder of at least one physical consequence of sexual activity (Overdone and the gentlemen embody others).

As is the case with Juliet's presence in both 1.2 and 5.1, the changes in 1.2 evidently led on to other, related alterations involving the roles of Lucio, the Bawd, and the Clown. Whereas Lucio's part in bringing the news of Claudio's arrest to Isabella undoubtedly belongs to the original text, his presence is suspect in 2.2, the scene in which Isabella first visits Angelo. It seems likely that some of the Provost's speeches were transferred to Lucio, and that some of his lines, such as those at 2.2.132, 135, and 159, were written in by Middleton. Lucio's fervent yet cynical support for Isabella both augments his role in the play and adds a note of ironic detachment to the intensity of her debate with Angelo.

More speculatively, the objective of highlighting Lucio's role in the early scenes may have affected the sequence of the scenes at the end of Act 1. As is explained in the commentary note to 1.3(b), there are indications that Shakespeare would originally have staged Lucio's interview with Isabella before the Duke's conversation with the Friar. Once again, an act break is implicated, for the final text puts Lucio on stage just before the first act interval. There may also have been considerations of doubling actors' roles (see commentary note to 1.3(a)).

The Bawd is both a disreputable figure, like Lucio and his companions, and probably a role for a boy actor, like Juliet and the singing boy. As has already been suggested, her first appearance in 1.2, like Lucio's, must belong to the adaptation. What was added to her role elsewhere was probably her name, Mistress Overdone, and the lines that make reference to it at 2.1.79–81, 2.1.187–94, and 4.3.1–38. Shakespeare's Bawd was probably nameless, like her equivalent in *Pericles* (and like other roles in many other Shakespeare plays, including, in *Measure*, the Duke—named nowhere in the dialogue, speech-prefixes and stage directions—and the Provost). The name is itself distinctively Middletonian. It can scarcely be coincidence that in *No Wit* a significant character who is a sexually decrepit gentleman is called Master Overdone. In principle, the influence between *Measure* and *No Wit* could run in either direction, but the *type* of name is also in Middleton's vein. He frequently coins names that involve a compound, and names that indicate a Jonsonian character-type. More specifically, his names often suggest a sexual identity: *Mistress Newcut*, *Mistress Cleveland*, *Mistress Openwork*, *Castiza*, *Kix*, *Whorehound*, *Touchwood*, *De Flores*, and so on. Shakespeare examples are far fewer, and they tend to include a forename; 'Mistress Kate Keepdown' in *Measure* itself is one example. A particularly striking Middleton parallel that involves a sexual identity constructed on 'Mistress' followed by the antithesis of *Over* followed by a monosyllable ending in 'n' is *Mistress Underman* in *Chaste Maid*. If the name is not in itself sufficient to prove Middleton's intervention, the inference is effectively confirmed by textual dislocations in all three passages mentioning it, as can be seen in the commentary notes.

The passages in 2.1 are brief enough, but the mention of Mistress Overdone in 4.3 falls within a substantial speech that can be demonstrated on other grounds to have been written by Middleton. As an entirely separate set-piece for a clown, this speech is characteristic of the kind of material that might be added during the adaptation of any play. In this case, the element of allusive social satire accords fully with Middleton, the device of the catalogue of representative figures has a close parallel elsewhere in his writing, and the speech contains a proliferation of words and phrases that are strikingly in Middleton's vein. The addition is consistent with other changes to the play, and adaptations more generally, in that it augments the role of a comic figure. It develops the play's picture of a violent and decadent society, using a comic mode of delivery to offer harsh glances at urban vices.

Another passage probably added by Middleton helps to counterpoise this added emphasis on the play's lawless characters. It is the brief and far from distinctively Shakespearean exchange between Escalus and the Justice at the end of 2.1, in which the need to restrain vice firmly is given almost choric articulation. The passage is, like Pompey's speech, separable from the rest of the action. It introduces a character, the Justice, who, like the two Gentlemen, appears nowhere else in the play. It contains sentiments that are surprising from Escalus, to the effect that mercy and pardon are dangerous and cannot be extended to Claudio. We might think of Escalus elsewhere as the voice of a Shakespearean tolerance; the more judgemental attitude of this brief dialogue might accord with the Calvinist temper found in Middleton, and, like the exposure of vice in 1.2, it modifies the play's opposition to puritanism. If the Duke's laxity has been extreme, the extension of secular law to punish moral lapses severely can accordingly be justified.

Even as the adaptation makes the action more rooted in a city that closely resembles London, it adds an urgent relevance to the play's setting in Vienna. This location would have had little special relevance in 1603–4, and in some respects is decidedly unexpected. None of the play's recognized sources or analogues is set in Vienna, and Shakespeare elsewhere shows virtually no interest in either Vienna or Austria. Moreover, in contradiction of the linguistically Germanic setting, the personal names in *Measure* are consistently Italian. Some of the analogues refer to the Duke of Ferrara. 'Ferrara' is metrically identical with 'Vienna', and is mentioned in Shakespeare and John Fletcher's *All is True*, 3.2.324 (in a passage usually attributed to Shakespeare). There are reasons to suppose that Shakespeare set the play in Italian Ferrara, and that Middleton altered the setting specifically in order to establish the Thirty Years War as a backdrop.

We suggest that Italian names were deleted from the dialogue in three places to make the change of location less obvious. At 1.1.2, and perhaps also elsewhere, defective metre suggests that Shakespeare may have given the Duke the personal name Vincentio—otherwise mysteriously absent, and preserved only in 'The Names of All the Actors'. Similar considerations apply to Francisca in 1.4: she is named in the opening stage direction but not the dialogue, and the verse at 1.4.2 is metrically defective. Earlier, Middleton seems to have reflected *Measure*'s pairing of Isabella and Francisca when he made characters with the same names sisters-in-law in *The Witch*. Francisca in that play is therefore equivalent to Juliet in *Measure*, and, similarly, is pregnant: an unchaste sister-in-law rather than a member of a holy 'sisterhood'.

The adaptation may have introduced more substantial cuts. The extant text is one of the longer Shakespeare comedies, so the grounds for supposing extensive cutting are far slighter than in the case of *Macbeth*, which is conspicuously short for a Shakespeare tragedy. Nevertheless, any metrical irregularity or discontinuity in sense might hypothetically be the result of cutting. At 1.1.8–9 there is a crux that involves both sense and metre. Rather than emend, as in the Oxford Shakespeare text, we have here suggested a lacuna resulting from a cut.

Even before adaptation, *Measure* would have been amongst the most Middletonian of Shakespeare's plays. With the possible exception of the Plautine *Comedy of Errors*, *Measure* is Shakespeare's only strictly urban comedy. It has affinities of tone and subject matter with verse satire and satiric prose pamphlets, both of which are exemplified in Middleton's work. In the first instance Shakespeare was responding to writers of Middleton's ilk—witty, harsh, satiric, city-oriented. No other dramatist of the period is so persistently concerned with the politics of the libido and the economics of sexual exchange.

Measure itself seems to have influenced Middleton long before he adapted it. Though both Middleton and Fletcher had collaborated with Shakespeare, Middleton's predilections would certainly have made him the more obvious choice to adapt *Measure*. He had already adapted *Macbeth*, and indeed is the only person known to have adapted a Shakespeare play for the professional theatre (other than Shakespeare himself) before Sir William Davenant turned his hand to the trade after the Restoration. Davenant began, by coincidence or otherwise, with the very plays adapted by Middleton: *Measure*, adapted as *The Law against Lovers* (1662), and *Macbeth* (1663).

From the point of view of the King's Men and Middleton, *Measure* must have seemed pointedly significant in 1621 on account of its concern with justice. The word occurs considerably more often in this than any other Shakespeare play, and *Measure* shows justice as a principle whose enactment is both problematic and subject to considerable abuse. In 1621 the Lord Chancellor, Sir Francis Bacon, was impeached by Parliament on charges of bribery and corruption. Though the offences urged against him were financial rather than sexual, his impeachment drew attention to a conflict between personal gratification and the exercise of the highest judicial office in the land. As Bacon's adversary Sir Edward Coke declared, 'nothing is of so much moment as the taking away of corrupt judges'. The principles and morality of justice had therefore become specific matters of public concern and discussion in the very year *Measure* was evidently revived. In this edition we identify (on other grounds) Angelo's 'What knows the law | That thieves do pass on thieves?' (2.1.21–2) as Middleton's addition, and there may be other, less attributable, alterations of this kind. One can only speculate as to whether passages such as Isabella's offer to 'bribe' Angelo around 2.2.148 might have been slightly sharpened during adaptation. Few readers will doubt, however, that Isabella's explanation at 2.2.152–8 belongs to the original text. The Shakespearean play's concern with judicial process would have made it sharply pertinent in 1621 before any adaptation.

The new passage in 1.2 contained lines that were intensely topical to the early 1620s in other ways, and that both added to and thematized the play's participation in public debate. Lucio's conversation with his companions supplies a sensationalizing but localizing environment variously for the Duke's supposed urgent affairs out of Vienna, for Claudio's sexual misdemeanour as a topic for rumour-mongering, and for Lucio's role as news-bringer to Isabella in the convent, not to mention the rumours he later promotes about the Duke's sexual conduct.

The 'poverty' of 1.2.78 alludes to the economic depression of 1619–24, perhaps the severest England had experienced to that time, and another matter of debate in the 1621 Parliament. The opening lines refer to pirates. Only as of about 1609 did pirates become a regular menace to English shipping. Between 21 October 1620 and 22 September 1621 Sir Robert Mansell was at sea leading an expedition to strike against pirate bases in the Mediterranean, but with little success, and on 20 October 1621 John Chamberlain recorded news that pirates had captured no less than fifty-seven British merchant vessels.

Given the likelihood that Middleton switched the location from Ferrara to Vienna, the allusions to the Thirty Years War are especially significant. A few years later, in *A Game at Chess*, Middleton was to take a militant Protestant stance against the ambitions of Counter-Reformation diplomacy. He probably alludes to the Palatinate wars in that play, and certainly does so in *World Tossed at Tennis* (878–9) and *Quiet Life* (5.1.112). At the opening of 1.2 of *Measure* Middleton seizes on the significance of Vienna to the moment of the revival, as the seat of the Catholic Emperor Ferdinand II, and as a city at war. The Hungarian prince Bethlen Gábor (known to the English as Bethlehem Gabor or as Gabriel) had joined the Protestant alliance; as a gesture of defiance towards the Emperor's title of King of Hungary, he was elected King in 1620, so making a 'King of Hungary' an enemy of Vienna. His troops made incursions against Austrian strongholds in Bohemia, and into Austria itself; by mid-September 1621 they lay within sight of the walls of Vienna.

War in Europe prompted the innovation of newspapers, in the form of news-sheets or 'corantos' presenting regular reports from Vienna and other centres of conflict. The early issues (2 December 1620 to 2 September 1621) were printed in Holland, but production soon shifted to London. The news-sheets of 1621 gave constant reminders of the Hungarian troops' progress, new cities besieged, new villages burnt. But dispatches from Vienna in the news-sheets of 12 September and 6 October note a new move towards peace. Bethlen had begun working towards a separate peace with the Emperor, which materialized as the Treaty of Nikolsburg. By 13 December Hungarian forces in Bohemia had surrendered to the Emperor; the treaty was signed on 31 December, and by 11 February 1622 the Spanish ambassador in London, Count Gondomar, had declared that 'all the affairs of Hungary are settled'.

Measure was probably revised after 6 October, when the news-sheet was issued with details of lords of the Catholic League negotiating with Bethlen. If so, Middleton was writing at a time when the outcome was in the balance. Bethlen was in the midst of a rapid about-turn that could lead to a settlement. King James and others in England were dismayed by the alliance between James's son-in-law Frederick, the Elector Palatine, and Bethlen, as a prince supported by the Turks, and they were anxious for peace generally. A treaty between the Hungarians and Vienna would, however, be a deep disappointment to those who favoured a united military campaign against the Catholic Empire. In the mean time Bethlen's troops continued to raid and burn, and, as he had used similar negotiations earlier in the year merely to buy time whilst awaiting Turkish aid, a successful conclusion to the peace-talks was far from assured.

Lucio and the gentlemen are at once soldiers and, as JAGGARD's list of roles describes them, fantastics ('*Lucio, a fantastique.* | 2. *Other like Gentlemen*'). As soldiers they have a vested interest in the continuance of war: 'There's not a soldier of us all that in the thanksgiving before meat do relish the petition well that prays for peace'. Similarly, as frequenters of brothels they have a vested interest in Mistress Overdone and the domestic news she brings about Claudio's arrest. The adapted scene in *Measure* recognizes a double existence of news: on the one hand, a means whereby urgent external realities are negotiated (Parliament itself discussed the options of war and peace in late 1621); on the other hand, a trivial commodity-object in itself. When these gentlemen chat about war and plunder abroad, and then lechery and venereal disease at home, they have a high stake in the issues. But this does not prevent them from reducing mortal matters to topics for point-scoring and cynical banter, assigning to an item of news a value equivalent to an item of fashionable dress.

The instability of news in being at once important and ephemeral relates to the ambiguity of Vienna as a place of the here-and-now, like the audience's London, and as a faraway stronghold of an enemy power. Middleton's Vienna is a city at war with an immediacy that does not apply to London, and yet the actual Vienna, unlike England, was not in any obvious way a state whose well-being was threatened by pirates; unlike London, it was not a maritime city from which sailors would regularly put forth to sea. The references are eclectic; the effect is to locate the play both here and there. This 'here' and 'there' is defined by a particular textual transmission that runs from news-sheet correspondent to reader, and by a particular physical transmission along vulnerable trade routes from central Europe to the Low Countries and so to England. News of the peace negotiations is one of the very few things in the play to come from outside Vienna. Likewise, for the audience, the representation of news from afar is a thin slit of a window not only onto the London outside the theatre but also onto the distant city of Vienna itself. The momentous ephemerality of news is here absorbed to the stage, so as to correlate with the momentous ephemerality of theatre itself.

The revision was concerned not only to make the play topical, but also to intervene to make the play's structure, style, and fascinations match the dramaturgy of an indoor hall theatre in the early 1620s. The revision might have introduced all the act intervals, and Middleton approached the whole task of revision with a strong sense of structure. Critics have described the moment when the Duke steps forward in 3.1 to take control of Isabella's destiny as a crucial hinge that divides the play in two: between the predominance of Isabella and the Duke, verse and prose, passion and manipulation, the tragic and comic faces of tragicomedy. This structure has affinities with the emphatic division of *Winter's Tale* or *The Changeling* into two contrasted phases. But *Winter's Tale* interrupts the action with a Chorus who draws attention to the passage of seventeen years, and *The Changeling* introduces an extravagant dumb-show at the beginning of Act 4 to divide Beatrice-Joanna's maidenhood from her adulterous marriage; in contrast, the hinge moment in *Measure* is formally unmarked. It happens quite near the beginning of an exceptionally long sequence of action. From the point of view of a reviser establishing a five-part act structure, the hinge was unusable. The introduction of a unique song at the beginning of the new fourth act imposes a new two-part structure in which the song is a formal marker, like the Chorus in *Winter's Tale*, or the dumb-show in *The Changeling*. The act-interval moats the grange from Vienna; the song that follows it reinforces that separation and affirms a new turning point.

As the example of *Macbeth* shows, it was not unusual for revivals to introduce new songs into a play, and Middleton followed this practice. The revival of *A Fair Quarrel* similarly introduced (as the second-issue title-page of 1617 advertises) the new addition of the Bawd's song. At one stroke this combines salient features of the adaptation of *Measure* in 1.2, with the bawd, and in 4.1, with the song. Middleton adapted and shortened another writer's song at the beginning of a scene in *Trick* (4.5.1–4), where the initial spectacle is of Audrey spinning while either she or the Boy sings; Dampit's entry is a discovery. Middleton probably also cut a stanza from his own 'Venus is Cupid's only joy' when adapting it from *Masque of Cupids* to *More Dissemblers*. The dramatic technique compares strikingly with the 'melancholy strains' of the song 'To be chaste is woman's glory' at the beginning of *More Dissemblers*. This is sung offstage to give an emotive impression of the feelings and predicament of another woman, the Duchess in *More Dissemblers*. Her vows of celibacy after the death of her husband can be compared with Mariana's loyalty to the memory of the man who abandoned her. The Duchess, like Mariana (and indeed Dampit), is peculiarly isolated from the world of the court and city, and the song is one means whereby that isolation is expressed. Both songs are, moreover, strong moments of initiation. They introduce a new female character without any preceding dialogue, and in *More Dissemblers* the song begins not only an act but the entire play.

The new act-break and song in *Measure* pre-colour the action that follows. 'Take, O take those lips away' presents in tableau fashion the new figure of the jilted Mariana, who will unravel the plot whilst tangling up efficacy with ethics. The song highlights a romantic languor later celebrated in Alfred Tennyson's poem (1830) and Pre-Raphaelite paintings by Sir John Everett Millais and Dante Gabriel Rossetti, and so opens on a realm of experience remote from Vienna's rigorous nexus between sexual crime and punishment. Though all will not be well from here on, the song offers a prospect that a spirit of romantic tragicomedy might, perhaps, prevail. In this respect the adaptation is modish to the early 1620s, as is clearly suggested by the use of a song by Fletcher from a moment in *Rollo* of high emotional sensationalism.

Mariana's role as a keynote figure for the final two acts of the play corresponds with that of Lucio for the first three acts. In this respect the interpolated episode near the beginning of the play works in a remarkably similar way to the interpolated song. In the earlier episode too, a minor figure, Lucio, is presented so as to give him representative status, and the mode of dramatic writing is again almost exaggeratedly appropriate to the role. Here too, nothing much happens in the episode, but it gives a strong colouration to our view of the play's world; this is, after all, our first introduction to Vienna's street-life. The two major interventions, despite their differences of method and the contrast in their tone, are therefore of a piece.

In relocating and underscoring the play's 'hinge', Middleton identified and remedied an important but disconcerting aspect of its organization, and stressed the altered configurations that become possible once Mariana enters the play. Both in 1.2 and in the more local changes to the comic roles elsewhere, the adapted text gives a fuller impression of time, place, and manners, showing vice at home and warfare abroad as constituents of a newly vibrant and potentially subversive public discourse. These changes addressed important peripheries. They neither perceptibly added to nor perceptibly detracted from the roles of Isabella, Angelo, and the Duke (notwithstanding the latter's moved speeches). Yet the adaptation touches upon virtually every major aspect of *Measure*. Our engagement with the play is in some part Middleton's engagement with Shakespeare's play, and in some part our engagement with Middleton.

The text that follows highlights the changes that are thought to have been introduced (mostly or wholly) in 1621. Except in the case of the duplication in 1.2, where JAGGARD prints both passages, the adapted text broadly corresponds with JAGGARD. To indicate the changes attributed to the adaptation, text posited to have been deleted for the adaptation is printed in grey type, and added text is printed in bold type. Transposed lines are therefore printed in grey at their posited original position and printed in bold at the point to which they were relocated. Of course the presentation cannot allow for the varying shades of certainty with which the features of the adaptation can be identified; it is based on a balance of probability that includes everything from the reasonably likely to the almost certain. The commentary relinquishes the usual focus on glossing the text, in favour of providing further detail in support of the Middleton context that has been presented in this Introduction.

SEE ALSO

Music: *Companion*, 167
Textual introduction and apparatus: *Companion*, 681
Authorship and date: *Companion*, 417
Other Middleton–Shakespeare works: *Timon*, 467; *Macbeth*, 1165

WILLIAM SHAKESPEARE, adapted by THOMAS MIDDLETON

Measure for Measure

[for the King's Men]

THE NAMES OF ALL THE ACTORS

Vincentio, the DUKE
ANGELO, his deputy
ESCALUS, an ancient lord
CLAUDIO, a young gentleman
LUCIO, a fantastic
Two other like GENTLEMEN
PROVOST
Thomas, Peter, two FRIARS
ELBOW, a simple constable
FROTH, a foolish gentleman
Pompey, a CLOWN

ABHORSON, an executioner
BARNARDINE, a dissolute prisoner
JUSTICE
BOY

ISABELLA, sister to Claudio
MARIANA, betrothed to Angelo
JULIET, beloved of Claudio
Francisca, a NUN
Mistress Overdone, a BAWD

Varrius and other lords, officers, citizens, servants

1.1

Sc. 1 **1.1**
Incipit Actus Primus
Enter Duke, Escalus, lords

DUKE Escalus.

ESCALUS My lord Vincentio.

DUKE
Of government the properties to unfold
Would seem in me t' affect speech and discourse,
Since I am put to know that your own science
Exceeds in that the lists of all advice
My strength can give you. Then no more remains
But that [ ]
To your sufficiency, as your worth is able,
And let them work. The nature of our people,
Our city's institutions and the terms
For common justice, you're as pregnant in
As art and practice hath enrichèd any
That we remember.
[*He gives Escalus papers*]
There is our commission,
From which we would not have you warp.
[*To a lord*] Call hither,
I say bid come before us, Angelo. [*Exit lord*]
[*To Escalus*] What figure of us think you he will bear?—
For you must know we have with special soul
Elected him our absence to supply,
Lent him our terror, dressed him with our love,
And given his deputation all the organs
Of our own power. What think you of it?

ESCALUS
If any in Ferrara **Vienna** be of worth

This is a 'genetic' edition of the play: the text is presented to show the play's development from one state to another. The two states are the reconstructed Shakespearian original of 1603–4 and the Middletonian adaptation of 1621. See Critical Introduction, final paragraph.

Persons This list is based on that appended to the text in the 1623 Folio (JAGGARD), which gives prominence to Vienna as the location by printing *'The Scene Vienna.'* above 'The names of all the Actors'. The 1623 list omits both the Justice of 2.3 and the Boy who sings the song in 4.1. These are the only speaking or singing parts not to be mentioned, which suggests that the list had its origin in a pre-adaptation document, and offers some support for the view that these roles are late additions. But there are characteristics of the adaptation present, for the list includes the '2. *Other like Gentlemen*' who accompany Lucio in the revised version of 1.2 and names '*Mistris Ouer-don*'.

6 **Two other like GENTLEMEN** '[Number] other like [plural noun]' is unique in pre-1640 drama except for *Nice Valour* 5.1.79.1, '*Four other like fools*'.

1.1.0.1 *Sc. 1* **1.1** JAGGARD's system of act-breaks belongs to the adapted text. In 1603–4 the play would have been performed without act intervals. We provide both through-scene numbers (to reflect the structure of 1603–4 performance), and act-scene numbers (as a feature of the adaptation).

2 Vincentio See Introduction.

8 **But that** [ ] Difficulty in sense and irregular metre are possibly evidence of a cut.

23 Ferrara **Vienna** See Introduction.

To undergo such ample grace and honour,
It is Lord Angelo.
Enter Angelo
DUKE Look where he comes.
ANGELO
Always obedient to your grace's will,
I come to know your pleasure.
DUKE Angelo,
There is a kind of character in thy life
That to th' observer doth thy history
Fully unfold. Thyself and thy belongings
Are not thine own so proper as to waste
Thyself upon thy virtues, they on thee.
Heaven doth with us as we with torches do,
Not light them for themselves; for if our virtues
Did not go forth of us, 'twere all alike
As if we had them not. Spirits are not finely touched
But to fine issues; nor nature never lends
The smallest scruple of her excellence
But, like a thrifty goddess, she determines
Herself the glory of a creditor,
Both thanks and use. But I do bend my speech
To one that can my part in him advèrtise.
Hold therefore, Angelo.
In our remove be thou at full ourself.
Mortality and mercy in Ferrara **Vienna**
Live in thy tongue and heart. Old Escalus,
Though first in question, is thy secondary.
Take thy commissïon.
ANGELO Now good my lord,
Let there be some more test made of my metal
Before so noble and so great a figure
Be stamped upon it.
DUKE No more evasïon.
We have with leavened and preparèd choice
Proceeded to you; therefore take your honours.
[*Angelo takes his commission*]
Our haste from hence is of so quick condition
That it prefers itself, and leaves unquestioned
Matters of needful value. We shall write to you,
As time and our concernings shall impòrtune,
How it goes with us—and do look to know
What doth befall you here. So fare you well.
To th' hopeful execution do I leave you
Of your commissions.
ANGELO Yet give leave, my lord,
That we may bring you something on the way.
DUKE My haste may not admit it;
Nor need you, on mine honour, have to do
With any scruple. Your scope is as mine own,
So to enforce or qualify the laws
As to your soul seems good. Give me your hand.
I'll privily away. I love the people,
But do not like to stage me to their eyes.
Though it do well, I do not relish well
Their loud applause and *aves* vehement;
Nor do I think the man of safe discretion
That does affect it. Once more, fare you well.
ANGELO
The Lord **heavens** give safety to your purposes!
ESCALUS
Lead forth and bring you back in happiness!
DUKE I thank you. Fare you well. *Exit*
ESCALUS
I shall desire you, sir, to give me leave
To have free speech with you; and it concerns me
To look into the bottom of my place.
A power I have, but of what strength and nature
I am not yet instructed.
ANGELO
'Tis so with me. Let us withdraw together,
And we may soon our satisfaction have
Touching that point.
ESCALUS I'll wait upon your honour.
Exeunt

Enter Lucio, and two other Gentlemen 1.2

LUCIO **If the Duke with the other dukes come not to composition with the King of Hungary, why then, all the dukes fall upon the King.**

74 Lord **heavens** This is the first of a number of notes explaining conjecturally restored profanity in the original text. There is no Shakespeare parallel for 'The heavens give'.

1.2.0.1–1.2.79h ***Enter*...him** JAGGARD prints 1.2.0.1–1.2.76, then the Bawd's speech 'Thus...custom-shrunk' (77–9), then 'How now? what's the newes with you.' as part of the same speech, then '*Enter Clowne.*', then the remainder of the passage that is marked in our text as for cancellation. The opening dialogue is strongly Middletonian, and seems designed to replace the brief passage in which the Clown announces Claudio's imprisonment for 'Groping for trouts in a peculiar river'.

0.1–1.2.76 ***Enter*...the truth of it.** *The Puritan* also begins its second scene with a seedy, joking, and topical conversation in prose between characters, one of whom is a soldier, on the subject of war and peace. As in *Measure*, the dialogue is followed by the entry of a guarded prisoner passing over the stage on his way to prison, an event watched and discussed by the earlier conversants. Lucio's 'Away; let's go learn the truth of it' compares with Pieboard's 'but come; let's follow after to the prison, and know the nature of his offence'. The conversation also recalls that between the Captain and the '*soldiering fellows*' in *Phoenix* Sc. 2. The staging, and the inconsequentiality of the episode, may be compared with *Women Beware* 4.1.1–22, where Bianca chats bawdily with two unnamed Ladies who appear nowhere else in the play.

0.1 ***and two other Gentlemen*** The list of 'The names of all the Actors' describes Lucio as a '*fantastique*', and the Gentlemen, who appear only in this scene, as '*Other like Gentlemen*'. Lucio no doubt stands out as the extravagantly-dressed fop amongst fops.

1–5 **If...Hungary's** An allusion to events of the Thirty Years War in and around Vienna in 1621; see Introduction.

1–2 **come...with** An unShakespearean idiom, but compare *Solomon* 1.80.

FIRST GENTLEMAN **Heaven grant us its peace, but not the King of Hungary's!**

SECOND GENTLEMAN **Amen.**

LUCIO **Thou conclud'st like the sanctimonious pirate, that went to sea with the Ten Commandments, but scraped one out of the table.**

SECOND GENTLEMAN **'Thou shalt not steal'?**

LUCIO **Ay, that he razed.**

FIRST GENTLEMAN **Why, 'twas a commandment to command the captain and all the rest from their functions: they put forth to steal. There's not a soldier of us all that in the thanksgiving before meat do relish the petition well that prays for peace.**

SECOND GENTLEMAN **I never heard any soldier dislike it.**

LUCIO **I believe thee, for I think thou never wast where grace was said.**

SECOND GENTLEMAN **No? A dozen times at least.**

FIRST GENTLEMAN **What, in metre?**

LUCIO **In any proportion, or in any language.**

FIRST GENTLEMAN **I think, or in any religion.**

LUCIO **Ay, why not? Grace is grace despite of all controversy; as for example, thou thyself art a wicked villain despite of all grace.**

FIRST GENTLEMAN **Well, there went but a pair of shears between us.**

LUCIO **I grant—as there may between the lists and the velvet. Thou art the list.**

FIRST GENTLEMAN **And thou the velvet. Thou art good velvet: thou'rt a three-piled piece, I warrant thee. I had as lief be a list of an English kersey as be piled as thou art pilled, for a French velvet. Do I speak feelingly now?**

LUCIO **I think thou dost, and indeed with most painful feeling of thy speech. I will out of thine own confession learn to begin thy health, but whilst I live forget to drink after thee.**

FIRST GENTLEMAN **I think I have done myself wrong, have I not?**

SECOND GENTLEMAN **Yes, that thou hast, whether thou art tainted or free.**

Enter Bawd

LUCIO **Behold, behold, where Madam Mitigation comes! I have purchased as many diseases under her roof as come to—**

SECOND GENTLEMAN **To what, I pray?**

LUCIO **Judge.**

SECOND GENTLEMAN **To three thousand dolours a year?**

FIRST GENTLEMAN **Ay, and more.**

LUCIO **A French crown more.**

FIRST GENTLEMAN **Thou art always figuring diseases in me, but thou art full of error—I am sound.**

LUCIO **Nay not, as one would say, healthy, but so sound as things that are hollow—thy bones are hollow, impiety has made a feast of thee.**

FIRST GENTLEMAN ***[to Bawd]*** **How now, which of your hips has the most profound sciatica?**

BAWD **Well, well! There's one yonder arrested and carried to prison was worth five thousand of you all.**

SECOND GENTLEMAN **Who's that, I prithee?**

BAWD **Marry sir, that's Claudio, Signor Claudio.**

4 **its** There is only one other Shakespeare example of possessive *its* in a play written before 1609. *Its* occurs regularly in Middleton works, especially from *c.*1614 onwards.

7–14 **Thou ... steal** See Introduction for the topicality of pirates in 1621. For the Middletonian idea of deleting 'Thou shalt not steal' from the Ten Commandments, see *Five Gallants* 3.4.106–10, and compare *The Puritan* 1.4.143–55; for more general contempt to the Commandments, see *Hubburd* 505–8, *Trick* 1.4.17–18, and *Revenger* 1.2.160–2. The phrase 'Thou shalt not steal' is not found in Shakespeare, and outside Middleton is probably without example in early modern drama.

7 **sanctimonious** The ironic usage suggesting false piety is Middletonian. *Measure* is the earliest instance recorded in *OED*.

18 **I believe thee** A phrase found in Middleton but not Shakespeare.

18–21 **I think ... metre** There is a metrical grace spoken in *Timon* at 2.61–70, in a passage attributed to Middleton.

22 **any language** A phrase found in two Middleton plays of the 1620s (*Game at Chess* 1.1.147, *Women Beware* 3.2.138) and probably in no earlier extant English play. The jibe is at the Catholic use of Latin, a common subject of hostile comment in Middleton.

23–5 **religion ... controversy** The Thirty Years War was fought between Catholics and Protestants.

24–5 **controversy** Middleton elsewhere refers to religious dispute as 'controversy'.

25 **as for example** An idiom found at least six times in Middleton.

34 **speak feelingly** Found also in *Dissemblers* 5.2.87.

37 **begin** The required sense, 'initiate a toast', is common in Middleton (see especially *Entertainments* 1.84.2, 85).

43 **Behold, behold** Compare *Solomon* 6.152–3, 9.13–14, etc.

Madam Mitigation The ironic title compares with 'fine Madam Tiptoes' in *Microcynicon* 3.89 and other Middleton examples. *Mitigation* is not elsewhere in Middleton.

44 **purchased as many diseases** *Patient Man* 9.63–4 has 'To purchase | A filthy, loathed disease'. The passage attacks prostitution, and refers to pox as a 'French infant' (compare 34).

48 **dolours** The pun *dolours/dollars* is Shakespearean (see *Tragedy of King Lear*, 2.2.229–30, and *Tempest* 2.1.17–21), but is found elsewhere too. The sense of *dolours* required here, 'physical pains, diseases', is Middletonian, but is not found in Shakespeare.

51–2 **diseases ... full of error** Compare *Heroes* 34, 'Full of diseases'.

51–4 **diseases ... bones** Middleton parallels include *Quiet Life* 3.1.123–7, ''Twill breed diseases in you', collocated with 'profoundly' and 'relish' (compare 15); *Michaelmas* 2.1.164, 'Diseases gnaw thy bones'; *Tennis* 582, 'To call diseases early into my bones'.

54–5 **impiety has made a feast of thee** The idea that the body of the self-indulging sinner ironically becomes itself the object of devouring by an abstracted figure such as Impiety (or Destruction, or Lust and Forgetfulness) is characteristic of Middleton. Verbal parallels include *Mad World* 2.4.65, 'Pox feast you'; *Tennis* 806, 'With fat and filthy gain thy lust may feast'.

59 **worth ... all** That this is a Middleton idiom is suggested by *Roaring Girl* 8.15, 'worth a thousand of your headborough's lanterns'; *Trick* 4.4.212, 'worth ten of her'; *No Wit* 6.135–6, 'worth a hundred of your sons and heirs'; *Changeling* 5.1.93, 'He's worth 'em all'.

FIRST GENTLEMAN **Claudio to prison? 'Tis not so.**

BAWD **Nay, but I know 'tis so. I saw him arrested, saw him carried away; and, which is more, within these three days his head to be chopped off.**

LUCIO **But after all this fooling, I would not have it so. Art thou sure of this?**

BAWD **I am too sure of it, and it is for getting Madam Julietta with child.**

LUCIO **Believe me, this may be. He promised to meet me two hours since and he was ever precise in promise-keeping.**

SECOND GENTLEMAN **Besides, you know, it draws something near to the speech we had to such a purpose.**

FIRST GENTLEMAN **But most of all agreeing with the proclamation.**

LUCIO **Away; let's go learn the truth of it.**

Exit [Lucio, with Gentlemen]

BAWD **Thus, what with the war, what with the sweat, what with the gallows, and what with poverty, I am custom-shrunk.**

Sc. 2

Enter Clown [and Bawd, meeting]

[BAWD] How now, what's the news with you?

CLOWN Yonder man is carried to prison.

BAWD Well! What has he done?

CLOWN A woman.

BAWD But what's his offence?

CLOWN Groping for trouts in a peculiar river.

BAWD What, is there a maid with child by him?

CLOWN No, but there's a woman with maid by him.

[CLOWN] You have not heard of the proclamation, have you?

BAWD What proclamation, man?

CLOWN All houses in the suburbs of Ferrara **Vienna** must be plucked down.

BAWD And what shall become of those in the city?

CLOWN They shall stand for seed. They had gone down too, but that a wise burgher put in for them.

BAWD But shall all our houses of resort in the suburbs be pulled down?

CLOWN To the ground, mistress.

BAWD Why, here's a change indeed in the commonwealth. What shall become of me?

CLOWN Come, fear not you. Good counsellors lack no clients. Though you change your place, you need not change your trade. I'll be your tapster still. Courage, there will be pity taken on you. You that have worn your eyes almost out in the service, you will be considered.

[A noise within]

BAWD **What's to do here, Thomas Tapster? Let's withdraw!**

Enter Provost, Claudio, Juliet, officers, Lucio and two Gentlemen

CLOWN **Here comes Signor Claudio, led by the Provost to prison; and there's Madam Juliet.**

Exeunt Bawd and Clown

77–9 **Thus...custom-shrunk** Compare the Bawd's similar complaint that he is ruined by the 'poverty', the Devil's lengthy sceptical response, and the Bawd's insistence '*What with* this long vacation...Pierce was never so penniless as poor Lieutenant Frig-beard', in *Black Book* 375–7. The same passage also includes an allusion to syphilis comparable with the Bawd's reference to its cure by 'the sweat', in 'Monsieur Dry-bone the Frenchman' (368). See also commentary to 4.3.17.

78 **poverty** The adaptation was prepared at a time of the severest economic depression in living memory. As the depression was fuelled by a slump in exports, it was largely an effect of trade with Europe, and so the allusion fits in with the European consciousness of the episode.

79 **custom-shrunk** Middleton repeatedly uses the verb *shrink* to indicate male withdrawal from, or incapacity for, sexual activity (*No Wit* 7.119, *Weapons* 1.1.241, *Women Beware* 3.1.100).

99–102 BAWD...**Juliet** Probably added for the adaptation. JAGGARD's 'and there's Madam *Iuliet*' has to be an addition if Juliet is herself an addition, and this brings both speeches into question. The clumsy sequence of a natural exit point ('you will be considered'), then an interruption leading to a new exit point ('let's withdraw'), then a speech suggesting interest in the approaching figures ('Here comes...'), then an exeunt, is more likely to result from the disjunctions of a revised staging than to belong to the original text. In the fuller, more complex staging of the adapted text, the added lines establish the identities of the three characters entering for the first time.

100.1–2 ***Enter...Gentlemen*** The adaptation creates much more of a public shaming ritual. Lucio and the Gentlemen look on for a while before Lucio addresses Claudio. The Gentlemen have no part in the 1603–4 text, and serve in the adapted text only to change the emphasis of the staging. Without them, Lucio is redundant until he greets Claudio.

100.1 ***Juliet*** She has no part in the scene other than to appear visually as the observed, in a manner that contrasts in appearance and gender with the similarly silent but observing Gentlemen. Her theatrical function must be to be inscribed as visibly pregnant, 'With character too gross', and she may well have worn the gown of penance imposed on detected fornicators. It seems characteristic of the adaptation to add to and emblematize the presence of women: the expanded Bawd's role and Juliet in 1.2, Mariana (accompanied by a singing boy-actor) in 4.1, and Juliet in 5.1, where she makes another silent appearance. Pregnant unmarried women appear on stage to supply a visual and sometimes silent serio-comic comment on their misdeeds in *No Wit* (Grace), *Witch* (Francisca), *Quarrel* (Jane), *Nice Valour* (the 'Cupid') and *Dissemblers* (the 'Page'). ***officers*** The officers merely accompany Juliet and are unmentioned in the dialogue. The Clown announces that Claudio is simply 'led by the Provost', and at the end of the scene Claudio tells a single officer—the Provost again—'Come, officer, away'.

102 **Madam Juliet** The word 'madam' is found elsewhere in the play only in the Middletonian part of 1.2: when the Bawd is mocked as 'Madam Mitigation' at 1.2.43 and when Juliet herself is mentioned as 'Madam Julietta' at 1.2.68–9.

62 *Measure for Measure.*

Scena Secunda.

Enter Lucio, and two other Gentlemen.

Luc. If the *Duke*, with the other Dukes, come not to composition with the King of *Hungary*, why then all the Dukes fall vpon the King.

1. *Gent.* Heauen grant vs its peace, but not the King of *Hungaries*.

2. *Gent.* Amen.

Luc. Thou conclud'st like the Sanctimonious Pirat, that went to sea with the ten Commandements, but scrap'd one out of the Table.

2. *Gent.* Thou shalt not Steale?

Luc. I, that he raz'd.

1. *Gent.* Why? 'twas a commandement, to command the Captaine and all the rest from their functions: they put forth to steale: There's not a Souldier of vs all, that in the thanks-giuing before meate, do rallish the petition well, that praies for peace.

2. *Gent.* I neuer heard any Souldier dislike it.

Luc. I beleeue thee: for I thinke thou neuer was't where Grace was said.

2. *Gent.* No? a dozen times at least.

1. *Gent.* What? In meeter?

Luc. In any proportion. or in any language.

1. *Gent.* I thinke, or in any Religion.

Luc. I, why not? Grace, is Grace, despight of all controuersie: as for example; Thou thy selfe art a wicked villaine, despight of all Grace.

1. *Gent.* Well: there went but a paire of sheeres betweene vs.

Luc. I grant: as there may betweene the Lists, and the Veluet. Thou art the List.

1. *Gent.* And thou the Veluet; thou art good veluet; thou'rt a three pild-peece I warrant thee: I had as liefe be a Lyst of an English Kersey, as be pil'd, as thou art pil'd, for a French Veluet. Do I speake feelingly now?

Luc. I thinke thou do'st: and indeed with most painfull feeling of thy speech: I will, out of thine owne confession, learne to begin thy health; but, whilst I liue forget to drinke after thee.

1. *Gen.* I think I haue done my selfe wrong, haue I not?

2. *Gent.* Yes, that thou hast; whether thou art tainted, or free. *Enter Bawde.*

Stage direction on same line as speech saves space

Luc. Behold, behold, where Madam *Mitigation* comes. I haue purchas'd as many diseases vnder her Roofe,
As come to

2. *Gent.* To what, I pray?

Luc. Iudge.

2. *Gent.* To three thousand Dollours a yeare.

1. *Gent.* I, and more.

Luc. A French crowne more.

1. *Gent.* Thou art alwayes figuring diseases in me; but thou art full of error, I am sound.

Luc. Nay, not (as one would say) healthy: but so sound, as things that are hollow; thy bones are hollow; Impiety has made a feast of thee.

1. *Gent.* How now, which of your hips has the most profound Ciatica?

Bawd. Well, well: there's one yonder arrested, and carried to prison, was worth fiue thousand of you all.

2. *Gent.* Who's that I pray'thee?

Bawd. Marry Sir, that's *Claudio*, Signior *Claudio*.

1. *Gent.* *Claudio* to prison? 'tis not so.

Bawd. Nay, but I know 'tis so: I saw him arrested: saw him carried away: and which is more, within these three daies his head to be chop'd off.

Luc. But, after all this fooling, I would not haue it so: Art thou sure of this?

Bawd. I am too sure of it: and it is for getting Madam *Iulietta* with childe.

Luc. Beleeue me this may be: he promis'd to meete me two howres since, and he was euer precise in promise keeping.

2. *Gent.* Besides you know, it drawes somthing neere to the speech we had to such a purpose.

1. *Gent.* But most of all agreeing with the proclamatiō.

Luc. Away: let's goe learne the truth of it. *Exit.*

Reduced indent and shortened form of 'proclamation' save space

Bawd. Thus, what with the war; what with the sweat, what with the gallowes, and what with pouerty, I am Custom-shrunke. How now? what's the newes with you. *Enter Clowne.*

Stage direction on same line as speech saves space

Clo. Yonder man is carried to prison.

Baw. Well: what has he done?

Clo. A Woman.

Baw. But what's his offence?

Clo. Groping for Trowts, in a peculiar Riuer.

Baw. What? is there a maid with child by him?

Clo. No: but there's a woman with maid by him: you haue not heard of the proclamation, haue you?

Passage intended for deletion but actually printed takes extra space

Baw. What proclamation, man?

Clow. All howses in the Suburbs of *Vienna* must bee pluck'd downe.

Bawd. And what shall become of those in the Citie?

Clow. They shall stand for seed: they had gon down to, but that a wise Burger put in for them.

Bawd. But shall all our houses of resort in the Suburbs be puld downe?

Clow. To the ground, Mistris.

Bawd. Why heere's a change indeed in the Commonwealth: what shall become of me?

Clow. Come: feare not you: good Counsellors lacke no Clients: though you change your place, you neede not change your Trade: Ile bee your Tapster still; courage, there will bee pitty taken on you; you that haue worne your eyes almost out in the seruice, you will bee considered.

Bawd. What's to doe heere, *Thomas* Tapster? let's withdraw?

Clo. Here comes Signior *Claudio*, led by the Prouost to prison: and there's Madam *Iuliet*. *Exeunt.*

Scena Tertia.

Cramped spacing around scene heading saves space

Enter Prouost, Claudio, Iuliet, Officers, Lucio, & 2. Gent.

Cla. Fellow, why do'st thou show me thus to th'world?
Beare me to prison, where I am committed.

Pro. I do it not in euill disposition,
But from Lord *Angelo* by speciall charge.

Clau. Thus can the demy-god (Authority)
Make vs pay downe, for our offence, by waight
The words of heauen; on whom it will, it will,
On whom it will not (soe) yet still 'tis iust.

Luc. Why how now *Claudio*? whence comes this restraint.

Cla. From too much liberty, (my *Lucio*) Liberty
As surfet is the father of much fast,
So euery Scope by the immoderate vse
Turnes to restraint: Our Natures doe pursue

Like

Measure for Measure sig. F1[v], showing space loss caused by duplication and compositorial space saving in 1.2

Sc. 3
Enter Provost, Claudio

CLAUDIO
Fellow, why dost thou show me thus to th' world?
Bear me to prison, where I am committed.

PROVOST
I do it not in evil disposition,
But from Lord Angelo by special charge.

CLAUDIO
Thus can the demigod Authority
Make us pay down for our offence, by weight,
The bonds of heaven. On whom it will, it will;
On whom it will not, so; yet still 'tis just.
[*Enter Lucio*]

LUCIO
Why, how now, Claudio? Whence comes this restraint?

CLAUDIO
From too much liberty, my Lucio, liberty.
As surfeit is the father of much fast,
So every scope, by the immoderate use,
Turns to restraint. Our natures do pursue,
Like rats that raven down their proper bane,
A thirsty evil; and when we drink, we die.

LUCIO If I could speak so wisely under an arrest, I would send for certain of my creditors. And yet, to say the truth, I had as lief have the foppery of freedom as the morality of imprisonment. What's thy offence, Claudio?

CLAUDIO
What but to speak of would offend again.

LUCIO
What, is't murder?

CLAUDIO No.

LUCIO Lechery?

CLAUDIO Call it so.

PROVOST Away, sir; you must go.

CLAUDIO
One word, good friend.
[*Provost shows assent*]
Lucio, a word with you.

LUCIO
A hundred, if they'll do you any good.
[*Claudio and Lucio speak apart*]
Is lechery so looked after?

CLAUDIO
Thus stands it with me. Upon a true contract,
I got possession of Julietta's bed.
You know the lady; she is fast my wife,
Save that we do the denunciation lack
Of outward order. This we came not to
Only for propagation of a dower
Remaining in the coffer of her friends,
From whom we thought it meet to hide our love
Till time had made them for us. But it chances
The stealth of our most mutual entertainment
With character too gross is writ on Juliet.

LUCIO
With child, perhaps?

CLAUDIO Unhapp'ly even so.
And the new deputy now for the Duke—
Whether it be the fault and glimpse of newness,
Or whether that the body public be
A horse whereon the governor doth ride,
Who, newly in the seat, that it may know
He can command, lets it straight feel the spur—
Whether the tyranny be in his place,
Or in his eminence that fills it up—
I stagger in. But this new governor
Awakes me all the enrollèd penalties
Which have, like unscoured armour, hung by th' wall
So long that fourteen zodiacs have gone round,
And none of them been worn; and, for a name,
Now puts the drowsy and neglected act
Freshly on me. 'Tis surely for a name.

LUCIO I warrant it is; and thy head stands so tickle on thy shoulders that a milkmaid, if she be in love, may sigh it off. Send after the Duke, and appeal to him.

CLAUDIO
I have done so, but he's not to be found.
I prithee, Lucio, do me this kind service.
This day my sister should the cloister enter,
And there receive her approbatïon.
Acquaint her with the danger of my state.
Implore her in my voice that she make friends
To the strict deputy. Bid herself assay him.
I have great hope in that, for in her youth
There is a prone and speechless dialect
Such as move men; beside, she hath prosperous art
When she will play with reason and discourse,
And well she can persuade.

LUCIO I pray she may—
as well for the encouragement of thy like, which else would stand under grievous imposition, as for the enjoying of thy life, who I would be sorry should be thus foolishly lost at a game of tick-tack. I'll to her.

CLAUDIO I thank you, good friend Lucio.

102.2 Sc. 3 Noting the continuity of action, editors have removed the scene break printed in JAGGARD. Given the staging in the adapted text, it makes sense for the entry to happen before the Clown and Bawd withdraw, so that the Clown can identify the newcomers more effectively for the audience. But in JAGGARD, as marked in the present text of the original version, the entry follows the clearing of the stage that makes the scene-break. In the original staging the two speeches that establish continuity preceding JAGGARD's scene-header were probably absent.

111 **Why...restraint** Lucio's ignorance here is consistent with the postulated original 1603–4 text. In it, the Bawd would not previously have told Lucio of Claudio's imprisonment, as she has in the revised text.

LUCIO
Within two hours.
CLAUDIO Come, officer; away.
Exeunt [Lucio and gentlemen at one door;
Claudio, Juliet, Provost, and officers at another]

1.3(a) *1.3*
Enter Duke and Friar Thomas

DUKE
No, holy father, throw away that thought.
Believe not that the dribbling dart of love
Can pierce a complete bosom. Why I desire thee
To give me secret harbour hath a purpose
More grave and wrinkled than the aims and ends
Of burning youth.
FRIAR May your grace speak of it?
DUKE
My holy sir, none better knows than you
How I have ever loved the life removed,
And held in idle price to haunt assemblies
Where youth and cost a witless bravery keeps.
I have delivered to Lord Angelo—
A man of stricture and firm abstinence—
My absolute power and place here in Vienna;
And he supposes me travelled to Poland—
For so I have strewed it in the common ear,
And so it is received. Now, pious sir,
You will demand of me why I do this.
FRIAR Gladly, my lord.
DUKE
We have strict statutes and most biting laws,
The needful bits and curbs to headstrong weeds,
Which for this fourteen years we have let slip,
Even like an o'ergrown lion in a cave
That goes not out to prey. Now, as fond fathers,
Having bound up the threat'ning twigs of birch
Only to stick it in their children's sight
For terror, not to use, in time the rod
More mocked becomes than feared: so our decrees,
Dead to infliction, to themselves are dead;
And Liberty plucks Justice by the nose,
The baby beats the nurse, and quite athwart
Goes all decorum.
FRIAR It rested in your grace
To unloose this tied-up Justice when you pleased,
And it in you more dreadful would have seemed
Than in Lord Angelo.
DUKE I do fear, too dreadful.
Sith 'twas my fault to give the people scope,
'Twould be my tyranny to strike and gall them
For what I bid them do—for we bid this be done
When evil deeds have their permissive pass,
And not the punishment. Therefore indeed, my father,
I have on Angelo imposed the office,
Who may in th'ambush of my name strike home,
And yet my nature never in the fight
T'allow in slander. And to behold his sway,
I will as 'twere a brother of your order
Visit both prince and people. Therefore, I prithee,
Supply me with the habit, and instruct me
How I may formally in person bear
Like a true friar. More reasons for this action
At our more leisure shall I render you.
Only this one: Lord Angelo is precise,
Stands at a guard with envy, scarce confesses
That his blood flows, or that his appetite
Is more to bread than stone. Hence shall we see
If power change purpose, what our seemers be.
Exit [with Friar]

Sc. 4 *1.4* 1.4
Enter Isabella, and Francisca, a nun

ISABELLA
And have you nuns no farther privileges,
Holy Francisca?
NUN Are not these large enough?
ISABELLA
Yes, truly. I speak not as desiring more,
But rather wishing a more strict restraint
Upon the sisterhood, the votarists of Saint Clare.
LUCIO (*within*)
Ho, peace be in this place!
ISABELLA [*to Francisca*] Who's that which calls?
NUN
It is a man's voice. Gentle Isabella,
Turn you the key, and know his business of him.
You may, I may not; you are yet unsworn.
When you have vowed, you must not speak with men
But in the presence of the prioress.
Then if you speak, you must not show your face;
Or if you show your face, you must not speak.
[*Lucio calls within*]
He calls again. I pray you answer him.
[*She stands aside*]
ISABELLA
Peace and prosperity! Who is't that calls?
[*She opens the door. Enter Lucio*]
LUCIO
Hail, virgin, if you be—as those cheek-roses
Proclaim you are no less. Can you so stead me
As bring me to the sight of Isabella,
A novice of this place, and the fair sister
To her unhappy brother Claudio?

1.3(a) The scene was printed here in JAGGARD, in a position it was probably given for the adapted text. Shakespeare conjecturally first placed it after 1.4. The revised arrangement facilitates the doubling of boys' parts, by allowing the Nun or Isabella to double with Juliet, a role new to Act 1. The most likely distribution of roles is (*a*) Isabella, (*b*) Bawd and Mariana, (*c*) Juliet, Nun, and Boy. See Introduction, and note to 1.3(b).

1.4.2 Holy Francisca See Introduction.

ISABELLA
Why 'her unhappy brother'? Let me ask,
The rather for I now must make you know
I am that Isabella, and his sister.

LUCIO
Gentle and fair, your brother kindly greets you.
Not to be weary with you, he's in prison.

ISABELLA Woe me! For what?

LUCIO
For that which, if myself might be his judge,
He should receive his punishment in thanks.
He hath got his friend with child.

ISABELLA Sir, make me not your story.

LUCIO
'Tis true. I would not—though 'tis my familiar sin
With maids to seem the lapwing, and to jest
Tongue far from heart—play with all virgins so.
I hold you as a thing enskied and sainted
By your renouncement, an immortal spirit,
And to be talked with in sincerity
As with a saint.

ISABELLA
You do blaspheme the good in mocking me.

LUCIO
Do not believe it. Fewness and truth, 'tis thus:
Your brother and his lover have embraced.
As those that feed grow full, as blossoming time
That from the seedness the bare fallow brings
To teeming foison, even so her plenteous womb
Expresseth his full tilth and husbandry.

ISABELLA
Someone with child by him? My cousin Juliet?

LUCIO Is she your cousin?

ISABELLA
Adoptedly, as schoolmaids change their names
By vain though apt affection.

LUCIO She it is.

ISABELLA
O, let him marry her!

LUCIO This is the point.
The Duke is very strangely gone from hence;
Bore many gentlemen—myself being one—
In hand and hope of action; but we do learn,
By those that know the very nerves of state,
His giving out were of an infinite distance
From his true-meant design. Upon his place,
And with full line of his authority,
Governs Lord Angelo—a man whose blood
Is very snow-broth; one who never feels
The wanton stings and motions of the sense,
But doth rebate and blunt his natural edge
With profits of the mind, study, and fast.
He, to give fear to use and liberty,
Which have for long run by the hideous law
As mice by lions, hath picked out an act
Under whose heavy sense your brother's life
Falls into forfeit. He arrests him on it,
And follows close the rigour of the statute
To make him an example. All hope is gone,
Unless you have the grace by your fair prayer
To soften Angelo. And that's my pith
Of business 'twixt you and your poor brother.

ISABELLA
Doth he so seek his life?

LUCIO Has censured him already,
And, as I hear, the Provost hath a warrant
For's executiön.

ISABELLA Alas, what poor
Ability's in me to do him good?

LUCIO Assay the power you have.

ISABELLA My power? Alas, I doubt.

LUCIO Our doubts are traitors,
And makes us lose the good we oft might win,
By fearing to attempt. Go to Lord Angelo;
And let him learn to know, when maidens sue,
Men give like gods, but when they weep and kneel,
All their petitions are as freely theirs
As they themselves would owe them.

ISABELLA I'll see what I can do.

LUCIO
But speedily.

ISABELLA I will about it straight,
No longer staying but to give the Mother
Notice of my affair. I humbly thank you.
Commend me to my brother. Soon at night
I'll send him certain word of my success.

LUCIO
I take my leave of you.

ISABELLA Good sir, adieu.

Exeunt [*Isabella and Nun at one door, Lucio at another door*]

Finis Actus Primus

50–1 **Bore . . . action** This rumour-mongering is vague enough to be reasonably consistent with the adaptation at 1.2.1–3.

1.3(b) *Sc. 5*
Enter Duke and Friar Thomas

DUKE
No, holy father, throw away that thought.
Believe not that the dribbling dart of love
Can pierce a complete bosom. Why I desire thee
To give me secret harbour hath a purpose
More grave and wrinkled than the aims and ends
Of burning youth.

FRIAR May your grace speak of it?

DUKE
My holy sir, none better knows than you
How I have ever loved the life removed,
And held in idle price to haunt assemblies
Where youth and cost a witless bravery keeps.
I have delivered to Lord Angelo—
A man of stricture and firm abstinence—
My absolute power and place here in Ferrara;
And he supposes me travelled to Poland—
For so I have strewed it in the common ear,
And so it is received. Now, pious sir,
You will demand of me why I do this.

FRIAR Gladly, my lord.

DUKE
We have strict statutes and most biting laws,
The needful bits and curbs to headstrong weeds,
Which for this fourteen years we have let slip,
Even like an o'ergrown lion in a cave
That goes not out to prey. Now, as fond fathers,
Having bound up the threat'ning twigs of birch
Only to stick it in their children's sight
For terror, not to use, in time the rod
More mocked becomes than feared: so our decrees,
Dead to infliction, to themselves are dead;
And Liberty plucks Justice by the nose,
The baby beats the nurse, and quite athwart
Goes all decorum.

FRIAR It rested in your grace
To unloose this tied-up Justice when you pleased,
And it in you more dreadful would have seemed
Than in Lord Angelo.

DUKE I do fear, too dreadful.
Sith 'twas my fault to give the people scope,
'Twould be my tyranny to strike and gall them
For what I bid them do—for we bid this be done
When evil deeds have their permissive pass,
And not the punishment. Therefore indeed, my father,
I have on Angelo imposed the office,
Who may in th'ambush of my name strike home,
And yet my nature never in the fight
T'allow in slander. And to behold his sway,
I will as 'twere a brother of your order
Visit both prince and people. Therefore, I prithee,
Supply me with the habit, and instruct me
How I may formally in person bear
Like a true friar. More reasons for this action
At our more leisure shall I render you.
Only this one: Lord Angelo is precise,
Stands at a guard with envy, scarce confesses
That his blood flows, or that his appetite
Is more to bread than stone. Hence shall we see
If power change purpose, what our seemers be.
Exit [with Friar]

❀

Sc. 6 **2.1** 2.1
Incipit Actus Secundus
Enter Angelo, Escalus, and servants; ***Justice***

ANGELO
We must not make a scarecrow of the law,
Setting it up to fear the birds of prey,
And let it keep one shape till custom make it
Their perch, and not their terror.

ESCALUS Ay, but yet
Let us be keen, and rather cut a little
Than fall and bruise to death. Alas, this gentleman
Whom I would save had a most noble father.
Let but your honour know—
Whom I believe to be most strait in virtue—
That in the working of your own affections,
Had time cohered with place, or place with wishing,
Or that the resolute acting of your blood
Could have attained th'effect of your own purpose—
Whether you had not sometime in your life
Erred in this point which now you censure him,

1.3(b) In the original Shakespeare version this scene probably appeared here. With this sequence, the action is more strongly knitted and dramatically urgent in several ways. Lucio's agreement to speak to Isabella is followed immediately by him doing as anticipated. Their interview in 1.4 is not cushioned, as it is in the adapted text, by the audience's awareness that the disguised Duke will be keeping an eye on things. Isabella more intelligibly enters the nunnery seeking 'strict restraint' immediately after Lucio regrets the consequences to her brother of 'a game of tick-tack' at the end of 1.2. When placed before 1.3, the end of 1.4, with its reference to 'the Mother' of the nunnery, anticipates the opening line of 1.3, with its address to the 'holy father'; the novice nun's resolution to leave the nunnery to petition the Duke's deputy contrasts with the Duke's intention to take 'secret harbour' (as it at first seems) in the monastery. At the end of 1.3 the Duke determines to 'see | If power change purpose, what our seemers be', a couplet that strongly anticipates and frames the first entry of Angelo at the beginning of 2.1, and is effectively placed just before that entry. Moreover, the Duke's lament over the consequences 'When evil deeds have their permissive pass' in 1.3 finds quick uptake in Angelo's opening line, 'We must not make a scarecrow of the law'. The introduction of act-breaks would have considerably lessened the extent to which the latter considerations of sequence apply.

2.1.0.3 ***Justice*** Evidently tacked on after the original stage direction had been written; see Introduction.

And pulled the law upon you.
ANGELO
'Tis one thing to be tempted, Escalus,
Another thing to fall. I not deny
The jury passing on the prisoner's life
May in the sworn twelve have a thief or two
Guiltier than him they try. **What knows the law**
That thieves do pass on thieves? What's open made to justice,
That justice seizes. 'Tis very pregnant:
The jewel that we find, we stoop and take't
Because we see it, but what we do not see
We tread upon and never think of it.
You may not so extenuate his offence
For I have had such faults; but rather tell me,
When I that censure him do so offend,
Let mine own judgement pattern out my death,
And nothing come in partial. Sir, he must die.
ESCALUS
Be it as your wisdom will.
ANGELO Where is the Provost?
Enter Provost
PROVOST
Here, if it like your honour.
ANGELO See that Claudio
Be execute by nine tomorrow morning.
Bring him his confessor, let him be prepared,
For that's the utmost of his pilgrimage.
[*Exit Provost*]
ESCALUS
Well, heaven forgive him, and forgive us all!
Some rise by sin, and some by virtue fall.
Some run from breaks of ice, and answer none;
And some condemnèd for a fault alone.
Enter Elbow, Froth, Clown, officers

ELBOW Come, bring them away. If these be good people in a commonweal, that do nothing but use their abuses in common houses, I know no law. Bring them away.

ANGELO
How now, sir? What's your name? And what's the matter?

ELBOW If it please your honour, I am the poor Duke's constable, and my name is Elbow. I do lean upon justice, sir; and do bring in here before your good honour two notorious benefactors.

ANGELO
Benefactors? Well! What benefactors are they?
Are they not malefactors?

ELBOW If it please your honour, I know not well what they are; but precise villains they are, that I am sure of, and void of all profanation in the world that good Christians ought to have.

ESCALUS [*to Angelo*] This comes off well; here's a wise officer!

ANGELO Go to, what quality are they of? Elbow is your name? Why dost thou not speak, Elbow?

CLOWN He cannot, sir; he's out at elbow.

ANGELO What are you, sir?

ELBOW He, sir? A tapster, sir, parcel bawd; one that serves a bad woman whose house, sir, was, as they say, plucked down in the suburbs; and now she professes a hot-house, which I think is a very ill house too.

ESCALUS How know you that?

ELBOW My wife, sir, whom I detest before God **heaven** and your honour—

ESCALUS How, thy wife?

ELBOW Ay, sir, whom I thank heaven is an honest woman—

ESCALUS Dost thou detest her therefor?

ELBOW I say, sir, I will detest myself also, as well as she, that this house, if it be not a bawd's house, it is pity of her life, for it is a naughty house.

ESCALUS
How dost thou know that, constable?

ELBOW Marry, sir, by my wife, who, if she had been a woman cardinally given, might have been accused in fornication, adultery, and all uncleanliness there.

ESCALUS By this man's **the woman's** means?

ELBOW Ay, sir, by Master Froth's **Mistress Overdone's** means. But as she spit in his face, so she defied him.

CLOWN [*to Escalus*] Sir, if it please your honour, this is not so.

21–2 **What . . . on thieves?** The line, printed after 'seizes' (23) in JAGGARD, seems to be a misplaced addition. As such, it potentially belongs to the adaptation. The picture of Law as an ideal abstraction that is crucially separated from its highly imperfect execution by corrupt individuals is Middletonian. See in particular *Phoenix* 4.200–30 and 12.195–200.

37–40 ESCALUS . . . **alone**. R. V. Holdsworth argues that this passage is 'a strong candidate' as an addition by Middleton, providing convincing Middleton parallels for the diction, imagery, thought, and rhymes. He effectively dismisses the case for the commonly accepted emendation of 'Ice' to 'vice', showing that a contrast between serious *breaks* in the *ice* of virginity and a mere *fault* or flaw is consistent with the temper and imagery of Middleton's writing.

66 God **heaven** 'Before God' appears 21 times elsewhere in Shakespeare; 'before heaven' occurs only once, in *The Tempest* (written after the 1606 Act outlawing profanity on stage).

79–80 **the woman's . . . Mistress Overdone's** The Bawd's name, and lines mentioning it, probably belong to the adaptation. As Samuel Johnson first noted, some mention of Froth seems necessary here. In the speech as printed in JAGGARD and therefore as in the adaptation, it is far from clear whom Elbow is talking about when he says 'as she spit in his face, so she defied him'. Even if this is allowable as comic confusion, it remains hard if at all possible to infer what Froth's misconduct is, why he has been brought before Angelo and Escalus, and why Elbow's wife spits in his face. Moreover, the spitting suggests a joke on his name, though this is far from apparent in JAGGARD as his name has not been mentioned. It seems that Mistress Overdone has been rather awkwardly substituted for Froth, perhaps to prepare for the joke on her name at 191–3.

ELBOW Prove it before these varlets here, thou honourable man, prove it.

ESCALUS [*to Angelo*] Do you hear how he misplaces?

CLOWN Sir, she came in great with child, and longing—saving your honour's reverence—for stewed prunes. Sir, we had but two in the house, which at that very distant time stood, as it were, in a fruit dish—a dish of some threepence; your honours have seen such dishes; they are not china dishes, but very good dishes.

ESCALUS
Go to, go to, no matter for the dish, sir.

CLOWN No, indeed, sir, not of a pin; you are therein in the right. But to the point. As I say, this Mistress Elbow, being, as I say, with child, and being great-bellied, and longing, as I said, for prunes; and having but two in the dish, as I said, Master Froth here, this very man, having eaten the rest, as I said, and, as I say, paying for them very honestly; for, as you know, Master Froth, I could not give you threepence again.

FROTH No, indeed.

CLOWN Very well. You being, then, if you be remembered, cracking the stones of the foresaid prunes—

FROTH Ay, so I did indeed.

CLOWN Why, very well.—I telling you then, if you be remembered, that such a one and such a one were past cure of the thing you wot of, unless they kept very good diet, as I told you—

FROTH All this is true.

CLOWN Why, very well then—

ESCALUS Come, you are a tedious fool. To the purpose. What was done to Elbow's wife that he hath cause to complain of? Come me to what was done to her.

CLOWN Sir, your honour cannot come to that yet.

ESCALUS No, sir, nor I mean it not.

CLOWN Sir, but you shall come to it, by your honour's leave. And I beseech you, look into Master Froth here, sir, a man of fourscore pound a year, whose father died at Hallowmas—was't not at Hallowmas, Master Froth?

FROTH All Hallow Eve.

CLOWN Why, very well. I hope here be truths. He, sir, sitting, as I say, in a lower chair, sir—'twas in the Bunch of Grapes, where indeed you have a delight to sit, have you not?

FROTH I have so, because it is an open room, and good for winter.

CLOWN Why, very well then. I hope here be truths.

ANGELO
This will last out a night in Russïa,
When nights are longest there. [*To Escalus*] I'll take
my leave,
And leave you to the hearing of the cause,
Hoping you'll find good cause to whip them all.

ESCALUS
I think no less. Good morrow to your lordship.
Exit Angelo

Now, sir, come on, what was done to Elbow's wife, once more?

CLOWN Once, sir? There was nothing done to her once.

ELBOW I beseech you, sir, ask him what this man did to my wife.

CLOWN I beseech your honour, ask me.

ESCALUS Well, sir, what did this gentleman to her?

CLOWN I beseech you, sir, look in this gentleman's face. Good Master Froth, look upon his honour. 'Tis for a good purpose. Doth your honour mark his face?

ESCALUS Ay, sir, very well.

CLOWN Nay, I beseech you, mark it well.

ESCALUS Well, I do so.

CLOWN Doth your honour see any harm in his face?

ESCALUS Why, no.

CLOWN I'll be supposed upon a book his face is the worst thing about him. Good, then—if his face be the worst thing about him, how could Master Froth do the constable's wife any harm? I would know that of your honour.

ESCALUS He's in the right, constable; what say you to it?

ELBOW First, an it like you, the house is a respected house; next, this is a respected fellow; and his mistress is a respected woman.

CLOWN [*to Escalus*] By this hand, sir, his wife is a more respected person than any of us all.

ELBOW Varlet, thou liest; thou liest, wicked varlet. The time is yet to come that she was ever respected with man, woman, or child.

CLOWN Sir, she was respected with him before he married with her.

ESCALUS Which is the wiser here, justice or iniquity? [*To Elbow*] Is this true?

ELBOW [*to Clown*] O thou caitiff, O thou varlet, O thou wicked Hannibal! I respected with her before I was married to her? [*To Escalus*] If ever I was respected with her, or she with me, let not your worship think me the poor Duke's officer. [*To Clown*] Prove this, thou wicked Hannibal, or I'll have mine action of batt'ry on thee.

ESCALUS If he took you a box o'th' ear you might have your action of slander too.

ELBOW Marry, I thank your good worship for it. What is't your worship's pleasure I shall do with this wicked caitiff?

ESCALUS Truly, officer, because he hath some offences in him that thou wouldst discover if thou couldst, let him continue in his courses till thou know'st what they are.

ELBOW Marry, I thank your worship for it.—Thou seest, thou wicked varlet now, what's come upon thee. Thou art to continue now, thou varlet, thou art to continue.

ESCALUS [*to Froth*] Where were you born, friend?

FROTH Here in Ferrara **Vienna**, sir.

ESCALUS Are you of fourscore pounds a year?

FROTH Yes, an't please you, sir.

ESCALUS So. **[*To Clown*] What trade are you of, sir?**

188–94 **What . . . Nine?—** This short passage is discontinuous with Escalus's address to Froth at both ends, and the language is Middletonian in every respect. The overt sexual joking is entirely in his vein.

CLOWN A tapster, a poor widow's tapster.

ESCALUS Your mistress's name?

CLOWN Mistress Overdone.

ESCALUS Hath she had any more than one husband?

CLOWN Nine, sir—Overdone by the last.

ESCALUS Nine?—Come hither to me, Master Froth. Master Froth, I would not have you acquainted with tapsters. They will draw you, Master Froth, and you will hang them. Get you gone, and let me hear no more of you.

FROTH I thank your worship. For mine own part, I never come into any room in a tap-house but I am drawn in.

ESCALUS Well, no more of it, Master Froth. Farewell.

[*Exit Froth*]

Come you hither to me, Master Tapster. What's your name, Master Tapster?

CLOWN Pompey.

ESCALUS What else?

CLOWN Bum, sir.

ESCALUS Troth, and your bum is the greatest thing about you; so that, in the beastliest sense, you are Pompey the Great. Pompey, you are partly a bawd, Pompey, howsoever you colour it in being a tapster, are you not? Come, tell me true; it shall be the better for you.

CLOWN Truly, sir, I am a poor fellow that would live.

ESCALUS How would you live, Pompey? By being a bawd? What do you think of the trade, Pompey? Is it a lawful trade?

CLOWN If the law would allow it, sir.

ESCALUS But the law will not allow it, Pompey; nor it shall not be allowed in Ferrara **Vienna**.

CLOWN Does your worship mean to geld and spay all the youth of the city?

ESCALUS No, Pompey.

CLOWN Truly, sir, in my poor opinion they will to't then. If your worship will take order for the drabs and the knaves, you need not to fear the bawds.

ESCALUS There is pretty orders beginning, I can tell you. It is but heading and hanging.

CLOWN If you head and hang all that offend that way but for ten year together, you'll be glad to give out a commission for more heads. If this law hold in Ferrara **Vienna** ten year, I'll rent the fairest house in it after threepence a bay. If you live to see this come to pass, say Pompey told you so.

ESCALUS Thank you, good Pompey; and in requital of your prophecy, hark you. I advise you, let me not find you before me again upon any complaint whatsoever; no, not for dwelling where you do. If I do, Pompey, I shall beat you to your tent, and prove a shrewd Caesar to you; in plain dealing, Pompey, I shall have you whipped. So for this time, Pompey, fare you well.

CLOWN I thank your worship for your good counsel; [*aside*] but I shall follow it as the flesh and fortune shall better determine.
Whip me? No, no; let carman whip his jade.
The valiant heart's not whipped out of his trade.

Exit

ESCALUS Come hither to me, Master Elbow; come hither, Master Constable. How long have you been in this place of constable?

ELBOW Seven year and a half, sir.

ESCALUS I thought, by the readiness in the office, you had continued in it some time. You say seven years together?

ELBOW And a half, sir.

ESCALUS Alas, it hath been great pains to you. They do you wrong to put you so oft upon't. Are there not men in your ward sufficient to serve it?

ELBOW Faith, sir, few of any wit in such matters. As they are chosen, they are glad to choose me for them. I do it for some piece of money, and go through with all.

ESCALUS Look you bring me in the names of some six or seven, the most sufficient of your parish.

ELBOW To your worship's house, sir?

ESCALUS To my house. Fare you well. [*Exeunt*]

[*Exeunt Elbow and officers*]

189 **poor widow's tapster** Shakespeare nowhere else uses the possessive *widow's* with a qualifying adjective; Middleton not only does so, but he uses the same qualifier *poor*, and the referent is, as here, a man: 'poor old widow's son', *Women Beware* 4.1.165.

192 **any more than one** Not found anywhere in Shakespeare, but occurs exactly in Middleton in *Michaelmas* 3.4.49.
one husband Shakespeare never uses this phrase; Middleton does so at least three times: *Five Gallants* 5.1.14, *Michaelmas* 1.2.272–3, and *Dissemblers* 1.3.5. In the example from *Five Gallants* the implication is the same as in the Clown's comment: 'You broke the back of one husband already ...'.

193 **Nine** Middleton uses the number *nine*, in contrast with *one*, as a measure of excess in relation to sex and family relationships in *Chaste Maid* 2.1.178–80, 'There's a gentleman, | I haply have his name too, that has got | Nine children by one water that he useth'. (Mistress Overdone is again associated with *nine* in the passage evidently added at the beginning of 4.3, where *nine score* appears two lines below her name.)
by the last Shakespeare never uses the phrase; Middleton does so. Moreover, he uses it with an anteceding referent, and with a verbal element expressing augmentation of what was begun by the first: '*Begun by yon first king, which does increase | Now by the last;*' (*Aries* 206–7, where the mildly erotic imagery surrounding the line of kings in their relation to the city and nation compares with the overtly sexual implication of Mistress Overdone's line of nine husbands).

203 **Pompey** Compare Shakespeare's *Love's Labour's Lost* 5.2, where the clownish Costard plays 'Pompey the Huge', and Middleton's *Weapons*, in which a major role is a clown called Pompey Doodle.

What's o'clock, think you?
JUSTICE **Eleven, sir.**
ESCALUS **I pray you home to dinner with me.**
JUSTICE **I humbly thank you.**
ESCALUS
It grieves me for the death of Claudio,
But there's no remedy.
JUSTICE **Lord Angelo is severe.**
ESCALUS **It is but needful.**
Mercy is not itself that oft looks so;
Pardon is still the nurse of second woe.
But yet, poor Claudio! There is no remedy.
Come, sir. *Exeunt*

2.2

Sc. 7 **2.2**
Enter Provost, Servant

SERVANT
He's hearing of a cause; he will come straight.
I'll tell him of you.
PROVOST Pray you do. [*Exit Servant*]
I'll know
His pleasure; maybe he will relent. Alas,
He hath but as offended in a dream.
All sects, all ages, smack of this vice; and he
To die for't!
Enter Angelo
ANGELO Now, what's the matter, Provost?
PROVOST
Is it your will Claudio shall die tomorrow?
ANGELO
Did not I tell thee yea? Hadst thou not order?
Why dost thou ask again?
PROVOST Lest I might be too rash.
Under your good correction, I have seen
When after execution judgement hath
Repented o'er his doom.
ANGELO Go to; let that be mine.
Do you your office, or give up your place,
And you shall well be spared.
PROVOST I crave your honour's pardon.
What shall be done, sir, with the groaning Juliet?
She's very near her hour.
ANGELO Dispose of her
To some more fitter place, and that with speed.
[*Enter Servant*]
SERVANT
Here is the sister of the man condemned
Desires access to you.
ANGELO Hath he a sister?
PROVOST
Ay, my good lord, a very virtuous maid,
And to be shortly of a sisterhood,
If not already.
ANGELO Well, let her be admitted.
[*Exit Servant*]
See you the fornicatress be removed.
Let her have needful but not lavish means.
There shall be order for't.
Enter Lucio and Isabella
PROVOST God save **'Save** your honour.
ANGELO
Stay a little while. [*To Isabella*] You're welcome.
What's your will?
ISABELLA
I am a woeful suitor to your honour.
Please but your honour hear me.
ANGELO Well, what's your suit?
ISABELLA
There is a vice that most I do abhor,
And most desire should meet the blow of justice,
For which I would not plead, but that I must;
For which I must not plead, but that I am
At war 'twixt will and will not.
ANGELO Well, the matter?
ISABELLA
I have a brother is condemned to die.
I do beseech you, let it be his fault,
And not my brother.
PROVOST [*aside*] God **Heaven** give thee moving graces!
ANGELO
Condemn the fault, and not the actor of it?
Why, every fault's condemned ere it be done.
Mine were the very cipher of a function,
To fine the faults whose fine stands in record,
And let go by the actor.
ISABELLA O just but severe law!
I had a brother, then. God **Heaven** keep your honour.
PROVOST **LUCIO** [*aside to Isabella as she is going*]
Give't not o'er so. To him again; entreat him.

262–73 **What's . . . sir.** This passage, with its contrived dramaturgy and a character who appears nowhere else in the play, looks very much like an interpolation (see Introduction). The mixture of verse and prose is unShakespearean, but is Middletonian, and resembles that of the interpolation in 4.1. It also shares with that passage talk about the arrangements for and the timing of meetings (2.1.262–5, 4.1.7–9 and 17–25), clichés of thanks or apology, some sententious moralizing, and a couplet with exactly the same rhyme (*so/woe*).

269 **It is but needful** Similarly *Hengist* 1.3.75, 'that's but needful'.

271 **nurse of second woe** This phrase, with its theological connotations, has a good Middleton parallel in 'hope of second pity' (*Women Beware* 2.1.175). There is no other comparable phrase in early modern English drama.

2.2.25.1 ***Lucio*** Probably introduced into this scene as part of the adaptation. Most of his speeches could have originally been spoken by the Provost, but those at 132, 135, and 159 are likely to be Middleton's additions.

25, 163 God save **'Save** The apostrophe and the irregular metre both point to expurgation.

36 God **Heaven** 'Heaven give' occurs in Shakespeare only twice elsewhere, both times in expurgated texts.

42 God **Heaven** In such phrases Shakespeare's usage is 'God', not 'heaven'. The formulation here is echoed at 2.2.159 and 2.4.34.

Kneel down before him; hang upon his gown.
You are too cold. If you should need a pin,
You could not with more tame a tongue desire it.
To him, I say!

ISABELLA [*returning to Angelo*] Must he needs die?

ANGELO Maiden, no remedy.

ISABELLA
Yes, I do think that you might pardon him,
And neither God **heaven** nor man grieve at the mercy.

ANGELO
I will not do't.

ISABELLA But can you if you would?

ANGELO
Look what I will not, that I cannot do.

ISABELLA
But might you do't, and do the world no wrong,
If so your heart were touched with that remorse
As mine is to him?

ANGELO He's sentenced; 'tis too late.

PROVOST **LUCIO** [*aside to Isabella*] You are too cold.

ISABELLA
Too late? Why, no; I that do speak a word
May call it again. Well, believe this,
No ceremony that to great ones 'longs,
Not the king's crown, nor the deputed sword,
The marshal's truncheon, nor the judge's robe,
Become them with one half so good a grace
As mercy does.
If he had been as you and you as he,
You would have slipped like him, but he, like you,
Would not have been so stern.

ANGELO Pray you be gone.

ISABELLA
I would to God **heaven** I had your potency,
And you were Isabel! Should it then be thus?
No; I would tell what 'twere to be a judge,
And what a prisoner.

PROVOST **LUCIO** [*aside to Isabella*]
Ay, touch him; there's the vein.

ANGELO
Your brother is a forfeit of the law,
And you but waste your words.

ISABELLA Alas, alas!
Why, all the souls that were were forfeit once,
And He that might the vantage best have took
Found out the remedy. How would you be
If He which is the top of judgement should
But judge you as you are? O, think on that,
And mercy then will breathe within your lips,
Like man new made.

ANGELO Be you content, fair maid.
It is the law, not I, condemn your brother.
Were he my kinsman, brother, or my son,
It should be thus with him. He must die tomorrow.

ISABELLA
Tomorrow? O, that's sudden! Spare him, spare him!
He's not prepared for death. Even for our kitchens
We kill the fowl of season. Shall we serve God **heaven**
With less respect than we do minister
To our gross selves? Good good my lord, bethink you:
Who is it that hath died for this offence?
There's many have committed it.

PROVOST **LUCIO** [*aside*] Ay, well said.

ANGELO
The law hath not been dead, though it hath slept.
Those many had not dared to do that evil
If the first that did th'edict infringe
Had answered for his deed. Now 'tis awake,
Takes note of what is done, and, like a prophet,
Looks in a glass that shows what future evils,
Either raw, or by remissness new conceived
And so in progress to be hatched and born,
Are now to have no sùccessive degrees,
But ere they live, to end.

ISABELLA Yet show some pity.

ANGELO
I show it most of all when I show justice,
For then I pity those I do not know
Which a dismissed offence would after gall,
And do him right that, answering one foul wrong,
Lives not to act another. Be satisfied.
Your brother dies tomorrow. Be content.

ISABELLA
So you must be the first that gives this sentence,
And he that suffers. O, it is excellent
To have a giant's strength, but it is tyrannous
To use it like a giant.

PROVOST **LUCIO** That's well said.

ISABELLA Could great men thunder
As Jove himself does, Jove would never be quiet,
For every pelting petty officer
Would use his heaven for thunder, nothing but
thunder.
Merciful heaven,
Thou rather with thy sharp and sulphurous bolt
Split'st the unwedgeable and gnarlèd oak
Than the soft myrtle. But man, proud man,
Dressed in a little brief authority,
Most ignorant of what he's most assured,
His glassy essence, like an angry ape
Plays such fantastic tricks before high heaven
As makes the angels weep, who, with our spleens,
Would all themselves laugh mortal.

PROVOST **LUCIO** [*aside*]
O, to him, to him, wench! He will relent.
He's coming; I perceive't.

51 God **heaven** JAGGARD's 'heauen' hides a comparison between an anthropomorphic God and man.

69 God **heaven** JAGGARD gives an un-Shakespearean usage.

87 God **heaven** JAGGARD's 'serve heauen' appears elsewhere in Shakespeare only in another expurgated text.

PROVOST **[*aside to Lucio*]**
Pray God **heaven** she win him!

ISABELLA
We cannot weigh our brother with ourself.
Great men may jest with saints; 'tis wit in them,
But in the less, foul profanatïon.

LUCIO **[*aside to Isabella*]**
Thou'rt i'th' right, girl. More o' that.

ISABELLA
That in the captain's but a choleric word,
Which in the soldier is flat blasphemy.

LUCIO **[*aside to Isabella*] Art advised o' that? More on't.**

ANGELO
Why do you put these sayings upon me?

ISABELLA
Because authority, though it err like others,
Hath yet a kind of medicine in itself
That skins the vice o'th' top. Go to your bosom;
Knock there, and ask your heart what it doth know
That's like my brother's fault. If it confess
A natural guiltiness, such as is his,
Let it not sound a thought upon your tongue
Against my brother's life.

ANGELO [*aside*] She speaks, and 'tis such sense
That my sense breeds with it. [*To Isabella*] Fare you well.

ISABELLA Gentle my lord, turn back.

ANGELO
I will bethink me. Come again tomorrow.

ISABELLA
Hark how I'll bribe you; good my lord, turn back.

ANGELO How, bribe me?

ISABELLA
Ay, with such gifts that God **heaven** shall share with you.

PROVOST **LUCIO** [*aside to Isabella*] You had marred all else.

ISABELLA
Not with fond shekels of the tested gold,
Or stones whose rate are either rich or poor
As fancy values them; but with true prayers,
That shall be up at heaven and enter there
Ere sunrise, prayers from preservèd souls,
From fasting maids whose minds are dedicate
To nothing temporal.

ANGELO Well, come to me
Tomorrow.

LUCIO **[*aside to Isabella*] Go to; 'tis well; away.**

ISABELLA God **Heaven** keep your honour safe.

ANGELO [*aside*] Amen;
For I am that way going to temptation,
Where prayer is crossed.

ISABELLA At what hour tomorrow
Shall I attend your lordship?

ANGELO At any time fore noon.

ISABELLA
God save **'Save** your honour.

ANGELO [*aside*] From thee; even from thy virtue.
[*Exeunt Isabella, Lucio, Provost*]
What's this? What's this? Is this her fault or mine?
The tempter or the tempted, who sins most, ha?
Not she; nor doth she tempt; but it is I
That, lying by the violet in the sun,
Do, as the carrion does, not as the flower,
Corrupt with virtuous season. Can it be
That modesty may more betray our sense
Than woman's lightness? Having waste ground enough,
Shall we desire to raze the sanctuary,
And pitch our evils there? O, fie, fie, fie!
What dost thou, or what art thou, Angelo?
Dost thou desire her foully for those things
That make her good? O, let her brother live!
Thieves for their robbery have authority,
When judges steal themselves. What, do I love her,
That I desire to hear her speak again,
And feast upon her eyes? What is't I dream on?
O cunning enemy, that, to catch a saint,
With saints dost bait thy hook! Most dangerous
Is that temptation that doth goad us on
To sin in loving virtue. Never could the strumpet
With all her double vigour—art and nature—
Once stir my temper; but this virtuous maid
Subdues me quite. Ever till now
When men were fond, I smiled, and wondered how.
Exit

Sc. 8 **2.3** 2.3

Enter [*at one door*] *Duke,* [*disguised as a friar,*] *and* [*at another door*] *Provost*

DUKE
Hail to you, Provost!—so I think you are.

PROVOST
I am the Provost. What's your will, good friar?

DUKE
Bound by my charity and my blest order,
I come to visit the afflicted spirits
Here in the prison. Do me the common right
To let me see them, and to make me know
The nature of their crimes, that I may minister
To them accordingly.

PROVOST
I would do more than that, if more were needful.
Enter Juliet
Look, here comes one, a gentlewoman of mine,

128 God **heaven** 'Pray God' is common in Shakespeare, and demonstrably expurgated seven times. 'Pray heaven' occurs only once in an unexpurgated text.

132 **Thou'rt...that;** 135 **Art...on't;** 159 **Go...away** These speeches, unlike most of Lucio's other lines in the scene, sound unlikely to have been originally spoken by the Provost; the intrusion of prose and of cynical humour instead suggest interpolation by Middleton.

150 God Likely to be the original reading as it gives an echo of the biblical *gift(s) of God*, which was especially common in the Geneva bible; there are no occurrences of *gift(s) of heaven*.

159 God **Heaven** See note to 2.2.42.

Who, falling in the flaws of her own youth,
Hath blistered her report. She is with child,
And he that got it, sentenced—a young man
More fit to do another such offence
Than die for this.

DUKE When must he die?

PROVOST As I do think, tomorrow.
[*To Juliet*] I have provided for you. Stay a while,
And you shall be conducted.

DUKE
Repent you, fair one, of the sin you carry?

JULIET
I do, and bear the shame most patiently.

DUKE
I'll teach you how you shall arraign your conscience,
And try your penitence if it be sound
Or hollowly put on.

JULIET I'll gladly learn.

DUKE Love you the man that wronged you?

JULIET
Yes, as I love the woman that wronged him.

DUKE
So then it seems your most offenceful act
Was mutually committed?

JULIET Mutually.

DUKE
Then was your sin of heavier kind than his.

JULIET
I do confess it and repent it, father.

DUKE
'Tis meet so, daughter. But lest you do repent
As that the sin hath brought you to this shame—
Which sorrow is always toward ourselves, not heaven,
Showing we would not spare heaven as we love it,
But as we stand in fear—

JULIET
I do repent me as it is an evil,
And take the shame with joy.

DUKE There rest.
Your partner, as I hear, must die tomorrow,
And I am going with instruction to him.
God's grace go with you. *Benedicite!* *Exit*

JULIET
Must die tomorrow? O injurious law,
That respites me a life whose very comfort
Is still a dying horror!

PROVOST 'Tis pity of him. *Exeunt*

2.4 *Sc. 9* **2.4**

Enter Angelo

ANGELO
When I would pray and think, I think and pray
To several subjects: God **heaven** hath my empty words,
Whilst my invention, hearing not my tongue,
Anchors on Isabel; God **heaven** in my mouth,
As if I did but only chew his name,
And in my heart the strong and swelling evil
Of my conception. The state whereon I studied
Is like a good thing, being often read,
Grown seared and tedious. Yea, my gravity,
Wherein—let no man hear me—I take pride,
Could I with boot change for an idle plume
Which the air beats in vain. O place, O form,
How often dost thou with thy case, thy habit,
Wrench awe from fools, and tie the wiser souls
To thy false seeming! Blood, thou art blood.
Let's write 'good angel' on the devil's horn—
'Tis now the devil's crest.

Enter Servant

How now? Who's there?

SERVANT One Isabel, a sister, desires access to you.

ANGELO
Teach her the way. [*Exit Servant*]
O heavens,
Why does my blood thus muster to my heart,
Making both it unable for itself,
And dispossessing all my other parts
Of necessary fitness?
So play the foolish throngs with one that swoons—
Come all to help him, and so stop the air
By which he should revive—and even so
The general subject to a well-wished king
Quit their own part and, in obsequious fondness,
Crowd to his presence, where their untaught love
Must needs appear offence.

Enter Isabella

How now, fair maid?

ISABELLA I am come to know your pleasure.

ANGELO [*aside*]
That you might know it would much better please me
Than to demand what 'tis. [*To Isabella*] Your brother cannot live.

ISABELLA Even so. God **Heaven** keep your honour.

ANGELO
Yet may he live a while, and it may be
As long as you or I. Yet he must die.

ISABELLA Under your sentence?

ANGELO Yea.

ISABELLA
When, I beseech you?—that in his reprieve,
Longer or shorter, he may be so fitted
That his soul sicken not.

ANGELO
Ha, fie, these filthy vices! It were as good

2.3.41 **grace** The metrical irregularity might point to expurgation of 'God's' here and at 5.1.393.

2.4.2, 4 God **heaven** In the Eucharist, the body of Christ is symbolically taken in the mouth. In *Basilikon Doron* (1599), to which *Measure* alludes elsewhere, the future James I wrote 'Keep God more sparingly in your mouth, but abundantly in your heart'. Consistency is probably required between 2 and 4.

34 God **Heaven** See note to 2.2.45.

To pardon him that hath from nature stol'n
A man already made, as to remit
Their saucy sweetness that do coin God's **heaven's**
image
In stamps that are forbid. 'Tis all as easy
Falsely to take away a life true made
As to put metal in restrainèd moulds,
To make a false one.

ISABELLA
'Tis set down so in heaven, but not in earth.

ANGELO
Say you so? Then I shall pose you quickly.
Which had you rather: that the most just law
Now took your brother's life, or, to redeem him,
Give up your body to such sweet uncleanness
As she that he hath stained?

ISABELLA Sir, believe this.
I had rather give my body than my soul.

ANGELO
I talk not of your soul. Our còmpelled sins
Stand more for number than for account.

ISABELLA How say you?

ANGELO
Nay, I'll not warrant that, for I can speak
Against the thing I say. Answer to this.
I now, the voice of the recorded law,
Pronounce a sentence on your brother's life.
Might there not be a charity in sin
To save this brother's life?

ISABELLA Please you to do't,
I'll take it as a peril to my soul
It is no sin at all, but charity.

ANGELO
Pleased you to do't at peril of your soul
Were equal poise of sin and charity.

ISABELLA
That I do beg his life, if it be sin,
Heaven let me bear it. You granting of my suit,
If that be sin, I'll make it my morn prayer
To have it added to the faults of mine,
And nothing of your answer.

ANGELO Nay, but hear me.
Your sense pursues not mine. Either you are ignorant,
Or seem so craftily, and that's not good.

ISABELLA
Let me be ignorant, and in nothing good
But graciously to know I am no better.

ANGELO
Thus wisdom wishes to appear most bright
When it doth tax itself: as these black masks
Proclaim an enshield beauty ten times louder
Than beauty could, displayed. But mark me.
To be receivèd plain, I'll speak more gross.
Your brother is to die.

ISABELLA So.

ANGELO
And his offence is so, as it appears,
Accountant to the law upon that pain.

ISABELLA True.

ANGELO
Admit no other way to save his life—
As I subscribe not that nor any other—
But, in the loss of question, that you his sister,
Finding yourself desired of such a person
Whose credit with the judge, or own great place,
Could fetch your brother from the manacles
Of the all-binding law, and that there were
No earthly mean to save him, but that either
You must lay down the treasures of your body
To this supposed, or else to let him suffer—
What would you do?

ISABELLA
As much for my poor brother as myself.
That is, were I under the terms of death,
Th'impression of keen whips I'd wear as rubies,
And strip myself to death as to a bed
That longing have been sick for, ere I'd yield
My body up to shame.

ANGELO Then must your brother die.

ISABELLA And 'twere the cheaper way.
Better it were a brother died at once
Than that a sister, by redeeming him,
Should die for ever.

ANGELO
Were not you then as cruel as the sentence
That you have slandered so?

ISABELLA
Ignominy in ransom and free pardon
Are of two houses; lawful mercy
Is nothing kin to foul redemptïon.

ANGELO
You seemed of late to make the law a tyrant,
And rather proved the sliding of your brother
A merriment than a vice.

ISABELLA
O pardon me, my lord. It oft falls out
To have what we would have, we speak not what we
mean.
I something do excuse the thing I hate
For his advantage that I dearly love.

ANGELO
We are all frail.

ISABELLA Else let my brother die—
If not a federy, but only he,
Owe and succeed thy weakness.

ANGELO Nay, women are frail too.

ISABELLA
Ay, as the glasses where they view themselves,
Which are as easy broke as they make forms.
Women? Help, heaven! Men their creation mar

45 God's **heaven's** Humans were made in God's image, not heaven's (Genesis 1:27).

In profiting by them. Nay, call us ten times frail,
For we are soft as our complexions are,
And credulous to false prints.

ANGELO I think it well,
And from this testimony of your own sex,
Since I suppose we are made to be no stronger
Than faults may shake our frames, let me be bold.
I do arrest your words. Be that you are;
That is, a woman. If you be more, you're none.
If you be one, as you are well expressed
By all external warrants, show it now,
By putting on the destined livery.

ISABELLA
I have no tongue but one. Gentle my lord,
Let me entreat you speak the former language.

ANGELO Plainly conceive, I love you.

ISABELLA
My brother did love Juliet,
And you tell me that he shall die for't.

ANGELO
He shall not, Isabel, if you give me love.

ISABELLA
I know your virtue hath a licence in't,
Which seems a little fouler than it is,
To pluck on others.

ANGELO Believe me, on mine honour,
My words express my purpose.

ISABELLA
Ha, little honour to be much believed,
And most pernicious purpose! Seeming, seeming!
I will proclaim thee, Angelo; look for't.
Sign me a present pardon for my brother,
Or with an outstretched throat I'll tell the world aloud
What man thou art.

ANGELO Who will believe thee, Isabel?
My unsoiled name, th'austereness of my life,
My vouch against you, and my place i'th' state,
Will so your accusation overweigh
That you shall stifle in your own report,
And smell of calumny. I have begun,
And now I give my sensual race the rein.
Fit thy consent to my sharp appetite.
Lay by all nicety and prolixious blushes
That banish what they sue for. Redeem thy brother
By yielding up thy body to my will,
Or else he must not only die the death,
But thy unkindness shall his death draw out
To ling'ring sufferance. Answer me tomorrow,
Or by the affection that now guides me most,
I'll prove a tyrant to him. As for you,
Say what you can, my false o'erweighs your true.
Exit

ISABELLA
To whom should I complain? Did I tell this,
Who would believe me? O perilous mouths,
That bear in them one and the selfsame tongue
Either of condemnation or approof,
Bidding the law make curtsy to their will,
Hooking both right and wrong to th' appetite,
To follow as it draws! I'll to my brother.
Though he hath fall'n by prompture of the blood,
Yet hath he in him such a mind of honour
That had he twenty heads to tender down
On twenty bloody blocks, he'd yield them up
Before his sister should her body stoop
To such abhorred pollution.
Then Isabel live chaste, and brother die:
More than our brother is our chastity.
I'll tell him yet of Angelo's request,
And fit his mind to death, for his soul's rest. *Exit*

Finis Actus Secundus

Sc. 10 ***3.1*** 3.1

Incipit Actus Tertius

Enter Duke, [disguised as a friar,] Claudio, and Provost

DUKE
So then you hope of pardon from Lord Angelo?

CLAUDIO
The miserable have no other medicine
But only hope.
I've hope to live, and am prepared to die.

DUKE
Be absolute for death. Either death or life
Shall thereby be the sweeter. Reason thus with life.
If I do lose thee, I do lose a thing
That none but fools would keep. A breath thou art,
Servile to all the skyey influences
That dost this habitation where thou keep'st
Hourly afflict. Merely thou art death's fool,
For him thou labour'st by thy flight to shun,
And yet runn'st toward him still. Thou art not noble,
For all th'accommodations that thou bear'st
Are nursed by baseness. Thou'rt by no means valiant,
For thou dost fear the soft and tender fork
Of a poor worm. Thy best of rest is sleep,
And that thou oft provok'st, yet grossly fear'st
Thy death, which is no more. Thou art not thyself,
For thou exist'st on many a thousand grains
That issue out of dust. Happy thou art not,
For what thou hast not, still thou striv'st to get,
And what thou hast, forget'st. Thou art not certain,
For thy complexion shifts to strange effects
After the moon. If thou art rich, thou'rt poor,
For like an ass whose back with ingots bows,
Thou bear'st thy heavy riches but a journey,
And death unloads thee. Friend hast thou none,
For thine own bowels, which do call thee sire,
The mere effusion of thy proper loins,
Do curse the gout, serpigo, and the rheum,
For ending thee no sooner. Thou hast nor youth nor age,
But as it were an after-dinner's sleep
Dreaming on both; for all thy blessèd youth

Becomes as agèd, and doth beg the alms
Of palsied eld; and when thou art old and rich,
Thou hast neither heat, affection, limb, nor beauty,
To make thy riches pleasant. What's in this
That bears the name of life? Yet in this life
Lie hid more thousand deaths; yet death we fear
That makes these odds all even.

CLAUDIO I humbly thank you.
To sue to live, I find I seek to die,
And seeking death, find life. Let it come on.

ISABELLA [*within*]
What ho! Peace here, grace, and good company!

PROVOST
Who's there? Come in; the wish deserves a welcome.

Enter Isabella

DUKE [*to Claudio*]
Dear sir, ere long I'll visit you again.

CLAUDIO Most holy sir, I thank you.

ISABELLA
My business is a word or two with Claudio.

PROVOST
And very welcome.—Look, signor, here's your sister.

DUKE
Provost, a word with you.

PROVOST As many as you please.

DUKE
Bring me to hear them speak where I may be concealed.

[*Exeunt*]

CLAUDIO Now sister, what's the comfort?

ISABELLA
Why, as all comforts are: most good, most good indeed.
Lord Angelo, having affairs to heaven,
Intends you for his swift ambassador,
Where you shall be an everlasting leiger.
Therefore your best appointment make with speed.
Tomorrow you set on.

CLAUDIO Is there no remedy?

ISABELLA
None but such remedy as, to save a head,
To cleave a heart in twain.

CLAUDIO But is there any?

ISABELLA Yes, brother, you may live.
There is a devilish mercy in the judge,
If you'll implore it, that will free your life,
But fetter you till death.

CLAUDIO Perpetual durance?

ISABELLA
Ay, just, perpetual durance; a restraint,
Though all the world's vastidity you had,
To a determined scope.

CLAUDIO But in what nature?

ISABELLA
In such a one as you consenting to't
Would bark your honour from that trunk you bear,
And leave you naked.

CLAUDIO Let me know the point.

ISABELLA
O, I do fear thee, Claudio, and I quake
Lest thou a feverous life shouldst entertain,
And six or seven winters more respect
Than a perpetual honour. Dar'st thou die?
The sense of death is most in apprehension,
And the poor beetle that we tread upon
In corporal sufferance finds a pang as great
As when a giant dies.

CLAUDIO Why give you me this shame?
Think you I can a resolution fetch
From flow'ry tenderness? If I must die,
I will encounter darkness as a bride,
And hug it in mine arms.

ISABELLA
There spake my brother; there my father's grave
Did utter forth a voice. Yes, thou must die.
Thou art too noble to conserve a life
In base appliances. This outward-sainted deputy,
Whose settled visage and deliberate word
Nips youth i'th' head and follies doth enew
As falcon doth the fowl, is yet a devil.
His filth within being cast, he would appear
A pond as deep as hell.

CLAUDIO The precise Angelo?

ISABELLA
O, 'tis the cunning livery of hell
The damnedest body to invest and cover
In precise guards! Dost thou think, Claudio:
If I would yield him my virginity,
Thou might'st be freed!

CLAUDIO O heavens, it cannot be!

ISABELLA
Yes, he would give't thee, from this rank offence,
So to offend him still. This night's the time
That I should do what I abhor to name,
Or else thou diest tomorrow.

CLAUDIO Thou shalt not do't.

ISABELLA O, were it but my life,
I'd throw it down for your deliverance
As frankly as a pin.

CLAUDIO Thanks, dear Isabel.

ISABELLA
Be ready, Claudio, for your death tomorrow.

CLAUDIO
As God's my judge Yes. Has he affections in him
That thus can make him bite the law by th' nose
When he would force it? Sure it is no sin,
Or of the deadly seven it is the least.

3.1.107 As God's my judge **Yes** 'Yes' is used with anomalous frequency in *Measure*, and substitution for profanity is one obvious cause. 'As God's my judge' makes up a short line to a pentameter, and is thematically appropriate to the play as a whole and the passage in particular.

ISABELLA Which is the least?

CLAUDIO
If it were damnable, he being so wise,
Why would he for the momentary trick
Be pèrdurably fined? O Isabel!

ISABELLA What says my brother?

CLAUDIO Death is a fearful thing.

ISABELLA And shamèd life a hateful.

CLAUDIO
Ay, but to die, and go we know not where;
To lie in cold obstruction, and to rot;
This sensible warm motion to become
A kneaded clod, and the dilated spirit
To bathe in fiery floods, or to reside
In thrilling region of thick-ribbèd ice;
To be imprisoned in the viewless winds,
And blown with restless violence round about
The pendent world; or to be worse than worst
Of those that lawless and incertain thought
Imagine howling—'tis too horrible!
The weariest and most loathèd worldly life
That age, ache, penury, and imprisonment
Can lay on nature is a paradise
To what we fear of death.

ISABELLA Alas, alas!

CLAUDIO Sweet sister, let me live.
What sin you do to save a brother's life,
Nature dispenses with the deed so far
That it becomes a virtue.

ISABELLA O, you beast!
O faithless coward, O dishonest wretch,
Wilt thou be made a man out of my vice?
Is't not a kind of incest to take life
From thine own sister's shame? What should I think?
God **Heaven** shield my mother played my father fair,
For such a warpèd slip of wilderness
Ne'er issued from his blood. Take my defiance,
Die, perish! Might but my bending down
Reprieve thee from thy fate, it should proceed.
I'll pray a thousand prayers for thy death,
No word to save thee.

CLAUDIO Nay, hear me, Isabel.

ISABELLA O fie, fie, fie!
Thy sin's not accidental, but a trade.
Mercy to thee would prove itself a bawd.
'Tis best that thou diest quickly.
[*She parts from Claudio*]

CLAUDIO O hear me, Isabella.

[*Enter Duke*]

DUKE
Vouchsafe a word, young sister, but one word.

ISABELLA What is your will?

DUKE Might you dispense with your leisure, I would by and by have some speech with you. The satisfaction I would require is likewise your own benefit.

ISABELLA I have no superfluous leisure; my stay must be stolen out of other affairs; but I will attend you a while.

DUKE [*standing apart with Claudio*] Son, I have overheard what hath passed between you and your sister. Angelo had never the purpose to corrupt her; only he hath made an assay of her virtue, to practise his judgement with the disposition of natures. She, having the truth of honour in her, hath made him that gracious denial which he is most glad to receive. I am confessor to Angelo, and I know this to be true. Therefore prepare yourself to death. Do not falsify your resolution with hopes that are fallible. Tomorrow you must die. Go to your knees and make ready.

CLAUDIO Let me ask my sister pardon. I am so out of love with life that I will sue to be rid of it.

DUKE Hold you there. Farewell.
[*Claudio joins Isabella*]
Provost, a word with you.

[*Enter Provost*]

PROVOST What's your will, father?

DUKE That now you are come, you will be gone. Leave me a while with the maid. My mind promises with my habit no loss shall touch her by my company.

PROVOST In good time. *Exit* [*with Claudio*]

DUKE The hand that hath made you fair hath made you good. The goodness that is cheap in beauty makes beauty brief in goodness; but grace, being the soul of your complexion, shall keep the body of it ever fair. The assault that Angelo hath made to you fortune hath conveyed to my understanding; and but that frailty hath examples for his falling, I should wonder at Angelo. How will you do to content this substitute, and to save your brother?

ISABELLA I am now going to resolve him. I had rather my brother die by the law than my son should be unlawfully born. But O, how much is the good Duke deceived in Angelo! If ever he return and I can speak to him, I will open my lips in vain, or discover his government.

DUKE That shall not be much amiss. Yet as the matter now stands, he will avoid your accusation: he made trial of you only. Therefore fasten your ear on my advisings. To the love I have in doing good, a remedy presents itself. I do make myself believe that you may most uprighteously do a poor wronged lady a merited benefit, redeem your brother from the angry law, do no stain to your own gracious person, and much please the absent Duke, if peradventure he shall ever return to have hearing of this business.

ISABELLA Let me hear you speak farther. I have spirit to do anything that appears not foul in the truth of my spirit.

DUKE Virtue is bold, and goodness never fearful. Have you not heard speak of Mariana, the sister of Frederick, the great soldier who miscarried at sea?

142 God **Heaven** 'Heaven shield' occurs nowhere else in Shakespeare; 'God shield' (or 'God ield') occurs six times.

ISABELLA I have heard of the lady, and good words went with her name.

DUKE She should this Angelo have married, was affianced to her oath, and the nuptial appointed; between which time of the contract and limit of the solemnity, her brother Frederick was wrecked at sea, having in that perished vessel the dowry of his sister. But mark how heavily this befell to the poor gentlewoman. There she lost a noble and renowned brother, in his love toward her ever most kind and natural; with him, the portion and sinew of her fortune, her marriage dowry; with both, her combinate husband, this well-seeming Angelo.

ISABELLA Can this be so? Did Angelo so leave her?

DUKE Left her in her tears, and dried not one of them with his comfort; swallowed his vows whole, pretending in her discoveries of dishonour; in few, bestowed her on her own lamentation, which she yet wears for his sake; and he, a marble to her tears, is washed with them, but relents not.

ISABELLA What a merit were it in death to take this poor maid from the world! What corruption in this life, that it will let this man live! But how out of this can she avail?

DUKE It is a rupture that you may easily heal, and the cure of it not only saves your brother, but keeps you from dishonour in doing it.

ISABELLA Show me how, good father.

DUKE This forenamed maid hath yet in her the continuance of her first affection. His unjust unkindness, that in all reason should have quenched her love, hath, like an impediment in the current, made it more violent and unruly. Go you to Angelo, answer his requiring with a plausible obedience, agree with his demands to the point; only refer yourself to this advantage: first, that your stay with him may not be long; that the time may have all shadow and silence in it; and the place answer to convenience. This being granted in course, and now follows all. We shall advise this wronged maid to stead up your appointment, go in your place. If the encounter acknowledge itself hereafter, it may compel him to her recompense; and hear, by this is your brother saved, your honour untainted, the poor Mariana advantaged, and the corrupt deputy scaled. The maid will I frame and make fit for his attempt. If you think well to carry this, as you may, the doubleness of the benefit defends the deceit from reproof. What think you of it?

ISABELLA The image of it gives me content already, and I trust it will grow to a most prosperous perfection.

DUKE It lies much in your holding up. Haste you speedily to Angelo. If for this night he entreat you to his bed, give him promise of satisfaction. I will presently to Saint Luke's; there at the moated grange resides this dejected Mariana. At that place call upon me; and dispatch with Angelo, that it may be quickly.

ISABELLA I thank you for this comfort. Fare you well, good father. *Exit*

Enter Elbow, Clown, officers

ELBOW Nay, if there be no remedy for it but that you will needs buy and sell men and women like beasts, we shall have all the world drink brown and white bastard.

DUKE O heavens, what stuff is here?

CLOWN 'Twas never merry world since, of two usuries, the merriest was put down, and the worser allowed by order of law, a furred gown to keep him warm—and furred with fox on lambskins too, to signify that craft, being richer than innocency, stands for the facing.

ELBOW Come your way, sir.—God bless 'Bless you, good father friar.

DUKE And you, good brother father. What offence hath this man made you, sir?

ELBOW Marry, sir, he hath offended the law; and, sir, we take him to be a thief, too, sir, for we have found upon him, sir, a strange picklock, which we have sent to the deputy.

DUKE [*to Clown*] Fie, sirrah, a bawd, a wicked bawd!
The evil that thou causest to be done,
That is thy means to live. Do thou but think
What 'tis to cram a maw or clothe a back
From such a filthy vice. Say to thyself,
'From their abominable and beastly touches
I drink, I eat, array myself, and live'.
Canst thou believe thy living is a life,
So stinkingly depending? Go mend, go mend.

CLOWN Indeed it does stink in some sort, sir. But yet, sir, I would prove—

DUKE
Nay, if the devil have given thee proofs for sin,
Thou wilt prove his.—Take him to prison, officer.
Correction and instruction must both work
Ere this rude beast will profit.

ELBOW He must before the deputy, sir; he has given him warning. The deputy cannot abide a whoremaster. If he be a whoremonger and comes before him, he were as good go a mile on his errand.

DUKE
That we were all as some would seem to be—
Free from our faults, or faults from seeming free.

ELBOW His neck will come to your waist: a cord, sir.

Enter Lucio

CLOWN I spy comfort, I cry bail. Here's a gentleman, and a friend of mine.

LUCIO How now, noble Pompey? What, at the wheels of Caesar? Art thou led in triumph? What, is there none of Pygmalion's images newly made woman to be had now, for putting the hand in the pocket and extracting clutched? What reply, ha? What sayst thou to this tune,

278, 341 God bless **'Bless** The apostrophe in JAGGARD at 278 hints at an expurgation. 'God bless' is Shakespeare's preferred form, and elsewhere was demonstrably expurgated.

matter, and method? Is't not drowned i'th' last rain, ha? What sayst thou, trot? Is the world as it was, man? Which is the way? Is it sad and few words? Or how? The trick of it?

DUKE Still thus and thus; still worse!

LUCIO How doth my dear morsel thy mistress? Procures she still, ha?

CLOWN Troth, sir, she hath eaten up all her beef, and she is herself in the tub.

LUCIO Why, 'tis good, it is the right of it, it must be so. Ever your fresh whore and your powdered bawd; an unshunned consequence, it must be so. Art going to prison, Pompey?

CLOWN Yes, faith, sir.

LUCIO Why 'tis not amiss, Pompey. Farewell. Go; say I sent thee thither. For debt, Pompey, or how?

ELBOW For being a bawd, for being a bawd.

LUCIO Well then, imprison him. If imprisonment be the due of a bawd, why, 'tis his right. Bawd is he doubtless, and of antiquity too—bawd born. Farewell, good Pompey. Commend me to the prison, Pompey. You will turn good husband now, Pompey; you will keep the house.

CLOWN I hope, sir, your good worship will be my bail?

LUCIO No, in faith **indeed**, will I not, Pompey; it is not the wear. I will pray, Pompey, to increase your bondage. If you take it not patiently, why, your mettle is the more. Adieu, trusty Pompey.—God bless **'Bless** you, friar.

DUKE And you.

LUCIO Does Bridget paint still, Pompey, ha?

ELBOW [*to Clown*] Come your ways, sir, come.

CLOWN [*to Lucio*] You will not bail me then, sir?

LUCIO Then, Pompey, nor now.—What news abroad, friar, what news?

ELBOW [*to Clown*] Come your ways, sir, come.

LUCIO Go to kennel, Pompey, go.

[*Exeunt Elbow, Clown, and officers*]

What news, friar, of the Duke?

DUKE I know none. Can you tell me of any?

LUCIO Some say he is with the Emperor of Russia; other some, he is in Rome. But where is he, think you?

DUKE I know not where; but wheresoever, I wish him well.

LUCIO It was a mad, fantastical trick of him to steal from the state, and usurp the beggary he was never born to. Lord Angelo dukes it well in his absence; he puts transgression to't.

DUKE He does well in't.

LUCIO A little more lenity to lechery would do no harm in him. Something too crabbed that way, friar.

DUKE It is too general a vice, and severity must cure it.

LUCIO Yes, in good faith **sooth**, the vice is of a great kindred, it is well allied. But it is impossible to extirp it quite, friar, till eating and drinking be put down. They say this Angelo was not made by man and woman, after this downright way of creation. Is it true, think you?

DUKE How should he be made, then?

LUCIO Some report a sea-maid spawned him, some that he was begot between two stockfishes. But it is certain that when he makes water his urine is congealed ice; that I know to be true. And he is a motion ungenerative; that's infallible.

DUKE You are pleasant, sir, and speak apace.

LUCIO Fore God **Why**, what a ruthless thing is this in him, for the rebellion of a codpiece to take away the life of a man! Would the Duke that is absent have done this? Ere he would have hanged a man for the getting a hundred bastards, he would have paid for the nursing a thousand. He had some feeling of the sport, he knew the service, and that instructed him to mercy.

DUKE I never heard the absent Duke much detected for women; he was not inclined that way.

LUCIO O sir, you are deceived.

DUKE 'Tis not possible.

LUCIO Who, not the Duke? 'Sblood **Yes**, your beggar of fifty; and his use was to put a ducat in her clack-dish. The Duke had crochets in him. He would be drunk too, that let me inform you.

DUKE You do him wrong, surely.

LUCIO Sir, I was an inward of his. A shy fellow was the Duke, and I believe I know the cause of his withdrawing.

DUKE What, I prithee, might be the cause?

LUCIO No, pardon, 'tis a secret must be locked within the teeth and the lips. But this I can let you understand. The greater file of the subject held the Duke to be wise.

DUKE Wise? Why, no question but he was.

LUCIO A very superficial, ignorant, unweighing fellow.

DUKE Either this is envy in you, folly, or mistaking. The very stream of his life, and the business he hath helmed, must, upon a warranted need, give him a better proclamation. Let him be but testimonied in his own bringings-forth, and he shall appear to the envious a scholar, a statesman, and a soldier. Therefore you speak unskilfully, or, if your knowledge be more, it is much darkened in your malice.

LUCIO Sir, I know him and I love him.

363 faith **sooth** Lucio uses the very phrase Hotspur mocks in *1 Henry IV* 3.1.242–52 as a protestation fit only for 'Sunday citizens' or 'a comfit-maker's wife'. Before the 1606 Act against profanity, it was used in Shakespeare only by Lady Percy, in the instance Hotspur mocks, Rosalind (*As You Like It* 3.2.378), and Pandarus, by way of demonstrating effete courtly diction (*Troilus* 3.1.55). In expurgated Shakespeare texts, 'faith' is twice weakened to 'sooth'. 'In good faith' is spoken by Feste, Lavatch, and the First Clown in the grave-digger scene of *Hamlet*, and seems appropriate to a cynical comic.

376 **Why** Lucio's claims become steadily more outrageous, and it might be expected that his oaths would follow a similar course. A profanity such as 'fore God' may have been expurgated.

385 **O** An oath such as 'By the mass' might have been deleted.

387 'Sblood **Yes** 'Yes' is weak; a strong oath would be a comically offensive way of addressing the supposed friar, and ''Sblood' alliterates with 'beggar'.

DUKE Love talks with better knowledge, and knowledge with dearer love.

LUCIO Swounds Come, sir, I know what I know.

DUKE I can hardly believe that, since you know not what you speak. But if ever the Duke return, as our prayers are he may, let me desire you to make your answer before him. If it be honest you have spoke, you have courage to maintain it. I am bound to call upon you; and I pray you, your name?

LUCIO Sir, my name is Lucio, well known to the Duke.

DUKE He shall know you better, sir, if I may live to report you.

LUCIO I fear you not.

DUKE O, you hope the Duke will return no more, or you imagine me too unhurtful an opposite. But indeed I can do you little harm; you'll forswear this again.

LUCIO I'll be hanged first. Thou art deceived in me, friar. But no more of this. Canst thou tell if Claudio die tomorrow or no?

DUKE Why should he die, sir?

LUCIO Why? For filling a bottle with a tundish. I would the Duke we talk of were returned again; this ungenitured agent will unpeople the province with continency. Sparrows must not build in his house-eaves, because they are lecherous. The Duke yet would have dark deeds darkly answered: he would never bring them to light. Would he were returned. Marry, this Claudio is condemned for untrussing. Farewell, good friar. I prithee pray for me. The Duke, I say to thee again, would eat mutton on Fridays. He's not past it yet, and, I say to thee, he would mouth with a beggar, though she smelt brown bread and garlic. Say that I said so. Farewell. *Exit*

DUKE
No might nor greatness in mortality
Can censure scape; back-wounding calumny
The whitest virtue strikes. What king so strong
Can tie the gall up in the slanderous tongue?
Enter Escalus, Provost, and Bawd
But who comes here?

ESCALUS [*to Provost*]
Go, away with her to prison.

BAWD Good my lord, be good to me. Your honour is accounted a merciful man, good my lord.

ESCALUS Double and treble admonition, and still forfeit in the same kind! This would make mercy swear and play the tyrant.

PROVOST A bawd of eleven years' continuance, may it please your honour.

BAWD My lord, this is one Lucio's information against me. Mistress Kate Keepdown was with child by him in the Duke's time; he promised her marriage. His child is a year and a quarter old come Philip and Jacob. I have kept it myself; and see how he goes about to abuse me.

ESCALUS That fellow is a fellow of much licence. Let him be called before us. Away with her to prison. Go to, no more words. Provost, my brother Angelo will not be altered; Claudio must die tomorrow. Let him be furnished with divines, and have all charitable preparation. If my brother wrought by my pity, it should not be so with him.

PROVOST So please you, this friar hath been with him and advised him for th'entertainment of death.

[*Exeunt Provost and Bawd*]

ESCALUS Good even, good father.

DUKE Bliss and goodness on you.

ESCALUS Of whence are you?

DUKE
Not of this country, though my chance is now
To use it for my time. I am a brother
Of gracious order, late come from the See
In special business from his Holiness.

ESCALUS What news abroad i'th' world?

DUKE None, but that there is so great a fever on goodness that the dissolution of it must cure it. Novelty is only in request, and it is as dangerous to be aged in any kind of course as it is virtuous to be inconstant in any undertaking. There is scarce truth enough alive to make societies secure, but security enough to make fellowships accursed. Much upon this riddle runs the wisdom of the world. This news is old enough, yet it is every day's news. I pray you, sir, of what disposition was the Duke?

ESCALUS One that, above all other strifes, contended especially to know himself.

DUKE What pleasure was he given to?

ESCALUS Rather rejoicing to see another merry than merry at anything which professed to make him rejoice; a gentleman of all temperance. But leave we him to his events, with a prayer they may prove prosperous, and let me desire to know how you find Claudio prepared. I am made to understand that you have lent him visitation.

DUKE He professes to have received no sinister measure from his judge, but most willingly humbles himself to the determination of justice. Yet had he framed to himself, by the instruction of his frailty, many deceiving promises of life, which I, by my good leisure, have discredited to him; and now is he resolved to die.

ESCALUS You have paid the heavens your function, and the prisoner the very debt of your calling. I have laboured for the poor gentleman to the extremest shore of my modesty, but my brother-justice have I found so severe that he hath forced me to tell him he is indeed Justice.

DUKE If his own life answer the straitness of his proceeding, it shall become him well; wherein if he chance to fail, he hath sentenced himself.

ESCALUS I am going to visit the prisoner. Fare you well.

412 Swounds **Come** The Duke's 'You'll forswear this again' implies that Lucio has sworn the truth of his slanders. In expurgated Shakespeare plays where the original text can be compared, 'Come' is used three times to substitute for 'Swounds'.

DUKE Peace be with you. [*Exit Escalus*]
O place and greatness, millions of false eyes
Are stuck upon thee; volumes of report
Run with these false and most contrarious quests
Upon thy doings; thousand escapes of wit
Make thee the father of their idle dream,
And rack thee in their fancies.
Enter Isabella
Very well met.
He who the sword of heaven will bear
Should be as holy as severe,
Pattern in himself to know,
Grace to stand, and virtue go,
More nor less to others paying
Than by self-offences weighing.
Shame to him whose cruel striking
Kills for faults of his own liking!
Twice treble shame on Angelo,
To weed my vice, and let his grow!
O, what may man within him hide,
Though angel on the outward side!
How may likeness made in crimes
Make my practice on the times
To draw with idle spiders' strings
Most ponderous and substantial things?
Craft against vice I must apply.
With Angelo tonight shall lie
His old betrothèd but despisèd.
So disguise shall, by th' disguisèd,
Pay with falsehood false exacting,
And perform an old contracting. *Exit*
Finis Actus Tertius

❁

Incipit Actus Quartus 4.1
Mariana and Boy singing [discovered]
Song

[BOY]
Take, O take those lips away
That so sweetly were forsworn,
And those eyes, the break of day
Lights that do mislead the morn;
But my kisses bring again, bring again,
Seals of love, though sealed in vain, sealed in vain.
Enter Duke, [disguised as a friar]

MARIANA
Break off thy song, and haste thee quick away.
Here comes a man of comfort, whose advice
Hath often stilled my brawling discontent.
[*Exit Boy*]
I cry you mercy, sir, and well could wish
You had not found me here so musical.
Let me excuse me, and believe me so:
My mirth it much displeased, but pleased my woe.

DUKE
'Tis good; though music oft hath such a charm
To make bad good, and good provoke to harm.
I pray you tell me, hath anybody enquired for me here today? Much upon this time have I promised here to meet.

MARIANA **You have not been enquired after; I have sat here all day.**
Enter Isabella

DUKE **I do constantly believe you; the time is come even now. I shall crave your forbearance a little. Maybe I will call upon you anon, for some advantage to yourself.**

MARIANA **I am always bound to you.** ***Exit***

513c **Run ... quests** JAGGARD's 'Run with these false, and most contrarious Quest' can be emended 'these' to 'their' or 'Quest' to 'quests'. The first alternative is accepted in the present edition where the speech is printed in the same place as in JAGGARD, at 4.1.60, so that 'their' refers to 'false eyes'. 'These' quests refers to Lucio's slanders; the reading therefore works much more persuasively given the envisaged position of the speech before the adaptation took place, as here, after the Duke's encounter with Lucio and conversation with Escalus about his reputation.

514–35 **He who ... contracting** JAGGARD prints the Duke's soliloquy 'He who the sword of heaven will bear' here, and the shorter 'O place and greatness' after 4.1.56. The adaptation probably introduced this arrangement by transposing the two speeches in the original text, to provide a longer and stronger close at the new act-break (see Introduction).

4.1 Before adaptation, the Duke would presumably have remained on stage, and the action would therefore have moved directly from his soliloquy to his meeting Isabella; Mariana would have first entered at 4.1.49.1. There would therefore have been no scene-break between the beginning of JAGGARD's 3.1 and the end of JAGGARD's 4.1.

1–6 **Take ... vain** The song seems to have been added as part of the adaptation. The second stanza in the composer John Wilson's manuscript, and similarly most other texts including *Rollo, Duke of Normandy*, reads:

> Hide, O hide those hills of snow
> That thy frozen bosom bears,
> On whose tops the pinks that grow
> Are yet of those that April wears;
> But first set my poor heart free,
> Bound in those icy chains by thee.

This makes it certain that the addressee is a woman, whereas in *Measure* the song expresses Mariana's feelings towards Angelo. For the dramatic technique, see Introduction; for a musical setting, see *Companion*, p. 167.

8–9 **Here ... discontent** Perhaps an inconsistency, as the Duke has evidently only recently assumed disguise as a friar.

8 **comfort** A key Middleton word and concept, often equivocating between the spiritual and the physical.

12–15 **so ... woe ... charm ... harm** Compare the rhyme-sequence 'show ... harm ... woe ... charm' in *Solomon* 13.97–100, where 'Striving to heal himself, did himself harm' has a similar thought and chiastic structure to 4.1.15.

14–18 **'Tis ... meet** The alternation between verse and prose within a single speech is Middletonian.

14–15 **music ... harm** Middleton repeatedly refers to the evil potential of music (see for instance *Witch* 5.2.82–6, commenting on *A charm song*, and *Ghost* 346–52).

22 **a little** Printed in JAGGARD as one word, as it also appears in works by Middleton.

Added

Transposed

Meaſure for Meaſure. 75

Actus Quartus. Scœna Prima.

Enter Mariana, and Boy ſinging.

Song. *Take, oh take thoſe lips away,*
that ſo ſweetly were forſworne,
And thoſe eyes: the breake of day
lights that doe miſlead the Morne;
But my kiſſes bring againe, bring againe,
Seales of loue, but ſeal'd in vaine, ſeal'd in vaine.

Enter Duke.

Mar. Breake off thy ſong, and haſte thee quick away,
Here comes a man of comfort, whoſe aduice
Hath often ſtill'd my brawling diſcontent.
I cry you mercie, Sir, and well could wiſh
You had not found me here ſo muſicall.
Let me excuſe me, and beleeue me ſo,
My mirth it much diſpleaſ'd, but pleaſ'd my woe.

Duk. 'Tis good; though Muſick oft hath ſuch a charme
To make bad, good; and good prouoake to harme.
I pray you tell me, hath any body enquir'd for mee here to day; much vpon this time haue I promiſ'd here to meete.

Mar. You haue not bin enquir'd after: I haue ſat here all day.

Enter Iſabell.

Duk. I doe conſtantly beleeue you: the time is come euen now. I ſhall craue your forbearance alittle, may be I will call vpon you anone for ſome aduantage to your ſelfe.

Mar. I am alwayes bound to you. *Exit.*

Duk. Very well met, and well come:
What is the newes from this good Deputie?

Iſab. He hath a Garden circummur'd with Bricke,
Whoſe weſterne ſide is with a Vineyard back't;
And to that Vineyard is a planched gate,
That makes his opening with this bigger Key:
This other doth command a little doore,
Which from the Vineyard to the Garden leades,
There haue I made my promiſe, vpon the
Heauy midle of the night, to call vpon him.

Duk. But ſhall you on your knowledge find this way?

Iſab. I haue t'ane a due, and wary note vpon't,
With whiſpering, and moſt guiltie diligence,
In action all of precept, he did ſhow me
The way twice ore.

Duk. Are there no other tokens
Betweene you 'greed, concerning her obſeruance?

Iſab. No: none but onely a repaire ith' darke,
And that I haue poſſeſt him, my moſt ſtay
Can be but briefe: for I haue made him know,
I haue a Seruant comes with me along
That ſtaies vpon me; whoſe perſwaſion is,
I come about my Brother.

Duk. 'Tis well borne vp.
I haue not yet made knowne to *Mariana*

Enter Mariana.

A word of this: what hoa, within; come forth,
I pray you be acquainted with this Maid,
She comes to doe you good.

Iſab. I doe deſire the like.

Duk. Do you perſwade your ſelfe that I reſpect you?

Mar. Good Frier, I know you do, and haue found it.

Duke. Take then this your companion by the hand
Who hath a ſtorie readie for your eare:
I ſhall attend your leiſure, but make haſte
The vaporous night approaches.

Mar. Wilt pleaſe you walke aſide. *Exit.*

Duke. Oh Place, and greatnes: millions of falſe eies
Are ſtucke vpon thee: volumes of report
Run with theſe falſe, and moſt contrarious Queſt
Vpon thy doings: thouſand eſcapes of wit
Make thee the father of their idle dreame,
And racke thee in their fancies. Welcome, how agreed?

Enter Mariana and Iſabella.

Iſab. Shee'll take the enterprize vpon her father,
If you aduiſe it.

Duke. It is not my conſent,
But my entreaty too.

Iſa. Little haue you to ſay
When you depart from him, but ſoft and low,
Remember now my brother.

Mar. Feare me not.

Duk. Nor gentle daughter, feare you not at all:
He is your husband on a pre-contract:
To bring you thus together 'tis no ſinne,
Sith that the Iuſtice of your title to him
Doth flouriſh the deceit. Come, let vs goe,
Our Corne's to reape, for yet our Tithes to ſow. *Exeunt.*

Scena Secunda.

Enter Prouoſt and Clowne.

Pro. Come hither ſirha; can you cut off a mans head?

Clo. If the man be a Bachelor Sir, I can:
But if he be a married man, he's his wiues head,
And I can neuer cut off a womans head.

Pro. Come ſir, leaue me your ſnatches, and yeeld mee a direct anſwere. To morrow morning are to die *Claudio* and *Barnardine*: heere is in our priſon a common executioner, who in his office lacks a helper, if you will take it on you to aſſiſt him, it ſhall redeeme you from your Gyues: if not, you ſhall haue your full time of impriſonment, and your deliuerance with an vnpittied whipping; for you haue beene a notorious bawd.

Clo. Sir, I haue beene an vnlawfull bawd, time out of minde, but yet I will bee content to be a lawfull hangman: I would bee glad to receiue ſome instruction from my fellow partner.

Pro. What hoa, *Abhorſon*: where's *Abhorſon* there?

Enter Abhorſon.

Abh. Doe you call ſir?

Pro. Sirha, here's a fellow will helpe you to morrow in your execution: if you thinke it meet, compound with him by the yeere, and let him abide here with you, if not, vſe him for the preſent, and diſmiſſe him, hee cannot plead his eſtimation with you: he hath beene a Bawd.

Abh. A Bawd Sir? fie vpon him, he will diſcredit our myſterie.

Pro. Goe too Sir, you waigh equallie: a feather will turne the Scale. *Exit.*

Clo. Pray ſir, by your good fauor: for ſurely ſir, a good fauor you haue, but that you haue a hanging look: Doe you call ſir, your occupation a Myſterie?

G 2 *Abh.* I,

Measure for Measure sig. G2, showing the added lines at the start of 4.1 and the lines transposed from 3.1

DUKE **Very well met, and welcome.**
What is the news from this good deputy?
ISABELLA He hath a garden circummured with brick,
Whose western side is with a vineyard backed;
And to that vineyard is a plankèd gate,
That makes his opening with this bigger key.
This other doth command a little door
Which from the vineyard to the garden leads.
There have I made my promise
Upon the heavy middle of the night
To call upon him.
DUKE
But shall you on your knowledge find this way?
ISABELLA
I have ta'en a due and wary note upon't.
With whispering and most guilty diligence,
In action all of precept, he did show me
The way twice o'er.
DUKE Are there no other tokens
Between you 'greed concerning her observance?
ISABELLA
No, none, but only a repair i'th' dark,
And that I have possessed him my most stay
Can be but brief, for I have made him know
I have a servant comes with me along
That stays upon me, whose persuasion is
I come about my brother.
DUKE 'Tis well borne up.
I have not yet made known to Mariana
A word of this.—What ho, within! Come forth!
Enter Mariana
[*To Mariana*] I pray you be acquainted with this maid.
She comes to do you good.
ISABELLA I do desire the like.
DUKE [*to Mariana*]
Do you persuade yourself that I respect you?
MARIANA
Good friar, I know you do, and so have found it.
DUKE
Take then this your companion by the hand,
Who hath a story ready for your ear.
I shall attend your leisure; but make haste,
The vaporous night approaches.
MARIANA [*to Isabella*] Will't please you walk aside?
Exit [*with Isabella*]
DUKE
He who the sword of heaven will bear
Should be as holy as severe,
Pattern in himself to know,
Grace to stand, and virtue go,
More nor less to others paying
Than by self-offences weighing.
Shame to him whose cruel striking
Kills for faults of his own liking!
Twice treble shame on Angelo,
To weed my vice, and let his grow!
O, what may man within him hide,
Though angel on the outward side!
How may likeness made in crimes
Make my practice on the times
To draw with idle spiders' strings
Most ponderous and substantial things?
Craft against vice I must apply.
With Angelo tonight shall lie
His old betrothed but despisèd.
So disguise shall, by th' disguisèd,
Pay with falsehood false exacting,
And perform an old contracting.
DUKE
O place and greatness, millions of false eyes
Are stuck upon thee; volumes of report
Run with their false and most contrarious quest
Upon thy doings; thousand escapes of wit
Make thee the father of their idle dream,
And rack thee in their fancies.
Enter Mariana and Isabella
Welcome. How agreed?
ISABELLA
She'll take the enterprise upon her, father,
If you advise it.
DUKE It is not my consent,
But my entreaty too.
ISABELLA [*to Mariana*]
Little have you to say
When you depart from him but, soft and low,
'Remember now my brother'.
MARIANA Fear me not.
DUKE
Nor, gentle daughter, fear you not at all.
He is your husband on a pre-contract.
To bring you thus together 'tis no sin,
Sith that the justice of your title to him
Doth flourish the deceit. Come, let us go.
Our corn's to reap, for yet our tilth's to sow. *Exeunt*

Sc. 11 **4.2** 4.2

Enter Provost and Clown

PROVOST Come hither, sirrah. Can you cut off a man's head?

CLOWN If the man be a bachelor, sir, I can; but if he be a married man, he's his wife's head, and I can never cut off a woman's head.

PROVOST Come, sir, leave me your snatches, and yield me a direct answer. Tomorrow morning are to die Claudio and Barnardine. Here is in our prison a common executioner, who in his office lacks a helper. If you will take it on you to assist him, it shall redeem you from your gyves; if not, you shall have your full time of imprisonment, and your deliverance with an unpitied whipping; for you have been a notorious bawd.

25 **and welcome** The words are metrically redundant, and the half-pun 'wel met... welcome (well come)' is a characteristic Middleton tick.

57a–4.1.63 **He...fancies** See note to 3.1.514–35.

60 **their...quest** See note to 3.1.513c.

CLOWN Sir, I have been an unlawful bawd time out of mind, but yet I will be content to be a lawful hangman. I would be glad to receive some instruction from my fellow partner.

PROVOST What ho, Abhorson! Where's Abhorson there?

Enter Abhorson

ABHORSON Do you call, sir?

PROVOST Sirrah, here's a fellow will help you tomorrow in your execution. If you think it meet, compound with him by the year, and let him abide here with you; if not, use him for the present, and dismiss him. He cannot plead his estimation with you; he hath been a bawd.

ABHORSON A bawd, sir? Fie upon him, he will discredit our mystery.

PROVOST Go to, sir, you weigh equally; a feather will turn the scale. *Exit*

CLOWN Pray, sir, by your good favour—for surely, sir, a good favour you have, but that you have a hanging look—do you call, sir, your occupation a mystery?

ABHORSON Ay, sir, a mystery.

CLOWN Painting, sir, I have heard say is a mystery; and your whores, sir, being members of my occupation, using painting, do prove my occupation a mystery. But what mystery there should be in hanging, if I should be hanged I cannot imagine.

ABHORSON Sir, it is a mystery.

CLOWN Proof.

ABHORSON Every true man's apparel fits your thief—

CLOWN If it be too little for your thief, your true man thinks it big enough. If it be too big for your thief, your thief thinks it little enough. So every true man's apparel fits your thief.

Enter Provost

PROVOST Are you agreed?

CLOWN Sir, I will serve him, for I do find your hangman is a more penitent trade than your bawd—he doth oftener ask forgiveness.

PROVOST [*to Abhorson*] You, sirrah, provide your block and your axe tomorrow, four o'clock.

ABHORSON [*to Clown*] Come on, bawd, I will instruct thee in my trade. Follow.

CLOWN I do desire to learn, sir, and I hope, if you have occasion to use me for your own turn, you shall find me yare. For truly, sir, for your kindness I owe you a good turn.

PROVOST
Call hither Barnardine and Claudio.
Exit [Clown with Abhorson]
Th'one has my pity; not a jot the other,
Being a murderer, though he were my brother.

Enter Claudio

Look, here's the warrant, Claudio, for thy death.
'Tis now dead midnight, and by eight tomorrow
Thou must be made immortal. Where's Barnardine?

CLAUDIO
As fast locked up in sleep as guiltless labour
When it lies starkly in the travailer's bones.
He will not wake.

PROVOST Who can do good on him?
Well, go prepare yourself.
[*Knocking within*]
But hark, what noise?
God **Heaven** give your spirits comfort! [*Exit Claudio*]
[*Knocking again*]
By and by!
I hope it is some pardon or reprieve
For the most gentle Claudio.

Enter Duke, [disguised as a friar]

Welcome, father.

DUKE
The best and wholesom'st spirits of the night
Envelop you, good Provost! Who called here of late?

PROVOST None since the curfew rung.

DUKE Not Isabel?

PROVOST No.

DUKE They will then, ere't be long.

PROVOST What comfort is for Claudio?

DUKE There's some in hope.

PROVOST It is a bitter deputy.

DUKE
Not so, not so; his life is paralleled
Even with the stroke and line of his great justice.
He doth with holy abstinence subdue
That in himself which he spurs on his power
To qualify in others. Were he mealed with that
Which he corrects, then were he tyrannous;
But this being so, he's just.
[*Knocking within*]
Now are they come.
[*Provost goes to a door*]
This is a gentle Provost. Seldom when
The steelèd jailer is the friend of men.
[*Knocking within*]
[*To Provost*] How now, what noise? That spirit's possessed with haste
That wounds th'unlisting postern with these strokes.

PROVOST
There he must stay until the officer
Arise to let him in. He is called up.

DUKE
Have you no countermand for Claudio yet,
But he must die tomorrow?

PROVOST None, sir, none.

DUKE
As near the dawning, Provost, as it is,
You shall hear more ere morning.

PROVOST Happily
You something know, yet I believe there comes
No countermand. No such example have we;
Besides, upon the very siege of justice
Lord Angelo hath to the public ear
Professed the contrary.

4.2.67 God **Heaven** See note to 2.2.36.

Enter a Messenger

This is his lordship's man.

DUKE And here comes Claudio's pardon.

MESSENGER [*giving a paper to Provost*] My lord hath sent you this note, and by me this further charge: that you swerve not from the smallest article of it, neither in time, matter, or other circumstance. Good morrow; for, as I take it, it is almost day.

PROVOST I shall obey him. *Exit Messenger*

DUKE [*aside*] This is his pardon, purchased by such sin
For which the pardoner himself is in.
Hence hath offence his quick celerity,
When it is borne in high authority.
When vice makes mercy, mercy's so extended
That for the fault's love is th'offender friended.—
Now sir, what news?

PROVOST I told you: Lord Angelo, belike thinking me remiss in mine office, awakens me with this unwonted putting-on; methinks strangely, for he hath not used it before.

DUKE Pray you let's hear.

The letter

PROVOST [*reading*] 'Whatsoever you may hear to the contrary, let Claudio be executed by four of the clock, and in the afternoon Barnardine. For my better satisfaction, let me have Claudio's head sent me by five. Let this be duly performed, with a thought that more depends on it than we must yet deliver. Thus fail not to do your office, as you will answer it at your peril.'
What say you to this, sir?

DUKE What is that Barnardine, who is to be executed in th'afternoon?

PROVOST A Bohemian born, **but here nursed up and bred**; one that is a prisoner nine years old.

DUKE How came it that the absent Duke had not either delivered him to his liberty or executed him? I have heard it was ever his manner to do so.

PROVOST His friends still wrought reprieves for him; and indeed his fact, till now in the government of Lord Angelo, came not to an undoubtful proof.

DUKE It is now apparent?

PROVOST Most manifest, and not denied by himself.

DUKE Hath he borne himself penitently in prison? How seems he to be touched?

PROVOST A man that apprehends death no more dreadfully but as a drunken sleep; careless, reckless, and fearless of what's past, present, or to come; insensible of mortality, and desperately mortal.

DUKE He wants advice.

PROVOST He will hear none. He hath evermore had the liberty of the prison. Give him leave to escape hence, he would not. Drunk many times a day, if not many days entirely drunk. We have very oft awaked him as if to carry him to execution, and showed him a seeming warrant for it; it hath not moved him at all.

DUKE More of him anon. There is written in your brow, Provost, honesty and constancy. If I read it not truly, my ancient skill beguiles me. But in the boldness of my cunning, I will lay myself in hazard. Claudio, whom here you have warrant to execute, is no greater forfeit to the law than Angelo who hath sentenced him. To make you understand this in a manifested effect, I crave but four days' respite, for the which you are to do me both a present and a dangerous courtesy.

PROVOST Pray sir, in what?

DUKE In the delaying death.

PROVOST Alack, how may I do it, having the hour limited, and an express command under penalty to deliver his head in the view of Angelo? I may make my case as Claudio's to cross this in the smallest.

DUKE By the vow of mine order, I warrant you, if my instructions may be your guide, let this Barnardine be this morning executed, and his head borne to Angelo.

PROVOST Angelo hath seen them both, and will discover the favour.

DUKE **O, death's a great disguiser, and you may add to it**. Shave the head and tie the beard, and say it was the desire of the penitent to be so bared before his death; you know the course is common. If anything fall to you upon this more than thanks and good fortune, by the saint whom I profess, I will plead against it with my life.

PROVOST Pardon me, good father, it is against my oath.

DUKE Were you sworn to the Duke or to the deputy?

120.1 ***The letter*** The same heading is used in the autograph Trinity manuscript of *Game at Chess* at 2.1.15 and 3.1.33.

131 **but...bred** *Bohemian* potentially relates to the location in Vienna and the references to the Thirty Years War. King James's son-in-law Ferdinand and daughter Elizabeth were crowned King and Queen of Bohemia in 1619; their forces were decisively beaten at the Battle of the White Mountain, near Prague, in 1620. It is perhaps possible that in the original version of the play Barnardine was an inhabitant of somewhere else, closer to Italy. A Switzer, for instance, might be thought of as wearing a grisly beard, rough dress, and a large codpiece (Sugden, p. 495). However, in the light of English support for Protestant Bohemia in 1621, it seems unlikely that the revision of *Measure* would turn the dissolute and anti-religious Barnardine into a Bohemian. Indeed it is the comment 'but here nursed up and bred' that might have been added, in order to distance Barnardine from Bohemia. In a text without sensitivity to the religious politics of 1621, this qualification curiously neutralizes the point about Barnardine's origin. In 1603–4, 'a Bohemian born', without such qualification, would have offered a simple implied explanation of Barnardine's barbarity. In 1621, 'a Bohemian born, but here nursed up and bred' might have suggested, contrariwise, that despite his birth in a good Protestant country Barnardine had been debauched by his upbringing in Catholic and dissolute Vienna. Shakespeare never used the expression *nurse up*, but Middleton did (*Solomon* 6.85).

174 **O...it** Possibly added by Middleton, the only dramatist in the period elsewhere to use *disguiser* (Holdsworth, private communication). In *Tennis*, Persons.15, it is again alliterative and personifying: 'Deceit, the disguiser'. Compare 'great disguiser' with 4.3.17, 'great doers', in a nearby speech that is attributed to Middleton and that accentuates death.

PROVOST To him and to his substitutes.

DUKE You will think you have made no offence if the Duke avouch the justice of your dealing?

PROVOST But what likelihood is in that?

DUKE Not a resemblance, but a certainty. Yet since I see you fearful, that neither my coat, integrity, nor persuasion can with ease attempt you, I will go further than I meant, to pluck all fears out of you. [*Showing a letter*] Look you, sir, here is the hand and seal of the Duke. You know the character, I doubt not, and the signet is not strange to you?

PROVOST I know them both.

DUKE The contents of this is the return of the Duke. You shall anon over-read it at your pleasure, where you shall find within these two days he will be here. This is a thing that Angelo knows not, for he this very day receives letters of strange tenor, perchance of the Duke's death, perchance entering into some monastery; but by chance nothing of what is writ. Look, th'unfolding star calls up the shepherd. Put not yourself into amazement how these things should be. All difficulties are but easy when they are known. Call your executioner, and off with Barnardine's head. I will give him a present shrift, and advise him for a better place. Yet you are amazed; but this shall absolutely resolve you. Come away, it is almost clear dawn. *Exit* [*with Provost*]

4.3

Enter Clown

CLOWN **I am as well acquainted here as I was in our house of profession. One would think it were Mistress Overdone's own house, for here be many of her old customers. First, here's young Master Rash; he's in for a commodity of brown paper and old ginger, nine score and seventeen pounds, of which he made five marks ready money. Marry, then ginger was not much in request, for the old women were all dead. Then is there here one Master Caper, at the suit of Master Threepile the mercer, for some four suits of peach-coloured satin, which now peaches him a beggar. Then have we here**

4.3.1–18 **I . . . sake** This survey of the former brothel-customers who are now prison inmates (mostly disreputable young gentlemen rather than professional criminals) seems to belong to the adaptation. See Introduction. In the following notes the phrase is not found in Shakespeare unless noted otherwise. Neutral evidence is not mentioned.

1 **as well acquainted here** Compare *Owl* 18–19, 'as well acquainted'; *Roaring Girl* 3.18, 'familiarly acquainted there'.

2 **One would think** Found in *Trick* 1.1.141, *Phoenix* 10.64.

2–4 **One . . . customers** For the sequence '[a woman's] own . . . many of her old customers', compare *Women Beware* 1.1.92–3: 'Not the licentious swinge of *her own* will, | Like *some of her old* schoolfellows'. For 'own . . . old' collocated with a derivative of 'acquaint' and a metonymic form of 'our house', referring to a brothel, compare *Patient Man* 6.303–4, 'If yourself like *our roof*, such as it is, | Your *own acquaintance* may be as *old* as his'.

4 **First, here's** A similar catalogue occurs in *His Lordship's Entertainment*, where a descriptive list of artisans is 'read in the clerk's book' (66); it begins 'First, here's . . . ' (there 'are six hundred more' in the clerk's book; compare 17). 'First, here's', found nowhere in Shakespeare, occurs also at *Dissemblers* 4.2.165; compare too *Five Gallants* 5.1.136, 'first here be'. The listing of imaginary characters could be based on a stage property, 'the book where all the prisoners' names stand' (*Roaring Girl* 7.154).

young Master Rash The phrase and name-type resemble *Michaelmas* 1.2.43 and 118, 'Young Master Easy'.

4–6 **for . . . pounds** Similar in thought and phrasing to *Quiet Life* 1.1.97–9, '*For* tissue, cloth of gold, velvets and silks, about fifteen hundred *pounds*. | Your *money* is *ready*'. The phrase 'a commodity of brown paper and old ginger' is very strongly paralleled in *Michaelmas* 2.3.219–20, 'commodities in hawks' hoods and brown paper'. Other collocations of *commodity* with other words in the passage occur in '*Here's* a coil for a *dead commodity*.— 'Sfoot, *women* when they are alive are but *dead commodities*' (*Patient Man* 1.91–2; scene perhaps of mixed authorship); *Michaelmas* 2.3.202–3, '*a commodity of* two hundred *pounds*' worth of cloth'; *Mad World* 2.6.54–5, 'the *commodity of* keeping open *house*'. The sum 'nine score and seventeen pounds' is echoed in *Lady* 2.3.5, 'three *score and seventeen*'. Shakespeare never has a sum amounting to a *score and* over.

6 **five marks** Also in *Penniless Parliament* 44 and *Five Gallants* 1.1.296.

7 **ready money** Also in *Penniless Parliament* 93, *Michaelmas* 2.3.233, and *Quiet Life* 4.1.14.

7–8 **then ginger was not much in request** Compare *Quarrel* 2.2.232, 'then was wrestling in request'; *Owl* 1722–3, 'finally . . . much in request . . . because'; also *Old Law* 3.1.135, 'were never in more request', repeated at 139–40, where the phrase is collocated with 'commodities' (144). 'Not much in' occurs at *Game of Chess* 1.1.128.

9 **Master Caper** A similar dancing name is 'Signor Cinquepace', *Dissemblers* 5.1.92.

9–10 **Master Threepile the mercer** *Mercer* is common in Middleton but not found in Shakespeare. More specific parallels are *Michaelmas* 2.1.84, 'Master Gum, the mercer', and 2.3.152, 'Master Gum or Master Profit, the mercer'. *Three-piled* in *Measure* at 1.2.32 gives a specific cross-reference to another adapted passage.

10 **peach-coloured satin** 'Peach-coloured' occurs in *2 Henry IV* 2.2.14, referring to silk stockings. But compare *Five Gallants* 3.4.162, '*peach colour* . . . watchet *satin*'; *Michaelmas* 4.1.81, 'peach-colour'; *Patient Man* 8.33–4, 'flame-*coloured* doublet, red *satin* hose'.

11 **peaches him** Middleton uses the verb transitively in *Phoenix* 15.249, 'peach 'em'. It is only intransitive in Shakespeare.

12 **Dizzy** Shakespeare does not use the word disparagingly to characterize a giddy-minded person. Middleton does so in *Mad World* 5.2.113–14, '*dizzy constables*', and *Phoenix* 2.156, 'dizzy pates of fifteen attorneys'.

Deepvow Middleton has 'deep oath' (*Nice Valour* 2.1.165). His references to *deep* pledges repeatedly imply that they were made while the participants were drinking deeply (*Revenger* 1.2.180 and *No Wit* 9.563, 'deep healths'; *Patient Man* 5.160, 'I'll pledge them deep'; *Witch* 2.1.202–4, 'We'll have one health . . . Ay, sir, a deep one, | Which you shall pledge too'), and there is a similar cynical connotation here. As a character name, 'Master Deepvow' can be compared with 'Corporal Oath' in *Puritan*.

12–13 **Master Copperspur** In *Meeting* there is a character similarly called Signor Jinglespur.

13 **Starve-lackey** Compare *Hengist* 1.3.204, 'starve the guard'. A role in *Phoenix* is that of 'Lackey'.

13–14 **rapier and dagger man** This compares closely with *Phoenix*, 9.186, 'rapier and dagger men'.

young Dizzy, and young Master Deepvow, and Master Copperspur and Master Starve-lackey the rapier and dagger man, and young Drop-heir that killed lusty Pudding, and Master Torchlight the tilter, and brave Master Shoe-tie the great traveller, and wild Half-can that stabbed Pots, and I think forty more, all great doers in our trade, and are now 'for the Lord's sake'.

Sc. 12

Enter Abhorson and Clown

ABHORSON Sirrah, bring Barnardine hither.

CLOWN Master Barnardine! You must rise and be hanged, Master Barnardine!

ABHORSON What ho, Barnardine!

BARNARDINE (*within*) A pox o' your throats! Who makes that noise there? What are you?

CLOWN Your friends, sir; the hangman. You must be so good, sir, to rise and be put to death.

BARNARDINE Away, you rogue, away! I am sleepy.

ABHORSON Tell him he must awake, and that quickly too.

CLOWN Pray, Master Barnardine, awake till you are executed, and sleep afterwards.

ABHORSON Go in to him and fetch him out.

CLOWN He is coming, sir, he is coming. I hear his straw rustle.

ABHORSON Is the axe upon the block, sirrah?

CLOWN Very ready, sir.

Enter Barnardine

BARNARDINE How now, Abhorson, what's the news with you?

ABHORSON Truly, sir, I would desire you to clap into your prayers, for, look you, the warrant's come.

BARNARDINE You rogue, I have been drinking all night. I am not fitted for't.

CLOWN O, the better, sir; for he that drinks all night, and is hanged betimes in the morning, may sleep the sounder all the next day.

Enter Duke, [disguised as a friar]

ABHORSON [*to Barnardine*] Look you, sir, here comes your ghostly father. Do we jest now, think you?

DUKE [*to Barnardine*] Sir, induced by my charity, and hearing how hastily you are to depart, I am come to advise you, comfort you, and pray with you.

BARNARDINE Friar, not I. I have been drinking hard all night, and I will have more time to prepare me, or they shall beat out my brains with billets. I will not consent to die this day, that's certain.

DUKE
O sir, you must; and therefore, I beseech you,
Look forward on the journey you shall go.

BARNARDINE Fore God, **I swear** I will not die today, for any man's persuasion.

DUKE But hear you—

BARNARDINE Not a word. If you have anything to say to me, come to my ward, for thence will not I today. *Exit*

DUKE
Unfit to live or die. O gravel heart!
After him, fellows; bring him to the block.
[Exeunt Abhorson and Clown]

14 **young Drop-heir** Compare *Michaelmas* 1.2.287–8, 'to shame my blood, | And *drop* my staining birth'; also 'young heir', *Hengist* 5.1.126 and five instances in *Women Beware*: 'lawful heirs' (1.2.79), 'Now, young heir!' (2.2.79), 'the young heir his ward' (2.2.173), 'this young heir' (3.2.113), and 'young heir' (3.2.176).

14–15 **Drop-heir ... Pudding** Elements of the two names combine in *Quarrel* 4.1.221, 'thy pudding drop' (Rowley). 'Lusty Pudding' compares with another character named after a pudding, Captain Plumporridge in *Heroes*; he is described as 'lusty' at 56.

15 **Master Torchlight the tilter** Middleton never elsewhere uses the word *tilter*, but there is a character in *Roaring Girl* called Master Tiltyard, and *Tilting* has an explicit sexual connotation in that play at 7.35 and 9.173. *Tilter* itself has a sexual innuendo in Webster: *White Devil* 3.1.13, *Westward Ho!* 3.4.77, *Northward Ho!* 3.1.7.

Torchlight The misprint 'Forthlight' is usually emended to non-Middletonian 'Forthright'. The emended phrase favours Shakespeare's authorship, in that he elsewhere uses *forthright* whereas Middleton does not. But the reading is at least as likely to have been the Middletonian and alliterative 'Torchlight', which conjures up a figure of flaming and smoky temper, and perhaps suggests that his form of tilting involves sexual debauchery (specifically at court) of a kind Middleton elsewhere associates with torchlight. 'Torchlight' would be a valid and perhaps preferable alternative reading in any context, and is certainly to be preferred in the context of Middleton. Compare other character names that are compounded and have connotations of fire, such as Touchwood (again with a sexual implication), and Firestone.

16 **the great traveller** Compare *Mad World* 5.2.11, 'great travellers'.

16–17 **Half-can ... Pots** Elements of these two drinking names combine in *Roaring Girl* 2.211, 'drink half-pots'.

17 **and I think forty** The phrase 'and I think' immediately followed by a number occurs in *Quiet Life* 5.2.78–8, 'and I think two'—near 'all' and '*trades*man'.

forty more Also at *Women Beware* 1.3.51.

17–18 **all ... sake'** For the summative *all* followed by *our trade* followed by a quotation of the appropriate catchphrase, compare *Michaelmas* 2.3.462–5: 'they're *all* willing to, because 'tis good for *our trade* ... and indeed 'tis the fittest for a citizen's son, for our word is, "What do ye lack?"'. There are no instances of *our trade* in Shakespeare.

17 **great doers** John Davies of Hereford describes 'two queans' as 'good doers' in *Wit's Bedlam* (1617), Epi. 315. Middleton writes of the 'doings' in the trade of prostitution at *Black Book* 212–13 (punning on *undone*) and *Widow* 4.2.24. The latter occurs in a set-piece soliloquy in which a criminal (the thief Latrocinio) describes how his various victims are tricked into coming to him 'here i' my chamber', and is collocated with other phrases recalling Pompey's speech: '*all trades* ... have their *dead* time' (21–2), 'his trade' (29), and 'travellers' (21). The soliloquy in *Widow* correlates the effect of poverty on thieving and prostitution, and so offers an analogue also to the Bawd's speech at 1.2.77–9.

56 Fore God, **I swear** 'I swear' is unexpectedly tame for a man of Barnardine's temperament, and probably results from expurgation.

Enter Provost

PROVOST
Now, sir, how do you find the prisoner?

DUKE
A creature unprepared, unmeet for death;
And to transport him in the mind he is
Were damnable.

PROVOST Here in the prison, father,
There died this morning of a cruel fever
One Ragusine, a most notorious pirate,
A man of Claudio's years, his beard and head
Just of his colour. What if we do omit
This reprobate till he were well inclined,
And satisfy the deputy with the visage
Of Ragusine, more like to Claudio?

DUKE
O, 'tis an accident that heaven provides.
Dispatch it presently; the hour draws on
Prefixed by Angelo. See this be done,
And sent according to command, whiles I
Persuade this rude wretch willingly to die.

PROVOST
This shall be done, good father, presently.
But Barnardine must die this afternoon;
And how shall we continue Claudio,
To save me from the danger that might come
If he were known alive?

DUKE Let this be done:
Put them in secret holds, both Barnardine and Claudio.
Ere twice the sun hath made his journal greeting
To yonder generation, you shall find
Your safety manifested.

PROVOST I am your free dependant.

DUKE
Quick, dispatch, and send the head to Angelo.
Exit [*Provost*]
Now will I write letters to Angelo—
The Provost, he shall bear them—whose contents
Shall witness to him I am near at home,
And that by great injunctions I am bound
To enter publicly. Him I'll desire
To meet me at the consecrated fount
A league below the city, and from thence,
By cold gradation and well-balanced form,
We shall proceed with Angelo.

Enter Provost, [with Ragusine's head]

PROVOST
Here is the head; I'll carry it myself.

DUKE
Convenient is it. Make a swift return,
For I would commune with you of such things
That want no ear but yours.

PROVOST I'll make all speed. *Exit*

ISABELLA (*within*) Peace, ho, be here!

DUKE
The tongue of Isabel. She's come to know
If yet her brother's pardon be come hither;
But I will keep her ignorant of her good,
To make her heavenly comforts of despair
When it is least expected.

ISABELLA [*within*] Ho, by your leave!

Enter Isabella

DUKE
Good morning to you, fair and gracious daughter.

ISABELLA
The better, given me by so holy a man.
Hath yet the deputy sent my brother's pardon?

DUKE
He hath released him, Isabel, from the world.
His head is off and sent to Angelo.

ISABELLA
Nay, but it is not so.

DUKE It is no other.
Show your wisdom, daughter, in your close patience.

ISABELLA
O, I will to him and pluck out his eyes!

DUKE
You shall not be admitted to his sight.

ISABELLA [*weeping*]
Unhappy Claudio! Wretched Isabel!
Injurious world! Most damnèd Angelo!

DUKE
This nor hurts him, nor profits you a jot.
Forbear it, therefore; give your cause to heaven.
Mark what I say, which you shall find
By every syllable a faithful verity.
The Duke comes home tomorrow—nay, dry your eyes—
One of our convent, and his cònfessor,
Gives me this instance. Already he hath carried
Notice to Escalus and Angelo,
Who do prepare to meet him at the gates,
There to give up their power. If you can pace your wisdom
In that good path that I would wish it go,
And you shall have your bosom on this wretch,
Grace of the Duke, revenges to your heart,
And general honour.

ISABELLA I am directed by you.

DUKE
This letter, then, to Friar Peter give.
'Tis that he sent me of the Duke's return.
Say by this token I desire his company
At Mariana's house tonight. Her cause and yours
I'll perfect him withal, and he shall bring you
Before the Duke, and to the head of Angelo
Accuse him home and home. For my poor self,
I am combinèd by a sacred vow,
And shall be absent. [*Giving the letter*] Wend you with this letter.
Command these fretting waters from your eyes
With a light heart. Trust not my holy order
If I pervert your course.

Enter Lucio

Who's here?

LUCIO Good even.
Friar, where's the Provost?

DUKE Not within, sir.

LUCIO O pretty Isabella, I am pale at mine heart to see thine eyes so red. Thou must be patient. I am fain to dine and sup with water and bran; I dare not for my head fill my belly; one fruitful meal would set me to't. But they say the Duke will be here tomorrow. By my troth, Isabel, I loved thy brother. If the old fantastical Duke of dark corners had been at home, he had lived. *[Exit Isabella]*

DUKE Sir, the Duke is marvellous little beholden to your reports; but the best is, he lives not in them.

LUCIO Friar, thou knowest not the Duke so well as I do. He's a better woodman than thou tak'st him for.

DUKE Well, you'll answer this one day. Fare ye well.

LUCIO Nay, tarry, I'll go along with thee. I can tell thee pretty tales of the Duke.

DUKE You have told me too many of him already, sir, if they be true; if not true, none were enough.

LUCIO I was once before him for getting a wench with child.

DUKE Did you such a thing?

LUCIO Fore God **Yes, marry**, did I; but I was fain to forswear it. They would else have married me to the rotten medlar.

DUKE Sir, your company is fairer than honest. Rest you well.

LUCIO By my troth, I'll go with thee to the lane's end. If bawdy talk offend you, we'll have very little of it. Nay, friar, I am a kind of burr; I shall stick. *Exeunt*

Sc. 13 **4.4** 4.4

Enter Angelo and Escalus

ESCALUS Every letter he hath writ hath disvouched other.

ANGELO In most uneven and distracted manner. His actions show much like to madness. Pray God **heaven** his wisdom be not tainted. And why meet him at the gates, and redeliver our authorities there?

ESCALUS I guess not.

ANGELO And why should we proclaim it in an hour before his entering, that if any crave redress of injustice, they should exhibit their petitions in the street?

ESCALUS He shows his reason for that—to have a dispatch of complaints, and to deliver us from devices hereafter, which shall then have no power to stand against us.

ANGELO
Well, I beseech you let it be proclaimed.
Betimes i'th' morn I'll call you at your house.
Give notice to such men of sort and suit
As are to meet him.

ESCALUS I shall, sir. Fare you well.

ANGELO Good night. *Exit [Escalus]*
This deed unshapes me quite, makes me unpregnant
And dull to all proceedings. A deflowered maid,
And by an eminent body that enforced
The law against it! But that her tender shame
Will not proclaim against her maiden loss,
How might she tongue me! Yet reason dares her no,
For my authority bears off a credent bulk,
That no particular scandal once can touch
But it confounds the breather. He should have lived,
Save that his riotous youth, with dangerous sense,
Might in the times to come have ta'en revenge
By so receiving a dishonoured life
With ransom of such shame. Would yet he had lived.
Alack, when once our grace we have forgot,
Nothing goes right; we would, and we would not.
Exit

Sc. 14 **4.5** 4.5

Enter Duke, [in his own habit,] and Friar Peter

DUKE
These letters at fit time deliver me.
The Provost knows our purpose and our plot.
The matter being afoot, keep your instruction,
And hold you ever to our special drift,
Though sometimes you do blench from this to that
As cause doth minister. Go call at Flavio's house,
And tell him where I stay. Give the like notice
To Valentinus, Rowland, and to Crassus,
And bid them bring the trumpets to the gate.
But send me Flavius first.

FRIAR PETER It shall be speeded well.
[Exit]

Enter Varrius

DUKE
I thank thee, Varrius; thou hast made good haste.
Come, we will walk. There's other of our friends
Will greet us here anon. My gentle Varrius! *Exeunt*

Sc. 15 **4.6** 4.6

Enter Isabella and Mariana

ISABELLA
To speak so indirectly I am loath—
I would say the truth, but to accuse him so,
That is your part—yet I am advised to do it,
He says, to veil full purpose.

MARIANA Be ruled by him.

ISABELLA
Besides, he tells me that if peradventure
He speak against me on the adverse side,
I should not think it strange, for 'tis a physic
That's bitter to sweet end.

Enter Friar Peter

MARIANA I would Friar Peter—

ISABELLA O, peace; the friar is come.

166 Fore God **Yes, marry** The Duke later says 'I have heard him swear himself there's one | Whom he begot with child' (5.1.509–10). A strong profanity seems required.

4.4.3 God **heaven** See note to 2.2.128.

FRIAR PETER
Come, I have found you out a stand most fit,
Where you may have such vantage on the Duke
He shall not pass you. Twice have the trumpets sounded.
The generous and gravest citizens
Have hent the gates, and very near upon
The Duke is ent'ring; therefore hence, away. *Exeunt*
Finis Actus Quartus

5.1 *Sc. 16* ***5.1***
Incipit Actus Quintus
Enter Duke, Varrius, lords; Angelo, Escalus, Lucio, citizens; at several doors

DUKE [*to Angelo*]
My very worthy cousin, fairly met.
[*To Escalus*] Our old and faithful friend, we are glad to see you.

ANGELO *and* ESCALUS
Happy return be to your royal grace.

DUKE
Many and hearty thankings to you both.
We have made enquiry of you, and we hear
Such goodness of your justice that our soul
Cannot but yield you forth to public thanks,
Forerunning more requital.

ANGELO
You make my bonds still greater.

DUKE
O, your desert speaks loud, and I should wrong it
To lock it in the wards of covert bosom,
When it deserves with characters of brass
A forted residence 'gainst the tooth of time
And razure of oblivion. Give me your hand,
And let the subject see, to make them know
That outward courtesies would fain proclaim
Favours that keep within. Come, Escalus,
You must walk by us on our other hand,
And good supporters are you.
[*They walk forward.*]
Enter Friar Peter and Isabella

FRIAR PETER
Now is your time. Speak loud, and kneel before him.

ISABELLA [*kneeling*]
Justice, O royal Duke! Vail your regard
Upon a wronged—I would fain have said, a maid.
O worthy prince, dishonour not your eye
By throwing it on any other object,
Till you have heard me in my true complaint,
And given me justice, justice, justice, justice!

DUKE
Relate your wrongs. In what? By whom? Be brief.
Here is Lord Angelo shall give you justice.
Reveal yourself to him.

ISABELLA
O worthy Duke,
You bid me seek redemption of the devil.
Hear me yourself, for that which I must speak
Must either punish me, not being believed,
Or wring redress from you. Hear me, O hear me, hear!

ANGELO
My lord, her wits, I fear me, are not firm.
She hath been a suitor to me for her brother,
Cut off by course of justice.

ISABELLA [*standing*]
By course of justice!

ANGELO
And she will speak most bitterly and strange.

ISABELLA
Most strange, but yet most truly, will I speak.
That Angelo's forsworn, is it not strange?
That Angelo's a murderer, is't not strange?
That Angelo is an adulterous thief,
An hypocrite, a virgin-violator,
Is it not strange, and strange?

DUKE
Nay, it is ten times strange!

ISABELLA
It is not truer he is Angelo
Than this is all as true as it is strange.
Nay, it is ten times true, for truth is truth
To th' end of reck'ning.

DUKE
Away with her. Poor soul,
She speaks this in th'infirmity of sense.

ISABELLA
O prince, I conjure thee, as thou believ'st
There is another comfort than this world,
That thou neglect me not with that opinion
That I am touched with madness. Make not impossible
That which but seems unlike. 'Tis not impossible
But one, the wicked'st caitiff on the ground,
May seem as shy, as grave, as just, as absolute,
As Angelo; even so may Angelo,
In all his dressings, characts, titles, forms,
Be an arch-villain. Believe it, royal prince,
If he be less, he's nothing; but he's more,
Had I more name for badness.

DUKE
By mine honesty,
If she be mad, as I believe no other,
Her madness hath the oddest frame of sense,
Such a dependency of thing on thing
As e'er I heard in madness.

ISABELLA
O gracious Duke,
Harp not on that, nor do not banish reason
For inequality; but let your reason serve
To make the truth appear where it seems hid,
And hide the false seems true.

DUKE
Many that are not mad
Have sure more lack of reason. What would you say?

ISABELLA
I am the sister of one Claudio,
Condemned upon the act of fornication
To lose his head, condemned by Angelo.
I, in probation of a sisterhood,
Was sent to by my brother, one Lucio
As then the messenger.

LUCIO
That's I, an't like your grace.

I came to her from Claudio, and desired her
To try her gracious fortune with Lord Angelo
For her poor brother's pardon.

ISABELLA
That's he indeed.

DUKE [*to Lucio*]
You were not bid to speak.

LUCIO
No, my good lord,
Nor wished to hold my peace.

DUKE
I wish you now, then. Pray you take note of it;
And when you have a business for yourself,
Pray God **heaven** you then be perfect.

LUCIO
I warrant your honour.

DUKE
The warrant's for yourself; take heed to't.

ISABELLA
This gentleman told somewhat of my tale—

LUCIO Right.

DUKE
It may be right, but you are i' the wrong
To speak before your time. [*To Isabella*] Proceed.

ISABELLA
I went
To this pernicious caitiff deputy—

DUKE
That's somewhat madly spoken.

ISABELLA
Pardon it;
The phrase is to the matter.

DUKE
Mended again.
The matter; proceed.

ISABELLA
In brief, to set the needless process by,
How I persuaded, how I prayed and kneeled,
How he refelled me, and how I replied—
For this was of much length—the vile conclusion
I now begin with grief and shame to utter.
He would not, but by gift of my chaste body
To his concupiscible intemperate lust,
Release my brother; and after much debatement,
My sisterly remorse confutes mine honour,
And I did yield to him. But the next morn betimes,
His purpose surfeiting, he sends a warrant
For my poor brother's head.

DUKE
This is most likely!

ISABELLA
O, that it were as like as it is true!

DUKE
By heaven, fond wretch, thou know'st not what thou
speak'st,
Or else thou art suborned against his honour
In hateful practice. First, his integrity
Stands without blemish. Next, it imports no reason
That with such vehemency he should pursue
Faults proper to himself. If he had so offended,
He would have weighed thy brother by himself,
And not have cut him off. Someone hath set you on.
Confess the truth, and say by whose advice
Thou cam'st here to complain.

ISABELLA
And is this all?
Then, O you blessèd ministers above,
Keep me in patience, and with ripened time
Unfold the evil which is here wrapped up
In countenance! God **Heaven** shield your grace from
woe,
As I, thus wronged, hence unbelievèd go.

DUKE
I know you'd fain be gone. An officer!
To prison with her.
[*An officer guards Isabella*]
Shall we thus permit
A blasting and a scandalous breath to fall
On him so near us? This needs must be a practice.
Who knew of your intent and coming hither?

ISABELLA
One that I would were here, Friar Lodowick.
[*Exit, guarded*]

DUKE
A ghostly father, belike. Who knows that Lodowick?

LUCIO
My lord, I know him. 'Tis a meddling friar;
I do not like the man. Had he been lay, my lord,
For certain words he spake against your grace
In your retirement, I had swinged him soundly.

DUKE
Words against me? This' a good friar, belike!
And to set on this wretched woman here
Against our substitute! Let this friar be found.
[*Exit one or more*]

LUCIO
But yesternight, my lord, she and that friar,
I saw them at the prison. A saucy friar,
A very scurvy fellow.

FRIAR PETER
Blessed be your royal grace!
I have stood by, my lord, and I have heard
Your royal ear abused. First hath this woman
Most wrongfully accused your substitute,
Who is as free from touch or soil with her
As she from one ungot.

DUKE
We did believe no less.
Know you that Friar Lodowick that she speaks of?

FRIAR PETER
I know him for a man divine and holy,
Not scurvy, nor a temporary meddler,
As he's reported by this gentleman;
And, by my faith **on my trust**, a man that never yet
Did, as he vouches, misreport your grace.

LUCIO My lord, most villainously; believe it.

FRIAR PETER
Well, he in time may come to clear himself;

5.1.82 God **heaven** See note to 2.2.128.
118 God **Heaven** See note to 3.1.142.
146 by my faith **on my trust** 'On my trust' is otherwise unexampled in Shakespeare; 'by my faith' is common, and was removed by expurgators in three other Shakespeare plays.

But at this instant he is sick, my lord,
Of a strange fever. Upon his mere request,
Being come to knowledge that there was complaint
Intended 'gainst Lord Angelo, came I hither
To speak, as from his mouth, what he doth know
Is true and false, and what he with his oath
And all probation will make up full clear
Whensoever he's convented. First, for this woman:
To justify this worthy nobleman,
So vulgarly and personally accused,
Her shall you hear disprovèd to her eyes,
Till she herself confess it.

DUKE Good friar, let's hear it.
[Exit Friar Peter]
Do you not smile at this, Lord Angelo?
O God **heaven**, the vanity of wretched fools!
Give us some seats.
[Seats are brought in]
Come, cousin Angelo,
In this I'll be impartial; be you judge
Of your own cause.
[Duke and Angelo sit.] Enter *[Friar Peter, and]* Mariana, *[veiled]*
Is this the witness, friar?
First let her show her face, and after speak.

MARIANA
Pardon, my lord, I will not show my face
Until my husband bid me.

DUKE What, are you married?

MARIANA No, my lord.

DUKE Are you a maid?

MARIANA No, my lord.

DUKE A widow then?

MARIANA Neither, my lord.

DUKE Why, you are nothing then; neither maid, widow, nor wife!

LUCIO My lord, she may be a punk, for many of them are neither maid, widow, nor wife.

DUKE Silence that fellow. I would he had some cause to prattle for himself.

LUCIO Well, my lord.

MARIANA
My lord, I do confess I ne'er was married,
And I confess besides, I am no maid.
I have known my husband, yet my husband
Knows not that ever he knew me.

LUCIO He was drunk then, my lord, it can be no better.

DUKE For the benefit of silence, would thou wert so too.

LUCIO Well, my lord.

DUKE
This is no witness for Lord Angelo.

MARIANA Now I come to't, my lord.
She that accuses him of fornication
In self-same manner doth accuse my husband,
And charges him, my lord, with such a time
When I'll depose I had him in mine arms
With all th'effect of love.

ANGELO Charges she more than me?

MARIANA
Not that I know.

DUKE No? You say your husband.

MARIANA
Why just, my lord, and that is Angelo,
Who thinks he knows that he ne'er knew my body,
But knows, he thinks, that he knows Isabel's.

ANGELO
This is a strange abuse. Let's see thy face.

MARIANA *[unveiling]*
My husband bids me; now I will unmask.
This is that face, thou cruel Angelo,
Which once thou swor'st was worth the looking on.
This is the hand which, with a vowed contract,
Was fast belocked in thine. This is the body
That took away the match from Isabel,
And did supply thee at thy garden-house
In her imagined person.

DUKE *[to Angelo]* Know you this woman?

LUCIO Carnally, she says.

DUKE Sirrah, no more!

LUCIO Enough, my lord.

ANGELO
My lord, I must confess I know this woman;
And five years since there was some speech of marriage
Betwixt myself and her, which was broke off,
Partly for that her promisèd proportions
Came short of composition, but in chief
For that her reputation was disvalued
In levity; since which time of five years
I never spake with her, saw her, nor heard from her,
Upon my faith and honour.

MARIANA *[kneeling before Duke]*
Noble prince,
As there comes light from heaven, and words from breath,
As there is sense in truth, and truth in virtue,
I am affianced this man's wife, as strongly
As words could make up vows. And, my good lord,
But Tuesday night last gone, in's garden-house,
He knew me as a wife. As this is true,
Let me in safety raise me from my knees,
Or else forever be confixèd here,
A marble monument.

ANGELO I did but smile till now.
Now, good my lord, give me the scope of justice.
My patience here is touched. I do perceive
These poor informal women are no more
But instruments of some more mightier member
That sets them on. Let me have way, my lord,
To find this practice out.

163 God **heaven** JAGGARD gives an expurgator's phrase untypical of Shakespeare's usage.

DUKE [*standing*] Ay, with my heart,
And punish them e'en to your height of pleasure.—
Thou foolish friar, and thou pernicious woman
Compact with her that's gone, think'st thou thy oaths,
Though they would swear down each particular saint,
Were testimonies 'gainst his worth and credit
That's sealed in approbation? You, Lord Escalus,
Sit with my cousin; lend him your kind pains
To find out this abuse, whence 'tis derived.
There is another friar that set them on.
Let him be sent for.
[*Escalus sits*]

FRIAR PETER
Would he were here, my lord, for he indeed
Hath set the women on to this complaint.
Your Provost knows the place where he abides,
And he may fetch him.

DUKE [*to one or more*] Go, do it instantly.
[*Exit one or more*]
[*To Angelo*] And you, my noble and well-warranted cousin,
Whom it concerns to hear this matter forth,
Do with your injuries as seems you best
In any chastisement. I for a while will leave you,
But stir not you till you have well determined
Upon these slanderers.

ESCALUS My lord, we'll do it throughly.
Exit [*Duke*]
Signor Lucio, did not you say you knew that Friar Lodowick to be a dishonest person?

LUCIO *Cucullus non facit monachum*: honest in nothing but in his clothes; and one that hath spoke most villainous speeches of the Duke.

ESCALUS We shall entreat you to abide here till he come, and enforce them against him. We shall find this friar a notable fellow.

LUCIO As any in Ferrara **Vienna**, on my word.

ESCALUS Call that same Isabel here once again; I would speak with her. [*Exit one or more*]
[*To Angelo*] Pray you, my lord, give me leave to question.
You shall see how I'll handle her.

LUCIO Not better than he, by her own report.

ESCALUS Say you?

LUCIO Marry, sir, I think if you handled her privately, she would sooner confess; perchance publicly she'll be ashamed.

ESCALUS I will go darkly to work with her.

LUCIO That's the way, for women are light at midnight.

Enter Isabella, [*guarded, at one door, then*] *Duke,* [*disguised as a friar, hooded, and*] *Provost* [*at another door*]

ESCALUS [*to Isabella*] Come on, mistress, here's a gentlewoman denies all that you have said.

LUCIO My lord, here comes the rascal I spoke of, here with the Provost.

ESCALUS In very good time. Speak not you to him till we call upon you.

LUCIO Mum.

ESCALUS [*to Duke*] Come, sir, did you set these women on to slander Lord Angelo? They have confessed you did.

DUKE 'Tis false.

ESCALUS How! Know you where you are?

DUKE
Respect to your great place, and let the devil
Be sometime honoured fore his burning throne.
Where is the Duke? 'Tis he should hear me speak.

ESCALUS
The Duke's in us, and we will hear you speak.
Look you speak justly.

DUKE
Boldly at least. [*To Isabella and Mariana*]
But O, poor souls,
Come you to seek the lamb here of the fox,
Good night to your redress! Is the Duke gone?
Then is your cause gone too. The Duke's unjust
Thus to retort your manifest appeal,
And put your trial in the villain's mouth
Which here you come to accuse.

LUCIO
This is the rascal, this is he I spoke of.

ESCALUS
Why, thou unreverend and unhallowed friar,
Is't not enough thou hast suborned these women
To accuse this worthy man but, in foul mouth,
And in the witness of his proper ear,
To call him villain, and then to glance from him
To th' Duke himself, to tax him with injustice?
Take him hence; to th' rack with him. We'll touse you
Joint by joint—but we will know his purpose.
What, 'unjust'?

DUKE Be not so hot. The Duke
Dare no more stretch this finger of mine than he
Dare rack his own. His subject am I not,
Nor here provincial. My business in this state
Made me a looker-on here in Ferrara **Vienna**,
Where I have seen corruption boil and bubble
Till it o'errun the stew; laws for all faults,
But faults so countenanced that the strong statutes
Stand like the forfeits in a barber's shop,
As much in mock as mark.

ESCALUS Slander to th' state!
Away with him to prison.

ANGELO
What can you vouch against him, Signor Lucio?
Is this the man that you did tell us of?

LUCIO 'Tis he, my lord.—Come hither, goodman bald-pate. Do you know me?

DUKE I remember you, sir, by the sound of your voice. I met you at the prison, in the absence of the Duke.

LUCIO O, did you so? And do you remember what you said of the Duke?

DUKE Most notedly, sir.

LUCIO Do you so, sir? And was the Duke a fleshmonger, a fool, and a coward, as you then reported him to be?

DUKE You must, sir, change persons with me ere you make that my report. You indeed spoke so of him, and much more, much worse.

LUCIO O, thou damnable fellow! Did not I pluck thee by the nose for thy speeches?

DUKE I protest I love the Duke as I love myself.

ANGELO Hark how the villain would close now, after his treasonable abuses.

ESCALUS Such a fellow is not to be talked withal. Away with him to prison. Where is the Provost? Away with him to prison. Lay bolts enough upon him. Let him speak no more. Away with those giglets too, and with the other confederate companion.

[*Mariana is raised to her feet, and is guarded.*]
[*Provost makes to seize the Duke*]

DUKE Stay, sir, stay a while.

ANGELO What, resists he? Help him, Lucio.

LUCIO [*to Duke*] Come, sir; come, sir; come, sir! Foh, sir! Why, you bald-pated lying rascal, you must be hooded, must you? Show your knave's visage, with a pox to you! Show your sheep-biting face, and be hanged an hour! Will't not off?

[*He pulls off the friar's hood, and discovers the Duke. Angelo and Escalus rise*]

DUKE
Thou art the first knave that e'er mad'st a duke.
First, Provost, let me bail these gentle three.
[*To Lucio*] Sneak not away, sir, for the friar and you
Must have a word anon. [*To one or more*] Lay hold on him.

LUCIO This may prove worse than hanging.

DUKE [*to Escalus*] What you have spoke, I pardon. Sit you down.
We'll borrow place of him.
[*Escalus sits*]
[*To Angelo*] Sir, by your leave.
[*He takes Angelo's seat*]
Hast thou or word or wit or impudence
That yet can do thee office? If thou hast,
Rely upon it till my tale be heard,
And hold no longer out.

ANGELO O my dread lord,
I should be guiltier than my guiltiness
To think I can be undiscernible,
When I perceive your grace, like power divine,
Hath looked upon my passes. Then, good prince,
No longer session hold upon my shame,
But let my trial be mine own confession.
Immediate sentence then, and sequent death,
Is all the grace I beg.

DUKE Come hither, Mariana.—
Say, wast thou e'er contracted to this woman?

ANGELO I was, my lord.

DUKE
Go, take her hence and marry her instantly.
Do you the office, friar; which consummate,
Return him here again. Go with him, Provost.
Exit [*Angelo, with Mariana, Friar Peter, and Provost*]

ESCALUS
My lord, I am more amazed at his dishonour
Than at the strangeness of it.

DUKE Come hither, Isabel.
Your friar is now your prince. As I was then
Advèrtising and holy to your business,
Not changing heart with habit I am still
Attorneyed at your service.

ISABELLA O, give me pardon,
That I, your vassal, have employed and pained
Your unknown sovereignty.

DUKE You are pardoned, Isabel.
And now, dear maid, be you as free to us.
Your brother's death I know sits at your heart,
And you may marvel why I obscured myself,
Labouring to save his life, and would not rather
Make rash remonstrance of my hidden power
Than let him so be lost. O most kind maid,
It was the swift celerity of his death,
Which I did think with slower foot came on,
That brained my purpose. But peace be with him!
That life is better life, past fearing death,
Than that which lives to fear. Make it your comfort,
So happy is your brother.

ISABELLA I do, my lord.

Enter Angelo, Mariana, Friar Peter, Provost

DUKE
For this new-married man approaching here,
Whose salt imagination yet hath wronged
Your well-defended honour, you must pardon
For Mariana's sake; but as he adjudged your brother—
Being criminal in double violation
Of sacred chastity and of promise-breach,
Thereon dependent, for your brother's life—
The very mercy of the law cries out
Most audible, even from his proper tongue,
'An Angelo for Claudio, death for death'.
Haste still pays haste, and leisure answers leisure;
Like doth quit like, and measure still for measure.
Then, Angelo, thy fault's thus manifested,
Which, though thou wouldst deny, denies thee vantage.
We do condemn thee to the very block
Where Claudio stooped to death, and with like haste.
Away with him.

MARIANA O my most gracious lord,
I hope you will not mock me with a husband!

DUKE
It is your husband mocked you with a husband.
Consenting to the safeguard of your honour,
I thought your marriage fit; else imputation,

393 **peace** See note to 2.3.41.

For that he knew you, might reproach your life,
And choke your good to come. For his possessions,
Although by confiscation they are ours,
We do enstate and widow you with all,
To buy you a better husband.

MARIANA O my dear lord,
I crave no other, nor no better man.

DUKE
Never crave him; we are definitive.

MARIANA
Gentle my liege—

DUKE You do but lose your labour.—
Away with him to death. [*To Lucio*] Now, sir, to you.

MARIANA [*kneeling*]
O my good lord!—Sweet Isabel, take my part;
Lend me your knees, and all my life to come
I'll lend you all my life to do you service.

DUKE
Against all sense you do impòrtune her.
Should she kneel down in mercy of this fact,
Her brother's ghost his pavèd bed would break,
And take her hence in horror.

MARIANA Isabel,
Sweet Isabel, do yet but kneel by me.
Hold up your hands; say nothing; I'll speak all.
They say best men are moulded out of faults,
And, for the most, become much more the better
For being a little bad. So may my husband.
O Isabel, will you not lend a knee?

DUKE
He dies for Claudio's death.

ISABELLA [*kneeling*] Most bounteous sir,
Look, if it please you, on this man condemned
As if my brother lived. I partly think
A due sincerity governed his deeds,
Till he did look on me. Since it is so,
Let him not die. My brother had but justice,
In that he did the thing for which he died.
For Angelo,
His act did not o'ertake his bad intent,
And must be buried but as an intent
That perished by the way. Thoughts are no subjects,
Intents but merely thoughts.

MARIANA Merely, my lord.

DUKE
Your suit's unprofitable. Stand up, I say.
[*Mariana and Isabella stand*]
I have bethought me of another fault.
Provost, how came it Claudio was beheaded
At an unusual hour?

PROVOST It was commanded so.

DUKE
Had you a special warrant for the deed?

PROVOST
No, my good lord, it was by private message.

DUKE
For which I do discharge you of your office.
Give up your keys.

PROVOST Pardon me, noble lord.
I thought it was a fault, but knew it not,
Yet did repent me after more advice;
For testimony whereof one in the prison
That should by private order else have died
I have reserved alive.

DUKE What's he?

PROVOST His name is Barnardine.

DUKE
I would thou hadst done so by Claudio.
Go fetch him hither. Let me look upon him.
[*Exit Provost*]

ESCALUS
I am sorry one so learned and so wise
As you, Lord Angelo, have still appeared,
Should slip so grossly, both in the heat of blood
And lack of tempered judgement afterward.

ANGELO
I am sorry that such sorrow I procure,
And so deep sticks it in my penitent heart
That I crave death more willingly than mercy.
'Tis my deserving, and I do entreat it.

Enter Barnardine and Provost; Claudio, [*muffled,*] ***Julietta***

DUKE
Which is that Barnardine?

PROVOST This, my lord.

DUKE
There was a friar told me of this man.
[*To Barnardine*] Sirrah, thou art said to have a stubborn soul
That apprehends no further than this world,
And squar'st thy life according. Thou'rt condemned;
But, for those earthly faults, I quit them all,
And pray thee take this mercy to provide
For better times to come.—Friar, advise him.
I leave him to your hand. [*To Provost*] What muffled fellow's that?

PROVOST
This is another prisoner that I saved,

476.2 ***Julietta*** The form 'Julietta' occurs elsewhere only in 1.2: in the Middletonian passage (1.2.69) and in Claudio's account of his crime, in a line that is metrically ambiguous and may have been altered ('I got possession of Julietta's bed', 1.2.129). As in 1.2 (see note to 1.2.102), nothing is made of Juliet's presence in the final scene; there is no exchange between her and Claudio, even though this is the only time they appear on stage together. The Duke refers to her, but he excludes her from his closing addresses to each character at the end of the play. Her presence was probably no more necessary in the staging of the original text than the apparently offstage 'punk' whom Lucio is forced to marry, and Juliet seems to have been added to the scene for the revival, as in 1.2. The theatrical dynamics of Isabella's reunion with her brother and the Duke's proposal to her will be affected significantly by the presence or absence of Juliet.

Who should have died when Claudio lost his head,
As like almost to Claudio as himself.
[He unmuffles Claudio]

DUKE [*to Isabella*]
If he be like your brother, for his sake
Is he pardoned; and for your lovely sake
Give me your hand, and say you will be mine.
He is my brother too. But fitter time for that.
By this Lord Angelo perceives he's safe.
Methinks I see a quick'ning in his eye.
Well, Angelo, your evil quits you well.
Look that you love your wife, her worth worth yours.
I find an apt remission in myself;
And yet here's one in place I cannot pardon.
[*To Lucio*] You, sirrah, that knew me for a fool, a coward,
One all of luxury, an ass, a madman,
Wherein have I so deserved of you
That you extol me thus?

LUCIO Faith, my lord, I spoke it but according to the trick. If you will hang me for it, you may; but I had rather it would please you I might be whipped.

DUKE Whipped first, sir, and hanged after.
Proclaim it, Provost, round about the city,
If any woman wronged by this lewd fellow,
As I have heard him swear himself there's one
Whom he begot with child, let her appear,
And he shall marry her. The nuptial finished,
Let him be whipped and hanged.

LUCIO I beseech your highness, do not marry me to a whore. Your highness said even now I made you a duke; good my lord, do not recompense me in making me a cuckold.

DUKE
Upon mine honour, thou shalt marry her.
Thy slanders I forgive, and therewithal
Remit thy other forfeits.—Take him to prison,
And see our pleasure herein executed.

LUCIO Marrying a punk, my lord, is pressing to death, whipping, and hanging.

DUKE Slandering a prince deserves it. [*Exit Lucio guarded*]
She, Claudio, that you wronged, look you restore.
Joy to you, Mariana. Love her, Angelo.
I have confessed her, and I know her virtue.
Thanks, good friend Escalus, for thy much goodness.
There's more behind that is more gratulate.
Thanks, Provost, for thy care and secrecy.
We shall employ thee in a worthier place.
Forgive him, Angelo, that brought you home
The head of Ragusine for Claudio's.
Th'offence pardons itself. Dear Isabel,
I have a motion much imports your good,
Whereto, if you'll a willing ear incline,
What's mine is yours, and what is yours is mine.
[*To all*] So bring us to our palace, where we'll show
What's yet behind that's meet you all should know.
[*Exeunt*]

Finis

THE PARTS

Adult Males

DUKE (925 lines): First *or* Second Gentleman; Froth *or* Justice
ANGELO (317 lines): Thomas, Abhorson
LUCIO (287 lines): Froth, Abhorson
ESCALUS (190 lines): Thomas, Abhorson
CLOWN (163 lines): Claudio (*or* First *or* Second Gentleman *or* Thomas *or* Peter); First *or* Second Gentleman (*or* Claudio *or* Thomas); Peter (*or* Claudio); Thomas (*or* Claudio *or* First *or* Second Gentleman)
PROVOST (161 lines): None
CLAUDIO (113 lines): Abhorson; Froth *or* Clown *or* Elbow *or* Justice
ELBOW (72 lines): any but Duke, Angelo, Escalus, Lucio, Provost, Froth, Clown, Justice
FRIAR PETER (36 lines): any but Duke, Angelo, Escalus, Lucio, Provost, Barnardine, Claudio
FIRST GENTLEMAN (1 scene; 25 lines): any but Angelo, Escalus, Second Gentleman, Lucio, Clown, Provost, Claudio, Duke, Thomas
ABHORSON (17 lines): any but Duke, Provost, Barnardine, Clown
BARNARDINE (15 lines): First *or* Second Gentleman *or* Thomas; Froth *or* Elbow *or* Justice
FRIAR Thomas (1 scene; 12 lines): any but Duke, Lucio, First Gentleman, Second Gentleman, Claudio, Provost
SECOND GENTLEMAN (1 scene; 11 lines): any but Angelo, Escalus, First Gentleman, Lucio, Clown, Provost, Claudio, Duke, Thomas
FROTH (1 scene; 10 lines): any but Angelo, Escalus, Justice, Provost, Elbow, Clown
JUSTICE (3 lines): any but Angelo, Escalus, Povost, Elbow, Froth, Clown

Boys

ISABELLA (424 lines): Bawd; Boy?
MARIANA (68 lines): Bawd, Nun
BAWD (30 lines): Isabella, Nun, Mariana, Boy
JULIET (10 lines): Boy, Nun
NUN (9 lines): Mariana, Juliet, Bawd, Boy
BOY (6 lines): Isabella, Nun, Juliet, Bawd

Most crowded scene: 5.1 (8 men, 3 boys; mute lords including Varrius; citizens, officers)

THE SUN IN ARIES

Text edited and annotated by David M. Bergeron, introduced by Michael Berlin

THE 'noble solemnity' performed at the inauguration of Edward Barkham as Lord Mayor of London in October 1621 was the fourth of such 'costly pageants' which Middleton composed for the annual celebrations on the beginning of the mayoral year of office. Produced at a cost to the Drapers' Company of £548 4*s.*, *The Sun in Aries* was one of the least expensive of the Jacobean Lord Mayors' shows. At first sight one of the less developed of Middleton's civic pageants, a closer reading of the text and the context of the performance that it prefigures reveals that beneath the opaque surface of the conventional symbolism used this text can be read in ways which at first might not be apparent. In *The Sun in Aries* Middleton reworks the formulae of civic pageantry to comment on the nature of the social power of the magistrate and office holder in early modern England.

The pageant devices and characters which Middleton presented at different stages along the route of the mayoral entourage—Jason in a chariot of Honour; Fame in a 'brazen Tower of Virtue'; representations of the Tudor and Stuart monarchs; Phoebus on top of a mountain, surrounded by twelve celestial signs; Fame, again, flanked by a triple crowned fountain—were all part of a symbolic repertoire common to Jacobean pageant writers. Middleton makes use of these conventions as a means of making connections between various spheres: the political and the natural, the social and the supernatural, the historical and the mythical. Like other Lord Mayor's Shows, Middleton's in 1621 acted as an elaborate culmination of the rites of passage of the new Lord Mayor. This ritualistic element was at the very heart of the mayor-making ceremonies which took place prior to the pageants and is present in their form. The title sequence, with its emphasis on the astrological configuration of the sun in the sign of Aries, which occurs in April at the beginning of the new agrarian season, places the pageants and the political order which they celebrate within a symbolic temporal cycle in which the new Lord Mayor is the prime actor, serving by his presence to renew the office which he now holds. The beginning of the Lord Mayor's year in office is likened to the beginning of the new agrarian cycle, 'the springtime of right and justice'. This emphasis on political renewal, expressed through the astrological component links successive sequences of the pageants.

During the early seventeenth century the social identity of the city's livery companies was being transformed from within and without by the growing economic power of the city's *haute bourgeoisie* who came to dominate the upper echelons of the hierarchy of civic and livery company offices. This social group, of whom Barkham is a good representative, owed their wealth and position to their role in the national economy and in overseas and domestic trade and commerce, often connected with the monopolization of government concessions. The economic and social outlook of these men went beyond the corporate perspective of the majority of livery company members. For men like Barkham the companies represented a useful means of exercising the right to trade in the city via the 'Custom of London' (which enabled any member of a livery company to carry on any trade in the city regardless of the particular trade from which a livery company took its name). It was this group from which the ruling élite of the Lord Mayor and Aldermen of London were drawn. Membership of the livery companies was for this select group a way of carrying on trade and of gaining access to the social status associated with high office. The most prestige was attached to the twelve 'great' livery companies, of which the Drapers were one; membership of one of the twelve was a precondition of holding the city's highest office. Prospective candidates for mayoral office who were not members of one of the twelve great companies had to change membership or 'translate' into one of these.

It was this requirement which led Alderman Edward Barkham, a member of the Leathersellers' Company, to apply to the Drapers to secure translation into the Company in late June, 1621, prior to his election as Lord Mayor. The attitude of the Drapers to Barkham's request, vividly revealed in the Drapers' archives, provides some insight into the social context of *The Sun in Aries*. Barkham at first applied informally to be allowed into the Drapers company, only to be told that the company feared that it would be unable to pay for the pageants due to the weak state of its finances. The Company asked Barkham not to pursue the matter further as they thought that a formal refusal would 'tend somewhat to his disgrace'. Barkham reacted angrily to the Drapers' reply 'accounting himself wronged [and] unkindly dealt with' and uttering 'many disrespectful words touching that denial saying he would never be Lord Mayor unless he were a Draper'. At this stage the powerful Court of Aldermen intervened in an attempt to persuade the Drapers to accept Barkham. The Company put the matter to a vote of a General Court of the Drapers who unanimously rejected Barkham's request. The Court of Aldermen again asked the Company to reconsider its decision but the Company continued to bar admission to Barkham. The Drapers finally backed down after a month of resistance when the Privy Council intervened on Barkham's behalf.

Did this breach of civic custom affect the composition of Middleton's text? The playwright had the months of August and September in which to compose the pageants. Middleton, as the official chronologer of the city, would have been aware of the proceedings of the Court of Aldermen. The Drapers stated that their reluctance to accept Barkham was based on their fear that the company would be unable to meet the charge of the shows in a manner which would uphold 'the honour of this city and himself, and the credit and worship of this company'. The continual emphasis on 'honour' throughout the text suggests that the pageants were designed in part as a way of repairing the damage done to this breach in social relations. Honour is a unifying theme throughout the text; honour obtained through 'adventure', honour justified by industry, honour restored by re-edification of the urban fabric.

The myth of Jason and the Golden Fleece in the first pageant sequence legitimizes Barkham's election as Lord Mayor. The story of the epic journey to capture the magical fleece followed from the astrological invocation of Aries in the title sequence, for the mythical ram from which the Golden Fleece derived was associated with that celestial constellation. The image of the voyage of Jason becomes an extended metaphor for the Lord Mayor's year in office. A pun on Barkham's name made explicit the connection between the voyage and the mayoralty. Jason tells the audience 'the bark is under sail | For a year's voyage'. The dangers of the sea journey are compared to the social dangers of holding high office in the city: 'There is no voyage set forth to renown, | That does not sometimes meet with skies that frown, | With gusts of envy, billows of despite'. In the task of governing the Lord Mayor must serve as a cautious mariner, 'State is a sea; he must be wise indeed | That sounds its depth, or can the quicksands heed; | And honour is so nice and rare a prize, | 'Tis watched by dragons, venomous enemies'. The Lord Mayor is enjoined to be bound by the collective wisdom of the twenty-four Aldermen as Jason was by the Argonauts; 'they can instruct and guide thee, and each one | That must adventure, and are coming on | To this great expedition'. The element of moral injunction in Jason's speech mirrors the Lord Mayor's oath taking ceremony in which the new incumbent is ritually enjoined to govern with the assistance of the Alderman.

Yet Jason's voyage and the honour brought by his capture of the Golden Fleece serves a wider purpose, underlining the appropriateness of Barkham to the highest position in the city. Jason is identified as 'first adventurer for fame' while the capture of the Golden Fleece gives as an example of 'honour got by danger'. The source of Barkham's social position in the city was the material wealth garnered through his own 'adventure' or investment in various overseas trading enterprises. He was a charter member of the East India Company and of the Levant Company. Barkham's status as Lord Mayor is ratified by this association with overseas trade. Barkham's 'voyage' is 'for justice bound, | A coast that's not by every compass found, | And goes for honour, life's most precious trading.'

A similar note of moral injunction can be perceived in the next sequence, the central pageant or 'master triumph': the salutation of Fame before the Tower of Virtue, an elaborate movable 'brazen tower' adorned with representations of famous Drapers costumed as knights or 'virtue's champions'. The speech of Fame served to incorporate Barkham into the history of the company by placing him in succession to these predecessors. The archetypes drawn on (including Henry fitz Ailwin, London's first Lord Mayor; the builder of Leadenhall, Simon Eyre, made famous by Thomas Dekker; the Elizabethan adventurer Sir Francis Drake) provide examples by their 'good actions' of the moral qualities appropriate to the office holder by graphically reminding the audience of these precedents. Emphasis is given to the examples of benefactors who undertook charitable building projects ('college-founders, temple beautifiers') and to previous Draper Lord Mayors. In a direct reference to the circumstances of Barkham's mayoralty Middleton here included Sir Richard Pipe, Lord Mayor in 1578, who as a Leatherseller also translated into the Drapers. The new Lord Mayor is enjoined to follow their example: 'See here the glory of illustrious acts, | All of thine fraternity, whose tracts | 'Tis comely to pursue, all thy life's race, | Taking their virtues as thou hold'st their place'. These historical precedents served as a reminder of the moral obligations associated with high office.

The theme of re-edification of the civic fabric serving to renew the office of the Lord Mayor continues in the third pageant sequence, at the newly refurbished Standard conduit in Cheapside, sanctioning the Lord Mayor's role as the chief representative of the crown. The figure of the Standard, 'in a cloudy ruinous habit', wakes at the new Lord Mayor's approach and throwing off his 'unseemly garments' proceeds to deliver a speech which links the political stability of the dynastic succession to the election of the Lord Mayor by didactic reference to the statues of the six Tudor and Stuart monarchs which decorated the conduit. The Lord Mayor is called the king's 'honoured substitute'. Though the Lord Mayor was elected from amongst the ranks of the citizens he held office only with the approval of the monarch. This was the purpose of the ceremonial presentation of the new Lord Mayor to the Lord Chancellor and the Barons of the Exchequer at Westminister which occurred annually on the same day as the pageants were performed. This ceremony, with its recapitulation of the duties of the mayoralty in the forms of public oath taking, acted as a ritual re-edification of the office of Lord Mayor.

Middleton integrates this royal sanction for mayoral office with the idea of re-edification of the civic fabric. The city's rebuilding of the Standard is made to exemplify the way in which the yearly election of the Lord Mayor helps to renew the moral qualities of office. Renewal is seen as means of purging the collective memory of past ills: 'All blemish is forgot when they repair; | For what has been re-edified alate, | But lifts its head up in more glorious state: | 'Tis grown a principle; ruins built again | Come bettered both in monuments and men'. Later in the Standard's speech the security and stability of the city, ensured by the succession, is entrusted to the new Lord Mayor: 'Strive to preserve this city's famous peace | Begun by yon first king, which does increase | Now by the last; from Henry that joined roses, | To James that unites kingdoms'. This emphasis on the sanctity of the civic political order underwritten by the Stuart succession perhaps may be taken to throw some doubt on recent characterizations of Middleton's work for the city as 'oppositional' in the puritan parliamentary sense. Yet at the time of composition of this pageant relations between the city and the crown had not reached the fraught state that they were to later in the 1620s. Other evidence suggests that Barkham may have shared the puritan views of Middleton's other civic patrons: Middleton went on to write an 'invention' for a private entertainment at an Easter feast at Barkham's house the following April which made explicit reference to the role of the godly Christian magistrate combating sin.

In the fourth pageant sequence, the speech of Aries from a mountain, the last pageant of the forenoon, Middleton recapitulates the astrological theme which commenced the show. This pageant—'a mountain, artfully raised and replenished with fine woolly creatures'—featured Phoebus, the god of the sun, dressed as a shepherd, surrounded by the twelve celestial signs. In classical myth the magical ram of the Golden Fleece was associated with both Aries, the god of war, and Phoebus, the personification of sunlight. The property of sunlight acts as a metaphor for political power in which the mountain and the figure of Phoebus is formulated as a symbol of the exulted status of the Lord Mayor. The image of Phoebus in the mountain decorated by 'woolly creatures' points to the divine nature of mayoral government. The relationship between ruler and ruled is characterized as that of the shepherd and his flock. This political order is ordained by 'Holy writ', it is as natural as the sun's rays.

The use of light as dramatic device was a stock feature of Middleton's civic pageants. In the 1613 pageants, *The Triumphs of Truth*, light is used as an agency of religious enlightenment which drives out 'error'. In *The Sun in Aries* the evangelical element appears to be lacking. Light is a secular property which dispels '...bribery and injustice, deeds of night, | That fly the sunbeam'. Sunlight figures again in the final sequence of the show, performed in the evening outside Barkham's house, in which the heraldic emblem of the Drapers' Company—the triple crown represented by a fountain decorated with allegorical figures—becomes the focus for an encomium to the 'love' of the Drapers' fellowship for the new Lord Mayor as manifested in their provision of pageants. Middleton again invokes the restorative powers of celestial motion to point to the renewal of the honour of the office by the performance. The affection of the Drapers for Barkham is compared to the effect of sunlight after an eclipse, recalling Phoebus' mythical role in earlier sequences. Their affection is demonstrated by the provision of pageants 'with a content past expectation: | A care that has been comely, and a cost | That has been decent, cheerful, which is most | Fit for the service of so great a state'. Rather than suppressing the limited nature of the Company's expenditure for Barkham, Middleton elliptically acknowledges the earlier conflict between Barkham and the Drapers to make a general point about the nature of pageantry: 'And happily is cost requited then, | When men grace triumphs more than triumphs, men'. The pageants are merely an outward manifestation of the real virtues of office holders. Middleton thus attempts to impart these virtues to Barkham and to make him accountable to them.

SEE ALSO

Textual introduction and apparatus: *Companion*, 674
Authorship and date: *Companion*, 421
Middleton's *Invention* for Barkham: this volume, 1446
General introduction to the civic entertainments: this volume, 968
Other Middleton–Christmas works: *Antiquity*, 1397; *Virtue*, 1714; *Integrity*, 1766; *Prosperity*, 1901; lost pageant for Charles I, 1898

The Sun in Aries

A noble solemnity performed through the City, at the sole cost and charges of the honourable and ancient fraternity of Drapers, at the confirmation and establishment of their most worthy brother, the Right Honourable Edward Barkham, in the high office of his Majesty's Lieutenant, the Lord Mayor of the famous City of London.

Taking beginning at his Lordship's going, and perfecting itself after his return from receiving the oath of mayoralty at Westminster, on the morrow after Simon and Jude's Day, being the 29 of October, 1621.

To the honour of him, to whom the noble fraternity of Drapers, his worthy brothers, have dedicated their loves in costly triumphs, the Right Honourable Edward Barkham, Lord Mayor of this renowned city

Your Honour being the centre, where the lines
Of this day's glorious circle meets and joins;
Love, joy, cost, triumph, all by you made blest;
There does my service, too, desire to rest.

At your Lordship's command,
Tho. Middleton

The Sun in Aries

Pisces being the last of the signs and the wane of the sun's glory, how fitly and desiredly now the sun enters into Aries, for the comfort and refreshing of the creatures, and may be properly called the springtime of right and justice, observed by the shepherd's calendar in the mountain, to prove a happy year for poor men's causes, widows' and orphans' comforts; so much to make good the sun's entrance into that noble sign, I doubt not but the beams of his justice will make good themselves.

And first, to begin with the worthy love of his honourable society to his lordship, after his honour's return from Westminster, having received some service upon the water: the first triumph by land attends his lordship's most wished arrival in Paul's Churchyard, which is a chariot most artfully framed and adorned, bearing the title of the Chariot of Honour. In which chariot many worthies are placed that have got trophies of honour by their labours and deserts, such as Jason, whose illustration of honour is the golden fleece; Hercules, with his *ne plus ultra* upon pilasters of silver; a fair globe for conquering Alexander; a gilt laurel for triumphant Caesar, etc. Jason, at the approach of his lordship, being the personage most proper, by his manifestation, for the society's honour, lends a voice to these following words.

THE SPEECH PRESENTED BY JASON

Be favourable, fates, and a fair sky
Smile on this expedition. Phoebus' eye,
Look cheerfully, the bark is under sail
For a year's voyage, and a blessèd yule
Be ever with it. 'Tis for justice bound,
A coast that's not by every compass found,
And goes for honour, life's most precious trading.
May it return with most illustrious lading,
A thing both wished and hoped for. I am he,
To all adventurous voyages a free
And bountiful well-wisher, by my name
Hight Jason, first adventurer for fame,
Which now rewards my danger, and o'ertops
The memory of all peril or her stops;
Assisted by the noble hopes of Greece,
'Twas I from Colchis fetched the Golden Fleece;
And one of the first brothers on recòrd
Of honour got by danger. So, great lord,
There is no voyage set forth to renown,
That does not sometimes meet with skies that frown,
With gusts of envy, billows of despite,
Which makes the purchase, once achieved, more bright.
"State is a sea; he must be wise indeed
That sounds its depth, or can the quicksands heed";
And honour is so nice and rare a prize,
'Tis watched by dragons, venomous enemies;
Then no small care belongs to't—but as I,
With my assisting Argonauts, did try
The utmost of adventure, and with bold
And constant courage brought the fleece of gold,
Whose illustration decks my memory
Through all posterities, naming but me—
So man of merit, never faint or fear;
Thou hast th'assistance of grave senators here,
Thy worthy brethren, some of which have passed
All dangerous gulfs, and in their bright fames placed,
They can instruct and guide thee, and each one
That must adventure, and are coming on
To this great expedition; they will be
Cheerful and forward to encourage thee;
And blessings fall in a most infinite sum
Both on those past, thyself, and those to come.

Passing from this, and more to encourage the labour of the magistrate, he is now conducted to the master triumph, called the Tower of Virtue, which for the strength, safety, and perpetuity, bears the name of the Brazen Tower;

5 **Edward Barkham** Sheriff, 1611–12; died 1634.
27 **shepherd's calendar** almanac
34–5 **service . . . water** refers to the entertainment on the river Thames
40 **Jason** mythological figure noted for his conquest of the Golden Fleece, leader of the Argonauts
41 ***ne plus ultra*** no further; highest point capable of being attained
42 **pilasters** square or rectangular column or pillar
45 **manifestation** i.e., the Golden Fleece
54 ***lading*** freight
58 ***Hight*** called
77 ***decks*** attires, clothes
80 ***senators*** i.e., the Aldermen

of which Integrity keeps the keys, virtue being indeed as a brazen wall to a city or commonwealth; and to illustrate the prosperity it brings to a kingdom, the top turrets or pinnacles of this Brazen Tower shine bright like gold. And upon the gilded battlements thereof stand six knights, three in silvered and three in gilt armour, as virtue's standard-bearers or champions, holding six little streamers or silver bannerets, in each of which are displayed the arms of a noble brother and benefactor, Fame sounding forth their praises to the world, for the encouragement of after-ages, and Antiquity, the register of Fame, containing in her golden legend their names and titles: as that of Sir Henry fitz Ailwin, Draper, lord mayor four-and-twenty years together; Sir John Norman, the first that was rowed in barge to Westminster with silver oars at his own cost and charges; Sir Francis Drake, the son of fame, who in two years and ten months, did cast a girdle about the world; the unparalleled Sir Simon Eyre, who built Leadenhall at his own cost, a storehouse for the poor, both in the upper lofts and lower; the generous and memorable Sir Richard Champion and Sir John Milborne, two bountiful benefactors; Sir Richard Hardell, in the seat of magistracy six years together; Sir John Poultney, four years, which Sir John founded a college in the parish of St Lawrence Poultney, by Candlewick Street; John Hinde, a re-edifier of the parish church of St Swithin by London Stone; Sir Richard Pipe, who being free of the Leathersellers, was also from them translated to the ancient and honourable Society of Drapers; and many whose names for brevity's cause I must omit and hasten to the honour and service of the time present. From the tower, Fame, a personage properly adorned, thus salutes the great master of the day and triumph.

THE SALUTATION OF FAME

Welcome to Virtue's fortress, strong and clear.
Thou art not only safe but glorious here;
It is a tower of brightness. Such is truth,
Whose strength and grace feels a perpetual youth;
The walls are brass, the pyramids fine gold,
Which shows 'tis safety's and prosperity's hold;
Clear conscience is lieutenant, providence there,
Watchfulness, wisdom, constancy, zeal, care,
Are the six warders; keep the watch-tower sure,
That nothing enters but what's just and pure;
For which effect, both to affright and shame
All slothful bloods that blush to look on Fame,
An ensign of good actions each displays,
That worthy works may justly own their praise;
And which is clearliest to be understood,
Thine shines amidst thy glorious brotherhood,
Circled with arms of honour by those passed,
As now with love's arms by the present graced;
And how thy word does thy true worth display:
Fortunæ mater, Diligentia,
Fair Fortune's mother, all may read and see,
Is diligence, endeavouring industry.
See here the glory of illustrious acts,
All of thy own fraternity, whose tracts
'Tis comely to pursue, all thy life's race,
Taking their virtues as thou hold'st their place;
Some, college-founders, temple-beautifiers,
Whose blest souls sing now in celestial choirs;
Erecters some of granaries for the poor,
Though now converted to some rich men's store
(The more the age's misery), some so rare
For this famed city's government and care,
They kept the seat four years with a fair name;
Some, six; but one, the miracle of fame,
Which no society or time can match,
Twenty-four years complete; he was truth's watch,
He went so right and even, and the hand
Of that fair motion bribe could ne'er make stand.
And as men set their watches by the sun,
Set justice but by that which he has done,
And keep it even; so, from men to men,
No magistrate need stir the work again:
It lights into a noble hand today,
And has passed many; many more it may.

By this Tower of Virtue, his lordship being gracefully conducted toward the new Standard, one in a cloudy, ruinous habit, leaning upon the turret, at a trumpet's sounding suddenly starts and wakes, and in amazement throws off his unseemly garments.

NEW STANDARD

What noise is this wakes me from ruin's womb?
Ha! bless me, Time, how brave am I become!
Fame fixed upon my head. Beneath me, round,
The figures of illustrious princes, crowned

98 **gilt** golden
105 **Henry fitz Ailwin** London's first elected mayor (1189–1212)
106 **John Norman** mayor, 1453–54; Middleton repeats the error about Norman's being the first to go by barge to Westminster; he may have been the first to go at his own cost.
108 **Francis Drake** famous English navigator and sailor; admitted to the Drapers in 1588
110 **Simon Eyre** mayor, 1445–56; built Leadenhall in 1419; Dekker makes Eyre a Shoemaker in his play, but Eyre was a Draper.
113 **Richard Champion** mayor, 1565–66; several times Master of the Drapers
John Milborne mayor, 1521–22; built some fourteen alms houses
114 **Richard Hardell** mayor, 1254–58; first name was Ralph
115 **John Poultney** mayor, 1330–32, 1336–37; Stow in his *Survey* (1598) says that Poultney left many 'legacies long to rehearse'.
117–18 **John Hinde** mayor, 1391–92, 1402–05
119 **Richard Pipe** mayor, 1578–79; like Barkham he had first been a Leatherseller
130 ***pyramids*** structures of pyramidal form
138 ***ensign*** banner, coat of arms
140 ***clearliest*** most clear; form not attested in *OED*
149 ***tracts*** course of action
159 ***but one*** i.e., Henry fitz Ailwin
171 **new Standard** rebuilt in Cheapside in 1620–21, statue of Fame on top; served as water conduit
172 **ruinous** decayed, dilapidated

As well for goodness as for state by birth,
Which makes 'em true heirs both to heaven and earth.
Just six in number and all blessèd names,
Two Henrys, Edward, Mary, Eliza, James,
That joy of honest hearts; and there behold
His honoured substitute, whom worth makes bold
To undergo the weight of this degree,
Virtue's fair edifice, raised up like me:
Why, here's the city's goodness, shown in either,
To raise two worthy buildings both together;
For when they made that lord's election free,
I guess that time their charge did pèrfect me;
Nay, note the city's bounty in both still;
When they restore a ruin, 'tis their will
To be so noble in their cost and care,
All blemish is forgot when they repair;
For what has been re-edified o' late,
But lifts its head up in more glorious state:
"'Tis grown a principle; ruins built again
Come bettered both in monuments and men":
The instance is apparent. On then, lord;
E'en at thy entrance thou'dst a great man's word,
The noblest testimony of fair worth
That ever lord had, when he first stood forth
Presented by the city: lose not then
A praise so dear, bestowed not on all men;
Strive to preserve this famous city's peace,
Begun by yon first king, which does increase
Now by the last; from Henry that joined roses,
To James that unites kingdoms, who encloses
All in the arms of love, maliced of none;
Our hearts find that, when neighbouring kingdoms groan;
Which in the magistrate's duty may well move
A zealous care, in all, a thankful love.

After this, for the full close of the forenoon's triumph, near St Lawrence Lane stands a mountain, artfully raised and replenished with fine woolly creatures; Phoebus on the top, shining in a full glory, being circled with the twelve celestial signs. Aries, placed near the principal rays, the proper sign for illustration, thus greets his lordship.

ARIES

Bright thoughts, joy, and alacrity of heart
Bless thy great undertakings. 'Tis the part
And property of Phoebus with his rays
To cheer and to illumine good men's ways;
Eagle-eyed actions, that dare behold
His sparkling globe depart, tried all like gold;
'Tis bribery and injustice, deeds of night,
That fly the sunbeam, which makes good works bright;
Thine look upon't, undazzled; as one beam
Faces another, as we match a gem
With her refulgent fellow, from thy worth
Example sparkles as a star shoots forth.
This mount, the type of eminence and place,
Resembles magistracy's seat and grace;
The sun the magistrate himself implies;
These woolly creatures, all that part which lies
Under his charge and office; not unfit,
Since kings and rulers are in holy writ
With shepherds paralleled, nay, from shepherds reared,
And people and the flock as oft cohered.
Now, as it is the bounty of the sun
To spread his splendours and make gladness run
Over the drooping creatures, it ought so
To be his proper virtue that does owe
To justice his life's flame shot from above
To cheer oppressèd right with looks of love;
Which nothing doubted; Truth's reward light on you,
The beams of all clear comforts shine upon you.

The great feast ended, the whole state of the triumph attends upon his lordship, both to Paul's and homeward; and near the entrance of his lordship's house, two parts of the triumph stand ready planted, viz. the Brazen Tower and the triple-crowned Fountain of Justice, this fountain being adorned with the lively figures of all those graces and virtues which belong to the faithful discharging of so high an office: as Justice, Sincerity, Meekness, Wisdom, Providence, Equality, Industry, Truth, Peace, Patience, Hope, Harmony, all illustrated by proper emblems and expressions; as, Justice by a sword; Sincerity by a lamb; Meekness by a dove; Wisdom by a serpent; Providence by an eagle; Equality by a silvered balance; Industry by a golden ball, on which stands a Cupid, intimating that industry brings both wealth and love; Truth with a fan of stars, with which she chases away Error; Peace with a branch of laurel; Patience a sprig of palm; Hope by a silvered anchor; Harmony by a swan; each at night holding a bright-burning taper in her hand, as a manifestation of purity. His lordship being in sight and drawing near to his entrance, Fame, from the Brazen Tower, closes up the Triumph, his lordship's honourable welcome, with the noble demonstration of his worthy fraternity's affection, in this concluding speech.

FAME

I cannot better the comparison
Of thy fair brotherhood's love than to the sun
After a great eclipse. For as the sphere
Of that celestial motion shines more clear

182 ***Henrys . . . James*** Henry VII, Henry VIII, Edward VI, Queen Mary, Queen Elizabeth, King James I
207–8 ***Henry . . . James*** from Henry VII who united the Yorks and Lancasters to King James I who united Scotland and England
214 **St Lawrence Lane** in Cheapside offering access to the Guildhall
215 **Phoebus** the god Apollo, god of sun and poetry
216–17 **twelve celestial signs** the twelve signs of the zodiac
224 ***tried*** refined
229 ***refulgent*** radiant, gleaming
238 ***cohered*** combined, made analogous
248 **Paul's** St Paul's Cathedral
251 **triple-crowned** refers to the three crowns in the arms of the Drapers
261–2 **Truth . . . Error** Compare the central battle between these two figures in *The Triumphs of Truth* (1613).

After the interposing part is spent,
Than to the eye before the darkness went
Over the bright orb, so their love is shown
With a content past expectation:
A care that has been comely, and a cost
That has been decent; cheerful, which is most,
Fit for the service of so great a state,
So famed a city, and a magistrate
So worthy of it; all has been bestowed
Upon thy triumph, which has clearly showed
The loves of thy fraternity as great
For thy first welcome to thy honoured seat;
And happily is cost requited then,
"When men grace triumphs more than triumphs, men:
Diamonds will shine though set in lead; true worth
Stands always in least need of setting forth."
What makes less noise than merit or less show
Than virtue? 'Tis the undeservers owe
All to vain-glory and to rumour still,
Building their praises on the vulgar will;
All their good is without 'em, not their own;
When wise men to their virtues are best known.
Behold yon fountain with the tripled crown,
And through a cloud the sunbeam piercing down;
So is the worthy magistrate made up;
The triple crown is charity, faith, and hope,
Those three celestial sisters; the cloud too,
That's care, and yet you see the beam strikes through;
A care discharged with honour it presages,
And may it so continue to all ages.
It is thy brotherhood's arms; how well it fits
Both thee and all that for Truth's honour sits.
The time of rest draws near; triumph must cease;
Joy to thy heart, to all a blessèd peace.

FINIS.

For the framework of the whole triumph, with all the proper beauties of workmanship, the credit of that justly appertains to the deserts of Master Garret Christmas, a man excellent in his art, and faithful in his performances.

298 ***cloud the sunbeam*** refers to the heraldic arms of the Drapers

312 **Garret Christmas** artificer whom Middleton regularly praises in the pageant texts

ANYTHING FOR A QUIET LIFE

Edited by Leslie Thomson

IN *Anything for a Quiet Life* (*c.*1621), Middleton returned to the world of his earlier city comedies, and of his audience: commercial London. Together with John Webster, he created an intriguing combination of the immediately topical and timelessly theatrical—the one complementing and commenting on the other. Central to this mix is cloth, as a commodity and as clothing. Consequently, disguise and discovery, which often symbolize the deceptive difference between appearance and reality in plays of the period, are here not only effective and entertaining theatrical devices but also the means of putting visual and verbal focus on the cloth trade itself. With scenes about the buying and selling of fabric literally at the heart of the action, the numerous references to clothing, cloth, and even yarn, gain in significance until the conclusion, when clothes signal the resolution to each of the plots.

For those Londoners who came to Blackfriars Theatre to watch the King's Men perform the play, this emphasis on cloth and clothing would have been especially satisfying, since there could hardly have been anyone in the audience not somehow affected by the sharp decrease in the wool trade which had begun after 1614. By 1621, about when *Anything for a Quiet Life* was being written, the unhappy consequences of a disastrous change in the control of England's cloth trade with the Continent had become distressingly apparent. Middleton and Webster produced a play that in its comic business, wordplay and symbolism seems implicitly to acknowledge the importance of cloth in the real world of their audience.

Following the Anglo-Spanish treaty of 1604, the English trade in woollens (or cloth) grew rapidly—peace meant profit. Under the Merchant Adventurers' monopoly, production in the provinces, warehousing and distribution in London, and export of cloth to the Continent were organized and regulated largely by one group. New kinds of fabric, being produced in the Low Countries and Germany especially, were beginning to threaten the dominance of English woollens both at home and abroad, but more than ten years of growth in trade had fostered stability and complacency among domestic producers, merchants, and exporters. In 1614, however, the Cokayne project precipitated disastrous changes in England's major domestic and export businesses. Until then, the Merchant Adventurers had shipped mostly undyed, undressed cloth to Germany and the Low Countries to be finished. Alderman William Cokayne, a merchant, sold James on his plan to finish cloth before it was exported, and in December 1614 a proclamation abruptly ended the Merchant Adventurers' monopoly by giving a group led by Cokayne control over the export of cloth. The project was a fiasco. Evidence indicates that the new company, the King's Merchant Adventurers, never really intended to make the project a reality. No plans were put into place to dye and dress cloth, with the result that stocks accumulated in London, unfinished and unsold. The full story is long and complex, but the consequences were painfully simple. Before long, investment capital evaporated and the effects began to be felt in the provinces, where workers were laid off, and in the city, where distributors could not afford to warehouse unfinished stock and exporters were prevented from selling it. Almost simultaneously came a shift in domestic and foreign demand from the better quality, heavier wool England produced to the so-called 'new draperies' being manufactured on the continent. By 1617, when the Merchant Adventurers' monopoly was restored, conditions had changed irrevocably; by 1620 the English textile industry was at the beginning of a severe four-year depression (Supple). In 1621, Londoners could not but have had the cloth trade on their minds; in *Anything for a Quiet Life* Middleton and Webster can be seen to have simultaneously acknowledged and capitalized on very real and immediate social and economic concerns by writing a play focusing on cloth, clothing, and a clothseller.

The play's dramatis personae list indicates the importance of clothing as a silent but always visible signifier of function and class in society and therefore on the stage. Especially for spectators still influenced by earlier sumptuary laws, nuances of dress were infinite and telling, offering the playwrights a visual shorthand of implication and the audience a means of placing the various characters. *Anything for a Quiet Life* is populated by figures from virtually every level of early seventeenth-century London society, something their dress would have emphasized visually. Lord Beaufort would have worn expensive fabrics and trimmings to reflect his noble status, and Lady Cressingham's rich attire would have indicated her materialism and aspirations. Down the ladder in class and in dress—if not in morality—come the other characters. The audience would have seen clothing suitable for a knight and his wife, a country gentleman, a sea captain, a citizen and wife, a lawyer and wife, a page, a steward, a surveyor, a barber, a sergeant, a yeoman, apprentices, and a bawd.

But clothing is more than just a way of conveying information about characters; it is also given a central role both structurally and thematically through the shop of Walter Camlet, the mercer. On the unlocalized stage for which the play was written, this shop would have been the only fictional place with a physical presence. Bolts of cloth and possibly a counter in front of a tiring-house opening would have created the mercer's shop where several important scenes are staged. Perhaps these props were removed when the action was located elsewhere, but perhaps not; and if not, the ever-present shop would have provided a suggestive backdrop for the other plots which, although not about the cloth trade specifically, keep the audience's attention on clothing as a commodity, a symbol of status, and a means of deception.

The play has only just begun when references to cloth or clothing become a device of more specific characterization. Beaufort condemns Sir Francis Cressingham's folly in marrying a much younger woman with the judgement that: 'one new gown of hers | When 'tis paid for will eat you out the keeping | Of a bountiful Christmas' (1.1.12–14). Soon after, Walter Camlet tells Cressingham that his wedding purchases of 'tissue, cloth of gold, velvets and silks' will cost the enormous sum of 'about fifteen hundred pounds' (1.1.97–8). This impression of Lady Cressingham as a wife whose clothing purchases will bankrupt her husband is confirmed when she complains to Camlet that his fabrics are inferior, and says she plans to buy imported material instead—which seems likely to have earned her the condemnation of spectators feeling the real consequences of this attitude.

References to clothing elsewhere convey in material terms a character's questionable morality. The high-living Young Franklin protests that the salary offered by Beaufort will not keep him in 'scarlet and gold lace' (1.1.195). The despicable Knavesbe tries to persuade his wife to become Beaufort's mistress by using the analogy of his beaver hat, which he brushes first the wrong and then the right way: 'Look, this is all—smooth and keeps fashion still' (2.1.106–7). Beaufort begins his lustful advance on Sib Knavesbe by admiring her 'habit' and removing her glove; Sib makes Selenger her sexual 'captive' with a skein of symbolically gold thread, and says she will become Beaufort's mistress because he will put her 'into brave clothes and rich jewels' (2.1.188). To escape Sib, Selenger says he must serve Beaufort, 'or else I forfeit my recognizance, | The cloth I wear of his' (3.1.19–20). And Margarita, the bawd, is stigmatized as a 'French-hood' (4.1.333, 342; 4.2.27). These and similar plot-related images contribute to the play's distinctive language of the mercer, emphasizing the focus on Walter Camlet, the innocent and sympathetic victim. Given the hardship endured by men like him in the world of the audience, he is perhaps also representative of those victimized by Cokayne's fabrications.

Midway through *Anything for a Quiet Life*, Camlet, George and Ralph enter in the shop, the two apprentices singing a song advertising the kinds of cloth they have to sell. In the scene, Camlet is deceived by George Cressingham (Sir Francis's son) and Young Franklin, disguised as tailor and knight—clothing dupes the man who sells the fabric which makes it. Further, in the initial exchange between Rachel Camlet and the apprentice George, the bawdy wordplay on 'yard' uses the language of Camlet's trade to connect the play's concerns with sex and clothing. 'Yard' as a measure of cloth and as slang for penis is also central to the suggestive physical comedy of 2.4, when Ralph and the Barber talk at cross-purposes about his 'ware', another word with the same double meaning. The gulling of Camlet and his apprentices by George Cressingham and Young Franklin revolves around a lengthy transaction in which Young Franklin as Sir Andrew buys an inexpensive piece of cloth in order to trick Camlet into allowing him to have a more costly fabric on credit. Besides being good theatre, the scene presents a merchant and his apprentices at work: the bargaining, with its specific references to cloth quality and prices, would have given the action an everyday reality recognizable by spectators who frequented such shops, bargained for such fabrics.

During this transaction the importance of George, Camlet's apprentice, becomes apparent. He, not his master, does most of the negotiating, and as Camlet's problems grow so does the role of George. In a play concerned with social class and relationships of duty, obedience, and service, the role given this apprentice has thematic implications. As a character, George combines convention and invention. He has his origins in the crafty slave of Latin New Comedy: by trickery he reunites the bickering Camlets and helps restore order. But he is also very much a seventeenth-century London apprentice, with particular obligations and duties to his master. In attempting to serve Camlet, George earns the enmity of Rachel Camlet and is sent away before his time of service is completed. Defying Rachel's command to stop singing his song of wares, George insists on the reciprocity of his relationship to Camlet: 'Shall I not follow my trade? I'm bound to't, and my master bound to bring me up in't' (2.2.27–8). After Rachel has left him Camlet uses the same language in pleading with his apprentice to get her back: 'I love her, George, and I am bound to do so' (3.2.197). As both an abstract and concrete symbol of right service, George is a standard to set against the uncertain and inverted relationships of the play.

The deceptions of *Anything for a Quiet Life* are not only of some characters by others but also of the audience. Indeed, the play has been criticized for what have been seen as arbitrary reversals in character and plot. But the idea of thwarted expectations is set out in the first lines, when Beaufort scolds Francis Cressingham: 'you have in this one act | Overthrown the reputatïon the world | Held of your wisdom' (1.1.2–4). And when Cressingham tries to defend his wife Beaufort says, 'Come, come, you read | What you would have her to be, not what she is' (1.1.48–9)—a warning critics might also heed about the play. Near the end of the action, that same wife tells both her stepson, George Cressingham, and the audience, 'I will not be | The woman to you hereafter you expected' (5.1.251–2), anticipating her surprise reversal—one of several making up a series of unexpected and overtly ironic resolutions. Much of the action in the intervening scenes depends on visual and verbal deceptions, or defeated expectations. And several of these are achieved by disguises—changes of clothing—visual business more apparent to an audience than a reader. In particular, the deception which can be seen as a paradigm of the others, the gulling of Camlet and Ralph: (*a*) depends on the disguises of both Young Franklin and George Cressingham; (*b*) involves the theft of cloth; and (*c*) is successful because the Barber has been led to expect one thing, Ralph another.

Clothing, disguise, and defeated expectations are interwoven through *Anything for a Quiet Life*, indicating that Middleton and Webster worked together closely to dramatize certain themes, a process which culminates in the play's several surprise resolutions. Act 5 begins with the entrance of Old Franklin '*in mourning*' and Young Franklin '*disguised like an old serving man*'. After having tricked his son's creditors into accepting half of what they are owed, Old Franklin removes his supposedly dead son's disguise, bringing him 'back to life' (5.2.368)—a 'rebirth' that stretches the conventions of tragicomedy so far as to parody them. Perhaps the audience's expectations were fulfilled rather than thwarted by the discovery that Young Franklin was not dead; we cannot know how effective his disguise was meant to be. But in the case of Selenger, nothing in the stage directions or dialogue indicates that an audience was intended to realize before the end that the boy actor dressed as a page and seduced by Sib Knavesbe is really a woman in the fiction of the play. When in the last scene Selenger enters '*as a woman*' (5.2.215.1), the clothes say it all (indeed, the actor does not speak in this scene; the character is literally a 'quiet wife'). Merely by standing there Selenger would have represented the many deceptions of both characters and audience. Of these, the surprise reversal by Lady Cressingham is probably the most disconcerting. Clothing is again the means by which this change is first conveyed: '*Enter Lady Cressingham in civil habit, Saunder, and* [*the two*] *children, very gallant*' (5.2.260.1–2). Where before she has been extravagantly dressed, now she is in subdued clothes; conversely, Cressingham's two children, who have been shabbily clothed, are now in costly attire. Finally, in a notably different use of clothing, George the apprentice is rewarded for his service to the Camlets with 'two new suits' (5.2.329).

Each of the unexpected and therefore memorable resolutions somehow dramatizes the idea expressed in the prologue that men will do anything for a quiet life. At the play's end Beaufort, having avoided the censure he deserves, complacently describes a comic conclusion: 'Discorded friends atoned, men and their wives | This hope proclaims your after quiet lives.' This might seem merely a neatly rhymed summary of each plot—quiet wife equals quiet life—but in fact the verbal symmetry disguises some decidedly forced and ironic returns to 'quiet'. Of all the male characters, only Camlet achieves a quiet life without compromising himself; the rest are only too willing to do 'anything', pay any moral price, for marital or financial peace. Sir Francis Cressingham is prepared to sign away his children's inheritance to keep his wife in expensive clothes and houses. Knavesbe eagerly makes a deal with Beaufort to be cuckolded for leases and income. George Cressingham allows his wife to be employed by Beaufort—temporarily 'selling her', her name suggests. Old Franklin easily pretends his son is dead to avoid paying his debts in full. And Young Franklin enlists a prostitute to ensure the success of the second of his three self-enriching disguises. Even George lies to reunite his master and mistress, thereby regaining his job—and earning those two new suits.

Near the beginning of the action, Camlet accurately sums up Francis Cressingham's folly and his own attitude: 'He's tied to a new law, and a new wife, | Yet to my old proverb: "anything for a quiet life"' (1.1.312–13). The phrase certainly has a proverbial ring to it, but this may be the first time it was written down—in a sense it *is* Camlet's. There is a ballad with the same title printed about 1621—perhaps in acknowledgement of the play—which relates the story of a browbeaten husband and concludes by advising men to avoid marriage for as long as possible. The ballad's stereotypes emphasize the individuality of the play's characters, of whom the women are particularly effective embodiments of deception and its consequences. Not surprisingly, given the complex and memorable female characters created by both Middleton and Webster in other plays, each of the women in *Anything for a Quiet Life* is a means of dramatizing the movement from deception to reversal and discovery that is the action of the play. Because Lady Cressingham deceives her husband, he sends his two younger children to live with the Camlets. This leads Rachel Camlet to deceive herself into the belief that they are her husband's illegitimate progeny. As a consequence, Rachel threatens to leave Camlet and destroy his business by spreading rumours that his cloth is inferior. Also as a result of Lady Cressingham's deception, George Cressingham is effectively disinherited, leading him to disguise himself as a tailor to gull Camlet, and his wife, Selenger, to disguise herself as a page and work for Beaufort. This lord's sexual advances prompt Sib Knavesbe to deceive him and the audience into thinking she will become his mistress; as well, Sib is fooled by Selenger's disguise into propositioning 'him'. Finally, because Camlet believes that Margarita has helped him—when actually she has duped him by confirming Young Franklin's Frenchman disguise—Camlet offers to reward her. When George attempts to unite his master and mistress by tricking Rachel into believing that Camlet is about to marry Margarita, Rachel becomes violently jealous. Significantly, Walter Camlet, the unconventionally honest mercer and husband, is eventually the victim of most of these deceptions, which make his wife—and therefore his life—unquiet.

Camlet's shop is the Holy Lamb in Lombard Street, a telling combination of the sacred and profane; or perhaps of the innocent and mercantile—or mercenary. Amid the ironic ambiguities of the play's conclusion, Camlet gets the quiet wife and life he seeks, and deserves—a happy conclusion crafted by George, Camlet's paragon of an apprentice. In the rest of the action Old Franklin, George's country acquaintance, helps restore peace and order—quiet—with implications that seem decidedly more ambiguous. The *deus ex machina* quality of Old Franklin's sudden appearance at the play's end highlights the unexpectedness of the reversals. Lady Cressingham's surprising about-face and Knavesbe's unconvincing reformation are clear indications that it is still a fallen world. Middleton's conclusions are invariably ironic reminders that perfection can be achieved only at the price of incredulity. Because he never pretends otherwise, the endings of his plays are, or should be, disturbing; but if we think they are inexplicable, we are deceiving ourselves—pulling the wool over our own eyes.

SEE ALSO

Textual introduction and apparatus: *Companion*, 1160
Authorship and date: *Companion*, 422
Other Middleton–Webster works: *Caesar's Fall*, 328; *Magnificent*, 219; *'The Duchess of Malfi'*, 1886

THOMAS MIDDLETON and JOHN WEBSTER

Anything for a Quiet Life

[*for the King's Men at The Blackfriars*]

THE PERSONS OF THE PLAY

Lord BEAUFORT
Sir Francis CRESSINGHAM, an alchemist
OLD FRANKLIN, a country gentleman
YOUNG CRESSINGHAM, son to Sir Francis
YOUNG FRANKLIN, a sea captain, son to Old Franklin, and companion to Young Cressingham
Master Walter CAMLET, a citizen and mercer
KNAVESBE, a lawyer, and pander to his wife
SELENGER, page to Lord Beaufort
SAUNDER, steward to Sir Francis
GEORGE, an apprentice to Walter Camlet
RALPH, an apprentice to Walter Camlet
A SURVEYOR
Sweetball, a BARBER-SURGEON
Barber's BOY
FLESHHOOK, a yeoman
COUNTERBUFF, a sergeant
Two CHILDREN of Sir Francis, boarded out to Walter Camlet
LADY CRESSINGHAM, wife to Sir Francis
RACHEL, wife to Walter Camlet
SIB, wife to Knavesbe
MARGARITA, a French bawd
3 or 4 Citizens (CREDITORS)

Prologue

Howe'er th'intents and appetites of men
Are different as their faces how and when
T'employ their actions, yet all without strife
Meet in this point: anything for a quiet life.
Nor is there one, I think, that's hither come
For his delight, but would find peace at home
On any terms. The lawyer does not cease
To talk himself into a sweat with pain,
And so his fees buy quiet, 'tis his gain;

Prologue.4 anything . . . life proverbial, but this is perhaps the first printed occurrence of the phrase. There is also a ballad, 'Any thing for a quiet life; Or the married man's bondage to a cursed wife' (*c.*1620); and see *The Stonyhurst Pageants* (*c.*1610–25): 'For he that doth intend to live & lead a quiet life | Must ever more contented be to be ruled by his wife'. When, as in JOHNSON and commonly at the time, 'any thing' is two words, the bawdy implications are more apparent. The play's title and action are also summed up in another proverb: 'Better enjoy a little with quietness than possess much with trouble'.
quiet the word and its variants occur twenty-six times in the play, emphasizing the desire for peace and order at three levels: familial, social, political
5 **hither** to the theatre

The poor man does endure the scorching sun,
And feels no weariness his day-labour done,
So his wife entertain him with a smile,
And thank his travail, though she slept the while.
This being in men of all conditions true
Does give our play a name, and if to you
It yield content and usual delight,
For our parts we shall sleep secure tonight.

1.1 *Incipit Actus Primus*
Enter the Lord Beaufort, and Sir Francis Cressingham

BEAUFORT
Away! I am ashamed of your proceedings,
And seriously you have in this one act
Overthrown the reputatïon the world
Held of your wisdom.
CRESSINGHAM Why, sir?
BEAUFORT Can you not see
Your error? That having buried so good a wife
Not a month since, one that, to speak the truth,
Had all those excellencies—which our books
Have only feigned to make a complete wife—
Most exactly in her in practice, and to marry
A girl of fifteen, one bred up i'th' court,
That by all consonancy of reason is like
To cross your estate. Why, one new gown of hers
When 'tis paid for will eat you out the keeping
Of a bountiful Christmas. I am ashamed of you,
For you shall make too dear a proof of it,
I fear, that in the election of a wife,
As in a project of war, to err but once
Is to be undone for ever.
CRESSINGHAM Good my lord,
I do beseech you let your better judgement
Go along with your reprehension.
BEAUFORT So it does,
And can find naught to extenuate your fault
But your dotage. You are a man well sunk in years
And to graft such a young blossom into your stock
Is the next way to make every carnal eye
Bespeak your injury. Troth, I pity her too;
She was not made to wither and go out
By painted fires that yields her no more heat
Than to be lodged in some bleak banqueting house
I'th' dead of winter. And what follows then?
Your shame and the ruin of your children, and there's
The end of a rash bargain.
CRESSINGHAM With your pardon,
That she is young is true, but that discretion
Has gone beyond her years and overta'en
Those of maturer age does more improve
Her goodness. I confess she was bred at court,
But so retiredly that—as still the best
In some place is to be learnt there—so her life
Did rectify itself more by the court chapel
Than by the Office of the Revels. Best of all virtues
Are to be found at court, and where you meet
With writings contrary to this known truth,
They are framed by men that never were so happy
To be planted there to know it. For the difference
Between her youth and mine, if you will read
A matron's sober staidness in her eye
And all the other grave demeanour fitting
The governess of a house, you'll then confess
There's no disparity between us.
Enter Master Walter Camlet
BEAUFORT Come, come, you read
What you would have her to be, not what she is.—
O, Master Walter Camlet, you are welcome.
CAMLET
I thank your lordship.
BEAUFORT And what news stirring in Cheapside?
CAMLET
Nothing new there, my lord, but the Standard.
BEAUFORT O, that's

13 **travail** labour, with a probable pun on 'travel'
17 **our parts** (*a*) ourselves; (*b*) our roles
1.1 attributed to Webster
0.2 ***Beaufort*** perhaps ironic; French: *beau*: suitor, *fort*: strong
3 **reputatïon** good opinion
7–8 **books... complete wife** perhaps a specific allusion to Thomas Overbury's poem, 'The Wife' (1613), possibly edited by Webster; but the plural suggests the numerous domestic guidebooks popular at the time, such as *The English Housewife. Containing the inward and outward virtues which ought to be in a complete woman*, by Gervaise Markham (1615)
8 **feigned** fictitiously invented
12 **cross** deplete
16 **election** choice
17–18 **project... for ever** proverbial
20 **reprehension** rebuke
21 **extenuate** lessen
23 **stock** (*a*) trunk of a tree; (*b*) line of descent
24 **carnal** worldly
25 **Bespeak your injury** talk about your cuckolding (?)
27 **painted fires** pictures of fires rather than real ones; likely a euphemism for Cressingham's impotence: lack of 'fire'
28 **banqueting house** a semi-permanent building in Jacobean gardens, frequently used by lovers as meeting places
32 **discretion** judgement
34 **improve** prove
38 **rectify** improve
38–9 **court chapel... Office of the Revels** she has spent more time at prayer than at masques
45 **staidness** stability
48.1 ***Walter Camlet*** suggests 'watered camlet', a fabric with a wavy surface; 'camlet' was a name originally applied to a beautiful and costly eastern fabric, afterwards to more common imitations and substitutes; 'Water' is a variant of 'Walter'. Citizen: a man admitted to the freedom of the city through membership in a guild, a tradesman as opposed to a gentleman; mercer: a cloth merchant
51 **Cheapside** the chief commercial street of London, from St Paul's to the Poultry. Merchants such as clothsellers were located in streets running off Cheapside.
52 **Standard** The Standard in Cornhill was a square pillar with a fountain, statues around the sides, and the image of Fortune at the top.

A monument your wives take great delight in.
I do hear you are grown a mighty purchaser;
I hope shortly to find you a continual resident upon
The north aisle of the Exchange.

CAMLET Where? With the Scotsmen?

BEAUFORT
No sir, with the aldermen.

CAMLET Believe it, I am a poor commoner.

CRESSINGHAM
Come, you are warm, and blessed with a fair wife.

CAMLET
There's it; her going brave has the only virtue
To improve my credit in the subsidy book.

BEAUFORT But, I pray, how thrives your new plantation of silkworms, those I saw last summer at your garden?

CAMLET They are removed, sir.

BEAUFORT Whither?

CAMLET This winter my wife has removed them home to a fair chamber where divers courtiers use to come and see them, and my wife carries them up. I think shortly, what with the store of visitants, they'll prove as chargeable to me as the morrow after Simon and Jude—only excepting the taking down and setting up again of my glass windows.

BEAUFORT That a man of your estate should be so gripple-minded and repining at his wife's bounty!

CRESSINGHAM There are no such ridiculous things i'th' world as those love money better than themselves. For though they have understanding to know riches, and a mind to seek them, and a wit to find them, and policy to keep them, and long life to possess them, yet commonly they have withal such a false sight, such bleared eyes, all their wealth when it lies before them does seem poverty. And such a one are you.

CAMLET Good Sir Francis, you have had sore eyes too—you have been a gamester—but you have given it o'er, and to redeem the vice belonged to't now you entertain certain parcels of silenced ministers, which I think will equally undo you. Yet should these waste you but lenitively, your devising new watermill for recovery of drowned land and certain dreams you have in alchemy to find the philosopher's stone will certainly draw you to th' bottom. I speak freely, sir, and would not have you angry, for I love you.

CRESSINGHAM I am deeply in your books for furnishing my late wedding. Have you brought a note of the particulars?

CAMLET No sir, at more leisure.

CRESSINGHAM What comes the sum to?

CAMLET For tissue, cloth of gold, velvets and silks, about fifteen hundred pounds.

CRESSINGHAM Your money is ready.

CAMLET Sir, I thank you.

CRESSINGHAM And how do my two young children, whom I have put to board with you?

BEAUFORT Have you put forth two of your children already?

CRESSINGHAM 'Twas my wife's discretion to have it so.

BEAUFORT Come, 'tis the first principle in a mother-in-law's chop-logic to divide the family, to remove from forth your sight the object that her cunning knows

53 **monument...delight in** with bawdy implications, given the shape of the Standard
54 **purchaser** a money maker
56 **Exchange** the Royal Exchange built in London by Sir Thomas Gresham in 1566, where merchants assembled
Scotsmen probably a reference to the many who had followed King James from Scotland when he became king and had been given knighthoods or had otherwise benefited from association with the court
57 **aldermen** the chief officers of a city ward. Camlet's social position and allegiances are being defined.
58 **warm** financially comfortable
59 **brave** expensively dressed
virtue power
60 **subsidy book** tax roll
61–2 **plantation of silkworms** The implication is that she lured men to her. Cf. *The Fair Maid of the Inn* (*BEPD* 668), 2.2.43: 'In England you have several adamants, to draw in spurs and rapiers; one keeps silkworms in a gallery...'.
66 **use to come** are in the habit of coming
67 **carries** escorts
68 **store** large number
69 **chargeable** costly. Silkworms should be a source of income for Camlet rather than a cost incurred by his wife.
69–70 **Simon and Jude** the feast of Saints Simon and Jude, October 28, in honour of the two apostles martyred while preaching in Persia. October 29 was Lord Mayor's Day, when the new Lord Mayor of London assumed office. The livery company to which the Mayor belonged organized the costly celebrations, meeting expenses by levying a tax on its members.
70–1 **excepting...glass windows** Perhaps this is a general comment on the expense of removing and installing the windows in the upper level(s) of Camlet's shop building; but it may refer to the fact that people came to his house to watch the Lord Mayor's Day parade from the upper windows, necessitating their removal and reinstallation.
72–3 **gripple-minded** niggardly
73 **repining** grumbling
bounty liberality
77 **policy** prudence
79 **false** distorted
bleared eyes poor perception
82 **sore eyes** from lack of sleep; see 2.1.104
83 **gamester** a womanizer, or a gambler, probably the dominant meaning here
84 **redeem** atone for
85 **parcels** a set or pack; said contemptuously
silenced ministers nonconformists forbidden to preach
86 **waste** destroy
87 **lenitively** gently
watermill a reference to a scheme to use watermills to drain the fens, a costly, impossible project
89 **philosopher's stone** a supposed solid substance or preparation believed by alchemists to possess the property of changing other metals into gold or silver, the discovery of which was the aim of alchemy
92 **deeply...books** indebted
97 **tissue** a rich cloth, often interwoven with gold or silver, perhaps suggesting that his wife was dressing above his social class
98 **fifteen hundred pounds** Conversion into today's dollars is difficult, but a pound in the early 1600s would roughly equal between \$100 and \$150 today; Cressingham has spent an extravagant amount on his wedding.
102 **put to board** boarded out
104 **discretion** choice
105–6 **mother-in-law's** step-mother's
106 **chop-logic** sophistical or contentious argument

would dull her insinuation. Had you been a kind father, it would have been your practice every day to have preached to these two young ones carefully your late wife's funeral sermon. 'Las, poor souls, are they turned so soon a-grazing?

Enter Young Cressingham and Young Franklin

CAMLET My lord, they are placed where they shall be respected as mine own.

BEAUFORT
I make no question of it, good Master Camlet.
See here your eldest son, George Cressingham.

CRESSINGHAM
You have displeased and grieved your mother-in-law,
And till you have made submission and procured
Her pardon, I'll not know you for my son.

YOUNG CRESSINGHAM
I have wrought her no offence, sir. The difference
Grew about certain jewels which my mother—
By your consent—lying upon her deathbed,
Bequeathed to her three children. These I demanded,
And being denied these, thought this sin of hers
To violate so gentle a request
Of her predecessor was an ill foregoing
Of a mother-in-law's harsh nature.

CRESSINGHAM Sir, understand
My will moved in her denial. You have jewels
To pawn—or sell them! Sirrah, I will have you
As obedient to this woman as to myself.
Till then you are none of mine.

CAMLET O, Master George,
Be ruled, do anything for a quiet life;
Your father's peace of life moves in it too.
I have a wife, when she is in the sullens,
Like a cook's dog that you see turn a wheel,
She will be sure to go and hide herself
Out of the way dinner and supper. And in
These fits Bow bell is a still organ to her.
When we were married first, I well remember,
Her railing did appear but a vision
Till certain scratches on my hand and face
Assured me it was substantial. She's a creature
Uses to waylay my faults, and more desires
To find them out than to have them amended.
She has a book, which I may truly nominate
Her Black Book, for she remembers in it in
Short items all my misdemeanours, as:
Item, such a day I was got foxed with foolish metheglin in the company of certain Welsh chapmen. Item, such a day being at the Artillery Garden one of my neighbours in courtesy to salute me with his musket set afire my fustian-and-apes breeches. Such a day I lost fifty pound in hugger-mugger at dice at the quest-house. Item, I lent money to a sea captain, on his bare 'Confound him, he would pay me again the next morning', and suchlike.
For which she railed upon me when I should sleep,
And that's, you know, intolerable, for indeed
'Twill tame an elephant.

YOUNG CRESSINGHAM 'Tis a shrewd vexation,
But your discretion, sir, does bear it out
With a month's sufferance.

CAMLET Yes, and I would wish you
To follow mine example.

YOUNG FRANKLIN [*aside to Young Cressingham*]
Here's small comfort,
George, from your father.—Here's a lord whom I
Have long depended upon for employment; I will see
If my suit will thrive better. [*To Beaufort*] Please your lordship,
You know I am a younger brother, and my fate
Throwing me upon the late ill-starred voyage
To Guiana, failing of our golden hopes,
I and my ship addressed ourselves to serve
The Duke of Florence.

108 **insinuation** stealing into the favour or affections by subtle means
112 **a-grazing** The analogy to animals suggests the seriousness of what Cressingham has done in farming out his young children.
112.1 ***Franklin*** A franklin was a landowner of free but not noble birth; the term also implied a liberal host.
116 **George Cressingham** George is the name of two characters, one the son of a knight, the other an apprentice; the duplication would not be as apparent in performance as on the page, but it is probably intentional, perhaps suggesting underlying similarities.
118 **made submission** yielded
129 **Sirrah** a term of reprimand, assumption of authority
138 **Bow bell** the bells of Bow Church (St Mary-le-Bow) in Cheapside, so called from the 'bows' or arches that supported its steeple
still silent
140 **railing** abusive language
143 **Uses to waylay** has the habit of lying in wait for
146 **Black Book** (*fig.*) a book recording the names and crimes of those liable to censure or punishment; here a list of Camlet's follies, which suggest that he is a natural victim
remembers records
148 **Item** an entry in an account or register
foxed drunk
metheglin a liquor made by fermenting honey and water
149 **chapmen** merchants
150 **Artillery Garden** the soldiers' practising ground, outside Bishopsgate, London
151 **salute** greet
musket a shotgun
152 **fustian-and-apes** cotton velvet; a corruption of 'fustian of Naples'
153 **in hugger-mugger** secretly
quest-house a house where inquests in a ward or parish were held; also, apparently, a place for illegal gambling
159 **shrewd** severe
160 **discretion** prudence
bear it out endure
161 **sufferance** indulgence
162 **small comfort** literally, no money
167 **late ill-starred voyage** In June 1617, Sir Walter Ralegh departed on his second trip to Guiana, which was plagued by bad weather, disease, and attempted mutiny; when Ralegh returned to England in June 1618 without the gold he had agreed to deliver in return for freedom from imprisonment in the Tower, he was executed.
168 **Guiana** now part of north-eastern Venezuela along the Orinoco River
failing of with the failure of

BEAUFORT Yes, I understood so.

YOUNG FRANKLIN
Who gave me both encouragement and means
To do him some small service 'gainst the Turk.
Being settled there both in his pay and trust,
Your lordship, minding to rig forth a ship
To trade for the East Indies, sent for me.
And what your promise was, if I would leave
So great a fortune to become your servant,
Your letters yet can witness.

BEAUFORT Yes, what follows?

YOUNG FRANKLIN
That for aught I perceive, your former purpose
Is quite forgotten. I have stayed here two months
And find your intended voyage but a dream,
And the ship you talk of as imaginary
As that the astronomers point at in the clouds.
I have spent two thousand ducats since my arrival.
Men that have command, my lord, at sea, cannot live
Ashore without money.

BEAUFORT Know, sir, a late purchase
Which cost me a great sum has diverted me
From my former purpose. Besides, suits in law
Do every term so trouble me by land
I have forgot going by water. If you please
To rank yourself among my followers
You shall be welcome, and I'll make your means
Better than any gentleman's I keep.

YOUNG FRANKLIN
Some twenty mark a year! Will that maintain
Scarlet and gold lace, play at th'ordinary,
And bevers at the tavern?

BEAUFORT I had thought
To prefer you to have been captain of a ship
That's bound for the Red Sea.

YOUNG FRANKLIN What hinders it?

BEAUFORT
Why, certainly the merchants are possessed
You have been a pirate.

YOUNG FRANKLIN Say I were one still?
If I were past the line once, why, methinks
I should do them better service.

Enter Knavesbe

BEAUFORT Pray forbear;
Here's a gentleman whose business must
Engross me wholly.

[*Beaufort and Knavesbe talk apart*]

YOUNG CRESSINGHAM [*to Young Franklin*]
What's he? Dost thou know him?

YOUNG FRANKLIN
A pox upon him! A very knave and rascal
That goes a-hunting with the penal statutes,
And good for naught but to persuade their lords
To rack their rents and give o'er housekeeping.
Such caterpillars may hang at their lords' ears
When better men are neglected.

YOUNG CRESSINGHAM What's his name?

YOUNG FRANKLIN
Knavesbe.

YOUNG CRESSINGHAM
Knavesbe!

YOUNG FRANKLIN One that deals in a tenth share
About projections. He and his partners, when
They have got a suit once past the seal, will so
Wrangle about partitïon, and sometimes
They fall to th'ears about it, like your fencers
That cudgel one another by patent. You shall see him
So terribly bedashed in a Michaelmas term
Coming from Westminster that you would swear
He were lighted from a horse race. Hang him, hang him!
He's a scurvy informer, has more cozenage

172 **the Turk** the Turkish forces
174 **rig forth** ready [a ship] for the sea
175 **East Indies** probably a specific reference to the East India Company, a trading company formed in 1600
182–3 **ship...clouds** the constellation Argo
184 **two thousand ducats** A ducat was a gold coin worth about 9*s.*; the context indicates a considerable amount of money.
189 **term** one of the three or four periods in the year when law courts were in session
194 **twenty mark** A mark was an amount, not a coin; it was two-thirds of a pound, 13*s.* 4*d.*
195 **Scarlet and gold lace** expensive clothing
play at th'ordinary a gambling game at an eating-house
196 **bevers** drinks or snacks
199 **possessed** informed
200 **pirate** This characterizes Young Franklin as a threat to trade. In October 1620 a fleet had been sent out to scatter pirates preying on English ships; it was only partly successful.
201 **line** equator
204 **Engross** occupy
205 **pox upon him** an exclamation of irritation
knave an unprincipled man; a base and crafty rogue
206 **a-hunting...penal statutes** uses the law to entrap
208 **rack...rents** charge an extortionate rent for land
housekeeping hospitality
209 **caterpillars** (*fig.*) extortioners
hang at their lords' ears have influence
212 **projections** business deals
213 **past the seal** approved by the authorities
214 **partitïon** division into shares
215 **fall to th'ears** said of animals fighting; hence of persons, to disagree violently
215–16 **fencers...patent** The lawyers put on a false show to distract clients from their collusion, just as fencers fought fixed bouts with harmless weapons.
217 **bedashed** splattered with mud. In *Trick* 1.4.42–45, Dampit, who bears a considerable resemblance to Knavesbe, describes himself in similar terms.
Michaelmas term a High Court term beginning soon after Michaelmas (29 September)
218 **Westminster** Westminster Hall, site of the law courts
220 **scurvy** contemptible
cozenage fraud

In him than is in five travelling lotteries.
To feed a kite with the carrion of this knave
When he's dead, and reclaim her—O, she would prove
An excellent hawk for talon. H'as a fair creature
To his wife too, and a witty rogue it is,
And some men think this knave will wink at small faults.
But, honest George, what shall become of us now?

YOUNG CRESSINGHAM
'Faith I am resolved to set up my rest
For the Low Countries.

YOUNG FRANKLIN To serve there?

YOUNG CRESSINGHAM Yes, certain.

YOUNG FRANKLIN There's thin commons;
Besides, they have added one day more to th' week
Than was in the creation. Art thou valiant,
Art thou valiant, George?

YOUNG CRESSINGHAM
I may be, an I be put to't.

YOUNG FRANKLIN O, never fear that.
Thou canst not live two hours after thy landing
Without a quarrel. Thou must resolve to fight,
Or like a sumner thou'lt be bastinadoed
At every town's end. You shall have gallants there
As ragged as the fall o'th' leaf, that live
In Holland where the finest linen's made
And yet wear ne'er a shirt. These will not only
Quarrel with a newcomer when they are drunk,
But they will quarrel with any man has means
To be drunk afore them. Follow my counsel, George;
Thou shalt not go o'er, we'll live here i'th' city.

YOUNG CRESSINGHAM
But how?

YOUNG FRANKLIN
How? Why as other gallants do
That feed high and play copiously yet brag
They have but nine pound a year to live on. These
Have wit to turn rich fools and gulls into quarter-days
That bring them in certain payment. I have a project
Reflects upon yon mercer. Master Camlet
Shall put us into money.

YOUNG CRESSINGHAM What is't?

YOUNG FRANKLIN Nay,
I will not stale it aforehand; 'tis a new one.
Nor cheating amongst gallants may seem strange,
Why, a reaching wit goes current on th'Exchange.

Exeunt Young Cressingham and Young Franklin

KNAVESBE [*to Beaufort*] O, my lord, I remember you and I were students together at Cambridge, but believe me you went far beyond me.

BEAUFORT When I studied there I had so fantastical a brain that like a fieldfare, frighted in winter by a birding-piece, I could settle nowhere: here and there a little of every several art, and away.

KNAVESBE Now my wit, though it were more dull, yet I went slowly on, and, as divers others, when I could not prove an excellent scholar, by a plodding patience I attained to be a petty lawyer. And I thank my dullness for't—you may stamp in lead any figure, but in oil or quicksilver nothing can be imprinted, for they keep no certain station.

BEAUFORT O, you tax me well of irresolution. But say, worthy friend, how thrives my weighty suit which I have trusted to your friendly bosom? Is there any hope to make me happy?

KNAVESBE 'Tis yet questionable, for I have not broke the ice to her. An hour hence come to my house, and if it lie in man, be sure, as the law phrase says, I will create you Lord Paramount of your wishes.

BEAUFORT O, my best friend, and one that takes the hardest course i'th' world to make himself so. [*Exit Knavesbe*]
[*To Cressingham*] Sir, now I'll take my leave.

CRESSINGHAM Nay, good my lord, my wife is coming down.

221 **travelling lotteries** There were 'standing' lotteries in London and other large towns from the mid-sixteenth century, then from 1618–21 there were the Virginia Running Lotteries, 'running' or 'ring' lotteries which travelled from one locality to another, organized for raising money in the provinces to support new-world settlement; the lotteries in general, and these in particular, were unsuccessful and perceived as scams.
222 **kite** a bird of prey
carrion carcass
223 **reclaim** tame
224 **talon** a bird's hind claw
226 **will wink at small faults** is willing to be cuckolded, probably with a *double entendre*; 'fault': female genitals
228 **rest** a metaphor from the game of primero, meaning to stand upon the cards you have in your hand in hopes they may prove better than your adversary's; to take a chance
229 **Low Countries** The Netherlands, Belgium and Holland, where England had retained a military base after settling the war with Spain in 1604
230 **thin commons** Soldiers serving in the Low Countries were poorly paid.
231 **added . . . week** a reference to the unpunctuality of soldiers' pay. Irregular payments allowed the captain to keep back more of his men's pay.
232 **valiant** brave
234 **an** if
237 **sumner** one who summoned people to appear in court
bastinadoed beaten with a stick
238 **town's end** the outskirts of town
245 **city** both greater London and the business district which included Cheapside
247 **feed high** eat to excess
248 **nine pound a year** not enough to live in style
249 **quarter-days** the due dates of rents and other quarterly charges; hence, sources of income
251 **Reflects** casts blame upon
255 **reaching** far-reaching; perhaps suggesting 'overreaching'
goes current is common
259 **fantastical** impulsive
260 **fieldfare** a species of thrush
birding-piece a weapon for shooting birds
262 **art** a university subject
266 **petty lawyer** one who handles minor cases
dullness mental slowness
268 **quicksilver** mercury
269 **station** place
271 **weighty suit** important request
277 **Lord Paramount** one who has supreme power or jurisdiction, likely with the bawdy implication of being 'on top'

Enter Lady Cressingham and Saunder

BEAUFORT [*to Cressingham*] Pray, pardon me, I have business so importunes me o'th' sudden I cannot stay. Deliver mine excuse, and in your ear this: let not a fair woman make you forget your children. [*Exit*]

LADY CRESSINGHAM [*to Camlet*] What? Are you taking leave too?

CAMLET Yes, good madam.

LADY CRESSINGHAM The rich stuff which my husband bought of you, the works of them are too common. I have got a Dutch painter to draw patterns which I'll have sent to your factors, as in Italy, at Florence and Ragusa where these stuffs are woven, to have pieces made for mine own wearing of a new invention.

CAMLET You may, lady, but 'twill be somewhat chargeable.

LADY CRESSINGHAM Chargeable! What of that? If I live another year I'll have my agents shall lie for me at Paris and at Venice and at Valladolid in Spain for intelligence of all new fashions.

CRESSINGHAM Do sweetest, thou deservest to be exquisite in all things.

CAMLET [*to Lady Cressingham*] The two children to which you are mother-in-law would be repaired too; 'tis time they had new clothing.

LADY CRESSINGHAM I pray sir, do not trouble me with them. They have a father indulgent and careful of them.

CRESSINGHAM [*to Camlet*] I am sorry you made the motion to her.

CAMLET [*to Cressingham*] I have done. [*Aside*] He has run himself into a pretty dotage. [*To Lady Cressingham*] Madam, with your leave.
[*Aside*] He's tied to a new law, and a new wife,
Yet to my old proverb: 'anything for a quiet life'.
Exit

LADY CRESSINGHAM Good friend, I have a suit to you.

CRESSINGHAM Dearest self, you most powerfully sway me.

LADY CRESSINGHAM That you would give o'er this fruitless, if I may not say this idle, study of alchemy. Why, half your house looks like a glass-house.

SAUNDER And the smoke you make is a worse enemy to good housekeeping than tobacco.

LADY CRESSINGHAM Should one of your glasses break it might bring you to a dead palsy.

SAUNDER My Lord, your quicksilver has made all your more solid gold and silver fly in fume.

CRESSINGHAM [*to Lady Cressingham*] I'll be ruled by you in anything.

LADY CRESSINGHAM Go Saunder, break all the glasses.

SAUNDER I fly to't. *Exit*

LADY CRESSINGHAM Why, noble friend, would you find the true philosopher's stone indeed, my good housewifery should do it. You understand I was bred up with a great courtly lady. Do not think all women mind gay clothes and riot; there are some widows living have improved both their own fortunes and their children's. Would you take my counsel, I'd advise you to sell your land.

CRESSINGHAM My land!

LADY CRESSINGHAM Yes, and the manor house upon't, 'tis rotten. O, the new fashioned buildings brought from the Hague—'tis stately! I have intelligence of a purchase, an the title sound, will, for half the money you may sell yours for, bring you in more rent than yours now yields you.

CRESSINGHAM If it be so good a pennyworth, I need not sell my land to purchase it. I'll procure money to do it.

LADY CRESSINGHAM Where sir?

CRESSINGHAM Why, I'll take it up at interest.

LADY CRESSINGHAM Never did any man thrive that purchased with use-money.

CRESSINGHAM How come you to know these thrifty principles?

LADY CRESSINGHAM How? Why, my father was a lawyer and died in the commission, and may not I by a natural instinct have a reaching that way? There are on mine own knowledge some divines' daughters infinitely affected with reading controversies, and that, some think, has been a means to bring so many suits into the spiritual court. Pray, be advised, sell your land and purchase more. I knew a pedlar by being merchant this way is become lord of many manors. We should look to lengthen our estates as we do our lives.

Enter Saunder

And though I am young, yet I am confident
Your able constitutïon of body
When you are past fourscore shall keep you fresh
Till I arrive at the neglected year

289 **stuff** a woven woollen material with no nap
290 **works** weaving; ornamentation. Lady Cressingham's desire for imported fabric would have made her unpopular with many in the audience.
291 **Dutch painter** The Dutch had a reputation for fine craftsmanship; these references to foreigners again indicate the threat that Lady Cressingham poses to the domestic cloth trade.
292 **factors** agents
293 **Ragusa** an ancient seaport and trade centre on the east coast of the Adriatic where silk and woollen goods were manufactured
294 **new invention** the latest fashion
295 **chargeable** costly
297 **lie...at** i.e. visit these places to work
298 **Valladolid** in Spain; a textile manufacturing centre
307 **motion** suggestion
312 **new law** new way of doing things (?)
318 **glass-house** a glass-making works. There was one in Blackfriars, near the theatre.
322 **dead palsy** paralysis
324 **fume** smoke
332 **mind** desire
338–9 **the Hague** The city was said to be the most attractive and best built in the Netherlands.
343 **pennyworth** bargain
346 **take...interest** borrow money at interest
348 **use-money** money borrowed at interest
352 **in the commission** as a justice of the peace
353 **reaching** ability
354 **divines** clergymen
355 **controversies** religious disputes
357 **spiritual court** the ecclesiastical courts, which had jurisdiction in matrimonial cases
364 **neglected** unthought of

That I am past childbearing. And yet even then
Quick'ning our faint heats in a soft embrace,
And kindling divine flames in fervent prayers,
We may both go out together, and one tomb
Quit our executors the rites of two.

CRESSINGHAM
O, you are so wise and so good in everything.
I move by your direction.

SAUNDER [*aside*] She has caught him!

Exeunt

Finis Actus Primus

❀

2.1 *Incipit Actus Secundus*
A table [and chair]. Enter Knavesbe and his wife Sib Knavesbe

KNAVESBE
Have you drunk the eggs and muscadine I sent you?

SIB KNAVESBE
No, they are too fulsome.

KNAVESBE Away, you're a fool.
[*Aside*] How shall I begin to break the matter to her?
—I do long, wife.

SIB KNAVESBE Long, sir?

KNAVESBE Long infinitely.
Sit down.

[*She sits*]

There is a penitential motion in me
Which, if thou wilt but second, I shall be
One of the happiest men in Europe.

SIB KNAVESBE What might that be?

KNAVESBE
I had last night one of the strangest dreams.
Methought I was thy confessor, thou mine,
And we revealed between us privately
How often we had wronged each other's bed
Since we were married.

SIB KNAVESBE Came you drunk to bed?
There was a dream with a witness.

KNAVESBE No, no witness.
I dreamt nobody heard it but we two.
This dream, wife, do I long to put in act;
Let us confess each other, and I vow
Whatever thou hast done with that sweet corpse
In the way of natural frailty, I protest
Most freely I will pardon.

SIB KNAVESBE Go sleep again.
Was there ever such a motion?

KNAVESBE Nay, sweet woman,
An thou wilt not have me run mad with my desire
Be persuaded to't.

SIB KNAVESBE Well, be it your pleasure.

KNAVESBE
But to answer truly.

SIB KNAVESBE O, most sincerely.

KNAVESBE Begin then, examine me first.

SIB KNAVESBE Why, I know not what to ask you.

KNAVESBE Let me see. Your father was a captain—demand of me how many dead pays I am to answer for in the musterbook of wedlock by the martial fault of borrowing from my neighbours.

SIB KNAVESBE Troth, I can ask no such foolish questions.

KNAVESBE Why then, open confession I hope, dear wife, will merit freer pardon. I sinned twice with my laundress, and last circuit there was at Banbury a she-chamberlain that had a spice of purity, but at last I prevailed over her.

SIB KNAVESBE O, you are an ungracious husband.

KNAVESBE I have made a vow never to ride abroad but in thy company. O, a little drink makes me clamber like a monkey. Now, sweet wife, you have been an out-lier too—which is best feed, in the forest or in the purlieus?

SIB KNAVESBE A foolish mind of you i' this.

KNAVESBE Nay, sweet love, confess freely; I have given you the example.

SIB KNAVESBE Why, you know I went last year to Sturbridge Fair.

KNAVESBE Yes.

SIB KNAVESBE And being in Cambridge, a handsome scholar, one of Emmanuel College, fell in love with me.

KNAVESBE [*trying to embrace her*] O, you sweet-breathed monkey.

SIB KNAVESBE [*pushing him away*] Go hang—you are so boisterous.

KNAVESBE But did this scholar show thee his chamber?

371 **caught** deceived
2.1 attributed to Webster
1 **eggs and muscadine** an aphrodisiac; muscadine is muscatel wine
2 **fulsome** cloying
5 **penitential motion** impulse to confess
17 **corpse** living body
18 **natural frailty** human predisposition to sin
27 **dead pays** salary continued in the name of a soldier or sailor actually dead or discharged and appropriated by the officer
28 **musterbook** book in which military forces are registered
martial characteristic of soldiers; a continuation of the military imagery
33 **circuit** the journey of judges and lawyers like Knavesbe from town to town to hold court
Banbury a puritan market town in Oxfordshire
33–4 **she-chamberlain** chambermaid at an inn
34 **spice** trace
37 **ride** (*a*) travel; (*b*) have sexual intercourse
38–9 **clamber . . . monkey** Monkeys typified lechery; possibly this also describes Knavesbe's actions here.
39 **out-lier** one who sleeps away from home
40 **feed** (*a*) food; (*b*) sexual intercourse
purlieus (*a*) land on the border of a forest; (*b*) 'to hunt, follow one's game in the purlieus': to seek illicit sex
44–5 **Sturbridge Fair** just north of Cambridge, the annual fair ran from 19 September for two weeks
48 **Emmanuel College** in Cambridge University, which was decidedly puritan at the time
50 **monkey** In Sidney's *Arcadia* the monkey's sweet breath is said to be one of the gifts from beasts to women.
52 **boisterous** exuberant; perhaps describing Knavesbe's actions

SIB KNAVESBE Yes.

KNAVESBE And didst thou like him?

SIB KNAVESBE Like him! O, he had the most enticingest straw-coloured beard, a woman with black eyes would have loved him like jet. He was the finest man with a formal wit, and he had a fine dog that sure was whelped i'th' college, for he understood Latin.

KNAVESBE Pue wawe! This is nothing till I know what he did in's chamber.

SIB KNAVESBE He burnt wormwood in't to kill the fleas i'th' rushes.

KNAVESBE But what did he to thee there?

SIB KNAVESBE Some five-and-twenty years hence I may chance tell you. Fie upon you! What tricks, what crotchets are these? Have you placed anybody behind the arras to hear my confession? I heard one in England got a divorce from's wife by such a trick. Were I disposed now I would make you as mad. You shall see me play the changeling.

KNAVESBE No, no, wife; you shall see me play the changeling. Hadst thou confessed, this other suit I'll now prefer to thee would have been dispatched in a trice.

SIB KNAVESBE And what's that, sir?

KNAVESBE Thou wilt wonder at it four-and-twenty years longer than nine days.

SIB KNAVESBE I would very fain hear it.

KNAVESBE There is a lord o'th' court, upon my credit a most dear, honourable friend of mine, that must lie with thee. Do you laugh? 'Tis not come to that you'll laugh when you know who 'tis.

SIB KNAVESBE Are you stark mad?

KNAVESBE
On my religion, I have passed my word for't—
'Tis the Lord Beaufort. Thou art made happy for
ever—
The generous and bountiful Lord Beaufort.
You being both so excellent, 'twere pity
If such rare pieces should not be conferred
And sampled together.

SIB KNAVESBE Do you mean seriously?

KNAVESBE
As I hope for preferment.

SIB KNAVESBE And can you loose me thus?

KNAVESBE Loose you! I shall love you the better. Why, what's the viewing any wardrobe or jewel-house without a companion to confer their likings? Yet now I view thee well methinks thou art a rare monopoly, and great pity one man should enjoy thee.

SIB KNAVESBE This is pretty!

KNAVESBE Let's divorce ourselves so long, or think I am gone to th'Indies, or lie with him when I am asleep—for some familists of Amsterdam will tell you it may be done with a safe conscience. Come, you wanton, what hurt can this do to you? I protest, nothing so much as to keep company with an old woman has sore eyes—no more wrong than I do my beaver when I try it thus. [*He brushes the fur of his hat the wrong way, then smooths it*] Look, this is all—smooth, and keeps fashion still.

SIB KNAVESBE
You are one of the basest fellows.

KNAVESBE I looked for chiding.
I do make this a kind of fortitude
The Romans never dreamt of—an 'twere known,
I should be spoke and writ of when I am rotten,
For 'tis beyond example.

SIB KNAVESBE But, I pray, resolve me;
Suppose this done, could you ever love me after?

KNAVESBE
I protest I never thought so well of thee
Till I knew he took a fancy to thee—like one
That has variety of choice meat before him,
Yet has no stomach to't until he hear
Another praise.

Knock within

Hark, my lord is coming.

SIB KNAVESBE [*aside*] Possible?

KNAVESBE And my preferment comes along with him. Be wise, mind your good, and to confute all reason in the world which thou canst urge against it, when 'tis done

59 **formal wit** theoretical knowledge
61 **Pue wawe** a version of phew or pooh; an expression of impatience, or disdain; particular to Webster
63 **wormwood** a bitter tasting plant, the leaves and tops of which were used to protect clothes and bedding from moths and fleas
64 **rushes** Green rushes were strewn on floors.
68 **crotchets** whimsical fancies, perverse conceits
69 **arras** a hanging screen of tapestry placed around the walls of a room (and on the tiring-house wall of the stage)
74 **changeling** (*a*) a changeable person; (*b*) a half-wit, imbecile. Knavesbe means the former but the audience might hear the latter as well.
78–9 **wonder . . . days** a variant of the proverb, 'a wonder lasts but nine days'
80 **fain** eagerly
90 **conferred** brought together
91 **sampled** matched
92 **preferment** advancement in status
loose set free, release. 'Loose' and 'lose' were not differentiated by spelling and Knavesbe's response suggests that both verbs are active here; i.e. in loosing her, he would lose her.
95 **confer** compare
99 **divorce** separate
101 **familists of Amsterdam** the Family of Love, a puritan sect which originated in Holland and gained many followers in England during this period. The sect's theology scorned scripture and learning in favour of 'our most holy Service of Love', a tenet easily twisted into accusations of 'free love' by opponents of the sect.
104 **old woman . . . sore eyes** The analogy is between an old woman who cannot sleep and Beaufort, but the specific meaning is unclear.
105 **beaver** a beaver-skin hat
110 **Romans** proverbially stoic
112 **resolve** answer
117 **stomach** appetite
120 **preferment** advancement
121 **confute** disprove

we will be married again wife, which some say is the only *supersedeas* about Limehouse to remove cuckoldry.

Enter Beaufort

BEAUFORT Come, are you ready to attend me to the court?

KNAVESBE Yes, my lord.

BEAUFORT Is this fair one your wife?

KNAVESBE At your lordship's service. I will look up some writings and return presently. *Exit*

SIB KNAVESBE [*aside*] To see an the base fellow do not leave's alone too!

BEAUFORT 'Tis an excellent habit this. Where were you born, sweet?

SIB KNAVESBE I am a Suffolk woman, my lord.

BEAUFORT Believe it, every country you breathe on is the sweeter for you. Let me see your hand. [*He removes her glove*] The case is loath to part with the jewel. Fairest one, I have skill in palmistry. [*He studies her palm*]

SIB KNAVESBE Good my lord, what do you find there?

BEAUFORT In good earnest I do find written here all my good fortune lies in your hand.

SIB KNAVESBE You'll keep a very bad house then, you may see by the smallness of the table.

BEAUFORT Who is your sweetheart?

SIB KNAVESBE Sweetheart!

BEAUFORT Yes, come, I must sift you to know it.

SIB KNAVESBE I am a sieve too coarse for your lordship's manchet.

BEAUFORT Nay, pray you tell me, for I see your husband is an unhandsome fellow.

SIB KNAVESBE O, my lord, I took him by weight not fashion. Goldsmith's wives taught me that way of bargain, and some ladies swerve not to follow the example.

BEAUFORT But will you not tell me who is your private friend?

SIB KNAVESBE Yes, an you'll tell me who is yours.

BEAUFORT Shall I show you her?

SIB KNAVESBE Yes, when will you?

BEAUFORT Instantly. [*He hands her a mirror*] Look you—there you may see her.

SIB KNAVESBE I'll break the glass. 'Tis now worth nothing.

BEAUFORT Why?

SIB KNAVESBE You have made it a flattering one.

BEAUFORT I have a summer-house for you, a fine place to flatter solitariness. Will you come and lie there?

SIB KNAVESBE No, my lord.

BEAUFORT Your husband has promised me. Will you not?

SIB KNAVESBE I must wink, I tell you, or say nothing.

BEAUFORT So, I'll kiss you and wink too. Midnight is cupid's holiday.

Enter Knavesbe

KNAVESBE [*aside*] By this time 'tis concluded.—[*To Beaufort*] Will you go my lord?

BEAUFORT [*to Sib Knavesbe*] I leave with you my best wishes till I see you.

KNAVESBE [*aside to Beaufort*] This now—if I may borrow our lawyers' phrase—is my wife's *imparlance*; at her next appearance she must answer your *declaration*.

BEAUFORT
You follow it well, sir. *Exeunt Beaufort and Knavesbe*

SIB KNAVESBE Did I not know my husband
Of so base, contemptible nature I should think
'Twere but a trick to try me. But it seems
They are both in wicked earnest, and methinks
Upon the sudden I have a great mind to loathe
This scurvy unhandsome way my lord has ta'en
To compass me. Why, 'tis for all the world
As if he should come to steal some apricots
My husband kept for's own tooth, and climb up
Upon his head and shoulders. I'll go to him;
He will put me into brave clothes and rich jewels.
'Twere a very ill part in me not to go;
His mercer and his goldsmith else might curse me.
And what I'll do there, o' my troth, yet I know not.
Women though puzzled with these subtle deeds,
May, as i'th' spring, pick physic out of weeds. *Exit*

Enter (a shop being discovered) Walter Camlet; two apprentices, George and Ralph 2.2

GEORGE

What is't you lack, you lack, you lack?
Stuffs for the belly or the back?
Silk-grograms, satins, velvet fine,
The rosy-coloured carnadine,
Your nutmeg hue, or gingerline,

124 ***supersedeas*** a writ commanding the stay of legal proceedings which ought otherwise to have proceeded, or suspending the power of an officer; so called from the occurrence of the word in the writ; (*fig.*) a prevention or remedy
Limehouse a district on the north side of the Thames, between Wapping and Poplar, opposite Cuckold's Haven; the locale of prostitutes

132 **habit** outfit

134 **Suffolk** a largely puritan county on the east coast of England; a cloth-making centre

142 **keep . . . house** be inhospitable

143 **table** in palmistry, the quadrangle between the lines of Head, Heart, Fate and Apollo

146 **sift** question closely

148 **manchet** the finest flour

155 **friend** lover

164 **summer-house** a garden house used for clandestine meetings

168 **wink** i.e. be complaisant

176 ***imparlance*** (*fig.*) an extension of time to put in a response in pleading a law case

177 ***declaration*** (*fig.*) the plaintiff's statement of claim

184 **compass** encompass

186 **tooth** eating

188 **brave** fine

190 **mercer** seller of cloth and other goods

191 **o' my troth** in truth

193 **physic** medicine

2.2 attributed to Middleton

0.1 ***a shop being discovered*** Probably a curtain was pulled to reveal an area at the back of the stage or in the lower level of the tiring-house equipped with a few props to represent a mercer's shop.

1 **What is't you lack** a traditional street-vendor's cry. The song, with its focus on the cloth trade, is unique.

3 **Silk-grograms** coarse silk fabrics, often stiffened with gum

4 **carnadine** red fabric

5 **nutmeg** brown
gingerline probably a shade of violet red

Cloth of tissue, or tobine,
That like beaten gold will shine
In your amorous lady's eyne,
Whilst you their softer silks do twine.

Enter Rachel Camlet

What is't you lack, you lack, you lack?

RACHEL CAMLET I do lack content, sir, content I lack. Have you or your worshipful master here any content to sell?

GEORGE If content be a stuff to be sold by the yard, you may have content at home and never go abroad for't.

RACHEL CAMLET Do cut me three yards, I'll pay for 'em.

GEORGE There's all we have i'th' shop. We must know what you'll give for 'em first.

CAMLET
Why Rachel, sweet Rachel, my bosom Rachel,
How didst thou get forth? Thou wert here, sweet Rac,
Within this hour, even in my very heart.

RACHEL CAMLET
Away—or stay still—I'll away from thee.
One bed shall never hold us both again,
Nor one roof cover us. Didst thou bring home—

GEORGE What is't you lack, you lack, you lack?

RACHEL CAMLET Peace, bandog, bandog, give me leave to speak or I'll—

GEORGE Shall I not follow my trade? I'm bound to't, and my master bound to bring me up in't.

CAMLET
Peace, good George, give her anger leave;
Thy mistress will be quiet presently.

RACHEL CAMLET
Quiet! I defy thee and quiet too.
Quiet thy bastards thou hast brought home.

GEORGE *and* RALPH What is't you lack, you lack? etc.

RACHEL CAMLET
Death! Give me an ell; has one bawling cur
Raised up another? Two dogs upon me?
An the old bear-ward will not succour me,
I'll stave 'em off myself. Give me an ell, I say!

GEORGE Give her not an inch, master; she'll take two ells if you do.

CAMLET
Peace, George and Ralph, no more words I charge
you.
And Rachel, sweet wife, be more temperate;
I know your tongue speaks not by the rule
And guidance of your heart when you proclaim
The pretty children of my virtuous
And noble kinswoman—whom in life you knew
Above my praises' reach—to be my bastards.
This is not well. Although your anger did it,
Pray chide your anger for it.

RACHEL CAMLET Sir, sir, your gloss
Of kinswoman cannot serve turn, 'tis stale
And smells too rank. Though your shop wares you
vend
With your deceiving lights, yet your chamber stuff
Shall not pass so with me. I say, and I will prove

GEORGE What is't you lack?

Enter Cressingham's two children

CAMLET Why, George, I say—

RACHEL CAMLET
Lecher, I say. I'll be divorced from thee;
I'll prove 'em thy bastards and thou insufficient.
Exit

FIRST CHILD
What said my angry cousin to you, sir?
That we were bastards?

SECOND CHILD I hope she meant not us.

CAMLET No, no, my pretty cousins, she meant George and Ralph. Rage will speak anything, but they are ne'er the worse.

GEORGE Yes indeed, forsooth, she spoke to us, but chiefly to Ralph because she knows he has but one stone.

RALPH No more of that if you love me, George; this is not the way to keep a quiet house.

FIRST CHILD
Truly, sir, I would not for more treasure
Than ever I saw yet, be in your house
A cause of discord.

SECOND CHILD And do you think I would, sister?

FIRST CHILD No indeed, Ned.

Enter Young Franklin [*disguised as Sir Andrew, a knight*] *and Young Cressingham disguised* [*as Gascoine, a tailor*]

SECOND CHILD
Why did you not speak for me with you then,
And said we could not have done so?

CAMLET No more, sweet cousins, now.—Speak, George; customers approach. [*Exit children*]

[*Young Cressingham and Young Franklin talk apart*]

YOUNG CRESSINGHAM Is the barber prepared?

6 **tobine** silk taffeta
9 **softer silks** undergarments
twine embrace
9.1 *Rachel* a name popular with Puritans; perhaps an allusion to the biblical Rachel who was for so long barren (*Gen.* 29)
11 **content** (*a*) happiness; (*b*) sexual fulfilment
13 **yard** (*a*) length of fabric; (*b*) penis. The bawdy wordplay continues in the exchange between George and Rachel Camlet.
25 **bandog** literally a chained, barking dog
27 **bound** As an apprentice George is under a contract, or indenture, to serve Camlet for at least seven years; the word is used elsewhere in the play to refer to the ties of marriage.
34 **ell** a measuring rod of forty-five inches
36 **bear-ward** the keeper of a bear, who leads it about for public exhibition of its tricks
48 **gloss** explanation
51 **deceiving lights** London shopkeepers proverbially darkened their shops to deceive customers. In *Michaelmas Term* Quomodo, another clothseller, has an assistant named Falselight.
chamber stuff illegitimate children. 'Stuff' is also the term for a kind of cloth.
56 **insufficient** incompetent
63 **stone** testicle

YOUNG FRANKLIN With ignorance enough to go through with it; so near I am to him we must call cousins. Would thou wert as sure to hit the tailor.

YOUNG CRESSINGHAM If I do not steal away handsomely let me never play the tailor again.

GEORGE What is't you lack? etc.

YOUNG FRANKLIN Good satins, sir.

GEORGE The best in Europe, sir. [*He shows a cloth*] Here's a piece worth a piece, every yard of him; the King of Naples wears no better silk. Mark his gloss, he dazzles the eye to look upon him.

YOUNG FRANKLIN Is he not gummed?

GEORGE Gummed! He has neither mouth nor tooth, how can he be gummed?

YOUNG FRANKLIN Very pretty.

CAMLET An especial good piece of silk. The worm never spun a finer thread, believe it, sir.

YOUNG FRANKLIN [*to Young Cressingham*] Gascoine, you have some skill in it.

CAMLET Your tailor, sir?

YOUNG FRANKLIN Yes sir.

YOUNG CRESSINGHAM A good piece, sir, but let's see more choice.

RALPH Tailor, drive through; you know your bribes.

YOUNG CRESSINGHAM [*aside to Ralph*] Mum. He bestows forty pounds if I say the word.

RALPH [*aside to Young Cressingham*] Strike through. There's poundage for you then.

YOUNG FRANKLIN Ay, marry! I like this better, what sayest thou, Gascoine?

YOUNG CRESSINGHAM A good piece indeed, sir.

GEORGE The great Turk has worse satin at's elbow than this, sir.

YOUNG FRANKLIN The price?

CAMLET Look on the mark, George.

GEORGE O. Souse, and P., by my facks, sir.

CAMLET The best sort then—sixteen a yard, nothing to be bated.

YOUNG FRANKLIN Fie, sir, fifteen's too high—yet so, for how many yards will serve for my suit, sirrah?

YOUNG CRESSINGHAM Nine yards; you can have no less, Sir Andrew.

YOUNG FRANKLIN But I can, sir, if you please to steal less; I had but eight in my last suit.

YOUNG CRESSINGHAM You pinch us too near, in faith, Sir Andrew.

YOUNG FRANKLIN Yet can you pinch out a false pair of sleeves to a freezado doublet.

GEORGE No, sir, some purses and pin-pillows perhaps. A tailor pays for his kissing that ways.

YOUNG FRANKLIN Well, sir, eight yards, eight fifteens I give, and cut it.

CAMLET I cannot, truly, sir.

GEORGE My master must be no subsidy man, sir, if he take such fifteens.

YOUNG FRANKLIN I am at highest, sir, if you can take money.

CAMLET Well, sir, I'll give you the buying once; I hope to gain it in your custom. Want you nothing else, sir?

YOUNG FRANKLIN Not at this time, sir.

YOUNG CRESSINGHAM Indeed but you do, Sir Andrew. I must needs deliver my lady's message to you; she enjoined me by oath to do it. She commanded me to move you for a new gown.

YOUNG FRANKLIN Sirrah, I'll break your head if you motion it again.

YOUNG CRESSINGHAM I must endanger myself for my lady, sir. You know she's to go to my Lady Trenchmore's wedding, and to be seen there without a new gown—she'll have ne'er an eye to be seen there for her fingers in 'em. Nay, by my fack, sir, I do not think she'll go, and then the cause known, what a discredit 'twill be to you!

YOUNG FRANKLIN Not a word more, goodman Snipsnapper, for your ears. [*To Walter Camlet*] What comes this to, sir?

CAMLET Six pound, sir.

YOUNG FRANKLIN There's your money. [*To Young Cressingham, giving him the cloth*] Will you take this and be gone and about your business presently?

YOUNG CRESSINGHAM Troth, sir, I'll see some stuffs for my lady first. I'll tell her at least I did my good will. [*To George*] A fair piece of cloth of silver, pray you now.

76 **near** friendly; seemingly such close kin
77 **hit** represent successfully
78 **handsomely** cleverly. Tailors were proverbially untrustworthy.
83 **piece** the second use of the word refers to a gold coin worth twenty-two shillings
88 **gummed** Velvet and taffeta were sometimes stiffened with gum, which soon was rubbed out revealing the inferior quality.
92 **Gascoine** gaskin, a kind of breeches or hose from Gascony, where the fashion originated
93 **skill** knowledge
98 **drive through** bring to a settlement, conclude
102 **poundage** a commission or fee, of so much a pound
109 **mark** a price code
110 **O. Souse, and P.** a price code; see 2.2.203; cf. Rowley, *A New Wonder* (*BEPD* 460) A2^{v}, and anon. *Pedantius* (*BEPD* L9), ll. 2610–2614 and note
facks faith
111 **sixteen** i.e. shillings
112 **bated** bargained
121 **pinch out** eke out
false simulated
122 **freezado doublet** a close-fitting garment of coarse woollen cloth
124 **pays for his kissing** makes small gifts for his girlfriends by skimping on material
128 **subsidy man** a man wealthy enough to pay taxes
130–1 **if...money** He offers to pay cash rather than buying on credit.
133 **custom** future business
142 **Trenchmore's** (*fig.*) a boisterous country dance
144–5 **eye...fingers in 'em** she will cry and rub her eyes; or she will pretend to cry
149 **for your ears** if you value your ears; an allusion to the punishment of cropping felons' ears

GEORGE Or cloth of gold, if you please, sir, as rich as ever the Sophy wore.

YOUNG FRANKLIN You are the arrantest villain of a tailor that ever sat cross-legged. What do you think a gown of this stuff will come to?

YOUNG CRESSINGHAM Why, say it be forty pound, sir; what's that to you? Three thousand a year I hope will maintain it.

YOUNG FRANKLIN It will, sir, very good, you were best be my overseer. Say I be not furnished with money, how then?

YOUNG CRESSINGHAM A very fine excuse in you—which place of ten now will you send me for a hundred pound, to bring it presently?

CAMLET Sir, sir, your tailor persuades you well. 'Tis for your credit, and the great content of your lady.

YOUNG FRANKLIN 'Tis for your content, sir, and my charges. [*To Young Cressingham*] Never think, goodman Falsestitch, to come to the mercer's with me again. Pray, will you see if my cousin Sweetball the barber—he's nearest hand—be furnished, and bring me word instantly.

YOUNG CRESSINGHAM I fly, sir. *Exit*

YOUNG FRANKLIN You may fly, sir; you have clipped somebody's wings for it to piece out your own. An arrant thief you are.

CAMLET Indeed, he speaks honestly and justly, sir.

YOUNG FRANKLIN You expect some gain, sir, there's your cause of love.

CAMLET Surely I do a little, sir.

YOUNG FRANKLIN [*examining another cloth*] And what might be the price of this?

CAMLET This is thirty a yard; but if you'll go to forty, here's a nonpareil.

YOUNG FRANKLIN So, there's a matter of forty pound for a gown cloth.

CAMLET Thereabouts, sir. Why sir, there are far short of your means that wear the like.

YOUNG FRANKLIN Do you know my means, sir?

GEORGE By overhearing your tailor, sir—three thousand a year—but if you'd have a petticoat for your lady, here's a stuff. [*He shows another cloth*]

YOUNG FRANKLIN Are you another tailor, sirrah? Here's a knave—what are you?

GEORGE You are such another gentleman. But for the stuff, sir, 'tis L. SS. and K. For the turn stript o' purpose, a yard and a quarter broad too, which is the just depth of a woman's petticoat.

YOUNG FRANKLIN And why stript for a petticoat?

GEORGE Because if they abuse their petticoats, there are abuses stript; then 'tis taking them up, and they may be stript and whipt too.

YOUNG FRANKLIN Very ingenious.

GEORGE Then it is likewise stript standing, between which is discovered the open part, which is now called the placket.

YOUNG FRANKLIN Why, was it ever called otherwise?

GEORGE Yes, while the word remained pure in his original, the Latin tongue, who have no Ks, it was called the *placet*, a *placendo*—a thing or place to please.

Enter Young Cressingham [still disguised as a tailor]

YOUNG FRANKLIN Better and worse still. [*To George Cressingham*] Now, sir, you come in haste. What says my cousin?

YOUNG CRESSINGHAM Protests, sir. He's half angry that either you should think him unfurnished or not furnished for your use—there's a hundred pound ready for you. He desires you to pardon his coming, his folks are busy and his wife trimming a gentleman, but at your first approach the money wants but telling.

YOUNG FRANKLIN He would not trust you with it. I con him thanks for that—he knows what trade you are of. [*To Camlet*] Well sir, pray cut him patterns; he may in the mean time know my lady's liking. Let your man take the pieces whole, with the lowest prices, and walk with me to my cousin's.

CAMLET With all my heart, sir. Ralph, your cloak, and go with the gentleman; look you give good measure.

YOUNG CRESSINGHAM Look you carry a good yard with you.

RALPH The best i'th' shop, sir, yet we have none bad. You'll have the stuff for the petticoat too?

YOUNG FRANKLIN No, sir, the gown only.

YOUNG CRESSINGHAM By all means, sir. Not the petticoat? That were holiday upon working day, i'faith.

YOUNG FRANKLIN You are so forward for a knave, sir.

YOUNG CRESSINGHAM 'Tis for your credit and my lady's both I do it, sir.

YOUNG FRANKLIN Your man is trusty, sir?

CAMLET O, sir, we keep none but those we dare trust, sir. Ralph, have a care of light gold.

RALPH I warrant you, sir, I'll take none.

159 **Sophy** the Shah of Persia
160 **arrantest** worst
160–1 **villain ... cross-legged** Tailors sat cross-legged to sew.
164 **Three thousand a year** pounds; a considerable income
maintain afford
191 **nonpareil** unequalled
203 **L. SS. and K.** a price code; see 2.2.110
stript striped; but also stripped, revealed
208 **abuses stript** an allusion to George Wither's satiric poem, *Abuses Stript and Whipt* (1613). In the section on 'Vanitie', Wither specifically satirizes the demand for 'foreign trash' such as 'grosgrains, camlets, rash'.
taking them up gathering the cloth
209 **whipt** trimmed, ornamented; but also 'whipped'. Whipping was the usual punishment for prostitutes.
213 **placket** (*a*) the opening or slit at the top of a skirt or petticoat; (*b*) the pudendum, especially the vulva
217 ***placet*** Latin: he, she, it pleases
placendo Latin: pleasing; with bawdy innuendo
222–3 **furnished** provided with money
224 **pardon his coming** excuse him from coming
folks employees
226 **telling** counting
234–5 **give good measure ... carry a good yard** with *doubles entendres*
240 **holiday upon working day** (*fig.*) a fancy dress over a plain petticoat
246 **light gold** debased or clipped coins

YOUNG FRANKLIN [*to Young Cressingham*] Come, sirrah. [*To Camlet*] Fare you well, sir.

CAMLET Pray know my shop another time, sir.

YOUNG FRANKLIN That I shall, sir, from all the shops i'th' town. 'Tis the Lamb in Lombard Street.

Exeunt Young Franklin, Young Cressingham and Ralph

GEORGE A good morning's work, sir. If this custom would but last long you might shut up your shop and live privately.

CAMLET O, George, but here's a grief that takes away all the gains and joy of all my thrift.

GEORGE What's that, sir?

CAMLET Thy mistress, George, her frowardness sours all my comfort.

GEORGE Alas, sir, they are but squibs and crackers; they'll soon die. You know her flashes of old.

CAMLET But they fly so near me that they burn me, George; they are as ill as muskets charged with bullets.

GEORGE She has discharged herself now, sir; you need not fear her.

CAMLET No man can live without his affliction, George.

GEORGE As you cannot without my mistress.

CAMLET Right, right, there's harmony in discords. This lamp of love, while any oil is left, can never be extinct. It may—like a snuff—wink and seem to die, but up he will again and show his head. I cannot be quiet, George, without my wife at home.

GEORGE And when she's at home you're never quiet I'm sure. A fine life you have on't. Well, sir, I'll do my best to find her and bring her back if I can.

CAMLET

Do, honest George. At Knavesbe's house, that
 varlet's—
There's her haunt and harbour—who enforces
A kinsman on her and she calls him cousin.
Restore her, George, to ease this heart that's vext,
The best new suit that e'er thou wor'st is next.

GEORGE I thank you aforehand, sir. *Exeunt*

Enter Young Franklin [disguised as Sir Andrew], George Cressingham [disguised as a tailor], Ralph, Sweetball the barber, Boy 2.3

BARBER Were it of greater moment than you speak of, noble sir, I hope you think me sufficient, and it shall be effectually performed.

YOUNG FRANKLIN I could wish your wife did not know it, coz. Women's tongues are not always tuneable. I may many ways requite it.

BARBER Believe me, she shall not, sir; which will be the hardest thing of all.

YOUNG FRANKLIN Pray you dispatch him then.

BARBER With the celerity a man tells gold to him.

YOUNG FRANKLIN [*aside*] He hits a good comparison! [*To Ralph*] Give my waste-good your stuffs, and go with my cousin, sir; he'll presently dispatch you.

RALPH Yes, sir. [*He gives the cloth to Young Cressingham*]

BARBER Come with me, youth, I am ready for you in my more private chamber. *Exeunt Barber and Ralph*

YOUNG FRANKLIN [*to Young Cressingham*] Sirrah, go you show your lady the stuffs and let her choose her colour. Away, you know whither. [*To Barber's boy*] Boy, prithee lend me a brush i'th' mean time. [*To Young Cressingham*] Do you tarry all day now?

YOUNG CRESSINGHAM [*aside*] That I will, sir, and all night too, ere I come again. *Exit*

BOY Here's a brush, sir.

YOUNG FRANKLIN A good child.

BARBER (*within*) What, Toby!

BOY Anon, sir.

BARBER (*within*) Why, when, goodman Picklock?

BOY I must attend my master, sir. [*To Barber*] I come. *Exit*

YOUNG FRANKLIN

Do, pretty lad.—So, take water at Cole Harbour,
An easy mercer and an innocent barber. *Exit*

Enter Sweetball the barber, Ralph, Boy 2.4

BARBER So, friend, I'll now dispatch you presently. Boy, reach me my dismembering instrument and let my cauterizer be ready, and hark you, snipsnap—

252 **Lamb in Lombard Street** The street runs from the Mansion House on the south of the Royal Exchange, to Gracechurch Street; a street of merchants; Camlet's shop would have a sign with a lamb on it.

255 **privately** retired

259 **frowardness** perversity

261 **squibs** (*fig.*) fireworks with a slight explosion

crackers (*fig.*) fireworks with a sharp report

262 **flashes** (*fig.*) explosions, outbursts

271 **snuff** the nozzle of a lamp in which a wick burns

272 **quiet** peace

277 **varlet's** knave's

278–9 **enforces | A kinsman on her** insists that he is her relative. There is nothing to either contradict or confirm this accusation; when later Knavesbe calls Rachel Camlet 'cousin' she does not protest; see 2.2.44–6 and 4.1.346.

2.3 attributed to Middleton

0.3 ***Sweetball*** a ball of aromatic substance placed in a barber's basin to provide lather

6 **requite** repay

10 **celerity** speed

tells counts out

12 **waste-good** spendthrift

21 **tarry** delay

30 **take water** travel by boat

Cole Harbour originally Cold Harbour; a sanctuary for vagrants and debtors composed of a number of small tenements in Upper Thames Street

31 **easy** easily fooled; cf. the gull Easy in *Michaelmas Term*

2.4 attributed to Middleton

2 **dismembering instrument** Fooled into thinking Ralph has venereal disease, Sweetball prepares to remove Ralph's penis. From the time of Henry VIII, barber-surgeons had been restricted to barbering and dentistry, thus it would seem that Sweetball is going beyond the law. Since, however, nothing is made of this, it may be that, in fact, barbers were still performing surgery at this time. Other plays also represent the barber's double occupation, especially the treatment of venereal diseases.

3 **cauterizer** a heated metallic instrument used for burning or searing organic tissue. In his use of the terminology related to his craft, Sweetball resembles the Surgeon in *Quarrel* 4.2, and the Lawyer in Webster's *White Devil* 3.2. Like the other two, Sweetball is often

BOY Ay, sir.

BARBER See if my *lixivium*, my *fomentation* be provided first, and get my rollers, bolsters, and pledgets armed.

RALPH Nay, good sir, dispatch my business first. I should not stay from my shop.

BARBER You must have a little patience, sir, when you are a patient. If *preputium* be not too much perished you shall lose but little by it, believe my art for that.

RALPH What's that, sir?

BARBER Marry, if there be exulceration between *preputium* and *glans*, by my faith, the whole *penis* may be endangered as far as *os pubis*.

RALPH What's this you talk on, sir?

BARBER If they be gangrened once, *testiculi*, *vesica* and all may run to mortification.

RALPH What a pox does this barber talk on?

BARBER O fie, youth, 'pox' is no word of art. *Morbus gallicus* or *neopolitanus* had been well. Come, friend, you must not be nice; open your griefs freely to me.

RALPH Why, sir, I open my grief to you: I want my money.

BARBER Take you no care for that. Your worthy cousin has given me part in hand and the rest I know he will upon your recovery, an I dare take his word.

RALPH 'Sdeath! Where's my ware?

BARBER Ware! That was well, the word is cleanly, though not artful. Your ware it is that I must see.

RALPH My tobine and cloth of tissue?

BARBER You will neither have tissue nor issue if you linger in your malady. Better a member cut off than endanger the whole microcosm.

RALPH Barber, you are not mad?

BARBER I do begin to fear you are subject to *subeth*, unkindly sleeps, which have bred oppilations in your brain. Take heed the *symptoma* will follow, and this may come to frenzy. Begin with the first cause, which is the pain of your member.

RALPH [*showing his measuring-stick*] Do you see my yard, barber?

BARBER Now you come to the purpose; 'tis that I must see indeed.

RALPH You shall feel it, sir. Death! Give me my fifty pounds or my ware again, or I'll measure out your anatomy by the yard.

BARBER Boy, my cauterizing iron, red hot.

Exit Boy, [*and re-enter with iron*]

BOY 'Tis here, sir.

BARBER If you go further, I take my dismembering knife.

RALPH Where's the knight, your cousin the thief, and the tailor with my cloth of gold and tissue?

BOY The gentleman that sent away his man with the stuffs is gone a pretty while since; he has carried away our new brush.

BARBER O, that brush hurts my heart's side. Cheated! Cheated! He told me that your *virga* had a burning fever.

RALPH Pox on your *virga*, barber.

BARBER And that you would be bashful and ashamed to show your head.

RALPH I shall so hereafter. [*He removes his hat*] But here it is, you see yet my head, my hair, and my wit, and here are my heels that I must show to my master if the cheaters be not found. And, barber, provide thee plasters; I will break thy head with every basin under the pole. *Exit*

BARBER

Cool the *lixivium*, and quench the cauterizer.
I am partly out of my wits, and partly mad.
My razor's at my heart. These storms will make
My sweetballs stink, my harmless basins shake.

Exeunt

Finis Actus Secundus

Incipit Actus Tertius 3.1

Enter Selenger and Sib Knavesbe

SELENGER You're welcome, mistress—as I may speak it—but my lord will give it a sweeter emphasis. I'll give him knowledge of you. *Exiturus*

SIB KNAVESBE Good sir, stay; methinks it sounds sweetest upon your tongue. I'll wish you to go no further for my welcome.

incomprehensible, a fact called attention to by those to whom he speaks. As a result, it is impossible to know if the errors in spelling and pronunciation in JOHNSON are the barber's, the writer's or the compositor's. The Textual Notes give the original of words corrected.

5 ***lixivium*** a solution of water and alkaline salts
fomentation medicinal substance
6 **rollers** long rolled bandages
bolsters compresses
pledgets small medicated compresses
10 ***preputium*** Latin: prepuce, the foreskin
13 **exulceration** a sore
14 ***glans*** Latin: the head of the penis
15 ***os pubis*** Latin: pubic bone
17 ***vesica*** Latin: bladder
18 **mortification** the death of a part of the body while the rest is living
20 **pox** syphilis
20–1 ***Morbus gallicus*** **or** ***neopolitanus*** syphilis
22 **nice** shy
29 **ware** Ralph means the cloth he brought; Sweetball means Ralph's penis.
30 **tobine** silk taffeta
33 **microcosm** the body
35 ***subeth*** unhealthy sleep
36 **oppilations** obstructions
37 ***symptoma*** Latin: symptoms
38 **frenzy** temporary insanity
39 **member** penis
40 **yard** Ralph means his yardstick; Sweetball means Ralph's penis.
56 ***virga*** Latin: rod, also slang for penis
60 **head** glans
65 **plasters** a healing substance applied to a cloth used for closing a wound
66 **pole** barber's pole
70 **sweetballs** probably with a *double entendre*: testicles
3.1 attributed to Middleton
1 **mistress** ironic wordplay on the two meanings
3 ***Exiturus*** Latin: about to exit

SELENGER Mine! It seems you never heard good music that commend a bagpipe; hear his harmony.

SIB KNAVESBE Nay, good now, let me borrow of your patience. I'll pay you again before I rise tomorrow—if it please you.

SELENGER What would you, forsooth?

SIB KNAVESBE Your company, sir.

SELENGER My attendance you should have, mistress, but that my lord expects it, and 'tis his due.

SIB KNAVESBE And must be paid upon the hour! That's too strict. Any time of the day will serve.

SELENGER Alas, 'tis due every minute, and paid, 'tis due again, or else I forfeit my recognizance, the cloth I wear of his.

SIB KNAVESBE Come, come, pay it double at another time and 'twill be quitted. I have a little use of you.

SELENGER Of me? Forsooth, small use can be made of me. If you have suit to my lord, none can speak better for you than you may yourself.

SIB KNAVESBE O, but I am bashful.

SELENGER So am I, in troth, mistress.

SIB KNAVESBE Now I remember me, I have a toy to deliver your lord that's yet unfinished, and you may further me. Pray you your hands, while I unwind this skein of gold from you. 'Twill not detain you long.

[*She puts a skein of wool around Selenger's hands and begins to wind it onto a bobbin*]

SELENGER You wind me into your service prettily. With all the haste you can, I beseech you.

SIB KNAVESBE If it tangle not I shall soon have done.

SELENGER No, it shall not tangle if I can help it, forsooth.

SIB KNAVESBE If it do I can help it. Fear not this thing of long length; you shall see I can bring you to a bottom.

SELENGER I think so too; if it be not bottomless this length will reach it.

SIB KNAVESBE It becomes you finely. But I forewarn you, and remember it, your enemy gain not this advantage of you—you are his prisoner then. For look you, you are mine now, my captive manacled—I have your hands in bondage.

[*She*] *grasps the skein between his hands*

SELENGER 'Tis a good lesson, mistress, and I am perfect in it; another time I'll take out this and learn another. Pray you, release me now.

SIB KNAVESBE I could kiss you now spite of your teeth if it please me.

SELENGER But you could not, for I could bite you with the spite of my teeth if it pleases me.

SIB KNAVESBE Well, I'll not tempt you so far; I show it but for rudiment.

SELENGER When I go a-wooing, I'll think on't again.

SIB KNAVESBE
In such an hour I learnt it. Say I should—
In recompense of your hands' courtesy—
Make you a fine wrist-favour of this gold,
With all the letters of your name embossed
On a soft tress of hair, which I shall cut
From mine own fillet, whose ends should meet and close
In a fast true-love knot. Would you wear it
For my sake, sir?

SELENGER I think not, truly, mistress.
My wrists have enough of this gold already;
Would they were rid on't yet. Pray you, have done;
In troth, I'm weary.

SIB KNAVESBE And what a virtue
Is here expressed in you, which had lain hid
But for this trial. Weary of gold, sir!
O, that the close engrossers of this treasure
Could be so free to put it off of hand,
What a new-mended world would here be!
It shows a generous condition in you,
In sooth I think I shall love you dearly for't.

SELENGER
But if they were in prison, as I am,
They would be glad to buy their freedom with it.

SIB KNAVESBE
Surely, no. There are that rather than release
This dear companion do lie in prison with it—
Yes, and will die in prison too.

Enter Beaufort

SELENGER 'Twere pity but the hangman did enfranchise both.

BEAUFORT Selenger, where are you?

SELENGER E'en here, my lord.—Mistress, pray you my liberty, you hinder my duty to my lord.

Beaufort puts off his hat

BEAUFORT Nay, sir, one courtesy shall serve us both at this time. You're busy, I perceive. When your leisure next serves you I would employ you.

SELENGER You must pardon me, my lord, you see I am entangled here. Mistress, I protest I'll break prison if you free me not—take you no notice?

SIB KNAVESBE [*to Beaufort*] O, cry your honour mercy. [*To Selenger, as she releases her hold on the skein of wool*] You are now at liberty, sir.

8 **bagpipe** an inferior instrument, musically and socially
12 **forsooth** truly
19 **recognizance** a bond of service
28 **remember me** remember
37 **bottom** a bobbin, around which wool is wound
44.1 **[*She*]...*hands*** By this action Sib seems to handcuff Selenger.
48 **spite...teeth** in defiance of your opposition
53 **rudiment** a first step
56 **your hands' courtesy** courtesy in offering your hands
57 **wrist-favour** a bracelet given to a lover
59 **tress** a long lock of hair
60 **fillet** a headband
68 **close engrossers** stingy monopolizers
69 **put it off of hand** relinquish exclusive use
78 **but** unless
enfranchise set free

SELENGER And I'm glad on't. I'll ne'er give both my hands at once again to a woman's command. I'll put one finger in a hole rather.

BEAUFORT Leave us.

SELENGER Free leave have you, my lord. [*Aside*] So I think you may have.—Filthy beauty, what a white witch thou art! *Exit*

BEAUFORT Lady, you're welcome.

SIB KNAVESBE
I did believe it from your page, my lord.

BEAUFORT
Your husband sent you to me.

SIB KNAVESBE
He did, my lord,
With duty and commends unto your honour,
Beseeching you to use me very kindly.
By the same token your lordship gave him grant
Of a new lease of threescore pounds a year,
Which he and his should forty years enjoy.

BEAUFORT
The token's true, and for your sake, lady,
'Tis likely to be bettered. Not alone the lease,
But the fee-simple may be his and yours.

SIB KNAVESBE
I have a suit unto your lordship too,
Only myself concerns.

BEAUFORT
'Twill be granted sure,
Though it out-value thy husband's.

SIB KNAVESBE
Nay, 'tis small charge:
Only your good will and good word, my lord.

BEAUFORT
The first is thine confirmed, the second then
Cannot stay long behind.

SIB KNAVESBE
I love your page, sir.

BEAUFORT
Love him! For what?

SIB KNAVESBE
O, the great wisdoms that
Our grandsires had! Do you ask me reason for't?
I love him because I like him, sir.

BEAUFORT
My page!

SIB KNAVESBE
In mine eye he's a most delicate youth,
But in my heart a thing that it would bleed for.

BEAUFORT
Either your eye is blinded or your remembrance broken.
Call to mind wherefore you came hither, lady.

SIB KNAVESBE
I do my lord, for love, and I am in profoundly.

BEAUFORT
You trifle sure. Do you long for unripe fruit?
'Twill breed diseases in you.

SIB KNAVESBE
Nothing but worms
In my belly, and there's a seed to expel them.
In mellow falling fruit I find no relish.

BEAUFORT
'Tis true, the youngest vines yields the most clusters,
But the old ever the sweetest grapes.

SIB KNAVESBE
I can taste of both, sir.
But with the old I am the soonest cloyed;
The green keep still an edge on appetite.

BEAUFORT
Sure you are a common creature.

SIB KNAVESBE
Did you doubt it?
Wherefore came I hither else? Did you think
That honesty only had been immured for you
And I should bring it as an offertory
Unto your shrine of lust? As it was, my lord,
'Twas meant to you had not the slippery wheel
Of fancy turned when I beheld your page.
Nay, had I seen another before him
In mine eyes' better grace, he had been forestalled.
But as it is, all my strength cannot help—
Beseech you your good will and good word, my lord;
You may command him, sir—if not affection,
Yet his body—and I desire but that. Do't
And I'll command myself your prostitute.

BEAUFORT
You're a base strumpet. I succeed my page!

SIB KNAVESBE
O, that's no wonder, my lord; the servant oft
Tastes to his master of the daintiest dish
He brings to him. Beseech you, my lord—

BEAUFORT
You're a bold mischief—and to make me your spokesman,
Your procurer to my servant!

SIB KNAVESBE
Do you shrink at that?
Why, you have done worse without the sense of ill,
With a full free conscience of a libertine.
Judge your own sin:
Was it not worse with a damned broking-fee
To corrupt a husband, state him a pander
To his own wife by virtue of a lease
Made to him and your bastard issue—could you get 'em.
What a degree of baseness call you this?

93–4 **put one finger in a hole** The idea is that he would do anything to avoid being caught this way again. Hole: rectum, as in 'sit on my thumb', or do nothing (?)

97 **white witch** probably suggesting the proverb, 'the white witch is worse than the black', because more difficult to recognize

105 **threescore** sixty

109 **fee-simple** absolute ownership

121 **remembrance broken** memory is faulty

124 **unripe fruit** (*fig.*) young men

125 **worms** from eating unripe fruit

126 **seed** a child

130 **cloyed** surfeited

134 **immured** secluded

135 **offertory** Communion offerings

140 **In mine eyes' better grace** more appealing

151 **procurer** a pander
shrink recoil

155 **broking-fee** payment for service as procurer

156 **state** to give a person the status of (usually complimentary)

158 **bastard issue** illegitimate children (by her)

'Tis a poor sheep-steal provoked by want
Compared unto a capital traitor. The master
To his servant may be recompensed, but the husband
To his wife, never.

BEAUFORT Your husband shall smart for this.
Exit

SIB KNAVESBE
Hang him, do; you have brought him to deserve it.
Bring him to the punishment; there I'll join with you.
I loathe him to the gallows. Hang your page too;
One mourning-gown shall serve for both of them.
This trick hath kept mine honesty secure.
Best soldiers use policy. The lion's skin
Becomes not the body when 'tis too great,
But then the fox's may sit close and neat. *Exit*

3.2 *Enter Fleshhook, Counterbuff, and Sweetball the barber*

BARBER Now, Fleshhook, use thy talon—set upon his right shoulder—thy sergeant Counterbuff at the left, grasp in his *jugulars* and then let me alone to tickle his *diaphragma*.

FLESHHOOK You are sure he has no protection, sir?

BARBER A protection to cheat and cozen! There was never any granted to that purpose.

FLESHHOOK I grant you that too, sir, but that use has been made of 'em.

COUNTERBUFF Marry has there, sir. How could else so many broken bankrupts play up and down by their creditors' noses, and we dare not touch 'em?

BARBER That's another case, Counterbuff; there's privilege to cozen. But here cozenage went before, and there's no privilege for that. To him boldly; I will spend all the scissors in my shop, but I'll have him snapped.

COUNTERBUFF Well, sir, if he come within the length of large mace once, we'll teach him to cozen.

BARBER Marry, hang him. Teach him no more cozenage; he's too perfect in't already. Go gingerly about it; lay your mace on gingerly and spice him soundly.

COUNTERBUFF He's at the tavern, you say?

BARBER At the Man in the Moon, above stairs. So soon as he comes down, and the Bush left at his back, Ralph is the dog behind him. He watches to give us notice. Be ready then, my dear bloodhounds. You shall deliver him to Newgate, from thence to the hangman. His body I will beg of the sheriffs, for at the next lecture I am likely to be the master of my anatomy. Then will I vex every vein about him. I will find where his disease of cozenage lay, whether in the *vertebrae*, or in *os coxendix*. But I guess I shall find it descend from *humour* through the *thorax*, and lie just at his fingers' ends.

Enter Ralph

RALPH Be in readiness, for he's coming this way—alone too. Stand to't like gentleman and yeoman; so soon as he is in sight I'll go fetch my master.

BARBER I have had a *conquassation* in my *cerebrum* ever since the disaster, and now it takes me again. If it turn to a migraine I shall hardly abide the sight of him.

RALPH My action of defamation shall be clapped on him too. I will make him appear to't in the shape of a white sheet all embroidered over with *peccavis*. Look about, I'll go fetch my master. [*Exit*]

Enter Young Franklin

COUNTERBUFF I arrest you, sir.

YOUNG FRANKLIN *Ha! Qui va là? Que pensez-vous faire, messieurs? Me voulez-vous dérober? Je n'ai point d'argent. Je suis un pauvre gentilhomme français.*

BARBER Whoop! Pray you, sir, speak English. You did when you bought cloth of gold at six *nihils* a yard, when Ralph's *preputium* was exulcerated.

YOUNG FRANKLIN *Que voulez-vous? Me voulez-vous tuer? Les français ne sont point ennemis. Voilà ma bourse; que voulez-vous d'avantage?*

163 **smart** suffer
168 **trick** stratagem
169 **policy** dissimulation
169–71 **The lion's skin...neat** a variant of the proverbial, 'if the lion's skin cannot, the fox's shall'; i.e., the lion's strength must be combined with the fox's cunning
3.2 attributed to Middleton
0.1 ***Fleshhook*** a hook for removing meat from a pot; also slang for 'constable'; yeoman: a sergeant's subordinate
Counterbuff a blow given in return, or an encounter where blows are exchanged
1 **talon** (*fig.*) hand
3 ***jugulars*** neck
tickle ironic: beat
4 ***diaphragma*** (*fig.*) the chest
5 **protection** a document guaranteeing immunity from prosecution
6 **cozen** defraud
11–12 **play...noses** take advantage of; cheat
13 **privilege** a right
14 **went before** preceded
16 **snapped** captured
18 **mace** (*a*) a club; (*b*) a spice, with puns following
23 **Man in the Moon** a tavern in Cheapside
above stairs upstairs
24 **Bush** (*a*) the sign of a tavern; (*b*) with 'dog', allusions to the man in the moon whose props these were
27 **Newgate** a prison
29 **master of my anatomy** in charge of dissecting the next corpse at the barber-surgeons' hall
31 ***os coxendix*** Latin: hip bone
32 ***humour*** a disease resulting from the dominance of one humour (blood, phlegm, yellow bile, black bile), or lack of balance among them. The idea is that an excess of one causes Franklin to steal.
33 ***thorax*** Latin: chest
fingers' ends because he is a thief
37 ***conquassation*** agitation
cerebrum Latin: brain
38 **the disaster** the trick played on him
40 **clapped** served
41 **appear to't** appear in court
41–2 **shape...*peccavis*** wearing a gown with 'peccavi' (Latin: 'I have sinned') written on it
43.1 ***Franklin*** He is not disguised visually, only verbally; and his name likely hints at this deception: Frank: 'French'. The French spoken here is as colloquial as the English of the rest of the play and the translations aim at conveying this while remaining reasonably literal.
45–7 ***Ha!...français.*** Ha! Who's there? What do you think you're doing, sirs? Do you want to rob me? I have no money. I'm a poor French gentleman.
49 ***nihils*** Latin: nothings
51–3 ***Que...d'avantage?*** What do you want? Do you want to kill me? The French are not at all enemies. Here is my purse—what else do you want?

COUNTERBUFF Is not your name Franklin, sir?

YOUNG FRANKLIN *Je n'ai point de joyaux que ceux-ci. Et c'est à monsieur l'ambassadeur; il m'envoie à ses affaires et vous empêchez mon service.*

Enter Camlet and Ralph hastily

COUNTERBUFF [*to Camlet*] Sir, we are mistaken for aught I perceive.

CAMLET So, so, you have caught him; that's well.—How do you, sir?

YOUNG FRANKLIN *Vous semblez être un homme courtois. Je vous prie entendez mes affaires. Il y a ici deux ou trois canailles qui m'ont assiégé, un pauvre étranger qui ne leur ai fait nul mal, ni donné mauvaise parole, ni tiré mon épée. L'un me prend par une épaule, et me frappe deux livres pesant. L'autre me tire par le bras. Il parle je ne sais quoi. Je leur ai donné ma bourse, et s'ils ne me veulent point laisser aller, que ferai-je, monsieur?*

CAMLET This is a Frenchman it seems, sirs.

COUNTERBUFF We can find no other in him, sir, and what that is we know not.

CAMLET He's very like the man we seek for, else my lights go false.

BARBER In your shop they may, sir, but here they go true. This is he.

RALPH The very same, sir; as sure as I am Ralph, this is the rascal.

COUNTERBUFF Sir, unless you will absolutely challenge him the man, we dare not proceed further.

Enter Margarita, a French bawd

FLESHHOOK I fear we are too far already.

CAMLET I know not what to say to't.

MARGARITA *Bonjour, bonjour, gentilhommes.*

BARBER How now! More news from France?

YOUNG FRANKLIN *Cette femme ici est de mon pays.—Madame, je vous prie leur dire mon pays. Ils m'ont retardé, je ne sais pourquoi.*

MARGARITA *Etes-vous de France, monsieur?*

YOUNG FRANKLIN *Madame, vrai est que je les ai trompés, et suis arrêté, et n'ai nul moyen d'échapper qu'en changeant mon langage. Aidez-moi en cette affaire. Je vous connais bien, où vous tenez un bordel. Vous et les vôtres en serez de mieux.*

MARGARITA *Laissez-faire à moi. Etes-vous de Lyon, dites-vous?*

YOUNG FRANKLIN *De Lyon, ma chère dame.*

MARGARITA *Mon cousin! Je suis bien aise de vous voir en bonne disposition.*

[*They*] *embrace and compliment*

YOUNG FRANKLIN *Ma cousine!*

CAMLET This is a Frenchman sure.

BARBER If he be, 'tis the likest an Englishman that ever I saw, all his dimensions, proportions! Had I but the dissecting of his heart, in *capsula cordis* could I find it now, for a Frenchman's heart is more *quassative* and subject to tremor than an Englishman's.

CAMLET Stay, we'll further enquire of this gentlewoman. Mistress, if you have so much English to help us with—as I think you have, for I have long seen you about London—pray tell us, and truly tell us, is this gentleman a natural Frenchman or no?

MARGARITA Ey begar, de Frenchman, born *à Lyon*, my cozin.

CAMLET Your cousin? If he be not your cousin, he's my cousin sure.

MARGARITA Ey connosh his *père*, what you call his fadre? He sell *poissons*.

BARBER Sell poisons? His father was a pothecary then.

MARGARITA No, no, *poissons*, what you call, fish, fish.

BARBER O, he was a fishmonger.

MARGARITA *Oui, oui.*

CAMLET Well, well, we are mistaken I see. Pray you so tell him, and request him not to be offended. An honest man may look like a knave and be ne'er the worse for't. The error was in our eyes and now we find it in his tongue.

55–7 ***Je . . . service.*** I have no other jewels but these. And these belong to the ambassador; he sent me on his business and you are hindering my service.

62–9 ***Vous . . . monsieur?*** You seem to be a courteous man. I beg you to listen to my troubles. Here are two or three ruffians who have besieged me, a poor stranger who has done them no harm at all, nor spoken an ill word, nor drawn my sword. One takes me by one shoulder and strikes me two heavy blows. The other pulls me by the arm. He says I don't know what. I have given them my purse, and if they don't want to let me go, what shall I do, sir?

80.1 ***bawd*** prostitute

83 ***Bonjour . . . gentilhommes.*** Good day, good day, sirs.

84 **news from France** an allusion to short pieces by Thomas Overbury: 'News from Court', 'News from France', 'News from Rome', 'News from my Lodging'

85–7 ***Cette . . . pourquoi.*** This woman here is from my country.—Madame, I beg you to tell them my country. They have detained me, I don't know why.

88 ***Etes-vous . . . monsieur?*** Are you from France, sir?

89–93 ***Madame . . . mieux.*** Madame, the truth is that I have cozened them and am detained, and have no means of escaping except by changing my language. Help me in this business. I know you well, where you have a brothel. You and yours will benefit.

94 ***Laissez-faire . . . dites-vous?*** Leave it to me. You are from Lyon, you say?

94, 95 **Lyon** Lyon was a clothmaking city, but perhaps it was also chosen for the bawdy pun when the pronunciation is anglicized: 'Lie on'.

95 ***De . . . dame.*** From Lyon, my dear woman.

96–7 ***Mon . . . disposition.*** My cousin! I'm so pleased to see you in good health.

97.1 ***compliment*** a ceremonious greeting, probably they bow

98 ***Ma cousine!*** My cousin!

102 ***capsula cordis*** Latin: the centre of his heart

103 **quassative** inclined to shake

110 **Ey begar** a corruption of 'Yes, by God' ***à Lyon*** at Lyon

113 **cousin** punning on 'cozen', cheat

114 **connosh** a corruption of '*connais*', to know

118 **fishmonger** (*a*) seller of fish; (*b*) pimp

MARGARITA *J'essayerai encore une fois, monsieur cousin, pour votre sauveté.* [*He offers her money*] *Allez-vous en. Votre liberté est suffisante. Je gagnerai le reste pour mon devoir, et vous aurez votre part à mon école. J'ai une fille qui parle un peu français. Elle conversera avec vous à la Fleur-de-Lice en* Turnbull Street. *Mon cousin, ayez soin de vous-même, et trompez ces ignorans.*

YOUNG FRANKLIN *Cousine, pour l'amour de vous, et principalement pour moi, je suis content de m'en aller. Je trouverai votre école, et si vos écoliers me sont agréables, je tirerai à l'épée seule. Et si d'aventure je la rompe, je payerai dix sous. Et pour ce vieux fol et ces deux canailles, ce poulain* Snipsnap, *et l'autre bonnet rond, je les verrai pendre premier que je les vois.* *Exit*

CAMLET So, so, she has got him off. But I perceive much anger in his countenance still. And what says he, madam?

MARGARITA Moosh moosh anger, but ey connosh heere lodging shall cool him very well. Dere is a kinse-womans can moosh allay heere heat and heere spleene. She shall do for my saka, and he no trobla you.

CAMLET [*giving her money*] Look, there is earnest, but thy reward's behind. Come to my shop, the Holy Lamb in Lombard Street; thou hast one friend more than e'er thou hadst.

MARGARITA Tank u *monsieur*. Shall visit u. Ey make all *pacifie—à votre service très humblement.* [*Aside*] Tree, four, five fool of u. *Exit*

CAMLET What's to be done now?

COUNTERBUFF To pay us for our pains, sir, and better reward us that we may be provided against further danger that may come upon 's for false imprisonment.

CAMLET All goes false I think. What do you, neighbour Sweetball?

BARBER I must phlebotomize, sir, but my almanac says the sign is in Taurus. I dare not cut my own throat, but if I find any precedent that ever barber hanged himself I'll be the second example.

RALPH This was your ill *lixivium*, barber, to cause all to be cheated.

COUNTERBUFF [*to Camlet*] What say you to us, sir?

CAMLET

Good friends, come to me at a calmer hour.
My sorrows lie in heaps upon me now.
What you have, keep; if further trouble follow
I'll take it on me. I would be pressed to death.

COUNTERBUFF Well, sir, for this time we'll leave you.

BARBER I will go with you, officers. I will walk with you in the open street though it be a scandal to me. For now I have no care of my credit; a cacochymy is run all over me.

Exeunt Sweetball the barber, Counterbuff and Fleshhook

CAMLET What shall we do now, Ralph?

Enter George

RALPH Faith, I know not, sir. Here comes George, it may be he can tell you.

CAMLET And there I look for more disaster still. Yet George appears in a smiling countenance. Ralph, home to the shop; leave George and I together.

RALPH I am gone, sir. *Exit*

CAMLET Now, George, what better news eastward? All goes ill t'other way.

GEORGE I bring you the best news that ever came about your ears in your life, sir.

CAMLET Thou puttest me in good comfort, George.

GEORGE My mistress, your wife, will never trouble you more.

CAMLET Ha? Never trouble me more? Of this, George, may be made a sad construction; that phrase we sometimes use when death makes the separation. I hope it is not so with her, George?

GEORGE No, sir, but she vows she'll never come home again to you, so you shall live quietly. And this I took to be very good news, sir.

CAMLET

The worst that could be, this—candied poison.

125–31 ***J'essayerai . . . ignorans.*** I'll try once more, mister cousin, for your safety. *He offers her money*. Go away! Your freedom is enough. I'll earn the rest for my duty, and you'll have your share at my school. I have a girl who speaks some French. She'll talk with you at the *Fleur-de-Lice* in Turnbull Street. My cousin, take care of yourself—and cheat these fools.

128 ***école*** a euphemism for brothel

128–9 ***une fille qui parle un peu français*** a prostitute

129 ***conversera*** 'Talk' is a euphemism.
Fleur-de-Lice There was a tavern called the Fleur-de-Lis in Turnbull Street; the original spelling has been retained since it probably indicates pronunciation and implication: lice: fleas.

132–8 ***Cousine . . . vois.*** Cousin, for the love of you, and principally for me, I'm willing to go. I'll find your school, and if your students please me I'll draw one sword only. And if perchance I break it, I'll pay ten sous. And for this old fool and these two scoundrels, this snip-snapping colt and the other round hat, the next time I see them I'll see them hanged.

134–5 ***tirerai à l'épée seule*** with a *double entendre*: sword: penis

136–7 ***ce vieux fol . . . bonnet rond*** Franklin refers to Camlet, Counterbuff and Fleshhook, Sweetball, and Ralph.

146 **earnest** a sum of money paid as an instalment, especially to secure a bargain or contract

147 **behind** still to come

151 ***pacifie . . . humblement*** peaceful—at your very humble service

159 **phlebotomize** practise phlebotomy, or bloodletting
almanac a book of astrological charts

169 **pressed to death** the painful punishment for those who refused to plead either guilty or not guilty, of having the body pressed by heavy weights. Unlike the comparatively painless punishment of hanging, this saved forfeiture of the victim's goods to the crown.

172 **scandal** damaging his reputation because people will know he has been cheated (?)

173 **credit** reputation
cacochymy an unhealthy state of the humours or bodily fluids; see 3.2.32–3.

182 **eastward** (*fig.*) from elsewhere

I love her, George, and I am bound to do so.
The tongue's bitterness must not separate
The united souls. 'Twere base and cowardly
For all to yield to the small tongue's assault.
The whole building must not be taken down
For the repairing of a broken window.

GEORGE Ay, but this is a principle, sir. The truth is she will be divorced, she says, and is labouring with her cousin Knave—what do you call him?—I have forgotten the latter end of his name.

CAMLET Knavesbe, George.

GEORGE Ay, Knave or Knavesbe; one I took it to be.

CAMLET Why neither rage nor envy can make a cause, George.

GEORGE Yes, sir, not only at your person, but she shoots at your shop too. She says you vend ware that is not warrantable, braided ware, and that you give not London measure. Women, you know, look for more than a bare yard. And then you keep children in the name of your own which she suspects came not in at the right door.

CAMLET She may as well suspect immaculate truth to be cursèd falsehood.

GEORGE Ay, but if she will, she will; she's a woman, sir.

CAMLET 'Tis most true, George. Well, that shall be redressed. My cousin Cressingham must yield me pardon; the children shall home again and thou shalt conduct 'em, George.

GEORGE That done, I'll be bold to venture once more for her recovery since you cannot live at liberty, but because you are a rich citizen you will have your chain about your neck. I think I have a device will bring you together by th'ears again, and then look to 'em as well as you can.

CAMLET
O, George, amongst all my heavy troubles this
Is the groaning weight. But restore my wife.

GEORGE
Although you ne'er lead hour of quiet life?

CAMLET
I will endeavour't, George, I'll lend her will
A power and rule to keep all hushed and still.
Eat we all sweetmeats we are soonest rotten.

GEORGE
A sentence! Pity't should have been forgotten.

Exeunt

Finis Actus Tertius

Incipit Actus Quartus 4.1

Enter Sir Francis Cressingham and a surveyor [severally]

SURVEYOR Where's Master Steward?

CRESSINGHAM Within.—What are you, sir?

SURVEYOR A surveyor, sir.

CRESSINGHAM And an almanac-maker, I take it. Can you tell me what foul weather is toward?

SURVEYOR Marry, the foulest weather is that your land is flying away. *Exit*

CRESSINGHAM A most terrible prognostication! All the resort, all the business to my house is to my lady and Master Steward, whilst Sir Francis stands for a cipher. I have made away myself and my power as if I had done it by deed of gift. Here comes the controller of the game.

Enter Saunder [the steward]

SAUNDER What, are you yet resolved to translate this unnecessary land into ready money?

CRESSINGHAM Translate it?

SAUNDER The conveyances are drawn and the money ready. My lady sent me to you to know directly if you meant to go through in the sale. If not, she resolves of another course.

CRESSINGHAM Thou speakest this cheerfully methinks, whereas faithful servants were wont to mourn when they beheld the lord that fed and cherished them is by cursed enchantment removed into another blood. Cressingham of Cressingham has continued many years, and must the name sink now?

SAUNDER All this is nothing to my lady's resolution. It must be done or she'll not stay in England. She would know whether your son be sent for that must likewise set his hand to th' sale. For otherwise the lawyers say there cannot be a sure conveyance made to the buyer.

197 **bound** by marriage; also suggesting 'destined'
209 **cause** the case of one party in a suit for divorce
211–12 **shoots at** censures
213 **warrantable** guaranteed as genuine
braided ware goods that have changed colour, tarnished, or faded
214 **London measure** London clothsellers gave a certain amount above the standard yard in their measurements. Another bawdy pun on 'yard' follows.
216–17 **came not in at the right door** (*fig.*) are illegitimate; a variant of the proverb, 'To come in at the window'
226 **at liberty** free
227 **chain** worn by rich citizens, with an ironic glance at Rachel as Camlet's chain or restraint, threatening his business and therefore his social status
228 **device** scheme
229 **by th'ears** ironic; The phrase means to be at variance; also alluding to the loudness of Rachel Camlet's voice.
236 **all** only
sweetmeats sweets
237 **sentence** a maxim; a variant of the proverb, 'A little with quiet is the only diet'
4.1 attributed to Webster
4 **I take it** Perhaps the Surveyor is carrying charts.
6–7 **foulest . . . away** punning on 'fowlest'
8 **prognostication** prediction
9 **resort** visitors
10 **cipher** zero; (*fig.*) a thing of no value
16 **conveyances** documents transferring property ownership
22–3 **is . . . removed . . . blood** has lost the privileges of birth and rank
28–9 **set his hand to** authorize

CRESSINGHAM Yes, I have sent for him. But I pray thee think what a hard task 'twill be for a father to persuade his son and heir to make away his inheritance.

SAUNDER Nay, for that use your own logic. I have heard you talk at the sessions terribly against deer stealers, and that kept you from being put out of the commission. *Exit*

Enter Young Cressingham [as himself]

CRESSINGHAM [*aside*] I do live to see two miseries: one to be commanded by my wife, the other to be censured by my slave.

YOUNG CRESSINGHAM [*kneeling*] That which I have wanted long and has been cause of my irregular courses, I beseech you, let raise me from the ground.

CRESSINGHAM Rise, George. [*George rises*] There's a hundred pounds for you, and my blessing; with these your mother's favour. But I hear your studies are become too licentious of late.

YOUNG CRESSINGHAM [*aside*] He's heard of my cozenage.

CRESSINGHAM What's that you are writing?

YOUNG CRESSINGHAM Sir, not anything.

CRESSINGHAM Come, I hear there's something coming forth of yours will be your undoing.

YOUNG CRESSINGHAM Of mine?

CRESSINGHAM Yes, of your writing; somewhat you should write will be dangerous to you.—I have a suit to you.

YOUNG CRESSINGHAM Sir, my obedience makes you commander in all things.

CRESSINGHAM
I pray, suppose I had committed some fault
For which my life and sole estate were forfeit
To the law, and that some great man near the king
Should labour to get my pardon on condition
He might enjoy my lordship. Could you prize
Your father's life above the grievous loss
Of your inheritance?

YOUNG CRESSINGHAM Yes, and my own life at stake too.

CRESSINGHAM
You promise fair; I come now to make trial of it.
You know I have married one whom I hold so dear
That my whole life is nothing but a mere estate
Depending upon her will and her affections to me.
She deserves so well I cannot longer merit
Than *durante beneplacito*. 'Tis her pleasure.
And her wisdom moves in't too—of which I'll give you
Ample satisfaction hereafter—that I sell
The land my father left me. You change colour!
I have promised her to do't and should I fail
I must expect the remainder of my life
As full of trouble and vexation
As the suit for a divorce. It lies in you
By setting of your hand unto the sale
To add length to his life that gave you yours.

YOUNG CRESSINGHAM
Sir, I do now ingeniously perceive
Why you said lately somewhat I should write
Would be my undoing, meaning—as I take it—
Setting my hand to this assurance. O, good sir,
Shall I pass away my birthright? O, remember
There is a malediction denounced against it
In holy writ. Will you, for her pleasure,
The inheritance of desolation leave
To your posterity? Think how compassionate
The creatures of the field that only live
On the wild benefits of nature are
Unto their young ones. Think likewise you may
Have more children by this woman, and by this act
You undo them too. 'Tis a strange precedent this,
To see an obedient son labouring good counsel
To the father! But know, sir, that the spirits
Of my great-grandfather and your father moves
At this present in me; and what they bequeathed you,
On your deathbed they charged you not to give away
In the dalliance of a woman's bed. Good sir,
Let it not be thought presumption in me that
I have continued my speech unto this length.
The cause, sir, is urgent; and, believe it, you
Shall find her beauty as malevolent unto you
As a red morning that doth still foretell
A foul day to follow. O, sir, keep your land;
Keep that to keep your name immortal and you shall see
All that her malice and proud will procures
Shall show her ugly heart, but hurt not yours.

CRESSINGHAM
O, I am distracted and my very soul
Sends blushes into my cheeks.

Enter George with [Cressingham's] two children

YOUNG CRESSINGHAM See here an object
To beget more compassion.

GEORGE O, Sir Francis, we have a most lamentable house at home, nothing to be heard in't but separation and divorces, and such a noise of the spiritual court as if it were a tenement upon London Bridge and built upon the arches.

35 **sessions** the periodical sittings of justices of the peace
36 **commission** the Commission of Peace; Cressingham is a Justice of the Peace
45 **favour** preference
46 **licentious** unrestrained by law or morality
66 **estate** condition
69 ***durante beneplacito*** Latin: during her good pleasure
79 **ingeniously** cleverly
84–5 **malediction ... holy writ** *Gen.* 27
108 **distracted** disturbed
111 **lamentable** mournful
113 **noise** threatening talk
spiritual court the court with religious and ecclesiastical jurisdiction
114 **tenement upon London Bridge** The bridge from the Tower across the Thames had houses and shops along its length on both sides.
115 **arches** a reference to the noisy arches of London Bridge, and an allusion to the Court of Arches where divorces were tried

CRESSINGHAM What's the matter?

GEORGE All about boarding your children, my mistress is departed.

CRESSINGHAM Dead?

GEORGE In a sort she is, and laid out too, for she is run away from my master.

CRESSINGHAM Whither?

GEORGE Seven miles off, into Essex. She vowed never to leave Barking while she lived till these were brought home again.

CRESSINGHAM O, they shall not offend her. I am sorry for't.

FIRST CHILD I am glad we are come home, sir, for we lived in the unquietest house!

SECOND CHILD The angry woman methought grudged us our victuals. Our new mother is a good soul and loves us and does not frown so like a vixen as she does.

FIRST CHILD I am at home now, and in heaven methinks. What a comfort 'tis to be under your wing!

SECOND CHILD Indeed my mother was wont to call me your nestlecock, and I love you as well as she did.

Enter Saunder, Knavesbe, and Surveyor

CRESSINGHAM You are my pretty souls.

YOUNG CRESSINGHAM Does not the prattle of these move you?

SAUNDER [*to Cressingham*] Look you, sir; here's the conveyance and my lady's solicitor. Pray resolve what to do; my lady is coming down.—How now, George, how does thy mistress that sits in a waistcoat gown like a citizen's lure to draw in customers? O, she's a pretty mousetrap!

GEORGE She's ill-baited though to take a Welshman—she cannot away with cheese.

CRESSINGHAM And what must I do now?

KNAVESBE Acknowledge a fine and recovery of the land, then for possession the course is common.

CRESSINGHAM Carry back the writings, sir; my mind is changed.

SAUNDER Changed! Do not you mean to seal?

Enter Lady Cressingham

CRESSINGHAM No sir, the tide's turned.

SAUNDER [*aside to Lady Cressingham*] You must temper him like wax or he'll not seal.

LADY CRESSINGHAM [*to the children*] Are you come back again? [*To Cressingham*] How now, have you done?

FIRST CHILD How do you, Lady Mother?

LADY CRESSINGHAM You are good children. [*To George*] Bid my woman give them some sweetmeats.

FIRST CHILD Indeed, I thank you. Is not this a kind mother?

[*Exit George with children*]

YOUNG CRESSINGHAM Poor fools, you know not how dear you shall pay for this sugar.

LADY CRESSINGHAM [*to Cressingham*] What, ha'n't you dispatched?

CRESSINGHAM
No sweetest. I am dissuaded by my son
From the sale o'th' land.

LADY CRESSINGHAM Dissuaded by your son!

CRESSINGHAM
I cannot get his hand to't.

LADY CRESSINGHAM Where's our steward?
[*To Saunder*] Cause presently that all my beds and hangings
Be taken down. Provide carts, pack them up;
I'll to my house i'th' country. [*To Cressingham*] Have I studied
The way to your preferment and your children's
And do you cool i'th' upshot?

YOUNG CRESSINGHAM With your pardon,
I cannot understand this course a way
To any preferment; rather a direct
Path to our ruin.

LADY CRESSINGHAM
O, sir, you are young-sighted.

[*To Knavesbe*] Show them the project of the land I mean to buy in Ireland that shall out-value yours three thousand in a year.

[*Knavesbe shows a*] *map*

KNAVESBE Look you, sir, here is Clangibbon, a fruitful country and well wooded.

CRESSINGHAM What's this, marsh ground?

KNAVESBE No these are bogs, but a little cost will drain them. This upper part that runs by the Blackwater is the Cusacks' land, a spacious country and yields excellent profit by the salmon and fishing for herring. Here runs

120 **laid out** (*a*) prepared for burial; (*b*) spent, expended, (usually referring to money)
123 **Essex** a mostly agricultural county on the east coast of England
124 **Barking** a town in Essex; with a pun on 'barking'
129 **grudged** begrudged
130 **victuals** food
131 **vixen** shrew
135 **nestlecock** the last hatched bird or weakling of a brood, hence a mother's pet
137 **prattle** childish chatter
142 **waistcoat** a short, elaborate garment worn by women on the upper part of the body. To wear the waistcoat with no outer gown was disreputable; prostitutes were called 'waist-coaters'.
145–6 **Welshman ... cheese** The Welsh were said to be especially fond of cheese.
146 **away with** tolerate
148 **fine and recovery** A fine was an agreement of a suit, real or fictitious, whereby the lands in question were acknowledged to belong to one party ('fine' because final). Recovery was a complicated method of making a conveyance of fee-simple or lands held in tail.
149 **common** Court of Common Pleas
152 **seal** ratify the agreement
154–5 **temper ... wax** (*fig.*) manipulate carefully
165 **dispatched** completed the transaction
180 **Clangibbon** There was a Clangibbon in the south-west of Ireland, in Limerick County.
184 **Blackwater** There was a Blackwater river in the south-east of Ireland, in Waterford County.
185 **Cusacks'** Cusack or Cussack is a well-known Irish name.

the Kernesdale, admirable feed for cattle, and here about is St Patrick's Purgatory.

YOUNG CRESSINGHAM Purgatory! Shall we purchase that too?

LADY CRESSINGHAM
Come, come, will you dispatch th'other business?
We may go through with this?

CRESSINGHAM My son's unwilling.

LADY CRESSINGHAM
Upon my soul, sir, I'll never bed with you
Till you have sealed.

CRESSINGHAM Thou hearest her. On thy blessing
Follow me to th' court and seal.

YOUNG CRESSINGHAM Sir, were it my death, were't to th' loss of my estate, I vow to obey you in all things. Yet with it remember there are two young ones living that may curse you. I pray dispose part of the money on their generous educations.

LADY CRESSINGHAM Fear not you, sir.—[*She calls*] The caroche there! [*To Cressingham*] When you have dispatched, you shall find me at the scrivener's where I shall receive the money.

YOUNG CRESSINGHAM [*aside*] She'll devour that mass too.

LADY CRESSINGHAM [*to Saunder*] How likest thou my power over him?

SAUNDER Excellent.

LADY CRESSINGHAM
This is the height of a great lady's sway,
When her night-service makes her rule i'th' day.

Exeunt, manet Knavesbe

Enter Knavesbe's wife [*unseen by him*]

KNAVESBE Not yet, Sib? My lord keeps thee so long thou'rt welcome I see then, and pays sweetly too. A good wench, Sib, thou'rt, to obey thy husband. [*He sees her*] She's come. A hundred mark a year. [*He embraces her*] How fine and easy it comes into mine arms now! Welcome home—what says my lord, Sib?

SIB KNAVESBE My lord says you are a cuckold.

KNAVESBE Ha, ha, ha, ha! I thank him for that bob, i'faith. I'll afford it him again at the same price a month hence, and let the commodity grow as scarce as it will. 'Cuckold' says his lordship! Ha, ha,
I shall burst my sides with laughing, that's the worst.
Name not a hundred a year, for then I burst.
It smarts not so much as a fillip on the forehead by five parts. What has his dalliance taken from thy lips? 'Tis as sweet as e'er 'twas—let me try else. [*He tries to kiss her*] Buss me, sugar-candy.

SIB KNAVESBE [*pushing him away*]
Forbear; you presume to a lord's pleasure!

KNAVESBE How's that?
Not I, Sib?

SIB KNAVESBE
Never touch me more.
I'll keep the noble stamp upon my lip,
No underbaseness shall deface it now.
You taught me the way, now I am in I'll keep it.
I have kissed ambition and I love it.
I loathe the memory of every touch
My lip hath tasted from thee.

KNAVESBE
Nay, but sweet Sib, you do forget yourself.

SIB KNAVESBE
I will forget all that I ever was,
And nourish new, sirrah. I am a lady.

KNAVESBE
Lord bless us, Madam.

SIB KNAVESBE I have enjoyed a lord,
That's real possessïon, and daily shall,
The which all ladies have not with their lords.

KNAVESBE But with your patience, madam, who was it that preferred you to this ladyship?

SIB KNAVESBE
'Tis all I am beholden to thee for;
Thou'st brought me out of ignorance into light.
Simple as I was, I thought thee a man
Till I found the difference by a man.
Thou art a beast, a hornèd beast, an ox.

KNAVESBE
Are these ladies' terms?

SIB KNAVESBE For thy pander's fee,
It shall be laid under the candlestick;
Look for't, I'll leave it for thee.

KNAVESBE A little lower,
Good your ladyship, my cousin Camlet
Is in the house. Let these things go no further.

SIB KNAVESBE
'Tis for mine own credit if I forbear,

187 **Kernesdale** or the dale of the Kernes, poor Irish footsoldiers or, more generally, rustics or boors. There was a Kearne near the Bay of Galway.

188 **St Patrick's Purgatory** It was in the north-west of Ireland, in Ulster. The places named are widely separated, implying that Lady Cressingham's plan is impossible.

189 **purchase** a reference to the sale of indulgences or pardons by the church

202 **caroche** a luxurious coach

210 **night-service** sexual intercourse

210.1 ***Exeunt, manet Knavesbe*** While the fictitious location changes to Knavesbe's house here, because Knavesbe remains on stage the scene does not change; from here to the end of the scene is attributed to Middleton.

214 **A hundred mark a year** about $1000 today

218 **bob** a taunt

220 **commodity** sexual favours

224 **fillip** a flick of the finger

224–5 **five parts** four fingers and a thumb

226 **else** to see if it isn't true

227 **Buss** kiss

248 **beast...ox** a cuckold; Sib Knavesbe has not committed adultery, but wants her husband to think she has

250 **laid under the candlestick** an allusion to the proverb, 'It is good to set a candlestick before the devil'. Sib means that Knavesbe has done the devil's work.

252 **Camlet** Rachel Camlet

Not thine, thou bugle-browed beast, thou.

Enter George with rolls of paper [*seeming not to see the Knavesbes*]

GEORGE [*to himself*] Bidden, bidden, bidden, bidden. So, all these are passed, but here's as large a walk to come. If I do not get it up at the feast, I shall be leaner for bidding the guests, I'm sure.

KNAVESBE How now! Who's this?

GEORGE [*reading to himself*] 'Doctor Glister, *et*', what word's this? f-u-x-o-r? O, '*uxor*', the Doctor and his wife. 'Master Body *et uxor* of Bow Lane, Master Knavesbe *et uxor*.'

KNAVESBE [*to his wife*] Ha! We are in, whatsoever the matter is.

GEORGE Here's forty couple more in this quarter. But there the provision bringing in, that puzzles me most. 'One ox'—that will hardly serve for beef too—'five muttons, ten lambs'—poor innocents they'll be devoured too—'three gross of capons.'

KNAVESBE Mercy upon us! What a slaughterhouse is here!

GEORGE 'Two bushels of small birds: plovers, snipes, woodcocks, partridge, larks'—then for baked meats.

KNAVESBE George, George, what feast is this? 'Tis not for St George's Day?

GEORGE Cry you mercy sir, you and your wife are in my roll; my master invites you his guests tomorrow dinner.

KNAVESBE Dinner, sayest thou? He means to feast a month sure.

GEORGE Nay, sir, you make up but a hundred couple.

KNAVESBE Why, what ship has brought an India home to him that he's so bountiful? Or what friend dead—unknown to us—has so much left to him of arable land that he means to turn to pasture thus?

GEORGE Nay, 'tis a vessel, sir; a good estate comes all in one bottom to him, and 'tis a question whether ever he find the bottom or no. A thousand a year, that's the uppermost.

KNAVESBE A thousand a year!

GEORGE To go no further about the bush, sir—[*aside*] now the bird is caught—my master is tomorrow to be married, and amongst the rest invites you a guest at his wedding dinner the second.

KNAVESBE Married!

GEORGE There is no other remedy for flesh and blood, that will have leave to play whether we will or no, or wander into forbidden pastures.

KNAVESBE Married! Why he is married, man—his wife is in my house now—thy mistress is alive, George.

GEORGE She that was, it may be, sir, but dead to him. She played a little too rough with him and he has discarded her. He's divorced, sir.

KNAVESBE He divorced! Then is her labour saved, for she was labouring a divorce from him.

GEORGE They are well parted then, sir.

KNAVESBE But wilt thou not speak with her? I'faith, invite her to't.

GEORGE 'Tis not in my commission; I dare not. Fare you well, sir; I have much business in hand and the time is short.

KNAVESBE Nay, but George, I prithee, stay. May I report this to her for a certain truth?

GEORGE Wherefore am I employed in this invitation, sir?

KNAVESBE Prithee, what is she, his second choice?

GEORGE Truly a goodly presence, likely to bear great children and great store. She never saw five and thirty summers together in her life by her appearance, and comes in her French hood. By my fecks, a great match 'tis like to be. I am sorry for my old mistress but cannot help it. Pray you excuse me now, sir, for all the business goes through my hands, none employed but myself.

Exit

KNAVESBE Why here is news that no man will believe but he that sees.

SIB KNAVESBE This and your cuckoldry will be digestion throughout the city dinners and suppers for a month together; there will need no cheese.

Enter Rachel Camlet [*unseen by the Knavesbes*]

KNAVESBE No more of that, Sib. I'll call my cousin Camlet and make her partaker of this sport. [*He sees her*] She's come already. Cousin, take't at once, you're a free woman—your late husband's to be married tomorrow.

RACHEL CAMLET Married! To whom?

KNAVESBE To a French-hood, byrlakins, as I understand. Great cheer prepared and great guests invited, so far I know.

RACHEL CAMLET What a cursed wretch was I to pare my nails today, a Friday too. I looked for some mischief.

KNAVESBE Why, I did think this had accorded with your best liking: you sought for him what he has sought for you, a separation, and by divorce too.

RACHEL CAMLET I'll divorce 'm! Is he to be married to a French-hood? I'll dress it the English fashion. Ne'er a

255 **bugle-browed** horned
256 **bidden** invited
258 **get it up** eat well
261 **Glister** a suppository or enema
262 **f-u-x-o-r** phonetically, 'fucks 'er'
uxor Latin: wife
263 **Bow Lane** a street in Cheapside, formerly Cordwayner's Street, from the shoemakers who had shops there
267 **quarter** district
274 **baked meats** meat pies
276 **St George's Day** 23 April. St George was the patron saint of England. At 3.2.159–60 Sweetball says 'the sign is in Taurus' (20 April–20 May), so Knavesbe makes a reasonable assumption. Taurus is the Bull, another allusion to cuckoldry.
282 **India** proverbial for its wealth in gold and gems
287 **bottom** (*a*) a ship; (*b*) an end
291–2 **bush . . . caught** alluding to the proverb, 'a bird in the hand is worth two in the bush'
319 **French hood** a hood of softly pleated fabric; also possibly a headdress worn by women when punished for unchastity
325 **digestion** (*fig.*) after-dinner talk
331 **late** past
333 **byrlakins** an expletive; a contraction of 'by our ladykin' (the Virgin Mary)
337 **Friday . . . mischief** because Friday was associated with Catholicism (?)
342 **the English fashion** the latest fashion

coach to be had with six horses to strike fire i'th' streets as we go?

KNAVESBE Will you go home then?

RACHEL CAMLET Good cousin, help me to whet one of my knives while I sharp the t'other; give me a sour apple to set my teeth an edge. I would give five pound for the paring of my nails again. Have you e'er a bird-spit i'th' house, I'll dress one dish to the wedding.

KNAVESBE This violence hurts yourself the most.

RACHEL CAMLET I care not who I hurt. O, my heart, how it beats o' both sides! Will you run with me for a wager into Lombard Street now?

KNAVESBE I'll walk with you, cousin, a sufficient pace. Sib shall come softly after. I'll bring you through Bearbinder Lane.

RACHEL CAMLET Bearbinder Lane cannot hold me. I'll the nearest way over St Mildred's Church. If I meet any French-hoods by the way I'll make black patches enough for the rheum. *Exeunt, manet Sib Knavesbe*

SIB KNAVESBE

So, 'tis to my wish, Master Knavesbe.
Help to make peace abroad, here you'll find wars,
I'll have a divorce too, with locks and bars. *Exit*

4.2 *Enter George, Margarita [at Camlet's shop]*

GEORGE Madam, but stay here a little; my master comes instantly. I heard him say he did owe you a good turn and now's the time to take it. I'll warrant you a sound reward ere you go.

Enter Camlet

MARGARITA Ey tank u *de bon coeur, monsieur*.

GEORGE Look, he's here already. [*Aside*] Now would a skilful navigator take in his sails, for sure there is a storm towards. *Exit*

CAMLET O, Madam, I perceive in your countenance I am beholden to you—all is peace?

MARGARITA All quiet, goor frendsheep, ey mooch a do, ey strive wid him, give goor worda for you, no more speak a de matra. All es undone—u no more trobla.

Enter Rachel Camlet and Knavesbe [unseen by the others]

CAMLET [*giving her money*] Look, there's the price of a fair pair of gloves, and wear 'em for my sake.

RACHEL CAMLET [*aside to Knavesbe*] O, O, O, my heart's broke out of my ribs!

KNAVESBE Nay, a little patience.

MARGARITA [*to Camlet*] Ey tank u 'eartily, shall no bestow en gloves, shall put moosh more to dees and bestow your shop. *Regardez* dees stofa my petticoat—u no soosh anodre. Shall deal wid u for moosh. Take in your hand.

CAMLET [*taking up her petticoat*] I see it, mistress, 'tis good stuff indeed, 'tis a silk rash—I can pattern it.

RACHEL CAMLET [*aside*] Shall he take up her coats before my face? [*Coming forward*] O, beastly creature! French-hood! French-hood! I will make your hair grow through!

CAMLET My wife returned!—O, welcome home, sweet Rachel.

RACHEL CAMLET I forbid the banns! Lecher and strumpet, thou shalt bear children without noses.

MARGARITA O, *pardonnez-moi*, by my trat ey mean u no hurta; wat u meant by dees?

RACHEL CAMLET I will have thine eyes out, and thy bastards shall be as blind as puppies.

CAMLET Sweet Rachel. [*To Knavesbe*] Good cousin, help to pacify.

RACHEL CAMLET I forbid the banns, adulterer.

CAMLET [*to Knavesbe*] What means she by that, sir?

KNAVESBE [*restraining Rachel Camlet*] Good cousin, forbid your rage awhile. Unless you hear, by what sense will you receive satisfaction?

RACHEL CAMLET [*trying to free herself*] By my hands and my teeth, sir—give me leave. Will you bind me whiles mine enemy kills me?

CAMLET Here all are your friends, sweet wife.

RACHEL CAMLET Wilt have two wives? Do and be hanged, fornicator. I forbid the banns. Give me the French hood; I'll tread it under feet in a pair of pantofles.

MARGARITA Begar, shall save hood, head and all; shall come no more heer, ey warran u. *Exit*

KNAVESBE

Sir, the truth is, report spoke it for truth,
You were tomorrow to be marrièd.

RACHEL CAMLET

I forbid the banns.

CAMLET Mercy deliver me—
If my grave embrace me in the bed of death,
I would to church with willing ceremony.
But for my wedlock-fellow—here she is,
The first and last that e'er my thoughts looked on.

KNAVESBE [*to Rachel Camlet*]

Why law you, cousin; this was naught but error

346–7 **one of my knives** an allusion to a pair of knives worn at the girdle by a bride; see *Edward III* 2.2.171
350 **dress** cook
353 **run . . . wager** (*fig.*) race me for a prize
358 **Bearbinder Lane** a narrow street in Cheapside, now called George Street, running into Lombard Street
359 **St Mildred's Church** a church in London on the north side of the Poultry, a street connecting Cheapside and Cornhill
360–1 **black patches . . . rheum** Black patches were worn to hide signs of disease; here they are bruises.
4.2 attributed to Middleton
5 ***de bon coeur, monsieur*** from the bottom of my heart, sir
11 **goor** good; This 'franglais' is similar to that of a couplet in *Black Book* 497–8.
13 **matra** matter
21 **stofa** stuff, material
24 **rash** a smooth fabric
pattern copy
27–8 **make your hair grow through** The implication seems to be that Rachel will tear holes in Margarita's hood.
31 **banns** the proclamation in church of an intended marriage, in order that those who know of any impediment may object
32 **children without noses** as a result of syphilis
33 **trat** troth, truth
36 **blind as puppies** puppies are blind at birth
50 **pantofles** high-heeled, cork-soled slippers

Or an assault of mischief.

CAMLET Whose report was it?

KNAVESBE
Your man George's, who invited me to the wedding.

Enter George

CAMLET
George? And was he sober? Good sir, call him.

GEORGE
It needs not, sir; I am here already.

CAMLET
Did you report this, George?

GEORGE Yes, sir, I did.

CAMLET And wherefore did you so?

GEORGE For a new suit that you promised me, sir, if I could bring home my mistress—and I think she's come with a mischief.

RACHEL CAMLET Give me that villain's ears!

GEORGE I would give ear if I could hear you talk wisely.

RACHEL CAMLET Let me cut off his ears!

GEORGE I shall hear worse of you hereafter then. Limb for limb, one of my ears for one of your tongues, and I'll lay out for my master.

CAMLET
'Twas knavery with a good purpose in't,
Sweet Rachel. This was e'en George's meaning—
A second marriage 'twixt thyself and me;
And now I woo thee to't. A quiet night
Will make the sun like a fresh bridegroom rise
And kiss the chaste cheek of the rosy morn,
Which we will imitate and like him create
Fresh buds of love, fresh spreading arms, fresh fruit,
Fresh wedding robes, and George's fresh new suit.

RACHEL CAMLET [*looking at a cloth*]
This is fine stuff; have you much on't to sell?

GEORGE
A remnant of a yard.

CAMLET Come, come, all's well.
[*To Knavesbe*] Sir, you must sup instead of tomorrow's dinner.

Exeunt, [*manet Knavesbe*]

KNAVESBE
I follow you—no, 'tis another way,
My lord's reward calls me to better cheer,
Many good meals a hundred marks a year.
My wife's transformed a lady—tush, she'll come
To her shape again. My lord rides the circuit.
If I ride along with him, what need I grutch?
I can as easy sit, and speed as much. *Exit*

Finis Actus Quartus

Incipit Actus Quintus 5.1

Enter Old Franklin, in mourning; Young Cressingham with Young Franklin disguised like an old servingman

YOUNG CRESSINGHAM
Sir, your son's death which has apparelled you
In this darker wearing is a loss wherein
I have ample share; he was my friend.

OLD FRANKLIN
He was my nearest and dearest enemy,
And the perpetual fear of a worse end
Had he continued his former dissolute course,
Makes me weigh his death the lighter.

YOUNG CRESSINGHAM Yet, sir, with your pardon,
If you value him every way as he deserved,
It will appear your scanting of his means,
And the Lord Beaufort's most unlordly breach
Of promise to him, made him fall upon
Some courses to which his nature and mine own—
Made desperate likewise by the cruelty of
A mother-in-law—would else have been as strange
As insolent greatness is to distressed virtue.

OLD FRANKLIN
Yes, I have heard of that too—your deceit
Made upon a mercer. I style it modestly;
The law intends it plain cozenage.

YOUNG CRESSINGHAM 'Twas no less,
But my penitence and restitution may
Come fairly off from't. It was no impeachment
To the glory won at Agincourt's great battle,
That the achiever of it in his youth
Had been a purse-taker—this with all reverence
To th' great example. Now to my business,
Wherein you have made such noble trial of
Your worth that in a world so dull as this—
Where faith is almost grown to be a miracle—
I have found a friend so worthy as yourself
To purchase all the land my father sold
At the persuasion of a riotous woman,
And charitable to reserve it for his use
And the good of his three children. This, I say,
Is such a deed shall style you our preserver
And owe the memory of your worth and pay it
To all posterity.

OLD FRANKLIN Sir, what I have done
Looks to the end of the good deed itself,
No other way i'th' world.

69 **mischief** vengeance
75 **lay out** give one of his ears
92 **circuit** the journey of judges through the provinces for the purpose of holding court; probably also used figuratively to indicate Beaufort's infidelities ('ride')
93 **grutch** complain
5.1 probably mostly by Webster
4 **dearest** most injurious
15 **strange** unfamiliar, distant
18 **style** name
modestly moderately
19 **intends** interprets
21 **Come . . . off** result
impeachment detriment
22–4 **Agincourt's . . . purse-taker** George Cressingham likens himself to Prince Hal, whose youthful prodigality and eventual succession are dramatized in Shakespeare's second tetralogy; Agincourt is a battlefield in France, the site of Henry's victory in *Henry V*.
31 **riotous** troublesome, extravagant

YOUNG CRESSINGHAM But would you please
Out of a friendly reprehensïon
To make him sensible of the weighty wrong
He has done his children? Yet I would not have it
Too bitter for he undergoes already
Such torment in a woman's naughty pride
Too harsh reproof would kill him.

OLD FRANKLIN Leave you that
To my discretion. I have made myself
My son's executor and am come up
On purpose to collect his creditors,
And where I find his pennyworth conscionable
I'll make them in part satisfactïon.—

Enter George

O, this fellow was born near me and his trading here i'th' city may bring me to the knowledge of the men my son owed money to.

GEORGE Your worship's welcome to London; and, I pray, how does all our good friends i'th' country?

OLD FRANKLIN They are well, George. How thou art shot up since I saw thee! What, I think thou art almost out of thy time?

GEORGE I am out of my wits, sir. I have lived in a kind of Bedlam these four years. How can I be mine own man then?

OLD FRANKLIN Why, what's the matter?

GEORGE I may turn soap-boiler—I have a loose body—I am turned away from my master.

OLD FRANKLIN How! Turned away!

GEORGE I am gone, sir—not in drink, and yet you may behold my indentures.

[He shows the] indenture

O, the wicked wit of woman—for the good turn I did bringing her home she ne'er left sucking my master's breath like a cat—kissing him I mean—till I was turned away!

OLD FRANKLIN I have heard she's a terrible woman.

GEORGE Yes, and the miserablest! Her sparing in housekeeping has cost him somewhat, the Dagger pies can testify. She has stood in's light most miserably—like your fasting days before red letters in the almanac—saying the pinching of our bellies would be a mean to make him wear scarlet the sooner. She had once persuaded him to have bought spectacles for all his servants that they might have worn 'em dinner and supper.

OLD FRANKLIN To what purpose?

GEORGE Marry, to have made our victuals seem bigger than't was. She shows from whence she came, that my wind-colic can witness.

OLD FRANKLIN Why, whence came she?

GEORGE Marry, from a courtier, and an officer too, that was up and down I know not how often.

OLD FRANKLIN Had he any great place?

GEORGE Yes, and a very high one, but he got little by it. He was one that blew the organ in the court chapel. Our puritans, especially your puritans in Scotland, could ne'er away with him.

OLD FRANKLIN Is she one of the sect?

GEORGE 'Faith, I think not, for I am certain she denies her husband the supremacy.

OLD FRANKLIN Well, George, your difference may be reconciled. I am now to use your help in a business that concerns me. Here's a note of men's names here i'th' city unto whom my son owed money, but I do not know their dwelling.

GEORGE Let me see, sir. *[Reading]* 'Fifty pound ta'en up at use of Master Water Thin, the brewer.'

OLD FRANKLIN What's he?

GEORGE An obstinate fellow, and one that denied payment of the groats till he lay by th' heels for't. I know him. *[Reading]* 'Item, fourscore pair of provant breeches o'th'

39 **reprehensïon** reprimand
48 **pennyworth conscionable** a reasonable amount
49 **satisfactïon** repayment
55–7 **shot up ... time** George has grown so much he looks old enough to have almost completed his period of indenture as an apprentice (but if he has served only four years, he has at least three remaining).
59 **Bedlam** a madhouse; from Bethlehem, a hospital for the insane
62 **soap-boiler** Soap was used for suppositories.
loose body because not bound to a master, with a pun on 'soap'
63 **turned** sent
66 **indentures** the contract by which an apprentice is bound to a master who undertakes to teach him his trade
72 **sparing** niggardliness
73 **Dagger pies** pies from the Dagger, a tavern in Cheapside famous for its ale and pies, where George was forced to go for food
74 **stood in's light** (*fig.*) harmed his interests
75 **fasting days ... almanac** Fasting preceded important feasts and saints' days. In almanacs and ecclesiastical calendars such days were printed in red, other days in black.
77 **wear scarlet** become an alderman
83 **from whence she came** probably an allusion to the court of James I, in which corruption and scandal were pervasive
84 **wind-colic** intestinal gas
87 **up and down** had a place at court and lost it
88 **great place** powerful position
89 **got little by it** did not make money from it
91 **puritans in Scotland** This suggests that the Scottish puritans were the most extreme of the sect in their hatred of music.
92 **away with** tolerate
93 **sect** a puritan
94–5 **denies ... supremacy** Puritan teaching insisted on the traditional family hierarchy; here there is probably a bawdy pun on 'supremacy': the uppermost position.
101–2 **ta'en up at use of** borrowed at interest
105 **groats** (*a*) hulled grain, chiefly oats, but also wheat, maize, and barley, of which beer is made; (*b*) a coin worth 4*p*.
lay by th' heels literally, was put in irons or the stocks; but also, imprisoned
106 **fourscore** eighty
provant breeches breeches supplied to soldiers; provant: soldiers' allowance

new fashion to Pinch Buttock, a hosier in Birchin Lane', so much.

OLD FRANKLIN What the devil did he with so many pair of breeches?

YOUNG FRANKLIN [*disguised as an old servingman*] Supply a captain, sir, a friend of his went over to the Palatinate.

GEORGE 'Item, to my tailor, Master Weatherwise, by St Clement's Church.'

YOUNG CRESSINGHAM Who should that be? It may be 'tis the new prophet, the astrological tailor.

YOUNG FRANKLIN No, no, no, sir; we have nothing to do with him.

GEORGE Well, I'll read no further; leave the note to my discretion. Do not fear but I'll enquire them all.

OLD FRANKLIN Why, I thank thee, George. [*To George Cressingham*] Sir, rest assured I shall in all your business be faithful to you, and at better leisure find time to imprint deeply in your father the wrong he has done you. *Exeunt Old Franklin, George, and Young Franklin*

YOUNG CRESSINGHAM [*to the departing Old Franklin*] You are worthy in all things.

Enter Saunder

Is my father stirring?

SAUNDER Yes, sir; my lady wonders you are thus chargeable to your father and will not direct yourself unto some gainful study may quit him of your dependence.

YOUNG CRESSINGHAM What study?

SAUNDER Why, the law, that law that takes up most o'th' wits i'th' kingdom—not for most good but most gain. Or divinity—I have heard you talk well and I do not think but you'd prove a singular fine churchman.

YOUNG CRESSINGHAM I should prove a plural better, if I could attain to fine benefices.

SAUNDER My lady, now she has money, is studying to do good works. She talked last night what a goodly act it was of a countess—Northamptonshire breed belike, or thereabouts—that to make Coventry a corporation rode through the city naked, and by daylight.

YOUNG CRESSINGHAM I do not think but you have ladies living would discover as much in private to advance but some member of a corporation.

Enter Sir Francis Cressingham

SAUNDER Well, sir, your wit is still goring at my lady's projects. Here's your father.

CRESSINGHAM Thou comest to chide me, hearing how like a ward I am handled since the sale of my land.

YOUNG CRESSINGHAM No, sir, but to turn your eyes into your own bosom.

CRESSINGHAM Why, I am become my wife's pensioner, am confined to a hundred mark a year, t'one suit, and one man to attend me.

SAUNDER And is not that enough for a private gentleman?

CRESSINGHAM Peace, sirrah; there is nothing but knave speaks in thee. And my two poor children must be put forth to prentice.

YOUNG CRESSINGHAM
Ha! To prentice! Sir, I do not come
To grieve you but to show how wretched your
Estate was that you could not come to see order
Until foul disorder pointed the way to't—
So inconsiderate yet so fruitful still
Is dotage to beget its own destruction.

CRESSINGHAM
Surely I am nothing, and desire to be so.
[*To Saunder*] Pray thee, fellow, entreat her only to be quiet;
I have given her all my estate on that condition.

SAUNDER
Yes, sir; her coffers are well lined, believe me.

CRESSINGHAM
And yet she is not contented. We observe
The moon is ne'er so pleasant and so clear
As when she is at the full.

YOUNG CRESSINGHAM You did not use
My mother with this observance. You are like
The frogs, who, weary of their quiet king,
Consented to the election of the stork,
Who in the end devoured them.

CRESSINGHAM You may see

107 **new fashion** the latest fashion
hosier one who sells hose, stockings; more generally a men's outfitter, haberdasher
Birchin Lane a street running from Lombard Street to Cornhill, where drapers and secondhand clothes dealers were located

112 **Palatinate** a German protectorate. James's daughter Elizabeth was married to the Elector of the Palatinate. English volunteers for its defence embarked in July 1620.

113 **Master Weatherwise** also the name of a character in *No Wit*

113–14 **St Clement's Church** actually St Clement Danes church, at the east end of the Strand

116 **new prophet . . . tailor** probably the prophet Ball, a Puritan tailor

127.1 ***Enter Saunder*** Although the stage is not cleared, the fictional location seems to have changed to Cressingham's house.

130 **chargeable** burdensome

138 **plural** a reference to the ecclesiastical practice of priests holding several benefices, or positions in different locations

139 **benefices** ecclesiastical livings or positions

140 **studying** planning

141–2 **act . . . of a countess** According to legend, Lady Godiva (1040–80) implored her husband Leofric to reduce Coventry's heavy taxes. He agreed on the condition that she ride naked through the city. She did so, with her hair covering all her body except her legs. On her return Leofric issued a charter freeing Coventry 'from servitude'. An annual procession in her honour was held in Coventry. St George headed the procession and Lady Godiva was represented.

142 **Northamptonshire** the county adjacent to Warwickshire, where Coventry is

146 **discover** uncover
advance put forward in rank

147 **corporation** city administration

148 **goring at** sneering, scoffing at

151 **ward** a person, usually a minor, subject to a guardian

166 **dotage** (*a*) infatuation; (*b*) senility

170 **coffers** boxes or chests for keeping money or valuables

175–7 **frogs . . . them** a folktale

How apt man is to forfeit all his judgement
Upon the instant of his fall.

YOUNG CRESSINGHAM Look up, sir.

CRESSINGHAM
O, my heart's broke. Weighty are injuries
That come from an enemy, but those are deadly
That come from a friend for we see commonly
Those are ta'en most to heart. She comes.

Enter Lady Cressingham

YOUNG CRESSINGHAM
What a terrible eye she darts on us.

CRESSINGHAM O, most natural for lightning to go before the thunder.

LADY CRESSINGHAM What? Are you in council? Are ye levying faction against us?

CRESSINGHAM Good friend—

LADY CRESSINGHAM Sir, sir, pray come hither. There is winter in your looks, a latter winter. Do you complain to your kindred? I'll make you fear extremely to show you have any cause to fear. [*To Saunder*] Are the bonds sealed for the six thousand pounds I put forth to use?

SAUNDER Yes, madam.

LADY CRESSINGHAM The bonds were made in my uncle's name?

SAUNDER Yes.

LADY CRESSINGHAM 'Tis well.

CRESSINGHAM 'Tis strange, though.

LADY CRESSINGHAM Nothing strange. You'll think the allowance I have put you to as strange, but your judgement cannot reach the aim I have in't. You were pricked last year to be high sheriff, and what it would have cost you I understand now. All this charge and the other by the sale of your land, and the money at my dispose, and your pension so small will settle you in quiet, make you master of a retired life. And our great ones may think you a politic man and that you are aiming at some strange business, having made all over.

CRESSINGHAM I must leave you. Man is never truly awake till he be dead. *Exeunt Cressingham and Saunder*

YOUNG CRESSINGHAM What a dream have you made of my father!

LADY CRESSINGHAM Let him be so, and keep the proper place of dreams, his bed, until I raise him.

YOUNG CRESSINGHAM Raise him! Not unlikely 'tis you have ruined him.

LADY CRESSINGHAM You do not come to quarrel?

YOUNG CRESSINGHAM No, certain, but to persuade you to a thing that in the virtue of it nobly carries its own commendation—and you shall gain much honour by it, which is the recompense of all virtuous actions—to use my father kindly.

LADY CRESSINGHAM Why? Does he complain to you, sir?

YOUNG CRESSINGHAM Complain! Why should a king complain for anything but for his sins to heaven? The prerogative of husband is like to his—over his wife.

LADY CRESSINGHAM
I am full of business, sir, and will not mind you.

YOUNG CRESSINGHAM
I must not leave you thus. I tell you, mother,
'Tis dangerous to a woman when her mind
Raises her to such height it makes her only
Capable of her own merit, nothing of duty.
O, 'twas a strange, unfortunate o'erprising
Your beauty brought him—otherwise discreet—
Into the fatal neglect of his poor children.
What will you give us of the late sum you received?

LADY CRESSINGHAM
Not a penny. Away! You are troublesome and saucy.

YOUNG CRESSINGHAM
You are too cruel. Denials, even from princes—
Who may do what they list—should be supplied
With a gracious verbal usage, that though they do
Not cure the sore they may abate the sense of't.
The wealth you seem to command over is his,
And he I hope will dispose of't to our use.

LADY CRESSINGHAM
When he can command my will.

YOUNG CRESSINGHAM Have you made him
So miserable that he must take a law from his wife?

LADY CRESSINGHAM
Have you not had some lawyers forced to groan
Under the burden?

YOUNG CRESSINGHAM
O! But the greater the women
The more visible are their vices.

LADY CRESSINGHAM
So, sir, you have been so bold. By all can bind
An oath, and I'll not break it, I will not be
The woman to you hereafter you expected.

YOUNG CRESSINGHAM
Be not; be not yourself; be not my father's wife;
Be not my Lady Cressingham, and then
I'll thus speak to you. But you must not answer

179 **Look up** cheer up
188 **faction** opposition
194 **put forth to use** loaned at interest
204 **pricked** A prick was made next to the selected names in the list of those eligible.
210 **made all over** put everything in his wife's name
213 **dream** She has made him into a 'dream come true'.
217–18 **Raise ... ruined** with a pun on 'raze'; also, with the reference to bed, probably a double entrendre on 'raise'
228 **prerogative** right of supremacy
233 **Capable** able to perceive
234 **o'erprising** overestimating, overvaluing
240 **list** please
242 **sense** (*a*) feeling; (*b*) meaning
247 **some lawyers** a probable reference to the quarrels of Sir Edward Coke and his wife Elizabeth Hatton over property and the intended marriage of their daughter Frances to Sir John Villiers. Both husband and wife appeared before the Privy council in a famous series of confrontations. This allusion to a contemporary marriage that symbolized disorder is particularly apposite.

In your own person.

LADY CRESSINGHAM A fine puppet play!

YOUNG CRESSINGHAM
Good madam, please you pity the distress
Of a poor gentleman that is undone
By a cruel mother-in-law. You do not know her,
Nor does she deserve the knowledge of any good one,
For she does not know herself. You would sigh for her
That e'er she took your sex if you but heard
Her qualities.

LADY CRESSINGHAM
This is a fine crotchet.

YOUNG CRESSINGHAM
Envy and pride flow in her painted breasts,
She gives no other suck. All her attendants
Do not belong to her husband. His money is hers;
Marry, his debts are his own. She bears such sway
She will not suffer his religion be his own
But what she please to turn it to.

LADY CRESSINGHAM And all this while
I am the woman you libel against.

YOUNG CRESSINGHAM I remember
Ere the land was sold you talked of going to Ireland,
But should you touch there you would die presently.

LADY CRESSINGHAM
Why, man?

YOUNG CRESSINGHAM
The country brooks no poison. Go—
You'll find how difficult a thing it is
To make a settled or assured estate
Of things ill gotten. When my father's dead
The curse of lust and riot follow you—
Marry some young gallant that may rifle you!
Yet add one blessing to your needy age,
That you may die full of repentance.

LADY CRESSINGHAM Ha, ha, ha!

YOUNG CRESSINGHAM
O! She's lost to any kind of goodness. *Exeunt*

Enter Lord Beaufort and Knavesbe 5.2

BEAUFORT
Sirrah, be gone, you're base.

KNAVESBE Base, my good lord?
'Tis a ground part in music, trebles, means,
All is but fiddling—your honour bore a part,
As my wife says, my lord.

BEAUFORT Your wife's a strumpet.

KNAVESBE
Ah, ha! Is she so? I am glad to hear it;
Open confession, open payment.
The wager's mine then—a hundred a year my lord—
I said so before and staked my head against it.
Thus after darksome night the day is come, my lord.

BEAUFORT
Hence, hide thy branded head. Let no day see thee,
Nor thou any but thy execution day.

KNAVESBE
That's the day after washing day, once a week,
I see 't at home, my lord.

BEAUFORT Go home and see
Thy prostituted wife—for sure 'tis so—
Now folded in a boy's adultery.
My page, on whom the hot-reined harlot dotes—
This night he hath been her attendant—my house
he's fled from
And must no more return. Go, and make haste, sir
Lest your reward be lost for want of looking to.

KNAVESBE
My reward lost? Is there nothing due
For what is passed, my lord?

BEAUFORT
Yes, pander, wittol, macrio, basest of knaves,
Thou bolster-bawd to thine own infamy!
Go! I have no more about me at this time.
When I am better stored thou shalt have more
Where'er I meet thee.

KNAVESBE Pander, wittol, macrio, base knave, bolster-bawd; here is but five mark toward a hundred a year. This is poor payment if lords may be trusted no better than thus! I will go home and cut my wife's nose off;

256 **puppet play** popular entertainment
263 **crotchet** whimsical fancy; perverse notion
264 **painted** coloured with cosmetics
273 **country ... poison** St Patrick, according to legend, purged Ireland of venomous creatures.
278 **rifle** rob thoroughly
5.2 attributed substantially to Middleton
1 **base** morally low; leads to musical pun
2 **ground part** the plain-song or melody on which a descant is raised
means the middle or intermediate part in any harmonized composition or performance, especially the tenor and alto
3 **fiddling** (*a*) playing the violin; (*b*) having illicit sexual intercourse
bore a part cooperated, with a *double entendre*
8 **staked my head** with the usual wordplay on 'horns'
10 **branded** marked
12 **day after washing day** perhaps meaning that executions (seizures of goods for debt) were made on clean linen every week in Knavesbe's house (?)
16 **hot-reined** lustful
22 **wittol** contented cuckold
macrio mackerel, from French: '*maquereau*': a pimp
23 **bolster-bawd** pimp; bolster: pillow
27–35 **Pander ... *primo*** These lines might be spoken as an aside as Knavesbe exits, but he is angry enough not to care if Lord Beaufort hears him.
28 **five mark** with a pun on 'mark', since Beaufort hurls five insults at Knavesbe, and perhaps strikes him five times
30 **cut ... off** probably a twisted version of 'cutting one's nose off to spite one's face'; similar confusions follow

I will turn over a new leaf and hang up the page; lastly I will put on a large pair of wet-leather boots and drown myself. I will sink at Queenhithe and rise again at Charing Cross contrary to the statute in *Edwardo primo*. *Exit*

Enter Old Franklin, Young Franklin still disguised as an old servingman, George, three or four citizens (creditors)

OLD FRANKLIN Good health to your lordship.

BEAUFORT Master Franklin, I heard of your arrival and the cause of this your sad appearance.

OLD FRANKLIN And 'tis no more than as your honour says—indeed, appearance—it has more form than feeling sorrow, sir. I must confess there's none of these gentlemen—though aliens in blood—but have as large cause of grief as I.

FIRST CREDITOR No, by your favour, sir, we are well satisfied. There was in his life a greater hope, but less assurance.

SECOND CREDITOR Sir, I wish all my debts of no better promise to pay me thus; fifty in the hundred comes fairly homewards.

YOUNG FRANKLIN [*in disguise*] Considering hard bargains and dead commodities, sir.

SECOND CREDITOR Thou sayest true, friend, and from a dead debtor too.

BEAUFORT And so you have compounded and agreed all your son's riotous debts?

OLD FRANKLIN There's behind but one cause of worse condition; that done, he may sleep quietly.

FIRST CREDITOR Yes, sure, my lord; this gentleman is come a wonder to us all that so fairly with half a loss could satisfy those debts were dead even with his son, and from whom we could have nothing claimed.

OLD FRANKLIN I showed my reason, I would have a good name live after him because he bore my name.

SECOND CREDITOR May his tongue perish first—and that will spoil his trade—that first gives him a syllable of ill.

Enter Camlet

BEAUFORT Why, this is friendly.

CAMLET My lord!

BEAUFORT Master Camlet! Very welcome.

CAMLET Master Franklin, I take it—these gentlemen I know well, good Master Pennystone, Master Phillip, Master Cheyney! I am glad I shall take my leave of so many of my good friends at once. [*To Beaufort, shaking his hand*] Your hand first, my lord, fare you well, sir. [*To others*] Nay, I must have all your hands to my pass. [*They shake hands*]

GEORGE Will you have mine too, sir?

CAMLET Yes, thy two hands, George, and I think two honest hands of a tradesman, George, as any between Cornhill and Lombard Street.

GEORGE Take heed what you say, sir; there's Birchin Lane between 'em.

BEAUFORT But what's the cause of this, Master Camlet?

CAMLET I have the cause in handling now, my lord. George, honest George, is the cause, yet no cause of George's. George is turned away one way and I must go another.

BEAUFORT And whither is your way, sir?

CAMLET
E'en to seek out a quiet life, my lord.
I do hear of a fine peaceable island.

BEAUFORT
Why 'tis the same you live in.

CAMLET No, 'tis so famed,
But we th'inhabitants find it not so.
The place I speak of has been kept with thunder,
With frightful lightnings, amazing noises,
But now—th'enchantment broke—'tis the land of peace,
Where hogs and tobacco yield fair increase.

BEAUFORT This is a little wild, methinks.

CAMLET [*starting to leave*] Gentlemen, fare you well, I am for the Bermudas.

BEAUFORT Nay, good sir, stay—and is that your only cause, the loss of George?

CAMLET The loss of George, my lord! Make you that no cause? Why but examine, would it not break the stout heart of a nobleman to lose his george? Much more the tender bosom of a citizen.

31 **hang up the page** In a printing house a newly printed page was hung to dry; 'page' is also a reminder of Selenger.

32 **wet-leather** waterproof; which would seem to prevent, not permit, drowning

33 **Queenhithe** a quay on the north bank of the Thames west of Southwark Bridge, which was a landing place for goods brought to London by sea

34 **Charing Cross** the cross erected by Edward I in honour of Eleanor, his queen, at the then village of Charing Cross between London and Westminster

34–5 **contrary . . . *Edwardo primo*** According to legend, Eleanor, queen of Edward I, denied her guilt in the murder of the Lady Mayoress of London, praying that the earth might swallow her if she lied. She sank immediately to the spot where Charing Cross was later erected and rose again at Queenhithe. She died later, after confessing to all her crimes. Note that contrary to this, Knavesbe intends to sink at Queenhithe and rise at Charing Cross.

42 **aliens in blood** not related to Young Franklin

48 **fifty in the hundred** half of what is owed

51 **dead commodities** unsaleable goods

54 **compounded** settled

56 **behind** not yet mentioned

57 **sleep quietly** rest in peace

70 **Pennystone** or penistone, a coarse woollen cloth manufactured in the Yorkshire town of that name

70–1 **Master Phillip, Master Cheyney** 'Philip and Cheyney' was the name for a worsted material.

79 **Cornhill** a street in London running east from the end of the Poultry past the Royal Exchange to Leadenhall

80 **Birchin Lane** 'To send a person to Birchin Lane' was a proverbial phrase ordering him to be whipped or otherwise punished.

83 **in handling** he holds George's hands

92–5 **The place . . . increase** a probable allusion to Shakespeare's *Tempest*

98 **Bermudas** The islands symbolized tempests and enchantments.

103 **george** the jewelled figure of St George, part of the insignia of the Order of the Garter

BEAUFORT Fie, fie, I'm sorry your gravity should run back to lightness thus. You go to the Bermoothes!

OLD FRANKLIN Better to Ireland, sir.

CAMLET The land of ire—that's too near home. My wife will be heard from Helbre to Divelin.

OLD FRANKLIN Sir, I must of necessity awhile detain you; I must acquaint you with a benefit that's coming towards you. You were cheated of some goods of late. Come, I'm a cunning man and will help you to the most part again, or some reasonable satisfaction.

Enter Rachel Camlet [neither husband nor wife seeing the other]

CAMLET That's another cause of my unquiet life, sir. Can you do that, I may chance stay another tide or two. [*he sees his wife*]—My wife!—[*To Old Franklin*] I must speak more private with you. By forty foot pain of death I dare not reach her. No words of me, sweet gentlemen. (*Slips behind the arras*)

GEORGE I had need hide too. [*Slips behind the arras*]

RACHEL CAMLET O, my lord, I have scarce tongue enough yet to tell you—my husband, my husband's gone from me. Your warrant, good my lord, I never had such need of your warrant—my husband's gone from me.

BEAUFORT Going he is, 'tis true; has ta'en his leave of me and all these gentlemen, and 'tis your sharp tongue that whips him forwards.

RACHEL CAMLET A warrant, good my lord.

BEAUFORT You turn away his servants, such on whom his estate depends, he says, who know his books, his debts, his customers. The form and order of all his affairs you make orderless; chiefly, his George you have banished from him.

RACHEL CAMLET My lord, I will call George again.

GEORGE (*within*) Call George again.

BEAUFORT Why, hark you how high-voiced you are that raise an echo from my cellarage which we with modest loudness cannot.

RACHEL CAMLET My lord, do you think I speak too loud?

GEORGE (*within*) Too loud.

BEAUFORT Why hark, your own tongue answers you and reverberates your words into your teeth.

RACHEL CAMLET I will speak lower all the days of my life. I never found the fault in myself till now. Your warrant, good my lord, to stay my husband.

BEAUFORT Well, well, it shall o'ertake him ere he pass Gravesend, provided that he meet his quietness at home, else he's gone again.

OLD FRANKLIN And withal to call George again.

RACHEL CAMLET I will call George again.

GEORGE [*within*] Call George again.

BEAUFORT See, you are raised again; the echo tells you.

RACHEL CAMLET I did forget myself indeed, my lord; this is my last fault. I will go make a silent enquiry after George; I will whisper half a score porters in the ear that shall run softly up and down the city to seek him. Be wi' ye, my lord; bye all gentlemen. *Exit*

[*George and Camlet come out from behind the arras*]

BEAUFORT George, your way lies before you now; cross the street and come into her eyes. Your master's journey will be stayed.

GEORGE I'll warrant you bring it to better subjection yet. [*Exit*]

BEAUFORT
These are fine flashes—how now, Master Camlet?

CAMLET
I had one ear lent to you-ward, my lord,
And this o'th' t'other side; both sounded sweetly.
I have whole recovered my late losses, sir;
Th'one half paid, the t'other is forgiven.

BEAUFORT Then your journey is stayed?

Enter Barber and Knavesbe

CAMLET
Alas, my lord, that was a trick of age,
For I had left never a trick of youth
Like it to succour me.

BEAUFORT [*seeing Barber and Knavesbe*] How now? What new object's here?

BARBER The next man we meet shall judge us.

KNAVESBE Content, though he be but a common council man.

BEAUFORT The one's a knave; I could know him at twelve-score distance.

OLD FRANKLIN And t'other's a barber-surgeon, my lord.

KNAVESBE I'll go no further; here is the honourable lord that I know will grant my request. My lord—

BARBER Peace, I will make it plain to his lordship. My lord, a covenant by *jus jurandum* is between us: he is to

106 **Bermoothes** a contemporary spelling and pronunciation; also the name of a brothel district in the neighbourhood of Covent Garden

109 **Helbre to Divelin** Helbre: a small island in the mouth of the river Dee off West Kirby. Divelin: an old form of Dublin. With *doubles entendres* in 'Hell-bre' and 'Devil-in'. Rachel's strident voice will carry across the Irish sea.

113 **cunning** skilful, ingenious. But a 'cunning-man' was one who was thought to possess magical knowledge or skill, a quality in keeping with Old Franklin's surprise appearance and plot resolution.

118–19 **By forty foot … reach her** i.e. 'On pain of death I must not come within forty feet of her'; a reference in *Doctor Faustus* 2.19 suggests that the distance of forty feet from the gallows has particular significance

131 **books** accounts

137 **high-voiced** loud

148 **Gravesend** a port in Kent on the south bank of the Thames, thirty miles below London; the limit of the Port of London

150 **withal** as well

158 **Be wi' ye** elliptical form of 'God be with you'

162 **subjection** control, submission

163 **flashes** empty phrases, vulgarisms (?)

171 **succour** assist

175 **common council** the administrative body of London

183 ***jus jurandum*** Latin: oath

suffocate my respiration by his *capistrum* and I to make incision so far as mortification by his jugulars.

BEAUFORT This is not altogether so plain neither, sir.

BARBER I can speak no plainer, my lord, unless I wrong mine art.

KNAVESBE I can, my lord; I know some part of the law. I am to take him in this place where I find him and lead him from hence to the place of execution and there to hang him till he dies. He in equal courtesy is to cut my throat with his razor, and there's an end of both on's.

BARBER There is the end, my lord, but we want the beginning. I stand upon it to be strangled first, before I touch either his *gula* or *cervix*.

KNAVESBE I am against it, for how shall I be sure to have my throat cut after he's hanged?

BEAUFORT Is this a condition betwixt you?

KNAVESBE A firm covenant, signed and sealed by oath and handfast, and wants nothing but agreement.

BEAUFORT A little pause—what might be the cause on either part?

BARBER My passions are grown to putrefaction and my griefs are gangrened. Master Camlet has scarified me all over, besides the loss of my new brush.

KNAVESBE I am kept out of mine own castle, my wife keeps the hold against me; your page, my lord, is her champion. I summoned a parle at the window, was answered with defiance. They confess they have lain together, but what they have done else I know not.

BEAUFORT Thou canst have no wrong that deserves pity, thou art thyself so bad.

KNAVESBE I thank your honour for that; let me have my throat cut then.

Enter Selenger as a woman, and Sib Knavesbe

CAMLET Sir, I can give you a better remedy than his *capistrum*—your ear a little.

[*Camlet and Barber talk apart*]

SIB KNAVESBE
I come with a bold innocence to answer
The best and worst that can accuse me here.

BEAUFORT
Your husband.

SIB KNAVESBE He's the worst; I dare his worst!

KNAVESBE
Your page, your page!

SIB KNAVESBE We lay together in bed,
It is confessed. You and your ends of law
Makes worser of it; I did it for reward.

BEAUFORT I'll hear no more of this.—Come gentlemen, will you walk?

Enter Young Cressingham

YOUNG CRESSINGHAM
My lord, a little stay. You'll see a sight
That neighbour amity will be much pleased with.

Enter Cressingham [in rich new clothing]

'Tis come already—my father, sir.

BEAUFORT
There must be cause certain for this good change.
Sir, you are bravely met; this is at the best
I ever saw you.

CRESSINGHAM
My lord, I am amazement to myself.
I slept in poverty and am awake
Into this wonder. How I came thus brave
My dreams did not so much as tell me of.
I am of my kind son's new making up.
It exceeds the pension much—that yesternight
Allowed me—and my pockets centupled.
But I am my son's child, sir; he knows of me
More than I do myself.

YOUNG CRESSINGHAM Sir, you yet have
But earnest of your happiness, a pinnace
Foreriding a goodly vessel, by this near anchor,
Bulked like a castle and with jewels fraught—
Joys above jewels, sir, from deck to keel.
Make way for the receipt, empty your bosom
Of all griefs and troubles, leave not a sigh
To beat her back again, she is so stored
Ye 'ad need have room enough to take her lading.

CRESSINGHAM
If one commodity be wanting now,
All this is nothing.

YOUNG CRESSINGHAM
Tush, that must out too,
There must be no remembrance, not the thought
That ever youth in woman did abuse you,
That e'er your children had a stepmother,
That you sold lands to please your punishment,
That you were circumscribed and taken in,
Abridged the large extendure of your grounds
And put into the pinfold that belonged to't,
That your son did cheat for want of maintenance.
That he did beg, you shall remember only,
For I have begged off all these troubles from you.

Enter Lady Cressingham in civil habit, Saunder, and [the two] children, very gallant

BEAUFORT This was a good week's labour.

YOUNG CRESSINGHAM
Not an hour's, my lord, but 'twas a happy one—
See, sir, a new day shines on you.

184 ***capistrum*** Latin: halter
195 **stand upon** insist on
196 ***gula*** Latin: throat
cervix Latin: neck
201 **handfast** the joining of hands in making a bargain
205 **scarified** scarred, covered with scratches
209 **parle** parley: conference
230 **bravely met** finely dressed
241 **pinnace** a small boat
248 **lading** loading
255 **circumscribed** *fig.* confined
256 **Abridged** deprived of
extendure extent
257 **pinfold** (*fig.*) a place of confinement
260.1 **civil habit** sober, subdued clothes, presumably in contrast to her previous apparel. The two children are now in fine clothing whereas before they were poorly dressed.

LADY CRESSINGHAM O, sir,
Your son has robbed me.
CRESSINGHAM Ha! That way I instructed?
YOUNG CRESSINGHAM
Nay, hear her, sir.
LADY CRESSINGHAM
Of my good purpose, sir;
He hath forced out of me what lay concealed,
Ripened my pity with his dues of duty.
Forgive me, sir, and but keep the number
Of every grief that I have pained you with—
I'll tenfold pay with fresh obedience.
CAMLET
O, that my wife were here to learn this lesson.
LADY CRESSINGHAM [*to Cressingham*]
Your state is not abated. What was yours
Is still your own. And take the cause withal
Of my harsh seeming usage. It was to reclaim
Faults in yourself—the swift consumption
Of many large revenues; gaming that
Of not much less speed—burning up house and land,
Not casual but cunning fire, which though
It keeps the chimney and outward shows
Like hospitality, is only devourer on't—
Consuming chemistry. There I have made you
A flat bankrupt—all your stillatories
And labouring minerals are demolished;
That part of hell in your house is extinct.
Put out your desire with them and then these feet
Shall level with my hands; until you raise
My stooped humility to higher grace
To warm these lips which love and duty do
To every silver hair, each one shall be
A senator to my obedience.
CRESSINGHAM
All this I know before; whoever of you
That had but one ill thought of this good woman,
You owe a knee to her and she is merciful
If she forgive you.

Enter George and Rachel Camlet

BEAUFORT That shall be private penance, sir; we'll all joy in public with you.

GEORGE [*to Rachel Camlet*] On the conditions I tell you, not else.

RACHEL CAMLET Sweet George, dear George, any conditions.

CAMLET My wife!

OLD FRANKLIN Peace—George is bringing her to conditions.

CAMLET Good ones, good George.

GEORGE You shall never talk your voice above the key, sol, sol, sol.

RACHEL CAMLET Sol, sol, sol. Ay, George.

GEORGE Say 'welcome home, honest George', in that pitch.

RACHEL CAMLET Welcome home, honest George.

GEORGE Why, this is well now.

CAMLET That's well indeed, George.

GEORGE 'Rogue' nor 'rascal' must never come out of your mouth.

RACHEL CAMLET They shall never come in, honest George.

GEORGE Nor I will not have you call my master plain husband, that's too coarse, but as your gentlewomen in the country use, and your parsons' wives in the town. 'Tis comely and shall be customed in the city: call him Master Camlet at every word.

RACHEL CAMLET At every word, honest George.

GEORGE Look you, there he is, salute him then.

RACHEL CAMLET Welcome home, good Master Camlet.

CAMLET Thanks and a thousand, sweet wife—I may say, honest George?

GEORGE Yes sir, or bird, or chuck, or heart's ease, or plain Rachel, but call her Rac no more, so long as she is quiet.

CAMLET God-a-mercy, shalt have thy new suit o' Sunday, George.

RACHEL CAMLET George shall have two new suits, Master Camlet.

CAMLET God-a-mercy, i'faith, chuck.

BARBER Master Camlet, you and I are friends, all even betwixt us?

CAMLET I do acquit thee, neighbour Sweetball.

BARBER I will not be hanged then—Knavesbe do thy worst—nor I will not cut thy throat.

KNAVESBE I must do't myself.

BARBER If thou comest to my shop and usurpest my chair of maintenance I will go as near as I can, but I will not do't.

YOUNG CRESSINGHAM No, 'tis I must cut Knavesbe's throat for slandering a modest gentlewoman—and my wife—in shape of your page, my lord. In her own I durst not place her so near your lordship.

BEAUFORT No more of that sir. If your ends have acquired their own events, crown 'em with your own joy.

YOUNG CRESSINGHAM Down o' your knees, Knavesbe, to your wife; she's too honest for you.

BARBER Down, down, before you are hanged; 'twill be too late afterwards and long thou canst not scape it.

Knavesbe kneels

SIB KNAVESBE You'll play the pander no more, will you?

KNAVESBE O, that's an inch into my throat.

SIB KNAVESBE And let out your wife for hire?

KNAVESBE O, sweet wife, go no deeper.

SIB KNAVESBE Dare any be bail for your better behaviour?

281 **chemistry** his alchemy
282 **stillatories** distilleries
283 **labouring minerals** chemicals which Sir Francis used
304 **sol** the note G in the natural scale of C major
324 **chuck** an endearment
heart's ease (*a*) tranquillity, peace of mind; (*b*) a common name for the pansy
325 **Rac** or 'rack': (*a*) a loud noise; (*b*) an iron bar to which prisoners were secured; here with an additional pun on 'wrack'
338–9 **chair of maintenance** the source of his livelihood, the barber's chair
343 **shape** disguise
345–6 **ends...events** intentions... outcomes

BEAUFORT Yes, yes, I dare; he will mend one day.
SIB KNAVESBE And be worse the next.
KNAVESBE
Hang me the third then, dear merciful wife,
I will do 'anything for a quiet life'.
BEAUFORT All then is reconciled?
BARBER Only my brush is lost, my dear new brush.
OLD FRANKLIN I will help you to satisfaction for that too, sir.
BARBER O, *spermaceti*, I feel it heal already.
OLD FRANKLIN Gentlemen, I have fully satisfied my dead son's debts?
OMNES All pleased, all paid, sir.
OLD FRANKLIN
Then once more, here I bring him back to life,
From my servant to my son.
[*He removes his son's disguise*]
Nay, wonder not—
I have not dealt by fallacy with any;
My son was dead. Whoe'er outlives his virtues
Is a dead man, for when you hear of spirits
That walk in real bodies to the amaze
And cold astonishment of such as meet 'em,
And all would shun, those are men of vices
Who nothing have but what is visible;
And so by consequence they have no souls;
But if the soul return he lives again,
Created newly. Such my son appears
By my blessing rooted, growing by his tears.
OMNES You have beguiled us honestly, sir.
YOUNG FRANKLIN And you shall have your brush again.
BARBER My basins shall all ring for joy.
BEAUFORT
Why, this deserves a triumph, and my cost
Shall begin a feast to't to which I do
Invite you all. Such happy reconcilements
Must not be passed without a health of joy.
Discorded friends atoned, men and their wives,
This hope proclaims your after quiet lives. *Exeunt*

Finis

Epilogue

I am sent t'enquire your censure, and to know
How you stand affected. Whether we do owe
Our service to your favours, or must strike
Our sails—though full of hope—to your dislike.
Howe'er, be pleased to think we purposed well,
And from my fellows thus much I must tell,
Instruct us but in what we went astray,
And to redeem it, we'll take any way.

THE PARTS

Adult Males

CAMLET (284 lines): Surveyor
YOUNG CRESSINGHAM (276 lines): Surveyor; Fleshhook, *or* Counterbuff
KNAVESBE (256 lines): Surveyor; Fleshhook, *or* Counterbuff
GEORGE (238 lines): Surveyor; Fleshhook, *or* Counterbuff
BEAUFORT (226 lines): Surveyor; Fleshhook, *or* Counterbuff
YOUNG FRANKLIN (213 lines): Surveyor
CRESSINGHAM (176 lines): Fleshhook, *or* Counterbuff
BARBER (125 lines): Surveyor
OLD FRANKLIN (78 lines): Surveyor; Fleshhook, *or* Counterbuff, *or* Ralph
SAUNDER (49 lines): Surveyor; Fleshhook, *or* Counterbuff
RALPH (46 lines): Surveyor; creditor (5.2)
COUNTERBUFF (3.2; 19 lines): any adult male but Camlet, Young Franklin, Ralph, George, Sweetball, Fleshhook
Three or Four CREDITORS (5.2; 14 lines): Fleshhook; Counterbuff; Ralph; *or* Surveyor
FLESHHOOK (3.2; 4 lines): any adult male but Camlet, Young Franklin, Ralph, George, Sweetball, Counterbuff
SURVEYOR (4.1; 4 lines): any adult male but Old Cressingham

Youths

SELENGER (45 lines): [Prologue, Epilogue]

Boys

SIB KNAVESBE (230 lines): Barber's boy
LADY CRESSINGHAM (150 lines): Margarita; Barber's boy
RACHEL CAMLET (86 lines): Margarita; Barber's boy
MARGARITA (37 lines): First Child, *or* Second Child; Barber's boy
FIRST CHILD (12 lines): Margarita; Barber's boy
SECOND CHILD (9 lines): Margarita; Barber's boy
Barber's BOY (2.3, 2.4; 8 lines): any woman or child

Most crowded scene: 5.2: 13 speaking parts (+ 6 or 7 mute)

364 ***spermaceti*** a fatty substance from the sperm whale, used medicinally
369.1 ***He . . . disguise*** The dialogue suggests that some such action occurs.
371–7 **Whoe'er . . . souls** According to church doctrine, a living person could, through acts of treachery, lose possession of his soul before he died; then the devil inhabits the body until its natural death.
Epilogue.1 **censure** judgement

THE CHANGELING

Text edited and annotated by Douglas Bruster, introduced by Annabel Patterson

The Changeling has been, for at least a century, alive and well in the theatre as well as the classroom. Like *Hamlet*, as the play without which Shakespeare is unimaginable, it has defined Middleton's canon around itself. It has enhanced the otherwise slim reputation of William Rowley, Middleton's collaborator. Though most frequently performed in English-speaking countries, it is known in Europe, having been translated into French (1948, 1956, 1966), Italian (1946), Hungarian (1961), and Spanish (1973); and it has even entered the territory of general literacy. In a 1994 television series, *To Play the King*, De Flores's cynical line, 'Some women are odd feeders', was complacently quoted by the evil British Prime Minister. Like *Hamlet*, *The Changeling* is powered by a toxic brew of domestic violence, sexual obsession and madness. Unlike *Hamlet*, however, *The Changeling* locates those threats to 'normality' in the protagonist's consummated sexual relationship, whose electric charge disables or at least disrupts our evaluative reflexes.

One might not have written such a sentence fifty years ago; but films like *Blue Velvet* (1986), *The Draughtsman's Contract* (1982), and *The Night Porter* (1973) have inured us to studies in sexual obsession. *The Night Porter*, though the earliest of these deliberate shockers, is the most pertinent analogy, since it shows how a criminal record in the past (of a concentration camp official and his Jewish concubine) binds together in the postwar present the hotel servant and the beautiful aristocrat, their social roles reversed, their rediscovered passion entirely self-destructive and entirely convincing. What has come over the film industry, however, is only one of several changes that make it time for a new account of *The Changeling*, one that might beg to differ from N. W. Bawcutt's brilliant and humane introduction to his Revels edition in 1958.

Criticism of Jacobean drama was then predominantly ethical in tone. Bawcutt declared that 'the moral world' of the play 'is the orthodox Christian universe of sin and punishment', and at the end, as the betrayed husband offers his father-in-law the filial duty that his daughter had withheld, 'moral order is finally established'. Today, ethical judgement seems more complicated, and readers and audiences will have contradictory responses. For example, the tendency of feminism to see women as the victims of the system can produce a protagonist who merely overreacted to being forced to marry according to her father's will, not hers. But the critique of dynastic marriage seems less pertinent here, where the daughter suddenly changes *her* mind about whom she desires as a husband, than in *Women, Beware Women*, where Middleton himself writes a passionate speech (for the Isabella of that play) attacking it. And though Vermandero and Alsemero will now appear to share more of the blame, even today those who arrange for the murder of an inconvenient mate may send shudders down our spines. Horror, however, will not prevent us from identifying more readily with guilty, scheming Beatrice-Joanna than with the cool, hands-off Isabella of the hospital plot, or from imagining what De Flores would be like as a lover. Middleton added to his source the bad skin and 'dogface' that at some level attracts Beatrice as much as it repels her, and, more importantly, makes it clear from what De Flores says that his name matches his belief in defloration as the quintessential form of sexual possession. But would these reactions not have been equally possible for Jacobean audiences? Our answer today may be different from those who in the mid-century defined the 'moral temper' of Jacobean tragedy; but it will likewise be only a guess.

We can speak more securely about the moral temper of literary criticism, which has certainly changed. The Christian-ethical vocabulary has been forgotten by readers accustomed to Freudian and Lacanian psychoanalysis, for whom sexuality is *the* power to which we owe allegiance. This assumption competes with a renewed curiosity about the sociopolitical circumstances in which the English public theatre appeared and spread like some fabulous alien growth. The extent to which *The Changeling* was specifically a play for 1622 is now again an interesting question; a political explanation may actually be necessary for otherwise mysterious additions to the plot and inexplicable remarks. And whereas Marxist and feminist approaches, which may claim that *The Changeling* interrogates hierarchical assumptions in the state and the family, *reverse* the traditionally negative evaluations of characters who breach them, a more narrowly historical approach will not necessarily steer audience sympathy in the same direction. Ideally, one would want to acknowledge all these possibilities, while remaining sensitive to the play's capacity to make us believe in its characters and their predicament—the quality for which it continues to be successfully revived.

The Changeling was a late work of both Middleton and Rowley, and both seem to have profited from years of experience in a theatre where writerly collaboration was, as we sometimes forget, as common as individual authorship. It has been common practice since P. G. Wiggin's 1897 study to attribute to Middleton most of the castle plot, while to Rowley are assigned the hospital plot and the opening and closing scenes of the play. And one strain of modern criticism deriving from T. S. Eliot has wished the hospital plot entirely away. Samuel Schoenbaum, himself engaged in recuperating Middleton as a tragic writer, declared it 'stupid and tedious, and the treatment of insanity... offensive to the modern reader'. Others, however, have been sensitive to the parallel-with-difference structure, whereby Isabella's successful resistance of her two disguised suitors and the leering warder Lollio is the normative foil to Beatrice-Joanna's betrayals. Several striking verbal analogies between the two plots suggest how closely Middleton and Rowley intended them to be related. Thus the famous moment when De Flores picks up Beatrice-Joanna's gloves and visibly 'thrust[s his] | ... fingers into her sockets' (1.1.237–8) is followed in the next scene by the sexual banter between Lollio and his employer Alibius, who keeps the madhouse and who is also Isabella's newly-married and insanely jealous husband. Will he manage to keep his new 'ring' on his own finger? 'If it but lie by,' sneers Lollio, 'one or other will be thrusting into't' (1.2.30–1).

It seems obvious now that the madness and folly which are literal in the hospital plot metaphorically indict the behaviour of *all* the castle-plot characters; not least because an antemasque of madmen and idiots is to be included in the wedding festivities for Alsemero and Beatrice-Joanna. But Alibius's speech describing his commission suggests a still more mysterious relation between the two plots:

> Only an unexpected passage over,
> To make a frightful pleasure, that is all—
> But not the all I aim at. Could we so act it
> To teach it in a wild distracted measure,
> Though out of form and figure, breaking Time's
> head—
> (It were no matter, 'twould be healed again
> In one age or other, if not in this). (3.3.280–6)

This enigmatic statement, so out of character for the profit-conscious entrepreneur, is reminiscent of Hamlet's advice to the players that the purpose of theatre is to 'show the very age and body of the time his form and pressure' (3.2.25). Its strangeness plausibly gives these playwrights an alibi for defining *their* larger purpose. For while 'frightful pleasure' implies the sexual Sublime, to break time's head and to imagine its healing in another era suggests not self-destruction but reconstructive zeal.

The two plots explicitly converge in the last scene, where Alsemero explicates the play's title by listing the 'changes' or exchanges they have witnessed; of Beatrice-Joanna into a whore, of De Flores into a murderer, of Diaphanta for her mistress in the nuptial bed, of Tomazo the avenger into a reasonable person. But he concludes with the wide-open question, 'Are there any more on's?' This permits the addition of not one but three changelings from the hospital plot, Antonio, Franciscus and Alibius, whose change, as Isabella points out, 'is still behind', by which she means ahead. The title is therefore retroactively rendered plural, *The Changelings*, and may even have extension into the world outside the play.

One should be wary, however, of taking Alsemero's complacent categories at face value, since he stands self-accused of substituting skin-deep for inner beauty, as also of susceptibility (as victim of a bed-trick) to the cynical view that all cats are grey in the dark. As for his remarkable observation that 'servant-obedience' has changed in the person of De Flores to 'a master-sin: imperious murder', it logically implies that murder is the privilege of the aristocracy. This locution might support a class-based analysis of the play such as proposed by Jonathan Dollimore and modified by Cristina Malcolmson; but it makes better sense in the context of a highly specific political interpretation.

The most strenuous effort to provide this appears in a 1990 collaborative study by A. A. Bromham and Zara Bruzzi, who read the entire play as a 'hieroglyph' of its times, specifically the 'years of crisis' from 1619 to 1624. This is specificity indeed. But they can rightly claim that Middleton signalled his general intentions by topical allusion to the scandalous divorce of Frances Howard, Countess of Essex, from Robert Devereux, third earl of Essex, and her remarriage to Robert Carr, Earl of Somerset, the King's current favourite. The divorce was achieved by the claim of non-consummation, confirmed by a panel of matrons who examined the Countess internally. There was widespread scepticism about this test, including rumours that an actual virgin had been substituted for the Countess, who insisted on remaining veiled. When Beatrice-Joanna, terrified lest Alsemero will discover on their wedding night that she is no longer intact, engages Diaphanta as her substitute, and experiments on her with the medical test intended for herself, Diaphanta mutters in an aside: 'She will not search me, will she, | Like the forewoman of a female jury?' (4.1.102–3).

This odd remark was acknowledged by A. H. Bullen in 1885 and by Margot Heinemann in 1980 as an unmistakable allusion to the Somerset scandal; but in the Modernist criticism of the interim its importance was submerged. For Schoenbaum the whole episode of the virginity test was 'ridiculous'. Bawcutt saw it as fantastic, and wondered whether Middleton himself 'took it very seriously'. But we should remember that while the *name* of De Flores appeared in Middleton's source, John Reynolds's *The Triumphs of God's Revenge against the Crying and Execrable Sin of Murder*, there is no such emphasis there on defloration. Middleton added the entire episode of the tests and the bed-trick, thereby making virginity and its overvaluation a central theme of his tragedy.

In 1616, Howard and Somerset were tried for the murder of a courtier, Sir Thomas Overbury, who had strenuously opposed the divorce and remarriage. They were found guilty; their accomplices were executed, but their own sentences were commuted by James, and in January 1622 they were released from their none-too-uncomfortable restraint in the Tower. In that year it would also, therefore, have been just possible to hear another topical allusion in Alsemero's strange remark about Vermandero: 'How shall I dare to venture in his castle

| When he discharges murderers at the gate?' (1.1.226–7). Editors gloss this remark with the information that 'murderers' was a contemporary term for small cannon, but the remark still seems unwarranted. Later, a textual echo reinforces the more commonplace meaning—Vermandero's discovery that Antonio and Franciscus have been missing from his retinue since the day of Piracquo's murder: 'The time accuses 'em; a charge of murder | Is brought within my castle gate' (4.2.10–11).

It may be that Middleton used these allusions as discreet reparation for his earlier response to the Howard–Somerset marriage, the *Masque of Cupids* written to celebrate it, of which no text survives. But by using the Somerset affair as their key to interpretation, Bromham and Bruzzi went far beyond seeing such hints at abuse of power and privilege. They constructed a huge allegorical edifice, in which almost every detail of the play text is pressed into service. Middleton becomes a Puritan propagandist like Thomas Scott, obsessed by the fear of Roman Catholicism, which the Howard family were suspected of promoting, but also packing his play with the language of contemporary propaganda against Arminianism, the halfway house of conservative theology. Popular opposition to the so-called Spanish marriage—James's plan to marry Prince Charles to the Spanish Infanta and so promote his dream of a Europe reunited by dynastic ties—also becomes part of this frame, as does the crisis in the Palatinate, where James's own daughter Elizabeth and her husband Frederick, the Elector Palatine of Bohemia, had been driven out by Spanish forces. The nature and fate of *A Game at Chess* proves that Middleton was concerned with these issues. In what follows I want to distinguish between that reasonable hypothesis and the manner in which Bromham and Bruzzi stretch it beyond plausibility; not least because they cite my own theories of how literature responds to censorship as encouragement for their methods.

That recent European history *was* supposed to be part of the interpretive context is signalled in the opening scene, where Alsemero and Vermandero identify themselves as Spaniards and hence as enemies of the Protestant Dutch. Vermandero refers to the death of Alsemero's father at the Battle of Gibraltar in 1607, in which 'those rebellious Hollanders' defeated the Spanish fleet, and Alsemero responds, 'Whose death I had revenged... had not the late league | Prevented me' (1.1.186–9). This locates the action as occurring shortly after the Treaty of the Hague in 1609, which provided for a twelve-year truce between Spain and the United Provinces. By the time *The Changeling* was staged, the truce had lapsed (in 1621), and those same 'rebellious Hollanders' had provided a haven for the King and Queen of Bohemia.

This opening gambit presented *The Changeling* to audiences of 1622 as a contemporary play about 'Spanish' values in the context of international relations; but 'Spain' is also in some sense England. In explaining to Beatrice-Joanna that he is not rash in declaring his love for her instantaneously, Alsemero compares his eyes to the House of Commons, his judgement to the Lords, their agreement to the legislative consent of both Houses, *her* agreement to the royal concurrence (1.1.78–82). This witticism, a combination of Rowley's punsterism with Middleton's mordant irony, would remind an alert audience not of the smooth functioning of a limited monarchy, but of the currently deadlocked relation between James I and his Parliament. In 1621 the Commons had petitioned the King to abandon his pro-Spanish policy and the Spanish marriage negotiations, and to engage instead in a war *against* Spain, which would also constitute positive intervention in the fate of the Palatinate. In response, the King, who had already prohibited discussion of these matters in the press or the pulpit, cut short official debate by dissolving his Parliament.

From 1620 to 1624, when Parliament reconvened, there were therefore unusually strong motives for the theatre to take up the foreign policy debate. Both Jerzy Limon and Thomas Cogswell have shown how censorship and resistance to it, in the form of libels, sermons and unlicensed pamphlets, were intensified in these years. In *A Game at Chess* Middleton asks a telling question:

> Whose policy was't to put a silenced muzzle
> On all the barking tongue-men of the time?
> Made pictures, that were dumb enough before,
> Poor suff'rers in that politic restraint? (3.1.102–105)

And one of the strongest points made by Bromham and Bruzzi is that John Reynolds, the author whose story Middleton borrowed for *The Changeling*, was himself an anti-Spanish propagandist who suffered from this 'politic restraint', being unable to publish his *Vox Coeli* until 1624, and then finding himself in prison in consequence. Was *The Triumph of God's Revenge*, entered in the Stationers' Register on 7 June 1621, an alternative way of 'picturing' support for the Puritan/Protestant faction in England? The tone of this collection, its focus on murderers, and its prefatory reference to writers 'cautious to disguise and maske their Acts, under the vayles of other names' (sig. B2^{v}) would seem to answer yes. But there is nothing in Reynolds's version of Middleton's tragic plot that matches the political entry codes I have just observed in *The Changeling*.

Other evidence from theatre history supports the hypothesis of a European-political subtext. *The Changeling* was licensed for performance on 7 May 1622 by Sir John Astley. The theatre was the Phoenix, the company the Lady Elizabeth's, otherwise known as the Queen of Bohemia's, which had just been reconstituted for London business in 1621 or 1622. After the disruptive plague of 1625 some of its members would merge with the remnant of the Palsgrave's (the Elector Palatine's ancestor) in the King and Queen of Bohemia's Company. The company, then, implied an allegiance. *The Changeling* was the first of the plays licensed to the new company; and on 4 January 1624, Sir Henry Herbert recorded its court performance 'by the Queene of Bohemias company,... the prince only being there'. This special performance before

Prince Charles, just back (in October) from his abortive courtship of the Spanish Infanta, was probably a sign that Charles and Buckingham had already switched their policy from Hispanophilia to its opposite. Ironically, then, Charles himself became one of the many 'changelings' whose inconstancy the play either feared or encouraged.

But the most that can be argued from this collage of internal signposts and stage historical detail is that *The Changeling* permitted its original audiences to intuit a connection between Spanish/Catholic interests, crimes of violence, and sexuality out of control. Even at the level of allusion to the Somerset scandal, if one extends the analogy and imagines Somerset as De Flores, or James I himself as Vermandero, discomfort sets in. While early modern audiences expected only a loose fit between fiction and recent history (and I have elsewhere argued that Jacobean drama often employed inexact analogy for the purposes of deniability), Bromham and Bruzzi strain credibility when they turn *The Changeling* into a hostile political allegory of Jacobean foreign and domestic policy.

And in so far as we must assess the claims of different interpretive approaches, it is important to recognize that in *The Changeling*, as is not the case in *A Game at Chess*, an anti-Catholic agenda runs athwart an audience's tendency to identify emotionally with the most doomed and interesting characters. Such an agenda is logically incompatible with Marxist or feminist claims that the play supports its rebels against convention, even if only temporarily and before recontainment; but it is *almost* compatible with the old-fashioned moralism by which Beatrice is condemned, in Bawcutt's terminology, as 'selfish, proud, self-righteous to the point of complacency, and in the later scenes hard and unscrupulous' (lv).

This interpretive impasse can be, if not resolved, rendered less trivial if we imagine that Middleton and Rowley deliberately created it. What makes *The Changeling* work, both on the page and on the stage, is something less schematic and more accessible to a mixed audience than political allegory (though it can certainly have political dimensions). That something is ethical undecidability, an experience much attested to in the seventeenth century, and almost endemic today. The reciprocal exchange of meaning between the two plots, with its broad suggestion that the madhouse is coextensive with the nation, is only part of the story. Another is simply the quality of the writing, the 'frightful pleasure' of the perfect blank verse line in appalling circumstances:

> I have within mine eye all my desires (2.2.8)
> Methinks I feel her in mine arms already (2.2.149)
> I could not get the ring without the finger (3.4.29)
> This fellow has undone me endlessly (4.1.1)

More subliminal still is the unusual system of linguistic bonding that Middleton and Rowley devised for this play, the structure of keywords that stand for, and lock together, those major issues (then and now) that otherwise might tend to separate out and dominate a reading or production. Christopher Ricks wrote a brilliant essay on 'moral and poetic' structure as deducible from the play's vocabulary; but his method can be extended to question, once again, the explanatory power of an exclusively moral thematics. Obviously 'change' (with nineteen occurrences) is a keyword in *The Changeling*, and 'choice', 'judgement' and 'will' (emphases noted, tellingly, by both Bawcutt and Bromham/Bruzzi) belong to the realm of ethical decision-making or its failure. But 'service', with seventeen occurrences, also demands attention. It belongs ambiguously to the territories of formalized Petrarchan courtship, copulation, and class hierarchy. 'Danger' and 'secrets' and their cognates are unsurprising in a Jacobean melodrama, but 'blood', with its double reference to aristocratic birth and butchery, is here used with absolute clarity to signify analytical confusion. 'Push, you forget yourself!' says De Flores to Beatrice-Joanna when she reacts with horror to his proposition, 'A woman dipped in blood, and talk of modesty?' (3.4.128–9). Bleeding from the fatal stab De Flores has given her, she cries to her father at the end, 'I am that of your blood was taken from you | For your better health' (5.3.150–1), alluding to the end of the dynasty as well as to the medical practice of blood-letting.

Ricks noted these significances in 'blood' and 'service', but not that 'poison' appears no less than thirteen times, a strange verbal obsession in a play in which (unlike *Women, Beware Women*) no literal poison is used. The word runs secretly through the veins of this text until we can feel it burning; and though to some in 1622 it might have suggested poor Sir Thomas Overbury poisoned in the Tower, Alsemero glosses it as phobia. Thus in a world of flawed personalities, wine, oil and the scent of roses may all be poisonous to someone, and Beatrice does well to ask, 'And what may be *your* poison, Sir?' (1.1.127). As for 'pleasure', poison's opposite, we have already seen it rendered sublime and oxymoronic in Alibius's 'frightful pleasure'; but a careful reader can discover that elsewhere in the play it is *always* sexual, and especially a sign of De Flores's priorities. 'The wealth of all Valencia shall not buy,' he says, forcing Beatrice-Joanna to recognize the colour of the coin in which she must pay for murder, 'My pleasure from me' (3.4.163–4). 'Yes,' he cries defiantly in the last scene, 'and her honour's prize | Was my reward. I thank life for nothing | But that pleasure' (5.3.167–9). So much for the primacy of the economic.

In the live theatre, of course, we cannot count words to discover subliminal thematics, and such balancing acts as I have just performed between *The Changeling*'s preoccupations are usually impossible for a director. But in one respect the performance history of *The Changeling* actually intensifies the dilemma of the scholarly interpreter, at least when a historicizing criticism is at issue. For if we are correct in inferring from the text an 'oppositional' agenda in the earliest seventeenth-century productions, how long could it have lasted? What could the play have meant to a Restoration audience? In 1659 John Rhodes, a former actor who sensed another change of the political winds, assembled a new Duke of York's Company which included

The Changeling in its repertoire. We do not know to what qualities Samuel Pepys referred when he recorded seeing it at the Whitefriars on 23 February 1661, with Thomas Betterton playing De Flores, and reported that 'it takes exceedingly'. Joost Daalder records a court performance on 30 November 1668; but this could scarcely have carried the same message as the one before Charles II's father forty-six years earlier.

The 1668 performance was the last recorded before the revivals of the twentieth century, where the universities were considerably ahead of the professional theatre. The first modern production recorded by Marilyn Roberts was a Yale University student performance in May 1924, when most of the hospital plot was cut. But this strategy seems to have been more typical of university, radio or television productions than for the professional theatre. For instance, the first professional stage performance, in 1961, was directed by Tony Richardson for the English Stage Company at the Royal Court. Richardson set the play in the period of Goya's Spain, and spent considerable effort in making the hospital plot integral. In 1970, Peter Stein's production at the Schauspielhaus in Zurich made it symbolic of a bleak modernity illuminated by blue neon, and illustrating, so Dieter Sturm wrote for the programme, our vacillation between 'Herrschaft and Sexualität,... sozialer Ordnung und psychischer Unterdrückung'. Although one reviewer of the 1977 production by the Wiesbaden Theatre reminded his readers of English Hispanophobia in the 1620s, stage revivals unsurprisingly tend to favour the broader categories of psycho-social analysis over historical reconstruction. In Peter Gill's 1978 production at the Riverside Studios, Hammersmith, the audience seating was raised on scaffolding, creating an underground world in which the lunatics were allowed to roam like wild animals; while Terry Hands's production of the same year focused primarily on the sexuality of Beatrice-Joanna, emphasized the multiple sexual puns in the text, and created a stylized moral colour scheme of red and black, which is not so different, finally, from the black and white of an earlier ethical tradition.

But in Richard Eyre's notorious production for the Lyttleton Theatre in June 1988, the distinction between stage and study seems to have been deliberately, if confusingly, abrogated. The impact of new academic styles of criticism—Marxist, feminist and ethnic (and their competition)—was rendered explicit. The programme featured a portrait of Miranda Richardson as Beatrice-Joanna, with primitive symmetrical gashes on both cheeks, an effect repeated for De Flores. The Eyre programme also became a work of cross-cultural (and often self-contradictory) theory, featuring mini-essays on class and race, enforced dynastic marriage, the early modern madhouse, and the rise of capitalism. Eyre himself was quoted as saying: 'I have tried to make this [Jacobean] interdependence of rank and money visibly apparent, by transposing the play to a Spanish slave colony of the nineteenth century'. By way of Ronald Harwood's *All the World's a Stage*, readers were invited to locate the play specifically in early seventeenth-century England, and to imagine *it* imagining 'the internecine rage of the Civil War to come'. But this prophetic turn was itself compared to the nightmares of psychiatric patients in the 1920s and 1930s which Jung diagnosed as previews of Fascist horrors. We come full circle, then, to the world of *The Night Porter*.

Despite its confusions, one sentence in this medley will serve us well. 'Sometimes a nation', wrote Harwood, 'will choose the theatre to do its collective dreaming.' Provided we see them as sharing with us the diagnosis as well as the symptoms, it would be hard to write a better sentence in which to condense Middleton and Rowley's achievement, and to explain why *The Changeling* seems so disturbingly familiar today.

SEE ALSO

Textual introduction and apparatus: *Companion*, 1094
Authorship and date: *Companion*, 422
Other Middleton–Rowley works: *Weapons*, 980; *Quarrel*, 1209; *Old Law*, 1331; *Tennis*, 1405; *Gypsy*, 1723

WILLIAM ROWLEY and THOMAS MIDDLETON

The Changeling

[*for Lady Elizabeth's Men at The Phoenix*]

THE PERSONS OF THE PLAY

BEATRICE-Joanna, *Daughter to Vermandero*
DE FLORES, *Servant to Vermandero*
ALSEMERO, *A Nobleman, afterwards married to Beatrice*
JASPERINO, *His friend*
DIAPHANTA, *Beatrice's Waiting-woman*
VERMANDERO, *A Noble captain, father to Beatrice*
TOMAZO de Piracquo, *A Noble lord*
ALONZO de Piracquo, *His brother, suitor to Beatrice*
ISABELLA, *Wife to Alibius*
ALIBIUS, *A jealous doctor*
LOLLIO, *His man*
ANTONIO, *A Gallant, and counterfeit fool*
FRANCISCUS, *A Gallant, and counterfeit madman*
PEDRO, *Friend to Antonio*
MADMEN
SERVANTS
Gentlemen
Gentlewomen
Gallants

1.1 *Incipit Actus Primus*
Enter Alsemero

ALSEMERO
'Twas in the temple where I first beheld her,
And now again the same; what omen yet
Follows of that? None but imaginary.
Why should my hopes of fate be timorous?
The place is holy, so is my intent:
I love her beauties to the holy purpose,
And that, methinks, admits comparison
With man's first creation, the place blest,
And is his right home back, if he achieve it.
The church hath first begun our interview
And that's the place must join us into one;
So there's beginning and perfection too.

Enter Jasperino

JASPERINO
O sir, are you here? Come, the wind's fair with you,
You're like to have a swift and pleasant passage.

ALSEMERO
Sure you're deceivèd, friend; 'tis contrary
In my best judgement.

JASPERINO
What, for Malta?
If you could buy a gale amongst the witches,
They could not serve you such a lucky pennyworth
As comes o' God's name.

Title Although Antonio is identified as 'the' changeling in the *dramatis personae* of the 1653 quarto, this may well have been a later interpolation. The word 'changeling' had numerous meanings, many of them applicable here: (*a*) a retarded (here 'foolish') or ugly child left in place of another child by fairies; (*b*) a fickle, inconstant person (compare Tilley C234), often with implications of sexual infidelity; (*c*) any person substituted for another. During the late 1610s and early 1620s 'changeling' began to be applied with increasing frequency to those who had changed and otherwise altered gender roles. Patrick Hannay's 1618/19 *Happy Husband*, for example, complains of a man 'so womaniz'd turn'd Dame, | As place 'mongst *Ovids* changlings he might claime'; and in *The Spanish Gypsy* (1623), Pretiosa vows to 'play the changeling', altering her shape, posture, and voice a thousand ways as she cross dresses (as a man) (2.1.106 ff).

1.1.6 **the holy purpose** marriage

8–12 **the place ... perfection too** Alsemero persuades himself that his love of Beatrice-Joanna is as holy as the place where it began ('the temple'); that it is directed ('my intent') toward marriage ('the holy purpose'), a state comparable to that of Adam and Eve before the Fall ('man's first creation', where the Garden of Eden—'the place blessed'—is man's 'right home back'); and, because they will be married there, the church is the fitting place first to have seen each other.

10 **interview** literally: mutual view, sight of each other

14 **like** likely

15 **contrary** against him (a wind which blows away from Alicante (and Beatrice) is 'contrary' to his wishes)

17 **buy ... witches** In Renaissance folklore, witches were believed to have power over the weather, especially that which could affect ships at sea.

18 **lucky pennyworth** bargain

19 **o' God's name** without charge—the grace of God not for sale.

ALSEMERO Even now I observed
The temple's vane to turn full in my face,
I know 'tis against me.

JASPERINO Against you?
Then you know not where you are.

ALSEMERO Not well indeed.

JASPERINO
Are you not well, sir?

ALSEMERO Yes, Jasperino;
Unless there be some hidden malady
Within me, that I understand not.

JASPERINO And that
I begin to doubt, sir: I never knew
Your inclinations to travels at a pause
With any cause to hinder it till now.
Ashore you were wont to call your servants up,
And help to trap your horses for the speed;
At sea I have seen you weigh the anchor with 'em,
Hoist sails for fear to lose the foremost breath,
Be in continual prayers for fair winds,
And have you changed your orisons?

ALSEMERO No, friend;
I keep the same church, same devotion.

JASPERINO
Lover I'm sure you're none; the stoic
Was found in you long ago—your mother
Nor best friends, who have set snares of beauty
(Ay, and choice ones too), could never trap you that way.
What might be the cause?

ALSEMERO Lord, how violent
Thou art! I was but meditating of
Somewhat I heard within the temple.

JASPERINO Is this violence?
'Tis but idleness compared with your haste yesterday.

ALSEMERO
I'm all this while a-going, man.

Enter Servants

JASPERINO Backwards,
I think, sir.—Look, your servants.

FIRST SERVANT The seamen call; shall we board your trunks?

ALSEMERO
No, not today.

JASPERINO 'Tis the critical day,
It seems, and the sign in Aquarius.

SECOND SERVANT [*aside*] We must not to sea today? This smoke will bring forth fire.

ALSEMERO
Keep all on shore; I do not know the end,
Which needs I must do, of an affair in hand
Ere I can go to sea.

FIRST SERVANT Well, your pleasure.

SECOND SERVANT [*aside*] Let him e'en take his leisure, too; we are safer on land. *Exeunt Servants*

Enter Beatrice-Joanna, Diaphanta, and Servants.
[*Alsemero greets Beatrice and kisses her*]

JASPERINO [*aside*] How now! The laws of the Medes are changed, sure. Salute a woman? He kisses too: wonderful! Where learnt he this? And does it perfectly too; in my conscience he ne'er rehearsed it before. Nay, go on; this will be stranger and better news at Valencia than if he had ransomed half Greece from the Turk.

BEATRICE
You are a scholar, sir.

ALSEMERO A weak one, lady.

BEATRICE
Which of the sciences is this love you speak of?

ALSEMERO
From your tongue I take it to be music.

BEATRICE
You are skilful in't, can sing at first sight.

ALSEMERO
And I have showed you all my skill at once.
I want more words to express me further,
And must be forced to repetition:
I love you dearly.

BEATRICE Be better advised, sir:
Our eyes are sentinels unto our judgements,
And should give certain judgement what they see;
But they are rash sometimes, and tell us wonders
Of common things, which when our judgements find,
They can then check the eyes, and call them blind.

ALSEMERO
But I am further, lady; yesterday

30 **trap** harness, put trappings on
for the speed to speed up the process
31 **'em** the servants
34 **orisons** prayers
36 **the stoic** The stoic philosophers were believed to have shunned emotion and sentiment in favour of rational, dispassionate existence.
42 **Somewhat** something
48 **critical** (astrologically) crucial
49 **Aquarius** in the zodiac, the water sign—propitious for sailing
50–1 **This smoke...fire** proverbial: 'No smoke without some fire' (Tilley, Dent S569). The Second Servant hints at some hidden meaning behind the order not to board ship.
57.1 ***Beatrice-Joanna*** Etymologically, 'Beatrice' means 'one who blesses/makes happy', and 'Joanna' means 'the Lord's grace'. But a strong pejorative sense also obtained in each case: Beatrice was a common nickname for a brazen woman, and Joanna for a common one.
Diaphanta (from the Greek), 'transparent', 'light-revealing', 'glowing (red-hot)'.
58 **laws of the Medes** proverbially constant; compare Daniel 6:8: 'the law of the Medes & Persians, which altereth not'.
59 **Salute** greet, address
61 **in my conscience** truly, to my knowledge
62 **Valencia** capital of the province of Valencia, on the east coast of Spain.
63 **than if...Turk** (Greece was at this time controlled by Turkey)
67 **sing at first sight** sight-read (both love and music)—i.e. You waste no time. With understated bawdy.
69 **want** lack
75 **Of** concerning
76 **check** rebuke, censure
77 **I...further** I'm past that stage

Was mine eyes' employment, and hither now
They brought my judgement, where are both agreed.
Both Houses then consenting, 'tis agreed,
Only there wants the confirmation
By the hand royal—that's your part, lady.

BEATRICE O, there's one above me, sir.
[*Aside*] For five days past to be recalled!
Sure mine eyes were mistaken: this was the man was
meant me.
That he should come so near his time, and miss it!

JASPERINO [*aside*] We might have come by the carriers from Valencia, I see, and saved all our sea-provision; we are at farthest, sure. Methinks I should do something too; I meant to be a venturer in this voyage. Yonder's another vessel; I'll board her: if she be lawful prize, down goes her topsail.

[*He crosses to and greets Diaphanta*]
Enter De Flores

DE FLORES
Lady, your father—

BEATRICE
Is in health, I hope.

DE FLORES
Your eye shall instantly instruct you, lady:
He's coming hitherward.

BEATRICE
What needed, then,
Your duteous preface? I had rather
He had come unexpected; you must stall
A good presence with unnecessary blabbing:
And how welcome for your part you are,
I'm sure you know.

DE FLORES [*aside*] Will't never mend, this scorn,
One side nor other? Must I be enjoined
To follow still whilst she flies from me? Well,
Fates do your worst, I'll please myself with sight
Of her at all opportunities,
If but to spite her anger. I know she had
Rather see me dead than living, and yet
She knows no cause for't but a peevish will.

ALSEMERO
You seemed displeased, lady, on the sudden.

BEATRICE
Your pardon, sir, 'tis my infirmity,
Nor can I other reason render you,
Than his or hers, of some particular thing
They must abandon as a deadly poison,
Which to a thousand other tastes were wholesome;
Such to mine eyes is that same fellow there,
The same that report speaks of the basilisk.

ALSEMERO
This is a frequent frailty in our nature;
There's scarce a man amongst a thousand found
But hath his imperfection: one distastes
The scent of roses, which to infinites
Most pleasing is, and odoriferous;
One oil, the enemy of poison;
Another wine, the cheerer of the heart,
And lively refresher of the countenance.
Indeed this fault, if so it be, is general:
There's scarce a thing but is both loved and loathed.
Myself, I must confess, have the same frailty.

BEATRICE
And what may be your poison, sir? I am bold with
you.

ALSEMERO
What might be your desire, perhaps—a cherry.

BEATRICE
I am no enemy to any creature
My memory has but yon gentleman.

80–2 **Both Houses ... hand royal** political metaphor drawing on the two 'Houses' of parliament ('eyes', 'judgement'), which could propose a measure to which the monarch ('hand royal') might assent; Alsemero implies he wants her hand in marriage.
83 **one above me** i.e. her father
84 **five days past** apparently the length of time since her betrothal, upon which she now wishes to recant
87 **by the carriers** i.e. by land (thus slowly) instead of by sea
89 **at farthest** at the end (i.e. of one's journey, abilities, or wits). Perhaps here: 'we are surely out of our minds'.
90 **a venturer** a partner in the commercial 'venture' of the voyage (here metaphorical: 'venture' = love, wooing)
91 **vessel** ship (= Diaphanta), continuing the nautical metaphor.
board come alongside (i.e. accost)
lawful prize Sea adventurers were supposed to obey certain laws in taking plunder; the metaphor is one of 'boarding' Diaphanta, which may depend on her marital status.
92 **topsail** A lowered sail signalled surrender; here of the woman to her accoster.
92.2 ***De Flores*** both 'of the flowers' and 'the deflowerer'
95 **What needed, then** what need was there, then, for
97 **unexpected** i.e. unannounced
stall (*a*) 'to bring to a standstill, render unable to proceed' (*OED v.* III. 11a) (*b*) 'to take away (a person's) appetite' (*OED v.* III. 12a) (*c*) = *in*stall, with play on political sense of 'presence' (l. 98), 'to place in a high office or dignity' (*OED v.* II. 7a)
98 **A good presence** more desirable company (i.e. of Vermandero)
blabbing babbling
101 **One side nor other** one way or another (see 'side' *OED sb.*[1] III.2)
enjoined ordered (by the 'fates' of l. 103)
102 **still** always
110–11 **reason ... Than his or hers, of** than any other person's (i.e. idiosyncratic) reasons concerning
111–13 **some ... wholesome** compare the proverb: 'One man's meat is another man's poison' (Tilley M483)
112 **abandon** reject
113 **were** would be
114 **that same fellow** i.e. De Flores; here 'fellow' = a man of low worth
115 **report** legend, myth
basilisk a mythological serpent which could kill by its look
118 **distastes** dislikes
119 **infinites** an infinite number of people
121 **One** i.e. one man
122 **cheerer of the heart** proverbial
123 **countenance** demeanour toward others as expressing good or ill will (*OED sb.* 7)
127–8 **poison ... a cherry** probably a kiss of her cherry-like lips, hence instrument of her 'desire'—where 'poison' = her influence in love, greatly exaggerated for effect. But perhaps with bawdy as well.
130 **yon gentleman** i.e. De Flores

ALSEMERO
He does ill to tempt your sight, if he knew it.

BEATRICE
He cannot be ignorant of that, sir:
I have not spared to tell him so; and I want
To help myself, since he's a gentleman
In good respect with my father, and follows him.

ALSEMERO He's out of his place then now. [*They talk apart*]

JASPERINO [*to Diaphanta*] I am a mad wag, wench.

DIAPHANTA So methinks; but for your comfort I can tell you, we have a doctor in the city that undertakes the cure of such.

JASPERINO Tush, I know what physic is best for the state of mine own body.

DIAPHANTA 'Tis scarce a well-governed state, I believe.

JASPERINO I could show thee such a thing with an ingredient that we two would compound together, and if it did not tame the maddest blood i'th' town for two hours after, I'll ne'er profess physic again.

DIAPHANTA A little poppy, sir, were good to cause you sleep.

JASPERINO Poppy? I'll give thee a pop i'th' lips for that first, and begin there. [*He kisses her*] Poppy is one simple indeed, and cuckoo what-you-call't another. I'll discover no more now; another time I'll show thee all.
They talk apart

Enter Vermandero and Servants

BEATRICE My father, sir.

VERMANDERO O Joanna, I came to meet thee.
Your devotion's ended?

BEATRICE For this time, sir.
[*Aside*] I shall change my saint, I fear me; I find
A giddy turning in me.—Sir, this while
I am beholden to this gentleman,
Who left his own way to keep me company,
And in discourse I find him much desirous
To see your castle: he hath deserved it, sir,
If ye please to grant it.

VERMANDERO With all my heart, sir.
Yet there's an article between: I must know
Your country; we use not to give survèy
Of our chief strengths to strangers. Our citadels
Are placed conspicuous to outward view
On promonts' tops; but within are secrets.

ALSEMERO
A Vàlencìan, sir.

VERMANDERO A Vàlencìan?
That's native, sir; of what name, I beseech you?

ALSEMERO
Alsemero, sir.

VERMANDERO Alsemero? Not the son
Of John de Alsemero?

ALSEMERO The same, sir.

VERMANDERO
My best love bids you welcome.

BEATRICE [*aside*] He was wont
To call me so, and then he speaks a most
Unfeignèd truth.

VERMANDERO O sir, I knew your father:
We two were in acquaintance long ago,
Before our chins were worth Iülan down,
And so continued till the stamp of time
Had coined us into silver. Well, he's gone;
A good soldier went with him.

ALSEMERO You went together in that, sir.

VERMANDERO No, by Saint Jaques, I came behind him.
Yet I have done somewhat too. An unhappy day
Swallowèd him at last at Gibraltar,
In fight with those rebellious Hollanders.
Was it not so?

ALSEMERO Whose death I had revenged,
Or followed him in fate, had not the late league
Prevented me.

VERMANDERO Ay, ay, 'twas time to breathe.

131 **tempt** test
133–4 **want | To help myself** lack means to correct this (by banishing him)
135 **respect** repute
follows serves
136 **He's ... now** therefore he's in the wrong place (Vermandero being absent)
139 **doctor** i.e. Alibius (presented in the following scene)
141 **Tush** a Rowleyan interjection
physic medicine
state Diaphanta plays on the metaphor of state as 'body politic'.
144–5 **I could ... together** Under cover of medicinal discourse, Jasperino hints plainly at his need for sexual gratification.
144 **such a thing** i.e. his penis
144–5 **ingredient** with bawdy play on the etymological sense of ingredient as 'a thing which enters in or penetrates' (*OED sb.* 2)
145 **compound** (*a*) mix (*b*) copulate. Jasperino plays on the sexual symbolism of the mortar and pestle
146 **blood** the seat of passion and desire
148 **poppy** a sleep-inducing, opiate plant
152 **simple** medicine or herb
cuckoo what-you-call't probably the plant called the 'cuckoo-pintle' (wild arum) used medicinally. 'Pintle' was slang or dialectal for 'penis'—thus Jasperino's leading 'what-you-call't'.
153 **discover** reveal
158 **saint** here (and later) a pun on saint as (*a*) religious figure and (*b*) lover; compare 5.3.53
165 **article** this metaphor turns on the notion of a legal contract which has a prior condition to be met.
166 **use not** are not accustomed
survèy observation
169 **promonts'** promontories'
174–6 **He was ... truth** i.e. because I am my father's 'best love' (174), he truthfully says that his best love bids Alsemero welcome
178 **Iülan down** referring to the *Aeneid*'s youthful Iulus Ascanius, whose name may have come from the Greek word for 'first growth of the beard' (= 'down')
180 **coined us into silver** made our hair silvery grey
181 **A good ... him** i.e. when he died, a good soldier died.
182 **went ... that** were as fine a soldier as he
183 **Saint Jaques** St James the Greater, patron saint of Spain
185–6 **Gibraltar ... Hollanders** referring to the 1607 siege of the fortress called Gibraltar on the south coast of Spain
187 **had** would have
188 **the late league** The treaty of the Hague in 1609 brought peace between Spain and the Netherlands for twelve years.
189 **breathe** i.e. take a respite from fighting

O Joanna, I should ha' told thee news:
I saw Piracquo lately.

BEATRICE [*aside*] That's ill news.

VERMANDERO
He's hot preparing for this day of triumph;
Thou must be a bride within this sevennight.

ALSEMERO [*aside*] Ha!

BEATRICE
Nay, good sir, be not so violent. With speed
I cannot render satisfactïon
Unto the dear companion of my soul,
Virginity, whom I thus long have lived with,
And part with it so rude and suddenly;
Can such friends divide, never to meet again,
Without a solemn farewell?

VERMANDERO Tush, tush, there's a toy.

ALSEMERO [*aside*]
I must now part, and never meet again
With any joy on earth.—Sir, your pardon,
My affairs call on me.

VERMANDERO How, sir? By no means.
Not changed so soon, I hope? You must see my castle
And her best entertainment ere we part;
I shall think myself unkindly used else.
Come, come, let's on: I had good hope your stay
Had been a while with us in Alicante;
I might have bid you to my daughter's wedding.

ALSEMERO [*aside*]
He means to feast me, and poisons me beforehand.—
I should be dearly glad to be there, sir,
Did my occasions suit as I could wish.

BEATRICE
I shall be sorry if you be not there
When it is done, sir—but not so suddenly.

VERMANDERO
I tell you, sir, the gentleman's complete:
A courtier and a gallant, enriched
With many fair and noble ornaments;
I would not change him for a son-in-law
For any he in Spain—the proudest he,
And we have great ones, that you know.

ALSEMERO He's much
Bound to you, sir.

VERMANDERO He shall be bound to me,
As fast as this tie can hold him; I'll want
My will else.

BEATRICE [*aside*]
I shall want mine if you do it.

VERMANDERO
But come; by the way I'll tell you more of him.

ALSEMERO [*aside*]
How shall I dare to venture in his castle
When he discharges murderers at the gate?
But I must on, for back I cannot go.

BEATRICE [*aside, seeing De Flores*]
Not this serpent gone yet? [*She drops glove*]

VERMANDERO Look, girl: thy glove's fall'n;
Stay, stay.—De Flores, help a little.

[*Exeunt Vermandero, Alsemero, Jasperino and Servants*]

DE FLORES [*retrieving glove*] Here, lady.

BEATRICE
Mischief on your officious forwardness!
Who bade you stoop? They touch my hand no more:
[*She throws down the other glove*]
There, for t'other's sake I part with this.
Take 'em and draw thine own skin off with 'em.

Exeunt [*all but De Flores*]

DE FLORES Here's a favour come with a mischief!
Now I know she had rather wear my pelt tanned
In a pair of dancing pumps than I should thrust
My fingers into her sockets here.
[*He thrusts his hand into the glove*]
I know
She hates me, yet cannot choose but love her.

191 **I saw...ill news** invoking the proverb 'Ill news comes too soon' (Tilley N14)
192 **hot** excitedly
193 **sevennight** week (probably pronounced 'sénnight')
201 **toy** trifle
209 **Alicante** a seaport of Valencia on the eastern coast of Spain, where the play's action is laid
210 **I might have** I would, then, have been able to
211 **poisons** here figuratively, but with (unconsciously) ominous overtones
215 **When it...so suddenly** Beatrice has a double meaning; for Alsemero she hints that she hopes the wedding is postponed long enough so that he is the groom. Holdsworth suggests 'When it is done' carries a sexual connotation.
216 **complete** perfect, accomplished. 'Complete gentleman' was a popular phrase: compare Henry Peacham's 1622 *The Complete Gentleman.*
218 **ornaments** qualities
220 **he** i.e. man
221 **that you know** you know that to be true
221–2 **He's...sir** i.e. He would thank you, if he were here, for that handsome compliment. But Vermandero answers with wordplay on 'bound' in the sense of 'attached through matrimony'.
223 **this tie** i.e. Beatrice
223–4 **I'll...else** Otherwise ('else') my wishes will be unfulfilled.
224 **want** Beatrice may play on 'want' in the double sense of 'lack' and 'desire'.
227 **murderers** literally, small canon mounted at the entries to fortifications; here used figuratively
233 **t'other's** the other's
234 **Take...'em** i.e. If you put my gloves on your hands, may they stick to your skin and thus strip you raw. (Perhaps following from 'serpent' (229), which would shed its skin.)
235 **favour** generally, any good thing; more specifically: a love token, often worn on the body of the beloved. Here the glove, perhaps dropped for Alsemero—De Flores's presence has prevented them from talking.
with a mischief with a vengeance
238 **sockets** the finger sockets of the glove, but with connotation of her sexual body.

No matter: if but to vex her, I'll haunt her still;
Though I get nothing else, I'll have my will. *Exit*

1.2 *Enter Alibius and Lollio*

ALIBIUS
Lollio, I must trust thee with a secret,
But thou must keep it.

LOLLIO I was ever close to a secret, sir.

ALIBIUS
The diligence that I have found in thee,
The care and industry already past,
Assures me of thy good continuance.
Lollio, I have a wife.

LOLLIO Fie, sir, 'tis too late to keep her secret: she's known to be married all the town and country over.

ALIBIUS
Thou goest too fast, my Lollio. That knowledge,
I allow, no man can be barred it;
But there is a knowledge which is nearer,
Deeper and sweeter, Lollio.

LOLLIO Well, sir, let us handle that between you and I.

ALIBIUS
'Tis that I go about, man; Lollio,
My wife is young.

LOLLIO So much the worse to be kept secret, sir.

ALIBIUS
Why, now thou meet'st the substance of the point;
I am old, Lollio.

LOLLIO No sir, 'tis I am old Lollio.

ALIBIUS
Yet why may not this concòrd and sympathise?
Old trees and young plants often grow together,
Well enough agreeing.

LOLLIO Ay, sir. [*He makes horns*] But the old trees raise themselves higher and broader than the young plants.

ALIBIUS Shrewd application! There's the fear, man;
I would wear my ring on my own finger:
Whilst it is borrowed it is none of mine,
But his that useth it.

LOLLIO You must keep it on still, then; if it but lie by, one or other will be thrusting into't.

ALIBIUS
Thou conceiv'st me, Lollio; here thy watchful eye
Must have employment: I cannot always be at home.

LOLLIO I dare swear you cannot.

ALIBIUS I must look out.

LOLLIO I know't: you must look out, 'tis every man's case.

ALIBIUS
Here, I do say, must thy employment be:
To watch her treadings, and in my absence
Supply my place.

LOLLIO I'll do my best, sir; yet surely I cannot see who you should have cause to be jealous of.

ALIBIUS Thy reason for that Lollio?
'Tis a comfortable question.

LOLLIO We have but two sorts of people in the house, and both under the whip: that's fools and madmen. The one has not wit enough to be knaves, and the other not knavery enough to be fools.

ALIBIUS
Ay, those are all my patients, Lollio.
I do profess the cure of either sort;
My trade, my living 'tis, I thrive by it.
But here's the care that mixes with my thrift:

241 **will** Throughout, this word has the connotations of volition, wilfulness, and sexual desire.

1.2.0.1 **Alibius** Latin: 'being in another place, elsewhere'. Probably a topical satire of Dr Hilkiah Crooke, appointed keeper of Bedlam in 1619. He was notoriously absent from his duties there, and was investigated as early as 1625; both he and his steward were put on trial in 1632 for fraud and misappropriation of funds. Like Lollio, his steward apparently took bribes and otherwise cheated his charges monetarily.
Lollio see previous note

3 **close to a secret** literally, good at keeping a secret; but with a hint (which Alibius misses) at the sexual sense of 'secret' as in 'secret parts' (compare l. 8 below)

6 **good continuance** continual trustworthiness

8 **to keep her secret** literally, 'to hide knowledge of her', but Lollio may pun bawdily. The punning on 'knowledge' as sexual knowledge continues in ll. 10–12.

12 **knowledge** i.e. 'carnal' or sexual knowledge, intercourse

13 **Deeper and sweeter** proverbial (Dent D188), with sexual suggestion here

14 **handle** with a sexual connotation

17 **the worse** i.e. more difficult

20 **I am old Lollio** With the choplogic banter of servants, Lollio deliberately misunderstands Alibius's address to him in l. 19.

21 **this** i.e. our (Isabella's and Alibius's) disparate ages. He has ignored or not heard Lollio's response.

26 **application** Alibius finds his metaphor well applied to the situation by Lollio; here Alibius's age makes it more likely that his wife will give him cuckold's horns, thus making him 'higher and broader' than her.

27–9 **I would wear . . . useth it** While rings were a token of the trothplight in marriage that legitimates sex, the 'finger in the ring' metaphor was a common way of configuring sexual intercourse itself.

30 **lie by** (*a*) lie aside somewhere (*b*) facilitate an untruth (here, adultery). This pun is prominent in Middleton's practice; compare 4.1.15, 5.1.1.

32 **conceiv'st** understand (but the word has a sexual resonance in the context of this discussion)

33 **employment . . . at home** words often used with sexual suggestion (and compare 'employment' in l. 37 below)

35 **look out** go out and about (Lollio, though, plays on the sense of 'look[ing] out' for cuckoldry—'every man's case')

36 **case** This word could signify the vagina.

38 **treadings** literally, footsteps—but with overtones of 'sexual motion'; the word 'tread' is often used of copulating birds

39 **Supply my place** replace me. Here as elsewhere Alibius unwittingly invites Lollio to understand a sexual sense.

43 **comfortable** comforting (in that an answer is likely to placate or flatter)

45 **fools and madmen** separate categories: fools were born 'foolish', madmen those who had lost their wits.

48 **are all** the extent so far as 'sorts' go

49 **profess** have as my occupation, profession
either sort both sorts

51 **my thrift** my living, earnings, prosperity—that which Alibius 'thrive[s] by' (50).

The daily visitants that come to see
My brainsick patients I would not have
To see my wife. Gallants I do observe
Of quick enticing eyes, rich in habits,
Of stature and proportion very comely:
These are most shrewd temptations, Lollio.

LOLLIO They may be easily answered, sir. If they come to see the fools and madmen, you and I may serve the turn, and let my mistress alone: she's of neither sort.

ALIBIUS
'Tis a good ward. Indeed, come they to see
Our madmen or our fools, let 'em see no more
Than what they come for. By that consequent
They must not see her; I'm sure she's no fool.

LOLLIO And I'm sure she's no madman.

ALIBIUS
Hold that buckler fast, Lollio; my trust
Is on thee, and I account it firm and strong.
What hour is't, Lollio?

LOLLIO Towards belly-hour, sir.

ALIBIUS Dinner-time? Thou mean'st twelve o'clock.

LOLLIO Yes, sir, for every part has his hour: we wake at six and look about us, that's eye-hour; at seven we should pray, that's knee-hour; at eight walk, that's leg-hour; at nine gather flowers and pluck a rose, that's nose-hour; at ten we drink, that's mouth-hour; at eleven lay about us for victuals, that's hand-hour; at twelve go to dinner, that's belly-hour.

ALIBIUS
Profoundly, Lollio. It will be long
Ere all thy scholars learn this lesson, and
I did look to have a new one entered.—Stay,
I think my expectation is come home.

Enter Pedro, and Antonio like an idiot

PEDRO
Save you, sir. My business speaks itself:
This sight takes off the labour of my tongue.

ALIBIUS Ay, ay, sir,
'Tis plain enough you mean him for my patient.

PEDRO
And if your pains prove but commodious,
To give but some little strength to the sick
And weak part of nature in him, these are
But patterns to show you of the whole pieces
That will follow to you, beside the charge
Of diet, washing, and other necessaries
Fully defrayed. [*He gives money*]

ALIBIUS
Believe it, sir, there shall no care be wanting.

LOLLIO Sir, an officer in this place may deserve something; the trouble will pass through my hands.

PEDRO
'Tis fit something should come to your hands then,
sir. [*He gives money*]

LOLLIO Yes, sir: 'tis I must keep him sweet, and read to him. What is his name?

PEDRO His name is Antonio. Marry,
We use but half to him: only Tony.

LOLLIO Tony? Tony? 'Tis enough, and a very good name for a fool. [*To Antonio*] What's your name, Tony?

ANTONIO Hee, hee, hee! Well, I thank you cousin; hee, hee, hee!

LOLLIO Good boy! Hold up your head!—[*To Pedro*] He can laugh; I perceive by that he is no beast.

PEDRO Well, sir,
If you can raise him but to any height,
Any degree of wit, might he attain
(As I might say) to creep but on all four
Towards the chair of wit, or walk on crutches,
'Twould add an honour to your worthy pains,
And a great family might pray for you,
To which he should be heir, had he discretion
To claim and guide his own; assure you, sir,
He is a gentleman.

52 **visitants** At Bethlehem ('Bedlam') hospital outside London (see 1.2.209–10, 3.3.24 and notes) people of leisure—including the 'gallants' that Alibius especially fears (l. 54)—often came to divert themselves by viewing the residents.

55 **habits** dress, apparel

57 **shrewd** (*a*) wicked (as it pertains to Isabella, morally; *OED a.* 1a) (*b*) mischievous, irksome (in so far as the possibility of Isabella succumbing to such temptation troubles Alibius; *OED a.* 6a). That he follows his references to business and prosperity (ll. 49–51) with a moralistic cliché like 'shrewd temptations' (see *OED a.* 6b) suggests his affinity with contemporary puritanism.

59–60 **serve the turn** answer to the occasion (with play on being 'turn-keys', or jailors); compare also the (unintended) implication that he and Lollio might stand in as fools and madmen

61 **ward** defensive guard or pose taken in fencing

63 **By that consequent** as a result of that

66 **buckler** shield (used here metaphorically)

74 **pluck a rose** with suggestion of a common meaning for this phrase, to urinate

75–6 **lay about** search around

80 **entered** enrolled

81.1 ***Enter . . . Antonio like an idiot*** perhaps illustrated in the frontispiece to Francis Kirkman's *The Wits, or Sport upon Sport* (1662), where a figure labelled 'Changling' wears a long coat and pointed dunce's cap, and has a hornbook hanging from his wrist. Antonio is perhaps in the tradition of 'wise fools' associated with St Anthony.

82 **Save you, sir** i.e. 'God save you', a form of salutation

83 **This sight** i.e. of Antonio

86 **commodious** useful, beneficial

89 **patterns** samples

90 **charge** expense. It was customary to pay the expenses of private inmates at Bedlam.

97 **sweet** clean

101–2 **good name for a fool** 'good' because 'tony' seems by this time to have meant both (*a*) a foolish person, ninny, or madman (*OED sb.*[1]), and (*b*) (as verb) to make a fool of, to fool, cheat, or swindle (*OED v.*). Rowley himself may have played a fool named 'Tony' in Fletcher's *Wife for a Month* in 1624.

103 Antonio answers as though Lollio had asked 'How are you?'

106 **no beast** Since Aristotle, it had been thought that the ability to laugh separated humanity from the beasts.

116 **gentleman** More specific than today, 'gentleman' implied a high social status, a man of good family, rank, or breeding, also a land owner.

LOLLIO Nay, there's nobody doubted that; at first sight I knew him for a gentleman: he looks no other yet.

PEDRO
Let him have good attendance and sweet lodging.

LOLLIO As good as my mistress lies in, sir; and as you allow us time and means, we can raise him to the higher degree of discretion.

PEDRO
Nay, there shall no cost want, sir.

LOLLIO He will hardly be stretched up to the wit of a magnifico.

PEDRO O, no, that's not to be expected;
Far shorter will be enough.

LOLLIO I'll warrant you I'll make him fit to bear office in five weeks; I'll undertake to wind him up to the wit of constable.

PEDRO
If it be lower than that it might serve turn.

LOLLIO No, fie! To level him with a headborough, beadle, or watchman were but little better than he is: constable I'll able him. If he do come to be a justice afterwards, let him thank the keeper. Or I'll go further with you: say I do bring him up to my own pitch, say I make him as wise as myself?

PEDRO
Why, there I would have it.

LOLLIO Well, go to: either I'll be as arrant a fool as he, or he shall be as wise as I, and then I think 'twill serve his turn.

PEDRO Nay, I do like thy wit passing well.

LOLLIO Yes, you may. Yet if I had not been a fool, I had had more wit than I have too: remember what state you find me in.

PEDRO I will, and so leave you:
[*To Alibius*] Your best cares, I beseech you.

ALIBIUS
Take you none with you; leave 'em all with us.

Exit Pedro

ANTONIO O, my cousin's gone! Cousin, cousin, O!

LOLLIO Peace, peace, Tony! You must not cry, child; you must be whipped if you do. Your cousin is here still: I am your cousin, Tony.

ANTONIO Hee, hee, then I'll not cry, if thou beest my cousin, hee, hee, hee!

LOLLIO I were best try his wit a little, that I may know what form to place him in.

ALIBIUS
Ay, do, Lollio, do.

LOLLIO I must ask him easy questions at first. Tony, how many true fingers has a tailor on his right hand?

ANTONIO As many as on his left, cousin.

LOLLIO Good; and how many on both?

ANTONIO Two less than a deuce, cousin.

LOLLIO Very well answered. I come to you again, cousin Tony: how many fools goes to a wise man?

ANTONIO Forty in a day sometimes, cousin.

LOLLIO Forty in a day? How prove you that?

ANTONIO All that fall out amongst themselves, and go to a lawyer to be made friends.

LOLLIO A parlous fool! He must sit in the fourth form at least, I perceive that. I come again, Tony: how many knaves make an honest man?

ANTONIO I know not that, cousin.

LOLLIO No, the question is too hard for you. I'll tell you cousin: there's three knaves may make an honest man—a sergeant, a jailer, and a beadle; the sergeant catches him, the jailer holds him, and the beadle lashes him; and if he be not honest then, the hangman must cure him.

ANTONIO Ha, ha, ha, that's fine sport, cousin!

ALIBIUS This was too deep a question for the fool, Lollio.

LOLLIO Yes, this might have served yourself, though I say't. Once more and you shall go play, Tony.

ANTONIO Ay, play at push-pin, cousin; ha, hee!

LOLLIO So thou shalt. Say how many fools are here—

ANTONIO Two, cousin: thou and I!

LOLLIO Nay, you're too forward there, Tony. Mark my question: how many fools and knaves are here—A fool

---

118 **he looks...yet** (*a*) his madness hasn't affected his innately superior appearance (*b*) he doesn't look as foolish as he evidently wants to. (Lollio may see through Antonio's disguise quite early).

121 **means** i.e. money

121–2 **raise...discretion** (*a*) teach him more discernment (*OED* 3) (*b*) make him behave more discretely

123 **there...want** all your expense will be reimbursed

125 **magnifico** generally, a person of high standing in any social sphere.

131 **serve turn** suffice

132 **headborough** akin to a village-mayor; the lowest parochial authority
beadle the lowest judicial authority (and public whipper)

133 **watchman** the lowest civil authority
constable notoriously dim-witted and incompetent

134 **able him** make him capable of
justice frequently portrayed as stupid (compare 4.1.130, note).

136 **pitch** level, height (in a figurative sense)

143–4 **Yet...too** i.e. If I'd had enough sense to turn down this job, I'd be smarter today. (Implying that the company of fools and madmen lowers his intelligence or 'wit'.)

144 **what state** i.e. my status as keeper of fools and madmen (and, perhaps, my financial condition).

149 **cousin** a term for a close relative. In ll. 151, Lollio may also hint at 'couzen', to cheat (a common pun).

159 **true fingers has a tailor** Antonio's answer of zero ('two less than a deuce', l. 162) depends on tailors' proverbial dishonesty. See Dent T16.01, T16.11.
right with play on 'honest'

164 **goes to** Lollio means 'constitute'; Antonio takes it as 'visit' (as indicated by his next speech in ll. 167–8).

167–8 **All that...friends** compare Tilley L130

169 **A parlous** (*a*) (as *adv.*) thoroughly a, excessively a (*b*) a cunning, shrewd

181 **Yes...say't** (*a*) this would have stumped even you (*b*) such a question involves you, as it concerns knaves

183 **push-pin** a child's game (here with sexual innuendo: he would like to play at 'push-pin' with Isabella)

before a knave, a fool behind a knave, between every two fools a knave; how many fools, how many knaves?

ANTONIO I never learnt so far, cousin.

ALIBIUS
Thou putt'st too hard questions to him, Lollio.

LOLLIO I'll make him understand it easily. Cousin, stand there.

ANTONIO Ay, cousin.

LOLLIO Master, stand you next the fool.

ALIBIUS [*at Antonio's side*] Well, Lollio?

LOLLIO [*at Alibius' side*] Here's my place. Mark now, Tony: there's a fool before a knave.

ANTONIO That's I, cousin.

LOLLIO Here's a fool behind a knave—that's I—and between us two fools there is a knave—that's my master. 'Tis but 'we three', that's all.

ANTONIO We three, we three, cousin!

Madmen within

FIRST MADMAN Put's head i'th' pillory; the bread's too little!

SECOND MADMAN Fly, fly, and he catches the swallow!

THIRD MADMAN Give her more onion, or the devil put the rope about her crag!

LOLLIO You may hear what time of day it is, the chimes of Bedlam goes.

ALIBIUS [*to Madmen within*] Peace, peace, or the wire comes!

THIRD MADMAN Cat-whore, cat-whore, her parmesant, her parmesant!

ALIBIUS Peace, I say!—
Their hour's come, they must be fed, Lollio.

LOLLIO There's no hope of recovery of that Welsh madman, was undone by a mouse that spoiled him a parmesant; lost his wits for't.

ALIBIUS
Go you to your charge, Lollio; I'll to mine.

LOLLIO Go you to your madmen's ward; let me alone with your fools.

ALIBIUS
And remember my last charge, Lollio. *Exit*

LOLLIO [*after Alibius*] Of which your patients do you think I am? Come, Tony: you must amongst your schoolfellows now. There's pretty scholars amongst 'em, I can tell you; there's some of 'em at *stultus, stulta, stultum*.

ANTONIO I would see the madmen, cousin, if they would not bite me.

LOLLIO No, they shall not bite thee, Tony.

ANTONIO They bite when they are at dinner, do they not, coz?

LOLLIO They bite at dinner indeed, Tony. Well, I hope to get credit by thee; I like thee the best of all the scholars that ever I brought up, and thou shalt prove a wise man, or I'll prove a fool myself. *Exeunt*

Finis Actus Primus

Incipit Actus Secundus **2.1**

Enter Beatrice and Jasperino severally

BEATRICE
O sir, I'm ready now for that fair service
Which makes the name of friend sit glorious on you.
Good angels and this conduct be your guide.
[*She gives him a paper*]
Fitness of time and place is there set down, sir.

JASPERINO
The joy I shall return rewards my service. *Exit*

BEATRICE
How wise is Alsemero in his friend!
It is a sign he makes his choice with judgement.
Then I appear in nothing more approved
Than making choice of him,
For 'tis a principle: he that can choose
That bosom well, who of his thoughts partakes,
Proves most discreet in every choice he makes.
Methinks I love now with the eyes of judgement,

202 **'we three'** comic situation defined by a sign saying 'We Three', with only two fools'- or asses'-heads depicted: the viewer's was the third.

203.1 ***within*** i.e. behind the main stage

204–5 **Put's head . . . little** a complaint about the size of a loaf of bread.

206 **Fly . . . swallow** proverbial: 'Fly and you will catch the swallow' (Tilley S1024).

207–8 **onion . . . rope** (*a*) the onion string ('rope') (*b*) a hangman's noose

208 **crag** neck

209–10 **chimes of Bedlam** bells of Bedlam, here used figuratively to describe the madmen's cries. See 1.2.52, note.

211 **wire** whip. Whipping appears to have been the discipline of choice at Bedlam; compare ll. 45, 151–2 above.

213 **Cat-whore . . . parmesant** the cat is called a 'whore' because she failed to stop a mouse from stealing 'parmesant' cheese

her stage Welsh for 'the' or 'my'

217–18 **Welsh . . . parmesant** the Welsh were thought abnormally fond of cheese—thus 'undone' (driven mad) by a mouse who stole ('spoiled') from him a portion of 'parmesant' (cheese)

223 **last charge** final instruction (to watch Isabella)

224–5 **Of which . . . I am?** Do you think I'm a fool or a madman? (Lollio seems perturbed that Alibius should think he would forget.)

227 ***stultus, stulta, stultum*** Latin for 'foolish' or 'stupid', here referring to the declensions repeated from memory at Renaissance grammar schools.

232 **coz** shortened form of the familiar 'cousin', sometimes used for any relative, friend, or familiar; see note above at l. 151

234 **get credit** gain recognition (perhaps money)

2.1.0.2 ***severally*** from different sides of the stage (indicating a change of place; here an arranged meeting)

3–5 **Good angels . . . service** Beatrice may invoke the common pun on 'angels' as coins, offering Alsemero's friend money for delivering the letter; Jasperino's reply indicates that the joy he will bring Alsemero (with the letter) (and, perhaps, to Beatrice, when he returns again) is sufficient reward.

3 **conduct** note containing instructions (i.e. time and place—for a clandestine meeting with Alsemero)

And see the way to merit, clearly see it.
A true deserver like a diamond sparkles:
In darkness you may see him that's in absence
(Which is the greatest darkness falls on love),
Yet is he best discerned then
With intellectual eyesight. What's Piracquo
My father spends his breath for? And his blessing
Is only mine, as I regard his name,
Else it goes from me, and turns head against me,
Transformed into a curse. Some speedy way
Must be remembered. He's so forward too,
So urgent that way, scarce allows me breath
To speak to my new comforts.

Enter De Flores

DE FLORES [*aside*] Yonder's she.
What ever ails me, now o' late especially?
I can as well be hanged as refrain seeing her;
Some twenty times a day—nay, not so little—
Do I force errands, frame ways and excuses
To come into her sight, and I have small reason for't,
And less encouragement; for she baits me still
Every time worse than other, does profess herself
The cruellest enemy to my face in town,
At no hand can abide the sight of me,
As if danger or ill luck hung in my looks.
I must confess my face is bad enough,
But I know far worse has better fortune,
And not endured alone, but doted on;
And yet such pig-haired faces, chins like witches',
Here and there five hairs, whispering in a corner,
As if they grew in fear one of another,
Wrinkles like troughs, where swine-deformity swills
The tears of perjury that lie there like wash
Fallen from the slimy and dishonest eye—
Yet such a one plucked sweets without restraint,
And has the grace of beauty to his sweet.
Though my hard fate has thrust me out to servitude,
I tumbled into th' world a gentleman.
She turns her blessèd eye upon me now,
And I'll endure all storms before I part with't.

BEATRICE [*aside*] Again!
This ominous ill-faced fellow more disturbs me
Than all my other passions.

DE FLORES [*aside*] Now't begins again;
I'll stand this storm of hail though the stones pelt me.

BEATRICE
Thy business? What's thy business?

DE FLORES [*aside*] Soft and fair!
I cannot part so soon now.

BEATRICE [*aside*] The villain's fixed.—
Thou standing toad-pool!

DE FLORES [*aside*] The shower falls amain now.

BEATRICE
Who sent thee? What's thy errand? Leave my sight.

DE FLORES
My lord your father charged me to deliver
A message to you.

BEATRICE What, another since?
Do't, and be hanged then. Let me be rid of thee.

DE FLORES
True service merits mercy.

BEATRICE What's thy message?

DE FLORES
Let beauty settle but in patïence,
You shall hear all.

BEATRICE A dallying, trifling torment!

DE FLORES
Signor Alonzo de Piracquo, lady,
Sole brother to Tomazo de Piracquo—

BEATRICE
Slave, when wilt make an end?

DE FLORES [*aside*] Too soon I shall.

BEATRICE
What all this while of him?

15–19 **A true . . . eyesight** Even as a luminous diamond can shine in the absence of external light, one who truly deserves something can make his presence felt though absent—separation being, to him and his love, like night to a precious jewel (i.e. in that lustre [their love] increases with the external light [each other's company]). (Middleton alters the proverb 'A true friend is a great treasure' (Tilley F719) to work in a form of his keyword 'serve'.)

19 **With intellectual eyesight** in the imagination, with one's 'mind's eye'

20–3 **And his blessing . . . into a curse** My father's good will toward me exists only while I obey him ('as I regard his name'); otherwise it turns on me and becomes a curse.

24 **remembered** devised
He's Vermandero (who so adamantly urges the marriage with Piracquo)

26 **my new comforts** i.e. Alsemero

27 **o' late** lately, of late

32 **baits** torments (as in animal 'baiting'; compare ll. 81–2, note, below)

35 **At no hand** never, by no means

38 **I know far worse** This begins what may be a topical allusion to some well-known individual 'in town' (l. 34)—a specific phrase for the fashionable society of a locality, increasingly used with reference to London. See his continued comparisons at ll. 46, 83 ff., and compare Middleton's topical satire in *Game*.

39 **alone** only

43–4 **swine-deformity . . . wash** Like swine that gorge themselves on 'wash' (= kitchen swill or brewery refuse: *OED* *sb.* 11), the deformity De Flores castigates here seems to thrive on perjured tears that trickle down the trough-like wrinkles of this ugly face.

45 **dishonest** unchaste, lascivious

46 **plucked sweets** gained sweethearts (with sexual suggestion: compare 3.4.149, note)

47 **of beauty** associated with beauty
to his sweet (*a*) in the eyes of his lover (*b*) as his sweetheart

55 **this storm** compare the proverb 'After a Storm comes a calm (fair weather)' (Tilley S908)

56–7 **Soft . . . now** Calling on the proverb 'Soft and fair goes far' (Tilley, Dent S601), De Flores counsels himself that patience may bring what he wants.

58 **standing** stagnant, foul (referring to his face)
amain at full force

61 **another since** another message so soon

63 **mercy** (*a*) forbearance (*b*) reward, thanks (with play on French *merci*)

67 **Tomazo** perhaps with a sense of 'doubting Thomas' (compare John 20:25)

DE FLORES The said Alonzo,
With the foresaid Tomazo—
BEATRICE Yet again?
DE FLORES
—Is new alighted.
BEATRICE Vengeance strike the news!
Thou thing most loathed, what cause was there in this
To bring thee to my sight?
DE FLORES
My lord your father charged me to seek you out.
BEATRICE
Is there no other to send his errand by?
DE FLORES
It seems 'tis my luck to be i'th' way still.
BEATRICE Get thee from me!
DE FLORES [*moving aside*]
So. [*Aside*] Why, am not I an ass to devise ways
Thus to be railed at? I must see her still!
I shall have a mad qualm within this hour again,
I know't, and like a common Garden-bull,
I do but take breath to be lugged again.
What this may bode I know not: I'll despair the less,
Because there's daily precedents of bad faces
Beloved beyond all reason; these foul chops
May come into favour one day 'mongst his fellows:
Wrangling has proved the mistress of good pastime;
As children cry themselves asleep, I ha' seen
Women have chid themselves abed to men.
Exit De Flores
BEATRICE
I never see this fellow but I think
Of some harm towards me. Danger's in my mind still;
I scarce leave trembling of an hour after.
The next good mood I find my father in,
I'll get him quite discarded. O, I was
Lost in this small disturbance and forgot
Affliction's fiercer torrent that now comes
To bear down all my comforts.

Enter Vermandero, Alonzo, Tomazo
VERMANDERO [*to Alonzo and Tomazo*]
You're both welcome,
But an especial one belongs to you, sir,
To whose most noble name our love presents
The addition of a son, our son Alonzo.
ALONZO
The treasury of honour cannot bring forth
A title I should more rejoice in, sir.
VERMANDERO
You have improved it well.—Daughter, prepare;
The day will steal upon thee suddenly.
BEATRICE [*aside*]
Howe'er, I will be sure to keep the night,
If it should come so near me.
[*Beatrice and Vermandero talk apart*]
TOMAZO Alonzo.
ALONZO Brother?
TOMAZO
In troth I see small welcome in her eye.
ALONZO
Fie, you are too severe a censurer
Of love in all points: there's no bringing on you.
If lovers should mark everything a fault,
Affection would be like an ill-set book,
Whose faults might prove as big as half the volume.
BEATRICE [*to Vermandero*]
That's all I do entreat.
VERMANDERO It is but reasonable;
I'll see what my son says to't.—Son Alonzo,
Here's a motion made but to reprieve
A maidenhead three days longer; the request
Is not far out of reason, for indeed
The former time is pinching.
ALONZO Though my joys
Be set back so much time as I could wish
They had been forward, yet since she desires it,
The time is set as pleasing as before;
I find no gladness wanting.
VERMANDERO
May I ever meet it in that point still:

69–70 **said . . . foresaid** De Flores uses the rhetoric of legal documents to prolong his time with Beatrice.
80 **qualm** fit
81 **Garden-bull** bulls were regularly 'baited' (set upon by dogs for public sport) at the Paris Garden baiting ring on the south bank of the Thames
82 **lugged** dragged, pulled down by the ear (as bulls were)
85 **chops** cheeks
87 **Wrangling** noisy quarrelling
89 **have chid** who have chided, argued
92 **of** for
98 **one** i.e. welcome
100 **The addition of a son** (*a*) the benefit of a son-in-law (*b*) his heraldic mark ('addition' *OED* 5) added to our family's coat of arms (compare 'treasury of honour', l. 101, 'title', l. 102)
103 **improved** established
105–6 I will be in charge of what happens at night if that time (or situation) should get so close to actually happening
105 **night** i.e. night watch
109 **points** probably a pun on 'point' meaning 'a dot or small mark used in writing' (*OED sb.*[1] 3), or perhaps simply 'punctuation mark' (3.a), so as to form part of the extended metaphor, from proof-correction, in the speech (Holdsworth)
bringing on persuading, leading forward or on (perhaps with a legal undertone, as in *Hamlet*, 3.1.9)
110–12 **fault . . . faults** defect, imperfection . . . misprints
111 **ill-set** badly set (for printing, by the compositor or typesetter)
113 **That's . . . entreat** In private conversation, Beatrice has been urging her father to delay the marriage; he now accedes, and puts the proposition before Alonzo.
115 **motion** proposal
118 **former time** schedule we formerly agreed to (for the marriage)
123 **May . . . point still** may I always find the time ('it'; and compare l. 121) 'set' (l. 121) to that 'point' (i.e. moment, instant: *OED sb.*[1] 24) that causes you such gladness. But 'in that point' may also suggest the phrase 'in point' (compare French *à propos*), meaning 'apposite, appropriate' (*OED* D.4d).

You're nobly welcome, sirs.
Exeunt Vermandero and Beatrice

TOMAZO
So, did you mark the dullness of her parting now?

ALONZO
What dullness? Thou art so exceptious still!

TOMAZO
Why, let it go then: I am but a fool
To mark your harms so heedfully.

ALONZO
Where's the oversight?

TOMAZO
Come, your faith's cozened in her, strongly cozened.
Unsettle your affection with all speed
Wisdom can bring it to; your peace is ruined else.
Think what a torment 'tis to marry one
Whose heart is leaped into another's bosom.
If ever pleasure she receive from thee,
It comes not in thy name, or of thy gift;
She lies but with another in thine arms,
He the half-father unto all thy children
In the conception—if he get 'em not,
She helps to get 'em for him in his absence.
And how dangerous
And shameful her restraint may go in time to,
It is not to be thought on without sufferings.

ALONZO
You speak as if she loved some other, then.

TOMAZO
Do you apprehend so slowly?

ALONZO
Nay, an that
Be your fear only, I am safe enough.
Preserve your friendship and your counsel, brother,
For times of more distress. I should depart
An enemy, a dangerous, deadly one,
To any but thyself, that should but think
She knew the meaning of inconstancy,
Much less the use and practice. Yet we're friends;
Pray let no more be urged. I can endure
Much till I meet an injury to her,
Then I am not myself. Farewell, sweet brother.
How much we're bound to heaven to depart lovingly.
Exit

TOMAZO
Why, here is love's tame madness: thus a man
Quickly steals into his vexatïon. *Exit*

Enter Diaphanta and Alsemero 2.2

DIAPHANTA
The place is my charge. You have kept your hour,
And the reward of a just meeting bless you.
I hear my lady coming. Complete gentleman,
I dare not be too busy with my praises,
They're dangerous things to deal with. *Exit*

ALSEMERO
This goes well.
These women are their ladies' cabinets;
Things of most precious trust are locked into 'em.
Enter Beatrice

BEATRICE
I have within mine eye all my desires.
Requests that holy prayers ascend heaven for,
And brings 'em down to furnish our defects,
Come not more sweet to our necessities
Than thou unto my wishes.

ALSEMERO
We're so like
In our expressions, lady, that unless I borrow
The same words, I shall never find their equals. [*They embrace*]

BEATRICE
How happy were this meeting, this embrace,
If it were free from envy! This poor kiss,
It has an enemy, a hateful one,
That wishes poison to't: how well were I now
If there were none such name known as Piracquo,
Nor no such tie as the command of parents!
I should be but too much blessed.

ALSEMERO
One good service
Would strike off both your fears, and I'll go near it too,
Since you are so distressed. Remove the cause,
The command ceases; so, there's two fears blown out
With one and the same blast.

BEATRICE
Pray let me find you, sir.
What might that service be, so strangely happy?

125 **dullness** slowness to respond (especially from lack of interest)
126 **exceptious** contrary, contradictory
129 **cozened** cheated, deceived
131 **bring it to** effect
139 **absence** Tomazo implies that by thinking of her adulterous lover during sex with her husband, an adulterous woman effectively 'gets' (i.e. conceives and bears) a child for and of that lover. It was commonly thought that a woman's imagination could influence the body of a child at conception.
141 **her restraint** (*a*) her keeping (restraining) her true passions to herself (*b*) her being restrained (by you)—as in 4.3.73
144 **an** if
145 **your fear only** your only fear
2.2.1 **charge** responsibility
4 **I dare ... with my praises** Diaphanta here flirts with Alsemero.
6 **women** i.e. maidservants
ladies' cabinets cabinets into which women locked their most personal and otherwise valuable possessions
10 **And ... defects** and brings down the things we pray for in order to supply us with what we desire
'em i.e. requests
16 **envy** ill will
16–18 **This poor kiss ... poison to't** i.e. Piracquo would wish the kiss I gave you were poisoned, if he knew.
22 **strike off** (*a*) cancel (as if by the stroke of a pen) an item from a list or record (*b*) remove (e.g. fetters or bonds) with a sharp blow
I'll go near it (*a*) I'll be explicit about what it is (*b*) I won't shirk doing it
23–4 **the cause ... ceases** The 'cause' is Alonzo, the 'command' Vermandero's wishes. Alsemero alters the Latin proverb *Ablata causa, tollitur effectus*, often paraphrased 'Remove the cause, and the effect ceases to be' (Dent, Tilley C202).
25 **same blast** breath (here blowing out two flames at once)
find understand
26 **strangely** extremely, unexpectedly

ALSEMERO
The honourablest piece 'bout man: valour.
I'll send a challenge to Piracquo instantly.
BEATRICE
How? Call you that extinguishing of fear
When 'tis the only way to keep it flaming?
Are not you ventured in the action,
That's all my joys and comforts? Pray, no more, sir.
Say you prevailed—your dangers and not mine,
then—
The law would claim you from me, or obscurity
Be made the grave to bury you alive.
I'm glad these thoughts come forth. O, keep not one
Of this condition, sir. Here was a course
Found to bring sorrow on her way to death:
The tears would ne'er 'a' dried till dust had choked
'em.
Blood-guiltiness becomes a fouler visage.
[*Aside*] And now I think on one. I was to blame:
I ha' marred so good a market with my scorn;
'T'ad been done questionless! The ugliest creature
Creation framed for some use, yet to see
I could not mark so much where it should be!
ALSEMERO
Lady—
BEATRICE [*aside*]
Why, men of art make much of poison,
Keep one to expel another. Where was my art?
ALSEMERO
Lady, you hear not me.
BEATRICE I do especially, sir.
The present times are not so sure of our side
As those hereafter may be. We must use 'em, then,
As thrifty folks their wealth: sparingly, now,
Till the time opens.
ALSEMERO You teach wisdom, lady.
BEATRICE
Within there: Diaphanta!
Enter Diaphanta
DIAPHANTA Do you call, madam?
BEATRICE
Perfect your service, and conduct this gentleman
The private way you brought him.
DIAPHANTA I shall, madam.
ALSEMERO
My love's as firm as love e'er built upon.
Exeunt Diaphanta and Alsemero [*one way; at another*] *enter De Flores*
DE FLORES [*aside*]
I have watched this meeting, and do wonder much
What shall become of t'other; I'm sure both
Cannot be served unless she transgress. Happily,
Then, I'll put in for one; for if a woman
Fly from one point, from him she makes a husband,
She spreads and mounts then like arithmetic:
One, ten, a hundred, a thousand, ten thousand—
Proves in time sutler to an army royal.
Now do I look to be most richly railed at,
Yet I must see her.
BEATRICE [*aside*] Why, put case I loathed him
As much as youth and beauty hates a sepulchre,
Must I needs show it? Cannot I keep that secret
And serve my turn upon him? See, he's here.—
De Flores!
DE FLORES [*aside*]
Ha, I shall run mad with joy!
She called me fairly by my name, De Flores,
And neither 'rogue' nor 'rascal'!
BEATRICE What ha' you done
To your face o' late? You've met with some good
physician;
You've pruned yourself, methinks.
You were not wont to look so amorously.
DE FLORES [*aside*] Not I;
'Tis the same phys'nomy to a hair and pimple,
Which she called scurvy scarce an hour ago:
How is this?
BEATRICE Come hither. Nearer, man.
DE FLORES [*aside, crossing to her*]
I'm up to the chin in heaven!
BEATRICE Turn, let me see.

37–8 **Here was a course | Found** this would be a way, indeed
38 **sorrow . . . death** i.e. not only to make me sorrowful but to push me toward death
41 **one** i.e. one 'fouler visage' (l. 40: De Flores)
42 **marred . . . market** spoiled such a good opportunity
my scorn my scornful behaviour toward De Flores
44 **Creation . . . use** a commonplace held that everything in nature had been created for some purpose ('use')
46 **men of art** doctors, apothecaries. 'Art' here means learning, knowledge.
46–7 **make much . . . another** proverbial: 'One poison expels another' (Tilley P457)
47 **art** cunning (in contrast to the learned 'art' of the 'men' in l. 46)
49–50 **are not . . . may be** are not as certainly favourable to us as we can hope future times may be
52 **time opens** the right moment reveals itself
54 **Perfect** finish, make complete
58 **t'other** the other (Alonzo)
59 **served** looked after (with strong sexual overtones)
Happily perhaps, haply (as it was probably pronounced)
60 **put in for one** enter my own bid (i.e. as one of those seeking 'favours' from Beatrice-Joanna); with salacious overtones (compare 4.3.36)
61 **Fly . . . point** break away from a single position (i.e. constancy); with pun on decimal 'point', the woman shifts from 1.0 to 10.0, etc.
62 **spreads and mounts** lifts her wings and rises (but with a strong sense of 'spreads her legs and mounts men')
64 **sutler** provisioner (with play on 'prostitute')
66 **put case** suppose (as in presenting a hypothesis (often legal in nature); *OED* 12)
69 **serve my turn upon him** manipulate him to my advantage
74 **pruned** preened, groomed
75 **amorously** attractive; like a lover
76 **phys'nomy** physiognomy

[*She touches him*] Faugh, 'tis but the heat of the liver, I perceive't.
I thought it had been worse.

DE FLORES [*aside*]
Her fingers touched me! She smells all amber.

BEATRICE
I'll make a water for you shall cleanse this
Within a fortnight.

DE FLORES
With your own hands, lady?

BEATRICE
Yes, mine own, sir; in a work of cure, I'll
Trust no other.

DE FLORES [*aside*]
'Tis half an act of pleasure
To hear her talk thus to me.

BEATRICE [*aside*]
When we're used
To a hard face, 'tis not so unpleasing.—
It mends still in opinion, hourly mends,
I see it by experience.

DE FLORES [*aside*]
I was blessed to light upon this minute:
I'll make use on't.

BEATRICE
Hardness becomes the visage of a man well;
It argues service, resolution, manhood,
If cause were of employment.

DE FLORES
'Twould be soon seen,
If e'er your ladyship had cause to use it.
I would but wish the honour of a service
So happy as that mounts to.

BEATRICE
We shall try you—
O my De Flores!

DE FLORES [*aside*]
How's that?
She calls me hers already, 'my De Flores'!—
You were about to sigh out somewhat, madam.

BEATRICE
No, was I? I forgot—O!

DE FLORES
There 'tis again—
The very fellow on't.

BEATRICE
You are too quick, sir.

DE FLORES
There's no excuse for't, now I heard it twice, madam.
That sigh would fain have utterance: take pity on't
And lend it a free word; 'las, how it labours
For liberty! I hear the murmur yet
Beat at your bosom.

BEATRICE
Would creation—

DE FLORES
Ay, well said, that's it.

BEATRICE
Had formed me man!

DE FLORES
Nay, that's not it.

BEATRICE
O, 'tis the soul of freedom!
I should not then be forced to marry one
I hate beyond all depths; I should have power
Then to oppose my loathings, nay, remove 'em
Forever from my sight.

DE FLORES
O blest occasion!—
Without change to your sex, you have your wishes.
Claim so much man in me.

BEATRICE
In thee, De Flores?
There's small cause for that.

DE FLORES
Put it not from me;
It's a service that I kneel for to you. [*He kneels*]

BEATRICE
You are too violent to mean faithfully:
There's horror in my service, blood and danger.
Can those be things to sue for?

DE FLORES
If you knew
How sweet it were to me to be employed
In any act of yours, you would say then
I failed, and used not reverence enough
When I receive the charge on't.

BEATRICE [*aside*]
This is much, methinks.
Belike his wants are greedy, and to such
Gold tastes like angels' food.—Rise.

DE FLORES
I'll have the work first.

BEATRICE [*aside*]
Possible his need is strong upon him.—
[*She gives him money*] There's to encourage thee.
As thou art forward and thy service dangerous,
Thy reward shall be precious.

DE FLORES
That I have thought on;
I have assured myself of that beforehand
And know it will be precious: the thought ravishes.

BEATRICE
Then take him to thy fury!

80 **Faugh** an interjection of impatience
82 **all amber** like ambergris (a waxy substance from sperm whales, used in perfumes)
83 **water** lotion; perhaps with bawdy as well
86 **act of pleasure** sexual act
89 **mends still in opinion** continually becomes more acceptable
95–8 **'Twould . . . to** De Flores says she has only to test his resolution and ability, but his response also puns on the sexual implications of 'Hardness' (l. 93 = ''Twould', 'it'), 'use it' (l. 96), 'service' (l. 97), and 'mounts' (l. 98).
103 **quick** perceptive (with, perhaps, a hint of 'too quick to take up my words')
106 **And . . . word** give it utterance
108 **creation** i.e. the process of my creation
109 **that's it** i.e. 'creation', which De Flores understands as 'procreation'
110 **O . . . freedom** i.e. being a man
114 **occasion** opportunity
117 **small cause for** i.e. little reason for thinking so
119 **too . . . faithfully** too eager truly to mean (i.e. have had time to consider fully) what you say
123 **any act of yours** with ambivalent sexual suggestion; see note at l. 86 above
125 **the charge on't** the orders you give me
126 **Belike** perhaps
127 **angels' food** manna from heaven; compare Psalm 78:25
work commission
128 **Possible** possibly
130 **forward** bold
131 **reward** Beatrice means financial 'reward'; De Flores makes it plain to the audience that he thinks in sexual terms (compare 'ravishes', l. 133).

DE FLORES I thirst for him.
BEATRICE Alonzo de Piracquo!
DE FLORES [*rising*]
His end's upon him; he shall be seen no more.
BEATRICE
How lovely now dost thou appear to me!
Never was man dearlier rewarded.
DE FLORES I do think of that.
BEATRICE
Be wondrous careful in the execution.
DE FLORES
Why, are not both our lives upon the cast?
BEATRICE
Then I throw all my fears upon thy service.
DE FLORES
They ne'er shall rise to hurt you.
BEATRICE When the deed's done,
I'll furnish thee with all things for thy flight;
Thou mayst live bravely in another country.
DE FLORES
Ay, ay: we'll talk of that hereafter.
BEATRICE [*aside*] I shall rid myself
Of two inveterate loathings at one time:
Piracquo and his dog-face. *Exit*
DE FLORES O my blood!
Methinks I feel her in mine arms already,
Her wanton fingers combing out this beard,
And being pleased, praising this bad face.
Hunger and pleasure: they'll commend sometimes
Slovenly dishes, and feed heartily on 'em;
Nay, which is stranger, refuse daintier for 'em.
Some women are odd feeders!—I'm too loud;
Here comes the man goes supperless to bed,
Yet shall not rise tomorrow to his dinner.
Enter Alonzo
ALONZO
De Flores.
DE FLORES
My kind, honourable lord.
ALONZO
I am glad I ha' met with thee.
DE FLORES Sir?
ALONZO Thou canst show me
The full strength of the castle?
DE FLORES That I can, sir.
ALONZO
I much desire it.
DE FLORES And if the ways and straits
Of some of the passages be not too tedious for you,
I will assure you, worth your time and sight, my lord.
ALONZO
Puh, that shall be no hind'rance.
DE FLORES I'm your servant, then.
'Tis now near dinner-time; 'gainst your lordship's
rising
I'll have the keys about me.
ALONZO Thanks, kind De Flores.
DE FLORES [*aside*]
He's safely thrust upon me beyond hopes. *Exeunt*
Finis Actus Secundus

3.1
Incipit Actus Tertius
Enter Alonzo and De Flores
(*In the Act time, De Flores hides a naked rapier*)
DE FLORES
Yes, here are all the keys. I was afraid, my lord,
I'd wanted for the postern; this is it.
I've all, I've all, my lord.
[*He shows a large key*]
This for the sconce.
ALONZO
'Tis a most spacious and impregnable fort.
DE FLORES
You'll tell me more, my lord. This descent
Is somewhat narrow. We shall never pass
Well with our weapons; they'll but trouble us.
ALONZO
Thou sayst true. [*They disarm*]
DE FLORES Pray let me help your lordship.
ALONZO
'Tis done. Thanks, kind De Flores.
DE FLORES Here are hooks, my lord,
To hang such things on purpose.
[*He hangs up the rapiers*]
ALONZO Lead, I'll follow thee.
Exeunt at one door and enter at the other

3.2
DE FLORES
All this is nothing. You shall see anon
A place you little dream on.
ALONZO I am glad
I have this leisure. All your master's house
Imagine I ha' taken a gondola.
DE FLORES
All but myself, sir—[*aside*] which makes up my
safety.—

140 **execution** performance (with a grisly pun)
141 **cast** i.e. of the dice
145 **bravely** splendidly, openly
148 **his** i.e. De Flores's
blood the inciter of sexual desire (for which it stands here)
155 **are odd feeders** have strange tastes
156–7 **Here . . . dinner** Here's the man who, though going to bed without eating, won't be rising tomorrow to eat.
165 **'gainst** in anticipation of
3.1.0.3 **Act time** interval between the Acts, when often music was played
2 **I'd . . . postern** that I was lacking the key for the small gate
3 **sconce** small fortification. Later, the word takes on the meaning of 'head', making for a grisly pun at 3.2.13–17.
5 **You'll tell me more** i.e. when you've seen the rest you'll praise it even more strongly
10.2 ***at one door and . . . the other*** implying a change of place (compare 2.1.0.2)

My lord, I'll place you at a casement here
Will show you the full strength of all the castle.
Look, spend your eye a while upon that object.

ALONZO
Here's rich variety, De Flores.

DE FLORES Yes, sir.

ALONZO
Goodly munition.

DE FLORES Ay, there's ordnance, sir—
No bastard metal—will ring you a peal
Like bells at great men's funerals; keep your eye straight, my lord,
Take special notice of that sconce before you:
There you may dwell awhile.

ALONZO I am upon't.

DE FLORES
And so am I.
[*He clubs him with key*]

ALONZO De Flores, O De Flores!
Whose malice hast thou put on?

DE FLORES [*retrieving rapier*]
Do you question a work of secrecy?
I must silence you.
[*He stabs him*]

ALONZO O, O, O!

DE FLORES I must silence you. [*He stabs him*]
So, here's an undertaking well accomplished.
This vault serves to good use now.—Ha! what's that
Threw sparkles in my eye? O, 'tis a diamond
He wears upon his finger. It was well found:
This will approve the work.
[*He struggles with the ring*]
What, so fast on?
Not part in death? I'll take a speedy course then:
Finger and all shall off. [*He cuts off the finger*] So, now I'll clear
The passages from all suspèct or fear. *Exit with body*

3.3

Enter Isabella and Lollio

ISABELLA
Why, sirrah, whence have you commissïon
To fetter the doors against me? If you
Keep me in a cage, pray whistle to me,
Let me be doing something.

LOLLIO You shall be doing, if it please you; I'll whistle to you if you'll pipe after.

ISABELLA
Is it your master's pleasure, or your own,
To keep me in this pinfold?

LOLLIO 'Tis for my master's pleasure, lest being taken in another man's corn, you might be pounded in another place.

ISABELLA
'Tis very well, and he'll prove very wise.

LOLLIO He says you have company enough in the house, if you please to be sociable, of all sorts of people.

ISABELLA
Of all sorts? Why, here's none but fools and madmen.

LOLLIO Very well: and where will you find any other, if you should go abroad? There's my master and I to boot, too.

ISABELLA
Of either sort one, a madman and a fool.

LOLLIO I would e'en participate of both, then, if I were as you. I know you're half mad already; be half foolish too.

ISABELLA
You're a brave, saucy rascal! Come on, sir:
Afford me then the pleasure of your Bedlam.
You were commending once today to me,
Your last-come lunatic—what a proper
Body there was without brains to guide it,
And what a pitiful delight appeared
In that defect, as if your wisdom had found
A mirth in madness. Pray, sir, let me partake
If there be such a pleasure.

3.2.6 **casement** (window) recess
10 **munition** (*a*) fortifications (*b*) ammunition, military stores
ordnance cannon
11 **bastard metal** probably referring to small cannon called 'bastards' (i.e. 'bastard culverin'), but perhaps with a sense of corrupt, adulterated (hence weaker), second-rate metal
13 **sconce** with pun on 'head'; compare 3.1.3, note
14 **dwell** look (with pun on 'reside'); De Flores's stratagem is to get Alonzo to look the other way
upon't fixed upon it with my gaze. But De Flores replies with a grim joke: I'm about this business of killing you.
21 **vault** probably a hidden recess, with play on vault as 'burial chamber'; yet 'vault' could also mean 'a covered conduit for carrying away water or filth; a drain or sewer' (*OED* 4a); 'a privy' (*OED* 4c); or 'a deep hole or pit' (*OED* 5)
22 **Threw** that just threw
24 **approve** confirm my completion of
27 **suspèct** suspicion
3.3.3 **whistle to me** i.e. as you would to caged bird
4 **Let...doing something** Isabella means only 'let me go about my business', but Lollio in his reply wilfully puts a sexual interpretation on 'doing'.
5–6 **whistle...pipe** 'To dance after a person's pipe' can suggest sexual activity.
8 **pinfold** kennel, cage, 'pound' (compare l. 10)
9–10 **in another man's corn** in another man's (grain) field—i.e. arms
10–11 **pounded in another place** locked up, *im*pounded elsewhere—with joke (continuing the grain metaphor) on 'screwed somewhere else'
12 Isabella speaks ironically; this is far from well, and her husband is a fool.
19 **Of either sort one** one of each kind
20 **participate** partake (with sexual suggestion)
21 **I know...foolish** Lollio hints that she might take him, a fool, as her lover; because Isabella is the 'better half' of the mad Alibius, their marriage is 'half mad'.
23 **brave** daring, presumptuous
24 **Bedlam** lunatic asylum in London, often used generically (as a form of 'Bethlehem' Hospital) for 'madhouse'; compare 1.2.0.1, 1.2.52, notes
26 **last-come lunatic** the madman who has most recently arrived (Franciscus)
proper handsome, attractive

LOLLIO If I do not show you the handsomest, discreetest madman—one that I may call the understanding madman—then say I am a fool.

ISABELLA Well, a match, I will say so.

LOLLIO When you have had a taste of the madman, you shall (if you please) see Fools' College, o'th' other side. I seldom lock there: 'tis but shooting a bolt or two, and you are amongst 'em.

Exit. Enter presently [*with Franciscus*]

Come on, sir, let me see how handsomely you'll behave yourself now.

FRANCISCUS How sweetly she looks! O, but there's a wrinkle in her brow as deep as philosophy. [*To Lollio; he mimes giving him a cup*] Anacreon, drink to my mistress' health, I'll pledge it. Stay, stay, there's a spider in the cup! No, 'tis but a grape-stone. Swallow it; fear nothing, poet. So, so, lift higher. [*Lollio laughs*]

ISABELLA [*to Lollio*]
Alack, alack, 'tis too full of pity
To be laughed at. How fell he mad? Canst thou tell?

LOLLIO For love, mistress. He was a pretty poet too, and that set him forwards first; the muses then forsook him, he ran mad for a chambermaid, yet she was but a dwarf neither.

FRANCISCUS [*approaching Isabella*] Hail, bright Titania!
Why standst thou idle on these flow'ry banks?
Oberon is dancing with his Dryades;
I'll gather daisies, primroses, violets,
And bind them in a verse of poesy.

LOLLIO Not too near! You see your danger. [*He shows a whip*]

FRANCISCUS O, hold thy hand, great Diomed; thou feedst thy horses well, they shall obey thee. [*He kneels like a horse*] Get up, Bucephalus kneels.

LOLLIO You see how I awe my flock: a shepherd has not his dog at more obedience.

ISABELLA
His conscience is unquiet—sure that was
The cause of this. A proper gentleman.

FRANCISCUS [*rising*] Come hither, Aesculapius; hide the poison.

LOLLIO [*putting up whip*] Well, 'tis hid.

FRANCISCUS Didst thou never hear of one Tiresias, a famous poet?

LOLLIO Yes, that kept tame wild-geese.

FRANCISCUS That's he! I am the man.

LOLLIO No!

FRANCISCUS Yes! But make no words on't; I was a man seven years ago.

LOLLIO A stripling, I think you might say.

FRANCISCUS Now I'm a woman, all feminine.

LOLLIO I would I might see that.

FRANCISCUS Juno struck me blind.

LOLLIO I'll ne'er believe that; for a woman, they say, has an eye more than a man.

FRANCISCUS I say she struck me blind.

LOLLIO And Luna made you mad. You have two trades to beg with.

FRANCISCUS
Luna is now big-bellied, and there's room
For both of us to ride with Hecatë;
I'll drag thee up into her silver sphere,
And there we'll kick the dog (and beat the bush)

35 **a match** an agreement, compact (i.e. 'that's a deal')
37 **Fools' College** the madmen and fools are kept apart; see 1.2.44, 221. As Bedlam hospital was divided into two wings, perhaps an actual practice is here referred to.
38 **shooting a bolt** sliding back the bolt on a door (but compare also the proverb 'A fool's bolt is soon shot' (Tilley, Dent F515), where 'bolt' = arrow).
44 **Anacreon** Greek lyric poet famous for his songs of love and wine-drinking. Franciscus's mad speech, unlike that of the 'Bedlam' madmen, continually centres on classical references; this may play on contemporary tavern culture.
45–6 **spider in the cup** It was thought that, seen in a cup, spiders had the power to poison.
46 **grape-stone** Anacreon was believed to have died from choking on the stone of a dried grape while drinking wine.
47 **lift higher** presumably Franciscus refers to lifting a cup higher while drinking. Here Lollio may indulge him by miming Anacreon drinking a 'health', or Franciscus may merely address an empty part of the stage.
51 **set him forwards first** first gave him a tendency (to madness)
52–3 **yet . . . neither** even though she was nothing but a dwarf
54–6 **Titania . . . Oberon** the queen and king of fairy land, known best from *A Midsummer Night's Dream*
56 **dancing . . . Dryades** sporting with his wood-nymphs. Franciscus uses the cover of madness to hint to Isabella that Alibius is 'dancing' (= copulating) with other women.
61 **Diomed** In mythology, Diomedes was king of the Bistones, in Thrace, whose mares (compare 'horses', l. 62) ate human flesh. (But compare also the *Iliad* 5, 10, where (another) Diomedes is associated with horses.)
63 **Bucephalus** horse of Alexander the Great, which only he could ride
67 **this** i.e. his madness
68 **Aesculapius** (Greek) patron divinity of medicine
69 **poison** Lollio's whip (compare ll. 94–5 below)
71 **Tiresias** mythological Theban soothsayer who, having been changed into a woman for seven years, was blinded by Juno as a punishment for revealing that women enjoy sex more than men do
71–2 **famous poet** Tiresias was a prophet, 'poet' in so far as prophets and seers were so considered.
73 **tame wild-geese** possibly a joke on 'goose' as slang for prostitute; the oxymoron seems also connected with the gender inversion of Tiresias as man and woman
77 **seven years ago** see note at l. 71.
78 **stripling** youth
81 **Juno** Juno was responsible for striking Tiresias blind.
83 **an eye more** sexual joke on the vagina as 'eye'
85 **Luna** the moon, and cause of 'lunacy'
85–6 **two trades to beg with** i.e. being blind and mad (beggars often pretended to be both)
87 **big-bellied** (*a*) full (*b*) pregnant
88 **Hecatë** a witch goddess, associated with the moon and black magic—here seen as a source of (supernatural) transportation
90 **dog . . . bush** The Man in the Moon was thought to have a dog and a bush.

That barks against the witches of the night;
The swift lycanthropi that walks the round,
We'll tear their wolvish skins, and save the sheep.
[*He attempts to seize Lollio*]

LOLLIO Is't come to this? [*He flourishes the whip*] Nay, then, my poison comes forth again, mad slave! Indeed, abuse your keeper!

ISABELLA
I prithee, hence with him, now he grows dangerous.

FRANCISCUS (*sings*)
Sweet love, pity me,
Give me leave to lie with thee.

LOLLIO No, I'll see you wiser first. To your own kennel.

FRANCISCUS (*sings*)
No noise—she sleeps,
Draw all the curtains round;
Let no soft sound
Molest the pretty soul;
But love, and love,
Creeps in at a mouse-hole. *Exit Franciscus*

LOLLIO [*after him*] I would you would get into your hole. Now, mistress, I will bring you another sort: you shall be fooled another while. Tony! Come hither, Tony!

Enter Antonio

Look who's yonder, Tony.

ANTONIO Cousin, is it not my aunt?

LOLLIO Yes, 'tis one of 'em, Tony.

ANTONIO Hee, hee! How do you, uncle?

LOLLIO Fear him not, mistress: 'tis a gentle nidget; you may play with him, as safely with him as with his bauble.

ISABELLA How long hast thou been a fool?

ANTONIO Ever since I came hither, cousin.

ISABELLA
Cousin? I'm none of thy cousins, fool.

LOLLIO O mistress, fools have always so much wit as to claim their kindred.

MADMAN (*singing, within*)
Bounce! Bounce!
He falls! He falls!

ISABELLA
Hark you, your scholars in the upper room
Are out of order.

LOLLIO [*shouting offstage*] Must I come amongst you there?—Keep you the fool, mistress. I'll go up and play left-handed Orlando amongst the madmen. *Exit*

ISABELLA Well, sir.

ANTONIO [*removing disguise*]
'Tis opportuneful now, sweet lady! Nay,
Cast no amazing eye upon this change.

ISABELLA Ha!

ANTONIO
This shape of folly shrouds your dearest love,
The truest servant to your powerful beauties,
Whose magic had this force thus to transform me.

ISABELLA
You are a fine fool indeed.

ANTONIO O, 'tis not strange:
Love has an intellect that runs through all
The scrutinous sciences; and like
A cunning poet, catches a quantity
Of every knowledge, yet brings all home
Into one mystery, into one secret
That he proceeds in.

ISABELLA You're a parlous fool.

ANTONIO
No danger in me: I bring naught but love
And his soft-wounding shafts to strike you with.
Try but one arrow; if it hurt you,
I'll stand you twenty back in recompense. [*He kisses her*]

ISABELLA
A forward fool too!

ANTONIO This was love's teaching:
A thousand ways she fashioned out my way,

92 **lycanthropi** wolf-men
walks the round walk a regular circuit as a sentinel
95 **slave** rascal
100 **your own kennel** i.e. in contrast to those of the 'dog' (l. 90) and 'lycanthropi' (l. 92) he has threatened. ('kennel' = room, cell)
105–6 **love … mouse-hole** i.e. love creeps in at any little crevice; with sexual innuendo of the vagina. 'Mouse' = diminutive for woman or sweetheart.
107 **hole** i.e. cell
109 **fooled** (*a*) amused by a fool (*b*) deceived
111 **aunt** 'Aunt' could mean 'bawd' or 'prostitute' as well as 'relative'; 'One of my aunts' (compare 112) was proverbial bawdy (see Tilley A398).
113 **uncle** If Antonio's 'aunts' and 'cousins' (ll. 118–19) are prostitutes, then his 'uncle' is likely to be an 'uncle Pandarus', as in *Troilus and Cressida*.
114 **nidget** idiot
116 **bauble** a toy or trifle. Technically, a bauble was a stick or baton with a carved ass's head and ears on top, used by a fool or court jester: see *OED* 4. Here it possesses a sexual sense.
118 **cousin** As Isabella realizes, like 'aunt' (l. 111), 'cousin' could refer to a prostitute or easy woman.
122 **Bounce** bang, the sound of a gun.
127 **Keep you** take care of
128 **left-handed Orlando** a clumsy, parodic, or perhaps even sinister version of the violent, mad hero of Ariosto's *Orlando Furioso*
130 **opportuneful** convenient. Antonio here drops his feigned madness to woo Isabella.
131 **amazing** amazed
136 **fine** proper; also: intricate, complex. Isabella speaks sardonically, with suggestion that Antonio is making a fool of himself in love.
138 **scrutinous sciences** searching, prying fields of learning
141 **mystery** secret (as in the following line), but also with a sense of a science, or special branch of learning or training
143 **naught** nothing
love i.e. Cupid
145 **one arrow** Antonio may mean 'arrow' (i.e. of Cupid) as 'kiss'; it may also have a buried meaning of 'penis'.
146 **stand you twenty back** take twenty back from you in return. ('Stand' often had a connotation of male sexual arousal.)

And this I found the safest and the nearest
To tread the Galaxia to my star.

ISABELLA
Profound, withal! Certain you dreamed of this:
Love never taught it waking.

ANTONIO
Take no acquaintance of these outward follies;
There is within a gentleman that loves you.

ISABELLA
When I see him, I'll speak with him. So, in the mean
time,
Keep your habit; it becomes you well enough.
As you are a gentleman, I'll not discover you;
That's all the favour that you must expect:
When you are weary, you may leave the school,
For all this while you have but played the fool.

Enter Lollio

ANTONIO [*disguising himself*]
And must again;—
[*As Tony*] Hee, hee! I thank you, cousin! (*sings*)
I'll be your Valentine
Tomorrow morning.

LOLLIO How do you like the fool, mistress?

ISABELLA Passing well, sir.

LOLLIO Is he not witty, pretty well for a fool?

ISABELLA If he hold on as he begins, he is like to come to something.

LOLLIO Ay, thank a good tutor. You may put him to't; he begins to answer pretty hard questions. Tony: how many is five times six?

ANTONIO Five times six is six times five.

LOLLIO What arithmetician could have answered better? How many is one hundred and seven?

ANTONIO One hundred and seven is seven hundred and one, cousin.

LOLLIO This is no wit to speak on. Will you be rid of the fool now?

ISABELLA By no means!—Let him stay a little.

MADMAN (*within*) Catch there! Catch the last couple in hell!

LOLLIO Again? Must I come amongst you?—Would my master were come home! I am not able to govern both these wards together. *Exit*

ANTONIO
Why should a minute of love's hour be lost?

ISABELLA
Fie, out again? I had rather you kept
Your other posture: you become not your tongue
When you speak from your clothes.

ANTONIO
How can he freeze
Lives near so sweet a warmth? Shall I alone
Walk through the orchard of the Hesperides
And, cowardly, not dare to pull an apple?
This with the red cheeks I must venture for.

[*He kisses her*]

Enter Lollio above

ISABELLA Take heed, there's giants keep 'em.

[*He kisses her again*]

LOLLIO [*aside*] How now, fool: are you good at that? Have you read Lipsius? He's past *Ars Amandi*; I believe I must put harder questions to him, I perceive that.

ISABELLA
You are bold without fear too.

ANTONIO
What should I fear,
Having all joys about me? Do you but smile,
And love shall play the wanton on your lip,
Meet and retire, retire and meet again;
Look you but cheerfully, and in your eyes
I shall behold mine own deformity,
And dress myself up fairer. I know this shape
Becomes me not, but in those bright mirrors

150 **Galaxia** Milky Way

151 **withal** in addition to (or on top of) everything else, also

152 **waking** while you were awake (and presumably in possession of your rational faculties)

156 **habit** costume; with a glance at 'role' **becomes** suits

157 **discover** uncover, give you away

168–9 **If he ... come to something** An ambiguous line: Antonio/Tony may 'come to something', signifying (*a*) to Lollio, that 'Tony' promises to advance in his education; and perhaps (*b*) to Antonio, that she may be open to his advances; and (*c*) to herself, that he may eventually come to grief, or ridicule. See following note.

170–1 **Ay ... hard questions** On the surface, Lollio understands Isabella's response (ll. 168–9) to deal with his tutoring of 'Tony'—where 'put him to't' means 'put him to his examination, test his knowledge'; yet with 'pretty *hard* questions' ('hard' = erect), this line takes on a bawdy meaning.

178 **no wit to speak on** i.e. not a remarkable example of wit

181–2 **Catch the last couple in hell** In the outdoor (courting) game of barley-break, referred to again at 5.3.163, one couple would join hands within a marked-off, circular area called 'hell', and attempt to catch others as they ran through the circle. Those caught had to replace the original pair in 'hell'.

187 **out** i.e. of your role as a fool

188–9 **you become not ... clothes** when Antonio speaks differently from how he is dressed (he is dressed as a fool), he does not adorn decorously ('becomes' *OED* III) the body ('yourself') that wears fool's clothes. Compare l. 156 above, and note

189–90 **How ... warmth?** (*a*) how could anyone not respond to you amorously? (*b*) how can Alibius be so old and passionless?

191 **Hesperides** three mythological nymphs whose orchard contained golden apples

193 **This** i.e. this golden apple (Isabella)

194 **giants** The Hesperides were the daughters of Atlas, a giant who placed a dragon guard over the golden apples.

195 **that** i.e. kissing or making love

196 **Lipsius** Lipse, a Renaissance humanist best known for his Latin epigrams and translations; here the joke is on the 'Lips' in his name.
Ars Amandi Latin title of Ovid's *Arts of Love*; Lollio sardonically jests that Antonio appears to have graduated beyond Ovid's famous treatise. In view of the preceding pun on lips, 'Ars' here is probably a pun on 'arse'.

199 **Do you but** if you will only

205 **mirrors** i.e. of Isabella's eyes

I shall array me handsomely.

LOLLIO Cuckoo! Cuckoo!

Exit [Lollio. Antonio embraces Isabella. Lollio re-enters presently with] Madmen above, some as birds, others as beasts. [Antonio and Isabella part]

ANTONIO
What are these?

ISABELLA Of fear enough to part us.
Yet are they but our schools of lunatics,
That act their fantasies in any shapes
Suiting their present thoughts—if sad, they cry;
If mirth be their conceit, they laugh again.
Sometimes they imitate the beasts and birds,
Singing, or howling, braying, barking; all
As their wild fancies prompt 'em.

[*Exeunt Madmen, above*]

Enter Lollio

ANTONIO
These are no fears.

ISABELLA But here's a large one: my man.

ANTONIO [*as Tony*] Ha, hee! That's fine sport indeed, cousin.

LOLLIO I would my master were come home. 'Tis too much for one shepherd to govern two of these flocks; nor can I believe that one churchman can instruct two benefices at once—there will be some incurable mad of the one side, and very fools on the other. Come, Tony.

ANTONIO Prithee cousin, let me stay here still.

LOLLIO No, you must to your book now; you have played sufficiently.

ISABELLA Your fool is grown wondrous witty.

LOLLIO Well, I'll say nothing; but I do not think but he will put you down one of these days.

Exeunt Lollio and Antonio

ISABELLA Here the restrainèd current might make breach,
Spite of the watchful bankers. Would a woman stray,
She need not gad abroad to seek her sin;
It would be brought home one ways or other.
The needle's point will to the fixèd north,
Such drawing arctics women's beauties are.

Enter Lollio

LOLLIO How dost thou, sweet rogue?

ISABELLA How now?

LOLLIO Come, there are degrees; one fool may be better than another.

ISABELLA What's the matter?

LOLLIO Nay, if thou giv'st thy mind to fool's-flesh, have at thee! [*He tries to kiss her*]

ISABELLA
You bold slave, you!

LOLLIO I could follow now as t'other fool did:
'What should I fear,
Having all joys about me? Do you but smile,
And love shall play the wanton on your lip,
Meet and retire, retire and meet again;
Look you but cheerfully, and in your eyes
I shall behold my own deformity,
And dress myself up fairer; I know this shape
Becomes me not—'
And so as it follows. But is not this the more foolish way? Come, sweet rogue; kiss me, my little Lacedemonian. Let me feel how thy pulses beat. Thou hast a thing about thee would do a man pleasure.—I'll lay my hand on't.

[*He tries to embrace her*]

ISABELLA
Sirrah, no more! I see you have discovered
This love's knight-errant, who hath made adventure
For purchase of my love. Be silent, mute—
Mute as a statue—or his injunction
For me enjoying shall be to cut thy throat;
I'll do it, though for no other purpose,
And be sure he'll not refuse it.

LOLLIO My share, that's all. I'll have my fool's part with you.

ISABELLA
No more: your master.

207 **Cuckoo! Cuckoo!** Lollio signals Alibius's cuckoldry by mimicking the cuckoo bird (which appropriates other birds' nests for its own use).
208 **Of fear enough** fearful enough, threatening enough
212 **conceit** thought, whim
216 **no fears** nothing to be afraid of
here's a large one: my man 'one' = fear; 'man' = servant, i.e. Lollio. As Rowley the actor specialized in fat clown roles, 'large' may indicate that he intended to take the part of Lollio himself.
217 **That's fine sport** i.e.(*a*) watching the madmen (*b*) kissing Isabella
221–2 **two benefices at once** A single clergyman appointed to (and enjoying the income from, without paying full attention to) separate churches or livings ('benefices') was long a problem in England.
229 **put you down** i.e. in a battle of wits; but with a sexual sense of 'laying' a woman
230–1 **restrainèd current . . . bankers** i.e. the water might get through the dam even though some (e.g. Alibius) have taken precautions. A 'banker' is a labourer who makes earthen banks.
234 **needle's point** compass needle, with innuendo of penis
fixèd north magnetic North
235 **Such . . . are** women's beauties are just such North Poles with their attracting qualities
246–52 **Do . . . not** By quoting Antonio's wooing at ll. 199–205, Lollio reveals to Isabella that he has witnessed the attempted seduction. He now offers this information as sexual blackmail.
253 **And so as it follows** i.e. *et cetera*, and so forth
253–4 **more foolish way** (*a*) Antonio's (foolish) love poetry (*b*) what I (a fool) will do next: accost you
254–5 **Lacedemonian** (*a*) one of few words, 'laconic' of speech (*b*) slang for loose woman or whore
256 **thing about thee** i.e. between her legs
259 **love's knight-errant** (romantic) adventurer in the service of love
263 **though . . . purpose** i.e. as if for the act's sake itself
265 **part** share, portion

Enter Alibius

ALIBIUS Sweet, how dost thou?

ISABELLA
Your bounden servant, sir.

ALIBIUS Fie, fie, sweet heart:
No more of that.

ISABELLA You were best lock me up.

ALIBIUS
In my arms and bosom, my sweet Isabella, [*He embraces her*]
I'll lock thee up most nearly.—Lollio,
We have employment; we have task in hand.
At noble Vermandero's, our castle captain,
There is a nuptial to be solemnized—
Beatrice-Joanna, his fair daughter bride,
For which the gentleman hath bespoke our pains:
A mixture of our madmen and our fools,
To finish (as it were) and make the fag
Of all the revels, the third night from the first.
Only an unexpected passage over,
To make a frightful pleasure, that is all—
But not the all I aim at. Could we so act it
To teach it in a wild distracted measure,
Though out of form and figure, breaking Time's head—
(It were no matter, 'twould be healed again
In one age or other, if not in this).
'Tis this, Lollio: there's a good reward begun,
And will beget a bounty be it known.

LOLLIO This is easy, sir, I'll warrant you: you have about you fools and madmen that can dance very well, and 'tis no wonder—your best dancers are not the wisest men; the reason is, with often jumping they jolt their brains down into their feet, that their wits lie more in their heels than in their heads.

ALIBIUS
Honest Lollio, thou giv'st me a good reason,
And a comfort in it.

ISABELLA You've a fine trade on't:
Madmen and fools are a staple commodity.

ALIBIUS O wife, we must eat, wear clothes, and live.
Just at the Lawyer's Haven we arrive;
By madmen and by fools we both do thrive. *Exeunt*

Enter Vermandero, Alsemero, Jasperino, and Beatrice 3.4

VERMANDERO
Valencia speaks so nobly of you, sir,
I wish I had a daughter now for you.

ALSEMERO
The fellow of this creature were a partner
For a king's love.

VERMANDERO I had her fellow once, sir,
But heaven has married her to joys eternal;
'Twere sin to wish her in this vale again.
Come, sir: your friend and you shall see the pleasures
Which my health chiefly joys in.

ALSEMERO
I hear the beauty of this seat largely.

VERMANDERO
It falls much short of that. *Exeunt. Manet Beatrice*

BEATRICE So, here's one step
Into my father's favour. Time will fix him.
I have got him now the liberty of the house;
So wisdom by degrees works out her freedom,
And if that eye be darkened that offends me—
I wait but that eclipse—this gentleman

268 **bounden servant** obligated servant; compare 1 Corinthians 7:39, and 'bounden duty and service' (*Book of Common Prayer* (1559), Holy Communion). With a suggestion that Isabella considers herself under undeserved duress and constraint—where 'bounden' = imprisoned, fettered.
271 **nearly** tightly
276 **bespoke our pains** solicited our services
278 **fag** end, as in 'fag end'
280 **passage over** Alibius anticipates that the madmen and fools will 'pass over' a stage-like area.
282–6 **Could ... this** If we could perform this part of the revels with our madmen, presenting our show in a wild and distracted measure, even though this would be formless and disordering of Time itself it wouldn't matter, for it would all mend itself sooner or later.
284 **breaking Time's head** Alibius talks himself into a cuckold joke (a cuckold's head would be 'broken' by his horns), only to dismiss it.
287–8 **'Tis ... known** We've already started to make money with our madmen and fools; once our show is seen ('known'), we will make even more.
297 **staple** most valuable (said with irony by Isabella)
299–300 **Just ... thrive** Alibius responds to his wife's sarcasm by his own wry observation: we thrive by the aid of madmen and fools much as we see in the law courts ('Lawyer's Haven'—here ironic; a similar proverbial location was called 'Cuckold's Haven').
300 **we both** (*a*) both we and the lawyers (*b*) you and I (i.e. Alibius and Isabella)
3.4.3 **The fellow ... creature** a woman equal to Beatrice (Alsemero hides his desire for Beatrice by saying he would give anything for a woman just like her)
4 **I had her fellow once** Vermandero probably refers to Beatrice's (dead) mother.
6 **in this vale** i.e. on earth, in this 'vale of tears'
9 **seat** residence (often of a person of authority)
largely widely
10 ***Manet*** remains
11 **fix him** i.e. make Alsemero more permanent in
14 **that eye ... offends me** i.e. Alonzo's. Compare Matthew 18:9: 'And if thine eye offend thee, pluck it out, and cast it from thee'. Beatrice is offended by *another's* eye and plans to have it plucked out. With 'darkened', and 'eclipse' in the following line, 'eye' here has an astrological resonance: the sun or 'eye' of heaven, here to be eclipsed.

Shall soon shine glorious in my father's liking,
Through the refulgent virtue of my love.
Enter De Flores

DE FLORES [*aside*]
My thoughts are at a banquet for the deed.
I feel no weight in't; 'tis but light and cheap
For the sweet recompense that I set down for't.

BEATRICE
De Flores.

DE FLORES
Lady.

BEATRICE
Thy looks promise cheerfully.

DE FLORES All things are answerable: time,
Circumstance, your wishes, and my service.

BEATRICE
Is it done, then?

DE FLORES
Piracquo is no more.

BEATRICE
My joys start at mine eyes; our sweet'st delights
Are evermore born weeping.

DE FLORES
I've a token for you.

BEATRICE
For me?

DE FLORES
But it was sent somewhat unwillingly:
I could not get the ring without the finger.
[*He shows her the finger*]

BEATRICE Bless me! What hast thou done?

DE FLORES
Why, is that more than killing the whole man?
I cut his heart strings:
A greedy hand thrust in a dish at court
In a mistake hath had as much as this.

BEATRICE
'Tis the first token my father made me send him.

DE FLORES And I made him send it back again
For his last token; I was loath to leave it,
And I'm sure dead men have no use of jewels.
He was as loath to part with't, for it stuck
As if the flesh and it were both one substance.

BEATRICE
At the stag's fall the keeper has his fees;
'Tis soon applied: all dead men's fees are yours, sir.
I pray, bury the finger, but the stone
You may make use on shortly: the true value,
Take't of my truth, is near three hundred ducats.

DE FLORES
'Twill hardly buy a capcase for one's conscience, though,
To keep it from the worm, as fine as 'tis.
Well, being my fees I'll take it;
Great men have taught me that, or else my merit
Would scorn the way on't.

BEATRICE
It might justly, sir.
Why, thou mistak'st, De Flores: 'tis not given
In state of recompense.

DE FLORES
No, I hope so, lady:
You should soon witness my contempt to't then.

BEATRICE
Prithee, thou look'st as if thou wert offended.

DE FLORES
That were strange, lady: 'tis not possible
My service should draw such a cause from you.
Offended? Could you think so? That were much
For one of my performance, and so warm
Yet in my service.

BEATRICE
'Twere misery in me to give you cause, sir.

DE FLORES
I know so much, it were so: misery
In her most sharp condition.

BEATRICE
'Tis resolved then.
Look you, sir: here's three thousand golden florins;
[*She gives him money*]
I have not meanly thought upon thy merit.

17 **refulgent** bright, radiant
virtue This word continues the astrological metaphor of ll. 14–17, since 'virtue' can mean power, influence—here in an astrological sense. The irony of the word's moral inappropriateness to Beatrice's plan is no less apparent.

18 **are . . . deed** feast on the imagining of what I have done

20 **For** in comparison with
set down for't (*a*) set down in my imaginary account book as what I shall be paid for the murder (*b*) placed down as a wager

22 **answerable** correspondent, responsive to (Beatrice's) desire

25 **start at mine eyes** make me begin to weep

33 **at court** i.e. where, in a communal dish, it might be cut off by another hurried or greedy eater

41 **At the stag's fall . . . fees** proverbial: A traditional courtesy in hunting gave the gamekeeper the skin (and, often, horns) of a fallen stag.

42 **applied** brought to bear; compare 1.2.26, note

43 **stone** i.e. ring (by metonymy)

45 **three hundred ducats** The word 'ducat' could refer to many gold and silver coins. Here, perhaps, a good yearly income.

46–7 **a capcase for one's conscience . . . worm** a case, bag, box, or other receptacle—here 'coffin' is strongly suggested, hence 'worm' in the following line ('the worm of conscience' was proverbial). There may also be a pun on 'case of conscience', a matter or question on which one's conscience may be in doubt (see 'case' *OED sb.*[1] 7).

48–9 **Well . . . that** (*a*) I've learned that one must accept favours from aristocrats and seem to do so gratefully (*b*) 'Great men' have taught me, by their example, to take such unethical 'fees'.

49–50 **or else . . . on't** i.e. otherwise, my sense of self worth would reject this subservience

50 **It might justly** i.e. your merit is indeed real enough that you might show your true feeling about gifts

56 **cause** accusation, blame (*OED* 9; from Latin *causa*)

61–2 **I know . . . condition** (*a*) I believe what you're saying (i.e. it would cause misery indeed) (*b*) I know so much (to your discredit) that it would indeed mean 'misery' for you (i.e. were I to reveal it)

63 **three thousand golden florins** Like 'ducat', 'florin' could refer to one of many coins. This amount is probably meant to sound like much more than the value of the ring (compare 'golden').

DE FLORES
What, salary? Now you move me.
BEATRICE How, De Flores?
DE FLORES
Do you place me in the rank of verminous fellows
To destroy things for wages? Offer gold
For the life-blood of man? Is any thing
Valued too precious for my recompense?
BEATRICE
I understand thee not.
DE FLORES I could ha' hired
A journeyman in murder at this rate,
And mine own conscience might have lain at ease,
And have had the work brought home.
BEATRICE [*aside*] I'm in a labyrinth!
What will content him? I would fain be rid of him.—
I'll double the sum, sir.
DE FLORES You take a course
To double my vexation, that's the good you do.
BEATRICE [*aside*]
Bless me! I am now in worse plight than I was;
I know not what will please him!—For my fears' sake,
I prithee make away with all speed possible.
And if thou be'st so modest not to name
The sum that will content thee, paper blushes not:
Send thy demand in writing. It shall follow thee,
But prithee take thy flight.
DE FLORES You must fly too, then.
BEATRICE I?
DE FLORES
I'll not stir a foot else.
BEATRICE What's your meaning?
DE FLORES
Why, are not you as guilty, in, I'm sure,
As deep as I? And we should stick together.
Come, your fears counsel you but ill. My absence
Would draw suspèct upon you instantly;
There were no rescue for you.
BEATRICE [*aside*] He speaks home.
DE FLORES
Nor is it fit we two engaged so jointly
Should part and live asunder. [*He kisses her*]
BEATRICE How now, sir?
This shows not well.
DE FLORES What makes your lip so strange?
This must not be betwixt us.
BEATRICE [*aside*] The man talks wildly.
DE FLORES
Come, kiss me with a zeal now.
BEATRICE [*aside*] Heaven, I doubt him!
DE FLORES
I will not stand so long to beg 'em shortly.
BEATRICE
Take heed, De Flores, of forgetfulness;
'Twill soon betray us.
DE FLORES Take you heed first.
Faith, you're grown much forgetful; you're to blame
in't.
BEATRICE [*aside*]
He's bold, and I am blamed for't!
DE FLORES I have eased you
Of your trouble. Think on't: I'm in pain,
And must be eased of you. 'Tis a charity.
Justice invites your blood to understand me.
BEATRICE
I dare not.
DE FLORES Quickly!
BEATRICE O, I never shall!
Speak it yet further off, that I may lose
What has been spoken and no sound remain on't.
I would not hear so much offence again
For such another deed.
DE FLORES Soft, lady, soft:
The last is not yet paid for. O, this act
Has put me into spirit; I was as greedy on't
As the parched earth of moisture, when the clouds
weep.
Did you not mark? I wrought myself into't,
Nay, sued and kneeled for't: why was all that pains
took?
You see I have thrown contempt upon your gold:
Not that I want it not, for I do—piteously.
In order I will come unto't, and make use on't,
But 'twas not held so precious to begin with.
For I place wealth after the heels of pleasure;
And were I not resolved in my belief
That thy virginity were perfect in thee,
I should but take my recompense with grudging,
As if I had but half my hopes I agreed for.

71 **journeyman** workman for hire
73 **brought home** done (by an agent); here with a figurative sense, as in thrusting 'home' a sharp object. See note at l. 90.
78 **For... sake** on account of my fears (i.e. of what may happen when the murder is discovered)
90 **home** to the point (painfully so)
91 **engaged... jointly** brought together in collaboration (with a compelling undertone of erotic engagement)
93 **strange** distant, cold, unfriendly (*OED a.* 11)
95 **doubt him** (*a*) fear him (*b*) am apprehensive about his motives
96 **I... so long** i.e. I will not wait so long (with pun on sexual sense of 'stand'; compare 3.3.146, note).
'em i.e. kisses
97 **forgetfulness** i.e. of (*a*) propriety (*b*) the difference between our ranks
99 **forgetful** i.e. of what you've had me do
100 **I... for't** i.e. He is the one who's forward, yet I am blamed.
103 **blood** supposed seat of the emotions and passions
108–9 **Soft... for** ironic: slow down, we've yet to settle for the last murder I committed.
110 **put me into spirit** excited me; probably sexual excitement
112 **wrought myself into't** (*a*) worked my way into position to perform the act ('work' *OED v.* 33b) (*b*) fashioned myself into your instrument (*OED v.* 3)
116 **In order** in proper sequence (according to rank, importance, etc.; *OED sb.* 27)

BEATRICE
Why, 'tis impossible thou canst be so wicked,
Or shelter such a cunning cruelty;
To make his death the murderer of my honour!
Thy language is so bold and vicïous
I cannot see which way I can forgive it
With any modesty.

DE FLORES Push! You forget yourself.
A woman dipped in blood, and talk of modesty?

BEATRICE
O misery of sin! Would I had been bound
Perpetually unto my living hate
In that Piracquo than to hear these words.
Think but upon the distance that creation
Set 'twixt thy blood and mine, and keep thee there.

DE FLORES
Look but into your conscience; read me there.
'Tis a true book; you'll find me there your equal.
Push! Fly not to your birth, but settle you
In what the act has made you. You're no more now;
You must forget your parentage to me.
You're the deed's creature; by that name you lost
Your first condition, and I challenge you,
As peace and innocency has turned you out,
And made you one with me.

BEATRICE With thee, foul villain?

DE FLORES Yes, my fair murd'ress. Do you urge me?
Though thou writ'st 'maid', thou whore in thy
affection,
'Twas changed from thy first love, and that's a kind
Of whoredom in thy heart; and he's changed now,
To bring thy second on, thy Alsemero,
Whom (by all sweets that ever darkness tasted),
If I enjoy thee not, thou ne'er enjoy'st.
I'll blast the hopes and joys of marrïage.
I'll confess all; my life I rate at nothing.

BEATRICE De Flores!—

DE FLORES [*aside*]
I shall rest from all lovers' plagues then;
I live in pain now: that shooting eye
Will burn my heart to cinders.

BEATRICE O sir, hear me!

DE FLORES
She that in life and love refuses me,
In death and shame my partner she shall be.

BEATRICE
Stay, hear me once for all. [*She kneels, weeping*] I make
thee master
Of all the wealth I have in gold and jewels;
Let me go poor unto my bed with honour,
And I am rich in all things.

DE FLORES Let this silence thee:
The wealth of all Valencia shall not buy
My pleasure from me.
Can you weep fate from its determined purpose?
So soon may you weep me.

BEATRICE [*aside*] Vengeance begins;
Murder, I see, is followed by more sins.
Was my creation in the womb so cursed,
It must engender with a viper first?

DE FLORES
Come, rise, and shroud your blushes in my bosom;
[*Beatrice rises*]
Silence is one of pleasure's best receipts:
Thy peace is wrought for ever in this yielding.
'Las, how the turtle pants! Thou'lt love anon
What thou so fear'st and faint'st to venture on.

Exeunt

Finis Actus Tertius

Incipit Actus Quartus 4.1
[*Dumb Show*]
Enter Gentlemen, Vermandero meeting them with action of wonderment at the flight of Piracquo. Enter Alsemero, with Jasperino and Gallants; Vermandero points to him, the Gentlemen seeming to applaud the choice. [*Exeunt in procession Vermandero,*] *Alsemero, Jasperino, and Gentlemen,* [*Gallants*]*; Beatrice the bride following in great state, accompanied with Diaphanta, Isabella, and other Gentlewomen; De Flores after all, smiling at the accident. Alonzo's ghost appears to De Flores*

125 **honour** chastity, reputation
128 **Push** an interjection preferred by Middleton
133 **creation** (*a*) Nature (*b*) God (compare 2.2.108)
139 **parentage** family, birth, rank
to me (*a*) with me, in your new relation to me, when you talk to me (*b*) in favour of
140 **the deed's creature** what the deed has made you
141 **Your first condition** original innocence
141–3 **I challenge... one with me** I lay claim to you, inasmuch as peace and innocence have abandoned you, leaving you my partner (see 'challenge' *OED v.* 5).
143 **one with me** like me; also: my partner
144 **urge** provoke (*OED v.* 7)
145 **affection** lust, inclination
146 **'Twas changed** your affection changed
147 **he's changed now** Alonzo's now dead (changed from life to death, and exchanged for Alsemero).
149 **by all sweets... tasted** i.e. by all the acts of lust ever performed at night
151 **blast** ruin, destroy
155 **shooting eye** i.e. Beatrice's; see note to 3.3.82
159–62 **I make... things** Holdsworth points out the echoes here of 2 Corinthians 6:8–10.
167 **Murder... sins** proverbial: '(Every) sin brings in another' (Dent S467.1)
168 **my creation** the act of my begetting
cursed (*a*) wicked (*b*) put under God's curse (i.e. 'cursed')
169 **It... first** i.e. that I must sleep first with a snake like De Flores (before doing so with a man)
170 **shroud** conceal
171 **receipts** (*a*) results (*b*) rewards
173 **turtle** turtle-dove (an emblem of perfect love and constancy—with irony here)
4.1.0.2 *Dumb Show* a unit of silent ('dumb') movement and activity on stage, often encapsulating events for which dialogue was redundant and otherwise undramatic
0.12 **accident** scene, event

in the midst of his smile, startles him, showing him the hand whose finger he had cut off. They pass over in great solemnity [*and so exeunt*]

Enter Beatrice

BEATRICE

This fellow has undone me endlessly;
Never was bride so fearfully distressed.
The more I think upon th'ensuing night,
And whom I am to cope with in embraces—
One that's ennobled both in blood and mind,
So clear in understanding (that's my plague now),
Before whose judgement will my fault appear
Like malefactors' crimes before tribunals,
There is no hiding on't—the more I dive
Into my own distress. How a wise man
Stands for a great calamity! There's no venturing
Into his bed, what course soe'er I light upon,
Without my shame, which may grow up to danger.
He cannot but in justice strangle me
As I lie by him—as a cheater use me.
'Tis a precious craft to play with a false die
Before a cunning gamester. Here's his closet,
The key left in't, and he abroad i'th' park.
Sure 'twas forgot. I'll be so bold as look in't.
[*She unlocks the closet*]
Bless me! A right physician's closet 'tis,
Set round with phials—every one her mark too.
Sure he does practise physic for his own use,
Which may be safely called your great man's wisdom.
What manuscript lies here? 'The Book of Experiment,
Called *Secrets in Nature*'. [*She reads*] So 'tis, 'tis so:
'How to know whether a woman be with child or no.'
I hope I am not yet. If he should try, though!
Let me see. 'Folio forty-five.' Here 'tis,
The leaf tucked down upon't, the place suspicious:
'If you would know whether a woman be with child or not, give her two spoonfuls of the white water in Glass C—'
Where's that Glass C? O, yonder I see't now.
'—and if she be with child, she sleeps full twelve hours after; if not, not.'
None of that water comes into my belly!
I'll know you from a hundred. I could break you now,
Or turn you into milk, and so beguile
The master of the mystery, but I'll look to you.
Ha! That which is next is ten times worse:
'How to know whether a woman be a maid or not.'
If that should be applied, what would become of me?
Belike he has a strong faith of my purity,
That never yet made proof; but this he calls
'A merry sleight, but true experiment,
The author Antonius Mizaldus':
'Give the party you suspect the quantity of a spoonful of the water in the Glass M, which—upon her that is a maid—makes three several effects: 'twill make her incontinently gape, then fall into a sudden sneezing, last into a violent laughing, else dull, heavy, and lumpish.'
Where had I been?
I fear it, yet 'tis seven hours to bed-time.

Enter Diaphanta

DIAPHANTA

Cuds, madam; are you here?

BEATRICE [*aside*] Seeing that wench now,
A trick comes in my mind—'Tis a nice piece
Gold cannot purchase.—I come hither, wench,
To look my lord.

DIAPHANTA [*aside*]

Would I had such a cause to look him, too!—
Why, he's i'th' park, madam.

BEATRICE There let him be.

1 **fellow** (*a*) man of low rank—a meaning she has called on thrice before to describe him: 1.1.114, 2.1.52–3, 2.1.90; (*b*) counterpart, twin, double—an unintended meaning, but prepared for by De Flores (2.1.86, 2.2.13), Alsemero (3.4.3), and Vermandero (3.4.4).
undone ruined; with a sense here as well (from 'endlessly') of 'sexually exhausted'
4 **cope with** (*a*) contend with (*b*) couple, copulate with
5–7 **mind . . . understanding . . . judgement** (Beatrice's first line to Alsemero described him as a 'scholar', 1.1.64.)
11 **Stands for** represents—here 'threatens me with (a calamity)'
15 **As . . . me** treat me as a cheater on my vows
lie by (*a*) tell an untruth; and (*b*) recline next to. Middleton often puns on 'lie by': compare 1.2.30, 5.1.1 and notes.
21 **her** its
23 **Which . . . wisdom** i.e. because it gives him advantages (as the following experiments hint)
24 **The Book of Experiment** probably Alsemero's personal title for his 'book'—evidently either a commonplace book containing transcriptions of various 'experiments', or verbatim transcript of the book mentioned next
25 ***Secrets in Nature*** Antoine Mizauld (Antonius Mizaldus), l. 46, wrote a book of this title (*De Arcanis Naturae*), which has chastity tests; an experiment similar to this one can also be found in his *Centuriae IX. Memorbilium* (1566/1613).
28 **Folio** leaf (Beatrice is reading a table of contents)
31 **Glass** phial
36 **water . . . into my belly** (*a*) I'll avoid drinking that (*b*) an (unconscious) semen joke set up by 'white water' in l. 31; see also 2.2.83, note
38 **turn you into milk** i.e. replace you with (harmless) milk
39 **master of the mystery** expert of the science, craft
look to watch out for
43 **Belike** probably, possibly
44 **That . . . proof** (*a*) (reading 'That' as 'he') who has not yet tested my virginity (*b*) (reading 'That' as 'purity') which has not passed any of the tests it has already been put to
45 **sleight** trick, device
50 **incontinently** immediately
gape yawn, or stare with an open-mouth
51 **else** then, after that
52 **Where had I been?** what trouble would I have been in (had I not seen this)?
54 **Cuds** a mild oath (a periphrasis for 'God's')
here i.e. in Alsemero's chamber before the wedding
55 **piece** i.e. Diaphanta, where 'nice piece' could mean (*a*) scrupulous woman, or (*b*) good-looking wench (i.e. 'piece' = piece of flesh)
56 **Gold . . . purchase** Compare the proverb 'Money will do anything' (Tilley M1084).
57 **look** seek, search for

DIAPHANTA
Ay, madam, let him compass
Whole parks and forests, as great rangers do;
At roosting time a little lodge can hold 'em.
(*Sings*) Earth-conquering Alexander,
That thought the world too narrow for him,
In the end had but his pit-hole.
BEATRICE
I fear thou art not modest, Diaphanta.
DIAPHANTA
Your thoughts are so unwilling to be known, madam;
'Tis ever the bride's fashion towards bed-time
To set light by her joys, as if she owed 'em not.
BEATRICE
Her joys? Her fears, thou wouldst say.
DIAPHANTA Fear of what?
BEATRICE
Art thou a maid, and talkst so to a maid?
You leave a blushing business behind:
Beshrew your heart for't.
DIAPHANTA Do you mean good sooth, madam?
BEATRICE
Well, if I'd thought upon the fear at first,
Man should have been unknown.
DIAPHANTA Is't possible?
BEATRICE
I will give a thousand ducats to that woman
Would try what my fear were, and tell me true
Tomorrow, when she gets from't. As she likes
I might perhaps be drawn to't.
DIAPHANTA Are you in earnest?
BEATRICE
Do you get the woman, then challenge me,
And see if I'll fly from't. But I must tell you
This, by the way: she must be a true maid,
Else there's no trial; my fears are not hers else.
DIAPHANTA
Nay, she that I would put into your hands, madam,
Shall be a maid.
BEATRICE You know I should be shamed else,
Because she lies for me.
DIAPHANTA [*aside*] 'Tis a strange humour.—
But are you serious still? Would you resign
Your first night's pleasure, and give money too?
BEATRICE
As willingly as live. [*Aside*] Alas, the gold
Is but a by-bet to wedge in the honour.
DIAPHANTA [*aside*]
I do not know how the world goes abroad
For faith or honesty: there's both required in this.—
Madam, what say you to me, and stray no further?
I've a good mind, in troth, to earn your money.
BEATRICE You're too quick, I fear, to be a maid.
DIAPHANTA
How? Not a maid? Nay, then you urge me, madam:
Your honourable self is not a truer
With all your fears upon you—
BEATRICE [*aside*] Bad enough then!
DIAPHANTA
—than I with all my lightsome joys about me.
BEATRICE
I'm glad to hear't, then. You dare put your honesty
Upon an easy trial?
DIAPHANTA Easy? Anything!
BEATRICE
I'll come to you straight. [*She crosses to the closet*]
DIAPHANTA [*aside*] She will not search me, will she,
Like the forewoman of a female jury?
BEATRICE [*aside*]
Glass M. Ay, this is it.—Look, Diaphanta:
You take no worse than I do. [*She drinks*]
DIAPHANTA And in so doing
I will not question what 'tis, but take it. [*She drinks*]
BEATRICE [*aside*] Now if the experiment be true,
'Twill praise itself, and give me noble ease—[*Diaphanta yawns*]
Begins already: there's the first symptom,
And what haste it makes to fall into the second—
[*Diaphanta sneezes*]
There by this time! Most admirable secret!

61 **rangers** those who range
62 **roosting time** bedtime, lodging time
little lodge small cabin (with 'vagina' strongly suggested)
65 **pit-hole** grave, with innuendo on 'sexual orifice'
66 **modest** chaste, virginal
67 **Your ... known** perhaps you're not being entirely candid with yourself about love
69 **set light by** make light of
owed 'em not were not responsible for them ('owed' = 'owned')
71 **maid** virgin
73 **Beshrew** shame (a mild rebuke)
Do you mean good sooth are you in earnest
75 **Man ... unknown** I would never have become engaged (with ironic subtext, perhaps intended by Beatrice: she has already 'known' De Flores)
78 **gets from't** finishes it
80 **Do you ... me** go ahead and find a woman willing to do this, then try me
84 **she** Diaphanta means herself
86 **lies for** (*a*) lies down in place of (*b*) performs an untruthful action for. Compare 'lie by' and 4.1.15, note.
humour turn of mood
90 **by-bet** side bet
wedge in solidify, confirm
91 **the world ... abroad** the common run of behaviour
95 **quick** eager, with pun on 'quick' = pregnant
96 **urge me** press, push me (to speak)
98 **Bad enough then** i.e. that comparison is bad enough
99 **lightsome** frivolous, flirtatious
100 **honesty** chastity
102 **search** examination—including a gynecological search as might be performed by a female 'forewoman' in a criminal case (l. 103). Such a search was performed in the divorce case of Frances Howard in 1613; claiming non-consummation of the marriage, she was subsequently examined physically for her virginity by a group of sixteen matrons and noblewomen.
106 **I will not ... take it** compare the proverb 'Maids say nay and take it' (Dent M34)
108 **noble** splendid, with a sense of the dignity which her falsely-confirmed virginity will restore to her

On the contrary, it stirs not me a whit,
Which most concerns it.

DIAPHANTA
Ha, ha, ha!

BEATRICE [*aside*]
Just in all things, and in order,
As if 'twere circumscribed; one accident
Gives way unto another.

DIAPHANTA
Ha, ha, ha!

BEATRICE
How now, wench?

DIAPHANTA
Ha, ha, ha! I am so—so light at heart—Ha, ha, ha!—so pleasurable!
But one swig more, sweet madam!

BEATRICE
Ay, tomorrow;
We shall have time to sit by't.

DIAPHANTA
Now I'm sad again.

BEATRICE [*aside*]
It lays itself so gently too.—Come, wench,
Most honest Diaphanta I dare call thee now.

DIAPHANTA
Pray tell me, madam, what trick call you this?

BEATRICE I'll tell thee all hereafter. We must
Study the carriage of this business.

DIAPHANTA
I shall carry't well, because I love the burden.

BEATRICE
About midnight you must not fail to steal forth gently,
That I may use the place.

DIAPHANTA
O fear not, madam:
I shall be cool by that time. [*Aside*] The bride's place,
And with a thousand ducats! I'm for a justice now;
I bring a portion with me. I scorn small fools.

Exeunt

4.2 *Enter Vermandero and Servant*

VERMANDERO
I tell thee knave, mine honour is in question—
A thing till now free from suspicïon—
Nor ever was there cause.
Who of my gentlemen are absent?
Tell me and truly how many, and who.

SERVANT Antonio, sir, and Franciscus.

VERMANDERO
When did they leave the castle?

SERVANT
Some ten days since, sir—
The one intending to Briamata,
Th'other for Valencia.

VERMANDERO
The time accuses 'em; a charge of murder
Is brought within my castle gate: Piracquo's murder.
I dare not answer faithfully their absence;
A strict command of apprehensïon
Shall pursue 'em suddenly, and either wipe
The stain off clear, or openly discover it.
Provide me wingèd warrants for the purpose.

Exit Servant [*one way, at another*] *enter Tomazo*

See, I am set on again.

TOMAZO
I claim a brother of you.

VERMANDERO
You're too hot;
Seek him not here.

TOMAZO
Yes, 'mongst your dearest bloods,
If my peace find no fairer satisfaction;
This is the place must yield account for him,
For here I left him, and the hasty tie
Of this snatched marriage gives strong testimony
Of his most certain ruin.

VERMANDERO
Certain falsehood!
This is the place indeed. His breach of faith
Has too much marred both my abusèd love—
The honourable love I reserved for him—
And mocked my daughter's joy. The prepared morning
Blushed at his infidelity. He left
Contempt and scorn to throw upon those friends
Whose belief hurt 'em. O, 'twas most ignoble
To take his flight so unexpectedly,
And throw such public wrongs on those that loved him.

TOMAZO
Then this is all your answer?

113 **Which most concerns it** whom it most concerns
114 **Just** correct
115 **circumscribed** pre-ordained, bound to this exact order
accident incident; here 'symptom'
119 **sit by't** spend as much time with it as we desire
120 **lays itself** allays, subsides
121 **honest** chaste
125 **carry't well** (*a*) carry off the business successfully (*b*) bear the weight ('burden', l. 125) of Alsemero
127 **use** assume, get into
128 **cool** i.e. sexually spent
129 **for a justice** i.e. wealthy enough to marry a judge
130 **portion** marriage portion, dowry
small fools (*a*) socially inferior men (*b*) men less foolish than judges (compare 1.2.134 above, and note)
4.2.8 **Briamata** In this play's source, Briamata is a house ten leagues from Alicante.
12 **answer faithfully** account trustfully for
13 **command of apprehensïon** order for their arrest
15 **discover** reveal
17 **set on again** harassed once more (a metaphor from animal baiting; compare 2.1.81–2 above, and notes)
19 **bloods** relatives, or young men (also, with the following lines, 'the blood your family and you will shed')
20 **peace** i.e. peace of mind
satisfaction a technical term, meaning recompense for the dishonour I have received
23 **snatched** overly hasty. Tomazo is a type of the avenger in the Elizabethan revenge play. See *Hamlet* 1.2.177–80.
24 **Certain falsehood** i.e. that of Alonzo de Piracquo (whom Vermandero believes has voluntarily absconded from the castle)
28 **prepared morning** morning appointed for the wedding ceremony
29 **Blushed** with play on the natural 'blush' of sunrise
31 **Whose . . . 'em** who were hurt by trusting him too much

VERMANDERO 'Tis too fair
For one of his alliance; and I warn you
That this place no more see you.
Exit Vermandero one way, at another enter De Flores

TOMAZO [*aside*] The best is,
There is more ground to meet a man's revenge on.—
Honest De Flores!

DE FLORES That's my name indeed.
Saw you the bride? Good sweet sir, which way took
she?

TOMAZO
I have blessed mine eyes from seeing such a false one.

DE FLORES [*aside*]
I'd fain get off; this man's not for my company.
I smell his brother's blood when I come near him.

TOMAZO
Come hither, kind and true one. I remember
My brother loved thee well.

DE FLORES O purely, dear sir.
[*Aside*] Methinks I am now again a-killing on him;
He brings it so fresh to me.

TOMAZO Thou canst guess, sirrah
(One honest friend has an instinct of jealousy)
At some foul guilty person?

DE FLORES 'Las, sir:
I am so charitable, I think none
Worse than myself—You did not see the bride, then?

TOMAZO
I prithee name her not. Is she not wicked?

DE FLORES
No, no, a pretty, easy, round-packed sinner,
As your most ladies are, else you might think
I flattered her; but sir, at no hand wicked,
Till they're so old their chins and noses meet,
And they salute witches. I am called, I think, sir.
[*Aside*] His company e'en o'erlays my conscience.
Exit

TOMAZO
That De Flores has a wondrous honest heart;
He'll bring it out in time, I'm assured on't.
O, here's the glorious master of the day's joy.
'Twill not be long till he and I do reckon.
Enter Alsemero
Sir!

ALSEMERO
You are most welcome.

TOMAZO You may call that word back:
I do not think I am, nor wish to be.

ALSEMERO
'Tis strange you found the way to this house then.

TOMAZO [*aside*]
Would I'd ne'er known the cause!—I'm none of
those, sir,
That come to give you joy, and swill your wine:
'Tis a more precious liquor that must lay
The fiery thirst I bring.

ALSEMERO Your words and you
Appear to me great strangers.

TOMAZO Time and our swords
May make us more acquainted. This the business:
I should have a brother in your place.
How treachery and malice have disposed of him,
I'm bound to enquire of him which holds his right,
Which never could come fairly.

ALSEMERO You must look
To answer for that word, sir.

TOMAZO Fear you not;
I'll have it ready drawn at our next meeting.
Keep your day solemn. Farewell; I disturb it not.
I'll bear the smart with patience for a time. *Exit*

ALSEMERO
'Tis somewhat ominous this, a quarrel entered
Upon this day. My innocence relieves me,
Enter Jasperino
I should be wondrous sad else.—Jasperino!
I have news to tell thee, strange news.

JASPERINO I ha' some too,
I think as strange as yours; would I might keep

35 **alliance** family
37 **There...on** (*a*) this insult I've just received gives further grounds to justify my revenge (*b*) there are other places ('more ground') where I can exact my vengeance
38 **Honest** at this time, a word of multiple meanings and resonances—compare 'honest Iago' in *Othello*
40 **I have...one** I have prayed that my eyes might be prevented from seeing one so false as Beatrice.
47 **jealousy** suspicion, apprehension
49–50 **I...myself** De Flores's speech is laden with ironic meaning.
52 **easy** easily persuaded, tractable; with hint of sexual availability
round-packed sinner one who is surrounded ('round-packed') by sin; with suggestion also of 'voluptuously shaped sinner'
53 **your most** most of your
55–6 **Till...salute witches** De Flores describes toothless old crones who (*a*) hail or (*b*) bring bad luck to ('salute') witches by kiss, word, other physical gesture, or merely their presence—perhaps just from the growing together of their 'chins and noses'.
57 **o'erlays** lays heavy upon, oppresses
59 **bring it out** (*a*) reveal the truth (compare 5.3.98–9) (*b*) reveal the contents of his heart
60 **the glorious...joy** i.e. the bridegroom (ironic: it is the wedding day of Beatrice and Alsemero)
61 **reckon** come to an accounting of or understanding about (i.e. through a duel) what Alsemero has done
65 **the cause** the reason he has found his way to this house (i.e. his brother's disappearance)
67 **precious liquor** i.e. (Alsemero's) blood
68–9 **Your...strangers** (*a*) I have neither seen you before nor know what you mean (*b*) what you are saying appears unsuited to your rank
73 **which holds his right** who has usurped his place, what is rightfully his
74 **Which...fairly** which could never have been achieved legitimately, justly
76 **I'll...drawn** (*a*) I'll have the contract between us drawn up (*b*) I'll have my sword out of its sheath
77 **solemn** ceremoniously (hence undisturbed)
79 **ominous** continuing the superstition with which Alsemero began the play: compare 1.1.2

Mine, so my faith and friendship might be kept in't!
Faith sir, dispense a little with my zeal
And let it cool in this.

ALSEMERO
This puts me on,
And blames thee for thy slowness.

JASPERINO
All may prove nothing;
Only a friendly fear that leapt from me, sir.

ALSEMERO
No question it may prove nothing: let's partake it
though.

JASPERINO
'Twas Diaphanta's chance—for to that wench
I pretend honest love, and she deserves it—
To leave me in a back part of the house,
A place we chose for private conference.
She was no sooner gone, but instantly
I heard your bride's voice in the next room to me;
And, lending more attention, found De Flores
Louder than she.

ALSEMERO
De Flores? Thou art out now.

JASPERINO
You'll tell me more anon.

ALSEMERO
Still, I'll prevent thee:
The very sight of him is poison to her.

JASPERINO
That made me stagger too, but Diaphanta
At her return confirmed it.

ALSEMERO
Diaphanta!

JASPERINO
Then fell we both to listen, and words passed
Like those that challenge interest in a woman.

ALSEMERO
Peace! Quench thy zeal! 'Tis dangerous to thy bosom.

JASPERINO
Then truth is full of peril.

ALSEMERO
Such truths are.—
O, were she the sole glory of the earth,
Had eyes that could shoot fire into kings' breasts,
And touched, she sleeps not here! Yet I have time,
Though night be near, to be resolved hereof;
And prithee do not weigh me by my passions.

JASPERINO
I never weighed friend so.

ALSEMERO
Done charitably. [*He gives a key*]
That key will lead thee to a pretty secret,
By a Chaldean taught me, and I've spent
My study upon some. Bring from my closet
A glass inscribed there with the letter M,
And question not my purpose.

JASPERINO
It shall be done, sir.
Exit

ALSEMERO
How can this hang together? Not an hour since,
Her woman came pleading her lady's fears,
Delivered her for the most timorous virgin
That ever shrunk at man's name, and so modest,
She charged her weep out her request to me,
That she might come obscurely to my bosom.

Enter Beatrice

BEATRICE [*aside*]
All things go well. My woman's preparing yonder
For her sweet voyage, which grieves me to lose.
Necessity compels it: I lose all else.

ALSEMERO [*aside*]
Push! Modesty's shrine is set in yonder forehead.
I cannot be too sure, though.—My Joanna!

BEATRICE
Sir, I was bold to weep a message to you;
Pardon my modest fears.

ALSEMERO [*aside*]
The dove's not meeker:
She's abused, questionless.—

Enter Jasperino [*with phial*]

O, are you come, sir?

BEATRICE [*aside*]
The glass, upon my life! I see the letter.

JASPERINO
Sir, this is M.

ALSEMERO
'Tis it.

BEATRICE [*aside*]
I am suspected.

84 **so** provided
85 **dispense a little with** pardon
86 **in** i.e. in light of
puts me on whets me on
89 **No question ... though** certainly it will turn out to be nothing—yet let's hear it. (Alsemero's asperity shows his resistance to what he senses Jasperino is about to tell him.)
91 **pretend** make, offer (with no sense of deception or falsity)
97 **out** wide of the mark
98 **You'll ... anon** you'll be even more angry when you hear fully what I have to tell
prevent anticipate (and thus forestall)
100 **stagger** (*a*) to reel, totter (*b*) to begin to doubt or waver in opinion, to become less confident or determined (*OED v.* 2).
103 **challenge interest** (*a*) lay claim to (i.e. De Flores's words lay a claim of his own to Beatrice; compare *OED v.* 5, and 3.4.141 above) (*b*) call in question, dispute (the words disputed Alsemero's claim to (his 'interest' in) Beatrice; compare *OED v.* 4). The effect of both readings is the same.
104 **'Tis ... bosom** i.e. you're risking death for speaking such slander
105 **Then ... are** Jasperino stoically says that the truth is to be told no matter what the personal risk. Alsemero answers angrily that 'truths' like this are dangerous because they are lies.
108 **touched** tainted, corrupted
110 **weigh me by my passions** judge my value as a man by my passionate outbursts
111 **Done** (you have) acted
113 **Chaldean** here an epithet for one especially learned in the quasi-scientific experiments which Alsemero admires; in Daniel 2:2 ff., used as an occupational description alongside 'magicians', 'astrologers', and 'sorcerers'
114 **some** i.e. secrets
119 **Delivered her for** represented her as
121 **charged her** commanded Diaphanta to
122 **she** i.e. Beatrice
obscurely in darkness (Beatrice has by this time arranged for the 'bed-trick')
128 **I ... you** I earlier sent a tearful message to you (via Diaphanta; compare ll. 117–22)
131 **the letter** i.e. M

ALSEMERO
How fitly our bride comes to partake with us!
[*He offers a glass*]

BEATRICE
What is't, my lord?

ALSEMERO
No hurt.

BEATRICE
Sir, pardon me:
I seldom taste of any composition.

ALSEMERO
But this, upon my warrant, you shall venture on.
[*He gives her the glass*]

BEATRICE
I fear 'twill make me ill.

ALSEMERO
Heaven forbid that.

BEATRICE [*aside*]
I'm put now to my cunning; th'effects I know,
If I can now but feign 'em handsomely. [*She drinks*]

ALSEMERO [*aside to Jasperino*]
It has that secret virtue it ne'er missed, sir,
Upon a virgin.

JASPERINO
Treble-qualitied?
[*Beatrice gapes, then sneezes*]

ALSEMERO
By all that's virtuous, it takes there, proceeds!

JASPERINO
This is the strangest trick to know a maid by.

BEATRICE Ha, ha, ha!
You have given me joy of heart to drink, my lord.

ALSEMERO
No, thou hast given me such joy of heart,
That never can be blasted.

BEATRICE
What's the matter, sir?

ALSEMERO [*to Jasperino*]
See, now 'tis settled in a melancholy;
Keeps both the time and method. [*He crosses to Beatrice*] My Joanna:
Chaste as the breath of heaven, or morning's womb,
That brings the day forth; thus my love encloses thee.
[*He embraces her, and*] *Exeunt*

4.3

Enter Isabella [*with a letter,*] *and Lollio*

ISABELLA [*aside, as she reads*]
O heaven! Is this the waning moon?
Does love turn fool, run mad, and all at once?—
Sirrah, here's a madman, akin to the fool too—
A lunatic lover.

LOLLIO No, no, not he I brought the letter from.

ISABELLA [*giving letter*]
Compare his inside with his out, and tell me.

LOLLIO The out's mad, I'm sure of that; I had a taste on't. [*He reads*] 'To the bright Andromeda, chief chambermaid to the Knight of the Sun, at the sign of Scorpio, in the middle region, sent by the bellows-mender of Aeolus. Pay the post.' This is stark madness.

ISABELLA Now, mark the inside.
[*She takes the letter from Lollio and reads*]
'Sweet lady, having now cast off this counterfeit cover of a madman, I appear to your best judgement a true and faithful lover of your beauty.'

LOLLIO He is mad still.

ISABELLA 'If any fault you find, chide those perfections in you, which have made me imperfect: 'tis the same sun that causeth to grow, and enforceth to wither—'

LOLLIO O rogue!

ISABELLA '—shapes and trans-shapes, destroys and builds again. I come in winter to you dismantled of my proper ornaments; by the sweet splendour of your cheerful smiles, I spring and live a lover.'

LOLLIO Mad rascal still!

ISABELLA 'Tread him not under foot that shall appear an honour to your bounties. I remain mad till I speak with you, from whom I expect my cure. Yours all, or one beside himself, Franciscus.'

LOLLIO You are like to have a fine time on't. My master and I may give over our professions; I do not think but you can cure fools and madmen faster than we—with little pains too.

ISABELLA Very likely.

134 **What is't** i.e. what is this you'd have me drink?
135 **composition** compound, such as medicine or drink
140 **It has . . . missed** it has so secret a property or power ('virtue') that it has never failed
141 **Treble-qualitied?** with three effects?
142 **virtuous** (*a*) efficacious (*b*) chaste
149 **time and method** pace and quality (of the drink's effects)
4.3.1 **waning moon** Isabella may mean that the 'lunatic' (l. 4) activity in the hospital changes with time (i.e. the more she learns about it), even as the moon does when it wanes.
3 **here's** referring to Franciscus within, as author of this letter
6 **inside . . . out** (*a*) what it says on the outside of the envelope in contrast to what the letter itself says (*b*) his appearance and behaviour versus his real self
7 **out's** outside (indicating the name and superscription) is
8–11 **Andromeda . . . Aeolus** more of Franciscus's classical references, perhaps made superficially meaningless to prevent Lollio from reading the inside
8 **Andromeda** in mythology, the beloved of Perseus, who rescued her from the rock to which she had been bound as sacrifice to a sea monster
9 **Scorpio** a sign of the zodiac, governing the genitals
10 **middle region** astronomically, the region governing the year's middle months, but with bawdy quibble on the 'middle region' of the body = the genital area
10–11 **bellows-mender of Aeolus** In mythology, Aeolus was god of the winds; following 'middle region', 'bellows-mender' may be a bawdy quibble, gathering both 'bellies' and 'billows' (compare ll. 121–2 and note).
11 **Pay the post** i.e. 'postage due'; a deliberately bathetic close to the salutation
21 **trans-shapes** metamorphoses
22 **dismantled** stripped
24 **spring** grow, with pun on the season (compare 'in winter', l. 22)

LOLLIO One thing I must tell you, mistress: you perceive that I am privy to your skill. If I find you minister once and set up the trade, I put in for my thirds. I shall be mad or fool else.

ISABELLA
The first place is thine, believe it, Lollio,
If I do fall—

LOLLIO I fall upon you.

ISABELLA So.

LOLLIO Well, I stand to my venture.

ISABELLA
But thy counsel now: how shall I deal with 'em?

LOLLIO Why, do you mean to deal with 'em?

ISABELLA
Nay, the fair understanding: how to use 'em.

LOLLIO Abuse 'em! That's the way to mad the fool, and make a fool of the madman, and then you use 'em kindly.

ISABELLA
'Tis easy: I'll practise. Do thou observe it;
The key of thy wardrobe.

LOLLIO There, fit yourself for 'em, and I'll fit 'em both for you. [*He gives a key*]

ISABELLA
Take thou no further notice than the outside. *Exit*

LOLLIO [*after her*] Not an inch. I'll put you to the inside.

Enter Alibius

ALIBIUS
Lollio, art there? Will all be perfect, think'st thou?
Tomorrow night, as if to close up the solemnity,
Vermandero expects us.

LOLLIO I mistrust the madmen most; the fools will do well enough: I have taken pains with them.

ALIBIUS
Tush, they cannot miss; the more absurdity,
The more commends it, so no rough behaviours
Affright the ladies; they are nice things, thou know'st.

LOLLIO You need not fear, sir; so long as we are there with our commanding pizzles, they'll be as tame as the ladies themselves.

ALIBIUS
I will see them once more rehearse before they go.

LOLLIO I was about it, sir: look you to the madmen's morris, and let me alone with the other; there is one or two that I mistrust their fooling. I'll instruct them, and then they shall rehearse the whole measure.

ALIBIUS
Do, do; I'll see the music prepared. But Lollio—
By the way, how does my wife brook her restraint?
Does she not grudge at it?

LOLLIO So so. She takes some pleasure in the house, she would abroad else. You must allow her a little more length: she's kept too short.

ALIBIUS
She shall along to Vermandero's with us;
That will serve her for a month's liberty.

LOLLIO What's that on your face, sir?

ALIBIUS
Where, Lollio? I see nothing.

LOLLIO Cry you mercy, sir: 'tis your nose; it showed like the trunk of a young elephant.

ALIBIUS
Away, rascal! I'll prepare the music, Lollio. *Exit*

LOLLIO Do, sir, and I'll dance the whilst. Tony, where art thou, Tony?

Enter Antonio

ANTONIO Here, cousin; where art thou?

LOLLIO Come, Tony: the footmanship I taught you.

ANTONIO I had rather ride, cousin.

LOLLIO Ay, a whip take you; but I'll keep you out. Vault in; look you, Tony: [*He sings and dances*] fa, la, la, la, la.

ANTONIO [*imitating him*] Fa, la, la, la, la.

LOLLIO There, an honour.

ANTONIO Is this an honour, coz? [*He bows*]

36 **I am privy to** (*a*) I recognize (*b*) I share

36–7 **If . . . thirds** Lollio says, literally, that if Isabella ever sets up in the business of curing (see 'minister') madmen, he wants a 'third' share, but the subtext of 'the trade' as whoring—an exaggeration of Isabella's potential infidelity—is too strong for her to miss. (Compare De Flores at 2.2.60, 'I'll put in for one'.)

41 **I fall upon you** Lollio responds with coarse wordplay to Isabella's suggestion, 'If I do fall', in l. 40. He will leap upon her.

43 **I stand to** sexual wordplay: (*a*) I stand by (*b*) I will be sexually aroused

45 **deal with 'em** Lollio deliberately interprets Isabella's remark sexually.

46 **Nay . . . 'em** i.e. nay, interpret my meaning charitably: I meant I will make use of them, not deal sexually with them.

47 **Abuse** Deceive

49 **kindly** (*a*) tenderly (*b*) according to their 'kind', as they deserve

50 **practise** (*a*) rehearse (i.e. theatrically) (*b*) act cunningly, scheme

52 **fit** make ready, but with suggestive wordplay: 'get yourself ready for these men, and I'll match you with them'.

54 **Take . . . outside** (*a*) don't pry into this affair; take it at face value (*b*) notice only the disguise I'll be wearing, not the person underneath

55 **put you to the inside** (*a*) get special access or accommodations for you (*b*) arrange it so that I or others can have sex with you

57 **close . . . solemnity** provide a finale for the wedding festivities

63 **nice** delicate, fastidious

65 **pizzles** whips made from dried bull penises (with obvious bawdy play on the 'pizzles' taming the 'ladies')

69 **morris** a festive dance sometimes put on for money during this period; here perhaps used generally, to refer to a group dance.

69–70 **one or two** i.e. Antonio and Franciscus

71 **measure** dance

77 **short** i.e. on too short a leash, with obvious bawdy undertones on Alibius's sexual inadequacy as a husband

79 **liberty** (*a*) freedom (*b*) lack of sexual restraint

82 **Cry you mercy** I beg your pardon

82–3 **nose . . . elephant** an insulting suggestion that Alibius has a big nose, with a cuckold joke (where nose = horn) at Alibius's expense. To 'put one's nose out of joint' was to cuckold him.

90 **out** i.e. out of those bad habits; with secondary meaning of: keep you away from Isabella

94 **honour** a curtsy, bow

LOLLIO [*returning bow*] Yes, an it please your worship.

ANTONIO Does honour bend in the hams, coz?

LOLLIO Marry, does it; as low as worship, squireship—nay, yeomanry itself sometimes, from whence it first stiffened. There, rise: a caper.

ANTONIO Caper after an honour, coz?

LOLLIO Very proper; for honour is but a caper, rises as fast and high, has a knee or two, and falls to th' ground again. You can remember your figure, Tony? *Exit*

ANTONIO Yes, cousin, when I see thy figure, I can remember mine.

Enter Isabella [like a madwoman]

ISABELLA Hey, how she treads the air: Shoo! shoo! t'other way! He burns his wings else. [*She pulls Antonio down*] Here's wax enough below, Icarus, more than will be cancelled these eighteen moons.

[*She rises, (singing)*] He's down, he's down,
What a terrible fall he had!
Stand up, thou son of Cretan Dedalus,
And let us tread the lower labyrinth;
I'll bring thee to the clue. [*She raises him*]

ANTONIO
Prithee, coz, let me alone.

ISABELLA Art thou not drowned?
About thy head I saw a heap of clouds
Wrapped like a Turkish turban; on thy back, [*She touches him*]
A crook'd chameleon-coloured rainbow hung
Like a tiara down unto thy hams. [*She kneels*]
Let me suck out those billows in thy belly;
Hark how they roar and rumble in the straits!
Bless thee from the pirates.

ANTONIO [*pulling free*] Pox upon you! Let me alone.

ISABELLA
Why shouldst thou mount so high as Mercury,
Unless thou hadst reversion of his place?
Stay in the moon with me, Endymion, [*She touches him*]
And we will rule these wild rebellious waves
That would have drowned my love.

ANTONIO I'll kick thee if again thou touch me,
Thou wild unshapen antic; I am no fool,
You bedlam.

ISABELLA [*rising*]
But you are, as sure as I am—mad.
Have I put on this habit of a frantic,
With love as full of fury, to beguile
The nimble eye of watchful jealousy
And am I thus rewarded? [*She reveals herself*]

ANTONIO
Ha! Dearest beauty—

ISABELLA No, I have no beauty now,
Nor never had, but what was in my garments.
You, a quick-sighted lover? Come not near me.
Keep your caparisons; you're aptly clad,
I came a feigner to return stark mad. *Exit*

Enter Lollio

ANTONIO [*after Isabella*] Stay, or I shall change condition,
And become as you are.

LOLLIO Why, Tony, whither now? Why, fool?

ANTONIO
Whose fool, usher of idiots? You coxcomb!
I have fooled too much.

LOLLIO You were best be mad another while then.

ANTONIO
So I am, stark mad; I have cause enough,

98 **Marry, does it** i.e. by (the Virgin) Mary it does

98–9 **low as...sometimes** i.e. as low as these degrees of society traditionally bow to their social superiors

99 **yeomanry** compare the bawdy pun (on the vagina) by Jaques, played by Rowley, in *All's Lost by Lust* 1.3.14–15.

100 **stiffened** (*a*) grew rigid—perhaps with play on making rigid with starch, as in the starched ruffs and collars of the aristocracy (see *OED v.* 1) (*b*) assumed a permanent character (*OED v.* 2b, though not attested until 1697) (*c*) with bawdy pun on 'yeomanry' (see previous note)
caper leap

102–4 **honour...again** honour is something insubstantial (like a jump or energetic dance step): it goes up, then it goes down

104 **figure** (dance) routine; also: visage, physiognomy

105–6 **when...mine** when I see how foolish you are, it's easy for me to remember how to be a fool

107–29 Isabella parodies Franciscus's learned nonsense, but in doing so stresses: a myth of male arrogance (Icarus, who flew too close to the sun, ll. 107 ff.); one in which a male hero depends on a woman to help him (Theseus and Ariadne, ll. 114–15); and one in which a goddess (Selene, the Moon, ll. 127–9) effectively feminizes an attractive man (Endymion) for her enjoyment.

109–10 **wax...cancelled** to 'cancel' was to obliterate or otherwise damage (*OED v.* 1a, b); punning on the waxen wings of Icarus, Isabella refers to the wax seals of legal bonds or deeds which come to grief in the human society 'below' Icarus

115 **clue** literally, the secret thread which led Theseus out of Minos's labyrinth; but with obvious bawdy undertones.

117–20 **About thy head...thy hams** Isabella describes a (flying) Icarus touched by clouds and a rainbow. In Greek mythology, Icarus was given wings of feathers and wax with which to escape from where Minos, king of Crete, had imprisoned him with his father, the inventor Dedalus (compare l. 113). Enjoying the powers of flight, Icarus flew too close to the sun, which melted his wings and plunged him into the ocean.

120 **tiara** ceremonial headdress
hams knee-joints

121 **suck out...belly** drain the (sea) water that drowned you (with an innuendo of oral sex: as Daalder points out, 'billows' was often a homonym for 'bellows' = penis: see 4.3.10–11 and note)

125–6 **Why...place?** (*a*) why should you fly as high as Mercury unless you had claim to his role? (*b*) why should you take the sexual place (with play on 'Mount') of my husband unless you had legitimate claim to it?

126 **reversion of** claim to

131 **antic** grotesque figure, clown

133 **habit** costume
frantic mad person

140 **caparisons** rags, rough cloth

141 **I came...mad** i.e. I came in pretending to be a madwoman, but now I leave maddened and angered by your foolishness.

143 **as you are** i.e. actually mad (from unrequited love)

145 **usher** keeper
coxcomb fool

147 **another while** a different time

And I could throw the full effects on thee,
And beat thee like a fury!

LOLLIO Do not, do not: I shall not forbear the gentleman under the fool, if you do. Alas, I saw through your fox-skin before now. Come, I can give you comfort: my mistress loves you, and there is as arrant a madman i'th' house as you are a fool—your rival, whom she loves not. If after the masque we can rid her of him, you earn her love, she says, and the fool shall ride her.

ANTONIO May I believe thee?

LOLLIO Yes, or you may choose whether you will or no.

ANTONIO
She's eased of him; I have a good quarrel on't.

LOLLIO Well, keep your old station yet, and be quiet.

ANTONIO
Tell her I will deserve her love.

LOLLIO And you are like to have your desire.

[*Exit Antonio one way.*] *Enter* [*at another*] *Franciscus*

FRANCISCUS [*singing*]
Down, down, down a-down a-down.
And then with a horse-trick
To kick Latona's forehead,
And break her bowstring.

LOLLIO [*aside*] This is t'other counterfeit: I'll put him out of his humour.—[*He retrieves the letter and reads*] 'Sweet lady, having now cast off this counterfeit cover of a madman, I appear to your best judgement a true and faithful lover of your beauty.' This is pretty well for a madman.

FRANCISCUS Ha! What's that?

LOLLIO 'Chide those perfections in you which have made me imperfect.'

FRANCISCUS [*aside*] I am discovered to the fool.

LOLLIO [*aside*] I hope to discover the fool in you, ere I have done with you.—'Yours all, or one beside himself, Franciscus.' This madman will mend, sure.

FRANCISCUS What do you read, sirrah?

LOLLIO Your destiny, sir: you'll be hanged for this trick, and another that I know.

FRANCISCUS Art thou of counsel with thy mistress?

LOLLIO Next her apron strings.

FRANCISCUS Give me thy hand.

LOLLIO Stay, let me put yours in my pocket first. [*He puts up letter*] Your hand is true, is it not? It will not pick? I partly fear it, because I think it does lie.

FRANCISCUS Not in a syllable.

LOLLIO So, if you love my mistress so well as you have handled the matter here, you are like to be cured of your madness.

FRANCISCUS And none but she can cure it.

LOLLIO Well, I'll give you over then, and she shall cast your water next.

FRANCISCUS [*giving money*] Take for thy pains past.

LOLLIO I shall deserve more, sir, I hope. My mistress loves you, but must have some proof of your love to her.

FRANCISCUS There I meet my wishes.

LOLLIO That will not serve; you must meet her enemy and yours.

FRANCISCUS He's dead already.

LOLLIO Will you tell me that, and I parted but now with him?

FRANCISCUS Show me the man.

LOLLIO Ay, that's a right course now. See him before you kill him in any case, and yet it needs not go so far, neither: 'tis but a fool that haunts the house—and my mistress—in the shape of an idiot. Bang but his fool's coat well-favouredly, and 'tis well.

FRANCISCUS Soundly, soundly!

LOLLIO Only, reserve him till the masque be past, and if you find him not now in the dance yourself, I'll show you. In, in! My master!

Enter Alibius

FRANCISCUS He handles him like a feather. Hey!

[*Exit, dancing*]

ALIBIUS Well said! In a readiness, Lollio?

151–2 **I shall not ... fool** I will not spare you for the gentleman you are under your disguise of fool.
153 **fox-skin** disguise—foxes were proverbially wily
157 **ride** (*a*) control, enjoy (*b*) have sex with
160 **She's ... on't** she can forget about him; he's as good as dead (I have a good excuse to pick a quarrel with him and do him in)
161 **old station** disguise as a fool
163 **And ... desire** with ironic double meaning: (*a*) you're in a fair way to being favoured with her love (*b*) you're going to get what's coming to you
164 **Down, down** a burden or refrain common to several popular ballads
165–7 **horse-trick ... bowstring** on the surface, mad nonsense. But a 'horse trick' was an energetic dance step or kick, and Franciscus perhaps puns bawdily as well. Latona (Greek, 'Leto') is here probably an epithet for the chaste Artemis/Diana, who, as a hunter, used a bow.
177–8 **discovered ... discover** wordplay: revealed in my identity ... uncover, expose
183 **another that I know** Lollio perhaps knows of the warrant issued for their arrest.
184 **of counsel with** a confidant of
186–7 **hand ... yours** Lollio puns in response to Franciscus's offering of a handshake with a jest about the hand that picks pockets. If he puts Franciscus's 'hand' ((handwritten) letter) in his pocket, won't that hand pick his pocket?
188 **true** honest
pick pick pockets
192–3 **you are like ... madness** Lollio puns: (*a*) you're likely to be cured by obtaining your wish, the lack of which has driven you mad (*b*) you're likely to be cured by not getting her at all, which will remove the cause of your distemper. Franciscus's reply indicates he hears only the first, as Lollio intends.
195–6 **cast your water** (*a*) diagnose your urine, acting as your doctor to cure you (*b*) throw it and you away, throw you over (*c*) make you ejaculate (compare 2.2.83, 4.1.36 and notes)
201–2 **her enemy and yours** i.e. Antonio
203 **He's dead already** he's as good as dead
204–5 **Will ... him?** Lollio jokingly takes Franciscus literally: Here you tell me he's already dead; why have I just seen him alive?
217 **Well said!** Well done!

LOLLIO Yes, sir.

ALIBIUS
Away then, and guide them in, Lollio;
Entreat your mistress to see this sight.
Hark, is there not one incurable fool
That might be begged? I have friends.

LOLLIO [*exiting*]
I have him for you, one that shall deserve it too.
[*Enter Isabella, then Lollio with Madmen and Fools*]

ALIBIUS Good boy, Lollio.
The Madmen and Fools dance [*to music*]
'Tis perfect; well, fit but once these strains,
We shall have coin and credit for our pains. *Exeunt*
Finis Actus Quartus

5.1 *Incipit Actus Quintus*
Enter Beatrice. A clock strikes one

BEATRICE
One struck, and yet she lies by't.—O my fears!
This strumpet serves her own ends, 'tis apparent now,
Devours the pleasure with a greedy appetite,
And never minds my honour or my peace,
Makes havoc of my right; but she pays dearly for't,
No trusting of her life with such a secret,
That cannot rule her blood to keep her promise.
Beside, I have some suspicion of her faith to me,
Because I was suspected of my lord,
And it must come from her.—Hark! By my horrors:
Strike two
Another clock strikes two.
Enter De Flores

DE FLORES Pist! Where are you?

BEATRICE
De Flores?

DE FLORES Ay—Is she not come from him yet?

BEATRICE As I am a living soul, not.

DE FLORES
Sure the devil hath sowed his itch within her.
Who'd trust a waiting-woman?

BEATRICE I must trust somebody.

DE FLORES Push! They are termagants,
Especially when they fall upon their masters
And have their ladies' first-fruits. They're mad whelps;
You cannot stave 'em off from game royal then.
You are so harsh and hardy, ask no counsel,
And I could have helped you to a pothecary's daughter
Would have fall'n off before eleven, and thanked you too.

BEATRICE
O me, not yet? This whore forgets herself.

DE FLORES
The rascal fares so well. Look, you're undone:
The day-star, by this hand! See Phosphorus plain yonder.

BEATRICE
Advise me now to fall upon some ruin,
There is no counsel safe else.

DE FLORES Peace, I ha't now:
For we must force a rising, there's no remedy.

BEATRICE
How? Take heed of that.

DE FLORES Tush, be you quiet,
Or else give over all.

BEATRICE Prithee, I ha' done then.

DE FLORES
This is my reach: I'll set some part a-fire
Of Diaphanta's chamber.

BEATRICE How? Fire, sir?
That may endanger the whole house!

DE FLORES
You talk of danger when your fame's on fire?

BEATRICE
That's true; do what thou wilt now.

DE FLORES Push! I aim
At a most rich success strikes all dead sure;
The chimney being a-fire, and some light parcels
Of the least danger in her chamber only;
If Diaphanta should be met by chance then,

221–2 **is there . . . friends** Alibius asks if there isn't an incurable fool somewhere they might ask for, to help in their entertainment. But 'begging' a fool also meant applying for legal guardianship of an insane person: their guardians stood to inherit or control any wealth which the fools had coming to them.

223 **I have him** Lollio means Franciscus

225 **strains** strains of music

5.1.1 **she** i.e. Diaphanta (but see 5.1.67 below, and note)

9 **of** by

10 **And it . . . from her** i.e. Diaphanta must be the source of this damning information.

10.1 ***Strike two*** probably an imperative, directing a stage hand to 'strike two' on a gong or bell

16 **termagants** Termagant was thought to be a violent, blustering god of the Muslims. This word came to mean 'an overbearing, quarrelsome woman' (*OED* 2b).

18 **first-fruits** first produce of the year (thus the property of a privileged few), with innuendo of 'taking their virginity'

18–19 **mad whelps . . . royal** i.e. they are like young dogs that disobey commands to leave animals owned by the monarch alone ('game royal' has a sexual suggestion as well)

20 **harsh and hardy** rash and daring

25 **Phosphorus** the 'daystar', the planet Venus which appeared before the sun in the morning

26 **fall upon some ruin** come across some desperate plan

28 **force a rising** make it necessary for everyone to get out of bed

31 **reach** plan

34 **fame's** reputation's

36 **success** outcome
strikes all dead sure i.e. (which) makes everything a dead certainty; with ominous overtones

37–8 **light . . . only** some small things (least likely to produce a large fire) in her lodgings alone

Far from her lodging—which is now suspicious—
It would be thought her fears and affrights then
Drove her to seek for succour; if not seen
Or met at all (as that's the likeliest),
For her own shame she'll hasten towards her lodging.
I will be ready with a piece high-charged,
As 'twere to cleanse the chimney: there 'tis proper now,
But she shall be the mark.

BEATRICE I'm forced to love thee now,
'Cause thou provid'st so carefully for my honour.

DE FLORES
'Slid, it concerns the safety of us both,
Our pleasure and continuance.

BEATRICE One word now, prithee.
How for the servants?

DE FLORES I'll dispatch them,
Some one way, some another in the hurry
For buckets, hooks, ladders. Fear not you.
The deed shall find its time, and I've thought since
Upon a safe conveyance for the body too.
How this fire purifies wit! Watch you your minute.

BEATRICE
Fear keeps my soul upon't, I cannot stray from't.

Enter Alonzo's ghost

DE FLORES
Ha! What art thou that tak'st away the light
'Twixt that star and me? I dread thee not!
'Twas but a mist of conscience. All's clear again.
[*Exit De Flores*]

BEATRICE
Who's that, De Flores? Bless me! It slides by.
[*Exit ghost*]
Some ill thing haunts the house; 't'as left behind it
A shivering sweat upon me: I'm afraid now.
This night hath been so tedious. O this strumpet!
Had she a thousand lives, he should not leave her
Till he had destroyed the last.

Struck three o'clock

List! O my terrors:
Three struck by Saint Sebastian's.

VOICES (*within*) Fire! Fire! Fire!

BEATRICE
Already? How rare is that man's speed!
How heartily he serves me! His face loathes one,
But look upon his care, who would not love him?
The east is not more beauteous than his service.

VOICES (*within*) Fire! Fire! Fire!

Enter De Flores, Servants

DE FLORES
Away, dispatch! Hooks, buckets, ladders!

[*The Servants*] *pass over. Ring a bell*

That's well said.
The fire-bell rings, the chimney works, my charge;
The piece is ready.

Exit [*De Flores, one way.*]
Enter [*at another*] *Diaphanta*

BEATRICE
Here's a man worth loving.—[*To Diaphanta*] O, you're a jewel.

DIAPHANTA Pardon frailty, madam;
In troth I was so well I e'en forgot myself.

BEATRICE
You've made trim work.

DIAPHANTA What?

BEATRICE Hie quickly to your chamber:
Your reward follows you.

DIAPHANTA I never made
So sweet a bargain. *Exit*

Enter Alsemero

ALSEMERO O my dear Joanna:
Alas, art thou risen too? I was coming,
My absolute treasure.

BEATRICE
When I missed you, I could not choose but follow.

ALSEMERO
Thou'rt all sweetness! The fire is not so dangerous.

BEATRICE
Think you so, sir?

ALSEMERO I prithee, tremble not:
Believe me, 'tis not.

Enter Vermandero, Jasperino

VERMANDERO
O bless my house and me!

ALSEMERO [*to Beatrice*] My lord your father.

Enter De Flores with a piece

VERMANDERO
Knave, whither goes that piece?

DE FLORES To scour the chimney.
Exit [*another way*]

40 **suspicious** unlikely, doubtful. De Flores thinks it unlikely that Diaphanta will be found far from her lodging; if she is, he's ready with a plausible story as to why she would have been there.
45 **piece high-charged** gun, heavily loaded
48 **honour** The word expresses an unconscious irony.
49 **'Slid** an oath: by God's eyelid
50 **continuance** (*a*) continued relationship (*b*) survival.
54 **The deed** i.e. Diaphanta's murder
65 **he** i.e. De Flores
67 **Three struck by Saint Sebastian's** three chimes from the bell tower of the local church, which would sound the passing hours
69 **loathes** is loathsome to
71 **The east** The rising sun and the Far East were both associated with the beauty of orient pearls.
73 **well said** well done, good
79 **You've made trim work** ironic: (*a*) you've done a fine job (*b*) you've had a fine time at your sexual pleasure (where 'trim work' plays on the meaning of 'to trim' = to copulate)
80 **Your reward follows you** grim comic irony: (*a*) you're about to receive your reward for faithful service (*b*) you'll get what's coming to you. Beatrice's joke is much like Lollio's at 4.3.163.
84 **I...follow** ironically echoed at 5.3.108

VERMANDERO O well said, well said!
That fellow's good on all occasïons.
BEATRICE
A wondrous necessary man, my lord.
VERMANDERO
He hath a ready wit. He's worth 'em all, sir.
Dog at a house of fire, I ha' seen him singed ere now.
The piece goes off
Ha, there he goes.
BEATRICE 'Tis done.
ALSEMERO
Come, sweet; to bed now. Alas, thou wilt get cold.
BEATRICE Alas, the fear keeps that out.
My heart will find no quiet till I hear
How Diaphanta, my poor woman, fares:
It is her chamber, sir, her lodging chamber.
VERMANDERO How should the fire come there?
BEATRICE
As good a soul as ever lady countenanced,
But in her chamber negligent and heavy:
She 'scaped a ruin twice.
VERMANDERO Twice?
BEATRICE Strangely, twice, sir.
VERMANDERO
Those sleepy sluts are dangerous in a house,
An they be ne'er so good.
Enter De Flores [*with corpse of Diaphanta, covered*]
DE FLORES O poor virginity!
Thou hast paid dearly for't.
VERMANDERO Bless us! What's that?
DE FLORES
A thing you all knew once: Diaphanta's burnt.
BEATRICE
My woman! O, my woman!
DE FLORES Now the flames
Are greedy of her. Burnt, burnt, burnt to death, sir!
BEATRICE
O my presaging soul!
ALSEMERO Not a tear more;
I charge you by the last embrace I gave you
In bed before this raised us.
BEATRICE Now you tie me.
Were it my sister now she gets no more.
Enter Servant
VERMANDERO How now?
SERVANT
All danger's past. You may now take your rests,
My lords, the fire is throughly quenched.
Ah, poor gentlewoman, how soon was she stifled!
BEATRICE
De Flores, what is left of her inter,
And we as mourners all will follow her:
I will entreat that honour to my servant,
E'en of my lord himself.
ALSEMERO Command it, sweetness.
BEATRICE
Which of you spied the fire first?
DE FLORES 'Twas I, madam.
BEATRICE
And took such pains in't too? A double goodness!—
'Twere well he were rewarded.
VERMANDERO He shall be.—
De Flores, call upon me.
ALSEMERO And upon me, sir.
Exeunt [*all but De Flores*]
DE FLORES
Rewarded? Precious, here's a trick beyond me!
I see in all bouts, both of sport and wit,
Always a woman strives for the last hit. *Exit*

5.2

Enter Tomazo
TOMAZO
I cannot taste the benefits of life
With the same relish I was wont to do.
Man I grow weary of, and hold his fellowship
A treacherous bloody friendship; and because
I am ignorant in whom my wrath should settle,
I must think all men villains, and the next
I meet—whoe'er he be—the murderer
Of my most worthy brother.
Enter De Flores, passes over the stage
Ha! What's he?
O, the fellow that some call honest De Flores,
But methinks honesty was hard bestead
To come there for a lodging, as if a queen
Should make her palace of a pest-house.
I find a contrariety in nature
Betwixt that face and me. The least occasion
Would give me game upon him. Yet he's so foul
One would scarce touch him with a sword he loved
And made account of. So most deadly venomous,

94 **Dog at** keen, hot on the trail of—the metaphor from dogs pursuing other animals
of on
103 **countenanced** favoured
104 **heavy** sluggish
106 **sluts** servant women (no sexual sense implied)
107 **An . . . good** be they ever so good
107–8 **O poor virginity! . . . for't** De Flores seems to be suggesting, publicly, that Diaphanta has tempted the Fates too much through the perfection of her chastity; on another level, though, he speaks of the 'bargain' her virginity has led her to enter into with Beatrice.
112 **O my presaging soul** With some irony, Beatrice pretends to have had intuition of Diaphanta's death ('presaging' = prophetic). Compare *Hamlet* 1.5.41: 'O my prophetic soul!'
118 **throughly** thoroughly
128 **here's . . . beyond me** i.e. she's outdone me; my pupil has outsmarted me as her master in this kind of duplicity (by arranging that both Alsemero and Vermandero will now reward me for my 'service')
5.2.10 **hard bestead** poorly accommodated (thus sorely pressed)
12 **pest-house** hospital for those with infectious diseases (especially the plague)
15 **give me game upon** offer me a chance to provoke
16 **he** i.e. the one who owns the sword

He would go near to poison any weapon
That should draw blood on him—one must resolve
Never to use that sword again in fight,
In way of honest manhood, that strikes him;
Some river must devour't, 'twere not fit
That any man should find it.

Enter De Flores

What, again?
He walks o' purpose by, sure, to choke me up,
To infect my blood.

DE FLORES
My worthy noble lord!

TOMAZO
Dost offer to come near and breathe upon me? [*He strikes him*]

DE FLORES [*drawing his rapier*]
A blow?

TOMAZO
Yea, are you so prepared?
I'll rather like a soldier die by th' sword
Than like a politician by thy poison. [*He draws his rapier*]

DE FLORES
Hold, my lord, as you are honourable.

TOMAZO
All slaves that kill by poison are still cowards.

DE FLORES [*aside*]
I cannot strike. I see his brother's wounds
Fresh bleeding in his eye, as in a crystal!—[*He sheathes rapier*]
I will not question this: I know you're noble.
I take my injury with thanks given, sir,
Like a wise lawyer; and as a favour
Will wear it for the worthy hand that gave it.
[*Aside*] Why this from him, that yesterday appeared
So strangely loving to me?
O, but instinct is of a subtler strain;
Guilt must not walk so near his lodge again.
He came near me now. *Exit*

TOMAZO [*sheathing rapier*]
All league with mankind I renounce for ever,
Till I find this murderer. Not so much
As common courtesy but I'll lock up:
For in the state of ignorance I live in,
A brother may salute his brother's murderer.
And wish good speed to th' villain in a greeting.

Enter Vermandero, Alibius, and Isabella

VERMANDERO
Noble Piracquo!

TOMAZO
Pray keep on your way, sir.
I've nothing to say to you.

VERMANDERO
Comforts bless you, sir.

TOMAZO
I have forsworn compliment; in troth I have, sir:
As you are merely man, I have not left
A good wish for you, nor any here.

VERMANDERO
Unless you be so far in love with grief
You will not part from't upon any terms,
We bring that news will make a welcome for us.

TOMAZO
What news can that be?

VERMANDERO
Throw no scornful smile
Upon the zeal I bring you. 'Tis worth more, sir.
Two of the chiefest men I kept about me
I hide not from the law or your just vengeance.

TOMAZO Ha!

VERMANDERO
To give your peace more ample satisfaction,
Thank these discoverers.

TOMAZO
If you bring that calm,
Name but the manner I shall ask forgiveness in
For that contemptuous smile upon you:
I'll perfect it with reverence that belongs
Unto a sacred altar. [*He kneels*]

VERMANDERO
Good sir, rise:
Why, now you overdo as much o' this hand,
As you fell short o' t'other.—Speak, Alibius.

ALIBIUS
'Twas my wife's fortune—as she is most lucky
At a discovery—to find out lately
Within our hospital of fools and madmen
Two counterfeits slipped into these disguises,
Their names Franciscus and Antonio.

VERMANDERO
Both mine, sir, and I ask no favour for 'em.

ALIBIUS
Now that which draws suspicion to their habits:
The time of their disguisings agrees justly
With the day of the murder.

TOMAZO [*rising*]
O blest revelation!

VERMANDERO
Nay, more; nay, more, sir: I'll not spare mine own
In way of justice. They both feigned a journey
To Briamata, and so wrought out their leaves.
My love was so abused in't.

TOMAZO
Time's too precious
To run in waste now. You have brought a peace

18 **He** De Flores
29 **politician** i.e. cunning plotter
33 **crystal** reflecting surface, such as a glass or ball, here used to see the past
35–6 **I take ... lawyer** compare the proverb 'A good lawyer must be a great liar' (*ODEP*, p. 447)
36 **favour** see I.1.235, note.
43 **league** alliance
44–5 **Not so ... lock up** I'll repress and avoid even the most common of courteous greetings
46–7 **For ... murderer** Tomazo speaks with an irony of which he is unaware: 'in my state of ignorance, I might, for all I know, actually give a good morning greeting to my brother's murderer'. (Tomazo has just been talking to the very man.)
56 **will** i.e. which will
63 **discoverers** revealers of the news (i.e. Alibius and Isabella)
68 **o' this hand** in this direction
70–1 **as she ... discovery** probably an unintentional joke on 'discovery' = dis- or uncovering a body of its clothing
76 **draws ... habits** makes their disguises (especially) suspicious
81 **wrought out** obtained

The riches of five kingdoms could not purchase.
Be my most happy conduct; I thirst for 'em:
Like subtle lightning will I wind about 'em
And melt their marrow in 'em. *Exeunt*

5.3 *Enter Alsemero and Jasperino*

JASPERINO
Your confidence, I'm sure, is now of proof.
The prospect from the garden has showed enough
For deep suspicion.

ALSEMERO The black mask
That so continually was worn upon't
Condemns the face for ugly ere't be seen.
Her dèspite to him, and so seeming bottomless—

JASPERINO
Touch it home then! 'Tis not a shallow probe
Can search this ulcer soundly; I fear you'll find it
Full of corruption. 'Tis fit I leave you:
She meets you opportunely from that walk;
She took the back door at his parting with her.
Exit Jasperino

ALSEMERO
Did my fate wait for this unhappy stroke
At my first sight of woman?
Enter Beatrice
She's here.

BEATRICE
Alsemero!

ALSEMERO
How do you?

BEATRICE How do I?
Alas, how do you? You look not well.

ALSEMERO
You read me well enough. I am not well.

BEATRICE
Not well, sir? Is't in my power to better you?

ALSEMERO
Yes.

BEATRICE
Nay, then you're cured again.

ALSEMERO
Pray resolve me one question, lady.

BEATRICE If I can.

ALSEMERO None can so sure. Are you honest?

BEATRICE
Ha, ha, ha! That's a broad question, my lord.

ALSEMERO
But that's not a modest answer, my lady.
Do you laugh? My doubts are strong upon me.

BEATRICE
'Tis innocence that smiles, and no rough brow
Can take away the dimple in her cheek.
Say I should strain a tear to fill the vault,
Which would you give the better faith to?

ALSEMERO
'Twere but hypocrisy of a sadder colour,
But the same stuff. Neither your smiles nor tears
Shall move or flatter me from my belief:
You are a whore.

BEATRICE What a horrid sound it hath!
It blasts a beauty to deformity.
Upon what face soever that breath falls,
It strikes it ugly. O, you have ruined
What you can ne'er repair again.

ALSEMERO
I'll all demolish, and seek out truth within you,
If there be any left. Let your sweet tongue
Prevent your heart's rifling, there I'll ransack
And tear out my suspicion.

BEATRICE You may, sir;
'Tis an easy passage. Yet, if you please,
Show me the ground whereon you lost your love.
My spotless virtue may but tread on that
Before I perish.

ALSEMERO Unanswerable,
A ground you cannot stand on! You fall down
Beneath all grace and goodness when you set
Your ticklish heel on't. There was a visor
O'er that cunning face, and that became you;
Now impudence in triumph rides upon't.
How comes this tender reconcilement else
'Twixt you and your despite—your rancorous loathing,
De Flores? He that your eye was sore at sight of,

85 **conduct** document ensuring safe passage
'em i.e. Franciscus and Alonzo, who Tomazo believes to have murdered his brother

86–7 **lightning ... marrow** proverbial: 'Lightning (thunder) bruises the tree (melts the marrow) but breaks not the bark (skin)' (Tilley, Dent L280).

5.3.1 **Your ... of proof** your suspicion is now confirmed

2 **from the garden** Jasperino and Alsemero appear to have spied on Beatrice and De Flores sometime since 5.1.

3 **black mask** Beatrice's pretence of loathing De Flores

7 **Touch** strike

7–8 **probe ... ulcer** A 'probe' was a blunt surgical instrument, typically metal, for exploring the depth and direction of wounds and sinuses.

13 **At ... woman** i.e. at my first insight into what women are really like. (Alsemero's image reprises the Garden of Eden conceit from the play's first speech.)

14 **How do you?** a deliberately cool greeting (especially for newlyweds)

18 **Nay ... again** i.e. if all that's needed to make you well again is for me to offer my help, consider it done

20 **honest** (*a*) truthful (*b*) chaste

21 **broad** (*a*) general (hence vague) (*b*) bawdy (a sense Alsemero picks up in 'modest', l. 22)

26 **vault** (*a*) the cavity of her dimple (l. 25)—but 'vault' could mean drain, sewer, or privy (compare 3.2.21 and note)

28 **sadder** darker

32 **blasts ... to** (violently) transforms ... into

37–8 **Let ... rifling** i.e. Even if your sweet tongue tries to forestall me, I'll ransack your heart to learn the truth.

41 **ground** (*a*) spot, place (*b*) grounds, basis. Beatrice continues the metaphor with 'tread' in the next line, and Alsemero picks it up in l. 44, saying 'You have no basis on which to defend yourself honourably'.

46 **ticklish** (*a*) slippery (*b*) lascivious, wanton

50 **despite** contempt

He's now become your arm's supporter,
Your lip's saint!

BEATRICE
Is there the cause?

ALSEMERO
Worse, your lust's devil,
Your adultery!

BEATRICE
Would any but yourself say that,
'Twould turn him to a villain.

ALSEMERO
'Twas witnessed
By the counsel of your bosom, Diaphanta.

BEATRICE
Is your witness dead then?

ALSEMERO
'Tis to be feared
It was the wages of her knowledge, poor soul;
She lived not long after the discovery.

BEATRICE
Then hear a story of not much less horror
Than this your false suspicion is beguiled with,
To your bed's scandal. I stand up innocence,
Which even the guilt of one black other deed
Will stand for proof of: your love has made me
A cruel murd'ress.

ALSEMERO
Ha!

BEATRICE
A bloody one.
I have kissed poison for't, stroked a serpent.
That thing of hate, worthy in my esteem,
Of no better employment, and him most worthy
To be so employed, I caused to murder
That innocent Piracquo, having no
Better means than that worst, to assure
Yourself to me.

ALSEMERO
O, the place itself e'er since
Has crying been for vengeance, the temple
Where blood and beauty first unlawfully
Fir'd their devotion, and quenched the right one;
'Twas in my fears at first; 'twill have it now,
O, thou art all deformed!

BEATRICE
Forget not, sir,
It for your sake was done! Shall greater dangers
Make the less welcome?

ALSEMERO
O, thou shouldst have gone
A thousand leagues about to have avoided
This dangerous bridge of blood! Here we are lost.

BEATRICE
Remember I am true unto your bed.

ALSEMERO
The bed itself's a charnel, the sheets shrouds
For murdered carcasses. It must ask pause
What I must do in this; meantime you shall
Be my prisoner only. Enter my closet.
[*Exit Beatrice into closet*]
I'll be your keeper yet. O, in what part
Of this sad story shall I first begin?
Enter De Flores
Ha! This same fellow has put me in.—De Flores!

DE FLORES
Noble Alsemero!

ALSEMERO
I can tell you news, sir:
My wife has her commended to you.

DE FLORES
That's news indeed, my lord; I think she would
Commend me to the gallows if she could,
She ever loved me so well, I thank her.

ALSEMERO
What's this blood upon your band, De Flores?

DE FLORES
Blood? No, sure. 'Twas washed since.

ALSEMERO
Since when, man?

DE FLORES
Since t'other day I got a knock
In a sword-and-dagger school. I think 'tis out.

ALSEMERO
Yes, 'tis almost out, but 'tis perceived though.
I had forgot my message. This it is:
What price goes murder?

DE FLORES
How, sir?

ALSEMERO
I ask you, sir.
My wife's behindhand with you, she tells me,
For a brave bloody blow you gave for her sake
Upon Piracquo.

DE FLORES [*aside*]
Upon? 'Twas quite through him, sure.—
Has she confessed it?

ALSEMERO
As sure as death to both of you,
And much more than that.

DE FLORES
It could not be much more:
'Twas but one thing, and that is she's a whore.

ALSEMERO
It could not choose but follow. O cunning devils!

53 **Is there the cause?** (*a*) is that what you are so exercised about? (*b*) is that the accusation? (compare 3.4.56, note)
53–4 **Worse...adultery** And what's worse, he, De Flores, is your tempter to lust and adultery
58 **wages of** price paid for
62 **stand up innocence** am innocent
64 **your love** love of you
71 **than that worst** i.e. than De Flores
75 **Fir'd...one** set afire their devotion and extinguished (i.e. suppressed) the proper one (i.e. to God: compare 'devotion' at 1.1.157)
76 **'twill have it now** probably 'the place' (l. 72), which has been 'crying for vengeance' (l. 73), and will now get it
87 **keeper** 'Keeper' here has resonances of (*a*) jailor (*b*) (with pun) keeper of prostitutes, pimp (*c*) keeper of lunatics (as at 1.2.134, 3.3.95).
89 **put me in** (*a*) put me in mind of (*b*) given me an idea or cue (theatrical)
95 **band** i.e. collar (of garment)
98–9 **out...out** with bitter wordplay: drawn...revealed
102 **behindhand with** in debt to (also suggesting 'behind' in the sense of backing up, conspiring with, 'in back of')
103 **brave** splendid, daring
104 **Upon...Upon** grim punning: on the body of...on the surface (as distinguished from all the way through)
106 **And...than that** much more than death—eternal damnation. In his reply, De Flores misunderstands or deliberately twists Alsemero's meaning, taking it to refer to how much Beatrice has confessed to.

How should blind men know you from fair-faced saints?
BEATRICE (*within*) He lies! The villain does belie me!
DE FLORES
Let me go to her, sir.
ALSEMERO Nay, you shall to her.
[*To Beatrice*] Peace, crying crocodile, your sounds are heard!
Take your prey to you.—Get you in to her, sir.
[*Exit De Flores into closet. Alsemero locks them in*]
I'll be your pander now; rehearse again
Your scene of lust, that you may be perfect
When you shall come to act it to the black audience
Where howls and gnashings shall be music to you.
Clip your adulteress freely; 'tis the pilot
Will guide you to the *Mare Mortuum*,
Where you shall sink to fathoms bottomless.
Enter Vermandero, Alibius, Isabella, Tomazo, Franciscus, and Antonio
VERMANDERO
O, Alsemero, I have a wonder for you.
ALSEMERO
No, sir. 'Tis I, I have a wonder for you.
VERMANDERO
I have suspicion near as proof itself
For Piracquo's murder.
ALSEMERO Sir, I have proof
Beyond suspicion for Piracquo's murder.
VERMANDERO
Beseech you hear me: these two have been disguised
E'er since the deed was done.
ALSEMERO I have two other
That were more close disguised than your two could be,
E'er since the deed was done.
VERMANDERO You'll hear me! These mine own servants—
ALSEMERO Hear me! Those nearer than your servants
That shall acquit them, and prove them guiltless.
FRANCISCUS
That may be done with easy truth, sir.
TOMAZO
How is my cause bandied through your delays!
'Tis urgent in my blood, and calls for haste.
Give me a brother alive or dead:
Alive, a wife with him; if dead, for both
A recompense—for murder and adultery.
BEATRICE (*within*)
O, O, O!
ALSEMERO
Hark, 'tis coming to you.
DE FLORES (*within*)
Nay, I'll along for company!
BEATRICE (*within*) O, O!
VERMANDERO What horrid sounds are these?
ALSEMERO [*unlocking closet*]
Come forth, you twins of mischief.
Enter De Flores, bringing in Beatrice, [*wounded*]
DE FLORES
Here we are. If you have any more
To say to us, speak quickly: I shall not
Give you the hearing else. I am so stout yet,
And so, I think, that broken rib of mankind.
VERMANDERO
An host of enemies entered my citadel
Could not amaze like this. Joanna! Beatrice-Joanna!
BEATRICE
O come not near me, sir. I shall defile you.
I am that of your blood was taken from you
For your better health. Look no more upon't,
But cast it to the ground regardlessly;
Let the common sewer take it from distinction.
Beneath the stars, upon yon meteor
Ever hung my fate, 'mongst things corruptible.
I ne'er could pluck it from him; my loathing
Was prophet to the rest, but ne'er believed.
Mine honour fell with him, and now my life.

111 **Let ... shall to her** more grim punning: De Flores asks to be united with Beatrice, to which Alsemero answers that De Flores will share her fate.
Nay Indeed
112 **crying crocodile** The crocodile was thought to cry false tears to trap its prey, and to cry hypocritically as it devoured it.
116 **black audience** i.e. devils in hell
117 **howls and gnashings** compare Matthew 13:42: (in Hell) 'there shall be wailing and gnashing of teeth'
118 **Clip** embrace
119–20 ***Mare Mortuum*... bottomless** Alsemero alludes to hell with its rivers. The Dead Sea was thought, like hell, to be bottomless.
127 **two other** i.e. Franciscus and Antonio (to whom Vermandero likely gestures here)
134 **bandied** tossed aside (hence ignored)
138 **adultery** Presumably Tomazo regards Beatrice as his brother's 'wife' (l. 137), hence her marriage to Alsemero is adulterous.
139 **O, O, O!** It is strategically unclear what transpires in the closet; along with their implication of violence, Beatrice's cries (and those of De Flores) are apt to remind the audience of the sounds lovers make in their passionate embrace. Alsemero's 'Hark, 'Tis coming to you' in l. 139 helps prepare for this sexual suggestion.
'tis i.e. Tomazo's 'recompense' (l. 138)
145 **stout** (*a*) strong (i.e. strong enough to hear a brief speech) (*b*) defiant, uncompromising
146 **that** i.e. is that
broken rib of mankind i.e. Beatrice. De Flores speaks misogynistically of Beatrice as a daughter of Eve, the first woman, whom God made out of Adam's rib (Genesis 2:21–2).
150–1 **I am that ... better health** I have been taken from you this way to remove the contamination which I now infect you with. (The metaphor is from blood-letting, a standard medical procedure at the time. Beatrice describes herself as a phial of tainted blood which Vermandero should immediately discard.)
152 **it** your blood; me
153 **common sewer** With 'defile' in l. 149 and 'cast' in l. 152, compare Matthew 15:17–20 (Rheims).
take it from distinction sweep it away where it will be indistinguishable from all the wasted matter of this corrupted world
154 **yon meteor** i.e. De Flores, who is like an ill-omened meteor beneath the constant and pure 'stars' (proverbial).
156 **him** De Flores
157 **the rest** i.e. subsequent events

Alsemero, I am a stranger to your bed;
Your bed was cozened on the nuptial night,
For which your false-bride died.

ALSEMERO Diaphanta!

DE FLORES
Yes, and the while I coupled with your mate
At barley-break; now we are left in hell.

VERMANDERO We are all there. It circumscribes us here.

DE FLORES
I loved this woman in spite of her heart;
Her love I earned out of Piracquo's murder.

TOMAZO
Ha! My brother's murderer!

DE FLORES Yes, and her honour's prize
Was my reward. I thank life for nothing
But that pleasure, it was so sweet to me
That I have drunk up all, left none behind
For any man to pledge me.

VERMANDERO Horrid villain!
Keep life in him for further tortures.

DE FLORES No,
I can prevent you: here's my penknife still;
It is but one thread more—
[*He cuts himself*]
—and now 'tis cut.
Make haste, Joanna, by that token to thee:
Canst not forget, so lately put in mind,
I would not go to leave thee far behind. (*Dies*)

BEATRICE
Forgive me, Alsemero, all forgive:
'Tis time to die when 'tis a shame to live. (*Dies*)

VERMANDERO
O, my name is entered now in that record
Where till this fatal hour 'twas never read.

ALSEMERO
Let it be blotted out; let your heart lose it,
And it can never look you in the face,
Nor tell a tale behind the back of life
To your dishonour. Justice hath so right
The guilty hit, that innocence is quit
By proclamation, and may joy again.
Sir, you are sensible of what truth hath done;
'Tis the best comfort that your grief can find.

TOMAZO
Sir, I am satisfied: my injuries
Lie dead before me. I can exact no more
Unless my soul were loose, and could o'ertake
Those black fugitives that are fled from thence,
To take a second vengeance; but there are wraths
Deeper than mine, 'tis to be feared, about 'em.

ALSEMERO
What an opacous body had that moon
That last changed on us! Here's beauty changed
To ugly whoredom; here, servant-obedience
To a master-sin: imperious murder!
I, a supposèd husband, changed embraces
With wantonness, but that was paid before.
[*To Tomazo*] Your change is come too: from an ignorant wrath
To knowing friendship.—Are there any more on's?

ANTONIO Yes, sir: I was changed too, from a little ass as I was, to a great fool as I am; and had like to ha' been changed to the gallows, but that you know my innocence always excuses me.

FRANCISCUS
I was changed from a little wit to be stark mad,
Almost for the same purpose.

ISABELLA [*to Alibius*] Your change is still behind,
But deserve best your transformatïon.
You are a jealous coxcomb; keep schools of folly,
And teach your scholars how to break your own head.

ALIBIUS
I see all apparent, wife, and will change now
Into a better husband, and never keep
Scholars that shall be wiser than myself.

ALSEMERO [*to Vermandero*]
Sir, you have yet a son's duty living;
Please you accept it. Let that your sorrow
As it goes from your eye, go from your heart;
Man and his sorrow at the grave must part.

163 **barley-break . . . hell** see 3.3.181–2, note
164 **It circumscribes us here** compare *Doctor Faustus*, 5.121–2 (A-text): 'Hell hath no limits, nor is circumscribed | In one self place; for where we are is hell, | And where hell is, must we ever be'.
165 **in spite of her heart** (*a*) despite her disposition toward me (*b*) despite her inconstant heart
167 **her honour's prize** her virginity
175 **token** probably his wound—perhaps the gesture of cutting himself
180 **that record** i.e. the heavenly book listing earthly rights and wrongs
186–7 **quit | By proclamation** acquitted or absolved by public proclamation
188–90 **Sir . . . Sir** Alsemero may address either Vermandero or Tomazo; Tomazo may address Vermandero or Alsemero.
192 **loose** freed
193 **black fugitives . . . thence** i.e. sooty or evil devils (here = the souls of) (Beatrice and De Flores), newly departed from their bodies ('thence'). See 5.3.116 and note.
194–5 **there . . . about 'em** divine vengeance, more profound even than mine, is perhaps even now encompassing them
196 **opacous** shadowy, not illuminating
201 **but . . . before** but that monstrous charge has already been paid for (by the deaths of Beatrice, Diaphanta, and De Flores)
207 **innocence** (*a*) guiltlessness (*b*) idiocy
209 **still behind** yet to come
212 **break your own head** crack your skull; with clear suggestion of cuckoldry
215 **that shall** i.e. who may seem to be
216 **son's duty living** (*a*) the duty of a son-in-law, still alive (*b*) continuing fealty from someone once your son
217 **Let . . . sorrow** let that which sorrows you
218 **from your eye** i.e. as tears

The Changeling.

Epilogue [*Spoken by Alsemero*]
All we can do to comfort one another,
To stay a brother's sorrow for a brother,
To dry a child from the kind father's eyes,
Is to no purpose; it rather multiplies.
Your only smiles have power to cause re-live
The dead again, or in their rooms to give
Brother a new brother, father a child:
If these appear, all griefs are reconciled.
Exeunt omnes [*with the bodies*]

Finis

THE PARTS

BEATRICE (541 lines): Madmen
DE FLORES (422 lines): Jasperino, Pedro, Madmen, Servants, Diaphanta
LOLLIO (324 lines): Tomazo *or* Alonzo *or* Servants *or* Diaphanta *or* Gentlemen *or* Gallants or Gentlewomen
ALSEMERO (284 lines): Alonzo *or* Lollio *or* Pedro *or* Madmen
VERMANDERO (148 lines): Pedro; Madmen (4.3)
ISABELLA (146 lines): Jasperino, Pedro, Servants
TOMAZO (128 lines): Jasperino; Lollio *or* Pedro; Madmen; Servants; Diaphanta *or* Gentlemen *or* Gallants *or* Gentlewomen
ALIBIUS (124 lines): Jasperino; Servants; Alonzo *or* Diaphanta *or* Gentlemen *or* Gallants *or* Gentlewomen
ANTONIO (102 lines): Alonzo, Jasperino, Servants, Diaphanta, Gentlemen, Gallants, Gentlewomen
JASPERINO (89 lines): any but Alsemero, Servants, Beatrice, Diaphanta, Isabella, De Flores, Lollio, Alonzo, and Gentles (4.1)
DIAPHANTA (63 lines): Alibius, Lollio, Pedro, Antonio, Franciscus, Madmen, Servants
FRANCISCUS (59 lines): Alonzo, Jasperino, Pedro, Servants, Diaphanta, Gentlemen, Gallants, Gentlewomen
ALONZO (48 lines): Alibius *or* Lollio *or* Pedro *or* Antonio *or* Franciscus *or* Madmen *or* Servants
PEDRO (31 lines; 1.2): any but Lollio, Alibius, Antonio
4? MADMEN and FOOLS (11 lines; 1.2, 3.3, and 4.3): any but Alibius, Lollio, Antonio, Isabella
Vermandero's First SERVANT (7 lines; 1.1, 4.2, and 5.1): any but Alsemero, Jasperino, Vermandero's Second Servant, Beatrice's First Servant, Beatrice's Second Servant, Beatrice, Diaphanta, De Flores, Vermandero, Tomazo
Alsemero's SECOND SERVANT (4 lines; 1.1): any but Alsemero, Jasperino, Alsemero's First Servant, Beatrice, Diaphanta
Alsemero's FIRST SERVANT (3 lines; 1.1): any but Alsemero, Jasperino, Alsemero's Second Servant, Beatrice, Diaphanta
Vermandero's Second SERVANT (no lines; 1.1 and 5.1): any but Alsemero, Jasperino, Vermandero's First Servant, Beatrice's First Servant, Beatrice's Second Servant, Beatrice, Diaphanta, De Flores, Vermandero
Beatrice's First SERVANT (no lines; 1.1): any but Alsemero, Jasperino, Beatrice's Second Servant, Vermandero's First Servant, Vermandero's Second Servant, Beatrice, Diaphanta, De Flores, Vermandero
Beatrice's Second SERVANT (no lines; 1.1): any but Alsemero, Jasperino, Beatrice's First Servant, Vermandero's First Servant, Vermandero's Second Servant, Beatrice, Diaphanta, De Flores, Vermandero
2? GENTLEMEN (dumb show, 4.1): Tomazo; servants; Alibius *or* Lollio *or* Pedro *or* Antonio *or* Franciscus
2? GALLANTS (dumb show, 4.1): Tomazo; servants; Alibius *or* Lollio *or* Pedro *or* Antonio *or* Franciscus
2? GENTLEWOMEN (dumb show, 4.1): Tomazo; Alibius *or* Lollio *or* Pedro *or* Antonio *or* Franciscus

Most crowded scene: 4.1, Dumb show: 8 characters (+2? mute gentlemen, 2? mute gallants, 2? mute gentlewomen)

Missing from 4.1 dumb show (characters who would have a narrative reason to be present): Alibius, Lollio
Missing from 5.3 (characters who would have a narrative reason to be present): Lollio, Jasperino

Epilogue.2 **stay** eradicate, forestall
5 **Your only** i.e. Only your
6 **their rooms** their place

THE NICE VALOUR; OR, THE PASSIONATE MADMAN

Text introduced and annotated by Susan Wiseman, edited by Gary Taylor

The Nice Valour is an enigmatic play. Who wrote it, the date of composition, and the circumstances of its theatrical production—for the prologue and epilogue do imply that it was not only performed but revived—have all been disputed. But no such uncertainties surround its publication. It first appeared in print—in the folio *Comedies and Tragedies* attributed to Francis Beaumont and John Fletcher—in 1647, a time of famines and disorders as the Civil War dragged to a close (the last royalist castle, at Harlech, fell only in March 1647); Charles I was in custody, unable to raise an army in the field. It could be said that the war on the battlefield gave way to cultural polemic, and certainly books were read as partisan. Momentarily, in 1648, there were seventeen newspapers. The 'Beaumont and Fletcher' folio occupied a special place in the royalist publication drive and, following the various strictures against theatres after the closure of 1642, theatre had come to occupy an overtly politicized and contested position, with the composite name 'Beaumont and Fletcher' signalling the 'true' and élite value of royalist culture, aligned with 'romance' rather than city comedy. The composite name might well also have connoted the idealized royalist understanding of masculine friendship and honour—implications which echo some of the concerns of *Valour*. Such values, of course, were far from 'purely' 'literary' or ideal: throughout the Civil War and Interregnum genre and proper name were aesthetic capital in political debate.

In Civil War invocations of the writers valued by royalists, Middleton is notably absent. For example, *The Famous Tragedy of Charles I* (1649) includes a 'Prologue to the Gentry' which invokes the names of 'Jonson, Shakespeare, Goffe, and Davenant, | Brave Suckling, Beaumont, Fletcher, Shirley', claiming that they are 'loathed, by the Monsters of the times'—thereby constructing both the desired audience for the play and articulating in full the royalist claim to cultural capital. Middleton is missing. Although the writers claimed in this list were not, necessarily, producers of plays which simply served the dominant ideology of the pre-war period and the threatened royalist position of the Civil War period, Middleton's output differs from theirs in terms, simply, of the number of his plays which deal with the city in whatever terms. This made Middleton's an unlikely name to conjure royalism. As Martin Butler and Margot Heinneman have argued, his influence can be traced in the emplotment of political satire, and he probably influenced interregnum political playlets: Samuel Sheppard's *The Committee Man Curried*, for instance, transposes the conventions of city comedy to Civil War London. But with regard to the printing of *Valour* in a book designed, as the 'Beaumont and Fletcher' folio in part was, as royalist cultural capital, the value of Middleton's name—even assuming his connection with the play was remembered—would have been trivial or even, possibly, negative. So the Civil War circumstances may have aided the effacement of authorship, and thereby facilitated *Valour*'s cultural disappearance into the quantity argument for royalist values exemplified by the folio 'Beaumont and Fletcher', a claim reiterated in the 1679 edition's claim to reprint 'fifty plays'.

To the extent that the publication of the Beaumont and Fletcher folio relied on the 'content' of the texts that it contained rather than invoking their totemic status as produced by the co-opted 'royalists' Beaumont and Fletcher, as a tragicomedy *Valour* could also be read as shaping experience in terms of the restitution of a questioned social order; such tragicomic shaping was to become crucial to royalist dramatic production during the 1650s. And royalist associations also encircle one aspect of *Valour* which certainly did have a cultural afterlife in mid-century: the song sung by the Passionate Lord in 3.3, 'Hence all you vain delights', more often anthologized than any other lyric from the early modern English stage. Although it appears in manuscript miscellanies dating from as early as 1624, it is especially common in Oxford miscellanies of the troubled decades from 1630 to 1660. In the overtly royalist anthology *Wit Restored* (1658), the song reappears after political poems of the 1640s and 1650s, suggesting that the play's most famous moment was incorporated into the cultural capital of royalist publication.

But most scholars now agree that Middleton wrote much (and probably all) of the play, and he certainly wrote it years before Charles I polarized English politics into royalist and roundhead. The associations which have governed all previous readings of the printed text are therefore, at best, anachronistic. *Valour* is not Fletcherian but Middletonian, not Caroline but Jacobean. And what it meant to its author and first audiences would have depended, in part, on exactly when in the reign of James I it premièred. The previously conjectured date of composition ('1615–16') has recently been reassessed by Gary Taylor, who concludes that the play was written in the summer or autumn of 1622. Taylor reads 'Hence all you vain delights' as an epitome of melancholy in contrast to Robert Burton's sprawling *Anatomy of Melancholy* (1621); he also argues that the play adopts and adapts the innovative technique of John Barclay's internationally acclaimed political romance *Argenis* (1621), allegorizing the contemporary British court as Barclay had allegorized its French counterpart. Taylor's redating of the play's composition radically changes *Valour*'s place in the sequence of Middleton's works, bringing it much closer to the date of *A Game at Chess*. Taylor's argument grounds the plot in relation to the court of King James and, in doing so, gives the play a cultural context unavailable when *Valour* was lost among the 'fifty plays' of the amorphous 'Beaumont and Fletcher canon'.

Valour uses a genre of court tragicomedy to articulate problems about the codification, meaning and regulation of violence and desire. Though the level of detail of court events known to the dramatist or recognized by spectators remains a matter of speculation, it does seem likely that *Valour* responds to events at court in the last decade of the reign of King James. In doing so it uses figures in the grip of the passions to represent threats to the stability of the social order and to illuminate the tendency of the rules supporting that order—such as the rules of honour—to generate the very antisocial behaviour they are imagined as regulating. The play's first scenes suggest both the analogy with James's court and the dramatic use of emotional excess to make a point about the rules shaping social behaviour. The Duke returns to court from hunting (James's favourite sport); there he meets his dear friend Chamont (who has the kind of relationship with his sovereign that James's court favourite enjoyed). Chamont is a close adherent of the code of honour, which required the individual male to police all social actions, relations and bodily boundaries for possible infringements; he is contrasted with the Duke's kinsman, 'the Passionate Lord' (associated by Taylor with the Duke of Buckingham's mentally unstable brother), who systematically violates physical boundaries. Chamont and the Passionate Lord both observe Chamont's brother, 'the Soldier', making love to a chaste court Lady (the Duke's sister), an object of the Passionate Lord's promiscuous desires and of Chamont's fantasies about honour and chastity. While Chamont stands in a jealous reverie the Duke enters and, attempting to catch his attention, taps him with a switch—thereby initiating the potentially tragic second part of the action. Mortally wounded in his honour but unable to challenge his sovereign to a duel, Chamont, evading the Duke's many attempts to call him back, retreats to the country. As Baldwin Maxwell suggested, this way of configuring the question of honour and status may draw on an incident when James I kicked one of his courtiers. In the play, it precipitates the Duke's dismissal of his entire entourage (which resembles the major upheavals in court personnel between 1616 and 1622). Apparently shocked at the effect of the code of honour on the interrelationship of 'worth' and 'blood', the Duke decides to employ solely lowly 'grooms'. Thus it is the Duke, keystone of hierarchy, who in the end challenges social status—an example of the play's critical attention to the way in which the rules which apparently shape society generate their own transgression.

The play again twins issues of violence and status in the actions of the Soldier (whom Taylor associates with English involvement in the Thirty Years War). When the Passionate Lord sends men to beat the Soldier, he responds by running the Lord through, apparently killing him. The Duke's sister pleads for the Soldier's pardon (unsuccessfully); the First Gentleman of the Duke's bedchamber posts to Chamont's retreat and persuades him to come and plead for his brother (successfully). However, in the tragicomic denouement the Passionate Lord reappears, not only alive but cured. The conflict between honour and status is reconciled through the exchange of women; as Mario DiGangi argues, heterosexuality here serves the needs of an overwhelmingly homosocial male court. The disciplining of the antisocial promiscuous desire of the Passionate Lord and the hypermasculine militarism of the Soldier and Chamont is dramatized in a classic 'comic' conclusion of betrothal: the Passionate Lord marries the Cupid, Chamont marries the Lady. That ending could be read or staged as reintroducing gender relations (which permits an ideological rather than a physical regulation of masculine violence) or as imposing marital contracts on a play which derives its energy from the intimate violence produced by contradictory masculine codes.

Each of the plot's three strands concerns both 'proper' masculine behaviour and the passions, with the relationship between the two organized by violence. The figure of Chamont suggests that honour is a highly codified form of violence. The excesses of the Passionate Lord—licensed by the Duke—call attention to the problematic interrelationship of individual conduct (even under the sign of 'madness') and state regulation of violence. And the masochistic social climber Lepet—busy formulating and printing a code of submission, and turning blows to pragmatic and economic ends—presents a 'cowardly' counter-logic in which the violence generated by social relations is absorbed, literally, by the bodies of social inferiors.

In voicing questions about status, violence and 'worth', the text deploys a complex range of references which find more and less precise resonance in issues, incidents and figures of significance in Jacobean England. For example, 'Frenchness' in the plot might draw on the French wars of religion—'La Nove' (5.2.24) was the name of a Protestant commander in those wars. Considered in terms of their relationship to violence, the warlike eponym La Nove—potentially tragic—contrasts with the Italian and comic 'wetness' of Galoshio. However, 'Frenchness' has further connotations: the office of Gentlemen of the Bedchamber (referred to, for example, by Lepet's wife at 1.1.178–9) was a French as well as English office of courtly nobility, and its representation seems to hint at a theme of sexual licence when the Passionate Lord calls for Margaret of Valois and two of her waiting women (2.1.142). Margaret de Valois (who married Henry IV to produce the mixing of Catholic and Protestant dynasties in France) was accused by her brother, Henry III, of having affairs; he arrested and had interrogated two of her attendants—Dame de

Béthune and Dame de Duras—who were denounced as improper company for the queen. De Valois (who died in 1615) might have sprung to mind because she was divorced at the time of her death and, after 1615, any association of divorce and sexual excess might well have recalled the murder scandal around Sir Thomas Overbury, poisoned by Frances Howard because of his opposition to her divorce. While *Valour* indeed seems to use 'topical' material, the way it shapes such material contrasts markedly with *A Game at Chess*, working by implication rather than direct political analogy.

Middleton in 1614 had written *Masque of Cupids* in celebration of the marriage of the couple later convicted for Overbury's murder—Robert Carr and Frances Howard, the Earl and Countess of Somerset. Carr was then (like Chamont) the acknowledged favourite of his sovereign, and Chamont's petulance recalls the 'strange streams of unquietness, passion, fury, and insolent pride' which King James condemned in Carr, who at times seemed to assume that the king 'dare not offend you or resist your appetites'. The appearance of Cupid in *Valour*, now in ruined or disgraced form, might be read as a return to the idea of Cupid in the later context of the couple's disgrace. Like the masquers of the Stuart court, Cupid attempts to turn a device or apparently playful disguise not only towards a 'cure' of the Passionate Lord but significantly towards her own needs. However, like Aurelia, the mistress disguised as a page in *More Dissemblers Beside Women*, this Cupid is pregnant, and her swollen figure increasingly threatens to destroy her disguise. As Bruce Smith has noted, such uses of 'female' disguise configure gender very differently from the gender-ambiguous page. The growing bigness of the Cupid invites a reading of the body (penetrated, bruised, mixed) as the place in which the transgression of social codes might become visible.

Here and elsewhere, the play investigates assessments of female chastity and moral fortitude. Except in the case of Chamont, where the integrity of the male body itself becomes explicitly the locus of dispute, women provide the focus, or pretext, of violent relations between men. They are repeatedly exchanged between men (like the Cupid), competed for (like the Lady) or used as a pretext or face-saving device (as Lepet uses his wife). The Passionate Lord—apparently unable to distinguish men from women in masculine dress—'sees' the First Gentleman as a woman disguised; this bawdy episode is symptomatic of the place of female figures in the play as a whole. Typically, it situates women as promiscuous and sexually desiring. Though this construction of femininity is promulgated by the Passionate Lord, it is shared by other men—hence Chamont's implicit surprise at, and corresponding overvaluation of, the Lady's chastity.

As suggested by the importance the play accords to female chastity and to the borders of the male body, *Valour* traces a sequence of quarrels between men which hover on the borders between 'private' and 'public' acts and the implications of border violation. This is significantly explored (as Taylor also argues) in the play's treatment of duelling. Duels had been the object of much royal attention and subject to three royal actions by 1615, but scandalous duels involving important courtiers continued throughout James I's reign. James may have found duels personally repellent, but (as David Wilson Harris notes) they were also 'an affront to public justice', because the aristocratic implications of their rule-dominated structure for controlling violence both challenged and replicated or mimicked government authority.

Historians suggest that the challenge to a duel implied claims to status which contrasted with the 'killing affray' in a hierarchy of violence—both, notably, outside government control. Challenging someone to duel itself asserted a particular social position: in *Valour* duels appear most specifically at 4.1, where social hierarchy is rendered problematic by the ambiguity of dress codes and the return of blows. The question of redress is crucial, too, where the code of honour is brought into direct conflict with the state through Chamont's conflict with his ruler.

The on-stage circulation of violence takes place in tandem with continued questioning of the meaning or stability of social codes and hierarchy. The question of violence is worked out in terms of a contrast between Chamont's code of honour and Lepet's reverse code of cowardice: Lepet links pragmatic responses to violence with social and financial gain, and his book codifies cowardice in a way that mimics the code of honour. Disrupting this binary contrast is the Passionate Lord's violence: apparently random, but authorized by his social status. The play reserves the label 'madman' for this perpetrator of acts which lack codification. But of course, as Sander Gilman argues, the representation of madness acts as a sign of difference, a function of 'historical and cultural continuity, rather than any quality of the process of insanity or of the actual individual' represented. In the theatre, madness can, as here, stand as a shorthand for crises in social relations. Specifically, in *Valour* madness localizes a crisis in the enforcement of rules: in the rule-bound court the rule for this figure is rulelessness. In the 'case' of the Passionate Lord the passions follow each other sequentially, as he transgresses various court codes and—particularly—violates social boundaries around the body. Not only has the Lord impregnated the Cupid, but he also keeps the clown Galoshio as a 'carcass' to beat: as Gilman notes, in seventeenth-century iconography 'the pinwheel, the cudgel (which the madman mounts like a hobby-horse), and the disordered clothing' all signify the madman. In *The Passions of the Mind in General* (1604), Thomas Wright compared human passions to the desires of animals: 'as we see beasts hate, love, fear and hope,' and that they act 'seducing the will, inducing ... to vice, and commonly withdrawing from virtue', whereas properly governed passions enable a man to make the world productive for himself. The theatrical and signifying nature of passion described by Wright—'Extraordinary apparel of body declareth well the apparel of the mind'—resembles *Valour*'s staging of excess in the Passionate Lord's defence of loose garments. The Passionate Lord is coded in stage directions in terms of that iconography of madness, putting into circulation the question of the relationship between reason and passion, a psychological hierarchy related to social hierarchies.

As a relative of the Duke (a 'cousin'), the Passionate Lord is not restrained but humoured. (Even the First Gentleman enters into cross-gendered wordplay with him.) But when he crosses the Soldier and sends a group of bravos to beat him, he precipitates the revenge scenario which dominates Acts 4 and 5. Thus the Passionate Lord is, like Chamont, placed in a problematic relationship to the twin discourses of hierarchy and violence; his passionate outbursts question the boundaries of courtesy and hierarchy. The implication of the Passionate Lord's licence is that at court the passions are allowed to reign: the courtiers are controlled by one who is in turn controlled by his passions, and who exceeds decorum in dress, speech, sexual appetite and violent behaviour.

Seen this way, the Passionate Lord once again invokes the paradox of blood and worth, posed also by the touchy honour and violence of Chamont, and taken up again in Lepet's receipts for receiving blows and his willingness to give up his newly bought title of gentleman for profit and a place in the Duke's service. Where Chamont insists on observing the code of honour to the letter, the Passionate Lord refuses to observe any form of propriety; his acts of violence are sanctioned by his relative, the Duke, and therefore by his 'blood'. Chamont sticks to the code of personal valour, but the Passionate Lord sends a group to beat up the Soldier.

The complexity and confusion of the relationship between worth and blood reaches a climax in 4.1. The Duke, the supreme hierarchical authority, nevertheless apologizes to Chamont in terms of his offended honour: 'So that, what you in tenderness of honour, | Conceive to be loss to you... | I'll restore again'. When scornfully rejected by Chamont ('O miserable satisfaction, | Ten times more wretched than the wrong itself'), the Duke dismisses all the gentlemen of his chamber, saying 'Your worths will find you fortunes'. This claim, demonstrating his adherence to the elaborate code of honour articulated by Chamont, draws out the code's full implications: 'worth' can actually replace 'blood' (that is, inherited social status) in the establishment of individual fortune—an implication questioned by the dismissed gentlemen. The complexity is increased when we find that the comparison to Chamont is not, precisely, that the gentleman should have behaved like him, but that the Duke seeks men of lower social status—'Men more insensible of reputation' (worth), 'grooms' who are less ambiguously situated in the social hierarchy—so that 'if my anger chance let fall a stroke, | ...it may pass...undisputed.'

The possibility that value might centre on the individual, bypassing social forms and hierarchical expectations, is hinted at here. 'Worth' (worthiness) is also understood as an expression of the hierarchy which ought to generate it and which it, circularly, seems to uphold: although the play teases out the implicit contradictions between 'merit' and 'lineage' implicit in Stuart society, those contradictions are not, here, in open conflict. 'Worth' literally retreats in a direct conflict with 'blood' when the altercation between Chamont and the Duke causes Chamont's retirement. Like the disgraced Earl of Essex (who in order to secure Frances Howard's divorce was publicly declared impotent), the humiliated Chamont will remain available for the defence of his country, but he will no longer participate in court life.

The Duke calls for men of lower social status, assuming that they, at least, will be below the social ladder of honour and personal affront. Likewise, by subordinating concerns of 'worth' *and* blood to economic questions, Lepet finds employment receiving the blows which are forbidden by social custom and which—as the revenge of the Soldier on the Passionate Lord suggests—lead to combat between men of rank. In the second part of the same scene, when the First Gentleman is attempting to find the Duke new servants, violence passes down the social hierarchy. The Gallant provokes the First Gentleman, who challenges him; the Gallant backs down; emboldened by this success, the Gentleman next encounters a Plain Fellow and jostles him. However, rather than accede to the right to do violence as conferred by visible social position, the Plain Fellow returns the blow—indicating once again the instability of social hierarchy marked by dress ('Who would ha' thought this would prove a gentleman?'). The Plain Fellow poses a further problem about the code of honour: its lack of transparency. Is he responding outside the code of challenges and outside the code of elaborately hierarchized court violence, returning impromptu an affront?—or does he (as the First Gentleman interprets him) by the blow assert his claim to be a gentleman? In this instance, the blow *itself* is taken as proof of social status.

Finally, Lepet enters—the play's funniest and most original character. Lepet's coward's code rejects both 'worth' and 'blood'. He eschews the code of honour to absorb the blows of other men; he has purchased the rank of gentleman, but would surrender it for money. Moreover, Lepet's behaviour, like that prescribing rules for duels and court etiquette, is about to be printed in a book setting out the rules for cowards; albeit comically, this radical cowardice is articulated as a systematic (if unmasculine) set of responses to violence. In this inverted code life and limb are preserved overall—though worn and bruised. The preservation rather than expenditure of life is linked to the exchange value which Lepet ascribes to the body in service: under this code the individual, by electing to eschew all ideal values, is free to attempt to turn all social interaction to his own gain outside any intertwining of worth, blood and place. Thus, Lepet's worthlessness, his lack of attachment to the social hierarchy (which he is nevertheless attempting to climb), render him the codifier of laws of ignobility which might be made productive by individuals with no integral place in the social system. Lepet's book begins to articulate the social code of those placed by behaviour beyond both worth and blood and, therefore, outside the binary competition between them.

Lepet receives blows—and produces texts. He corrects proofs and guides readers to particular passages of his book; he belongs to Middleton's gallery of satirical portraits of authorship, always 'implicated' and 'never innocent' (Taylor 1994). The innovative subject position embodied in Lepet, inside the market but outside of 'blood' and 'worth', is, according to Middleton, the not so nice status of an author.

SEE ALSO

Music and dance: *Companion*, 169
Textual introduction and apparatus: *Companion*, 1070
Authorship and date: *Companion*, 423

The Nice Valour

Or, The Passionate Madman

THE PERSONS

A DUKE
CHAMONT, a gentleman, the Duke's favourite
A SOLDIER, Chamont's brother
A LADY, the Duke's Sister, Chamont's beloved

A PASSIONATE LORD, the Duke's distracted kinsman
CUPID, personated by a lady, affecting the Passionate Lord
Two BROTHERS to the Cupid
BASE, the Passionate Lord's jester

First GENTLEMAN of the Duke's Chamber
Three other GENTLEMEN of the Duke's Chamber
LEPET, an author and a gentleman about the court
CLOWN (named Galoshio), another tried piece of man's flesh, later servant to Lepet
Lepet's WIFE
POLTROT, MOULEBAISER } two mushroom courtiers
A GALLANT of the same temper

FIRST WOMEN MASQUER
A PLAIN FELLOW
A PRIEST
A HUNTSMAN
Two SERVANTS
EPILOGUE
Dancers, Court Officers, five other woman masquers

1.1 *Incipit Actus Primus*

[*Enter*] *Duke, Chamont, and Four Gentlemen* [*of the Chamber*]

DUKE
Chamont, welcome. We have missed thee long,
Though absent but two days: I hope your sports
Answered your time and wishes.

CHAMONT
Very nobly, sir:
We found game worthy your delight, my lord,
It was so royal.

DUKE
I've enough to hear on't.
Prithee bestow't upon me in discourse.

[*They walk apart*]

FIRST GENTLEMAN
What is this gentleman, coz? You are a courtier,
Therefore know all their insides.

SECOND GENTLEMAN
No farther than the taffeta goes, good coz,
For the most part, which is indeed the best part
Of the most general inside. Marry, thus far
I can with boldness speak this one man's character,
And upon honour pass it for a true one:

Title Nice either 'excessively fastidious' (like Chamont) or 'effeminate, unmanly' (like Lepet)

Persons.1 DUKE No dukedom is specified, but the play's combination of French and Italian names might have suggested Savoy, then an independent state.

9 **GENTLEMAN of the Duke's Chamber** (an important office at court, with direct and intimate access to the sovereign)

1.1.5 **royal** magnificent (but literally 'appropriate to a king', like James I, who was an avid huntsman)

12 **character** as in Sir Thomas Overbury's *Characters*: description of a type

He has that strength of manly merit in him,
That it exceeds his sovereign's power of gracing.
He's faithfully true to valour, that he hates
The man from Caesar's time, or farther off,
That ever took disgraces unrevenged:
And if he chance to read his abject story,
He tears his memory out, and holds it virtuous
Not to let shame have so much life amongst us.
There is not such a curious piece of courage
Amongst man's fellowship, or one so jealous
Of honour's loss or reputation's glory:
There's so much perfect of his growing story.

FIRST GENTLEMAN
'Twould make one dote on virtue, as you tell it.

SECOND GENTLEMAN
I ha' told it to much loss, believe it, coz.

THIRD GENTLEMAN [*to Fourth Gentleman*]
How the Duke graces him! What is he, brother?

FOURTH GENTLEMAN
Do you not yet know him? A vainglorious coxcomb
As proud as he that fell for't.
Set but aside his valour—which is indeed
No virtue, and not fit for any courtier—
And we his fellows are as good as he,
Perhaps as capable of favour too,
For one thing or another, if 'twere looked into.
Give me a man, were I a sovereign now,
Has a good stroke at tennis and a stiff one,
Can play at equinoctium with the line
As even as the thirteenth of September,
When day and night lie in a scale together:
Or may I thrive as I deserve at billiards,
No otherwise at chess or at primero.
These are the parts required; why not advanced?

DUKE [*to Chamont*]
Trust me, it was no less than excellent pleasure,
And I'm right glad 'twas thine.—How fares our
kinsman?
Who can resolve us best?

FIRST GENTLEMAN I can, my lord.

DUKE
There if I had a pity without bounds,
It might be all bestowed—a man so lost
In the wild ways of passion that he's sensible
Of naught but what torments him.

FIRST GENTLEMAN True, my lord,
He runs through all the passions of mankind,
And shifts 'em strangely too: one while in love—
And that so violent, that for want of business
He'll court the very prentice of a laundress,
Though she have kibed heels—and, in's melancholy
again,
He will not brook an empress, though thrice fairer
Than ever Maud was, or higher-spirited
Than Cleopatra or your English Countess.
Then on a sudden he's so merry again,
Outlaughs a waiting-woman, before her first child;
And in the turning of a hand, so angry—
He's almost beat the northern fellow blind,
That is for that use only. If that mood hold, my lord,
He'd need of a fresh man; I'll undertake
He shall bruise three a month.

DUKE I pity him dearly.
And let it be your charge, with his kind brother,
To see his moods observed. Let every passion
Be fed ev'n to a surfeit, which in time
May breed a loathing. Let him have enough
Of every object that his sense is rapt with;
And being once glutted, then the taste of folly
Will come into disrelish.

FIRST GENTLEMAN I shall see

20 **his memory** i.e. the pages which recall the man who acted ignobly

22 **curious** (*a*) precise in the maintenance of standards (here of courage) (*b*) overly fastidious

25 **growing story** unfolding or continuing life story

29 **coxcomb** foolish person (term derived from the cap worn by a professional fool, like a cock's comb in shape)

30 **he ... for't** Satan, whose pride led him to challenge God

38 **equinoctium** equinox; equality between day and night. Here suggesting even-handedness but also the temporizing or fence-sitting talents of the courtier.

39 **thirteenth of September** day in the unreformed English calendar (ten days behind the correct Gregorian calendar) on which day and night were of equal length

40 **in a scale** equally weighted, without one exceeding the other

42 **primero** card and gambling game in which each player received four cards and each card had three times its usual value

49 **passion** regarded as intensifying feelings which might already be present in the psychological 'humours': see Thomas Wright, *Passions of the Mind* (1601). The Passionate Lord articulates the moods generated by humoural dispositions with a passionate immoderacy.

52 **one while** at one moment, for a time

53 **want of business** lack of (sexual) opportunity, or exercise

54 **laundress** (such a lowly occupation that it did not have a guild and therefore had no formal apprenticeships)

55 **kibed** with chilblains; may imply a woman with sores from venereal disease

57 **Maud** or Matilda (1102–1167), the daughter of Henry I. Named as her father's heir to English throne but eventually gave up her claim to her son, Henry II.

58 **English Countess** Frances Howard, Countess of Somerset, who divorced the Earl of Essex to marry Robert Carr. See Introduction.

62 **northern fellow** probably the clown Galoshio, regularly beaten by the Passionate Lord. 'Northern' seems to imply that he comes from the north of England (or Scotland)

66 **kind brother** (a ghost character who does not appear on stage)

67 **his moods observed** The Duke's treatment of such passions is unusual in permitting rather than forcibly restraining them; contrast the Soldier's reaction and its effect on the Passionate Lord.

Your charge, my lord, most faithfully effected.
Exit [*Duke and other gentlemen*]
And how does noble Chamont?
CHAMONT Never ill, man,
Until I hear of baseness; then I sicken.
I am the healthfull'st man i'th' kingdom else.
FIRST GENTLEMAN
Be armed then for a fit.
Enter Lepet [*aloof off*]
Here comes a fellow
Will make you sick at heart, if baseness do't.
CHAMONT
Let me be gone. What is he?
FIRST GENTLEMAN Let me tell you first.
It can be but a qualm; pray, stay it out, sir.
Come, you've borne more than this.
CHAMONT Borne? Never anything
That was injurious.
FIRST GENTLEMAN Ha, I am far from that.
CHAMONT
He looks as like a man as I have seen one.
What would you speak of him? Speak well, I prithee,
Even for humanity's cause.
FIRST GENTLEMAN You'd have it truth, though?
CHAMONT
What else, sir? I have no reason to wrong heav'n
To favour nature; let her bear her own shame
If she be faulty.
FIRST GENTLEMAN
Monstrous faulty there, sir.
CHAMONT
I'm ill at ease already.
FIRST GENTLEMAN Pray, bear up, sir.
CHAMONT
I prithee, let me take him down with speed then,
Like a wild object that I would not look upon.
FIRST GENTLEMAN
Then thus: he's one that will endure as much
As can be laid upon him.
CHAMONT That may be noble.
I'm kept too long from his acquaintance.
FIRST GENTLEMAN O sir,
Take heed of rash repentance; you're too forward
To find out virtue where it never settled.
Take the particulars first of what he endures:
Videlicet, bastinadoes by the great.
CHAMONT How!
FIRST GENTLEMAN
Thumps by the dozen and your kicks by wholesale.
CHAMONT No more of him.
FIRST GENTLEMAN
The twinges by the nostril he snuffs up,
And holds it the best remedy for sneezing.
CHAMONT Away.
FIRST GENTLEMAN
He's been thrice switched from seven o'clock till nine,
Yet with a cart-horse stomach fell to breakfast,
Forgetful of his smart.
CHAMONT Nay, the disgrace on't;
There is no smart but that. Base things are felt
More by their shames than hurts.
[*Chamont meets Lepet*]
Sir, I know you not,
But that you live an injury to nature
I'm heartily angry with you.
LEPET
Pray give your blow or kick, and begone then:
For I ne'er saw you before, and indeed
Have nothing to say to you, for I know you not.
CHAMONT
Why, wouldst thou take a blow?
LEPET I would not, sir,
Unless 'twere offered me; and if from an enemy—
I'd be loath to deny it from a stranger.
CHAMONT What, a blow?
Endure a blow? And shall he live that gives it?
LEPET
Many a fair year—why not, sir?
CHAMONT Let me wonder!
As full a man to see too, and as perfect—
I prithee, live not long.
LEPET How?
CHAMONT Let me entreat it.
Thou dost not know what wrong thou dost mankind
To walk so long here, not to die betimes.
Let me advise thee, while thou hast to live here,
Ev'n for man's honour's sake, take not a blow more.
LEPET
You should advise them not to strike me then, sir,
For I'll take none, assure you, 'less they are given.
CHAMONT
How fain would I preserve man's form from shame
And cannot get it done!—However, sir,
I charge thee live not long.
LEPET This is worse than beating.

76 **kingdom** (here as elsewhere suggesting that the play's real locale is the kingdom of England, not an unnamed dukedom)
else otherwise
86–7 **wrong . . . nature** lie (before God) to protect man (nature)
87 **her** (nature was often more or less definitely personified as a female being)
91 **wild object** something beyond the laws of nature and culture, excessive, implicitly monstrous
98 ***Videlicet*** 'that is to say', or 'namely' (Latin); introduces amplification or explanation
bastinadoes blows with sticks or cudgels
by the great at a fixed price for the whole amount
99 **How** (expression of shock)
100 **your** one's, anyone's
102 **twinges . . . nostril** physical abuse with the implication of social provocation
105 **switched** hit with a switch
106 **cart-horse stomach** with huge and hearty appetite
124 **betimes** forthwith, speedily

CHAMONT
Of what profession art thou—tell me, sir—
Besides a tailor? For I'll know the truth.

LEPET
A tailor? I'm as good a gentleman—
Can show my arms and all.

CHAMONT How black and blue they are?
Is that your manifestation? Upon pain
Of pounding thee to dust, assume not wrongfully
The name of gentleman—because I am one,
That must not let thee live.

LEPET I have done, I have done, sir!
If there be any harm, beshrew the herald.
I'm sure I ha' not been so long a gentleman
To make this anger; I have nothing nowhere
But what I dearly pay for.

CHAMONT Groom, begone! *Exit Lepet*
I never was so heartsick yet of man.

Enter Lady (the Duke's sister) and Lepet's wife

FIRST GENTLEMAN
Here comes a cordial, sir, from t'other sex,
Able to make a dying face look cheerful.

CHAMONT [*to Lady*]
The blessedness of ladies—

LADY You're well met, sir.

CHAMONT
The sight of you has put an evil from me,
Whose breath was able to make virtue sicken.

LADY
I'm glad I came so fortunately. What was't, sir?

CHAMONT
A thing that takes a blow, lives and eats after it,
In very good health; you ha' not seen the like, madam.
A monster worth your sixpence, lovely worth.

LADY
Speak low, sir; by all likelihoods 'tis her husband,
That now bestowed a visitation on me.
Farewell, sir. *Exit*

CHAMONT
'Husband'? Is't possible he has a wife?
Would any creature have him? 'Twas some forced match.
If he were not kicked to th' church o'th' wedding day,
I'll never come at court. Can be no otherwise.
Perhaps he was rich.—Speak, Mistress Lepet, was it not so?

WIFE Nay, that's without all question.

CHAMONT
O ho! He would not want kickers enough then.
If you are wise, I much suspect your honesty,
For wisdom never fastens constantly
But upon merit. If you incline to fool,
You are alike unfit for his society.
Nay, if it were not boldness in the man
That honours you, to advise you—troth, his company
Should not be frequent with you.

WIFE 'Tis good counsel, sir.

CHAMONT
O I am so careful where I reverence—
So just to goodness and her precious purity,
I am as equally jealous and as fearful
That any undeservèd stain might fall
Upon her sanctified whiteness, as of the sin
That comes by wilfulness.

WIFE Sir, I love your thoughts,
And honour you for your counsel and your care.

CHAMONT [*bowing*]
We are your servants.

WIFE [*aside*] He's but a gentleman
O'th' chamber; he might have kissed me. Faith,
Where shall one find less courtesy than at court?
Say I have an undeserver to my husband;
That's ne'er the worse for him. Well, strange-lipped men,
'Tis but a kiss lost; there'll more come again. *Exit*

Enter the Passionate Lord (the Duke's kinsman), makes a congee or two to nothing

FIRST GENTLEMAN [*aside to Chamont*]
Look who comes here, sir. His love fit's upon him.
I know it by that set smile and those congees.
How courteous he's to nothing—which, indeed,
Is the next kin to woman; only shadow
The elder sister of the twain, because 'tis seen too.
See how it kisses the forefinger still—
Which is the last edition, and (being come

133 **tailor** (term of abuse or ridicule; also suggests he is fashionably dressed)
135 **arms** coat of arms, to indicate his rank
136 **manifestation** demonstration or revelation of qualities; suggests the heraldic display of arms; emblem. Pun on 'man'.
140 **herald** herald at arms who regulated the devices of the gentry and aristocracy
141–3 **I ha' . . . for** (he has only recently been elevated to the gentry and has paid for the privilege)
143 **Groom** (insult because of the groom's low social status; the dominant modern sense of 'one who attends horses' was only used contextually)
145 **cordial** invigorating, medicinal thing; heartening
153 **monster . . . sixpence** (freaks were displayed at fairs for profit)
lovely worth (sarcastic: 'and what a charming thing you see for your money')
154 **low** softly
158 **forced match** 'arranged marriage' or 'shotgun wedding'
164 **honesty** chastity
179 **chamber** reception room in a palace and therefore a court office
kissed social greeting (refers to gentleman of l. 178)
180 **courtesy** (pun on 'court')
182 **strange-lipped** unwilling to be kissed
183.2 ***congee*** bow, in courtesy
186–8 **nothing . . . too** although, like a shadow, woman is effectively nothing—yet she is visible
189 **it** derogatory term for 'him'
kisses . . . forefinger (fashionable behaviour)
190 **Which . . . edition** courtesy learnt from courtesy books of the latest edition—i.e. fashion. (Also possibly the Passionate Lord is kissing his fingers, and this refers to the last finger before the thumb.)

So near the thumb) every cobbler has got it.
CHAMONT
What a ridiculous piece humanity
Here makes itself!
FIRST GENTLEMAN Nay, good, give leave a little, sir,
You're so precise a manhood—
CHAMONT It afflicts me
When I behold unseemliness in an image
So near the Godhead; 'tis an injury
To glorious eternity.
FIRST GENTLEMAN Pray use patience, sir.
PASSIONATE LORD [*to First Gentleman*]
I do confess it freely, precious lady—
And love's suit is so, the longer it hangs
The worse it is; better cut off, sweet madam.
O that same drawing-in your nether lip there
Foreshows no goodness, lady. Make you question on't?
Shame on me but I love you.
FIRST GENTLEMAN Who is't, sir,
You are at all this pains for? May I know her?
PASSIONATE LORD
For thee thou fairest, yet the falsest woman,
That ever broke man's heartstrings.
FIRST GENTLEMAN How? How's this, sir?
PASSIONATE LORD
What, the old trick of ladies, man's apparel?
Will't ne'er be left amongst you? steal from court in't?
FIRST GENTLEMAN [*to Chamont*]
I see the fit grows stronger.
PASSIONATE LORD Pray, let's talk a little.
CHAMONT
I can endure no more.
FIRST GENTLEMAN Good, let us alone a little.
You are so exact a work: love light things somewhat, sir.
CHAMONT
They're all but shames.
FIRST GENTLEMAN [*to Passionate Lord*]
What is't you'd say to me, sir?
PASSIONATE LORD
Can you be so forgetful to enquire it, lady?
FIRST GENTLEMAN
Yes, truly, sir.
PASSIONATE LORD
The more I admire your flintiness.
What cause have I given you, illustrious madam,
To play this strange part with me?
FIRST GENTLEMAN Cause enough.
Do but look back, sir, into your memory,
Your love to other women. O lewd man,
It's almost killed my heart! You see I'm changed with it;
I ha' lost the fashion of my sex with grief on't,
When I have seen you courting of a dowdy,
Compared with me, and kissing your forefinger
To one o'th' blackguard's mistresses. Would not this
Crack a poor lady's heart, that believed love,
And waited for the comfort? But 'twas said, sir,
A lady of my hair cannot want pitying.
The country's coming up; farewell to you, sir.
PASSIONATE LORD
Whither intend you, sir?
FIRST GENTLEMAN A long journey, sir.
The truth is, I'm with child, and go to travel.
PASSIONATE LORD
With child? I never got it.
FIRST GENTLEMAN I heard you were busy
At the same time, sir, and was loath to trouble you.
PASSIONATE LORD
Why, are not you a whore then, excellent madam?
FIRST GENTLEMAN
O, by no means! 'Twas done, sir, in the state
Of my belief in you, and that quits me;
It lies upon your falsehood.
PASSIONATE LORD Does it so?—
You shall not carry her though, sir; she's my contract.
CHAMONT
I prithee, thou four elements ill-brewed,
Torment none but thyself. Away, I say,

191 **thumb** (biting the thumb implied aggressive intention)
cobbler manual labourer (thumbs are associated with work and with measurement at work)
194 **precise** punctilious about
195–6 **image... Godhead** (alluding to the idea that man is made in God's image)
198 **lady** (he assumes the First Gentleman is a woman in disguise)
200 **cut off** 'abridged, abrupt' (declaration of love) or 'castrated'
201 **nether lip** lower lip (also suggesting vulva; the tightness of the lips suggests she will not be sexually open)
208 **steal from court** possibly referring to Arabella Stuart's escape from the court in 1610
221 **dowdy** shabby or unattractively dressed woman
223 **blackguard's** criminal, vagabond, idler
225 **comfort** consolation (here the consolation or invigorating influence of knowing oneself to be loved, with an ambiguity about whether the anticipated consolation is spiritual or physical, sexual)
226 **hair** appearance, type
want lack
227 **country's coming up** people (here presumably potential suitors) are coming to London to attend court
228 **sir** (a possible form of address to females as well as males)
229 **travel** pun on 'travail' (labour, childbirth)
233–5 **'Twas... falsehood** (the logic of this claim seems to be that because 'she' was in a state of belief in, or fantasy about, the Passionate Lord when the child was conceived, the conception does not constitute unfaithfulness)
236 **contract** bargain, property (also implying 'contracted' to be married)
237 **four elements** in humoural theory earth, water, air, and fire were seen as the elements which constituted personality, and imbalance in the elements (as in the case of the Passionate Lord) was seen as causing behavioural patterns and changes

Thou beast of passion, as the drunkard is
The beast of wine; dishonour to thy making,
Thou man in fragments.

PASSIONATE LORD [*kneeling to First Gentleman*]
Hear me, precious madam.

CHAMONT
Kneel for thy wits to heaven.

PASSIONATE LORD Lady, I'll father it,
Whoe'er begot it; 'tis the curse of greatness.

CHAMONT How virtue groans at this!

PASSIONATE LORD
I'll raise the court, but I will stay your flight.
Exit Passionate Lord

CHAMONT
How wretched is that piece!

FIRST GENTLEMAN He's the Duke's kinsman, sir.

CHAMONT
That cannot take away a passion, sir,
Nor cut a fit but one poor hour shorter.
He must endure as much as the poor'st beggar
That cannot change his money; there's the equality
In our impartial essence.
Enter a Servant
What's the news now?

SERVANT
Your worthy brother, sir, has left his charge,
And come to see you.
Enter Chamont's brother (a soldier)

CHAMONT [*embracing him*]
O the noblest welcome
That ever came from man meet thy deservings!
Methinks I've all joy's treasure in mine arms now.

SOLDIER
You are so fortunate in prevention, brother,
You always leave the answerer barren, sir;
You comprehend in few words so much worth—

CHAMONT
'Tis all too little for thee. Come, thou'rt welcome.
So I include all: take especial knowledge, pray,
Of this dear gentleman (my absolute friend)
That loves a soldier far above a mistress,
Though excellently faithful to 'em both;
But love to manhood owns the purer troth. *Exeunt*

❁

[*Incipit*] *Actus Secundus* 2.1

[*Chairs.*] *Enter Chamont's brother (a Soldier) and a Lady (the Duke's sister)*

LADY
There should be in this gallery—O they're here.
[*She sits*]
Pray, sit down; believe me, sir, I'm weary.

SOLDIER
It well becomes a Lady to complain a little
Of what she never feels. Your walk was short,
madam.
You can be but afraid of weariness
(Which well employs the softness of your sex);
As for the thing itself, you never came to't.

LADY
You're wondrously well read in ladies, sir.

SOLDIER
Shall I think such a creature as you, madam,
Was ever born to feel pain, but in travail?
There's your full portion,
Besides a little toothache in the breeding,
Which a kind husband too takes from you, madam.

LADY
But where do ladies, sir, find such kind husbands?
Perhaps you have heard
The rheumatic story of some loving chandler now,
Or some such melting fellow, that you talk
So prodigal of men's kindness. I confess, sir,
Many of those wives are happy their ambition
Does reach no higher than to love and ignorance,
Which makes an excellent husband, and a fond one.
Now sir, your great ones aim at height and cunning,
And so are oft deceived. Yet they must venture it;
For 'tis a lady's cóntumely, sir,
To have a lord an ignorant; then the world's voice
Will deem her for a wanton ere she taste on't.
But to deceive a wise man, to whose circumspection
The world resigns itself (with all his envy),
'Tis less dishonour to us then to fall,
Because his believed wisdom keeps out all.

SOLDIER
Would I were the man, lady, that should venture
His wisdom to your goodness.

LADY You might fail
In the return, as many men have done, sir.
I dare not justify what is to come of me,

242 **father** act as the male parent and therefore give his name
245 **raise** arouse, alert, disturb
stay your flight prevent your escape
246 **wretched** (*a*) miserable (*b*) base, contemptibly low in status
piece man, creature (as in 'piece of flesh')
250 **change his money** transform his fortunes
258 **comprehend** sum up
264 **owns** has a claim to being
2.1.12 **toothache** (considered a side effect of pregnancy)
breeding (*a*) pregnancy (*b*) sexual intercourse
13 **kind husband** the husband removes her 'ache', perhaps implying her desire
16 **rheumatic** tearful, weeping
chandler maker or seller of candles
17 **melting** sentimental, drippy
22 **height and cunning** high position and cleverness (here qualities seen as incompatible with male marital fidelity)
24 **cóntumely** reproach, insult
25 **ignorant** idiot
31–2 **venture... goodness** risk his wisdom in trusting to her sexual fidelity and deserved good name
33 **return** profit which comes back from on commodities risked in a trading 'venture' (the outcome of taking a risk on a woman's 'goodness')

Because I know it not, though I hope virtuously;
Marry, what's past or present, I durst put
Into a good man's hand, which if he take
Upon my word for good, it shall not cozen him.

SOLDIER
No, nor hereafter?

LADY
It may hap so too, sir.
A woman's goodness, when she is a wife,
Lies much upon a man's desert, believe it, sir.
If there be fault in her, I'll pawn my life on't,
'Tis first in him, if she were ever good.
That makes me, knowing not a husband yet,
Or what he may be, promise no more virtues
Than I may well perform, for that were cozenage.

SOLDIER
Happy were he that had you with all fears!
That's my opinion, lady.

Enter Chamont and a servant list'ning. [*They talk apart*]

SERVANT
What say you now, sir?
Dare you give confidence to your own eyes?

CHAMONT
Not yet, I dare not.

SERVANT
No?

CHAMONT
Scarce yet, or yet—
Although I see 'tis he. Why, can a thing
That's but myself divided be so false?

SERVANT
Nay, do but mark how the chair plays his part too;
How amorously 'tis bent.

CHAMONT
Hell take thy bad thoughts!
For they are strange ones; never take delight
To make a torment worse.—Look on 'em, heaven,
For that's a brother. Send me a fair enemy,
And take him; for a fouler fiend there breathes not.
I will not sin, to think there's ill in her
But what's of his producing.
Yet goodness, whose enclosure is but flesh,
Holds out oft times but sorrily. But as black, sir,
As ever kindred was, I hate mine own blood,
Because it is so near thine. Live without honesty,
And mayst thou die with an unmoistened eye,
And no tear follow thee. *Exeunt Chamont, Servant*

LADY
You're wondrous merry, sir;
I would your brother heard you.

SOLDIER
Or my sister;
I would not out o'th' way let fall my words, lady,
For the precisest humour.

Enter Passionate Lord

PASSIONATE LORD [*aside*]
Yea, so close?

SOLDIER
They're merry; that's the worst you can report on 'em;
They're neither dangerous nor immodest.

PASSIONATE LORD
So, sir,
Shall I believe you, think you?

SOLDIER
Who's this, lady?

LADY
O, the Duke's cousin; he came late from travel, sir.

SOLDIER
Respect belongs to him.

PASSIONATE LORD
For as I said, lady,
'They're merry; that's the worst you can report on 'em.
They're neither dangerous nor immodest.'

SOLDIER
How's this?

PASSIONATE LORD
And there I think I left.

SOLDIER [*aside*]
Abuses me!

[*The Soldier stands apart*]

PASSIONATE LORD
Now to proceed, lady. Perhaps I swore I loved you;
If you believe me not, you're much the wiser.

SOLDIER [*aside*]
He speaks still in my person, and derides me.

PASSIONATE LORD
For I can cog with you.

LADY
You can all do so.
We make no question of men's promptness that way.

PASSIONATE LORD
And smile, and wave a chair with comely grace too,
Play with our tassel gently, and do fine things
That catch a lady sooner than a virtue.

SOLDIER [*aside*]
I never used to let man live so long that wronged me.

PASSIONATE LORD
Talk of battalions, woo you in a skirmish,
Divulge my mind to you, lady, and (being sharp set)
Can court you at half-pike, or name your weapon—
We cannot fail you, lady.

Enter First Gentleman [*behind*]

SOLDIER [*aside*]
Now he dies
Were all succeeding hopes stored up within him.

38 **cozen** deceive

43 **'Tis . . . good** i.e., if a woman ever had any virtue, her fall from it must have occurred because she was corrupted by some man, who fell before she did

44 **That makes me** i.e, the foregoing logic is why I

53 **chair** (seems to imply that Soldier is leaning towards the Lady, using a chair as an aid to flirtation)

62 **sorrily** feebly

67 **would** wish that
sister sister-in-law (assuming she will marry Chamont)

68–9 **I . . . humour** (A precisian is exact in observing forms, so perhaps the Soldier is suggesting that he would be unhappy for his words to wander 'out of the way', the strict path, followed by the most correct and exact observer of forms—as Chamont might be said to be.)

75–6 **They're . . . immodest** (Passionate Lord mimics the Soldier's manner.)

81 **cog** play or deal dishonestly

84 **tassel** (*a*) part of clothing (*b*) penis (*c*) 'tassel gentle'—the male hawk

88 **sharp set** (*a*) set on edge, having an appetite (*b*) prepared with a sharp weapon

89 **weapon** (*a*) military skill (*b*) penis

91 **succeeding hopes** 'hopes of succession', i.e. chances for the continuation of the ruling line

[He draws his sword]
FIRST GENTLEMAN *[to Soldier]*
O fie, i'th' court, sir?
SOLDIER I most dearly thank you, sir.
[He sheathes his sword]
FIRST GENTLEMAN
'Tis rage ill spent upon a passionate madman.
SOLDIER
That shall not privilege him for ever, sir.
A madman call you him? I have found too much reason
Sound in his injury to me to believe him so.
FIRST GENTLEMAN
If ever truth from man's lips may be held
In reputation with you, give this confidence;
And this' his love-fit, which we observe still,
By's flattering and his fineness: at some other time,
He'll go as slovenly as heart can wish.
The love and pity that his highness shows to him
Makes every man the more respectful of him:
Has never a passion, but is well provided for—
As this of love. He is full fed in all;
His swinge, as I may term it. Have but patience,
And ye shall witness somewhat.
SOLDIER Still he mocks me,
Look you, in action, in behaviour.
[The Soldier addresses the Passionate Lord]
Sir,
Hold still the chair, with a grand mischief to you,
Or I'll set so much strength upon your heart, sir—
PASSIONATE LORD
I feel some power has restrained me, lady.
If it be sent from love, say, I obey it,
And ever keep a voice to welcome it.
[The Passionate Lord sings]
Thou deity, swift-wingèd love,
Sometimes below, sometimes above,
Little in shape, but great in power,
Thou that mak'st a heart thy tower,
And thy loop-holes, ladies' eyes,
From whence thou strik'st the fond and wise.
Did all the shafts in thy fair quiver
Stick fast in my ambitious liver,
Yet thy power would I adore
And call upon thee to shoot more.
Shoot more, shoot more.
Enter one like a Cupid offring to shoot at him
I prithee hold though, sweet celestial boy.
I'm not requited yet with love enough
For the first arrow that I have within me.
And if thou be an equal archer, Cupid,
Shoot this lady, and twenty more for me.
LADY Me, sir?
FIRST GENTLEMAN
'Tis nothing but device; fear it not, lady.
You may be as good a maid after that shaft, madam,
As e'er your mother was at twelve and a half.
'Tis like the boy that draws it; 't'as no sting yet.
CUPID *(aside)*
'Tis like the miserable maid that draws it,
That sees no comfort yet, seeing him so passionate.
PASSIONATE LORD
Strike me the Duchess of Valois in love with me,
With all the speed thou canst, and two of her women.
CUPID
You shall have more. *Exit*
PASSIONATE LORD Tell 'em I tarry for 'em.
FIRST GENTLEMAN *[to Soldier]*
Who would be angry with that walking trouble now
That hurts none but itself?
SOLDIER I am better quieted.
PASSIONATE LORD
I'll have all womenkind struck in time for me
After thirteen once.
—I see this Cupid will not let me want;
And let him spend his forty shafts an hour,
They shall be all found from the Duke's exchequer.
He's come already.
Enter again the same Cupid, two Brothers, six women Masquers, Cupid's bow bent all the way towards them, the first woman singing and playing; a Priest
FIRST WOMAN MASQUER *(sings)*
O turn thy bow!
Thy power we feel and know;
Fair Cupid, turn away thy bow.

92 **i'th' court** (where drawing of weapons was forbidden)
99 **this'** this is
100 **By's** by his, visible in his
102 **his highness** i.e. the Duke (although the title is usually reserved for kings)
106 **swinge** (*a*) blow (*b*) scope or free course to indulge one's inclinations
108 **action** gesture
115 **below ... above** (*a*) devilish ... heavenly (*b*) ethereal, intellectual ... physical (*c*) on the upper parts of the body ... on the lower parts
116 **Little** alluding to the small size of (*a*) Cupid (*b*) a penis
118 **loop-holes** vertical opening in fortification to allow the firing of missiles
119 **fond** foolish
121 **liver** organ which secretes bile; the seat of violent passion
128 **equal** impartial
131 **device** conceit, or play-acting elaborating a symbolic story
132 **shaft** pun on (*a*) stalk of Cupid's arrow (*b*) penis in sexual intercourse
133 **twelve and a half** (too young to have had intercourse)
134 **sting** (*a*) power to hurt, or 'bite' (*b*) pole used as a weapon, or organ used to insert poisonous fluid—hence, 'erect penis'
137 **Duchess of Valois** See Introduction.
142 **in time** (*a*) eventually (*b*) at an appropriate time
143 **After thirteen once** For the audience this picks up and twists the first gentleman's words to the Lady: he intends to have sex once with every female who has passed her thirteenth birthday (normal age of puberty)
146 **They ... exchequer** i.e. they will be paid for out of the national treasury

They be those golden arrows
Bring ladies all their sorrows,
And till there be more truth in men
Never shoot at maid again.

PASSIONATE LORD
What a felicity of whores are here!
And all my concubines, struck bleeding new.
A man can in his lifetime make but one woman,
But he may make his fifty queans a month.
[*Cupid, two Brothers, and Priest talk apart*]

CUPID
Have you remembered a priest, honest brothers?

FIRST BROTHER
Yes, sister, and this is the young gentleman.
Make you no question of our faithfulness.

SECOND BROTHER
This growing shame, sister, provokes our care.

PRIEST
He must be taken in this fit of love, gentlemen.

FIRST BROTHER
What else, sir? He shall do't.

SECOND BROTHER Enough.

FIRST BROTHER Be cheerful, wench.

A dance, Cupid leading

PASSIONATE LORD
Now by the stroke of pleasure (a deep oath),
Nimbly hopped, ladies all. What height they bear, too!
A storey higher than your common statures—
A little man must go up stairs to kiss 'em.
What a great space there is
Betwixt love's dining chamber and his garret!
I'll try the utmost height—the garret stoops, methinks.
The rooms are made all bending, I see that,
And not so high as a man takes 'em for.

CUPID
Now, if you'll follow me, sir, I've that power
To make them follow you.

PASSIONATE LORD Are they all shot?

CUPID
All, all, sir, every mother's daughter of 'em.

PASSIONATE LORD
Then there's no fear of following; if they be once shot,
They'll follow a man to th' devil.—
[*To Soldier*] As for you, sir—
Exit with the Lady and the Masquers,
[*Cupid, two Brothers, and the Priest*]

SOLDIER Me, sir?

FIRST GENTLEMAN Nay, sweet sir.

SOLDIER
A noise, a threat'ning; did you not hear it, sir?

FIRST GENTLEMAN
Without regard, sir; so would I have you.

SOLDIER
This must come to something. Never talk of that, sir;
You never saw it otherwise.

FIRST GENTLEMAN Nay, dear merit—

SOLDIER
Me, above all men?

FIRST GENTLEMAN Troth, you wrong your anger.

SOLDIER [*calling to Passionate Lord*]
I will be armed, my honourable lecher!

FIRST GENTLEMAN O fie, sweet sir!

SOLDIER [*calling to Passionate Lord*]
That devours women's honesties by lumps
And never chew'st thy pleasure.

FIRST GENTLEMAN What do you mean, sir?

SOLDIER
What does *he* mean? T'engross all to himself?
There's others love a whore, as well as he, sir.

FIRST GENTLEMAN
O, an that be part o'th' fury, we have a city
Is very well provided for that case.
Let him alone with them, sir; we have women
Are very charitable to proper men
And to a soldier that has all his limbs.
Marry, the sick and lame gets not a penny:
Right women's charity, and the husbands follow't too.

155 **felicity of whores** a propitiously large number of prostitutes, enough to make the Passionate Lord happy (like a 'pride of lions')

157 **make** mate, honestly marry

158 **queans** prostitutes. The joke works in three ways: (*a*) the Passionate Lord implies that he can 'make' prostitutes in the sense of having sexual intercourse with them but (*b*) also in the sense of making women into prostitutes by taking their virginity; (*c*) there is also a pun on queans/queens with the joke here being that of the relative status and sexual availability of queens and prostitutes.

162 **growing shame** i.e. her increasingly visible pregnancy, which (since she is umarried) shames her and her relatives

170 **dining chamber . . . garret** a downstairs room for eating, and a room in the uppermost floor, suggesting a physical analogy between the sexual body below and the intellectual head above

171 **height** (*a*) loftiness, in accordance with the Platonic conventions of the court masque (*b*) physical tallness (because the women were in fact played by males)
garret stoops (*a*) masquer curtsies (*b*) building leans

172 **bending** (*a*) like a crooked building (*b*) curved, curvaceous (*c*) morally 'bent' rather than straight; another comment on female chastity

173 **high** pun on (*a*) physical height (*b*) moral elevation

175 **shot** i.e. pierced by Cupid's darts (punning on sexual ejaculation, believed to occur in both sexes)

179.1–2 ***Exit with . . . the Priest*** (for the Priest will marry them, offstage)

187 **by lumps** (suggesting immoderate greed and lack of table manners)

189 **T'engross** to require the whole use of something, or to monopolize it

191 **an** if
city City of London (by contrast to, but also physically adjoining, the Court)

194 **charitable** ironic: willing to 'give generously' of their sexual favours
proper complete, perfect

Here comes his highness, sir.

Enter Duke, and Lords [among them, the second, third, and fourth Gentlemen]

SOLDIER I'll walk to cool myself. *Exit*

DUKE
Who's that?

FIRST GENTLEMAN
The brother of Chamont.

DUKE
He's brother then
To all the court's love—they that love discreetly,
And place their friendliness upon desert.
As for the rest, that with a double face
Look upon merit (much like Fortune's visage,
That looks two ways, both to life's calms and storms),
I'll so provide for him, chiefly for him,
He shall not wish their loves, nor dread their envies.
And here comes my Chamont.

Enter Chamont [speaking to himself]

CHAMONT
That lady's virtues are my only joys,
And he to offer to lay siege to them?

DUKE [*to Chamont*] Chamont.

CHAMONT
Her goodness is my pride; in all discourses,
As often as I hear rash-tongued gallànts
Speak rudely of a woman, presently
I give in but her name, and they're all silent.
O, who would lose this benefit?

DUKE [*to Chamont*] Come hither, sir.

CHAMONT
'Tis like the gift of healing, but diviner,
For that but cures diseases in the body;
This works a cure on fame, on reputation—
The noblest piece of surgery upon earth.

DUKE Chamont!—He minds me not.

CHAMONT A brother do't?

DUKE Chamont, I say.

He gives him a touch with his switch

CHAMONT Ha?
If he be mortal, by this hand he perishes.

[He draws his sword]

Unless it be a stroke from heaven, he dies for't.

DUKE
Why, how now, sir? 'Twas I.

CHAMONT
The more's my misery.

DUKE
Why, what's the matter, prithee?

CHAMONT
Can you ask it, sir?
No man else should. Stood forty lives before him,
By this I would have oped my way to him.
It could not be you, sir; excuse him not,
Whate'er he be. Speak, as you're dear to honour,
That I may find my peace again.

DUKE
Forbear, I say.
Upon my love to truth, 'twas none but I.

CHAMONT
Still miserable!

DUKE
Come, come, what ails you, sir?

CHAMONT
Never sat shame cooling so long upon me
Without a satisfaction in revenge,
And heaven has made it here a sin to wish it.

DUKE Hark you, sir.

CHAMONT
O you've undone me.

DUKE
How?

CHAMONT
Cruelly undone me!
I have lost my peace and reputation by you.
Sir, pardon me, I can never love you more. *Exit*

DUKE What language call you this, sirs?

FIRST GENTLEMAN
Truth my Lord, I've seldom heard a stranger.

SECOND GENTLEMAN
He is a man of a most curious valour,
Wondrous precise and punctual in that virtue.

DUKE
But why to me so punctual? My last thought
Was most entirely fixed on his advancement.
Why, I came now to put him in possession
Of his fair fortunes—what a misconceiver 'tis!—
And from a Gentleman of our Chamber merely
Make him Vice-Admiral. I was settled in't;
I love him next to health. Call him, gentlemen.

Exit First Gentleman

Why, would not you, or you ha' taken as much
And never murmured?

SECOND GENTLEMAN Troth, I think we should, my lord,
And there's a fellow walks about the court
Would take a hundred of 'em.

DUKE
I hate you all for't,
And rather praise his high-pitched fortitude,
Though in extremes for niceness. Now I think on't,
I would I had never done't.

Enter First Gentleman

Now, sir, where is he?

FIRST GENTLEMAN
His suit is only, sir, to be excused.

203 **Fortune's visage** i.e. Fortune's 'double face' may smile or frown
229 **this** (*a*) now (*b*) this sword
244 **curious** particular, precise
245 **punctual** exact in every point; accurate, superscrupulous
250 **merely** both 'only' (referring backward to 'Gentleman of our Chamber', an office of personal attendance on the sovereign, without official function in governance) and 'actually' (referring forward to 'Make him . . .')
251 **Vice-Admiral** naval position second to admiral or commander of a national fleet. (Buckingham, James I's favourite, was Admiral of England.)
258 **niceness** fastidiousness

DUKE
He shall not be excused. I love him dearlier.
Say we entreat him; go, he must not leave us.
Exit two Gentlemen
So virtue bless me, I ne'er knew him paralleled.
Why, he's more precious to me now than ever.
Enter two Gentlemen and Chamont [*who stands apart*]

SECOND GENTLEMAN
With much fair language, sir, we've brought him.

DUKE Thanks.
Where is he?

SECOND GENTLEMAN
Yonder, sir.

DUKE [*to Chamont*] Come forward, man.

CHAMONT
Pray, pardon me. I'm ashamed to be seen, sir.

DUKE
Was ever such a touchy man heard of?—
Prithee, come nearer.

CHAMONT More into the light?
Put not such cruelty into your requests, my Lord,
First to disgrace me publicly, and then draw me
Into men's eyesight, with the shame yet hot
Upon my reputation.

DUKE What disgrace, sir?

CHAMONT What?
Such as there can be no forgiveness for,
That I can find in honour.

DUKE That's most strange, sir.

CHAMONT
Yet I have searched my bosom to find one,
And wrestled with my inclinatïon,
But 'twill not be. Would you had killed me, sir!
With what an ease had I forgiven you then!
But to endure a stroke from any hand
Under a punishing angel's (which is justice),
Honour disclaim that man, for my part chiefly:
Had it been yet the malice of your sword,
Though it had cleft me, 't had been noble to me;
You should have found my thanks paid in a smile
If I had fell unworded. But to shame me,
With the correction that your horse should have,
Were you ten thousand times my royal lord,
I cannot love you, never, nor desire to serve you
more.
If your drum call me, I am vowed to valour,
But peace shall never know me yours again,
Because I've lost mine own. I speak to die, sir.
Would you were gracious that way to take off shame
With the same swiftness as you pour it on:
And since it is not in the power of monarchs
To make a gentleman (which is a substance
Only begot of merit), they should be careful
Not to destroy the worth of one so rare
Which neither they can make; nor, lost, repair.
Exit [*behind*]

DUKE [*to Chamont*]
You've set a fair light, sir, before my judgement,
Which burns with wondrous clearness; I acknowledge
it,
And your worth with it. But then, sir, my love,
My love—what, gone again?

FIRST GENTLEMAN And full of scorn, my lord.

DUKE
That language will undo the man that keeps it,
Who knows no difference 'twixt contempt and man-
hood.
Upon your love to goodness, gentlemen,
Let me not lose him long.
Enter a huntsman
How now?

HUNTSMAN The game's at height, my lord.

DUKE
Confound both thee and it! Hence, break it off!
[*Exit Huntsman*]
He hates me brings me news of any pleasure.
I felt not such a conflict since I could
Distinguish betwixt worthiness and blood. *Exeunt*

❁

[*Incipit*] *Actus Tertius* 3.1
Enter the two Brothers, First Gentleman, with those that were the Masquers, and the Cupid

FIRST GENTLEMAN
I heartily commend your project, gentlemen.
'Twas wise and virtuous.

FIRST BROTHER 'Twas for the safety
Of precious honour, sir, which near blood binds us to.
He promised the poor easy fool there marriage.
There was a good maidenhead lost i'th' belief on't.

281 **punishing angel's** angel employed by deity to exact retribution
282 **disclaim** disown
287 **your horse** (Buckingham was the King's Master of the Horse.)
288 **my royal lord** (like 'monarchs' at l. 301, encouraging the audience to think of a king rather than a 'Duke')
290 **drum** military drum, used to summon soldiers to combat
292 **mine own** i.e. my inner peace
speak to die (*a*) request death (*b*) speak so bluntly that I may be executed for it
295–6 **it...gentleman** A paradoxical claim, since a monarch can enoble even a commoner. But 'gentleman' is here considered a category of intrinsic personal worth and accomplishment ('merit'), which cannot be bestowed by anyone else.
308 **game's** hunt's
309–10 **Confound...pleasure** (a reaction in striking contrast to King James, who refused to interrupt his hunting when told of the Spanish attack on his son-in-law's territory)
3.1.1–2 **your project...'Twas** The 'project' here spoken of in the past tense is the marriage of the Passionate Lord and Cupid, apparently offstage during the interval between Acts 2 and 3; the Cupid is now legally married, but must still win her new husband's 'love, the main point' (3.1.13).
3 **near blood** close kinship

Beshrew her hasty confidence!

FIRST GENTLEMAN O, no more, sir,
You make her weep again!—Alas, poor Cupid.—
Shall she not shift herself?

FIRST BROTHER O by no means, sir:
We dare not have her seen yet. All the while
She keeps this shape, 'tis but thought device,
And she may follow him so, without suspicion—
To see if she can draw all his wild passions
To one point only, and that's love, the main point.
So far his highness grants, and gave at first
Large approbation to the quick conceit,
Which then was quick indeed.

FIRST GENTLEMAN You make her blush, in sooth.

FIRST BROTHER
I fear 'tis more the flag of shame than grace, sir.

FIRST GENTLEMAN
They both give but one kind of colour, sir.
If it be bashfulness in that kind taken,
It is the same with grace—and there she weeps again.
In truth you're too hard, much much too bitter, sir,
Unless you mean to have her weep her eyes out,
To play a cupid truly.

FIRST BROTHER Come, ha' done then.
We should all fear to sin first; for 'tis certain,
When 'tis once lodged, though entertained in mirth,
It must be wept out, if it e'er come forth.

FIRST GENTLEMAN
Now 'tis so well, I'll leave you.

FIRST BROTHER Faithfully welcome, sir.
[*Exit First Gentleman*]
Go, Cupid, to your charge. He's your own now;
If he want love, none will be blamed but you.

CUPID
The strangest marriage and unfortunat'st bride
That ever human memory contained!
I cannot be myself for't. *Exit* [*Cupid and Masquers*]

Enter the Clown

CLOWN
O gentlemen!

FIRST BROTHER
How now, sir, what's the matter?

CLOWN
His melancholy passion is half spent already;
Then comes his angry fit at the very tail on't.
Then comes in my pain, gentlemen; he's beat me
E'en to a cullis. I am nothing, right worshipful,
But very pap and jelly: I have no bones.
My body's all one burstness. They talk of ribs
And chines most freely abroad i'th' world;
Why, I have no such thing. Whoever lives
To see me dead, gentlemen, shall find me all mummy,
Good to fill gallipots and long dildo-glasses.
I shall not have a bone to throw at a dog.

AMBO
Alas, poor vassal, how he goes!

CLOWN O, gentlemen,
I am unjointed; do but think o' that.
My breast is beat into my maw, that what I eat
I am fain to take't in all at mouth with spoons
(A lamentable hearing)—and 'tis well known, my belly
Is driven into my back.
I earned four crowns a month most dearly, gentlemen,
And one he must have when the fit's upon him;
The privy purse allows it, and 'tis thriftiness.
He would break else some forty pounds in casements,
And in five hundred years undo the kingdom:
I have cast it up to a quarrel.

FIRST BROTHER There's a fellow
Kicked about court; I would he had his place, brother,
But for one fit of his indignation.

SECOND BROTHER
And suddenly I have thought upon a means for't.

FIRST BROTHER
I prithee, how?

SECOND BROTHER
'Tis but preferring, brother,
This stockfish to his service, with a letter
Of commendations, the same way he wishes it.
And then you win his heart: for o' my knowledge
He has laid wait this half-year for a fellow
That will be beaten; and with a safe conscience
We may commend the carriage of this man in't.
No servants he has kept, lusty tall feeders,

8 **shift** change her costume (i.e. put on a woman's clothes again)
15 **quick conceit** rapidly imagined joke or device (of disguising her as Cupid)
16 **quick** pregnant
23 **truly** accurately, i.e. by being blind, like Cupid
26 **wept out** (alluding again to pains of childbirth, but also to repentance more generally)
28 **your own** i.e., your husband
37 **cullis** a thick broth with meat
38 **pap** soft, semi-liquid food
40 **chines** spine; also used of joints of meat using the spine
42 **mummy** ointment used in making mummy; the flesh of the mummy, embalmed
43 **gallipots** earthenware vessels used by apothecaries
dildo-glasses cylindrical glasses (but also a reference to the penis as meat without a bone)
45 **goes** walks
51 **crowns** coins worth five shillings apiece
52 **one** i.e. someone to beat
53 **privy purse** (*a*) budget for the personal expenses of the sovereign and his household entourage (*b*) official responsible for that budget
54 **He . . . casements** (apparently alluding to a notorious fit of madness in which Buckingham's elder brother, John Villiers, broke windows with his bare hands)
56 **cast . . . quarrel** calculated to the cost of a square pane in a casement (a 'quarrel')
57–8 **he . . . his . . . his** Lepet . . . the Clown's . . . the Passionate Lord's
61 **stockfish** codfish, split open and beaten before cooking (i.e. the Clown)
his Lepet's
67 **tall feeders** large eaters

But they have beat him, and turned themselves away.
Now one that would endure is like to stay,
And get good wages of him—and the service too
Is ten times milder, brother; I would not wish it else.
I see the fellow has a sore crushed body,
And the more need he has to be kicked at ease.

CLOWN
Ay, sweet gentlemen, a kick of ease—
Send me to such a master.

SECOND BROTHER No more, I say;
We have one for thee, a soft-footed master,
One that wears wool in's toes.

CLOWN O gentlemen,
Soft garments may you wear,
Soft skins may you wed,
But as plump as pillows,
Both for white and red.
And now will I reveal a secret to you,
Since you provide for my poor flesh so tenderly:
He's hired mere rogues, out of his chamber window,
To beat the soldier, Monsieur Chamont's brother—

FIRST BROTHER
That nothing concerns us, sir.

CLOWN —For no cause, gentlemen,
Unless it be for wearing shoulder points
With longer tags than his.

SECOND BROTHER Is not that somewhat?
By'rlakin, sir, the difference of long tags
Has cost many a man's life, and advanced other some.
Come, follow me. *[Exeunt two Brothers]*

CLOWN See what a gull am I!
O every man in his professïon.
I know a thump now as judiciously
As the proudest he that walks; I'll except none.
Come to a tag, how short I fall!—I'm gone. *[Exit]*

3.2 *Enter Lepet*

LEPET
I have been ruminating with myself
What honour a man loses by a kick.
Why, what's a kick? The fury of a foot,
Whose indignation commonly is stamped
Upon the hinder quarter of a man—
Which is a place very unfit for honour;
The world will confess so much.
Then what disgrace, I pray, does that part suffer
Where honour never comes? I'd fain know that.
This being well forced and urged, may have the power
To move most gallants to take kicks in time,
And spurn out the *duelloes* out o'th' kingdom.
For they that stand upon their honour most
When they conceive there is no honour lost—
As by a table, that I have invented
For that purpose alone, shall appear plainly,
Which shows the vanity of all blows at large,
And with what ease they may be took of all sides,
Numbering but twice o'er the letters 'Patience',
From *P.* to *E.* I doubt not but in small time
To see a dissolution of all bloodshed,
If the reformed kick do but once get up.
For what a lamentable folly 'tis,
If we observe't, for every little jostle
(Which is but the ninth part of a sound thump,
In our meek computation) we must fight forsooth, yes,
If I kill, I'm hanged; if I be killed myself,
I die for't also. Is not this trim wisdom?
Now for the *con*: a man may be well beaten,
Yet pass away his fourscore years smooth after.
I had a father did it, and to my power
I will not be behind him.
Enter Chamont

CHAMONT O, well met.

LEPET *[aside]*
Now a fine punch or two, I look for't duly.

CHAMONT
I've been to seek you.

LEPET Let me know your lodging, sir;
I'll come to you once a day and use your pleasure, sir.

CHAMONT
I'm made the fittest man for thy society:
I'll live and die with thee. Come, show me a chamber;
There is no house but thine, but only thine,
That's fit to cover me. I've took a blow, sirrah.

LEPET
I would you had indeed. Why, you may see, sir;
You'll all come to't in time, when my book's out.

CHAMONT
Since I did see thee last, I've took a blow.

LEPET
Pha, sir! That's nothing; I ha' took forty since.

68 **But they** except that they—i.e. they have all taken this course
turned themselves away left his service
71 **milder** less violent (than waiting on the Passionate Lord)
73 **at ease** in comfortable circumstances (comparatively)
87 **shoulder points** ties, here on the shoulders, using thread etc., to join garments
88 **longer tags** (*a*) pointed hanging pieces for fastening or metal points at the end of a lace to insert through an eye; (*b*) trivial matters over which quarrels might start
89 **By'rlakin** oath: by Our Lady (i.e. Virgin Mary)
difference... tags (*a*) disputes over such accessories, or other trivial matters (*b*) differences in penis size
91 **gull** person easily deceived
92 **in his professïon** to his own business
95 **short I fall** (*a*) fall short of being fully informed (*b*) small my penis hangs down
3.2.4 **stamped** (*a*) kicked (*b*) officially marked and validated (used of coins and printing presses)
9 **fain** be glad to
12 ***duelloes*** duels (Italian)
15 **table** engraved picture or chart
19 **letters 'Patience'** (possible pun on Letters Patent)
22 **reformed** (word with strong connotations of a project of social and religious reformation)
29 ***con*** abbreviated form of Latin preposition 'contra'; the other side of the coin, the argument against

CHAMONT
What? and I charged thee thou shouldst not?
LEPET
Ay, sir,
You might charge your pleasure, but they would give't me,
Whether I would or no.
CHAMONT
O, I walk
Without my peace; I've no companion now.
Prithee resolve me, for I cannot ask
A man more beaten to experience
Than thou art in this kind: what manner of blow
Is held the most disgraceful or distasteful?
For thou dost only censure 'em by the hurt,
Not by the shame they do thee: yet having felt
Abuses of all kinds, thou mayst deliver,
Though't be by chance, the most injurious one.
LEPET
You put me to't, sir. But to tell you truth,
They're all as one with me, little exception.
CHAMONT
That little may do much; let's have it from you.
LEPET
With all the speed I may. First, then, and foremost,
I hold so reverently of the bastinado, sir,
That if it were the dearest friend i'th' world,
I'd put it into his hand.
CHAMONT Go to, I'll pass that then.
LEPET You're the more happy, sir.
Would I were past it too! But being accustomed to't,
It is the better carried.
CHAMONT
Will you forward?
LEPET
Then there's your souse, your wherret, and your douse,
Tugs on the hair, your bob o'th' lips, a whelk on't—
I ne'er could find much difference. Now your thump
(A thing derived first from your hemp-beaters)
Takes a man's wind away, most spitefully:
There's nothing that destroys a colic like it,
For't leaves no wind i'th' body.
CHAMONT
On, sir, on.
LEPET
Pray, give me leave; I'm out of breath with thinking on't.
CHAMONT
This is far off yet.
LEPET
For the twinge by th' nose,
'Tis certainly unsightly—so my table says—
But helps against the headache, wondrous strangely.
CHAMONT Is't possible?
LEPET
O your crushed nostrils slakes your opilation
And makes your pent powers flush to wholesome sneezes.
CHAMONT
I never thought there had been half that virtue
In a wrung nose before.
LEPET
O, plenitude, sir!
Now come we lower, to our modern kick,
Which has been mightily in use of late,
Since our young men drank coltsfoot: and I grant you
'Tis a most scornful wrong, cause the foot plays it.
But mark again, how we that take't, requite it
With the like scorn, for we receive it backward—
And can there be a worse disgrace retorted?
CHAMONT
And is this all?
LEPET
All but a lug by th' ear,
Or such a trifle.
CHAMONT
Happy sufferer!
All this is nothing to the wrong I bear.
I see the worst disgrace thou never felt'st yet.
It is so far from thee, thou canst not think on't;
Nor dare I let thee know, it is so abject.
LEPET
I would you would, though, that I might prepare for't,
For I shall ha't at one time or another.
If't be a thwack, I make account of that;
There's no new-fashioned swap that e'er came up yet,
But I've the first on 'em, I thank 'em for't.
Enter the Lady and Servants
LADY
Hast thou inquired?
FIRST SERVANT
But can hear nothing, madam.
CHAMONT [*aside, to Lepet*]
If there be but so much substance in thee
To make a shelter for a man disgraced,
Hide my departure from that glorious woman
That comes with all perfectïon about her,
So noble, that I dare not be seen of her,
Since shame took hold of me. Upon thy life,
No mention of me!
LEPET [*aside, to Chamont*]
I'll cut out my tongue first,
Before I'll lose my life; there's more belongs to't.
[*Exit Chamont*]

60 **bastinado** blow with a stick or cudgel
67 **souse** blow
wherret a box on the ear or slap in the face
douse heavy blow, given with force and noise
68 **bob** blow with the fist (see also 4.1.340–1)
whelk pimple, pustule, cold sore
70 **hemp-beaters** those who pound the thick fibre into tractable material
79 **slakes** slackens, relaxes, makes less intense and painful
opilation obstruction
80 **flush** rush, start, spring
85 **drank** (*a*) swallowed (*b*) inhaled
coltsfoot an infusion made from leaves of the plant; also smoked as a cure for asthma. Lepet suggests that the medicine conveys to its users the fondness for kicking characteristic of colts.
89 **retorted** turned against an opponent, with the back turned to the giver
99 **swap** sudden harsh blow

LADY
See there's a gentleman, inquire of him.

SECOND SERVANT
For Monsieur Chamont, madam?

LADY
For whom else, sir?

FIRST SERVANT
Why, this fellow dares not see him.

LADY
How?

FIRST SERVANT
Chamont, madam?
His very name's worse than a fever to him,
And when he cries, there's nothing stills him sooner.
Madam, your page of thirteen is too hard for him;
'Twas tried i'th' woodyard.

LADY
Alas, poor grievèd merit!
What is become of him? If he once fail,
Virtue shall find small friendship. Farewell, then,
To ladies' worths, for any hope in men.
He loved for goodness, not for wealth or lust,
After the world's foul dotage; he ne'er courted
The body but the beauty of the mind,
A thing which common courtship never thinks on.
All his affections were so sweet and fair,
There is no hope for fame if he despair.

Exeunt Lady and Servants

Enter the Clown [*behind*]. *He kicks Lepet* [*and presents a letter*]

LEPET
Good morrow to you again most heartily, sir.
[*Lepet kicks Clown*]
Cry you mercy, I heard you not; I was somewhat busy.

CLOWN [*aside*]
He takes it as familiarly as an *Ave*,
Or precious salutation. I was sick
Till I had one, because I am so used to't.

LEPET
However you deserve, your friends and mine here
Give you large commendations i' this letter.
They say you will endure well.

CLOWN
I'd be loath
To prove 'em liars: I've endured as much
As mortal pen and ink can set me down for.

LEPET
Say you me so?

CLOWN
I know and feel it so, sir.
I have it under black and white already;
I need no pen to paint me out.

LEPET [*aside*]
He fits me,
And hits my wishes pat, pat. I was ne'er
In possibility to be better manned,
For he's half-lamed already; I see't plain,
But take no notice on't, for fear I make
The rascal proud and dear, to advance his wages.—
First, let me grow into particulars with you.
What have you endured of worth? Let me hear.

CLOWN
Marry, sir, I'm almost beaten blind.

LEPET
That's pretty well for a beginning,
But many a mill-horse has endured as much.

CLOWN
Shame o' the miller's heart for his unkindness then!

LEPET Well, sir, what then?

CLOWN
I've been twice thrown down stairs, just before supper.

LEPET
Puh, so have I; that's nothing.

CLOWN
Ay, but sir,
Was yours, pray, before supper?

LEPET
There thou passest me.

CLOWN
Ay, marry, that's it; 'thad been less grief to me,
Had I but filled my belly, and then tumbled.
But to be flung down fasting, there's the dolour.

LEPET
It would have grieved me, that, indeed. Proceed, sir.

CLOWN
I have been plucked and tugged by th' hair o'th' head
About a gallery, half an acre long.

LEPET
Yes, that's a good one, I must needs confess,
A principal good one that, an absolute good one.
I have been trod upon, and spurned about,
But never tugged by th' hair, I thank my fates.

CLOWN
O 'tis a spiteful pain.

LEPET
Peace, never speak on't,
For putting men in mind on't.

CLOWN
To conclude,
I'm bursten, sir. My belly will hold no meat.

LEPET
No? That makes amends for all.

CLOWN
Unless't be puddings,
Or such fast food. Any loose thing beguiles me;
I'm ne'er the better for't.

LEPET
Sheepheads will stay with thee?

CLOWN
Yes, sir, or chaldrons.

LEPET
Very well, sir:

116 **woodyard** place where wood was chopped etc., presumably a lowly location at court (here, a place for a fight, where Lepet was bested by a thirteen-year-old)
128 **it** i.e. a kick as a form of greeting
Ave from 'Ave Maria', salutation to the Virgin Mary used as a part of devotional address, still familiar by the Latin name after the Reformation. A penance prescribed to follow confession and said by rote because the words are so familiar.
139 **pat** exactly
156 **dolour** pain
165 **men . . . on't** the idea in people's heads
166 **meat** food
168 **fast** stodgy, binding
169 **Sheepheads** dish consisting of the head of a sheep; also a fool or simpleton
170 **chaldrons** entrails, offal

Any your bursten fellows must take heed of surfeits.
Strange things, it seems, you have endured.

CLOWN Too true, sir.

LEPET
But now the question is: what you will endure
Hereafter in my service?

CLOWN Anything
That shall be reason, sir, for I'm but froth,
Much like a thing new-calved, or (come more nearer, sir),
You've seen a cluster of frog-spawns in April?
E'en such a starch am I, as weak and tender
As a green woman yet.

LEPET Now I know this,
I will be very gently angry with thee,
And kick thee carefully.

CLOWN O ay, sweet sir.

LEPET
Peace, when thou art offered well, lest I begin now.
Your friends and mine have writ here, for your truth
They'll pass their words themselves, and I must meet 'em.

CLOWN Then have you all. *Exit Lepet*
As for my honesty, there is no fear of that,
For I have ne'er a whole bone about me. *Exit*

3.3

Music. Enter the Passionate cousin, rudely and carelessly apparelled, unbraced and untrussed, [and] the Cupid following

CUPID
Think upon love, which makes all creatures handsome,
Seemly for eyesight; go not so diffusedly.
There are great ladies purpose, sir, to visit you.

PASSIONATE LORD
Grand plagues! Shut in my casements, that the breaths
Of their coach-mares reek not into my nostrils;
Those beasts are but a kind of bawdy forerunners.

CUPID It is not well with you,
When you speak ill of fair mistresses.

PASSIONATE LORD
Fair mischiefs! Give me a nest of owls and take 'em.
Happy is he, say I, whose window opens
To a brown baker's chimney; he shall be sure there
To hear the bird screech sometimes after twilight.
What a fine thing 'tis, methinks, to have our garments
Sit loose upon us thus, thus carelessly.
It is more manly and more mortifying,
For we're so much the readier for our shrouds—
For how ridiculous were't, to have death come
And take a fellow pinned up like a mistress?
About his neck a ruff like a pinched lantern,
Which schoolboys make in winter, and his doublet
So close and pent, as if he feared one prison
Would not be strong enough to keep his soul in,
But's tailor makes another.
And trust me—for I knew't when I loved, Cupid—
He does endure much pain for the poor praise
Of a neat-sitting suit.

CUPID One may be handsome, sir,
And yet not pained, nor proud.

PASSIONATE LORD There you lie, Cupid,
As bad as Mercury. There is no handsomeness
But has a wash of pride and luxury,
And you go there too, Cupid. Away, dissembler!
Thou tak'st the deed's part which befools us all;
Thy arrowheads shoot but sinners. Hence, away!
And after thee I'll send a powerful charm
Shall banish thee forever.

CUPID Never, never,
I am too sure thine own. *Exit Cupid*

PASSIONATE LORD (*sings*)

Hence, all you vain delights,
As short as are the nights
Wherein you spend your folly.
There's naught in this life sweet,
If men were wise to see't,
But only melancholy,
O sweetest melancholy.

Welcome folded arms and fixèd eyes,
A sigh that piercing mortifies,
A look that's fastened to the ground,
A tongue chained up without a sound,
Fountain-heads and pathless groves
(Places which pale passion loves),

171 **surfeits** eating to excess provoking nausea
179 **green** young unripe pre-sexual
187 **whole bone** (*a*) unbroken bone (*b*) hole-bone, hard penis
3.3.0.2 ***unbraced*** without clothes fastenings, or with clasps undone
untrussed pantsless. (Trusses were close-fitting breeches or drawers covering buttocks and tops of thighs.)
3 **purpose** intend
4 **Grand plagues** i.e. great ladies
9 **nest of owls** collection of melancholy ominous nightbirds (which would be worth having in exchange for beautiful women)
12 **bird** i.e. owl
18 **pinned...mistress** enclosed or confined by tight or complex clothing
19 **ruff** neck decoration made of stiffly starched linen or muslin
pinched closely covered
20 **doublet** close-fitting garment for male body
23 **But's** unless his
28 **Mercury** messenger of gods; associated with news, furtiveness, oratorical ability and trickery
29 **luxury** sumptuous enjoyment, lechery
31 **deed's** sexual act's
36–54 **Hence...melancholy** (This poem is more widely anthologized, in manuscript and print, than any theatrical song of the period; it was particularly popular from the mid-1620s to the 1650s, in private manuscript anthologies as well as printed ones. For musical settings, see *Companion*, 169.)
36 **vain** (*a*) proud (*b*) futile
38 **spend** (*a*) expend, pass away (*b*) ejaculate

Moonlight walks, when all the fowls
Are warmly housed, save bats and owls.
A midnight bell, a parting groan,
These are the sounds we feed upon.
Then stretch our bones in a still gloomy valley:
Nothing's so dainty sweet as lovely melancholy.
Exit [at one door]

3.4 *Enter at another door Lepet, the Cupid's Brothers watching his coming*

FIRST BROTHER
So, so, the woodcock's ginned; keep this door fast, brother.

SECOND BROTHER
I'll warrant this.

FIRST BROTHER I'll go incense him instantly;
I know the way to't.

SECOND BROTHER Will't not be too soon,
Think you, and make two fits break into one?

FIRST BROTHER
Pah, no, no. The tail of his melancholy
Is always the head of his anger, and follows
As close as the report follows the powder.
[Exeunt Brothers, at separate doors]

LEPET
This is the appointed place, and the hour struck.
If I can get security for's truth,
I'll never mind his honesty. Poor worm,
I durst lay him by my wife, which is a benefit
Which many masters ha' not. I shall ha' no maid
Now got with child, but what I get myself,
And that's no small felicity; in most places
They're got by th' men, and put upon the masters.
Nor shall I be resisted when I strike,
For he can hardly stand. These are great blessings.

PASSIONATE LORD (*within*)
I want my food; deliver me a varlet.

LEPET
How now: from whence comes that?

PASSIONATE LORD [*within*] I am allowed
A carcass to insult on: where's the villain?

LEPET
He means not me, I hope.

PASSIONATE LORD [*within*] My maintenance rascals,
My bulk, my exhibition!

LEPET Bless us all,
What names are these? Would I were gone again.

The passionate man enters in fury, with a truncheon

PASSIONATE LORD (*sings*)
A curse upon thee for a slave!
Art thou here, and heard'st me rave?
Fly not sparkles from mine eye
To show my indignation nigh?
Am I not all foam and fire?
With voice as hoarse as a town-crier?
How my back opes and shuts together
With fury, as old men's with weather!
Couldst thou not hear my teeth gnash hither?

LEPET
No, truly, sir, I thought 'thad been a squirrel,
Shaving a hazelnut.

PASSIONATE LORD
Death, hell, fiends, and darkness!
I will thrash thy mangy carcass.
[He beats Lepet]

LEPET O sweet sir!

PASSIONATE LORD
There cannot be too many tortures
Spent upon those lousy quarters.
[He beats Lepet]

LEPET
Hold, O!
[Lepet] falls down for dead

PASSIONATE LORD
Thy bones shall rue, thy bones shall rue.
[He] sings again
Thou nasty, scurvy, mongrel toad,
Mischief on thee! Light upon thee
All the plagues that can confound thee
Or did ever reign abroad:
Better a thousand lives it cost
Than have brave anger spilt or lost. *Exit*

LEPET
May I open mine eyes yet, and safely peep?
I'll try a groan first—O!—Nay, then, he's gone.
There was no other policy but to die;
He would ha' made me else. Ribs, are you sore?
I was ne'er beaten to a tune before.
Enter the two Brothers

FIRST BROTHER
Lepet—

LEPET Again?
[He] falls again

FIRST BROTHER [*to Second Brother*]
Look, look, he's flat again,
And stretched out like a corpse, a handful longer

49 **fowls** birds
51 **parting** (*a*) dying (*b*) departing
53 **stretch our bones** (*a*) lie down on the ground (*b*) die
still (*a*) quiet (*b*) perpetually
3.4.1 **woodcock's** edible bird, fool; person ensnared by trickery
ginned snared; a gin is a sprung trap
2 **warrant** guarantee
7 **report...powder** noise follows the shot
22 **bulk** heap or cargo; also applied to the belly
exhibition allowance
30–1 **my...weather** my body twisted in anger resembles the spinal misshaping caused by age
39 **lousy** infested with lice; valueless
54 **handful longer** i.e. stretched out flat

Than he walks; trust me, brother.—Why, Lepet!—
I hold my life we shall not get him speak now.—
Monsieur Lepet!—It must be a privy token,
If any thing fetch him; he's so far gone.—
We come to pass our words for your man's truth.

LEPET [*rising*]
O gentlemen, you're welcome: I have been thrashed,
i'faith.

SECOND BROTHER
How? thrashed, sir?

LEPET Never was Shrove-Tuesday bird
So cudgelled, gentlemen.

FIRST BROTHER Pray, how? by whom, sir?

LEPET
Nay, that I know not.

FIRST BROTHER Not who did this wrong?

LEPET
Only a thing came like a walking song.

FIRST BROTHER
What, beaten with a song?

LEPET Never more tightly, gentlemen.
Such crotchets happen now and then, methinks;
He that endures well, of all waters drinks. *Exeunt*

4.1 [*Incipit*] *Actus Quartus*
Enter Chamont's Brother (*the Soldier*), [*having been beaten*], *and First Gentleman*

SOLDIER
Yes, yes, this was a madman, sir, with you,
'A passionate madman'.

FIRST GENTLEMAN Who would ha' looked for this, sir?

SOLDIER
'And must be privileged'. A pox privilege him!
I was never so dry-beat since I was born—
And by a litter of rogues, mere rogues. The whole
twenty
Had not above nine elbows 'mongst 'em all too;
And the most part of those left-handed rascals—
The very vomit, sir, of hospitals,
Bridewells, and spital-houses—such nasty smellers,
That if they'd been unfurnished of club-truncheons,
They might have cudgelled me with their very stinks;
It was so strong and sturdy. And shall this,
This filthy injury, be set off with madness?

FIRST GENTLEMAN
Nay, take your own blood's counsel, sir, hereafter;
I'll deal no further in't. If you remember,
It was not come to blows when I advised you.

SOLDIER
No, but I ever said, 'twould come to something,
And 'tis upon me, thank him. Were he kin
To all the mighty emperors upon earth,
He has not now in life three hours to reckon;
I watch but a free time.

Enter Chamont

FIRST GENTLEMAN
Your noble brother, sir; I'll leave you now. *Exit*

CHAMONT
Soldier, I would I could persuade my thoughts
From thinking thee a brother, as I can
My tongue from naming on't. Thou hast no friend
here
But fortune and thy own strength; trust to them.

SOLDIER
How? What's the incitement, sir?

CHAMONT Treachery to virtue,
Thy treachery, thy faithless circumvention.
Has Honour so few daughters—never fewer—
And must thou aim thy treachery at the best?
The very front of virtue? that blest lady?
The Duke's sister?
Created more for admiration's cause
Than for love's ends; whose excellency sparkles
More in divinity than mortal beauty;
And as much difference 'twixt her mind and body
As 'twixt this earth's poor centre and the sun.
And couldst thou be so injurious to fair goodness
Once to attempt to court her down to frailty?
Or put her but in mind that there is weakness,
Sin, and desire, which she should never hear of?
Wretch, thou'st committed worse than sacrilege
In the attempting on't, and oughtst to die for't.

SOLDIER
I rather ought to do my best to live, sir.
Provoke me not, for I've a wrong sits on me
That makes me apt for mischief. I shall lose
All respects suddenly of friendship, brotherhood,
Or any sound that way.

CHAMONT But 'ware me most,
For I come with a two-edged injury:
Both my disgrace and thy apparent falsehood,
Which must be dangerous.

SOLDIER I courted her, sir:
Love starve me with delays when I confess it not—

CHAMONT There's nothing then but death
Can be a penance fit for that confession.

57 **privy token** something of intimate significance

61–2 **Never ... cudgelled** (referring to a Shrovetide amusement in which people throw cudgels at a cock until he is killed)

66 **crotchets** idiosyncracies (punning on musical sense)

67 **well** (punning on wells as a source of water)

4.1.8 **hospitals** charitable institutions for housing those who are destitute or ill

9 **Bridewells** places of correction or forced labour, like the London prison so named **spital-houses** lower class of hospital, associated with 'unclean' diseases such as leprosy

14 **blood's** (used in a range of ways in this scene; temper, temperament, kinship: see ll. 82, 113)

29 **daughters** women who as the children of Honour (personified) are therefore honourable themselves

31 **front** forehead as well as foremost part; therefore the part of the body on which virtue can be read

SOLDIER
—But far from any vicious taint.

CHAMONT O, sir,
Vice is a mighty stranger grown to courtship.

SOLDIER
Nay, then, the fury of my wrong light on thee.
[*They draw*]
Enter First Gentleman, and other [*gentlemen*]

FIRST GENTLEMAN
Forbear, the Duke's at hand, here, hard at hand,
Upon my reputation.

SOLDIER I must do something now. *Exit Soldier*

CHAMONT I'll follow you close, sir.

FIRST GENTLEMAN
We must entreat you must not, for the Duke
Desires some conference with you.

CHAMONT Let me go,
As you're gentlemen.

SECOND GENTLEMAN Faith, we dare not, sir.

CHAMONT
Dare ye be false to honour, and yet dare not
Do a man justice? give me leave—

FIRST GENTLEMAN Good, sweet sir,
He's sent twice for you.

CHAMONT Is this brave, or manly?

FIRST GENTLEMAN
I prithee be conformed.

CHAMONT Death!—
Enter Duke

SECOND GENTLEMAN Peace, he's come in truth.

CHAMONT
O, have you betrayed me to my shame afresh?
How am I bound to loathe you!

DUKE Chamont, welcome.
I sent twice.

SECOND GENTLEMAN
But, my lord, he never heard on't.

CHAMONT [*to Duke*]
Pray, pardon him for his falseness; I did, sir,
Both times. I'd rather be found rude than faithless.

DUKE
I love that bluntness dearly: [*aside*] ha's no vice,
But is more manly than some other's virtue,
That sets it out only for show or profit.

CHAMONT [*to First Gentleman*]
Will't please you quit me, sir? I've urgent business.
[*Exeunt Gentlemen*]

DUKE
Come, you're so hasty now; I sent for you
To a better end.

CHAMONT And if it be an end,
Better or worse, I thank your goodness for't.

DUKE
I've ever kept that bounty in condition
And thankfulness in blood, which well becomes
Both prince and subject, that where any wrong
Bears my impression, or the hasty figure
Of my repented anger, I'm a law
Ev'n to myself, and doom myself most strictly
To justice and a noble satisfaction.
So that, what you in tenderness of honour
Conceive to be loss to you—which is nothing
But curious opinion—I'll restore again,
Although I give you the best part of Genoa
And take to boot but thanks for your amends.

CHAMONT
O miserable satisfactïon,
Ten times more wretched than the wrong itself!
Never was ill better made good with worse.
Shall it be said that my posterity
Shall live the sole heirs of their father's shame?
And raise their wealth and glory from my stripes?
You have provided nobly, bounteous sir,
For my disgrace, to make it live for ever,
Outlasting brass or marble.
This is my fear's construction, and a deep one,
Which neither argument nor time can alter;
Yet I durst swear, I wrong your goodness in't, sir,
And the most fair intent on't, which I reverence
With admiration, that in you (a prince)
Should be so sweet and temperate a condition
To offer to restore where you may ruin,
And do't with justice, and in me (a servant)
So harsh a disposition that I cannot
Forgive where I should honour, and am bound to't.
But I have ever had that curiosity
In blood, and tenderness of reputation,
Such an antipathy against a blow—
I cannot speak the rest. Good sir, discharge me.
It is not fit that I should serve you more,
Nor come so near you. I'm made now for privacy
And a retired condition; that's my suit,
To part from court for ever, my last suit.
And as you profess bounty, grant me that, sir.

DUKE
I would deny thee nothing.

CHAMONT Health reward you, sir.
Exit

DUKE
He's gone again already, and takes hold
Of any opportunity; not riches
Can purchase him, nor honours, peaceably,
And force were brutish. What a great worth's gone
with him—
And but a gentleman? Well, for his sake,
I'll ne'er offend more those I cannot make:
They were his words, and shall be dear to memory.
Say I desire to see him once again?

85–6 **I'm . . . myself** (refers in paradoxical fashion to the question of whether the King is above the law or vice versa. The Duke argues that the ruler as law-giver should punish himself.)
106 **prince** monarch

Yet stay: he's so well forward of his peace
'Twere pity to disturb him. He would groan
Like a soul fetched again, and that were injury,
And I've wronged his degree too much already.—
Call forth the gentlemen of our chamber instantly.

FIRST SERVANT (*within*)
I shall, my lord.

DUKE I may forget again,
And therefore will prevent. The strain of this
Troubles me so, one would not hazard more.

Enter First Gentleman and divers others [*including the other three Gentlemen*]

GENTLEMEN
Your will, my lord?

DUKE Yes, I discharge you all.

SECOND GENTLEMAN My lord—

DUKE
Your places shall be otherwise disposed of.

FOURTH GENTLEMAN
Why, sir?

DUKE Reply not; I dismiss you all.
You're gentlemen; your worths will find you fortunes.
Nor shall your farewell tax me of ingratitude;
I'll give you all noble remembrances
As testimonies 'gainst reproach and malice,
That you departed loved.

THIRD GENTLEMAN This is most strange, sir.

FIRST GENTLEMAN [*to Duke*]
But how is your grace furnished, these dismissed?

DUKE Seek me out grooms,
Men more insensible of reputation,
Less curious and precise in terms of honour,
That if my anger chance let fall a stroke
(As we are all subject to impetuous passions),
Yet it may pass unmurmured, undisputed,
And not with braver fury prosecuted.

FIRST GENTLEMAN
It shall be done, my lord. [*Exit Duke*]

THIRD GENTLEMAN Know you the cause, sir?

FIRST GENTLEMAN
Not I, kind gentlemen, but by conjectures,
And so much shall be yours, when you please.

FOURTH GENTLEMAN Thanks, sir.

THIRD GENTLEMAN
We shall i'th' mean time think ourselves guilty
Of some foul fault, through ignorance committed.

FIRST GENTLEMAN
No, 'tis not that, nor that way.

FOURTH GENTLEMAN For my part,
I shall be disinherited; I know so much.

FIRST GENTLEMAN
Why, sir, for what?

FOURTH GENTLEMAN My sire's of a strange humour:
He'll form faults for me, and then swear 'em mine—
And commonly he first begins with lechery;
He knows his own youth's trespass.

FIRST GENTLEMAN Before you go,
I'll come and take my leave, and tell you all, sirs.

THIRD GENTLEMAN
Thou wert ever just and kind.

FIRST GENTLEMAN That's my poor virtue, sir,
And parcel valiant; but it's hard to be perfect.
[*Exeunt other gentlemen*]

The choosing of these fellows now will puzzle me,
Horribly puzzle me—and there's no judgement
Goes true upon man's outside; there's the mischief.
He must be touched and tried, for gold or dross;
There is no other way for't, and that's dangerous too.
But since I'm put in trust, I will attempt it:
The Duke shall keep one daring man about him.

Enter a Gallant

Soft, who comes here? A pretty bravery this.
Everyone goes so like a gentleman,
'Tis hard to find a difference, but by th' touch.
I'll try your mettle sure.
[*He boxes the Gallant's ear*]

GALLANT Why, what do you mean, sir?

FIRST GENTLEMAN
Nay, an you understand it not, I do not.

GALLANT Yes, would you should well know,
I understand it for a box o'th' ear, sir.

FIRST GENTLEMAN
And o' my troth, that's all I gave it for.

GALLANT
'Twere best it be so.

FIRST GENTLEMAN [*aside*]
This is a brave coward,
A jolly threat'ning coward; he shall be captain.—
Sir, let me meet you an hour hence i'th' lobby.

GALLANT
Meet you? The world might laugh at me then, i'faith.

FIRST GENTLEMAN
Lay by your scorn and pride—they're scurvy qualities—
And meet me, or I'll box you while I have you,
And carry you gambrelled thither like a mutton.

GALLANT
Nay, an you be in earnest, here's my hand
I will not fail you.

FIRST GENTLEMAN 'Tis for your own good.

148 **grooms** men of inferior social position, serving-men
150 **curious** punctilious
168 **parcel** in part, in portion—having valour as one of his constituent parts
172 **touched and tried** as a touchstone tries, or tests, gold
178 **touch** (*a*) testing of metal (*b*) physical contact
179 **mettle** nature, quality (pun on 'metal')
180 **an** if
185 **captain** The gallant's particularly cowardly response suits him to be a leader in the Duke's army: he is suitable to be a captain in the ranks of cowardice.
186 **meet** seemingly, a challenge to a duel; here, an arrangement to enter the Duke's service
190 **gambrelled** hung upon a stick like a large piece of meat

GALLANT Away!

FIRST GENTLEMAN
Too much for your own good, sir—a pox on you!

GALLANT
I prithee curse me all day long so.

FIRST GENTLEMAN Hang you!

GALLANT [*aside*]
I'll make him mad; he's loath to curse too much to me.
Indeed, I never yet took box o'th' ear
But it redounded; I must needs say so.

FIRST GENTLEMAN
Will you be gone?

GALLANT Curse, curse, and then I go.
[*Aside*] Look how he grins. I've angered him to th' kidneys.

Exit

FIRST GENTLEMAN
Was ever such a prigging coxcomb seen?
One might have beat him dumb now in this humour,
And he'd ha' grinned it out still.

Enter a Plain Fellow

O, here's one
Made to my hand; methinks looks like a craven.
Less pains will serve his trial—some slight jostle.
[*He jostles the Plain Fellow*]

PLAIN FELLOW
How? Take you that, sir:
[*He cuffs the First Gentleman*]
And if that content you not—

FIRST GENTLEMAN
Yes, very well, sir; I desire no more.

PLAIN FELLOW
I think you need not, for you have not lost by't.

Exit

FIRST GENTLEMAN
Who would ha' thought this would have proved a gentleman?
I'll never trust long chins and little legs again—
I'll know 'em sure for gentlemen hereafter.
A gristle but in show, but gave his cuff
With such a fetch and reach of gentry,
As if he'd had his arms before the flood.
I have took a villainous hard task upon me;
Now I begin to have a feeling on't.

Enter Lepet [with proofs], and Clown his servant, and so habited

O, here comes a tried piece, now, the reformed kick.
The millïons of punches, spurns, and nips
That he has endured! His buttock's all black lead;
He's half a negro backward. He was past a Spaniard
In eighty-eight, and more Egyptian-like.
His table and his book come both out shortly,
And all the cowards in the town expect it.
So, if I fail of my full number now,
I shall be sure to find 'em at church corners,
Where Dives and the suff'ring ballads hang.

LEPET [*to Clown*]
Well, since thou art of so mild a temper,
Of so meek a spirit, thou mayst live with me
Till better times do smile on thy deserts.
I am glad I am got home again.

CLOWN
I am happy in your service, sir;
You'll keep me from the hospital.

LEPET
So, bring me the last proof; this is corrected.
[*Lepet gives proofs to Clown*]

CLOWN
Ay, you're too full of your correction, sir.

LEPET
Look I have perfect books within this half hour.

CLOWN Yes, sir.

LEPET
Bid him put all the thumps in pica roman—
And with great T's, you vermin, as thumps should be.

CLOWN
Then in what letter will you have your kicks?

LEPET
All in *italica*—your backward blows
All in *italica*, you hermaphrodite.
When shall I teach you wit?

193 **Away** quit talking nonsense
200 **grins** grimaces
to th' kidneys to the depth of his constitution
201 **prigging** haggling, over-precise (used of thieves)
coxcomb foolish, showy, conceited person
204 **craven** cock that is not game to fight; hence, coward
212 **gristle** cartilage, unformed bones as in infancy
213 **fetch** sweep, sweeping movement
214 **arms** (*a*) coat of arms (*b*) limbs
flood Biblical flood survived by Noah
219 **black lead** graphite
220 **a negro** i.e., so bruised and beaten that he looks like a black man (punning on heraldic discourse)
Spaniard i.e. more dark-complexioned than an Englishman
221 **eighty-eight** the year of the Armada
225 **church corners** the outside, rather than the inside, of churches used for the displaying of wares for sale. It suggests St Paul's churchyard, the main bookselling district in London.
226 **Dives** rich man in the parable (Luke 16). Here suggests the titles or topics of printed sermons (a very popular genre at the time).
the suff'ring ballads The ballads—very cheap but also very popular commodities—may be suffering because they are pinned up for sale, or because ballads often describe sensational tragedies.
233 **proof** sheets of printed book sent for examination and correction before it is finally published
237 **pica roman** (a common typeface)
238 **great T's** capital letter T, or T in a larger typeface
239 **letter** typeface
240 ***italica*** italic (a kind of type in which the letters slope towards the right)
backward blows blows to the backside—with connotations of sodomy (associated with Italy)
241 **hermaphrodite** person in whom the characteristics of both sexes are combined

CLOWN [*aside*] O, let it alone,
Till you have some yourself, sir.
LEPET You mumble?
CLOWN
The victuals are locked up; I'm kept from mumbling.
Exit
LEPET
He prints my blows upon pot-paper too, the rogue,
Which had been proper for some drunken pamphlet.
FIRST GENTLEMAN
Monsieur Lepet? How the world rings of you, sir!
Your name sounds far and near.
LEPET A good report it bears
For an enduring name—
FIRST GENTLEMAN What luck have you, sir!
LEPET
Why, what's the matter?
FIRST GENTLEMAN I'm but thinking on't.
I've heard you wish this five year for a place.
Now there's one fall'n, and freely without money too,
And empty yet—and yet you cannot have't.
LEPET
No? What's the reason? I'll give money for't
Rather than go without, sir.
FIRST GENTLEMAN That's not it, sir.
The truth is, there's no gentleman must have it
Either for love or money; 'tis decreed so.
I was heartily sorry when I thought upon you.
Had you not been a gentleman, I had fitted you.
LEPET
Who, I, a gentleman? A pox! I'm none, sir.
FIRST GENTLEMAN
How?
LEPET
How? Why, did you ever think I was?
FIRST GENTLEMAN What? Not a gentleman?
LEPET
I would thou'dst put it upon me, i'faith.
Did not my grandfather cry cony-skins?
My father aqua vitae? (A hot gentleman.)
All this I speak on i' your time and memory too;
Only a rich uncle died and left me chattels.
You know all this so well too—
FIRST GENTLEMAN Pray, excuse me, sir,
Ha' not you arms?
LEPET Yes, a poor couple here,
That serve to thrust in wild-fowl.
FIRST GENTLEMAN Herald's arms,
Symbols of gentry, sir: you know my meaning.
They've been shown and seen.
LEPET They have?
FIRST GENTLEMAN I'fax, have they.
LEPET
Why, I confess, at my wife's instigation once
(As women love these herald's kickshaws, naturally)
I bought 'em—but what are they, think you? Puffs.
FIRST GENTLEMAN
Why, that's proper to your name, being Lepet,
Which is 'Le Fart', after the English letter.
LEPET
The herald, sir, had much ado to find it.
FIRST GENTLEMAN And can you blame him?
Why, 'tis the only thing that puzzles the devil.
LEPET
At last he looked upon my name again,
And having well compared it, this he gave me:
The two colics playing upon a wind instrument.
FIRST GENTLEMAN
An excellent proper one: but I pray tell me,
How does he express the colics? They are hard things.
LEPET
The colics? With hot trenchers at their bellies.
There's nothing better, sir, to blaze a colic.
FIRST GENTLEMAN
And are not you a gentleman by this, sir?
LEPET No, I disclaim't.
No bellyache on earth shall make me one.
He shall not think to put his gripes upon me,
And wring out gentry so, and ten pound first.
If the wind instrument will make my wife one,
Let her enjoy't, for she was a harper's grandchild;
But sir, for my particular, I renounce it.
FIRST GENTLEMAN
Or to be called so?
LEPET Ay, sir, or imagined.
FIRST GENTLEMAN
None fitter for the place. Give me thy hand.

244 **mumbling** (*a*) muttering (*b*) chewing
245 **pot-paper** poor quality paper
246 **drunken pamphlet** cheap, insignificant, publication which was rhetorically crazy or about drinking and, for either reason, might appropriately be printed on 'pot-paper' (punning on 'drinking pot')
248 **report** sound (alluding to his name, 'the fart')
251 **place** position at court
264 **cry** sell as a street vendor
cony-skins rabbit-skins (possibly implying that his grandfather was a poacher)
265 **aqua vitae** general term for distilled spirits; alcohol
hot choleric—both needing liquid to cool him and 'spiritedly' hot in temperament
269 **arms** (*a*) coat of arms as a sign of gentility (*b*) physical arms as employed in the lowest kind of work—cleaning out the gizzards of wild-fowl
272 **I'fax** in faith (but *fax* also means 'waste, excrement' and so carries on the joke)
274 **kickshaws** trifles
275 **Puffs** air, emptiness, nothing
280 **'tis . . . devil** (proverbial)
283 **colics** bellyaches, intestinal pains (one for each colon)
286 **trenchers** plates
287 **blaze** blazon, demonstrate or symbolize as in heraldry (with a pun on the burning sensations of indigestion)
291 **gripes** (*a*) stomach pains (*b*) greedy, gripping hands
294 **harper's** one who plays upon a harp, of low social status

LEPET
A hundred thousand thanks—beside a bribe—sir.

FIRST GENTLEMAN
You must take heed of thinking toward a gentleman,
now.

LEPET
Pish, I am not mad, I warrant you. Nay more, sir,
If one should twit me i'th' teeth that I'm a gentleman,
Twit me their worst, I am but one since Lammas;
That I can prove, if they would see my heart out.

FIRST GENTLEMAN
Marry, in any case, keep me that evidence.

Enter Clown [*with proofs*]

LEPET
Here comes my servant, sir, Galoshio.
Has not his name for naught; he will be trod upon.—
What says my printer now?

CLOWN
Here's your last proof, sir.
You shall have perfect books now in a twinkling.

LEPET
These marks are ugly.

CLOWN
He says, sir, they're proper:
Blows should have marks, or else they are nothing
worth.

LEPET
But why a pilcrow here?

CLOWN
I told 'im so, sir:
A scare-crow had been better.

LEPET
How, slave? Look you, sir,
Did not I say, this wherret and this bob
Should be both pica roman?

CLOWN
So said I sir,
Both pikèd Romans, and he has made 'em Welsh bills;
Indeed, I know not what to make on 'em.

LEPET
Hey-day! A souse, *italica*?

CLOWN
Yes, that may hold, sir.
Souse is a bona-roba; so is Flops too.

LEPET
But why stands bastinado so far off here?

CLOWN
Alas, you must allow him room to lay about him, sir.

LEPET
Why lies this spurn lower than that spurn, sir?

CLOWN
Marry, this signifies one kicked down stairs, sir;
The other, in a gallery.
I asked him all these questions.

FIRST GENTLEMAN
Your book's name?
Prithee, Lepet, mind me; you never told me yet.

LEPET Marry, but shall, sir:
'Tis called *The Uprising of the Kick*
And the Downfall of the Duello.

FIRST GENTLEMAN
Bring that to pass, you'll prove a happy member,
And do your country service. Your young bloods
Will thank you then, when they see fourscore.

LEPET
I hope
To save my hundred gentlemen a month by't,
Which will be very good for the private house.

CLOWN
Look you, your table's finished, sir, already.

LEPET [*to First Gentleman*]
Why, then, behold my masterpiece. See, see, sir:
Here's all your blows and blow-men whatsoever,
Set in their lively colours—givers and takers.

FIRST GENTLEMAN
Troth, wondrous fine, sir.

LEPET
Nay, but mark the postures.
The standing of the takers I admire
More than the givers: they stand scornfully,
Most contumeliously. I like not them.
O here's one cast into a comely figure.

CLOWN [*to First Gentleman*]
My master means him there that's cast down headlong.

LEPET
How sweetly does this fellow take his douse?
Stoops like a camel, that heroic beast,
At a great load of nutmegs. And how meekly
This other fellow here receives his wherret!

CLOWN
O master, here's a fellow stands most gallantly,
Taking his kick in private behind the hangings,
And raising up his hips to't. But O, sir,
How daintily this man lies trampled on?
Would I were in thy place, whate'er thou art.
How lovely he endures it!

301 **twit** mock, taunt provokingly
302 **Lammas** 1 August
303 **see my heart out** (referring to the punishment for traitors, who were disembowelled and had their hearts torn out)
305 **Galoshio** galoshes (Italian)
307 **last proof** final stop-press proofsheet, made during the actual printing
309 **marks** (*a*) printer's characters (*b*) marks on the body made by a blow
311 **pilcrow** paragraph
315 **pikèd** carrying pikes, weapons with long shafts and pointed heads
Welsh bills offensive weapons, like halberds
317 **souse** strike suddenly as a bird strikes prey
318 **bona-roba** prostitute (Italian)
Flops (*a*) bump or thud, heavy movement (*b*) name of prostitute (like 'Souse')
321 **spurn** part of a type, or letter, which descends below the line
329 **happy member** useful limb of the body politic, fortunate member of Parliament
333 **private house** an enclosed London theatre, such as the Blackfriars, which charged more than open air theatres like the Globe, and so depended upon a more élite clientele
345–6 **camel . . . nutmegs** i.e. kneeling, front lowered first, or sway-backed yet also lumpy-backed, like an overladen camel. Nutmeg may be suggested by the pageants of Lord Mayors' Shows (honouring the Grocers' Company).
349–50 **Taking . . . to't** (suggesting sodomy)

FIRST GENTLEMAN
But will not these things, sir, be hard to practise,
think you?
LEPET
O, easy, sir: I'll teach 'em in a dance.
FIRST GENTLEMAN
How? In a dance?
LEPET
I'll lose my new place else,
Whate'er it be; I know not what 'tis yet.
FIRST GENTLEMAN
And now you put me in mind, I could employ it well,
For your grace specially, for the Duke's cousin
Is by this time in's violent fit of mirth,
And a device must be sought out for suddenly
To overcloy the passion.
LEPET
Say no more, sir.
I'll fit you with my scholars, new practitioners,
Endurers of the time.
CLOWN
Whereof I am one, sir.
FIRST GENTLEMAN
You carry it away smooth; give me thy hand, sir.
Exeunt

❀

5.1 [*Incipit*] *Actus Quintus*
Enter the Two Brothers
PASSIONATE LORD (*within*) Ha, ha, ha.
SECOND BROTHER Hark, hark! How loud his fit's grown.
PASSIONATE LORD [*within*] Ha, ha, ha.
FIRST BROTHER
Now let our sister lose no time, but ply it
With all the power she has.
FIRST BROTHER
Her shame grows big, brother;
The Cupid's shape will hardly hold it longer.
'Twould take up half an ell of China damask more,
And all too little: it struts per'lously.
There is no tamp'ring with these Cupids long;
The mere conceit with womankind works strong.
PASSIONATE LORD [*within*]
Ha, ha, ha.
SECOND BROTHER
The laugh comes nearer now.
'Twere good we were not seen yet.
Exeunt Brothers [*at one door*]
Enter Passionate Lord and Base (*his jester*) [*at another door*]
PASSIONATE LORD
Ha, ha, ha.
And was he bastinadoed to the life? Ha, ha, ha.
I prithee say, Lord General, how did the rascals
Entrench themselves?
BASE
Most deeply, politicly, all in ditches.
PASSIONATE LORD Ha, ha, ha.
BASE
'Tis thought he'll ne'er bear arms i'th' field again;
Has much ado to lift 'em to his head, sir.
PASSIONATE LORD I would he had.
BASE
On either side round truncheons played so thick
That shoulders, chines, nay flanks were paid to th'
quick.
PASSIONATE LORD
Well said, Lord General: ha, ha, ha.
BASE
But pray, how grew the difference first betwixt you?
PASSIONATE LORD
There was never any, sir; there lies the jest, man.
Only because he was taller than his brother,
There's all my quarrel to him—and methought
He should be beaten for't; my mind so gave me, sir.
I could not sleep for't. Ha, ha, ha, ha.
Another good jest quickly, while 'tis hot now.
Let me not laugh in vain. Ply me, O ply me,
As you will answer't to my cousin Duke.
BASE [*to the spectators*] Alas, who has a good jest?
PASSIONATE LORD I fall, I dwindle in't.
BASE [*to the spectators*] Ten crowns for a good jest!
Enter Servant
Ha' you a good jest, sir?
SERVANT A pretty moral one.
BASE
Let's ha't, whate'er it be.
SERVANT
There comes a Cupid
Drawn by six fools.
BASE
That's nothing.
PASSIONATE LORD
Help it, help it, then!
BASE
I ha' known six hundred fools drawn by a Cupid.
PASSIONATE LORD
Ay, that, that! That's the smarter moral—ha, ha, ha.
Now I begin to be song-ripe methinks.
BASE
I'll sing you a pleasant air, sir, before you ebb.
Song
PASSIONATE LORD [*sings*]
O how my lungs do tickle! ha, ha, ha!
BASE [*sings*]
O how my lungs do tickle! ho, ho, ho!

363 **scholars** those who are learning his new code
5.1.1 **Ha, ha, ha** (a stage direction for laughter)
7 **ell** measurement of length, e.g. of cloth **damask** rich silk fabric woven with designs
8 **struts** walks like someone with a great belly
10 **conceit** (*a*) idea with an additional implication of (*b*) conception
34 **I fall . . . in't** my mirthful humour is fading
39 **Drawn . . . fools** (*a*) pulled as in a cart drawn by fools (*b*) attracted by the presence of the fools, ready victims for Cupid's arrows
40 **six . . . Cupid** hundreds of people directed by sexual passion
42 **song-ripe** ready to sing

PASSIONATE LORD [*sings*]
Set a sharp jest
Against my breast;
Then how my lungs do tickle!
As nightingales
And things in cambric rails
Sing best against a prickle.
Ha, ha, ha, ha!

BASE [*sings*]
Ho, ho, ho, ho, ha!

PASSIONATE LORD [*sings*]
Laugh,

BASE [*sings*]
Laugh,

PASSIONATE LORD [*sings*]
Laugh,

BASE [*sings*] Laugh,

PASSIONATE LORD [*sings*] Wide,

BASE [*sings*] Loud,

PASSIONATE LORD [*sings*] And vary!

BASE [*sings*]
A smile is for a simpering novice,

PASSIONATE LORD [*sings*]
One that ne'er tasted caviary,

BASE [*sings*]
Nor knows the smack of dear anchóvies.

PASSIONATE LORD [*sings*]
Ha, ha, ha, ha, ha!

BASE [*sings*]
Ho, ho, ho, ho, ho!

PASSIONATE LORD [*sings*]
A giggling waiting wench for me,
That shows her teeth how white they be:

BASE [*sings*]
A thing not fit for gravity,
For theirs are foul and hardly three.

PASSIONATE LORD [*sings*]
Ha, ha, ha!

BASE [*sings*]
Ho, ho, ho!

PASSIONATE LORD [*sings*]
Democritus, thou ancient fleerer,
How I miss thy laugh, and ha' since!

BASE [*sings*]
There you named the famous jeerer
That ever jeered in Rome, or Athens.

PASSIONATE LORD [*sings*]
Ha, ha, ha!

BASE [*sings*]
Ho, ho, ho!

PASSIONATE LORD [*sings*]
How brave lives he that keeps a fool,
Although the rate be deeper!

BASE [*sings*]
But he that is his own fool, sir,
Does live a great deal cheaper.

PASSIONATE LORD [*sings*]
Sure I shall burst, burst, quite break; thou art so witty.

BASE [*sings*]
'Tis rare to break at court, for that belongs to th' city.

PASSIONATE LORD [*sings*]
Ha, ha, my spleen is almost worn to the last laughter.

BASE [*sings*]
O keep a corner for a friend: a jest may come hereafter.

Enter Lepet and Clown, and four other like fools, dancing, the Cupid leading, and bearing his Table, and holding it up to Lepet at every strain, and acting the postures

[*First strain*]

LEPET
Twinge all, now; twinge, I say.

Second strain

Souse upon souse.

Third strain

Douses single.

Fourth strain

Jostle sides.

Fifth strain

Knee belly.

Sixth strain

Kicksy buttock.

Seventh strain

Down derry.

Enter Soldier (Chamont's brother), his sword drawn

SOLDIER
Not angry law nor doors of brass shall keep me
From my wrong's expiation. To thy bowels

50 **rails** upper garment or jacket worn by women
51 **prickle** (*a*) thorn (*b*) penis
55 **novice** (*a*) probationer in religious house (*b*) amateur, inexperienced laugher
56 **caviary** caviar (rhymes with 'vary'), as an example of exquisiteness of taste (in mirth)
57 **anchóvies** (rhymes with novice)
66 **Democritus** 'the laughing philosopher' who laughed at the follies of men (often opposed to Heraclitus, who wept)
fleerer jeerer, scorner
67 **since** long since
68 **famous** most famous
77 **break** become bankrupt
78 **spleen** organ understood as seat of melancholy and morose feelings, thereby associated with laughter
last laughter death throes
79 **hereafter** (cue for entry of Lepet's masque)
79.1 ***like*** dressed as, similar
79.2 ***leading*** drawing in behind them: see l. 39
79.4 ***the postures*** (*a*) physical positions indicated in Lepet's table (*b*) title of 'Aretino's postures', a famous set of pornographic images; hence, the dance postures may be suggestively sexual
84 **Knee belly** (which would cause them to bend over in agony, thus preparing them to be kicked in the butt)
85 **Kicksy** (invented word, perhaps suggesting French pronunciation 'kick zhe' = kick the)
86 **Down derry** possibly refers to a final posture, flat on the floor as after the impact of a kick

[*He stabs the Passionate Lord*]
I return my disgrace, and after turn
My face to any death that can be sentenced.
[*He throws down and tramples upon Lepet and Clown, and exit*]

BASE
Murder, O murder, stop the murderer there!
[*Exeunt Base and four dancers, following Soldier*]

LEPET
I am glad he's gone; he's almost trod my guts out.
Follow him who list. For me, I'll ha' no hand in't.

CLOWN
O 'twas your luck and mine to be squelched, master.
He's stamped my very puddings into pancakes.
[*Exeunt Lepet and Clown at another door*]

CUPID [*calling*]
O brothers!—O, I fear 'tis mortal.—Help! O help!—
I'm made the wretched'st woman, by this accident,
That ever love beguiled.
Enter two Brothers

SECOND BROTHER We are undone, brother;
Our shames are too apparent.—Away, receptacle
Of luxury and dishonour! Most unfortunate,
To make thyself but lackey to thy spoil,
After thy sex's manner.—Lift him up, brother.
He breathes not to our comfort; he's too wasted
Ever to cheer us more. A surgeon speedily!—
Hence, the unhappiest that e'er stepped aside!—
She'll be a mother ere she's known a bride.
[*Exeunt Brothers carrying Passionate Lord*]

CUPID [*to her unborn child*]
Thou hadst a most unfortunate conception,
Whate'er thou prov'st to be. In midst of mirth
Comes ruin, for a welcome, to thy birth. [*Exit*]

5.2

Enter Chamont

CHAMONT
This is a beautiful life now: privacy,
The sweetness and the benefit of essence.
I see there is no man but may make his paradise,
And it is nothing, but his love and dotage
Upon the world's foul joys, that keeps him out on't.
For he that lives retired in mind and spirit
Is still in paradise, and has his innocence
Partly allowed for his companion too,
As much as stands with justice. Here no eyes
Shoot their sharp-pointed scorns upon my shame;
They know no terms of reputation here,
No punctual limits or precise dimensions.
Plain downright honesty is all the beauty
And elegance of life found amongst shepherds;
For knowing nothing nicely, or desiring it,
Quits many a vexation from the mind,
With which our quainter knowledge does abuse us;
The name of envy is a stranger here,
That dries men's bloods abroad, robs health and rest;
Why, here's no such fury thought on. No, nor false-
hood,
That brotherly disease, fellow-like devil,
That plays within our bosom and betrays us.
Enter First Gentleman

FIRST GENTLEMAN
O are you here?

CHAMONT La Nove, 'tis strange to see thee.

FIRST GENTLEMAN
I ha' rid one horse to death, to find you out, sir.

CHAMONT [*going*]
I am not to be found of any man
That saw my shame, nor seen long.

FIRST GENTLEMAN Good, your attention:
You ought to be seen now, and found out, sir,
If ever you desire before your ending
To perform one good office—nay, a dear one;
Man's time can hardly match it.

CHAMONT Be't as precious
As reputation, if it come from court
I will not hear on't.

FIRST GENTLEMAN You must hear of this, sir.

CHAMONT
Must?

FIRST GENTLEMAN
You shall hear it.

CHAMONT I love thee, that thou'lt die.

FIRST GENTLEMAN 'Twere nobler in me,
Than in you living: you will live a murderer
If you deny this office.

CHAMONT Ev'n to death, sir.

FIRST GENTLEMAN
Why, then you'll kill your brother.

CHAMONT How?

FIRST GENTLEMAN Your brother, sir.
Bear witness, heaven: this man destroys his brother
When he may save him, his least breath may save
him.
Can there be wilfuller destructiön?—
He was forced to take a most unmanly wrong,

95 **puddings** entrails, guts
100 **luxury** lechery
101 **lackey** servant
spoil ruin
5.2.7 **Is . . . paradise** remains in an unfallen, prelapsarian world
7–8 **innocence . . . companion** (in contrast with Adam, whose companion was not innocence but Eve)
17 **quainter** more sophisticated
20 **fury** (*a*) rage (*b*) avenging infernal deity
21 **brotherly** close, similar yet unlike (envy); here, associated with his brother (whom he believes false)
33 **shall** will, must (whether you want to or not)—a very provocative idiom for an inferior to use to a superior
34 **thou'lt die** i.e. you are willing to die (as indicated by your acting in a way that will make me kill you, in defence of my honour)
35–6 **'Twere . . . living** nobler for First Gentleman to die than for Chamont to live
37 **Ev'n to** (I will deny it) even if it results in, even to the extent of

Above the suffering virtue of a soldier;
He's killed his injurer—a work of honour,
For which (unless you save him) he dies speedily.
My conscience is discharged. I'm but a friend;
A brother should go forward where I end. *Exit*

CHAMONT Dies?
Say he be naught; that's nothing to my goodness,
Which ought to shine through use, or else it loses
The glorious name 'tis known by. He's my brother.
Yet peace is above blood. Let him go. Ay,
But where's the noblesse of affection then?
That must be cared for too, or I'm imperfect.
The same blood that stood up in wrath against him
Now in his misery runs all to pity.
I'd rather die than speak one syllable
To save myself; but living as I am,
There's no avoiding on't; the world's humanity
Expects it hourly from me. Curse of fortune!
I took my leave so well, too.—Let him die;
'Tis but a brother lost. So pleasingly
And swiftly I came off, 'twere more than irksomeness
To tread that path again, and I shall never
Depart so handsomely.—But then where's posterity?
The consummation of our house and name?
I'm torn in pieces betwixt love and shame. *Exit*

5.3 *Enter Lepet, Clown [with books], Poltrot, Moulebaiser, and others, the new Court Officers*

LEPET
Good morrow, fellow Poltrot, and Moulebaiser;
Good morrow, fellows all.

POLTROT Monsieur Lepet!

LEPET
Look, I've remembered you; here's books apiece for you.
[*Lepet gives books to them all*]

MOULEBAISER
O sir, we dearly thank you.

LEPET So you may.
There's two impressions gone already, sirs.

POLTROT
What? No! In so short a time?

LEPET 'Tis as I tell you, sir.
My *Kick* sells gallantly, I thank my stars.

CLOWN
So does your table; you may thank the moon, too.

LEPET
'Tis the book sells the table.

CLOWN But 'tis the bookseller
That has the money for 'em; I'm sure o' that.

LEPET
'Twill much enrich the Company of Stationers.
'Tis thought 'twill prove a lasting benefit,
Like *The Wise Masters* and the almanacs,
The Hundred Novels and *The Book of Cookery*—
For they begin already to engross it
And make it a stock-book, thinking indeed
'Twill prove too great a benefit and help
For one that's new set up; they know their way,
And make him Warden ere his beard be grey.

MOULEBAISER
Is't possible such virtue should lie hid,
And in so little paper?

LEPET How? Why, there was *The Carpenter*,
An unknown thing, an odoriferous pamphlet,
Yet no more paper, by all computation,

53 **noblesse** nobility
65 **handsomely** (Chamont is congratulating himself on the elegance of his departure from court.)
where's posterity what about future generations of his family (what will they think of him, or will they even exist)
66 **consummation** (*a*) perfection (*b*) death, end
5.3.0.1 ***Poltrot*** coward (French)
0.1–2 ***Moulebaiser*** mussel-kisser (French slang for 'pussy-kisser')
5 **impressions gone** printings sold-out (i.e. his book is in its third edition)
8 **moon** (apparently influencing lunatics to buy the table; almanacs included tables showing the lunar months)
9–10 **bookseller...'em** (Authors did not receive royalties; the wholesale and retail booksellers therefore pocketed all profits)
11 **Company of Stationers** trade association of booksellers and printers
13 ***Wise Masters*** probably *The Wise Masters of Rome*, a popular sixteenth-century collection
almanacs books published annually containing tables of months and days with astronomical and astrological data, predictions and information—very popular, and profitable to booksellers
14 ***Hundred Novels*** Boccaccio's *Decameron*—or the popular jestbook *A Hundred Merry Tales*
Book of Cookery (probably indicating a popular genre, rather than any particular title)
16 **stock-book** part of 'the English Stock', a set of profitable titles jointly owned by a monopoly of wealthy booksellers
18 **one...up** a young member of the company only recently having finished his apprenticeship and set up in business
19 **Warden** elected member of the governing body of the Stationers' Company, under the authority of the Master
20 **virtue...hid** (an echo of the parable of the talents, Matthew 25)
21 ***The Carpenter*** probably *A Little Tractate, entitled The Carpenter*
22 **odoriferous** having a scent or fragrance, here ironically 'smelly'
23–4 **no...once** (*a*) no more toilet paper than Ajax would use to wipe himself (*b*) no more paper than used in the small print run of an edition of an ancient Greek play

Than *Ajax Telamon* would use at once.
Your *Herring* proved the like, able to buy
Another Fisher's Folly, and your *Pasquil*
Went not below the madcaps of that time—
And shall my elaborate *Kick* come behind, think you?

CLOWN
Yes, it must come behind; 'tis in *italica* too,
According to your humour.

LEPET Not in sale, varlet.

CLOWN
In sale, sir? It shall sail beyond 'em all, I trow.

LEPET [*looking over the shoulder of a reader*]
What have you there now? O, page 21.

CLOWN
That page is come to his years, he should be a servingman.

LEPET [*to his readers*]
Mark how I snap up *The Duello* there.
One would not use a dog so,
I must needs say; but's for the common good.

CLOWN
Nay sir, your commons seldom fight at sharp,
But buffet in a warehouse.

LEPET [*to his readers*] This will save
Many a gentleman of good blood from bleeding, sirs.
I have a curse from many a barber-surgeon;
They'd give but too much money to call't in.
Turn to page 45. See what you find there.

CLOWN O, out upon him!
Page, 45? That's an old thief indeed.

Enter Duke, the Lady (his sister), First Gentleman

LEPET [*to his readers*]
The duke! Clap down your books.—Away, Galoshio!

CLOWN
Indeed, I am too foul to be i'th' presence;
They use to shake me off at the chamber door still.

Exit

LADY [*kneeling to Duke*]
Good my lord, grant my suit; let me not rise
Without the comfort on't. I have not often
Been tedious in this kind.

DUKE Sister, you wrong yourself,
And those great virtues that your fame is made of,
To waste so much breath for a murderer's life.

LADY
You cannot hate th'offence more than I do, sir,
Nor the offender. The respect I owe
Unto his absent brother makes me a suitor,
A most importunate sister. Make me worthy
But of this one request.

DUKE I am deaf
To any importunacy, and sorry
For your forgetfulness. You never injured
Your worth so much; you ought to be rebuked for't.
Pursue good ways; end as you did begin.
'Tis half the guilt to speak for such a sin.

LADY [*rising*]
This is love's beggary right, that now is ours:
When ladies love, and cannot show their powers.

Exit

DUKE
La Nove?

FIRST GENTLEMAN
My lord.

DUKE Are these our new attendants?

LEPET
We are, my lord, and will endure as much
As better men, my lord—and more, I trust.

DUKE [*to First Gentleman*]
What's he?

FIRST GENTLEMAN
My lord, a decayed gentleman,
That will do any service.

DUKE A decayed one?

24 ***Ajax Telamon*** (*a*) tragedy of Sophocles in which 'the madman' scourges a ram which he thinks is Ulysses (*b*) punning on 'a jakes' or 'lavatory', as in Harington's *Metamorphosis of Ajax*

25 ***Herring*** Probably Thomas Nashe's *Lenten Stuff, containing a Description and first Procreation and Increase of the town of Great Yarmouth in Norfolk; With a new Play, never printed before, of the praise of the Red Herring.*

26 **Fisher's Folly** (*a*) a well-known house sold in July 1616 to Lady Harrington (*b*) punning on 'Fisher' in relation to 'Herring' (*c*) perhaps punning on the Jesuit named Fisher, allegedly responsible for converting Buckingham's mother to Catholicism
Pasquil satirical text—probably the series of best-selling pamphlets by Nicholas Breton: *Pasquil's Madcap, The Second Part of Pasquil's Madcap, Pasquil's Fools-cap* (all 1600)

28 **come behind** (*a*) fall short of the example of these other books (*b*) punning on a kick on the backside

30 **in sale** ('come behind') in the sense of not selling so many copies

32–3 **page . . . page** page of his book . . . boy or adolescent in personal attendance on a person of high rank

33 **That . . . years** (Pages of the Bedchamber in the court of James I often kept their positions as adults. See l. 44.)

34 **snap up** take up sharply in an argument (using the figurative sense drawn from biting or snapping)
The Duello (*a*) duelling (*b*) John Selden's *The Duello* (1610). Publication on duelling in France and Italy was intense: see for instance Pierre de Boissat, *Recherches sur les Duels* (Lyon, 1610) and Charles Bodin, *Discours contre les Duels* (Paris, 1618).

37 **commons** (*a*) lower orders (*b*) members of the House of Commons, involved in incidents of hitting and shoving in the Parliament of 1621
at sharp with pointed weapons (as in a duel)

40 **barber-surgeon** Of lower status than a physician who dealt with medicine, barber-surgeons dealt with surgery, and so were likely to be called to attend to wounds caused in duelling; hence, a decline in duelling would reduce their business.

41 **call't in** take the book off the market (like Lady Mary Wroth's *Urania* of 1621)

46–7 **too foul . . . door** (equating himself with the galoshes for which he is named)
presence . . . chamber Presence Chamber, where suitors and ambassadors were formally admitted into the King's presence

FIRST GENTLEMAN
A renounced one, indeed; for this place only.
DUKE
We renounce him then. Go, discharge him instantly.
He that disclaims his gentry for mere gains,
That man's too base to make a vassal on.
LEPET [*to First Gentleman*]
What says the Duke?
FIRST GENTLEMAN Faith, little to your comfort, sir.
You must be a gentleman again.
LEPET How?
FIRST GENTLEMAN There's no remedy.
LEPET
Marry, the fates forfend!—Ne'er while I breathe, sir.
FIRST GENTLEMAN
The Duke will have it so; there's no resisting.
He spied it i' your forehead.
LEPET My wife's doing.
She thought she should be put below her betters now,
And sued to ha' me made a gentleman again.
FIRST GENTLEMAN And very likely, sir.
Marry, I'll give you this comfort: when all's done,
You'll never pass but for a scurvy one.
That's all the help you have. Come, show your pace.
LEPET
The heaviest gentleman that e'er lost place.
Bear witness: I'm forced to't. *Exit*
DUKE [*to the remaining officers*]
Though you have a coarser title yet upon you
Than those that left your places without blame,
'Tis in your power to make yourselves the same.
I cannot make you gentlemen; that's a work
Raised from your own deservings; merit, manners,
And inborn virtue does it. Let your own goodness
Make you so great, my power shall make you greater.
And more t'encourage you, this I add again:
There's many grooms now exact gentlemen.
Enter Chamont [and stands aloof]
CHAMONT
Methinks 'tis strange to me to enter here.
Is there in nature such an awful power
To force me to this place, and make me do this?
Is man's affection stronger than his will?
His resolution? Was I not resolved
Never to see this place more? Do I bear
Within my breast one blood that confounds th'other?
The blood of love and will, and the last weakest?
Had I ten millions, I would give it all now
I were but past it, or 'twould never come;
For I shall never do't, or not do't well,
But spoil it utterly betwixt two passions.
Yonder's the Duke himself.—I will not do't now,
Had twenty lives their several sufferings in him. *Exit*
DUKE
Who's that went out now?
POLTROT I saw none, my lord.
DUKE
Nor you?
MOULEBAISER
I saw the glimpse of one, my lord.
DUKE
Whate'er it was, methought it pleased me strangely,
And suddenly my joy was ready for't.
Did you not mark it better?
POLTROT *and* MOULEBAISER Troth, my lord,
We gave no great heed to't.
Enter Chamont
CHAMONT [*aside*] 'Twill not be answered;
It brings me hither still, by main force hither.
Either I must give over to profess humanity
Or I must speak for him.
DUKE 'Tis here again:
[*Aside*] No marvel 'twas so pleasing: 'tis delight
And worth itself, now it appears unclouded.
CHAMONT My lord—
[*Aside*] He turns away from me. By this hand,
I am ill-used of all sides! 'Tis a fault
That fortune ever had, t'abuse a goodness.
DUKE
Methought you were saying somewhat.
CHAMONT [*aside*] Mark the language:
As coy as fate. I see 'twill ne'er be granted.
DUKE
We little looked, in troth, to see you here yet.
CHAMONT [*aside*]
Not till the day after my brother's death, I think.
DUKE
Sure some great business drew you.
CHAMONT No, in sooth, sir:
Only to come to see a brother die, sir,
That I may learn to go too—and if he deceive me not,
I think he will do well in't of a soldier,
Manly and honestly. And if he weep then,
I shall not think the worse on's manhood for't,
Because he's leaving of that part that has it.
DUKE
He's slain a noble gentleman; think on't, sir.
CHAMONT
I would I could not, sir.
DUKE Our kinsman, too.

80 **spied...forehead** saw it written on your noble brow (with a suggestion of cuckoldry, taken up implicitly in Lepet's response)

81 **put below** (*a*) given a lower rank than (*b*) sexually mounted by. (There may be an allusion to a dispute about precedence in the 1621 Parliament.)

86 **show your pace** a command to leave (perhaps—given Lepet's earlier display of 'the postures'—an opportunity for the actor to display a characteristic 'funny walk' in his exit)

87 **heaviest** saddest (but perhaps alluding to the size of the comic actor William Rowley, who was a gentleman, and may have originated the role)

104 **blood** the competing codes of conduct, association and family which bind society together

111 **him** the Soldier

CHAMONT
All this is but worse, sir.
DUKE When 'tis at worst,
Yet seeing thee, he lives.
CHAMONT My lord—
DUKE He lives.
Believe it as thy bliss; he dies not for't.
Will this make satisfaction for things past?
CHAMONT [*kneeling*]
O, my lord—
DUKE Will it? Speak.
CHAMONT
With greater shame to my unworthiness.
DUKE
Rise then; we're ev'n. I never found it harder
To keep just with a man. My great work's ended.
I knew your brother's pardon was your suit, sir,
However your nice modesty held it back.
CHAMONT
I take a joy now to confess it, sir.
Enter First Gentleman
FIRST GENTLEMAN
My lord—
DUKE Hear me first, sir, whate'er your news be:
Set free the soldier instantly.
FIRST GENTLEMAN 'Tis done, my Lord.
DUKE
How?
FIRST GENTLEMAN
In effect. 'Twas part of my news too.
There's fair hope of your noble kinsman's life, sir.
DUKE
What sayst thou?
FIRST GENTLEMAN And the most admirèd change
That living flesh e'er had: he's not the man, my lord.
Death cannot be more free from passions, sir,
Than he is at this instant. He's so meek now,
He makes those seem passionate were never thought of.
And for he fears his moods have oft disturbed you, sir,
He's only hasty now for his forgiveness—
And here behold him, sir.
Enter Passionate Lord [*bandaged*], *the Cupid, and two Brothers*
DUKE Let me give thanks first.
Our worthy cousin—
PASSIONATE LORD Your unworthy trouble, sir—
For which, with all acknowledged reverence,
I ask your pardon. And for injury
More known and wilfull, I have chose a wife,
Without your counsel or consent, my lord.
DUKE
A wife? Where is she, sir?
PASSIONATE LORD [*introducing the Cupid*]
This noble gentlewoman.
DUKE How?
PASSIONATE LORD
Whose honour my forgetful times much wronged.
DUKE [*to First Gentleman*]
He's madder than he was.
FIRST GENTLEMAN I would ha' sworn for him.
DUKE The Cupid, cousin?
PASSIONATE LORD Yes, this worthy lady, sir.
DUKE [*to First Gentleman*] Still worse and worse.
FIRST BROTHER
Our sister, under pardon, my lord.
DUKE What?
SECOND BROTHER
Which shape love taught her to assume.
DUKE Is't truth then?
FIRST GENTLEMAN
It appears plainly now below the waist, my lord.
DUKE
Chamont, didst ever read of a she-Cupid?
CHAMONT
Never in fiction yet, but it might hold, sir,
For desire is of both genders.
Enter [*Lady*] (*the Duke's sister*)
DUKE Make that good here:
He joins Chamont's hand and his sister's
I take thee at thy word, sir.
CHAMONT O my lord,
Love would appear too bold and rude from me.
Honour and admiration are her rights;
Her goodness is my saint, my lord.
DUKE I see,
You're both too modest to bestow yourselves.
I'll save that virtue still; 'tis but my pains. Come,
It shall be so.
CHAMONT
This gift does but set forth my poverty.
LADY
Sir, that which you complain of is my riches.
Enter Chamont's brother (*the Soldier*)
DUKE
Soldier, now every noise sounds peace, thou'rt welcome.
SOLDIER [*kneeling*]
Sir, my repentance sues for your blest favour—
Which, once obtained, no injury shall lose it.
I'll suffer mightier wrongs.
DUKE [*raising Soldier*] Rise, loved and pardoned.
For where hope failed—nay, art itself resigned—

156 **not the man** no longer who he used to be
166–7 **I ... consent** (as did Kit Villiers, Buckingham's brother)
171 **madder** more deluded (because he has just called the apparently male Cupid a woman)
180 **desire ... genders** i.e. the Cupid could have been female for, although Cupid traditionally is represented as male, yet both men and women experience sexual desire

Thou'st wrought that cure which skill could never
find;
Nor did there cease, but to our peace extend.
Never could wrongs boast of a nobler end. *Exeunt*

Epilogue [*Enter*] *the Epilogue*

Our poet bid us say, for his own part,
He cannot lay too much forth of *his* art,
But fears our over-acting passions may,
As not adorn, deface his laboured play.
Yet still he is resolute for what is writ
Of nicer valour, and assumes the wit:
But for the love-scenes (which he ever meant
Cupid, in's petticoat, should represent)
He'll stand no shock of censure. The play's good;
He says he knows it (if well understood).
But we (blind god) beg, if thou art divine,
Thou'lt shoot thy arrows round; this play was thine.
[*Exit*]

Epilogue.0.1 *Enter the Epilogue* Who speaks this final speech will strongly affect its interpretation: it could plausibly be spoken by Lepet (an author speaking for the author, who is offstage at play's end and could enter as the others exit), or by Chamont, the Soldier, Passionate Lord, or Cupid.

1 **part** (punning on 'actor's role')

2 **lay...of** (*a*) boast too much about (*b*) bet too much money on (*c*) reveal too much about

3 **over-acting passions** (paradoxically applying action to what is passive)

4 **laboured play** playing on labour and 'play'; the play, designed to give delight, on which he has worked so hard (and which contains a pregnant woman)

5 **writ** scripted (what the writer did in contrast to what the actors did)

6 **assumes** claims as his own

11 **blind god** Cupid

12 **Thou'lt...round** You will shoot your arrows at the circle of spectators (and so make them fall in love with us, the actors)

thine (i.e. not the author's work, or the actors')

THE TRIUMPHS OF HONOUR AND VIRTUE

Text edited and annotated by David M. Bergeron, introduced by Ania Loomba

The Triumphs of Honour and Virtue, Middleton's third pageant for the Company of Grocers, encapsulates crucial aspects of the cultural politics of English overseas expansion during the early seventeenth century, some of which are neglected by Renaissance criticism today. It was commissioned to celebrate the inauguration of Sir Peter Proby as Lord Mayor of London in 1622; Middleton collaborated with Garret Christmas for its production, and they received £220 as gross payment for it. At first glance, one might be tempted to dismiss it as a collage of snippets of Middleton's earlier pageants, or as an undistinguished example of the formula followed by most Lord Mayor's shows. But the ways in which this pageant follows, adds to, and departs from the pattern of both Middleton's pageants and other mayoral shows through the seventeenth century indicates some of the ideological parameters within which English trade was conducted.

The opening paragraph is identical to that of *The Triumphs of Love and Antiquity* which Middleton had written in 1619 for the Skinners' Company. Middleton is confident that his pageant, 'where invention flourishes,' will be popularly received, because even inferior triumphs, 'wherein art hath been weakly imitated and most beggarly worded' have been successful (24–5). It is significant, however, that Middleton claims that these inferior pageants have been applauded by 'foreign nations'; by implication, his own shows are designed for a more discerning English audience. This nationalistic appeal is appropriate in the context of the mayoral pageants, which celebrated not only the civic organization of London, and the livery companies that controlled it, but also the colonial possibilities of trade and commerce. The Grocers, it should be recalled, were then the second most powerful of the twelve major livery companies of London. *Honour and Virtue* enacts aspects of the colonial drama which were yet to unfold; it canvasses for a national pride which was both the necessary condition for colonial ventures and their outcome.

From the 1619 pageant Middleton also transported the figure of Antiquity, who, in both shows, traces the lineage of the company in question. Such an exercise reminds us of the negotiations between ascendant mercantile capital and the Crown: not only is the 'family tree' of the company an appropriation of feudal and royal practices, it also seeks to demonstrate the connections between the merchants and the nobility by including the names of royal and noble patrons of the livery companies. The heritage of the morality play is evident in this, as in all the mayoral shows, with the newly appointed mayor cast as a sort of Everyman who must resist temptation in order to govern well. The prolonged moral see-saw of the more lavishly produced *The Triumphs of Truth*, Middleton's second show for the Grocers, however, is truncated here because there is no personification of evil and therefore no elaborate temptations are enacted. Its four major figures are all 'good': Honour, Virtue, Antiquity, and 'a black personage representing India, called, for her odours and riches, the Queen of Merchandise' and 'attended by Indians in antique habits: Commerce, Adventure and Traffic' (41–6).

This last figure is what makes this pageant remarkable—even though she is not unique. Visual entertainments and pageants, from at least the first decade of the sixteenth century, had repeatedly featured an enormous variety of racial outsiders as well as personifications of lands with which there was real or desired trade. The praise of an uncivilized outsider for the ruler was obviously an effective way to indicate the power of the latter. During the entertainments for Elizabeth at Kenilworth Castle in 1575, for example, it was arranged that a *Hombre Salvagio* or wild man should testify to the Queen's 'glorie' (Bergeron). The *King's Entertainment* written for James in 1604 by Dekker, features 'Arabia Britannica' represented as a woman in white, who is sad until the arrival of the King. Jonson's *The Masque of Blackness* (1605) had Queen Anne and her ladies in blackface as the daughters of the River Niger. Blacks and other outsiders were represented even more insistently in the Jacobean mayoral shows: their presence, either within the spectacle or in processions preceding it, signified the new territories that held the promise of commercial expansion for the Companies that sponsored the pageants. In Anthony Munday's *The Triumphs of Re-United Britannia* (1605), for example, an Indian King and Queen come to England, bringing with them 'no mean quantity of Indian Gold'; in his show for the Ironmongers in 1609, a whale is featured with a 'Black More' in its mouth; and in *Chruso-thrambos, The Triumphs of Gold* (written by Munday in 1611), a 'King of Moors' appears 'gallantly mounted on a golden leopard, he hurling gold and silver every way about him' and accompanied by 'six tributarie kings'.

Middleton's Indian Queen, then, not only resembles his King of Moors who appears in *The Triumphs of Truth*, but is part of a pattern which was to continue throughout the century. To take a few examples just from pageants sponsored by the Grocers, Middleton's *The Triumphs of Honour and Industry* (1617) contains a personification of India, 'the seat of merchandise'; in John Squire's *The*

Triumphs of Peace (1620) the figures of America, Asia, and Africa crown Europe as Empress of the earth; John Tatham's *London's Triumph* (1659) depicts 'several of the places or countries, in which the commodities belonging to the Grocers Trade do grow, and the natives disporting therein, in habits of each nation'; Thomas Jordan's *London Triumphant* (1672), also written for the Grocers, includes an Indian Emperor, 'negroes in Indian habits' and the figure of America; *London in its Splendour* (1673) by the same writer again shows 'two negroes properly mounted, in East Indian shapes' and Jordan's *The Triumphs of London* (1678) has an East Indian deity 'called Opulenta, a representative of all the intrinsic treasure in the Oriental Indies' whom the 'idolatrous natives' worship 'with pagan piety, and diabolical devotion'. Opulenta is accompanied by 'three black Indian princes, viz., Animalia, Mineralia and Vegetabilia'. The Grocers' shows routinely began with black boys, mounted on griffins or camels, strewing the streets with the 'delicious traffic of the Grocers Company': company records show payments for '50 sugar loaves, 36 pounds of nutmegs, 24 pounds of dates and 114 pounds of ginger' which were used for this purpose in the 1617 show (Heath). Middleton is the first, to the best of my knowledge, to give blacks a speaking part in the civic pageants, although Jonson's *Masque of Blackness* had done so earlier with respect to courtly shows.

Given the expansion of English overseas trade during this period, as also the fact that these shows were sponsored by companies who had a direct stake in the trade, the recurrence of such figures is not surprising. Various cultural and racial 'others'—the natives of different parts of the New World, Africans and Asians—are often confused with each other so we get composite figures that seem to belong to no specific place; at other times they are represented as the same so that in certain respects there is no distinction between the King of Moors and the Indian Queen. These blurrings, as well as the specificity of each figure, are important for unravelling the politics of English trade and colonial contact during the period. The Indian Queen in *Honour and Virtue*, like the Moorish King in *Truth*, offers her own conversion to Christianity as a justification for English trading practices overseas. She asks the viewer to observe her 'with an intellectual eye', to see beyond her native blackness, which was commonly associated with the devil, with depravity, sin and filth, and to perceive her inner goodness, which, she suggests, is made possible by her new faith (55–8).

The impossibility of 'washing the Ethiope white' was an old idea (the Moorish servant girl Zanche in Webster's *The White Devil* calls it a 'sunburnt proverb') which was commonly used to indicate the difficulty of changing outward realities like one's physique as well as inner qualities, such as one's disposition and faith. Both variants show up in contemporary emblem books, which influenced the imagery and iconography of Middleton's pageants. Thomas Palmer's *Two Hundred Posies* (1565), England's earliest known emblem book, depicts, under the title 'Impossible things', two white men washing a black man. The accompanying lines specifically refer to the impossibility of religious conversions:

Ripa's emblem for 'wasted labour'.

> Why washest thou the man of Inde? . . .
> Indurat heart of heretics
> Much blacker than the mole;
> With word or writte who seeks to purge
> Starke dead he blows the coal.

Geoffrey Whitney's *A Choice of Emblems* (1586), reproduces a similar picture, under the title 'Æthiopem laure', and advises that it is useless to battle against the power of Nature and whiten the 'blackamore'. Cesare Ripa's influential *Iconologia*, various editions of which were issued from different places on the Continent beginning in 1593, also depicts a black figure or 'More' as the emblem for 'wasted labour', with an explanatory legend that echoes Palmer and Whitney. In Middleton's representation of India, what was once impossible is now rendered feasible by English merchants. Commerce can whiten the 'indurat heart of heretikes' but in order to do so, skin colour must be unyoked from moral qualities. (In Jonson's *Masque of Blackness* such unyoking is seen as a possibility because Niger's black daughters are 'bright' within. But Niger in that pageant wants to restore them to their original white exteriors and hence match the outside with the inside.) It is ironic, and even paradoxical, that mercantilist-colonialist discourse, which was to help institutionalize, rationalize, and circulate such a variety of racial prejudice, should in its infancy need to posit such a divorce.

India's speech in Middleton's pageant intricately mixes the language of religion with that of commerce. 'Blest commerce' is literally a crusader for Christianity and 'settles such happiness' on the Indian Queen that the English merchants' cargo of 'gums and fragrant spices', indeed all 'the riches and the sweetness of the east', are only fair exchange for the 'celestial knowledge' that is now hers (62–80). This is again a theme that runs through the Mayoral shows where a variety of colonized people celebrate the civilizational and moral qualities of English trading practices and contrast them to the barbarity of the Dutch, the Portuguese, and the Spanish.

This contrast, and indeed the fact that it is *traders* who are agents of religious conversion, reminds us of the context in which these pageants were being enacted. In the mayoral shows, most of the black, brown, and tawny figures that praise the might of London, England, and English trade are not simply savage or wild peoples: more often than not they are emperors, queens, or other representatives of riches, plenitude, and exotic grandeur. They are born of the newly established spice trade during the period, which brought the British into contact with the highly stratified societies of Asia, with their sophisticated courts and long standing commercial and trading histories, in contrast to the societies they encountered in the New World which were more tribal, and hence more readily regarded as primitive and uncultured. In the East, the first English travellers like Ralph Fitch found cities 'much greater then London' (Ramsay). Thomas Coryat wrote home in 1615 that Lahore, part of the Mughal empire in India, was 'one of the largest cities of the whole universe' (Purchas). Here the English had to literally beg for favours from potentates who were wealthier and at least as whimsical as European monarchs. The Turkish Sultan, the Sultan of Achin, and the powerful Mughal rulers, for example, had to be approached with deference, with expensive gifts (no glass beads would do in the face of their own huge treasuries and developed economies), and with patience. After spending many years at the court of Jehangir 'The Great Mogor', William Hawkins found that his efforts to secure trading privileges had come to naught. Hawkins, Nicholas Dounton, Thomas Roe, and other pioneering English merchant-sailors were also frustrated by the layers of bureaucracy that they had to negotiate with before they could even approach the kings (Purchas).

It is no accident, then, that the Indian woman in *Honour and Virtue*, like so many other related figures, is both royal and compliant to the English will: the splendour and wealth that the East promised the English but had not yet delivered is in this way rendered available. Representations of exotic royalty in city pageants had a precedent in countries which had a longer history of contact with the East. The triumphal arches and pedestals erected in Lisbon when Philip of Spain made his formal entry there in 1581 depicted personifications of various territories in the East which had been conquered by Portugal, all offering their products to the new king. Goa, Portugal's main outpost in India, was represented as 'Queen of the East' and occupied a central position in the show. Even though the Spanish, the English, the Dutch, and the Portuguese were bitter rivals in their dealings overseas, there was a flow of information and of materials such as travelogues and paintings and art objects from one country to another, just as there was the attempt to guard them from each other (Lach).

The literature produced during the period of the spice trade, including the mayoral pageants, both invoked medieval images of India (and the East generally), and recast these according to the newer dynamics of contact (Hahn). In recent writing on early modern Europe, this history of the 'old world' contact has been neglected in favour of the new world expansion, which has therefore become the dominant model for most work on colonial discourse during the period. Middleton's Indian Queen is a useful reminder of the other half of the picture.

The Grocers' Company, Middleton's patron for this show, had an obvious connection with Eastern trade: its founders had once been known as the Pepperers, and following a treaty between Elizabeth I and Sultan Murad II of Turkey, the Levant Company was established in 1581. The Grocers had control over all druggists, confectioners, tobacconists, and tobacco cutters, and the founders of the East India Company included such well known Grocers as Sir John Moore and Middleton's famous namesake Sir Thomas Myddelton. England had remained remarkably tardy in acquiring information generated by European, especially Portuguese, ventures into Asia so that the Tudor image of India was largely one derived from ancient Greek and medieval sources as a land of monsters, heathens, and untold splendour and wealth. But several parallel developments towards the end of the sixteenth century changed all that. Firstly, new materials began to circulate. The English translation of the Dutch Jan van Linschoten's work *Itinerario* in 1598 made a great impact on English merchants, as did Theodor de Bry's lavish travel collection, *Collectiones peregrinationum in Indiam Orientalem et Occidentalims*, (issued from Frankfurt between 1590 and 1634). Richard Hakluyt had hardly touched on Asian materials in the first edition of *Principall Navigations*, but after 1590 he became one of the most assiduous collectors of information on Asia, reproducing travel narratives with the object of providing the first fleets bound for India with as much authoritative data as possible. He also took an active part in the founding of the East India Company: a memorial written in 1600, probably by him, is called 'Certain Reasons Why the English Merchants May Trade into the East Indies', and it argued for trade with the East in the same way as his 'Discourse on Western Planting' pleaded for colonization in the New World. Hakluyt persuaded Ralph Fitch, who had returned from India in 1599, to write his 'wonderful travailes', which became the first English account of India. The final edition of *Principall Navigations* (1598–1600) carried that account, as well as a translation of the Venetian merchant Cesare

Fedrici's book on India, along with John Newberry's letters from that country and other related documents (Hakluyt). The other pioneering English collector of travel accounts, Richard Eden, was similarly interested in stimulating interest in expansion (Lach).

Secondly, travel narratives were complemented by the goods and profits gleaned from actual voyages which also served to reopen the Orient for the English. Trading stations sprang up all over the Ottoman Empire following the Anglo-Turkish treaty which generated firsthand accounts of the East. In March 1588, *The Hercules* returned from Tripoli in Syria, 'the richest ship of English merchant goods that ever was known to come into this realme' as John Eldred described it (Hakluyt). Its cargo included 'silk from Persia, indigo and cotton from India, cinnamon from Ceylon, pepper from Sumatra and nutmegs, cloves and mace from the Moluccas', convincing sceptics about the viability of trade in the East Indies. The huge profits made by the Dutch East India Company, the defeat of the Armada, and the continual and steep rise in pepper prices between 1592 and 1599, all contributed to the initiation of direct English trade with India. The East India Company was set up (only four years after its Dutch counterpart), on the last day of 1600, with a capital of £50,000. Elizabeth I granted monopoly of trade with the east to the Company 'for the honour of our nation, the welfare of the people, the increase of our navigation, and the advancement of lawful traffic to the benefit of the commonwealth'. Unlike the contact with America, which rested almost entirely on colonization, the English presence in India remained, through the century, largely mercantile. The East India Company's profits averaged over 101 per cent for the first five voyages. By 1620, the Company possessed factories in Sumatra, India, Japan, Java, Borneo, Malacca, Celebes, Siam, and Malabar. The specificity of these places was blurred in their representation as 'the spice islands', a blurring that is reflected in the mayoral pageants where we have 'negroes in Indian clothes', or the word 'Moor' applied to everyone. But the confusion also testifies to the bewildering variety of peoples that Europeans actually found in India, where, in addition to the internal variegation of peoples, Arabs, Ethiopians, and Persians mingled with Kaffirs from Mozambique, Turks, and Jews (Lach).

The Portuguese had justified their eastward expansion by seeing it as an extension of the Crusades: India, it was argued, was being colonized by Moors and needed to be saved. But they had had very limited success in this regard. The British, in contrast, had little crusading zeal in India initially. Thus it is especially significant that the Indian Queen in *Honour and Virtue*, and indeed many other 'black' figures in the pageants, should cast English trading practices as achieving missionary ends. In reality, Oriental populations, let alone the monarchs, were hardly as tractable as Middleton's Indian Queen or King of Moors. The Mughal emperors, for example, were intellectually interested in Christianity, thanks to the established presence of the Jesuits in India. Akbar even

Ripa's figures of Asia, Africa, Europe, and America.

tried to experiment with a composite faith that would synthesize Hinduism, Islam, and Christianity, and his son Jehangir, according to Thomas Coryat, 'speaketh very reverently of our saviour'. But none of them came even remotely close to converting, and Jehangir, Coryat says, regarded all conversions as evidence of fickleness.

Nor was English trade quite as secure as the shows might lead us to believe. It is true that in 1622, the same year that Middleton wrote this pageant, the East India Company defeated the Portuguese at Ormuz in the Persian Gulf and negotiated to become the maritime auxiliary of the Mughals. But in the same year too, on 11 February, many English traders had been massacred by the Dutch in Amboyna, an event about which there was much publicity and 'much complaint in England', according to Purchas. Since 1606, the merchants of the East India Company had petitioned the Privy Council to authorize use of force against the Dutch; in 1609 and 1611 they complained to the Lord Treasurer about Portuguese and Dutch behaviour. Later pageants castigated the Dutch and Spanish trading practices as barbaric, in contrast with the English merchants, who are 'Peacable and kind | Full of Humanity' (*London Triumphant*, 1672). While Middleton may not be as explicit, his Queen does insist that she is 'by English merchants first enlightened' (62). Moreover, his selective use of recent events is significant. It is Ormuz rather than Amboyna that resonates in his pageant, not only because it marked a rare victory for the English over their rivals but because in 1586, its Queen had come to Goa to be converted to Christianity after her marriage to a Portuguese. Middleton's pageant for the Grocers then is clearly meant to assuage very real anxieties and bolster hopes that were, in reality, rather far from being realized.

The Indian Queen is not just a generalized seventeenth-century trope for a feminized Orient but marks a specific playing with specific histories. Of course, routine representations of Asia as female in books such as Ripa's *Iconologia* must certainly have contributed to the way in which she was presented in the actual pageant. One can only speculate what other factors might have contributed to the image: Elizabeth herself had often dressed in Oriental garb. In 1599 she received Thomas Platter at Nonsuch Castle wearing 'a gown of pure white satin, gold-embroidered with a whole bird of paradise', and thus showing 'her continental visitor that she, like any ruler of the distant Moluccas, knew how to wear a plumage headdress of the rare bird of paradise found only in the East' (Lach). The representation may also have been influenced by other contemporary images of Oriental women: Cesare Vecellio's *Habiti antichi et moderni di tutto il mondo* (1598) offered remarkably detailed pictures of African, Asian, and American as well as European peoples, classified according to both class and gender.

In the last part of *Honour and Virtue*, the throne of Virtue is joined by 'the Globe of Honour', a contraption that must have called for much expense and ingenuity, for it flies open into eight parts revealing eight personifications of moral qualities such as Clear Conscience and Peace of Heart, and four 'cardinal virtues, Wisdom, Justice, Fortitude, and Temperance' who display the arms of the City of London, the Grocers, the Mayor, and the 'Noble East India Company' (232–63). The Globe itself includes 'that prosperous plantation in the Colony Of Virginia and the Bermudas, with all good wishes to the Governors, Traders, and Adventurers unto those Christianly reformed islands' (266–9). The Pageant, then, develops from a specific representation of British trade, via the genealogy of worthy merchants (some of whom had colonial connections) to an image of global victory for English trade. Beginning with a moral victory over the interiority of the colonized woman, it moves to a very physical image of victory, with Honour mounted over the globe.

The mayoral pageants are testimonies to the almost oligarchic power of the livery companies, and hymns to the new god of mercantilism. And yet the new religion was still far from secure: James had renewed the charter of the East India Company in 1607, but was drawn into making huge concessions to the Dutch, who, along with the Portuguese, were still creating difficulties for English trade in India. The Company of Grocers had their own problems: James sought to take away certain privileges from them in favour of the Apothecaries. He did so in a language that still disdained the ascendant commercial spirit, calling the Grocers 'but Merchants' who are lacking 'the mystery' of the Apothecaries, and accusing them

Vecellio's 'Donna Indiana Orientale Di Conditione'.

of bringing 'home rotten wares from the Indies, Persia and Greece' and of thinking that 'no man must control them' (Rees). Some of the triumphs of *The Triumphs of Honour and Virtue*, then, were real, some merely wishful thinking, and some yet to come. In putting on a show for Sir Peter Proby, Middleton created a fantasy that enacts the possibilities of contemporary colonial trading practices, and thereby mobilizes the national pride and commercial optimism necessary for such ventures.

SEE ALSO

Textual introduction and apparatus: *Companion*, 676
Authorship and date: *Companion*, 427
General introduction to the civic entertainments: this volume, 963
Other Middleton–Christmas works: *Antiquity*, 1397; *Aries*, 1586; *Integrity*, 1766; *Prosperity*, 1901; lost pageant for Charles I, 1898

The Triumphs of Honour and Virtue

A noble solemnity, performed through the City, at the sole cost and charges of the Honourable Fraternity of Grocers, at the confirmation and establishment of their most worthy brother, the Right Honourable Peter Proby, in the high office of His Majesty's lieutenant, Lord Mayor and chancellor of the famous City of London.

Taking beginning at his lordship's going and perfecting itself after his return from receiving the oath of mayoralty at Westminster, on the morrow after Simon and Jude's Day, being the 29 of October 1622.

To the honour of him, to whom the noble Fraternity of Grocers, his worthy brothers, have dedicated their loves in costly triumphs, the Right Honourable Peter Proby, Lord Mayor of this renowned city

To be his servant that hath served
Two royal princes and deserved
So worthily of both; the same
Call not service, rather fame.

At your lordship's command:
Tho. Middleton.

The Triumphs of Honour and Virtue

If foreign nations have been struck with admiration at the form, state, and splendour of some yearly triumphs, wherein art hath been but faintly imitated, there is fair hope that things where invention flourishes, clear art and her graceful proprieties, should receive favour and encouragement from the content of the spectator, which, next to the service of his Honour and honourable society, is the principal reward it looks for; then, not despairing of that common favour, this takes delight to present itself.

And first, to begin with the worthy love of his noble fraternity, after his Honour's return from Westminster, having received some service upon the water, by the conduct of two artful triumphs, viz., the Throne of Virtue and the Continent of India, which also by land attends his lordship's most wished arrival, accompanied with the whole body of the triumph, which, near upon the time of his Honour's approach, are decently and distinctly placed; the first, bearing the title of the Continent of India, a triumph replenished with all manner of spice-plants and trees bearing odour, attends his Honour's arrival in Paul's Churchyard: a black personage representing India, called, for her odours and riches, the Queen of Merchandise, challenging the most eminent seat, advanceth herself upon a bed of spices, attended by Indians in antique habits: Commerce, Adventure and Traffic, three habited like merchants, presenting to her view a bright figure, bearing the inscription of Knowledge, a sun appearing above the trees in brightest splendour and glory. The black Queen before mentioned lending a voice to these following words.

THE SPEECH OF THE BLACK QUEEN

You that have eyes of judgement and discern
Things that the best of man and life concern,
Draw near: this black is but my native dye,
But view me with an intellectual eye,
As wise men shoot their beams forth, you'll then find
A change in the complexion of the mind:
I'm beauteous in my blackness. O ye sons
Of fame and honour, through my best part runs
A spring of living waters, clear and true,
Found first by knowledge, which came first by you,
By you, and your examples, blessed commerce,
That by exchange settles such happiness.
Of gums and fragrant spices I confess,
My climate heaven does with abundance bless,
And those you have from me; but what are they
Compared with odours whose scent ne'er decay?
And those I have from you, plants of your youth,
The savour of eternal life, sweet truth,
Exceeding all the odoriferous scent,
That from the beds of spices ever went:
I that command (being prosp'rously possessed)
The riches and the sweetness of the east,
To that famed mountain Taurus spreading forth
My balmy arm, whose height does kiss the north,
And in the Sea Enos lave this hand,
Account my blessings not in those to stand,
Though they be large and fruitful, but confess
All wealth consists in Christian holiness.
To such celestial knowledge I was led,
By English merchants first enlightenèd
In honour of whose memory only three
I instance here, all of this brotherhood free;
To whose fames the great honour of this hour
Aptly belongs, but to that man of power
The first and chiefest, to whose worth so clear,
Justice hath given her sword up for a year:
And as yon sun his perfect splendour shows,
Cheering the plants, and no clouds interpose
His radiant comforts, so no earthy part,
Which makes eclipses in a ruler's heart,
(As in that glorious planet) must come nigh
The sun of justice: all such mists must fly.

4 **Peter Proby** (1565–1625), born in Chester; Sheriff 1614–15; served also as Member of Parliament
16 **Two royal princes** Elizabeth and James
41–2 **Paul's Churchyard** area at the east end of St Paul's Cathedral
45 **antique** ancient, possibly old-fashioned
70 ***odoriferous*** fragrant
74 ***Taurus*** mountain chain in southern Turkey
76 ***Sea Enos*** an apparent reference to the Gulf of Enos, an inlet of the Aegean Sea, in Turkey
lave wash

You're in an orb of brightness placed and fixed,
And with no soil must honour be commixed:
So to your worthy progress zeal commends
Your lordship, with your grave and noble friends.

The speech being ended, to add a little more help to the fainter apprehensions, the three merchants placed in the Continent have reference to the lord mayor and sheriffs, all three being this year brothers of this ancient and honourable society, which triple or threefold honour happened to this worthy company in the year 1577, Sir Thomas Ramsay being then lord mayor, and Master Nicholas Backhouse and Master Francis Bowyer, sheriffs; having coherence with this year's honour, matched and paralleled with these three their as worthy successors: the Right Honourable Peter Proby, and the generous and nobly affected Master John Hodges, and Sir Humphrey Handford, sheriffs and aldermen.

By this time his lordship being gracefully conducted toward the Chariot of Fame, which awaits his Honour's approach near the Little Conduit in Cheap, Antiquity, a grave and reverend personage with a golden register-book in his hand, gives life to these words.

THE SPEECH OF ANTIQUITY

Objects of years and reverence greet mine eye,
A sight most pleasing to Antiquity.
I never could unclasp this book of fame
Where worthies dwell by a distinguished name,
At a more comely season I shall tell
Things sprung from truth, near kin to miracle.
With that of later days I first begin,
So back into the deeper times again:
I only touch thy memory (which I know
In thankfulness can never be found slow)
With Heaven's miraculous mercy to thy health
After so long a sickness: all the wealth
Which thou with an unusuring hand hast got,
Which is not the least wonder-worthy note,
(Truth makes me speak things freely) cannot be
A greater work than thy recovery.
Nine brethren-senators, thy seniors all,
Whose times had been before thee, Death did call
To their eternal peace from this degree,
Leaving their earthly honour now to thee;
Think and be thankful still, this seems the more.
Another observation kept in store,
For seventeen senators since thy time were chose,
And to this minute not one dead of those.
Those are not usual notes; nor here it ends,
The court and city, two most noble friends,
Have made exchange o'late: I read from hence,
There has gone some most worthy citizens
Up to the court's advance; in lieu of that,
You have a courtier now your magistrate,
A servant to Elizabeth the blest,
Since to King James that reigns with Solomon's breast;
Kept the recòrds for both; from the Queen took
Charge of three hundred horse, three thousand foot.
Four attributes cleaves to this man of men,
A scholar, soldier, courtier, citizen:
These are no usual touches, to conclude
(Like to his life with blessings so endued)
He's chose his brotherhood, men of that fame
For bounty, amity, and honoured name,
The city bounds transcend not in their place,
And their word makes 'em prosper, God grant grace.
Honour they never wanted: when was't seen,
But they had senators to their brethëren?
Nay, one recòrd here to make joy more glad,
I find seventeen that were in scarlet clad,
All at one time of this fraternity;
Now five, for this hour's honour brings forth three,
Fame triple will make triple virtue strive
At whose triumphant throne you next arrive.

For farther illustration, there are contained in Antiquity's golden legend the names of many worthies of ancient time, by whom this noble fraternity has received much honour; such as were the worthy and famous Sir Andrew Bockerell, who was lord mayor of this city the sixteenth year of King Henry the Third, and continued in the magistracy seven years together; also the noble Allen de la Zouch, who for his good government in the time of his mayoralty, was by King Henry the Third created both a Baron of this realm, and Lord Chief Justice of England. Also that famous worthy, Sir Thomas Knowles, twice lord mayor of this honourable city, which said Sir Thomas began at his own charge that famous building of Guildhall in London, and other memorable works both in the city and in his own company, re-edifying also St Anthony's Church, with many others that are fair ornaments to memory, viz., Sir William Sevenock, Sir Robert Chichsley, Sir Stephen Browne, Sir Henry Keble, Sir William Laxton, etc. Who by those virtues that they were most addicted unto in their lifetime, are illustrated by persons of brightness in the Throne of Virtue, the next part of triumph that presents itself. Next beneath Antiquity sits Authority, placed between Wisdom and Innocence, holding a naked sword, a serpent wound about the blade thereof, two doves standing upon the crossbar of the hilt,

109 **John Hodges** Grocer, Alderman of Cordwainer Street; died 1629
109–10 **Humphrey Handford** (1565–1625), Grocer, Alderman of Castle Baynard
113 **Little Conduit** water source located in Cheapside, frequently used as a place of dramatic representation in the mayoral pageants
147 ***Solomon's*** wise Biblical king of Israel
157 ***God grant grace*** motto of the Grocers
169–70 **Andrew Bockerell** mayor for seven years, 1231–37
172–3 **Allen de la Zouch** mayor, 1267–68
176 **Thomas Knowles** mayor 1399 and 1410, began to build the Guildhall
181 **St Anthony's Church** St Anthony, patron saint of the Grocers; church located in Cordwainer Street ward
182–4 **William Sevenock . . . Laxton** William Sevenock, mayor 1418; Robert Chichley, mayor 1411 and 1421; Stephen Browne, mayor 1438; Henry Keble, mayor 1510; William Laxton, mayor 1544

and two hands meeting at the pummel, intimating Mercy and Justice; accompanied with Magistracy, who holds in his hand a key of gold, signifying both the key of Knowledge and of Confidence, the city magistrate taking into his trust the custody of the King's chamber, the proper title of the City; and which key of gold also stands in his lordship's crest, viz., an ostrich holding a key of gold in his mouth, his neck circled with a golden crown.

His lordship, by this time arriving at the Throne of Virtue, placed near St Lawrence Lane end, receives this greeting from her deity.

THE SPEECH OF VIRTUE

I see great power approach, here makes a stand;
Would it with Virtue ought? for some command
Seems so complete in self-opinion's eye,
It will scarce look on me, but passes by;
As if the essence of my deity
Were raised by power, and not power raised by me:
But let such rulers know that so command,
They build the empire of their hopes on sand.
Still this remains, with eye upon me fixed
As if he sought to have his splendours mixed
With these of mine, which makes authority meek,
And I'm so sick of love to those that seek
I cannot choose but yield; nor does it wrong
Great power to come to Virtue to be strong,
Being but a woman, merciful and mild:
Therein is Heaven with greater glory styled
That makes weak things, as clemency and right,
Sway power, which would else rule all by might.
It may be said you but late pass by
Some part of triumph that spake virtuously,
And one such speech suffices: 'tis not so
In taking of your office; there you go
From court to court before you be confirmed
In this high place, which praetorship is termed.
From Virtue, if to Virtue you resort,
It is but the same course you have in court
In settling of your honour, which should be
Redoubled rather; that I hope to see:
So power and virtue, when they fill one seat,
The city's blessed, the magistrate complete.

At the close of the speech, this Throne of Virtue with all her celestial concomitants and the other parts of the triumph take leave of his lordship for that time, and till after the feast at Guildhall rests from service; but the feast ended, the whole state of the triumph attends upon his lordship, both to St Paul's and homeward. And in Soper Lane two parts of the triumph stand ready planted; viz., the Throne of Virtue and the Globe of Honour, which Globe, suddenly opening and flying into eight cants or distinct parts, discovers in a twinkling eight bright personages most gloriously decked, representing (as it were) the inward man, the intentions of a virtuous and worthy breast by the graces of the mind and soul, such as Clear Conscience, Divine Speculation, Peace of Heart, Integrity, Watchfulness, Equality, Providence, Impartiality, each expressed by its proper illustration. And because man's perfection can receive no constant attribute in this life, the cloud of frailty, ever and anon shadowing and darkening our brightest intentions, makes good the morality of those cants, or parts, when they fall and close into the full round of a globe again, showing, that as the brightest day has his overcastings, so the best men in this life have their imperfections; and worldly mists oftentimes interprose the clearest cogitations, and yet that but for a season, turning in the end, like the mounting of this engine, to their everlasting brightness, converting itself to a canopy of stars. At the four corners below are placed the four cardinal virtues, Wisdom, Justice, Fortitude, and Temperance, by each of them fixed a little streamer or banner in which are displayed the arms of this honourable city, the Lord Mayor's, the Grocers', and the noble East India Company's. The outparts of the Globe, showing the world's type in countries, seas and shipping, whereon is depicted or drawn ships that have been fortunate to this kingdom by their happy and successful voyages; as also that prosperous plantation in the colony of Virginia and the Bermudas, with all good wishes to the governors, traders, and adventurers unto those Christianly reformed islands.

The speech at night presented by Honour, a personage mounted on the top of this unparalleled masterpiece of invention and art, the Globe or Orb of Honour.

HONOUR

By Virtue you came last, and who brings home
True Honour must by Virtue always come;
The right path you have took then, still proceed,
For 'tis continuance crowns each worthy deed.
Behold this Globe of Honour; every part
It is composed of, to a noble heart
Applies instruction. When 'tis closed and round,
It represents the world, and all that's found
Within the labouring circle of man's days,
Adventures, dangers, cares, and steepy ways;
Which when a wiseman thinks on, straight he mounts
To heavenly cogitations and accounts
The vexing spirit of care and labour vain,
Lifting himself to his full height again.
And as this engine does in eight parts rise
Discovering eight bright figures, so the wise,

200 **St Lawrence Lane** street in Cheapside providing access to the Guildhall
225 ***praetorship*** chief magistrate, mayor
237–8 **Soper Lane** named for the soap-makers who lived there; street now called Queen Street
268 **Bermudas** Sir George Somers helped establish the settlement in Bermuda, which he discovered in 1609 on his way to Virginia.

From this life's slumber roused (which time deludes)
Opens his heart to eight beatitudes:
And as I, Honour, overtopping all,
Here fix my foot on this orbicular ball,
Over the world expressing my command;
As I in this contemptuous posture stand,
So every good and understanding spirit
Makes but use only of this life t'inherit
An everlasting living; making friends
Of Mammon's heaps got by unrighteous ends;
Which happy thou stand'st free from, the more white
Sits Honour on thee, and the cost more bright
Thy noble brotherhood this day bestows:
Expense is graced when substance follows shows.
Now to no higher pitch of praise I'll come;
Love brought thee forth, and Honour brings thee home.

For the body of the whole triumph, with all the proper graces and ornaments of art and workmanship, the reputation of those rightly appertain to the deserts of Master Garret Christmas, an exquisite master in his art and a performer above his promises.

FINIS

291 ***eight beatitudes*** from the New Testament Sermon on the Mount in St Matthew's gospel, chapter 5

293 ***orbicular*** round as a circle

295 ***contemptuous posture*** defiant, disdainful

299 ***Mammon's*** god of wealth, money

309 **Garret Christmas** artificer who now regularly assists Middleton in the Lord Mayor's Shows

THE SPANISH GYPSY

Text edited and annotated by Gary Taylor, introduced by Suzanne Gossett

The Spanish Gypsy is a play of rape transcended and revenge averted—and a play complexly intertwined with Anglo-Spanish relations in the fraught year of 1623. Based upon two classics of Spanish Golden Age literature, its immediate theatrical success was envied by contemporaries; it was revived at the Restoration, and became the only Middleton play produced in the nineteenth century (Steen).

Unfortunately, for much of the twentieth century critical discussion of the play was dominated by disputes about authorship. *Gypsy* was first published in 1653 as the work of Middleton and Rowley, but in 1924 H. Dugdale Sykes argued that the play was 'substantially, if not wholly, from the pen of John Ford' (183). This edition accepts the conclusion reached by Taylor, that the play was co-written by four authors. Ford was probably responsible for the rape plot (1.3, 1.5.1–73, 2.2.1–118, 3.2.242–300, 3.3, 5.1.1–126, 5.3.1–95). Thomas Dekker is most evident in 2.1, 2.2.119–75, 3.1, the songs in 3.2 (82–113, 197–217), and 4.1.1–148. Rowley seems to have written 4.3, and may also be responsible for parts of Soto's role. Middleton's hand has been most confidently identified in 1.5.73–127, 3.2.114–94, 4.1.149–210, and 4.2, but he may be responsible for other elements of the Don Juan/Preciosa plot (1.4, 2.1.104–13). As this summary makes clear, Dekker and Ford apparently did more of the writing than Middleton or Rowley. But Middleton is the most likely candidate for composing the 'plot' or scenario for the play, linking its four narratives into a polyphonic whole, and then assigning scenes and subscenes to the playwright best suited to each. The details of the attribution are discussed in the *Companion*; this introduction will instead attempt to imagine what *Gypsy* meant to its authors and audiences in 1623.

Structure and Interpretation

The play is built on four plots, derived from different sources but intricately interconnected. Each centres on a young man who becomes temporarily involved with the newly-arrived Gypsies and is ultimately reunited with a father. Although these plots vary in density and importance—Levin identifies the action of the foolish gentleman Sancho and his man Soto as a typical 'clown subplot' (110)—they are united by parallels between four prodigal sons (Burlebach 38) and between three young women whose gendered role in marriage arrangements varies from powerlessness to abuse of power. Reading the play as a moral structure the Kistners find a repeated pattern of sin, repentance, and rebirth; tracing tragicomic form reveals that each young man is brought to a moment of maximum danger or terror before being released to happiness.

Cervantes's novella *La Fuerza de la Sangre* inspired the rape plot which dominates the first scenes. The play's opening is startling and effective. Roderigo and his friends Luis and Diego encounter Clara and her parents on a dark street. Despite protestations that they will only do what is 'fit for gentlemen', the friends accept Roderigo's assurance that 'for a wench, man, any course is honourable' and restrain the parents while Roderigo abducts Clara (1.1.10, 32). These hot-blooded aristocrats are a pack of hoodlums. The rape's only motivation is sexual infatuation, and for the first time in all the rape plots of the Elizabethan stage, neither party knows the other's identity.

Gypsy is the last of three Jacobean plays—the others are *The Queen of Corinth* and *Women, Beware Women*—in which the heroine, in a striking rejection of the Lucrece and Philomel models that had previously determined the course and aftermath of rape on the English stage, survives and marries the rapist (Gossett, 'Best Men'). It is also the first to put the action into a Christian context. Oddly enough, this play, in which rape actually takes place, is less prurient than Fletcher and Rowley's *Maid in the Mill*, where violation is repeatedly threatened, or *The Queen of Corinth*, where two rapes are elaborately prepared. By the time the moon rises on Clara in the third scene of *Gypsy*, the unseen act has been accomplished: the remainder of the play concentrates on consequences. The crucifix that Clara steals in this scene, ultimately leading to Roderigo's identification, is symbolic of the faith that sustains her in her trial. Though she at first asks Roderigo to kill her, and later marvels that she survives (3.3.55–7), she does not contemplate suicide. Her parents' belief in a providential solution is fulfilled when Clara is accidentally brought back to Roderigo's house. Belief in heaven-dealt justice is also present in Roderigo's father, who learns of the rape, arranges for Roderigo to marry Clara without recognizing her, and then tricks him into confessing by telling him that his new wife is wanton, certainly the punishment for some sin of his: 'Impossible that justice should rain down | In such a frightful horror without cause' (5.1.20–1).

One reason Clara does not kill herself is that (unlike the heroines of other rape plays) she is genuinely unsure that she is stained. St Augustine had argued that if Lucrece's will did not consent, she remained chaste and ought not to have killed herself, and Clara, despite moments of doubt (2.2.1–4), seems assured that her tears have 'washed off the leprosy' (1.3.62–3). The authors prepare the audience to accept the final marriage by emphasizing, instead of the pollution and dishonour of the heroine, the moral development of the rapist. Roderigo begins as lustful and heedless, unaware that the girl he proposes to abduct is his friend Luis's beloved. Furthermore, the son of 'the great *corregidor*' (2.2.53) has no need to ravish—the word comprehends both abduction and sexual violation—a young woman to gain control of her or her property. Indeed, after the rape Roderigo tries to deny the nature of the transaction by offering Clara money. But innovations begin when Roderigo experiences guilt and repentance before discovery. Clara's cry that her blood is infected 'by your soul-staining lust' (1.3.10) suggests that his soul is as stained as hers, and the third act opens with a soliloquy in which Roderigo berates himself in religious terms—'what vile prisons | Make we our bodies to our immortal souls!' (3.1.1–2). When informed of the rape, his father considers his 'till-now-untainted blood and honour' (3.3.87) corrupted not by a woman's dishonour but by a man's sin. Roderigo's weakest moment comes when he ignores his feelings of guilt and marries the unrecognized Clara, but when Fernando extracts his confession and tells him 'young man, thou shouldst have married her', he agrees (5.1.34). The final marriage becomes the desire of both parties.

The tragicomic ending dismays modern audiences because it requires Clara to accept her victimization and become 'the happiest woman, being married' (5.1.39) to the man she begged to be a 'gentle ravisher, | An honourable villain' (1.3.7–8). Like her predecessor Bianca of *Women, Beware Women*, she displays 'the classic pattern of the victim succumbing to and embracing the inevitability of redefined power relations' (Dawson 312). For an early modern English audience the ending required ignoring English law, according to which the abduction of an heiress was a felony, even if she consented afterwards and married the man. It also required a major change from the Cervantes source. In *La Fuerza* seven years go by, during which the heedless hero travels and the rape victim raises the child of that encounter. The mother only discovers the identity of her violator when, following an accident, she finds her son in the chamber where he was conceived. Modifying the plot avoids an awkward time gap for the drama, but there was a more profound ideological reason. On the basis of Galenic medical theory—embodied in such gynecological texts as *Aristotle's Masterpiece* and repeated in convenient legal summaries like Michael Dalton's *The Country Justice* (1618)—it was widely believed that a woman who was raped could not conceive. Conversely, 'If at the time of rape supposed, the woman conceive child, there is no rape, for none can conceive without consent' (*The Lawes Resolutions of Womens Rights*, 396). Transposition from the Spanish Catholic setting to the mental world of Jacobean London thus necessitated that Clara demonstrate her full innocence by not becoming pregnant.

The rape plot is complexly connected to the other three. Three young men—Roderigo, Don Juan, and Sancho—flee father figures in a pattern that can be read generically as a prodigal son tale and psychoanalytically as exposing unresolved Oedipal feelings. Determined to resist his father's power, Roderigo assures himself that Fernando is 'not the king of Spain' (4.2.102); Sancho tells his guardian Don Pedro (Clara's father) to be hanged; to join the Gypsies Don Juan loses 'father, friends, | Birth, fortunes' (4.1.18–19). Father-son hostility is foregrounded in the playlet that Fernando requests of the disguised Roderigo. The play-father complains that 'he that should prop me is mine overthrow' and Roderigo, playing the 'rake-hell' prodigal, questions his father's paternity and orders his man to 'carbonado thou the old rogue my father' (4.3.35, 68–9).

Unlike many comedies *Gypsy* sides with the fathers. None of the plots can resolve until the sons have returned to their proper positions. Indeed, several of the most effective dramatic moments occur in confrontations between Roderigo and the Corregidor, who asserts that 'Fathers have eagles' eyes' (4.3.190) and manœuvres Roderigo into marriage and confession. Outwitted and overwhelmed, Roderigo finally assures his 'Fathers both' (5.1.56) that he will redeem himself. Similarly, Don Juan and Preciosa depend on identification with and of their fathers for their union. Don Juan escapes punishment for his attack on Diego because of his caste (in Cervantes the equivalent figure is pardoned for murder). In a parody of such logic, when the Gypsies are threatened with imprisonment the terrified Sancho and Soto creep back to Don Pedro for protection.

The scenes involving the play's fourth young man—Luis de Castro (Roderigo's friend and Clara's suitor)—are also constructed around conflicting filial emotions. Luis burns with desire to revenge the death of his father; by the end of the play, Luis instead attains peace by accepting a substitute. Thus the central figures in the two potentially tragic plots both extract what Clara required: 'A noble satisfaction, though not revenge' (3.3.96).

Sources and Contexts

The intertwined histories of Luis and Don Juan indicate how *Gypsy* was constructed from a combination of sources and familiar romantic and dramatic tropes. The names Luis de Castro and Roderigo the authors found in Mateo Aleman's popular picaresque novel *Guzman de Alfarache*, translated in 1622 by James Mabbe (Part II, Book I, Chapter 4). But the play borrows only the names, and Luis's disappointment in love. Shanti Padhi demonstrates that Aleman is also the source for many of the Gypsy Father's proverbs (cxxix–cxxx). The heart of the Juan/Preciosa/Cardochia plot comes from another of Cervantes's *Novellas Exemplars*, *La Gitanilla*.

The play's Gypsies have a complicated ancestry. Middleton had put Gypsies on the stage in *More Dissemblers Besides Women*. But the vogue for Gypsies exploded after

Ben Jonson's wildly successful masque *The Gypsies Metamorphosed*, produced three times in three separate venues for the King in August and September of 1621. This masque stimulated not only *The Spanish Gypsy* in 1623, but the relicensing of *More Dissemblers* in 1623 and its production at court in January 1624, as well as the 1622 court production of Fletcher and Massinger's *Beggar's Bush*, where the scenes of the beggars' tricks parallel Jonson's masque. *The Spanish Gypsy* takes from *Gypsies Metamorphosed* the premise that all the Gypsies—rather than, as in Cervantes, merely a few noble runaways—are aristocrats in disguise. An explicit structural imitation occurs in 3.2, when the Gypsies come to the home of the noble Francisco, sing, dance, and tell the company's fortunes. Similarly pointed fortune telling at Burley and Windsor had especially pleased King James and could give the private theatre audience a sense of inclusion.

Gypsy is densely imbricated in the drama of its period. These interconnections, emerging from the collective memory of four experienced playwrights, tie the play not only to others on rape but to such dramatic topoi as feuding, honour, and duels; stolen children; and hidden nobility (see Gossett, 'Resistant'). For example, the quarrel between Luis's father and Alvarez, which sprung 'From a mere trifle first, a cast of hawks, | Whose made the swifter flight, whose could mount highest' (2.2.78–9), is modelled on the sub-plot of Thomas Heywood's *A Woman Killed With Kindness*, while Luis's obsession with honour and his confrontation with Alvarez are related to Middleton and Rowley's scenes between Captain Ager and the Colonel in *A Fair Quarrel*.

Gypsy was presumably composed in the spring and early summer of 1623, immediately before it was licensed on 9 July. It was probably performed later that summer by the Lady Elizabeth's Men at the Phoenix, and was certainly performed at Whitehall on 5 November, 'the prince being there only'—that is, for Prince Charles and his guests, without the King (Bentley, IV, 893). But the play's significance changed as the year progressed, because in this period attitudes towards Spain divided the country and evolved rapidly.

King James dearly desired to marry his remaining son, Charles, to the Spanish Infanta, thereby balancing the Protestant alliance of his daughter Elizabeth (wife of Frederick the Elector Palatine, deposed King of Bohemia). However, negotiations progressed slowly. Frustrated by the delay, on 17 February 1623 Charles and Buckingham left, in disguise, for Spain. The king was frightened for their safety, and large sections of the anti-Spanish, anti-Catholic English populace were displeased by the absence of the heir and by the open toleration of Catholics (Cogswell, 41). Once in Madrid the twenty-two-year-old Charles, having persuaded himself he was in love, was annoyed by the protocol that kept him from the Infanta; in June he leapt the wall of the Casa del Campo, where the Infanta was taking the air, and 'advanced towards his lady-love, who responded by running in the opposite direction, shrieking for her virtue' (Carlton, 43). By July Charles and Buckingham had doubts about the Spanish demands; when Charles departed on 30 August he left a proxy for the marriage, but gave the ambassador orders not to deliver it. In early November, with James very ill, Charles and Buckingham met with the Spanish ambassadors and demanded a commitment to restore the Palatinate. Though James tried to reconcile the men with a masque on 16 November, his purpose was thwarted, as the Spanish were 'represented by actions worthy of laughter' (Cogswell, 86, citing Tillières, 16 November 1623.) In general, November 1623 'was one of the most uncomfortable periods in Charles's life' (Cogswell, 109), climaxed only a week after the performance of *Gypsy* by the dispatch of four different messengers to Spain to ensure that no proxy wedding take place. By the end of 1623 Buckingham and Charles were opening marriage negotiations with France and preparing for war with Spain. The masque intended for Twelfth Night 1624, *Neptune's Triumph for the Return of Albion* (in which Jonson reversed the position he had taken in *The Gypsies Metamorphosed* and celebrated Charles's escape from the 'sirens'), was cancelled, ostensibly because of a dispute over precedence between the French and Spanish ambassadors but no doubt because of dissension in the court about the marriage.

The Spanish Gypsy, while not a systematic allegory, seems calculated to keep Anglo-Spanish politics present in the minds of audiences while the outcome of the match remained uncertain and largely feared. Details of Cervantes are rewritten to create flashes of specific reference: the play's action is now confined to Madrid (mentioned ten times), and the horseman whose accident frightens Clara becomes 'the jester that so late arrived in court' (3.2.246), that is, King James's fool Archy, who had a similar accident in the Prince's entourage (see Taylor, 2008). The Catholicism of the setting is emphasized: Clara steals the crucifix, Diego and Louis agree to meet at the Inquisition chapel (1.4). Three young men flee secretly from their fathers to the Gypsies, like Prince Charles and Buckingham galloping off to Spain, but only one, John, is ultimately successful, and even he suffers a frightening imprisonment that recalls Spain's enforced retention of Charles. In what may be wishful thinking, John's prize, Pretiosa, proves to be not 'really' a Gypsy and consequently John does not really 'convert'. But Sancho and his sidekick Soto are satirized as wasteful fools, while the son of the Corregidor, a marriageable young aristocrat like Prince Charles, carries out an impetuous and brutal rape. With appropriate stage action the impressive Corregidor chiding his hot-headed son could suggest James objecting to Charles's voyage. Furthermore, repeated criticism of English Gypsies resonates oddly with *The Gypsies Metaphormosed* where, as everyone knew, these had turned out to be the country's chief courtiers.

All four authors shadow contemporary events. Ford probably writes the passage referring to Archy, Rowley and Dekker satirize Sancho and Soto, Middleton controls the Don John plot. Julia Gasper argues that Dekker's *Match Me in London*, another play with an attempted rape, relicensed in August 1623 for the Lady Elizabeth's Men, was an attack on the Spanish match by the militantly protestant Dekker (166–189). By the summer of 1624, Middleton was openly inviting anti-Spanish allegorical readings in *A Game at Chess*; apparently Dekker was doing so before the Prince and Buckingham returned from Spain. Several of the plays with which the Prince distracted himself once he did return—*The Maid in the Mill*, which he saw on November 1 and again with the King on December 26, *The Spanish Gypsy*, on November 5, and *The Changeling*, on January 4—had Spanish sources and settings. *The Changeling* depicts Spain as corrupt politically and sexually, and Bromham and Bruzzi suggest that the Prince requested the January 1624 performance to make an anti-Spanish foreign policy statement (5). *The Spanish Gypsy* is protected by its romantic form from such close political reading, but its hostility towards a culture that tolerates rape, duels, blackmail, and discussion of trust in 'the word royal' (3.2.26–32) could easily be inferred, by Prince and public alike.

Theatre, Music, and Appropriations

According to the title-page *Gypsy* was acted 'with great applause' at 'the Privat House in Drury-Lane, and at Salisbury Court'. The private (play)house was the Phoenix (also called the Cockpit). The Lady Elizabeth's Men had been brought there by Christopher Beeston in 1622. Their predilection for plays with a 'gentlemanly concern for questions of honour and love' soon made the theatre a rival of the Blackfriars (Gurr, 407). The theatre itself, designed by Inigo Jones after a visit to Italy, was appealingly modern, a compromise between 'designs based on Vitruvius and Palladio and the usual style of a Jacobean theatre', with an elegant stage façade (Foakes, 66). The play's popularity at the Phoenix is attested to in the backhanded compliment of W. B. (William Bagnall?). His commendatory verses to Massinger's *The Bondman* (produced in the same theatre by the same company in the same season) sneer at 'Gypsy jigs... drumming stuff... dances [and] other trumpery to delight' (Steen). At court the play may have been produced in the Cockpit-at-court or the Great Hall, perhaps metatheatrically suggested by the 'great chamber' (4.2.28) in which the play-within-the-play is given (Padhi, clxxvii).

Performances at Salisbury Court must have occurred after November 1630, when that theatre opened (Bentley, VI, 87). *Gypsy* was one of the plays protected for Christopher Beeston and his new boys' company in 1639. Apparently Beeston owned the play, and 'none of the companies who performed at the Cockpit ever took their plays away with them when they left his playhouse' (Gurr, 425). Bentley concludes that performance at the Salisbury Court must have been by Queen Henrietta's men, for no other company occupied both houses (I, 255), but the Queen Henrietta's at Salisbury Court was the remnants of the earlier company, forced out of the Cockpit by Beeston in the plague closing of 1636–7.

Shortly after the Restoration the play was again revived. Reading it, Pepys thought it 'not very good, though commended much' (16 June 1661). On 7 March 1668, 'the second time of acting, and the first that I saw it', he liked it no better than he had *A Midsummer Night's Dream*, finding *Gypsy* 'a very silly play' somewhat redeemed by its performance elements: 'only, great variety of dances, and those most excellently done' (Steen). Yet he had judged Brome's 1641 *The Jovial Crew*—a reworking of many elements of *Gypsy*—also revived in 1661, 'full of mirth' (Bentley, III, 71). Later, Francis Manning's *All for the Better or, the Infallible Cure* was based on *Gypsy*, along with a reconsultation of Cervantes (Hogg).

One of the most remarkable aspects of the play is its music. The quarto marks five songs but there may have been seven. Although it was unusual for gentry to sing on stage (Austern, 153), Sancho sings four songs and also 'set[s] out a throat' for 'O that I were a bee to sing' (2.1.176–93). The other identified singer is the Gypsy leader, who sings a verse of Sancho's 'Now that from the hive' (3.2.205–16) and would be appropriate for at least the first stanza of the unassigned 'Come, follow your leader, follow' (3.2.82–4). Sections of Don Juan's initiation into the Gypsies and his betrothal to Preciosa (4.1) may also have been sung.

Apparently the music was partly borrowed, partly original. Some of the wordless dances may have copied music and choreography from Jonson's *Gypsies Metamorphosed*, and 'Trip it, Gypsies, trip it fine' was probably composed to fit the 'The Gypsies' Round' by William Byrd. Playford's *The Dancing Master* (1651) contains music and choreography for a dance called 'The Spanish Gypsy'; Chappell thought it derived from 'Come, follow your leader, follow' (3.2.82–113), but its directions, for four couples who 'turn back-to-back' but eventually unite, seem more appropriate to the final dance. In the Roxburghe Collection is a black letter ballad, called 'The brave English Jipsie. To the tune of The Spanish Jipsie', published by John Trundle (died 1626). This ballad patriotically reverses Alvarez's praise of Spanish Gypsies: 'Who ere hath been in Spaine, | And seene there Jipsies vaine, | Shall soone the difference find, | Else judgement makes him blind. | So, Spanish Jipsies all, adue! | For English equall are to you' (Chappell, *Roxburghe*, 333).

The songs and dances, concentrated in the middle acts, are a significant factor in creating the play's tragicomic form. The dark first act closes with Roderigo's comment that 'Pleasure and Youth like smiling evils woo us | To taste new follies' (1.5.126–7); the second opens on pleasure and youth without evil. Sancho's first song reduces rape to melodious double entendre: 'O that I were a bee to sing | Hum buz, buz, hum! I first would bring | Some honey to your hive, and there leave my sting' (2.1.178–80). The songs in 3.1 reiterate the Gypsies' scorn for cutting purses, celebrating a mad world that anticipates the final reversal where 'Beggars would on cock-horse ride' (3.1.127). The Gypsy 'army' sings and dances between Luis's treacherous determination to take revenge, and the accident which returns Clara to the fatal bedroom.

Also controlling the tone is the play's metatheatricality, which weakens the intense audience engagement of the opening scenes. Theatrical distancing occurs most obviously in the play-within-the-play, which Fernando asks the Gypsies to perform on 'some slight plot', like the Italian or French *commedia* (4.2.41). Preciosa has a nine-line aria beginning 'How? not a changeling? | Yes, father, I will play the changeling.... None but myself shall play the changeling' (2.1.105–13), clearly intended to alert the audience to another of the youthful actor's roles, and the Gypsy Father foregrounds her cross-dressing: 'A-many dons | Will not believe but that thou art a boy | In woman's clothes' (98–100). Roderigo ruefully acknowledges he has 'writ... a tragedy' (3.1.73–5). Nineteenth-century objections to the play (Steen) were based on a sense that the happy ending is both immoral and unprepared; such readings ignore the power of the music and distancing to mitigate the effect. Indeed, twice we hear that the Gypsies will bring a 'merry tragedy' (4.2.37, 39).

In the end the very character of *The Spanish Gypsy*, with its disturbing mixture of rape and Gypsies, duels and disguising, is a product of the mysterious alchemy of collaboration. The balance between Clara's seriousness and Preciosa's charm, between the sinfulness of Roderigo and Cardochia and the merely high-spirited waywardness of Don Juan and Sancho, between the romance of the lost child and the potential tragedy of violation and revenge, is a theatrical tour de force based on the various strengths of four professional playwrights—including, it seems clear, those to whom the play was first attributed, Middleton and Rowley.

SEE ALSO

Music and dance: *Companion*, 172 ('The Gypsies' Round'), 174 ('The Spanish Gypsy')
Textual introduction and apparatus: *Companion*, 1105
Authorship and date: *Companion*, 433
Other Middleton–Dekker works: *Caesar's Fall*, 328; *Gravesend*, 128; *Meeting*, 183; *Magnificent*, 219; *Patient Man*, 280; *Banquet*, 637; *Roaring Girl*, 721
Other Middleton–Rowley works: *Weapons*, 980; *Quarrel*, 1209; *Old Law*, 1331; *Tennis*, 1405; *Changeling*, 1632

JOHN FORD, THOMAS DEKKER, THOMAS MIDDLETON, and WILLIAM ROWLEY

The Spanish Gypsy

[*for Lady Elizabeth's Men at The Phoenix*]

DRAMATIS PERSONAE

Don FERNANDO de Azevedo, *Corregidor* of Madrid
RODERIGO, his young son
Don LUIS de Castro, Roderigo's friend, suitor to Clara
DIEGO, a friend of Luis

PEDRO de Cortes, an old don
MARIA, his wife
CLARA, his daughter
SANCHO, his ward, a foolish gentleman
SOTO, Sancho's man, a merry fellow

Count FRANCISCO de Carcamo, an old don
Don JUAN, his son, suitor to Preciosa

The old FATHER of the Gypsies
EUGENIA, the old Mother of the Gypsies
PRECIOSA, a young Spanish Gypsy girl
CARLO, ANTONIO, CHRISTIANA } Gypsies
Juana CARDOCHIA, young hostess to the Gypsies

Servants

1.1 *Incipit Actus Primus*

Enter Roderigo, Luis, and Diego, [as at night]

LUIS Roderigo!

DIEGO [*to Roderigo*] Art mad?

RODERIGO Yes!—not so much with wine: it's as rare to see a Spaniard a drunkard as a German sober, an Italian no whoremonger, an Englishman to pay his debts. I am no *boraccio*: sack, malaga, nor canary breeds the *calentura* in my brains. Mine eye mads me, not my cups.

LUIS What wouldst have us do?

RODERIGO Do?

DIEGO So far as 'tis fit for gentlemen we'll venture.

RODERIGO I ask no more. I ha' seen a thing has bewitched me: a delicate body, but this [*showing the size by a sign*] in the waist, foot and leg tempting; the face I had scarce a glimpse of, but the fruit must needs be delicious, the tree being so beautiful.

LUIS Prithee, to the point.

RODERIGO Here 'tis: an old gentleman (no matter who he is), an old gentlewoman (I ha' nothing to do with her)—but a young creature that follows them, daughter or servant or whatsoever she be, her I must have. They are coming this way. Shall I have her? I must have her.

DIEGO How, how?

LUIS Thou speak'st impossibilities.

RODERIGO Easy, easy, easy! I'll seize the young girl; stop you the old man; stay you the old woman.

LUIS How then?

RODERIGO I'll fly off with the young bird, that's all. Many of our Spanish gallants act these merry parts every night. They are weak and old, we young and sprightly. Will you assist me?

LUIS Troth, Roderigo, anything in the way of honour.

RODERIGO For a wench, man, any course is honourable.

LUIS Nay, not any. Her father, if he be her father, may be noble.

RODERIGO I am as noble.

LUIS Would the adventure were so!

RODERIGO Stand close, they come.

[*They stand aloof, cover their faces, and draw their swords.*] *Enter Pedro, Maria, and Clara* [*veiled*]

PEDRO 'Tis late. Would we were in Madrid!

MARIA Go faster, my lord.

PEDRO Clara, keep close.

[*Luis, Diego, and Roderigo*] *seize them*

CLARA Help, help, help!

RODERIGO Are you crying out? I'll be your midwife.

Exit with Clara

PEDRO What mean you, gentlemen?

MARIA Villains! thieves! murderers!

PEDRO Do you know me? I am De Cortes, Pedro de Cortes.

LUIS De Cortes?—Diego, come away.

Exeunt [*Luis and Diego*]

PEDRO
Clara!—Where is my daughter?

MARIA Clara!—These villains
Have robbed us of our comfort and will, I fear,
Her of her honour.

PEDRO This had not wont
To be our Spanish fashion; but now our gallants,
Our gentry, our young dons, heated with wine
(A fire our countrymen do seldom sit at),
Commit these outrages.—Clara!—Maria,
Let's homeward. I will raise Madrid to find
These traitors to all goodness.—Clara!

MARIA Clara! *Exeunt*

1.2 *Enter Luis and Diego* [*as at night*]

LUIS
O Diego, I am lost, I am mad!

DIEGO So we are all.

LUIS
'Tis not with wine. I'm drunk with too much horror,
Inflamed with rage, to see us two made bawds
To Roderigo's lust. Did not the old man
Name De Cortes, Pedro de Cortes?

DIEGO Sure he did.

LUIS
O Diego! As thou lov'st me, nay, on the forfeit
Of thine own life or mine, seal up thy lips:
Let 'em not name De Cortes.—Stay, stay, stay:
Roderigo has into his father's house
A passage through a garden—

DIEGO Yes, my lord.

LUIS
Thither I must find Roderigo out

1.1.6 ***boraccio*** drunkard (literally, bag in which Spaniards keep wine)
sack...canary sweet wines from Spain and its islands
calentura sunstroke, delirium
7 **cups** (as in 'beercan' or 'shot glass')
9 **Do** (perhaps suggesting the sexual sense 'fuck')
11 **thing** lascivious plaything (suggesting the slang sense 'genitals')
12 **but this** i.e. 'only this big', small
13–14 **face...glimpse** (because, like other respectable Spanish women, she was veiled. His not seeing or recognizing her face is crucial to the plot.)
13 **scarce** scarcely, barely
14–15 **fruit...tree** proverbially, a tree is known by its fruit (Matthew 12:33)
25 **stay you** you stop
27 **bird** (*a*) girl (*b*) prey. (Wild birds were trapped and eaten as a regular part of the early modern diet.)
37 **close** (*a*) together (*b*) hidden, secretively
38 **Madrid** (Not the setting in Cervantes, but where Prince Charles stayed in 1623.)
39 **Go** walk
42 **crying out** calling for help (but also used of the cries of a woman in labour)
be your midwife (*a*) minister to your distress (*b*) help you bring a child to birth, i.e. by impregnating you
43 **mean you** are your intentions
49 **had not wont** did not use
51 **dons** aristocrats
54 **raise** alert, call out
1.2.9 **Stay** wait

And check him, check him home; if be but dare—
No more!—Diego, along! My soul does fight
A thousand battles blacker than this night. *Exeunt*

1.3 [*A bed.*] *Enter Roderigo and Clara* [*as at night*]

CLARA
Though the black veil of night hath overclouded
The world in darkness, yet ere many hours
The sun will rise again, and then this act
Of my dishonour will appear before you
More black than is the canopy that shrouds it.
What are you? Pray, what are you?

RODERIGO Husht!—a friend, a friend.

CLARA
A friend? Be then a gentle ravisher,
An honourable villain: as you have
Disrobed my youth of nature's goodliest portion,
My virgin purity, so with your sword
Let out that blood which is infected now
By your soul-staining lust.

RODERIGO Pish!

CLARA Are you noble?
I know you then will marry me. Say!

RODERIGO Umh.

CLARA
Not speak to me? Are wanton devils dumb?
How are so many harmless virgins wrought
By falsehood of prevailing words to yield
Too easy forfeits of their shames and liberty,
If every orator of folly plead
In silence, like this untongued piece of violence?
You shall not from me.
[*She holds him*]

RODERIGO Phew!—no more.

CLARA You shall not.
Whoe'er you are—disease of nature's sloth,
Birth of some monstrous sin, or scourge of virtue,
Heaven's wrath and mankind's burden—I will hold you.
I will. Be rough, and therein merciful;
I will not loose my hold else.

RODERIGO [*offering money*] There. 'Tis gold.

CLARA
Gold? Why, alas, for what? The hire of pleasure
Perhaps is payment; mine is misery.
I need no wages for a ruined name
More than a bleeding heart.

RODERIGO Nay, then, you're troublesome.
[*He shakes her off*]
I'll lock you safe enough.
Exit [*locking the door behind him*]

CLARA They cannot fear
Whom grief hath armed with hate and scorn of life.
Revenge, I kneel to thee!—Alas, 'gainst whom?
By what name shall I pull confusion down
From justice on his head that hath betrayed me?
I know not where I am. Up, I beseech thee,
Thou lady regent of the air, the moon,
And lead me by thy light to some brave vengeance!
It is a chamber, sure. The guilty bed
(Sad evidence against my loss of honour)
Assures so much. What's here, a window-curtain?
[*She opens the curtain*]
O heaven, the stars appear too! Ha, a chamber?
A goodly one. Dwells rape in such a paradise?—
Help me, my quickened senses! 'Tis a garden
To which this window guides the covetous prospect,
A large one and a fair one; in the midst
A curious alabaster fountain stands,
Framed like—like what? No matter. Swift, remembrance!
Rich furniture within too—and what's this?
A precious crucifix!
[*She takes the crucifix, and conceals it in her sleeve*]
I have enough.
[*She closes the curtain*]
Assist me, O you powers that guard the innocent!
Enter Roderigo

RODERIGO
Now—

CLARA Welcome, if you come armed in destruction:
I am prepared to die.

RODERIGO Tell me your name
And what you are.

CLARA You urge me to a sin
As cruel as your lust; I dare not grant it.
Think on the violence of my defame
And, if you mean to write upon my grave
An epitaph of peace, forbear to question
Or whence or who I am. I know the heat
Of your desires are (after the performance
Of such a hellish act) by this time drowned
In cooler streams of penance, and for my part

13 **check** obstruct, rebuke
home thoroughly
1.3.2 **ere** before
5 **canopy** (*a*) sky (*b*) covering over a bed
shrouds covers (like the wrappings around a corpse)
6 **friend** (slang for 'illicit lover')
11 **infected** stained (according to a belief that rape polluted even an innocent victim)
14 **dumb** mute
15 **wrought** made
24 **Be rough** i.e. kill me
25 **loose** let go of
26 **hire** salary, recompense
28 **name** reputation
33 **confusion** destruction
36 **regent** ruler during absence of the monarch (the sun)
38 **chamber** bedroom, private room
43 **quickened** roused, sharpened (but also suggesting 'pregnant')
44 **covetous prospect** greedy eye
46 **curious** exquisitely wrought
49 **precious** 'made of solid silver' (Cervantes)
53 **what** what class or kind of person
55 **defame** defamation, ruined reputation
58 **Or whence** either from where

I have washed off the leprosy that cleaves
To my just shame in true and honest tears.
I must not leave a mention of my wrongs,
The stain of my unspotted birth, to memory.
Let it lie buried with me in the dust,
That never time hereafter may report
How such a one as you have made me live.
Be resolute, and do not stagger; do not,
For I am nothing.

RODERIGO Sweet, let me enjoy thee
Now with a free allowance.

CLARA Ha, enjoy me?
Insufferable villain!

RODERIGO Peace! Speak low.
I mean no second force. And since I find
Such goodness in an unknown frame of virtue,
Forgive my foul attempt, which I shall grieve for
So heartily that, could you be yourself
Eyewitness to my constant vowed repentance,
Trust me, you'd pity me.

CLARA Sir, you can speak now.

RODERIGO
So much I am the executioner
Of mine own trespass that I have no heart
Nor reason to disclose my name or quality;
You must excuse me that. But, trust me, fair one,
Were this ill deed undone, this deed of wickedness,
I would be proud to court your love like him
Whom my first birth presented to the world.
This for your satisfaction: what remains,
That you can challenge as a service from me,
I both expect and beg it.

CLARA First, that you swear,
Neither in riot of your mirth, in passion
Of friendship, or in folly of discourse,
To speak of wrongs done to a ravished maid.

RODERIGO
As I love truth, I swear!

CLARA Next, that you lead me
Near to the place you met me, and there leave me
To my last fortunes, ere the morning rise.

RODERIGO
Say more.

CLARA Live a new man. If e'er you marry—
O me, my heart's a-breaking!—but if e'er
You marry, in a constant love to her
That shall be then your wife, redeem the fault
Of my undoing. I am lost for ever.
Pray, use no more words.

RODERIGO You must give me leave
To veil you close.

CLARA Do what you will. No time
Can ransom me from sorrows or dishonours.
[*Roderigo veils her*]
Shall we now go?

RODERIGO My shame may live without me,
But in my soul I bear my guilt about me.
Lend me your hand; now follow. *Exeunt*

Enter Luis, Diego, and a servant [*as at night*] 1.4

LUIS [*to servant*] Not yet come in, not yet?

SERVANT
No, I'll assure your lordship; I've seldom known him
Keep out so long; my lord usually observes
More seasonable hours.

LUIS What time of night is't?

SERVANT On the stroke of three.

LUIS
The stroke of three? 'Tis wondrous strange! Dost hear?

SERVANT
My lord?

LUIS Ere six I will be here again.
Tell thy lord so: ere six. A must not sleep;
Or if a do, I shall be bold to wake him.
Be sure thou tell'st him, do.

SERVANT My lord, I shall. *Exit*

LUIS Diego,
Walk thou the street that leads about the Prado;
I'll round the west part of the city; meet me
At the Inquisition chapel. If we miss him,
We'll both back to his lodgings.

DIEGO At the chapel?

LUIS
Ay, there we'll meet.

DIEGO Agreed.—I this way.
Exit Luis [*at one door*]

Enter Don Juan [*at another door*]

JUAN (*reading*)
'She is not noble, true; wise nature meant
Affection should ennoble her descent,
For love and beauty keeps as rich a seat
Of sweetness in the mean-born as the great.'
—I am resolved. *Exit*

62 **leprosy** (conventionally attributed to promiscuous women)
cleaves adheres
70 **enjoy** sexually possess
72 **low** quietly
75 **attempt** assault
78 **speak** i.e. reveal your identity (as she had asked at l. 6)
81 **quality** rank, status
86 **what** whatever
87 **challenge** demand, claim
94 **last fortunes** final fate (suggesting imminent death, or at least that he will never see her again)
99 **my undoing** your ruin of me
101 **close** closely, securely
103 **My ... without me** 'I may be able to live without the presence of shame' (which is social, and—in contrast to *guilt*—depends on whether others know what he has done)
1.4.1 **in** home
2 **him** Roderigo
9 **A** he
12 **Prado** then a place of recreation in eastern Madrid, frequented by the nobility
14 **Inquisition chapel** (in the centre of Madrid; for Protestants, emblematic of Catholic tyranny)
18 **Affection** love, i.e. marriage
descent lineage, pedigree

DIEGO 'Tis Roderigo certainly.
Yet his voice makes me doubt; but I'll o'erhear him.
Exit [*following Juan*]

1.5 *Enter Luis* [*as at night*]

LUIS
That I, ay, only I should be the man
Made àccessary and a party both
To mine own torment, at a time so near
The birth of all those comforts I have travailed with
So many, many hours of hopes and fears,
Now at the instant—
Enter Roderigo
Ha! Stand! Thy name,
Truly and speedily.
RODERIGO Don Luis?
LUIS The same.
But who art thou? Speak!
RODERIGO Roderigo.
LUIS Tell me,
As you're a noble gentleman, as ever
You hope to be enrolled amongst the virtuous,
As you love goodness, as you wish t'inherit
The blessedness and fellowship of angels,
As you are my friend, as you are Roderigo,
As you are anything that would deserve
A worthy name: where have you been tonight?
O, how have you disposed of that fair creature
Whom you led captive from me? Speak, O speak!
Where, how, when, in what usage have you left her?
Truth, I require all truth.
RODERIGO Though I might question
The strangeness of your importunity,
Yet, 'cause I note distraction in the height
Of curiosity, I will be plain
And brief.
LUIS I thank you, sir.
RODERIGO Instead of feeding
Too wantonly upon so rich a banquet,
I found, even in that beauty that invited me,
Such a commanding majesty of chaste
And humbly glorious virtue, that it did not
More check my rash attempt than draw to ebb
The float of those desires, which in an instant
Were cooled in their own streams of shame and folly.
LUIS Now all increase of honours
Fall in full showers on thee, Roderigo,
The best man living!
RODERIGO You are much transported
With this discourse, methinks.
LUIS Marry, I am.
She told ye her name too?
RODERIGO I could not urge it
By any importunity.
LUIS Better still!
Where did you leave her?
RODERIGO Where I found her; farther
She would by no means grant me to wait on her.
O Luis, I am lost!
LUIS This selfsame lady
Was she to whom I have been long a suitor,
And shortly hope to marry.
RODERIGO
She your mistress then? Luis, since friendship
And noble honesty conjures our loves
To a continued league, here I unclasp
The secrets of my heart. O, I have had
A glimpse of such a creature that deserves
A temple! If thou lov'st her—and I blame thee not,
For who can look on her and not give up
His life unto her service?—if thou lov'st her,
For pity's sake conceal her. Let me not
As much as know her name; there's a temptation in't.
Let me not know her dwelling, birth, or quality,
Or anything that she calls hers, but thee;
In thee, my friend, I'll see her. And t'avoid
The surfeits and those rarities that tempt me,
So much I prize the happiness of friendship
That I will leave the city—
LUIS Leave it?
RODERIGO Speed me
For Salamanca, court my studies now
For physic 'gainst infection of the mind.
LUIS
You do amaze me.
RODERIGO Here to live, and live
Without her, is impossible and wretched.
For heaven's sake, never tell her what I was,
Or that you know me! And when I find that absence
Hath lost her to my memory, I'll dare
To see ye again. Meantime, the cause that draws me
From hence shall be to all the world untold;
No friend but thou alone, for whose sake only
I undertake this voluntary exile,
Shall be partaker of my griefs. Thy hand.
[*They shake hands*]
Farewell. And all the pleasures, joys, contents
That bless a constant lover, henceforth crown thee
A happy bridegroom!
LUIS You have conquered friendship
Beyond example.
Enter Diego
DIEGO Ha, ha, ha! Some one
That hath slept well tonight, should a but see me

1.5.4 **travailed with** had labour pains for
21 **distraction** madness
28 **check** rebuke (but suggesting 'obstruct, prevent')
attempt assault (but suggesting 'unsuccessful intention')
29 **float** flood-tide
33 **transported** rapt
42 **mistress** beloved
58 **Salamanca** site of a famous Spanish university founded in 1200 (172 miles from Madrid)
59 **physic** medical treatment
73 **example** precedent

Thus merry by myself, might justly think
I were not well in my wits.
LUIS Diego?
DIEGO Yes,
'Tis I, and I've had a fine vagary,
The rarest wild-goose chase!
LUIS 'T'as made thee melancholy.
DIEGO
Don Roderigo here? 'Tis well you met him—
For though I missed him, yet I met an accident
Has almost made me burst with laughter.
LUIS How so?
DIEGO
I'll tell you: as we parted, I perceived
A walking thing before me, strangely tickled
With rare conceited raptures. Him I dogged,
Supposing 't'ad been Roderigo landed
From his new pinnace, deep in contemplation
Of the sweet voyage he stole tonight.
RODERIGO You're pleasant.
LUIS Prithee, who was't?
RODERIGO
Not I.
DIEGO
You're i' the right, not you indeed;
For 'twas that noble gentleman Don Juan,
Son to the Count Francisco de Carcámo.
LUIS
In love, it seems?
DIEGO Yes, peppered, o' my life.
Much good may't do him! I'd not be so limed
For my cap full of double pistolets.
LUIS
What should his mistress be?
DIEGO That's yet a riddle
Beyond my resolution—but o' late
I have observed him often to frequent
The sports the Gypsies newly come to th' city
Present.
LUIS 'Tis said there is a creature with 'em,
Though young of years, yet of such absolute beauty,
Dexterity of wit, and general qualities,
That Spain reports of her, not without admiration.
DIEGO Have you seen her?
LUIS Never.
DIEGO Nor you, my lord?
RODERIGO I not remember.
DIEGO
Why then, you never saw the prettiest toy
That ever sung or danced.
LUIS Is she a Gypsy?
DIEGO
In her condition, not in her complexion.
I tell you once more, 'tis a spark of beauty
Able to set a world at gaze: the sweetest,
The wittiest rogue! Shall's see 'em? They have fine
gambols,
Are mightily frequented; court and city
Flock to 'em, but the country does 'em worship.
This little ape gets money by the sackful;
It trolls upon her.
LUIS [*to Roderigo*] Will ye with us, friend?
RODERIGO
You know my other projects; sights to me
Are but vexations.
LUIS O, you must be merry!—
Diego, we'll to th' Gypsies.
DIEGO Best take heed
You be not snapped.
LUIS How snapped?
DIEGO By that little fairy.
'T'as a shrewd tempting face and a notable tongue.
LUIS I fear not either.
DIEGO Go, then.
LUIS [*to Roderigo*] Will you with us?
RODERIGO I'll come after. *Exeunt Luis and Diego*
Pleasure and Youth like smiling evils woo us
To taste new follies; tasted, they undo us. *Exit*

77 **vagary** wander, meander
78 **wild-goose chase** (proverbial)
melancholy hysterical
84 **conceited** far-fetched poetic
85 **landed** disembarked, dismounted
86 **pinnace** small light vessel, often in attendance on a larger one—hence 'bit on the side', 'light woman' that a man 'boards' and rides
87 **voyage** sexual adventure
stole secretly and dishonestly acquired, 'snuck'
You're pleasant 'very funny' (sarcastic), or 'you're drunk'
92 **peppered** (*a*) pounded, physically punished (*b*) infected with venereal disease
93 **limed** (*a*) trapped, as birds are by birdlime (*b*) mated sexually
94 **double pistolets** Spanish gold coins
98 **sports** pastimes, amusements (perhaps also 'sexual dalliance')
101 **qualities** (*a*) natural talents (*b*) learned accomplishments
102 **reports of** (*a*) describes (*b*) resounds with talk about
109 **condition** (*a*) circumstances (*b*) behaviour
complexion 'skin colour' (Gypsies being considered darker than the English) and 'temperament' (of which skin colour was thought to be symptomatic)
111 **at gaze** gazing, in dazed spectatorship
112 **Shall's** shall we
gambols leaping tricks, child-like frolics, toys
114 **country** rural population (stereotypically ignorant and superstitious)
does 'em worship pays them homage (as if they were people of high rank, instead of outcasts), reveres them
115 **ape** (comparing Preciosa to a performing animal, mimic)
116 **trolls** rolls in, flows down (but also suggesting 'sings'—the means by which she gets it, in Cervantes)
120 **snapped** suddenly bitten, snatched
fairy diminutive supernatural enchantress (Preciosa)
121 **'T'as** it has ('it' being used of fairies and children)
shrewd dangerously, sharply (perhaps punning on 'shrewish')
notable remarkable (but punning on 'note-able', capable of musical notes)
tongue (for singing, witty conversation, or sexual pleasure; but also the chief attribute of a nagging 'shrew', which a man might fear)
126 **Pleasure and Youth** (like characters in allegorical plays or masques)
evils crimes, sins, diseases

2.1 *Incipit Actus Secundus*

Enter the old Father of the Gypsies, Carlo, and Antonio [all properly habited as Gypsies]

FATHER Come, my brave boys! The tailor's shears has cut us into shapes fitting our trade.

CARLO A trade free as a mason's.

ANTONIO A trade brave as a courtier's—for some of them do but shark, and so do we.

FATHER Gypsies, but no tanned ones; no red-ochre rascals umbered with soot and bacon as the English Gypsies are, that sally out upon pullen, lie in *emboscado* for a rope of onions, as if they were Welsh freebooters. No, our style has higher steps to climb over: Spanish Gypsies, noble Gypsies!

CARLO
I never knew nobility in baseness.

FATHER Baseness? The arts of *Cocoquismo* and Germania, used by our Spanish *picaros*—I mean filching, foisting, nimming, lifting—we defy. None in our college shall study 'em; such graduates we degrade.

ANTONIO
I am glad Spain has an honest company.

FATHER
We'll entertain no mountebanking stroll,
No piper, fiddler, tumbler through small hoops,
No ape-carrier, baboon-bearer;
We must have nothing stale, trivial, or base.
Am I your *mayordomo*, your *teniente*,
Your captain, your commander?

ANTONIO Who but you?

FATHER So then: now being entered Madrid, the enchanted circle of Spain, have a care to your new lessons.

BOTH [CARLO *and* ANTONIO] We listen.

FATHER Plough deep furrows, to catch deep root in th'opinion of the best, *grandes*, dukes, marquesses, *condes* and other *titulados*; show your sports to none but them. What can you do with three or four fools in a dish, and a blockhead cut into sippets?

ANTONIO Scurvy meat!

FATHER The Lacedemonians threw their beards over their shoulders, to observe what men did behind them as well as before; you must do so.

BOTH [CARLO *and* ANTONIO] We shall never do't. Our muzzles are too short.

FATHER Be not English Gypsies, in whose company a man's not sure of the ears of his head, they so pilfer! No such angling; what you pull to land, catch fair. There is no iron so foul but may be gilded, and our Gypsy profession (how base soever in show) may acquire commendations.

CARLO Gypsies, and yet pick no pockets?

FATHER Infamous and roguy! So handle your webs, that they never come to be woven in the loom of justice. Take anything that's given you (purses, knives, handkerchiefs, rosaries, tweezers, any toy, any money); refuse not a *maravedi*, a blank. Feather by feather birds build nests; grain pecked up after grain makes pullen fat.

2.1.0.2 ***Father*** leader, elder
0.3 ***habited*** dressed
1 **brave** fine
boys lads (younger than him, with not much hair on their chins; imagined in college, taking lessons)
3 **free... mason's** master stone-workers, free to travel wherever there were major building projects
5 **but shark** only sponge off others, behave in a predatory way
6–7 **tanned... bacon** (allusions to stereotypical reddish-brown Gypsy complexion)
7 **umbered** (artificially) darkened (like actors pretending to be Gypsies)
bacon smoked ham
8 **sally out** make a military sortie (ironic)
pullen poultry
emboscado ambush (Spanish)
9 **rope** string
onions (stereotypical Welsh cuisine)
freebooters pirates, adventurers
10 **style** (punning on 'stile')
11 **noble Gypsies** oxymoron ('aristocratic homeless vagrants', 'magnanimous crooks'), but also alluding to the English noblemen who played Gypsies in Jonson's masque (see Introduction).
13 ***Cocoquismo* and Germania** jargon of Gypsies and thieves. (Like many phrases in this scene, taken from James Mabbe's translation of Mateo Aleman's classic picaresque novel, *Guzman de Alfarache*.)
14 ***picaros*** wanderers, rogues
foisting picking pockets
15 **nimming** seizing
lifting stealing
defy denounce, renounce
college (treating the Gypsy band as an elect fraternity with strict rules and hierarchy)
16 **degrade** (punning on '*grad*uates')
17 **company** trade association like the London guilds. (Spain's only 'honest company' is a band of Gypsies?)
18–20 **We'll... baboon-bearer** (satirizing the repertoire of the rival Hope Theatre)
18 **entertain** host, welcome
mountebanking stroll itinerant charlatan
20 **ape-carrier, baboon-bearer** trainers who taught primates to perform tricks to amuse paying spectators
22 ***mayordomo*** steward (Spanish)
teniente lieutenant (Spanish)
24–5 **enchanted circle** circle drawn by a conjurer, summoning spirits or devils, to keep them out (or in)
28 ***grandes*** aristocrats (Spanish)
29 ***condes*** counts (Spanish)
titulados people with grand titles (jocular Spanish)
30 **fools** (*a*) foolish people, professional jesters (*b*) custards
31 **blockhead** dummy (but imagined as a kind of meat, like a baked boar's head, or a bird called the blackhead)
sippets small pieces, esp. bits of fried or toasted bread served with soup, etc.
32 **Scurvy meat** rotten food
33 **Lacedemonians** inhabitants of ancient Sparta
37 **muzzles... short** chins don't have enough long hair on them
40 **angling** using a fishing-line to steal sheets and clothes (but punning on 'Angland')
45 **webs** hands (compared to webbed feet of a duck, or spiderwebs); but punning on 'woven fabric'
46 **woven in the loom** i.e. entangled in the machine, which catches loose yarn and fixes it in a tight weave
48 **rosaries** (specifically Catholic devotional beads, here grouped with various worthless trifles)
49 ***maravedi*** very small Spanish copper coin worth sixpence
blank small silver coin

ANTONIO The best is, we Spaniards are no great feeders.

FATHER If one city cannot maintain us, away to another! Our horses must have wings. Does Madrid yield no money? Seville shall. Is Seville close-fisted? Valladolid is open; so Cordova, so Toledo. Do not our Spanish wines please us? Italian can then, French can. Preferment's bow is hard to draw; set all your strengths to it. What you get, keep: all the world is a second Rochelle. Make all sure, for you must not look to have your dinner served in with trumpets.

CARLO No, no, sack-butts shall serve us.

FATHER When you have money, hide it. Sell all our horses but one.

ANTONIO Why one?

FATHER 'Tis enough to carry our apparel and trinkets, and the less our ambler eats, our cheer is the better. None be sluttish, none thievish, none lazy; all bees, no drones, and our hives shall yield us honey.

Enter Eugenia, Preciosa, and Christiana [in new Gypsy clothes], and Cardochia

PRECIOSA
See, father, how I'm fitted! How do you like
This our new stock of clothes?

FATHER My sweet girl, excellent!—
[*To Cardochia*] See their old robes be safe.

CARDOCHIA That, sir, I'll look to.
Whilst in my house you lie, what thief soever
Lays hands upon your goods, call but to me,
I'll make thee satisfaction.

FATHER Thanks, good hostess!

CARDOCHIA
People already throng into the inn
And call for you into their private rooms.

FATHER No chamber comedies! Hostess, ply you your tide; flow let 'em to a full sea, but we'll show no pastime till after dinner, and that in a full ring of good people, the best, the noblest. No closet sweetmeats; pray, tell 'em so.

CARDOCHIA I shall. *Exit*

FATHER
How old is Preciosa?

EUGENIA Twelve and upwards.

PRECIOSA I am in my teens, assure you, mother. As little as I am, I have been taken for an elephant, castles and lordships offered to be set upon me, if I would bear 'em; why, your smallest clocks are the prettiest things to carry about gentlemen.

EUGENIA Nay, child, thou wilt be tempted.

PRECIOSA Tempted? Though I am no mark in respect of a huge butt, yet I can tell you, great bibbers have shot at me, and shot golden arrows. But I myself gave aim, thus: 'Wide, four bows!'—'Short, three and a half!' They that crack me shall find me as hard as a nut of Galicia. A parrot I am, but my teeth too tender to crack a wanton's almond.

FATHER
Thou art my noble girl! A-many dons
Will not believe but that thou art a boy
In woman's clothes—and to try that conclusion,
To see if thou be'st alchemy or no,
They'll throw down gold in musses. But, Preciosa,

52 **Spaniards . . . feeders** alluding to the notoriously skimpy Spanish diet (subject of many English complaints in 1623; satirized in *Game at Chess* 5.3)
58 **bow . . . draw** (alluding to the bow of Odysseus, which no one but himself could draw)
59 **Rochelle** characterized in *Guzman* as a place for self-seekers who 'keep what they get'
62 **sack-butts** cask of Spanish wine (126 gallons)—but punning on 'sackbuts' (musical instruments resembling a trumpet, with a slide like a modern trombone)
serve satisfy
63–4 **horses but one** (stereotypically, several Gypsies rode on a single horse)
67 **cheer** (*a*) food supply (*b*) frame of mind
68 **sluttish** (*a*) slovenly (*b*) sexually immoral
bees (traditional image of ideal community)
73 **house** public house, inn
78 **chamber comedies** bedroom farces
ply . . . tide (*a*) 'use the tide' to work a ship upriver, to windward, etc. (*b*) take advantage of your opportunity (*c*) assiduously keep offering your wine (to customers)
80 **ring** circle (as in outdoor amphitheatres and innyards)
81 **closet** private room, bedroom
sweetmeats (*a*) candy or sugared pastry (*b*) 'goodies', delicious lascivious bodies, sexual favours
84 **Preciosa** 'precious' (Spanish)
Twelve and upwards (the age of the Infanta of Spain; Preciosa is fifteen in Cervantes)
86 **elephant** (often pictured with a 'castle'—roofed wooden structure, enclosing its riders—on its back)
87 **bear 'em** support their weight (sexually), bare them
88 **smallest clocks** personal timepieces, watches (new and fashionable)
92 **butt** (*a*) archery target (*b*) wine cask (*c*) buttock
bibbers heavy drinkers, imbibers
93 **golden arrows** i.e. offers of money
gave aim measured how far the arrows fell from their target
94 **bows** bow-lengths
96 **Galicia** area of north-west Spain (most famous in 1623 as the home of Gondomar, hated Spanish ambassador to Britain, satirized as the Black Knight in *Game at Chess*)
parrot i.e. small brightly-decorated creature, who has been taught to repeat words (in her case, songs)
97 **wanton's** lecher's
almond (proverbially, food for which parrots would perform; here, offered by a 'wanton' seducer to tempt the 'parrot' Preciosa)
98 **A-many** many, a great number of
99 **Will . . . but** insist on believing, refuse to believe anything but
thou . . . boy (literally true, because the part would have been played by a boy actor)
100 **try** test
101 **alchemy** (*a*) metal which imitates gold (*b*) marvellous or magical transformation
102 **musses** heaps to scramble for

Let these proud sakers and gyrfalcons fly;
Do not thou move a wing. Be to thyself
Thyself, and not a changeling.

PRECIOSA How! Not a changeling?
Yes, father, I will play the changeling:
I'll change myself into a thousand shapes
To court our brave spectators; I'll change my postures
Into a thousand different variations
To draw even ladies' eyes to follow mine;
I'll change my voice into a thousand tones
To chain attention. Not a changeling, father?
None but myself shall play the changeling.

FATHER
Do what thou wilt, Preciosa.

A beating within

What noise is this?

Enter Cardochia

CARDOCHIA
Here's gentlemen swear all the oaths in Spain
They have seen you, must see you, and will see you.

FATHER To drown this noise, let 'em enter.

[*Cardocchia opens the door.*] *Enter Sancho and Soto*

SANCHO 'Swounds! Is your playhouse an inn? A gentleman cannot see you without crumpling his taffeta cloak.

SOTO Nay, more than a gentleman, his man being a diminutive don too.

SANCHO Is this the little ape does the fine tricks?

PRECIOSA 'Come aloft, Jack-little-ape!'

SANCHO Would my jack might come aloft! Please you to set the watermill with the ivory cogs in't a-grinding my handful of purging comfits.

[*He offers her comfits*]

SOTO My master desires to have you loose from your company.

PRECIOSA Am I a pigeon, think you, to be caught with cumin seeds? a fly to glue my wings to sweetmeats, and so be ta'en?

SANCHO [*to Father*] When do your gambols begin?

FATHER Not till we ha' dined.

SANCHO 'Sfoot! Then your bellies will be so full, you'll be able to do nothing.—Soto, prithee, set a good face on't, for I cannot, and give the little monkey that letter.

SOTO Walk off and hum to yourself.

[*Sancho stands aloof. Soto delivers a letter to Preciosa, reading from its superscription*]

'I dedicate, sweet destiny (into whose hand every Spaniard desires to put a distaff), these lines of love—'

EUGENIA What, 'love'? What's the matter?

SOTO Grave Mother Bumby, the mark's out o' your mouth.

FATHER What's the paper? From whom comes it?

SOTO The commodity wrapped up in the paper are verses; the warming-pan that puts heat into 'em, yon fire-brained bastard of Helicon.

SANCHO Hum, hum.

FATHER [*to Soto*] What's your master's name?

SOTO His name is Don Tomazo Portocarrero, nuncle to young Don Hortado de Mendonça, cousin-german to the *Conde* de Tendilla, and natural brother to Francisco de Bovadilla, one of the *comendadors* of Alcantara, a gentleman of long standing.

FATHER And of as long a style.

PRECIOSA Verses? I love good ones; let me see 'em.

SANCHO [*advancing*] Good ones? If they were not good ones, they should not come from me; at the name of verses I can stand on no ground.

103 **sakers** peregrine hawks
gyrfalcons large northern falcons

104 **Do . . . wing** (Preciosa is imagined as a small vulnerable bird, whom the predators will spot and pounce upon if she moves; she should remain still, constant, unmoved by attempts to move her.)

105–13 **not a changeling . . . play the changeling** (apparently an allusion to Middleton and Rowley's *The Changeling*, performed by the same company)

105 **changeling** (*a*) fickle, inconstant person (*b*) child stolen in infancy (*c*) one person substituted for another

114.1 ***beating*** (pounding on a door or playing a drum)

117.1 ***Sancho*** (name of a famous comic character in *Don Quixote*; first appearance of the name in an extant English play)

117.2 ***Soto*** (suggesting *sot*, 'fool, drunkard')

118 **'Swounds** by God's wounds (a very strong oath, referring to the crucifixion)

120 **man** servant

122 **this** (Preciosa)

123 **Come . . . Jack-little-ape** (playing on 'come aloft, jackanapes', the ape-trainer's command for an animal to begin performing tricks)

124 **Would . . . aloft** i.e. I wish I could get an erection

125 **ivory cogs** i.e. white teeth, compared to the 'cogs' of the mill-wheel

126 **purging** laxative
comfits sweets, candied fruit

127 **loose** (*a*) free, detached (*b*) with loose bowels (*c*) naked (*d*) sexually lax, promiscuous

130 **cumin seeds** (*a*) used to lure pigeons to a dove-cote (*b*) alluding to Matthew 23:23 ('hypocrites . . . pay tithe of . . . cummin, and have omitted the weightier matters of the law')

134 **'Sfoot!** by God's foot (strong oath)

135 **face** appearance, explanation

136 **I cannot** (because he does not have a 'good face')

139 **distaff** staff used in spinning, emblem of 'destiny' (because the Fates of classical mythology spun the web of a man's destiny) and of female domestic labour; here, the context also suggests 'erect penis'
lines (punning on 'loins')

140 **matter** subject (but also suggesting 'female genitals')

141 **Mother Bumby** (famous fortune-teller; title character of Lyly's *Mother Bombie*)
the mark's . . . mouth you are too old (comparing the old woman to a horse, whose age can be determined by examining the gums)

145 **Helicon** Greek mountain sacred to the muses

148–51 **Don . . . Alcantara** (Spaniards were often satirized for their pride in lineage; this haphazard string of grandiose titles is collected from *Guzman*.)

148 **nuncle** uncle (colloquially incongruous here)

150 **natural** (*a*) bastard (*b*) idiot

156 **verses** (perhaps punning on the legal term *versus*)

156–7 **I . . . ground** (*a*) I can stand even when there is nothing to stand on (*b*) my claims are groundless

PRECIOSA [*opening the paper*] Here's gold too!—Whose is this?

SANCHO Whose but yours? If there be any fault in the verses, I can mend it extempore; for a stitch in a man's stocking, not taken up in time, ravels out all the rest.

SOTO [*aside*] Botcherly poetry, botcherly!

PRECIOSA Verses and gold! These then are golden verses.

SANCHO Had every verse a pearl in the eye, it should be thine.

PRECIOSA A pearl in mine eye! I thank you for that; do you wish me blind?

SANCHO Ay, by this light do I, that you may look upon nobody's rhymes but mine.

PRECIOSA I should be blind indeed then.

FATHER [*to Sancho*] Pray, sir, read your verses.

SANCHO Shall I sing 'em or say 'em?

FATHER Which you can best.

SOTO [*aside*] Both scurvily.

SANCHO I'll set out a throat then.

SOTO Do, master, and I'll run division behind your back.

SANCHO [*sings*]
O that I were a bee to sing
Hum, buzz, buzz, hum! I first would bring
Home honey to your hive, and there leave my sting.

SOTO [*sings*]
He maunders.

SANCHO [*sings*]
O that I were a goose, to feed
At your barn-door! Such corn I need;
Nor would I bite, but goslings breed.

SOTO [*sings*]
And ganders.

SANCHO [*sings*]
O that I were your needle's eye!
How through your linen would I fly
And never leave one stitch awry!

SOTO [*sings*]
He'll touse ye.

SANCHO [*sings*]
O would I were one of your hairs,
That you might comb out all my cares
And kill the nits of my despairs!

SOTO [*sings*]
O lousy!

SANCHO How? 'Lousy'! Can rhymes be lousy?

OMNES No, no, they're excellent.

FATHER [*to Sancho*] But are these all your own?

SANCHO Mine own? Would I might never see ink drop out of the nose of any goose-quill more, if velvet cloaks have not clapped me for 'em! Do you like 'em?

PRECIOSA Past all compare!
They shall be writ out; when you've as good or better,
For these and those, pray, book me down your debtor.
Your paper is long-lived, having two souls,
Verses and gold.

SANCHO Would both those were in thy pretty little body, sweet Gypsy!

PRECIOSA A pistolet and this paper? 'Twould choke me.

SOTO No more than a bribe does a constable. The verses will easily into your head; then buy what you like with the gold, and put it into your belly. I hope I ha' chewed a good reason for you.

SANCHO Will you chew my jennet ready, sir?

SOTO And eat him down, if you say the word. *Exit*

SANCHO Now the coxcomb my man is gone, because you're but a country company of strolls, I think your stock is threadbare; here, mend it with this cloak...

[*He gives them his cloak*]

FATHER What do you mean, sir?

SANCHO [*giving them*]...this scarf, this feather, and this hat.

OMNES Dear senor!

SANCHO If they be never so dear—pox o' this hot ruff!—Little Gypsy, wear thou that.

[*He gives his ruff to Preciosa*]

FATHER Your meaning, sir?

SANCHO My meaning is: not to be an ass, to carry a burden when I need not. If you show your gambols forty leagues hence, I'll gallop to 'em. [*To Father*]

161–2 **a stitch...rest** (proverbial: a stitch in time saves nine)
161 **stitch** (punning on 'distich', Latin for 'couplet')
163 **botcherly** botched, badly made (but punning on *botcher*, 'tailor')
165 **pearl** (*a*) jewel (*b*) cataract
177 **division** ornamentation of a melodic line, or rhythmic accompaniment
180 **sting** (comparing intercourse to an insect's sting—which involves penetration, followed by swelling)
181 **maunders** (*a*) mutters (*b*) begs
182 **goose** (*a*) proverbially stupid fowl (*b*) simpleton
183 **barn-door** (suggesting 'bairn-door', aperture where babies enter the world, i.e. vagina)
184 **goslings** (*a*) young geese (*b*) fools
185 **ganders** he would breed (*a*) male geese (*b*) fools
186 **needle's eye** (punning on 'needles, I' or 'ay': *needle* was slang for 'penis')
187 **linen** underwear
189 **touse** dishevel, rumple, tumble, indelicately horse-play with
192 **nits** eggs of lice
193 **lousy** (*a*) infested with lice (*b*) contemptible, obscene
195 OMNES (Latin for 'All')
198 **nose** (suggested by 'neb', both the nib of a pen and the snout/nose of a human/animal)
goose-quill pen made from the wing-feathers of a goose (which, in the context, suggests 'fool's pen')
velvet cloaks (people wearing) expensive clothing
199 **clapped** (*a*) applauded (*b*) imprisoned
201 **writ out** copied down
202 **book me down** write me down in your account books
207 **pistolet** (*a*) Spanish coin (*b*) small pistol
207–8 **choke...constable** obstruct [Preciosa's] windpipe...'perturb' or 'silence' a law officer
210 **put...belly** (proverbial)
chewed 'chewed over', ruminated upon
211 **reason** (punning on 'raisin')
212 **chew** (nonsense-verb, perhaps punning on 'shew' and 'shoe')
jennet small Spanish horse
215 **strolls** vagabonds (comparing Gypsies to provincial touring actors)
stock (*a*) capital (*b*) theatrical wardrobe (*c*) stocking, sock
221 **dear** expensive

Farewell, old greybeard; [*to Eugenia*] adieu, Mother Mumble-crust; [*to Preciosa*] morrow, my little wart of beauty. *Exit*

Enter Don Juan, muffled, [*behind them*]

FATHER
So, harvest will come in! Such sunshine days
Will bring in golden sheaves, our markets raise.
Away to your task!

Exeunt [*Gypsies*]. *Don Juan pulls Preciosa back*

PRECIOSA Mother! Grandmother!

JUAN Two rows of kindred in one mouth?

EUGENIA [*returning*] Be not uncivil, sir. Thus have you used her thrice.

JUAN Thrice? Three thousand more! May I not use mine own?

PRECIOSA Your own! By what tenure?

JUAN Cupid entails this land upon me. I have wooed thee; thou art coy. By this air, I am a bull of Tarifa, wild, mad for thee! You trowed I was some copper coin; I am a knight of Spain, Don Francisco de Cárcamo my father, I Don Juan his son. This paper [*giving her a paper*] tells you more.—Grumble not, old granam; [*giving Eugenia money*] here's gold. For I must, by this white hand, marry this cherry-lipped, sweet-mouthed villain.

PRECIOSA There's a thing called *quando*.

JUAN Instantly.

EUGENIA [*to Preciosa*] Art thou so willing?

JUAN Peace, threescore and five!

PRECIOSA Marry me? Eat a chicken ere it be out o'th' shell? I'll wear no shackles. Liberty is sweet; that I have, that I'll hold. Marry me? Can gold and lead mix together? a diamond and a button of crystal fit one ring? You are too high for me, I am too low; you too great, I too little.

EUGENIA [*to Juan*] I pray, leave her, sir, and take your gold again.

PRECIOSA [*to Juan*] Or if you dote, as you say, let me try you: do this.

JUAN Anything; kill the great Turk, pluck out the Mogul's eye-teeth! In earnest, Preciosa, anything!

PRECIOSA Your task is soon set down: turn Gypsy for two years. Be one of us. If in that time you mislike not me, nor I you, here's my hand. Farewell. [*Exit*]

EUGENIA There's enough for your gold. [*Aside*] Witty child! *Exit*

JUAN
Turn Gypsy! for two years! A capering trade,
And I in th'end may keep a dancing school,
Having served for't. Gypsy I must turn.
O beauty, the sun's fires cannot so burn! *Exit*

Enter Clara **2.2**

CLARA
I have offended. Yet, O heaven, thou know'st
How much I have abhorred, even from my birth,
A thought that tended to immodest folly!
Yet I have fallen. Thoughts with disgraces strive,
And thus I live, and thus I die alive.

Enter Pedro and Maria

PEDRO
Fie, Clara, thou dost court calamity too much.

MARIA
Yes, girl, thou dost.

PEDRO
Why should we fret our eyes out
With our tears' weary complaints? 'Tis fruitless, childish
Impatience—for when mischief hath wound up
The full weight of the ravisher's foul life
To an equal height of ripe iniquity,
The poise will, by degrees, sink down his soul
To a much lower, much more lasting ruin
Than our joint wrongs can challenge.

MARIA
Darkness itself
Will change night's sable brow into a sunbeam
For a discovery; and be thou sure,
Whenever we can learn what monster 'twas
Hath robbed thee of the jewel held so precious,
Our vengeance shall be noble—

PEDRO
royal, anything!
Till then let's live securely; to proclaim
Our sadness were mere vanity.

CLARA
A needs not.
I'll study to be merry.

PEDRO
We are punished,
Maria, justly; covetousness to match
Our daughter to that matchless piece of ignorance,

227–8 **Mother Mumble-crust** toothless old woman (character in Nicholas Udall's *Ralph Roister Doister*, 1576)
239 **tenure** legal title, right
240 **entails** bestows as an inalienable possession (but punning on the sexual sense of 'tail')
241 **Tarifa** town in southern Spain, just west of Gibraltar, famed for wild bulls used in bull-fights
242 **trowed** believed
copper (less valuable than gold or silver)
246 **this** (Preciosa's)
248 ***quando*** when (Spanish), time when it should be done
250 **so willing** willing it should be so
256 **low … little** (conflating her size and social status)
261 **great Turk** sultan of the Ottoman empire
Mogul's potentate of India's
262 **In earnest** (*a*) seriously (*b*) as a down payment
269 **served** passed my apprenticeship
turn become (but punning on the gyrations of Gypsy dancing)
270 **sun's … burn** (*a*) sun does not generate as much heat [as beauty generates sexual passion] (*b*) sunburn could not turn his complexion as dark as a Gypsy's [but love of her beauty can]
2.2.3 **immodest folly** sexual indiscretion
12 **poise** weight
14 **challenge** claim
18 **jewel** i.e. her virginity
21 **A** it
23 **match** marry
24 **matchless** (*a*) unparalleled (*b*) unmarriable

Our foolish ward, hath drawn this curse upon us.
MARIA
I fear it has.
PEDRO Off with this face of grief:
Enter Luis and Diego
Here comes Don Luis.—Noble sir!
LUIS My lord,
I trust I have you and your lady's leave
T'exchange a word with your fair daughter.
PEDRO Leave
And welcome.—Hark, Maria.—Your ear too.
DIEGO Mine, my lord?
[*Pedro, Maria, and Diego talk apart*]
LUIS
Dear Clara, I have often sued for love,
And now desire you would at last be pleased
To style me yours.
CLARA Mine eyes ne'er saw that gentleman
Whom I more nobly in my heart respected
Than I have you; yet you must, sir, excuse me,
If I resolve to use awhile that freedom
My younger days allow.
LUIS But shall I hope?
CLARA
You will do injury to better fortunes,
To your own merit, greatness, and advancement,
Which I beseech you not to slack.
LUIS Then hear me:
If ever I embrace another choice,
Until I know you elsewhere matched, may all
The chief of my desires find scorn and ruin.
CLARA
O me!
LUIS Why sigh you, lady?
CLARA 'Deed, my lord,
I am not well.
LUIS Then all discourse is tedious.
I'll choose some fitter time. Till when, fair Clara—
CLARA
You shall not be unwelcome hither, sir.
That's all that I dare promise. [*Exit*]
LUIS Diego!
DIEGO My lord?
LUIS
What says Don Pedro?
DIEGO He'll go with you.
LUIS Leave us.
[*Exit Diego*]
[*To Pedro*] Shall I, my lord, entreat your privacy?
PEDRO
Withdraw, Maria; we'll follow presently.
Exit [*Maria*]
LUIS
The great *corregidor* (whose politic stream
Of popularity glides on the shore
Of every vulgar praise) hath often urged me
To be a suitor to his Catholic Majesty
For a repeal from banishment for him
Who slew my father; compliments in vows
And strange well-studied promises of friendship;
But what is new to me, still as he courts
Assistance for Alvarez, my grand enemy,
Still he protests how ignorant he is
Whether Alvarez be alive or dead.
Tomorrow is the day we have appointed
For meeting, at the lord Francisco's house,
The earl of Cárcamo. Now, my good lord,
The sum of my request is, you will please
To lend your presence there, and witness wherein
Our joint accord consists.
PEDRO You shall command it.
LUIS
But first, as you are noble, I beseech you
Help me with your advice what you conceive
Of great Fernando's importunity,
Or whether you imagine that Alvarez
Survive or not?
PEDRO It is a question, sir,
Beyond my resolution. I remember
The difference betwixt your noble father
And *Conde de* Alvarez, how it sprung
From a mere trifle first, a cast of hawks,
Whose made the swifter flight, whose could mount highest,
Lie longest on the wing; from change of words
Their controversy grew to blows, from blows
To parties, thence to faction and, in short,
I well remember how our streets were frighted
With brawls, whose end was blood—till, when no friends
Could mediate their discords, by the king
A reconciliation was enforced,
Death threatened to the first occasioner
Of breach, besides the confiscatïon
Of lands and honours; yet at last they met
Again, again they drew to sides, renewed
Their ancient quarrel—in which dismal uproar
Your father hand to hand fell by Alvarez.
Alvarez fled, and after him the doom
Of exile was sent out. He (as report

25 **ward** an orphaned minor, heir to an estate, whose legal guardian had the right to arrange a marriage, which the ward could not refuse without paying financial compensation: a system much abused in early modern England. (Sancho is Pedro's ward.)
28 **leave** permission
45 **'Deed** indeed
47 **Till when** until which time
56 **his Catholic Majesty** the King of Spain
78 **cast** couple
hawks trained hunting birds (kept by aristocrats, who made bets on their performance)
82 **parties** rival groups

Was bold to voice) retired himself to Rhodes;
His lands and honours by the king bestowed
On you, but then an infant.

LUIS
Ha, an infant?

PEDRO
His wife, the sister to the *corregidor*,
With a young daughter and some few that followed
her,
By stealth were shipped for Rhodes, and by a storm
Shipwrecked at sea. But for the banished *Conde*,
'Twas never yet known what became of him.
Here's all I can inform you.

LUIS
A repeal?
Yes, I will sue for't, beg for't, buy it, anything
That may by possibility of friends
Or money, I'll attempt.

PEDRO
'Tis a brave charity.

LUIS
Alas, poor lady, I could mourn for her!
Her loss was usury more than I covet.
But for the man, I'd sell my patrimony
For his repeal, and run about the world
To find him out; there is no peace can dwell
About my father's tomb till I have sacrificed
Some portion of revenge to his wronged ashes.
You will along with me?

PEDRO
You need not question it.

LUIS
I have strange thoughts about me. Two such furies
Revel amidst my joys as well may move
Distraction in a saint: vengeance and love.
I'll follow, sir.

PEDRO
Pray, lead the way, you know it.—

Exit Luis

Enter Sancho [*without his cloak, scarf, feather, hat, ruff, or rapier*], *and Soto*

How now? From whence come you, sir?

SANCHO From flaying myself, sir.

SOTO [*to Pedro*] From playing with fencers, sir—and they have beat him out of his clothes, sir.

PEDRO [*to Sancho*]
Cloak, band, rapier, all lost at dice?

SANCHO Nor cards neither.

SOTO [*to Pedro*] This was one of my master's dog-days, and he would not sweat too much.

SANCHO [*to Pedro*] It was mine own goose, and I laid the giblets upon another coxcomb's trencher. You are my guardian: best beg me for a fool now.

SOTO [*aside*] He that begs one begs t'other.

PEDRO [*to Sancho*]
Does any gentleman give away his things thus?

SANCHO Yes, and gentlewomen give away their things too.

SOTO [*to Pedro*] To gulls sometimes, and are cony-catched for their labour.

PEDRO [*to Sancho*] Wilt thou ever play the coxcomb?

SANCHO If no other parts be given me, what would you have me do?

PEDRO
Thy father was as brave a Spaniärd
As ever spoke the haught Castilian tongue.

SANCHO
Put me in clothes, I'll be as brave as he.

PEDRO
This is the ninth time thou hast played the ass,
Flinging away thy trappings and thy cloth
To cover others, and go nak'd thyself.

SANCHO I'll make 'em up ten, because I'll be even with you.

PEDRO
Once more your broken walls shall have new
hangings.

SOTO To be well hung is all our desire.

PEDRO And what course take you next?

SANCHO What course? Why, my man Soto and I will go make some maps.

PEDRO What maps?

SOTO Not such maps as you wash houses with, but maps of countries.

SANCHO I have an uncle in Seville, I'll go see him; an aunt in Siena in Italy, I'll go see her.

105 **may** may be done
108 **usury** interest (an addition to the principal debt he is owed)
117 **Distraction** madness
121 **playing** (*a*) exercising (*b*) gambling
122 **beat** (*a*) thrashed (*b*) out-gambled
125 **dog-days** hottest and unhealthiest days of the year
129 **beg...fool** apply to be my guardian (after I have been certified a lunatic)
130 **He...t'other** whoever asks for Sancho asks for a fool
131 **things** possessions (punning on 'genitals')
133 **gulls** dupes (like Sancho and Soto)
cony-catched cheated, duped (punning on *cony*, slang for *con*, 'cunt': cunt-catched)
134 **labour** (*a*) trouble (*b*) child-birth
135 **play** (*a*) behave like (*b*) act the part of
136 **parts** (*a*) faculties (*b*) roles. (A joke about the type-casting of the actor.)
138 **brave** courageous
139 **haught** elevated, arrogant
Castilian tongue i.e. Spanish language
140 **brave** well-dressed
142 **trappings** (*a*) decorative accessories placed over a saddle (*b*) fancy clothes
cloth (*a*) cloth placed under a saddle (*b*) clothes
144 **even** square, fair, quits (but punning on 'even number')
146 **hangings** tapestries (used to cover walls)
147 **well hung** (*a*) supplied with large genitals (*b*) thoroughly hanged on the gallows
152 **maps** (punning on 'mops')
154 **uncle** (proverbially, someone to visit when you need food, or to escape sexual trouble)
in Seville in the richest city of Spain, disembarkation point for gold from America, distributed from there to European financial networks (punning on 'incivil'?)
aunt (slang for 'prostitute' or 'procuress', especially associated with Italy)
155 **in Siena** (punning on Italian 'anziana', ancient?)

SOTO A cousin of mine in Rome, I'll go to him with a mortar.

SANCHO There's a courtesan in Venice, I'll go tickle her.

SOTO Another in England, I'll go tackle her.

PEDRO So, so!—and where's the money to do all this?

SANCHO If my woods, being cut down, cannot fill this pocket, cut 'em into trapsticks.

SOTO [*to Pedro*] And if his acres, being sold for a *maravedi* a turf for larks in cages, cannot fill this pocket, give 'em to gold-finders.

PEDRO You'll gallop both to the gallows. So fare you well. *Exit*

SANCHO [*to Pedro*] And be hanged you! New clothes, you'd best!

SOTO [*to Pedro*] Four cloaks!—[*to Sancho*] that you may give away three, and keep one.

SANCHO We'll live as merrily as beggars; let's both turn Gypsies.

SOTO By any means. If they cog, we'll lie; if they toss, we'll tumble.

SANCHO Both in a belly, rather than fail.

SOTO Come, then, we'll be Gypsified.

SANCHO And tipsified too.

SOTO
And we will show such tricks and such rare gambols
As shall put down the elephant and camels. *Exeunt*

3.1 *Incipit Actus Tertius*

Enter Roderigo disguised like an Italian

RODERIGO
A thousand stings are in me. O what vile prisons
Make we our bodies to our immortal souls!
Brave tenants to bad houses: 'tis a dear rent
They pay for naughty lodging. The soul, the mistress;
The body, the caroche that carries her;
Sins, the swift wheels that hurry her away;
Our will, the coachman rashly driving on
Till coach and carriage both are quite o'erthrown.
My body yet 'scapes bruises; that known thief
Is not yet called to th' bar. There's no true sense
Of pain but what the law of conscïence
Condemns us to; I feel that. Who would lose
A kingdom for a cottage? an estate
Of perpetuity for a man's life
For annuity of that life (pleasure)?—a spark
To those celestial fires that burn about us,
A painted star to that bright firmament
Of constellations which each night are set
Lighting our way. Yet thither how few get!
How many thousand in Madrid drink off
The cup of lust (and laughing) in one month?—
Not whining as I do! Should this sad lady
Now meet me, do I know her? Should this temple,
By me profaned, lie in her ruins here,
The pieces would scarce show her me. Would they
did!
She's mistress to Don Luis; by his steps,
And this disguise, I'll find her. To Salamanca
Thy father thinks thou'rt gone; no, close here stay.
Where'er thou travell'st, scorpions stop thy way.
Faith, what are these?

Enter Sancho and Soto as Gypsies

SANCHO Soto, how do I show?

SOTO Like a rusty armour new scoured. But, master, how show I?

SANCHO Like an ass with a new piebald saddle on his back.

156 **cousin** (punning on *cozen*, 'cheat'—like someone who would claim to 'walk... mortar')

156–7 **Rome... mortar** (apparently alluding to the proverbially impossible feat of walking—or hopping—all the way to Rome with a mortar-bowl on one's head, without it falling off)

156 **go** walk

158 **Venice** (famous for its courtesans)
tickle (*a*) excite, pleasure (*b*) amuse, make laugh

159 **tackle** equip with necessary accessories (like the tackle of the ships for which England was famous); also punning, after *tickle*, on 'tick-tack'

161 **fill** (i.e. 'with money from the sale of the timber', but ludicrously suggesting the literal 'with trees')

162 **trapsticks** (used in the game of trap-ball)

163 ***maravedi*** Spanish copper coin worth sixpence

164 **turf** sod of grass, small slab of earth and vegetation pared from the surface
cages (Traditionally, the bottom of the birdcage was lined with freshly cut turf.)

165 **gold-finders** people who scavenge through dung, looking for anything salvagable

173 **cog** (*a*) cheat (*b*) jest (*c*) brake
lie (*a*) tell lies (*b*) lie down (*c*) lie still, stop
toss (*a*) move about restlessly (*b*) drink (*c*) punish by tossing in a blanket

174 **tumble** (*a*) perform acrobatic tricks (*b*) toss, be tossed (*c*) stumble, fall

175 **belly** womb (like twins; but here suggesting that they will take turns falling into, or performing acrobatic tricks in, the same vagina)

176 **Gypsified** turned into Gypsies (made-up word)

177 **tipsified** intoxicated (made-up word)

179 **put down** outclass
elephant and camels (*a*) exotic performing animals (*b*) gift of an elephant and five camels, given to King James by the King of Spain in 1623

3.1.3 **Brave** excellent
bad houses (suggesting 'whorehouses')

4 **naughty** (*a*) inferior, poor quality (*b*) immoral
mistress woman in authority, female head of household (but suggesting 'kept woman, illicit sexual partner')

5 **caroche** luxurious coach (urban status symbol)

7 **will** desire (but punning on the nickname 'Will')

8 **carriage** (*a*) what is being carried (*b*) behaviour, bodily deportment

10 **bar** place in court where the accused stands

15 **annuity** yearly allowance

19 **way** path (to heaven)

23 **temple** body (1 Corinthians 3:16)

24 **her ruins** her (Clara's) despoiled condition, ruined reputation

26 **mistress to** beloved by

30 **Faith** (by my) faith (a mild oath)

31 **show** look

34 **piebald** black streaked with white

SOTO If the devil were a tailor, he would scarce know us in these gaberdines.

SANCHO If a tailor were the devil, I'd not give a louse for him, if he should bring up this fashion amongst gentlemen and make it common.

RODERIGO
The freshness of the morning be upon you both!

SANCHO
The saltness of the evening be upon you single!

RODERIGO
Be not displeased that I abruptly thus
Break in upon your favours. Your strange habits
Invite me with desire to understand
Both what you are and whence, because no coun-
try—
And I have measured some—shows me your like.

SOTO Our like? No, we should be sorry we or our clothes should be like fish: new, stale, and stinking in three days.

SANCHO [*to Roderigo*] If you ask whence we are, we are Egyptian Spaniards; if what, we are—[*singing*] 'ut, re, mi, fa, sol'—jugglers, tumblers, anything, anywhere, everywhere.

RODERIGO
A good fate hither leads me by the hand.
Your quality I love. The scenical school
Has been my tutor long in Italy
(For that's my country); there have I put on
Sometimes the shape of a comedian,
And now and then some other.

SANCHO
A player! A brother of the tiring-house!

SOTO
A bird of the same feather!

SANCHO [*to Roderigo*] Welcome! Wou't turn Gypsy?

RODERIGO
I can nor dance nor sing; but if my pen
From my invention can strike music tunes,
My head and brains are yours.

SOTO A calf's head and brains were better for my stomach.

SANCHO A rib of poetry!

SOTO A modicum of the Muses! A horseshoe of Helicon!

SANCHO [*to Roderigo*] A magpie of Parnassus! Welcome again! I am a fire-brand of Phoebus myself; we'll invoke together—so you will not steal my plot.

RODERIGO 'Tis not my fashion.

SANCHO But nowadays 'tis all the fashion.

SOTO [*to Roderigo*] What was the last thing you writ—a comedy?

RODERIGO
No, 'twas a sad, too sad a tragedy.
[*Aside*] Under these eaves I'll shelter me.
[*Enter the old Father of the Gypsies, Eugenia, Preciosa, and the Gypsies*]

SANCHO See, here comes our company. [*To Gypsies*] Do our tops spin as you would have 'em?

SOTO [*to Gypsies*] If not, whip us round.

SANCHO [*to Father*] I sent you a letter to tell you we were upon a march.

FATHER And you are welcome.—[*Aside to Eugenia*] Yet these fools will trouble us!

EUGENIA [*aside to Father*] Rich fools shall buy our trouble.

SANCHO Hang lands! It's nothing but trees, stones, and dirt.—Old father, I have gold to keep up our stock.—Precious Preciosa (for whose sake I have thus transformed myself out of a gentleman into a Gypsy), thou shalt not want sweet rhymes, my little musk-cat—for besides myself, here's an Italian poet, on whom I pray throw your welcomes.

OMNES He's welcome!

35 **devil . . . tailor** (associated because a tailor's discarded cloth box was called 'hell')
36 **gaberdines** coarse loose frocks with long sleeves
41 **saltness** lecherousness (but suggested by the contrast between 'fresh' and 'salt' water, or fresh food and food artifically preserved in salt)
single (*a*) alone (*b*) unmarried
48–9 **fish . . . three days** (proverbial: Tilley F310)
51 **Egyptian** Gypsy (because of the false belief that they originated in Egypt)
51–2 **ut . . . sol** i.e. musicians, identified by the first five notes of the musical scale (perhaps singing William Byrd's song of that title)
55 **quality** profession
scenical school *commedia dell'arte*
58 **comedian** (*a*) actor (*b*) playwright
60 **player** actor
brother fellow-member of a guild
tiring-house backstage area, dressing room
61 **bird . . . feather** (proverbial—but here also suggesting the notorious affection of actors for fine clothes, epitomized by fashionable and expensive feathers)
Wou't wouldst thou
62 **can nor** can neither
65 **calf's . . . brains** (*a*) part of the early modern diet (*b*) stupid person
66 **rib of poetry** (as in 'rib of pork' or 'rib of poultry', perhaps punning on Latin *porcaria*)
67 **modicum** small quantity of food (punning on Latin *modus*, musical or grammatical mode, mood, measure)
horseshoe (because the fountain of the muses allegedly sprung from the hoof-print of the winged horse Pegasus, but also perhaps alluding to a plant of that name)
Helicon stream associated with the muses of Greek mythology, who inspired poets
68 **magpie** (bird famous for chattering and pilfering)
Parnassus mountain in Greece, sacred to Apollo and the muses; hence, literature, poetry
69 **fire-brand** piece of wood kindled by the fire, person inspired by the power (but also 'person who is doomed to burn in hell')
Phoebus Apollo, god of poetry and the sun
invoke pray for inspiration, intone
75 **tragedy** i.e. his rape of Clara
78 **tops** (*a*) spinning tops (*b*) foretop, forelock (object of a recurrent comic routine of the clown Rowley)
82 **Yet** still
89 **musk-cat** i.e. courtesan (an insult, though Sancho uses it as though it were a complement)

PRECIOSA [*to Roderigo*]
Sir, you're most welcome; I love a poet,
So he writes chastely. If your pen can sell me
Any smooth quaint romances which I may sing,
You shall have bays and silver.
RODERIGO Pretty heart, no selling;
What comes from me is free.
SANCHO And me too.
FATHER [*to Roderigo*]
We shall be glad to use you, sir. Our sports
Must be an orchard, bearing several trees
And fruits of several taste; one pleasure dulls.
A time may come when we, besides these pastimes,
May from the *grandes* and the dons of Spain
Have leave to try our skill even on the stage—
And then your wits may help us.
SANCHO And mine too.
RODERIGO [*to Father*]
They are your servants.
PRECIOSA [*to all*] Trip softly through the streets
Till we arrive (you know at whose house, father).
Song
SANCHO [*sings*]
Trip it, Gypsies, trip it fine,
Show tricks and lofty capers!
At threading needles we repine,
And leaping over rapiers:
Pindy-pandy rascal toys!
We scorn cutting purses.
Though we live by making noise,
For cheating none can curse us.

Over high ways, over low,
And over stones and gravel
Though we trip it on the toe
And thus for silver travel,
Though our dances waste our backs,
At night fat capons mend 'em;
Eggs (well brewed in buttered sack),
Our wenches say, befriend 'em.

O that all the world were mad!
Then should we have fine dancing.
Hobby-horses would be had
And brave girls keep a-prancing;
Beggars would on cock-horse ride
And boobies fall a-roaring
And cuckolds (though no horns be spied)
Be one another goring.

Welcome, poet, to our ging!
Make rhymes; we'll give thee reason.
Canary bees thy brains shall sting;
Mulled sack did ne'er speak treason.
Peter-see-me shall wash thy noll
And malaga glasses fox 'ee.
If, poet, thou toss not bowl for bowl,
Thou shalt not kiss a doxy. *Exeunt* [*dancing*]

Enter Fernando, Francisco de Cárcamo, Don Juan, Pedro, Maria, Luis, and Diego 3.2

FERNANDO
Luis de Castro, since you circled are
In such a golden ring of worthy friends,
Pray, let me question you about that business
You and I last conferred on.
LUIS My lord, I wish it.
FERNANDO
Then, gentlemen, though you all know this man,
Yet now look on him well, and you shall find
Such mines of Spanish honour in his bosom
As but in few are treasured.
LUIS O, my good lord—
FERNANDO
He's son to that De Castro o'er whose tomb
Fame stands, writing a book, which will take up
The age of time to fill it with the stories
Of his great acts, and that his honoured father
Fell in the quarrel of those families,
His own and Don Alvarez de Castilla's.
FRANCISCO
The volume of those quarrels is too large

94 **So** if
95 **romances** Spanish verse genre (like English historical ballad)
96 **bays** laurel (traditional reward of poets)
100 **several taste** distinct flavour
106.1 ***Song*** For the music, see *Companion*, p. 172.
107 **Trip** dance, move nimbly
108 **capers** frolics, leaps
109 **threading needles** (an old-fashioned child's dance/game, but also conventional domestic work for women)
110 **leaping over rapiers** (a feature of folk-dances, but also suggesting the conventional male work of warfare)
111 **Pindy-pandy** refrain of a child's game involving switching hands or places (like 'handy-dandy')
118 **travel** (*a*) roam (*b*) work, travail
121 **Eggs** (considered an aphrodisiac)
sack Spanish wine
125 **Hobby-horses** (*a*) in the English morris dance, the figure of a horse, worn by a dancer (*b*) a child's toy horse (*c*) a promiscuous woman
127 **on cock-horse ride** (*a*) achieve an exalted social position, riding a stallion (*b*) ride on a toy horse (instead of a real one)
128 **boobies** nincompoops
129 **horns** (popularly associated with cuckolds)
131 **ging** gang
132 **rhymes...reason** (proverbially contrasted)
133 **Canary** Spanish wine
134 **Mulled sack** heated wine mixed with sugar, spices, eggyolk, etc.
ne'er speak treason (because *in vino veritas*, 'in wine there is truth')
135 **Peter-see-me** Spanish wine (named for Pedro Ximene)
noll head, noddle
136 **fox** intoxicate
'ee thee
137 **bowl** large drinking cup
138 **doxy** harlot (specifically, a Gypsy's mistress)
3.2.7 **mines** (associated with Spain because of precious metals mined in the Spanish New World)
12 **that** (Fame stands writing) that

And too wide printed in our memory.
LUIS
Would it had ne'er come forth!
OMNES So wish we all.
FERNANDO
But here's a son as matchless as the father,
For he mends bravery. He lets blood his spleen,
Tears out the leaf in which the picture stands
Of slain De Castro, casts a hill of sand
On all revenge, and stifles it.
OMNES 'Tis done nobly!
FERNANDO
For I by him am courted to solicit
The king for the repeal of poor Alvarez,
Who lives a banished man—some say, in Naples.
PEDRO
Some say, in Aragon.
LUIS No matter where.
That paper folds in it my hand and heart,
Petitioning the royalty of Spain
To free the good old man and call him home.
But what hope hath your lordship that these beams
Of grace shall shine upon me?
FERNANDO The word royal.
OMNES And that's enough.
LUIS
Then since this sluice is drawn up to increase
The stream, with pardon of these honoured friends
Let me set ope another, and that's this:
That you, my lord Don Pedro, and this lady
Your noble wife, would in this fair assembly—
If still you hold me tenant to your favour—
Repeat the promise you so oft have made me,
Touching the beauteous Clara for my wife.
PEDRO
What I possess in her, before these lords
I freely once more give you.
MARIA And what's mine,
To you (as right heir to it) I resign.
OMNES [*to Luis*] What would you more?
LUIS
What would I more? The tree bows down his head
Gently to have me touch it, but—when I offer
To pluck the fruit—the top branch grows so high,
To mock my reaching hand, up it does fly.
I have the mother's smile, the daughter's frown.
OMNES
O, you must woo hard!
FERNANDO [*to Luis*] Woo her well; she's thine own.
JUAN [*aside*]
That law holds not 'mongst Gypsies. I shoot hard,
And am wide off from the mark.
Flourish [*within*]
FERNANDO [*to Francisco*]
Is this, my lord, your music?
FRANCISCO None of mine.
Enter Soto [*as a Gypsy*], *with a cornet in his hand*
SOTO
A crew of Gypsies with desire
To show their sports are at your gates a-fire.
FRANCISCO
How, how, my gates a-fire, knave?
JUAN [*aside*] Art panting?
I am a-fire, I'm sure!
FERNANDO [*to Soto*] What are the things they do?
SOTO
They frisk, they caper, dance and sing,
Tell fortunes too (which is a very fine thing).
They tumble—how? not up and down,
As tumblers do, but from town to town.
Antics they have and Gypsy-masquing,
And toys which you may have for asking.
They come to devour nor wine nor good cheer
But to earn money, if any be here.
(But being asked, as I suppose,
Your answer will be, 'in your t'other hose'.)
For there's not a Gypsy amongst 'em that begs,
But gets his living by his tongue and legs.
If therefore you please, dons, they shall come in:
Now I have ended, let them begin.
OMNES Ay, ay, by any means.
FRANCISCO But, fellow, bring you music along with you too?
SOTO Yes, my lord, both loud music and still music: the loud is that which you have heard, and the still is that which no man can hear. *Exit*
FERNANDO
A fine knave!
FRANCISCO There is report of a fair Gypsy,
A pretty little toy, whom all our gallants
In Madrid flock to look on: this she, trow?
JUAN
Yes, sure 'tis she. [*Aside*] I should be sorry else.
Enter the old Father of the Gypsies, Eugenia, Preciosa, Roderigo [*disguised as an Italian*],

16 **wide printed** (*a*) widely reprinted (*b*) printed in large type or on large pages
17 **come forth** (*a*) happened (*b*) been published
19 **mends** (*a*) amends, reforms, improves upon (*b*) mends, patches
bravery (*a*) bragging, machismo (*b*) extravagant apparel
lets blood bleeds, drains blood from (in order to reduce a perceived excess)
spleen (considered the source of anger and resentment)
20 **leaf** page (of the imaginary printed book)
62 **Antics** fantastic dances
Gypsy-masquing (an allusion to Ben Jonson's court masque, *The Gypsies Metamorphosed*. See Introduction.)
67 **in your t'other hose** proverbial excuse for niggardliness
75 **still music** quiet music (usually flutes and recorders), but punning on 'silent'
78 **fair** beautiful, but also (paradoxically) with a pale complexion
80 **trow** do you think

Sancho, Soto, and all the Gypsies, [singing this] song

[FATHER]
Come, follow your leader, follow!
Our convoy be Mars and Apollo!
The van comes brave up here;

ANSWER
As hotly comes the rear.

OMNES
Our knackers are the fifes and drums.
Sa, sa, the Gypsies' army comes!

[SECOND GYPSY]
Horsemen we need not fear;
There's none but footmen here.
The horse sure charge without—
Or, if they wheel about,

OMNES
Our knackers are the shot that fly,
Pit-a-pat rattling in the sky.

[THIRD GYPSY]
If once the great ordnance play
(That's laughing), yet run not away
But stand the push of pike:
Scorn can but basely strike.

OMNES
Then let our armies join and sing,
And pit-a-pat make our knackers ring.

[FOURTH GYPSY]
Arm, arm! What bands are those?
They cannot be sure our foes.
We'll not draw up our force
Nor muster any horse—

OMNES
For since they pleased to view our sight,
Let's this way, this way give delight.

[FIFTH GYPSY]
A council of war let's call!
Look either to stand or fall.
If our weak army stands,
Thank all these noble hands,

OMNES
Whose gates of love being open thrown,
We enter, and then the town's our own,
Whose gates of love being open thrown,
We enter, and then the town's our own.

FERNANDO
A very dainty thing!

FRANCISCO
A handsome creature!

PEDRO
Look what a pretty pit there's in her chin!

JUAN [*aside*]
Pit? 'Tis a grave to bury lovers in.

RODERIGO [*aside*] My father?—Disguise guard me!

SANCHO [*aside to Soto*] Soto, there's De Cortes my guardian, but he smells not us.

SOTO [*aside to Sancho*] Peace, brother Gypsy. [*To nobles*] Would anyone here know his fortune?

OMNES Good fortunes, all of us!

PEDRO [*to Soto*]
'Tis I, sir, needs a good one. Come, sir, what's mine?
[*Soto reads his palm*]

MARIA
Mine and my husband's fortunes keep together;
Who is't tells mine?

SANCHO I, I. Hold up, madam; fear not your pocket, for I ha' but two hands.
[*He reads her palm*]
You are sad, or mad, or glad
For a couple of cocks that cannot be had;
Yet when abroad they have picked store of grain,
Doodle-doo they will cry on your dunghills again.

MARIA
Indeed I miss an idle gentleman
And a thing of his, a fool—but neither sad
Nor mad for them. Would that were all the lead
Lying at my heart!

PEDRO [*to Soto*] What look'st thou on so long?

SOTO So long! Do you think good fortunes are fresh herrings, to come in shoals? Bad fortunes are like mackerel at midsummer. You have had a sore loss o' late.

PEDRO I have indeed; what is't?

SOTO I wonder it makes you not mad, for—

82 FATHER The stanzas are numbered '1' to '5', and in each case a single voice is answered by a chorus; it seems logical that the Gypsy's leader should sing 'follow your leader', but who sings each of the remaining stanzas is anyone's guess.
83 **Mars and Apollo** gods of war and poetry
84 **van** vanguard
86 **knackers** castanets
89 **footmen** (*a*) infantry (*b*) dancers
96 **pike** spear-like weapon
100 **bands** troops
114 **thing** Preciosa (who has presumably been conspicuous in the singing and/or dancing)
115 **pit** dimple
121 **Would...know** does...wish to know
121–94 **fortune...eyes** (alludes to the fortune-telling in Jonson's *Gypsies Metamorphosed*)
129 **cocks** (*a*) roosters (*b*) spirited men (*c*) penises
130 **picked** (*a*) pecked (*b*) stolen **store** plenty
131 **Doodle-doo** cry of a rooster (but perhaps punning on *doodle* as noodle-head: see Pompey Doodle in *Weapons*) **dunghills** proverbially, every rooster is proud of his own dunghill; domesticated 'dunghill cocks' are cowardly (by comparison with fighting cocks)
132 **miss** do not know the whereabouts of (without any sense of emotional bereavement)
134 **lead** heaviness
137–8 **like...midsummer** i.e. plentiful
138 **sore loss** Soto means his own disappearance; Pedro means Clara's rape

Through a gap in your ground thence late have been stole
A very fine ass and a very fine foal.
Take heed, for I speak not by habs and by nabs:
Ere long you'll be horribly troubled with scabs.

PEDRO
I am now so; go, silly fool.

SOTO [*aside*] I ha' gi'n't him.

SANCHO [*aside*] O Soto, that ass and foal fattens me!

FERNANDO
The mother of the Gypsies, what can she do?
I'll have a bout with her.
[*He goes to Eugenia, who reads his palm*]

JUAN I, with the Gypsy daughter.

FRANCISCO To her, boy.
[*Juan goes to Preciosa, who reads his palm*]

EUGENIA [*reading Fernando's palm*]
From you went a dove away,
Which ere this had been more white
Than the silver robe of day;
Her eyes, the moon has none so bright.
Sat she now upon your hand,
Not the crown of Spain could buy't;
But 'tis flown to such a land,
Never more shall you come nigh't.—
Ha! Yet, if palmistry tell true,
This dove again may fly to you.

FERNANDO
Thou art a lying witch; I'll hear no more.

SANCHO If you be so hot, sir, we can cool you with a song.

SOTO [*to Fernando*] And when that song's done, we'll heat you again with a dance.

LUIS [*to Pedro*]
Stay, dear sir; send for Clara, let her know
Her fortune.

MARIA 'Tis too well known.

LUIS 'Twill make her merry
To be in this brave company.

PEDRO Good Diego,
Fetch her. *Exit Diego*

FRANCISCO [*to Gypsies*]
What's that old man? Has he cunning too?

OMNES
More than all we!

LUIS Has he? I'll try his spectacles.
[*He goes to the Father of the Gypsies, who reads his palm*]

FERNANDO [*aside*]
Ha! Roderigo there? Forsooth, the scholar
That went to Salamanca!—takes he degrees
I'th' school of Gypsies? Let the fish alone,
Give him line. This is the dove—the dove?—the raven
That beldam mocked me with.

LUIS [*to Father*] What worms pick you out there now?

FATHER
This: when this line the other crosses,
Art tells me 'tis a book of losses.—
Bend your hand thus.—O, here I find
You've lost a ship in a great wind.

LUIS
Lying rogue, I ne'er had any.

FATHER Hark: as I gather,
That great ship was 'De Castro' called (your father).

LUIS
And I must hew that rock that split him. Vengeance!

FATHER Nay, an you threaten—
[*He goes away from Luis*]

FRANCISCO
And what's, Don Juan, thy fortune?—[*To Preciosa*]
Thou'rt long fumbling at it.

JUAN
She tells me tales of the moon, sir.

PRECIOSA [*to Francisco*]
And now 'tis come to the sun, sir.
Your son would ride, the youth would run,
The youth would sail, the youth would fly!

142 **late** lately
stole stolen (but playing on 'stole away', sneaked off)
143 **fine** (*a*) excellent (*b*) well-dressed
ass (*a*) donkey (*b*) dumbass, fool
foal colt (but punning on 'fool')
144 **by habs...nabs** at random
145 **scabs** (*a*) itching disease (*b*) scoundrels
147 **gi'n't him** 'given it to him': (*a*) delivered the prophecy (*b*) given him a good beating, lambasted him
149 **mother** female elder (Eugenia)
150 **bout** (*a*) turn (*b*) sexual encounter
153 **dove** (often used for an innocent woman or child; but also suggesting the dove Noah sent out, which returned with an olive branch, and thus became an emblem of peace: see Genesis 8:8–12)
154 **white** white-haired, old
155 **silver robe** (emblematic attire of the sun-god)
156 **moon** personified as the goddess Cynthia or Diana
157 **upon your hand** (like a tame bird)
159 **flown** (playing on the sense 'fled')
160 **nigh't** near it (the land, or the dove)
161 **Yet** (*a*) nevertheless (*b*) still, at some future time
palmistry palm-reading, fortune-telling
164 **hot** angry
170 **cunning** (*a*) occult knowledge (*b*) cleverness
171 **all we** all of us
spectacles magical instruments for seeing the unseen
174 **school...fish** (punning)
175 **raven** Presumably Roderigo is dressed in black; he is certainly morally black, in contrast to the whiteness of the innocent dove.
176 **beldam** (*a*) old woman (*b*) hag, witch
worms (as though the sustained attention to his palm were for the purpose of picking out parasites)
178 **Art** technical knowledge, science
book of losses record of suffering, debit account
182 **great ship** warship
186 **moon** (*a*) something unattainable, insubstantial, fantastic (*b*) goddess of chastity
187 **sun** (punning on 'son'). This initiates an allusion to Phaeton, son of the sun-god, who borrowed his father's chariot to ride/fly across the sky (disastrously).
188 **ride** (*a*) go on a journey on horseback or by coach, as the sun-god was imagined riding across the sky (*b*) mount sexually
189 **fly** (*a*) travel through the air (*b*) run away

He's tying a knot will ne'er be done.
He shoots, and yet has ne'er an eye;
You have two, 'twere good you lent him one—
And a heart too, for he has none.

FRANCISCO Hoyday! Lend one of mine eyes?

SANCHO [*to the Gypsies*] They give us nothing; we'd best put on a bold face and ask it.

[*He sings a*] *song*

Now that from the hive
You gathered have the honey,
Our bees but poorly thrive
Unless the banks be sunny;
Then let your sun and moon
(Your gold and silver) shine.
My thanks shall humming fly to you,

OMNES [*sing*]
And mine, and mine, and mine.

FATHER [*sings*]
See, see, you Gypsy-toys,
You mad girls, you merry boys,
A *bon voyage* we've made.
Loud peals must then be had.
If I a Gypsy be,
A crack-rope I'm for thee:
O, here's a golden ring!
Such clappers please a king,

OMNES [*sing*]
Such clappers please a king.

FATHER [*sings*]
You (pleased) may pass away;
Then let your bell-ropes sway:
Now chime, 'tis holiday.

OMNES [*sing*]
Now chime, 'tis holiday.

PRECIOSA
No more of this, pray, father; fall to your dancing.

[*Gypsy*] *dance*

LUIS
Clara will come too late now.

FERNANDO [*to Gypsies*] 'Tis great pity,
Besides your songs, dances, and other pastimes,
You do not, as our Spanish actors do,
Make trial of a stage.

FATHER We are, sir, about it—
So please your high authority to sign us
Some warrant to confirm us.

FERNANDO My hand shall do't,
And bring the best in Spain to see your sports.

FATHER
Which to set off, this gentleman, a scholar—

RODERIGO [*aside*]
Pox on you!

FATHER Will write for us.

FERNANDO [*to Roderigo*] A Spaniard, sir?

RODERIGO
No, my lord, an Italian.

FERNANDO [*aside*] Denies
His country too? My son sings Gypsy-ballads!—
Keep as you are. We'll see your poet's vein,
And yours for playing: time is not ill spent
That's thus laid out in harmless merriment.

Exit Gypsies dancing

PEDRO [*to Francisco*]
My lord of Cárcamo, for this entertainment
You shall command our loves.

FRANCISCO You're nobly welcome.

PEDRO
The evening grows upon us: lords, to all
A happy time of day.

FERNANDO The like to you,
Don Pedro.

LUIS [*to Maria*]
To my heart's sole lady
Pray let my service humbly be remembered;
We only missed her presence.

MARIA I shall truly
Report your worthy love. *Exit Pedro, Maria*

FERNANDO You shall no further;
Indeed, my lords, you shall not.

FRANCISCO With your favour,
We will attend you home.

Enter Diego

DIEGO Where's Don Pedro?—
O sir!

LUIS Why, what's the matter?

DIEGO The lady Clara,
Passing near to my lord *corregidor*'s house,
Met with a strange mischance.

FERNANDO How? What mischance?

DIEGO
The jester that so late arrived at court

190 **knot** wedding knot, wedlock
done ended (because marriage is an eternal relationship) or completed (because she does not intend to consummate it, or 'do' it, sexually)
191 **shoots** (*a*) fires a gun or shoots an arrow (*b*) ejaculates
eye (*a*) ability to see well (*b*) vagina
192 **lent...one** (to 'give' or 'lend an eye' = to keep watch)
193 **heart...none** (*a*) he's heartless (*b*) she has not given him her heart
200 **banks** (*a*) rural slopes (*b*) riversides, particularly of the Thames in London
210 **crack-rope** rogue (likely to hang)
211 **golden ring** wealthy circle (or a gift given by one of the onstage spectators)
212 **clappers** bells (but perhaps also 'beggars', who begged with a dish called a clapper)
king (not in the dramatis personae, but alluding to the pleasure King James took in Jonson's masque of Gypsies)
215 **sway** swing
229 **Gypsy-ballads** ballads were the most despised of literary forms (as Gypsies were a despised class of people)
246 **jester** King James's court jester, Archy Armstrong, visited Madrid as part of the entourage of Prince Charles and the Duke of Buckingham: on 16 May 1623 Joseph Mead reported a rumour that 'Archy the King's fool, fell there' [in Madrid] 'from an horse and is killed.' (He survived.)

(And there was welcome for his country's sake),
By importunity of some friends, it seems,
Had borrowed from the Gentleman of your Horse
The backing of your mettled Barbary—
On which being mounted, whilst a number gazed
To hear what jests he could perform on horseback,
The headstrong beast (unused to such a rider)
Bears the press of people back before him;
With which throng the lady Clara meeting
Fainted, and there fell down—not bruised, I hope,
But frighted and entranced.

LUIS Ill-destined mischief!

FERNANDO [*to Diego*]
Where have you left her?

DIEGO At your house, my lord.
A servant coming forth, and knowing who
The lady was, conveyed her to a chamber.
A surgeon, too, is sent for.

FERNANDO Had she been my daughter,
My care could not be greater than it shall be
For her recure.

LUIS But if she miscarry,
I am the most unhappy man that lives. *Exit*

FERNANDO
Diego, coast at once about the fields,
And overtake Don Pedro and his wife;
They newly parted from us.

DIEGO I'll run speedily. *Exit*

FERNANDO
A strange mischance!—But what I have, my lord
Francisco, this day noted, I may tell you:
An accident of merriment and wonder.

FRANCISCO
Indeed, my lord?

FERNANDO I have not thoughts enough
About me to imagine what th'event
Can come to. 'Tis, indeed, about my son;
Hereafter you may counsel me.

FRANCISCO Most gladly.—

Enter Luis

How fares the lady?

LUIS Callèd back to life,
But full of sadness.

FERNANDO Talks she nothing?

LUIS Nothing—
For when the women that attend on her
Demanded how she did, she turned about,
And answered with a sigh. When I came near
And by the love I bore her begged a word
Of hope to comfort me in her well-doing,
Before she would reply, from her fair eyes
She greets me with a bracelet of her tears—
Then wished me not to doubt she was 'too well',
Entreats that she may sleep without disturbance
Or company until her father came.
And thus I left her.

FRANCISCO Sir, she's past the worst.
Young maids are oft so troubled.

Enter Pedro and Maria

FERNANDO Here come they
You talk of.—Sir, your daughter, for your comfort,
Is now upon amendment.

MARIA O, my lord,
You speak an angel's voice!

FERNANDO Pray, in and visit her;
I'll follow instantly. *Exit Pedro, Maria*
You shall not part
Without a cup of wine, my lord.

FRANCISCO 'Tis now
Too troublesome a time.—Which way take you,
Don Luis?

LUIS No matter which; for till I hear
My Clara be recovered, I am nothing.—
My lord *corregidor*, I am your servant
For this free entertainment.

FERNANDO You have conquered me
In noble courtesy.

LUIS O, that no art
But love itself can cure a love-sick heart! *Exeunt*

3.3

Clara [*discovered*] *in a chair, Pedro and Maria* [*standing*] *by her*

MARIA
Clara, hope of mine age!

PEDRO Soul of my comfort!
Kill us not both at once. Why dost thou speed
Thine eye in such a progress 'bout these walls?

CLARA Yon large window
Yields some fair prospect. Good my lord, look out
And tell me what you see there.

PEDRO Easy suit.

[*He opens the curtain*]

Clara, it overviews a spacious garden,
Amidst which stands an alabaster fountain,
A goodly one.

CLARA Indeed, my lord!

MARIA Thy griefs grow wild,
And will mislead thy judgement through thy weakness,
If thou obey thy weakness.

CLARA
Who owns these glorious buildings?

247 **his country's** i.e. England's
249 **Gentleman . . . Horse** steward of your stable
250 **backing** saddling and riding
mettled spirited
Barbary famous breed of horse, associated with North Africa
254 **Bears . . . back** forces . . . backward
263 **recure** recovery
miscarry perish
270 **accident** incident
272 **th'event** the outcome
281 **well-doing** well-being
283 **bracelet** little pair (*brace* + diminutive suffix *-let*, like 'ringlet')
290 **upon amendment** improving
298 **free entertainment** liberal hospitality
3.3.3 **progress** (royal) journey

PEDRO
Don Fernando
De Azevedo, the *corregidor*
Of Madrid, a true noble gentleman.

CLARA
May I not see him?

MARIA
See him, Clara? Why?

CLARA [*to Pedro*]
A truly noble gentleman, you said, sir?

PEDRO
I did.
Enter Fernando
Lo, here he comes in person.—
We are, my lord, your servants.

FERNANDO
Good, no compliment.—
Young lady, there attends below a surgeon
Of worthy fame and practice; is't your pleasure
To be his patient?

CLARA [*rising*]
With your favour, sir,
May I impart some few but needful words
Of secrecy to you, to you yourself,
None but yourself?

FERNANDO
You may.

PEDRO
May I not hear 'em?

MARIA
Nor I?

CLARA
O yes.—Pray, sit, my lord.
[*Fernando sits*]

FERNANDO
Say on.

CLARA
You have been married?

FERNANDO
To a wife, young lady,
Who (whiles the heavens did lend her me) was fruitful
In all those virtues which styles woman good.

CLARA
And you had children by her?

FERNANDO
'Had'—'tis true;
Now have but one, a son, and he yet lives.
The daughter (as if in her birth the mother
Had pèrfected the errand she was sent for
Into the world) from that hour took her life
In which the other that gave it her lost hers;
Yet shortly she—unhappily, but fatally—
Perished at sea.

CLARA
Sad story!

FERNANDO
Roderigo,
My son—

CLARA
How is he called, sir?

FERNANDO
Roderigo.
He lives at Salamanca—and I fear
That neither time, persuasions, nor his fortunes
Can draw him thence.

CLARA
My lord, d'ye know this crucifix?
[*She reveals the crucifix*]

FERNANDO
You drive me to amazement! 'Twas my son's,
A legacy bequeathed him from his mother
Upon her deathbed, dear to him as life.
On earth there cannot be another treasure
He values at like rate as he does this.

CLARA
O, then I am a cast-away!

MARIA
How's that?

PEDRO
Alas, she will grow frantic!

CLARA [*to Fernando*]
In my bosom,
Next to my heart, my lord, I have laid up,
In bloody characters, a tale of horror.
[*She gives him a paper, written with blood*]
Pray, read the paper—and if there you find
Aught that concerns a maid undone and miserable,
Made so by one of yours, call back the piety
Of nature to the goodness of a judge,
An upright judge, not of a partial father;
For do not wonder that I live to suffer
Such a full weight of wrongs, but wonder rather
That I have lived to speak them. Thou, great man,
Yet read, read on, and as thou read'st consider
What I have suffered, what thou ought'st to do,
Thine own name, fatherhood, and my dishonour:
Be just as heaven and fate are, that by miracle
Have in my weakness wrought a strange discovery.
Truth copied from my heart is texted there.
Let now my shame be throughly understood;
Sins are heard farthest when they cry in blood.

FERNANDO
True, true, they do not cry but holler here.
This is the trumpet of a soul drowned deep
In the unfathomed seas of matchless sorrows.—
I must lock fast the door. *Exit*

MARIA
I have no words
To call for vengeance.

PEDRO
I am lost in marvel.
Enter Fernando

FERNANDO [*to Clara*]
Sit, pray, sit as you sat before.
[*Clara sits*]
White paper,
This should be innocence; these letters gules
Should be the honest oracles of revenge.
What's beauty but a perfect white and red?
Both here (well mixed) limn truth so beautiful

14 **true** honest, truly
18 **Good** (vocative, 'you good person')
32 **pèrfected** completed
35 **unhappily** by bad luck, sadly
fatally by destiny
40 **d'ye** do you
47 **frantic** insane
49 **characters** letters
54 **not of** not (the goodness or piety) of
60 **Thine** (consider) your (or a line may have been accidentally omitted)
64 **throughly** thoroughly
72 **gules** red (heraldic term)
74 **white and red** (conventional Petrarchan ideal of female complexion)
75 **limn** draw, paint

That to distrust it, as I am a father,
Speaks me as foul as rape hath spoke my son.
'Tis true?

CLARA 'Tis true.

FERNANDO [*kneeling*]
Then mark me how I kneel
Before the high tribunal of your injuries.
Thou too-too-much-wronged maid, scorn not my tears,
For these are tears of rage, not tears of love.—
Thou father of this too-too-much-wronged maid,
Thou mother of her counsels and her cares,
I do not plead for pity to a villain.
O, let him die as he hath lived, dishonourably,
Basely and cursèdly! I plead for pity
To my till-now-untainted blood and honour.
Teach me how I may now be just and cruel—
For henceforth I am childless.

CLARA Pray, sir, rise.
You wrong your place and age.

FERNANDO [*rising*] Point me my grave
In some obscure by-path, where never memory
Nor mention of my name may be found out.

CLARA
My lord, I can weep with ye, nay, weep for ye,
As you for me; your passions are instructions,
And prompt my faltering tongue to beg at least
A noble satisfaction, though not revenge.

FERNANDO
Speak that again.

CLARA Can you procure no balm
To heal a wounded name?

FERNANDO O, thou'rt as fair
In mercy as in beauty! Wilt thou live,
An I'll be thy physician?

CLARA I'll be yours.

FERNANDO Don Pedro, we'll to counsel;
This daughter shall be ours.
[*Fernando sits Clara in the chair*]
Sleep, sleep, young angel!
My care shall wake about thee.

CLARA Heaven is gracious,
And I am eased.

FERNANDO We will be yet more private.
Night curtains o'er the world; soft dreams rest with thee!
The best revenge is to reform our crimes:
Then time crowns sorrows, sorrows sweeten times.
Exeunt

❁

4.1
Incipit Actus Quartus
A shout within. Enter [at one door] the old Father of the Gypsies, Sancho, Soto, Antonio, Carlo, Eugenia, Preciosa, Christiana, and [at another door] Don Juan

OMNES [*to Juan*] Welcome, welcome, welcome!

SOTO More sacks to the mill.

SANCHO More thieves to the sacks.

FATHER Peace!

PRECIOSA [*to Juan*]
I give you now my welcome without noise.

JUAN 'Tis music to me.
He offers to kiss her

OMNES O sir!

SANCHO [*to Juan*] You must not be in your mutton before we are out of our veal.

SOTO [*to Juan*] Stay for vinegar to your oysters; no opening till then.

EUGENIA [*to Juan*]
No kissing till you're sworn.

JUAN Swear me then quickly.
I have brought gold for my admissïon.

FATHER [*taking the gold*]
What you bring, leave—and what you leave, count lost.

SANCHO I brought all my teeth, two are struck out; them I count lost, so must you.

SOTO I brought all my wits; half I count lost, so must you.

JUAN [*to Preciosa*]
To be as you are, I lose father, friends,
Birth, fortunes, all the world.—What will you do
Wi'th' beast I rode on hither?

SANCHO A beast? Is't a mule? Send him to Mullah Crag-a-whee in Barbary.

SOTO [*to Juan*] Is't an ass? Give it to a lawyer, for in Spain they ride upon none else.

JUAN
Kill him by any means—lest, being pursued,
The beast betray me.

SOTO He's a beast betrays any man.

SANCHO Except a bailiff to be pumped.

90 **place** (high) social position
Point appoint
4.1.8 **in** (*a*) partaking of (*b*) sexually penetrating
mutton (*a*) flesh of an adult sheep (*b*) flesh of a sexually active woman (*c*) woman's genitals
9 **are...veal** have finished all our veal (flesh of a calf, tenderer and more desirable than *mutton*, and therefore eaten first)
10 **oysters** (slang for 'female genitals')
21 **Mullah** Islamic spiritual leader (punning on 'mule')
21–2 **Crag-a-whee** (nonsense-name, suggesting mountainous terrain and stage Welsh)
23 **ass** (*a*) donkey (*b*) fool
28 **bailiff** (whom it is legitimate to betray, because they betray others)
pumped (*a*) roughly punished by being dunked (*b*) drained of money or information

JUAN [*to the Gypsies*]
Pray, bury the carcass and the furniture.

SANCHO Do, do; bury the ass's household stuff, and in his skin sew any man that's mad for a woman.

FATHER
Do so then; bury it. [*To Juan*] Now to your oath.

EUGENIA All things are ready.

FATHER
Thy best hand lay on this turf of grass.
There thy heart lies; vow not to pass
From us two years for sun nor snow,
For hill nor dale, howe'er winds blow.
Vow the hard earth to be thy bed
With her green cushions under thy head,
Flow'r banks or moss to be thy board,
Water thy wine—

SANCHO And drink like a lord.

OMNES [*sing*]
Kings can have but coronations;
We are as proud of Gypsy-fashions.
Dance, sing, and in a well-mixed border
Close this new brother of our order.

FATHER
What we get, with us come share;
You to get must vow to care—
Nor strike Gypsy, nor stand by
When strangers strike, but fight or die.
Our Gypsy-wenches are not common;
You must not kiss a fellow's leman—
Nor to your own (for one you must)
In songs send errands of base lust.

OMNES [*sing*]
Dance, sing, and in a well-mixed border
Close this new brother of our order.

JUAN
On this turf of grass I vow
Your laws to keep, your laws allow.

OMNES A Gypsy! a Gypsy! a Gypsy!

EUGENIA
Now choose what maid has yet no mate:
She's yours.

JUAN Here then fix I my fate.

[*He*] *offers to kiss* [*Preciosa*]

SANCHO Again fall to before you ha' washed?

SOTO Your nose in the manger before the oats are measured, jade so hungry?

FATHER
Set foot to foot; those garlands hold.
Teach him how. Now mark what more is told.
By cross arms (the lover's sign),
Vow—as these flowers themselves entwine,
Of April's wealth building a throne
Round—so your love to one or none.
By those touches of your feet,
You must each night embracing meet,
Chaste, howe'er disjoined by day;
You the sun with her must play,
She to you the marigold,
To none but you her leaves unfold.
Wake she or sleep, your eyes so charm,
Want, woe, nor weather do her harm.

CARLO
This is your market now of kisses:
Buy and sell free each other blisses.

JUAN Most willingly.
[*Juan and Preciosa kiss*]

OMNES [*sing*]
Holidays, high days, Gypsy fairs,
When kisses are fairings, and hearts meet in pairs.

FATHER [*to Juan*]
All ceremonies end here. Welcome, brother Gypsy!

SANCHO And the better to instruct thee, mark what a brave life 'tis all the year long.

Song

Brave Don, cast your eyes
On our Gypsy fashions:
In our antic hay-de-guys
We go beyond all nations.
Plump Dutch
At us grutch;
So do English, so do French.
He that lopes
On the ropes,
Show me such another wrench.

29 **furniture** trappings (but also 'household stuff')
30–1 **in ... woman** (in contrast to the folktale in which a nagging wife is sown up inside an animal's skin)
36 **for** despite
40 **board** dinner table
42 **but** only
44 **well-mixed** gender-mixing, combining men and women
45 **Close** enclose
brother fraternal member
order monastic or aristocratic society
51 **leman** bedfellow
52 **one you must** you must have (only) one wench
59 **what** whatever
maid young woman, virgin
61 **fall to** (*a*) start eating (*b*) lie down for sex
62 **nose** (slang for 'penis')
manger (*a*) trough (*b*) sumptuous dish
oats (punning on 'oaths')
63 **jade** good-for-nothing (*a*) horse (*b*) person
66 **cross** crossed, crossing (conventional lover's gesture)
73 **play** act the part of
74 **marigold** (which opens when the sun rises, and is hence an emblem of fidelity)
77 **Want** dearth, poverty
82 **fairings** presents bought at a fair
88 **antic** grotesque, comic (but also 'ancient')
hay-de-guys (a rustic dance)
91 **grutch** murmur, grudge
93–4 **He ... ropes** the rope-dancer (popular entertainment, often at the rival Hope Theatre)
93 **lopes** leaps
95 **wrench** twist of the torso (a dancer's or an acrobat's)

We no camels have to show,
  Nor elephant with grout head—
We can dance; he cannot go,
  Because the beast is corn-fed—
    No blind bears
    Shedding tears
For a collier's whipping,
    Apes nor dogs
    Quick as frogs
Over cudgels skipping.

Jack-in-boxes, nor decoys,
  Puppets, nor such poor things—
Nor are we those roaring boys
  That cozen fools with gilt rings;
    For an ocean,
    No such motion
As the city Nineveh.
    Dancing, singing,
    And fine ringing:
You these sports shall hear and see.

Come now, what shall his name be?

PRECIOSA
His name shall now be Andrew.—Friend Andrew, mark me:
Two years I am to try you. Prove fine gold,
The uncracked diamond of my faith shall hold.

JUAN
My vows are rocks of adamant.

PRECIOSA
Two years you are to try me: black when I turn,
May I meet youth and want, old age and scorn!

JUAN
Kings' diadems shall not buy thee.

CARLO
Do you think
You can endure the life, and love it?

JUAN
As usurers doat upon their treasure.

SOTO
But when your face shall be tanned
Like a sailor's work-a-day hand—

SANCHO
When your feet shall be galled
And your noddle be mauled—

SOTO
When the woods you must forage,
And not meet with poor pease-porridge—

SANCHO
Be all to-bedabbled, yet lie in no sheet—

SOTO
With winter's frost, hail, snow, and sleet,
What life will you say it is then?

JUAN As now, the sweetest.

DIEGO (*within*) Away! Away! The *corregidor* has sent for you.

SANCHO (*sings*)
Hence merrily fine to get money!
Dry are the fields, the banks are sunny,
Silver is sweeter far than honey.

Hence bravely, boys! Fly like swallows!
We for our conies must get mallows.
Who loves not his dell, let him die at the gallows.

Hence, bonny girls! Foot it trimly!
Smug up your beetle-brows; none look grimly.
To show a pretty foot, O 'tis seemly!

Smug up your beetle-brows; none look grimly.
To show a pretty foot, O 'tis seemly!

Exeunt [*dancing*]

Enter Cardochia, stays Soto

CARDOCHIA
Do you hear—you, Gypsy, Gypsy?

SOTO
Me?

CARDOCHIA
There's a young Gypsy newly entertained;
Sweet Gypsy, call him back for one two-words,
And here's a jewel for thee.

96–7 **camels ... elephant** (exotic animals people would pay to see)
97 **grout** great
98 **go** walk
99 **corn-fed** i.e. overfed, overweight
100 **blind bears** (alluding to the tormenting of captive bears in bear-baiting arenas)
102 **For ... whipping** as a result of being whipped by a coal miner
105 **cudgels** (the trainer's stick, over which animals were taught to jump)
106 **decoys** swindlers
107 **Puppets** (lower class popular entertainments)
108 **roaring boys** noisy bullies
109 **cozen** cheat
gilt covered with gold paint (which the customer takes for solid gold)
111 **motion** puppet show
112 **Nineveh** biblical city, whose destruction was a popular theme for puppet shows (rhymes with 'see')
114 **ringing** music produced by bells (here, worn on the bodies of dancers)
117 **Andrew** (the patron saint of Scotland, and hence a popular Scots name; like his father, Prince Charles was born in Scotland)
118 **try** test
fine high quality
119 **faith** sexual fidelity (but perhaps suggesting 'religion', since the Infanta's Catholicism was a major political issue)
121 **black** corrupt, tarnished (but also suggesting the traditional racial stereotyping of Gypsy and Spanish complexions)
129 **noddle** head
131 **pease-porridge** split yellow peas boiled into a pudding (poor man's diet)
132 **to-bedabbled** wet with dirty liquid
138 **fine** finely
142 **conies** (*a*) rabbits (*b*) lovers (pronounced 'cunnies', slang for 'cunts')
mallows a common wild herb (poor man's diet)
143 **dell** (*a*) young unmarried vagrant female, sexually available wench (*b*) natural hollow, wooded vale
144 **bonny** pretty, cheerful
145 **Smug** spruce, smarten
beetle-brows conspicuously dark, large, or sullen eyebrows
146 **show ... foot** (usually considered indecorous exhibitionism)
seemly (*a*) handsome (*b*) decorous
150 **entertained** welcomed
151 **two-words** i.e. brief conversation

[She gives Soto a jewel]
SOTO I'll send him.
CARDOCHIA What's his name?
SOTO Andrew. *Exit*
CARDOCHIA
A very handsome fellow. I've seen courtiers
Jet up and down in their full bravery,
Yet here's a Gypsy worth a drove of 'em.
Enter Don Juan
JUAN
With me, sweetheart?
CARDOCHIA Your name is Andrew?
JUAN Yes.
CARDOCHIA
You can tell fortunes, Andrew?
JUAN I could once,
But now I've lost that knowledge; I'm in haste,
And cannot stay to tell you yours.
CARDOCHIA I cannot
Tell yours then—and 'cause you're in haste, I'm quick.
I am a maid—
JUAN So, so, a maid quick?
CARDOCHIA Juana Cardochia,
That's mine own name. I am my mother's heir
Here to this house, and two more.
JUAN I buy no lands.
CARDOCHIA
They shall be given you, with some plate and money,
And free possession during life of me,
So the match like you—for so well I love you
That I, in pity of this trade of Gypsying
(Being base, idle, and slavish), offer you
A state to settle you, my youth and beauty,
(Desired by some brave Spaniards), so I may call you
My husband. Shall I, Andrew?
JUAN 'Las, pretty soul,
Better stars guide you! May that hand of Cupid
Ache, ever shot this arrow at your heart!
Sticks there one such indeed?
CARDOCHIA I would there did not,
Since you'll not pluck it out.
JUAN Good sweet, I cannot.
For marriage, 'tis a law amongst us Gypsies
We match in our own tribes. For me to wear you,
I should but wear you out.
CARDOCHIA I do not care.
Wear what you can out, all my life, my wealth:
Ruin me, so you lend me but your love,
A little of your love!
JUAN Would I could give it,
For you are worth a world of better men
For your free noble mind! All my best wishes
Stay with you; I must hence.
CARDOCHIA Wear for my sake
This jewel.
[She offers him a necklace]
JUAN I'll not rob you, I'll take nothing.
CARDOCHIA
Wear it about your neck but one poor moon;
If in that time your eye be as 'tis now,
Send my jewel home again, and (I protest)
I'll ne'er more think on you. Deny not this.
Put it about your neck.
JUAN *[putting it on]* Well then, 'tis done.
CARDOCHIA
And vow to keep it there.
JUAN By all the goodness
I wish attend your fortunes, I do vow it. *Exit*
CARDOCHIA
Scorned! Thou hast tempered poison to kill me
Thyself shall drink. Since I cannot enjoy thee,
My revenge shall.
Enter Diego
DIEGO Where are the Gypsies?
CARDOCHIA Gone.
Diego, do you love me?
DIEGO Love thee, Juanna?
Is my life mine? It is but mine so long
As it shall do thee service.
CARDOCHIA
There's a young Gypsy newly entertained.
DIEGO
A handsome rascal. Marry, what of him?
CARDOCHIA
That slave in obscene language courted me,
Drew *reals* out, and would have bought my body,
Diego, from thee.
DIEGO
Is he so itchy? By my troth, I'll cure him.

155 **Jet** strut
bravery bravado, finery
156 **drove** herd
163 **maid quick** 'pregnant virgin'
166 **house** (*a*) dwelling (*b*) inn
167 **plate** (*a*) bullion (*b*) gold or silver utensils
168 **free** unlimited freehold for life (legal terminology, but here with added sexual referent)
169 **So** if
172 **state** estate
174 **'Las** alas
177 **Sticks...such** does one of those stick in your heart
179–80 **marriage...tribes** Those who objected to the proposed Spanish Match felt that Protestants should marry Protestants.
180 **wear** (*a*) possess sexually (*b*) damage, waste, devalue (*c*) exhaust physically
182 **what** whatever (suggesting an explicitly physical, sexual friction)
183 **Ruin** (*a*) impoverish (*b*) make disrespectable sexually and socially
but just, only
184 **give** (in contrast to her request that he merely 'lend')
189 **moon** month
196 **Thou** (shifting immediately from 'you', as an expression of her change of attitude)
tempered mixed
197 **Thyself** (which) you yourself
enjoy (*a*) take pleasure in (*b*) possess sexually, make use of
204 **slave** contemptible lower class villain
205 ***reals*** Spanish gold coins

[He draws his sword]

CARDOCHIA
Thou shalt not touch the villain; I'll spin his fate.
Woman strikes sure, fall the blow ne'er so late.

DIEGO
Strike on since: by'r Lady, thou wilt be a striker.
Exeunt

4.2 *Enter Fernando, Francisco, Pedro, and Luis*

FERNANDO See, Don Luis; an arm,
The strongest arm in Spain, to the full length
Is stretched to pluck old Count Alvarez home
From his sad banishment.

LUIS With longing eyes,
My lord, I expect the man. Your lordship's pardon:
Some business calls me from you.

FERNANDO Prithee, Don Luis,
Unless th'occasion be too violent,
Stay and be merry with us. All the Gypsies
Will be here presently.

LUIS I will attend your lordship
Before their sports be done.

FERNANDO Be your own carver.
Exit Luis
[To Francisco] Not yet shake off these fetters? I see a son
Is heavy when a father carries him
On his old heart.

FRANCISCO Could I set up my rest
That he were lost or taken prisoner,
I could hold truce with sorrow; but to have him
Vanish I know not how, gone none knows whither,
'Tis that mads me.

PEDRO You said he sent a letter.

FRANCISCO
A letter? A mere riddle: he's 'gone to seek
His fortune in the wars'. What wars have we?
Suppose we had, goes any man to th' field
Naked, unfurnished both of arms and money?

FERNANDO
Come, come, he's gone a-wenching. We in our youth
Ran the self-same bias.

Enter Diego

DIEGO The Gypsies, my lord, are come.

FERNANDO Are they? Let them enter. *Exit Diego*
My lord De Cortes, send for your wife and daughter.
Good company is good physic: take the pains
To seat yourselves in my great chamber.
Exit Pedro [with Francisco]

Enter the old Father of the Gypsies, Don Juan, Roderigo [wearing a visor], Antonio, Carlo, Eugenia, Preciosa, Christiana, Sancho, and Soto

See, they are here. *[To Gypsies]* What's your number?

SANCHO The figure of nine casts us all up, my lord.

FERNANDO
Nine? Let me see—you are ten, sure.

SOTO *[pointing to Roderigo]* That's our poet; he stands for a cipher.

FERNANDO
Ciphers make numbers.—What plays have you?

FATHER Five or six, my lord.

FERNANDO It's well, so many already.

SOTO We are promised a very merry tragedy, if all hit right, of Cobby Nobby.

FERNANDO
So, so, a 'merry tragedy'! There is a way
Which the Italians and the Frenchmen use:
That is, on a word given, or some slight plot,
The actors will extempore fashion out
Scenes neat and witty.

FATHER We can do that, my lord:
Please you bestow the subject.

FERNANDO Can you? *[To Roderigo]* Come hither,
You master poet. To save you a labour,
Look you, against your coming I projected
This comic passage:
[He gives Roderigo a paper]
your drama; that's the scene.

RODERIGO Ay, ay, my lord.

FERNANDO I lay't in our own country, Spain.

RODERIGO 'Tis best so.

FERNANDO
Here's a brave part for this old Gypsy; look you,
The father. Read the plot: this young she-Gypsy,
This lady. Now the son—play him yourself.

208 **spin** (comparing herself to the three sisters of classical mythology, who spun each man's fate)
209 **strikes** (playing on the sense 'fornicates')
210 **since** then (= sithence), but perhaps punning on 'sins'
by'r Lady by our lady, the Virgin Mary
wilt are determined or destined to
4.2.10 **Be...carver** suit yourself (proverbial)
11 **fetters** chains (of grief)
12 **carries** (like a pregnant mother)
13 **set...rest** be convinced enough to bet my final reserves (metaphor from card games)
19 **What...we** (an ironic comment, in the context of the ongoing Thirty Years War; England was officially still at peace)
20 **field** battlefield
21 **Naked** without accessories
arms armour, weapons
22 **a-wenching** chasing women
23 **Ran...bias** followed the same curving or irregular path (metaphor from bowling)
27 **physic** medicine
28 **great chamber** large formal room
30 **figure of** numeral
casts us all up sums us up (but probably punning on 'vomits us')
32–3 **poet...cipher** playwright...nonentity
34 **Ciphers...numbers** zeros, added to another numeral, greatly increase the number
38 **Cobby Nobby** (nonsense name, compounded of words with low-class associations: *cob*, *nob*)
40–3 **Italians...witty** (referring to *commedia dell'arte*)
41 **plot** outline, scenario (technical theatrical term for list of entrances and exits)
46 **against** anticipating
49 **lay't** set it (the play)

RODERIGO
My lord, I am no player.
FERNANDO Pray, at this time
(The plot being full), to please my noble friends
(Because your brains must into theirs put language),
Act thou the son's part. I'll reward your pains.
RODERIGO
Protest, my lord—
FERNANDO Nay, nay, shake off protesting.
When I was young, sir, I have played myself.
SANCHO Yourself, my lord? You were but a poor company then.
FERNANDO
Yet full enough, honest fellow.—Will you do it?
RODERIGO I'll venture.
FERNANDO
I thank you. [*To Father*] Let this father be a don
Of a brave spirit. Old Gypsy, observe me.
FATHER Yes, my lord.
FERNANDO
Play him up high—not like a pantaloon,
But hotly, nobly, checking this his son,
Whom make a very rake-hell, a debauched fellow.—
This point, I think, will show well.
RODERIGO This of the picture?
It will indeed, my lord.
SANCHO My lord, what part play I?
FERNANDO What parts dost use to play?
SANCHO If your lordship has ever a coxcomb, I think I could fit you.
FERNANDO I thank your coxcombship.
SOTO Put a coxcomb upon a lord!
FERNANDO
There are parts to serve you all. Go, go, make ready,
And call for what you want. *Exit*
FATHER [*to Roderigo*]
Give me the plot. Our wits are put to trial.
What's the son's name? 'Lorenzo': that's your part.
Look only you to that; these I'll dispose.
'Old Don Avero', mine. 'Hialdo, Lollio,
Two servants': [*to Sancho and Soto*] you for them.
SANCHO
One of the foolish knaves give me.
I'll be Hialdo.
SOTO And I, Lollio.
SANCHO Is there a banquet in the play? We may call for what we will.
RODERIGO Yes, here is a banquet.
SANCHO I'll go then and bespeak an ocean of sweetmeats, marmalade, and custards.
FATHER Make haste to know what you must do.
SANCHO Do? Call for enough—and when my belly is full, fill my pockets.
SOTO To a banquet there must be wine. Fortune's a scurvy whore, if she makes not my head sound like a rattle and my heels dance the canaries.
FATHER
So, so, dispatch, whilst we employ our brains
To set things off to th' life.
RODERIGO I'll be straight with you.
[*Exeunt all except Roderigo*]
Why does my father put this trick on me?
Spies he me through my visor? If he does,
He's not the king of Spain, and 'tis no treason.
If his invention jet upon a stage,
Why should not I use action? 'A debauched fellow'!
'A very rake-hell'! This reflects on me—
And I'll retort it. Grown a poet, father?
No matter in what strain your play must run,
But I shall fit you for a roaring son. *Exit*

Enter Francisco, Pedro, Fernando, Diego, Maria, and Clara. Flourish 4.3

FERNANDO
Come, ladies, take your places.—This' their music?
'Tis very handsome. O, I wish this room

54 **player** actor
55 **plot** roster of roles
59 **played myself** personally acted (but taken as 'impersonated myself' or 'acted alone, all by myself')
60 **company** acting troupe
62 **Yet full** but wealthy, satisfactory
63 **venture** try, take the risk
64 **don** aristocrat
67 **pantaloon** skinny, bespectacled, foolish old man in *commedia dell'arte*
68 **hotly** angrily
checking rebuking
69 **rake-hell** scoundrel
70 **point** detail
74 **coxcomb** fool, clown
75 **fit** satisfy
77 **lord** (Sancho)
79 **want** lack, need
87 **banquet** feast (consisting mostly of desserts)
88 **will** like, want
90 **bespeak** reserve, order in advance
sweetmeats goodies
97 **canaries** Spanish dance, allegedly derived from Canary islanders (but punning on the name of the Spanish wine)
99 **straight** immediately
101 **visor** mask, disguise (as an Italian actor)
102 **'tis no treason** Roderigo's disguise, or his lying to his father, is not illegal (but perhaps also linked to next line, since it would be illegal to represent the king of Spain on stage)
103 **jet** strut
104 **action** theatrical gestures
105 **reflects on** (*a*) represents (*b*) insults
106 **retort** repay, retaliate
poet (usually associated with youth, and inappropriate for a 'father' and aristocrat; possibly alluding to James I's verses, in February 1623, replying to anonymous verse criticisms, and his sonnet in March 1623 'of Jack and Tom')
107 **strain** (*a*) tone (*b*) melody (*c*) sophistry (*d*) offspring, lineage (*e*) kind of person
play (*a*) stage play (*b*) playing on a musical instrument (*c*) game (*d*) sexual performance
108 **roaring son** playing on 'roaring boy' (urban adolescent behaving outrageously) and on 'roaring' in contrast to music
4.3.0.2 ***Flourish*** (trumpet call, signalling that a theatrical performance is about to begin)
1 **This'** this is

Were fretted but with gold works, noble friends,
As are to you my welcomes!
Flourish
Begin there, masters!

SANCHO (*within*) Presently, my lord; we want but a cold capon for a property.

FERNANDO
Call, call for one!
[*Flourish*]
Now they begin.

Enter Sancho (the Prologue)

SANCHO
Both short and sweet, some say, is best.
We will not only be sweet, but short.
Take you pepper in the nose, you mar our sport.

FERNANDO By no means pepper.

SANCHO
Of your love measure us forth but one span.
We do, though not the best, the best we can. *Exit*

FERNANDO A good honest Gypsy!

Enter the old Father of the Gypsies [as Don Avero] and Soto [as Lollio]

FATHER [*as Avero*] Slave, where's my son Lorenzo?

SOTO [*as Lollio*] I have sought him, my lord, in all four elements: in earth (my shoes are full of gravel), in water (I drop at nose with sweating), in air (wheresoever I heard noise of fiddlers, or the wide mouths of gallon pots roaring), and in fire (what chimney soever I saw smoking with good cheer—for my master's dinner, as I was in hope).

FATHER [*as Avero*]
Not yet come home? Before on this old tree
Shall grow a branch so blasted, I'll hew it off,
And bury it at my foot! Didst thou inquire
At my brother's?

SOTO [*as Lollio*] At your sister's.

FATHER [*as Avero*]
At my wife's father's?

SOTO [*as Lollio*] At your uncle's mother's.
No such sheep has broke through their hedge; no such calf as your son sucks or bleats in their ground.

FATHER [*as Avero*]
I am unblessed to have but one son only,
One staff to bear my age up, one taper left
To light me to my grave, and that burns dimly;
That leaves me darkling hid in clouds of woe.
He that should prop me is mine overthrow.

FERNANDO
Well done, old fellow!—Is't not?

OMNES Yes, yes, my lord.

SOTO [*as Lollio*] Here comes his man Hialdo.

Enter Sancho [as Hialdo]

FATHER [*as Avero, to Sancho*]
Where's the prodigal your master, sirrah?

SANCHO [*as Hialdo*] Eating acorns amongst swine, draff amongst hogs, and gnawing bones amongst dogs. He's lost all his money at dice, his wits with his money, and his honesty with both—for he bumfiddles me, makes the drawers curvet, pitches the plate over the bar, scores up the vintner's name in the Ram-head, flirts his wife under the nose—
And bids you, with 'a pox', send him more money.

FATHER [*as Avero*]
Art thou one of his curs to bite me too?
To nail thee to the earth were to do justice.

SANCHO [*as Hialdo*]
Here comes Bucephalus, my prancing master.
Nail me now who dares.

3 **fretted** decorated (used of musical elaboration and architectural ornament), but playing on the sense 'irritated'
but only
gold works (*a*) architectural ornamentation with gold leaf (*b*) golden actions, superb literary or musical compositions, 'good works'
noble (perhaps punning on the 'gold' coin)
4 **masters** skilled workmen, masters of their trade
5 ***within*** (perhaps poking his head out through a curtain or stage window)
Presently immediately
want but lack only
6 **capon** (cooked castrated) chicken
property prop
7.2 ***Prologue*** (conventionally dressed in a long black velvet cloak)
8 **short and sweet** (proverbial)
10 **Take you** if you take
pepper ... nose offence (proverbial)
12 **span** hand's length, small amount (but 'hand' perhaps alluding to applause)
16–17 **four elements** (earth, water, air, fire: regarded as the basic materials from which everything else was formed)
18 **drop at nose** have a runny nose
19 **noise** (*a*) cacophonous din (*b*) rumour, talk (*c*) company of musicians
19–20 **gallon pots** drinking vessels so large they can hold a gallon of liquid
21 **cheer** food
28 **uncle's mother's** (a ridiculous way of saying) 'grandmother's'
29 **sheep** (*a*) domesticated sheep (*b*) feckless person (*c*) lost sheep, lost soul
30 **calf** (*a*) infant cow (*b*) fool
sucks (*a*) nourishes itself at its mother's teat (*b*) smokes tobacco
bleats (*a*) makes a sheep's cry (*b*) talks or sings with a high-pitched voice
32 **staff** crutch, support
taper candle
34 **darkling** in the dark, getting dark
38–9 **prodigal ... swine** (alluding to the parable of the Prodigal Son at Luke 15:11–32)
39 **swine** (*a*) pigs (*b*) lecherous degraded persons
39–40 **draff ... hogs** (proverbial)
39 **draff** refuse
40 **hogs** (*a*) castrated pigs intended for early slaughter (*b*) coarse gluttonous filthy persons
dogs (*a*) canines (*b*) despicable cowardly persons
42 **bumfiddles** plays on my buttocks (beats, cheats, or sodomizes)
43 **drawers** employees who serve wine in a tavern
curvet leap like horses
pitches the plate throws the tableware (but probably also 'ejaculates')
43–4 **scores up** writes, etches (but playing on 'marks the tab, records the bill')
44 **Ram-head** name of a tavern, or a room in one (but punning on the sense 'cuckold' or 'list of cuckolds')
flirts jerks, strikes, insults
46 **with 'a pox'** (*a*) swearing an oath (*b*) with venereal disease
47 **curs** dogs
49 **Bucephalus** (famous horse of Alexander the Great)

Enter Roderigo [as Lorenzo]

RODERIGO [*as Lorenzo*] I sit like an owl in the ivy-bush of a tavern. 'Swounds, Hialdo, I have drawn red wine from the vintner's own hogshead.

SANCHO [*as Hialdo, pointing to the others*]
Here's two more; pierce them too.

RODERIGO [*as Lorenzo, to Avero*]
Old Don, whom I call father: am I thy son?
If I be, flesh me with gold, fat me with silver!
Had I Spain in this hand, and Portugal in this,
Puff it should fly.—Where's the money I sent for?
[*Aside*] I'll tickle you for a rake-hell!

SANCHO [*as Hialdo*]
Not a *mar'vedi*.

FATHER [*as Avero*]
Thou shalt have none of me.

SOTO [*as Lollio, to Avero*] Hold his nose to the grindstone, my lord.

RODERIGO [*as Lorenzo, to Avero*]
I shall have none?

FATHER [*as Avero, to Lollio*]
Charge me a case of pistols.
What I have built I'll ruin. Shall I suffer
A slave to set his foot upon my heart?
A son? A barbarous villain! Or if heaven save thee
Now from my justice, yet my curse pursues thee.

RODERIGO [*as Lorenzo*] Hialdo, carbonado thou the old rogue my father.

SANCHO [*as Hialdo*] Whilst you slice into collops the rusty gammon his man there.

RODERIGO [*as Lorenzo, to Avero*] No money? Can taverns stand without 'anon, anon'? fiddlers live without scraping? taffeta girls look plump without pampering? If you will not lard me with money,
Give me a ship, furnish me to sea.

FATHER [*as Avero*]
To have thee hanged for piracy?

SANCHO [*as Hialdo*] Trim, tram, hang master, hang man!

RODERIGO [*as Lorenzo*] Then send me to the West Indies, buy me some office there.

FATHER [*as Avero*]
To have thy throat cut for thy quarrelling?

RODERIGO [*as Lorenzo*] Else send me and my ningle Hialdo to the wars.

SANCHO [*as Hialdo*] A match! We'll fight dog, fight bear.

Enter Antonio [as Hernando]

FATHER [*as Avero*]
O dear Hernando, welcome!—Clap wings to your heels,
And pray my worthy friends bestow upon me
Their present visitation.— [*Exeunt Soto and Sancho*]

ANTONIO [*as Hernando*]
Lorenzo, see the anger of a father:
Although it be as loud and quick as thunder,
Yet 'tis done instantly. Cast off thy wildness.

FATHER [*as Avero, to Lorenzo*]
Be mine, be mine—for I to call thee home
Have (with my honoured friend here, Don Hernando)
Provided thee a wife.

RODERIGO [*as Lorenzo*] A wife! Is she handsome? Is she rich? Is she fair? Is she witty? Is she honest?—Hang honesty!—Has she a sweet face, cherry cheek, strawberry lip, white skin, dainty eye, pretty foot, delicate legs?—as there's a girl now.

ANTONIO [*as Hernando*]
It is a creature both for birth and fortunes,
And for most excellent graces of the mind,
Few like her are in Spain.

RODERIGO [*as Lorenzo*] When shall I see her?
Now, father, pray take your curse off.

FATHER [*as Avero*] I do. The lady
Lives from Madrid very near fourteen leagues,
But thou shalt see her picture.

RODERIGO [*as Lorenzo*] That, that! Most ladies in these days are but very fine pictures.

Enter Carlo, Don Juan, Eugenia, Preciosa, Christiana [as friends of Avero], Sancho and Soto [as Hialdo and Lollio]

FATHER [*as Avero*]
Ladies, to you first, welcome.—My lords (Alonzo,
And you, worthy marquis), thanks for these honours.—
Away, you! [*Exeunt Sancho and Soto*]
To th' cause now of this meeting. My son Lorenzo
(Whose wildness you all know) comes now to th' lure,

51 **sit ... ivy-bush** resemble a painted owl in a tavern sign (proverbial)
owl emblematic of (*a*) wisdom (*b*) staying up all night
52 **'Swounds** by God's wounds (a particularly profane oath, appropriate to a 'rake-hell')
red wine (playing on the sense 'blood')
53 **hogshead** (*a*) large wine cask (*b*) head of a piggish person
59 **tickle** (*a*) amuse (*b*) beat
for as
61 **Hold ... grindstone** (proverbial)
63 **Charge** load
case pair
68 **carbonado** cut into slices for broiling
70 **collops** pieces
70–1 **rusty gammon** smoked ham
73 **stand** remain in business
'anon, anon' 'just a second' (conventional reply of waiters to impatient customers)
74 **taffeta girls** well-dressed prostitutes
75 **lard** fatten, enrich
78 **Trim ... man** (playing on the proverb 'Trim, tram, like master like man')
79 **West Indies** (Spanish colonies)
82 **Else** otherwise
ningle catamite, passive homosexual partner
84 **fight ... bear** (cry of spectators at bear-baiting arenas)
85 **Clap ... heels** fly (like Mercury, messenger of the gods)
90 **done** finished, extinguished
95 **fair** light-skinned, blonde
honest chaste
98 **as ... girl** (referring to Clara, in the onstage audience)
105–6 **ladies ... pictures** (because they use so much make-up, which was called 'painting')
109 **Away, you** get out (presumably because they are clowning around)
111 **comes ... lure** returns home (like a trained hawk)

Sits gently, has called home his wandering thoughts,
And now will marry.

PRECIOSA A good wife fate send him!

EUGENIA
One staid may settle him.

RODERIGO [*as Lorenzo, to Avero*]
Fly to the mark, sir.
Show me the wench, or her face, or any thing
I may know 'tis a woman fit for me.

FATHER [*as Avero*]
She is not here herself, but here's her picture.
[He draws the curtain, and shows] a picture

FERNANDO
My lord de Cárcamo, pray, observe this.

FRANCISCO
I do, attentively.—Don Pedro, mark it.
Enter Soto

SOTO [*aside to Juan*]
If you ha' done your part, yonder's a wench
Would ha' a bout with you. *Exit*

JUAN [*aside*] Me? *Exit*

DIEGO [*aside*] A wench? *Exit*

FATHER [*as Avero, to Lorenzo*]
Why stand you staring at it? How do you like her?

RODERIGO [*as Lorenzo*]
Are you in earnest?

FATHER [*as Avero*] Marry, sir, in earnest.

RODERIGO [*as Lorenzo*]
'Snails, I am not so hungry after flesh
To make the devil a cuckold.

ANTONIO [*as Hernando*]
Look not upon the face, but on the goodness
That dwells within her.

RODERIGO [*as Lorenzo*] Set fire on the tenement!

FATHER [*as Avero*] She's rich; nobly descended.

RODERIGO [*as Lorenzo*] Did ever nobility look so scurvily?

FATHER [*as Avero*]
I'm sunk in fortunes; she may raise us both.

RODERIGO [*as Lorenzo*] Sink, let her, to her grannam! Marry a witch? Have you fetched a wife for me out of Lapland? An old midwife in a velvet hat were a goddess to this. That, a red lip?

PRECIOSA There's a red nose.

RODERIGO [*as Lorenzo*] That, a yellow hair?

EUGENIA Why, her teeth may be yellow.

RODERIGO [*as Lorenzo*] Where's the full eye?

CHRISTIANA She has full blubber cheeks.

FATHER [*as Avero, to Lorenzo*]
Set up thy rest: her marriest thou, or none.

RODERIGO [*as Lorenzo*] None then: were all the water in the world one sea, all kingdoms one mountain, I would climb on all four up to the top of that hill, and headlong hurl myself into that abyss of waves, ere I would touch the skin of such rough haberdine—foh! The breath of her picture stinks hither.

A noise within. Enter Don Juan, Diego [bleeding], Cardochia, Sancho, and Soto, [all] in a hurry

FERNANDO What tumult's this?

SANCHO *and* SOTO Murder, murder, murder! One of our Gypsies is in danger of hanging, hanging!

PEDRO
Who is hurt?

DIEGO 'Tis I, my lord, stabbed by this Gypsy.

JUAN
He struck me first, and I'll not take a blow
From any Spaniard breathing.

PEDRO Are you so brave?

FERNANDO [*to Gypsies*]
Break up your play.—Lock all the doors.

DIEGO I faint, my lord.

FRANCISCO
Have him to a surgeon.— [*Exeunt some with Diego*]
How fell they out?

CARDOCHIA
Faith, my good lord, these Gypsies when they lodged
At my house, I'd a jewel from my pocket
Stolen by this villain.

JUAN 'Tis most false, my lords.
Her own hands gave it me.

PRECIOSA She that calls him villain,
Or says he stole—

FERNANDO Hoyday! We hear your scolding.

CARDOCHIA
And the hurt gentleman, finding it in his bosom,
For that he stabbed him.

FERNANDO Hence with all the Gypsies!

PEDRO
Ruffians and thieves—to prison with 'em all!

FATHER
My lord, we'll leave engagements, in plate and money,
For all our safe forthcomings. Punish not all
For one's offence. We'll prove ourselves no thieves.

SANCHO [*aside*] O Soto, I make buttons!

114 **Fly ... mark** get to the point (like an arrow shot at a target)
115 **any thing** (sexually suggestive)
116 I (so that) I
120 **done your part** finished your role
121 **bout** sexual wrestle
123 **in earnest** serious
124 **'Snails** by God's nails (a strong oath, also relevant to the devil, often represented with cloven feet)
125 **devil a cuckold** (implying that the woman in the picture is a fit wife only for the devil—who, already having horns, is a natural cuckold)
128 **Set ... tenement** burn the house down (playing on 'dwells')
132 **Sink** i.e. down to hell
133 **witch** (traditionally hideously ugly)
Lapland (traditionally associated with witches)
140 **blubber** fat, swollen
141 **Set ... rest** make your final bid
146 **haberdine** dried salted fish
foh (exclamation of nausea or disgust)
153 **brave** defiant, insolent
161 **bosom** breast pocket
162 **he** Juan
164 **engagements** security, bail
165 **forthcomings** appearance (at trial)
167 **make buttons** am so afraid my 'buttocks go a twitter-twatter'

SOTO [*aside*] Would I could make some, and leave this trade!

FERNANDO
Iron him then, let the rest go free.—But stir not one foot
Out of Madrid. Bring you in your witness.
[*Exeunt at one door Don Juan to prison, and at another door the old Father of the Gypsies, Antonio, Carlo, Eugenia, Preciosa, Christiana*]

SOTO [*aside to Sancho*] Prick him with a pin, or pinch him by the elbow—anything.

SANCHO My lord Don Pedro, I am your ward. We have spent a little money to get a horrible deal of wit, and now I am weary on't.

PEDRO
My runaways turned jugglers, fortune-tellers?

SOTO No great fortunes.

FERNANDO
To prison with 'em both! A gentleman, play the ass?

SANCHO If all gentlemen that play the ass should to prison, you must widen your jails.—Come, Soto, I scorn to beg. Set thy foot to mine, and kick at shackles.

FERNANDO So, so—away with 'em!

SOTO Send all our company after, and we'll play there, and be as merry as you here.
Exeunt [*Sancho and Soto to prison*]

FERNANDO
Our comedy turned tragical!—Please you, lords, walk.
This actor here and I must change a word,
And I come to you.

OMNES Well, my lord, your pleasure.
Exeunt. [*Manent Fernando and Roderigo*]

FERNANDO
Why? Couldst thou think in any base disguise
To blind my sight? Fathers have eagles' eyes.
But pray, sir, why was this done? Why, when I thought you
Fast locked in Salamanca at your study,
Leaped you into a Gypsy?

RODERIGO Sir, with your pardon,
I shall (at fit time) to you show cause for all.

FERNANDO
Meantime, sir, you have got a trade to live by.
Best to turn player. An excellent ruffian, ha!
But know, sir, when I'd found you out, I gave you
This project of set purpose. 'Tis all myself;
What the old Gypsy spoke must be my language.
Nothing are left me but my offices
And thin-faced honours—and this very creature,
By you so scorned, must raise me by your marrying her.

RODERIGO
You would not build your glory on my ruins?

FERNANDO
Marry, the rascal has belied the lady;
She is not half so bad. All's one: she's rich.

RODERIGO
O, will you sell the joys of my full youth
To dunghill muck? Seek out some wretch's daughter,
Whose soul is lost for gold then. You're more noble
Than t'have your son, the top-branch of your house,
Grow in a heap of rubbish. I must marry a thing
I shall be ashamed to own, ashamed to bring her
Before a sunbeam.

FERNANDO I cannot help it, sir.
Resolve upon't, and do't.

RODERIGO And do't? And die!
Is there no face in Spain for you to pick out
But one to fright me? When you sat the play here,
There was a beauty, to be lord of which
I would against an army throw defiance.

FERNANDO
She? Alas!

RODERIGO How? She!—at every hair of hers
There hangs a very angel. This!—I'm ready
To drop down looking at it. Sir, I beseech you:
[*He kneels*]
Bury me in this earth (on which I'm humbled
To beg your blessing on me) for a Gypsy,
Rather than—O, I know not what to term it!
Pray, what is that young pensive piece of beauty?
Your voice for her: I eyed her all the scene.

FERNANDO
I saw you did.

RODERIGO Methought 'twas a sweet creature.

FERNANDO
Well, though my present state stands now on ice,
I'll let it crack and fall, rather than bar thee
Of thy content. This lady shall go by then.

RODERIGO
Hang let her there, or anywhere!

FERNANDO That young lannard
Whom you have such a mind to, if you can whistle her

168 **make some** become a button-maker (as an alternative profession)
170 **Iron him** place him in irons, chains
171 **witness** testimony, evidence
172–3 **Prick ... anything** do anything to get Don Pedro's attention
182 **Set ... mine** (shoulder to shoulder)
kick at defy
184 **company** (*a*) companions (*b*) theatrical troupe
play (*a*) perform (*b*) enjoy ourselves
188 **I** then I will
190 **eagles** (remarkably sharp-sighted, overseeing their prey; believed to be able to look directly at the sun)
193 **Leaped ... into** eagerly changed positions, identities (as though 'Gypsy' were a saddle into which he jumped)
198 **of set** with premeditated
201 **thin-faced** worn out, thin-veneered
204 **rascal** i.e. painter
belied slandered
211 **own** acknowledge mine
215 **sat** attended
216 **a beauty** i.e. Clara
229 **This lady** (in the picture)
230 **Hang** (like a picture on the wall, or a criminal on the gallows)
lannard hawk
231 **whistle** call

To come to fist, make trial; play the young falconer.
I will nor mar your marriage, nor yet make.
Beauty, no wealth; wealth, ugliness—which you will, take.

RODERIGO
I thank you, sir. [*Exit Fernando*]
Put on your mask, good madam:
The sun will spoil your face else.
[*He closes the curtain on the picture.*] *Exit*

❀

5.1 *Incipit Actus Quintus*
Enter Fernando, Pedro, Roderigo, Clara [*in a bridal gown*] *and Maria, as from church,* [*passing*] *over the stage:* [*as the others exeunt*] *Fernando stays Roderigo*

FERNANDO
Thou hast now the wife of thy desires.

RODERIGO
Sir, I have—
And in her every blessing that makes life
Loath to be parted with.

FERNANDO
Noble she is,
And fair; has (to enrich her blood and beauty)
Plenty of wit, discourse, behaviour, carriage.

RODERIGO
I owe you duty for a double birth,
Being in this happiness begot again—
Without which I had been a man of wretchedness.

FERNANDO
Then henceforth, boy, learn to obey thy fate.
'Tis fall'n upon thee; know it, and embrace it.
Thy wife's a wanton.

RODERIGO A wanton?

FERNANDO
Examine through the progress of thy youth
What capital sin, what great one 'tis—for 'tis
A great one—thou'st committed.

RODERIGO
I, a great one!

FERNANDO
Else heaven is not so wrathful to pour on thee
A misery so full of bitterness.
I am thy father; think on't, and be just.
Come, do not dally.

RODERIGO
Pray, my lord—

FERNANDO
Fool, 'twere
Impossible that justice should rain down
In such a frightful horror without cause.
Sir, I will know it. Rather blush thou didst
An act thou dar'st not name, than that it has
A name to be known by.

RODERIGO
Turn from me then,
And as my guilt sighs out this monster—rape—
O, do not lend an ear!

FERNANDO
Rape? Fearful!

RODERIGO
Hence,
Hence springs my due reward.

FERNANDO
Thou'rt none of mine—
Or if thou be'st, thou dost belie the stamp
Of thy nativity.

RODERIGO
Forgive me!

FERNANDO
Had she
(Poor wrongèd soul, whoe'er she was) no friend,
Nor father, to revenge? Had she no tongue
To roar her injuries?

RODERIGO
Alas, I know her not.

FERNANDO
Peace! Thou wilt blaze a sin beyond all precedent.
Young man, thou shouldst have married her; the devil
Of lust that riots in thy eye should there
Have let fall love and pity, not on this stranger
Whom thou hast doted on.

RODERIGO
O, had I married her,
I had been then the happiest man alive!
Enter Clara, Maria, and Pedro, from behind the arras

CLARA
As I the happiest woman, being married.
Look on me, sir.

PEDRO [*to Roderigo*]
You shall not find a change
So full of fears as your most noble father,
In his wise trial, urged.

MARIA [*to Roderigo*]
Indeed you shall not,
The forfeit of her shame shall be her pawn.

RODERIGO
Why, pray, d'ye mock my sorrows? Now, O now,
My horrors flow about me!

FERNANDO
No, thy comforts,
Thy blessings, Roderigo.

CLARA [*showing the crucifix to Roderigo*]
By this crucifix
You may remember me.

RODERIGO
Ha! Art thou
That lady wronged?

CLARA
I was, but now am I
Righted in noble satisfactïon.

RODERIGO
How can I turn mine eyes, and not behold

232 **fist** the gloved hand of the falconer
trial attempt, effort
234 **which you will** whichever you prefer
235 **Put...mask** cover your face
236 **sun...face** (Suntans were considered ugly.)
5.1.0.3–4 ***passing...stage*** entering at one door and exiting out another
0.5 ***stays*** stops
5 **carriage** deportment
11 **wanton** slut
15 **I** (or 'Ay')
28 **stamp** legitimizing seal (conception being imagined as the impressing of male form upon waxen female substance)
33 **blaze** (*a*) proclaim, publish (*b*) blazon, describe heraldically
38.2 ***arras*** curtain
40 **change** transformation (into a 'wanton')
43 **pawn** pledge, guarantee

On every side my shame?
FERNANDO No more. Hereafter
We shall have time to talk at large of all.
Love her that's now thine own; do, Roderigo.
She's far from what I charactered.
CLARA [*to Roderigo*] My care
Shall live about me to deserve your love.
RODERIGO
Excellent Clara!
[*They embrace*]
Fathers both, and mother,
I will redeem my fault.
FERNANDO, PEDRO, *and* MARIA
Our blessings dwell on ye!
Enter Luis and Francisco
LUIS
Married to Roderigo?
FRANCISCO Judge yourself:
See where they are. *Exit*
LUIS [*to Clara*] Is this your husband, lady?
CLARA
He is, sir. Heaven's great hand, that on recòrd
Fore-points the equal union of all hearts,
Long since decreed what this day hath been pèrfected.
LUIS
'Tis well then. I am free, it seems.
CLARA Make smooth,
My lord, those clouds, which on your brow deliver
Emblems of storm. I will (as far as honour
May privilege) deserve a noble friendship,
As you from me deserve a worthy memory.
LUIS
Your husband, faith, has proved himself a friend
Trusty and tried; he's welcome, I may say,
From th'university.
RODERIGO To a new school
Of happy knowledge, Luis.
LUIS Sir, I am
Not so poor-spirited to put this injury up.
The best blood flows within you is the price.
RODERIGO
Luis, for this time calm your anger,
And if I do not give you noble satisfaction,
Call me to what account you please.
LUIS So, so.—
[*To Fernando*] I come for justice t'ye, and you shall grant it.
FERNANDO
Shall and will.
LUIS With speed, too:
My poor friend bleeds the whiles.
FERNANDO You shall yourself,
Before we part, receive the satisfaction
You come for.—Who attends?
SERVANTS (*within*) My lord?
FERNANDO The prisoner!
SERVANTS (*within*)
He attends your lordship's pleasure.
Enter Preciosa, Eugenia, and the old Father of the Gypsies
LUIS What would this girl?—
Foh, no tricks! Get you to your cabin, hussy;
We have no ear for ballads.
FERNANDO Take her away.
CLARA
A wondrous lovely creature!
PRECIOSA Noble gentlemen,
If a poor maid's (a Gypsy-virgin's) tears
May soften the hard edge of angry justice,
Then grant me gracious hearing. As you're merciful,
I beg my husband's life!
FERNANDO Thy husband's, little one?
PRECIOSA
Gentle sir, our plighted troths are chronicled
In that white book above, which notes the secrets
Of every thought and heart. He is my husband;
I am his wife.
LUIS Rather his whore.
PRECIOSA Now, trust me,
You're no good man to say so. I am honest;
'Deed, la, I am—a poor soul, that deserves not
Such a bad word. Were you a better man
Than you are, you do me wrong.
LUIS The toy grows angry!
CLARA [*to Roderigo*]
And it becomes her sweetly. Troth, my lord,
I pity her.
RODERIGO I thank you, sweet.
LUIS [*to Preciosa*] Your husband,
You'll say, is no thief—
PRECIOSA Upon my conscience,
He is not.
LUIS Dares not strike a man—
PRECIOSA Unworthily,
He dares not; but if trod upon, a worm
Will turn again.
LUIS That turning turns your worm
Off from the ladder, minion.

54 **charactered** described
61 **Fore-points** appoints in advance
63 **free** released of his commitment to her (ironic)
69 **tried** tested
72 **put...up** accept this insult
82 **would this girl** does this girl want
83 **cabin** tent, hut, cave
84 **ballads** (popular songs, despised by educated contemporaries, and often sad)
86 **Gypsy-virgin's** (paradoxical, according to early modern prejudice)
90 **plighted troths** pledged betrothals
chronicled recorded and dated (like other historical facts)
91 **white book** divine register
94 **honest** chaste
95 **'Deed, la** indeed (very mild ladylike oath)
97 **toy** plaything
102–3 **if...turn** (proverbial justification for revenge)
103–4 **turns...ladder** i.e. hangs him

PRECIOSA Sir, I hope
You're not his judge; you are too young, too choleric,
Too passionate. The poise of life or death
Requires a much more grave consideration
Than your years warrant. Here sit they, like gods,
Upon whose heads the reverend badge of time
Hath sealed the proof of wisdom; to these oracles
Of riper judgement, lower in my heart
[She kneels]
Than on my knees, I offer up my suit,
My lawful suit, which begs they would be gentle
To their own fames, their own immortal stories.
O, do not think, my lords, compassion thrown
On a base low estate, on humble people,
Less meritorious than if you had favoured
The faults of great men (and indeed great men
Have oftentimes great faults). He whom I plead for
Is free; the soul of innocence itself
Is not more white. Will you pity him?
I see it in your eyes. 'Tis a sweet sunbeam;
Let it shine out—and to adorn your praise,
The prayers of the poor shall crown your days
(And theirs are sometimes heard).
FERNANDO Beshrew the girl,
She has almost melted me to tears!
LUIS Hence, trifler!—Call in my friend!
Enter Don Juan [in irons], Diego, and Cardochia
[*To Diego*] What hope of ease?
DIEGO Good hope, but still I smart;
The worst is in my pain.
LUIS The price is high
Shall buy thy vengeance. To receive a wound
By a base villain's hand, it mads me.
JUAN
Men subject to th'extremity of law
Should carry peace about 'em to their graves;
Else, were you nobler than the blood you boast of
Could any way (my lord) derive you, know
I would return sharp answer to your slanders.
But it suffices, I am none of aught
Your rage misterms me.
LUIS None of 'em? No rascal?
JUAN
No rascal.
LUIS Nor no thief?
JUAN
Ask her that's my accuser. Could your eyes
Pierce through the secrets of her foul desires,
You might (without a partial judgement) look into
A woman's lust and malice.
CARDOCHIA My good lords,
What I have articled against this fellow,
I justify for truth.
JUAN On then, no more.
This being true she says, I have deserved
To die.
FERNANDO
We sit not here to bandy words,
But minister the law, and that condemns thee
For theft unto the gallows.
PRECIOSA O my misery!
Are you all marble-breasted? Are your bosoms
Hooped round with steel? To cast away a man
More worthy life and honours than a thousand
Of such as only pray unto the shadow
Of abused greatness!
JUAN 'Tis in vain to storm.
My fate is here determinèd.
PRECIOSA Lost creature,
Art thou grown dull too? Is my love so cheap
That thou court'st thy destruction 'cause I love
thee?—
My lords, my lords!—Speak, Andrew, prithee, now,
Be not so cruel to thyself and me.
One word of thine will do't.
FERNANDO Away with him!
Tomorrow is his day of execution.
JUAN
Even when you will.
PRECIOSA Stay, man, thou shalt not go;
Here are more women yet.—Sweet madam, speak.
You, lady, you methinks should have some feeling
Of tenderness; you may be touched as I am.
Troth, were't your cause, I'd weep with you, and join
In earnest suit for one you held so dear.
CLARA [*to Roderigo*]
My lord, pray speak in his behalf.
RODERIGO I would,
But dare not; 'tis a fault so clear and manifest.
LUIS
Back with him to his dungeon!
JUAN Heaven can tell
I sorrow not to die, but to leave her
Who whiles I live is my life's comforter.
CARDOCHIA [*aside*] Now shall I be revenged!
[*Exeunt Don Juan, Diego, and Cardochia*]

105 **choleric** full of choler, angry
106 **poise** balance
108 **they** (Fernando and Pedro)
109 **badge** insignia (= white hair)
114 **stories** histories, biographies
120 **free** fault-free, faultless
123 **shine out** (eyes were believed to see by projecting eye-beams, like sunbeams)
125 **Beshrew** damn
129 **smart** hurt, wince
135 **Else** otherwise
145 **articled** particularized in the indictment
147 **This being** (*a*) since this is (*b*) if this is
148 **bandy** toss back and forth
149 **minister** administer
151 **marble-breasted** hard-hearted
154 **pray...shadow** (*a*) kneel down at the feet of, in the shadow of (*b*) worship the appearance rather than reality
155 **abused** deceived
157 **dull** senseless
161 **One word** i.e. his real name (which he has sworn to conceal, in becoming a Gypsy for two years)
166 **touched** affected, moved

PRECIOSA
O me unhappy!
[*She swoons*]
FERNANDO See, the girl falls!
Some one look to her.
CLARA 'Las, poor maid!
EUGENIA Preciosa!—
She does recover. Mine honourable lord—
FERNANDO In vain, what is't?
EUGENIA
Be pleased to give me private audience;
I will discover something shall advantage
The noblest of this land.
FERNANDO Well, I will hear thee.
Bring in the girl. *Exeunt.* [*Father stays Luis*]
LUIS Aught with me? What is't?
I care not for thy company, old ruffian.
Rascal, art impudent?
FATHER To beg your service.
LUIS
Hang yourself!
FATHER By your father's soul, sir, hear me!
LUIS
Dispatch.
FATHER First promise me you'll get reprieve
For the condemnèd man, and by my art
I'll make you master of what your heart on earth
Can wish for or desire.
LUIS Thou li'st; thou canst not.
FATHER
Try me.
LUIS Do that, and then (as I am noble)
I will not only give thy friend his life
But royally reward thee, love thee ever.
FATHER
I take your word. What would you?
LUIS If thou mock'st me,
'Twere better thou wert damned.
FATHER Sir, I am resolute.
LUIS
Resolve me, then, whether the Count Alvarez,
Who slew my father, be alive or dead?
FATHER
Is this the mighty matter? The count lives.
LUIS
How?
FATHER
The count lives.
LUIS O fate! Now tell me where,
And be my better genius.
FATHER I can do't.
In Spain a lives; more, not far from Madrid—
But in disguise, much altered.
LUIS Wonderful scholar!
Miracle of artists! Alvarez living?
And near Madrid too? Now, for heaven's sake, where?
That's all, and I am thine.
FATHER Walk off, my lord,
To the next field; you shall know all.
LUIS Apace, then!
I listen to thee with a greedy ear.
The miserable and the fortunate
Are alike in this, they cannot change their fate.
Exeunt at one door.

Enter [*the old Father and Luis*] *presently at the other* [*door*] 5.2

FATHER
Good, good: you would fain kill him, and revenge
Your father's death?
LUIS I would.
FATHER Bravely, or scurvily?
LUIS
Not basely, for the world!
FATHER We are secure.
[*He discovers*] *two swords*
Young Luis, two more trusty blades than these
Spain has not in her armory. With this,
Alvarez slew thy father; and this other
Was that the king of France wore when great Charles
In a set battle took him prisoner.
Both I resign to thee.
LUIS This is a new mystery.
FATHER
Now see this naked bosom. Turn the points
Of either on this bulwark, if thou covet'st
(Out of a sprightly youth and manly thirst
Of vengeance) blood; if blood be thy ambition,
Then call to mind the fatal blow that struck
De Castro, thy brave father, to his grave.
Remember who it was that gave that blow,
His enemy Alvarez: hear, and be sudden.
Behold Alvarez.
LUIS Death, I am deluded!
FATHER
Thou art incredulous. As fate is certain,
I am the man.
LUIS Thou, that butcher?

175, 182 **girl** (two syllables)
180 **discover** reveal
advantage profit
186 **Dispatch** be quick about it
187 **art** black magic (associated with Gypsies)
199 **better genius** guardian angel
200 **a** he
202 **artists** magicians
205 **Apace** quickly
5.2.0.1 ***presently*** immediately
1 **fain** like to
3.1 ***discovers*** reveals, produces (probably from the trapdoor, as though they had been buried in this 'field')
4 **trusty** reliable
7–8 **king...prisoner** worn by Francis I at the battle of Pavia (1525), where he was defeated by the Holy Roman Emperor and King of Spain, Charles V (1500–1558), the most powerful monarch in sixteenth-century Europe
11 **bulwark** defensive barrier (i.e. his chest)
19 **As...certain** (proverbial)

FATHER
Tremble not, young man. Trust me, I have wept
Religiously to wash off from my conscience
The stain of my offence. Twelve years and more,
Like to a restless pilgrim I have run
From foreign lands to lands to find out death.
I'm weary of my life. Give me a sword.
That thou mayst know with what a perfect zeal
I honour old De Castro's memory,
I'll fight with thee; I would not have thy hand
Dipped in a wilful murder. I could wish
For one hour's space I could pluck back from time
But thirty of my years, that in my fall
Thou might'st deserve report. Now if thou conquer'st,
Thou canst not triumph; I'm half dead already.
Yet I'll not start a foot.

LUIS Breathes there a spirit
In such a heap of age?

FATHER O, that I had
A son of equal growth with thee, to tug
For reputation! By thy father's ashes,
I would not kill thee for another Spain.
Yet now I'll do my best. Thou art amazed;
Come on.

LUIS Twelve tedious winters' banishment—
'Twas a long time.

FATHER Could they redeem thy father?
Would every age had been twelve ages, Luis,
And I for penance every age a-dying!
But 'tis too late to wish.

LUIS I am o'ercome.
Your nobleness hath conquered me. Here ends
All strife between our families, and henceforth
Acknowledge me for yours.

FATHER O, thou reviv'st
Fresh horrors to my fact—for in thy gentleness
I see my sin anew.

LUIS Our peace is made.
Your life shall be my care. 'Twill be glad news
To all our noble friends.

FATHER Since heaven will have it so,
I thank thee, glorious majesty! My son—
For I will call thee son—ere the next morrow
Salute the world, thou shalt know stranger mysteries.

LUIS
I have enough to feed on. Sir, I'll follow ye. *Exeunt*

5.3 *Enter Eugenia, Fernando, and Preciosa*

FERNANDO
Don Juan, son to the count of Cárcamo?
Woman, take heed thou trifle not.

EUGENIA Is this,
My lord, so strange?

FERNANDO Beauty in youth, and wit
To set it forth, I see, transforms the best
Into what shape love fancies.

PRECIOSA Will you yet
Give me my husband's life?

FERNANDO Why, little one,
He is not married to thee.

PRECIOSA In his faith
He is—and faith and troth I hope bind faster
Than any other ceremonies can.
Do they not, pray, my lord?

FERNANDO Yes, where the parties
Pledged are not too unequal in degree,
As he and thou art.

PRECIOSA This is new divinity.

EUGENIA
My lord, behold this child well. In her face
You may observe, by curious insight, something
More than belongs to every common birth.

FERNANDO
True, 'tis a pretty child.

EUGENIA The glass of misery
Is (after many a change of desperate fortune)
At length run out. You had a daughter,
Called Constanza.

FERNANDO Ha!

EUGENIA A sister, Guiomare,
Wife to the Count Alvarez.

FERNANDO Peace, O, peace!

EUGENIA
And to that sister's charge you did commit
Your infant daughter—in whose birth your wife,
Her mother, died.

FERNANDO Woman, thou art too cruel!

PRECIOSA
What d'ye mean, grannam? 'Las, the nobleman
Grows angry!

FERNANDO Not I, indeed I do not.—
But why d'ye use me thus?

EUGENIA Your child and sister,
As you supposed, were drowned.

FERNANDO Drowned, talking creature!
'Supposed'?

EUGENIA They live. Fernando, from my hand,
Thy sister's hand, receive thine own Constanza,
The sweetest, best child living.

PRECIOSA Do you mock me?

FERNANDO
Torment me on—yet more, more yet, and spare not.

33 **report** reputation
35 **start** budge
39 **another Spain** (Spanish conquests in the Americas were called 'New Spain')
49 **fact** crime
5.3.3–4 **Beauty ... forth** i.e. Preciosa
5 **what** whatever
7 **faith** fidelity, commitment
8 **troth** betrothal, promise, truth
11 **degree** class, status
12 **divinity** theology
16 **glass** hourglass
21 **charge** care
27 **creature** (as though she were not human, but something else that was nevertheless—as only humans should be—capable of speech)

My heart is now a-breaking, now!
EUGENIA O brother,
Am I so far removed off from your memory
As that you will not know me? I expected
An other welcome home. Look on this casket,
[She shows] a casket
The legacy your lady left her daughter
When to her son she gave her crucifix.
FERNANDO
Right, right, I know ye now.
EUGENIA In all my sorrows,
My comfort has been here; she should be yours,
Because born yours.—Constanza, kneel, sweet child,
To thy old father.
PRECIOSA *[kneeling]*
How? my father?
FERNANDO Let not
Extremity of joys ravish life from me
Too soon, heaven, I beseech thee!—Thou art my sister,
My sister Guiomare. How have mine eyes
Been darkened all this while! 'Tis she!
EUGENIA 'Tis, brother—
And this Constanza, now no more a stranger,
No 'Preciosa' henceforth.
FERNANDO My soul's treasure,
Live to an age of goodness, and so thrive
In all thy ways that thou mayst die to live!
PRECIOSA
But must I call you father?
FERNANDO Thou wilt rob me else
Of that felicity, for whose sake only
I am ambitious of being young again.
Rise, rise, mine own Constanza!
PRECIOSA *[rising]* 'Tis a new name,
But 'tis a pretty one. I may be bold
To make a suit t'ye?
FERNANDO Anything.
PRECIOSA O father,
An if you be my father, think upon
Don Juan, my husband. Without him, alas,
I can be nothing!
FERNANDO As I without thee;
Let me alone, Constanza.—Tell me, tell me,
Lives yet Alvarez?
EUGENIA In your house.
FERNANDO Enough.
Cloy me not; let me by degrees digest
My joys.—Within! My lords! Francisco, Pedro!
Enter Francisco, Pedro, Maria, Roderigo, Clara
Come all at once! I have a world within me.
I am not mortal sure, I am not mortal.—
My honourable lords, partake my blessings.
Count Alvarez lives, here in my house;
Your son, my lord Francisco, Don Juan, is
The condemned man, falsely accused of theft;
This, my lord Pedro, is my sister Guiomare;
Madam, this is Constanza, mine own child,
And I'm a wondrous merry man.—Without!
The prisoner!
Enter the old Father (Alvarez), Luis, Don Juan, Diego, Sancho, Soto, and Cardochia
LUIS Here, free, and acquitted
By her whose folly drew her to this error—
And she for satisfaction is assured
To my wronged friend.
CARDOCHIA I crave your pardons.
He whose I am speaks for me.
DIEGO We both beg it.
FERNANDO
Excellent, admirable!—My dear brother!
[Fernando and the old Father Alvarez embrace]
FATHER
Never a happy man till now. Young Luis
And I are reconciled.
LUIS For ever, faithfully,
Religiously.
OMNES *[to Alvarez]*
My noble lord, most welcome!
FATHER
To all my heart pays what it owes, due thanks.—
[To Luis] Most, most, brave youth, to thee!
JUAN I all this while
Stand but a looker-on, and though my father
May justly tax the violence of my passions,
Yet if this lady (lady of my life)
Must be denied, let me be as I was,
And die betimes.
PRECIOSA *[to Fernando]*
You promised me—
FERNANDO I did.—
My lord of Cárcamo, you see their hearts
Are joined already; so let our consents
To this wished marriage.
FRANCISCO *[to Juan]* I forgive thine errors.
Give me thy hand.
FERNANDO *[to Preciosa]*
Me, thine.—But wilt thou love
My daughter, my Constanza?
JUAN As my bliss.
PRECIOSA *[to Juan]*
I thee as life, youth, beauty, anything
That makes life comfortable.

35 **other** different
39–40 **yours . . . yours** your comfort . . . your child
41 **How** what
42 **ravish** abduct
47 **treasure** (playing on the name 'Preciosa')
49 **live** survive eternally in heaven
71 **Without** outside, out there
74 **assured** affianced, engaged
77 **admirable** amazing
87 **betimes** soon, early
89 **so** likewise (be joined)

FERNANDO [*joining their hands*]
Live together
One, ever one!

OMNES And heaven crown your happiness!

PEDRO [*to Sancho*] Now, sir, how like you a prison?

SANCHO As gallants do a tavern, being stopped for a reckoning: scurvily.

SOTO Though you caged us up never so close, we sung like cuckoos.

FERNANDO Well, well, you are yourself now.

SANCHO Myself?—Am I out of my wits, Soto?

FERNANDO
Here now are none but honourable friends.
Will you, to give a farewell to the life
You've led as Gypsies—these being now found none,
But noble in their births, altered in fortunes—
Give it a merry shaking by the hand,
And cry adieu to folly?

SANCHO We'll shake our hands and our heels, if you'll give us leave.

A dance

FERNANDO
On, brides and bridegrooms! To your Spanish feasts
Invite with bent knees all these noble guests. *Exeunt*

THE PARTS

Adult Males

FERNANDO (367 lines)
RODERIGO (306 lines)
LUIS (289 lines)
FATHER OF THE GYPSIES (288 lines)
SANCHO (268 lines)
SOTO (149 lines)
PEDRO (119 lines)
JUAN (105 lines)
DIEGO (95 lines)
FRANCISCO (40 lines)
ANTONIO (15 lines)
CARLO (8 lines)
SERVANT (1.4; 8 lines): *any but* Roderigo, Luis, Diego
Servants (5.1, within; 2 lines): *any but* Fernando, Roderigo, Luis, Francisco, Pedro, Father of the Gypsies

Boys

CLARA (182 lines)
PRECIOSA (159 lines)
CARDOCHIA (69 lines)
EUGENIA (64 lines)
MARIA (38 lines)
CHRISTIANA (1 line)

Most crowded scene: 4.3 (12 men, 6 boys)

98 **reckoning** bill to be paid

110.1 ***dance*** For the music and choreography of this dance, see *Companion*, p. 174.

111 **Spanish feasts** (ironic, given the notorious Spanish frugality experienced by the English in 1623)

112 **noble guests** aristocrats on stage (but also alluding, in court performance, to the audience)

THE TRIUMPHS OF INTEGRITY
with THE TRIUMPHS OF THE GOLDEN FLEECE

Edited by David M. Bergeron

ADDRESSING Parliament on 31 March 1607, James I warmed to a compelling metaphor: 'I would heartily wish my breast were a transparent glass for you all to see through, that you might look into my heart, and then would you be satisfied of my meaning.' He opened his March 1610 parliamentary address with the same metaphor. We know, of course, that James often went to great lengths to remain obscure and unknowable. In the 1623 mayoral pageant Middleton seizes the metaphor of transparency and links it to the concept of integrity, needed in both royal and city government. The idea and allegorical figure of Integrity provide a bridge in the pageant by which the memorable past crosses into present politics and by which mayoral celebration gives rise to royal politics. And *The Triumphs of Integrity* constructs a bridge by which Anthony Munday enters explicitly into authorial collaboration with Middleton.

Garret Christmas and Middleton received £150 for 'making and setting out of the pageants and Shows' in 1623. But one also finds in the records of the Drapers' Company, the sponsoring guild, a payment to Munday of £35 'for an Argoe', confirming his nearly ubiquitous participation in Jacobean Lord Mayor's shows, especially in the pageant writing of Middleton. At moments indeed it may be difficult to separate the two writers. But in 1623 their collaboration takes a rather different turn, resulting—uniquely—in two different texts for the mayoral pageant: Middleton's *The Triumphs of Integrity* and Munday's *The Triumphs of the Golden Fleece*.

Early in his text Middleton writes about the show that occurred on the river as the new mayor made his way to Westminster, describing it as 'a proper and significant masterpiece of triumph called the Imperial Canopy, being the ancient arms of the company, an invention neither old nor enforced' (36–9). This 'same glorious and apt property' (39) joined the four land devices. Since Munday wrote the river entertainment, Middleton presumably refers to that contribution, in fact in rather glowing terms. Munday in his text provides a brief device on the river that does not include any speeches. The 'argoe' depicts Jason and his Argonauts, all appropriate to the Drapers' arms and all taken from Munday's 1615 pageant, *Metropolis Coronata*. Middleton's characterization of the device as 'neither old nor enforced' seems at best inaccurate.

From at least the fifteenth century London mayors had made the obligatory trip to Westminster by river. This journey regularly included several boats, appropriately decorated with banners that reflected the guilds and the city. Eyewitness accounts focus on the spectacle of the river procession. In 1591 George Peele's *Descensus Astraeae* became the first pageant text to record the river entertainment. Only in *The Triumphs of Love and Antiquity* (1619) does Middleton record the river festivities, principally Love's speech. John Squire's 1620 mayoral pageant, *The Triumphs of Peace*, offers one of the most elaborate river entertainments. Munday, more often than not, includes in his texts some account of the river pageant. *Metropolis Coronata*, for example, portrays, in addition to Jason, a person representing Henry fitz Ailwin, London's first mayor. In a hundred-line speech he explicates the relevance of the Golden Fleece to the Drapers and finally insists to the new mayor: 'You are our Jason.'

For ten years Munday and Middleton have encountered each other in the process of writing mayoral pageants. Munday (1560–1633), poet, dramatist, historian, and translator, had been recognized by Francis Meres in *Palladis Tamia* as 'our best plotter'. Between 1602 and 1623 he had at least a hand in fifteen Lord Mayor's shows. In 1602 Middleton and Munday had collaborated, along with Dekker, Drayton, and Webster, on a play, *Caesar's Fall*, for Henslowe's company (see the further discussion in 'Lost Plays', p. 328). Since William Gifford's edition of Ben Jonson (1816) editors and commentators have referred to their 'rivalry', noting how Middleton in his pageant texts speaks 'slightingly' or 'disparagingly' of his rival Munday, who apparently regularly nips at Middleton's artistic heels. Little reliable evidence exists to confirm that Middleton thought Munday his inferior: we need only recall his praise of Munday at the end of *The Triumphs of Truth*. Instead, their unpleasant rivalry emerges as a nineteenth-century invention, which has become by now both 'old' and 'enforced'. Their separate texts in 1623, an aberration, confirm cooperation, not some personal rivalry. 'Collaboration' seems a far better, more nearly accurate, term to characterize much of the relationship between Middleton and Munday. In 1623 we do not have to scour guild records or glean some hint from Middleton's text to know of Munday's involvement. Here Munday's independently printed text, his last pageant, stands alongside Middleton's, evidence of his participation in the mayoral pageant and a necessary text if we would gain the complete picture of the mayoral festivities.

In *Integrity* Middleton moves from ancient shepherds to more recent former Lord Mayors in order to represent the past. The speaker Memory, reviewing the contribution of past mayors, comments that 'shows, pomp, nor a house of state | Curiously decked' (178–9) do not make a magistrate; rather, wisdom, justice, and care define him. At the same time, however, the indulgence in shows, pomp, and pageants calls attention to the virtues required of a magistrate; and this awareness leads to the Temple of Integrity where the realistic examples of the past give way to a mystification of virtue and an allegorizing of politics.

Of all playwrights from the mid-sixteenth to the mid-seventeenth century only Middleton represents Integrity. In *Sun in Aries* (1621) he cites Integrity as the one who keeps the keys to the Tower of Virtue; in *Triumphs of Honour and Virtue* (1622) he represents the allegorical figure Integrity as one of the eight parts that constitute the inward man, symbolized in the Globe of Honour. By 1623 Integrity has evolved into the titular character for the pageant. Middleton's concept of Integrity corresponds to the opening lines of Horace's Ode 22 of Book 1: 'The man of upright life and free from sin, | requires no Moorish spears nor bow | and quiver laded with poisoned | arrows.' Middleton plays off the idea that integrity means both whole and morally upright.

Middleton refers to the Temple of Integrity as 'an unparalleled masterpiece of art' (190); and he may be right, based on the tantalizing description. Through some kind of crystal one could see Integrity with 'all her glorious and sanctimonious concomitants' (192–3). In order to provide 'content' for the spectators and to express 'the invention and the art of the engineer' (194–5), this crystal temple 'is made to open in many parts, at fit and convenient times' (196–7). It has gold columns and silver battlements, 'the whole fabric for the night triumph adorned and beautified with many lights, dispersing their glorious radiances on all sides through the crystal' (199–202). We have to imagine what Integrity looked like, for Middleton only refers to her 'immaculate self' (192) without providing more specific information.

Integrity in her speech urges, 'Look and look through me' (207), possibly suggesting that she wears a garment of glass. Nothing hides her actions, no disguise or veil, 'only a crystal, which approves me clear', she says (214). Integrity instructs the new mayor: 'so must thy acts | Be all translucent' (231–2), and he must leave behind 'worthy tracts | For future times to find' (232–3). Such accomplishment would make him worthy of Memory's recollection, joining the impressive list of Drapers. When Integrity says to the mayor that his 'very breast' should be 'Transparent, like this place wherein I rest' (233–4), she recalls James I's metaphor in the parliamentary speeches. Paradoxically, one not only sees through Integrity, but also one gains a reflection, 'the crystal glass | By which wise magistracy sets his face', according to Orpheus in *The Triumphs of Love and Antiquity* (113–4).

Through a transparent glass we also gaze into current royal politics, refracted with a topical twist in the pageant's last device, the Canopy of State. The tableau has 'three imperial crowns cast into the form and bigness of a triumphal pageant, with cloud and sunbeams' (256–8), all derived from the Drapers' arms, as also in the 1621 pageant. These sunbeams 'mount and spread like a golden and glorious canopy over the deified persons' under them (259–60). The persons, eight in number, represent the scriptural Beatitudes, as in the 1622 pageant, taken from the Sermon on the Mount. To enhance the device, Middleton has added James's 'word or motto', '*Beati pacifici*', 'set in fair great letters near the uppermost of the three crowns' (263–4). The Drapers' crowns intersect with the King's word even as his word joins the Word of God of the Beatitudes. Middleton justifies the reference to the King by drawing an architectural analogy: just as great buildings may have the king's arms affixed to them, so this triumph that celebrates the mayor should contain 'some remembrance of honour' that reflects 'upon his majesty, by whose peaceful government, under heaven, we enjoy the solemnity' (269–71). The king's arms attached to a building make a 'frontispiece' (266), just as such pageant devices often resemble title-pages of a book, and vice versa. Fair great letters produce the King's word; Middleton's words produce a book.

The speech, which has a three-part structure, begins by justifying the reference to 'that royal peacemaker our king' (274) and noting the contribution of the guild which has thrice 'crowned their goodness this one day, | With love, with care, with cost' (280–1). The second part leads to an extended interpretation of the symbolism of the tableau: the crowns, the cloud, the sunbeams. The crowns, for example, may also imply the three kingdoms of England, Scotland, and Ireland, 'swayed by the meek hand | Of blest James' (291–2). The three crowns may refer to the 'threefold honour [that] makes the royal suit, | In the king, prince, and the king's substitute' (303–4). Middleton links the mayor with the King and Prince in a triumvirate of power. In his last pageants Middleton gives voice to the concept of the mayor as the king's substitute, an idea absent from earlier Jacobean Lord Mayor's shows. Certainly in terms of civic shows and pageants the Lord Mayor of London has virtually usurped the king's place, suggesting the rising power of the city and the diminished economic and cultural power of the sovereign. Therefore, even in the midst of celebrating the peacemaker king, Middleton returns to the bracing idea that London's mayor rivals the king, takes his place. He had in fact at the beginning of *Integrity* referred to the city's preparations to receive 'his Majesty's great substitute into his honourable charge' (26–7).

The immediate, topical nature of royal politics arises in the third part of the speech, which begins with this assertion: 'We have the crown of Britain's hope again, | Illustrious Charles our prince' (298–9). If we have the prince *again*, where has he been? Charles had been to Spain, this same prince whose investiture as Prince of Wales Middleton had celebrated. Twenty-three years old, Charles had reached the time to marry. But negotiations with Spain, the leading contender, had somewhat bogged down; therefore, Charles determined to go to Spain himself, complete the negotiations, and bring the Infanta with him to England to marry. In a somewhat hare-brained scheme he and the Duke of Buckingham, complete with disguises, set out on 28 February 1623 for Spain. Finally, at the end of August, King Philip IV and the English delegation signed an agreement; and Charles left Spain shortly thereafter. But he did not take the Infanta with him; the Spanish would not consent to such.

On 5 October 1623, Charles, Buckingham, and the others safely landed at Plymouth; they arrived in London the next day to universal rejoicing. Sir Simonds D'Ewes reports in his diary that he had never before seen so many bonfires, 335 just between Whitehall and Temple Bar. A few days later the Prince and the Duke had a tearful but joyful reunion with James at Royston. Such celebration continues into the Lord Mayor's show. Charles's return may itself be a triumph of integrity. Clearly Middleton prepares the pageant and this final commemoration of Charles in light of his recent return: 'We have the crown of Britain's hope again.'

SEE ALSO

The Triumphs of the Golden Fleece: 1772
Textual introduction and apparatus: *Companion*, 679
Authorship and date: *Companion*, 438
General introduction to the civic entertainments: this volume, 963
Other Middleton–Christmas works: *Antiquity*, 1397; *Aries*, 1586; *Virtue*, 1714; *Prosperity*, 1901; lost pageant for Charles I, 1898
Other Middleton–Munday works: *Caesar's Fall*, 328

The Triumphs of Integrity

A noble solemnity, performed through the city, at the sole cost and charges of the Honourable Fraternity of Drapers, at the confirmation and establishment of their most worthy brother, the Right Honourable Martin Lumley, in the high office of his Majesty's Lieutenant, Lord Mayor and Chancellor of the famous City of London.

Taking beginning at his lordship's going, and perfecting itself after his return from receiving the oath of mayoralty at Westminster, on the morrow after Simon and Jude's Day, being the 29 of October 1623.

To the honour of him, to whom the noble Fraternity of Drapers, his worthy brothers have consecrated their loves, in costly triumphs; the Right Honourable Martin Lumley, Lord Mayor of this renowned city.

Thy descent worthy, fortune's early grace
Sprung of an ancient and most generous race
Matched with a virtuous lady, justly may
Challenge the honour of so great a day.

Faithfully devoted to the worthiness of you both,
Tho. Middleton

The Triumphs of Integrity,
or, a noble solemnity through the City.

Of all solemnities by which the happy inauguration of a subject is celebrated, I find none that transcends the state and magnificence of that pomp prepared to receive his Majesty's great substitute into his honourable charge, the City of London, dignified by the title of the King's Chamber Royal; which that it may now appear no less heightened with brotherly affection, cost, art, or invention, than some other preceding triumphs—by which of late times the city's honour hath been more faithfully illustrated—this takes its fit occasion to present itself.

And first to specify the love of his noble fraternity, after his lordship's return from Westminster, having received some service upon the water by a proper and significant masterpiece of triumph called the Imperial Canopy, being the ancient arms of the company, an invention neither old nor enforced; the same glorious and apt property, accompanied with four other triumphal pegmes, are in their convenient stages planted to honour his lordship's progress through the city: the first, for the land, attending his most wished arrival in Paul's Churchyard, which bears the inscription of a Mount Royal, on which mount are placed certain kings and great commanders, which ancient history produces, that were originally sprung from shepherds and humble beginnings: only the number of six presented; some with crowns, some with gilt laurels, holding in their hands silver sheephooks; viz. Viriat, a prime commander of the Portugals, renowned amongst the historians, especially the Romans, who, in battles of fourteen years' continuance, purchased many great and

5 **Martin Lumley** (*c.*1560–1634); serving as Alderman by 1614
17 **race** a possible reference to Lumley's Italian ancestry
18 **virtuous lady** reference to Lumley's wife
36 **service...water** refers to Munday's *Triumphs of the Golden Fleece*, performed on the Thames (see p. 1772)
40 **pegmes** pageant structures
43 **Paul's Churchyard** eastern end of St Paul's Cathedral
49 **Viriat** or Viriathus; between *c.*145 and 139 BC gained control of the Iberian peninsula

honourable victories; Arsaces, king of the Parthians, who ordained the first kingdom that ever was amongst them, and in the reverence of this king's name and memory all others his successors were called Arsacides after his name, as the Roman emperors took the name of Caesar for the love of great Caesar Augustus; also Marcus Julius Lucinus; Bohemia's Primislaus; the emperor Pertinax; the great victor Tamburlaine, conqueror of Syria, Armenia, Babylon, Mesopotamia, Scythia, Albania, etc. Many honourable worthies more I could produce, by their deserts ennobling their mean originals. But for the better expression of the purpose in hand, a speaker lends a voice to these following words.

THE SPEECH IN THE MOUNT ROYAL

They that with glory-inflamed hearts desire
To see great worth deservingly aspire,
Let 'em draw near and fix a serious eye
On this triumphant Mount of Royalty;
Here they shall find fair virtue and her name
From low, obscure beginnings raised to fame,
Like light struck out of darkness. The mean wombs
No more eclipse brave merit than rich tombs
Make the soul happy; 'tis the life, and dying
Crowns both with honour's sacred satisfying;
And 'tis the noblest splendour upon earth
For man to add a glory to his birth,
All his life's race with honoured acts commixed,
Than to be nobly born, and there stand fixed,
As if 'twere competent virtue for whole life
To be begot a lord: 'tis virtuous strife
That makes the cómplete Christian, not high place,
As true submission is the state of grace.
'The path to bliss lies in the humblest field;
Who ever risse to heaven that never kneeled?'
Although the roof hath supernatural height,
Yet there's no flesh can thither go upright.
All this is instanced only to commend
The low condition whence these kings descend.
David. *I spare the prince of prophets in this file,*
And preserve him for a far holier style,
Who, being king anointed, did not scorn
To be a shepherd after. These were born
Shepherds and risse to kings; took their ascending
From the strong hand of virtue, never ending
Where she begins to raise, until she place
Her love-sick servants equal with her grace:
And by this day's great honour it appears
She's much prevailed amongst the reverend years
Of these grave senators; chief of the rest,
Her favour hath reflected most and best
Upon that son whom we of honour call;
And may't successively reflect on all.

From this Mount Royal, beautified with the glory of deserving aspirers, descend we to the modern use of this ancient and honourable mystery, and there we shall find the whole livery of this most renowned and famous city, as upon this day, and at all solemn meetings furnished by it; it clothes the honourable senators in their highest and richest wearings, all courts of justice, magistrates, and judges of the land.

By this time his lordship and the worthy company being gracefully conducted toward the Little Conduit in Cheap, there another part of the triumph waits his honour's happy approach, being a chariot artfully framed and properly garnished. And on the conspicuous part thereof is placed the register of all heroic acts and worthy men, bearing the title of Sacred Memory, who, for the greater fame of this honourable fraternity, presents the never-dying names of many memorable and remarkable worthies of this ancient Society, such as were then famous for state and government: Sir Henry fitz Ailwin, knight, who held the seat of magistracy in this city twenty-four years together; he sits figured under the person of Government; Sir John Norman, the first lord mayor rowed in barge to Westminster with silver oars at his own cost and charges, under the person of Honour; the valiant Sir Francis Drake, that rich ornament to memory, who in two years and ten months' space did cast a girdle about the world, under the person of Victory; Sir Simon Eyre, who at his own cost built Leadenhall, a granary for the poor, under the figure of Charity; Sir Richard Champion and Sir John Milborne, under the person of Munificence or Bounty: Sir Richard Hardell and Sir John Poultney, the one in the seat of magistracy six years, the other four years together, under the figures of Justice and Piety, that Sir John being a college-founder in the parish of St Lawrence Poultney, by Candlewick Street; *et sic de ceteris*. This Chariot drawn by two pelleted lions, being the proper supporters of the company's arms; those two upon the lions presenting Power and Honour, the one in a little streamer or banneret bearing the Lord Mayor's arms, the other the company's.

THE SPEECH IN THE CHARIOT BY MEMORY

I am all Memory, and methinks I see
Into the farthest time, act, quality,

53 **Arsaces** obscure first king of Parthia, *c.*250 BC; reigned two years before being assassinated
58–9 **Marcus Julius Lucinus** possibly Valerius Licinianus Licinius, a Dacian peasant who became Augustus, AD 308–24
59 **Primislaus** Premysl, legendary founder of the Premyslid dynasty; originally a ploughman and later a noted lawgiver
Pertinax supposedly son of a weaver, became distinguished general under Marcus Aurelius (Burridge)
60 **Tamburlaine** immortalized in Marlowe's two plays about him
90 ***file*** catalogue or list
90.n **David** Old Testament king, former shepherd
106 **mystery** guild
107 **livery** all the guilds
122–34 **Henry ... Poultney** identified in the 1621 pageant, *Aries*
138 ***et sic de ceteris*** and so forth
139 **pelleted lions** marked with heraldic pellets

As clear as if 'twere now begun again,
The natures, dispositions, and the men.
I find to goodness they bent all their powers,
Which very name makes blushing times of ours;
They heaped up virtues long before they were old;
This age sits laughing upon heaps of gold.
We by great buildings strive to raise our names,
But they more truly wise built up their fames,
Erected fair examples, large and high,
Patterns for us to build our honours by:
For instance only, Memory relates
The noblest of all city magistrates,
Famous fitz Ailwin; naming him alone,
I sum up twenty-four lord mayors in one,
For he, by free election and consent,
Filled all those years with virtuous government;
Custom and time requiring now but one,
How ought that year to be well dwelt upon;
It should appear an abstract of that worth
Which former times in many years brought forth.
Through all the life of man this is the year
Which many wish and never can come near;
Think, and give thanks; to whom this year does come,
The greatest subject's made in Christendom.
This is the year for whom some long prepared,
And others have their glorious fortune shared,
But serious in thanksgiving; 'tis a year
To which all virtues, like the people here,
Should throng and cleave together, for the place
Is a fit match for the whole stock of grace.
And as men gather wealth 'gainst the year comes,
So should they gather goodness with their sums;
For 'tis not shows, pomp, nor a house of state
Curiously decked, that makes a magistrate,
'Tis his fair, noble soul, his wisdom, care,
His upright justness to the oath he sware
Gives him complete; when such a man to me
Spreads his arms open, there my palace be.
He's both an honour to the day so graced,
And to his brotherhood's love, that sees him placed;
And in his fair deportment there revives
The ancient fame of all his brothers' lives.

After this, for the full close of the forenoon's triumph, near St Lawrence Lane his lordship receives an entertainment from an unparalleled masterpiece of art, called the Crystal Sanctuary, styled by the name of the Temple of Integrity, where her immaculate self with all her glorious and sanctimonious concomitants sit, transparently seen through the crystal; and more to express the invention and the art of the engineer, as also for motion, variety, and the content of the spectators, this Crystal Temple is made to open in many parts, at fit and convenient times, and upon occasion of the speech. The columns or pillars of this Crystal Sanctuary are gold, the battlements silver, the whole fabric for the night triumph adorned and beautified with many lights, dispersing their glorious radiances on all sides through the crystal.

THE SPEECH FROM THE SANCTUARY BY INTEGRITY

Have you a mind, thick multitude, to see
A virtue near concerns magistracy?
Here on my temple throw your greedy eyes,
See me, and learn to know me, then you're wise;
Look and look through me, I no favour crave,
Nor keep I hid the goodness you should have;
'Tis all transparent what I think or do,
And with one look your eye may pierce me through;
There's no disguise or hypocritic veil,
Used by adulterous beauty set to sale,
Spread o'er my actions for respect or fear,
Only a crystal, which approves me clear.
Would you desire my name? Integrity,
One that is ever what she seems to be;
So manifest, perspicuous, plain, and clear,
You may e'en see my thoughts as they sit here;
I think upon fair equity and truth,
And there they sit crowned with eternal youth;
I fix my cogitations upon love,
Peace, meekness, and those thoughts come from above.
The temple of an upright magistrate
Is my fair sanctuary, throne, and state;
And as I dare detraction's evill'st eye,
Sore at the sight of goodness, to espy
Into my ways and actions, which lie ope
To every censure, armed with a strong hope.
So of your part ought nothing to be done,
But what the envious eye might look upon:
As thou art eminent, so must thy acts
Be all translucent, and leave worthy tracts
For future times to find, thy very breast
Transparent, like this place wherein I rest.
Vain doubtings; all thy days have been so clear,
Never came nobler hope to fill a year.

At the close of this speech this crystal Temple of Integrity with all her celestial concomitants and the other parts of triumph take leave of his lordship for that time and rest from service till the great feast be ended; after which the whole body of the triumph attends upon his honour, both towards Saint Paul's and homeward, his lordship accompanied with the grave and honourable senators of the city, amongst whom the two worthy consuls, his lordship's grave assistants for the year, the worshipful and generous Master Ralph Freeman and Master Thomas

181 ***sware*** past tense of swore
185 ***brotherhood's*** members of the Drapers
193 **sanctimonious concomitants** holy companions
203 ***thick multitude*** crowd
212 ***adulterous*** false
214 ***approves*** proves
217 ***perspicuous*** translucent, transparent
221 ***cogitations*** thoughts, meditations
232 ***tracts*** pamphlets; deeds form books
246 **Ralph Freeman** became mayor, 1633–34; honoured in Thomas Heywood's Lord Mayor's Show; died in office
246–7 **Thomas Moulson** became mayor in 1634 upon Freeman's death

Moulson, sheriffs and aldermen, ought not to pass of my respect unremembered, whose bounty and nobleness will prove best their own expressers.

Near the entrance of Wood Street, that part of triumph being planted to which the concluding speech hath chiefly reference, and the rest about the Cross, I thought fit in this place to give this its full illustration, it being an invention both glorious and proper to the company, bearing the name of the thrice-royal Canopy of State, being the honoured arms of this fraternity, the three imperial crowns cast into the form and bigness of a triumphal pageant, with cloud and sunbeams, those beams, by enginous art, made often to mount and spread like a golden and glorious canopy over the deified persons that are placed under it, which are eight in number, figuring the eight Beatitudes. To improve which conceit, *Beati pacifici*, being the King's word or motto, is set in fair great letters near the uppermost of the three crowns; and as in all great edifices or buildings the king's arms is especially remembered, as an honour to the building and builder, in the frontispiece, so is it comely and requisite in these matters of triumph, framed for the inauguration of his great substitute, the Lord Mayor of London, that some remembrance of honour should reflect upon his majesty, by whose peaceful government, under heaven, we enjoy the solemnity.

THE SPEECH, HAVING REFERENCE TO THIS IMPERIAL CANOPY, BEING THE DRAPERS' ARMS

The blessedness, peace, honour, and renown,
This kingdom does enjoy, under the crown
Worn by that royal peacemaker our king,
So oft preserved from dangers menacing,
Makes this arms, glorious in itself, outgo
All that antiquity could ever show;
And thy fraternity hath strived t'appear
In all their course worthy the arms they bear;
Thrice have they crowned their goodness this one day,
With love, with care, with cost; by which they may,
By their deserts, most justly these arms claim,
Got once by worth, now trebly held by fame.
Shall I bring honour to a larger field
And show what royal business these arms yield?
First, the three crowns affords a divine scope,
Set for the graces, charity, faith, and hope,
Which three the only safe combiners be
Of kingdoms, crowns, and every company;
Likewise, with just propriety they may stand
For those three kingdoms swayed by the meek hand
Of blest James: England, Scotland, Ireland.
The cloud that swells beneath 'em may imply
Some envious mist cast forth by heresy,
Which, through his happy reign and heaven's blest will,
The sunbeams of the Gospel strikes through still;
More to assure it to succeeding men,
We have the crown of Britain's hope again,
Illustrious Charles our prince, which all will say
Adds the chief joy and honour to this day;
And as three crowns, three fruits of brotherhood,
By which all love's worth may be understood,
To threefold honour makes the royal suit,
In the king, prince, and the king's substitute;
By th'eight Beatitudes ye understand
The fullness of all blessings to this land,
More chiefly to this city, whose safe peace
Good angels guard, and good men's prayers increase.
May all succeeding honoured brothers be
With as much love brought home as thine brings thee.

For all the proper adornments of art and workmanship in so short a time, so gracefully setting forth the body of so magnificent a triumph, the praise comes, as a just due, to the exquisite deservings of Master Garret Christmas, whose faithful performances still take the upper hand of his promises.

FINIS.

250 **Wood Street** runs north off of Cheapside between Cutter Lane and Milk Street
252 **Cross** The Cheapside Cross stood opposite the end of Wood Street.
258 **enginous** clever, ingenious; or having the nature of an engine
261 **eight Beatitudes** used by Middleton in the previous year's pageant, *Virtue*
262 ***Beati pacifici*** 'Blessed are the peacemakers', the motto of King James
266 **frontispiece** entrance of a building
274 ***king*** King James I
275 ***preserved . . . menacing*** refers probably to King James's escapes from death in the Gowrie Conspiracy of 1600 and the Gunpowder Plot of 1605
287 ***graces*** the Theological Graces found in the New Testament, 1 Corinthians 13
292 ***Ireland*** trisyllabic

ANTHONY MUNDAY

The Triumphs of the Golden Fleece

Edited by David M. Bergeron

Performed at the cost and charges of the ancient and honourable Society of the Drapers, for the instalment of their worthy brother Master Martin Lumley in the mayoralty of London.

On Wednesday, being the nine and twentieth day of October, 1623.

To the worshipful and worthy gentlemen, Master John Gualter, Master John Foster, Master Robert Aubrey, Master Walter Coventrey, the masters, wardens, bachelors, and their assistant brethren, of the ancient and honourable company of the Drapers

To you worthy gentlemen, whose provident care and liberal cost hath run through the troublesome travail of so serious an employment, do I justly (and as no more than is your due) dedicate this poor pains of mine, which might have been more, had time so favoured; but such as it is, take you the honour of my best endeavour, in this day's Triumphs of the Golden Fleece, and what service else you shall please to command me.

Your poor loving brother,
A. Munday

Gracing the triumph day, for the inauguration of the Drapers' worthy brother, Master Martin Lumley, in the mayoralty of London, for the year ensuing.

First, for the water service in the morning, when his lordship taketh barge for his convoy to Westminster, accompanied with the knights and aldermen, his worthy brethren of several societies and all the other companies in their triumphal barges with drums, fifes, trumpets, and other jovial instruments. There is readily mounted on a barge of apt conveyance a beautiful and curious argo, shaped after the old Grecian antique manner, not with masts and sails, as prepared for rough and boisterous seas, but like to the Grecian argos, for carriage of passengers, in time of calm and gentle weather, having banks for men to sit and row with oars, for more quick and agile passage on the seas.

This argo, figureth that of so great fame and renown, wherein Prince Jason and his valiant Argonauts of Greece passed to Colchis, to fetch from thence the Golden Fleece, which is the crest of the Drapers' armory, and therefore the main motive of our employing the invention, alluding to that famous moral and ancient history.

We suppose this argo to be returned from Colchis, purposely to honour this triumphal day by the rare art of Medea the enchantress that kept the fleece there so long a time, and wherewith she was now the more willing to part, in regard of her affection to the Drapers company, to whom she gave it freely for an honour and ornament to their arms.

And to make the triumph the more full of majesty, she vouchsafed to come herself in person, attended with the fair Queen Irene her daughter, and accompanied with the famous princes Jason, Hercules, Telamon, Orpheus, Castor, and Pollux, all armed with fair gilt armours, and bearing triumphal lances, wreathed about with gilded laurel and curious shields, all carrying the impress of the Golden Fleece.

Six tributary Indian kings, holding their several dominions of Medea and living in vassalage to her, are commanded by her to row the argo, all of them wearing their tributary crowns, and antiquely attired in rich habiliments.

The service being performed upon the water, the like is done on the land, all the rest of the day following, always attending his honour's service, and for adding the more splendour to the triumph's solemnity.

Whatsoever credit or commendation (if any at all) may attend on the artful performance of this poor device, it belongeth to the arts-masters Richard Simpson and Nicholas Sotherne; and freely I give it to them.

A. M.

FINIS.

26 **convoy** escorted journey
30 **jovial** merry
39 **Jason** See Munday's treatment of the Jason story in his 1615 Lord Mayor's Show, *Metropolis Coronata*. Jason succeeded in getting the Golden Fleece with the help of Medea and his fellow Argonauts.
46 **Medea** noted for her witchcraft, she helped Jason secure the Golden Fleece and fled with him, becoming his wife
54–5 **Hercules . . . Pollux** Mythological figures who accompanied Jason on his quest. Hercules possessed great strength, and accomplished the twelve great labours imposed on him. Telamon helped Hercules in the battle against Troy, and was first to scale the walls of Troy. Orpheus was a superb musician; compare Middleton's treatment of him in *Antiquity*. Castor and Pollux were brothers, and later the patron deities of mariners.
57 **impress** emblem or device
70–1 **Richard Simpson . . . Nicholas Sotherne** The names of these artificers do not appear in other records or texts of pageant entertainments.

A GAME AT CHESSE: AN EARLY FORM

Edited by Gary Taylor

A Game at Chess is an English history play—a play about history, which also made history. It stimulated more immediate commentary than any play, masque, or pageant of its age. Accounts of it were dispatched to Brussels, Dublin, Florence, Madrid, Paris, and Venice. In England, it was rumoured to have received a secret performance at court; certainly, it provoked action by the King, the Earl of Pembroke, and the Privy Council, which not only closed down the play but (for a while) closed down all the London theatres, fined the King's Men, ordered a manhunt for Middleton, interrogated his son, and eventually jailed the author in the Fleet prison. (See 'Occasional Poems'.) Its text survives in many more manuscripts than any other play of the period; it was published in more illicit editions than any other play; it was the first individual play published with an engraved title-page—and was then published again in another edition with yet another engraved title-page. Almost forty years later, in 1663, William Davenant still expected audiences to remember it as the exorbitant high-water mark of theatrical popularity (Steen, 63).

The play that made literary history dramatizes a pivotal period of English, and indeed European, history: the major political and foreign policy crises of 1620–24. It might be entitled *The Troublesome Reign of King James*. It brought onto the stage representations of King James I, Prince Charles, the Duke of Buckingham, King Felipe IV of Spain, the Archbishop of Spalato, the Conde de Gondomar, and various other participants in the conflict between Protestant England and Catholic Spain at the beginning of the Thirty Years' War.

Like every other history play, *A Game at Chess* sometimes sacrifices documentary detail to the foreshortening demands of dramatic form. Shakespeare, for instance, conflates separate historical individuals into a single fictional character, routinely manufactures persons, invents or distorts motives and events. Likewise, Middleton's White King's Pawn combines elements of several unpopular courtiers, and satirizes not an individual, but a pattern of court corruption increasingly visible in Jacobean England (Peck); many characters cannot be confidently identified with historical individuals, but instead personify tendencies or institutions.

From Aristotle to Sir Philip Sidney, poetry had been celebrated as 'more philosophical and more studiously serious than history', precisely because it was not bound to the 'bare *was*' of chronicle particulars. Political critics then and since have sometimes complained about 'inaccuracy' in *A Game at Chess*; such objections are themselves a tribute to the play's uniquely persuasive historicity-effect. But all histories are stories. Even the most rigorously academic monographs on English politics in the 1620s cannot help but deploy (like Middleton's play) the rhetorics of fiction—emphasis, selection, connection, speculation.

If, in such respects, *A Game at Chess* resembles all other histories and plays, it does differ from the more familiar history plays of the 1590s, praised and epitomized by Thomas Nashe:

> How would it have joyed brave Talbot (the terror of the French) to think that, after he had lain two hundred years in his tomb, he should triumph again on the stage, and have his bones new embalmed

with the tears of ten thousand spectators at least, at several times, who, in the tragedian that represents his person, imagine they behold him fresh bleeding.

That is not how anyone has ever reacted to *A Game at Chess*. Its radical originality can be seen in the two features of Nashe's prescription which it conspicuously rejects: the focus on individual prowess, and the representation of a distant past.

There is, in *A Game at Chess*, no personal political protagonist. Like other Middleton plays, his last play emphasizes ensemble; it is not built around a single dominant 'star'. Middleton does not represent politics in terms of charismatic individuality, and he never created supermen like Marlowe's Tamburlaine, Shakespeare's Henry V, or Chapman's Duke of Byron. The insistence upon magnetic individuals (good or bad), which pervades earlier history plays, reflects and helps to perpetuate a political system defined by factions. The politics of faction is organized around loyalty to individuals. There are no stable political parties, no fundamentally ideological motives or groupings, only a complex network of interlocking personal relationships, shifting alliances and rivalries, within a relatively small ruling group.

Faction (as Conrad Russell, Kevin Sharpe, and other revisionist historians have demonstrated) still dominated English governance in the 1620s. Indeed, the Spanish Match—which is in one sense the subject of *A Game at Chess*—epitomizes the politics of faction. James I sought to cement an alliance between Catholic Spain and Protestant England by marrying the Prince of Wales to the sister of Felipe IV; as a result of this alliance, James expected Spanish help in restoring his son-in-law Frederick to his hereditary domain (the Palatinate), from which he had been ousted by Felipe IV's uncle (the Holy Roman Emperor Frederick II). This sort of dynastic diplomacy translated faction onto an international scale: personal alliances between ruling families determined the fate of nations.

The Spanish Match was never consummated. It was aborted by a combination of the old politics of faction and a new politics of ideology and race. Returning from Madrid in October 1623 after months of frustrating negotiations, Prince Charles and the Duke of Buckingham—in what contemporaries called a 'blessed revolution'—quickly created a new factional alliance against the King's pro-Spanish foreign policy. The heir to the throne and the royal favourite, working in concert, formed a formidable nexus of political patronage. But that localized personal power was, in 1624, allied to a more widespread and impersonal nexus of opposition, in a brief moment of national unity which *A Game at Chess* celebrates (Cogswell). Most of the King's subjects wanted anti-Catholic foreign and domestic policies; they did not want a Catholic Spanish Queen of England. A majority of public and Parliament believed that foreign policy should be dictated, not by personal family alliances (which might unite the Habsburg and the Stuart dynasties), but by ideological convictions (which bitterly divided their subjects).

The protagonist of *A Game at Chess* is not a person but a party: 'the White cause'. In his four plays on the reigns of Henry VI and Richard III (printed for the first time together in November 1623), Shakespeare had dramatized 'the contention' between 'the House of York' and 'the House of Lancaster', two rival factions with no discernible ideological differences, eventually reconciled by a marriage which unites the two dynasties. Middleton instead represents the contention between the House of Stuart and the House of Habsburg as a struggle between the White House and the Black House. Familial relationships, so central to the politics of faction and the history plays of Shakespeare, are ignored: though Prince Charles was James I's son, the White King is not characterized as the White Knight's father. Shakespeare used white and red roses as props, to clarify shifting factional alliances; Middleton uses white and black for the same purpose, but he also saturates clothing and skin-colour with meaning. And Middleton's audience celebrates the fact that a contracted marriage is never consummated.

In *A Game at Chess*, political conflict is ideologically (and racially) organized. That is one reason why the play's historical figures are translated into chess pieces. This conceit is usually explained as a ruse that helped Middleton slip an incendiary play past the censor. But the chess game is not just a disguise; it is also, in itself, a powerful signifier. Chess, which formalizes conflict into a binary opposition between polarized teams, articulates an emergent political system.

The organizational politics of party opposition did not crystallize until the crises of the 1640s, and did not develop into the familiar two-party Parliamentary system until the 1670s; historians are right to criticize anachronistic readings of the political turmoil of the 1620s in terms of simple divisions between a 'court party' and a 'country party', or 'government' and 'opposition'. But Middleton has here *envisaged* party politics. In 1624 Thomas Scott called the divisions between Englishmen over continental politics '*the seminary of a civil war*' (*Vox Regis*, 22; his italics). Echoes of Middleton's 1624 play can be heard in the civil war of the early 1640s and then again in the party-political street-theatre of the Exclusion Crisis which preceded the Glorious Revolution. In March 1641 a 'Game at Chess' (possibly Middleton's play) was performed at Oxford before Prince Charles (the future Charles II); the prologue, specially written for the occasion, warned that 'The King had best look to't, ere't be too late. | He has had sufficient checks; now, 'ware the mate.' In a polemical pamphlet entitled *The Game at Chess: a metaphorical discourse showing the present state of this kingdom* (1643), King Charles I—the White Knight of Middleton's play—has become, instead, the Black King, and the White side 'betokens the Parliament's army'. In 1680 'The Devil in the habit of a Jesuit' seduced a nun before audiences at Bartholomew and Southwark Fairs; later, '*The Scene*

This 1624 title-page illustrates Gondomar's special chair, litter, and cane. The cane is not mentioned in Middleton's text, but may have been used in performance, as were the chair and litter.

suddenly draws off, and discovers Hell full of Devils, Popes and Cardinals'. *A Game at Chess* was the first, and is still the most evocative and complex, characterization of a recognizably modern political world.

Its modernity was its most scandalous feature. Unlike Talbot, Middleton's White King had not 'lain two hundred years in his tomb' before the players showed him 'on the stage'. The events dramatized in *A Game at Chess* were very recent history. The major players were all still alive. Gondomar's actual litter and special chair were brought on stage; the comedian who played him wore a discarded suit of Gondomar's clothes, and mimicked his personal mannerisms.

Other history plays worked to familiarize the far-away, to make the past present; Middleton's play sets out, instead, to re-present the present to itself. *A Game at Chess* applies to national and international politics an artistic agenda Middleton had perfected in the insistent present tensing of city comedies and Yorkshire tragedies, annals and almanacs. As in his Lord Mayor's shows, this 'Angle of the world' (Induction.1) at the same time represents and *is* London—a place where the fictive and the actual coalesce, where 'anie in the Assemblie' deceived by Jesuit misrepresentations (5.78–9) may be fictive persons in a fictive theatre, and/or real persons in Parliament, Privy Council, the Convocation of the Church of England, and/or ourselves now.

But re-presenting the present is not as easy as it may sound. Long before Bertold Brecht, Middleton realized the need to defamiliarize familiar material, as a way of forcing audiences to perceive freshly what they had always seen and therefore never noticed. That is one function of metaphor, and one function of chess in Middleton's 'epic theatre'. Chess is an alienation device: the most important political events of recent months and years were translated into a series of moves in a game. Every disguise signifies. Formalizing politics re-focused it.

Annabel Patterson has argued that the indirection, irony, and polyphony which epitomize what we call 'literature' originated in early modern England as a way of communicating past or through a censor; censorship created in authors and readers a hermeneutical habit, which located encoded meanings beneath the surface or between the lines. Deciphering this code (using techniques first advocated by the right-wing philosopher Leo Strauss), left-wing critics have discerned fragments of subversion in almost every early modern play and poem. But by finding resistance everywhere, this critical programme has tended to homogenize the very real political differences between texts and authors, and thus to obscure the demonstrable uniqueness—political and literary—of Middleton's play.

No doubt, censorship contributed to Middleton's double-focus. But such displacement is not just a response to censorship, and did not originate in early modern England. Comparable techniques can be found in the uncensored democratic comedies of Aristophanes (which Middleton could have read, and to which *A Game at Chess* has often been compared). Artistic displacement exists independently of censorship. Moreover, censorship does not necessarily produce dense or intense displacements. It takes little wit for an author to make a fictive character complain about a fictive ruler's failure to appreciate and reward his fictive soldiers (as Massinger did in 1623 in the superfluous subplot of *The Bondman*), and little wit in an interpreter to realize that such complaints apply to the English government's treatment of its own veterans. The doubled meanings of *A Game at Chess* are altogether more complicated, politically and artistically.

With or without censors, the doubling created by metaphor, metonymy, and irony multiply the intellectual and emotional content which can be packed into a single unit of text: they increase information density, thereby intensifying the pleasures of interpretation. One of its earliest interpreters, John Holles, ended his eyewitness description of *A Game at Chess* with the teasing assurance that 'Every particular will bear a large paraphrase.' This density, intensity, and variety multiply the markets to which a text may appeal. John Chamberlain reported that Middleton's play was 'frequented by all sorts of people: old and young, rich and poor, masters and servants, papists and puritans'. Perceived by contemporaries as simultaneously the most subversive and the most commercially successful play of its era, for both historians and literary critics *A Game at Chess* sets the standard by which the political force of early modern literature must be measured.

A Game at Chess made news—appropriately enough, because Middleton's play was made *from* news. Formally, it drew upon a long native tradition of anti-Catholic polemic, which ranged in substance from Donne's erudite *Ignatius his Conclave* to popular ballads and broadsides ridiculing the pope or celebrating the constancy of Protestant women (Watt). Factually, though, the sources for the play's political details were not magnificent old folios of official history, but rough pamphlets about recent events (extensively cited in the commentary).

More generally, Middleton transformed ephemera into art. In the early 1620s there was (as Joseph Frank, Richard Cust, Thomas Cogswell, and other historians have shown) an explosive proliferation of mechanisms—oral and textual, informal and institutionalized—for collecting and communicating political information. They included the gossip shop around St Paul's cathedral, the manuscript newsletters and Parliamentary reports regularly sent by London agents to their country patrons, the country inns and alehouses where merchants and pedlars retailed texts and re-told stories to local communities, the cheap news-sheets ('*corantos*'), printed in hundreds or thousands of copies. News had become, for the first time, a routine commodity, part of the long-distance traffic organized by merchants like Richard Fishbourne (to whom Middleton had dedicated the 1620 issue of *The Two Gates of Salvation*). By such means, the details of royal policy at home and abroad—what Tacitus had called *arcana imperii*, what James I labelled 'my prerogative, or mystery of state'—were exposed to the uncontrolled scrutiny of a wider public.

The 'genesis of the bourgeois public sphere', theorized by Jürgen Habermas, was actually consolidated in the early 1620s—the years in which, and about which, *A Game at Chess* and its sources were written. Not accidentally, the beginning of news coincides with the beginning of parties. Most of the products of the English printing industry, for a century, had been religious texts, ranging from expensive polemical theology to cheap popular piety. The press helped to create an ideological reading public, which in turn created a growing demand for ideological news.

Royal officials and apologists were quick to execrate this democratizing of information. Sir Francis Bacon, dismissing poetry as 'nothing else but *feigned history*', argued that 'ministers and great officers... and those who have handled the helm of government, and been acquainted with the difficulties and mysteries of state business' were the only people qualified to interpret political chronicles, and in 1622 his *History of the Reign of King Henry the Seventh* offered itself as a new model of historicity. In his 1620 court masque, *News from the New World Discovered in the Moon*, Ben Jonson ridiculed the 'printers of news' and 'factors of news' who manufactured 'news, news, news', selling lies to 'the common people'; in 1626, Jonson's play *The Staple of News* expanded this satire of the age's 'hunger and thirst after published pamphlets of news'. One explicit object of Jonson's scorn was *A Game at Chess*.

Not content to complain, the government did its best to restrain the growing 'inordinate liberty of unreverent speech'. Royal proclamations of 1620 and 1621 forebade 'excess of lavish and licentious speech in matter of state'. The English Reformation had laboured to create a learned clergy, but the success of that effort had now produced a cadre of ideological intellectuals, many of them openly critical of government policy; in response, the King's 1622 'Directions concerning Preaching' specifically constrained the freedom of ministers. This crackdown on the press and the pulpit, putting 'a silencst Muzzle, on all the Barking Tongmen of the Time', Middleton attributes, not inaccurately, to the 'policie' of Gondomar (3.21–2). Before the play begins, the White Bishop's Pawn—a faithful servant of the Calvinist White Bishop—has been gelded by a member of the Black House; castration was a popular Protestant metaphor for censorship of spiritual texts by an absolutist, despotic regime (Taylor, *Castration*, 75–91).

But Middleton's play does more than condemn censorship: it also anticipates that it will be censored. For nine days the actors played 'nothing else, knowing their time cannot be long' (Sir Francis Nethersole, 14 August). Spectators waited for hours and paid higher prices to see *A Game at Chess* precisely because 'it is thought it will be called in' (George Lowe, 7 August) and 'it is feared it will be [suppressed] ere long' (John Woolley, 11 August) and 'it is believed... that it will be prohibited' (Amerigo Salvetti, 13 August)—a crackdown which, when it came, simply confirmed the play's accusations. The nascent news media did not just supply Middleton with sources; they also supplied him with a vehicle. The expected and then actual suppression of performances made *A Game at Chess* news, creating a demand for performances and reports, for manuscripts, for printed editions. Middleton turned the censorship of news against itself, creating a text designed to make news of censorship.

James I died on 27 March 1625, and by May readers could buy an illicit edition of *A Game at Chess*, which claimed to have been printed in the Netherlands. The timing was not coincidental, and like the play's other disguises the false imprint is, in itself, a signifier: it aligned the play with the pamphlets of Thomas Scott and other radical Protestant critics of the Stuart regime. James had sought a *rapprochement* with the Spanish because, as an hereditary monarch, he detested the republican alternative offered by the Dutch. In 1621, James was outraged by a Parliamentary speech which compared his

Contemporary English statesmen in council on 21 April 1624: notice the chessboard pattern on the floor of this 1624 broadside.

ministers to those of Edward II: 'To reckon me with such a prince is to esteem me a weak man' (and—though neither he nor his critics dared openly say so—a sodomite). In *A Game at Chess*, James is again 'paralleled and scandalized', and weakness—the accusation he found most intolerable—suffuses the portrait. In chess, kings are inevitably weak, and the White House is saved, not by its King, but by its Knight, Duke, Bishop, and Pawns. Although everyone in the audience knows the truth, the White King, duped by the Black Knight, cannot see it (2.388–416). As recent historians (Elliott, Lockyer, Pursell, Redworth) have shown, James I's diplomatic strategy was based upon a fundamental misperception: Spain could not deliver the Palatinate, and would not deliver the Infanta on terms which England could accept. When his own minister, the White King's Pawn, turns out to be an enemy agent (3.203–27), the White King treats it as a personal (not an ideological) betrayal, still playing the game in terms of faction rather than party.

A Game at Chess, in portraying the weakness of James I, also demonstrated it. When he finally learned of the play, the King was outraged that none of his own officers or courtiers had informed him earlier. From the beginning, some critics have assumed that Middleton must have had a patron or protector at court: the Earl of Pembroke (Margot Heinemann), the Duke of Buckingham and Prince Charles (Louis B. Wright), the 'war party' (Thomas Cogswell, Jerzy Limon). There is no evidence for any of these connections, and given the King's diminishing authority no reason to search for one (Yachnin 1987). By positing a patron, critics have tried to explain away Middleton's application of private reason to public affairs: they have tried to fold the play back into the old politics of faction, when in fact it heralds the new politics of ideology. One of Middleton's probable sources, Thomas Scott's 1624 pamphlet *Vox Regis*, begins with a prolonged defence of his criticisms of the Jacobean regime, arguing that it was an individual's *duty* to write in defence of his faith and his nation. Scott's pamphlets were authorized by his own conscience, nothing else. The same is almost certainly true of Middleton's play.

Like Scott's pamphlets, *A Game at Chess* champions an ideology of resistance. As in the Elizabethan history play, communal self-identity is here defined by opposition

The reunion of King James and Prince Charles, with public celebrations in the background (1623). Compare the reunion of White King and White Knight in the play's final scene.

to a demonized Other. Nashe had celebrated Talbot as 'the terror of the French'; the White Knight proves himself equally terrible to the Spanish. The Habsburg empire was the world's first global power, and Middleton's White Kingdom resembles Cold War Cuba more than postwar America: a small island uncomfortably close to an aggressive proselytizing imperial superpower, whose victims include not only Protestants but Catholics and non-Christians (5.262–88). Against such an opponent, the author of *The Peacemaker* does not, even here, advocate war; he urges, instead, vigilant independence, exposure, 'discovery'. The besieged nationalism of *A Game at Chess* is not the expansionist ethic of conqueror or colonist. It is characterized, above all, by resistance to efforts to impose upon the world a single 'universal monarchy'.

But that repeated association of 'monarchy' and 'hierarchy' with the enemy had implications for domestic politics: 'a foul injury to Spain', eyewitness John Holles reported, Middleton's satire also did 'no great honour to England'. In an inversion of dramatic and political hierarchy, the play's most important White character is not a male king, but a female pawn. The story of the White Queen's Pawn is, among other things, an attack on the principle of obedience—the very principle of absolutism which the King, and royal apologists like Donne and Jonson, had loudly reiterated during the crackdown on dissent (Taylor, 'Forms of Opposition'). Such obedience was as important to the church as to the monarchy. The ritual of 5.23–42 satirizes both Spanish Catholicism and the Arminian party in England (Taylor, 'Divine'). As early as 1615, King James had decisively sided with the Arminians—led by the future Archbishop of Canterbury, William Laud—against his own Calvinist Archbishop George Abbot (Cranfield and Fincham); by the early 1620s, as Nicholas Tyacke and Peter Lake have demonatrated, Arminians were increasingly visible within the English episcopate.

'No bishop, no king', James had insisted in the first year of his reign. A satire against empire, episcopacy, and obedience is not likely to strengthen royal absolutism; the imperial pretensions of Stuart court culture (Smuts) are not enhanced by a text which cites Pliny, Scaliger, Athenaeus, and the *Scriptores Historiae Augustae* to document the carnal excesses of an imperial élite (5.185–232)—and then goes on to suggest that the heir to the English throne is a greedy liar, and the King's own favourite a sodomite. Life at court is characterized as a game—and games are, by definition, not natural but artificial. What makes this denaturalizing of hierarchy even worse is the presence of kings, dukes, and bishops on both sides; one hierarchy mirrors the other. But one side represents an evil which the audience rejects. Thus, there can be no intrinsic dignity or authority in bishops or dukes or kings, who may, as individuals, be either good or bad, worthy of obedience or deserving of disrespect. The repetition of the figure destroys its exemplarity.

This unravelling by repetition is only part of the play's sustained destruction of the cultural distance which legitimates inequality. Power is dependent on the perception of power: in the formula of Clifford Geertz, 'the real is as imagined as the imaginary'. That is why Queen Elizabeth banned cheap reproductions of her portrait, and why King James prohibited actors from portraying living kings: both monarchs tried to limit and control the *external* circulation of representations of sovereignty. At the same time, both encouraged an increasingly elaborate and costly *internal* circulation of representations of sovereignty—epitomized by the masque, in which the court offered itself an image of its own power. In masques, allegorical roles disguised real courtiers; the characteristic climax is a 'discovery', in which a change of perception precipitates a change of state. *A Game at Chess*, by transferring these conventions into a public space, radically transforms their significance. When Buckingham and other courtiers performed as Gypsies in Jonson's most popular masque, *The Gypsies Metamorphosed* (1621), their audacious will to play demonstrated and enhanced their privileged status; when Buckingham and other courtiers are portrayed as chessmen in *A Game at Chess*, they are robbed of the privilege of self-portrayal, and suffer rather than command the will to play.

A Game at Chess demystifies, by its undignified representing of the present, the very authority of authority. If William Hazlitt had been reading it, instead of *Coriolanus*, he might not have concluded so quickly that 'The language of poetry naturally falls in with the language of power'; if Stephen Greenblatt had been reading it, instead of *Henry V*, he might not have despaired that all 'subversive doubts...serve paradoxically to intensify the power of the king'. Instead of the absolutist glamour of theatricality found in earlier history plays, this last great chronologer's drama reduces majesty to a mannerism and foreign policy to a farcical plot. Even as it defends a besieged form of Christianity, it simultaneously de-sacralizes the state (Moretti). Politics here is explicitly a mere game, which some people play better than others. In this 'Machiavellian moment', Middleton celebrates discovery: that is, news, journalism, the abolition of distance, the public stripping away of authoritative disguises—by characters, but also by spectators and readers. In the uncontrollable laughter of those audiences, in the uncontrollable circulation among readers of the news and texts of *A Game at Chess*, the authority of an *ancien régime* began to dissolve. As Napoleon said of *The Marriage of Figaro*, so we might say of *A Game at Chess*: 'C'est déjà la revolution'.

SEE ALSO

A Game at Chess: A Later Form, 1825
Occasional Poems, 1886
'Lives and Afterlives', 25
General textual introduction: *Companion*, 712
List of works cited: *Companion*, 848
Textual introduction and apparatus: *Companion*, 874
Authorship and date: *Companion*, 439

A GAME at CHESSE

Compoŝde by Tho: Middleton

Induction *The Induction!*

(·.·)

Ignatius discouerd, Error asleepe.

Ign—Hah? where? what Angle of the world is this?
that I can neyther see the politick face
nor wth my refinde Nostrills taste the Footesteps
of anie my disciples, Sonnes and heyres
as well of my designes as Institution,
I thought theyde spread ouer the world by this time
couerd the Earths face and made darke the Land

This text represents the earliest extant version of the play, in the spelling, punctuation, capitalization, and other manuscript conventions of Middleton, so far as these can be represented in print. (See illustrations, pp. 1780 and 1791.) No attempt is made here to preserve variant letter-forms (such as the distinction between italic and secretary letters within words); word-spacing has been standardized. This commentary is primarily historical; it concentrates upon political allusions, conventions of early modern English usage, Middleton's sources, his process of composition and revision, and evidence of censorship. For a modern-spelling text with a literary and theatrical commentary, see *A Later Form*.

Title *A GAME at CHESSE* The play was licensed by the Master of the Revels, Sir Henry Herbert, on 12 June 1624, for the usual fee of one pound; the King's Men claimed that he had licensed the text they played, and produced the manuscript to prove it. The first complete draft, represented here, draws upon pamphlets not published until mid-May. The first performance—of the revised text—occurred on August 5 (the anniversary of James I's escape from the Gowrie Conspiracy against his life). Between June and October, the actors normally played to primarily city audiences, while the provincial gentry and aristocracy returned to their estates in the country. King James and his court had begun a state progress through the Midlands on July 18. The earliest surviving manuscript is dated August 13.

Compoŝde Middleton's apostrophes were often placed over rather than between letters. He often used the verb 'composed' to describe his activity as a writer.

Middleton The author's identity—though known to the actors, the censor, and those who read the play in manuscript—was not known by any of the extant early witnesses to the play's performances, and was not indicated in the printed texts.

Induction.0.1 ***The Induction*** John Gee's *New Shreds of the Old Snare* (1624), one of Middleton's probable sources, begins with 'The Induction', which refers to 'the great seducing *Masters*, especialy the *Iesuites*' and their '*Loiolan*' tricks, which are described—in the trope Gee uses in both his books of 1624—in terms of the '*tyring house*' and the 'stage': 'Come and heare a Iesuits play'. This is immediately followed by an account of the efforts of two 'Iesuites' and a female recusant to convert a 'yong woman' in London 'some three years since.' For the prologue Middleton later added, see *Later*.

0.3 ***Ignatius*** St Ignatius Loyola (1491–1556), Catholic and Spaniard; author of *Spiritual Exercises*, a guide to self-examination, deeply influential in the Counter-Reformation, and related to the Jesuit emphasis on confession (see 1.77, etc.). Subject of a 'Comedie' projected for Ash Wednesday at Trinity College, Cambridge (Joseph Mead, 22 February 1623, f. 289).

Error often associated with Catholicism by Protestants, as in Spenser's *Faerie Queene* I.i.13–26

1 ***Ign*** Middleton normally abbreviated speech prefixes (but did not indent or italicize them, as this edition consistently does).

Angle 'that angle of the world *England*' (Thomas Scott, *The Second Part of Vox Populi* (1624), 26)

3 **wth** with (a common abbreviation)

refinde Middleton often spelled the monosyllabic past participle 'de'.

6 **theyde** Middleton often omitted the apostrophe in contractions. Here, his preferred 'de' ending occurs, even though the elided word is 'had'.

ouer over. Early modern English normally used 'u' as a medial letter (for either consonant or vowel) and 'v' for an initial letter (even when it represented a vowel, as at l. 12, 'Vnperfect').

7–8 **couerd . . . Grassehoppers** Rumour greatly exaggerated the magnitude of Jesuit infiltration: Walter Yonge in 1622 estimated the number in England and Ireland at 12,000, while Thomas Scott claimed to know of 255 in London alone (*2 Vox Populi*, 30).

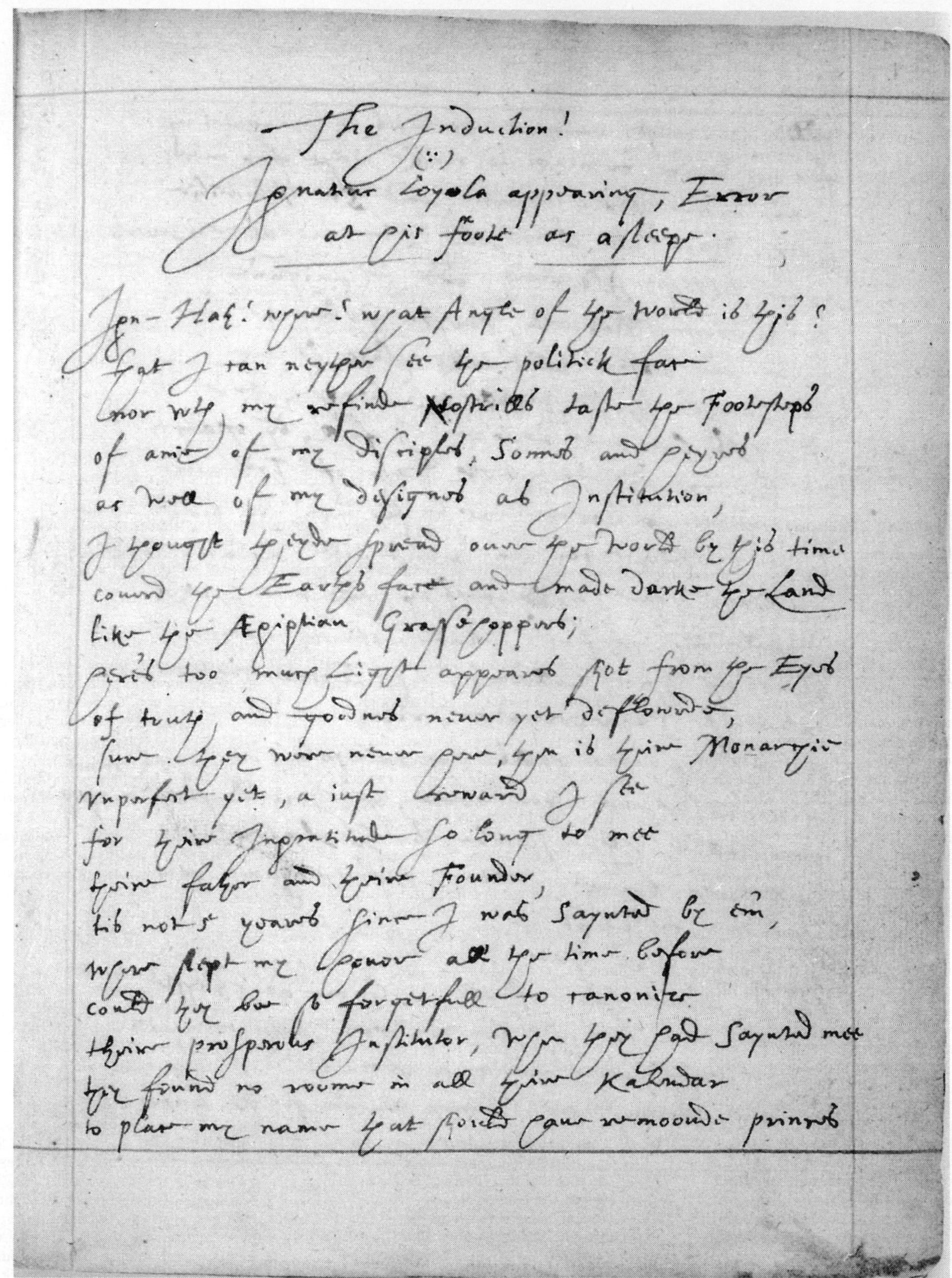

The Induction.
(:)
Ignatius Loyola appearing, Error
at his foote as asleepe.

Ign. Hah! where? what Angle of the world is this?
that I can neyther see the politick face
nor with my refinde Nostrills taste the Footesteps
of anie of my disciples, Sonnes and heires
as well of my designes as Institution,
I thought theyde spread over the world by this time
covered the Earths face and made darke the Land
like the Ægiptian Grassehoppers;
heres too much Light appeares shot from the Eyes
of truth and goodnes never yet deflowred,
sure they were never here, then is their Monarchie
vnperfect yet, a iust reward I see
for their Ingratitude so long to mee
their father and their Founder,
tis not 5 yeares since I was Sainted by em,
where slept my honor all the time before
could they be so forgetfull to canonize
their prosperous Institutor, when they had Sainted mee
they found no roome in all their Kalendar
to place my name that should have removde princes

A Game at Chesse in Middleton's own handwriting (actual size), showing the opening stage direction and the first twenty lines of the first speech. The edited text of 'An Early Form', printed here, represents an earlier version of the play, which differs from this authorial manuscript in many details: notice the differences in the wording of the opening stage direction. No attempt is made here to preserve variant letter forms: notice, in the photograph of the fourth line of the speech, the two different forms of the letter 's' in the word that our edition prints as 'disciples'. The manuscript does not distinguish stage directions or speech prefixes by using italic handwriting; our printed edition consistently uses italic for those features, and also consistently makes speech prefixes jut out into the left margin (which the manuscript does not). We also normalize the indenting of stage directions: notice the differences in indentation in the three initial lines of stage direction in the manuscript. The four long lines that form a ruled box around the central text-area of the page are hand-drawn in red ink.

like the Ægiptian Grassehoppers;
heres too much Light appeares shot from the Eyes
of truth and goodnes neuer yet deflowrde,
sure they were neuer here, then is theire Monarchie
Vnperfect yet, a iust reward I see
for theire Ingratitude so long to mee
theire father and theire Founder,
tis not 5 Yeares since I was Saynted by em̃,
where slept my honor all the time before
could they bee so forgetfull to canonize
theire prosperous Institutor, when theyde Saynted mee
they found no roome in all theire Kalendar
to place my name that should haue remooude princes
pulde the most eminent prelates by the rootes up
for my deere coming to make waye for mee,
lett euerie pettie Martir, and St Homilie,
Roch, Main, and petronell, Itch and ague-Curers
youre Abbesse Aldegund, and Cunigund
the widdowe Marcell, vicar Policarpe
Sislie and Vrslie, all take place of mee,
and but for the Bissextill, or leape-Yeare
and thats but one in three, I fall by chance
into the nine and twentith daye of Februarie
there were no Roome else for mee, see theire Loue
theire Conscience too, to thrust mee a lame souldier
into leape Yeare, my Wraths up, and mee thinkes
I could wth the first Sillable of my name
blowe up theire Colledges, up, Error, wake,

8 **Ægiptian** The Jesuits '(like the Caterpillers of Egypt) doe eate vp the fat and best fruits of the Land' (Thomas Robinson, *The anatomy of the English nunnery at Lisbon* (1622), 13).

12 **iust** just. Early modern English made little use of 'j'; 'i' served as vowel or consonant.

15 **not 5 Yeares** Loyola was beatified in 1609, canonized on 12 March 1622. Protestants believed in direct address to God, without the intercession of saints.
em̃ Middleton always centres the apostrophe over the 'm' in this contraction, and often places apostrophes at what seems to modern readers the 'wrong' place.

19 **Kalendar** the subject of much theological dispute. The Church of England calendar still preserved some saints' days; Puritans believed only the Sabbath should be celebrated. James I regularly vetoed Sabbatarian bills passed by Parliament. Finding a place for Loyola in the Catholic calendar had caused controversy, as recorded in Joseph Mead's letter of 1 February 1623: 'In France the Iesuites hauing putt St Germane out of the Almanack (in the end of October) to putt in Ignatius Loyola, (who was this yeare sollemly canonized for a saint) were complained of to the Lieutenants Ciuill (Iudge in such causes at Paris) by the Chanons of St Germane (in whose parish the Kinges Paliace is. & sentence was giuen, that the Fathers should prouide another place for Loyola, & their copies thus printed should be confiscate & burnt' (Harleian 389).

24 **Roch . . . petronell** In a passage discussing Loyola, a fictional Catholic claimed that 'God hath assigned to euery other Saint the cure of some one disease or other, as to St. *Roch* the plague, to St. *Petronel* the feuer, to St. *Main* the itch' (*State Mysteries of the Iesuites*, tr. Peter Gosselin, (1623), 11).

25 **Aldegund** St Aldegundis (*c.*635–84). Although I have found a few contemporary references to her, none identifies her as an 'Abbesse', or treats her satirically.
Cunigund St Cunegund (*c.*978–1033) (perhaps punning on 'cunny', cunt). 'The like story we read of one Cunegunda . . . in whose chamber the divell (in the likenesse of a youngman, with whom she was suspected to be too familiar in court) was often seen coming in and out' (Reginald Scot, *Discouerie of Witchcraft*, Book 16, chap. 5; a source Middleton used for *Witch*).

26 **Marcell** St Marcella (*c.*410). I have not discovered Middleton's source for identifying her as a 'widdowe', or treating her satirically.
vicar (later altered to 'Parson'). 'Vicar' might suggest criticism of the hierarchy of the English church, much resented by Puritans; 'Parson', by contrast, would imply non-established clergy.
Policarpe St Polycarp, martyred bishop of Smyrna (*c.*69–155), one of the 'primitive' fathers of the Church, recognized in the Geneva Bible notes, John Foxe's 'Book of Martyrs', and many other Protestant sources: in Middleton's lifetime, the most immediately recognizable and admirable name in this satirical list of saints.

27 **Sislie** St Cecilia, martyr and patron saint of musicians (third century), mentioned in English accounts of visits to Rome (Anthony Munday's *English Roman Life*, Morrison's *Itinerary*, etc.) The colloquial 'Sislie' is the name of a maid in two plays: Thomas Heywood's *A Woman Killed with Kindness* (1602) and Gervase Markham's *The Dumb Knight* (1608).
Vrslie St Ursula (fourth century), daughter of a British king: the English nunnery at Lisbon claimed to possess 'the head of S. *Vrsula*' (Gee, *New Shreds*, Q3).

28 **Bissextill** so called because in the Julian Calendar the sixth day before the Kalends of March was counted twice: hence, 'double sixth'. The title-pages of all London almanacs for 1624 noted that it was the 'bissextill, or leape-yeare' (John Rudston, *New Almanack*).

29 **one in three** In a Latin epigram by Raphael Thorius (written *c.*1623), prompted by the French dispute over the calendar of saints, God offered Ignatius the leap-year feast-day—meaning he would be ignored 'three' years for every 'one' year he was celebrated. (Loyola's actual feast day is 31 July.)

32 **a lame souldier** '*Ignatius Loiola*, a lame souldier' (Robinson, *English nunnery*, 10). Although the exact phrase seems unique to Robinson and Middleton, Loyola's lameness is mentioned in many Protestant books on the Jesuits, always unsympathetically (and thus unlike Middleton's use of it).

34 **first Sillable** 'Ign' (as in the abbreviated speech prefixes) suggesting *ignis* (Latin for 'fire'): 'his name taketh its signification from fire' (Gosselin, 6).

35 **Colledges** seminaries. The Society of Jesus was the first Catholic order founded specifically for the purpose of teaching.

father of Supererogation, rize,
it is Ignatius calls thee, Loyola!

Er—what haue you donne, oh I could sleepe in ignorance
immortallie, the slumber is so pleasing,
I sawe the brauest setting for a game now
that euer my Eye fixt on;

Ign: what Game prethee?

Er—the noblest Game of all, a Game at Chesse
twixt our side and the Whitehouse, the men sett
in theire iust order readie to goe to't;

Ign: were anie of my Sonnes placst for the Game,?

Er—yes, and a daughter too, a secular daughter
that playes the Black Queenes pawne, hee the Bl.
Bishops,

Ign—if euer power could showe a Mastrie in thee
lett it appeare in this,

Er—tis but a dreame a uision you must thinke

Ign—I care not what
so I behold the children of my cunning
and see what ranck they keepe

Er—you haue youre Wish,
behold theres the full Number of the Game,
Kings, and theire pawnes, Queenes, Bishops, Knights
& dukes,

Ig: Dukes? theire cald Rookes by some,

Er—Corruptiuelye?
Le Roc the Word, Custode de La Roche
the Keeper of the Forts, in whome both Kings
repose much Confidence, and for theire trust sake
Courage and Worth, do Well deserue those Titles,

Ign—the Answeres high, I see my Sonne and daughter,

Enter the Bl. Qu^{s} pawne and Bl. Bps.

36 **Supererogation** overpayment, specifically in Catholic doctrine works performed over and above God's commands, a surplus—usually accumulated by saints—which the Church might use (through indulgences) for the salvation of souls who fell short of God's standard. Luther's attack on supererogation—directly related to his attack on the mediation of the saints (see 1.15–31), and the sale of indulgences (see 4.255)—was central to the Reformation: 'No saint had adequately fulfilled God's commandments in this life. Consequently the saints have done absolutely nothing which is superabundant. Therefore they have left nothing to be allocated through indulgences' (*Explanation of 'The Ninety-Five Theses'*, 1518). *Tom Tell-Troath* (1622) attacked King James I's persistence in pursuing peace, when all his enemies had resorted to war against his 'children', as 'such a strange peace of Supererogation / as will serve to astonish the present Age / and that to come' (7).

41–2 **that ... prethee** a single verse line. Early texts do not indicate verse structure by indenting the second half-line, as do most modern editions. Compare ll. 54–5, 58–9, etc.

42 **Game** Geopolitical and ideological rivalries were often visualized as games: see 'Lives', Ill. 1, p. 26.

44 **Whitehouse** See G.B.'s translation of Vida's sixteenth-century Latin poem on chess, *Ludus Scacchiae: Chesse-play* (1597): 'One side much like the white-facde *Galles*,' [i.e. ancient Gauls, northern European Germanic tribes] 'thus standing in aray, To fight against the *Black-amoores*'. The classical contrast between white northern Europeans and black sub-saharan Africans was originally, in Greek and Roman medical theory, a criticism of both extremes, from the perspective of the 'temperate', balanced reddish-brown complexions of Mediterranean peoples; white northerners were thought to be phlegmatic barbarians, less quick-witted than Mediterraneans (as the White King is initially outwitted by the Black Knight). Although Middleton characterized the English as white, that term was at the time still used for many inhabitants of Asia (China, Korea, Japan) and for the native peoples of North America; it distinguished between northern and southern Europeans, not between Europeans and all other peoples. For the emergence of modern racial meanings of the word *white*, see Taylor, *Buying Whiteness*.
men 'as for the fashion of the peeces, that is according to the fantasie of the workman ... Some make them like men' (G. B., *Ludus Scacchiae*).

47 **secular** living in the world (i.e. not in the seclusion of a nunnery)

48 **Black** 'Sin of itself is black' (*Solomon* 17.29); see also *The Black Book*. For the racial contrast with 'white', see Induction.44. Black was systematically associated, in Christian mythology, with night, hell, and death.
Bl. Black. Designations of pieces are regularly abbreviated in dialogue, stage directions, and speech prefixes.

51 **tis ... thinke** This single manuscript line combines two verse part-lines: 'tis but a dreame' completes the iambic pentameter begun by 'let it appeare in this', and 'a uision you must thinke' begins a new iambic pentameter line, which will be completed by 'I care not what'. Middleton often writes two half-lines together in this way, to save paper (which was very expensive).
tis but a dreame King James, in his opening speech to Parliament on 19 February 1624, describing his change of policy in relation to negotiations with Spain, said 'I awaked as a man out of a dreame' (Folger MS V.b.303, p. 335).
uision vision. (Middleton, idiosyncratically, began words with minuscule 'u' even when a consonant was intended; he used initial 'V' only when the word was capitalized.)

58 **Dukes?** 'Duke' enables identification of the white rook as the Duke of Buckingham. The argument justifying the term 'Duke' for 'rook' is taken from J. Barbier's revision of the first book on chess by an Englishman, Arthur Saul's *The Famous Game of Chesse-Play* (1618): 'the Rooke is called of some the Duke ... wee may allow them that Name, in the sense that the *French* seemes to inferre, by their denomination of this Piece, which they call, *Le Roc*, or *Le custode de la Roche*, (that is to say) the Rocke or keeper of the Rocke: intending thereby, the Gouernor of a Prouince, which commonly is resident in the strongest castle in the Countrey ... and they are commonly Dukes. So that although these Dukes seeme remote from the King and Courte, yet in theyr substitution and trust on them reposed, they may be accounted in worth and power next to the King. In this sense (I say) may the Rookes bee called Dukes' (C3^{v}–C5).
theire they're

59 ? (often used where modern English calls for an exclamation mark)

62 **trust** trust's. (Genitive apostrophes and redundant sibilants are often omitted.)

64.1 ***Bl. Qu^{s} ... Bl. Bps.*** Black Queen's ... Black Bishop's. This minimal original stage direction was later revised to bring on 'both houses' in their entirety (requiring more theatrical resources than are presumed by the first draft).

Er—those are 2 pawnes the bl.Q$^{s.}$ and the Bishops

Ign—pawnes argue but poore Spirits, & slight præfermnts,
not Worthie of the name of my Disciples,
if I had stood so nigh, I would haue cut
that Bishops Throate but Ide haue had his place
and told the Queene a Loue-tale in her Eare
would make her best pulse dance, theres no Elixir
of brayne or Spirit amongst em̃;

Er—why would you haue em̃ playe agaynst themselues,
thats quite agaynst the Rule of Game, Ignatius;

Ign—push, I would rule my selfe, not obserue rule,

Er—why then yoůde playe a Game all by youre selfe,

Ign—I would doo anye thing to rule alone,
Tis rare to haue the world reignd in by one;

Er; See em̃ anon, and marke em̃ in theire playe,
Obserue, as in a dance, they glide awaye,

Ign—Oh wth what longings will this brest bee tost,
Vntill I see this Great Game wun and lost. *exeunt*

Actus Primi, Scæna prima.
Enter from the Black-house, a Weoman-pawne in Black, and from the whitehouse, a Weoman-pawne in white;

Act 1

Bl.p. I ne're see that face but my pittie rizes,
when I behold so cleere a Mr-peice
of heauens Art, wrought out of dust and Ashes,
and at next thought to giue her lost æternallie,
(in being not ours but the daughter of Ignorance)
my soule bleedes at mine Eyes;

wh.p. where should Truth speake
if not in such a sorrowe⸮ theire teares playnelie,
beshrewe mee if shee weepe not heartilie,
what is my peace to her to take such paynes in't,
if I wander to losse and wth broad Eyes
yet misse the path shee can run blindefold in,
(through often exercize) why should my oursight
though in the best Game that er'e Christian Lost
rayse the least Spring of pittie in her Eye,
tis doubtlesse a great charitie, and no Vertue
could win mee surer;

66 **præfermnts** preferments
73 **agaynst themselues** 'So vices do ruffle among themselues, and vsurp one another' (William Camden, *Remains concerning Britain*, 1614).
78 **reignd** reined (but punning on 'reigned')
1.0.2 ***Enter from the Black-house*** At Induction.64.1, Black Queen's Pawn was the first chess piece to enter; here, her movement toward the White Queen's Pawn initiates the game. This independent mobility, especially in travelling back and forth between the Black and White house, is the most striking feature of the role. In Acts 2 and 5, her offstage movements interrupt the action between White Queen's Pawn and Black Bishop's Pawn; in the first scene of Act 2, the action requires her to enter and exit at least three times, and she reveals the secret passage that allows unobserved entrances and exits; in the first scene of Act 3, her entrance is the turning point in the action; in Act 3, and twice in Act 4, she leads the Black Bishop's Pawn and White Queen's Pawn on and off stage. This mobility was the most controversial feature of the religious order of 'Jesuitesses' founded by Mary Ward (1585–1645). George Abbot, Archbishop of Canterbury, considered Ward more dangerous than six Jesuits (Wallace, 'Mary Ward', 407).
pawne in Black . . . pawne in white 'a Pawne in white . . . another Pawne in blacke' (G. B., *Ludus Scacchiae*, D1).
0.2–3 ***Weoman-pawne in Black*** identified more precisely in later texts as the Black Queen's Pawn (confirming she is the same character/piece specified in the Induction). Some scholars have speculated that she represents Donna Luisa de Carvajal, 'a Spanish woman from Valladolid', resident in London, but the source of her speech at 5.160–2 specifically identifies her as an Englishwoman, and a member of the order of wandering female Jesuits established by Mary Ward. There is nothing in the text, the sources, or early responses, to suggest that the character impersonated an identifiable historical person, or was understood allegorically as anything other than a female Jesuit.
in Black 'Their Apparell is commonly a blacke . . . cloake, coule, and vaile' (Gee, *New Shreds*, concluding his discourse of 'English Nunnes', including a list of 'inlarged, vnclostred, vbiquitary' nuns, ending with '*Black Besse*').
0.3–4 ***Weoman-pawne in white*** identified more precisely in later texts as the White Queen's Pawn (although not so specified in dialogue until l. 310, after she has left the stage). There is nothing in the text, the sources, or early responses, to suggest that the character impersonated an identifiable historical figure, or was understood allegorically as anything other than a young Protestant Englishwoman, vulnerable to temptation by Catholics. Like any fictional character, she can be understood as 'representative', in this case perhaps—within the morality play tradition—as 'Everyman'. Here 'Everyman' is 'Everywoman': in the frontispiece of the 1611 edition of Richard Hooker's *Of the Laws of Ecclesiastical Polity*, the divine light falls on the King, the Church, and a female figure apparently representing the individual soul. However, the chess framework gives Every(wo)man here a specific social status (as pawn, commoner) and a political identity (as Protestant and English).
0.4 ***in white*** The account of the Jesuit attempt to seduce/convert a young woman in London at the beginning of Gee's *New Shreds* includes the appearance of 'a woman all in white'. A second story, of an attempt by Jesuits to convert 'a young Gentlewoman' in Surrey, also involves the appearance of '*a beautifull Virgin like your selfe, all in white*'. Summing up such incidents, Gee complains of the 'Actors having little or no vaietie of disguise. In all these three or foure Playes, none comes in Acting but *A Woman, A Woman, A Woman*, arrayed in *white, white, white*' (D2^{v}).
1 **ne're** ne'er, never
2 **Mr-peice** masterpiece
8 ⸮ (Middleton's unusual combination of query and comma)
12 **path . . . blindefold** Thomas Scott criticizes 'such as seeme to haue warrant for their *wayes*' but in fact are guided entirely by tradition or the opinion of friends and neighbours: 'by imitation and example of others whome wee reverence for knowledge or deuotion, by the custome and consent of times and places, wee are led as it were blindfold' (*The High-wayes of God and the King* (1623), 59).
13 **exercize** practice (but also suggesting Loyola's *Spiritual Exercises*)

Bl.p. blessed things præuayle wth't,
if euer Goodnes made a gratious promise
it is in yonder looke, what Litle paynes
would build a Fort for Vertue to all memorie
in that sweete Creature were the Ground-Worke firmer,

wh.p. it ha's beene all my glorie to bee firme
in what I haue profest,

Bl.p. that is the Enimie
that steales youre strenght awaye, and fights agaynst you,
disarmes youre Soule een' in the heate of battayle,
Youre Firmnes that waye makes you more infirme
for the right Christian Conflict, there I spied
a Zealous Primatiue Sparckle, but now flewe
from youre deuoted Eye, able to blowe up all the Errors
that euer sate in Councell wth youre Spirit,
Enter Bl B.s p.
and here comes hee whose Sanctimonious breath
will make that Sparke a Flame, list to him, Virgin,
at whose first Entrance, princes will fall prostrate,
weomen are weaker Vessells,

wh.p. by my pœnitence
a comlye præsentation, and the habit
to admiration reuerend,

Bl.p. but the heart, the heart, Ladie,
so meeke, that as you see good charitie picturde still
wth yong Ones in her Armes, so will hee cherish
all his yong Tractable sweete obedient daughters
een' in his bosome, in his owne deare bosome;
I am my selfe a Secular Iesuite
as manye Ladies are of wealth and Greatnes,
a second sort are Iesuites in Voto,
giuing theire Vowe in to the Father Generall
thats the black Bishop of our house, whose pawne
this Gentleman now stands for, to receiue
the Colledge habit at his holie pleasure

wh.p. but how are those in Voto employde, Ladie,
till they receiue the habit,

Bl.p. they̓re not idle,
hee findes em̓ all true Labourers in the Worke
of th' Vniuersall Monarchie, wch hee
and his Disciples principallie ayme at,
those are mayntaynde in manie Courts and palaces,
and are induc'st by noble personages
into great princes Seruices, and prooue
some Counsellors of State, some Secretaries
all seruing in Notes of Intelligence,
(as parish clearkes theire mortuarie Bills)
to the Father Generall, so are designes
oft times præuented, and Important Secretts
of State discouerd, yet no Author found
but those suspected oft that are most sound,
this Mysterie is too deepe yet for youre Entrance
and I offend to sett youre Zeale so back,
checkt by obedience wth desire to hasten
youre progresse to perfection, I commit you
to the great workers hands, to whose graue worth

23 **ha's** has. (Middleton often places a superfluous apostrophe in this word.)

30 **Primatiue** primitive, original. Catholics claimed to preserve 'the old religion', condemning the Reformation as a novel departure from well-established doctrines; Protestants claimed to be returning to authentic early doctrines, corrupted by the intervening medieval papacy.

31–2 **blowe ... Councell** (reminiscent of the Gunpowder Plot: four Jesuits were implicated in the 1605 Catholic conspiracy to blow up King James and Parliament—regarded by them as heretics)

32 **Councell** (*a*) private deliberation (*b*) gathering of church leaders, like the 1619 Synod of Dort, which brought together Protestants from much of Europe (*c*) gathering of political leaders, like the 1605 meeting of King James with his Parliament

32.1 ***Bl B.s p.*** Black Bishop's Pawn, a Jesuit, and therefore naturally dressed in the black vestments of his order.

33 **breath** 'there is admirable power in a Priests *breath*' (Gee, *Foot out of the Snare*, 1624)

42–4 **cherish ... bosome** Describing 'our Recusants daughters in *England*', Robinson explains how the Jesuits 'will cherish and nourish them, euen in their owne bosomes' (*English nunnery*, 9).

45 **Secular Iesuite** member of a female religious order founded in England by Mary Ward. These 'wandring Nuns ... observe the *Ignatian* habit, and go clad very like the Jesuits; in this onely differing from other Nuns, that they walk abroad the world, and preach the Gospel (as they call it) to their Sex in *England* and else-where' (James Wadsworth, *Memoirs*, published 1679, describing events in the 1620s).

46 **manye Ladies** The order founded by Ward was often called the 'English Ladies'. Prominent Catholic Englishwomen of the 1620s, besides Ward, included Lady Falkland (Elizabeth Carey, author of *The Tragedy of Mariam*) and the mother of the Duke of Buckingham (the royal favourite).

47–58 **second sort ... palaces** 'The second sort is, of men alone ... these make a vowe to receiue a habite of the society, at the pleasure of the Father Generall; and therfore they are called Iesuits in *Voto*: and by the labors of these men, the Iesuites wondrously auaile themselues in the fabricke of their Monarchy. For they maintaine in all kingdoms and Prouinces, in all courts of Princes, and Pallaces of great men, such of these as shall serue them' (*An exact and sound Discovery of the cheife mysteries of Iesuiticall iniquity*, trans. Isaac Bargrave (1619), B8^{v}–B9).

56 **Vniuersall Monarchie** See *The Spaniard's Perpetual Designs to an Universal Monarchy* (1624); similar claims about Spanish and/or papal intentions are made in *Vox Populi* and many other polemical tracts.

65–6 **Secretts of State** Gondomar credits English 'Priests and Iesuits' for the Spanish knowledge of 'the secrets of their State' (Scott, *2 Vox Populi*, 30).

66–7 **no ... sound** For ten years King James tried, through his ambassador in the Netherlands, to identify and punish the author of *Isaaci Casauboni Corona Regia* (1615), a slanderous depiction of the king which pretended to praise as virtues what were in fact vices; James wrongly believed it was written by Erycius Puteanus.

I fitt my Reuerence, as to you my wishes
Bl-Bs·p. doo you finde her supple?
Bl.p. ther'es a litle passage;
weomens poore Arguments make but Wimble holes,
the Augur is the mans.— *exit*
Bl.Bs·p. lett mee contemplate
wth holie wonder season my Accesse,
and by degrees approach the Sanctuarie
of unmacht bewtie sett in grace and Goodnes,
amongst the Daughters of men I haue not found
a more catholicall Aspect, that Eye
do's promise single life and meeke Obedience
uppon those lips the sweete fresh Buds of youth
the holie Dewe of prayer lyes like pearle
dropt from the opening Eyelids of the Morne
uppon the bashfull Rose; how bewteouslie
a gentle Fast not rigorouslie imposde
would looke uppon that cheeke, and how delightfullie
the curteous phisick of a tender pennance
whose Vtmost Crueltie should not exceede
the first feare of a Bride to beate downe frayltie
would worke to sound health youre Long festerd Iudgm̃t,
and make youre Merit, wch through erring Ignorance
appeares but spotted Righteousnes to mee
far cleerer then the Innocence of Infants:
wh.p. to that good worke I bowe, and will become
Obedience humblest daughter, since I finde
th' assistance of a sacred Strenght to ayde mee
the labour is as easie to serue Vertue
the right waye, since tis shee I euer serude
in my desire, though I transgrest in Iudgment:
Bl.Bs:p. thats easilie absolud amongst the rest
You shall not finde the Vertue that you serue now
a sharpe and cruell Mistris, her Eares open
to all youre Supplications, you maye boldlie
and safelie let in the most secret Sin
into her knowledge, wch Like uanisht man
neuer returnes into the world agen,
Fate locks not up more trulier
wh.p. to the Guiltie
that maye appeare some benefit,
Bl.Bs·p. who is so Innocent
that neuer stands in neede on't, in some Kinde,
if euerie thought were blabd thats so confest
the uerie Ayre wee breathe would bee unblest:
now to the worke indeed wch is to catch
her Inclination, thats the spetiall use
wee make of all our practise in all Kingdomes,
for by disclosing theire most secret Frayltties
things, wch once ours, they must not hide from us
thats the first article in the Creede wee teach em'
finding to what poynt theire bloud most enclines
Knowe best to apt them then to our Designes:
Daughter! the sooner you disperse youre Errors
the sooner you make haste to youre Recouerie
You must part wth em̃, to bee nice or modest
toward this good Action, is to imitate
the Bashfullnes of one conceales an Vlcer
for the uncomlie parts the Tumor uexes
til't bee past Cure, Resolue you thus far, Ladie,
the priuat'st thought that runs to hide It selfe
in the most secret Corner of youre heart nòw
must bee of my Acquayntance, so familiarlye
neuer shee frend of youre Night-Councell neerer,

74 **doo . . . supple** (spoken aside to Black Queen's Pawn; asides are seldom marked in early modern scripts)
76–7 **weomens . . . mans** These lines appear only in *Early*.
77 ***exit*** (leaving the White Queen's Pawn and Black Bishop's Pawn alone together, creating the privacy normative for the Catholic sacrament of confession.) Confessionals, as a special structure within churches, were introduced after the Council of Trent (1564), but were not yet universal, even in Catholic countries.
89 **Fast** generally rejected by Protestants, but favoured by Catholics and Arminians: Bishop Launcelot Andrewes encouraged 'works of chastisement of the body, as fasting' (26 February 1623).
91 **curteous** courteous
pennance expression of penitence, imposed by a priest, after he has heard a sinner's confession
94 **Iudgm̃t** judgement
97 **then** than
98 **good worke** emphasized by Catholics as the basis for salvation, but rejected by Calvinists: 'man hath no workes whereof he may glorie before God . . . he is iustified by only faith' (Jean Calvin, *The Institute of Christian Religion*, tr. (1561), fol. 201). England was the largest market for vernacular translations of Calvin's works.
102 **serude** served
104 **absolud** absolved, purged. Catholic priests had the power to absolve sinners, as part of the sacrament of confession; Protestants generally denied such sacerdotal authority, but some Arminians believed that 'Purging was ever the priest's office' (Bishop Andrewes, 25 December 1612; also 30 March 1600); confession and priestly absolution was also defended (pp. 83–5) in Richard Montagu's controversial Arminian *A Gagg for the new Gospell* (1624), which provoked a Parliamentary protest.
111 **more trulier** (double comparative, often used for emphasis)
118–25 **now . . . Designes** (an aside, confirming Protestant suspicions of auricular confession: 'by way of confession my master is able to unlock the secrets of every Prince, and to withdraw their subjects allegiance' (Scott, *Vox Populi*, A4))

wh.p. I stand not much in feare of anie Action
guiltie of that black time (most noble Holines)
I must confesse, as in a sacred Temple
throngd wth an Auditorie, some come rather
to feede on humayne obiect, then to taste
of Angells Foode; so in the congregation of quick thoughts
wch are more infinite then such assemblies
I cannot wth truths safetie speake for all,
some haue beene wanderers, some fond, some sinfull,
but those found euer but poore Entertaynment
theyde small encouragement to come agen,
the single life wch stronglie I professe now,
heauen pardon mee, I was about to part from;

Bl.Bs.p. then you haue past through Loue?

wh.p. but left no Stayne
in all my passage (S^{ir}) no print of Wrong
for the most chast Mayde that maye trace my footsteps;

Bl.Bs.p. how came you off so cleere?

wh.p. I was dischargd
by an inhumayne Accident, wch modestie
forbids mee to putt anie Language to:

Bl.Bs.p. how you forgett youre selfe, all actions
clad in theire proper language, though most sordid
my Eare is bound by dutie to lett in
and lock up euerlastinglie, shall I helpe you
hee was not found to answere his Creation,
a uestall Virgin in a Slip of prayer
could not deliuer mans losse modestlier,
twas the white Bishops pawne;

wh.p. the same blest S^{ir},

Bl.B$^{s.}$p. a Puritane well pickled,

wh.p. by base trecherie
and Violence præparde by his Competitor
the black Knights pawne, whome I shall euer hate fort

Bl.Bs.p. twas of Reuenges the unmanliest waye
that euer Riuall tooke, a Villanie
that for youre sake Ile ner'e absolue him off,

wh.p. I wish it not so heauie,

Bl.Bs.p. hee must feele it
I neuer yet gaue absolution
to anie Crime of that unmanning Nature;
it seemes then you refusde him for defect,
therein you stand not pure from the desire
that other weomen haue in ends of marriage
pardon my boldnes, if I sift youre goodnes
to the last grayne;

wh.p. I reuerence youre paynes (S^{ir})
and must acknowledge custome to enioye
what other weomen challenge and possesse
more rulde mee then desire, for my desires
dwell all in ignorance, and Ile ne're wish
to knowe that fond waye maye redeeme em̃ thence,

BlB$^{s.}$p. I neuer was so taken, besett doublie
now wth her Iudgment, what a strenght it putts forth
I bring worke neerer to you, when yau'e seene
a Mr-peice of man, composde by heauen
for a Great princesse fauour, Kingdomes Loue
so exact Enuie could not finde a place
to stick a Blot on person or on fame;
haue you not found Ambition swell youre Wish then?
and desire steere youre Bloud?

wh.p. by Vertue neuer,
Iue onelie in the dignitie of the Creature
admirde the Makers Glorie;

Bl.B$^{s.}$p. shees impregnable;
a Second Seige must not fall off so tamelie,
shees one of those must bee informde to knowe
a daughters dutie, wch some take untaught;
her modestie brings her behinde hand much
my ould meanes I must flye to, yes, tis it;
please you peruse this small Tract of obedience

138 **black time** night; but also suggesting 'black lust' (*Women Beware* 4.2.66). Conversion from the White to the Black House also suggests sexual corruption: 'Thou first mad'st me black', a prostitute complains to a customer (*Honest Whore* 15.477).

141 **humayne** human. ('Humane' and 'human' were not distinct words.)

142 **Angells Foode** literally, manna (as at *Solomon* 16.184); figuratively, the eucharist, 'food of angels' (Bishop Andrewes, 25 December 1618)

163 **uestall** vestal

167 **Puritane** a presbyterian, or more generally anyone who believed that the Church of England retained too many Roman Catholic features. (Later altered by censorship to the less specific 'heretic'.) This variant suggests that the White Bishop's Pawn might have been represented, on stage, in a manner which recognizably mimicked 'the godly'.

169 **Violence** 'The Papists here everywhere assault and insult upon our poor brethren in the ministry' (Joseph Mead, 5 September 1623).

170 **fort** for't, for it

171 **Reuenges** The play does not explain why the gelding is characterized as revenge (here and at 4.30). Middleton may have been thinking of the vengeful castration of the theologian Peter Abelard by his lover's uncle. The first editions of the letters of the fourteenth-century lovers Abelard and Heloise, and of Abelard's autobiography, were published in France in 1616.

173 **off** of

193 **princesse** princess's, alluding to (*a*) the Spanish princess, Donna Maria, to whom Prince Charles was almost married (*b*) the English princess, Elizabeth Stuart, married to the Elector Palatine, and afterward Queen of Bohemia

199 **Iue** I've

207 **Tract of obedience** 'their ghostly father hath composed sundry Treatises for [these silly women] of Obedience, wherein hee pronounceth no lesse then damnation for the least scruple or hesitation in the performance of their Superiours commands... And this is a principall furtherance to his sacrilegious lusts: for I am verily perswaded that not one amongst them will (for feare of being disobedient) refuse to come to his bed whensoeuer he commands them: and

twill helpe you forward well,

wh.p. Sir, thats a Vertue
Iue euer thought on wth espetiall Reuerence

Bl.Bs.p. you will conceiue by that, my power, youre dutie,

wh.p. the knowledge will bee prætious of both Sir,
Enter wh: Bps. pawne

wh:Bsp. What makes yo'nd troubler of all christian Waters
so neere that blessed Spring, but that I knowe
her Goodnes is the Rock from whence it issues
unmoueable as Fate, twould more afflict mee
then all my suffrings for her, wch, so long
as shee holds constant to the house shee comes of
the whitenes of the cause, the side, the Qualitie,
are Sacrifices to her worth, and Vertue,
and though confinde, in my relligious Ioyes
I marrie her and possesse her,
Enter Bl Kts pawne

Bl.Bs.p. behold Ladie,
the 2 inhumayne Enimies, the black Knights pawne
and the white Bishops,

wh.p. there's my greefe, my hate,

Bl.Kts.p. what in the Iesuites fingers, by this hand
I'le giue my part now for a parrots feather
shee neuer returnes Vertuous, tis impossible,
Ile undertake more wagers will bee layde
uppon a Vsurers returne from hell
then uppon hers from him now; haue I bin guiltie
of such base malice that my uerie Conscience
shakes at the memorie of, and when I looke
to gather fruite finde nothing but the Sauin Tree
too frequent in Nuns Orchards, and there planted
by all Coniecture to destroye fruite rather,
I will bee resolude now, most noble Virgin

wh.p. Ignoble Villayne! dare that unhallowed tong
laye hold uppon a Sound so gratious?
whats Noblenes to thee? or Virgin Chastitie
theyr̃e out of thy Acquayntance, talke of Violence
that shames creation, deeds would make night blush
thats companie for thee, hast thou the Impudence
to court mee wth a leprosie uppon thee
able t' infect the walls of a great Building

Bl Bs.p. Sonne of offence, forbeare, goe, sett youre euill
before youre Eyes, a pœnitentiall Vesture
would better become yòu, some shirt of hayre,

Bl.Kts.p. and you a 3 pound Smock, stead of an Albe
an Epicœne Cassible, this holie Fellon
robs safe and closse, I feele a sting thats worse too,
white pawne! hast so much charitie to accept
a Reconcilement make thy owne Conditions
for I begin to bee extreamelie burdned

that they doe so, I haue manifestly seene and knowne' (Robinson, *English nunnery*, 18–19). In 1622, in order to silence criticism of his foreign policy, James I ordered the reprinting (for the first time in thirty years) of the homily 'Against Disobedience'; John Donne's sermon defending 'religious obedience' was 'by commandement of his Majesty Published' the same year (*Sermons*, IV: 178, 209).

212.1 ***wh: Bps. pawne*** White Bishop's Pawn; as a servant of the White Bishop, presumably represented as an English clergyman. Coloma reported that 'the first act ... was played by their ministers [in Spanish, "*ministros*"], impersonated by the white pieces, and the Jesuits, by the black ones' (suggesting one set of clerics against another). See notes to 1.166–7, 169.

219 **the cause** (used specifically for 'the Puritan cause' in the Martin Marprelate pamphlets as early as 1588)

221 **confinde** (perhaps alluding to the imprisonment, in the early 1620s, of ministers who criticized the Spanish Match)

222.1 ***Bl Kts pawne*** Black Knight's Pawn, not identified with any particular person or group: apparently a Catholic commoner and layman. The play thus contains two examples of 'Everyman': one female, Protestant, and English; the other male, Catholic, and Spanish.

225 **Bishops** (Middleton later added 'the gelder and the gelded', to clarify the nature of the White Bishop's Pawn's injury. Pope John XIII was accused of having 'gelded *Iohn* an Archdeacon' (Patrick Simson, *The historie of the Church* (1624), 655); Pope Honorius III was said to have hanged 400 Scots, 'and gelded their children, to extinguish their race for euer' (Goad, *Friers chronicle*, H4v). Eunuchs had been singing in papal choirs since the mid-sixteenth century. Less literally, Catholic censorship and suppression of religious texts was often characterized as castration: Catholics 'gelt ... their Writers, when they meete with any thing that makes not for their turne' (Gee, *Foot*, I4v–I5). See particularly (for the combination of two elements of the context here): 'beeing gelded [by a Jesuit] as the other bookes of Obedience were' (Robinson, *English nunnery*, 18) and 'how the Auncient *Fathers* haue beene shauen, clipt ... gelt, and mutilated' (Scott, *High-wayes of God*, 36–7). Taylor cites further examples from William Fulke, William Crashaw, John Donne, and others (*Castration* 82, 265), and the trope also appears in Robert Sanderson's *Two Sermons* (1622), 77, and Montagu's *Gagg* (1624), 135. Scott compared the storming of the Palatinate, and the persecution of Protestants in France and Switzerland, to 'the cauterizing and cutting off our owne members' (*The Belgick Pismire* (1622), 89). All these metaphors involve Catholic violence against Protestants who see themselves as legitimately reproducing the 'seed' of the Gospels.)

228 **parrots feather** A European market for ornamental feathers developed in the sixteenth century, supplied in large part by exotic birds from Spanish and Portuguese tropical possessions; by the early seventeenth century oversupply had diminished the initial wonder.

235 **Sauin Tree** See *A Gagge for the Pope and the Iesuits* (1624): 'in the Orchards of their Frieries and Nunneries ... they haue whole trees of *Sauine*, and to what vse that serues, *Physicians* and *Mid-wiues* know too well' (14), i.e. 'the property of *Sauine* is to destroy any thing condensed in the wombe' (Goad, *Friers Chroicle*, E2).

wh.B$^{s.}$p. no truth, or peace of that black house protested
is to bee trusted, but for hope of quittance
and warnd by diffidence I maye entrap him soonest,
I admit Conference;

Bl.K$^{ts.}$p. it is a Noblenes
that makes confusion cleaue to all my meritts *exit*

Bl·Bs.p. that treatise will instruct You fullie:
Enter Bl: K^{t}

Bl.K$^{t.}$ so, so,
the Busines of the Vniuersall Monarchie
goes forward well now, the great Colledge pott
that should bee alwayes boyling, wth the fuell
of all Intelligences possible
thorough the Christian Kingdomes, is this fellowe
our prime Incendiarie? and one of those
that promist the white Kingdome 7 yeare since
to our black house? putt a new daughter to him
the great worke stands, hee mindes nor Monarchie
nor Hierarchie
diuiner principalitye; I haue bragd lesse,
but Iue donne more then all the Conclaue on em,
take theire Assistant fathers in all parts
I, and theire father Generall in to boote,
and what Iue donne, I ha' donne facetiouslie,
wth pleasant subteltie and bewitching Courtship
abusde all my Beleiuers wth delight
they tooke a Comfort to bee coosned by mee,
to manie a Soule, Iue let in mortall poyson
whose cheekes haue crackt wth laughter to receiue it,
I could so rowle my pills in sugred sillables
and strewe such kindlie Mirth ore all my mischeifs,
they tooke theire Bane in waye of Recreation
as pleasure steales Corruption into Youth
hee spyes mee now, I must uphold his reuerence
espetiallie in publick, though I knowe
Priapus, Guardian of the Cherrie Gardens
Bacchus and Venus Chit, is not more Vitious

Bl.Bs.p. Blessings Accumulation keepe wth you, S^{ir},

Bl.K$^{t.}$ Honors dissimulation bee youre due, S^{ir},

wh.p. how deepe in dutie his Obseruance plundges
his charge must needs bee reuerend,

Bl.B$^{s.}$p. I am confessor
to this black K$^{t.}$ too, you see Deuotioñs fruitfull
sh'as manye Sonnes and daughters,

256–7 **no . . . trusted** (the view of those who opposed James I's efforts to secure the return of the Palatinate through a peace treaty with Spain)

262.1 ***Bl: K^{t}*** Black Knight, an impersonation of Don Diego Sarmiento de Acuña, Conde de Gondomar (1567–1626), Spain's resident ambassador in England from 1613 to 1622. The identification is confirmed by many contemporary witnesses, and by the title-page engravings. The actors 'counterfeited his person to the life, with all his graces and faces, and had gotten (they say) a cast sute of his apparell for the purpose' (John Chamberlain, 21 August 1624).

265–9 **great . . . Incendiarie** 'besides the care we prouidently take, that the great pot may be alwayes boyling . . . we exercise the trade of incendaries' (Gosselin, *State Mysteries*, 8).

269 **Incendiarie** 'those incendiaries of Rome, and professed engines of Spain, the priests and Jesuits' (House of Commons petition to King James, April 24 (*Journals* III, 289)).

270 **7 yeare** Sir John Digby had been sent to Madrid to negotiate a marriage treaty in 1617: 'The Duke [of Buckingham] replied . . . that the Match had need be firm and strong; it had been seven years in soldering' (House of Commons *Journal . . . 1624*, III, 226).

271 **our black house** here first defined, by Gondomar's presence, as not only religious (Jesuit Catholicism), but specifically political ('the House of Austria', as it is defined in Buckingham's 1624 'Relation' to Parliament, and many other Protestant sources). Emphasis on the 'House of Austria' elided differences between the Habsburg King of Spain and the Habsburg Holy Roman Emperor; it presupposed that Spain could order the Emperor to return the Palatinate and Bohemia to Protestant control. The play 'describes Gondomar and all the Spanish proceedings very boldly and broadly' (George Lowe, 7 August). As contemporary portraits reveal, Spaniards often dressed in black.

272 **Hierarchie** episcopacy, the rule of bishops, cardinals, and ultimately the Pope; the English church retained many elements of ecclesiastical hierarchy, to the dismay of more radical Protestants.

274 **donne more** Gondomar had 'effected more by his wit and policy, then could have beene wrought by the strength of many Armies' (Scott, *2 Vox Populi*, 58)

275 **Assistant fathers** a Jesuit appointed 'to informe the *Father Generall* of all accidents of State, which occur in that Prouince or Kingdome, of which he is Assistant' (Bargrave, *Iesuiticall iniquity*, B2).

276 **I** ay, yes

289 **Priapus** Roman god of sexuality, usually represented by an erect penis: St Augustine objects to the worship of 'his monstrous and unmentionable member' (*City of God*, 1610). Thomas Cooper's *Theseaurus Linguae Romanae et Britannicae* (1578) defines 'Priapus' as 'An Idole, vnto whome the Paynyms commited their gardeyns to keepe.' Middleton could have found the garden association in Ovid's *Fasti*, I, 415, or Catullus 18, or several English poets; none specifies cherries. Pausanius identifies him as the son of Dionysus and Aphrodite (9.31.2); 'Of Venus and Bacchus, Priapus was borne' (Abraham Fraunce, *The third part of the Countesse of Pembrokes Iuychurch* (1592), O1).

290 **Vitious** vicious

295–6 **confessor . . . K$^{t.}$** Gondomar did have a Spanish confessor, Fray Diego de la Fuente (Padre Maestro), despatched to England in 1618, and involved in negotiations for the marriage treaty. But no contemporary observer identified the Black Bishop's Pawn as de la Fuente (who was a Dominican, not a Jesuit). The character compounds elements from various sources. See 5.0.4.

Bl.Kt. I doo this the more
t 'amaze our Aduersaries to behold
the reuerence wee giue these Guitenens,
and to beget a sound opinion
of Holines in them and Zeale in us,
as also to enuite the like Obedience
in other Pusills, by our meeke Example,
so, is youre Trifle uanisht?

Bl.Bs·p. Trifle call you her? tis a good pawne Sir
sure shees the sccond pawne in the whitehouse,
and to the opening of the Game I hold her,

Bl Kt· I you hold well for that I Knowe youre playe of ould
if there were more Qs: pawnes youde plye the Game
a great deale harder, (now Sir weere in priuate,
but what for the mayne worke, the great Existence
the Hope monarchall,

Bl. Bs·p. it goes on in this,

Bl.Kt· in this? I cannot see'te,

Bl.Bs·p. you maye denye so
a dyalls motion, cause you cannot see
the hand moue, or a winde that rends the Cedar,

Bl Kt· where stops the Current of Intelligence,
youre father Generall Bishop a'th black-house
complaynes for want of worke;

Bl.Bs·p. heres from all parts
sufficient to employe him, I receiude
a packet from th' Assistant Fathers latelie,
Looke you, theres Anglica, this Gallica,

Bl Kt· I marrie Sir, theres some quick flesh in this

Bl.Bs·p. Germanica!

Bl.Kt· thinke theyue seald this wth Butter,

Bl.Bs·p. this Italica!

Bl.Kt· theyue putt theire pens the Hebrewe waye mee thinkes

Bl.Bs·p. Hispanica here!

Bl.Kt· Hispanica, blinde worke tis,
the Iesuite ha's writt this wth Iuice of Lemmans sure
it must bee held closse to the fire of Purgatorie
er't can bee read.

Bl. Bs·p. you will not Loose youre Iest Knight
though't wounded youre owne name,

Enter wh. Ks pawne

Bl Kt· Curanda Pecuniâ;

Bl.Bs·p. take heede Sr, weere entrapt the wh. Kings pawne!

Bl.Kt· hees made our owne (man) halfe in Voto yours,
his hearts in the black house, leaue him to mee,
most of all frends endeerde, prætiouslie spetiall;

298–302 **I doo . . . us** Thomas Scott has Gondomar describe his attendance on Father Baldwin, released from the Tower in 1613: 'I behaved my self after so lowly & hūble a maner, that our adversaries stood amazed to behold the reverence we give to our ghostly fathers. And this I did . . . to beget an extraordinary opinion of holinesse in the person, & pietie in us, and also to provoke the English Catholiques to like devout obedience' (*Vox Populi*, C4v).

303 **enuite** invite

305 **uanisht** The exit of the White Queen's Pawn is not indicated (the first of several unmarked departures in *Early*). Even promptbooks often omitted exits.

311 **weere** we're
in priuate 'Publique persons should do publique actions in publique, in the *Gates of the City*, in the *Kings high-way*, in the eye of all. For chamber-workes are suspicious, and carry a shew of priuacy and parciality' (Scott, *High-wayes of God*, 69–70).

312 **great Existence** See Massinger's *Renegado* (licensed for performance 17 April 1624): 'thou great Existence' (a prayer addressed to God by a Jesuit).

318 **Cedar** emblem of James I

325–31 **Anglica . . . Hispanica** provinces into which Jesuits divided their missions

328 **theyue** they've
Butter alluding not only to the northern European fondness for butter, but to news-sheets reporting on the Catholic–Protestant wars in Germany and the Palatinate, published by Nathaniel Butter

333 **Iuice of Lemmans** (*a*) juice of lemons (*b*) juice of lemans, lovers. For *juice* = female sexual juices, see *Michaelmas* 1.3.5 and Williams, *Dictionary*, 2:750. For the pun lemons/lemans see *Owl's Almanac* 323 and Williams, 2:799.
Lemmans Father Henry Garnett (1555–1606), superior of the Jesuits in England until his execution for participation in the Gunpowder Plot, often wrote secret letters with ink made from lemon (or orange) juice, which is illegible unless heated.

335 **er't** ere't, before it

336 **Loose** lose

337.1 ***wh. Ks pawne*** White King's Pawn, combining features of several Jacobean courtiers. By 1622 several of the King's ministers—including Secretary of State Sir George Calvert, Sir Richard Weston, and Francis Cottington (secretary of the Prince of Wales)—were crypto-Catholics. Sir Toby Matthew (1577–1655), who converted to Catholicism in 1606 and was ordained a priest in 1614, was sent to Madrid in 1623 to advise Prince Charles and the Duke of Buckingham in negotiations for the Spanish marriage. Subsequent revisions—see *Later* 1.1.319–24—incorporated allusions relevant to the Earl of Middlesex. Nevertheless, an eyewitness identified the character as Sir John Digby, 1st Earl of Bristol (1580–1653), ambasssador to Madrid 1610–17, 1618, 1622–4 (Holles, 11 August); in 1624 Digby was widely (wrongly) perceived as a treasonous Catholic and Spanish sympathizer. Middleton's pawn compounds elements of several historical figures.

338 ***Curanda Pecuniâ*** Like most university-educated writers, Middleton wrote an elegant italic script, and mixed italic letter forms with secretary forms; but very few words are written entirely in italic. Here it distinguishes Latin.

340 **(man)** vocative, addressed to the Black Bishop's Pawn

wh.Ks.p. you see my outside, but you knowe my heart,
Kt.,
great difference in the Colour, theres some Intelligence
and as more ripens, so youre knowledge still
shall prooue the richer, and my selfe youre Frend:
I dare not longer of this Theame discusse,
the Eare of State is quick and Iealious:

Bl.Kt. Excellent Estimation, thou art Valued
abouc the Fleete of Gold, that came short home,
poore Iesuite ridden Soule, how art thou foolde
out of thy Fayth, from thy Alleagance drawen
wch path so ere̓ thou tak'st thour̕t a lost pawne.
exit

Finit Actus primus.

Act 2

Incipit Secundi.
Enter White-weoman pawne wth a booke in her hand;

Wh.p. and here agen it is the daughters dutie
to obaye her Confessors command in all things
wthout exception, or expostulation,
tis the most generall Rule that I erẻ read of,
Yet when I thinke how boundlesse Vertue is
Goodnes and Grace, tis gentlie reconcilde
and then it appeares well to haue the power
of the dispenser as uncircumscribd
Enter Bl.Bs.p.

Bl.Bs.p. shee's hard uppoǹt, twas the most modest Key
that I could use to open my Intents,
what litle or no paynes goes to some people,
hah? a Seald Note, whence this?
to the black Bishops pawne these, how? to mee?
strange, who subscribes it? the Black King? what
would hee?
(·:)
pawne! sufficientlie holic, but unmeasureablie politick; wee had late intelligence from our most industrious Seruant famous in all parts of Europe (,our Knight of the black house, that you haue at this instant in chace, the white Queenes pawne, and uerie liklie by the carriage of youre Game to entrap and take her, these are therefore to require you by the burning affection I beare to the Rape of Deuotion, that speedilie uppon the

343 **outside...heart** Elizabeth, Queen of Bohemia, wrote that 'I think I can easily guess who it is that doth chieflie hinder the King in resolving, but I am sure that though they have English bodies they have Spanish hartes' (Pursell, *Winter King*, 109).

344–6 **theres...richer** A number of court officials, including members of the Privy Council, had been on Spanish pensions since the peace treaty of 1604; when this became public knowledge in 1620, many observers concluded that Gondomar 'knowes your [James I's] secrets before the greatest part / and most faithfull of your councel. And which is worse / they saye your Majestie knowes it; and therfore suspect that your selfe is bribed against your selfe' (*Tom Tell-Troath*, 4).

346 **and...Frend** 'To doe this I had many Agents, first divers Courtiers who were hungrie and gaped wide for Spanish gould' (Scott, *Vox Populi*); '(replyed *Gondomar*)...our best intelligencers... we haue had in times past many friends, euen in the Parliament House' (Scott, *2 Vox Populi*, 37). As late as January 1624, five members of the King's council were known to be still supporting the Spanish marriage (despite the aggressive opposition of Charles and Buckingham): John Williams (Lord Keeper of the Privy Seal), the Earl of Middlesex (Lord Treasurer), the Earl of Arundel, Sir Richard Weston, and Sir George Calvert. The added lines at *Later* 1.1.323–4—'keepe all Supplies back both in meanes and men | that may rayse strenght against you'—clearly refer to the military effort to defend the Palatine territories of Elizabeth and Frederick against the Spanish army.

350 **Fleete of Gold** Spanish treasure fleet, bringing gold from their New World colonies (about 5 million pesos per year in the 1620s); responsible for making Spain the richest power in Europe, with military resources that threatened all other European powers.

came short home Between 1618 and 1624 Spanish ships were increasingly harassed by privateers. On 14 February 1623 Joseph Mead reported 'There is no siluer come yet from the West Indies into Spaine, nor to be expected before May; the Admirall & 2 others are sunk, & the rest returned to the Hauana' (f. 286).

351–3 **poore...lost pawne** Act 1 dramatizes the link between personal and political salvation: it begins with an apolitical white lay woman, tempted by a female Jesuit who passes her to a male Jesuit, who reveals himself to be the agent of a Spanish diplomat, who ends Act 1 gloating over the treason of a converted white layman. The ending of Act 1 raises the question: will the White Queen's Pawn become, like the White King's Pawn, a 'poore...lost pawne' who betrays her religion and her country?

2.0.1 ***Incipit*** This Latin formula for beginning an act is rare in English plays: in printed drama before Middleton it occurs only in the sixteenth-century Protestant morality plays of John Bale (eleven examples in two plays).

0.2 ***White-weoman*** This compound idiom does not appear in later texts, and has therefore not been recorded. The first use of *white* in its modern racial sense in English drama occurs at *Truth* 407–8, 'I see amazement set upon the faces Of these white people' (spoken to the London crowd by the Black King). The racial sense of 'white' is not spoken or explicit in this stage direction, but the play's colour coding was interpreted racially by the Spanish ambassador Coloma, who reported indignantly that Felipe IV was represented as 'the king of the blacks' (*negros*) and James I as 'the king of the whites' (*blancos*), words with unambiguous racial meanings in Spain. See Induction.44 and 3.213–16.

booke 'Printing presses and booksellers almost in every corner' had flooded England with 'swarms of [Catholic] books' in the early 1620s (Gee, *Foot*); 'wee saw euery pocket stuft with popish pamphlets' (Scott, *Vox Dei* (1624). 69).

4 **erẻ** e'er, ever

8 **uncircumscribd** (a word first recorded in Healey's 1610 translation of Augustine's *City of God*; there, it describes God)

15 **politick** 'The fourth sort is of Politicke Iesuites, through whose handes passeth the whole gouernement of religion; and these are they, who...labour to reduce their society to an absolute Monarchy, and to place the head thereof at *Rome*' (Bargrave, *Iesuiticall iniquity*, B9v–B10).

6

10

Actus Secundi Scæna prima.

Enter Wh: Qs. pawne wth a booke in her hand.

Wh: Qs. p. and here agen it is the daughters dutie
to obey her Confessors command in all things
without exception, or expostulation,
tis the most generall Rule that ere I read of,
yet when I thinke how boundlesse vertue is
Goodnes and Grace, tis gentlie reconcild
and then it appeares well, to haue the power
of the dispenser as uncircumscribd.

Enter Bl. Bs. p.

Bl. Bs. p. Shee has upon't, twas the most modest Key
that I could use to open my Intents,
what little or no paynes goes to some people,
hah! a Seald Note, whence this?
to the black Bishops pawne these, how! to me!
strange, who subscribes it? the Black King: what would (hee?

the letter

Pawne! sufficientlie holie, but unmeasurablie poli=
tique; wee had late intelligence from our most indus=
trious Seruant famous in all parts of Europe (our
Knight of the black house) that you haue at this instant
in chace, the white Queenes Pawne, and verie likelie
by the carriage of your Game to entrap and take
her, these are therefore to require you by the burning

A Game at Chesse in Middleton's handwriting (actual size), showing the beginning of Act 2. Notice the spatial contrast between the opening stage direction of the scene (top) and the mid-scene entrance of the Black Bishop's Pawn (midpage, right), which is boxed with horizontal lines to call attention to it. Our printed edition does not preserve this visual distinction between different kinds of stage directions. Below line 2.8, our printed edition preserves the horizontal line, called a 'speech rule', that separates one speech from another, but it gives all those speech rules the same length, rather than reproducing the exact length of each one. Notice also (at line 2.14) the way that the manuscript deals with a verse line that is too long to fit within the margins: it puts the extra word 'hee?' above the line, to the right, with an opening parenthesis before it (whereas our edition puts the extra words 'would hee?' on the line below, indented). In the prose at the bottom, our printed text does not break the lines in exactly the same places that the manuscript does.

surprizall of her, by all watchfull aduantage you make
some attempt uppon the white Queenes person whose
fall or prostitution our Lust most uiolentlie rages for,
S^{ir} after my desire ha's tooke a Iulepp
for it's owne Inflammation, that yet scorches mee,
I shall haue cooler time to thinke of yours:
shȧs past the generall Rule, the large Extent
of our præscriptions for obedience
and yet wth what Alacritie of Soule
her Eye moues on the Letters;

wh.p. Holie S^{ir},
too long Iue mist you, oh youre absence starues mee,
hasten for times redemption worthie S^{ir}
laye youre commands as thick and fast uppon mee
as you can speake em̃, how I thirst to heare em̃,
sett mee to worke uppon this spatious Vertue
wch the poore Span of lifes too narrowe for
Boundlesse Obedience, the humblest yet the mightiest
of all duties
well here set downe a Vniuersall Goodnes;

Bl. B$^{s.}$p. by holines of Garment her safe Innocence
ha's frighted the full meaning from it selfe,
Shees farder off from understanding now
the language of m'Intent then at first meeting;

wh.p. for Vertues sake, good sir, command mee somthĩg,
make tryall of my dutie in some small seruice
and as you finde the fayth of my obedience there,
then trust it wth a greater;

Bl.B$^{s.}$p. you speake sweetelie,
I do command you first then—

wh.p. wth what ioye
I do præpare my dutie,

Bl.B$^{s.}$p. to meete mee
and seale a Kisse of Loue uppon my Lip,

wh.p. hah?

Bl.B$^{s.}$p. at first disobedient, in so litle too,!
how shall I trust you wth a greater then,
wch was youre owne request;

wh.p. praye send not back
my Innocence to wound mee, bee more curteous,
I must confesse much like an ignorant plantiffe
who præsuming on the fayre path of his meaning
goes rashlie on, till on a suddayne brought
into the wildernes of Lawe, by words
dropt unaduisedlie, hurts his good cause
and giues his aduersarie aduantage by't
applie it you can best (S^{ir}) if m'obedience
and youre command can finde no better waye
Fond men command, and wantons best obaye;

Bl.Bs.p. If I can at that distance send you a blessing,
is it not neerer to you in mine Armes?
it flyes from these Lips dealt abroad in parcells,
and I to honor thee aboue all daughters
enuite thee home to th' house, where thou mayst
surfet
on that, wch others miserablie pine for,
a fauour wch the daughters of great Potentates
would looke of Enuies colour but to heare,

wh.p. Goodmen maye err somtimes, you are mistooke sure,
if this bee Vertues path, tis a most strange one,
I neuer came this waye before,

Bl.B$^{s.}$p. thats youre ignorance,
and therefore shall that Ideot still conduct you
that knowes no waye but one, nor euer seekes it,
if there bee twentie wayes to some poore Village
tis strange that Vertue should bee putt to one,
youre feare is wondrous faultie, cast it from you
twill gather else in Time a Disobedience
too stubborne for my pardon,

wh.p. haue I lockt my selfe at unawares into Sins seruitude
wth more desire of Goodnes;? is this the Top
of all strickt Order,? and the holiest
of all societies, the 3 uowde people
for pouertie, obedience, chastitie,
the last the most forgot, when a Virgins ruinde
I see the great worke of obedience
is better then halfe finisht;

30 **obedience** James I's later court was characterized, to its critics, by 'a blind Jesuitical obedience' (John Holles, 18 July 1617); 'Let a Protestant king . . . be never so notoriously wicked in his person nor so enormous in his government,' nevertheless 'the Reformed Religion . . . tyes the subject to such wonderfull patience and obedience' that it 'makes men obey Kings as the Angels of God' (*Tom Tell-Truth*, 26).

40 **Boundlesse . . . duties** Middleton often writes a line and a half of verse as a single manuscript line, to save paper. Compare Induction.51.

44 **farder** farther

45 **m'Intent** my Intent (an unusual elision)

46 **somthĩg** something

55–71 **Kisse . . . blessing** 'When any of the Priests knauery was discouered, there were excuses enough ready to defend them; yea, when they were found kissing of a woman; the answer was, You must suppose he did it to print a blessing on her lips' (Thomas Goad, *The Friers Chronicle* (1623), $C1^{v}$).

64 **suddayne** sudden

79 **Goodmen** (often treated as a compound, like 'handyman' or 'doorman')

85–6 **if . . . one** This relativism is contradicted by many contemporary assertions of the singularity of truth; for instance, 'I never showed thee yet more paths than one' (*Truth* 330), or 'such a deade luke-warme indifferencie, a dow-baked zeale, as if . . . all wayes were alike to vs' (Scott, *High-wayes of God*, 81).

94 **pouertie, obedience, chastitie** vows taken by members of the Society of Jesus (all three, according to Protestant polemicists, systematically violated)

Bl.Bs.p. what a Stranger
are you to dutie growen, what distance keepe you?
must I bid you come forward to a happines
youre selfe should sue for,? twas neuer so wth mee,
I dare not let this Stubbornes bee knowen
twould bring such feirce hate on you, yet presume not
to make that curteous care a priuiledge
for willfull disobedience, it turnes then
into the blacknes of a Curse uppon you,
come, come, bee neerer,

wh.p. neerer?

Bl.Bs.p. was that Scorne?
I would not haue it prooue so, for the hopes
of the grand Monarchie, if it were like it
let it not dare to stir abroad agen
a stronger Ill Will coape wth't,

wh.p. blesse mee, threatnens mee
and quite dismayes the good strenght that should helpe mee,
I neuer was so doubtfull of my safetie,

Bl.Bs.p. twas but my Iealousie, forgiue mee Sweetnes
Yon'd is the house of Meeknes and no Venom liues
under that Roofe, bee neerer, why so fearefull?
neerer the Altar the more safe and sacred

wh.p. but neerer to the Offrer oft more wicked

Bl.Bs.p. a playne and most insufferable Contempt,
my glorie I haue lost uppon this weoman
in freelie offring that shee should haue kneelde
a Yeare in Vayne for, my respect is darkned
giue mee my Reuerence thou hast robd mee of
in thy repulse, thou shalt not carrie't hence

wh.p. Sir,

Bl.Bs.p. thou'rt too great a winner to depart
and I too great a Looser to giue waye to't

wh.p. oh heauen!

Bl.Bs.p. laye mee downe Reputation
before thou stirst, thy nice Virginitie
is recompence too litle for my Loue
tis well if I accept of that for both
thy losse is but thine owne, theres Art to helpe thee
and fooles to passe thee to, in my discouerie
the whole Societie suffers, and in that
the hope of Absolute Monarchie eclipst,
assurance thou can'st make none for thy Secrecie
but by thy honors losse, that Act must awe thee,

wh.p. oh my distrest Condition!

Bl.Bs.p. do'st thou weepe?
if thou hadst anie pittie this necessitie
would wring it from thee, I must else destroye thee
wee must not trust the policie of Europe
uppon a weomans tong;

wh.p. then take my life sir,
and leaue my honor for my guide to heauen,

Bl.Bs.p. take heede I take not both, wch Iue uowde since;
if Longer thou resist mee,

wh.p. helpe, oh helpe—
a noyse wthin

Bl.Bs.p. art thou so cruell for an honors Bubble
t'undoo a whole Fraternitie, and disperse
the secretts of most princes lockt in us;

wh.p. for heauen and Vertues sake;

Bl.Bs.p. must force confound noyse?
hah? whats that? silence if fayre worth bee in thee

wh.p. Ile uenture my Escape uppon all dangers now;

Bl.Bs.p. who comes to take mee let mee see that pawns face
or his proud tympanous Mr sweld wth state winde
wch being once prickt ith Conuocation house
the corrupt Ayre puffs out and hee falls shriueld,

wh.p. I will discouer thee Arch hIpocrite
to all the Kinreds of the earth

Bl.Bs.p. Confusion! in that Voyce rings the Alarum of my undoing
how? wch waye scapte shee from mee?
Enter Black weoman-pawne

Bl.p. are you mad?
can Lust infatuate a man so hopefull,
no patience in youre bloud the Dogstar reignes sure
time and fayre Temper would haue wrought her pleasant,
I spied a pawne ath whitehouse walke neere us
and made that Noyse a purpose to giue warning
for mine owne turne, wch end in all I worke for,

111 **grand Monarchie** 'the Iesuites are wont to call their Religion, *A Grand-Monarchy*; as if they gouerned all Princes and their ministers at their pleasure' (Bargrave, *Iesuiticall iniquity*, C5v).
114 **threatnens** threatens
161 **Mr** master
164 **I will discouer thee** In the play, this anticipates the political 'Checkmate by discouerye' (5.356); but it also reflects the exposure of Catholic malpractice by former Catholics like Thomas Robinson (1622) and John Gee (1624). Several of Gee's anecdotes involve women who turn against the Jesuits.
170 **Dogstar** Sirius, in the constellation of the Great Dog, the brightest of the fixed stars; its astrological influence was thought to be most debilitating during the 'dog days', said by 1624 almanacs to begin on July 19. The first performances of *Game* took place during the Dogstar's reign, traditionally associated with rage, madness, and other dangerous or evil behaviour.
172 **ath** o'th', of the
173 **a** o', on

Bl.B$^{s.}$p. mee thinkes I stand ouer a powder-Vault
and the Match now a kindling, whats to bee donne?

Bl.p. Aske the black Bishops councell youre his pawne
tis his owne case, hee will defend you maynelie

Enter Bl. Bp, and Bl.K$^{t.}$

and happilie here hee comes wth the Bl. Knight too,

Bl.B. oh yau'e made noble worke for the whitehouse
yonder,
this Act will fill the Aduersaries mouth
and blowe the Hugonites cheeke tillt crack agen,

Bl.K$^{t.}$ this will aduance the great Monarchall busines
in all parts well, and helpe the Agents forward,
what I in 7 yeare labourd to accomplish
one Minute setts back by some Codpeice Colledge still

Bl.B$^{s.}$p. I dwell not, S^{ir}, alone in this default
the blackhouse yeilds mee partners;

Bl.B: all more cautelous;

Bl. K$^{t.}$ Qui cautè, castè, thats my Motto euer
I haue trauayld wth that word ouer most kingdomes
and layne safe wth most Nations, of a leaking bottome
I haue beene as often tost on Venus seas
as trimmer fresher Barkes, when sounder Vessells
haue layne at Anchor, that is, kept the doore;

Bl.B. shee ha's no wittnesse then?

Bl.B$^{s.}$p. None, none,

Bl.Kt. grosse! wittnesse! when went a man of his Societie
to mischeife wth a wittnesse,

Bl.B. I haue don't then,
awaye, uppon the Wings of Speede, take posthorse
cast 30 leagues of earth behind thee suddenlie
leaue letters Antedated wth our house
ten dayes at least from this,

Bl.K$^{t.}$ Bishop I tast thee,
good strong Episcopall Councell, take a bottle on't
twill serue thee all the Iourney,

Bl.B$^{s.}$ p. but good S^{ir}
how for my getting forth, unspied?

Bl.K$^{t.}$ theres check agen,

Bl.p. no, Ile helpe that!

Bl.Kt. well sayde my litle Iesuitesse,

Bl.p. there lyes a secret Vault,

Bl.Kt. awaye, make haste then,

Bl.B$^{s.}$p. run for my Cabinet of Intelligences
for feare they search the house, good Bishop burne em̃
rather
I cannot stand to pick em̃, now,

Bl.B. bee gon,
the dangers all in you,

Bl.K$^{t.}$. let mee see Queenes pawne,
how formallie ha's packt up his Intelligences,
ha's layde em̃ all in Truckle beds mee thinkes,
and like Court-Harbingers ha's writt theire names
in Chalke uppon theire Chambers, Anglica!
oh this is the English house, what newes there tro?
hah? by this light, most of these are bawdie Epistles

175 **powder-Vault** almost inevitably suggesting, to English Protestants, the Gunpowder Plot. 'Blush, blush, (O *Iesuites*) *England* knowes too well, | Your Counsell furthered most this worke of *Hell*' (Francis Herring, *Mischeefes Mysterie... The Powder-plot*, tr. John Vicars (1617), 109). See also Induction.34, 1.269.

177 **youre** you're

178.1 ***Bl. Bp*** Black Bishop: the Father General, or head, of the Society of Jesus: see 1.48–9, 320.

182 **Hugonites** Huguenots. In May 1624 English ambassadors arrived in Paris to negotiate a marriage between Prince Charles and a French (Catholic) princess, so any reference to persecuted French protestants would be politically dangerous; all subsequent texts read 'Lutherans' (*Later* 2.1.166). In 1624, 'Lutherans' might easily suggest Germany (the home of Lutheranism), and specifically Bohemia.

tillt till't, until it

190 **Qui cautè, castè** Lecherous Jesuits, caught in bed with their nuns, forgot 'the old caueat, *Cautè si non castè*' (Robinson, *English nunnery*, 19). Middleton transforms 'Careful, if not chaste' into 'Whoever is cautious, is'—that is, has the reputation for being—'chaste'.

191 **trauayld** travelled (not distinguished from 'travailed', laboured)

192 **leaking bottome** (Gondomar suffered from a fistula; his rectal leak is here conflated with a not-watertight ship's hull.)

193 **tost** tossed

200 **don't** done't

206 **Episcopall** (gratuitously negatively used here, at 2.334, and at *Later* 3.1.29)

212 **Iesuitesse** A rare word, used since 1616 to describe the followers of Mary Ward (Sir Dudley Carlton, *Letters*, 68); in 1611 Ward decided that her order of 'English Ladies' should follow the same constitution as the (male) Society of Jesus. The word is used often of them in the next two decades: see '*English Iesuitesses*' (Lewis Owen, *The Running Register*, 8), and 'English Iesuitesses, (a new inuented Order)' (William Prynne, *A Briefe Suruay and Censure* (1628), 39).

215–51 **Cabinet... Expulse** After the 'expulsion' of the Jesuits from Venice, in part because of their 'dangerous abuse of that great instrument of State, Auricular confession', a 'search' by state officials discovered 'a *Scrinio* (as they call it here) with partitions of their addresses to and from all parts, As *England*, *France*, *Spaine*, *Flaunders*, *Germany*, *Poland*, *Russia*, *etc*.... And in this *Scrinio* they had left rather through vanity then hast, a great and incredible heape of the very ashes and tynder of their dispatches' (*A Declaration of the Variance between the Pope and the Signiory of Venice* (1606), 33–4).

225 **what newes there** 'Letters of News' had become an increasingly common and important form of correspondence, either commercial (Thomas Gainsford, John Pory, Ralph Starkey) or personal (John Chamberlain, Joseph Mead, and many others).

tro trow

time they were burnt indeed, whole Bundles on em̃
heres from his daughter Blanch, and daughter bridget
from theire safe Sanctuarie in the Whitefriers,
these from 2 tender Sisters of Compassion
in the bowells of Bloomsburie;
3 from the Nunnerie wthout Temple Bar,
a fire, a fire, good Iesuitesse, a fire, what haue you
there

Bl.B. a note Sir of State=policie
and one exceeding safe one,

Bl.Kt. praye letts see't sir,—
to sell awaye all the powder in a Kingdome
to præuent blowing up, thats safe Ile able it,
heres a facetious Obseruation now
and suites my humour better, hee writes here
some wiues in England will committ Adulterie,
and then send to Rome for a Bull for theire hous-
bands,

Bl.B. haue they those Shifts?

Bl.Kt. oh theres no Female breathing
sweeter and subteller, here wench take these papers
scortch em̃ mee soundlie, burne em̃ to French Russet
and putt em̃ in agen,

Bl.B. why whats youre Mysterie?

Bl.Kt. oh Sir twill mock the Aduersarie strangelye
if eře the house bee searchd twas donne in Venice
uppon the Iesuiticall Expulse there
when the Inquisitors came all spectacled
to pick out Sillables ont ath Dung of Treason
as children pick out Cherriestones, yet found none
but what they made themselues wth ends of Letters,
doo as I bid you, pawne, *exeunt*

Bl.p. feare not, in all,
I loue Roguerie too well to lett it fall,
Enter Bl.Kts. pawn,
how now? what newes wth you?

Bl.Kts.p. the Sting of Conscience
afflicts mee so, for that inhumayne Violence
on the White Bishops pawne, it takes awaye
my Ioye, my rest;

Bl.p. this tis to make an Eunuch
you made a Sport on't then,

Bl.Kts.p. ceasse Aggrauation,
I come to bee absolude fort, where's my Confessor?
why do'st thou poynt toth' Ground?

Bl.p. cause hee went that waye, *Bl.Kts.p.* what's that?

Bl.p. come, helpe in wth this Cabinet
and after I haue singd these papers throughlie
Ile tell thee a strange storie;

Bl.Kts.p. if't bee sad
tis welcome,

Bl.p. tis not troubled wth much mirth, Sir; *exeunt*

228 **bridget** The English nunnery in Lisbon (the subject of Robinson's spectacular exposé) belonged to an order founded by 'Saint *Briget* and her daughter' (6, 12), Bridget having been 'miserably seduced' by her confessor (6).

229 **Whitefriers** a district associated with both prostitutes and Catholics, encouraging the slang description of whores as nuns: a prodigal keeps 'his most delicate drab' in 'Whitefriars nunnery' (*Father Hubburd's Tales* 600–1); a customer visits 'his nun in Whitefriars' (Thomas Dekker, *Westward Ho*, 1604).

231 **Bloomsburie** 'about *Bloomesbury* . . . take heed of a Iesuite' (Gee, *Foot*, H1v–H2)

232 **wthout Temple Bar** just outside the western limits of the jurisdiction of the City of London. 'Temple Bar' directs suspicion at the legal profession. The phrase was later altered, probably by censorship, to 'in Drury Lane'. Gee describes Father Townsend as 'a Iesuite, a little black fellow, very compt and gallant, lodging about the midst of *Drury-Lane* acquainted with collapsed Ladies' (*Foot*, P1v). 'In Drury Lane there are three family of Papists residing there for one of Protestants; insomuch that it may well be called little Rome' (House of Commons, 5 June 1628).

237–8 **to sell . . . up** Chamberlain reported rumours that Gondomar had transported gunpowder out of the kingdom (13 February 1619). A 1621 Parliamentary committee investigated the export of English ordnance, most probably to Spain.

253 **ont ath** of it, from the: 'of [treason], from the'

253–4 **Dung . . . Cherriestones** 'coquins de village qui fougent et escharbottent la merde des petitz enfans, en la saison des cerises et guignes, pour trouver les noyaulx et iceulx vendre es drogeurs' (Rabelais, *Gargantua et Pantagruel*, bk. 2, ch. 34); 'the poor rogues of a village, that are busy in stirring up and scraping in the ordure and filth of little children, in the season of cherries and guinds, and that only to find the kernels, that they may sell them to the druggists' (first English translation, 1653).

264 **to make an Eunuch** 'For there are some Eunuches . . . which were made Eunuches of [= by] men' (Matthew 19:12, 1611 translation). Eunuch-making was practised in Islamic societies, and among the 'heathen' peoples of the Americas, Africa, and Asia; as such, it typified alien despotism and tyranny. After the Reformation, Protestants (including Luther and Calvin) used the eunuch metaphor to characterize Roman Catholicism, with its 'tyrannical law of celibacy' (Taylor, *Castration*, 76–9).

269 **cause . . . that** (two part lines, one linking backward and the other linking forward, spoken by two different speakers, on the same manuscript line: compare Induction.51)

271 **singd** (past tense of 'singe')
throughlie thoroughly

275 ***exeunt*** The clearing of the stage here ends the first scene of Act 2, but scene breaks and scene numbers are not indicated in the authorial manuscript. For a text with the conventional scene-breaks, see *Later*.

Enter wh. King: Q: Bp. Duke. Knight: pawnes: and Qs.pawne: and Bl. King Q.Bp. &c.

Wh.Q. Is this my pawne? shee that should guard our person?
or some pale Fygure of Deiection
her shape usurping? sorrowe and affrightment
ha's præuaylde strangelie wth her;

wh.p. King of Integritie!

275.1 ***Enter*** For Middleton's addition, introducing a major new character, see *Later* 2.2.0.1–95. The Fat Bishop impersonated Antonio De Dominis, Archbishop of Spalato (1566–1624), as the title-page likenesses and contemporary reports confirm. But the vices Middleton gave his 'Fat Bishop' were not limited to De Dominis (who had left England two years earlier). His theology was closely connected to the Arminianism of some English clerics (including the Bishops of Chichester, Durham, London, Rochester, St David's, and Winchester), who—like King James—were also sympathetic to his contention that the religion of Catholics and Protestants 'is in the maine essentials and fundamentals the very same' (*A Sermon Preached in Italian* (1617), 31). The legitimacy of the Jacobean episcopate, which De Dominis defended, had been polemically contested in at least a dozen pamphlets since 1606. Ben Jonson satirized young men who were obsessed with foreign news and domestic politics, and would ''gainst the Bishops . . . rail' ('The New Cry', 1616). A 'Fat Bishop' could have reminded audiences of John Jegon, who was called 'our short, fat Lord Bishop' of Norwich. The practice of clerical pluralism—in which a single person holds two benefices—was attacked in Parliament in 1621 and 1625; it was particularly prevalent among the episcopate and court clergy. Theophilus Field, made Bishop of Llandaff through Buckingham's patronage in 1619, was impeached in 1621 by Parliament for bribery and brocage; Richard Corbet was satirized in 1623 for his overt courting of Buckingham in pursuit of additional benefices. In a widely circulated anonymous manuscript poem, the pro-Spanish Bishop John Williams, Lord Keeper, was accused of having a sexual affair with the Countess of Buckingham (converted to Catholicism in 1623): 'She loves the fucking game | He's her cunt-keeper' ('All the News', with the refrain 'These are they, bear the sway'). Lewes Bayly—'Bishop of Bang-whore' [Bangor]—was repeatedly accused (1619, 1621, 1626) of promiscuity, and of fathering several bastards. And Spalato was not the only 'turncoat Bishop': John King, Bishop of London, was alleged, in pamphlets of 1621 and 1623, to have made a deathbed conversion to Catholicism (an incident discussed in Middleton's lost *Farrago*).

275.1–2 ***wh. King . . . Qs.pawne*** This scene brings on stage, for the first time, the entire White House (King, clergy, lords, and commons), and its action resembles the Parliament of 1621, where King James rejected complaints by the Commons against Catholic infiltration in England and against Spanish aggression in northern Europe. This does not mean that the White Queen's Pawn personifies Bohemia or the Palatinate (an allegory that cannot be consistently applied). But the structure and emotion of the scene, and various verbal details, would have reminded many spectators of the crisis three years earlier.

275.1 ***wh. King*** Explicitly or implicitly identified, by contemporaries, as King James I; given the universal recognition of the Black Knight as Gondomar, the identity of the two kings was indisputable. It is not clear whether performances made any specific attempt at impersonation. 'His Mastie remembers well there was a commaundment and restraint giuen against the representinge of anie moderne Christian kings in those Stage-playes, and wonders much . . . at the boldnes nowe taken by that Companie' (Sir Edward Conway, Secretary of State, to the Privy Council, 12 August 1624).

275.2–2.276 ***Bl. . . . &c.*** Although the Black House enters here, the first 47 lines are spoken by White characters: the Black House are characterized as observers of English domestic politics.

275.2 ***Bl. King*** Identified—by Don Carlos Coloma (Spanish ambassador to England), and by Woolley, Conway, Pembroke, and Holles—as Felipe IV of Spain, 'because of his youth, dress, and other details' (Coloma). Notably, he does not speak until l. 440, after the White House has left the stage.

275.2–2.276 ***&c.*** including Black Knight and Black Duke (who both speak) and some black pawns (but not the Black Bishop's Pawn, who is absent)

276 ***Wh.Q.*** White Queen, who presumably wears some sort of crown or tiara, and stands adjacent to the White King. She is not specifically identified in any surviving contemporary response, but probably represents Elizabeth Stuart, Queen of Bohemia. Queen Anne had died early in 1619, before any of the other events dramatized in the play take place; the only living Stuart Queen, and Europe's most conspicuous Protestant Queen, was Elizabeth, who is a 'White Queen' not only because of her association with the White (English, Protestant, Stuart) cause, but because she was called 'the Winter Queen', whose army had been defeated at the Battle of White Mountain in November 1620. The first report of the play's performance compared it to 'Vox popoly' (John Wooley, 6 August 1624); Scott's *2 Vox Populi* (May 1624) was dedicated to Elizabeth, '*Queene of Bohemia*', and her husband Frederick, and she is at the centre of the frontispiece of Scott's *Vox Regis* (1624), kneeling in front of King James, pleading her '*Iust cause*'. The Venetian ambassador said that *Game* contained 'several representaitons under different names of many of the circumstances about the marriage with the Infanta' (30 August); all English accounts of the Spanish Match linked it directly to the fate of the Queen of Bohemia. John Holles called the play 'a representation of all our spannishe traffike' (11 August), and Sir Francis Nethersole said that in the play 'the whole Spanish business is ripped vp to the quicke' (14 August); it could not have been as comprehensive as they claim ('all', 'whole') without representing the Queen of Bohemia. Even to identify Elizabeth as 'Queen' was dangerous, because King James consistently refused to recognize Frederick and Elizabeth's claim to Bohemia.

Is . . . person In chess and life, a Queen is more powerful than a pawn/servant/gentlewoman. The Queen's Pawn stands before the Queen at the opening of the game, blocking any immediate direct attack upon her. In the 1620s many Protestants argued that the English people, and particularly the House of Commons—which appropriated funds, and was therefore essential to military action—had a natural obligation ('should') to defend the Queen of Bohemia, as a Protestant and a member of the English royal family.

our person (royal plural, in this first speech by the White Queen, confirming for the audience that she belongs to the royal family)

277–8 **Deiection . . . sorrowe** Although White Queen's Pawn was certainly frightened in the preceding scene, and is righteously angry in this scene, 'sorrow' and 'dejection' seem more relevant to the emotions of Protestant supporters of the Queen of Bohemia in the early 1620s.

280 ***wh.p.*** i.e. White Queen's Pawn

Queene of the same, and all the house professors
of noble Candor, uncorrupted Iustice
and truth of heart, through my alone discouerie
my life and honor wondrouslie præserude
I bring into youre Knowledge wth my suffrings
(fearefull affrightments, and heart-killing Terrors)
the great Incendiarie of Christendome,
the absolutst Abuser of true Sanctitie
fayre peace and holie Order, can bee found
in anie part a'th Vniucrsall Globe
who making meeke Deuotion keepe the doore
his lips being full of holie Zeale at first,
would haue committed a fowle Rape uppon mee,

wh.Q. hah?

wh. King—a Rape? thats fowle indeed, the uerie sound
to our Eare fowler then the offence it selfe
to some Kings of the Earth;

wh.p. Sir, to proceede,
gladlie I offerd life to præserue honor
wch would not bee accepted wthout both
the cheife of his ill Ayme being at mine honor,
till heauen was pleasde by some unlookte for accident
to giue mee courage to redeeme my selfe

Wh. K. when wee finde desperate Sins in Ill mens companies,
wee place a charitable Sorrowe there
but custome and theire leprous Inclination
quitts us of wonder, for our expectation
is answerd in theire liues, but to finde Sin
I, and a Mrpeice of darknes, shelterd
under a Robe of Sanctitie, is able
to drawe all wonder to that Monster onelie
and leaue created Monsters wthout any;
the pride of him that tooke first fall for pride
is to bee Angell shapte, and imitate
the forme from whence hee fell, but this offender
far baser then Sins Master, fixt by Vowe
to holie Order, wch is Angells method
takes pride to use that Shape to bee a Deuill
it greiues mee that my knowledge must bee taynted
wth his infested Name; oh rather wth thy finger poynt him out,

wh.p. the place wch hee should fill is uoyde, my L.,
his Guilt ha's ceazde him; the Bl. Bishops pawne, Sir,

Bl.B. hah? mine? my pawne? the Glorie of his Order;
the prime and præsident Zelot of the Earth,
Impudent pawne! for thy sake at this minute
modestie suffers, all thats Vertuous blushes
and Truths selfe like the Sun uext wth a mist
lookes red wth Anger,

wh.B. bee not you drunck wth rage too,

Bl.B. sober Synceritye! nor you a Cup
Spic'st wth Hypocrisie;

wh.Kt. you name there Bishop
but youre owne Christmas Bowle, youre mornings draught
next youre Episcopall heart all the i2 dayes
wch Smack you cannot leaue all the Yeare following

281 **Queene of the same** i.e., Queen of Integrity (not necessarily 'Queen of the same kingdom'). The White Queen is identified as a queen, in dialogue, within seconds of her first appearance on stage. For the very different treatment of the Black Queen, see 2.441.
all the house the House of Commons, and/or the kingdom of England, and/or the Stuart dynasty of England's king. Holles observed that 'The whole play is a chess board, England ye whyt hows' (11 August). When Prince Charles returned safely from Spain, a service of thanksgiving was observed at St Paul's Cathedral, based upon Psalm 114, 'When Israel came out of Egypt, and the house of Jacob from among the barbarous people'.

295–7 **Rape . . . Earth** As an example of recent outrages committed by Spanish soldiers in northern Protestant Europe, Scott claims that they were permitted 'to rauish yong girles not aboue eight or ten yeares of age' (*2 Vox Populi*, 48).

311 **onelie** only

322 **ceazde** seized

323 **Order** Middleton often uses the word ironically, playing on the double sense exploited (unironically) in Donne's sermon on obedience: 'I am glad that our *Ministery* is called *Orders*; that when we take this calling, we are said to take *Orders* . . . for giving example of obedience to Orders . . . . *Men of Orders* . . . ought to be most ready of all others to obey' (*Sermons* IV: 198).

329 ***wh.B.*** White Bishop, representing the Church of England. No surviving contemporary report identifies him more specifically, but the likeliest candidate is George Abbot (1562–1633), Archbishop of Canterbury, who vigorously opposed Catholicism, Arminianism, and the Spanish marriage (and who had overlapped with Middleton at Oxford). Abbot strongly supported the Queen of Bohemia and tighter restrictions on Jesuits in England.

330–1 **sober Synceritye . . . Hypocrisie** (words frequently associated with 'Puritans', which with the rise of Arminianism came increasingly to include Calvinists like Abbot)

331 **Hypocrisie** Abbot was especially vulnerable to this charge after July 1621, when in a hunting accident with a crossbow he killed a gamekeeper (Fincham, *DNB*). This incident exposed him to 'the rejoycing of the papist, the insulting of the puritan'; it was difficult for a 'man of blood' (i.e. with blood on his hands), taunted by some as a 'murderer', to criticize the sins of others—particularly 'rage'. The accusation temporarily silences the White Bishop, and he does not again directly confront the Black Bishop until the end of Act 4.

332 ***wh.Kt.*** White Knight, representing Charles, Prince of Wales (1600–49), as numerous contemporary references to the play make clear. His trip to Madrid was characterized by contemporaries as gallant knight-errantry: 'the voyage of the Knights of Adventure' (Secretary of State Conway, 3 March 1623), with Charles and Buckingham as 'venturous knights, worthy to be put into a new romance' (King James, 27 February 1623); Charles 'there did . . . imitate one of Prince *Arthurs* Knights, in seeking adventures through forraigne Princes territories' (Sir Antony Weldon, *The Court and Character of King James* (1651), 133). Middleton had celebrated the investiture of Charles as a Knight of the Order of the Garter in *Civitatis Amor*, and *Tennis* was written for him.

Bl.K$^{t.}$ a shrewde Retort! ha's made our Bishop smell of burning to,
would I stood farder off, wer't no Impeachment
to my honor or the Game, would the'yde playe faster;
White Knight! there is acknowledgd from our house
a Reuerence to you, and a Respect
to that lo'ude Duke stands next you, wth the fauour
of the white king, and th'aforenamde Respected
I combate wth this cause, if wth all speede
waste not one Sillable (unfortunate pawne)
of what I speake, thou do'st not pleade distraction
a plea wch will but fayntlie take thee off neyther
from this Leuiathan Scandall, that lyes rowling
uppon the Crystall Waters of Deuotion,
or what maye quitt thee more, though ynough, nothing,
fall downe and foame, and by that Pang discouer
the uexing Spirit of Falshood strong wthin thee,
make thy selfe readie for Perdition,
there's no Remoue in all the Game to scape it,
this pawne, or this, the Bishop or my selfe
will take thee in the end playe how thou can'st;

wh.p. Spite of Sins glorious ostentation
and all lowde threats those Thundercraks of pride
ushring a Storme of malice, house of Impudence
Craft and Æquiuocation, my true cause
shall keepe the path it treads in

Bl-Kt. I playe thus then;
now in the hearing of this high assemblie
bring forth the Time of this Attempts conception

wh.p. Conception? Lord how tenderlie you handle it,

Wh.B. it seemes black Knight you are afrayde to touch it,

Bl.K$^{t.}$ well, its Eruption, will shee haue it so then,
or you white Bishop for her, the uncleaner
Vile and more Impious, that you urge the strayne to
the greater will her Shames heape showe ith end
and the wrongd meekemans glorie, the time, pawne?

wh.p. yesterdayes cursed Euening,—

Bl.K$^{t.}$ oh the treasure of my Reuenge I can't spend all on thee,
Ruine ynough to spare for all thy Kinred,
for honors sake calle in more Slanderers
I haue such plentifull confusion
I knowe not how to waste it, Ile bee nobler yet
and putt her to her owne house, king of meekenes
take the cause to thee, for our hands too heauie
our proofes will fall uppon her like a Tower
and grinde her Bones to powder;

wh.p. what new Engine
ha's the Deuill raysde in him now?

Bl.K$^{t.}$ is it hee?
and that the Time, stand firme now to youre Scandall
praye do not shift youre Slander,

Wh.p. Shift youre Trecheries
theyůe worne one Suite too long

Bl.K$^{t.}$ that holie Man
so wrongfullie accusde by this lost pawne,
ha's not beene seene these 10 dayes in these parts,

wh: K$^{t.}$ how?

Bl.K$^{t.}$ naye at this instant 30 leagues from hence,

Wh.p. Fadomelesse Falshood will it scape unblasted!

wh.K$^{t.}$ can you make this appeare?

Bl.K$^{t.}$ light is not cleerer,
by his owne Letters, most Impartiall Monarch!

wh.K$^{s.}$p. how wrongfullie maye sacred Vertue suffer? S^{ir},

Bl.K$^{t.}$ Bishop! wee haue a Iewell of that false heart,

wh.K. step forth and reach those proofes;

wh.p. amazement couers mee,
Can I bee so forsaken of a cause
so strong in truth and æquitie? will uertue
send mee no Ayde in this hard time of Frendship?

336 ***Bl.K$^{t.}$*** The perceived influence of Gondomar, a foreign ambassador, on the outcome of the 1621 Parliament was particularly resented. He dominates the remainder of the scene, and reverses its direction.

347 **rowling** rolling

349 **ynough** enough

350–1 **fall . . . thee** suggesting symptoms of demonic possession (which had been discredited as frauds by Bishop John Harsnet and other Anglican authorities, and repudiated by King James)

357 **lowde** loud

359 **Æquiuocation** practice of making a 'mental reservation' which, when added to a false statement, makes it true: for instance, mentally adding the word 'not' to a sentence spoken aloud. Made famous by Father Henry Garnett's defence in 1606, when on trial for complicity in the Gunpowder Plot.

373 **all thy Kinred** The family of the White Queen's Pawn is not elsewhere identified, but the most sensitive political issue in the 1620s was the familial relationship between the King of England and the Queen of Bohemia.

393 **Fadomelesse** fathomless

396 **most Impartiall Monarch** King James prided himself on being the 'British Solomon'; Solomon was famous for his impartiality (1 Kings 3). In 1619, arbitrating a dispute between Lady Roos and Lady Frances Howard, James 'compared himself to Salomon that was to judge between two women . . . for which purpose he came furnished with all fit instructions wherby he might informe himself, but specially with equitie and unpartiall affection' (Chamberlain, 2:211). Buckingham was heard to 'say merrely, that the King had need be another Salomon to judge between the harlots'. As the White King condemns the White Queen's Pawn, James condemned Lady Roos 'for putting in a crosse slaunderous bill into the court' (214).

397 ***wh.K$^{s.}$p.*** Reflecting on the events of the abortive Parliament of 1621, Thomas Scott observed 'how much more easie it was *for a few* who had the Kings *eare*, to hinder, then *for many*, though they had the Kings *heart*, to helpe' (*Vox Regis*, 48).

398 **Iewell** jewel, later revised to 'treasure', suggesting the Earl of Middlesex (Lord Treasurer, 1621–4)

Bl.Kt. theres an Infallible Staff, and a *Red Hat*
wh.Ks.p. oh Sir endeerde,
Bl.Kt. theres a State figg for you now,
wh.K. behold all,
how they cohære in one, I alwayes held a charitie so good
to holines profest, I euer beleiude rather
the accuser false then the profession uitious,
Bl.Kt. a charitie like all youre Vertues else
most gratious and glorious,
Wh. K. where settles th' offence
let the faults punishment bee deriude from thence
wee leaue her to youre censure,
Bl.Kt. most iust maiestie;
wh.p. Calamitie of Vertue! my Queene leaue mee too;
I am cast off as th' Oliue casts her Flower
poore Frendlesse Innocence art thou left a Prey
to the Deuourer?
wh.Kt. no, thou art not lost
let em' putt on theire bloudiest Resolutions
If the fayre policie I ayme at prospers,
thy Councell Noble Duke?
wh.D. for that most cheerefullie,
wh.Kt. a man for speede now?
Wh.Bs.p. let it bee my honor, Sir,
make mee that Flight that owes her my lifes Seruice,
exeunt
Bl.Kt. was not this brought about well for our honors,
Bl.B. push, that Galician Skonce can worke out wonders,
Bl.Kt. letts use her, as uppon the like discouerie
a mayde was usde in Venice, euerie one
bee readie wth a pennance, begin Maiestie,
Vessell of foolish Scandall! Take thy freight
had there beene in that Cabinet of Nicenes
halfe the Virginities of th' earth lockt up
and all swept at one cast by the Dexteritie
of a Iesuiticall Gamster, tåd not Valued
the least part of that generall worth thou'st tayntd,

404–5 **theres . . . endeerde** For an expansion of this passage, see *Later* 2.2.211–14.

404 **Staff . . . *Hat*** Sir Toby Matthew had advocated restoration of Catholic bishoprics in England. An 'Oxford man', chaplain to Archbishop Abbot, at a Visitation Sermon complained 'The hope of a crosier-staffe or a Cardinalls hatt would make many a scholler in England beat his braine to reconcile the Church of Rome & England &c &c &c' (Joseph Mead, 25 April 1623). There may also be an implicit contrast with a 'fallible staff' the White King's Pawn already holds (perhaps the white staff of office of the Lord Treasurer).

407–15 **behold . . . censure** Eyewitness John Holles reported how Gondomar (the Black Knight) 'sett ye Kings affayrs as a clock, backward & forward, made him belieue, & vn=believe as stood best with [Gondomar's] busines, be ye caws neuer so cleere' (11 August). 'They cannot tear Count Gondomar so much by revealing his fashion of dealing, without . . . consequently reflecting weakness on those that gave him credence, and that daily dealt with him' (Florentine ambassador, 13 August). 'The worst is in playeng [Gondomar], they played somebody els . . .' (Chamberlain, 21 August). 'The Spaniards are touched from their tricks being discovered, but the king's reputation is affected much more deeply by representing the ease with which he was deceived' (Venetian ambassador, 30 August).

410 **uitious** vicious

411 **youre** In transcribing this passage Middleton first wrote 'his' here, suggesting he was thinking of someone outside the dramatic fiction (King James).

415 **wee . . . censure** In 1620, when Spanish troops invaded the Palatinate, Sir John Digby reported that 'many people were saying that the King must want his daughter and grandchildren taken prisoner to Spain, since he was doing nothing to help them' (Pursell, *Gondomar*, 9).

417 **my Queene leaue** The Queen of Bohemia first left Bohemia, then the Palatinate, settling in exile in the Hague, while her supporters in those countries suffered invasion and persecution.

419 **frendlesse** (*a*) without friends, supporters (*b*) without family, orphaned. Protestant critics of James I argued that he had abandoned his own child.

421–3 **no . . . prospers** Charles had long advocated more active English intervention to support his sister, the Queen of Bohemia.

422 **bloudiest** The Spanish were claimed to believe that 'except our victories be drowned in blood, we cannot tast them' (Scott, *2 Vox Populi*, 48). The adjective is more appropriate to the European wars than to the onstage context.

425 ***wh.D.*** White Duke, identified by Thomas Salisbury (1 December 1624) as George Villiers, Duke of Buckingham, favourite of King James, political ally of Prince Charles in the 1621 Parliament, his companion on the trip to Madrid to forward the Spanish marriage, then on their return his partner in repudiating it.

428 **Flight** arrow shot from a bow. The Bishop in chess was sometimes called the Archer (for example, in *Ludus Scacchiae*, A2v, A3v), so it makes sense for his Pawn to be imagined as an arrow. For the particular relevance of these associations to the White Bishop, see 2.331.

430 **Galician Skonce** 'King *Iames* loues [*Gondomar*] so well, as he esteemes his speeches Oracles and Scriptures', and Gondomar's '*Castillian*, or rather *Galitian* braine, hath now brought matters to this passe, that no cinsere advise, honest Letter . . . can point at the King of Spaine, but they are called in; and their Authors imprisoned (instead of rewarded) though never so honest and loyall Subiects' (Reynolds, *Vox Coeli* (1624), 60). In Middleton and Reynolds the reference to Gondomar's 'Galician Skonce' is associated with the imprisonment of an honest subject who is willing to 'point' at Catholic treachery.

438 **Iesuiticall Gamster** 'the *Master-Gamesters* the *Iesuites*' (Gee, *New Shreds*, 23)
tåd it had

Bl K. first I enioyne thee to a 3 dayes fast fort
Bl.Q. youre too penurious S^{ir}, Ile make it 4,
Bl.B. I, to a i2 howers Kneeling at one time,
Bl Kt. and in a Roome fild all wth Aretines pictures
more then the twice i2 labours of Luxurie
thou shalt not see so much as the chast Pummell
of Lucrece Dagger peeping, naye, Ile punnish thee
for a Discouerer, Ile torment thy modestie,
Bl.D. after that 4 dayes Fast to th' Inquisition house
Strenghtned wth bread and Water for worse pennance,
Bl.K$^{t.}$ why well sayde Duke of our house Noblie aggrauated;
wh.p. Vertue! to showe her Influence more strong,
Fitts mee wth patience mightier then my Wrong.
exeunt

Finit Actus Secundi

Incipit tercij Act 3

(·.·)

Enter Bl.k$^{t.}$

lett mee a litle solace my designes
wth the remembrance of some braue ones past
to cherish the futuritie of Proiect
whose motion must bee restlesse, till that great worke
cald the possession of the world bee ours.,
was it not I procurde a prætious safeguard
from the White Kingdome to secure our Coasts
gaynst th' Infidell Pyrates, under prætext
of more necessitous Expedition;
who made the Iayles flie open (wthout miracle)
and let the Locusts out, those dangerous Flies
whose propertie is to burne Corne wth touching,
the Heretique Granaries feele it to this minute,
and now theyue got amongst the Countrie-Crops

440 **enioyne** enjoin
fort for't, for it

441 ***Bl.Q.*** Black Queen. She is not called 'Queen' anywhere in the dialogue of the *Early* text, though her dress and position next to the Black King immediately indicate her royal status. (Contrast the White Queen at 2.281.) Woolley identified her as the Infanta Donna Maria (6 August), and Holles also referred to the Infanta in his account of the play (11 August). English writers paid almost no attention to the actual Queen of Spain, but were obsessed with the possibility that the Infanta Maria might become Queen of England. Her first action in the play is to punish another woman (an innocent English Protestant) by enforced kneeling.

443 **Roome...pictures** Art-collecting had become increasingly popular among influential Jacobean courtiers, particularly the Earl of Arundel and the Duke of Buckingham.
Aretines pictures *I Modi*, a set of pornographic images of sexual positions, painted by Giulio Romano, engraved by Marcantonio Raimondi, and published in 1524; later editions, with woodcuts replacing the engravings, included caption-sonnets by Pietro Aretino. Suppressed by Pope Clement VII, they continued to be surreptitiously printed, associated with Aretino rather than their unnamed artists.

444 **i2 labours** (alluding to the twelve labours, or tasks, of Hercules). Aretino calls attention to the extreme strenuousness of some of the depicted sexual positions; the figures are classical rather than modern, and thus encouraged mythological comparisons.

446 **Lucrece** For the representation and significance of this figure, see *Ghost of Lucrece*.

448 ***Bl.D.*** Black Duke. Not particularized in *Early*; at *Later* 5.3.213 he is specifically identified as Don Gaspar de Guzman, Conde-Duque de Olivares (1587–1645), Philip IV's favourite, and Buckingham's antagonist in Madrid.
Inquisition Catholic judicial system, particularly used for persecuting 'heretics'; 'the dangerous practices and most horrible executions of the Spanish Inquisition'—including 'the villainous and shameless tormenting of naked women beyond all humanity'—had been a recurrent focus of Protestant fear and propaganda for more than half a century (*A Discovery and playne Declaration of sundry subtill practises of the Holy Inquisition of Spayne*, trans. Thomas Skinner, 1568).

452 **my Wrong** the wrong done to me. The end of Act 1 hints at the political consequences of conversion of a single 'lost pawn' (White King's Pawn); at the end of Act 2, that traitor and the larger political struggle between leaders of the two houses leads directly to the imprisonment of a faithful pawn (perhaps echoing the end of the 1621 Parliament, when King James imprisoned five Members and sent five others out of England). For the conspicuous failure of justice here, see Scott's *High-wayes of God and the King*: 'how haps it then, that there are...crying sinnes...as if there were no King, no Lawe, no Priest, no Iudge in *England?*' (73). Scott cites, from Judges:21, 'the rape of certaine virgins by fraude and force, who came out, without feare of trechery, securely trusting to their owne innocence, and the peace of the State. The reason of these disorders is giuen as before, *Then ther was no King in Israel*...There was a Lawe, but there was none designed to execute it.' (73) Scott's sermon was addressed to judges: 'Iudges, who know you haue a King aboue you too....though all scarlet sinnes, & crying crimes be kept from his eyes and eares artificially' (84).

3.0.3 ***Enter*** Middleton later expanded this scene to include the Fat Bishop: see *Later* 3.1.0.1–81, 283–305.

1 **lett** The solitary entrance direction doubles as a speech prefix.

2 **remembrance...past** The projects Gondomar describes here all occurred in the years 1618–21 (before conclusion of the second session of the 1621 Parliament).

6–9 **procurde...Expedition** Gondomar 'procured a gallant Fleete to secure the coast of *Spaine*, against the Turkish Pyrates' (Reynolds, *Vox Coeli*, 57). The fleet sailed in October 1620 and returned in September 1621. In place of 'prætious safeguard', *Later* 3.1.87 has 'gallant fleet', reverting to the wording of Reynolds.

6 **prætious** 'valuable' (to the Spanish, in protecting their coasts) but also 'expensive' (to the English, who paid for the fleet) and ultimately 'good-for-nothing' (because it did not stop piracy against English merchant ships)
safeguard defence, armed naval escort (compared to an expensive outer garment worn by women to protect their skirts when riding)

10–11 **made...out** 'the King has consented to deliver [74 imprisoned priests] to the...Conde de Gondomar, to go abroad' (*Calendar of State Papers*, 5 June 1618)

10 **Iayles** jails, gaols

11 **Locusts** (a common metaphor for Jesuits: see Gee, *Snare*, sig. E2)

13 **Granaries...minute** This may allude to the bad English harvest of 1622, as though Gondomar's success in releasing imprisoned Jesuits before 1621 were responsible for the subsequent dearth. But the outbreak of war in 1620 also produced famines in Germany and France.

they stick so fast to the conuerted Eares
the lowdest Tempest that Authoritie rayses
will hardlie shake em̃ off, they haue theire Dens
in Ladies Couches, there's safe Groues and Fens,
naye were they followed and found out byth' Scent
Palme-Oyle will make a Purseuant relent;
whose policie wa'st to putt a silencst Muzzle,
on all the Barking Tongmen of the Time,
made pictures, that were dumbe ynough before
poore Suffrers in that politick Restraynt
my light Spleene skips and shakes my Ribs to thinke
on't
whilst our drifts walkte uncensurde but in thought
a whistle or a whisper would bee questiond,
in the most fortunate Angle of the world, Venice
the Court ha's held the Cittie by the Hornes
whilst I haue milkt her, I haue got good soapes too
from Countrie Ladies for theire Liberties,
from some for theire most uaynelie hopde preferments
high offices ith Ayre, I should not liue
but for this Mell Aerium, this Mirth-Manna:
Enter Bl. pawne:
my pawne! how now? the Newes!

Bl.p. expect none uerie pleasing
that comes S^{ir} of my bringing, Ime for sad things,

Bl.K$^{t.}$ thy Conscience is so tender-hoofte alate
euerie nayle pricks it,

Bl.p. this maye prick yours too
if there bee anye quick Flesh in a Yard on't,

Bl.K$^{t.}$ mine? mischeife must finde a deepe Nayle, and a
Driuer
beyond the strenght of anye Machiauill
the politick Kingdomes fatten, to reach mine;
prethee Compunction! needle prickt a Litle
unbinde this sore wound;

Bl.p. Sir, youre plotts discouerd;

Bl.K. wch of the twentie thousand and nine hundred
threescore and fiue, can'st tell?

Bl.p. blesse us, so manie?
how do's poore Countrimen haue but one plott
to keepe a Cowe on, yet in Lawe for that;
you cannot Knowe em' all sure by theire Names, S^{r},

Bl-K$^{t.}$ yes, were the Number trebled, thou hast seene
a Globe stands on the Table in my Closett?

20 **Purseuant** pursuivant. 'And yet when these *Pursevants* had greatest authoritie, a small bribe in the Countrey would blinde their eyes' (Scott, *Vox Populi* (1620), C4^{v}). Chamberlain recorded 'the censuring of a pursevant in the Star-chamber for making a trafficke of taking priests and letting them go for monie' (8 July 1620).

21–4 **policie... Restraynt** 'I saw... Scots loyall *Vox Populi, D. Whiting, D. Everard, & Claytons* zealous Sermons, and others, suppress'd and silenced, as also *Wards* faithfull picture, which yet was so innocent, as it onely breathed forth his fidelity to *England* in silent Rethorique, and dumbe eloquence' (Reynolds, *Vox Coeli*, A4^{v}).

21–2 **Muzzle... Barking** Gondomar explains that the English clergy 'are muzled for barking, when ours may both barke and bite too' (Scott, *Vox Populi*, C3^{v}).

23 **pictures** Samuel Ward, 'a special preacher of Ipswich', was imprisoned in 1621 for the engraving *1588 Deo Trin-vni Brittaniae... 1605*; it combined images of the Spanish Armada and the Gunpowder Plot.

28 **Venice** This extrametrical word, present only in the earliest manuscript, distracts attention from the obvious interpretation of 'most fortunate Angle' as England: see Induction.1.

29 **Court... Cittie** James I had repeatedly given monopolies to courtiers, at the expense of various commercial interests of the City of London. Collection of customs was farmed out to various syndicates throughout the reign ('a great discouragment to [merchants] in their trades', according to a 1612 report to the Privy Council). The Cokayne monopoly (1614–17) was disastrous for the Merchant Adventurers; the gold and silver thread monopoly was adamantly opposed by the Goldsmiths' Company, Lord Mayor, and aldermen, and led to Sir Giles Mompesson's impeachment by the 1621 Parliament; there were also successful attacks on monopolies in the 1624 Parliament.

30 **milkt** 'these other tyme-servers... milk the estate and keep it poore' (Scott, *Vox Populi*); 'him that is the cause of all this, and that's the *Courtly Thiefe*... the milking of the state by priuate *Monopolies*... Looke vpon the highest, if they make any other account of the poore then of their tame cattell' (Scott, *High-wayes of God*, 79–81).
her (London, frequently personified as female)
soapes sops, pieces of bread dipped in liquid before being eaten

32 **uaynelie hopde** vainly hoped

34 **Mell Aerium** (alluding to the beginning of Virgil's Fourth Georgic: 'Protinus aerii mellis caelestia dona...' Gondomar thus equates the gifts/bribes he receives with the honey produced by hard-working bees, which Virgil describes as 'heaven's gift'; that image leads in turn to the image of Biblical 'manna' (Exodus 16:15, etc.) which 'came down from heaven' (Job 6:58))

35 **the Newes** John Taylor complained that he 'cannot pass the streets but I am continually stayed by one or other, to know what news' (*Taylor's Travels to Prague*, 1620). The subtitle of Scott's *Vox Populi* is 'Newes from Spayne'.

36 ***Bl.p.*** Black Pawn, just identified as 'my pawne', i.e. Black Knight's Pawn. With no other pawn on stage, the abbreviation is unambiguous.

38–9 **tender-hoofte... nayle** Compare Horace *Odes* 3.6.24: *de tenero ungui*, 'from the tender nail' [= from early youth].

43 **Machiauill** The subtitle of Scott's *2 Vox Populi* was 'Gondomar appearing in the likenes of Matchiauell'. The works of Niccolò Machiavelli (1469–1627) were banned in much of Europe; *The Prince* was not published in English until 1640. Privately, his works circulated widely, and his name became a label for atheism, amoral cunning, and political ambition. He appears as the Prologue to Marlowe's *Jew of Malta*, and influenced characters like Shakespeare's Richard III, who promises 'to set the murderous Machiavel to school' (*Duke of York* 3.2.193).

48 ***Bl.K.*** Black Knight. (With no King on stage, the abbreviation is unambiguous.)

55 **Globe** a rare and expensive object at the time, and a reminder of Spain's global ambitions

Bl.p. a thing Sir full of Cuntryes, and hard words,
Bl.K. true, wth lines drawen some tropicall, some Oblique,
Bl.p. I scarce can reade I was brought up in Blindnes;
Bl.K. iust such a thing (if e're my Skull bee opend)
will my braynes looke like,
Bl.p. like a Globe of Cuntryes,
Bl.Kt. I, and some Mr-Polititian
that ha's sharpe State Eyes will goe neere to pick out
the plotts, and euerie Clymate where they fastned
twill puzzle em̃ too;
Bl.p. Ime of youre minde for that S^{ir},
Bl.K$^{t.}$ theyle finde em̃ to fall thick uppon some Coũtryes
theyde neede use Spectacles, but I turne to you now,
what plott is that discouerd?
Bl.p. youre last Brat, S^{ir}
begot twixt the Black Bishop and youre selfe
youre Antedated letters 'bout the Iesuite,
Bl.K$^{t.}$ discouerd? how?
Bl.p. the White Knights policie
ha's out stript yours it seemes,
ioynd wth th' Assistant Councell of his Duke
the Bishops white pawne undertooke the Iourney
who as they saye dischargd it like a Flight
I made him for the Businesse fitt and light
Bl.Kt. tis but a bawdie pawne out a'th waye a litle
Enter Bl.Bishop and the Wh. house and Bl. house.
enow of them in all parts
Bl.B. you haue heard all?
Bl.Kt. the Wonders past wth mee, but some shall downe fort,
wh.K. Set free the Vertuous pawne from all her wrongs
let her bee brought wth honor to the face
of her malitious Aduersaries,
Bl.K$^{t.}$ good!
wh.K. Noble chast Knight, a Title of that Candor
the greatest prince on earth wthout impeachment
maye haue the dignitie of his worth comprizde in,
this fayre deliuering Act uertue will register
in that white Booke of the defence of Virgins
where the cleere Fames of all præseruing Knights
are to æternall memorie consecrated,
and wee embrace as partner of that honor
this worthie peice the Councell of the Act
whome wee shall euer place in our respect,

56 **Cuntryes** countries
58 **scarce can reade** 'many priests could scarce read Latine' (Goad, *Friers Chronicle*, F3^{v}). Literacy rates were higher in northern than southern Europe. The Reformation emphasized the need for direct individual access to the Word of God; Protestants (especially Calvinists) owned many more books than Catholics.
59 **if . . . opend** (suggesting images of human dissection popularized by sixteenth-century anatomy textbooks)
67 **Coũtryes** countries
72 **Antedated letters** (a device elsewhere attributed to the Jesuits Robert Parsons and Henry Garnett, and to the Earl of Middlesex)
76 **ioynd** joined
78 **Flight** For the archery metaphor, see 2.428. But 'flight' also can refer to a flock: eunuchs were compared to angels by several early Church Fathers, including Basil of Ancyra, Jerome, and Augustine (Taylor, *Castration*, 44, 257).
79 **I . . . fitt** 'By gelding him, I increased his ability to thwart our plans.' Castration, routinely performed on domesticated animals and widely performed on human males since antiquity, produced a being custom-made for certain purposes: royal service, singing, or dedication to God. In Matthew 19:12, Jesus referred to men who 'made themselves eunuchs for the kingdom of heaven's sake', and it was widely known that Origen and some other early Christians were castrated; the first convert to Christianity was a eunuch (Acts 8:26–40), who was praised as exemplary in Charles Sonibancke's *The Eunuche's Conuersion. A Sermon preached at Paules Crosse* (1617) and in a sermon by John Donne (*Sermons* 5:35–36, undated, probably before 1623). **light** This claim in part depends on an implicit pun: 'I made him . . . light' by gelding him, i.e. by removing his testicles, normally called 'stones'; stones are heavy, and in particular 'stone' is a measure of weight (fourteen pounds). The same pun-complex ('light' because gelded and deprived of 'stones') is explicit in Edward Sharpham's *Cupid's Whirligig*, Philip Massinger's *The Renegado*, and Richard Brome's *The Court Beggar*.
80.1 ***the Wh. house*** The second entry of the entire house. (See 2.275.1–2.) But the fictional action of this scene cannot be so easily related to a Parliamentary session, because the Black House is already present, and is immediately addressed; many Black characters speak while the White House is on stage. Black and White Houses now interact across the whole board, as it were, like the two dynasties/religions/nations manœuvring in mid-game on the larger chessboard of Europe.
81 **enow** enough
86 **malitious** malicious
88–105 **Noble . . . fidelitie** The King's praise of White Knight and Duke echoes popular enthusiasm for Prince Charles and Buckingham after their return from Spain; they persuaded King James to call another Parliament, beginning in February 1624, which reversed many of the royal policies of 1621–3, accepted earlier accusations against Spain, and supported a crackdown on Jesuits in England. In other respects it resembles the popular welcome of the Earls of Oxford and Essex in November 1620, who 'arrived safe at London, being newly returned from their dangerous and successless expedition into the Palatinate. Their return was the more joyed at, because their families were great and noble, and they had yet no issue, nor were married' (D'Ewes, *Autobiography*, I:156).
88 **chast** chaste. Prince Charles was, by all accounts, still a virgin; it was particularly important to Protestants that he returned from Spain unmarried.
88–90 **Title . . . in** (probably alluding to Prince Charles's status as a Knight of the Order of the Garter—a ceremonial title celebrated in Middleton's *Civitatis Amor*—and justifying representation of the heir to the throne as a mere knight)
89 **impeachment** disparagement (but also suggesting Parliamentary impeachment of government officials, a practice spectacularly revived in 1621 and 1624)
92 **that white Booke** (in contrast to Middleton's *Black Book*, or perhaps more recently what *Tom Tell-Troath* called 'the black booke of the Court')
96 **peice** (later revised to 'Duke', for clarity)

wh.D. most blest of Kings! throand in all royall Graces
euerie good Deed sends back its owne reward
into the bosome of the Enterprizer,
but you t'expresse youre selfe as well to bee
King of Munificence as Integritie
adds glorie to the Gift,
Enter wh.Qs. pawne

wh.K. thy desert claymes it
Zeale, and fidelitie, appeare thou bewtie
of truth and Innocence, best ornament
of patience, thou that makes thy suffrings glorious,

Bl.Kt. Ile take no knowledge on't, what makes shee here?
how dares yon'd pawne unpennanc'st, wth a cheeke
fresh as her Falshood yet, where Castigation
ha's left no pale print of her uisiting Anguish
appeare in this assemblie, lett mee alone
Sin must bee bold, thats all the Grace tis borne to,

wh.Kt. whats this!

wh:K. Ime wonderstruck;

wh.p. assist mee Goodnes
I shall to prison agen,

Bl.Kt. at least Iue mazde em̃,
scatterd theire Admirations of her Innocence,
as the firde Ship putt in, seuerd the Fleete
in 88, Ile on wth't, Impudence
is mischeifes patrimonie, is this Iustice?
is iniurde Reuerence no sharplier righted,
I euer held that Maiestie Impartiall
that like most æquall heauen lookes on the manners
not on the shapes they shroud in;

wh.K. this black Knight
will neuer take an answere, tis a Victorie
to make him understand hee do's amisse
when hee knowes in his owne cleere understanding
that hee do's nothing else, showe him the testimonie
confirmd by goodmen, how that fowle Attempter
got but this morning to the place, from whence
hee dated his forgd Lines for io dayes past:

Bl.Kt. why maye not that Corruption sleepe in this
by some Conniuence, as you haue wakte in ours
by too rash Confidence,

wh.D. Ile undertake
that Knight shall teach the deuill how to lye

wh.Kt. if Sin were halfe as wise as impudent,
She'ede ner'e seeke farder for an Aduocate:
Enter Bl.Qs.p.

Bl.p. now to act Trechrie Wth an Angells tong
since alls come out, Ile bring him in agen;
where is this iniurde Chastitie, this Goodnes
whose worth no Transitorie peice can Value
this Rock of constant and inuincible Vertue
that made Sins Tempest wearie of his Furie;

Bl.Q. what is my pawne distracted

Bl.Kt. I thinke rather
there is some notable Mr-prize of Roguerie
this Drum strikes up for,

Bl.p. lett mee fall wth reuerence
before this blessed Altar,

Bl.Q. this is madnes,

Bl.Kt. well, marke the end I stand for Roguerie still
I will not change my Side

Bl.p. I shall bee taxt I knowe
I care not what the Blackhouse thinkes on mee,

Bl.Q. what saye you now?

Bl.Kt. I will not bee unlayde yet;

Bl.p. how anie censure flyes, I honor Sanctitie
that is my obiect I entend no other;
I sawe this glorious and most Valiant Vertue
fight the most noblest Combate wth the Deuill

Bl.Kt. if both the Bishops had beene there for seconds
tad beene a compleate Duell;

wh.K. then thou heardst
the Violence entended,

Bl.p. tis a truth I ioye to iustifie, I was an agent
on Vertues part; and raysde that confusde noyse,
that startled his Attempt, and gaue her libertie,

wh.p. oh tis a righteous Storie shee ha's told, Sir,)
my life and Fame stand mutuallie engagde,
both to the truth and Goodnes of this pawne

wh.K. do's it appeare to you yet: cleere as the Sun?

Bl.Kt. lasse I beleiude it long before twas donne

Bl.K. Degenerate!

Bl.Q. Base

Bl.B. perfidious

Bl.D. traytrous pawne;

118 **mazde** 'mazed, amazed
120–1 **as ... 88** as the English fireships, on 28 July 1588, scattered the Spanish Armada in the English Channel off Calais. The singular 'Ship' is probably Middleton's error; it is corrected in *Later*.
127–31 **this ... else** (perhaps alluding specifically to Gondomar's remarkable evasive calm when King James angrily accused him of deception regarding Spanish plans to invade the Palatinate)
136 **Conniuence** connivance
141 **ner'e** ne'er, never
145 **Value** equal in value (changed at *Later* 3.1.211 to 'equal')
150 **Mr-prize** master-prize, masterpiece (Middleton coinage)
151–68 **Drum ... Combate ... Violence** (military language, suggesting the warfare in Germany as much as the attempted rape of the White Queen's Pawn)
161 **how** however, no matter how
166 **tad** it had
176 **lasse** 'las, alas

Bl.p. what are you all beside youre selues?
Bl Kt. but I,
remember that pawne?
Bl.p. maye a fearefull Barrennes
blast both my hopes and pleasures, if I brought not
her Ruine in my pittie, a new Trap
for her more sure Confusion,
Bl.K$^{t.}$ haue I wun now?
did not I saye twas Craft and Machination
I smelt Conspiracie all the waye it went
although the Messe were couerd, Ime so usde too'te,
Bl.K. that Queene would I fayne finger,
Bl.K$^{t.}$ youre too hott S^{ir}
if shee were tooke, the Game would bee ours quicklie
my Aymes at that White Knight, entrap him first
that peice will followe too,
Bl.B. I would that Bishop
were in my Diocesse, Ide soone change his Whitenes,
Bl.K$^{t.}$ S^{ir}, I could whip you up a pawne immediatlie
I knowe where my Game stands,
Bl.K. doo'te suddenlye
aduantage least must not bee lost in this playe
Bl.Kt. pawne, thou art ours,
wh.K$^{t.}$ hees taken by default
by willfull negligence, guard the sacred persons
looke well to the white Bishop, for that pawne
gaue Guard to th' Queene and him in the 3^{d} place;
Bl.K$^{t.}$ see what sure peice you lock youre confidence in
I made this pawne here by Corruption ours
as soone as honor by Creation yours,
this whitenes uppon him, is but the Leprousie
of pure dissimulation, View him now
his upper garment taken of, he appeeres Black underneath
hir heart, and his Intents are of our Colour,
wh.K$^{t.}$ most dangerous Hypocrite

186 **a new Trap** In the second session of the 1621 Parliament, Sir John Digby, after his diplomatic mission to Vienna as 'an Agent' of King James, publicly confirmed the duplicity of the Emperor Ferdinand (21 November 1621). Although this convinced many Englishmen in and out of Parliament that only war could restore the Palatinate and Bohemia to Queen Elizabeth, it had a different effect on King James: the failure of diplomacy in Vienna persuaded him that the Spanish Match was the only possible solution, and in February 1622 Digby was dispatched to Spain to reconvene the marriage negotiations (in abeyance since 1618). Likewise, the Black Queen's Pawn's confirmation of the attempted rape leads directly to her central role in the marriage plot: see 3.232, 248–52.

192 ***Bl.K.*...finger** Elizabeth Stuart (b. 1596), called the 'queen of hearts', was still young and attractive; her decolletage provoked gossip in Prague; she attracted the chivalric romantic devotion of Christian of Halberstadt, whose battle standards carried the motto 'All for God and for her'. She was therefore a plausible object of the lust of a young Spanish King with a reputation for sexual exploits. Politically, Spanish troops were instrumental in evicting Queen Elizabeth of Bohemia from the Palatinate; she was chased across Europe from Prague to the Hague.

193 **youre too hott** 'You must not be too hastie to play' ('Certaine generall rules', G.B., *Ludus Scacchiae*). In chess, an early ill-prepared frontal assault on the Queen is seldom successful; Black Knight instead proposes a more indirect strategy.

194 **if...quicklie** Protestant supporters of the Queen of Bohemia argued that, if the Habsburgs were allowed to conquer Bohemia, the Palatinate, and all of Germany, England would be fatally isolated, politically, economically, and militarily.

195 **my...Knight** This is the first indication that Gondomar (and the Spanish more generally) have targeted Prince Charles as the key to the game; it follows directly from discussion of the White Queen, implying that the entrapment of Charles 'first' will make it easier to take the Queen.

196 **that peice** ambiguous: the context suggests 'the White Queen', but the phrase was subsequently changed to 'The Duke' (*Later* 3.1.249).

206–7 **pawne...place** 'the Kings Pawn giueth guard to the third House before the Queene, and to the third house before the kings Byshop' (Saul, *Chesse-Play*, C2^{v}).

207 **3^{d}** third

212.1 ***of*** off

213 **hir** All other texts change 'hir' to 'his' (*Later* 3.1.263), but 'her' could refer to the White Queen's Pawn (whom he has repeatedly slandered) or the White Queen, or the Black Queen's Pawn, who has apparently crossed over to the White side: in taking the White King's Pawn, the Black Knight wants to confound the White House, by making them doubt the loyalty of their own members.

213–16 **our Colour...theire Complexion** The language here suggests that the 'blackness' of the Spanish characters refers not just to their costumes but to their skin colour. A Spanish speaker in Scott's *2 Vox Populi* admits that 'many of vs are discended of the Moorish race' (13), and another refers to the 'insolent and african pride' of the Spanish (23). The history of invasion from North Africa, and the importing of slaves from sub-Saharan Africa to the Iberian peninsula since the 1440s, had made Spaniards and Portuguese particularly vulnerable to such claims. A manuscript invective against Gondomar alleged 'a Spanish Moore's thy mother' (Rosenbach 1083/16, p. 297). Pawns from the Black House are compared to 'the Deuill' (3.289), 'a Black-bird' (291), 'a Monckey' (312), 'Russet woodcocks' (318), and associated with 'Slauerie' (298); the Black House is twice associated with Egyptians (Induction.8, 3.264); the Black Duke is said to be 'sunburnt' and 'Oliue-Colourd' (*Later* 5.3.213–14). For the racial contrast with 'White' see Induction.44 and 2.0.2.

214 **Hypocrite** This image of hypocrisy (white on the outside, black on the inside) derives from the paradox of the 'white devil', which originated in Luther's commentary on Galatians (the most popular of his works in England), and was repeated and elaborated in Pierre Vivet's *The Worlde possessed with Deuils* (1583) and in a Paul's Cross sermon by Thomas Adams, *The White Deuil, or The Hypocrite Vncased* (1613). The earliest example in English drama is *Revenger* 3.5.146, 'white devil'; see also the 'hypocrite' called 'white-fac't Diuell' (*Tennis* 719, 724) and the 'white-fac't hyppocrite, Lady Sanctity' (*Tennis* 391). For the merging of this religious image of white hypocrisy with tropes of racial whiteness, see Taylor, *Castration*, 243–49, 310.

wh.D. one made agaynst us,

wh.Q. his Truth of theire Complexion!

wh.K. ha's my Goodnes
Clemencie, loue, and fauour gratious rousd thee
and grafted thee into a Branch of honor
and do'st thou fall from the Top-bough by th'
rottennes
of thy alone Corruption, like a Fruite
thats ouer ripend by the beames of Fauour,
lett thy owne weight reward thee, I haue forgot thee,
Integritie of life is so deere to mee
where I finde falshood or a crieng Trespasse
bee it in anye whome our Grace shines most on
Ide teare em̃ from my heart,

Wh.B. spoke like heauens Substitute;

wh.K. you haue him, wee can spare him, & his shame
will make the rest looke better to theire Game;
exeunt

Bl.K. the more cunning wee must use then;

Bl.Kt. wee shall match you
playe how you can, perhaps and mate you too;

wh.p. I rest uppon you, Knight, for my Aduancement now,

Bl.Kt. oh for the Staff Sir, the strong Crosier-Staff
and the red Hat fitt for the Guiltie Mazard
into the emptie Bagg, knowe thy first waye
pawnes that are lost, are euer out of playe:

wh.p. howes this?

Bl.Kt. no Replications, you knowe mee,
no doubt ere long youle haue more companie
the Bagg is big ynough twill hold us all *exeunt*

wh.Qs.p. I sue to thee, prethee bee one of us,
let my loue win thee, thou'st donne truth this daye,
and yesterdaye my honor noble Seruice
the best pawne of our house could not transcend it

Bl.p. my pittie flamde wth Zeale, espetiallie
when I forsawe youre Marriage, then it mounted

wh.Qs.p. how? marriage?

Bl.p. that contaminating Act
would haue spoyld all youre Fortunes, a Rape! blesse
us

wh.Qs.p. thou talkst of marriage,

Bl.p. yes, yes, you doo marrie,
I sawe the man;

wh.Qs.p. the Man?

Bl.p. an Absolute handsome Gentleman, a Compleate one,
you'le saye so when you see him, heyre to 3 Red
hatts
besides his generall hopes in the black house

wh.Qs.p. why sure thour̃t much mistaken for this Man;
Iue promist single life to all my Affections

Bl.p. promise you what you will or I or all on's
there's a Fate rules and ouerrules us all mee thinkes,

wh.Qs.p. why how came you to see, or knowe this
Mysteric!

219 **grafted...honor** united him with an honourable family (a standard reward for successful courtiers)
thee Three lines added here (*Later* 3.1.267–69) seem to refer to the Earl of Middlesex, who had left school at fifteen to become apprenticed to a grocer, and thus had been lifted by the King from 'labour' and the 'hazards' of life as a merchant.
224–7 **Integritie...heart** Recalling the disgrace of several high officials to whom King James had shown extraordinary favour: the Earl of Somerset (royal favourite, 1615, for murder), the Earl of Suffolk (Lord Treasurer, 1619, for corruption), Sir Francis Bacon (Lord Chancellor, 1621, for bribery), the Earl of Middlesex (Lord Treasurer, 1624, for corruption), and the Earl of Bristol (long-time ambassador to Spain, 1624, for treason).
225 **crieng** crying
228 **heauens Substitute** James I believed that kings were God's lieutenants (*Speech to the Lords and Commons*, 1610); 'Kings are properly judges, and judgement properly belongs to them from God, for kings sit in the Throne of God' (speech to Star Chamber, 1616). His view was endorsed by many clerical authorities.
231 **more cunning** This suggests that the next Black move will be even more clever and dangerous than any in the first half of the play. See next note.
232–3 **match...mate** the first use in the play of either verb. Both clearly suggest the 'Spanish Match', which would 'mate'—marry—Prince Charles to a Spanish princess. See 3.176, 248–53.
235 **oh...Crosier-Staff** 'Oh blessed...his sacred *Crozier-staffe*' (Gee, *New Shreds*, 33)
242 **the Bagg...all** 'And after death like Chesmen hauing stood | In play for Bishops, some for Knights, and Pawnes, | We all together shall be tumbled vp, into one bagge' (John Marston, *Jack Drum's Entertainment*, 1600?).
248–53 **Marriage...marriage...marriage...marrie** The reiteration emphasizes the structural significance of this moment: the second half of the play will dramatize the Spanish Match. (See 3.186, 231–2.) The Venetian ambassador described the play as 'several representations under different names of many of the circumstances about the marriage with the Infanta' (30 August 1624). In the action initiated here, a naïve English Protestant virgin is deceived, and led to the brink of marriage with a dishonest foreign Catholic, as a result of a cynical plot by supporters of the Spanish and Catholic cause; the play's colour contrast suggests not only inter-faith marriage but miscegenation.
257–8 **heyre...house** Like the Spanish Infanta, the proposed spouse promises exceptional wealth and power (which is delusory: no one could inherit three cardinalships). The three hats might suggest the crowns of the kingdoms of Spain and Portugal and the Holy Roman Empire (all held by Habsburgs).
261 **on's** of us

Bl.p. a magicall Glasse I bought of an Ægiptian
whose Stone retaynes that Speculatiue Vertue
præsented the Man to mee, youre name brings him
as often as I use it, and mee thinkes
I neuer haue ynough, person and postures
are all so pleasing,

wh.Qs.p. this is wondrous strange
the faculties of soule are still the same,
I can feele no one Motion tend that waye,

Bl.p. wee do not alwayes feele our fayth wee liue by,
nor euer see our Growth, yet both worke upward,

wh.Qs.p. twas well resolud, but maye I see him too,

Bl.p. surelie you maye wthout all doubt or feare
Obseruing the right use as I was taught it,
not looking back, nor questioning the Specter,

wh.Qs.p. thats no hard Obseruation, trust it wth mee,
ist possible? I long to see this man,

Bl.p. praye followe mee then and Ile ease you instantlie;
exeunt

Enter Bl. Iesting pawne

Bl.Iestp. I would so fayne take one of these white pawnes now,
Ide make him doo all under Drudgerie,
Feede him wth Asses Milke crumbd wth Goates cheese
and all the Whitmeates could bee deuisde for him,
Ide make him my White Iennet when I praun'cst
after the black Knights Litter;

Enter a Wh: pawne,

wh.p. and youde looke then
iust like the Deuill striding or̓e a Night-Mare
made of a Millers daughter.

Bl.p. pox on you were you so neere, Ime taken like a Black-bird
in the great Snowe, this white pawne grinning ouer mee,

wh.p. and now because I will not fowle my Cloaths
euer hereafter, for white quicklie soyles, you knowe,

Bl.p. I prethee gett thee gon then I shall smut thee

wh.p. no Ile putt that to Venture now I haue snapt thee
thou shalt doo all the Drudgerie, and durtie Busines
that Slauerie was ere̓ putt to,

Bl.p. I shall coozen you
you maye chance come and finde youre worke undonne then
for Ime too proud to labour, Ile starue first
I tell you that before hand

wh.p. I will fitt you then
wth a black whip that shall not bee behinde hand

Bl.p. puh, I haue beene usde to whipping I haue
whipt my selfe 3 mile out of Towne in a morning and
I can fast a fortnight and make all youre meate stinck
and lye a youre hands?

wh.p. to præuent that youre foode shall bee Blackberries
and uppon Gawdie dayes a pickled Spyder
cut out like an Anchouis, Ime not to learne
a Monckeys Ordnarie, come sir, will you friske?

Enter 2 Black pawne.

2 Bl.p. soft, soft you, you haue no such bergayne ont
if you looke well about you,

wh.p. by this hand—
I am snapt too, a Black pawne in the Breech of mee,
wee 3 looke like a Birdspit, a white Chick
between 2 Russet woodcocks;—

i.Bl.p. Ime so glad of this

wh.p. but you shall haue small cause, for Ile firke you

2 Bl.p. then Ile firke you agen,

wh. p. and Ile firke him agen,

Bl.p. masse, here will bee ould firking; I shall haue
the worst ont I can firke no bodie, wee drawe
together now for all the world, like 3 Flyes
wth one Strawe in theire Buttocks. *exeunt*

264 **Ægiptian** Egyptian, or gypsy. The Egyptian Hermes Trismegistus was believed to be the author of a number of early mystical, neoplatonic, and alchemical texts. 'Common opinion' derived gypsies (also called 'counterfeit moors') 'from Egypt' (Sir Thomas Browne, *Pseudodoxia Epidemica*); for their reputation for dishonesty, see *Dissemblers*.

281–327 **praye . . . this** The jesting pawn scene was later cut, and the text slightly modified to ease the transition: see *Later* 3.1.345–46.

287 **black Knights Litter** See 5.0.2.

291 **Ime taken** A midgame pawn-exchange: after Black takes a White Pawn (at 3.203–42), White here takes a Black Pawn (possibly the Black King's Pawn).

294 **white quicklie soyles** 'Black was commonly worn, and soiled garments could be dyed . . . white, however, was not much used either in the theatre or in practical life . . . all-white costumes do not occur in Revels inventories. When the King's Men needed white costumes for Middleton's play, they probably had to have most or all of them made.' Costumes for the White King, Queen, Knight, Duke, and Bishop 'seem likely to have translated clothes worn by the real persons into white satin, velvet, and cloth of tissue, fabrics of decorum for those of high rank' (MacIntyre, 317).

305–6 **whipping . . . morning** 'on the papists Goode Friday there were great dooings at the Spanish ambassadors, and many Ladies and others invited to see the ceremonie or tragedie of their whipping, among whom an English baron or vicount was saide to be of the number' (Chamberlain, 30 March 1622). 'This last *Good-Fryday*, this present yeere 1624, they made some of you in the morning, before day, goe in *Procession* to *Tiburne*, in penitentiall manner; the form of which . . . is for a man to *walke naked from the girdle vpward, and scourge himselfe with a whip* . . . . you made one whip himselfe so long, till he swouned' (Gee, *Foot*, N4^{v}–O1).

308 **a** on

Enter Bl.Qs.p. and wh.Qs.p.

Bl.p. this is the Roome hee did appeare to mee in
and looke you this the Magicall glasse that showde
him,

wh.p. I finde no Motion yet, what should I thinke on't,
a Suddayne feare inuades mee, a faynt trembling
under this omen, as is oft felt the panting of a Turtle
under a Stroaking hand

Bl.p. that boades good luck still,
signe you shall change state speedilie, for that
trembling
is alwayes the first Symptome of a Bride
for anie Vayner feares that maye accompanie
his Apparition, by my truth to Frendship
I quit you of the least, neuer was obiect
more gracefullie præsented, the uerie Ayre
conspires to doo him honor, and creates
sweete Vocall Sounds as if a Bridegroome enterd
wch argues the blest Harmonie of youre Loues:

wh.p. and will the using of my name produce him,?

Bl.p. naye of yours onelie else the Wonder halted,
to cleere you of that doubt Ile putt the diffrence
in practise the first thing I doo, and make
his Inuocation in the names of others

wh.p. twill satisfye mee much that

Bl.p. it shall bee donne

(·.·)

Thou whose gentle Forme and face
fild latelie this Ægiptick glasse
by th'Imperious-powerfull name
and the uniuersall Fame
of the mightie black-house Queene
I coniure thee to bee seene: what? you see nothing
yet?

wh.p. not anie part;
praye try another,

Bl.p. you shall haue youre will
I double my command and power
and at the Instant of this hower
inuoke thee in the white Queenes Name
wth staye for Time, and Shape the same: what see
you yet?

wh.p. there's nothing showes at all

Bl.p. my Truth reflects the cleerer, then now fixe,
and blesse youre fayre Eye wth youre owne for euer,
Thou well composde, by Fates hand drawen
to enioye the white Queenes pawne,
of whome thou shalt by Vertue met
manye gracefull Issues gett,
by the bewtie of her Fame
by the whitenes of her Name,
by her fayre and fruitfull Loue
by her Truth that mates the Doue
by the Meeknes of her Minde
by the softnes of her kinde
by the Lustrë of her Grace *Musique,*
by all these thou art summond to this place,
enters Bl. B^{s}. pawne in rich attire like an Apparition
Harke, how the Ayre enchanted wth youre prayses
and his approach those words to sweete Notes rayses:

wh.p. oh lett him staye awhile, alitle longer,

Bl.p. thats a good hearing;

wh.p. if hee bee mine why should hee part so soone?

Bl.p. why this is but the shadowe of yours; how do you?

wh.p. oh I did ill to giue consent to see it;
what certayntie is in our bloud or State
what wee still write is blotted out by Fate,
Our Wills are like a cause that is Lawe-tost,
what one Court orders is by another crost

Bl.p. I finde no fitt place for this passion here,
tis meerelie an Intruder, hees a Gentleman
most wishfullie composde honor growes on him
and wealth pilde up for him, ha's youth ynough too
and yet in the Sobrietie of his Countenance
graue as a Tetrarch, wch is gratious
ith eye of modest pleasure, where's the emptines?
what can you more desire?

wh.p. I do not Knowe
what answere yet to make? it do's require
a Meeting twixt my feare and my desire,

328 **Magicall glasse** 'The great Magitian *Merlin*' allegedly devised a 'looking glasse' that showed everything that 'to the looker appertaynd' (Spenser, *Faerie Queene*, III.ii.18–19). In William Rowley's *A Shoemaker a Gentleman* (1608?), a woman persuades a man to look in a 'magic' glass to see the woman 'who must be [his] wife'; she stands so that he sees her own reflection.

351 **fild** filled

354 **black-house Queene** The first invocation, in relation to the proposed marriage, is of a member of the Spanish royal family: the terms of praise fit the Infanta Maria (whose 'Fame' in England was universal, and whose 'name' powerful) better than the actual Queen of Spain (who was relatively unknown in England, and politically unimportant).

359 **double** repeat (but perhaps also because Elizabeth Stuart had two titles: Princess Palatine and Queen of Bohemia)

361 **white Queenes Name** The play's first verbal pairing/doubling of the two Queens, who never address or refer to one another: they are here linked in relation to the marriage plot (as their political destinies were linked by negotiations for the Spanish Match).

377.1 ***in rich attire*** If 'thou meet a good smug Fellow in a gold-laced suit, a cloke lined thorow with veluet, one that hath . . . Rings on his fingers, a Watch in his pocket . . . a very broad-laced Band, a Stiletto by his side, . . . then take heed of a Iesuite' (Gee, *Foot*, sig. H2).

392 **pilde** piled

Bl.p. shees caught, and wch is strange, by her most wronger *exeunt*
Finit Actus Tercij

Act 4
Incipit Quarti.
Enter Bl.K^{ts} pawne meeting the Black B^{s} pawne.

Bl.K$^{ts.}$p. Tis hee, my Confessor! hee might ha' past mee
7 yeare together, had I not by chance
aduancd mine Eye uppon that litterate hattband
the Iesuiticall Symbole to bee Knowen by
worne by the braue Colledgians by Consent;
this a strange habit for a holie Father
a præsident of pouertie espetiallie,
but wee the Sonnes and daughters of Obedience
dare not once thinke awrie, but must confesse ourselues
as humblie to the Father of that Fether
Long Spur and poniard, as to the Albe and Altar,
and happie weere so highlye gracde t'attayne to't,
holie and Reuerend!

Bl.B$^{s.}$p. how hast found mee out?

Bl.K$^{ts.}$p. oh S^{ir}, putt on the Sparklingst Trim of glorie
perfection will shine formost, and I knewe you
by the Vniuersall Marke you weare about you,
the Marke aboue youre forehead;

Bl.B$^{s.}$p. are you growen
so ambitious in youre obseruance? well, youre busines?
I haue my Game to followe,

Bl.K$^{ts.}$p. I haue a worme
followes mee so that I can followe no Game,
the most faynt-hearted pawne if hee could see his playe
might snap mee up at pleasure, I desire S^{ir},
to bee absolude, my Conscience being at ease
I could then wth more courage plie my Game

Bl.B$^{s.}$p. twas a base Fact

Bl.K$^{ts.}$p. twas to a Schismatick pawne

Bl.B$^{s.}$p. whats that to the Nobilitie of Reuenge
suffizes, I haue neyther will nor power
to giue you absolution for that Violence
make youre Petition to the Pennance-Chamber,
if the Taxe-Register releiue you in't
by the black Bishops clemencie, you haue wrought out
a singular peice of fauour wth youre monie,
thats all youre refuge now;

Bl.K$^{ts.}$p. the sting shootes deeper *exit*
Enter wh.Qs p. and Bl.Qs.p.

Bl.B^{s}p. yonders my Game, wch like a politick Chesse M^{r}:
I must not seeme to see;

wh.Q$^{s.}$p. oh my heart!

Bl.Q$^{s.}$p. that tis!

wh.Qs.p. the uerie selfe same, that the magicall Mirror præsented latelie to mee,

Bl.Qs.p. and how like
a most regardlesse Stranger hee walkes by
meerelie ignorant of his Fate, you are not minded
the principallst part of him, what strange Mysteries
inscrutable Loue workes by!

wh.Q$^{s.}$p. the time you see
Is not yet come!

Bl.Qs.p. but tis in our power now
to bring time neerer, Knowledge is a Mastrie,
and make it obserue us, and not wee it:

wh.Qs.p. I would force nothing from its proper Vertue,
let time haue his full course, Ide rather die
the modest death of undiscouerd Loue
then haue heauens least and lowest Seruant suffer
or in his motion receiue Check for mee;
how is my Soules Growth alterd, that single Life
the fittest garment that peace euer made fort
is growen too streight, too stubborne on the suddayne;

Bl.Q$^{s.}$p. hee comes this waye agen

wh.Qs.p. oh theres a Traytor
Leapt from my heart into my cheeke alreadie
that will betraye all to his powerfull eye
if it but glance uppon him,

Bl.Qs.p. by my Veritie
looke, hees past by agen, drownd in neglect
wthout the prosperous hin't of so much happines
to looke uppon his fortune, how closse Fate
seales up the Eye of humayne Vnderstanding
till like the Suns Flower Time and Loue uncloses it,
twere pittie hee should dwell in ignorance Longer.

400 **wronger** (echoing the reference to her 'wrongs' at the end of Act 2)

4.3 **litterate hattband** 'the Iesuite hath a superlatiue cognizance whereby they know one another . . . a gold Hatband studded with letters or Characters' (Gee, *Foot*, sig. H2).

6 **this** this', this is
strange habit See note to 3.377.1.

7 **pouertie** 'This man hath vowed *pouerty*' (Gee, *Foot*, sig. H2, sarcastically summing up his description of the richly dressed Jesuit).

10 **Fether** See 1.228.

11 **Albe and Altar** (associated with the ceremonialism of English Arminians, as well as Catholics)

39 **Chesse M^{r}** In 1622–3 the Calabrian chess-master Gioacchino Greco visited England, defeating London's best players in exhibition games. For more than a century chess had been dominated by players from the Iberian peninsula (Damiano, López, Ceron) or Spanish-ruled parts of Italy (Boi, Carrera, Greco, Leonardo di Boni, Salvio), and some were priests (Carrera, López).

wh.Qs.p. what will you doo?

Bl.Q$^{s.}$p. yes, dye a bashfull Death, doo,
and let the remedie passe by unusde still
youre changd ynough alreadie, and youd'e looke intoote,
Absolute S^{ir}, wth youre most noble pardon
for this my rude Intrusion, I am bold
to bring the Knowledge of a Secret neerer
by manie dayes (S^{ir}) then it would arriue
in its owne proper reuelation wth you,
praye turne, and fixe, do you Knowe yon'd Noble goodnes

Bl.Bs.p. tis the first minute my Eye blest mee wth her,
and cleerelie showes how much my Knowledge wanted
not Knowing her till now;

Bl.Q$^{s.}$p. shees to bee likte then,
praye uiew aduisedlie, there is strong reason
that Ime so bold to urge it, you must ghesse
the worke concernes you neerer then you thinke for

Bl.B$^{s.}$p. her glorie, and the Wonder of this Secret
putts a Reciprocall amazement on mee,

Bl.Qs.p. and tis not wthout worth, you 2 must bee
better acquaynted;

Bl.B$^{s.}$p. is there cause? Affinitie?
or anie Curteous helpe Creation ioyes in
to bring that forward,

Bl.Qs.p. yes, yes, I can showe you
the neerest waye to that perfection
of a most uertuous one, that Ioye erẻ found,
praye marke her once agen, then followe mee
and I will showe you her must bee youre Wife, Sr,

Bl.B$^{s.}$p. the Mysterie extends, or else Creation
ha's sett that admirable peice before us
to chuse our chast delights by

Bl.Q$^{s.}$p. please you followe, S^{ir},

Bl.B$^{s.}$p. what Art haue you to putt mee on an Obiect
and cannot gett mee off, tis payne to part fromt;
exit

wh.Q$^{s.}$p. if there prooue no Check in that Magicall glasse now
but my proportion come as fayre and full
into his Eye, as his into mine latelie,
then Ime confirmde hee is mine owne for euer,

Enter agayn.

Bl.B$^{s.}$p. the uerye selfe same that the Mirror blest mee wth
from head to foote, the bewtie and the Habit;
Kept you this place still? did you not remoue, Ladie?

wh.Q$^{s.}$p. not a foote farder, S^{ir}

Bl.Bs.p. ist possible,
I would haue sworne Id'e seene the substance yonder,
twas to that Lustrë, to that life præsented

wh.Qs.p. ee'n so was yours to mee, S^{ir},

Bl.Bs.p. sawe you mine?

wh.Qs.p. perfectlie cleere, no sooner my Name usde
but yours appearde

Bl.Bs.p. iust so did yours at mine now;

Bl.Q$^{s.}$p. why stand you idle, will you lett time coosen you
protracting Time, of those delitious benefitts
that Fate hath markte to you, you modest payre
of blushing Gamsters and you S^{ir} the bashfulst,
I can not flatter a fowle fault in anie,
can you bee more then man and wife assignde,
and by a power the most irreuocable?
Others that bee aduenturers in delight
maye meete wth Crosses, Shame, or Seperation
theire Fortunes hid, and the Euents lockt from e'm,
you Knowe the minde of Fate you must bee coupled:

Bl.B$^{s.}$p. shee speakes but truth in this, I see no reason then
that wee should misse the rellish of this night
but that wee are both shamefacst

wh.Qs.p. how? this night, S^{ir},
did not I Knowe you must bee mine, and therein
youre priuiledge runs strong, for that loose Motion
you neuer should bee; is it not my fortune
to match wth a pure minde, then am I miserable,
the Doues and all chast louing winged Creatures
haue theire payres fitt, theire desires iustlie mated;
is weoman more Vnfortunate? a Virgin
the Maye of weoman! Fate that ha's ordaynde Sir
wee should bee man and wife, hås not giuen warrant
for anie Act of Knowledge till wee are so,

Bl.B$^{s.}$p. tender-eyde Modestie, how it giues at this
Ime as far off for all this strange Imposture
as at first Enteruiew, where lyes our Game now?
you Knowe I cannot marrie by my Order;

78 **and** an, if
88 **likte** liked
90 **ghesse** guess (with a strong pause at the end of the line: Middleton often regarded the line break itself as a form of punctuation)
151 **giues** yields, gives way, collapses (subsequently changed to 'grieves' at *Later* 4.1.131)
154 **I... Order** members of the Society of Jesus were sworn to celibacy (unlike Anglican ministers)

Bl.Qs.p. I knowe you cannot, S^{ir,} yet you maye Venture
uppon a Contract,

Bl.B$^{s.}$p. hah?

Bl.Qs.p. surelie you maye S^{ir},
wthout all question so Far, wthout danger
or anie Stayne to youre Vowe, and that maye take her,
naye doo'te wth speede sheele thinke you meane the
better too;

Bl.B$^{s.}$p. Bee not so lauish of that blessed Spring
youȗe wasted that uppon a cold occasion now
would wash a sinfull soule white, by our Loue-Ioyes
that motion shall neře light uppon my Tong more
till weere contracted then I hope youre mine

wh.Qs.p. in all iust dutie euer,

Bl.Qs.p. then, do you question it?
push, then youre man and wife all but Church
Ceremony,
praye letts see that donne first, shee shall doo reason
then,

exeunt

Enter Bl. K$^{t.}$ wth his pawne

(·.·))

Pawne I haue spoke to the black Bishop for thee,
I'le gett thee Absolution from his owne mouth;
Reach mee my Golden Stoole, my Stoole of coosnage
7 thousand pound in weoman reach mee that
I loue a life to sitt uppon a Banck
of heretique Gold, oh soft and gentlie, sirrah,
theres a fowle Flawe ith Bottome of my Drum; P.
I ner'e shall make sound Souldier, but sound Trecher
wth anie hee in Europe, how now, Qualme!
thou hast the pukingst Soule that e're I met wth
it cannot beare one Suckling Villanie,
mine can digest a Monster wthout cruditie
a Sin as Weightie as an Elephant
and neuer wamble fort;

Paw. I, you haue beene usde toote, S^{ir},
thats a great helpe, the swallowe of my Conscience
ha's but a narrowe passage you must thinke yet
it lyes ith pœnitent pipe and will not downe
if I had got 7 thousand pound by offices
and guld downe that, the Boare would haue bin
bigger;

Bl.K$^{t.}$ naye, if thou proousṭ facetious I shall hugg thee
can a soft Reare, poore-pocht Iniquitie
so ride uppon thy Conscience Ime ashamde of thee,
hadst thou betrayde the Whitehouse to the black
beggard a Kingdome by dissimulation
Vnioynted the fayre frame of peace and Traffique,
poysond Alleagance, sett fayth back, and wrought

156 **Contract** promise of marriage, legally binding. Although moralists disapproved, between the contract and the church ceremony perhaps as many as half of all couples had sexual relations: 20–30% of brides gave birth less than nine months after the wedding, and many court records describe women abandoned by their promised bridegrooms, after sexual consummation but before marriage. Henry Mason, in *The New Arte of Lying, Couered By Iesuites vnder the Vaile of Equiuocation, Discouered and Disproued* (1624), listing 'in what cases it is allowed' (41) by the Jesuits, includes cases where a man is forced 'to promise marriage to a woman' (50) and where a man has 'contracted himselfe to a woman … by words *de praesenti*' (51).

161 **doo'te … sheele** do it … she'll

166 **weere … youre** we're … you're

169 **man and wife** In July 1623, James I and his council approved the terms of the Spanish treaty, thereby formalizing the contract of marriage: at that point, one letter-writer concluded, 'we account [Charles] as good as married,' and after this espousal 'he may lie if he please with his mistress' (James Beaulieu, 18 and 25 July 1623). In Scott's *2 Vox Populi* Gondomar says that Prince Charles thought 'nothing had beene wanting to the absolute comsummation of the marriage, but the Rites of the Church …'

170.1 ***exeunt*** For the expanded ending of this scene, see *Later* 4.1.148–9.

171 **Pawne** (The vocative makes it clear that the speaker is the only other character on stage, the Black Knight who has just entered. Compare 3.1.)

173 **Golden Stoole** later revised to 'chair of ease', a chair specially designed for the comfort of Gondomar's tender posterior: 'his chayre, wherein he sat vpon two downe pillowes' (Scott, *2 Vox Populi*, 7).
coosnage cozenage

175 **a life** o' life
Banck bench

177 **P.** pawn

185 **I** ay, yes

190 **guld** gulled
Boare bore
bin been

192 **Reare** rare, barely cooked at all
poore-pocht poor-poached

195 **beggard a Kingdome** Between 1619 and 1624 England suffered one of the worst economic depressions in its history.

196 **Vnioynted** unjointed
peace England had been at peace with Spain since 1604. But Spanish troops had helped drive James I's daughter and son-in-law out of the Palatine and Bohemia; the Spanish truce with the Dutch Republic expired in 1621.
Traffique trade, particularly overseas trade, badly disrupted by the Cokayne monopoly (1614–17), then by the war in central Europe (1619–24); James I had also intervened, under pressure from Gondomar, to stop English ventures into the Caribbean and Brazil.

197 **poysond Alleagance** In 1613—the year of Gondomar's arrival in England—the loyal (and vehemently anti-Catholic) Sir Thomas Overbury was poisoned, allegedly by Frances Howard (of the powerful Catholic family headed by the Earl of Northampton); in 1616 she was convicted of the murder, and disgraced, along with her husband the Earl of Somerset, in one of the most notorious court scandals of the seventeenth century. Poisoning was described as 'an Italian comfit for the court of Rome' (Sir Francis Bacon, prosecuting Somerset), and Overbury's murder was described as part of a larger treasonous plot: 'the wickedness of poisoning, had it not been prevented in time, although it began in Overbury, would have not ceased with his destruction; but that his Majesty's person, the Queen, and the whole state should have felt thereof' (Sir Lawrence Hyde, prosecuting an alleged accomplice).

197–8 **wrought … Malice** 'I left behinde mee such an instrument composed artifically of a secular understanding and a religious profession, as hee is every way adapted to serue himself into the closet of the heart, and to worke upon feminine leuity, who in that country haue masculine spirits to command and pursue their plots unto death' (Scott, *Vox Populi*, C1). One of Frances Howard's convicted accomplices was female (and allegedly Catholic).

weomens soft soules eeñ up to masculine Malice
to pursue truth to death if the cause rowzd em̃,
that Stares and Parrotts are first taught to curse thee,

Paw. I marrie S^{ir,} heres swapping Sins indeed

Bl.Kt. all these and io times trebled, ha's this Brayne
beene parent to, they are my offsprings all,

Paw. a goodlie broode!

Bl.Kt. yet I can iest as titelie,
laugh and tell stirring Stories to Court Maddames
daughters of my Seducement wth alacritie
as high and heartie, as youths time of Innocence
that neuer knewe a Sin to shape a sorrowe by
I feele no tempest not a Leafe winde stirring
to shake a fault my Conscience is becalmd rather

Paw. Ime sure there is a Whirlwinde huffs in mine S^{ir},

Bl.Kt: Sirrah, I ha' sold the Groome ath Stoole 6 times,
and receiude monye of 6 seuerall Ladies
ambitious to take place of Barronets Wiues,
to 3 ould Mummie-Matrons I haue promist
the Mothership ath Maydes, Iue taught o^{r} frends too
to conuey Whitehouse Gold to our black Kingdome
in cold bakte Pasties and so coozen Searchers,
for Venting hallowed Oyle, Beads, Meddalls, Pardons,
pictures, Veronicaes heads in priuate presses,
thats donne by one ith habit of a Pedler
Letters conuayde in roules, Tobacco-balls
when a Restraynt comes by my politick Councell
some of our Iesuites turne gentlemen Vshers,
some Faulkners, some Park Keepers, & some huntsmen,
one tooke the Shape of an ould Ladies Cooke once
and dispacht 2 Chares in a Sundaye morning
the Altar and the Dresser,? praye what use
putt I my Summer Recreation to?
but more t'informe my knowledge in the State
and strenght of the White Kingdome! no Fortificatiõ,
Hauen, Creeke, Landing place 'bout the White Coast
but I got draught and platforme, learnd the depth
of all theire Channells, knowledge of all Sands
Shelues, rocks, and riuers for inuasion properst
a Catalogue of all the Nauie Royall
the burden of each ship, the Brassie Murderers,
the number of the men, to what Cape bound;

201 **swapping** 'snatcheth vp a whole Elephant at a stoope, and swappes him vp at a bit' (John Healey, tr., *Discovery of a New World*, 1609). For the elephant see l. 183.

213–17 **I . . . Maydes** 'I borrowed of the good old Lady *W.* of the parish in St. *Martins* in the Feilds 300 pounds, or thereabouts, promising to make her repayment . . . so soone as *Donna Maria*, the *Infanta* should arriue in *England*, and for the vse hereof, I promised to make her mother of her maydes . . . I sold moreouer, the place of Groomesse, of her highnesse Stoole, to six seuerall English Ladyes, who were eager of it, only cause be [= because] they might take place before their fellowes' (Scott, *2 Vox Populi*, B3).

213 **sold** 'oh root of all euil to Church and Commonwealth, when authorities and offices of Iustice shall bee bought and solde' (Samuel Ward, *Iethro's Iustice of Peace*, (1618), 11).
Groome ath Stoole an officer in the royal Bed Chamber

217 **Mothership ath Maydes** post of supervisor of the royal maids, in the Queen's household. Since Queen Anne had died in 1619, this post would only be filled with the arrival of a new queen, the Spanish Infanta, as an eyewitness understood: 'how many Ladies brybed him to be groome of ye stool to ye Infanta, how many to be mother of ye mayds' (John Holles, 11 August 1624).

217–23 **taught . . . Tobacco-balls** 'If you would at any time convey over any Silver or Gold, the Searcher commonly may be couzoned, if you send it over in Pasties baked, provided that you haue some of flesh onely to eate or giue away, as a cullor for the rest. For the venting of hallowed Oyle, Beades, *Agnus Deies*, Meddalles, Pardons, Crucifixes, &c. You may doe it, by some one poore yet trustie Catholique or two, to goe vp and downe the Countrie in the habit and nature of Pedlers; this also is a good way to hold intelligence with friends in many places. I haue knowne some vnder the cullour of selling *Tobacco*, have carried Letters handsomly, privily in the balls or roules' (Scott, *2 Vox Populi*, 56–57).

217 **o^{r}** our

218 **Whitehouse Gold** In 1621 and 1624 members of Parliament blamed the economic depression on the export of English gold. 'Bullion is the very body and blood of kings' (Gerard Malynes, *The Centre of the Circle of Commerce*, 1623).

221 **Veronicaes . . . presses** 'a small rouling presse for little Pictures of Saints, *Veronica*'s heads' (Scott, *2 Vox Populi*, 57)

224 **Restraynt** Jesuits and priests were officially banished from England in 1604, 1606, 1610, and again on 6 May 1624; from Ireland in 1614 and 1623.

225–9 **some . . . Dresser** 'for the better avoyding suspition, and concealing themselues, some [Catholiques] will turne Schoole-maisters in priuate mens houses . . . some Gentleman Vshers unto Collapsed Ladies are . . . Some *Falconers* . . . one I was acquainted withall, who was the Keeper of a Parke, and a good Huntsman . . . I know another Priest who . . . the better to colour his absence from the Church, learned the arte of Cookery, and is growne so expert therein . . . that hee is able to dresse a Dinner with such arte . . . and his manner is, when hee hath layed his meate to the fire, to goe and say Masse, which finished by that time, or soone after his meate is boyled or roasted, which . . . he serueth vp to his old Mistresse' (Scott, *2 Vox Populi*, 29–30).

228 **Chares** chores

229–39 **praye . . . bound** Scott gives Gondomar a speech explaining how 'in sommer, time vnder the colour of taking the ayre, I would take view of the countrey) I had perfect knowledge of the state of the whole Land; for there was no Fortification, Hauen, Creeke, or Landing-place about the Coast of *England*, but I got a platforme and draught thereof, I learned the depth of all their Channels, I was acquainted with all Sands, Shelues, Rockes, Riuers that might impeach or make for inuasion, I had perpetually in a Role the names of all the Ships of King *Iames* his Nauy Royall, I knewe to a haire of what burthen euery ship was, what Ordinance she carried, what number of Saylors, who were the Captaines, for what places they were bound' (*2 Vox Populi*, 15).

then, for the discouerie of the Inlands,
neuer a Sheire but the state better knowen
to mee then to her brest Inhabitants
what power of men and horse, Gentries reuennues,
who well affected to our Side, who ill
who neyther well nor ill, all the Neutrallitie,
thirtie eight thousand Soules haue beene seducd, P.
since the Iayles Vomited wth the pill I gaue em̄.

Paw. sure you putt Oyle of toade into that phisick, S^{r},

Bl.K$^{t.}$ Imc now about a Mr:peice of playe
t'entrap the white Knight and wth false allurements
entice him to the black house, more will followe
whil'st our Black Bishop setts uppon the Queene
then will our Game lye sweetelye;
Enter Bl. Bishop,

Paw. hees come now S^{ir},

Bl.B. heres Taxa pœnitentiaria, Knight;
the Booke of generall pardons of all prices
I haue beene searching for his Sin this halfe hower,
and cannot light uppont,

Bl.K$^{t.}$ thats strange, let mee see't,

Paw. pawne wretched that I am, ha's my rage donne that
there is no præsident of pardon for,

Bl.K^{t}—for wilfull murder, 13 pound 4 shillings and
sixepence—thats reasonable cheape, for Killing, Killing,
Killing, Killing, heres nothing but Killing Bishop of this
side,

Bl.B. turne the Sheete ouer, you shall finde Adulterie
and other triuiall Sins,

Bl.K$^{t.}$ Adultrie? oh Ime at it now, for Adulterie
2 Shillings, and for fornication fiuepence,
masse, these are 2 good penniworths, I cannot
see how a man can mend him selfe,—for Lieng
wth mother, Sister, and daughter—I marrie S^{ir},
33 pound, 3 shilling, 3 pence,—
the Sins gradation right payde all in threes,

Bl.B. y'aue read the Storie of that Monster S^{ir},
that got his daughter, Sister and his wife
of his owne Mother

Bl.K$^{t.}$ Simonie, 9 pound
Sodomie sixpence, you should putt that Summe
euer on the Backside of youre Booke;

Bl.B. theres fewe on̄s uerie forward S^{ir}

Bl.Kt. whats here S^{ir}; 2 ould præsidents of Encouragement,

Bl.B. I, those are Antient Notes

Bl.K$^{t.}$ Giuen as a gratuitie for Killing of an hæreticall
prince wth a poysond Knife 5 thousand ducketts

240–5 **then . . . Neutrallitie** Scott's Gondomar continues: 'I was no less diligent for the discouery of the Inland, then for the Shores and Sea-coasts; for there was neuer a Sheire in *England*, but I better knew the estate, power and quality thereof then the Inhabitants, euen the best of them themselues did. I could in particular relate the nature of the soyle, what power of men and horse they were able to raise, who were the chiefe and of most ability and credit in the Countrey, who the most antient Gentlemen, what they were worth in their reuenues and estates, how they stood affected in Religion, who were Puritanes, and who Catholiques, and among Catholiques who stood for us, and who (for such there were) were indifferent or against vs' (*2 Vox Populi*, 16–17).

246–7 **thirtie . . . em̄** 'the number of soules which they haue gained into the bosome of the Church since the remission of the penall Lawes against them, and their freedom by my meanes obtained, amounteth to the number of eight and thirty thousand and odde' (*2 Vox Populi*, 18).

246 **Soules . . . seducd** Many Protestants complained of 'the seducements of priests and papists' (*Acts of the Privy Council*, 19 February 1615); Catholic persuasions were pervasively characterized as seduction.

250 **allurements** (suggesting the sexual allure of the White Knight's proposed bride, a subject never explicitly mentioned in the play but known to all spectators as the reason for his trip to Madrid)

252 **Black** later revised to 'Fat', giving the Fat Bishop the role originally assigned to the Black Bishop in this act: see *Later* 4.2.80.

255 **Taxa pœnitentiaria** *Taxa Sacra Pœnitentiaria Apostolica*, a catalogue of ecclesiastical pardons for sins, published in Rome in 1510; the first English translation, by William Crashaw, was not published until 1625, and its sums bear no relation to Middleton's.

261 **præsident** precedent

264 **of** on

271 **Lieng** lying

272 **I** ay

275 **Storie** (told in Marguerite of Navarre's *Heptameron* (1559, trans. 1597) and Matteo Bandello's 1554 *Novelle*). This reference makes explicit the association of Catholicism with incest, implicit in the sexual pursuit of 'tractable daughters' by their Jesuit 'Father', and a common theme in Protestant polemics, which often cited Pope Alexander VI's incestuous relationship with his own daughter.

278 **Simonie** 'They serue not Iesus Christ, but their belly. And this is done not in one place, nor in one Citie, but throughout England' (Henry Burton, *A Censure of Simonie* (1624), 'Epistle Dedicatorie'). Similar complaints were made by Thomas Scott and many other zealous Protestants. During his impeachment in 1626, Buckingham was accused of selling bishoprics.

279 **Sodomie** a sexual practice associated with Catholics—'the catamites of Babel's scarlet whore' ('On the Powder Treason')—but also with the Buckingham faction and family: Sir Anthony Ashley, 'who never liked any but boys', when forced to marry is said to have sodomized Lady Philippa Sheldon's 'blackarse hole' ('All the News'; both poems in Yale manuscript Osborne b.197).

284–5 **Giuen . . . Knife** Henri IV was assassinated with a dagger by François Ravaillac in 1610, allegedly prompted by Jesuits.

Bl.B. true S^{ir}, that was payde

Bl.K$^{t.}$ promised also to Doctor Lopez for poysoning the Mayden Queene of the white Kingdome 20 thousand, wch sayde Summe was afterwards giuen as a meritorious Almes to the Nunnerie at Lisbon, hauing at this present io thousand pound more at Vse in the Townehouse of Antwerpe!

Paw—whats all this to my Conscience, worthie Holines,
I sue for pardon, I haue brought monye wth mee,

Bl.B. you must depart, you see there is no præsident
of anie price or pardon for youre fact,

Paw. most miserable, are fowler sins permitted?
Killing, naye willfull murder;

Bl.B. true, theres instance,
were you to Kill him I would pardon you
theres præsident for that and price sett downe,

Paw. I haue pickt out Vnderstanding now for euer
out of that Cabalistique bloudie Riddle
Ile make awaye all my estate and Kill him *exit*
Enter Bl. King

why Bishop,! Knight! wheres youre Remoues? youre Traps?
stand you now idle in the heate of Game?

Bl.K$^{t.}$ my life for yours, black Soueraigne, the Games ours
I haue wrought under hand for the white Knight,
and his braue Duke and finde em̄ coming both

Bl.B. then for theire sanctimonious Queenes surprizall, S^{ir},
in that State puzzle and distracted hurrie
trust my Arch subteltie wth,

Bl K. oh Eagle pride
neuer was Game more hopefull of our Side: *exeunt*
Musique.
Enter Bl. Queenes pawne wth Lights, Conducting the White to a Chamber, and then the Bl. Bishops pawne to another and exit. {*Dumb showe*
Enter white Knight, and wh. Duke.

Wh.K$^{t.}$ True Noble Duke, fayre Vertues most endeerd one
lett us præuent theire ranck Insinuation
wth truth of cause and courage, meete theire Plotts
wth confident goodnes that shall strike em̄ grouling

wh.D. S^{ir} all the Iins, Traps and alluring snares
the Deuill ha's beene at worke since 88 on
are layde for the Great Hope of this Game onlie,

wh.K$^{t.}$ S^{ir} the more Noble will truths Triumph bee,
when they haue woond about our constant Courages
the glistringst Serpent that e're falshood fashiond
and glorieng most in his resplendent poysons
iust heauen can finde a bolt to bruize his head;
Enter Bl. Knight

wh.D. looke, will you see distruction lye a sunning
in yonder smile sitts bloud and Trecherie basking
in that perfidious Modell of Face-Falshood
Hell is drawen grinning,

287–92 **promised...Antwerpe** 'they haue ten thousand pound at vse in the Towne-house of *Antwerp*...Likewise when they remained in *France*, they had the custodie of no small summe of money, which was sent to them to keepe for Doctor *Lopez* the Portugese, as his reward for poysoning our late Queene *Elizabeth* of famous memorie, which after that Traitor (hauing missed of his intent) was executed, was remitted vnto them as an almes' (Robinson, *English nunnery*, 9–10).

287 **Lopez** Roderigo Lopez, member of the Royal College of Physicians, chief physician to Elizabeth I, executed in 1594 for alleged complicity in a plot to assassinate her by poison

288 **Mayden Queene** Elizabeth I, the focus of considerable nostalgia among critics of James I: 'some there are that find such fault with your Majesties gouernmēt as they wish Q. Elizabeth were aliue againe' (*Tom Tell-Troath*, 2).

292 **Townehouse of Antwerpe** seminary in Catholic Netherlands, where Jesuit missionaries to England were trained

301 **downe** Middleton later added 'but none for gelding', again clarifying the nature of the crime (as at 1.225)

304 **him** For a line subsequently added see *Later* 4.2.134.

305 **why** The entrance direction doubles as a speech prefix: compare 3.1.

310 **sanctimonious** holy. (More appropriate to the conspicuously Protestant Elizabeth of Bohemia than to Queen Anne, who was better known for masques than piety.)
surprizall seizure (most often used in a military sense, of a sudden attack on a fort, city, or army—like the Catholic assaults on strongholds in the Palatinate, and their efforts to capture Elizabeth and her husband)

311 **distracted** 'divided' (as King James was divided from his heir and favourite, during their residence in Madrid) and 'crazy' (implying criticism of the trip to Madrid)
hurrie haste, rush (another possible criticism of the trip)

314.2.n ***Dumb showe*** mimed action without dialogue. The Black Queen's Pawn deceives the Black Bishop's Pawn, putting herself in his bed, instead of the White Queen's Pawn. This kind of 'bed-trick' occurred 26 times in extant plays from 1598 to 1624, but also allegedly occurred outside the theatre. In Madrid in 1623, Buckingham 'made court to *Conde Olivares* wife, a very handsom Lady. But it was so plotted betwixt the Lady, her Husband, and [the Earl of] *Bristol* that, instead of that beauty, [Buckingham] had a notorious Stewsbird [prostitute] sent him' (Weldon, *King James*, 135).

314.5 ***Enter white Knight*** His first appearance since his exit at 3.230.1, and the Black Knight's threat of 'match' and 'mate' (3.232–3). The play separates the White Knight's trip to the Black House (dramatized here, and in the first and last scenes of Act 5) from the deceptive marriage plot (initiated at 3.248–53).

315 ***Wh.K$^{t.}$*** Here as elsewhere in the play, White Knight initiates action, which White Duke merely supports. The idea of visiting Madrid originated with Prince Charles, as King James told Parliament: 'being of fit age and ripeness for marriage...[Prince Charles] urged me to know the certainty in a matter of so great weight' (*Journals of the House of Lords* III, 209). James also mentioned this in a letter to Charles—'it was upon your earnest entreaty' (June 1623)—and it is reiterated in the court diaries of Godfrey Goodman and John Hacket.

319 **Iins** jins, gins: (en)gines, traps

320 **88** 1588, the *annus mirabilis* of the defeat of the Spanish Armada, 'wherein the black night of our threatened destruction was beaten backe by the puissance of our Prince praying' (William Leigh, *Queene Elizabeth, paraleld* (1612), 96)

323 **woond** wound (past participle of *wind*)

325 **glorieng** glorying

wh.Kt. what a payne it is
for Truth to fayne a litle,

Bl.Kt. oh fayre Knight!
the rising Glorie of that house of Candor,
haue I so manie Protestations lost,
lost, lost, quite lost, am I not worth youre confidence?
I that haue uowde the Faculties of soule
life, spirit, and Brayne to youre sweete Game of youth
youre noble fruitfull Game, can you mistrust
anie fowle playe in mee, that haue beene euer
the most submisse Obseruer of youre Vertues
and no waye taynted wth Ambition
saue onelie to bee thought youre first Admirer,
how often haue I changd for youre delight
the reall præsentation of my place
into a Mimick Iester, and become
(for youre sake and th'expulsion of sad thoughts
of a graue State-Sire a light Sonne of pastime
made 3 score yeares a Tomboye, a meere wanton
Ile tell you what I told a Sauoye Dame once,
new wed, high, plumpe and lusting for an Issue,
wthin the yeare I promist her a childe
if shee could stride ouer St Rombauts breeches
a Rellique kept at Mechlin, the next morning
one of my followers ould hose was conuayde
into the chamber where shee tryde the Feate,
by that and a Court Frend after grewe great

wh.Kt. why who could bee wthout thee

Bl.Kt. I will change
to anye shape to please you, and my Ayme
ha's beene to win youre loue in all this Game

wh.Kt. thou hast it Noblie, and wee Long to see
the Black house pleasure State and dignitie

Bl.Kt. of honor you'le so surfett and delight
youle ner'e desire agen to see the White: *exeunt*

Enter wh: Q.

wh.Q. my loue, my hope, my deerest, oh hees gon,
ensnarde, entrapt, surprizde amongst the Black-ones
I neuer felt Extreamitie like this
thick Darknes dwells uppon this hower Integritie
like one of heauens bright Luminaries now
by Errors dullest Element interposde,
suffers a black Eclips—I neuer was
more sick of loue then now I am of horror
I shall bee taken, the Games lost, Ime sett uppon
the Bishop of the blackhouse, hauing watcht
th' aduantage of his playe, comes now to ceaze on
mee

Enter Bl. Bp.

oh Ime hard besett distrest most miserablye

Bl.B. tis uaine to stir, remoue wch waye you can
I take you now, this is the time weeue hopde for,
Queene you must downe:

332 **fayne** feign, dissemble

338–9 **sweete . . . youth . . . fruitfull** (suggesting the game of courtship and marriage, designed to produce royal offspring)

346 **Iester** jester, gesture

350 **Sauoye Dame** woman married in the Hospital of St John the Baptist in the former Savoy Palace on the north bank of the Thames. The chapel was often used for irregular marriages (and hence raises, again, the subject of marriage).

351–4 **new wed . . . Mechlin** Among 'miracles done in *England*' which 'are meere impostures', Thomas Scott includes claims 'that a young married wife shall haue a child the same yeare if she can stride ouer at once Saint *Rombauts* breeches at *Mechlin*' (2 *Vox Populi*, 38–39).

357 **Court Frend** lover at court. The Jacobean court was often accused of sexual licentiousness. In a sermon preached to King James and the court in 1621, Francis Mason identified 'carnal concupiscence and politic practices' as the two sins most 'likely to be found in princes' courts'. Courtiers 'invited the citizens' wives to those [masques and plays at Whitehall], on purpose to defile them' (Sir Edward Peyton).

362–5 **wee . . . White** In February 1623 Prince Charles (accompanied by Buckingham) left England and travelled to Madrid, to supervise personally negotiations for his marriage to Donna Maria, Infanta of Spain.

366–77 **my loue . . . miserablye** Queen Elizabeth of Bohemia was especially distressed about Prince Charles's trip to Madrid, with the prospect of a Spanish marriage that would leave her territories occupied by Catholic troops: 'I hope his majesty will one day see the falsood of our ennemies, but I pray God send my dear brother safe in England againe and then I shall be more quiet in my minde' (Pursell, 'Spanish Match', 720).

366 **my hope** Given the resistance of King James, the Queen of Bohemia was almost entirely dependent on the support of her brother (and heir to the throne), Prince Charles. From the perspective of anyone else, Elizabeth and Frederick were an alternative 'hope', since she would become heir to the throne in the event of her brother's death.
deerest 'our hearts were filled with astonishment, doubt, despayre; wee gavu them for lost, and our selues with them, and with them and vs, our lawes, libertyes, land, and (what was dearest) our religion' (Scott, *Vox Dei*, 59).

372 **Eclips** A partial eclipse of the moon—visible throughout England, Germany, Spain, and most of Europe—occurred on 15 April 1623, while Charles and Buckingham were in Madrid.

373 **sick of loue** lovesick, sick as a result of love. But the rest of the line suggests that *sick* has the stronger sense 'nauseated, dangerously weak, close to fainting or losing consciousness'. Elizabeth of Bohemia was famously fertile and often pregnant, so the image might refer to morning sickness (caused by 'loue'), or to her being sickened by Prince Charles's apparent 'loue' for the Infanta.
then than

374 **sett uppon** attacked. Protestants feared that, once they had conquered Germany, Catholic armies would be free to attack the Dutch Republic (where the Queen of Bohemia was living in exile).

375 **Bishop . . . blackhouse** Jesuit influence was widely blamed for the military aggression of the (Habsburg) Holy Roman Emperor Ferdinand, and for the brutal repression of Protestantism in conquered territories like Bohemia and the Palatinate. (In *Later* the Black Bishop's role in this scene is transferred to the Fat Bishop.)

376 **ceaze** seize

378 **remoue . . . can** Elizabeth, Queen of Bohemia, was forced to move repeatedly as a result of the series of military defeats that began with the battle of White Mountain in 1620.

wh.Q. no rescue no deliuerer
Bl.B. the Black Kings bloud burnes for thy Prostitution
and nothing but the Spring of thy Chast Vertue
can coole his Inflammation, instantlie
hee dyes uppon a plurisie of Luxurie
Enter Wh: Bishop.
if hee deflower thee not—
wh Q. oh streight of miserie;
wh.B. and is youre holines his diuine procurer
Bl.B. the Deuills int, Ime taken by a Ring-doue,
where stood this Bishop that I sawe him not
Wh B. you were so ambitious you lookte ouer mee
you aymde at no lesse person then the Queene
the glorie of the Game if shee were wun
Enter wh. King
the waye were open to the Mr:check
wch, looke you, hee or his Liues to giue you;
honor and Vertue guide him in his Station
wh Q. oh my safe Sanctuarie
wh K. lett heauens blessings
bee mine no longer then I am thy sure one,
the Doues house is not safer in the Rock
then thou in my firme bosome;
wh:Q. I am blest int
wh K. Bishop; thou hast donne our white house gratious
Seruice
and worthie the fayre Reuerence of thy place
For thee (black holines) that workst out thy Death
as the blinde Mole, the properst Sonne of earth
who in the casting his Ambitious hills up
is often taken, and destroyde ith midst
of his aduanced worke, twere well wth thee
if like that Verminous Labourer, wch thou imitatst
in hills of pride and malice, when death putts thee up
the silent Graue might prooue thy Bagg for euer
no deeper pitt then that, for thy uaine hope
of the white Knight, and his most firme assistant
2 princelye Peices wch I knowe thy thoughts
giue lost for euer now, my strong assurance
of theire fixt Vertues, could you lett in Seas
of populous untruths agaynst that fort
twould burst the proudest Billowes,
wh.Q. my feares past then,
wh K. Feare? you were neuer guiltie of an Iniurie
to goodnes, but in that
wh Q. it stayde not wth mee, S^{ir},
wh K. it was too much if it usurpd a thought
place a good Guard there
wh Q. confidence is sett, sir;
wh K. Take that prize hence Goe Reuerend of men
putt couetousnes, into the Bagg agen *exeunt*
Finit Actus Quarti.

382 **Prostitution** sexual commodification (reducing a 'pure' Protestant to the same status as the Roman Catholic 'Whore of Babylon'), degradation, prostration

383 **Chast** sexually virtuous (applied to faithful wives, like the Queen of Bohemia; it need not mean 'celibate')

386 **deflower** violate, ravage, desecrate, spoil (in addition to its literal meaning, 'sexually penetrate')

388 **wh.B.** Archbishop Abbot was one of the strongest English supporters and allies of the Queen of Bohemia.

393–4 **if shee ... Mr:check** Opposition Protestants argued that the defeat of the Queen of Bohemia and the Protestant cause in Germany would lead to the conquest of the Netherlands and Britain, and Catholic victory throughout Europe.

395 **hee or his** King James *or* his family (or his supporters)—which leaves open the possibility that King James might have nothing to do with the prophesied Protestant triumph. At *Later* 4.4.76 'or' is changed, significantly, to 'and'.

396 **honor ... guide him** Discussing the national disgrace caused by the King's failure to defend his daughter and son-in-law in Bohemia and the Palatinate, *Tom Tell-Troath* flatly told King James that 'there is no way to recouer your losses and vindicate your honour, but with fighting with him that hath cozened you'. In what the title-page called '*a patheticall discourse, presented to the King ... to perswade his Majestie to drawe his royall sword, for the restoring of the Pallatynat*', John Reynolds—'speaking in the behalf of the forsaken ... sorowfull Princesse your onlie Daughter'—argued that permitting his daughter and son-in-law to be ruined would 'eclipse' the King's honor: 'Doe I speake of Dishonnor, O then I beseech your Majestie to consider, how long Honor is purchasing, how soon lost' (*Votivæ Angliæ* (1624), A1–A1^{v}). Reynolds reiterates the same theme, in the same language of 'honour', in *Vox Coeli* (also 1624).

397 **Sanctuarie** King James refused 'to receyue and harbour them' [his daughter Elizabeth and her husband] 'into the Sanctuarie of [his] Kingdom'—a refusal for which Reynolds, among many other Englishmen, rebuked him (*Votivæ Anglicæ*, A4^{v}). The White Queen's exclamation is therefore unavoidably ironic, whether she speaks it to the White King or—even more subversively—to the White Bishop.

398–9 **lett ... one** This statement makes the legitimacy of King James dependent upon his support of the White Queen. Middleton here, like Thomas Scott in *Vox Regis*, quotes King James, apparently in praise, but with an implicit threat.

401 **bosome** i.e. he keeps her in his 'heart' (not in his 'kingdom')

406 **Mole** (a creature who works underground, like the Jesuits hiding in their priest-holes, or placing gunpowder in the vaults under Parliament)

420 **my feares** Elizabeth of Bohemia, and many English and European Protestants, were afraid that Prince Charles would convert to Catholicism while in Madrid, or that he would be kept prisoner in Spain, or that as part of the marriage treaty he would agree to legalize Catholicism in England, and/or allow his heirs to be raised as Catholics.

421–4 **you ... thought** The King here echoes the official version of events, articulated in Buckingham's widely-distributed relation to Parliament in February 1624: that there was never any danger of Charles succumbing to Spanish pressure, and that the entire trip was a cunning trap to force Spain to reveal its treachery.

421 **neuer guiltie** (typically extravagant praise for the Queen of Bohemia)

Act 5

Incipit Quintus et Vltimus.
Lowde Musique, Enter Bl.K. Q. D. wth pawnes and Black Knight meeting the wh. Knight and Duke: (the Bl.Bps.pawne aboue Entertaynes them wth this Lattin Oration)

(∴)

Si quid mortalibus unquam oculis hilarem et gratum aperuit diem, si quid peramantibus amicorum animis gaudium attulit, peperituè lætitiam (Eques Candidissime prælucentissime) fœlicem profectò tuum a domo Candoris ad domum Nigritudinis accessum, promisisse, peperisse, attulisse fatemur. Omnes aduentus tui conflagrantissimi, Omni qua possumus, lætitià, gaudio, congratulatione, acclamatione, animis obseruantïssimis, affectibus diuotissimis, obsequiis uenerabundis, te sospitem congratulamur.

Bl.K. Sir in this short Congratulatorie Speech
you maye conceiue how the whole house affects you,

Bl.Kt. the Colledges and sanctimonious Seedeplotts,

wh.Kt. tis cleere, and so acknowledgd, Royall Sir

Bl.K. What honors, pleasures, rarities, delights
youre noble thought can thinke

Bl.Q. youre fayre Eye fix on;
thats comprehended in the spatious circuit
of our black Kingdome, theyre youre seruants all

wh.Kt. how amplie you endeere us

wh.D. they are fauours that æquallye enrich the royall giuer
as the receiuer in the free Donation

Bl.Kt. Harke, to enlarge youre welcome, from all parts
is heard sweete sounding Ayres, abstruse things open,
Musique
of Voluntarie Freenes, and yon'd Altar
an Altar discouerd richlie adornd and diuers Statues standing on each Side
the Seate of Adoration, seemes t'adore

5.0.2 ***Enter*** Middleton revised the beginning of this scene to provide an individual entrance and dialogue for the Black Knight and his litter: see *Later* 5.1.1–10. Gondomar was often 'carried in his litter or bottomless chair, the easiest seat for his fistula' (Wilson, *Life and Reign of James I*). The Spanish ambassador objected that the actors had brought Gondomar 'on to the stage in his little litter almost to the life' (10 August 1624); John Chamberlain reported that the actors 'had gotten ... his Lytter' (21 August).

0.4 ***Bl.Bps.pawne*** Gondomar's confessor, Fray Diego de la Fuente (who had lived in London several years), was present in Madrid, and conspicuously interacted with the English there, in 1623 (Redworth, 130). See 1.295–6.

1–6 **Si ... fatemur** This speech undeniably establishes that the play's last act represents the Charles–Buckingham visit to Spain. Taken from 'A gratulatory Oration made by a Iesuite vnto the Prince at Madrid' (29), it is included in *The Popes Letter To the Prince* (1623), in the original Latin, followed by an English translation: '*Si quid mortalibus unquam oculis hilarem & gratum aperuit diem, si quid peramantibus subditorum tuorum animis gaudium attulit, peperitvè lætitiam, si quid salutem Patriæ, fœlicitatem Civium, securitatem Imperij, Christianæ Reipublicæ pacem & incolumitatem promisit nobis unquã, nobis unquã spospondit (clarissime & serenissime Princeps) fœlicem profectò tuum ad Hesperias oras accessum, fœlicem in Hispaniam adventum novum utrumq; & inauditum, promisisse, peperisse, attulisse, fatemur*' (29). (For a translation of the whole speech, see *Later* 5.1.10–19.)

6–10 **Omnes ... congratulamur** '*Accipe singulorum obsequium, singulorum amorem, pium & constantem singulorum affectum. Omni quâ possumus, lætitiâ, gaudio, congratulatione, acclamatione, sospitem tuum & fœlicem congratulamur tibi adventum; maxime quo licet, obsequio, amore, affectu, omnia tibi nostra & nosmet ipsos tradimus .... hæc omnia & singula (auspicatissime Princeps) observantissimis animis, divotissimis affectibus, venerabundis obsequiis, ad lætas & augustas tuas fortunas, ... dirigimus*' (*Popes Letter*, 32–3).

17 **Eye fix on** 'I have seen the Prince [Charles] have his eyes immovably fixed upon the *Infanta* half an hour together .... I have seen him watch a long hour together in a close Coach in the open street to see her as she went abroad' (James Howell, *Familiar Letters* (1673), 119–20, printing a letter from Madrid dated 10 July 1623). Significantly, this remark is spoken by the Black Queen.

21 **æquallye** equally

24.1 ***Musique*** played by hidden musicians, but clearly meant to suggest a celestial harmony: unseen music was used, from the late sixteenth century, to mystify not only papal but also royal power, as for instance in Jacobean court masques. John Buckeridge (Bishop of Rochester) claimed that, during the consecration of the eucharist, 'the heavenly powers do raise up cries and the place near the altar is filled with the choirs of angels' (*A Sermon Preached before His Maiesty ... Touching Prostration, and Kneeling*, 1618).

25.1 ***Altar*** characteristic of Catholics, but also perhaps suggesting the formalist/Arminian wing of the English church. Buckeridge argued that the sacrifice of the eucharist required an altar, not a table. (See preceding note.) About thirty polemical pamphlets, debating the legitimacy of Church ceremonies, were published between 1618 and 1624, including David Calderwood's *Altar of Damascus* (1621), critical of the Anglican hierarchy. In 1639 at the Fortune Theatre an altar and candlesticks were set up on stage, and the gesture of genuflection mocked in a clownish manner (*Calendar of State Papers Domestic*)—a parody clearly aimed at the emphasis on church ceremony, under the Arminian faction which began to dominate the Anglican episcopate in the 1620s.

25.1–5.36 **richlie adornd ... Tapors** King James sent to Madrid in March 1623 'all stuff and ornaments fit for the service of God', including candlesticks, and ordered that a room be set aside 'chappellwise with an altar ... pallls, lynnen coverings, [and] demy carpett' (Loomis, 2:186). Calderwood objected to the practice of covering English communion tables 'in imitation of the popish rich altar clothes' (*Altar of Damascus*, 211).

the Vertues you bring wth you,

wh.K^{t}, theres a taste
of the ould Vessell still,

wh.D. th' erroneous rellish.

Song.

Wonder worke some strange delight
this place was neuer yet wthout
to welcome the fayre Whitehouse Knight,
and to bring our hopes about
maye from the Altar flames aspire
those Tapors set themselues afire
maye sencelesse things our Ioyes approoue
and those Brazen Statuës moue

The Statues moue, and dance.

Quickned by some power aboue
or what more strange to showe our Loue:

Bl.K$^{t.}$ a happie omen waites uppon this hower
all moue portentouslie, the right hand waye;

Bl:K. Come letts set free all the most choyse delights
that euer adornd dayes or quickned Nights *exeunt*

Enter wh.Qs.p. and Bl.Bps.pawne (in his reuerend habit) meeting her

Wh. Qs:p. I see twas but a tryall of my Dutie now,
ha's a more modest minde, and in that Vertue
most worthilie h'as Fate prouided for mee!
hah? tis the bad man in the reuerend habit
dares hee bee seene agen, Traytor to Holines,
oh marble Fronted Impudence! and Knowes
how ill ha's usde mee, Ime ashamde hee blushes not,

Bl.B^{s}*p.* arc you yet storde wth anie Weomans pittie
are You the Mris of so much deuotion
Kindnes and charitie as to bestowe
an Almes of Loue on youre poore Suffrer yet
for youre sake onelie;

wh.Qs.p. Sir, for the reuerend respect you ought
to giue to Sanctitie though none to mee
in being her Seruant uowde and weare her Liuerie
if I might councell you You should nere speake
the Language of Vnchastnes in that habit
you would not thinke how ill it do's wth you!
the worlds a Stage on wch all parts are playde
youde thinke it most absurd to see a deuill
presented there not in a deuills shape
or wanting one to send him out in yours
youde rayle at that for an Absurditie
no Colledge erѐ committed, for decorums sake then
for pitties cause, for Sacred Vertues honor,
if youle persist still in youre Deuills part
present him as you should doo, and lett one
that carries up the Goodnes of the playe
come in that habit and Ile speake wth him,
then will the parts bee fitted and the Spectators
Knowe wch is wch, they must haue cunning
Iudgments
to finde it else for such a one as you
is able to deceaue a mightie Audience,
naye those you haue seducst if there bee anie
in the Assemblie, if they see what manner
you playe youre Game wth mee they cannot loue you;
is there so litle hope of you to smile S^{ir};?

Bl.B$^{s.}$*p.* yes, at youre feares, at th' Ignorance of youre
power,
the litle use you make of Time, youth, Fortune,
Knowing you haue a housband for Lusts Shelter,
You dare not yet make bold wth a Frends comfort
this is the plauge of Weaknes,

wh.Qs.p. so hott-burning
the Sillables of Sin flie from his Lips,
as if the Letter came new cast from hell;

28–9 **taste...still** Catholicism was still called, by many Englishmen, 'the old religion'; but Spain, the dominant defender of Catholicism, preserved more than a 'taste' of that religion, and 'still' (yet, even after all this time) suggests the lingering of Catholic sentiment in England itself. Since 1617, Arminians had been appointed to a succession of deaneries and bishoprics; on 6 July 1622 Joseph Mead heard a sermon preached 'totally for Arminianisme, wonderfully boldly & peremptorily' (f. 213); in 1623, Charles was accompanied to Madrid by two Arminian chaplains; early in 1624, royal chaplain Richard Montagu's Arminian pamphlet *A Gagg for the New Gospel* provoked a Parliamentary protest.

30.1 ***Song*** Play scripts often did not specify who sang a song. Songs were usually sung by boy actors, and the only boy actor present in this scene was the one playing the Black Queen.

33 **the** (may mean 'thee')

38.1 ***Statues moue*** 'Concerning coozening deuices: Are not yet men liuing, that can remember the knauerie of Priests to make the Roodes and Images of the Churches in *England*...to goggle with their eyes, and shake their hands: yea, with Wiers to bend the whole body' (Goad, *Friers Chronicle*, B3^{v}).

dance In Francis Beaumont's *Masque of the Inner Temple and Gray's Inn*, 'four statues of gold and silver' were made to 'dance for joy of these great nuptials' (1613)—i.e., the wedding of Princess Elizabeth to the Elector Palatine. The combination of music, dance, and special effects strongly suggests the Jacobean court masque.

53 **Mris** (abbreviation of 'Mistris', mistress)

59 **uowde** vowed

60 **nere** ne'er, never

63 **the worlds a Stage** '*Totus mundus agit histrionem*' (motto displayed on the sign of the Globe theatre)

67–8 **Absurditie...Colledge** Jesuit seminaries at St Omer and Douay, the Jesuitess schools founded by Mary Ward, and Oxford and Cambridge colleges, regularly performed academic dramas (which unlike plays in London's commercial theatres usually observed 'decorums' based on Greek and Roman dramatic practice).

68 **decorums sake** 'What *Decorum* is it', Gee asks, criticizing Jesuit con-games, 'the spectator being a Woman' and 'the *Iesuites* being or having *Actors* of such dexteritie, I see no reason but that they should set vp a company for themselues, which surely will put down *The Fortune, Red-Bull, Cock-pit, & Globe*' (*New Shreds*, 17–19).

84 **housband** husband

86 **plauge** plague

Bl.B$^{s.}$p. well, setting aside the dish you loathe so much
Wch ha's beene heartilie tasted by youre Betters
I come to marrie you to the Gentleman
that last enioyde you, 'hope that pleases you;
theres no immodest rellish in that office;
wh.Q$^{s.}$p. strange! of all men hee should first light on him
to tye that holie Knott that sought t'undoo mee,
were you requested to performe that busines S^{ir}?
Bl.B$^{s.}$p. I name you a sure Token;
wh.Qs.p. as for that S^{ir};—
now youre most welcome, and my fayre hopes of you
You'le neuer breake the Sacred Knott you tye once
by anye lewde solliciting hereafter,
Bl.Bs.p. but all the Crafts in getting of it Knitt,
youre all a fire to make youre coosning market
I am the marrier and the man do you Knowe mee?
do you Knowe mee Nice Iniquitie, strickt Luxurie
and holie Whoredome that would clap on Marriage
Wth all hott Speede to soader up youre Game,
see what a Scourge Fate ha's prouided for thee,
you were a Mayde, sweare still, youre no worse now,
I left you as I found you, haue I startled you,
Ime quit wth you now for my discouerye
youre Outcryes and youre cunnings, farewell Brokage[2]
wh.Qs.p. naye staye, and heare mee but giue thankes a Litle
if youre Eare can endure a worke so gratious,
then You maye take Youre pleasure,
Bl.Bs.p. I haue donne that;
wh.Qs.p. that power that hath preserud mee from this Deuill
Bl.B$^{s.}$p. how?
wh.Qs.p. this, that maye challenge the cheif chayre in hell
and sitt aboue his Master;
Bl.B$^{s.}$p. bring in merït?
Wh.Qs.p. that suffredst him through blinde Lust to bee lead
last night to th' Actïon of some Common bed;
Bl.Qs.p wthin
Intus. not ouercommon neyther!
Bl.B$^{s.}$p. hah. what Voyce is that;
wh.Qs.p. of Virgins bee thou euer honored:
now you maye goe you heare Iue giuen thankes S^{ir}
Bl.B$^{s.}$p. this a strange Game, did not I lye wth you?
Intus. Noh!
Bl.Bps p. what a deuill art thou
wh.Qs.p. Ile not answere you S^{ir}
after thanksgiuing;
Bl.Bs.p. you made promise to mee
after the Contract;
Intus yes—
Bl.B$^{s.}$p. mischeife confound thee
I speake not to thee,—and thou didst præpare thy selfe
and sett thy Ioyes more high—
Intus—then you could reach S^{ir};
Bl.B$^{s.}$p. tis a bawdie Voyce Ile slit the throate ont,
Enter Bl.Qs.p.
Bl.Qs.p. what? offer Violence to youre bedfellowe?
to one that workes so Kindlie wthout Rape?
Bl.B$^{s.}$p. my bedfellowe?
Bl.Qs.p. do you plant youre Scorne agaynst mee?
why when I was probationer at Bruxells
there Was no such Engine Knowen, then Adoration
fild up the place and Wonder was in fashion
ist turnd to th' Wilde Seede of Contempt so soone?
Can 5 Yeares stampe a Bawde? praye Looke uppon mee S^{ir}
Iue Youth ynough to take it, tis no longer
Since you were cheife Agent for the Transportation
of Ladies daughters, if you bee remembred
some of theire portions I can name, Who purst em, too
they Were soone dispossest of Worldlie cares
that came into youre fingers?

104 **coosning** cozening
108 **soader** solder
125 ***Intus*** inside, within (Latin). Very rare as a stage direction or speech prefix in English.
146 **Bruxells** Brussels (a Spanish Catholic stronghold, and site of an English nunnery)
152–3 **cheife . . . daughters** 'there lurketh in *England* an arch-Traytor, one *Henry Flood* a Iesuit, who is the chiefe Agent for the transporting of Nunnes, both to *Bruxels*, *Greueling*, *Lisbon*, or any other place' (Robinson, *English nunnery*, 8).
154–6 **some . . . fingers** '*Father Floud* Iesuit, their prime *Procurator*, and others) haue boasted . . . [of] the rich portions which many of our English women carry ouer with them . . . those that haue a good round summe for their dowry (as 1000 or 2000 pounds, which some good customers cary hence), such are stamped for Bruxels, where the hungry Iesuits (who sometimes meet with as good booties as the Merchants of Argier) dispossess them of all worldly cares and vanities' (Gee, *New Shreds* Q2^{v}–3). Gee paraphrases a similar paragraph in Robinson's *English nunnery* (p. 9); only Gee has the plural 'portions', but both have the phrase 'dispossess . . . cares', and Robinson alone has 'quickly dispossesse'.

Bl.Bs.p. Shall I heare her?

Bl.Qs.p. Holie Derision! yes! till thy Eare swell
wth thy owne Venom, thy prophane Lifes Vomit!
whose Neice was shee you poysond wth childe, twice?
and gaue her out possest wth a fowle Spirit
when twas indeed youre Bastard;
Enter white Bs.p. wth white Queene.

Bl.Bs.p. I am taken
in myne owne Toyles;

wh.Bs.p. yes, and tis iust you should bee;

wh.Q. and thou lewde pawne the Shame of weomanhood;

Bl.Bsp. Ime lost of all hands;

Bl.Qs.p. and I cannot feele
the weight of my perdition now hees taken
tås not the burden of a Grashopper,

Bl.Bs.p. thou whore of Order, Cockatrice in Voto;
Enter Bl.Kts.p.

Yond's the white Bishops pawne, Ile playe at's heart
now!

wh.Qs.p. how now, Black Villayne, wouldst thou heape a
murder
on thy first fowle offence, oh merciles Bloudhound
tis time that thou wer't taken;

Bl.Kts.p. Death! præuented!

wh.Qs.p. for thy sake, and that partner in thy shame,
Ile neuer knowe man farder, then by name. *exeunt*

Scæna Vltima.

Enter Bl.K.Q. Kt. Duke and pawnes wth white Kt. and Duke

wh.Kt. You haue enricht my Knowledge, Royall Sir)
and my Content together;

Bl.Kt. stead of Riot
wee sett you onelie welcome, Surfet is
a thing wee seldome heare off in these parts:

wh.Kt. I heare of the more Vertue when I misse ońt,

Bl.Kt. wee doo not use to burie in our Bellyes
2 hundred thowsand ducketts and then boast ońt
or exercize th' ould Romane paynfull-Idlenes
wth care of fetching Fishes far from home,
the Golden-headed Coracine out of Ægipt

160–2 **whose . . . Bastard** 'A certaine *Catholick collapsed Lady* . . . about some two or three yeeres since, departed from her Husband (yet liuing) and went ouer to *Bruxels*, and was admitted into the order of *Nunnery*, I meane a *Nunne* at large, one of the uncloystred sisters of *the order* of Saint *Clare*'—that is, the order of mobile female Jesuits founded by Mary Ward—'and there shee remained a while, till there appeared in her some passion incompatible with *Nunship*. Shee came ouer into *England*, a companion with a *religious Iesuite*, since of great note, *F.D.*'—[Father Drury]—'and remaining afterwards an inlarged *Nun* in *London*, was (as it seemeth) more visibly taken with a disease befalling that sexe, called *flatus uterinus:* and thereupon, that this matter might bee carried the more cleanly, it was giuen out, that shee was possessed with an euill spirit, which did make her belly swell like a woman with child' (Gee, *Snare*). This is immediately followed by description of 'a certaine Iesuite (whom I could also name)' as 'a smug, spruce, liquorish' [= lecherous] 'young fellow, a fit man to be called *Father* (forsooth)'—thus making explicit the double meaning of 'father' (religious and biological).

160 **Neice** Heloise was the niece of Fulbert, who ordered the castration of Abelard; she had a bastard child by Abelard. (See note to 1.171).

170 **tås** it has

178 **Ile . . . name** Heloise, after the castration of Abelard, became a nun. Protestants generally doubted the human capacity for celibacy, and regarded vows of celibacy as a remnant of pagan religious practices (like the castration of priests of Cybele); but they did recognize voluntary abstinence as 'a rare and special gift given only to some' (William Perkins, *Works*, 1612). Throughout the seventeenth century there were various proposals—from Margaret Cavendish and Mary Astell, among others—to establish what amounted to English Protestant nunneries, where women could have independence and an education sequestered from men.

181–239 **stead . . . hereafter** There were many English complaints about 'the scarcity of victuall' (*2 Vox Populi*, 22) during the visit to Spain: 'As if the Prince had ventured there his life | To make a famine, not to fetch a wife' (Richard Corbet, 'A Letter to the Duke of Buckingham, being with the Prince in Spain', 1623).

186 **2 hundred thowsand ducketts** a colossal sum, perhaps suggested by '*tribus milibus sestertium*', the cost of banquets thrown by the Roman emperor Heliogabalus: see 5.201. 'That supper which was of least price did commonly cost thirty pound weight of gold, which (after our computation) might amount to the value of above a thousand pounds sterling; and there were some which did cost threescore thousand crowns' ('Heliogabulus', in Edward Grimestone, *The Imperial History, from the first foundation of the Roman monarchy to this present tyme*, 1623).

187 **ould Romane** characteristic of (*a*) the old Roman empire (*b*) the Roman Catholic church (*c*) the Holy Roman Empire, ruled by the Habsburgs. Sir John Digby, on a diplomatic mission to Emperor Ferdinand in Vienna, remarked that the 'imperio Romano . . . is so often here in theyr mouthes, as if the imperatore romano were in better estate then Augustus Cæsar' (5 August 1621). The final scene's pervasive classical allusions have an early modern political and religious significance.

189–92 **the Golden-headed . . . Aquitayne** See Pliny's *Naturall Historie*, tr. Philemon Holland (1601): 'the Coracinus in Ægypt carrieth the name for the best fish. At Gades in Spaine, the Doree or Goldfish . . . About the isle Ebusus, the Stock fish is much called for; . . . In the countrey of Aquitaine or Guienne in Fraunce, the river Salmon passeth all other sea Salmons whatsoever' (1:246–7, IX:17). The following lines draw upon ten widely separated chapters of Pliny, which Middleton could have read in Latin.

189 **Coracine** (four syllables, as in the Latin of the source)

the Salpa from Ebusis, or the pelamis
wch some call Summer-whiting from Calcedon,
Salmons from Aquitayne, Helops from Rhodes,
Cockles from Chios, franckt and Fatted up
wth Far and Sapa flower and cockted wine,
Wee cramb no Birds, nor Epicurean-Like
Enclose some Creekes a'th Sea, as Sergius Crata did
hee that inuented the first Stewes for Oysters
and other Sea-Fish, who beside the pleasure
of his owne Throate got large Reuennewes by
th 'Inuention;
whose Fat Example the Nobilitie followed;
nor do wee imitate that arch-Gurmundizer
wth 2 and twentye Courses at one dinner
and betwixt euerie course hee and his Guesse
washt and usde weomen then sate downe and
strenghtnd;
Lust swimming in theire Dishes; wch no sooner
Was tasted but was readie to bee Vented:

Wh:K^{t}. most Impious Epicures?

Bl.K$^{t.}$ wee commend rather
of 2 Extreames the parsimonie of pertinax
who had Halfe Lettices sett up to serue agen,
or his Successor Iulian that would make
3 Meales of a Leane hare, and often supp
wth a greene Figg and Wipe his Beard as wee can;
the ould bewaylers of Excesse in those dayes,
complaynde there Was more coyne bid for a Cooke
then for a Warhorse, but now Cookes are purchasde
after the Rate of Triumphs, and some dishes
after the Rate of Cookes, wch must needs make
some of youre Whitehouse Gurmundizers, spetiallie
youre Wealthie plumpe-plebeians, like the Hoggs
wch Scalliger cites that could not moue for Fat,
so insensible of eyther Prick or Goade
that Mice made Holes to Needle in theire Buttocks
and they not felt em; there was once a Ruler
Cyrenès Gouernor, choackte wth his owne Paunch

190 **Salpa from Ebusis** 'Circa Ebusum salpa' (Pliny)

190–1 **pelamis...Calcedon** 'These fishes, togither with the old Tunies and the young, called Pelamides.... neare to Chalcedon' (Pliny 1:243, IX:15).

191 **Summer-whiting** Italian *palamite*, 'a fish called a tunny; before it be a year old, a summer-whiting' (John Florio, *New World of Words*, 1611)

192 **Helops from Rhodes** '*elops Rhodi*' (Pliny IX:54), 'the Elops at Rhodes' (1:267).

193 **Cockles from Chios** (The source for this detail has not been identified; it is not in volume one of Holland's translation of Pliny.)

193–4 **franckt...wine** 'to feed them fat, namely, with a certaine past made of cuite and wheate meale...that the gluttons table might be served plentifully with home-fed and franked great Winkles also' (Pliny 1:267, IX:56). Pliny elsewhere identifies 'the bearded wheat Far' (2:138, XXII:25) and explains that 'the Cuit named in Latine Sapa...is, but Must or new wine boiled' (2:157, XXIII:2).

195 **cramb no Birds** 'Who first devised to cram Hens' (Pliny 1:297, X:50).

196–200 **Enclose...followed** 'The first that invented stewes and pits to keepe oysters in, was *Sergius Orata*...And this the man did not for his belly and to maintain gourmandise, but of a covetous mind for verie gaine. And by this and such wittie devises, hee gathered great revenues....somewhat before *Orata*, *Licinius Murena* devised pooles and stewes for to keepe and feed other fishes: whose example noble men followed...[*Lucullus*] let in an arme of the sea into his fish-pools' (Pliny, 1:246–7, IX:54).

201 **arch-Gurmundizer** the Roman emperor Heliogabalus (d. 222) who '*exhibuit aliquando et tale convivium ut haberet viginti et duo fercula ingentium epularum, sed per singula lavarent et mulieribus uterentur et ipse et amici*' (Aelius Lampridius, xxx, in *Scriptores Historiae Augustae*, not translated into English in Middleton's time, but often edited and reprinted between 1518 and 1620 by humanist scholars, including Erasmus and Isaac Casaubon). 'Occasionally he gave a banquet in which he would serve twenty-two courses of extraordinary viands, and between each course he and his guests would wash, and use women.' (This detail is not in Grimestone.)

209 **pertinax** Roman emperor (d. 193): '*dimidiatas lactucas et cardus...conviviis adponerat...etiam in alium diem differebat*' (Julius Capitolinus, xii, in *Scriptores*): 'at his banquets he served lettuce and edible thistle in half portions...he would defer using it until another day'.

211 **Iulian** Didius Julianus, Roman emperor (d. 193): '*Iulianus tantae parsimoniae fuisse...ut per triduum porcellum, per triduum leporem divideret...saepe autem...holeribus leguminibusque contentus sine carne cenaverit*' (Aelius Spartianus, iii, *Scriptores*): 'Julianus was so parsimonious...that he divided a sucking pig for three days, a hare for three days...often, moreover...he was content to dine on cabbages and beans without meat'.

214–18 **the ould...of Cookes** 'those, who in their reproofes of gluttonie and gourmandise, complained, that a cooke carried a greater price in the market than a good horse of service. For now adaies a cooke will cost as much as the charge of a triumph: and one fish as deere as a cooke' (Pliny 1:246, IX:17).

219 **Whitehouse Gurmundizers** Buckingham's banquet at York House on his return from Madrid in 1623 served 3000 dishes of meat (Joseph Mead, f. 385, 21 November 1623). Sir James Hay, one of James I's Scottish favourites, regularly spent £2–3000 on individual banquets, on one occasion employing a hundred cooks for eight days to cook larks, Muscovy salmon, swans, and pheasants (Chamberlain, 2:57–8, 333–4).

220 **plumpe-plebeians** (suggesting rich merchants of the City of London, rather than the 'patricians' of the court)

220–4 **like...em** 'Pinguescit autem longe magis sus: adeoque pinguescit, ut pene totus immobile reddatur. Neque enim fabulosum est: in eorum clunibus excavare sibi mures foveas; non quidem ut nidificent, sed ut saginentur' (Julius Caesar Scaliger, *Exotericarum Exercitationum liber quintus decimus de Subtilitate, ad Hieronymum Cardanum*, often reprinted between 1557 and 1612). Middleton and/or his audience may have confused this 'Scaliger' with his more famous son, the great Protestant scholar J. J. Scaliger (1540–1609).

224–5 **there...Paunch** Athenaeus, *Deipnosophistae* (available in Latin translations since 1553), XII.550: 'Magam...Cyrenes Regem per annos quinquaginta...obesum esse factum, ac ita praeter aequum iuxta extremum aetatis, ut ob corporis ignauiam ipsa crassitudine sit suffocatus, tum propter nutrimenti copiam' (1556 Latin tr.): 'Magas, who reigned over Cyrene for fifty years...was weighted down with monstrous masses of flesh in his last days; in fact he choked himself to death because he was so fat'.

Wch death Fat Sanctius K. of Castile fearing
through his Infinite Masse of Bellie, rather chose
to bee Kild suddenlie, by a pernitious Herbe
taken to make him Leane, wch ould Corduba
K. of Morocco counceld his feare to
then hee would hazard to bee stunck to death
as that huge Cormorant that was choackte before
him;

wh.Kt. well, youre as sound a Spokesman, S^{r}, for parsimony
cleane Abstinence, and scarce one meale a daye
as euer spake wth Tong;

Bl.King—censure him meekelie, S^{ir},
twas but to finde discourse

Bl.Q. heele rayst of anie thing

wh.K$^{t.}$ I shall bee halfe afrayde to feede hereafter

wh.D. or I, beshrewe my heart for I feare Fatnes
the Fogg of Fatnes as I feare a Dragon
the Comlines I wish for thats as glorious;

wh.Kt. youre course is wondrous strickt, I should transgresse
sure,
were I to change my side as y'aue much wrought mee
to't:

Bl.Kt. how you misprize; this is not meant to youward
You that are woond up to the height of Feeding
by Clime and Custome are dispencst wthall;
You maye eate Kid, Cabrito, Calfe and Ton's
naye the Franckt Hen, fattend wth milke and Corne
a Riot, wch th' Inhabitants of Delos
Were first Inuenters of, or the Crambd Cockle

Wh.Kt. Well, for the Foode Ime happilie resolude in,
but for the Diett of my Disposition
there comes a trouble, you will hardlie finde
foode to please that;

Bl.K$^{t.}$ it must bee a strange nature
wee cannot finde a dish for, hauing policie
the Mr-Cooke of Christendome to dresse it,
praye name Youre Natures diett,

wh.K$^{t.}$ the first Messe
is hott Ambition!

Bl.Kt. thats but serude in puff paste
alasse the meanest of our Cardinalls Cookes
can dresse that dinner; youre Ambition S^{ir}
can fetch no farder compasse then the world;?

wh:K$^{t.}$ thats certayne Sir;

Bl.Kt. weere about that alreadie;
and in the Large Feast of our Vast Ambition
wee count but the white Kingdome whence you came
from
the garden of our Cooke to pick his Salletts;
the Foode's leane France larded wth Germanie,

226–30 **Fat...to** No source of this anecdote has been found. In all hitherto-identified versions of the story, Sancho was cured by his trip to Corduba. The confusion over Corduba—a kingdom, rather than a king—might be related to a line in Gee's *New Shreds* which refers to '*Corduba* King of the *Moores*' (p. 68).

229 **Corduba** (perhaps reminding English audiences of Don Gonzalo Fernándes de Cordoba, the Spanish general in command of the occupying forces in the Palatinate)

238 ***Bl.Q.*** These five words—complaining about a man's verbosity—are the Black Queen's only speech until after checkmate (when she speaks another three). Her silence in this scene may suggest the Spanish refusal to give Prince Charles opportunities to speak with the Infanta: 'restrayning him from that liberall accesse and converse, (not denied elsewhere to a meane person) with the Lady *Maria Infanta* his Mistress... with whom in all the time of his being here, he had not aboue twice talked' (Scott, 2 *Vox Populi*, 23).
rayst of raise't of, raise't off, utter 'discourse' on [any subject] or from [any stimulus]

240 **I feare Fatnes** Sir James Hay, like Buckingham one of James I's intimates, remembered that 'the mode was to appear very small in the waist; I remember I was drawn up from the ground by both hands whilst the tailor with all his strength buttoned on my doublet' (*The Autobiography of Thomas Raymond*). In 1621 Sir Simonds D'Ewes described Buckingham as 'full of delicacy and handsome features; yea, his hands and face seemed to me, especially, effeminate and curious' (*Autobiography*, 1:166–7).

246–8 **You...Ton's** In Spain, the English for their supper could get only 'perhaps a piece of leane Kid, or Cabrito, a Tripe, Tone's or such like... we were faine to send seaventeene miles off for a Calfe... how should our [Spanish] dyet agree with their [English] stomackes, who are accounted the greatest feeders of the World' (Scott, 2 *Vox Populi*, 22).

253–354 **Diett...euer** This catalogue of confessed vices resembles the vices of 'a Protestant King I meane one that rules ouer a people of that profession' (i.e. King James) in *Tom Tell-Troath*, who 'may solace himselfe as securely in his bed-chamber as the *Grand Signor in his Seraglio*, have Lords Spiritual for his Mates / Lords Temporall for his Eunuchs / and whom hee will for his Incubus. There may hee kisse his minions without shame' (25).

258 **Mr-Cooke** 'The King's Master-Cook' was an actual court official (*Civitatus* 391); he appears as a major character in Ben Jonson's masque for Christmas 1623, *Neptune's Triumph for the Return of Albion* (an allegory of the trip to Madrid).

264–5 **Ambition...world** Spain 'is the same Nation, whose ambitions to satisfie, the East and West *Indies* are not sufficient, nor all *Europe*: but all the earth must become slaues to their pride... as if all other men and places had beene made for them' (Scott, *Vox Regis*, 13).

268 **Large Feast** Gondomar's list in Scott's *Vox Populi* includes Naples, Francc, Navarre, Portugal, Savoy, Venice, the Low-countries, and Bohemia (B1).

271 **Foode's** main dish is. France was Catholic; the religion of Germany (the birthplace of the Reformation) was being contested militarily. Germany and France were central to control of Europe; England was geographically marginal, and militarily insignificant (hence its status as 'salad').
leane (Bad harvests and interrupted grain imports from Danzig produced scattered food shortages in the early 1620s in France and other Mediterranean countries.)
France France, although Catholic, had been the chief obstacle to Habsburg domination of Europe, and much more tolerant of religious difference than Spain; but in 1615 Louis XIII had been united by marriage to Spain, and in 1620 he began a series of military campaigns against French Protestants.
larded garnished with strips of bacon, or greased with melted fat (appropriate to the German taste for boar, and to the Spanish piecemeal conquest of various German Protestant towns and territories in the 1620s)
Germanie not a nation but a series of duchies and principalities, within the boundaries of the Holy Roman Empire; site of extensive Catholic–Protestant

before wch comes the Graue-Chast Seigniorie
of Venice serude in Capon-Like in whitebroath
from our Cheife Ouen Italie the Bakemeates,
Sauoye the Salt, Geneua the Chipt Manchet,
belowe the Salt the Netherlands are placst
a Common Dish at Lower end ath Table
for meaner pride to fall to, for our second Course
a Spit of portugalls serude in for plouers
Indians and Moores for Blackbirds, all this while
Holland stands readie melted to make Sawce
On all Occasions; when the Voyder comes
and wth such cheere our full Hopes wee suffize
Zealand sayes Grace, for fashion, then wee rize:

wh.Kt. heres meate ynough a conscience for Ambition!

Bl Kt. if there bee anie want there's Switzerland
Polonia, and such pickled things will serue
to furnish out a Table;

wh.Kt. You saye well Sir:
but heres the mistrie I tell you in priuate:

Bl.Kt. oh weere youre Cabinets.

warfare, 1619–24. It included Bohemia (mentioned by Gondomar in *Vox Populi*) and the Palatinate (the key point of contention in negotiations between Spain and England in 1621–24, and the reason given by Charles and Buckingham for the final breakdown of negotiations). The Palatinate is conspicuously *not* named here: 'I dare not speake of the *Palatinate*' (Michael Drayton, *Works*, 3:206).

272–3 **Graue-Chast . . . Venice** Venice was a 'mayden city . . . never conquered' (Thomas Coryat, *Coryat's Crudities*, 1611); for theorists of republicanism, its city-state government was an epitome of 'moderation' and 'temperance' (Gasparo Contarini, *The Commonwealth and Government of Venice*, tr. Lewes Lewkenor, 1599). Although Catholic, Venice resisted the Counter-Reformation papacy (to the extent of being excommunicated in 1606–7) and the Habsburg empire (at war with them in 1613–17, and violently crushing an attempted Spanish coup in 1618).

273 **Capon-Like** like a castrated chicken. Venetian sea-power, once dominant in the Mediterranean, became insignificant after 1590, even in the Adriatic; its economy and trade were in rapid decline.

274 **our . . . Italie** Spain had ruled southern Italy and Sicily for more than a century; Milan was also in its possession, and Genoa an ally.
Cheife Ouen (because Rome is the centre of Catholicism, and the Italian climate much hotter than the English)

275 **Sauoye** The independent Duchy of Savoy, in what is currently south-eastern France and north-western Italy; in 1623 it formed an alliance with France and Venice against the Habsburgs. Gondomar's catalogue of European states includes 'Sauoy (that hardly slipt from us)' (Scott, *Vox Populi*, B1).
Salt salt-cellar, a large and often ornate utensil at the centre of the table, as salt was at the centre of European diet (probably double modern consumption), food-preservation (esp. meat and fish), and trade (Catholic countries exported salt, Protestants imported). The customs tax on exported salt was a major source of income for the Dukes of Savoy (*The Estates, Empires, and Principalities of the World*, trans. Edward Grimestone, 1615). The salt-cellar was passed around the table, as Savoy changed its allies.
Geneua formerly part of Savoy, but since the mid-sixteenth century an independent republican city; beseiged in 1602–3 by a Catholic military alliance. Geneva was the birthplace and international centre of Calvinism; the 'Geneva Bible' was still the favourite personal Bible of English Protestants.
Manchet the finest white bread, used figuratively for religious purity: 'In so much that I am the wheate of God, I am to be grinded by the teeth of beastes, that I may be founde pure breade, or fine manchet' (Meredith Hanmer, trans., *The Ancient Ecclesiastical Histories written by Eusebius* (1577), III:32; echoed by subsequent writers).

276 **Netherlands** The Spanish Netherlands (modern Belgium), after the death of Archduke Albert in 1621, was increasingly subservient to Spain; a twelve-year truce between Spain and the Dutch (the United Provinces of the northern Netherlands) had expired in 1621. Whereas Elizabeth I had formed a Protestant military alliance with the Dutch against Spain, James I and Prince Charles were suspicious of the Dutch Republic (because of its hostility to monarchy), and hence favoured an alliance with Catholic Spain or France.

277 **Common** (because, unlike England, Spain, and most other European states, the United Provinces had a republican government)

279 **portugalls** Portuguese. (Portugal had been ruled by the king of Spain since 1578.)

280 **Indians . . . Blackbirds** Spain effectively enslaved the dark-skinned peoples of its colonies in the Americas; in 1609–10 it had driven the dark-skinned Moriscos (Moors converted to Christianity) from the Iberian peninsula, but continued to be deeply engaged with the Ottoman empire, as Mediterranean neighbours and rivals.

281 **Holland** a province of the northern Netherlands, 'readie melted' because so much of it is under water; famous for its dairy products, and hence its sauces

284 **Zealand** another province of the northern Netherlands, particularly associated with puritans, including English dissenters in exile

286 **Switzerland** most famous for its mercenary soldiers, who could be used to supply any 'want' in a nation's own military forces, and were employed by French and Spanish armies in the 1620s. In the early 1620s Spanish forces invaded the south-eastern Swiss cantons of the Valtelline (modern Italian Vatellina).

287 **Polonia** Poland, a major European power, recently at war with Russia and the Ottoman empire

290–1 **mistrie . . . Cabinets** 'They that fly higher and fixe theyr speculations uppon the Mysteries of the Court doe apparently perceive that . . . Gondemar . . . hath at his command / and is maister of your Cabinett without a key' (*Tom Tell-Troath*, 4). (This passage, unique to the earliest text, was probably censored elsewhere, because the exchange establishes Gondomar as the confidant of the Prince of Wales, and the entire Black House as intimate advisors of the British royal family.)

290 **mistrie** mystery, *arcana imperii* (Tacitus, *Annales*), often invoked by James I in defence of what he called 'my prerogative, or mystery of state', to justify the secrecy of his foreign policy. *Tom Tell-Troath* berates what 'the Polititians call / *Arcana imperij*' (14).

291 **Cabinets** chests in which personal treasures could be locked up and hidden away (but also suggesting 'private apartments', especially those used for 'cabinet counsels', advice given to the monarch by courtiers who were admitted into his bedchamber)

wh.Kt. when I haue stopt my mouth
of one Vice theres another gapes for Foode,
I am as Couetous as a Barren wombe
the Graue, or whats more rauennous,

Bl.Kt. wee are for you S^{ir};
Call you that haynous thats good housbandrie,
why wee make monye of our fayths our prayers
wee make the uerie deathbed buy her Comforts
most deerelie paye for all her pious Counsells
leaue rich Reuennewes for a fewe weake Orisons
or else they passe unreconcilde wthout em;
did you but uiew the Vaults wthin our Monasterys
Youde sweare then, Plutus wch the Fiction calls
the Lord of Riches were entombd wthin em̃,
you cannot walke for Tuns?

wh.K$^{t.}$ ist possible;

Wh.D. but how shall I bestowe the Vice I bring S^{ir},
you neuer mind mee, I shall bee shut out
by youre strickt Key of Life;

Bl.K$^{t.}$ is Yours so fowle Sir;

wh.D. fayth, some thats pleasde to make a Wanton oňt
call it infirmitie of bloud, Flesh-Frayltie,
but certayne theres a worse Name in youre bookes fort;

Bl.Kt. the Trifle of all Vices, the meere Innocent
the uerie Nouice of this house of Claye,;
if I but hugg thee hard I showe the worst oňt,
tis all the Fruite wee haue here after Supper;
naye at the Ruines of a Nunnerie once
6 thousand Infants heads found in a Fishpond:

wh.D. how?

Bl.Kt. I how? how came they thether thinke you?
Huldrick Bishop of Ausburge ins Epistle
to Nicholas the first can tell you how
maye bee hee Was at clensing of the Pond;
I can but laugh to thinke how it would puzzle
all Mother-Maydes that euer liude in that place
to Knowe theire owne childes head, but is this all?

Bl.D. are you ours yet?

Wh.Kt. one more, and I am silencst,
but this that comes now will diuide us questionlesse,
tis 10 times 10 times worse then the Forerunners;

Bl:K$^{t.}$ is it so uilde there is no name ordaynde fort
Toades haue theire Titles, and Creation gaue
Serpents and Adders those names to bee knowen by

Wh.Kt. this of all Vices beares the hiddenst Venom
the smoothest poyson,—Ime an Archdissembler S^{r},

Bl.Kt. how?

294 **Couetous** King James and his son Charles repeatedly clashed with Parliament over the ever-expanding royal demand for money. In 1621 Parliament raised taxes to support a war to recover the Palatinate, only to have the money spent for such items as £15,356 in new jewels for King James (Cogswell, '1621', 40). In 1623 the King sent Prince Charles in Madrid (for display and generosity) jewels valued between £80,000 and £200,000 (Redworth, 96).

298–305 **why...em̃** (The Catholic sale of absolution had been the immediate impetus for the Reformation.)

298 **fayths** individual professions of faith

304 **Plutus** 'Plutus, the god of gold' (*Timon* 1.1.280); in medieval and Renaissance Europe, the most widely known and performed play ('fiction') of Aristophanes was his *Plutus*.

312 **fayth** (an oath which Sir Henry Herbert, Master of the Revels, routinely censored; present only in the earliest manuscript)

313 **infirmitie of bloud** sexual indulgence, thought to reflect an imbalance in the blood. Buckingham had a reputation for profligacy: in Madrid 'he did a little offend in his wantonness' (Godfrey Goodman, *The Court of King James the First*). 'These are they spend the day in drink and swiving' ('All the News').

314 **a worse Name** perhaps 'sodomy', a crime punishable by execution. 'The love the king [James I] showed [his male favourites] was as amorously conveyed, as if he had mistaken their sex, and thought them ladies.... the king's kissing them after so lascivious a mode in public, and upon the theatre (as it were) of the world, prompted many to imagine some things done in the tiring house that exceed my expressions no less than they do my experience' (Francis Osborne, *Historical Memoires*, 1658). In 1619 Sir Francis Bacon imprisoned Isaac Shingleton, an Oxford scholar, 'who preaching in Paules on May day... declaimed bitterly against his court, and glaunced (they say) somwhat scandalously at him and his Catamites as he called them' (Chamberlain, 2:243). On 24 April 1623 Joseph Mead heard a chaplain to Archbishop Abbot 'speak wondrous plainly & vehemently against the fearfull or flattering silence of our Clergie viz... Who dare call the Great ones Princes of Sodom &c?' (f. 318^{v}).

319–24 **at...how** John Foxe reproduces 'A learned epistle of Hulderike bishop of Augsburg, sent to Pope Nicholas the first', describing how the Pope 'sent unto his fishpond to haue fish, and did see more than six thousand infants' heads brought unto him'; the infanticide is attributed to 'the wicked decree of the single life of priests' (*Acts and Monuments*, 'The Book of Martyrs'); often subsequently cited by polemicists such as Sampson Price (*A Heavenly Proclamation*, 1612) and Samuel Hieron, who calls it 'The fruits of monkish lechery' (*Sermons*, 1624).

323 **Ausburge** free imperial city in Bavaria (modern Augsburg), famous for waterworks, artificial ponds, and mining. (The armies of the Catholic Maximilian of Bavaria had recently evicted Elizabeth Stuart from the Palatinate.)

337 **Ime...Archdissembler** 'Some paralleled [James I] to Tiberius for dissimulation' (Arthur Wilson, *Life and Reign of James I*, 1653); his motto was allegedly '*Qui nescit dissimulate, nescit regnare*', 'Who does not know how to dissemble, does not know how to rule' (Weldon, *King James*, 95).

wh.Kt. tis my Natures Brand, turne from mee, Sir,
the time is yet to come that I er'e spake
what my heart meant!

Bl Kt. and call you that a Vice!
auoyde all prophanation I beseech you
the onelie prime-State-Vertue uppon earth
the policie of Empires! oh take heede Sir;
for feare it take displeasure and forsake you,
tis like a Iewell of that prætious Value
whose worths unknowen but to the skillfull Lapidarie,
the Instrument that picks ope princes hearts,
and locks up ours from them wth the same Motion;
you neuer Yet came neere our Soules till now

Bl.D. now youre a Brother to us,

Bl.Kt. what wee haue donne
ha's beene dissemblance euer,

Wh.Kt. there you Lye then
and the Games ours—wee giue thee Checkmate by discouerye;
the Noblest Mate of all;

Bl.Kt. Ime lost, Ime taken;

Wh.Kt. Ambitious, Couetous, luxurious
Falshood—Dissembler includes all, *Flourish.*

Bl.Q. all hopes confounded

Bl.K. miserable Condition!

Enter White King Q. Bishop white pawnes.

Wh.King: oh let mee blesse mine Armes wth this deere treasure
Truths glorious Masterpeice! see, Queene of Meekenes,
hees in my bosome safe, and this fayre Structure
of Comlie honor, his true-blest Assistant,

Wh.Q. maye theire Integrities euer possesse
that peacefull Sanctuarie;

Wh.Kt. twas a Game (Sir)
Wun wth much hazard, so wth much more Triumph,
I gaue him Check-Mate by discouerie Sir;

Wh.K. Obscuritie is now the fittest fauour
Falshood can sue for, it well suites perdition
tis theire best course that so haue Lost theire fame
to putt theire Heads into the Bagg of Shame; *exeunt*

T.m.

Finit Actus Quinti

(·.·)

347 **prætious** precious

356–7 **Checkmate . . . all** 'Many other wayes may a discoverie bee brought to passe, and oftentimes a Mate giuen by it, which is the noblest Mate of all' (Saul, *Chess-Play*, E5).

356 **Checkmate** (English Protestants celebrated the checking of mate: the 'prevention, stopping' of a Spanish 'marriage'.)

358 **taken** (The revised text adds a stage direction here for 'A great shout and flourish' (*Later* 5.3.162.1). When Prince Charles returned from Spain, 'all London . . . resounded all over with such shouts, as is not well possible to express' (Francis Ryves, 1623); the air 'was filled with the shouts and acclamations of people' (Taylor, *Prince Charles his Welcome*).)

361 **hopes** hope's, hope is. See Zechariah 9:5 ('her hope is confounded, and the king shall perish.') The Black Queen—the Spanish Infanta Donna Maria—appropriately responds to the loss specifically of her 'hope' (implying, from the English perspective, her sexual desire for the English prince).

363–71 **oh . . . Sir** 'the Conclusion expresseth his H: [Prince Charles's] returne [from Spain]' (John Woolley, 6 August).

366 **true-blest Assistant** the White Duke. Of the Duke of Buckingham, Thomas Scott wrote 'How many curses did fill his sayles goeing towards Spain? . . . But now how many blessings and prayers attend his prosperity, from the same hearts, & mouthes, since his returning, when they finde, he hath showne himself more faithfull to God, to the King, Prince, and his Countrey, then the first Scene of that Act . . . could either assure vs, or suffer vs to imagine' (*Vox Dei*, 59).

371 **I . . . discouerie** 'the Prince of *Wales* by comming in Person discovered our plot, and found how faire so euer wee pretended, wee meant nothing lesse' (Scott, 2 *Vox Populi*, 22).

375 **Shame** For Middleton's expanded new ending, see *Later* 5.3.179–Epilogue.10.

A GAME AT CHESS: A LATER FORM

Edited by Gary Taylor

A Game at Chess is a famously complicated literary work which is also famously easy to comprehend immediately. 'Middleton's most comprehensive play' (Howard-Hill) had the longest consecutive run of any English play before the Restoration, and that run would certainly have continued if the play had not been suppressed. In nine days in August 1624, *A Game at Chess* was seen by perhaps one-seventh of the total population of London, and many more who did not see it heard about it, or heard the 'extraordinary applause' and 'extraordinary concourse' of its audiences. One contemporary says that, in order to meet the unprecedented demand, it was played twice a day; certainly, for every performance the large Globe theatre was packed to capacity: 'There was such merriment, hubbub and applause that' even if someone 'had been many leagues away it would not have been possible' not to have noticed it. The play made the King's Men an unparalleled, scandalous amount of money: '£100 a day' or '£200 a day', or 'near a thousand pound' in five days, or '£1500' in all, according to rumours circulating at the time.

But this play, so deliciously transparent to early audiences, has often baffled later readers. In 1877 Anthony Trollope (an industrious man who seldom started a job he did not finish) simply gave up, and confessed 'I have found that it was impossible to read this piece'. In 1927 T. S. Eliot (a more difficult writer than Trollope, with a tooth for more difficult texts) called the play 'that perfect piece of literary-political art', but elsewhere he lamented that no critic had yet appreciated or described its 'literary and dramatic merit'. Even now, *A Game at Chess* remains, for most critics, an enigma, as unclassifiable as it was two centuries ago to the theatre historian Charles Dibdin, who described it as 'anything you please but a play'.

But what makes *A Game at Chess* hard to read? Stylistically, it is neither difficult nor dull. In the localities of image and phrase *A Game at Chess* is as varied, strong, and immediate, as surprising-convincing, as any poem or play in English. Its satirical virtuosity ranges from the low physical ('the fistula of Europe') to the high metaphysical ('Thou whore of order!'). It can draw deep and complicated laughter from the simplest question ('Did I not lie with you?'). It relishes both the starkest of contrasts ('I'm taken like a blackbird In the great snow') and the smallest of conjunctions ('Like three flies with one straw thorough their buttocks'). It plays games with every sexual nuance of ordinary language, including particularly and systematically 'game' and 'play', whose chords are sounded in its first sentence; 'work' works in complicated counterpoint to both. The Black House is characterized by leitmotifs of fire and soot, but those flames do not, as we might expect, foreshadow the conventional ecology of hell; here, hell is—simply, unforgettably—a shapeless overcrowded bag. What Sartre laboured a whole play to say, Middleton compressed into a single theatrical image: hell is other people. The bag image, effortlessly dense and lucid at the same time, epitomizes the play's metaphorical compounding of ideas in things ('the swallow of my conscience Has but a narrow passage'). The resulting sentences can be brusque and brutal ('Fat cathedral bodies Have very often but lean little souls'). But they can also be lingeringly beautiful:

> Upon those lips (the sweet fresh buds of youth)
> The holy dew of prayer lies like pearl
> Dropped from the op'ning eyelids of the morn
> Upon the bashful rose.

Milton stole from this when writing *Lycidas* (1637):

> Together both, ere the high lawns appeared
> Under the opening eyelids of the morn,
> We drove afield...

But what is in Milton merely an inert poeticism belongs in Middleton to a sustained intertwining of sanctity, eroticism, and pain. The romantic resonances of Elizabethan love poetry (virgin lips are rosebuds, not yet opened, red because blushing) and classical allusion (the goddess Aurora rising from her lover's bed) are replayed with an assurance as haunting as ever—but something's wrong. The description, conventional enough in a sonneteer, is here spoken by a priest, and the dew of prayer becomes a precious tear running from the eyes to the lips of a devout young daughter observed by her father awakening in bed. The 'eyelids of the morn' open to realize what they have done the night before, and that moment of embarrassed, pained awakening is precisely what the observer relishes. He goes on to imagine 'How beauteously A gentle fast, not rigorously imposed, Would look upon that cheek', and to recommend ('to beat down frailty') a penance 'Whose utmost cruelty should not exceed The first fear of a bride' (1.1.77–85). What excites him, what he turns into exquisite poetry, is a vision of purity shamed and beauty in just a little pain.

No doubt, reading *A Game at Chess* is more difficult than reading *Lycidas*, not because Middleton's language is more complex but simply because all plays are harder to read than poems. But that forever-everywhere difference between script and performance will not account for this particular play's unique, often-remarked resistance to legibility. That resistance is most often attributed to the passage of time: modern readers, it is said, do not understand the complicated historical context of the play. But the play also proved illegible to its two earliest known readers. If the censor, Sir Henry Herbert, had fully understood the manuscript of *A Game at Chess*, the play would almost certainly never have been licensed for performance. The first known reader of the play in a printed edition—a Cambridge intellectual named Joseph Mead—was equally confused. In a letter dated 25 May 1625, Mead wrote that 'The play called the game at chess is in print, but because I have no skill in the game I understand it not.' Mead's correspondence demonstrates that he assiduously followed domestic and foreign politics and gossip; indeed, I sometimes cite his letters in my historical commentary on the *Early* text. His difficulty, like the censor's, cannot have been due to ignorance of the play's political background.

Mead attributed his incomprehension to the fact that he had 'no skill in the game,' that is, he did not know how to play chess. But it is impossible to believe that all those tens of thousands of spectators in August 1624 were chessmasters. The difference between early readers and early spectators results, instead, from the difference in what was visible to each. A spectator at the play simply *saw* a series of recognizable historical figures (the Spanish Ambassador Gondomar, the Archbishop of Spalato, King James, Prince Henry, the Duke of Buckingham, King Felipe) and *saw* individuals who belonged to recognizable social categories (a Jesuit priest, a lay Jesuitess, an English Protestant minister). Twelve different contemporary witnesses identify Gondomar as the main character; indeed, the play was sometimes called 'Gondomar', as though that were its title. In performances of *A Game at Chess* (and in the *Later* text, which follows this introduction), the literal visible sense was political and social; the chess game was a secondary trope. By contrast, in early texts of the play (and in the *Early* text, which precedes this introduction), in order to evade the censor the political sense had to be deliberately veiled, and the chess game was instead the only visible sense.

A reader of the early texts (or the *Early* text) encounters a series of actions and speeches attributed to characters identified as WQP, BQP, BBP, WBP, etc. This system of abbreviated signs creates an almost insuperable problem of reference; in order to understand the action, a series of cryptic shifting initials first has to be translated into the sign system of chess (White Queen's Pawn, Black Queen's Bishop's Pawn, etc.). Modern editions usually expand the initials, but that does not in itself solve the problem.

The play's characters are at least as fully realized as those in Middleton's other late masterpieces; in fact, some of them—like Black Knight or Fat Bishop—might be described as hyperindividualized. But it is easier for readers to keep track of a character labelled 'Beatrice' or 'Isabella' than of one labelled 'White Queen's Pawn'. In a game of chess, there can only be a single White Queen's Pawn; the designator specifies a unique individual, precisely located in relation to others. But, as a textual label, 'White Queen's Pawn' (unlike 'Isabella') achieves its individuality by the combination of a series of markers which are not themselves individualized: there are two queens, many pawns, and even more whites. Most readers must consciously work to keep differentiating 'White Queen's Pawn' from 'White King's Pawn', 'Black Queen's Pawn', etc. And even when we can keep track, the labels do not sound human.

In part, this confusion is anachronistic. Renaissance chess pieces had not yet been reduced to their standardized modern abstract shapes; the figures were often individualized. All the pieces, moreover, represented recognizable social classes—just like the unnamed pages, ladies, knights, bishops, and dukes in other Middleton plays. On the stage of the Globe, White Bishop would have looked like a real bishop, not like a Staunton chess piece. The signs for 'real bishop' and 'chess bishop' were not distinct.

Moreover, in performance—in London (1624), at Oxford (1971), and Cambridge (1973)—the body and voice of the player make each character immediately recognizable and obviously human. But these facts remove only a part of the difficulty. The more fundamental problem is that the play forces us to imagine characters who are both persons and pieces. At any given moment, we can interpret their actions either in terms of chess, or in terms of life. Moreover, because some (or all?) characters impersonate identifiable individuals, we must decide whether to interpret their actions in terms of local facts or universal fictions. At any given moment, is Fat Bishop a chess piece, the historical Archbishop of Spalatro, a caricature of the Jacobean episcopate, the familiar actor (and playwright) William Rowley, a conventional fat fool, or an epitome of hypocritical careerism in any age?

The word 'chess' referred, not only to the familiar board game, but more generally to 'layers' or 'tiers' or 'rows' (*OED sb*[2]). Which layer is in play? Chess? History? Theatre? Literary convention? Human nature? In chess, everything signifies. There are no meaningless positions. Moreover, meaning is positional; it belongs—like language, or politics, or character, or the label 'White Queen's Pawn'—to a system, and has meaning only within that system. The problem for players is to remain aware of all the multiplying combinations of systematic significance created by successive moves.

A Game at Chess creates similar problems. *There is too much meaning.* Readers can begin to feel overwhelmed by possibilities, frustrated by the sense that we cannot hold suspended all the meanings in play. This frustration is intensified by the impression that the play is—as various critics have called it—a 'simple' morality play, or a 'transparent' political allegory, which ought to be easy enough to understand. (As the modern grandmaster Capablanca observed, 'apparently simple moves are in reality of a very complicated nature'.)

This is more than the usual hermeneutic problem created by what an Elizabethan critic called 'the courtly figure *allegoria*'. Allegories—like Spenser's *Faerie Queene*, which also begins with a character named 'Error'—always force readers to sort various orders of meaning, and to be intelligible at all an allegory must supply a set of translation-codes, or make use of a set already widely known. In the case of Middleton's divine comedy, the protocols of reading were provided by what Arthur Saul called *The Famous Game of Chess Play* (1614, 1618). By contrast with the play's historical subject matter, that game is transhistorical, and still familiar to millions of readers; Lewis Carroll, Stefan Zweig, and Vladimir Nabokov have taken chess as metaphor or matter for major modern novels. As in *A Game at Chess*, the daughter-heroine of *Through the Looking Glass* is a White Queen's Pawn; the contest of ideologies played out by Middleton and Zweig can be seen in representations of chess since a Spanish illuminated manuscript of 1283, which pits Christian against Moslem (Schafroth, 36–7); the sexual politics of the game, as important to Middleton as to Nabokov, appear as early as fourteenth-century images of Tristan and Isolde (Schafroth, 52, 58–9). Middleton may have been influenced by the 'living chess game' in Rabelais's *Gargantua et Pantagruel* and by the related 'game in which the vices fight a pitched battle with the virtues' in Thomas More's *Utopia*. More generally, as Paul Yachnin has demonstrated, he drew upon—and significantly altered—a long tradition of chess allegory. In plays and paintings, chess had already been used as an emblem of contest, sexual (as in Fletcher and Massinger's *The Spanish Curate*) or political (as in Chapman's *Bussy D'Ambois*); *A Game at Chess* combines both, exploring the intertwined relationship between seduction and conversion. But Middleton also, for the first time, turns the colour-coded game into an emblem of modern racial politics: the Spanish ambassador indignantly objected that the King of Spain was represented in the play as 'the king of the blacks', while the Anglo leader of the 'White House' was 'the king of the whites' (Taylor 2005).

But the allegorical key provided by chess, though it contributes to the play's proliferation of meanings, does not solve all our difficulties; in fact, it creates new difficulties. Chess applies strict rules to a strictly ruled space. But the play repeatedly breaks the rules. In fact, its first two lines lead us to expect discrepancies between game and play: 'What of the game called chess-play can be made To make a stage-play shall this day be played'. Playing on the verb *make*—to compel, and to create—Middleton announces that the creation of his play depends upon doing violence to chess. The conventions of Renaissance theatre cannot accommodate all the conventions of chess. More fundamentally, the conventions of chess cannot accommodate the realities of either sex or politics. Rape is not a possible move in chess. Neither is betrayal.

A Game at Chess is not only an allegory, but also a critique, of chess. Chess depends upon absolute distinctions, upon the maintenance of fixed visible categories created by precise rules. Like Nabokov's *The Defence*, Middleton's *A Game at Chess* combines this totally ordered universe with the disordered world of 'a dream' (Induction.49). Dreams have no rules and no fixed categories. The very clarity and regularity of chess provides a background against which irregularities are conspicuously foregrounded. In chess, for instance, the distinction between Black House and White House is always absolutely clear. In Middleton's dream-play, it is not. White King's Pawn and Fat Bishop appear to be white, but are in fact black. It is possible, in bed, simply to substitute Black Queen's Pawn for White Queen's Pawn; Black Bishop's Pawn cannot tell the difference. And in the final scene, both White Knight and White Duke are guilty of 'dissemblance'; they deliberately pretend to belong to a category to which they do not belong. This is the sin which they expose in the Black House. The 'discovery' which makes possible a final and systematic distinction between White House (which wins and is saved) and Black House (which loses and is damned) is the result of an action which blurs that very distinction.

In chess, players ought to obey the rules. But what if it were impossible to obey them? This is exactly what the Protestant Reformation supposes: that sin is damnable and inevitable. Luther and Calvin objected to the Roman Catholic view that people could earn salvation by obedience to moral laws. No one, Luther insisted, can avoid mixing the categories of good and evil—not even a White Knight in shining armour. Christ had come to save us from the law, to offer a new covenant in which salvation was determined not by human merit (obeying the rules) but by divine grace (forgiveness for breaking the rules). *A Game at Chess* dramatizes the central philosophical problem of the Reformation: how are the categories 'saved' and 'damned' constructed? Which is to say: how is any category constructed?

Categories are constructed by laws, by rules, by what Jacques Derrida calls 'the law of genre'. Black House is distinguished from White House by the Black belief that the category salvation is constructed by obedience to certain rules. But if people can merit the right to be sorted into the 'saved' category, what determines whether they have done enough to deserve admission? Not surprisingly, the dominant emotion of the Black pieces—especially evident in Loyola, Fat Bishop, and Black Queen's Pawn—is resentment: their good works, they believe, have not been properly rewarded. As belief in 'merit' (a word only used by Black pieces) leads to resentment, so belief in obedience leads to rebellion. 'Boundless obedience' (2.1.39)—an unbounded imposition of boundaries, an unrestrained restraining—is an impossible and self-defeating paradox. The insistence upon obedience to a human superior leads, in practice, to rebellion against a divine law, in this case the law against fornication.

The Black House in fact desires the kind of fornication which most fundamentally mixes categories: incest. In 2.1, White Queen's Pawn—whom Black Bishop's Pawn repeatedly calls his 'daughter'—is asked to give herself, sexually, to her spiritual 'father'. Black Bishop's Pawn demands sexual satisfaction as proof of 'a daughter's duty', an obedience owed to him simply as a function of his paternal status; indeed, he characterizes his invitation to intercourse not as an abuse of power, but as a special favour, demonstrating his intention 'to honour [her] above all daughters'. When White Queen's Pawn refuses—when she objects to his mixing of the genres of fatherly divinity and Petrarchan love poetry—he abuses her verbally for her disobedience, which must be punished. The punishment consists of the forced satisfaction of the very desire she has refused to satisfy voluntarily. The request for sex in the name of obedience, when denied, justifies rape. Continued paternal authority can only be guaranteed if 'all his young tractable sweet obedient daughters' remain silent about the father's illicit desire; her silence can only be guaranteed if she herself is made guilty of fornication, the very crime of which she would accuse the father. After a daughter is raped, she can only accuse the father by admitting that she is no longer a virgin, and has committed incest: to accuse him is to accuse herself. In Middleton the priest's sexual abuse of his parishioner is heterosexual, but it springs from the same confusion of sexual and sacred authority found in our contemporary Church scandals.

This daughter is fortuitously saved, when the father is momentarily distracted by his own fear of 'discovery'. (The rape of a daughter depends on the privacy of a 'Black House', a privileged circumscribed space in which the father can act with impunity, undetected by others.) The father's fear of discovery allows the daughter to escape, and later she publicly accuses the would-be rapist. But, as often happens, the daughter's accusation is not believed, is categorized as slander of an innocent man with a spotless reputation; consequently, the would-be rapist escapes, and the abused daughter is punished. The White King concludes—as would Sigmund Freud, in rejecting testimony of incestuous abuse—'I ever believed rather the accuser false Than the professor vicious' (2.2.218–19). By the orders of the ultimate male authority in the White House, the almost-raped daughter is punished, characteristically, by being returned to the very House in which she was earlier threatened with rape, and where she will now be tormented by being locked in a room full of pornographic pictures (Taylor 2000).

Middleton clearly expects us to reject the category 'Boundless obedience'. But the Black House is defeated, not because of its programmatic regime of obedience, but because individual black pieces seek their own advantage; they are not obedient enough.

ERROR

> Why, would you have 'em play against themselves?
> That's quite against the rule of game, Ignatius.

IGNATIUS

> Push! I would rule myself, not observe rule.

The Black House is the category, simultaneously, of unruly individuality and unbounded obedience. The insistence upon rules ends in the dissolution of all boundaries, sexual and political—a world epitomized by the jumbled chaos of the 'bag'.

If obedience ends in the bag, it begins in the act of confession, staged in the play's first scene. The Black House demands that initiates confess their sins:

> The privat'st thought that runs to hide itself
> In the most secret corner of your heart now
> Must be of my acquaintance (1.1.124–6).

Everyone must obey this command, which records the breaking of commandments. The rule of confession demands that people categorize themselves by means of the categories of rule they have broken. Confession earns people salvation, by revealing that they have not earned salvation.

Middleton demonstrated, long before Michel Foucault, that confession is an instrument of power, by which the boundaries between one person and another—between private self and public authority—are broken down. In *A Game at Chess* confessions are cynically exploited, for political and sexual advantage, by the confessors of the Black House. We know this because the confessor tells us so, in an aside (1.1.109–16). But what is an aside? A theatrical confession. *A Game at Chess* is full of asides and soliloquies; pieces repeatedly unabashedly reveal their own 'most secret frailties' to the audience; in the final scene, the Black House voluntarily confesses all its vices to the White Knight, White Duke, and (presumably) White Audience. *A Game at Chess* opposes confession, and depends upon it. Confession makes possible the play's extraordinary transparency. As in chess, everything is visible, and victory depends, not upon force, but upon a change of perception: 'discovery'.

Most remarkably, the play even manages to stage invisibility. Who is moving the pieces in *A Game at Chess*? They believe they are free agents, making their own moves, but the very conceit of a chess game implies the existence of at least one, usually two, players. We cannot see any, but does that mean they do not exist? 'You may deny so A dial's motion, cause you cannot see The hand move, or a wind that rends the cedar' (1.1.292–4).

Theologically, the onstage pieces are being moved by God and the devil, or by the one invisible God of Calvinism, who alone wills both salvation and damnation. But theatrically, the onstage pieces are being moved by an offstage author. This similarity between plotting playwright and plotting God was and is familiar enough to readers and audiences acquainted with *Measure for Measure* and *The Tempest*, but Middleton, in contrast to Shakespeare, never brings his creator on stage. He refuses to visualize the invisible. By refusing, of course, he leaves open the possibility that God is not there at all.

Instead of an onstage impersonation of God, we get a Fat Bishop (author of satirical books) and a Black Knight (a director as 'facetious' as Middleton himself was said to be). John Russell Brown has denied that directors existed in the Elizabethan theatre, which emphasized instead the improvisational freedom of actors. But the complex logistics of a Lord Mayor's show clearly demanded a director, and in 1617 Middleton began directing (as well as writing) those shows. Pageant speeches were normally delivered by child actors; Middleton had written for companies of child actors at the Blackfriars and Paul's; for the adult companies, he wrote plays particularly remarkable for female roles played by boy actors. Adult actors may have insisted upon their interpretive freedom, but children—like the puppets of *The Revenger's Tragedy* and *Wit at Several Weapons*—took direction. Shakespeare and Rowley were actors; Middleton was a director.

In *A Game at Chess*, the most spectacular play of its period, Middleton successfully transferred onto the public stage the 'total theatre' of Lord Mayors' shows. This impulse can be seen, earlier, in the songs and machines of *The Witch* and *Macbeth*, in *Hengist*'s spectacular fiery conclusion, in the stage-masque of *World Tossed at Tennis*, in the extraordinarily complicated final scene of *Women, Beware Women*. The individual components of this stagecraft are not new; what is new is the concentration and concatenation of effects which require an extraordinarily precise control of *every* element of the *whole* theatrical space, both within and outside of the spectator's view. More than any other play of its time, *A Game at Chess*—with its transformation of stage into chessboard, uniformed oppositions of costuming and colour, formalization of space and movement, exploitation of particulars of impersonation, specially designed and unreusable properties—is a director's play.

It is also a play which, more than any other of its time, demystifies and opposes obedience. But this critique of obedience could only be performed through repeated acts of obedience. White Queen's Pawn is given a text which instructs her in obedience to her spiritual director; the child actor playing White Queen's Pawn was given a script containing instructions for speech and action. If the actor had not obeyed Middleton's written and spoken directions—if, like the character, he had rejected the book's demands—the play could not have been performed.

Likewise, the play rejects dissemblance, but depends upon it. Actors are, by definition, people who deliberately pretend to belong to categories to which they do not really belong. When the Black Knight says, 'What we have done Has been dissemblance ever' (5.3.157–8), he speaks for both the character and the actor. In this sense, *all* the actors, on both sides of the chessboard, belong to the Black House. Dissemblance and obedience—the generic marks of the Black House—are also the generic marks of the Play House.

So is the unnatural mixing of sexual categories. White Queen's Pawn was played by a boy actor. Boy actors were instructed, by an older male, to dress up in women's clothes and enact scenes of seduction, involving sexual innuendo, touching, fondling, kissing. The male actor playing White Queen's Pawn pretends not to have a penis; the male actor playing White Bishop's Pawn pretends to have been castrated.

A Game at Chess depends upon what it rejects: chess, obedience, confession, dissembling, totalizing power, sexual mismatching. Its most irresistible roles, for both actors and audiences, are the Fat Bishop and Black Knight. We enjoy what we repudiate. We enjoy them in part because we know they will lose. They are confined, contained, within the boundaries of a 'game'. *A Game at Chess* belongs, not simply to the genre of chess literature, but to the much larger genre of game literature. But the category 'game' is itself, as Wittgenstein insisted, fundamentally unstable. It is also surprisingly close to the category 'philosophy'—as James I complained, when he called chess a 'philosophic . . . folly'. *A Game at Chess* belongs to a genre of philosophical game also played by Aristophanes, Calderon, Goethe, and Beckett.

In the end, the world is divided into two simple categories, as all the Black pieces are swept from the board. But this finality and simplicity, like all the play's other categories, self-deconstructs. Ezra Pound's poem 'The Game of Chess' ends with the phrase 'Renewal of contest'. Middleton's apocalyptic play—which begins, in its title, with the word 'a'—ends with the word 'again'. This is only one game; there will be others. But, despite the play's characteristic modesty about its own merit, there will never be another play quite like this. It belongs to a category of one.

SEE ALSO

A Game at Chesse: An Early Form, 1773
General textual introduction: *Companion*, 712
List of works cited: *Companion*, 848
Textual introduction and apparatus: *Companion*, 912
Authorship and date: *Companion*, 439
Related poems: 'To the worthily accomplished Master William Hammond', 1896; 'To the King', 1895; 'The Picture plainly explained, after the manner of the chess play', 1897

A Game at Chess

as it was acted nine days together by the King's Men at the Globe on the bankside

[PERSONS AND PIECES OF THE PLAY

The whole play is a chessboard.

THE BLACK HOUSE, Spain

THE WHITE HOUSE, England

BLACK KNIGHT GONDOMAR (Black Queen's Knight), Don Diego Sarmiento de Acuña, Conde de Gondomar, ambassador from Black King Felipe to the White House; suffers from an anal fistula, which is public knowledge, and which requires him to sit in a special chair and be carried in a special litter

JESUIT BLACK BISHOP'S PAWN (Black Queen's Bishop's Pawn), a lecherous Jesuit priest in England; confessor to the Black Knight, Black Knight's Pawn, Black Queen's Pawn, and White Queen's Pawn (whom he wishes to seduce)

VIRGIN WHITE QUEEN'S PAWN, a devout unmarried English lady; literate, young, and fair; formerly betrothed to the White Bishop's Pawn before he was castrated

JESUITESS BLACK QUEEN'S PAWN, a member of the society of female Jesuits; formerly seduced by the Black Bishop's Pawn

FAT BISHOP OF SPALATO (White King's Bishop), gluttonous, lecherous, greedy, polemical author; former Catholic, recently converted to the Protestant cause, now resident in the White House; played by the acting company's leading clown

WHITE KING JAMES, King James I of England, aging political leader of the White House, father of White Knight Charles, patron of the Fat Bishop of Spalato and the White King's Counsellor Pawn

BLACK KNIGHT'S PAWN GELDER (Black Queen's Knight's Pawn), a Catholic servant of the Black Knight and unsuccessful suitor to the White Queen's Pawn; responsible for castrating his sexual rival, the White Bishop's Pawn

WHITE KNIGHT CHARLES (White Queen's Knight), Charles Stuart, Knight of the Order of the Garter, English Protestant champion, young son and heir of White King James, companion and ally of White Duke of Buckingham

Ghost of Saint IGNATIUS LOYOLA, Spanish Catholic, former soldier, lame; founder of the Jesuit Order, a missionary society dedicated to resisting the Protestant Reformation

JESUIT BLACK BISHOP (Black Queen's Bishop), Father General of the Society of Jesus, ecclesiastical superior of all Jesuits

WHITE DUKE OF BUCKINGHAM (White Queen's Duke), companion and ally of White Knight Charles; court favourite of White King James

WHITE QUEEN [OF BOHEMIA], daughter of White King James, sister of White Knight Charles, patron of the White Queen's Pawn; object of Black King Felipe's desire

ERROR, a personification of deviance

BLACK QUEEN MARIA, Spanish princess, sister of the Black King, proposed bride of White Knight Charles, and thus intended as a future Queen of the White House

BLACK KING FELIPE, King Felipe IV of Habsburg Spain, young lecherous Spanish Catholic; political leader of the Black House

WHITE BISHOP'S GELDED PAWN (White Queen's Bishop's Pawn), a Protestant minister; formerly betrothed to the White Queen's Pawn, before he was castrated by his rival (the Black Knight's Pawn Gelder)

This commentary focuses on literary and theatrical matters, including Biblical allusions (which many spectators and readers would recognize). For historical commentary see *Early*.

Title ***together*** in a row

bankside area on the south bank of the Thames

Persons Probably for reasons of censorship, no early text contains a list of characters. This list is editorial, but all information not in square brackets comes from the text itself or an early witness. The order of characters is based on the number of words in each role, from most to least.

2–3 BLACK ... WHITE (words with racial as well as moral meanings, then as now: Spaniards were typically darker-skinned than Englishmen, ruled over an empire with many black and brown peoples, and had imported many slaves from tropical regions.)

28 SPALATO Italian name for Split, in modern Croatia; in 1624, part of the Venetian empire

WHITE KING'S COUNSELLOR PAWN, a trusted political adviser of White King James, secretly working for the Black House

WHITE BISHOP [OF CANTERBURY] (White Queen's Bishop), religious leader of the White House; an ardent Protestant, patron of the White Bishop's Pawn

PROLOGUE

BLACK DUKE OLIVARES (Black Queen's Duke), dark-skinned Spanish Catholic, court favourite (and lover) of Black King Felipe

BLACK PAWN, a servant in the Black House

FAT BISHOP'S PAWN (White King's Bishop's Pawn), a servant in the White House

Dancing Statues]

Prologue *[Enter] the Prologue [in a black cloak]*

PROLOGUE

What of the game called chess-play can be made
To make a stage-play shall this day be played.
First you shall see the men in order set,
States and their pawns, when both the sides are met;
The houses well distinguished; in the game
Some men entrapped and taken, to their shame,
Rewarded in their play; and in the close
You shall see checkmate given to virtue's foes.
But the fair'st jewel that our hopes can deck
Is so to play our game t'avoid your check. *[Exit]*

Induction *The Induction. Ignatius Loyola [in his black Jesuit habit] appearing, Error at his foot as asleep*

IGNATIUS LOYOLA

Ha? Where? What angle of the world is this?
That I can neither see the politic face
Nor with my refined nostrils taste the footsteps
Of any my disciples, sons and heirs
As well of my designs as institution.
I thought they'd spread over the world by this time,
Covered the earth's face and made dark the land
Like the Egyptian grasshoppers.
Here's too much light appears shot from the eyes
Of truth and goodness never yet deflow'red;
Sure they were never here. Then is their monarchy
Unperfect yet—a just reward, I see,
For their ingratitude so long to me,
Their father and their founder.
It's not five years since I was sainted by 'em.
Where slept my honour all the time before?
Could they be so forgetful to canònise
Their prosperous institutor? When they'd sainted me,
They found no room in all their calendar
To place my name (that should have removed princes,
Pulled the most eminent prelates by the roots up

69 PROLOGUE (could be doubled with any roles except Loyola and Error)
76 DANCING STATUES (the only other roles in the play that might have been doubled, perhaps by the actors who played Loyola and Error, perhaps by the White King, Queen, Bishop, or Bishop's Pawn)
Prologue.1–2 **made To make** compelled to fashion
2 **this day** today (but especially pointed here, when actors and audiences were aware that the play might be banned by tomorrow)
played (mixing the senses 'playing a game' and 'performing a play')
3 **men** (*a*) persons (*b*) chess pieces
order (*a*) positions required at the outset of a chess game (*b*) hierarchical relationship of real persons
4 **States** offices of importance and power (i.e. bishop, duke, etc.)
are met (*a*) have encountered one another (*b*) are encountered by the audience
5 **houses** (*a*) families, lineages, races (*b*) place of abode of a religious fraternity (*c*) opposing sides in chess. Perhaps also (*d*) 'mansions' (since each side was associated with a separate stage entrance: see 1.1.0.2–4).
well distinguished (*a*) recognizably distinguishable from one another (*b*) socially and politically eminent
7 **Rewarded** (*a*) recompensed (*b*) punished
9 **our ... deck** can decorate, crown, our hopes
10 **check** rebuke (punning on technical meaning, in chess)
Induction.0.1 ***Ignatius Loyola*** (not named on stage until l. 37, but presumably dressed as a Jesuit)
0.2 ***appearing*** (perhaps rising through the trapdoor, as if coming from hell)
Error (may be female, as in Spenser's *Faerie Queene*, or male, as in *Truth*, where Error wears a 'garment of ash-colour silk, his head rolled in a cloud, over which stands an owl, a mole on one shoulder, a bat on the other, all symbols of blind ignorance and darkness, mists hanging at his eyes')
1 **angle** corner (punning on England, 'Angle-Land')
2 **politic** manipulating, deliberate, not spontaneous but consciously deployed for political advantage
5 **institution** i.e., the Society of Jesus, founded by Loyola
8 **Egyptian grasshoppers** (Exodus 10:14)
9–10 **light ... goodness** (Exodus 24:17, Daniel 10:6, Psalms 19:8, Revelation 1:14)
9 **eyes** (thought to actively radiate light, not just passively receive it)
10 **deflow'red** (*a*) deprived of its originary state of intactness (*b*) raped
11 **they** 'my disciplines'
15 **sainted** canonized, officially enrolled in the calendar of saints
17 **to canònise** about canonizing
18 **prosperous institutor** successful founder, founder of a rich institution

For my dear coming, to make way for me),
Let every petty martyr, and saint homily,
Roch, Maine, and Petronill (itch- and ague-curers),
Your Abbess Aldegund, and Cunigund,
The widow Marcell, parson Polycarp,
Cic'ly and Urs'ly, all take place of me,
And but for the bissextile, or leap year—
And that's but one in three—I fall by chance
Into the nine-and-twenti'th day of February.
There were no room else for me. See their love,
Their conscience too, to thrust me, a lame soldier,
Into leap year. My wrath's up, and methinks
I could with the first syllable of my name
Blow up their colleges.—Up, Error, wake!
Father of supererogation, rise!
It is Ignatius calls thee: Loyola.

ERROR
What have you done? O I could sleep in ignorance
Immortally, the slumber is so pleasing.
I saw the bravest setting for a game now
That ever my eye fixed on.

IGNATIUS LOYOLA 'Game'? What game?

ERROR
The noblest game of all, a game at chess
'Twixt our side and the White House, the men set
In their just order ready to go to't.

IGNATIUS LOYOLA
Were any of my sons placed for the game?

ERROR
Yes, and a daughter too, a secular daughter
That plays the Black Queen's Pawn, he the Black
Bishop's.

IGNATIUS LOYOLA
If ever pow'r could show a mast'ry in thee,
Let it appear in this.

ERROR It's but a dream,
A vision, you must think.

IGNATIUS LOYOLA I care not what,
So I behold the children of my cunning
And see what rank they keep.

Music. Enter severally the White House and Black House, as in order of the game

ERROR You have your wish.
Behold, there's the full number of the game,
Kings and their pawns, queens, bishops, knights and
dukes.

IGNATIUS LOYOLA
'Dukes'? They're called 'rooks' by some.

ERROR Corruptively.
Le Roc the word, *Custode de la Roche*,
The Keeper of the Forts, in whom both kings
Repose much confidence, and for their trust' sake,
Courage and worth, do well deserve those titles.

IGNATIUS LOYOLA
Thy answer's high. I see my son and daughter.

ERROR
Those are two pawns, the Black Queen's and Black
Bishop's.

IGNATIUS LOYOLA
Pawns argue but poor spirits and slight preferments,
Not worthy of the name of my disciples.
If I had stood so nigh, I would have cut
That Bishop's throat but I'd have had his place
And told the Queen a love tale in her ear
Would make her best pulse dance. There's no elixir
Of brain or spirit amongst 'em.

ERROR
Why, would you have 'em play against themselves?

23 **Let** they allow (continuing grammar of l. 19)
saint homily 'Saint Sermon', holy preacher

24 **ague** (*a*) fever (*b*) fit
itch (*a*) skin disease (*b*) restless propensity, appetite

25 **Your** colloquial collective pronoun (= 'one's')

27 **Cic'ly . . . Urs'ly** nicknames for Cecilia and Ursula (usually lower-class)
take place demonstrate their higher social status, by claiming a more desirable location
of from

28 **bissextile** leap-year or leap-day (Latin)

29 **one in three** one leap-year, for every three normal years

32 **lame** crippled (therefore ill-equipped to 'leap')

34 **first syllable** *ignis* (Latin), 'fire'

35 **colleges** seminaries, monasteries

36 **supererogation** (*a*) overpayment (*b*) a Catholic doctrine, regarded by Protestants as a fundamental theological error (*c*) suggesting 'super-error'

39 **Immortally** literally, 'without ever dying', but here it is only 'sleep' which is eternally uninterrupted (by contrast with saved Christians, who do not sleep forever, but wake and rise from their graves at the Second Coming)

40 **bravest** most splendid

42 **noblest game** Chess represents in game form the pursuits of the most powerful and admired families (courtiership, diplomacy, war).

47 **plays** impersonates, takes the role of

48 **mast'ry** expert proficiency

52.1 ***Music*** 'Invisible' music—played by offstage musicians—was often used to suggest magical or supernatural effects; it probably continues until the pieces exit, at l. 76.1.

52.1–2 ***Enter . . . House*** 'Living chess'—chess played with human beings as pieces, moving on a giant board—has been recorded since the fifteenth century. A full board would require 32 pieces (in addition to the two observers), but only five of the eight main pieces of each house speak (King, Queen, Queen's Bishop, Queen's Knight, Queen's Rook); if each has a pawn, this moment would require only 22 performers (a more manageable total). The choice of the Queen's side emphasizes the political and symbolic importance of the two contrasting Queens.

52.1 ***severally*** separately. In chess the Queen's side is on the left for Black, on the right for White, so the White House probably enters on the right, the Black House on the left, the 'sinister side' associated with the damned (Ecclesiastes 10:2).

56 ***Le Roc . . . Roche*** 'the rock . . . the keeper of the rock' (French), with 'rock' imagined as the site of a fortress; a conjectural etymology of 'rook'—the commoner title for the chess piece here called 'duke'.

60 **high** dignified, high in value, appropriate for someone of high rank
my . . . daughter (recognizably dressed as Jesuits)

64 **nigh** close

67 **elixir** quintessence, precious juice

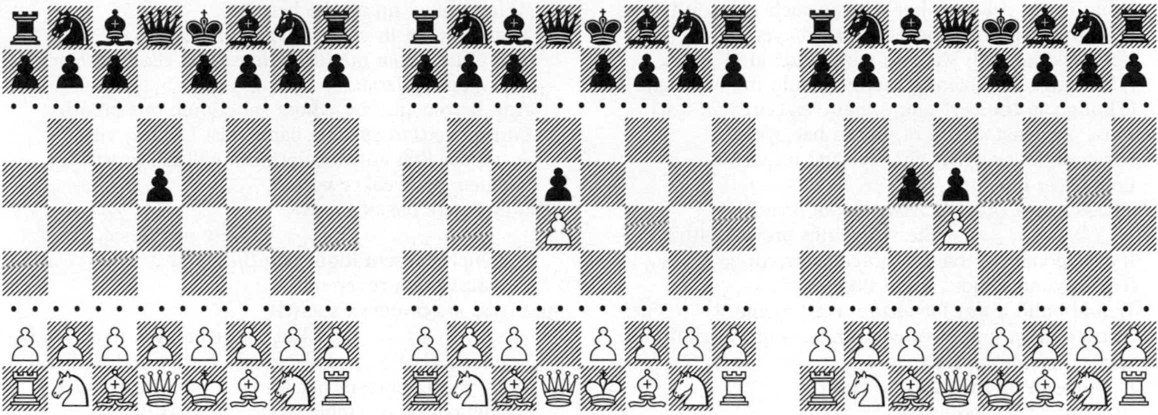

At 1.1.0.2–4 Black Queen's Pawn enters (*a*); at 1.1.0.3–5 White Queen's Pawn enters (*b*); then at 1.1.30.1–2 Black Bishop's Pawn enters, threatening White Queen's Pawn (*c*). In these diagrams of the opening, the pieces above the upper dotted line or below the lower dotted line are not visible to the audience.

That's quite against the rule of game, Ignatius.

IGNATIUS LOYOLA
Push! I would rule myself, not observe rule.

ERROR
Why then you'd play a game all by yourself.

IGNATIUS LOYOLA
I would do anything to rule alone.
It's rare to have the world reined in by one.

ERROR
See 'em anon, and mark 'em in their play.
Observe: as in a dance they glide away.
[*Exeunt both houses*]

IGNATIUS LOYOLA
O with what longings will this breast be tossed
Until I see this great game won and lost! *Exeunt*

[*Incipit*] *Actus Primus* 1.1

Enter from the Black House the Jesuitess Black Queen's Pawn (a woman-pawn in black), [*then*] *from the White House the Virgin White Queen's Pawn (a woman-pawn in white)*

JESUITESS BLACK QUEEN'S PAWN [*as to herself*]
I ne'er see that face but my pity rises.
When I behold so clear a masterpiece
Of heaven's art, wrought out of dust and ashes,
And at next thought to give her lost eternally
(In that not ours, but the daughter of heresy),
My soul bleeds at mine eyes.

VIRGIN WHITE QUEEN'S PAWN [*aside*]
Where should truth speak
If not in such a sorrow? They're tears plainly.
Beshrew me if she weep not heartily.

71 **Push** pish (meaningless expletive; but also slang for 'fuck')
74 **reined in** controlled (but also suggesting 'reigned')
reined...one Judges 9:12, Romans 5:17
75 **mark** pay attention to
76 **dance** Chess had been associated with dance since Francesco Colonna's chess allegory (1467) and the fifth book of Rabelais's *Gargantua* (1564).
78 **won and lost** won [by one side] and [consequently] lost [by the other], as in chess; but the phrase paradoxically conflates winning and losing
Exeunt (perhaps spectacularly: according to an eyewitness account, Loyola here 'vanisheth')
1.1.0.2–4 ***from...from*** This formula suggests that each 'house' was identified with a separate door for its exits and entrances, a staging device associated with classical drama and English morality plays.
0.2–3 ***Black Queen's Pawn*** initiating a well-known chess opening (Queen's Gambit Declined): see Illustrations. Black Queen's Pawn (named first in the stage direction, and speaking first) moves forward first, followed by White Queen's Pawn, then Black Bishop's Pawn (l. 30.1); she could take the Black Bishop's Pawn, but does not, and instead the next forward move is the entrance of the White Bishop's Pawn (l. 195.1), followed by the Black Knight's Pawn (l. 205.1–1.1.205.2). Chess games usually begin with pawn play, and in Act 1 only a single non-pawn appears (the Black Knight).
0.3 ***in*** dressed in
1 ***as to herself*** (she pretends to be speaking to herself, but intends to be overheard—thus deliberately manipulating the theatrical conventions of aside and soliloquy)
that (the White Queen's Pawn's)
2 **clear** (*a*) evident (*b*) fair, light-coloured (in contrast to 'dust and ashes')
3 **heaven's art** divine workmanship. (All creatures were made by the Creator; but here implying a contrast with 'merely human craft' and 'devilish artfulness'.)
dust and ashes Genesis 3:19, 18:27, Job 30:19, 42:5: 'ashes to ashes, dust to dust' ('Order for the Burial of the Dead', *Book of Common Prayer*)
4 **give** concede, acknowledge
lost (*a*) damned (*b*) forfeited in a game
5 **daughter of** woman who embodies an abstract quality (Biblical idiom)
6 **My...eyes** (tears being to the soul as blood is to the body)
8 **Beshrew** curse, damn

What is my peace to her to take such pains in't?
If I wander to loss and with broad eyes
Yet miss the path she can run blindfold in
(Through often exercise), why should my oversight
(Though in the best game that e'er Christian lost)
Raise the least spring of pity in her eye?
It's doubtless a great charity, and no virtue
Could win me surer.

JESUITESS BLACK QUEEN'S PAWN [*as to herself*]
Blessèd things prevail with't.
If ever goodness made a gracious promise,
It is in yonder look. What little pains
Would build a fort for virtue to all memory
In that sweet creature, were the ground-work firmer.

VIRGIN WHITE QUEEN'S PAWN
It has been all my glory to be firm
In what I have professed.

JESUITESS BLACK QUEEN'S PAWN
That is the enemy
That steals your strength away and fights against you,
Disarms your soul e'en in the heat of battle.
Your firmness that way make you more infirm
For the right Christian conflict. There I spied
A zealous primitive sparkle but now flew
From your devoted eye
Able to blow up all the heresies
That ever sat in council with your spirit,

Enter [from the Black House] the Black Bishop's Pawn (a Jesuit)

And here comes he whose sanctimonious breath
Can make that spark a flame. List to him, virgin—
At whose first entrance princes will fall prostrate;
Women are weaker vessels.

VIRGIN WHITE QUEEN'S PAWN
By my penitence,
A comely presentation, and the habit
To admiration reverend.

JESUITESS BLACK QUEEN'S PAWN
But the heart, the heart, lady—
So meek, that as you see good Charity pictured still
With young ones in her arms, so will he cherish
All his young tractable sweet obedient daughters
E'en in his bosom, in his own dear bosom.
I am myself a secular Jesuitess,
As many ladies are of worth and greatness;
A second sort are Jesuits *in voto*,
Giving their vow in to the Father General
(That's the Black Bishop of our House, whose pawn
This gentleman now stands for) to receive
The college habit at his holy pleasure.

9 **peace** spiritual tranquillity
10 **broad** wide-open
11 **Yet** (*a*) nevertheless (*b*) still, continually
the path biblical image for the right way of life, as in Psalm 16:11 ('Thou show'st me the path of life'); typically, 'strait is the gate, and narrow is the way' (Matthew 7:14), versus the 'broad' way in which sinners lose their moral compass and 'wander'.
blindfold (used in many child and adult games, and by virtuoso chessmasters, who could play the game blindfolded, so long as they were told where each opposing piece was moved)
12 **often** frequent
exercise practice (but suggesting Loyola's famous 'Spiritual Exercises')
oversight failure to see (source of all errors in chess, where everything is visible)
14 **spring of pity** natural wellhead or fountain of compassionate water (= tears)
16 **'t** it (pity, or charity, or 'her', the neuter pronoun suggesting that the White Queen's Pawn is child-like or childish)
win (*a*) win over, persuade (*b*) defeat
surer more certainly
17–18 **goodness . . . look** (reflecting the neo-Platonic belief that beauty was a sign of virtue)
19 **all** (*a*) eternal (*b*) universal
20 **firmer** more secure, better founded
21 **firm** constant, loyal
22–6 **enemy . . . conflict** (Christian allegory of psychomachia, or internal war between opposing personified aspects of the individual: here, stubborn loyalty to a mistaken theology fights against 'right Christian' inclinations.)
25 **infirm** (*a*) weak; (*b*) unhealthy—the first of many images equating spiritual error with physical disease
27 **primitive** original (therefore authentic)
sparkle light emitted by the eye (as at Induction.9), imagined as an incendiary spark
but just
30 **council** (*a*) private deliberation (*b*) synod of church leaders (*c*) gathering of political leaders
30.1–2 ***Black Bishop's Pawn*** Since pawns are taken by diagonally adjacent pawns, an exposed and unsupported Queen's Pawn is threatened by an opposing Queen's Bishop's Pawn, if she does not immediately take him.
31 **sanctimonious** holy (not necessarily suggesting hypocrisy)
breath speech (imagined as breath, blowing upon embers, to raise a fire); but also suggesting intimate or 'breathy' speech
32 **List . . . virgin** (suggesting a comparison with the Virgin Mary, impregnated by the breath of God: at the Annunciation. Mary listened to a divinely-appointed messenger who informed her of her elect status)
33 **entrance** (*a*) appearance (*b*) movement onto the stage (but also suggesting 'physical penetration')
fall prostrate lie face-down on the floor in deference to his reverence (but also suggesting a passive position inviting sexual penetration)
34 **weaker vessels** (1 Peter 3:7)
weaker less able to resist physical force or spiritual temptation
35 **presentation** manner of presenting [himself]
habit (*a*) clothing associated with a religious order (*b*) deportment
36 **To . . . reverend** respected to the point of amazement
38 **young ones** infants, emblematic of Charity's attention to people who are helpless, and of Charity's fruitfulness, one act of kindness generating others (but soon suggesting the immature women whose vulnerability the Black Bishop's Pawn will exploit, and whose fruitfulness will be illicitly literal)
39 **tractable** shapable, movable, unresisting
40 **bosom** heart, centre of tender emotions (but also suggesting a naked chest)
41 **secular** living in the world, not confined to a religious house or its daily routines
43 ***in voto*** 'by vow' (Latin), having taken vows as novices, but not yet fully invested
44 **General** universal (but also suggesting 'military commander')
46 **stands for** represents (as at Induction.47)
47 **college habit** vestments of the Jesuit Order (associated with academic vestments)
pleasure discretion (but also suggesting sensual delight)

VIRGIN WHITE QUEEN'S PAWN
But how are those *in voto* employed, lady,
Till they receive the habit?
JESUITESS BLACK QUEEN'S PAWN
They're not idle.
He finds 'em all true labourers in the vineyard
Of th'universal monarchy, which he
And his disciples principally aim at.
Those are maintained in many courts and palaces
And are induced by noble personages
Into great princes' services, and prove
Some counsellors of state, some secretaries,
All serving in notes of intelligence
(As parish clerks their mortuary bills)
To th' Father General. So are designs
Oft times prevented and important secrets
Of state discovered, yet no author found,
But those suspected oft that are most sound.
[Jesuit Black Bishop's Pawn gestures to Jesuitess Black Queen's Pawn]
—This mystery is too deep yet for your entrance
And I offend to set your zeal so back.
Checked by obedience, with desire to hasten
Your progress to perfection, I commit you
To the great worker's hands, to whose grave worth
I fit my reverence, as to you my wishes.
[Jesuitess Black Queen's Pawn does obeisance to Jesuit Black Bishop's Pawn]
JESUIT BLACK BISHOP'S PAWN *[aside to Black Queen's Pawn]*
Dost find her supple?
JESUITESS BLACK QUEEN'S PAWN *[aside to Black Bishop's Pawn]*
There's a little passage made. *Exit*
JESUIT BLACK BISHOP'S PAWN Let me contemplate,
With holy wonder season my access,
And by degrees approach the sanctuary
Of unmatched beauty set in grace and goodness.
Amongst the daughters of men I have not found
A more catholical aspèct. That eye
Does promise single life and meek obedience,
Upon whose lips (the sweet fresh buds of youth)
The holy dew of prayer lies like pearl
Dropped from the op'ning eyelids of the morn

50 **He** the Black Bishop (but also perhaps Loyola)
labourers ... vineyard (Matthew 20:8)
51 **th'universal monarchy** global imperium, in which the whole world is ruled by a single person, who combines absolute political and religious power
51–2 **monarchy ... at** (in contrast to Jesus, who when tempted in the desert rejected worldly power: Luke 4:4–8)
53 **courts** (*a*) royal entourages (*b*) judicial institutions
54 **induced** inducted, introduced
personages Very Important Persons (but also 'dramatic characters, theatrical impersonations', like those of *Game* itself)
55 **prove** turn out to be
56 **secretaries** (*a*) trusted personal assistants to powerful individuals (*b*) bureaucrats, government officials (as in 'Secretary of State')
57 **serving in** sending in as an act of service
intelligence information, fruits of espionage
58 **parish clerks** (person in each parish responsible for recording births, marriages, and deaths)
mortuary bills weekly lists of deaths caused by plague (which if they reached a dangerous level triggered government action—just as espionage reports might do)
60 **prevented** anticipated; forestalled
61 **discovered** exposed
author (*a*) cause, person responsible (*b*) writer [of the text which reveals state secrets]
62 **sound** reliable, uninfected
62.1 ***Jesuit ... Pawn*** (some such stage action would explain her sudden abandonment of this topic, and the claim that she has been 'Checked by obedience')
63 **mystery** occupational or religious secret
too ... entrance unfathomable to the newly initiated, like yourself (like water too deep for an inexperienced swimmer to wade into)
65 **Checked** (*a*) rebuked (*b*) stopped (*c*) placed in check, in chess, necessitating a defensive move to save oneself
66 **progress to perfection** Hebrews 6:1 ('let us go on unto perfection')
66–7 **I ... hands** 'Into thine hand I commit my spirit' (Psalm 31:5), 'into thy hands I commend my spirit' (Luke 23:46). The 'hands' here are more literal and less holy.
67 **great worker** i.e. Black Bishop's Pawn (but Exodus 14:31 attributes 'the great work' to God)
69 **supple** pliable
70 **passage** movement, transition; opportunity to enter (but also suggesting 'physical entrance', in a sexual sense more explicit in *Early* 1.1.75–7)
Exit (Here and throughout, theatrical conventions conflict with chess conventions: once pawns advance, they cannot retreat. Her withdrawal gives the Black Bishop's Pawn privacy—a freedom from human observation crucial to the fallen human world, as opposed to the transparent chess world.)
71–3 **Let ... sanctuary** (mimicking the language of Catholic meditation)
72 **season** render fit for use; acclimatize; discipline
access approach
73 **degrees** gradations (but also suggesting the literal 'steps' by which a Catholic priest approaches a raised altar)
73–4 **sanctuary ... beauty** Psalms 96:6
74 **unmatched** unparalleled (but also 'unmarried', and inexperienced at sex and chess)
set in (*a*) placed in the middle of (*b*) fixed firmly in
grace (*a*) the favour of God (*b*) physical gracefulness
75 **daughters of men** Genesis 6:2
76 **catholical** (*a*) universal—in so far as the White Queen's Pawn represents the individual soul ('Everyman'), she is the play's most universal character (*b*) Roman Catholic (*c*) universally effective, a panacea that heals all patients or satisfies all desires
77 **single life** unmarried celibacy
78–86 **Upon ... frailty** See Introduction. The classic Petrarchan imagery here is appropriate, since Petrarch was himself a member of the Catholic clergy, who broke his vows of chastity and fathered several illegitimate children.
78 **whose** (*a*) White Queen's Pawn's (*b*) Obedience's
buds rose-buds (suggesting the Petrarchan image of woman as flower, who when still a virgin is in bud, before she 'opens')
79 **holy** (because dew was imagined to descend from heaven)
dew literally, something wet and pearly on the 'lips', suggesting tears ('dropped from the' eyes) or semen
prayer In *The Book of Common Prayer*, a recommended 'Morning Prayer' asks God for 'the continual dew of thy blessing'.
lies (*a*) rests (*b*) falsifies
pearl (thought to result from a hardening of 'dew' in shellfish)
80 **morn** (personified as a female opening her eyelids, like the classical deity Aurora, famous for rising unwillingly from the bed of her lover)

Upon the bashful rose. How beauteously
A gentle fast (not rigorously imposed)
Would look upon that cheek, and how delightfully
The courteous physic of a tender penance
(Whose utmost cruelty should not exceed
The first fear of a bride) to beat down frailty
Would work to sound health your long festered judgement
And make your merit (which, through erring ignorance,
Appears but spotted righteousness to me)
Far clearer than the innocence of infants.

VIRGIN WHITE QUEEN'S PAWN
To that good work I bow, and will become
Obedience' humblest daughter, since I find
Th'assistance of a sacred strength to aid me,
The labour is as easy to serve virtue
The right way, since it's she I ever served
In my desire, though I transgressed in judgement.

JESUIT BLACK BISHOP'S PAWN
It's easily absolved amongst the rest.
You shall not find the virtue that you serve now
A sharp and cruel mistress. Her ear's open
To all your supplications. You may boldly
And safely let in the most secret sin
Into her knowledge, which like vanished man
Never returns into the world again.
Fate locks not up more trulier.

VIRGIN WHITE QUEEN'S PAWN To the guilty
That may appear some benefit.

JESUIT BLACK BISHOP'S PAWN Who is so innocent
That never stands in need on't, in some kind?
If every thought were blabbed that's so confessed,
The very air we breathe would be unblessed.
[*Aside*] Now to the work indeed, which is to catch
Her inclination. That's the special use
We make of all our practice in all kingdoms,
For by disclosing their most secret frailties
(Things which, once ours, they must not hide from us;
That's the first article in the creed we teach 'em),
Finding to what point their blood most inclines,
Know best to apt them then to our designs.—
Daughter, the sooner you disperse your errors,
The sooner you make haste to your recovery.
You must part with 'em. To be nice or modest
Toward this good action is to imitate
The bashfulness of one conceals an ulcer
For the uncomely parts the tumor vexes
Till't be past cure. Resolve you thus far, lady:
The privat'st thought that runs to hide itself
In the most secret corner of your heart now

81 **bashful** shy, embarrassed (because the rose's colour was associated with blushing)
rose literally, the 'lips' of l. 78

82 **fast** religious abstention from food, particularly associated with Roman Catholics; theologically justified as elevating the soul over the bodily appetites, here its purpose is to improve a woman's looks

84 **courteous** 'gracious' (characterizing the actions of a superior to an inferior) but also 'typical of courtiers'
physic (*a*) prescribed physical regimen—which might include regular sexual intercourse, considered healthy, and especially necessary for virgin females (*b*) enema (widely practised medical treatment to purge the body of physical or emotional ailments). As the 'fast' prevents new food from entering the body, the 'physic' removes everything already in the alimentary tract.
penance cathartic act of self-mortification imposed by a priest upon a penitent after confession, as part of the Roman Catholic sacrament of penance (not recognized by Protestants)

86 **The first...bride** what a virgin bride primarily fears, the pain of being penetrated for the first time, and having her hymen broken (implicitly compared to penetration of rectum by enema pipe)
to...frailty Compare 'to beat down Satan' (litany, *Book of Common Prayer*); rather than Satan, he wishes to overthrow the White Queen's Pawn.
beat down (*a*) overthrow (*b*) batter down (like a penis ramming the hymen)
frailty weakness of the human soul, susceptible to temptations of the body (which fast and physic will weaken); but here suggesting the physical and moral frailty of a woman resisting a man's sexual advances

87 **festered** corrupted, wounded, poisoned

88 **merit** worthiness. (Protestants believed that no mortal could merit salvation, which was earned not by correct 'judgement' but by faith in God's mercy.)
through...ignorance ambiguous: he means *her* ignorance, but it can be understood as *his*.

89 **spotted** blemished (Genesis 30:33)

91 **good work** (suggesting the Catholic belief that good works—rather than faith—can earn salvation)
bow kneel, submit, express obeisance or reverence (first sign of her idolatrous move toward Catholicism)

92 **Obedience** (Jesuits were distinguished from other religious orders by their vow of obedience.)

92–3 **since I...aid me** (a hinge phrase, which can apply to either the preceding or following sentence)

97 **absolved** forgiven by a priest, in the Catholic sacrament of absolution

99 **mistress** (Christianity had always gendered the Church female; for Protestants, the Roman Church was 'the whore of Babylon'.)

101 **let in** admit to (but suggesting 'welcome in')

102 **vanished** disappeared, dead

107 **thought** (not only acts but thoughts had to be confessed; thus, confession resulted in the articulation and expression of otherwise unvoiced evil)
blabbed indiscreetly blurted out

109 *Aside* (a confession to the audience, exposing the Catholic confessional)

111 **practice** (*a*) habitual action, profession, exercise (*b*) machinations

113 **ours** they belong to us

114 **creed** summary of essential Christian beliefs (here contrasting with the Apostle's Creed and other venerated early statements of Christian belief, which did not require auricular confession)

115 **blood** carnal appetite

116 **Know** (we) know (how)
apt adapt, make fit

117 **Daughter** term of affectionate address from a male religious superior (usually older) to a lay woman, originating in its use by Jesus at Matthew 9:22
disperse (*a*) dispel, rid yourself of (*b*) publish, disseminate (through confession)

119 **nice** overly scrupulous

121 **ulcer** suppurating open sore

122 **uncomely parts** 1 Corinthians 12:23 (where it seems to refer to both genital and excretory organs)
tumor any abnormal morbid swelling

125 **secret...heart** Kings 10:2, 2 Chronicles 9:1

Must be of my acquaintance, so familiarly
Never she-friend of your night-counsel nearer.

VIRGIN WHITE QUEEN'S PAWN
I stand not much in fear of any action
Guilty of that black time, most noble holiness.
I must confess, as in a sacred temple
Thronged with an auditory, some come rather
To feed on human object than to taste
Of angels' food;
So in the congregation of quick thoughts
Which are more infinite than such assemblies
I cannot with truth's safety speak for all.
Some have been wanderers, some fond, some sinful—
But those found ever but poor entertainment;
They'd small encouragement to come again.
The single life, which strongly I profess now,
Heaven pardon me, I was about to part from.

JESUIT BLACK BISHOP'S PAWN
Then you have passed through love?

VIRGIN WHITE QUEEN'S PAWN
But left no stain
In all my passage, sir, no print of wrong
For the most chaste maid that may trace my footsteps.

JESUIT BLACK BISHOP'S PAWN
How came you off so clear?

VIRGIN WHITE QUEEN'S PAWN
I was discharged
By an inhuman accident, which modesty
Forbids me to put any language to.

JESUIT BLACK BISHOP'S PAWN
How you forget yourself! All actïons
Clad in their proper language, though most sordid,
My ear is bound by duty to let in
And lock up everlastingly. Shall I help you?
'He was not found to answer his creation.'
A vestal virgin in a slip of prayer
Could not deliver man's loss modestlier.
'Twas the White Bishop's Pawn.

VIRGIN WHITE QUEEN'S PAWN
The same, blest sir.

JESUIT BLACK BISHOP'S PAWN [*aside*]
A Puritan well pickled.

VIRGIN WHITE QUEEN'S PAWN
By base treachery
And violence prepared by his competitor,
The Black Knight's Pawn, whom I shall ever hate
for't.

JESUIT BLACK BISHOP'S PAWN
'Twas of revenges the unmanliest way
That ever rival took—a villainy
That, for your sake, I'll ne'er absolve him of.

VIRGIN WHITE QUEEN'S PAWN
I wish it not so heavy.

JESUIT BLACK BISHOP'S PAWN
He must feel it.
I never yet gave absolutïon
To any crime of that unmanning nature.
It seems then you refused him for defèct.
Therein you stand not pure from the desire
That other women have in ends of marriage.
Pardon my boldness, if I sift your goodness
To the last grain.

VIRGIN WHITE QUEEN'S PAWN
I reverence your pains, sir,
And must acknowledge custom to enjoy
What other women challenge and possess

126 **familiarly** (*a*) intimately (*b*) habitually

127 **she-friend** (with whom a woman might frankly discuss sexual desires, etc.)
night-counsel conversation, advice (*a*) at night (*b*) about things done at night

129 **Guilty** worthy, deserving
black (*a*) dark (*b*) damnable

130 **sacred temple** i.e. a cathedral like St Paul's, where people often met for secular purposes: see *Meeting of Gallants*.

131 **auditory** assembly of listeners. (Protestantism stressed listening to sermons, rather than contemplating visual images, in church.)

132 **feed on** feast their eyes upon, gratify themselves with (but for the literal sense compare *Bloody Banquet* 5.1)

133 **angels' food** manna, which fell from heaven to feed the Israelites in the wilderness (Psalm 78:25); hence, the Lord's Supper (eucharist)

134 **congregation** gathering (a word often preferred by Protestants for its lack of hierarchical associations, where Catholics used 'Church')
quick living, lively, brisk, rapid, pregnant

137 **Some ... wanderers** some [of her thoughts] have strayed
fond foolish, infatuated

138 **entertainment** welcome

141 **I ... from** i.e. she was about to marry the White Bishop's Pawn

142 **stain** (Sex produces literal stains on clothes and sheets, and symbolic stains on the soul.)

143 **print** impression or discoloured indentation left on something by physical contact with something else (finger, foot, stamp, etc); printing punches black ink into white paper

146 **inhuman** (*a*) done by someone brutal (*b*) producing someone who is not fully human
accident unexpected unusual incident (but also, in grammar, a change to a word due to gender, tense, etc.; the gelding of the White Bishop's Pawn changed his gender, and affects her 'language')

152 **answer** (*a*) justify (*b*) repay (*c*) repeat, return in kind (*d*) match exactly
his creation (*a*) God's creation of mankind generally, and of the White Bishop's Pawn in particular, which imposes a reciprocal obligation to 'go forth and multiply' (*b*) his state when new-born

153 **vestal virgin** (*a*) priestess of the Roman goddess Vesta, vowed to chastity (*b*) nun
slip inadvertent mistake in speaking (as in 'Freudian slip'); but also 'instance of moral weakness, evasion, counterfeit'

154 **deliver** report (but suggesting 'give birth to')
man's loss (*a*) loss of manhood (*b*) damnation of mankind

155 **blest sir** (can refer to White Bishop's Pawn or Black Bishop's Pawn)

156 **Puritan** (contemptuous way of referring to zealous Protestants)
pickled (*a*) 'in a pickle,' in a bad situation (*b*) drunk, mischievous (*c*) steeped in salt or other solution to preserve it; thus, saturated with indelible heresy (but also suggesting the marinating of his amputated body parts, as something edible, like the testicles of various domesticated animals)

165 **for defèct** because of his genital deficiency

170–2 **custom ... desire** i.e. her interest in marriage was not driven by heterosexual desire or biological instinct, but by a wish to be like other women, with the customary social rights and possessions accorded a wife and mother

171 **challenge** claim

More ruled me than desire, for my desires
Dwell all in ignorance, and I'll ne'er wish
To know that fond way may redeem them thence.

JESUIT BLACK BISHOP'S PAWN [*aside*]
I never was so taken, beset doubly
Now with her judgement. What a strength it puts
forth!—
I bring work nearer to you. When you've seen
A masterpiece of man (composed by heaven
For a great princess' favour, kingdom's love,
So exact envy could not find a place
To stick a blot on person or on fame)
Have you not found ambition swell your wish then
And desire stir your blood?

VIRGIN WHITE QUEEN'S PAWN
By virtue, never.
I've only in the dignity of the creature
Admired the Maker's glory.

JESUIT BLACK BISHOP'S PAWN [*aside*]
She's impregnable.
A second siege must not fall off so tamely.
She's one of those must be informed to know
A daughter's duty, which some take untaught;
Her modesty brings her behindhand much.
My old means I must fly to; yes, 'tis it.—
[*He takes a book from his pocket*]
Please you peruse this small tract of obedience;
[*He gives the book to her*]
'Twill help you forward well.

VIRGIN WHITE QUEEN'S PAWN Sir, that's a virtue
I've ever thought on with especial reverence.

JESUIT BLACK BISHOP'S PAWN
You will conceive by that my pow'r, your duty.

VIRGIN WHITE QUEEN'S PAWN
The knowledge will be precious of both, sir.
[*She reads.*] *Enter* [*from the White House*] *White Bishop's Gelded Pawn*

WHITE BISHOP'S GELDED PAWN [*aside*]
What makes yon troubler of all Christian waters
So near that blessèd spring? But that I know
Her goodness is the rock from whence it issues
Unmovable as fast, 'twould more afflict me
Than all my suff'rings for her—which (so long
As she holds constant to the House she comes of,
The whiteness of the cause, the side, the quality)
Are sacrifices to her worth and virtue,
And (though confined) in my religious joys
I marry her and possess her.
Enter [*from the Black House*] *Black Knight's Pawn Gelder* [*opposite White Bishop's Gelded Pawn*]

172–3 **my ... ignorance** her appetites are limited by ignorance of male bodies and sexual acts

174 **fond** foolish, infatuated
redeem ransom, bring back and release from captivity

175 **taken** smitten with desire (but suggesting the capture of a chess piece)

176 **judgement** intelligence (in addition to her beauty)

179 **princess'** (or 'prince's')

180 **exact** perfect, accomplished, astute in observation and conduct

181 **fame** reputation

185 **impregnable** untakable (like a besieged fortress which holds out against all attacks), impossible to impregnate

188 **daughter's duty** 'duty of woman in the Church to be guided by her religious superiors,' but strongly suggesting filial duty, here defined as obedience to the sexual demands of her 'father'.
which (transforming the abstract 'duty' into its physical correlative, which some daughters 'take' without needing instructions)

189 **behindhand** lagging behind spiritually (but also 'not forward' sexually)

194 **conceive** understand (but suggesting 'become pregnant')

195.1–2 ***White ... Pawn*** Probably dressed as a minister (natural subordinate to a Bishop), whose clerical gown is an ambiguous sexual sign; perhaps played by a boy actor (because eunuchs resembled boys or women). Middleton described him as 'a Puritan', and he might look like one. Adjacent to the White Queen's Pawn at the start of the game, and as her close companion plausibly betrothed to her initially; but also a natural piece to move forward to back up and thereby protect an endangered Queen's Pawn (because he could take any piece which took her).

196 **makes** business has

197 **near** (In order to give her the book, the Black Bishop's Pawn must have come within reaching distance of the White Queen's Pawn; he is now perhaps going over the book with her.)

197–8 **blessèd ... issues** suggesting the spring which issued from the rock struck by Moses (Exodus 17:6)

197 **spring** source, natural fountain of pure water (but also suggesting 'youth', 'dawn', season of the year)

198 **it** the 'blessed spring', here equated with her purity (of soul and body), still 'clear' as the divine source of her soul

199 **fast** fixed, constant, loyal (the rock, her goodness); rapid (the flow of the spring)
'twould the Black Bishop's Pawn's closeness to her would

202 **whiteness** (*a*) purity, here equated with (*b*) white colour of one half the chess pieces, and (*c*) pale complexion
the cause (*a*) their purpose, goal (*b*) position upheld by the White House (*c*) specifically, 'the Puritan cause'
quality (*a*) party, faction (*b*) nature, attribute (*c*) social rank (*d*) profession, esp. acting profession, role played by an actor

203 **sacrifices** (*a*) offerings to a deity, sometimes literally a living body or parts of a body (*b*) something willingly lost for the sake of something considered more important

204 **confined** restricted, limited (i.e., to a relationship short of a consummated marriage)
joys blessings, happiness (in contrast to the slang sense 'sexual pleasures, orgasms')

205 **marry** am united to (in contrast to actual matrimony, legally forbidden because of his castrated state)
possess her (*a*) strongly influence her, permeate her thoughts; in implicit contrast to (*b*) 'own' her, as a patriarchal husband's property, or (*c*) 'have sex with her'.

205.1–2 ***Black Knight's Pawn*** He has come to 'court' (l. 227) the White Queen's Pawn, and may be dressed up or accessoried accordingly (ll. 230–1). He and the White Bishop's Pawn are in adjoining files, and thus each is naturally vulnerable to diagonal attack by the other; only by attacking a White Queen's Bishop's Pawn and thereby moving into his file could a Black Queen's Knight's Pawn adjoin or take a White Queen's Pawn.

205.2 ***opposite*** (presumably entering from the left side, upstage)

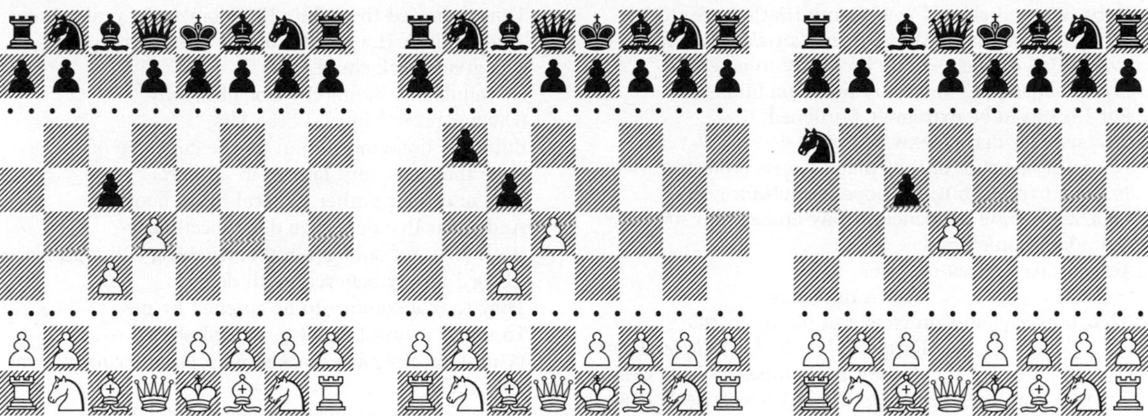

At 1.1.195.1–2 White Bishop's Pawn enters, protecting White Queen's Pawn (*a*); at 1.1.205.1–2 Black Knight's Pawn enters, protecting Black Bishop's Pawn (*b*). Notice that the Black Queen's Pawn is no longer on the visible part of the board. Then at 1.1.243.1 Black Knight enters, protecting Black Bishop's Pawn (*c*); notice that the Bishop's Pawns are no longer visible.

JESUIT BLACK BISHOP'S PAWN Behold, lady,
The two inhuman enemies: the Black Knight's Pawn
And the White Bishop's, the gelder and the gelded.
VIRGIN WHITE QUEEN'S PAWN There's my grief, my hate.
BLACK KNIGHT'S PAWN GELDER [*aside*]
What, in the Jesuit's fingers? By this hand,
I'll give my part now for a parrot's feather,
She never returns virtuous. 'Tis impossible.
I'll undertake more wagers will be laid
Upon a usurer's return from hell
Than upon hers from him now. Have I been guilty
Of such base malice that my very conscience
Shakes at the memory of it, and when I look
To gather fruit find nothing but the savin tree?—
Too frequent in nuns' orchards, and there planted
By all conjecture to destroy fruit rather.
I will be resolved now. [*To her*] Most noble virgin—
VIRGIN WHITE QUEEN'S PAWN
Ignoble villain! Dare that unhallowed tongue
Lay hold upon a sound so graciöus?
What's nobleness to thee? or virgin chastity?
They're not of thy acquaintance. Talk of violence
That shames creation, deeds would make night
blush—
That's company for thee. Hast thou the impudence
To court me with a leprosy upon thee
Able t'infect the walls of a great building?
JESUIT BLACK BISHOP'S PAWN [*to Black Knight's Pawn Gelder*]
Son of offence, forbear, go, set your evil
Before your eyes. A penitential vesture
Would better become ye, some shirt of hair.
BLACK KNIGHT'S PAWN GELDER
And you a three-pound smock 'stead of an alb,
An epicene chasuble. [*Aside*] This holy felon

207 **gelder** castrator. Protestants compared the doctrine of clerical celibacy to castration, equating Roman Catholicism with the pagan cult of Cybele, a goddess who (like the 'Whore of Babylon') was worshipped by castrated priests
gelded castrated; literally, having had his testicles cut off, and therefore incapable of fathering children; hence, gelding was often used as a metaphor for censorship (which prevents dissemination of the 'seed' of the Gospel)
208 **my grief, my hate** i.e. she grieves for the White Bishop's Pawn, and hates the Black Knight's Pawn
210 **part** (*a*) role, station (*b*) genitals
215 **that** which (modifying 'malice')
217 **fruit** (*a*) reward, consequence of my actions (*b*) offspring, fruit of a woman's womb
savin tree a bush that does not produce edible fruit, but was used to induce miscarriages of unwanted pregnancies
218 **nuns** (widely regarded as promiscuous: see Aretine's *Dialogues*, among many literary sources)
220 **resolved** (*a*) resolute, in approaching her (*b*) freed from doubt, by determining the real state of affairs
227 **leprosy** polluted and polluting sinfulness—religious metaphor from the disease which covers the body with white scales (appropriate for a member of the Black House who is attempting a veneer of piety) and which rots the body, eventually causing appendages to fall off (an appropriate punishment for a castrator)
228 **t'infect . . . building** (Leviticus 14:33–53 describes the spread of leprosy to human dwellings)
229 **Son of** man who embodies an abstract quality (like 'daughter of', l. 5); after his crime, he is 'the deed's creature' (*Changeling* 3.4.140).
232 **three-pound smock** expensive woman's undergarment, slip
alb white tunic worn by priests, falling to the feet
233 **epicene** characteristic of both sexes, hermaphroditic, bisexual, effeminate (alluding to the similarity between male clerical vestments and women's dresses)
chasuble sleeveless mantle worn over the alb by a priest celebrating mass
holy felon sacred criminal (paradox)

Robs safe and close. I feel a sting that's worse too.
[He turns to the White Bishop's Gelded Pawn]
White Pawn! Hast so much charity to accept
A reconcilement? Make thy own conditions,
For I begin to be extremely burdened.

WHITE BISHOP'S GELDED PAWN *[aside]*
No truth or peace of that Black House protested
Is to be trusted; but, for hope of quittance
And warned by diffidence, I may entrap him soonest.
—I admit conference.

BLACK KNIGHT'S PAWN GELDER
It is a nobleness
That makes confusion cleave to all my merits.
Exeunt White Bishop's Gelded Pawn and Black Knight's Pawn Gelder

JESUIT BLACK BISHOP'S PAWN *[to Virgin White Queen's Pawn]*
That treatise will instruct you fully.
[She reads.] Enter Black Knight Gondomar [from the Black House, behind]

BLACK KNIGHT GONDOMAR *[aside]* So, so,
The business of the universal monarchy
Goes forward well now, the great college pot
That should be always boiling with the fuel
Of all intelligences possible
Thorough the Christian kingdoms. Is this fellow
Our prime incendiary? one of those
That promised the White Kingdom sev'n years since
To our Black House? Put a new daughter to him,
The great work stands;
He minds nor monarchy nor hierarchy
(Diviner principality). I brag less,
But have done more than all the conclave of 'em,
Take their assistant fathers in all parts,
Yea, and their Father General in, to boot—
And what I've done I've done facetiously
With pleasant subtlety and bewitching courtship
Abused all my believers with delight;
They took a comfort to be cozened by me.
To many a soul I've let in mortal poison
Whose cheeks have cracked with laughter to receive it.
I could so roll my pills in sugared syllables
And strew such kindly mirth o'er all my mischief,
They took their bane in way of recreation
As pleasure steals corruption into youth.—
He spies me now. I must uphold his reverence,
Especially in public, though I know
Priapus, guardian of the cherry gardens,
Bacchus' and Venus' chit, is not more vicious.

JESUIT BLACK BISHOP'S PAWN
Blessing's accumulation keep with you, sir.

234 **close** covertly, secretly
sting inward pain caused by sin or shame (compared to the sting of a serpent, or Satan), in this case 'worse' than the sting of lust

239 **quittance** requital

240 **diffidence** distrust (of others), suspicion

242 **confusion** (*a*) destruction, ruin, damnation (*b*) embarrassment (*c*) perplexity (*d*) chaos, disorder
cleave stick

243.1 ***Enter Black*** (Another recurring clash between theatrical conventions and the rules of chess: a Black piece enters, though there has been no intervening White move since the entrance of the Black Knight's Pawn. As the play progresses, it becomes harder for an audience to follow the exact sequence of chess moves, in part because the actors are probably moving on stage, between entrances; and the exits of three pawns have already disrupted the game's symmetries. For both exits and entrances it is black pieces who first break the rules.)
Black Knight Like the chess piece, capable of rapid, unexpected and 'devious' action (jumping over obstacles, and not moving in a straight line or symmetrical jump). Because Knights can skip over pawns, they are often active early in the game. Of the three possible initial moves of the chess piece, two would protect the Black Bishop's Pawn, one would threaten the White Queen's Pawn; all three would place him in a rank behind the Black Bishop's Pawn.

243.2 ***behind*** (in the chess sense, not advanced so far forward)

245 **great college pot** Jesuit receptacle, compared to a pot in a college kitchen, big enough for cooking communal meals (perhaps also punning on 'chamber pot')

247 **intelligences** espionage

248 **Thorough** throughout

249 **prime** (*a*) principle (*b*) sexually aroused (*c*) priming, laying gunpowder in preparation for firing
incendiary (*a*) inflammatory agitator (*b*) arsonist

250 **since** ago

252 **stands** (*a*) stands still (*b*) stands up, sexually erects

253 **hierarchy** ecclesiastical authority: rule of the state by the church, and rule of the church by prelates (rather than congregations), allegedly modelled upon the hierarchy of angels

254 **principality** (*a*) supreme authority (*b*) one of the ranks of angels
I brag less (He then proceeds to brag for another twelve lines, confirming the stereotype of Spanish arrogance.)

255 **conclave** assembly of prelates (especially cardinals)

256 **assistant fathers** (*a*) subordinate priests (*b*) local Jesuits, reporting to the Father General of the Order (*c*) men who assist in fathering children, i.e. who have sex with other men's wives

257 **to boot** in addition

258 **facetiously** wittily

259 **With . . . courtship** (another hinge phrase, working grammatically with both the preceding and following clauses)

260 **Abused** (*a*) deceived (*b*) misused, badly treated (*c*) sexually violated
my believers (*a*) people who trusted me (*b*) believers in my religion
delight pleasure (to them and to me)

261 **cozened** swindled, double-crossed

262 **mortal** fatal

266 **bane** poison, ruin

267 **steals** secretly insinuates

270 **Priapus** Roman god of fertility and guardian of gardens, usually represented by a huge erect penis
cherry cherry-tree (slang for the male genitals) or fruit (metaphor for female lips or nipples)

271 **Bacchus . . . chit** i.e. the offspring of an adulterous union between the god of wine and goddess of lust is a male erection
chit animal offspring (whelp, cub)
vicious addicted to vice, impure

BLACK KNIGHT GONDOMAR
Honour's dissimulation be your due, sir.
[He kneels to the Jesuit Black Bishop's Pawn]
VIRGIN WHITE QUEEN'S PAWN [*aside*]
How deep in duty his observance plunges.
His charge must needs be reverend.
JESUIT BLACK BISHOP'S PAWN I am confessor
To this Black Knight too. You see devotion's fruitful;
Sh'as many sons and daughters.
BLACK KNIGHT GONDOMAR [*aside*] I do this the more
T'amaze our adversaries to behold
The reverence we do these *guitonens*
And to beget a sound opiniön
Of holiness in them and zeal in us,
As also to invite the like obedience
In other pucelles by our meek example.
[Exit Virgin White Queen's Pawn]
So, is your trifle vanished?
JESUIT BLACK BISHOP'S PAWN
'Trifle' call you her? It's a good pawn, sir.
Sure she's the second pawn of the White House,
And to the op'ning of the game I hold her.
BLACK KNIGHT GONDOMAR
Ay, you hold well for that. I know your play of old:
If there were more Queen's Pawns you'd ply the game
A great deal harder. Now, sir, we're in private.
But what for the main work, the great existence,
The hope monarchal?
JESUIT BLACK BISHOP'S PAWN
It goes on in this.
BLACK KNIGHT GONDOMAR
In this? I cannot see't.
JESUIT BLACK BISHOP'S PAWN
You may deny so
A dial's motion 'cause you cannot see
The hand move, or a wind that rends the cedar.
BLACK KNIGHT GONDOMAR
Where stops the current of intelligence?
Your Father General, Bishop o'th' Black House,
Complains for want of work.
JESUIT BLACK BISHOP'S PAWN Here's from all parts
Sufficient to employ him. I received
A packet from th'assistant fathers lately;
Look you, there's *Anglica*, this *Gallica*—
[He gives papers to Black Knight Gondomar]
BLACK KNIGHT GONDOMAR
Ay, marry, sir, there's some quick flesh in this.
JESUIT BLACK BISHOP'S PAWN [*giving paper*] *Germanica*—
BLACK KNIGHT GONDOMAR
'Think they've sealed this with butter.
JESUIT BLACK BISHOP'S PAWN [*giving paper*] *Italica*, this—
BLACK KNIGHT GONDOMAR
They put their pens the Hebrew way, methinks.
JESUIT BLACK BISHOP'S PAWN [*giving paper*]
Hispanica here.
BLACK KNIGHT GONDOMAR
Hispanica? Blind work, this.
The Jesuit has writ this with juice of lemons sure.
It must be held close to the fire of purgatory
Ere't can be read.
JESUIT BLACK BISHOP'S PAWN
You will not lose your jest, knight,
Though't wounded your own fame.

274 **his observance** the Black Knight's act of ritual deference
275 **His charge** Black Bishop Pawn's pastoral duties
279 ***guitonens*** vagrants, vagabonds (Middleton coinage: Spanish *guiton*): Jesuits were missionaries
283 **pucelles** (*a*) girls, young women, virgins (*b*) sluts
284 **trifle** (*a*) thing of little value or importance (*b*) worthless person (*c*) toy (*d*) dessert made from cake, wine, and cream
285 **pawn** (*a*) chess piece (*b*) security for a debt, investment
286 **second pawn** pawn second in importance only to the White King's Pawn
287 **op'ning ... game** opening up the chess board (an important objective of initial pawn play); but suggesting 'opening for sexual entrance'
288 **I ... old** (One of many indications that this game has been played many times before—and that the characters are all imagined as players, not just pieces.)
play (*a*) way of playing a game, using a weapon (*b*) tricks (*c*) playing around, idleness (*d*) sexual sport
289 **ply** (*a*) work at (*b*) assiduously assail (*c*) solicit persistently
game (*a*) contest (*b*) sexual sport (*c*) prey
290 **harder** (*a*) more vigorously (*b*) with a stiffer penis
291 **existence** state of affairs, source and focus of life (usually applied to God, as absolute and eternal being)
292 **hope monarchal** (*a*) sovereign ambition (*b*) desire for absolute power
294 **dial's** time-piece's
295 **rends the cedar** Zechariah 11:23
298 **want** lack
301 ***Anglica*** England (first of a series of Latin—hence Catholic—geographical terms)
Gallica France (associated with promiscuity)
302 **quick** (*a*) vital (*b*) highly sensitive (*c*) pregnant
flesh 'meat', i.e. (*a*) substance (*b*) sexual bodies
303 ***Germanica*** countries speaking High or Low German (modern Germany, Netherlands, Austria, etc.)
304 **butter** alluding to (*a*) Germanic fondness for dairy products (*b*) English newspapers on events in northern Europe published by Nathaniel Butter
305 ***Italica*** various Italian-speaking states (but also alluding to 'italic' handwriting)
306 **pens** (*a*) writing implements (*b*) penises
Hebrew (written right to left; hence 'backwards'; hence alluding to alleged Italian fondness for anal intercourse)
307 ***Hispanica*** Spanish-speaking world
Blind (*a*) unseeing (*b*) unseen
308 **juice of lemons** used for writing secret messages (because invisible, unless heated)
309 **purgatory** intermediate state of the afterlife, where souls were punished for venial sins, before becoming eligible for heaven (Catholic belief, not shared by Protestants)
311 **fame** reputation (Gondomar is Spanish himself)

Enter [from the White House] White King's Counsellor Pawn

BLACK KNIGHT GONDOMAR *Curanda pecunia.*

JESUIT BLACK BISHOP'S PAWN
Take heed, sir, we're entrapped. The White King's Pawn!

BLACK KNIGHT GONDOMAR
He's made our own, man, half *in voto* yours.
His heart's in the Black House. Leave him to me.
[Exit Jesuit Black Bishop's Pawn]
Most of all friends endeared, preciously special!

WHITE KING'S COUNSELLOR PAWN
You see my outside, but you know my heart, knight;
Great difference in the colour. There's some intelligence,
[Gives papers to Black Knight Gondomar]
And as more ripens, so your knowledge still
Shall prove the richer. There shall nothing happen,
Believe it, to extenuate your cause
Or to oppress her friends, but I will strive
To cross it with my counsel, purse and power,
Keep all supplies back both in means and men
That may raise strength against you. We must part.
I dare not longer of this theme discuss;
The ear of state is quick and jealïous.

BLACK KNIGHT GONDOMAR
Excellent estimation, thou art valued
Above the fleet of gold that came short home.
Exit White King's Counsellor Pawn
Poor Jesuit-ridden soul, how art thou fooled
Out of thy faith, from thy allegiance drawn,
Which way soe'er thou tak'st, thou'rt a lost pawn.
Exit

Finit Actus Primus

❁

Incipit Actus Secundus 2.1

Enter Virgin White Queen's Pawn [from the White House] with a book in her hand

VIRGIN WHITE QUEEN'S PAWN
And here again: (*reading*) 'it is the daughter's duty
To obey her confessor's command in all things
Without exception or expostulation.'
It's the most general rule that e'er I read of.
Yet when I think how boundless virtue is,
Goodness and grace, it's gently reconciled,
And then it appears well to have the power
Of the dispenser as uncircumscribed.
[She reads silently.] Enter [from the Black House] Jesuit Black Bishop's Pawn [apart]

JESUIT BLACK BISHOP'S PAWN *[aside]*
She's hard upon't. 'Twas the most modest key
That I could use to open my intents.
What little or no pains goes to some people!
[He finds a paper]
Ha? What have we here? A sealed note. Whence this?
'To the Black Bishop's Pawn, these.' How? to me?
Strange. Who subscribes it? 'The Black King'? What would he?
[He reads] the letter

'Pawn! sufficiently holy, but unmeasurably politic. We had late intelligence from our most industrious servant famous in all parts of Europe (our Knight of the Black House) that you have at this instant in chase the White Queen's Pawn, and very likely by the carriage of your game to entrap and take her. These are therefore to require you, by the burning affection I bear to the rape of devotion, that speedily upon the surprisal of her by all watchful advantage you make some attempt upon the White Queen's person, whose fall or prostitution our lust most violently rages for.'

Sir, after my desire has took a julep

311.1–2 ***White...Pawn*** (combining features of various pro-Spanish historical persons in the King's government)
311 ***Curanda pecunia*** 'watch the money' (Latin). White King's Pawn may be the White King's Treasurer; he is certainly being bankrolled by the Black House.
312 **entrapped** endangered unawares. (A Black Knight could not be trapped at this point, if he has stood still since his first entrance move; he could, however, in three moves have occupied a square threatened by the first move of the White King's Pawn, and the actor could have been moving restlessly.)
313–14 **He's...House** (Betrayal, though common in politics, is of course not possible in chess: see Introduction.)
320 **extenuate** emaciate, weaken
322 **cross** thwart
purse financial resources. (See '*pecunia*', l. 311.)
324 **raise...you** Isaiah 29:3, 49:6; Amos 6:14
325 **theme** subject
326 **quick** swift, sensitive
jealïous suspicious
327 **estimation** assessment, judgement
328 **fleet of gold** treasure fleet
short not as full as expected
330 **from...drawn** (a hinge-phrase, which makes sense with either the preceding or following sentence)
331.1 *Exit* (thereby clearing the stage/board, something that does not happen in chess)
331.2 ***Finit...Primus*** (Music was usually played during the interval between acts.)
2.1.4 **general** comprehensive
6 **reconciled** harmonized (with reason)
8 **dispenser** bestower (of virtue, goodness, and grace); steward (of God)
as so
uncircumscribed unboundaried (normally used of God)
9 **modest** (*a*) unobtrusive (*b*) not offensive to decency
11.1 ***a paper*** (left on stage during the act-break)
15 **politic** (*a*) politically astute (*b*) cunningly manipulative (*c*) *politique*, indifferent to religion, secular
19 **carriage** conduct
20 **take** (*a*) capture (a chess piece) (*b*) captivate, charm (*c*) seize, sexually possess
These these letters, instructions
22 **surprisal** unexpected attack, ambush
23 **attempt** (*a*) violent sexual assault (*b*) temptation
24 **fall** (*a*) destruction (*b*) moral ruin (*c*) defeat by being thrown to the floor in wrestling (*d*) lying down for sexual purposes
prostitution (*a*) transformation into a whore (*b*) defilement (*c*) prostration
26 **julep** cool sweet drink

For its own inflammation that yet scorches me,
I shall have cooler time to think of yours.
She's passed the general rule, the large extent
Of our prescriptions for obedience,
And yet with what alacrity of soul
Her eye moves on the letters.

VIRGIN WHITE QUEEN'S PAWN Holy sir,
Too long I've missed you. O your absence starves me.
Hasten for time's redemption, worthy sir,
Lay your commands as thick and fast upon me
As you can speak 'em. How I thirst to hear 'em!
Set me to work upon this spacious virtue
Which the poor span of life's too narrow for,
Boundless obedience,
The humblest yet the mightiest of all duties,
Well here set down a universal goodness.

JESUIT BLACK BISHOP'S PAWN [*aside*]
By holiness of garment her safe innocence
Has frighted the full meaning from itself.
She's farther off from understanding now
The language of my intent than at first meeting.

VIRGIN WHITE QUEEN'S PAWN
For virtue's sake, good sir, command me something.
Make trial of my duty in some small service,
And as you find the faith of my obedience there,
Then trust it with a greater.

JESUIT BLACK BISHOP'S PAWN You speak sweetly.
I do command you first then—

VIRGIN WHITE QUEEN'S PAWN With what joy
I do prepare my duty.

JESUIT BLACK BISHOP'S PAWN
To meet me
And seal a kiss of love upon my lip.

VIRGIN WHITE QUEEN'S PAWN Ha?

JESUIT BLACK BISHOP'S PAWN
At first disobedient, in so little too?
How shall I trust you with a greater then?—
Which was your own request.

VIRGIN WHITE QUEEN'S PAWN Pray send not back
My innocence to wound me. Be more courteous.
I must confess, much like an ignorant plaintiff
Who, presuming on the fair path of his meaning,
Goes rashly on, till on a sudden brought
Into the wilderness of law by words
Dropped unadvisedly, hurts his own cause
And gives the adversary advantage by't—
Apply it you can best, sir. If my obedience
And your command can find no better way,
Fond men command, and wantons best obey.

JESUIT BLACK BISHOP'S PAWN
If I can at that distance send you a blessing,
Is it not nearer to you in my arms?
It flies from these lips dealt abroad in parcels,
And I to honour thee above all daughters
Invite thee home to th' house, where thou mayst surfeit
On that which others miserably pine for,
A favour which the daughters of great potentates
Would look of Envy's colour but to hear.

VIRGIN WHITE QUEEN'S PAWN
Good men may err sometimes. You are mistaken, sure,
If this be virtue's path, 'tis a most strange one.
I never came this way before.

JESUIT BLACK BISHOP'S PAWN That's your ignorance—
And therefore shall that idiot still conduct you
That knows no way but one? nor ever seeks it?
If there be twenty ways to some poor village,
'Tis strange that virtue should be put to one.
Your fear is wondrous faulty. Cast it from you.
'Twill gather else in time a disobedience
Too stubborn for my pardon.

VIRGIN WHITE QUEEN'S PAWN Have I locked myself
At unawares into sin's servitude
With more desire of goodness? Is this the top
Of all strict order? and the holiest
Of all Societies, the three-vowed people
For poverty, obedience, chastity

27 **For** as a cure for
29 **passed** i.e. already read
34 **Hasten ... redemption** hurry to make up for lost time
39 **Boundless obedience** unbounded binding, an unlimited imposing of limits (paradox)
41 **set down** termed, defined
42 **holiness of garment** 'garment of holiness' (Ecclesiasticus 50:11)
safe (*a*) secure from harm (*b*) morally sound
innocence (*a*) sinlessness (*b*) ignorance
52 **seal** (associated with kissing because the seal's pressure on hot wax, usually at a juncture of two edges, resembles the pressing of joined lips together; also, because seals ratified contracts, as kisses confirmed intimate relationships)
53 **Ha?** This might indicate a nervous laugh, or an expression of disbelief (as in modern 'huh?').
57 **innocence** (imagined as a projectile, rebounding to harm its user)
58 **confess** acknowledge as a mistake or sin, that
59 **meaning** intention
62 **hurts** (he) hurts
63 **the adversary** (*a*) his opponent (*b*) Satan
64 **Apply ... best** i.e. you can figure out how to complete my incomplete sentence, by comparing her to the 'ignorant plaintiff'
65 **no better way** no alternative better than the command you have just given, [then it is evident that]
66 **Fond** unwise, infatuated, crazy
wantons (*a*) spoiled brats (*b*) undisciplined unmanageable animals or persons (*c*) sluts
best obey i.e. epitomize obedience
67 **distance** (indicative of the stage blocking of this scene: see also ll. 93–4, 101, 110. It is White's move, so he must ask her to voluntarily 'Be nearer', because he cannot move toward her himself: unless she comes closer, he cannot take her.)
69 **parcels** (*a*) small portions (*b*) passages of Scripture
74 **of ... colour** i.e. pale with envy
hear (*a*) hear about (*b*) overhear
75 **Good men** 'virtuous persons', but also suggesting *goodmen* ('heads of household' and 'persons of substance, below the rank of gentlemen')
sure surely
85 **sin's servitude** (*a*) enslavement to sin (*b*) sin's essence or correlative, slavery
89 **poverty ... chastity** the three vows taken by Jesuits

(The last the most forgot)? When a virgin's ruined
I see the great work of obedience
Is better than half finished.

JESUIT BLACK BISHOP'S PAWN
What a stranger
Are you to duty grown! What distance keep you!
Must I bid you come forward to a happiness
Yourself should sue for? 'Twas never so with me.
I dare not let this stubbornness be known;
'Twould bring such fierce hate on you. Yet presume not
To make that courteous care a privilege
For wilful disobedience. It turns then
Into the blackness of a curse upon you.
Come, come, be nearer.

VIRGIN WHITE QUEEN'S PAWN
Nearer?

JESUIT BLACK BISHOP'S PAWN
Was that scorn?
I would not have it prove so, for the hopes
Of the great monarchy. If it were like it,
Let it not dare to stir abroad again;
A stronger ill will cope with't.

VIRGIN WHITE QUEEN'S PAWN
Bless me! Threatens me
And quite dismays the good strength that should help me.
I never was so doubtful of my safety.

JESUIT BLACK BISHOP'S PAWN
'Twas but my jealousy. Forgive me, sweetness.
Yon is the house of meekness, and no venom lives
Under that roof. Be nearer. Why so fearful?
Nearer the altar, the more safe and sacred.

VIRGIN WHITE QUEEN'S PAWN
But nearer to the off'rer, oft more wicked.

JESUIT BLACK BISHOP'S PAWN
A plain and most insufferable contempt!
My glory I have lost upon this woman
In freely off'ring that she should have kneeled
A year in vain for. My respect is darkened.
Give me my reverence again thou'st robbed me of
In thy repulse; thou shalt not carry't hence.

VIRGIN WHITE QUEEN'S PAWN
Sir—

JESUIT BLACK BISHOP'S PAWN
Thou'rt too great a winner to depart so
And I too deep a loser to give way to't.

VIRGIN WHITE QUEEN'S PAWN
O heaven!

JESUIT BLACK BISHOP'S PAWN
Lay me down reputatïon
Before thou stir'st. Thy nice virginity
Is recompense too little for my love.
'Tis well if I accept of that for both.
Thy loss is but thy own; there's art to help thee
And fools to pass thee to. In my discovery
The whole Society suffers, and in that
The hope of absolute monarchy eclipsed.
Assurance thou canst make none for thy secrecy
But by thy honour's loss; that act must awe thee.

VIRGIN WHITE QUEEN'S PAWN
O my distressed condition!

JESUIT BLACK BISHOP'S PAWN
Dost thou weep?
If thou hadst any pity this necessity
Would wring it from thee. I must else destroy thee.
We must not trust the policy of Europe
Upon a woman's tongue.

VIRGIN WHITE QUEEN'S PAWN
Then take my life, sir,
And leave my honour for my guide to heaven.

JESUIT BLACK BISHOP'S PAWN
Take heed I take not both, which I've vowed since
If longer thou resist me.

94 **come forward** (*a*) approach me (*b*) advance to more prominence
96 **I...known** I must conceal this to protect (*a*) you, but also (*b*) myself
103 **great monarchy** ultimate sovereignty (single rule over the whole world)
105 **cope with't** battle your scorn
107 **doubtful** apprehensive
108 **jealousy** (*a*) righteous indignation, characteristic of God (*b*) eagerness to protect something valuable from harm (*c*) anxiety over sexual rivalry
109 **Yon** (gesturing toward the Black House, which pretends to be meek)
no venom (suggesting a serpent, commonly associated with Satan and therefore with the Black House)
111 **altar** (associated with Roman Catholic religious practice; Protestants preferred 'the Lord's table')
112 **off'rer** (*a*) person who officiates at a religious sacrament, especially communion (*b*) person who offers something, propositions someone
114 **glory** (*a*) renown (*b*) bliss in heaven
116 **respect** (*a*) deference due to me (*b*) social status (*c*) appearance
117 **reverence** (*a*) respect (*b*) holiness
119–20 **Thou'rt...to't** (as when a big winner wants to leave before the other gamblers have a chance to recoup some of their losses)
119 **great** big (but also often suggesting 'eminent' or 'high' rank or status; in contrast to the downward 'deep')
120 **deep** (*a*) big (*b*) hell-bound (*c*) financially embarrassed, having to dig deep in my purse (*d*) cunning (*e*) deep-voiced
121 **Lay me down** (*a*) deliver to me, by (*b*) lying down
reputatïon respectability (based, in a woman's case, upon chastity)
122 **stir'st** (*a*) make the slightest move (*b*) leave the building (*c*) cause trouble
nice shy, fastidious, delicate, minute, thin, unimportant
125 **art** (*a*) cunning (*b*) medical skill (to conceal her lack of virginity, or to end a pregnancy)
126 **fools** i.e. men too stupid to realize she's not a virgin, or foolishly willing to overlook her indiscretion
discovery exposure
127 **Society** (*a*) Society of Jesus, Jesuit organization (*b*) commonwealth, political alliance, confederation
130 **act** sexual act (which will give him the power of sexual blackmail)
awe (*a*) intimidate (*b*) inspire with appropriate reverence
132 **necessity** compelling need (sexual and political)
134 **policy** (*a*) government (*b*) statecraft, diplomacy
135 **a woman's tongue** proverbially, 'always in motion' (and unable to keep secrets)
137 **Take...both** (either by violating and then killing her, or killing and then violating: compare the necrophilia of *Lady*)
vowed since already vowed

VIRGIN WHITE QUEEN'S PAWN
Help, O help!

JESUIT BLACK BISHOP'S PAWN
Art thou so cruel for an honour's bubble
T'undo a whole fraternity, and disperse
The secrets of most nations locked in us?

VIRGIN WHITE QUEEN'S PAWN
For heaven and virtue's sake—

JESUIT BLACK BISHOP'S PAWN Must force confound noise?

A noise within

Ha! What's that? Silence, if fair worth be in thee.

VIRGIN WHITE QUEEN'S PAWN [*aside*]
I'll venture my escape upon all dangers now.

JESUIT BLACK BISHOP'S PAWN
Who comes to take me? Let me see that pawn's face
Or his proud tympanous master swelled with state wind
Which being once pricked i'th' convocation house
The corrupt air puffs out and he falls shriveled.

VIRGIN WHITE QUEEN'S PAWN
I will discover thee, arch-hypocrite,
To all the kindreds of the earth. *Exit*

JESUIT BLACK BISHOP'S PAWN Confusion!
In that voice rings th'alarum of my undoing.
How? Which way scaped she from me?

Enter Black Queen's Pawn [*from the Black House*]

JESUITESS BLACK QUEEN'S PAWN Are you mad?
Can lust infatuate a man so hopeful?
No patience in your blood? The dog-star reigns sure.
Time and fair temper would have wrought her pliant.
I spied a pawn of the White House walk near us,
And made that noise on purpose to give warning
(*Aside*) For mine own turn, which end in all I work for.

JESUIT BLACK BISHOP'S PAWN
Methinks I stand over a powder-vault
And the match now a-kindling. What's to be done?

JESUITESS BLACK QUEEN'S PAWN
Ask the Black Bishop's counsel. You're his pawn.
It's his own case. He will defend you mainly,

Enter Jesuit Black Bishop and Black Knight Gondomar [*from the Black House*]

And haply here he comes with the Black Knight too.

JESUIT BLACK BISHOP [*to his Pawn*]
O you've made noble work for the White House.
This act will fill the adversary's mouth
And blow the Luth'ran's cheek till't crack again.

BLACK KNIGHT GONDOMAR
This will advance the great monarchal business
In all parts well and help the agents forward.
What I have sev'n years laboured to accomplish

139 **bubble** something insubstantial and fragile: compared to *honour* because reputation is air, blown from the mouth like bubbles, and because the hymen is a thin membrane which when broken releases liquid

142 **confound** (*a*) confute (*b*) dumbfound
noise (*a*) shouting (*b*) slander. (But he may also mean 'a woman', whom he has reduced and objectified to the misogynist stereotype of 'noise-maker'; in which case *confound* could also mean 'ruin, overthrow, sully'.)

144 **venture...dangers** risk any danger for the sake of escape

145 **Who comes to take me?** Black Bishop's Pawn in this position could be attacked directly by White Knight's Pawn, a character who does not appear in the play; he more probably suspects White Bishop's Pawn (her former fiancè), which could move into position to take him if he dared take White Queen's Pawn—as he was just about to do.

146–8 **Or...shriveled** The implied image is of (white) sheep swollen from eating tansy weed, who will die if their abdomens are not punctured to release the 'corrupt air'.

146 **tympanous** resembling (*a*) abdominal swelling due to gas (*b*) false pregnancy, tumorous swelling in the womb (*c*) a hollow drum, which makes noise but has no substance (Middleton coinage)
master (probably the White Bishop)
state (*a*) exalted, dignified, ceremonial (*b*) a critically extreme case of
wind (*a*) speech (*b*) flatulence (*c*) vain notions

147 **convocation house** place where clergymen in the Church of England assemble; ecclesiastical Parliament

149 **discover** expose
arch-hypocrite (in contrast to 'archbishop'; he has probably just been talking about the White Bishop/Archbishop of Canterbury)

150 **kindreds** families, clans, peoples (emphasizing the 'incestuous' quality of his attempted rape)
Exit (In chess, she would become invulnerable to him by moving forward, past him. In any case, his fear of being taken by another piece prevents him from taking her when he has the chance.)

153 **hopeful** ambitious, promising

154 **dog-star** Sirius, most prominent in the heat of summer; astrologically associated with excess 'heat' (lust, rage, madness)

155 **temper** (*a*) temperament (*b*) moderation (*c*) tempering
pliant compliant, pliable, easily bent into the position desired

156 **I...us** (implying that some chess movements on the board are not visible on the stage, thus 'explaining' certain apparent irregularities in the alternation of moves: a white piece allegedly moved between the entrances of Black Bishop's Pawn and of Black Queen's Pawn.)

158 **turn** advantage
end...for purpose I work for in all my actions

159 **powder-vault** gunpowder-vault (recalling the 1605 Jesuit conspiracy to blow up the English Parliament)

162 **his...case** (*a*) a matter that concerns him (*b*) a lawsuit in which he will be a party or lawyer
mainly vigorously, loudly

162.1 ***Black Bishop and Black Knight*** (adjacent pieces, associated here and in 2.2, 3.1, and the *Early* version of 4.2)

163 **haply** (*a*) by chance (*b*) happily

164 **noble** (sarcastic)

165 **fill...mouth** be in the mouths of, talked about by, all our adversaries

166 **blow** inflate
Luth'ran's (dismissive Catholic term for all Protestants)
crack make an explosive noise as it splits in two, i.e. laugh
again once more (because Protestants have had little to smile about lately, after a series of defeats by Catholics)

167–8 **advance...forward** (sarcastic)

One minute sets back by some codpiece college still.
JESUIT BLACK BISHOP'S PAWN
I dwell not, sir, alone in this default.
The Black House yields me partners.
JESUIT BLACK BISHOP All more cautelous.
BLACK KNIGHT GONDOMAR
Qui cauté, casté. That's my motto ever.
I've travelled with that word over most kingdoms
And lain safe with all nations. Of a leaking bottom,
I have been as often tossed on Venus' seas
As trimmer fresher barques, when sounder vessels
Have lain at anchor (that is, kept the door).
JESUIT BLACK BISHOP [*to his Pawn*]
She has no witness then?
JESUIT BLACK BISHOP'S PAWN
None, none.
BLACK KNIGHT GONDOMAR Gross! witness?
When went a man of his Society
To mischief with a witness?
JESUIT BLACK BISHOP [*to his pawn*]
Be it thus then.
Away! Upon the wings of speed, take post-horse,
Cast thirty leagues of earth behind thee suddenly,
Leave letters antedated with our House
Ten days at least from this.
BLACK KNIGHT GONDOMAR Bishop, I taste thee.
Good strong episcopal counsel.—Take a bottle on't;
'Twill serve thee all the journey.
JESUIT BLACK BISHOP'S PAWN But, good sir,
How for my getting forth unspied?
JESUIT BLACK BISHOP There's check again.
JESUITESS BLACK QUEEN'S PAWN
No, I'll help that!
BLACK KNIGHT GONDOMAR
Well said, my bouncing Jesuitess!
JESUITESS BLACK QUEEN'S PAWN
There lies a secret vault.
[*She reveals a trapdoor*]
BLACK KNIGHT GONDOMAR [*to Jesuit Black Bishop's Pawn*]
Away, make haste then!
JESUIT BLACK BISHOP'S PAWN [*to Black Queen's Pawn*]
Run for my cabinet of intelligences
For fear they search the house.
[*Exit Jesuitess Black Queen's Pawn*]
Good Bishop, burn 'em rather.
I cannot stand to pick 'em now.
JESUIT BLACK BISHOP Be gone!
The danger's all in you.
Exit Jesuit Black Bishop's Pawn [*by the trapdoor.*
Enter Jesuitess Black Queen's Pawn from the Black
House with a cabinet]
BLACK KNIGHT GONDOMAR
Let me see, Queen's Pawn.
[*She gives him the cabinet*]
How formally he's packed up his intelligences!
He's laid 'em all in truckle-beds methinks,
And like court-harbingers he's writ their names
In chalk upon their chambers. *Anglica*!

170 **codpiece** baggy appendage to male trousers, in front of the genitals, often conspicuous and ornamented; hence, male genitalia, male lust. (The White Bishop's Pawn's 'cods', or testicles, were removed when he was castrated.)
college institutionalized association of clergymen (like the Society of Jesus) or scholars (also all male)
171 **default** culpable neglect of duty
172 **cautelous** crafty and cautious (and therefore less likely to get caught)
173 ***Qui . . . casté*** 'Whoever [is] discreet, [is] chaste' (i.e., if you're careful people will think you're virtuous)
174 **word** maxim
175 **lain** (*a*) resided (*b*) had sex
all (alluding to the Spanish global empire, and their reputation for indiscriminate miscegenation)
nations (*a*) races (*b*) classes
Of Despite being of, having
bottom hull, keel of a ship; but here a metaphor for his anal fistula
176 **tossed** (suggesting both the movement of a ship in rough water and a man moving up and down on top of a woman)
Venus' seas seas of lust. (In classical mythology, the goddess of love was born from the sea.)
177 **trimmer** better-made, better-equipped, better looking
fresher (*a*) not as old (*b*) not as overused, more vigorous
barques small ships (more manœuvrable than big ones)
sounder (*a*) more seaworthy (*b*) healthier, less diseased (*c*) more orthodox theologically (*d*) more ethical
vessels ships (but also in the Biblical senses 'persons' and 'bodies', both being seen as receptacles of the soul or of God's purposes)
178 **at anchor** (*a*) going nowhere (*b*) with a hanging prosthesis, like a detumescent penis
kept guarded (like a pimp)
182 **post-horse** fast horse, available for hire
184 **antedated** given an earlier, counterfeit date
185 **taste** (*a*) have a fore-taste or hint of what is to come (*b*) relish
186 **counsel** advice (but alluding to Catholic belief in the twelve 'Counsels' of Christ, not commandments but recommendations, as at Matthew 19:21)
bottle (comparing the Bishop's advice to a bottle of wine for the Pawn, or a bundle of hay for his horse)
on't of it
188 **forth** 'away' or specifically 'out' (of a residence), thus suggesting that the stage is here imagined as an indoor locale: the subsequent 'vault', 'cabinet', etc., reinforce this impression.
unspied (difficult, if he were outdoors now)
check (*a*) an obstacle, sudden interruption of movement (*b*) a threat to our king. (Black King would not be literally checked by taking of the Black Bishop's Pawn at this point, but politically the scandal would check his power, and require a response, either defensive evasion or counterattack.)
189 **bouncing** dancing, thumping, interjecting loudly (incongruous for a nun)
190 **vault** (*a*) underground room (*b*) burial chamber (*c*) deep pit; all these meanings, and theatrical terminology for the space under the stage, suggest (*d*) hell
191 **cabinet** case for safe storage of jewels, documents
intelligences news reports, secret documents
192 **they** i.e. the White House
193 **stand** remain
pick carefully select, cull
195 **formally** neatly
196 **truckle-beds** low beds stored below a higher bed (suggesting a cabinet with multiple drawers, one below another)
197 **court-harbingers** officers sent ahead of a royal progress to arrange lodgings
198 ***Anglica*** England (famous for its 'chalk' cliffs)

O, this is the English House. What news there, trow?
Ha? By this hand, most of these are bawdy epistles.
Time they were burnt indeed, whole bundles of 'em.
Here's from his daughter Blanch and daughter Bridget
From their safe sanctuary in the Whitefriars;
These from two tender Sisters of Compassion
In the bowels of Bloomsbury;
These from the nunnery without Temple Bar.
A fire, a fire—go, Jesuitess, a fire!
[Exit Jesuitess Black Queen's Pawn]
What have you there?

JESUIT BLACK BISHOP A note, sir, of state policy,
And an exceeding safe one.

BLACK KNIGHT GONDOMAR Pray, let's see't, sir.
'To sell away all the powder in the kingdom
To prevent blowing up.' That's safe; I'll able it.—
Here's a facetious observation now
That suits my humour better. He writes here
Some wives in England will commit adult'ry
And then send to Rome for a bull for their husbands.

JESUIT BLACK BISHOP
Have they those shifts?
[Enter Jesuitess Black Queen's Pawn from the Black House with fire]

BLACK KNIGHT GONDOMAR
O, no familiar breathing
Sweeter and subtler!—Here, wench, take these papers.
Scorch me 'em soundly, burn 'em to French russet,
And put 'em in again.

JESUIT BLACK BISHOP Why, what's your mystery?

BLACK KNIGHT GONDOMAR
O, sir, 'twill mock the adversary strangely
If e'er the house be searched. 'Twas done in Venice
Upon the Jesuitical expulse there,
When the inquisitors came all spectacled
To pick out syllables out of the dung of treason
As children pick their cherrystones, yet found none
But what they made themselves with ends of letters.—
Do as I bid you, pawn.
Exeunt [Black Knight Gondomar and Jesuit Black Bishop]

JESUITESS BLACK QUEEN'S PAWN
Faith, not in all.
I love roguery too well to let it fall.
Enter Black Knight's Pawn Gelder [from the Black House]
How now, what news with you?

BLACK KNIGHT'S PAWN GELDER The sting of conscience
Afflicts me so for that inhuman violence
On the White Bishop's Pawn, it takes away
My joy, my rest.

JESUITESS BLACK QUEEN'S PAWN
This 'tis to make an eunuch.
You made a sport on't then.

BLACK KNIGHT'S PAWN GELDER
Cease, Aggravation.
I come to be absolved for't. Where's my confessor?
Why dost thou point to th' ground?

JESUITESS BLACK QUEEN'S PAWN
'Cause he went that way.
Come, come help me in with this cabinet,
And after I have singed these papers throughly
I'll tell thee a strange story.

BLACK KNIGHT'S PAWN GELDER
If't be sad,
It's welcome.

199 **trow** hey (meaningless expletive)
200 **epistles** letters (but suggesting by contrast the New Testament epistles)
202 **Blanch** white (especially, white face paint; here suggesting a woman whose purity is artificial, a 'painted woman'); to whitewash; to cheat
Bridget (St Bridget founded a community of nuns named after her.)
203 **Whitefriars** district in London (and the 'White House') associated with (*a*) Catholics, and (*b*) prostitutes
204 **Sisters of Compassion** (*a*) nuns (*b*) women who take pity on men, and relieve their sexual frustrations ('nuns of the pity-fuck')
205 **bowels** centre, interior (but also the body organ associated with compassion)
206 **nunnery** (*a*) convent (*b*) brothel (a 'nunnery without temple', without a chapel or church)
without beyond
Temple Bar a gate marking the limit of the jurisdiction of the City of London, at the west end of Fleet Street; beyond it was the increasingly fashionable then-suburban 'West End' (associated with lawyers and courtiers) and Westminster (associated with Parliament)
208 **state policy** (*a*) government action (*b*) political cunning
209 **exceeding** exceptionally
210 **powder** gunpowder
211 **able** (*a*) enable, make possible (*b*) vouch for
213 **humour** mood, inclination
215 **bull** papal decree (in this case, to dissolve a marriage); but also suggesting that the 'horns' of the bull will belong to the husband/cuckold
216 **shifts** tricks, evasions, jokes
216.2 ***fire*** (emblematic of lust and damnation)
216 **familiar** (*a*) member of family or household (*b*) intimate acquaintance (*c*) officer of the Inquisition (*d*) familiar spirit, attendant devil
218 **me** for me
French russet the colour of imported coarse reddish-brown garments
219 **mystery** (*a*) secret purpose (*b*) state secret (*c*) theological doctrine, sacrament
222 **Jesuitical expulse** expulsion of the Jesuits
223 **inquisitors** (*a*) legal investigators (*b*) officials of the Catholic Inquisition (*c*) inquisitive persons
spectacled be-spectacled, wearing glasses, carrying magnifying glasses
224 **dung of treason** (*a*) brown mass deposited by traitors (*b*) shittiness of treason
225 **cherrystones** (which are not digested, and hence pass through the body into the excrement)
226 **ends of letters** alphabetical fragments
227 **all** everything
229 **sting of conscience** John 8:9
232 **make an eunuch** 'some are made eunuchs' (Matthew 19:12)
233 **sport on't** joke of it
Aggravation (using the abstract noun as though it were her name)
234 **absolved** forgiven by a priest (Catholic sacrament)
235 **point...ground** (a gesture which would usually indicate that someone was dead or in hell)
236 **in** go in
237 **singed** toasted
throughly thoroughly

JESUITESS BLACK QUEEN'S PAWN
'Tis not troubled with much mirth, sir.
Exeunt [with cabinet and fire]

2.2 *Enter Fat Bishop of Spalato [from the White House, dressed in white, followed by his servant,] a [white] Pawn*

FAT BISHOP OF SPALATO Pawn!
FAT BISHOP'S PAWN
I attend at your great holiness's service.
FAT BISHOP OF SPALATO
For 'great' I grant you, but for 'greatly holy',
There the soil alters. Fat cathedral bodies
Have very often but lean little souls,
Much like the lady in the lobster's head,
A great deal of shell and garbage of all colours,
But the pure part that should take wings and mount—
That's at last gasp, as if a man should gape
And from this huge bulk let forth a butterfly,
Like those big-bellied mountains which the poet
Delivers, that are brought to bed with mouse-flesh.
Are my books printed, Pawn? My last invectives
'Gainst the Black House.
FAT BISHOP'S PAWN Ready for publication,
For I saw perfect books this morning, sir.
FAT BISHOP OF SPALATO
Fetch me a few, which I will instantly
Distribute 'mongst the White House.
FAT BISHOP'S PAWN With all speed, sir.
Exit Fat Bishop's Pawn
FAT BISHOP OF SPALATO
It's a most lordly life to rail at ease,
Sit, eat, and feed upon the fat of one kingdom
And rail upon another with the juice on't.
I have writ this book out of the strength and marrow
Of six-and-thirty dishes at a meal.
Of all things I commend the White House best
For plenty and variety of victuals.
When I was one of the Black House professed,
My flesh fell half a cubit; time to turn
When my own ribs revolted. But to say truth,
I've no preferment yet that's suitable
To th' greatness of my person and my parts.
I grant I live at ease, for I am made
The Master of the Beds, the long-acre of beds,
But there's no marigolds that shuts and opens,
Flower-gentles, Venus-baths, apples of love,
Pinks, hyacinths, honeysuckles, daffadowndillies.
There was a time I'd more such drabs than beds;
Now I've more beds than drabs.
Yet there's no eminent trader deals in hole-sale
But she and I have clapped a bargain up,
Let in at watergate, for which I've racked
My tenants' purse-strings that they've twanged again.
Enter [from the Black House] Black Knight Gondomar with Jesuit Black Bishop [aloof off]
Yonder's Black Knight, the fistula of Europe,
Whose disease once I undertook to cure

2.2.0.1 *Fat Bishop* (from the outset he violates the rules of chess, by having changed sides from Black to White)
3 **'great'** very large
4 **cathedral bodies** (*a*) bodies as big as a cathedral, relative to a small parish church (*b*) bodies of bishops
6 **lady...head** calcareous structure in lobster, thought to resemble a seated woman
7 **garbage** entrails
8 **pure part** soul
9 **gape** (*a*) open the mouth wide to eat (*b*) gasp in pain (*c*) yawn
11 **the poet** Horace, criticizing a pompous author: 'mountains will labour; to birth will come a laughter-rousing mouse' (*Art of Poetry*)
12 **Delivers** reports (but punning on 'give birth', 'act as midwife')
bed child-bed
13 **last** latest (but they will also prove to be 'final')
15 **perfect** complete, finished
18–20 **It's...on't** (true both of the character and the actor)
19 **fat...kingdom** Genesis 41:4
20 **rail upon** (*a*) verbally abuse or attack (*b*) make jokes about
21 **marrow** vitality (but suggesting 'bone marrow', a delicacy)
22 **Of** given by, resulting from
meal See Additional Passage A.
26 **fell** shrank
cubit ancient measure of length (18–22 inches)
turn (*a*) reverse direction (*b*) repent, convert to a different religion (*c*) desert, change sides
29 **greatness** magnitude
person (*a*) identity, personality (*b*) body (*c*) character I am playing as an actor
parts (*a*) body parts (*b*) talents (*c*) roles played by an actor
31 **Master...Beds** governor of a hospital (a sinecure)
long-acre (*a*) long narrow field (*b*) disreputable street in London
beds (*a*) furniture associated with illness or sex (*b*) flower-beds
32–4 **marigolds...daffadowndillies** (flowers used as metaphors for women)
32 **marigolds** 'Mary's flowers' (which 'open' or 'spread' when the sun shines on them)
opens (*a*) florally (*b*) sexually
33 **Flower-gentles** floramour, 'flower of love' (amaranthus)
Venus-baths wild teasel (noted for their pricking)
apples of love tomatoes (but 'apples' is also slang for 'women' or 'breasts')
34 **Pinks** (*a*) *dianthus* (*b*) beautiful women (*c*) whores
honeysuckles (*a*) flowers from which honey can be sucked (*b*) woodbine, which entwines itself like ivy (*c*) persons to whom one addresses endearments (*d*) those who suck 'honey' = semen
daffadowndillies daffodils (in context, punning on 'down' as a female sexual position)
35 **drabs** strumpets
37 **trader** (*a*) pimp (*b*) dealer
hole-sale (*a*) sale of vaginas or other orifices (*b*) wholesale
38 **clapped** (*a*) copulated (*b*) shaken hands
39 **watergate** (*a*) vulva, entrance for water = semen (*b*) gate giving access to the Thames
racked (*a*) pulled tight (*b*) tortured
41 **fistula** suppurating pipe-like ulcer

With a High Holborn halter. When he did
Vouchsafe to peep into my privileged lodgings,
He found good store of plate there, and rich hangings.
He knew I brought none to the White House with me.
I have not lost the use of my profession
Since I turned White House Bishop.

Enter [Fat Bishop's] Pawn [from the White House] with books

BLACK KNIGHT GONDOMAR [*apart to Jesuit Black Bishop*]
Look, more books yet!
Yonder greasy gormandizing prelate
Has wrought our House more mischief by his scripts,
His fat and fulsome volumes,
Than the whole body of the adverse party.

JESUIT BLACK BISHOP
O 'twere a masterpiece of serpent subtlety
To fetch him on this side again.

BLACK KNIGHT GONDOMAR And then damn him
Into the bag for ever, or expose him
Against the adverse part (which now he feeds upon),
And that would double-damn him. My revenge
Has prompted me already. I'll confound him
On both sides for the physic he prescribed
And the base surgeon he provided for me.
I'll tell you what a most uncatholic jest
He put upon me once, when my pain tortured me:
He told me he had found a present cure for me,
Which I grew proud of and observed him seriously.
What think you 'twas? Being execution day,
He showed the hangman to me out at window,
The common hangman.

JESUIT BLACK BISHOP O insufferable!

BLACK KNIGHT GONDOMAR
I'll make him the balloon-ball of the churches,
And both the sides shall toss him. He looks like one,
A thing swelled up with mingled drink and urine,
And will bound well from one side to another.
Come, you shall write: our second Bishop absent
(Which has yet no employment in the game,
Perhaps nor ever shall—it may be won
Without his motion; it rests most in ours),
He shall be flattered with *sede vacante*.
Make him believe he comes into his place,
And that will fetch him with a vengeance to us,
For I know powder is not more ambitious
When the match meets it than his mind for mounting;
As covetous and lecherous—

JESUIT BLACK BISHOP No more now, sir.

Enter [from] the White House [White King James, White Queen of Bohemia, White Bishop of Canterbury, White Knight Charles, White Duke of Buckingham, and white pawns,] and [from] the Black House [Black King Felipe, Black Queen Maria, Black Duke Olivares, and black pawns]

Both the sides fill.

43 **High...halter** elevated hangman's rope (as in 'hang 'em high') **High Holborn** London street which runs from Newgate prison to the Tyburn gallows
44 **privileged lodgings** (*a*) exceptionally luxurious home (*b*) ecclesiastical sanctuary, where he cannot be seized or arrested
45 **good store** abundant supplies **plate** silver or gold kitchen utensils (useful for a glutton), but also 'bullion' and 'body armour' **hangings** draperies for a room or bed (useful for a lecher, but also in contrast to 'halter')
47 **use** (*a*) utilization for its intended purpose (*b*) sexual exploitation (*c*) revenue, especially passive income which does not require any work by the recipient **profession** (*a*) religious vows (*b*) religious beliefs (*c*) vocation, career
49 **greasy** (*a*) smeared with grease, from sloppy eating (*b*) anointed with chrism, as a former Roman Catholic priest (*c*) obscene **gormandizing** gluttonous
50 **wrought...mischief** caused...damage **scripts** writings
51 **fat** (*a*) obese (*b*) substantial (*c*) yielding a good return on investment (*d*) slow-witted, 'thick', lazy **fulsome** (*a*) full, plump, abundant (*b*) coarse (*c*) cloying (*d*) stinking (*e*) disgusting (*f*) morally filthy, obscene
52 **body** aggregate, corporation (but suggesting 'body politic', with the Fat Bishop as a single 'member' of the whole) **adverse party** opposed side (in a dispute, contest, game), faction (but also playing on the sense 'part, fraction' in opposition to earlier 'whole')
53 **serpent subtlety** Genesis 3:1
55 **bag** sack in which chess pieces were placed as they were captured; allegorically, often used as an image of the universality of death, which does not distinguish between social classes; Middleton makes it instead an image of hell. **expose** imperil, expose to danger
56 **Against** in opposition to
57 **double-damn** doubly condemn
58 **prompted** (*a*) incited (*b*) given a cue to **confound** (*a*) ruin (*b*) shame
60 **surgeon** (of lower prestige than other physicians, at the time, because of the messy manual nature of their work)
61 **uncatholic** (*a*) not universally applicable; specific to one person or patient (*b*) unusual (*c*) unsympathetic (*d*) unChristian (*e*) Protestant
63 **present** instant
64 **grew proud of** became elated about **observed** respectfully paid attention to
67 **common** ordinary (used for common criminals, not aristocrats or state officials)
68 **balloon-ball** large heavy inflated ball of strong double leather, used in a competitive game (very different from chess, whose rules Fat Bishop consistently violates)
71 **bound** bounce, rebound
72 **second Bishop** i.e. Black King's Bishop, probably representing the Bishop of Rome (= the Pope)
73 **Which** which position (of Black King's Bishop, or Pope), rather than 'which person', because the papacy was filled by a succession of different persons (and the same is imagined of the chess piece)
75 **motion** (*a*) activity (*b*) movement (of a chess piece)
76 **He** i.e. Fat Bishop ***sede vacante*** vacant seat (Latin), i.e. bishop's see, or papacy
78 **with a vengeance** (*a*) violently, emphatically (*b*) with a curse (*c*) in revenge
79 **ambitious** eager to rise to a higher position (literal, in the case of gunpowder)
80 **mounting** (*a*) rising socially and politically (*b*) riding, sexually (redefining 'match' as sexual)
82 **Both...fill** All the chess pieces cannot move at once; rather, this stage movement brings into view of the audience the full array, which has not been visible since the Induction.

[*Fat Bishop of Spalato presents his book to White King James*]

WHITE KING JAMES
This has been looked for long.

FAT BISHOP OF SPALATO
The stronger sting it shoots into the blood
Of the Black adversary. I'm ashamed now
I was theirs ever. What a lump was I
When I was led in ignorance and blindness!
I must confess, I've all my lifetime played
The fool till now.

BLACK KNIGHT GONDOMAR [*to Jesuit Black Bishop*]
And now he plays two parts: the fool and knave.

FAT BISHOP OF SPALATO [*to White King James*]
There's my recantation in the last leaf,
Writ like a Ciceronian in pure Latin.

WHITE BISHOP [OF CANTERBURY]
Pure honesty, the plainer Latin serves then.

BLACK KNIGHT GONDOMAR [*to Jesuit Black Bishop*]
Plague of those pestilent pamphlets! Those are they
That wound our cause to th' heart.

Enter Virgin White Queen's Pawn [*from the White House*]

JESUIT BLACK BISHOP
Here comes more anger.

BLACK KNIGHT GONDOMAR
But we come well provided for this storm.

WHITE QUEEN [OF BOHEMIA]
Is this my pawn? she that should guard our person?
Or some pale figure of dejectïon,
Her shape usurping? Sorrow and affrightment
Has prevailed strangely with her.

VIRGIN WHITE QUEEN'S PAWN
King of integrity,
Queen of the same, and all the House professors
Of noble candor, uncorrupted justice
And truth of heart, through my alone discovery—
My truth and honour wondrously preserved—
I bring into your knowledge with my suff'rings
(Fearful affrightments and heart-killing terrors)
The great incendiary of all Christendom,
The absolut'st abuser of true sanctity,
Fair peace and holy order, can be found
In any part o'th' universal globe,
Who—making meek devotion keep the door,
His lips being full of holy zeal at first—
Would have committed a foul rape upon me.

WHITE QUEEN [OF BOHEMIA] Ha?

WHITE KING JAMES
A rape? That's foul indeed, the very sound
To our ear fouler than the offence itself
To some kings of the earth.

VIRGIN WHITE QUEEN'S PAWN
Sir, to proceed:
Gladly I offered life to preserve honour,
Which would not be accepted without both,
The chief of his ill aim being at my honour,
Till heaven was pleased by some unlooked-for accident
To give me courage to redeem myself.

WHITE KING JAMES
When we find desp'rate sins in ill men's company,
We place a charitable sorrow there,
But custom and their leprous inclination
Quits us of wonder, for our expectation
Is answered in their lives; but to find sin—
Yea, and a masterpiece of darkness—sheltered
Under a robe of sanctity is able
To draw all wonder to that monster only
And leave created monsters unadmired.
The pride of him that took first fall for pride
Is to be angel-shaped and imitate
The form from which he fell, but this offender—
Far baser than sin's master, fixed by vow
To holy order (which is angels' method)—
Takes pride to use that shape to be a devil.
It grieves me that my knowledge must be tainted
With his infested name.
O rather with thy finger point him out.

VIRGIN WHITE QUEEN'S PAWN [*pointing*]
The place which he should fill is void, my lord;

82.1–2 ***Fat Bishop*...*King*** (a natural juxtaposition, since this second Bishop occupies the space adjacent to the King)
82 **looked for** expected
83 **stronger** (i.e., because anticipation increases desire, and therefore the public impact of his statement)
85 **I...ever** that there was ever a time when I was theirs (but also, ironically, 'that I have always been theirs')
lump (*a*) slow, dull person (*b*) mass of clay without shape or soul: God has the power 'of the same lump to make one vessel unto honour, and another unto dishonour' (Romans 9:21)
86 (punning on 'lead', heavy, non-precious metal)
87–8 **played | The fool** (*a*) acted like an idiot (*b*) acted the role of the clown in plays
88 **fool** (at the time, an alternative name for the Bishop in chess)
90 **leaf** sheet
91 **Ciceronian** imitator of the florid prose style of the Roman orator Cicero
pure classical (as opposed to medieval Latin, stigmatized as decadent by humanist scholars)
92 **plainer** i.e. more like Seneca or Tacitus, whose leaner prose style influenced writers like Francis Bacon and Middleton
98 **shape** (*a*) physical form (*b*) theatrical role, part
affrightment fear
100 **professors** adherents, advocates (but also, ironically, 'people who pay lip-service to')
101 **candor** (*a*) brilliant whiteness (*b*) purity, innocence
102 **alone** i.e. unassisted
103 **honour** (*a*) good reputation (*b*) virginity
108 **can** (that) can
110 **keep the door** i.e. serve the function of a pimp
121 **redeem** save, regain, free (physically and spiritually)
124 **custom** (*a*) their habitual sinfulness (*b*) our experience of them
leprous diseased (see 1.1.227)
125 **Quits** rids
wonder astonishment (negative or positive)
130 **created monsters** bizarre animals created by God (as opposed to artificial human monstrous behaviour)
unadmired not wondered at
131 **him...pride** Lucifer

His guilt has seized him—the Black Bishop's Pawn.
JESUIT BLACK BISHOP
Ha? Mine? My Pawn? The glory of his Order,
The prime and president zealot of the earth?
Impudent Pawn! For thy sake at this minute
Modesty suffers, all that's virtuous blushes,
And truth's self (like the sun vexed with a mist)
Looks red with anger.
WHITE BISHOP [OF CANTERBURY]
Be not thou drunk with rage too.
JESUIT BLACK BISHOP
Sober sincerity!—nor you a cup
Spiced with hypocrisy.
WHITE KNIGHT CHARLES
You name there, Bishop,
But your own Christmas bowl, your morning's draught
Next your episcopal heart all the twelve days,
Which smack you cannot leave all the year after.
BLACK KNIGHT GONDOMAR
White Knight, there is acknowledged from our House
A reverence to you, and a respect
To that loved Duke stands next you. With the favour
Of the White King and th'aforenamed respected,
I combat with this cause. [*To her*] If with all speed—
Waste not one syllable, unfortunate Pawn,
Of what I speak—thou dost not plead distraction
(A plea which will but faintly take thee off neither
From this leviathan scandal that lies rolling
Upon the crystal waters of devotion)
Or, what may quit thee more—though enough, nothing—
Fall down and foam, and by that pang discover
The vexing spirit of falsehood strong within thee,
Make thyself ready for perditïon.
There's no remove in all the game to 'scape it.
This Pawn, or this, the Bishop or myself,
Will take thee in the end, play how thou canst.
VIRGIN WHITE QUEEN'S PAWN
Spite of sin's glorious ostentatïon
And all blood-threats (that thunder cracks of pride,
Ush'ring a storm of malice), House of impudence,
Craft and equivocation, my true cause
Shall keep the path it treads in.
BLACK KNIGHT GONDOMAR
I play thus then:
Now in the hearing of this high assembly,
Bring forth the time of this attempt's conception.
VIRGIN WHITE QUEEN'S PAWN
'Conception'? Lord! How tenderly you handle it!
WHITE BISHOP [OF CANTERBURY]
It seems, Black Knight, you are afraid to touch it.
BLACK KNIGHT GONDOMAR
Well, its 'eruption'—will you have it so then?
Or you, White Bishop, for her? The more unclean,
Vile and impious, that you urge the strain to,
The greater will her shames' heap show i'th' end
And the wronged meek man's glory. The time, Pawn?
VIRGIN WHITE QUEEN'S PAWN
Yesterday's cursèd evening—
BLACK KNIGHT GONDOMAR
O the treasure
Of my revenge I can't spend all on thee;
Ruin enough to spare for all thy kindred too.
For honour's sake, call in more slanderers.
I have such plentiful confusïon,

143 **prime** first, foremost
president presiding, taking precedence over others
147 **drunk with rage** (because either drunkenness or anger could make a person red-faced)
148–9 **Sober sincerity ... hypocrisy** (qualities for which Puritans were often mocked)
148 **Sober** (*a*) not intoxicated (*b*) grave, serious (*c*) not showily dressed
cup (*a*) cupful of wine (*b*) chalice, eucharistic wine
150 **Christmas bowl** large drinking vessel (festive, rather than particularly Christian, and in contrast to the eucharist)
draught drink
151 **twelve days** (of Christmas)
152 **smack** flavour, relish
153 **White Knight** See Additional Passage B.
155 **favour** permission
157 **combat with** take arms against, oppose
cause (*a*) agent (*b*) accusation, legal charge (*c*) side of a controversy
159 **distraction** insanity
160 **faintly** (*a*) imperceptibly, scarcely (*b*) deceitfully (*c*) timidly, like a coward
take thee off remove you
161 **leviathan** (*a*) sea monster of enormous size, hence 'huge' (*b*) enemy of the Lord (Isaiah 27:1), hence Satan
scandal slanderous imputation (but also 'behaviour of a member of a religious order which discredits religion')
rolling (*a*) turning over on its axis, like a whale (*b*) coiling, like a snake (*c*) meditating, plotting. See also Psalms 37:5 'Roll thy way upon the Lord'.
162 **crystal** i.e. as transparent as ice or crystal
163 **quit** acquit
enough, nothing nowhere near enough
164 **foam** foam at the mouth
pang spasm
discover reveal
165 **spirit ... thee** demon who has strongly possessed you, and filled you with falsehood (since the devil was 'father of lies')
166 **Make ... ready** (then) prepare yourself
perditïon (*a*) destruction (*b*) damnation
167 **remove** move
168 **This ... this** (probably indicating Jesuitess Black Queen's Pawn and Black Knight's Pawn Gelder)
169 **how** however
170 **Spite of** despite
glorious (*a*) illustrious, impressive (*b*) boastful
ostentatïon (*a*) showing off (*b*) false show (*c*) presaging
172 **House of impudence** Ezekiel 3:7 ('all the house of Israel are impudent')
176 **Bring forth** reveal (but also suggesting 'give birth to')
attempt (*a*) violent assault upon a person, sexual assault (*b*) temptation
conception origin, initiation (but suggesting her literal 'impregnation'). In English law, sexual intercourse which resulted in pregnancy was regarded as consensual, and hence not rape.
178 **touch** handle directly (rather than point at, euphemistically allude to)
179 **eruption** bursting out (suggesting 'ejaculation')
181 **strain** (*a*) style (*b*) Biblical passage (*c*) injury (*d*) compulsion (*e*) strained interpretation
182 **shames' heap** mass of shame, collection of causes of shame (but also suggesting the grotesque image of a 'pile of human genitals', as in Rabelais's *Gargantua*)
188 **confusïon** (*a*) destruction of an adversary (*b*) confounding, refutation of an argument

I know not how to waste it. I'll be nobler yet
And put her to her own House.—King of meekness,
Take the cause to thee, for our hand's too heavy.
Our proofs will fall upon her like a tower
And grind her bones to powder.

VIRGIN WHITE QUEEN'S PAWN What new engine
Has the devil raised in him now?

BLACK KNIGHT GONDOMAR Is it he?
And that the time? Stand firm now to your scandal;
Pray, do not shift your slander.

VIRGIN WHITE QUEEN'S PAWN Shift your treacheries.
They've worn one suit too long.

BLACK KNIGHT GONDOMAR That holy man,
So wrongfully accused by this lost Pawn,
Has not been seen these ten days in these parts.

WHITE KNIGHT CHARLES How!

BLACK KNIGHT GONDOMAR
Nay, at this instant thirty leagues from hence.

VIRGIN WHITE QUEEN'S PAWN
Fathomless falsehood! Will it 'scape unblasted?

WHITE KING JAMES [*to Black Knight Gondomar*]
Can you make this appear?

BLACK KNIGHT GONDOMAR Light is not clearer.
By his own letters, most impartial monarch.

WHITE KING'S COUNSELLOR PAWN [*to White King James*]
How wrongfully may sacred virtue suffer, sir.

BLACK KNIGHT GONDOMAR [*aside to Jesuit Black Bishop*]
Bishop, we have a treasure of that false heart.

WHITE KING JAMES [*to White King's Counsellor Pawn*]
Step forth and reach those proofs.
[*White King's Counsellor Pawn advances toward Black Knight Gondomar*]

VIRGIN WHITE QUEEN'S PAWN [*aside*]
Amazement covers me.
Can I be so forsaken of a cause
So strong in truth and equity? Will virtue
Send me no aid in this hard time of friendship?

BLACK KNIGHT GONDOMAR [*aside to White King's Pawn*]
There's an infallible staff and a red hat
Reserved for you.
[*Black Knight Gondomar gives letters to White King's Counsellor Pawn*]

WHITE KING'S COUNSELLOR PAWN [*aside to Black Knight*]
O, sir endeared!

BLACK KNIGHT GONDOMAR [*aside to White King's Pawn*]
A staff
That will not eas'ly break, you may trust to't—
[*White King's Counsellor Pawn delivers letters to White King James*]
[*Aside*] And such a one had your corruption need of.
There's a state fig for you now.

WHITE KING JAMES Behold all,
How they cohere in one.
I always held a charity so good
To holiness professed, I ever believed rather
The accuser false than the profession vicious.

BLACK KNIGHT GONDOMAR
A charity like all your virtues else,
Gracious and glorious.

WHITE KING JAMES Where settles the offence,
Let the fault's punishment be derived from thence.
We leave her to your censure.

BLACK KNIGHT GONDOMAR Most just majesty!
[*Exeunt all the White House but White Knight Charles, White Duke of Buckingham, and White Bishop's Gelded Pawn, who stand aloof with the Virgin White Queen's Pawn*]

VIRGIN WHITE QUEEN'S PAWN
Calamity of virtue! My Queen leave me too?
Am I cast off as th'olive casts her flower?
Poor friendless innocence, art thou left a prey
To the devourer?

WHITE KNIGHT CHARLES
No, thou art not lost.

189 **waste** spend, use
190 **put her to** leave her to be judged by
191 **for our hand's** because our hand is
193 **engine** (*a*) device (*b*) ingenuity (*c*) large offensive weapon (*d*) trap
195 **to your scandal** (*a*) to the scandalous charge you've made (*b*) with the result that you will be engulfed by scandal
196 **shift ... slander** change your story, transfer your slander to another object
Shift change, rid yourself of (but also suggesting 'change clothes')
202 **unblasted** (*a*) not struck with lightning (*b*) not blighted by astrological influences (*c*) not discredited
203 **appear** evident, demonstrably so
207 **Amazement** consternation
208 **of a cause** (*a*) in a case (*b*) by a cause
209 **equity** (*a*) fairness, impartiality (*b*) jurisprudence based on general 'natural' principles, which overrule the letter of specific statute laws when those would produce an unjust result (a distinctive feature of English law, institutionalized in the Court of Chancery)
210 **of** for
211 **infallible** (*a*) certain, guaranteed (*b*) credited with the doctrinal infallibility which the Catholic church claimed for itself
staff ... hat insignia of office of Catholic cardinal
212 **staff** (playing on the sense 'means of support')
214 **corruption** (*a*) moral depravity (*b*) corrupt administration of public office
215 **state** political, pompous, high-class (sarcastic, as in modern 'royal')
fig (*a*) contemptuous gesture, thrusting the thumb between closed fingers (*b*) poisoned fig (method of assassination, associated with Italy and Spain)
217 **they** i.e. the letters, as internally consistent evidence against White Queen's Pawn
218 **charity** willingness to interpret actions charitably, sympathetically
219 **professed** vowed (but suggesting 'claimed, pretended')
220 **profession** (*a*) declaration, vow (*b*) religious order, religious community (*c*) occupation, vocation
222 **Where** wherever
224 **We leave her** (thus stranded, surrounded by Black pieces, she is an exposed pawn which can be taken at any point, and whose capture most of the White pieces will clearly do nothing to prevent or revenge)
226 **cast ... flower** Job 15:33 ('cast off his flower as the olive')
228–31 **WHITE KNIGHT ... WHITE DUKE** (adjoining chess pieces, who collaborate here and for the remainder of the play)

Let 'em put on their bloodiest resolutions,
If the fair policy I aim at prospers.—
Thy counsel, noble Duke?

WHITE DUKE OF BUCKINGHAM
For that work, cheerfully.

WHITE KNIGHT CHARLES
A man for speed now!

WHITE BISHOP'S GELDED PAWN
Let it be my honour, sir.
Make me that flight, that owes her my life's service.
[*Exeunt White Knight Charles, White Duke of Buckingham, and White Bishop's Gelded Pawn*]

BLACK KNIGHT GONDOMAR [*to Black House*]
Was not this brought about well for our honours?

JESUIT BLACK BISHOP
Push! That Galician brain can work out wonders.

BLACK KNIGHT GONDOMAR
Let's use her, as upon the like discovery
A maid was used at Venice: everyone
Be ready with a penance. Begin, majesty.—
[*To her*] Vessel of foolish scandal! Take thy freight.
Had there been in that cabinet of niceness
Half the virginities of th'earth locked up,
And all swept at one cast by the dexterity
Of a Jesuitical gamester, 't'ad not valued
The least part of that general worth thou'st tainted.

BLACK KING FELIPE [*to Virgin White Queen's Pawn*]
First, I enjoin thee to a three days' fast for't.

BLACK QUEEN MARIA
You're too penurious, sir. I'll make it four.

JESUIT BLACK BISHOP
I, to a twelve hours' kneeling at one time.

BLACK KNIGHT GONDOMAR
And in a room filled all with Aretine's pictures,
More than the twice twelve labours of luxury.
Thou shalt not see so much as the chaste pommel
Of Lucrece' dagger peeping. Nay, I'll punish thee
For a discoverer: I'll torment thy modesty.

BLACK DUKE OLIVARES
After that four days' fast, to th' Inquisition house,
Strengthened with bread and water, for worse penance.

BLACK KNIGHT GONDOMAR
Why, well said, Duke of our House, nobly aggravated!

VIRGIN WHITE QUEEN'S PAWN
Virtue, to show her influence more strong,
Fits me with patience mightier than my wrong.
Exeunt [*into the Black House*]

Finit Actus Secundus

Incipit Actus Tertius 3.1
Enter Fat Bishop of Spalato [*from the White House, dressed in white*]

FAT BISHOP OF SPALATO
I know my pen draws blood of the Black House.
There's ne'er a book I write but their cause bleeds.
It has lost many an ounce of reputation
Since I came of this side. I strike deep in
And leave the orifex gushing where I come.

229 **bloodiest** (probably alluding to Spanish and Catholic military attacks on Bohemia, the Palatinate and other Protestant strongholds in Germany)
231 **Thy counsel** (can I count on) your (*a*) advice (*b*) confidentiality, secrecy
233 **that** who
flight long, well-feathered arrow for long-distance shooting. (In chess, the Bishop was also called 'the Archer'; hence his pawn or instrument might be imagined as an arrow the archer shoots.)
235 **Push** (exclamation: 'fuck')
Galician belonging to Galicia, a north-western region of Spain
236 **use** treat (but suggesting 'sexually exploit')
discovery revelation
237 **maid** virgin
Venice (resisted Jesuits and the Inquisition; also associated with sexual license, and for thirty years the home of Pietro Aretino: see l. 248)
238 **penance** (*a*) act of self-mortification imposed by religious authority as consequence of sin (*b*) legal punishment
239 **Vessel** See 1.1.34.
foolish scandal (*a*) her naïve accusation (*b*) Black Bishop's Pawn's unwise scandalous behaviour
freight burden (of punishment), but also suggesting 'cargo' (of her sea-going 'vessel')
240 **niceness** fastidiousness, delicacy
242 **swept** (*a*) violently removed (*b*) taken up wholesale (of winnings from a gambling table)
cast (*a*) throw of an opponent in wrestling (*b*) glance (*c*) throw of the dice
dexterity (*a*) adroitness (*b*) base cunning (*c*) manual skill, use of the right hand
243 **gamester** (*a*) game-player (*b*) gambler (*c*) wrestler (*d*) happy-go-lucky person (*e*) playboy
245 **three days** i.e. the Black House does not 'take' the exposed pawn immediately (as they could do), because they assume it can be taken whenever they want
245–7 **fast . . . kneeling** (Catholic religious practices)
248 **Aretine's pictures** sixteen Italian images with caption-poems by Pietro Aretino, showing classical figures in various sexual positions
249 **twelve labours** (suggesting the labours of Hercules, imposed on him as a punishment)
luxury lust
250 **pommel** knob at end of hilt
251 **Lucrece** Roman wife who killed herself after having been raped (see *Ghost of Lucrece*)
252 **discoverer** (*a*) whistle-blower (*b*) person who exposes something that others want hidden (and who is therefore properly punished by being exposed to something she doesn't want to see)
253 **Inquisition** Catholic ecclesiastical tribunal for investigation of heretics; notorious for brutality of its interrogations and punishments
257 **my wrong** the wrong done to me
3.1.1 **of** (*a*) from (*b*) belonging to
pen (*a*) writing (*b*) quill for writing, its tip sharpened with a knife (*c*) stylus, tool for cutting designs in metal (*d*) penis
draws (*a*) extracts, as from an inkwell or artery (*b*) delineates
blood (*a*) life-blood (*b*) rage, passion (*c*) murder (*d*) sexual passion
3 **ounce** measure of fluids (like ink, blood) or solids (like the Fat Bishop)
4 **of** onto
strike penetrate
5 **orifex** orifice
gushing spouting (blood or sexual fluids)
come (punning on 'have an orgasm')

But where is my advancement all this while
I ha' gaped for't?
I'd have some round preferment, corpulent dignity
That bears some breadth and compass in the gift on't.
I am persuaded that this flesh would fill
The biggest chair ecclesiastical
If it were put to trial.
To be made master of a hospital
Is but a kind of diseased bedrid honour,
Or dean of the poor alms-knights that wear badges.
There's but two lazy beggarly preferments
In the White Kingdom, and I've got 'em both.
My merit does begin to be crop-sick
For want of other titles.

Enter [from the Black House] Black Knight Gondomar [aloof off]

BLACK KNIGHT GONDOMAR [*aside*]
O, here walks
His fulsome holiness. Now for the master-trick
T'undo him everlastingly (that's put home)
And make him hang in hell most seriously
That jested with a halter upon me.

FAT BISHOP OF SPALATO [*aside*]
The Black Knight! I must look to my play then.

BLACK KNIGHT GONDOMAR [*coming forward with a letter*]
I bring fair greetings to your reverend virtues
From Cardinal Paulus, your most princely kinsman.

FAT BISHOP OF SPALATO
Our princely kinsman, sayst thou? We accept them.
[*Fat Bishop of Spalato takes the letter*]
Pray, keep your side and distance; I am chary
Of my episcopal person.
I know the Knight's walk in this game too well;
He may skip over me, and where am I then?

BLACK KNIGHT GONDOMAR [*aside*]
There where thou shalt be shortly, if art fail not.

FAT BISHOP OF SPALATO (*reads the letter*) 'Right reverend and noble'—meaning ourself—'our true kinsman in blood, but alienated in affection, your unkind disobedience to the mother cause proves at this time the only cause of your ill fortune. My present remove by general election to the papal dignity had now auspiciously settled you in my *sede vacante*'—ha? had it so?—'which at my next remove by death might have proved your step to supremacy.'
How? All my body's blood mounts to my face
To look upon this letter.

BLACK KNIGHT GONDOMAR [*aside*]
The pill works with him.

FAT BISHOP OF SPALATO (*reads the letter*) 'Think on't seriously, it is not yet too late then, through the submiss acknowledgement of your disobedience to be lovingly received into the brotherly bosom of the conclave.'
This was the chair of ease I ever aimed at.
I'll make a bonfire of my books immediately.
All that are left against that side I'll sacrifice,
Pack up my plate and goods and steal away
By night at watergate. It is but penning
Another recantation and inventing
Two or three bitter books against the White House
And then I'm in o' t'other side again
As firm as e'er I was, as fat and flourishing.—
Black Knight, expect a wonder ere't be long.
You shall see me one of the Black House shortly.

BLACK KNIGHT GONDOMAR
Your holiness is merry with the messenger.
Too happy to be true; you speak what should be,
If natural compunction touched you truly.

8 **round** (*a*) financially generous (*b*) vigorously physical (*c*) honest, straightforward (*d*) plump
corpulent (*a*) big bulky (*b*) corporeal, in contrast to spiritual
dignity (*a*) high office (*b*) gravity
9 **compass** (*a*) scope (*b*) girth
10 **persuaded** convinced
11 **biggest chair** (*a*) most important office (*b*) largest seat
12 **put to trial** tried, given the chance
13 **master** governor
hospital any institution dedicated to unselfish physical and spiritual charity: place for (*a*) treatment of the ill or insane (*b*) lodging pilgrims (*c*) housing the destitute (*d*) educating the young
14, 16 **but** only
15 **dean of** ecclesiastical officer entrusted with pastoral care of
alms-knights military pensioners (derogatory Middleton coinage)
badges (*a*) identifying emblems of a knight (*b*) licences to beg
16 **lazy beggarly** (expressing the Fat Bishop's opinion of the people he is supposed to care for, but also describing his soliciting of undemanding but rewarding preferments)
18 **crop-sick** having something wrong with your craw or throat, or something stuck in your throat which causes you to gag (Middleton coinage)
19 **want** lack
20 **master-trick** (Middleton coinage, as in 'masterpiece')
21 **that's** (*a*) (modifying 'him') who is (*b*) (modifying 'undo') that is, meaning
put home (*a*) restored to his home, the Black House (*b*) brought back to his natural condition (*c*) put to death
23 **upon** (*a*) (modifying 'jested') about (*b*) (modifying 'halter') placed on
28 **side** half of the chessboard
chary careful about the preservation
30 **Knight's walk** unique movement of a knight in chess: two spaces in one direction and one space in a second direction, at a right angle to the first. Perhaps also suggesting that the actor playing Gondomar mimicked his way of walking (affected by his fistula? with his cane?).
31 **skip over** jump over (knights being the only chess pieces which can skip over others), jump up and onto
36 **mother cause** cause of Mother Church
45 **submiss** submissive
48 **chair of ease** comfortable ecclesiastical position offered by the *sede vacante* (but punning on the sense 'toilet')
59 **merry** joking
60 **happy** fortunate (as in 'too good to be true')
61 **compunction** compassion, remorse for sin (literally, the 'pricking' of conscience: hence 'touched')

O you've drawn blood, life blood—yea, blood of
 honour—
From your most dear, your primitive mother's heart.
Your sharp invectives have been points of spears
In her sweet tender sides. The unkind wounds
Which a son gives, a son of reverence 'specially,
They rankle ten times more than th'adversary's.
I tell you, sir, your reverend revolt
Did give the fearful'st blow to adoration
Our cause e'er felt. It shook the very statues,
The urns and ashes of the sainted sleepers.

FAT BISHOP OF SPALATO
Forbear, or I shall melt i'th' place I stand
And let forth a fat bishop in sad syrup.
Suffices, I am yours when they least dream on't.
Ambition's fodder (pow'r and riches) draws me.
When I smell honour that's the lock of hay
That leads me through the world's field every way.
Exit

BLACK KNIGHT GONDOMAR
Here's a sweet paunch to propagate belief on,
Like the foundation of a chapel laid
Upon a quagmire. I may number him now
'Mongst my inferior policies and not shame 'em.
But let me a little solace my designs
With the remembrance of some brave ones past
To cherish the futurity of project
Whose motion must be restless till that great work
Called the possession of the world be ours.
Was it not I procured a gallant fleet
From the White Kingdom to secure our coasts
'Gainst th'infidel piràte, under pretext
Of more necessitous expeditïon?
Who made the jails fly open, without miracle,
And let the locusts out—those dangerous flies
Whose property is to burn corn with touching?
The heretic granaries feel it to this minute,
And now they've got amongst the country crops
They stick so fast to the converted ears
The loudest tempest that authority rouses
Will hardly shake 'em off. They have their dens
In lady's couches; there's safe groves and fens.
Nay, were they followed and found out by th' scent,
Palm-oil will make a pursuivant relent.
Whose policy was't to put a silenced muzzle
On all the barking tongue-men of the time?
Made pictures, that were dumb enough before,
Poor suff'rers in that politic restraint?
My light spleen skips and shakes my ribs to think on't.
Whilst our drifts walked uncensured but in thought,
A whistle or a whisper would be questioned
In the most fortunate angle of the world

63 **primitive mother** true original mother (the Church)

64–5 **spears . . . sides** When Christ was on the cross, 'one of the soldiers with a spear pierced his side, and forthwith came there out blood and water' (John 20:34). Black Knight's image substitutes the Church for Christ (as Protestants accused Catholicism of doing).

69 **adoration** worship (not of God but of the Church, epitomized by its idolatrous statues and saints)

71 **sainted sleepers** dead saints ('sleeping' until the general resurrection)

72 **melt** 'dissolve in tears of compassion' (Psalms 119:28, Joshua 2:11, etc.); but also suggesting 'sweat excessively' (sweat was thought to be melted excess body fat)

73 **fat bishop** bishop entirely composed of lard (like the food sculptures popular in Renaissance banquets)
sad (*a*) massive, heavy (*b*) sorrowful
syrup thick liquid, usually sweet

74 **Suffices** suffice (to say)

75–7 **Ambition's . . . way** i.e. his ambition is an appetite which leads him by the nose, like a horse or donkey hungry for a small parcel of hay

78 **propagate** breed

81 **inferior policies** lesser stratagems
shame humiliate (by comparing to something unworthy)

82 **solace** comfort

83 **brave ones past** former splendid plots

84 **cherish** foster
project speculative scheming (political or commercial)

89 **infidel piràte** Ottoman raiders (based in the Mediterranean)

91 **jails . . . miracle** St Peter (Acts 12:4–11) and St Paul (Acts 16:23–6) were miraculously released from prison

92 **locusts** i.e. parasitic Catholic clergy, especially Jesuits, often compared (because of their alleged numbers, rapid movements, and destructiveness) to the plague of locusts in Exodus 10:1–20 and Revelation 9:3–7
flies (*a*) winged insects (*b*) flatterers, spies (*c*) devils, familiars which take the form of small insects infesting a human body

93 **burn** ruin, cause to wither as if scorched

94 **heretic** Protestant, English

95, 112 **country** i.e. rural areas which remained loyal to Catholicism longer than the cities

96 **converted** 'changed in religious belief' and 'illegally appropriated' (first occurrence)
ears i.e. listeners, people paying attention to Catholic propaganda (but punning on 'ears of corn')

98 **dens** (*a*) lairs (*b*) hideouts (Matthew 21:13: 'My house shall be called the house of prayer; but ye have made it a den of thieves'.)

99 **couches** (*a*) beds (*b*) lairs (*c*) floor or frame on which grain is laid for processing
there's (*a*) there exist (*b*) in lady's couches are

100 **scent** smell of a man or animal, tracked by hunting dogs

101 **Palm-oil** 'oil of angels' applied to an outstretched hand: a bribe (first occurrence)
pursuivant official with an arrest warrant

102 **muzzle** (*a*) face (*b*) contrivance which prevents an animal from biting

103 **barking** making noises like an angry dog: warning, rebuking
tongue-men public speakers, preachers (first occurrence)

104 **pictures** allegorical engravings, political cartoons

105 **politic restraint** clever crack-down on political dissidents

106 **light spleen** supposed anatomical source of laughter (as opposed to 'dark spleen', causing melancholy)

107 **drifts** intentions, plots (compared to a migratory herd)
uncensured but uncriticized, unprosecuted, uncensored except

109 **In the . . . world** in England (punning on Angle-land). The phrase goes with both the preceding and following sentence.

The court has held the city by the horns
Whilst I have milked her. I have got good sops too
From country ladies for their liberties—
From some, for their most vainly hoped preferments,
High offices i'th' air. I should not live
But for this *mel aerium*, this mirth-manna.

Enter Black Knight's Pawn Gelder [*from the Black House*]

My Pawn! How now? the news?

BLACK KNIGHT'S PAWN GELDER
Expect none very pleasing
That comes, sir, of my bringing. I'm for sad things.

BLACK KNIGHT GONDOMAR
Thy conscience is so tender-hoofed of late
Every nail pricks it.

BLACK KNIGHT'S PAWN GELDER
This may prick yours too,
If there be any quick flesh in a yard on't.

BLACK KNIGHT GONDOMAR Mine?
Mischief must find a deep nail and a driver
Beyond the strength of any machiavel
The politic kingdoms fatten to reach mine.
Prithee, Compunction, needle-pricked a little,
Unbind this sore wound.

BLACK KNIGHT'S PAWN GELDER
Sir, your plot's discovered.

BLACK KNIGHT GONDOMAR
Which of the twenty thousand and nine hundred
Fourscore and five? canst tell?

BLACK KNIGHT'S PAWN GELDER Bless us! so many?
How do poor countrymen have but one plot
To keep a cow on, yet in law for that?
You cannot know 'em all sure by their names, sir.

BLACK KNIGHT GONDOMAR
Yes, were their number trebled. Thou hast seen
A globe stands on the table in my closet?

BLACK KNIGHT'S PAWN GELDER
A thing, sir, full of countries and hard words?

BLACK KNIGHT GONDOMAR
True, with lines drawn some tropical, some oblique.

BLACK KNIGHT'S PAWN GELDER
I can scarce read; I was brought up in blindness.

BLACK KNIGHT GONDOMAR
Just such a thing, if e'er my skull be opened,
Will my brains look like.

BLACK KNIGHT'S PAWN GELDER
Like a globe of countries?

BLACK KNIGHT GONDOMAR
Yes, and some master politicïan
That has sharp state-eyes will go near to pick out
The plots and every climate where they fastened;
'Twill puzzl'em too.

BLACK KNIGHT'S PAWN GELDER
I'm of your mind for that, sir.

BLACK KNIGHT GONDOMAR
They'll find 'em to fall thick upon some countries;
They'd need use spectacles. But I turn to you now:
What plot is that discovered?

BLACK KNIGHT'S PAWN GELDER
Your last brat, sir,
Begot 'twixt the Black Bishop and yourself:
Your antedated letters 'bout the Jesuit.

BLACK KNIGHT GONDOMAR Discovered? How?

BLACK KNIGHT'S PAWN GELDER
The White Knight's policy has outstripped yours, it seems,
Joined with th'assistant counsel of his Duke.

110 **court . . . city** government has restrained the free enterprise and political action of urban capitalists
horns (suggesting the horns of citizen cuckolds, whose wives have been seduced by courtiers)

111 **milked** exploited, drained dry financially
sops literally, 'pieces of bread soaked in milk or wine'; figuratively, 'bribes'—alluding to the sops Aeneas threw to Cerberus, the dog who guarded hell, in order to pacify and distract him (first occurrence)

112 **country** rural (but punning on 'cunt': see next note)
liberties immunities (from prosecution for their Catholicism), but ironically suggesting 'licentiousness' and 'spiritual freedom from sin'

113 **vainly** futilely, arrogantly

113–14 **preferments . . . air** pie-in-the-sky promotions to important positions

115 **manna** divine bread which God sent to feed the children of Israel (Exodus 16)
mel aerium airy honey (an allusion to Virgil's *Georgics*, perhaps prompted by 'country' three lines earlier)

119, 122 **nail** (alluding to the Crucifixion)

120 **quick** sensitive
yard three feet—but punning, like 'prick', on the normal English word for 'penis' (which is thus equated with 'conscience')

122 **driver** hammer

125 **Compunction** 'Mr Remorse' (sarcastic; also suggesting the allegorical personal names used by Puritans)
needle-pricked (*a*) having suffered a very tiny puncture (*b*) with a small penis

128 **tell** (*a*) report (*b*) count

129 **plot** piece of land

130 **in law for** legally embroiled over

133 **closet** private room

135 **tropical** latitudinal (like the Tropics of Cancer and Capricorn); but also suggesting the Spanish global empire, and characterizing Black Knight's 'troped, figurative, not plain or literal' brain
oblique slanting downwards at something other than a right angle (like longitudinal lines on a globe); but also characterizing Black Knight's 'indirect, deviant' brain

136 **I . . . read** (Catholics did not encourage literacy, or personal Bible-reading, as Protestants did.)
blindness (standard Protestant characterization of Catholicism)

140 **state-eyes** (first occurrence)

141 **every climate** all the world's five climatic zones (again suggesting the global nature of Spain's empire and ambition)

146 **Begot . . . yourself** (suggesting male-male fornication)

The Bishop's White Pawn undertook the journey
Who, as they say, discharged it like a flight.
(I made him, for the business, fit and light.)

BLACK KNIGHT GONDOMAR
It's but a bawdy pawn out of the way a little.
Enough of them in all parts.

Enter Jesuit Black Bishop, [followed by Black King Felipe, Black Queen Maria, Black Duke Olivares, and pawns from] the Black House and [White King James, White Queen of Bohemia, White Bishop of Canterbury, White Knight Charles, White Duke of Buckingham, and pawns from] the White House

JESUIT BLACK BISHOP You have heard all then?

BLACK KNIGHT GONDOMAR
The wonder's past with me, but some shall down for't.

WHITE KING JAMES [*to Black House*]
Set free that virtuous Pawn from all her wrongs.
Let her be brought with honour to the face
Of her malicious adversary.

BLACK KNIGHT GONDOMAR Good! [*Exit a pawn*]

WHITE KING JAMES [*to White Knight Charles*]
Noble chaste knight (a title of that candor
The greatest prince on earth without impeachment
May have the dignity of his worth comprised in),
This fair delivering act virtue will register
In that white book of the defence of virgins,
Where the clear fame of all preserving knights
Are to eternal memory consecrated—
And we embrace, as partner of that honour,
This worthy Duke, the counsel of the act,
Whom we shall ever place in our respect.

WHITE DUKE OF BUCKINGHAM
Most blest of kings, throned in all royal graces,
Every good deed sends back its own reward
Into the bosom of the enterpriser,
But you t'express yourself as well to be
King of munificency as integrity
Adds glory to the gift.

Enter Virgin White Queen's Pawn [from the Black House]

WHITE KING JAMES Thy deserts claim it,
Zeal and fidelity.—Appear, thou beauty
Of truth and innocence, best ornament
Of patience, thou that mak'st thy suff'rings glorious.

BLACK KNIGHT GONDOMAR [*aside*]
I'll take no knowledge on't.—What makes she here?
How dares yon Pawn unpenanced (with a cheek
Fresh as her falsehood yet, where castigation
Has left no pale print of her visiting anguish)
Appear in this assembly? [*Aside*] Let me alone.
Sin must be bold; that's all the grace 'tis born to.

WHITE KNIGHT CHARLES
What's this?

WHITE KING JAMES
I'm wonderstruck.

VIRGIN WHITE QUEEN'S PAWN Assist me, goodness!
I shall to prison again.

BLACK KNIGHT GONDOMAR [*aside*]
At least I've 'mazed 'em,
Scattered their admiration of her innocence,
As the fired ships put in severed the fleet
In '88. I'll on with't. Impudence
Is mischief's patrimony.—Is this justice?
Is injured reverence no sharplier righted?
I ever held that majesty impartial
That like most equal heaven looks on the manners,
Not on the shapes they shroud in.

WHITE KNIGHT CHARLES That Black Knight
Will never take an answer. 'Tis a victory
To make him understand he does amiss
When he knows, in his own clear conscïence,
That he does nothing else. Show him the testimony,
Confirmed by good men, how that foul attempter
Got but this morning to the place from whence
He dated his forged lines for ten days past.

BLACK KNIGHT GONDOMAR
Why may not that corruption sleep in this
By some connivance, as you have waked in ours
By too rash confidence?

152 **flight** company of angels, dive of a trained hawk, volley of arrows
153 **I...light** i.e., by castrating him I relieved him of the weight of his testicles (called 'stones'), and thereby transformed him into a faster and more obedient animal (like geldings among horses), with the powers of angels (God's eunuch messengers, capable of flight)
business mission (but ironically suggesting, by contrast, the 'sexual business' which castration had made him *not* 'fit' to do)
fit (*a*) well adapted, qualified (*b*) inclined, disposed
light (*a*) quick (*b*) not heavy (but ironically suggesting 'lascivious')
159 **adversary** (the meaning of 'Satan', in Hebrew)
161 **impeachment** disparagement
163–6 **This...consecrated** i.e. his exoneration of Virgin White Queen's Pawn will be commemorated like the deeds of chivalric heroes
172 **enterpriser** person who attempts it
173 **you** i.e. for you
174 **munificency** splendid generosity
178 **mak'st...glorious** (like martyrs)
179 **take...on't** i.e. not admit to knowing about it
makes she is she doing
180 **unpenanced** who has not performed penance for her sin (only occurrence)
182 **visiting** punishing
186 **'mazed** astonished, confused
188–9 **fired...'88** English fireships scattered the Spanish Armada at Calais in 1588.
191 **sharplier** more keenly
193 **equal** equitable
manners behaviour
194 **shroud in** shelter under, are dressed or buried in. (Housing, clothing, and burial rituals all reflect class, status, and social allegiance, which are irrelevant to God.)
195 **take an answer** acknowledge a rebuttal
199 **attempter** would-be rapist
200 **but** only
202–3 **that...as** the same...which
202 **sleep in this** lie undetected in this (account of events)
204 **confidence** trust

WHITE DUKE OF BUCKINGHAM [*to White House*]
I'll undertake
That Knight shall teach the devil how to lie.

WHITE KNIGHT CHARLES
If sin were half as wise as impudent,
She'd ne'er seek farther for an advocate.

Enter Jesuitess Black Queen's Pawn [from the Black House]

JESUITESS BLACK QUEEN'S PAWN (*aside*)
Now to act treach'ry with an angel's tongue.
Since all's come out, I'll bring him strangely in again.—
Where is this injured chastity? this goodness,
Whose worth no transitory prize can equal?
This rock of constant and invincible virtue
That made sin's tempest weary of his fury?

BLACK QUEEN MARIA
What, is my Pawn distracted?

BLACK KNIGHT GONDOMAR [*aside*]
I think rather
There's some notable masterpiece of roguery
This drum strikes up for.

JESUITESS BLACK QUEEN'S PAWN
Let me fall with reverence
Before this blessèd altar.

[*She falls before Virgin White Queen's Pawn*]

BLACK QUEEN MARIA This is madness.

BLACK KNIGHT GONDOMAR [*aside*]
Well, mark the end. I stand for roguery still.
I will not change my side.

JESUITESS BLACK QUEEN'S PAWN [*to White House*]
I shall be taxed, I know.
I care not what the Black House thinks of me.

BLACK QUEEN MARIA [*to Black Knight Gondomar*]
What say you now?

BLACK KNIGHT GONDOMAR
I will not be unlaid yet.

JESUITESS BLACK QUEEN'S PAWN
However censure flies, I honour sanctity.
That is my object; I intend no other.
I saw this glorious and most valiant virtue
Fight the most noblest combat with the devil.

BLACK QUEEN MARIA
If both the Bishops had been there for seconds,
'T'ad been a complete duel.

WHITE KNIGHT CHARLES [*to Jesuitess Black Queen's Pawn*]
Then thou heard'st
The violence intended?

JESUITESS BLACK QUEEN'S PAWN
'Tis a truth
I joy to justify. I was an agent, sir,
On virtue's part, and raised that confused noise
That startled him and gave her liberty.

VIRGIN WHITE QUEEN'S PAWN [*to White Knight Charles*]
O 'tis a righteous story she has told, sir.
My life and fame stand mutually engaged
Both to the truth and goodness of this Pawn.

WHITE KNIGHT CHARLES [*to Black Knight Gondomar*]
Does it appear to you yet clear as the sun?

BLACK KNIGHT GONDOMAR
'Las, I believed it long before 'twas done.

[*The Black House speaks apart*]

BLACK KING FELIPE [*to Jesuitess Black Queen's Pawn*]
Degenerate!

BLACK QUEEN MARIA [*to Jesuitess Black Queen's Pawn*]
Base!

JESUIT BLACK BISHOP [*to Jesuitess Black Queen's Pawn*]
Perfidious!

BLACK DUKE OLIVARES [*to Jesuitess Black Queen's Pawn*]
Trait'rous Pawn!

JESUITESS BLACK QUEEN'S PAWN
What, are you all beside yourselves?

BLACK KNIGHT GONDOMAR But I:
Remember that, Pawn.

JESUITESS BLACK QUEEN'S PAWN
May a fearful barrenness
Blast both my hopes and pleasures, if I brought not
Her ruin in my pity, a new trap
For her more sure confusion.

BLACK KNIGHT GONDOMAR [*to Black House*]
Have I won now?
Did not I say 'twas craft and machination?
I smelt conspiracy all the way it went,
Although the mess was covered, I'm so used to't.

undertake bet
209 **him** Jesuit Black Bishop's Pawn
212 **rock** (in contrast to the 'rock', Peter, who founded the Roman church)
214 **distracted** deranged
216–17 **fall ... altar** (Protestants characterized such actions as an excessive, insane Catholic worship of merely human virtue.)
218 **mark the end** pay attention to the outcome
219 **taxed** criticized
221 **unlaid** moved from the position I've taken
222 **However ... flies** no matter how people rush to criticize
226–7 **If ... duel** (seconds sometimes fought in duels, as well as the principals; but duelling would be outrageously inappropriate for bishops)
233 **mutually** reciprocally, equally
236 **'Las ... done** (ambiguous)
238 **But I** except me
242 **Have I won** (The preceding exchanges resemble the gambling between spectators at exhibition chess matches: Black Knight, having seen the pawn ploy, wins the bet.)
245 **mess** dish of food

BLACK DUKE OLIVARES
That Queen would I fain finger.
BLACK KNIGHT GONDOMAR You're too hasty, sir.
If she were took, the game would be ours quickly.
My aim's at that White Knight, t'entrap him first:
The Duke will follow too.
JESUIT BLACK BISHOP I would that Bishop
Were in my diocese; I'd soon change his whiteness.
BLACK KNIGHT GONDOMAR
Sir, I could whip you up a pawn immediately.
I know where my game stands.
JESUIT BLACK BISHOP Do't, suddenly!
Advantage least must not be lost in this play.
[*Black Knight Gondomar takes White King's Counsellor Pawn*]
BLACK KNIGHT GONDOMAR
Pawn, thou art ours.
WHITE KNIGHT CHARLES [*to White House*]
He's taken by default,
By wilful negligence. Guard the sacred persons.
Look well to the White Bishop, for that Pawn
Gave guard to th' Queen and him in the third place.
BLACK KNIGHT GONDOMAR
See what sure piece you lock your confidence in.
I made this Pawn here by corruption ours,
As soon as honour by creation yours.
This whiteness upon him is but the leprosy
Of pure dissimulation. View him now:
His upper garment being taken off [*the White King's Counsellor Pawn*], *he appears black underneath*
His heart and his intents are of our colour.
WHITE KING JAMES
Most dangerous hypocrite!
WHITE QUEEN [OF BOHEMIA]
One made against us!
WHITE DUKE OF BUCKINGHAM
His truth of their complexion!
WHITE KING JAMES [*to White King's Counsellor Pawn*]
Has my goodness,
Clemency, love and favour gracious, raised thee
From a condition next to popular labour?
Took thee from all the dubitable hazards
Of fortune, her most unsecure adventures,
And grafted thee into a branch of honour?
And dost thou fall from the top bough by th' rottenness
Of thy alone corruption?—like a fruit
That's over-ripened by the beams of favour?
Let thy own weight reward thee. I ha' forgot thee.
Integrity of life is so dear to me,
Where I find falsehood or a crying trespass,
Be it in any whom our grace shines most on,
I'd tear 'em from my heart.
WHITE BISHOP [OF CANTERBURY]
Spoke like heaven's substitute.
WHITE QUEEN [OF BOHEMIA] [*to Black House*]
You have him, we can spare him, and his shame
Will make the rest look better to their game.
BLACK KNIGHT GONDOMAR
The more cunning we must use then.
WHITE KNIGHT CHARLES We shall match you,
Play how you can—perhaps and mate you too.
FAT BISHOP OF SPALATO
Is there so much amazement spent on him
That's but half black? There might be hope of that man,
But how will this House wonder if I stand forth
And show a whole one? instantly discover
One that's all black, where there's no hope at all?
WHITE KING JAMES
I'll say thy heart then justifies thy books.
I long for that discovery.

246 DUKE (The speech is spoken by Black King in *Early*. The Duke of Bavaria specifically, and the Habsburg dynasty more generally, wanted possession of the Palatinate, the territory ruled by the Queen of Bohemia and her husband.)
246–53 **That ... play** (Kibitzing—a public debate about the next move—was permitted in early chess matches.)
246 **fain** gladly
finger (*a*) steal (*b*) sexually handle (but also literally picking up with the fingers a captured chess piece)
246–9 **You're ... follow too** (Black Knight rebukes Black Duke for imagining that a chess game against a skilful opponent can be won by immediately attacking the opponent's Queen, before a single piece has been captured. He instead proposes a long-term, indirect strategy.)
246 **hasty** (Good chess players think before they move, rather than leaping at the first opportunity, which may be a trap.)
249–50 **Bishop ... diocese** (Black Queen's Bishop and White Queen's Bishop are on different coloured squares; one can never take the other.)
250 **diocese** (punning on 'dye')
253 **play** (*a*) game (*b*) theatrical performance
255 **sacred persons** i.e. White King and Queen
257 **Gave ... place** (because a pawn can attack diagonally to the left or right, a stationary White King's Pawn defends the third rank in front of both the White Queen and White King's Bishop)
258 **sure** reliable
260 **honour ... yours** investiture with a title (made him) yours
265 **complexion** (*a*) nature (*b*) skin colour. Anti-Spanish propaganda emphasized their dark skin, as a sign of their mixture with Arabs, Jews, and Africans.
268 **dubitable** doubtful
269 **fortune** chance
adventures risks (of business, in particular)
270 **grafted ... honour** united you with an honourable family (using the metaphor of a 'family tree')
272 **alone** unique
274 **weight** (which will cause him to fall: from power, and more generally downwards toward hell, at the centre of the earth)
276 **crying** crying out for punishment
278 **'em** 'them' or 'him'
heaven's substitute God's deputy on earth
280 **better** more carefully (crucial in chess, where everything is visible, and failure results from inattention)
281 **match** equal (but also alluding to the proposed 'match' linking White House England to Black House Spain)
282 **mate** checkmate (but also suggesting 'marry')

FAT BISHOP OF SPALATO Look no farther then.
Bear witness all the House, I am the man,
And turn myself into the Black House freely.
[*Fat Bishop of Spalato crosses to the Black House*]
I am of this side now.

WHITE KING JAMES Monster ne'er matched him!

FAT BISHOP OF SPALATO [*to Black Knight Gondomar*]
This is your noble work, Knight.

BLACK KNIGHT GONDOMAR [*aside*] Now I'll halter *him.*

FAT BISHOP OF SPALATO [*to White House*]
Next news you hear, expect my books against you
Printed at Douai, Brussels, or Spalato.

WHITE KING JAMES [*to White House*]
See his goods seized on.

FAT BISHOP OF SPALATO 'Las, they were all conveyed
Last night by water to a tailor's house,
A friend of the Black cause.

WHITE KNIGHT CHARLES A prepared hypocrite!

WHITE DUKE OF BUCKINGHAM
Premeditated turncoat!
Exeunt [*all of White House but Virgin White Queen's Pawn and White King's Counsellor Pawn*]

FAT BISHOP OF SPALATO [*to the departing White House*]
Yes, rail on!
I'll reach you in my writings when I'm gone.

BLACK KNIGHT GONDOMAR [*aside to Black House*]
Flatter him awhile with honours, till we put him
Upon some dangerous service and then burn him.

BLACK KING FELIPE [*to Fat Bishop of Spalato*]
This came unlooked for.

BLACK DUKE OLIVARES [*to Fat Bishop of Spalato*]
How we joy to see you!

FAT BISHOP OF SPALATO
Now I'll discover all the White House to you.

BLACK DUKE OLIVARES
Indeed, that will both reconcile and raise you.
[*Exeunt Fat Bishop of Spalato with all of Black House but Black Knight Gondomar and Jesuitess Black Queen's Pawn*]

WHITE KING'S COUNSELLOR PAWN [*to Black Knight Gondomar*]
I rest upon you, Knight, for my advancement.

BLACK KNIGHT GONDOMAR
O for the staff, the strong staff, that will hold
And the red hat fit for the guilty mazard?
Into the empty bag! Know thy first way.
Pawns that are lost are ever out of play.

WHITE KING'S COUNSELLOR PAWN
How's this?

BLACK KNIGHT GONDOMAR
No replications. You know me.
No doubt ere long you'll have more company.
The bag is big enough; 'twill hold us all.
Exeunt [*Black Knight Gondomar, taking off White King's Counsellor Pawn*]

VIRGIN WHITE QUEEN'S PAWN [*to Black Queen's Pawn*]
I sue to thee: prithee, be one of us.
Let my love win thee. Thou'st done truth this day,
And yesterday my honour, noble service.
The best Pawn of our house could not transcend it.

JESUITESS BLACK QUEEN'S PAWN
My pity flamed with zeal, especially
When I foresaw your marriage—then it mounted.

VIRGIN WHITE QUEEN'S PAWN
How, marriage, sayst thou?

JESUITESS BLACK QUEEN'S PAWN
I saw the man.

VIRGIN WHITE QUEEN'S PAWN The man?

JESUITESS BLACK QUEEN'S PAWN
An absolute honest gentleman, a complete one—
You'll say so when you see him—heir to three red hats,
Besides his general hopes in the Black House.

VIRGIN WHITE QUEEN'S PAWN
Sure thou art much mistaken for this man.
Why, I have promised single life to all my affections.

JESUITESS BLACK QUEEN'S PAWN
Promise you what you will, or I, or all on's,
There's a fate rules, and overrules, us all, methinks.

VIRGIN WHITE QUEEN'S PAWN
How came you to see or know this mystery?

JESUITESS BLACK QUEEN'S PAWN
A magical glass I bought of an Egyptian
(Whose stone retains that speculative virtue)
Presented the man to me. Your name brings him
As often as I use it, and methinks
I never have enough—person and postures
Are all so pleasing.

VIRGIN WHITE QUEEN'S PAWN
This is wondrous strange.
The faculties of soul are still the same.
I cannot feel one motion tend that way.

JESUITESS BLACK QUEEN'S PAWN
We do not always feel the faith we live by,
Nor ever see our growth, yet both work upward.

VIRGIN WHITE QUEEN'S PAWN
'Twas well applied. But may I see him too?

293 **halter *him*** hang him, instead of me (in contrast to the Fat Bishop's joke about hanging the Black Knight, at 2.2.63–7)
305 **raise** promote
306 **rest** depend
307 **staff...hold** Jeremiah 48:17 ('How is the strong staff broken!')
308 **mazard** head (literally, 'drinking cup')
311 **replications** rejoinders (legal term)
313 **'twill** 'it is big enough to' (but also an unintentionally ironic prediction: 'it will') **us all** all of the Black House (who will be damned), or all of humanity (who will die)
320 **marriage** See Additional Passage C.
322 **heir...hats** (as though cardinalships were inherited, like earldoms)
326 **on's** of us (humans)
329 **glass** mirror **Egyptian** gypsy (famous for fortune-telling)
330 **stone** polished surface **speculative virtue** image-making power
335 **faculties** dispositions
336 **motion** (*a*) stirring, inclination, desire (*b*) working of God within the soul

JESUITESS BLACK QUEEN'S PAWN

Surely you may, without all doubt or fear—
Observing the right use, as I was taught it,
Not looking back or questioning the spectre.

VIRGIN WHITE QUEEN'S PAWN

That's no hard observation. Trust it with me.
Is't possible? I long to see this man.

JESUITESS BLACK QUEEN'S PAWN

Why then, observe: I'll ease you instantly.
This is the room he did appear to me in,
[*She reveals a large mirror*]
And—look you—this, the magical glass that showed him.

VIRGIN WHITE QUEEN'S PAWN

I find no motion yet. What should I think on't?
A sudden fear invades me, a faint trembling
Under this omen,
As is oft felt the panting of a turtle
Under a stroking hand.

JESUITESS BLACK QUEEN'S PAWN

That bodes good luck still—
Sign you shall change state speedily, for that trembling
Is always the first symptom of a bride.
For any vainer fears that may accompany
His apparition, by my truth to friendship
I quit you of the least. Never was object
More gracefully presented. The very air
Conspires to do him honour and creates
Sweet vocal sounds, as if a bridegroom entered
(Which argues the blest harmony of your loves).

VIRGIN WHITE QUEEN'S PAWN

And will the using of my name produce him?

JESUITESS BLACK QUEEN'S PAWN

Nay, of yours only, else the wonder halted.
To clear you of that doubt, I'll put the diff'rence
In practice, the first thing I do, and make
His invocation in the name of others.

VIRGIN WHITE QUEEN'S PAWN

That will satisfy me much.

JESUITESS BLACK QUEEN'S PAWN

It shall be done.
[*She speaks*] *the invocation*
Thou whose gentle form and face
Filled lately this Egyptic glass,
By th'imperious pow'rful name
And the universal fame
Of the mighty Black House Queen,
I conjùre thee to be seen.
What, see you nothing yet?

VIRGIN WHITE QUEEN'S PAWN

Not any part.
Pray, try another.

JESUITESS BLACK QUEEN'S PAWN

You shall have your will.
[*She speaks the invocation*]
I double my command and power
And at the instant of this hour
Invoke thee, in the White Queen's name,
With stay for time, and shape the same.
What see you yet?

VIRGIN WHITE QUEEN'S PAWN

There's nothing shows at all.

JESUITESS BLACK QUEEN'S PAWN

My truth reflects the clearer. Then now fix
And bless your fair eyes with your own forever.
[*She speaks the invocation*]
Thou well-composed, by fate's hand drawn
To enjoy the White Queen's Pawn,
Of whom thou shalt (by virtue met)
Many graceful issues get:
By the whiteness of her name,
By her fair and fruitful love,
By her truth that mates the dove,
By the meekness of her mind,
By the softness of her kind,
By the lustre of her grace,
Music
By all these thou art summoned to this place.

341 **right use** proper ceremony
342 **spectre** apparition
343 **observation** observance, rule
345–6 **Why . . . This** For a scene apparently omitted in performance, see Additional Passages.
351 **turtle** dove
353 **state** social condition, marital status
357 **quit** relieve
object spectacle
363 **else** otherwise
wonder (*a*) miracle (*b*) admiration, amazement
halted (*a*) limped (*b*) faltered, failed, proved false
366 **His invocation** invocation of him
368 **gentle** well-born, noble
369 **Egyptic** Egyptian, gypsy
370 **imperious** (*a*) imperial, majestic (*b*) tyrannical, domineering
371 **fame** (*a*) reputation (*b*) infamy
379 **stay** pause
381 **Then** therefore
fix focus, fasten
383 **well-composed** well-balanced, harmoniously combining the essential physiological elements ('humours')
drawn (*a*) sketched, created (*b*) pulled, moved
385–6 **Of . . . get** on whom you will beget many beautiful children
387 **whiteness** unspottedness
name reputation (but also, here, literal cognomen)
389 **truth** fidelity
mates (*a*) matches, equals (*b*) marries
dove (proverbially monogamous)
391 **kind** i.e. sex, gender (women being traditionally physically softer and emotionally more 'tender' than men)
392 **lustre** luminous beauty, glory
grace attractiveness (but also God-given virtue)
392.1 ***Music*** Offstage instrumental music, because it came from an invisible source, often suggested or accompanied supernatural effects.
393 **By** (*a*) in the name of (*b*) by means of

Hark how the air, enchanted with your praises
And his approach, those words to sweet notes raises.

The Jesuit Black Bishop's Pawn comes like an apparition, in rich attire, and presents himself before the glass; then exit

VIRGIN WHITE QUEEN'S PAWN
O let him stay awhile! a little longer!
JESUITESS BLACK QUEEN'S PAWN That's a good hearing.
VIRGIN WHITE QUEEN'S PAWN
If he be mine, why should he part so soon?
JESUITESS BLACK QUEEN'S PAWN
Why, this is but the shadow of yours. How do you?
VIRGIN WHITE QUEEN'S PAWN
O I did ill to give consent to see it.
What certainty is in our bloods, our states?
What we still write is blotted out by fates.
Our wills are like a cause that is law-tossed:
What one court orders, is by another crossed.
JESUITESS BLACK QUEEN'S PAWN
I find no fit place for this passion here.
It's merely an intruder. He's a gentleman,
Most wishfully composed. Honour grows on him
And wealth piled up for him; has youth enough too,
And yet in the sobriety of his countenance,
Grave as a tetrarch—which is gracïous
I'th' eye of modest pleasure. Where's the emptiness?
What can you more request?
VIRGIN WHITE QUEEN'S PAWN I do not know
What answer yet to make. It does require
A meeting 'twixt my fear and my desire. *Exit*
JESUITESS BLACK QUEEN'S PAWN
She's caught—and (which is strange) by her most wronger. *Exit*

Finit Actus Tertius

Incipit Actus Quartus 4.1

Enter [from the Black House] Black Knight's Pawn Gelder meeting the Jesuit Black Bishop's Pawn (in his gallant habit, richly accoutred)

BLACK KNIGHT'S PAWN GELDER [*aside*]
It's he, my confessor. He might ha' passed me
Sev'n years together, had I not by chance
Advanced mine eye upon that lettered hatband,
The Jesuitical symbol to be known by,
Worn by the brave collegians with consent.
It's a strange habit for a holy Father,
A president of poverty, especially;
But we the sons and daughters of obedience
Dare not once think awry, but must confess ourselves
As humbly to the Father of that feather,
Long spur and poniard, as to the alb and altar
(And happy we're so highly graced t'attain to't).—
Holy and reverend!
JESUIT BLACK BISHOP'S PAWN
How hast found me out?
BLACK KNIGHT'S PAWN GELDER
O sir, put on the sparkling'st trim of glory,

394 **enchanted** (*a*) charmed, delighted (*b*) literally bewitched, deluded
your praises words praising you
395 **sweet** harmonious (and therefore associated with both love and God)
raises (*a*) rouses (*b*) utters with force and animation (*c*) elevates [implying the superiority of music to words]
395.1–2 ***comes...apparition*** (not 'dressed like' a ghost or spirit, but apparently 'moving like' one)
395.2 ***in rich attire*** i.e. disguised (a move not permissible in chess: one piece cannot pretend to be another)
395.2–3 ***presents...glass*** i.e., stands in such a way that White Queen's Pawn sees his reflection in the mirror (without realizing that it is only a reflection)
398 **part** leave
399 **but** only
shadow foreshadowing, image (but also literally 'reflection' and 'delusion', and a darkness cast by interception of light)
401 **bloods** (*a*) emotions (*b*) physical desires, lusts (*c*) pedigrees
states (*a*) physical, mental, spiritual conditions (*b*) social status (*c*) governments, courts (*d*) nations
402 **still** continually
fates (*a*) three mythological goddesses of destiny (*b*) predestined events
403 **wills** intentions, desires (but suggesting the literal 'last will and testament')
cause legal dispute, case
404 **crossed** obstructed, cancelled
405 **passion** (*a*) emotion (*b*) outburst
407 **grows on** is increasingly bestowed upon
410 **Grave** sober, serious
tetrarch subordinate governor (Roman history)
411 **I'th'...pleasure** i.e. when observed by someone whose pleasures are bashful and restrained—in implicit contrast to 'inside the eye of immodest pleasure' (in the vagina)
eye (*a*) organ of vision (*b*) slang for 'vagina'
modest (a virtue prized in women, whose desires would be considered more decent if they were attracted to 'sober-looking' men)
4.1.0.4 ***in...habit*** disguised like a rich man-about-town or lady's man
1–3 **He...hatband** (He recognizes him only because of a secret sign, which the White Queen's Pawn does not know.)
2 **together** in a row
3 **that...hatband** a gold hatband, studded with coded letters
5 **brave** well-dressed, dolled-up
collegians students or graduates of a Jesuit seminary
with consent by mutual agreement
6 **holy Father** priest (but continuing the play on 'father' and 'daughter' which makes Black Bishop Pawn's sexual pursuit of White Queen's Pawn seem incestuous)
7 **president** leading example, model or precedent to inspire others
poverty (one of the Jesuit vows)
9 **think awry** 'have even an erring thought' (since sinful thoughts as well as actions had to be confessed) or 'think differently' (than the Catholic Church demands)
10 **feather** (frivolous expensive fashionable ornament)
11 **Long** (i.e. decorative)
poniard dagger (duelling weapon, inappropriate for a priest)
alb and altar ecclesiastical accessories associated with Catholics (suggesting a worship of things, rather than a direct relationship to God)
12 **happy** delighted, lucky
14 **trim** fancy dress: 'And when thou shalt be destroyed, what wilt thou do?... thou shalt trim thyself in vain' (Jeremiah 4:30)

Perfection will shine foremost—and I knew you
By the Catholical mark you wear about you,
The mark above your forehead.

JESUIT BLACK BISHOP'S PAWN
Are you grown so ambitious
In your observance? Well, your busïness?
I have my game to follow.

BLACK KNIGHT'S PAWN GELDER
And I have a worm
Follows *me* so that I can follow *no* game.
The most faint-hearted Pawn (if he could see his play)
Might snap me up at pleasure. I desire, sir,
To be absolved. My conscience being at ease,
I could then with more courage ply my game.

JESUIT BLACK BISHOP'S PAWN
'Twas a base fact.

BLACK KNIGHT'S PAWN GELDER
'Twas to a schismatic Pawn, sir.

JESUIT BLACK BISHOP'S PAWN
What's that to the nobility of revenge?
Suffices I have neither will nor power
To give you absolution for that violence.
Make your petition to the Penance Chamber.
If the tax register relieve you in't,
By the Black Bishop's clemency, you have wrought
out
A singular piece of favour with your money.
It's all your refuge now.

BLACK KNIGHT'S PAWN GELDER
This sting shoots deeper.
Exit

Enter [aloof off] Virgin White Queen's Pawn and Jesuitess Black Queen's Pawn

JESUIT BLACK BISHOP'S PAWN [*aside*]
Yonder's my game, which (like a politic chessmaster)
I must not seem to see.

VIRGIN WHITE QUEEN'S PAWN
O my heart! 'Tis he.

JESUITESS BLACK QUEEN'S PAWN That 'tis.

VIRGIN WHITE QUEEN'S PAWN
The very self-same that the magical mirror
Presented lately to me.

JESUITESS BLACK QUEEN'S PAWN
And how like
A most regardless stranger he walks by,
Merely ignorant of his fate! You are not minded,
The principal'st part of him. What strange mysteries
Inscrutable love works by!

VIRGIN WHITE QUEEN'S PAWN
The time, you see,
Is not yet come.

JESUITESS BLACK QUEEN'S PAWN
But 'tis in our pow'r now
To bring time nearer—knowledge is a mast'ry—
And make *it* observe *us*, and not we it.

VIRGIN WHITE QUEEN'S PAWN
I would force nothing from its proper virtue.
Let time have his full course. I'd rather die
The modest death of undiscovered love
Than have heaven's least and lowest servant suffer,
Or in his motion receive check for me.
How is my soul's growth altered, that single life

16–17 **mark ... mark** (perhaps suggesting 'a mark ... in their foreheads ... the mark of the beast' (Revelation 13:16–17))
18 **observance** (*a*) observation (*b*) attendance on a superior (which should therefore not be 'ambitious')
19 **game to follow** (*a*) strategic work to do (*b*) prey to pursue
worm gnawing grief, remorse (compared to a parasite in the body, or the serpent/dragon that continually preys on the damned in hell: Mark 9:48, Isaiah 66:24)
21 **play** move (in the game), tactical opportunity
25 **base fact** despicable crime
schismatic heretic, sectarian
26 **nobility of revenge** (Contrast the classic Christian condemnation of revenge, as at Romans 12:19: 'Vengeance is mine, ... saith the Lord'.)
27 **will** desire (to forgive a man who seems genuinely penitent)
27–8 **power ... absolution** (ironic: Protestants denied the power of Catholic priests to absolve sins)
29 **Penance Chamber** ecclesiastical office that dealt with penitents (sometimes, in Protestant propaganda, a prison or torture chamber)
30 **tax register** *Taxa Sacra Poenitentiaria* (brought on stage in 4.2)
32 **singular** extraordinary, unique
33 **all your** your only
sting (comparing his guilt to the pain caused by the poison of an insect or snake, like the serpent Satan)
34 **game** (*a*) prize awarded to the winner (*b*) prey (*c*) amusement
34–5 **which ... see** (a clever chess player will give no sign of noticing that his opponent is making a bad move, because any reaction might alert his opponent to the mistake)
34 **politic** (*a*) prudent (*b*) political (*c*) scheming
38 **Presented** (*a*) ceremoniously introduced (*b*) showed (*c*) represented (*d*) offered, gave
39 **regardless** careless, inattentive; literally, 'not looking' (but ironically suggesting 'not worth anyone's attention')
stranger (*a*) unknown person (*b*) foreigner (*c*) newcomer
40 **Merely** wholly
fate i.e. his allegedly fated marriage (but also, ironically, his predestined damnation)
minded (*a*) noticed (*b*) remembered
41 **part** duty, allotment (but also suggesting woman's creation from Adam's rib)
mysteries (*a*) enigmas (*b*) revealed religious truths (*c*) sacraments (*d*) state secrets
42 **love** (*a*) emotional and/or sexual attraction (*b*) 'God is love' (1 John 4:16)
time right moment
44 **mast'ry** (*a*) control, power (*b*) victory in competition (*c*) achievement
45 **observe** (*a*) watch (*b*) attend (*c*) obey (*d*) defer to
46 **proper** (*a*) appropriate (*b*) private, particular
virtue (*a*) ethical conduct (*b*) chastity (*c*) particular inherent quality
48 **modest death** (by contrast to the 'immodest death', sexual orgasm)
undiscovered not revealed, not detected
50 **motion** actions or feelings (but also suggesting the movement of a clock or watch, as a measurement of time)
check (*a*) stop, delay (*b*) rebuke. The chess sense is also ironically present.
51 **single** unmarried, celibate

(The fittest garment that peace ever made for't)
Is grown too strait, too stubborn on the sudden?

JESUITESS BLACK QUEEN'S PAWN
He comes this way again.

VIRGIN WHITE QUEEN'S PAWN
O there's a traitor
Leaped from my heart into my cheek already
That will betray all to his powerful eye
If it but glance upon me.

JESUITESS BLACK QUEEN'S PAWN
By my verity,
Look, he's passed by again, drowned in neglect,
Without the prosperous hint of so much happiness
To look upon his fortunes. How close fate
Seels up the eye of human understanding
Till (like the sun's flow'r) time and love uncloses it!
'Twere pity he should dwell in ignorance longer.

VIRGIN WHITE QUEEN'S PAWN
What will you do?

JESUITESS BLACK QUEEN'S PAWN
Yes, die a bashful death, do,
And let the remedy pass by unused still.
You're changed enough already, if you'd look into't.
[Jesuitess Black Queen's Pawn goes to the Jesuit Black Bishop's Pawn]
Absolute sir, with your most noble pardon
For this my rude intrusion, I am bold
To bring the knowledge of a secret nearer
By many days, sir, than it would arrive
In its own proper revelation with you.
Pray, turn and fix. Do you know yon noble goodness?

JESUIT BLACK BISHOP'S PAWN
'Tis the first minute my eye blessed me with her,
And clearly shows how much my knowledge wanted,
Not knowing her till now.

JESUITESS BLACK QUEEN'S PAWN
She's to be liked then?
Pray, view advisedly. There is strong reason
That I'm so bold to urge it, you must guess:
The work concerns you nearer than you think for.

JESUIT BLACK BISHOP'S PAWN
Her glory and the wonder of this secret
Puts a reciprocal amazement on me.

JESUITESS BLACK QUEEN'S PAWN
And 'tis not without worth. You two must be
Better acquainted.

JESUIT BLACK BISHOP'S PAWN
Is there cause? Affinity?
Or any courteous help creation joys in
To bring that forward?

JESUITESS BLACK QUEEN'S PAWN
Yes, yes, I can show you
The nearest way to that perfectïon
(Of a most virtuous one) that joy e'er found.
Pray, mark her once again, then follow me,
And I will show you her must be your wife, sir.

JESUIT BLACK BISHOP'S PAWN
The mystery extends, or else creation

52 **fittest** (*a*) most appropriate (*b*) best-fitting
peace tranquillity (but playing on 'piece' of cloth)

53 **strait** (*a*) honest, virtuous (*b*) tight
stubborn (*a*) unyielding (*b*) stiff, rigid
on the all of a

54 **a traitor** i.e. her blush, which reveals all her secret feelings when blood rushes from her heart to her cheeks (but also, ironically, literally, the Black Bishop's Pawn)

56 **his** (*a*) Black Bishop's Pawn's (*b*) God's
powerful eye (*a*) attention of a powerful viewer (*b*) piercing vision: eyes were thought to actively emit beams, so an eye capable of emitting stronger beams would see more

57 **but** only, just
verity (*a*) truthfulness, honesty (*b*) true faith, religious belief (*c*) God, Christ

58 **neglect** negligence

59 **prosperous** auspicious, prospering
happiness (*a*) felicity (*b*) good luck

60 **fortunes** (*a*) fate (*b*) wealth, goods
close (*a*) closely, tightly (*b*) secretive, niggardly

61 **Seels** stitches (like the eyes of hawks, sewn shut to tame them)

62 **sun's flow'r** sunflower (*a*) implicitly compared to the open human eye (*b*) often a symbol for the soul, turning toward God
time and love (implicitly compared to the sun, characterized by both the warmth/heat of love and the regularity of time)

63 **dwell** remain

65 **remedy** i.e. the man who, by making love to her, would cure her of the anemia (or greensickness) which was thought to afflict female virgins

67 **Absolute** (*a*) perfect (*b*) independent, unattached (but also ironically suggesting 'despotic')

71 **proper** intrinsic, self-actuated (but also ironically suggesting 'appropriate, respectable, ethical')

72 **fix** rivet (your eyes, your attention)

74 **wanted** lacked

78 **think for** expect

79 **glory** unearthly beauty (often used of saints, angels, etc.)

80 **reciprocal** corresponding (to the 'wonder' and 'glory')

82 **Affinity** kinship (by blood or marriage): 'should I become better acquainted with her because she is a member of my family?'

83–4 **any . . . forward?** 'anything that would make her a member of my family?' (Since he knows the White Queen's Pawn knows the answer to his question, he uses religious circumlocution; for the audience, who also knows the answer, his complex evasive language is characteristically Jesuitical.)

83 **courteous** gracious, polite, courtly (a product of human artifice—like the magic mirror—rather than divine 'creation'). A sexual favour could be described as a *courtesy*.
help (God created Eve, and marriage, to be a 'help' for Adam: Genesis 2:18.)
creation joys in (*a*) that the world created by God celebrates (*b*) that enjoys procreation. See Mark 10:6 ('from the beginning of the creation God made them male and female').

84 **that** 'affinity' (by marriage)

85 **perfectïon** consummation (i.e. marriage, understood as the perfect mature union of the immature incompleteness of two complementary individuals)

86 **most virtuous** (modifying and correcting 'nearest way', which otherwise might be understood as 'the quickest route to intercourse')
joy (*a*) happiness (*b*) sexual pleasure

87 **mark** observe

89 **extends** widens, deepens
or else unless [the explanation for your mysterious *non sequitur* is that]
creation (*a*) God's act of creation (*b*) the entire created natural world; fallen nature

Has set that admirable piece before us
To choose out chaste delight by.

JESUITESS BLACK QUEEN'S PAWN Please you follow, sir.

JESUIT BLACK BISHOP'S PAWN
What art have you to put me on an object
And cannot get me off? 'Tis pain to part from't.

Exeunt [Jesuit Black Bishop's Pawn, following Jesuitess Black Queen's Pawn]

VIRGIN WHITE QUEEN'S PAWN
If there prove no check in that magical glass,
But my proportion come as fair and full
Into his eye as his into mine lately,
Then I'm confirmed he is mine own for ever.

Enter again Jesuit Black Bishop's Pawn [with Jesuitess Black Queen's Pawn]

JESUIT BLACK BISHOP'S PAWN
The very self-same that the mirror blessed me with,
From head to foot, the beauty and the habit.
Kept you this place still? Did you not remove, lady?

VIRGIN WHITE QUEEN'S PAWN
Not a foot farther, sir.

JESUIT BLACK BISHOP'S PAWN
Is't possible?
I would have sworn I'd seen the substance yonder.
'Twas to that lustre, to that life presented.

VIRGIN WHITE QUEEN'S PAWN
E'en so was yours to me, sir.

JESUIT BLACK BISHOP'S PAWN Saw you mine?

VIRGIN WHITE QUEEN'S PAWN
Perfectly clear: no sooner my name used
But yours appeared.

JESUIT BLACK BISHOP'S PAWN
Just so did yours at mine now.

JESUITESS BLACK QUEEN'S PAWN
Why stand you idle? Will you let time cozen you,
Protracting time, of those delicious benefits
That fate has marked to you? You modest pair
Of blushing gamesters—and you, sir, the bashfull'st:
I cannot flatter a foul fault in any—
Can you be more than man and wife assigned,
And by a power the most irrevocable?
Others that be adventurers in delight
May meet with crosses, shame, or separation;
Their fortune's hid, and the event's locked from 'em.
You know the mind of fate. You must be coupled.

JESUIT BLACK BISHOP'S PAWN *[to Virgin White Queen's Pawn]*
She speaks but truth in this. I see no reason then
That we should miss the relish of this night,
But that we are both shamefaced.

VIRGIN WHITE QUEEN'S PAWN How, this night, sir?
Did not I know you must be mine, and therein
Your privilege runs strong, for that loose motion
You never should be. Is it not my fortune
To match with a pure mind? Then am I miserable.
The doves and all chaste loving wingèd creatures
Have their pairs fit, their desires justly mated;
Is woman more unfortunate? A virgin,
The May of woman? Fate—that has ordained, sir,
We should be man and wife—has not given warrant
For any act of knowledge till we are so.

[She weeps]

JESUIT BLACK BISHOP'S PAWN
Tender-eyed modesty! How it grieves at this!

[Jesuit Black Bishop's Pawn and Jesuitess Black Queen's Pawn speak apart]

I'm as far off, for all this strange imposture,
As at first interview. Where lies our game now?
You know I cannot marry, by my Order.

JESUITESS BLACK QUEEN'S PAWN
I know you cannot, sir; yet you may venture
Upon a contract.

JESUIT BLACK BISHOP'S PAWN
Ha?

---

90 **piece** masterpiece—but also suggesting the derogatory slang sense 'sexual object' (used of the genitals, or of a woman defined as a 'piece of ass')
before us (literally true of the genitals)

91 **choose out** select, pick out
chaste delight i.e. procreative sexual pleasure within marriage (but also suggesting 'chased pleasure')

92 **put me on** incite me to, set me to study (but suggesting 'put me on top of', a literal sense sustained in 'off' and 'part' and 'it')
object (*a*) goal (*b*) admirable spectacle (*c*) thing

93 **from't** i.e. from the White Queen's Pawn, defined as his 'object' (but also suggesting the sexual sense of 'it')

94 **check** obstruction, detour, false target (but suggesting the chess sense)

95 **proportion** shape, image which reproduces the harmonious proportions of the original
fair beautiful, pale, unblemished, unfraudulent
full complete, replete, perfect

99 **habit** outfit

100 **remove** move

102 **substance** real thing (instead of the mere 'shadow' reflected in the mirror)

107 **cozen** cheat

108 **Protracting** prolonging

109 **marked** assigned, indicated

110 **gamesters** sexual players, gamblers

111 **flatter** praise falsely, like a flatterer (ironically, since bashful modesty is not usually considered a 'foul fault')

112 **more . . . assigned** anything more legitimately married than you already are
assigned appointed

113 **power** i.e. God

114 **adventurers** gamblers, players, investors

115 **crosses** trials, afflictions, obstacles

116 **fortune's hid** destiny is hidden
event's outcome is (meaning 'the outcome of their desire' but suggesting 'death', the outcome of all human life, as in Ecclesiastes 9:2–3)
locked from 'em i.e. unknown to them, like something kept in a locked room

117 **coupled** (*a*) joined in marriage (*b*) sexually united

118 **but** only

119 **relish** enticing taste

122 **privilege** prerogative
loose motion lascivious proposal

128 **May** springtime, prime

130 **knowledge** carnal knowledge, sexual intercourse

134 **by my Order** because of the vow of chastity he made as a Jesuit

136 **contract** a betrothal or verbal 'precontract' (producing a marriage of uncertain legal validity; often the justification for premarital intercourse)

JESUITESS BLACK QUEEN'S PAWN
Surely you may, sir,
Without all question so far, without danger
Or any stain to your vow, and that may take her.
Nay, do't with speed. She'll think you mean the better too.

JESUIT BLACK BISHOP'S PAWN [*to Virgin White Queen's Pawn*]
Be not so lavish of that blessèd spring.
You've wasted that, upon a cold occasion now,
Would wash a sinful soul white. By our love-joys,
That motion shall ne'er light upon my tongue more
Till we're contracted. Then, I hope, you're mine?

VIRGIN WHITE QUEEN'S PAWN
In all just duty ever.

JESUITESS BLACK QUEEN'S PAWN [*to Black Bishop's Pawn*]
'Then'? Do you question it?
Push! then you're man and wife—all but church ceremonies.
Pray, let's see that done first. [*Aside to him*] She shall do reason then.—
[*Aside*] Now I'll enjoy the sport, and cozen 'em both.
My blood's game is the wages I have worked for.
Exeunt

4.2 *Enter Black Knight Gondomar with his Pawn [from the Black House]*

BLACK KNIGHT GONDOMAR
Pawn, I have spoke to the Fat Bishop for thee.
I'll get thy absolution from his own mouth.
Reach me my chair of ease, my chair of coz'nage,
Sev'n thousand pounds in women, reach me that.
[*Black Knight's Pawn Gelder fetches*] *Gondomar's golden chair with a hole in it*
I love, o' life, to sit upon a bank
Of heretic gold—O soft and gently, sirrah!
[*Black Knight Gondomar sits*]
There's a foul flaw i'th' bottom of my drum, Pawn;
I ne'er shall make sound soldier, but sound treacher
With any he in Europe. How now, qualm?
Thou hast the puking'st soul that e'er I met with.
It cannot bear one suckling villainy.
Mine can digest a monster without crudity,
A sin as weighty as an elephant,
And never wamble for't.

BLACK KNIGHT'S PAWN GELDER
You have been used to't, sir;
That's a great help. The swallow of my conscience
Has but a narrow passage. You must think yet
It lies i'th' penitent pipe, and will not down.
If I had got sev'n thousand pounds by offices,
And gulled down that, the bore would have been bigger.

BLACK KNIGHT GONDOMAR
Nay, if thou prov'st facetious, I shall hug thee.
Can a soft, rare, poor-poached iniquity
So ride upon thy conscience? I'm ashamed of thee.
Hadst thou betrayed the White House to the Black,
Beggared a kingdom by dissimulation,
Unjointed the fair frame of peace and traffic,
Poisoned allegiance, set faith back, and wrought
Women's soft souls e'en up to masculine malice
To pursue truth to death if the cause roused 'em,

140 **lavish of** excessively generous in dispensing from
that blessèd spring i.e. her eyes, from which spring tears, blessed because they are a sign of her modesty and virtue, too precious to be wasted
141 **that** i.e. the warm water of her tears
cold dead, stale, weak, incapable of stimulating
occasion fleeting circumstance
142 **wash…white** (Tears, as a sign of repentance, would be more effective than Catholic 'holy water' in cleansing the soul.)
love-joys future sexual pleasure (not a very religious oath)
143 **light** alight (like a moving bird)
146 **Push** (exclamation: euphemism for 'fuck')
147 **Pray** please (but the religious sense haunts the line, right after 'church ceremonies')
that i.e. the pre-contract
do reason behave reasonably, i.e. surrender
149 **blood's** lust's, anger's
game fun, sex, prey, diversion (opposite of 'work', and alluding to chess)
is the wages 'The wages of sin is death' (Romans 6:23)

4.2.1 **spoke** spoken
3 **me** for me
chair of ease Gondomar used a specially designed chair, which allowed him to sit comfortably despite his painful fistula. See illustration, p. 1775.
coz'nage trickery
4 **Sev'n…women** i.e. (*a*) paid for with £7000 I received from women (*b*) worth as many women as I could buy with £7000. The hole in the chair probably suggested the comparison of women to holes he uses to 'ease' himself.
5 **o' life** as much as life (swearing 'on my life')
bank (*a*) bench (*b*) pile
6 **heretic gold** (implying that he acquired the gold from English suitors: see l. 18)
7 **foul…bottom** disgusting crack in the ass (his anal fistula)
drum (comparing buttocks to something tight beaten with a stick, suggesting sodomy)
8 **sound** reliable (but punning on the sound of a drum)
soldier (suggested by the military 'drum', and contrasting the courageous loyalty of soldiers with the cowardly self-aggrandizement of politicians)
8–9 **sound treacher With** 'I shall make as reliable a cheat and traitor as' (oxymoron) and/or 'I sound out and announce myself as a cheater and traitor to'
9 **he** man
qualm bellyache, scruple (i.e., Black Bishop's Pawn)
10 **puking'st** most easily nauseated
11 **suckling** baby (but suggesting tender meat, like veal, which should be easy to digest)
12 **crudity** indigestion
14 **wamble** (*a*) feel nausea (*b*) totter, reel
15 **swallow** gorge
17 **It** his sin (castrating the White Bishop's Pawn)
lies…pipe sticks in the throat of penitence
18 **by offices** by means of holding or selling official positions
19 **gulled** (*a*) guzzled (*b*) tricked
20 **facetious** witty
21 **rare** barely cooked (but castration is also 'unusual')
poor-poached underboiled (comparing his sin to an almost-raw egg, easy to swallow)
25 **traffic** trade, business

That stares and parrots are first taught to curse
thee—

BLACK KNIGHT'S PAWN GELDER

Ay, marry, sir, here's swapping sins indeed!

BLACK KNIGHT GONDOMAR

All these, and ten times trebled, has this brain
Been parent to; they are my offsprings all.

BLACK KNIGHT'S PAWN GELDER

A goodly brood.

BLACK KNIGHT GONDOMAR

Yet I can jest as lightly,
Laugh and tell stirring stories to court madams
(Daughters of my seducement) with alacrity
As high and hearty as youth's time of innocence,
That never knew a sin to shape a sorrow by.
I feel no tempest, not a leaf-wind stirring
To shake a fault; my conscience is becalmed, rather.

BLACK KNIGHT'S PAWN GELDER

I'm sure there's a whirlwind huffs in mine, sir.

BLACK KNIGHT GONDOMAR

Sirrah, I ha' sold the Groom o'th' Stool six times,
And received money of six several ladies
Ambitious to take place of baronets' wives;
To three old mummy-matrons I have promised
The Mothership o'th' Maids. I've taught our friends
too
To convey White House gold to our Black Kingdom
In cold baked pasties, and so cozen searchers;
For venting hallowed oil, beads, medals, pardons,
Pictures, Veronica's heads in private presses,
That's done by one i'th' habit of a pedlar;
Letters conveyed in rolls, tobacco balls.
When a restraint comes, by my politic counsel
Some of our Jesuits turn gentlemen-ushers,
Some falc'ners, some park-keepers, and some
huntsmen.
One took the shape of an old lady's cook once
And dispatched two chores in a Sunday morning:
The altar and the dresser. Pray, what use
Put I my summer recreation to?
But more t'inform my knowledge in the state
And strength of the White Kingdom. No fortification,
Haven, creek, or landing place 'bout the White coast
But I got draught and platform, learned the depth
Of all their channels, knowledge of all sands,
Shelves, rocks, and rivers for invasion prop'rest,
A catalogue of all the navy royal,
The burden of the ships, the brassy murderers,
The number of the men, to what cape bound.
Again, for the discovery of the inlands,
Never a shire but the state better known
To me than to her best inhabitants:
What pow'r of men and horse, gentry's revènues,
Who well affected to our side, who ill,
Who neither well nor ill, all the neutrality.
Thirty-eight thousand souls have been seduced, Pawn,
Since the jails vomited with the pill I gave 'em.

BLACK KNIGHT'S PAWN GELDER

Sure you put oil of toad into that physic, sir.

BLACK KNIGHT GONDOMAR

I'm now about a masterpiece of play
T'entrap the White Knight and with false allurements
Entice him to the Black House—more will follow—
Whilst our Fat Bishop sets upon the Queen.
Then will our game lie sweetly.

Enter Fat Bishop of Spalato [from the Black House, in his black habit, with a book]

BLACK KNIGHT'S PAWN GELDER He's come now, sir.

29 **stares** starlings (which, like parrots, can be 'taught to' mimic speech)
30 **swapping** (*a*) whopping huge (*b*) devouring (*c*) exchanging
33 **lightly** merrily, easily, carelessly, often, lewdly
34 **stirring** exciting, sexually arousing
madams (*a*) ladies (*b*) whores, bawds
35 **Daughters . . . seducement** young women he has seduced, sexually and/or ideologically (a Biblical idiom, as in 'daughters of Zion', 'daughters of music')
37 **shape . . . by** cause remorse
38 **tempest** storm (sign of divine wrath), physical or psychological
41 **sold** i.e., taken a bribe to secure someone's appointment to
Groom o'th' Stool 'Minister of the Royal Toilet' (prized court appointment to the royal Privy Chamber, with direct access and personal influence)
42 **several** separate
43 **take place of** secure precedence over
44 **mummy-matrons** i.e. madams as shrivelled and ancient as a mummy
45 **Mothership o'th' Maids** Chief Gentlewoman of the Queen's Privy Chamber, supervising her Maids of Honour
48 **venting** selling
48–9 **hallowed . . . heads** (Catholic religious paraphernalia)
48 **beads** rosary/prayer beads
medals metal disk stamped with image or inscription, believed to be blessed
pardons indulgences, bought for remission of sins
49 **Pictures** i.e. of saints or Bible scenes (as opposed to the Protestant emphasis on Biblical texts rather than images)
Veronica's heads i.e. images of Christ, like that allegedly produced when St Veronica wiped his face on his way to crucifixion
private presses secret cupboards
50 **habit** clothes
51 **rolls** first suggesting rolls of paper, scrolls, but in fact 'cylinder of tobacco'
52 **restraint** crackdown [on Catholic activities]
53 **gentlemen-ushers** gentlemen working as ushers/servants to people of even higher rank
57 **dresser** sideboard where food is prepared for serving (a secular version of the altar, where communion bread and wine were prepared)
59 **But** only
62 **draught** (*a*) drawing (*b*) water current
platform (*a*) chart, map (*b*) surface area
66 **burden** capacity
brassy (*a*) brass (*b*) pitiless, impudent
murderers small cannon
69 **shire** county
75 **vomited** suddenly involuntarily ejected their disgusting contents (i.e. Catholic prisoners)
76 **oil of toad** an imaginary medical ingredient: essence of a creature considered loathsome, hence nauseating (particularly if crushed to produce oil)
physic purgative medical treatment
81 **lie** be set (but playing on 'tell untruths')

FAT BISHOP OF SPALATO
Here's *Taxa Pœnitentiaria*, Knight,
The book of general pardons of all prices.
I have been searching for his sin this half hour
And cannot light upon't.

BLACK KNIGHT GONDOMAR
That's strange. Let me see't.

BLACK KNIGHT'S PAWN GELDER
Pawn wretched that I am, has my rage done that
There is no precedent of pardon for?

BLACK KNIGHT GONDOMAR [*reads*] 'For wilful murder, thirteen pound four shillings and sixpence.' That's reasonable cheap. 'For killing—killing—killing—killing—killing—killing'—
Why, here's nothing but 'killing', Bishop, on this side.

FAT BISHOP OF SPALATO
Turn the sheet over, you shall find adultery
And other trivial sins.

BLACK KNIGHT GONDOMAR
Adultery?
O I'm in't now. [*Reading*] 'For adultery, a couple of shillings, and for fornication fivepence'.—Mass, those are two good pennyworths. I cannot see how a man can mend himself.—'For lying with mother, sister, and daughter'—ay, marry, sir—'thirty-three pounds, three shillings, threepence.'
The sins' gradation right, paid all in threes, too.

FAT BISHOP OF SPALATO
You've read the story of that monster, sir,
That got his daughter, sister, and his wife
Of his own mother.

BLACK KNIGHT GONDOMAR [*reads*]
'Simony, nine pounds.'

FAT BISHOP OF SPALATO
They may thank me for that: 'twas nineteen
Before I came. I've mitigated many of the sums.

BLACK KNIGHT GONDOMAR [*reads*]
'Sodomy, sixpence.'—You should put that sum
Ever on the backside of your book, Bishop.

FAT BISHOP OF SPALATO
There's few on's very forward, sir.

BLACK KNIGHT GONDOMAR
What's here, sir?
[*Reads*] 'Two old precedents of encouragement.'

FAT BISHOP OF SPALATO Ay, those are ancient notes.

BLACK KNIGHT GONDOMAR [*reads*] 'Given as a gratuity for the killing of an heretical prince with a poisoned knife, ducats five thousand.'

FAT BISHOP OF SPALATO True, sir, that was paid.

BLACK KNIGHT GONDOMAR [*reads*] 'Promised also to Doctor Lopez for poisoning the Maiden Queen of the White Kingdom, ducats twenty thousand; which said sum was afterwards given, as a meritorious alms, to the nunnery at Lisbon, having at this present ten thousand pounds more at use in the townhouse of Antwerp.'

BLACK KNIGHT'S PAWN GELDER
What's all this to my conscience?—Worthy holiness,
I sue for pardon. I have brought money with me.

FAT BISHOP OF SPALATO
You must depart; you see there is no precedent
Of any price of pardon for your fact.

BLACK KNIGHT'S PAWN GELDER
Most miserable! Are fouler sins remitted?
Killing? Nay, wilful murder?

FAT BISHOP OF SPALATO
True, there's instance.
Were you to kill him, I'd pardon you.
There's precedent for that, and price set down;
But none for gelding.

BLACK KNIGHT'S PAWN GELDER
I have picked out understanding now forever
Out of that cabalistic bloody riddle.

84 **his sin** i.e. the Black Knight's Pawn's castration of the White Bishop's Pawn
89 **pound** (equivalent to 20 shillings) **shillings** (equivalent to 12 pence)
90–2 **killing . . . killing** (multiple listings for different kinds of murder)
95 **I'm in't now** (*a*) I've found it in the book (*b*) I'm an adulterer myself
96 **Mass** by the Mass (Catholic oath)
97 **pennyworths** bargains
98 **can mend himself** can reform (when it's so cheap to continue sinning) **lying** having sex with
98–9 **mother . . . daughter** (either three separate sinners, or one sinner who committed all three forms of incest)
99 **ay, marry** (affirmative interjections, suggesting enthusiastic interest)
101 **sins'** (or 'sin's': aurally ambiguous) **gradation** rhetorical sequence and financial scale (as though a man proceeded from incest with mother to incest with sister and then incest with daughter; also suggesting that one pays thirty pounds for the mother, three shillings for the sister, and only threepence for the daughter) **threes** (mirroring the three kinds of incest, and the fact that two incestuous people act the roles that would normally require three: the mother's son also acting as her husband, etc.)
103–4 **got . . . mother** i.e. got his mother pregnant with a daughter (therefore his half-sister), whom he later married
108 **backside** reverse side of a sheet of paper, left-hand page of an open book (but punning on 'buttocks')
109 **on's** of us (i.e. Catholics, or Italians, or priests—all accused of routinely practising sodomy) **forward** (*a*) zealous (*b*) inclined to sex with the forward-facing vagina rather than the 'backside'/anus
113 **prince** i.e. Henri IV of France (assassinated in 1610)
117 **Lopez** Roderigo Lopez, royal physician
117–18 **Maiden . . . Kingdom** i.e. the unmarried 'Virgin Queen' Elizabeth I of England, target of an alleged assassination attempt in 1594
119 **afterwards** i.e. after Lopez was executed
120 **Lisbon** (because Lopez was Portuguese)
121 **townhouse of Antwerp** seminary in the Spanish Netherlands
122 **What's all this** how is any of this relevant
125 **fact** deed, crime
127 **instance** precedent
131 **picked out** (*a*) found, selected (*b*) disentangled
132 **cabalistic** secretive, obscure, mystical (but also suggesting 'Jewish, magical') **riddle** i.e. the paradox of forgiveness for murder but none for castration

I'll make away all my estate and kill him,
And by that act obtain full absolution. *Exit*

Enter Black King Felipe [from the Black House]

BLACK KING FELIPE
Why, Bishop, Knight, where's your removes? your traps?
Stand you now idle in the heat of game?

BLACK KNIGHT GONDOMAR
My life for yours, Black Sovereign, the game's ours.
I have wrought underhand for the White Knight
And his brave Duke, and find 'em coming both.

FAT BISHOP OF SPALATO
And for their sanctimonious Queen's surprisal,
In that state-puzzle and distracted hurry,
Trust my arch-subtlety with't.

BLACK KING FELIPE O eagle pride!
Never was game more hopeful of our side.

Exeunt [Black King Felipe and Fat Bishop of Spalato]

BLACK KNIGHT GONDOMAR
If Bishop Bull-beef be not snapped next bout
As the game stands, I'll never trust art more. *Exit*

4.3

Recorders [within, playing soft music]. Enter the Jesuitess Black Queen's Pawn with a taper in her hand, as conducting the Virgin White Queen's Pawn in her night attire to one chamber, then—fetching in the Black Bishop's Pawn (the Jesuit), in his night habit—conveys him into another chamber; [then shuts the door, pauses,] puts out the candle, and follows him [into the second chamber].

4.4

Enter White Knight Charles and White Duke of Buckingham [from the White House]

WHITE KNIGHT CHARLES
True, noble Duke, fair virtue's most endeared one,
Let us prevent their rank insinuation
With truth of cause and cunning, meet their plots
With confident goodness that shall strike 'em grov'ling.

WHITE DUKE OF BUCKINGHAM
Sir, all the gins, traps, and alluring snares
The devil has been at work since '88 on
Are laid for the great hope of this game only.

WHITE KNIGHT CHARLES
Why, the more noble will truth's triumphs be!
When they have wound about our constant courages
The glitt'ring'st serpent that e'er falsehood fashioned
And glorying most in his resplendent poisons,
Just heaven can find a bolt to bruise his head.

Enter [from the Black House] Black Knight Gondomar [aloof off]

WHITE DUKE OF BUCKINGHAM
Look, would you see destruction lie a-sunning?
In yonder smile sits blood and treachery basking;
In that perfidious model of face-falsehood
Hell is drawn grinning.

WHITE KNIGHT CHARLES What a pain it is
For truth to feign a little.

BLACK KNIGHT GONDOMAR [*coming forward*]
O fair Knight!
The rising glory of the House of candor!
Have I so many protestations lost,

133 **make away** dispose of
estate (which would be confiscated if he were convicted of murder; by giving it away in advance, he outwits the authorities—but also proves that the murder was premeditated)
134 **by...absolution** by committing murder buy forgiveness for all my sins
135 **removes** (*a*) chess moves (*b*) murders (*c*) changes of residence
139 **coming** (*a*) amenable, persuadable (*b*) literally, moving toward us
140 **sanctimonious** holy
surprisal seizure, ambush
141 **state-puzzle** confusing political and diplomatic problem (caused by the 'coming' of Charles and Buckingham to the Black House/Spain)
distracted (*a*) crazed, insane (*b*) divided
hurry (*a*) political tumult (*b*) mental and emotional agitation
142 **eagle** considered the king of birds, associated with 'pride' because high-soaring; also the emblem of the Holy Roman Empire (ruled by the Habsburgs, including King Felipe)
144 **Bull-beef** bull-meat (term of abuse: 'meathead', 'big ox')
snapped suddenly seized, taken, bitten (suggesting the snapping of dogs at a bull in bull-baiting)
145 **art** (*a*) political cunning (*b*) gamesmanship (*c*) literature, aesthetic form
4.3.0.1–9 ***Enter...chamber*** sexual bait-and-switch: the Black Queen's Pawn deceives both other pawns, putting herself—instead of the White Queen's Pawn—in the Black Bishop's Pawn's bed. (The absolute indoor darkness of moonless nights in the pre-electric world made such substitutions plausible; they were very common in folklore, drama, etc.)
0.1 ***Enter*** (probably from the central door)
0.2 ***taper*** candle
0.4 ***one chamber*** (probably through the 'White House' door)
0.6 ***habit*** clothes
0.6–7 ***another chamber*** (probably through the 'Black House' door)
4.4.1 **True, noble** (aurally ambiguous: 'Yes, noble' and 'Truly-noble' and 'Honest, reliable, noble')
fair beautiful (allegorically of 'virtue', literally of Buckingham)
2 **prevent** anticipate, preempt, forestall
their the Black House's
rank swift, abundant, gross, corrupt, lewd, transparent
insinuation (*a*) ingratiating behaviour (*b*) subtle penetration (*c*) covert allegation
3 **cunning** (paradoxically paired with 'truth')
5 **gins** engines, machinations, schemes
6 **'88** 1588, the year the English defeated the Spanish Armada
7 **laid** lying in wait, set in place
9 **they** the Black House
our constant (contrasting their paired male fidelity with the paired inconstancy of Adam and Eve)
10–11 **glitt'ring'st...resplendent** (*a*) like the serpent in Eden, before God cursed him for tempting Eve (*b*) like the Spanish court, fabulously enriched by its global empire
10–12 **serpent...head** Genesis 3:1–15 (the serpent's temptation of Eve) and Revelations 20:2 ('that old serpent, which is the devil and Satan')
11 **glorying** rejoicing proudly. (1 Corinthians 5:6: 'Your glorying is not good.')
his the serpent's, i.e. Gondomar's
12 **bolt** lightning bolt
13 **a-sunning** sunning itself (like a snake)
14 **blood** bloodshed, lust
17 **feign** lie, pretend (paradoxical)
18 **candor** (*a*) brilliant whiteness (*b*) purity
19 **lost** wasted

Lost, lost, quite lost? Am I not worth your confidence?
I that have vowed my faculties of soul,
Life, spirit, and brain, to your sweet game of youth,
Your noble fruitful game—can you mistrust
Any foul play in me, that have been ever
The most submiss observer of your virtues,
And no way tainted with ambitiön
Save only to be thought your first admirer?
How often have I changed for your delight
The royal presentation of my place
Into a mimic jester?—and become
(For your sake, and th'expulsion of sad thoughts),
Of a grave state-sire, a light son of pastime?
Made threescore years a tomboy, a mere wanton?
I'll tell you what I told a Savoy dame once,
New-wed, high, plump, and lusting for an issue:
Within the year I promised her a child
If she could stride over Saint Rombaut's breeches
(A relic kept at Mechlin). The next morning
One of my follower's old hose was conveyed
Into her chamber, where she tried the feat;
By that (and a court friend), after grew great.

WHITE KNIGHT CHARLES
Why, who could be without thee?

BLACK KNIGHT GONDOMAR
I will change
To any shape to please you, and my aim
Has been to win your love in all this game.

WHITE KNIGHT CHARLES
Thou hast it nobly, and I long to see
The Black House' pleasure, state, and dignity.

BLACK KNIGHT GONDOMAR
Of honour you'll so surfeit and delight
You'll ne'er desire again to see the White. *Exeunt*

Enter White Queen [of Bohemia from the White House, as they go into the Black House]

WHITE QUEEN [OF BOHEMIA]
My love, my hope, my dearest—O he's gone,
Ensnared, entrapped, surprised amongst the Black ones.
I never felt extremity like this.
Thick darkness dwells upon this hour. Integrity—
Like one of heaven's bright luminaries now
By error's dullest element interposed—
Suffers a black eclipse. I never was

Enter [from the Black House] Fat Bishop of Spalato [in black]

More sick of love than now I am of horror.
I shall be taken. The game's lost, I'm set upon.
O 'tis the turncoat Bishop, having watched
Th'advantage of his play, comes now to seize on me.
O I'm hard beset, distressed most miserably!

FAT BISHOP OF SPALATO
'Tis vain to stir: remove which way you can,
I take you now. This is the time we've hoped for.
Queen, you must down.

WHITE QUEEN [OF BOHEMIA]
No rescue, no deliverer?

FAT BISHOP OF SPALATO
The Black King's blood burns for thy prostitution,
And nothing but the spring of thy chaste virtue

22 **game of youth** i.e. interest in sex-play
23 **fruitful** rewarding (but also suggesting 'producing offspring', particularly important for a 'noble' family)
mistrust suspect
25 **submiss** submissive
observer (*a*) spectator (*b*) deferential follower
27 **first** chief
29 **place** official position, status
30 **mimic jester** mimed gesture, comic mime, clown specializing in impersonation (like the comic actor mimicking Gondomar's gestures)
31 **sad** serious
32 **Of** instead of
state-sire senior statesman
light frivolous, lascivious
pastime entertainment
33 **tomboy** boisterous kid (but also suggesting 'immodest girl', transgressive sex-switching)
mere wanton (*a*) totally spoiled child (*b*) total slut
34 **Savoy** former London palace turned chapel, sanctuary, and hospital; famous for irregular marriages
35 **high** high-class, upper class, highfalutin, high-pitched, intoxicated
issue offspring
37 **Saint Rombaut** (martyred *c*.775)
breeches pants (making fun of the Catholic fondness for attributing miraculous qualities to objects associated with saints)
38 **Mechlin** city in Spanish Catholic Belgium, home of St Rombaut's cathedral ('Malines' in French)
39 **hose** (worn by men and women)
41 **friend** (*a*) patron (*b*) lover
great 'big with child', pregnant (but playing on 'politically important')
47 **surfeit** excessively indulge, eat till you're sick
delight (*a*) of delight (*b*) you'll so delight
49 **gone** 'lost forever', because departed into enemy territory (the Black House, Spain)
50 **surprised** ambushed
52 **Thick darkness** Job 38:9
darkness dwells upon Job 3:5, 38:19
53 **luminaries** (*a*) astronomical lights: sun, moon, planets (*b*) leaders
54 **error** See Induction, and *Triumphs of Truth*. (Literally, *error* comes from Latin for 'wandering', errant; 'planet' comes from the Greek word with the same meaning.)
dullest element i.e. earth (the heaviest of the traditional four elements: fire, air, water, earth)
dullest (*a*) heaviest, most dense (*b*) stupidest
interposed blocked
55 **black** i.e. total (but also suggesting 'evil', and referring to the 'Black House', in the astrological sense of the 'night house' of the signs of the seven planets)
eclipse (widely interpreted as a bad omen, particularly for nations and their leaders)
56 **of** with
57 **set upon** attacked
58 **watched** watched out for
59 **advantage** opportunity
60 **hard beset** violently hemmed in
61 **remove which** move whichever
63 **down** fall (in political, sexual, and chess senses)
64 **Black King** (*a*) King Felipe (*b*) Satan
blood (one of the four fundamental 'humours' of the body, associated with rage and lust; semen was considered a distillation of blood)
burns (associated with lust and pain)
prostitution (not mere rape, but complete transformation into a debased commodity—as in Protestant descriptions of the Catholic church as the 'whore of Babylon', based on 'the great whore' of Revelations 17:1–16)
65 **spring** (associated with 'chastity' because the water rises from underground, apparently uncontaminated)
chaste sexually virtuous (including marital fidelity as well as premarital virginity)

Can cool his inflammation. Instantly
He dies upon a pleurisy of luxury
If he deflower thee not.

Enter [from the White House] White Bishop [of Canterbury]

WHITE QUEEN [OF BOHEMIA]
O strait of misery!

[White Bishop of Canterbury takes Fat Bishop of Spalato]

WHITE BISHOP [OF CANTERBURY]
And is your holiness his divine procurer?

FAT BISHOP OF SPALATO
The devil's in't. I'm taken by a ring-dove.
Where stood this Bishop all this while that I saw him not?

WHITE BISHOP [OF CANTERBURY]
O you were so ambitious you looked over me.
You aimed at no less person than the Queen,
The glory of the game. If she were won,

Enter White King James [from the White House]

The way were open to the master-check,
Which, look you, he and his live to give you.
Honour and virtue guide him in his station.

WHITE QUEEN [OF BOHEMIA] [*to White King James*]
O my safe sanctuary!

WHITE KING JAMES Let heaven's blessings
Be mine no longer than I am thy sure one.
The dove's house is not safer in the rock
Than thou in my firm bosom.

WHITE QUEEN [OF BOHEMIA] I am blessed in't.

WHITE KING JAMES
Is it that lump of rank ingratitude
Swelled with the poison of hypocrisy?
Could he be so forgetful has partaken
Of the sweet fertile blessings of our kingdom?
—Bishop, thou hast done our White House gracious service,
And worthy the fair reverence of thy place.—
For thee, Black holiness, that work'st out thy death
As the blind mole, the proper'st son of earth,
Who in the casting his ambitious hills up
Is often taken, and destroyed i'th' midst
Of his advancèd work, 'twere well with thee
If (like that verminous labourer, which thou imitat'st
In hills of pride and malice) when death puts thee up,
The silent grave might prove thy bag forever—
No deeper pit than that. For thy vain hope
Of the White Knight and his most firm assistant
(Two princely pieces, which I know thy thoughts
Give lost forever now), my strong assurance
Of their fixed virtues, could you let in seas
Of populous untruths against that fort,
'Twould burst the proudest billows.

WHITE QUEEN [OF BOHEMIA] My fear's past then.

WHITE KING JAMES
Fear? You were never guilty of an injury
To goodness but in that.

WHITE QUEEN [OF BOHEMIA]
It stayed not with me, sir.

WHITE KING JAMES
It was too much if it usurped a thought.
Place a strong guard there.

WHITE QUEEN [OF BOHEMIA] Confidence is set, sir.

66 **inflammation** (*a*) physical morbid hot red swelling—here, of the penis (*b*) passion
67 **pleurisy** (*a*) excess, in this case of overheated blood (*b*) inflammation of the side or chest, often fatal
luxury lust
68 **deflower** violate, ravage. (The victim need not be a virgin.)
strait tight difficult place (but also 'tubular passage in the body', like the vagina)
68.3–4 ***White . . . Spalato*** Protestant episcopacy defeats Catholic episcopacy, and protects princely Anglo-German Protestantism (the first White capture of a Black piece in this version).
69 **procurer** pimp (first recorded use in this sense)
70 **The devil's in't** 'What the hell!'
ring-dove common wood-pigeon. (A ring is a bishop's mark of office, doves are proverbially peaceful; for doves as messengers of God, see Noah's dove at Genesis 8:8–12, and the Holy Spirit at Matthew 3:16, etc.)
72 **looked over** overlooked (the chief source of mistakes in chess, especially when a player focuses on his own attack on a major piece)
73 **Queen** (the most powerful chess piece)
75 **master-check** supreme check, i.e. checkmate (but also suggesting a progression from female Queen to male master/King)
76 **you** you all (the Black House)
he and his the White King and his people. (The King alone cannot check an opponent.)
77 **Honour . . . station** (either a declarative statement or a wishful imperative: 'they do guide him' or 'may they guide him!')
station (*a*) official capacity (*b*) game position
79 **thy sure one** (*a*) dependably yours (*b*) your reliable sanctuary
80 **dove's . . . rock** 'O my dove that art in the clefts of the rock' (Song of Solomon 2:14).
rock 'Upon this rock I will build my church' (Matthew 16:18). The King was Defender of the Faith and leader of the English Church.
82 **rank** (*a*) corrupt (*b*) gross, puffed up
84 **has** (*a*) he who has (*b*) that he has
88 **Black holiness** (paradox)
work'st . . . death 'the motions of sins . . . did work . . . to bring forth fruit unto death' (Romans 7:5).
89 **blind** (literally or spiritually)
mole (symbolic of the devil, since hell was located in underground darkness)
proper'st . . . earth i.e. epitome of a soulless material being
90–2 **casting . . . work** i.e. his molehills make it easy to find and kill him
94 **puts . . . up** removes you (from life, or the chess board)
95 **silent grave** total oblivion (instead of howling torment)
bag (*a*) shroud, winding sheet (*b*) small sack in which chess pieces are stored
99 **Give lost** consider (*a*) captured, taken (*b*) damned
101 **populous** numerous
fort (*a*) my conviction of their integrity (*b*) their integrity
102 **burst** pop, resist
proudest billows highest-swelling waves

WHITE KING JAMES [*to White Bishop of Canterbury*]
Take that prize hence, you reverend of men:
Put covetousness into the bag again.

FAT BISHOP OF SPALATO
The bag had need be sound, or it goes to wrack.
Sin and my weight will make a strong one crack.

Exeunt

Finit Actus Quartus

5.1

Incipit Actus Quintus et Ultimus
Loud music. Enter Black Knight Gondomar in his litter [carried by Black Pawns], as passing in haste over the stage, and the Jesuit Black Bishop's Pawn above [in his reverend habit]

BLACK KNIGHT GONDOMAR (*calls*) Hold, hold!
[*The litter stops*]
Is the Black Bishop's Pawn, the Jesuit,
Planted above for his concise oration?

JESUIT BLACK BISHOP'S PAWN
Ecce triumphanti me fixum Caesaris arce.

BLACK KNIGHT GONDOMAR Art there, my holy boy? Sirrah,
Bishop Tumbrel is snapped i'th' bag by this time.

JESUIT BLACK BISHOP'S PAWN
Haeretici pereant sic.

BLACK KNIGHT GONDOMAR
All Latin?
Sure the oration has infected him.—
Away, make haste, they're coming!
[*Exeunt Black Pawns carrying his litter*]
Oboes again!

Oboes. Enter [from] the Black House Black King Felipe, Black Queen Maria, Black Duke Olivares, [Jesuit Black Bishop], with Pawns, meeting White Knight Charles and White Duke of Buckingham [who enter from the White House]. The Jesuit Black Bishop's Pawn (above) entertains them with this Latin oration

JESUIT BLACK BISHOP'S PAWN *Si quid mortalibus unquam oculis hilarem et gratum aperuit diem, si quid peramantibus amicorum animis gaudium attulit peperitvè lætitiam (Eques candidissime prælucentissime), felicem profecto tuum a Domo Candoris ad Domum Nigritudinis accessum promisisse, peperisse, attulisse fatemur. Omnes adventus tui conflagrantissimi, omni qua possumus lætitia, gaudio, congratulatione, acclamatione, animis observantissimis, affectibus devotissimis, obsequiis venerabundis, te sospitem congratulamur.*

BLACK KING FELIPE [*to White Knight Charles*]
Sir, in this short congratulatory speech
You may conceive how the whole House affects you.

BLACK KNIGHT GONDOMAR [*to White Knight Charles*]
The colleges and sanctimonious seed-plots.

WHITE KNIGHT CHARLES [*to Black King Felipe*]
'Tis clear, and so acknowledged, royal sir.

BLACK KING FELIPE
What honours, pleasures, rarities, delights,
Your noble thought can think—

BLACK QUEEN MARIA [*to White Knight Charles*]
Your fair eye fix on,
That's comprehended in the spacious circuit
Of the Black Kingdom, they're your servants all.

WHITE KNIGHT CHARLES
How amply you endear us!

WHITE DUKE OF BUCKINGHAM [*to Black House*]
They are favours
That equally enrich the royal giver

107 **reverend . . . men** most reverend man
108 **covetousness** excessive desire, possessive greed (i.e., the Fat Bishop, as if he were a personified vice)
again (Like the last word of the play, this emphasizes the recurring nature of the game.)
109 **sound** secure
wrack ruin
5.1.0.1 ***Actus . . . Ultimus*** fifth and last act (Latin)
0.2–5 ***Enter . . . above*** (This scene represents the arrival of Charles and Buckingham in Madrid; the staging may indicate the Black House, or Spain.)
4 ***Ecce . . . arce*** Behold me, fixed on the triumphing citadel of the emperor. (A Latin hexameter: 'Caesar' because the Habsburgs were Holy Roman emperors, 'citadel' because the White Knight and Duke are about to enter the most heavily fortified centre of the enemy empire.)
6 **Tumbrel** dung-cart, drunk
7 ***Haeretici . . . sic*** May all heretics perish so!
9 **Oboes** (Early modern oboes were larger and louder than the modern instrument; in the theatre they were often used for royal entries or supernatural effects.)
9.2–8 ***Enter . . . oration*** (White Knight and Duke are surrounded by a Black crowd; the theatre has become the inside of a citadel. In chess, an attacking knight and rook can enter deep into enemy territory, but in doing so they make themselves highly vulnerable to capture.)
9.8 ***Latin*** (associated with Catholicism, and with important official occasions generally)
10–19 ***Si . . . congratulamur*** 'If anything hath unto mortal eyes ever opened a glad and welcome day, if anything hath unto the loving souls of friends brought any joy, or given birth to gladness (most white, most shining Knight), your happy coming from the House of Whites to the House of Blacks, we confess, has promised it, given birth to it, brought it. We all, most inflamed by your coming, with all possible rejoicing, joy, gladness, acclamation, with most respectful souls, with most devout affections, with most obsequious veneration, congratulate you on your safety.'
21 **affects** loves
22 **colleges** religious orders, monasteries
sanctimonious seed-plots holy seed-beds, i.e. seminaries (Latin for 'seed-bed'), but suggesting 'hypocritical breeding ground for political plots'
25 **think . . . Your** (It is shockingly indecorous for a woman to interrupt a man, or for anyone to interrupt a king.)
eye fix on (suggesting that the White Knight has his eyes fixed on the Black Queen, as Prince Charles stared at the Infanta Maria)
26 **spacious circuit** huge circle (referring to Spain's global empire)
27 **servants** (a word often used of sexual relationships)
28 **endear us** (*a*) make us feel important (*b*) make yourself dear to us
favours (perhaps gifts that the Black Queen gives the White Knight, as women gave tokens to their suitors)

As the receiver in the free donation.
Music

BLACK KNIGHT GONDOMAR
Hark! To enlarge your welcome, from all parts
Is heard sweet-sounding airs; abstruse things open
Of voluntary freeness, and yon altar
An altar discovered, richly adorned, with tapers on it, and divers statues standing on each side
(The seat of adoration) seems t'adore
The virtues you bring with you.

WHITE KNIGHT CHARLES [*aside to White Duke*]
There's a taste
Of the old vessel still.

WHITE DUKE OF BUCKINGHAM [*aside to White Knight*]
Th'erroneous relish.

[BLACK QUEEN MARIA] ([*sings a*] *song*)
Wonder, work some strange delight—
This place was never yet without—
To welcome thee, fair White House Knight,
And to bring our hopes about.
May from the altar flames aspire,
Those tapers set themselves on fire.
May senseless things our joys approve
And those brazen statues move,
The statues move
Quickened by some power above,
Or what more strange, to show our love.
The statues dance

BLACK KNIGHT GONDOMAR
A happy omen waits upon this hour:
All move portentously the right-hand way.

BLACK KING FELIPE
Come, let's set free all the most choice delights
That ever adorned days or quickened nights.
Exeunt [*into the Black House*]

Enter Virgin White Queen's Pawn [*from the White House*] 5.2

VIRGIN WHITE QUEEN'S PAWN
I see 'twas but a trial of my love now.
H'as a more modest mind, and in that virtue
Most worthily has fate provided for me.

30.1–5.1.46.1 ***Music*** . . . ***dance*** (The combination of offstage musicians, dance, and spectacle suggests a court masque, rather than religious observance.)

31 **from all parts** (indicating that the music is performed offstage, and therefore produced by invisible and dispersed instruments—an effect associated with royal absolutism, magic, and the supernatural)

32–3 **abstruse** . . . **freeness** secret things reveal themselves freely and voluntarily (perhaps playing on the sexual meanings of 'things' and 'open': the Infanta Maria was being used as sexual bait)

33.1 ***discovered*** revealed (probably by pulling back a curtain, displaying a central alcove, which would look like a small side chapel)
richly . . . ***tapers*** (characteristic of Catholic altars, by contrast with plainer Protestant communion tables)

33.2 ***divers statues*** several separate religious statues, probably of saints

34 **seat** residence, home
adoration worship (but in context suggesting idolatry)

35 **taste** hint, taint

36 **erroneous relish** (*a*) wrong flavour (*b*) relishing of error, appetite for heresy
old (as in 'the old religion', Catholicism)
vessel receptacle (suggesting the ornate Catholic communion cup)

37 [BLACK QUEEN] (not specified in early texts, but songs were usually sung by onstage boy actors, and the only onstage boy is the one playing the Black Queen. She indecorously woos him with this climactic song, ending with the word 'love'.)
Wonder (The song invokes 'amazement' rather than God.)
work (A 'wonder-work' was a miracle, a 'wonder-worker' a miracle-worker or magician. Protestants argued that miracles had ceased.)
strange extraordinary, exotic, perverse
delight (more often associated with sex than God)

39 **thee** (shifting from the formal 'you' to the more intimate 'thee')

40, 46 **our** (*a*) the Black House's (*b*) my (a royal plural)

40 **our hopes** i.e. Spanish hopes to 'take' Prince Charles by converting him to Catholicism

41 **aspire** rise (but suggesting incendiary ambition)

42 **tapers** . . . **fire** (a theatrical 'magic' trick: the candles light themselves)

43 **senseless** inanimate
approve confirm, demonstrate

44 **brazen** (*a*) brass (*b*) shameless

44.1 ***statues move*** (Working water-driven automatons had been spectacularly demonstrated in Catholic, and more technologically advanced, Italy; in the English theatre statues were performed by actors.)

45 **Quickened** (*a*) given life (*b*) speeded up
some power above (The indefinite 'some' is blasphemous: Christians recognized only a single heavenly power. It may suggest that the statues are really puppets.)

46 **what** . . . **strange** (*a*) quickened by something even stranger than some power above (*b*) may the statues do something even stranger than moving (a cue for their dance)

46.1 ***dance*** (Dancing around an altar is outrageously profane, especially if the statues represent Biblical figures and saints.)

47 **happy** lucky
waits upon accompanies

48 **portentously** in a way that foretells something momentous
right-hand propitious, virtuous (as opposed to 'left-hand', sinister). If the statues are all moving to the right, they are presumably dancing in a circle, clock-wise.

49–50 **free** . . . **delights** . . . **quickened nights** (Words with sexual meanings: the 'delights' are not culinary, as 5.3 makes clear.)

50.1 ***Exeunt*** . . . ***House*** (A complex symbolic exit. The alcove must close, concealing the altar. The statues might return to the alcove, or they could, as in the court masque, take aristocratic partners and exeunt with them, dancing. Since it is a large group, they could all exit through the centre doors, past the altar. Black Queen Maria might exit alongside White Knight Charles.)

5.2.0.1–2 ***Enter*** . . . ***House*** (alone, and in contrast to the exiting Black Queen)

1 **I** . . . **now** I now realize that the pre-contract was simply a test (i.e., that is why the Black Bishop's Pawn did not come to her bedroom in 4.3)

2 **H'as** he (the Black Bishop's Pawn) has
more modest more chaste (than to engage in pre-marital sex, even after their betrothal)

Enter [from the Black House] the Jesuit Black Bishop's Pawn in his reverend habit, meeting her

Yonder's the bad man in the reverend habit.
Dares he be seen again?—traitor to holiness,
O marble-fronted impudence!—and knows
How much he's wronged me? I'm ashamed he blushes not.

JESUIT BLACK BISHOP'S PAWN

Are you yet stored with any woman's pity?
Are you the mistress of so much devotion,
Kindness, or charity, as to bestow
An alms of love on your poor suff'rer yet
For your sake only?

VIRGIN WHITE QUEEN'S PAWN

Sir, for the reverence and respect you ought
To give to sanctity—though none to me—
In being her servant vowed and wear her livery,
If I might counsel you, you should ne'er speak
The language of unchasteness in that habit.
You would not think how ill it does with you.
The world's a stage, on which all parts are played.
You'd count it strange to have a devil
Presented there not in a devil's shape,
Or—wanting one—to send him out in yours;
You'd rail at that for an absurdity
No college e'er committed. For decorum's sake, then,
For pity's cause, for sacred virtue's honour,
If you'll persist still in your dev'lish part,
Present him as you should do, and let one
That carries up the goodness of the play
Come in that habit, and I'll speak with him.
Then will the parts be fitted, and the spectators
Know which is which; they must have cunning judgements
To find it else, for such a one as you
Is able to deceive a mighty auditory.
Nay, those you have seduced—if there be any
In the assembly—when they see what manner
You play the game with me, they cannot love you.
Is there so little hope of you to smile, sir?

JESUIT BLACK BISHOP'S PAWN

Yes, at your fears, at th'ignorance of your power,
The little use you make of time, youth, fortune.
Knowing you have a husband for lust's shelter,
You dare not yet make bold with a friend's comfort—
Which is the plague of weakness.

VIRGIN WHITE QUEEN'S PAWN So hot-burning
The syllables of sin fly from his lips
As if the letter came new-cast from hell.

JESUIT BLACK BISHOP'S PAWN

Well, setting by the dish you loathe so much
(Which has been heartily tasted by your betters),
I come to marry you to th' gentleman
That last enjoyed you. Hope that pleases you.
There's no immodest relish in that office.

VIRGIN WHITE QUEEN'S PAWN [*aside*]

Strange, of all others he should light on him
To tie that holy knot that sought t'undo me.—
Were you requested to perform that office?

JESUIT BLACK BISHOP'S PAWN

I named you a sure token.

VIRGIN WHITE QUEEN'S PAWN

As for that, sir,
Now you're most welcome, and my fair hope's of you
You'll never break the sacred knot you tie once

4 **reverend habit** (She immediately recognizes him because he has reverted to his priestly vestments; the last time she saw him—in 4.1—he wore his secular 'gallant' disguise.)
6 **marble-fronted** stone-faced, cold and hard
8 **pity** compassion (thought to be particularly characteristic of women); often invoked as a reason to accept a man's sexual advances
9 **devotion** religious (or romantic) dedication
10 **Kindness ... charity** (both with the slang sense 'willingness to do sexual favours')
11 **alms** small charitable donation
11–12 **your poor ... only** the poor man (me) who suffers only for you
15 **her** sanctity's
livery uniform
17 **habit** outfit
18 **does with** suits
21 **shape** costume
22 **wanting** lacking
out from backstage out onto the stage
24 **college** (like those at Oxford and Cambridge, or the Jesuit seminaries in Europe, which performed academic plays which obeyed critical rules in ways that commercial plays did not)
28 **carries** holds
29 **that habit** i.e. your priestly vestments
30 **fitted** outfitted, supplied with necessary (theatrical) equipment
32 **it else** which is which, otherwise
33 **mighty** (*a*) large (*b*) powerful, important
auditory audience
35 **assembly** i.e., the current audience of *A Game at Chess*
37 **you** i.e., your salvation
to smile i.e., that you respond to my earnest advice by grinning ironically
38 **th'ignorance ... power** (*a*) your ignorance of your own power (*b*) your ignorant power
40 **for ... shelter** 'to cover your ass' (i.e., if you get pregnant as a result of your lecherous behaviour, everyone will think your husband is the father)
41 **friend's comfort** lover's attention
44 **letter** typeface, movable types used by printing presses
new-cast newly thrown, new-made (by pouring hot liquid metal into molds)
45 **the dish** sexually attractive person, 'good enough to eat', or sexual organ (i.e., him, or his penis)
47–8 **th' ... you** i.e. himself (because he thinks he has had sex with her—though he knows that *she* does not realize he is the man she betrothed herself to)
48 **last** most recently (implying she's had other lovers)
Hope I hope
49 **no ... office** nothing that smacks of immodesty in that sacrament (of marriage)
50 **he ... him** her fiancé ... the Jesuit (but the confusing pronouns ironically remind the audience that the two men are the same)
light on happen to pick, randomly choose
51 **tie ... knot** perform the marriage ceremony (but also, ironically, 'marry')
t'undo to sexually ruin (by raping her)
53 **named ... token** specified clear evidence (in his previous speech): he refers to the phrase 'last enjoyed you', but she interprets it as a reference to the fact that she is to be married to a gentleman
55 **break ... tie** violate the union that you as priest sanctify (but also, ironically, 'violate your marriage vows')

With any lewd solicitings hereafter.
JESUIT BLACK BISHOP'S PAWN
But all the craft's in getting of it knit.
You're all on fire to make your coz'ning market.
I am the marrier—and the man. Do you know me?
Do you know me, nice iniquity, strict luxury,
And holy whoredom? Ay, would clap on marriage
With all hot speed to solder up the game?
See what a scourge fate has provided for thee.
You were a 'maid,' swear still, you're no worse now.
I left you as I found you. Have I startled you?
I'm quit with you now for my discovery,
Your outcries and your cunnings. Farewell, brokage.
VIRGIN WHITE QUEEN'S PAWN
Nay, stay and hear me but give thanks a little,
If *your* ear can endure a work so gracious;
Then you may take your pleasure.
JESUIT BLACK BISHOP'S PAWN I have done that!
VIRGIN WHITE QUEEN'S PAWN [*kneels, praying*]
That pow'r that has preserved me from this devil—
JESUIT BLACK BISHOP'S PAWN How?
VIRGIN WHITE QUEEN'S PAWN [*praying*]
This, that may challenge the chief chair in hell
And sit above his master—
JESUIT BLACK BISHOP'S PAWN
Bring in merit!
VIRGIN WHITE QUEEN'S PAWN [*praying*]
That suffered'st him, through blind lust, to be led
Last night to th'action of some common bed—
JESUITESS BLACK QUEEN'S PAWN (*within*)
Not over-common neither.
JESUIT BLACK BISHOP'S PAWN
Ha! What voice is that?
VIRGIN WHITE QUEEN'S PAWN [*praying*]
Of virgins be thou ever honourèd.—
[*She rises and addresses Black Bishop's Pawn*]
Now you may go; you hear I've given thanks, sir.
JESUIT BLACK BISHOP'S PAWN
Here's a strange game indeed. Did not I lie with you?
JESUITESS BLACK QUEEN'S PAWN (*within*) No.
JESUIT BLACK BISHOP'S PAWN
What a devil art thou?
VIRGIN WHITE QUEEN'S PAWN
I'll not answer you, sir,
After thanksgiving.
JESUIT BLACK BISHOP'S PAWN
Why, you made a promise to me
After the contract.
JESUITESS BLACK QUEEN'S PAWN (*within*)
Yes.
JESUIT BLACK BISHOP'S PAWN
A pox confound thee!
I speak not to thee.—And you were prepared for't,
And set your joys more high—
JESUITESS BLACK QUEEN'S PAWN (*within*)
—than you could reach, sir.
JESUIT BLACK BISHOP'S PAWN
'Slid, 'tis a bawdy voice. I'll slit the throat on't.
Enter Jesuitess Black Queen's Pawn [*from the Black House*]
JESUITESS BLACK QUEEN'S PAWN
What, offer violence to me, your bedfellow?

57 **craft** skill, trick
it knit the marriage tied up
58 **all on fire** desperate, hurrying, oversexed (like someone with their 'pants on fire')
coz'ning cheating (because, he believes, she has falsely pretended to be a virgin)
market bargain (with the idea that she is trying to sell herself on 'the marriage market')
59 **marrier** officiating priest (punning on 'merrier'?)
man bridegroom (as in 'man and wife'), but also 'the man who had you'
59–60 **know . . . know** (*a*) recognize (*b*) have carnal knowledge of
60–1 **nice . . . whoredom** (he intends these paradoxes to apply to 'you', but they really apply to 'me')
60 **nice** scrupulous, fastidious, bashful
luxury lechery
61–2 **Ay . . . game** (*a*) 'yes, would you get married in a hurry in order to legitimate the sexual game you play?' (*b*) 'I would marry you right away in order to legitimate the sexual game I wanted to play?'
61 **Ay** (*a*) yes, you know me (*b*) yes, that's what kind of woman you are (described in the preceding phrases). But 'ay' also puns on 'I'.
62 **hot** impetuous, oversexed (but literally looking forward to 'solder')
solder up repair (specifically suggesting the re-sealing of a broken maidenhead)
63 **scourge** divine punishment (literally, a whip, like that used to lash convicted prostitutes)
64 **a 'maid'** (she had implicitly or explicitly called herself a 'maid' or 'virgin' repeatedly in earlier scenes)
swear still keep swearing (*a*) that you *were* a virgin (*b*) that you *are still* a virgin
you're . . . now (He means this ironically, but it is truer than he knows.)
65 **I . . . found you** i.e., you were not a virgin before or after I had sex with you; I 'found' you, at a first encounter, already without an intact hymen. (In fact he had sex with the Black Queen's Pawn, not the White Queen's Pawn: see 4.3.)
66 **quit** even, quits
my discovery exposing me (her publicly accusing him of rape in 2.2)
67 **brokage** insulting epithet for the White Queen's Pawn, referring to (*a*) pimping, dealing with go-betweens to gain sexual access to a prostitute (*b*) a broken hymen
70 **take . . . pleasure** do what you like (but he interprets it sexually)
71 **That pow'r** i.e. God (to whom all her speeches are addressed, until 'honourèd' at l. 78)
72 **How?** either a question ('in what way?') or an exclamation ('what!')
73 **This** this devil
challenge lay claim to, compete for
74 **his master** i.e. Satan
Bring in merit 'fetch someone deserving' or 'don't forget qualifications' (i.e., I deserve to fill the chief chair)
76 **action** i.e. sexual activity
common public, like 'common' land, available for anyone to use
77 ***within*** offstage
80 **lie** go to bed, have sex
84 **pox** venereal disease
85 **prepared for't** ready for intercourse (i.e., 'wet')
86 **set . . . high** had orgasms more powerful (suggesting also high-pitched exclamations during sex)
reach equal, satisfy
87 **'Slid** by God's eyelid (a strong oath)
bawdy lewd, smutty
on't of the invisible speaker (but playing on the relationship between 'throat' and 'voice')
88 **violence** (looking backward to 'slit the throat' and forward to 'rape')

To one that works so kindly, without rape?
JESUIT BLACK BISHOP'S PAWN
My bedfellow?
JESUITESS BLACK QUEEN'S PAWN
Do you plant your scorn against me?
Why, when I was probationer at Brussels,
That engine was not seen; then adoration
Filled up the place, and wonder was in fashion.
Is't turned to th' wild seed of contempt so soon?
Can five years stamp a bawd?—Pray, look upon me,
sir;
I've youth enough to take it.—'Tis no more
Since you were chief agent for the transportation
Of ladies' daughters, if you be remembered;
Some of their portions I could name; you pursed 'em,
too.
They were soon dispossessed of worldly cares
That came into your fingers.
JESUIT BLACK BISHOP'S PAWN Shall I hear her?
JESUITESS BLACK QUEEN'S PAWN
Holy derision, yes, till thy ear swells
With thy own venom, thy profane life's vomit.
Whose niece was she you poisoned with child, twice?
—Then gave her out 'possessed with a foul spirit'?
When 'twas indeed your bastard.
Enter White Bishop's Gelded Pawn with White Queen [*of Bohemia from the White House*]
JESUIT BLACK BISHOP'S PAWN I am taken
In mine own toils.
WHITE BISHOP'S GELDED PAWN
Yes, and 'tis just you should be.
[*White Bishop's Pawn takes Black Bishop's Pawn*]
WHITE QUEEN [OF BOHEMIA]
And thou, lewd Pawn, the shame of womanhood.
[*White Queen takes Black Queen's Pawn*]
JESUIT BLACK BISHOP'S PAWN
I'm lost of all hands.
JESUITESS BLACK QUEEN'S PAWN
And I cannot feel
The weight of my affection, now he's taken;
'T'as not the burden of a grasshopper.

89 **works so kindly** (*a*) behaves so obligingly (*b*) performs the 'deed of kind', gives you a sexual workout

90 **My bedfellow?** (He still does not realize who was in bed with him in 4.3.)
plant ... against (as though 'scorn' were cannon, or projectiles fired from the cannons of the eyes)

91 **probationer** a novice in a religious order
Brussels (in the Catholic Spanish Netherlands)

92 **engine** (*a*) trick (*b*) heavy artillery used in siege warfare

94 **wild seed** bastard offspring
of (*a*) called (*b*) created by

95 **five years** (presumably the time that has passed since she was a probationer that he seduced)
stamp make by means of stamping (suggesting a coin or medallion, but also with the implied metaphor of intercourse, and of impregnation as the male stamping a form on female matter)
bawd pimp, procuress. (As prostitutes aged and became less attractive to customers, they turned into managers of brothels; he has tried to use her to help him seduce the White Queen's Pawn, thereby turning his former mistress into his pimp.)
look upon me (indicating that the shamed Black Bishop's Pawn is trying to avoid eye contact; she might physically force him to look at her, here)
sir (a deliberately formal, cold way to address a lover; like modern 'mister', used to address strangers, appropriately for a bawd accosting a potential customer)

96 **I've ... it** 'I'm young enough that I can still endure close scrutiny'
take it (perhaps punning on sexual sense)
no more i.e. no more than five years

97–8 **chief ... daughters** i.e. responsible for helping aristocratic young women secretly leave England to go to nunneries in Catholic countries

98 **be remembered** remind yourself (sarcastic: she then proceeds to remind him herself)

99 **portions** inheritances, share of their family's wealth
pursed 'em pocketed them (the women's money, the women themselves)

100 **dispossessed** relieved (sarcastic)
worldly cares (*a*) secular burdens (*b*) financial assets

101 **came into** (punning on 'had an orgasm upon')
fingers (suggesting pick-pocketing and sexual groping)
Shall ... her i.e. should I continue to endure listening to this woman? should I, like a court, admit her plea?

102 **Holy derision** saintly scorn (ironic), mockery of holiness
ear swells (compare the idea that your ears burn, when someone is talking about you: here, in contrast with her swelling womb)

103 **venom** poison (sometimes administered through the ear)

104–6 **Whose niece ... bastard** (A rhetorical question: he knows she is referring euphemistically to herself: she is too ashamed to use the first person singular.)

104 **niece** (*a*) female relative (*b*) euphemism for 'mistress, whore' (especially a priest's)
poisoned with child impregnated (comparing his semen to 'venom' and 'vomit')

105 **gave her out** reported she (I) was
possessed ... spirit 'a victim of demonic possession' (thus providing a bogus supernatural explanation for her abdominal swelling, later presumably exorcised when she secretly gave birth); but playing on 'sexually possessed' and 'spirit' (= semen)

106 **'twas indeed** the 'foul spirit' was in fact

106.1–2 ***White Queen*** (Having been saved by the White Bishop, the most powerful White piece now gives the White pawns a decisive advantage over the Black pawns: the capture of three adjacent black pawns exposes the Black Queen flank and prepares for the endgame of 5.3.)

107 **toils** traps

107.1 ***White Bishop's ... Pawn*** Protestant clergy defeats Catholic clergy (a plausible late move, if one or the other piece has already taken another pawn earlier in the game, and thereby moved into an adjacent file). Alternatively, he might be taken by White Queen's Pawn, his intended target, or by White Queen.

108.1 ***White Queen ... Pawn*** Protestant womanhood defeats Catholic womanhood (a plausible late move, and safer after Black Queen's Bishop's Pawn has been taken, since that piece might otherwise retaliate). Alternatively, she might be taken by White Queen's Pawn.
Black Queen's Pawn (who may have deliberately conspicuously forfeited her move, signalling her approval of his capture)

109 **of all hands** on all sides (but also suggesting the hands that move chess pieces)

110 **affection** love (for him)

111 **burden ... grasshopper** Ecclesiastes 12:5 ('the grasshopper shall be a burden').
burden weight

JESUIT BLACK BISHOP'S PAWN
Thou whore of order! Cockatrice *in voto*!
Enter Black Knight's Pawn Gelder [from the Black House, with a weapon]
BLACK KNIGHT'S PAWN GELDER [*aside*]
Yonder's the White Bishop's Pawn. Have at his heart
now!
VIRGIN WHITE QUEEN'S PAWN
Hold, monster-impudence! Wouldst heap a murder
On thy first foul attempt? O merciless bloodhound!
'Tis time that thou art taken.
[*White Queen's Pawn takes Black Knight's Pawn*]
BLACK KNIGHT'S PAWN GELDER
Death! prevented?
VIRGIN WHITE QUEEN'S PAWN
For thy sake, and yon partner in thy shame,
I'll never know man farther than by name. *Exeunt*

5.3 *Enter [from] the Black House Black King Felipe, Black Queen Maria, Black Duke Olivares, Jesuit Black Bishop, Black Knight Gondomar, with White Knight Charles and his White Duke of Buckingham*

WHITE KNIGHT CHARLES [*to Black King Felipe*]
You've both enriched my knowledge, royal sir,
And my content together.
BLACK KING FELIPE
Stead of riot,
We set you only welcome. Surfeit is
A thing that's seldom heard of in these parts.
WHITE KNIGHT CHARLES
I hear of the more virtue when I miss on't.
BLACK KNIGHT GONDOMAR
We do not use to bury in our bellies
Three hundred thousand ducats, and then boast on't,
Or exercise th'old Roman painful idleness
With care of fetching fishes far from home:
The golden-headed coracinë out of Egypt,
The salpa from Ebusus, or the pelamis
(Which some call 'summer whiting') from Chalcedon,
Salmons from Aquitaine, ellops from Rhodes,
Cockles from Chios, franked and fatted up
With *far* and *sapa*, flour and cocted wine.
We cram no birds, nor (Epicurean-like)
Enclose some creeks o'th' sea, as Sergius Orata did—
He that invented the first stews for oysters
And other sea-fish, who (besides the pleasure
Of his own throat) got large revènues by th'invention,
Whose fat example the nobility followed.
Nor do we imitate that arch-gormandizer

112 **whore of order** prostitute (*a*) of a religious order (*b*) on demand (*c*) of ordure, excrement, filth (but also a complex paradox, since 'whore' epitomizes sexual and moral *dis*order)
Cockatrice mythical monster, a serpent with a rooster's head, whose look was poisonous (like the 'evil eye' of a menstruating woman); slang for 'low-class prostitute'
in voto See 1.1.43; here, having sworn eternal fornication instead of eternal celibacy (playing on the slang equation of 'nun' and 'whore').

112.1–2 ***Enter*...*House*** (Black responds to White's successful pawn attack.)

112.2 ***weapon*** (probably a sword or knife: a phallic weapon that must be theatrically taken from him when he is 'prevented': perhaps suggesting symbolic—or even literal—genital amputation)

113 **Have** aim
his heart now (in contrast to 'his testicles, earlier' when Black Knight's Pawn gelded him, in his 'first foul attempt')

115 **attempt** assault

116.1 ***White Queen's*...*Pawn*** Protestant female innocence defeats Catholic male malice (a plausible mid-game move in chess, if either piece has already taken another pawn earlier, and thereby moved into an adjacent file). Alternatively, he might be taken by White Bishop's Pawn or White Queen.

117 **yon**...**shame** i.e. Black Bishop's Pawn (his confessor)

118 **I'll**...**name** I'll never have carnal knowledge of any man (i.e., like Heloise after the castration of Abelard, she vows to remain celibate for life). The White Queen was sometimes called 'the Amazon' (invoking a female community without men).

5.3.0.1–4 ***Enter*...*Buckingham*** (endgame: a less crowded and spectacular scene than 5.1, with fewer black pieces surrounding White Knight and Duke)

0.2 ***Black Queen*** (speaks only six words in this scene: male political negotiations take over, and the promised bride is kept firmly away from Charles)

0.3 ***Black Bishop*** (says nothing in this scene—perhaps simply blocking access to Black Queen Maria)

2 **riot** extravagance (particularly 'noisy feasting' and 'sexual abandon'). The spectacular public promises of 5.1 are replaced, behind the scenes, by tight-fisted reserve.

3 **Surfeit** excess (particularly of food or sex)

6 **We**...**use** it is not our custom
bellies (*a*) stomachs (*b*) wombs

7 **Three**...**ducats** i.e., things worth millions of dollars

8 **old** classical, patrician
painful idleness (oxymoron: 'idleness made possible by the painful labour of slaves'—or 'it takes a lot of work to be this lazy'—or 'laziness is unhealthy and uncomfortable')

9 **care** expense, worry
fetching...**home** importing exotic food. (Proverbially, 'far-fetched and dear bought is good for ladies', and 'fish' has various sexual meanings: Prince Charles went far to fetch home an exotic dish.)

10 **coracinë** black Nile fish, resembling perch

11 **salpa** salt-water fish
Ebusus Roman name for the Spanish island now called Ibiza (at the opposite end of the Mediterranean from Egypt)
pelamis young or small tuna

12 **Chalcedon** city in north-west Turkey, on the Black Sea and the Bosphorus (also the title of the provisional leader of Catholics in Protestant England—an association which would also place it very far from Rome)

13 **Aquitaine** (south-west coast of France)
ellops (unknown fish, mentioned by ancient writers)
Rhodes famous island off the south-west coast of Turkey

14 **Cockles** common shellfish
Chios Greek island in the north Aegean
franked stuffed

15 ***far* and *sapa*** flour and boiled wine

16 **cram** stuff
Epicurean-like like a follower of the Greek hedonist philosopher Epicurus (d. 270 BCE)

17 **Sergius Orata** (*c.*98 BCE)

18 **stews** fish-farms, ponds for breeding specially prized varieties (but suggesting 'brothels')

22 **arch-gormandizer** super-glutton (Middleton coinage); This seemingly refers to Orata, but is based historically on the Emperor Heliogabalus (d. 222), famous for sexual and financial extravagance

With two-and-twenty courses at one dinner,
And betwixt every course he and his guests
Washed, and used women, then sat down and strengthened,
Lust swimming in their dishes—which no sooner
Was tasted, but was ready to be vented.

WHITE KNIGHT CHARLES
Most impious epicures!

BLACK KNIGHT GONDOMAR
We commend rather,
Of two extremes, the parsimony of Pertinax,
(Who had half lettuces set up to serve again)
Or his successor Julian (that would make
Three meals of a lean hare, and often sup
With a green fig and wipe his beard, as I can).
The old bewailers of excess in those days
Complained there was more coin bid for a cook
Than for a warhorse, but now cooks are purchased
After the rate of triumphs, and some dishes
After the rate of cooks—which must needs make
Some of your White House gormandizers ('specially
Your wealthy plump plebeians) like the hogs
Which Scaliger cites, that could not move for fat,
So insensible of either prick or goad
That mice made holes to needle in their buttocks
And they ne'er felt 'em. There was once a ruler,
Cyrene's governor, choked with his own paunch—
Which death fat Sanctius (King of Castile) fearing
Through his infinite mass of belly, rather chose
To be killed suddenly—by a pernicious herb
Taken to make him lean, which old Cordoba
(King of Morocco) counselled his fear to—
Than he would hazard to be stunk to death
As that huge cormorant that was choked before him.

WHITE KNIGHT CHARLES
Well, you're as sound a spokesman, sir, for parsimony,
Clean abstinence, and scarce one meal a day,
As ever spoke with tongue.

BLACK KING FELIPE
Censure him mildly, sir.
'Twas but to find discourse.

BLACK QUEEN MARIA
He'll talk of anything.

WHITE KNIGHT CHARLES
I shall be half afraid to feed hereafter.

WHITE DUKE OF BUCKINGHAM
Or I, beshrew my heart, for I fear fatness,
The fog of fatness, as I fear a dragon.
The comeliness I wish for, that's as glorious.

WHITE KNIGHT CHARLES [*to Black House*]
Your course is wondrous strict. I shall transgress sure,
If I should change my side (as you've much wrought me to't).

BLACK KNIGHT GONDOMAR
How you misprize! This is not meant to you-ward.
You, that are wound up to the height of feeding
By clime and custom, are dispensed withal.
You may eat kid, *cabrito*, calf, and tunas—
Eat, and eat every day, twice, if you please—
Nay, the franked hen fattened with milk and corn
(A riot which th'inhabitants of Delos
Were first inventors of), or the crammed cockle.

WHITE KNIGHT CHARLES
Well, for the food I'm happily resolved on.
But for the diet of my disposition
There comes a trouble; you will hardly find
Food to please that.

25 **used** (sexually)
strengthened got stronger, intensified
27 **vented** 'expressed' and 'expelled from the body' (as in urinating, vomiting, ejaculating, farting)
28 **epicures** gluttons, drunkards, lechers, atheists
29 **parsimony** (*a*) thriftiness (*b*) stinginess
Pertinax Roman emperor (d. 193)
30 **set...again** elevated to a second term of public office (i.e. served as left-overs)
31 **Julian** Roman emperor (d. 193)
32–3 **sup...fig** (It was rare for aristocrats to eat a meal without meat.)
33 **wipe his beard** (to signify the meal was over)
can know how to do
34 **bewailers** critics
37 **triumphs** (*a*) public spectacles after military victories (*b*) London Lord Mayor's pageants
40 **plebeians** commoners (not born gentlemen or aristocrats)
41 **Scaliger** Julius Caesar Scaliger (1484–1558), famous Italian humanist scholar
42 **prick** puncture
goad spike for driving cattle
43 **needle** bore, tunnel
45 **Cyrene's governor** Magas, king of Greek colony of Cyrene in North Africa (d. 258 BCE)
choked with suffocated by, unable to breathe because of
paunch gut, fat
46 **fat Sanctius** 'gluttonous holiness': Sancho I, king of Leon (956–65)
47 **Through** because of
49–50 **Cordoba...Morocco** (Cordoba—the name of a southern Spanish kingdom rather than its king—belonged, like Morocco, to the Islamic world, and Sancho I went there for advanced medical treatment.)
51 **Than...death** rather than risk dying squalidly (i.e. so overweight that he was bedridden and incontinent)
52 **As...him** i.e. like Cyrene's governor
cormorant large, voracious sea-bird that swallows more than it can immediately digest, and regurgitates it for later feeding: hence, bulimic glutton
53 **sound** (*a*) reliable (*b*) healthy
54 **Clean** total
56 **discourse** conversation, subject matter
59 **fog** flab (but suggesting 'dangerous mist')
fear (*a*) am afraid of (*b*) frighten
60 **comeliness** handsomeness
as glorious i.e. as glorious as fearing or frightening a dragon
62 **change my side** (*a*) personally convert (*b*) convert the whole White House
wrought me to't worked on me to do
63 **misprize** misunderstand
to you-ward to apply to you all
64 **wound up** (like a watch, or a musical instrument being set to a high pitch)
65 **clime** climate (based on the medical theory that national characteristics were determined by distance from the equator)
dispensed withal excused from this. (Characteristic of the Catholic tradition of granting exceptions to ethical rules.)
66 **kid** baby goat
cabrito (Spanish for 'baby goat')
calf i.e. veal
67 **twice** (a joke, since the English ate three or four times a day)
69 **Delos** (Greek island famous in antiquity)
71 **happily...on** happy to accept
72 **diet** (*a*) food (*b*) regulation
disposition personality

BLACK KNIGHT GONDOMAR
It must be a strange nature
We cannot find a dish for, having policy
(The master cook of Christendom) to dress it.
Pray, name your nature's diet.

WHITE KNIGHT CHARLES
The first mess
Is hot ambition.

BLACK KNIGHT GONDOMAR
That's but served in puff-paste.
Alas, the meanest of our cardinals' cooks
Can dress that dinner. Your ambition, sir,
Can fetch no farther compass than the world?

WHITE KNIGHT CHARLES
That's certain, sir.

BLACK KNIGHT GONDOMAR
We're about that already,
And in the large feast of our vast ambition
We count but the White Kingdom (whence you came from)
The garden for our cook to pick his salads.
The food's lean France, larded with Germany,
Before which comes the grave chaste signory
Of Venice, served in (capon-like) in whitebroth;
From our chief oven Italy, the bake-meats;
Savoy, the salt; Geneva, the chipped manchet.
Below the salt the Netherlands are placed,
A common dish at lower end o'th' table
For meaner pride to fall to. For our second course,
A spit of Portugals served in for plovers,
Indians and Moors for blackbirds. All this while
Holland stands ready melted to make sauce
On all occasions; when the voider comes
And with such cheer our crammed hopes we suffice,
Zealand says grace, for fashion, then we rise.

WHITE KNIGHT CHARLES
Here's meat enough, in conscience, for ambition.

BLACK KNIGHT GONDOMAR
If there be any want, there's Switzerland,

76 **dress** prepare for eating, cook
77 **mess** course, dish (as in military 'mess-hall')
78 **hot** (*a*) eager, passionate, sexually aroused (*b*) according to the medical theory of humours, containing an excess of the element of fire (*c*) heated, spicy
but only
puff-paste fine, rich, flaky flour (i.e. light, frivolous, unsubstantial dishes or persons)
79 **meanest** worst, lowest-class
81 **compass** (*a*) measurement, sphere (*b*) instrument for making maps (*c*) navigational instrument (*d*) policy, stratagem (all relevant to the Spanish global empire)
82 **about that** (*a*) have begun compassing the world (*b*) around the globe
83–103 **large feast . . . table** (The allegorical menu parodies elaborate court feasts—where dishes were sometimes sculpted to represent persons or places—and expensive allegorical court masques.)
84–5 **but . . . salads** i.e. 'England just a small piece of ground used for growing the least substantial part of the feast'
85 **to . . . salads** to do something trivial (proverbial)
86 **food's** real meal, main course, sustenance is
lean (*a*) muscular, not fatty—as in 'lean meat' (*b*) famished (referring to recent French famines)
larded garnished with strips of bacon, or greased with melted fat (appropriate to the German taste for pork)
Germany (site of extensive Catholic–Protestant warfare, 1619–24)
87 **Before which** i.e. as an appetizer, soup
grave dignified, respected (also suggesting the age of Venetian senators)
chaste (Venice was a 'maiden' city, never conquered; but given its reputation for prostitution, this may be ironic)
signory (*a*) domain (*b*) city-state ruled by a collective of male 'signors' rather than a monarch
88 **capon-like** like a castrated chicken
whitebroth thin soup, whitened with flour or milk (like a sea, in which the capon sits like the island city of Venice)
89 **our . . . Italy** (Spain had ruled southern Italy and Sicily for more than a century; Milan was also in its possession, and Genoa an ally.)
chief oven (because Rome is the centre of Catholicism, and the Italian climate much hotter than the English)
bake-meats meat pies (as in Genesis 50:17, 'bake-meats for Pharaoh')
90 **Savoy** independent duchy in what is currently south-eastern France and north-western Italy (major source of salt exports)
salt salt-cellar, a large and often ornate utensil at the centre of the table. (The salt-cellar was passed around the table, as Savoy changed its allies.)
Geneva (birthplace and international centre of Calvinism)
chipped having had the hard dry outer crust removed, leaving only the highly-valued interior of the loaf
manchet the finest white bread (often used figuratively to suggest 'religious purity', but perhaps here pronounced 'man-cheat')
91 **Below the salt** (*a*) at the inferior end of the table, below the salt-cellar (*b*) below sea-level
Netherlands (Spanish territory, but its northern Protestant provinces had been in revolt for decades)
92 **common** (because the Dutch had a non-monarchical government)
lower (*a*) socially inferior (*b*) below sea-level
93 **meaner pride** humbler self-importance (oxymoron), self-respect of social inferiors
fall to (*a*) chow down on (*b*) descend socially to (*c*) submerge in
94 **spit** skewer-full
Portugals Portuguese (ruled by Spain)
94, 95 **for** in place of
94 **plovers** lapwings (a bird commonly eaten at the time)
95 **Indians** natives of the New World or southern Asia (both belonging to the Spanish empire)
Moors (*a*) Africans (*b*) Moslems (*c*) Moriscos (Spanish Moors who had publicly converted to Christianity, but were nevertheless collectively expelled in 1609)
blackbirds (another bird commonly eaten at the time, suggesting the dark skin of Amerindians, Africans, Arabs, and southern Asians)
96 **Holland** a province of the northern Netherlands, 'ready melted' because so much of it is under water; famous for its dairy products, and hence its sauces
97 **voider** tray or basket for clearing table of dirty utensils and leftover food
98 **such cheer** food, entertainment I have just described
suffice satisfy
99 **Zealand** another province of the northern Netherlands, particularly associated with puritans, including English dissenters in exile (playing on 'zeal-land')
for fashion as a mere formality (implying the hypocrisy of Dutch puritans)
100 **meat . . . conscience** (*a*) enough food for any conscience (*b*) enough food, by my conscience (an oath)
101 **any want** anything missing, anyone left with an appetite
Switzerland most famous for its mercenary soldiers, who could be used to supply any 'want' in a nation's own military forces

Polonia, and such pickled things will serve
To furnish out the table.

WHITE KNIGHT CHARLES You say well, sir.
But here's the myst'ry—I tell you in private.

BLACK KNIGHT GONDOMAR
O, we're your cabinets.

WHITE KNIGHT CHARLES When I ha' stopped the mouth
Of one vice, there's another gapes for food.
I'm as covetous as a barren womb,
The grave, or what's more ravenous.

BLACK KNIGHT GONDOMAR We're for you, sir.
Call you that heinous that's good husbandry?
Why, we make money of our faith, our prayers.
We make the very deathbed buy her comforts,
Most dearly pay for all her pious counsels,
Leave rich revènues for a few sale-orisons—
Or else they pass unreconciled without 'em.
Did you but view the vaults within our monasteries
You'd swear then Plutus (whom the fiction calls
The lord of riches) is entombed within 'em.

WHITE KNIGHT CHARLES
Is't possible?

BLACK DUKE OLIVARES
You cannot pass for tuns.

WHITE DUKE OF BUCKINGHAM
But how shall I bestow the vice I bring, sirs?
You quite forget me. I shall be locked out
By your strict key of life.

BLACK KNIGHT GONDOMAR
Is yours so foul, sir?

WHITE DUKE OF BUCKINGHAM
Faith, some that's pleased to make a wanton on't
Call it infirmity of blood, flesh-frailty;
But certain there's a worse name in your book for't.

BLACK KNIGHT GONDOMAR
The trifle of all vices, the mere innocent,
The very novice of this house of clay. Venery?
If I but hug thee hard, I show the worst on't.
It's all the fruit we have here after supper;
Nay, at the ruins of a nunnery once
Six thousand infants' heads found in a fishpond.

WHITE KNIGHT CHARLES
How?

BLACK KNIGHT GONDOMAR
How? Ay, how? How came they thither, think you?
Ulric, bishop of Augsburg, in's epistle
To Nicholas the First, can tell you how.
Maybe he was at cleansing of the pond.
I can but smile to think how it would puzzle
All mother-maids that ever lived in those parts
To know their own child's head. But is this all?

BLACK DUKE OLIVARES [*to White Knight Charles*]
Are you ours yet?

WHITE KNIGHT CHARLES
One more, and I am silenced.
But this that comes now will divide us questionless.
'Tis ten times ten times worse than the forerunners.

BLACK KNIGHT GONDOMAR
Is it so vile there is no name ordained for't?
Toads have their titles, and creation gave
Serpents and adders those names to be known by.

WHITE KNIGHT CHARLES
This of all vices bears the hidden'st venom,
The secret'st poison. I'm an arch-dissembler, sir.

BLACK KNIGHT GONDOMAR
How!

102 **Polonia** Poland
pickled (*a*) preserved in brine, like condiments at a meal (*b*) drunk (*c*) variegated—like the uniform of Swiss soldiers, or the linguistically and theologically diverse populations of both countries

104 **myst'ry** (*a*) private enigma (*b*) state secret

105 **we're . . . cabinets** we are the repositories of your most precious documents and secret discussions

107 **womb** (often described as a mouth, hungry for insemination, and not satisfied until pregnant)

108 **grave** (often described as a mouth which gaped for all mankind)
what's whatever else is

109 **husbandry** household financial management

111 **the very . . . comforts** i.e. even someone on their deathbed pay for their soul's spiritual consolation

112 **her . . . counsels** all the religious advice given to her (the soul)

113 **Leave . . . revènues** bequeath (to the Church) huge estates
sale-orisons (*a*) purchased prayers (*b*) prayers for money

114 **pass unreconciled** die without being reconciled to God or the Church

116 **fiction** myth, pagan religion

117 **lord** god

118 **pass for tuns** walk through because the passage is blocked by so many large casks of wine or huge chests of gold

119 **bestow** dispose of

120–1 **locked . . . life** i.e. excluded by your rigorous code of conduct—echoing the Biblical references to 'the key of David' (Isaiah 22:22, Revelations 3:7) and 'the key to the bottomless pit' (Revelations 9:1, 20:1)

122 **make . . . on't** treat it as something trifling

123 **infirmity . . . flesh-frailty** See 'infirmity of flesh' (Romans 6:19, Galatians 4:13) and 'the spirit indeed is willing, but the flesh is weak' (Matthew 26:41).
blood (in humoural medical theory, the source of lust)

124 **a worse name** i.e. 'lust' or 'adultery' or 'sodomy'

125 **trifle** littlest
mere innocent complete child, simpleton, harmless person

126 **novice** beginner (especially in a monastic 'house')
house of clay i.e. the human body (Job 4:19, etc.)
Venery sex (but also 'sport of hunting', to which King James and his favourites were addicted)

127 **If . . . hard** (one man closely embracing another, with the sexual suggestion of 'hard')

128 **It's . . . fruit** the only dessert is sex (perhaps specifically sodomy, of which Catholics were often accused); the sex we have does not bear fruit (= produce children)

132 **Ulric** St Ulric (890–973)
epistle letter (widely cited by Protestant propagandists)

133 **Nicholas the First** Pope St Nicholas I (d. 867)

136 **mother-maids** alleged virgins who are actually mothers (a blasphemous version of the Virgin birth)

142 **Toads** i.e., even toads (considered poisonous and repulsive)
titles names (but suggesting aristocratic or royal rank)

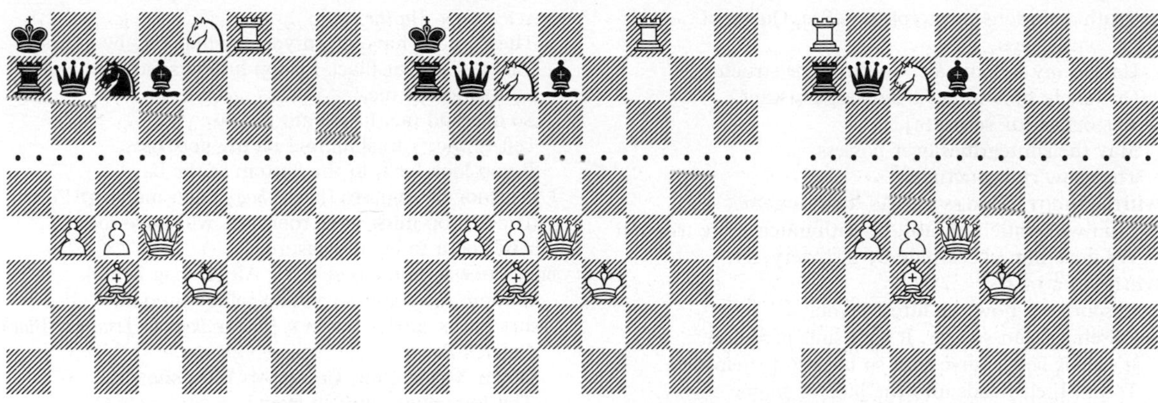

In the endgame, White Duke is behind White Knight, protecting him, deep in the Black House (*a*). At 5.3.161.1 White Knight takes Black Knight, opening up White Duke's threat to Black King (*b*): White Knight could be taken, or Black Duke could be blocked, but either response would still leave Black King vulnerable to attack by the other piece. Black realizes that the cause is lost, and at 5.3.162 White Duke takes Black King (*c*). In all three diagrams, the White pieces below the dotted line are invisible to the audience, and their positions are completely speculative (and irrelevant to the staging).

WHITE KNIGHT CHARLES
It's my nature's brand. Turn from me, sir.
The time is yet to come that e'er I spoke
What my heart meant.
BLACK KNIGHT GONDOMAR
And call you that a vice?
Avoid all profanation, I beseech you.
The only prime state-virtue upon earth,
The policy of empires—O take heed, sir,
For fear it take displeasure and forsake you.
It is a jewel of that precious value
Whose worth's not known but to the skilful lapidary:
The instrument that picks ope princes' hearts
And locks up ours from them with the same motion.
You never came so near our souls till now.
BLACK DUKE OLIVARES [*to White Knight Charles*]
Now you're a brother to us.
BLACK KNIGHT GONDOMAR [*to White Knight Charles*]
What we have done
Has been dissemblance ever.
WHITE KNIGHT CHARLES There you lie then,
And the game's ours. We give thee checkmate by
Discovery, King—the noblest mate of all.
[*White Knight Charles takes Black Knight Gondomar, and White Duke of Buckingham takes Black King Felipe*]
BLACK KING FELIPE I'm lost, I'm taken!
A great shout and flourish
WHITE KNIGHT CHARLES
Ambitious, covetous, luxurious falsehood!
WHITE DUKE OF BUCKINGHAM Dissembler!—that includes all.
BLACK KNIGHT GONDOMAR All hope's confounded.
BLACK QUEEN MARIA Miserable condition!
Enter [*from the White House*] *White King James, White Queen* [*of Bohemia*], *White Bishop* [*of Canterbury*], *with their White Pawns*
WHITE KING JAMES [*embracing White Knight Charles*]
O let my arms be blessed with this dear treasure,

146 **brand** mark of infamy
149 **Avoid . . . profanation** don't be blasphemous (by calling dissembling a vice). Contrast Psalm 26:4, 'neither will I go in with dissemblers'.
150 **state** political, diplomatic
157 **You . . . now** (*a*) you were never so closely connected to us as you are now (*b*) you never understood our insides as well as you do now
158 **brother** soul-mate, fellow Christian, fellow monk. (If he had married the Infanta, White Knight Charles would have become literally the 'brother' (= brother-in-law) of Black King Felipe).
159 **lie** (*a*) are positioned (*b*) tell lies
161 **Discovery** public exposure (of your lies and other vices). In chess, 'checkmate by discovery' occurs when the movement of one piece (here, the White Knight) clears a path by which another piece (here, the White Duke) places the opposing King in check. A knight and duke can place an opposing king in check only if his freedom of movement is blocked by other pieces.
noblest mate most impressive form of checkmate (but in contrast to the other meaning of the words, the 'royal marriage' proposed between Charles and Maria)
163 **Ambitious . . . falsehood** (the four vices which the Black House confesses in this scene)
luxurious lecherous
165–6 **hope's . . . Miserable** Wisdom 3:11 ('For whoso despiseth wisdom and nurture, he is miserable, and their hope is vain')
166 BLACK QUEEN (The object of the 'Spanish Match' appropriately speaks the last speech by the Black House, acknowledging the complete collapse of their strategy.)
Miserable (*a*) unhappy, wretched (*b*) contemptible, pathetic
condition situation, position (but playing on 'contract, treaty', i.e. the proposed diplomatic dynastic marriage)

Truth's glorious masterpiece.—See, Queen of sweetness,
He's in my bosom safe, and this fair structure
Of comely honour his true-blest assistant.

WHITE QUEEN [OF BOHEMIA]
May their integrities ever possess
That pow'rful sanctuary.

WHITE KNIGHT CHARLES As 'twas a game, sir,
Won with much hazard, so with much more triumph
We gave him checkmate by discovery, sir.

WHITE KING JAMES
Obscurity is now the fittest favour
Falsehood can sue for. It well suits perdition.
It's their best course that so have lost their fame
To put their heads into the bag for shame—
The bag opens, and the Black lost [pieces] appear in it. The Jesuit Black Bishop slides in it
And there, behold! The bag, like hell-mouth, opens
To take her due, and the lost sons appear
(Greedily gaping for increase of fellowship
In infamy—the last desire of wretches),
Advancing their perdition-branded foreheads
Like Envy's issues or a bed of snakes.

JESUIT BLACK BISHOP'S PAWN [*in the bag*]
'Tis too apparent. The game's lost, King taken.

FAT BISHOP OF SPALATO [*in the bag*]
The White House has given us the bag, I thank 'em.

BLACK PAWN [*in the bag*]
They'd need have given you a whole bag by yourself.
'Sfoot! This Fat Black Bishop has so squelched and squeezed me,
So overlaid me, I have no verjuice
Left in me. You shall find all my goodness,
If you look for't, in the bottom of the bag.

FAT BISHOP OF SPALATO [*in the bag*] Thou malapert Pawn!
The Bishop must have room, he will have room,
And room to lie at pleasure.

BLACK PAWN [*in the bag*] All the bag I think
Is room too scant for your Spalato paunch.

JESUIT BLACK BISHOP'S PAWN [*in the bag, to Jesuitess Black Queen's Pawn*]
Down, viper of our Order! Art thou showing
Thy impudent whorish front?

JESUITESS BLACK QUEEN'S PAWN [*in the bag*]
Yes, monster holiness!

WHITE KNIGHT CHARLES
Contention in the bag? Is hell divided?

WHITE KING JAMES [*to Black pieces in the bag*]
You'd need have some of majesty and power
To keep good rule amongst you. Make room, Bishop.
[*White King James puts Black King Felipe in the bag*]

FAT BISHOP OF SPALATO [*in the bag*]
I'm not so easily moved when I'm once set.
I scorn to stir for any king on earth.

170 **comely** lovely
assistant i.e. White Duke of Buckingham

174 **We** (emphasizing their cooperation, as at l. 160)

175 **Obscurity** (*a*) darkness, as in the eternal darkness of hell (*b*) inconspicuousness, making it possible to hide (*c*) unintelligibility, as a defence against being caught in a lie
favour reward, mercy

176 **perdition** (*a*) utter ruin (*b*) damnation

177 **fame** good reputation

178 **put ... bag** i.e. hide, conceal their faces
bag sack in which chess pieces are stored (allegorically, death, or hell), but also suggesting the 'game-bag' in which hunters put killed game

178.1 ***bag opens*** (probably by opening a trapdoor, with what appears to be the open top of a huge bag sticking out of it: see the illustrated title-pages, pp. 27 and 1773)
Black ... appear (The Fat Bishop and three captured pawns speak, but not all need appear simultaneously: the dialogue emphasizes their struggling for position within the chaotic bag.)

178.2 ***Jesuit ... slides*** (perhaps because the trapdoor opens under him)

179 **like hell-mouth** (similar—but not identical—to the old-fashioned theatrical representation of the entrance to hell, with devils and painted flames)

180 **lost sons** See John 17:12 (translated 'son of perdition' or 'lost child')

181–2 **Greedily ... wretches** (proverbially, 'misery loves company')

183 **Advancing ... foreheads** raising their heads up (presumably the only part of their bodies visible to the audience)
perdition-branded Genesis 4:15 ('the Lord set a mark upon Cain', who killed his brother Abel out of envy), or 1 Timothy 4:2 ('Speaking lies in hypocrisy, having their conscience seared with a hot iron')

184 **Envy's issues** children of envy (one of the seven deadly sins). See Wisdom 2:24 ('through envy of the devil came death into the world'); the serpent in Eden was often said to have been motivated by envy.
snakes (often associated with Envy)

186 **given ... bag** bagged us (but playing on the colloquial senses 'given us the money-bags' and 'cheated us, left us holding an empty bag')

187 BLACK PAWN (originally the Black Jesting Pawn, in a scene cut from this version: see Additional Passages. Here, perhaps Black Knight's Pawn or White King's Pawn.)

188 **'Sfoot** by God's foot (a strong oath, referring to the feet of Jesus, nailed to the cross)

188–91 **This ... bottom** (possibly suggesting sodomy, the Fat Bishop having drained the Pawn sexually)

189 **overlaid** laid on top of
verjuice acidic juice squeezed from sour fruit (hence, 'life-juices', but perhaps playing on 'vir' meaning 'man' and 'juice' meaning 'semen')

190 **goodness** (Ironic: normally 'virtue', but here 'best part, physically'; slang for sexual prowess)

192 **malapert** impudent

193 **room** (punning on 'Rome': he wanted to become the Pope, which Protestants called 'the Bishop of Rome')

194 **lie** (*a*) lie down (*b*) tell untruths

196 **viper** poisonous snake (alluding to the fable of a frozen viper that a man revived by placing it in his shirt, who was then killed when it bit him: hence, 'treacherous ingrate')
our Order i.e. the Jesuits

197 **front** forehead, face (which should be blushing, if she were not so shameless)
monster holiness (oxymoron, playing on the title 'Your Holiness')

WHITE QUEEN [OF BOHEMIA]
Here comes the Queen. What say you then to her?
[White Queen of Bohemia puts Black Queen Maria in the bag]

FAT BISHOP OF SPALATO *[in the bag]*
Indeed a quean may make a bishop stir.

WHITE KNIGHT CHARLES
Room for the mightiest machiavel politician
That e'er the devil hatched of a nun's egg.
[White Knight Charles beats and kicks Black Knight Gondomar into the bag]

FAT BISHOP OF SPALATO *[in the bag]*
He'll peck a hole i'th' bag and get out shortly.
But I shall be the last man that creeps out,
And that's the misery of greatness ever.—
Foh! the politician is not sound i'th' vent;
I smell him hither.

WHITE DUKE OF BUCKINGHAM
Room for a sunburnt, tansy-faced beloved,
An olive-coloured Ganymede.
[White Duke of Buckingham puts Black Duke Olivares in the bag]
And that's all
That's worth the bagging.

FAT BISHOP OF SPALATO *[in the bag]*
Crowd in all you can,
The Bishop will be still uppermost man,
Maugre King, Queen, or politicïan.

WHITE KING JAMES
So let the bag close now (the fittest womb
For treachery, pride, and malice),
[The bag closes]
whilst we winner-like,
Destroying through heaven's power what would destroy,
Welcome our White Knight with loud peals of joy.
Exeunt

Epilogue. [*Enter*] *the Virgin White Queen's Pawn* **Epilogue**

VIRGIN WHITE QUEEN'S PAWN *[bowing]*
My mistress, the White Queen, hath sent me forth
And bade me bow thus low to all of worth
That are true friends of the White House and cause,
Which she hopes most of this assembly draws.
For any else—by envy's mark denoted,
To those night glow-worms in the bag devoted—
Where'er they sit, stand, and in corners lurk,
They'll be soon known by their depraving work.
But she's assured, what they'd commit to bane
Her White friends' hands will build up fair again.
[Exit]

ADDITIONAL PASSAGES

A Apparently omitted in performance; between 2.2.22 and 23 in a speech by the Fat Bishop.

But most on't out of cullis of cock-sparrows.
'Twill stick and glue the faster to the adversary;
'Twill slit the throat of their most calvish cause,

204 **quean . . . stir** (*a*) prostitute can arouse a bishop sexually (*b*) queen, the most powerful chess piece, can make a chess bishop flee
205 **machiavel** machiavellian
209 **greatness** i.e. overweightness (which makes it difficult for him to squeeze through a little hole—but also, more generally, equating 'Very Important People' with 'Very Fat People')
210 **Foh** (expression of disgust, presumably accompanied by stage business: hell is when someone farts in a crowded phonebooth)
sound . . . vent healthy in the anus (referring to Gondomar's stinking fistula)
212 **sunburnt** dark-skinned (referring not just to a suntan, but to the belief that dark complexions were caused by living closer to the equatorial sun: Ethiopians were called 'sunburnt')
tansy-faced yellow to brownish-orange complexion (like varieties of tansy flower)
213 **olive-coloured** (Olives range in colour from green to brown to black; here punning on the name 'Olivares')
Ganymede In Greek mythology, a youngster and court cupbearer, sodomized by Zeus; hence, catamite, passive homosexual lover. (The relationship between Black King and Black Duke mirrors that rumoured between White King and White Duke.)
216 **Maugre** despite
217 **womb** (*a*) stomach (*b*) uterus (i.e., either the place that eats evil, or the one that gives birth to it)
220 **peals** traditional celebratory bell-ringing (which perhaps accompanies the exit)
Epilogue.3 **House and cause** dynasty and ideology (not always united)
4 **most . . . draws** attracts most of this audience (but *assembly* also suggests 'Parliament' and 'congregation')
5 **envy's mark** (Envy's traditional characteristics were pallor, leanness, hollow eyes, sidelong glances. But perhaps also 'the mark of Cain', again.)
6 **night** dark (referring to the Black House, the darkness of sin or hell, and the underground worm-world)
glow-worms shiny monsters (referring to the common Biblical images of 'worm' for death and the devil)
bag (where fishermen might keep worms for bait)
devoted (*a*) dedicated (*b*) destined
7 **sit . . . corners** (all possible for spectators in the Globe theatre)
9 **bane** poison, death, ruin (perhaps alluding to the massive destruction of Protestant territories in Germany, esp. the Palatinate)
10 **hands** (a cue for applause)
build . . . again beautifully rebuild
again (recognizing that the game will keep being played)
A.1 **cullis** rich broth
cock-sparrows small birds (a regular part of the English diet), notorious for lechery, and eaten as aphrodisiacs
3 **calvish** (*a*) stupid (*b*) idolatrous, worshipping the Biblical golden calf (a Protestant charge against Catholics)

And yet I ate but little butcher's meat
In the conception.

B Apparently omitted in performance; at the beginning of the Black Knight's speech at 2.2.148.

BLACK KNIGHT GONDOMAR [*aside*] A shrewd retort!
He's made our Bishop smell of burning too.
Would I stood farther off, were't no impeachment
To my honour or the game. Would they'd play faster!—

C In place of 3.1.320.

VIRGIN WHITE QUEEN'S PAWN
How, marriage?
JESUITESS BLACK QUEEN'S PAWN
That contaminating act
Would have spoiled all your fortunes. A rape? God bless us!
VIRGIN WHITE QUEEN'S PAWN
Thou talk'st of marriage?
JESUITESS BLACK QUEEN'S PAWN
Yes, I saw the man.
VIRGIN WHITE QUEEN'S PAWN The man?

D Apparently omitted in performance, perhaps because its original comic function had been superseded by addition of the Fat Bishop; in place of 3.1.345–6.

Pray, follow me then, and I'll ease you instantly.
Exeunt

[3.2]
Enter a Black Jesting Pawn [from the Black House]
BLACK JESTING PAWN
I would so fain take one of these White Pawns now.
I'd make him do all under-drudgery,
Feed him with asses' milk (crumbed with goats' cheese)
And all the whitemeats could be devised for him;
I'd make him my white jennet when I pranced
After the Black Knight's litter.
Enter a White Pawn [from the White House]
WHITE PAWN And you'd look then
Just like the devil, striding o'er a night-mare
Made of a miller's daughter.
[*White Pawn takes Black Jesting Pawn*]
BLACK JESTING PAWN A pox on you!
Were you so nigh? I'm taken like a blackbird
In the great snow, this White Pawn grinning over me.
WHITE PAWN
And now because I will not foul my clothes
Ever hereafter (for white quickly soils, you know)—
BLACK JESTING PAWN
Ay, prithee get thee gone, I shall smut thee.
WHITE PAWN
Nay, I'll put that to venture: now I have snapped thee
Thou shalt do all the dirty drudgery
That slavery was e'er put to.
BLACK JESTING PAWN I shall cozen you.
You may chance come and find your work undone then,

5 **conception** imagining, composition (of the book)
B.2 **burning** (*a*) burnt flesh, as in hellfire, or in heretics burned at the stake (*b*) rage
3 **farther off** i.e. not next to the Bishop, as the Knight is in the opening array of a chess game
impeachment (*a*) damage (*b*) impediment
4 **Would** I wish
faster (Like a chessmaster, he is bored by the slow play of amateur moves he can already anticipate.)
D.0.1 ***Black Jesting Pawn*** (not precisely identified, but perhaps the Black King's Pawn, to be captured soon after White King's Pawn). Could be doubled with Black Knight's Pawn, Ignatius, or Error.
1 **fain** gladly
take capture (a chess piece), seize sexually
2 **under-drudgery** (unique Middleton compound, 'under' suggesting both 'menial' and 'sexually subordinate')
3 **asses' milk** (normally used medicinally, not as nourishment)
asses (proverbially clumsy, stupid beast of burden)
milk (proverbially, 'as white as milk')
crumbed with topped with crumbs of
goats' cheese (typically white, unlike most cheese made from cows' milk; not a delicacy, but associated with poor, mountainous regions like Wales and Scotland)
goats (proverbially lecherous; also, by allusion to Matthew 25:32–33, the damned, in contrast to the sheep who are saved)
4 **whitemeats** dairy products
5 **jennet** small Spanish horse—hence 'ridden' by his master (suggesting sexual mounting, but also perhaps the famous scene in *Tamburlaine* when the prisoner Bajazet is turned into a beast of burden)
6.1 ***White Pawn*** (not precisely identified; could be doubled with any characters except the two other pawns in this scene, Black Queen's Pawn, or White Queen's Pawn)
7 **devil** (traditionally black: see title-page of *World Tossed at Tennis*)
striding o'er straddling
night-mare Bad dreams were thought to be caused by a female spirit or goblin (night-mare), which sat upon the dreamer's chest and produced a feeling of suffocation; here, punning on *mare*, 'female horse', which the male devil/pawn rides
8 **Made of** created by a spell which transformed
miller (proverbially, covered with white flour)
8.1 ***White...Pawn*** (the first White capture of a black piece, in almost exactly the middle of the play, so far dominated by aggressive Black moves)
9 **nigh** near
9–10 **blackbird...snow** a blackbird frozen to death or immobilized, conspicuous and easily collected (by a man also presumably covered with snow)
10 **grinning** (*a*) grimacing, baring his fangs (*b*) smiling exaggeratedly, like an idiot
12 **white quickly soils** (why acting companies normally avoided white costumes—which made *Game at Chess* an unprecedented spectacle)
13 **smut** smudge, defile
14 **put...venture** risk that
snapped snatched, bitten or seized quickly
16 **cozen** cheat

For I'm too proud to labour. I'll starve first.
I tell you that beforehand.

WHITE PAWN And I'll fit you then
With a black whip—that shall not be behindhand.

BLACK JESTING PAWN Push, I ha' been used to whipping, I have whipped myself three miles out of town in a morning, and I can fast a fortnight, and make all your meat stink and lie upon your hands.

WHITE PAWN
To prevent that, your food shall be blackberries,
And upon gaudy-days a pickled spider,
Cut out like an anchovy. I'm not to learn
A monkey's ordinary. Come, sir, frisk!

Enter a second Black Pawn [from the Black House]

SECOND BLACK PAWN
Soft, soft you. You have no such bargain on't,
If you look well about you.

[Second Black Pawn takes White Pawn]

WHITE PAWN By this hand,
I'm snapped too, a Black Pawn in the breech of me!
We three look like a bird-spit: a white chick
Between two russet woodcocks.

BLACK JESTING PAWN I'm so glad of this.

WHITE PAWN
But you shall have but small cause, for I'll firk you.

SECOND BLACK PAWN
Then I'll firk *you* again.

WHITE PAWN And I'll firk *him* again.

BLACK JESTING PAWN
Mass, here will be old firking. I shall have
The worst on't, for I can firk nobody.
We draw together now, for all the world
Like three flies with one straw thorough their buttocks.

Exeunt

[3.3]

Enter Jesuitess Black Queen's Pawn and Virgin White Queen's Pawn

JESUITESS BLACK QUEEN'S PAWN
This is the room he did appear to me in,

18 **too...labour** (Protestants condemned the 'idleness' of Catholic clergy, nuns, and monks.)
proud (stereotypical Spanish vice)
starve Compare the satire on Spain's niggardly diet in 5.3.
19 **beforehand** in advance
fit fix, suit, be prepared for
20 **behindhand** in arrears (usually of payments on a debt, here of 'payment' as punishment, 'paid' promptly)
22 **whipped myself** (referring to Catholic ritual self-flagellation)
23 **fast** (another Catholic ritual—which means a Catholic servant can ignore a master who attempts to punish or intimidate him by withholding food)
fortnight two weeks
24 **meat** food
stink go bad, rot
25 **blackberries** (commonest wild fruit in England, therefore plentiful and cheap)
26 **gaudy-days** holidays, feast-days
27 **anchovy** small brown fish (usually pickled)
not to learn i.e., don't need to be taught
28 **monkey** (Imported black monkeys were sometimes kept as pets, and were notoriously lecherous.)
ordinary diet, daily meal; but also suggesting (*a*) order of divine service, esp. in the Roman Catholic mass (*b*) heraldic device (like Middleton's coat of arms, which included a monkey)
frisk move briskly, dance
28.1 ***second Black Pawn*** (not precisely identified)
30.1 ***Second...Pawn*** (pawn-exchange)
31 **breech** (*a*) britches, trousers (*b*) buttocks, arse (*c*) breach, fissure, gap in fortifications
32 **bird-spit** shish kebab, birds skewered for roasting
chick young chicken (also a term of endearment, 'child, young thing')
33 **woodcocks** (*a*) large migratory birds, often eaten (*b*) idiots, 'dodos'
34 **firk** whip, lash (often suggesting modern 'screw')
36 **Mass** by the mass (an appropriate oath for a Catholic)
old grand, plentiful, traditional
37 **on't** of it
39 **three...buttocks** (perhaps suggesting insects used for fishing bait, or mounted for display in a 'cabinet of curiosities')
flies not just houseflies, but any flying insects, including (white) moths; common and unappreciated, like pawns or commoners
thorough through
39.1 ***Exeunt*** (presumably like a three-man train, each thrusting against the one in front of him—an opportunity for obscene stage business)

OCCASIONAL POEMS, 1619–25

Edited by Gary Taylor

THOUGH Oscar Wilde was famous for his wit, without historical testimony it would be almost impossible to prove that any particular *bon mot* was a genuine Oscarism. Because Middleton never published a collection of the shorter products of his 'witty muse', we will never know how many small poems he wrote. With longer works, we can confidently identify Middleton's distinctive style, but as the size of the data sample shrinks the statistical reliability of such stylistic fingerprinting also diminishes. Many anonymous early modern poems might be Middleton's, but his name did not adhere to them because the name would have been irrelevant to readers or dangerous for the author. It hardly seems a coincidence that no satirical political poems are attributed to Middleton (one of the great Renaissance satirists), despite the survival of hundreds of libellous verses written in his lifetime: if he had written such poems, he would have had every incentive to conceal his authorship. 'The Picture Plainly Explained' was printed as part of an edition of *A Game at Chess* that concealed the name not only of the author but also of the printer, engraver, and publisher. That anonymity itself announced something about the nature of the work.

Notably, for several of the poems explicitly attributed to Middleton in early documents, his authorship is part of the poem's meaning. A playwright praises an actor, or another playwright; the imprisoned author of *A Game at Chess* petitions for his release; a gift identifies the giver. But other poems belong to what Marcy North calls the 'Anonymous Renaissance'. Many of Middleton's contemporaries made conscious use of the diverse possibilities created by the absence of a name. Middleton almost certainly wrote the epitaph on Sir George Bolles and the poem celebrating the opening of the Chapel of St James—he is historically linked to the occasion for both poems, and stylistically they resemble him more than any rival candidate—but the meaning of those two poems, for early readers, was not in any way affected by who wrote them. Attribution would not only have been irrelevant; it could have detracted from the seemingly impersonal authority of the text. Middleton, as the official Chronologer of London, was being paid to praise Bowles and Barker, and any acknowledgement of his authorship might have diminished each poem's credibility.

Whether attributed or anonymous, all Middleton's uncollected verses are public artifacts, not simulated autobiography. He wrote in many once-popular genres: epitaph, prison poem, verse caption to a painting or a printed image. The verses celebrating the christening of St James church might be included in Middleton's *Honourable Entertainments*, though they are not attributed to a dramatic persona and deliberately make no gestures toward theatrical illusion. The commendatory poem was the most common genre of literary criticism before the Restoration (Chandler); at least 4,748 commendatory poems were printed in British books between 1478 and 1641 (Williams). Middleton's praise of Webster's *Duchess of Malfi* will stand comparison with any rival example, including Ben Jonson's famous commendation of Shakespeare. 'Every particular will bear a large paraphrase', eyewitness John Holles said of Middleton's *A Game at Chess*, and the same might be said of his occasional poems.

None of them are love poems, or lust poems. Middleton's plays include many song lyrics, including the enormously popular 'Hence, all you vain delights' (*Valour* 3.3.36–54), with its speaker/singer's evocative, paradoxical praise of the deliciousness of melancholy. But, like other seventeenth-century poets from Jonson to Dryden, Middleton abandoned the belated Petrarchanism which had dominated sixteenth-century English verse from Wyatt to Shakespeare; sonnets gave way to epigrams. But Jonson's epigrams can still give the impression of being deeply personal poems, representing his reaction to the death of his son or an invitation to dinner. Even when it treats less intimate material, Jonson's verse focuses our attention squarely on the poet himself, on Jonson rhetorically constructing his own cultural authority. The contrast with Middleton is evident in Jonson's epigram to the great Elizabethan actor Edward Allen (usually spelled 'Alleyn'):

> If Rome so great, and in her wisest age,
> Feared not to boast the glories of her stage—
> As skilful Roscius and grave Aesop, men
> Yet crowned with honours (as with riches, then),
> Who had no less a trumpet of their name
> Than Cicero, whose every breath was fame—
> How can so great example die in me,
> That, Allen, I should pause to publish thee?—
> Who both their graces in thyself hast more
> Outstripped, than they did all that went before,
> And present worth in all dost so contract,
> As others speak, but only thou dost act.
> Wear this renown. 'Tis just, that who did give
> So many poets life, by one should live.

Jonson rhymes 'thee' with 'me', and the poem tells us more about its author than its subject. The comparison of Alleyn to Roscius and Aesop praises the actor, but it also displays the poet's own learning, which was central to Jonson's self-made reputation. Roscius and Aesop give place to Cicero, with whom Jonson (in the next line) implicitly compares himself. Jonson praises an actor who surpasses the actors Cicero praised, thus implying that Jonson's judgement actually outstrips Cicero's. After the complex twelve-line-long first sentence, the simple imperative 'Wear this renown' assumes that 'this' little poem by Jonson itself constitutes and guarantees fame. At the pinnacle of the hierarchical final conceit, emphatically saved for last, stands the unique poet Jonson ('one') who gives life to the actor who gives life to 'many' unnamed other 'poets'. Jonson's binaries—Rome/England, actor/author, many/one—create a structure which defines and affirms Jonson's unparalleled, world-historically significant me me me.

Middleton also uses 'me' as a rhyme word, and also defines himself as 'one' in the final line of a poem. But Middleton's authorial 'one', at the end of his plea 'To the King', is diminutive, not aggrandizing: 'but...one man'. Even 'man' is minuscule: this is not Pico della Mirandola's or Jacob Burckhardt's god-like Renaissance Man, but Middleton's self-deflating pun on 'man' as chess piece and personal servant. Middleton defines himself as just a single man (in a kingdom that contains perhaps two million of the King's male subjects), just a single chess piece (on a board containing thirty-two), and just a pawn, a servant to some other more important piece/person. Unlike Jonson's 'me', Middleton's 'me' is an explanatory afterthought: he does not assume that the King even knows who he is, but explicates 'one man' by appending 'that's me', and then his signature.

Jonson's poem on the actor Alleyn differs even more remarkably from Middleton's poem on the actor Burbage, where the first person pronoun does not appear at all, and the reader's eyes are focused wholly on Burbage. Middleton's poem is, typically, much smaller than Jonson's, just as Middleton's plays are shorter than Jonson's, as Middleton's body was less bulky than Jonson's. Middleton's tight style nevertheless packs as much punch in four lines as Jonson manages in fourteen. This may not at first be obvious, because Middleton's lines seem so characteristically, disarmingly simple.

> Astronomers and star-gazers this year
> Write but of four eclipses; five appear,
> Death interposing Burbage—and their staying
> Hath made a visible eclipse of playing.

Middleton does not begin with the greatness of Rome. He does not invoke millennia of praise. He doesn't say 'I'm like Cicero.' Instead, he begins with ephemera, implicitly compares himself to the nameless writers of almanacs, and limits himself to 'this year'. His subject is not eternity. His subject, he announces, is only his (our) own little moment. Jonson explicitly compares modern London to ancient Rome. Middleton also situates modern London in a larger cultural context, but his allusion is subtler. 'Astronomers and star-gazers' echoes Isaiah 47:13: 'Let now the astrologers, the star-gazers, the prognosticators, stand up, and save thee from these things that shall come upon thee.' That's the translation in the Geneva Bible (1560), the most popular personal Bible of the time; the King James translation (1611) is identical, except that it adds 'monthly' before 'prognosticators'. This verse, prescribed by the Book of Common Prayer, had been read to congregations every December 20 for sixty years, so it would have been familiar to many of Middleton's contemporaries. But Middleton's art, like Burbage's, was not exclusive or elitist. You can miss this allusion entirely and still make sense of the poem. Middleton's word *astronomers* may be a synonym for *astrologers*, but in any case the Greek word is more learned, and suggests a more educated activity, than the dismissive Anglo-Saxon 'star-gazers', which can refer to anyone who looks up at the sky, gaping in ignorance and wonder, in the way that groundlings at the Globe might have looked up at Burbage on the raised stage. Connoisseurs and amateurs alike, this year, mourn Burbage.

The clustered consonants (str, nd|st, rg, rs|th, s|y), the four stresses in the last five syllables, make this first line difficult to articulate. Part of the decorum of epitaphs, part of their function, is to slow us down, make us stop, think. The poem comes to a sharp stop twice in its second line: abruptly, 'five appear'. Astrologers, astronomers, and almanacs fascinate Middleton because they epitomize the overwhelming human desire to predict the future, an obsession writers and Calvinists share with farmers, businessmen, theatre owners and actors. Eclipses should be predictable; four of them have been predicted, to the day and hour. Then, unexpectedly, we face a fifth. Disturbingly, the universe refuses to be scheduled. And another unexpectedness attends this fifth eclipse. 'When beggars die,' Shakespeare tells us, 'there are no comets seen; the heavens themselves blaze forth the death of princes.' Queen Anna had died eleven days before Burbage, at Hampton Court, and her body was lying in state at Denmark House during the days when Burbage died and was buried. The royal expiration inspired poets like Patrick Hannay to declare that 'general darkness all the world o'erspreads'. We might therefore expect, any reader in March 1619 might expect, the third line to read, 'Death interposing Anna'. Middleton interposes Burbage where we would expect Anna, as an eclipse interposes one thing where we expect another. In context, Middleton's epitaph implicitly claims that the death of a mere actor was more important than the death of the Queen of England, Scotland, and Ireland.

'Five appear' announces a new eclipse, and the first word of the next line links that eclipse to 'Death'. Eclipses were traditionally regarded as omens, warnings, or signs of disaster. Middleton could have claimed that the prophecy written in the skies by those four eclipses of 1619 was being fulfilled by the death of Burbage (or Queen Anne, or both). But he does not claim that. Four eclipses are not enough; Middleton adds a fifth. Or rather, Death adds a fifth, 'interposing' that fifth eclipse, slipping it in between the other four. With great tact—which is to say, by sleight of hand introducing an outrageous idea in such a way that it seems natural—'Death interposing Burbage' transforms the actor's death into an eclipse, transforms Burbage himself into a heavenly body. The fifth eclipse at first seems to be, but then is not, the usual pathetic fallacy: unlike us, the universe is not convulsed by grief when someone we love dies. Middleton is not Shakespeare's Cleopatra, exclaiming that 'there should be now a huge eclipse Of sun and moon' as the macrocosm registers the death of microcosmic Mark Antony. The verb *interpose*—'to place between'—was often used in a technical sense, describing the movement of the moon into a position where it blocked the sun (or of the earth into a position between sun and moon). Since the eclipse has already been introduced, 'interposing Burbage' represents the actor as an astronomical object large enough to eclipse the sun or moon. Behind this metaphysical conceit lies a recurrent theme in classical mythology, echoed in many Renaissance texts: extraordinary individuals get transformed, at death, into stars. Burbage, though, is not just a star; Burbage is big enough to block the sun; Burbage is, we might say—thinking of the theatre where he had acted his greatest roles for two decades—'the Globe'.

But the poem does not explicitly say any of that. We are saved from the absurdity of this image by the verb's more common, less technical sense: Death blocks Burbage, Death gets in his way. Death is an unexpected interruption. Death intercepts, obstructs Burbage, creating an eclipse by blocking the light that Burbage normally emanates. Depending on how we interpret the participle, Burbage is obstructing or obstructed. In either reading, the phrase puts Burbage in motion. If Burbage is 'placed between', then he is an actor, set in motion by someone else. Death, then, is the playwright, the writer of the final script that Burbage performs. If Burbage is 'interrupted', then Death's unscripted interposing denies the actor his last opportunity to 'enter, posing'.

But 'Death interposing Burbage' is itself only an interruption, a participial phrase between two simple sentences. The third line's first three words link personification to Latinate technical verb to unusual proper name; its last three words link the commonest of all conjunctions to a common pronoun and a common Anglo-Saxon verb. Two consecutive unstressed syllables ('-age, and') throw the weight of the line forward onto two consecutive stressed syllables ('their stay'), and the consonant conjunctions (nd | th . . . r | st) force us to slow down to articulate the spondee. Those two stressed syllables make, despite their simplicity, two complicated claims. Why 'their'? Why the plural instead of the singular? Epitaphs are usually all about singularity. And why 'stay'? Epitaphs are poems about people who have left us. What slows us down is not only the consonants and the stresses, but the unexpectedness of these words, these claims.

Whose stay? Death's and Burbage's. Death and Burbage, at opposite ends of the verb in the preceding phrase, are now coupled: no longer subject and object, active and passive, but united, as in an eclipse two formerly distinct objects become one. And what is this new odd couple doing? They stay. Or rather, they are staying. Middleton could easily have written 'stay', and rhymed it with 'play' in the last line, but he prefers the present participial noun, with its sense of renewed continuing activity: not a single stay, but a stretched-out staying.

The most famous epitaph on Burbage is the notorious, anonymous, snide quip, 'Exit Burbage'. Middleton's 'their staying' characterizes Burbage's death in exactly the opposite way. The sense is not, 'Burbage has left the stage' but rather, 'We are waiting for Burbage to enter, and he keeps not appearing, he keeps staying backstage.' The eclipse refuses to end. The Earl of Pembroke—the Lord Chamberlain, responsible for formal entertainments at court—wrote on 20 May (more than two months after Burbage's funeral) that he could not bear to attend a court performance of *Pericles* by the King's Men 'so soon after the loss of my old acquaintance Burbage'. Watching *Pericles* would have been painful because Pembroke would keep expecting to see Burbage enter, and Burbage would keep staying away. This is, I think, how many of us are affected by the death of someone we love. We cannot really imagine eternity; we cannot imagine that someone has exited, forever. Intellectually, we may know this; but cognition and emotion clash. What repeatedly pains us, after someone's death, is that we keep being startled by their failure to arrive. It is not that someone has gone away: the people we love leave our sight routinely, every day; the problem is that, this time, they have stopped returning. We keep expecting them to come around the corner or enter the room or step on stage, and they don't. It is as though Burbage, slower in his old age, has simply missed his cue, or been slow responding to his cue. Someone, backstage, has intercepted him.

But the poem continues, across the temporary 'staying' of the line-break. Middleton usually prefers the colloquial 'has', but the last line begins with the more formal, solemn, old-fashioned, Biblical 'hath'. Again, the cluster of consonants ('th | m') slows us down. 'Hath made' what? Made us cry, made us grieve, made us think about our own mortality? No, their staying makes another paradox: a 'visible eclipse'. The adjective *visible* enforces the implicit or submerged oxymoron in the earlier verb *appear*: in an eclipse what appears is the failure of light to appear, what's visible is the sudden invisibility of what we expect to see. Again, Middleton's language has a technical meaning: a visible eclipse is one visible at our latitude and longitude, but it is also an eclipse that is less than total, that leaves part of the disk of the sun or moon still visible. Having compared Burbage's death to an eclipse, Middleton now precisely qualifies that hyperbole: it is only an eclipse *here*, at the meridian of London, and even here it is not total.

And the last two words further qualify that image: it is only an eclipse 'of playing'. The fifth eclipse, announced earlier, is not an astronomical convulsion, but just a local interruption of theatrical activity. Out of (enforced) respect for the memory of Queen Anne, the theatres were closed until her funeral on 13 May. By instead attributing the all-too-visible eclipse of playing to Burbage's death, Middleton again implicitly claims that it was more important than the death of the Queen. Finally, the word 'playing' summons up all the more general senses of play, merriment, joy, spontaneity. It also announces an eclipse of 'feigning', pretending. The actor's death is not fiction, is not feigning, is not acting; this time, the death is real.

But it is also temporary. It is only an eclipse, a momentary interruption of light. It is only one eclipse out of five, one death among many deaths, and our grief for Burbage's death, our memory of his life, are as brief as an eclipse, or a temporary closure of the theatres, or an ephemeral almanac, thrown away at the end of its year, 'this year', the traditional period of formal rituals of mourning. Our grief is as brief as our own lives. Or perhaps it is death that is brief, only an eclipse, only a momentary blocking of the light, which will in due course return, in the promised resurrection of the dead. Middleton lets us choose how to interpret this eclipse.

With the exception of this 'elegant' epitaph, the tributes to Burbage after his death 'were notable for quantity rather than quality' (Edmond). Theatre historians often quote the others, because they tell us which roles Burbage played, or how he played them; we quote them as evidence, as archival records, not as poems. Middleton's four lines tell us nothing about Burbage's performances, but they are the most beautiful and moving tribute in English to any actor. There is no 'I' in this poem, but it takes three to eclipse: an observer, a light, and something that gets between the observer and the light. Middleton is quietly present among those implied observers, the communal 'we' of theatre people and theatre audiences, the community of mourners for any death, temporarily unable to see.

SEE ALSO

Textual introduction and apparatus: *Companion*, 992
Authorship and date: 'Burbage', *Companion*, 404; 'Bolles', 416; 'St James', 427; 'Malfi', 438; 'To the King', 441; 'Hammond', 441; 'Picture', 442

Occasional Poems, 1619–25

Burbage

On the death of that great master in his art and quality, painting and playing: Richard Burbage

Astronomers and star-gazers this year
Write but of four eclipses; five appear,
Death interposing Burbage—and their staying
Hath made a visible eclipse of playing.

Burbage See Critical Introduction. Next to our edited text we reproduce the source: the only surviving copy, in a personal manuscript miscellany compiled about 1630 by Robert Bishop.

Title ***quality*** profession (especially used of acting)
painting Burbage was a painter, but also an expert in face-painting, i.e. actor's make-up.
playing acting
Richard Burbage Burbage was buried on 16 March 1619 in the London parish of St Leonard Shoreditch; he died on a Saturday in Lent, 13 March.

1 **Astronomers** (not distinguished from what we now call 'astrologers')

2 **Write** (in the very popular annual almanacs: Thomas Bretnor's London *Almanac*, writing 'Of Eclipses of this year 1619', notes that 'Although we in England shall see no eclipse at all this year, yet will our neighbouring dwellers and lunar inhabitants behold the luminaries four times eclipsed', and then goes on to describe where and when the four eclipses will occur.)

3 **interposing** (*a*) intruding, placing between [the other eclipses] (*b*) intruding, placing between [the sun and the earth, or the sun and the moon] (*c*) interrupting
their Death's and Burbage's

4 **visible** apparent, evident; but also in the technical sense 'partial, not creating total darkness'
playing (*a*) acting, dancing, theatre (*b*) free movement, live mobility (*c*) amusement, merriment

Bolles [*On Sir George Bolles*]

Honour, integrity, compassïon:
Those three filled up the lifetime of this man.
Of honour: the grave praetorship he bare,
Which he discharged with conscience, truth, and care.
He possessed earth, as he might heaven possess:
Wise to do right, but never to oppress.
His charity was better felt than known,
For when he gave there was no trumpet blown.
What more can be comprised in one man's fame
To crown a soul and leave a living name?
All his just praise in her life may be read,
The true wife of his worth as of his bed.

Honour, Integrity,
Compaſſion,
Thoſe three fil'd up
the life time of this man:
Of Honour, the grave
Prætorſhip he bare,
Which he diſcharg'd with
Conſcience, Truth, and Care,
He poſſes'd Earth,
as he might Heaven poſſeſſe,
Wiſe to doe right,
but never to oppreſſe.

His Charity was better
felt than knowne,
For when he gave,
there was no Trumpet blown.
What more can be compriz'd
in one mans fame,
To crowne a ſoule,
and leave a living name?
All his juſt praiſe
in her life may be read,
The true Wife of his worth
as of his bed.

Bolles Sir George Bolles (1538–1621) was Lord Mayor of London in 1617–18; Middleton wrote *The Triumphs of Honour and Industry* to celebrate his inauguration. He was buried in the parish church of St Swithin, with 'A very fair monument on the south side of the chancel, with this inscription' (*Survey of London*, 1633). The church was destroyed in the Great Fire of London (1666).

The source is a revised and expanded edition of John Stow's *Survey of London*, edited by Anthony Munday and others, published in 1633. Each verse line is divided into two type lines, because the full line would not fit in the narrow column of the double-column page.

1 **compassïon** (four syllables: Middleton often treated '-ion' as two syllables, particularly at the end of a verse line)

2 **filled up** (perhaps punning on his name, which could be pronounced 'bowls')
man (rhyming with 'compassïon'—a typical Middleton rhyme)

3 **praetorship** i.e. office of Lord Mayor (associating the government of London with that of ancient Rome)
bare bore, carried the burden of

5 **possessed earth** (*a*) owned land (*b*) inhabited a body
as (*a*) in the same way that (*b*) in a way that would make it likely that

7–8 **His ... blown** i.e. his acts of charity were anonymous, were not publicly trumpeted or bragged about (playing on the phrase 'blow your own trumpet', brag about yourself)

10 **living** ever-living, surviving
name reputation

12 **true** (*a*) genuine, real (*b*) sexually faithful, chaste
wife The funeral monument 'was erected at the sole cost and charges of Joan, Lady Bolles, in memory of her late dear and worthy husband... which Lady Joan was the eldest daughter of that worthy and famous deceased Knight, Sir John Hart, sometimes likewise Lord Mayor of the said City of London' (*Survey of London*).

As David *could*
his eyes no rest afford,
Till he had found
a place out to the Lord,
To build an Altar:
So this man of worth,
The mirrour which
these later dayes brings forth,
Barkham *the worthie,*
whose immortall name,
Marble's too weake to hold,
for this workes fame.
He never ceast
in industrie and care,
From ruines to
redeeme this House of Praier;
Following in this
the holy Patriarks waies,
That ready were
him Altars still to raise,
Where they receiv'd a blessing:
So this Lord,
Scarce warme in Honours seat,
did first accord
To this most pious worke,
in which is shewne,
Gods blessing, and his thanks
met both in one.
The charge
the honourable Citie beares,
whose bounty
in ful Noblenesse appeares
To acts of best condition,
in such wise,

St James

[*The Temple of St James*]

[*I*]

As David could his eyes no rest afford
Till he had found a place out to the Lord
To build an altar, so this man of worth,
The mirror which these later days bring forth,
Barkham the worthy, whose immortal name
Marble's too weak to hold, for this work's fame.
He never ceased in industry and care
From ruins to redeem this house of prayer,
Following in this the holy patriarchs' ways,
That ready were Him altars still to raise
Where they received a blessing; so this lord,
Scarce warm in honour's seat, did first accord
To this most pious work, in which is shown
God's blessing and his thanks met both in one.
The charge the honourable City bears,
Whose bounty in full nobleness appears
To acts of best condition, in such wise

St James These verses were written to celebrate the consecration of the 'very beautiful and comely parish church' of St James, in Aldgate Ward just inside London's old north-east wall, on 2 January 1623; the City of London had paid for the church's restoration, and the Mayor, both Sheriffs, and sixteen aldermen were present. The church was destroyed in the Great Fire of London, rebuilt, and then completely demolished in 1874.

The source is the same edition of *Survey of London* that contains 'Bolles'.

I 'On a fair table [i.e., tablet] hanging in the chancel are these verses depicted' (*Survey of London*, 1633)

1–3 **As David . . . altar** 2 Samuel 24:18–25, 1 Chronicles 21:18–29. (This is the beginning of the construction of the Temple in Jerusalem.)

4 **mirror** exemplary ideal
later days (Seventeenth-century Christians believed that they lived in the world's old age.)
bring forth (*a*) give birth to (*b*) bring to public attention

5 **Barkham** Edward Barkham, Lord Mayor of London 1621–22; Middleton celebrated his inauguration in *The Sun in Aries*

8 **house of prayer** (a phrase that occurs seven times in the King James Bible)

9 **patriarchs** Noah, Abraham, Jacob, Moses, and Joshua

12 **Scarce . . . seat** i.e., immediately after becoming Lord Mayor
accord agree

14 **his** Barkham's

15 **charge** expense

That all things, bettering by their ruin, rise.
Two noble faithful supervisors then
(Amongst a Senate of religious men)
Selected were, to whom the care they gave:
Generous Hamersley, and Campbell the grave,
Each being a masterpiece of zeal and care
Towards God's own temple, fit for truth's affair.
Now at the blessèd foundress I arrive,
Matilda, whom Henry the First did wive.
The christendom she gave it held the same
Till James our sovereign gave it his own name.
And since I touch antiquity so near,
Observe what notes remarkable appear:
An alderman of London was at first
Prime prior of this church; falling to worst,
It is now raised by encouragement and care
Of a Lord Mayor of London, which is rare

That all things, bettering
by their ruine, rise.
Two noble faithfull
Supervisors then,
Amongst a Senate
of religious men,
Selected were,
to whom the care they gave,
Generous Hamersley,
and Cambell *the grave,*
Each being a master-piece
of zeale and care
Towards Gods owne Temple,
fit for truths affaire.
Now at the blessed Foundresse
I arrive,

Matilda, *whom*
Henry *the first did wive,*
The Christendome she gave it
held the same,
Till James *our Soveraigne*
gave it his owne name.
And since I touch
Antiquity so neere,
Observe what notes
remarkable appeare:
An Alderman of London
was at first
Prime Prior of this Church.
Falling to worst,
It is now rais'd
by encouragement and care
Of a Lord Maior of London,
which is rare,

18 **bettering . . . ruin** improving as a result of their deterioration (paradox): the new church is not only restored, but converted from Catholic to Protestant worship
bettering (perhaps pronounced as two syllables, 'bett'ring')

20 **Senate** (comparing the Aldermen of London to the Senators of ancient Rome)

22 **Hamersley . . . Campbell** Hugh Hamersley and James Campbell, Aldermen (named in the dedication to *Entertainments*, 12–13)

24 **affair** business (since both were business-men)

26 **Matilda** Matilda 'the good Queen' (1080–1118), famous for her piety and her patronage of religious foundations, first wife of Henry I (1069–1135), youngest son of William the Conqueror; she founded the Priory in 1108.

27 **christendom** christening, giving of a Christian name
held remained

31–2 **alderman . . . prior** 'Norman, the first prior, was made an alderman of London, and rode with them on solemn days, but in an ecclesiastical habit' (marginal note, *Survey of London*). Norman was 'the first canon regular in all England' (*Survey*, p. 145).

And worth obſerving.
Then, as I began,
I end beſt with
the honour of the man.
This Cities firſt Lord Maior
lies buried here,
Fitz-Alwine,
of the Drapers Company,
And the Lord Maior,
whoſe fame now ſhines ſo cleere,
Barkham,
is of the ſame Society.

And worth observing. Then, as I began,
I end best with the honour of the man.
This city's first Lord Mayor lies buried here,
  Fitz Ailwin, of the Drapers' Company,
And the Lord Mayor, whose fame now shines so clear,
  Barkham, is of the same society.

The riſing here
of the cleere Goſpels Sunne,
Is through the Senates
free donation.
The Globe of that bright Sunne,
the God of might,
Chriſt Ieſus is the riſing
and the light.
The heat the bleſſed Spirit
of Truth and Right;
And as theſe three,
the Globe, the light, the heat,
Are all one Sunne,
ſo Three One God compleat:
Thrice Allelujah
ſpeakes about the rayes,
That Three in One
may onely have the praiſe.

[*II*]

The rising here of the clear Gospel's sun
Is through the Senate's free donatïon.
The globe of that bright sun, the God of might;
Christ Jesus is the rising and the light;
The heat, the blessèd Spirit of truth and right.
And as these three (the globe, the light, the heat)
Are all one sun, so three one God complete.
Thrice 'Alleluia' speaks about the rays
That three in one may only have the praise.

38 **Fitz Ailwin** Henry fitz Ailwin (d. 1212), who held a lifetime appointment as Mayor, traditionally said to have begun in 1189
40 **society** association, guild
II 'there is a fair monument in the east end of the chancel, made in resemblance of a golden sun, with beams and rays very ingeniously formed, charactering these verses in and among them' (*Survey of London*). These verses are separated from the preceding forty. The nine lines—three times three—formally mirror their subject (the Trinity).
2 **free donatïon** (a phrase usually referring to the Emperor Constantine's act, making Christianity the state religion of Rome; here, 'Senate' contrasts with Emperor, and the English church 'here' with the Roman one)
3 **God of might** God the Father (a phrase used in John Hopkin's *The Whole Book of Psalms* (1562) and in Matthew Parker's translation of *The Whole Psalter* (1567?), Psalm 2, 24, 77, 95, 146, and often thereafter)
5 **Spirit** Holy Spirit
9 **three in one** the Holy Trinity, the Christian notion of one God in three aspects (Father, Son, Holy Spirit), alluding to the church's medieval name (the Priory of the Holy Trinity, called Christchurch) and to its temporary name during the rebuilding ('Trinity Christ's Church')

[III]

This sacred structure, which this Senate fames,
Our King hath styled 'The Temple of St James'.

This Sacred Structure,
which this Senate fames,
Our King hath stil'd,
The Temple of S. James.

Malfi

In the just worth of that well-deserver,
Master John Webster,
and upon this masterpiece of tragedy
[The Duchess of Malfi]

In this thou imitat'st one rich and wise,
That sees his good deeds done before he dies;
As he by works, thou by this work of fame
Hast well provided for thy living name.
To trust to others' honorings is worth's crime;
Thy monument is raised in thy lifetime.
And 'tis most just, for every worthy man
Is his own marble, and his merit can
Cut him to any figure and express
More art than death's cathedral palaces,
Where royal ashes keep their court. Thy note
Be ever plainness; 'tis the richest coat.
Thy epitaph only the title be:
Write 'Duchess', that will fetch a tear for thee—
For who e'er saw this duchess live and die,
That could get off under a bleeding eye?

In Tragœdiam
Ut lux ex tenebris ictu percussa Tonantis,
Illa, ruina malis, claris fit vita poetis.

In the iust VVorth, of that well Deseruer,
Mr. IOHN WEBSTER, *and Vpon this*
Maister-peece of Tragœdy.

IN this Thou imitat'st one Rich, and Wise,
That sees His Good Deedes done before he dies;
As He by workes, Thou by this worke of Fame,
Ha'st well prouided for thy Liuing Name;
To trust to others Honorings, is Worth's Crime,
Thy Monument is rais'd in thy Life Time;
And 'tis most iust; for euery Worthy Man
Is his owne Marble; and his Merit can
Cut Him to any Figure, and expresse
More Art, then Deaths Cathedrall Pallaces,
Where Royall Ashes keepe their Court: thy Note
Be euer Plainnes, 'tis the Richest Coate:
Thy Epitaph onely the Title *bee,*
Write, Dutchesse, *that will fetch a teare for thee,*
For who e're saw this Dutchesse *liue, and dye,*
That could get off vnder a Bleeding Eye.

In Tragædiam.

Vt Lux ex Tenebris ictu percussa TONANTIS;
Illa, (*Ruina Malis*) *claris fit Vita Poetis.*

Thomas Middletonus,
Poëta & Chron:
Londinensis.

III This couplet is separated from the preceding verses by prose, which identifies the Mayor and Aldermen who constitute 'this Senate'.

1 **which . . . fames** (*a*) which they make famous (*b*) which makes them famous

2 **Our King** James I, who personally authorized the building of the new church, in response to a petition from George Abbot, Archbishop of Canterbury
styled named, given the title

Malfi The poem appears in the first edition (1623) of Webster's play, after Webster's dedication and before shorter commendatory poems by William Rowley and John Ford (with whom Middleton collaborated that year on *Gypsy*). The play was printed by Nicholas Okes, who also printed most of Middleton's pageants and the first edition of *A Game at Chess*. In this and other copies of the printed quarto, ink from the other side of the page shows through. Italic type is used for the Dedication and for all the commendatory poems.

1 **this** (*a*) writing this play (*b*) publishing this play

4 **living name** ever-living reputation

6 **Thy monument . . . lifetime** (comparing Webster to people who build their own tombs before they die)

8 **marble** monument, statue

9 **Cut** sculpt

10–11 **cathedral . . . court** (probably referring to Westminster Abbey, where King James in 1612 had buried his son Prince Henry and re-interred his mother Mary, Queen of Scots; most recently, Queen Anne was buried there in 1619)

16 **get off under** escape, get away with a payment less than
bleeding eye (imagining tears as drops of blood: compare *Game* 1.1.6, 'My soul bleeds at mine eyes')

17–19 ***In . . . poetis*** 'To Tragedy: | As light from darkness springs at the Thunderer's stroke, | So is life to the famous poet, ruin to the bad.' Tragedy is gendered female in Latin.

18 ***lux ex tenebris*** (later motto of the Freemasons)
Tonantis (from *Tonans*, Thunderer, a common classical and neo-Latin epithet for the supreme deity: 'Jupiter the Thunderer' occurs at *Duchess of Malfi* 2.2.19)

19 ***malis*** (*a*) evildoers (*b*) bad poets
claris both 'famous' and 'clear' (glancing back toward the praise of 'plainness')

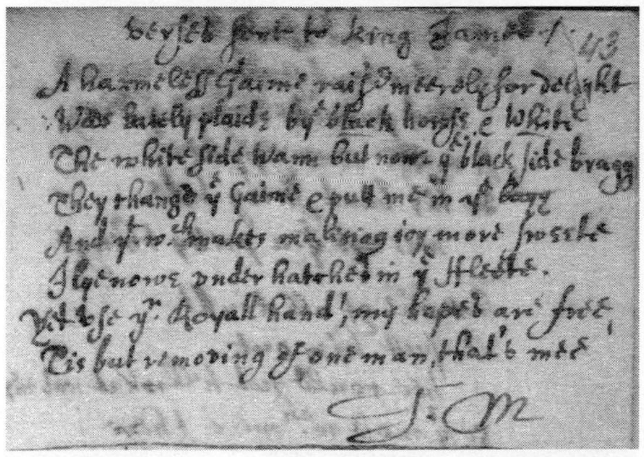
verses sent to King James / 43
A harmless Gaime raisd merely for delight
Was lately plaid by ye black house & White
The white side wan but now ye black side bragg
They changd ye Gaime & put me in ye bagg
And yt wch makes malicious joy more sweete
I lye nowe under hatches in ye Fleete.
Use but yr Royall hand, my hopes are free
Tis but removing of one man, that's mee
T.M

To the King

King

A harmless game, raised merely for delight,
Was lately played by the Black House and White.
The White side won, but now the Black House brag
They changed the game and put me in the bag—
And that which makes malicious joy more sweet,
I lie now under hatches in the Fleet.
Use but your royal hand, my hopes are free;
'Tis but removing of one man—that's me,

Tho. Middleton

King Several texts of the poem identify the King as James I, who died on 27 March 1625. A warrant for Middleton's arrest was issued on 30 August 1624.

These couplets belong to a long tradition of poems written in prison. Ovid's *Tristia*, written during his exile, were an important classical antecedent; particularly relevant to Middleton's poem here was Ovid's Book II, which contains poems addressed to the Emperor Augustus (who had exiled Ovid, as King James had imprisoned Middleton). The most famous early specimens of the genre in Britain were written in the fifteenth century by Charles D'Orleans and James I of Scotland. The genre has continued to be popular in modern times (Daniel Berrigan, Dietrich Bonhoeffer, Joseph Brodsky, Dennis Brutus, Nazim Hikmet, Etheridge Knight, Ho Chi Minh, Ezra Pound, Bobby Sands, and Jimmy Santiago Baca standing out among the many twentieth-century examples).

We reproduce two of the five early copies of the poem, one (top) in a miscellany compiled by Sir Thomas Dawes *c.*1624–8, the other (bottom) in a miscellany compiled by Sir Thomas Hulse *c.*1624–40s.

1 **game** (*a*) contest (*b*) quarry (*c*) *A Game at Chess*, performed from 5–14 August 1624. We do not know when Middleton was found, or how long he was imprisoned; this poem might have been written before the dedicatory poem to Hammond.

raised 'mounted' (used of theatrical performances), but also 'startled, roused from its hiding place' or 'bred' (a hunting term, used of prey). James I's favourite hobby was hunting.

merely only, entirely

2 **played** (*a*) acted (*b*) hunted

3–4 **Black House... bag** The play was closed and Middleton arrested as a result of complaints by the Spanish ambassador.

4 **changed the game** (*a*) reversed the outcome of the game (*b*) changed the kind of game being played (*c*) substituted a different quarry

put... in the bag bagged (like lost chess pieces, or dead game)

me (in contrast to the Black pieces spectacularly bagged in Middleton's play)

6 **under hatches** below deck (i.e. in the lower wards or dungeons), like the Black characters in the play, peering out the trapdoor from under the stage

the Fleet a London prison (but punning on the naval sense)

7 **but** only

hand power (but also literally 'handwriting', signing the papers for Middleton's release, and the hand that moves a chess piece)

my hopes are free (in anticipation, or as a consequence, of the King's pardon: even when his body is imprisoned, his hopes are at liberty)

8 **removing** taking out (of prison, of the bag); but also re-moving, moving again

man (*a*) person (*b*) chess piece (*c*) servant

Hammond

To the worthily accomplished
Master William Hammond

This—which nor stage nor stationer's stall can show;
The common eye may wish for, but ne'er know—
Comes in its best love with the New Year forth
As a fit present to the hand of worth.

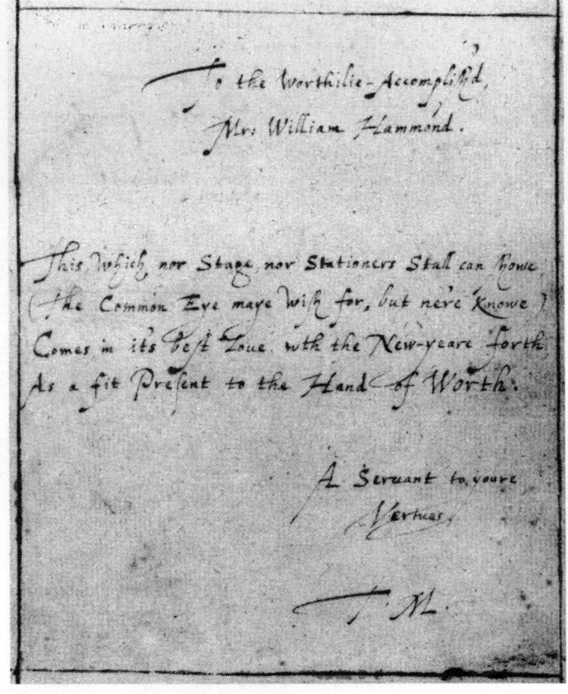

To the Worthilie-Accomplish'd,
Mr: William Hammond.

This, which nor Stage, nor Stationers Stall can showe,
(The Common Eye maye wish for, but ne're knowe)
Comes in its Best Love, with the New-yeare forth,
As a fit Present to the Hand of Worth.

A Servant to youre
Vertues.

T. M.

Hammond Probably addressed to the wealthy William Hammond who lived in the London parish of Allhallows on the Wall, where he was buried on 10 January 1635; he was a friend of Richard Fishborne, to whom Middleton dedicated the 1620 edition of *Two Gates*.

The unique source is depicted, part of a manuscript of *A Game at Chess* prepared in late 1624 by the professional scribe Ralph Crane. Crane occasionally worked for the King's Men, and also prepared two other surviving manuscripts of *A Game at Chess* (one of them the unique copy of the *Early* form), the only surviving manuscripts of *The Witch* and 'An Invention', and the manuscripts from which Middleton's adaptation of *Measure for Measure* and Webster's *Duchess of Malfi* were printed in 1623. He worked closely with Middleton in the 1620s.

This is the only page in Middleton's handwriting, and the deliberate waste of space (a whole page for a four-line poem) announces the deluxe nature of the gift: given the high cost of paper, the amount of blank space on this page represents 'conspicuous consumption'. What seems to have been the original binding was also pointedly expensive: parchment with gilt stamps and holes for tie-strings or ribbons.

1 **This** *A Game at Chess*: Middleton's gift to Hammond was this manuscript copy of the play.
nor stage . . . stall (Further performances of the play had been banned, and it did not appear in print until May 1625.)
stationer's bookseller's

3–4 **New Year . . . present** (It was common to give gifts on New Year's Day, rather than Christmas.)

The Picture plainly explained, after the manner of the Cheſſe-play.

A Game at Cheſse is here diſplayde,
Betweene the *Blacke* and *White-Houſe* made,
Wherein Crowne-thirſting Policy,
For the *Blacke-Houſe* (by Falacy)
To the *White-Knight*, checke, often giues,
And, to ſome ſtraites, him thereby driues;
The *Fat-Blacke-Biſhop* help's alſo,
With faithleſſe heart to giue the blow:
Yet (maugre all their craft) at length,
The *White Knight*, with wit-wondrous ſtrength;
And circumſpectiue Prudency,
Giues Check-mate by Diſcouery
To the *Blacke-Knight*; and ſo at laſt
The Game (thus) won, the *Blacke-Houſe* caſt
Into the Bagge, and therein ſhut,
Finde all their plumes and Cockes-combes cut.
Plaine-dealing (thus) by wiſedomes guide,
Defeates the cheates of Craft and Pride.

The Picture plainly explained,
after the manner of the chess play **Picture**

A game at chess is here displayed
Between the Black and White House made,
Wherein crown-thirsting policy
For the Black House (by fallacy)
To the White Knight check often gives,
And to some straits him thereby drives.
The Fat Black Bishop helps also
With faithless heart to give the blow.
Yet (maugre all their craft) at length
The White Knight, with wit-wondrous strength
And circumspective prudency,
Gives checkmate by discovery
To the Black Knight; and so at last,
The game thus won, the Black House—cast
Into the bag, and therein shut—
Find all their plumes and coxcombs cut.
Plain-dealing thus by wisdom's guide
Defeats the cheats of craft and pride.

Picture The most famous example of this genre—a poem commenting on an illustrated title-page or frontispiece—is Ben Jonson's poem on the engraved portrait of Shakespeare in his *Comedies, Histories, and Tragedies* (1623). But there were many other poems of this kind written in the period, including Jonson's 'The Mind of the Frontispiece to a Book', Richard Crashaw's 'On the Frontispiece of Isaacson's *Chronology Explained*', George Wither's 'The Meaning of the Frontispiece' and 'The Meaning of the Title-page', and Michael Drayton's 'Upon the Frontispiece' to *Poly-Olbion*. Immediately relevant political parallels for the genre can be found in Thomas Scott's *Vox Dei* (1623) and *Vox Regis* (1624). More generally, the genre of caption poem is connected to the Renaissance fondness for emblem books, anthologies of symbolic images with an explanatory poem attached to each; *A Game at Chess* 2.2.248 alludes to one of the most notorious anthologies of picture poems—'Aretine's pictures', Pietro Aretino's sixteenth-century collection of poems about a series of pornographic woodcuts.

The source is a copy of the illicit edition of *A Game at Chess*, printed in 1625 by Nicholas Okes, who also printed Middleton's poem on *The Duchess of Malfi*. The poem was placed (above the Prologue) on a page facing the illustrated title-page (reproduced in 'Lives and Afterlives', p. 27).

3 **crown-thirsting** hungry for (*a*) other king's crowns, kingdoms (*b*) coin, money
policy machiavellian political scheming

4 **fallacy** (*a*) deceit, deception (*b*) error

5 **White Knight** Check is given to the King, not the Knight, and 'Knight' might be an error. But Middleton imagines his characters as both pieces and players, and in the play the chief direct target of the Black House is the White Knight (Prince Charles, prominently depicted on the engraved title-page, who by the time the picture and poem were printed had become King Charles).

6 **straits** difficulties (but perhaps punning on the 'narrow seas' which Prince Charles crossed and re-crossed in his 1623 visit to Spain, represented in Acts 4 and 5 of the play)

7 **Fat Black Bishop** Marc'Antonio di Dominis, prominently depicted on the title-page; the play's Fat Bishop begins on the White side but later switches to Black.

9 **maugre** despite
craft craftiness, cunning

10 **wit-wondrous** amazingly clever

11 **circumspective** cautious, looking in all directions (as a good chess player should do): apparently a Middleton coinage
prudency prudence, wisdom, foresight

13 **Black Knight** See l. 5. The chief Black player is Count Gondomar, prominently depicted on the title-page: Charles's trip to Madrid undid all the diplomatic schemes of the Spanish ambassador, and the poem portrays the play as a chess game played by Charles against Gondomar.

15 **bag** sack for holding discarded chess pieces, spectacularly represented at the end of the play, and visible in the background of the engraving

16 **plumes** pretentious ornament suggesting high rank, military arrogance, or the latest fashions
coxcombs caps worn by fools, hence 'fools' (but suggesting the literal sense of a rooster's crest)
cut 'cut down to size' (but ironic, given that the Black House is responsible for castrating a White character)

18 **pride** arrogance (often attributed to the Spanish; Spanish chess players dominated the game, and Spanish power still dominated Europe and much of the globe)

LOST PAGEANT FOR CHARLES I: A BRIEF ACCOUNT

Gary Taylor

On 27 March 1625, James I died. The next month the Aldermen of the City of London began making plans so 'that the citizens of this City may show and perform their loyalties and bounden duties towards his most excellent Majesty at his passage through the same in preparing of pageants and other shows and things necessary toward the solemnization of that his royal coronation in as stately and sumptuous manner as hath been heretofore performed by this City unto any his noble progenitors.' Soon after the Chamberlain was authorized to make payments to the workmen employed for the 'intended shows'. One of those workmen was Middleton, although he was not named until later. Indeed, Middleton is the only writer ever named in connection with these pageants, intended to equal *The Whole Royal and Magnificent Entertainment*, which had officially welcomed James I into London.

The London authorities were advised, by the court, 'to prepare and erect, in several places within the city, sundry pageants for the fuller and more significant expression of your joys upon his Majesty's and his royal consort's intended entrance through your said city'. That entrance could never have been celebrated before the state funeral on May 7. But the reign of the second Stuart king, like the reign of the first, began with a devastating outbreak of plague. Plague deaths had reached thirty by the week ending 5 May, and forty-five by the week ending 12 May (Bentley). Deaths did not abate till November.

Nevertheless, preparations for the pageants did not immediately stop. On April 22, the Venetian ambassador reported 'The plague grows worse in the city. All the best inhabitants are leaving it'; nevertheless, 'The coronation will take place,' including 'the festivities, illuminations and the dispensation of wine, beer and bread.' On May 6, Londoner John Chamberlain wrote, 'Here is great preparation for shows and pageants.' The same day the Cambridge scholar Joseph Mead, in a letter written from London, reported that 'The coronation is put off till September.' Eight days later, still in London, Mead relayed rumours circulating about the postponement: 'Why the coronation is deferred so long we know not, but some imagine some mystery in it, besides the present businesses and the danger of infection.' The present businesses included Charles I's marriage to the French princess Henrietta Maria, performed by proxy in Paris on May 1 (London dating), and preparations for the new Queen's imminent arrival in England. But on 21 May Mead wrote that 'The pageants howsoever go forward at London', despite seventy-one plague deaths that week. Apparently, Middleton and others were still working on the pageants; the projected delay until September may simply have given them time to prepare a more magnificent royal entry. The Venetian ambassador reported, 'Everything is prepared for the entry into this city, although they will delay the time in order to perfect the apparatus they are making, which will be very costly, both publicly and privately.' He also had an explanation for the delay: 'The coronation has apparently been deferred to September for various reasons, such as the plague and the expense, but perhaps even more the claim of Scotland to come first in order and not agreeing to the union of the two kingdoms.' By June 27, he had heard that 'the public celebrations' were 'postponed until the time of the coronation' (September no longer being specified), and that 'the Scots are dissatisfied since the death of the late king, for they have no hope of the chief influence, and absolutely require his Majesty's coronation in Scotland'. (The King's royal entry into Edinburgh was in fact delayed until 1633.)

I have found no further references to the pageants until December, which is not surprising given the severity of the plague in London during the intervening months. On 10 September, Mead quoted a letter sent to him from a doctor in London: 'The want and misery is the greatest here that ever any man living knew; no trading at all, the rich all gone; housekeepers and apprentices of manual trades begging in the streets, and that in such lamentable manner as will make the strongest heart to yearn.' The annual Lord Mayor's show, which should have taken place on October 29, was cancelled.

The London theatres re-opened the last week of November or the first week of December. City authorities were still worried about the plague for several weeks, but by 12 December Mead had heard that plans were still in place for the King and Queen to arrive at the Tower of London at the end of the month, and then 'the first of February to ride through London; the second, to be crowned'. On 26 December 1625 the Earl of Arundel and Surrey, acting in his capacity as Earl Marshal, informed the Lord Mayor and Council that 'his Majesty is resolved to have his royal coronation solemnized on Candlemas Day next [February 2], and therefore intendeth to make his solemn entry from the Tower of London unto Westminster on the day before, being the first of February'; he expected that the Mayor and Council would resolve 'that such preparations of triumph as you have thought convenient for the honouring of his Passage through London' should be in 'absolute readiness', and added 'I know that your Lordship will have care that all diligence shall be used for the dignity and honour of the same, in regard of the great concourse of strangers [i.e., foreigners] that will be present' for the occasion. London could expect a spectacular royal pageant to attract many visitors from outside the city—with a resulting economic windfall for inns, taverns, and retail shopkeepers.

Responding to the renewed royal command, in January 1626 the Common Council set up a committee 'for the preparing, appointing, and ordering of such shows, pageants, and triumphs as against his Majesty's said passage through this city should be thought fit'. This group was to meet with a similar group of Aldermen and to 'take care also for the disbursing of such moneys and charges... touching the preparing, ordering, and fitting of the said triumphs and shows... and likewise to consider what course and means they conceive most fittest to be taken for the levying and raising of moneys already disbursed or to be disbursed in and about the same'.

As the formation of this new committee suggests, a lot had changed in the intervening months. The City of London was governed by a committee of twenty-six aldermen, who served for life; in the nine months between early April and the end of December, eighteen new Aldermen took the places of predecessors who had died (Beaven, Pearl). Three more were elected in January, and another five by early June. This unusual instability in the City government meant that the plans approved by one group of aldermen were eventually judged by a very different group (including a new Mayor).

Middleton might have had to revise some of the material he had written the previous spring, in order to satisfy the new aldermen and to take account of intervening events. The word 'triumphs', used here and in other documents, had become bitterly ironic: purpose-built triumphal arches, harking back to the Roman ritual for celebrating military victories, could certainly have become embarrassing after the huge, useless expedition against Cadiz returned in December. Moreover, the long delay, the economic and personal disruption caused by the plague, and the London winter cannot have been good for the arches that had been partially or wholly erected the previous spring. At some point in January 1626 the Court of Aldermen received 'information' from 'the Master and Wardens of the Company of Painter-stainers of London,' reporting 'abuses and bad workmanship in and about the contriving and painting of the pageants'. The Aldermen appointed men 'to view the pageants, also the Cross in Cheap, and the work done in the Exchange, and sufficiently to inform themselves of the abuses any way committed in and about the workmanship thereof'. These problems obviously involved construction and decoration, which were not Middleton's personal responsibility. But the records do tell us that, in addition to the pageants, Middleton had planned events at Cheapside and the Royal Exchange.

On January 12, the Venetian ambassador reported that, 'On account of the mourning, the plague and present expenses, they will not prepare all the usual splendour. However the public and private expenses will be very heavy.' In London the next day, Mead had heard 'It's said the King and Queen's riding through London is put off till May,' but that the coronation would be performed 'in a private manner to save the charge of £60,000 in scarlet, which the King should otherwise have been at.' The King's financial difficulties were also emphasized by the Venetian ambassador, in a dispatch filed the same day: 'the entry is postponed until May to allow time for the display, and perhaps to prevent that from being too great, the expense being lessened by having the coronation only'. Chamberlain had heard a different explanation: 'the solemn entry... is put off till May, when the King means to go into Scotland to be crowned'. By 21 January a London friend had told Mead that the pageants were not the only thing being postponed: 'We hear neither of the Parliament nor coronation to be deferred, but only the crowning of the Queen and solemnity of riding through London to be put off.' The postponement of the Queen's coronation resulted from the Catholic Henrietta Maria's refusal to be crowned by a Protestant prelate. Six days later, Mead advised a friend in the country, 'The sight of the coronation will not be worthy of your journey to London, for the King rides not in state through the city until May.' On 2 February, Charles I detoured around the streets of London, going by water from the Tower to Westminster, and he went without his wife, Queen Henrietta having refused even to attend the ceremony. A new Parliamentary session began on February 6.

Although the public pageants were still being postponed, the royal court found time and money for private theatricals. The first court masque of the new reign, Seigneur de Racan's *Artenice*, took place on 21 February at Somerset House on a stage specially constructed by Inigo Jones, with a proscenium arch, perspective scenery, and changing scenes after the French fashion. Queen Henrietta Maria, who would not participate in the coronation, not only danced but also acted in the masque, with various ladies playing male roles. 'The performance was conducted as privately as possible', the Florentine ambassador reported; but although the audience was limited to those with special invitations, that did not stop rumours from circulating, or prevent English disapproval of the Queen (behaving like a common actor), or her transvestite female companions (playing with gender).

This first Caroline masque created, for its tiny circle of chosen actors and spectators, what Stephen Orgel calls 'the illusion of power'. By contrast, the official entry into London would have been a massive public display, celebration, and confirmation of royal power. On 25 May 1626, the Mayor of London received another letter from court—but not from the Earl of Arundel, who had been arrested on 5 March; a House of Lords petition for Arundel's release had been rejected by the King the previous week. The King's new messenger was William Herbert, Earl of Pembroke and Lord Chamberlain, who on May 25 directed the Lord Mayor 'to remove the said pageants which, besides the particular charge they cause in the city, do choke and hinder the passages of such as in coaches, or with their carriages, have occasion to pass up and down'. The pageants were to be torn down because they were obstructing traffic flow for London's wealthiest inhabitants. On May 26, the day after Pembroke's letter, the House of Lords voted not to consider any other business until Arundel was released. On 6 June, the London Aldermen ruled that 'Mr Christmas and Mr Middleton referring themselves to this Court, no further moneys shall be paid unto either of them, but that Mr Christmas shall forthwith cause the said pageants to be taken down, and to have the same for his full satisfaction.' Christmas was allowed to sell off the building materials, by way of reimbursement; Middleton got nothing, although 'no further moneys' indicates that he had been paid earlier, presumably for writing the speeches that should have been delivered, and perhaps for inventing the symbolism of the pageants themselves.

Charles I dissolved Parliament on June 15. To raise the money he could not get from Parliament, he asked a convocation of three hundred of London's wealthiest citizens to contribute £100,000; they refused. But the Court of Aldermen, so tight-fisted with Middleton, immediately gave the King £20,000. By 8 July, Mead had heard from 'some from London' that 'The money which the Aldermen gave the King, they presented neither in the name of a loan nor of their own proper gift, but as that which was intended for a present to his Majesty if he had rode through the city.' This might seem the end of the story, but in fact the cost of the aborted pageants haunted the London government for years. In September 1627—two months after Middleton's death—the Council established a committee to 'take consideration of such moneys as have been disbursed and paid out of the Chamber as well for and touching the making of the pageants and other solemnities and shows, and work for the beautifying of this city against the late intended time of his Majesty's passage through the same'. The investigation revealed that £4,300 had been spent (more than three times the cost of Middleton's *Triumphs of Truth*). That money had come directly from City funds, without any corresponding revenues to balance the books; the committee recommended levying this sum against the companies. But London citizens were increasingly reluctant to pay for the aldermen's generosity to the crown. As late as 26 August 1630, more than £973 remained to be raised (Withington), for pageants *not* performed in 1626.

The royal entry is not the only entertainment Middleton wrote for the city of London that is now lost: on 2 September 1623 he was paid twenty marks 'for and towards the charges of the service, lately performed by him at the shooting at Bunhill before the Lord Mayor and Aldermen, and for his service to be performed at the Conduit heads'. But those entertainments, and others, were at least performed, if not published. The text of the much more elaborate royal entry pageant—which would have eaten up more of his time, energy, and anxiety between April 1625 and May 1626—was never even heard.

Middleton's frustration must have been shared by many others. 'Owing to the scarcity of money,' the Venetian ambassador had reported on 26 May 1626, 'the King has given up his procession through London which was arranged for his coronation. Accordingly five most superb arches in the streets, two erected by the citizens and three by divers other nations, at an expense of many thousands of ducats, will prove useless and they have already begun to dismantle them amid the murmurs of the people and the disgust of those who spent the money.' Anthony Weldon also noted that 'some have taken as an ill omen' the fact that Charles I did not ride through the city in state, 'although the same triumphs were provided for him, as sumptuous as for any others'. An anonymous poem lamenting the cancellation of the 1625 Lord Mayor's show suggests what many ordinary people, in and out of London, must have felt about cancellation of the repeatedly promised and postponed entry pageant:

For lo the sport of that great day,
In which the Mayor hath leave to play,
    and with him all the town;
His flag and drum and fife released,
And he forbid to go a feast-
    ing in his scarlet gown;
No fife must on the Thames be seen . . .

The pageants, and the painted cost
Bestowed on them, are all quite lost . . .

And 'mongst themselves they much complain
That this Lord Mayor, in first of reign,
    should do them so much wrong
As to suppress by message sad
The feast for which they all have had
    their marchpane dream so long.

Middleton's most elaborate pageant fell victim to problems that would continue to beset Charles I: lack of money, military failure, discontent in Scotland, clashes with Parliament, and the influence of his French Catholic wife. But the repeated postponement and then cancellation of the pageant were also, in themselves, a public relations disaster. On 13 May 1626, Mead reported that the King had been overheard saying, in private, 'I have . . . lost the love of my subjects.' He may finally have cancelled the pageant because he feared that the crowds would be less jubilant, in 1626, than they would have been the year before—or than they had been when he returned from Spain in October 1623. A riot at the Fortune Theatre on May 15, and a threatened riot at the Globe later that week, could not have increased his confidence in the stability of his people. Whatever the motives for his final decision, it can only have further disappointed the hopes of many of his subjects, Middleton among them.

SEE ALSO

Lost Plays: A Brief Account: this volume, 328
Lost Political Prose, 1620–7: A Brief Account: this volume, 1907
General introduction to the civic entertainments: this volume, 968
Other Middleton–Christmas works: *Antiquity*, 1397; *Aries*, 1586; *Virtue*, 1714; *Integrity*, 1766; *Prosperity*, 1901
List of works cited: *Companion*, 442

THE TRIUMPHS OF HEALTH AND PROSPERITY

Edited and annotated by David M. Bergeron, introduced by Bryan Reynolds

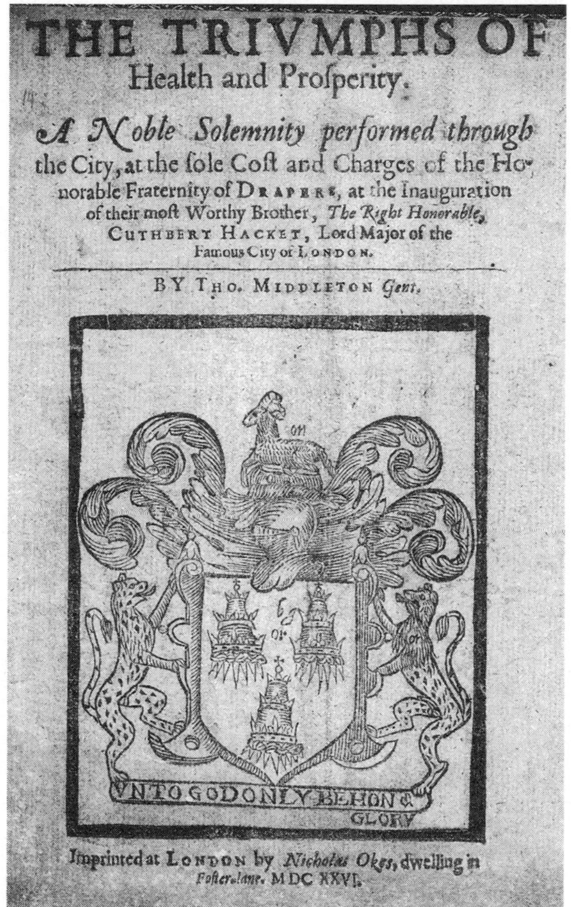

THE TRIVMPHS OF
Health and Proſperity.

A Noble Solemnity performed through the City, at the ſole Coſt and Charges of the Honorable Fraternity of DRAPERS, at the Inauguration of their moſt Worthy Brother, *The Right Honorable*, CUTHBERT HACKET, Lord Major of the Famous City of LONDON.

BY THO. MIDDLETON *Gent.*

VNTO GOD ONLY BE HON & GLORY

Imprinted at LONDON by *Nicholas Okes*, dwelling in *Foſter-lane*. MDC XXVI.

SIXTEENTH and seventeenth century Europe experienced a number of momentous historical sea changes: the Reformation, acceptance of the Copernican system of planetary motion, nascent capitalism, colonial expansion. Another important conceptual revolution, which has been largely overlooked, links all these revolutions. I refer to the evolution of the concept of place, especially as it relates to the concept of space. While the transformation was multifaceted and far-reaching, one particular aspect of it has been charted for the history of ideas by philosopher Edward Casey as a shift toward a downplaying of the concept of place as it had been construed in Aristotelian/Ptolemaic and Christian philosophical traditions. For Aristotle, 'place' is both an abstraction of containment—that which is contained—and a significant interpretive category by which to process the interconnectedness among things, experiences, and events. Moving into the sixteenth century, the concept was enlarged with respect to Christian theology that viewed God as omnipresent, with place sometimes seen as having power in itself, and sometimes regarded as a sentient being (Casey).

By 1626, when Thomas Middleton wrote *The Triumphs of Health and Prosperity* to celebrate the inauguration of Cuthbert Hacket as Lord Mayor, place's status had significantly changed. Although still granted its relation to the immeasurability of God, place was being subsumed within an idea of infinite space that was more scientific and mathematical, and that became synonymous with the infinitude of God; place was thus understood less and less as individuated or proper. Robert Weimann noted in 2000 that this important topic had not been treated at much length in scholarship on early modern English drama, but Henry S. Turner and others have begun to repair this gap. Place became a mere mark on the expanse of a grid, like the identical squares of *A Game at Chess*, which Martin Brückner and Kristen Poole have related to early modern surveying. Place was therefore commensurately devalued as something without any particular power, and neutralized in effect by this historical move toward a scientific as opposed to a religious form of relativism. For instance, Middleton and Rowley's *The Changeling*, as Donald Hedrick and Bryan Reynolds have shown, embodies this historical shift in its remarkable reaction to the decay of the local, which is so pronounced as to suggest that the play may constitute a conscious exploration of the fugitive concept of place-in-drift. The play pursues its own transversal investigation, moving investigative-expansively across various fields of knowledge and kinds of phenomena, by which a place may be creatively altered—interpretively and experientially—in response to the openness and reduction of definition that constitutes new ideas of an overarching, subsuming, or all-encompassing space-time.

Although in an abbreviated form, Middleton's *The Triumphs of Health and Prosperity* similarly reflects anxiety over the diminishing material presence of place vis-à-vis a concept of space-time beyond the cognitive scope and physical control of humans. It gestures toward a return to an understanding of place itself, when virtuously occupied, as idiosyncratic, possessing sentience, affective presence, and the capacity to proliferate. More importantly, *Prosperity* insists on an understanding of place that requires a return to the—at this time—historically reactionary notion that God occupies specific places; by extension, it suggests that humans, because they are designed in God's image, may also.

The pageant begins with a bold assertion that epitomizes implicitly Middleton's concern over the value or stature of place and the subjective particularity it affords:

> If you should search all chronicles, histories, records, in what language are letter soever; if the inquisitive man should waste the dear treasure of his time and eyesight, he shall conclude his life only with this certainty, that there is no subject upon earth received into the place of his government with the like state and magnificence as is his Majesty's great substitute into his honourable charge, the City of London, bearing the inscription of the Chamber Royal . . . (17–25)

All the methods by which humans attempt to contain time—'chronicles, histories, records'—cannot stand in for the City of London's affective presence, its 'delight to present itself' as a combined material, symbolic, and imaginary force of social power (Bryan Reynolds); the City inhabits experientially by 'magnificence', causing the transformation of space into place through activities designated, mapped, and thereby made proper (Michel de Certeau; Joseph Fitzpatrick and Bryan Reynolds). The Lord Mayor, the King's representative, by legitimate connection, via a chain of proper God-given links, enjoys the City as his 'great substitute in his honourable charge'. The City is strategically organized, mapped properly, as 'the most pleasant garden in England', a specific place (44).

But this nomination must not be taken for granted: 'A cloud of grief hath showered upon the face | Of this sad city, and usurped the place . . .' (60–1). All is saved because the new Lord Mayor arrives just in time to bring health and prosperity to 'this garden [that] was o'erflown' (64), so that one may 'Behold what figure now the city bears, | Like gems unvalued, her best joys she wears' (66–7); now 'Fixed in the king's great substitute: delight, | Triumph, and pomp, had almost lost their right: | The garden springs again' (70–2). Now the City requires 'Care and uprightness in the magistrate's place, | And in all men obedience, truth, and grace' (80–1). These declarations of redemption, the City revived with particularity and purpose, come not without warning, disinterred in the heroic account of 'that most famous and renowned brother of this company' of drapers (85–6), an explorer who has given the world a map, or rather, given a cartographic explanation of the world, with proper names and places, to a population possibly afraid of being nothing but dust in the wind of infinite sky, particles in space without direction or end:

> Sir Francis Drake, who in two years and ten months did encompass the whole world, deserving an eminent remembrance in this sanctuary [the City of London], who never returned to his country without the Golden Fleece of honour and victory. (86–9)

Drake confirms, *Prosperity* opines, not only the placefullness of the world, itself a now comprehensible place, but also the priority and privilege of the particular place, the City of London, on which Londoners stand.

With a pronounced self-consciousness about the ever-expanding world, and thus potentially unwieldy world-view, Middleton discloses poignant concern over the precariousness and uncertainty that such placelessness may precipitate, 'For worth unmatched, danger unparalleled' (103), and seeks to mitigate these destabilizing forces with assurance of particularity, authority, righteousness, and propriety:

> With just propriety does the city stand,
> As fixed by fate, i'th' middle of the land;
> It has, as in the body, the heart's place,
> Fit for her works of piety and grace;
> The head her sovereign, unto whom she sends
> All duties that just service comprehends. (144–9)

Shot through with anxieties about loss of place combined with over-determined rhetoric underscoring the substitutive and synecdochical relations in a line of divine influence from God to Monarch to Lord Mayor to City of London to Londoners, *Prosperity* is a desperate attempt to convince its London audience that 'The place where now you are' (158) is together an exemplary site of collaboration with the monarchy, 'the king and you his substitute' (175).

Unfortunately, the 'prosperity' of Middleton and his collaborator Garret Christmas was not much enhanced by their work, because as late as 31 December 1626—more than two months after the performance—they had still not been paid:

> Item: the payment of Mr Middleton and Mr Christmas for the pageants, and others for the fireworks and providing of chambers, being hitherto put off, in regard of the ill performance thereof, is now referred to the Wardens Bachelors of this Company, who are willing to compound and agree with the parties the best they may be, giving them contentment as the business shall deserve and as shall be fit the credit of this Company.

The claim of 'ill performance' may be an excuse: having had to finance three of the last five mayoral pageants (during years of economic depression, capped by the financial catastrophe of the 1625 plague), the Drapers were broke, and the Minutes of the Court of Assistants here acknowledge that the delay in payment may be detrimental to the company's 'credit'. In any case, the complaint concerned the pageant's 'performance', not Middleton's text and design, which would have been approved in advance;

the published text was the first mayoral pageant to bear the arms of the sponsoring company on the title-page. *Prosperity* was the cheapest pageant since 1609—when there had also been complaints (Robertson and Gordon). It cost less than half the previous pageant, John Webster's *Monuments of Honour* (1624), and the contrast must have been obvious to everyone. Even more obvious to Middleton would have been the contrast with his previous shows: the Grocers had raised, for *The Triumphs of Truth* in 1613, 237 per cent of what the Drapers paid to produce *The Triumphs of Health and Prosperity*. Then as now, decisions about how much to spend on a spectacle are made by the producer, not the writer. Whatever the causes of its failings or successes, Middleton's text remains an important testimony to the period's concerns over the displacement of the concept of place by the concept of space.

SEE ALSO

Textual introduction and apparatus: *Companion*, 1010
Authorship and date: *Companion*, 337
General introduction to the civic entertainments: this volume, 968
Other Middleton–Christmas works: *Antiquity*, 1397; *Aries*, 1586; *Virtue*, 1714; *Integrity*, 1766; lost pageant for Charles I, 1898

The Triumphs of Health and Prosperity

A noble solemnity performed through the City, at the sole cost and charges of the honourable fraternity of Drapers, at the inauguration of their most worthy brother, the Right Honourable Cuthbert Hacket, Lord Mayor of the famous City of London.

To the honour of him, to whom the noble fraternity of Drapers, his worthy brothers have consecrated their loves in magnificent triumphs, the Right Honourable Cuthbert Hacket, Lord Mayor of the City of London

The city's choice, thy company's free love,
This day's unlooked-for triumph, all three prove
The happiness of thy life to be most great;
Add to these, justice, and thou art complete.

At your lordship's command,
Thomas Middleton

The Triumphs of Health and Prosperity

If you should search all chronicles, histories, records, in what language or letter soever; if the inquisitive man should waste the dear treasure of his time and eyesight, he shall conclude his life only with this certainty, that there is no subject upon earth received into the place of his government with the like state and magnificence as is his Majesty's great substitute into his honourable charge, the City of London, bearing the inscription of the Chamber Royal; which, that it may now appear to the world no less illustrated with brotherly affection than former triumphal times have been partakers of, this takes delight to present itself.

And first to enter the worthy love of his honourable society for his lordship's return from Westminster, having received some service by water, by the triumphant Chariot of Honour, the first that attends his lordship's most wished arrival bears the title of the Beautiful Hill or Fragrant Garden, with flowery banks, near to which lambs and sheep are a-grazing. This platform, so cast into a hill, is adorned and garnished with all variety of odoriferous flowers; on the top, arched with an artificial and curious rainbow, which both shows the antiquity of colours, the diversity and nobleness, and how much the more glorious and highly to be esteemed, they being presented in that blessed covenant of mercy, the bow in the clouds; the work itself encompassed with all various fruits, and bears the name of the most pleasant garden of England, the noble City of London, the flowers intimating the sweet odours of their virtue and goodnesses, and the fruits of their works of justice and charity, which have been both honourable brothers and bounteous benefactors of this ancient fraternity, who are presented in a device following under the types and figures of their virtues in their lifetime, which made them famous then and memorable for ever. And since we are yet amongst the woolly creatures that graze on the beauty of this beautiful platform, come we to the modern use of this noble mystery of ancient drapery, and we shall find the whole livery of this renowned and famous city furnished by it; it clothes the honourable senators in their highest and chiefest wearing, all courts of justice, magistrates, and judges of the land. But for the

4–5 **Cuthbert Hacket** had been a member of the Dyers company; translated to the Drapers in order to become mayor in 1626; served as Alderman until his death in 1631

16–217 **Health** ... ***Health*** (in contrast to the 35,000 plague deaths of 1625)

31 **service by water** pageant entertainment on the Thames

35 **a-grazing** archaic form

36 **odoriferous** sweet, fragrant

41 **covenant** ... **bow** refers to Old Testament story of Noah (Genesis 9); rainbow, symbol of God's covenant of mercy

53 **mystery** guild

better expression of the purpose in hand a speaker gives life to these following words.

THE SPEECH IN THE HILL WHERE THE RAINBOW APPEARS

A cloud of grief hath showered upon the face
Of this sad city, and usurped the place
Of joy and cheerfulness, wearing the form
Of a long black eclipse in a rough storm;
With showers of tears this garden was o'erflown,
Till mercy was, like the blest rainbow, shown.
Behold what figure now the city bears,
Like gems unvalued, her best joys she wears;
Glad as a faithful handmaid to obey
And wait upon the honour of this day,
Fixed in the king's great substitute: delight,
Triumph, and pomp, had almost lost their right:
The garden springs again; the violet beds,
The lofty flowers bear up their fragrant heads;
Fruit overlade their trees, barns crack with store;
And yet how much the heavens wept before,
Threat'ning a second mourning. Who so dull
But must acknowledge mercy was at full?
In these two mighty blessings what's required?
That which in conscience ought to be desired:
Care and uprightness in the magistrate's place,
And in all men obedience, truth, and grace.

After this, awaits his lordship's approach a masterpiece of triumph, called the Sanctuary of Prosperity; on the top arch of which hangs the Golden Fleece, which raises the worthy memory of that most famous and renowned brother of this company, Sir Francis Drake, who in two years and ten months did encompass the whole world, deserving an eminent remembrance in this sanctuary, who never returned to his country without the golden fleece of honour and victory. The four fair Corinthian columns or pillars imply the four principal virtues: wisdom, justice, fortitude, temperance, the especial upholders of kingdoms, cities, and honourable societies.

THE SPEECH IN THE SANCTUARY UPON THE FLEECE

If Jason, with the noble hopes of Greece,
Who did from Colchis fetch the golden fleece,
Deserve a story of immortal fame,
That both the Asias celebrate his name,
What honour, celebration, and renown,
In virtue's right, ought justly to be shown
To the fair memory of Sir Francis Drake?
England's true Jason, who did boldly make
So many rare adventures, which were held
For worth unmatched, danger unparalleled;
Never returning to his country's eye
Without the golden fleece of victory.
The world's a sea, and every magistrate
Takes a year's voyage when he takes this state.
Nor on these seas are there less dangers found
Than those on which the bold adventurer's bound;
For rocks, gulfs, quicksands, here is malice, spite,
Envy, detraction of all noble right;
Vessels of honour, those do threaten more
Than any ruin between sea and shore.
Sail, then, by th' compass of a virtuous name,
And, spite of spites, thou bring'st the fleece of fame.

Passing from this, and more to encourage the noble endeavours of the magistrate, his lordship and the worthy company is gracefully conducted toward the Chariot of Honour. On the most eminent seat thereof is Government illustrated, it being the proper virtue by which we raise the noble memory of Sir Henry fitz Ailwin, who held

60 ***cloud of grief*** reaction to death of King James in March 1625 and to the 1625 plague, which had caused the cancellation of the mayoral pageant that year

70 ***substitute*** that is, the mayor

71 ***Triumph ... right*** no Lord Mayor's Show in 1625 (because of the plague) and no pageant to celebrate the official entry into London of the new king and queen (postponed for more than a year, then cancelled)

74 ***barns ... store*** (in contrast to the dearth of 1622–23)

78 ***two mighty blessings*** end of the plague in 1626 and abundant harvest (Burridge)

83 **Prosperity** (in contrast to the devastating economic effects of the plague the previous year: see Lost Royal Pageant, p. 1898)

87 **encompass ... world** (an image Middleton probably picked up from Samuel Purchas)

89–90 **never ... victory** (in striking contrast to the 1625 naval expedition against Spain: see 'Lost Political Prose', p. 1909)

90 **Corinthian columns** the most ornate of the three orders of Greek architecture, with bell-shaped capitals

91 **principal virtues** the Cardinal Virtues

95 ***golden fleece*** Drake is prominently featured in William Vaughan's *The Golden Fleece, divided into three parts, under which are discovered the errors of religion, the vices and decays of the kingdom, and lastly the ways to get wealth and to restore trading, so much complained of* (1626).

97 ***both the Asias*** Asia Minor and Asia Major

100 ***Sir Francis Drake*** Drake is briefly mentioned in the prose of *Aries* (1621) and *Integrity* (1623), but here is the subject of one of the pageant's four speeches. Unlike Jason (who speaks in *Aries*), Drake was not primarily a merchant; he was instead famous for his military exploits against Spain. References to Drake acquired a strong political meaning in the mid-1620s, amid Protestant calls for a naval war against Spain, as a way of forcing the Habsburgs to relinquish the Palatinate. Because Drake had successfully attacked Cadiz in 1587, any mention of him in 1626 would recall the humiliating failure of the late 1625 expedition against Cadiz (which had cost *c.*£250,000, and achieved nothing). Alongside extended historical accounts, in John Smith's *General History of Virginia* (1624), *Purchas his Pilgrims* (1625) and William Camden's *Annals* (1625), Drake in the mid-1620s was lauded in texts with a more obvious agenda, like Philip Nichols's *Sir Francis Drake Revived, calling upon this dull or effeminate age, to follow his noble steps* (1626) and Bishop George Carleton's *A Thankful Remembrance of God's Mercies* (1624). Drake was also invoked polemically in some of Middleton's possible sources for *A Game at Chess*: the anonymous *Experimental Discovery of Spanish Practises* (1623), John Reynolds's *Votivæ Angliæ* (1624) and *Vox Coeli* (1624).

115 ***spite of spites*** notwithstanding, despite (*OED*)

121–6 **Henry fitz Ailwin ... Simon Eyre** cf. their descriptions in earlier pageants, *Aries* (1621) and *Integrity* (1623)

the seat of magistracy in this city twenty-four years together, a most renowned brother of this company: in like manner, the worthy Sir John Norman first rowed in barge to Westminster with silver oars, under the person of Munificence: Sir Simon Eyre that built Leadenhall, a granary for the poor, under the type of Piety; *et sic de ceteris*. This chariot drawn by two golden pelleted lions, being the proper supporters of the company's arms; those two that have their seats upon the lions presenting Power and Honour, the one in a little streamer or banneret bearing the arms of the present lord mayor; the other of the late, the truly generous and worthy Sir Allen Cotton, knight, a bounteous and a noble housekeeper, one that hath spent the year of his magistracy to the great honour of the city, and by the sweetness of his disposition, and the uprightness of his justice and government, hath raised up a fair lasting memory to himself and his posterity forever; at whose happy inauguration, though triumph was not then in season—death's pageants being only advanced upon the shoulders of men—his noble deservings were not thereby any way eclipsed: *Est virtus sibi marmor, et integritate triumphat.*

THE SPEECH OF GOVERNMENT

With just propriety does this city stand,
As fixed by fate, i'th' middle of the land;
It has, as in the body, the heart's place,
Fit for her works of piety and grace;
The head her sovereign, unto whom she sends
All duties that just service comprehends;
The eyes may be compared, at wisdom's rate,
To the illustrious counsellors of state,
Set in that orb of royalty, to give light
To noble actions, stars of truth and right;
The lips, the reverend clergy, judges, all
That pronounce laws divine or temporal;
The arms to the defensive part of men.
So I descend unto the heart again,
The place where now you are; witness the love,
True brotherhood's cost and triumph, all which move
In this most grave solemnity; and in this
The city's general love abstracted is:
And as the heart, in its meridian seat,
Is styled the fountain of the body's heat,
The first thing receives life, the last that dies,
Those properties experience well applies
To this most loyal city, that hath been
In former ages, as in these times seen,
The fountain of affection, duty, zeal,
And taught all cities through the commonweal;
The first that receives quick'ning life and spirit
From the king's grace, which still she strives to inherit,
And, like the heart, will be the last that dies
In any duty toward good supplies.
What can express affection's nobler fruit,
Both to the king and you his substitute?

At the close of this speech, this Chariot of Honour and Sanctuary of Prosperity, with all her graceful concomitants, and the two other parts of triumph, take leave of his lordship for that time, and rest from service till the great feast at Guildhall be ended; after which the whole fabric of the triumph attends upon his honour both toward Saint Paul's and homeward, his lordship accompanied with the grave and honourable senators of the city, amongst whom the two worthy sheriffs, his lordship's grave assistants for the year, the worshipful and generous master Richard Fen and master Edward Brumfield, ought not to pass of my respect unremembered, whose bounty and nobleness for the year will no doubt give the best expression to their own worthiness. Between the Cross and the entrance of Wood Street, that part of triumph being planted, being the Fragrant Garden of England with the rainbow, to which the concluding speech hath chiefly reference, there takes its farewell of his lordship, accompanied with the Fountain of Virtue, being the fourth part of the Triumph.

THE LAST SPEECH

Mercy's fair object, the celestial bow,
As in the morning it began to show,
It closes up this great triumphal day,
And by example shows the year the way,
Which if power worthily and rightly spend,
It must with mercy both begin and end.
It is a year that crowns the life of man,
Brings him to peace with honour, and what can
Be more desired? 'Tis virtue's harvest time,
When gravity and judgement's in their prime;
To speak more happily, 'tis a time given

127–8 ***et sic de ceteris*** and so forth
128 **pelleted lions** marked with heraldic pellets
133 **Allen Cotton** elected Lord Mayor in 1625, but because of the plague there was no Lord Mayor's Show
142–3 ***Est . . . triumphat*** virtue is marble unto itself and triumphs through its integrity (Burridge)
146 ***as in the body*** This passage rewrites a classic comparison of a political community to a human body, the 'body politic': Shakespeare's version of the comparison in *Coriolanus* is now the most familiar, but Middleton would have been equally familiar with versions in Plutarch, Livy, Erasmus, Machiavelli, and William Camden's *Remains*. The emphasis on the body is particularly appropriate, given the theme of 'health' and the sickness of the previous year. ***heart's*** Middleton focuses on the heart (London), rather than the belly.
149 ***All . . . comprehends*** i.e., only those duties which would be included in the category of 'just service' to the sovereign. (Which services were legal and appropriate was a matter of dispute between the King and Parliament.)
151 ***illustrious counsellors*** the Privy Council
162 ***meridian*** locality or situation distinct from others (*OED*)
177–8 **concomitants** companions
185–6 **Richard Fen** or Venn, became mayor in 1637
186 **Edward Brumfield** Leatherseller and Fishmonger, became mayor in 1636
189 **Cross** located in Cheapside at end of Wood Street
195 ***celestial bow*** rainbow
203 ***harvest time*** (alluding to the date of the Lord Mayor's Show, October 29)

To treasure up good actions fit for heaven.
To a brotherhood of honour thou art fixed,
That has stood long fair in just virtue's eye;
For within twelve years' space thou art the sixt
That has been lord mayor of this company.
This is no usual grace, being now the last;
Close the work nobly up, that what is past,
And known to be good in the former five,
May in thy present care be kept alive.
Then is thy brotherhood for their love and cost
Requited amply, but thy own soul most.
Health and a happy peace fill all thy days;
When thy year ends, may then begin thy praise.

For the fabric or structure of the whole triumph, in so short a time so gracefully performed, the commendation of that the industry of master Garret Christmas may justly challenge; a man not only excellent in his art, but faithful in his undertakings.

FINIS

209 *sixt* six Drapers had been mayor since 1614

LOST POLITICAL PROSE, 1620–7: A BRIEF ACCOUNT

Thomas Cogswell

IN 1735, two manuscript volumes of Thomas Middleton's work as Chronologer for the City of London appeared at an auction, where the curious were able to peruse them. A quick inspection revealed that the first of these, *The Annales*, dealt with a series of notable 'Passages and Occurrences' in the city from 1620 to 1622: the death of the Bishop of London, the imprisonments of Viscount St Albans and Sir Edward Coke, and the fiery destruction of the Fortune Theatre. The other volume, lacking the precise focus on the metropolis, was aptly dubbed *Middleton's Farrago*. Among the charges and counter-charges between the earl of Essex and Viscount Wimbledon was an account of Henrietta Maria's marriage contract and two sections tersely entitled 'Parliamentary Matters, 1625–26' and 'Habeas Corpus 1627'. The owner of these works, hopeful of cashing in on Middleton's name, 'puffed up' the price. But when the market proved less enthusiastic than expected, he withdrew the *Annales* and the *Farrago* from the auction—and ultimately from scholarly view.

Aside from this tantalizing description, there is no other surviving information on these two major prose works of Thomas Middleton. Since a willingness to explore the boundaries of the politically acceptable was a hallmark of Middleton's plays and entertainments, it is tempting to speculate that he might have done the same as City Chronologer. Yet the basic fact of the matter is that we can now say very little about these two lost works with any degree of confidence. The only certainty in this otherwise murky business concerns the main themes of the *Annales* and the *Farrago*, which were noted at the auction house in 1735. Fortunately these tell us a great deal about Middleton's lost histories.

It could well be assumed that the disappearance of these two volumes was not a major calamity, since they may well have been thoroughly anodyne. After all, history was one of the literary genres to which the Stuart regime exhibited a hypersensitivity. Given that assessments of medieval kings often earned their authors an uncomfortable encounter with the Privy Council, contemporaries interested in more recent history could be confident that their efforts would receive a thorough inspection at Whitehall. Indeed after 1620 there was a 'political' licensor, specially charged to review 'any matters of newes relations histories or other things in prose or in verse that have reference to matters and affairs of State'. Little wonder then that when a team of writers decided to continue John Stow's popular *Annales* into the 1620s, they wisely erred on the side of extreme caution. After tersely noting the disastrous Ré expedition in 1627, the editor advised his readers that 'what more may be said of this voyage and action, I refer you unto other books written to that purpose'. The coverage of the 1626 Parliament was even more laconic; all the editor noted about this highly significant session was that 'a Parliament began at Westminster and continued until Thursday the 15th of January next following, and then was dissolved by Commission'. Chronologies in other words generally gave a wide berth to anything even remotely controversial.

In his chronicle Middleton may well have run true to the cautious form of the genre. But before endorsing that judgement, it is vital to remember an important mitigating factor: Middleton was only writing a manuscript history, which was not intended for publication. To be sure, the government was not wholly oblivious to the 'underground' trade in manuscripts, and it did sometimes prosecute the authors of controversial poems and tracts. Nevertheless the frankness with which authors writing in this medium regularly discussed the most sensitive contemporary issues would have been simply unimaginable in print. Consequently the basic fact that Middleton did not have to secure official authorization for his work accorded him considerable leeway. The main themes of his two works, furthermore, suggest that Middleton availed himself of this comparative freedom. Of all the themes, only one—the destruction of the Fortune Theatre—was a thoroughly mundane matter, devoid of political significance. All the others dealt with issues of the first importance, which had riveted the nation's attention. By contrast, in the continuation of Stow's *Annales*, sensational topics were apt to receive a non-committal sentence, if the editors did not pass over them in complete silence.

Unfortunately, the comparative audacity of Middleton's reportage is now hidden by the obscurity of the events themselves, some of which are murky even to scholars on the field. Therefore, in order to arrive at a fuller appreciation of the contemporary significance of the topics which Middleton handled, the present essay will examine them in some detail.

I. *Annales*

The crisis atmosphere which hung over the realm in the early 1620s is clearly apparent in Middleton's *Annales*. In the years after 1618, warfare erupted between the Habsburgs and Protestants in central Europe. At the centre of this conflict was James I's daughter, Princess Elizabeth, who had married the leading Calvinist protagonist, Frederick V of the Palatinate. Unfortunately for the Protestant militants, early hopes for resounding victory quickly evaporated as Imperial armies easily bested their opponents and so revived fears of a Habsburg 'universal monarchy'. Meanwhile James I, the 'Defender of the Faith', refused to become militarily involved. Instead he diligently sought a diplomatic solution to the international crisis, the centrepiece of which was the projected marriage of his heir to a Spanish princess. Had such a match simply been a matter of finding a suitable bride for Prince Charles, it would not have aroused as much anxiety as it did among English contemporaries. But everyone suspected—and with good reason—that the Habsburgs would insist on a de facto toleration of English Catholics. Such an action seemed especially foolhardy; given the Catholic reputation for rebellion and aggressive proselytizing, toleration appeared a prescription for the imminent subversion of the Church of England and indeed of England itself.

These apprehensions surfaced at the death of John King. After a long and distinguished clerical career as Dean of Christ Church, Vice-Chancellor of Oxford and ultimately Bishop of London, King died on 31 March 1621. Yet the solemnity of his funeral was soon marred by reports of a deathbed conversion to Catholicism. Although apparently untrue, the charges flourished in part because of the kindness he had shown to imprisoned priests. Such actions speak well for King's sense of Christian charity, but when religious war had erupted on the continent, they were all too easily misinterpreted. Furthermore, as Bishop of London, King had played a major role in checking zealous metropolitan preachers who criticized James's pacifism. In any event, the rumour of his conversion made enough sense to enough people that it clung to his name; in fact, later in the year, a Protestant tract urging renewed vigilance against resurgent Catholicism calmly cited King's conversion as common knowledge. Nor was the rumour simply a useful tool for radical Protestants; Catholic controversialists also trumpeted the news. King's son found the situation so embarrassing that in an effort to redeem the good name of the Church of England and his father, he directly confronted these reports in a sermon at Paul's Cross. Middleton therefore lavished attention on an incident in which a local bishop's reputation had become a casualty in James I's campaign for accommodation with Spain.

Those alarmed at the prospect of a Catholic revival found refuge in hopes for a Parliament, whose members by and large had scant sympathy for a Spanish match in general and for a relaxation of the penal laws in particular. Unfortunately, after an impressive display of devotion to the institution early in James's English reign, the king had become irritated with the Parliament-men's refusal to vote new subsidies with either the generosity or the frequency that James thought appropriate. Thus aside from a brief 'addled' session in 1614, James summoned no Parliaments between 1610 and 1621. In the interim, moral as well as fiscal corruption seemed to overwhelm the administration. Admittedly a few outrageous examples like the Overbury murder and the earl of Suffolk's light fingers forced James to intervene. Yet until matters reached such extraordinary heights, the king appeared distressingly tolerant of embezzlement and extortion. The situation in the law courts seemed most alarming, with widespread reports of corruption among the senior judges. Consequently, when the continental crisis eventually forced James to summon a new Parliament in 1621, many contemporaries hoped that the new session would belatedly clean up internal abuses as well as steer the king away from a Spanish match.

These hopes explain the attention which Middleton accorded Viscount St Albans's commitment to the Tower. In the opening weeks of the session, the Parliament-men in an extraordinary action immediately voted a handsome subsidy bill. Since in normal circumstances they would only have done so at the end of the session, James was delighted with their action, vowing in response to 'meet with his Subjects more than halfway' in their demands. A few months later he learned the cost of such generosity, for what the House of Commons most desired was revival of the medieval practice of impeaching royal ministers. The first court grandee to suffer at the hands of an early modern Parliament was Francis Bacon, the Lord Chancellor. Initially James attempted to save him, but ultimately a full set of witnesses, all recounting multiple tales of bribery, proved too much even for his lax moral standards. With Bacon's fall, justice at last appeared done, and many across the country rejoiced. Yet more importantly, Parliament had played a major role in the legal drama, and having established a precedent, many were understandably eager to have Parliament send more corrupt officials to keep Bacon company in the Tower. Thomas Locke perhaps best caught the mood: 'they have begun at the highest, and they meane to come downwards, Westminster Hall was never so made clean as it is like to be this year'.

Events soon proved that James had no intention of permitting such extensive cleaning. Nevertheless, when the Lord Chancellor was himself committed to the Tower on 28 May 1621, many contemporaries regarded it as an obvious red-letter day. Equally obvious is the next item in *The Annales*, which concerned Parliament and another commitment to the Tower of London. But this time the imprisonment had nothing to do with either corruption or impeachment.

Late in 1621, as Imperial forces were poised to overrun all of the Palatinate, the home of Frederick V and Elizabeth, James again turned to Parliament. Additional parliamentary funds were essential, he argued, in order to maintain an army of mercenaries until plans for a negotiated settlement could be completed. Although many in the House of Commons were interested in a more bellicose response, the more they thought about James's proposal the less they fancied it. Chief among their worries was the wisdom of committing English taxpayers, if not English soldiers, to a limited war against some elements of the House of Austria, while remaining at peace and indeed planning a wedding with the rest of the family. All these fears came out into the open after an unclear message from Court apparently suggested that James was at last ready for a more belligerent policy. In the unrestrained debate which followed, some members proposed open war against Spain and the breach of the Spanish match. Once word of these developments reached Court, James and Charles were furious, and in an effort to forestall a major incident with Spain, the king ordered the Commons to cease any further discussion of foreign affairs.

Unfortunately while the royal order made logical diplomatic sense, it initiated a quarrel with the House over a matter about which it was tetchiest—its privileges. Earlier in the year, the Parliament-men had been deeply suspicious about royal efforts to subvert the House's customary freedom of speech. A brief royal message had been enough to alleviate this apprehension, but with James's order at the end of the year forbidding any discussion of affairs of state, the suspicion arose again. Rather than back down, the House dug in its heels, formally reminding James in its 'Protestation', that 'every Member of the House of Parliament hath, and of right, ought to have freedom of speech'. Rather than accept this position, James dissolved the Parliament even though the lack of parliamentary subsidies hamstrung his diplomatic efforts. Once the session was over, the king signalled his contempt for the House's vaunted freedom of speech by ripping the 'Protestation' out of the Commons Journals with his own hands. He also imprisoned several leaders of the Commons for their words at the end of the session. Most prominent among the imprisoned was Sir Edward Coke, former Lord Chief Justice and erstwhile Privy Counsellor. In sharp contrast to St Albans's brief stay in the Tower in some of the more salubrious rooms, Coke and his fellow Parliament-men spent over half a year there in almost complete isolation. Thus, the bland summary excerpted from *The Annales* for 27 December 1621, 'Sir Edward Coke Committed to the Tower', referred to an event easily as constitutionally important and as politically dramatic as the revival of impeachment.

II. *Farrago*

We do not know how long Middleton continued working on the *Annales*. But the Aldermen and the Common Councillors eventually decided he was no longer earning his annual fee of £10. On 1 February 1626, the Common Council of London resolved to end Middleton's salary, 'unless he give this Court satisfaction according as was intended he should do when the said pension was first granted him'. All things considered, Middleton's work for the city was comparatively easy money, and it speaks volumes about his financial position in 1626 that he decided to resume his duties.

In doing so, he displayed his deference to a patron. Yet as a cursory examination of the main categories of *Annales* and *Farrago* reveals, Middleton's understanding of his duties as City Chronologer had shifted radically between 1622 and 1626. The death of the Bishop of London, the imprisonment of two men in the Tower and a fire at a London theatre were all events which, at least in the first instance, took place in the metropolis. In *The Farrago*, however, Middleton adopted a much wider and a more distinctly national focus. The city hence found itself underwriting someone much more interested in imitating William Camden than John Stow.

Middleton's interest in larger themes becomes apparent with the first item in *The Farrago*: the charges and counter-charges between the earl of Essex and Viscount Wimbledon. Late in 1625, after many delays, Charles I initiated open war against Spain with a bold *coup de main*; he dispatched Wimbledon with an enormous Anglo-Dutch fleet of over a hundred vessels and 12,000 troops to capture Cadiz. With a force that size, it seemed impossible that Wimbledon could fail to do something which would redeem the battered honour of the realm. Yet he did fail. On his ignominious return in December, Wimbledon blamed the inadequate supplies, the weather and bad luck for the debacle. His subordinate officers led by the earl of Essex were quick to point to a more crippling problem: Wimbledon's indecision and timidity, they alleged, verged on cowardice. In turn, Wimbledon denounced his own officers: Lord Cromwell he termed a drunkard, Lord Valentia a common embezzler, Colonel Horwood a mutineer, and as for Essex, 'an evil spirit hath got possession of you'. Thus the bitterest irony about the opening of the long awaited military intervention on the continent was that the hottest skirmishes were between the general and his officers.

Plainly these bickerings through the first half of 1626 attracted widespread popular interest, but they did not monopolize it. Rather the second of Middleton's topics did. Within weeks of assuming the throne, Charles I finally wed a Bourbon rather than a Habsburg princess. Amid the celebrations over the marriage, many of his subjects hoped and prayed that Henrietta Maria would follow the ecclesiastical eclecticism of her father, Henri IV, and decide that London was worth an Anglican service. Events soon proved the futility of such hopes, for far from being a politique, she was a zealous Catholic devot. Indeed, it would have been hard for her to be anything else, given the size of her clerical retinue. In turn, the presence of a bishop and twenty priests moving through London in full clerical garb naturally excited suspicions that something had gone seriously wrong in the negotiations for a French match.

Thanks to James's insistence on organizing a broad non-denominational front against the Habsburgs, a Bourbon bride for Charles made the most diplomatic sense. Yet many at home were alarmed over the prospect that France would insist on de facto toleration just as much as Spain had. To allay these fears, Prince Charles had solemnly vowed to the 1624 Parliament that he would never agree to any marriage terms which required the suspension of English laws. In subsequent negotiations with the French, however, he and his father agreed to a separate codicil, the Ecrit Particular, granting an English toleration of Catholics in return for French military support against the Habsburgs. This clause of course remained secret. On the other hand, it did not require detailed inside information to deduce that Charles had violated the spirit, if not the letter, of his promise to Parliament; the spectacle of thousands of English Catholics openly flouting the penal laws was enough to create considerable interest in the precise terms of the marriage treaty.

In the face of the mounting curiosity, the government stonewalled. Only after high-level negotiators had agreed on the terms was John Beaulieu, the king's French Secretary, able to secure the full text, which he forwarded to the king's Agent in Brussels; these details, Beaulieu added, 'I can assure you are yet made very dainty here amongst us, for the reasons which shall but too plainly appear unto you in the reading of the same.' And for those less well connected, the exact terms were to remain a very precious commodity. In light of Middleton's fondness for tackling sensitive issues, it is only natural that he should have written a section on 'the Treaty and Articles of Marriage between Prince Charles and Henrietta Maria'. But it is worth noting that he had at last entered the innermost chamber of the arcana imperii, the same one whose discussion in 1621 had earned Coke and his colleagues a stint in the Tower.

Having at last directly tackled one of the most sensitive 'affairs of state', he continued to do so with his last two themes. Of all the parliamentary sessions which Middleton had witnessed, none matched those of 1625 and 1626 for sheer emotional drama and political intensity. Early in his reign, Charles I hurriedly summoned a new Parliament in order to vote new funding for the war. But between the plague then raging in the metropolis and the massive French wedding party which had arrived with the new queen, the administration temporarily forgot about the new session. When its attention returned, the regime found that the Parliament-men, eager to flee the infected capital, had already passed the subsidy bill. Closer calculations revealed that the amount voted was inadequate for Charles's requirements. Therefore, a few weeks after adjourning the Westminster session, he met a second one at Oxford where he pressed for an extraordinary second vote of supply in one year. There, for the first time, direct criticism of the duke of Buckingham emerged. Some Parliament-men voiced grave reservations about his ability to direct the nascent war effort, citing everything from the French match to the massive fleet which Wimbledon was then gathering for the Cadiz expedition. 'Let us lay the fault where it is,' Sir Francis Seymour told his colleagues, 'the Duke of Buckingham is trusted.' Rather than endure further complaint, Charles dissolved the Parliament.

Although such abrupt action was hardly a prescription for future harmony, Charles and Buckingham hoped that early in 1626 they could meet a new Parliament armed with domestic reforms, like the enforcement of the penal laws, and victories which Wimbledon's fleet would surely gain. Unfortunately, as the quarrelling among Wimbledon and staff testified, hopes of presenting Parliament with a splendid triumph proved vain. The cessation of the Catholic toleration, while a shrewd political act, was offset by the loan of English vessels to Louis XIII, who, thanks to another administrative mistake, was able to use them *against* the Huguenots of La Rochelle. In short, in the half year between the two Parliaments, Buckingham succeeded in eroding rather than improving his credibility.

Consequently in the 1626 Parliament, renewed criticism of the duke quickly turned into a move to impeach him; additional parliamentary funds, a majority agreed, were only certain to be wasted with Buckingham at the helm. Meanwhile Charles I dug in his heels, refusing to consider cashiering the duke. The result was a four-month-long confrontation between king and Parliament. In the end, although it meant financially sabotaging the war effort, Charles dissolved his second Parliament. But before he did so, enough dirt emerged from various parliamentary investigations to shatter forever any popular enthusiasm for Buckingham. Amid the flood of revelations was one which can only have fixated Middleton: armed with a bundle of diplomatic documents, the earl of Bristol quite convincingly argued that Buckingham's relation of the trip to Madrid in 1623, the heroic account which Middleton enshrined in *A Game at Chess*, in fact played fast and loose with the truth. Thus in less than two years after Middleton's greatest triumph, the White Duke had taken on decidedly more somber hues.

The last item in *Farrago*, 'Habeas Corpus 1627', arose as a direct consequence of Charles's decision to dissolve the Parliament of 1626. This action preserved Charles's poverty as well as his prerogative, and in the midst of a Spanish war, this condition was, to say the least, extremely dangerous. In desperation, the regime sought to raise money through a series of extra-parliamentary levies. First Charles and Buckingham asked for a nationwide benevolence; this in the end produced only trifling amounts after the ratepayers rejected the request with cries of 'a Parliament, a Parliament!' Better luck attended a more finely crafted appeal in the 'forced loan' campaign of 1626–7. Carefully presented to small groups and individuals and surrounded by an array of royal concessions, this campaign stressed the repayment of the loan as well as the king's promise not to make this non-parliamentary tax the first of many others. On these terms, the government at last managed to extract an impressive amount of money, albeit grudgingly, from the ratepayers.

Although a majority paid, a significant minority refused, alleging that the levy, notwithstanding all the concessions and conditions, was illegal. What further heightened the drama of these refusals was the fact that many of the 'recusants' were godly Protestants, gentlemen like the earl of Essex, committed to the war against Spain. For them, their eagerness to grapple with the Habsburg Antichrist did not extend to subverting the 'ancient constitution' at home. In response, the government adopted a hard line. In extreme cases, some of the lower orders who refused were actually impressed for foreign service. Those of higher rank were stripped of local office and imprisoned indefinitely pending the King's pleasure. Although this practice was common enough—Coke and his colleagues had suffered it after the 1621 session—its legal standing was dubious. Therefore, in 1627 five of the knights then imprisoned resolved to challenge the government on this point. Some of the best attorneys in the realm then argued that the practice of indefinite imprisonment without charge, much less a trial, violated the venerable legal principles enshrined in the writ of habeas corpus. Hence, the plaintiff's counsel urged the Court to see that this practice 'cannot stand with the laws of the realm or that of Magna Carta'. This result was one of the great cases in seventeenth-century constitutional law, easily equal to Bate's case in 1606 and the Ship Money case of 1636. It would not be surprising if the Five Knights Case had fascinated Middleton, whose usurping tyrant in *Hengist, King of Kent*, Vortiger, indignantly asked

What's all our greatness
If we that prescribe bounds to meaner men
Must not pass these ourselves? (3.1.98–100)

Regrettably Middleton was unable to hear the answer to Vortiger's question. He died in July 1627 before either the judges found for the king or Charles reluctantly accepted in the following years the Petition of Right, which explicitly prohibited the practice. Nevertheless the date of his passing only underscores the importance which he set on his chronicle and on this issue. Since the opening rounds of the legal proceedings in the Five Knights Case had only begun a few days before his demise, Middleton died in a thoroughly appropriate manner: even from his deathbed he was busy following developments in a case which represented, in Sir Robert Phelips's words, 'the greatest thing that ever was about the liberty of the subject'.

III.

With much of the mystery removed from the main topics in the *Annales* and the *Farrago*, the importance of these works should now be clearer. To be sure, we are still unable to deduce how Middleton handled these matters, and it is even possible that he might have been sympathetic to the government on some issues. Yet the one fact about Middleton's chronicles is indisputable: his post with the City of London did not make him any less audacious in grappling with controversial issues than he was in other genres. As we have seen, the topics which tended to attract Middleton's attention were either sensitive 'affairs of state' or controversies involving the liberties of the subject, and as the decade progressed, this tendency hardened into a habit.

This conclusion, it must be conceded, supports the somewhat unusual notion that a major dramatist might have enjoyed writing contemporary history. Yet in Middleton's case, this is on mature reflection not entirely surprising. In *A Game at Chess*, the Black Queen's Pawn boasted of the thorough Spanish penetration of the bureaucracy at Whitehall; indeed Catholic moles were so ubiquitous that

so are designs
Oft times prevented and important secrets
Of states discovered. (1.1.59–61)

It is not hard to imagine that Middleton enjoyed turning tables on the Jesuits and the Spaniards. All the evidence from the *Annales* and the *Farrago* indicates that he was eager to try his hand at discovering secrets of state, even if he was only working for the Corporation of London.

SEE ALSO

Lost Plays: A Brief Account: this volume, 328
Lost Pageant for Charles I: A Brief Account: this volume, 1898
Authorship and date: *Annales*, *Companion*, 438; *Farrago*, *Companion*, 443
List of works cited: *Companion*, 1166

JUVENILIA 1597–1601

THE WISDOM OF SOLOMON PARAPHRASED

Edited and annotated by G. B. Shand, introduced by Debora Shuger

The Wisdom of Solomon Paraphrased, Middleton's earliest known work, appeared in print in 1597, probably between March and June of that year. Although perhaps loosely modelled on Henry Lok's metrical paraphrase, *Ecclesiastes, Otherwise Called the Preacher* (1597), Middleton's poem relies principally on the Geneva Bible's translation of the Apocryphal *Sapientia Solomonis* (also known as the *Liber Sapientiae*), along with the Latin translation included in the Protestant Junius-Tremellius Bible and possibly the Great Bible or a pre-Clementine Vulgate (see the commentary note to 10.89–120). Middleton, however, apparently did not enlist the assistance of any commentary, since he makes elementary errors of interpretation in dealing with passages clearly and correctly explicated by all patristic, medieval, and Renaissance exegetes (see the commentary on 10.89–120, 16.43–54, and 19.204).

As the handful of scholars who have attempted to read *The Wisdom of Solomon Paraphrased* uniformly report, it is a very bad poem, committing some of the most execrable lines extant in the corpus of English verse, my favourites being 'Fishes are oft deceivèd by the bait. | The bait, deceiving fish, doth fish deceive' (4.127–8) and 'Old time is often lost in being bald: | Bald because old, old because living long' (12.13–14). G. B. Shand (1983) summarizes the critical tradition with admirable concision: the poem is 'a stupefying read'. Yet it is not uniformly bad, or, more accurately, despite its often wretched versification, *The Wisdom of Solomon* has a striking and problematic weirdness that awakens scholarly curiosity—a decent and customary substitute for aesthetic pleasure.

Lily Bess Campbell's *Divine Poetry and Drama in Sixteenth-Century England* (1961) richly documents the Elizabethan vogue for biblical paraphrases, particularly of the Psalms and the canonical books attributed to Solomon (Canticles, Ecclesiastes, Proverbs). Yet at first glance the *Sapientia Solomonis* (I use the Latin title to distinguish the biblical text from Middleton's poem) seems an unlikely subject for an English Protestant poet. While part of the Vulgate Old Testament, all Protestant Bibles reject *Sapientia*'s canonical status, lumping it with other post-exilic texts in the Apocrypha, which both the Geneva Bible and Thirty-Nine Articles define as extra-canonical books written by 'godly men' but having no doctrinal authority. From Jerome on, most exegetes, both Catholic and Protestant, recognized that the *Sapientia Solomonis* should not be attributed to Solomon but probably originated in the Alexandrian Jewish community sometime between the third century BC and the first century AD, perhaps—given its syncretic Platonism—a work of Philo Judeus.

Sapientia thus lacks, particularly for Protestants, any firm claim to divine inspiration. But Middleton may have considered it attractive for a couple of reasons. First, the thirteenth chapter of *Sapientia* closely parallels the beginning of Paul's Epistle to the Romans—the central text of Reformed theology. Moreover, the book's precarious status may have made it more accessible to literary experimentation; in *Biblical Drama in England* (1968), Murray Roston notes that Protestant biblical drama avoids tampering with canonical Scripture, preferring instead to adapt the less fearfully sacred material found in the Apocrypha and the first-century Jewish historian Josephus. Although the same tacit interdict did not fall so heavily on non-dramatic biblical poetry, Middleton may have been more comfortable with drastically rewriting a non-canonical text than with embroidering the Word of God. For *The Wisdom of Solomon* spills over the confines of paraphrase, more than sixty per cent of the poem having no biblical equivalent; even where Middleton's lines do have some recognizable basis in *Sapientia*, their relation tends to be aggressively contrapuntal rather than faithfully paraphrastic. Middleton's liberties with his ostensible source increase in the latter half of the poem, an independence signalled by a shift in speaker from the fictional 'Solomon' of *Sapientia* to the authorial 'I' that suddenly intrudes at 10.67. One might more accurately describe the poem as a creative misreading than a strict paraphrase.

Shand has suggested a general political context for the poem, noting that Middleton several times hints at parallels between Elizabeth and Wisdom, particularly his depiction of the latter as Astraea, a queen, and as 'barren' (6.1–18, 8.1–7, 4.12). The remainder of what little scholarship exists on *The Wisdom of Solomon* focuses rather narrowly on the poem's rhetoric. Norman Brittin's 1946 dissertation treats the work as a typically Elizabethan academic exercise in figural hyperactivity. However, Brittin's staggering enumeration of schemes and tropes does not convey the peculiar flavour of Middleton's verse, which differs radically from the 'Platonic', metaphysical splendour suffusing *Sapientia*'s celebration of Wisdom's radiance and majesty. Middleton is at his worst when trying to evoke cosmic glory: compare the Geneva Bible's 'for while all things were in quiet silence, and the night was in the midst of her swift course, Thine almighty word leaped down from heaven out of thy royal throne' (18:14–15) with Middleton's ponderous

When Phoebe's axletree was limned with pale,
Pale which becometh night, night which is black
Hemmed round about with gloomy-shining veil,
Borne up by clouds, mounted on silence' back;
And when night's horses, in the running wain,
O'ertook the middest of their journey's pain;

Thy word, O Lord, descended from thy throne....
(18.157–63)

Instead, *The Wisdom of Solomon* shows clear affinities to Renaissance emblems; the poetry is static, pictorial, and sententious. The descriptions of the 'fruitful tree' in 1.169–74 and the contrast between the cedar and the mushroom at 2.128–32 are typical, if rather flat, examples of Middleton's allegorical emblems.

Often these images have a grotesque vividness. Bizarre figures peer from the stanzas: the voracious demon-lover of 1.109–12, the 'hungry cannibals' who 'suck your pelican to death' (19.121–6), the dying men digging their graves with their own tears (19.13–18). Pastoral and macabre merge disconcertingly in Middleton's comparison of death to 'Sol bestrid[ing] his golden mountain's top, | Lightening heaven's tapers with his living fire' (2.43–4) and his description of divine vengeance as resembling 'dew-distilling drops [that] fall from the morn' (11.167). The finest of Middleton's images have the morbid beauty one associates with Jeremy Taylor, evoking haunting scenes of bodily decay where 'Man, being grass, is hopped and grazed upon, | With sucking grasshoppers of weeping dew' (16.73–4) and dying swans fill 'the choir of waves with laving pain, | Yet dancing in their wail' (19.183–4). At times the poetry has an almost surreal quality: the strange 'icy jaw of Phoebe's hair' (19.202) and 'dead carcass of descending spirit' (1.134). The rhetorical exemplum dissolves into the resonant illogic of dreams.

A bewilderingly unstable landscape, indistinct chronology, and grammatical ambiguities intensify one's sense of surreal dislocation. Pronouns often have no discernible referent. Who, for example, is the 'Thou' that suddenly appears at 4.67 or the 'You' in 10.171–4? Similarly, spatio-temporal indicators point enigmatically into a referential miasma. Beginning at 5.181, Middleton seems to be describing an impending apocalypse, in which 'All heaven shall be in arms against earth's world'; the remainder of this chapter continues in the future tense, but the following chapter unexpectedly begins, 'After this conflict between God and man, | Remorse took harbour in God's angry breast' (6.1–2). Future metamorphizes into past; one cannot tell whether the conclusion to Chapter 5 depicts the Apocalypse or the Deluge or some unknown historical event. Similarly, 3.87–8 describes 'here' as a place void of 'justice,' the habitation of 'woe and sorrow', but at 18.103–4 Middleton declares that 'Now righteousness bears sway, and vice put down, | Virtue is queen, treading on mischief's head'. Again, we do not know whether 'here' and 'now' refer to Elizabethan England, a biblical episode, a moment in allegorical time, or nothing in particular. In place of consistent chronology or spatial orientation, the poem unfurls a sequence of images that mysteriously surface and recede: a nameless, dead 'face, heaving her heavy eyelids up | From forth the chamber of eternal night' (5.7–8), the demonic 'empress of the night' (10.46), the strange 'newly created beasts' that march past 'profane, ill-limned, pale spectacles' (11.127–34), the bodiless 'tigers' jaws' (16.43), an unidentified father bound in prison, facing imminent death (2.211–16). This procession of obscure creatures gives the poem a phantasmagoric atmosphere, like a nightmarish dream-vision or Spenser on acid.

The disorientation increases in the latter half of the poem (Chapters 10–19), which in *Sapientia* rehearses the Old Testament stories of the Israelites' providential deliverance from their enemies. Middleton either omits or confuses the historical allusions, so that the reader cannot possibly tell that the passages refer to Abraham, Moses, Joseph, and Jacob. Instead, historical events become psychological allegory, symbols of fear, horror, and misery. The seventeenth chapter of *Sapientia* recounts the plague of darkness afflicting the Egyptians; in Middleton, both plague and Egyptians disappear, leaving only a terrifying darkness where 'grief's pris'ners... | Slept in night's dungeon insupportable, | Lodged in night's horror too endurable' (17.136–8). The darkness turns into a troubled sleep, a 'hollow cave where visions come and go, | Where serpents hiss, where mandrakes groan and creep!' (17.141–2)—nightmares reminiscent of the 'dire and dreadful dreams' Calvin ascribes to the wicked (*Institutes* 1.3.2). The 'hollow cave' is one of a series of images of caverns, tombs, and concavities recurring throughout Middleton's poem as figures of the obscure centre of personality, from whose darkness arise monstrous visions and agonized cries: 'sobs' piercing the 'deep cistern of the centre's breast', 'vaults [that] | Sound and resound their old-new-weeping faults' (18.109–20). *Sapientia* celebrates the power of God over Israel's enemies; Middleton writes about the nightmares tormenting the evil conscience.

The Wisdom of Solomon's erasure of Old Testament history seems surprising, given the centrality of these narratives in Reformed theology. In other respects, however, the poem follows the ideological contours of sixteenth-century English Protestantism. Sometimes—as in the stanzas on social justice and the responsibilities of rulers (6.61–96, 217–28)—these *loci* approximate the corresponding biblical passage (6:9–11, 24); at other times they seem Middleton's additions. To this latter category belong the emphases on obedience, discipline, and submission to God (1.161, 6.55–6, 8.25–36, 9.61–6). One also occasionally notes an implicit anti-Romanist bias, most evidently in Middleton's reference to idols as 'saints' (13.111) and his total omission of *Sapientia*'s account of the redemptive, mediating role of the Aaronic priesthood (18:21–24), which Middleton turns into an encomium on the divine Word (18.223–46). The same theological animus may explain the curious removal of all typological allusions from the poem (see note to 2.211–16). Roman Catholic exegetes defended *Sapientia*'s canonicity on the ground that its second chapter prophesies Christ's torture and death at the hands of his enemies (2:12–21). Middleton, conversely, may have been uncomfortable with the notion that an apocryphal text could attain prophetic vision and therefore alters the passage to make its Christological implications unrecognizable.

The Wisdom of Solomon, in fact, consistently rewrites *Sapientia*, often in a Calvinist direction but at times with implications less easy to categorize. The assertion that 'God made thy thought' (1.67) seems an oblique reference to predestination; the description of God at 12.97–102 shows the marks of Protestant voluntarism. Likewise 13.49–60 replaces the biblical affirmation that 'by the greatness and beauty of the creatures proportionably the maker of them is seen' (13:5 in the Authorized Version; the Geneva translation is garbled here) with a defence of the absolute freedom of God *vis-à-vis* his creation; the non-analogical relation between 'workman' and 'hand-work' replaces *Sapientia*'s ontological correspondences.

The most overt and drastic misreading, however, comes at 10.89–132, where Middleton takes the Bible's periphrastic allusions to Jacob as a continuation of the story of Cain begun earlier in the tenth chapter. That is, he assimilates the first murderer and the godly patriarch into a single figure, who becomes the type of the repentant and redeemed sinner. Cain was 'fetched again by wisdom's power, | Had pardon for his deed, love for his lower' (10.95–6). This assimilation produces a narrative model of radical conversion effected by God's gratuitous mercy. This paradigm recurs repeatedly in Middleton's poem. Whereas *Sapientia* consistently *contrasts* the righteous and the wicked—usually the Egyptians and Hebrews—Middleton conflates the opposing figures, treating them as a single referent, as 'man' in general: 'man' who, although wicked, receives pardon, who is both punished and redeemed, whose corrupt nature is restored by divine grace (8.187–201, 11.73–108, 12.13–60, 12.121–32, 16.1–66, 18.13–36). Middleton's revisions tend to stress the total depravity of human nature, since the vices *Sapientia* attributes to the Egyptians become universal human characteristics, and simultaneously to underscore the radical otherness of a grace that redeems such creatures almost in spite of themselves. We are 'pressed down with vice's weights and mischief's gins' but God's 'pity is without a bound, | And sparest them which in some faults be found' (12.124–32).

The wedge Middleton drives between nature and grace—a polarity foreign to *Sapientia*—gives the poem a generally Calvinist structure. This label, however, while accurate, seems not quite adequate. A radical dualism pervades the whole poem, opposing nature to grace, mortality to eternity, earth to heaven. Middleton's additions to his biblical material often betray a sharp revulsion from the body, temporality, and the terrible burden of existence (7.1–60, 8.37–42, 8.187–96, 16.34). Echoes of Job announce

> Happy is he that lives, twice he that dies,
> Thrice happy he which neither lived nor died,
> Which never saw the earth with mortal eyes,
> Which never knew what miseries are tried. (4.85–8)

In Middleton's hands, in fact, the distinction between nature and grace takes a curious, almost gnostic, turn, where nature at moments seems an autonomous, demiurgic force opposed to divine wisdom (7.77–84). The creation of Adam described in the opening stanzas of Chapter 10 thus appears to involve two stages: first nature produces a rough, 'unfashioned' creature, who then needs to be, as it were, licked into shape by Wisdom. The poem never speaks of nature as a law or instrument of God; it (or she) denotes a separate power, the principle at once of generation and mortality: a mother who 'loves the issues of her womb' and 'makes her lap their quiet-sleeping tomb' (11.181–3). Nature also, Middleton several times suggests, determines 'moral' character, making some persons bad, some good, in the same sense that it makes some trees oaks and some poplars (2.163–8, 3.19–21, 4.25–30, 5.145–54). Hence sin results from biology rather than wrong choice; the opening stanzas of Chapter 13, which debate whether evil derives from man or from nature, conclude: 'Why blame I men? 'Tis she [nature]... that weaves, | That weaves, that wafts unto destruction's pen'.

A related quasi-gnostic anthropology informs Middleton's representation of the relation between body and soul. The body seems an alien shell or burden, enclosing and weighing down a divine emanation-spirit; the speaker thus equates Wisdom with 'my pure soul, locked in my body's grave' (8.106; cf. 7.13–24, 8.187–92, 10.151–4, 12.1–6, 12.229–30, 15.71–2, 16.133). At one point he describes Wisdom as his 'face' or 'form' (9.101–3), apparently a reflection or mirror of the self apprehended as an external and yet interior presence—as both 'my map' and 'shape of my thought'. Wisdom—one's 'pure soul' or conscience—seems less part of the self than a divine being who enters and transforms what Middleton terms our 'clayey lumps of pain' (12.114).

Hence in this life the righteous are strangers in a strange land, apparently unable or unwilling to act; they have 'no deeds', 'no show of store', but simply 'wait death's hour', knowing 'death to be the way to rest' (4.78–83). In an extraordinary passage, Middleton compares the good man to a fatally wounded lion, who in his agony rends 'the harbour of his body's cage; | Scorning the base-housed earth, mounts to the sky' (16.97–101). The soul claws with suicidal violence at its mortal prison. Innocent III might have appreciated such sentiments, but they scarcely suggest the ethical, reforming temper of urban Protestantism.

These disquieting and not-quite-orthodox oppositions between the realms of nature and spirit culminate in the concluding apocalypse of 19.163–210. In *Sapientia*, the corresponding passage (19:18–22) forms a rather obscure coda, apparently intended to give a 'scientific' explanation for such miracles as the parting of the Red Sea and the ten plagues by comparing these disruptions of natural phenomena to rearranging a sequence of musical notes. Middleton, however, excises the reference to Exodus, evoking instead a fantastic vision where each creature undergoes metamorphosis, so that sparrows sing like larks, nightingales fall silent, eagles fly below sparrows, and so forth. The irruption of supernatural power inverts natural law—or rather, as Middleton puts it, at the approach of God, 'nature slew herself' (19.205). This apocalypse thus repeats on a cosmic scale the individual's drastic conversion as divine Wisdom penetrates its sinful flesh, for grace does not perfect nature but shatters it.

One more topic deserves consideration. While it seems futile to comb *The Wisdom of Solomon* for anticipations of Middleton's mature style, the work's repeated evocations of 'tragedy' and the 'tragic' are not without interest in light of the poet's subsequent career. Although Middleton's later understanding of tragedy need not be identical to his youthful intuitions, his earlier use of the term may elucidate the trajectory linking the Elizabethan biblical poet to the Stuart dramatist.

The word first occurs in the beginning of the second chapter, as part of the long prosopopoeia spoken by the ungodly. They defend their libertine pursuit of momentary pleasures on the ground that 'our life [is] but our life's tragedy, | Extinguished in a momentary time' by the bleak finality of death (2.31–2). Thus, for unbelievers, mortality is tragedy. In *Wisdom*, this is almost always tragedy's primary sense. At 4.6, 'tragedy' means simply 'death'. At 17.161 the speaker commands 'Pull in thy head, thou sorrow's tragedy', and then goes on to define this (apparently snail-like) tragedy in what may be the only wholly successful stanza of the poem:

> The merry shepherd cannot walk alone,
> Tuning sweet madrigals of harvest's joy,
> Carving love's roundelays on every stone,
> Hanging on every tree some amorous toy,
>   But thou with sorrow interlines his song,
>   Opening thy jaws of death to do him wrong.

Et in Arcadia ego. The intrusion of death gives all plots their tragic endings—the snap-shut of tragedy's fatal jaws. Middleton further adumbrates 'sorrow's tragedy' in the following stanza, where this grotesque allegorical figure (a cross between a snail and a tyrannosaur?) metamorphizes into a second image of death-in-life. The nightmare visions that well up from the 'hollow cave' (17.133–56) and the toothy monster lying in wait for the merry shepherd are 'poisoned buds from Acherontic stalk'—hell-flowers pushing up into the garden and infecting the air with a miasmic and 'gloomy darkness' (17.171–2).

Again at 18.128 Middleton evokes the tragic implications of mortality. Here, however, tragedy signifies less the impinging of death upon life than the meaninglessness of individual achievement and status in the face of universal mortality. King, subject, and slave become undifferentiated 'dead carcasses' in a charnel 'dead scene' that bows down before 'the tragic cypress of lament', as though the tombs were suppliants prostrating themselves before the towering, funereal trees. The syntax of the passage is confusing, but Middleton seems to suggest that the tragic lament records the 'knowledge' of death's brutal levelling—that this knowledge constitutes the laments of the dead, whose sobs and weeping issue from their tombs (18.109–20).

The dead here seem to be the damned. As Middleton conflates nature and evil, so he makes no firm distinction between mortality and eternal punishment; for unbelievers, 'Earth is their hell' (11.78) or rather earth and hell together constitute a realm of pain, wickedness, and despair, cut off from the consoling radiance of supernal Wisdom. Hence Middleton at times associates tragedy with the penal agony of the damned and the suffering of sinners, a suffering at once the consequence of their own wickedness and a punishment imposed by divine justice (5.13–14, 13.153–4, 18.73–6). The tragic darkness shadowing this composite realm of nature and sin appears most starkly at 10.25–34, which recounts the murder of Abel. The murder is itself 'death's tragedy', but Middleton pursues the theatrical metaphor, making the earth the tragic chorus, as it were, for 'A weeping part had earth in that same play, | For she did weep herself to death that day'. But the earth's tears, 'distilled from millions of her eyes', cause the Flood, making 'her womb an overflowing clime'. The mother-earth who weeps for her lost children also destroys them; she is both source and grave for, in Yeats's words, 'those dying generations'. The tragic play that climaxes in the Flood simultaneously enacts divine vengeance against sin and nature's ineluctable cycles of birth and death. Mortality is, it would seem, its own punishment.

Middleton's notion of tragedy thus differs radically from the typical definitions given in Renaissance poetics. For Middleton, tragedy does not involve extraordinary calamities nor the fall of princes nor Fortune's caprice; it has no politics and no heroes. Instead, in *The Wisdom of Solomon* 'tragedy' signifies something close to the Calvinist state of fallen nature. The opening chapter of the *Institutes* thus defines the human condition as a composite of 'miseries . . . infamies . . . unhappiness . . . ignorance, vanity, poverty, infirmity . . . depravity and corruption'. So too Middleton's tragic creatures are sinful, hopeless, and agonizingly mortal. The 'gnostic' undertones in Middleton's poem are less un-Calvinist than selectively Calvinist: the result of his obsessive focus on the ruined world of *homo naturalis*, a nightmare shadow-world that is only briefly and sporadically punctured by an alien transcendence bringing pardon and renewal. Hence, for all the syntactic and prosodic defects of its style, *The Wisdom of Solomon*'s surreal and murky allegorical imagery has, at least in certain passages, its own peculiarly haunting power as the decorous symbol for this tragic universe of unbelief in which vermilion worms and 'grasshoppers of weeping dew' suck on corpses (16.73–8) and the 'often-weeping eyes of dry lament | ... pour forth burning water of despair' (16.157–8).

SEE ALSO

Textual introduction and apparatus: *Companion*, 461
Authorship and date: *Companion*, 335

The Wisdom of Solomon Paraphrased

A Jove surgit opus.

Epistles *To the right honourable and my very good lord, Robert Devereux, Earl of Essex and Ewe, Viscount of Hereford, Lord Ferrers of Chartley, Bourcher, and Louvaine, Master of Her Majesty's Horse and Ordnance, Knight of the Honourable Order of the Garter, and one of Her Majesty's most honourable Privy Council*

The summer's harvest, right honourable, is long since reaped, and now it is sowing time again. Behold, I have scattered a few seeds upon the young ground of unskilfulness. If it bear fruit, my labour is well bestowed, but if it be barren, I shall have less joy to set more. The husbandman observes the courses of the moon, I the forces of your favour; he desireth sunshine, I cheerful countenance, which once obtained, my harvest of joy will soon be ripened. My seeds as yet lodge in the bosom of the earth like infants upon the lap of a favourite, wanting the budding springtime of their growth, not knowing the east of their glory, the west of their quietness, the south of their summer, the north of their winter. But if the beams of your aspects lighten the small moiety of a smaller implanting, I shall have an everyday harvest, a fruition of content, a branch of felicity.

Your Honour's, addicted in all observance,
Thomas Middleton

To the Gentlemen Readers

Gentlemen, I give you the surveyance of my new-bought ground, and will only stand unto your verdicts. I fear me, that the acres of my field pass the ankers of my seed. If wanting seed, then I hope it will not be too much seeded. This is my bare excuse. But trust me, had my wit been sufficient to maintain the freedom of my will, then both should have been answerable to your wishes. Yet nevertheless think of it as a willing, though not a fulfilling moiety. But what mean I? While I thus argue, Momus and Zoilus, those two ravens, devour my seed because I lack a scarecrow. Indeed, so I may have less than I have, when such foul-gutted ravens swallow up my portion. If you gape for stuffing, hie you to dead carrion carcasses, and make them your ordinaries. I beseech you, gentlemen, let me have your aid, and as you have seen the first practice of my husbandry in sowing, so let me have your helping hands unto my reaping.

Yours, devoted in friendship,
Thomas Middleton

Epigraph ***A Jove surgit opus.*** Of God the work arises. First half of the Ovidian phrase (*Fasti* 5.111) with which Middleton will devoutly close the poem at 19.216.1; later the epigraph to the manuscript version of *Hubburd*. The intermingling of classical with Christian elements, from passing representations of the sun as Phoebus or Titan, to extended passages as when Astraea's voice replaces that of Solomon in Chapter Six, is not unusual; sometimes, as in *Ghost* (see 479–562 and Introduction), it may embody telling thematic complexity or conflict.

Epistles.2 Robert Devereux, Earl of Essex ambitious favourite of Elizabeth I, executed for his ill-fated rebellion against the Queen in February 1601

4 **Master ... Ordnance** director of the Queen's military stores and artillery; Essex was appointed to the post 18 March 1597, just prior to the composition of this dedication.

12 **husbandman** farmer

20 **aspects** favourable looks or glances, as from the sun

moiety portion

28 **my field** the Apocryphal *Sapientia Solomonis*, identified as *Geneva* in this commentary

ankers dry measures; *OED* records no other occurrence of this sense.

29 **If wanting seed** if lacking in creative invention

30 **seeded** gone to seed; overgrown

34 **Momus** Greek god of ridicule, criticism

35 **Zoilus** acerbic Greek critic

36 **scarecrow** apparently, a protective patron, though the figure is less than flattering

so thus

37 **you** Momus and Zoilus

39 **ordinaries** tavern meals

Chapter One

Verse 1 Wisdom, elixir of the purest life,
Hath taught her lesson to judicial views,
To those that judge a cause and end a strife,
Which sits in judgement's seat, and justice use:
  A lesson worthy of divinest ear,
  Quintessence of a true divinest fear.

Unwilling that exordium should retain
Her life-infusing speech, doth thus begin:
'You,' quoth she, 'that give remedy or pain,
Love justice, for injustice is a sin.
  Give unto God his due, his reverent style,
  And rather use simplicity than guile.

Verse 2 'For him, that guides the radiant eye of day,
Sitting in his star-chamber of the sky,
The horizons and hemispheres obey,
And winds, the fillers of vacuity.
  Much less should man tempt God, when all obey,
  But rather be a guide, and lead the way.

'For tempting argues but a sin's attempt.
Temptation is to sin associate.
So doing, thou from God art clean exempt,
Whose love is never placed in his love's hate.
  He will be found not of a tempting mind,
  But found of those which he doth faithful find.

Verse 3 'Temptation rather separates from God,
Converting goodness from the thing it was,
Heaping the indignation of his rod
To bruise our bodies like a brittle glass:
  For wicked thoughts have still a wicked end,
  In making God our foe, which was our friend.

'They muster up revenge, encamp our hate,
Undoing what before they meant to do,
Stirring up anger and unlucky fate,
Making the earth their friend, the heaven their foe:
  But when heaven's guide makes manifest his power,
  The earth, their friend, doth them like foes devour.

'O foolish men, to war against your bliss! Verse 4
O hateful hearts, where wisdom never reigned!
O wicked thoughts, which ever thought amiss!
What have you reaped? What pleasure have you gained?
  A fruit in show, a pleasure to decay:
  This have you got by keeping folly's way.

'For wisdom's harvest is with folly nipped,
And, with the winter of your vice's frost,
Her fruit all scattered, her implanting ripped,
Her name decayèd, her fruition lost:
  Nor can she prosper in a plot of vice,
  Gaining no summer's warmth, but winter's ice.

'Thou barren earth, where virtues never bud, Verse 5
Thou fruitless womb, where never fruits abide,
And thou dry withered sap which bears no good,
But the dishonour of thy proud heart's pride:
  A seat of all deceit, deceit deceived,
  Thy bliss a woe, thy woe of bliss bereaved.

'This place of night hath left no place for day.
Here never shines the sun of discipline,
But mischief, clad in sable night's array,
Thought's apparition, evil angel's sign:
  These reign enhousèd with their mother, night,
  To cloud the day of clearest wisdom's light.

'O you that practise to be chief in sin, Verse 6
Love's hate, hate's friend, friend's foe, foe's follower,
What do you gain? What merit do you win,
To be blaspheming vice's practiser?
  Your gain is wisdom's everlasting hate,
  Your merit grief, your grief your life's debate.

'Thou canst not hide thy thought. God made thy thought.
Let this thy caveat be for thinking ill.
Thou know'st that Christ thy living freedom bought,
To live on earth according to his will.
  God being thy creator, Christ thy bliss,
  Why dost thou err? Why dost thou do amiss?

1 The Judges of the earth are enjoined by Wisdom to seek God, to refrain from death-dealing slander and complaint, to know justice and righteousness from vice. (The summary headnotes to each chapter are editorial.)

Convenient compendia of the exegetical tradition on the *Sapientia Solomonis* can be found in the *Biblia Sacra* (1617), which gives patristic and medieval glosses; Cornelius a Lapide's *Commentarius in librum Sapientiae* (1627), which summarizes patristic, medieval, and Tridentine readings; and the *Critici sacri* (1698), which reprints the major scholarly commentaries from the mid-fifteenth through the mid-seventeenth centuries (D.S.).

6 **fear** of God, which is traditionally the beginning of wisdom

7 **exordium** introductory portion of a discourse
retain restrain, hinder

10 **justice** 'righteousness' (*Geneva*)

12 **simplicity** freedom from deceit; sincerity

14 **star-chamber** playing on the name of the judicial court at Westminster

15 **horizons and hemispheres** earth and heaven

21 **exempt** cut off, excluded

23 **of** by

25 **Temptation** 'wicked thoughts' (*Geneva*)

29 **still** always, constantly

31 **encamp** organize into a military camp (continuing the figure initiated by 'muster')

43 **folly** 'a wicked heart' (*Geneva*)

56 **sun** 'holy Spirit' (*Geneva*)
discipline instruction in the mysteries of faith

57 **mischief** harm or evil caused by a particular agent; often, as perhaps here, a hurtful character

68 **caveat** warning (regularly disyllabic in this text)

69 **Christ** not, of course, in *Geneva*

72 **err** go astray; sin

Verse 7 'He is both judge and witness of thy deeds.
He knows the volume which thy heart contains.
Christ skips thy faults, only thy virtue reads,
Redeeming thee from all thy vice's pains.
  O happy crown of mortal man's content,
  Sent for our joy, our joy in being sent!

'Then sham'st thou not to err, to sin, to stray,
To come to composition with thy vice,
With new-purged feet to tread the oldest way,
Lending new sense unto thy old device?
  Thy shame might flow in thy sin-flowing face,
  Rather than ebb to make an ebb of grace.

Verse 8 'For he which rules the orb of heaven and earth,
And the inequal course of every star,
Did know man's thoughts and secrets at his birth,
Whether inclined to peace or discord's jar.
  He knows what man will be ere he be man,
  And all his deeds in his life's living span.

'Then 'tis unpossible that earth can hide
Unrighteous actions from a righteous God,
For he can see their feet in sin that slide,
And those that lodge in righteousness' abode.
  He will extend his mercy on the good,
  His wrath on those in whom no virtues bud.

Verse 9 'Many there be that after trespass done
Will seek a covert for to hide their shame,
And range about the earth, thinking to shun
God's heavy wrath and meritorious blame.
  They, thinking to fly sin, run into sin,
  And think to end, when they do new begin.

'God made the earth; the earth denies their suit,
Nor can they harbour in the centre's womb.
God knows their thoughts although their tongues be mute,
And hears the sounds from forth their bodies' tomb.
  Sounds? Ah, no sounds, but man himself he hears,
  Too true a voice of man's most falsest fears.

Verse 10 'O see destruction hovering o'er thy head,
Mantling herself in wickedness' array,
Hoping to make thy body as her bed,
Thy vice her nutriment, thy soul her prey.
  Thou hast forsaken him that was thy guide,
  And see what follows to assuage thy pride.

'Thy roaring vices' noise hath cloyed his ears.
Like foaming waves they have o'erwhelmed thy joy.
Thy murmurings, which thy whole body bears,
Hath bred thy wail, thy wail thy life's annoy.
  Unhappy thoughts, to make a soul's decay!
  Unhappy soul, in suffering thoughts to sway!

'Then, sith the height of man's felicity Verse 11
Is plunged within the puddle of misdeeds,
And wades amongst discredit's infamy,
Blasting the merit of his virtue's seeds,
  Beware of murmuring, the chiefest ill,
  From whence all sin, all vice, all pains distill.

'O heavy doom, proceeding from a tongue!
Heavy-light tongue, tongue to thy own decay!
In virtue weak, in wickedness too strong,
To mischief prone, from goodness gone astray;
  Hammer to forge misdeeds, to temper lies,
  Selling thy life to death, thy soul to cries.

'Must death needs pay the ransom of thy sin Verse 12
With the dead carcass of descending spirit?
Wilt thou of force be snarèd in his gin,
And place thy error in destruction's merit?
  Life, seek not for thy death; death comes unsought,
  Buying the life which not long since was bought.

'Death and destruction never needs a call:
They are attendants on life's pilgrimage,
And life to them is as their playing ball,
Grounded upon destruction's anchorage.
  Seek not for that which unsought will betide.
  Ne'er wants destruction a provoking guide.

'Will you needs act your own destructïon? Verse 13
Will you needs harbour your own overthrow?
Or will you cause your own eversïon,
Beginning with despair, ending with woe?
  Then dye your hearts in tyranny's array,
  To make acquittance of destruction's pay.

'What do you meditate but on your death?
What do you practise but your living fall?
Who of you all have any virtue's breath,
But ready armèd at a mischief's call?
  God is not pleasèd at your vice's savour,
  But you best pleasèd when you lose his favour.

73 **He** 'the Spirit of the Lord' (*Geneva*)
80 **come to composition** enter into a compromising agreement
82 **device** wilful invention; embedded in this stanza ('err', 'stray', 'way', 'device') is the language of the Elizabethan General Confession.
88 **jar** dissension
100 **meritorious** merited
104 **centre's womb** midpoint of the earth
109–10 **O see destruction . . . array** This emblematic description repeats the elements of the presentation of 'mischief' at 57.
117 **murmurings** grumblings
118 **annoy** vexation, trouble
121 **sith** since
124 **Blasting** ruining, discrediting
126 **distill** trickle; gently flow
127 **doom** judgement
proceeding . . . tongue 'The mouth that speaketh lies, slayeth the soul' (*Geneva*).
133 **needs** necessarily; emphatic when combined with 'must'
135 **gin** snare, trap, device
143 **betide** happen
147 **eversïon** overthrow

Verse 14 'He made not death to be your conqueror,
But you to conquer over death and hell;
Nor you to be destruction's servitor,
Enhousèd there where majesty should dwell.
God made man to obey at his behest,
And man to be obeyed of every beast.

'He made not death to be our labour's hire,
But we ourselves made death through our desert.
Here never was the kingdom of hell-fire
Before the brand was kindled in man's heart.
Now man defieth God, all creatures man;
Vice flourisheth, and virtue lieth wan.

Verse 15 'O fruitful tree, whose root is always green,
Whose blossoms ever bud, whose fruits increase,
Whose top celestial virtue's seat hath been,
Defended by the sovereignty of peace!
This tree is righteousness. O happy tree,
Immortalizèd by thine own decree!

'O hateful plant, whose root is always dry,
Whose blossoms never bud, whose fruits decrease,
On whom sits the infernal deity
To take possession of so foul a lease!
This plant is vice. O too unhappy plant,
Ever to die, and never fill death's want!

Verse 16 'Accursèd in thy growth, dead in thy root,
Cankered with sin, shaken with every wind,
Whose top doth nothing differ from the foot,
Mischief the sap, and wickedness the rind:
So the ungodly, like this withered tree,
Is slack in doing good, in ill too free.

'Like this their wicked growth, too fast, too slow:
Too fast in sloth, too slow in virtue's haste.
They think their vice a friend when 'tis a foe:
In good, in wickedness, too slow, too fast.
And as this tree decays, so do they all,
Each one copartner of the other's fall.'

Chapter Two

Verse 1 Indeed they do presage what will betide,
With the misgiving verdict of misdeeds.
They know a fall will follow after pride,
And in so foul a heart grows many weeds.
'Our life is short,' quoth they. No, 'tis too long,
Lengthened with evil thoughts and evil tongue.
A life must needs be short to them that dies,
For life once dead in sin doth weakly live.
These die in sin, and mask in death's disguise,
And never think that death new life can give.
They say life dead can never live again.
O thoughts, O words, O deeds: fond, foolish, vain!

Vile life, to harbour where such death abodes, Verse 2
Abodes worse than are thoughts, thoughts worse than words,
Words half as ill as deeds, deeds sorrow's odes,
Odes ill enchanters of too ill records:
Thoughts, words, and deeds conjoinèd in one song,
May cause an echo from destruction's tongue.

Quoth they, ''tis chance whether we live or die,
Born or abortive, be or never be.
We worship fortune, she's our deity.
If she denies, no vital breath have we.
Here are we placèd in this orb of death.
This breath once gone, we never look for breath.

'Between both life and death, both hope and fear, Verse 3
Between our joy and grief, bliss and despair,
We here possess the fruit of what is here,
Born ever for to die, and die death's heir.
Our heritage is death annexed to life,
Our portion death, our death an endless strife.

'What is our life but our life's tragedy,
Extinguished in a momentary time?
And life to murder life is cruelty,
Unripely withering in a flow'ry prime.
An urn of ashes pleasing but the shows,
Once dry, the toiling spirit wand'ring goes.

'Like as the traces of appearing clouds Verse 4
Gives way when Titan resalutes the sea,
With new-changed flames gilding the ocean's floods,
Kissing the cabinet where Thetis lay,
So fares our life, when death doth give the wound:
Our life is led by death, a captive bound.

'When Sol bestrides his golden mountain's top,
Light'ning heaven's tapers with his living fire,
All gloomy powers have their diurnal stop,
And never gains the darkness they desire:
So perisheth our name when we are dead,
Ourselves ne'er called to mind, our deeds ne'er read.

159 **servitor** manservant
161 **behest** command
163 **hire** wages
168 **wan** sickly; gloomy
188 **sloth** laziness, often in matters of faith (hence the merger of sloth with despair as one of the seven deadly sins)
2 The wicked speak out against the faithful, but their speech is envious imaginings.
1 **they** 'the ungodly' (*Geneva*)
presage predict
betide happen
2 **misgiving** apprehensive
13–14 **abodes,** | **Abodes** shifting awkwardly from the verbal ('forebodes') to the substantive ('forebodings') for the sake of the *anadiplosis*
16 **enchanters** chanters, or singers
records musical notes
34 **prime** springtime; state of perfection
38 **Titan** the sun
40 **cabinet** boudoir
Thetis one of the Nereids; *fig.* the sea
43 **Sol** the sun
45 **diurnal** daily

Verse 5 'What is the time we have? What be our days?
No time, but shadow of what time should be;
Days in the place of hours which never stays,
Beguiling sight of that which sight should see.
As soon as they begin they have their fine,
Ne'er wax, still wane, ne'er stay, but still decline.

'Life may be called the shadow of effect,
Because the cloud of death doth shadow it;
Nor can our life approaching death reject;
They both in one for our election sit.
Death follows life in evëry degree,
But life to follow death you never see.

Verse 6 'Come we, whose old decrepit age doth halt
Like limping winter, in our winter, sin.
Faulty we know we are. Tush, what's a fault?
A shadowed vision of destruction's gin.
Our life begun with vice, so let it end;
It is a servile labour to amend.

'We joyed in sin, and let our joys renew.
We joyed in vice, and let our joys remain.
To present pleasures future hopes ensue,
And joy once lost, let us fetch back again.
Although our age can lend no youthful pace,
Yet let our minds follow our youthful race.

Verse 7 'What though old age lies heavy on our back,
Anatomy of an age-crookèd clime?
Let mind perform that which our bodies lack,
And change old age into a youthful time.
Two heavy things are more than one can bear:
Black may the garments be, the body clear.

'Decaying things be needful of repair.
Trees eaten out with years must needs decline.
Nature in time with foul doth cloud her fair,
Begirting youthful days with age's twine.
We live, and while we live, come let us joy:
To think of afterlife, 'tis but a toy.

Verse 8 'We know God made us in a living form,
But we'll unmake, and make ourselves again:
Unmake that which is made, like winter's storm,
Make unmade things to aggravate our pain.
God was our maker, and he made us good,
But our descent springs from another blood.

'He made us for to live, we mean to die.
He made the heaven our seat, we make the earth.
Each fashion makes a contrariety,
God truest God, man falsest from his birth.'
Quoth they, 'This earth shall be our chiefest heaven,
Our sin the anchor, and our vice the haven.

'Let heaven in earth, and earth in heaven consist. Verse 9
This earth is heaven, this heaven is earthly heaven.
Repugnant earth, repugnant heaven resist:
We joy in earth, of other joys bereaven.
This is the paradise of our delight:
Here let us live, and die in heaven's spite.

'Here let the monuments of wanton sports
Be seated in a wantonness' disguise,
Closed in the circuit of venereal forts
To feed the long-starved sight of amour's eyes.
Be this the chronicle of our content,
How we did sport on earth till sport was spent.

'But in the glory of the brightest day, Verse 10
Heaven's smoothest brow sometime is furrowèd,
And clouds usurp the clime in dim array,
Dark'ning the light which heaven had borrowèd.
So in this earthly heaven we daily see
That grief is placèd where delight should be.

'Here lives the righteous, bane unto their lives.
O sound from forth the hollow cave of woe.
Here lives age-crookèd fathers, widowed wives,
Poor, and yet rich in fortune's overthrow.
Let them not live, let us increase their want,
Make barren their desire, augment their scant.

'Our law is correspondent to our doom. Verse 11
Our law to doom, is dooming law's offence.
Each one agreeth in the other's room
To punish that which strives and wants defence.
This, cedar-like, doth make the shrub to bend,
When shrubs doth waste their force but to contend.

'The weakest power is subject to obey:
The mushrooms humbly kiss the cedar's foot,
The cedar flourishes when they decay,
Because her strength is grounded on a root.
We are the cedars, they the mushrooms be,
Unabled shrubs unto an abled tree.

'Then sith the weaker gives the stronger place, Verse 12
The young the elder, and the foot the top,
The low the high, the hidden powers the face,
All beasts the lion, every spring his stop,
Let those which practise contrariety
Be joined to us with inequality.

53 **fine** ending
54 **wax** grow, increase
still wane constantly decrease
82 **Begirting** encircling
93 **contrariety** opposition
97 **consist** co-exist
99 **Repugnant** Opposed
100 **bereaven** bereft
103 **monuments of wanton sports** 'some token of our pleasure' (*Geneva*)
105 **venereal** pertaining to sexual desire (from Venus, goddess of love)
106 **amour's** amorous; or possibly love's; pronounced with the stress on the first syllable in the 15th-17th centuries
115 **bane** destroyer
120 **scant** need

'They say that we offend. We say they do.
Their blame is laid on us, our blame on them.
They strike, and we retort the strucken blow:
So in each garment there's a differing hem.
  We end with contraries as they begun,
  Unequal sharing of what either won.'

Verses 13, 14 In this long conflict between tongue and tongue,
Tongue new beginning what one tongue did end
Made this cold battle hot in either's wrong,
And kept no pausing limits to contend.
  One tongue was echo to the other's sound,
  Which breathèd accents between mouth and ground.

He which hath virtue's arms upon his shield
Draws his descent from an eternal king.
He knows discretion can make folly yield,
Life conquer death, and vice a captive bring.
  The other, tutored by his mother, sin,
  Respects nor deeds nor words, but hopes to win.

Verse 15 The first, first essence of immortal life,
Reproves the heart of thought, the eye of sight,
The ear of hearing ill, the mind of strife,
The mouth of speech, the body of despite.
  Heart thinks, eyes sees, ears hears, minds meditate,
  Mouth utters both the soul and body's hate.

But nature, differing in each nature's kind,
Makes differing hearts, each heart a differing thought.
Some hath she made to see, some folly-blind,
Some famous, some obscure, some good, some naught.
  So these which differeth in each nature's reason,
  Had nature's time, when time was out of season.

Verse 16 Quoth they, 'He doth reprove our heart of thinking,
Our eyes of sight, our ears of hearing ill,
Our minds, our hearts in meditation linking,
Our mouths in speaking of our bodies' will.
  Because heart, sight, and mind do disagree,
  He'd make heart, sight, and mind of their decree.

'He says our heart is blinded with our eyes,
Our eyes are blinded with our blinded heart,
Our bodies on both parts defilèd lies,
Our mouths the trumpets of our vices' smart.'
  Quoth he, 'God is my father, I his son:
  His ways I take, your wicked ways I shun.'

Verse 17 As meditated wrongs are deeper placed
Within the deep cave of a wrongèd mind,
So meditated words is never passed
Before their sounds a settled harbour find.
  The wicked, answering to the latter words,
  Begins to speak as much as speech affords:

'One tongue must answer other tongue's reply.
Beginning boasts requires an ending fall.
Words lively spoke do sometimes wordless die:
If not, live echoes unto speeches call.
  Let not the shadow smother up the deed:
  The outward leaf differs from inward seed.

'The shape and show of substance and effect Verse 18
Doth shape the substance in the shadow's hue,
And shadow, put in substance, will neglect
The wonted shadow of not being true.
  Let substance follow substance, show a show,
  And let not substance for the shadow go.

'He that could give such admonitïon,
Such vaunting words, such words confirming vaunts,
As if his tongue had mounted to ambitïon,
Or climbed the turrets which vainglory haunts,
  Now let his father, if he be his son,
  Undo the knot which his proud boasts have spun.

'We are his enemies, his chain our hands, Verse 19
Our words his fetters, and our heart his cave;
Our stern embracements are his servile bonds:
Where is the helper now which he should have?
  In prison like himself, not to be found:
  He wanteth help himself to be unbound.

'Then sith thy father bears it patiently,
To suffer torments, grief, rebuke, and blame,
'Tis needful thou shouldst bear equality,
To see if meekness harbour in thy name.
  Help, father, for thy son in prison lies!
  Help, son, or else thy helpless father dies!'

Thus is the righteous God and righteous man Verse 20
Drowned in oblivion with this vice's reign.
'God wanteth power,' say they, 'of what we can:
The other would perform that which is vain.
  Both faulty in one fault, and both alike
  Must have the stroke which our law's judgements
    strike.

'He calls himself a son, from heaven's descent.
What can earth's force avail 'gainst heaven's defence?
His life by immortality is lent:
Then how can punishment his wrath incense?
  Though death herself in his arraignment deck,
  He hath his life's preserver at a beck.'

139 **They** 'the righteous' (*Geneva*, where it is singular)
196 **wonted** usual
199 **He... admonitïon** the righteous or godly man; Christ
203–16 **Now let... dies!** The words of the wicked apparently echo the taunting of the crucified Christ.
207 **servile** enslaving
211–16 The corresponding biblical passage (2:13–20) does not mention an imprisoned father. Virtually all pre-modern commentaries (including the notes to *Geneva*) take the passage, which describes the suffering of the righteous man at the hands of the wicked, as the prophecy of Christ's passion. Middleton's addition of the unnamed 'father' effectively eliminates any typological resonances (D.S.).
220 **The other** the righteous or godly man
228 **beck** tiny gesture of command

Verse 21 As doth the basilisk with poisoned sight
Blind every function of a mortal eye,
Disarm the body's powers of vital might,
Rob heart of thought, make living life to die,
So doth the wicked with their vice's look
Infect the spring of clearest virtue's brook.

This basilisk, mortality's chief foe,
And to the heart's long-knitted artery,
Doth sometime perish at her shadow's show,
Pois'ning herself with her own poisoned eye.
Needs must the sting fall out with over-harming,
Needs must the tongue burn out in over-warming.

Verse 22 So fares it with the practisers of vice:
Laden with many venomous adders' stings,
Sometimes are blinded with their own device,
And tunes that song which their destruction sings.
Their mischief blindeth their mischievous eyes,
Like basilisks which in their shadow dies.

They go, and yet they cannot see their feet,
Like blinded pilgrims in an unknown way:
Blind in perceiving things which be most meet,
But need nor sight nor guide to go astray.
Tell them of good, they cannot understand;
But tell them of a mischief, that's at hand.

Verses 23, 24 The basilisk was made to blind the sight,
The adder for to sting, the worm to creep,
The viper to devour, the dog to bite,
The nightingale to wake when others sleep.
Only man differs from his maker's will,
Undoing what is good, and doing ill.

A godlike face he had, a heavenly hue,
Without corruption, image without spots,
But now is metamorphosèd anew,
Full of corruption, image full of blots,
Blotted by him that is the plot of evil:
Undone, corrupted, vanquished by the devil.

Chapter Three

Verse 1 But every cloud cannot hide Phoebus' face,
Nor shut the casement of his living flame,
Nor is there every soul which wanteth grace,
Nor every heart seduced with mischief's name.
Life cannot live without corruptïon;
World cannot be without destructïon.
Nor is the body all corrupt, or world
Bent wholly unto wickedness' assault.
The adder is not always seen uncurled,
Nor every soul found guilty in one fault.
Some good, some bad: but those whom virtues guard,
Heaven is their haven, comfort their reward.

Thrice-happy habitation of delight! Verse 2
Thrice-happy step of immortality!
Thrice-happy souls, to gain such heavenly sight,
Springing from heaven's perpetuity!
O peaceful place! But O, thrice-peaceful souls,
Whom neither threats, nor strife, nor wars controls!

They are not like the wicked, for they live; Verse 3
Nor they like to the righteous, for they die.
Each of their lives a differing nature give:
One thinks that life ends with mortality,
And that the righteous never live again,
But die as subjects to a grievous pain.

What labouring soul refuseth for to sweat, Verse 4
Knowing his hire, his payment, his reward,
To suffer winter's cold and summer's heat,
Assurèd of his labour's due regard?
The bee with summer's toil will load her hive,
In winter's frost to keep herself alive.

And what divinest spirit would not toil,
And suffer many torments, many pains,
This world's destruction, heavy labour's foil,
When heaven is their hire, heaven's joy their gains?
Who would not suffer torments for to die,
When death's reward is immortality?

Pain is the entrance to eternal joy. Verse 5
Death endeth life, and death beginneth life:
Beginneth happy, endeth in annoy,
Begins immortal peace, ends mortal strife.
Then, seeing death and pains bring joy and heaven,
What need we fear death's pain when life is given?

Say sickness or infirmity's disease
(As many harms hang over mortal heads)
Should be his world's reward, yet heaven hath ease,
A salve to cure, and quiet resting beds.
God maketh in earth's world lament our pleasure,
That in heaven's world delight might be our treasure.

Fair may the shadow be, the substance foul. Verse 6
After the trial followeth the trust.
The clearest skin may have the foulest soul.
The purest gold will sooner take the rust.

229 **basilisk** fabulous reptile whose look was reputed to be fatal
236 **long-knitted** interlaced, intertwined; the arteries were considered to bear both blood and vital spirits.
243 **are** they are
249 **meet** fitting, suitable
263 **plot** type, representation; *OED* records this sense only in *Solomon*.
3 While the righteous and faithful are assured of eternal peace after worldly suffering, the ungodly are punished eternally.
1 **Phoebus** the sun
2 **casement** hinged window
33 **foil** defeat; also, as at 54, muck
45 **his** death's

The brook, though ne'er so clear, may take some soil.
The heart, though ne'er so strong, may take some foil.

Wouldst thou be counted just? Make thyself just.
O purify thy mire-bespotted heart!
For God doth try thy actions ere he trust,
Thy faith, thy deeds, thy words, and what thou art.
He will receive no mud for clearest springs,
Nor thy unrighteous words for righteous things.

Verse 7 As God is perfect God and perfect good,
So he accepteth none but perfect minds.
They ever prosper, flourish, live, and bud,
Like blessèd plants, far from destruction's winds:
Still bud, ne'er fade, still flourish, ne'er decay,
Still rise, ne'er fall, still spring, ne'er fade away.

Who would not covet to be such a plant?
Who would not wish to stand in such a ground,
Sith it doth neither fruit nor blessing want,
Nor aught which in this plant might not be found?
They are the righteous which enjoy this earth,
The figure of an ever-bearing birth.

Verse 8 The small is always subject to the great,
The young to him which is of elder time,
The lowest place unto the highest seat,
And pale-faced Phoebe to bright Phoebus' clime.
Vice is not governor of virtue's place,
But blushes for to see so bright a face.

Virtue is chief, and virtue will be chief:
Chief good, and chief Astraea, justice' mate,
Both for to punish and to yield relief,
And have dominion over every state,
To right the wrongs which wickedness hath done,
Delivering nations from life-lasting moan.

Verse 9 O you whose causes plungeth in despair,
Sad-faced petitioners with grief's request,
What seek you? Here's nor justice nor her heir,
But woe and sorrow with death's dumb arrest.
Turn up your woe-blind eyes unto the sky:
There sits the judge can yield you remedy.

Trust in his power. He is the truest God:
True God, true judge, true justice, and true guide.
All truth is placèd in his truth's abode,
All virtues seated at his virtuous side.
He will regard your suit, and ease your plaint,
And mollify your misery's constraint.

Then shall you see the judges of the earth *Verse 10*
Summonèd with the trumpet of his ire,
To give account and reck'ning from their birth,
Whe'er worthy or unworthy of their hire.
The godly shall receive their labour's trial,
The wicked shall receive their joy's denial.

They which did sleep in sin, and not regarded
The poor man's fortune, prostrate at their feet,
Even as they dealt, so shall they be rewarded,
When they their toilèd souls' destruction meet:
From judges they petitioners shall be,
Yet want the sight which they do sue to see.

That labour which is grounded on delight, *Verse 11*
That hope which reason doth enrich with hap,
That merit which is placed in wisdom's might,
Secure from mischief's bait or folly's clap,
Wit's labour, reason's hope, and wisdom's merit,
All three in one make one thrice-happy spirit.

Why set I happiness fore mortal eyes,
Which covets to be drenched in misery,
Mantling their foolish minds in folly's guise,
Despising wisdom's perpetuity?
Sin's labour, folly's hope, and vice's merit:
These three in one make a thrice-cursèd spirit.

Vain hope must needs consist in what is vain. *Verse 12*
All foolish labours flows from folly's tears.
Unprofitable works proceed from pain,
And pain ill labour's duest guerdon bears.
Three vanities in one, and one in three,
Make three pains one, and one uncertainty.

A wicked king makes a more wicked land.
Heads once infected soon corrupts the feet.
If the tree falls, the branches cannot stand,
Nor children, be their parents indiscreet.
The man infects the wife, the wife the child,
Like birds which in one nest be all defiled.

The field which never was ordained to bear *Verse 13*
Is happier far than a still-tillèd ground:
This sleeps with quietness in every year,
The other cursed if any tares be found.
The barren happier than she that bears:
This brings forth joy, the other tares and tears.

The eunuch never lay in vice's bed. *Verse 14*
The barren woman never brought forth sin.
These two in heaven's happiness are led:
She fruit in soul, he fruit in faith doth win.

76 **Phoebe** the moon
80 **Astraea** goddess of justice, associated with Virgo; sometimes a complimentary persona of Elizabeth I
96 **mollify** soften
constraint affliction, distress; but also continuing the legal imagery of 'suit' and 'plaint' in 95
106 **toilèd** exhausted; trapped as in a toil or net
108 **sight . . . see** heaven
110 **hap** good fortune
112 **clap** stroke, blow
124 **duest guerdon** most deserved reward
138 **tares** weeds
139 **never . . . bed** 'with his hands hath not wrought iniquity, nor imagined wicked things against God' (*Geneva*)

O rare and happy man, forever blest!
O rare and happy woman, heaven's guest!

Verse 15 Who seeks to reap before the corn be ripe?
Who looks for harvest among winter's frost?
Or who in grief will follow pleasure's pipe?
What mariner can sail upon the coast?
That which is done in time is done in season,
And things done out of time is out of reason.

The glorious labour is in doing good,
In time's observance, and in nature's will,
Whose fruit is also glorious for our food,
If glory may consist in labour's skill,
Whose root is wisdom, which shall never wither,
But spring, and sprout, and love, and live together.

Verse 16 But every ground doth not bear blessèd plants,
Nor every plant brings forth expected fruit.
What this same ground may have, another wants,
Nor are all causes answered with one suit.
That tree whose root is sound, whose grounding strong,
May firmly stand when others lie along.

View nature's beauty, mark her changing hue:
She is not always foul, nor always fair.
Chaste and unchaste she is, true and untrue,
And some springs from her in a lustful air.
And these adulterers be, whose seed shall perish:
Never shall lust and wickedness long flourish.

Verse 17 Although the flint be hard, the water soft,
Yet is it mollified with lightest drops.
Hard is the water when the wind's aloft,
Small things in time may vanquish greatest stops.
The longer grows the tree, the greater moss,
The longer soil remains, the more the dross.

The longer that the wicked lives on earth,
The greater is their pain, their sin, their shame,
The greater vice's reign and virtue's dearth,
The greater goodness' lack and mischief's name.
When in their youth no honour they could get,
Old age could never pay so young a debt.

Verses 18, 19 To place an honour in dishonour's place,
Were but to make disparagement of both.
Both enemies, they could not brook the case,
For honour to subvert dishonour's growth.
Dishonour will not change for honour's room:
She hopes to stay after their bodies' doom.

Or live they long, or die they suddenly,
They have nor hope, nor comfort of reward.
Their hope of comfort is iniquity,
The bar by which they from their joys are barred.
O old-new end, made to begin new grief!
O new beginning, end of old relief!

Chapter Four

If happiness may harbour in content, *Verse 1*
If life in love, if love in better life,
Then unto many happiness is lent,
And long-departed joy might then be rife:
Some happy if they live, some if they die,
Happy in life, happy in tragedy.

Content is happiness because content.
Bareness and barrenness is virtue's grace:
Bare because wealth to poverty is bent,
Barren in that it scorns ill fortune's place.
The barren earth is barren of her tares,
The barren woman barren of her cares.

The soul of virtue is eternity, *Verse 2*
All-filling essence of divinest rage,
And virtue's true eternal memory
Is barrenness, her soul's eternal gage.
O happy soul, that is engagèd there,
And pawns his life that barren badge to wear!

See how the multitude, with humble hearts,
Lies prostrate for to welcome her return.
See how they mourn and wail when she departs.
See how they make their tears her trophy's urn.
Being present, they desire her; being gone,
Their hot desire is turned to hotter moan.

As everyone hath not one nature's mould, *Verse 3*
So everyone hath not one nature's mind.
Some think that dross which others take for gold.
Each difference cometh from a differing kind.
Some do despise what others do embrace,
Some praise the thing which others do disgrace.

The barren doth embrace their barrenness,
And hold it as a virtue worthy meed.
The other calls conception happiness,
And hold it as a virtue-worthy deed.
The one is firmly grounded on a rock,
The other billows game and tempests mock.

147 **follow pleasure's pipe** dance to wanton tunes
160 **causes** cases in law
166 **some . . . air** some people are naturally born lecherous
172 **stops** obstacles
174 **dross** impure matter
187 **Or . . . or** Whether . . . or
190 **bar** obstacle; objection which completely invalidates a legal claim or plea
4 Of the salvation of the righteous, despite the lures of worldly pleasure, and of the spiritual blindness of the unrighteous, whose hearts cannot see God's grace.
4 **rife** flourishing, abundant, common, free
14 **rage** creative fervour
16 **gage** pledge, security, badge
22 **trophy's** memory's?
32 **meed** reward
36 **game** make sport of

Verse 4 Sometime the nettle groweth with the rose.
The nettle hath a sting, the rose a thorn.
This stings the hand, the other pricks the nose,
Harming that scent which her sweet birth had borne.
Weeds among herbs, herbs among weeds are found:
Tares in the mantle of a corny ground.

The nettle's growth is fast, the rose's slow.
The weeds outgrow the herbs, the tares the corn.
These may be well compared to vice's show,
Which covets for to grow ere it be born.
As greatest danger doth pursue fast going,
So greatest danger doth ensue fast growing.

Verse 5 The tallest cedar hath the greatest wind.
The highest tree is subject unto falls.
High-soaring eagles soon are strucken blind.
The tongue must needs be hoarse with many calls.
The wicked, thinking for to touch the sky,
Are blasted with the fire of heaven's eye.

So, like ascending and descending air,
Both dusky vapours from two humorous clouds,
Lies witherèd the glory of their fair,
Unpleasant branches wrenched in folly's floods:
Unprofitable fruits like to a weed,
Made only to infect, and not to feed.

Verse 6 Made for to make a fast, and not a feast,
Made rather for infection than for meat,
Not worthy to be eaten of a beast,
Thy taste so sour, thy poison is so great:
Thou mayst be well comparèd to a tree,
Because thy branches are as ill as thee.

Thou hast begot thine own confusïon,
The witnesses of what thou dost begin,
Thy doomers in thy life's conclusïon,
Which will unasked and asked reveal thy sin.
Needs must the new-hatched birds bewray the nest,
When they are nursèd in a stepdame's breast.

Verse 7 But righteousness is of another sect.
Her root is from an everlasting seed.
No weak, unable grounding doth connect
Her never-limited memorial's deed.
She hath no branches for a tempest's prey,
No deeds but scorns to yield unto decay.

She hath no withered fruit, no show of store,
But perfect essence of a còmplete power.
Say that she dies to world, she lives the more,
As who so righteous but doth wait death's hour?
Who knows not death to be the way to rest?
And he that never dies is never blest.

Happy is he that lives, twice he that dies, Verse 8
Thrice happy he which neither lived nor died,
Which never saw the earth with mortal eyes,
Which never knew what miseries are tried.
Happy is life, twice happy is our death,
But three times thrice he which had never breath.

Some thinks that pleasure is achieved by years,
Or by maintaining of a wretched life,
When, out alas, it heapeth tears on tears,
Grief upon grief, strife on beginning strife.
Pleasure is weak, if measurèd by length:
The oldest ages hath the weaker strength.

Three turnings are contained in mortal course: Verse 9
Old, mean, and young. Mean and old brings age.
The youth hath strength, the mean decaying force.
The old are weak, yet strong in anger's rage.
Three turnings in one age: strong, weak, and weaker;
Yet age nor youth is youth's or age's breaker.

Some says that youth is quick in judging causes.
Some says that age is witty, grave, and wise.
I hold of age's side with their applauses,
Which judges with their hearts, not with their eyes.
I say grave wisdom lies in greyest heads,
And undefilèd lives in age's beds.

God is both grave and old, yet young and new: Verse 10
Grave because agèd, agèd because young.
Long youth may well be callèd age's hue,
And hath no differing sound upon the tongue.
God old, because eternities are old,
Young, for eternities one motion hold.

Some in their birth, some dies when they are born.
Some born, and some abortive, yet all die.
Some in their youth, some in old age forlorn,
Some neither young nor old, but equally.
The righteous, when he liveth with the sinner,
Doth hope for death, his better life's beginner.

37–51 **Sometime . . . blind** intensely proverbial: 39 glances at Tilley N134: 'It is better to be stung by a nettle than pricked by a rose', and 49–50 make up a version of Tilley C208: 'High cedars fall . . . when low shrubs remain.'
42 **Tares** weeds, but playing on 'tears' (rips) **corny** fruitful
51 **High-soaring . . . blind** direct contradiction of the proverb, 'Only the eagle can gaze at the sun' (Tilley E3)
56 **humorous** moist
68 **witnesses** 'For all the children that are born of the wicked bed, shall be witness of the wickedness against their parents when they be asked' (*Geneva*).
69 **doomers** judges
71 **bewray** foul
73 **righteousness** 'the righteous' (*Geneva*); in shifting to the virtue, Middleton also shifts to the feminine from *Geneva*'s masculine.
88 **tried** undergone
102 **breaker** destroyer, violator
119 **The righteous** Middleton seems to pass over *Geneva*'s allusion to Enoch: 'He pleased God, and was beloved of Him, so that whereas he lived among sinners, He translated him.'

Verse 11 The swine delights to wallow in the mire,
The giddy drunkard in excess of wine.
He may corrupt the purest reason's gyre,
And she turn virtue into vice's sign.
  Mischief is mire, and may infect that spring
  Which every flow and ebb of vice doth bring.

Fishes are oft deceivèd by the bait.
The bait, deceiving fish, doth fish deceive.
So righteous are allured by sin's deceit,
And oft enticèd into sinners' weave.
  The righteous be as fishes to their gin,
  Beguiled, deceived, allurèd into sin.

Verse 12 The fisher hath a bait, deceiving fish.
The fowler hath a net, deceiving fowls.
Both wisheth to obtain their snaring wish,
Observing time like night-observing owls.
  The fisher lays his bait, fowler his net:
  He hopes for fish, the other birds to get.

This fisher is the wicked, vice his bait.
This fowler is the sinner, sin his net.
The simple righteous falls in their deceit,
And like a prey, a fish, a fowl beset.
  A bait, a net, obscuring what is good,
  Like fish and fowl took up for vice's food.

Verse 13 But baits nor nets, gins nor beguiling snares,
Vice nor the vicious sinner, nor the sin,
Can shut the righteous into prison's cares,
Or set deceiving baits to mew them in.
  They know their lives' deliverer, heaven's God,
  Can break their baits and snares with justice' rod.

Verse 14 When vice abounds on earth, and earth in vice,
Then virtue keeps her chamber in the sky,
To shun the mischief which her baits entice,
Her snares, her nets, her guiles, her company.
  As soon as mischief reigns upon the earth,
  Heaven calls the righteous to a better birth.

Verse 15 The blinded eyes can never see the way.
The blinded heart can never see to see.
The blinded soul doth always go astray.
All three want sight, in being blind all three.
  Blind and yet see, they see and yet are blind.
  The face hath eyes, but eyeless is the mind.

They see with outward sight God's heavenly grace,
His grace, his love, his mercy on his saints.
With outward-facèd eye and eyèd face,
Their outward body inward soul depaints.
  Of heart's chief eye they chiefly are bereft,
  And yet the shadow of two eyes are left.

Some blinded be in face, and some in soul. Verse 16
The face's eyes are not incurable;
The other wanteth healing to be whole,
Or seems to some to be endurable.
  Look in a blinded eye, bright is the glass,
  Though brightness banishèd from what it was.

'So,' quoth the righteous, 'are these blinded hearts:
The outward glass is clear, the substance dark.
Both seem as if one took the other's parts,
Yet both in one have not one brightness' spark.
  The outward eye is but destruction's reader,
  Wanting the inward eye to be the leader.

'Our body may be called a commonweal, Verse 17
Our head the chief, for reason harbours there.
From thence comes heart's and soul's united zeal,
All else inferiors be which stand in fear.
  This commonweal, ruled by discretion's eye,
  Lives likewise if she live, dies if she die.

'Then how can weal or wealth, common or proper,
Long stand, long flow, long flourish, long remain,
When wail is weal's, and stealth is wealth's chief stopper,
When sight is gone, which never comes again?'
  The wicked sees the righteous lose their breath,
  But know not what reward they gain by death.

Though blind in sight, yet can they see to harm, Verse 18
See to despise, see to deride and mock;
But their revenge lies in God's mighty arm,
Scorning to choose them for his chosen flock.
  He is the shepherd, godly are his sheep;
  They wake in joy, these in destruction sleep.

The godly sleep in eyes, but wake in hearts. Verse 19
The wicked sleep in hearts, but wake in eyes.
These ever-wake eyes are no sleepy parts.
These ever sleep, for sleep is heart's disguise.
  Their waking eyes do see their heart's lament,
  While heart securely sleeps in eyes' content.

If they awake, sleep's image doth molest them, Verse 20
And beats into their waking memories.
If they do sleep, joy waking doth detest them,
Yet beats into their sleeping arteries.
  Sleeping or waking, they have fear on fear,
  Waking or sleeping, they are ne'er the near.

If waking, they remember what they are,
What sins they have committed in their waking.
If sleeping, they forget tormenting's fare,
How ready they have been in mischief's making.

123 **gyre** circle, revolution
128 **deceiving fish** in the form of, or consisting of, a deceiving fish
148 **mew** confine
153 **her baits** vice's lures
166 **depaints** depicts
191 **the righteous** 'the wise' (*Geneva*)
205 **molest** trouble, grieve
207 **joy waking** the pleasure they indulged in while awake
detest curse; denounce
208 **Yet . . . arteries** yet taints or infects their forgetful hearts
210 **near** nearer

When they awake, their wickedness betrays them,
When they do sleep, destructïon dismays them.

Chapter Five

Verse 1 As these two slumbers have two contraries,
One slumber in the face, one in the mind,
So their two casements two varieties,
One unto heaven, and one to hell combined.
The face is flattery, and her mansion hell.
The mind is just, this doth in heaven dwell.

The face, heaving her heavy eyelids up
From forth the chamber of eternal night,
Sees virtue hold plenty's replenished cup,
And boldly stand in God's and heaven's sight.
She, opening the windows of her breast,
Sees how the wicked rest in their unrest.

Verse 2 Quoth she, 'Those whom the curtain of decay
Hath tragically summonèd to pain,
Were once the clouds and clouders of my day,
Depravers and deprivers of my gain.'
The wicked hearing this descending sound,
Fear struck their limbs to the pale-clothèd ground.

Verse 3 Amazèd at the freedom of her words,
Their tongue-tied accents drove them to despair,
And made them change their minds to woe's records,
And say within themselves, 'Lo what we are:
We have had virtue in derision's place,
And made a parable of her disgrace.

Verse 4 'See where she sits enthronized in the sky.
See, see her labour's crown upon her head.
See how the righteous live which erst did die,
From death to life with virtue's lodestar led.
See those whom we derided, they are blest:
They heaven's, not hell's, we hell's, not heaven's guest.

'We thought the righteous had been fury's son,
With inconsiderate speech, unstayèd way.
We thought that death had his dishonour won,
And would have made his life destruction's prey.
But we were mad, they just, we fools, they wise:
We shame, they praise, we loss, they have the prize.

'We thought them fools, when we ourselves were fools. *Verse 5*
We thought them mad, when we ourselves were mad.
The heat which sprang from them our folly cools.
We find in us which we but thought they had.
We thought their end had been dishonour's pledge;
They but surveyed the place, we made the hedge.

'We see how they are blessed, how we are curst,
How they accepted are, and we refused,
And how our bonds are tied, their bonds are burst,
Our faults are hourly blamed, their faults excused.
See how heavens gratulate their welcome sight,
Which comes to take possession of their right.

'But O, too late we see our wickedness! *Verse 6*
Too late we lie in a repentant tomb!
Too late we smooth old hairs with happiness!
Too late we seek to ease our bodies' doom!
Now falsehood hath advanced her forgèd banner,
Too late we seem to verify truth's manner.

'The sun of righteousness, which should have shined,
And made our hearts the cabins of his east,
Is now made cloudy night through vice's wind,
And lodgeth with his downfall in the west.
That summer's day, which should have been night's bar,
Is now made winter in her icy car.

'Too much our feet have gone, but never right. *Verse 7*
Much labour have we took, but none in good.
We wearièd ourselves with our delight,
Endangering ourselves to please our mood.
Our feet did labour much: 'twas for our pleasure.
We wearièd ourselves: 'twas for our leisure.

'In sin's perfection was our labour spent.
In wickedness' preferment we did haste.
To suffer perils we were all content,
For the advancement of our vices past.
Through many dangerous ways our feet have gone,
But yet the way of God we have not known.

'We which have made our hearts a sea of pride, *Verse 8*
With huge risse billows of a swelling mind,
With tossing tumults of a flowing tide,
Leaving our laden bodies plunged behind,
What traffic have we got? Ourselves are drowned,
Our souls in hell, our bodies in the ground.

5 The belated recognition of the unrighteous that they have wandered in darkness and that their passing leaves no trace; for they put their faith in worldly nature, which God will bring to chaos and confusion.
1 **two slumbers** of the unrighteous and the righteous
3 **casements** windows; *fig.* eyes
11 **She** virtue
24 **parable** proverbial story; here, a mocking story
25 **enthronized** enthroned
27 **erst** earlier; not long ago
28 **lodestar** guiding star
31–4 **son...his** reverting momentarily to *Geneva*'s singular
32 **unstayèd** unstable
40 **which** that which; i.e., dishonour
41 **pledge** hostage, pawn
42 **made the hedge** entrapped ourselves
47 **gratulate** greet joyfully
56 **cabins** dwellings
east rising
59 **bar** barrier
60 **car** triumphal chariot
68 **preferment** furtherance, promotion
74 **risse** risen
77 **traffic** saleable commodities; *fig.* benefit

Verse 9 'Where are our riches now? Like us, consumed.
Where is our pomp? Decayed. Where's glory? Dead.
Where is the wealth of which we all presumed?
Where is our profit? Gone. Ourselves? Misled.
All these are like to shadows what they were:
There is nor wealth, nor pomp, nor glory here.

Verse 10 'The dial gives a caveat of the hour.
Thou canst not see it go, yet it is gone.
Like this the dial of thy fortune's power,
Which fades by stealth till thou art left alone.
Thy eyes may well perceive thy goods are spent,
Yet can they not perceive which way they went.

'Lo, e'en as ships sailing on Tethys' lap
Ploughs up the furrows of hard-grounded waves,
Enforcèd for to go by Aeol's clap,
Making with sharpest tine the water graves,
The ship once past, the trace cannot be found,
Although she diggèd in the water's ground;

Verse 11 'Or as an eagle with her soaring wings,
Scorning the dusty carpet of the earth,
Exempt from all her clogging jesses, flings
Up to the air, to show her mounting birth,
And every flight doth take a higher pitch,
To have the golden sun her wings enrich;

'Yet none can see the passage of her flight,
But only hear her hovering in the sky,
Beating the light wind with her being light,
Or parting through the air where she might fly;
The ear may hear, the eye can never see
What course she takes, or where she means to be;

Verse 12 'Or as an arrow which is made to go
Through the transparent and cool-blowing air,
Feeding upon the forces of the bow,
Else forceless lies in wanting her repair;
Like as the branches when the tree is lopped
Wanteth the forces which they forceless cropped;

'The arrow, being fed with strongest shot,
Doth part the lowest elemental breath,
Yet never separates the soft air's knot,
Nor never wounds the still-foot winds to death;
It doth sejoin and join the air together,
Yet none there is can tell or where or whither;

Verse 13 'So are our lives: now they begin, now end,
Now live, now die, now born, now fit for grave.
As soon as we have breath, so soon we spend,
Not having that which our content would have.
As ships, as birds, as arrows, all as one,
Even so the traces of our lives are gone.

'A thing not seen to go, yet going seen,
And yet not showing any sign to go:
Even thus the shadows of our lives have been,
Which shows to fade, and yet no virtues show.
How can a thing consumed with vice be good?
Or how can falsehood bear true virtue's food?'

Vain hope, to think that wickedness hath bearing, Verse 14
When she is drownèd in oblivion's sea,
Yet can she not forget presumption's wearing,
Nor yet the badge of vanity's decay.
Her fruits are cares, her cares are vanities:
Two, both in one destruction's liveries.

Vain hope is like a vane turned with each wind.
'Tis like a smoke scattered with every storm,
Like dust, sometime before, sometime behind,
Like a thin foam made in the vainest form.
This hope is like to them, which never stay,
But comes and goes again all in one day.

View nature's gifts: some gifts are rich, some poor, Verse 15
Some barren grounds there are, some clothed with fruit,
Nor hath all nothing, nor hath all her store,
Nor can all creatures speak, nor are all mute.
All die by nature, being born by nature,
So all change feature, being born with feature.

This life is hers. This dead, dead is her power.
Her bounds begins and ends in mortal state.
Whom she on earth accounteth as her flower,
May be in heaven condemned of mortal hate,
But he whom virtue judges for to live,
The Lord his life and due reward will give.

The servant of a king may be a king, Verse 16
And he that was a king, a servile slave.
Swans before death a funeral dirge do sing,
And waves their wings against ill fortune's wave.
He that is lowest in this lowly earth
May be the highest in celestial birth.

The rich may be unjust in being rich,
For riches do corrupt and not correct.
The poor may come to highest honour's pitch,
And have heaven's crown for mortal life's respect.
God's hands shall cover them from all their foes,
God's arm defend them from misfortune's blows.

85 **dial** sundial
91 **Tethys' lap** the lap of the sea-goddess; Tethys is often figurative for the sea
93 **Aeol's** Aeol is Aeolus, god of winds
clap forceful blow
94 **tine** iron tooth of a harrow
99 **clogging** encumbering
jesses straps fastened to the legs of a hawk used in falconry
112 **repair** return
114 **cropped** fed upon
116 **lowest elemental breath** slightest material breeze
118 **still-foot** stable
119 **sejoin** separate, disjoin
123 **spend** pass away
133 **bearing** fruition

Verses 17, 18 His hand eternity, his arm his force,
His armour zealousy, his breastplate heaven,
His helmet judgement, justice and remorse,
His shield is victory's immortal steven,
The world his challenge, and his wrath his sword,
Mischief his foe, his aid his gospel's word.

Verses 19, 20 His arm doth overthrow his enemy,
His breastplate sin, his helmet death and hell,
His shield prepared against mortality,
His sword 'gainst them which in the world do dwell:
So shall vice, sin and death, world and the devil,
Be slain by him which slayeth every evil.

Verse 21 All heaven shall be in arms against earth's world.
The sun shall dart forth fire commixed with blood.
The blazing stars from heaven shall be hurled.
The pale-faced moon against the ocean flood.
Then shall the thund'ring chambers of the sky
Be lightened with the blaze of Titan's eye.

The clouds shall then be bent like bended bows
To shoot the thund'ring arrows of the air.
Thick hail and stones shall fall on heaven's foes,
And Tethys overflow in her despair.
The moon shall overfill her horny hood
With Neptune's ocean's overflowing flood.

Verse 22 The wind shall be no longer kept in caves,
But burst the iron cages of the clouds,
And Aeol shall resign his office staves,
Suffering the winds to combat with the floods.
So shall the earth with seas be palèd in,
As erst it hath been overflowed with sin.

Thus shall the earth weep for her wicked sons,
And curse the concave of her tirèd womb,
Into whose hollow mouth the water runs,
Making wet wilderness her driest tomb.
Thus, thus iniquity hath reigned so long
That earth on earth is punished for her wrong.

Chapter Six

Verse 1 After this conflict between God and man,
Remorse took harbour in God's angry breast.
Astraea to be pitiful began,
All heavenly powers to lie in mercy's rest.
Forthwith the voice of God did redescend,
And his Astraea warned all to amend.

'To you I speak,' quoth she, 'Hear, learn, and mark, Verse 2
You that be kings, judges, and potentates.
Give ear, I say. Wisdom, your strongest ark,
Sends me as messenger, to end debates.
Give ear, I say, you judges of the earth.
Wisdom is born: seek out for wisdom's birth.

'This heavenly ambassage from wisdom's tongue, Verse 3
Worthy the volume of all heaven's sky,
I bring as messenger to right your wrong,
If so her sacred name might never die.
I bring you happy tidings: she is born,
Like golden sunbeams from a silver morn.

'The Lord hath seated you in judgement's seat.
Let wisdom place you in discretion's places.
Two virtues one will make one virtue great,
And draw more virtues with attractive faces.
Be just and wise, for God is just and wise:
He thoughts, he words, he words and actions tries.

'If you neglect your office's decrees, Verse 4
Heap new lament on long-tossed miseries,
Do and undo by reason of degrees,
And drown your sentences in briberies,
Favour and punish, spare and keep in awe,
Set and unset, plant and supplant the law,

'O be assured, there is a judge above, Verse 5
Which will not let injustice flourish long.
If tempt him, you your own temptation move,
Proceeding from the judgement of his tongue.
Hard judgement shall he have, which judgeth hard,
And he that barreth others shall be barred.

'For God hath no respect of rich from poor, Verse 6
For he hath made the poor and made the rich.
Their bodies be alike, though their minds soar,
Their difference naught but in presumption's pitch.
The carcass of a king is kept from foul,
The beggar yet may have the cleaner soul.

'The highest men do bear the highest minds.
The cedars scorn to bow, the mushrooms bend.
The highest often superstition blinds,
But yet their fall is greatest in the end.
The winds have not such power of the grass,
Because it lowly stoopeth whenas they pass.

170 **zealousy** zealousness? *OED* records only this occurrence of such usage, and *Geneva* reads 'jealousy'.

172 **steven** voice; but at 7.282 (as also in *Ghost*, 503) 'steven' evidently means crown, from the Greek *stephanos*.

191 **horny hood** presumably with reference to the two horns of the crescent moon; but possibly Tethys's headdress?

195 **staves** rods or wands, carried as badges of authority

197 **palèd** fenced

6 Astraea exhorts the judges of the earth to seek wisdom through discipline, love, and God's law, and cautions them that God has higher expectations of the mighty.

3 **Astraea** goddess of justice, associated with Virgo, and sometimes a complimentary type for Queen Elizabeth I; substituted here for *Geneva*'s Solomon, and including the personification of virtue from Chapter Five

9 **ark** chest, coffer, particularly as receptacle for divine law

13 **ambassage** message

Verses 7, 8 'The old should teach the young observance' way,
But now the young doth teach the elder grace.
The shrubs do teach the cedars to obey.
These yield to winds, but these the winds outface.
Yet he that made the winds to cease and blow,
Can make the highest fall, the lowest grow.

'He made the great to stoop as well as small,
The lions to obey as other beasts.
He cares for all alike, yet cares for all,
And looks that all should answer his behests.
But yet the greater hath the sorer trial,
If once he finds them with his laws' denial.

Verse 9 'Be warned, you tyrants, at the fall of pride.
You see how surges change to quiet calm,
You see both flow and ebb in folly's tide,
How fingers are infected by their palm.
This may your caveat be: you, being kings,
Infect your subjects, which are lesser things.

'Ill scents of vice, once crept into the head,
Doth pierce into the chamber of the brain,
Making the outward skin disease's bed,
The inward powers as nourishers of pain.
So if that mischief reigns in wisdom's place,
The inward thought lies figured in the face.

Verse 10 'Wisdom should clothe herself in king's attire,
Being the portraiture of heaven's queen,
But tyrants are no kings, but mischief's mire,
Not sage, but shows of what they should have been.
They seek for vice, and how to go amiss,
But do not once regard what wisdom is.

'They which are kings by name are kings by deed,
Both rulers of themselves and of their land.
They know that heav'n is virtue's duest meed,
And holiness is knit in holy bond.
These may be rightly callèd by their name,
Whose words and works are blazed in wisdom's flame.

Verse 11 'To nurse up cruelty with mild aspèct
Were to begin, but never for to end.
Kindness with tigers never takes effect,
Nor proffered friendship with a foe-like friend.
Tyrants and tigers have all natural mothers:
Tyrants her sons, tigers the tyrants' brothers.

'No words' delight can move delight in them,
But rather plough the traces of their ire,
Like swine that take the dirt before the gem,
And scorns that pearl which they should most desire,
But kings, whose names proceed from kindness' sound,
Do plant their hearts and thoughts on wisdom's ground:

'A grounding ever moist, and never dry, Verses 12, 13
An ever-fruitful earth, no fruitless way,
In whose dear womb the tender springs do lie,
Which ever flows, and never ebbs away.
The sun but shines by day: she day and night
Doth keep one stayèd essence of her light.

'Her beams are conducts to her substance' view.
Her eye is adamant's attractive force.
A shadow hath she none, but substance true,
Substance outliving life of mortal course.
Her sight is easy unto them which love her,
Her finding easy unto them which prove her.

'The far-fet chastity of female sex Verse 14
Is nothing but allurement into lust,
Which will forswear and take, scorn and annex,
Deny and practise it, mistrust and trust.
Wisdom is chaste, and of another kind:
She loves, she likes, and yet not lustful blind.

'She is true love, the other love a toy.
Her love hath eyes, the other love is blind.
This doth proceed from God, this from a boy.
This constant is, the other vain combined.
If longing passions follow her desire,
She offereth herself as labour's hire.

'She is not coyish she, won by delay Verse 15
With sighs and passions, which all lovers use,
With hot affection, death, or life's decay,
With lovers' toys, which might their loves excuse.
Wisdom is poor, her dowry is content.
She nothing hath because she nothing spent.

'She is not wooed to love, nor won by wooing,
Nor got by labour, nor possessed by pain.
The gain of her consists in honest doing.
Her gain is great in that she hath no gain.
He that betimes follows repentance' way
Shall meet with her his virtue's worthy pay.

'To think upon her is to think of bliss. Verse 16
The very thought of her is mischief's bar.
Depeller of misdeeds which do amiss,
The blot of vanity, misfortune's scar.
Who would not think, to reap such gain by thought?
Who would not love, when such a life is bought?

81 **duest meed** most deserved reward
84 **blazed** published
91 **No words' delight** 'set your delight upon my words' (*Geneva*)
102 **stayèd** fixed
104 **adamant's** magnet's
106 **course** journey; and glancing at 'corse', corpse
109 **far-fet** far-fetched, elaborate; this jaded assessment of female chastity as mere coyness has no parallel in *Geneva*.
111 **annex** take over
117 **boy** Cupid
118 **combined** as in marriage
131 **betimes** while there is still time
135 **Depeller** one who drives out

'If thought be understanding, what is she?
The full perfection of a perfect power,
A heavenly branch from God's immortal tree,
Which death nor hell nor mischief can devour.
  Herself is wisdom, and her thought is so.
  Thrice happy he which doth desire to know.

Verse 17 'She manlike woos, men womenlike refuses.
She offers love, they offered love deny,
And hold her promises as love's abuses
Because she pleads with an indifferent eye.
  They think that she is light, vain, and unjust,
  When she doth plead for love and not for lust.

Hard-hearted men, quoth she, can you not love?
Behold my substance: cannot substance please?
Behold my feature: cannot feature move?
Can substance nor my feature help or ease?
  See heaven's joy defigured in my face:
  Can neither heaven nor joy turn you to grace?

Verses 18, 19 'O, how desire sways her pleading tongue,
Her tongue her heart, her heart her soul's affection!
Fain would she make mortality be strong,
But mortal weakness yields her plea's rejection.
  Her care is care of them, they careless are.
  Her love loves them, they neither love nor care.

'Fain would she make them clients in her law,
Whose law's assurance is immortal honour,
But them nor words nor love nor care can awe,
But still will fight under destruction's banner.
  Though immortality be their reward,
  Yet neither words nor deeds will they regard.

Verse 20 'Her tongue is hoarse with pleading, yet doth plead,
Pleading for that which they should all desire.
Their appetite is heavy, made of lead,
And lead can never melt without a fire.
  Her words are mild, and cannot raise a heat,
  Whilst they with hard repulse her speeches beat.

'Requested they, for what they should request.
Entreated they, for what they should entreat.
Requested to enjoy their quiet rest,
Entreated like a sullen bird to eat.
  Their eyes behold joy's maker, which doth make it,
  Yet must they be entreated for to take it.

Verse 21 'You whose delight is placed in honour's game,
Whose game in majesty's imperial throne,
Majestic portraitures of earthly fame,
Relievers of the poor in age's moan:
  If your content be seated on a crown,
  Love wisdom, and your state shall never down.

'Her crowns are not as earthly diadems,
But diapasons of eternal rest.
Her essence comes not from terrestrial stems,
But planted on the heavens' immortal breast.
  If you delight in sceptres and in reigning,
  Delight in her, your crown's immortal gaining.

Verse 22 'Although the shadows of her glorious view
Hath been as accessory to your eyes,
Now will I show you the true substance' hue,
And what she is, which without knowledge lies,
  From whence she is derived, whence her descent,
  And whence the lineage of her birth is lent.

'Now will I show the sky, and not the cloud,
The sun, and not the shade, day, not the night,
Tethys herself, not Tethys in her flood,
Light, and not shadow of suppressing light.
  Wisdom herself, true type of wisdom's grace,
  Shall be apparent before heart and face.

Verse 23 'Had I still fed you with the shade of life,
And hid the sun itself in envy's air,
Myself might well be callèd nature's strife,
Striving to cloud that which all clouds impair.
  But envy, haste thee hence: I loathe thy eye,
  Thy love, thy life, thyself, thy company.

'Here is the banner of discretion's name,
Advanced on wisdom's ever-standing tower.
Here is no place for envy or her shame,
For Nemesis or black Megaera's power.
  He that is envious is not wisdom's friend:
  She ever lives, he dies when envies end.

Verse 24 'Happy, thrice-happy land, where wisdom reigns!
Happy, thrice-happy king, whom wisdom sways!
Where never poor laments, or souls complains,
Where folly never keeps discretion's ways.
  That land, that king, doth flourish, live, and joy,
  Far from ill fortune's reach, or sin's annoy.

Verse 25 'That land is happy, that king fortunate,
She in her days, he in his wisdom's force,
For fortitude is wisdom's sociate,
And wisdom truest fortitude's remorse.
  Be therefore ruled by wisdom, she is chief,
  That you may rule in joy and not in grief.'

155 **defigured** portrayed
166 **banner** pronounced (and spelled) 'bonner'
175 **Requested they** they are requested
176 **Entreated they** they are entreated
188 **diapasons** consonance of the top and bottom notes of a musical octave; hence heavenly concords? But Middleton evidently misunderstands the term, here and at 18.252, as the name of some sort of crown.
194 **accessory** contributory
201 **Tethys herself** the sea-goddess, as opposed to the sea
214 **Nemesis** goddess of retribution
Megaera's Megaera was one of the avenging Furies.
222 **annoy** vexation
225 **sociate** associate (obs.); preserved for metre, as also at 10.66
226 **remorse** force

Chapter Seven

Verse 1 What am I? Man. O what is man? O naught.
What am I? Naught. Yes. What? Sin and debate,
Three vices all in one, of one life bought.
Man am I not. What then? I am man's hate.
Yes, man I am: man because mortal, dead;
Mortality my guide, by mischief led.

Man because like to man, man because born;
In birth no man, a child; child because weak;
Weak because weakened by ill fortune's scorn;
Scorned because mortal, mortal in wrong's wreak.
My father, like myself, did live on earth.
I, like myself and him, follow his birth.

Verse 2 My mother's matrix was my body's maker.
There had I this same shape of infamies.
Shape? Ah, no shape, but substance, mischief's taker,
In ten months' fashion. Months? Ah, miseries.
The shame of shape, the very shape of shame,
Calamity myself, lament my name.

I was conceived with seed, deceived with sin:
Deceived because my seed was sin's deceit.
My seed deceit because it closed me in,
Hemmed me about for sin's and mischief's bait.
The seed of man did bring me into blood,
And now I bring myself... in what? No good.

Verse 3 When I was born, when I was, then I was.
Born? When? Yet born I was, but now I bear:
Bear mine own vices, which my joys surpass,
Bear mine own burden full of mischief's fear.
When I was born, I did not bear lament,
But now, unborn, I bear what birth hath spent.

When I was born, my breath was born to me,
The common air which airs my body's form.
Then fell I on the earth with feeble knee,
Lamenting for my life's, ill fortune's, storm,
Making myself the index of my woe,
Commencing what I could, ere I could go.

Verse 4 Fed was I with lament as well as meat.
My milk was sweet, but tears did make it sour.
Meat and lament, milk and my tears I eat,
As bitter herbs, commixed with sweetest flower.
Care was my swaddling clothes as well as cloth,
For I was swaddled and clothèd in both.

Why do I make myself more than I am? *Verse 5*
Why say I, I am nourishèd with cares,
When everyone is clothèd with the same,
Sith as I fare myself, another fares?
No king had any other birth than I,
But wailed his fortune with a wat'ry eye.

Say what is mirth? An entrance unto woe. *Verse 6*
Say what is woe? An entrance unto mirth.
That which begins with joy doth not end so,
These go by change, because a changing birth.
Our birth is as our death, both barren, bare:
Our entrance wail, our going out with care.

Naked we came, into the world as naked.
We had nor wealth nor riches to possess.
Now differ we, which difference riches makèd,
Yet in the end we naked ne'ertheless.
As our beginning is, so is our end:
Naked and poor, which needs no wealth to spend.

Thus weighing in the balance of my mind *Verse 7*
My state, all states, my birth, all births alike,
My meditated passions could not find
One freèd thought which sorrow did not strike.
But knowing every ill is cured by prayer,
My mind besought the Lord, my grief's allayer.

Wherefore I prayed, my prayer took effect,
And my effect was good, my good was gain,
My gain was sacred wisdom's bright aspèct,
And her aspèct in my respect did reign.
Wisdom, that heav'nly spirit of content,
Was unto me from heav'n by prayer sent.

A present far more worthy than a crown, *Verse 8*
Because the crown of an eternal rest;
A present far more worthy than a throne,
Because the throne of heav'n, which makes us blest;
The crown of bliss, the throne of God is she,
Comparèd unto heav'n, not, earth, to thee.

Her footstool is thy face, her face thy shame,
Thy shame her living praise, her praise thy scorn,
Thy scorn her love, her love thy merit's blame,
Thy blame her worth, her worth thy being born.
Thyself art dross to her comparison,
Thy valour weak unto her garrison.

7 Solomon, no longer replaced by Astraea, asserts his decaying physical humanity, wherefore he has prayed for and received the gifts of wisdom, knowledge, reason, and discretion.

1–12 **What... birth** 'I myself am also mortal and a man like all other, and am come of him that was first made of the earth' (*Geneva*). These lines seem almost experimental, the poet seeking an internalized dialogic way to articulate a conflict not evident in the *Geneva* version, where Solomon merely tells of his common humanity.

2 **Yes** denying 'Naught'; see the similar antithesis between 4 and 5, also turning on 'Yes'.

10 **wreak** retributive pain or punishment

13 **matrix** womb

16 **ten months'** usual Elizabethan measurement of human gestation, equating 'month' with the 28-day lunar cycle, rather than with the longer calendar units

39 **eat** ate

57 **makèd** made

78 **Comparèd** comparable, equal

83 **dross** impure matter

84 **garrison** means of defence

Verse 9 To liken gold unto her radiant face
Were likening day to night, and night to day,
The king's high seat to the low subject's place,
And heav'n's translucent breast to earthly way;
  For what is gold? Her scorn. Her scorn? Her ire,
  Melting that dross with naught but anger's fire.

In her respect 'tis dust. In her aspècts
Earth. In respect of her 'tis little gravel.
As dust, as earth, as gravel she rejects
The hope, the gain, the sight, the price, the travail.
  Silver, because inferior to the other,
  Is clay, which two she in one look doth smother.

Verse 10 Her sight I callèd health, herself my beauty:
Health as my life, and beauty as my light;
Each in performance of the other's duty,
This curing grief, this leading me aright.
  Two sovereign eyes, belonging to two places:
  This guides the soul, and this the body graces.

The heartsick soul is cured by heart-strong health.
The heart-strong health is the soul's brightest eye.
The heartsick body healed by beauty's wealth,
Two sunny windolets of either's sky,
  Whose beams cannot be clouded by reproach,
  Nor yet dismounted from so bright a coach.

Verse 11 What dowry could I wish, more than I have?
What wealth, what honour, more than I possess?
My soul's request is mine, which I did crave
For sole redress: in soul I have redress.
  The bodily expenses which I spend,
  Is lent by her which my delight doth lend.

Then I may call her author of my good,
Sith good and goods are portions for my love.
I love her well. Who would not love his food,
His joy's maintainer, which all woes remove?
  I richest am, because I do possess her;
  I strongest am, in that none can oppress her.

Verse 12 It made me glad to think that I was rich,
More gladder for to think that I was strong,
For lowest minds do covet highest pitch,
As highest braves proceed from lowest tongue.
  Her first arrival first did make me glad,
  Yet ignorant at first, first made me sad.

Joyful I was, because I saw her power.
Woeful I was, because I knew her not.
Glad that her face was in mine eyes' locked bower,
Sad that my senses never drew her plot.
  I knew not that she was discretion's mother,
  Though I professed myself to be her brother.

Like a rash wooer feeding on the looks, *Verse 13*
Digesting beauty, apparition's show,
Viewing the painted outside of the books,
And inward works little regards to know,
  So I, feeding my fancies with her sight,
  Forgot to make inquiry of her might.

External powers I knew, riches I had;
Internal powers I scarcely had discerned.
Unfeignèdly I learnèd to be glad;
Feigning I hated, verity I learned.
  I was not envious, learnèd to forsake her,
  But I was loving, learnèd for to take her.

And had I not, my treasure had been lost, *Verse 14*
My loss my peril's hazard had proclaimed,
My peril had my life's destruction tossed,
My life's destruction at my soul had aimed:
  Great perils hazarded from one poor loss,
  As greatest filth doth come with smallest dross.

This righteous treasure, whoso rightly useth
Shall be an heir in heav'n's eternity.
All earthly fruits her heritage excuseth,
All happiness in her felicity.
  The love of God consists in her embracing,
  The gifts of knowledge in her wisdom's placing.

I speak as I am prompted by my mind, *Verse 15*
My soul's chief agent, pleader of my cause.
I speak these things, and what I speak I find
By heaven's judgement, not mine own applause.
  God he is judge; I next, because I have her.
  God he doth know; I next, because I crave her.

Should I direct, and God subvert, my tongue,
I worthy were of an unworthy name:
Unworthy of my right, not of my wrong,
Unworthy of my praise, not of my shame;
  But seeing God directs my tongue from missing,
  I rather look for clapping than for hissing.

He is the prompter of my tongue and me. *Verse 16*
My tongue doth utter what his tongue applies.
He sets before my sight what I should see.
He breathes into my heart his verities.
  He tells me what I think, or see, or hear:
  His tongue a part, my tongue a part doth bear.

94 **travail** pronounced 'travel'
101 **sovereign** efficacious in curing
106 **windolets** small windows; *OED* records this item only in the 1590s
124 **braves** boasts, vaunts; not recorded as a substantive sense in *OED*
129 **bower** habitation; chamber
130 **plot** representation
132 **brother** Solomon has apparently reclaimed his role from Astraea.
153 **heritage** inheritance
excuseth forgives, as in the case of a debt
168 **clapping . . . hissing** audience expressions of approval and disapproval in the theatre; the theatre imagery continues in the next stanza, with 'prompter' and 'part'.
170 **applies** apparently, 'speaks'; from the transitive sense 'address, direct (words) to'?

Our words he knows in telling of our hearts.
Our hearts he knows in telling of our words.
All in his hands, words, wisdom, works, and arts,
And every power which influence affords.
He knows what we will speak, what we will do,
And how our minds and actïons will go.

Verse 17 The wisdom which I have is heaven's gift.
The knowledge which I have is God's reward.
Both presents my forewarnèd senses lift,
And of my preservation have regard.
This teaches me to know, this to be wise;
Knowledge is wit's, and wit is knowledge' guise.

Verse 18 Now know I how the world was first created,
How every motion of the earth was framed,
How man was made, the devil's pride abated,
How time's beginning, midst, and end was named.
Now know I time, time's change, time's date, time's show,
And when the seasons come, and when they go.

Verse 19 I know the changing courses of the years,
And the division of all differing climes,
The situation of the stars and spheres,
The flowing tides and the flow-ebbing times.
I know that every year hath his four courses,
I know that every course hath several forces.

Verse 20 I know that nature is in everything:
Beasts furious, winds rough, men wicked are,
Whose thoughts their scourge, whose deeds their judgement's sting,
Whose words and works their peril and their care.
I know that every plant hath difference;
I know that every root hath influence.

Verse 21 True knowledge have I got in knowing truth,
True wisdom purchasèd in wisest wit.
A knowledge fitting age, wit fitting youth,
Which makes me young, though old with gain of it.
True knowledge have I, and true wisdom's store,
True hap, true hope: what wish, what would I more?

Known things I needs must know, sith not unknown.
My ear is knowledge, she doth hear for me.
All secrets know I more because not shown.
My wisdom secret is, and her I see.
Knowledge hath taught me how to hear known causes;
Wisdom hath taught me secrecy's applauses.

Knowledge and wisdom known in wisest things Verse 22
Is reason's mate, discretion's sentinel.
More than a trine of joys from virtues springs,
More than one union, yet in union dwell:
One for to guide the spring, summer the other,
One harvest's nurse, the other winter's mother.

Four mounts, and four high mounters, all four one: Verse 23
One holy union, one begotten life,
One manifold affection, yet alone,
All one in peace's rest, all none in strife;
Sure, stable, without care, having all power,
Not hurtful, doing good; as one all four.

This peaceful army of four knitted souls Verse 24
Is marching unto peace's endless war.
Their weapons are discretion's written rolls,
Their quarrel love, and amity their jar.
Wisdom director is, captain, and guide;
All other take their places, side by side.

Wisdom divides the conflict of her peace
Into four squadrons of four mutual loves,
Each bent to war, and never means to cease.
Her wings of shot her disputation moves.
She wars unseen, and pacifies unseen;
She is war's victory, yet peace's queen.

She is the martial trumpet of alarms, Verse 25
And yet the quiet rest in peace's night.
She guideth martial troops, she honours arms,
Yet joins she fight with peace, and peace with fight.
She is the breath of God's and heaven's power,
Yet peace's nurse, in being peace's flower.

A flowing in of that which ebbeth out,
An ebbing out of that which floweth in;
Presumption she doth hate in being stout.
Humility, though poor, her favours win.
She is the influence of heaven's flow:
No filth doth follow her, where'er she go.

She is that spring which never hath an ebb, Verse 26
That silver-coloured brook which hath no mud,
That loom which weaves and never cuts the web,
That tree which grows and never leaves to bud.
She constant is, inconstancy her foe;
She doth not flow and ebb, nor come and go.

Phoebus doth weep when wat'ry clouds approach;
She keeps her brightness everlastingly.
Phoebe, when Phoebus shines, forsakes night's coach;
Her day is night and day immortally:
The undefilèd mirror of renown,
The image of God's power, her virtue's crown.

175 **telling** instructing
176 **telling** prompting
195 **spheres** concentric transparent celestial globes imagined, by the older astronomy, to revolve around the earth
219 **trine** group of three
225 **alone** playing on 'all one'
231 **rolls** muster lists (of troops)
232 **jar** dissension
238 **wings of shot** flanking divisions, armed with bows or firearms, in battle array
256 **leaves** ceases; also playing on the plural of 'leaf'

Verse 27 Discretion, knowledge, wit, and reason's skill,
All four are places in one only grace.
They wisdom are, obedient to her will.
All four are one, one in all four's place.
And wisdom being one, she can do all,
Sith one hath four, all subject to one call.

Verse 28 Herself, remaining self, the world renews,
Renewing ages with perpetual youth,
Ent'ring into the souls which death pursues,
Making them God's friends, which were friends to truth.
If wisdom doth not harbour in thy mind,
God loves thee not, and that thy soul shall find.

Verse 29 For how canst thou be led without thy light?
How can thy eyeless soul direct her way,
If wanting her which guides thy steps aright,
Thy steps from night into a path of day
More beautiful than is the eye of heaven,
Gilding herself with her self-changing steven?

Verse 30 The stars are twinkling handmaids to the moon.
Both moon and stars handmaids to wisdom's sun.
These shine at middest night, this at mid-noon.
Each new begins their light when each hath done.
Pale-mantled night follows red-mantled day;
Vice follows both, but to her own decay.

Chapter Eight

Verse 1 Who is the empress of the world's confine,
The monarchess of the four-cornered earth,
The princess of the seas, life without fine,
Commixer of delight with sorrow's mirth?
What sovereign is she, which ever reigns,
Which queen-like governs all, yet none constrains?

Verse 2 Wisdom. O fly my spirit with that word!
Wisdom. O lodge my spirit in that name!
Fly soul unto the mansion of her lord,
Although thy wings be singèd in her flame.
Tell her my blackness doth admire her beauty;
I'll marry her in love, serve her in duty.

Verse 3 If marry her, God is my father God,
Christ is my brother, angels are my kin,
The earth my dowry, heaven my abode,
My rule the world, my life without my sin.
She is the daughter of immortal Jove,
My wife in heart, in thought, in soul, in love.

Happy forever he, that thought in heart.
Happy forever he, that heart in thought.
Happy the soul of both which bears both part.
Happy that love which thought, heart, soul hath sought.
The name of love is happiest, for I love her;
Soul, heart, and thoughts, love's agents are to prove her.

Ye parents that would have your children ruled, Verse 4
Here may they be instructed, ruled, and taught.
Ye children that would have your parents schooled,
Feeding their wanton thirst with folly's draught,
See here the school of discipline erected;
See here how young and old are both corrected.

Children, this is the mistress of your bliss,
Your schoolmistress, reformer of your lives.
Parents, you that do speak, think, do amiss,
Here's she which loves, and life's direction gives.
She teacheth that which God knows to be true;
She chooseth that which God would choose for you.

What is our birth? Poor, naked, needy, cold. Verse 5
What is our life? Poor as our birth hath been.
What is our age? Forlorn in being old.
What is our end? As our beginning's scene.
Our birth, our life, our age, our end is poor:
What birth, what life, what age, what end hath more?

Made rich it is with vanity's vain show.
If wanting wisdom, it is folly's game;
Or like a bended or unbended bow,
Ill fortune's scoff it is, good fortune's shame.
If wisdom be the riches of thy mind,
Then can thy fortune see; not seeing, blind.

Then if good fortune doth begin thy state, Verse 6
Ill fortune cannot end what she begins.
Thy fate at first will still remain thy fate,
Thy conduct unto joys, not unto sins.
If thou the bridegroom art, wisdom the bride,
Ill fortune cannot swim against thy tide.

Thou marrying her dost marry more than she: Verse 7
Thy portion is not faculties, but bliss.
Thou need'st not teaching, for she teacheth thee;
Nor no reformer, she thy mistress is.
The lesson which she gives thee for thy learning
Is every virtue's love, and sin's deserving.

Dost thou desire experience for to know? Verse 8
Why, how can she be less than what she is?
The growth of knowledge doth from wisdom grow.
The growth of wisdom is in knowing this.
Wisdom can tell all things: what things are past,
What done, what undone, what are doing last.

282 **steven** crown; voice
285 **middest** the very middle of
8 How Wisdom, the beloved schoolmistress, teaches all the higher virtues; marriage with her achieves both worldly glory and joyful immortality.
3 **fine** ending
24 **prove** verify, validate
32 **reformer** amender; glancing at the leaders of the 16th-century religious reformation?
49 **good fortune** 'prudency' (*Geneva*)
56 **faculties** powers of the mind
60 **every virtue's** 'soberness and prudency, righteousness and strength' (*Geneva*)

Nay more, what things are come, what are to come,
Or words, or works, or shows, or actïons;
In her brain's table-book she hath the sum,
And knows dark sentences' solutïons.
She knows what signs and wonders will ensue,
And when success of seasons will be new.

Verse 9 Who would not be a bridegroom? Who not wed?
Who would not have a bride so wise, so fair?
Who would not lie in such a peaceful bed,
Whose canopy is heav'n, whose shade the air?
How can it be that any of the skies
Can there be missing where heav'n's kingdom lies?

If care-sick, I am comforted with joy.
If surfeiting on joy, she bids me care.
She says that overmuch will soon annoy:
Too much of joy, too much of sorrow's fare.
She always counsels me to keep a mean,
And not with joy too fat, with grief too lean.

Verse 10 Fain would the shrub grow by the highest tree.
Fain would the mushroom kiss the cedar's bark.
Fain would the seely worm a-sporting be.
Fain would the sparrow imitate the lark.
Though I a tender shrub, a mushroom be,
Yet covet I the honour of a tree.

And may I not? May not the blossoms bud?
Doth not the little seed make ears of corn?
Doth not a sprig, in time, bear greatest wood?
Doth not young ev'nings make an elder morn?
For wisdom's sake, I know, though I be young,
I shall have praises from my elders' tongue.

Verse 11 And as my growth doth rise, so shall my wit;
And as my wit doth rise, so shall my growth.
In wit I grow; both growths grow to be fit;
Both fitting in one growth be fittest both.
Experience follows age, and nature youth:
Some agèd be in wit, though young in ruth.

The wisdom which I have springs from above.
The wisdom from above is that I have.
Her I adore, I reverence, I love;
She's my pure soul, locked in my body's grave.
The judgement which I use from her proceeds,
Which makes me marvelled at in all my deeds.

Although mute silence tie my judgement's tongue, *Verse 12*
Sad secretary of dumb actïon,
Yet shall they give me place though I be young,
And stay my leisure's satisfactïon,
Even as a judge which keeps his judgements mute,
When clients have no answer of their suit.

But if the closure of my mouth unmeets,
And dives within the freedom of my words,
They like petitioners' tongues welcome greets,
And with attentive ear hears my accords.
But if my words into no limits go,
Their speech shall ebb, mine in their ebbing flow.

And what of this vain world, vain hope, vain show, *Verse 13*
Vain glory, seated in a shade of praise,
Mortality's descent, and folly's flow,
The badge of vanity, the hour of days?
What glory is it for to be a king,
When care is crown, and crown is fortune's sling?

Wisdom is immortality's alline,
And immortality is wisdom's gain.
By her the heaven's lineage is mine.
By her I immortality obtain.
The earth is made immortal in my name;
The heav'ns are made immortal in my fame.

Two spacious orbs of two as spacious climes *Verse 14*
Shall be the heritage which I possess:
My rule in heav'n, directing earthly times,
My reign in earth, commencing earth's redress.
One king made two, one crown a double crown;
One rule two rules, one fame a twice renown.

What heaven is this, which every thought contains?
Wisdom my heav'n, my heav'n is wisdom's heav'n.
What earth is this, wherein my body reigns?
Wisdom my earth, all rule from wisdom giv'n.
Through her I rule, through her I do subdue;
Through her I reign, through her my empire grew.

A rule, not tyranny; a reign, not blood; *Verse 15*
An empire, not a slaughterhouse of lives;
A crown, not cruelty in fury's mood;
A sceptre which restores, and not deprives;
All made to make a peace, and not a war,
By wisdom, concord's queen and discord's bar.

69 **table-book** pocket notebook or memorandum-book
70 **dark sentences** difficult problems, enigmas
85 **Fain** Gladly
87 **seely** innocent, harmless
a-sporting playing happily
88 **imitate the lark** by singing beautifully
102 **ruth** pity
110 **Sad** sober
secretary one entrusted with secret matters
111 **they** 'great men' (*Geneva*)
115 **unmeets** is unsuitable (not recorded in *OED*)
118 **accords** agreements between parties; so, judicious pronouncements?
119–20 **But if... flow** 'If I talk much, they [the great men] shall lay their hands upon their mouths' (*Geneva*).
127 **alline** ally or kin, presumably; apparently Middleton's coining (not in *OED*)
150 **bar** barrier

The coldest word oft cools the hottest threat,
The tyrant's menaces the calms of peace.
Two colds augmenteth one, two heats one heat,
And makes both too extreme, when both increase.
My peaceful reign shall conquer tyrants' force:
Not arms, but words, not battle, but remorse.

Verse 16 Yet mighty shall I be, though war in peace;
Strong, though ability hath left his clime;
And good, because my wars and battles cease,
Or at the least lie smothered in their prime.
The sense, once diggèd up with fear's amaze,
Doth rage untamed with folly's senseless gaze.

If wisdom doth not harbour in delight,
It breaks the outward passage of the mind.
Therefore I place my war in wisdom's might,
Whose heavy labours easy harbours find.
Her company is pleasure, mirth, and joy,
Not bitterness, not mourning, not annoy.

Verse 17 When every thought was balancèd by weight
Within the concave of my body's scale,
My heart and soul did hold the balance straight,
To see what thought was joy, what thought was wail;
But when I saw that grief did weigh down pleasure,
I put in wisdom to augment her treasure.

Verse 18 Wisdom, the weight of immortality.
Wisdom, the balance of all happiness.
Wisdom, the weigher of felicity.
Wisdom, the paragon of blessedness.
When in her hands there lies such plenty's store,
Needs must her heart have twice as much and more.

Verse 19 Her heart have I conjoinèd with her hand.
Her hand hath she conjoinèd with my heart.
Two souls one soul, two hearts one body's bond,
And two hands made of four by amour's art.
Was I not wise in choosing earthly life?
Nay, wise, thrice wise, in choosing such a wife!

Verse 20 Was I not good? Good, then the sooner bad.
Bad, because earth is full of wickedness,
Because my body is with vices clad,
Anatomy of my sin's heaviness.
As doth unseemly clothes make the skin foul,
So the sin-inkèd body blots the soul.

Thus lay my heart plunged in destruction's mire. Verse 21
Thus lay my soul bespotted with my sin.
Thus lay myself consumed in my desire.
Thus lay all parts ensnarèd in one gin.
At last my heart, mounting above the mud,
Lay between hope and death, mischief and good.

Thus panting, ignorant to live or die,
To rise or fall, to stand or else to sink,
I cast a fainting look unto the sky,
And saw the thought which my poor heart did think;
Wisdom my thought, at whose seen sight I prayed,
And with my heart, my mind, my soul, I said:

Chapter Nine

O God of fathers, Lord of heav'n and earth, Verse 1
Mercy's true sovereign, pity's portraiture,
King of all kings, a birth surpassing birth,
A life immortal, essence ever pure,
Which, with a breath ascending from thy thought,
Hast made the heav'ns of earth, the earth of naught,

Thou which hast made mortality for man, Verses 2, 3
Beginning life to make an end of woe,
Ending in him what in himself began,
His earth's dominion, through thy wisdom's flow,
Made for to rule according to desert,
And execute revenge with upright heart:

Behold a crown, but yet a crown of care, Verse 4
Behold a sceptre, yet a sorrow's guise,
More than the balance of my head can bear,
More than my hands can hold, wherein it lies:
My crown doth want supportance for to bear,
My sceptre wanteth empire for to wear.

A legless body is my kingdom's map,
Limping in folly, halting in distress.
Give me thy wisdom, Lord, my better hap,
Which may my folly cure, my grief redress.
O let me not fall in oblivion's cave;
Let wisdom be my bail, for her I crave.

Behold thy servant pleading for his hire, Verse 5
As an apprentice to thy gospel's word.
Behold his poor estate, his hot-cold fire.
His weak-strong limbs, his merry woes record.
Born of a woman, woman-like in woe:
They weak, they feeble are, and I am so.

156 **remorse** pity, compassion
170 **concave** hollow, cavity
scale playing secondarily on the rare sense of 'scale' as surface, exterior
181 **conjoinèd** linked (in the preceding couplet); in the next line it means married
187–96 **Was...gin** Nothing in *Geneva* 8:20, 21 parallels the self-loathing given to Solomon here. Middleton apparently motivates the transition to prayer by plunging his speaker into remorse for the self-congratulatory worldliness of 185–6.
9 Solomon, on behalf of sinning humanity, prays for wisdom's correction, that his works may be acceptable, his governance righteous.
12 **revenge** 'judgement' (*Geneva*)
29–30 **Born of a woman...I am so.** 'I thy servant, and son of thine handmaid, am a feeble person' (*Geneva*); the attribution of weakness and feebleness to women is Middleton's.

My time of life is as an hour of day;
'Tis as a day of months, a month of years.
It never comes again but fades away,
As one morn's sun about the hemispheres.
Little my memory, lesser my time,
But least of all my understanding's prime.

Verse 6 Say that my memory should never die;
Say that my time should never lose a glide;
Say that myself had earthly majesty,
Seated in all the glory of my pride;
Yet if discretion did not rule my mind,
My reign would be like fortune's, folly-blind;

My memory a pathway to my shame,
My time the looking-glass of my disgrace,
Myself resemblance of my scornèd name,
My pride the puffèd shadow of my face:
Thus should I be remembered, not regarded;
Thus should my labours end, but not rewarded.

Verse 7 What were it to be shadow of a king?
A vanity. To wear a shadowed crown?
A vanity. To love an outward thing?
A vanity. Vain shadows of renown.
This king is king of shades, because a shade,
A king in show, though not in action made.

His shape have I, his cognizance I wear,
A smoky vapour hemmed with vanity.
Himself I am, his kingdom's crown I bear,
Unless that wisdom change my livery.
A king I am, God hath inflamèd me,
And lesser than I am I cannot be.

Verse 8 When I command, the people do obey,
Submissive subjects to my votive will.
A prince I am, and do what princes may:
Decree, command, rule, judge, perform, fulfil.
Yet I myself am subject unto God,
As are all others to my judgement's rod.

As do my subject honour my command,
So I at his command a subject am.
I build a temple on Mount Zion's sand,
Erect an altar in thy city's name.
Resemblances these are, where thou dost dwell,
Made when thou framèd'st heaven, earth, and hell.

All these three casements were contained in wit: *Verse 9*
'Twas wisdom for to frame the heaven's sky,
'Twas wisdom for to make the earth so fit,
And hell within the lowest orb to lie;
To make a heav'nly clime, an earthly course,
And hell, although the name of it be worse.

Before the world was made, wisdom was born:
Born of heav'n's God, conceivèd in his breast,
Which knew what works would be, what ages worn,
What labours life should have, what quiet rest,
What should displease and please, in vice, in good,
What should be clearest spring, what foulest mud.

O make my sinful body's world anew; *Verse 10*
Erect new elements, new airs, new skies.
The time I have is frail, the course untrue,
The globe unconstant, like ill fortune's eyes.
First make the world, which doth my soul contain,
And next my wisdom, in whose power I reign.

Illumine earth with wisdom's heav'nly sight.
Make her ambassador to grace the earth.
O let her rest by day and lodge by night
Within the closure of my body's hearth,
That in her sacred self I may perceive
What things are good to take, what ill to leave.

The body's heat will flow into the face, *Verse 11*
The outward index of an outward deed.
The inward sins do keep an inward place:
Eyes, face, mouth, tongue, and every function feed.
She is my face. If I do any ill,
I see my shame in her repugnant will.

She is my glass, my type, my form, my map,
The figure of my deed, shape of my thought,
My life's charàcter, fortune to my hap,
Which understandeth all that heart hath wrought.
What works I take in hand, she finisheth,
And all my vicious thoughts diminisheth.

My facts are written in her forehead's book, *Verse 12*
The volume of my thoughts, lines of my words.
The sins I have she murders with a look,
And what one cheek denies, th'other affords.
As white and red, like battles and retreats,
One doth defend the blows, the other beats.

34 **hemispheres** heavens
36 **prime** state of perfection
38 **glide** step
55 **His shape** the 'king in show' of the preceding line
cognizance emblem, coat of arms
59 **God** The shift to speaking of God rather than to him is Middleton's. *Geneva* in this chapter is unvarying in its direct prayerful address. Middleton returns to addressing God only at 69–72, and in *Verse 10*. And see note to 163.
62 **votive** expressive of a vow, desire
67 **subject** collective singular for subjects of a realm
69 **Mount Zion's** Mount Zion is a sacred hill in Jerusalem
72 **framèd'st** created
72–84 **hell...mud** The stress on hell, vice, and foulness is Middleton's.
73 **casements** here, apparently, creations or constructions, suggested by 'framèd'st' in the preceding line
86 **Erect...skies** Build a whole new creation, from this material world, to the air above it, to the upper regions or heavens.
102 **repugnant** opposing
103 **type** representation, image
105 **charàcter** emblem, cipher
109 **facts** evil deeds; like 'vicious thoughts' in 108, this detail has no counterpart in *Geneva*

So is her furious mood commixed with smile.
Her rod is profit, her correction mirth.
She makes me keep an acceptable style,
And govern every limit of the earth.
  Through her the state of monarchy is known;
  Through her I rule, and guide my father's throne.

Verse 13 Mortality itself, without repair,
Is ever falling feebly on the ground:
Submissive body, heart above the air,
Which fain would know, when knowledge is not found.
  Fain would it soar above the eagle's eye,
  Though it be made of lead, and cannot fly.

The soul and body are the wings of man.
The soul should mount, but that lies drowned in sin,
With leaden spirit, but doth what it can,
Yet scarcely can it rise when it is in.
  Then how can man so weak know God so strong?
  What heart from thought, what thought from heart
    hath sprung?

Verse 14 We think that every judgement is alike,
That every purpose hath one final end.
Our thoughts, alas, are fears; fears horrors strike;
Horrors our life's uncertain course do spend.
  Fear follows negligence, both death and hell:
  Unconstant are the paths wherein we dwell.

Verse 15 The hollow concave of our bodies' vaults,
Once laden up with sin's eternal graves,
Straight bursts into the soul the slime of faults,
And overfloweth like a sea of waves.
  The earth, as neighbour to our privy thought,
  Keeps fast the mansion which our cares have bought.

Verse 16 Say, can we see ourselves? Are we so wise?
Or can we judge our own with our own hearts?
Alas, we cannot. Folly blinds our eyes,
Mischief our minds, with her mischievous arts.
  Folly reigns there where wisdom should bear sway,
  And folly's mischief bars discretion's way.

O weak capacity of strongest wit!
O strong capacity of weaker sense!
To guide, to meditate, unapt, unfit,
Blind in perceiving earth's circumfluence.
  If labour doth consist in mortal skill,
  'Tis greater labour to know heaven's will.

The toiling spirit of a labouring man Verse 17
Is tossed in casualties of fortune's seas.
He thinks it greater labour than he can,
To run his mortal course without an ease.
  Then who can gain or find celestial things,
  Unless their hopes a greater labour brings?

What volume of thy mind can then contain
Thoughts, words, and works, which God thinks, speaks,
    and makes,
When heav'n itself cannot such honour gain,
Nor angels know the counsel which God takes?
  Yet if thy heart be wisdom's mansïon,
  Thy soul shall gain thy heart's made mentïon.

Who can in one day's space make two days' toil? Verse 18
Or who in two days' space will spend but one?
The one doth keep his mean in overbroil,
The other under mean because alone.
  Say, what is man without his spirit sways him?
  Say, what's the spirit if the man decays him?

An ill-reformèd breath, a life, a hell,
A going out worse than a coming in.
For wisdom is the body's sentinel,
Set to guard life which else would fall in sin.
  She doth correct and love, sways and preserves,
  Teaches and favours, rules and yet observes.

Chapter Ten

Correction follows love, love follows hate, Verse 1
For love in hate is hate in too much love.
So chastisement is preservation's mate,
Instructing and preserving those we prove.
  So wisdom first corrects, then favoureth,
  But fortune favours first, then wavereth.

139 **concave** cavity
  vaults sewers
143 **privy** secret or intimate; with a glance at the substantive sense, a latrine
147–8 **Folly . . . Mischief** not implied by *Geneva*
154 **circumfluence** flowing around; apparently here, activity; *OED*'s first record of this item is from 1888
160 **ease** relief
163 **thy mind** another instance of the poem's instability concerning addressor–addressee: where *Geneva*'s Solomon prays to God, Middleton's speaker now addresses either himself or some undefined listener.
168 **made mentïon** mention-making; i.e., commemoration
171 **keep his mean in overbroil** To keep one's mean is to observe moderation; a broil is a tumult, quarrel, tempest; overbroil is presumably an intensified state of agitation, disorder; and so the sense is apparently that the one keeps his cool in desperate situations.
172 **under mean** below average; of low regard
173 **without** unless
10 From the five books of Moses: the deliverance of the righteous, and the destruction of the unrighteous, all effected by wisdom. In order, the stories of Adam, Cain, Noah, Lot, Cain again (probably in error for Jacob), Joseph, and the durance and flight of the Israelites, culminating in the central miracle of this work, the parting and closing of the Red Sea.
1 **Correction** like 'chastisement' in 3, not implied by *Geneva*
4 **prove** try, test

First, the first father of this earthly world,
First man, first father called for after time,
Unfashionèd and like a heap was hurled,
Formed and reformed by wisdom out of slime.
By nature ill reformed, by wisdom purer:
She mortal life, she better life's procurer.

Verse 2 Alas, what was he but a clod of clay?
Whatever was he but an ashy cask?
By wisdom clothèd in his best array,
If better may be best, to choose a task.
One gave him time to live, she power to reign,
Making two powers one, one power twain.

Verse 3 But O, malign, ill-boding wickedness,
Like bursting gulfs o'erwhelming virtue's seed,
Too furious wrath forsaking happiness,
Losing ten thousand joys with one dire deed:
Caïn could see, but folly struck him blind,
To kill his brother in a raging mind.

Verse 4 O too unhappy stroke, to end two lives!
Unhappy actor in death's tragedy!
Murd'ring a brother, whose name murder gives,
Whose slaying action, slaughter's butchery.
A weeping part had earth in that same play,
For she did weep herself to death that day.

Water distilled from millions of her eyes
Upon the long-dried carcass of her time.
Her wat'ry conduits were the weeping skies,
Which made her womb an overflowing clime.
Wisdom preserved it, which preserves all good,
And taught it how to make an ark of wood.

Verse 5 O that one board should save so many lives
Upon the world's huge billow-tossing sea!
'Twas not the board, 'twas wisdom which survives:
Wisdom that ark, that board, that fence, that bay.
The world was made a water-rolling wave,
But wisdom better hope's assurance gave.

And when pale malice did advance her flag
Upon the raging standard of despite,
Fiend's sovereign, sin's mistress, and hell's hag,
Dun Pluto's lady, empress of the night,
Wisdom, from whom immortal joy begun,
Preserved the righteous as her faultless son.

The wicked perishèd, but they survived. *Verse 6*
The wicked were ensnared, they were preserved.
One kept in joy, the one of joy deprived,
One feeding, fed, the other feeding, starved.
The food which wisdom gives is nourishment,
The food which malice gives is languishment.

One feeds, the other feeds, but choking feeds:
Two contraries in meat, two differing meats.
This brings forth hate, and this repentance' seeds,
This war, this peace, this battles, this retreats.
And that example may be truly tried,
These lived in Sodom's fire, the other died.

The land will bear me witness they are dead, *Verse 7*
Which for their sakes bears nothing else but death,
The witness of itself with vices fed,
A smoky testimony of sin's breath.
This is my witness, my certificate,
And this is my sin-weeping sociate.

My pen will scarce hold ink to write these woes,
These woes, the blotted inky lines of sin.
My paper wrinkles at my sorrow's shows,
And like that land will bring no harvest in.
Had Lot's unfaithful wife been without fault,
My fresh-inked pen had never called her salt.

But now my quill, the tell-tale of all moans, *Verse 8*
Is savoury bent to aggravate salt tears,
And wets my paper with salt-water groans,
Making me stick in agonizing fears.
My paper now is grown to billows' might;
Sometimes I stay my pen, sometimes I write.

O foolish pilot I, blind-hearted guide!
Can I not see the cliffs, but rend my bark?
Must I needs hoist up sails 'gainst wind and tide,
And leave my soul behind, my wisdom's ark?
Well may I be the glass of my disgrace,
And set my sin in other sinners' place.

7 **first father** Adam
10 **Formed . . . slime** The original for this line is omitted from *Geneva* and the Junius–Tremellius versions; it appears, however, in pre-1592 editions of the Vulgate (*eduxit illum de limo terrae*) and in the Coverdale, Matthew, and Great Bibles ('took him out of the mould of the earth') (D.S.).
reformed amended
27 **name** linking 'Cain' metonymically with 'murder'
34 **clime** region
40 **bay** embankment, dam
46 **Dun** dark, murky
Pluto's lady Persephone or Hecate, queen of hell
48 **the righteous** The reference in *Geneva* is to Abraham; but Middleton evidently treats the term as plural in his next line.
60 **Sodom's** Sodom was one of the cities destroyed by fire for carnal wickedness (Genesis 19).
67 **My pen** replacing Solomon's voice with that of the poet
71 **Lot's unfaithful wife** turned into a pillar of salt when fleeing the destruction of Sodom
72 **salt** see 71; but playing on the adjectival sense, lecherous
74 **savoury** playing on two senses: the religious one, savouring of holiness, and the culinary one, describing tastes distinct from sweet
aggravate intensify
80 **bark** sailing vessel
82 **ark** chest, coffer, particularly as receptacle for divine law
83 **glass** emblematic mirror

Verse 9 But why despair I? Here comes wisdom's grace,
Whose hope doth lead me unto better hap,
Whose presence doth direct my fore-run race,
Because I serve her as my beauties' map.
Like Caïn I shall be restored to heaven,
From shipwreck's peril to a quiet haven.

Verse 10 When that by Caïn's hand Abel was slain,
His brother Abel, brother to his ire,
Then Caïn fled, to fly destruction's pain,
God's heavy wrath, against his blood's desire;
But being fetched again by wisdom's power,
Had pardon for his deed, love for his lower.

Verse 11 By his repentance he remission had,
And relaxation from the clog of sin.
His painful labour labour's riches made,
His labouring pain did pleasure's profit win.
'Twas wisdom, wisdom made him to repent,
And newly placed him in his old content.

His body, which was once destruction's cave,
Black murder's territory, mischief's house,
By her these wicked sins were made his slave,
And she became his bride, his wife, his spouse,
Enriching him which was too rich before:
Too rich in vice, in happiness too poor.

Verse 12 Megaera, which did rule within his breast,
And kept foul Lerna's fen within his mind,
Both now displease him, which once pleased him best,
Now murd'ring murder with his being kind.
These which were once his friends are now his foes,
Whose practice he retorts with wisdom's blows.

Yet still lie they in ambush for his soul,
But he, more wiser, keeps a wiser way.
They see him, and they bark, snarl, grin and howl,
But wisdom guides his steps, he cannot stray:
By whom he conquers, and through whom he knows
The fear of God is stronger than his foes.

Verse 13 When man was clad in vice's livery,
And sold as bondman unto sin's command,
She, she forsook him not for infamy,
But freed him from his heart's imprisoned bond,
And when he lay in dungeon of despite,
She interlined his grief with her delight.

Though servile she with him, she was content. Verse 14
The prison was her lodge as well as his,
Till she the sceptre of the world had lent
To glad his fortune, to augment his bliss,
To punish false accusers of true deeds,
And raise in him immortal glory's seeds.

Say, shall we call her wisdom by her name? Verse 15
Or new invent a nominating style,
Reciting ancient worth to make new fame,
Or new-old hierarchy from honour's file?
Say, shall we file out fame for virtue's store,
And give a name not thought nor heard before?

Then should we make her two, where now but one.
Then should we make her common to each tongue.
Wisdom shall be her name, she wise alone.
If alter old for new, we do old wrong.
Call her still wisdom, mistress of our souls,
Our lives' deliverer from our foes' controls.

To make that better which is best of all, Verse 16
Were to disarm the title of the power,
And think to make a raise, and make a fall,
Turn best to worst, a day unto an hour.
To give two sundry names unto one thing,
Makes it more commoner in Echo's sling.

She guides man's soul: let her be called a queen.
She enters into man: call her a sprite.
She makes them godly which have never been:
Call her herself, the image of her might.
Those which for virtue plead, she prompts their tongue,
Whose suit no tyrant nor no king can wrong.

She stands as bar between their mouth and them. Verse 17
She prompts their thoughts. Their thoughts prompts speeches' sound.
Their tongue's reward is honour's diadem,
Their labour's hire with duest merit crowned.
She is as judge and witness of each heart,
Condemning falsehood, taking virtue's part.

A shadow in the day, star in the night:
A shadow for to shade them from the sun,
A star in darkness for to give them light.
A shade in day, a star when day is done:
Keeping both courses true, in being true,
A shade, a star, to shade and lighten you.

89 **Caïn** All premodern commentaries and glosses on the corresponding biblical passage (10:10–12), including the marginal cross-reference in *Geneva*, note that it refers to Jacob (D.S.); but *Genesis Rabbah*, oddly, illustrates divine mercy by recounting Adam's encounter with a repentant and forgiven Cain (22:13).
96 **lower** reward, recompense
109 **Megaera** one of the avenging Furies
110 **Lerna's** Lerna was a swampy Argolian river, home of the hydra.
121 **man** Joseph, son of Jacob; he was sold to the Egyptian Potiphar, falsely accused of sexual harassment by Potiphar's wife, and thrown into prison, where he prospered.
133 **we** the righteous people
136 **file** catalogue, roll
137 **file out** erase
150 **Echo's sling** figurative explanation for the nymph's ability to throw sound back to its source
152 **sprite** spirit
168–75 **lighten you . . . your craves** Evidently the poem turns here briefly to direct address of Moses and the Israelites.

Verses 18, 19 And had she not, the sun's hot-burning fire
Had scorched the inward palace of your powers,
Your hot affection cooled your hot desire.
Two heats once met make cool distilling showers.
So likewise, had not wisdom been your star,
You had been prisoner unto Phoebe's car.

She made the Red Sea subject to your craves,
The surges calms, the billows smoothest ways.
She made rough winds sleep silent in their caves,
And Aeol watch, whom all the winds obeys.
Their foes, pursuing them with death and doom,
Did make the sea their church, the waves their tomb.

Verses 20, 21 They furrowed up a grave to lie therein,
Burying themselves with their own handy deed.
Sin digged a pit itself to bury sin.
Seed plowèd up the ground, to scatter seed.
The righteous, seeing this same sudden fall,
Did praise the Lord, and seized upon them all.

A glorious prize, though from inglorious hands!
A worthy spoil, though from unworthy hearts!
Tossed with the ocean's rage upon the sands,
Victorious gain, gainèd by wisdom's arts:
Which makes the dumb to speak, the blind to see,
The deaf to hear, the babes have gravity.

Chapter Eleven

Verse 1 What he could have a heart, what heart a thought,
What thought a tongue, what tongue a show of fears,
Having his ship balànced with such a fraught,
Which calms the ever-weeping ocean's tears,
Which prospers every enterprise of war,
And leads their fortune by good fortune's star?

Verses 2, 3 A pilot on the seas, guide on the land,
Through uncouth, desolate, untrodden way,
Through wilderness of woe, which in woes stand,
Pitching their tents where desolation lay,
In just revenge encount'ring with their foes,
Annexing wrath to wrath, and blows to blows.

Verse 4 But when the heat of overmuch alarms
Had made their bodies subject unto thirst,
And broiled their hearts in wrath's allaying harms
With fiery surges which from body burst,
That time had made the total sum of life,
Had not affection strove to end the strife.

Wisdom, affectionating power of zeal,
Did cool the passion of tormenting heat
With water from a rock, which did reveal
Her dear dear love, placed in affection's seat.
She was their mother twice, she nursed them twice,
Mingling their heat with cold, their fire with ice.

From whence received they life? From a dead stone? Verse 5
From whence received they speech? From a mute rock?
As if all pleasure did proceed from moan,
Or all discretion from a senseless block?
For what was each but silent, dead, and mute,
As if a thorny thistle should bear fruit?

'Tis strange how that should cure which erst did kill,
Give life in whom destruction is enshrined.
Alas, the stone is dead, and hath no skill.
Wisdom gave life and love: 'twas wisdom's mind.
She made the stone, which poisonèd her foes,
Give life, give cure, give remedy to those.

Blood-quaffing Mars, which washed himself in gore, Verse 6
Reigned in her foes' thirst slaughter-drinking hearts,
Their heads the bloody storehouse of blood's store,
Their minds made bloody streams disbursed in parts.
What was it else but butchery and hate,
To prize young infants' blood at murder's rate?

But let them surfeit on their bloody cup, Verse 7
Carousing to their own destruction's health.
We drink the silver-streamèd water up,
Which unexpected flowed from wisdom's wealth,
Declaring by the thirst of our dry souls
How all our foes did swim in murder's bowls.

What greater ill than famine? Or what ill Verse 8
Can be comparèd to the fire of thirst?
One be as both, for both the body kill,
And first brings torments in tormenting first:
Famine is death itself, and thirst no less,
If bread and water do not yield redress.

174 **Phoebe's car** the moon
175 **made the Red Sea subject** when the Israelites fled through the parted waters, which then closed to swallow up the pursuing Egyptians
craves needs; prayers; *OED* records no substantive form before 1707
178 **Aeol** Aeolus, god of the winds
179 **Their foes** the Egyptians
182 **handy** manual
11 The many miracles done for Israel in the flight out of Egypt; God's vengeance against the unrighteous and idolatrous, and the guarantee of God's mercy to the repentant righteous.
3 **balànced** common Elizabethan error for ballasted; retained here for metre
fraught cargo, freight (obs., retained for rhyme); wisdom
13 **alarms** calls to arms
15 **broiled** embroiled, involved in hostility; seared, charred
allaying tempering by fire
18 **affection** (divine) love
19 **affectionating** regarding with affection
21 **water from a rock** Moses's miracle in Kadesh
25 **dead stone** anticipating the discussion of idolatry in Chapter 13
31 **erst** at first, formerly
37 **Blood-quaffing Mars** god of war; the phrase appears in Marlowe's *Hero and Leander*, 151 (first published in 1598)
38 **thirst** thirsty?

Yet this affliction is but virtue's trial,
Proceeding from the mercy of God's ire,
To see if it can find his truth's denial,
His judgement's breach, attempts contempt's desire.
But O, the wicked, sleeping in misdeed,
Had death on whom they fed, on whom they feed.

Verse 9 Adjudged, condemned, and punished in one breath,
Arraigned, tormented, tortured in one law,
Adjudged like captives with destruction's wreath,
Arraigned like thieves before the bar of awe:
Condemned, tormented, tortured, punishèd,
Like captives bold, thieves unastonishèd.

Say God did suffer famine for to reign,
And thirst to rule amongst the choicest heart,
Yet father-like he eased them of their pain,
And proved them how they could endure a smart;
But as a righteous king condemned the others,
As wicked sons unto as wicked mothers.

Verse 10 For where the devil reigns, there sure is hell,
Because the tabernacle of his name,
His mansion-house, the place where he doth dwell,
The coal-black visage of his nigrum fame.
So, if the wicked live upon the earth,
Earth is their hell, from good to worser birth.

If present, they are present to their tears,
If absent, they are present to their woes,
Like as the snail, which shows all that she bears,
Making her back the mountain of her shows:
Present to their death, not absent to their care,
Their punishment alike, where'er they are.

Verse 11 Why, say they mourned, lamented, grieved, and wailed,
And fed lament with care, care with lament:
Say, how can sorrow be with sorrow bailed,
When tears consumeth that which smiles hath lent?
This makes a double prison, double chain,
A double mourning and a double pain.

Captivity, hoping for freedom's hap,
At length doth pay the ransom of her hope,
Yet frees her thought from any clogging clap,
Though back be almost burst with iron's cope.
So they endured the more, because they knew
That never till the spring the flowers grew;

Verse 12 And that by patience cometh heart's delight,
Long-sought-for bliss, long-far-fet happiness.
Content they were to die for virtue's right,
Sith joy should be the pledge of heaviness.
When unexpected things were brought to pass,
They were amazed, and wondered where God was.

He whom they did deny, now they extol.
He whom they do extol, they did deny;
He whom they did deride, they do enrol
In register of heav'nly majesty.
Their thirst was ever thirst. Repentance stopped it.
Their life was ever dead. Repentance propped it.

And had it not, their thirst had burned their hearts, *Verse 13*
Their hearts had cried out for their tongues' reply,
Their tongues had raisèd all their bodies' parts,
Their bodies, once in arms, had made all die.
Their foolish practices had made them wise:
Wise in their hearts, though foolish in their eyes.

But they, alas, were dead to worship death,
Senseless in worshipping all shadowed shows,
Breathless in wasting of so vain a breath,
Dumb in performance of their tongues' suppose.
They in adoring death, in death's behests,
Were punishèd with life, and living beasts.

Thus for a show of beasts they substance have, *Verse 14*
The thing itself against the shadow's will,
Which makes the shadows, sad woes in life's grave,
As naught impossible in heaven's skill.
God sent sad Os for shadows of lament.
Lions and bears in multitudes he sent,

Newly created beasts, which sight ne'er saw, *Verse 15*
Unknown, which neither eye nor ear did know,
To breathe out blasts of fire against their law,
And cast out smoke with a tempestuous blow,
Making their eyes the chambers of their fears,
Darting forth fire as lightning from the spheres.

Thus marching one by one, and side by side, *Verse 16*
By the profane, ill-limned, pale spectacles,
Making both fire and fear to be their guide,
Pulled down their vain-adoring chronicles;
Then staring in their faces, spit forth fire,
Which heats and cools their frosty-hot desire:

Frosty in fear, unfrosty in their shame,
Cool in lament, hot in their powers' disgraces,
Like lukewarm coals, half kindled with the flame,
Sate white and red must'ring within their faces.
The beasts themselves did not so much dismay them,
As did their ugly eyes' aspècts decay them.

56 **the mercy of God's ire** merging and compressing what 11:8 keeps separate in *Geneva*: 'For when they were tried and chastised with mercy, they knew how the ungodly were judged and punished in wrath.'
58 **attempts** tries with afflictions or temptations
61 **Adjudged** sentenced, doomed
70 **proved** tested
73 **devil** no comparable mention in *Geneva*
74 **tabernacle** dwelling-place
76 **nigrum** black (*Latin*)
87 **bailed** liberated
93 **clogging clap** encumbering imprisonment
94 **cope** cloak; vaulted covering
98 **long-far-fet** far-fetched, i.e., fetched from afar
134 **ill-limned** poorly-painted
142 **Sate** apparently for sated, or satiate, i.e., glutted

Verse 17 Yet what are beasts but subjects unto man,
By the decree of heav'n, degree of earth?
They have more strength than he, yet more he can,
He having reason's store, they reason's dearth;
  But these were made to break subjection's rod,
  And show the stubbornness of man to God.

Had they not been ordained to such intent,
God's word was able to supplant their powers,
And root out them which were to mischief bent,
With wrath and vengeance, minutes in death's hours;
  But God doth keep a full, direct, true course,
  And measures pity's love with mercy's force.

Verse 18 The wicked thinks God hath no might at all,
Because he makes no show of what he is,
When God is loath to give their pride a fall,
Or cloud the day wherein they do amiss;
  But should his strength be shown, his anger rise,
  Who could withstand the sun-caves of his eyes?

Verse 19 Alas, what is the world against his ire?
As snowy mountains 'gainst the golden sun,
Forced for to melt and thaw with frosty fire,
Fire hid in frost, though frost of cold begun.
  As dew-distilling drops fall from the morn,
  So new destruction's claps fall from his scorn.

Verse 20 But his revenge lies smothered in his smiles.
His wrath lies sleeping in his mercies' joy,
Which very seldom rise at mischief's coils,
And will not wake for every sinner's toy.
  Boundless his mercies are, like heaven's grounds:
  They have no limits, they, nor heav'n no bounds.

The promontory-top of his true love
Is like the end of never-ending streams,
Like Nilus' water-springs which inward move,
And have no outward show of shadows' beams.
  God sees, and will not see, the sins of men,
  Because they should amend. Amend? O when?

Verse 21 The mother loves the issues of her womb,
As doth the father his begotten son.
She makes her lap their quiet-sleeping tomb.
He seeks to care for life which new begun.
  What care hath he, think then, that cares for all,
  For agèd and for young, for great and small?

Is not that father careful, filled with care,
Loving, long-suffering, merciful and kind,
Which made with love all things that in love are,
Unmerciful to none, to none unkind?
  Had man been hateful, man had never been,
  But perished in the springtime of his green.

But how can hate abide where love remains? Verses 22, 23
Or how can anger follow mercy's path?
How can unkindness hinder kindness' gains?
Or how can murder bathe in pity's bath?
  Love, mercy, kindness, pity, either's mate,
  Doth scorn unkindness, anger, murder, hate.

Had it not been thy will to make the earth
It still had been a chaos unto time;
But 'twas thy will that man should have a birth,
And be preserved by good, condemned by crime.
  Yet pity reigns within thy mercies' store.
  Thou spar'st and lov'st us all. What would we more?

Chapter Twelve

When all the elements of mortal life Verse 1
Were placèd in the mansion of their skin,
Each having daily motion to be rife,
Closed in that body which doth close them in,
  God sent his holy spirit unto man,
  Which did begin when first the world began.

So that the body, which was king of all, Verse 2
Is subject unto that which now is king,
Which chast'neth those whom mischief doth exhale
Unto misdeeds from whence destructions spring.
  Yet merciful it is, though it be chief,
  Converting vice to good, sin to belief.

Old time is often lost in being bald: Verse 3
Bald because old, old because living long.
It is rejected oft when it is called,
And wears out age with age, still being young.
  Twice children we, twice feeble and once strong,
  But being old, we sin and do youth wrong.

The more we grow in age, the more in vice.
A house-room long unswept will gather dust.
Our long unthawèd souls will freeze to ice,
And wear the badge of long imprisoned rust.
  So those inhabitants in youth twice born,
  Were old in sin, more old in heaven's scorn,

Committing works as inky spots of fame, Verse 4
Commencing words like foaming vice's waves,
Committing and commencing mischief's name,
With works and words sworn to be vice's slaves:
  As sorcery, witchcraft, mischievous deeds,
  And sacrifice, which wicked fancies feeds.

162 **sun-caves of his eyes** 'power of thine arm' (*Geneva*)
171 **coils** confused noises
177 **Nilus' water-springs** sources of the Nile, thought by Europeans to be obscure
12 How God is merciful toward even murderers and idol-worshippers, giving them leisure to repent; but his wise and just punishment of the unrepentant, especially the idolatrous, is extreme; how they are first derided and shamed, then damned.
3 **rife** flourishing
9 **exhale** drag out
23 **those inhabitants** 'those old inhabitants of the holy land' (*Geneva*), from whom the Israelites would reclaim it

Verse 5 Well may I call that wicked which is more.
I rather would be low than be too high.
O wondrous practisers, clothed all in gore,
To end that life which their own lives did buy!
More than swine-like, eating man's bowels up,
Their banquet's dish, their blood their banquet's cup.

Verses 6, 7 Butchers unnatural, worse by their trade,
Whose house the bloody shambles of decay,
More than a slaughter-house which butchers made,
More than an Eastcheap, seely bodies prey;
Thorough whose hearts a bloody shambles runs:
They do not butcher beasts, but their own sons.

Chief murd'rers of their souls which their souls bought,
Extinguishers of light which their lives gave,
More than knife butchers they, butchers in thought,
Sextons to dig their own begotten grave,
Making their habitations old in sin,
Which God doth reconcile and new begin.

Verse 8 That murd'ring place was turned into delight,
That bloody slaughter-house to peace's breast,
That lawless palace to a place of right,
That slaught'ring shambles to a living rest,
Made meet for justice, fit for happiness,
Unmeet for sin, unfit for wickedness.

Verse 9 Yet the inhabitants, though mischief's slaves,
Were not dead-drenched in their destruction's flood.
God hoped to raise repentance from sins' graves,
And hoped that pain's delay would make them good.
Not that he was unable to subdue them,
But that their sins' repentance should renew them.

Verse 10 Delay is took for virtue and for vice.
Delay is good, and yet delay is bad.
'Tis virtue when it thaws repentance' ice.
'Tis vice to put off things we have or had.
But here it followeth repentance' way,
Therefore it is nor sin's nor mischief's prey.

Delay in punishment is double pain,
And every pain makes a twice-double thought,
Doubling the way to our lives' better gain,
Doubling repentance, which is single bought;
For fruitless grafts, when they are too much lopped,
More fruitless are, forwhy their fruits are stopped.

Verse 11 So fares it with the wicked plants of sin,
The roots of mischief, tops of villainy:
They worser are with too much punishing,
Because by nature prone to injury;
For 'tis but folly to supplant his thought,
Whose heart is wholly given to be naught.

These seeded were in seed. O cursèd plant!
Seeded with other seed. O cursèd root!
Too much of good doth turn unto good's want,
As too much seed doth turn to too much soot:
Bitter in taste, presuming of their height,
Like misty vapours in black-coloured night.

But God, whose powerful arms one strength doth hold, Verse 12
Scorning to stain his force upon their faces,
Will send his messengers both hot and cold,
To make them shadows of their own disgraces.
His hot ambassador is fire, his cold
Is wind, which two scorn for to be controlled.

For who dares say unto the king of kings,
What hast thou done which ought to be undone?
Or who dares stand against thy judgement's stings?
Or dare accuse thee for the nations' moan?
Or who dare say, revenge this ill for me?
Or stand against the Lord with villainy?

What he hath done he knows. What he will do Verse 13
He weigheth with the balance of his eyes.
What judgement he pronounceth must be so,
And those which he oppresseth cannot rise.
Revenge lies in his hands. When he doth please,
He can revenge and love, punish and ease.

The carvèd spectacle which workmen make
Is subject unto them, not they to it.
They which from God a lively form do take,
Should much more yield unto their maker's wit,
Sith there is none but he which hath his thought,
Caring for that which he hath made of naught.

The clay is subject to the potter's hands, Verse 14
Which with a new device makes a new mould,
And what are we, I pray, but clayey bonds,
With ashy body joined to cleaner soul?
Yet we, once made, scorn to be made again,
But live in sin like clayey lumps of pain.

Yet if hot anger smother cool delight,
He'll mould our bodies in destruction's form,
And make ourselves as subjects to his might,
In the least fuel of his anger's storm.
Nor king nor tyrant dare ask or demand,
What punishment is this thou hast in hand?

38 **shambles** meat market
40 **Eastcheap** London meat-market area
seely bodies prey innocent bodies [their] prey
41 **Thorough** through; retained for metre
46 **Sextons** church officers whose duties include digging graves
72 **forwhy** because
74 **tops** green growth above ground
78 **naught** immoral, vicious
79 **seeded were in seed** were gone to seed at the very outset; 'it was a cursed seed from the beginning' (*Geneva*)
82 **soot** gardener's term for a substance of sooty appearance or nature
83 **presuming** aspiring; rank, overgrown
102 **ease** relieve
103 **carvèd spectacle** idol; not suggested here by *Geneva*, but anticipating the discussion in Chapter 13

Verse 15 We all are captives to thy regal throne.
Our prison is the earth, our bonds our sins,
And our accuser our own bodies' groan,
Pressed down with vice's weights and mischief's gins.
Before the bar of heav'n we plead for favour,
To cleanse our sin-bespotted bodies' savour.

Thou righteous art; our pleading then is right.
Thou merciful; we hope for mercy's grace.
Thou order'st everything with look-on sight:
Behold us, prisoners in earth's wand'ring race.
We know thy pity is without a bound,
And sparest them which in some faults be found.

Verse 16 Thy power is as thyself, without an end,
Beginning all to end, yet ending none,
Son unto virtue's son, and wisdom's friend,
Original of bliss to virtue shown,
Beginning good which never ends in vice,
Beginning flames which never end in ice.

For righteousness is good in such a name.
It righteous is; 'tis good in such a deed.
A lamp it is, fed with discretion's flame;
Begins in seed, but never ends in seed.
By this we know the Lord is just and wise,
Which causeth him to spare us when he tries.

Verse 17 Just, because justice weighs what wisdom thinks;
Wise, because wisdom thinks what justice weighs.
One virtue maketh two, and two more links.
Wisdom is just, and justice never strays.
The help of one doth make the other better,
As is the want of one the other's letter.

But wisdom hath two properties in wit,
As justice hath two contraries in force.
Heat added unto heat augmenteth it,
As too much water bursts a water-course.
God's wisdom too much proved doth breed God's hate;
God's justice too much moved breeds God's debate.

Verse 18 Although the ashy prison of fire-dust
Doth keep the flaming heat imprisoned in,
Yet sometime will it burn, when flame it must,
And burst the ashy cave where it hath been.
So if God's mercy pass the bounds of mirth,
It is not mercy then, but mercy's dearth.

Yet how can love breed hate, without hate's love?
God doth not hate to love, nor love to hate.
His equity doth every action prove,
Smoth'ring with love that spiteful envy's fate.
For should the teen of anger trace his brow,
The very puffs of rage would drive the plow.

But God did end his toil when world begun. Verse 19
Now like a lover studies how to please,
And win their hearts again whom mischief won,
Lodged in the mansion of their sin's disease.
He made each mortal man two ears, two eyes,
To hear and see; yet he must make them wise.

If imitation should direct man's life,
'Tis life to imitate a living corse.
The thing's example makes the thing more rife.
God loving is. Why do we want remorse?
He put repentance into sinful hearts,
And fed their fruitless souls with fruitful arts.

If such a boundless ocean of good deeds Verse 20
Should have such influence from mercy's stream,
Kissing both good and ill, flowers and weeds,
As doth the sunny flame of Titan's beam,
A greater Tethys then should mercy be,
In flowing unto them which loveth thee.

The sun which shines in heav'n doth light the earth. Verse 21
The earth which shines in sin doth spite the heaven.
Sin is earth's sun, the sun of heav'n sin's dearth:
Both odd in light, being of height not even.
God's mercy then, which spares both good and ill,
Doth care for both, though not alike in will.

Can vice be virtue's mate, or virtue's meat? Verse 22
Her company is bad, her food more worse.
She shames to sit upon her better's seat,
As subject beasts, wanting the lion's force.
Mercy is virtue's badge, foe to disdain;
Virtue is vice's stop, and mercy's gain.

Yet God is merciful, to mischief flows,
More merciful in sin's and sinners' want.
God chast'neth us, and punisheth our foes,
Like, sluggish drones amongst, a labouring ant.
We hope for mercy at our bodies' doom;
We hope for heav'n, the bail of earthly tomb.

What hope they for? What hope have they of heaven? Verse 23
They hope for vice, and they have hope of hell,
From whence their souls' eternity is given,
But such eternity which pains can tell.
They live, but better were it for to die,
Immortal in their pain and misery.

121 **thy** resuming, until 143, *Geneva*'s direct conversation with God
124 **gins** traps, fetters, instruments of torture
136 **Original** originator, source
150 **letter** hinderer, obstructor
155 **proved** tested
156 **debate** strife, contention
167 **teen** vexation, irritation; perhaps with a play on 'tine' (tooth of a harrow, as at 5.94)
176 **corse** obsolete form of 'corpse', retained for rhyme
198 **stop** set-back, loss
202 **drones** in bees, the non-worker males; hence idlers, sluggards; the line is evidently inverted for the sake of both metre and rhyme, logically reading 'Like a labouring ant among sluggish drones.'
204 **bail** release

Hath hell such freedom to devour souls?
Are souls so bold to rush in such a place?
God gives hell power of vice, which hell controls.
Vice makes her followers bold with armèd face.
  God tortures both, the mistress and the man,
  And ends in pain that which in vice began.

Verse 24 A bad beginning makes a worser end,
Without repentance meet the middle way,
Making a mediocrity their friend,
Which else would be their foe because they stray.
  But if repentance miss the middle line,
  The sun of virtue ends in west's decline.

So did it fare with these, which strayed too far,
Beyond the measure of the mid-day's eye,
In error's ways, led without virtue's star,
Esteeming beast-like powers for deity;
  Whose heart no thought of understanding meant,
  Whose tongue no word of understanding sent:

Verse 25 Like infant babes, bearing their nature's shell
Upon the tender heads of tend'rer wit,
Which tongue-tied are, having no tale to tell
To drive away the childhood of their fit;
  Unfit to tune their tongue with wisdom's string,
  Too fit to quench their thirst in folly's spring.

But they were trees to babes, babes sprigs to them,
They not so good as these, in being naught;
In being naught, the more from vice's stem,
Whose essence cannot come without a thought.
  To punish them is punishment in season:
  They children-like, without or wit or reason.

Verse 26 To be derided is to be half dead.
Derision bears a part 'tween life and death.
Shame follows her with misery half fed,
Half-breathing life, to make half life and breath.
  Yet here was mercy shown: their deeds were more
  Than could be wiped off by derision's score.

This mercy is the warning of misdeeds,
A trumpet summoning to virtue's walls,
To notify their hearts which mischief feeds,
Whom vice instructs, whom wickedness exhales.
  But if derision cannot murder sin,
  Then shame shall end, and punishment begin.

For many shameless are, bold, stout in ill. Verse 27
Then how can shame take root in shameless plants,
When they their brows with shameless furrows fill,
And plows each place, which one plow-furrow wants?
  Then being armed 'gainst shame with shameless face,
  How can derision take a shameful place?

But punishment may smooth their wrinkled brow,
And set shame on the forehead of their rage,
Guiding the fore-front of that shameless row,
Making it smooth in shame, though not in age.
  Then will they say that God is just and true;
  But 'tis too late, damnation will ensue.

Chapter Thirteen

The branch must needs be weak, if root be so. Verse 1
The root must needs be weak, if branches fall.
Nature is vain, man cannot be her foe,
Because from nature, and at nature's call.
  Nature is vain, and we proceed from nature:
  Vain therefore is our birth, and vain our feature.

One body may have two diseases sore.
Not being two, it may be joined to two.
Nature is one itself, yet two and more,
Vain, ignorant of God, of good, of show,
  Which not regards the things which God hath done,
  And what things are to do, what new begun.

Why do I blame the tree, when 'tis the leaves? Verse 2
Why blame I nature for her mortal men?
Why blame I men? 'Tis she, 'tis she that weaves,
That weaves, that wafts unto destruction's pen.
  Then being blameful both, because both vain,
  I leave to both their vanity's due pain.

To prize the shadow at the substance' rate,
Is a vain substance of a shadow's hue;
To think the son to be the father's mate,
Earth to rule earth because of earthly view;
  To think fire, wind, air, stars, water, and heaven,
  To be as gods, from whom their selves are given.

Fire as a god? O irreligious sound! Verse 3
Wind as a god? O vain, O vainest voice!
Air as a god, when 'tis but dusky ground?
Star as a god, when 'tis but Phoebe's choice?
  Water a god, which first by God was made?
  Heaven a god, which first by God was laid?

218 **Without** unless
240 **or . . . or** either . . . or
250 **exhales** drags off
13 Derision of idolators, who worship nature or their own impermanent handiwork, ignoring the eternal Creator who first made all nature and all humankind.
3 **vain** ineffectual
6 **feature** creation
7 **sore** grievous, severe
16 **wafts** carries, transports
17 **both** nature and men
22–30 **Earth . . . laid?** drawing on a conventional anatomy of the created world, ascending from the four elements (earth, air, fire, water) to the winds, the stars in their spheres, and heaven itself
27 **dusky ground** the dim or obscure lower level of creation (wanting 'God's bright excellence of brightest day'—33)

Say all hath beauty, excellence, array,
Yet beautified they are, they were, they be,
By God's bright excellence of brightest day,
Which first implanted our first beauty's tree.
If then the painted outside of the show
Be radiant, what is the inward row?

Verse 4 If that the shadow of the body's skin
Be so illumined with the sun-shined soul,
What is the thing itself which is within,
More rinsed, more cleansed, more purified from foul?
If elemental powers have God's thought,
Say what is God, which made them all of naught?

It is a wonder for to see the sky,
And operation of each airy power;
A marvel that the heav'n should be so high,
And let fall such a low distilling shower.
Then needs must he be high, higher than all,
Which made both low and high with one tongue's call.

Verse 5 The workman mightier is than his hand-work,
In making that which else would be unmade.
The ne'er-thought thing doth always hidden lurk,
Without the maker in a making trade.
For had not God made man, man had not been,
But nature had decayed and ne'er been seen.

The workman never showing of his skill
Doth live unknown to man, though known to wit.
Had mortal birth been never in God's will,
God had been God, but yet unknown in it.
Then having made the glory of earth's beauty,
'Tis reason earth should reverence him in duty.

Verse 6 The savage people have a supreme head,
A king, though savage as his subjects are;
Yet they with his observances are led,
Obeying his behests whate'er they were.
The Turks, the infidels, all have a lord,
Whom they observe in thought, in deed, in word.

And shall we, differing from their savage kind,
Having a soul to live and to believe,
Be rude in thought, in deed, in word, in mind,
Not seeking him which should our woes relieve?
O no, dear brethren, seek our God, our fame;
Then if we err, we shall have lesser blame.

How can we err? We seek for ready way. *Verse 7*
O that my tongue could fetch that word again,
Whose very accent makes me go astray,
Breathing that erring wind into my brain.
My word is passed, and cannot be recalled;
It is like agèd time, now waxen bald.

For they which go astray in seeking God,
Do miss the joyful narrow-footed path;
Joyful, thrice joyful way to his abode,
Naught seeing but their shadows in a bath.
Narcissus-like, pining to see a show,
Hind'ring the passage which their feet should go.

Narcissus' fantasy did die to kiss. *Verses 8, 9*
O sugared kiss, dyed with a poisoned lip!
The fantasies of these do die to miss.
O tossèd fantasies, in folly's ship!
He died to kiss the shadow of his face;
These live and die to life's and death's disgrace.

A fault without amends, crime without ease,
A sin without excuse, death without aid;
To love the world, and what the world did please,
To know the earth, wherein their sins are laid;
They knew the world, but not the Lord that framed it;
They knew the earth, but not the Lord that named it.

Narcissus drowned himself for his self's show; *Verse 10*
Striving to heal himself, did himself harm.
These drowned themselves on earth with their selves' woe,
He in a water-brook by fury's charm.
They made dry earth wet with their folly's weeping,
He made wet earth dry with his fury's sleeping.

Then leave him to his sleep. Return to those
Which ever wake in misery's constraints,
Whose eyes are hollow caves and made sleep's foes,
Two dungeons dark with sin, blind with complaints.
They callèd images which man first found
Immortal gods, for which their tongues are bound.

Gold was a god with them, a golden god:
Like children in a pageant of gay toys,
Adoring images for saints' abode.
O vain, vain spectacles of vainer joys!
Putting their hope in blocks, their trust in stones,
Hoping to trust, trusting to hope in moans.

31 **array** condition of being specially fitted out for display
36 **row** ray, beam
61 **savage** non-Christian
69 **rude** ignorant, untutored
71 **dear brethren** The addressee becomes a virtual Puritan congregation here.
78 **waxen** grown
80 **narrow-footed** having a narrow footway
82 **bath** spring of water (anticipating the Narcissus image of the next line)
83 **Narcissus-like** in Greek mythology, Narcissus is the beautiful youth who died of self-love (the essence of idolatry), adoring his own image in a pool
87 **these** the misguided people who seek God in his material world
100 **fury's** Fury is inspired frenzy, passionate obsession.
107 **found** founded? i.e., cast, moulded, as in a foundry
111 **saints' abode.** This reference makes explicit the underlying anticatholicism of the poem's assault on idolatry.

Verses 11, 12 As when a carpenter cuts down a tree,
Meet for to make a vessel for man's use,
He pareth all the bark most cunningly,
With the sharp shaver of his knife's abuse,
  Ripping the seely womb with no entreat,
  Making her woundy chips to dress his meat;

Verse 13 Her body's bones are often rough and hard,
Crooked with age's growth, growing with crooks,
And full of weather-chinks which seasons marred,
Knobby and rugged, bending in like hooks;
  Yet knowing age can never want a fault,
  Encounters it with a sharp knife's assault,

Verse 14 And carves it well, though it be self-like ill,
Observing leisure, keeping time and place,
According to the cunning of his skill,
Making the figure of a mortal face,
  Or like some ugly beast in ruddy mould,
  Hiding each cranny with a painter's fold.

Verses 15, 16 It is a world to see, to mark, to view,
How age can botch up age with crooked thread,
How his old hands can make an old tree new,
And dead-like he can make another dead;
  Yet makes a substantive able to bear it,
  And she, an adjective, nor see nor hear it.

A wall it is itself, yet wall with wall
Hath great supportance, bearing either part.
The image, like an adjective, would fall,
Were it not closèd with an iron heart.
  The workman, being old himself, doth know
  What great infirmities old age can show.

Verse 17 Therefore, to stop the river of extremes,
He burst into the flowing of his wit,
Tossing his brains with more than thousand themes,
To have a wooden stratagem so fit:
  Wooden, because it doth belong to wood;
  His purpose may be wise, his reason good.

His purpose wise? No, foolish, fond, and vain.
His reason good? No, wicked, vile, and ill,
To be the author of his own life's pain,
To be the tragic actor of his will,
  Praying to that which he before had framed,
  For welcome faculties, and not ashamed;

Calling to folly for discretion's sense, *Verse 18*
Calling to sickness for sick body's health,
Calling to weakness for a stronger fence,
Calling to poverty for better wealth;
  Praying to death for life, for this he prayed,
  Requiring help of that which wanteth aid;

Desiring that of it which he had not, *Verse 19*
And for his journey that which cannot go,
And for his gain her furth'rance, to make glad
The work which he doth take in hand to do.
  These windy words do rush against the wall;
  She cannot speak, 'twill sooner make her fall.

Chapter Fourteen

As doth one little spark make a great flame, *Verse 1*
Kindled from forth the bosom of the flint,
As doth one plague infect with its self name,
With wat'ry humours making bodies' dint:
  So, even so, this idol worshipper
  Doth make another idol practiser.

The shipman cannot team dame Tethys' waves
Within a wind-taut cap'ring anchorage,
Before he prostrate lies, and suffrage craves,
And has a block to be his fortune's gage:
  More crooked than his stern, yet he implores her;
  More rotten than his ship, yet he adores her.

Who made this form? He that was formed and made. *Verse 2*
'Twas avarice, 'twas she that found it out.
She made her craftsman crafty in his trade,
He cunning was in bringing it about.
  O, had he made the painted show to speak,
  It would have called him vain, herself to wreak.

It would have made him blush alive, though he *Verses 3, 4*
Did dye her colour with a deadly blush.
Thy providence, O Father, doth decree
A sure, sure way amongst the waves to rush,
  Thereby declaring that thy power is such,
  That though a man were weak, thou canst do much.

117 **cunningly** skilfully
120 **woundy** characterized by wounds; *OED*'s earliest example is from 1660
129 **cunning** knowledge, craft
132 **fold** wrapping, covering
134 **botch up** patch, repair
137 **substantive** *fig.* an independent person or thing
138 **she** the idol, consistently neuter in *Geneva*
adjective *fig.* a dependent person or thing: 'he setteth it in a wall, and maketh it fast with iron, providing so for it lest it fall' (*Geneva*), 15–16.
145 **river of extremes** journey toward death
148 **wooden** playing on the sense 'mad'
156 **faculties** personal attributes, such as the 'discretion' and 'health' of the next stanza
14 Of idol-worshipping at sea; idolatry and vice; the origins and spreading of idolatry, and the evils proceeding from it.
3 **self** very, own (emphatic adj.)
4 **humours** mists; bodily fluids
dint stroke, blow
7 **team** harness, yoke; but perhaps an error for 'tame'
8 **wind-taut** holding wind tautly; usually applied to a dangerous excess of sail or rigging
cap'ring dancing
9 **suffrage** assistance; intercession
10 **block** of wood
11 **her** the block or idol; again feminizing *Geneva*'s neutral object; see gloss on 67, and note especially 235–40.
15 **crafty** skilful; cunning
18 **wreak** avenge

Verse 5 What is one single bar to double death,
One death in death, the other death in fear?
This single bar, a board, a poor board's breadth,
Yet stops the passage of each Neptune's tear.
To see how many lives one board can have!
To see how many lives one board can save!

How was this board first made? By wisdom's art,
Which is not vain but firm, not weak but sure.
Therefore do men commit their living heart
To planks which either life or death procure,
Cutting the storms in two, parting the wind,
Plowing the sea till they their harbour find;

Verse 6 The sea whose mountain billows, passing bounds,
Rusheth upon the hollow-sided bark,
With rough-sent kisses from the water grounds,
Raising a foaming heat with rage's spark.
Yet sea nor waves can make the shipman fear:
He knows that die he must, he cares not where.

For had his timorous heart been dyed in white,
And sent an echo of resembling woe,
Wisdom had been unknown in folly's night,
The sea had been a desolation's show;
But one world's hope lay hovering on the sea,
When one world's hap did end with one decay.

Yet Phoebus drownèd in the ocean's world,
Phoebe disgraced with Tethys' billow-rolls,
And Phoebus' fiery-golden wreath uncurled,
Was seated at the length in brightness' souls.
Man, tossed in wettest wilderness of seas,
Had seed on seed, increase upon increase.

Verses 7, 8 Their mansion-house a tree upon a wave:
O happy tree, upon unhappy ground!
But every tree is not ordained to have
Such blessedness, such virtue, such abound:
Some trees are carvèd images of naught,
Yet godlike reverenced, adored, besought.

Verse 9 Are the trees naught? Alas, they senseless are.
The hands which fashion them condemn their growth,
Cuts down their branches, vails their forehead bare.
Both made in sin, though not sin's equal both:
First God made man, and vice did make him new,
And man made vice from vice, and so it grew.

Now is her harvest greater than her good,
Her wonted winter turned to summer's air,
Her ice to heat, her sprig to cedar's wood,
Her hate to love, her loathsome filth to fair.
Man loves her well, by mischief new created;
God hates her ill, because of virtue hated.

O foolish man, mounted upon decay, *Verse 10*
More ugly than Alastor's pitchy back,
Night's dismal summoner, and end of day,
Carrying all dusky vapours hemmed in black,
Behold thy downfall, ready at thy hand!
Behold thy hopes wherein thy hazards stand!

O spurn away that block out of thy way,
With virtue's appetite and wisdom's force,
That stumbling block of folly and decay,
That snare which doth ensnare thy treading corse!
Behold, thy body falls! Let virtue bear it.
Behold, thy soul doth fall! Let wisdom rear it.

Say, art thou young or old, tree or a bud? *Verse 11*
Thy face is so disfigurèd with sin,
Young I do think thou art. In what? In good,
But old I am assured by wrinkled skin.
Thy lips, thy tongue, thy heart, is young in praying,
But lips and tongue and heart is old in straying:

Old in adoring idols, but too young
In the observance of divinest law;
Young in adoring God, though old in tongue,
Old and too old, young and too young in awe:
Beginning that which doth begin misdeeds,
Inventing vice which all thy body feeds.

But this corrupting and infecting food, *Verse 12*
This caterpillar of eternity,
The foe to bliss, the canker unto good,
The new accustomed way of vanity:
It hath not ever been, nor shall it be,
But perish in the branch of folly's tree.

As her descent was vanity's alline, *Verse 13*
So her descending like to her descent:
Here shall she have an end, in hell no fine.
Vainglory brought her vainly to be spent.
You know all vanity draws to an end,
Then needs must she decay, because her friend.

Is there more folly than to weep at joy? *Verse 14*
To make eyes wat'ry when they should be dry?
To grieve at that which murders grief's annoy?
To keep a shower where the sun should lie?
But yet this folly-cloud doth oft appear,
When face should smile and wat'ry eye be clear.

27 **board** ship; *fig.* providence
28 **Neptune's** sea-god's
47 **one world's hope** Noah (who built his ark guided by divine wisdom), and his living cargo
48 **hap** luck, chance
58 **abound** abundance (not otherwise recorded)
63 **vails** lowers submissively
67 **her** vice's
74 **Alastor's** belonging to the Greek spirit of vengeance
82 **corse** obsolete form of corpse, here with the sense (also obsolete) of a living body (hence, of life in death?)
98 **caterpillar** rapacious parasite; like 'moth', much stronger in Middleton's usage than in ours
101 **ever** always
103 **alline** ally, kin
105 **fine** ending
111 **annoy** vexation

The father mourns to see his son life-dead,
But seldom mourns to see his son dead-lived.
He cares for earthly lodge, not heaven's bed,
For death in life, not life in death survived,
Keeping the outward shadow of his face
To work the inward substance of disgrace;

Keeping a show to counterpoise the deed;
Keeping a shadow to be substance' heir,
To raise the thing itself from shadow's seed,
And make an element of lifeless air;
Adoring that which his own hands did frame,
Whose heart invention gave, whose tongue the name.

Verses 15, 16 But could infection keep one settled place,
The poison would not lodge in every breast,
Nor feed the heart, the mind, the soul, the face,
Lodging but in the carcass of her rest;
But this idolatry, once in man's use,
Was made a custom then without excuse.

Nay more: it was at tyranny's command,
And tyrants cannot speak without a doom,
Whose judgement doth proceed from heart and hand,
From heart in rage, from hand in bloody tomb,
That if through absence any did neglect it,
Presence should pay the ransom which reject it.

Then to avoid the doom of present hate,
Their absence did perform their presence' want,
Making the image of a kingly state,
As if they had new seed from sin's old plant;
Flatt'ring the absence of old mischief's mother,
With the like form and presence of another;

Verse 17 Making an absence with a present sight,
Or rather presence with an absent view;
Deceiving vulgars with a day of night,
Which know not good from bad, nor false from true:
A craftsman cunning in his crafty trade,
Beguiling them with that which he had made.

Like as a vane is turned with every blast,
Until it point unto the windy clime,
So stand the people at his word aghast.
He making old-new form in new-old time,
Defies and deifies all with one breath,
Making them live and die, and all in death.

They, like to Tantalus, are fed with shows, *Verse 18*
Shows which exasperate and cannot cure.
They see the painted shadow of suppose.
They see her sight, yet what doth sight procure?
Like Tantalus they feed, and yet they starve.
Their food is carved to them, yet hard to carve.

The craftsman feeds them with a starving meat,
Which doth not fill but empty hunger's gape.
He makes the idol comely, fair, and great,
With well-limned visage and best-fashioned shape,
Meaning to give it to some noble view,
And feign his beauty with that flatt'ring hue.

Enamoured with the sight, the people grew *Verse 19*
To divers apparitions of delight.
Some did admire the portraiture so new,
Hewed from the standard of an old tree's height.
Some were allured through beauty of the face,
With outward eye to work the soul's disgrace.

Adorèd like a god, though made by man!
To make a god of man, a man of god,
'Tis more than human life or could or can,
Though multitudes' applause in error trod:
I never knew since mortal life's abode,
That man could make a man, much less a god.

Yes, man can make his shame without a maker, *Verse 20*
Borrowing the essence from restorèd sin.
Man can be virtue's foe, and vice's taker,
Welcome himself without a welcome in.
Can he do this? Yea, more. O shameless ill:
Shameful in sin, shameless in wisdom's will!

The river of his vice can have no bound,
But breaks into the ocean of deceit,
Deceiving life with measures of dead ground,
With carvèd idols, disputation's bait;
Making captivity, clothed all in moan,
Be subject to a god made of a stone.

Too stony hearts had they which made this law. *Verse 21*
O, had they been as stony as the name,
They never had brought vulgars in such awe,
To be destruction's prey, and mischief's game.
Had they been stone-dead both in look and favour,
They never had made life of such a savour.

115 **life-dead** deprived of life
116 **dead-lived** living in a condition of spiritual death
119 **outward shadow** the father's idolatrous image of his dead son, viewed as one of the possible origins of idolatry
132 **without excuse** no one was excused from idol-worship, not the servants of the mourning father, not the subjects of the tyrant: 'this wicked custom prevailed, and was kept as a law, and idols were worshipped by the commandment of tyrants' (*Geneva*)
134 **doom** sentence of punishment
140 **Their absence** the absence of tyrants (whose images were worshipped in their stead)
151 **vane** weathervane
157 **Tantalus** mythical king of Phrygia, condemned never to gain the ever-receding food and drink just beyond his reach
158 **exasperate** increase the fierceness of appetite
164 **gape** wide-open mouth
166 **well-limned** well painted, portrayed
177 **or . . . or** either . . . or
179 **abode** temporary stay
193 **they . . . law** the tyrants who commanded idol-worshipping
195 **vulgars** common or uneducated people

Yet was not this a too sufficient doom,
Sent from the root of their sin-o'ergrown tongue,
To cloud God's knowledge with hell-mischief's gloom,
To overthrow truth's right with falsehood's wrong:
But daily practisèd a perfect way,
Still to begin, and never end to stray.

Verse 22 For either murder's paw did grip their hearts,
With whisp'ring horrors drumming in each ear,
Or other villainies did play their parts,
Augmenting horror to new-strucken fear,
Making their hands more than a shambles' stall,
To slay their children ceremonial.

Verse 23 No place was free from stain of blood or vice.
Their life was marked for death, their soul for sin,
Marriage for fornication's thawèd ice,
Thought for despair, body for either's gin.
Slaughter did either end what life begun,
Or lust did end what both had left undone.

Verses 24, 25 The one was sure, although the other fail,
For vice hath more competitors than one.
A greater troop doth evermore avail,
And villainy is never found alone.
The bloodhound follows that which slaughter killed,
And theft doth follow what deceit hath spilled.

Corruption's mate to infidelity,
For that which is unfaithful is corrupt.
Tumults are schoolfellows to perjury,
For both are full when either one hath supped.
Unthankfulness, defiling, and disorders,
Are fornication's and uncleanness' boarders.

Verse 26 See what a sort of rebels are in arms,
To root out virtue, to supplant her reign,
Opposing of themselves against all harms,
To the deposing of her empire's gain.
O double knot of treble miseries!
O treble knot, twice, thrice in villainies!

O idol-worshipping, thou mother art,
She-procreatress of a he-offence.
I know thee now. Thou bear'st a woman's part.
Thou nature hast of her, she of thee sense.
These are thy daughters, too too like the mother:
Black sins, I damn you all with inky smother.

Verse 27 My pen shall be officious in this scene,
To let your hearts' blood in a wicked vein,
To make your bodies clear, your souls as clean,
To cleanse the sinks of sin with virtue's rain.
Behold your coal-black blood, my writing ink,
My paper's poisoned meat, my pen's foul drink.

New-christened are you with your own new blood,
But mad before, savage and desperate,
Prophesying lies, not knowing what was good,
Living ungodly, evermore in hate;
Thund'ring out oaths, pale sergeants of despair;
Swore and forswore, not knowing what you were.

Now look upon the spectacle of shame, *Verse 28*
The well-limned image of an ill-limned thought.
Say, are you worthy now of praise or blame,
That such self-scandal in your own selves wrought?
You were heart-sick before I let you blood,
But now heart-well since I have done you good.

Now wipe blind folly from your seeing eyes,
And drive destruction from your happy mind.
Your folly now is wit, not foolish-wise;
Destruction, happiness, not mischief blind.
You put your trust in idols, they deceived you.
You put your trust in God, and he received you.

Had not repentance grounded on your souls, *Verse 29*
The climes of good or ill, virtue or vice,
Had it not flowed into the tongue's enrols,
Ascribing mischief's hate with good advice,
Your tongue had spilled your soul, your soul your tongue,
Wronging each function with a double wrong.

Your first attempt was placèd in a show:
Imaginary show without a deed.
The next attempt was perjury, the foe
To just demeanours, and to virtue's seed.
Two sins, two punishments, and one in two,
Makes two in one, and more than one can do.

Four scourges from one pain, all comes from sin, *Verse 30*
Single yet double, double yet in four.
It slays the soul. It hems the body in.
It spills the mind. It doth the heart devour,
Gnawing upon the thoughts, feeding on blood,
Forwhy, she lives in sin, but dies in good.

She taught their souls to stray, their tongues to swear,
Their thought to think amiss, their life to die,
Their heart to err, their mischief to appear,
Their head to sin, their feet to tread awry.
This scene might well have been destruction's tent,
To pay with pain what sin with joy hath spent.

209 **shambles'** meat market's
222 **spilled** destroyed
225 **Tumults** riots; mental agitation
236 **She-procreatress . . . he-offence** 'For the worshipping of idols . . . is the beginning and the cause and the end of all evil' (*Geneva*); 'a he-offence' is presumably the highest sort in the patriarchal hierarchy of gender.
241 **My pen . . . scene** casting himself as something like the author of a stage satire; by the end of Verse 28, he will sound more like a healing evangelist
266 **climes** regions
267 **enrols** registers, lists; *fig.* prayers of confession, lists of sins
269 **spilled** destroyed
271 **attempt** temptation, seduction
a show an idol
277 **scourges** instruments of divine chastisement, agents of calamity
282 **Forwhy** Because

Chapter Fifteen

Verse 1 But God will never dye his hands with blood,
His heart with hate, his throne with cruelty,
His face with fury's map, his brow with cloud,
His reign with rage, his crown with tyranny.
  Gracious is he, long-suffering and true,
  Which ruleth all things with his mercy's view.

Gracious, for where is grace but where he is:
The fountain-head, the ever-boundless stream?
Patient, for where is patience in amiss,
If not conducted by pure grace's beam?
  Truth is the moderator of them both,
  For grace and patience are of truest growth.

Verse 2 For grace-beginning truth doth end in grace,
As truth-beginning grace doth end in truth.
Now patience takes the moderator's place,
Young-old in suffering, old-young in ruth.
  Patience is old in being always young,
  Not having right, nor ever offering wrong.

So this is moderator of God's rage,
Pardoning those deeds which we in sin commit,
That if we sin, she is our freedom's gage,
And we still thine, though to be thine unfit.
  In being thine, O Lord, we will not sin,
  That we thy patience, grace, and truth may win.

Verse 3 O grant us patience, in whose grant we rest,
To right our wrong, and not to wrong the right.
Give us thy grace, O Lord, to make us blest,
That grace might bless, and bliss might grace our sight.
  Make our beginning and our sequel truth,
  To make us young in age, and grave in youth.

We know that our demands rest in thy will,
Our will rests in thy word, our word in thee,
Thou in our orisons, which dost fulfil
That wishèd action which we wish to be.
  'Tis perfect righteousness to know thee right;
  'Tis immortality to know thy might.

Verses 4, 5 In knowing thee, we know both good and ill:
Good to know good and ill, ill to know none.
In knowing all, we know thy sacred will,
And what to do, and what to leave undone.
  We are deceived, not knowing to deceive;
  In knowing good and ill, we take and leave.

The glass of vanity, deceit, and shows,
The painter's labour, the beguiling face,
The divers-coloured image of suppose,
Cannot deceive the substance of thy grace;
  Only a snare to those of common wit,
  Which covets to be like, in having it.

The greedy lucre of a witless brain, Verse 6
This feeding avarice on senseless mind,
Is rather hurt than good, a loss than gain,
Which covets for to lose, and not to find.
  So they were colourèd with such a face,
  They would not care to take the idol's place.

Then be your thoughts coherent to your words,
Your words as correspondent to your thought.
'Tis reason you should have what love affords,
And trust in that which love so dearly bought.
  The maker must needs love what he hath made,
  And the desirer's free of either trade.

Man, thou wast made. Art thou a maker now? Verse 7
Yes, 'tis thy trade, for thou a potter art,
Temp'ring soft earth, making the clay to bow,
But clayey thou dost bear too stout a heart.
  The clay is humble to thy rigorous hands,
  Thou clay too tough against thy God's commands.

If thou want'st slime, behold thy slimy faults.
If thou want'st clay, behold thy clayey breast.
Make them to be the deepest centre's vaults,
And let all clayey mountains sleep in rest.
  Thou bear'st an earthly mountain on thy back,
  Thy heart's chief prison-house, thy soul's chief wreck.

Art thou a mortal man, and mak'st a god? Verse 8
A god of clay, thou but a man of clay.
O suds of mischief, in destruction sod!
O vainest labour in a vainer play!
  Man is the greatest work which God did take,
  And yet a god with man is naught to make.

He that was made of earth would make a heaven,
If heaven may be made upon the earth.
Sin's heirs the airs, sin's plants the planets seven,
Their god a clod, his birth true virtue's dearth.
  Remember whence you came, whither you go:
  Of earth, in earth, from earth to earth in woe.

15 But by God's mercy and grace, and by learning to know good and ill, the faithful avoid idolatry. The potter who worships a clay image of his own making is again derided, as are those who worship senseless animals.
16 **ruth** pity
19 **this** mercy
21 **gage** warrant, guarantee
33 **orisons** prayers
41 **We . . . deceive** Not knowing how to deceive, we are easily deceived.
43 **glass** mirror
45 **suppose** fancy, imagination
49 **lucre** monetary profit
53 **So** So long as
55 **coherent** consistent
61 **thou** the potter (third person in *Geneva*)
69 **vaults** sewers
72 **wreck** pronounced, and spelled, 'wrack' in SIMMES
75 **suds** filth, dregs
sod stewed

Verse 9 'No,' quoth the potter, 'as I have been clay,
So will I end with what I did begin.
I am of earth, and I do what earth may.
I am of dust, and therefore will I sin.
My life is short. What then? I'll make it longer.
My life is weak. What then? I'll make it stronger.

'Long shall it live in vice, though short in length,
And fetch immortal steps from mortal stops.
Strong shall it be in sin, though weak in strength,
Like mounting eagles on high mountains' tops.
My honour shall be placèd in deceit,
And counterfeit new shows of little weight.'

Verse 10 My pen doth almost blush at this reply,
And fain would call him wicked to his face,
But then his breath would answer with a lie,
And stain my ink with an untruth's disgrace.
Thy master bids thee write. The pen says, 'No.'
But when thy master bids, it must be so.

Call his heart ashes. O, too mild a name!
Call his hope vile. More viler than the earth!
Call his life weaker than a clayey frame;
Call his bespotted heart an ashy hearth.
Ashes, earth, clay, conjoined to heart, hope, life,
Are feature's love, in being nature's strife.

Verse 11 Thou mightst have chose more stinging words than these,
For this he knows he is, and more than less.
In saying what he is, thou dost appease
The foaming anger which his thoughts suppress.
Who knows not, if the best be made of clay,
The worst must needs be clad in foul array?

Thou, in performing of thy master's will,
Dost teach him to obey his lord's commands.
But he repugnant is, and cannot skill
Of true adoring, with heart-heaved-up hands.
He hath a soul, a life, a breath, a name,
Yet is he ignorant from whence they came.

Verse 12 'My soul,' saith he, 'is but a map of shows,
No substance, but a shadow for to please.
My life doth pass even as a pastime goes,
A momentary time to live at ease;
My breath a vapour, and my name of earth,
Each one decaying of the other's birth.

'Our conversation best, for there is gains,
And gain is best in conversation's prime.
A mart of lucre in our conscience reigns,
Our thoughts as busy agents for the time.
So we get gain, ensnaring simple men,
It is no matter how, nor where, nor when.

'We care not how, for all misdeeds are ours. Verse 13
We care not where, if before God or man.
We care not when, but when our crafts have powers,
In measuring deceit with mischief's fan.
For wherefore have we life, form, and ordaining,
But that we should deceive, and still be gaining?

'I, made of earth, have made all earthen shops,
And what I sell is all of earthy sale.
My pots have earthen feet, and earthen tops,
In like resemblance of my body's veil.
But knowing to offend the heavens more,
I made frail images of earthy store.'

O bold accuser of his own misdeeds! Verse 14
O heavy clod, more than the earth can bear!
Was never creature clothed in savage weeds,
Which would not blush when they this mischief hear!
Thou told'st a tale which might have been untold,
Making the hearers blush, the readers old.

Let them blush still that hears, be old that reads;
Then boldness shall not reign, nor youth in vice.
Thrice miserable they which rashly speeds,
With expedition to this bold device:
More foolish than are fools, whose misery
Cannot be changed with new felicity.

Are not they fools which live without a sense? Verse 15
Have not they misery which never joy?
Which takes an idol for a god's defence,
And with their self-willed thoughts themselves destroy?
What folly is more greater than is here?
Or what more misery can well appear?

Call you them gods which have no seeing eyes,
No noses for to smell, no ears to hear,
No life but that which in death's shadow lies,
Which have no hands to feel, no feet to bear?
If gods can neither hear, live, feel, nor see,
A fool may make such gods of every tree.

97 **My pen** The poem's voice shifts again to the persona of the poet. The pen's submission to the will of the poet in the following four stanzas mirrors the idol's subjection to its maker.
108 **feature's** that which is created, made
115 **Thou** the pen
116 **him** the potter
117 **repugnant** resistant, hostile
skill have knowledge
127 **Our conversation** living with others, society; in *Geneva*, the verse harks back to the greedy idol-making craftsmen of 15:9
gains material profit
129 **mart** market
136 **fan** instrument for winnowing grain; mischief was sometimes personified as a corn-thresher, as in the 15th-century morality play *Mankind*
140 **sale** with a play on French *sale*, dirty?
142 **veil** i.e., apparently, that which veils the soul

Verse 16 And what was he that made them but a fool,
Conceiving folly in a foolish brain,
Taught and instructed in a wooden school,
Which made his head run of a wooden vein?
'Twas man which made them; he his making had.
Man, full of wood, was wood, and so ran mad.

He borrowèd his life, and would restore
His borrowed essence to another death.
He fain would be a maker, though before
Was made himself, and God did lend him breath.
No man can make a god like to a man.
He says he scorns that work; he further can.

Verse 17 He is deceived, and in his great deceit,
He doth deceive the folly-guided hearts.
Sin lies in ambush, he for sin doth wait:
Here is deceit deceived in either parts.
His sin deceiveth him, and he his sin;
So craft with craft is mewed in either gin.

The craftsman mortal is, craft mortal is,
Each function nursing up the other's want.
His hands are mortal, deadly what is his,
Only his sins buds in destruction's plant.
Yet better he than what he doth devise,
For he himself doth live; that ever dies.

Verse 18 Say, call you this a god? Where is his head?
Yet headless is he not, yet hath he none.
Where is his godhead? Fled. His power? Dead.
His reign? Decayèd. And his essence? Gone.
Now tell me, is this god the god of good,
Or else Silvanus, monarch of the wood?

There have I pierced his bark, for he is so:
A wooden god, feigned as Silvanus was.
But leaving him, to others let us go,
To senseless beasts their new adoring glass:
Beasts which did live in life, yet died in reason;
Beasts which did seasons eat, yet knew no season.

Verse 19 Can mortal bodies and immortal souls
Keep one knit union of a living love?
Can sea with land, can fish agree with fowls?
Tigers with lambs, a serpent with a dove?
O no, they cannot. Then say, why do we
Adore a beast which is our enemy?

What greater foe than folly unto wit?
What more deformity than ugly face?
This disagrees, for folly is unfit,
The other contrary to beauty's place.
Then how can senseless heads, deformèd shows,
Agree with you, when they are both your foes?

Chapter Sixteen

O call that word again! They are your friends, Verse 1
Your lives' associates, and your loves' content.
That which begins in them, your folly ends.
Then how can vice with vice be discontent?
Behold, deformity sits on your heads:
Not horns, but scorns; not visage, but whole beds.

Behold, a heap of sins your bodies pale,
A mountain-overwhelming villainy.
Then tell me, are you clad in beauty's veil,
Or in destruction's pale-dead livery?
Their life demònstrates, now alive, now dead,
Tormented with the beasts which they have fed.

You like to pelicans have fed your death Verses 2, 3
With folly's vain-let blood from folly's vein,
And almost starved yourselves, stopped up your breath,
Had not God's mercy helped, and eased your pain.
Behold, a new-found meat the Lord did send,
Which taught you to be new, and to amend.

A strange-digested nutriment, even quails,
Which taught them to be strange unto misdeeds.
When you implore his aid, he never fails
To fill their hunger whom repentance feeds.
You see, when life was half at death's arrest,
He new-created life at hunger's feast.

Say, is your god like this, whom you adored, Verse 4
Or is this God like to your handy-frame?
If so, his power could not then afford
Such influence which floweth from his name.
He is not painted, made of wood and stone,
But he substantial is, and rules alone.

171 **wooden** playing on the adjectival sense of 'wood' meaning mad
177 **fain** willingly
180 **he further can** [he says] he is capable of more [than the mere creation of man]
186 **mewed** confined
gin cunning stratagem *fig.*
190 **his sins buds** his sins spring forth, begin to grow
193 **Say ... god** to the maker of the idol; the implicit dialogue of the next few rhetorical questions shows Middleton's poetic persona at its dramatic best.
198 **Silvanus** Pan
204 **seasons** seasonings, i.e., herbs?
season moderation
16 Continuing to chastise the idolatrous: those who repent are guaranteed God's mercy and divine nourishment; the unrepentant idolators and ungodly suffer plagues, fires and tempests; God's people endure torments but are finally safe, nourished with angelic food and with the word of the Lord.
1 **that word** 'foes'
6 **beds** of vice, as in 17.1
7 **pale** fence in
11 **Their** reverting momentarily to *Geneva*'s third-person designation of the idolatrous
13 **pelicans** reputed to nourish their young self-sacrificially, with blood pecked from their own breasts
19 **quails** referring to the miraculous feeding of the grumbling Israelites in the wilderness (Numbers 11:31 ff.); the quail is a small relative of the partridge
20 **strange** reserved, uncomplying
26 **handy-frame** handiwork

He can oppress and help, help and oppress
The sinful incolants of his made earth.
He can redress and pain, pain and redress
The mountain-miseries of mortal birth.
  Now, tyrants, you are next, this but a show,
  And merry index of your after-woe.

Verses 5, 6 Your hot-cold misery is now at hand:
Hot because fury's heat, and mercy's cold;
Cold because limping, knit in frosty bond,
And cold and hot in being shamefast-bold.
  They cruel were. Take cruelty their part,
  For misery is but too mean a smart.

But when the tigers' jaws, the serpents' stings,
Did summon them unto this life's decay,
A pardon for their faults thy mercy brings,
Cooling thy wrath with pity's sunny day.
  O tyrants, tear your sin-bemirèd weeds!
  Behold your pardon, sealed by mercy's deeds!

Verse 7 That sting which painèd could not ease the pain.
Those jaws that wounded could not cure the wounds.
To turn to stings for help, it were but vain,
To jaws for mercy, which wants mercy's bounds.
  The stings, O Saviour, were pulled out by thee,
  Their jaws clasped up in midst of cruelty.

Verse 8 O sovereign salve, stop to a bloody stream!
O heavenly care and cure, for dust and earth!
Celestial watch to wake terrestrial dream,
Dreaming in punishment, mourning in mirth:
  Now knows our enemies that it is thee,
  Which helps and cures our grief and misery.

Verse 9 Our punishment doth end, theirs new begins.
Our day appears, their night is not o'erblown.
We pardon have, they punishment for sins.
Now we are raised, now they are overthrown.
  We with huge beasts oppressed, they with a fly;
  We live in God, and they against God die.

A fly! Poor fly to follow such a flight!
Yet art thou fed, as thou wast fed before,
With dust and earth feeding thy wonted bite,
With self-like food from mortal earthly store.
  A mischief-stinging food, and sting with sting,
  Do ready passage to destruction bring.

Man, being grass, is hopped and grazed upon, *Verse 10*
With sucking grasshoppers of weeping dew.
Man, being earth, is worms' vermilïon,
Which eats the dust, and yet of bloody hue.
  In being grass, he is her grazing food;
  In being dust, he doth the worms some good.

These smallest actors were of greatest pain,
Of folly's overthrow, of mischief's fall,
But yet the furious dragons could not gain
The life of those whom verities exhale.
  These folly overcame, they foolish were;
  These mercy cured and cures, these godly are.

When poisoned jaws and venenated stings *Verse 11*
Were both as opposite against content,
Because content with that which fortune brings,
They easèd were, when thou thy mercies sent.
  The jaws of dragons had not hunger's fill,
  Nor stings of serpents a desire to kill.

Appalled they were, and struck with timorous fears,
For where is fear but where destruction reigns?
Aghast they were, with wet eye-standing tears,
Outward commencers of their inward pains.
  They soon were hurt, but sooner healed and cured,
  Lest black oblivion had their minds inured.

The lion, wounded with a fatal blow, *Verse 12*
Is as impatient as a king in rage;
Seeing himself in his own bloody show,
Doth rend the harbour of his body's cage;
  Scorning the base-housed earth, mounts to the sky,
  To see if heaven can yield him remedy.

O sinful man! Let him example be,
A pattern to thine eye, glass to thy face,
That God's divinest word is cure to thee,
Not earth but heaven, not man but heavenly grace.
  Nor herb nor plaster could help teeth or sting,
  But 'twas thy word, which healeth everything.

32 **incolants** inhabitants; the earliest known occurrence of this rare latinate item (*OED*)
made created
41 **They** The person shifts; the referent remains the tyrants of line 35.
43–54 **But... cruelty** The exegetical tradition on the corresponding (and obscure) biblical passage (16:7) associates it with the brazen serpent (Numbers 21:9). Middleton does not appear to have grasped the allusion (D.S.). 'For when the cruel fierceness of the beasts came upon them, and they were hurt with the stings of cruel serpents, | Thy wrath endured not perpetually, but they were troubled for a little season, that they might be reformed, having a sign of salvation, to remember the commandment of thy Law. | For he that turned toward it, was not healed by the thing that he saw, but by thee, O Saviour of all' (*Geneva* 5–7).
65 **they with a fly** 'For the biting of grasshoppers and flies killed them' (*Geneva*).
69 **wonted** habitual
75 **vermilïon** red earth; glancing at Latin *vermis*, worm
81 **furious dragons** 'the teeth of the venomous dragons could not overcome thy children' (*Geneva*)
82 **exhale** drag out
85 **venenated** envenomed, poisonous; according to *OED*, Middleton's is the earliest recorded occurrence of any form of this item created from Latin *venenare*
96 **inured** hardened
97 **lion** proverbial? Compare Marlowe's *Edward II*, 5.1.11–14, on which Middleton seems to depend here.

Verse 13 We fools lay salves upon our body's skin,
But never draw corruption from our mind.
We lay a plaster for to keep in sin;
We draw forth filth, but leave the cause behind.
With herbs and plasters we do guard misdeeds,
And pare away the tops, but leave the seeds.

Away with salves, and take our Saviour's word.
In this word Saviour lies immortal ease.
What can thy cures, plasters and herbs afford,
When God hath power to please and to displease?
God hath the power of life, death, help, and pain;
He leadeth down, and bringeth up again.

Verses 14, 15 Trust to thy downfall, not unto thy raise:
So shalt thou live in death, not die in life.
Thou dost presume, if give thyself the praise,
For virtue's time is scarce, but mischief's rife.
Thou mayst offend, man's nature is so vain.
Thou, now in joy, beware of after-pain.

First cometh fury, after fury thirst,
After thirst blood, and after blood a death.
Thou mayst in fury kill whom thou loved'st first,
And so, in quaffing blood, stop thine own breath;
And murder done can never be undone,
Nor can that soul once live whose life is gone.

Verse 16 What is the body but an earthen case,
That subject is to death, because earth dies?
But when the living soul doth want God's grace,
It dies in joy, and lives in miseries.
This soul is led by God, as others were,
But not brought up again, as others are.

This stirs no provocation to amend,
For earth hath many partners in one fall,
Although the Lord doth many tokens send,
As warnings for to hear when he doth call.
The earth was burned and drowned with fire and rain,
And one could never quench the other's pain.

Verse 17 Although both foes, God made them then both friends,
And only foes to them which were their foes.
That hate begun in earth what in them ends,
Sin's enemies they which made friends of those.
Both bent both forces unto single earth,
From whose descent they had their double birth.

'Tis strange that water should not quench a fire,
For they were heating-cold, and cooling-hot.
'Tis strange that wails could not allay desire,
Wails water's kind, and fire desire's knot.
In such a cause, though enemies before,
They would join friendship to destroy the more.

Verse 18 The often-weeping eyes of dry lament,
Doth pour forth burning water of despair,
Which warms the caves from whence the tears are sent,
And, like hot fumes, do foul their nature's fair.
This, contrary to icy water's vale,
Doth scorch the cheeks, and makes them red and pale.

Here fire and water are conjoined in one,
Within a red-white glass of hot and cold;
Their fire like this, double and yet alone,
Raging and tame, and tame and yet was bold:
Tame when the beasts did kill and felt no fire,
Raging upon the causers of their ire.

Verse 19 Two things may well put on two several natures,
Because they differ each in nature's kind.
They differing colours have, and differing features:
If so, how comes it that they have one mind?
God made them friends, let this the answer be.
They get no other argument of me.

What is impossible to God's command?
Nay, what is possible to man's vain ear?
'Tis much, he thinks, that fire should burn a land,
When mischief is the brand which fires bear.
He thinks it more, that water should bear fire;
Then know it was God's will. Now leave t'inquire.

Verse 20 Yet mightst thou ask, because importunate,
How God preserved the good. Why? Because good.
Ill fortune made not them infortunate.
They angels were, and fed with angels' food.
Yet mayst thou say—for truth is always had—
The rain falls on the good as well as bad.

And say it doth: far be the letter P
From R, because of a more reverent style.
It cannot do without suppression be.
These are two bars against destruction's wile:
Pain without changing P cannot be rain;
Rain without changing R cannot be pain.

Verse 21 Both sun and rain are portions to the ground,
And ground is dust, and what is dust but naught?
And what is naught is naught, with alpha's sound,
Yet every earth the sun and rain hath bought.
The sun doth shine on weeds as well as flowers;
The rain on both distills her weeping showers.

111 **plaster** poultice; remedy applied to the body on fabric or a bandage
120 **down** 'unto the gates of hell' (*Geneva*)
135 **want** lack
145 **both foes** of one another
153 **wails** associated with weeping, and thence with water
167 **felt no fire** 'For some time was the fire so tame, that the beasts, which were sent against the ungodly, burnt not' (*Geneva*).
169–80 **Two things . . . t'inquire**. There is no comparable throwing up of the hands in *Geneva*.
187–92 **And . . . pain** The point of this whimsy is that rain may be destructive to the damned, benevolent to the saved.
193 **portions** the proper destiny
195 **naught** worthless
198 **distills** pours

Yet far be death from breath, annoy from joy,
Destruction from all happiness' allines.
God will not suffer famine to destroy
The hungry appetite of virtue's signs.
  These were in midst of fire, yet not harmed,
  In midst of water, yet but cooled and warmed.

Verse 22 And water-wet they were, not water-drowned;
And fire-hot they were, not fire-burned.
Their foes were both, whose hopes destruction crowned,
But yet with such a crown which ne'er returned.
  Here fire and water brought both joy and pain:
  To one disprofit, to the other gain.

The sun doth thaw what cold hath freezed before,
Undoing what congealèd ice hath done,
Yet here the hail and snow did freeze the more,
In having heat more piercing than the sun;
  A mournful spectacle unto their eyes,
  That as they die, so their fruition dies.

Verses 23, 24 Fury, once kindled with the coals of rage,
Doth hover unrecalled, slaughters untamed.
This wrath on fire, no pity could assuage,
Because they pitiless which should be blamed;
  As one in rage, which cares not who he have,
  Forgetting who to kill and who to save.

One deadly foe is fierce against the other,
As vice with virtue, virtue against vice,
Vice heartenèd by death, his heartless mother,
Virtue by God, the life of her device.
  'Tis hard to hurt or harm a villainy;
  'Tis easy to do good to verity.

Verse 25 Is grass man's meat? No, it is cattle's food,
But man doth eat the cattle which eats grass,
And feeds his carcass with their nursed-up blood,
Length'ning the lives which in a moment pass.
  Grass is good food, if it be joined with grace,
  Else sweeter food may take a sourer place.

Verse 26 Is there such life in water and in bread,
In fish, in flesh, in herbs, in growing flowers?
We eat them not alive, we eat them dead.
What fruit then hath the word of living powers?
  How can we live with that which is still dead?
  Thy grace it is, by which we all are fed.

Verses 27, 28 This is a living food, a blessèd meat,
Made to digest the burden at our hearts,
That leaden-weighted food which we first eat,
To fill the functions of our bodies' parts:
  An indigested heap, without a mean,
  Wanting thy grace, O Lord, to make it clean.

That ice which sulphur vapours could not thaw,
That hail which piercing fire could not bore,
The cool-hot sun did melt their frosty jaw,
Which neither heat nor fire could pierce before.
  Then let us take the springtime of the day,
  Before the harvest of our joys' decay.

A day may be divided, as a year, *Verse 29*
Into four climes, though of itself but one:
The morn the spring, the noon the summer's sphere,
The harvest next, evening the winter's moon.
  Then sow new seed in every new day's spring,
  And reap new fruit in day's old evëning.

Else, if too late, they will be blasted seeds;
If planted at the noontide of their growing,
Commencers of unthankful, too late deeds,
Set in the harvest of the reaper's going;
  Melting like winter ice against the sun,
  Flowing like folly's tide, and never done.

Chapter Seventeen

O fly the bed of vice, the lodge of sin! *Verse 1*
Sleep not too long in your destruction's pleasures!
Amend your wicked lives, and new begin
A more new, perfect way to heaven's treasures!
  O, rather wake and weep than sleep and joy!
  Waking is truth, sleep is a flatt'ring toy.

O take the morning of your instant good!
Be not benighted with oblivious eye.
Behold the sun which kisseth Neptune's flood,
And resalutes the world with open sky.
  Else sleep and ever sleep. God's wrath is great,
  And will not alter with too late entreat.

Why wake I them which have a sleeping mind? *Verse 2*
O words, sad sergeants to arrest my thoughts!
If waked, they cannot see, their eyes are blind,
Shut up like windolets which sleep hath bought.
  Their face is broad awake, but not their heart;
  They dream of rising, yet are loath to start.

These were the practisers how to betray
The simple-righteous with beguiling words,
And bring them in subjection to obey
Their irreligious laws and sin's accords;
  But night's black-coloured veil did cloud their will,
  And made their wish rest in performance' skill.

200 **allines** allies
208 **which ne'er returned** which remained with them permanently
226 **device** design
240 **grace** 'word' (*Geneva*)
243 **leaden-weighted food** Adam's sin?
254 **climes** seasons
263 **Melting . . . ice** 'For the hope of the unthankful shall melt as the winter ice, and flow away as unprofitable waters' (*Geneva*).
17 How the unrighteous are forgetful of their salvation; how they think to sleep hidden in the bed of vice, but are plagued with hellish darkness, with uncontrollable fears and visions.
9 **Neptune's** sea-god's
16 **windolets** small windows
24 **rest . . . skill** incapable of performance

Verse 3 The darksome clouds are summoners of rain,
In being something black and something dark;
But coal-black clouds makes it pour down amain,
Darting forth thunderbolts, and lightning's spark.
Sin of itself is black, but black with black
Augments the heavy burden of the back.

They thought that sins could hide their sinful shames,
In being demi-clouds and semi-nights;
But they had clouds enough to make their games,
Lodged in black coverings of oblivious nights.
Then was their vice afraid to lie so dark,
Troubled with visions from Alastor's park.

Verse 4 The greater poison bears the greater sway.
The greatest force hath still the greatest face.
Should night miss course, it would infect the day
With foul-risse vapours from a humorous place.
Vice hath some clouds, but yet the night hath more,
Because the night was framed and made before.

That sin which makes afraid was then afraid,
Although enchambered in a den's content.
That would not drive back fear which comes repaid,
Nor yet the echoes which the visions sent.
Both sounds and shows, both words and actïon,
Made apparitions' satisfactïon.

Verse 5 A night in pitchy mantle of distress,
Made thick with mists, and opposite to light,
As if Cocytus' mansion did possess
The gloomy vapours of suppressing sight;
A night more ugly than Alastor's pack,
Mounting all nights upon his night-made back.

The moon did mourn in sable-suited veil.
The stars, her handmaids, were in black attire.
All nightly visions told a hideous tale.
The screech-owls made the earth their dismal choir.
The moon and stars denied their twinkling eyes,
To lighten vice, which in oblivion lies.

Verse 6 Only appeared a fire in doleful blaze,
Kindled by furies, raised by envious winds,
Dreadful in sight, which put them to amaze,
Having before fury-despairing minds.
What hair in reading would not stand upright?
What pen in writing would not cease to write?

Fire is God's angel, because bright and clear,
But this an evil angel, because dread:
Evil to them which did already fear,
A second death to them which were once dead,
Annexing horror to dead-strucken life,
Connecting dolour to live nature's strife.

Deceit was then deceived, treason betrayed, Verse 7
Mischief beguiled, a night surpassing night.
Vice fought with vice, and fear was then dismayed,
Horror itself appalled at such a sight.
Sin's snare was then ensnared, the fisher caught;
Sin's net was then entrapped, the fowler fought.

Yet all this conflict was but in a dream,
A show of substance, and a shade of truth,
Illusions for to mock in flatt'ring theme,
Beguiling mischief with a glass of ruth,
For boasts require a fall, and vaunts a shame,
Which two vice had, in thinking but to game.

Sin told her creditors she was a queen, Verse 8
And now become revenge, to right their wrong,
With honey-mermaid's speech alluring seen,
Making new-pleasing words with her old tongue:
'If you be sick,' quoth she, 'I'll make you whole.'
She cures the body, but makes sick the soul.

Safe is the body when the soul is wounded.
The soul is joyful in the body's grief.
One's joy upon the other's sorrow grounded,
One's sorrow placèd in the one's relief.
Quoth sin, 'Fear nothing, know that I am here,'
When she, alas, herself was sick for fear.

A promise worthy of derision's place, Verse 9
That fear should help a fear when both are one.
She was as sick in heart, though not in face,
With inward grief, though not with outward moan;
But she clasped up the closure of the tongue,
For fear that words should do her body wrong.

Cannot the body weep without the eyes?
Yes, and frame deepest canzons of lament.
Cannot the body fear without it lies
Upon the outward show of discontent?
Yes, yes, the deeper fear sits in the heart,
And keeps the parliament of inward smart.

So sin did snare in mind, and not in face, Verse 10
The dragon's jaw, the hissing serpent's sting.
Some lived, some died, some ran a fearful race,
Some did prevent that which ill fortunes bring.
All were officious servitors to fear,
And her pale cognizance in heart did wear.

36 **Alastor's park** Alastor is the Greek spirit of vengeance.
40 **foul-risse** foul-risen
humorous moist
51 **Cocytus'** belonging to hell's river of lamentation
58 **screech-owls** birds of ill omen
73 **Deceit was then deceived** *Geneva*'s marginal note on Verse 7 links it to the triumph of Moses and Aaron over the sorcerers of Pharaoh (Exodus 7, 8).
85 **creditors** believers
104 **canzons** songs

Malice condemned herself guilty of hate,
With a malicious mouth of envious spite,
For Nemesis is her own cruel fate,
Turning her wrath upon her own delight.
We need no witness for a guilty thought,
Which to condemn itself a thousand brought.

Verse 11 For fear deceives itself in being fear.
It fears itself in being still afraid.
It fears to weep, and yet it sheds a tear.
It fears itself, and yet it is obeyed:
The usher unto death, a death to doom,
A doom to die in horror's fearful tomb.

Verse 12 His own betrayer, yet fears to betray,
He fears his life by reason of his name.
He fears lament, because it brings decay,
And blames himself in that he merits blame.
He is tormented, yet denies the pain;
He is the king of fear, yet loath to reign.

Verse 13 His sons were they which slept and dreamt of fear,
A waking sleep, and yet a sleepy waking,
Which passed that night more longer than a year,
Being grief's pris'ners, and of sorrow's taking;
Slept in night's dungeon insupportable,
Lodged in night's horror too endurable.

O sleep, the image of long-lasting woe!
O waking image of long-lasting sleep!
The hollow cave where visions come and go,
Where serpents hiss, where mandrakes groan and creep!
O fearful show, betrayer of a soul,
Dying each heart in white, each white in foul!

Verse 14 A guileful hole, a prison of deceit,
Yet nor deceit nor guile in being dead;
Snare without snarer, net without a bait,
A common lodge, and yet without a bed;
A hollow-sounding vault, known and unknown,
Yet not for mirth, but too too well for moan.

Verse 15 'Tis a free prison, a chained liberty,
A freedom's cave, a sergeant and a bail.
It keeps close prisoners, yet doth set them free,
Their clogs not iron, but a clog of wail.
It stays them not, and yet they cannot go;
Their chain is discontent, their prison woe.

Still it did gape for more, and still more had, *Verse 16*
Like greedy avarice without content;
Like to Avernus, which is never glad
Before the dead-lived wicked souls be sent.
Pull in thy head, thou sorrow's tragedy,
And leave to practise thy old cruelty.

The merry shepherd cannot walk alone,
Tuning sweet madrigals of harvest's joy,
Carving love's roundelays on every stone,
Hanging on every tree some amorous toy,
But thou with sorrow interlines his song,
Opening thy jaws of death to do him wrong.

O now I know thy chain, thy clog, thy fetter, *Verse 17*
Thy free-chained prison, and thy cloggèd walk!
'Tis gloomy darkness, sin's eternal debtor.
'Tis poisoned buds from Acherontic stalk.
Sometime 'tis hissing winds which are their bonds,
Sometime enchanting birds which binds their hands.

Sometime the foaming rage of water's stream, *Verse 18*
Or clatt'ring down of stones upon a stone,
Or skipping beasts at Titan's gladsome beam,
Or roaring lion's noise at one alone,
Or babbling Echo, tell-tale of each sound,
From mouth to sky, from sky unto the ground.

Can suchlike fears follow man's mortal pace, *Verses 19, 20*
Within dry wilderness of wettest woe?
It was God's providence, his will, his grace,
To make midnoon midnight in being so.
Midnight with sin, midnoon where virtue lay:
That place was night, all other places day.

The sun, not past the middle line of course,
Did clearly shine upon each labour's gain,
Not hind'ring daily toil of mortal force,
Nor clouding earth with any gloomy stain.
Only night's image was apparent there,
With heavy-leaden appetite of fear.

Chapter Eighteen

You know the eagle by her soaring wings, *Verse 1*
And how the swallow takes a lower pitch.
You know the day is clear, and clearness brings,
And how the night is poor, though gloomy-rich.
This eagle virtue is, which mounts on high;
The other sin, which hates the heavens' eye.

117 **Nemesis** goddess of retribution
142 **mandrakes** poisonous plants whose forked roots were thought to have human properties
154 **clogs** blocks attached to the leg or neck to prevent escape
159 **Avernus** sulphurous central Italian lake, thought to be the entrance to (and thus synonymous with) hell
164 **madrigals** part songs for three or more voices
165 **roundelays** simple songs with refrains
172 **Acherontic** hellish; pertaining to one of the rivers of hell
179 **Echo** nymph, reduced to disembodied voice
187 **middle line of course** the midpoint of its daily journey, noon; literally, the celestial meridian which the sun crosses at noon
18 Triumphs of virtue and wisdom over mischief and vice: how Moses was preserved, for the later salvation of the repentant Israelites; how God struck down the firstborn of the Egyptians, his punishment falling equally on master and servant; how the word of God plagued the ungodly with fearful visions of their guilt and punishment; how even the Israelites were plagued, until divine wisdom, through Aaron, put death to flight.

This day is wisdom, being bright and clear.
This night is mischief, being black and foul.
The brightest day doth wisdom's glory wear.
The pitchy night puts on a blacker roll.
  Thy saints, O Lord, were at their labour's hire,
  At whose heard voice the wicked did admire.

Verse 2 They thought that virtue had been clothed in night,
Captive to darkness, prisoner unto hell,
But it was sin itself, vice, and despite,
Whose wishèd harbours do in darkness dwell.
  Virtue's immortal soul had midday's light;
  Mischief's eternal soul had midday's night.

For virtue is not subject unto vice,
But vice is subject unto virtue's seat.
One mischief is not thawed with other's ice,
But more adjoined to one, makes one more great.
  Sin virtue's captive is, and kneels for grace,
  Requesting pardon for her rude-run race.

Verse 3 The tongue of virtue's life cannot pronounce
The doom of death, or death of dying doom.
'Tis merciful, and will not once renounce
Repentant tears to wash a sinful room.
  Your sin-shine was not sun-shine of delight,
  But shining sin in mischief's sunny night.

Now by repentance you are bathed in bliss,
Blessed in your bath, eternal by your deeds.
Behold, you have true light, and cannot miss
The heav'nly food which your salvation feeds.
  True love, true life, true light, your portions true:
  What hate, what strife, what night can danger you?

Verse 4 O happy, when you pared your o'ergrown faults,
Your sin, like eagle's claws, past growth of time,
All underminèd with destruction's vaults,
Full of old filth, proceeding from new slime;
  Else had you been deformèd like to those
  Which were your friends, but now become your foes.

Those which are worthy of eternal pain,
Foes which are worthy of immortal hate,
Dimming the glory of thy children's gain
With cloudy vapours set at darkness' rate:
  Making new laws, which are too old in crime;
  Making old-wicked laws serve a new time.

Wicked? No, bloody laws. Bloody? Yea, worse, *Verse 5*
If any worse may have a worser name.
Men? O no, murd'rers, not of men's remorse,
For they are shameful, these exempt from shame.
  What, shall I call them slaughter-drinking hearts?
  Too good a name for their too ill deserts.

Murder was in their thoughts, they thought to slay.
And who? Poor infants, harmless innocents.
But murder cannot sleep. It will betray
Her murd'rous self with self-disparagements.
  One child, poor remnant, did reprove their deeds,
  And God destroyed the bloody murd'rers' seeds.

Was God destroyer then? No, he was just, *Verse 6*
A judge severe, yet of a kind remorse;
Severe to those in whom there was no trust,
Kind to the babes which were of little force.
  Poor babes, half murdered in whole murder's thought,
  Had not one infant their escaping wrought.

'Twas God which breathed his spirit in the child,
The lively image of his self-like face.
'Twas God which drowned their children, which defiled
Their thoughts with blood, their hearts with murder's
    place;
  For that night's tidings our old fathers joyed,
  Because their foes by water were destroyed.

Was God a murd'rer in this tragedy? *Verse 7*
No, but a judge how blood should be repaid.
Was't he which gave them unto misery?
No. 'Twas themselves which miseries obeyed.
  Their thoughts did kill and slay within their hearts,
  Murd'ring themselves, wounding their inward parts.

When shines the sun, but when the moon doth rest?
When rests the sun, but when the moon doth shine?
When joys the righteous? When their foes are least.
And when doth virtue live? When vice doth pine.
  Virtue doth live when villainy doth die;
  Wisdom doth smile when misery doth cry.

The summer days are longer than the nights. *Verse 8*
The winter nights are longer than the days.
They show both virtue's loves and vice's spites,
Sin's lowest fall, and wisdom's highest raise.
  The night is foe to day, as naught to good;
  The day is foe to night, as fear to food.

10 **roll** portion of a head dress
11 **labour's hire** reward
12 **admire** wonder, marvel
33 **true light** the 'burning pillar of fire' (*Geneva*) which led the Israelites in the wilderness
39 **vaults** sewers
43 **Those…pain** Pharaoh and the Egyptians
59 **One child** Moses
67–70 **'Twas God…place** This seems closer to blasphemy than Calvinism. The passage is theologically defensible only if one interprets the second 'which' as referring to 'their'. God, that is, drowned the children of those who defiled their thoughts with blood. This would be stretching a point, except that Middleton's syntax is frequently ungrammatical (D.S.).
69 **drowned their children** 'thou hast taken away the multitude of their children and destroyed them all together in the mighty water' (*Geneva*, 18:5); there is no comparable event in Exodus
89 **naught** mischief, vice

A king may wear a crown, but full of strife,
The outward show of a small-lasting space.
Mischief may live, but yet a deadly life.
Sorrow may grieve in heart and joy in face.
Virtue may live disturbed with vice's pain;
God sends this virtue a more better reign.

Verse 9 She doth possess a crown, and not a care,
Yet cares, in having none but self-like awe.
She hath a sceptre without care or fear,
Yet fears the Lord, and careth for the law.
As much as she doth rise, so much sin falls,
Subject unto her law, slave to her calls.

Now righteousness bears sway, and vice put down,
Virtue is queen, treading on mischief's head,
The law of God sancited with renown,
Religion placed in wisdom's quiet bed.
Now joyful hymns are tunèd by delight,
And now we live in love, and not in spite.

Verse 10 Strong-hearted vice's sobs have pierced the ground,
In the deep cistern of the centre's breast,
Wailing their living fortunes with dead sound,
Accents of grief, and actions of unrest.
It is not sin herself, it is her seed,
Which, drowned in sea, lies there for sea's foul weed.

It is the fruit of murder's bloody womb,
The lost fruition of a murd'rous race,
A little stone which would have made a tomb
To bury virtue with a sin-bold face.
Methinks I hear the echoes of the vaults
Sound and resound their old-new-weeping faults.

Verse 11 View the dead carcasses of human state,
The outsides of the soul, case of the hearts.
Behold the king, behold the subject's fate,
Behold each limb and bone of earthen arts.
Tell me the difference then of every thing,
And who a subject was, and who a king.

The self-same knowledge lies in this dead scene,
Vailed to the tragic cypress of lament.
Behold that man, which hath a master been,
That king, which would have climbed above content.
Behold! Their slaves, by them upon the earth,
Have now as high a seat, as great a birth.

Verse 12 The ground hath made all even which were odd,
Those equal which had inequality;
Yet all alike were fashionèd by God,
In body's form, but not in heart's degree.
One difference had, in sceptre, crown, and throne,
Yet crowned, ruled, placed in care, in grief, in moan.

For it was care to wear a crown of grief,
And it was grief to wear a crown of care;
The king death's subject, death his empire's thief,
Which makes unequal state, and equal fare:
More dead than were alive, and more to die
Than would be buried with a mortal eye.

O well-fed earth with ill-digesting food! *Verse 13*
O well-ill food, because both flesh and sin!
Sin made it sick, which never did it good.
Sin made it well. Her well doth worse begin.
The earth, more hungry than was Tantal's jaws,
Had flesh and blood held in her earthen paws.

Now could belief some quiet harbour find,
When all her foes were mantled in the ground,
Before their sin-enchantments made it blind,
Their magic arts, their necromantic sound.
Now truth hath got some place to speak and hear,
And whatsoe'er she speaks, she doth not fear.

When Phoebe's axletree was limned with pale, *Verse 14*
Pale which becometh night, night which is black,
Hemmed round about with gloomy-shining veil,
Borne up by clouds, mounted on silence' back;
And when night's horses, in the running wain,
O'ertook the middest of their journey's pain;

Thy word, O Lord, descended from thy throne, *Verses 15, 16*
The royal mansion of thy power's command,
As a fierce man of war in time of moan,
Standing in midst of the destroyèd land,
And brought thy precept as a burning steven,
Reaching from heaven to earth, from earth to heaven.

Now was the night far spent, and morning's wings *Verse 17*
Flew thorough sleepy thoughts and made them dream,
Hying apace to welcome sunny springs,
And give her time of day to Phoebus' beam.
No sooner had she flown unto the east,
But dreamy passage did disturb their rest.

And then, like sleepy-waking hearts and eyes,
Turned up the fainting closures of their faces,
Which between day and night in slumber lies,
Keeping their waky and their sleepy places;
And lo, a fearing dream and dreaming fear
Made every eye let fall a sleepy tear.

97 **She** virtue, righteousness
103 **Now** after the Passover, the destruction of the firstborn of Egypt, the subsequent plague; what follows is a triumphant moralizing of the scene of death.
105 **sancited** established; evidently a Middleton coinage, from Latin *sancire*
117 **stone** fruit pit (following from 'seed', 'fruit', 'fruition')
128 **Vailed** lowered in deference
cypress fine black mourning kerchief
149 **Tantal's** belonging to Tantalus (mythical king of Phrygia, condemned never to gain the ever-receding food and drink just beyond his reach)
157 **axletree** axle; axis of revolution
limned painted
161 **wain** wagon
167 **steven** voice
171 **Hying apace** speeding swiftly
176 **closures** *fig.* eyes?

Verses 18, 19 A tear half-wet from they themselves half-lived,
Poor dry-wet tear, too moist a wet-dry face;
A white-red face, whose red-white colour strived
To make anatomy of either place;
Two champions, both resolved in face's field,
And both had half, yet either scorned to yield.

They which were wont to mount above the ground
Hath leaden, quick-glued sinews, forced to lie,
One here, one there, in prison, yet unbound,
Heart-striving life and death to live and die;
Nor were they ignorant of fate's decree,
In being told before what they should be.

Verse 20 Their falsest visions showed the truest cause,
False because fantasies, true because haps;
For dreams, though kindled by sleep-idle pause,
Sometime true indices of danger's claps,
As well doth prove in these sin-sleeping lines
That dreams are falsest shows, and truest signs.

By this time death had longer pilgrimage,
And was encagèd in more living breasts.
Now every ship had fleeting anchorage.
Both good and bad were punished with unrests.
But yet God's heavy plague endured not long,
For anger quenched herself with her self wrong.

Verse 21 Not so, for heat can never cool with heat,
Nor cold can warm a cold, nor ice thaw ice.
Anger is fire, and fire is anger's meat.
Then how can anger cool her hot device?
The sun doth thaw the ice with melting harm;
Ice cannot cool the sun which makes it warm.

It was celestial fire, terrestrial cold.
It was celestial cold, terrestrial fire.
A true and holy prayer which is bold
To cool the heat of anger's hot desire,
Pronouncèd by a servant of thy word,
To ease the miseries which wraths afford.

Verse 22 Weapons and wit are double links of force.
If one unknit, they both have weaker strength.
The longer be the chain, the longer course,
If measured by duplicity of length.
If weapons fail, wit is the better part;
Wit failing, weapons have the weaker heart.

Prayer is weak in strength, yet strong in wit,
And can do more than strength, in being wise.
Thy word, O Lord, is wisdom, and in it
Doth lie more force than forces can surprise.
Man did not overcome his foes with arms,
But with thy word, which conquers greater harms.

That word it was with which the world was framed, *Verse 23*
The heavens made, mortality ordained.
That word it was with which all men were named,
In which one word there are all words contained:
The breath of God, the life of mortal state,
The enemy to vice, the foe to hate.

When death pressed down the sin-dead-living souls,
And drew the curtain of their seeing day,
This word was virtue's shield, and death's controls,
Which shielded those which never went astray;
For when the dead did die and end in sin,
The living had assurance to begin.

Are all these deeds accomplished in one word? *Verse 24*
O sovereign word, chief of all words and deeds!
O salve of safety, wisdom's strongest sword,
Both food and hunger, which both starves and feeds:
Food unto life, because of living power,
Hunger to those whom death and sins devour.

For they which lived were those which virtue loved,
And those which virtue loved did love to live.
Thrice happy these whom no destruction moved;
She present there, which love and life did give.
They bore the mottoes of eternal fame
On diapasons of their father's name.

Here death did change his pale to purple hue, *Verse 25*
Blushing, against the nature of his face,
To see such bright aspècts, such splendent view,
Such heav'nly paradise of earthly grace,
And hid with life's quick force his ebon dart
Within the crannies of his meagre heart;

Descending to the place from whence he came,
With rich-stored chariot of fresh-bleeding wounds,
Sore-grievèd bodies from a soul's sick name,
Sore grievèd souls, in bodies' sin-sick sounds.
Death was afraid to stay where life should be,
For they are foes, and cannot well agree.

184 **anatomy** skeleton, especially one prepared for examination; from *Geneva*'s 'shewed the cause of his death'
194 **haps** unfortunate events, mishaps
196 **claps** blows
204 **self** own
215 **servant of thy word** Aaron
220 **duplicity** doubleness
226 **surprise** overcome, overpower
252 **diapasons** again, as at 6.188, Middleton misunderstands the musical term; he uses it here for *Geneva*'s 'diadem'.
255 **splendent** extremely brilliant
257 **ebon** black
258 **meagre** emaciated
19 Despite all these torments, and despite apparent repentance, the Egyptians still persecuted the Israelites, broke faith and pursued them to the Red Sea and their own destruction; God, both merciful and vengeful, fed his starving people with quails, but plagued the Egyptians for their persecutions; at last the whole earth is miraculously transformed by God in aid of his faithful people.

Chapter Nineteen

Verses 1, 2 Avaunt, destroyer, with thy hungry jaws,
Thy thirsty heart, thy longing ashy bones!
The righteous live. They be not in thy laws,
Nor subjects to thy deep oppressing moans.
Let it suffice that we have seen thy show,
And tasted but the shadow of thy woe.

Yet stay, and bring thy empty car again:
More ashy vessels do attend thy pace.
More passengers expect thy coming wain.
More groaning pilgrims long to see thy face.
Wrath now attends the passage of misdeeds,
And thou shalt still be stored with souls that bleeds.

Verse 3 Some lie half-dead, while others dig their graves
With weak-forced tears to moist a long-dry ground;
But tears on tears in time will make whole waves,
To bury sin with overwhelming sound.
Their eyes for mattocks serve, their tears for spades,
And they themselves are sextons by their trades.

What is their fee? Lament. Their payment? Woe.
Their labour? Wail. Their practice? Misery.
And can their conscience serve to labour so?
Yes, yes, because it helpeth villainy.
Though eyes did stand in tears, and tears in eyes,
They did another foolishness devise.

Verse 4 So that what prayer did, sin did undo,
And what the eyes did win, the heart did lose.
Whom virtue reconciled, vice did forego.
Whom virtue did forego, that vice did choose.
O had their hearts been just, eyes had been winners!
Their eyes were just, but hearts new sin's beginners.

Verse 5 They digged true graves with eyes, but not with hearts,
Repentance in their face, vice in their thought.
Their delving eyes did take the sexton's parts.
The heart undid the labour which eyes wrought.
A new strange death was portion for their toil,
While virtue sat as judge to end the broil.

Verse 6 Had tongue been joined with eyes, tongue had not strayed.
Had eyes been joined to heart, heart then had seen.
But O, in wanting eyesight it betrayed
The dungeon of misdeeds where it had been.
So, many living in this orb of woe
Have heaved-up eyes, but yet their hearts are low.

This change of sin did make a change of feature,
A new strange death, a misery untold,
A new reform of every old-new creature,
New-serving offices which time made old:
New-living virtue from an old-dead sin,
Which ends in ill what doth in good begin.

When death did reap the harvest of despite, *Verse 7*
The wicked ears of sin and mischief's seed,
Filling the mansion of eternal night
With heavy-leaden clods of sinful breed,
Life sowed the plants of immortality,
To welcome old-made new felicity.

The clouds, the gloomy curtains of the air,
Drawn and redrawn with the four-wingèd winds,
Made all of borrowed vapours, darksome fair,
Did overshade their tents, which virtue finds.
The Red Sea's deep was made a dry-trod way,
Without impediment, or stop, or stay.

The thirsty winds, with overtoiling puffs, *Verses 8, 9*
Did drink the ruddy ocean's water dry,
Tearing the zone's hot-cold, whole-ragged ruffs,
With ruffling conflicts in the field of sky;
So that dry earth did take wet water's place,
With sandy mantle and hard grounded face.

That way, which never was a way before,
Is now a trodden path, which was untrod,
Through which the people went as on a shore,
Defended by the stretched-out arm of God,
Praising his wondrous works, his mighty hand,
Making the land of sea, the sea of land.

That breast where anger slept is mercy's bed. *Verse 10*
That breast where mercy wakes is anger's cave.
When mercy lives, then Nemesis is dead,
And one for either's corpse makes other's grave.
Hate furrows up a grave to bury love,
And love doth press down hate; it cannot move.

This breast is God, which ever wakes in both.
Anger is his revenge, mercy his love.
He sent them flies instead of cattle's growth,
And multitudes of frogs for fishes strove.
Here was his anger shown, and his remorse,
When he did make dry land of water-course.

The sequel proves what actor is the chief. *Verse 11*
All things beginning knows, but none their end.
The sequel unto mirth is weeping grief,
As doth mishaps with happiness contend;
For both are agents in this orb of weeping,
And one doth wake when other falls a-sleeping.

1 **Avaunt** Depart
destroyer death
8 **ashy vessels** dead carcasses
9 **wain** wagon
17 **mattocks** tools for dislodging roots and stones
18 **sextons** gravediggers
24 **another foolishness** the pursuit of the Israelites
35 **portion** payment
36 **broil** quarrel
63 **zone's** sky's
ruffs fringes, ruffles; clouds, continuing the figure from 55
64 **ruffling** blustering, turbulent
75 **Nemesis** goddess of retribution
79 **both** mercy and anger
83 **remorse** pity
85 **sequel** outcome
actor agent

Yet, should man's eyes pay tribute every hour,
With tributary tears to sorrow's shrine,
He would all drown himself with his own shower,
And never find the leaf of mercy's line.
They in God's anger wailed, in his love joyed;
Their love brought lust ere love had lust destroyed.

Verse 12 The sun of joy dried up their tear-wet eyes,
And sat as lord upon their sobbing heart,
For when one comfort lives, one sorrow dies,
Or ends in mirth what it begun in smart.
What greater grief than hunger-starvèd mood?
What greater mirth than satisfying food?

Quails from the fishy bosom of the sea
Came to their comforts which were living-starved,
But punishments fell in the sinners' way,
Sent down by thunderbolts which they deserved.
Sin-fed these sinners were, hate-cherishèd;
According unto both they perishèd.

Verse 13 Sin-fed, because their food was seed of sins,
And bred new sin with old-digested meat;
Hate-cherishèd, in being hatred's twins,
And sucking cruelty from tiger's teat:
Was it not sin to err and go astray?
Was it not hate to stop a stranger's way?

Was it not sin to see and not to know?
Was it not sin to know and not receive?
Was it not hate to be a stranger's foe,
And make them captives which did them relieve?
Yes, it was greatest sin first for to leave them,
And it was greatest hate last to deceive them.

Verse 14 O hungry cannibals which know no fill,
But still do starving feed, and feeding starve!
How could you so deceive? How could you spill
Their loving selves which did yourselves preserve?
Why did you suck your pelican to death,
Which fed you too too well with his own breath?

O, say that cruelty can have no law,
And then you speak with a mild-cruel tongue;
Or say that avarice lodged in your jaw,
And then you do yourselves but little wrong.
Say what you will, for what you say is spite
'Gainst ill-come strangers which did merit right.

You lay in ambush. O deceitful snares, *Verse* 15
Enticing baits, beguiling sentinels!
You added grief to grief, and cares to cares,
Tears unto weeping eyes where tears did dwell.
O multitudes of sin, legions of vice,
Which thaws with sorrow sorrow's frozen ice!

A banquet was prepared, the fare deceit,
The dishes poison, and the cup despite,
The table mischief, and the cloth a bait,
Like spinner's web t'entrap the strange fly's flight.
Pleasure was strewed upon the top of pain,
Which, once digested, spread through every vein.

O ill conductors of misguided feet, *Verse* 16
Into a way of death, a path of guile!
Poor pilgrims which their own destruction meet
In habitations of an unknown isle!
O had they left that broad deceiving way,
They had been right, and never gone astray!

But mark the punishment which did ensue
Upon those ill-misleading villainies:
They blinded were themselves with their self view,
And fell into their own-made miseries,
Seeking the entrance of their dwelling places
With blinded eyes and dark misguided faces.

Lo, here was snares ensnared, and guiles beguiled, *Verse* 17
Deceit deceived, and mischief was misled.
Eyes blinded sight, and thoughts the hearts defiled.
Life, living in aspècts, was dying-dead.
Eyes thought for to mislead, and were misled;
Feet went to make mistreads, and did mistread.

At this proud fall the elements were glad,
And did embrace each other with a kiss.
All things were joyful which before were sad:
The pilgrims in their way, and could not miss.
As when the sound of music doth resound
With changing tune, so did the changèd ground.

The birds forsook the air, the sheep the fold. *Verse* 18
The eagle pitchèd low, the swallow high.
The nightingale did sleep, and uncontrolled
Forsook the prickle of her nature's eye.
The seely worm was friends with all her foes,
And sucked the dew-tears from the weeping rose.

94 **leaf of mercy's line** the written line (containing his salvation) on mercy's page, or in mercy's book (*fig.*); compare *Timon*, 14.118: 'not within the leaf of pity writ'.

103 **Quails** relatives of the partridge; despite the authority of Numbers 11:31, quails are not sea-birds

105 **sinners'** apparently, the Egyptians' (supported by *Geneva*'s marginal note); Exodus at this point tells the story of the forgetful Israelites and their subsequent sins and punishments.

114 **to stop a stranger's way** to place the Israelites (strangers or foreigners) in bondage

125 **pelican** the Israelites; but most often associated emblematically with Christ, from the belief that the adult pelican feeds its (ungrateful) young with its own blood from a wound pecked in its breast

142 **spinner's** spider's
strange foreign

160 **aspècts** looks, glances

The sparrow tuned the lark's sweet melody.
The lark in silence sung a dirge of dole.
The linnet helped the lark in malady.
The swans forsook the choir of billow-roll.
The dry-land fowl did make the sea their nest;
The wet-sea fish did make the land their rest.

Verse 19 The swans, the choristers which did complain
In inward feeling of an outward loss,
And filled the choir of waves with laving pain,
Yet dancing in their wail with surge's toss,
Forsook her cradle-billow-mountain bed,
And hies her unto land, there to be fed.

Her sea-fare now is land-fare of content.
Old change is changèd new, yet all is change.
The fishes are her food, and they are sent
Unto dry land, to creep, to feed, to range.
Now coolest water cannot quench the fire,
But makes it proud, in hottest hot desire.

Verse 20 The ev'ning of a day is morn to night.
The ev'ning of a night is morn to day.
The one is Phoebe's clime, which is pale-bright,
The other Phoebus in more light array.
She makes the mountains limp in chill-cold snow;
He melts their eyes and makes them weep for woe.

His beams, ambassadors of his hot will,
Through the transparent element of air,
Doth only his warm ambassage fulfil,
And melts the icy jaw of Phoebe's hair;
Yet those, though fiery flames, could not thaw cold,
Nor break the frosty glue of winter's mould.

Here nature slew herself, or, at the least, *Verse* 21
Did tame the passage of her hot aspècts.
All things have nature to be worst or best,
And must incline to that which she affects.
But nature missed herself in this same part,
For she was weak, and had not nature's heart.

'Twas God which made her weak and makes her strong,
Resisting vice, assisting righteousness,
Assisting and resisting right and wrong,
Making this epilogue in equalness.
'Twas God, his people's aid, their wisdom's friend,
In whom I did begin, with whom I end.

A Jove surgit opus; de Jove finit opus.

178 **forsook . . . billow-roll** abandoned the sea
183 **laving** washing, bathing
186 **her** the swan's; Middleton's abrupt change of number is awkward, but it does restore parallelism with the singular birds in Verse 18.
195 **Phoebe's clime** the moon's territory
204 **frosty glue** Premodern commentaries identify this ('which seemed to be ice, and was of a nature that would melt, and yet was an immortal meat' in *Geneva* 19:21) with manna, not snow; again Middleton appears to have misunderstood the text (D.S.).
216.1 ***A Jove . . . finit opus.*** See note to the Epigraph. Now, echoing 216, Middleton completes the Ovidian phrase and with it ends his labours: Of God the work arises; in God the work ends.

MICROCYNICON: SIX SNARLING SATIRES

Edited by Wendy Wall

Microcynicon is chiefly famous because it was publicly burned on 4 June 1599 shortly after its publication. Three days earlier the Archbishop of Canterbury and the Bishop of London ordered the suppression of ten books including Middleton's, and banned the publication of all satires, presumably because the genre was scurrilous and dangerously topical. Lynda Boose has argued that it was satire's status as a new brand of self-loathing pornography that attracted the Archbishop's attention. Whether the texts were censored primarily for moral or political reasons remains unclear. Joseph Hall's influential precursor text, *Virgidemiarum*, also included in the order, was mysteriously spared from the flames. While some writers ignored the order and continued to write satires, Middleton, like John Marston, mainly directed his satirical energies toward the commercially-promising stage. *Microcynicon* disappeared and was not reprinted in the seventeenth century. By leaving *Microcynicon* in the ashes of obscurity for almost the next four hundred years, many critics have unwittingly validated the censor's notion that the text was better left unknown. Its spectacularly controversial inauguration, however, highlights how this diminutive octavo volume exemplifies the conventions and contradictions of late sixteenth-century satire.

Satire always ushers the reader into a degenerate world of rogues, liars, panders and sinners. *Microcynicon* is no exception. It shows us snippets of London life—from the dinner table of the haughty Superbia, to Droone's elaborate schemes to trick a gull in a tavern, to the cross-dressed Pyander's titillating sexual deceptions in public streets. In this work, as in all of its kind, the satirist holds up for our censure a world gone awry. Each of *Microcynicon*'s six poems targets a specific vice: usury, prodigality, pride, cheating, cross-dressing, foolishness. As in *The Nightingale and the Ant* and *The Black Book*, Middleton writes here in a didactic genre designed to prevent threats to the social and moral order. *Microcynicon*, however, shows us Middleton's only foray into the genre of formal verse satire, a form established by Horace, Juvenal, and Persius.

Middleton was inspired to write *Microcynicon* by the outpouring of English satires at the turn of the century, primarily by Hall's *Virgidemiarum* (1597–8), and Marston's two 'snarling' satires, *Pygmalion's Image and Certain Satires* (1598) and *The Scourge of Villainy* (1598), but also by Everard Guilpin's *Skialetheia* (1598), William Rankins's *Seven Satires* (1598); and John Donne's manuscript *Satires* (1593?). In these works, the speakers display little of the marked humility prevalent in the medieval *Piers Plowman*. Instead writers deploy a combative rhetoric which can be, as Hall describes, 'unpleasing both to the unskilful and over-musical ear'. Middleton places his work squarely in these literary circles by imitating Hall's preface, echoing Marston's indignant language, presenting conventional satire themes (the spendthrift heir, the hermaphrodite), and toying with a genre seen as appropriate for launching a poet's career in the 1590s literary milieu. Joining contemporary writers who abandoned Petrarchan and Ovidian love traditions in favour of the emergent Jacobean impulse toward burlesque and parody, he nevertheless departs from Marston's furious tone of rebuke and Hall's Horatian and urbane criticism of literary style. Instead Middleton presents character sketches focusing on social follies rather than invective fuelled by disdain for poetic practices.

In formal satire, the (male) speaker displays his intimate knowledge of human frailty. For this reason, as Alvin Kernan notes, the satiric persona can appear as unsavoury as his subject matter. Given this dilemma, the suppression of *Microcynicon* brilliantly demonstrates one of the strange tensions surrounding satiric writing: in engaging a self-professed 'low' genre that denounces low social modes, the satirist is always in danger of absorption into the world of vice. Indeed the issue of self-incrimination is a prevalent theme in *Microcynicon*.

Written in rhymed iambic couplets, *Microcynicon* moves from the discursive style of classical satire in the first two poems to narrative vignettes in the next three. In effect, Middleton wanders from the declamatory to the dramatic. In keeping with the expected obscure style of the genre, the first poem opens with the metaphysical world of the avaricious usurer Cron. After mourning the decline of the golden age, the speaker places Cron at the London Exchange and elliptically describes Cron's various fallacious rationalizations for greed: money constitutes heaven, hell, and earth in his cosmology of gold. The second satire vivifies the ironic wages of Cron's sin by showing how his wastrel heir Zodon lavishly spends the miser's hoard. A typical Renaissance social climber, Zodon has pretensions that lead him to financial ruin. Middleton specifically mocks Zodon's haughty demands for material pampering and social respect. When Zodon's extravagance blurs into lust, we see Middleton's awareness of the conceptual linkages between monetary and sexual circulation. The second satire thus demonstrates the Renaissance tendency to express social problems through the language of eroticism.

In Satires Three, Four, and Five, the speaker appears to abandon his moral stance and instead to revel in the

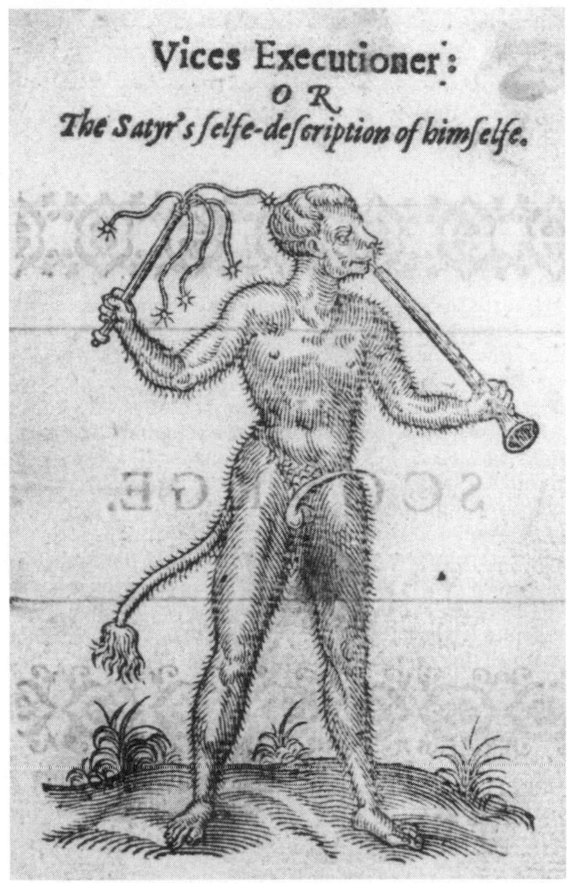

Vice's Executioner, from George Wither, *Abuses Stript and Whipt* (1617).

energy revealed by his character sketches of Superbia, Droone, and Pyander. In the satire on pride, Superbia decides to kill herself in the wake of a spectacularly lavish luncheon because she sees someone more beautiful than she. After deftly conveying the seductive delights of the meal, Middleton shifts from Superbia's narcissism to a related sketch of Lady Tiptoes, who pitches a temper tantrum because she detects a spot on her gorgeous frock. Middleton follows Renaissance convention both in gendering pride as female and in exemplifying it as the fetishization of food and clothing. Critiques of courtly foppery, fastidiousness, and what Puritan-influenced conduct books call 'prodigal nicety' and 'dainty-mouthed' behaviour were often directed at women or labelled as effeminate traits. Barnaby Rich, for instance, notes that 'Far-fetched and dear bought is good for Ladies'. If Zodon represents the hubristic male social climber who is punished for acquisitiveness, Superbia embodies the paralysis that can ensue from the overvaluation of creature comforts.

Satire Four offers its readers a foray into rogue literature by presenting a single continuous narrative about Droone's triumph in wining, dining, and pickpocketing a gullible dinner companion. Here Middleton contributes to the vogue for cony-catching pamphlets popularized by Robert Greene. These works make visible the operations of a powerful underground of cheaters and thieves who trade on human greed and self-interest. The most striking element of this satire is the liveliness of the poetic style, the cohesion of the story, and the one-line moral that is remembered only in the final line. Satire Four thus dramatizes how the satirist can become intrigued by the moral flaws that he condemns.

This problem reaches its pinnacle in the fifth satire when we enter the world of the transvestite Pyander, for here the speaker confesses that he has actually frequented bawdy-houses and lusted after this cross-dressed boy. The speaker coyly feigns reluctance at exposing Pyander's secret, but eventually decides to publicize the boy's duplicity:

> And shall I then procure eternal blame
> By secret cloaking of Pyander's shame,
> And he not blush?
> By heaven I will not! I'll not burn in hell
> For false Pyander, though I loved him well.

Middleton's singular use of the half-line accentuates the drama of this confession. In the Prologue the speaker narrates his wild origins; it is no coincidence that the speaker's complicity in vice is established in the fifth satire in peculiarly sexual terms: the satirist, like the lustful mythological satyr to which he was falsely linked etymologically, is known for his physicality. Elizabethans speculated that satire had its origins in satyr plays in which actors assumed the character of woodland creatures to launch savage attacks. 'A satire is . . . a very railing, only ordained to rebuke vice . . . . The Satires had their name of uplandish gods, that were rude, lascivious and wanton of behaviour', Thomas Langley declared in 1546. In *Microcynicon* the speaker appropriately confesses his sordid motive of revenge in the satire most explicitly connected with sexuality. If satire always turns on inherent contradictions in the moral but beastly persona, as Kernan argues, then that persona is one peculiarly linked to eroticism. In *Abuses Stript and Whipt* (1617), for instance, George Wither's satyr-speaker readily admits his own sexual culpability: 'An Executioner am I, | Of Lust, and wanton Venery. | Thus are the vices scourg'd by me, | Yet my self from vice not free'.

The fifth satire is also conventional in establishing the theme of homoeroticism. Marston, Hall, Rankins, and Weever all describe the allure of the seductive boy 'Ganymede'. Middleton's reference to Sodom makes clear that his satire is not just about Pyander's gender trickery, but also about what we now understand as homosexual desire. In fact, Pyander's 'trick' becomes emblematic of satire's instability: the desire for (moral or sexual) difference erodes into a familiar sameness. The satirist's efforts to stand apart from the arena of sin only expose his immersion within it, and the distinction between high and low moral worlds collapse. The result is a 'crisis of categories', of which, Marjorie Garber argues, the transvestite is a favourite cultural symbol. Neither male nor female, Pyander exists to point to the general breakdown of cultural categories. Middleton neatly describes Pyander's undecideable nature:

Sometimes he jets it like a gentleman,
Otherwhiles much like a wanton courtesan.
But truth to tell a man or woman whether,
I cannot say, she's excellent in either.
But if report may certify a truth,
She's neither of either, but a cheating youth.

Unsurprisingly critics have downplayed these homoerotic elements. In John Payne Collier's mock dialogue about *Microcynicon*, for instance, the characters decide that this satire reveals the author's negative view of women; they further determine that Pyander's 'ingling' (the word for sodomizing) is throughout the text a misprint for 'jugling'. Sodomy, however, was understood in the Renaissance as a channelling of sexual energy for purposes other than reproduction, an excess of desire. Homoeroticism thus ties neatly into the writer's understanding of satire's indebtedness to the Bacchanalian wild man; and *Microcynicon* exposes how eroticism pervades the issues of social critique and self-incrimination central to the genre.

The final satire presents an intentionally confusing dialogue between a fool and a satirist. In a self-conscious moment, the satirist finds himself satirized by an 'Innocent' who steps into the poem to interrogate him about his writing. The difficulty that the reader has in disentangling the speakers is deliberate: ascertaining the boundaries between satirist and fool (both of whom are called an 'ass') becomes part of the game. Verifying Juvenal's famous credo, '*Difficile est saturam non scribere*' (it is difficult not to write satire), the speaker suggests that his writing is involuntary: 'It is impossible, streams that are barred their course, | Swell with more rage, and far more greater force, | Until their full-stuffed gorge a passage makes'. The fool's response, 'A resolute ass!', deflates this high-blown rhetoric and ironically points toward the future suppression of the poem. The reversals that have hovered around the other satires become the subject of this last poem, where a supposed critique of wise (foolish) innocence becomes the satirist's own trial. Middleton thus ends *Microcynicon* with a direct comment on the problem ever-present in satire: its failed attempt to maintain stable ethical boundaries between moralist and immoral world.

We are not surprised by the poem's final twist because Middleton has already drawn attention to the satirist's inextricable relationship to the disorderly world that is his subject. In the Prologue, the speaker suggests that he develops a vengeful and hostile tone simply in response to the malice of society; satire merely returns the world's vices to itself. Drawing on a grotesquely vivid image of regurgitation, he defies his critics in terms that far exceed a simple mirroring of vice to itself:

Your devilish venom cannot me affright.
It is a cordial of a candy taste,
I'll drink it up, and then let't run at waste.
...
I'll belch into your throats all open wide,
Whose gaping swallow nothing runs beside.
And it if venom, take it as you list:
He spites himself, that spites a satirist.

The text's concluding motto, however, highlights anxieties about satire: '*Qui color albus erat, nunc est contrarius albo*' ('its colour, that once was white, is now the very opposite'). Drawn from Ovid's *Metamorphoses*, this passage refers to the transformation of the spotlessly white raven who turned black because it chattered too much. Middleton's allusion addresses the world's general degeneration through a story that hints at the more particular problem of representation. Describing evil through satire can infect both writer and reader, transforming them into the black colour that defines the speaker's project. In the Prologue, Middleton claims that his pen drinks up sin (which blackens his ink) and spits it back at detractors. The poem becomes a 'black defying embassy' (Prologue.21) sent out to travel the 'deserts of black sin' (1.11). Blackness is thus linked explicitly to the satirist's embittered invective and the flaws that he seeks to remedy. The final motto indicates that the text itself may have blackened the world, as 'nigrum' ink (Defiance.16) metaphorically spills into the reading public—polluting it with knowledge of its own sordid nature and marking the poem as a figure for the impurity it condemns.

Middleton's symbolic use of ink underscores his general attention to the materiality of his books. As Gary Taylor notes, Middleton chooses a title for this satire that self-referentially highlights the small size of the book object. While the octavo format was not uncommon to satire, Middleton makes the size part of the text's wit: penned by the youthful 'little cynic' and small enough to rest comfortably in a hand or pocket, the book humbly names its ambitious project and suggests an uneasy intimacy with its readers. In essence, Middleton cleverly renders the conventional humility espoused by satirists (Horace called his satires 'little books') into physical form. *Microcynicon* calls attention to the text's physicality to convey satire's 'lowly' power to hold a microscope to the world's grand foibles.

Through his book's title and format, Middleton also defines *Microcynicon* as an abbreviated project. The chapter headings clearly promise to present more than one 'book' (chapter), in keeping with conventions established by other writers: Hall's first three books included twenty-two satires, and Marston's *Scourge* boasted three books of ten satires. Middleton's allusion to further books issues a promise that his last satire teasingly cancels. By calling his readers' attention to the relative brevity of his six satires, Middleton implies both his ability and his disinclination to write grander volumes. In fact, the book object's incomplete status could register the speaker's disgust and frustration with the unpleasant and difficult task of satire writing.

Middleton's references to satyrs also help us to understand *Microcynicon*'s theatrical nature, for Renaissance etymology linked formal satire to satyr plays. Unlike popular satires of its day, *Microcynicon* is prefaced with a list of persons. Middleton follows Hall in writing a prologue, but he is the only satirist to further this motif by adding an epilogue. This theatricalization of the text is intensified by the fact that the poem is not dedicated to a patron. Instead the list of characters becomes the text's primary defining feature, appropriate because each poem is devoted principally to a single character. Departing from the model of Hall's and Marston's more excursive satires, Middleton offers relatively continuous dramatic narratives. While other satirists rail elliptically at vice, Middleton tells stories about particular characters who embody certain traits. And unlike Marston's and Hall's interest in specific contemporary poets and styles, Middleton makes no reference to the literary scene. Instead of topical references that document his inclusion in an élite circuit of writers, Middleton shapes this work through theatrical techniques, as he does later in *The Black Book*. *Microcynicon* thus looks appropriately ahead to Middleton's career in theatre.

Critics have generally considered satire to be an inferior literary form because of its topicality and harsh style. Unlike epic or romance, satire emphasizes its social referentiality; that is, it points explicitly to details of contemporary life. Certainly *Microcynicon*'s themes are not new to the Renaissance: the world's enslavement to sex, money, greed, and vanity were all topics familiar to Horace, Persius, and Juvenal. But *Microcynicon* gives these satirical staples a local cast and colour. For this reason, satire has been seen as a wayward form in need of close regulation from authorities. For this reason as well, satire has been neglected by critics who felt that it did not properly transcend its own social moment to meditate on universal truths. As literary criticism has increasingly become aware of the historical embeddedness of all literary forms, however, it has made way for a new appreciation of this genre. In an age in which we now commonly recognize that all works of literature are intricately tied to their social moment, satire's topicality is no longer perceived as a critical shortcoming.

Satire has also been devalued because it cuts against the grain of aesthetic standards. Derived from *satura*, 'satire' means a medley, a heterogeneous compilation of disparate forms. *Microcynicon* is perfectly in keeping with its genre in its fragmentary form and rapidly changing caricatures. Collating proverbs, Biblical verse, and classical satire with contemporary description, Middleton places a premium on capturing features of English life in quick and broad lines rather than developing principles of cohesion. He also shows himself capable of adopting the rough poetic style and truculent persona established by Juvenal and perfected by Marston. Hence Everard Guilpin primes his Muse to sing as a 'foul-mouth Jester'; and Middleton says in his conclusion, 'For jocund wit of force must jangling be'. This impropriety is precisely what bothered the text's second nineteenth-century editor, Bullen, who noted *Microcynicon*'s 'barbarous phraseology' and predicted that '"Brief, but tedious" will be the censure of most readers'. Middleton followed other satirists in deploying jangling rhymes and metrical irregularities; thus the indecorous and hybrid quality that some of the poem's readers have so disliked are fundamental and self-conscious elements of satire.

Microcynicon is also conventional in reflecting cultural anxieties about shifts in the social order, particularly the instability of class and of gender relations. *Microcynicon* patrols the ground of social distinction by scapegoating Superbia as the emblem of pride, by mocking Pyander's 'deviant' sexual behaviour and by denouncing Zodon's social mobility as lustful debauchery. Like many contemporary satires, it announces itself as a 'low' form that consolidates the high world of moral value, as Greg Bredbeck suggests. But the impulse to establish social orthodoxy fractures visibly in Satire Five where Pyander's homosexuality is not at moments as troublesome as his false advertising, and in Satire Four where Droone's tactics are amusingly condoned. As in so much Renaissance writing, the text exceeds its own easy morals and instead offers a complex picture of the problems that arise when one attempts to hold on to fixed cultural and ethical boundaries. In doing so, the work makes visible a truism: satire always teeters on the brink of becoming its opposite. Thus it is no surprise that the avowedly moral *Microcynicon* could be burned in its own time. It is itself commentary on the troubling energy of satire. The last poem ends up parodying the fate of *Microcynicon* when the fool/satirist is forced to disappear. It was just a short time until the censors made the text do the same.

SEE ALSO

Textual introduction and apparatus: *Companion*, 465
Authorship and date: *Companion*, 336

Microcynicon

Six Snarling Satires

Persons

Insatiate *Cron*
Prodigal *Zodon*
Insolent *Superbia*
Cheating *Droone*
Ingling *Pyander*
Wise *Innocent*

Adsis pulcher homo canis hic tibi pulcher emendo

His Defiance to Envy

Envy, which mask'st thyself in common guise,
To haunt deservers and to hunt deserts,
Hard-soft, cold-hot, well-evil, foolish-wise,
Miscontrarieties, agreeing parts,
Avaunt I say! I'll anger thee enough,
And fold thy fiery eyes in thy smazky snuff.

Defiance, resolution and neglects,
True trine of bars against thy false assault,
Defies, resolves defiance, and rejects
Thy interest to claim the smallest fault.
Thou lawless landlady, poor prodigal,
Sour solace, credit's crack, fear's festival.

More angry satire-days I'll muster up
Than thou canst challenge letters in thy name,
My nigrum true-born ink no more shall sup
Thy stainèd blemish, charàctered in blame.
My pen's two nebs shall turn unto a fork,

This commentary focuses upon intertextual relationships.

Title ***Microcynicon*** Translated as 'having to do with a churlish dog or a cynic', the title alludes to the relationship between the satirist and the cynic, as well as referring to the general association of satire with the fury of dogs. Compare Hall's 'biting satires', Goddard's *A Mastiff Whelp with other Rough-Island-like Curs*, and Marston's reference to himself as a 'barking' and 'sharp-fang'd satirist' (*Pygmalion*, 262 and *The Scourge of Villainy*, Satire IX, 362). In the first satire, Middleton refers to his 'snarling muse' (14). In this text, dogs become representative of both evil and the project that is necessary to drive away viciousness; this image thus marks a collapse in the dichotomies that underpin satire (see notes to 1.4 and 1.100). The title also calls attention to the text's small 'micro' size. Because satire was perceived to be an unheroic genre, writers often humbly speak of their works as diminutive: Horace, for instance, refers to his 'little books' (Satire I:4) and his 'little volume' (Satire I:10). Through his title, Middleton shows that he has transformed a rhetorical ploy into a physical object.

Persons.7 ***Adsis . . . emendo*** This phrase is obscure, but it might translate as 'Come here, good-looking man—and I, a good-looking dog, will amend you'. Irwin admits difficulty in translating this phrase, but guesses: 'Draw near, handsome man: I, a handsome dog, publish [these things] for you here'. No source is known, although the scansion could be classical hexameter. Whatever the meaning of this motto, it furthers the link between satire writing and bestiality established by the title.

Defiance This conventional address to potential critics is written specifically in imitation of Joseph Hall's *Virgidemiarum* (1597). Middleton replicates Hall's rhyme scheme, stanzaic form, and title, the *Defiance to Envy*.

2 **mask'st . . . guise** The masquerade imagery follows Hall's *Prologue* to *Virgidemiarum*, which denounces envy and hypocrisy: 'The world's eye bleared with those shameless lies, | Mask'd in the show of meal-mouth'd poesies. | Go, daring Muse, on with thy thankless task, | And do the ugly face of Vice unmask'. Marston also introduces the satirist as someone who unmasks the world's 'masked shows' (*Pygmalion*, 262).

5 **Miscontrarieties** false contraries; the double negative contributes to the tone created by the extensive use of oxymoron in this stanza. These figures call attention to the duplicitous way in which Envy works to appear as its opposite as well as its tendency to levy contrarieties.

6 **Avaunt** go away

7 **smazky** The precise meaning of this word is unclear; perhaps 'smeechy', as Dyce suggests (blackened and smoky); or a variant of 'smaikry', meaning contemptible behaviour or roguery.

snuff candle end, used to signify something of little value or on the point of extinction. Here the term is part of an unusual and obscure phrase which calls attention to the self-destructive nature of envy.

12–13 **Thou . . . festival** This series of inappropriately yoked words indicate Envy's contradictions.

13 **crack** boast

14 **satire-days** punning on 'Saturdays', continuing the holiday imagery of 'festival'. In his address to detractors, Marston imagines his critics as part of a common crowd gathered sadistically at the 'festival' of poetry (*Scourge*, 301).

16 **nigrum** black. Middleton uses this obscure term in *Solomon* to describe the devil: 'the coal-black visage of his nigrum fame' (11.76). As in this passage, Middleton calls attention to the physical nature of writing in *The Black Book* where the devil links the blackness of ink to the evil nature of the objects he satirizes: 'Am I black enough, think you, dressed up in a lasting suit of ink? Do I deserve my dark and pitchy title?' (824–6). In *Microcynicon* Middleton calls his text a 'black defying embassy' (Prologue.21) sent out to travel over the deserts of 'black sin' (1.11). In *Solomon* Middleton employs an extended version of the frightening image called forth in these lines, as the satirist's pen drinks up the black sins of the world to serve as the ink through which he will excoriate vice: 'Black sins, I dim you all with inky smother. | My pen shall be officious in this scene, | To let your hearts blood in a wicked vein; | . . . Behold your coal-black blood, my writing-ink, | My paper's poison'd meat, my pen's foul drink' (14.240–6). Following Hall, who notes that poets write in 'black condemning coal' (Book I, Satire III), and Marston, who refers to the satirist's 'ink-black fist' (*Scourge*, 322), Middleton associates blackness both with the satirist's caustic rebuke and with the evil he excoriates.

18 **nebs** the points of pens. Satirists conventionally described writing as an act of violence. In *Skialetheia*, for instance, Everard Guilpin figures satirical writing as a physical attack: 'Holding my pen, my Rapier in my fist: | I know I shall wide-gaping Momes convince' (Conclusion, 23–24).

Chasing old Envy from so young a work;
I, but the author's mouth, bid thee avaunt,
He more defies thy hate, thy hunt, thy haunt.
T.M. Gent.

The Author's Prologue

Book 1

Dismounted from the high-aspiring hills,
Which the all-empty airy kingdom fills,
Leaving the scorchèd mountains threat'ning heaven
From whence fell fiery rage my soul hath driven,
Passing the down-steep valleys all in haste,
Have tripped it through the woods; and now, at last,
Am veilèd in a stony sanctuary,
To save my ire-stuffed soul lest it miscarry,
From threat'ning storms o'erturning verity,
That shames to see truth's refinèd purity.
Those open plains, those high sky-kissing mounts,
Where huffing winds cast up their airy accounts
Were too too open, shelter yielding none,
So that the blasts did tyrannize upon
The naked carcass of my heavy soul,
And with their fury all my all control.
But now, environed with a brazen tower,
I little dread their stormy raging power.
Witness this black defying embassy,
That wanders them before in majesty,
Undaunted of their bugbear threat'ning words,
Whose proud aspiring vaunts, time past records.
Now windy parasites or the slaves of wine,
That wind from all things save the truth divine,
Wind, turn, and toss into the depth of spite,
Your devilish venom cannot me affright.
It is a cordial of a candy taste,
I'll drink it up, and then let't run at waste—
Whose druggy lees mixed with the liquid flood
Of muddy fell defiance as it stood,—
I'll belch into your throats all open wide,
Whose gaping swallow nothing runs beside.
And if it venom, take it as you list:
He spites himself, that spites a satirist.

The First Book

Satire 1

Insatiate Cron

Cur eget indignus quisquam, te divite

Time was, when down-declining toothless age,
Was of a holy and divine presage,
Divining prudent and foretelling truth,
In sacred points instructing wand'ring youth.
But O detraction of our latter days,

20 **but** only

Prologue.2 *Book 1* By referring to subsequent books, Middleton imitates and revises Hall's *Virgidemiarum*, which advertised six books of satires but delivered only the first three. The remaining satires were published in the following year. But Middleton playfully alters the presentation of Hall's incomplete text in two important ways. First, he uses the reference to highlight the small size of his 'micro' collection. Hall's first three books included twenty-two satires, Horace's work contained two books of eighteen satires, and Marston's *Scourge* boasted three books of ten satires. By calling his readers' attention to the relative brevity of his six satires, Middleton creates the impression that he could write grand volumes if he so desired. While placing his work in relation to prominent satires, his allusion to further books issues a promise that his last satire teasingly cancels, for the sixth satire ends with the satirist blending into the fool who is 'carried away' by wit. The satire seems to be unexpectedly broken off in the middle. Such an ending, Middleton hints, appropriately signifies the trauma of satire in a world where the satirist's vantage point continuously erodes.

6 **fell** savage. Middleton imitates Marston's trademark fury, a style derived primarily from Juvenal.

11 **verity** truth. The speaker describes his descent from a place associated with both elevated thoughts and openness. He retreats to a secure site from which satire can be written, a place safe from both moral vice and critical pressures against expression (both of which can lead to the poet's 'miscarriage').

19 **with** within

brazen strong, as made of brass

23 **bugbear** imagined as dreadful

26 **wind** unfolds; turning and winding are words that indicate movement away from the straight and narrow; as the word 'error' means to turn. Middleton picks up on the word 'windy' in the preceding line.

28 **affright** frighten

31 **lees** the basest part, the dregs

33 **belch** The imagery of regurgitation is a subset of the more general body imagery common to satire, a genre obsessed with the vices of the flesh and the often violent curative procedures necessary to purge sin. Middleton deploys images of vomiting throughout *Solomon*.

35 **venom** is poisonous

36 **satirist** The original spelling 'Satyrist' hints at the erroneous Renaissance etymology for the word, derived from the licentious goat-man satyr and signalling the satirist's beastly persona. See introduction.

1.3 *Cron* a shortened version of Cronus, the mythological Titan who rebelled against his father in order to gain power, or a pun on 'crone'. Satire One is one of the more difficult satires; it uses the cosmographical imagery of earth, heaven, and hell to establish the domain of devilish greed and its fallacies. The satire is more fragmentary than the next four because it rapidly moves through various sketches of the usurer and his foibles.

4 ***Cur . . . divite*** 'Why should any decent man be in need when you are rich?' (Horace, *Satires*, Book II. 2, 103). Horace's speaker is a poor peasant named Ofellus who argues for the simple life. In this passage, Ofellus urges a rich young man to share his wealth. The allusion to this particular satire is telling because Ofellus deploys dog imagery in representing the miser.

5 **toothless** harmonious; but also a common reference to satire. Hall's *Virgidemiarum*, which is subtitled *The First Three Books of Toothless Satires*, opens its last book with the theme that establishes Middleton's first satire: 'Time was, and that was term'd the time of gold, | When world and time were young that now are old'. Hall's satire laments the passing of an age of natural simplicity into a time of wasteful luxury.

6 **presage** an utterance foretelling future events

How much from verity this age estrays!
Ranging the briery deserts of black sin,
Seeking a dismal cave to revel in.
This latter age, or member of that time
Of whom my snarling muse now thund'reth rhyme,
Wandered the brakes until a hidden cell
He found at length and still therein doth dwell.
The house of gain insatiate it is,
Which this hoar-agèd peasant deems his bliss.
O that desire might hunt amongst that fur!
It should go hard but he would loose a cur
To rouse the fox hid in a bramble bush,
Who frighteth conscience with a wry-mouthed 'Push!'
But what need I to wish or would it thus,
When I may find him starting at the Burse,
Where he infecteth other pregnant wits,
Making them co-heirs to his damnèd fits?
There may you see this writhen-facèd mass
Of rotten mould'ring clay, that prating ass
That riddles wonders (mere compact of lies)
Of heaven, of hell, of earth and of the skies.
Of heaven thus he reasons: heaven there's none,
Unless it be within his mansïon.
O there is heaven. Why? Because there's gold,
That from the late to this last age controlled
The massy sceptre of earth's heavenly round,
Exiling forth her silver-pavèd bound
The leaders, brethren, brazen counterfeits
That in this golden age contempt begets.
'Vaunt then immortal I, I only king,
And golden god of this eternal being.'
Of hell Cimmerian thus Avarus reasons:
'Though hell be hot, yet it observeth seasons.'
Having within his kingdom residence,
O'er which his godhead hath preeminence,
An obscure angel of his heaven it is,
Wherein's contained that hell-devouring bliss.
Into this hell sometimes an angel falls,
Whose white aspect black forlorn souls appalls,
And that is when a saint believing gold,
Old in that heaven, young in being old,
Falls headlong down into that pit of woe,
Fit for such damnèd creature's overthrow.
To make this public that obscurèd lies,
And more apparent vulgar secrecies,
To make this plain, harsh unto common wits,
Simplicity in common judgement sits.
This down-cast angel or declining saint
Is greedy Cron, when Cron makes his complaint,
For his poor creditors—fall'n to decay,
Being bankërupts—take heels and run away.
Then frantic Cron, galled to the very heart,
In some by-corner plays a devil's part,
Repining at the loss of so much pelf,
And in a humour goes and hangs himself.
So of a saint, a devil Cron is made.
The devil lov'd Cron, and Cron the devil's trade.
Thus may you see such angels often fall,
Making a working day a festival.
Now to the third point of his deity,
And that's th'earth, thus reasons credulity:
Credulous Cron, Cron credulous in all,
Swears that his kingdom is in general.
As he is regent of this heaven and hell,
So of the earth all others he'll expel.
The sky's at his dispose, the earth his own,
And (if Cron please) all must be overthrown.
Cron, Cron, advise thee, Cron with the copper nose,
And be not ruled so much by false suppose,
Lest Cron's professing holiness turn evil,
And of a false god prove a perfect devil.
I prithee, Cron, find out some other talk,

10 **estrays** strays
11 **briery** thorny
12 **cave** Cron's refuge uneasily echoes the satirist's own 'stony sanctuary' (Prologue.9)
15 **brakes** clumps of bushes
17 **insatiate** never satisfied
18 **hoar-agèd** white-haired. Middleton puns on 'age' when he shifts from a description of a righteous past age to the elderly Cron.
19–22 **O . . . 'Push!'** These lines are obscure, but they generally express a wish that the usurous fox, whose insidious goading tempts people to 'push' ahead greedily, could be routed out of his hiding place by correct desire. The speaker imagines that frightening the fox into action would give him a dose of his own medicine.
19 **fur** either a forest of fir-trees (picking up on 'brakes' in l. 15), or the typical usurer's garment which was lined with fur.
20 **cur** dog
21 **bramble bush** a briery shrub that the fox uses to entangle others, now serving as his defence
22 **wry-mouthed** with a twisted smile
24 **Burse** the Royal Exchange in London, a place of national and international financial trade
25 **pregnant** swelling
27 **writhen-facèd** contorted
28 **mould'ring** decaying
prating chattering or bragging
29 **riddles** used as a verb
mere compact composed wholly
33–5 **gold . . . round** with a pun on the mythic golden age now literalized as money in the present time
36 **bound** boundary; gold exiles out of its limits the people listed in the next line; with a possible secondary meaning of 'bond' (lowly and base peasants) in which case 'bound' would refer not to the limits but to the exiled elements.
39 **Vaunt** boast
41 **Cimmerian** fabled place of intense darkness and gloom
Avarus Latin for avarice, with the accent on the second syllable
43 **Having . . . residence** Hell has residence within Avarice's heaven; this designation is part of Avarice's false reasoning that reinterprets the entire theological cosmology as within his domain of greed.
44 **godhead** divine nature
45 **angel** pun on a gold coin
48 **appalls** dims or fades, as well as dismays
59–60 **For . . . away** For Cron's suicide because of his creditors' flight, compare *Trick* 4.4.22–23.
63 **Repining** complaining
pelf money or property, usually tainted
70 **credulity** Cron's over-readiness to believe
72 **in general** universal
77 **copper nose** brazen, rash; a red nose caused by intemperance
78 **suppose** supposition

Make not the Burse a place for spirits to walk,—
For doubtless if thy damnèd lies take place,
Destruction follows; farewell, sacred grace.
Th'Exchange for goodly merchants is appointed;
'Why not for me?' says Cron, 'and mine anointed?
Can merchants thrive and not the usurer nigh?
Can merchants live without my company?'
No, Cron helps all, and Cron hath help from none,
What others have is Cron's, and Cron's his own.
And Cron will hold his own, or't shall go hard,
The devil will help him for a small reward.
The devil's help—O 'tis a mighty thing!
If he but say the word, Cron is a king.
O then the devil is greater yet then he?
I thought as much—the devil would master be.
'And reason too,' saith Cron, 'for what care I,
So I may live as God, and never die?'
Yea, golden Cron, death will make thee away,
And each dog, Cron, must have a dying day.
And with this resolution I bequeath thee
To God or to the devil, and so I leave thee.

Satire 2

Prodigal Zodon

Who knows not Zodon? Zodon, what is he?
The true born child of insatiety.
If true born, when? If born at all, say where?
Where conscience begged in worst time of the year.
His name young Prodigal, son to greedy gain,
Let blood by folly in a contrary vein.
For scraping Cron, seeing he needs must die,
Bequeathèd all to prodigality.
The will once proved and he possessed of all,
Who then so gallant as young Prodigal?
Mounted aloft on flattering fortune's wings,
Where like a nightingale secure he sings,
Floating on seas of scarce prosperity,
Engirt with pleasure's sweet tranquillity.
Suit upon suit, satin too too base,—
Velvet, laid on with gold or silver lace,
A mean man doth become, but he must ride
In cloth of finèd gold, and by his side
Two footmen at the least, with choice of steeds,
Attirèd when he rides in gorgeous weeds.
Zodon must have his chariot gilded o'er,
And when he triumphs, four bare before
In pure white satin to usher out his way
To make him glorious on his progress day.
Vail bonnet he that doth not passing by,
Admiring on that sun-enriching sky,
Two days encaged at least in strongest hold;
Storm he that list, he scorns to be controlled.
What, is it lawful that a mounted beggar
May uncontrollèd thus bear sway and swagger?—
A base-born issue of a baser sire,
Bred in a cottage, wand'ring in the mire
With nailèd shoes and whipstaff in his hand,
Who with a 'hey and ree' the beasts command,
And being seven years practised in that trade,

85 **Th'Exchange** the Burse or Royal Exchange

87 **usurer** someone who lends money with interest; one of the main targets of satire and social critique in early modern England. The devilish Cron here coyly points to the often unacknowledged relationship between demonized usurers and the more socially-acceptable rising merchant class.

100 **And...day** a bleak revision of the proverb: 'Every dog has his day' (Tilley, D464). This dog imagery hearkens back to the motto on the title-page and the title.

101–2 **And...thee** This section appropriately ends with the satirist's mock legacy, which counters Cron's reluctance to accept his mortality and draw up a will, and which sets up the next satire in which Cron has unwisely bequeathed his money to the spendthrift Zodon.

2.2 ***Zodon*** The extravagant heir is a theme treated by Hall in Book IV, Satire II of *Virgidemiarum*, Rankins in *Seven Satires*, and Marston in the third satire of *The Scourge of Villainy*. Irwin speculates that Zodon refers to the Greek phrase for a carved or painted figure. The second satire is clearly concerned with preserving established socioeconomic divisions within the social order, as it denounces the extravagance and lechery of the unlicensed social climber.

8 **Let blood** medical practice whereby blood was drained in order to balance the humours that constituted bodily fluids. Middleton uses the image of a mistaken blood-letting to indicate Cron's fallacy in leaving money to the spendthrift Zodon.

9 **scraping** miserly

16 **Engirt** encircled

17–18 **Suit...lace** clothing imagery signals Zodon's inappropriate presumption to class status. Sumptuary laws regulated the clothing that each class could wear. Zodon's finery indicates his attempt to ignore such laws and climb above his station. Zodon far surpasses the ostentatious people that Hall mocks for wearing 'satin sleeves' (Book III, Satire IV). Throughout the poem, Middleton uses clothing imagery to signal various improprieties—for instance, Superbia's over-investment in her gown in Satire 3 and Pyander's transvestism in Satire 5.

19 **mean** lowly
become become himself, suffice for himself

22 **weeds** clothes

23 **gilded** painted gold

24 **triumphs** to enter a city victoriously in a lavish procession. Middleton authored a series of pageants called *Triumphs* designed for use in the civic life of London.
bare horses without saddles

26 **progress** a ceremonial procession or journey by a king of queen; picking up on the pageant imagery from l. 24

27 **Vail** to tip a hat in deference. This expression is seen, for instance, in Book III, Satire V of *Virgidemiarum* when Hall mocks the exaggerated courtesy of the gallant who keeps 'his bonnet vailed' (60). Middleton here suggests that Zodon will strenuously punish anyone who neglects to show respect for him.

30 **list** desires

35 **nailèd shoes** cheap shoes. In *Black Book* Middleton uses the image of the 'hard naily soles' of swains' shoes in order to signal their plodding natures (84).

36 **'hey and ree'** Irwin: 'terms used in driving horses, oxen, etc: "hey" (haw)—turn to the left; "ree" (gee)—turn to the right'

At seven years' end by Tom a journey's made
Unto the city of fair Troynovant,
Where through extremity of need and want
He's forced to trot with fardel at his back
From house to house, demanding if they lack
A poor young man that's willing to take pain
And mickle labour, though for little gain.
Well, some kind Trojan, thinking he hath grace,
Keeps him himself or gets some other place.
The world now—God be thankèd!—'s well amended:
Want, that erewhile did want, is now befriended,
And scraping Cron hath got a world of wealth.
Now what of that? Cron's dead. Where's all his pelf?
Bequeathèd to young Prodigal. That's well:
His god hath left him, and he's fled to hell.
See, golden souls, the end of ill-got gain!
Read and mark well; to do the like refrain.
This youthful gallant, like the prince of pleasure,
Floating on golden seas of earthly treasure
(Treasure ill-got by minist'ring of wrong),
Made a fair show, but endur'd not long.
Ill-got, worse spent; gotten by deceit,
Spent on lascivious wantons which await
And hourly expect such prodigality,
Lust-breathing lechers given to venery.
No day expired but Zodon hath his trull.
He hath his tit, and she likewise her gull.
Gull he, trull she: O 'tis a gallant age!
Men may have hackneys of good carrïage,
Provided that there rain a golden shower.
Then come whos' will at the appointed hour.
Hour me no hours; hours break no square.
Where gold doth rain, be sure to find them there.
Well, Zodon hath his pleasure: he hath gold,
Young in his golden age, in sin too old.—
Now he wants gold; all his treasure's done.
He's banishèd the stews; pity finds none.
Rich yesterday in wealth, this day as poor,
Tomorrow like to beg from door to door.
See, youthful spendthrifts, all your bravery
Even in a moment turned to misery.

Satire 3

Insolent Superbia

List, ye profane fair painted images,
Predestinated by the destinies
At your first being to fall eternally
Into Cimmerian black obscurity.
Ill-favoured idols, pride's anatomy,
Foul-coloured puppets, balls of infamy,
Whom zealous souls do racket to and fro,
Sometimes aloft ye fly, otherwhiles below,
Bandied into the air's loose continent,
Where hard upbearing winds hold parliament.
For such is the force of down-declining sin,
Where our short-feathered peacocks wallow in,
That when sweet motions urge them to aspire
They are so bathèd o'er by sweet desire
In the odiferous fountain of sweet pleasure,
Wherein delight hath all embalmed her treasure—
I mean where sin, the mistress of disgrace,
Hath residence and her abiding place.
And sin, though it be foul, yet fair in this,

38 **journey's** journeyman's; a journeyman is an employee who can earn wages after a period of apprenticeship; but also a pun on the journey undertaken to London (Troynovant), both of which signal potentially disruptive social shifts
39 **Troynovant** nickname for London, because supposedly founded by Brutus the Trojan. The myth of Troy surfaces frequently in Renaissance dramatists' descriptions of London.
41 **fardel** bundle or parcel
42 **demanding** asking
44 **mickle** great quantity
45 **Trojan** see above, 2.39
47 **The . . . amended** proverbial: 'The world is well amended with him' (Tilley, W902), used sarcastically to indicate Zodon's inflated importance
53 **ill-got gain** proverbial: 'Ill-gotten goods never prosper'; 'Ill-gotten gods thrive not to the third heir' (Tilley, G301, G305).
62 **Lust-breathing** excited by lust. Irwin points to Shakespeare's *Rape of Lucrece* (1594): 'Lust-breathèd Tarquin leaves the Roman host' (3).
venery lechery
63 **trull** prostitute or concubine
64 **tit** young woman of loose character
gull dupe
66 **hackneys** horses for hire; slang for prostitutes or other people who rent themselves for cash
68 **whos'** whosoever
68–9 **hour . . . square** make me no set timetables, for hours are unimportant. 'Break no square' was a common phrase for 'ought not to matter'.
70 **rain** with a pun on reign
74 **banishèd** banished from
stews red-light districts
77 **bravery** finery
3.2 ***Superbia*** in excess. The haughty and overly-materialistic woman is the subject of much Renaissance literature. In making woman the figure of pride, Middleton contributes to the well-worn convention of aligning women with rampant consumerism and narcissism. In Marlowe's parade of seven deadly sins in *Doctor Faustus*, for instance, Pride identifies himself in two central ways: through his imitation of a lady's extravagant fashions and thus his conquest of her naked body, and through his haughty demands to be pampered (vi.114–122).
3 **List** listen
4 **Predestinated** predestined
6 **Cimmerian** see 1.41
7 **anatomy** medical term for dissection applied metaphorically to the act of laying something bare. Here Superbia strips away the surface of Pride to expose it explicitly and thoroughly. The title of Stephen Gosson's *Anatomy of Abuses* is a common example of how the term signalled an exhaustive description or an exposure of something hidden.
8 **puppets** dolls, commonly used contemptuously to describe women who use cosmetics. See Guilpin's *Skialetheia*: 'Why they are Idols, Puppets, Exchange babies, | And yet (thou fool) tak'st them for goodly Ladies' (Satire II, 11–12).
balls tennis balls conventionally imply inconstancy, as they are linked to the vicissitudes of fortune. In this passage, Superbia travels aimlessly on the whims of her own self-gratification.
11 **continent** space
12 **upbearing** supportive
14 **peacocks** creatures concerned with excessive display
17 **odiferous** fragrant

In being painted with a show of bliss.
For what more happy creature to the eye
Than is Superbia in her bravery?
Yet who more foul disrobèd of attire?—
Pearled with the botch as children burnt with fire,
That for their outward cloak upon the skin,
Worser enormities abound within.
Look they to that; truth tells them their amiss,
And in this glass, all-telling truth it is.
When welcome spring had clad the hills in green
And pretty whistling birds were heard and seen,
Superbia abroad 'gan take her walk
With other peacocks for to find her talk.
Kyron, that in a bush lay closely couched,
Heard all their chat, and how it was avouched.
'Sister,' says one, and softly packed away,
'In what fair company did you dine to day?'—
''Mongst gallant dames'—and then she wipes her lips,
Placing both hands upon her whalebone hips,
Puffed up with a round circling farthingale;
That done, she 'gins go forward with her tale:
'Sitting at table carved of walnut tree,
All coverèd with damasked napery,
Garnished with salts of pure beaten gold,
Whose silver-plated edge of rarest mould
Moved admiration in my searching eye
To see the goldsmith's rich artificy;
The butler's placing of his manchets white,
The plated cupboard, for our more delight,
Whose golden beauty glancing from on high
Illuminated other chambers nigh;
The slowly pacing of the servingmen
Which were appointed to attend us then,
Holding in either hand a silver dish
Of costly cates of far-fetched dainty fish,
Until they do approach the table nigh,
Where the appointed carver carefully
Dischargeth them of their full-freighted hands,
Which instantly upon the table stands.
The music sweet, which all that while did sound,
Ravish the hearers, and their sense confound.
This done, the master of that sumptuous feast
In order 'gins to place his welcome guest.
Beauty first seated in a throne of state,
Unmatchable, disdaining other mate,
Shone like the sun, whereon mine eyes still gazed,
Feeding on her perfections that amazed.
But O her silver-framèd coronet
With low down-dangling spangles all beset,
Her sumptuous periwig, her curious curls,
Her high-prized necklace of entrailèd pearls,
Her precious jewels wondrous to behold,
Her basest gem framed of the purest gold!
O I could kill my self for very spite,
That my dim stars give not so clear a light.
Heart-burning ire new kindled bids despair,
Since beauty lives in her, and I want fair.
O had I died in youth, or not been born,
Rather than live in hate, and die forlorn.
And die I will—' Therewith she drew a knife
To kill herself, but Kyron saved her life.
See here, proud puppets, high-aspiring evils,
Scarce any good, most of you worse than devils,
Excellent in ill, ill in advising well,
Well in that's worst, worse than the worst in hell.
Hell is stark blind; so blind most women be,
Blind, and yet not blind when they should not see.
Fine Madam Tiptoes in her velvet gown,
That quotes her paces in charàcters down,
Valuing each step that she had made that day,
Worth twenty shillings in her best array.
And why, forsooth, some little dirty spot

22 **painted** In condemning them for their use of cosmetics, Renaissance writers conventionally transformed women into a central emblem of hypocrisy and duplicity. The second satire of Guilpin's *Skialetheia* is devoted entirely to this subject.
26 **Pearled** ornamented, sprinkled with pearl-like shapes
botch boils and sores
30 **glass** The speaker follows medieval convention in holding up a mirror to the vices of the age. Interestingly the satirist's use of the glass to expose vice resembles one of the vices themselves: women's conventional association with vanity.
31 **clad** dressed
35 **Kyron** Irwin suggests that the name alludes to Chiron, the centaur who trained various mythological figures to be heroes; here used parodically to underscore Superbia's failed moral education.
37 **packed away** to bring a fellow conspirator into a plot; here to incite Superbia
40 **whalebone** the material used to stiffen the midriff of women's dresses
41 **farthingale** hooped petticoat
44 **damasked** richly-figured designs, usually on fine cloth
napery table linen
45 **salts** salt shakers
49 **manchets** loaves of the finest wheat bread
50 **plated cupboard** a sideboard either overlaid with a thin trim of gold or silver, or used to hold the china
56 **cates** delicacies
64 **guest** guests
69 **coronet** decorative headdress
71 **periwig** wig
72 **entrailèd** entwined
74 **basest** cheapest
78 **want fair** lack beauty; 'fair', or light-coloured features, is the ideal of feminine beauty during this time
83 **puppets** contemptuous term for people, usually women, suggesting that they are dressed like dolls
89 **Tiptoes** Middleton shifts here to a related character sketch about Lady Tiptoes, whose name indicates her disdain and haughtiness. In *The Scourge of Villainy* Marston uses the term to indicate presumption: 'O how on tip-toes proudly mounts my muse! | Stalking a loftier gait than satires use' (Satire III, 362). In *Christ's Tears over Jerusalem* Thomas Nashe calls forth a similar image: 'Delicacy is the sin of our London Dames. So delicate are they in their diet, so dainty and pulling fine in their speech, so tiptoe-nice in treading on the earth' (*Works*, II, 144–45).
90 **quotes ... down** remembers in detail her steps and writes them down

Hath fell upon her gown or petticoat.
Perhaps that nothing much, or something little,
Nothing in many's view, in hers a mickle,
Doth thereon surfeit, and some day or two
She's passing sick, and knows not what to do.
The poor handmaid, seeing her mistress wed
To frantic sickness, wishes she were dead,
Or that her devilish tyrannizing fits
May mend, and she enjoy her former wits.
For whilst that Health thus counterfeits Not-well,
Poor Here-at-Hand lives in the depth of hell.
'Where is this baggage? where's this girl? what ho!'
Quoth she, 'was ever woman troubled so?
What, hussy Nan!' And then she 'gins to brawl.
Then in comes Nan, 'Sooth mistress did you call?'—
'Out on thee, quean! now by the living God'—
And then she strikes, and on the wench lays load.
Poor silly maid, with finger in the eye,
Sighing and sobbing takes all patiently.
Nimble Affection, stung to the very heart
To see her fellow mate sustain such smart,
Flies to the Burse gate for a match or two,
And salves th'amiss, there is no more to do.
Quickfooted kindness, quick as itself thought,
With that well-pleasing news but lately bought
By love's assiduate care and industry,
Into the chamber runs immediately,
Where she unloads the freight of sweet content.
The haggler pleased doth rise incontinent.
Then thought of sickness is not thought upon;
Care hath no being in her mansïon.
But former peacock pride, grand insolence,
Even in the highest thought hath residence.
But it on tiptoe stands: Well, what of that?
It is more prompt to fall and ruinate.
And fall it will when death's shrill clamorous bell
Shall summon you unto the depth of hell.
Repent, proud princocks. Cease for to aspire,
Or die to live with pride in burning fire.

Satire 4

Cheating Droone

There is a cheater by professïon
That takes more shapes than the chameleon.
Sometimes he jets it in a black furred gown,
And that is when he harbours in the town.
Sometimes a cloak to mantle hoary age,
Ill-favoured like an ape in spiteful rage,
And then he walks in Paul's a turn or two,
To see by cheating what his wit can do.
Perhaps he'll tell a gentlemen a tale
Will cost him twenty angels in the sale,
But if he know his purse well-lined within,
And by that means he cannot finger him,
He'll proffer him such far-fet courtesy
That shortly in a tavern neighb'ring by
He hath encaged the silly gentleman,
To whom he proffers service all he can.
'Sir, I perceive you are of gentle blood;
Therefore I will our cates be new and good.
For well I wot, the country yieldeth plenty,
And as they diverse be, so are they dainty.
May it please you then a while to rest you merry?
Some cates I will make choice of and not tarry.'
The silly cony blithe and merrily
Doth for his kindness thank him heartily.
Then hies the cheater very hastily
And with some peasant, where he is in fee,
Juggles, that dinner being almost ended,
He in a matter of weight may then be friended.
The peasant, for an angel then in hand,
Will do whate'er his worship shall command,
And yields, that when a reckoning they call in,
To make reply there's one to speak with him.
The plot is laid. Now comes the cheater back,
And calls in haste for such things as they lack.
The table freighted with all dainty cates,
Having well fed, they fall to pleasant chats,
Discoursing of the mickle difference
'Twixt perfect truth and painted eloquence.

104 **Here-at-Hand** nickname for her maid
109 **quean** ill-behaved and impudent woman
111 **finger in the eye** derisive term for weeping
113 **Nimble Affection** probably a fellow maid
115 **match** Dyce glosses this as 'pattern', meaning a piece of cloth, but Irwin suggests that it could imply as well a love match, a morsel of gossip.
119 **assiduate** constant
121 **unloads** pronounced 'unlades'
122 **incontinent** without self-restraint
131 **princocks** a proud, conceited and pert young boy. In abruptly shifting from Superbia as a feminized figure of pride to the masculine coxcomb, Middleton anticipates the gender-crossing created by Pyander's 'painted' counterfeiting in Satire 5.
4.2 *Droone* a loafer, someone idle
4 **more ... chameleon** proverbial. See Tilley, C221.
5 **jets** struts or parades
7 **mantle** conceal
hoary grey-haired
9 **Paul's** the courtyard of St Paul's Cathedral, scene of commerce and social gathering
12 **angels** coins, with a common pun on losing virtue
13 **his** the gentleman's
15 **far-fet** far-fetched
21 **wot** know
25 **cony** dupe. 'Cony-catching' pamphlets describing the ruses and tricks of rogues were popular at the turn of the century. Middleton's fourth satire partakes more of this genre than of traditional satire. Here as in the most prominent cony-catching works—Robert Greene's *A Disputation Between a He Cony-Catcher and a She Cony-Catcher*, *The Black Book's Messenger*, and *The Defence of Cony-Catching*—the writer exposes with relish the ingenious practices of the cheater.
27 **hies** hastens
28 **in fee** beholden to; from a medieval term indicating feudal obligation
29 **Juggles** plays tricks, plans to cheat
38 **chats** pronounced 'chates'

Plain truth that harbours in the country swain,
The cony stands defendant; the cheater's vein
Is to uphold an eloquent smooth tongue,
To be truth's orator righting every wrong.
Before the cause concluded took effect,
In comes a crew of fiddling knaves abject,
The very refuse of that rabble rout,
Half shoes upon their feet torn round about—
Save little Dick the dapper singing knave.
He had a threadbare coat to make him brave,
(God knows, scarce worth a tester, if it were
Valued at most; of seven it was too dear).
Well, take it as they list, Shakerag came in,
Making no doubt but they would like of him,
An 'twere but for his person, a pretty lad,
Well-qualified, having a singing trade.
Well, so it was the cheater must be merry,
And he a song must have, called 'hey-down-derry'.
So Dick begins to sing; the fiddlers play.
The melancholy cony replies, 'Nay, nay,
No more of this!' The other bids, 'Play on!
'Tis good our spirits should something work upon—
Tut, gentle sir; be pleasant, man,' quoth he,
'Yours be the pleasure; mine the charge shall be.
This do I for the love of gentlemen.
Hereafter happily if we meet again,
I shall of you expect like courtesy,
Finding fit time and opportunity.'
'Or else I were ungrateful,' quoth the cony,
'It shall go hard, but we will find some money,
For some we have, that some well used gets more,
And so in time we shall increase our store.'
'Mean time', said he, 'employ it to good use,
For time ill-spent doth purchase time's abuse.'
With that, more wine he calls for, and intends
That either of them carouse to all their friends.
The cony nods the head, yet says not 'Nay!'
Because the other would the charge defray.
The end tries all, and here begins the jest,
My gentleman betook him to his rest.
Wine took possession of his drowsy head,
And cheating Droone hath brought the fool to bed.
The fiddlers were discharged and all things whist,
Then pilf'ring Droone 'gan use him as he list.
Ten pounds he finds, the reckoning he doth pay,
And with the residue passeth sheer away.
Anon the cony wakes, his coin being gone,
He exclaims against dissimulatïon.
But 'twas too late; the cheater had his prey.
Be wise, young heads: care for an afterday.

Satire 5

Ingling Pyander

Age hath his infant youth, old trees their sprigs,
O'erspreading branches their inferior twigs.
Old beldam hath a daughter or a son,
True born or illegitimate, all's one.
Issue she hath. The father? ask you me?
The house wide open stands; her lodging's free.
Admit myself for recreatïon
Sometimes did enter her possessïon,
It argues not that I have been the man
That first kept revels in that mansïon.
No, no, the haggling common place is old;
The tenement hath oft been bought and sold.

41 **swain** gentleman; here suggesting the simple man
42 **stands defendant** offers a defence of
47 **rabble rout** disorderly crowd
49 **dapper** trim and neat
50 **brave** handsome in appearance
51 **tester** slang term for a sixpence
53 **Shakerag** a beggarly and disreputable person
55 **An** If
58 **'hey-down-derry'** both a common refrain and a tune, often associated in seventeenth-century songbooks and ballads with frivolous and bawdy songs
71 **that some** a pun on 'sum'
78 **defray** pay
79 **tries** determines
83 **whist** silenced
84 **pilf'ring** thieving
90 **Be . . . afterday** In compressing the entire moral lesson into this final line, the speaker reveals his departure from conventional satire. Interestingly, he seems to forget his role as righteous commentator for most of the poem and to neglect the moral that justifies his rollicking description of vice.
5.2 **Ingling** An ingle was a sodomite, hermaphrodite, or someone who engaged in homosexual practices. When the term was used more generally to suggest trickery, fondling, or cozening, it still carried this sexual connotation. Marston's satires refer numerous times to the lustful gallant's boy-lover, and to the English love of dainty fashions that filled the London streets with apparent hermaphrodites (*Pygmalion*, Satires II and III; and *Scourge*, Satires III, VII and VIII). See also Weever's poem on Pontus, the woman-man (*Epigrams*, Fifth Week, 14); William Rankins's satire on the duplicitous practices of inglers (*Seven Satires*, 30–31); Brathwaite's dedication to catamites in *Strappado for the Devil*; and Donne's reference to the 'prostitute boy' in his first satire. Middleton lists inglers in his array of vices in *Black Book* (339).
5 **beldam** old woman, with slightly pejorative meaning
9 **Admit** meaning 'I admitted myself into the house' or 'I do admit that I did enter'
13 **haggling** wrangling, suggesting perhaps the bickering over prices common in such a house
common place with a pun on 'commonplace', a truism
14 **tenement** house, usually rented

'Tis rotten now ('earth to earth, dust to dust').
Sodom's on fire, and consume it must,
And wanting second reparatïons
Pluto hath seized the poor reversïons.
But that hereafter worlds may truly know
What hemlocks and what rue there erst did grow,
As it is Satan's usual policy,
He left an issue of like quality,
The still memorial, if I aim aright,
Is a pale chequered black hermaphrodite.
Sometimes he jets it like a gentleman,
Otherwhiles much like a wanton courtesan.
But truth to tell a man or woman whether,
I cannot say, she's excellent in either.
But if report may certify a truth,
She's neither of either, but a cheating youth.
Yet Troynovant, that all-admirèd town,
Where thousands still do travel up and down,
Of beauty's counterfeits affords not one
So like a lovely smiling paragon
As is Pyander in a nymph's attire,
Whose rolling eye sets gazers' hearts on fire,
Whose cherry lip, black brow and smiles procure
Lust-burning buzzards to the tempting lure.
What, shall I cloak sin with a coward fear,
And suffer not Pyander's sin appear?
I will, I will.—Your reason?—Why, I'll tell,
Because time was I loved Pyander well.
True love indeed will hate love's black defame;
So loathes my soul to seek Pyander's shame.
O but I feel the worm of conscience sting,
And summons me upon my soul to bring
Sinful Pyander into open view,
There to receive the shame that will ensue.
O this sad passion of my heavy soul
Torments my heart and senses do control.
Shame thou, Pyander, for I can but shame;
The means of my amiss by thy means came.
And shall I then procure eternal blame
By secret cloaking of Pyander's shame,
And he not blush?
By heaven I will not! I'll not burn in hell
For false Pyander, though I loved him well.
No, no, the world shall know thy villainy,
Lest they be cheated with like roguery.
Walking the city as my wonted use,
There was I subject to this foul abuse;
Troubled with many thoughts pacing along,
It was my chance to shoulder in a throng,
Thrust to the channel I was, but crowding her,
I spied Pyander in a nymph's attire.
No nymph more fair than did Pyander seem,
Had not Pyander then Pyander been.
No lady with a fairer face more graced,
But that Pyander's self himself defaced.
Never was boy so pleasing to the heart
As was Pyander for a woman's part.
Never did woman foster such another,
As was Pyander, but Pyander's mother.
Fool that I was in my affectïon,
More happy I had it been a visïon.
So far entangled was my soul by love
That force perforce I must Pyander prove,
The issue of which proof did testify
Ingling Pyander's damnèd villainy.
I loved indeed and to my mickle cost;

15 **'earth ... dust'** See the penalty exacted on Adam when ousted from the garden of Eden: 'In the sweat of thy face shalt thou eat bread, till thou return unto the ground, for out of it wast thou taken: for dust thou art, and unto dust shalt thou return' (Genesis 3:19). *The Book of Common Prayer* paraphrases this verse in its instructions for 'The Burial of the Dead': 'I commend thy soul to God, the almighty, and thy body to the ground—earth to earth, ashes to ashes, dust to dust'.

16 **Sodom's** Sodom was the famous Biblical city of wickedness destroyed by God because of its sexual corruption (see Genesis 18–19). Bredbeck describes how Renaissance writers frequently allude to Sodom to conjure up a host of sexual sins that threaten the integrity of the social world, but he emphasizes the danger of erasing the specific homoerotic meanings implied by the term. The reference to Sodom indicates that this satire is not just about Pyander's gender trickery, but also concerned with homosexuality.

18 **Pluto** god of Hades, the underworld for the dead
reversïons the return of an estate to its original owner after the holder's death; the remainder or legacy

20 **hemlocks** poisonous plants
rue plant associated with bitterness and contrition

22 **issue** offspring

23 **still** secret; but also continuing

24 **pale chequered black** contrast of colours on either Pyander's clothing or his face
hermaphrodite both male and female

27–8 **But ... either** Compare Marston's call for clarification in *Pygmalion*: 'lay the substance out, | Or else, fair Briscus, I shall stand in doubt | What sex thou art, since such hermaphrodites, | Such Protean shadows so delude our sights' (Satire II, 274).

31 **Troynovant** see 2.39

34 **paragon** thing of supreme excellence

36 **rolling eye** wandering eye; often represented as a seductive and dangerous quality of feminine beauty. See, for instance, Shakespeare's Sonnet 20 where the poet's praise for his beloved is similarly implicated in a story of gender confusion: 'A woman's face, with nature's own hand painted | Hast thou, the master-mistress of my passion; | A woman's gentle heart, but not acquainted | With shifting change as it false women's fashion; | An eye more bright than theirs, less false in rolling, | Gilding the object whereupon it gazeth'. Adams compares this line to *Ghost of Lucrece*: 'Raging to see beauty's enrollèd themes | Writ in her eye-rolls' (624–5).

55 **And ... blush?** the only partial line in the text, used to accentuate the confession and resolve of the satirist

59 **roguery** trickery, mischief

60 **wonted** customary

63 **shoulder** to rub shoulders, move between people
throng crowd

64 **channel** sewer

77 **force perforce** of necessity; because of a peculiarly binding power
prove test (sexually)

I loved Pyander, so my labour lost.
Fair words I had, for store of coin I gave,
But not enjoyed the fruit I thought to have.
O so I was besotted with her words,—
His words, that no part of a she affords;
For had he been a she, injurious boy,
I had not been so subject to annoy.
A plague upon such filthy gullery!
The world was ne'er so drunk with mockery.
Rash-headed cavaliers, learn to be wise,
And if you needs will do, do with advice.
Tie not affection to each wanton smile,
Lest doting fancy truest love beguile.
Trust not a painted puppet as I have done,
Who far more doted than Pygmalïon.
The streets are full of juggling parasites
With the true shape of virgins' counterfeits,
But if of force you must a hackney hire,
Be curious in your choice; the best will tire.
The best is bad; therefore hire none at all.
Better to go on foot than ride and fall.

Satire 6

Wise Innocent

'Way for an innocent, ho!'—'What, a pure fool?'—
'Not so, pure ass'—'Ass, where went you to school?'—
'With innocents.'—'That makes the fool to prate.'—
'Fool, will you any? Yes, the fool shall ha't.'—
'Wisdom, what shall he have?'—'The fool, at least.
Provender for the ass, ho! Stalk up the beast!'—
'What, shall we have a railing Innocent?'—
'No, gentle gull, a wise man's precedent.'—
'Then forward, Wisdom!'—'Not without I list;
Twenty to one, this fool's some satirist.'—
'Still doth the fool haunt me. Fond fool be gone!'—
'No, I will stay, the fool to gaze upon.'—
'Well, fool, stay still.'—'Still shall the fool stay? No!'—
'Then pack simplicity.'—'Good Innocent, why so?'—
'Nor go nor stay: what will the fool do then?'—
'Vex him that seems to vex all other men!'—
'It is impossible; streams that are barred their course
Swell with more rage and far more greater force

81 **labour lost** proverbial phrase (Tilley, L9), punning also on the sexual meaning of 'labour'

83 **But . . . have** This line leaves somewhat ambiguous the exact extent of Pyander's 'trial'. Either the speaker did not find sexual gratification at all because of Pyander's sex, or the speaker merely did not find the kind of sexual gratification that he expected.

84 **besotted** infatuated

90 **cavaliers** swaggering sprightly gentlemen

91 **do** have sexual relations

95 **Pygmalïon** mythic artist who fell in love with the statue that he created. His story is detailed in Ovid's general account of sexual perversities in *Metamorphoses*. The speaker here asserts the strength of his devotion by referring to Pygmalion, who often exemplified the persistent lover. But Middleton secondarily follows Renaissance sonnet writers who use this myth to evoke intensely frustrated desire. Influenced by Marston's *The Metarmorphosis of Pygmalion's Image*, in which the central character finds himself 'deceived' because he believes the object of his desire to be a 'real' woman (101), Middleton represents his speaker as an unfulfilled but equally ardent Pygmalion. Middleton also implicitly refers to the literary controversy surrounding Marston's *Pygmalion*: Marston claimed that his text parodies Ovidian poetry, while others read it as unironic, and accused him of contradicting his own denunciations of lust. This reference is thus appropriate for a speaker who rails at the hermaphrodite boy that he himself has desired.

98 **hackney** prostitute (see 2.66); because the phrase denotes a horse for hire, it suggests the bawdy connotations of riding

99 **curious** careful, discriminating
tire weary

6.2 ***Wise*** foolish. This obscure satire is written as a mock dialogue between an innocent and a satirist, in which the two speakers play with the terms 'fool', 'innocent', and 'ass' in their debate over who is truly the fool. By having a character step forth to challenge the poet who has written the previous five satirical pieces, this poem self-consciously emphasizes the satirist's precarious moral ground. As the satire continues, it becomes almost impossible to distinguish the speakers.
Innocent someone deficient in intelligence or sense. When the Innocent introduces himself in the opening lines, however, he intends the term to mean someone guileless.

5 **prate** chatter; echoing Proverbs 10:8: 'The wise in heart will receive commandements: but a prating fool shall fall.' Marston similarly closes his book of satires by echoing a phrase from this verse: 'Lord, how I laugh to hear the pretty fool | How it will prate!' (*Scourge*, Satire XI, 380).

6 **'Fool . . . ha't.'** The Innocent answers his own question by suggesting that the real fool will indeed receive some of his words

8 **Provender** provisions. Middleton uses this word to establish the satire's playful puns on packing, carrying and bearing—all of which suggest the burden endured by the person who has to listen to the fool. (See 16, 31–3, and 38.) The Innocent also alludes to the proverb, 'a proud horse that will not carry his own provender' (Tilley, H683), suggesting that the Satirist must dispense with his pride and take on the intellectual equipment he needs in order to carry out his tasks.
Stalk The central meaning here is to stock or provide goods, but the word also suggests other meanings: to pursue stealthily and to walk with stiff, high and haughty steps. With this command, the Innocent sarcastically calls for preparations for the burdensome task of having the fool unleash his thoughts.

11 **list** listen

17 **'Nor . . . then?'** Through his exasperated response, the satirist pretends that the Innocent's designation of the satirist as a fool in fact only constitutes his refusal to leave or stay.

19–20 **streams . . . force** A common Renaissance image suggesting that prohibition increases desire. See Shakespeare's *Rape of Lucrece* when Tarquin tells Lucrece that her protests merely increase his desire to rape her: 'my uncontrollèd tide | Turns not, but swells the higher by this let [barrier]' (645–46). Indirectly alluding to Juvenal's famous credo, 'Difficile est saturam non scribere' (it is difficult not to write satire), the speaker uses this image to explain the involuntary nature of his writing. Citing Juvenal explicitly, Marston similarly claims: 'I cannot hold . . . my rage must freely run' (*Scourge*, Satire II, 311–12). The text's allusion to prohibition increases the irony of *Microcynicon*'s subsequent censorship and the prohibition on satire-writing.

Until their full-stuffed gorge a passage makes
Into the wide maws of more scopious lakes.
Spite me? Not spite itself can discontent
My steelèd thoughts or breed disparagement.
Had pale-faced coward fear been resident
Within the bosom of me, Innocent,
I would have housed me from the eyes of ire,
Whose bitter spleen vomits forth flames of fire.'—
'A resolute ass! O for a spurring rider,
A brace of angels!'—'What? Is the fool a briber?
Is not the ass yet weary of his load?'—
'What? With once bearing of the fool abroad?
Mount again, fool!'—'Then the ass will tire
And leave the fool to wallow in the mire.'—
'Dost thou think otherwise?'—'Good ass, then, be
gone!'—
'I stay but till the Innocent get on.'—
'What, wilt thou needs of the fool bereave me?
Then pack, good foolish ass, and so I leave thee.'

Epilogue to the last Satire of the First book

Thus may we see by folly oft the wise
Stumble and fall into fool's paradise,
For jocund wit of force must jangling be.
Wit must have his will, and so had he.
Wit must have his will, yet parting of the fray
Wit was enjoined to carry the fool away.

Qui color albus erat, nunc est contrarius albo

FINIS

21 **gorge** narrow ravine, but also implying a vomiting forth of matter
22 **maws** voracious stomach-like space
scopious spacious
27 **housed** sheltered
29 **rider** gold coin embossed with the image of a horseman
30 **brace** a couple, with possible puns on the spiritual embrace which lends security and defence (another meaning for brace)
briber either an extortioner or a general term for a scoundrel
31–2 **Is... abroad?** alludes to the proverb: 'the wise man must carry the fool upon his shoulders' (Apperson, 697)
31 **load** the Innocent's term for the speaker's diatribe, which the Satirist interprets in the next lines as his burdensome task of carrying the listener by having to explain the world to him
35–8 **'Dost... thee.'** Although the Innocent probably has the last word in sending the Satirist away, the speakers in these lines cannot with any certainty be assigned. Instead Middleton deliberately ends his satire with the Satirist blending indistinguishably into one of his targets.
37 **bereave** deprive
38 **pack** leave
Epilogue.1 As in 1.2 and Prologue.2, Middleton indicates that he has written more books. His Epilogue suggests, however, that he cannot bring them forth, since both wit and the satirist have been lost in the process of writing. Middleton could also imply that his abbreviated *Microcynicon*, unlike classical and contemporary satires containing more than one book in a single volume, gets at the heart of satire, a genre designed to self-destruct or to be left unfinished.
3 **Stumble and fall** common biblical phrase for sin. See, for instance, Jeremiah 50:32, 'And the most proud shall stumble and fall.'
fool's paradise proverbial (Tilley, F523)
4 **jocund** merry; but Marston's references to his satires as 'jocund' often turns into an assertion of their discordant nature. See *Scourge*, 367 and 371.
of force necessarily
jangling noisy and discordant
5 **Wit... will** proverbial
6 **fray** skirmish
8 ***Qui... albo*** 'its colour, that once was white, is now the very opposite' (Ovid, *Metamorphoses*, Book II, 541). Middleton refers to the transformation of the spotlessly white raven who turned black because it chattered too much. The citation provides textual symmetry because it alludes to the world's sweeping degeneration, the idea which opens Satire One. It also suggests that representing and exposing vice has possibly infected both writer and reader, transforming them into the black colour that defines the speaker's project (see Defiance.16 and the introduction).

THE GHOST OF LUCRECE

Edited by G. B. Shand

From the moment it is summoned up to perform its history on the poet's 'round stage' (35) until its final containment in the 'hall of hell' (597), the mutilated body of the raped and self-slaughtered Lucrece is the central geographical feature of Middleton's *The Ghost of Lucrece* (1600). Onto that copiously weeping, bleeding, and lamenting body is inscribed a poet's and an age's dramatically impacted masculine ambivalence about chastity and rape, guilt and shame, holy dying and suicide, salvation and damnation, Christianity and paganism. Lucrece, the classical paragon of female chastity, has been eternally polluted by the fact of rape. Riddled with a complex of Christian guilt and pagan shame (translated into concern for her stained soul on the one hand, for her stained honour on the other), she has committed suicide, both the ultimate damnable act of despair and the ultimate laudable act of reclamation. In consequence, she has descended into an underworld which is the inevitable destination of her pagan spirit, but which is imaged as a fiery hell of eternal torment, rendered unbearably tragic by her 'Christian' longing for redemption.

The history of the Lucrece myth's many transformations is concisely traced by Ian Donaldson; and Stephanie Jed persuasively situates the myth at the centre of the rise and formation of Humanism. The basic story is quickly summarized: during a lull in the Roman siege of Ardea (509 BC), young Prince Tarquin and some noble friends rode home in secret to spy into the behaviour of their wives. Only Collatine's wife, Lucrece, was found virtuously at home, spinning wool with her maids and longing for her husband's safe return; the others were all abroad, dancing and revelling. So Lucrece was judged the most chaste, and the night visitors rode back to Ardea. But ironically, Ovid tells us, blind love for Lucrece had suddenly infected Prince Tarquin. The more unachievable she seemed, the more hotly he desired her. So he returned secretly to Collatine's residence, where Lucrece chastely welcomed him as both kinsman and guest. At night, he sneaked into Lucrece's bedchamber, raped her, and fled. Lucrece summoned her husband and father from the siege, told them of the rape, and stabbed herself to death. She thus became the catalyst for the resultant banishment of the Tarquins, and the establishment of the republic.

Although viewed as the epitome of chaste virtue, Lucrece nevertheless also became a highly problematic interpretative nexus on two counts: first, she did not physically resist the rape, but yielded to fear of infamy when Tarquin threatened to kill both her and a slave and to claim he had caught them together; and second, she subsequently committed what most Renaissance Christian commentators saw as the terrible crime of self-murder. The inherent contradictions between deep personal sympathy for her history and deep moral concern for its implications rendered her a compelling and unstable signifier.

While some English versions of Lucrece's story, such as Thomas Heywood's 1607 play, come near to effacing her personal tragedy beneath the project of dramatizing its political implications, Middleton, like Shakespeare before him, seizes the opportunity to personalize an icon of violated chastity, taking an important early step toward the sympathetic evocation of the female subject which marks some of his later work. Yet Middleton's unquestioned sympathy for the plight of Lucrece is nonetheless compromised and problematic. He uses intrusive exposure of her body as a major strategy for articulating the impotent humiliation of the modest raped woman. He begins by staging her publicly, summoning her from hell to perform her wretchedness amidst a cast of Tarquins, 'Black spirits, hard hearts, thick thoughts, souls boiled in lust' (44). Her nominal audience is to be female soul-mates:

> Enrollèd vestals, Dian's hemispheres,
> Rape-slaughtered Lucreces, all martyred graces, (39–40)

but the dominant spectating gaze is actually male: the attending poet, and his implicitly male readership, from the Baron Compton to whom the poem is dedicated, to the admirers of her hair, her eyes, her breasts, all mapped and controlled by the concluding blazon. Shortly after her exposure on the Prologue's stage, her location is reconfigured as 'this world below' (69), and for the remainder of the poem Lucrece's ghostly body seems suspended in a virtually unlocalized desert place, its only reference points a distant Milky Way, the competing starry figures of Venus and Vesta, and the nearby 'hall of hell' (597). All features of a stable or identifiable surrounding worldly landscape are erased, leaving her alone in the unbroken objectifying gaze of poet and reader. The focal stare thus imposed on the female subject paradoxically enforces her object status, and silently informs every word of Lucrece's lament. It is one of Middleton's main achievements in the poem, but it depends on a calculated act of intrusion for its success.

Lucrece's foregrounded body is rendered a hyperbolic site of instability by the poem's most obvious imagistic technique, the intensive use of liquid imagery stemming from Ovid's 'fluunt lacrimae more perennis aquae' ('her tears flowed like a running stream'). Weeping and wounded, the body is figured as a copiously flowing vessel or source, awash in incessantly shifting tides, floods, fountains, rivers, streams and baths of tears and blood. The common Renaissance trope of the leaky vessel, and 'the potential shamefulness of the association of women with water' (Paster), are everywhere evident. Lucrece figures the recreated moment of her suicide as a 'tide of blood' opening the sluices of her spirit (122). Then, in a latently incestuous gesture, Lucrece exhorts the spirit of Tarquin to quaff his bloody fill at the ivory bowl of her wounded breast:

Thou art my nurse-child, Tarquin, thou art he.
Instead of milk, suck blood and tears and all.
In lieu of teats, Lucrece thy nurse, even she,
By tragic art seen through a crystal wall,
Hath carvèd with her knife thy festival.
  Here's blood for milk; suck till thy veins run over,
  And such a teat which scarce thy mouth can cover.
    (136–42)

This horribly leaking embodiment of lust's dominion is set against the distant milky white of chaste Vesta, of the *Via Lactea*, of an unattainable heaven, all equally realized in images of liquidity:

'Twas thou, O chastity, that gild'st the sky
With beams of virtue. It is thou dost dwell
In that white milken crystal silver cell,
  Thou laundress to the gods and goddesses,
  Washing their souls in fonts of holiness. (509–13)

Tarquin's ardent lust, on the other hand, is thoroughly figured in images of dry heat and fire. Jonathan Bate points out that Ovid misses the opportunity to pun from *Ardea* to *ardent*, and that if Shakespeare yields to the pun it is very discreetly. Not so Middleton:

Tarquin from Ardea posts. Hence sprang the fire,
For Ardea's name sounds ardent hot desire. (148–9)

So heated is Tarquin's ardour that it is capable of igniting Lucrece's blood, causing her fall, and turning her shame into an ever-burning beacon (73–9). The poem's larger irony is that, at least in Lucrece's assessment, none of her floods of tears and blood will finally dampen the fiery dust and ashes of Tarquin's lechery, nor quench the flames of hell where she is doomed to meet with him for eternity. Middleton's stand on Lucrece's story may be troubled, but his indictment of the blindly destructive force of male desire is unmistakable.

Lucrece's fluent properties are not limited to tears and blood. She flows in eloquence as well. Framed by the dignified measures of rhyme-royal, which Gascoigne characterized as 'a royal kind of verse, serving best for grave discourses', Lucrece's lament is in a near-theatrical language, reminiscent of early Marlowe, or of the self-conscious rhetoric of Kyd's *Spanish Tragedy*. Its frequent repetitive patterning, manifesting the reverberative quality typical of 'female complaints', is particularly remarkable. Sometimes this takes the form of highly rhythmic alliteration and assonance, or playful echoic clotting: 'Like beams of morning, to a mourning cloud' (54), 'To show that Tarquin's planet plants in me' (76), or 'From beauty's wrist so wrest that golden rod' (609). At other times the repetition may take the form of *anadiplosis*, where the word or phrase ending one line anticipates the beginning of the next:

But O my heaven, shall I forget thy spheres?
O spheres of heaven, shall I let pass your skies?
O skies which wears out time... (479–81)

(This passage also typifies the poem's use of repeated apostrophe.)

Sometimes this repetitive patterning is much more dilated. In her formal *vituperatio* against Tarquin (115–261), Lucrece pursues an *anaphora* (repetition of the beginning of a line, clause, or sentence) through twenty occurrences in fourteen stanzas, tolling out the name of the rapist: 'Tarquin the ravisher', 'Tarquin the Roman', 'Tarquin my kinsman', 'Tarquin the prince', 'Tarquin the traitor', 'Tarquin the lecher', and at last, six times, and with an effect of ominous physical presence, 'Tarquin the night-owl' (143–240).

And finally, the varied tools of repetition may inform an amplification with presentational bravura, as in this remarkable imagistic elaboration (*peristasis*) when Lucrece displays her blood- and tear-stained knife:

Behold this blade, varnished with blood and tears,
Blood from my heart, tears from my stilling eyes.
Behold, I say, this knife, whereon appears
Vesta's vermilion, melting from her skies,
And tears of pearls in bloody mysteries.
  This is the tragic knife. Here you may see
  Tears strive for fame, and blood for chastity.
    (101–7)

Such insistent patterning might seem at first to distance the reader from Lucrece's experience, conferring on it a ritual elegance which mutes its emotional intensity. But the verse has an orality which silent reading may obscure. Spoken aloud, it can spring into life, its inexorable repetitive beats becoming the driving pulse of the speaker herself, as was observed in a remarkable 1996 staging of the poem at the Bear Gardens in London's Globe Education Centre. Directed by Claire van Kampen, with Joy Richardson as Lucrece, and Mark Rylance playing the young poet in the act of writing her, this production effectively claimed a significant new female role for the Elizabethan stage repertoire. Richardson's Lucrece, reliving her rape, suicide, and damnation, was a compelling vocal and emotional presence, her performance derived organically from Middleton's instinctively theatrical provision of text which readily embodies a living subject.

Not that Lucrece's personal ownership of that text is uncomplicated. The voice of Middleton's poem might be described as a sometimes indeterminate vocal mosaic, formed from a combination of several 'female' voices identified as Lucrece's, but significantly contained and permeated by the male voice of the attendant poet, who does not confine himself to the framing Prologue and Epilogue. Instead he intervenes unannounced in Lucrece's lament on several occasions. Assigning voice is complicated by the fact that Simmes's edition provides no typographical marker to indicate changes of speaker. In Claire van Kampen's staging, Mark Rylance's poet intervened eight times from his dominant position in a study on the upper level, bringing to life the poem's latent tension between its creating poet and the violated subject of his creation. Rylance spoke the first half of 143, 241–7, 260–1, 332–8, 360–94, 402–36, 478, and 556–62.

Only a few of these masculine interruptions of the female voice are clear textual obligations. At 241–7, an unmistakable intervention, the poet contrives to elide Lucrece's description of the actual rape by entering as a kind of controlling playwright to transform the moment of violation into two discreetly emblematic dumb shows:

Now enters on the stage of Lucrece' heart
Black appetites in flamed habiliments.
When they have acted all, then they depart.
Rape ent'ring next, armèd in murder's tents,
Racks Vesta's tenants and takes all her rents.
  This shows that Vesta's deity is poor:
  She hath the stalk, but Venus hath the store.

At 302, almost as if to remind us that Lucrece's chaste domestic behaviour on the night before her rape was an object of male spying, and indeed that Lucrece's very words are contained by male reportage, he intrudes briefly, and entirely unexpectedly into her own description of her speech to her maids:

Yet was my heart so light that still I said,
'Sing merrily, my maids, our wheels go round.
Who would not sing and spin and be a maid,
To serve so sweet a goddess, and be bound
Apprentice where such mistresses abound?
  Sing merrily, my maids,' (again she says)
  'For Vesta is the goddess of our lays.' (297–303)

A third likely intrusion of the attendant poet occurs at 402–36, where he seems goaded into a personal excoriation of Tarquin, and of masculine desire more generally. This moment is harder to be certain about. While it identifies a writer whose pen has been burnt to ashes by the sulphurous fire of Tarquin's lust (and indeed, while the collocation of 'lust' with 'pen of mine' (402) may ironically turn back in self-condemnation upon a male speaker through the common Elizabethan interplay of 'pen' and 'penis'), no inverted commas or parentheses signal the advent of a new speaker, and in any case, Lucrece has already begun to present herself as writer at 396–7, a transformation she will complete at 563, where she entirely reshapes herself from the staged speaker of the beginning of her lament into the epistolary plainant who finishes it off. So the reader may be justifiably uncertain as to who the writing 'I' is when Tarquin is attacked at 402. But if the speaker here is in fact taken to be the attendant poet, there is an effect almost like duet as the voice of Lucrece re-enters at 437, seamlessly taking over the poet's apostrophe to lust, and making it explicitly her own in the reference to 'my ghost' at 438. That the status of these possible poetic interventions remains dubious suggests how blurred is the poem's line between the 'female' subject and her objectifying male presenter.

As has been suggested above, Lucrece's own status in the poem shifts from staged speaker of her lament to writer of the plaining '*Lines of Blood and Flame*' which she directs to Tarquin at 574. Her voice undergoes other variations as well, most notably into the scathing tones of a turn-of-the-century satirist, crying out for vengeance to a corrupt and thus unhearing world. At 164–77 she launches an attack on Rome which might seem, in its references to the 'triple crown' (172) and to 'Roman devils' (170), to transcend Lucrece's pagan age, glancing at the papacy and at Elizabethan anti-Catholic animosity. Later, at 360–94 (lines assigned to the poet in Claire van Kampen's production), the satirical target is enlarged: not just Tarquin's masculine lust, but an apparently current iron age, and an iniquity-ridden prince's court which may not be restricted to the world of the Tarquins. This voice, sometimes more anticipatory of Vindice in *The Revenger's Tragedy* than reminiscent of the typical female plainant, carries such compelling weight that at least one observer (Bromley) has read the entire poem as satire.

Though the poem's satirical and vengeful impulses are strong, however, the impotent stasis of Lucrece's circumscribed condition is even stronger: there is no avenger to hear her hell-bound ghost, and in any event Tarquin is already dead and damned with her. Her potential is confined to lament. Thus *The Ghost of Lucrece* is most fruitfully characterized as 'female complaint', a broadly inclusive genre extending back to Ovid's *Heroides*, and much explored in the English Middle Ages and Renaissance by poets, mainly men, drawn to its capacity for staging the solitary 'female' voice in a heightened condition of grievance over abandonment, loss or violation (Kerrigan). For his Lucrece, Middleton draws importantly on Shakespeare's Lucrece, and on Ovid's in the *Fasti*. He also appears familiar with versions in Livy's *Historia*, perhaps as translated by William Painter in *The Palace of Pleasure* (1566) or by Philemon Holland in *The Roman History* (1600, but licensed in 1598). And, as recorded in Adams's edition, he does recycle phrasing and imagery from Robert Greene's *Ciceronis Amor* (1598), a work which probably caught his attention because of an incidental Lucrece-like narrative in which the Roman conqueror of a castle finds its lord and chaste lady in bed, she having committed suicide to prevent her certain rape. But the formal kin of Middleton's poem are works like Samuel Daniel's *Complaint of Rosamond* (1592), Thomas Churchyard's lament of Jane Shore from *The Mirror for Magistrates* (reprinted as 'The Tragedy of Shore's Wife' in 1593), and Michael Drayton's *Matilda* (1594). Like so many earlier 'female complaints' (and like Shakespeare's *The Rape of Lucrece* for that matter), all these works are couched formally in rhyme-royal. All feature a powerless plaining female ghost. And all are mediated in some fashion by an attendant male poet whose voice inevitably complicates and even contains the 'female' voice of the poem's subject.

The troubled containment of Middleton's Lucrece ultimately goes beyond the fact that she is a male construction, extending to her eternal confinement in a Christian hell. Middleton tacitly accepts a Calvinist reading of her damnation. Where Shakespeare's Lucrece, at her suicide, releases an 'immaculate and spotless' soul from the 'polluted prison' of her body, bequeathing it 'unto the clouds', Middleton's heroine has gone to hell, and her lament in no way challenges the appropriateness of this fate. Instead, she characterizes herself as culpable, indeed complicit, in having been deceived by Tarquin: 'I left sweet verdure for a flattering voice' (457).

Middleton does not directly foreground the debate, joined famously by Saint Augustine in *De civitate dei*, as to whether Lucrece's damnation is for self-slaughter, or for the sexual pollution she so relentlessly claims. Instead, he virtually neutralizes it, implying that, whatever her faults, as a pagan her soul's exclusion from salvation is automatic. This Christian colouring of classical materials is at the heart of the poem's climax, as Middleton exploits the central paradox of a pre-Christian (and therefore damned) Lucrece who nonetheless has compelling Christian instincts. He renders her thoroughly contrite, and yearning for Christian salvation. At 479, Lucrece addresses heaven. She begins with two stanzas of rhetorical questions berating herself for having forsaken chastity. Then, beginning at 514, she is given five entire stanzas of apostrophe to chastity, figured as 'Saint' Vesta (the Roman goddess of the household). This single-sentence apostrophe is grammatically closed only at 549, beginning a climactic stanza where at last she prays for explicit Christian redemption, through the elements of the Eucharist ('blood divine', 'food angelical') and through the gift of the Holy Spirit ('silver dove'). Abruptly, however, the following stanza (556–62) pulls back to assert her pagan ineligibility, either in her own voice or in that of the poet, ending with:

> Lucrece, I say, how canst thou Lucrece be,
> Wanting a God to give a life to thee?

The force of this moment is devastating. As the words of rejection were spoken by Mark Rylance's poet at the Globe, Joy Richardson's Lucrece shrank perceptibly, her entire demeanour instantly transformed from beseeching penitence to resigned and bitter hellishness. For after such knowledge, Lucrece can entertain no hope. She bitterly consecrates her lament to Tarquin, and her mortified body is pulled from the poem's stage by Melpomene, the muse of tragedy, sinking in despair to partner the ghost of Tarquin 'in the hall of hell' (597). The poetic persona now closes off the poem with a wistful, even chagrined funereal blazon of Lucrece's physical beauties as they are transformed by Death: her hair, her eyes, her tongue, her breath, her breasts. He thus contains Lucrece's body, her 'female' voice, her very subjectivity, in a specifically objectifying masculine frame. Indeed, the bracketing of her lament between the male poet's Prologue and Epilogue is of a piece with Lucrece's strait confinement not only in hell, but in a world of overwhelming male desire which inevitably imposes pollution, destruction, and damnation, even on the most chaste.

SEE ALSO

Textual introduction and apparatus: *Companion*, 467
Authorship and date: *Companion*, 337

The Ghost of Lucrece

To the Right Honourable and my very bountiful good Lord,
my Lord Compton, T.M. wisheth the fruit of eternal fruition.
Comptus honos, honor est Comptono, et Compton honore.

Thou, that rock'st comely honour in thine arms,
Thou patron to the child-house of my vein,
Thou hive unto the muses' honey swarms,
And godfather to th' issue of my brain:
To thee, baptiser of mine infant lines
With golden water in a silver font,
Thy bounty gold, thy fingers silver twins,
Silvering my paper's ink as they were wont;
To thee, the bloody crystal of a ghost
Wrapt in a fiery web I spin to thee;
To thee, the thawer of Diana's frost,
Tarquin the hot in Lucrece' tragedy;
To thee I consecrate these ashy fires,
She quenched in blood, he burnt in his desires.
Bound by your honour's bounty,
T.M.

Castissimo, purissimoque Lucretiae Spiritui: Thomas Medius
et Gravis Tonus primum Surge vociferat
Tu castitatis imago,
Surgito! Tarquinium Phlegetontis imagine notum,
Noscito! Tu coeptis—nam te mutavit et illum—
Adspirato meis! Postremo tempore mundi,
Ad sua perpetuum deducito crimina carmen.
Castissimo Spiritui tuo addictissimus,
T.M.

The Prologue

Reach me a quill from the white angels' wings,
My paper from the *Via Lactea*,
My ink from Jove's high nectar-flowing springs,
My muse from Vesta. Awake, Rhamnusia!
Call up the ghost of gored Lucretia.
Thrice hath the trumpet of my pen's round stage
Sounded a '*Surge!*' to her bloody age.

Sad spirits, soft hearts, sick thoughts, souls sod in tears,
Well-humoured eyes, quick ears, tear-wounded faces,
Enrollèd vestals, Dian's hemispheres,
Rape-slaughtered Lucreces, all martyred graces,
Be ye the audience, take your tragic places.
Here shall be played the miseries that immures
Pure diamond hearts in crystal covertures.

Black spirits, hard hearts, thick thoughts, souls boiled in lust,
Dry fiery eyes, dull ears, high bloody looks
Made of hot earth, moulded in fire and dust,

2 **Compton** William, second Baron Compton (later first Earl of Northampton), *c.*1568–1630. Peele's *Polyhymnia*, in which he figures as one of the champions of the Virgin Queen, was dedicated to him in 1590, and he was the recipient of some half-dozen dedications after *Ghost*. He married the wealthy Elizabeth Spencer, 18 April 1599, over the strenuous objections of her father, Sir John Spencer. When the Comptons' first child, Spencer, was born *c.*5 May 1601, the Queen personally worked a reconciliation between the couple and Sir John.

Ghost may have been dedicated to Compton simply to capitalize on his popularity with the Queen, his recent marriage, or the fabulous dowry rumoured to have accompanied his wife. While there is no indisputable sign that the dedication produced favour, the wording sounds like gratitude, implying that bounty from Compton had preceded publication. Nonetheless Adams speculates that Middleton received nothing for his pains, and that he subsequently pilloried Compton as Sir Christopher Clutchfist in *Hubburd*.

3 ***Comptus ... honore.*** Beautified honour, honour is one with Compton, and Compton one with honour.

4 **honour in thine arms** This may glance at Compton's honorial arms, whose main elements were a lion passant gardant or, between three helmets argent.

5 **child-house** nursery (apparently Middleton's coinage)
vein literary aptitude

10 **twins** Given the baptismal context, the reference is apparently to the two-fingered gesture of blessing. SIMMES's spelling, 'twines', makes the meaning strings or strands an alternate possibility.

12 **crystal** (*a*) glass, mirror (*b*) ice, glancing at Lucrece's chastity (*c*) with a possible glance at 'chrysalis' (collocating with 'web' and 'spin')

13 **Wrapt** modifying 'ghost'

14 **Diana's** goddess of chastity and the moon, as well as of the hunt

20–8 ***Castissimo*** ... T.M. To the most chaste and pure Ghost of Lucrece: Thomas, in a moderate and weighty voice [with a pun (*Medius ... Tonus*) on 'Middleton'], cries out the first 'Arise'.

O thou, the image of chastity, arise! Acknowledge Tarquin, branded with the mark of Phlegethon! Favour these my beginnings (which have transformed both you and him)! In this the world's worst age, launch my tireless poetry against his crime.

Totally devoted to your most chaste ghost, T.M.

23 ***Phlegetontis*** Phlegethon is one of the rivers of fire in Hades.

25 ***Postremo tempore mundi*** the iron age (see 335, 364)

31 ***Via Lactea*** Milky Way

33 **Vesta** Goddess of the hearth and household, and, by extension, of domestic union and chastity. The Vestal Virgins maintained the eternal fire in the temple of Vesta in Rome.
Rhamnusia Nemesis (associated with revenge)

35 **Thrice** In the public theatres, the last of three trumpet sounds signalled the start of the prologue.
round stage a metonymy for 'theatre'

36 **'Surge'** Arise (disyllabic)
age era, looking ahead to the idea that Lucrece's rape manifests the Iron Age

37 **sod** seethed, steeped

38 **Well-humoured** moistened
quick alive, lively

39 **hemispheres** followers

45 **Dry fiery eyes** as opposed to the 'Well-humoured eyes' of the audience (38). Widespread physiological theory held that the body was chiefly composed of four fluids or humours, their relative proportions creating personal qualities and temperaments: blood (sanguine, hot-moist), yellow bile (choleric, hot-dry), black bile (melancholic, cold-dry), phlegm (phlegmatic, cold-moist).

Desire's true graduates read in Tarquin's books,
Be ye our stage's actors. Play the cooks:
 Carve out the daintiest morsel—that's your part—
 With lust-keen falchion, even in Lucrece' heart.

Now weepeth Lucrece with a trine of eyes,
Quenching the fire of lust with tears and blood,
Changing those eye-lamps, which were wont to rise
Like beams of morning, to a mourning cloud,
Her heart, the purest eye, to a red sea-flood.
 Her ghost the idea of her soul resumes,
 Which Phoenix-wise burns in her own perfumes.

The Ghost of Lucrece

Medea's magic, and Calypso's drugs,
Circe's enchantments, Hecatë's triform
Weans my soul, sucking at revenge's dugs,
To feed upon the air. What wind, what storm
Blew my dissevered limbs into this form,
 And from the virgin paradise of death
 Conjures my ghost with poetizing breath?

The candle of my shame burns in the sky,
Set on the cross-poles of the firmament
To fear away divine virginity
And light this world below, that being bent
To follow me, they go not as I went.
 But when I hope to see the candle wane,
 Then Tarquin's spirit falls on the snuff again,

So that the snuff, the savour of my shame
That stinks before the throne of chastity,
Is still rekindled with venereal flame
To show that Tarquin's planet plants in me
The root of fiery blood and luxury,
 First forcing with his breath one flame's retire,
 Then takes my blood for oil, his lust for fire.

Now burns the beacon of my soul indeed
Too high for fame, but low enough for fume.
Saints, keep your cloister-house. Vesta, make speed,
Take in thy flowers, for fear the fire consume
Thy eternal sweet virginity-perfume.
 For lust and blood are mingled in one lamp
 To seal my soul with rape and murder's stamp.

Before my shame, yon candle had no fire,
Vestals nil feared me, the world saw me not.
Shame was the tinder, and the flint desire
That struck in Tarquin's bosom and begot
A child of fire, a firebrand, and so hot
 That it consumed my chastity to dust,
 And on my heart painted the mouth of lust.

Was I the cradle, O my chastity,
To rock and lull this bastard firebrand,
Nursed with my blood, weaned with my tragedy,
Fed at my knife's sharp point upon my hand,
Born and reborn where'er my spirits stand?
 I was the cradle. See the fiery dart
 That burns Diana's temples in my heart.

Behold this blade, varnished with blood and tears,
Blood from my heart, tears from my stilling eyes.
Behold, I say, this knife, whereon appears
Vesta's vermilion, melting from her skies,
And tears of pearls in bloody mysteries.
 This is the tragic knife. Here you may see
 Tears strive for fame, and blood for chastity.

Right hand, thou act'st revenge's hand aright.
This knife and thou have sworn to kiss my breast.
Thou art my Vesta's antidote, to fright
Lust from the bed of Collatinus' rest.
Performer of thy vow, hand, be thou blest,
 For thou in this hast shown me what thou art,
 Driving the foe from scaling of my heart.

47 **read** learned
50 **falchion** sword
51 **Now weepeth Lucrece** The implication is that she has arisen to the stage by this point.
trine threesome (her actual eyes, and the wound to her heart)
55 **sea-flood** tide
56 **idea** perfect form. (The sense is that Lucrece's soul inhabits, for the moment, the apparition of her deceased body, 'ghost' being the inverted object of 'resumes'.)
resumes puts on anew
57 **Which** The referent is presumably 'Her ghost.'
Phoenix-wise Phoenix: mythical Arabian bird, reincarnated from its own ashes
perfumes odorous fumes or vapour given off by the burning of any substance
59 **Medea's** vengeful sorceress of Greek mythology, responsible for numerous deaths, including those of her own children
Calypso's nymph who held Odysseus enthralled for seven years
60 **Circe's** enchantress who turned Odysseus's companions to swine
Hecatë's goddess of the moon, and Persephone's underworld attendant, with power to conjure dreams, phantoms and spirits; often represented with three heads or bodies (hence 'triform')
67 **cross-poles** transverse supports, as of a high roof
69 **bent** inclined, tempted
70 **they** i.e., chaste women, those who comprise 'divine virginity' (68)
72 **snuff** burnt or burning portion of a candle-wick
75 **still** constantly
76 **Tarquin's planet** Venus
77 **luxury** lechery
81 **fame** here, modest female reputation, which, in Elizabethan prescriptions, keeps a low profile
fume (*a*) smoke (which dirties it) (*b*) anger
88 **nil** not at all
91 **firebrand** i.e., Tarquin's lust (literally, flaming kindling, but figuratively (*a*) one who enflames the passions (*b*) one who is doomed or deserves to burn in Hell)
93 **mouth of lust** i.e., her death-wound?
102 **stilling** trickling (aphetic form of 'distilling')
104 **vermilion** scarlet pigment
105 **pearls** associated with purity
mysteries rites
108–14 At some point immediately before or during this stanza, Lucrece appears to reenact her suicide, stabbing herself once again. Joy Richardson, in the 1996 Globe production, used the force of the verb 'Driving' in 114, plunging the imagined dagger into her breast as she spoke the word.
111 **Collatinus** Collatine, Lucrece's husband

Come, spirit of fire, bred in a womb of blood,
Forged in a furnace by the smith of hell,
Begot and formèd in that burning flood
Where Pluto's Phlegethontic tenants dwell,
And scalded spirits in their fiery cell
Breathes from their soul the flame of luxury.
From that luxurious clime I conjure thee.

Now is my tide of blood. Come, quench thy soul.
The sluices of my spirit now runs again.
Come, I have made my breast an ivory bowl
To hold the blood that streameth from my vein.
Drink to my chastity, which thou hast slain.
But woe the while, that labour is in vain,
To drink to that which cannot pledge again.

Quaff thine own fill and let that lustful flame
That circuits in the circle of thy spirit
Pledge thy desire, carousing off my shame
Which swims amidst my blood and doth inherit
The portion of my soul without a merit.
And if this spring of blood cannot suffice,
I'll rain down tears from my elemental eyes.

Thou art my nurse-child, Tarquin, thou art he.
Instead of milk, suck blood and tears and all.
In lieu of teats, Lucrece thy nurse, even she,
By tragic art seen through a crystal wall,
Hath carvèd with her knife thy festival.
Here's blood for milk; suck till thy veins run over,
And such a teat which scarce thy mouth can cover.

Tarquin the ravisher: O, at that name
See how mine eyes dissolveth into tears!
Tarquin the Roman: I describe my shame.
From Rome it came, a Roman name it bears.
Tarquin my guest: lo, here began my fears.
Tarquin from Ardea posts. Hence sprang the fire,
For Ardea's name sounds ardent hot desire.

Tarquin my kinsman: O divinity,
Where art thou fled? Hast thou forsook thy sphere?
Where's virtue, knighthood and nobility?
Faith? Honour? Piety? They should be near,
For 'kinsman' sounds all these. They are not here.
Tarquin my kinsman: was it thou didst come
To sack my Collatine's Collatium?

Tarquin my kinsman: too unkindly done,
And by a kinsman too, my ghost avers it.
Doth therefore that same name of kindred run
To see their kin red, and with blood prefers it?
O enemy to faith, that still defers it!
Had Tarquin never lustful Tarquin been,
Lucrece the chaste should have chaste Lucrece seen.

Tarquin the prince: had Rome no better heirs?
Thou mistress of the world, no better men?
Thou prodigality of nature's fairs,
Are tigers kings? Mak'st thou thy throne a den?
Thy silver glittering streams black Lerna's fen?
Thy seven hills that should o'erlook thy evils
Like seven hells to nurse up Roman devils?

To thee, that mak'st the moon thy looking-glass
To view thy triple crown and seven-fold head,
To thee, I say, the ghost of what I was
Plains me and it, sith thou so long hast fed
The ravisher and starved the ravishèd.
If Vesta's lines were ever writ in thee,
Then weigh the blotting of those lines in me.

115–261 This attack on Tarquin is in the form of a *vituperatio*, an ironic inversion of the methods of rhetorical praise. As an exercise it was common in Renaissance schools and universities, and is therefore not surprising in a young poet. It is in three parts: an exordium (115–42), an ironic genus of Tarquin (143–240), and the presentation of his vicious achievement (241–61).

115 **Come, spirit of fire** conjuring Tarquin, who ascends the imagined stage between 121 and 122

116 **smith of hell** i.e., Vulcan

118 **Pluto's** god of the underworld

122 **tide** (*a*) high tide (*b*) time

135 **elemental** Water is one of the four elements, of course, but 'elemental' may also mean 'pertaining to the sky'; see 253 and 340, where 'elements' are celestial spheres, and 502, where 'element' appears to mean 'sky'.

136 **nurse-child** child breast-fed by its nurse

139 **crystal wall** again figuring Lucrece's gored ghost as an observed glass or mirror, as in the dedicatory sonnet, line 12. (John Jowett suggests, alternatively, an echo of the crystal pavement of Venus' temple in Marlowe's *Hero and Leander*, I.144–5: 'There might you see the gods in sundry shapes, | Committing heady riots, incests, rapes'.)

140 **festival** (*a*) apparently a feeding place (*b*) feast

148 **Ardea** town 23 miles south of Rome, site of the siege by the Roman army (including both Tarquin and Collatine)

150 **kinsman** Lucius Tarquinius Collatinus (Collatine) and Sextus Tarquinius were second cousins.

153 **near** quibbling on 'closely related'

156 **Collatium** here, Lucrece herself, figured conventionally as the patriarchal property of Collatine (his house, city, fortress)

157 **unkindly** unnaturally, not befitting a relative
done with a play on the sexual sense

159 **Doth...run** i.e., Do kindred run to see their kin red (with blood, shame)? SIMMES, in 159, uses the usual Elizabethan spelling 'kinred', setting up the wordplay.

160 **prefers** promotes

161 **defers** sets aside

163 **Lucrece...seen** exploiting the duality between the gored ghost and the voice of its presenter (see 174)

166 **fairs** beauties

168 **Lerna's** a marsh in Argolis (a region of ancient Greece), traditional home of the many-headed Hydra slain by Hercules

169 **o'erlook** (*a*) keep watch over (*b*) wink at, ignore

172 **triple crown** signifying imperial rule over Europe, Asia and Africa; perhaps also glancing at the papal crown

174 **Plains** laments, complains

175 **starved** killed, destroyed (playing on 'fed' in the previous line)

176 **lines** (*a*) lineaments (*b*) lines of writing

177 **weigh** ponder

Tarquin the prince: sham'st thou to hear thy name?
Rome, 'tis thy heir. Sham'st thou to call him son?
Tarquin the prince: lo, I'll repeat thy shame.
A Roman heir, from him to thee I run.
I'll shame you both before my shame be done.
  Tarquin the prince, Tarquin the Roman heir:
  Thus will I haunt and hunt you to despair.

Tarquin the traitor: bid my spirit rise
And call up all the senses of my soul,
For treason should be guarded with more eyes
Than was Jove's Io under his control,
For treason's guile doth win the traitor's goal.
  Tarquin the traitor: watch when time's in season,
  For treason doth betray all things to treason.

Tarquin the lecher: virgin chastity
Melts at the heat of that luxurious word,
Like maiden snow upon a promontory,
Kissing the sun, her heavenly lovely lord,
Then dies, and melts into a wat'ry ford.
  So did my chastity's white-snow attire
  Dissolve in blood at Tarquin's lustful fire.

Tarquin the night-owl: chastity, beware.
Thou art beset with millions of deceits.
Thy eyes have leaden lids, they take no care;
Thy senses, rocked asleep, and thy conceits,
Tempered with silence, fear nor snares nor baits.
  Only the vestal pureness of thy soul
  Bade me beware that night-observing owl.

Tarquin the night-owl: in whose flaming eyes
Lust and desire bandied their balls of blood,
Chasing my spirit with fiery mysteries
Unto the hazard where destruction stood
Ready to strike my soul into a cloud,
  So, when the sun had seen my vapour rise,
  Then with his beams to dash me from the skies.

Tarquin the night-owl: watch destructïon.
What, hath the eyes of lust no lids at all,
Or do they hover for confusïon,
Answering in silence when affections call?
When lust awakes, the eyelids never fall,
  But, like a courser holding reason's rein,
  Doth shut the eyes and opens them again.

Tarquin the night-owl: Vesta, look about.
The fourth alarum of my fears now rings,
And yet the hour of dread is scarce run out,
For midnight's face more force of terror brings.
To think on that, my sinews shake like strings,
  And chastity, which yet had spirit and breath,
  Lay quavering at my heart to tune her death.

Tarquin the night-owl: turn the glass again.
Five times my tongue, the hammer of my soul,
That beats upon my breath and strikes a strain
Sounding all quavers—that's the song of dole—
Five times my tongue did even my tongue control,
  For fear is such a slave and coward elf,
  That, fearing others, runs and fears himself.

Tarquin the night-owl: enter treachery.
Sextus Tarquinius, this sixth hour is thine.
Farewell my life, farewell my chastity,
Farewell, though not mine now, that which was mine.
Thy grapes are now devoured. Alas, poor vine.
  The tyrant, with his force of luxury,
  Tires me an aunt, through imbecility.

Now enters on the stage of Lucrece' heart
Black appetites in flamed habiliments.
When they have acted all, then they depart.
Rape ent'ring next, armèd in murder's tents,
Racks Vesta's tenants and takes all her rents.
  This shows that Vesta's deity is poor:
  She hath the stalk, but Venus hath the store.

187 **with** by
188 **Io** Seduced by Jove and then transformed into a heifer, she was guarded by Argus of the hundred eyes.
under his control The pronoun refers, without explicit antecedent, to Argus.
194 **promontory** mountain ridge
196 **ford** stream
202 **conceits** imaginings
207 **Lust...blood** i.e., Tarquin's eyeballs are figured as bloody with lust and desire. 'bandied', meaning tossed back and forth, as with rackets, introduces a series of tennis references: once chased to the 'hazard' or in-play area of a tennis court (209), Lucrece's soul is struck or served (210) and dashed or devastatingly returned (212) in an exchange between destruction (209) and the sun (211).
213 **watch** (*a*) watch for (*b*) stay awake
218 **reason's rein** that rein which reason properly should hold. (The conventional image of the rider reason controlling the horse of the passions is reversed here.)
219 **Doth shut** The apparent agent is 'lust' (217), and the sense is that lust takes control of sight, as with Tarquin's 'flaming eyes' (206).
221 **alarum** peal or chime of warning bell or clock (here referring to the anaphora 'Tarquin the night-owl', which is repeated six times)
224 **strings** of a musical instrument
226 **quavering** (*a*) playing or singing quavers, i.e., eighth notes (*b*) trembling
227 **glass** hourglass
228 **hammer** as of a bell
232 **elf** demon
239 **tyrant** SIMMES prints 'Tyr-ant' to set up the pun in 240.
240 **Tires** attires
aunt whore
imbecility weakness, impotence
242 **flamed** flaming. Specifically (*a*) burning (*b*) decorated with flame-like streaks or slashes (*c*) flame-coloured (as often was the attire of strumpets)
habiliments (*a*) garments (*b*) armour
244 **tents** (*a*) intents, purposes (*b*) tents of war
247 **stalk** (*a*) stem (*b*) chaff
store that which is stored; i.e. the grain. (In *A Lover's Complaint*, 147, Shakespeare's abandoned maid 'Reserv'd the stalk and gave him all my flower.')

This is the tragic scene. Bleed heart, weep eyes,
Fly soul from body, spirit from my veins.
Follow my chastity where'er it lies,
Which my unhallowed body now refrains.
Look to the lamp of chastity, it wanes.
The star which guided all my elements
Pulls in her head and leaves the firmaments.

Rape, in his paws of blood and fangs of lust,
Hath stained th' immaculate lily of my field,
And hath sepùlchred in the shade of dust
Diana's milken robe, and Vesta's shield.
When tigers prey, the seely lambs must yield;
When Tarquin posts from Ardea, by and by
Lucrece must lose her life and chastity.

O Collatine, where sleeps thy troubled spirit?
What new-come Morpheus hath arrested thee?
Doth thy heart soundly sleep? Doth nothing stir it?
Dear Collatine, awake! Wert thou with me,
The arches of mine eyes would waken thee,
For tears like waves rush at my eyelids' door,
Striving together who should go before.

Come, Collatine, the foe hath sacked thy city.
Collatium goes to wrack. Come, Collatine.
Come, Collatine, all piety and pity
Is turned to petty treason. What is thine
Is seized upon long since, and what is mine
Carried away. True man, thou sleep'st at Rome
Even while a Roman thief robs thee at home.

Come, Collatine, 'tis Lucrece bids thee come,
Or shall I send my pursuivant of groans
Unto proud Rome from poor Collatium
To make all private means by public moans,
Discoursing my black story to the stones?
Come, Collatine, 'tis Tarquin's dreadful drum
That conjures me to call, and thee to come.

Thy Lucrece' bed, which had fair canopies
Spangled with stars like to the firmament,
And curtains wrought with many deities,
Resembling Jove's white lacteal element,
Are stainèd now by lust and ravishment,
The stars out-stared, the deities defied.
These I had stored, the other deified.

The night before Tarquin and lust came hither—
Ill token for a chaste memorial—
My maids and I, poor maid, did spin together
Like the three sisters which the fates we call,
And fortune lent us wheels to turn withal.
Round goes our wheels like worlds. On mine alone
Stood fortune reeling on a rolling stone.

Yet was my heart so light that still I said,
'Sing merrily, my maids, our wheels go round.
Who would not sing and spin and be a maid,
To serve so sweet a goddess, and be bound
Apprentice where such mistresses abound?
Sing merrily, my maids,' (again she says)
'For Vesta is the goddess of our lays.

'Maidens,' quoth I, 'but think what maidens be:
They are the very string that ties their hearts,
The pillars of their souls' pure purity,
The distillations of th' essential parts,
Both good deservers and the good deserts.
Then, seeing Vesta hath so many trades,
Go round, our wheels. Sing merrily, my maids.

'What nimble fingers hath virginity,
To twist the thread and turn the wheel about!
O virgins, that same pearl of chastity
Shines like the moon to light your thoughts throughout.
Pure cogitations never harbours doubt,
But like the fairest purest chrysolite,
Admits no bruise without a crack with it.

'Spin merrily, my maiden paradise.'
Thus with a merry cheer I whirled their wheels,
And made them rid at once more than at twice.
Such pretty pleasure true affection feels
That time's old head runs swifter than his heels,
For mirth's fledged wings are of so quick a flight
That makes the morn seem noon, the noon seem night.

251 **refrains** avoids (here transitive, the object being 'body')
252 **lamp of chastity** i.e., the Moon
253 **elements** (*a*) basic components of body (and soul); but playing here on the secondary meaning (*b*) celestial spheres
254 **firmaments** heavens; the plural is quite unusual
256 **lily of my field** chastity. (The phrase, though not the sense, may derive from Matthew 6:28.)
259 **seely** innocent
263 **Morpheus** god of dreams
266–7 **arches . . . waves** Probably refers to the arches of London Bridge, famed for the noise of the water rushing through them.
273–4 **seized . . . Carried away** probably from the standard English gloss of Latin *rapio, rapere*: to seize, carry off, drag away
277 **pursuivant** herald
279 **means** laments
286 **Jove's . . . element** the Milky Way
289 **These . . . deified.** The sense of the line seems to be that Lucrece had decorated her canopies and curtains herself.
stored accumulated
deified created as gods
291 **Ill . . . memorial** i.e., an evil way of identifying a chaste occasion
296 **reeling** (*a*) whirling unsteadily (*b*) winding up thread (as Collatine should have been present to do—355)
stone ball
305–8 **They . . . deserts** The essential quality of maidens, namely virgin chastity, is the very string that ties the hearts of maidens, it is the pillar of their purity, and so on; finally, in line 308, virtue is its own reward.
316 **chrysolite** greenish gemstone such as zircon, topaz
320 **rid** accomplish (more in one hour than others might in two)

'My maids, those airy sinews in your hands
Were of a finer thread than that you spin.
It was a merry age in golden bands
When Saturn sowed the earth and did begin
To teach bad husbands a new way to win.
  Then was true labour exercised and done,
  When gods did reel what goddesses had spun.'

Those times are waxen bald. A prouder air
Blows in the heaven and breathes upon the earth.
That age is out of date. Another heir
Claims his possession by an iron birth,
And in an iron throne of death and dearth
  Rules this young age, sucking until it whine
  Even at the dugs of Pluto's Proserpine.

Thus, like Diana by a lily fount,
Sat I amidst my vestal elements.
Thus did myself still with myself account,
To free my thoughts from chainèd discontents
And stir up mirth, the nurse of nourishments.
  Thus with a lightsome spirit and soul's carouse,
  I like a housewife cherished up my house.

When Roman dames, tickled with pride and lust,
Ravished with amorous philosophy,
Printed the measures of their feet in dust,
Temp'ring their blood with music's harmony—
The very synod-house of venery—
  Then I at home, instead of melody,
  Grated my wheel upon the axletree.

How like Arachne turnèd I my wheel!
Each of my maids how like a shepherdess!
Had Collatine, my shepherd, held the reel,
We four might well have made a country mess.
But one abroad makes one at home the less.
  My Collatine, my shepherd, was at Rome,
  And left poor me to feed his flock at home.

Is Venus made a laundress to the court?
Cupid, her son, elected for a page?
No marvel if Diana's stars do sport
With Venus' planets upon Cupid's stage.
Iron must have fire. This is an iron age.
  Our souls, like smiths, with anvils of desire,
  Beat on our flesh, and still we sparkle fire.

The prince's court is ev'n a firmament
All wrought with beams by day and stars by night;
The prince himself the sunny element
From whence all beams and stars do borrow light
To paint their faces with a red and white;
  Those beams ambassadors of his bright array,
  Those stars his counsellors by night and day.

How comes it then—speak, speak, iniquity,
Thou blur of kingdoms and thou blot of kings,
Thou metamorphosis of purity,
That shap'st the greater things to lesser things—
How comes it then that Cupid's bow-string swings
  About the heels of time? Iniquity,
  It is the halter of thy luxury.

Thou hast burnt out the humour of thy bones,
And made them powders of impiety
To strew about the earth as thick as stones,
Like wombs of lust in tombs of lechery;
And all thy sinews, O iniquity,
  Are so dried up, and now so slender spun,
  That Venus makes them bow-strings for her son.

327 **merry age in golden bands** the golden age, the first and best age of the world, when Saturn, the Roman god of the harvest, reigned benignly, and introduced agriculture

329 **husbands** husbandmen, farmers
win earn, as through harvest

332 **bald** i.e., old, decrepit

334 **heir** Vulcan?

335 **iron** referring, as at 364, to the iron age, the last and worst age of the world, a period of wickedness, debasement

338 **Proserpine** goddess of fertility, queen of the underworld

340 **elements** celestial spheres, i.e., chaste maids (proceeding from the association of Diana with the moon); see 'Diana's stars' (below, 362)

343 **nurse of nourishments** Middleton is particularly fond of this brand of etymological wordplay

347 **Ravished with amorous philosophy** enraptured by practical wisdom or disputation on the art of love (i.e., 'Seduced by love talk')

348 **measures** playing on the sense 'dances'

349 **Temp'ring** (*a*) blending (*b*) heating

350 **synod-house** (*a*) ecclesiastical council-chamber; but (*b*) a 'synod' is also an astrological conjunction, and 'house' may be used in a loosely astrological sense, suggesting that the other Roman wives, carried away by love-talk, dance and music, were under the planetary influence of Venus, as at 363. (In either case, wanton dance—the conjunction of 'blood' with 'music'—is a site of 'venery' or sexual indulgence.)

352 **Grated** underlining the contrast with the sounds of dance music
axletree (*a*) axle (of the spinning-wheel) (*b*) imaginary axis-line of any heavenly body, or the pole of the heavens (compare previous note)

353 **Arachne** unfortunate weaver who angered Athena with her depictions of the gods' amours, and was transformed into a spider

356 **mess** company of four (Lucrece, her two maids, and Collatine)

360 **laundress** here, a prostitute (but not at 512)

361 **page** male whore

367 **prince's** i.e., the ideal prince, ironically contrasted with Prince Tarquin

369 **sunny element** the sun itself

371 **red and white** conventional figure for beauty

372 **array** courtly assembly (and playing on 'ray')

378–9 **Cupid's ... time** Cupid's bow is now the possession of time; love has become temporal, debased. Compare the situation of beauty at 466.

380 **It ... luxury** Cupid's bowstring (love) has become subject to Iniquity's lust.

381 **humour** juice, perhaps even marrow; probably alluding to the effects of syphilis

382 **powders** ashes

Where is the spring of blood's virginity
That wont to serve thy veins like conduit heads
And cleanse thy cistern of iniquity
With maiden humours from chaste Flora's meads?
Then slept'st thou like a lord in honour's beds.
  Then virtue was thy bedfellow. Now know,
  As great an ebb follows as great a flow.

Lo, under that base type of Tarquin's name
I cipher figures of iniquity.
He writes himself the shamer, I the shame,
The actor he, and I the tragedy.
The stage am I, and he the history,
  The subject I, and he the ravisher.
  He, murd'ring me, made me my murderer.

O lust, this pen of mine that writes thee 'lust'
Lies blasted at the sulphur of thy fire.
The quill and feathers, burnt to ashy dust,
Like dust and ashes flies before desire,
Unable to endure thy flamed attire;
  For, in the sky of contrariety,
  The winner's life is when the losers die.

If I proceed, O fiery incolants
Of that vast hell which Pluto terms his hall,
Tarquin's companions, ye, I say, that haunts
The banks of burning baths, to you I call:
Send me Prometheus' heart t' indite withal,
  And from his vulture's wings a pen of blood
  Thrice steeped and dipped in Phlegethontic flood.

Then shall I stamp the figure of the night
On Tarquin's brow, and mark him for her son,
The heir of darkness, bastard of the light,
The cloud of heaven, th' eclipser of the sun,
The stain in Vesta's cheeks which first begun
  In Tarquin's flesh, begot of fiery dust.
  O thou the hell of love, untutored lust!

It bribes the flesh to war against the spirit
With tickling blood must'ring in every vein.
It weans the conscience from her heavenly merit,
Depraving all chaste thoughts, her maiden train.
It makes the heart think and unthink again.
  It taints the breath with fire, the brain with blood,
  And sets a devil where a god had stood.

Being in the eye, lust is a cockatrice,
Hemlock in taste, a canker in the thought,
And in the life a moth, which in a trice
Consumes that treasure which so dear was bought
And cost so many drops of blood, for naught;
  So many streams of blood and baths of sweat,
  To bathe our spirits and to quench our heat.

O hell-eyed lust, when I behold thy face
Prefigured in my ghost, drawn in my mind,
I think of Sidon's flowers that grow apace
And favour thee by quality and kind:
They look like faith before, and fame behind,
  But if thou savour these well-favoured evils,
  They have the sight of gods, the scent of devils.

If I had, like a curious herbalist,
Measured thy quantity by quality,
Or Aesculapius-wise, on reason's fist
Had planted virtue by the property,
Or with the lapidary's policy
  Made choice by insight—that's the note of wit,
  And not by outward hue to judge of it—

Then, like that skilful Aesculapius,
Setting apart the colour of deceit,
I might have known Tarquin from Tereus,
And Lucrece' bed from Philomela's bait.
Vesta conceived what Venus did conceit,

389 **thy** Tarquin and iniquity becoming one; see 395–6
391 **maiden humours** pure streams
Flora's goddess of flowers
395 **type** symbol
396 **cipher** express (as with characters, or in a cryptogram)
399 **history** (*a*) story (*b*) play
402 **this pen of mine** either a temporary refiguring of Lucrece as the epistolary writer of her own lament (see 413 ff., and 563 ff.); or, as in the 1996 Globe production, an interjection in the voice of the poet
409 **incolants** inhabitants (possibly a Middleton coinage; cf. *Solomon*, 16.32)
412 **burning baths** Phlegethon (river of fire in Hell)
413 **Prometheus' heart** Prometheus was a Titan, chained to a mountain by Zeus for giving fire and arts to humankind. His liver was devoured over and over by a vulture. In asking for his heart, Lucrece asks for his strength and endurance.
indite write
422 **untutored** uncontrolled, undisciplined
427 **think and unthink** i.e., be unsteadfast
430 **cockatrice** fabulous serpent, said to kill with its glance, like the basilisk
432 **moth** used figuratively for something that eats away, gnaws or wastes gradually and silently
433 **treasure which so dear was bought** the soul, bought (saved) by the Crucifixion
438 **Prefigured** represented
439 **Sidon's flowers** Sidon was an ancient Phoenician seaport on what is now the coast of Lebanon. The image, from *Ciceronis Amor* (7.123), is evidently Greene's invention: 'the flowers in *Sidon* as they are precious in the sight so they are pestilent in savour.'
440 **favour** resemble
441 **fame** virtuous reputation
442 **savour** smell
443 **sight** appearance
444 **curious** careful, attentive
445 **quantity** worth
446 **Aesculapius-wise** legendary Greek physician who could revive the dead; god of medicine, associated through his father Apollo with truth and prophecy
reason's fist Tarquin's forcible persuasion, perhaps reflecting an oratorical hand gesture; Lucrece's apparent point is that she did not put the 'virtue' of Tarquin's argument to a sufficiently wise test; 'fist' may also carry its sense of 'stench, fart', picking up 'the scent of devils' above (443), and setting up the subsequent opposition between 'sweet verdure' and 'a flattering voice' (457).
449 **note** (*a*) mark (*b*) regard, notice (thus 'note of wit' would mean 'wit's manner of taking note')
453 **from** by the example of
Tereus Thracian king, rapist of Philomela
454 **bait** temptation
455 **Vesta...conceit** Vesta (unlike me) understood what Venus was planning.

But, wanting Aesculapius in my choice,
I left sweet verdure for a flattering voice.

Did beauty, that same bavin's blaze, incense thee,
That flower of time, which buds with vanity,
That string of fortune's wheel, which doth commence
thee
The graduate of hell-born iniquity?
Was beauty made the mark of luxury?
Then, heavens, from henceforth let the world behold
Beauty in lead, deformity in gold.

Say beauty's beams dazzled thy cloudy eyes;
This beauty hangs but at the heels of time,
And when time's wings a loftier measure flies
Then beauty like poor Icarus must climb,
Or plunge into the puddle of her slime;
For beauty's limbs are of a waxen frame,
And melts like Icarus' wings at every flame.

Saw'st thou the colours which quaint Phidias drew
In dead-live pictures with a touch of art?
Such red and white hath beauty being new,
Made only to amaze th' amazer's heart.
Yet Phidias' colours, piercing like a dart,
Were stained with every breath, and lost their prime.
So beauty's blot drops from the pen of time.

But O my heaven, shall I forget thy spheres?
O spheres of heaven, shall I let pass your skies?
O skies which wears out time, and never wears,
Shall I make dim the tapers of your eyes?
O eyes of heaven, sun, moon, and stars that rise
To wake the day, and free imprisoned night,
Shall my oblivious vapour cloud your light?

'Tis thou, O chastity. Shall I forsake thee,
Or drown thy memory in my bloody stream?
Remember, O my soul, did she not make thee
Out of Diana's ribs? Did not that beam
Which glisters in thy spirit like Jove's eye-gleam
Reflect from Vesta's face upon thy heart,
Like Phoebus' brow, the pride of heaven's art?

O thou that mak'st the *Via Lactea* whiter,
That virgin gallery of majestic Jove,
Fair Juno's maze—to foot it doth delight her—
The silver path of heaven, and bath of love;
There sits the lamb, the swan, the turtle dove,
Ensigns of peace, of faith, and chastity:
O silver stage to golden harmony.

That choir of saints in virgin ornament
Where angels sing like choristers of heaven,
Where all the martyrs kneel, the element
Where Cynthia's robe and great Apollo's steven
Hangs at the altar of this milken haven—
And to conclude, not able to begin,
I write of that which flesh hath never seen.

'Twas thou, O chastity, m' eternal eye,
The want of thee made my ghost reel to hell.
'Twas thou, O chastity, that gild'st the sky
With beams of virtue. It is thou dost dwell
In that white milken crystal silver cell,
Thou laundress to the gods and goddesses,
Washing their souls in fonts of holiness.

O thou that deck'st our Phoebus in the east,
Circling his temples with spiritual beams,
And guides his vestal chariot to the west
Through that pure crystal track of lacteal streams,
Silvering his wheels with alabaster gleams,
Then temp'ring the bright porphyry of his face
With chaste Endymion's blush, the dye of grace,

That doing duty to his father Jove
Upon his knee of fire, bids him arise,
And blessing all his beams with kissing love,
Like a majestic father gilds his eyes
To add a rarer shine unto the skies,
Then takes his chariot with a brighter pride,
And cries aloud, 'Saint Vesta be my guide!'

457 **verdure** odour
458 **bavin's blaze** a 'bavin' is a bundle of kindling
incense set on fire; inflame with passion
460 **string** Middleton evidently overlaps Fortune's wheel with the spinning wheel of the Fates; 'string' thus becomes something like the thread of life. The collocation with 'commence' and 'graduate' suggests a secondary glance at the special sense of 'string' at Oxford: a pat logical argument passed down from undergraduate to undergraduate for use in examinations.
commence admit to a university degree
462 **mark** target
468 **Icarus** son of Daedalus who flew too near the sun on waxen wings which melted, plunging him to death in the sea
469 **slime** original ooze; moral filth
472 **Phidias** considered the greatest artist of ancient Greece
477 **prime** newness
489 **Diana's ribs** echoing the creation of Eve
492 **Phoebus** Apollo, god of light, the arts, etc.; associated, as here, with the sun
493 **thou** chastity
495 **Juno's** wife of Jupiter; protectress of women
foot (*a*) walk (*b*) dance
497 **the lamb, the swan, the turtle dove** respectively, the 'faith', 'chastity', and 'peace' of the following line. (The context implies constellations or stars, particularly as Cygnus (The Swan), one of the Ptolemaic constellations, is located in the Milky Way, and poetically linked to the rape of Leda. But Columba (The Dove), a minor southern constellation, was almost unknown in the 16th century, and I find no heavenly body associated with the lamb.)
502 **element** sky
503 **Cynthia's** moon goddess
steven probably here understood by Middleton to mean 'crown', as in *Solomon*, 7.282. See 622–3.
507 **m' eternal** my eternal, presumably with play on 'maternal'
519 **temp'ring** modifying
porphyry hard rock consisting of red or white crystals in a red ground-mass
520 **Endymion's** young Greek shepherd, beloved of the Moon
522 **bids** The subject appears to be Jove; at 'takes' (526), it appears to revert to Phoebus.

Saint Vesta, O thou sanctifying saint,
That lends a beam unto the clearest sun,
Which else within his fiery course would faint
And end his race ere he had half begun,
Making the world believe his power were done,
His oil burnt out, his lamp returned to slime,
His fires extinguished by the breath of time,

O thou, the pearl that hangs on Juno's brow,
Like to the moon, the massy pearl of night,
Thou jewel in the ear of Jove, to show
The pride of love, the purity of light,
Thou Atlas of both worlds, umpire of right,
Thou haven of heaven, th' assigner of each sign,
Sanctity's saint, divinity's divine,

O thou, the silver taper of the moon,
Set in an alabaster candlestick
That by the bed of heaven at afternoon
Stands like a lily which fair virgins pick
To match it with the lily of their cheek,
Thou lily lamb, thou crystal-feathered dove
That nestles in the palace of thy Jove,

O touch my veins again, thou blood divine.
O feed my spirit, thou food angelical,
And all chaste functions with my soul combine.
Colour my ghost with chastity, whose all
Feeds fat lean death and time in general.
Come, silver dove, heaven's alabaster nun,
I'll hug thee more than ever I have done.

Lucrece, alas, thou picture of thyself,
Drawn poor and pale by that old painter, time,
And overdashed by death, that meagre elf
Which dries our element of blood to thyme,
And temp'reth our old ashes with new slime;
Lucrece, I say, how canst thou Lucrece be,
Wanting a god to give a life to thee?

Bleed no more lines, my heart. This knife, my pen,
This blood, my ink, hath writ enough to lust.
Tarquin, to thee, thou very devil of men,
I send these lines. Thou art my fiend of trust.
To thee I dedicate my tomb of dust.
To thee I consecrate this little-most
Writ by the bloody fingers of my ghost.

This little scroll of fire that burns my hand
In repetition of thy fiery name
I fold upon my heart, my bloody land,
And to thy ghost my ghost doth send the same,
Intitulèd *The Lines of Blood and Flame*:
The ghost of Lucrece, that's the ghost of blood;
The ghost of Tarquin, that's the fiery flood.

Now for thy title and deservèd style,
In dedication to thy worthiness:
To thee the second of Cocytus' isle,
Chief seignior to the Phlegethontic mess,
High steward unto Pluto's holiness,
Temp'rer of flames, the Lord Tisiphone,
My bloody fires begs patronage of thee.

Now lack I nothing but the post of hell
To fly like Vesta's arrow from my bow
With these my red-hot news, and then to tell
How many times my heart did ebb and flow
Like seas, with tears above and blood below.
And from poor Lucrece' mouth tell Tarquin thus,
That Philomel hath writ to Tereus.

Here stops the stream of tragic blood and fire,
And now Melpomene hales my spirit in.
The stage is down, and Philomela's choir
Is hushed from pricksong. Acheron's bells begin
To call our ghosts, clad in the spirits of sin.
Now Tereus meets with ravished Philomel,
Lucrece with Tarquin in the hall of hell.

The Epilogue

Rhamnusia in a chariot of revenge,
Heaped up with ghosts of blood and spirits of fire,
Hath pilled up Lucrece' ghost, so to avenge
Her chaste untimely blood of flamed desire.
Now at the bar of hell, revenge's choir,
Pleads Lucrece with a tongue of tears and bloods.
First speaks her heart, and then her eyes in floods.

539 **Atlas** Titan condemned to stand at the western end of earth and hold up the sky
541 **divine** priest, cleric
555 **hug** cherish
558 **overdashed** (*a*) splashed over (*b*) destroyed, overthrown (*c*) cancelled out
559 **thyme** described by herbalists as particularly hot and dry
566 **of trust** trusted
572 **fold** (*a*) roll up (*b*) clasp
577 **style** designation
579 **Cocytus** like Phlegethon and Acheron, a river of Hell; Middleton uses all three interchangeably with 'hell'. See line 594 below.
580 **seignior** lord
582 **Lord Tisiphone** Middleton has apparently given the avenging fury a sex-change, and made the new lord, figuring Tarquin, very like Vulcan.
592 **Melpomene hales my spirit in** the muse of tragedy drags my spirit offstage (or beneath the stage)
593 **The stage is down** the play is over, the hangings struck
594 **pricksong** a written descant or counterpoint (with punning allusions to Philomela's thorn, and to the violating male organ)
600 **of blood** bloody
601 **pilled** plucked, pulled, torn
602 **of** upon
603 **bar** as in a courtroom, the wooden rail marking off the judge's seat
revenge's choir in apposition to 'the bar of hell', 'choir' meaning, figuratively, the judgement place where revenge is seated

Can death, that shrimp of spirits, that bony wretch,
That meagre element, that beggar god,
From Lucrece' sky such heavenly colours fetch,
From beauty's wrist so wrest that golden rod
Which makes all red and white disperse abroad?
  Death's power is come, and beauty's triumph past.
  She was as chaste as fair, as fair as chaste.

Her hair, which in Arachne's finest loom
Was kissed with silver shuttles, O that hair
Which made Collatium shine in spite of Rome,
Combing her tresses like Jove's golden heir—
He made Rome bright, she made Collatium fair—
  That hair which danced in beams before her breath
  Serves now to stuff the gaping ribs of death.

Her eyes, the curious fabric of her world,
Apollo's touchstones where he tried his beams,
And when her eyes outmatched his fires he hurled
His crown of splendour into quenching streams,
Raging to see beauty's enrollèd themes
  Writ in her eye-rolls; but alas, those eyes
  Which lived in beauty, now in beauty dies.

Her tongue, which Orpheus tuned before he died,
And strung before he journeyed unto hell,
That new Parnassus by a river's side,
Where music sojourns and the muses dwell,
O tongue of hers, Diana's silver bell,
  That rung chaste prayers to the church of heaven,
  Now she of it, and it of her bereaven.

Her breath, which had a violet perfume
Tempered with rose all verdure, O her breath
Through discord of her tongue did all consume.
Unto the air of earth she did bequeath
That pension of her life, from life to death.
  How ill was this bestowed on death, that elf
  Which robs all others, yet still poor itself.

Her teats, twixt whom an alabaster bridge
Parts each from other, like two crystal bowls
Standing aloof upon the body's ridge,
Bears chastity's white nectar-flowing souls.
O valley decked with Flora's silver rolls,
  Why giv'st thou suck to death? It will be fed,
  For know, death must not die till all be dead.

And to conclude, her all in every sphere,
That like the sun on crystal elements
Did shine in clearness bright, in brightness clear,
Her head her skies, her soul her firmaments,
Now stained by death, before by ravishments:
  First Tarquin-life clad her in death's array.
  Now Tarquin-death hath stol'n her life away.

FINIS

608 **fetch** carry off
609 **rod** sceptre
610 **Which... abroad** which defeats or scatters all other beauty
616 **Jove's golden heir** Phoebus
620 **curious fabric** elaborately wrought construction; perhaps with a glance at 'curious' meaning especially observant, often collocating with 'eyes'
624 **enrollèd** celebrated
625 **eye-rolls** (*a*) the rounds or disks of her eyes (*b*) rollings of the eyes (*c*) punning on 'roll' meaning parchment scroll
627 **Orpheus** mythological musician-poet whose lyre charmed even the gods of Hell
629 **Parnassus** mountain sacred to the muses, and thus to the arts
river's side Orpheus's dying song echoed from the riverbank. This ironic 'new Parnassus' is presumably hell, with the dead Lucrece situated beside the river Phlegethon in a bitter revision of the conventional riverside placement of the speaker of a female complaint.
635 **verdure** fragrance
637 **air** punning on 'heir'?
645 **rolls** (*a*) round ornamental pads (*b*) *fig.* breasts

THE PENNILESS PARLIAMENT OF THREADBARE POETS

Edited by Swapan Chakravorty

THE first extant edition of *The Penniless Parliament of Threadbare Poets* appeared in 1604 as the concluding part of a jestbook called *Jack of Dover, His Quest of Inquiry for the Veriest Fool in England.* William Ferbrand, the publisher, had entered *The Second Part of Jack of Dover* in the Stationers' Register on 3 August 1601, and *Penniless* was probably first published later that year. Hayward Townshend's *Megalopsychy* (1682) reports that on 16 December 1601, Henry Doyley complained to the Commons against 'The Assembly of Fools', a book published by one living '*right over* Guild-Hall-Gate', an address which agrees with Ferbrand's. The Privy Council dismissed the libel charge, having found the work 'a mere toy...an old book, entitled, *The Second Part of Jack of Dover*' (Wilson, p. 316).

The Assembly of Fools was possibly a mock-parliament, a fact that provoked the literal-minded Doyley into moving the Commons. Jack's name in the reported title suggests that *Penniless*, perhaps then called 'Assembly of Fools', was printed as part of the jestbook in 1601. A probable reference to the first Fortune, completed by the end of 1600 (Orrell, p. 127), as the 'new playhouse' (ll. 247–8) also favours 1601 as the date of composition.

F. P. Wilson pointed out in 1938 that *Penniless* was a revision of Simon Smellknave's *Fearful and Lamentable Effects of Two Dangerous Comets*, a mock-prognostication for 1591 influenced by Adam Foulweather's *A Wonderful Strange and Miraculous Prognostication* published the same year. It was Smellknave's tract from which Middleton borrowed passages for *Plato's Cap*, and which Anthony Nixon recycled two years later in *The Black Year* (Wilson, pp. 267–72). The reviser's opening lines—'all such as buys this book' (l. 2)—show that *Penniless* was intended for separate publication, and it was so printed in 1608, 1637, and 1649. Its integrity indicates a revision in two stages. The first turned *Comets* into *Penniless*; the second recast Jack's first-person report of his search (which survives unrevised in six jests) into his encounter with a group of poor poets in St Paul's Cathedral, so that a pretext was provided for joining the parliament to the jests. It is hard to tell if Middleton was involved in retouching the jests. But the new material in *Penniless* shows an undoubted concentration of Middleton traits.

In 1601 Middleton was nearly a penniless poet himself, dependent on odd jobs for Henslowe and the popular press. The comic almanac or prophecy, credited to pseudonymous authors who borrowed from one another, was one form of fast and cheap publishing which suited his satiric talents. He might have been interested in *Comets* if, as seems possible, 'Simon Smellknave' was a pseudonym of Thomas Nashe. Middleton, whose *Microcynicon* was banned at the same time as Nashe's books, seems to have viewed himself as Nashe's literary heir (Rhodes, pp. 57–61). Not only did he defend Nashe in *The Ant and the Nightingale*; he also wrote *The Black Book* as a sequel to *Pierce Penniless*. The words 'Penniless' and 'Threadbare' in the title invoke *Pierce Penniless* and Nashe's self-description in *Have With You to Saffron Walden* as a poet in a 'threadbare cloak' (III, 26.16). The idea of having penniless poets as legislators (at a time when only freeholders worth at least forty shillings a year could vote) agrees with the self-regarding portrayal in Middleton's early work of the talented but indigent scholar-poet as an instance of social injustice. It is also consistent with his sympathy, deeper than Nashe's, for the socially disadvantaged. More generally, the change from a mock forecast to a comic parliament, the reviser's most significant contribution, turned a socially neutral parody into a potentially disruptive satire.

The composition of literary 'parliaments' varied from the councils of birds and beasts in medieval texts to *The Parliament of Devils*, published in 1509. The medieval instances of the ancient convention were allied to that of the debate or colloquy (Bennett, p. 140), but Chaucer's *Parliament of Fowls* exploited the dual connotation of the word as a parley and as a political institution (Dean, p. 19). Middleton may have had Chaucer's poem in mind in the choice of metaphor and title, the latter including the formulaic caption, 'Here beginneth' (l. B.10), present in the headline to a Cambridge University Library manuscript (Gg. 4.27) of *The Parliament of Fowls*. The conciliar form, however, was ruled out by the nature of Middleton's source, and he had thus to use 'parliament' in the exclusive sense of a legislative body.

If *The Assembly of Fools* was an earlier title for *Penniless*, the jury might originally have been one of fools rather than of poets. The 1615 edition of the jestbook printed by John Beale has a chapter-title that reads 'How the Fool of Hereford was chosen Foreman of the Jury, and of the speech he uttered to the rest of his fellows' (A4). There is no such event or speech in the tale, and the caption is clearly a survival from an earlier version. Fools, in any case, had long been associated with mock forecasts. The first leaf of *A Merry Prognostication* (1544), the oldest known example in English, shows a costumed fool making prophecies, the block being borrowed from Richard Pynson's 1509 edition of Barclay's *The Ship of Fools*.

Doyley's suspicion may not have been altogether idle, especially since mock-parliaments figured in oppositional polemics starting from the anonymous *An Heavenly Act of Parliament concerning how Man shall Live* (first published from Amsterdam *c.*1547) to Thomas Scott's *The Second Part of Vox Populi* (1624). His complaint must surely have alerted publishers to the political resonances of the metaphor. As a title, *Penniless Parliament* should have had a resilient topicality throughout a period in which Parliament's presumed duty to relieve the king's debts was a major divisive issue (Harriss), and the extant editions were marketed at some of the climactic moments in the contest between Crown and Commons. In 1601 the demand for the withdrawal of monopolies occasioned what Robert Cecil thought was unprecedented 'levity and disorder' in Parliament (Elton, p. 324). In 1604 disputes between the new king and the Commons over religious and fiscal reforms had resulted in an assertion of parliamentary privileges in the celebrated 'Apology'. In 1608 the Commons was refusing to vote the additional taxes proposed after the Court of Exchequer had upheld the royal prerogative of levying poundage. Beale bought his rights in *Penniless* in 1614, the year James I summoned and dissolved the Addled Parliament (which had again attacked the 1608 impositions). Beale printed another edition in 1637, when the discontent over Charles I's refusal to call Parliament was sharpened by the Ship Money case and the enforcing of a new liturgy in Scotland. The 1649 edition followed Pride's Purge and appeared in the year the Rump Parliament executed the king.

In ll. 258–9 the reviser changed the phrase 'these times' (*Comets*, C1) to 'these dangerous times'. The adjective suits 1601, the year that saw the rebellion of the Earl of Essex to whom Middleton had dedicated *Solomon*. The change from 'King of Spain' ($C3^v$) to 'Tyrone' (ll. 177–8) recalls Essex's embarrassing truce with the rebel after his failed Irish expedition (1599–1600), as might the revised text in ll. 283–4 which mentions those who 'go to the wars and get nothing'. There may be a sly glance at the depositions made in the February trial of Essex and Southampton in ll. 318–20, where an allusion to illiterate forgers is altered to those who may 'forswear themselves' as 'boldly' as the lettered. Through such minor changes made to an 'old book', Middleton was able to produce social and political satire even after the bishops' 1599 edict against the genre.

The adaptation certainly made *Penniless* a more popular work than *Comets*. While *Comets* is known to have had only one edition, *Penniless* had at least six between 1601 and 1649. Only five copies of these early printings survive: one each for the 1604, 1637, and 1649 editions, and two for the 1608 quarto. There is no copy of the 1601 edition, and in the only extant copy of the 1615 quarto of *Jack of Dover*, the *Penniless* section is missing, though advertised on the title-page. The low survival-rate is that of such fast-selling ephemera as jestbooks, ballads, and almanacs (Wilson, p. 284), and it is possible that other editions were printed of which no copies remain.

Astrological prognostications had a mass circulation in Europe throughout the Renaissance, even when written by distinguished scholars such as Agostino Nifo and Peter Martyr (Febvre and Martin, p. 277). The *Pronosticatio* (1488) of the Rhenish astrologer Johan Lichtenberger, for instance, had fourteen editions in German, Italian, and Latin by 1500, and about fifty by the middle of the sixteenth century (Mandrou, p. 51). The English astrological writers parodied by Foulweather and Smellknave were thus reworking the material of a genre that had always needed to combine its esoteric pedigree with the demands of a large lay readership.

The same paradox characterizes European examples of mock prophecies, the earliest German example dating as far back as 1480. The genre attracted humanists such as Jacob Henrichmann, Rabelais, and Aretino, yet the parodies show little regard for authorial rights (Wilson, pp. 259–61). English mock-prophecies also recycled earlier material. A work such as W. W.'s *A Merry and Pleasant Prognostication by Four Witty Doctors* (1577), for example, derives most of its material from the rhymed *Merry Prognostication* of 1544 (Wilson, pp. 262–3, 283–4).

A feature of genres which commanded large press runs was their symbiotic contact with oral culture and, hence, the collective nature of their authorship. Sermons, news, ballads, jests, riddles, recipes, and rogue literature stimulated the oral circulation of the material they sought to preserve (Neuburg, pp. 50–1), inducing demand for further reprintings and redactions. The writer needed to exploit this market spiral as much as the publisher, while he could hope for a fair deal only by claiming his intellectual property rights. The paradox is reflected in the way educated but indigent authors such as Nashe would write anonymous or pseudonymous pamphlets one day and abuse authors of popular genres the next. In *Have with You to Saffron Walden*, Nashe ridicules Gabriel Harvey for ghosting the almanacs of Gabriel Frende: 'What, a grave Doctor a base John Doleta, the almanac-maker, Doctor Deus-ace and Doctor Merry-man?' (III, 72.8–9). The name-calling suggests that the writer of mock almanacs was as much a hack as the authors he parodied, and it was under the pseudonym of 'Doctor Merryman' that Beale published the 1637 edition of *Penniless*.

The mock prophecies of Foulweather and Smellknave, however, were rather different from the ones Nashe derides. Their parodic quibbles demand a more lettered readership, and their involvement in the Marprelate and Harvey–Nashe controversies means that they were designed to address a knowledgeable coterie. The decision to print *Penniless* as a sequel to an anonymous jestbook marks the extent to which Middleton was able to convert such a coterie text into a recyclable bestseller, or what he later called a 'stock-book' (*Valour*, 5.3.16). Since 'stock-books' such as almanacs were priced according to size (Bosanquet, p. 10), a detachable piece of work like *Penniless* gave publishers the option of printing it separately in cheaper editions. This adaptability to market segments is reflected in at least one typographical decision in the independent quarto of 1608: the change from the roman type of 1604 to the parodic use of black letter, the standard font for printed Parliamentary decrees and royal proclamations. Judging by the equal division of the six known editions into the two formats, *Penniless* appears to have been successful both as a sequel and as a discrete work.

Penniless reduces its source by a little over 30 per cent. The examples of *Macbeth* and *Measure for Measure* show that Middleton was chosen to adapt important texts by others, and the Malone manuscript of *A Game at Chess* is evidence that he could skilfully abridge his own. The latter omits 787 lines by cutting long speeches, interjections, explanatory digressions, and secondary motifs such as the story of the Black Knight's Pawn. That it yet manages to disguise the jumps, justify the metre, and even speed up the action suggests that the reviser had considerable experience with such editorial work.

That manuscript, of course, was a gift for one distinguished reader and not an adaptation for mass circulation. With Smellknave, Middleton's editorial method was similar to that by which the Troyes printers of the early seventeenth century adjusted texts from lettered French culture to the demands of lowbrow publishing. These texts of the *bibliothèque bleue*, often titles first published in more reputable formats, modernized the vocabulary, pruned allusions and digressions, and broke up sentences and paragraphs into shorter, repetitive, and formulaic units which were easier to read and remember (Chartier, pp. 248–50). Some of these features were already present in Smellknave, since he was mimicking a popular genre. The change to the parliamentary metaphor, however, enabled Middleton to add to the text's appeal a durable dimension missing in Nixon's *Black Year*, which also recalls some of the verbal and lexical formulae of the *bibliothèque bleue*.

One may derive some idea of the abridgement and rewriting demanded by the revision from the following passage in *Comets*, B2v–B3:

> Plato, the prince of philosophers, with others, looking into the successive alteration of states, saith that, generally, Comets do appear when some dangerous change is to follow. And Aristotle, a man of rare and exquisite judgement, thinketh that *Crinite Comets* have their particular working in private houses, as well as in commonweals. For which cause, let those married men of weakest wit and worst courage provide themselves of good weapons to defend them from assaults, for about the hour and year appointed shall this feminine Comet appear, putting such masculine courage in all wives that they who have had their will to this hour, will (if they may choose) have the mastery all the year after. But at this instant their value shall be doubled, for they who shall not valiantly resist them are awarded to pay a sheep's head to their neighbour in penance of their folly.
>
> It shall be wonderful to behold (through this sinister influence) how men that are deaf shall hear no more than those that are dead; and such as are without teeth shall chew as little as babes new born. Women that every morning taste a pint of malmsey and oil shall chide as well as they that drink small beer all the winter; and those that have no regard of their honesty, may strain a point beyond modesty.
>
> Erra Pater with provident judgement, looking into these lamentable miseries incident in these westerly parts, saith that oil of holly is a present remedy for a shrewd housewife, calling Socrates flat fool that suffered his wife to crown him with a pisspot.

When this passage is adapted for *Penniless* (ll. 139–55), the new conceit has no use for such conventions of comic forecasts as citing authorities from Plato to Erra Pater, and the distinctions made between the two comets and their respective effects. Traces of the annual forecast are erased (except in the phrase 'all the year after'); 'shall' in l. 145 avoids the clumsy repetition of 'will' as noun and verb; deft substitutions ('about midnight', 'ordaining that all those that give their wives their own wills to be fools', 'those husbands') sharpen the jokes; the remark on chiding women is shifted to fit an earlier context (ll. 19–21); and the deletions considerably shorten the passage. The future tense of prophecies lends itself easily to the imperative of statutes. Phrases effecting the change occasionally transpose words from the source. The praises of Aristotle and Erra Pater, for example, are given to the legislators (ll. 139–40, 149). The dependence suggests a conscious exercise of the parodist's skill in altering sense without changing too many words. Elsewhere, the revision resituates lines from Smellknave's prefatory epistle (A2; ll. 7–12), and paraphrases verse, moving them to new contexts (C3v–D1v; ll. 375–7, 379–82).

In most cases, the changes enrich the quibbles. Thus the phrase 'horse-nightcap' introduces the 'horse/whores' pun, extending the meaning of 'clip' (ll. 20–3), brought over from a different context in *Comets* (A4), to include 'embrace' as well as the more obvious ones ('steal' and 'pare the edges of gold and silver coins'). The phrase 'Footman's Inn' for prison furthers the pun on 'lattice' (l. 208), since lattices were a feature of inns, and the addition of 'Salisbury Plain' creates a new quibble on 'plain dealing' (ll. 341–5). The added passages ease the entry into the parliamentary metaphor, besides importing new jokes such as the pun on 'stocks' (l. 329–30). Of the omissions, perhaps the most significant is Smellknave's censure of players—'as famous in idleness, as dissolute in living' (B2).

Prophecies such as Richard Harvey's *Astrological Discourse upon the Conjunction of Saturn and Jupiter* (1583), a possible target of Smellknave's satire, centred on the fear of the prodigious 'in these latter days' when the end of the world was expected shortly (Nashe, V, 167) and when harvest-failures, wars, and the plague were breeding chiliastic hallucinations (Clark, p. 44). The mock prophecy's weapon for deflating that sensationalism was the pun. Keeping the tone but twisting its import, the pun laboured the banal and brought the reader back to the unexceptional and the familiar. By a further turn of conceit, *Penniless* legislates the average and the corrupt, the triteness of which mocks the idealism of the text's legal refrains. While the comic forecast predicted the predictable, the saturnalian conceit of *Penniless* indicts that dullness as the image of a society indifferent to true merit. This transition to a satire with a pronounced class animus is typical of Middleton, even if his verbal contribution only amounts to roughly 35 per cent of the text.

As long as its dependence on *Comets* went undetected, *Penniless* was regarded as a document of some curiosity value. The headnote in the *Harleian Miscellany* (1744), in which it was included by William Oldys, saw it as a 'jocose reproof' of contemporary 'vices and follies'. Thomas Wright reprinted *Jack of Dover* and *Penniless* for the Percy Society in 1842, as did Charles Hindley in 1872. But Wilson's discovery of its borrowings led to disesteem of *Penniless* and its sources. These were to be treated, to recall Edward Young's distinction, not as 'originals', but 'Imitations . . . wrought up by those mechanics, art and labour, out of pre-existent materials not their own' (Young, p. 274). In 1617, in *Satires and Satirical Epigrams*, Henry Fitzgeffrey declared that he did not wish 'each peasant, each mechanic ass' to buy his verse; he included 'A Quest of Inquiry (Jack of Dover's)' (A8–8v) in a list of works from which he wished to distance his own poetry. Since Beale printed a composite edition in 1615, Fitzgeffrey was probably thinking of *Penniless* as well. Similar suspicion of, if not distaste for, popular success may still haunt academic appraisals. Thus Foulweather and Smellknave are branded 'pseudonymous scribblers' by Sandra Clark (p. 29), who finds *Comets* 'dull and laboured' (p. 270) and who, following Wilson, dismisses *Penniless* as a purloined text.

Distinguished contemporaries of Foulweather and Smellknave, however, did not deem their work unworthy of notice. In *Pierce's Supererogation* (1593) Gabriel Harvey chose to describe Andrew Perne, the Vice Chancellor of Cambridge whom Nashe held in high regard, as 'a fair prognostication of a foul weather' (Harvey, *Works*, II, 300). John Florio mentions those that 'prognosticate of fair, of foul, and of smelling weather' (A2) in the dedication to his *Second Fruits* (1591). Ironically, such attention is a witness to the works' ephemeral and coterie appeal. *Penniless*, on the other hand, retains, even furthers, the genre's strengths while removing its dependence on the annual and the topical.

The biggest tribute to *Penniless* and its source comes from Middleton himself. Not only did he find *Comets* worth borrowing from in *Plato* and, less directly, in *Owl*; he also quarried its quibbles and jokes for his mature plays (Chakravorty). It is not surprising that the vigorous current of anonymous, collaborative, and popular writing of which *Penniless* is part should be such a vital presence in the signed texts of a self-repeating author with a paradoxical flair for self-erasure.

SEE ALSO

Textual introduction and apparatus: *Companion*, 469
Authorship and date: *Companion*, 337

'SIMON SMELLKNAVE', adapted by THOMAS MIDDLETON

The Penniless Parliament of Threadbare Poets

First of all, for the increase of every fool in his humour, we think it necessary and convenient that all such as buys this book and laughs not at it before he hath read it over shall be condemned of melancholy, and be adjudged to walk over Moorfields twice a week in a foul shirt and a pair of boots, but no stockings.

It is also agreed upon that long-bearded men shall seldom prove the wisest, and that a niggard's purse shall scarce bequeath his master a good dinner. And because water is like to prove so weak an element in the world that men and women will want tears to bewail their sins, we charge and command all gardeners to sow more store of onions, for fear widows should want moisture to bewail their husbands' funerals.

In like manner we think it fit that red wine should be drunk with oysters, and that some maidens shall blush more for shame than for shamefastness. But men must have care, lest conversing too much with red petticoats they banish their hair from their heads and, by that means, make the poor barbers beggars for want of work.

Furthermore, it is lawful for those women that every morning taste a pint of muscadine with eggs to chide as well as they that drink small beer all the winter, and those that clip that they should not shall have a horse-nightcap for their labour. Gentlemen that sell land for paper shall buy penury with repentance. And those that have most gold shall have least grace; some that mean well shall fare worse; and he that hath no credit shall have less commodity.

It is also ordered and agreed upon that such as are choleric shall never want woe and sorrow, and they that lack money may fast upon Fridays by the statute. And it shall be lawful for them that want shoes to wear boots all the year, and he that hath never a cloak may without offence put on his best gown at midsummer (witness old Prime, the keeper of Bedlam dicing house).

This commentary notes major departures from Middleton's source, Simon Smellknave's *Fearful and Lamentable Effects of Two Dangerous Comets* (1591). It does not record every variant, and ignores the verbal formulae added to turn the forecasts into statutes.

1–5 **First . . . stockings** (an addition)

1 **every . . . humour** a possible reference to Jonson's plays, *Every Man in His Humour* (1598), and *Every Man out of His Humour* (1599)

2 **buys this book** (evidence that *Penniless* was conceived as a work independent of *Jack of Dover*)

4 **melancholy** Melancholia, a mental disease, was caused by an excess of black bile, a 'humour' in the sense in which the word is used in l. 1.

Moorfields Field for public recreation outside Bishopsgate and adjoining the hospital of St Mary of Bethlehem or Bedlam. The safer lunatics roamed and begged in Moorfields; hence, its association with melancholy (Tilley, M1134).

5 **but no stockings** The bedlam-beggar, and the 'abraham man' posing as one, went bare-legged. See John Awdely, *The Fraternity of Vagabonds* (1561): 'An abram-man is he that walketh bare-armed, and bare-legged, and feigneth himself mad'.

6 **long-bearded men** Pun on 'long beard' or 'the man with the beard', a round drinking jug with a narrow neck. The line in *Comets*, A4, followed the definition of the first comet as 'barbata' or 'bearded'.

8 **like** likely

9 **want** lack

11 **store** supply

onions (often associated with false tears)

13–14 **red . . . oysters** an aphrodisiac

15 **shamefastness** modesty

16 **red petticoats** 'Venus' (*Comets*, A4). Red velvet petticoats were worn by the more expensive prostitutes. See Deloney, *Thomas of Reading* (1598–9): 'no meat pleased him so well as mutton, such as was laced in a red petticoat' (218).

16–17 **banish . . . heads** as an effect of syphilis

20 **pint . . . eggs** 'pint of malmsey and oil' (*Comets*, B3). Muscatel wine with eggs was a reputed aphrodisiac.

21–2 **those . . . not** The clause 'such as clip that they should not' occurs in a different passage in *Comets*, A4. 'Clip' could mean pare the edges of gold and silver coins or steal by cutting. The additional sense of embrace (*Mad World* 4.5.53) is introduced by the 'horse/whores' pun in ll. 21–2.

22 **shall . . . labour** (An addition.) As punishment for those who 'clip', *Comets*, A4, mentioned the 'cord', here altered to 'horse-nightcap', meaning a halter or hangman's noose.

horse-nightcap (punning on 'whores')

24 **grace** lustre; also blush, shame

25 **credit** Solvency, inverting the senses of honour and reputation as in the proverb, 'He that has lost his credit is dead to the world' (Tilley, C817).

26 **commodity** goods, profit

27 **choleric** irascible, having choler as the dominant humour

28 **and sorrow** (an addition)

29 **fast upon Fridays** Sale of meat was banned since 1548 on Fridays to help the fish trade.

by the statute The phrase 'by statute', otherwise formulaic for the mock-parliament, was present in the source line in *Comets*, A4[v]. Smellknave may have been referring to either of two Elizabethan statutes on fasting days passed in 1562 and 1585.

29–32 **And . . . house** (an addition)

30 **boots** Worn by gallants even when not riding. Middleton hints at cheats who wore boots to hide money as well as their bare legs (see ll. 4–5).

31 **midsummer** the period of the summer solstice, supposed to worsen madness

32 **old Prime** (1) an actual person? (2) a possible play on 'prime', the third best hand at primero, consisting of four cards all of different suits; (3) Priam of Troy

In like manner it is agreed upon that what day soever Paul's Church hath not in the middle aisle of it either a broker, masterless man, or a penniless companion, the usurers of London shall be sworn by oath to bestow a new steeple upon it. And it shall be lawful for cony-catchers to fall together by the ears about the four knaves at cards which of them may claim superiority, and whether false dice or true be of the most antiquity.

Furthermore, we think it necessary and lawful for the husband and wife to fall at square for superiority in such sort as the wife shall sit playing above in the chamber while the husband stands painting below in the kitchen. Likewise we mark all brokers to be knaves by letters patents. And usurers, for five marks apiece, shall lawfully be buried in the chancel, though they have bequeathed their souls and bodies to the devil in hell.

In like manner it is thought good that it shall be lawful for muscadines in vintners' cellars to indict their masters of commixtion, and sergeants shall be contented to arrest any man for his fees. Alewives shall sell flesh on Fridays without licence, and such as sell beer in halfpenny pots shall utter bread and cheese for money through the whole year. And those that are past honesty and shame shall smile at sin; and they that care not for God, prefer money before conscience.

Furthermore, it shall be lawful for footstools (by the help of women's hands) to fly about without wings. And poor men shall be accounted knaves without occasions. Those that flatter least shall speed worst. And pigs by the statute shall dance the antics with bells about their necks to the wonder and amazement of all swineherds.

In like manner it is convenient that many men shall wear hoods that have little learning, and some surfeit so much upon wit and strive so long against the stream as their necks shall fail them. Some shall build fair houses by bribes, gather much wealth by contention, and, before they be aware, heap up riches for another and wretchedness for themselves.

Furthermore, it shall be established for the benefit of increase that some shall have a tympany in their bellies which will cost them a child-bearing, and, though the father bear all the charges, it shall be a wise child that shall know his own father.

It shall be lawful for some to have a palsy in their teeth in such sort as they shall eat more than ever they will be able to pay for, some such a migrain in their eyes as they shall hardly know another man's wife from their own, some such a stopping in their hearts as they shall be utterly obstinate to receive grace, some such a buzzing in their ears as they shall be enemies to good counsel, some such a smell in their noses as no feast shall escape without their companies. And some shall be so needy as neither young heirs shall get their own, nor poor orphans their patrimony.

Also it is enacted and decreed that some shall be so humorous in their walks as they cannot step one foot from a fool, some so consumed in mind as they shall keep never a good thought

34 **middle aisle** central aisle of St Paul's, a haunt of idlers and cheats on weekdays, when the cathedral was used as a market
broker (1) pawnbroker; (2) second-hand dealer
34–5 **masterless man** unemployed servant
35–6 **shall . . . oath** 'have sworn' (*Comets*, B3)
36 **new steeple** The spire of St Paul's Cathedral was destroyed by lightning on 4 June 1561. The restoration, not started until 1633, remained incomplete when the church was destroyed in the fire of 1666. The delay provoked satiric attacks.
36–7 **And . . . about** (an addition)
37 **fall . . . ears** quarrel
38 **knaves** (1) jacks in a deck of cards; (2) villains
superiority (The cards are of course equal.)
38–9 **whether . . . antiquity** The fairness of diceplay in antiquity is discussed in Gilbert Walker, *A Manifest Detection of Dice Play* (1552).
40–1 **the . . . square** 'we shall have a dreadful war betwixt the wife and husband' (*Comets*, A4^{v})
41 **at square** to quarrelling
42 **playing** (1) playing a musical instrument; (2) having sex (with someone other than her husband)
chamber bedroom
43 **painting** Face-painting was common among fashionable Elizabethan males. (A possible quibble on 'panting'.)
below . . . kitchen 'beneath' (*Comets*, A4^{v})
brokers (1) pawnbrokers; (2) middlemen; (3) pimps
44 **letters patents** statutory documents
marks A mark was worth 13*s*. 4*d*.
45 **lawfully . . . chancel** an allusion to rich citizens buying their burials in parish churches
46 **souls . . . hell** 'souls to the devil' (*Comets*, A4^{v})
48–9 **commixtion** dilution (common complaint against vintners)
49 **sergeants** 'bailiffs' (*Comets*, A4^{v}); sheriff's officers
50 **fees** bribes
Alewives . . . Fridays Alewives appear to have dodged the Friday ban on the sale of meat.
sell flesh (alluding to prostitution)
51 **utter** sell
51–2 **bread . . . money** 'mutton and faggots for silver' (*Comets*, A4^{v}). Smellknave's hint that alehouses dodged the lenten ban is destroyed by the change.
52–3 **honesty and** (an addition)
55–6 **(by . . . hands)** Added to clarify the joke on flying footstools which in *Comets*, B1 (as in Foulweather, *Prognostication*, III, 389, ll. 17–22) followed a forecast of tempests.
57 **occasions** reasons
58 **speed** fare
pigs drunkards
antics the performance of burlesque dancers, themselves called 'antics'
59 **bells** A feature of 'antics' as of morris-dancers; see the play on 'bell' in *Gravesend*, 1064–5: 'And all these antics dressed in hell, | To dance about the passing bell'.
61 **hoods** university bachelors' caps
62 **surfeit . . . wit** overuse their cheating skills
63 **strive . . . stream** Allusion to the proverb, 'It is folly to strive against the stream' (Tilley, S927).
their . . . them (i.e., they shall be hanged or beheaded)
65 **contention** litigation
before . . . aware 'ere they are aware' (*Comets*, B1)
67 **increase** breeding
68 **tympany . . . bellies** swelling because of pregnancy
70 **it . . . father** proverbial (Tilley, C309)
73–4 **hardly . . . wife** 'not know a poor man's franktenant' (*Comets*, B1). The change draws on Foulweather, *Prognostication*, III, 390, ll. 17–19: 'and men shall be troubled with such pain in the eyes that they shall not know their own wives from other women'.
74 **stopping** obstruction
75 **grace** (1) divine favour; (2) pardon
77 **noses** 'nostrils' (*Comets*, B1)
78 **companies** 'presence' (*Comets*, B1)
so needy 'hidebound so near themselves' (*Comets*, B1)
80 **humorous** 'altered' (*Comets*, B1)
81 **foot** 'pace' (*Comets*, B1). The alliterative substitution introduces a pun on 'foot' (step, measure of distance).
82 **keep** 'find' (*Comets*, B1)

to bless themselves, some so disguised in purse as they count it fatal to have one penny to buy their dinners on Sundays, some so burdened in conscience as they count wrongful dealing the best badge of their occupation.

But, amongst other laws and statutes by us here established, we think it most necessary and convenient that poulters shall kill more innocent poultry by custom than their wives and maids can sell with a good conscience. Also it is ordered and agreed upon that bakers, woodmongers, butchers and brewers shall fall to a mighty conspiracy so that no man shall either have bread, fire, meat or drink without credit or ready money.

Sycophants by the statute shall have great gifts, and good and godly labours shall scarce be worth thanks. It is also thought necessary that maids about midnight shall see wondrous visions to the great heart-grief of their mothers.

Furthermore, it is marked and set down that, if lawyers plead poor men's causes without money, Westminster Hall shall grow out of custom, to the great impoverishing of all nimmers, lifters and cutpurses. Those that sing bases shall love good drink by authority, and trumpeters that sound trebles shall stare by custom. Women that wear long gowns may lawfully raise dust in March. And they that keep a temperate diet shall never die on surfeits.

In like manner it shall be lawful for sailors and soldiers to spend at their pleasures what they get by their swords. And if the treasurer pay them anything beyond count and reckoning, if they build not an hospital therewith, they may bestow it in apparel by the statute.

It is further established and agreed upon that they that drink too much Spanish sack shall about July be served with a *fiery facias*. But oh you ale-knights, you that devour the marrow of the malt and drink whole aletubs into consumptions, that sing *Queen Dido* over a cup and tell strange news over an alepot, how unfortunate are you who shall piss out that which you have swallowed down so sweetly. You are under the law, and shall be awarded with this punishment: that the rot shall infect your purses and eat out the bottoms ere you be aware.

It is also agreed upon and thought necessary that some women's lips shall swell so big as they shall long to kiss other men beside their husbands. Others' cheeks shall be so monstrous out of frame as they cannot speak in a just cause without large fees. Some with long tongues shall tell all things which they hear; some with no brains shall meddle much and know little. And those that have no feet may by the statute go on crutches.

Furthermore, it is convenient and thought meet that Ale shall exceed so far beyond his bounds as many stomachs shall be drowned in liquor, and thereupon will follow the dropsy to the great benefit of all physicians. It is lawful for some to take such purgative drugs that, if nature help not, the worms in the churches in London shall keep their Christmas at midsummer in their bellies. But tailors by this means shall have more conscience, for, where they were wont to steal but one quarter of a cloak, they shall have due commission to nick their customers in the lace, and, beside their old fees, take more than enough for new fashions' sake. But now touching these following articles, we are to advise old men to look with spectacles lest in finding over-many wise lines they wax blind with reading.

But now touching the benefit of private houses, by our rare and exquisite judgements, we think it very commodious that those

83 **disguised** altered (to a new fashion)
84 **fatal** 'impious' (*Comets*, B1)
85 **burdened** 'consumed' (*Comets*, B1). The change avoids the repetition of 'consumed', used in ll. 81–2.
88–9 **poulters . . . poultry** (alluding to the supposedly English excess in slaughtering poultry)
93 **meat** 'flesh' (*Comets*, B1^{v})
94–5 **good . . . thanks** 'virtuous and godly labours shall be scarce worth gramercies' (*Comets*, B1^{v})
96 **maids . . . visions** Maids' nocturnal visions were almost invariably accounted sexual.
99 **Westminster Hall** seat of the chief London law courts such as the Chancery, the King's Bench, and the Star Chamber
99–100 **grow . . . custom** 'be little troubled with rich men' (*Comets*, B1^{v})
100 **nimmers** pilferers
lifters thieves, cheats
101 **sing bases** a probable quibble on 'base' = bastard, also the name for a sweet Spanish wine
102 **trumpeters** braggarts
sound trebles boast
stare boast and threaten
104 **on** of
106 **what . . . swords** (an addition)
107 **treasurer** purser
count and reckoning computed dues
108 **hospital** (for injured soldiers and sailors)
bestow 'employ' (*Comets*, B1^{v})
111 **sack** white wine, usually imported from Spain
111–12 ***fiery facias*** quibble on the red faces of drunkards and *fieri facias*, a writ of attachment against debtors
112 **ale-knights** votaries of the ale-house
112–13 **marrow . . . malt** malt-extract
113 **consumptions** wasting diseases (which supposedly drained the 'marrow')
114 ***Queen Dido*** *In Crete when Dedalus* (*Comets*, B1^{v}). Probably a bawdy song; note the pun on 'quean' = a whore, and on 'die' = have an orgasm + 'do' = copulate. Compare *Roaring Girl*, 6.62. Or it could be William Byrd's song on Dido ('When by first by force of fatal destiny') printed in *Songs of Sundry Natures* (1589).
strange 'Spanish' (*Comets*, sig. B1^{v}); (1) unusual; (2) foreign
117 **rot** A wasting disease. The context suggests an allusion to the 'rot' or liver-inflammation in sheep.
118 **purses** (1) money-bags; (2) scrotums
ere . . . aware (an addition)
120 **swell** The context in *Comets*, B2, was a forecast of the disease 'mumpsimus', a mock-Latinism for mumps.
121–32 **Others' . . . bellies** Abbreviates forecast of various monsters in *Comets*, B2.
121–2 **shall . . . frame** 'to swell so monstrously' (*Comets*, B2)
124 **meddle . . . little** Proverbially, 'Fools will be meddling' (Tilley, F546).
126 **meet** fit, proper
Ale The word is capitalized elsewhere as well, but here the capitalization suggests the metaphor of the river.
128–9 **to . . . physicians** (an inserted phrase, anticipating the idea in ll. 339–40)
130 **worms . . . churches** maggots in graves
131 **keep** celebrate
132 **bellies** (comparing a round belly to the vault of the church)
133 **steal . . . cloak** (a familiar complaint against tailors)
134–5 **nick . . . lace** (1) snip lace of clothes they made for customers; (2) rob their customers in overcharging for lace
136 **But . . . articles** (phrase added to justify retaining ll. 136–8, which ended the section on the first comet in *Comets*, B2)
touching concerning
138 **wax** 'were' (*Comets*, B2)
139 **private houses** In *Comets*, B2^{v}, the second comet was a crinite comet, supposed to affect domestic matters as well as state affairs.
140 **commodious** convenient, profitable

married men of weakest wit and worse courage should provide themselves of good weapons to defend themselves from assaults which shall assail them about midnight. And it shall be lawful for all wives to have a masculine courage in such sort that they who have had their wills to this hour shall have the mastery all the year after. And those husbands which doth not valiantly resist them shall be awarded to pay a sheep's head to their next neighbour in penance for their folly.

As by our provident judgements we have seen into these lamentable miseries incident in these parts of the world, so for the reformation thereof we do ordain and enact that the oil of holly shall prove a present remedy for a shrewd housewife, accounting Socrates for a flat fool that suffered his wife to crown him with a pisspot, ordaining that all those that give their wives their own wills to be fools by act of Parliament.

Also it is further established and agreed upon that Essex calves shall indict butchers' knives of wilful murder, and whosoever will prove a partial juryman shall have a hot sheep's skin for his labour. Bow Bell in Cheapside (if it break not) shall be warranted by letters patents to ring well. And, if the conduit heads want no water, the tankard bearers shall have one custard more to their solemn dinners than their usual custom.

Moreover, it is thought good that it shall be lawful for all tripe-wives to be exquisite physicians, for in one offal they shall find more simples than ever Galen gathered since he was christened. Beside, if dancers keep not tide and time in their measures, they shall forfeit a fat goose to their teacher for their slender judgement. The French *morbus* by commission shall be worth three weeks' diet. And they who have but one shirt to shift them withal may by the law strain courtesy to wear a foul one upon the Sunday. Also our commission shall be sent forth for the increase of hemp, as not only upland grounds shall be plentifully stored therewith, but also it shall so prosper in the highways as the stalks thereof shall touch the top of Tyburn.

In like manner we think it necessary and convenient that there shall be great noise of wars in taverns, and wine shall make some so venturous as they will destroy Tyrone and all his power at one draught. Also we think it meet that there be craft in all occupations (and those that are penitent in this world shall have comfort in a better). Silk weavers by the statute shall prosper well if they wash their hands clean on fasting days, for otherwise in soiling their work they shall lose their work-masters. Daws by authority shall leave building in steeples and dwell in cities. And such as are cunning in music shall know a crotchet from a quaver. But let

142 **of** with
weapons (i.e., penises)
143 **about midnight** (an addition)
143–6 **And . . . after** Revised version of the forecast in *Comets*, B2^{v}, concerning the second comet, which, although hairy ('crinite'), was 'feminine'.
144–5 **they . . . wills** Proverbially, 'Women will have their wills' (Tilley, W723).
146 **And . . . doth** 'for they who shall' (*Comets*, B2^{v})
147 **sheep's head** (referring to the cuckold's horned head)
150 **parts . . . world** 'westerly parts' (*Comets*, B3, since the second comet was to appear in the west)
151 **oil of holly** a whipping, traditionally prescribed for a scold
152 **shrewd** shrewish
153–4 **Socrates . . . pisspot** The story of Socrates comparing the urine poured on him by Xanthippe to rain following thunder is told in *Merry Tales, Witty Questions and Quick Answers* (1567). The same story is told in *Jack of Dover*, B4–4^{v}, where Socrates's place is taken by 'a certain poor labouring man in Lincoln' (B4). (Xanthippe throws water, not urine, in the source in Diogenes Laertius, *Lives of Eminent Philosophers*, II, 36.)
153 **flat** slow-witted
154–5 **ordaining . . . Parliament** (an addition)
155 **wills** (1) powers of choice (2) penises
156 **Essex calves** (1) finest calves (2) dupes
157 **of wilful murder** (an addition)
158 **juryman** 'Juror' (*Comets*, B3)
hot sheep's skin New parchment bonds. The phrase suggests that the calves and butchers refer to rich heirs and loan sharks (the skin is 'hot' since the victim has been just slaughtered).
159 **Bow . . . Cheapside** 'The bells of Barking' (*Comets*, B3). The great bell at the church of St Mary Bow in Cheapside, rung every night at nine, had a reputation for being late and loud.
160 **conduit heads** London's chief source of fresh water were the nine conduits.
161 **tankard bearers** water carriers
custard open pie
161–2 **solemn dinners** The 'bake-house', where the tankard bearers had their meals, were, like the conduits, a notorious centre of gossip, and here not 'solemn' at all.
162 **than . . . custom** (an addition)
163–4 **tripe-wives** tripe-sellers
164 **offal** entrails
165 **simples** medicines made of one ingredient (with a possible hint of 'simpletons' who will trust in the medicinal value of offal)
Galen Claudius Galenus (*c.*129–99), Graeco-Roman medical writer (not Christian or 'christened')
166 **dancers** (commonly associated with sexual licence)
tide and time The joke in *Comets*, B3, followed a forecast on tides.
167 **fat** (in contrast to 'slender' in l. 167–8)
goose (1) blockhead; (2) whore
168 ***morbus*** 'pox' (*Comets*, B3); syphilis
169 **three weeks' diet** standard three weeks' treatment for syphilis
shift them (1) use as a shirt; (2) manage their affairs
171 **Sunday** (when one could normally wear one's best clothes)
171–2 **Also . . . hemp** (an addition)
172 **hemp** material used in making ropes, including hangman's nooses
upland grounds high ground, with a quibble linking it to 'highways' in l. 173–4, the way to the gallows for highwaymen
174 **Tyburn** site for public hangings (in what is now Connaught Square)
176 **noise** (1) confused sound; (2) a band of musicians (who often played at taverns)
wars (1) brawling; (2) battles, recounted by veterans
177 **Tyrone** 'the King of Spain' *Comets*, B3^{v}. Hugh O'Neill, Earl of Tyrone led an Irish uprising in Ireland in 1595. Routed by Mountjoy's Irish expedition, Tyrone formally surrendered in April 1603. See Critical Introduction.
power army
178 **craft** (1) skill; (2) dishonesty
occupations Trades; proverbially, 'There is knavery in all trades' (Tilley, K152).
179–80 **shall . . . better** i.e., they can expect no reward in this world
181 **wash . . . days** referring to the stink of fish, the statutory diet for fasting days
on fasting days 'this Lent' (*Comets*, C3^{v}: removing a trace of the annual forecast; see ll. 249–50, 306–7)
182 **work-masters** master workmen, employers
Daws (1) birds; (2) fools
184 **cunning** learned, skilful
crotchet (1) quarter note; (2) whim
quaver (1) half a crotchet; (2) shaking movement

such men as instruct youth be very circumspect, for, if they learn more than their masters can teach them, they shall forfeit their wits to those that bring them up.

Furthermore, we think it most necessary and convenient that the generation of Judas should walk about the world in these our latter days and sell his neighbour for commodity to any man. But the usurers shall be otherwise disposed, for, having monthly taken but a penny in the shilling ever since they began first their occupation, shall now with a good conscience venture upon threepence with the advantage. Besides, many men shall prove themselves apparently knavish and yet in their own opinions will not be so. And many women shall imagine that there are none fairer than themselves.

Moreover, for the further increase of foolish humours, we do establish and set down that fantastic devices shall prove most excellent, and some shall so long devise for other men that they will become barren themselves. Some shall devise novelties to their own shames, and some snares to entrap themselves within.

In like manner we think it most necessary that those that be fortune-tellers shall shut a knave in a circle and, looking about for the devil, shall find him locked in their own bosoms. Atheists by the law shall be as odious as they are careless, and those that depend on destiny and not on God may chance look through a narrow lattice at Footman's Inn. But my dear friends the grocers are plentifully blessed, for their figs and reasons may allure fair lasses by authority. Yea, many men by the statute shall be so kind-hearted that a kiss and an apple shall serve to make them innocents.

It is further agreed upon and established that many strange events shall happen in those houses where the maid is predominant with her master and wants a mistress to look narrowly unto her.

Also we think it convenient that some shall take their neighbour's bed for their own, some the servant for the master, and (if candles could tell tales) some will take a familiar for a flea. Also we think it meet that there should be many fowlers who instead of larks shall catch lobcocks. And many for want of wit shall sell their freehold for tobacco pipes and red petticoats. Likewise we think it convenient that there should be many takers—for some would be taken for wise men who indeed are very fools, for some will take cracked angels of poor debtors, and a quart of malmsey when they cannot get a pottle.

But stay a while, whither are we carried, leaving the greatest laws unpublished and establishing the less? Therefore we enact and ordain as a necessary statute that there shall great contentions fall between soldiers and archers, and, if the fray be not decided at a pot of ale and a black pudding, great bloodshed is like to ensue. For some shall maintain that a Turk can be hit at twelve score pricks in Fiendsbury Fields, *ergo* the bow and shafts won Boulogne. Others shall say that a pot gun is a dangerous

185 **they** (i.e., the youths)
186 **forfeit** lose as penalty (for breach of engagement)
189–90 **the generation . . . days** 'Judas shall walk about the world this latter time' (*Comets*, B3^{v}). The return of Judas was linked in *Comets* to the imminent end of the world. The revision expands the sense to mean usurers in general.
190 **commodity** profit
191 **usurers** 'Jews' (*Comets*, B3^{v})
192–4 **a . . . advantage** The Act against Usury in the thirteenth year of Elizabeth's reign fixed the legal rate of interest at ten per cent. Three pence in the shilling monthly is an extortionate rate.
192 **shilling** ten pence
192–3 **ever . . . occupation** 'this six year' (*Comets*, B3^{v})
194 **advantage** gain
194–7 **many . . . themselves** Abbreviates a passage on self-love in *Comets*, B3^{v}–B4.
199 **fantastic devices** (1) swindling tricks; (2) remarkable inventions
201 **barren** (1) unproductive; (2) dull
202 **their own shames** 'shame themselves' (*Comets*, B4)
204 **circle** conjuror's circle for raising and confining the devil
206 **careless** (1) thoughtless; (2) carefree
207 **chance** happen to (alluding to the atheist belief in chance rather than divine providence)
208 **narrow lattice** prison bars
at Footman's Inn (an addition); in a prison, playing on 'lattice' in l. 208, since lattices were a feature of inns
209 **figs** (thought to be aphrodisiacs)
reasons (punning on 'rasins')
211 **kind-hearted** (1) benevolent; (2) cheated (literally, have their teeth extracted, since 'kind-heart' meant a tooth-drawer)
apple harlot (but also suggesting Eve's apple in Eden)
212 **innocents** fools, dupes
214 **maid** 'Virgo' (*Comets*, B4); (1) maid servant; (2) virgin
215 **wants** lacks
narrowly suspiciously
218 **some . . . master** i.e., some women will have sex with their male servants instead of their husbands
218–19 **(if . . . tales)** Variant of the proverb, 'If the bed could tell all it knows it would put many to the blush' (Tilley, B190).
219 **familiar** attendant spirit
220 **fowlers** (1) trappers of wild birds; (2) cheats, fool-takers
221 **lobcocks** bumpkins, simpletons
for . . . wit 'to the West of the North' (*Comets*, B4^{v})
222 **freehold** estate held in fee-simple, fee-tail or for life
tobacco . . . petticoats 'peas pottage' (*Comets*, B4^{v})
223 **many takers** The theme of 'takers' unites the paragraph, and the source of this sentence was at its start in *Comets*, B4^{v}.
224 **would . . . fools** 'one would be taken for wise, who is an idiot' (*Comets*, B4^{v})
225 **cracked angels** Dud coins, the crack extending from the edge to the ring within which the sovereign's head was stamped. An angel was a gold coin worth about 50 pence.
malmsey 'a nipcrust' (*Comets*, B4^{v}). Malmsey is a sweet wine.
226 **pottle** two quarts
227 **stay a while** 'alas' (*Comets*, B4^{v})
228 **laws . . . the** 'wonders unreckoned, and relying on the' (*Comets*, B4^{v})
230–2 **archers . . . ensue** 'archers (if the fray be not decided) at a pot of ale and a black pudding' (*Comets*, B4^{v}). The changed construction makes 'at' follow 'decided' rather than 'contention' as in the source.
232 **Turk** dummy target in archery
233 **twelve score pricks** 120 paces (the standard archery range)
Fiendsbury Fields i.e., Finsbury Fields (used for archery practice; also a notorious promenade)
234 **Boulogne** 'Granado' (where the Moors were defeated by the Christians) (*Comets*, B4^{v}). Boulogne was captured by Henry VIII in 1544 after a two-month siege.
pot gun mortar (quibbling on 'pot', a drinking vessel)
234–5 **dangerous . . . against** 'perilous weapon at' (*Comets*, B4^{v}). The artillery charge against a city wall is here reduced to drunkards defacing walls by urinating against them.

weapon against a mud wall and an enemy to the painter's work. Amongst these controversies we will send forth our commission to god Cupid, being an archer, who shall decide the doubt and prove that archery is heavenly, for in meditation thereof he hath lost his eyes.

O gentle fellow soldiers, then leave your controversies if you love a woman, for I will prove it that a mince pie is better than a musket. And he that dare gainsay me, let him meet me at the Dagger in Cheap with a case of pewter spoons, and I will answer it. And, if I prove not that a mince pie is the better weapon, let me dine twice a week at Duke Humphrey's table.

It is furthermore established that the four knaves at the cards shall suddenly leap from out the bunch and desperately prank about the new playhouse to seek out their old master Captain Cropear. Also it is thought meet that some men (in these days) shall be politic beyond reason, and write more in one line than they can prove in an age. It shall be lawful for some to study which way they may walk to get them a stomach to their meat, whilst other are as careful to get meat to put in their bellies. Likewise there shall be great persecution in the commonweal of kitchen fees, so that some desperate women shall boil, try and seethe poor tallow to the general commodity of all the whole company of tallow chandlers.

Alas, alas, how are we troubled to think on these dangerous times? For tailors by act of Parliament may lawfully invent new fashions. And he that takes Irish aqua vitae by the pint may by the law stumble without offence and break his face. And it shall be thought convenient that some be so desperate bent as they shall go into my Lord Mayor's buttery when all the barrels be full without either sword or dagger about them. Many men shall be so vent'rously given as they shall go into Petticoat Lane and yet come out again as honestly as they went first in.

In like manner it shall be lawful for Thames water to cleanse as much as ever it did in times past, and if the brewers of London buy store of good malt, poor bargemen at Queenhithe shall have a whole quart for a penny. St Thomas onions shall be sold by the rope at Billingsgate by the statute. And sempsters in the Exchange shall become so conscionable that a man without offence may buy a falling band for twelve pence.

It shall be lawful for smiths to love good ale. And, if it be possible to have a frost of three weeks long in July, men shall not be afraid of a good fire at midsummer. Porters' baskets shall

238–9 **in . . . eyes** i.e., love is blind, like someone who stares too long at the sun (heaven)

241 **mince pie** an expensive delicacy (but also suggesting the slang sense of *pie* as 'female pubic triangle')

243 **Dagger in Cheap** 'Woolsack' (*Comets*, C1). The change helps the wordplay (see 'weapon' in ll. 244–5). The Dagger in Foster Lane in Cheapside specialized in minced pies: see *Quiet Life*, 5.1.73.
pewter spoons (instead of pistols, normally carried in a case and used in duels)

243–4 **answer it** (1) prove it; (2) answer his challenge to a duel

244–5 **prove . . . table** 'say not that a gun is the better weapon, he shall never be bound to serve with bow and arrows while he liveth' (*Comets*, C1). 'To dine with Duke Humphrey's' was to go without dinner (Tilley, D637). The tomb of Sir John Beauchamp (d. 1358) in the south aisle of St Paul's, taken to be that of Duke Humphrey of Gloucester (1391–1447), was the rendezvous of debtors seeking sanctuary.

246 **knaves** See l. 38 above.

248 **about . . . playhouse** 'it on the stage' (*Comets*, C1). The change shifts the censure from players to the crooks in the audience. The playhouse was probably the Fortune, built in 1600.

248–9 **to . . . Cropear** (An addition.) Allusion to the common punishment at the pillory, involving a pun on the 'ear' of the corn.

249 **some . . . days)** 'Men this year' (*Comets*, C1)

250 **politic** clever, affecting worldly wisdom

252 **get** 'catch' (*Comets*, C1)
a stomach an appetite

253 **other** (i.e., poorer people)
careful anxious, painstaking
put . . . bellies 'fill their maw' (*Comets*, C1)

254 **persecution** quest

254–5 **kitchen fees** drippings, a perquisite of the cook

255 **try** extract oil from fat by heating
seethe boil

256 **tallow** animal fat, used for making candles
commodity profit

256–7 **the . . . of** (an addition)

258–9 **are . . . times** 'am I perplexed to think on these times' (*Comets*, C1; see Critical Introduction). The paragraph abbreviates and rearranges the source.

260–1 **And . . . face** 'Irish aqua vitae abundantly taken about this time, shall make a man stumble' (*Comets*, C1).

260 **aqua vitae** whisky, brandy

262 **desperate** 'desperately' (*Comets*, C1)

263 **buttery** cellar
barrels wine barrels (but suggesting 'gun barrels' of defensive fortifications)

265 **given . . . Lane** 'disposed, that they shall go into brothel houses' (*Comets*, C1). Petticoat Lane (Middlesex Street, formerly Hog Lane) was a haunt of prostitutes.

266 **come . . . in** i.e., come out with their reputation intact (with a bawdy quibble suggesting copulation)

268 **in times past** 'before' (*Comets*, B4^{v})
brewers of London 'brewer of Putney' (*Comets*, C1); allusion to the practice of diluting beer with water

269 **poor . . . Queenhithe** 'they about Richmond and Mortlake' (*Comets*, C1). Queenhithe was a quay in Upper Thames Street near Southwark Bridge.

270 **whole . . . penny** In 1591 (date of *Comets*), beer was 6*s.* 8*d.* per barrel of 32 (or 36) gallons, and small ale 3*s.* 4*d.*

270–1 **St Thomas . . . rope** There is a multiple quibble involving St Thomas à Waterings on Kent Road, an execution site. 'Waterings' would thus be linked to false tears (and, therefore, to onions; see ll. 10–12) as in *Puritan*, 1.1.124–5, and the hangman's rope to the 'rope' or string of onions as in *Changeling*, 1.2.208.

271 **Billingsgate** A London wharf in Thames Street. Stow mentions onions among the cargo unloaded at Billingsgate (p. 185).
sempsters (1) seamstresses; (2) prostitutes
Exchange Old Exchange, near St Paul's, a centre for shopping and trade

273 **falling band** Flat collar for men which became fashionable at the end of the sixteenth century. There is a bawdy innuendo in 'falling'.

274 **smiths . . . ale** Proverbially, 'The smith has always a spark in his throat' (Tilley, S562).

275 **frost . . . long** (possibly another reference to the three weeks' routine treatment for syphilis as in l. 169 above)

have authority to hold more than they can honestly carry away. And such a drought shall come amongst cans at Bartholomew Fair in Smithfield that they shall never continue long filled.

The images in the Temple Church (if they rise again) shall have a commission to dig down Charing Cross with their falchions. And millers by custom shall have small mind to morning prayer if the wind serve them in any corner on Sundays. Those that go to the wars and get nothing may come home poor by authority. And those that play fast and loose with women's apron-strings may chance make a journey for a Winchester pigeon, for prevention thereof, drink every morning a draught of *Noli me tangere* and by that means thou shalt be sure to escape the physician's purgatory.

But amongst all other decrees and statutes by us here set down, we ordain and command that three things (if they be not parted) ever to continue in perpetual amity: that is, a louse in an old doublet, a painted cloth in a painter's shop, and a fool and his bauble. Furthermore, it shall be lawful for bakers to thrive by two things (that is, scores well paid and millers that are honest); physicians, by other men's harms; and churchyards, by often burials. Also we think it necessary for the commonwealth that the salmon shall be better sold in Fish Street than the beer shall be at Billingsgate. And heartsease amongst the company of herb-wives shall be worth as much money as they can get for it by the statute.

It is further enacted and agreed upon that those that run fourscore mile afoot on a winter's day shall have a sore thirst about seven of the clock in the evening. And such as are inclined to the dropsy may be lawfully cured, if the physicians know how. Also we ordain and appoint that (if there be no great store of tempests) two halfpenny loaves shall be sold for a penny in Whitechapel. Chaucer's books (by act of Parliament) shall in these days prove more witty than ever they were, for there shall so many sudden or rather sodden wits step abroad that a flea shall not frisk forth unless they comment on her.

O what a detestable trouble shall be among women about fourscore and ten years old, for such as have more teeth about them than they can well use shall die for age if they live not by miracle. Also it shall be lawful for bees, if the summer show not, to go on pilgrimage, and fly so far in one day as whoso sets up a landmark where they first light shall come to us and have a pound weight of gold for his diligence and labour.

Moreover, we think it necessary that those that have two eyes in their head shall sometime stumble, and they that can neither

277 **they . . . away** 'their masters can carry' (*Comets*, C1^{v}); (i.e., porters will steal)
278 **cans** drinking vessels
278–9 **at Bartholomew . . . Smithfield** 'about Cape S. Vincent' (*Comets*, C1^{v}). The change to 'Smithfield' quibbles on 'smiths' in l. 274. On 24 August, the Feast of St Bartholomew, a civic fair was held at Smithfield.
280 **images . . . Church** images of crusading Knights Templars buried in the Temple Church
281 **Charing Cross** A possible reference to the legend that Eleanor of Castile (d. 1290), queen of Edward I, sank into the ground at Charing Cross. The legend is told in George Peele's *Edward I* which was probably first produced in 1591. Peele transfers a scandal involving Eleanor of Aquitaine, queen of Henry II, to Eleanor of Castile. Smellknave may have been led by the play to confuse the two queens, since William Marshal (one of the Knights Templars buried in Temple Church) was instrumental in freeing Eleanor of Aquitaine from prison in 1189.
falchions broad, curved swords
282 **morning prayer** (The avoidance of Sunday morning prayers was a common complaint against citizens.)
283 **serve them** i.e., turn their mills
corner direction
283–4 **Those . . . may** 'They that ride to the westward of *Flowers* and *Corns*, if they catch not Brazil men, shall' (*Comets*, C1^{v}). See Critical Introduction.
284–8 **And . . . purgatory** (an addition)
285 **fast and loose** A cheating game in which a string or belt was so arranged that the viewer would think that he could make it fast by placing a stick through its folds, while the operator could pull it away.
286 **Winchester pigeon** (1) a prostitute; (2) a swelling in the groin caused by syphilis (so called because the Bishop of Winchester owned most of the land in the Southwark red-light area)
287 ***Noli me tangere*** literally, touch me not (John 20:17; Tilley, N202); a species of balsam
288 **physician's purgatory** (referring to the treatment of syphilis by inducing salivation with mercury, like Purgatory, uncomfortably hot, but temporary)
289–91 **amongst . . . amity** 'among all these changes, three things shall continue in perpetual amity if they be not severed' (*Comets*, C1^{v})
291–2 **louse . . . doublet** Proverbially, 'A rogue's wardrobe is harbour for a louse' (Tilley, R161).
292 **doublet** sleeveless upper garment
painted cloth imitation tapestry, used as hangings
293 **bauble** Familiar pun on *bauble* (fool's sceptre), and *babble*. Proverbially, 'A fool will not give his bauble for the Tower of London' (Tilley, F476).
294 **scores** accounts, bills
millers . . . honest Proverbially, 'The miller is a thief' (Tilley, M955).
297 **salmon . . . Street** 'cod shall be better sold than the bean' (*Comets*, C2). 'Salmon' and 'cod's head' both meant a gull, and 'salmon' was also a name for a prostitute. Old and New Fish Streets, in Queenhithe Ward and Bridge Ward Within respectively, were known for alehouses and whores.
297–8 **than . . . Billingsgate** (an addition)
298 **heartsease** (1) a pansy; (2) an endearment, a lover
herb-wives herb-sellers
299 **much money** 'much' (*Comets*, C2)
301 **sore thirst** (probably as a result of the sweating sickness, a febrile disease)
303 **dropsy** morbid accumulation of fluids in tissues and internal cavities
304 **great store** excess
305 **tempests** Storms and bad weather were likely to push up wheat prices and, therefore, reduce the statutory weight of the baker's loaf.
halfpenny loaves The baker's halfpenny loaf seems expected to weigh six ounces, although statutory weights varied with wheat prices. Bakers often dodged the law.
306 **Whitechapel** the central market district around St Paul's Cathedral
Chaucer's books The text of Chaucer familiar at the time of *Comets* was the folio edited by William Thynne, which had 10 editions between 1532 and 1561; but a new edition by Speght was published in 1598.
306–7 **in these days** 'this year' (*Comets*, C2)
308 **sudden** ready, quick
sodden (1) dull; (2) drunk
308–9 **a . . . forth** i.e., the most trivial thing shall not be spared
312 **for age** of old age
314 **whoso** whoever
315 **light** alight, land
315–16 **come . . . gold** 'have a talent' (*Comets*, C2). The reward could be for tracking honey or because swarms had to be reclaimed, usually by beating on pots and pans.

write nor read may as boldly forswear themselves as they that can. And it shall be lawful for almanac-makers to tell more lies than true tales. And they that go to sea without victuals may suffer penury by the statute.

In like manner it shall be lawful for any man to carry about him more gold than iron, if he can get it. But they that are given to a sullen complexion (if they be females) must be more circumspect for, if they repent their hidden sins too much, they may chance catch heaven for their labour. Therefore let maidens take heed how they fall on their backs, lest they catch a forty weeks' fever. And he that hath once married a shrew, and by good chance bury her, beware how he come into the stocks again.

Further, it shall be lawful for those that be rich to have many friends, and they that be poor may by authority keep money, if they can get it honestly.

Also we command and charge all such as have no conscience to do their worst, lest they die in the devil's debt. As for the rest, they that have more money than they need may help their poor neighbours if they will.

In like manner it shall be lawful for such as are subject to hot rheums to drink cold drink, and those that have a mind to enrich physicians to be never without diseases.

Also soldiers that have no means to thrive by plain dealing may by the statute swallow down an ounce of the syrup of subtlety every morning, and, if they cannot thrive that ways, we think it necessary that four times in the year they go a-fishing on Salisbury Plain.

Furthermore, for the benefit and increase of foolish humours, we think it necessary that those our dear friends which are sworn true servitors to women's pantables should have this order set down that you suit yourselves handsomely against goose feast, and if you meet not a fair lass betwixt Paul's and Stratford that day, we will bestow a new suit of satin upon you, so you will bear all the charges.

But as for you, dear friends and scholars, thus much we favour you, for you shall dine upon wit by authority, and, if you pay your hostess well, it is no matter though you score it up till it come to a good round sum.

In like manner it shall be lawful for maid's milk to be good physic for kibed heels, and a cup of sack to bedward a present remedy for the rheum. Such as are sick in the spring may take physic by the statute, and those that are cold may wear more clothes without offence. It is best to ride in long journeys lest a man be weary with going afoot, and more comely to go in broken stockings than barelegged.

Further, it shall be lawful for some to be lean because they cannot be fat. Some by the statute shall love beef passing well because they can come by no better meat, and other some simper it with an egg at dinner that dare manfully set upon a shoulder of veal in the afternoon.

Some shall be sad when they want money, and in love with widows rather for their wealth than their honesties. It is also thought necessary that some shall suspect their wives at home because they themselves play false abroad. And some love bowling alleys

319 **forswear . . . can** 'quit themselves of forgery' (*Comets*, C2^{v}). See Critical Introduction.

320 **almanac-makers** 'Such as have skill in physiognomy' (*Comets*, C2^{v})

321 **true tales** 'truth' (*Comets*, C2^{v})

321–2 **go . . . penury** 'will sail without compass, may have shipwreck without remedy' (*Comets*, C2^{v}). Middleton may have been remembering Ralegh's stranded and starving crew, of which his stepfather was a member, brought back by Drake from Roanoke Island in 1586.

324 **more . . . iron** more money than sword and armour

324–5 **given . . . complexion** (1) Dull skinned; (2) sullen tempered. The quibble followed from the forecast for the saturnine in *Comets*, C3^{v}. Unchaste women supposedly had pale complexions.

327 **catch heaven** Attain salvation. The verb contrasts with 'catch' in l. 328.

327–8 **take . . . they** 'beware to' (*Comets*, C3^{v}; part of a longer sentence which also involved men who seduced them)

328 **forty weeks' fever** pregnancy

329–30 **And . . . again** (an addition)

330 **stocks** (1) instrument of punishment; (2) frame to which a horse is confined for shoeing

331 **to . . . many** 'let them be sure of' (*Comets*, C4)

333 **honestly** (an addition)

335 **do** 'spit' (*Comets*, C4)

337 **if they will** (an addition)

339 **rheums** 'humours' or tempers

342 **subtlety** (1)an ornamental device or dressing made of sugar; (2) guile

343–5 **we . . . Plain** (An addition, introducing the 'plain dealing-Salisbury Plain' quibble.) Salisbury Plain was a flat region in the central south-west of England. 'Freshwater mariners', who swindled people with tales of shipwreck or piracy, were described by Thomas Harman in *A Caveat for Common Cursitors* (1566) as those whose 'ships were drowned in the plain of Salisbury' (p. 84). The phrase here would thus mean a cheat who 'fished' for dupes by pretending to be a ruined sailor.

347–8 **which . . . pantables** 'that are born under this kind goddess' (i.e. Venus) (*Comets*, C4^{v}). Compare Massinger, *A New Way to Pay Old Debts*, 1.1.137: 'And yet sworn servant to the pantofle'.

348 **servitors** servants

pantables pantofles, shoes with high cork heels

349 **against** in preparation for

goose feast (1) Greengoose Fair at Stratford Bow in Whitsun week; (2) ('goose' = prostitute)

354 **dine upon wit** Live by cunning. Proverbially, 'He lives by his wits' (Tilley, W581).

pay (1) recompense financially; (2) satisfy sexually

355 **score it up** (1) run up a bill; (2) copulate

356 **round** (pun on the 'roundness' of pregnancy)

357 **maid's milk** *lac virginis*, a medicinal cosmetic using monoxide of lead, red lead, white vinegar, and common salt

358 **physic for** 'to heal' (*Comets*, D1)

kibed affected by chilblains

sack (considered a preventive against catarrh)

360 **may wear** 'get' (*Comets*, D1)

361 **without offence** (an addition)

362 **broken** tattered

363 **barelegged** See ll. 4–5 above.

365 **beef** considered the favourite meat of the stupid

366 **other some** some other

366–7 **simper it** eat daintily with mouth shut

367 **dinner** principal meal, had usually around midday

manfully set upon 'make incision in' (*Comets*, D2). The change links the eating of veal to setting upon a 'veal', i.e., a gull, by the sergeant or robber for bribe or booty. Clapping on the shoulder is frequently associated with arresting officers.

370 **honesties** sexual modesty

372 **bowling** a disreputable pastime like dicing and drinking

better than a sermon. But, above all other things, sprites with aprons shall much disturb your sleeps about midnight.

Furthermore, it shall be lawful for him that marries without money to find four bare legs in his bed. And he that is too prodigal in spending shall die a beggar by the statute.

In like manner we think it necessary that he that is plagued with a cursed wife to have his pate broke quarterly, as he pays his rent. Likewise he that delights in subtlety may play the knave by custom. And he that hath his complexion and courage spent may eat mutton on fasting days by the law.

And, to conclude, since there are ten precepts to be observed in the art of scolding, we humbly take our leave of Duke Humphrey's Ordinary, and betake us to the Chapel of Ill Counsel, where a quart or two of fine Trinidado shall arm us against the gunshot of tongue-mettle and keep us safe from the assaults of Sir John Findfault. *Vale*, my dear friends, till my next return.

FINIS

ADDITIONAL PASSAGES

A

Jack of Dover's Quest of Inquiry

When merry Jack of Dover had made his privy search for the fool of all fools, and making his inquiry in most of the principal places in England, at his return home was adjudged to be the fool himself. But now wearied with the motley coxcomb, he hath undertaken in some place or other to find out a verier fool than himself. But first of all, coming to London he went into Paul's Church, where, walking very melancholy in the middle aisle with Captain Thingut and his fellows, he was invited to dine at Duke Humphrey's Ordinary, where, amongst many other good stomachs that repaired to his bountiful feast, there came in a whole jury of penniless poets who, being fellows of a merry disposition (but as necessary in a commonwealth as a candle in a straw bed), he accepted of their company. And as from poets cometh all kinds of foolery, so he hoped by their good directions to find out this fool of all fools so long looked for. So thinking to pass away the dinner time with some pleasant chat, lest being overcloyed with too many delicates they should surfeit, he discovered to them his merry meaning, who being glad of so good an occasion of mirth, instead of a cup of sack and sugar for digestion, these men of little wit began to make inquiry and to search for this aforesaid fool...

B

'Well,' quoth one of the jury, 'if we cannot find the fool we look for amongst these fools before named, one of us will be the fool, for, in my mind, there cannot be a verier fool in the world than is a poet. For poets have good wits, but cannot use them; great store of money, but cannot keep it; and many friends, till they lose them. Therefore we think fit to have a Parliament of poets, and to enact such laws and statutes as may prove beneficial to the commonwealth of Jack of Dover's motley-coated fools.'

Here beginneth the Penniless Parliament of Threadbare Poets

373–4 **sprites... midnight** 'as all the crinite comets in Christendom cannot disturb us of our sleeps, (I mean such comets as wear aprons...)' (*Comets*, D2)
373 **sprites** spirits (i.e., women)
375–6 **for... bed** Adapts four verse lines in *Comets*, C3^{v}: 'Whoso marries without money, | in midst of his dread: | Shall at night if he please, | Find four bare legs in his bed.' Allusion to the proverb, 'There goes more to matrimony than four bare legs in a bed.'
376–7 **And... statute** Adapts four verse lines in *Comets*, C3^{v}: 'He that is prodigal, | And lets his crowns fly: | If he spare not in time, | shall a beggar die.'
378–80 **he... rent** (An addition.) There is a quibble on 'quarterly' (broken into quarters, quarterly payment of rent). Smellknave predicted the appearance of the comets on 25 March, the legal quarter-day for rent payment.
379 **cursed** shrewish
380–1 **Likewise... custom** Adapts two verse lines in *Comets*, D1: 'Whoso in craft and subtlety delight, | Can play the knaves by day as well as night.'
381–2 **And... days** Adapts four verse lines in *Comets*, D1^{v}: 'That a man whose complexion | and courage is spent: | May instead of red herrings, | eat mutton in Lent.' See l. 29 above.
383–8 **And... return** (an addition)
383–4 **ten... scolding** Borrows from the Epilogue in *Comets*, D3: '*here are the ten precepts to be observed in the art of scolding*'. The 'precepts' or 'commandments' were the shrew's ten fingernails (Tilley, C553).
384–5 **Duke Humphrey's Ordinary** See ll. 244–5 above.
385 **Chapel of Ill Counsel** apparently a tobacconist's shop
386 **fine Trinidado** Trinidad tobacco, considered the finest
387 **tongue-mettle** mettle = spirit (continuing the metaphor of 'gunshot' and punning on 'metal')
387–8 **Sir John Findfault** any carping critic
388 ***Vale*** farewell

A *Penniless* was published in 1604 as the second part of *Jack of Dover*; this paragraph was added at the start of the previously-published text of *Jack of Dover* to account for the new part.
2 **privy** private, secret
6 **motley** fool's parti-coloured dress
coxcomb jester's cap
7 **verier** truer
10 **Thingut** (i.e., a starveling)
10–11 **dine... Ordinary** See ll. 244–5 above.
12 **bountiful feast** (ironic)
14–15 **as necessary... straw bed** Borrows the censure of poets in *Comets*, B2: 'as necessary in a Commonweale, as a candle in a strawbed' (i.e., useless, adapting Mark 4:21, but also suggesting the sense of dangerous).
20 **delicates** tasty dishes (ironic)
surfeit be sick from overeating (ironic)
discovered disclosed
B This is the transition from the existing text of *Jack of Dover* into the text of *Penniless*, as it appears in the 1604 edition.

ACKNOWLEDGEMENTS

John Lavagnino and I have overseen everything in the edition. I am responsible for commissioning the editorial team. However, each work was assigned to a specific general editor (or in some cases two), who did much of the detailed work of proofreading and commenting on the edited text, critical introduction, and commentary (including the relevant sections in Parts II and III of the *Companion*).

MacDonald P. Jackson: *Michaelmas Term, Weapons, Widow, Macbeth, Quiet Life, Changeling, Valour, Gypsy*, and *Poems*
John Jowett: *Honest Whore, Trick, Yorkshire, Revenger, Gallants, Chaste Maid, Tennis, Hengist*, and *Game*
Gary Taylor: *Black Book, Magnificent Entertainment, Banquet, Sherley, Two Gates, Lady, Cupids, Dissemblers, Owl, Peacemaker, Old Law, Hengist, Measure, Solomon, Ghost*, and *Penniless*
Valerie Wayne: *Phoenix, Father Hubburd, Mad World, Timon, Puritan Widow, Roaring Girl, No Wit, Lady, Quarrel, Witch, Heroes*, and *Women Beware*
Adrian Weiss: *Meeting, Plato, Truth, Civitatis, Industry, Antiquity, Entertainments, Aries, Virtue, Integrity, Prosperity, Microcynicon*, and *Penniless*

This table underestimates the extensive collaborative contribution of the Associate General Editors, who generously gave their time and expertise, assisting and advising on many aspects of the edition, large and small. My own introductory essays ('How to Use This Book', 'Lives and Afterlives', and—in the *Companion*—'Textual Proximities', 'The Order of Persons', and the General Textual Introduction to *A Game at Chess*) have benefited enormously from the general-editing of Jackson, Jowett, Lavagnino, Wayne, and Weiss. Even these Fantastic Five could not always save me from myself, but they have certainly worked overtime to minimize my fallibility. I have also received personal help and feedback from many—indeed, most—of the other contributors, and every one of them has enhanced my understanding of Middleton. R. V. Holdsworth has advised on this project from the outset, and although in the end he did not edit any of the works he has so generously shared his own exceptionally wide and detailed knowledge of Middleton with so many of us that we have listed him among the Contributors to both volumes.

A few pages cannot adequately express twenty years of gratitude for help given to seventy-five scholars on three continents. These overdue moral debts are both institutional and personal. The edition could never have been completed without the resources of the great archival collections that house the earliest texts of Middleton's works and the early records of his life, most particularly the British Library, the Folger Shakespeare Library, the Huntington Library, the Houghton Library at Harvard University, the Bodleian Library at the University of Oxford, the Public Record Office, and the library of Trinity College, Cambridge. Oxford University Press has, like Penelope, faithfully waited for two decades; its promise has sustained us through the long dark haul—and unlike Penelope it has been often present and helpful, a companion as well as an aspiration. Many other institutions have provided invaluable assistance with particular items, as can be seen in the list of illustrations, and in the individual acknowledgements recorded below. Each of these 'institutions' consists, in fact, of particular living individuals, who have personally helped one (or many) of us. But each of those institutions also represents particular individuals no longer living, who were instrumental in accumulating and preserving the cultural capital that has been invested in this enterprise.

The same is true of the institutions that have provided salaries and travel grants, technical support, and intellectual stimulation to all the scholars who have invested their lives in this edition. Institutional affiliations are acknowledged in the List of Contributors; each such affiliation represents a complex network of resources and individuals. As general editors, we could not have completed our own work without the generous research support of Florida State University, King's College London, and (at earlier stages of the project) Brandeis University and the University of Alabama. This sustained assistance has been supplemented by individual research fellowships awarded to me by the John Simon Guggenheim Foundation, the National Endowment for the Humanities, and the Folger Shakespeare Library.

Gary Taylor

My biggest debt is to my department at King's College London, which has supported my efforts since 1998 and in particular gave me a year's leave. Reiko Takeda made it possible for me to complete my work. Of the many scholars who have come to my aid, I want to thank especially Mac Pigman, Richard Proudfoot, Peter Robinson, Paul Vetch, and my fellow editors. The British Library provided the ideal environment for research.

For their advice and help during earlier years of the project, I am grateful to many people at Brandeis University, the Smithsonian Astrophysical Observatory, Brown University, and Texterity Inc. These organizations did not employ me to work on this edition, but they all found ways to make that work possible; Scott Magoon, Kelly Chance, and Martin Hensel were particularly generous. The Employment and Training Administration of the United States Department of Labor kept me going during one year; Leslie Brown provided every kind of support for many years. I created part of the production system for the edition in collaboration with Dominik Wujastyk, and with the financial support of the California Institute of Technology.

I am grateful to many people at Oxford University Press for their efforts on our behalf. I didn't think we could finish the edition without Frances Whistler, but she took us far enough along that we managed. Paul Luna's initial design was adapted and extended by Paul Cleal, Bryony Newhouse, Liz Powell, and Ruth Vincent; my thanks to all of them for making us look good.

John Lavagnino

All editors and readers of Middleton are indebted to Roger V. Holdsworth; I am especially so. I owe great thanks to G. Blakemore Evans and to David Bevington for expert advice and comments. I am grateful to D. H. Craig, Marjorie Garber, Scott Paul Gordon, Philip Gossett, Lisa Jardine, Elizabeth D. Scala, G. B. Shand, and Debbie Shen. I am also thankful to M. J., J. L., G. T., and A. W.

Douglas Bruster

I wish to thank Dr Amlan Das Gupta of Jadavpur University, Calcutta, and Professor C. S. Lim and his Department of English at the University of Malaya, Kuala Lumpur, for their generous help at various stages of this work.

Swapan Chakravorty

The present edition owes a great deal to the work of twelve student actors who performed the play in the 1991 James Madison University production. Working from Xerox copies of Eld's quarto, these actors became, in effect, RAC's twelve assistant editors. And who better to help in decisions about inflection, meaning, and movement than actors, the people who, as a good playwright knows from the start, are going to reconstruct the play with their performance? Their choices as actors inform the present text. Here are their names alphabetically and the parts they played:

Caryn Baker: *a gentleman and the Boy*
Tenley Bank: *First Courtesan, a drawer, Tiffany's servant, Marmaduke*
Tapio Christiansen: *Tailby*
Jen DeMayo: *Second Courtesan, Jack the Vintner, Piamont*
Karen Hester: *the Novice, Cleveland's servant, a drawer, a gentleman*
Tod Kovner: *Fitzgrave*
Nicholas McDowell: *Frip*
Kara McLane: *Arthur, Mistress Newcut, Fulk, Newblock's servant, a constable*
Erick Pinnick: *Goldstone*
C. Charles Scheeren: *Pursenet*
Trissy Sincavage: *a gentleman, Katherine, Bungler, a constable*
J. Steven Smith: *Primero, Tailby's servant, a tailor*

Ralph Alan Cohen

We would like to thank Nancy Selleck for her help in compiling the doubling list. Ivo Kamps would like to thank the Graduate School at the University of Mississippi for a summer grant that allowed him to work on *The Phoenix*.

Lawrence Danson and Ivo Kamps

I have incurred four principal debts in producing this edition. The first is to the play's two modern editors, Iain Sharp and Robert Kean Turner; the second is to MacDonald Jackson, in his capacity as a General Editor of the present edition; the third is to the American Philosophical Society, who supported my own work on the play with a very welcome summer fellowship; and the fourth is to the staff of the Lilly Library in Bloomington, Indiana, from whose exceptionally handsome copy of the 1647 Beaumont and Fletcher folio, formerly the property of Richard Brinsley Sheridan, I have prepared this edition.

Michael Dobson

For this edition of *A Fair Quarrel* I am grateful for help received from Roger Holdsworth, Stephanie McIntyre, Marguerite Barrett, Fr. Frans Jozef Van Beeck, S.J., and Adrian Weiss.

Suzanne Gossett

I wish to thank the trustees of the Folger Shakespeare Library and the University of Nottingham Library for permission to reprint the manuscripts of *Hengist, King of Kent*. I also thank the Henry E. Huntington Library, the British Academy, and the Folger Shakespeare Library for their generous awards of fellowships to support the completion of this edition. Special thanks are also owed to Peter Beal, Peter Blayney, the late Fredson Bowers, S. P. Cerasano, R. A. Foakes, R. V. Holdsworth, William Ingram, Alan H. Nelson, G. R. Proudfoot, James Riddell, Adrian Weiss, and Laetitia Yeandle for advice and support during the preparation of this edition.

Grace Ioppolo

My work has been facilitated by a period of leave and research funding from the University of Auckland and by an Edwin Mellon Fellowship at the Henry E. Huntington Library. I am grateful to the Librarians of Magdalen College and Worcester College, Oxford, and of Dulwich College, London, for making special arrangement to enable me to collate copies of *The Revenger's Tragedy*. Thanks are also due, for help of various kinds, to Ken Larsen, Roger Holdsworth, and the late Don McKenzie.

MacDonald P. Jackson

We acknowledge the generous support of Yves Peyré (University of Montpellier III). He is the author of *La Voix des mythes dans la tragédie élisabéthaine* (Paris: CNRS, 1996). We are also extremely grateful to Jane Kingsley-Smith (Roehampton University, London) for her expert advice on Cupids in the literature of the period. Finally, we wish to thank James R. Sewell, City Archivist of the Corporation of London Records Office, for his invaluable assistance with the manuscript of the Court of Aldermen proceedings.

M. T. Jones-Davies and Ton Hoenselaars

I would like to record here my debt to various institutions and individuals who have assisted me during my editing of Moseley's three 1657 Middleton plays over a number of years. The British Academy provided a grant towards study at the Folger Shakespeare Library in 1986, and the University of Waikato in New Zealand contributed towards a similar period at the Huntington Library in 1988. Wolfson College, Oxford, facilitated a spell of research in 1991 by awarding a Visiting Scholarship. Staff at the University of Waikato Library were constantly generous and efficient in their help. I am grateful to the hospitality of the Bodleian Library, the British Library, the Folger Shakespeare Library, and the Henry Huntington Library. Ken O. Arvidson and Marshall Walker were unflinchingly supportive Heads of the English Department at Waikato. Various people have provided me with information, advice, or encouragement: Nigel Bawcutt, Robert Cummings, Ton Hoenselaars, Roger Holdsworth, Grace Ioppolo, Robert Irish, MacDonald P. Jackson, Liz Ketterer, Johan Koppenol, Robert Maslen, Alan Riach, Kim Walker, and Helen Wilcox. Vanessa Byrnes, Helen Miller, and others at Waikato sustained my enthusiasm for Middleton. Kristin Lucas was my best reader.

John Jowett

I am grateful to Paul Mulholland for supplying me with a photographic copy of the Princeton copy of Okes. I also wish to thank Sue-Ellen Case for giving me a copy of her adaptation of *The Roaring Girl*; David Bergeron and Jean E. Howard for reading the Critical Introduction; Kim Colwell, Sianne Ngai, and Garrett Sullivan for invaluable help in preparing the edition; Christine Buckley of Oxford University Press; Gary Taylor, for generous support both editorial and moral; Peter Blayney, for sharing his discovery of new legal records concerning Mary Frith; and Brown University, for research funding.

Coppélia Kahn

I would like to thank Neil Fraistat, Joan Rachel Goldberg, John Lavagnino, Gail Kern Paster, Gary Taylor, and Adrian Weiss for their help and encouragement.

Theodore B. Leinwand

The commentaries on *Honour and Industry* and the Busino Account have benefitted from the help of Prof. Stephen Booth, Dr Christopher Gales and Prof. Donald M. Friedman. Prof. Paul Seaver has been extremely generous in sharing his research into the membership of the Grocers' Company, as well as information about the personal income of various individuals and professions; I am most grateful. Tudi Sammartini, Paolo G. Sissa and Mark di Suvero provided invaluable assistance with (respectively) obtaining access to the Busino manuscript, with transcribing it, and with my translation. I am especially indebted to Prof. Louise George Clubb, who reviewed both transcription and translation, offering her expert advice on paleographic and interpretive problems.

Kate D. Levin

The editing of this text could not have been completed without the collaboration of two resourceful research assistants Nicholas Hoffman (commentary) and Eric Wilson (textual introduction and notes); additional assistance was provided by Jeremy Faro and Marco Torres. I am also grateful to: Marjorie Garber and Gregory Nagy for assistance with classical allusions; Thomas L. Berger, Barbara K. Lewalski, Barbara A. Mowat, and Wendy Wall, for discussions of editorial method; the Renaissance Doctoral Colloquium at Harvard University; students in English 90dl (Spring 1993, Harvard), particularly Will Schoettle; the Clark, Rollins, and Robinson Research Funds (Harvard) and the Weinberg College of Arts and Sciences (Northwestern University); the staffs of the Chapin, Folger, Houghton, Huntington, and Newberry Libraries (in particular Susan Halpert at the Houghton and Paul Saenger at the Newberry); the department of Special Collections, Northwestern University Library; Gary Taylor for his patience, his suggestions and productive resistances, and his guidance; and Jay Grossman, who saved me from (at least *some*) editorial fallacies.

Jeffrey Masten

Besides many of the other Middleton editors, I am especially grateful to the following for the generous assistance they have given me at various stages of this project: Peter Blayney, Roman Dubinski, Rosalind Hays, Derek Keene, Jean Miller, Barbara Mowat, Donna Penrose, Thomas Sloane, Paul Stevens, Abigail Young, St Jerome's University, and the libraries holding copies of *Tennis*, particularly the Folger Shakespeare Library, which provided photographs of the title-page and cast-list of the masque and gave permission for their reproduction.

C. E. McGee

I would like to acknowledge the help of John Astington, Susan Cerasano, Andrew Gurr, and Laurie Maguire.

Scott McMillin

I am happy to record debts of gratitude to many who have assisted the preparation of editions of *The Patient Man and the Honest Whore*, *The Two Gates of Salvation*, and *The Peacemaker*. No editor of *The Patient Man and the Honest Whore* can fail to benefit from the labours of previous editors and other scholars; among those deserving of particular mention in this regard are Fredson Bowers and Cyrus Hoy. Special thanks are due to Valerie Wayne, who generously apprised me of research on her edition of *A Trick to Catch the Old One*; to Peter W. M. Blayney for freely sharing with me his own bibliographical investigations on the play and *The Two Gates*; to Laurie Maguire and to the production's director, Gordon Anderson, for accounts and observations on the 1992 London revival; and to John Jowett, who at an early stage provided extensive and valuable advice and suggestions.

In respect to *The Two Gates of Salvation* and *The Peacemaker* I am glad of the opportunity to extend thanks to several individuals: Bernard Katz and Padraig O'Cleirigh, each of whom made helpful contributions to recondite, stubborn, and knotty commentary matters; and Adrian Weiss, who graciously and unstintingly responded to a number of bibliographical queries. I wish also to express my gratitude to my General Editor, Gary Taylor, for beneficial thoughts and advice on all aspects of these editions and to G. B. (Skip) Shand for much-appreciated support and probing discussion. Any errors or infelicities that remain are my own. Thanks go also to librarians of various institutions and collections who made available early printed copies of the respective texts, microfilms, photocopies, and other research materials, and who have been unfailingly helpful in providing assistance.

I am grateful to the University of Guelph Research Advisory Board and the Social Sciences and Humanities Research Council of Canada for research grants without which the editions could not have been completed.

Paul Mulholland

For assistance with manuscripts, thanks to Dr Bruce C. Barker Benfield, Department of Western Manuscripts, Bodleian Library, Oxford, and to Dr Ceridwen Lloyd-Morgan, Department of Manuscripts and Records, National Library of Wales, Aberystwyth. For elucidating particular points of text or context, thanks to: Professor Gordon Campbell, University of Leicester; Professor Patrick Collinson, Trinity College, Cambridge; Professor Richard Dutton, University of Lancaster; Professor (Emeritus) Eric Poole, University of Kent at Canterbury; Ms Anne Seller, University of Kent at Canterbury; and Ms Sheila Sweetinburgh, University of Kent at Canterbury. For locating visual materials, thanks to: Dr Kenneth Fincham, University of Kent at Canterbury; Dr Volker Krahn, Preusserkulturbesitz, Berlin; Dr Elisabeth McGrath, Warburg Institute, University of London; and Dr Thomas Sorge, Berlin. For sharing editorial expertise and theatrical experience, thanks to: Professor Al Braunmuller, University of California at Los Angeles; Dr Elizabeth Schafer, Royal Holloway, University of London; and Professor Martin White, University of Bristol. For conferring long-term benefits, more than can be noted here, thanks to Professor Anne Lancashire, University College, University of Toronto and to Professor John C. Meagher, St. Michael's College, University of Toronto.

Marion O'Connor

I would like to thank Gary Taylor and Valerie Wayne for their helpful readings of earlier versions of my introduction.

Sharon O'Dair

The present editor is most grateful to T. W. Craik and D. E. L. Crane for help in the preparation of the text, and to Gary Taylor, John Jowett and Roger Holdsworth for supplying many of the verbal parallels in Canon and Chronology.

Neil Rhodes

I am grateful to Standish Henning for microfilms and encouragement at the start of this project. Frank Atkinson of the St Paul's Cathedral Library, Dr Heslop of the University of Birmingham Library, and the staffs at the British Library and the Beinecke Library at Yale were helpful in tracking down books and nearly-forgotten dissertations. The staff of Baker Library at Dartmouth College, especially Patricia Carter and her colleagues in Interlibrary Loan, devoted much time to my aid. Collaborating with Celia Daileader has been instructive to us both. The advice of Harry Beskind came at a crucial time. My deepest debt is to James L. Steffensen, upon whose editorial experience and personal support I have placed the greatest reliance.

Peter Saccio

Charlene Liska and Anne Russell provided invaluable assistance with the early textual work on this edition of *The Wisdom of Solomon Paraphrased*. Textual research was made possible by grants from the Social Sciences and Humanities Council of Canada and the Huntington Library.

Paul Mulholland kindly read and advised on the early stages of *The Ghost of Lucrece*.

John Jowett and Gary Taylor made many helpful suggestions for the Commentary and the Critical Introduction. The textual work was supported by a grant from Glendon College.

Thanks to Paul Yachnin and Andrew Gurr for assistance and advice. Research for this edition of *The Black Book* was aided by grants from the Folger Shakespeare Library, the Canada Council, The British Council, and Glendon College.

G. B. Shand

I would like to thank my colleague at the University of Massachusetts Boston, Joseph Shork, for his generous and patient assistance in translating Latin that did not derive from standard classical texts, and Kenneth Rothwell and Robert Maher for additional advice on other problems relating to classical references or Latin translation. Sabrina Baron of the University of Chicago helped with the identification of some of the more obscure court officers in the processional Order. For Dekker's text I derived valuable assistance from the commentaries of Cyrus Hoy. Gary Taylor provided patient and invaluable assistance throughout the project. Any mistakes that remain are, of course, entirely my own responsibility.

R. Malcolm Smuts

My thinking about *The Widow* has been much influenced by graduate students at Brandeis University and the University of Alabama. Special thanks also to Raphael Seligmann and Leslie Thomson. The Georgia Shakespeare Festival on 1 April 2001 gave me the chance to direct a reading of the play by professional actors, which confirmed and enhanced my sense of its rich theatrical potential: I am indebted to everyone involved. Michael Warren's generous collaboration extended beyond the commentary to consistently insightful input on both the text and the introduction.

My edition of *Macbeth* is much indebted to the work of the two previous Oxford editors, Stanley Wells and Nicholas Brooke.

The careful proofreading eye and mind of Ronald A. Tumelson contributed greatly to the accuracy of the text and apparatus of both *The Bloody Banquet* and *The Nice Valour*. Suzanne Gossett played the part of a general editor for my work on *Gypsy*, as did Robert Maslen for my work on *Gravesend*. David Kathman, Bill Lloyd, and Tiffany Stern contributed useful information to 'The Order of Persons'. Doug Bruster, Larry Danson, and Paul Mulholland helped expedite urgent illustration requests. Kay Picart answered urgent questions about contemporary dance theory, and Scott Kopel was routinely, cheerfully indispensable.

My work on *A Game at Chess* is most heavily indebted to Trevor Howard-Hill, who generously provided me with advance access to much of his own work. Graduate students in seminars and readings at Brandeis University, the University of Alabama, and Florida State University have taught me a lot about the literary and dramatic potential of the play. Trish Henley spent many hours of work turning my hand-drawn (and re-drawn and re-drawn) stemmata into intelligible printed images. The assiduous repeated proofreading of John Jowett, Molly Hand, Trish Henley, John Lavagnino, Emily Rendek, Brandie Siegfried, and Ronald A. Tumelson made the texts and apparatus much more accurate than they would otherwise have been. Jowett provided invaluable editorial feedback on a colossal amount of material; Jackson, Wayne, and Weiss also contributed helpful local feedback.

My institutional debts for twenty years of work on all parts of the edition are recorded above. John Lavagnino has overseen every detail of my work (and everyone else's); his sense of humour, his intellectual range and acuity, his superb organizational and managerial skills, his ability to detect inconsistencies and connect hitherto-unconnected dots (not to mention his London apartment), sustained me through a task that would otherwise have succumbed to the despair of a sprinter miscast in a marathon. My first conversations with Celia R. Daileader were about Middleton, and we have continued talking about him for fifteen years; I owe much of my understanding of each to the other.

Gary Taylor

I am grateful to Peter W. M. Blayney for numerous helpful suggestions, answers to questions, and solutions to problems. Thanks are also due to Richard Proudfoot for his corrections and suggestions and to David Carnegie who generously shared insights gained when editing the play for the Cambridge edition of Webster. A much-appreciated release-time grant from the Social Sciences and Humanities Research Council of Canada gave me the valuable time necessary to work on this edition.

Leslie Thomson

My thanks to Barbara Newman and Helen Deutsch for their suggestions about translation. I also wish to thank Joel Kaplan for generously sharing his preliminary work on *Microcynicon* with me.

Wendy Wall

I wish to thank the Huntington Library for granting me an Andrew W. Mellon Fund Fellowship which enabled me to prepare my contributions to the commentary while in residence there; and the Committee on Research of the Academic Senate, University of California, Santa Cruz, for its support of this work.

Michael Warren

It is a pleasure to acknowledge the help of many people in the preparation of this edition, beginning with all of the general editors: thank you Gary, John L., John J., Mac and Adrian for being such knowledgeable and genial colleagues. With remarkably good humour, George Watson loaned me his own annotated copy of the Oxford B.Litt. thesis he prepared on this play, from which I learned a great deal. With equal enthusiasm, Adrian Weiss shared his written analysis of the text of *Trick* and his knowledge of bibliography; the textual introduction is much improved by his vigorous response. In preparing this edition, I have benefitted from communications with *Trick*'s future editor, Paul Mulholland, with John Astington about illustrations, with David Gants about paper, with Leslie Thomson about the Folger copy of the first edition, and with Gail Kern Paster about early modern medicine. For help on the critical introduction, I am grateful to Susan Amussen and Fran Dolan for advice on rape and the law; to Barbara Hodgdon for introducing me to Mary Carleton; to Margo Hendricks for assistance with Aphra Behn; and to my students for their varied and astute responses to the play, especially Joan Perkins and Jill Sprott. Paula Reeve did a thorough job of collating commentaries from previous editions; her work was funded by a grant from the University of Hawaiʻi Office of Women's Research. My university's Office of Research Relations also provided their support in two separate grants, and the NEH funded a summer stipend. My final and deepest thanks go to Richard Tillotson and Sarah Wayne Callies for their willing engagement with this play and related concerns, which in our family are often simultaneously dramatic and domestic.

Valerie Wayne

The collating of the scattered manuscripts of 'Hence, all you vain delights' has been done by various members of the Middleton team: Michael Dobson (Oxford), Lori Anne Ferrell (Huntington), Suzanne Gossett and Valerie Wayne (Folger), Grace Ioppolo (Cambridge and London), Lawrence Manley (Yale), Robert Maslen (Aberdeen), and Gary Taylor (Harvard, Nottingham, London). For advice and assistance more generally, we wish to thank Tim Armstrong, Greg DeRocher, Gordon McMullan, and Marion O'Connor.

Susan Wiseman and Gary Taylor

For my edition of *A Chaste Maid in Cheapside*, I gratefully acknowledge the financial assistance of the Social Science and Humanities Research Council of Canada, whose generous grant enabled me to employ a series of excellent research assistants, Linda Sinclair, Kimberley McLean-Fiander, and Faith Nostbakken, to whom I am very grateful. The edition, and especially the lineation and commentary, are indebted to the fine work of the play's many good previous editors and critics, especially R. B. Parker, David L. Frost, Charles Barber, Alan Brissenden, Richard J. Wall, Margery Fisher, and David F. George.

Linda Woodbridge

Penelope Rensley assisted diligently and accurately in the initial editing of *Meeting* and *Plato*. R. V. Holdsworth and Gary Taylor helped make this version of both texts better than they would otherwise have been. I am grateful for their astute and rigorous suggestions. I am also grateful to the Social Sciences and Humanities Research Council of Canada and the Huntington Library, San Marino, California, for their generous support.

Paul Yachnin